Tyndale Bible Dictionary

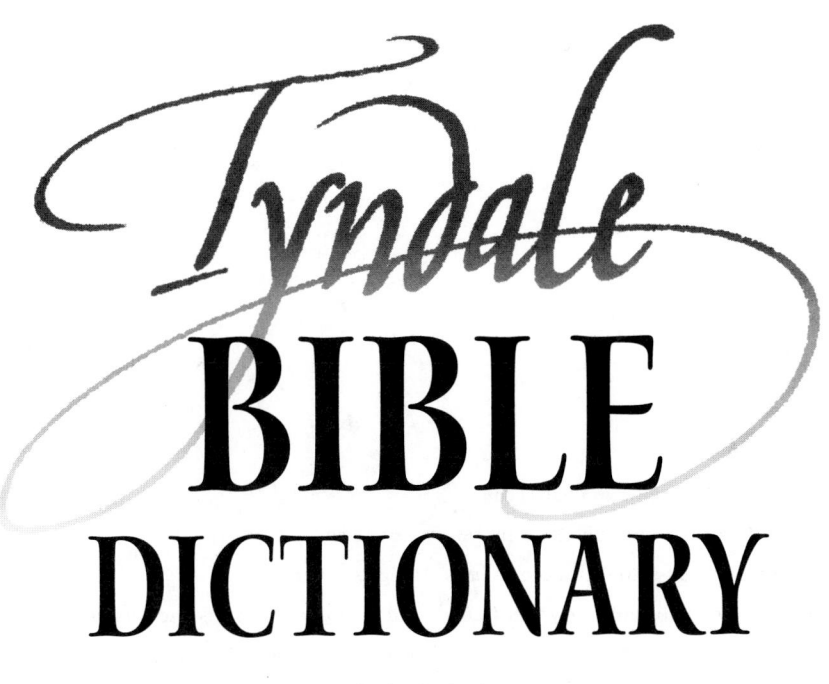

BIBLE DICTIONARY

◆◆◆◆◆

EDITORS

Walter A. Elwell, Ph. D.

AND

Philip W. Comfort, Ph. D.

Tyndale House Publishers

WHEATON, ILLINOIS

Visit Tyndale's exciting Web site at www.tyndale.com

Designed by Timothy R. Botts

Library of Congress Cataloging-in-Publication Data

Tyndale Bible dictionary / editors, Philip W. Comfort, Walter A. Elwell.
    p. cm. — (The Tyndale reference library)
  ISBN 0-8423-7089-7 (alk. paper)
  1. Bible—Dictionaries. I. Title: Bible dictionary. II. Comfort, Philip Wesley. III.
Elwell, Walter A. IV. Series.

  BS440 .T96 2001
  220.3—dc21   2001034697

Printed in the United States of America

08 07 06 05 04 03 02
9   8   7   6   5   4   3   2

PERMISSIONS

PERMISSIONS FOR ILLUSTRATIONS
We recognize the following institutions for permission to reproduce
photographs in this volume:

British Library
Frontispiece of the Authorized King James Version: Bible
Tyndale's Version, The Ending of Matthew's Gospel: Bible

British Museum
Papyrus Oxyrhynchus 654: Apocrypha, Gospel of Thomas

Egypt Exploration Society
Papyrus Oxyrhynchus 1166: Bible, Old Testament Manuscripts
Papyrus Oxyrhynchus 1786: Music
Papyrus Oxyrhynchus 2684: Amulet; Jude
Papyrus Oxyrhynchus 3522: Job
Papyrus Oxyrhynchus 3523: Bible, New Testament Manuscripts
Papyrus Oxyrhynchus 3525: Apocrypha, Gospel of Mary
Papyrus Oxyrhynchus 4404: Matthew
Papyrus Antinoopolis 12: John, Epistles of

Foundation Martin Bodmer
Bodmer Papyrus II (P66): John; Spirit
Bodmer Papyrus XIV-XV (P75): Bible; Luke

Franklin Trask Library, Andover Newton Theological Seminary
Papyrus Oxyrhynchus 1230: Revelation

Institut für Alterumskunde der Universität zu Köln
Köln Papyrus 12 (P87): Philemon

Israel Antiquities Authority
Dead Sea Scroll of Deuteronomy, 4QDeut^n: Deuteronomy
Dead Sea Scroll of Exodus, 4QpaleoExod^m: Exodus
Dead Sea Scroll of Habakkuk, 1QpHab: Tetragrammaton; God, Names of
Dead Sea Scroll of Isaiah, 1QIsa^b: Isaiah
Dead Sea Scroll of Leviticus, 11QpaleoLev: Leviticus
Dead Sea Scroll of 1 Samuel, 4QSam^a: 1 Samuel

PERMISSIONS FOR WRITTEN WORKS

Some of the articles in this dictionary have been adapted from other works published by Tyndale House Publishers, particularly *The Origin of the Bible* and *Who's Who in Christian History*. In preparing several other articles, the editor, Philip Comfort, made some adaptions from his own previously published works, now no longer in print. These works are as follows: *New Commentary on the Whole Bible* (New Testament volume); *I Am the Way; Opening the Gospel of John* (with W. Hawley); *The Complete Guide to Bible Versions; The Quest for the Original Text of the New Testament; Early Manuscripts and Modern Translations of the New Testament;* and *The Inspired Word.*

INTRODUCTION
TYNDALE BIBLE DICTIONARY

Our primary aim throughout the writing and editing process of this volume has been to provide our readers with a comprehensive Bible dictionary. We believe we have reached that goal. The *Tyndale Bible Dictionary* includes all the significant people, places, and terms in the Bible. The dictionary also has comprehensive articles on all the books of the Bible, significant words in the Bible, translations of the Bible, manuscripts of the Bible, and the canon of Scripture (including articles on apocryphal and pseudepigraphal books). Furthermore, you will find informative articles on the life and times of various nations that existed during Bible times as well as comprehensive articles on plants, animals, musical instruments, clothing, and other everyday objects. Key Bible themes and concepts such as redemption, justification, holiness, and righteousness are explained in depth. Difficult-to-understand subjects such as the "sin unto death" are also covered.

BIBLE VERSIONS
This dictionary can be used with any of the major Bible translations, including the New Living Translation, King James Version, Revised Standard Version, New International Version, New American Standard Bible, New English Bible, New Jerusalem Bible, Revised English Bible, Today's English Version, American Standard Version, and the English Revised Version. Special effort has been made to list terms (usually with unique spellings) found only in the King James Version and then to refer the reader to the modern term.

ASTERISKS
One of our foremost goals in the creation of the *Tyndale Bible Dictionary* was to include as many terms and topics as possible while being careful to ensure the relevance of every entry. Part of this goal included presenting terms from a variety of Bible versions. Though the New Living Translation is the primary Bible version used, hundreds of terms appear in the dictionary that do not appear in the NLT. All dictionary entries marked with an asterisk (*) are words that are not found in the New Living Translation but do appear in other versions such as the King James Version and Revised Standard Version.

CROSS-REFERENCES
Two types of cross-references are utilized in this dictionary:
- **"See" references** point to one or more articles that contain information considered necessary for a complete understanding of the topic in question.
- **"See also" references** point to one or more articles that contain information considered interesting but not essential.

Both "See" and "See also" references refer to articles by topic name. When a topic name appears in a cross-reference in quotes and refers to a specific page number, the reference is to a text box that occurs on that page.

PHOTOGRAPHS

One of the features that sets the *Tyndale Bible Dictionary* apart from other Bible dictionaries is the inclusion of over one hundred new photographs of the Holy Lands, supplied by Barry Beitzel, a well-known geographer of the Holy Lands. These unique aerial-view photos provide a visual perspective to the topics presented in the dictionary. Also included are nearly one hundred photographs of ancient biblical manuscripts and artifacts as well as dozens of hand-drawn illustrations of Bible life and times.

MAPS

Over fifty maps of the Holy Lands are included in the *Tyndale Bible Dictionary* in an attempt to better acquaint you with the layout of the land about which you are reading. In addition, twelve full-color pages of detailed maps appear in the center of the dictionary.

ABBREVIATIONS

Apocryphal Books

Add Est	Additions to Esther	Jdt	Judith
Bar	Baruch	1 Macc	1 Maccabees
1 Esd	1 Esdras	2 Macc	2 Maccabees
2 Esd	2 Esdras	Pss of Sol	Psalms of Solomon
4 Ezr	4 Ezra	Tb	Tobit
Ecclus	Sirach (Ecclesiasticus)	Wisd of Sol	Wisdom of Solomon

Dead Sea Scrolls (Non-Canonical)

CD	Cairo Damascus Document	2QS	Manual of Discipline
1QM	War Scroll	1QSa	Rule of the Congregation

Other Writings

Antiquities	Josephus, *Antiquities of the Jews*	*Prol Gal*	Jerome, *Prologue to Galatians*
Apion	Josephus, *Against Apion*	Strabo	Strabo, *Biography*
Dio Cassius	Dio Cassius, *Roman History*	Tacitus	Tacitus, *Histories*
Eusebius	Eusebius, *Historia Ecclesiastica*	*War*	Josephus, *The Jewish War*
		Eph	Ephesians

Books of the Bible

Gn	Genesis	Est	Esther			Mi	Micah
Ex	Exodus	Jb	Job			Na	Nahum
Lv	Leviticus	Ps(s)	Psalms			Hb	Habbakkuk
Nm	Numbers	Prv	Proverbs			Zep	Zephaniah
Dt	Deuteronomy	Eccl	Ecclesiastes			Hg	Haggai
Jos	Joshua	Sg	Song of Songs			Zec	Zechariah
Jgs	Judges	Is	Isaiah			Mal	Malachi
Ru	Ruth	Jer	Jeremiah			Mt	Matthew
1 Sm	1 Samuel	Lam	Lamentations			Mk	Mark
2 Sm	2 Samuel	Ez	Ezekiel			Lk	Luke
1 Kgs	1 Kings	Dn	Daniel			Jn	John
2 Kgs	2 Kings	Hos	Hosea			Acts	Acts
1 Chr	1 Chronicles	Jl	Joel			Rom	Romans
2 Chr	2 Chronicles	Am	Amos			1 Cor	1 Corinthians
Ezr	Ezra	Ob	Obadiah			2 Cor	2 Corinthians
Neh	Nehemiah	Jon	Jonah			Gal	Galatians

Eph	Ephesians	2 Tm	2 Timothy	2 Pt	2 Peter
Phil	Philippians	Ti	Titus	1 Jn	1 John
Col	Colossians	Phlm	Philemon	2 Jn	2 John
1 Thes	1 Thessalonians	Heb	Hebrews	3 Jn	3 John
2 Thes	2 Thessalonians	Jas	James	Jude	Jude
1 Tm	1 Timothy	1 Pt	1 Peter	Rv	Revelation

Bible Versions

ASV	American Standard Version	NJB	New Jerusalem Bible
ERV	English Revised Version	NLT	New Living Translation
JB	Jerusalem Bible	NRSV	New Revised Standard Version
KJV	King James Version	RSV	Revised Standard Version
NASB	New American Standard Bible	REB	Revised English Bible
NEB	New English Bible	TEV	Today's English Version
NIV	New International Version	TLB	The Living Bible

Other Abbreviations

approx.	approximately	MS, MSS	manuscript, manuscripts
c.	circa—approximately	Mt	Mountain, Mount
cf.	compare	MT	Masoretic Text
ch, chs	chapter, chapters	NT	New Testament
d.	died	OT	Old Testament
ed	edition, editions; editor, editors	p, pp	page, pages
e.g.,	for example,	St	Saint
et al.	and others	TR	Textus Receptus
etc.	and so forth	v, vv	verse, verses
i.e.,	that is,	vid	Latin for "it appears [to read as such]"
lit.	literal, literally		
LXX	Septuagint	vol, vols	volume, volumes
mg	a variant reading noted in the margin or footnote of a translation	yr., yrs.	year, years

AUTHORSHIP OF ARTICLES

Many writers contributed to this volume, either by writing articles or editing and rewriting articles substantially. Because so many articles were worked on by so many different hands in the editorial process, it is impossible to assign authorship to each article. Furthermore, if we noted authorship for some articles while excluding others, our acknowledgments would be uneven and therefore unfair. Consequently, we have listed all of the contributors beginning on page xi.

We pray that this volume will help you, the reader, in your study of God's Word, and that such study will enrich your appreciation for the inspired Scriptures.

Philip W. Comfort, Ph.D.
Walter Elwell, Ph.D.

CONTRIBUTORS

GENERAL EDITORS
Philip W. Comfort
Walter A. Elwell

COORDINATING EDITOR
Jeremy P. Taylor

PHOTOGRAPHY
Barry Beitzel

WRITERS
Wallace Alcorn
Robert L. Alden
L. C. Allen
Ronald Allen
James F. Babcock
Clarence B. Bass
Barry Beitzel
W. Wilson Benton, Jr.
Gilbert Bilezikian
E. M. Blaiklock
George Blankenbaker
Gerald L. Borchert
Manfred T. Brauch
Kenneth J. Bryer
H. Douglas Buckwalter
George E. Cannon
J. Knox Chamblin
Philip W. Comfort
Roger Douglass Congdon
Mark T. Coppenger
David Cornell
John Crandall
Robert D. Culver
Peter H. Davids
Bruce A. Demarest
Carl E. DeVries
Paul H. DeVries
James C. DeYoung
Raymond B. Dillard
J. D. Douglas

James D.G. Dunn
J. J. Edwards
John Elliott
Walter A. Elwell
H. K. Farrell
Paul F. Feiler
David A. Fields
Charles L. Feinberg
Harvey E. Finley
John Fischer
Francis Foulkes
Louis Goldberg
Wesley L. Gerig
Robert Guelich
D. L. Hall
J. Gordon Harris
R. K. Harrison
Ginnie Hearn
Walter Hearn
Paul Helm
Carl Wayne Hensley
Andrew E. Hill
Harold W. Hoehner
James M. Houston
E. Margaret Howe
F. B. Huey, Jr.
Philip Edgcumbe Hughes
David K. Huttar
Edgar C. James
Jakob Jocz

Paul Kaufman
Donald Kenney
William Nigel Kerr
Eugene F. Klug
George E. Ladd
William Lane
William Sanford LaSor
F. Duane Lindsey
Robert W. Lyon
W. Harold Mare
James L. Mason
Gerald L. Mattingly
Paul K. McAlister
Jim McClanahan
Thomas E. McComiskey
J. Gordon McConville
Wayne O. McCready
Lee McDonald
Douglas J. Miller
Robert H. Mounce
W. Robert Myers
Roger Nicole
Mark R. Norton
Grant Osborne
Daniel Partner
Hazel W. Perkin
John Piippo
John Piper
Gary Pollitt
Austin H. Potts

A

AARON Moses' brother and Israel's first high priest. In the books of Exodus, Leviticus, and Numbers, Aaron was Moses' spokesman and assistant during the Israelites' exodus from Egypt. Aaron was three years older than Moses and was 83 when they first confronted the pharaoh (Ex 7:7). Their sister, Miriam (Nm 26:59), must have been the eldest child, old enough to carry messages when the infant Moses was found by the pharaoh's daughter (Ex 2:1-9). Aaron's mother was Jochebed and his father was Amram, a descendant of the Kohath family of Levi's tribe (Ex 6:18-20).

Aaron and his wife, Elisheba, had four sons (Ex 6:23), who were to follow him in the priesthood (Lv 1:5). Two of them, Nadab and Abihu, violated God's instructions by performing a sacrilegious act while burning incense and were burned to death as a result (Lv 10:1-5). The priesthood was then passed on through the other two sons, Eleazar and Ithamar, who also sometimes failed to carry out God's instructions precisely (10:6-20).

Aaron's prominence in the events of the exodus arose partly from the fact that he was Moses' brother. When Moses tried to avoid becoming Israel's leader on the grounds of having a speech impediment, Aaron's ability as a speaker was recognized and used by God (Ex 4:10-16).

Events of Aaron's Life The Hebrew people were slaves in Egypt at the beginning of Aaron's life. Raised as an Egyptian by one of the pharaoh's daughters, Moses had fled into the Midian Desert after killing a cruel Egyptian taskmaster (Ex 1–2). When God sent Moses back as a liberator (chs 3–4), he also sent Aaron out to meet Moses in the desert (4:27). Moses was a stranger to his people after so many years of exile, so Aaron made contact with Israel's elders for him (4:29-31). When Moses and Aaron went to see the pharaoh, God told the Egyptian monarch through the two of them to let the Israelites go (Ex 5:1). When the pharaoh made life even more miserable for the Hebrew slaves, God began to show his power to the Egyptian ruler through a series of miracles (chs 5–12). God performed the first three miracles through Aaron, using a rod (probably a shepherd's staff). The pharaoh had his palace sorcerers do similar tricks. After God brought a plague of gnats (KJV "lice") over all Egypt, the Egyptian magicians admitted defeat and said, "This is the finger of God!" (Ex 8:19, NLT). Then God brought on more plagues through Moses, culminating in the deaths of all the Egyptians' firstborn sons. Aaron was with Moses (12:1-28) when God revealed how he would "pass over" the properly marked homes of the Israelites, sparing their children on the night the Egyptian children died. That event was the origin of the Passover feast still observed by Jews today (13:1-16).

After God led the Israelites to safety and destroyed the pursuing Egyptians, Aaron participated with Moses in governing the people on their long wilderness journey to the Promised Land (Ex 16:1-6). Later, battling against Amalek's army, Aaron helped hold up Moses' weary arms in prayer to maintain God's blessing (17:8-16). Although always subordinate to Moses, Aaron seems to have been recognized as an important leader (18:12). God summoned him to be with Moses when God gave the law on Mt Sinai (19:24). Aaron was among the representatives of the people who ratified God's statutes in the Book of the Covenant (24:1-8). Aaron went with those leaders partway up the holy mountain and saw the vision of the God of Israel (24:9-10). With Hur, he was left in charge when Moses was with God on the mountaintop (vv 13-14).

AARON THE PRIEST
Because it marked the beginning of the priesthood in Israel, the consecration of Aaron to his office was both instructive and solemn. Nothing was left to human ingenuity; all was precisely commanded of God. There were three ceremonies: washing, clothing, and anointing. When the tabernacle was finished, Aaron and his sons were set apart to the priesthood by washing (to signify purification), clothing with official garments (for beauty and glory), and anointing with oil (to picture the need of empowering by the Spirit; cf. Ex 28; 40:12-15; Lv 8). Aaron thus became the first high priest, serving nearly 40 years. The character of his office was hereditary; this is attested to by his sons' wearing his garments (to signify purification), to the office of high priest (Ex 29:29-30; Nm 20:25-28). Although all priests were anointed with oil, the anointing of Aaron and his successors was distinct from that of the ordinary priests (Ex 29:7; 40:12-15; Lv 8:12). Because the priesthood was inherited, all subsequent priests had to trace their ancestry back to Aaron (Ezr 7:1-5; Lk 1:5). Also, a sharp distinction was always drawn between the family of Aaron and the rest of the Levites (cf. Nm 3:5). Thus, the high priest was designated as the anointed priest in a special sense (Lv 4:3-4; 6:20-22; 21:10).

Because of Aaron's priestly role, the NT looks upon him as prefiguring the Messiah of Israel. Jesus Christ was appointed High Priest (Heb 3:1-2) in the same way God chose Aaron (Heb 5:1-5), but he was described as a greater high priest than Aaron (Heb 7:11-28).

Moses was gone for over a month, and in a moment of weakness, Aaron gave in to the people's request for an idol to worship. He melted down their gold ornaments to make a golden image of a calf (Ex 32:1-4). (The Israelites had probably been influenced in Egypt by the cult of Apis, a fertility god in the form of a bull.) At first, Aaron seemed to think he might be doing something acceptable to God (v 5), but things got out of hand and a drunken sex orgy took place around the idol (v 6). God was angry enough to destroy the people, but Moses interceded, reminding God of his promise to multiply Abraham's descendants (Ex 32:7-14). Moses furiously confronted Aaron about the immorality and idolatry, which Aaron blamed on the people without admitting any guilt of his own (vv 21-24). Although the idolators were punished by death (Ex 32:25-28) and the whole camp by a plague (v 35), Aaron was evidently not punished. In a retelling of the events, Moses said that Aaron was in great danger but was spared because he had prayed for him (Dt 9:20).

In their second year of nomadic wilderness life, Aaron helped Moses carry out a census (Nm 1:1-3, 17-18). Eventually, Aaron may have become jealous of Moses' position of leadership, for Miriam and Aaron began to slander their brother, even though the elderly Moses was by then more humble than any man on earth (Nm 12:1-4). God's anger toward the two was averted by Moses' prayer, although Miriam did suffer for her sin (12:5-15). Aaron again seems to have escaped punishment entirely. With Moses, Aaron opposed a rebellion at Kadesh (14:1-5). He stood with Moses against a later revolt (ch 16). After a final incident at Meribah, where the Israelites almost revolted again, God accused Moses and Aaron of having failed to take him at his word and denied them entry into the Promised Land (20:1-12). Aaron died at the age of 123 on Mt Hor, after Moses had removed his elaborate priestly garments and put them on Aaron's son Eleazar (Nm 20:23-29; 33:38-39).

See also Israel, History of; Exodus, The; Wilderness Wanderings; Priests and Levites; Levi, Tribe of; Aaron's Rod.

AARONITES* Collective name for the priests who descended from Aaron through his sons Eleazar and Ithamar. The term is used twice in the KJV to refer to the 3,700 men who supported David against Saul (1 Chr 12:27) and of whom Zadok later became leader (1 Chr 27:17). Both "house of Aaron" (Pss 115:10, 12; 118:3; 135:19) and "Aaron" (1 Chr 27:17, RSV) are used to refer to the Aaronites.

See also Aaron.

AARON'S ROD* Staff belonging to Moses' brother, Aaron, symbolizing the two brothers' authority in Israel. When the Israelites were wandering in the wilderness, a threat against Moses and Aaron's leadership was led by Korah, Dathan, and Abiram (Nm 16:1-40). In spite of the Lord's destruction of those rebels and their followers, the rest of the people of Israel turned against Moses and Aaron, saying that they had killed the people of the Lord (16:41). In order to restore respect for the divinely appointed leadership, the Lord told Moses to collect a rod from each tribe and have the leader of the tribe write his name on it. Aaron was told to write his name on the rod of Levi. The rods were placed in the inner room of the tabernacle, in front of the ark (of the covenant). In the morning, Aaron's rod had sprouted blossoms and had produced ripe almonds. The rod was then kept there as a continual sign to Israel that the Lord had established the authority of Moses and Aaron (Nm 17:1-11; cf. Heb 9:4).

Following that incident the people of Israel entered the wilderness of Zin, but there was no water for them and their flocks. Again the people argued with Moses and Aaron. The Lord instructed Moses to get the rod and, in the presence of Aaron and the rest of the people, command a particular rock to bring forth water. Taking the rod, Moses asked dramatically, "Must we bring you water from this rock?" (Nm 20:10, NLT) and struck the rock twice. Water gushed out and the people drank. Yet Moses

and Aaron were forbidden to enter the Promised Land because they did not sanctify the Lord in the people's eyes (Nm 20:12-13). An earlier event had provided evidence that the Lord was able to provide needed water in that manner (Ex 17:1-7).

See also Aaron.

AB* Month in the Hebrew calendar, about mid-July to mid-August. See Calendars, Ancient and Modern.

ABADDON Hebrew word that means "place of destruction." The word occurs six times in the OT, generally referring to the place of the dead (Jb 26:6; 28:22; 31:12; Ps 88:11; Prv 15:11; 27:20). It serves as a synonym for Sheol and is variously translated "hell," "death," "the grave," or "destruction." The same Hebrew word occurs once in the NT in its Greek equivalent, Apollyon (Rv 9:11). Here the idea of destruction is personified as the "angel from the bottomless pit," so the word is often translated "destroyer." Abaddon (or Apollyon) was the angel reigning over the realm of the dead, who appeared after the fifth trumpet in John's vision (Rv 9:1).

See also Sheol.

ABAGTHA One of the seven eunuchs commanded by King Ahasuerus to bring Queen Vashti to his drunken party (Est 1:10).

ABANA Syrian river (modern Barada) running through the city of Damascus. Although Naaman thought the Abana would be more effective than the Jordan River in curing leprosy, he obeyed the prophet Elisha, washed in the Jordan, and was cured (2 Kgs 5:9-14; "Amana" is an alternate textual reading in 5:12).

See also Amana.

ABARIM* Mountainous area located east of the Jordan River and the Dead Sea, and extending northward from the plains of Moab. From the highest point on Mt Nebo, called Pisgah, located in Abarim (2,643 feet; 805 meters), Moses looked into the Promised Land shortly before he died (Dt 32:48-50; 34:1-6).

ABBA Aramaic word for "father," which is applied to God in Mark 14:36; Romans 8:15; and Galatians 4:6. The name expresses a very intimate and inseparable relationship between Christ and the Father and between believers (children) and God (Father).

ABDA
1. Adoniram's father. Adoniram was superintendent of public works under King Solomon (1 Kgs 4:6).
2. Shammua's son, who was a Levite leader in Jerusalem after the exile (Neh 11:17). The same father and son are elsewhere identified as Shemaiah and Obadiah (1 Chr 9:16).

ABDEEL Shelemiah's father. Shelemiah was an officer sent by King Jehoiakim of Judah to arrest Jeremiah and Baruch after the king had read and burned their prophetic scroll (Jer 36:26).

ABDI
1. Member of the Merari clan of Levites. Abdi's grandson Ethan was a musician in David's time (1 Chr 6:44; 15:17).
2. Levite whose son Kish served in Hezekiah's time (2 Chr 29:12). This Abdi has sometimes been confused with Abdi #1.

3. Member of the Elam clan in Ezra's time. This Abdi is listed as one of the Israelites who married a foreign wife after the exile (Ezr 10:26).

ABDIEL Guni's son and father of Ahi (1 Chr 5:15). Ahi was a clan leader in Gad's tribe during the reigns of King Jotham of Judah and King Jeroboam II of Israel (1 Chr 5:15-17).

ABDON (Person)
1. Hillel's son who judged Israel for eight years (Jgs 12:13-15). Abdon was a very wealthy man, as indicated by reference to the 70 donkeys he owned.
2. Shashak's son from Benjamin's tribe who lived in Jerusalem (1 Chr 8:23, 28).
3. Jeiel's oldest son from Benjamin's tribe who lived in Gibeon. This Abdon is mentioned in Saul's genealogy (1 Chr 8:30; 9:36).
4. Micah's son (2 Chr 34:20), also called Acbor, son of Micaiah. See Acbor #2.

ABDON (Place) One of four cities in Asher's territory given to the Levites after the conquest of Canaan, the Promised Land (Jos 21:30; 1 Chr 6:74). Abdon is probably the same as Ebron (Jos 19:28). Today Abdon is called Khirbet 'Abdeh.

ABEDNEGO One of Daniel's three friends who was sentenced to death by Nebuchadnezzar but was protected in the fiery furnace by an angel (Dn 1:7; 3:12-30). See Shadrach, Meshach, and Abednego; Daniel, Additions to (Prayer of Azariah).

ABEL (Person) Second male child of Adam and Eve (Gn 4:2). The name is probably related to Sumerian and Akkadian words meaning "son" and was thus used as a generic term for the human race.

Abel's older brother, Cain, was engaged in agriculture, but Abel himself was a shepherd. When both brothers brought offerings, God accepted Abel's animal sacrifice but rejected Cain's vegetable offering. As a result, Cain became jealous of Abel and killed him.

The narrative indicates that Abel's character was more worthy of God's blessing; hence his offering was accepted and Cain's was not (Gn 4:7). There is no scriptural evidence that cereal or vegetable offerings were less effective as either sin offerings or fellowship meals than offerings involving the shedding of blood, since in later Mosaic law both were prescribed. In the NT Abel is regarded as the first martyr (Mt 23:35; Lk 11:51; Heb 11:4).

ABEL (Place) Fortified border city in upper Galilee to which King David's general Joab pursued the rebel Sheba. After a wise woman of the city negotiated with Joab, the citizens executed Sheba and threw his head over the wall. Joab then called off the siege 2 Sm 20:13-22). The city was later conquered by the Syrian Ben-hadad during a continuing war between King Asa of Judah and King Baasha of Israel. When Asa persuaded Ben-hadad to break a treaty with Baasha, Ben-hadad took a large amount of territory, including Abel, or Abel-beth-maacah, as it was also called (1 Kgs 15:16-20). Still later, Abel-beth-maacah (sometimes called simply Abel of Beth-maacah, or Abel of Beth-maachah) was conquered by Tiglath-pileser III, and its inhabitants were taken captive to Assyria (2 Kgs 15:29). The same city is called Abel-maim ("meadow of water"), emphasizing the productivity of the region (2 Chr 16:4). The town has been identified with modern Tell Abil-el-Qamh.

ABEL-BETH-MAACAH (MAACHAH*) Alternate name for Abel, a fortified city in upper Galilee in 1 Kings 15:20 and 2 Kings 15:29. It was also called Abel of Beth-Maacah (Maachah) in 2 Sm 20:14-15. See Abel (Place).

ABEL-KERAMIM City taken by Jephthah the Israelite judge when he conquered the Ammonites (Jgs 11:33). It was located south of the Jabbok River.

ABEL-MAIM* Alternate name for Abel, a fortified city in upper Galilee, in 2 Chronicles 16:4. See Abel (Place).

ABEL-MEHOLAH Birthplace of the prophet Elisha (1 Kgs 19:16). Here Elijah found Elisha plowing and threw his coat over Elisha's shoulders, symbolizing God's call to Elisha to become a prophet (1 Kgs 19:19-21). The town is earlier mentioned as one place to which the Midianites fled from Gideon's 300 warriors (Jgs 7:22). It is also mentioned in a list of administrative districts set up by King Solomon (1 Kgs 4:12). The most likely modern identification is Khirbet Tell el-Hilu.

ABEL-MIZRAIM Alternate name for Atad, a place in Canaan, in Genesis 50:11. See Atad.

ABEL-SHITTIM Alternate name for Shittim, a place on the plains of Moab, in Numbers 33:49. See Shittim (Place).

ABEZ* KJV form of Ebez, a place in Issachar's territory, in Joshua 19:20. See Ebez.

ABI* Shortened form of Abijah, the name of the mother of Judah's King Hezekiah (2 Kgs 18:2). See Abijah #4.

ABIA*
1. KJV rendering of Abijam, Rehoboam's son and king of Judah, in 1 Chronicles 3:10 and Matthew 1:7. See Abijam.
2. KJV rendering of Abijah in Luke 1:5. See Abijah #6.

ABIAH*
1. KJV translation for Abijah, Samuel's son, in 1 Samuel 8:2 and 1 Chronicles 6:28. See Abijah #1.
2. KJV translation of a Hebrew word in 1 Chronicles 2:24, which renders it as a proper name referring to the wife of Hezron. Most modern translations render it "his father": "Caleb went in to Ephrathah, the wife of Hezron his father" (RSV). The Hebrew is difficult, with different textual families evidently preserving variant readings and thus accounting for the divergences between the versions.
3. KJV translation for Abijah, Becher's son, in 1 Chronicles 7:8. See Abijah #5.

ABI-ALBON Alternate name of Abiel in 2 Samuel 23:31. See Abiel #2.

ABIASAPH Alternate form of Ebiasaph, a descendant of Korah, in Exodus 6:24. See Ebiasaph.

ABIATHAR One of two high priests during the reign of King David. The other high priest was Zadok, who evidently was appointed by David after his conquest of Jerusalem.

Only Abiathar escaped when the priestly families at Nob were massacred at the instigation of King Saul. The priests of Nob had given food and Goliath's sword to David during his escape from the wrath of Saul, thus earning Saul's hatred (1 Sm 21–22). When Abiathar joined David he brought the ephod, which David then used in determining the will of God (1 Sm 23:6, 9-11; 30:7-8). Abiathar was one of the first persons from Saul's administration to support David. His support was formidable because he represented the priesthood of the old tribal league of the line of Eli.

During the last days of David's kingship, his sons struggled for the throne. The two major rivals were Adonijah and Solomon. Abiathar the high priest supported Adonijah's claim to the throne, probably because Adonijah was David's oldest living heir and because David's general Joab, one of the strongest men in the kingdom, supported Adonijah (1 Kgs 1:5-7). Zadok supported Solomon, who actually succeeded David on the throne. Having fallen out of favor with the new king, Abiathar was banished to his estate in Anathoth (1 Kgs 2:26-27), a village about four miles (6.4 kilometers) northeast of Jerusalem.

The relationship of Abiathar to Ahimelech is confusing. Ahimelech could have been the name of both Abiathar's father (1 Sm 22:20; 23:6) and son (2 Sm 8:17; 1 Chr 18:16; 24:6). If each of the references was to the same Ahimelech, then the names were reversed in the later passages. In the NT, Abiathar is mentioned as the high priest when David came to Nob needing food and weapons (Mk 2:26). The OT account says that Ahimelech was the priest at that time (1 Sm 21:1-2). The apparent discrepancy may have resulted from a copyist's error or from the fact that Abiathar as high priest was more prominent than Ahimelech.

ABIB* Canaanite name of the Hebrew month Nisan, about mid-March to mid-April. *See* Calendars, Ancient and Modern.

ABIDA One of Midian's sons. Midian was Abraham's son by his concubine Keturah (Gn 25:2, 4; 1 Chr 1:33).

ABIDAN Gideoni's son and leader of Benjamin's tribe when the Israelites were wandering in the Sinai wilderness after their escape from Egypt (Nm 1:11; 2:22). As leader, he presented his tribe's offering at the consecration of the tabernacle (Nm 7:60-65).

ABIEL

1. Father of Kish and Ner and grandfather of King Saul, according to 1 Samuel 9:1 and 14:51. Other genealogies in 1 Chronicles list Ner, instead of Abiel, as Kish's father and Saul's grandfather (1 Chr 8:33; 9:39). This confusion is due either to a copyist's error or to the possibility that Saul had two relatives named Ner, a great-grandfather and an uncle.
2. Warrior among David's mighty men who were known as "the thirty" (1 Chr 11:32), also called Abi-albon the Arbathite (2 Sm 23:31).

ABIEZER

1. Descendant of Manasseh (Jos 17:1-2). Although Abiezer's father is not named, Abiezer is listed with the descendants of his mother's brother, Gilead (1 Chr 7:18). In Numbers 26:30, Abiezer's name is shortened to Iezer (KJV "Jeezer"), and the family is called Iezerites (KJV "Jeezerites"). Abiezer's family, to which Gideon belonged, was the first clan to respond to Gideon's call to fight the Midianites (Jgs 6:34). Abiezer's descendants were referred to as Abiezrites (Jgs 6:11, 24, 34; 8:32).
2. Member of Benjamin's tribe from Anathoth and warrior among David's mighty men, known as "the thirty" (2 Sm 23:27; 1 Chr 11:28). This Abiezer was commander of the ninth division of the army in the rotation system established by David (1 Chr 27:12).

ABIEZRITE* Member of Abiezer's family (Jgs 6:11, 24, 34; 8:32). *See* Abiezer #1.

ABIGAIL

1. Nabal's wife, who later became the wife of David (1 Sm 25:2-42). Nabal was a wealthy sheep owner whose holdings had been protected by David's men. When David requested provisions in return for that protection, Nabal refused. Enraged, David set out with 400 armed men to destroy Nabal and his house. Abigail had been informed of her husband's behavior and met David with many provisions, taking the blame for her foolish husband. David thanked God for using Abigail to restrain his anger.

   When Nabal woke from a drunken stupor the next morning and learned what had happened, he had a stroke from which he died 10 days later. Abigail then married David and shared his adventurous life among the Philistines (1 Sm 27:3). She was captured by the Amalekites and rescued by David (1 Sm 30:1-19). Abigail went with David to Hebron when he became king of Judah (2 Sm 2:2), and she bore his second son, Chileab (2 Sm 3:3), also called Daniel (1 Chr 3:1).
2. David's sister, who married Jether and gave birth to Amasa (1 Chr 2:16-17). There appears to be confusion as to the ancestry of this Abigail. In 1 Chronicles 2:13-17 she is listed as a daughter of Jesse. However, in 2 Samuel 17:25, her father is identified as Nahash. The discrepancy could be due to scribal error, or Nahash may be another name for Jesse, or the widow of Nahash could have married Jesse.

ABIGAL* RSV rendering of Abigail, David's sister, in 2 Samuel 17:25. *See* Abigail #2.

ABIHAIL Name used for both men and women in the OT.

1. Zuriel's father and a leader of the Merari family of Levites in Israel's wilderness community (Nm 3:35).
2. Abishur's wife, and mother of Ahban and Molid (1 Chr 2:29).
3. Huri's son, a descendant of Gad, living in Gilead and Bashan (1 Chr 5:14).
4. Woman named in 2 Chronicles 11:18 whose relationship to King Rehoboam is not clear from the Hebrew text. In some translations, Abihail seems to be the second wife of Rehoboam. However, only one wife is mentioned at first, so Abihail was probably the mother of Rehoboam's first wife, Mahalath. This Abihail was thus a daughter of Eliab, David's eldest brother. She married her cousin Jerimoth, one of David's sons.
5. Esther's father, and uncle of Mordecai (Est 2:15; 9:29).

ABIHU Second son of Aaron and Elisheba (Ex 6:23; Nm 26:60; 1 Chr 6:3). Abihu and his brother Nadab joined Moses, Aaron, and the 70 elders of Israel in worshiping the glory of God on Mt Sinai (Ex 24:1-11). The four sons of Aaron were made priests along with their father (Ex 28:1), but later Abihu and Nadab were burned to death for offering "a different kind of fire" before the Lord (Lv 10:1, NLT; see also Nm 3:2-4; 26:61; 1 Chr 24:1-2).

ABIHUD One of Bela's nine sons (1 Chr 8:3). Abihud should not be confused with the Abiud of Matthew's genealogy of Christ in the NT.

ABIJAH

1. Samuel's second son who, with his older brother, Joel, was a corrupt judge in Beersheba. Because of the corruption, Israel's leaders demanded to be ruled instead by a king (1 Sm 8:2; 1 Chr 6:28).
2. Son of Jeroboam I of the northern kingdom of Israel. The boy's illness impelled his family to seek guidance from the prophet Ahijah at Shiloh (1 Kgs 14:1-2).
3. Alternate name for Abijam, king of Judah, in 2 Chronicles 12:16–14:1 and Matthew 1:7. *See* Abijam.
4. Ahaz's wife, and mother of King Hezekiah (2 Kgs 18:2, short form "Abi"; 2 Chr 29:1). This Abijah was Zechariah's daughter.
5. Becher's son from Benjamin's tribe (1 Chr 7:8).
6. Levite who headed the eighth of 24 priestly divisions established in David's time (1 Chr 24:10; Lk 1:5).
7. Head of a priestly family who signed Ezra's covenant of faithfulness to God with Nehemiah and others after the exile (Neh 10:7).
8. Head of a priestly family who returned to Jerusalem with Zerubbabel after the exile (Neh 12:4). Perhaps of the same family as #7.

ABIJAM

Rehoboam's son and successor as king of Judah, 913–910 BC (1 Chr 3:10; alternately called "Abijah" in 2 Chr 11:18-22; 12:16; 13:1-22; 14:1). A major focus of Abijam's reign was his war with King Jeroboam I of Israel (2 Chr 13:1-3). Before a decisive battle, Abijam stood on Mt Zemaraim and shouted condemnation of Jeroboam's political divisiveness and religious idolatry (2 Chr 13:4-12). Abijam and his army then prayed for God's help in their precarious military position. Against two-to-one odds, they fought their way out of an ambush and won a stunning victory over Jeroboam (2 Chr 13:13-19). Abijam's reign in the southern kingdom of Judah was summed up rather unfavorably in 1 Kings 15:1-8: "He committed the same sins as his father before him, and his heart was not right with the LORD his God, as the heart of his ancestor David had been" (v 3, NLT). But God had promised to keep David's descendants on the throne in Jerusalem (1 Kgs 11:36), so Abijam's son Asa succeeded him. Being of David's line, Abijam was an ancestor of Jesus, the Christ (Mt 1:7, "Abijah").

See also Israel, History of; Chronology of the Bible (Old Testament); Genealogy of Jesus Christ.

ABILENE

Region on the east side of the Anti-Lebanon Mountains in Syria. The district took its name from the capital city of Abila, located about 18 miles (29 kilometers) from Damascus. At the time of John the Baptist, Abilene was governed by the tetrarch Lysanias (Lk 3:1).

ABIMAEL

One of the many sons or descendants of Joktan, and thus a descendant of Shem (Gn 10:28; 1 Chr 1:22).

ABIMELECH

Royal title for Philistine rulers, similar to the designation "pharaoh" among the Egyptians and "agag" among the Amalekites.

1. King of Gerar in Abraham's time. At Gerar, a city a few miles south of Gaza, Abraham presented his wife as his sister out of fear for his life (Gn 20:1-18), as he had once done in Egypt (Gn 12:10-20). Because of this, Sarah was taken into Abimelech's harem. But Abimelech was warned by God in a dream not to come near her on pain of death because she was a married woman, so she was restored to her husband. The same Abimelech and Abraham later entered into a treaty to clarify water rights in the Negev Desert at Beersheba (Gn 21:22-34).
2. King of Gerar in Isaac's time. Isaac, too, passed off his wife, Rebekah, as his sister at Gerar. Abimelech, perhaps remembering the near judgment on his predecessor, acted decisively to protect Rebekah's integrity. He proclaimed a death penalty on any who touched her or her husband (Gn 26:1-11). Abimelech asked Isaac to leave Philistine territory because of overcrowding and continuing dispute over water (Gn 26:12-22). Eventually, at Beersheba, Isaac and Abimelech ended their hostility by renewing the treaty made by Abraham and the earlier Abimelech (Gn 26:26-33).
3. Gideon's son by a concubine in Shechem (Jgs 8:31). After his father's death, Abimelech conspired with his mother's family to assassinate his 70 half brothers. Only one of them, Jotham, escaped (Jgs 9:1-5). In Abimelech's third year of rule, he cruelly suppressed a rebellion (Jgs 9:22-49). Eventually his skull was crushed by a millstone thrown down by a woman on a tower. Abimelech ordered his armor bearer to kill him with a sword so that no one could say he had been killed by a woman (Jgs 9:53-57).
4. Achish, king of the Philistine city of Gath (1 Sm 21:10-15).
5. Abiathar's son, a priest associated with Zadok in David's time (1 Chr 18:16).

ABINADAB

1. Resident of Kiriath-jearim to whose home the ark of God was brought on its return by the Philistines (1 Sm 6:21–7:2).
2. Jesse's second son, and brother of David (1 Sm 16:8; 17:13; 1 Chr 2:13). This Abinadab served in Saul's army for part of the Philistine war.
3. KJV form of Ben-abinadab, one of King Solomon's administrative officers in 1 Kings 4:11. *See* Ben-abinadab.
4. One of Saul's sons (1 Chr 8:33; 10:2).

ABINOAM

Barak's father. Barak was the companion of Deborah, an Israelite judge, in the war against the Canaanites (Jgs 4:6, 12; 5:1, 12).

ABIRAM

1. One of Eliab's two sons. Abiram and his brother Dathan joined in an uprising against Moses and Aaron. At Moses' word, the ground split open beneath the two rebellious brothers and everything associated with them was swallowed up in a massive earthquake (Nm 16:1-33).
2. Hiel's oldest son, who died prematurely when his father presumptuously rebuilt Jericho (1 Kgs 16:34). Joshua's prophetic curse was thereby fulfilled (Jos 6:26).

ABISHAG

Beautiful young woman from Shunem who was appointed to care for David during his last days (1 Kgs 1:1-4). After David's death, Adonijah asked permission from his half brother King Solomon to marry Abishag. In the ancient Near East, to claim the concubine of a deceased king was to claim the throne. Enraged, Solomon ordered Adonijah to be killed (1 Kgs 2:13-25).

ABISHAI

David's nephew, son of Zeruiah (by an unnamed father) and brother of Joab and Asahel (1 Chr 2:16). Abishai volunteered to accompany David to Saul's camp one night and would have killed the sleeping Saul if David had not restrained him (1 Sm 26:6-12). He also helped Joab kill Abner, Saul's general, in revenge for the death of another brother (2 Sm 3:30). Later Abishai won a victory over the Edomites (1 Chr 18:12-13) and was second in command in a decisive battle against the Ammonites (1 Chr 19:10-15). Often vengeful and cruel, Abishai wanted to behead the spiteful Shimei during Absalom's rebellion, but again David intervened (2 Sm 16:5-12; 19:21-23). When King David fled beyond the Jordan, Abishai was given command of one of David's three divisions that crushed the rebellion (2 Sm 18:1-15).

In a later battle with the Philistines, Abishai saved David's life by killing the giant Ishbi-benob (2 Sm 21:15-17). He ranked among David's bravest warriors (2 Sm 23:18-19; 1 Chr 11:20-21).

ABISHALOM* Alternate name for Absalom, King David's son, in 1 Kings 15:2, 10. *See* Absalom.

ABISHUA

1. Aaron's great-grandson, son of Phinehas and ancestor of Ezra (1 Chr 6:4-5, 50; Ezr 7:5). Abishua's name also appears in the apocryphal genealogy of Ezra (1 Esd 8:2; 2 Esd 1:2).
2. Bela's son, and grandson of Benjamin (1 Chr 8:4).

ABISHUR Shammai's son and the father of Ahban and Molid from Judah's tribe. Abishur's wife was Abihail (1 Chr 2:28-29).

ABITAL Mother of King David's fifth son, Shephatiah (2 Sm 3:4; 1 Chr 3:3).

ABITUB Son of Shaharaim and Hushim from Benjamin's tribe (1 Chr 8:11).

ABIUD Individual listed in Matthew's genealogy of Christ in the NT as Eliakim's father (Mt 1:13). *See* Genealogy of Jesus Christ.

ABNER Ner's son and Saul's cousin. Abner was commander of Saul's army (1 Sm 14:50; 17:55). Highly respected by Saul, he even ate at the king's table together with David and Jonathan (1 Sm 20:25).

Five years after Saul's death, Abner made Ishbosheth, Saul's son, king over Israel (2 Sm 2:8-9). War between Ishbosheth and David, who then was king over Judah, lasted for two years. Abner was in command of Ishbosheth's army, Joab of David's, in a series of skirmishes. David's position was generally stronger, but Abner became a powerful figure among Saul's followers.

Although only the king had a right to sexual relationships with the previous king's concubines, Abner slept with Saul's concubine Rizpah, perhaps planning to take over the kingdom himself at the first opportunity. When Ishbosheth rebuked him, Abner became so angry that he broke with Ishbosheth and came to terms with David. David showed him great respect, and in return, Abner promised to bring the whole of Israel over to David. Joab, however, feared Abner's influence with the king and killed him, claiming revenge for the death of his brother at Abner's hand in battle. Abner was honored with a public funeral and mourning, an honor given only to a ruler or great leader. King David wept aloud at the tomb, and even the people wept with him (2 Sm 3:7-34). David condemned Joab for murdering Abner.

See also David; Israel, History of.

ABOMINATION Repugnant or detestable act, person, or thing. The idea of abomination derives from the specific demands God's holiness makes upon his people.

Adjectives frequently used for abominations in the OT are "abhorrent," "loathsome," "unclean," and "rejected."

Of the four major Hebrew words translated "abomination," the one most frequently used indicates violation of an established custom or ritual that, in turn, brings the judgment of God. Examples range from defective sacrifices (Dt 17:1) to magic and divination (Dt 18:12) or idolatrous practices (2 Kgs 16:3). A second Hebrew word refers to the meat of certain kinds of animals that was ritually defiling, whether touched or eaten (Lv 11:10-13). A third word designates three-day-old sacrificial meat (Lv 7:18). A fourth word refers almost exclusively to idolatrous objects of pagan origin (Jer 4:1; 7:30). Apart from the specialized usage of "abomination of desolation," the Greek word for "abomination" is used infrequently in the NT (Lk 16:15; Rom 2:22; Ti 1:16; Rv 17:4-5; 21:8, 27) and is translated by many English words. The primary connotation is anything that is abhorrent to a holy God.

See also Cleanness and Uncleanness, Regulations Concerning; Dietary Laws (After Moses).

ABOMINATION OF DESOLATION

Phrase used in Daniel, 1 Maccabees, Matthew, and Mark to designate a detestable object of pagan idolatry so loathsome to God that he would enact desolating judgment.

In Daniel's vision of coming abomination, a detestable object would be set up in the temple in Jerusalem (Dn 11:31) 1,290 days after the beginning of a period of sacrilege (Dn 12:11), thus destroying the temple's holiness and rendering it unclean by ceremonial and ethical standards. In 1 Maccabees it is recorded that the Syrian Antiochus Epiphanes invaded Palestine (167 BC) and erected a desolating sacrilege, probably a statue of Zeus, upon the altar of burnt offering in the temple (1 Macc 1:54).

Jesus used the phrase "abomination of desolation" in answering the disciples' questions concerning the destruction of the temple and the general course of the age until his return (Mt 24:1-31; Mk 13:1-27; Lk 21:5-28). In alluding to the Daniel passages, Jesus predicted that something analogous to the destruction by Antiochus would occur. Jesus applied the prediction and fulfillment of Daniel's prophecy in part to the coming Roman desecration, which did take place in AD 70. Jesus warned that the erection of the abomination of desolation ("desolating sacrilege," RSV) was a signal to flee the city of Jerusalem (Mt 24:15-16; Mk 13:14).

The Greek version of the book of Ezekiel sometimes used "lawlessness" in place of abomination, leading to the association of "man of lawlessness" (man of abomination) with the detestable sacrilege of the Antichrist (2 Thes 2:3). A similar theme is reflected in the book of Revelation, where the image of the creature or beast from the sea symbolizes the power of the forces of evil demanding obedience and submission (Rv 13:1-10).

See also Antichrist; Daniel, Book of; Abomination.

ABRAHAM One of the Bible's most significant personalities, whom God called from the city of Ur to become patriarch of God's own people.

Abraham's name was originally Abram, meaning "[the] father is exalted." When he was given that name by his parents, they were probably participants in the

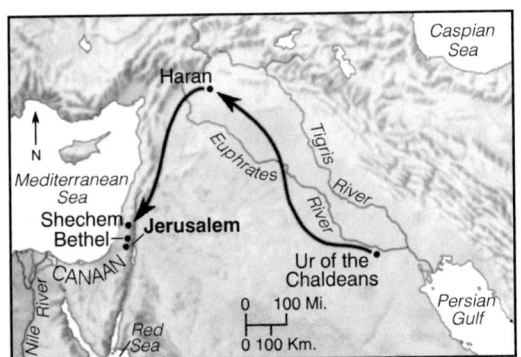

Abram's Journey to Canaan Abram, Sarai, and Lot traveled from Ur of the Chaldeans to Canaan by way of Haran.

moon cult of Ur, so the father deity suggested in his old name could have been the moon god or another pagan deity. God changed Abram's name to Abraham (Gn 17:5), partly, no doubt, to indicate a clear-cut separation from pagan roots. The new name, interpreted by the biblical text as meaning "father of a multitude," was also a statement of God's promise to Abraham that he would have many descendants, as well as a significant test of his faith in God—since he was 99 years old at the time and his childless wife was 90 (Gn 11:30; 17:1-4, 17).

Abraham's Life The story of Abram begins in Genesis 11, where his family relationships are recorded (Gn 11:26-32). Terah, Abram's father, was named after the moon deity worshiped at Ur. Terah had three sons, Abram, Nahor, and Haran. Haran, the father of Lot, died before the family left Ur. Terah took Lot, Abram, and Abram's wife, Sarai, from Ur to go to Canaan but settled at the city of Haran (v 31). It is stated in Acts 7:2-4 that Abraham heard the call of God to leave for a new land while he was still in Ur.

A note of major importance to the course of Abram's life is found in Genesis 11:30: "Sarai was not able to have any children" (NLT). The problem of Sarai's barrenness provided the basis for great crises of faith, promise, and fulfillment in the lives of Abram and Sarai.

ABRAHAM, THE FRIEND OF GOD
Referred to as the "friend of God" (2 Chr 20:7; Jas 2:23, NLT), Abraham played an important role in Hebrew history. Through Abraham's life, God revealed a program of "election" and "covenant," which culminated in the work of Jesus Christ. God said to Abraham, "All the families of the earth will be blessed through you" (Gn 12:3, NLT). Centuries later, the apostle Paul explained that the full import of God's promise was seen in the preaching of the gospel to all nations and the response of faith in Christ, which signifies believers from all families of the earth as sons of Abraham (Gal 3:6-9).

After Terah's death, God told Abram, "Leave your country, your relatives, and your father's house, and go to the land that I will show you." This command was the basis of a "covenant," in which God promised to make Abram the founder of a new nation in that new land (Gn 12:1-3, NLT). Abram, trusting God's promise, left Haran at the age of 74. Entering Canaan, he went first to Shechem, an important Canaanite royal city between Mt Gerizim and Mt Ebal. Near the oak of Moreh, a Canaanite shrine, God appeared to him (12:7). Abram built an altar at Shechem, then moved to the vicinity of Bethel and again built an altar to

the Lord (12:8). The expression "to call on the name of the LORD" (RSV) means more than just to pray. Rather, Abram made a proclamation, declaring the reality of God to the Canaanites in their centers of false worship. Later Abram moved to Hebron by the oaks of Mamre, where again he built an altar to worship God. Another blessing given in a vision (15:1) led Abram to exclaim that he was still childless and that Eliezer of Damascus was his heir (15:2). Discovery of the Nuzi documents has helped to clarify that otherwise obscure statement. According to Hurrian custom, a childless couple of station and substance would adopt an heir. Often a slave, the heir would be responsible for the burial and mourning of his adoptive parents. If a son should be born after the adoption of a slave-heir, the natural son would of course supplant him. Thus God's response to Abram's question is directly to the point: "No, your servant will not be your heir, for you will have a son of your own to inherit everything I am giving you" (Gn 15:4, NLT). God then made a covenant with Abram insuring an heir, a nation, and the land.

ABRAHAM'S BOSOM
Figure of speech probably derived from the Roman custom of reclining on one's left side at meals with the guest of honor at the bosom of his host (cf. Jn 13:23-25). It was used by Jesus in the story of Lazarus as a description of paradise (Lk 16:22-23). In rabbinical writings, as well as 4 Maccabees 13:17, righteous people were thought to be welcomed at death by Abraham, Isaac, and Jacob. Jesus, probably aware of this, was also alluding to the "messianic banquet," an image he used a number of times. Thus, in the world to come, the godly poor like Lazarus would not only be welcomed by Abraham but would occupy the place of honor next to him at the banquet.
See also Heaven; Paradise.

Abram was 86 years old when Ishmael was born. When Abram was 99, the Lord appeared to the aged patriarch and again reaffirmed his covenant promise of a son and blessing (Gn 17). Circumcision was added as the seal of covenantal relationship (17:9-14), and at that point the names Abram and Sarai were changed to Abraham and Sarah (17:5, 15). Abraham's response to the promise of another son was to laugh: "Then Abraham bowed down to the ground, but he laughed to himself in disbelief. 'How could I become a father at the age of one hundred?' he wondered. 'Besides, Sarah is ninety; how could she have a baby?'" (Gn 17:17, NLT).

Genesis 18 and 19 recount the total destruction of two cities of the Jordan plain, Sodom and Gomorrah. Chapter 18 begins with three individuals seeking comfort in the heat of the day. Abraham offered refreshment and a meal to his guests. They turned out to be no ordinary travelers, however, but the Angel of the Lord along with two other angels (18:1-2; 19:1). There is reason to believe that the Angel of the Lord was God himself (18:17, 33). Another announcement of a promised son made Sarah laugh in unbelief and then deny having laughed (18:12-15).

Genesis 21 to 23 form the climax of the story of Abraham. At long last, when Abraham was 100 years old and his wife 90, "the LORD did exactly what he had promised" (Gn 21:1, NLT). The joy of the aged couple on the birth of their long-promised son could not be contained. Both Abraham and Sarah had laughed in unbelief in the days of promise; now they laughed in joy as God had "the last laugh." The baby, born at the time God promised, was named Isaac ("he laughs!"). Sarah said, "God has brought me laughter! All who hear about this will laugh with me" (Gn 21:6, NLT).

The laughter over Isaac's birth subsided entirely in the test of Abraham's faith described in chapter 22, God's command to sacrifice Isaac. Only when one has experienced vicariously with Abraham the long 25 years of God's promise of a son can one imagine the trauma of such a supreme test. Just as the knife was about to fall, and only then, did the angel of God break the silence of heaven with the call, "Abraham!" (22:11). The name of promise, "father of a multitude," took on its most significant meaning when Abraham's son was spared and the test was explained: "I know that you truly fear God. You have not withheld even your beloved son from me" (Gn 22:12, NLT).

Those words were coupled with a promise implicit in the discovery of a ram caught in the thicket. The Lord provided an alternative sacrifice, a substitute. The place was named "the Lord will provide." Christian believers generally see the whole episode as looking ahead to God's provision of his only Son, Jesus Christ, as a sacrifice for the sins of the world.

See also Covenant; Patriarchs, Period of the; Israel, History of; "Abraham's Bosom" on page 7; Sarah #1.

ABRAM Original name of Abraham (Gn 11:26). *See* Abraham.

ABRON Brook or wadi mentioned in the book of Judith, located on the route of attack of Nebuchadnezzar's general, Holofernes (2:24). Some early commentators identified it with the biblical Jabbok (Nm 21:24). Others called it the Cherbon, possibly through a misreading of Habor (2 Kgs 17:6).

ABRONAH Place near Elath where the Israelites camped on their journey from Egypt to Canaan (Nm 33:34-35). *See* Wilderness Wanderings.

ABSALOM Son of King David and his wife Maacah (2 Sm 3:3). The name is also spelled Abishalom (1 Kgs 15:2, 10). Absalom was a handsome young prince who was noted for his long, full hair (2 Sm 14:25-26). He had a beautiful sister, Tamar, who was raped by their half brother Amnon. After dishonoring Tamar, Amnon refused to marry her (2 Sm 13:1-20).

Absalom took his dejected sister into his own house, expecting his father, David, to punish Amnon for his incestuous act. After two years of suppressed rage and hatred, Absalom plotted his own revenge. He gave a feast for King David and his princes at his country estate. Although David did not attend, Amnon did and was murdered by Absalom's servants after Absalom got him drunk. Then, afraid of King David's anger, Absalom fled across the Jordan River to King Talmai of Geshur, his mother's father (2 Sm 13:21-39).

After three years in exile, Absalom was called back to Jerusalem through the efforts of David's general, Joab, and a wise woman from Tekoa. After two years he was back in full favor with the king (2 Sm 14), and in that position he began to maneuver himself to gain the throne. He put on an impressive public relations campaign, in the process undermining confidence in his father, the king (2 Sm 15:1-6).

Eventually, Absalom plotted a rebellion against David, gathering supporters in Hebron from all over Israel. After Ahithophel, one of David's wisest counselors, joined Absalom, the prince announced his own kingship. By the time news of Absalom's conspiracy reached him, David was unable to do anything but flee from Jerusalem (2 Sm 15; Ps 3).

Absalom arrived in Jerusalem without a struggle, and Ahithophel asked permission to attack David immediately with 12,000 troops. But Hushai, David's secret agent in Absalom's court, advised Absalom instead to take the time to mobilize the entire nation against David. He also used flattery, suggesting that Absalom himself should lead the attack. Absalom preferred Hushai's advice, and Ahithophel out of desperation committed suicide. Meanwhile, Hushai sent word of Absalom's plans to David by two priests, Zadok and Abiathar. With this information, David crossed the Jordan and camped at Mahanaim (2 Sm 16–17).

Absalom led his forces across the Jordan to do battle in the forest of Ephraim. David's loyal forces were under the able generalship of Joab, Abishai, and Ittai the Gittite, who routed Absalom's forces. Absalom himself fled on a mule, but his long hair got caught in the branches of an oak tree, and he was left dangling helplessly. Joab, leading his men in pursuit, came upon Absalom and killed him. Joab's men threw the body in a pit and piled stones on it (2 Sm 18:1-18). Absalom's death stunned David, who had given explicit orders to keep Absalom from harm. David moaned: "O my son Absalom! My son, my son Absalom! If only I could have died instead of you! O Absalom, my son, my son!" (2 Sm 18:33, NLT). In his excessive grief, David took no notice that a serious rebellion had been crushed until Joab reminded him that David's followers had risked their lives for him (2 Sm 19:1-8). *See* David.

ABUBUS Ptolemy's father. Ptolemy was a military governor of Jericho who treacherously killed his father-in-law Simon Maccabeus and two of Simon's sons in 134 BC (1 Macc 16:11-17). *See* Maccabean Period.

ABYSS Bottomless, immeasurable deep or underworld. *See* Bottomless Pit.

ACACIA Palestinian wood used in the construction of the ark of the covenant (Ex 25:10). *See* Plants.

ACBOR
1. Father of the Edomite king Baal-hanan before the establishment of Israel's monarchy (Gn 36:38-39; 1 Chr 1:49).
2. Micaiah's son, courtier of King Josiah of the southern kingdom of Judah. Josiah sent Acbor in a delegation to ask Huldah the prophetess about the newly found Book of the Law (2 Kgs 22:12-14). Acbor was also referred to as Abdon, son of Micah (2 Chr 34:20). He was the father of Elnathan (Jer 26:22; 36:12).

ACCAD* One of the three cities (Babel, Erech, and Accad, RSV) in the plains between the Tigris and Euphrates Rivers said to have been founded by Nimrod (Gn 10:10). "Akkadian" (from Accad) has become a general designation for the Semitic language of Mesopotamia from the days of Sargon (c. 2360 BC) through Assyrian and Babylonian times.

ACCHO*, ACCO Major Palestinian port city from the earliest Canaanite period. The only clear OT reference to Acco is the statement that at the time of Israel's conquest of Canaan, Asher's tribe failed to drive out its inhabitants (Jgs 1:31). Acco is frequently mentioned in Middle and New Kingdom Egyptian texts and in Assyrian records. Presumably Acco came under Israelite control during David's reign and was among the 20 cities given by Solomon to King Hiram of Tyre (1 Kgs 9:11-14). In later centuries, Acco was captured by Alexander the Great of

Macedonia. It was eventually rebuilt and renamed Ptolemais (Acts 21:7).

ACCOS Name of Hakkoz in 1 Maccabees 8:17. *See* Hakkoz.

ACELDAMA* KJV form of Akeldama, meaning "Field of Blood," in Acts 1:19. *See* Blood, Field of.

Aerial View of Acco

ACHAIA Name generally used in NT times to refer to the entire Greek peninsula south of Thessalonica. *See* Greece, Greek.

ACHAICUS Early Christian convert in Corinth. Achaicus, Stephanas, and Fortunatus were visiting Paul in Ephesus when he wrote 1 Corinthians (1 Cor 16:17). It was probably Achaicus and his companions who brought Paul a letter from the Corinthian church (1 Cor 7:1) and returned with Paul's reply.

ACHAN, ACHAR* Member of Judah's tribe who kept some of the spoils from the Israelite victory at Jericho in violation of Joshua's order and God's command (Jos 6:1–7:1). A subsequent Israelite defeat at Ai, a weaker city than Jericho, revealed God's anger to Joshua. With God's help, Joshua determined which of the Israelites had been guilty of disobedience. Achan confessed that he had buried a robe and some gold and silver from Jericho in his tent (Jos 7:20-22). The recovered loot was taken to the valley of Achor (meaning "trouble," "calamity"), where Achan and his family were stoned. In the Hebrew text, 1 Chronicles 2:7 gives Achan's name as Achar ("disaster") because he "brought disaster on Israel by taking plunder that had been set apart for the LORD" (NLT).

ACHAZ* KJV form of Ahaz, Judah's king, in Matthew 1:9. *See* Ahaz #1.

ACHBOR* Alternate spelling for Acbor. *See* Acbor.

ACHIM* Descendant of Zerubbabel, listed in the NT as an ancestor of Jesus (Mt 1:14). *See* Genealogy of Jesus Christ.

ACHIOR The book of Judith introduces Achior as "leader of all the Ammonites" (5:5). The main part of Judith 5 is devoted to Achior's version of the history of Israel and culminates in his warning Holofernes that God would protect Israel. At this the hearers threatened to tear him limb from limb. Holofernes then handed Achior over to the Israelites and Uzziah provided his hospitality (Jdt 6:1ff.). After Holofernes' demise, Achior was brought to view the Assyrian general's severed head. Seeing this he threw himself at the feet of Judith, pro-

claimed her praise, recognized the mighty works of God, accepted circumcision, and was incorporated in the house of Israel forever (Jdt 14:6-10).

ACHISH King of the Philistine city of Gath. Although David had killed Goliath, Gath's champion (1 Sm 17), David later fled from Saul to Achish's court. Realizing his mistake, David pretended to be crazy in order to preserve his life. His feigned madness caused Achish to throw him out (1 Sm 21:10-15), but later when David came back to Gath with a band of 600 guerrilla fighters, Achish gave him the city of Ziklag as a base of operations (1 Sm 27:1-7). Achish thought David's men were raiding the Israelites, not realizing they were actually wiping out Philistine towns (1 Sm 27:8-12).

ACHMETHA* KJV form of Ecbatana, a Persian city, in Ezra 6:2. *See* Ecbatana.

ACHOR Valley that received its name when Achan, the troubler of Israel, was stoned and burned there (Jos 7:24-26; cf. 1 Chr 2:7). Achor was on the northern boundary of Judah's tribal allotment (Jos 15:7). Later, the valley is mentioned in prophecies of Israel's future blessings. A valley once known as the scene of Israel's trouble would become "a door of hope" and a place for joyful singing (Hos 2:15); a place of relative desolation would one day become a place for herds to lie down (Is 65:10). The valley of Achor is commonly identified as the Buqei'ah.

ACHSA*, ACHSAH* Caleb's daughter (1 Chr 2:49). Othniel, Caleb's nephew, accepted his uncle's challenge to capture Kiriath-sepher in order to marry Achsah. She persuaded Othniel to ask her father, Caleb, for a field, and she herself asked Caleb for two springs of water, a necessity for life in the desert (Jos 15:16-19; Jgs 1:12-15).

ACHSHAPH* Canaanite royal city in Joshua's time. Its king joined an alliance led by Jabin, king of Hazor, against Israel in a battle at the springs of Merom (Jos 11:1). After Israel's decisive victory, Achshaph's king was one of 31 Canaanite kings conquered by Joshua (Jos 12:20), fulfilling God's promise to deliver kings into Israel's hand (Dt 7:24). The city was subsequently assigned to Asher's tribe for an inheritance (Jos 19:25).

ACHZIB* KJV form of Aczib. *See* Aczib.

ACRA* Citadel of Jerusalem during the Seleucid and Hasmonean periods. The citadel was located on a high point near the temple. An exceptionally strong fortress, the Acra housed the garrison and controlled the city throughout the Maccabean wars. The Seleucid government considered the Acra a royal stronghold to be administered separately from the rest of Judea. At times, one armed force held the Acra and its opponent held the city itself, so that the fortress almost became an independent city. Josephus made mention of two forts called Acra. The earlier citadel was captured by Antiochus III in 198 BC. That Acra must be identical with the temple fortress of the Persian and Ptolemaic periods, the "castle" of Nehemiah 7:2 (RSV). The site later became the fortress called Antonia in the Roman period.

A new citadel, the Acra proper, was later built by the Seleucids. Antiochus IV Epiphanes (ruled 175–164 BC), after a humiliating defeat in Alexandria by the Romans, decided to abolish all Jewish worship practices. In 167 BC, he violated the most sacred Jewish laws by constructing an altar to the Greek god Zeus in the temple at Jerusalem and perhaps by sacrificing a pig on it (1 Macc 1:20-64;

The Acropolis in Athens with the Parthenon

2 Macc 6:1-6). The next year Antiochus sent a garrison to build the Acra and maintain his religious reforms, primarily to see that no aspect of the Jewish religion was practiced in the city. The Acra also served as a storehouse for food and loot plundered from the city. The Jews considered it "an ambush against the sanctuary, an evil adversary of Israel continually" (1 Macc 1:36).

Josephus reported that Simon, the second of the Maccabean brothers, captured the Acra in 142 BC and spent three years leveling both the fort and the hill on which it stood. Josephus's account is questioned, however, because other accounts mention Simon as ritually cleansing the citadel and using it to maintain the city's security (see 1 Macc 13:50; 14:37).

ACRABA Site where a contingent of the Edomite-Ammonite division of Holofernes' army was stationed during the siege of Bethulia (Jdt 7:18). Acraba was probably located about 10 miles (16 kilometers) southeast of Shechem, modern Nablus.

ACRE Measure of an area of land. Literally, the Hebrew word means "yoke" and probably refers to the amount of land a yoke of oxen could plow in a day. *See* Weights and Measures.

ACROCORINTH* Massive, precipitous hilltop 1,886 feet (575 meters) above sea level to the south of the ancient city of Corinth. It overlooked the Isthmus of Corinth and controlled land traffic between central Greece and the Peloponesus, as well as sea traffic from Italy passing to the east through the Gulf of Corinth and the Saronic Gulf.

The temple of Aphrodite on the summit was unjustly notorious in antiquity. The geographer Strabo (c. AD 20) said that 1,000 prostitutes served at the temple during Greece's golden age. The Athenians may have perpetuated the myth of Corinthian licentiousness. "Not every man's ship is bound for Corinth" was a common saying among the ancient Greeks. Modern scholars tend to discount Strabo's statement, though it still influences interpretation of Paul's letters to the Corinthians. It is possible that the Corinthians were no less moral than

the residents of other cities of mainland Greece. Even Strabo could find only a small temple of Aphrodite, of which there are virtually no archaeological remains.

ACROPOLIS* This term is a combination of the Greek *akros* ("highest") *polis* ("city"), which originally applied to any fortified natural stronghold or citadel in ancient Greece. The typical acropolis was built on a hill as a place of refuge. The slopes and base of the hill often became the site of a city. The acropolis of Athens was surmounted by the Parthenon, a Doric temple for Athena, Greek goddess of wisdom. Built in the fifth century BC, it is the masterpiece of Greek architecture. Acts 17:34 records that Paul preached at the Areopagus ("hill of Ares"), a low hill northwest of the acropolis and there converted a member of the Athenian council.

ACROSTIC* Poetic composition in which the first letters of successive lines or stanzas spell out the alphabet, a word, or a motto. The Hebrew prophets and poets often used an alphabetical acrostic as a poetic or mnemonic (memory) device (see Pss 9; 10; 25; 34; 37; 111; 112; 119; 145; Prv 31:10-31; Lam 1–4; Na 1).

ACSAH *See* Achsa, Achsah.

ACSHAPH *See* Achshaph.

ACTS OF THE APOSTLES, Book of the NT book presenting the history of the early church and written as a sequel to the Gospel of Luke. In the arrangement of the NT books, Acts comes after the four Gospels and before the Epistles.

PREVIEW
•Author
•Date, Origin, Destination
•Background and Content
•Purpose

Author The book of Acts does not state clearly who its writer is, but the general consensus is that Luke was its author.

Early church tradition from the second century states that Acts (as well as the third Gospel) was written by a traveling companion and fellow worker of the apostle Paul. That companion is identified in Colossians 4:14 as "Luke, the beloved physician" (NASB) and mentioned among Paul's coworkers (Col 4:10-17; see also 2 Tm 4:11; Phlm 1:24).

Strong support for the tradition that the author of Acts was a companion of Paul comes from the second half of the book recounting Paul's ministry. There, several narratives are told in the first person plural:

1. "That night Paul had a vision. He saw a man from Macedonia in northern Greece, pleading with him, 'Come over here and help us.' So we decided to leave for Macedonia at once, for we could only conclude that God was calling us to preach the Good News there" (16:9-10, NLT).
2. "They went ahead and waited for us at Troas . . . we boarded a ship at Philippi in Macedonia and five days later arrived in Troas, where we stayed a week" (20:5-6, NLT).
3. "When the time came, we set sail for Italy" (27:1, NLT).

These "we" sections (16:9-18; 20:5-21:18; 27:1-28:16) sound like part of a travel narrative or diary written by an eyewitness who accompanied Paul from Troas to Philippi on his second missionary journey; from Philippi to Miletus on the third; from Miletus to Jerusalem; and from Caesarea to Rome. Since the style and vocabulary of these travel narratives resemble those of the rest of the book, it is highly probably that the diarist was also the author of the entire book.

The sophisticated literary style and polished use of the Greek language in the book, as well as the fact that it is addressed to someone called Theophilus (possibly a high-ranking Roman official), provide strong support for the tradition that Luke was a gentile convert to Christianity. His consistent and frequent use of the Greek OT may indicate that he had been a gentile "God-fearer" before conversion to the new faith.

Date, Origin, Destination The question of the date and place of the origin of Acts continues to be debated.

There are no clear indications in the book itself. With regard to its destination, however, Luke did not leave any doubt. In the opening verse he addresses a certain Theophilus, to whom he had already written an earlier book about the life of Jesus. There can be no doubt that he was referring to the work we know as the Gospel of Luke. In the preface to that Gospel (Lk 1:1-4), Luke clearly stated his purpose for writing and addressed his account to the "most honorable Theophilus." It is not clear who that person was. Some interpreters think that Theophilus (which means "dear to God" or "lover of God") stands for Christian readers in general rather than any specific individual. However, the designation "most honorable" argues against such an assumption. That ascription was a common title of honor, designating a person with official standing in the Roman sociopolitical order (cf. use of the title for Felix, Acts 23:26; 24:2; and for Festus, 26:25). It is thus likely that Luke intended his two-volume work for an official representative of Roman society.

When was Acts written? Some scholars date it in the last quarter of the first century. Since the Gospel was written first, and since Luke based his story of Jesus on eyewitness accounts and written sources (among which was possibly the Gospel of Mark, probably written in the 60s), Acts should not be dated much before AD 85. Proponents of such a late date claim support from the theology of Acts, which they see as picturing a Christian church settled into history, adjusted to the prospect of a lengthy period before the Lord's return. Since expectation of the Lord's imminent return was fanned into a living flame by the Jewish revolt and the fall of Jerusalem in AD 70, time must be allowed for that flame to have died down a bit.

Other scholars date Acts around AD 70 or shortly thereafter. The Jewish rebellion of AD 66-70, which culminated in the destruction of Jerusalem, brought the Jewish faith—legal until then—into disrepute. The Christian movement, which had been accepted as a Jewish sect, became suspect. Christians were increasingly charged with being enemies of Rome. A study of Acts shows that among a number of purposes (see below), Luke seems to have been defending the Christians against the charge of hostility toward the state. He

Key Places in Acts The apostle Paul, whose missionary journeys fill much of this book, traveled tremendous distances as he tirelessly spread the gospel across much of the Roman Empire. His combined trips, by land and ship, equal more than 13,000 miles (20,917 meters).

Modern names and boundaries are shown in gray.

showed how Roman officials repeatedly testified to the complete innocence of Christians and above all else of Paul (16:39; 18:14-17; 19:37; 23:29; 25:25; 26:32). Luke also made it clear that Paul was allowed to carry on his mission with full approval of Roman officials in the very heart of the imperial capital (28:16-31).

A still earlier date, closer to Paul's Roman imprisonment (early 60s), has been advocated by a number of scholars. There are two compelling reasons: (1) The abrupt ending of Acts, describing Paul carrying on a ministry in Rome before his trial had commenced, may indicate that Luke was writing at that point. It is possible, of course, that Luke ended his story with Paul preaching the gospel in Rome because one of his purposes had been accomplished: namely, showing how the gospel spread from Jerusalem to Rome. But it seems highly unlikely that Luke would close his history without Paul's defense of the gospel before Caesar himself if that had already happened. (2) The most appropriate period for Luke's history, with its defense of the Christian movement against all kinds of accusations from both Jews and Gentiles, is the period when Christianity was becoming suspect but was not yet proscribed. That was the time before the start of the persecutions under Nero in AD 64. The early date would correspond with the contention that Luke was with Paul during his Roman imprisonment and that he wrote his history in Rome while waiting for Paul's trial to begin. It is possible that Luke's work was partially intended to influence the verdict. Luke presented a picture of Christianity and of Paul that he hoped would enable Paul to continue his work among the Gentiles.

Background and Content Luke grounds his documentary of the rapid expansion of Christianity in the history of the Roman Empire and Palestine during the three decades from AD 30 to 60. Some brief historical and geographical considerations will aid in understanding Luke's history.

Acts 1–12 reports the beginnings of the Christian movement within the imperial province of Syria, which included Judea and Samaria. In the first century AD, those regions were generally governed by Roman procurators or puppet kings. At the time of Jesus' death and resurrection (c. AD 30), Pontius Pilate was procurator in Judea and Samaria (AD 26–36). Galilee was ruled by King Herod Antipas (4 BC–AD 39). Tiberius was emperor of the Roman Empire (AD 14–37). The account of Acts 1–12 took place in the period AD 30–44.

The conversion of Saul (Acts 9) is generally dated in AD 33. After Saul's conversion and departure to his native Tarsus, the church evidently enjoyed a period of tranquility, consolidating its gains and growing steadily (9:31–11:26). It can be assumed, from Galatians 1:18-21 and the existence of Christian communities that Paul and Silas visited on the second missionary tour (Acts 15:40-41), that Paul was not idle during that decade, but intensely involved in the mission to the Gentiles. (After Acts 13:9, the name "Saul" is dropped from the narrative.)

In AD 41, Claudius became emperor of Rome and installed Herod Agrippa I as king of the Jews. (The procurator Pontius Pilate had been removed several years earlier for inept administration of the region.) Agrippa I was grandson of Herod the Great and his Jewish princess Mariamne. Because of his Jewish roots, he was more popular with his subjects than the former Herods. No doubt it was his desire to increase that popularity and gain the support of the Jewish religious authorities that led to a renewed outbreak of violence against the Jerusalem church. Acts 12 recounts the execution of James (the brother of the apostle John) and the imprisonment of Peter. The story of Agrippa I's death (12:20-23) is paralleled in an account by the Jewish historian Josephus, who dates the event in AD 44.

A second event providing a time reference for the unfolding story of the early church is the collection of famine relief in Antioch for Christians in Judea (11:27-29). Luke stated that a severe famine took place (v 28) during the reign of Emperor Claudius (AD 41–54). Josephus, writing his *Antiquities* at the end of the first century, spoke of a severe famine in Palestine between the years AD 44 and 48. According to Acts 12:25, Barnabas and Paul finished their mission to famine-stricken Christians in Judea after the death of Agrippa I, making it possible to date their mission about AD 45.

At that point in the narrative of Acts, Paul is launched officially into his mission to the Gentiles (13:1-3), for which the history and geography of the larger Roman Empire form the backdrop. The official Roman policy toward the various religions in the empire was one of toleration. That policy, plus use of the Greek language throughout the empire and a phenomenal network of roads and sea routes, paved the way for Paul's far-ranging missionary work.

The first tour (AD 46–47) took Paul and Barnabas through the island province of Cyprus in the northeastern tip of the Mediterranean Sea and into the province of Galatia, where churches were established in several cities of southern Galatia (Antioch of Pisidia, Iconium, Lystra, Derbe). Galatia is located in Asia Minor, bordered by the Black Sea, the Aegean Sea, and the Mediterranean Sea on its northern, western, and southern sides. Those cities, important colonial outposts for the Romans, contained mixed populations, including large Jewish communities. It was in the synagogues of those communities that Paul launched his missionary efforts, almost always meeting with considerable opposition (chs 13–14).

The deliberation of the Jerusalem Council about differences between Jewish and gentile Christians (ch 15) can be dated in the year AD 48. It was followed by Paul's second missionary journey, which led him through the already evangelized territory of his native Cilicia, Galatia, and through Troas on the Aegean coast to Macedonia and down into Achaia, the Greek Peninsula (15:40–18:22). Churches were established in the important Macedonian cities of Philippi, Thessalonica, and Beroea.

Paul's one and a half years in Corinth (18:11) can be dated with some certainty in AD 51–52. An ancient inscription among the ruins of Delphi, a city in central Greece, states that Gallio became proconsul of Achaia in 51. Acts 18:12-17 tells how Paul was accused by antagonistic Jews before Gallio. The implication is that Paul's adversaries in Corinth felt that a new proconsul could be persuaded to side with their cause. Thus, Paul's stay in Corinth can be dated around the beginning of Gallio's proconsulship.

Luke's account of Paul's return to Palestine and the beginning of his third missionary tour brings up a fascinating historical question about what happened to the followers of John the Baptist (13:13–19:7). Acts 18:24-28 refers to a learned Jew, Apollos, who was actively teaching about Jesus in the synagogue at Ephesus, but who was apparently not a member of a distinctively Christian community, not having been baptized in the name of Jesus. He was acquainted only with the baptism of repentance practiced by John the Baptist. After Apollos went to Corinth to minister to the young congregation that Paul founded the previous year, Paul went to Ephesus. There he met several disciples of Jesus who, like Apollos, had experienced John's baptism of repentance, but who had not been baptized as Christians.

Luke's reference to Apollos and those disciples, as well as several passages in the Gospels, indicate that the movement begun by John the Baptist did not simply come to an end when Jesus began his ministry. Evidently John continued to baptize until his death (Jn 3:22-24), and many of his disciples maintained John's work after his death. Probably both Apollos and the disciples at Ephesus were products of the continuing ministry of John's disciples. Eventually they were introduced to "the way of the Lord" (18:25). Their lack of knowledge about a distinctive Christian baptism or about the reality of the Holy Spirit (19:2-4) shows how much diversity in both belief and practice existed in early Christianity.

Paul's third missionary tour began with a three-year ministry in Ephesus (19:1–20:1), continued with a visit to churches established on the previous journey (20:2-12), and came to a climax with his arrest in Jerusalem (Acts 21). It took place in the mid-50s (AD 53–57). Paul's arrest in Jerusalem and arraignment before the provincial governor, Felix, in Caesarea (23:23–24:23) must be dated about 57. After Paul had spent two years under house arrest, no doubt prolonged by Felix to gain favor with Jewish subjects, Felix was replaced by Porcius Festus (AD 59–60). Josephus noted that Felix was recalled because of an outbreak of civil strife between Jewish and gentile inhabitants of Caesarea and Felix's unwise handling of the situation.

The new procurator, Festus, was uncertain about what to do with his prisoner. The Jewish leadership sought to seize that opportunity, aware of the desire of new procurators to gain popularity with their subjects (25:1-9). Realizing the threat, Paul appealed his case to the highest court of the empire, presided over by Caesar himself (25:10-12).

Festus was then left with a problem. He had to send with his prisoner a report to the emperor, clearly outlining the charges. Since he did not really comprehend the case (25:25-27), he sought the advice of Herod Agrippa II, who with his sister had come to Caesarea to pay their respects to the new imperial governor of Palestine (25:13). Agrippa II was the son of Herod Agrippa I and, at least in theory, a Jew. He ruled over parts of Palestine from AD 50 to 100 and had been given the right to appoint the Jewish high priests. His familiarity with Jewish religious traditions and the Law thus put him in a better position to understand Jerusalem's case against Paul. The outcome of Paul's appearance before Festus and Agrippa (26:1-29) was recognition of Paul's innocence (26:31). Yet Paul's appeal to Rome had to be honored; the law governing such cases had to be followed (26:32).

Paul's relative freedom during the next two-year period (28:30) seems unusual but was a rather common practice in Roman judicial proceedings, especially for Roman citizens who had appealed to the emperor. There is no good reason to believe that Paul was executed at the time when Luke's narrative ends (c. AD 61–62). The great fire of Rome and Nero's subsequent persecution of Christians were still a few years away (AD 64). It is likely that the case against Paul was dismissed, especially in light of the favorable verdict by Festus and King Agrippa. It is also likely that Paul was executed during the later, more general persecution of Christians. Such a sequence would correspond with the tradition cited by Eusebius, a fourth-century church historian, that Paul resumed his ministry and later suffered martyrdom under Nero.

Purpose In the preface to the Gospel, intended to cover the second volume also, Luke told Theophilus (and the audience he represented) that he had set out to write an accurate, orderly account about the beginnings of the Christian movement in the ministry of Jesus of Nazareth (Lk 1:1-4). The opening lines in Acts indicate that the narrative beginning with Jesus of Nazareth (vol 1) is continuing and that Luke's second volume intends to trace the story from Palestine to Rome (Acts 1:1-8).

While recounting this story, Luke attempted to defend the Christian movement against false charges brought against it. A number of misconceptions attended the birth and growth of the Christian movement. One concerned the relationship between the new faith and Judaism. Many, both within the church and among Roman officials, understood the Christian faith as no more than a particular expression of, or sect within, Judaism. Against that restricted notion, Luke-Acts strikes a universal note. The Gospel proclaims Jesus as Savior of the world (Lk 2:29-32). In Acts, Stephen's defense before the Jewish council (ch 7), Peter's experience in Joppa with Cornelius (ch 10), and Paul's speech at Athens (ch 17) all demonstrate that Christianity is not merely a Jewish sect, some narrow messianic movement, but rather a universal faith. Another problem was popular identification of the new faith with the various religious cults and mystery religions in the Roman Empire. The accounts of the early church's conflict with Simon the magician (ch 8) and of Paul and Barnabas's rejection of an attempt to worship them at Lystra (ch 14) undermine the popular charge of superstition. Also, Christianity is not a mystery cult in which esoteric, secret rites bring a worshiper into union with the divine. The Lord worshiped by Christians, said Luke, belongs to real history; he lived his life in Palestine in the then-recent past, openly, for all to observe (see the speeches of Peter and Paul in Acts 2; 10; 13).

Luke's major purpose, however, was defense of Christianity against the charge that it posed a threat to the order and stability of the Roman Empire. There were, of course, grounds for such suspicions. After all, the founder of the movement had been crucified on a charge of sedition by a Roman procurator, and the movement that claimed his name seemed to evoke tumult, disorder, and riots wherever it spread. Luke's account met those problems head-on. In the Gospel he presented the trial of Jesus as a serious miscarriage of justice. Pilate had handed Jesus over for crucifixion, but he had found Jesus not guilty. Herod Antipas likewise found no substance in the charges against Jesus (Lk 23:13-16; Acts 13:28). A neutral or even friendly attitude of Roman officials toward leading Christians and the movement as a whole is documented throughout Acts. The Roman proconsul of Cyprus, Sergius Paulus, gladly received Paul and Barnabas and responded positively to their message (Acts 13:7-12). The chief magistrate in Philippi apologized for the illegal beating and imprisonment of Paul and Silas (16:37-39). The proconsul of Achaia, Gallio, found Paul guiltless in the eyes of Roman law (18:12-16). In Ephesus the magistrate intervened in a crowd's attack on Paul and his companions, rejecting the charges against them (19:35-39). A tribune of the Roman military contingent in Jerusalem arrested Paul, but it turned out that he really saved the apostle from the wrath of a mob; in his letter to the procurator Felix, the tribune acknowledged that Paul was not guilty by Roman law (23:26-29). The same verdict was repeated after Paul's arraignment before Felix, his successor Festus, and Herod Agrippa II: "This man hasn't done anything worthy of death or imprisonment" (26:31, NLT). Luke climaxed his story by telling how Paul carried on his missionary activity in Rome, the very heart of the empire, and with the permission of the imperial guards (28:30-31). It is clear throughout Luke's defense that the strife that attended the beginnings and progress of Christianity was not due primarily to anything within the movement, but rather to Jewish opposition and falsification.

Within his lengthy apology for the integrity of Christianity, Luke's specific theological perspectives can be clearly seen. The two volume work presents a grand scheme of the history of redemption, extending from the *time of Israel* (Lk 1-2) through the *time of Jesus*, and continuing through the *time of the church*, when the good news for Israel is extended to all nations. Paralleling that emphasis is an insistence that God is present in the redemptive story through the Holy Spirit. In the Gospel, Jesus is presented as the Man of the Spirit; the reality of the Spirit empowered him for his work (Lk 3:22; 4:1, 14, 18). In Acts, the fellowship of Jesus' disciples is presented as the community of the Spirit (1:8; 2:1-8). What Jesus in the power of the Spirit had begun in his own ministry, the church in the power of the Spirit continues to do.

For Luke, the empowering presence of God's Spirit was a reality that gave the new faith its power, integrity, and perseverance. It enabled faithful witness (1:8) and created genuine community (2:44-47; 4:32-37), something for which the ancient world desperately longed. The Spirit in the new community produced courage and boldness (see Peter's defenses in chs 2-5), empowered for service (ch 6), overcame prejudice as in the mission in Samaria (ch 8), broke down walls as in the Cornelius episode (chs 10-11), and sent believers out on missions (ch 13).

The entire story is also punctuated by the centrality of Jesus' resurrection. Luke, like Paul (see 1 Cor 15:12-21), must have been convinced that without the resurrection of Jesus there would be no Christian faith at all. More than that, the resurrection put God's stamp of approval on Jesus' life and ministry, authenticating the truth of his claims. Luke announced his interest in that theme at the outset: the ultimate criterion for an apostolic replacement for Judas was that he must have been, with the other disciples, a witness to Jesus' resurrection. Throughout Acts, from Peter's Pentecost sermon and defenses before the Sanhedrin to Paul's speeches before Felix and Agrippa, the church is shown bearing witness to Jesus' resurrection as a great reversal executed by God (2:22-24, 36; 3:14-15; 5:30-31; 10:39-42).

Acts falls naturally into two parts, chapters 1-12, and 13-28. The first part, roughly speaking, contains the "acts of Peter." Part two is largely concerned with the "acts of Paul." In the first 12 chapters, Peter is the central figure who initiates the choosing of a replacement for Judas Iscariot (ch 1); addresses the multitudes at Pentecost (ch 2); interprets the significance of the healing of a lame man to a temple crowd (ch 3); delivers a defense of the Christian proclamation before the supreme Jewish council (ch 4); leads the apostles in a healing ministry and speaks for them (ch 5); stands in the forefront of conflict with a Samaritan magician, "Simon the Great" (ch 8); launches—though somewhat unwillingly—the movement of the gospel to the Gentiles through Cornelius (chs 10-11); and draws the fire of Herod's campaign against the church but is miraculously delivered from prison (ch 12).

Proclamation of the gospel to the Gentiles through Paul's ministry is the theme of part two of Acts (chs 13-28). The story primarily concerns three major missionary tours, each of which moved the gospel into yet untouched territory and expanded earlier missionary efforts. The account of Paul's life and work climaxes in

his arrest in Jerusalem (chs 21-22), a lengthy imprisonment in Caesarea (chs 23-26), and a voyage to Rome (chs 27-28).

Another way of getting at the structure and content of Acts is thematic. It has its starting point in Jesus' statement, "You shall receive power when the Holy Spirit has come upon you; and you shall be my witnesses in Jerusalem and in all Judea and Samaria and to the ends of the earth" (1:8). Acts can be seen as the story of the fulfillment of that "Great Commission," unfolding essentially in three stages: (1) witness to Judaism, focused in Jerusalem but also expanding into surrounding Judea and north into Galilee (chs 1-7); (2) witness to Samaria through Philip, Peter, and John (8:1-9:31); (3) witness to the gentile world, first haltingly through Peter (9:32-12:25), and then decisively through Paul (chs 13-28).

See also Luke (Person); Paul, The Apostle; Simon Peter; Theophilus #1; Chronology of the Bible (New Testament.)

ACZIB

1. City in Judah's territory (Jos 15:44). The prophet Micah listed it among cities that would be destroyed with Samaria (Mi 1:14). It was probably the same as Chezib (Gn 38:5) and Cozeba (1 Chr 4:22).
2. City in Asher's territory (Jos 19:29), one of seven from which the tribe failed to drive out the Canaanite inhabitants (Jgs 1:31). Recent excavations at Aczib (modern ez-Zib) show that the town was occupied almost continuously from the ninth to the third centuries BC.

ADADAH
One of 30 cities assigned to Judah's tribe in the Negev, or southern desert region (Jos 15:22). A Greek textual variant in the Septuagint is *Ararah*, which appears as "Aroer" in 1 Samuel 30:28. It may be modern Khirbet Ar'arah, located 12 miles (19 kilometers) south of Beersheba.

ADAH
1. One of Lamech's two wives, and mother of two sons, Jabal and Jubal (Gn 4:19-21, 23).
2. Esau's first wife, daughter of Elon the Hittite and mother of Eliphaz (Gn 36:2-16).

ADAIAH
1. Josiah's maternal grandfather. Josiah's mother, Jedidah, was Adaiah's daughter (2 Kgs 22:1).
2. Ethan's son, a Levite of the Gershon clan and an ancestor of Asaph the psalmist (1 Chr 6:41). He is sometimes identified with the Iddo of 1 Chronicles 6:21. *See* Iddo #2.
3. Shimei's son, a minor member of Benjamin's tribe (1 Chr 8:21).
4. Jeroham's son, a priest who returned to Jerusalem after the exile (1 Chr 9:12; Neh 11:12).
5. Maaseiah's father. Maaseiah was a captain under Jehoiada the priest (2 Chr 23:1).
6. Bani's son, who obeyed Ezra's exhortation to divorce his pagan wife after the exile (Ezr 10:29).
7. Son of a different Bani, who also obeyed that exhortation (Ezr 10:39).
8. Joiarib's son, descended from Perez, and an ancestor of Maaseiah (Neh 11:5).

ADALIA
Fifth of Haman's ten sons, all of whom were killed with their father when his plot to destroy the Jews was foiled (Est 9:8).

ADAM (Person)

ADAM (Person) First man and father of the human race. Adam's role in biblical history is important not only in OT considerations but also in understanding the meaning of salvation and the person and work of Jesus Christ.

The creation of Adam and the first woman, Eve, is recited in two accounts in the book of Genesis. The intent of the first account (1:26-31) is to present the first pair in their relationship to God and to the rest of the created order. It teaches that with regard to God the first humans were created male and female in God's image with his specific mandate to populate and rule over the earth. With regard to the rest of creation the first humans were, on one hand, part of it, being created on the same day as other land animals; on the other hand, they were distinctly above it, being the culmination of the creation process and sole bearers of God's image.

The intent of the second account is much more specific (2:4–3:24); it seeks to explain the origin of the present human condition of sin and death and to set the stage for the drama of redemption. The story treats in detail aspects of Adam's creation omitted from the first story. For example, it tells of the formation of Adam from the dust of the ground and of his receiving the breath of life from God (2:7). It recounts the planting of the Garden and the responsibility given to Adam to cultivate it (2:8-15). God's instruction to Adam that the fruit of every tree in the Garden was his for food, except one, is carefully recorded, as well as the solemn warning that the fruit of the "tree of the knowledge of good and evil" was never to be eaten, under the pain of death (2:16-17). Adam's loneliness after naming the animals and not finding a suitable companion is also described, thus introducing the creation of the first woman (2:18-22). The creation of Eve from Adam's rib poignantly portrays the essential unity of spirit and purpose of the sexes intended by God.

The story does not end on such a positive note, however. It moves on to record the great deception Satan played upon Eve through the serpent. By clever insinuations and distortion of God's original commandment (cf. 3:1 with 2:16-17), the serpent tricked Eve into eating the forbidden fruit and sharing it with Adam. Eve seems to have eaten because she was deceived (1 Tm 2:14), Adam out of a willful and conscious rebellion. Ironically, the two beings originally created in God's image and likeness believed that they could become "like" God by disobeying him (Gn 3:5).

The effects of their disobedience were immediate, though not at all what Adam had expected. For the first time a barrier of shame disrupted the unity of man and woman (3:7). More important, a barrier of real moral guilt was erected between the first couple and God. The story relates that when God came looking for Adam after his rebellion, he was hiding among the trees, already aware of his separation from God (3:8). When God questioned him, Adam threw the blame on Eve and, by implication, back on God: "It was the woman you gave me who brought me the fruit" (3:12, NLT). Eve in turn blamed the serpent (3:13).

According to the story in Genesis, God held all three responsible and informed each one of the calamitous consequences of their rebellion (3:14-19). The two great mandates, originally signs of pure blessing, became mixed with curse and pain—the earth could now be populated only through the woman's birth pangs and could be subdued only by the man's labor and perspiration (3:16-18). Further, the unity of man and woman would be strained by man's subjugation of her, or possibly by the beginning of a struggle for dominance between them (3:16b can be taken both ways). Finally, God pronounced the ultimate consequence: as he had originally warned, Adam and Eve were to die. Someday the breath of life would be taken from them, and their bodies would return to the dust from which they were made (3:19). That very day they also experienced a "spiritual" death; they were separated from God, the giver of life, and from the tree of life, the symbol of eternal life (3:22). God sent them out of Eden, and there was no way back. The entrance to paradise was blocked by the cherubim and flaming sword (3:23-24). Only God could restore what they had lost.

The story is not devoid of hope. God was merciful even then. He made them garments of skin to cover their bodies and promised that someday the power of Satan behind the serpent would be crushed by the woman's "seed" (Gn 3:15; cf. Rom 16:20). Many scholars consider that promise to be the first biblical mention of redemption.

The Significance of Adam

The Significance of Adam Adam's significance is based upon several assumptions, the first being that he was a historical individual. That assumption was made by many OT writers (Gn 4:25; 5:1-5; 1 Chr 1:1; Hos 6:7). The NT writers agreed (Lk 3:38; Rom 5:14; 1 Cor 15:22, 45; 1 Tm 2:13-14; Jude 1:14). Equally essential to Adam's significance is a second assumption, that he was more than an individual. To begin with, the Hebrew word *adam* (more correctly *'a–dha–m*) is not merely a proper name. Even in the Genesis story it is not used as a name until Genesis 4:25. The word is one of several Hebrew words meaning "man" and is the generic term for "human race." In the vast majority of cases it refers either to a male individual (Lv 1:2; Jos 14:15; Neh 9:29; Is 56:2) or to humanity in general (Ex 4:11; Nm 12:3; 16:29; Dt 4:28; 1 Kgs 4:31; Jb 7:20; 14:1). The generic, collective sense of the word *adam* is also behind the phrase "children (or sons) of men" (2 Sm 7:14; Pss 11:4; 12:1; 14:2; 53:2; 90:3; Eccl 1:13; 2:3). That phrase, literally "sons of *adam*," simply means "men" or "human beings," and when it is used the entire human race is in view. Indeed, the universalistic human connotation of the word *adam* indicates a concern in the OT going far beyond Israel's nationalistic hopes and its God—to all the earth's people and the Lord of all nations (Gn 9:5-7; Dt 5:24; 8:3; 1 Kgs 8:38-39; Pss 8:4; 89:48; 107:8-31; Prv 12:14; Mi 6:8).

It is no accident, then, that the first man was named "Adam" or "Man." The name intimates that to speak about Adam is somehow also to speak about the entire human race. Such usage can perhaps best be understood through the ancient concept of corporate personality and representation familiar to the Hebrews and other Near Eastern peoples. Modern thinking emphasizes the individual; existence of the social group and all social relationships has been seen as secondary to, and dependent upon, the existence and desire of the individual. The Hebrew understanding was quite different. Though the separate personality of the individual was appreciated (Jer 31:29-30; Ez 18:4), there was a strong tendency to see the social group (family, tribe, nation) as a single organism with a corporate identity of its own. Likewise the group representative was seen as the embodiment or personification of the corporate personality of the group. Within the representative the essential qualities and characteristics of the social group resided in such a way that the actions and decisions of the representative were binding on the entire group. If the group was a family, the father was usually considered the corporate representative; for good or for ill his family, and sometimes his descendants, received the results of his actions (Gn 17:1-8; cf. Gn 20:1-9, 18; Ex 20:5-6; Jos 7:24-25; Rom 11:28; Heb 7:1-10).

As the original man and father of humankind, in whose image all succeeding generations would be born (Gn 5:3), Adam was the corporate representative of humanity. The creation accounts themselves give the impression that the mandates of Genesis 1:26-30 (cf. Gn 9:1, 7; Pss 8:5-7; 104:14) as well as the curses of Genesis 3:16-19 (cf. Ps 90:3; Eccl 12:7; Is 13:8; 21:3) were meant not only for Adam (and Eve) but, through him, for the entire race.

In Romans 5:12-21 the apostle Paul contrasted the death and condemnation brought upon humanity by Adam's disobedience with the life and justification given to humanity through Christ's obedience. More explicitly, in 1 Corinthians 15:45-50 (RSV), Paul called Christ the "last Adam," "second man," and the "man of heaven" in juxtaposition to the "first Adam," the "first man," and the "man of dust."

For Paul, the human race was divided into two groups in the persons of Adam and Christ. Those who remain "incorporated" in Adam are the "old" humanity, bearing the image of the "man of dust" and partaking of his sin and alienation from God and Creation (Rom 5:12-19; 8:20-22). But those who are incorporated into Christ by faith become Christ's "body" (Rom 12:4-5; 1 Cor 12:12-13, 27; Eph 1:22-23; Col 1:18); they are recreated in Christ's image (Rom 8:29; 1 Cor 15:49; 2 Cor 3:18); they become one "new man" (Eph 2:15; 4:24; Col 3:9-10, KJV); and they partake of the new creation (2 Cor 5:17; Gal 6:15). The old barriers raised by Adam are removed by Christ (Rom 5:1; 2 Cor 5:19; Gal 3:27-28; Eph 2:14-16). For Paul, the functional similarity of Adam and Christ as representatives meant that Christ had restored what Adam had lost.

See also Eve; Man, Old and New; New Creation, New Creature.

ADAM (Place) City on the Jordan River. When Joshua led the Israelites across the river, the stretch of riverbed from this city to the Dead Sea dried up miraculously so the people could cross on dry land (Jos 3:16). Adam is identified with modern Tell ed-Damiyeh.

ADAM*, The Second Analogy that compares and contrasts the first man with the one he is seen to typify, the Lord Jesus Christ. Two essential passages develop the idea, which basically states that, while Adam's historically rooted sin caused horrible consequences for the human race, the perfect work of Jesus Christ provided the complete remedy for mankind's resultant condition (Rom 5:12-21; 1 Cor 15:22, 45-49). See Adam (Person).

ADAMAH One of the 19 fortified cities belonging to Naphtali's tribe (Jos 19:36). It is possibly identified with Qarn Hattin.

ADAMI*, ADAMI-NEKEB Names of a city located near the southern border of Naphtali's territory (Jos 19:33), although the KJV lists it as two cities. Adaminekeb is usually identified as modern Khirbet ed-Damiyeh.

ADAR (Month) Babylonian name for a Hebrew month (Ezr 6:15). See Calendars, Ancient and Modern.

ADAR* (Place) KJV form of Addar in Joshua 15:3. See Addar (Place).

ADASA
1. Town mentioned only in the period of the Maccabean revolt. Judas Maccabeus defeated the Syrian army under Nicanor in 161 BC at Adasa. The victory was celebrated annually on the 13th of Adar (1 Macc 7:40, 45, 49). The modern site is probably Khirbet 'Adassa, 7 miles (11 kilometers) from Beth-horon.
2. Leader of a group of Babylonian exiles returning to Judah who were unable to prove their Jewish ancestry (1 Esd 5:36). The same name, spelled Addon, seems to refer to an otherwise unidentified place in the Babylonian Empire (Neh 7:61).

ADDAN Persian city from which Israelite exiles returned with Ezra to Jerusalem (Ezr 2:59), probably named after a Babylonian god called Addu. The exiles returning from this city were unable to give evidence of their Jewish descent, having lost their genealogical credentials. Also spelled Addon (Neh 7:61).

ADDAR (Person) Alternate name for Ard, one of Benjamin's descendants, in 1 Chronicles 8:3. See Ard, Ardite.

ADDAR (Place) Town on Judah's southwest border, northwest of Kadesh-barnea (Jos 15:3). The towns Hezron and Addar were called Hazar-addar (Nm 34:4).

ADDER* Any of several kinds of poisonous and non-poisonous snakes, especially the common viper of Europe and Asia. See Animals.

ADDI
1. One whose descendants obeyed Ezra's exhortation to divorce their pagan wives after the exile (1 Esd 9:31). The parallel list of Ezra has Pahath-moab in place of Addi (Ezr 10:30).
2. Ancestor of Jesus, mentioned in Luke's genealogy (3:28). See Genealogy of Jesus Christ.

ADDON* Alternate form of Addan, a place in Babylonia, in Nehemiah 7:61. See Addan.

ADDUS One of Solomon's servants. His descendants were among those who returned with Zerubbabel from the exile (1 Esd 5:24). His name is not mentioned in parallel lists in Ezra or Nehemiah.

ADER* KJV form of Eder, Beriah's son, in 1 Chronicles 8:15. See Eder (Person) #1.

ADIDA Town fortified by Simon Maccabeus (1 Macc 12:38; 13:13). Adida was in the foothills of southern Judea four miles (6.4 kilometers) east of Lydda between the Mediterranean coastal plain and the central highlands. It was probably identical with Hadid (Neh 11:34).

ADIEL
1. Prince of Simeon's tribe who led some Simeonites to the entrance of Gedor to find pasture for their flocks (1 Chr 4:36-39).
2. Ancestor of Maasai, a priest of Israel who was among the first to return to Palestine following the Babylonian captivity (1 Chr 9:12).
3. Ancestor of Azmaveth. Azmaveth was in charge of King David's treasuries (1 Chr 27:25).

ADIN
1. Ancestor of a group of people who returned to Judah with Zerubbabel after the Babylonian exile. Compari-

son of various lists (Ezr 2:15; 8:6; Neh 7:20; 1 Esd 5:14; 8:32) shows that groups of Adin's descendants returned at different times.

2. Political leader who signed Ezra's covenant of faithfulness to God with Nehemiah and others after the exile (Neh 10:16).

ADINA Shiza's son and a warrior among David's mighty men who were known as "the thirty" (1 Chr 11:42).

ADINO* Possibly another name for Josheb-basshebeth, one of the top three of David's military heroes (2 Sm 23:8); he was also called Jashobeam (1 Chr 11:11). *See* Jashobeam #1.

ADITHAIM Town in the lowlands of Judah's territory (Jos 15:36).

ADLAI Father of Shaphat, the chief herdsman of the king's cattle in the valleys during David's reign (1 Chr 27:29).

ADMAH City associated with Sodom, Gomorrah, and Zeboiim (Gn 10:19; 14:2, 8) and thus probably destroyed in God's judgment of Sodom and Gomorrah (Dt 29:23; not specifically mentioned in Gn 19:28-29). A recent survey of the area east and south of the Dead Sea has revealed five early Bronze Age cities that probably correspond to the five "cities of the plain" spoken of in Genesis. Each city was located next to the valley of a river that flowed into the plain around the Dead Sea.

ADMATHA One of seven counselors of King Ahasuerus (Est 1:14). The king's counselors advised him to banish Queen Vashti for refusing his summons to appear at a drunken party.

ADMIN Ancestor of Jesus mentioned in Luke's genealogy (3:33). *See* Genealogy of Jesus Christ.

ADNA
1. Descendant of Pahath-moab who obeyed Ezra's exhortation to divorce his pagan wife after the exile (Ezr 10:30).
2. Priest under the high priest Joiakim who returned to Jerusalem with Zerubbabel after the exile (Neh 12:15).

ADNAH
1. Captain from Manasseh's tribe who left Saul to join David's army at Ziklag (1 Chr 12:20).
2. General under King Jehoshaphat of Judah (2 Chr 17:14).

ADONAI* Divine name translated as "Lord" signifying honor, majesty, and sovereignty. *See* God, Names of.

ADONI-BEZEK Title of the Canaanite king of Bezek, a city in northern Palestine. Soon after Joshua's death, the tribes of Judah and Simeon defeated Adoni-bezek and amputated his thumbs and big toes. Adoni-bezek himself had treated many captured kings that way, so he regarded his fate as divine retribution (Jgs 1:5-7). Some have suggested that he and Adoni-zedek (Jos 10:1) were the same person.

ADONIJAH
1. David's fourth son, born to Haggith at Hebron (2 Sm 3:4). After the deaths of his three older brothers (Amnon, Chileab, and Absalom), Adonijah was next in line for the throne. According to 1 Kings, David had promised his wife Bathsheba that their son Solomon would be the one to succeed him (1:17). When his elderly father seemed to be dying, Adonijah began preparations to crown himself king (1:1-10). Before the ceremonies could take place, David appointed Solomon as his successor (1:11-40). Adonijah kept out of Solomon's way at first (1:41-53) but eventually worked up enough courage to ask King Solomon for permission to marry Abishag, the woman from Shunem who was appointed to care for David during his last days. In the ancient Near East, to claim the concubine of a deceased king was to claim the throne. Enraged, Solomon ordered Adonijah to be killed (2:13-25).
2. Levite sent out by King Jehoshaphat of the southern kingdom of Judah to teach the people the law of the Lord (2 Chr 17:8).
3. Political leader who signed Ezra's covenant of faithfulness to God with Nehemiah and others after the exile (Neh 10:16).

ADONIKAM Head of a family whose descendants returned to Jerusalem with Zerubbabel after the Babylonian exile (Ezr 2:13; Neh 7:18). Ezra states the number of Adonikam's family returning as 666; Nehemiah gives the number as 667 (as does 1 Esd 5:14), probably a scribal variation.

ADONIRAM Important official in Israel during the reigns of David, Solomon, and Rehoboam (1 Kgs 4:6; 5:14). Adoniram is also referred to as Adoram, possibly a contraction of his name (2 Sm 20:24; 1 Kgs 12:18), and as Hadoram (2 Chr 10:18). While Solomon's temple was under construction, Adoniram was overseer of a labor force of 30,000 men (1 Kgs 5:13-14). Evidently David had instituted a system of forced Israelite labor that Solomon continued, not only for building the temple, but for many other projects.

When Rehoboam became king the people asked for relief, but Rehoboam announced that instead, he would increase the labor requirements (1 Kgs 12:1-15). When Adoniram was sent to enforce the king's orders, he was stoned to death by the rebellious people (12:16-19).

ADONI-ZEDEK Amorite king of Jerusalem at the time of the Israelite conquest of the Promised Land (Jos 10:1-5). A battle between the Amorites and Israelites for control of Gibeon was the occasion on which Joshua prayed for the sun to stand still (Jos 10:6-15). The Israelites won a decisive victory. Adoni-zedek and four other enemy kings were discovered hiding in a cave and were executed by Joshua (Jos 10:16-27).
See also Conquest and Allotment of the Land.

ADOPTION Theologically, the act of God by which believers become members of "God's family" with all the privileges and obligations of family membership. "Sons of God," a common KJV expression, includes individuals of both sexes numbered among God's children (Is 43:6; 2 Cor 6:18).

According to the NT, all persons are sinners by nature, and hence are called "children of wrath" (Eph 2:3, KJV); however, those upon whom God bestows his love become "children of God" by grace (1 Jn 3:1). The adoption through which this happens has its origin in God's love and its foundation in Jesus Christ who is uniquely the Son of God. Theologians regard the term "Son of God" as referring preeminently to Christ's deity (Mt 11:25-27; 16:16-17), for he is one in substance and glory with the Father. As the second person of the Trinity, Christ is distinguished from the Father as "the only begotten Son." Believers in Christ, although "adopted," are never seen as on a par with the uncreated, divine Son.

Nevertheless, in the beloved Son, sinners have been loved and predestined by God the Father to become his children by adoption (Eph 1:4-6). That adoption is secured by Christ the Redeemer; through his death and resurrection he destroyed sin and its death penalty, restoring the righteousness and life requisite for the status of sonship. Christ is the head of the "new covenant" as its mediator and guarantor. His brothers and sisters, as its beneficiaries, become God's heirs, and his joint heirs (Rom 8:17). God gives to them the Holy Spirit, the Spirit of his Son, as the Spirit of adoption (Rom 8:15; Gal 4:6). The indwelling Spirit gives believers assurance that they are indeed God's children and enables them to cry out to God as Father (Rom 8:15-16). Such intimacy with the Creator and Savior in prayer is one privilege of adoption.

Adoption was a privilege given to God's people under the "old covenant" (Rom 9:4). Both Israel as a whole and individual Israelites knew God as Father (Is 64:8-9; Hos 11:1). Since the NT regards adoption as ultimately possible only through Jesus Christ, Israel's adoption before the Incarnation was an under-age sonship comparable to the status of servanthood (Gal 4:1-7). In Jesus the privilege of mature sonship was extended to include both Jews and Gentiles (Gal 3:25-29). Though adoption is a benefit enjoyed in the present experience of God's people (1 Jn 3:1), its full extent is realized only at their resurrection from the dead (Rom 8:21-23).

ADORAIM City in the southern kingdom of Judah fortified by King Rehoboam (2 Chr 11:9). Adoraim and Mareshah later became the two principal cities of Idumea. In 1 Maccabees 13:20 it is called Adora. The modern identification is Dura, south of Hebron.

ADORAM* Alternate spelling of Adoniram in 2 Samuel 20:24 and 1 Kings 12:18. See Adoniram.

ADRAMMELECH
1. Son of the Assyrian monarch Sennacherib. This Adrammelech and his brother Sharezer killed their father in the temple of Nisroch in Nineveh (2 Kgs 19:37; Is 37:38). The nonbiblical *Babylonian Chronicles* also refers to this assassination but does not name the sons.
    See also Sennacherib.
2. Deity worshiped by the Syrians from Sepharvaim whom the Assyrians resettled in Samaria. Adrammelech was a god to whom children were sacrificed by the Sepharvites (2 Kgs 17:31).
    See also Mesopotamia; Syria, Syrians.

ADRAMYTTIUM Ancient port city in Asia Minor. En route to Rome as a prisoner, Paul embarked on a ship having Adramyttium as its home port (Acts 27:2). Today Adramyttium is the Turkish city of Edremit. Coins found in the area indicate that Adramyttium may have been a center for the worship of Castor and Pollux (twin sons of the pagan god, Zeus).

ADRIA The Adriatic Sea, an arm of the Mediterranean Sea bordered by Italy on the west and by Greece, Albania, and Yugoslavia on the east. The apostle Paul was tossed about in a ship for 14 days in a violent storm on this body of water (Acts 27:27). Other ancient literature attests to the violence of the Adriatic Sea. The Jewish historian Josephus was shipwrecked in the Adriatic in AD 64, and the Greek poet Homer made several references in his writings to the great storms on this sea.

ADRIEL Barzillai's son, to whom Saul gave his daughter Merab in marriage, although she had been promised to David (1 Sm 18:19). King David later handed over Adriel's five sons to the Gibeonites to execute in vengeance against Saul's family (2 Sm 21:1-9).

ADUEL Tobit's great-grandfather, otherwise unknown (Tb 1:1).

ADULLAM, ADULLAMITE Old Canaanite city between Lachish and Hebron, as well as a cave region nearby. The first biblical mention of the city is in the word "Adullamite" (someone from Adullam), used of Hirah, a friend of Judah. After acting as a ringleader in selling his brother Joseph into slavery, Judah left home and lived in Adullam with Hirah (Gn 38:1, 12, 20).

Adullam was in the lowlands of Judah's tribal territory (Jos 15:35). It was one of 31 Canaanite royal cities conquered by Joshua (Jos 12:15) and one of 15 cities later fortified by King Rehoboam of Judah (2 Chr 11:7). After the exiles' return from captivity in Babylon, Adullam was again resettled by Judah's tribe (Neh 11:30).

A cave near Adullam figured in several events in David's life. It was a refuge when he fled from King Saul (1 Sm 22:1) and a stronghold in his war against the Philistines (2 Sm 23:13-17; 1 Chr 11:15-19). The Hebrew superscriptions to Psalms 57 and 142 indicate that David wrote them at the time of his experiences in the cave. Adullam is identified as modern Tell esh-Sheikh Madhkur.

ADULTERY A breach of the unity of marriage. It describes any act of sexual intercourse between a married woman and a man other than her husband, and all sexual intercourse involving a married man and a woman other than his wife.

In OT times, polygamous unions were not considered adulterous (cf. Dt 21:15). Nor was a husband branded as an adulterer if he had intercourse with a slave woman (Gn 16:1-4; 30:1-5) or a prostitute (Gn 38:15-18)— though the latter was, of course, condemned as immoral (1 Cor 6:15).

Any imbalance between the sexes was dispelled by Jesus in his teaching on divorce and remarriage. While he did not rule out the possibility of divorce in cases of sexual unfaithfulness (Mt 5:32; 19:9), he warned that in all other circumstances remarriage involves both (ex-)husband and (ex-)wife in adultery. Paul added that the charge of adultery only applies if the remarried person's original partner is still alive (Rom 7:2-3).

Jesus also sharpened the OT's definition of adultery by applying it to a man's thought life. Any man who fantasizes in lust (as distinct from just being tempted) has committed adultery in mind and intention, even though there is no physical contact (Mt 5:27-28; cf. Jb 31:1, 9).

The Bible's condemnation of adultery is written into the heart of the OT law, prophecy, and wisdom literature. The Ten Commandments ban it unequivocally (Ex 20:14; Dt 5:18). The prophets list it among offenses that attract God's anger and judgment (Jer 23:11-14; Ez 22:11; Mal 3:5). And the book of Proverbs scorns it as a senseless act by which a man destroys himself (Prv 6:23-35; cf. 7:6-27).

The NT echoes that clear condemnation. Where there is no repentance, adultery excludes those who practice it from God's kingdom (1 Cor 6:9). It is the very opposite of love of one's neighbor (Rom 13:9-10), and it stands under the judgment of God himself (Heb 13:4).

In the OT the penalty for adultery is death—for both the man and the woman (Lv 20:10; Dt 22:22). The same applies if the woman is single but engaged to another man, assuming she has not been raped (in which case only the man is to be executed—Dt 22:23-27). The refrain "You will cleanse the land from evil" (22:24) shows that adultery was considered a serious threat to society's health, not simply an attack on the family lives of the two people involved.

With such serious consequences, it was important to establish guilt beyond doubt. In cases of serious suspicion but insufficient evidence, the wife concerned was put through an elaborate ritual test that included taking an oath and drinking bitter water. The result was not a matter of chance because she stood in the Lord's presence (Nm 5:11-31).

In both the OT and NT, the language of adultery is used figuratively to describe human unfaithfulness to God. The OT prophets likened God's covenant relationship with his people to marriage (Is 54:5-8; cf. Rv 21:2), so in their eyes the breaking of that relationship, especially by idolatry, was equivalent to spiritual adultery (Jer 5:7-8; 13:22-27; Ez 23:37).

Jesus used the same imagery to characterize those who either rejected his claims or showed their lack of faith in him by demanding unnecessary extra signs of his deity (Mt 12:39; 16:4; Mk 8:38). And in another vivid NT passage, James describes God as a loving, jealous husband coming to deal with his adulterous people who have become good friends with the world and its false standards (Jas 4:4).

This is the special theme of the prophet Hosea. God used the prophet's own experience of a marriage broken by adultery to teach the seriousness of his people's unfaithfulness to him (Hos 2:2-6) and his keen longing for a full reconciliation (3:1-5). Spiritual infidelity, like physical adultery, brings God's judgment. But in both cases his overwhelming desire is for a mended relationship following sincere repentance (Jer 3:1-14; Ez 16:1-63).

See also Divorce; Marriage, Marriage Customs; Fornication.

ADUMMIM Pass extending from the hill country into the Jordan Valley, which formed part of Judah's northern border (Jos 15:7). It is a reference point establishing the location of Geliloth on Benjamin's southern border (Jos 18:17). The road from Jerusalem to Jericho ran through this mountain pass. The church father Jerome felt that this place was the setting for Jesus' story of the Good Samaritan (Lk 10:30-37). The modern Arabic name means "ascent of blood." The Hebrew name Adummim ("red rocks") probably stems from the natural color of the rocks rather than from the fate of many travelers through the pass at the hands of robbers.

ADVENT OF CHRIST* *See* Incarnation; Jesus Christ, Life and Teachings of; Second Coming of Christ.

ADVERSARY Any foe, opponent, or enemy of God and his people. The apostle Peter's description of the devil as "your adversary" (1 Pt 5:8, KJV) has led to use of "the adversary" as a reference to Satan in literature and popular speech. *See* Satan.

ADVOCATE Translation for the Greek term *parakletos*, a term used for the Holy Spirit in John's Gospel and for Jesus in 1 John 2:1. *See* Spirit of God; Paraclete.

AEGEAN SEA* Extension of the Mediterranean Sea between Greece on the west and north and Turkey on the east. The large island of Crete is its traditional southern limit. On the northeast, the Aegean connects with the Black Sea by way of the Strait of Dardanelles and the Sea of Marmara. Approximately 200 miles (320 kilometers) wide and 400 miles (640 kilometers) long, the Aegean Sea has hundreds of islands, including Lesbos and Patmos (Rv 1:9). The sea was probably named for Aegeus, in Greek mythology a king of Athens and the father of Theseus.

The apostle Paul spent much time in the Aegean area on his second and third missionary trips. The three major modern cities on the Aegean are Athens (with its port of Pireaus), Salonika (biblical Thessalonica), both in Greece, and Izmir (biblical Smyrna) in Turkey.

AENEAS Bedridden paralytic in Lydda who was miraculously healed by the apostle Peter (Acts 9:33-35).

AENON Small town near the Jordan River. Scholars think Aenon may have been about 30 miles (48 kilometers) north of the Dead Sea. The Bible's one reference to the town merely states that John the Baptist baptized there (Jn 3:23).

AEON* Greek word for a long period of time or age, from which comes the English word "eon." *See* Age.

AESORA Town alerted to prepare for the invasion of Holofernes, Nebuchadnezzar's chief general (Jdt 4:4). Most ancient translators omitted this city and mentioned only Samaria, Jericho, and sometimes Beth-horon. From the context, Aesora was probably north-northeast of Jerusalem.

AFFLICTION *See* Suffering.

AGABUS Prophet of NT times who made two predictions referred to in the book of Acts. His prophecy of a severe famine was fulfilled in the time of Claudius (Acts 11:27-28). He also predicted that Paul would be turned over to the Gentiles by the Jews in Jerusalem if he went there (Acts 21:10-11).

AGAG
1. Name of an Amalekite king, or perhaps a general title for their kings (like the Egyptian "pharaoh"). Balaam prophesied that Israel's king would be greater than Agag (Nm 24:7).
2. Name of another Amalekite king. God told Samuel to send King Saul to wipe out the Amalekite nation down to the last sheep. Saul conquered them but spared Agag's life and the Amalekites' best sheep and oxen. Samuel then executed Agag and told Saul that, because of his disobedience, he could no longer be Israel's king (1 Sm 15).

AGAGITE Term used to describe Haman, "the enemy of all the Jews," in the Persian court of King Ahasuerus (Est 3:1; 9:24). Agag, an Amalekite king, had been Saul's mortal enemy.

AGAPE* English transliteration of the NT Greek word for "love" or "love feast." *See* Love.

AGATE Hard, semiprecious stone, a variety of chalcedony (a kind of quartz), with striped or clouded coloring. *See* Minerals and Metals; Stones, Precious.

AGE Long, but indefinite, period of time, past or future. The ages, past and future, make up the whole of time.

God is spoken of as existing and planning "before the ages" (1 Cor 2:7, rsv). He is the King of ages (1 Tm 1:17) and has a purpose that embraces the ages (Eph 3:11). The Bible speaks of what God will do at the close or consummation of the age(s) (Mt 13:39-49).

The NT, following on from earlier Jewish writings, speaks of the contrast between "the present age" (an "evil age," Gal 1:4) and "the age(s) to come" when, in God's judgment, wrongs will be righted, and his people will come into their full inheritance (Mk 10:30). There is a sense, however, in which it can be said that we are both living now in "the end of the ages" (1 Cor 10:11, rsv) and that we experience "the powers of the age to come" (Heb 6:5, rsv) and its life.

Two other words are sometimes connected with the word "age." One is "generation." Colossians 1:26 speaks of the mystery hidden "for ages and generations" (rsv, cf. Eph 3:21), though there is no basis in the scriptural use of these words for dividing biblical times into dispensations, each involving some fresh development of the redemptive purpose of God. The other is the word "world." Ephesians 2:2 speaks of unredeemed humanity as "following the course of this world" (rsv). Hebrews 1:2 and 11:3 speak of God's creation of the world.

The Bible often speaks of the age of men and women, reckoned in years or in other ways. Wisdom is seen as belonging especially to the aged (Jb 12:12), though not necessarily found there (Eccl 4:13). Age should be respected (Lv 19:32), and length of days is a blessing of God (Prv 16:31). At the same time, the frailty of old age is recognized (Eccl 12:1-6), and Psalm 90:10 speaks of 70 years as the allotted human span which, if it is extended to 80, may well be "trouble and sorrow." *See* Eternity.

AGEE Father of Shammah, one of the warriors among David's mighty men who were known as "the thirty" (2 Sm 23:11).

AGIA Jaddus's wife, mentioned in the Apocrypha (1 Esd 5:38-39) as a descendant of Barzillai the Gileadite (2 Sam 19:31-40). Her sons, who had assumed the priesthood, were excluded from serving as priests when the Jews returned from Babylon and demanded verification of priestly ancestry (Ezr 2:61-63; Neh 7:63-65).

AGORA* *See* Market, Marketplace.

AGRICULTURE* During Bible times agriculture took the same three main forms found in Palestine today. Emphasis on each of these has depended upon the social and technological status of the people.

PREVIEW
•Herding
•Field Cropping
•Fruit Raising
•Cultivating
•Harvesting

Herding Raising livestock is one of the first occupations mentioned in the Scriptures. Abel (Gn 4:2) and Jabal (Gn 4:20) were keepers of sheep or had cattle. This occupation fit the seminomadic life, providing both food and clothing while requiring a minimum of techniques and equipment.

The patriarchs were mainly herdsmen, pasturing their sheep and cattle on common land and generally neglecting to till the soil. Jacob and his sons entered Egypt as shepherds (Gn 47:3). Later this pastoral life is still found in the tribes of Reuben, Gad, and the half-tribe of

Manasseh in Transjordan (Nm 32:1) and in certain of the tribes dwelling in the western Palestinian hills (1 Sm 25:2). Herding continued to be a part of Hebrew agriculture even in postnomadic days, partly because the animals utilized less productive lands and partly because of the people's traditions. Important among these traditions were the sacrifices performed in the temple.

Olive Press

Field Cropping Most authorities agree that the Israelites learned field agriculture from the Canaanites, since contact with these people was contemporaneous with the settling of the Promised Land. The raising of grain is known to have existed before that time. Cain was a tiller of the soil (Gn 4:2), although it is uncertain what he raised. Archaeologists date the existence of grain farming to around 6800 bc in the Near East. Isaac sowed in Gerar (Gn 26:12), and Joseph dreamed of sheaves of grain (Gn 37:6-7). Joseph probably learned more about farming grain from the Egyptians, who raised it on the fertile soils of the Nile floodplain.

Yet it was from contact with the Canaanites that Israelites began to raise grain. The productivity of Canaan was reported by Joshua and Caleb at Kadesh-barnea (Nm 13:26), and the Canaanites, who were later conquered, were no doubt made to initiate their conquerors into agricultural practices. Probably such a relationship contributed to the continual Israelite lapses into idolatry (Jgs 9:27). How rapidly they made the transition from the purely nomadic life is not clear. Some tribes never did shed the nomadic way, but cultivation of the soil seems to have been common by the time of the kings (2 Sm 14:30).

Of the cereals raised, wheat was one of the most important. Solomon sent great amounts of it, along with barley and oil, to Hiram (2 Chr 2:10), and it continued to be a chief item of export (Ez 27:17). Barley was second in importance. In early times it was the chief ingredient of bread (Jgs 7:13); later it became an important food for the poorer classes (Jn 6:9, 13). It was also fed to cattle.

Other field crops were beans and lentils (2 Sm 17:28), which were ground into meal and sometimes used for bread (Ez 4:9). Leeks, garlic, and onions were raised for seasoning, and cumin, coriander, dill, mint, rue, and mustard for spices. Flax was important (Jos 2:6). Some cotton was grown (Is 19:9). The fiber supply was supplemented with wool. By Roman times cotton had become much more important than flax.

Fruit Raising When the Israelites became well settled, orchards and vineyards were planted and came to be symbols of prosperity. Vineyards supplied wine to drink. Olive orchards provided oil for cooking, cosmetics, and medicine. Figs and pomegranates were also grown. For all of these crops more skill and equipment became necessary.

Cultivating Throughout biblical times, much of the labor for agriculture came from the farmer himself. To plant for the first time, it was necessary to clear the land of forest (Jos 17:18), stones (Is 5:2), weeds, and thorns. Sometimes the thin soil on hillsides was terraced, and sometimes irrigation was employed. Such tasks limited the size of farms so that only the wealthy, such as Job and Boaz, had large holdings.

To till the land, farmers used oxen or cows to pull very primitive plows (Jgs 14:18; Am 6:12). Occasionally an ass was used (Dt 22:10). Clods were broken with a hoe or the driver's goad. The surface was evened by drawing a simple harrow, perhaps only a thornbush, or a stoneboat over it. Seed was sown by hand, sometimes carefully in the furrow, and covered lightly with the harrow or stoneboat. Weeds were controlled by the plow, harrow, or hoe.

Threshing Sledge This sledge, pulled by an ox, was dragged over the grain to separate the kernel from the chaff.

Implements did not change much during Bible times. The plow consisted of an upright J-shaped piece of hardwood so fixed to be drawn by oxen at one end and held by the driver at the other. Such a primitive device could break up only four to five inches (10 to 13 centimeters) of soil. After the exodus, iron became available for the tip of the plow (1 Sm 13:20), but this served mainly to cut down wear on the point.

The use of fertilizer was very limited on Palestinian farms. Of course, ceremonial law requiring that the soil

lie fallow every seventh year helped to replenish water and nutrients, or at least delay their depletion. Manuring of fields was not common because dung was used for fuel. However, there is some mention of this practice in Scripture (Lk 13:8, where dung is placed around trees). There is mention in the Mishnah of the use of wood ashes, leaves, blood of slaughtered animals, and oil scum for fertilizer.

Harvesting Seeding was done at the beginning of the rainy season and harvesting was begun at the end. Harvesting lasted at least seven weeks. Some crops were pulled up by the roots (pulse), others were dug with a hoe (some grain), but most were cut with a sickle. Iron sickles have been found in archaeological excavations, some with cutting edges set with flakes of flint. The cut grain was tied in sheaves (Ps 126:6) and cast into heaps to be transported to the threshing floor. Barley was harvested first and wheat last.

Small quantities of grain, dill, cumin, and other small crops were beaten out with a flail (Jgs 6:11; Ru 2:17), but most grain was threshed on a floor placed on high ground so that the wind would carry off the chaff. The usual method was to scatter the loosened bundles of straw on the floor and to drive oxen over them to dislodge the grains. Sometimes heavy implements were drawn over the straw (Is 28:27; 41:15). These were weighted by stones and ridden by the driver. The resulting bits of straw, or chaff, were separated from the grain by a tedious winnowing process that involved throwing the material in the air with a fork or shovel (Is 30:24; Jer 15:7). The lighter straw would be blown to the edge of the floor, and the grain would collect at the feet of the worker. The chaff was burned or used as fodder. Grain was sifted (Am 9:9), shoveled into a heap, and later stored in covered pits in the field (Jer 41:8). Sometimes storehouses or granaries were used (Dt 28:8).

See also Plants; Harvest; Palestine; Vines, Vineyard; Food and Food Preparation.

AGRIPPA Name of two Roman rulers of Judea from the Herodian family line. *See* Herod, Herodian Family.

AGUE* Intense fever marked by recurring chills, common in malaria. Our English word comes from the same stem as "acute." The "fever" (Dt 28:22) can cause "your eyes to fail and your life to ebb away" (Lv 26:16, NLT). Both passages describe punishments the Israelites would suffer if they disobeyed God's laws. Early translators of the Septuagint used the Greek word for jaundice to translate the Hebrew word for ague, no doubt from association of both symptoms with malaria.

See also Medicine and Medical Practice.

AGUR Jakeh's son. Although not an Israelite, he wrote or collected the sayings in Proverbs 30. Agur was from Massa (Prv 30:1), an area of northern Arabia evidently settled by a son of Ishmael (Gn 25:14; 1 Chr 1:30). *See* Proverbs, Book of.

AHAB
1. Eighth king of the northern kingdom of Israel, who reigned about 874–853 BC. His father, Omri, founded a dynasty that lasted 40 years, through the reigns of Ahab and his two sons, Ahaziah and Jehoram. Omri's dynasty had an impact beyond biblical history, being mentioned on the famous Moabite Stone and in several Assyrian inscriptions. According to 1 Kings, Omri was a general in the army of King Elah, son of Baasha.

When Elah was assassinated, Omri was acclaimed king by his own forces in the field (16:8-16). He prevailed in the resulting civil war and occupied Tirzah, the capital city (16:17-23). Soon he moved his capital to Samaria and built fortifications in the region (16:24). Omri also made an alliance with the Phoenicians, as David and Solomon had done, but was condemned for it by later generations. When Ahab succeeded his father (16:28), he pursued this alliance by marrying the Phoenician king's daughter, Jezebel (16:29-31).

Mediterranean Sea

N

Mount Carmel

Sea of Galilee

Kishon River

Jezreel

Samaria

Jordan River

ISRAEL

Jerusalem

Dead Sea

JUDAH

0   20 Mi.

0   20 Km.

The Showdown at Carmel In a showdown with the false prophets of Baal at Mt Carmel, Elijah set out to prove to Ahab that only the Lord is God. Elijah then killed the false prophets in the Kishon Valley and fled back to Jezreel.

Ahab's marriage to Jezebel, an immoral and fanatical pagan, strongly affected Israel (21:21-26) and had consequences even in the southern kingdom of Judah. Athaliah, their daughter, married Jehoram of Judah and the results of this marriage were disastrous (2 Kgs 8:17-18, 26-27; 11:1-20). Under Jezebel's influence Ahab gave up the worship of God and took up Baal worship. Ahab's new religion was a fertility cult that featured sexual unions between priests and temple "virgins," practices explicitly contrary to the laws of God. Even in marrying Jezebel, Ahab had violated the biblical prohibition of marriage to pagans (Dt 7:1-5).

The biblical narrative mentions that Ahab built many cities (1 Kgs 22:39) and fought a number of wars, but for the most part it centers on the great prophetic figure, Elijah (1 Kgs 17:1; 18:1; 19:1). Early in Ahab's reign, God sent Elijah to predict years of drought and famine as punishment for the king's sin (1 Kgs 17:1; 18:16-18). The drought lasted three and a half years and was such a remarkable period in Israel's history that it was remembered into NT times (Lk 4:25; Jas 5:17). It was a time of great suffering for both people and animals (1 Kgs 18:5). At the end of the three and a half years Elijah challenged Ahab to gather all the pagan prophets for a final confrontation between God and Baal. Elijah taunted the 450 prophets of Baal for not being able to attract the attention of their false god. Then he prayed to God, and fire fell from heaven on God's altar. The people shouted their belief in God and helped Elijah execute the pagan prophets (1 Kgs 18:16-40). The drought ended immediately (18:41-46).

When she heard what had happened to her prophets, Jezebel swore revenge. Elijah fled, and on Mt Horeb, God told him to anoint Jehu to become king of Israel in place of Ahab (1 Kgs 19:1-16). This assignment was carried out by the prophet's successor, Elisha (1 Kgs 19:19-21; 2 Kgs 9:1-10). Elijah then

challenged Ahab's acquisition of a vineyard owned by a man named Naboth (1 Kgs 21:1-16). When Naboth refused to sell his land to the king, Jezebel had false witnesses swear that Naboth had cursed God and the king. Naboth was stoned to death for blasphemy. Elijah denounced Ahab, saying that as a judgment God would bring a bloody end to his family (1 Kgs 21:17-24). Ahab's repentance caused God to postpone the judgment until after Ahab's death (1 Kgs 21:27-29; 2 Kgs 10:1-14).

During his reign Ahab had military encounters with King Ben-hadad II of Syria (Aram), largely provoked by the Syrians. In the first encounter Ben-hadad besieged Samaria, Israel's capital, and demanded heavy tribute. Ahab refused the demands and called a council of elders. As the Syrians were preparing to attack, a prophet advised Ahab to attack first (1 Kgs 20:1-14). The Syrians were routed and Ben-hadad barely escaped with his life (1 Kgs 20:15-22). The following year Ben-hadad mounted another attack on Ahab's forces, was again defeated, and eventually surrendered to Ahab (1 Kgs 20:23-33). Ben-hadad gave up some Israelite cities that had been overrun by his father and granted Israel trading posts in Damascus (20:34). God rebuked Ahab through a prophet for forming such an alliance with a pagan power (1 Kgs 20:35-43).

In Ahab's last war with Syria, he had the advantage of an alliance with the king of Judah, Jehoshaphat (1 Kgs 22:2-4; 2 Chr 18:1-3). That alliance had been fortified by the marriage of Ahab's daughter Athaliah to Jehoram, son of Jehoshaphat. Ahab proposed a campaign for the recovery of Ramoth-gilead in the northeast corner of Israel. When Jehoshaphat refused to believe the optimistic predictions of Ahab's 400 prophets, a prophet of God named Micaiah was called, who foretold Ahab's death (1 Kgs 22:5-28; 2 Chr 18:4-27).

For the battle with Syria, Jehoshaphat put on his royal robes. Ahab tried to disguise himself as an ordinary soldier, but a Syrian archer hit him between the joints of his armor. Ahab died that evening, and his troops gave up the battle. His chariot and armor were washed beside the pool of Samaria, where, as Elijah had prophesied, dogs licked Ahab's blood. The fallen king was succeeded by his son Ahaziah (1 Kgs 22:29-40; 2 Chr 18:28-34).

See also Elijah #1; Jezebel; Israel, History of; King; Kings, Books of First and Second; Chronology of the Bible (Old Testament).

AHAB'S FAILURE
The Bible's evaluation of Ahab is based not on his accomplishments as a warrior or politician but on his failure to lead Israel in devotion to God. He was worse than all the previous kings of Israel (1 Kgs 16:28-30), and his marriage to Jezebel and the introduction of Baal worship "did more to provoke the LORD, the God of Israel, to anger than all the kings of Israel who were before him" (1 Kgs 16:31-33, RSV).

---

2. Kolaiah's son, a notorious false prophet in the closing days of Judah. He was among the Jews taken to Babylon in the deportation of Jehoiachin (598–597 BC). This Ahab and his colleague Zedekiah were denounced by the prophet Jeremiah for lying in God's name and for their sexual immorality (Jer 29:21-23).

AHARAH Alternate name for Ahiram, Benjamin's third son, in 1 Chronicles 8:1. *See* Ahiram, Ahiramite.

AHARHEL Harum's son from Judah's tribe (1 Chr 4:8).

AHASAI* KJV form of Ahzai, the priest, in Nehemiah 11:13. *See* Ahzai.

AHASBAI Eliphelet's father. Eliphelet, from the city of Maacah, was a warrior among David's mighty men who were known as "the thirty" (2 Sm 23:34).

AHASUERUS

1. Persian king better known to Western readers as Xerxes I (486–465 BC); the son and successor of Darius I (Hystaspis). In Ezra 4:6 Ahasuerus is mentioned as receiving letters of accusation from enemies of the Jews about their rebuilding the temple.

   Ahasuerus played a role in biblical history in the book of Esther. According to the Greek historian Herodotus, in the third year of his reign Xerxes (Ahasuerus) convoked an assembly of his leaders to plan an invasion of Greece. The book of Esther begins with a banquet scene probably reflecting that situation. The Greek campaign, begun in 480 BC, was unsuccessful. Afterward, Xerxes turned to private matters, such as the events recorded in Esther. The Jewish heroine of that book was the second wife of Xerxes (Ahasuerus). She and her cousin Mordecai influenced the king to reverse an edict condemning all Jews to death. Ahasuerus hanged Haman, his chief minister, who had asked for the edict.

   Ahasuerus, who controlled an immense area "from India to Ethiopia" (Est 1:1), was celebrated for massive building projects at Susa and Persepolis. His rule ended in 465 BC when he was assassinated in his bedchamber. He is called the conqueror of Nineveh in Tobit 14:15, but this is manifestly impossible: Nineveh was destroyed in 612 BC, over a century before Ahasuerus was born. *See* Persia, Persians; Esther, Book of; Israel, History of.
2. Father of Darius the Mede (Dn 9:1). The identity of this father and son in secular history is uncertain.

AHAVA The name of the river (and possibly town) in Babylonia where Ezra added some Levites to the remnant of exiles. There he also declared a fast for the Jews to humble themselves before God and seek his protection before returning to Palestine (Ezr 8:15, 21, 31).

AHAZ

1. King of Judah (735–715 BC) who was especially remembered for his apostasy. The name Ahaz (Mt 1:9) is a shortened form of Ahaziah or Jehoahaz. The three main accounts of Ahaz (2 Kgs 16; 2 Chr 28; Is 7) treat him as one of the most evil rulers of the southern kingdom of Judah. Consequently, his burial was relatively dishonorable (2 Chr 28:27). He was succeeded by his son Hezekiah (2 Kgs 18:1).

   There is little agreement on the chronology of this section of the OT. The chronological system that seems to have the fewest problems would place Ahaz's accession in 735 BC. If he first came to the throne as co-regent with his father, Jotham, from 735 to 732 BC, his entire reign covered a span of approximately 20 years, ending in 715 BC.

   Ahaz reigned over Judah during a critical time in the history of the ancient Near East. The Assyrians were pushing westward, threatening the Syro-Palestinian area. Pekah, king of Israel, and Rezin,

king of Syria, adopted a policy of resistance against the Assyrians and invaded Judah in order to effect a solid coalition by deposing Ahaz.

Blatantly revealing a lack of trust in God, Ahaz appealed to Tiglath-pileser III, the Assyrian king, for help. That appeal brought the wrath of the prophet Isaiah upon Ahaz. The ensuing encounter (Is 7) led to Isaiah's prediction of the birth of Immanuel as a sign of the dissolution of the countries of Israel and Syria. Those two kingdoms were ultimately destroyed by Tiglath-pileser in a campaign that lasted about two years (734–732 BC).

AHAZ'S LACK OF FAITH
Ahaz's lack of trust in God seems to have stemmed from his complete rejection of the Mosaic or traditional Jewish faith rather than from the dangerous political situation. The book of 2 Chronicles describes him as erecting images for the Baals (deities who represented the god Baal, a Canaanite fertility deity). Ahaz is also described as engaging in human sacrifice by offering his sons in pagan worship. The chronicler cites such practices as God's reason for the invasion by Israel and Syria (2 Chr 28:5).

Before the two kingdoms to the north were conquered by Assyria, their invasion of Judah caused great turmoil (2 Chr 28:8). The invaders not only carried off much spoil but also attempted to depopulate portions of Judah by taking 200,000 people captive to Samaria. That attempt was protested by a prophet in Samaria named Obed, who condemned the act of slavery and ordered the captives returned (v 9). He was joined by several leaders of Israel (v 12), who succeeded in having the captives returned to Jericho with provisions from the spoil that had been taken.

During that time, the kingdom of Judah may have been threatened from the south as well. The Edomites, who had long been under the domination of Judah, may have taken advantage of Judah's growing internal weakness to assert their independence. The Masoretic Text of the OT refers to an invasion of the seaport town of Elath on the Red Sea by Aram, the Hebrew name for Syria (2 Kgs 16:6). The name Aram is quite similar to the name Edom in Hebrew, however, so many scholars think that invasion was actually by Edomites.

By virtue of the alliance he had made, Ahaz placed his country in a dangerous position of dependence on Assyria. The kingdom of Judah became essentially a vassal state under the tacit control of Tiglath-pileser. Ahaz went to Damascus, the capital of fallen Syria, to appear before Tiglath-pileser, possibly to assure his allegiance to the king to whom his nation had become tributary (2 Kgs 16:10).

While in Damascus, Ahaz saw an Assyrian altar, a model of which he sent back to Judah. Under the direction of Uriah the priest, a similar altar was built in Jerusalem, replacing the original bronze altar. Several other alterations were made in the temple by Ahaz, all indicating his turning away from Jewish religion.

The "dial of Ahaz" (2 Kgs 20:11; Is 38:8) later figured in a sign given to his son Hezekiah; the Hebrew word actually refers to a flight of stairs, no doubt built by Ahaz and used to tell time by the movement of a shadow across it.

See also King; Kings, Books of First and Second; Israel, History of; Sundial; Chronology of the Bible (Old Testament).

2. Micah's son and Jehoaddah's father, a descendant of Saul, otherwise unknown (1 Chr 8:35-36).

AHAZIAH

1. Ahab's son, who ruled the northern kingdom of Israel for two years as its ninth king (853–852 BC). He came to the throne when Ahab was killed while trying to recover Ramoth-gilead from Syrian control. Ahaziah was a contemporary of King Jehoshaphat of Judah and of Jehoshaphat's son Jehoram. Politically, his short reign was characterized by peace with Judah, in contrast with the days of Asa and Baasha (2 Chr 20:37; cf. 1 Kgs 22:48-49). No sooner had he become king than he was compelled to launch an expedition against Mesha of Moab, who had ceased paying tribute to Israel.

Evidently Ahaziah followed not only the corrupt religion of Jeroboam I but also the overt Baal worship of his parents, Ahab and Jezebel (1 Kgs 22:51-53). The first chapter of 2 Kings is devoted to Ahaziah's terminal illness. He fell from the second story of his palace and was seriously injured. Instead of turning to the Lord for aid, he turned to the god of Jezebel, "Baalzebub, the god of Ekron." When the prophet Elijah condemned the king for his actions, Ahaziah, enraged, tried to arrest him. Two groups of soldiers were consumed by fire from God, a sign of victory over Baal since Baal was worshiped as the god of fire and lightning by his followers. Ahaziah died as predicted in Elijah's pronouncement from God (2 Kgs 1:2-18). He was succeeded by his younger brother, Jehoram, at a time when Ahaziah's brother-in-law, also named Jehoram, was king of Judah.

2. The son of Jehoram of Judah, grandson of Jehoshaphat and nephew of the Ahaziah just described. He ruled as the sixth king of Judah for only one year (841 BC) at the age of 22 (2 Kgs 8:25-26). The apostasy of the northern kingdom of Israel reached into the southern kingdom of Judah partly because this Ahaziah was a grandson of Ahab and Jezebel (his mother, Athaliah, was their daughter).

Ahaziah joined his uncle Jehoram of Israel (sometimes abbreviated Joram) in a campaign against King Hazael of Syria. In the battle Jehoram was wounded and went to Jezreel to recover. When Ahaziah went to visit his fallen kinsman at the royal residence at Jezreel (2 Chr 22:7-9), the visit proved to be a fatal mistake. Jehu, the army commander, anointed by Elisha to destroy Ahab's descendants (2 Kgs 9:1-13), seized this opportunity to kill both Joram and Ahaziah together (9:14-29).

When Ahaziah's mother, Athaliah, learned of his death, she seized the throne for herself and tried to kill all of his children. One child, Joash, escaped death and eventually became king (2 Kgs 11:1-21). Ahaziah's name is sometimes given as Jehoahaz (2 Chr 21:17) or Azariah (2 Chr 22:6, KJV; cf. NLT mg).

See also Israel, History of; Kings, Books of First and Second; Chronology of the Bible (Old Testament); King.

AHBAN Son of Abishur and Abihail from Judah's tribe (1 Chr 2:29).

AHER Alternate name for Ahiram, Benjamin's third son, in 1 Chronicles 7:12. *See* Ahiram, Ahiramite.

AHI

1. Abdiel's son, a clan leader in Gad's tribe (1 Chr 5:15).
2. Shemer's brother and therefore a member of Asher's tribe (1 Chr 7:34). The word "Ahi" in this verse, however, is probably not a name and should be translated "brother," as in most modern translations.

AHIAH

1. KJV form of Ahijah. *See* Ahijah #1, #2, and #6.
2. Political leader who signed Ezra's covenant of faithfulness to God with Nehemiah and others after the exile (Neh 10:26).

AHIAM Sharar's son and a warrior among David's mighty men who were known as "the thirty" (2 Sm 23:33).

AHIAN One of Shemida's four sons from Naphtali's tribe (1 Chr 7:19).

AHIEZER

1. Ammishaddai's son, a leader of Dan's tribe when the Israelites were roaming in the Sinai wilderness after their escape from Egypt. As leader he presented his tribe's offering at the consecration of the tabernacle (Nm 1:12; 2:25; 7:66, 71; 10:25).
2. Shemaah's son, a leader of the warriors from Benjamin's tribe who joined David at Ziklag in his struggle against King Saul. Like his men, Ahiezer was an ambidextrous archer and slinger (1 Chr 12:2-3).

AHIHUD

1. Shelomi's son, a leader of Asher's tribe. Ahihud was appointed to help Eleazar and Joshua divide the territory of Canaan among the Israelites (Nm 34:17, 27).
2. According to some English versions (KJV, RSV), a leader in Benjamin's tribe whose father, Gera (also called Heglam), was exiled to Manahath (1 Chr 8:7). But according to the Hebrew Masoretic Text, this Ahihud's father was Ehud (1 Chr 8:6), while Gera was the one who exiled Ahihud and his mother to Manahath.

AHIJAH

1. Ahitub's son who served as priest at Shiloh and had charge of the ark of the covenant at Gibeah during Saul's last campaign (1 Sm 14:3, 18). This Ahijah was evidently either the same person as Ahimelech or closely associated with him (1 Sm 21:1-9; 22:9-20).
2. One of King Solomon's secretaries (1 Kgs 4:3).
3. Prophet of Shiloh who informed King Solomon's official, Jeroboam, of the approaching revolt of the 10 northern tribes. Before Solomon died, Ahijah acted out a prophecy before Jeroboam, giving him 10 pieces of his robe, which he had torn into 12 segments, saying that God would tear 10 tribes from Solomon and give them to Jeroboam (1 Kgs 11:29-39; 2 Chr 10:15). Later, when Jeroboam had been unfaithful to Israel's religion, he sent his wife to ask the prophet about their son Abijah's illness (1 Kgs 14:1-5). Aware of her identity although he was now old and blind, Ahijah predicted both the child's death and the fall of Jeroboam and his family (1 Kgs 14:6-17; 15:28-30). "The Prophecy of Ahijah from Shiloh" was evidently a written source for Solomon's biography (2 Chr 9:29).
4. Father of King Baasha of the northern kingdom of Israel (1 Kgs 15:27-28, 33; 21:22; 2 Kgs 9:9).
5. Jerahmeel's son from Judah's tribe (1 Chr 2:25).
6. Ehud's son (1 Chr 8:7). The Hebrew is difficult to translate; therefore, some English versions make Ahijah one of Ehud's sons, while others make Ahijah the one who carried Ehud's sons, Uzza and Ahihud, into exile.

7. Warrior among David's mighty men who were known as "the thirty" (1 Chr 11:36); also called Eliam the son of Ahithophel (2 Sm 23:34).
8. Levite who oversaw King David's temple treasury (1 Chr 26:20).
9. Ancestor of the prophet Ezra (2 Esd 1:2).

AHIKAM Shaphan's son, an officer of the court of King Josiah of Judah (2 Kgs 22:12). Ahikam was among the group sent to the prophetess Huldah to ask about the Book of the Law (2 Kgs 22:14-20). Later, under King Jehoiakim, Ahikam was able to prevent the prophet Jeremiah from being killed (Jer 26:24). Ahikam's son Gedaliah was left as governor of Judah after Nebuchadnezzar destroyed Jerusalem and took most of its citizens to Babylon in 586 BC (2 Kgs 25:22; Jer 39:14; 40:5-16; 41:1-18; 43:6).

AHILUD Father of the court historian Jehoshaphat. Jehoshaphat served under both David and Solomon (2 Sm 8:16; 20:24; 1 Kgs 4:3; 1 Chr 18:15). Probably Ahilud was also the father of Baana, one of Solomon's tax officials (1 Kgs 4:12).

AHIMAAZ
1. Father of Ahinoam, who was King Saul's wife (1 Sm 14:50).
2. Son of the high priest Zadok and father of Azariah (1 Chr 6:8-9, 53). Ahimaaz remained loyal to King David at the time of Absalom's rebellion. He and Jonathan, son of the priest Abiathar, served as couriers. News of Absalom's movements was sent from Zadok and Abiathar in Jerusalem to Ahimaaz and Jonathan in En-rogel and then communicated by them to David (2 Sm 15:27-29; 17:15-23). Ahimaaz was probably well known as a fast runner. He outran the official messenger bearing news to David of Absalom's defeat (2 Sm 18:19-33).
3. One of 12 officers appointed to requisition food for Solomon's household. This Ahimaaz, of Naphtali's tribe, married Basemath, one of Solomon's daughters (1 Kgs 4:15).

AHIMAN
1. One of Anak's three sons. The Ahimanites were one of the Anakim clans living in Hebron when the 12 Israelite spies scouted the land of Canaan (Nm 13:22; Jos 15:13-14; Jgs 1:10).
2. Levite gatekeeper in postexilic Jerusalem (1 Chr 9:17).

AHIMELECH
1. A priest at Nob who aided David in his flight from Saul (1 Sm 21:1-9). When he was asked for food, all he could provide was the holy bread in the tabernacle (Jesus referred to this incident in Mt 12:1-8). Doeg the Edomite subsequently reported this action to Saul, who ordered Ahimelech put to death. Saul's guards were unwilling to execute a priest, but the informer Doeg had no such inhibitions. He killed Ahimelech and 84 other priests, plus their families and livestock (1 Sm 22:9-19). Only Abiathar, Ahimelech's son, escaped and fled to David's protection (22:20-23). Psalm 52 was written by David as an indictment of Doeg's treachery.
2. Hittite who joined David's guerrilla force during his flight from Saul (1 Sm 26:6).
3. Son of Abiathar and grandson of #1 above. This Ahimelech aided his father in the priesthood under King David (2 Sm 8:17; 1 Chr 24:3, 5, 31; cf. 1 Chr 18:16, where some versions have Abimelech instead).

AHIMOTH Elkanah's son, a Levite in the family of Kohath (1 Chr 6:25).

AHINADAB Iddo's son and one of 12 officers appointed to requisition food for King Solomon's household. Ahinadab's headquarters were in Mahanaim (1 Kgs 4:14).

AHINOAM
1. Daughter of Ahimaaz and wife of King Saul (1 Sm 14:50).
2. Jezreelite woman who became David's wife after Saul took back his daughter Michal and gave her to Palti (1 Sm 25:43-44). In Hebron, Ahinoam became the mother of David's oldest son, Amnon (2 Sm 3:2; 1 Chr 3:1).

AHIO
1. Abinadab's son. With his brother Uzzah, Ahio drove the ox cart carrying the ark of the covenant to its new home at Jerusalem (2 Sm 6:3-4; 1 Chr 13:7).
2. Elpaal's son from Benjamin's tribe (1 Chr 8:14).
3. Son of Jeiel and his wife Maacah. This Ahio was a brother or an uncle of Kish, Saul's father (1 Chr 8:31; 9:36-37).

AHIRA Enan's son and the leader of Naphtali's tribe when the Israelites were roaming in the Sinai wilderness after their escape from Egypt. As leader he presented his tribe's offering at the consecration of the tabernacle (Nm 1:15; 2:29; 7:78, 83; 10:27).

AHIRAM, AHIRAMITE Benjamin's third son and the ancestral head of the Ahiramite clan (Nm 26:38; 1 Chr 8:1, "Aharah"). Two abbreviated forms of the name Ahiram in genealogies may be Ehi (Gn 46:21) and Aher (1 Chr 7:12).

AHISAMACH Father of the craftsman Oholiab, of Dan's tribe. Oholiab helped construct the tabernacle and its furnishings (Ex 31:6; 35:34; 38:23).

AHISHAHAR Bilhan's son and chief of the subclan of Jediael, of Benjamin's tribe, in the time of King David (1 Chr 7:10).

AHISHAR Overseer in charge of Solomon's palace affairs (1 Kgs 4:6).

AHITHOPHEL King David's trusted counselor who turned traitor and joined Absalom's conspiracy. Ahithophel's counsel was highly regarded, almost as though it were an oracle of God (2 Sm 16:23). On hearing about Ahithophel's defection to Absalom, David prayed, "O LORD, let Ahithophel give Absalom foolish advice!" (2 Sm 15:31, NLT). Ahithophel advised Absalom to take over the royal harem (2 Sm 16:20-22). Taking possession of the harem was a public act declaring a former king to be deceased and replaced. Since David was still alive, the act was meant to bring about a final cleavage between David and Absalom. It also fulfilled Nathan's prophecy to David that because David had taken another man's wife in secret, his own wives would be taken from him in public (2 Sm 12:7-12).

Ahithophel's second stratagem was to attack David quickly with 12,000 elite troops (2 Sm 17:1-3). Absalom rejected this advice, however, and accepted a counter suggestion by Hushai, David's spy in Absalom's palace. In a speech designed to inflate Absalom's ego and gain time for David, Hushai advised a full campaign

(2 Sm 17:4-14). When Ahithophel saw that his counsel was not followed, he went to his hometown and hanged himself (2 Sm 17:23).

AHITHOPHEL THE BETRAYER
Ahithophel was surely in David's mind in Psalm 41:9, "Even my best friend, the one I trusted completely, the one who shared my food, has turned against me" (NLT). In the NT the similarity of Judas to Ahithophel is seen by Jesus' use of Psalm 41:9 to describe his own situation (Jn 13:18).

AHITUB
1. Member of the priestly line of Aaron's youngest son, Ithamar. Ahitub was a descendant of Eli through Eli's son Phinehas and father of Ahijah and Ahimelech, who were priests during Saul's reign (1 Sm 14:3; 22:9-12, 20).
2. Member of the priestly line of Aaron's third son, Eleazar. Ahitub was Meraioth's grandson, Amariah's son, and father of Zadok (1 Chr 6:4-7). Zadok was a chief priest during David's reign (2 Sm 8:17).
3. Possibly the same as #2 above (the scribes sometimes mistakenly copied names twice), but more likely another member of the priestly line of Eleazar, seven generations after #2 (1 Chr 6:11-12). This Ahitub's father was also named Amariah and his son or grandson Zadok (1 Chr 9:11; Neh 11:11), but his grandfather was Azariah. Ahitub is listed as an ancestor of Ezra (Ezr 7:2; 1 Esd 8:2; 2 Esd 1:1).

AHLAB Canaanite city in Asher's territory. The Israelites failed to drive out its inhabitants in their conquest of Canaan (Jgs 1:31). It probably is identical with Mahalab in Joshua 19:29, modern Khirbet el-Mahalib near Tyre. *See* Mahalab.

AHLAI
1. Sheshan's daughter, a member of Judah's tribe (1 Chr 2:31, 34). In verse 31 some translations refer to Ahlai as a son.
2. Zabad's father or ancestor. Zabad was one of David's mighty men who were known as "the thirty" (1 Chr 11:41).

AHOAH, AHOHI*, AHOHITE* One of Bela's nine sons, a member of Benjamin's tribe (1 Chr 8:4). Ahoah's descendants were called Ahohites, and two of them were among King David's most effective warriors: Dodo ("son of Ahohi," 2 Sm 23:9; spelled "Dodai" in 1 Chr 27:4) and Zalmon the Ahohite (2 Sm 23:28; called "Ilai" in 1 Chr 11:29).

AHOLAH* KJV form of Oholah, the symbolic name for Samaria, capital of the northern kingdom of Israel, in Ezekiel 23. *See* Oholah and Oholibah.

AHOLIAB* KJV form of Oholiab (Ex 31:6), a craftsman from Dan's tribe. *See* Oholiab.

AHOLIBAH* KJV form of Oholibah, the symbolic name for Jerusalem in Ezekiel 23. *See* Oholah and Oholibah.

AHOLIBAMAH* KJV form of Oholibamah (Gn 36:2), a name associated with two members of Esau's family. *See* Oholibamah #1, #2.

AHUMAI Jahath's descendant from Judah's tribe (1 Chr 4:2).

AHUZAM*, AHUZZAM Son of Ashur and Naarah and a member of Judah's tribe (1 Chr 4:6).

AHUZZATH Royal advisor to Abimelech of Gerar. Ahuzzath accompanied Abimelech to Beersheba to make a treaty with Isaac (Gn 26:26).

AHZAI Priest of the order of Immer. Ahzai's descendant, Amashsai, was a leading priest in Jerusalem in Ezra's day (Neh 11:13). In all probability Ahzai and Jahzerah were the same person (1 Chr 9:12). *See* Jahzerah.

AI Canaanite city that was settled before the time of Abraham (Gn 12:8; 13:3). The name suggests a "ruin" of special significance or striking appearance. The inhabitants of Ai, as well as those of other Canaanite cities (Shechem, Bethel, Jerusalem), did not hinder Abraham in his meanderings in the hill country throughout the land. Abraham may have met with representatives of those cities and convinced their kings of his peaceful intentions. Or he may have presented such a strong front with his sizable entourage that he forestalled any Canaanite move against him.

The people of Israel, led by Joshua, entered Canaan, the Promised Land, with the intention of ridding it of its former occupants and claiming it as their inheritance. Ai, the second city to face them, withstood the first Israelite attack against it. After dealing with Achan, a disobedient soldier whose taking of booty from Jericho had caused their defeat, the Israelites attacked Ai a second time and defeated it (Jos 7:1–8:29). Joshua captured the king, executed him, and burned the city, leaving it a heap of ruins (Jos 10:1).

Ai, rebuilt and reoccupied under the monarchy (under Saul, David, and Solomon), seems to have been known under several names. It was evidently called Ayyah, one of the villages of Ephraim (1 Chr 7:28); Aiath, a village through which Assyrian armies marched toward Jerusalem (Is 10:28); and Aija, a village occupied by Benjamin's descendants during the exilic period (Neh 11:31).

See also Conquest and Allotment of the Land; Joshua, Book of.

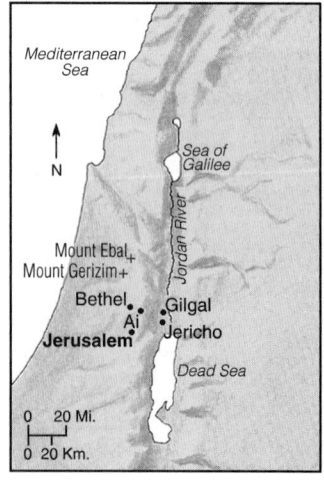

Joshua Conquers Ai After an unsuccessful first attempt, the Israelites attacked Ai again and were successful. Joshua sent one detachment of soldiers to lie in wait while he led a second group against the city. When the army of Ai attacked, Joshua's men occupied the enemy while the men lying in ambush moved in and burned the city.

AIAH
1. Zibeon's son, a Horite descended from Seir. Aiah is listed in Esau's genealogies (Gn 36:24; 1 Chr 1:35-40).
2. Father (or mother?) of Saul's concubine Rizpah (2 Sm 3:7; 21:8-11).

AIATH Alternate name for Ai, the Canaanite city, in Isaiah 10:28. See Ai.

AIJA Alternate name for Ai, the Canaanite city, in Nehemiah 11:31. See Ai.

AIJALON
1. City located in a valley 15 miles (24 kilometers) northwest of Jerusalem (at modern Yalo) and originally allotted to Dan's tribe (Jos 19:42). Aijalon was designated as one of four levitical cities in Dan's area (Jos 21:24) and was later made a city of refuge by Ephraim's tribe (1 Chr 6:69). Dan's tribe had by then migrated north, having been unable to occupy its southerly allotment, including Aijalon (Jgs 1:34-36). Near Aijalon, Saul and Jonathan won a victory over the Philistines (1 Sm 14:31). Members of Benjamin's tribe occupied it at one time (1 Chr 8:13).

When the kingdom was divided after Solomon's death, Aijalon, on the northwest border of the southern kingdom, was fortified by King Rehoboam (2 Chr 11:10). It was one of 65 cities claimed to have been conquered by the Egyptian pharaoh Shishak, who invaded Palestine around 924 BC (2 Chr 12:2-12). Much later, Aijalon was lost to the Philistines during the reign of Ahaz (2 Chr 28:18).

The valley of Aijalon was part of the geographical setting of Joshua's battle to control Gibeon (Jos 10:12, NLT). To make the Israelite victory complete, God answered Joshua's prayer to "let the sun stand still over Gibeon, and the moon over the valley of Aijalon" (Jos 10:12).
See also Cities of Refuge; Levitical Cities.
2. City in the territory of Zebulun, burial place of the judge Elon (Jgs 12:12).

AIJELETH SHAHAR* Hebrew phrase in the title of Psalm 22 (KJV), translated "according to The Hind of the Dawn" (RSV); perhaps a familiar ancient melody to which the psalm was sung. See Music.

AIN
1. City on the eastern border of Canaan, the Promised Land, northeast of the Sea of Galilee (Nm 34:11). The name means "well" or "spring." It may be modern Khirbet 'Ayyun.
2. Town in the territory of Simeon. Many (but not all) scholars consider the site to be En-rimmon (Jos 19:7; cf. Neh 11:29), implying a copyist's error that separated "Ain" from "Rimmon." See En-rimmon.
3. Place name in Joshua 21:16 resulting from another scribal mistake due to similarity of the words "Ain" and "Ashan" in Hebrew. The correct spelling is Ashan (cf. 1 Chr 6:59). See Ashan.

AJAH* KJV rendering of Aiah, Zibeon's son, in Genesis 36:24. See Aiah #1.

AJALON* KJV rendering of Aijalon in Joshua 10:12; 19:42; and 2 Chronicles 28:18. See Aijalon #1.

AKAN Alternate name for Jaakan, Ezer's son, in Genesis 36:27. See Jaakan.

AKELDAMA Name given to the field where Judas committed suicide after betraying Jesus; translated as "Field of Blood" (Acts 1:19). See Blood, Field of.

AKIBA*, Rabbi Jewish leader, prominent about AD 110–135. Akiba came from a humble background and began his scholarly training at the age of 40. Having

attained recognition in rabbinical study, he taught at his own school in Bene-berak, near Jaffa. During the Jewish uprising against the Romans in AD 132–135, Akiba was arrested for teaching the Jewish laws and willingly suffered a martyr's death. He had strongly supported the revolutionary leader Bar-Kochba, holding him to be the long-awaited Messiah. Akiba's rabbinical activities fall into three categories.

Akiba was at Jabneh (Jamnia) when discussions were held there (c. AD 90) concerning books to be included in the Jewish Scriptures and those to be left out. The discussions were less concerned with admitting new books than with reaffirming the canonical status of books that had come into question, especially Ecclesiastes and the Song of Solomon.

Akiba had a view of biblical interpretation that differed from other rabbis. For example, Rabbi Ishmael held that the language of Scripture was to be treated as ordinary human language, following the same grammar, word meanings, etc. In contrast, Akiba insisted that Scripture was to be interpreted in a way that was not applicable to ordinary language. Ordinary language might allow different spellings of the same word with no difference in meaning, for example; but if such a thing happened in Scripture, to Akiba there had to be some reason. Other schools of interpretation accused him of twisting language to force his own interpretations on Scripture. Akiba encouraged a scholar named Aquila to make a Greek translation of the Scriptures that would embody his principles of interpretation. Aquila's translation was therefore overliteral; because it disregarded standard principles of grammar, it cannot be said to be acceptable Greek.
See also Talmud; Bible, Canon of the.

AKIM See Achim.

AKKAD See Accad.

AKKADIANS See Sumerians.

AKKUB
1. One of Elioenai's seven sons and a distant descendant of David (1 Chr 3:24).
2. Ancestor of a family of Levite gatekeepers who returned to Jerusalem with Zerubbabel after the exile (Ezr 2:42; Neh 7:45). This family name was borne by two of his descendants (#3 and #6 below).
3. Descendant of #2 and head of a family of Levite gatekeepers who were among the first to return to Jerusalem after the Babylonian exile (1 Chr 9:17).
4. Ancestor of a group of temple assistants who returned to Jerusalem with Zerubbabel after the exile (Ezr 2:45).
5. Ezra's assistant who explained to the people passages from the law read by Ezra (Neh 8:7).
6. Descendant of #2 above and head of a family of Levite gatekeepers who lived in Jerusalem during the time of Ezra and Nehemiah (Neh 11:19; 12:25-26). He is perhaps the same as #5 above.

AKRABATTENE Place where Judas Maccabeus destroyed the strongholds of the "sons of Esau," from which they were harassing the Jews (1 Macc 5:3; 2 Macc 10:14-23). "In Idumea, at Akrabattene" probably refers to a northern Edomite enclave at or near Acraba (Jdt 7:18) rather than to an area in the Negev Desert as was formerly thought.

AKRABBIM* A mountain pass or slope in southern Palestine between the southwestern tip of the Dead Sea and the wilderness of Zin. The pass (Nm 34:4; Jgs 1:36) of Mt Akrabbim served as part of the southern border of the land given to Judah's tribe after the conquest of Canaan (Jos 15:3; KJV "Maaleh-acrabbim"). During the intertestamental period, Judas Maccabeus won an important victory over the Idumeans at this pass (1 Macc 5:3). Also called Scorpion Pass.

ALABASTER* White or translucent stone, sometimes veined, frequently used to make vases and flasks. *See* Minerals and Metals; Stones, Precious.

ALAMETH* KJV form of Alemeth, Becher's son, in 1 Chronicles 7:8. *See* Alemeth (Person) #1.

ALAMMELECH* KJV form of Allammelech in Joshua 19:26. *See* Allammelech.

ALAMOTH* Hebrew term in the title of Psalm 46 and also in 1 Chronicles 15:20. *See* Music.

ALCIMUS Treacherous high priest of the intertestamental period of Jewish history. A descendant of Aaron but not of the legitimate high-priestly family, Alcimus was declared high priest by the Syrian king Demetrius I, about 163 BC. However, since he was a Hellenist, the Maccabeans who controlled Jerusalem were violently opposed to him. Alcimus thus persuaded Demetrius to send General Bacchides to subdue Judah. Bacchides did so and "placed Alcimus in charge of the country, but Judas Maccabeus and his brothers waged guerrilla warfare against the traitors" (1 Macc 7:1-24). When Alcimus again sought help, Demetrius sent an army under Nicanor that was wiped out by the Maccabeans (1 Macc 7:25-50). Demetrius sent Bacchides back with an even stronger force. This time Judas Maccabeus was killed and Alcimus had free reign in Jerusalem (1 Macc 9:1-53). He "gave orders to tear down the wall of the inner court of the sanctuary," but before this sacrilege could be completed, he was stricken with paralysis; "Alcimus died at that time in great agony" (1 Macc 9:54-57), about 161 BC.

See also Maccabean Period.

ALEMA City in Gilead from which Judas Maccabeus liberated Jews who had been surrounded by hostile Gentiles (1 Macc 5:24-35). Most authorities place it some 25 to 35 miles (40 to 55 kilometers) east of the Sea of Galilee, perhaps at modern Alma in Gilead. Helam, scene of a decisive victory by David, might be the same site (2 Sam 10:16-17).

ALEMETH (Person)
1. Becher's son from Benjamin's tribe (1 Chr 7:8).
2. Son of Jehoaddah (1 Chr 8:36) or Jarah (1 Chr 9:42) and a descendant of King Saul.

ALEMETH (Place) Levitical city in the territory of Benjamin's tribe (1 Chr 6:60; NASB "Allemeth"); alternately called Almon in Joshua 21:18. Its site was at Khirbet 'Almit, about five miles (8 kilometers) northeast of Jerusalem. *See* Levitical Cities.

ALEXANDER
1. The Macedonian conqueror, Alexander the Great (356–323 BC), whose life has influenced history and culture for more than two millennia, down to the present time. He was a brilliant organizer and military strategist, but his greatest achievement was the Hellenization of the empire he won. This Greek cultural influence was a unifying element among many diverse peoples.

The introduction of the Greek language throughout this empire also had far-reaching effect. The OT was translated into Greek in Alexandria, Egypt, and the NT books were written in that language. The earliest Christian missionaries were bilingual, so that it was possible to bring the gospel "to the Jew first, and also to the Greek" (Rom 1:16).

Alexander was the son of an illustrious father, Philip II of Macedon. A seasoned military leader in his teens, Alexander succeeded to the throne at the age of 20 after the assassination of his father. After putting down the rebellions that broke out at his father's death, Alexander crossed the Dardanelles and conquered Asia Minor. In 333 BC, he met and defeated the vaunted Persian army of Darius III at Issus, in a battle that had a lasting historical significance. Moving down the Mediterranean coast, he captured Sidon, Tyre, and Gaza. Reaching Egypt in 332 BC, he was hailed by the oracle of Amon at Siwa as the divine pharaoh. He founded Alexandria, one of the more than 60 cities he established with this name, and then pushed on to the East. At Arbela (331 BC), he again defeated the Persians. When he reached Persia, he seized the cities of Susa, Persepolis, and Ecbatana. He forged eastward until he reached the Indus River; here, with his troops worn out and threatening mutiny, he turned back toward the West. He died in Babylon in 323 BC, a victim of fever, exhaustion, and dissipation, and master of an empire that stretched from the Danube to the Indus and south to the Egyptian Nile.

See also Greece, Greek; Hellenism; Hellenists; Judaism; Alexandria.

2. Brother of Rufus and son of Simon of Cyrene, the man who was passing by at the time Jesus was being led to Golgotha and whom the Roman soldiers compelled to carry the cross (Mk 15:21).
3. A member of the high-priestly family along with Caiaphas, Annas the high priest, and John (Acts 4:6). It was this group who summoned Peter and John to appear before them to account for the healing of the lame man at the Beautiful Gate of the temple (Acts 3).
4. Ephesian who was put forward by the Jews to serve as their spokesman when the silversmith Demetrius roused the Ephesians to riot (Acts 19:33). The preaching of the gospel by Paul and his companions had resulted in the conversion of many people, who left the worship of the goddess Artemis (Diana) and thus reduced the income of the silversmiths, whose revenue derived from the manufacture of images of this deity (Acts 19:23-41).
5. One who, with Hymenaeus, was mentioned as having shipwrecked his faith because of his rejection of conscience (1 Tm 1:20). Paul states that he had "turned them over to Satan so they would learn not to blaspheme God."
6. Coppersmith (2 Tm 4:14). Paul warns Timothy to beware of this man, who had done much harm to Paul and had strongly opposed the message of the gospel. Some scholars think this Alexander is the same as the Alexander of 1 Timothy 1:20 (#5 above).

ALEXANDER (BALAS) EPIPHANES Pretender who claimed to be the son of Antiochus IV Epiphanes. Alexander landed at Ptolemais in 152 BC and from 150 BC onward claimed to be the king. He sought the help of Jonathan Maccabeus to back him and in return appointed Jonathan high priest. Alexander attacked and defeated Syrian King Demetrius I, then strengthened his own position by marrying the daughter of Ptolemy VI of Egypt. In 147 BC, Alexander was challenged by Demetrius II and was overcome in 145 BC (1 Macc 10–11).

ALEXANDER JANNAEUS* (JANNEUS) Jewish ruler of the Hasmonean dynasty. *See* Hasmonean.

ALEXANDRA* Wife of the first Hasmonean to call himself king, Aristobulus (reigned 104–103 BC), and then of his brother Alexander Janneus (103–76 BC), probably through a "levirate" marriage. (Under certain circumstances a Jew was under obligation to marry his deceased brother's widow.) When Janneus died, Salome Alexandra became queen in accordance with her second husband's will. She was the only Jewish woman to rule as queen in the kingdom of Judah apart from the usurper Athaliah (841–835 BC). Janneus had advised his wife to make peace with the Pharisees who had rebelled against him. She took that advice, being the sister of a famous Pharisaic leader, Simon ben Shetach. Salome Alexandra reigned for almost a decade (76–67 BC), a peaceful period during which the Pharisees won considerable power and were first admitted to the Sanhedrin, the supreme Jewish assembly. By the time of Christ, the Pharisees had about equaled the Sadducees in power in the Sanhedrin. *See* Hasmonean.

ALEXANDRIA Egyptian city established by Alexander the Great in 331 BC. Alexandria was the capital city of Egypt through the Hellenistic and Roman periods and, next to Rome, was the most important city in the ancient world. It was built at the western edge of the Nile River delta on a peninsula between the mainland of Egypt and the Mediterranean Sea. Its harbor was protected by the island of Pharos, site of a huge lighthouse (the Pharos of Alexandria), one of the seven wonders of the ancient world. Pharos formed the top of a "T," the stem of which was a long mole running out from the peninsula; on both sides of the "T" lay the ancient harbor.

Alexander built the city to provide a military base, harbor facilities, and trading center with which to control Egypt and the East. The city was laid out in a grid, with two tree-lined streets, about 200 feet (61 meters) wide, that intersected in the middle. It was divided into three districts: Jews in the northeast, Egyptians in the west, and Greeks to the south.

Alexandria was famous in antiquity for its architecture: the lighthouse; the Museum, greatest library and learning center of the Hellenistic age; the mausoleum of Alexander, built by Ptolemy, one of his successors; the Serapeum, a temple to Pan (in the shape of a pine cone, according to the geographer Strabo); and the commercial buildings. Archaeological evidence of these structures of the ancient city is remarkably scarce. An earthquake damaged the lighthouse in AD 796, and it was completely destroyed some 500 years later. Only one scroll holder and a statue have been found from the Museum.

Alexandria played a key role in the history of the Greco-Roman world. When Alexander the Great died in 323 BC, Egypt fell to Ptolemy, one of his four generals. Ptolemy established a dynasty that continued until Cleopatra. Because of Alexander's destruction of Tyre, Alexandria became the Hellenistic center of commerce with the East and with central Egypt. Julius Caesar's romance with Cleopatra led to the end of the Ptolemaic dynasty.

The Museum, not a museum in the modern sense, was actually a university and library. Founded by Ptolemy Philadelphus, it made Alexandria the intellectual center of the Greek world, with emphasis on grammatical studies, literary criticism, and textual preservation. Before its partial destruction by Egyptians and Julius Caesar's forces in 47 BC, it reportedly housed 700,000 volumes, including carefully edited texts of the Greek classics. In the late Hellenistic and Roman periods, the Museum turned in the direction of the new sciences, exemplified by the building of a great lighthouse that could be seen by ingenious use of mirrors 20 miles (32 kilometers) at sea.

From its inception Alexandria had a large Jewish population. Under the patronage of the Ptolemies, Jewish scholars produced the Greek translation of the OT known as the Septuagint. Ethnic tension in the city grew as the Jewish populace increased and prospered. In AD 42 the tension erupted into riots by the Greeks and the expulsion of Jews from the gentile sections into which they had spread. Jewish commercial success, particularly in the wheat trade, led to intensified anti-Semitism.

There is little reference to Alexandria in Scripture. Stephen, who became the first Christian martyr, debated with "Jews from Alexandria" in Jerusalem concerning Jesus as the Messiah (Acts 6:9). Apollos, described as "an eloquent man, well versed in the scriptures," was a native of Alexandria (Acts 18:24). The apostle Paul made his sea journey to Rome aboard two Alexandrian ships (Acts 27:6; 28:11).

The earliest emphasis in biblical studies at Alexandria was Gnostic, under Basilides and continuing under his son Isidore. Later, an allegorizing school developed, with regular support by wealthy patrons and an organized curriculum. Clement and Origen are the names most often associated with this school. The teaching emphasized three levels of meaning in the Scriptures: historical, ethical, and spiritual.

Arianism, a powerful heresy, was later formulated in Alexandria by Arius, presbyter of Alexandria. This school of thought denied the eternality of Christ, arguing that since he was begotten he therefore had a beginning. The chief opponent of Arianism, Athanasius, was also from Alexandria. It was primarily through his efforts that the heretical teaching was dissipated in the fourth century and the Symbol of Nicaea confirmed at the Council of Constantinople in AD 381.

See also Alexander #1; Hellenism; Philo Judaeus; Hellenists.

ALEXANDRINUS*, Codex One of the three most important "codexes," or bound books, containing early copies of the whole Bible in Greek (the other two being the Vaticanus and Sinaiticus codexes). *See* Bible, Manuscripts and Text of the (New Testament).

ALGUM* Wood imported from Lebanon (2 Chr 2:8) and possibly Ophir (2 Chr 9:10-11) for the construction of the temple and the palace and for musical instruments. The term may be a copyist's error of transposition for "almug" tree. *See* Almug; Plants (Algum).

ALIAH* Alternate name for Alvah, Esau's descendant, in 1 Chronicles 1:51. *See* Alvah.

ALIAN* Alternate name for Alvan, Shobal's son, in 1 Chronicles 1:40. *See* Alvan.

ALIEN *See* Foreigner.

ALLAMMELECH Town in Asher's territory (Jos 19:26).

ALLEGORY* A method of interpretation ("allegorizing"), especially biblical interpretation, that seeks to find a deeper moral, theological, spiritual meaning behind the words and literal imagery of the text.

Allegory began among the ancient Greeks, for whom the writings of such epic poets as Hesiod and Homer provided the basis for religion and piety. Later developments in the understandings of life and the universe made these writings appear obsolete. Further, with the passage of time, the significance and identity of some literal expressions of historical, geographic, cultural, and social elements in the poets were lost. In order to maintain the validity of their traditions, interpreters began to employ ingenious schemes through which abiding truths and values were sought by using the objective, literal features of the texts as symbols pointing beyond themselves.

Hellenistic Judaism, best exemplified by the first-century Philo of Alexandria, used allegory to make the OT relevant in the Greco-Roman world. Later, a group of Christian interpreters centered around Alexandria employed allegory as their principal method of handling both the OT and NT. In one form or another allegory was the dominant interpretative method of the Middle Ages. It continues to be highly regarded by some pietistically and mystically oriented contemporary Christians, both Protestant and Roman Catholic.

Since allegorizing is a highly individualized interpretative method, its features widely differ from one practitioner to another. For all allegorists the obvious, literal, objective features and meaning of a text are either irrelevant or of only secondary importance; the significant or true meanings may well be dissociated from objective statements or the historical setting. In more advanced applications of the method the external and obvious are irrelevant and even the historicity of an account is of no consequence. Indeed, the understanding and intention of the original author may count for nothing in determining the "true," "spiritual" meaning of a biblical passage. External and obvious features of a writing are but clues pointing beyond themselves to spiritual meanings. Hence the allegorist makes free use of devices that establish arbitrary connections between ancient and contemporary events, seeks alleged meanings and derivations of word roots or the supposed relationship between similar words and sounds, and emphasizes prepositions. He assigns symbolic significance to individual parts such as persons, places, things, numbers, colors, and the like and may claim to discover truth hidden even in the shapes of letters.

Although the allegorical method has had a long history in the Christian church (and indeed is once specifically used by Paul in Gal 4:24, 26), it has inherent difficulties. These led the Reformers Luther and Calvin to reject allegory as a valid method of interpreting Scripture. The most serious problems include allegory's separation of the meaning of the text from its plain statements in their original historical-grammatical-cultural setting and its inability to provide a basis for evaluating competing, contradictory interpretations of the same passage. Allegory provides no "controls" to protect the interpreter from reading his own meanings into Scripture rather than drawing out the Scripture's more objective message.

See also Hellenism; Philo Judaeus.

ALLELUIA* KJV spelling for Hallelujah. See Hallelujah.

ALLEMETH* NASB rendering of Alemeth in 1 Chronicles 6:60. See Alemeth (Place).

ALLIANCE Close association of powerful individuals or nations for a common objective. Such alliances were ratified by various means, including gifts, oaths, dowries and marriages, and covenants.

In patriarchal times Israelites entered into alliances with foreign nations without hesitation. Abraham had an alliance with three Amorites: Mamre, Eshcol, and Aner (Gn 14:13, 24) and with Abimelech, king of Gerar (Gn 21:22-34). Isaac also made an alliance with Abimelech (Gn 26:26-31). Later, Moses forbade the Israelites to make alliances with the Canaanites (Ex 23:31-33; 34:12; Dt 7:1-4), primarily for religious rea-

sons. In the time of the judges the Israelites were reminded of that command (Jgs 2:1-3), but Joshua 9 tells how Israel was tricked into making an alliance with the Gibeonites.

During the period of the monarchy, various kings formed alliances and intermarried with foreigners. David (before he was king of all Israel) made an agreement with Achish, king of Gath, under which he was expected to fight with the Philistines against the Israelite army of Saul (1 Sm 27:1; 28:2). Solomon made alliances for the purpose of trade with Hiram of Tyre (1 Kgs 5:1-18; 9:26-28) and with the king of Egypt (1 Kgs 9:16). After the division of the kingdom, Asa formed an alliance with the king of Syria, Ben-hadad (1 Kgs 15:18-20). Shortly thereafter, Ahab, King of Israel, joined Jehoshaphat in fighting Syria (1 Kgs 22:1-4; 2 Chr 18:1-13). About a century later, King Pekah of Israel formed an alliance with Rezin, king of Syria, to fight Ahaz, king of Judah (Is 7:1-9), and Ahaz in turn made an alliance with Tiglath-pileser, king of Assyria, to fight against Pekah and Rezin (2 Kgs 16:7-9). The last king of Judah, Zedekiah, made an alliance with Egypt against the Babylonians (2 Kgs 24:20; Ez 17:1-21). In general these alliances brought foreign cults into Jerusalem (2 Kgs 16:10-18) and led the prophets to cry out against them (Hos 8:8-10; Is 30:1-3, 15-16; Jer 2:18).

ALLON (Person) Ziza's ancestor from Simeon's tribe (1 Chr 4:37).

ALLON* (Place) Landmark oak tree in Naphtali's territory, considered in some translations to be the name of a town (Jos 19:33, KJV). The NLT better reads "the oak at Zaanannim." See Zaanannim.

ALLON-BACHUTH*, ALLON-BACUTH* Oak tree near Bethel under which Deborah, Rebekah's aged nurse, was buried (Gn 35:8). The tree was named the "Oak of Weeping."

ALLOTMENT OF THE LAND Assignment of large territories of the Promised Land of Canaan to the 12 tribes of Israel following the Conquest. The specific territory in Canaan to be occupied by each of the 12 tribes of Israel was not left to their own initiative. They were not to possess whatever land they could wrest for themselves by military conquest. Rather, they were ordered to fight unitedly and then divide the total area by casting lots—a method analogous to drawing straws or tossing a coin. The same method was used at other times in Bible history as a means of determining the divine will. Besides avoiding arguments or intertribal fighting, the procedure had theological significance. The outcome was placed solely in God's hands (see Prv 16:33). The Lord thereby reminded his people that the land was his to apportion as he saw fit. In Numbers 26:52-56 the Lord's order for such a lottery was given (see also Nm 34). In Joshua chapters 13–19 the allotment was planned and carried out at Shiloh (19:51).

Assignment of the southern part of Transjordan to two and a half tribes had already been made by Moses (Nm 32). West of the Jordan the remaining nine and a half tribes received portions by lot after their faithful leader, Caleb, got his choice of the region around Hebron. The order in which the tribes were named somewhat follows their relative locations. The territory of the major southern tribe, Judah, included Caleb's lands and extended north to the yet unconquered Jerusalem. Next came the large central portions of the tribes of Ephraim and Manasseh, the patriarch Joseph's sons. Benjamin's area lay between Judah and Ephraim. Then Simeon's territory

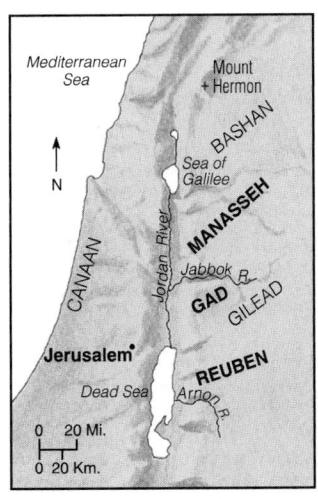

The Tribes East of the Jordan Joshua assigned territory to the tribes of Reuben, Gad, and the half-tribe of Manasseh on the east side of the Jordan. These tribes had asked Moses for land there because it was such wonderful livestock country (Nm 32:1-5).

The Tribes West of the Jordan Judah, Ephraim, and the other half-tribe of Manasseh were the first tribes to receive land west of the Jordan. The remaining seven tribes— Benjamin, Zebulun, Issachar, Asher, Naphtali, Simeon, and Dan—received their inheritance later because they were slow to conquer and possess the land allotted to them.

was named, lying in southern Judah. The remaining tribes listed in Joshua 19, with one exception, received territorial inheritance north of Manasseh. They were Zebulun, Issachar, Asher, Naphtali, and Dan. Dan's tribe drew an allotment west of Judah, but because the Philistines held the coastline, Dan's tribe migrated north and renamed the captured city of Lachish for their tribal ancestor, Dan (see Jgs 18). From then on, "from Dan to Beersheba" meant all of Israel.

Such a method of assigning real estate seems strange to present-day economics, yet with respect to the customs of that time, it made theological sense. Kings and emperors in the ancient Near East were considered sovereign representatives of their gods. They held the ownership right to all lands and gave portions to whomever they pleased. From the time of the exodus, Israel was a theocracy. God was king. No human authority was sovereign or possessed sovereign property rights. God was the Israelites' sole benefactor.

See also Conquest and Allotment of the Land; Israel, History of; Joshua, Book of; Chronology of the Bible (Old Testament).

ALMIGHTY Divine name found in several books of the Bible but particularly in the books of Job and Revelation. *See* God, Names of.

ALMODAD Son or descendant of Joktan in the family of Noah's son Shem (Gn 10:26; 1 Chr 1:20).

ALMON Alternate name for Alemeth in Joshua 21:18. *See* Alemeth (Place).

ALMOND *See* Plants.

ALMON-DIBLATHAIM Area in Moab where the Israelites camped during their 40 years of wandering (Nm 33:46-47). Some identify it with Beth-diblathaim (Jer 48:22).
See also Wilderness Wanderings.

ALMS Charitable gifts. The practice of giving alms to the poor. The English word "alms" comes from a longer Greek word used in the Septuagint (ancient Greek translation of the OT) to translate a Hebrew word for "righteousness." The Hebrew term, in general, is unrelated to almsgiving; consequently the OT has no literal reference to almsgiving. Nevertheless, the Israelites were expected to care for the unfortunate in their midst. The Mosaic

law contains many admonitions to treat the poor justly and humanely. Important among them is Deuteronomy 15:7-11, which, while recognizing the inevitable existence of poverty, commands Israel to take alleviating action. Thus, every seventh year all fields and gardens were to remain unharvested for the benefit of the poor and disadvantaged (Ex 23:10-11). Every third year one-tenth of all produce had to be given to the Levites (a Hebrew tribe that had no property), the sojourner, the fatherless, and the widow (Dt 14:28-29). Forgotten sheaves and the gleanings from grain fields at each harvest were left for the needy and the stranger (Lv 19:9; 23:22); from every vineyard and olive grove, any fallen fruit and the imperfect and topmost clusters were reserved for them (Lv 19:10; Dt 24:20-21). Likewise, festival pilgrims were expected to share food with those in need (Dt 16:11-14).

JESUS' VIEW ON ALMSGIVING
Jesus criticized the way in which many of his contemporaries gave alms (Mt 6:2-4; cf. Acts 3:2; 9:36; 10:2, 4, 31; 24:17). Jesus condemned the giving of alms when done in order to be praised by others. Those who gave for this reason, he said, would receive the reward of public recognition—but that was all. In contrast, God's blessing rested on those who contributed to the poor without drawing attention to themselves.

Several NT passages testify to the early church's continued concern. The needs of the poor in the Jerusalem church were supplied from a common pooling of resources (Acts 2:45; 4:32-35). The apostle Paul recognized the problems of the poor and was active in collecting contributions for them (Rom 12:13; 15:25-27; 1 Cor 16:1-4; 2 Cor 8:1-9, 15; Gal 2:10). James suggested that to demonstrate concern for widows and orphans was an example of pure religion (Jas 1:27). The apostle John warned that anyone who has the world's goods but refuses to share with another in need could hardly be considered a Christian (1 Jn 3:17).

The OT prophets continued to champion the theme of benevolent treatment for the poor. The strongest expressions of the social justice theme are found in Isaiah (1:23; 3:15; 10:1-2; 11:4-5; 58:5-10) and Amos (2:6-8; 4:1; 5:11; 8:4). Similarly, the Psalms and "Wisdom Literature" (Jb; Prv; Eccl) depict the plight of the poor, holding out hope to the afflicted and appealing to others to take up their cause or to improve their condition. The appeals were based on the conviction that all human beings are created by the one God, who had commanded Israel to deal with the unfortunate in their midst with a compassion that went beyond charity to justice.

During the intertestamental period the giving of alms acquired more importance. The general command to show loving-kindness (cf. Lv 19:18) became defined as specific individual acts believed to contribute to personal merit and security. Thus, "almsgiving atones for sin" (Ecclus 3:30) and "delivers from death" (Tb 4:10). Along with prayer and fasting, almsgiving was elevated as one of the most important expressions of Jewish piety (Tb 12:8-9).

ALMUG Wood imported from Ophir for the construction of the temple, the palaces, and for lyres and harps of the temple musicians (1 Kgs 10:11-12). *See* Algum; Plants (Algum).

ALOE Tree known for its fragrant wood; also a plant from which is pressed a juice used in embalming. *See* Plants.

ALOTH A place in one of Solomon's administrative districts (1 Kgs 4:16). *See* Bealoth #2.

ALPHA AND OMEGA Phrase used as a title in the NT for both God (Rv 1:8; 21:6) and Jesus Christ (Rv 22:13). The English equivalent is "the A and the Z." Similar epithets are "the beginning and the end" (Rv 21:6; 22:13) and "the first and the last" (Rv 1:17; 2:8; 22:13).

Alpha and Omega in Greek

Such affirmations, which have their counterpart in the OT (see Is 41:4; 44:6; 48:12), stress the unique and faithful sovereignty of God and his Son, Jesus. They serve as reminders to the Christian reader that the creation of the universe and the end of all human history are both under control of the living God. *See* God, Names of.

ALPHAEUS
1. Father of James, one of the 12 apostles (Mt 10:3; Mk 3:18; Lk 6:15; Acts 1:13), thought by some to be the same as Clopas of John 19:25.
2. Father of Levi, the tax collector (Mk 2:14) who is also known in the Gospels as Matthew (Mt 9:9).

ALTAR The platform upon which offerings are made to the deity. This may include a ritual sacrifice of animals or a burning of incense before God (Ex 30:1-10). The Hebrew word for altar and the verb "to slaughter" both derive from the same root word; they are terms used in connection with the ritual of sacrificing animals to God as a covering for sin. The Greek terms also point to sacrificing animals. The practice was not peculiar to Israel but was widely known in the ancient Middle East. Israel's immediate neighbors, the Canaanites, had their own altars and rituals. The altar was always a raised-up place.

The Bible refers to several altars built by the patriarchs. Noah offered burnt offerings (Gn 8:20). Abraham built an altar at Shechem (Gn 12:7), another at Bethel (Gn 12:8), and one on Mt Moriah (Gn 22:9). Isaac built an

altar at Beersheba (Gn 26:25), and Jacob at Shechem (Gn 33:20) and Bethel (Gn 35:7). Moses built one at Rephidim (Ex 17:15) and another at Horeb (Ex 24:4). In each case the altar was erected to commemorate an event in which God had helped the offerer.

Two altars were used in the tabernacle. One, measuring 5 by 5 by 3 cubits (7.5 by 7.5 by 4.5 feet; 2.3 by 2.3 by 1.4 meters), was made of acacia wood overlaid with bronze and used for burnt offerings (Ex 27:1-8; 38:1-7). The other, smaller one, the golden altar, was about 18 inches (45 centimeters) square and 3 feet (90 centimeters) high, and was used to burn incense before the veil (Ex 30:1-10; 40:5).

In Exodus 20:24-26, instructions were given to Israel to make an altar of earth or of unhewn stones, upon which burnt offerings and peace offerings were to be made in every place where God caused his name to dwell. This very general prescription seems to have allowed various individuals to erect an altar from time to time. Joshua built an altar on Mt Ebal (Jos 8:30-31); the Reubenites, Gadites, and the half-tribe of Manasseh built one in Transjordan (Jos 22:10-16); Gideon built one in Ophrah (Jgs 6:24); the family of David in Bethlehem (1 Sm 20:6, 29); David at the threshing floor of Araunah (2 Sm 24:25); and Elijah on Mt Carmel (1 Kgs 18:30). Apart from Elijah's altar these all predated Solomon's temple.

There were two altars in Solomon's temple. One was 20 cubits square (about 25 feet; 7.6 meters) and 10 cubits high (about 12.5 feet; 3.8 meters). It was made of bronze and used for burnt offerings. It remained the center of temple worship until the temple was destroyed, although in the days of King Ahaz it was removed from its place to the northern side of the temple at the command of the Assyrian ruler Tiglath-pileser (2 Kgs 16:14). It was later restored to its proper place by Hezekiah (2 Chr 29:18). The second, the incense altar, stood in front of the veil. It was made of cedar and overlaid with gold (1 Kgs 6:20-22).

During the exile, when the temple lay in ruins, Ezekiel had a vision of the restored temple in Jerusalem. There was an elaborate altar of burnt offering, rising in three terraces to a height of 10 cubits (17.5 feet; 5.3 meters) and resting on a base about 20 cubits (35 feet; 10.6 meters) square. Although the altar was visionary, it emphasized the need for atonement in Israel (Ez 43:13-17). No reference is made to an incense altar.

Zerubbabel built an altar of burnt offerings (Ezr 3:2) that Antiochus Epiphanes desecrated with a "desolating sacrilege," probably an image of Zeus (1 Macc 1:54).

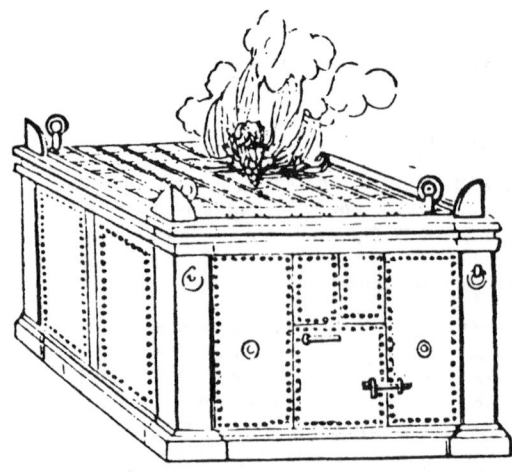

The Altar for Burnt Offerings

The Incense Altar

There was also an altar of incense. Antiochus Epiphanes carried off the golden altar (1 Macc 1:21) in 169 BC. Both were later restored by Judas Maccabeus (1 Macc 4:44-49).

In Christian worship no altar was required, since in the death of Jesus Christ the final sacrifice for sin had been made. There are numerous references to both the altar of burnt offering in the temple (Mt 5:23-24; 23:18-20, 35; Lk 11:51; 1 Cor 9:13; 10:18; Heb 7:13; Rv 11:1) and the altar of incense, both in the earthly temple (Lk 1:11) and in the heavenly temple (Rv 6:9; 8:5; 9:13).

See also Tabernacle; Temple.

AL-TASCHITH* Hebrew phrase in the titles of Psalms 57, 58, 59, and 75 (KJV), translated "Do Not Destroy!"; perhaps a familiar ancient melody to which the psalms were performed. *See* Music.

ALUSH Place where Israel encamped during the wilderness wanderings, mentioned as being between Dophkah and Rephidim (Nm 33:13-14) on the way to Mt Sinai.

See also Wilderness Wanderings.

ALVAH Esau's descendant and a chief of Edom (Gn 36:40); alternately called Aliah in 1 Chronicles 1:51.

ALVAN Shobal's son and a descendant of Esau (Gn 36:23); alternately spelled Alian in 1 Chronicles 1:40.

AMAD Town in northern Palestine near Mt Carmel, within the boundaries of Asher's territory (Jos 19:26).

AMAL Helem's son and a descendant of Asher (1 Chr 7:35).

AMALEK, AMALEKITES Amalek was the son of Eliphaz (Esau's son) by his concubine, Timna (Gn 36:12; 1 Chr 1:36). Descendants of this tribal chief of Edom were known as Amalekites. They settled in the Negev Desert and became allies of the Edomites, Ammonites, Moabites, Ishmaelites, and Midianites. The Amalekites were notable enemies of Israel. Amalek inherited the fra-

ternal feud that had begun with his grandfather Esau's antagonism toward Jacob. Since Jacob was one of the progenitors of Israel, the conflict between Amalek and Israel had both a theological and political basis.

The territory of the nomadic Amalekites in the Negev ranged at times from south of Beersheba to the southeast as far as Elath and Ezion-geber. They undoubtedly raided westward into the coastal plain, eastward into the Arabah wastelands, and possibly over into Arabia. In the Negev they blocked the path of the Israelites during the exodus (Ex 17:8-16).

Israel's first encounter with the warriors of Amalek came at Rephidim near Sinai. Moses stood on top of a hill and held up the rod of God until Israel won the battle, then built an altar and named it "The Lord Is My Banner" (Ex 17:1, 8-16). The Amalekites attacked stragglers during Israel's desert wanderings (Dt 25:17-18). After reaching the boundary of the Promised Land but rejecting Caleb and Joshua's report of it, the unbelieving and disheartened Israelites attacked the Amalekites and were defeated (Nm 14:39-45).

When Balaam was summoned by King Balak of Moab to curse Israel, he turned his curse upon Moab and in his last oracle predicted the end of Amalek's tribe (Nm 24:20). Moses, in his farewell speech, reminded the children of Israel that they had been harassed by Amalek's descendants and should blot out all remembrance of the name Amalek (Dt 25:17-19).

During the period of the judges Amalekites continued to occupy their traditional area and became associated with the Kenites (1 Sm 15:5-6), descendants of Moses' father-in-law, who settled in the Negev south of Arad (Jgs 1:16). The Amalekites, still associated with other nomadic tribes (Moabites, Ammonites, Midianites), were rallied by Eglon, king of Moab, to defeat Israel and seize Jericho (Jgs 3:12-14). The Song of Deborah cites Amalek as one of a coalition of tribes against Israel (Jgs 5:14, KJV). The name is omitted in a number of modern translations, and in others translated as "into the valley" (RSV). However, Amalekite harassment is referred to in other passages of the time of Deborah and Barak (Jgs 6:3, 33; 7:12). Gideon defeated the coalition (Jgs 7:12-25), but there is no evidence that the Amalekites were driven out of the Negev.

According to 1 Samuel, Saul sent his armies out against the Amalekites (14:47-48) and received a command from God to destroy them and all their possessions (15:1-3). He did attack their city (15:4-7) but did not kill their king, Agag (15:8). Saul distributed the choicest Amalekite livestock to his men (15:9), for which the Lord condemned him and sent Samuel to tell him that his kingship was ended because of his sin (15:10-31). Samuel then slaughtered Agag (15:32-35). A remnant of Amalekites must have escaped, since they appeared again as David's foes while he was still a young warrior (27:8). He rescued his two wives carried off by Amalekites and killed most of the raiding party (30:1-20). The Amalekites were Israel's sworn enemies throughout King David's reign (2 Sm 1:1). They are listed among the enemies of Israel (2 Sm 8:12; 1 Chr 18:11; Ps 83:7). Destruction of the few surviving Amalekites came several hundred years after David during the reign of Hezekiah of the southern kingdom of Judah (1 Chr 4:41-43).

AMALEKITES, Hill Country (Mount*) of the An area near Pirathon in Ephraim, probably about six miles (9.6 kilometers) west of Shechem (Jgs 12:15). It is mentioned in the Hebrew Bible but not in the Greek manuscripts of the OT. Some scholars find the reference confusing; however, it is possible that an argument based on Judges 5:14 and 12:15 can be made that there was a small Amalekite district in Ephraim.

AMAM Town in the southern part of the kingdom of Judah, along the border of Edom (Jos 15:26).

AMANA Mountain ridge, probably in the Anti-Lebanon range, mentioned along with Mt Senir and Mt Hermon (Sg 4:8). It is perhaps the source of the Abana (Amana) River (2 Kgs 5:12). *See* Abana.

AMARIAH Common OT name, meaning "the Lord has spoken" or "the Lord has promised."

1. Son of Meraioth in the line of Aaron's son Eleazer (1 Chr 6:7, 52).
2. High priest, Azariah's son and Ahitub's father (1 Chr 6:11; Ezr 7:3).
3. Hebron's second son and Kohath's grandson from Levi's tribe (1 Chr 23:19; 24:23).
4. Chief priest during the reign of Jehoshaphat of the southern kingdom of Judah (2 Chr 19:11).
5. Levite who served faithfully under King Hezekiah of Judah (2 Chr 31:14-15).
6. One of Binnui's sons, who obeyed Ezra's exhortation to divorce his pagan wife after the exile (Ezr 10:42).
7. Priest who returned from Babylon with Zerubbabel (Neh 12:2, 13) and who, with Nehemiah and others, signed Ezra's covenant of faithfulness to God after the exile (Neh 10:3).
8. Shephatiah's son, a descendant of Judah and ancestor of Athaiah. Amariah lived in Jerusalem after the exile (Neh 11:4).
9. Hezekiah's son and ancestor of the prophet Zephaniah (Zep 1:1).
10. Person mentioned in the Ezra genealogies of 1 Esdras 8:2 and 2 Esdras 1:2. In the first list he is Uzzi's son and Ahitub's father. In the second he is Azariah's son and Eli's father. He may be the same as Amariah #1 or #2 above, since both sources list him as Ahitub's father.

AMARNA TABLETS* Clay tablets, mostly letters from royal archives, the only cuneiform records ever found in Egypt. The 379 Amarna tablets were recovered from ruins located on a plain on the east bank of the Nile about 190 miles (305.7 kilometers) south of Cairo. The region is named after a tribe that settled there in modern times, the Beni Amran or Amarna tribe. The site of the ruins is mistakenly called Tell el-Amarna; *tell* is an Arabic word meaning "hill" or "mound," but this site lies on a plain. A village in the area bears the name "el-Till," and its name came to be annexed to the name el-Amarna.

The cuneiform script in which the tablets are written is a system that employs nail or wedge-shaped marks impressed into the writing material, usually clay, in many specific patterns. Each one of the patterns (called a "sign") represents a sound or, sometimes, a word. Cuneiform script could be used to represent a number of different languages, just as Latin script can be used to represent English, French, German, etc. The language of the Amarna tablets, with only three exceptions, is a certain dialect of Akkadian. Although its homeland was the general area of Mesopotamia, that Semitic language came to be the language of international correspondence and diplomacy in the Near East during the second millennium BC.

Twenty-nine of the tablets contain what appear to be copybook exercises for student scribes: lists of cuneiform signs, vocabulary lists, practice copies of sections of Mesopotamian mythological narratives. The other 350 texts are letters from the diplomatic correspondence of Amenophis III and Amenophis IV. The letters span a period of about 30 years, dating from sometime during the reign of Amenophis III to shortly after the death of Amenophis IV. They are mostly messages received from various local rulers and princes in Syria and Palestine, but there are also letters from monarchs of more powerful nations to the far north and east.

The letters show varying relationships between the Egyptian pharaoh and the writers. Some writers were considered as more or less equals of the pharaoh, the others as inferiors. Diplomatic relationships between the correspondents were often established by treaties and confirmed by marriages. Kings who were regarded as inferiors in their diplomatic relationship with the pharaoh referred to themselves as "your servant" and to the pharaoh as "my lord," "my sun," or sometimes as "my god." Modern-day researchers call such underling rulers "vassals" and their domains, "vassal states"; the pharaoh in such a relationship is referred to as a suzerain. Rulers regarded as relative equals of the pharaoh referred to themselves as "your brother" and to the pharaoh as "my brother," a relationship now described as a parity relationship.

The messages received by the pharaohs from their equals discuss such matters as exchange of gifts, negotiations for marriages, continuation of diplomatic ties, and promotion of commercial transactions. They also contain inventories of gifts sent or received and request presents, gold, or other goods. Such correspondence was received from rulers of the kingdoms of Babylonia, Mitanni, Assyria, Hatti (the Hittite kingdom), and Alashiya (Cyprus).

Of special interest are some letters from the Palestine area containing appeals for military assistance and references to military activity. Their mention of the "Habiru" was immediately connected with the word "Hebrew." The Habiru were said to be at several locations in Palestine and to be "plundering all the lands of the king." By fastening together several pieces of information, a conclusion was initially drawn that the Amarna letters came from the general period of the Hebrew exodus from Egypt and later invasion of Palestine under Joshua. Thus, some of the letters were taken to be firsthand reports of the invasion from the point of view of the inhabitants of Palestine.

However, reconsideration of the Amarna letters, along with other available information, soon showed that conclusion to be mistaken. The Habiru were not the invading Hebrews. The word "Habiru" is a dialect spelling of the word "Apiru." This term, in both the Amarna letters and other texts, describes a class of people that may be called "outlaws" or "renegades." People of various nationalities could be labeled "Apiru." A person was not born an Apiru; rather he could join the Apiru or, because of his actions, become an Apiru. The Apiru ranged throughout Syria and Palestine and had no special homesite. At times groups of them hired themselves out as mercenary troops; at other times they acted as brigands. *See* Inscriptions; Egypt, Egyptian.

AMASA

1. Son of Ithra (Jether) and David's sister Abigail (2 Sm 17:25; 1 Chr 2:17), and therefore David's nephew. Amasa was a captain who supported Absalom in his rebellion against his father, David. After Absalom was killed by David's general Joab, David pardoned Amasa

and replaced Joab with him (2 Sm 19:13). Greatly offended, Joab awaited his revenge and, as soon as he had opportunity, treacherously assassinated his unsuspecting rival (2 Sm 20:4-13). David was unable to punish Joab but instructed his son Solomon to see that Joab was executed for murdering Amasa and another of David's generals (1 Kgs 2:5-6, 28-34).

2. Hadlai's son from Ephraim's tribe. Amasa supported the prophet Oded's opposition to making slaves of women and children captured from the southern kingdom of Judah in the time of King Ahaz (2 Chr 28:8-13).

AMASAI

1. Elkanah's son (1 Chr 6:25) and Mahath's father (1 Chr 6:35), listed in the genealogy of Heman the singer.
2. Leader of 30 warriors who joined David at Ziklag after deserting King Saul (1 Chr 12:18).
3. Trumpeter priest in the procession when David brought the ark of God to Jerusalem (1 Chr 15:24).
4. Father of another Mahath. This Mahath was Hezekiah's contemporary and a participant in his revival (2 Chr 29:12).

AMASHAI*, AMASHSAI

Azarel's son and one of the leading priests who returned to Jerusalem after the Babylonian exile (Neh 11:13). Amashsai may possibly be identical with Maasai (1 Chr 9:12).

AMASIAH

Military leader in the time of Jehoshaphat, in charge of 200,000 men. Amasiah was Zichri's son and a man of unusual piety (2 Chr 17:16).

AMAW*

Region near the Euphrates River that included the city of Pethor, to which King Balak of Moab sent messengers in search of the soothsayer Balaam (Nm 22:5). The name Amaw appears in the Idrimi Inscription (1450 BC) and on the tomb of Qen-amun, who served under Amenophis II of Egypt in the latter part of the 15th century BC.

AMAZIAH

1. Ninth king of Judah (796–767 BC), who at age 25 succeeded his father, King Joash, when Joash was assassinated after a 40-year reign (2 Kgs 12:19-21). Amaziah's mother was Jehoaddin. He ruled Judah for 29 years before he too was killed by assassins (14:18-20). When Amaziah began his reign, another Joash was ruling the northern kingdom of Israel (14:1-2).

Amaziah was not like his ancestor David (2 Kgs 14:3). Like his father, Amaziah did things that pleased God, but he failed to remove the pagan shrines that were corrupting the nation's religious life. He himself was respectful of the law of Moses, at least at the beginning (14:4-6).

Amaziah was unwise in his dealings with the rival kingdom of Israel. To go to war against the Edomites, he hired 100,000 mercenaries from Israel. Warned by a prophet not to use them in battle, Amaziah discharged them. On their way out of Judah the angry soldiers raided cities and killed 3,000 people. Nevertheless, Amaziah's troops were victorious against the Edomites. At the Valley of Salt they killed 10,000 of the enemy in battle and executed another 10,000 prisoners (2 Chr 25:5-13).

Foolishly, Amaziah brought Edomite idols back with him after his conquest and was soon worshiping them. The Lord sent a prophet to announce Amaziah's doom for such spiritual rebellion (2 Chr 25:14-16).

Proud of his conquest of Edom, Amaziah soon declared war on King Joash of Israel. Joash warned him in a parable that Judah would be crushed like a thistle. Amaziah refused to back down, and the two armies met at Beth-shemesh in Judah. Amaziah's army was routed. Jerusalem was captured and the temple and palace looted. Amaziah was taken prisoner but was evidently left in Jerusalem. He outlived Joash of Israel by 15 years (2 Chr 25:17-26). Amaziah was murdered in Lachish, to which he had fled when he heard about a plot against him in Jerusalem. His body was brought back to the capital city and buried in the royal cemetery (2 Chr 25:27-28).

2. Father of Joshah, a member of Simeon's tribe (1 Chr 4:34).
3. Hilkiah's son, a Levite of Merari's clan (1 Chr 6:45).
4. Priest of Bethel in the days of Jeroboam II and an opponent of the prophet Amos (Am 7:10-17).

AMBASSADOR

Messenger or envoy officially representing a higher authority. In the OT, an ambassador was a messenger, envoy, or negotiator sent on a special, temporary mission as an official representative of the king, government, or authority who sent him. Examples include the ambassador of Pharaoh (Is 30:4, KJV), of the princes of Babylon (2 Chr 32:31), and of Neco, king of Egypt (2 Chr 35:21). In the letters of Paul, the apostle called himself an ambassador for Christ because he had an apostolic mission to convey the gospel of Christ to the Gentiles (2 Cor 5:20; Eph 6:20).

AMBER

Fossilized resin of certain cone-bearing plants. The resinous product of these conifers loses its volatile components and turns into a translucent yellow or orange solid. The word is used in the KJV to describe a color seen in visions of the Lord (Ez 8:2). The color is similar to that of polished brass or bronze (Ez 1:4, 27). *See* Color.

AMBUSH

See Warfare.

AMEN

Hebrew word meaning "so it is" or "let it be," derived from a verb meaning "to be firm or sure." Some translations of the Bible always retain the Hebrew word *amen* in the text. Others translate it by an expression such as "truly" or "I tell you the truth," or sometimes omit it altogether. Because of its use in the OT, "amen" was also used in Christian worship and religious writings, including the Greek NT.

"Amen" has much more significance than merely being the last word in a prayer. In fact, that practice is not evidenced in the Bible and was not especially frequent in ancient times. In the nearly 30 times it is used in the OT, "amen" almost always occurs as a response to what has preceded. The significance of the response is that with it the people adopted what had just been said as if it were their own. For example, in Deuteronomy 27:15-26 (where "amen" appears 12 times) the people responded with "amen" after each statement of a curse directed toward those who disobey God. Similarly, "amen" is used as a response after statements of promise (Jer 11:5) or of praise and thanksgiving (1 Chr 16:36), and as a conclusion to the first four of the five "books" of Psalms (Pss 41:13; 72:19; 89:52; 106:48). The only exceptions in the OT are two occurrences in Isaiah 65:16. There, the phrase "the God of amen" (or "the God of truth") stresses that God is the one who is "firm"; that is, he is completely trustworthy and faithfully fulfills his promises.

The use of "amen" as a response to a preceding statement is continued in the NT epistles and book of

Revelation. It appears after doxologies (Eph 3:21), benedictions (Gal 6:18), the giving of thanks (1 Cor 14:16), prophecy (Rv 1:7), and statements of praise (Rv 7:12). From 1 Corinthians 14:16 it is clear that a response of "amen" after a statement of thanks was a means for worshipers to participate by showing agreement with what had been said.

AMEN AND AMEN

Two uses of "amen" by the early church focused special attention on Jesus Christ. In 2 Corinthians 1:20 (cf. Rv 1:7) "amen" is used almost as an equivalent to "yes." Jesus is viewed as God's means of saying yes to us, fulfilling his promises. Jesus is also viewed as our means of saying yes to God; through Jesus the "amen" response of believers is presented for the glory of God. In Revelation 3:14, "the Amen" is used as a title of Christ to emphasize his reliability and the truth of what he says (cf. Is 65:16).

The use of "amen" in the Gospels, however, is entirely different from its use in the OT, the early church, or anywhere else in Jewish literature. Excluding Matthew 6:13 (KJV) and Mark 16:20 (both passages with textual uncertainty), all of the 100 occurrences of "amen" are spoken by Jesus and always precede what is said rather than coming after as a response. In the synoptic Gospels (Mt, Mk, Lk) the form is always "Amen, I say to you"; in John it is always the doubled form "Amen, amen, I say to you" (Jn 3:3, 5, etc.). That unique use of "amen" stresses both the authority with which he taught and his majesty: Jesus' words come with absolute certainty and are binding on all.

AMETHYST Purple variety of quartz used in jewelry. *See* Minerals and Metals; Stones, Precious.

AMI Official in Solomon's court whose descendants returned to Jerusalem after the exile (Ezr 2:57). Also spelled Amon in Nehemiah 7:59. *See* Amon (Person) #3.

AMILLENNIALISM* *See* Millennium.

AMINADAB* KJV form of Amminadab in Matthew 1:4 and Luke 3:33. *See* Amminadab #1.

AMITTAI Father of the prophet Jonah from Zebulun's tribe. Amittai came from the small village of Gath-hepher northeast of Nazareth (2 Kgs 14:25; Jon 1:1).

AMMAH Hill north of Jerusalem in the area of Gibeon. A battle fought there between David's troops under Joab and Ishbosheth's troops under Abner was the beginning of a long war between followers of Saul and followers of David (2 Sm 2:24-32; 3:1).

AMMI Hebrew word meaning "my people." The expression "people of God" is the most common designation for the nation of Israel in the OT. It originated in God's promise to Moses before the exodus: "I will make you my own special people (*'ammi*), and I will be your God" (Ex 6:7, NLT). For Israel to be called "my people" emphasized the unique personal nature of their religion in contrast with the idolatry of neighboring nations. The word represented God's love for them and his faithfulness to the promises he had made to their forefathers (Dt 4:37; 7:8). In return for the privileges the name implied, God required faithfulness and

obedience from Israel. Yet repeatedly the people of Israel failed, and repeatedly the prophets reminded them of their responsibility to God.

An example of such prophetic warning is found in the writings of Hosea. The prophet saw in his own marriage to an adulterous wife a picture of God's relationship to his people: God had joined himself to a people who had forsaken him for other gods. The names Hosea gave his children reflected God's attitude toward his unfaithful people. The first child was named Jezreel (Hos 1:4), a name with a double meaning. As the name of the place where King Ahab murdered Naboth (1 Kgs 21:1-16), it recalled a terrible experience in Israel's history. But the name also means "God sows," and expressed Hosea's hope that the people of Israel, despite all their failures, would soon return to God. A second child was named Lo-ruhamah ("Not pitied," Hos 1:6). That name expressed God's hatred for disobedience and his inclination to turn from an unrepentant people. Hosea's third child was named Lo-ammi ("Not my people," Hos 1:9). That name represented ultimate tragedy for Israel: dissolution of God's covenant relationship with them. God was saying to Israel, "Name him Lo-ammi—'Not my people'—for Israel is not my people, and I am not their God" (Hos 1:9). Although all seemed lost, Hosea's prophecy did not end on a note of doom. Rather, he foresaw that Israel would repent. In response, God would restore his covenant relationship with them: "And to those I called 'Not my people,' I will say, 'Now you are my people.' Then they will reply, 'You are our God!'" (Hos 2:23).

AMMIDIANS Name used in a list of towns identifying groups of exiles that returned from Babylon with Zerubbabel around 538 BC (1 Esd 5:20). Corresponding lists in Ezra 2:25-26 and Nehemiah 7:29-30 make no mention of a group from such a place.

AMMIEL

1. Gemalli's son, one of 12 men sent by Moses to spy out the land of Canaan. Ammiel represented Dan's tribe (Nm 13:12) and later died because of a plague (Nm 14:37).
2. Father of Machir of Lo-debar. Mephibosheth, Jonathan's son, was hidden from David in Machir's house (2 Sm 9:4-5). Machir later helped supply David in his war with Absalom (2 Sm 17:27-29).
3. Father of David's wife, Bath-shua (or Bathsheba, 1 Chr 3:5). Ammiel is also called Eliam (2 Sm 11:3).
4. Sixth son of Obed-edom, who, along with his family, served as gatekeeper in the temple during David's reign (1 Chr 26:5, 15).

AMMIHUD

1. Father of a leader of Ephraim's tribe, Elishama (Nm 1:10). Ammihud was Joshua's great-grandfather (1 Chr 7:26).
2. Father of Shemuel from Simeon's tribe. Shemuel helped Moses apportion the Promised Land (Nm 34:20).
3. Father of Pedahel from Naphtali's tribe. Pedahel also helped Moses apportion the Promised Land (Nm 34:28).
4. Father of King Talmai of Geshur. Talmai gave refuge to Absalom when he fled after murdering Amnon (2 Sm 13:37).
5. Omri's son and father of Uthai from Judah's tribe (1 Chr 9:4).

AMMINADAB

1. Father of Elisheba, who was Aaron's wife (Ex 6:23). Amminadab was also the father of Nahshon, Judah's tribal leader in the wilderness (Nm 1:7; 2:3; 7:12, 17; 10:14; 1 Chr 2:10). Amminadab is listed in the genealogy of David (Ru 4:18-22) and later in the genealogy of Jesus Christ (Mt 1:4; Lk 3:33). *See* Genealogy of Jesus Christ.
2. Alternate name for Izhar, one of Kohath's sons (1 Chr 6:22). *See* Izhar #1.
3. Levite contemporary of King David who helped bring the ark of the Lord to Jerusalem (1 Chr 15:1-4, 10-11).

AMMINADIB*

Word occurring in some English versions of the Song of Songs 6:12, "or ever I was aware, my soul made me like the chariots of Amminadib" (ASV mg, NASB mg). More recent translators have not regarded the term as a proper name. Some proposals for more accurate wording are: "among the chariots of my willing people" (ASV); "in a chariot beside my prince" (RSV); "over the chariots of my noble people" (NASB); and "in my princely bed with my beloved one" (NLT).

AMMISHADDAI

Ahiezer's father. Ahiezer was leader of Dan's tribe when the Israelites were wandering in the Sinai wilderness after their escape from Egypt (Nm 1:12; 2:25; 10:25). As leader he presented his tribe's offering at the consecration of the tabernacle (Nm 7:66, 71).

AMMIZABAD

Benaiah's son. Both Benaiah and Ammizabad were high-ranking officers in King David's army (1 Chr 27:5-6).

AMMON, AMMONITES

A Semitic people who occupied a fertile area northeast of Moab in Transjordan between the Arnon and Jabbok Rivers and extending eastward to the Syrian Desert. The chief city was Rabbah (Rabbath-ammon), modern Amman, capital of Jordan.

The Ammonites traced their ancestry to the younger daughter of Lot (Gn 19:38). Their name in Hebrew originally meant "son of my paternal clan," preserving the remembrance of an actual clan and personal name, and suggesting a kinship between the Ammonites and Israelites. The name occurred frequently in the ancient Near East from the middle of the second millennium on. One form was found in Assyrian inscriptions; other forms are seen in Ugaritic texts of the 15th century BC, in the Mari texts, in the Amarna tablets, and in the Alalakh tablets.

The Ammonites originated in the southern Transjordan region about the beginning of the second millennium BC. Though these people were of mixed ancestry, the languages they spoke were closely related to Hebrew. Ammonite was written in the old Canaanite-Phoenician script, which could probably be read and understood by Israelites. Ammonites intermarried with Hebrews (1 Kgs 14:21, 31; 2 Chr 12:13), and their personal names reflected early Arabic influences.

In language, ethnic background, and physical characteristics the Ammonites were difficult to distinguish from Amorites and were probably closely related. Both may have entered the land at about the same time, for when Joshua led the Israelites into Canaan, both the Ammonite kingdom and the Amorite kingdom of Heshbon were already well established.

The OT states that the territory of Ammon was once occupied by a race of giants called Rephaim or Zamzummim, about whom almost nothing is known (Dt 2:20-21; "Zuzim," Gn 14:5). The Genesis Apocryphon found among the Dead Sea Scrolls mentions them as one of the people defeated by the alliance of four kings (Gn 14:1, 5). The expedition of Chedorlaomer, king of Elam (Gn 14), broke the power of those giants and probably made the occupation of the land by Esau, Ammon, and Moab much easier. King Og was "of the remnant of the Rephaim" known to the Ammonites (Dt 3:11). His bed was evidently an object of veneration because of its unusual size.

When the Israelites arrived at Kadesh, they encountered the well-organized kingdom of Edom but were refused permission to pass through Edomite territory (Nm 20:14-21). They journeyed northward to Ammonite country, which was then occupied by the Amorite king Sihon. He also refused them permission to pass through his land, but the Israelites defeated him in battle and occupied his country (Nm 21:21-24). They were instructed by God through Moses not to try to occupy Ammonite territory, as it had already been given to the descendants of Lot (Dt 2:19, 37).

Continuing northward, the Israelites defeated King Og of Bashan (Dt 3:1-11), then went down to the Jordan Valley, where they camped on the plains of Moab. There Balak, king of Moab, hired a soothsayer, Balaam, to pronounce a curse on the Israelites, but Balaam pronounced a blessing each time instead (Nm 22–24). For supporting the Moabites in their actions, the Ammonites were excluded from the congregation of the Lord to the tenth generation (Dt 23:3; Neh 13:1-2).

The Israelite tribes of Gad and Reuben and the half-tribe of Manasseh were attracted to the fertile Transjordan region that had belonged to the Amorites and Bashan and decided to settle there on the Ammonite frontier (Nm 32; Dt 3:16; Jos 13:8-32). Subsequently they built an altar at the Jordan River, which the other tribes at first interpreted as an act of rebellion in that they appeared to be establishing a rival place of worship (Jos 22:10-34).

Before the Israelite conquest of Canaan, the Ammonites evidently had not attained the same level of political organization and settled life as the neighboring Moabites and Edomites. Even as late as the seventh century BC the nation was essentially nomadic. Shortly after Israel settled in Canaan, the Ammonites allied with the Moabites and Amalekites when King Eglon of Moab tried to regain former Moabite territory at the north end of the Dead Sea (Jgs 3:12-13).

By the end of the 12th century BC the Israelites, then securely established in the land of Canaan, angered God by their worship of the deities of the Syrians, Sidonians, Moabites, Ammonites, and Philistines (Jgs 10:6). The Ammonites, in their first recorded political expansion, launched an attack against Israel and were able to establish themselves in Gilead (Jgs 10:7-8). They then crossed the Jordan and attacked the tribes of Judah, Benjamin, and Ephraim (Jgs 10:9). In desperation the elders of Gilead turned for help to Jephthah, a social outcast but an able military leader (Jgs 11:1-11). He defeated the Ammonites so decisively that it was unnecessary for him to wage further campaigns against Ammonite settlements west of the Jordan (Jgs 11:12-33).

Near the end of the 11th century an Ammonite king named Nahash came to power, determined to reestablish Ammonite dominion over Israelite settlements in Transjordan. He launched an aggressive military campaign around 1020 BC that took him as far north as Jabesh-gilead. The inhabitants of the town were willing to surrender to him but delayed their surrender to appeal for help from Saul, the recently consecrated Israelite king. Saul quickly organized an army and decisively defeated the Ammonites (1 Sm 11:1-11). The victory ensured freedom from Ammonite domination in the

Jordan Valley for several centuries, although later in his reign Saul was forced to fight further battles with the enemies of Israel, including Ammonites (1 Sm 14:47-48).

When David became king, he took silver and gold from the Ammonites, Philistines, and Amalekites, either as spoils or as tribute (2 Sm 8:11-12; 1 Chr 18:11). Soon thereafter, David sent Joab at the head of a strong army to devastate the Ammonite countryside and besiege the capital city of Rabbah (2 Sm 11:1; 1 Chr 20:2). The siege lasted many months, but Joab weakened the city and David then completed its capture (2 Sm 12:26-29). In a ceremony of capitulation the Ammonite king's massive golden crown was placed on David's head (2 Sm 12:30; 1 Chr 20:1). The conquered city was plundered, and its inhabitants were enslaved. Other Ammonite cities were taken, and the nation was added to the growing number of vassal states of Israel (2 Sm 12:31; 1 Chr 20:3). David appointed a governor over the Ammonites from the Ammonite royal family. Shobi, another son of Nahash (and therefore Hanun's brother), became ruler of the Ammonites and aided David during his flight from Absalom's rebellion (2 Sm 17:27). One of David's best warriors was an Ammonite (2 Sm 23:37).

Ammonite relations with Israel remained generally peaceful during the reign of Solomon, David's successor, with the Ammonites undoubtedly sharing in the prosperity and wealth of that period. After the death of Solomon, the kingdom split apart under Rehoboam and was further weakened by a campaign of Shishak, king of Egypt, that swept through Palestine and also through Ammonite territory. Taking advantage of the situation, the Ammonites declared their independence from Israel and Judah. The Ammonites joined the Moabites and Meunites to make war against King Jehoshaphat of Judah (reigning 871–848 BC). In fear, Jehoshaphat sought help from God in prayer (2 Chr 20:1-12). The Ammonites and their allies began fighting among themselves and destroyed each other, leaving behind great spoils for Jehoshaphat and his people—which took three days to be carried away (2 Chr 20:22-25). Eventually the Ammonites recovered, so that by the end of the seventh century BC, Ammon had again become completely independent and was the dominant state of south Transjordan. Ammonite independence was short, however, for in 599 BC, according to the Babylonian Chronicle, Babylonian king Nebuchadnezzar led his troops into Syria and began raiding southern Palestine. In 593 BC, the Ammonites met in Jerusalem with King Zedekiah of Judah and representatives from Edom, Moab, Tyre, and Sidon in a conspiracy to rebel against Babylon (Jer 27:1-3). The prophet Jeremiah warned them that God would cause their plan to fail (Jer 27:4-22). Nebuchadnezzar sent an army to crush the rebellion and attacked Jerusalem, which he destroyed after a lengthy and bitter siege (586 BC), deporting many Jews to Babylonia. Ammon was not immediately invaded, however, and many Judeans sought refuge there (Jer 40:11), including a man named Ishmael (Jer 40:13-16). Ishmael plotted with Baalis, king of Ammon, to assassinate Gedaliah, whom Nebuchadnezzar had appointed governor over Judea, now reduced to a province of Babylonia. After carrying out the assassination, Ishmael escaped to Ammon (Jer 41:1-15). Nebuchadnezzar then sent troops that sacked Rabbah and took captive many of the Ammonites. Though the city was not destroyed, the destruction of the countryside was thorough. In the third century BC, Arab invaders poured in and destroyed the remaining organized political structure, thus marking the end of Ammon as a semi-independent state.

AMNON
1. David's oldest son by his wife Ahinoam, born in Hebron (2 Sm 3:2; 1 Chr 3:1). Amnon deceived and violated Tamar, his beautiful half sister, and was killed in revenge by Tamar's brother Absalom (2 Sm 13:1-33).
2. First son of Shimon from Judah's tribe (1 Chr 4:20).

AMOK Priest who returned to Jerusalem with Zerubbabel after the exile. Amok was the ancestor of Eber, a priest under Joiakim (Neh 12:7, 20).

AMON (Person)
1. Governor of the city of Samaria during the reign of Ahab in Israel (1 Kgs 22:26; 2 Chr 18:25). Amon imprisoned the prophet Micaiah while Ahab defied Micaiah's warning against attacking Ramoth-gilead.
2. King Manasseh's son, the 15th king of Judah (642–640 BC). Amon was 22 years old when he became king. He indulged in idolatry like his father and after a two-year reign was assassinated in a palace coup (2 Kgs 21:19-26; 2 Chr 33:20-25). See Israel, History of; Chronology of the Bible (Old Testament).
3. Official of Solomon; his descendants returned to Jerusalem after the exile (Neh 7:59). The spelling Ami (Ezr 2:57) is a variant of this name.
4. Egyptian god, probably a fertility deity (Jer 46:25).

AMON (Place) Part of the Hebrew name for Thebes, the capital of upper Egypt (Jer 46:25). See Thebes.

AMORITES Semitic people found throughout the Fertile Crescent of the Near East at the beginning of the second millennium BC. Amorites are first mentioned in the Bible as descendants of Canaan in a list of ancient peoples (Gn 10:16; cf. 1 Chr 1:13-16). Some of these nomadic people seem to have migrated from the Syrian Desert into Mesopotamia, others into Palestine.

Akkadian cuneiform inscriptions mention a relatively uncivilized people called Amurru (translation of the Sumerian Mar-tu), perhaps named for a storm god. They overran the Sumerians and eventually most of Mesopotamia. The city of Mari, on the upper Euphrates River, fell to them about 2000 BC; Eshunna a short time later; Babylon by 1830 BC; and finally Assur around 1750 BC.

Farther to the west, Amorites had been in Palestine and Syria as early as the third millennium BC. Egyptian texts of the early part of the 19th century BC show that additional waves of Amorite nomads were entering Canaan at that time. Many of their names are similar to the Amorite names from upper Mesopotamia. In fact, many names from the Mari tablets are identical with or similar to names in the patriarchal accounts in Genesis. People named Jacob, Abraham, Levi, and Ishmael were known at Mari, and names similar to Gad and Dan have been found there. Benjamin was known as the name of a tribe. Nahor was found to be the name of a city near Haran. According to Genesis, Abraham lived in Haran many years before going to Canaan. Jacob spent 20 years there and married two women from Haran.

Amorites appear prominently in the OT as major obstacles to the occupation of Canaan (the Promised Land) by the Israelites after the exodus. Calling Moses to lead Israel out of Egypt, the Lord spoke of Canaan, then occupied by Amorites and others, as a good land (Ex 3:8, 17; 13:5). When the Israelites were in the wilderness, God promised to destroy those nations (Ex 23:23) and drive them out of the land (Ex 33:2). The Hebrew people were warned not to make covenants with any of them, to intermarry with them, or to tolerate their idol worship (Ex 34:11-17).

Spies sent into the land found Amalekites in the south; Hittites, Jebusites, and Amorites in the northern mountains and to the west of the Jordan River; and Canaanites by the sea and along the Jordan (Nm 13:25-29). At that time there were Amorites east of the Jordan as well (Nm 21:13).

God had instructed Israel to go up from Horeb and conquer the mountain Amorites on the west side of the Jordan all the way to the Mediterranean Sea (Dt 1:7). When they arrived at Kadesh-barnea they were at the foot of those mountains (Dt 1:19-20). But the people murmured and complained that God had brought them from Egypt only to be slaughtered by the Amorites. From the spies' reports, they pictured the Amorites as an awesome people, greater and taller than the Israelites (Dt 1:26-28). At first they refused to trust God enough to go in, so God told them to turn around and head back into the wilderness. Then they changed their minds, stubbornly attacked the Amorites against God's command, and were badly beaten (Dt 1:34-44). Finally, after 38 additional years in the wilderness, the Israelites once again faced the Amorites, but this time on the east side of the Dead Sea (Nm 21:13). The Amorite king, Sihon, refused to let them pass through his land. The Israelites were drawn up at the Arnon River, which flows into the Dead Sea about two-thirds of the way up its eastern shore.

Transjordan was controlled by two Amorite kings, Sihon and Og. Israel had to face Sihon first. His city, Heshbon, lay due east of the north end of the Dead Sea (Nm 21:21-26). Sihon himself had taken this land from the Moabites. Moses knew of Sihon's reputation and quoted a poem that boasted of Sihon's victory over Moab (Nm 21:27-30). Nevertheless, the Israelites defeated Sihon and devastated his kingdom from Dibon, four miles (6.4 kilometers) north of the Arnon, to Medeba, seven miles (11.2 kilometers) south of Heshbon. King Og, farther to the north, received the same treatment (Nm 21:31-35). King Balak of Moab heard of the Israelite victories and was terrified (Nm 22:2-3).

Moses reminded the people that by relying on God's promises they had taken all of the land of the Amorites east of the Jordan (Dt 2:24–3:10). The conquered territory was given to the tribes of Gad and Reuben and to the half-tribe of Manasseh (Nm 32:33). Then, 40 years after the exodus began, Israel was standing on the east side of the Jordan, having dispossessed the two great Amorite nations there (Dt 1:1-4). But there were other Amorite kingdoms in the hills west of the Jordan, along with other nations (Dt 7:1-2). They were to be destroyed in the same way Sihon and Og had been defeated (Dt 31:3-6).

So famous was the victory of Israel east of the Jordan that Rahab and others in Jericho, west of the Jordan, knew of it and were frightened (Jos 2:8-11). The Israelites crossed the Jordan and took Jericho but were defeated at the smaller city of Ai in the hill country west of Jericho. They immediately assumed that they would be wiped out by the Amorites in those hills (Jos 7:7).

The Israelites regained God's favor, however, and defeated Ai. Their victory made an impression on the other kingdoms west of the Jordan in the hills, valleys, and coastlands up to Lebanon, who allied to fight Joshua (Jos 9:1-2). Gibeon, an Amorite city seven miles (11.2 kilometers) southwest of Ai, made peace with Israel, putting more fear in the hearts of the remaining kings (Jos 10:1-2). Adoni-zedek, king of Jerusalem, was evidently the leader of the Amorite kings west of the Jordan (Jos 10:3). Jerusalem was only eight miles (12.8 kilometers) southeast of Gibeon. Adoni-zedek called together the kings of Hebron, Jarmuth, Lachish, and Eglon, all within 50 miles (80.4 kilometers) of Jerusalem, to fight against Gibeon and Joshua (Jos 10:3-5).

Joshua came to Gibeon's defense and routed the Amorites, chasing them to the northwest and southwest. The Lord fought for Israel, raining hailstones on the Amorites at Azekah, southwest of Gibeon, and causing the sun to stand still in order to provide a longer battle day (Jos 10:6-14).

In the far north, Jabin, king of Hazor, rallied the Canaanites and remaining Amorites all the way north to Mt Hermon (Jos 11:1-5). But they too were overcome (Jos 11:10-23). Toward the end of Joshua's career, he reminded the people that it was the Lord who had given them the land of the Amorites (Jos 24:1-18).

After the occupation of Canaan by Israel, Amorites still present in the land chased Dan's tribe into the mountains and continued to live near Aijalon, 17 miles (27.4 kilometers) west of Jerusalem. They still held the slopes toward the south end of the Dead Sea as well (Jgs 1:34-36). In the period of the judges, the Amorites and their gods posed a constant threat to Israel's well-being (Jgs 6:10).

At the end of the period of the judges, relations between Israel and the Amorites improved (1 Sm 7:14). David continued to honor Joshua's treaty with the Amorite remnant of Gibeon (2 Sm 21:2-6). Solomon conscripted his labor forces from the Amorites and other peoples still surviving from Israelite conquest (1 Kgs 9:20-22).

The OT treats the deliverance of the Amorites and their land into the hands of Israel as a great event comparable with the exodus itself, a victory to be remembered and celebrated (Pss 135:9-12; 136:13-26). If the people forgot, the Lord reminded them through his prophets (Am 2:9-10). Long after Sihon and Og had been defeated, the area east of the Jordan was still remembered as the land of "Sihon king of the Amorites" (1 Kgs 4:19). When the kings of Israel and Judah began to fail God, the memory of the Amorites provided a standard of comparison of evil. The Jews' continuing fascination with idolatry led God to address Jerusalem, representing the Jewish people, through the prophet Ezekiel: "Your mother was a Hittite and your father an Amorite" (Ez 16:45). In the biblical view, the Amorites stood for everything that is abominable in the sight of God.

AMORITES, Hill Country (Mount*) of the Central mountainous region between the plains of Philistia, Sharon, and Phoenicia on the west and the valley of the Jordan on the east. While the KJV uses "mount," most modern translations use "hill country" because the phrase does not denote a single mountain but the range running north and south through Judah and Ephraim (Dt 1:7, 19-20).

AMOS (Person) Hebrew prophet of the eighth century BC. Nothing is known about Amos apart from the book that bears his name. He was a shepherd living in Tekoa, a village about 10 miles (16 kilometers) south of Jerusalem, when God spoke to him in a vision (Am 1:1-2). The kingdom was then divided, with Uzziah king of Judah in the south and Jeroboam II king of Israel in the north. In Amos's vision, the Lord was like a lion roaring out judgment on injustice and idolatry, especially among God's own people. The short biographical section of his writings shows Amos preaching only at Bethel, in Israel, about 12 miles (19 kilometers) north of Jerusalem and just over the border. Bethel had been made the royal religious sanctuary of Israel by Jeroboam I to rival Jerusalem in Judah. Amos prophesied that Israel would be overrun and its king killed. The priest of Bethel, Amaziah, called Amos a traitor and told him to go back to Judah and do his prophesying there. Amos replied, "I'm not one of your professional prophets. I certainly never trained to be one. I'm just a shepherd, and I take care of fig trees." But the Lord told him, "Go and prophesy to my people in Israel" (Am 7:10-15, NLT). Amos was evidently a God-fearing man who deeply felt the mistreatment of the poor by the privileged classes. He did not want to be identified with an elite group of professional prophets, who may have lost their original fervor. His writings reflect the earthy background of a shepherd (3:12). But he spoke with authority the message given him by the Lord God of Hosts: "I want to see a mighty flood of justice, a river of righteous living that will never run dry" (5:24, NLT). The message of Amos was a call to repentance of personal and social sins and a return to the worship of the one true God and to the covenantal standards that made the Jewish people a nation. *See* Amos, Book of; Prophet, Prophetess.

AMOS, Book of

AMOS, Book of Writings of the prophet Amos, one of the 12 minor prophets of the Hebrew OT. The book of Amos is called minor only because it is relatively short. Its message is as important as that of any of the major prophets. Indeed, Amos has one of the most powerful statements in the Bible of God's judgment against injustice, oppression, and hypocrisy. The book consists primarily of prophetic sermons preached by Amos at Bethel, royal sanctuary of the northern kingdom of Israel in the eighth century BC.

PREVIEW
•Author
•Date, Origin, and Destination
•Background
•Content
•Significance

Author The preacher of the sermons (or oracles) in the book was undoubtedly Amos, a herdsman and a dresser (farmer) of fig trees, from the village of Tekoa, south of Jerusalem. He received from God a vision of judgment on Israel and went north to Bethel, just across the border between Judah and Israel, to deliver his sermons. All we know about the prophet is contained in the superscription (1:1-2) and a biographical section (7:10-14) of the book of Amos, plus what can be learned about him from the style and content of the rest of the book.

Did Amos write down his prophecies himself? Although scholars have raised many questions about the authorship of Amos, there is no convincing reason to regard the book as the work of anyone else. Some have suggested that the sermons were passed on by word of mouth for a long time before they were written down in final form. The Hebrew text, however, is in much better shape than would be expected (had it come through prolonged oral transmission). The many first-person references and vigor of expression imply strongly that Amos himself put much of his prophecy into writing soon after delivering it at Bethel.

Another speculative proposal is that the visions described in the book (7:1-9; 8:1-3; 9:1-4) were compiled by Amos before he began his ministry to the northern kingdom, and the oracles (chs 1–6) were composed after that time. The two sections could have been joined into one book much later, during or after the Babylonian exile, with some sections inserted at that time. Other prophecies, however, such as Ezekiel and Jeremiah, contain both oracle and vision sections that scholars have not attempted to divide, and the internal evidence does not make such a division necessary with Amos. Both sections contain similar concerns; in both the visions

(7:1-3) and the oracles (5:1-7), Amos appears in the role of intercessor on behalf of Israel.

Date, Origin, and Destination According to the superscription, Amos prophesied during the reigns of Uzziah, king of Judah, and Jeroboam II, king of Israel (1:1), or between 792 and 740 BC. The content of his message fits what is known about the situation in Israel in that period. It is difficult to be more exact about the beginning and ending of Amos's prophetic ministry within that time span. The vision came to him "two years before the earthquake" (1:1), but another biblical reference to presumably the same earthquake places it during the days of King Uzziah of Judah (Zec 14:5). Archaeological excavations at Hazor seem to have yielded evidence for an earthquake, which has been dated at approximately 760 BC. Amos also contains a prophetic reference to a solar eclipse (8:9); such an eclipse has been calculated to have occurred about 763 BC. After King Uzziah was stricken with leprosy, he lived in isolation while Judah was under a co-regency (2 Chr 26:21). Therefore, Amos's mention of Uzziah as king (1:1) probably sets 760 BC as the latest possible date for Amos's ministry.

The doom that came upon Israel after Amos's prophecy was the conquest by the Assyrian king Tiglath-pileser III (745–727 BC). Although Amos referred to impending captivity, he never mentioned Assyria as the captor, although he did say that captivity would take Israel to a land east of Damascus (5:27). Probably Amos was not thinking specifically of the rising power of Assyria but only of the inevitable consequences of Israel's idolatry and hypocrisy. When all the evidence is taken into consideration, it seems reasonable to date the beginning of Amos's prophecies at Bethel to about 760 BC, or approximately the middle of the period during which both Uzziah and Jeroboam II were on their thrones. We do not know how long his ministry lasted; it may have been only a few months.

Amos had been caring for his flocks in the Judean hills south of Jerusalem when God told him, "Go and prophesy to my people in Israel" (7:15, NLT). He may have been familiar with the more urban north from earlier trips there to sell wool or fruit, or the pagan worship and social wrongs there may have made a sudden impact on him after his call to prophesy. At any rate, his writings reveal not only his rural Judean background but also a firsthand knowledge of conditions in the northern kingdom of Israel. Although his prophecies were directed primarily to Israel, he also denounced the sin of Judah, predicting that its capital, Jerusalem, would be burned (2:4-5). Several passages are directed at inhabitants of Samaria, capital of Israel (4:1, 11; 6:1), with which Amos was obviously familiar. He could have traveled on to Samaria from Bethel, or he could have learned of its splendors from the boasts of its citizens. He could have addressed them directly as they came from the capital city to worship at Bethel.

Background The eighth century BC was a critical time in Jewish history. Both kingdoms of the divided nation had risen to heights of economic affluence that had not been experienced since the days of Solomon. Yet internal religious decay was sapping the strength of both kingdoms, and their social fabric was being destroyed. A new wealthy class was benefiting from the affluence of the time, growing ever richer while poor people became poorer than ever.

In 803 BC, the conquest of Syrian Damascus by the Assyrian king Adad-nirari III had silenced one of Israel's major enemies. With the Syrians out of the picture, the kingdom of Israel was able to expand its borders under King Joash (2 Kgs 13:25), and for a time even the thrust of Assyrian power westward was diminished. Israel and Judah entered a period of rest from constant warfare and turned their attention to internal affairs.

Joash's son, Jeroboam II, became king of Israel in 793 and reigned until 753 BC. Uzziah was on the throne of Judah from 792 to 740 BC. Under these two kings, Judah and Israel controlled a territory that was almost as large as Solomon's empire had been. Their wealth had grown both from expansion of trade and from the booty of conquered territories.

Archaeology has yielded information about industrial activity within the nations, such as an impressive dyeing industry at Debir. Excavations at Samaria have produced large numbers of ivory inlays that confirm Amos's description of the wealthy in the capital city (6:4). The city of Samaria was protected by a huge double wall of unusual thickness. A palace, probably Jeroboam's, dominated the city with a massive tower.

The splendor and prosperity of the time, however, was masking the spread of internal decay. Oppression of the poor by many in the wealthy classes not only threatened the unity of the nation but also meant that God's laws were being violated. In his denunciations of the cruel treatment of the poor (5:11-13; 8:4-10), Amos warned of the inevitable punishment for disobeying God's laws.

The nation of Israel was guilty of more than social sins against the covenant. It was also adopting pagan religious practices. Canaanite religious influence intruded into the fabric of the nation of Israel. Excavation of a palace storehouse in Samaria uncovered many *ostraca* (pieces of broken pottery used for writing short messages such as letters, receipts, etc.) containing Hebrew names compounded with "Baal," a chief god of the Canaanite religion.

In spite of the gradual deterioration, false optimism seems to have prevailed. Amos found people desiring the Day of the Lord (5:18) and sought to correct their misunderstanding: the Day of the Lord prophesied in the Scriptures would be a time of judgment on all sinners. A more immediate judgment was to come, however. Assyria began to strengthen its position in the world and to resume its expansionist policies. Under the leadership of Tiglath-pileser III (745–727 BC), Assyria regained a position of world dominance. Eventually, Israel was attacked by Shalmaneser V of Assyria. Soon afterward, in 722 BC, Samaria was occupied. No doubt when the Assyrians were sweeping into Israel, many of the people who had ignored the message of Amos then realized that a prophet of God had been among them.

Content

Superscription (1:1) The prophet introduces himself as a shepherd, perhaps implying that it is more than sheep he wants to keep from straying.

Prophetic Oracles (1:2–6:14) This section begins with a picture of the great power of God, who acts in history to judge the nations (1:2).

➤ JUDGMENT ON SURROUNDING NATIONS (1:3–2:3) The prophet first speaks against Damascus, then moves on, pronouncing doom on various peoples in ever closer concentric circles, "homing in" on Israel. One may imagine the citizens of Israel applauding God's judgment on other nations until, with shocking effect, Amos accuses Israel of similar sins.

Damascus was the capital of Syria, northeast of Israel, and the center of Syrian influence. Syria had mistreated Israel during Hazael's reign in Damascus (842–806 BC). Hazael "whittled down" Israel in a number of campaigns

(2 Kgs 10:32-33; 13:3-5, 22-24). In their campaign into the territory of Gilead, the Syrians destroyed most of Israel's army as though they were dust on a threshing floor (2 Kgs 13:7). Hence, Amos denounces Syria for threshing Gilead as grain is threshed with iron rods (Am 1:3). He predicts that Syria will be destroyed and its people deported to Kir, which Amos understood to be their place of origin (9:7). (For the fulfillment of this prophecy, see 2 Kgs 16:9.)

Amos next turned to Gaza, a Philistine city in southwest Palestine. Gaza probably represents the Philistines as a whole, since three other of their five major cities are also mentioned (1:8). The fifth, Gath, had already been conquered by Hazael (2 Kgs 12:17). Amos denounced the Philistines for what must have been a border raid on Israel in which many were carried off into slavery (1:6).

The Phoenician city of Tyre is cited next. Tyre was on the Mediterranean, north of Israel and southwest of Damascus. Destruction of Tyre, like that of the Philistine cities, is predicted as punishment for making slaves of conquered Israelites.

Edom is next, south of the Dead Sea. Edom had perennially harassed the Israelites and is referred to in a negative light many times in the OT. Edom is said to have been pitiless toward Israel, his brother (1:11).

Ammon, just to the southeast of Israel, is also judged. The particularly violent incident referred to (1:13) evidently occurred in one of their many attempts to push northward into the Israelite territory of Gilead.

Moab is the last of the surrounding nations to be denounced, with reference to what may have been a well-known incident of desecration of the dead (2:1-3).

➤ ORACLES AGAINST ISRAEL AND JUDAH (2:4-16) Although Judah and Israel were at peace at the time, their enmity had continued after dissolution of the united kingdom. Amos accuses Judah of rejecting "the law of the Lord" and predicts the burning of Jerusalem.

The oracle against Israel is longer than the others. Amos carefully specifies the social nature of Israel's sin, making the point that Israel is no better than the surrounding nations. Israel deserves the same punishment. Just as some of the nations were guilty of taking people into slavery, Israel is selling her own poor who cannot repay their debts (2:6). Under Mosaic law it was illegal to keep overnight a garment pledged as security for a loan, since it might be the only source of warmth the debtor had (Ex 22:26-27). Rich people in Israel were attending religious feasts in such clothing "stolen" from the poor (2:8).

Amos reminds Israel of all the good things God has done for them (2:9-11). But because Israel has chosen to continue in disobedience, the nation will not escape impending judgment (2:12-16).

➤ DENUNCIATION OF AND WARNING AGAINST ISRAEL (3:1–6:14) Amos substantiates his prophetic authority with a lesson on cause and effect (3:1-8). A lion roars when it has prey, and people fear when a trumpet sounds an alarm. If calamity comes to a city, God has allowed it. God, who reveals his secrets to his prophets, has spoken Israel's doom, and Amos must proclaim it.

In a dramatic statement, Amos calls on Egypt and Assyria, great centers of oppression and cruelty, to witness Israel's crimes, as though even they will be amazed at what they see (3:9-10). Only a ragged remnant will survive the punishment to come (3:11-12). Judgment will fall on objects that symbolize Israel's religious disobedience (3:14) as well as on symbols of the wealth that led Israel away from the Lord (3:15).

Amos uses strong language to denounce luxurious and indolent living bought at the expense of the poor (4:1-3). Rich women whose love for luxuries drives their husbands to squeeze the needy still more are called "fat cows" who will someday be treated like cattle. Then Amos mocks those who worship at Bethel for going through the motions in the wrong spirit (4:4-5).

In the rest of the fourth chapter, Amos recalls incidents from Israel's history that were meant to call the people back to God: famine, drought, plagues, the destruction of some of their cities. Still they do not repent. "Prepare to meet your God!" warns the prophet, following his warning with a hymn to the mighty power of God (4:6-13).

The fifth chapter begins in the form of a funeral dirge, as though Israel were as good as dead already (5:1-2). There is no one to help Israel, whose own armies will be decimated when the disaster strikes (5:3). Of course, God is there to help: "Seek me and live" (5:4-6). The possibility of rescue, of "life," stands in sharp contrast to the nation's "death" pictured just before. Idols, as always, are a false hope (5:5). The call to seek the Lord is again followed by a hymn to his power (5:8-9).

In spite of the hope offered to Israel, Amos has to present a gloomy picture of what he sees (5:10-13). The judicial system is corrupt; taxes and high interest charges (usury) grind down the poor. Those injustices could be corrected if the people would "hate evil and love good" (5:15), but judgment is already on the way (5:16-17).

The people are full of hypocrisy, claiming to look forward to the Day of the Lord. That day will be a day of judgment on their sins, Amos says. Instead of empty gestures of offerings and praise, God wants to let justice roll down like waters, and righteousness like an everflowing stream (5:18-24). Their disobedient spirit goes back to the time of the exodus from Egypt, when God's own people were attracted to pagan gods. The Lord God of Hosts will send those false gods into captivity with the people who looked to them (5:25-27).

The self-satisfaction felt by the upper classes in Israel had evidently spread to Judah, since Jerusalem as well as Samaria receives some harsh words (6:1). Amos tells those who are lounging in luxury to take a look at three neighboring kingdoms on which judgment has already fallen: Calneh, Hamath, and Gath. Does Israel think it will escape, since they did not? When the Day of Judgment comes, the rich, who have gone "first-class," will be the first to go (6:2-7). The destruction will leave few survivors, but they will know that punishment came from God (6:8-11). Israel is behaving stupidly to be proud of themselves when they are actually so utterly self-deceived (6:12-14).

Prophetic Visions (7:1–9:10) By describing three visions God gave him, Amos then dramatically communicates God's revelation.

➤ISRAEL'S DESTRUCTION (7:1-9) The first vision is in three parts. In the first, Amos pictures the threat of a locust plague in which his prayer of intercession causes God to relent and withdraw the threat (7:1-3). Then he sees an all-consuming fire, and again his prayer averts a catastrophe (7:4-6). In the third part of the vision, Amos sees the Lord standing by a wall and holding a plumb line, implying that he has a standard for his people to live up to, an element missing from the two earlier images. This time, because the people have failed to measure up, the catastrophe cannot be averted (7:7-9).

➤HISTORICAL INTERLUDE (7:10-17) At this point, Amos encounters Amaziah, priest of Bethel, because he has said that the vision of the plumb line means destruction of the idol altars and temples of Israel and of the house of Jero-

boam with the sword. Amaziah sends word to Jeroboam that Amos is a traitor and tells Amos to go back to Judah. Amos disclaims any relationship with professional prophets, then specifically includes Amaziah's family in another prediction of Israel's disaster.

➤THE RIPE FRUIT (8:1-14) In the second vision, Amos is shown a basket of ripe (or summer) fruit. The Hebrew word for summer fruit is almost the same as the word for "end," so the play on words communicates that the nation is "ripe for punishment." Their ripeness is really moral rottenness. Greedy merchants can hardly wait for religious holidays to end so they can cheat the poor some more by using false weights, selling inferior goods, and foreclosing on debtors. When the captivity comes, their festivities will turn into funerals. A famine, not just of bread and water but of the words of the Lord, is coming upon them, causing even the strongest young people to drop to the ground.

➤DESTRUCTION OF THE TEMPLE (9:1-10) The third vision is of the Lord destroying the shrine at Bethel when it is thronged with people engaging in their empty worship. The place where they hoped to find security is where they find destruction. Those who are not inside will be destroyed, too, no matter where they try to flee. They won't be able to hide from God in Sheol or on the heights of Carmel or in the depths of the sea (9:1-4). Another hymn to God's power follows the vision (9:5-6).

The final words of denunciation in the book of Amos are found in 9:7-10, but they are a prelude to a message of hope. Amos shows that Israel is no better than any other nation in the eyes of God. Did he not bring Israel out of Egypt? Yes, but he also brought the Philistines from Caphtor and the Syrians from Kir. The religious significance of the exodus has been lost because of Israel's sin, so all but a faithful remnant will be lost.

The concept of the remnant was important in the prophetic preaching of the eighth century BC (cf. Is 6:12-13; Mi 6:7-9). It recalled God's promise to maintain the nation of Israel for the sake of the covenant given to the patriarchs (Lv 26:44-45). In Amos's prophecy, Israel is to be sifted by other nations like grain in a sieve; the ungodly "chaff" will be scattered across the world, but the true "grain" will be preserved.

Israel's Hope (9:11-15) The expression of hope is expanded in the last section of the book in a series of startling and beautiful metaphors.

➤RESTORATION OF THE CITY OF DAVID (9:11-12) The first metaphor is of the city (literally "house") of David, a house fallen into disrepair. The monarchy, which had crumbled from internal decay and external threats, is envisioned as being restored to its former glory. Further, an expansion of the Davidic kingdom will include all nations that belong to the Lord.

In the NT, this passage was quoted by James to support the inclusion of Gentiles in the promise (Acts 15:16-18). The wording in Acts is slightly different from that of Amos because it was based on an early Greek translation of the OT (called the Septuagint). Those called by God's name or belonging to God include not only geographical entities such as nations but also individuals in any nation who have a close relationship to God. James saw that Amos was predicting inclusion of Gentiles in the kingdom of God, a kingdom far greater than the early monarchy. This prophecy has been fulfilled in part in the Christian church.

➤RESTORATION OF ISRAEL'S FORTUNES (9:13-15) A series of pastoral metaphors closes the book of Amos. They depict the abundance of blessing in the coming kingdom. Israel's fortunes are to be restored, far beyond the dismal events of the century in which Amos is speaking. Theologians differ in their understanding of the application of this prophecy. If it refers to the present age of the Christian church, it pictures the blessings of the church now as "spiritual Israel." If it refers to the future, to the millennial reign of Christ, it depicts what will happen on earth at that time.

The concept of a rejuvenated earth is found elsewhere in the Bible (Rom 8:20-22). Micah uses language somewhat similar to that of Amos to describe restoration of what seems to be the literal city of Jerusalem (Mi 3:12–4:4). It may be best to apply the prophetic finale of Amos to the restoration to be effected at the ultimate return of Christ. Whatever the correct application, the remnant must include the followers of Jesus Christ, and the blessings should be seen as intended for all who belong to the kingdom of God.

Significance The major purpose of Amos in his prophecies was to denounce Israel's disobedience to the covenant. Although the covenant promise given to Abraham (Gn 22:15-18) and reiterated throughout the OT is not mentioned explicitly in Amos, it is implicit in the total message of the book. Amos upheld the spiritual nature of the covenant and emphasized that its blessing was mediated through obedience.

Looking around him, Amos saw not only disobedience but hypocrisy. A basic aspect of his ethical teaching was insistence that outward adherence to religious ceremonies without a heart response to the will of God (as expressed in the law) was wrong. The law contained many injunctions that sought to engender love of God and fellow human beings (Ex 23:1-13). In Amos's time, those social aspects of the law were being willfully disobeyed by the rich, who nevertheless clung to religious ritual. Amos saw what was in their hearts and condemned it. To him, religious obligations not observed in the proper spirit of responsibility to God could actually become sin (4:4). Religion could degenerate to the place where it becomes a curse, a mockery of the will of a holy God.

Amos saw the disobedience and hypocrisy of Israel as culminating in national disaster. Thus his prophecy served as a warning of impending doom to the nation. He saw that other nations besides Israel and Judah were held accountable to God because of their mistreatment of others (1:3–2:3). Their social sins were punished by God in history. Amos thus saw an aspect of the law extending beyond Israel and Judah to other nations. They were responsible to God under what might be called a universal moral law, and they were judged for their crimes against humanity.

The prophetic concept of the Day of the Lord, regarded by the people of Amos's day as a time of vindication for their nation, was seen by Amos as a time of punishment for all sinners. Such punishment would not exclude the nation of Israel.

Yet denunciation was not the sole purpose of Amos's prophetic activity. He proclaimed a future of hope for Israel in the reestablishment of the Davidic monarchy, evidently under Messiah, in a time that would be characterized by peace (9:8-15). The relationship of the Davidic kingdom to the messianic kingdom goes back to the promise given to David (2 Sm 7:8-16). Just as those in other nations participated by extension in the demands of the law and in judgment, so would those in other nations who belonged to God participate in the blessings of the promise (9:12).

The concepts of God drawn most sharply in the book of Amos are God's sovereignty and God's righteousness.

He is sovereign over all the nations of the world, typified by those surrounding Israel, and he brings them to judgment (1:3–2:3). He is also sovereign over nature, as recognized in his control of the universe (4:13; 5:8; 9:13-14). His righteousness demands that he cannot allow his law to continue to be violated without retribution. But his righteousness is also the guarantee of hope for the believing remnant of Israel. It binds him to keep his promise to preserve Israel as a nation (Lv 26:44-45).

Amos held out the possibility of averting the national catastrophe looming on the horizon of world events. However, from his gloomy description of social conditions and of the hardness of people's hearts at the time, it seems likely that he did not foresee any escape.

His message was presented in bold metaphors and vivid pictures that stick in the mind. That message is still relevant, for many of the sins that characterized the people of the prophet's day are still prevalent in modern society and in the lives of individuals. Mistreatment of fellow human beings is as much a feature of the 21st century AD as it was of the 8th century BC.

Today's reader of the book of Amos should note the prophet's insistence on the consequences of sin; his emphasis on the responsibility that always accompanies privilege; his presentation of God's faithfulness; and his message of hope, expressed in part today through the church.

If the book seems to be gloomy in its outlook, it should be remembered that the prophet faced a gloomy picture. He was watching a nation crumble because of its unfaithfulness to God. But beyond the dismal prospect that faced Israel, Amos saw a new kingdom emerging. It was a kingdom of peace in which the people of God would realize the fulfillment of God's promises. *See* Prophecy; Prophet, Prophetess; Israel, History of.

AMOZ Isaiah's father (2 Kgs 19:2; Is 1:1), not to be confused with the prophet Amos.

AMPHIPOLIS City in ancient Greece, once the home of the Thracian Edoni tribe. Amphipolis occupied a strategic location in a fertile area on the eastern bank of the Strymon River. Its name ("around city") may refer to its being surrounded on three sides by the river. Located about 30 miles (48.2 kilometers) from Philippi, it eventually became an important station on the Roman Via Egnatia. On his second missionary journey Paul passed through this commercial center en route to Thessalonica (Acts 17:1).

AMPLIAS*, AMPLIATUS Name of a Christian to whom the apostle Paul sent greetings at the end of his Letter to the Romans (16:8). Called "my beloved in the Lord" (RSV) by Paul, nothing further is known of this Christian who bore a common Roman name.

AMRAM

1. Kohath's son, a member of Levi's tribe. Amram married Jochebed and had three famous children: Aaron, Moses, and Miriam (Ex 6:16-20; Nm 26:58-59). During the Israelites' wilderness journey, the responsibility of the Amramites was to care for the ark and the table, lampstand, altars, and other furnishings used in the tabernacle (Nm 3:27, 31). Later, the Amramites were one of the groups in charge of offerings placed in the temple treasury (1 Chr 26:23-24).
2. Priest from Bani's family, who obeyed Ezra's exhortation to divorce his pagan wife after the exile (Ezr 10:34).
3. KJV form of Hamran, Dishon's son, in 1 Chronicles 1:41. Hamran itself is an alternate form of Hemdan (cf. Gn 36:26). *See* Hemdan.

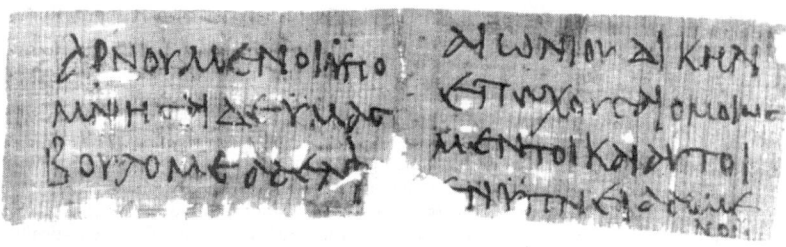

Christian Amulet This amulet shows Jude 1:4-8; the manuscript is known as P78, Papyrus Oxyrhynchus 2684.

AMRAMITE* Descendant of Amram, Kohath's son (Nm 3:27; 1 Chr 26:23). *See* Amram #1.

AMRAPHEL King of Shinar (Babylonia), who helped King Chedorlaomer of Elam quell a revolt of five vassal cities in Palestine (Gn 14:1-11).

AMULET* Small object worn by an individual, usually around the neck, as a charm or means of protection against evil, witchcraft, disease, or other physical and spiritual threats. The word is probably derived from either a Latin or Arabic term meaning "to carry." Amulets (also known as talismans) have been made of various substances and occur in many forms. Pieces of metal or strips of parchment with portions of sacred writings (even Scriptures), as well as herbs and animal preparations, have been used. Semiprecious gems were often inscribed with a magical formula.

No Hebrew or Greek word in the Bible is translated "amulet" with certainty. The practice of wearing amulets, however, is sometimes implied—generally with disapproval. The gold earrings worn by the Israelites escaping from Egypt, from which Aaron fashioned a golden calf, have been considered amulets (Ex 32:2-4). The prophet Isaiah condemned the ornaments worn by the women of his day (Is 3:16-23). Most scholars regard the phylacteries and mezuzahs used by the Jews as forms of amulets. *See* Phylactery; Magic; Frontlet.

AMZI
1. Merarite Levite and an ancestor of Ethan the musician (1 Chr 6:46).
2. Forefather of Adaiah and a priest of Malchijah's division (Neh 11:12).

ANAB Town in the hill country of Hebron inhabited by giant warriors. After Joshua eliminated the giants (Jos 11:21), Anab was allotted to Judah's tribe (Jos 15:50). Today Anab is known as Khirbet 'Anab el-Kebireh.

ANAEL Brother of Tobit (Tb 1:21-22). After the death of King Sennacherib (681 BC), Anael's son Ahikar was appointed by the Assyrian king Esarhaddon to a high court position in Nineveh.

ANAH
1. Son of Zibeon the Hivite and father of Oholibamah. Oholibamah was one of Esau's wives (Gn 36:2, 18).
2. Fourth son of Seir the Horite. Anah was a chief among the Horites who also had a daughter named Oholibamah (Gn 36:20, 25; 1 Chr 1:38, 41).
3. Son of Zibeon who found hot springs in the wasteland (Gn 36:24). This Zibeon was a brother to #2 above. *See* Zibeon.

ANAHARATH Town in the valley of Jezreel allotted to Issachar's tribe when the land was divided by Joshua (Jos 19:19).

ANAIAH
1. Priest and assistant of Ezra who explained to the people passages from the law read by Ezra (Neh 8:4).
2. Political leader who signed Ezra's covenant of faithfulness to God with Nehemiah and others after the exile (Neh 10:22). He is perhaps identical with #1 above.

ANAK, ANAKIM*, ANAKITES Ancestor of a race of giants in old Canaan. When Israel first reached Canaan, the Anakim were well established in Hebron. Ten of the 12 spies Moses sent into Canaan (Nm 13:17-22) were terrified by the size of the Anakim (Nm 13:31). Their terror led to a rebellion at Kadesh-barnea (Nm 14:39-45; Dt 1:19-46) and another 38 years of wandering. When the Israelites were finally ready to enter Canaan, God promised his help against the famed Anak giants (Dt 9:1-3).

The two spies who were not afraid of the Anakim were both involved in their defeat. Joshua defeated the Anakim living in Hebron, Debir, Anab, and all the region of Judah (Jos 11:21-23). Those who survived were left only in the Philistine cities of Gaza, Gath, and Ashdod. The other spy, Caleb, was responsible for the defeat of the Anakim chiefs Sheshai, Ahiman, and Talmai at Hebron; Caleb's nephew Othniel was the hero of Debir (Jos 15:14-17). Hebron had earlier been called Kiriath-arba for Anak's father Arba, a great hero of the Anakim (Jos 14:15; 21:11). The fact that the Anakim survived in the Philistine cities of Gaza, Gath, and Ashdod leads to the supposition that Goliath of Gath may have been a descendant of these giants (1 Sm 17:4-7).

See also Giants.

ANAMIM*, ANAMITES Unidentified group of people, possibly related to the Egyptians, mentioned in the biblical records of earliest nations (Gn 10:13; 1 Chr 1:11).

ANAMMELECH Deity associated with Adrammelech, who was worshiped by the people of Sepharvaim, whom the Assyrians relocated in Samaria after 722 BC. Anammelech is evidently the Hebrew rendering of the designation for a Mesopotamian deity, Anu-melek, meaning "Anu is King." Anu was the name of the chief god of Assyria, the sky god. The worship of this deity by the Sepharvites in Samaria included child sacrifice (2 Kgs 17:31). It is not certain whether the burning of children in the Anu cult was brought from Sepharvaim or was an innovation when the Sepharvites came to Canaan.

See also Mesopotamia; Syria, Syrians.

ANAN One of the chiefs of the people who set his seal on Ezra's covenant to keep God's law during the postexilic era (Neh 10:26).

ANANI One of seven sons of Elioenai, a descendant of David (1 Chr 3:24).

ANANIAH (Person) Azariah's grandfather. Azariah was one of three men who repaired the Jerusalem wall near their homes after the exile (Neh 3:23).

ANANIAH (Place) Town in Benjamin's territory after the exile (Neh 11:32) that may have become the Bethany of the NT ("Bethany" is a contraction of Beth-ananiah).

ANANIAS

1. Member of the early church in Jerusalem. Along with his wife, Sapphira, he was struck dead for attempted deception with regard to some money (Acts 5:1-5).
2. Early convert to Christianity who was living in Damascus when Saul of Tarsus (Paul) arrived there supposedly to arrest Christians. Ananias knew that Paul was a deadly enemy of Christians, but the Lord reassured him, explaining that Paul had been chosen as a special messenger of the gospel (Acts 9:13-16). The Lord sent Ananias to the newly converted Paul to restore his eyesight (Acts 9:17-19). Ananias told Paul the meaning of his unusual encounter with Christ on the road to Damascus (Acts 22:12-16) and probably introduced him to the church there as a new Christian brother rather than a persecutor. Various traditions say that Ananias later became one of the 70 disciples of Jerusalem, a bishop of Damascus, and a martyr.
3. High priest who presided over the Sanhedrin when the apostle Paul was arrested and questioned by that council in Jerusalem at the end of Paul's third missionary journey (Acts 22:30–23:10). Ananias was one of the witnesses who testified against Paul in Caesarea when he was on trial before Felix, the Roman governor (Acts 24:1). This Ananias was appointed high priest by Herod Agrippa II in AD 48 and served until AD 59. The Jewish historian Josephus wrote that he was wealthy, haughty, and unscrupulous. He was known for his collaboration with the Romans and for his severity and cruelty. Hated by nationalistic Jews, he was killed by them when war with Rome broke out in AD 66.

ANANIEL Grandfather of Tobit (Tb 1:1).

ANATH

1. Parent of Shamgar, one of the judges of Israel (Jgs 3:31; 5:6). Since the name Anath is feminine, it is likely that Anath was Shamgar's mother.
2. Canaanite goddess of fertility. See Canaanite Deities and Religion.

ANATHEMA* Greek word meaning "cursed" or "banned," and associated with destruction. See Curse, Cursed.

ANATHOTH (Person)

1. Becher's son from Benjamin's tribe (1 Chr 7:8).
2. Political leader who signed Ezra's covenant of faithfulness to God with Nehemiah and others after the exile (Neh 10:19).

ANATHOTH (Place), ANATHOTHITE*

Town in Benjamin's territory set aside for the Levites (Jos 21:18; 1 Chr 6:60). Anathoth may have been named by the Canaanites for their goddess Anath, or later by the Israelites for one of Benjamin's descendants (1 Chr 7:8). The town was probably located at Ras el-Karrubeh near the modern town of Anata three miles (4.8 kilometers) north of Jerusalem. Its residents were sometimes called Anethothites or Anetothites (2 Sm 23:27; 1 Chr 27:12). Abiezer, one of David's military leaders, was from Anathoth (1 Chr 11:28,

KJV "Antothite") as was the soldier Jehu (1 Chr 12:3) and the priest Abiathar (1 Kgs 2:26). It was also the hometown of the prophet Jeremiah (Jer 1:1), though some of its inhabitants violently opposed him (Jer 11:21, 23). Just before Judah fell to Babylon, Jeremiah bought a field in Anathoth as a sign that Israel would be restored to her land (Jer 32:7-9). Years later, 128 men of Anathoth returned from the exile, and the town was resettled (Neh 11:32).

ANCHOR Object used to keep a ship or boat stationary in the water. An anchor is attached to a ship by a cable or chain, and when thrown overboard, its weight and/or ability to dig into the sea bottom keeps the vessel from drifting. Anchors were used many centuries before the time of Christ, beginning as simple stone weights and evolving into wooden hooks weighted with lead or stone. Not long after the time of Christ, iron anchors of the familiar modern shape were used. Anchors are mentioned in Luke's account of the apostle Paul's voyage to Rome (Acts 27:13, 29-30, 40). Hebrews 6:19 uses "anchor" in a figurative sense to indicate the stability of God's promise of salvation to those who believe in him.

ANCIENT OF DAYS*, ANCIENT ONE Name of God used by Daniel to describe God as judge (Dn 7:9, 13, 22). See God, Names of.

ANDREAS Chief of the bodyguard of Egyptian king Ptolemy Philadelphus, sent by the king to Palestine to procure scribes to translate the OT into Greek (about 275 BC). The result was the translation known as the Septuagint. Eleazar, the Jewish high priest, praised Andreas as a good man, distinguished by his learning.

ANDREW, The Apostle One of Christ's 12 apostles. Andrew first appears in the NT as a disciple of John the Baptist (Jn 1:35, 40). After hearing John say, "Look, there is the Lamb of God!" (Jn 1:36), referring to Jesus, Andrew and another unnamed disciple followed Jesus and stayed with him for a day (Jn 1:36-39). Andrew then told his brother, Simon Peter, that he had found the Messiah and brought Peter to Jesus (Jn 1:40-42). From then on Andrew faded into the background, and his brother came into prominence. Whenever the relationship of the two is mentioned, Andrew is always described as the brother of Simon Peter and never the other way around (Mt 4:18; Mk 1:16; Jn 1:40; 6:8), although Andrew is also mentioned without reference to his relationship to Peter (Mk 1:29; 3:18; 13:3; Jn 12:22). Andrew's father was John (Mt 16:17; Jn 1:42; 21:15-17), and his hometown was Bethsaida (Jn 1:44), a village on the north shore of the Sea of Galilee.

The Gospel of John mentions disciples being with Jesus (2:2; 4:2), and it is likely that Andrew was one of that early group. Evidently, however, he returned to his activity as a fisherman on the Sea of Galilee, where he shared a house with Peter and his family in Capernaum (Mt 4:18-20; Mk 1:16-18, 29-33). While they were fishing, Andrew and Peter received a definite call to follow Jesus and become those who fish for people. From among the disciples of Jesus a group of 12 were later specially chosen as apostles. Andrew is always listed among the first four named, along with Peter and two other brothers, John and James (Mt 10:2-4; Lk 6:13-16; Acts 1:13).

Andrew is named in only three other contexts in the Gospels. At the feeding of the 5,000 he called attention to the boy who had five barley loaves and two fish (Jn 6:8-9). When certain Greeks came to Philip, asking to see Jesus, Philip told Andrew and then the two of them told

Jesus (Jn 12:20-22). Finally, Andrew is listed among those who were questioning Jesus privately on the Mt of Olives (Mk 13:3-4). The last NT mention of Andrew is in the list of apostles waiting in the upper room in Jerusalem for the promised outpouring of the Holy Spirit (Acts 1:12-14).

Various documents associated with Andrew, such as the Acts of Andrew mentioned by the early church historian Eusebius, are of doubtful value. Some traditions indicate that Andrew ministered in Scythia. According to the Muratorian Canon, Andrew received a revelation at night that the apostle John should write the fourth Gospel. Tradition is rather uniform that Andrew died at Patrae in Achaia. A story developed that he was martyred on an X-shaped cross (a "decussate" or "saltire" cross), which has become known as St Andrew's Cross. Another tradition is that an arm of the dead Andrew was taken into Scotland as a relic by Regulus, and thus Andrew became known as a patron saint of Scotland. On the calendar of saints of the Roman and Greek churches, Andrew's date is set as November 30. *See* Apocrypha (Specific Titles of Apocryphal Writings): Andrew, Acts of; Andrew, Story of; Andrew and Matthias, Acts of; Andrew and Paul, Acts of.

See also Apostle, Apostleship.

ANDRONICUS
1. Deputy of Seleucid king Antiochus Epiphanes. This Andronicus aroused the Jews by murdering Onias, the high priest, and was himself then executed by Antiochus (2 Macc 4:31-38).
2. Officer in charge of Gerizim after Antiochus Epiphanes sacked Jerusalem (2 Macc 5:21-23).
3. Christian greeted by the apostle Paul in his Letter to the Romans (16:7) but not mentioned elsewhere. Paul called Andronicus his kinsman. The word could mean fellow countryman, fellow Jew, member of Paul's own family, or other relative. Andronicus may also have been a fellow prisoner for the cause of Christ, perhaps even in the same prison with Paul (2 Cor 6:4-5; 11:23). Paul described him as a man of note among the apostles and recognized him respectfully as an "older" Christian.

ANEM Town in Issachar's territory given to the priestly family of Gershom (1 Chr 6:73). It was also called En-gannim (Jos 21:29) and was probably located southeast of Mt Tabor.

See also Levitical Cities; En-gannim #2.

ANEMONE* Plant of the buttercup family, with cup-shaped flowers that are usually white, pink, red, or purple. *See* Plants (Lily).

ANER (Person) Amorite ally of Abram and brother of Mamre and Eshcol (Gn 14:13). With his brothers, Aner helped Abram defeat a confederation of four kings who had plundered Sodom and Gomorrah and had captured Abram's nephew Lot (Gn 14:14-16, 21-24).

ANER (Place) Levitical city in Manasseh's territory (1 Chr 6:70). *See* Cities of Refuge.

ANETHOTHITE*, ANETOTHITE* KJV forms of Anathothite, a resident of Anathoth, in 2 Samuel 23:27 and 1 Chronicles 27:12, respectively. *See* Anathoth (Place), Anathothite.

ANGEL Messenger of God or supernatural being, either good or evil, with powers greater than humans possess.

The first kind of angels mentioned in the Bible are cherubim (plural of "cherub," a Hebrew word). They were celestial beings sent by God to guard the tree of life in the Garden of Eden (Gn 3:24). They were represented symbolically on the ark of the covenant (Ex 25:18-22), in the tabernacle (Ex 26:31) and temple (2 Chr 3:7), and seen by the prophet Ezekiel in a vision of the restored Jerusalem (Ez 41:18-20). Two angels, Gabriel and the chief, or archangel, Michael, are named in the Bible (Dn 8:16; 9:21; 10:13; Lk 1:19, 26; Jude 1:9; Rv 12:7-9).

ANGEL OF THE LORD
Angelic being mentioned in the Bible, more properly translated the "messenger" of the Lord. In the OT the angel of the Lord, as God's personal emissary, performed special functions at particular times in the history of Israel.

The OT references portray a variety of services rendered but a basic unity of purpose: the gracious intervention of the Lord toward his people, sometimes to an individual, sometimes on a national scale. The angelic figure served Israel positively as guide and protector (Ex 14:19) and companion in the wilderness wanderings (Ex 23:20; 33:2; Nm 20:16) or negatively as assassin or destroyer (2 Sm 24:16), yet always acted to preserve the sanctity of Israel's covenant with God. Certain individuals such as Hagar (Gn 16:7; 21:17), Balaam (Nm 22:21-22), and Abraham's servant (Gn 24:7, 40) were also confronted by the divinely commissioned messenger (cf. further references 1 Sm 29:9; 2 Sm 14:20; 19:27; 1 Kgs 19:7; 2 Kgs 19:35; 1 Chr 21:15; 2 Chr 32:21).

In certain texts, it seems impossible to distinguish between the angel of the Lord and the Lord himself (Gn 16:7-13; 21:17; 22:11-18; 24:7, 40; 31:11-13; 48:16; Ex 3:2-10; Jgs 6:12-14; 13:21-22). Sometimes the angel is depicted acting for the Lord and yet is addressed as the Lord. God says, "You may not look directly at my face, for no one may see me and live" (Ex 33:20, NLT). And yet Hagar (Gn 16:13), Jacob (Gn 32:30), and Moses (Ex 33:11) are said to have seen God "face-to-face" in view of their confrontation with this angel. God promises that his very presence will be among the Israelites, and yet it is the angel who goes with them (Ex 23:23). The commander of the army of God is given reverence equal to God's (Jos 5:13–6:2). The angel seems to possess the full authority and character of God. The presence of the messenger of the Lord, in whom God's "name" resides (Ex 23:20) assures the hearer-reader that it is one God who directs the course of history (Gn 16:7; 31:11; Ex 3:2).

In the Bible, angels are spiritual beings who serve primarily as messengers. The English word "angel" comes directly from a Greek word for messenger. In Luke 9:52, Jesus sent "messengers" ahead of him. Usually the same word is translated "angel" and is understood to mean a spiritual messenger from God. In the OT also, one Hebrew word can refer either to a human messenger or to a spiritual being. It is not always immediately clear which is meant, especially since angels sometimes appeared in human form. In certain passages, "the angel of God" or a similar phrase may refer to God delivering his own message (see Gn 18:2-15).

Angels appeared to many of God's people in the Bible to announce good news (Jgs 13:3), warn of danger (Gn 19:15), guard from evil (Dn 3:28; 6:22), guide and protect (Ex 14:19), nourish (Gn 21:14-20; 1 Kgs 19:4-7), or instruct (Acts 7:38; Gal 3:19). When Christ came to earth as the Savior, angels heralded his birth (Lk 2:8-15), guided and warned his parents (Mt 2:13), strengthened him when he was tempted (Mt 4:11) and in his last distress (Lk 22:43-44 in some manuscripts), and observed his resurrection (Mt 28:1-6). Jesus spoke about the guardian angels of little children (Mt 18:10). Philip was guided by an angel (Acts 8:26). Apostles were rescued from prison by an angel (Acts 5:19; 12:7-11). In a frightening situation, the apostle Paul was encouraged by an angel (Acts 27:21-25).

ANGELS OF THE SEVEN CHURCHES
This term is used in Revelation 1:20 and repeated in its singular form in 2:1, 8, 12, 18; 3:1, 7, 14. The word "angel" is translated from the Greek word *angelos* (one who delivers a message). Hence, some versions render this word as "messenger" in these chapters. The word could also be translated "guardian" or "representative" in this context. There is no consensus as to the significance of this term in the first three chapters of Revelation. In fact, although the seven churches addressed here were actual places where churches existed, some have suggested that they are symbolic of the various conditions of the church throughout her history. With this view, the angel of each church could be considered a human messenger, minister, or representative of the local church. However, some say that an angel here is simply the personification of the prevailing spirit of each church. A third opinion holds that consistent usage of the word elsewhere in the book provides a persuasive argument that the epistles of Revelation were addressed to a true spiritual guardian angel of each church.

The physical appearance of angels in biblical encounters was often unusual enough to distinguish them from ordinary people. The angel who moved the stone from the entrance to Jesus' tomb had an appearance like lightning and raiment white as snow (Mt 28:3). Many passages about angels are descriptions of dreams or visions. "Jacob's ladder" with angels ascending and descending (Gn 28:12) is an example. In another dream an angel spoke to Jacob (Gn 31:11). An angel appeared to Cornelius in a vision (Acts 10:1-3). Major passages of this type include Isaiah 6 (the seraphim), much of the book of Ezekiel (the cherubim), and much of Daniel and Zechariah. In the NT, over a third of the references to angels are in the book of Revelation. In most cases there, the angelic beings are glorious or grotesque figures seen in visions and are not to be confused with human persons. The language describing such visions is appropriately mystical, or at least metaphorical and difficult to interpret.

Angelology, or the doctrine of angels, is not a major theme in Christian theology in spite of the many references to angels in the Bible. Angels are included in descriptions of all that God created (Ps 148:2; Col 1:16). There are hints that they witnessed the creation of the world (Jb 38:7). No matter how close to God angels may be, they share with humankind the status of creatures. But as wholly spiritual creatures they are free from many human limitations, such as death (Lk 20:36). They do not marry (Mt 22:30), so they could be regarded as sexless. In all their appearances, angels in human form were taken to be men, never women or children. Their ability to communicate in human language and to affect human life in other ways is basic

to their role in the Bible. Their power and awesome appearance (Mt 28:2-4) sometimes tempted people to fear or worship them, but the NT does not condone the worship of angels (Col 2:18; Rv 22:8-9). Though angels are stronger and wiser than human beings, their power and knowledge are also limited by God (Ps 103:20; Mt 24:36; 1 Pt 1:11-12; 2 Pt 2:11). *See* Cherub, Cherubim; Seraph, Seraphim; Demon; Demon-possession; Satan.

ANGER The word normally used in the Bible to refer to rage, fury, and indignation. In most instances, anger is considered to be wrong. Psalm 37:8 (NLT), for example, commands: "Stop your anger! Turn from your rage!" Jesus paralleled anger with murder when he said, "If you are angry with someone, you are subject to judgment!" (Mt 5:22, NLT)—just as if the person had actually committed the murder he felt in his angry heart. Ephesians 4:31 and Colossians 3:8 both list anger, along with bitterness, wrath, malice, and slander, as attitudes that Christians must rid themselves of once and for all. In his list of attributes for a bishop or pastor of a church, the apostle Paul said that a Christian leader should not be prone to anger, that is, easily provoked (Ti 1:7).

The Bible recognizes that humans get angry; it does not condemn the anger in and of itself but what often happens as the result. Humans have a habit of letting their anger get the best of them, causing them to sin. That is why the apostle Paul said, "Don't sin by letting anger gain control over you" (Eph 4:26, NLT). The longer a person allows anger to continue, the greater the danger that it will develop sinful qualities, giving Satan a foothold (see Eph 4:27).

Anger of a good sort is also spoken of in the Bible. "Righteous indignation" refers to the extreme displeasure of a holy heart unable to tolerate sin of any kind. The anger of God contains this element: man should be good, yet he sins—and God is angry "because they forsook the covenant of the Lord, the God of their fathers, which he made with them when he brought them out of the land of Egypt, and went and served other gods and worshiped them, gods whom they had not known and whom he had not allotted to them" (Dt 29:25-26, RSV). It was in that sense also that Moses' anger burned on Mt Sinai and caused him to smash the tablets of the covenant on the ground when he saw the golden calf and Israel's idolatry (Ex 32:19).

In the NT, Mark says that Jesus looked with anger at the Pharisees, who were hoping to catch him breaking their law (Mk 3:5). Jesus' anger was also shown in his cleansing of the temple (Jn 2:13-22); it should have been a place of prayer but was being used as a place of business. So Jesus "entered the Temple and began to drive out the merchants and their customers. He knocked over the tables of the money changers and the stalls of those selling doves" (Mt 21:12, NLT). His holy indignation was neither a weakness nor a sin. Such anger is an appropriate response to iniquity and injustice, especially when they are apparently unpunished.

ANIAM Shemida's son from Naphtali's tribe (1 Chr 7:19).

ANIM One of 44 cities of the hill country given to Judah's tribe in the allotment of the land (Jos 15:50). Anim is probably modern Khirbet Ghowein et-Tahta.

ANIMALS In biblical usage, all members of the animal kingdom. Animals are mentioned throughout the Bible from Genesis to Revelation. Animals figured in many important biblical events, including the Creation, the fall of man, the Flood, the ten plagues in Egypt, the Hebrew worship system, and the life of Jesus Christ. The people of both OT and NT times lived close to the land and were well acquainted with various animals so that the scriptural writers and Jesus himself frequently used animals as object lessons.

The biblical approach to classification of animals is somewhat different from the system of classification used by biologists today. The present system of classification, which traces back to Carolus Linnaeus (an 18th-century Swedish botanist), is based on structure, both internal and external. The biblical basis of classification is habitat. Thus Genesis 1 speaks of aquatic organisms (v 20); aerial organisms (v 21); animals that crawl on the ground (v 24); cattle or domesticated animals (animals that live in association with humans) (v 24); and wild animals (v 24). The same system of classification is followed in Leviticus 11 and throughout Scripture.

Because of the divergence between systems of classification, the various animals of the Bible will be listed here in alphabetical order—including reptiles, fish, and even invertebrates such as insects, spiders, worms, and sponges. Birds are discussed in a separate article.

PREVIEW

•Adder	•Dragon	•Locust
•Ant	•Fish	•Mole
•Antelope	•Flea	•Moth
•Ape	•Fly	•Mouse
•Asp	•Fox	•Mule
•Ass	•Frog	•Pig
•Badger	•Gazelle	•Porcupine
•Bat	•Gecko	•Scorpion
•Bear	•Gnat	•Sheep
•Bee	•Goat	•Snail
•Behemoth	•Grasshopper	•Snake
•Camel	•Hare	•Spider
•Caterpillar	•Hippopotamus	•Sponge
•Cattle	•Horse	•Unicorn
•Chameleon	•Hyena	•Wasp
•Coral	•Jackal	•Whale
•Cricket	•Leech	•Wild Ox
•Crocodile	•Leopard	•Wolf
•Deer	•Leviathan	•Worm
•Dog	•Lion	
•Donkey	•Lizard	

Adder One of the 20 poisonous snakes found in Israel and surrounding countries, also referred to as cockatrice and viper. True vipers (genus *Cerastes, Echis colorata*, and *Vipera palestina*) also exist there, poisonous snakes with curved fangs that spring into position when the snake strikes. The horned viper *(Cerastes hasselquistii)* may attack horses. It is 12 to 18 inches (30 to 46 centimeters) long and often lies in ambush in the sand with only its eyes and the hornlike protrusions on its head visible.

Both Jesus and John the Baptist referred to the viper several times (Mt 3:7; 12:34; 23:33). The reference in Acts 28:3 is probably to a small viper *(Vipera aspis)* that strikes rapidly and is very pugnacious. It is found in southern Europe and hisses each time it inhales and exhales. The poison of vipers attacks the respiratory system and disintegrates red blood cells.

See also Snake (below).

Ant Mentioned only twice in the Bible, both times in the book of Proverbs. For many years Solomon was charged with a biological error when he referred to the

ant as providing her meat in the summer and gathering her food in the harvest (Prv 6:8). Critics of the Bible were quick to point out that, so far as was then known, ants do not store up food. They assumed that Solomon had probably kicked open an ant hill and mistaken the pupal cases (pods in which immature ants grow to maturity) for grain or had observed ants carrying bits of grain, leaves, and other matter to their nests.

At least three species of grain-storing ants are now known—two occur in Israel and the other in Mediterranean countries. The particular species referred to by Solomon (Prv 6:6-8; 30:24-25) is probably the harvester ant *(Messor semirufus)*. Its granaries are flat chambers connected by galleries irregularly scattered over an area about six feet (1.8 meters) in diameter and about a foot (.3 meter) deep in the ground. Seeds are collected from the ground or picked from plants. The head, or radicle, which is the softest part of the kernel, is bitten off to prevent germination, and the chaff and empty capsules are discarded on kitchen middens (refuse piles) outside the nest. Individual granaries may be 5 inches (12.7 centimeters) in diameter and a half inch (1.2 centimeters) high. Some nests are known to be 40 feet (12 meters) in diameter and 6 to 7 feet (approx. 2 meters) deep with several entrances.

Antelope Several antelope-like creatures are referred to in the Scriptures. One seems to be the white oryx *(Oryx leucoryx)*, referred to in Deuteronomy 14:5 (KJV "wild ox"; RSV "antelope") and Isaiah 51:20 (KJV "wild bull"; RSV "antelope"). The oryx was probably the antelope, commonly used for food because its long horns made it relatively easy to catch.

Another antelope mentioned in the Bible is the addax *(Addax nasomaculatus)*, probably the "pygarg" of Deuteronomy 14:5 (KJV). It is a native of North Africa with grayish white hinder parts, a white patch on the forehead, and twisted and ringed horns. The word "pygarg" comes from a Greek word meaning "white rump." The addax is about the size of a donkey. Its body is closely covered with short hair. It has a short mane on the underside of its neck that makes the head look somewhat like that of a goat. The hooves are broad and flat, and the tail resembles that of a donkey. It is common in Africa and in Arabia, where Arabs hunt it with falcons and dogs.

Antelopes are very graceful and run with their heads held high. Both sexes have long, permanent, hollow horns. With the oryx the horns go straight back; addax horns are twisted and ringed. Antelope are alert, wary, and keen sighted. They are usually found in herds of from two to a dozen. If injured or brought to bay, an antelope attacks with its head lowered so that the sharp horns point forward. Antelopes feed on grasses and shrubs, drinking from streams and water holes. When water is scarce, they eat melons and succulent bulbs. Both addax and oryx were ceremonially clean in Jewish law.

Ape Primate not native to Palestine. The two references to apes in the OT (1 Kgs 10:22; 2 Chr 9:21) refer to their importation by King Solomon with other treasures on board the ships of his mercantile fleet. There is some question concerning the origin of those primates. Some believe that the mention of "ivory" in the same verses suggests they came from East Africa and that they were indeed apes, that is, tailless primates. Others, believing they came from India or Ceylon, suggest that they were actually monkeys. There the baboon (genus *Papeio*), a large monkey, was considered sacred to the god Thoth. Males of that genus were kept in temples, and the more docile females were often kept as house pets. Such baboons frequently had some of their teeth removed or ground down to lessen the danger of their

Gazelle

Ancient Egyptian Horse

Antelope

Rock Badger

Ibex

biting. A number of mummified baboons have been found in Egypt, indicating the high regard in which they were held.

Asp Poisonous snake. Most biblical references to the asp (Dt 32:33) seem to be to the Egyptian cobra *(Naja haje)*, which conceals itself in holes, walls, and rocks and has the ability to expand its neck by raising its anterior ribs so as to enlarge the front of its breast into the shape of a flat disc. Its potent poison can cause death in 30 minutes. It attains a length of about 80 inches (2 meters). The fangs are permanently erect, not movable as in the vipers (the common poisonous snakes of North America; only the coral snake in America has permanently erect fangs). Cobra poison attacks the nervous system, causing muscular paralysis. The Egyptians looked upon it as a sacred creature; they regarded it as a protector since it fed on the rodents that ate their crops. The "fiery serpents" (Nm 21:6; Dt 8:15, both RSV) may have been cobras; "fiery" probably refers to the burning fever caused by their venom. Isaiah 14:29 and 30:6 ("flying serpent") may refer to the hood of the cobra.
See also Snake (below).

Ass *See* Donkey (below).

Badger Small hoofed mammal. What the KJV calls a "coney," modern translations name "rock badger" (Lv 11:5; Dt 14:7; Ps 104:18; Prv 30:26). The rock badger spoken of in the Bible is probably the Syrian rock hyrax *(Hyrax syriaca)*, the only species of hyrax found outside Africa. This small ungulate (having hooflike toenails) lives among rocks from the Dead Sea valley to Mt Hermon. It is strictly a herbivorous (plant-eating) animal about the size of a rabbit. It resembles a guinea pig more than a rabbit, having quite inconspicuous ears and a very small tail. It has broad nails with four toes on its forelegs and three on its hind legs, the toes being connected with skin almost like a web. Pads acting as sucking discs under its feet enable it to keep its footing on slippery rocks. With its yellow and brown fur, it is sometimes

called the bear rat because of its resemblance to a tailless rat. It is also equipped with black whiskers that may be seven inches (17.8 centimeters) long.

These rock badgers, or hyraxes, live together in colonies of from 6 to 50 animals, often sunning themselves on rocks. They are difficult to catch. Guards are posted, and if approaching danger is sighted, the whole group will scurry for cover, warned by the sharp whistles of the guards. Thus they are commended for taking refuge in the rocks (Ps 104:18) and are called wise for making "their houses in the rocks" (Prv 30:24, 26, KJV). The badger is not a ruminant (does not chew its cud), but the motion of its jaws may suggest that it chews its cud. That is probably why it was included with other cud-chewing animals in the Jewish food laws (Lv 11:5; Dt 14:7). It was forbidden to the Jews as food because it did not have cloven hooves. Some Arabs eat and even prize its meat.

Bat Flying mammals according to modern classification. They have hair and provide milk for their young. The Bible classifies them with other aerial creatures. Bats take shelter in caves, crevices, tree cavities, buildings, and also in exposed places on trees. In colder areas they hibernate or migrate. The normal resting position for a bat is hanging head downward. Bats "swim" through the air rather than fly because they move with their legs as well as with their wings.

The bat's thumb is free and terminates in a single hook claw used for climbing and hanging. The hind feet have five toes, all pointing the same way. The large chest accommodates the powerful muscles needed for flying. Because they orient themselves by echo location, the sense of hearing is very well developed.

Most bats are insect eaters, seizing insects in flight. Many insectivorous bats also eat some fruit. Other bats feed exclusively, usually in groups, on fruit and green vegetation. Fruit-eating bats generally live in the tropics where fruit is constantly ripening, although some have been found in the Holy Land. These bats tend to be larger than the insectivores, having a wingspread of up to five feet (1.5 meters).

A third group includes flower-eating bats that feed on pollen and nectar. These small bats with long pointed heads and long tongues are found only in tropical and semitropical regions. Three species of vampire bats, which do not occur in the Holy Land, eat blood by making a small incision and lapping it up. Carnivorous (meat-eating) bats prey on birds, lizards, and frogs. Fish-eating bats catch fish at or near the water surface.

Eight varieties of bats are known in the Holy Land. One of them, the little brown bat (genus *Myotis),* is worldwide in its distribution. It is insectivorous and probably has the widest distribution of any nonhuman terrestrial mammal. Brown bats are mostly cave dwellers. The females form maternity colonies that may number in the tens of thousands.

Two species of mouse-tailed bats (genus *Rhinopoma)* are found in the Holy Land. Their tails are nearly as long as the head and body combined. They are colonial, roosting in caves, rock clefts, wells, pyramids, palaces, and houses. Like the brown bat, they are insectivorous. The slit-faced or hollow-faced bats (genus *Nycteris)* are also found in the Holy Land. They are insectivorous and roost in groups from 6 to 20.

The bats found in the Holy Land vary in size from that of a mouse to the size of a rat; the largest species measures more than 20 inches (51 centimeters) across the wings. The bat was unclean to the Jews (Lv 11:19; Dt 14:18).

Bear Large, heavy, big-headed mammal with short, powerful limbs, a short tail, and small eyes and ears. Bears have a "plantigrade" walk: they walk on both the sole and heel as humans do. The Palestinian bear is a Syrian version of the brown bear *(Ursus arctos syriacus).* It can grow to a height of 6 feet (1.8 meters) and may weigh as much as 500 pounds (227 kilograms).

Bears have an excellent sense of smell but less developed senses of sight and hearing. They are omnivorous (eating any kind of food); they subsist largely on vegetation, fruits, insects, and fish.

Bears are usually peaceful and inoffensive, but if they think they must defend themselves (Lam 3:10) or their young (2 Sm 17:8; Prv 17:12; Hos 13:8), they may be formidable and dangerous adversaries. David boasted of his role as a bear killer (1 Sm 17:34-37). Since a blow from a bear's paw can be fatal, David's courage and strength as a young shepherd in running after a bear and wrenching one of his father's sheep from its jaws were noteworthy.

Some biblical passages seem to imply that bears attacked for no apparent reason (e.g., Prv 28:15; Am 5:19). At other times they were God's instruments of punishment, as in the story of Elisha and the two she-bears (2 Kgs 2:24). The bear and the lion, often mentioned together in the Bible (1 Sm 17:37), were the two largest and strongest beasts of prey in the Holy Land. Thus they symbolized both strength and terror (Am 5:19).

In biblical times bears seem to have roamed all over Palestine. Today they are found only in the Lebanon and Anti-Lebanon Mountains, and even there they are rare.

Bee One of two domesticated insects *(Apis mellifica),* the other being the silkworm. Bees gather nectar from flowers, transferring pollen from one flower to another in the process. It is believed that they convey the location of sources of nectar to other bees through a bee "dance," which may indicate both distance and direction. Bees are sensitive to four colors: blue-green, yellow-green, blue-violet, and ultra-violet (invisible to humans).

The wild bees of the Holy Land are especially noted for their ferocity in attack. Only the female "worker" bees sting people and animals, the virulence of their venom increasing in warm weather. A number of biblical passages allude to the irritable, vindictive nature of bees and to the painful stings they inflict (Dt 1:44; Ps 118:12; Is 7:18).

One reference calls attention to the fact that in semidesert regions a dead animal's carcass, stripped to the bone by jackals or vultures and dried in the sun, can provide wild bees an excellent place to start a new colony (Jgs 14:5-9).

The Egyptians considered the bee sacred. In ancient Greece candles were made from beeswax. In the Holy Land, beekeeping was probably not practiced until the Hellenistic period (second century BC), although Ezekiel 27:17 suggests that it may have been practiced earlier. If domestic honey was not available to the Hebrews, wild honey certainly was, and travelers would be on the lookout for caches of honey in rocky clefts and other likely places. The Philistines and the Hittites practiced beekeeping in their cities.

The Bible contains many references to bees and bee products. A bee swarm was a valuable asset, though the price of honey itself was low. Honey was sometimes eaten with the honeycomb (Sg 5:1). Honey also had uses other than food, e.g., in embalming.

The land of Israel was described as a land flowing with milk and honey. Honey was a major source of sweetening in the ancient Near East—hence, its importance (cf. Jgs 14:8-9). Actually the Hebrew word for "honey" may include not only bee honey but also the sweet syrup extracted from such fruits as figs, dates, and grapes. Thus "a land flowing with milk and honey" (Ex 3:8, RSV) does not necessarily stand for a land of bees but for a land rich in sweetness.

See also Food and Food Preparation; Honey.

Behemoth *See* Hippopotamus (below).

Camel Large beast of burden. Unintelligent, ill-natured, and quarrelsome, the camel *(Camelus dromedarius)* is nevertheless a blessing to people living in the desert and on its borders because it is especially adapted to that habitat. It has been called the ship of the desert. Having thick elastic pads of fibrous tissue on its feet, it can walk on hot desert sands. It can go without water for long periods and can subsist on vegetation growing on the saline soils. The camel's nostrils are pinched together and can be closed at will to prevent penetration of sand during violent sandstorms.

Camels are used for transporting both goods and people. A person riding a camel can cover from 60 to 75 miles (96.5 to 121 kilometers) in a day. A camel can carry a load weighing 600 pounds (272 kilograms) or more. Camels were used heavily in the spice trade (Gn 37:25) and traveled regularly in camel trains between Arabia, Egypt, and Assyria. They were also ridden in time of war (Jgs 6:5). A camel can even be hitched to a plow in areas where the land is cultivated.

The hair shed by camels during the early spring is preserved and used in weaving cloth and making tents. As much as 10 pounds (4.5 kilograms) of hair can be obtained from one camel. A rough cloak of camel's hair, as worn by John the Baptist (Mt 3:4), is still worn by Bedouins today. A camel's hair garment was also the sign of the prophetic office (Zec 13:4).

Two varieties of camel occur within the one-humped species, the slow burden-bearing camel referred to in Genesis 37:25 and the fast dromedary of 1 Samuel 30:17. The dromedary can stand seven feet (2.1 meters) tall and measure as much as nine feet (2.7 meters) from the muzzle to the tip of the tail. With its three-chambered stomach, which can hold from 15 to 30 quarts (14.2 to 28.4 liters) of liquid, it can go for as long as 5 days during the summer or 25 days in winter without drinking. The camel's hump is a reserve store of fat, making it possible for the animal to subsist on very little food during a desert journey.

Another species of camel, the Bactrian camel *(Camelus bactrianus)*, is also resident in the Holy Land. It has two humps. It is heavier, bigger, and has longer hair than the one-humped camel and is slower than the swift dromedary. Isaiah 21:7 may refer to the Bactrian camel; both kinds of camel are referred to in Esther 8:10 (KJV). Camels ranked in importance with sheep, cattle, and asses in OT times. A third of the 66 biblical references to the camel lists it with other animals.

Camels are ruminants (cud-chewing mammals) but do not have cloven hooves. Thus, they were included in the list of unclean beasts, forbidden by the Israelites as food (Lv 11:4; Dt 14:7). They are eaten by Arabs, however, who also drink their milk (cf. Gn 32:15).

Abraham had camels in Egypt (Gn 12:16). At first Job had 3,000 camels (Jb 1:3) and after his recovery, 6,000 (Jb 42:12). Although wide use of camels does not seem to have begun until shortly before 1000 BC (Jgs 6:5), Sumerian texts from the Old Babylonian period list camels and indicate that they had been domesticated. Camel bones and figurines have been found at various eastern archaeological sites dating from well before 1200 BC.

See also Travel.

Caterpillar Larval stage of insects characterized by complete metamorphosis. Such insects pass through four stages: egg, larva or caterpillar, pupa, and adult. Bees, flies, moths, and butterflies all pass through a larval or caterpillar stage.

The word "caterpillar" occurs three times in the NLT (1 Kgs 8:37; 2 Chr 6:28; Ps 78:46). In the book of Joel that same Hebrew word is translated "locust" (1:4; 2:25, NLT). The locust and grasshopper to which the Hebrew word refers have an incomplete type of metamorphosis with only three stages: egg, nymph, and adult. The nymph is a miniature adult in which the wings are not fully developed, though their outline may be present. There are several nymph stages known as instars. The reference is to one of the last instars, in which the wing structures are still folded together and enclosed in a sac but are nevertheless clearly recognizable. That form of the insect is about an inch (2.5 centimeters) long.

See also Locust (below).

Cattle Domestic animals of the bovine species *(Bos primigenius)*. The OT often emphasized the beauty of cattle. Egypt was rich in cattle, especially in the Nile River delta area (Goshen), where the Hebrews settled under Joseph.

Some scholars believe that milk rather than meat was the foremost consideration in the domestication of cattle and that in early civilizations meat supplies came chiefly from wild game. Cattle also supplied strong hides that supplanted wood in the manufacture of shields. Their dung was a source of fuel when wood was scarce (Ez 4:15). They were used as beasts of burden and for plowing. Development of wheeled transportation was associated more closely with cattle than with any other animal.

The biblical term "cattle" often refers to all domesticated animals or livestock (Gn 1:24; 2:20; 7:23; 47:6, 16-17; Ex 9:3-7; Nm 3:41, 45). Occasionally, the term was used to refer to all large domestic animals (Nm 31:9;

32:26), although sometimes the word as used in the KJV refers only to sheep and goats (Gn 30:32, 39, 43; 31:8, 10; Is 7:25; 43:23).

Probably several kinds of cattle were domesticated in the Holy Land. Small, short-legged, black or brown shorthorn cattle were found in the southern part of Judah; that type submitted easily to the yoke and was prominent in agricultural operations. Along the coast a larger variety was found, and the wild districts east of the Jordan River were populated with a breed of huge black cattle.

Cattle breeding was widely practiced by the patriarchs (cf. Gn 32:15; Jb 21:10). Strict laws in Mesopotamia, as well as in Israel, penalized the owner of a bull that gored a man or other cattle (Ex 21:28-36). Bulls were sometimes employed figuratively as pictures of strength or violence (Dt 33:17; Pss 22:12; 68:30; Is 10:13). For breeding purposes one bull is normally adequate for about 30 cows, but many more were kept since bulls were widely used in Israel for sacrifices. They might be used as a general sacrifice (Lv 22:23; Nm 23:1) or for special sacrifices (Jgs 6:25; 1 Sm 1:24). Particular sacrifices were offered at the consecration of priests (Ex 29:1), consecration of an altar (Nm 7), purification of the Levites (Nm 8), sin offerings (Lv 16), day of the new moon (Nm 28:11-14), Passover (Nm 28:19), Feast of Weeks (Nm 28:27), Feast of Trumpets (Nm 29:1-2), Day of Atonement (Nm 29:7-9), and the Feast of Tabernacles (Nm 29:12-38). The Feast of Tabernacles required the largest number of bulls for burnt offerings of all the annual feasts, with a total of 71 being slaughtered during the course of eight days.

Calves were sometimes referred to as "sons of the herd" in the original Hebrew (Gn 18:8; 1 Sm 6:7; 14:32). The calf, a symbol of peacefulness (Is 11:6), was also used figuratively to refer to the weak (Ps 68:30). A calf's head decorated the back of Solomon's throne (1 Kgs 10:19). Calves were sometimes fattened in stalls to keep them from running off weight in the field (Am 6:4; Mal 4:2; Lk 15:23) or were kept around the house; the witch of Endor kept a calf in her house that she killed and served to Saul and his men (1 Sm 28:24-25). Calves supplied veal (Gn 18:7), considered a delicacy by the wealthy; Amos referred to stall-fattened calves in a denunciation of luxurious and careless living (Am 6:4). Calves also supplied meat for all Saul's armies at the great slaughter of the Philistines (1 Sm 14:32). The "fatted calf" served roasted or boiled was gourmet fare, suitable for the finest banquet (Gn 18:7; Mt 22:4; Lk 15:23).

Cattle were subject to the law of firstlings (Ex 13:12). They were a mark of wealth (Gn 13:2) and were considered proper booty of war (Jos 8:2). Aaron, the first high priest, made a golden calf as a rival to the ark of the covenant (Ex 32; Dt 9:16, 21). Even though he represented the calf as an image of the invisible God, it was especially offensive because the calf was a fertility symbol related to Egyptian and Canaanite practices. Two calves were later made by Jeroboam I of Israel (930–909 BC) for his shrines at Bethel and Dan (1 Kgs 12:28-33). Hosea's prophetic denunciations of calf worship were directed at those shrines (Hos 8:5-6; 13:2).

An ox is an adult castrated bull. A steer is a young ox. Oxen were used to do work (Nm 7:3; Dt 22:10; 25:4), though for moving heavy objects, cows were typically favored over bulls because of their more docile nature. Oxen were also used as pack animals (1 Chr 12:40, although they did not have the endurance of the ass, camel, or mule. They usually fed on grass (Nm 22:4; Ps 06:20), but they also ate straw (Is 11:7) and salted fodder (Is 30:24) and could be kept in a stable (Lk 13:15). Oxen could not be offered as sacrifices because they had been castrated (Lv 22:24). They could be used for food but were rarely eaten. Possession of an ox and an ass was regarded as the bare minimum for existence in the ancient Palestinian agriculture economy (Jb 24:3; cf. Ex 20:17).

See also Agriculture; Food and Food Preparation; Offerings and Sacrifices.

Chameleon Lizard characterized by its ability to change color according to its surroundings (Chameleon vulgaris). To the Israelites the chameleon was ritually unclean (Lv 11:30). The Hebrew word for chameleon is derived from a word meaning "to pant." A lizard's lungs are very large, and in ancient times lizards were believed to live on air. A chameleon's eyes move independently of each other; so at times one eye may be turned upward and the other downward. Chameleons live in trees and bushes, clinging to branches with their long tails.

See also Lizard (below).

Coral Calcareous (lime-containing) skeletons of relatively simple marine organisms (Corallium rubrum). Red coral from the Mediterranean and Red Seas is widely used for jewelry and for medicinal purposes. While the animal is alive, the coral is green in color and shrublike in appearance, looking rather like an underwater plant since the coral animals are immobil. When the coral is removed from the water, it becomes hard and red in color.

In ancient times coral was sometimes used as money, along with precious stones, pearls, and gold. Some believe the biblical reference in Lamentations 4:7 (RSV) is to pearls rather than to coral, but it is probable that the references in Job 28:18 and Ezekiel 27:16 are to the red coral (see NLT).

Cricket Insect of the order Orthptera related to grasshoppers and locusts. According to Leviticus 11:22, the cricket was edible. The reference may be to one of the growth stages of the locust.

The KJV translates the Hebrew word as "beetle." Beetles are insects with chewing mouth parts and two pairs of wings, the fore pair being hard and sheathlike and the hind pair being membranous and folded under the fore pair. Some beetles are carnivorous, others are chiefly herbivorous. Some are aquatic, some produce a secretion that blisters the skin, some damage fabrics, some damage crops, and some feed on other insects that are harmful to humans. In ancient Egypt the beetle, or sacred scarab, was a symbol of the sun god Ra. Scarab seals and amulets were extremely popular in Egypt.

Crocodile Largest of all existing reptiles (Crocodilus vulgaris), attaining a length of well over 20 feet (6 meters). Crocodiles are characterized by large lizardlike bodies supported by short legs. The head terminates in a flattened snout armed with strong conical teeth, each of which is implanted in a distinct socket. New teeth growing from beneath continually replace those in use. The toes are webbed. The back and tail are protected by quadrangular horny shields of varying sizes arranged in regular rows and in contact with one another at the edges. The eyes are covered with movable lids that can be closed when the animal enters the water.

The crocodile spends most of its time in the water where it feeds mainly on fish but also on aquatic birds and even small animals that come down to the water's edge to drink. It is surprisingly fast and agile on dry land, even though its legs are so short that its belly and tail drag across the earth leaving a distinct path.

Until the beginning of the 20th century, the crocodile was found in the marshes and small coastal rivers of western Palestine. A first-century Roman writer, Pliny, referred to a place in the Holy Land called Crocodeilopolis ("crocodile city") to the south of Mt Carmel, and visitors to the Holy Land as late as the 19th century reported seeing crocodiles in that general region.

The description of "Leviathan" in Job 41 seems to be based on the crocodile (thus the translation of the NLT). The "dragon" of Ezekiel 29:3, used figuratively of the Egyptian pharaoh, may be a reference to the crocodile.

Deer Large ruminant (cud-chewing) animals. Only the males have antlers (branching horns). Deer antlers grow annually and are solid, in contrast to those of the antelope and the gazelle. Fully developed antlers are devoid of any covering of skin or horn and, for all practical purposes, may be regarded as a mass of dead bone carried for a certain time by the living animal.

The end of the deer's muzzle is naked in all species. The stomach is divided into a series of compartments, some of which are used to store partly chewed food. The food is later regurgitated, rechewed, and finally swallowed into a section of the stomach where true digestion takes place.

Three species of deer were known in Palestine: the red deer (Cervus elaphus), the Persian fallow deer (Dama mesopotamica), and the roe deer (Capreolus capreolus). All are now extinct there. The last deer were hunted in the Holy Land in 1914. The red deer referred to in the Bible as "hart" (male), "stag" (male), or "hind" (female) stood about four feet (1.2 meters) high at the shoulder. It was gregarious (living in herds or flocks), each group remaining in a definite territory. Red deer grazed and browsed during the morning and late afternoon (Lam 1:6). The sexes remained in separate herds. The red deer was known for its leaping (Is 35:6) and sure-footedness in the mountains (Ps 18:33; Sg 2:8-9, 17; 8:14; Hb 3:19).

The antlers of the Persian fallow deer (1 Kgs 4:23) were large, flattened, and palmated (shaped like an open palm with fingers extended), and its coat was a yellow-brown. It traveled in small groups, feeding mainly on grass in the morning and evening.

The roe deer (Dt 14:5; 1 Kgs 4:23) was a small, graceful animal, dark reddish brown in summer and yellowish gray in winter. Its antlers were about a foot (30.5 centimeters) long and had three points. The roe deer preferred sparsely wooded valleys and the lower slopes of mountains, grazing in open grasslands. It usually associated in family groups made up of the doe and her offspring. They were shy, yet very curious. The roe deer barked like a dog when disturbed, and they were excellent swimmers.

There is some question as to whether the roe deer is actually referred to in such passages as 1 Kings 4:23; references may be to the fallow deer, although that animal does not seem to have lived in the southern part of Palestine around the Sinai Desert because of its need for ample amounts of food and water. Fallow deer were found in northern Palestine.

The hart (the male red deer) was listed among the clean beasts that Jewish law permitted as food (Dt 12:15, 22; 14:5), but deer were not listed among the animals appropriate for sacrifice. The hind (female red deer) normally gave birth to one calf at a time, though twins were born with some degree of regularity (Jb 39:1; Ps 29:9, KJV; Jer 14:5). The gestation period was about 40 weeks. When it was about to give birth, the hind looked for a secure hiding place, preferably in the dense undergrowth of the forest where it could find natural protection for the tiny calf. During the first few days after birth, the mother never went far from her young. The fawn was able to stand on its own legs a few hours after birth. The solicitous care by the hind for her calf during the first days of its life is hinted at in a touching way in Jeremiah 14:4-5, where only a severe drought is said to drive the hind from her calf. Job 39:1-4 describes the calving of the hinds. The hind illustrated grace and charm (Gn 49:21; Prv 5:19), and its dark, gentle eyes and graceful limbs were used to describe the beauty of a woman (Prv 5:18-19).

Dog Probably the earliest domesticated animal (*Canis familiaris*), used very early in hunting. The modern dog is believed to have come from the Indian wolf (*Canis lupus pallipes*). The dogs of biblical times probably looked like a modern German shepherd, with short pointed ears, a pointed nose, and a long tail.

The dog was generally looked down upon in biblical times (Prv 26:11; 2 Pt 2:22). The biblical writers did not share modern sentiments about dogs being man's best friends. The dog was pictured as a scavenger, haunting streets and dumps (Ex 22:31; 1 Kgs 22:38; Mt 15:26; Lk 16:21). Human corpses could become the spoil of dogs (2 Kgs 9:35-36). In general, dogs served the same function as vultures and other birds of prey. Most of the 41 references in the Scriptures to dogs show strong disfavor. Dogs were considered cowardly, filthy creatures.

Dogs used in hunting occur in paintings in Egyptian tombs, and there is a reference to dogs herding sheep in Job 30:1. One good quality of dogs highly esteemed by the Israelites was watchfulness (Is 56:10). In general, however, in biblical times "dog" was a term of contempt (1 Sm 17:43; 2 Sm 16:9) and was used of overly submissive persons (2 Sm 9:8; 2 Kgs 8:13) and of evil persons (Is 56:10-11; Mt 7:6; Phil 3:2; Rv 22:15).

Dogs, like pigs, were voracious and omnivorous (eating any kind of food). In response to a Gentile woman's request that he heal her daughter, Jesus used the metaphor of throwing household food scraps to dogs (Mt 15:22-28; Mk 7:25-30). At the time of Jesus, the word "dog" was a standard Jewish term of contempt for Gentiles who, like dogs, were considered unclean, although the diminutive form of the word, used by Jesus, softened this considerably. Seeing her faith, Jesus granted the woman's request, giving a non-Jew some of "the children's bread."

Donkey Beast of burden. The donkey of the Holy Land (*Equus asinus*) was quite different from the European donkey of today, which is usually a small, stubborn animal. In biblical times the donkey was a beautiful, stately, friendly animal. Its color was usually reddish brown. Three wild races have been described, all from Africa. The race from northwest Africa is extinct; the one from northeast Africa, if not extinct, is close to extinction; the Somalian race, which survives, did not play an important part in domestication. The northeast African race, the Nubian donkey, was evidently domesticated in the Nile River region in early historic times. The donkey was used as a mount from the time of domestication on. It is first mentioned in the Bible among the animals that Abraham acquired in Egypt (Gn 12:16). The donkey was primarily a beast of burden, driven but not bridled. From the time of the Middle Kingdom on (c. 2040 BC), it was used for riding in Egypt, but only the Jews and Nubians rode donkeys regularly. The donkey was also used for threshing grain and for pulling the plow. In Arab countries today peasants plow with a donkey and a cow or camel hitched together. In Israel the law forbade plowing

with a donkey and an ox hitched together (Dt 22:10). Until the time of Solomon (960 BC), horses were not used in Palestine. From that time on, the horse was ridden by warriors; the donkey was used by those who were traveling peaceably.

The donkey was held in high regard by the Jews and was considered an economic asset. An individual had to have a donkey for minimum existence (Jb 24:3), and wealth was frequently counted by the number of donkeys one possessed (Gn 12:16; 24:35). The donkey was considered an acceptable gift (Gn 32:13-15). It was allowed to rest on the Sabbath (Dt 5:14). Women in biblical times often used the donkey as a riding animal (Jos 15:18; 1 Sm 25:23; 2 Kgs 4:24); often a special driver would help a woman guide the animal, running along at its side. If a married couple possessed only one donkey, the husband usually walked alongside while the wife rode (Ex 4:20).

The people of Israel returning from Babylon had ten times as many donkeys as horses and camels (Ezr 2:66-67; Neh 7:68-69). Job's wealth was indicated by the fact that he had 500 she-donkeys before catastrophe hit him (Jb 1:3); after his recovery he had 1,000 donkeys (Jb 42:12). Joseph's brothers used donkeys to transport the grain they purchased in Egypt (Gn 42:26; 43:24). Abigail transported food on donkeys to David and his troops during their conflict with Saul (1 Sm 25:18). David assigned one of the 12 managers of his royal estates to look after his donkeys exclusively (1 Chr 27:30).

The onager, or Syrian wild donkey (*Equus hemionus hemihippus,*) is an intermediate between the true horse and the true donkey. Its ears are longer than those of a horse but shorter than those of a donkey. The front hooves are narrow; there are chestnuts (callouslike spots on the inside of the knees) on the front legs only, and the tail is short haired for a long distance from its root so that it appears to be tufted.

The Sumerians (ancient Mesopotamians) were able to domesticate the onager, which was eventually replaced by the horse. It was used to draw chariots in Ur; a number of onagers were buried with their vehicles in a royal grave that dates from about 2500 BC. Later the wild onager was a favorite hunter's prize for Babylonian and Assyrian kings.

The onager was very common in the steppe lands near Israel, where it was described as a freedom-loving desert animal (Jb 24:5; 39:5-8; Ps 104:11; Is 32:14; Jer 2:24; Hos 8:9). Ishmael was described as "free and untamed as a wild donkey" (Gn 16:12, NLT)—that is, one who could not adjust to domestic life. Drought seems to have been responsible for the population decline of the onager in biblical times (Jer 14:6). The modern onager (*Equus hemionus onager*) is slightly larger than the Syrian wild donkey that is extinct.

See also Travel.

Dragon Any one of a number of monstrous land and sea creatures. In biblical usage, "dragon" does not refer to the huge, fire-breathing, winged reptile of European folklore. The translators of the KJV used the term to translate two Hebrew words that are usually rendered more precisely in modern translations. One word referred to desert animals; most scholars agree with the NIV that "jackals" is its proper meaning (Ps 44:19; Is 13:22; Jer 9:11; Mal 1:3). *See* Jackal (below).

The other Hebrew word translated "dragon" is harder to define. It was frequently used in reference to serpents (so translated in the RSV: Ex 7:9-12; Dt 32:33; Ps 91:13). In other RSV passages it is translated "sea monster" (Gn 1:21; Jb 7:12; Ps 148:7). The exact identity of such sea monsters is not known. Several RSV passages retain the English "dragon." In two of them (Ps 74:13; Is 27:1), the context indicates that sea monsters are meant. In three others (Is 51:9; Ez 29:3; 32:2) "dragon" seems to refer to the crocodile, a figurative reference to the Egyptian pharaoh at the time of the exodus. Jeremiah 51:34 (translated "monster" in the RSV) may also refer to a voracious creature such as a crocodile. *See* Crocodile (above).

Babylonian myths described monsters and dragons in primordial conflict with the god Marduk; they represented the principle of evil. In its figurative usages in Scripture, "dragon" has a similar significance, especially in the prophetic books. In the book of Revelation it is a symbol of Satan, the archenemy of God and his people (Rv 12:3-17; 13:2, 4, 11; 16:13; 20:2).

Fish Aquatic animals frequently mentioned in the Bible without names or descriptions that enable us to identify the particular species. Since time immemorial, fish have constituted one of the staple foods of humanity, and they still serve as the chief source of protein in many parts of the world. The trade in fish was highly developed in biblical times. For example, one of the gates in Jerusalem was called the Fish Gate (Neh 3:3; Zep 1:10). The law in Leviticus 11:9-12 permitted the Jews to eat fish, but only those having both fins and scales. Scaleless fish such as catfish were forbidden, even though they had fins.

Egyptian paintings depict various methods of fishing, and the Philistines fished in the Mediterranean Sea. Since the people of Israel were not a seafaring nation, it is safe to assume that most of their fish came from freshwater lakes and rivers, especially the Sea of Galilee. Some 36 species of fish have been identified in that lake, including varieties of perch, carp, barbel, "sardine," and catfish.

The method of fishing characteristic of NT times was the dragnet. After a boat had put out into the deep (Lk 5:4), a large net would be thrown out from it and then dragged toward shore by the rowers in the boat, possibly with the help of a crew in another boat. The catch was sorted out on shore (Mt 13:47-48). Fishing was usually carried out at night when the coolness of the water brought fish closer to the surface and when they could not see the approaching nets.

The Jews also fished by hook and line (Mt 17:27), a few by spear (Jb 41:7), and some by the throw net (Ez 47:10). Habakkuk refers to hook-and-line fishing, netting, and seining (1:15).

Very early in the history of the Christian church the fish became a symbol for Christ and the faith. It was scratched on the walls of Roman catacombs and may be seen today decorating walls, altars, pews, and vestments. The symbol came into use because the Greek word for "fish" *(ichthus)* is composed of the first letter of each word in the Greek phrase "Jesus Christ, Son of God, Savior." *See* Whale (below).

Flea Tiny, irritating insect (1 Sm 24:14; 26:20, NLT). Many species of fleas occur in Palestine, the most common being *Pulex irritans.* About a thousand species are known around the world. Fleas are wingless parasites that have sharp jaws and suck out blood from the bodies of humans and animals. The body is wedge shaped, enabling the flea to burrow into folds of skin and hide there. The eggs, laid by the female in dust heaps in the corners of rooms, hatch into small, white larvae that pupate (a nonfeeding stage) in a cocoon. Soon adult fleas appear that immediately attach themselves to the body of a host. The female requires blood for the development of her eggs.

A flea bite is painful and causes some swelling and itching. Fleas are attracted by warmth. With favorable moisture and temperature, adult fleas can live a year or longer without food, but they are voracious feeders. The most dangerous fleas are those of the rat that transmit the organism responsible for bubonic plague. There were 41 recorded epidemics of bubonic plague before the Christian era.

Fly Insects of the order Diptera, which have one pair of wings. Many winged insects of other orders, however, are also called flies, such as the dragonfly or butterfly.

As in almost all parts of the world, flies are abundant in Palestine. One of the most numerous is the common housefly *(Musca domestica),* found chiefly around dung heaps and garbage. The female lays her eggs, out of which emerge white maggots that feed on refuse. After a few days the maggot develops into a cocoon out of which emerges the adult housefly. In the summer the whole cycle lasts about 12 days, so that a fly can breed about 20 generations a year.

Another fly common to Palestine is the botfly (family Oestridae). It causes much discomfort among livestock by irritating them and spreading diseases. Tabanid flies (family Tabanidae), including the horsefly (genus *Tabanus*) and related species, are also found in Palestine. Both the botfly and horsefly are known as gadflies because of the persistent distress they inflict. Babylonian King Nebuchadnezzar is spoken of as a gadfly in view of his invasion of Egypt (Jer 46:20).

The fourth plague in Egypt just before the exodus featured "swarms of flies" (Ex 8:21-31, NLT; cf. Pss. 78:45; 105:31). Those swarms may have been made up of any or all the flies mentioned above. The maggots mentioned in Job 25:6 and Isaiah 14:11 and the worms in Exodus 16:24 and Job 7:5 and 17:14 were probably fly larvae.

A proverb quoted in Ecclesiastes 10:1 probably refers to the housefly, which would be attracted to an open, perfumed ointment bottle. Once inside it would drown and eventually decay, causing the ointment to spoil and stink. The fly is also referred to in Isaiah 7:18 where it symbolizes Egypt. Isaiah may have had in mind a horsefly *(Tabanus arenivagus)* that attacks both humans and animals.

Philistine inhabitants of the city of Ekron worshiped a god named Baal-zebul, meaning "Lord of the high places." The Hebrews mockingly spoke of Baal-zebub, meaning "Lord of the flies" (2 Kgs 1:2). The NT form is Beelzebub (e.g., Mt 10:25; 12:24, 27).

Fox Small, doglike carnivore with a bushy tail that is about half its body length. The red fox of the Holy Land *(Vulpes palaetinae)* is similar to the North American red fox; it is smaller than a wolf and is normally a nocturnal solitary animal. The omnivorous fox eats almost any kind of food—fruits, plants, mice, beetles, and birds—but seldom touches carrion. It loves the sweet juice of grapes, but it also burrows underground tunnels that can destroy the vines (Sg 2:15). The fox is intelligent and known for its slyness (Lk 13:32). It has considerable endurance and can run at speeds up to 30 miles (48 kilometers) per hour. The Jews rebuilding Jerusalem's wall were taunted by the wisecrack that even a fox jumping on their wall would knock it over (Neh 4:3).

The Egyptian fox *(Vulpes niloticus)* is found in the central and southern parts of the Holy Land. It is somewhat smaller than the common red fox. Its back is rust colored and its belly light. The Syrian fox *(Vulpes flavescens)* that lives in the northern part of the Holy Land is shiny gold in color.

Some OT references such as Psalm 63:10 and Lamentations 5:18 are translated "fox" in the KJV but probably refer to jackals. Jackals, not foxes, hunt in packs and tend to act as scavengers.

Frog Amphibian (genus *Rana*), living part of its life in the water and part on land.

Frogs and toads are covered with soft, hairless skin and lack a tail in the adult stage. The hind legs are much longer and more powerfully developed than the forelegs so that the animals are able to jump large distances. It has been suggested that the frog referred to in Scripture is an edible one, *Rana ridibunda,* one of the aquatic frogs found in Egypt and in the stagnant waters of the Holy Land.

The female frog lays her eggs in the water; after about a week the eggs hatch into tadpoles. Gradually through metamorphosis the tail is lost and limbs are acquired. Frogs must maintain a moist skin since they take oxygen through the skin as well as through their lungs; thus they must always remain close to water. They feed on insects and worms.

Frogs are found throughout the Palestinian lowlands, where their croaking is heard in the spring and on summer evenings. The Israelites seem to have associated frogs primarily with sliminess and foulness. They fell into the category of creeping or swarming creatures, which in general were ritually unclean (Lv 11:29-31). Since the frog was not specifically listed, however, rabbis did not consider it one of the animals that defiled human beings through contact.

In Revelation 16:13 certain foul spirits are said to look like frogs. The ancient Egyptians made the frog a symbol of life and birth and an image of Heqet, the patron goddess of birth. She is depicted with a frog's head giving life to the newborn. Thus that deity was discredited when the power of God afflicted Egypt in the second of the ten plagues on the Egyptians with the very animal that was her symbol (Ex 8:1-14; Pss 78:45; 105:30). The frog in question may have been the spotted frog of Egypt *(Rana punctata,* or *Rana ridibunda).*

See also Plagues upon Egypt.

Gazelle Small, dainty, graceful antelope with hollow recurved horns on both sexes. Two varieties exist in the Holy Land, the dorcas gazelle *(Gazella dorcas),* which is pale fawn in color and up to 22 inches (56 centimeters) tall, and the Arabian gazelle *(Gazella arabica),* which is a dark smoky color and up to 25 inches (63.5 centimeters) tall.

Gazelles are still quite common throughout the desert and steppe areas of the Holy Land, especially in the Negev Desert. Herds usually consist of from 5 to 10 animals, but some varieties assemble in large migratory herds in the fall to relocate to lower elevations and new feeding grounds. Gazelles are herbivorous (plant eating). They are very shy and post guards to warn the herd of approaching danger.

In biblical times the gazelle was probably the game animal most hunted by the Jews (Prv 6:5; Is 13:14). Pharaoh Tutankhamen hunted gazelles and ostriches. The gazelle is said to have graced Solomon's table (1 Kgs 4:23). Gazelles were not easy to catch because of their great speed (2 Sm 2:18; 1 Chr 12:8; Prv 6:5); they surpass the deer in swiftness. They were trapped in various ways—encircled with nets, driven into enclosures with pitfalls, or forced into narrow valleys and shot with arrows. The Bedouin hunt gazelle with falcons and dogs; the falcon annoys the gazelle, striking it on the head and injuring it so that the dogs can overtake it.

The gazelle is referred to in Song of Solomon 2:9, 17; 4:5; 7:3; 8:14, where it is an image of feminine beauty.

Gecko Reptile of the family Gekkonidae, referred to in Leviticus 11:30. In Jewish food law it was a ritually unclean lizard. There are seven species of geckos in the Holy Land (including *Hemidactylus turcicus* and *Ptyodactylus hasselquistii,* all insectivorous—insect eating). The gecko makes a low mourning sound by vibrating its tongue rapidly against the roof of its mouth. In legend the gecko was said to cause leprosy by crawling across a person's body.

Another name for the gecko is the wall lizard, so named because it can walk upside down on ceilings with the aid of the suction discs on its toes—but it often plops down into the middle of the home. Since it was considered unclean, such an intrusion would have been a disgusting nuisance to Jewish households (Lv 11:31-38).

See also Lizard (below).

Gnat Any very small fly, in common and biblical usage. According to the NLT, the third plague in Egypt before the exodus consisted of gnats (Ex 8:16-18; Ps 105:31). The KJV translates the Hebrew word there as "lice," but the breeding pattern described in Exodus 8—insects rising from the dust—seems to fit gnats better than lice. Since "gnat" is a general term, the small flies of that plague may have included several small species such as mosquitos, harvester gnats, midges, or sand flies.

The sand fly inflicts a far more painful bite than the mosquito. Further, it does not betray itself by a buzzing noise in flight and is so small that it penetrates most mosquito netting.

Gnats were drawn to wine while it was fermenting. The Pharisees in particular would strain their wine to avoid consuming unclean insects (Mt 23:24).

Goat Cloven-hooved mammals (genus *Capra*) with large eyes and big, floppy ears that constantly twitch. Both males and females have backward arching horns. The Palestinian goat is a ruminant (cud-chewing animal) of lighter build than the sheep.

The goat was probably the earliest ruminant to be domesticated. Its wild ancestor seems to have been the Gezoar goat *(Capra aegagrus).* Wild goats are believed to have been domesticated very early in Palestine. The goat of Bible times was probably the Syrian or Mamber variety *(Capra hircus mambrica).* Domesticated goats may have as many as four kids in a litter, whereas wild goats bear only one or two.

The Palestinian goat was commonly black. Speckled and spotted goats were a rarity, and for that reason Jacob's request for those goats in Genesis 30:32 appeared very modest. There may also have been red goats (cf. 1 Sm 16:12; 19:13, where goat's hair was used to imitate David's hair, which was "ruddy" or auburn).

Almost every part of the goat was used by the Israelites. The whole goat was used for sacrifice. Its flesh served as meat (Lv 7:23; Dt 14:4), and it was the principal source of milk (Prv 27:27). Goats were sheared in the late spring, and the goat hair was used for weaving tent cloth and for various domestic purposes (Ex 36:14; 1 Sm 19:13, 16). The tabernacle at Mt Sinai was made of goat's hair blankets (Ex 26:7).

Adult male goats were generally not eaten because of their strong flavor and toughness and also because they were necessary to insure the flock's increase. Young kids, however, were usually the chief meat for a feast and were offered to visitors as a symbol of hospitality. Goat milk is richer than the milk of cows and sheep and evidently had broader uses. A good goat gives three quarts of milk a day, from which a rich butter and buttermilk can be made. The average Hebrew family could have lived almost entirely on a single goat's production.

Goatskin was tanned as leather, and the whole hide was turned into a skin bottle by sewing shut leg and neck apertures (Gn 21:14; Jos 9:4). Goatskin had many uses, including the construction of Hebrew musical instruments. The nebal, a large harp, was made with goatskin for its base sound. Drums had goatskin coverings.

Goats were herded with sheep in biblical times, but each group remained separate following its own bell-laden leader. Jesus was evidently referring to their common herding in his description of the Last Judgment (Mt 25:31-46).

Because of their wool, sheep are valued more than goats. However, where pasture and water are scarce and thorny shrubs dominate over grass, sheep are difficult to keep and goats become important. They can live under conditions that suit neither cows nor sheep, producing large quantities of milk. The goat does not supply fat as the sheep does, and since its hair is coarse its wool is rather scarce. Goat-hair cloth called cilicium was used to make tents.

Goats have voracious appetites. They also were responsible for much damage done to the land of Palestine, breaking down terraces, destroying forests, and bringing about soil erosion by eating off all cover.

The goat was recognized as a form of wealth, subject to the law of firstlings (Nm 18:17). It had to be eight days old before it could be offered as a sacrifice. A year-old male goat was one of the animals offered at the Passover (28:22), and two goats were offered on the Day of Atonement (Lv 16:7-10). The goat was also used for other specific sacrifices.

The ibex, a type of wild goat *(Capra ibex nubiana)*, still lives in small numbers on the cliffs close to the Dead Sea. That it was known in ancient times is evident from rock carvings. It is distinguished from the true wild goat by having a more compact rump and horns that are slender and curved back. Its slender legs and sharp cloven hooves enable it to cling to narrow rock ledges, to jump between them, and to climb steep cliffs.

Usually the ibex is found in rugged mountain country among rocky crags and meadows just below the snow line (Ps 104:18). In Job 39:1 they are referred to as "mountain goats." They frequently gather in herds of 5 to 20. They graze and browse, being active in the afternoon and sometimes feeding through the night. The large horn of the ibex was at one period made into the shofar that was blown in the second Jerusalem temple to announce the new year and the jubilee year.

The goat was often used in a figurative and symbolic sense by the writers of the Bible: in Song of Solomon 4:1 and 6:5 for the bride's black hair; in Matthew 25:31-46 for the wicked; and in Ezekiel 34:17 and Daniel 8:5-8 for various human leaders.

Grasshopper Large insects of the Orthoptera order. They have chewing or biting mouth parts and two pairs of wings, the front pair of which is narrow and somewhat thickened and the hind pair membranous and used for flying. When not in use the flight wings are folded beneath the protective front wings like a fan against the body. By rubbing their wings together, male grasshoppers produce sounds that both males and females can detect. Grasshoppers pass through a partial metamorphosis; the egg hatches into a juvenile nymph that looks like an adult except for its smaller size and undeveloped wings. After several months the nymph becomes a winged adult.

The terms "grasshopper" and "locust" are often used interchangeably. Actually the locust is a kind of grasshopper. Also confusing is the fact that other insects such as cicadas are sometimes called locusts. The difference between grasshoppers and locusts depends more on behavior than appearance. Grasshoppers are individual insects that lead solitary lives and do not migrate. The same insects when migrating in a swarm are called migratory grasshoppers or locusts. Elimination of their food supply by drought, flood, or fire may lead to migration. Climatic factors such as a warm dry winter also stimulate migrations.

Grasshoppers and locusts have been a staple food in the Middle East and also among the Indians of the American Southwest. To the Israelites the grasshopper was considered ritually clean and could be eaten (Lv 11:22).

See also Locust (below).

Hare Animal of the genus and species *Lepus europaeus judaeus, Lepus capensis,* and *Lepus arabicus.* It is found in open country, often near or on cultivated lands, and in woods, usually deciduous rather than evergreen. It is an herbivorous rodent and is different from the rabbit, which is not found in Palestine. Although it is not a true ruminant according to modern classification (because it does not have a four-chambered stomach), the hare does rechew its food. It has a process of partial regurgitation of material too hard for the cells in the stomach to absorb initially; thus, the hare actually chews food previously swallowed.

Near Eastern hares have very long ears and large hind feet; their feet are well furred. They are similar to American jackrabbits, which are true hares. Hares do not dig or occupy burrows the way rabbits do. Hares are mainly nocturnal and spend their inactive hours hiding in vegetation. They eat grasses and herbaceous matter as well as twigs and young bark of woody plants. Hares breed with great rapidity—the young attaining sexual maturity at six months after birth.

The hare was ceremonially unclean (Lv 11:6; Dt 14:7), evidently because although it appeared to chew its cud, it did not have cloven hooves. Consumption of hares has also been forbidden among the Arabs, Chinese, and Lapps, but the hare was widely hunted by other people in ancient and modern times. Its great speed, prolific breeding, timidity, and caution have saved it from extermination by its many enemies.

Hippopotamus Large beast of problematic interpretation. Some early interpreters thought it referred to the elephant, others to the wild ox, the mammoth, or any large animal. It was called "behemoth" by the KJV translators. Today it is generally agreed that the reference is to the hippopotamus *(Hippopotamus amphibius),* a large, thick-skinned, amphibious mammal, an ungulate (having hooflike toenails) with a large head, a bulky, hairless body, and short legs.

The description in Job 40:15-24 fits closely the modern hippopotamus (see NLT), except for the depiction of the tail. At present the hippopotamus is found only in the rivers of Africa, but there is fossil evidence that it has existed in the Holy Land, perhaps in the swamps of northern Galilee and the Jordan Valley.

The hippopotamus has highly developed sense organs, placed in such a way that it can see, hear, and smell almost without being seen; its eyes, ears, and nostrils can reach above water while the rest of the animal lies submerged. It has a large mouth, large tusks, and a short, heavy throat. The strong legs are so short that the belly almost reaches the ground when the animal is on the land. The hippopotamus lives on plants and herbs growing in rivers, but if food is scarce there, it forages on land, usually at night. In spite of its heavy body it is surprisingly agile on land.

Horse Przewalski's horse (*Equus przewalskii,* an eastern race that roamed about Mongolia until modern firearms destroyed most of them after World War I) and the tarpan (a western race of southern Russia that became extinct in the Ukraine in 1851). The domesticated horse (*Equus caballus*) seems to have been derived from the tarpan. The original site of domestication is believed to have been Turkestan, a region north of Afghanistan and India, now in Russia. The horse differs from the donkey in that it has shorter ears, a longer mane with a forelock, a long hairy tail, and a soft, sensitive muzzle.

Horses were used in war not only for riding but also for pulling the heavy, springless war chariots. Two kinds of horses were needed for these different purposes, and the Hebrews distinguished between chariot horses and cavalry horses.

Hippodrome (Race Course for Horses) near Caesarea

The Lord warned the early Israelites against unnecessarily amassing military strength in the form of horses and thereby following the oppressive tactics of the powerful Egyptians (Dt 17:14-16), but the demands of war caused both David and Solomon to import horses from Egypt into their kingdoms and to breed them. Solomon greatly increased the number of horses in the Jewish kingdom and maintained large stables at various cities (1 Kgs 10:26) such as the regional defense centers of Megiddo, Hazor, and Gezer (1 Kgs 9:15-19). Ahab's horses are mentioned in 1 Kings 18:5, and records of Shalmaneser III state that Ahab furnished 2,000 chariots to a coalition against Assyria.

In early Israel, the horse was opposed as a symbol of pagan luxury and of dependence on physical power for defense (Dt 17:16; 1 Sm 8:11; Ps 20:7; Is 31:1). Horse trading, mentioned as early as Genesis 47:17, was carried on by Solomon between Egypt and the Syro-Hittite principalities (1 Kgs 10:28-29). Most biblical references to horses refer to their use in war, but horses were also used for transportation. Riding seems to have been less popular than the use of chariots. Cavalry units were not introduced until the 12th century BC by the Medes. Joseph rode in Pharaoh's second horse-drawn chariot (Gn 41:43), and Absalom made a display by riding a horse-drawn chariot (2 Sm 15:1). Naaman traveled by horse and chariot (2 Kgs 5:9). Later, horses were so common in Jerusalem that the royal palace had a special horse gate (2 Chr 23:15), and a gate of the city itself was known as the Horse Gate (Neh 3:28; Jer 31:40). Mordecai rode a royal horse of King Xerxes as a sign of honor (Est 6:8-11). Horses are often spoken of figuratively (Ps 32:9; "mare," Sg 1:9; "stallions," Jer 5:8; 12:5), especially in

the context of judgment (Hb 3:8; Zec 1:8; 6:1-8; Rv 6:2-8; 9:17; 19:11-16).

See also Warfare; Travel.

Hyena Stocky carnivore (*Hyaena hyaena*) with coarse hair, an erect mane, and long hairs along the neck and back. Hyenas live in holes among rocks and banks. They are mainly nocturnal but are ordinarily neither noisy nor aggressive. Their cry, however, is a disagreeable, unearthly sound. Hyenas usually feed on carrion, crushing bones with their powerful jaws. If the carrion supply is inadequate, they will kill sheep, goats, or other small animals. When threatened, hyenas growl and erect their mane, but they rarely fight. They are massively built with forelegs longer than the hind legs.

Known as scavengers in Africa, hyenas eat domestic refuse in the villages. In Palestine the striped hyena is a common predator, preferring rocky territory and even rock tombs. Since hyenas were notorious for raiding the graves of the dead, all Israelites who could afford it arranged for burial in tombs protected by massive stone doors. Absalom, King David's son who was killed by Joab in the wild, was buried under a huge pile of stones to protect his corpse from molestation by hyenas (2 Sm 18:17).

Jackal Carnivore (*Canis aureus*) smaller than the true wolf and with a shorter tail. It is similar to the fox but has a broader head, shorter ears, and longer legs. The fox is solitary; the jackal tends to be gregarious. Its tail can be drooping or erect, compared with the long horizontal tail of the fox. Jackals usually prowl at night, either singly, in pairs, or in packs through open savannah country. They eat small mammals, poultry, fruit, vegetables, and carrion. They spend their days in thickets and clumps of vegetation. Often they obtain scraps from kills by larger carnivores. Jackals can run at speeds of about 33 miles (53 kilometers) per hour.

The jackal can reach a height of about 20 inches (51 centimeters), roughly the size of a German shepherd dog. Its back is pale yellow with dark, almost black, flanks. Its lips are black and its ears white on the inside. The howl of the jackal sounds like the crying of a child or the heartrending wail of the bereaved (Mi 1:8; cf. Jb 30:29). To other jackals the howl is merely an invitation calling the pack together for its nocturnal hunting.

OT references are chiefly to jackals prowling around ruined cities and wilderness areas (Neh 2:13; Ps 44:19; Is 13:22; 34:13; 35:7; Jer 9:11; 14:6; 49:33; 51:37; Lam 4:3; 5:18; Mal 1:3). Many such references are translated "dragon" in the KJV, but "jackal" is more appropriate.

Leech Segmented worm (class Hirundinea) up to five inches (12.7 centimeters) long with a flat body equipped with suction pads at each end. The mouth, located at the bottom of the front suction pad, has three teeth that the leech uses to pierce the skin of its host. The leech feeds on blood, and its glands secrete an anticoagulant to prevent the blood from clotting. The ordinary medicinal leech (*Hirudo medicinalis*) is abundant in springs and ponds from the Negev Desert to Galilee. It adheres to the bodies of human beings and animals that submerge themselves in water, injects its anticoagulant, and sucks their blood.

The reference in Proverbs 30:15 is uncertain (see NLT) but may be to the parasitic and greedy nature of the horse leech (genus *Haemopis*). The small horse leech enters its host's mouth and nostrils from water while the animal is drinking. A leech weighing one-half ounce (14.2 grams) has been known to gorge itself with two and a half ounces (71 grams) of concentrated blood and then to exist for 15 months with no more to eat.

Leopard Called *Panthera pardus tulliana*, it is the most widespread of all the large wildcats. In rocky areas it lives in caves, but in forested regions it lives in thick vegetation. In OT times many lived in the vicinity of Mt Hermon (Sg 4:8).

The leopard is somewhat smaller than the tiger, measuring up to 5 feet (1.5 meters) in length with a tail of about 30 inches (.8 meter). Its body is better proportioned than that of the tiger. The leopard takes its victim by surprise from a silent ambush, often concealing itself near villages or watering places and waiting for its prey, remaining in one spot for long spans of time. The leopard is swift on the ground (Hb 1:8), agile in trees, and very graceful in its movements. Its color is yellowish speckled with black spots (Jer 13:23). Daniel and John saw visions in which leopards were symbols of world powers (Dn 7:6; Rv 13:2).

The leopard is a wary and cunning animal, formidable and ferocious (Jer 5:6; Hos 13:7; cf. Is 11:6). The leopard is dangerous not only to domestic animals but also to humans. With its natural camouflage it can hide on the forest floor, blending into the changing light and shadows. The Israelites were terrified of the leopard because it constantly ravaged their sheep and goats. Several biblical place names suggest that they were known for the leopards in their vicinity: Nimrah, Beth-nimrah, and Nimrim, a district northeast of the Dead Sea. It has survived in the Holy Land into the present century; a few leopards still exist in remote areas near Mt Tabor and Mt Carmel.

Leviathan Sea monster mentioned several times in the Bible (Pss 74:14; 104:26; Is 27:1, NLT). It may refer to any of the larger marine animals such as large jellyfish, whales, or sharks, or to a large reptile like the crocodile. Some scholars think "Leviathan" may refer to animals now extinct, such as ichthyosaurs and plesiosaurs (marine reptiles similar to dinosaurs). The scriptural term might also refer to certain dinosaurs that spent part of their lives half-submerged in shallow lakes and oceans. Other scholars believe that most of the references are to the crocodile.

See also Crocodile (above).

Lion Large, tawny-colored carnivore *(Panthera leo)* that preys chiefly on hoofed mammals and charges by a series of leaps and bounds. Within historic times the lion ranged in Africa, Europe, and the Holy Land. In ancient times the territories of the African and Persian lions met in the Middle East. The lion of the Holy Land was the Asiatic or Persian lion *(Panthera leo persica)*.

The males have heavy manes that stop at the shoulders but cover much of the chest. The Persian lion cannot climb and is mainly nocturnal, returning to its lair or a thicket by day (Jer 4:7; 25:38; Na 2:11-12). This lion is about 5 feet (1.5 meters) long with a tasseled tail 30 inches (.8 meter) or so long; its shoulders may reach a height of 35 inches (.9 meter). It is one of the smallest of the lion breeds.

Lions are usually found in pairs, though sometimes in larger numbers. A small group is known as a pride. They generally prefer open country but in Palestine evidently prowled the subtropical vegetation of the Jordan River valley. Lions, which usually hunt at dusk, kill smaller animals by a blow of the paw, larger ones by a bite in the throat. A lion does not remain in the same place for more than a few days. The animal is in its prime at about seven years of age, when it weighs from 400 to 600 pounds (181.6 to 272.4 kilograms).

The lion does not characteristically attack humans, though like other great cats it may become a man-eater (1 Kgs 13:24-28; 20:36; 2 Kgs 17:25-26; Ps 57:4; Dn 6:7-27). Ordinarily, it attacks only out of great hunger or in self-defense. A very young lion that attacks humans can become dangerous if it develops a taste for human flesh. A very old lion, expelled from the pride because it can no longer keep up in the pursuit of antelope or gazelles, may choose humans as a relatively slow-moving prey.

A lion generally roars only on a full stomach—that is, after it has consumed its prey (Ps 22:13; Ez 22:25; Am 3:4). Nevertheless, its roaring arouses fear (Am 3:8; 1 Pt 5:8). The lion is a bold (2 Sm 17:10; Prv 28:1), destructive animal (Ps 7:2; Jer 2:30; Hos 5:14; Mi 5:8), and the enemy of flocks (Am 3:12).

Lions were common in biblical times in all parts of the Holy Land. Hebrew has at least seven words for lion and young lion. The lion is referred to about 130 times in the OT—more than any other wild animal. Lions were evidently much less common in NT times. After gradually declining, they became extinct in Palestine shortly after AD 1300. The lion was present in Mesopotamia, however, until the end of the 19th century.

Lions played an important part in the political and religious symbolism of the Near East (1 Kgs 10:19-20). In Assyria and Babylonia the lion was regarded as a royal beast (Dn 7:4). Oriental monarchs maintained artificial lion pits as places of execution (Ez 19:1-9; Dn 6:7-16). Animals for these were captured in camouflaged nets or pits. To the Jews, the lion was the mightiest of beasts (Prv 30:29-31). Thus, it symbolized leadership (Gn 49:9-10; Nm 24:9) and hence eventually became a title for Christ (Rv 5:5). It was also the ensign of Judah's tribe and was used by King Solomon in the decoration of his house and the temple.

Lizard Reptiles of the suborder Lacertilia. Their skin is covered with scales. The lizard is a useful creature because it captures harmful insects and worms. Like other reptiles, it lays eggs with shells softer than those of a bird and with no clear division between the yolk and the white. Lizards are "cold-blooded" organisms without a temperature-maintenance mechanism; hence, they become inactive in cold weather.

Lizards can survive in barren parched countryside. In the Near East they are encountered in great numbers in the Arabian Desert, the Sinai Peninsula, and the Judean wilderness. There may be as many as 44 different species of lizards in the Holy Land.

The Dabb lizard (genus *Uromastyx*), which attains a length of about 24 inches (61 centimeters), is found in the Negev Desert. It is omnivorous, an unusual trait since most lizards are insectivorous. It has a hard, rough skin, green with brown spots; a short, rounded head; and a powerful tail encircled with a row of strong spines that it uses as a weapon of defense.

Lizards are listed as ceremonially unclean in Jewish law (Lv 11:29-31). The fact that lizards crawl on their bellies made them unclean. Contact with a lizard's carcass defiled a law-abiding Jew (Lv 11:32-36). The NLT translates the "lizards" of Leviticus 11 as "great lizard," "gecko," "monitor lizard," "sand lizard," and "chameleon." The monitor lizard is a large lizard that lives in the deserts of southern Palestine, Sinai, and Egypt. It is up to 55 inches (1.4 meters) long with a long snout and sharp teeth. Other translators and commentators render the original Hebrew in a wide variety of ways, including "tortoise," "ferret," "lizard," "snail," "mole," and even "water hen." The fact that most of the original Hebrew words occur only once in Scripture makes it very difficult to be certain about their appropriate translation.

See also Gecko (above).

Locust An insect of the family *Acridiidae*. It is referred to by at least 12 different names in Scripture. The various Hebrew words may refer to different stages of its development from larva to adult or to the type of damage that it causes. Locusts are characterized by swarming and mass migration. In modern times they have caused extensive and disastrous destruction to vegetation. Grasshoppers do not swarm or migrate en masse, differentiating them from the true locusts.

The OT mentions several different species of locusts. Leviticus 11:22 seems to refer to the slant-faced (bald) locust and also to the katydid, or long-horned grasshopper. The reference in Deuteronomy 28:42 may be to the mole cricket. In Joel 1:4 and 2:25 and in Nahum 3:16-17, successive stages of the insect's development are described. The cutting locust (KJV "palmerworm") of Joel is probably the first instar (stage of development), the swarming locusts (KJV "locust") are middle stages, and the hopping locusts (KJV "cankerworm") later instars but not yet fully matured insects. In the adult stage, called destroying locusts (KJV "caterpillar"), the color of the locust is reddish brown, which turns to yellow with a brownish network on the wings.

Only three of the hundreds of varieties of locusts found in Bible lands are capable of multiplying into great swarms, and only the desert locust (*Schistocerca gergaria*) can be considered widespread in all the Bible lands. The desert locust is native to the Sudan (Africa). It is a little over two inches (5 centimeters) long and has a wingspread of some five inches (12.7 centimeters). It shows two phases, a solitary phase and a gregarious phase, with a possible third phase known as transiens. There are differences in the immature and adult forms of the phases in color and physiology.

The quantity and distribution of rains are important factors in the extent of swarming. Moist soil is needed for depositing the eggs and permitting them to develop. Each female deposits from one to six egg pods, containing 28 to 146 eggs each. The larvae emerge in 15 to 43 days.

In the gregarious phase (from the second stage of metamorphosis onward), the locust is driven by a strong wandering instinct. Masses of them form a random procession of overflowing locust bodies that ignore any obstruction. They swarm over everything (Jl 2:4-9). The only regulator of their activities is temperature; they are immobilized by high or low temperatures. Taking to wing they may move 1,200 miles (1,930.8 kilometers) from their native home. They fly in compact formations large enough to blot out the light of the sun. Their movement seems to be controlled by hormones, but the direction is influenced by the wind. The swarms consume almost every plant in their path, sparing only the carob, sycamore, castor tree, and oleander bush.

A locust plague was one of the most severe evils to come upon the ancient world (Dt 28:38). Joel 2:1-11 describes a locust plague in graphic terms, using it as a symbol of God's destroying judgment. Special days of prayer, fasting, and trumpet blowing were prescribed to remove locust plagues (1 Kgs 8:37-38; 2 Chr 6:28-29; Jl 2:12-17). Locusts symbolized powerful and merciless enemies that completely destroyed the earnings of human toil (Jgs 6:5; Is 33:4; Jer 46:23; 51:27; Na 3:15).

Bedouins eat locusts raw, roasted, or boiled, preserving them by drying and threading. They are also crushed and ground, and the grist used in cooking or eaten with bread, sometimes mixed with honey and dates. Such was the diet of John the Baptist (Mk 1:6). The Greeks ground locusts in stone mortars to make flour of them.

The ancients considered the two large hind legs, or jumping legs, as separate limbs and had a special name for them. Hence locusts were described as having four legs, a reference to the four smaller walking legs. "Going on all fours" thus referred to creeping or walking as opposed to jumping and did not mean that the unclean insects had only four legs in all. Because of its two hind jumping legs, the locust was exempted from the prohibition against unclean insects (Lv 11:20-23).

See also Plagues upon Egypt.

Mole Rodent (*Spalax ehrenbergi*) from six to nine inches (15 to 23 centimeters) long, which burrows in any area where the soil is suitable for digging; it should be called a mole rat. Common in the Holy Land, large numbers are found in the vicinity of Jerusalem. Isaiah 2:20 refers to the mole, as does Leviticus 11:29-30 (NLT).

The mole rat has no tail and is molelike in appearance, but neither true moles nor shrews have ever been found in the Holy Land. The mole rat's teeth are strong and protruding like those of a squirrel. The neck is short and thick with a plump body shaped like a sausage. The short legs have broad paws with claws adapted for burrowing. The fur is soft, thick, and ashen gray. Its ears and almost sightless eyes, which are no larger than poppyseeds, are hidden in the fur. Folklore taught that touching a mole rat would result in blindness.

In the wet winter season the mole rat builds breeding mounds resembling those of pocket gophers. It builds less complex resting mounds in the summer, although both have rather elaborate tunnel systems. The mole rat feeds on roots, bulbs, tubers, and various other subterranean plant parts, often doing extensive damage to agriculture.

Moth Insect of the genus *Tineola* that lays its eggs on wool or furs, its larvae feeding on those materials. The destructive qualities of moths are referred to in several biblical passages (Jb 13:28; Ps 39:11; Is 50:9; Hos 5:12; Mt 6:19-20; Lk 12:33; Jas 5:2). In Isaiah 51:8 "worm" (NLT) refers specifically to the larva of the clothes moth. The moth symbolizes disintegration, decay, and weakening. It is only the larvae that do the damage. The adult is quite harmless and feeds mainly on the nectar of flowers. It is easily crushed (Jb 4:19). The clothes moth reproduces in May or June. It enters human dwellings in the evening. A week after the eggs are laid the larvae appear and immediately begin their work of destruction, eating anything within reach made of animal fibers.

The moth's destructive activity is done in secret without any sound and without any dramatic appearance, such as a swarm that blots out the sun. In an age when wealth was counted more in possessions than in money, and when among those possessions wool clothing was highly valued, moths could literally cause economic disaster; hence the words of Jesus in the Sermon on the Mount (Mt 6:19-20).

There are hundreds of species of moths other than the clothes moth in the Holy Land; they are harmless to leaves, flowers, fruit, trees, and seeds. As with the clothes moth, the larvae inflict the damage.

Mouse Rodent of the family Muridae, especially genus *Mus*. The mouse was regarded as unclean because, being short legged, it was considered one of the creeping creatures (Lv 11:29). Mice known as commensals live in dwellings and tend to have longer tails and to be darker in color than wild mice, which are active chiefly at night. Mice are good climbers and even good swimmers. Wild mice eat many kinds of vegetation, including seeds, fleshy roots, leaves, and stems. At times they store food.

The Hebrew word for "mouse" (Lv 11:29; 1 Sm 6:4-5; Is 66:17) is probably a general term for various rats and mice. The root meaning of the Hebrew word "mouse" is "destruction of corn," a reference to the damage mice do to field crops. At least 23 varieties of mouselike rodents are known in the Holy Land. They cause food spoilage, damage household articles, and transport the host fleas that spread typhus, spotted fever, and bubonic plague. Plague bacteria may have caused the tumors or swellings among the Philistines (1 Sm 6:5). Isaiah 66:17 refers to a pre-exilic Canaanite cultic practice in which mice were eaten; the reference may actually be to the hamster. A number of rodents are eaten by Arabs of the Near East; the gerbil is considered a special delicacy. *See* Mole (above).

Mule Hybrid offspring of a male ass and a female horse *(Equus asinus mulus)*, ordinarily sterile. The offspring of a female donkey and a stallion (male horse) is known as a hinny and is of little value because of its inferior size.

Because crossbreeding was forbidden in the law (Lv 19:19), the Israelites procured mules from the Gentiles, perhaps from the Phoenicians, since Tyre (a Phoenician seaport in what is now southern Lebanon) imported horses and mules (Ez 27:14). Mules did not appear in Israel until David's reign (2 Sm 13:29), possibly because of the rarity of horses among the Hebrews. Mules were used chiefly by members of the royal court and by other nobles. King David rode on a mule, and Solomon rode to his inauguration on King David's mule (1 Kgs 1:33). Absalom met his death riding on a mule (2 Sm 18:9). Mules were less common than horses, camels, and asses in the postexilic community (Ezr 2:66). In antiquity Asia Minor was especially noted for breeding fine mules.

Mules have long enjoyed a reputation for obstinacy, but that trait is not mentioned in the Bible. The mule is prized for riding and for carrying heavy burdens, especially in warm mountainous regions. They are surefooted and thrive best in hot, dry climates. The mule has the frugality, endurance, and steady gait of an ass along with the size, strength, swiftness, and courage of a horse. Mules are almost never sick. They live longer than horses. They can carry a load of up to 300 pounds (136 kilograms) as far as 30 miles (48.3 kilometers) a day.

See also Travel.

Pig Most properly, newborn swine. "Swine" is technically the better name for the species, but it is rarely used in common speech today. The domestic pigs of the Middle East derived from the wild pig *(Sus scrofa)*. The pig is the most prolific and abundant supplier of meat and fat for food. A thick layer of fat just under the skin is especially pronounced in domestic breeds. Pigs cannot be driven, so they are of value only to the settled farmer. The Hebrews were originally a nomadic people; therefore, they had little use for an animal closely associated with settled life. An Egyptian prince of about 1500 BC, however, is recorded as owning a herd of 1,500 swine.

The pig is clumsily built, yet lively and able to move with agility and speed. The most conspicuous characteristic of the pig is a truncated, mobile snout terminating in a disc-shaped surface on which the nostrils are located. Most pigs have large tusks in both jaws which grow continuously in life. The tusks of the upper jaw are unique in that they curve upward instead of pointing downward as in most animals. The excrement of a pig has an almost unbearable odor, which clings not only to the pig itself but also to swineherds, who can be identified a long way off.

Pigs were never raised in the Holy Land by Jews. The great herd into which Jesus drove the unclean spirits was encountered in the land of the Gadarenes, a non-Jewish area east of the Jordan. The Gadarene demons took refuge in a herd of pigs feeding on a bluff overlooking the Sea of Galilee (Mt 8:28-32).

Wild pigs were found in the Holy Land as in many countries today. Psalm 80:13 refers to the destructiveness of a wild boar (the male, or hog) attacking growing crops. A party of wild boars can destroy an entire vineyard or a field of crops in a single night. They devour, trample, and ravage everything within reach.

Boar hunts were common in ancient Mesopotamia. Wild boars do not attack unless molested, but they are dangerous when aroused. They travel in bands of from 6 to 50 and are most active in the evening and early morning hours. The body is covered with stiff bristles and usually some finer hair, but the body covering is often quite scanty. Wild pigs are mainly vegetarian, feeding on roots, nuts, grains, and plant stems. Wild boars were particularly abundant in the mountainous regions of Lebanon and Anti-Lebanon, in the Jordan River valley, and in wooded sections such as Mt Tabor.

Strict Jews would not even mention swine by name but would always substitute the term "the abomination." Israelites considered themselves polluted if they were even touched by a swine's bristle. To the Jews, the pig symbolized filth and ugliness. Pigs will eat fecal material, vermin, rodents, carrion, and the like (2 Pt 2:22). Proverbs 11:22 refers to the incongruity of a golden ring in the nose of an animal showing such characteristics. A similar metaphor occurs in Jesus' statement about casting pearls before swine (Mt 7:6). The prodigal son's degeneration was shown by his being forced in his poverty to feed pigs and eat their food (Lk 15:15-16).

Eating the flesh of pigs was forbidden to the Jews (Lv 11:7; Dt 14:8). The Canaanites in the Holy Land killed and ate pigs freely. In intertestamental times Antiochus IV (Epiphanes), a Syrian king whose territories included Israel, used the pig to "Hellenize" the Jews. He first tested their loyalty to the Jewish faith by requiring the consumption of pork, considered a delicacy by the Greeks (2 Macc 6:18). The act of desecration that drove the Jews to rebellion, however, was the sprinkling of pig blood on the temple altar in a sacrifice to Zeus (1 Macc 1:47).

Pigs were frequently used in pagan worship (Is 65:4; 66:3, 17), which may account for their being forbidden to the Jews as food. Evidence in the Holy Land shows that pigs were sacrificed long before Hellenistic times. Pig bones were found in a grotto below the rock-cut place of sacrifice at Gezer. A similar underground chamber with vessels containing piglet bones at Tirzah dates to the middle Bronze Age (about 2000 BC).

Alabaster fragments of a statuette of a pig ready to be sacrificed have been unearthed. Swine were sacrificed to Aphrodite (Venus) in Greece and Asia Minor. In addition, pigs were sacrificed in connection with oaths and treaties; in the *Iliad*, Agamemnon sacrificed a boar to Zeus and Helios. So it is not surprising that among the Jews the pig became a symbol of filthiness and paganism.

It is possible that eating pork was forbidden primarily because the pig may carry many worm parasites such as trichina, though that is also true of some "clean" animals. Another reason for forbidding their consumption may have been that pigs eat carrion. Some people are allergic to pork in hot weather—another suggested reason behind the Jewish taboo. The same taboo exists among the Muslims and existed in certain social strata in Egypt.

Porcupine Rodent, *Hystrix cristata*, which lives in forested areas, rocky hills, ravines, and valleys. The porcupine is still found in the Holy Land today. It has long quills that can be raised to give the appearance of a crest. It is almost entirely nocturnal. It burrows by day into a natural cavity or crevice. The Old World porcupine rarely climbed trees, although the New World porcupine frequently does. A porcupine may weigh as much as 60 pounds (27.2 kilograms). It eats fruit, bark, roots, and other vegetation, and carrion as well. Although its flesh is edible, the porcupine was not classed among the clean animals for the Israelites. The reference in Isaiah 34:11 (RSV) is probably to the porcupine, as is Isaiah 14:23 in the NLT. See Hedgehog.

Scorpion Arthropod of the same group as spiders (arachnids). A dozen species of scorpions (order Scorpionida) are found in the Holy Land, but 90 percent of the scorpions are yellow scorpions, usually three to five inches (7.6 to 12.7 centimeters) long. The rock scorpion, also common to the Holy Land, is as thick as a man's finger and from five to seven inches (12.7 to 17.8 centimeters) in length. Scorpions are slow, nocturnal invertebrates that rest beneath stones by day and prey on insects and other arachnids by night. At the end of its long tail the scorpion carries a poisonous sting that is fatal to most prey and extremely painful to humans (Rv 9:3, 5, 10; cf. 1 Kgs 12:11, 14). Scorpions symbolize Ezekiel's evil countrymen (Ez 2:6) and the demonic forces of Satan (Lk 10:19). The scorpion is referred to as frequenting the Sinai Desert (Dt 8:15).

A scorpion has from six to eight eyes. It has eight legs like a spider and two lobsterlike claws with which it catches and holds its prey. It feeds particularly on locusts and beetles. In many species the female scorpion eats the male after mating. Scorpions lay eggs that hatch very shortly after laying. Scorpions prefer warmer climates, and because of their desire for warmth, enter houses, especially at night, hiding in beds, blankets, footwear, and clothing.

Sheep Domestic animal, *Ovis orientalis*, referred to directly or by some term such as ewe, lamb, ram, or by some fact concerning them over 700 times in Scripture.

Sheep represented the chief wealth and total livelihood of pastoral peoples, providing food to eat, milk to drink, wool for the making of cloth, and hides and bones for other uses. In addition, the sheep was a medium of exchange and a sacrificial animal. The number of sheep raised in ancient times was prodigious. Mesha, king of Moab, paid a tribute annually of 100,000 lambs and the wool of 100,000 rams (2 Kgs 3:4). The Israelites took 250,000 sheep from the Hagrites (1 Chr 5:21).

Sheep shearing was often done for festivals (2 Sm 13:23). The sheep was held down on its side and its legs were tied together; then it lay docilely while its wool was clipped (Is 53:7). Sheep reserved for burnt offerings were not shorn; nothing could be held back from a sacrifice to the Lord.

Wool had to be processed before it could be used for clothing. First it was washed, sometimes while still on the sheep, then carded and perhaps weighed for the market. The spinning of wool was regarded as a woman's work (Prv 31:19), but weaving the spun thread into cloth on a loom was primarily a man's occupation.

The Bible reports that Abel kept sheep (Gn 4:2). The first sheep to be domesticated was probably the argali (*Ovis ammon*), a variety of the urial (*Ovis vignei*), a mountainous species still existing in Turkestan and Mongolia. Five breeds had reached Mesopotamia by 2000 BC; all were of the urial stock.

The sheep known in Israel was the broad-tailed sheep (*Ovis orientalis vignei* or *laticaudata)*, of which the tail weighs from 10 to 15 pounds (4.5 to 6.8 kilograms) and

has always been considered a delicacy. Thus the Lord asked for this choice part as a sacrifice (Ex 29:22-25).

Only the ram of the broad-tailed sheep has horns, but in other varieties of sheep in the Holy Land the ewe also has horns. The horns, two to three inches (5 to 8 centimeters) in diameter, can be potent weapons. Rams' horns could be used as trumpets (Jos 6:4) or as oil containers (1 Sm 16:1).

Although the sheep is very similar to the goat, it is differentiated by a lower forehead, its angulated spiral horns marked with transverse wrinkles and curved slightly outward, its covering of wool, and its lack of a "goatee." Most sheep are white (Ps 147:16; Is 1:18; Dn 7:9; Rv 1:14).

The flesh of sheep was a luxury in the biblical culture. King Solomon required a daily provision of 100 sheep for his table (1 Kgs 4:23), but the common people ate lamb or mutton only on festive occasions. A young ram was usually chosen because the ewes were more important to the future prospects of the herd. The meat was boiled in large caldrons. The milk of the sheep is extremely rich; in biblical times it was usually allowed to curdle before drinking. Possibly some Israelites kept lambs in their houses as pets (2 Sm 12:3-4).

To protect the flock at night against predatory attacks, the shepherd tried to provide a fold. In meadows near villages, folds were built and watchmen were hired to relieve the shepherds. The shepherds of the nativity story were out in the field (Lk 2:8); they had no fold but probably had set up a tent for shelter, consisting simply of goat-hair blankets spread across sapling supports. The scarcity of springs in the Holy Land made the watering of the flock a crucial problem for the shepherd (Gn 13:8-11).

Wild mountain sheep, varieties of *Ovis orientalis*, are known in the Mediterranean area (Dt 14:5). The Deuteronomy passage (KJV "chamois") might also refer to *Ovis traelaphus*, a sheep about five feet high (1.5 meters) with long, curved horns. Another possibility is the Barbary sheep that lives in small flocks in rugged mountain areas in Barbary, Egypt, and Mt Sinai. The true chamois is unknown in Palestine.

The sheep is also used figuratively in Scripture. The ram represented great strength and fittingly symbolized Medo-Persia in Daniel's vision (Dn 8:3). It is the nature of sheep to be gentle and submissive (Is 53:7; Jer 11:19), defenseless (Mi 5:8; Mt 10:16), and in constant need of guidance and care (Nm 27:17; Mt 9:36). Such qualities are regarded as desirable in the lives of believers in Christ; hence the many figurative references to sheep in the NT and to Jesus as shepherd (Mk 6:34; Jn 10:1-30; Rom 8:35-37; Heb 13:20-21; 1 Pt 2:25). The resurrected Christ told the apostle Peter to "feed my lambs" and "tend my sheep" (Jn 21:15-17).

See also Offerings and Sacrifices.

Snail Invertebrate gastropods (mollusks). Land snails are very numerous in the Near East. Some freshwater forms serve as hosts for the schistosome worm, the fluke parasite causing the dread disease bilharzia (schistosomiasis).

Purple dyes of all shades were highly valued in the ancient world. A royal purple dye was obtained from secretions of a sea snail *(Murex trunculus* and *Murex brandaris)*. Evidently, that process was developed by Phoenicians, Egyptians, and Assyrians as early as 1500 BC. The "purple" fishermen had their own guild during the time of the Roman Empire. The snails were harvested during the fall and winter seasons; in the spring, when egg laying took place, little dye was available. The snails tended to remain concealed in the summer. They inhabited the waters off Crete and Phoenicia. Tyrian purple, produced in the Phoenician city of Tyre, the center of the purple-dye industry, was obtained by a double dyeing. Large deposits of murex shells from dyeing operations have been found along the Mediterranean shoreline. The Israelites had to import purple goods (Ez 27:16). Lydia was a "seller of purple" or of cloth so dyed (Acts 16:14). Purple was a sign of distinction, royalty, and wealth (cf. Ex 25:4; 28:5-6, 15; Nm 15:38; 2 Chr 2:7; Est 8:15; Prv 31:22; Sg 3:10; Ez 27:7; Dn 5:7).

Exodus 30:34-35 refers to "onycha," which was an important ingredient of incense. Onycha is the horny, clawlike operculum (the plate that closes off the opening of its shell when a snail is retracted) of a Near Eastern member of the molluskan family Strombidae. The operculum is sometimes used for offense or locomotion as well as for defense. When burned, the operculum gives off a sharp, strong scent, and when mixed with more fragrant but less powerful substances is even more potent. The name "onycha" is derived from a Greek word *(onyx)* for a fingernail or a claw.

See also Dye, Dyeing, Dyer.

Snake Various species of snake, suborder Ophidia (Serpentes). In the Bible nine Hebrew words and four Greek ones refer to snakes. The most common Hebrew word is onomatopoeic—that is, it is an imitation of a snake hissing or of the sound it produces as it scrapes its scales along the ground (cf. Jer 46:22). Many types of snakes lay eggs (Is 59:5), although some retain the eggs in the body until ready to hatch.

Snakes are among the most widespread reptiles and are found on all continents except Antarctica; they decrease in numbers and species toward the poles but increase as one approaches the equator. Thirty-three species of snakes are known in Palestine and neighboring countries, 20 of which are poisonous. Two dangerous characteristics of the snake noted by biblical writers are its inconspicuous way of moving and the ease with which it hides itself.

Many snakes are able to swallow animals several times their own diameter because of their unusually flexible jaw mechanism. They lack not only legs but also movable eyelids. Snakes periodically shed their skins. The tongue is actually a hearing apparatus sensitive to airborne vibrations and probably to heat waves.

The venom of poisonous species is a clear, thin secretion, transmitted to the victim's bloodstream by means of fangs. Two types of venom are known: that of the vipers, which affects respiration and disintegrates red blood cells, and that of the cobras, which paralyzes the nervous system.

The "asp" referred to in the Bible is probably the cobra; the "adder" is the viper. The "cockatrice" (KJV) is probably the adder. Serpents were associated with worship in Canaanite religion and symbolized evil deities among many other peoples. Steles (upright stones bearing inscriptions) have been unearthed at several sites in the Holy Land and Syria depicting a god or worshiper with a snake winding about the legs or body. Because the Israelites were burning incense in pagan worship of Moses' bronze serpent (Nm 21:8-9), King Hezekiah destroyed it in his religious reform (2 Kgs 18:4).

Although snakes have been an object of veneration in some religions, in the Judeo-Christian tradition snakes represent evil and, more specifically, the devil. That association began in the Garden of Eden (Gn 3:1-15) and is also found in the book of Revelation (12:9; 20:2-3).

See also Adder (above); Asp (above).

Spider Animal of the order Araneida. Between 600 and 700 different species inhabit the Holy Land. Spiders are

different from insects in that, like scorpions, they have four pairs of legs instead of three. Spiders are equipped with poison glands—the effectiveness varying from species to species. A few can kill only insects, but others can also kill birds and mice.

Most spiders have a pair of spinnerets attached to silk glands on the underside of the abdomen; from them a web is extruded. In the Bible the spider's web is referred to as a symbol of frailty and insecurity (Jb 8:14; Is 59:5-6).

Sponge Simple marine animals, phylum Porifera. The term "sponge" also refers to those animals' skeletal remains. The sponge has a porous body composed of tubules and cells.

Sponge fishing was well known in the Mediterranean area in ancient times. It was practiced particularly along the Anatolian and Syrian coasts. Sponges were harvested by divers. The use of sponges in absorbing liquids is referred to in the Bible (Mt 27:48; Mk 15:36).

Unicorn *See* Wild Ox (below).

Wasp Insects of the family Vespidae. Hornets are social wasps that build large aerial apartment houses in which 1,000 or more individuals may live. In the Bible the hornet is used as a metaphor for God's use of military forces (Ex 23:28; Dt 7:20; Jos 24:12).

Whale Largest of all living creatures, including those that have become extinct. Whales are air-breathing mammals of the order Cetacea.

Two varieties of whales visit the shores of the Holy Land at times. The finback whale *(Balaenoptera physalus)* weighs about 200 tons (181 metric tons) and lives mainly in the Arctic region but sometimes passes through the Straits of Gibraltar to reach the eastern Mediterranean Sea. It feeds on small marine organisms that it strains through its whale bone; it does not have teeth. The finback whale's esophagus is narrow.

The sperm whale *(Physeter catodon)*, about 60 feet (18.3 meters) long, has a curiously shaped head that looks like a battering ram. The teeth in the lower jaw of the male sperm whale are about seven inches (17.8 centimeters) long. It feeds on big fish, even on sharks. It has a large throat opening.

Whales are referred to in Genesis 1:21 and Job 7:12 (KJV only). The "great fish" of Jonah 2:1 need not have been a whale but could have been a large shark, such as the whale shark *(Rhineodon)*, which grows 70 feet (21.3 meters) long and lacks the terrible teeth of other sharks. Whatever the actual marine organism, Jonah's deliverance was miraculous. The Greek word for "whale" is sometimes used as a general term for "sea monster" or huge fish and may be used in that sense in Matthew 12:40.

Wild Ox Large, fierce, fleet, intractable animal *(Bos primigenius)*. It had a long, lean rump with a straight back and a long, narrow head. The animal described in Job 39:9-12 is clearly the wild ox. The two horns (Dt 33:17), its outstanding characteristic, were straight and as long as the head (Nm 23:22; 24:8; Ps 22:21). Kings often symbolized their dominion by wearing a helmet with two wild ox horns (cf. Pss 92:10; 132:17-18). The horns were often used as drinking vessels by the Israelites; some were large enough to hold four gallons (15 liters).

Hunting the wild ox was a favorite sport of Assyrian kings. Tiglath-pileser I hunted it in the Lebanon Mountains about 1100 BC (cf. Ps 29:6). At one time the animal referred to in Job 39:9-12 was thought to be the oryx or antelope because of the similarity between the Hebrew

word in Job and the Arabian name for oryx. The translators of the KJV called the wild ox a "unicorn" because of
representations found on Babylonian mosaics and Egyptian drawings. Those representations showed it in strict
profile, showing only one horn—hence, "unicorn."
Jerome's Vulgate, a Latin Bible translation (fourth century AD) and Martin Luther's German version translated
it similarly.

Wolf Large doglike mammal (*Canis lupus*) that travels in
bands of up to 30 animals. From the nose to the rump,
the wolf measures about 3 feet (.9 meter); its drooping
tail is about 18 inches (.5 meter) long. It looks much like
a skinny German shepherd dog. The grayish yellow pelt
is coarse and short haired.

Wolves hunt singly or in relays, usually at night (Jer
5:6). Wolves have acute hearing and sight but rely chiefly
on scent and usually catch their prey in a swift, open
chase. The wolf has a reputation for boldness, fierceness,
and voracity (Gn 9:27; Hb 1:8). It commonly kills more
than it can eat or drag away and thus is known for its
greediness.

The wolf is a restless animal, always on the move;
hunger drives it from one place to another in constant
search of new hunting grounds. During spring and fall,
wolves usually roam singly or in pairs, whereas in summer they may travel in family groups. In winter, several
such groups may join to form a large pack. Wolves are
intelligent, social creatures, faithful to their own kind.
They mate for life. Individually, the wolf is a rather timid
animal; it would much rather avoid human beings. But
collectively wolves can be among the most dangerous
animals alive.

In Egypt, Rome, and Greece the wolf was considered
sacred. Wolves were well known in the Holy Land and
are still found there and also in many places in Asia
Minor. Shepherds continually battled with wolves that
plundered their flocks (Jn 10:12).

The Bible refers to wolves in a literal sense in only
three places (Is 11:6; 65:25; Jn 10:12), all other references being figurative. Usually the wolf is a symbol of
enemies or the wicked (e.g., Ez 22:27; Zep 3:3; Acts
20:29). Both the wolf's courage and its cruelty were
probably in the mind of the patriarch Jacob when he
predicted the fate of Benjamin's tribe (Gn 49:27).

Worm Actually insect larvae in most biblical references,
usually maggots, the larvae of flies (see Fly, above). For
example, maggots are evidently referred to in accounts of
worms feeding on spoiled manna (Ex 16:19-20), corpses
(Jb 21:26; Is 14:11), or open wounds (Jb 7:5). Mark 9:48
refers to a maggot that eats dead flesh. In Acts 12:23 a
fatal, worm-induced abdominal disease of King Herod is
mentioned. In other cases, the reference is to the larvae
of other insects (Is 51:8). In Deuteronomy 28:39 and
Jonah 4:7 the vine weevil (*Cochylis ambiguella*) is probably referred to; it destroys vines by boring into their
stems. Comparing a man to a worm is a metaphor for
abasement (Jb 25:6; Ps 22:6).

ANISE* KJV translation of dill in Matthew 23:23. *See*
Plants (Dill).

ANNA Phanuel's daughter from Asher's tribe and a
prophetess in Jerusalem when Jesus was a young child.
Advanced in years, she worshiped with prayer and fasting day and night in the temple. When Jesus was brought
by his parents and presented to the Lord in the temple,
she came up, thanking God and speaking of him to all
who were looking for the redemption of Jerusalem (Lk
2:36-38).

ANNAN Father of five sons who divorced their foreign
wives under the direction of Ezra (1 Esd 9:32), also
called Harim (Ezr 10:31).

ANNAS Jewish high priest from AD 7 to 15. Appointed
by Quirinius, Roman governor of Syria, Annas was put
out of office by Valerius Gratus, procurator of Judea.
Annas was succeeded by three minor figures before the
post was assumed by his son-in-law Caiaphas (Jn 18:13,
24). The tenure of Caiaphas extended from AD 18 to 36;
thus, he was high priest at the time of Jesus' public
ministry.

Evidently Annas's power and influence remained considerable even after his removal from that office. Like an
American Supreme Court justice, the high priest held a
lifetime appointment. Deposition of a high priest by the
pagan Romans would have been strongly resented by the
Jews. Consequently, Annas may still have been referred
to as high priest among the populace, as a sort of high
priest emeritus. Such a practice, evidenced in the writings
of the Jewish historian Josephus, tends to clear up those
references in the NT to Annas as high priest during the
same chronological period as Caiaphas (Lk 3:2; Jn 18:19,
22-24; Acts 4:6). The fact that Annas conducted a private
inquiry of Jesus after he was arrested (Jn 18:13, 19-24)
but before he was taken to Caiaphas, is a strong indication that Annas was still a person of considerable stature
among the Jewish religious leaders.

Annas is also mentioned in the NT account of an
investigation of the apostles Peter and John. Interestingly, the penalty imposed on the apostles was far less
severe than the one Jesus suffered (Acts 4:6-21).

ANNIAS Ancestor of a family of 101 sons that under-
took the rigorous migration from Babylon with
Zerubbabel, according to the Apocrypha (1 Esd 5:16).
Parallel canonical texts omit this family (Ezr 2:16-20;
Neh 7:21-25).

ANNIUTH Apocryphal name of Bani in 1 Esdras 9:48.
See Bani #10.

ANNUNCIATION* The angel Gabriel's announcement
to Mary that she would bear a son by the Holy Spirit (Lk
1:26-38).

In spite of the misunderstanding and hardship Mary
would have to endure because of her premarital pregnancy, Gabriel greeted her as one "highly favored" or
"richly blessed" (Lk 1:28). With fear characteristic of a
human being confronted by a heavenly being, Mary
"considered . . . what sort of greeting this might be"
(Lk 1:29, RSV). Reassuring her, Gabriel said the Lord had
chosen her to bring forth a son to be named Jesus.

"Jesus" is the Greek form of the Hebrew name
"Joshua," which means "the Lord is salvation." Matthew
described an angel's appearance to Joseph also to
announce that Mary was pregnant with a child conceived
by the Holy Spirit, who would be called Jesus, "for he
will save his people from their sins" (Mt 1:18-21, NLT).

Using figures of speech drawn from the OT, Gabriel
prophesied concerning the child that Mary would bear
(Lk 1:32-33). Like John the Baptist, Jesus would be great,
but Jesus' greatness would be of a different kind, for John
was to be "great in the sight of the Lord" (Lk 1:15, NASB),
but Jesus would be great and be "called the Son of the
Most High" (Lk 1:32, NLT).

Jesus would be given the throne of his father David
(Lk 1:32). He would receive the sovereignty promised in
the OT to the Messiah-King of David's line, but unlike

David, Jesus would reign forever (2 Sam 7:12-16; Pss 2:7; 89:26-29).

Mary's question, "How can this be, since I have no husband?" (Lk 1:34, RSV) did not express doubt, but curiosity as to the manner in which the event should take place. Gabriel explained that "the power of the Most High," the Holy Spirit, would "overshadow" Mary, and her child would be conceived by God's power, like no child before it. Gabriel's observation to Mary, "For with God nothing will be impossible" echoes the Lord's word to Sarah when he announced Isaac's birth (Gn 18:10-14). Because Jesus was conceived by the Holy Spirit, he would be called "holy" and would be recognized as "the Son of God" (Lk 1:35, NLT).

It required courage for Mary to reply to Gabriel, "I am the Lord's servant, and I am willing to accept whatever he wants" (Lk 1:38, NLT). As a handmaid, or slave, Mary could not but do the will of her master. However, as an unmarried pregnant woman, she faced the possibility of disgrace (Mt 1:19) and even the death penalty (Dt 22:20-24; see Jn 8:3-5). Still Mary realized that because of the mighty thing God would do in her, "generation after generation will call me blessed" (Lk 1:48, NLT).

Since December 25 is celebrated as the traditional date of Christ's birth, liturgical churches celebrate the Feast of the Annunciation (Incarnation) nine months earlier, on March 25.

See also Virgin Birth of Jesus.

ANNUNUS One of the men supplied by the Lord in response to Ezra's request for priests to serve in Jerusalem (1 Esd 8:48). Annunus was probably one of Jeshaiah's brothers (Ezr 8:19).

ANOINT To pour oil or ointment onto a person or object in a ritualistic fashion.

The Hebrew word for anoint first appears in Genesis 31:13, where it refers to Jacob pouring oil on the stone of Bethel (Gn 28:18-19). At a later time the ceremony was repeated (Gn 35:9-15). The ceremony was clearly religious, signifying induction into sacred use. As a religious act, the anointing was meant to endow the anointed one with the quality of the deity involved. From ancient times the Hebrews inaugurated officers of their national community by pouring special oil on the head of the person designated for office. The same practice was used to set objects apart for special divine use.

Scripture supplies few details of the ceremonial anointings of official things and persons. Jacob simply poured oil on a rock with an accompanying pronouncement. When anointing Israel's first king, the prophet-judge Samuel took Saul aside for instruction (1 Sm 9:25-27), then "took a vial of oil and poured it on his head, and kissed him and said, 'Has not the Lord anointed you to be prince over his people Israel'" (1 Sm 10:1, RSV). For anointing the tabernacle and its priests, a special oil was compounded and used only for that sacred purpose. Skilled perfume makers blended the choicest spices (myrrh, cinnamon, sweet cane, cassia) in olive oil (Ex 30:22-25). The Lord specified that everything set apart for God—the tabernacle, the ark, the table and its instruments, the lampstand and utensils, the incense altar and main altar, the washbasin—was to be anointed. Aaron the high priest and his sons the priests were also to be anointed (Ex 30:26-32). The result was a holy place with holy furnishings, holy implements of worship, and holy ministers.

The offices of prophet, priest, and king were those associated with anointing in the nation of Israel. Prophets were sometimes, but not invariably, inducted

by official anointing (1 Kgs 19:16). They could be referred to as God's anointed ones (1 Chr 16:22; Ps 105:115). At the institution of the levitical priesthood, all the priests were anointed to their offices, the sons of Aaron as well as Aaron himself (Ex 40:12-15; Nm 3:3). Afterward, anointing was not repeated at the consecration of ordinary priests, but was especially reserved for the high priest (Ex 29:29; Lv 16:32).

Before they had a king of their own, the Israelites were aware of anointing as a mode of inaugurating kings (Jgs 9:8,15). Anointing became a divinely ordained rite accompanying induction of all the kings of Judah and Israel (2 Kgs 9:1-6; 11:12) from Saul onward (1 Sm 10:1; 1 Kgs 1:39). David's anointing took place in three stages (1 Sm 16:1, 13; 2 Sm 2:4; 5:1-4). "The Lord's anointed" or some similar phrase became a common designation for Hebrew kings (1 Sm 12:3-5; 2 Sm 1:14-16; Ps 89:38, 51; Lam 4:20).

Anointing, however, had more than religious or ritualistic significance. Both the Egyptians and the Syrians practiced anointing for medical and cosmetic reasons, and the Scriptures indicate that such nonreligious practice was also a part of Israelite customs (2 Sm 12:20; Ru 3:3; Mi 6:15). In fact, failure to anoint or perfume oneself indicated mourning or distress (2 Sm 14:2; Dn 10:3; Mt 6:17).

In the NT, anointing of the sick accompanied by prayer for healing by local church elders is recommended when requested by a sick person (Jas 5:14-16). Anointing with oil was also a part of the apostles' healing ministry (Mk 6:12-13).

ANOINTED ONE, ANOINTED ONES In the NT, Jesus Christ is portrayed as fulfilling the three offices of prophet, priest, and king. He is, supremely, God's Anointed One. "Messiah" is the term for "anointed one" derived directly from the Hebrew word for anointed; "Christ" is the same title derived from the Greek word for "anointee." The true anointing of Messiah (Ps 2:2; Dn 9:25-26) is spiritual; that is, it is done by the Holy Spirit (Is 61:1; Lk 4:1, 18-19). That Jesus of Nazareth was indeed the Anointed One (Messiah) of OT prophecy was evidenced in his anointing by the Holy Spirit and by the miracles that followed (Jn 1:32-51; Lk 4:33-37). By extension, Christians also are said to be anointed by the Holy Spirit, enabling them to understand their faith and to live godly lives (2 Cor 1:21-22; 1 Jn 2:20, 27).

See also Messiah.

ANT Insect used as an example of industriousness for storing up food in the summer (Prv 6:6; 30:25). *See* Animals.

ANTEDILUVIAN* Name given to the whole period before the Flood of Noah's time. The adjective, which literally means "before the flood [deluge]," designates a major epoch in biblical history. The noun "antediluvians" refers to the people who lived in that time. Toward the end of the antediluvian period, society was characterized by great corruption that according to the Bible led to its God-ordained destruction by the Flood. *See* Flood, The.

ANTELOPE Swift, deerlike animal mentioned in Deuteronomy 14:5 and Isaiah 51:20. *See* Animals.

ANTHOTHIJAH Benjamite and Shashak's son (1 Chr 8:24).

ANTHROPOLOGY* In a theological sense, the study of what the Bible says about man and the relation in which he stands and should stand to God. *See* Man.

ANTICHRIST According to 1 John, anyone who denies that Jesus is the Christ, that he is the unique Son of God, or that he has come in the flesh. The biblical term, however, principally refers to a particular person in whom that denial reaches its consummate expression and who will play a key role in the final stage of history.

The word "antichrist" occurs only four times, all in John's epistles (1 Jn 2:18, 22; 4:3; 2 Jn 1:7). First John 2:18 refers also to "many antichrists." John assumed that his Christian readers knew about the Antichrist and had been taught to expect his coming (1 Jn 2:18-27). The presence of many antichrists, in fact, indicated that the end times had arrived. But John warned that a final Antichrist who, like the others, would deny that Jesus is the Christ, would yet make an appearance.

OTHER NAMES FOR THE ANTICHRIST
The concept of antichrist undoubtedly comes from the teaching of Jesus in the Gospels. A lengthy passage (Mk 13, paralleled in Mt 24–25, and Lk 21) records the instruction Jesus gave his disciples about the tragic events and persecution that they could expect before his return as the glorious Son of Man. His coming would be preceded by the appearance of many "deceivers" and "false Christs." The term "false Christs" is used only twice (Mt 24:24; Mk 13:22). Although it has obvious similarities to John's "antichrist," the Gospel passages do not refer to "a deceiver" or "false Christ" in the singular as do John's and Paul's writings.

In the book of Revelation, John's symbol for the Antichrist is probably "the beast" (Rv 13:1-18; 17:3, 7-17). The Beast is described, not only as an opposer of Christ, but more specifically as a satanically inspired Christ-counterfeit. Although the Beast (Antichrist) is clearly distinguishable from the Lamb (Christ), he receives worship from everyone except God's elect.

Another probable reference to the Antichrist is "the man of lawlessness" (2 Thes 2:3). The passage is difficult to interpret, but the person described seems to be the same person later designated by John as the Beast. Both the apostles Paul and John saw present events as leading up to the events of the future. Instructing the church at Thessalonica about the second coming of Christ (2 Thes 2:1-12), Paul stressed that the appearance and rebellion of the man of lawlessness must occur beforehand. That man would oppose the worship of any gods or God and even proclaim himself to be God (2 Thes 2:4). He would subsequently be destroyed by Christ at his return (2 Thes 2:8)—an indication that those events are set in the final days of history.

John further described any person or message that did not "confess Jesus" as being of the spirit of the antichrist (1 Jn 4:3). In his brief Second Epistle, John referred to "many deceivers" who would not acknowledge the coming of Jesus Christ in the flesh (2 Jn 1:7). Such a person, he wrote, was "the deceiver and the antichrist."

See also False Christs, False Messiahs; Mark of the Beast; Prophets, False; Beast; Revelation, Book of.

ANTIGONUS* Name of three Greek kings and two Hasmonean (Jewish) kings in the intertestamental period.

1. Antigonus I, also called Cyclops, the "one-eyed" (in Greek, *Monophthalmus*). Born in 382 BC, he served under Alexander the Great and became provincial governor of Phrygia in 333 BC. After Alexander's death in 323 BC, Antigonus spent most of his life battling various coalitions of the four generals who inherited Alexander's empire (cf. Dan 8:8; 11:3-4). Antigonus dreamed of uniting what had been the Alexandrian Empire, but Cassander (who ruled Macedonia), Lysimachus (who ruled Thrace and Asia Minor), Seleucus (who ruled Syria), and Ptolemy (who ruled Egypt) had the same aspirations. Antigonus was a brilliant military strategist and amassed considerable territory including much of Cassander's inheritance and the island of Cyprus. He lived to be 80 years old and was the founder of the Antigonid dynasty, to which the next two Antigonuses belonged.

2. Antigonus II (Gonatas). Born in 319 BC, he was a son of Demetrius I Poliorcetes and grandson of Antigonus I. His major achievement was to rout the Seleucid ruler Antiochus I from Syria and so eliminate any threat to his own rule over Macedonia (northern Greece). This Antigonus also lived to be 80.

3. Antigonus III, born to Demetrius the Fair in 263 BC and thus a half nephew of Antigonus II. He maintained the Antigonid dynasty and held Greece together through the Hellenic League (224 BC) against various efforts to dissolve its united parts.

4. Antigonus (135–104 BC), son of John Hyrcanus. His grandfather was Simeon and his great-grandfather Mattathias; therefore he was a grandnephew of the famous Jewish military leader Judas Maccabeus. The glory of the Hasmonean dynasty had faded before this Antigonus came on the scene. The dynasty deteriorated rapidly, virtually destroying itself with internal strife and mutual suspicion.

5. Antigonus II (Mattathias), last of the Hasmoneans, and a nephew of the above. Son of Aristobulus II, this Antigonus spent a good part of his life in Rome trying to convince Julius Caesar that he (Antigonus) rather than Antipater II should rule Judea. After Caesar's assassination in 44 BC, Antigonus made his way eastward and in the year 40 BC established a precarious and short-lived rule in Jerusalem. The routed King Herod eventually gathered enough Roman support to retake what Antigonus had conquered, and three years later Antigonus was beheaded by Mark Antony, the new Roman emperor.

See also Hasmonean.

ANTI-LEBANON Mountain range (Jdt 1:7) stretching from Mt Hermon, its southern extremity, toward the north-northeast, running parallel to the Lebanon range west of it. Drainage from the two ranges provides most of the water for the Jordan River. The range was known in OT times as Sirion (Dt 3:9; 4:48; Ps 29:6) or Senir (1 Chr 5:23; Sg 4:8; Ez 27:5).

ANTILEGOMENA* *See* "Antilegomena: The Books That Didn't Make It," page 175; Bible, Canon of the.

ANTIOCHIANS "Turncoat" Jews of the intertestamental period who had largely abandoned their Judaism for Greek ideas and practices. During the reign of the Syrian king Antiochus Epiphanes (second century BC), Palestine was subjected to an intensive "Hellenizing" program. Many citizens of Jerusalem compromised or disregarded their religious heritage under the strong social and economic pressure to "be Greek" in every possible way. Jason supplanted his brother Onias as high priest (through a bribe) and worked hand in hand with Antiochus Epiphanes to create a community of Greek-thinking people within Jerusalem. Jason

established a gymnasium (school) to further his indoc-
trination program and introduced new customs contrary to the Jewish practice. Many Jews corrupted
themselves at his prodding and left the faith of their
fathers. Even the priests neglected the sacrificial system
to sample the worldly pleasures offered by Jason and
his cohorts, "putting the highest value on Greek forms
of prestige" (2 Macc 4:15). In 2 Maccabees 4:9, this
group of turncoat Jews was referred to as "citizens of
Antioch" (the Syrian capital). *See* Maccabean Period;
Hasmonean.

ANTIOCHIS Concubine of the Syrian king Antiochus
Epiphanes (2 Macc 4:30). When the cities of Tarsus and
Mallus were given to Antiochis as a gift, their inhabitants
revolted in protest.

ANTIOCH OF PISIDIA City in Asia Minor between
the districts of Phrygia and Pisidia to which the apostle
Paul traveled to introduce the gospel. Paul was invited
by the elders of the synagogue in Antioch to deliver any
message of exhortation he might have at their Sabbath
meeting (Acts 13:14-15). According to the record in Acts,
many begged to hear more (13:42), but certain Jewish
leaders envied Paul's popularity and began to revile him
(13:45). Paul then turned to gentile listeners (13:46-48)
until Jewish persecutors forced him to leave the city
(13:50). The same Jews from Antioch continued harassing Paul as he traveled to Lystra (Acts 14:19). Paul
passed through Antioch a second time while en route to
Perga and Attalia (14:21).

The city of Antioch was founded around 300 BC by
Seleucus Nicator and was named for his son, Antiochus I.
As a result of the Roman conquest in 188 BC, the area
was declared free from the rule of the Seleucid kings,
and deliberate steps toward Romanization followed. In
about 36 BC, Antony made Antioch part of the domain
of the Galatian king, Amyntas. Upon the death of
Amyntas 11 years later, the city was elevated to colony
status and became Caesarea Antiochela, capital of
southern Galatia.

ANTIOCH OF SYRIA Principal city among 16 others
of the same name built about 300 BC by the Syrian
emperor Seleucus I in honor of his father Antiochus.
This Antioch (modern Antakya, Turkey) occupies a fertile plain in a western bend of the Orontes River that
terminates in the Mediterranean Sea. In ancient times
the population numbered half a million. Because of its
location on navigable waters reaching to a Mediterranean port 15 miles (24 kilometers) away and because
of its ready access through passes in the Taurus Mountains eastward to the interior, Antioch was a busy,
cosmopolitan center of trade, religious ferment, and
high levels of intellectual and political life. Under
Roman authority Antioch received lavish attention in
the form of beautiful public works, harbor improvements, and special trade advantages.

Side by side with a truly high culture were the degrading institutions of strange fertility religions, brutalizing
sports spectacles, and a variety of mystery religions. Two
other major influences were the large community of fully
franchised Jews who flourished there and the community of government functionaries. The Jewish community
supplied a number of Christian proselytes to the early
church in Antioch. The government officials provided
police protection, stability, and order, alternating with
seemingly insatiable appetites for lavish dissipations in
gambling, chariot races, brothels, exotic banquets, and
the like.

Antioch of Syria played an important role in the book
of Acts. A certain Nicholas from Antioch became one of
the first deacons in the early church (Acts 6:5). Jerusalem
Christians fled to Antioch from fierce persecution
(11:19). Acts 11 gives details of Barnabas and Paul's
teaching in the Antioch church and of the benevolent
gift of the believers there to suffering Christians in Jerusalem. The term "Christians" was first used in Antioch
(11:26). Acts 13 records that the first missionaries were
sent from there. The Jerusalem church council's statement on requirements for gentile believers was in part a
result of the work in Antioch among Gentiles (see Acts
15 and Gal 2).

From the third century to about the eighth century,
Antioch was an important center for the development of
Christian theology. The approach to Scripture and to the
nature of Christ taken in Antioch tended to be historical
and rational, in contrast to an overly spiritualized, allegorical approach taken in Alexandria (Egypt) by such
theologians as Origen and Clement.

ANTIOCHUS IV Hellenistic king called Epiphanes
meaning the "illustrious" or "god manifest"; he was the
eighth in the Seleucid dynasty (c. 215–164 BC). The year
189 BC found this younger son of Antiochus III the Great
hostage in Rome after the Battle of Magnesia. There he
was educated. Later, he seized the Syrian throne in
Antioch after the murder of his brother Seleucus IV and
ruled from 175 to 164 BC.

Antiochus Epiphanes is the most important of all the
Seleucid rulers as far as the biblical literature is concerned and is known as one of the cruelest tyrants of all
time. He was an enthusiastic believer in the Olympian
god Zeus and hoped to unify his territories by spreading
Hellenistic culture, law, and religion. In so doing he
came into violent conflict with the Jews in Judah. At the
beginning of his reign Antiochus IV meddled in the
appointment of Jewish high priests. From 171 to 168 BC,
he waged war against Egypt, defeating Ptolemy VI and
Ptolemy VII. He then captured Jerusalem, prohibited
Judaism with cruel persecution, looted the temple, and
tried to establish the worship of Greek gods by building
an altar to Zeus over the altar of burnt offering (1 Macc
1:10-62; 2 Macc 4:7-42). This altar is probably the
"abomination that makes desolate" of Daniel 11:31
(RSV). In fact, Antiochus IV plays a major role in the book
of Daniel. He is probably the "little horn" of 7:8; 8:9-14,
23-25 and the oppressor of the "saints of the Most High"
(7:25, RSV).

By Antiochus's edict, Judaism was made illegal under
pain of death and Jews were forced to participate in
heathen festivals. Open rebellion broke out in 167 BC
under the leadership of the Jewish priest Mattathias.
This occurred when a representative of the king was
enforcing compliance in a village named Modine near
Jerusalem and was slain by Mattathias who fled to the
surrounding hills. Although great slaughter fell upon
the priest's followers, Mattathias was eventually joined
by large numbers of the Hasidim, and guerrilla warfare
commenced.

After his death in 166 BC, Mattathias was succeeded by
his son Judas Maccabeus who escalated the war and
enjoyed repeated victories over the Syrian generals.
Antiochus was unable to personally lead the suppression
of the Jewish revolt because of serious rebellions in
Parthia and Armenia. He assigned this task to his regent
Lysias who was empowered to depopulate Judah, enslave
the Jews, and leave the land desolate. But this did not happen. Judas routed Gorgias at Emmaus, and the Syrians fled
from Judah. Then Lysias personally led a larger army

against the Maccabees but was severely defeated at Beth-zur. In 164 BC, Judas restored the temple and reintroduced the daily sacrifices. By 160 BC every vestige of the power of Antiochus IV had been erased from Jerusalem.

Antiochus Epiphanes was known to be frenetic and rash to the point of madness, and the success of Judas Maccabeus combined with the Syrian king's inability to personally suppress the Jewish revolt helped drive Antiochus to further madness. After these events he withdrew to Persia where it is said he died insane.

ANTIOCHUS V Called Antiochus Eupator, meaning "of a noble father" (173–162 BC), the son of Antiochus IV, and king of Syria from 163 to 162 BC. The boy king traveled with his regent Lysias to relieve the besieged Jerusalem in 163 BC. He eventually made peace with Judas Maccabeus. Returning to Antioch, Antiochus V was betrayed by his cousin Demetrius I who also claimed the throne. The young king and his regent were put to death in 162 BC.

ANTIOCHUS VII Called Antiochus Sidetes (c. 159–129 BC), was king of Syria from 139/138 to 129 BC, son of Demetrius I and brother of Demetrius II. After the capture of Demetrius II, he became the third husband of his brother's queen Cleopatra Thea and drove the usurper Trypho from the throne (139 BC). Antiochus VII was at war with the Jews from 138 to 134, destroyed part of Jerusalem, and caused John Hyrcanus to submit to his rule. He died while fighting in the Parthian War.

ANTIPAS
1. Early martyr in the church at Pergamum (Rv 2:13).
2. Son of Herod the Great. *See* Herod, Herodian Family.

Aerial View of Aphek ("fortress")

ANTIPATER
1. Goodwill ambassador sent out with Numenius to the Spartans and Romans by Jonathan, the high priest (1 Macc 12:16; 14:22).
2. Father of Herod the Great. *See* Herod, Herodian Family.

ANTIPATRIS City some 26 miles (41.8 kilometers) south of Caesarea rebuilt by Herod the Great in 9 BC in honor of his father, Antipater. Before its rebuilding, it was known as Aphek. Paul passed through Antipatris under Roman guard on his way from Jerusalem to Caesarea (Acts 23:31). Antipatris served as a Roman military relay station and marked the border between Judea and Samaria.
See also Aphek.

ANTITYPE* Fulfillment or resolution of a corresponding earlier type. *See* Type.

ANTOTHIJAH* KJV spelling of Anthothijah, Shashak's descendant, in 1 Chronicles 8:24. *See* Anthothijah.

ANTOTHITE* KJV form of Anathothite, a resident of Anathoth, in 1 Chronicles 11:28 and 12:3. *See* Anathoth (Place), Anathothite.

ANUB Koz's son from Judah's tribe (1 Chr 4:8).

APAME Concubine of Darius I of Persia (1 Esd 4:29).

APE Large, tailless primate. Apes, or perhaps other monkeys and baboons, were imported to Israel by King Solomon (1 Kgs 10:22; 2 Chr 9:21). *See* Animals.

APELLES Roman Christian who received special greetings from the apostle Paul and the complimentary assessment of being one who is "approved in Christ" (Rom 16:10, RSV).

APHAIREMA One of the cities taken from Samaria and added to Judea by Demetrius Nicator (the Conqueror), king of Syria (1 Macc 11:34). The name is thought by some scholars to be a corruption of Ephraim. Aphairema may be the modern et-Taiyibeh.

APHARSACHITES*, APHARSATHCHITES*, APHARSITES* Words used in the book of Ezra to designate certain groups of people in Samaria who joined in writing King Artaxerxes of Babylon to stop the rebuilding of the temple in Jerusalem. Apharsathchites (Ezr 4:9, KJV) could refer to a specific ethnic group or to government leaders; a similar Old Persian word meant "messengers." Apharsachites (Ezr 5:6; 6:6, KJV) could be a shortened form of Apharsathchites or could be derived from an old Persian word for "investigators." Apharsites (Ezr 4:9, KJV) is similar to the Hebrew word for "Persians" and has been translated that way.

APHEK
1. Canaanite city west of the Jordan River conquered by Israel (Jos 12:18) and later included in Ephraim's territory. It was located near the source of the Yarkon River in the plain of Sharon. Aphek was later captured by the Philistines (1 Sm 4:1; 29:1). In Roman times Herod the Great rebuilt the city and named it Antipatris, mentioned in Acts 23:31. Its modern name is Ras el-'Ain.
   See also Antipatris.
2. Place in Phoenicia (modern Lebanon) that remained unconquered after Joshua's campaigns (Jos 13:4). This Aphek was probably located near the source of the river Ibrahim, east of Byblos.
3. Town given to Asher's tribe in the distribution of conquered cities (Jos 19:30). Asher's tribe failed to drive out the pagan inhabitants (Jgs 1:31, where it is spelled "Aphik"). Aphek was located on the plain of Acco, at the present site of Tell Kurdaneh near the source of the river Na'main.
4. City east of the Jordan River, on the main highway between Damascus and the valley of Jezreel. The Syrian king Ben-hadad, defeated by King Ahab of Israel, retreated into Aphek, where a falling wall demolished the rest of his army (1 Kgs 20:26, 30). A century later Elisha prophesied to King Joash of Israel that he would defeat the Syrians in the same city (2 Kgs 13:17).

APHEKAH City in the hill country of Canaan given to Judah's tribe after the conquest of the Promised Land by Joshua (Jos 15:53).

APHIAH Ancestor of King Saul in Benjamin's tribe (1 Sm 9:1).

APHIK Alternate form of Aphek in Judges 1:31. *See* Aphek #3.

APHRAH* KJV for Beth-leaphrah, possibly the name of a Philistine city, in Micah 1:10. *See* Beth-leaphrah.

APHSES* KJV form of Happizzez, a priest in David's time, in 1 Chronicles 24:15. *See* Happizzez.

APOCALYPSE* Term meaning a "revelation" or a "disclosure." The books of Daniel and Revelation are the two apocalypses in the Bible. *See* Apocalyptic; Daniel, Book of; Revelation, Book of.

APOCALYPSES* Group of extra-canonical writings, apocalyptic in nature, and purported to be written by biblical characters. *See* Apocrypha (Apocalyptic Apocrypha).

APOCALYPTIC* Term derived from a Greek word meaning "revelation" and used to refer to a pattern of thought and to a form of literature, both dealing with future judgment (eschatology).

The literature designated "apocalyptic" consists of compositions that either are or purport to be divine revelations received by their authors. The revelations were usually received in the form of visions. They were recounted in detail and accompanied by an interpretation. The second half of Daniel (chs 7–12) is filled with such visions, as is the whole of Revelation. Although revelatory visions also occurred frequently in OT prophetic literature (e.g., Is 6; Am 7–9; Zec 1–6), they were particularly prominent in apocalyptic literature and determined the basic literary form and structure of such writings. Sometimes (as in Daniel) the revelatory message was received through a dream by the apocalyptic seer. In another form of vision (as in Revelation), the apocalyptist was caught up to the heavenly world, where he saw and heard things to be transmitted to the world of men (cf. Paul's experience, 2 Cor 12:1-4). Frequently, the apocalyptist was unable to understand the meaning of the visions he received. In such instances an "interpreting angel" clarified the meaning of the vision (Dn 8:15-26; 9:20-27; 10:18–12:4; Rv 7:13-17; 17:7-18).

Two primary patterns of eschatological thought are found in the Bible, both centered in the conviction that God will act in the near future to save his people and punish those who oppress them. In prophetic eschatology, the dominant form in the OT, God is expected to act within history to restore man and nature to the perfect condition that existed prior to man's fall. Apocalyptic eschatology, on the other hand, expects God to destroy the old imperfect order before restoring the world to paradise.

In Israel, apocalyptic eschatology evidently flourished under foreign domination. From the early sixth century BC, prophetic eschatology began to decline and apocalyptic eschatology became increasingly popular. The book of Daniel, written during the sixth century BC, is the earliest example of apocalyptic literature in existence. The prophetic book of Malachi, written sometime during the fifth century BC, was the last Israelite prophetic book. Thereafter, the prophetic voice became silent in Israel until the rise of Christianity. With the exception of Daniel, all the surviving Jewish apocalyptic literature was written from the third century BC to the early second century AD.

In apocalyptic literature, antagonism between God and Satan was sharply emphasized. All people, nations, and supernatural beings (angels, demons) were seen as allies of God or of Satan. Although Satan had always been thought of as the adversary of God and humanity (Gn 3:1-19; Jb 1:6-12; 2:1-8), his power was restrained as long as Israel remained faithful to the covenant law of God. When Israel began to experience the long national nightmare of subjugation by foreign enemies, the reality of Satan's temporary domination of the world was brought home with great force. Though apocalyptic writers dealt with particular nations dominating Israel during one or another epoch in its history, those nations were seen as servants of Satan whose opposition to God (and God's people) would inevitably spell their downfall.

Apocalyptic thought was dominated by the conviction that, no matter how bad circumstances might be at any given moment, God and his people would ultimately triumph over their enemies. Apocalyptic determinism was not a fatalistic conviction that everything happened by a kind of mindless necessity; rather, it clung to hope in a sovereign God who would cause his people to experience ultimate victory over all temporal and spiritual enemies. Many apocalypses contained predictions of the future historical experience of Israel (or of the Christian church), culminating in a final and decisive victory of God and his people. In Nebuchadnezzar's dream interpreted by Daniel, for example, a series of foreign empires was referred to under the symbolism of various parts of a gigantic image constructed of various materials; the image was destroyed by the kingdom of God, symbolized by a stone cut without hands from a mountain (Dn 2:31-45).

A major difference between apocalyptic eschatology and prophetic eschatology was that apocalypticism nearly always envisaged a cosmic catastrophe prior to the final, decisive victory of God. In some apocalypses, such as the book of Daniel, God was expected to intervene decisively in the course of history, subdue evil, and introduce the kingdom of God. In others, such as the Revelation of John, God would first destroy the old world before creating a wholly new one (Rv 21:1; cf. 2 Pt 3:10). The general view was that things would get much worse before they got better. During the golden age of Israelite independence (10th through 7th centuries BC), the notion of future catastrophe was understandably not given much emphasis. However, after the destruction of Jerusalem in 586 BC, apocalyptists thought the Jews' problems could be reversed only by decisive and climactic intervention of God into the affairs of men and of nations.

A common apocalyptic notion based on both dualism and pessimism was the concept of two "ages." "This age," which is present and evil, was dominated by Satan and his minions, but "the age to come" would bring the blessings of the kingdom of God. A constellation of eschatological events would serve to bring the old age to a close and inaugurate the new age. When Paul spoke of the "god of this evil world" (2 Cor 4:4), he was actually referring to Satan's domination of "this age."

Another characteristic of apocalypticism was its frequent expression of intense longing for God to shorten the present evil days and quickly usher in the kingdom of God. Just as Daniel could ask, "How long shall it be till the end of these wonders?" (Dn 12:6, RSV), so John could exclaim, "Come, Lord Jesus!" (Rv 22:20). The desire for God's speedy intervention and victory made it possible to maintain hope in thoroughly adverse circumstances and encouraged God's people to conduct their lives in a manner worthy of the coming kingdom (2 Pt 3:11-13; Rv 21:5-8).

The book of Daniel is the only apocalypse in the OT canon of Scripture, and the book of Revelation the only apocalypse within the NT canon. Many noncanonical Jewish and Christian apocalypses survive, however. The Jewish apocalypses were written between the late third century BC and the early second century AD; the existing Christian apocalypses, from the second through the fourth centuries AD. Further, many apocalyptic literary patterns and structures are found outside the formal category of apocalyptic literature. The Olivet discourse of Jesus, for example (Mk 13; Mt 24; Lk 21), has frequently been called a little apocalypse by biblical scholars. In general, most of the features enumerated below must be present for a literary work to be considered "an apocalypse."

With the exception of Daniel and Revelation, most of the surviving apocalypses are pseudonymous, that is, they were written under a false name. This characteristic is such a constant feature that apocalyptic literature has been commonly referred to as "pseudepigrapha" ("false writings"). A composite apocalypse (1 Enoch) written by several unknown authors from the second century BC to probably the first century AD claimed to have been written by the Enoch who was an early descendant of Adam (Gn 5:21-24). Other Jewish apocalypses were attributed to such important OT characters as Adam and Eve, Moses, Isaiah, Baruch, Solomon, and Ezra. Since all were written after the close of the OT canon, their real authors probably thought that identification with some important OT personage was necessary for favorable reception. Early Christian apocalypses often bore the names of such important figures as Peter, Paul, and Thomas.

See also Apocrypha for a discussion on each of the books just mentioned.

APOCRYPHA* Books excluded from the canon of Scripture.

PREVIEW
• Introduction
• Apocryphal Gospels
• Apocryphal Acts
• Apocryphal Epistles
• Apocalyptic Apocrypha
• Specific Titles of Apocryphal Writings

Introduction The writings of the Old and New Testaments tended to attract certain additional compositions in the form of books, parts of books, letters, "gospels," apocalypses, and so on. Most of the authors wrote anonymously, but some presented their writings to the public under the name of a familiar OT figure or member of the Christian church. Several of these compositions formed a small but important part of the great body of Jewish literature that emerged during the period between the Old and New Testaments. Much of it was the result of religious and political ferment, for the Jews felt their faith and their very existence threatened, first by the pagan influences of Hellenistic Greek culture, then by the oppression of invading Roman forces.

Most of the apocryphal books are also pseudepigrapha—that is, they are books ascribed to a pseudonymous author. In other words, the main characteristic of these writings is the fictitious claim that the author of the book was a biblical person (Enoch, Abraham, Moses,

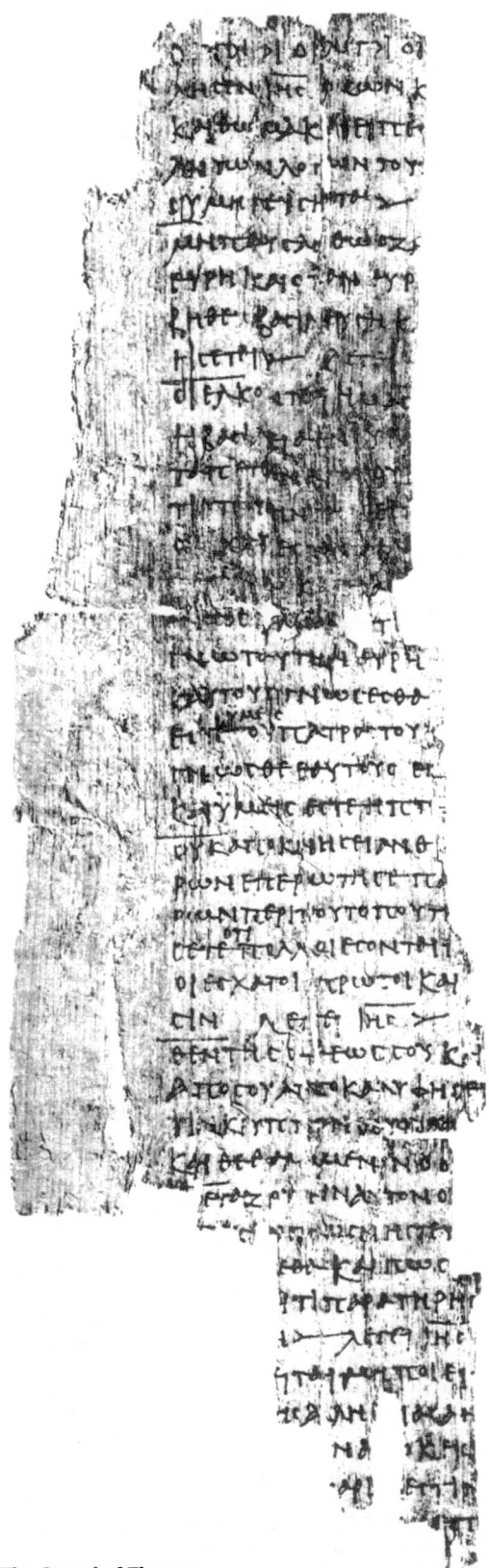

The Gospel of Thomas
Papyrus Oxyrhynchus 654,
third century

Solomon, Bartholomew, Thomas, etc.) or that the revelation contained in the book was originally given to a biblical character (Adam and Eve, Isaiah). Generally, the pseudepigrapha show a strong interest in the apocalyptic: the creation of the world, the future of Israel and the nations, the glory of God and his angels, the messianic kingdom, and life after death. Many of the pseudepigrapha are Jewish writings that were never accepted by the Jewish or Christian communities. They were written about the time of the Apocrypha (c. 200 BC–AD 110), but by the nature of the contents of the pseudepigrapha, they were only recognized by certain groups. Since some of these books approximated counterparts in the canonical Scriptures, there is no doubt that in some circles their authority and inspiration were regarded as similar to that of the scriptural compositions venerated by the Jews and later by Christians.

Other religious writings from that period made no claim to be scriptural. Such compositions preserved the familiar traditions of both Judaism and primitive Christianity, although on occasion they enriched or embellished them by means of legends and unhistorical narratives. Because very few books of any kind were in circulation at that time, the Palestinians tended to read whatever literary material came into their possession. Although the Torah, or law of Moses, had always been recognized as the standard of theological orthodoxy for the Jews, narratives of endurance under persecution or accounts of the way that the enemies of God's people received their just reward had an obvious attraction for those under the pressures of a pagan society.

In the same way, although the Gospels and Epistles—along with the OT—comprised the basic canon or approved list of Scriptures for Christians, many additional narratives claimed the attention of Christ's early followers. Those compositions often dealt with the supposed activities of Jesus and his followers, as well as with martyrdoms, revelations, and spiritual teachings. Some works contained material that was not only unhistorical but downright bizarre, but others reflected the spirit of Christ and the apostolic teachings to a certain extent. For the early Christians, as also for the Jews, the establishment of a formal canon of scriptural writings must have been prompted in part by a necessity to separate the record of revealed truth from other written forms of religious tradition as well as from actual heresy.

Writings that failed to gain acceptance into the OT and NT canons were described in the writings of some early Christian scholars by the term "apocrypha." The Greek word means "hidden things," and when applied to books it described those works that religious authorities wished to be concealed from the reading public. The reason was that such books were thought to contain mysterious or secret lore, meaningful only to the initiate and therefore unsuitable for the ordinary reader. But the word "apocrypha" was also applied in a less complimentary sense to works that deserved to be concealed. Such works contained harmful doctrines or false teachings calculated to unsettle or pervert rather than edify those who read them. The suppression of undesirable writings was comparatively easy at a time when only a few copies of any book were in circulation at a given time.

By the end of the first century AD, a clear distinction was being made in Jewish circles between writings that were suitable for use by the general public and esoteric works that were to be restricted to the knowledgeable and the initiated. Thus in 2 Esdras 14:1-6, the writer tells how Ezra was supposedly instructed by God to publish openly certain writings (among them the Torah), and

keep others secret (that is, apocalyptic traditions dealing with the coming end of the age). In 2 Esdras 14:42-46 reference is made to 70 books, evidently noncanonical material, written after the 24 books of the Hebrew Canon.

Use of the term "apocrypha" to mean "noncanonical" goes back to the fifth century AD, when Jerome urged that the books found in the Septuagint and in the Latin Bibles that did not occur in the canon of the Hebrew OT writings should be treated as apocryphal. They were not to be disregarded entirely, since they were part of the great contemporary outpouring of Jewish national literature. At the same time, they should not be used as sources for Christian doctrine but at best for supplementary reading of an uplifting or inspirational nature.

Protestant theologians generally have followed the tradition established by Jerome, regarding the OT apocrypha as the excess of the Septuagint canon over the Hebrew Scriptures. When the Hebrew Bible began to be translated into Greek in Egypt during the reign of Ptolemy II (285–246 BC), the scholars concerned included a number of books that, while remaining outside the generally accepted list of Hebrew canonical writings, still had a bearing upon Jewish history and society. That procedure reflected contemporary attitudes in Palestine, where many people did not attempt to separate canonical writings from other forms of religious literature. The decision made by Jewish authorities about what to regard as canonical Scripture naturally had a bearing on what would constitute OT apocrypha.

Textual evidence represented by certain manuscripts and fragments from the Dead Sea caves makes it reasonably certain that the last of the canonical Hebrew writings had been completed several decades before the time Alexander the Great (356–323 BC) began his conquests in the Near East. The process by which those compositions came to be accepted as canonical was more protracted, however. Only when they had been circulated, read, and assessed favorably by comparison with the spirituality of the Torah were they accorded general canonicity. Hence the distinction between the canonical and apocryphal writings came as much through usage and general consent on the part of orthodox Judaism as through any other manner. Earlier scholars suggested that the so-called Council of Jamnia, held in Palestine about AD 100, was responsible for drawing up a list of OT books suitable for use by the faithful. However, subsequent studies have thrown considerable doubt upon the historicity of such a council, at the same time showing that the Jewish authorities of that period considered their noncanonical writings to be more of an obstacle than a help to devotion.

The books the Jews regarded as being specifically outside the Canon, and therefore apocryphal, are as follows: 1 Esdras; 2 Esdras; Tobit; Judith; the additions to Esther; the Wisdom of Solomon; Ecclesiasticus; Baruch; the Letter of Jeremiah; the additions to the book of Daniel (the Prayer of Azariah and the Song of the Three Young Men, Susanna, Bel and the Dragon); the Prayer of Manasseh; 1 Maccabees; and 2 Maccabees. Several Septuagint manuscripts included some pseudohistorical material under the titles of 3 and 4 Maccabees. Therefore, even the Apocrypha varied somewhat in content, depending upon the manuscript tradition being followed. Among early Christian scholars there was also some difference of opinion about the precise limits of canonical Hebrew Scripture, and hence of apocryphal material. A serious break with Hebrew and rabbinic tradition came with the writings of Augustine, who advanced the view that the books of the Apocrypha were of equal authority with the other writings of the canonical Hebrew and Christian Scriptures. A few dissenting voices were raised in support of Jerome's position, but the views of Augustine were embraced by the Council of Trent (1546) and became official Roman Catholic teaching.

The Roman Catholic Church includes the following works as part of the Deuterocanonical Scriptures: Tobit; Judith; the additions to Esther; the Wisdom of Solomon; Ecclesiasticus, or the Wisdom of Jesus ben Sirach; Baruch; the additions to the book of Daniel (the Prayer of Azariah and the Song of the Three Young Men, Susanna, Bel and the Dragon); 1 Maccabees; and 2 Maccabees. (Articles on each of these are interspersed throughout this dictionary.)

Christians of the NT period were already familiar with Jewish apocryphal works, including the apocalyptic speculations found in 2 Esdras. Therefore, it was hardly surprising that a similar body of literature should grow up around their own Scriptures when they began to be composed and circulated. NT apocrypha, however, like its OT counterpart, could be considered only in relationship to an established canon of scriptural writings. Since the earliest catalog of NT writings, the Muratorian Canon, was not compiled until about AD 200, a considerable period of time elapsed before an official church statement could appear on what was to be considered NT apocrypha. In the meantime, a large assortment of materials of a predominantly religious nature appeared, purporting to be orthodox in nature and dealing with various aspects of historic Christianity. As events turned out, this apocryphal literature defeated the purposes it was intended to serve.

Apocryphal Gospels One major class of apocrypha are the apocryphal gospels. These writings preserved stories about Christ and some teachings, but being mostly fanciful in nature they never became canonical. There are three broad classes:

1. A type similar to the synoptic Gospels, represented by the Gospel of Peter and the Gospel of the Egyptians, as well as papyrus fragments including Oxyrhynchus 840 and Papyrus Egerton 2. Other papyrus collections of sayings show affinities with the canonical Gospels.
2. Gospels that disseminated Gnosticism, a second-century AD heresy stressing philosophical knowledge (*gnosis*) of the cosmos and man. They are often in the form of dialogues between Jesus and his disciples, such as the Coptic Gospel of Thomas, the Apocryphon of John, the Wisdom of Jesus Christ, and the Dialogue of the Redeemer. In this category also come those "gospels" attributed to the Twelve as a group, such as the Memoirs of the Apostles.
3. Infancy gospels, purporting to supply otherwise unknown information of a legendary nature about Christ's earliest years. Passion gospels also come into this category. These narratives were written to satisfy curiosity about Christ's birth and childhood or to embellish the canonical accounts of his crucifixion and resurrection.

  Because of the scarcity of information about such matters as the childhood, adolescence, and early manhood of Jesus, the "infancy" gospels purport to supply the reader with what was meant to pass for historical fact. Much of the material, however, was entirely within the realm of fantasy and could never have been accepted as fact by any intelligent reader. For example, in the Gospel of Thomas the five-year-old Jesus is accused of breaking the Sabbath by making sparrows of clay beside a stream. When his father Joseph investigates the situation, Jesus claps his hands and the clay birds come to life and fly away chirping.

"Passion" gospels were written to embellish the canonical accounts of Christ's crucifixion and resurrection. As supplements to Christian teaching, many of the apocryphal writings seemed to be proclaiming ideas that were actually outside the scope of NT doctrine. Attempts to fill in the "hidden years" of Christ's life had no foundation whatever in the traditions of the Gospels. Works dealing with the last state of unbelievers were embellished in a manner that went far beyond anything stated in the NT. In some notable instances, as in the writings of various Gnostic sects, the authors set out deliberately to propagate heretical teachings they had accepted under the authority of some apostolic figure. The Gospel of Thomas, recovered around 1945 from Nag Hammadi (Chenoboskion) near the Nile River, is an example of an attempt to perpetuate curious sayings and dogmas by attributing them to Jesus, so that they would receive wide currency and acceptance.

Apocryphal Acts There are also some apocryphal acts, which are purported to be accounts of apostolic achievements not recorded in Scripture. Such "acts" are the source of much tradition, such as Peter's being crucified upside down and Thomas's mission to India. The reliability of the traditions is questionable because the writings contain clearly unorthodox material. Yet small fragments of accurate information may be embedded in this mass of largely fictitious literature.

Because of their often heretical character, the church consistently reacted against such books, sometimes even demanding that they be burned (for example, at the Nicene Council of 787). The Acts of John pictured Jesus talking to John on the Mt of Olives during the crucifixion, explaining that it was only a spectacle. In the Acts of Thomas, Jesus appeared in the form of Thomas, exhorting a newly married couple to dedicate themselves to virginity. Sexual abstinence was a dominant theme, reflecting Platonic ideas, which disparaged the physical body.

Many scholars date the earliest work, the Acts of John, before AD 150. The major Acts (of John, Paul, Peter, Andrew, and Thomas) were probably written during the second and third centuries. These gave rise to other "acts" that were primarily miracle stories, written more to entertain than to teach.

Apocryphal Epistles A host of apocryphal works are classified as epistles. These generally pseudonymous works originated from many widely separated periods of time. Many other apocryphal works are apocalyptic in nature. These works are supplemented by material such as the Apostolic Constitutions and Canons. Added to these are the Gnostic compositions found at Nag Hammadi, which include works purporting to represent the teachings of Christ as well as "secret" instructions compiled by the Gnostic writers and a few apocryphal compositions.

Apocalyptic Apocrypha Another group could be called apocalyptic apocrypha. The term "apocalypse" means "disclosure" or "revelation," a term that was generally applied to Christian literature that resembled the Revelation of John, which designates itself an apocalypse in Revelation 1:1. The practice of writing under the name of an illustrious figure of the past, or pseudonymity, was a characteristic device used by most unknown authors of Jewish and Christian apocalypses (the Revelation of John is a striking exception). Jewish apocalypses were attributed to such ancient worthies as Adam, Enoch, Abraham,

Moses, Ezra, and others. Similarly, Christian apocalypses written in the second century AD and later were ascribed to such important early Christian figures as Peter, Thomas, James and others.

In NT times there emerged in Judaism certain circles that developed an apocalyptic view of history. They provided such writings as the five parts of 1 Enoch, the Assumption of Moses, 4 Ezra, and the Apocalypse of Baruch. These books are of importance to NT study, for they provide a bridge between the OT and the NT concepts of the kingdom of God.

The apocalypses were written to answer the problems of theodicy (the justice of God). After the days of Ezra, the law assumed a more important role in the life of the people than before. In prophetic times Israel again and again apostatized from the law and worshiped foreign gods. The primary message of the prophets was to challenge Israel to get right with God and to turn in repentance to keep the law. After Ezra and throughout NT times, Israel was obedient to the law as never before. The Jews abhorred idolatry and faithfully worshiped God. Still the kingdom did not come. Instead came the fearful persecution in the Maccabean times by Antiochus IV Epiphanes, the worldly rule of the Hasmoneans, Pompey and Roman hegemony, and in AD 66–70, the siege and destruction of Jerusalem. Where was God? Why did he not deliver his faithful people? Why did the kingdom not come? The apocalypses were written to answer questions like these.

One of the most important elements in apocalyptic religion is an explicit dualism, expressed as "this age" and "the age to come." The prophets contrasted the present time with the future when the kingdom of God would be established. The apocalyptists radicalized this contrast. Twice we find fragments of this idiom in 1 Enoch. We meet the fully developed idiom in 2 Esdras and the Apocalypse of Baruch (late first century AD). "The Most High has made not one age but two" (2 Esd 7:50); "the day of judgment shall be the end of this age and the beginning of the immortal age that is to come" (2 Esd 7:113); "this age the Most High has made for many but the age to come for few" (2 Esd 8:1; see also Apoc Bar 14:13; 15:7; *Pirke Aboth* 4:1, 21-22; 6:4-7). Furthermore, the transition from this age to the age to come can be accomplished only by a cosmic act of God. In the apocryphal Assumption of Moses there is no messianic personage; it is God alone who comes to redeem Israel. In the Similitudes of Enoch the transition is accomplished with the coming of a heavenly, preexistent Son of Man. In 4 Ezra we find a conflation of the concepts of Davidic Messiah and the Son of Man.

Apocalyptic differs from OT prophetic religion in that it is pessimistic about the present age. It would be wrong to describe the apocalypses as ultimately pessimistic, for their basic message is that in due time God will intervene and save his people. But for the present, as long as this age lasts, he has removed himself from intervening in Israel's affairs. The present age is under the power of evil angelic and demonic forces and is irretrievably evil. God has abandoned this age to evil; salvation can be expected only in the age to come.

The apocalyptists lost completely the tension between history and eschatology. They no longer expected any deliverance in this age. God had, in fact, become the God of the future, not of the present.

In the dream-visions of Enoch (1 Enoch 83–90), God faithfully guided Israel throughout its history. Then God withdrew his personal leadership, forsook the temple, and surrendered his people to be torn and devoured. God "remained unmoved, though he saw it, and rejoiced that they were devoured and swallowed and robbed, and left them to be devoured in the hand of all the beasts" (1 Enoch 89:58). After the Babylonian captivity God was conceived to be inactive in history. History was surrendered to evil. All salvation was thrust into the future.

Comparative studies have shown that the NT apocryphal writings preserve at best a series of debased traditions about the founder and teachings of early Christianity. At worst, the narratives are entirely devoid of historical value and in some respects are totally alien to NT spirituality. Even where they seem to support a tradition current in some part of the early church, the evidence they present is inferior to what can often be had from other sources. Sometimes the compositions are so trivial and inconsequential that it is difficult to account for their survival. Certain apocryphal writings did in fact become lost and are now known only in the form of quotations in larger works.

Nevertheless, the NT apocryphal compositions are important in indicating what was attractive to the ordinary people of the day. For them an element of the romantic seemed necessary to supplement the body of received spiritual truth. Certain of the stories recounted were vivid and imaginative, and others, such as the apocalypses, provided a form of escapism from harsh temporal realities. No matter what their nature, the NT apocryphal writings exerted an influence out of all proportion to their fundamental worth.

Specific Titles of Apocryphal Writings

Abdias, Apostolic History of Collection of material drawn from canonical and apocryphal writings concerning the lives of the apostles, including Paul. Abdias, an early bishop of Babylon, was supposedly the author of this history that more probably was collated from a variety of sources in the sixth century AD in France. This apocryphal "acts," divided into 10 books, originally circulated in Greek as individual volumes that were collected into one when a Latin version was made. The content is generally regarded as folklore or legend but is of some value where no other source is available.

Abdias, a contemporary of the apostles, may have seen Christ and supposedly traveled extensively with Simon and Jude. There is no historical basis for considering Abdias as the author of the Hebrew text, or for believing that his disciple Eutropius translated it into Greek or that Africanus translated the Greek into Latin—although the preface to the Latin version makes those claims.

Abgarus, Letters of Christ and Apocryphal work comprising two short letters, one supposedly written by the Syrian king Abgar (Abgarus), the other supposedly a reply from Jesus. Eusebius claimed to have found the material in the archives of Abgar at Edessa and translated it from Syrian to Greek together with an account of the exploits of the disciple Thaddaeus.

According to the legend, Abgar, suffering from a severe disease, hears of the miracles of Jesus and sends a messenger with a letter asking Jesus to come heal him. At the same time he offers Jesus sanctuary from the dangerous opposition of the Jews in Jerusalem. In a written reply (later altered to an oral one to comply with the tradition that no writings of Jesus existed), Jesus declines the offer of sanctuary but promises that after his ascension he will comply with Abgar's request for healing by sending a disciple to him. Thaddaeus, one of the Twelve, is dispatched to Edessa, the king is healed, and the community converts to Christianity. In a slightly different version in the Doctrina Addaei (about AD 400), an oral reply is given, and the messenger returns with a portrait of Jesus that is displayed prominently in Abgar's palace.

The legend is essentially similar to that described in the Greek Acts of Thaddaeus (fifth or sixth century AD), except that in the latter Ananias returns with a handkerchief on which is a miraculous imprint of the face of Christ.

Abraham, Apocalypse of Jewish document existing in old Slavonic texts that go back through Greek to a Hebrew or Aramaic original.

The Apocalypse of Abraham begins with Abraham turning from idolatry. Incorporating old rabbinical traditions of Abraham's youth, it describes his awakening to the call of God and his awareness that God was one and was holy. An angel named Jahoel, whose functions and powers are lifted from rabbinical lore, takes Abraham to the seventh heaven where he is shown things past and things yet to be. He sees the temptation of Adam and Eve through sexual sin, and the murder of Cain. Azazel, an evil being, plays Satan's role. These details probably reflect a tradition that Abraham was the author of the first documents of the Bible. The revelation then turns to the future and shows the destruction of the temple, plagues upon the heathen, and the coming of the Messiah. It is probable that the composite document took final form in the last generation of the first century AD.

True to his character as revealed in Genesis, Abraham raises the question of evil and why God tolerates the rebellious Azazel. He receives the answer that evil has its origin in the free will of man. This apocalypse shows how faithful Jews struggled to understand the problem of evil during a time of great suffering in Judaism. It also illustrates the curious "doctrine of angels" of that period. Both Gnostic and Christian editing of the text has been noted by some scholars.

Abraham, Testament of Jewish apocryphal writing describing the death of Abraham. In the testament, when the angel Michael comes to take Abraham's soul, Abraham refuses to die. Reluctant to insist on the old man's death, Michael accedes to his request to see all creation before he dies. The angel transports Abraham by chariot into the heavens so that he can observe mankind. Abraham is so shocked at the perfidy of humanity that he curses the sinners, who die immediately. He then observes the judgment of a soul, and although angels take part in the trial he notes that the presiding judge is Abel. The merits and demerits of the soul seem equally balanced, but because of the intervention of Abraham, the judgment is favorable. Abraham then realizes the severity of his cursing of sinners, but the angel informs him that the premature death of those whom he had cursed was the means of atonement for their sins.

After his return to earth, Abraham again refuses to die. Death appears in all his horror and kills 7,000 servants of Abraham (who are subsequently raised to life), but the aged saint still will not die. Finally, Death grasps Abraham's hand and the angels lift his spirit to the heavens.

The account is found in several Greek manuscripts, the oldest perhaps dating from the 13th century AD, as well as in Slavonic, Romanian, Arabic, Ethiopic, and Coptic. The original language was probably Hebrew, from the first century AD, with the work possibly translated into Greek by a Christian. The testament also exists in a shorter version in which God comes to lift up the soul of Abraham during a dream. There is no attempt in the work to make a theological statement, but the portrayal of the angel Michael and of Death are typical of Jewish thought of the first century.

Acts, Apocryphal Writings purported to be accounts of apostolic achievements not recorded in Scripture.

Acts of Pilate See Pilate, Acts of (below).

Adam, Apocalypse of One of the best examples of Gnostic apocalyptic literature. In 1946, a farm worker discovered a number of ancient texts in a cave about 6 miles (10 kilometers) north of the Egyptian city of Nag Hammadi. The discovery included 13 codexes (predecessors of bound books) of Christian and non-Christian origin. The discovery was not immediately disclosed, so it was not until 1958 that a French scholar, Jean Doresse, revealed the existence of the Apocalypse of Adam to the public. The apocalypse is written in Coptic and stands as the last of five works in Codex V.

Although the author's true identity is unknown, the subtitle spuriously attributes the book to Adam or Seth: "An Apocalypse that Adam revealed to his son Seth in the seven hundredth year." Seth was often cast in the role of transmitter of truth by the writers of Gnostic literature (for example, the Gospel of the Egyptians, the Paraphrase of Shem).

The earliest existing copy of the Apocalypse of Adam is dated around AD 300 to 350, although it may have been written long before. Its frequent Gnostic references, its dependence on Jewish history, and its allusions to baptism have led some scholars to postulate an origin in the Jewish baptist sects of the first and second centuries. Parallels also exist between this work and third-century Manichean (a brand of Gnosticism) literature.

The Apocalypse of Adam is of great importance to students of Christian origins. For many years scholars have debated whether the Gnostic religion was a heretical outgrowth of Christianity or whether it was a movement of independent origins. Some scholars have argued that the Apocalypse of Adam is an example of an early, independent Gnosticism. If this proves to be the case the debate will certainly be simplified.

In addition to its introduction and conclusion, the Apocalypse of Adam may be divided into three parts: Adam's summary of significant past events, predictions of attempts to eliminate mankind by the evil creator-god, and predictions about the coming of the Enlightener who will show his people the way to the true God.

The apocalypse opens with Adam, supposedly on his deathbed, revealing the future secrets of the Gnostic people to Seth. These have been mystically communicated to him by three angelic beings. Adam bemoans his condition of perpetual slavery to the evil creator-god, brought about by the fall and mankind's subsequent loss of *gnosis* (knowledge). Typical of Gnostic literature, a sharp distinction is drawn between the evil creator-god who rules the earth and the true God of the universe, knowledge of whom brings authentic life. Adam predicts that the creator-god will jealously attempt to destroy mankind by a flood (the story of Noah) and by fire (the story of Sodom and Gomorrah) and thus keep mankind from knowledge of the true God. These attempts, however, will be foiled by the intervention of angelic beings sent from the God of truth. Finally, the true God will send the Enlightener who will teach *gnosis* to mankind so that they might know him. The creator-god will try to defeat the Enlightener but will be able to harm only his physical body. With the message of the Enlightener prevailing, mankind will turn from the creator-god and seek the true God through *gnosis*.

See also Gnosticism.

Adam, Apocryphal Books of Account of the life and death of Adam and Eve recorded in Latin, and in a Greek version known as the Apocalypse of Moses. Other minor versions of early Christian origin also exist. Like other apocryphal writings, the work is fanciful and of unknown authorship.

According to the Latin account, after their expulsion from Paradise Adam and Eve are hungry and unable to find food for seven days. In desperation a penitent Eve, assuming responsibility for tasting the forbidden fruit, suggests that Adam kill her. He refuses, and after a search they survive by eating animals' food. Adam suggests that as a penance they should stand fasting in the river up to their necks for 40 days, he in the Tigris, she in the Jordan. After 18 days Satan comes to Eve in the guise of an angel, tells her that the Lord has accepted her penance, and persuades her to leave the river. Coming to the Tigris where Adam is, Eve realizes that it was Satan who had spoken to her. Satan then explains that the reason for his fall was his refusal to worship man, a lower being.

The archangel Michael is then sent to Adam with seeds so that he can learn to till the land. In a dream Eve sees Cain kill Abel, and in an attempt to prevent the murder by separating the brothers, Cain is made a farmer and Abel a shepherd. Subsequently a third son, Seth, is born. Adam receives a message from God that he is to die because he has obeyed the word of his wife rather than the instructions of God. When Adam is later in pain and close to death, he explains to Seth that Satan had tempted Eve to eat the forbidden fruit and that she in turn had persuaded him to taste it. Seth and Eve journey to the gates of Paradise to plead with God for Adam's life. On the way Seth is attacked and bitten by a snake. At Paradise, Michael explains to them that Adam must die. Seth observes the burial of Adam and Abel.

Before Eve's death the following week, she asks Seth to make a record of the lives of his parents on tablets of stone and clay, so that if the Lord shows his anger with the world by water, the clay will be dissolved and the stone remain; if by fire, the stone will be broken up and the clay baked hard. Eve also warns Seth to mourn for six days only and not on the Sabbath.

The text of the Greek version is similar to that of the Latin, except that the Greek version includes a description of Adam's resurrection (added later to the Latin) and a detailed account by Eve of her temptation and fall. The burial of Adam and the initial refusal of the earth to accept the body of the slain Abel are also elaborately described in the Greek account. Both versions are probably derived from Hebrew originals dating from the first century AD.

Ahikar, Book of Near Eastern folktale from the sixth or seventh century BC showing the reward of ingratitude. According to the story, Ahikar, secretary of Sennacherib, king of Assyria, was renowned for his wisdom. Childless even though he had 60 wives, Ahikar adopted his sister's son, Nadan, and reared him to be his successor in Sennacherib's court. Ahikar diligently educated his adopted son, who nevertheless turned out to be bad and even forged documents to have his benefactor condemned to death. Ahikar was spared through his friendship with the executioner and was concealed until the wrath of the king cooled. Later, when Sennacherib had occasion to wish for his wisdom, Ahikar was brought on the scene, long-haired, disheveled, and with fingernails like eagles' claws. Once again in the king's favor, Ahikar sternly rebuked his unscrupulous nephew. In response to Ahikar's rebuke, Nadan's body swelled up and his stomach burst open.

Ahikar's story has interesting parallels with OT wisdom books and also with some of the parables of Jesus. References to Ahikar occur in the apocryphal book of Tobit, in the Greek philosopher Democritus, in the apocalyptic Testaments of the Twelve Patriarchs, as well as in the Koran. The story, originally in Aramaic, also survives in Syriac, Arabic, Armenian, Ethiopic, and Greek, though with considerable variations in the versions.

Akhmim Fragment Document found in a tomb in Akhmim in Egypt and containing the apocryphal Gospel of Peter. *See* Peter, Preaching of (below).

Allogenes Supreme Gnostic work ("The Most High Stranger"), discovered in 1946 in an urn near Nag Hammadi (Egypt). The Neoplatonist historian Porphyry, as well as later Syriac Christian writings against heresy, mentioned the works of Allogenes (whose name means "foreigner" or "stranger"). Allogenes Supreme, a Gnostic "apocalypse" written in Coptic, contains an account of the creation of the higher world, exalting Barbelo the celestial mother. The existing copy was made during the fourth century, but the original may date back to the second century.

Andrew, Acts of Apocryphal work describing purported miracles and the martyrdom in Greece of the apostle Andrew, Peter's brother. Its theme is the virtue of turning away from materialism and the transitory values of the world to an asceticism associated with dedication of life to God. The earliest fragment available is in the Vatican. The original probably dated from the second century AD and was probably long, verbose, and tedious. Feeling that it had merit, Gregory of Tours in the sixth century wrote a concise account of the miracles of Andrew from an original, now lost. The account of the martyrdom of Andrew probably circulated separately.

Among the many miracles Gregory recorded was one concerning Exoōs, a noble youth from Thessalonica, who, having heard of Andrew's preaching and miracles, comes to him at Philippi, is converted, and remains with him. Finding bribery useless and refusing to listen to Andrew, the youth's parents set fire to the house where the Christians are staying. As the flames roar, Exoōs prays that the Lord will extinguish the fire and sprinkles it with water. Thereupon the flames die out. The parents and the crowd, claiming that the youth is now a sorcerer, climb ladders to enter the house and kill the inhabitants, but God blinds the intruders. Although it is night, a light shines out from the house, sight is restored to those who have been blinded, and all except the youth's parents are converted. The parents die soon afterward, and Exoōs remains with Andrew, spending his inheritance on the poor. Returning to Thessalonica, Exoōs heals a man who has been paralyzed for 23 years, and subsequently Exoōs and Andrew perform further miracles and preach to the people.

In Patrae the maidservant of Maximilla, wife of the proconsul Aegeates, comes to Andrew and implores him to heal her mistress, whose fever is so severe that her husband is standing at her bedside threatening to kill himself with a sword the moment she dies. Telling the proconsul to put up his sword, Andrew takes Maximilla's hand and the fever leaves her. Ordering food for her, Andrew then refuses Aegeates' offer of 100 pieces of silver. After performing many miracles in the city, Andrew receives a message from Maximilla to come and heal the slave of the proconsul's brother, Stratocles. The apostle restores the boy to health, and his master believes.

Maximilla, to the fury of her husband, spends considerable time listening to the preaching of Andrew and is also converted. She then refuses to sleep with her husband and one night even substitutes a servant for herself. Details of subsequent events are found in the account of the martyrdom. Aegeates, in anger, holds Andrew responsible for his wife's alienation and has him arrested. After preaching from prison, Andrew is taken to be crucified by the seashore. When the Christian Stratocles sees Andrew being manhandled by the soldiers, he fights his way through, and he and Andrew walk together to the place of crucifixion. Aegeates, fearing his brother, orders the soldiers not to interfere. At the seashore the soldiers follow the proconsul's command that Andrew be tied, not nailed, to the cross so that his death will be lingering and he will be eaten by dogs. After two days he is still speaking to people from the cross, and many come to Aegeates demanding Andrew's release. Arriving at the scene, the proconsul sees that Andrew is indeed alive, and Aegeates approaches the apostle to release him. Andrew demands that he be allowed to die and meet his Lord. As they watch, Andrew dies and the onlookers weep as Maximilla and Stratocles take down his body from the cross. Maximilla remains apart from her husband and continues as a Christian.

Andrew, Story of Legendary fragment existing only in the Coptic language. In the legend coming from the late second century AD, a woman kills her child in the desert and gives the remains to a dog. She flees when the apostle Andrew and Philemon approach, but the dog tells what happened. Andrew prays and the child, being vomited forth, is restored to life and laughs and cries.

Andrew and Matthias, Acts of Lengthy document of highly questionable authenticity, probably dating from the late second century AD. This book was one of many apocryphal "acts" intended to supplement the NT book of Acts by providing more information about the apostles. The fourth-century church historian Eusebius described this work and others like it as heretical, absurd, and spurious.

In this story, the apostles cast lots to determine where each should go. Matthias (Matthew in some versions) is sent to the country of the man-eaters, where he soon requires rescue from a cannibal feast. The Lord then sends Andrew to save him. Andrew arrives in time to do so, and Matthias is then carried off by a cloud. Now alone, Andrew is arrested and tortured, being dragged through the city that he nearly destroys by calling forth water from a statue. Eventually, impressed by Andrew's miracles, the people repent and release him. Andrew next draws a plan for a church, has it built, baptizes the people, and gives them the ordinances of the Lord.

Andrew and Paul, Acts of Fragmentary apocryphal story, existing only in Coptic fragments, about the arrival of the apostles Andrew and Paul by sea at a city. In the story, Paul, instructing Andrew to rescue him, visits the underworld. There he meets Judas, who explains that he worshiped Satan after Jesus had pardoned him for the betrayal. Andrew rescues Paul, who returns carrying a piece of wood. Although Andrew is asked to heal a child, some Jews are skeptical and the city gates remain closed to the apostles. Paul strikes the gates with his piece of wood, and the gates are swallowed up into the earth. Astonished at the miracle, 27,000 Jews are converted.

Apostles, Epistle of the Letter purporting to come from

the 11 apostles to the churches "of the east and the west, of the north and the south, declaring and imparting to you that which concerns our Lord Jesus Christ." Some believe that the epistle was written in Asia Minor about AD 160; others think that it originated in Egypt. It is probably to be dated near the middle of the second century. In existence are a mutilated Coptic manuscript of the fourth or fifth century, a complete version in Ethiopic, and a fragment in Latin. The epistle was unknown until the discovery in 1895 of the Coptic manuscript.

After an introduction there is a declaration that "our Lord and Redeemer Jesus Christ is God the Son of God who was sent of God the Lord of the whole world." Then follows a summary of a number of incidents from the Gospels, including a negative statement of the Golden Rule: "Love your enemies, and what you would not that man do to you, that do to no man." Chapter 24 introduces the subject of the resurrection followed by a series of questions by the disciples with answers by Jesus. A prophecy of the conversion of Paul appears in chapter 31. In chapter 43 the five wise virgins are identified as "Faith and Love and Grace and Peace and Hope"; the names of the foolish are "Knowledge, Understanding (Perception), Obedience, Patience, and Compassion." The question-and-answer format of a substantial part of the work is reminiscent of the style of some of the texts found in the Gnostic library at Nag Hammadi, especially the Apocryphon of John. However, warnings that Cerinthus and Simon (ch 7) are "enemies of our Lord Jesus Christ" make it clear that this is not a Gnostic document. The epistle contains numerous evidences of orthodox influence, along with clear indications of a departure from apostolic Christianity.

Apostles, Gospel of the Twelve One of a large number of heretical "gospels" circulating in the earliest centuries of the Christian church along with the Gospels of Matthew, Mark, Luke, and John. The Gospel of the Twelve Apostles was first mentioned by name in comments on Luke 1:1 by the Christian theologian Origen (c. AD 185–254). Some scholars think it may have been the same as the Gospel of the Ebionites, quoted in a few early Christian writings. Nothing is known directly of the Gospel of the Twelve Apostles.

Arabic Gospel of the Infancy One of several "gospels of the infancy" found in the apocryphal NT. This one from about the fifth century contains an account of the birth of Jesus, including the visits of the shepherds and the magi, the flight into Egypt, and miracles performed by Jesus as a boy. Details of the early period of Jesus' life are given, about which the canonical Gospels (Matthew, Mark, Luke, John) say nothing. An interesting facet of the miracle stories is the role in many of them of Mary, the mother of Jesus, in contrast to the record of the miracles in the canonical Gospels. The Arabic Gospel may have been written in Syriac and translated into Arabic. Some of its stories are also found in the Koran and other Islamic writings. Study of this apocryphal gospel reveals its sharp contrast with the canonical accounts, but it also indicates how much this and similar writings had to do with the growing veneration of the virgin Mary.

Arabic History of Joseph the Carpenter Fourth-century AD account of the life and death of Joseph—with information supposedly supplied by Jesus. According to this account, Joseph the carpenter becomes a widower after fathering four sons and two daughters (ch 2). He is entrusted with the care of Mary in his 90th year (ch 14).

Thus, according to this account, the brothers and sisters of Jesus are Joseph's children by a previous marriage. Joseph is said to have died at the age of 111 years. The document, which exists in both Arabic and Coptic versions, contains the statement that Mary "must look for the same end of life as other mortals" (ch 18). Hence, it has been dated as earlier than the fifth century, when the idea of the "assumption of Mary into heaven" was being promoted.

Aristeas, Letter of Early account of the relationships between Judaism and Hellenism in Egypt during the period when the Hebrew OT was translated into Greek (the Septuagint). The author, Aristeas, who identifies himself as an Alexandrian court attendant under Ptolemy Philadelphus II (ruled 283–247 BC), purports to give information about the translation procedures. The most probable date for the Letter of Aristeas (estimates vary from 200 BC to AD 50) is the end of the second century BC.

As part of his massive library project, King Ptolemy shows interest in the Jewish law. Aristeas uses the occasion to request the emancipation with remuneration of all Jewish slaves in the kingdom and King Ptolemy accedes to the request. The king asks that the high priest in Jerusalem select translators for the project. There follows a lengthy description of gifts sent to Eleazar, the high priest, with special emphasis upon an exquisite table. And then Aristeas describes the temple, the priests, the vestments of the high priest, and the defense system for the temple, followed by a brief description of Palestine and its environs.

In the next section, the high priest talks with Aristeas and the translators before their departure to Alexandria. A summary of his speech includes a careful defense of the law from a philosophical viewpoint. The king gives a lavish banquet for the 72 translators (6 from each tribe) when they arrive in Alexandria. Each translator gives a brilliant answer to the king's specific questions at the seven successive nights of celebration. The name of each translator and his question and answer are recorded. Then the work is completed on the island of Pharos in 72 days and is praised by the Alexandrian Jews and the king. The translators are dismissed with lavish gifts.

In the epilogue, the author claims to have been an eyewitness to the events and maintains that his report is accurate. This is not believed by modern scholars. Its embellished and legendary quality was recognized in the fifth century BC. Aristeas's discussion of the translation procedure was obviously a convenient literary frame on which to hang a defense of Judaism to the heathen world. Religious liberalism and loyalty to basic Jewish beliefs were skillfully combined to plead for political toleration for the Jews. Many specifics of the Letter of Aristeas are questionable, but its basic picture of how the Septuagint translation came to be made is credible. *See* the discussion of the Septuagint in Bible, Versions of the (Ancient).

Armenian Gospel of the Infancy Legendary account of the infancy and boyhood of Jesus Christ, one of many apocryphal gospels intended to supplement the four NT Gospels by providing more details about Jesus' early life. It was probably translated into Armenian from a Syriac original. Nestorian missionaries reportedly brought an "infancy gospel" into Armenia about AD 590, but evidently not the Armenian Gospel in its present form.

Sources for the Armenian Gospel included two books containing legendary material about Christ's infancy, the Protevangelium of James and the Infancy Gospel of Thomas. The Armenian Gospel amplifies the material of these two texts considerably, making many novel additions to the life of Jesus. For example, Joseph searches for a midwife and meets Eve, who has come to witness the fulfillment of the promised Redeemer-seed (Gn 3:15). Later the magi bring the testament Adam gave to Seth. Jesus, accused of causing a child's death, is cleared when the child is raised from the dead.

Ascension of Isaiah *See* Isaiah, Ascension of (below).

Ascents of James *See* James, Ascents of (below).

Asenath, Prayer of Jewish story about the wife of Joseph when he was in Egypt (Gn 41:45) and known by several titles—The Life and Confession of Asenath, The Book of Joseph and Asenath, and variations of the above. It was apparently very popular in the early and medieval Christian church. Latin, Syriac, Slavonic, Rumanian, and Ethiopic versions, in addition to 40 Armenian copies, have been found.

Modern scholars tend to see the source of the novel in the Hellenistic Judaism prevalent in Egypt from 100 BC to AD 100. Asenath seems to serve as a model for any proselyte to Judaism. If that understanding is correct, the story gives valuable insight into the less legalistic attitudes of a sector of pre-Christian Judaism. Repentant realization of the hopelessness of one's sinful condition and casting oneself upon the mercies of God play a large part in the story.

The original was probably written in Greek and is divided into two major parts. Part I deals with Asenath's pampered life prior to meeting Joseph, his initial rejection of her because of her idolatry, and her consequent repentance in ashes. Asenath calls upon God in prayer, and he sends an angel to her to announce her forgiveness and to say that her name is now written in the Book of Life. Joseph returns and marvels at Asenath's new beauty, rejoicing at her conversion. With Pharaoh's blessing they are married the next day.

Part II describes the period when Joseph's father, Jacob, and his family have come to Egypt. Desiring Asenath, the elder son of Pharaoh tempts Joseph's brothers Dan and Gad to help him kidnap her. The plan is foiled by Joseph's other brothers, who then wish to kill Dan and Gad, but Asenath pleads successfully for their lives. Pharaoh leaves the crown to Joseph, who rules 40 years and then returns the reign to Pharaoh's younger son.

Asher, Testament of *See* Testaments of the Twelve Patriarchs (below).

Assumption of Moses *See* Moses, Assumption of (below).

Barnabas, Acts of Document of one of several distinct cycles of tradition about Barnabas, the apostle Paul's companion, this one linking him with Cyprus. This work, whose full title is The Journeyings and Martyrdom of Saint Barnabas the Apostle, was probably composed in Cyprus at the end of the fifth or the beginning of the sixth century AD.

The book purports to be a first-person account written by John Mark. He claims to have left the apostles in Perga (cf. Acts 13:13) so he could sail to the West but was prevented. When he tried to rejoin them in Antioch, Paul prohibited him. Consequently, after some dispute, John Mark and Barnabas sailed for Cyprus. After preaching and healing many people, Barnabas encountered his old adversary, Bar-Jesus, who finally stirred up the Jews to capture him. Leading Barnabas out of the city of

Salamis, they circled around him and burned him alive. John Mark and some other believers escaped with his ashes and buried them in a cave along with scriptures Barnabas had received from Matthew. John Mark then left for Alexandria to minister there.

Barnabas, Epistle of This anonymous letter addresses a question commonly asked throughout the early church: What should Christianity's relationship be to Judaism? Clement of Alexandria quoted from this document frequently and ascribed it to "Barnabas, who himself also preached with the apostle [Paul]." Jerome believed the same. But the writer does not claim to be Barnabas, and the earliest claims of authorship come only from Alexandrian church leaders. The literary and interpretive style is entirely Alexandrian, so it is assumed that the epistle was written in Alexandria.

The author of this epistle unequivocally denies any connection between Judaism and the gospel of Jesus Christ. At the same time, he does not say that the OT opposes the NT; rather, he sees Christianity everywhere in the Law and the Prophets. He holds that all the Judaistic rites and ceremonies are mystical pointers to Christ and that an evil angel has blinded the Jews from understanding this.

The epistle mentions the destruction of Jerusalem, so it was not written before AD 70. There was a second devastation of Jerusalem in AD 132 that ended the revolt of Bar-Kochba. This defeat would have served the author's purposes so well that he would surely have referred to it if he were writing after the event. Many scholars suggest that the letter was composed around 130, since this was a period of strong Jewish nationalism. This nationalism would have pressured many Jewish Christians to return to Judaism, and so the author of the Epistle of Barnabas wrote to defend Christianity against Judaism.

The Epistle of Barnabas is composed of two parts. The first section (chs 1–17) contains allegorical interpretations of the OT. These highly spiritual and mystical interpretations are intended to oppose Jewish legalism and explain how the OT prophesied of Jesus Christ. The author concedes that righteous people, such as Moses, David, and the prophets, understood the true meaning of Mosaic law, but he contends that the rest of the nation of Israel had misconstrued God's covenant. Therefore, the Jews lost their claim to the covenant's blessings, which were transferred to the Christians instead. This allegorical style of interpretation was very popular among Alexandrian church leaders. The NT epistle of Hebrews also makes use of this type of interpretation. The author of the Epistle of Barnabas often quotes from the Septuagint, though the quotes are somewhat loosely recited.

A Latin version of the first section was all that was known of the Epistle of Barnabas until the discovery of Codex Sinaiticus in 1859. This codex contained the first known Greek version of the Epistle of Barnabas, which was appended to the books of the NT along with The Shepherd and the Didache. The Greek version contains a second section that begins, "Now let us pass on to quite a different sort of instruction." This section contains moral precepts that contrast the way of darkness with the way of light, much of which seems to be transcribed from the "Two Ways" of the Didache. It has little connection with the first section. This has led many scholars to conclude that the second section was added by another writer at some later date.

Barnabas, Gospel of Long Italian work actually written in the fourth century by a proselyte to Islam. He probably sought to capitalize on the mysterious mention of such a gospel in the Gelasian Decree, written not later than the sixth century AD. To date, no other evidence of an authentic gospel by Barnabas has been uncovered, a fact that has led many scholars to doubt whether it ever existed.

Bartholomew, Acts of Early Christian novel purporting to describe the last days and death of the apostle Bartholomew. The work is also known as The Martyrdom of the Holy and Glorious Apostle Bartholomew. It may date back to the fifth or sixth century AD and was evidently well received, for copies exist in Latin, Greek, Armenian, and Ethiopic.

In the Acts, Bartholomew goes to India, takes up residence in a pagan temple, and causes its false oracle to cease. Bartholomew then heals a demoniac, thus drawing the attention of King Polymius. Bartholomew also heals the king's demon-possessed daughter. Next, he casts the false god out of the temple. After this display of power, many believe the gospel. The king's brother, however, is enraged and has Bartholomew beaten and beheaded. His rash action is soon punished, for he is strangled to death by a demon. The good King Polymius becomes bishop and serves 20 years.

Bartholomew, Apocalypse of Fragmentary Coptic texts that have some similarities to the apocryphal Gospel of Bartholomew. A few scholars have felt that two works were represented in these fragments, a gospel and also an apocalypse. Though this hypothesis has been generally abandoned, references to the debatable Apocalypse of Bartholomew still appear.

See also Bartholomew, Gospel of (below).

Bartholomew, Book of the Resurrection of Christ by Apocryphal work existing only in Coptic and probably dating from the fifth or sixth century AD. Like many similar writings of doubtful authenticity, it claims to supplement the accounts of Jesus found in the biblical Gospels. The book was supposedly addressed by Bartholomew to his son, Thaddaeus, who was warned in it not to let this book "come into the hand of any man who is an unbeliever and a heretic." The book can hardly be regarded as a narrative; its aim is obviously the glorification of Bartholomew, who sees things that are hidden from others. The text contains many breaks; contradictions abound and a disregard of history is evident. Two different persons bury the body of Jesus: Joseph and Philogenes, father of a boy healed by Jesus. Mary, the mother of Jesus, is confused with Mary Magdalene. In the account of the Last Supper the author goes far beyond biblical statements about the bread and wine: "His Body was on the Table about which they were assembled; and they divided it. They saw the blood of Jesus pouring out as living blood down into the cup." Imaginative details also embellish the account of the resurrection. Christ, for example, brings Adam back with him from hades. The story of doubting Thomas has been greatly amplified.

The most complete text of the Book of the Resurrection is in the British Museum in London. Several other fragments exist, probably from an earlier version.

Bartholomew, Gospel of One of many apocryphal gospels appearing after the second century under the name of some illustrious figure. The early church was aware not only of the existence of these writings but also of their fictitious character. In the fourth century the church historian Eusebius described them as heretical, spurious, absurd, and impious. Later a Gospel of Bartholomew was mentioned by name, along with several other

Gnostic gospels, in the prologue of Jerome's commentary on Matthew's Gospel. However, there is no evidence that Jerome had seen such a book or that it actually existed.

A work called Questions of Bartholomew does exist in Greek, Latin, and Slavonic texts—the Greek dating possibly from the fifth or sixth century. Its text has Bartholomew asking Jesus where he went after the Crucifixion and Jesus telling him that he went into hades. Later Bartholomew is pictured as asking Mary to tell how she conceived the incomprehensible or bore him that cannot be carried. Mary warns him that if she began to tell them, fire would come forth from her mouth and consume all the world, but the apostle persists. As she tells the story of the angelic visitation and the Annunciation, fire comes from her mouth. The world is about to come to an end, but Jesus intervenes and places his hand over Mary's mouth. The apostles also ask to see the bottomless pit and "the things which are in the heavens." Bartholomew is shown the adversary of men, Beliar, restrained by 660 angels and bound with fiery chains. When Bartholomew treads upon his neck, Beliar explains that he had first been called Satanael and later Satan, describes the creation of the angels, and tells how he fell and how he was able to deceive Eve. Finally, Bartholomew is said to have asked Jesus about the greatest sin. Jesus replies that to say anything evil against a faithful worshiper of God is to sin against the Holy Spirit.

Baruch, Apocalypse of Two different pseudepigraphal works.

1. Pseudepigraphal Jewish document of 87 chapters, written in Hebrew and translated into Greek and from Greek into Syriac. Only a few lines of the Hebrew original still exist, quoted in rabbinic writings. The Syriac manuscript dates from the sixth or seventh century AD and is the only complete text. It shows evidence of multiple authorship and dependence on the book of 2 Esdras in the Apocrypha. Similarity of many expressions to those in the NT suggests that the original may have been composed in the last half of the first century or the first half of the second century.

   The text is in seven sections of unequal length containing both prose and poetic material. The subjects dealt with are the Messiah and his future kingdom, Israel's past woes, and the destruction of Jerusalem by the Babylonians. Theological questions such as sin and suffering, free will, the number of people to be saved by the Messiah, and the resurrection of the righteous are not always treated consistently within the text. Some passages paint an optimistic picture of Israel's future; others are deeply pessimistic. In general the world is a scene of corruption for which no remedy exists. A new and spiritual world is at hand: "Whatever is now is nothing, but that which shall be is very great. For everything that is corruptible shall pass away, and everything that dies shall depart and all the present time, which is defiled with evils." The alternating optimism and pessimism may reflect the changing fortunes of Judaism in the first and second centuries AD or simply the outlook of the different authors. The message of hope is directed to those who keep the law of Moses: "For the righteous justly hope for the end, and without fear depart from this habitation, because they have with Thee a store of works preserved in treasuries."

   The final section of the book is identified as "the epistle which Baruch, the son of Neriah, sent to the nine and a half tribes." It was sent by being "bound to the neck of the eagle," probably meaning that it was intended for the Jews scattered outside Palestine (the Diaspora).

   Baruch was the prophet Jeremiah's companion and secretary (Jer 36:4-8). His name was attached to a number of apocryphal and pseudepigraphal writings composed long after his death. The Syriac Apocalypse of Baruch is also called 2 Baruch to distinguish it clearly from the book of Baruch (1 Baruch) in the Apocrypha.

2. Pseudepigraphal document of 17 chapters, also called the Greek Apocalypse of Baruch or 3 Baruch. It is preserved in Greek, Ethiopic, Armenian, and Slavonic manuscripts. It was first published in Venice in 1609 and then in 1868, although its existence was suggested by the early Christian theologian Origen. Like 2 Baruch, this apocalypse seems to be a composite document of the second century AD but in contrast is a Christian document intended to warn unconverted Jews and to encourage Christians to be patient in dealing with them.

Basilides, Gospel of Polemic commentary on the Gospels by a second-century Gnostic. Basilides's writings remain only as allusions and fragments in later works by several church fathers. Basilides taught in Alexandria during the reign of the Roman emperor Hadrian (AD 117–138). His teacher, Glaucias, claimed to be a first-hand interpreter of the apostle Peter. Basilides asserted that his Gnostic scheme emerged from Peter's views on the relationship between God and Christ. He described God paradoxically as a nonexistent Being who "generated" three Sonships. Through successive ascents and enlightenments, the gospel of the supreme God (the Gospel of Light) eventually descended upon Jesus.

Origen stated that "Basilides dared to write a gospel According to Basilides." Clement of Alexandria and the writer of a fourth-century fragment, Acta Archelai, thought that Origen referred to an apocryphal gospel, the teaching of which was deduced from Irenaeus's account. Today, more in line with Hippolytus's understanding of Basilides, this work is regarded as merely a commentary on the Gospels. Basilides was probably not responsible for the magical rites and libertinism of the Basilidians, a Gnostic sect led by his son Isidore and continuing in Egypt to the end of the century.

Benjamin, Testament of See Testaments of the Twelve Patriarchs (below).

Birth of Mary An early Gnostic writing. "The Gnostics have a book which they call the Birth (or Descent) of Mary, in which are horrible and deadly things." So said the fourth-century bishop Ephiphanius in describing the Birth of Mary, a work that has not survived. The Birth of Mary claimed to reveal what Zechariah, father of John the Baptist, saw in the temple—namely, the Jewish god in the form of an ass. That Jews and Christians worshiped an ass-god was commonly held by their critics in those days. This blasphemous work should not be confused with the Gospel of the Birth of Mary, a fanciful but relatively harmless account of Mary's birth, early life, and marriage to Joseph.

Birth of Mary, Gospel of the Collection of legends purporting to tell Mary's story from birth to King Herod's slaughter of the children in Bethlehem. The earliest such manuscript is called Book of the Nativity of Mary or Gospel of James because it claimed to be written by James, half brother of Jesus. It was written by AD 150, since Justin, an early Christian writer, named it in his *Dialogues* (165). It was rediscovered for the West by Postel, who

Gospel of Mary Papyrus
Oxyrhynchus 3525, third century

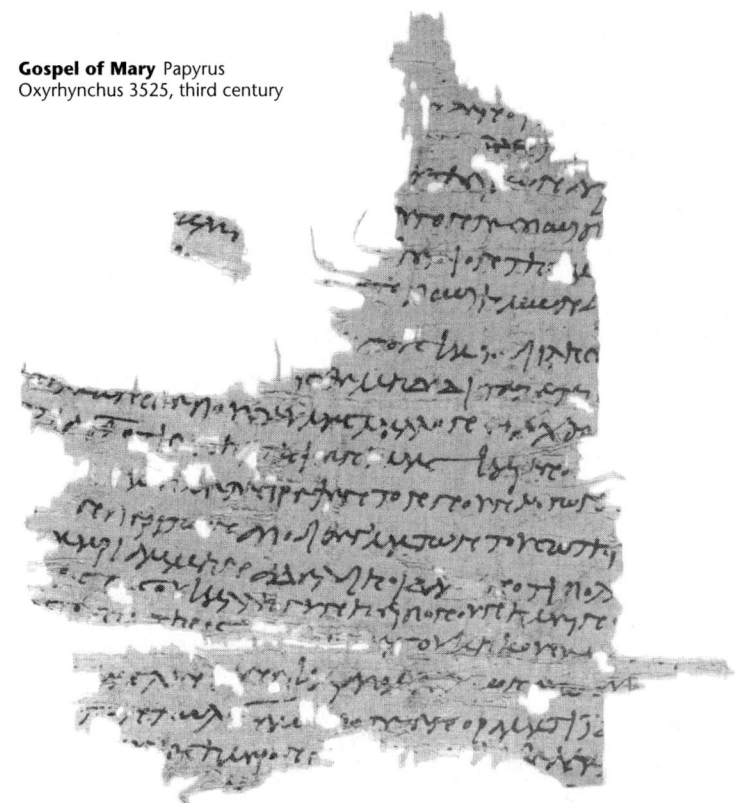

dinner. After Judas leaves the room, Jesus touches the cock and it comes to life. He instructs it to follow Judas and to report his dealings. The cock returns and tells about the forthcoming betrayal, mentioning Paul of Tarsus as one of those involved. The disciples weep. Jesus sends the cock to the sky for a thousand years.

A similar story exists as a fragment in Sahidic Coptic. In the Coptic version the resurrection of the cock is a symbol of the resurrection of Christ.

Coptic Lives of the Virgin Apocryphal works concerning Mary, the mother of Jesus, in the Egyptian language of Coptic. *See* Virgin, Life of the (below).

Corinthians, Third Apocryphal correspondence purporting to be between the apostle Paul and the Corinthian church. Written during the second century and known as 3 Corinthians, the work consists of three parts: an epistle allegedly from Stephanus of Corinth to Paul concerning two false apostles, Simon and Cleobius; a brief narrative telling of its delivery; and Paul's

translated it from Greek into Latin (*Protevangelium Jacobi*, 1552). Before it was lost, two major Latin revisions of it had been produced: Pseudo-Matthew and the Gospel of the Nativity of Mary, compiled around the sixth and ninth centuries respectively. These revisions amplified the Book of the Nativity of Mary with more fanciful legends and were the basis for the Golden Legends of James of Voragine (1230–1298), which in turn became instrumental in fostering veneration of Mary.

According to the Book of the Nativity of Mary, Mary is born to rich, barren parents (Joachim and Anna) through angelic response to their prayers. They dedicate Mary to the Lord. At six months Mary walks seven steps, so Anna makes her bedroom a sanctuary, allowing nothing unclean to enter, and vows that Mary will walk again only in the temple. At age three Mary is placed in the temple and receives food from an angel. On Mary's twelfth birthday the high priest asks God what to do and is told to marry her to a widower. Elderly Joseph is chosen when a dove springs from his rod. Months later, Mary "gives birth" to Jesus in Bethlehem's cave, through a light so bright that none can see; the light gradually withdraws and the Child appears at Mary's breast. The Book of the Nativity of Mary closes with the magi and Herod's slaughter of infants. Mary saves Jesus by wrapping him in swaddling clothes and laying him in a manger.

Recently another Greek fragment, this one from the Gospel of Mary, was found (see photo). The fragment is too little to tell us much about the content of this gospel.

Book of the Cock Apocryphal story preserved by the church of Ethiopia and still read there on the Thursday before Easter. According to the Book of the Cock, on the night of the Last Supper, Akrosina, wife of Simon the Pharisee, presents Jesus with a nicely prepared cock for

reply and refutation of the false doctrine. The sequence of letters was originally part of the Acts of Paul, a longer apocryphal document, but circulated on its own as well—it even found its way into the text of the Armenian Bible. It pretends to explain the reference in 2 Corinthians 2:4 to a letter written in great distress.

According to an early church father, Tertullian *(On Baptism)*, the author of 3 Corinthians was a presbyter (church leader) of Asia who forged it out of love for Paul shortly after AD 160. That presbyter's removal from office indicates the stern attitude of the early Christians toward the writing of documents falsely claiming apostolic origin.

Dan, Testament of *See* Testaments of the Twelve Patriarchs (below).

Dialogue of the Redeemer Christian Gnostic document, also called the Dialogue of the Savior. The document was found in the ancient Nag Hammadi Library at the modern city of Nag Hammadi (Upper Egypt) in 1946. The Dialogue is a fictitious account of a conversation between Jesus and some of his disciples in which they discuss questions about the universe, humanity, the end times, and salvation. The manuscript is in poor condition. Its authorship and origin are unknown, though it was possibly written in Egypt during the second or third centuries AD.

Discourse of Theodosius Coptic Boharic version of the Assumption of the Virgin and a main source for the Coptic form of that legend. *See* Virgin, Assumption of the (below).

Doctrina Addaei Expanded Syriac form of the Epistles of Christ and Abgarus, written about AD 400. The Doctrina Addaei tells a story about the contacts between Abgar

(Abgarus), king of Edessa, and Jesus Christ. King Abgar, suffering from an unspecified ailment, is said to have sent a messenger to Jesus bearing the king's written request for healing along with an offer of sanctuary for Jesus in his kingdom. Jesus responds orally, promising to send one of his followers to Abgar after his own ascension to heaven. Abgar's envoy also takes back a self-portrait of Jesus that becomes the pride of Edessa. Later Addai visits the kingdom, heals Abgar, and establishes Christianity there. *See* Abgarus, Letters of Christ and (above).

Ebionites, Gospel of the Gospel quoted by one early Christian writer, Epiphanius (fourth century), in a work against heresies. The Gospel of the Ebionites is possibly the same as the apocryphal Gospel of the Hebrews, although some scholars associate it with the Gospel of the Nazarenes. The Ebionites were vegetarians; Epiphanius's citations stress the vegetarian diets of John the Baptist and Jesus.

Egyptians, Gospel of the Two apocryphal works with the same name.

1. Apocryphal second-century AD Greek writing, mentioned by the early church writers, Clement and Origen. Used in Egypt, the composition seems to have contained and propagated Gnostic teachings, especially those advocated in Syria by Simon and Menander. According to these Gnostics, marriage, eating meat, and procreation were evil. Clement may have quoted from this writing to refute the beliefs of the Encratites, who broadly agreed with the Syrian Gnostics on those matters. The Gnostics' depreciation of women was reflected in the quotations Clement used.

2. Composition discovered in 1946 at Chenoboskion (Egypt) in the Nag Hammadi collection of Gnostic writing. The principal title of the work, described in the colophon as "Gospel of the Egyptians" was "Sacred Book of the Great Invisible Spirit." This work dealt with emanations from "the primal spirit of the cosmos" and perhaps was a product of the Barbelo Gnostic sect.

Eldad and Medad, Book of Pre-Christian pseudepigraphic composition containing the alleged prophecies of Eldad and Medad, two persons appointed as elders by Moses (Nm 11:26). Since the nature of their prophecy was not specified, it gave rise to a lost work that is quoted in the Shepherd of Hermas as follows: "The Lord is near to them who return to Him, as it is written in Eldad and Medad who prophesied to the people in the wilderness" (Vision II, ch 3). That is the only source of information concerning the lost book.

Eugnostos, Letter of Gnostic work. Found near the modern city of Nag Hammadi, the Letter of Eugnostos was written in Coptic by a teacher to his disciple. Both author and date of composition are unknown. An early example of non-Christian Gnostic writing, it perhaps served as the basis for a Christian Gnostic composition, "The Wisdom of Jesus Christ."

The Letter of Eugnostos attempts to prove the existence of an invisible spiritual realm. It also stresses God's remoteness from humanity.

Eve, Gospel of Gnostic and apocalyptic writings, known solely through a citation by Epiphanius, a late fourth-century metropolitan of Cyprus. Epiphanius quoted the Gospel of Eve in a biting refutation of Gnostic and Origenistic teachings. Evidently a cult had formed around Eve as if her name implied revelation

because the serpent had spoken to her in the Garden of Eden. Epiphanius's quotation from the Gospel of Eve roughly translates: "I stood on a high mountain and saw a giant and a feeble man, and I heard a voice like thunder. 'Come near me and listen,' and he spoke to me saying, 'I am you and you are me. Wherever you are, there I am. I am spread through all things, and any place you are able to retire into or take shelter in me; and, taking shelter in me, you take shelter in yourself.'"

Ezekiel, Apocryphal Noncanonical book of Ezekiel mentioned by Josephus, first-century Jewish historian. An apocryphal Ezekiel is cited in five early Christian writings and a recent archaeological discovery. Bishop Epiphanius (fourth century) cited an Ezekiel parable, in proof of the resurrection of the interdependent soul and body, about a blind man and a lame man collaborating to rob an orchard. Clement of Rome, writing to the Corinthians (AD 90?), and Clement of Alexandria in two of his writings (AD 200?) have noncanonical Ezekiel quotations. An Ezekiel apocryphon is mentioned in the pseudo-Athanasian canon (purporting to list canonical books of the Bible) and is named in the stichometry (prose written in rhythmic phrases) of Nicephorus, Patriarch of Constantinople (AD 806–815). In 1940 Campbell Bonner published Greek papyrus fragments that confirm the existence of an apocryphal Ezekiel.

Ezra, Fourth Book of Alternate name for the apocryphal book 2 Esdras. *See* Esdras, Second Book of.

Gad, Testament of *See* Testaments of the Twelve Patriarchs (below).

Genesis Apocryphon Name given to one of the seven large Dead Sea Scrolls recovered from the first Qumran cave in 1947. With three others it came into the possession of the Syrian archbishop of Jerusalem but could not be unrolled and photographed because it was badly preserved, having not been kept in an earthen jar like the others. Some small pieces were detached, however, and certain words on them indicated that it might be an apocryphal Aramaic work connected with the patriarch Enoch. Further scraps spoke of Lamech, however, thus the scroll was tentatively named for that ancient person.

Eventually it was unrolled and found to be not only damaged but incomplete; the beginning and the end were missing. The inner portion had been best preserved, but considerable damage had been done to the text by the ink it had been written with. The scroll not only dealt with Enoch and Lamech but with other persons mentioned in the book of Genesis. It proved to be an Aramaic form of parts of Genesis dealing with the patriarchs, but it included legends and other materials presented in memoir style, not found in the Hebrew Bible. That style was popular among pious Jews at the beginning of the Christian era, thus its original has been dated to the first century BC. The Qumran copy was probably made between 50 BC and AD 70.

The literary characteristics of the scroll have presented some classification problems. Free expansion and inclusion of nonbiblical material led certain scholars to call the scroll a "targum" or commentary-expansion of the Genesis text. Others have regarded it as a "midrash" or sermonic account of the Hebrew narrative. The scroll contains both elements and is best regarded as an independent recounting of certain Genesis stories, enriched by the inclusion of imaginative

material such as a description of the beauty of the patriarch Abraham's wife Sarah; dreams; and accounts of
plagues and journeys.

The Aramaic Apocryphon somewhat antedates the one
used in Palestine in the time of Christ. It contains some
Hebraisms but is mostly written in good Aramaic, much
of which parallels biblical Aramaic. The language of the
scroll, however, is later than the period of old Aramaic
(tenth to eighth centuries BC) or official Aramaic (Assyrian and Persian periods), as the presence of certain grammatical forms indicate. Most scholars have described the
language as middle Aramaic and have placed it between
the Aramaic of Daniel and later western Aramaic. Those
scholars generally assign a second-century BC date to
Daniel, but that conclusion needs to be modified
because the Qumran material shows that no canonical
work was composed later than about 350 BC. On any
evidence, the Aramaic of Daniel is earlier than that of the
Apocryphon and seems to fit properly into the period
when official Aramaic was the dominant form of the language. The Genesis Apocryphon presents no valid reasons for dating the Aramaic of Daniel or Ezra later than
the sixth to fifth centuries BC.

Gospel of Thomas *See* Thomas, Gospel of (below).

Isaiah, Ascension of Pseudepigraphal apocalyptic work
widely known to the early Christians; also known as the
Martyrdom of Isaiah, the Testament of Hezekiah, and
the Vision of Isaiah. It was rediscovered when an
Ethiopic version of part of the text was published in
1819. The full Ethiopic version is the only complete version in existence. A partial Latin text published in 1832
had actually been published in Venice over three centuries before. Slavonic and Coptic versions also exist. All
may be traced back to two Greek versions of the third,
fifth, and sixth centuries.

It is not clear whether the original was a single composition or even whether the authorship was Christian or
Jewish with later Christian editing. The final form may
date from the latter part of the second century. It was
known to Ambrose, Jerome, Origen, Tertullian, and possibly to Justyn Martyr. The contents fall under three
heads:

1. The Martyrdom of Isaiah. This material consists of
   prophetic utterances, including the prophet's prediction of his own death at the hands of King Manasseh
   of Judah. The document deals with the dark apostasy
   of the king, who, indwelt by Satan and following
   Beliar, leads his people into all manner of sin. Jerusalem, whose fall is prophesied, is called "Sodom" and
   its princes "Gomorrah." In the form of a midrash
   (devotional sermon), this section dwells on Isaiah's
   firm rejection of compromise or recantation. Isaiah's
   martyrdom by being "sawn in two" is the portion with
   which the church fathers seem to have been familiar.
2. The Testament of Hezekiah. This section is apocalyptic, a vision Isaiah passes on to his king. It speaks of
   the descent of "the Beloved," a title used in this document for the Messiah. The vision covers the Messiah's
   incarnation, life, death, resurrection, and ascension,
   then turns to the early history of the church and the
   apostasy that precedes the second coming of the Lord.
   The Antichrist is revealed as Beliar or Satan, who
   assumes human form and kills his mother (no doubt
   directed at the Roman emperor Nero, who murdered
   his mother, Agrippina). The whole section is based on
   Daniel and the biblical Apocalypse and was also influenced by Gnosticism. The conclusion of the vision
   (the Beloved's victory, the two resurrections, and the

final judgment) very closely parallels the consummation of all things in the NT book of Revelation.
3. The Vision of Isaiah. This section resembles #2 even
   linguistically but shows more Gnostic influence: Isaiah is lifted to the dwelling place of the Trinity, the
   seventh heaven, and shown many mysteries of Christ.
   Because of this vision Manasseh kills the prophet.
   Gnostic doctrine, as propagated by Cerinthus at the
   end of the first century, is evident. Jesus, earthly born,
   becomes the host of the Christ, who leaves his earthly
   tenement at the Crucifixion.

Historically, the value of the Ascension of Isaiah is to
show the welter of conflicting opinion which, claiming
authority and inspiration, besieged the minds of the
early Christians.

Isaiah, Martyrdom of *See* Isaiah, Ascension of (above).

Issachar, Testament of *See* Testaments of the Twelve
Patriarchs (below).

James, Apocalypse of There were two Gnostic apocalypses of James (designated "first" and "second"). The
first, covering over 20 pages of text, purports to be a revelation given by the Lord, some of it before the Crucifixion and some after it, to James, his brother, who was
also know as James the righteous. The two documents
referred to as the Apocalypse of James are in Codex V
of the Nag Hammadi literature discovered in 1945 in
Egypt just west of the Nile River opposite the city of
Chenoboskion and are distinct from the Apocryphon of
James, which is included in NT apocryphal writings. The
second apocalypse composed of 20 pages of Coptic text
is purportedly a speech delivered by James the Just on
the fifth step of the temple and contains many references
to or echoes of canonical Scriptures. The work ends with
the multitude casting James down from the temple and
stoning him in a manner reminiscent of the martyrdom
of Stephen.

James, Ascents of Lost book mentioned only by
Epiphanius (bishop of the Greek island of Salamis) in
his fourth-century work *Refutation of All the Heresies*.
According to Epiphanius, the Ascents of James was used
by the Ebionites, a rigidly ascetic sect of Jewish Christians. The book represented James, Jesus' brother, as having spoken against the temple and sacrifices. It declared
the apostle Paul to be a Greek who went to Jerusalem,
sought to marry the high priest's daughter, and to that
end became a proselyte and was circumcised. When he
did not win the young woman, he inveighed against the
Sabbath, the Law, and circumcision.

In a commentary on Galatians (1865), J. B. Lightfoot
suggested that the book's title referred to James's ascents
up the temple steps, from which he addressed the people. Lightfoot also suggested that James's death was the
grand climax of the ascents. According to a quote from
the early Christian writer Hegesippus (as recorded in
Eusebius's *Ecclesiastical History*), James was cast down to
his death from the pinnacle of the temple.

James, Protevangelium of This is an apocryphal "gospel" that tells of the token marriage and pregnancy of
Mary and of Jesus' birth, childhood, and adolescent
years. This apocryphal writing was discovered in the 16th
century by Guillaume Postel.

Job, Testament of Apocalyptic literature bearing resemblance to the biblical book of Job. The book was probably
written in Greek in the second century AD. Since it is
devoid of Christian thought, it was likely written by a Jew.

In chapters 1–45, Job is the speaker. He comes to

understand that a nearby temple has been desecrated by there having been offered in it sacrifices to Satan. When Job destroys it, Satan threatens him. Job's friends come to console him but their speeches are greatly abbreviated. Elihu is represented as Satan's mouthpiece and earns God's displeasure. But Job sacrifices for all three friends. He remarries and has seven sons and three daughters, who inherit his wealth. Chapters 46–51, in which Job's brother is the speaker, conclude the narrative.

John the Baptist, Life of A legendary account supposedly written by Serapion dealing with the early life of John the Baptist and especially with the death of his mother, Elizabeth. While Jesus was living with his parents in Egypt, Elizabeth dies on the same day as Herod the Great dies. John, who is but a small boy, does not know how to bury her. The clouds bring Jesus, Mary, and Salome who wash the body. The grave is dug by Michael and Gabriel, who also bring the souls of Zacharias and Simeon. John is then left to grow up in the desert under the care of the angels, while the clouds lift Jesus and Mary to Nazareth where they live.

John the Evangelist, Book of This writing was used most extensively by the Albigenses and was commonly regarded as stemming from the Bogomiles before them. It was written in the form of questions and answers propounded to have come from the apostle John while he leaned upon the breast of Jesus at the Last Supper. This pattern of questions and answers is found in other early Gnostic writings, especially the Gospel of Bartholomew.

The writing contains Gnostic theology. It portrays a world created by Satan and not by God. Christ was not born of Mary but was an angel sent forth to the earth. He "entered in by the ear and came forth by the ear" of Mary. John the Baptist was sent by Satan, and his disciples (the Roman Catholic Church) are not the disciples of Christ. Baptism and apparently the Lord's Supper are valueless.

The writing is preserved only in Latin and in its present form is not earlier than the 12th century. A convenient English translation may be found in M. R. James, *The Apocryphal NT* (1924).

Joseph, Prayer of Jewish apocalyptic work. The Prayer of Joseph won the commendation of Origen, an early church scholar, as a document "not to be despised." Origen's quotations provide almost the only surviving information about the work, so that its total content and significance are unclear. An ancient list of OT apocryphal and canonical writings puts the Prayer of Joseph third and mentions its length as 1,100 verses. Origen's quotations concern mainly Joseph's father, Jacob. Jacob exists in the form of an angel, bearing Jacob's given name Israel. He is the speaker in the quoted fragments and foretells the fate of humankind. He describes how he met Uriel on a journey to Mesopotamia and how Uriel wrestled with him, claiming to be the greatest of the angels. The apocalyptic poet had in mind the story of Jacob's mysterious wrestling at Jabbok (Gn 32:22-29) and passages such as Daniel 10:13. Because Jacob claims to be "the first born of all living beings" and therefore the chief of all angels, Uriel challenges him.

Joseph, Testament of *See* Testaments of the Twelve Patriarchs (below).

Joseph the Carpenter, History of Document glorifying Jesus' earthly father and promoting a cult of Joseph. Words in chapter 18 of the History of Joseph support a fourth-century date for it. There Jesus tells his mother,

"You, too, must look for the same end of life as other mortals." By the fifth century the doctrine of the "Assumption of the Virgin" was widely held.

The document, derived from the Protevangelium of James, was contaminated by both Gnosticism and other religious beliefs of Egypt, the country in which it was written. It is extant in Coptic and Arabic and also in a fourth-century translation of the Coptic text.

The History of Joseph the Carpenter claims to give an account of Joseph's life and his model death at the age of 111. The story is allegedly told by Jesus to his disciples on the Mt of Olives. Joseph, a carpenter (Mt 13:55), is a widower well advanced in years when he marries Mary, who is only 12. (He had six children by an earlier marriage.) Joseph is buried according to the rites of the Egyptian Osiris cult after Jesus pronounces an eulogy.

Jubilees, Book of Jubilees is a pseudepigraphal work from the last half of the second century BC during the Maccabean period. It is an invaluable source for understanding the environment in the age prior to the launching of the Christian church. Jubilees stands with the Book of Enoch and the Testaments of the Twelve Patriarchs as the most important Hebrew or Aramaic literature of the time. Like these it was translated into Greek and used by the church fathers. Most probably, Jubilees was written in Hebrew since it purported a Mosaic authorship and since its nationalistic Maccabean environment would demand it. Fragments of 10 manuscripts in Hebrew found at Qumran support the thesis that it was originally in that language.

The work is referred to by later Greek writers following Hebrew sources as "Jubilees" and "the little (lesser) Genesis." It is also entitled "The Apocalypse of Moses" and the "Testament of Moses." In revised forms it has been called "The Book of Adam's Daughters" and "The Life of Adam."

Complete, fifty-chapter manuscripts exist in six Ethiopian texts of which the texts of the fifth and sixth centuries are best. The Latin text is valuable but partial and only a few fragments of the Greek version remain. The Hebrew fragments found at Qumran are of special importance since they are from the period of original writing. The Bibliotheque Nationale has "Ethiopien 51" and "Ethiopien 160." The British Museum has *Kufale*, or *Liber Jubilaeorum*, and *Enoch*.

The author of Jubilees claims a direct revelational source for the teaching that he espouses. God had spoken to Moses in the Pentateuch the "lesser law" in this "little book of Genesis." At Sinai God communicated to Moses by the "Angel of the Presence" saying to the angel, "Write for Moses from the beginning of creation until my sanctuary has been built among them for all eternity" (1:27). This is supplementary to the "first law" (6:22).

Following a brief introduction Jubilees follows the text of Genesis and Exodus to 14:31. This midrashic treatment of the Pentateuchal material attempts to show that the patriarchy adhered to the law even prior to Moses. The author's aim is to strengthen classical Judaism in the face of the serious intrusions of Hellenistic culture among Jewish peoples. In doing this the author does not hesitate in adding and subtracting from Pentateuchal history. The patriarchs are adorned in every way. Anything that showed their weaknesses and sins was removed and legendary content inserted to glorify these fathers. The patriarchs are the fountainheads of culture. Enoch invented writing; Noah, medicine; Abraham, plowing.

Appealing to Leviticus 25:8-12, the work emphasizes

the importance of the number seven. History from Adam to Moses is arranged according to cycles of seven. This manner of compartmentalizing history into jubilee periods was revealed to Moses at Sinai and so has divine sanction and in fact is mandated. The philosophy of history that springs from this sees God acting sovereignly and uniquely in Israel in distinction to his relationship with the gentile world. The other nations are ruled by angels but not Israel, which is directly in God's charge (Jubilees 15:31ff.).

The polemic that Jubilees mounts against the lunar calendar (6:36-38) and its acceptance of the solar calendar is but another facet of the drive for a deep reform that will cleanse Israel. Israel is to be separated to God in every way with no intermingling in marriage or sitting at the table with Gentiles. There is a surprising stringency demanded in Sabbath keeping (50:1-13). The penalty of death is levied against those who travel, buy or sell, draw water, bear burdens, snare creatures, or have marital relations on the Sabbath. These go far beyond the biblical requirements and belong to that milieu that produced the Qumran community and the Essenes.

The apocalyptic declaration of the Angel of Presence contains a clear but limited eschatological truth. Jubilees does contain the expectation of an immediate establishment of the messianic age. The entire emphasis, however, is such that ethical and cultural purposes are preeminent.

Judah, Testament of *See* Testaments of the Twelve Patriarchs (below).

Judas Iscariot, Gospel of Very old Gnostic writing probably produced by the Cainite sect. As it is not preserved for us today, we know it only through quotations in the writings of early Christians, especially Irenaeus. Thus, it must have been written before the middle of the second century AD. It probably contained a body of secret doctrine purportedly revealed by Judas Iscariot, summarizing the truth of superior and perfect knowledge supposedly revealed to this sect of the Gnostics. The gospel sets forth the "mystery of the betrayal," explaining how Judas through his treachery made the salvation of all mankind possible. This was accomplished by his forestalling the destruction of the truth proclaimed by Christ or by his thwarting the designs of the evil powers, the Archons, who wished to prevent the crucifixion of Christ because they knew it would destroy their evil power.

Lentulus, Epistle of Lentulus, ostensibly a predecessor of Pontius Pilate, is said to have prepared a report to the Roman Senate known as the Letter (or Epistle) of Lentulus. In it he included a detailed description of Jesus: "tall and handsome, his countenance inspiring reverence along with love and fear, his hair dark, shining, curling, parted in the middle, his face with a delicate rudiness. . . ." The authenticity of the letter is extremely doubtful.

Levi, Testament of *See* Testaments of the Twelve Patriarchs (below).

Lives of Adam and Eve A general title given to a noncanonical writing extant in Greek and Latin. The book is Jewish in nature, though there is a Christian flavor that causes most scholars to date the original work to the beginning of the Christian era. The content of the book is an expansion on the biblical story of Adam and Eve.

The Greek version begins with the expulsion from

Eden. In a dream, Eve sees the murder of Abel. After Adam had fallen ill Seth and Eve went to obtain oil from the tree of life. Michael the archangel met Seth and told him that Adam would die. Upon his death, he was ultimately taken to the third heaven. Seth witnessed how the angels interred his father and received instructions on how to bury his mother, who died a week after Adam.

The Latin version gives additional information. After the expulsion from the Garden, Eve asked Adam to kill her but instead of that he suggested they both do an act of penitence. Adam went to stand in the Jordan for 40 days and Eve went to stand in the water of the Euphrates for 37 days. While there, she was again tempted by Satan, who was disguised as an angel of light but was eventually exposed by Adam. Satan now explained the reason for his hostility toward them: when the angels were commanded to worship the Lord, he refused to do obeisance to God and was consequently cast out of heaven.

Matthew, Martyrdom of Loosely organized tale of Matthew's martyrdom that borrows heavily from the "Acts of Andrew and Matthias" and assumes that Matthias was in fact Matthew. The document represents the low literary and theological impulse of the later apocryphal texts.

The story begins when Matthew is commissioned by Jesus to plant a staff in Myrna, the city of man-eaters. Matthew does so, after exorcising the demon Asmodeus from the king's wife and family. The staff becomes a tree overnight, Matthew preaches to the people, and they "become humanized." But Asmodeus seeks revenge by directing the king to burn Matthew. The fire consumes golden idols and many soldiers, then turns into a dragon and chases the king, who begs Matthew for help. But Matthew dies.

A somewhat repentant but not yet converted king places the body of Matthew in an iron casket and sinks it secretly in the sea. The next day Matthew appears on the sea in the presence of two shining men and a "beautiful" child. The king is finally converted, baptized, and accepted into the church. Matthew appears to confer on the king his own name and to ordain him a priest and his family, deacons and deaconesses. Then Matthew ascends to heaven with two angels.

Medad, Book of Eldad and *See* Eldad and Medad, Book of (above).

Moses, Assumption of A Jewish legend that Moses was taken bodily into heaven without dying. Probably written between AD 7 and 30, it may be a combination of two earlier works, and appears to borrow heavily from the book of Deuteronomy. The work was likely produced to provide a miraculous ending to Moses' outstanding earthly life, attributing to him an experience similar to Elijah's. But this Jewish legend is contrary to the OT account of Moses' death (Dt 32:48-50; 34:5-7).

➤THE LOST ASSUMPTION OF MOSES Three facts indicate that there once was an apocryphal book that contained the legend of the assumption of Moses: (1) early lists of apocryphal works mention a work by this title; (2) several church fathers refer to it; and (3) a few fragments in Greek have survived.

The following items appeared in the work. God commissioned the archangel Michael to bury Moses' body. Satan opposed Moses' burial because he claimed authority over all matter and because Moses was a murderer. Michael countered Satan's claims and charged him with tempting Eve in Eden. Joshua and Caleb then watched Moses' assumption occur in a strange way. As they watched, they saw Moses' dead body buried in the mountain, but they also saw Moses himself in the company of the angels. In effect Moses' body died, but Moses himself did not.

Though often stated that Jude (v 9) was quoted from the Assumption of Moses, this is impossible to prove, simply because the relevant portions of that work have not survived. The most one can say is that several church fathers, including Clement of Alexandria (d. AD 215) and Origen (c. 185–254), suggested that the Assumption of Moses was the source for the account in Jude 1:9. They had both works. We have only Jude, so we cannot check their conclusions. The matter is further complicated because there is another work (see next section) now called the Assumption of Moses. People often suppose that Jude 1:9 is a citation from that book. It is not.

►THE EXTANT ASSUMPTION OF MOSES This work, perhaps written during Jesus' lifetime, purports to be a description of Moses' predictions to Joshua of the destiny of the nation of Israel. It is similar to other apocryphal, nonhistorical writings that were written under the names of great Jewish leaders.

It was discovered quite by chance in 1861, in the Ambrosian Library in Milan, Italy. The manuscript, dated to the fifth century AD, is a very poor copy of a Latin translation, perhaps derived from a Greek translation of a Hebrew original. The beginning and the ending are lost. There are numerous spelling mistakes, and there is no space between words. Not surprisingly, scholars have long disputed the reading, interpretation, and translation even of whole verses.

The opening three lines have not survived, so the original title has been lost. When discovered, the work was assumed to be the long-lost Assumption of Moses, but this identification is now widely doubted. Even though the book is still called by this title, it is far more likely to be either the Testament of Moses (which is also mentioned, along with the Assumption of Moses, in early lists of apocryphal works) or a composite work resulting from the combination of the Testament and the Assumption into one work.

There is only one reference to Moses' assumption in the book, and it comes in connection with a mention of his death (10:12). Because the ending of the book is also lost, it is impossible to know the contents of the conclusion or to tell whether this one remaining reference to Moses' assumption is original or whether it has been added by a scribe by mistake or by an editor combining two different works. It is clear, however, that the author of the surviving section believed that Moses expected to die (1:15; 10:12-14) and that Joshua assumed that he would (11:4-8).

The work begins midsentence (three lines are missing) and dates Moses' following speech to 2,500 years after Creation (1:2-5). Expecting to die, Moses summons Joshua, encourages him, and tells him that God created the world for his people (the Israelites), who will repent before the consummation at the end of the days (1:6-18).

Then Moses foretells Israel's future. The people will inherit the land (Canaan) and be ruled by local magistrates, chiefs (judges?), and kings (2:1-3). The kingdom will divide, and the people will turn to idolatry (2:4-9). A king from the east (Nebuchadnezzar) will take two tribes into captivity for about 77 years, where they will recall Moses' warnings (3:1-14; cf. Jer 25:11-12; Dt 28:15-68; 30:15-20). Someone (Daniel) will pray for deliverance (cf. Dn 9:4-19), and God will persuade a king (Cyrus) to send the exiles home (4:1-6; cf. Is 45:1-6; Ezr 1:1-4). Some exiles will return to their appointed place (Jerusalem) and rewall it but be unable to offer [proper] sacrifices (4:7-8; contrast Ezr 3:1-7). Others will remain in exile but will increase in population (4:9). This concludes the OT period and begins the intertestamental period (c. 400 to 1 BC).

The widespread apostasy of the Seleucid period (c. 201–267 BC) is described, with special reference to priests and judges (4:1-6). The Maccabees, who gained and maintained political independence from Syria (in 164 BC) are not mentioned. Instead, the focus is on the kings (the Hasmoneans) who made themselves high priests (6:1). Next will come an insolent king (Herod the Great, 37–4 BC), who will rule ruthlessly (6:2-7). Then a powerful king of the West will conquer the people, take some captive, crucify others, and burn part of the temple (6:8-9).

From this point on, the author, having reached his own period, had to guess at the future, so the predictions that he put in Moses' mouth are general or obscure and often unfulfilled. The next rulers (Sadducees?) would be impious, treacherous, gluttons, deceitful, and worried about ritual uncleanness while living in luxury at the expense of the poor (7:1-10). An unprecedented time of wrath would follow, when a great king would persecute the Jews, torturing, imprisoning, and even crucifying them for practicing circumcision (8:1-5). During this persecution, one man, Taxo, a Levite with seven sons, would remain faithful to God and die rather than adopt Greek customs (8:1-7).

The next section (10:1-10), an apocalyptic poem (ten stanzas, each with three lines), is the only apocalyptic section of the book. The Lord's kingdom will appear, Satan will be no more, and the chief angel (Michael) will avenge Israel (10:1-2). "The Heavenly One will arise from His royal throne," and there will be miraculous signs on the earth and in the sky; even the ocean will drain away (10:3-6). The Most High, the Eternal God, will appear and punish the Gentiles, destroying their idols (10:7). But Israel will be happy and exalted, rejoicing at seeing her enemies in Gehenna (hell) and thankfully praising her Creator (10:8-10). With Moses' mention of his death and some consoling words for Joshua, the composition ends in an incomplete form.

The book must have been written after Herod died and Varus had subdued a rebellion in Judea (4 BC) and before the temple was destroyed (AD 70). The book predicts that Herod's sons will not rule as long as Herod himself did (34 years, 37–4 BC). This prediction may be based on the fact that one son, Archelaus, was deposed after a 10-year reign (4 BC–AD 6). If so, the book was written after AD 6. But two other sons (Philip and Antipas) actually ruled longer than their father. For the author not to know this requires that the book must have been written within 34 years of Herod's death—in other words, before AD 30. Therefore, the book was probably written sometime between AD 6 and 30. This also means that the book reflects Jewish thinking during Jesus' lifetime.

The author was evidently a Palestinian Jew, but it is doubtful whether he was a member of any known major sect of the times. He hates Roman rule (8:1–10:10) without advocating revolt, as the Zealots and their predecessors did. His interest in the temple (2:8-9; 5:3; 6:9; 8:5) is not typical of an Essene. He condemns the Sadducean lifestyle (7:3-10). And his use of apocalyptic writing (10:1-10) is thought to have been unusual for a Pharisee.

Naphtali, Testament of *See* Testaments of the Twelve Patriarchs (below).

Nicodemus, Gospel of Alternate title for the apocryphal work Acts of Pilate. *See* Pilate, Acts of (below).

Noah, Book of Allusion to the writing of Noah is made in the book of Jubilees where it is said "Noah wrote down all things in a book as we instructed him concerning every kind of medicine. Thus the evil spirits were precluded from (hurting) the sons of Noah" (10:13; see also 21:10). The book of Noah borrows heavily from the book of Enoch (see chs 6–11, 54–55, 60, 65–69, 106–110). The other sections relate to the Noachic flood and subjects about which Noah could be presumed to have knowledge. Unfortunately no separate manuscript of the book of Noah is known to be extant.

Odes of Solomon *See* Solomon, Psalms of (below).

Patriarchs, Testaments of the Twelve *See* Testaments of the Twelve Patriarchs (below).

Paul, Acts of *See* Paul and Thecla, Acts of (below).

Paul, Acts of Andrew and *See* Andrew and Paul, Acts of (above).

Paul and Thecla, Acts of The Acts of Paul and Thecla is one section of an apocryphal work known as the Acts of Paul. It was apparently written in the latter half of the second century AD by a church elder who lived in Asia. According to Tertullian (*On Baptism* 17.19-21), the motive for the writing was "love of Paul," but the presbyter was removed from office for producing this document. It is not clear whether the reason for his deposition was that he made a false claim to apostolic authorship, or whether it was that the viewpoints expressed in the document were considered heretical.

The story reads like a folktale. Paul arrives in Iconium after fleeing from Antioch. He is met by Onesiphorus, who welcomes Paul into his home. A group of people gather there to hear Paul's message. Beside the window of a neighboring house, Thecla is seated. She cannot see Paul, but she listens intently to his message. Her mother, Thecleia, exclaims, "My daughter, like a spider, is bound by his words to the window, seized by a new craving and a terrible passion." Paul is teaching that in order to "see God," a person must live a life of abstinence from sexual activity.

Thecla is engaged to be married, but she is so impressed with Paul's teaching that she determines she will break her engagement to Thamyris. Thamyris, in distress, appeals to the governor of the city, who arrests and imprisons Paul. Thecla bribes the jailer with bracelets and a silver mirror and enters Paul's cell. Again she is transfixed by his teaching. At the trial, Thecla is adamant in her refusal to marry Thamyris. Paul is banned from the city; Thecla is condemned to be burned to death. Miraculously her life is spared, and she is reunited with Paul and travels with him to Antioch.

In Antioch, Thecla rebuffs the advances of a nobleman, Alexander, and for a second time is condemned to death. But the wild beasts who are to devour her in the public arena instead lick her feet and protect her. When she throws herself into a water cistern to effect her baptism, she is again spared death—a lightning flash kills the fish lurking in the water, and they float lifeless to the surface. Queen Tryphaena, who has befriended Thecla, faints with shock as repeated attempts are made to take Thecla's life. Seeing this, Alexander finally begs the governor to set Thecla free.

Free once more, Thecla seeks Paul. She disguises herself as a man by putting on male attire. Arriving in Myra, she finds Paul and announces to him that she is returning to Iconium. Paul commands her to "teach the word of God." After teaching for a while in Iconium, Thecla travels on to Seleucia.

The remainder of Thecla's life is not well documented. Some manuscripts record that Thecla, being afraid of the people of Seleucia, withdrew to a mountain and resided in a cave. There she lived an ascetic life, taught certain women who came to her, and carried out a ministry of healing. Later she departed to Rome, seeking Paul. Paul, however, was already dead. When Thecla herself died, at 90 years of age, she was buried not far from the tomb of her beloved master.

Although this work is considered apocryphal and is excluded from the NT canon, there are some early writers who held it in high regard. The Acts of Paul, of which this document forms a part, is mentioned by Origen and by Hippolytus with respect. Eusebius was of the opinion that the document was spurious, but he distinguished it from inferior heretical works. There are two instances where details of information have found their way from the Acts of Paul into early manuscripts of canonical books (2 Tm 3:11; 4:19). It is probable that the viewpoints indicated in this document reflected popular religious traditions widely held in the second century AD.

Tertullian, however, argues that the document is quite out of harmony with Paul's attitudes as expressed in the canonical material. In particular, he objects to the role assumed by a woman in the Acts of Paul and Thecla. Paul, Tertullian says, would never have permitted a woman to teach and to baptize (*On Baptism* 17.21-23). The Acts of Paul and Thecla does differ from the Pauline stance, but not in the way indicated by Tertullian. The document depicts Paul as a proponent of the encratite viewpoint, teaching that celibacy is necessary for salvation. The canonical Paul taught that salvation is attained through faith alone, and that celibacy is a matter of special calling and certainly not the norm for every Christian (1 Cor 7:1-7). The Acts of Paul and Thecla suggests that a woman must assume male attire and must abstain from marriage if she is to exercise a leadership role. The canonical Paul instructed that a woman in a leadership position should dress as a woman (1 Cor 11:4-6), and he affirmed the ministerial function of married women (Rom 16:3). The Acts of Paul and Thecla emulates a woman whose motivating power was personal devotion to the apostle. The canonical writings suggest that Paul strongly discouraged such a show of personal allegiance to himself (1 Cor 1:12-17). Christ alone was to be the motivating influence in Christian service.

The Acts of Paul and Thecla provides us with a unique description of the physical appearance of Paul: "a man small of stature, with a bald head and crooked legs, in good state of body, with eyebrows meeting and nose somewhat hooked, full of friendliness; for now he appeared like a man, and now he had the face of an angel." This description is probably not reliable in any historical sense; more likely it pictures a typical Jew of the period. But because there is no other description preserved in early documents, this one has formed the basis for the many portraits of Paul that have come down through the centuries.

Paul, Apocalypse of This document, which originated in the late fourth century AD, pretends to be a written account of some of the experiences that the apostle Paul had when he was caught up to the third heaven, or paradise, according to 2 Corinthians 12:2-4. The fact that

Paul did not describe what he saw or heard during that revelatory vision excited the imagination of some unknown fourth-century Christian. Since the author describes with relish the tortures in hell experienced by a presbyter, bishop, and deacon (chs 34–36) and elsewhere approves of the devotion and piety of monks and nuns (chs 7–9) and of those who are virgins or chaste (ch 22), it is safe to conclude that he was a monk who disapproved of the insincere and hypocritical religiosity of his contemporaries, both laymen and clergy.

This book, originally written in Greek, survives in relatively complete form in Latin. A partial indication of the great popularity of this piece of religious fiction is the fact that it was translated into Ethiopic, Coptic, and Syriac as well as Latin.

The book is loosely structured in seven sections. The work begins with a short introductory section that attempts to explain why the book was unknown from the first to the fourth century (chs 1–2): during the consulate of (emperor) Theodosius Augustus the Younger and Cynegius (the document can thus be dated to AD 388), a respectable but nameless person received a revelation through an angel. The man happened to be living in Tarsus in a house once occupied by St Paul himself. The angel told the man to break up the foundations and publish whatever he found. After being pummeled by the angel for disobedience, he finally broke the foundations only to discover a marble box that he immediately delivered to the emperor. The emperor opened the box and found the original version of the Apocalypse of Paul (which he copies) and a pair of shoes used by Paul on his missionary journeys. The substance of the mysterious document then follows.

In chapters 3–6, Paul is said to have received a message from God announcing how all creation is subject to God with the exception of man himself. Chapters 7–10 relate how the guardian angels of each man and woman report every morning and evening to God concerning the deeds of those in their charge. Some are very good, while others are exceedingly wicked. In chapters 11–18, Paul is taken up in the Holy Spirit to the third heaven and asks to see the souls of the righteous and sinners as they leave the world. The angel accompanying Paul shows him a righteous man leaving the world, an ungodly man, and the soul of one who thought himself righteous but in fact was not.

Chapters 19–30 describe Paul being lifted up to the third heaven (cf. 2 Cor 12:2-4), where he saw a golden gate flanked by golden pillars upon which were mounted golden tablets containing the names of the righteous. Upon entering paradise he was greeted by Enoch and Elijah and shown things that he could not reveal to others (ch 21; cf. 2 Cor 12:4). From there he was taken to the second heaven and then to the firmament encircled by Ocean (ch 21). There he saw the milk white waters of Lake Acherusia where the city of Christ was located. He was brought to the city in a golden boat while 3,000 angels sang a hymn. At the river of honey he met Isaiah, Jeremiah, Ezekiel, and other prophets (ch 25); at the river of milk he saw the infants slain by Herod (ch 26); at the river of wine he met Abraham, Isaac, Jacob, Lot, and Job (ch 27); at the river of oil he met those completely dedicated to God (ch 28). At the center of the city, by a great altar, David sang the hallelujah to God.

Paul's tour of hell is described in chapters 31–44; it is a place of sorrow and distress in which flows a river boiling with fire. In the river, some of the damned were immersed to the knees, others to the navel or lips, depending on the severity of their sins (ch 31). Chapters 34–36 describe the tortures of a presbyter, bishop, and deacon. Throughout this section the most ghastly tortures imaginable are described in detail with great relish. Finally, in chapter 44, Christ decrees that for Paul's sake there will be no torture on Sundays henceforth.

Paul's angelic travel guide then escorts him to paradise (chs 45–51), where the righteous of all ages are anxious to meet him. He meets the Virgin Mary (ch 46), Abraham, Isaac, and Jacob as well as the 12 sons of Jacob (ch 47), Moses, who weeps for the unconverted Jews (ch 48), Isaiah, Jeremiah, and Ezekiel, each of whom describes his martyrdom, Lot and Job (ch 49), Noah (ch 50), Elijah, Elisha, Zechariah and his son, John the Baptist, and Adam (ch 51). The document either ended here or, in alternate versions, with Paul's miraculous trip to the Mt of Olives where he and the other disciples received the divine commission.

The document is filled with contradictions and inconsistencies and many of the translated versions do not agree with each other in all details. The chief importance of the document is in terms of its glimpses into the thinking of late fourth-century Christianity.

Paul, Passion of A revised Latin version of the apocryphal Martyrdom of Paul, which was part of a larger body of texts called the Acts of Paul. The original Martyrdom is the story of Paul's resuscitation of Patroclus, Nero's cupbearer, who had fallen from a window and died during one of Paul's sermons. Patroclus confesses his new loyalty to Christ before the stunned Nero, who moves quickly to round up all such "soldiers of the great king (Christ)." Paul is included in the purge. The Passion elaborates on the story to include a passage about Seneca's admiration for Paul and his writings, portions of which Seneca allegedly read to Nero. Also, Paul on the way to his death borrows a kerchief from Plautilla, promising to return it. When the returning soldiers mock her, she shows them the bloodied kerchief.

Paul, Passion of Peter and See Peter and Paul, Passion of (below).

Pearl, Hymn of the See Thomas, Acts of (below).

Peter and Paul, Passion of This writing comes to us in two forms, both of which are considered to have been written by Marcellus and date from the fifth century. The first form is essentially like the Acts of Peter and Paul. It lays emphasis upon Paul's journey to Rome. The second gives more attention to the men's residence in Rome with emphasis upon their stay in the home of a relative of Pontius Pilate. Both emphasize the close relationship between Peter and Paul and their continued and successful opposition to Simon Magus, who claims to be the Christ. Their death sentences are included in the writings but with only a brief account of their martyrdoms.

Peter, Gospel of See Akhmim Fragment (above).

Peter, Preaching of This document, which has survived only in fragments, appears to have been written early in the second century AD in Egypt. While the title does not explicitly claim Petrine authorship, it was understood by Clement of Alexandria (late second century AD) to have been an authentic composition by the apostle Peter (*Stromata* 2.15.68). The majority of the fragments of the Preaching of Peter are preserved in the form of brief quotations in the writings of Clement of Alexandria.

The fourth-century church historian Eusebius of Caesarea observed that the Preaching of Peter had not been accepted by any ancient authorities (*Historia Ecclesiastica* 3.3.1-4), though he was probably not aware of its acceptance by Clement. Even though only fragments of the document have survived, they are important in that they reveal a transitional stage in the history of early Christian literature. During the first century, Christian literature, including all of the NT, was written for the consumption of other Christians. During the second century, Christian writers began to feel the need to defend their faith against the criticisms of their pagan and Jewish opponents. A new kind of Christian literature, the apology (meaning "defense"), began to appear in the early second century with the writings of the earliest Christian apologists Quadratus and Aristides. The Preaching of Peter represents a transition from the kind of apologetic writing found in the Acts of the Apostles, the sermons that that book contains, and the writings of the early apologists.

Since Clement quotes randomly from the Preaching of Peter, it is not possible to determine the order in which any of the quotations appeared in the original composition. Some of the major emphases of the document will appear from the following summaries of the quotations of Clement. Peter, according to Clement, called the Lord both "Law and Word" in the "Preaching" (*Stromata* 1.29.182; 2.15.68). Mankind must recognize that *one* God created the beginning of all things and has the power to bring all things to an end (*Stromata* 6.5.39-41). The pagans, whom the author of the Preaching of Peter opposed, held that the universe was uncreated and eternal. God, the author contends, is invisible, incomprehensible, needs nothing, is inconceivable, everlasting, imperishable, and uncreated. This God must not be worshiped in the manner of the Greeks, for they have foolishly fashioned images of ordinary materials and worship them as gods. Further, they take animals that should be used for food and sacrifice them to these idols. The worship of the Jews should not be emulated either, for they revere angels, archangels, months, and the moon. If any of the nation of Israel should repent, they will find forgiveness (*Stromata* 6.5.43). In one place the Preaching of Peter narrates how the Lord sent disciples to preach the gospel throughout the world after the resurrection (*Stromata* 6.6.48), though the precise connection between this narrative and the preceding apologetic statements is not clear. It may be that the document began with a special version of the great commission. Elsewhere the document states that the OT prophets speak of Christ, sometimes in parables and enigmas, yet at other times very clearly and directly (*Stromata* 6.15.128). In fact, the major events of the life of Christ, his coming, torture, crucifixion, death, resurrection, and ascension into heaven were predicted in detail by the prophets.

The importance of the surviving fragments of the Preaching of Peter lies in the way in which they reveal how early second-century Christianity turned from a defensive to an offensive position in its proclamation of the gospel.

Peter, Slavonic Acts of An account of the later travels of Peter and his subsequent death in Rome preserved for us only in the Slavonic language. According to this account, a child (Jesus) comes to Peter and bids him to go to Rome. The angel Michael is captain of the ship taking them to Rome. After their arrival in Rome, Peter tells the child to catch some fish, whereupon he catches 12,000 in one hour. Then the child is sold to a Roman noble, Aravistus, for 50 pieces of gold. The child silences his teachers. After a vision of angels, the entire household is baptized. Nero arrests Peter, whereupon the child rebukes him. Many dead are raised, but the child sends them back to their graves to await the resurrection by Michael. Peter is crucified head downward. When the child reveals he is Jesus, the nails fall from Peter's body, he prays for the forgiveness of his execu-

tioners, and then he dies. Such apocryphal versions of the acts of early church leaders are characteristically filled with fanciful acts of the apostles and their contact with the Christ.

Peter's Letter to Philip This letter is part of the Christian Gnostic material discovered in 1947 at Nag Hammadi. It probably dates from the late second or early third century. The letter takes its name from a segment at the beginning of the tractate in which Peter claims to have sent the material to Philip. The letter is written in a dialogue form common in Gnostic literature. The body of the writing consists of a series of questions that are asked by the apostles of the risen Lord and the answers given by him. The questions provide a basis for the exposition of Gnostic philosophy about the structure of the world revealed by the Divine Light. That Light is the Christ, who is the heavenly Redeemer.

Pilate, Acts of This document is an apocryphal passion gospel that reached its present form by the middle of the fourth century AD. The first Christian writer to refer to the Acts of Pilate was Epiphanius, an ecclesiastical heresy hunter, who wrote a lengthy denunciation of various heresies in AD 375, in which he definitely mentioned the Acts of Pilate (*Heresies* 50.1). Much earlier, Justin Martyr had referred to Pilate's report to Tiberius regarding the trial of Jesus (*I Apology* 35; 48), but he does not seem to be referring to the Acts of Pilate. Toward the end of the second century AD, a generation after Justin, Tertullian referred to an account sent from Pilate to the emperor Tiberius, yet this cannot be the Acts of Pilate, since Jesus supposedly performed many miracles before the procurator. Although it is not improbable that an earlier version of the Acts of Pilate antedated the fourth century, the present version must be dated to the middle of that century. The original language of the Acts of Pilate was Greek, and translations of it were made into Latin, Coptic, and Armenian. Eusebius, the fourth-century church historian and bishop of Caesarea, condemns what he regarded as a blasphemous account of Pilate, apparently a pagan document calculated to defame Christ (*Historia Ecclesiastica*, 1.9.3; 9.5.1). The Christian Acts of Pilate was probably composed to counter the pagan document.

The Acts of Pilate is a composite document consisting of two main parts. The first part (chs 1–16) purports to be a translation from Hebrew to Greek of an account written by Nicodemus about the events surrounding the passion of Jesus. The second part (chs 17–27), also called "Christ's Descent into Hell," vividly describes Christ's descent into hades to liberate the righteous dead (an imaginative expansion of 1 Pt 3:19 which was itself transformed in the Apostles' Creed into the phrase "he descended into hell"). After the 14th century AD, the whole composition was commonly designated as the Gospel of Nicodemus because of the prominent place that character played in the passion.

In the prologue to the Acts of Pilate, a Roman soldier named Ananias claims to have found the Acts of Pilate in Hebrew and to have translated it into Greek in the 18th year of the reign of Emperor Flavius Theodosius (AD 425). A quotation of the entire document follows: In the 15th year of Tiberius Caesar (AD 29), Nicodemus wrote an account of the events that surrounded the passion, death, and resurrection of Jesus. The Jewish high priests accused Jesus of various religious crimes to Pilate and asked that he be tried. Though unwilling, Pilate sent for Jesus anyway, though in a most gracious manner. When Jesus arrived, the Roman standards bowed to him of their own accords (ch 1). In chapter 2 the Jewish charges against Jesus included: (1) that he was born of fornication, (2) that his birth meant the death of the children of Bethlehem, and (3) that Joseph and Mary fled to Egypt because they counted for nothing among the people of Israel. The charge of fornication was immediately refuted by 12 pious Jews who had witnessed the betrothal of Mary and Joseph. An interview between Pilate and Jesus (modeled after Jn 18:33-38) follows in chapter 3. The Jews charge Jesus with blaspheming God, and Pilate reluctantly turns Jesus over to them (ch 4). Nicodemus then stands up in the Jewish council and urges them to let Jesus go, for if he is not of God his movement will fail (cf. Acts 5:38-39), but the Jews oppose him (ch 5). Then three Jews healed by Jesus testify in his behalf (ch 6), followed by Bernice, the woman healed of the issue of blood (ch 7). The crowd proclaims Jesus a prophet (ch 8). When Pilate offers to release a prisoner, the Jews ask for Barabbas, and Pilate then washes his hands of the matter and has Jesus scourged and crucified with the two criminals, Dysmas and Gestas (ch 9). Jesus is mocked by the crowds, while one criminal (Gestas) is rebuked by the other (ch 10). Jesus' death is accompanied by a darkening of the sun, which the Jews regard as a normal eclipse (ch 11). Joseph of Arimathea is then seized by the Jews and imprisoned; when they come to execute him he has vanished (ch 12). The guards report the appearance of the angel at the tomb, but are bribed by the Jews to keep silence (ch 12). Three Jews then come from Galilee: Phineas, a priest; Adas, a teacher; and Angaeus, a Levite. They report that they have witnessed the great commission and ascension of Jesus on Mt Malich (ch 14). Nicodemus suggests that the surrounding mountains be checked to see if some spirit has not taken Jesus up only to dash him on the rocks; the Jews find nothing except Joseph of Arimathea in his hometown (ch 15). Joseph is summoned to testify before the council and reveals how the risen Jesus had appeared to him when he was imprisoned and set him free (ch 15). The council decides, after hearing other witnesses, that if Jesus is still remembered after 50 years, the stories must be true (ch 16).

The second document begins with an account of Joseph speaking to the council. Two brothers, he claims, had been raised at the same time as Jesus. The council summons them to give their stories (ch 17). While in hades, the brothers claimed, a great light appeared and Abraham and Isaiah became overjoyed (ch 18). Satan thought that Jesus could be restrained in hades (ch 20); but when the King of Glory arrived, the gates were broken down. Satan was handed over to the angels to be bound (ch 22) and was rebuked by hades for causing the ruin of his kingdom (ch 23). The King of Glory (Christ) then led Adam and the rest of the righteous dead out of hades (ch 24) and to paradise (ch 25), where even the repentant criminal was seen (ch 26). The two brothers claim that they have been sent by the angel Michael to preach the resurrection of Jesus to all mankind.

The Acts of Pilate is a pastiche (collection) of quotations and allusions from the four canonical Gospels, mingled with imaginative and even fantastic additions. It is basically an apologetic document that attempts to defend the truth of the resurrection of Jesus against the counterclaims of pagan and Jewish adversaries. Unfortunately, it has an anti-Semitic tone that was to characterize Christian dramatizations of the events of Passion Week from the fourth century through the end of the Middle Ages.

Pistis Sophia A fourth-century Coptic manuscript (Codex Askewanus) that represents one of the chief

Gnostic works extant today. The work, containing four chapters, derives its name from the heroine, Sophia, though only the first half of the work refers to her. This portion relates how Jesus, during the first 11 years after his resurrection, returned to teach his disciples the highest mystery of all: the Treasury of the Light. Jesus returned to the Mt of Olives where he is caught up through the aeons and on his journey comes to the thirteenth aeon where he finds Sophia. She is in sorrow because she has caught a glimpse of the Treasury of the Light but is deceived by Authades (the self-willed), who flashes a false brightness before her, causing her to fall into the hands of the powers of matter. She maintains her hope and faith, however, and after 12 prayers is delivered from Authades and chaos by Jesus who reinstates her at the lower limit of the thirteenth aeon.

The work is in dialogue form—with Jesus answering questions asked by his disciples. The theme is thoroughly Gnostic in its view of salvation that comes by a hidden doctrine that brings illumination.

Protevangelium of James *See* James, Protevangelium of (above).

Psalms of Solomon *See* Solomon, Psalms of (below).

Resurrection of Christ by Bartholomew, Book of the *See* Bartholomew, Book of the Resurrection of Christ by (above).

Reuben, Testament of *See* Testaments of the Twelve Patriarchs (below).

Sibylline Oracles A pseudepigraphal writing comprising originally 15 books, 12 of which are extant in late Greek manuscripts. The word *sibyl* is of Greek origin. It claimed to be an oracle of the gods and generally contained a message of a coming catastrophic event. Some Jews adopted and used this mode of writing for propagation purposes.

The sibyls came from the beginning of the Maccabean period (165 BC) and cover a period up to shortly after the destruction of the second temple (AD 76). The authors, presumably writing in Alexandria, Egypt, stressed the unity and sovereignty of God. God controlled all events, whereas pagan deities were useless, unable to do anything. "But God is one, most exalted of all, who has made the heaven, the sun, the stars and the moon. . . . He has constituted man as the Divinely appointed ruler of all. You men . . . be ashamed of making gods" (book 2). God controls the history of the nations. The sibyls outline the history of 10 generations from the Assyrian kingdom to the destruction of the second temple and the great earthquake (book 4.47ff.). The third book also contains a section on the devastation and troubles to be experienced before the great judgment. It includes two messianic passages wherein the Messiah introduces an era of peace and prosperity for the faithful: "He will raise up his kingdom for all ages over men. . . . For nothing but peace shall come upon the land of the good" (lines 767, 780). The eternal state is to be reserved for the faithful who will be raised from the dead in a bodily form: "But all who are godly shall live again on earth, when God gives breath and life and grace to them the godly" (book 4.187-190), whereas the ungodly are to be thrown into hell, "And all who have sinned with deeds of impiety a heap of earth shall cover again, and murky Tartarus and the black recesses of hell" (lines 183-186).

The express purpose of the authors of the sibyls was to demonstrate the reasonableness of the Jewish faith by casting their message in the form of the sibyl, introduced by the Greeks and appreciated by the Romans. In their emphasis on the God of Israel and their opposition to paganism, they nevertheless stand in the stream of the apocalyptic, the unveiling of God's secrets of past and future. The sibyl as divine oracle was, thus, used as a literary form in order to convey a message to the non-Jewish world.

Silvanus, Teachings of Literary work of the Gnostics, attributed to Silvanus, the companion of Peter and Paul. It was discovered at Chenoboskion in Upper Egypt in 1946.

Simeon, Testament of *See* Testaments of the Twelve Patriarchs (below).

Slavonic Acts of Peter *See* Peter, Slavonic Acts of (above).

Solomon, Psalms of The Psalms of Solomon are a collection of 18 songs attributed to Solomon. They are considered pseudepigrapha. The psalms were probably written by one author, who lived during the middle of the first century BC and wrote in Hebrew. The theological perspective of the author is Pharisaic in its views of the law, judgment, and the future of Israel. The Psalms of Solomon are derived from the canonical book of Psalms in their form and phraseology. One of the similarities in the form and phraseology is the emphasis on the antithesis between the righteous and the wicked. The wicked are the Gentiles who defile the holy things of the Lord (2:3) and apostate Jews who have fallen into sin (3:11, 13).

The character of the sinner is that of the fool, as opposed to the wise man (cf. Wisdom Literature). The fool has no concern for the Lord (4:1); his speech and deeds betray his unrighteousness (4:2ff.). He is known by his lies, judgment of others, false oaths, his immorality, lawlessness, and selfish ambitions at the cost of others (cf. 12). The righteous are the wise, who fear the Lord (4:26). He is not dismayed by bad dreams or perilous times (6:4-5). He is provoked with zeal for the Lord's righteousness, as he witnesses the desecration of the temple and the law (8:28). The Lord's love of him is expressed in discipline, and he responds to the Lord's rebuke with repentance for his sins. The author compares the righteous to the tree of life in Paradise. They are stable and will not be uprooted (14:2ff.). The wicked, on the other hand, will not be remembered in this life, and God will deal righteously with them by casting them into "Sheol and darkness and destruction" (14:6; 15:10).

The author views God as the King who mightily rules over the nations (2:34ff.) with readiness to judge his enemies and the enemies of the righteous (2:38ff.; 4:9) and to vindicate the righteous (2:39). As the Lord's care is demonstrated in his sustenance of nature (5:11-12), in his raising up kings, rulers, and nations (5:13), the author assures the reader that his care extends particularly to the poor and those who call upon him (5:2-3, 13). He is the hope of the righteous (8:37).

In view of the foregoing belief in the righteous kingship of God and in his protection of the righteous, the psalms abound in the conviction that evil will be overcome by God's intervention on behalf of the righteous. The particular context in which these psalms originated was Pompey's entrance into Jerusalem and his desecration of the temple (63 BC), and it was hoped that at the death of Pompey (48 BC, cf. 2:30ff.) the messianic era might be introduced. Therefore, the author reminds God of the covenant made with David (17:5) and asks God's forgiveness for Israel's sins in the past. Israel has suffered gentile invasions and control as the result of God's judgment (17:6). Since Pompey had died, the author prayed for the restoration of the theocracy under a Davidic king—"Behold, O Lord, and raise up unto them their king, the son of David. All the time in the which Thou seest, O God, that he may reign over Israel Thy servant" (17:23). By means of the Davidic Messiah the land will be purged of sinners, godless nations, and the righteous will be sanctified. The messianic rule extends only over the righteous remnant, who when restored to the land, will be divided into the 12 tribes; the Davidic Messiah will rule over the tribes and the other nations "in the wisdom of his righteousness" (17:29-31). The sojourner and the gentile nations will not share in the glory of the kingdom. Rather, their position will be that of servitude.

The hope of the glorious future of Israel is the apocalyptic element in the psalms. They arose in a historical context, but they anticipate a radically new future. The psalmist pronounced a benediction on all those who would witness God's judgment on the nations, the restoration of Israel, and the introduction of the messianic kingdom: "Blessed be they that shall be in those days, in that they shall see the good fortune of Israel which God shall bring to pass in the gathering together of the tribes. May the Lord hasten His mercy upon Israel! The Lord Himself is our king for ever and ever" (17:50-51).

Solomon, Testament of The Testament of Solomon is a second-century BC pseudepigraphal writing. The writing claims that Solomon was the writer of the testament. It is extant in Semitic manuscripts, and in some Greek texts.

The material is basically Christian with emphasis on the cross and the virgin birth but also contains Jewish material as well. The testament recounts how Solomon, by means of a ring given to him by the archangel Michael, is able to subdue and use the skills of demons to build his temple. After completing the temple, however, Solomon is led into idolatry on account of his lust for a Shunammite girl. His fall was taken by the author of the testament as an occasion to warn the readers of the power and shapes of the demons and the angels having power over them. The work is written in the form of a testament in order to let Solomon reflect (on his deathbed) how he succeeded and failed as a legacy to Israel.

Testaments of the Twelve Patriarchs Part of the Jewish pseudepigrapha. This particular composition is called a "testament" because it represents the deathbed speeches of each of the sons of Jacob. The testaments start with Reuben's speech to his sons and ends with Benjamin's testament to his heirs. Each patriarch is represented as gathering his sons around him and relating the important events of his life. During the speech the patriarch warns against particular vices and attitudes and recommends certain virtues. The advice and warnings of each patriarch often include insight and predictions concerning sin and salvation for his children. The account of the patriarch's life serves as a guide for the future of his descendants. At the end of the speech, each patriarch dies and is buried at Hebron.

It would appear that the concept of "testament" finds its orientation in Joshua 23–24, where Joshua summons the elders, heads, judges, and officers of Israel (Jos 23:2; 24:1) and gives them a charge before his death. First Kings 2:1-12 portrays David giving Solomon deathbed advice to walk in God's ways. The speeches of the patriarchs find further scriptural reference in Genesis chapter 49, where Jacob calls his sons together to hear about their future. At the end of the speech Jacob dies (Gn 49:33).

The present textual form (Slavonic, Armenian, and Greek versions) probably came about sometime during the second or third century AD. However, much of the material would appear to go back to the second or third century BC. The general scholarly consensus is that an original text in a Semitic language (either Hebrew or Aramaic) was composed by an author or authors sometime in the third or second century before the common era. At some later period, Christian sections were added to the original text. For examples of the Christian sections see Testament of Simeon 6:7; Testament of Levi 10:2; Testament of Dan 6:9; Testament of Naphtali 4:5; Testament of Asher 7:3-4; Testament of Joseph 19:11; Testament of Benjamin 3:8; 9:2-4. It would appear that the testaments may have been reworked by a Jewish writer(s) and by other Christian writers over the centuries. Thus we have a Jewish document from about the third century before the common era that has undergone both Jewish and Christian redactions over a long period of time. These testaments became quite popular in the tenth century, with special interest being displayed in the prophecies of the patriarchs and their secret knowledge.

The following is a summary of each of the testaments of the patriarchs. The excerpts are based on R. H. Charles's *Pseudepigrapha*, pp 282-367.

➤REUBEN The testament of Reuben is very much influenced by an overwhelming memory of defiling his father's bed. This refers to Reuben taking his father's concubine Bilhah while she was in a drunken stupor. Reuben has very strong opinions regarding what he considers to be negative attributes of women, and he warns his sons to be guarded in their relationship with women. His comments on women probably reflect the ill feelings that existed between himself and Jacob in regard to Bilhah. Reuben predicts that in the future his sons would be jealous of the sons of Levi but they would not be able to overthrow them. He admonishes his descendants to have respect and love for one another and to do truth to their neighbors. Reuben is buried at Hebron.

➤SIMEON The patriarch Simeon is presented as a strong warrior type. Reflecting the biblical account of Joseph being sold into slavery (Gn 37:25-28), Simeon testifies that he wanted to kill Joseph rather than sell him into slavery. As punishment for this attitude, God withered his right hand for seven days. Simeon warns his sons against envy, deceit, and fornication. He predicts that they will attempt to harm the sons of Levi but prophesies that the sons of Levi will remain superior. Simeon looked forward to a blissful era (6:4-7a), when the "Most High" would be blessed. Verse 7b is a Christian interpolation, "Because God has taken a body and eaten with men and saved men." He admonishes his sons to obey the sons of Levi and Judah, for it would be from them that their salvation would be accomplished. He predicts that a high priest would come from Levi and a king would descend from the lines of Judah. Simeon concludes his testament by predicting that all Gentiles (an interpolation) and Israel would be saved.

➤LEVI Levi's deathbed testament is in the form of dreams that he relates to his sons. He predicts that from his descendants and those of Judah the Lord would "appear among men" to save every race of men (2:11). The descendants of Levi would be "as the sun to all the

seed of Israel" (4:3b) and in one dream it is shown that the blessings of the priesthood would come to his sons (8:2-3). Levi predicts that a king would arise in Judah; this king would establish a new priesthood that ministers to both Jews and Gentiles. The tenth chapter has a Christian interpolation that because of ungodliness and transgression, the sons of Levi would wrong "the Savior of the world, Christ" (10:2) and that for this they would be scattered throughout the world. Chapter 13 has a number of wisdom themes with emphasis on the need to follow and obey the law. Chapter 16 introduces an eschatological prediction that the sons of Levi would go astray for 70 weeks. The following chapter gives a detailed account of the 70 weeks in which there would be a priesthood for each jubilee. The first priesthood would be great, and the priest's relationship to God would be such that God would be addressed as father. The second priesthood would "be conceived in the sorrow of beloved ones" (17:3), but this priesthood will be glorified by all. The following five priesthoods would be characterized by sorrow, pain, hatred, and darkness. However, a new priesthood would eventually arise and peace will be brought to all the earth (18:4); sin shall come to an end (18:9), for this new priesthood shall have a spirit of understanding and sanctification resting upon him. The testament closes with an admonition to choose either the law of the Lord or the work of Beliar (variant of Belial). The sons pledge themselves to the law, and following Levi's death they bury him at Hebron.

➤JUDAH At the beginning of the testament by Judah he tells his descendants that he had been promised by his father that he would be king. "And it came to pass, when I became a man, that my father blessed me, saying, You shall be a king, prospering in all things" (1:6). Judah reminisces about his early youth and his ability to conquer wild animals. He obeyed the commandments and did not give in to lust. He predicted that his descendants would fall into wickedness because of the love of money and the enticement of beautiful women (ch 17). In chapter 21 Judah predicts that the Lord would give the kingship to his descendants and the priesthood to the sons of Levi. Chapter 24 includes a Christian messianic redaction. It is predicted that from the star of Jacob one will arise that will be without sin and from it a rod of righteousness will grow to the Gentiles (24:6). The testament concludes with eschatological hope for the future when "they who are poor for the Lord's sake shall be made rich and they who are put to death for the Lord's sake shall awake to life" (25:4). Judah dies and is buried at Hebron.

➤ISSACHAR The last words of this patriarch are somewhat unique in that Issachar is depicted as being "upright" and without transgression (unlike many of his brothers). He predicts that the priesthood will come from Levi and the kingship will arise from the lineage of Judah. In chapter 6 Issachar predicts that his children will "cleave" after Beliar. If they recognize the mercy of God and follow Issachar's exemplary life, "every spirit of Beliar will flee from them." His final request is that he be buried at Hebron with his fathers.

➤ZEBULUN The patriarch Zebulun begins his testament by characterizing himself as a "good gift" to his parents. He, like Issachar, indicates that he is not conscious of sinning "except in thought" (and if he has any iniquity it is only the sin of ignorance). Zebulun claims that he did not support the actions taken against Joseph, and he would have told his father about Joseph's plight except that the other brothers agreed that if "anyone should declare the secret, he should be slain" (1:6). In 1:7 he declares that if it were not for him the other brothers would have killed Joseph. The brothers were so suspicious of Zebulun that they watched him until Joseph was sold. Verse 5:3 has a familiar theme that is found in the NT and in the rabbis: "Have compassion in your hearts, my children, because even as a man does to his neighbor, even so will the Lord do to him." Zebulun believes that this lesson is demonstrated in practical terms. The sons of the other brothers were sickened and died on account of the action taken against Joseph ("because they showed no mercy in their hearts," 5:5). The sons of Zebulun were preserved without sickness. He continues his wisdom teaching (8:3) by declaring that in the degree that a man has compassion upon his neighbor the Lord in the same degree will have mercy on him. Zebulun predicts the division between the northern and southern kingdoms and the eventual conquest of these kingdoms by the Gentiles. However, the people will repent and the Lord will bring them back to "the land" and Jerusalem (9:8). In chapter 10 Zebulun predicts that after his death he will "arise as a ruler in the midst of his sons" (10:2), and he promises reward for those who keep the laws and punishment for the ungodly. Zebulun dies at the end of his testament and is buried at Hebron.

➤DAN The patriarch Dan laments his jealousy of Joseph and indicates that he was controlled by the spirit of Beliar. He reveals that he wanted to kill Joseph so that he could have the love of his father. Dan warns against the spirits of lying and anger, and he exhorts his descendants to love truth and long-suffering. He admonishes them to keep the commandments and "love the Lord through all your life and one another with a true heart" (5:3). Dan predicts that his sons will "in the last days" depart from the Lord and thus provoke the anger of the sons of Levi. They also will fight against the sons of Judah. His sons will not win against the sons of Levi and Judah because an angel of the Lord will guide them. Dan is represented as having read in the book of Enoch (a favorite reference for the patriarchs) that Satan and all the spirits of wickedness and pride will cause the sons of Levi, Judah, and Dan to sin. They will be taken into captivity where they will receive the plagues of Egypt and all the evils of the Gentiles. However, when they return to the Lord they will receive mercy and be given peace. The prediction is such that there would be one who would arise from the tribe of Judah and Levi who is called "the salvation of the Lord." It would appear that the "one arising" would make war against Beliar and execute an "everlasting vengeance" against their enemies (5:10). Dan's final warning is to beware of Satan and his spirits and to draw near to God and the angel "that intercedes for you" (6:2). The last section admonishes Dan's sons to pass on to their children all that they have heard so that "the savior of the Gentiles may receive" them. There follows a Christian polemic about the savior being true, long-suffering, meek, and lowly (6:9). When Dan dies, he is buried near Abraham, Isaac, and Jacob.

➤NAPHTALI Naphtali is said to be 130 years old when he gives his last words. He is depicted as being in good health, but the morning after a feast realizes that he is going to die. Thus he gathers his sons about him. Naphtali has a very strong sense of order that contributes to the makeup and actions of man as well as the universe. He views the "Gentile problem" as their forsaking the Lord and changing their order so that they obeyed the "stocks and stones." The change of order was the problem at Sodom and it also caused the Flood.

Naphtali reads from the book of Enoch that his sons will depart from the Lord and walk "according to all lawlessness of the Gentiles" (4:1). He predicts that his descendants will be taken captive because of their sins and afterward a "few" will return to the Lord and he will bring them back to their land. After their return to the land, Naphtali predicts that his sons will forget the Lord and "become ungodly" with the result that they will be scattered all over the earth. They will remain in this state until the compassion of the Lord comes and a man working righteousness and mercy comes to them. Naphtali recounts two dreams that he had in his 40th year. In the first dream he saw the sun and moon stand still. Isaac told his grandsons to run and take hold of the sun and moon, each according to his strength. Levi took hold of the sun, and Judah seized the moon. Both of them were lifted up with the sun and moon. There appeared a bull in the dream with two great horns and eagle wings. The other sons attempted to seize this bull but could not. However, Joseph came and took hold of the bull and ascended "up with him on high" (5:7).

There follows a prediction that the 12 tribes of Israel would be taken into captivity by the Assyrians, Medes, Persians, Chaldeans, and Syrians. The other dream saw a ship sailing on the sea of Jamnia without sailors or pilot. Written on the ship was the inscription "The ship of Jacob" (6:2). Jacob and his sons were on the ship, and when a storm arose Jacob departed from their presence. Eventually the ship breaks up from the pounding of the sea, and while Joseph sails off in a little boat the rest of the brothers are divided among nine planks with Levi and Judah sharing a plank. It would appear that by the prayers of Levi all the brothers eventually land safely on the shore. When Naphtali relates these dreams to his father, Jacob responds that all these things must be fulfilled.

Naphtali admonished his sons to be united to Levi and Judah for through them "shall salvation arise to Israel" (8:2). Also through Levi and Judah the righteous of the Gentiles shall be gathered. Naphtali died and was buried at Hebron.

➤GAD The patriarch Gad is represented as hating Joseph because Joseph had told his father that Gad and some of the other brothers were eating from the best of the flocks while tending them. During his testament Gad confesses his sin of hatred to his sons and warns them against harboring hatred because it only brings anguish: "For as love would quicken even the dead and would call back them that are condemned to die, so hatred would slay the living and those that had sinned venially it would not suffer to live" (4:6).

Repentance is understood to give knowledge to the soul and leads the mind to salvation. Gad encourages his sons to honor the lineage of Levi and Judah, for therein is found the salvation of Israel. He predicts that his sons will walk in all wickedness and corruption and ends on a somewhat pessimistic note by asking to be buried near his fathers. Gad is buried at Hebron.

➤ASHER Asher is very conscious of good and evil spirits and the choice that man has to make between these two possibilities. Asher predicts that his descendants will act ungodly and not give heed to the law of God. Thus they will be delivered into the hands of their enemies and they will be scattered. They will exist in such a state until the "Most High" visits the earth "coming Himself [as man with men eating and drinking] . . . he shall save Israel and all the Gentiles" (7:3-4). This Christian interpolation is followed by a declaration that the Lord will gather them because of his mercy and for the sake of Abraham, Isaac, and Jacob. When Asher dies, he is buried at Hebron.

➤JOSEPH Joseph calls himself the "beloved of Israel," (1:2) and although he has seen envy and death, he did not go astray. During his testament he tells of his ordeal of being sold into slavery. The verses in chapter one are set in parallelism with the first half of the verse telling the plight of Joseph and the second half exalting the security of the Lord: "I was sold into slavery, and the Lord of all made me free: I was taken into captivity, and his strong hand succoured me. I was beset with hunger and the Lord himself nourished me" (1:5). Joseph details his experiences in Egypt with eight chapters being given to the temptations of the Egyptian woman. However, Joseph resisted her advances and the Lord rewarded him for his convictions. He admonishes his sons to have the fear of the Lord in all their works because whoever does the law of the Lord will be loved by him. This is the key to his success. Joseph encourages his children to do well to anyone who would do evil to them and pray for their enemies. He gives his attitude toward his brothers as an example of such a virtue.

Joseph admonishes his sons to observe the commandments of the Lord and honor Levi and Judah for "the Lamb of God, who takes away the sin of the world, who saves all the Gentiles and Israel" (19:11) shall arise from them. He predicts the enslavement in Egypt but also the eventual deliverance. He directs his sons to take his bones with them when they leave Egypt, and the testament indicates that Joseph was buried at Hebron.

➤BENJAMIN The last patriarch gives his testament when he is 125 years old. He encourages his children to love the Lord and keep his commandments. He urges them to follow the goodness of Joseph, for he did not want his brothers' actions against him to be counted as sin. Benjamin predicts that in Joseph shall the prophecy be fulfilled "concerning the Lamb of God and Savior of the world, and that a blameless one shall be delivered up for lawless men, and a sinless one shall die for ungodly men in the blood of the covenant, for the salvation of the Gentiles and of Israel and shall destroy Beliar and his servants" (3:8). One can immediately see how the Christian interpolation would find easy access for a polemic in this testament. Joseph is depicted as suffering in innocence and without remorse. Likewise the Christian messiah would suffer and die for ungodly men.

Benjamin believes that there are evildoers among his sons; from his reading of the book of Enoch he predicts that they will commit "fornication with the fornication of Sodom" and only a few will survive (9:1). There would appear to be a remnant from each tribe as the 12 tribes and the Gentiles will gather at the last temple. Their salvation will be a result of the "Most High" sending his only "begotten prophet" (9:2), and he will be lifted up upon a tree and the veil of the temple shall be rent and the Spirit of God shall be passed on to the Gentiles. Benjamin admonishes his sons that if they walk in holiness according to the commandments of the Lord, all of Israel will be gathered to the Lord. When Benjamin dies, he is buried at Hebron.

From the brief account of each patriarch, it is apparent that the testaments were subject to both Jewish and Christian redaction and go beyond mere interpolation. The text reflects such characteristics as two messiahs, a double love commandment, ethical and theological teachings, as well as universal salvation. However, it is most difficult to place these features within a particular time period or even religion.

Thaddeus, Acts of A sixth-century version and extension of the fifth-century Syriac Doctrina Addaei, or Legend of Abgar. The Legend contains a purported exchange of letters between Abgar, king of Edessa (AD 9–46), and Jesus. This exchange results in the sending of Thaddeus, one of Jesus' apostles, to Edessa. While there, he performs numerous miracles including the healing of Abgar. The Acts has Abgar healed when Ananias, his messenger, returns prior to the arrival of Thaddeus. The Acts focuses on the activity of Thaddeus in establishing the church in Edessa.

Thecla, Acts of Paul and *See* Paul and Thecla, Acts of (above).

Thomas, Acts of The Acts of Thomas is one of a cluster of acts of the apostles that have three common characteristics. They narrate the propagation of the gospel around the ancient world, promote the deeds and words of one of the apostles, and inevitably chronicle that apostle's martyrdom. The oldest of these "acts narratives" are those of Paul, John, Andrew, Peter, and Thomas. Acts of Thomas, like the others, is a blend of Christian piety, the popular Hellenistic romances of the day, and Jewish haggadic-type moralistic teachings.

Scholarly study of the Acts of Thomas suggests that it was probably written at the beginning of the third century. It was definitely written in Syriac first and probably by someone with strong tendencies toward the Gnostic heresy. It proved broadly popular among Gnostics, Manichees, and orthodox churches, so much so that it was quickly translated from the original Syriac into Arabic, Armenian, and several Greek translations. From these varied Greek versions, Coptic, Latin, and Ethiopic translations were made. Significant portions of the Coptic version were in turn retranslated back into Arabic, Ethiopic, and Greek, thus creating a most confusing textual tradition. Only one full early Syriac text survives, and it is considered less reliable than some of the extant Greek translations.

In the critical English edition of the Acts of Thomas, that of A. F. J. Klijn published in 1962, the narrative is divided into the traditional acts (praxeis). There are 13 of these numbered in 170 sequential chapters that include the concluding martyrdom of the apostle. Various liturgical pieces, sermon fragments, and hymns are inserted, including two particularly famous hymns in the early church—that of the "Song of the Bride" in act 1 and that of the "Song of the Pearl" in act 9. The first six acts are not woven together by any particular theme, and they record that Thomas went on board ship to go to India (act 3), which would imply a south Indian ministry. Yet the text speaks of ministry to the north Indian king, Gundaphoro (act 4). However, acts 7 through 13 and the martyrdom are set in the south Indian kingdom of Mazdai and are obviously written by one hand. It is probable that the first six acts represent earlier materials placed into the whole by the writer of the last seven acts and the martyrdom. This document is the first-known mention of the traditions that Thomas ministered in India, was martyred there, and that his bones were returned to Edessa. Acts of Thomas is written, as are all the apocryphal acts of the apostles, on the assumption that the world was divided among the apostles for evangelization and that India fell to Thomas.

Thomas is called Judas Thomas throughout these acts after the Syrian style of referring to that apostle. Thomas is spoken of as the twin of Jesus (the Didymus of the NT), as recipient of special divine revelations, and as being Jesus incarnate in the flesh again—in chapters 10, 11, 39, 47, and 48 of the Acts. Many historians think these are clear indications of Gnostic thought. Others think such ideas are expressions of Jesus' adaptation to human perception and identification with his apostles—features often found in early Christian literature. There seems to be no question but that Gnostic or Manichee tendencies were gradually edited out of Greek and Latin texts by orthodox copyists.

One quickly gets the feel for this narrative. The Acts of Thomas opens with Judas Thomas's refusing to go to India. He is then sold as a slave—in parallel to Christ's coming as a slave to redeem man. So Thomas reaches India as a carpenter (again the parallel with Jesus) and a builder of homes. He plays groomsman in a wedding at which miracles convince the flute player of Thomas's role as apostle of God; so the king asks Thomas to pray for his daughter. Great stress is placed on purity in Thomas's teaching, and this usually involves sexual abstinence as well. Finally, many are converted, including the king, and they form an assembly of believers in Sandaruk.

In the second act the king, Gundophor, gives Thomas a large sum of money to build a palace. After surprising the king by tracing the palace on the ground in winter, Thomas builds him a palace in heaven by giving the money to the poor. The king imprisons and decides to kill Thomas for the supposed deception; but the king's brother, Gad, dies and goes to heaven where he sees the palace and desires to buy it. Gad is then reunited with his body and tries to buy the palace from Gundophor, whereupon Gundophor learns that he cannot sell it, releases Thomas from prison, and advises Gad to arrange to have his own palace built in heaven. Thomas gives a great doxology (ch 25 of act 2), and the two brothers who have come to believe through all of this want to be baptized.

In these miracle narratives and teachings, all the books of the NT seem to be echoed, though there are relatively few direct quotations. Favorite miracle passages such as Balaam's talking donkey and Peter's release from prison are reexperienced in Thomas's life with vast embellishment. The talking ass enters a home and casts out a demon at Thomas's command; Thomas causes great consternation by repeatedly passing in and out of the securely closed prison. Such miracles, sufferings, and conversions make up acts 3 through 13 and continue to the climax of Judas Thomas's ministry. His martyrdom occurs (ch 168) at the hands of four soldiers with spears who have been ordered by the king of Mazdai to execute Thomas. He thereafter appears to his followers who have Thomas's bones removed to Edessa. Meantime, the son of the king of Mazdai becomes sick unto death. Desperate, the king goes to Thomas's tomb, thinking to get a relic to heal his son. Finding the body gone, he uses the very dust upon which Judas Thomas's body rested, and his son is healed. Thereafter the king becomes a believer and joins the community of believers.

Thomas, Gospel of A noncanonical and heretical gospel of Gnostic origin that probably dates from the second or third century AD. It is one of a large number of similar writings that flourished among early religious sects such as the Marcosians (a second-century group that built an elaborate sacramental system around numbers) and the Manicheans (a third-century dualistic heresy based on the primeval conflict between light and darkness). In fact, Cyril of Jerusalem, who died in AD 386 says the Gospel of Thomas was written by "one of those wicked disciples of Mani" (the founder of Manichaeism). Along with the Protevangelium of James, it is one of the oldest and most widely known of the more than 50 apocryphal gospels that circulated within the churches during the period of their early growth and expansion.

This Gospel of Thomas (sometimes referred to as an "infancy gospel") should not be confused with the Coptic version that was unearthed in 1945 near Nag Hammadi in Upper Egypt. The latter is a collection of 114 "sayings of Jesus," which shed a great deal of light on the influence of Gnosticism on Egyptian Christianity. They claim to be the "secret words" of Jesus transmitted by "Didymos Judas Thomas." The Gospel of Thomas, with which this article deals, is composed of a series of childhood miracles of Jesus and is preserved for us in four versions—two in Greek (one quite a bit longer than the other), one in Latin, and one in Syriac.

The Gospel of Thomas was apparently known as early as Hippolytus (AD 155–235), who quotes it as saying, "He who seeks me will find me in children from seven years old; for there will I, who am hidden in the fourteenth aeon, be found." Hippolytus claimed that it was used by the Naasenes (a Gnostic sect that worshiped the serpent) in support of their doctrine of the nature of the inward man. The quotation above is not found in the extant versions, but this is understandable because there is evidence from the Stichometry of Nicephorus (possibly fourth century) that an earlier version was over twice the length. The Gospel of Thomas was known both to Origen (c. AD 185–254) and Eusebius (c. AD 260–340). The latter classed it with the heretical writings and said it should be "rejected as altogether absurd and impious" (*Historia Ecclesiastica* 3.25).

The stories that make up the Gospel of Thomas emphasize the miraculous power and supernatural wisdom of the boy Jesus. Some scholars think they were originally fabricated by orthodox Christians in opposition to the Gnostic heresy that the "supernatural Christ" first came upon Jesus at the time of his baptism. It is much more likely, however, that they owe their origin to people's curiosity about what the boy Jesus must have been like. Some of the tales may have come from pagan sources.

Apart from three or four miracles, which could be classed as beneficial, the supernatural feats said to be performed by the boy Jesus were destructive. For example, when a certain child spoiled some pools made by Jesus, he was cursed by Jesus and totally withered up. Another boy who provoked Jesus by running into him "immediately . . . fell down and died." A teacher who struck Jesus on the head was straightway cursed and fell to the ground. The French writer Renan referred to the Jesus of the Gospel of Thomas as "a vicious little guttersnipe."

Throughout the gospel Jesus is presented as infinitely wise. He ridicules his teacher Zacchaeus saying, "You hypocrite, first, if you know it, teach the Alpha, and then we will believe you concerning the Beta." After Zacchaeus berates himself for being so inferior to the one he intended to take as a disciple, Jesus laughs and announces, "I am come from above that I may curse them." The text continues, "And no man after that dared to provoke him, lest he should curse him, and he should be maimed."

Other miracles include making 12 live sparrows out of clay, smiting his accusers with blindness, raising a child from the dead, healing a foot cut in two by an ax, carrying water in a cloth garment, reaping an enormous harvest from one kernal of wheat, stretching a piece of wood to its proper length, and healing his brother James who had been bitten by a viper while gathering fagots (sticks to use as firewood). More miracles may be found in the longer Latin version.

It comes as no surprise that the orthodox church has always rejected from its canon of sacred scripture the apocryphal Gospel of Thomas. It is, however, quoted in other later gospels of the same sort. For example, the Gospel of Pseudo-Matthew from chapter 18 on is based upon the Gospel of Thomas. Along with other apocryphal materials, it has exercised a significant influence on Christian art and literature, especially from the tenth century forward. For example, the account of Jesus making the 12 sparrows from clay shows up in the Koran.

Truth, Gospel of Around 1945 a group of Egyptian peasant farmers near modern Nag Hammadi inadvertently dug into a grave of the ancient village known as Shenesit-Chenoboskion and unearthed a jar containing 13 books (9 of which were largely complete) and 15 fragments of works. This find was the library of an ancient Gnostic sect and contained all or parts of 51 different Gnostic writings—all but two of which had never come into modern scholars' hands before. Now called the Nag Hammadi or Chenoboskion texts, these works were the first modern find of original Gnostic literature. All are Coptic translations of earlier Greek originals.

Codex I (titled the Jung Codex because it now is owned by the Jung Institute in Vienna) is unique among the 13 works because it is in Sub-Achimimic Coptic, while the rest of the works are in the more usual Sahidic Coptic. Codex I contains five works, two of which are the enormously controversial Gospel of Thomas and the Gospel of Truth.

The Gospel of Truth has no heading but rather draws its title from the incipit (first line of the text); it has no author; it contains no addressee. In fact, it is not a gospel at all, but rather a treatise expressive of Valentinian Gnosticism at its very earliest stage. Because the Gnosticism expressed in the Gospel of Truth is lacking all later-Valentinian mythological development and because it is stated simply and in almost orthodox Christian thought forms, the majority of modern scholars credit it to Valentinus himself, though no final proof of this has been discovered as yet. If Valentinus himself did not write this document, then it had to be someone in the immediate circle of his initial disciples.

Valentinus was born in Egypt around AD 100 to 110. He received a thorough education at Alexandria, became a Christian, and taught first in Egypt before moving to Rome around AD 136, where he stayed until 154 or 155. Tertullian, in his work against heresy, seems to imply that Valentinus was twice expelled from the Roman church; he states that Valentinus was a brilliant and eloquent man who had hopes of becoming a bishop in Rome at one time. Valentinus attracted able followers who later expanded his teachings almost beyond recognition. But when he left Rome sometime after 154 or 155, he had made a final break with orthodoxy and was teaching a form of Gnostic heresy the product of which was the Gospel of Truth, written by himself or someone of his immediate circle. There is a surviving statement that Valentinus taught subsequently in Cyprus, and then he vanishes into the mists of history.

Irenaeus said the Gospel of Truth is no gospel, for it is unlike the four Gospels (*Against Heresies* 3.2.9). Irenaeus was certainly correct, for the work is not a narrative. Nor does the Gospel of Truth contain any story about Jesus, any place name of any type, any date, or any mention of any person other than Jesus, who is only mentioned five times.

More than 60 times, this brief work uses the notions of knowledge or needing to know. This knowledge is born from within as the soul returns to itself, finding there what Deity deposited in it—or perhaps better, finding there the residue of Deity still entrapped within it. Thus whoever has Gnosis has simply taken what is his and can know where he or she comes from and for

where he or she is bound. Christ's role was to present the "Book of the Living" or the "Living Book." "Book" is understood, not as the gospel proclamation of the life and teachings of Jesus, but rather as the primordial gospel or truth that existed before creation. It was error and ignorance that rebelled against the Savior and nailed him to the tree. Implied in this, though not explicitly stated, is the Gnostic understanding that it was also divine error and ignorance out of which matter emerged or was created. Salvation for living beings entrapped in this matter comes with return to unalloyed Deity. The path of this return is Gnosis (knowledge). The Pleroma, the fullness of the Deity, went out into the depths of matter in search of the elect among beings by way of Jesus and the cross.

While these traits of Gnosticism are clear, this gospel is much closer to orthodoxy than most Gnostic Chenoboskion writings because it mentions only one Son of God, not several emanations; it does not split Jesus into a physical Jesus and a divine Christ; and most strikingly, Sophia, the usual central character in the Gnostic cosmic drama, does not appear at all. It is for these reasons among others that the Gospel of Truth is placed very close to Valentinus's break with orthodoxy.

The Gospel of Truth has assumed some degree of importance in NT studies beyond that warranted by its heretical content because it everywhere assumes our full NT canon. By some scholars' counts, there are no less than 83 places where the Gospel of Truth echoes NT canonical books—in spite of the fact it does not cite a single saying of Jesus directly. Most particularly, it relies heavily on the book of Revelation and the Epistle to the Hebrews.

Virgin, Assumption of the A widely circulated legend dealing with the death and translation of the Virgin Mary. None of the many versions is earlier than the fourth century. Most go back to Egypt. In the Coptic versions, Jesus himself appears to Mary before the apostles depart on their missionary labors; Jesus announces her coming death and translation. In the other form an angel makes the announcement. Mary requests the presence of all the apostles, who are miraculously brought on the clouds. Mary is transfigured, and many healings result from contact with her dead body. She is transported to heaven by Jesus shortly after her death.

This legend itself took on a new interest and importance when in 1950 "The Assumption of the Blessed Virgin" was made a part of official Roman Catholic dogma.

Virgin, Life of the There are a number of accounts of the early life and existence of the Virgin Mary. Most of them come to us through Coptic texts. They tell of the birth of Mary to Joachim (also called Cleopas) and Anna, who had been taunted by friends for having no children. Mary was born after a vision of a white dove. In some accounts Mary was dedicated to the Lord and then committed to the care of a man, Joseph. While she was in the house weaving on the veil of the temple, angels would come to minister to her. The annunciation by Gabriel is given at great length. The birth of Jesus is described in detail while Joseph is searching for a midwife, Salome. Other accounts go on to describe tender scenes between Mary and the child Jesus. In some of these versions, there is a reckless identification of the Virgin Mary with all of the other Marys of the Gospels.

Zebulun, Testament of *See* Testaments of the Twelve Patriarchs (above).

APOLLONIA Town located on the Egnatian Way in eastern Macedonia. Paul passed through Apollonia on his second missionary journey west from Philippi to

Thessalonica, a trip of about 90 miles (145 kilometers) (Acts 17:1). It is usually identified with modern Pollina.

APOLLONIUS Name of probably four different men in the Maccabean literature.

1. Apollonius of Tarsus, son of Menestheus (2 Macc 3:5-7; 4:4). According to the Greek historian, Polybius, this governor of Coelesyria and Phoenicia under Seleucus IV retired to Miletus when Antiochus IV began to rule. Apollonius's diplomatic expertise, however, was later utilized when he served as ambassador to Egypt (2 Macc 4:21). His son, another Apollonius (#4 below), served as governor under Demetrius II.
2. Apollonius, cruel captain of the Mysians sent by Antiochus IV to slaughter all adult Jewish males (1 Macc 1:29; 2 Macc 5:24). He met his death at the hands of Judas Maccabeus (1 Macc 3:10-12).
3. Apollonius, Gennaeus's son, petty governor who along with other local leaders continued to harass the Jews (2 Macc 12:2).
4. Apollonius, grandson of Menestheus. In 147 BC he began to serve as governor of Coelesyria, an office his father had held. Appointed by Demetrius II, this Apollonius led forces against Jonathan Maccabeus; Jonathan outmaneuvered him, overwhelmed his forces, and put him to flight (1 Macc 10:69-85).

See also Maccabean Period.

APOLLOPHANES Syrian warrior during the intertestamental period. Apollophanes was killed at a fortress named Gazara by the forces of Judas Maccabeus (2 Macc 10:37). His death occurred after a dramatic battle in which the Jewish forces relied on the Lord for victory, in contrast with the Syrians who "made rage their leader" (2 Macc 10:24-31).

APOLLOS Native of Alexandria (Egypt), a Christian Jew who was an eloquent preacher at the time of the apostle Paul's missionary journeys. The chief biblical passage about Apollos is Acts 18:24–19:1. From Alexandria, Apollos went to Ephesus in Asia Minor. Enthusiastic in spirit, learned and cultured in his ways, well versed in the OT Scriptures, and instructed in the way of the Lord, he began to speak boldly and openly in the synagogue there. Apollos knew and preached accurately about the coming of Jesus but knew of it only from the message of Jesus' forerunner, John the Baptist. Priscilla and Aquila, Paul's friends and former associates, heard Apollos speak in Ephesus and realized that he had not heard what had happened to Jesus. They took him aside privately and explained the way of God to him more accurately. Before that, he had been convinced of the value of John's baptism and John's message that Jesus was the Messiah. He was evidently uninformed, however, about such teachings as justification by faith in Christ or the work of the Holy Spirit in salvation. At such points, Priscilla and Aquila, having lived and worked with Paul, were able to help Apollos.

Soon after this instruction, Apollos left Ephesus for the Roman province of Achaia in Greece with letters from the Ephesian Christians, urging the disciples in Achaia to welcome him as a Christian brother. On arrival, he vigorously and publicly refuted the Jews, using his great knowledge of the OT Scriptures to prove that Jesus was the Messiah. Paul considered Apollos's work in Corinth, capital of Achaia, so valuable that he described him as waterer of the seed that Paul had planted as the founder of the church (1 Cor 3:5-11). From 1 Corinthians it is also clear that one of the factions dividing the Corinthian church was a clique centered around Apollos, although he was not directly responsible for it (1 Cor 1:12; 3:1-4). Paul had difficulty convincing Apollos that he should return to Corinth, perhaps because Apollos did not want to encourage the continuance of that little group (1 Cor 16:12).

APOLLYON Angel of the "bottomless pit," also called Abaddon (Rv 9:11). *See* Abaddon.

APOSTASY Turning against God, as evidenced by abandonment and repudiation of former beliefs. The term generally refers to a deliberate renouncing of the faith by a once sincere believer rather than a state of ignorance or mistaken knowledge. Apostasy is distinguished from heresy (denial of a part of the faith) and from transfer of allegiance from one religious body to another within the same faith. Also, it is possible to deny the faith, as Peter once did, and then at a later time reaffirm it.

Originally, "apostasy" meant literal rebellion. Thus the Jews were described as "rebels" against King Artaxerxes (1 Esd 2:23) and Jason as a "rebel against the laws" (2 Macc 5:6-8). OT descriptions of spiritual rebellion include departure from the law, forsaking temple worship, and willful disobedience toward God himself (Jos 22:22; 2 Chr 29:19; Jer 2:19). The prophetic writings of Isaiah and Jeremiah provide many examples of Israel's defections (Is 1:2-4; Jer 2:19). Israelite kings were often guilty of apostasy: Rehoboam (1 Kgs 14:22-24); Ahab (1 Kgs 16:30-33); Ahaziah (1 Kgs 22:51-53); Jehoram (2 Chr 21:6, 10); Ahaz (2 Chr 28:1-4); Manasseh (2 Chr 33:1-19); Amon (2 Chr 33:21-23).

In NT times many disciples withdrew from Christ (Jn 6:66)—the most notorious example being Judas Iscariot. The Greek word from which "apostasy" is derived appears in only two passages. The apostle Paul was accused of apostasy for teaching others "to turn their backs on the laws of Moses" (Acts 21:21, NLT). And apostasy is given an eschatological (end times) significance in 2 Thessalonians 2:3. Christians were warned not to be carried away and deceived in the widespread apostasy to come in the end times before the Lord's return. That apostasy is linked to the rise of a man of rebellion who will be Satan's tool (2 Thes 2:3-12; cf. 1 Tm 4:1-3).

WARNINGS AGAINST APOSTASY
Many NT passages, using different words, convey warnings against apostasy. In the last days, tribulation and persecution will cause many to "fall away" (Mt 24:9-10); false prophets will arise and "lead many astray" (Mt 24:11). Other causes of apostasy include temptation (Lk 8:13) and unbelief (Heb 3:12). Paul cited Hymenaeus and Alexander as examples of those who had rejected the faith (1 Tm 1:20). The writer of Hebrews referred to those who had believed and then departed from the faith as being in a hopeless state—with no possibility of further repentance (Heb 6:1-6). The consequences of willful sinning after receiving Christ are terrifying (Heb 10:26-31). The apostle Peter said that, for believers in Christ who knowingly turned away, "they are worse off than before" (2 Pt 2:20-22). The apostle John addresses this same problem (1 Jn 2:18-19).

APOSTLE, APOSTLESHIP Official designation given to certain leading individuals in the NT churches. Apostleship is the more comprehensive term, denoting the functions of the one who serves in such a capacity.

96 APOTHECARY

TYNDALE

Questions concerning origin, function, and history of the NT apostolate are much debated; one cannot speak of anything like consensus of opinion uniting the various church traditions. Some light is shed on our understanding of the terms by an examination of the possible linguistic and conceptual backgrounds.

The Greek word for "apostle" is not used outside the NT in the same sense as it is in the NT. It is derived from the verb "to send" and is at home in the language of the sea meaning a particular "ship" or "group of ships," a "marine expedition" or "the leader" of such. Its usage is almost always impersonal and thoroughly passive. There is no hint of personal initiative or authorization, merely the connotation of something being sent. Later papyri use the word to mean "bill" or "invoice" or even a "passport," continuing to reflect the vocabulary of maritime affairs.

In the NT, the word was used to designate those who had been sent by Jesus with the proclamation of the gospel. From among the wider group of those who followed him, Jesus selected 12 men (Mt 10:1-4; Mk 3:13-19; Lk 6:12-16) who maintained with him a particularly close relationship, receiving private instruction and witnessing his miracles and controversy with the Jewish authorities. On one occasion, Jesus sent these men out to preach the message of repentance, to cast out demons, and to heal the sick; that is, to minister in ways that were characteristic of his own work (Mt 10:1-15; Mk 6:7-13, 30; Lk 9:1-6). The same relationship is expressed in the saying "He who hears you hears me, and he who rejects you rejects me, and he who rejects me rejects him who sent me" (Lk 10:16, RSV; cf. Mt 10:40). It is clear that the Twelve are not merely to pass Jesus' teaching on but to represent his very person. After the resurrection, Jesus commissioned the Twelve (Mt 28; Lk 24; Jn 20-21) to proclaim God's act in Christ on behalf of all men. Only those who had been with Jesus from the beginning of his ministry to his resurrection were qualified to be his apostolic witnesses (Acts 1:21-22). Paul qualified because he had seen the risen Christ (1 Cor 15:4-10).

The Pauline writings demonstrate two characteristic usages of the word "apostle." On occasion, it refers to persons authorized by local congregations and entrusted with the safe delivery of specific gifts for other members of the Christian community (2 Cor 8:23; Phil 2:25). More important are those passages where "apostle" takes on a more technical sense through the qualifying phrase "of Jesus Christ" (1 Cor 1:1; 2 Cor 1:1; 11:13; Gal 1:1; Eph 1:1; Col 1:1; 1 Thes 2:6). The "sent one" is the "sent one of Jesus Christ" (Rom 16:7; 1 Cor 9:1, 5; 12:28; Gal 1:17-19). In the statements where Paul claims his own right to this title, he argues along lines assuming the same basic apostolic concept that Jesus had. He consistently links this claim to a specific event in the past in which the risen Lord had appeared to him (1 Cor 9:1; Gal 1:12, 16). This appearance he ranked alongside those of the resurrection appearances (1 Cor 15:3-8). Paul understood his experience outside Damascus (cf. Acts 9:1-19a; 22:6-16; 26:12-18; Gal 1:17) as a lifelong commission to preach the now-resurrected One (1 Cor 1:17; 2:1-2) chiefly among the Gentiles (Acts 9:15; 22:15; 26:17, 23; Gal 1:15-16). It was through his preaching ministry that Christ continued to work, creating the new people of God (1 Cor 9:1-2; Gal 2:8).

See also Acts of the Apostles, Book of the; Paul, The Apostle.

APOTHECARY*

KJV rendering of "perfumer" in Exodus 30:25, 35; 37:29; 2 Chronicles 16:14; Nehemiah 3:8; and Ecclesiastes 10:1.

APOTHEGM*

Short, pithy saying. As used by some biblical scholars, the term "apothegm" denotes brief stories in the Gospels that culminate in a saying of Jesus (e.g., Mt 8:18-22; 9:10-13; 16:1-4; Mk 2:18-22; 10:13-15; Lk 6:1-5; 11:37-44). Also known as "pronouncement stories," the apothegmata (plural) are devoid of a larger historical setting and contain only enough detail to make the saying of Jesus intelligible. Because such stories were used in worship, in the education of new Christians, and in the correction of false teachings, they were of great interest to the early church.

APPAIM

Nadab's son, and the father of Ishi in Judah's tribe (1 Chr 2:30-31).

APPEAL

Legal term meaning to request a higher court review of a decision by a lower one. OT law made no provision for appeals. In the NT the apostle Paul appealed to Caesar for a hearing after his arrest in Jerusalem (Acts 25:11). Because he was a Roman citizen, Paul could have his case removed from the Jewish courts where he feared an unfair trial.

See also Civil Law and Justice.

APPEARANCES OF CHRIST

Occasions on which Jesus Christ was seen by human witnesses after his resurrection. *See* Resurrection.

APPHIA

Christian woman in Colosse, possibly the wife or sister of Philemon. The apostle Paul greeted her in his letter to Philemon (v 2). According to tradition, she was martyred during Nero's persecution. On the saints' calendar of the Greek Orthodox Church, she is honored on November 22.

APPHUS

Nickname of Jonathan, one of Judas Maccabeus's four brothers (1 Macc 9:28-13:30). As with the other Maccabean nicknames (1 Macc 2:2-6), the meaning of the word apphus is uncertain. "Favorite," "beloved," or "desired" have been suggested as translations. *See* Jonathan #16.

APPIAN WAY

Main highway from Rome southward to the heel of the Italian peninsula. Originally the Appian Way terminated at Capua, but later it was extended to Brundisium, about 350 miles (560 kilometers) from Rome. It received its name from Appius Claudius Caecus, the Roman censor who began its construction in 312 BC. The Appian Way is referred to by the ancient writers Livy, Strabo, Horace, and others in a variety of contexts. Portions of the road still exist today south of Rome, with the original Roman paving intact in many places. Ruins of some structures built along the original road are also in evidence.

The apostle Paul traveled on the Appian Way on his journey to Rome after disembarking from a ship at Puteoli (Acts 28:13-15). Christians from Rome came out to meet him in the vicinity of Three Taverns and the Appii Forum ("marketplace of Appius"). These were two of eight major stations known to have existed along the Appian Way. The Appii Forum was located 43 miles (70 kilometers) from Rome in the middle of the Pontine Marshes. Horace, writing in 65-68 BC, complained of the noise and stench that assaulted those who stayed there. Three Taverns was located 10 miles (16 kilometers) closer to Rome.

As Paul traveled on, he would have passed Bovillae, a village located about 11 miles (18 kilometers) from Rome. This village was the ancestral home and cult center of the family of Caesar Augustus. Much of the Appian Way from Bovillae to Rome was lined with tombs.

Roman law forbade burials within the city of Rome, so it became common practice to bury the dead beside the major roads leading into the city.

The Appian Way The apostle Paul traveled on this road on his way to Rome.

APPIUS*, Forum of Marketplace mentioned in Acts 28:15 as the place where Christians met the apostle Paul when he came to appear before the caesar. It was apparently named for Appius Claudius, builder of the Appian Way (major artery of western Italy). Around the forum was a region of swamp and marsh, notorious in the ancient world for bad water, mosquitoes, expensive taverns for travelers, nighttime noisy traffic of cargoes and passengers on mule-drawn barges along a canal cut through the area. The Appian Way passes through the Appius Forum about 40 miles (64 kilometers) south of Rome.

See also Appian Way; Forum.

APPLE, APPLE TREE Fruit and tree not native to the Near East but used by some versions to translate certain references to fruit in the OT. *See* Plants (Apricot).

APRICOT* *See* Plants.

AQABA*, Gulf of Eastern branch (of two northern arms) of the Red Sea that penetrates northeast between Saudi Arabia and the Sinai Peninsula. The gulf varies in width from 12 to 17 miles (19 to 27 kilometers) and is 100 miles (161 kilometers) long. The port city of Elath (or Eloth), located at the northern end of the Gulf of Aqaba, is mentioned in the account of the Israelites' 40 years of wandering in the wilderness (Dt 2:8). From his port of Ezion-geber King Solomon sent ships down the Gulf of Aqaba to Ophir (1 Kgs 9:26-28).

AQUEDUCT Conduit or artificial channel for conducting water from a distance, usually by means of gravity; also a structure carrying a conduit or canal across a valley or over a river.

In Palestine most cities were situated near an abundant water supply so that in time of siege, water would be available. Ancient tunnels for the conveyance of water have been found at Gezer. The Jebusites, inhabitants of the area that later became Jerusalem, seem to have constructed some sort of aqueduct to bring rainwater into the city (2 Sm 5:8). By the time of King Hezekiah there existed a "conduit of the upper pool" (2 Kgs 18:17). In anticipation of throwing off the Assyrian yoke, Hezekiah made a 1,777-foot (541.4-meter) tunnel through the hill

of Ophel to carry water from the Gihon spring to the pool of Siloam (Is 22:9-11). The famous "Siloam inscription" describes how it was done.

It is also known that two aqueducts, 13 and 41 miles (21 and 66 kilometers) in length, brought water into Jerusalem. They merged at the Roman reservoirs near Bethlehem. On reaching the city, the water was carried to the temple area by means of underground pipes (cf. Ez 47:1; Jl 3:18). In NT times, the Jewish historian Josephus stated Pontius Pilate appropriated some "Corban" money from the temple treasury for work on an aqueduct. Three "pools of Solomon," which are of Roman design, were probably constructed with part of those funds.

Other cities of Bible times served by ancient aqueducts were Tyre, Samaria, Caesarea (Roman capital of the province), Jericho, and Ephesus in Asia Minor. The Romans brought the science of aqueduct engineering to a fine art. The Appia (312 BC) was 10.3 miles (16.6 kilometers) long, and the Ano Vetus (272 BC) was over 32 miles (51.5 kilometers) long. Both were underground channels that brought water into the city of Rome.

AQUILA Husband of Priscilla (Acts 18:2, 18, 26; Rom 16:3; 1 Cor 16:19; 2 Tm 4:19). *See* Priscilla and Aquila.

AR Capital city of Moab located on the northern border (Dt 2:18, 29) near the Arnon River (Nm 21:28). Ar was sometimes used figuratively to refer to all of Moab (Dt 2:9). The prophet Isaiah predicted the destruction of the Moabite cities Ar and Kir (Is 15:1).

ARA Son of Jether, a chief among Asher's tribe (1 Chr 7:38).

ARAB City in the hill country southwest of Hebron, given to Judah's tribe after the conquest of Canaan, the Promised Land (Jos 15:52).

ARABAH Great valley dividing eastern and western Palestine. The Arabah extends south from the Sea of Galilee through the Jordan River valley to the Dead Sea and the Gulf of Aqaba. Commonly known as the Rift Valley, the Arabah is about 6 miles (10 kilometers) wide and 200 miles (322 kilometers) long. The Dead Sea, located in the Arabah, is the lowest point on the earth's inland surface, 1,275 feet (388.5 meters) below sea level.

In general the Hebrew *arabah* means a wasteland or barren district. North of the Dead Sea to the Sea of Galilee, the valley is referred to by the Arabs as the Ghor ("depression") and south of the Dead Sea as the Arabah.

In the OT the name Arabah is sometimes applied to the entire length of the valley, though at times the southern portion is alluded to (Dt 1:1; 2:8), and elsewhere the northeast portion is indicated (Dt 3:17; 4:49; Jos 11:2). It could refer to the portion east of the Jordan River (Dt 4:49) or to the part west of the river (Jos 11:16) or to the Jordan River valley (2 Sm 4:7). In the Hebrew OT, the plural of Arabah (*Arboth*) is found 17 times, and its meaning is "plains"—referring to the portion of the Arabah near Jericho or Moab. The Dead Sea is sometimes referred to as the Sea of the Arabah or Sea of the Plain (2 Kgs 14:25). For the most part the section of the Arabah north of the Dead Sea was, and is today, fertile and productive.

It was from the Arabah that Joshua led the campaign to conquer Jericho. Abner fled to the northern Arabah after being defeated at Gibeon (2 Sm 2:29). The murderers of Ishbosheth crossed the area to bring his head to David at Hebron (2 Sm 4:7), and Zedekiah was fleeing to the area when he was captured by the Babylonians (2 Kgs 25:4; Jer 39:4).

The southern Arabah was the scene of Israel's wanderings before entering the Promised Land. Farther north, the Arabah was the site of the final acts of Moses (Nm 32–36), who died and was buried in the Arabah (Dt 1:1) in the plains of Moab east of the Dead Sea (Dt 34:1-6).

South of the Dead Sea there were deposits of iron and copper, and Deuteronomy 8:9 may allude to this general area when it speaks of "a land whose stones are iron, and out of whose hills you can dig copper." The land here is generally barren, though in ancient times careful use of irrigation made agriculture possible to a limited extent. Several important trade routes have passed through this area. The Arabah around the Dead Sea, prior to the destruction of Sodom and Gomorrah, was once an especially fertile area, "like the garden of the LORD" (Gn 13:10).

The rejuvenation of this area is one of the subjects of prophetic promise. Ezekiel speaks of a great river that will spring from the temple and go down into the Arabah, making the waters of the sea fresh and creating a healthy environment for fish and other living creatures (Ez 47:1-12; Jl 3:18; Zec 14:8). See Palestine.

ARABAH*, Brook of the Dry stream bed in southern Palestine (Am 6:14). See Brook of the Arabah.

ARABAH*, Sea of the Alternate name for the Dead Sea, since that body of water lies within the area of the land of Israel called Arabah (Dt 3:17; 4:49; Jos 3:16; 12:3; 2 Kgs 14:25). See Dead Sea.

ARABIA, ARABS Peninsula in southwestern Asia, surrounded by sea on three sides and by the Fertile Crescent on the fourth. Politically, the Arabian peninsula is bounded on the north by the modern Hashemite kingdom of Jordan and by Iraq and on the south by the Indian Ocean. The Persian Gulf forms its eastern boundary and the Red Sea its western boundary. Its area is just over a million square miles (1,609,000 square kilometers), about one-third the area of the United States.

Classical geographers such as Strabo followed the example set by the geographer Ptolemy in dividing Arabia into three divisions: *Arabia Petraea* (Rocky Arabia) in the northwest, which included Sinai, Edom, Moab, and Transjordan; *Arabia Deserta*, which included the Syrian Desert; and *Arabia Felix* (Happy Arabia), which included the southern section of the Arabian peninsula.

When "Arabia" is used as a geographical term in the Bible, it sometimes includes both northern and southern sections. For example, 2 Chronicles 9:14 says that the kings of Arabia brought gold to Solomon as tribute. At other times the name Arabia refers only to the northwestern *Arabia Petraea*. For example, Paul said that after his conversion he went away to the deserts of Arabia (Gal 1:17) and referred to Mt Sinai (4:25), which is in that northwestern area. Many places named in the Bible as being in Arabia are more specifically in *Arabia Petraea*. Such sites include Buz, Dedan, Dumah, Ephah, the Hazor of Jeremiah 49:28-33, Massa, Mesha, and Midian. Hazarmaveth, Ophir, Sabtah, Sephar, Sheba, and Uzal are in the south. Havilah and Parvaim are perhaps in the northeast, and authorities debate the location of Seba. The land of Uz, mentioned in the book of Job, is considered by many scholars to be located in the area between Edom and northern Arabia.

Arabia is thought by many to be one of the hottest countries. In some sections that conception is correct. The peninsula lies between seas on the east and west, but those bodies of water are too small to break the climatic continuity of the dry African-Asian continental masses. There are, however, some regions that enjoy temperate

and semitropical climate. In the south much of the land is sufficiently elevated to avoid the intensity of tropical heat. The lowlands along the coast have a semitropical environment. Fogs and dews are common in the humid regions, but over inner Arabia the sun shines the year round, obscured only by an occasional sandstorm or an even rarer rain shower.

Arabia has long been desired for natural resources. Pharaohs of the first dynasty operated turquoise mines in Sinai, and the gold of Ophir and the frankincense and myrrh of South Arabia were world renowned. The queen of Sheba brought such precious spices to Solomon (1 Kgs 10:2, 10), and trade between Israel and Arabia flourished. Solomon had a seaport at Ezion-geber on the Red Sea for his opulent commerce with Ophir (1 Kgs 9:26-28). King Jehoshaphat of Judah, who also received tribute from Arabs (2 Chr 17:11), tried to revive trade with Ophir but failed (1 Kgs 22:48).

Tribes associated with Arabia played a significant role in biblical history. The Ishmaelites or Midianites who took Joseph to Egypt (Gn 37:25-36) were Arabians. So were the Amalekites who waged war with Moses in the wilderness of *Arabia Petraea* (Ex 17:8-16). Moses' father-in-law, Jethro, was a Midianite (Ex 18:1). King Uzziah of Judah fought against Arabs (2 Chr 26:7); the Meunites mentioned in the same verse were probably also from Arabia. Geshem the Arab, known also from secular inscriptions, resisted the rebuilding of the Jerusalem wall (Neh 2:19; 6:1, 6).

Kedar was an important North Arab tribe condemned in Isaiah's message about Arabia (Is 21:13-17). Jeremiah also spoke against it, prophesying its destruction by Nebuchadnezzar, who conquered it (Jer 49:28-33). Close allies of the tribe of Kedar were the Nabatean Arabs (Is 60:7), who figure prominently in later history. They captured Petra, fulfilling the prophecy of Obadiah about Edom. References to Arabia and the Arabs in the Apocrypha and NT concern mostly the Nabatean Arabs (1 Macc 11:16; Gal 1:17).

In southern Arabia four kingdoms developed: the Sabean, Minean, Qataban, and Hadramaut. Around 115 BC the Himyarite kingdom gained control of southern Arabia, keeping it until about AD 300. Three centuries later the Arabian peninsula witnessed the birth of Islam.

ARAD (Person) Beriah's son, of Benjamin's tribe (1 Chr 8:15).

ARAD (Place) Name of a Canaanite settlement or region in the Negev Desert at the time of the Israelite conquest of Canaan. The king of Arad attacked the Israelites and was defeated (Nm 21:1-3; 33:40). Consequently the Israelites renamed the place Hormah ("destruction"). Arad was later conquered by Joshua (Jos 12:14).

Until recently archaeologists thought this Arad was the modern Tell Arad. Excavations at Tell Arad, however, have shown that this site was uninhabited at the time of the Israelite conquest of Canaan. Some scholars have suggested that the Arad mentioned in Numbers and Joshua was a region and not a specific place. Others say there were two Arads, the Canaanite city located possibly at Tell Malhata about 7.5 miles (12 kilometers) southwest of Tell Arad, and the Israelite city located at modern Tell Arad. This second suggestion is supported by an inscription of Shishak, an Egyptian pharaoh (940?–915 BC), which indicates that two cities named Arad existed during the early first millennium BC.

The only possible mention of modern Tell Arad is in Judges 1:16, where Arad is used as a reference point for the land settled by the Kenites. Tell Arad had been a large important city during the early Bronze Age, but after being destroyed around 2600 BC, it was not reoccupied until shortly before 1000 BC. From the time of King Solomon (970–930 BC) until the Jews were taken into exile, Tell Arad served as a fortified citadel on Judah's southern border.

Several interesting discoveries were made during the excavation of Tell Arad. An Israelite sanctuary was uncovered that is very similar in plan to the tabernacle and the temple, with an altar of the dimensions described in Exodus 27:1. It has been suggested that this sanctuary might have served as the worship center of the Kenite clan. Tell Arad has also provided us with a number of inscribed potsherds, called ostraca. One such ostracon contains a reference to the "house of Yahweh," a possible reference to the temple in Jerusalem.

Aerial View of an Iron Age Fort on Arad

ARADUS Greek name for the Phoenician city of Arvad. Aradus was one of the cities receiving a "letter of recommendation" for the Jews written by the Roman consul Lucius (1 Macc 15:16-23).
    See also Arvad, Arvadite.

ARAH
1. Ulla's son from Asher's tribe (1 Chr 7:39).
2. Ancestor of a group of people that returned to Jerusalem with Zerubbabel after the exile (Ezr 2:5; Neh 7:10).

ARAM (Person)
1. Shem's son and Noah's grandson (Gn 10:22-23; 1 Chr 1:17). Ancestor of the Arameans. *See* Syria, Syrians.
2. Kemuel's son, grandson of Abraham's brother Nahor (Gn 22:21).
3. Shemer's son from Asher's tribe (1 Chr 7:34).
4. The Aram occurring in the genealogy of Jesus Christ (Mt 1:3-4, KJV) is a mistranslation of the Greek word *Aram*, meaning "Ram"—an entirely different name (Ru 4:19). *See* Ram (Person) #1.

ARAM (Place)
Designation for the territory now called Syria. *See* Syria, Syrians.

ARAMAIC
One of the three original languages of the Bible, found in sections of the book of Daniel (2:4b–7:28) and Ezra (4:8–6:18; 7:12-26). Aramaic phrases and expressions also appear in Genesis (31:47), Jeremiah (10:11), and the NT.

Old Testament Use Aramaic is linguistically very close to Hebrew and similar in structure. Aramaic texts in the Bible are written in the same script as Hebrew. In contrast to Hebrew, Aramaic uses a larger vocabulary, including many loan words, and a greater variety of connectives. It also contains an elaborate system of tenses, developed through the use of participles with pronouns or with various forms of the verb "to be." Although Aramaic is less euphonious and poetical than Hebrew, it is probably superior as a vehicle of exact expression.

Aramaic has perhaps the longest continuous living history of any language known. It was used during the Bible's patriarchal period and is still spoken by a few people today. Aramaic and its cognate, Syriac, evolved into many dialects in different places and periods. Characterized by simplicity, clarity, and precision, it adapted easily to the various needs of everyday life. It could serve equally well as a language for scholars, pupils, lawyers, or merchants. Some have described it as the Semitic equivalent of English.

The origin of Aramaic is unknown, but it seems to have been closely related to Amorite and possibly to other ancient northwest Semitic dialects barely known to scholars. Although an Aramean kingdom as such never really existed, various Aramean "states" developed into influential centers. A few short Aramean inscriptions from that era (10th to 8th centuries BC) have been found and studied.

By the eighth century BC, King Hezekiah's representatives requested the spokesmen of the Assyrian king Sennacherib to "speak to your servants in Aramaic, since we understand it. Don't speak to us in Hebrew in the hearing of the people on the wall" (2 Kgs 18:26, NIV). By the Persian period, Aramaic had become the language of international trade. During their captivity, the Jews probably adopted it for convenience—certainly in commerce—while Hebrew became confined to the learned and to religious leaders.

Gradually, especially after the Babylonian exile, Aramaic influence pervaded the land of Palestine. Nehemiah complained that children from mixed marriages were unable to speak Hebrew (Neh 13:24). The Jews seem to have continued using Aramaic widely during the Persian, Greek, and Roman periods. Eventually the Hebrew Scriptures were translated into Aramaic paraphrases, called Targums, some of which have been found among the Dead Sea Scrolls.

New Testament Use In popular thought, Aramaic was the common language of Palestine during the time of Jesus. Yet that is by no means certain and probably is an oversimplification of the linguistic situation of that time. Names used in the NT reflect Aramaic (Bartholomew, Bar-Jonah, Barnabas), Greek (Andrew, Philip), and Latin (Mark), as well as Hebrew. There is no question that Aramaic was widely used, as were Greek and Hebrew. Latin was probably limited to military and governmental circles. Mishnaic Hebrew, a common kind of everyday Hebrew dialect, was also used in Jesus' day; Mishnaic Hebrew documents have been discovered among the Dead Sea Scrolls.

What was the "Hebrew" referred to in certain NT passages (Jn 5:2; 19:13, 17, 20; 20:16; Rv 9:11; 16:16)? The languages used for the inscription put on Jesus' cross were "Hebrew, Latin, and Greek" (Jn 19:19-20). Later, the apostle Paul was said to speak "Hebrew" (Acts 22:2; 26:14). The exact dialect he spoke may be debated, but as a Pharisee he was undoubtedly able to read the Hebrew of the OT. The Greek word for "Hebrew" is sometimes translated "Aramaic" and may be a general term for Semitic, or for a blend of Hebrew-Aramaic (as

Yiddish is German-Hebrew). At any rate, Aramaic served as a transition from Hebrew to Greek as the language spoken by Jews in Jesus' day. In that sense Aramaic connects OT Hebrew with NT Greek.

ARAMEANS People of Aram and predecessors of the Syrians. *See* Syria, Syrians.

ARAM-GESHUR* Small kingdom between Mt Hermon and Bashan bordering Argob. *See* Geshur, Geshurites.

ARAM-MAACAH (MAACHAH*) Alternate name for Maacah in 1 Chronicles 19:6. *See* Maacah, Maachah (Place).

ARAM-NAHARAIM Hebrew word meaning "Aram of the two rivers"; it refers to the area bounded by the upper Euphrates and the Habur Rivers. It is sometimes translated "Mesopotamia" (Dt 23:4, RSV). The major city of that area was Haran, where Terah and Abram stopped and where Terah died (Gn 11:31-32). A servant of Abraham (Abram) returned to the same region to seek a wife for Abraham's son Isaac (Gn 24:1-10). Isaac's son Jacob also returned to Haran to seek a wife (Gn 28:1-5; Paddan-aram is a synonym of Aram-naharaim). Aram-naharaim was the home of Balaam, the pagan prophet (Dt 23:4). One oppressor of Israel during the period of the judges was Cushan-rishathaim, king of Aram-naharaim (Jgs 3:8-11). Later, in King David's wars with Ammon, he had to confront mercenary charioteers hired from the Aramean centers of Aram-naharaim, Aram-maacah, and Zobah (1 Chr 19:6; cf. Ps 60 title). *See* Syria, Syrians.

ARAM OF DAMASCUS One of the several city-kingdoms in the land of Aram (Syria). This kingdom, whose principal city was Damascus, was conquered by King David (1 Chr 18:3-6). *See* Damascus.

ARAM-ZOBAH Syrian territory ruled in David's time by King Hadadezer, whom David defeated (2 Sm 8:3). This form of the name occurs in the title to Psalm 60. *See* Zoba, Zobah.

ARAN Dishan's son, grandson of Seir the Horite, and a descendant of Esau (Gn 36:28; 1 Chr 1:42).

ARARAT Name of a craggy, rugged range of mountains in Armenia (2 Kgs 19:37; Is 37:38). Ararat lies just south of the Black Sea and between it and the Caspian Sea. The region overlaps extreme eastern Turkey, the southern Caucasus of Georgian Russia, and the northern tip of Iran. The mountains of Ararat are cited as the resting

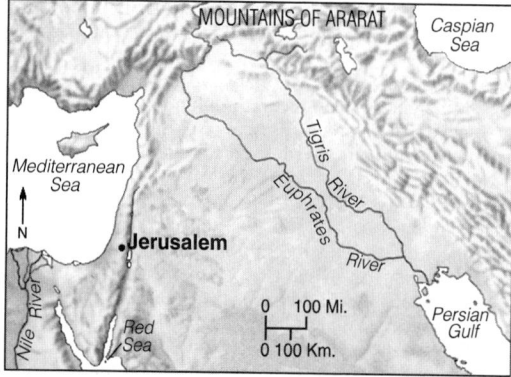

Ararat Mountains These mountains are located in present-day Turkey, near the Russian border.

place of Noah's ark when the floodwaters began to subside (Gn 8:4). Much speculation and several expeditions have stimulated considerable popular interest in that remote area.

No one can be dogmatic about making a precise location for a singular Mt Ararat, though a traditional site is pointed out between Lakes Van and Urmia in the heart of ancient Urartu (note the common consonants with Ararat), once a district of Assyria. Surrounding topography is a high plain of sparse vegetation, equally sparse habitation, and barren lava beds. Agri Dagh (Turkish for "Mountain of Trouble") is one peak 17,000 feet (5,180 meters) high to which local tribesmen have given the name Kohl Nu, that is, Mt of Noah. Hence, most of the searching for the ark is concentrated there. *See* Noah #1; Flood, The.

ARATUS* Greek poet (315?–245? BC). Born at Soli in Cilicia (region in Asia Minor), Aratus studied in Athens where he was influenced by Zeno, the father of Stoicism. Later, Aratus lived in the palace of Antigonus Gonatas of Macedonia and Antiochus I, king of Syria. Aratus's only existing work is a poem on astronomy, "Phaenomena," dedicated to Zeus. The apostle Paul quoted from that poem in his speech on the Aeropagus in Athens: "We are indeed his offspring" (Acts 17:28, RSV).

ARAUNAH Jebusite whose threshing floor was the scene of some significant events in biblical history. (Jebus was the ancient Canaanite city that later became Jerusalem.) Araunah's threshing floor marked the place where the Lord stopped an angel from further inflicting Israel with a pestilence after the death of 70,000 Israelites (2 Sm 24:15-16). The plague from the Lord had come upon Israel as a result of King David's prideful census. At the instruction of the prophet Gad, the repentant David purchased the floor and built an altar to the Lord (2 Sm 24:17-25). Araunah offered oxen and everything needed for the altar as a gift, but David insisted on paying him, saying, "I cannot present burnt offerings to the LORD my God that have cost me nothing" (2 Sm 24:24, NLT). A parallel account (1 Chr 21:15-16) uses the Hebrew form Ornan for the Jebusite's foreign name. David was in too much of a hurry to go to the tabernacle to make his sacrifice, the tabernacle and altar being farther away on the hill of Gibeon (1 Chr 21:27-30). David chose the threshing floor as the site for the temple (1 Chr 22:1), and Solomon built it there on Mt Moriah (2 Chr 3:1). It was the same area to which God commanded Abraham to go for the sacrifice of Isaac (Gn 22:2). Tradition locates the present-day Muslim mosque, the Dome of the Rock, on the site of Araunah's threshing floor.

ARBA Ancestor of the giant Anakim and a great hero among them (Jos 15:13; 21:11). Arba was the founder of Kiriath-arba (city of Arba), later known as Hebron (Jos 14:15).

ARBATHITE Resident of the city of Beth-arabah, and the hometown of Abi-albon (Abiel), one of David's 30 "mighty men" (2 Sm 23:31; 1 Chr 11:32).

ARBATTA Region south of the Esdraelon Valley in the southwest corner of Galilee. When its inhabitants were threatened by non-Jewish forces of Ptolemais, Tyre, and Sidon (1 Macc 5:15), they sent an urgent letter requesting help from Judas Maccabeus. Judas dispatched his brother Simon who, with 3,000 men, rescued the Galileans "and led them into Judea with great rejoicing" (1 Macc 5:23).

ARBELA Site of a great slaughter when General Bacchides invaded Judea from Syria (1 Macc 9:1-2). The site has not been positively identified, although the historian Josephus called it a city of Galilee and noted that the caves of Arbela in lower Galilee were fortified against marauding robbers. Possible identifications include Beth-arbel in Gilead and the Galilean Khirbet Irbid overlooking the wadi el-Hamam, west of the Sea of Galilee.

ARBITE* Title given to Paarai, warrior among David's 30 "mighty men" (2 Sm 23:35). The expression may indicate that he was a native of Arab, a village in southern Judah (Jos 15:52).

ARCH* Curved structure, usually of masonry, supporting the weight over a doorway or other open space. The capstone or keystone is the most important part of an arch and the last stone put in place. It ties the two curving sides together and distributes the weight evenly through them to the foundation.

Arches were not used in the architecture of ancient Israel and appear in the Bible only through mistranslation. The Hebrew word translated "arches" throughout Ezekiel's vision of the temple (Ez 40, KJV) refers to porches rather than arches.

See also Architecture.

ARCHAEOLOGY AND THE BIBLE* Simply defined, archaeology is the science that recovers and studies the relics of human antiquity. Biblical archaeology is concerned with the remains scattered across the Near East. Some lie buried at different levels in mounds; others survive as ruins or weathered monuments to past grandeur. Many of the artifacts bear inscriptions of sorts in a variety of ancient languages, some of which still need much study to be understood properly. Other artifacts comprise the material remains of everyday life; broken pottery bowls, charred timbers, trinkets, toys, ornaments, occasional fragments of cloth, rusted weapons, perhaps only the imprint of a woven mat. All must be interpreted carefully in the light of what is known about the period of history from which the objects have been recovered.

Many outstanding archaeological discoveries have been entirely accidental. At Ras Shamra in Syria, a peasant's plow struck a tomb that led to the discovery of the ancient site of Ugarit. A Bedouin in search of a lost goat discovered the cave at Qumran that contained the Dead Sea Scrolls. In 1887 an Egyptian woman found the Amarna tablets while seeking decomposed bricks for use as fertilizer. In 1945 Egyptians hunting bird manure in caves near Nag Hammadi discovered important Coptic Gnostic manuscripts. Such chance finds, however, are no substitute for systematic surveys.

In modern archaeology potential sites are surveyed carefully, generally photographed from the air, and tested for metals and other underground anomalies by the use of complex electronic equipment. Recovered artifacts are dated according to the level where they occurred in the site and by other methods, including radiocarbon dating. The purpose is to present a chronologically accurate picture of the artifacts and also of the site itself.

The archaeologist and the Near Eastern scholar look at this testimony to ancient life in the realization that they are dealing with factual, objective data. Although there is obviously room for some speculation or difference of opinion, the objects being handled are silent but nevertheless real witnesses to people and events of the past. The relics, therefore, need to be understood in their own right as evidence and must not be manipulated to suit the fancies of some speculative interpretation of history,

culture, or religion. Near Eastern archaeology is able to help us understand Scripture by providing objective background data. If, for example, an artifact containing pictographic or other forms of writing can be dated to around 3000 BC, that alone tells us that written communications in the locality date back to at least that period. The antiquity of writing is now known to be such that all the early authors of OT material could easily have composed and written down all the narratives credited to them. Thus it is no longer necessary to suppose that Moses could not have written the Pentateuch (first five books of the Bible) on the ground that writing had not been invented in his day. In fact, archaeological discoveries have shown that Moses could, and probably did, write in Egyptian hieroglyphics, Babylonian cuneiform, and several Canaanite dialects (of which biblical Hebrew is one). Any theory of Pentateuchal composition that ignores such factual information is obviously wrong in a fundamentally important area.

PREVIEW
•Archaeology and Daily Life
•Archaeology and Religion
•Archaeology and Warfare
•Archaeology and Literature
•Archaeology and Language

Archaeology and Daily Life The kind of housing in which the ancients lived has been revealed from excavations at many Near Eastern sites. Neolithic (late Stone Age) dwellings were often simple "wattle-huts" of interwoven sticks, though some showed evidence of artistic interior decoration. The elegant middle-class home at Ur in the time of Abram was attractive even by modern standards. The magnificence of ancient palaces at such sites as Knossos, Persepolis, Mari, and Qantir is abundantly evident even from the ruins. Weaving is now known to be one of the oldest human crafts; the two types of knots used today in making oriental rugs originated in Mesopotamia in the remote past. Of similar antiquity was the manufacture of pottery, glazed and unglazed, some plain and some decorated.

Obscure social customs in Scripture have been illustrated by archaeological discoveries. Abram's procreation of a child by Hagar, his wife's servant, was in conformity with local customs at Nuzi and was not regarded as immoral. The adoption of Eliezer by Abram (Gn 15:2-4) is clarified by texts from Nuzi that permitted childless couples to adopt sons who, in return for certain duties to the parents, would inherit the family estate. Such children had the inheritance rights of the firstborn, but their rights could be modified if the adopting parents subsequently had their own children. Texts from Nuzi, Ugarit, and Alalakh show that heads of families could disregard the natural order and choose any one of the sons to inherit firstborn rights (cf. Gn 48:13-22; 49:3-4). Nuzi tablets indicate that such rights could be traded between various members of the family, which accounts for the transaction between Esau and Jacob (Gn 25:31-34).

Work of all kinds in the biblical period has been illustrated from many sources. The Beni Hasan tableau (1900 BC) shows traveling Semites bringing goods to Egypt. On one of the animals is a set of portable bellows, suggesting that the travelers may have been metalworkers. Other trades and occupations illustrated from monuments and paintings include hunting, fishing, brick making, various types of agricultural work, pottery making, and other domestic crafts. Such sources also provide valuable information about the way the ancients dressed. Men pictured on the Beni Hasan tableau were bearded and wore short skirts and sandals. Women had long, multicolored dresses fastened at the shoulder with a clasp. They wore shoes and kept their flowing hair in place by means of bands. Another Egyptian painting, dated 500 years later and showing Semites bringing gifts to the pharaoh, indicates that clothing styles had barely changed at all. These illustrations come from lands other than Palestine; the Israelites were forbidden to make representations of human beings or God.

The most common traces of everyday life are potsherds, broken pottery pieces that were discarded in great quantities in settled areas and that can still be found today. Such fragments were often used as materials on which short messages were written, as illustrated by an important group of letters dating from the time of the prophet Jeremiah. The "Lachish letters" were actually military dispatches written in 587 BC from an outpost north of Lachish to one of the officers defending Lachish itself. Centuries later in NT times potsherds were still popular as writing materials because they were more durable than Egyptian papyrus and more convenient than waxed writing boards. Rectangular wooden palettes with a slot for the rush pens and rounded hollows for the little tablets of red and black ink have been found in Egypt. Remains of some of the ink actually used in writing the Dead Sea Scrolls have been recovered from the settlement at Qumran.

In antiquity, various games were played by children and adults alike. From a tomb at Beni Hasan (c. 2000 BC) came a painting of pigtailed Egyptian girls keeping several balls up in the air at once. A relief in a temple at Thebes showed Ramses III playing draughts (checkers) with a concubine. Egyptian children of a later period played a game using pebbles that was perhaps the ancestor of backgammon. From Megiddo came an ivory gaming board with holes, presumably for pegs (c. 1200 BC). Children's toys recovered from Near Eastern sites include whistles, leather-covered balls, model chariots, and animals on wheels, showing that tastes have changed very little over the ages. Adult sports such as wrestling, archery, and running were depicted in Egyptian tomb paintings.

The embalming of Jacob and Joseph (Gn 50:2-3, 26) represented a social custom of long standing in Egypt and is thoroughly consistent with the background of the narrative. Jacob was buried in the cave of Machpelah with Sarah, Abraham, and others; although the site is well known, it cannot be excavated because it is venerated by the Arabs as the sacred resting place of their ancestor Abraham.

An inscription associated with an ancient Hebrew burial site was found in the Russian Museum on the Mt of Olives in 1931. At some point it had been removed from the grave site. It reads, "Hither were brought the bones of Uzziah king of Judah—do not open." The inscription came from Christ's time, suggesting that the original tomb of the great ruler had been found during excavations in Jerusalem and that the remains had been transferred to another site. Archaeologists have shown that the kind of stone door covering the entrance to Christ's tomb was in fashion chiefly from about 100 BC to about AD 100, which is consistent with the Gospel records.

Archaeology and Religion Archaeological excavations have done much to indicate the nature of biblical religion and worship. Long before Abram left Ur at the command of the one true God, pagan Mesopotamian peoples worshiped individual gods and recognized them as celestial deities or "sky gods." There is thus nothing inherently impossible or improbable about the relationship of the Hebrew patriarchs to the God whom they served and venerated. The worship of heathen deities in portable shrines has been illustrated from a relief of Ramses II, which showed the divine tent in the middle of the Egyptian encampment. In addition, seventh-century BC Phoenician writings referred to a portable shrine pulled by oxen. The Israelite wilderness tabernacle thus fits properly into that kind of background and is not of comparatively late origin, as was once supposed.

The tradition of singers participating in preexilic worship has been verified by archaeological discoveries indicating that for centuries the Palestinians had been noted for their musical abilities. Tablets from Ras Shamra (Ugarit) are full of religious poetry, some of which contains phrases similar to expressions in the Hebrew psalms. Solomon's temple was built by Phoenician (Canaanite) workmen according to a ground plan (cf. 1 Kgs 6) similar to that of the eighth-century BC chapel found at Tel Tainat in Syria. The Wailing Wall in Jerusalem is thought to contain stones going back to Nehemiah's time, but no traces of Solomon's foundations have yet been uncovered in the city. Pieces of masonry from Herod's temple, demolished in AD 70, have come to light and furnish interesting factual information about the appearance of contemporary pillars and supporting structures. Though there were supposedly many synagogues in Palestine in Christ's time, few remains of any significance have survived.

Archaeology and Warfare Understanding of ancient warfare, a prominent biblical theme, has been assisted greatly by the work of archaeologists. Ancient Near Eastern peoples regarded war as conflict between the gods of the opposing nations. Military service was therefore regarded as a sacred calling, and soldiers were members of an honored profession. In his capacity as Lord of hosts, God was the commander in chief of the Hebrew army; he could order a city to be given up to the "ban," that is, to complete destruction (cf. Jos 6:17, 24). War was waged according to well-understood rules. An enemy threatening the safety of a city would normally send its inhabitants a demand for surrender. If it was accepted, all lives were spared, though property would be plundered. If the demand was rejected, the besieged city dwellers knew that if their defenses were breached, they might all be killed. Frontal assaults, spies, ambushes, and armed patrols were all used in warfare. Sometimes battles were decided by the outcome of combat between champions (1 Sm 17:38-54).

Ancient armor was pictured widely on reliefs and monuments, supplementing the artifacts that have been recovered. A magnificent golden helmet from Ur is an outstanding example of Sumerian military equipment, contrasting with the much smaller Hittite helmets depicted on a tomb wall at Karnak. Metal helmets (cf. 1 Sm 17:38) were worn initially only by leaders in the Israelite armies, but by Seleucid times all Hebrew soldiers were issued bronze helmets (1 Macc 6:35). Roman legionnaires commonly wore either leather or bronze helmets. The Hebrews used two kinds of shields: a large one protected the whole body and was designed for use by infantry; the other, smaller one was carried by archers (cf. 2 Chr 14:8). Such shields were generally of wood-and-leather construction, though occasionally made of bronze. Coats of scale armor (cf. Jer 46:4) were used in the Near East from at least the 15th century BC, as indicated by the recovery of such scales from Alalakh and Ugarit. Swords and spears, a normal part of Hebrew weaponry, came in a variety of shapes and sizes, as illustrated on monuments and bas-reliefs. Furnaces used for manufacturing swords were found at Gerar; Bronze Age daggers have been recovered from Lachish and Megiddo. The compound Asiatic bow, made of wood, horn, and tendons attached to iron limbs, was the successor of the Semitic weapon depicted on the Beni Hasan tableau. Discovery of names inscribed on arrowheads dating between 1300 and 900 BC seems to indicate the existence of companies of archers (cf. Is 21:17). Very little is said in the NT about contemporary military equipment.

Archaeology and Literature Many types of biblical literature have been paralleled in counterparts discovered in the Near East. Excavators at Ras Shamra found poetic and prose tablets that contain grammatical and literary forms occurring in the Hebrew psalms. It is now incorrect to suppose that detailed law codes such as those in the Pentateuch were not compiled until after the time of Moses, because fragmentary Sumerian codes dating from about the 19th century BC exhibit the same legislative tendencies. The code of the Babylonian ruler Hammurabi (18th century BC), based on earlier Sumerian legislation, expanded the principles of justice into nearly 300 sections. Hammurabi's code was an attempt to stabilize contemporary society on the basis of law and order. Its style is interesting; it commenced with a poetic prologue, followed by the prose legal section, and concluded with a prose epilogue. This three-part literary pattern also appears in the book of Job (prose-poetry-prose), as well as in more modern writings.

The covenant structure of Exodus 20:1-17 and its fuller form in Deuteronomy have been examined in light of the literary structure of second-millennium BC Hittite vassal treaties from Boghazkôy. The treaties were drawn up according to a standard pattern, the elements of which occur wholly or in part in the various OT covenantal passages (Ex 20:1-17; Lv 18:1-30; Dt 1:1–31:30; Jer 31:31-37).

What appear to be 11 Mesopotamian tablet forms in Genesis can be isolated by the recurrence of the phrase "these are the generations of" in the KJV and some modern versions. The phrase and its accompanying material correspond to the colophon (notation about a publication, often found on the very last page of modern books) of undamaged Mesopotamian tablets. Genealogical material such as occurs in Genesis was also found on clay tablets from Nuzi. The terse style of the earlier Genesis historical accounts is reminiscent of Sumerian history writing.

Hebrew wisdom literature such as Proverbs has been paralleled from Egypt by the "Instruction of Amenemope," where Proverbs 22:17–24:22 in particular is close in content to the Egyptian material. Scholars have yet to decide if one depended on the other, or if both went back to an even earlier source that has not survived.

The epistolary (letter) form was a common feature of the ancient world (2 Sm 11; 1 Kgs 21; 2 Kgs 5:10, 20; Ezr 4:6-7; Neh 2:7). Many collections of Egyptian papyri, such as the Zenon documents, consisted of letters. Among the Greeks the letter form dated back to Plato. His *Seventh Letter* (c. 354 BC) is interesting because it attempted to rebut contemporary misunderstandings of his teaching and personal behavior. Certain of the apostle Paul's letters (Corinthians, Galatians, Philippians, Thessalonians) also stand in that general tradition. Paul's Letter to Philemon corresponds closely to papyrus letters from Egypt of a purely personal nature.

Archaeology and Language Recovery of many ancient Near Eastern languages has done much to clarify our understanding of the OT. Expressions now known to be Sumerian and Akkadian occur not only in Genesis but elsewhere in the Scriptures. Thus in Genesis 1:1 the phrase "the heavens and the earth" is a Sumerian expression *(an-ki)* meaning "universe"; the pair of antonyms (words opposite in meaning) expresses totality. Revelation 22:13 uses this literary device to express the same concept in three different ways.

Ugaritic and Eblaic, both west Semitic dialects, are closely related to Hebrew and contain striking literary similarities. Reference to archaic Ugaritic expressions has made it possible to translate properly some obscure Hebrew poetic language that is now seen to have preserved genuine ancient Canaanite phraseology.

Aramaic, another northwest Semitic language, was spoken in the third millennium BC, and is represented in the OT principally by chapters in Ezra and Daniel. These were written in imperial Aramaic, as are the Elephantine papyri of the fifth and fourth centuries BC. It is now known, on the basis of the Aramaic used, to be linguistically incorrect to assign a late date to either Ezra or Daniel.

The NT was written in *koine,* or "common" Greek, the language of the Near East and the Roman Empire. NT common Greek differs from other Greek dialects in containing underlying Semitic expressions, which are frequently unrecognized and therefore mistranslated by the unwary.

From the foregoing it is evident that archaeological discoveries have done much to enlarge our knowledge of the ancient world. Even with the limited data at our disposal it is possible to see the men and women of Scripture as real persons, living mostly in times of stress and uncertainty but often enjoying a high degree of culture unmatched until modern times. We see such persons as they should be seen—not as mythical or legendary figures, but as true children of their age, grappling with life's problems and catching periodically a vision of God as all powerful and all holy, guiding the destinies of individuals and nations and bringing his purposes to pass in history. Archaeology has shown that the Hebrews must never be studied separately from other ancient Near Eastern peoples but instead must be seen as one element of a vast cultural complex that included such diverse peoples as the Sumerians and the Aegeans.

Such study must be pursued in a consistently objective fashion, arguing from relevant evidence to a proper understanding of biblical events and life. It is sometimes difficult to reconcile certain accepted interpretations of archaeological data and the evidence of Scripture. Such conflicts are few in number, however, and tend to diminish noticeably as new information is forthcoming. In principle the archaeologist has no particular interest in "proving the truth" of the Scriptures, and it is obviously impossible for a spade or a trowel to prove or disprove the spiritual revelations and assertions of Scripture. But it is fair to say that archaeology validates Hebrew history and explains many formerly obscure terms and traditions in both the OT and NT. It thus provides an authentic background for the prophecies culminating in Jesus Christ.

ARCHANGEL Chief angel; a title given to the angel Michael (Jude 1:9). *See* Angel.

ARCHELAUS Son of Herod the Great who followed his father in governing Idumea, Samaria, and Judea (Mt 2:22). *See* Herod, Herodian Family.

ARCHER, ARCHERY The archer used bow and arrows in peace and war. Nomads (Gn 21:20), hunters (Gn 27:3; Is 7:24), raiders (Gn 48:22; Jos 24:12), and warriors (Ez 39:9; Hos 1:7) used this weapon throughout the biblical period. The efficiency of the bow and the making of arrows improved tremendously over the centuries. The finest bow was the "composite bow," made from strips and bands of sinew glued to the parts furthermost from the core with animal horn glued to the inner surface. The best of these bows could fire arrows from 300 to 400 yards (274 to 366 meters). The archer needed to be a strong person to string and operate it.

While the archer used the bow for hunting, it was particularly useful in war. Saul and Jonathan fought with sword and bow (1 Sm 18:4), and David's army contained skilled bowmen (1 Chr 12:2). The kings of Israel equipped their troops with bows (2 Chr 17:17). Israel's enemies, the Egyptians, Syrians, Assyrians, Babylonians, Persians, Greeks, and Romans, all had strong contingents of archers, with excellent pictures still available on some of their bas-reliefs.

Job used the metaphor of God's archers round about him when describing his many bodily ailments (Jb 16:13). At times the archer's bow represents violence (Pss 11:2; 57:4) or divine judgment (Pss 7:13; 38:2; 64:7).

See also Armor and Weapons.

ARCHEVITES* KJV translation for the inhabitants of Erech (Uruk) in southern Babylonia who were transported to Samaria by Asnappar, the Assyrian King Ashurbanipal (Ezr 4:9-10). The Archevites were among the local residents who wrote to Artaxerxes of Persia, opposing the rebuilding of Jerusalem by the Jews who had returned from exile (Ezr 4:7-16).

ARCHIPPUS Contemporary of Paul whom the apostle encouraged to fulfill his ministry (Col 4:17) and referred to as a "fellow soldier" (Phlm 1:2).

ARCHI*, ARCHITE* A tribe descended from Canaan or a member of this tribe (Jos 16:2); also spelled "Arkite." Hushai, David's loyal adviser, was an Archite (2 Sm 15:32).

ARCHITECTURE Science, art, or profession of designing and constructing buildings, bridges, etc. Architecture is the practice of combining construction and art in order to produce "beauty with purpose." The architect's synthesis of creative imagination and technical skill produces structures of interest, unity, power, and convenience. When we look at a building, monument, or tomb, we are examining its art as well as its structure.

Special types of architecture are mentioned in Scripture, including houses, structures in particular cities, and, of course, the temples. All were influenced by the empires that dominated Israel at the time. It is therefore important to examine the architecture of empires associated with Bible history to understand the architecture of Palestine.

PREVIEW
- Sumerian Architecture
- Egyptian Architecture
- Assyrian and Hittite Architecture
- Greek Architecture
- Roman Architecture
- Palestinian Architecture

Sumerian Architecture Architecture was first developed by the Sumerians, a people of non-Semitic origin. They may have settled on the island of Bahrain in the Persian Gulf a thousand years before moving northward to the mainland. From the beginning of their culture the Sumerians regarded architecture as an important artistic endeavor. It found its fullest expression in the building of temples. The Sumerian ziggurat, or staged tower, became Mesopotamia's most distinctive contribution to architecture, both secular and sacred. The ziggurat has often been likened to a medieval European cathedral, the highest point of which might appear to be reaching upward to God as an expression of human religious aspirations. That, however, was not the concept the Sumerians held in building their shrines. For them, the ziggurat, standing on its mound or platform, represented a concentration of natural, life-giving forces. The god had already come down to his house, and it was the worshiper's duty to commune with him there.

By 2000 BC a Mesopotamian temple area commonly housed the ziggurat, several storehouses, shrines, workshops, and living quarters for priests. The ziggurat usually consisted of three stages: the inner walls of sun-dried mud brick, the outer walls of baked brick set in bitumen. The upper levels were reached by flights of stairs or ramps, and sometimes a small shrine to a local deity topped off the uppermost stage. In addition to devising decorated walls and columns, Sumerian architects discovered how to employ arches, domes, and vaults to give the impression of grandeur and space.

Sumerian domestic architecture was quite mixed in style. Most city houses were two-story dwellings built on three sides of a square, with the opening facing away from the narrow streets. Homes of the wealthy might contain 20 rooms; some included servants' quarters. Indoor bathroom facilities were connected by means of drainpipes to an underground cesspool. Many houses had a family burial vault in the basement. There seems little doubt that the Akkadians, Hittites, Egyptians, and Greeks all benefited in various ways from the architectural innovations of Sumer.

Egyptian Architecture The Egyptians achieved the most lasting architectural forms ever attempted by any civilization, and much of their architecture has been preserved. Such forms included temples, tombs, and pyramids. Huge stones to build those structures had to be brought from distant quarries. The Egyptians made use of slave labor and built their structures in honor of their rulers.

The outstanding examples of Egyptian architecture are the pyramids, virtually all of which were constructed in the Old Kingdom period (c. 2700–2200 BC). The Sumerian principle of the recessed niche was employed to accommodate the enormous stresses of stone masonry. Without that technique it would have been impossible to construct such a huge edifice as the Great Pyramid, the estimated weight of which is almost six million tons (5,448,000 metric tons). The Great Pyramid is one of the most perfectly oriented buildings on earth, being just a few seconds of one degree short of true north-south orientation. Many of the huge blocks of stone were cut and fitted together so accurately that it is impossible to insert the edge of a sheet of paper between them. The pyramids were meant to serve as tombs for the remains of the persons who ordered them constructed, but the structures themselves have become monuments to human creativity.

The major architectural style of the Egyptians was "post and lintel," with horizontal crosspieces resting on columns. As a result, buildings of any size became a forest of columns. Wall surfaces were covered with carvings, paintings, and hieroglyphics. Temples were planned on a long axis with almost perfect symmetry. The structures seem designed for imperial pageants and other ceremonies staged to impress the people with the power and authority of their rulers.

The Sphinx and Great Pyramids at Cairo, Egypt

Assyrian and Hittite Architecture The Assyrians followed the Sumerian pattern of temple construction but enlarged the ziggurats and added more stories. The great ziggurat at Borsippa was an outstanding example of seven-story temple construction. The foundation was about 272 feet (83 meters) square, and the building stood about 160 feet (49 meters) high. Each story was set back from the level beneath it in a terraced effect and painted with a different color of wash. Each story was intended to represent one of the planets. In accordance with later Sumerian practice the uppermost level had a small shrine built on its roof, where the god Nebo was thought to have taken up his residence. Many believe that the Tower of Babel, which God destroyed, was a ziggurat tower (Gn 11).

Assyrian royal palaces of the eighth and seventh centuries BC were large and elegant, decorated with enormous bas-reliefs depicting the king busily occupied with a variety of activities. Assyrian art was at its height in that period, and meticulous attention to detail brought a virile character to Assyrian architecture. Large stone sculptures of protective animals were stationed at entrances to public buildings. Similar statues were a feature of Hittite architecture in Anatolia, the eastern part of Asia Minor.

Hittite buildings excavated at Boghazkôy and elsewhere easily matched those of the Assyrians in extent and grandeur. Towering columns, long halls, and expansive rooms were typical of Hittite palace construction in the Bronze Age.

Hittite temple design followed what was common in Babylonia, with several buildings grouped around an open court. One difference was that the main sanctuary was approached through a series of entrances or porches extending beyond the length of adjacent buildings. The design enabled small windows to be placed at the top of the projection in order to give additional light in the sanctuary.

Greek Architecture Architecture rose to great achievements in the Greek world. Many factors combined to produce architectural beauty that has lasted for centuries. Those factors included the climate, setting, government, and people. Perhaps the most important factor was the people, who seemed free to imagine and develop designs and structures that have continued to excite our imaginations to this day.

The Greeks strove to attain beauty in their architecture. This worthy motive found its highest expression in the fifth century BC. In the time of Pericles (461–429 BC) the Parthenon and Propylea on the Acropolis were remodeled from earlier originals, and the Erechtheum was also built there. Subsequent temples in Athens included that of Hephaestus, which was a less graceful version of the Parthenon, and the shrine of Ares. Phidias, the sculptor who designed the Parthenon, was also responsible, with his students, for much of the fifth-century BC statuary. Although the Sumerians had been the first to execute rather stereotyped freestanding stone statues, they had done so largely with theological considerations in mind. For the Sumerian sculptors, the statue had represented an individual standing before a god, ready to be judged. For the Greeks, however, the objective of good statuary was the most realistic and accurate reproduction of human anatomy possible, and like the Assyrians', their sculptors studied anatomy. Eventually the Greeks became the world's most proficient sculptors.

Many Greek buildings featured appropriate combinations of structure and setting. For example, theaters were built on hills so that the structure could have tiers of seats and still have a beautiful background. Marble was used extensively. Buildings were placed so that shadows added to their beauty. All that structural beauty was seen by the apostle Paul when he visited the city of Athens, but "he was deeply troubled by all the idols he saw everywhere in the city" (Acts 17:16, NLT). Many of the most beautiful buildings, such as the Parthenon, were built in honor of pagan Greek gods. In response, Paul preached his famous sermon on the Areopagus (Mars Hill), a hill that overlooked the temples of Athens.

Roman Architecture The Romans were great builders who left their mark on the architecture of the world. Several factors influenced Roman architectural styles. First was the fact that the Romans took over earlier empires and earlier forms of architecture. Some Egyptian influence was seen, but the Greek eye for beauty and use of marble was more important. Another factor was the Roman discovery of cement made from volcanic earth which, when mixed with lime, formed a mortar of great cohesion. Cement enabled the Romans to build masonry arches without supporting columns. The effect was a sense of pomp and majesty. The use of cement also allowed the Romans to build structures of more than one story, such as the Colosseum.

Roman architects used central squares or public forums in the center of their cities. Around these were built public buildings, temples, shops, and porticoes. The central square contained arches and monuments commemorating victorious emperors. The Roman concept of municipal planning was copied throughout the Roman Empire, including Palestine.

The shortage of water in a number of countries over which the Romans ruled compelled them to devise means of transporting it overland. This led to the development of the aqueduct. Roman architects were faced with the problem of maintaining a sufficient degree of slope to enable water to flow by gravity. Cemented channels supported by stone arches provided much of the solution to the problem. The architectural design of aqueduct systems remained the same throughout the imperial period. Foundation piers were spanned by round arches. A stone channel was built on top of the archway, lined with cement, and frequently covered by a curved roof.

Palestinian Architecture For a generation the Israelites had been tent dwellers, living only semisedentary lives at best, without need of permanent structures of any kind. When the time came for them to settle down, they were handicapped by their lack of construction skills. Archaeological excavation at such sites as Shiloh, Bethel, and Debir have uncovered Israelite attempts to rebuild on earlier Canaanite foundations. Their standard of workmanship was noticeably inferior to that of the Canaanite builders, as exhibited especially in Canaanite royal cities. Until the fifth century BC, Israelite buildings tended to be small and narrow, partly because the architects had not devised any means of roofing a dwelling other than by laying beams across its width and placing a flat covering on top. The first vaulted arch in Palestine was built in the Persian period, but it was so innovative that the conservative Judeans refused to adopt it as an architectural style. Only in the Roman period did the arch and vault gain acceptance, due largely to the influence of Herod the Great.

Old Testament Architecture

➤CITIES In the OT era, cities were built on hills or mounds and surrounded with a wall for protection. Generally houses were placed in a random fashion with winding paths or alleys connecting them. People unable to afford city life lived in villages that surrounded the city. They would work the nearby fields and in time of danger flee to the city for protection.

Most essential to any city was an adequate water supply. For that reason cities were built on or near under-

ground springs. Some cities used plastered cisterns and catch basins to collect rainwater to supplement the regular water supply. Underground springs were protected by stepped tunnels for access when the city was besieged.

➤FORTIFICATIONS During much of OT times the Israelites used the techniques of the middle Bronze Age to defend their cities. The central feature was a wall made of stone or brick, 25 to 30 feet (7.6 to 9.1 meters) high. The wall was sometimes made with an artificial slope and a ditch at the bottom to fortify it against enemy battering rams.

During the Israelite monarchy, casemate walls were also built. These consisted of two parallel walls connected by a series of cross walls. The resulting rooms were then filled with dirt to give added protection against enemy battering rams (Ez 26:9). Sometimes walls 20 feet (6 meters) thick were built with overhangs so attackers could be subdued. The apostle Paul was let down off the wall of Damascus in a basket from a room in such a wall (Acts 9:25; 2 Cor 11:33).

Temple of Athena, Nike

➤GATES Most city walls had two gates. One of these was for camel caravans, chariots, and larger vehicles; the other, on the opposite side of the city, was used for pedestrians, donkeys, and small animals. Many gates consisted of double doors (Is 45:1; Neh 6:1) made of wood and overlaid with bronze plating (Is 45:2). The doors were secured with horizontal bars of wood, bronze (1 Kgs 4:13), or iron (Ps 107:16) that fit into openings in the gateposts (Jgs 16:3).

The location of the gates was important to the defense of the city. Often the road leading to the gate was laid out so that attackers, who carried their shields in their left hands, would have to face the wall of the city and its defenders on their right side. Sometimes the gate was part of a large tower (2 Chr 26:9). Occasionally, steps were constructed on the inside of the tower, so that sentinels could reach the top to stand watch (2 Kgs 9:17). At other times the gate was so positioned that it turned 90 degrees between the portals, in order to prevent enemy archers from making a straight shot through the gate.

➤HOUSES An above-average Israelite house consisted of several rooms facing an open courtyard (2 Sm 17:18). The largest room was for the family, another was for the family's cattle, and another was used as a general store-

The Parthenon in Athens

room. Sometimes the walls were made of stones, with the joints filled with mud. Sometimes the inside walls were plastered with mud, although more prosperous homes had cypress or cedarwood. Floors were made of clay or polished plaster stones. The flat roofs were supported by beams and made watertight with wood or brushwood. An outside stairway gave access to the roof, and some people built roof chambers that in effect made a two-story house (1 Kgs 17:19). The flat roofs of houses provided additional sleeping and recreational space for crowded households. The Mosaic law required these roofs to be surrounded by a protective parapet to prevent people falling to their deaths (Dt 22:8).

➤SOLOMON'S TEMPLE Probably the most important piece of Israelite architecture was King Solomon's temple. The building was located on the site where Abraham was supposed to have offered his son Isaac (Gn 22). It took seven and a half years to build and was notable for its beauty as well as its purpose. The plan of the temple was similar to that of the tabernacle, except that the dimensions were doubled and the height was tripled. The walls were made of stone overlaid with gold (1 Kgs 6:22), with gold also covering the ceilings and floor. The partition between the Holy of Holies and the Holy Place was made of gold-covered cedarwood. The entrance to the Holy of Holies consisted of a double door made of carved olive wood overlaid with gold. The doorway stood open but was veiled. Outside the temple were two courts, an inner court for the priests and an outer court for the people.

Lack of constructional expertise in Israel compelled Solomon to hire Phoenician workmen. The result was a typically Phoenician structure, the ground plan of which closely resembled that of an eighth-century BC Canaanite chapel excavated at Tell Tainat in Syria. Columns and porticoes were doubtless a feature of the temple of Solomon, though the precise function of the freestanding pillars named Jachin and Boaz is still far from certain. Carefully dressed masonry seems to have appeared in Israel initially in Solomon's time; excellent specimens of hewn and squared stone have been recov-

ered from Samaria. The Samaritan site, along with Megiddo, has also furnished interesting examples of a decorated pilaster capital that derived its design from Canaanite artistic representations.

When Babylon overthrew Jerusalem and leveled the city in 586 BC, the temple was plundered of its wealth and burned to the ground. After Israel returned from captivity, the temple was rebuilt, with the foundation being laid in 525 BC. However, that second temple was far less magnificent than Solomon's and was in great need of repair by the time of King Herod of Judea (37–4 BC).

Although OT tradition gives considerable prominence to the Solomonic temple and lauds its grandeur, the building was actually an adjunct to the royal palace, serving as a chapel. Only in the postexilic period was the temple freed from royal associations to become an independent shrine where people could observe the prescribed rituals. Both pre- and postexilic temples were quite small and narrow in their dimensions, their width being limited by the length of the wooden beams available for roofing purposes. The only way such a building could be enlarged was in the usual Near Eastern manner of attaching additional rooms to the exterior.

New Testament Architecture The architecture of NT times consisted of Greek and Roman structures, since those rulers had most recently dominated Israel. The Greek cities were architectural models, containing planned streets, arches, theaters, public baths, temples, and a central marketplace called the *agora*. Jewish homes, however, continued to remain small, with flat roofs over rooms facing a courtyard.

During Roman domination Herod the Great (37–4 BC) built some remarkable structures, including aqueducts, cisterns, dungeons, palaces, and whole cities (e.g., Caesarea). His greatest work was the rebuilding of the temple, a remarkable structure that took 83 years to complete. It lasted in its completed state only six years before it was destroyed by Titus in AD 70.

Herod's temple managed to blend the old with the new. Though it appeared to embody the latest Hellenistic architectural fashions in its colonnades, marble columns, and facades, it was still firmly rooted in the traditions of Phoenicia. The Herodian structure was an enlargement, and to some extent a rebuilding, of the sixth-century BC temple. A series of courts and porticoes surrounded the reconstructed shrine, which was given an illusion of grandeur by means of an enlarged entrance. In the middle of that porch stood an enormous doorway that gave access to the much smaller inner door of the shrine itself. Unfortunately, nothing of the building itself survived the destruction of AD 70, leaving us almost completely dependent upon Josephus's account. *See* City; Homes and Dwellings; Temple.

ARCHIVES *See* House of the Archives.

ARCTURUS* Constellation Ursa Major (the Great Bear), referred to in Job 9:9 and 38:32 (KJV) in connection with the constellation Orion and the Pleiades. *See* Astronomy.

ARD, ARDITE One of the nine sons of Bela (Nm 26:40), Benjamin's firstborn son (1 Chr 8:1). Ard is called Benjamin's son in the Hebrew sense, meaning descendant (Gn 46:21). He was the founder of the Ardite family, a subclan of Benjamin's tribe. The Ard/Addar transposition in 1 Chronicles 8:3 is probably a result of scribal error.

ARDON Caleb's third son by Azubah; a descendant of Judah (1 Chr 2:18).

ARELI, ARELITE One of Gad's seven sons (Gn 46:16). After the plague of Baal-peor, Areli's descendants, the Arelites, were numbered in Moses' census in preparation for war with the Midianites (Nm 25:6-18; 26:17).

AREOPAGITE* Member of the council or court of the Areopagus in Athens (Acts 17:34). *See* Dionysius.

AREOPAGUS* Hill northwest of the Acropolis in Athens overlooking the marketplace (Acts 17:19). "Areopagus" also refers to the Athenian council or court that met there. The irregular limestone outcropping was also known as Mars Hill, Mars being the Roman equivalent of the Greek god Ares. Paul was taken to the Areopagus after he had been reasoning with Jews and God-fearing Gentiles in the Athenian synagogue and marketplace *(agora)* for several days (Acts 17:16-21). Some Epicurean and Stoic philosophers involved in those discussions brought Paul before the council but evidently not for an official arraignment. Trials were held at the Areopagus; there, some five centuries earlier, Socrates had faced those who accused him of deprecating the Greek gods. By Paul's day the council of the Areopagus was responsible for various political, educational, philosophical, and religious matters, as well as for legal proceedings. The general tone of Paul's address does not suggest judicial proceedings. He spoke as an intelligent Christian believer who was able to meet the intellectual Athenians on their own ground (Acts 17:22-31). Some remained skeptical, but his address was convincing to a few who "joined him and became believers" (Acts 17:32-34).

ARETAS
1. Name of several kings of an Arabian people called the Nabateans, considered to be descendants of Nebaioth, Ishmael's oldest son (Gn 25:12-16; 1 Chr 1:29). According to the Jewish historian Josephus, Ishmael's descendants inhabited an area all the way from the Euphrates to the Red Sea, calling it Nabatene. Their capital city, Sela, was called Petra in NT times.
2. The Aretas of 2 Maccabees 5:8, before whom Jason the priest was accused, ruled about 170 BC. The Nabateans were evidently friendly toward the Maccabeans (1 Macc 5:24-28; 9:35). Josephus mentioned two other kings named Aretas. It was Aretas III, originally named Obodas, who extended Nabatean control and occupied Damascus during his reign (87–62 BC).
3. The NT contains a reference to still another Aretas. The apostle Paul had to escape from Damascus by being let down in a basket through a window in the wall because the governor there under King Aretas was guarding the city in order to seize him (2 Cor 11:32-33). That Aretas has been identified as Eneas, who took the title Aretas IV and ruled from 9 BC to AD 40. He attacked and defeated Herod Antipas over a boundary dispute and also as revenge. (Antipas had divorced Aretas's daughter in order to marry Herodias.)

ARGOB (Person) Individual supposedly killed with King Pekahiah of Israel in Pekah's revolt (2 Kgs 15:25). The early church father Jerome thought the name Argob (along with Arieh) referred to a place. Today some scholars think that Argob and Arieh may have been accidentally misplaced from a list of place names (2 Kgs 15:29) through scribal error.

ARGOB (Place) Region in Bashan won by the Israelites when they defeated King Og at Edrei (Nm 21:33-35; Dt 3:4). Argob was located east of the Sea of Chinnereth (later called Sea of Galilee), beyond the regions of Geshur and Maacah (Dt 3:14). Moses assigned all of Bashan, including Argob, to half of Manasseh's tribe (Dt 3:13-14). Jair, of that tribe, subdued the villages of Argob and named them Havvoth-jair ("the villages of Jair"). First Kings 4:13 distinguishes between Argob and the villages of Jair, that are said to be in Gilead, south of Argob. Deuteronomy 3:14 may represent a textual difficulty, or perhaps the location of the villages of Jair on the border between Argob and Gilead was responsible for the apparent discrepancy. That border could have shifted during the three centuries between the conquests of Jair and the reign of Solomon. By then, the name Havvoth-jair could even have referred to a different set of cities.

ARIARATHES King of Cappadocia in Asia Minor (163–130 BC). Educated in Rome, Ariarathes absorbed Roman ideas and became a close ally of the Romans. Because of his Roman ties, he declined a proposal to marry the sister of the Syrian king Demetrius Soter, who then declared war on him and drove him from his throne. After fleeing to Rome in 158 BC, Ariarathes was successful in eventually being restored to the throne of Cappadocia. In response to Simon Maccabeus, the Romans wrote to him and several other rulers in 139 BC that they should be kind to the Jews and "do them no harm, nor fight against them" (1 Macc 15:16-19, 22).

ARIDAI One of Haman's ten sons, who was killed with his father when Haman's plot to destroy the Jews was foiled (Est 9:7-10).

ARIDATHA One of Haman's ten sons, who was killed along with his father when Haman's plot to destroy the Jews was foiled (Est 9:7-10).

ARIEH Person mentioned along with Argob in 2 Kings 15:25 (KJV, NIV, NLT).

The Areopagus (Mars Hill) Inscription Paul's speech given on the Areopagus (see Acts 17:22-34)

ARIEL (Person)

1. Person or thing overcome in a heroic deed by Benaiah, chief of David's bodyguard (2 Sm 23:20; 1 Chr 11:22). It is not clear that the Hebrew word *ariel* is a proper name in these passages. Benaiah may have killed two "lionlike men" of Moab (KJV) or destroyed two Moabite altar hearths.
2. One of the men sent by Ezra to ask Iddo for Levitical priests to accompany the Jewish exiles returning to Jerusalem from Babylon (Ezr 8:16).

ARIEL (Place) Poetic designation for Jerusalem, used by the prophet Isaiah in a "woe" oracle warning people to turn from their wrongdoing (Is 29:1-2, 7). Jerusalem, location of the altar of burnt offering, was called Ariel ("hearth of God") by synecdoche, a poetic device in which a whole thing is referred to by naming one part. In a dramatic play on words Isaiah pronounced God's judgment: Jerusalem, city of the hearth of God, would become an ariel, a pagan altar hearth, when destroyed by her enemies.

ARIMATHEA Hometown of the Joseph who obtained Jesus' crucified body and buried it in his own tomb (Mt 27:57; Mk 15:43; Jn 19:38). The town's location is unknown, though it may be identical to the hill town of Ramathaim-zophim, the prophet Samuel's home (1 Sm 1:1), about 8 miles (12.9 kilometers) northwest of Jerusalem. Luke described the place as a Jewish town, and Joseph was himself a Jewish official (Lk 23:50).

ARIOCH

1. King of Ellasar, who with three other kings captured five cities and took a number of prisoners, including Abraham's nephew Lot (Gn 14:1-16).
2. Nebuchadnezzar's captain of the guard (KJV) or chief

executioner, who took Daniel to the Babylonian king to interpret his dream (Dn 2:14-25).

ARISAI One of Haman's ten sons, who was killed with his father when Haman's plot to destroy the Jews was foiled (Est 9:7-10).

ARISTARCHUS Companion of the apostle Paul; Macedonian from Thessalonica, possibly of Jewish ancestry. He is first mentioned as one of those seized by an angry mob in Ephesus (Acts 19:29). Later he accompanied Paul on the return from his third missionary journey (Acts 20:4) as well as to Rome to face Caesar (Acts 27:1-2). Paul described him as a coworker (Phlm 1:24) and fellow prisoner from whom he received great comfort (Col 4:10-11). Tradition says that Aristarchus was martyred in Rome under Nero.

ARISTOBULUS Name (of Greek origin, meaning "best advising") used in intertestamental times by ruling families in Palestine.

1. Jewish priest in Alexandria (Egypt) and teacher of Ptolemy (ruled 180–146 BC). A letter was sent to Aristobulus from the Judean Jews (2 Macc 1:10).
2. Aristobulus I. First king of the Maccabean (also called Hasmonean) family. *See* Hasmonean.
3. Aristobulus II. Son of Alexander Janneus (brother of Aristobulus I) and Salome Alexandra. In 67 BC Aristobulus II defeated his older brother, Hyrcanus II, and became king. *See* Hasmonean.
4. Aristobulus III. Grandson of Hyrcanus II and brother of Mariamne, wife of Herod the Great. Aristobulus was named high priest at the age of 17 (by Herod). When his acceptance as a Hasmonean by the people threatened Herod, Herod responded by arranging for his drowning (35 BC). *See* Hasmonean.
5. Younger of the two sons of Herod the Great and Mariamne. Aristobulus and Alexander became threats to Herod after he executed their mother in 29 BC. The two brothers were charged with attempting to poison their father in a trial before Caesar (12 BC) but were acquitted and reconciled to him. This Aristobulus was the father of Herod, king of Chalcis; Herod Agrippa I, of Judea; Aristobulus (see #6 below); and Herodias, wife of Herod Antipas. Later, Herod the Great ordered both Aristobulus and Alexander strangled at Sebaste (7 BC). *See* Herod, Herodian Family.
6. Son of Aristobulus (#5 above) and Bernice, mentioned by the Jewish historian Josephus for plotting against Herod Agrippa, his brother, and for opposing the plan of Petronius, governor of Syria, to erect a statue of Roman emperor Caligula in the temple in Jerusalem (AD 40).
7. Person whose family or household was greeted by the apostle Paul (Rom 16:10).

ARK*, Noah's *See* Noah #1.

ARKITE Name of a clan descended from Ham's son Canaan (Gn 10:17; 1 Chr 1:15). The Arkites were probably residents of Arqa, a Phoenician town north of Tripolis in Syria. According to an early inscription, Arqa was captured by the Assyrian Tiglath-pileser III in 738 BC. Possibly another branch of the tribe settled near Ataroth, a town on the border between Ephraim and Benjamin (Jos 16:2). *See also* Archi, Archites.

ARK OF THE COVENANT Most important piece of furniture in the wilderness tabernacle (tent-sanctuary) that God instructed Moses to build (Ex 25:10-22).

The Hebrew word for ark can also mean "chest" (2 Kgs 12:9-10) or "coffin" (Gn 50:26), but it is not the same word used for Noah's ark. The ark that Moses had Bezalel make was an oblong chest made of acacia wood (Ex 31:1-5; 37:1-9). The chest measured approximately 45 by 27 by 27 inches (114 by 69 by 69 centimeters), and was overlaid inside and out with gold. It was fitted with two pairs of rings through which poles were slid to make it portable. The ark would also serve as container for the two tablets of the covenant that would be given to Moses (Ex 25:16). Since the tablets were also called the "testimony," the ark was sometimes called the "ark of the testimony." Also in the ark were placed a pot of manna, the miraculous food provided by God (Ex 16:33), and Aaron's rod that had budded (Nm 17:10; Heb 9:4).

The lid of the ark was called the "mercy seat" or "place of mercy" (Ex 25:17). It was a slab of gold fitting over the top of the ark and having an importance of its own. Once a year the high priest was to make atonement for the people of Israel by sprinkling the mercy seat with the blood of bulls and goats (Lv 16:2-16). In fact, the English expression "mercy seat" is related to the Hebrew word for "atone." The lid was called a "seat" because the Lord was considered as enthroned between two cherubim (winged creatures) positioned opposite each other (Ps 99:1). The Lord spoke to Moses from between the cherubim (Nm 7:89).

The ark was sometimes referred to simply as the ark (Ex 37:1; Nm 3:31), at other times as the "ark of the covenant" (Nm 4:5; Jos 4:16). The Israelites were thus reminded that the ark's holiness was not magical but derived from the holy law of God contained inside it. That name also confronted the Israelites with their need to follow the commands God had given in his "covenant."

Those commands were given by the God of the covenant (or promise) who had rescued Israel from slavery in Egypt and who had promised to be the ever-present God of his people (Ex 6:6-7). Hence the ark was most widely known as the "ark of the covenant." Sometimes that name was expanded to "the Ark of the LORD's covenant" (1 Chr 28:18, NLT).

At times the ark was called "the Ark of God." It was a visible sign that the invisible God was dwelling in Israel's midst. It had a devastating and often deadly "holiness." The people of Beth-shemesh were severely punished after they had treated the ark without proper reverence (1 Sm 6:19). A man named Uzzah was killed by the Lord when he touched it with his hand to keep it from tumbling to the ground from a cart (2 Sm 6:6-9). The ark was dangerous to touch because it was the very symbol of God's presence. For this reason God commanded that the ark be placed in the Holy of Holies, separated from the rest of the tabernacle (and later the temple) by a heavy veil (Ex 26:31-33; Heb 9:3-5); no sinful man could look upon the glory of God above the ark and live (Lv 16:2).

History When the Israelites journeyed from Mt Sinai to Canaan, the ark accompanied them in their trek through the desert. It was to be a constant reminder of the holy presence of their God. The ark was spoken of in the accounts of that journey almost as though it were endowed with personal features (Nm 10:33-36). Although the wrapping and carrying of the sacred objects were carefully detailed (Nm 4), God's relationship with the ark was so close that the ark seemed to be "alive."

The ark clearly played a benevolent role during the desert journey. A group of Israelites rebelled and tried to invade Canaan on their own, although neither the ark nor Moses went with them (Nm 14:44). The result was defeat at the hands of their enemies (Nm 14:45). The ark

played an important role in the crossing of the Jordan (Jos 3:13-17; 4:9-10), the conquest of Jericho (Jos 6:6-11), and the life of the Israelites in their new land (Jos 8:33; Jgs 20:27). There is no hint of superstitious or magical use of the ark; it was not a fetish, talisman, or charm. Yet it had solemn significance as the container of God's "testimony" and as the pledge of his presence.

A sharp contrast to the role of the ark in Joshua's day is found in later times. In the days of Eli and his sons, that is, at the end of the period of the judges, religious life in Israel was at a low ebb. The ark was still venerated but looked upon as a fetish to ensure success or victory automatically. When losing a battle with the Philistines, the Israelites rushed the sacred chest to the battlefield, thereby hoping to gain a victory (1 Sm 4:1-10). But the Lord did not tolerate such flagrant misuse of the ark. He allowed it to be captured by the uncircumcised Philistines (1 Sm 4:11) and inflicted defeat on Israel and death on the house of the high priest Eli (1 Sm 4:13-22).

WHAT HAPPENED TO THE ARK?
Little is known about the ark's history after the time of Solomon. What happened to it when Judah was exiled to Babylon is a mystery. It may have been destroyed when Nebuchadnezzar destroyed the temple and the whole city of Jerusalem in 586 BC. The new temple built after return from the exile had no ark. There is a legend in the Apocrypha that Jeremiah hid the ark in a cave on Mt Nebo until a time when God would again restore his people (2 Macc 2:4-8).

The disappearance of the ark at the exile, however, was providential. For not only had the presence of God disappeared from above the mercy seat, but God had long since rejected worship as it was offered at the temple (Lam 2:6, 7; Is 1:11-14). Moreover, the very purpose and significance of the ark was ultimately to be fulfilled in the person and work of Jesus Christ.

With the coming of Jesus Christ, the yearly sprinkling of the mercy seat with the blood of bulls and goats was no longer necessary. Christ, with the shedding of his own blood, secured an eternal redemption (Heb 9:11-14). Consequently, those who trust in him are encouraged to come with boldness before the God of grace enthroned above the mercy seat (Heb 4:14-16). Whereas before, the veil hung as a barrier between men and the ark, Christ through his death tore the veil in two and passed through it (Mt 27:51; Heb 10:20), opening the way for all worshipers to see the ark of God's covenant (Rv 11:19).

At the same time, God vindicated the honor of the ark when it was offered to Dagon, the god of the Philistines. The account of the efforts of the pagan Philistines to get rid of the ark is humorous (1 Sm 5-6). The biblical writer dramatically illustrated that the holy ark could neither be treated superstitiously by God's people nor mocked by his enemies.

Samuel, a great reformer and prophet, made no attempt to restore the ark to a place of prominence after it was returned to Israel. He allowed it to remain in Kiriath-jearim (1 Sm 6:21; 7:2). Samuel first had to bring Israel back to obedience to God's covenant before the ark of the covenant could be of any use. David, described as a king after God's own heart and chosen to replace the disobedient Saul, exerted efforts to bring the ark back to a prominent place (2 Sm 6:1-17). It may have been to

David's political advantage to add prestige to his newly established capital, Jerusalem, formerly the Canaanite stronghold of Jebus. But Psalm 132 describes David's concern for the honor of God and for the ark. In a moment of great religious joy and enthusiasm he addressed God directly: "Arise, O LORD, and go to thy resting place, thou and the ark of thy might" (v 8, RSV). To restless David, the ark had also been "restless" as long as Israel had not yet obtained its "rest," that is, as long as Canaan had not been completely conquered. Some measure of peace had already come during Joshua's time (Jos 21:43-45), but much remained to be done. By conquering Jebus, David virtually completed the conquest of the Promised Land. Finally the land had rest and the Lord could then "dwell" in his temple, the suitable resting place for the ark. Nevertheless, David's desire to build a temple for the ark was not granted (2 Sm 7:1-17). He was told that his son Solomon would build a home for the ark and for the Lord. Solomon erected a magnificent temple with a place for the ark in the most holy part, behind the curtains (1 Kgs 8:1-11).

ARK'S COVER *See* Mercy Seat.

ARMAGEDDON Hebrew word in Revelation 16:16 meaning "Mount Megiddo." It is generally thought that the term refers to the town of Megiddo, strategically located between the western coastal area and the broad plain of Jezreel in northern Palestine. The area of Megiddo was important commercially and militarily and was the scene of many important battles in Israel's history. There the Lord routed Sisera before the armies of Deborah and Barak (Jgs 4-5); Gideon was victorious over the Midianites and Amalekites (Jgs 6-7); King Saul and his army were defeated by the Philistines (1 Sm 31); and King Josiah was slain in battle by the Egyptian army of Pharaoh Neco (2 Kgs 23:29). Because of that long history the name seems to have become symbolic of a battlefield. Such is the depiction in the book of Revelation.

Revelation 15 and 16 describe seven angels who pour out seven bowls of the wrath of God upon the earth. The sixth angel pours out his bowl upon the great river Euphrates, and its waters are dried up (Rv 16:12-16), preparing the way for the coming of the "kings of the East." Also three demonic spirits go forth to cause the kings of the whole world to gather for a battle on the great day of God the Almighty (16:13-14). Their gathering takes place at Armageddon (16:16). *See* Revelation, Book of.

HOW DO WE INTERPRET ARMAGEDDON?
Like most of Revelation the passage about Armageddon is difficult to interpret. A literal interpretation sees real armies gathered at an exact geographical location in the Near East. A more figurative interpretation sees John symbolically portraying a final worldwide conflict between wicked mankind and the Christ of God. Regardless of how literally or figuratively the passage is interpreted, it clearly describes a final battle in which Christ is victorious. That battle is known as the battle of Armageddon. The term has also passed into the secular vocabulary; for example, people now speak of the cataclismic end of the world as being "Armageddon."

ARMENIA* KJV translation of Ararat in 2 Kings 19:37 and Isaiah 37:38, mentioned as the place where Sennacherib's two sons fled after murdering their father. *See* Ararat.

ARMONI One of Saul's two sons by his concubine Rizpah. Seven of Saul's sons, including Armoni, were handed over to the Gibeonites by David to be killed to avenge Saul's slaughter of the Gibeonites (2 Sm 21:1, 8-9).

ARMOR AND WEAPONS Instruments of warfare.

The location of Palestine at the crossroads of three continents gave it a strategic importance in the ancient world quite out of proportion to its size. Surrounded by the great military powers (Egypt, Mesopotamia, the Hittites of Anatolia), that stretch of land was constantly the object of aggressive ambitions of other nations. The invention of different weapons, fortifications, and tactics exerted a profound reciprocal influence on other inventions. Tactical innovation by one side prompted new countertactics by the other.

The three basic elements of the art of warfare are mobility, firepower, and security. Weapons alone seldom determined the issue of battle, particularly when both sides were evenly matched. The skill with which strategy and tactics were deployed, the spirit of the commander in directing his troops, and the precision with which the troops handled their weapons were decisive factors in many of the battles mentioned in the Bible.

Attack Weapons The armory of a military commander in antiquity consisted of a variety of offensive weapons designed to engage the enemy at long, medium, and short range. The bow and the sling were the principal weapons developed for long-range firepower; the javelin and the spear for medium-range; the sword, the ax, and the mace for short-range.

Bow Early bows were fashioned from one piece of seasoned wood. No single type of bow wood, however, could provide the lightness, toughness, and elasticity required. Gradually the idea was conceived of combining several natural materials—wood, sections of animal horn, animal tendons and sinews, and glue—in the construction of a bow to meet all the demands placed on it. The resulting composite bow became a weapon of supreme importance. Composite structure gave a bow lightness, strength, and elasticity. Use of a double-convex form gave increased range and power of penetration.

The bowstring was made from bindweed, natural cord, hide, or the intestines of oxen or camels. The bow was strung by hand (2 Kgs 13:16), usually bending it with the foot, which required considerable strength (cf. 2 Sm 22:35; Jer 51:3). That may explain why archers were known as Obow treaders or as those who Otread a bow.

The form of the arrowhead was a response to the enemy's defense and armor. In the late Bronze period, for example, a battle arrowhead was generally of bronze and was thick in the middle, tapering to a spine. Its shape was dictated by the fact that the coats of mail in widespread use at the time could be penetrated only by a spined or ribbed arrowhead. The arrow shaft was usually made from reed, a material that combined strength with pliability.

Sling Complementing the bow was the sling, devised originally by shepherds to drive off animals molesting their flocks (cf. 1 Sm 17:40). It gradually assumed importance as a weapon of war, its supreme advantage being simple construction. Not only did a sling require little technical skill to produce, but the stones used as projectiles were readily available on the ground. In the hands of a trained slinger a missile could be hurled as far as 600 feet (183 meters) in any terrain. The sling's capacity for high-angled fire up a steep slope was particularly important in an assault on a fortified city. Its principal disadvantage was that strenuous training and experience were required to achieve accuracy in its operation (cf. Jgs 20:16).

A sling was commonly made from two leather thongs to which were attached a pocket for holding the stone. With the thongs pulled taut the pocket became a bag. The slinger held his arms above his head, the bag in his left hand and the ends of the taut thongs in his right hand. After swinging the sling several times around his head with great force to give it momentum, he suddenly released the end of one of the thongs to discharge the missile. Lead pellets as well as smooth stones were used as projectiles. They were carried in a bag or were piled conveniently at the slinger's feet.

The importance of the sling as a long-range weapon is evident in the familiar account of David's encounter with the Philistine champion, Goliath of Gath (1 Sm 17:40-51). At that time the Philistines possessed many advanced types of weapons, but the bow and sling were not among them. They depended on medium-range weapons like the javelin and short-range weapons like the sword (cf. 1 Sm 17:4-7, 45, 51). The sling gave David an advantage in range that was decisive against Goliath's superior weapons and armor (1 Sm 17:48-49).

Javelin and Spear Two weapons employed for medium-distance warfare were similar in appearance but different in length and operation. The javelin, generally lighter and shorter than the spear, was designed for throwing. It was like a large arrow that was hurled by the hand. Sumerian charioteers of the third millennium BC were armed with several javelins, carried like arrows in a quiver attached to the body of the chariot. Javelin heads were designed for penetration and altered in shape and material as enemy armor became more effective. A head fashioned with sharp hooks or barbs was difficult and painful to extract from a wound.

The spear was similar in appearance to the javelin but was larger, heavier, and designed primarily as a thrusting weapon (cf. Nm 25:7-8). The oldest military monuments known indicate that the spear was already well developed. On the Egyptian hunter's slate palette and on the black granite stele from Warka (c. 3000 BC), the warrior's personal weapon is a long staff tipped with a leaf-shaped blade with a sharp spine. Throughout the third millennium BC, the spear was standard equipment for heavy-armed infantry and the most effective weapon for both chariot and infantry charges. Excavations have shown that the spear was the common weapon of the seminomadic tribes who began pouring into Palestine from the north in the middle Bronze Age.

Another characteristic of spears in that early period was a metal tip attached to the butt of the shaft, enabling a spear to be stuck upright in the ground when not in use. That feature persisted into later periods and is mentioned specifically in reference to Saul's spear, which was stuck in the ground by his head while he slept (1 Sm 26:7). Occasionally the metal tip functioned as a thrusting weapon in its own right, as is evident in the account of the slaying of Asahel (2 Sm 2:23).

Sword One of the earliest objects made of iron was the sword. Swords were designed for either stabbing or striking. The stabbing sword developed as a long straight blade, tapered toward the point for piercing the body. Its tapered edges were sharpened so that it could also serve as a cutting instrument. The striking sword, on the other hand, had only one sharp edge, with the thickest part of the blade not along the center but along its blunt edge. Such a sword was often curved, sometimes to a degree that gave it the appearance of a sickle, but with the outer,

convex edge sharpened as the cutting blade. The earliest type of sickle sword appeared in the second half of the third millennium BC. Both the hilt, or handle, and the blade were fashioned from a single bar of metal. In the middle Bronze Age the curved striking sword functioned essentially as an ax, with a comparatively long hilt and short blade.

That type of sword completely disappeared in the late Bronze Age because it proved ineffective against the widespread use of the helmet and armor. In its place appeared a new design with the curved blade equal in length to the hilt and sometimes longer. It provided a cutting weapon in chariot fighting and against an enemy who possessed no armor. Widespread use of such long-bladed swords at that time explains the phrase repeatedly used in the Bible to describe Joshua's conquests of the Canaanites: Joshua smote them with the edge of the sword (e.g., Jos 8:24; 10:28-39). That expression would be inappropriate for the action of a short, straight, narrow sword designed as a thrusting weapon. A fine specimen of curved sword was found at Gezer in Palestine in the tomb of a nobleman, dating to the first half of the 14th century BC. The same type of blade is also depicted on a late 13th century BC ivory carving from Megiddo.

During those centuries advances made in the technology of forging iron were reflected in the development of the straight sword as well. The Sea Peoples, among whom were the Philistines, specialized in short-range arms. As early as the 13th century BC they began to make the straight blade more effective than the curved sickle-type sword.

By the time of Saul, the Philistines had used their technology to establish themselves as city dwellers and the dominant military presence in the land. Their military superiority was based on the chariot and on an infantry equipped with personal armaments of high quality. They carefully retained the forging of hard metal under their own supervision and kept the Israelites from developing forges of their own (cf. 1 Sm 13:19-22). Not until that situation was altered could the balance of power pass from the Philistines to Israel.

Mace and Ax The mace and the ax, developed as alternatives to the sword before hard metal could be forged, were designed for hand-to-hand fighting. They consisted of a comparatively short wooden handle, one end of which was fitted with a lethal head made of stone or metal. The weapons were swung like a hammer to deliver a striking blow. The critical detail was the secure fastening of the head to the handle to prevent its flying off when swung or breaking off when struck. The handle of both the mace and the ax was widened at the point of the grip, tapering toward the head, to prevent the weapon from slipping from the hand when swung. Such weapons were carried in the hand or attached to the wrist with a loop. The mace was designed to batter and smash, the ax to pierce and cut.

The mace was a very primitive weapon. The hieroglyphic sign for the infinitive *to fight* represents hands holding a mace and a medium-size shield. During the Chalcolithic and the first half of the early Bronze periods (3500–2500 BC), the mace was the primary weapon for personal combat. Because the helmet had not yet made its appearance, the striking power of the mace was devastating. Long after the mace had become obsolete as a personal weapon, it continued to serve as a symbol of sovereign authority for the king or deity (cf. Ps 2:9).

Complex technical problems taxed the ingenuity of armorers in the production of the ax. The blade had to be fixed securely to the handle. The cutting ax had a short blade and a wide edge. It was an effective weapon against an enemy unprotected by armor. It was also used for tearing down the wall of a besieged city, as in the wall painting at Saqqarah (23d century BC). But against armor the cutting ax was ineffective. Deeper power of penetration was achieved with the piercing ax, which had a long, narrow blade ending in a short, sharp edge.

Defensive Protection Without provision for personal protection of the individual soldier on the battlefield, the mobility and firepower of an army could be seriously compromised.

Shield Designed to provide a barrier between the body of a soldier and the weapon of his foe, the shield was one of the oldest means of security devised. In the time of the judges and the early Israelite kings, persons of rank were frequently protected by a very large shield. It was carried by a special shield bearer who remained constantly at the unprotected right side of the warrior to whom he was assigned as a bodyguard (cf. Jgs 9:54; 1 Sm 14:1; 17:7; 2 Sm 18:15). The right side of an armed combatant was unprotected because he carried his weapons in his right hand and his shield in his left. The shield bearer therefore had to stand by his master's vulnerable right side to protect him (1 Sm 17:41; cf. Ps 16:8). In that period the shield was ordinarily anointed as part of the consecration of an Israelite warrior and his weapons for battle (cf. 2 Sm 1:21).

Armor Personal armor protected the body of a combatant from injury while freeing his hands to use his weapons. The earliest type of body armor formed a substitute for the long shield. It consisted of a full-length tunic made from leather or some tough fiber. It was relatively simple to produce, was light enough to permit full mobility, and offered a measure of protection to the chest, abdomen, back, thighs, and legs. So equipped, a soldier required only a short shield to protect his arms and face.

The late Bronze period saw the development of the coat of mail. It consisted of hundreds of small pieces of overlapping metal joined together like fish scales and sewed to the surface of a cloth or leather tunic. Written documents from Nuzi state that from 400 to 600 large scales and several hundred smaller scales went into the production of a single coat. Smaller scales and narrower rows were used where greater flexibility was needed, as at the throat and neck. The resulting garment was relatively flexible, affording freedom of movement, while the hard metal scales gave far greater personal protection than leather or fiber could provide.

Helmet Since the greatest point of vulnerability for a soldier in combat was his head, concern for some form of protective helmet can be traced as far back as the end of the fourth millennium BC.

Bronze helmets were worn both by Goliath and by Saul (1 Sm 17:5, 38). Although the helmet was standard equipment for the heavily armed infantry of foreign armies for centuries, it does not seem to have been a common possession of soldiers in the Israelite army during the period of the united monarchy. Among military reforms introduced by King Uzziah in the ninth century BC was provision of helmets for the army of the southern kingdom of Judah (2 Chr 26:14).

See also Warfare.

ARMOR BEARER
One who carried the protective gear (armor) and weapons of a warrior. *See* Armor and Weapons.

ARMORY Storehouse for weapons; an arsenal (Jer 50:25). *See* Armor and Weapons.

ARMY Large organized body of soldiers for waging war, especially on land. *See* Warfare.

ARNAN Rephaiah's son and Obadiah's father, a descendant of David through Zerubbabel (1 Chr 3:21).

ARNI Ancestor of Jesus according to Luke's genealogy (3:33); also called Ram in Ruth 4:19 and 1 Chronicles 2:9-10.

ARNON River of Transjordan, the present Wadi el-Mojib, running from east to west through a canyon with walls 1,500 feet (457 meters) high into the Dead Sea. At the time of the Israelite conquest of Canaan, the gorge served as a natural border between Moab to the south and the Ammonite kingdoms to the north (Nm 21:13-15). After the division of the land under Joshua the river Arnon became the southern boundary of Reuben's territory (Dt 3:12, 16; Jos 13:16).

AROD*, ARODI, ARODITE Gad's sixth son, founder of the Arodite family (Nm 26:17). He is called Arodi in the list of those who went to Egypt with Jacob (Gn 46:16).

AROER
1. Transjordanian city existing from Moses' time until the fall of Jerusalem (586 BC). It was among the cities that Israel conquered from Sihon the Amorite and Og the Bashanite in an area assigned to the tribes of Gad and Reuben and to half of Manasseh's tribe. Aroer was on the southern border of that territory (Jos 13:9), on the northern rim of the large Arnon Canyon (Dt 2:36; 3:12; 4:48; Jos 13:9). Evidently the city was rebuilt after Israel destroyed it (cf. Jos 12:2; Nm 32:34).

   Aroer was the hub city for a number of villages (Jgs 11:26) and was the city from which the census began under King David (2 Sm 24:5). The Moabites gained control of it during the later monarchy and kept it until the time of Jeremiah (Jer 48:19). King Hazael of Damascus captured Aroer, assuring Syrian control of Transjordan (2 Kgs 10:33).

   Aroer has been identified with a mound beside the village 'Ara'ir, about three miles (4.8 kilometers) southeast of Dibon on the east side of the ancient north-south Transjordan highway.
2. City assigned to Gad's tribe (Jos 13:25), mentioned as a point of reference in Jephthah's victory over the Ammonites (Jgs 11:33). This Aroer has been tentatively placed in the area northwest of Amman and east of Rabbah.
3. City in the Negev Desert area of Judah. Aroer was one of the villages receiving spoil taken in David's victory over the Amalekites (1 Sm 30:28). Two of David's "mighty men" were sons of Hotham the Aroerite (1 Chr 11:44). This Aroer has been identified with Khirbet 'Ar'areh, located about 12 miles (19 kilometers) southeast of Beersheba.
4. City near Damascus (Is 17:2). The Hebrew text reads "the cities of Aroer," but the Septuagint (ancient Greek OT) has "her cities for ever" (a reading adopted by the RSV).

AROERITE* Resident of Aroer. The Aroerite Hotham, father of two of David's "mighty men," was a native of Aroer (1 Chr 11:44). *See* Aroer #3.

AROMATIC CANE* Species of fragrant reed used by the Israelites as a perfume (Sg 4:14) and as an ingredient of the anointing oil (Ex 30:23). *See* Plants (Cane).

ARPACHSHAD* Alternate spelling for Arphaxad. *See* Arphaxad.

ARPAD City in northern Syria. Arpad was overrun twice by the Assyrians: in 740 BC by Tiglath-pileser III and in 720 BC by Sargon II. The Assyrians used Arpad and Hamath as examples of the inability of any gods, including Israel's, to protect cities against Assyria's attacks (2 Kgs 18:34; 19:13; Is 10:9; 36:19; 37:13). Arpad and Hamath are also mentioned in a later prophecy against the Syrian city of Damascus (Jer 49:23). Arpad has been identified as modern Tell Erfad, north of Aleppo.

ARPHAXAD Shem's son and Noah's grandson, born two years after the Flood. Arphaxad's descendants were probably the Chaldeans (Gn 10:22-24; 11:10-13; 1 Chr 1:17-18, 24; Lk 3:36). Arphaxad was born two years after the Flood when his father was one hundred years old (Gn 11:10) and was the grandfather of Eber, whom some believe was ancestor of the Hebrews (1 Chr 1:17-25; Lk 3:35-36).

ARROW *See* Armor and Weapons.

ARSACES Title shared by Parthian rulers beginning with Arsaces I, founder of the kingdom (250? BC). The Parthian kingdom under Arsaces VI (Mithridates I) grew to include Media and Persia among other nations, thereby encroaching upon Seleucid territory. Syrian king Demetrius Nicator retaliated in 141 BC by invading the kingdom of Arsaces VI, an event recorded in the Apocrypha (1 Macc 14:1-3). Arsaces was one of the kings whom the Roman consul advised not to harm the Jews (1 Macc 15:15-22).

ARTAXERXES Name of three kings of the Persian Empire.

1. Artaxerxes I (465–424 BC), known as Macrocheir or Longimanus, son and successor of Xerxes I (486–465 BC). Xerxes I was the Ahasuerus of the book of Esther and Ezra 4:6. A few years after the succession of Artaxerxes I, the Greeks urged Egypt to revolt against Persia. Only in 454 BC was that movement crushed along with other dissension in the Persian Empire. By 449 BC, when peace was made between the Greeks and Persians by the treaty of Callias, Artaxerxes had gained full control over his empire, and a period of peace resulted.

   Artaxerxes I was the ruler who brought the rebuilding of Jerusalem to a temporary standstill (Ezr 4:7-23), and who commissioned Ezra to visit the city in the capacity of secretary of state of Jewish affairs in 458 BC (Ezr 7:8,11-26). In 445 BC Nehemiah went to Jerusalem as civil governor in the 20th year of Artaxerxes I (Neh 1:1; 2:1). By altering the text of Ezra 7:7 to read "thirty-seventh" instead of "seventh," some scholars have tried to show that Artaxerxes II was the Persian king under whom Nehemiah worked. The Elephantine papyri, however, indicate that Sanballat, governor of Samaria, was quite advanced in years in 408 BC, shortly before the death of Darius II (423–405 BC); hence Sanballat's opposition to Nehemiah must have occurred years earlier under Artaxerxes I. The dates of Ezra and Nehemiah thus fall within the lifetime of this monarch.

   Artaxerxes I was notable for his kindness toward the Jews in Persia, once matters of procedure had been established clearly; his support for the work of Ezra and Nehemiah is evident from their writings.

   See also Ahasuerus; Ezra, Book of; Nehemiah, Book of; Esther, Book of.

2. Artaxerxes II Mnemon (404–359 BC), grandson of Artaxerxes I and son of Darius II. His reign was a time of unrest in the Persian Empire, one result of which was the loss of Egypt about 401 BC. He constructed several splendid buildings and seems to have enlarged the palace at Susa.

3. Artaxerxes III Ochus (358–338 BC), son and successor of Artaxerxes II. He brought peace to the empire by shrewd diplomacy, but he was assassinated. Neither he nor his father is mentioned in the OT.

   See also Persia, Persians.

ARTEMAS Christian coworker with Paul, whom the apostle considered as a replacement for Titus on the island of Crete (Ti 3:12). Later tradition describes Artemas as bishop of Lystra.

ARTEMIS Greek goddess of the moon, wild animals, and hunting. The cult of Artemis at Ephesus, where she is called Diana by the Romans (Acts 19:23-41), regarded her especially as a fertility goddess.
   See also Diana.

ARTIFICER* KJV rendering of "craftsman" in Genesis 4:22; 1 Chronicles 29:5; 2 Chronicles 34:11; and Isaiah 3:3. *See* Work.

ARTISAN* Skilled craftsman working in the major mediums of wood, stone, metals, gems, and clay; important guild in the middle class of Hebrew society during the period of the monarchy. *See* Work.

ARUBBOTH Town that served as headquarters for one of King Solomon's 12 administrative districts (1 Kgs 4:10). Arubboth was probably in Manasseh's tribal territory, about nine miles (14.5 kilometers) north of Samaria, at the site of modern 'Aarabeh.

ARUMAH City where Gideon's son Abimelech lived after he was driven out of Shechem by its inhabitants (Jgs 9:1, 22-25, 31, 41); perhaps alternately called Rumah in 2 Kings 23:36.

ARVAD, ARVADITE Small fortified island about 2 miles (3.2 kilometers) off the coast of Syria (ancient Phoenicia) and 30 miles (48 kilometers) north of Tripolis. Arvad developed a large trading and fighting fleet, and the fame of its sailors was referred to in a description of the naval power of Tyre (Ez 27:8, 11). Egyptian records recount Arvad's fall to Thutmose III about 1472 BC. Assyrian records indicate the importance of Arvad and its recurrent conquest by foreign powers from the 11th to the 7th centuries BC.

   Arvad was later known as Aradus or Arados, and is referred to as such in 1 Maccabees 15:23. During the Persian and Hellenistic periods it was once again an important Mediterranean seaport, only to decline again. The Canaanite tribe of Arvadites (Gn 10:18; 1 Chr 1:16) possibly had an ethnic connection with the island Arvad. Today Arvad is known as Ruad.

ARZA Superintendent of the palace at Tirzah belonging to King Elah of the northern kingdom of Israel. The drunken king was murdered in Arza's home by Zimri, who then declared himself king (1 Kgs 16:9-10).

ASA

1. Third king of the southern kingdom of Judah (910–869 BC) after the split of Solomon's Empire into independent kingdoms. Solomon's son Rehoboam, Asa's grandfather, had neither Solomon's wisdom nor his tact. Rehoboam failed to use diplomacy to avoid an approaching explosion of popular resentment against Solomon's oppressive policies; in fact, Rehoboam actively precipitated the explosion. Asa came to the throne just after his father, Abijam (or Abijah), who reigned only briefly (913–910 BC). Asa thus inherited a shrunken, vulnerable kingdom. Moreover, he was thrust into a suddenly unstable political arena shaken by collapse of the great world empires of old Babylonia to the north and east in Mesopotamia, and of Egypt to the southwest. Hence until the emerging might of Assyria was firmly established (mid-ninth century BC), the small Palestinian states (Israel, Judah, Syria, the Arameans, and Phoenicians, and to some degree the peoples of Moab and Edom) were free to push and shove among themselves.

   The rival states had superficial similarities, especially Judah and Israel, but were divided by deep differences and intense self-interest. Borders were in perpetual dispute—never fully settled but seldom contested in all-out bloody conflict. Threats, expedience, bribes, payment of tribute, marriages purchased for power, and other cunning arts in the catalog of political kingcraft were employed to shift alliances. Since all were playing the same game, a kind of fluid balance resulted.

   At the beginning of King Asa's reign there was an initial decade of peace and prosperity. Then, however, he was called upon to face enemy threats and invasion. In those crises he trusted God and forced out or defeated all who attempted to conquer, divide, or destroy Judah (2 Chr 14:1-8). Further, he cleansed the land of pagan shrines and places of worship and even took away the royal prerogatives and standing of Maacah, his mother. She had erected an image of the fertility goddess Asherah (1 Kgs 15:10; 2 Chr 15:16).

   Nonetheless, later in his reign Asa abruptly abandoned his trust in God. By means of a huge gift that stripped the temple treasures, he entered an alliance with Ben-hadad, king of Damascus (Syria) in order to force Baasha, ruler of the northern kingdom of Israel, to withdraw from newly conquered territory in Judah. Asa had become heedless of God's faithful protection when Israel, Judah's mortal enemy, stood triumphant and strategically poised to strike, only five miles (8 kilometers) from Jerusalem. Asa's power play worked. Israel had to retire from the field in the south to meet Ben-hadad's threat from the north. When Hanani spoke plainly to Asa about his disbelief in God, Asa was infuriated and had Hanani thrown into prison (2 Chr 16:7-10).

   For the last years of his long 41-year reign, Asa was ill: "Even when the disease became life threatening, he did not seek the LORD's help but sought help only from his physicians" (2 Chr 16:12, NLT). He died and was buried with honor in the royal tombs (1 Kgs 15:24; 2 Chr 16:14).

   See also Israel, History of; Chronicles, Books of First and Second; Chronology of the Bible (Old Testament); King.
2. A Levite and Berechiah's father. Berechiah lived in one of the villages of the Netophathites after the exile (1 Chr 9:16).

ASAHEL

1. Warrior among David's mighty men known as "the thirty" (2 Sm 23:24; 1 Chr 11:26). Asahel was the son of David's half sister Zeruiah and the brother of Joab and Abishai (2 Sm 2:18; 1 Chr 2:16). In the battle of Gibeon, David's general Joab engaged the forces of Abner, leader of Ishbosheth's army. Asahel, who "could run like a deer," pursued Abner, but in the ensuing encounter Abner killed Asahel (2 Sm 2:18-23, 32).
2. One of the Levites sent out by King Jehoshaphat of Judah to teach the people the law of the Lord (2 Chr 17:8).
3. Temple aide appointed by King Hezekiah to take care of the tithed offerings given to support the Levites (2 Chr 31:13).
4. Father of Jonathan. Jonathan (not to be confused with Saul's son) opposed the appointment of a commission to take action concerning the foreign (pagan) wives of some of the Jews after the Babylonian exile (Ezr 10:15).

ASAHIAH*
KJV form of Asaiah, Josiah's servant, in 2 Kings 22:12, 14. See Asaiah #1.

ASAIAH

1. Royal servant sent by King Josiah of Judah to ask the prophetess Huldah about the meaning of the Book of the Law found in the renovation of the temple (2 Kgs 22:12, 14; 2 Chr 34:20).
2. Clan leader of Simeon's tribe who settled in Gedor (Gerar?) during Hezekiah's reign (1 Chr 4:36).
3. Levitical leader in the time of King David. Asaiah helped bring the ark to Jerusalem (1 Chr 6:30; 15:6, 11).
4. Shiloni's oldest son. Asaiah's family was among the first to resettle in Jerusalem after the exile (1 Chr 9:5). Perhaps the same as Maaseiah of Nehemiah 11:5. See Maaseiah #14.

ASAPH

1. Berechiah's son, an important tabernacle musician during King David's reign (1 Chr 6:31-32, 39). Along with Heman, the head singer, and Ethan, Asaph was appointed to sound bronze cymbals during the ceremony when the ark was brought to the new tabernacle (1 Chr 15:1-19). David appointed Asaph to serve "by giving constant praise and thanks to the Lord God of Israel" (1 Chr 16:4-5, TLB) and to lead Israel in a special psalm of praise (1 Chr 16:7-36). Along with his relatives he ministered daily before the ark (1 Chr 16:37; 25:6, 9; 1 Esd 1:15; 5:27, 59). He was also described as David's private prophet (1 Chr 25:1-2). Asaph's name appears in the superscriptions of Psalms 50 and 73-83 and in the guild he established, "the sons of Asaph" (1 Chr 25:1; 2 Chr 35:15; Ezr 2:41; Neh 7:44; 11:22).
2. Joah's father. Joah was the recorder (court historian or royal scribe) in King Hezekiah's administration (2 Kgs 18:18, 27; Is 36:33).
3. Temple guard or gatekeeper, seemingly the same person as Ebiasaph (1 Chr 9:18).
4. Keeper of the king's forest in Palestine under Artaxerxes I Longimanus (Neh 2:8). Nehemiah asked this Asaph for timber to rebuild the wall, gates, and structures of Jerusalem.

ASARAMEL
Enigmatic Hebrew word found in the dedicatory inscription honoring Simon, ruling high priest of Israel and brother of Judas Maccabeus (1 Macc 14:28). Plausible translations of the term are "prince of the people of God" or "court of the people of God." The Syriac version of the Apocrypha drops the "m" to give "Israel"—making the sentence read "in the third year of Simon the great high priest in Israel."

ASAREEL*, ASAREL Jehallelel's son from Judah's tribe (1 Chr 4:16).

ASARELAH Alternate form of Asharelah, Asaph's son, in 1 Chronicles 25:2. *See* Asharelah.

ASCALON Alternate form of Ashkelon in Judith 2:28. *See* Ashkelon.

ASCENSION OF CHRIST Transference of the resurrected body of Jesus from this world to heaven. Among the NT writers, only Luke described Jesus' ascension. Acts 1:9-11 pictures a scene in which Jesus was "taken up" and disappeared into a cloud. Luke 24:50-51 and Acts 1:12 locate that final event near Bethany, east of Jerusalem on the Mt of Olives.

Matthew concluded his history before Pentecost, but John suggested the Ascension in Jesus' own comments: Jesus has departed, but he will return (Jn 21:22); he cannot be touched, for he must ascend (20:17); many will believe without having seen him (20:29). Thus, the Gospels assume that (1) after the resurrection Jesus appeared to his disciples; (2) at some point in time those appearances ceased; and (3) although physically absent, Jesus is still spiritually present in his church. Other NT writings agree. The apostle Paul wrote that God raised Christ from the dead "and seated him in the place of honor at God's right hand in the heavenly realms" (Eph 1:20) or, as the writer of Hebrews put it, "in the place of honor at the right hand of the majestic God of heaven" (Heb 1:3).

The Ascension, however, is more than merely a past event. It has further significance in the NT that can be summarized under two headings: (1) its meaning for Christ and (2) its meaning for the Christian.

For Christ, the Ascension is the necessary entrance into his heavenly "glorification" in which he sits on the right hand of the Father until his enemies become his footstool (Ps 110:1—the OT text most quoted in the NT). The Ascension is proof of his glorification and his superiority over such OT heroes as David (Acts 2:33-36). By his ascension he rises over all and fills all (Eph 4:10), receiving "the name that is over every name" (Phil 2:9-11). For the author of the book of Hebrews the Ascension is also proof of Christ's superiority to angels; he sits enthroned while they are constantly being sent out to serve (Heb 1:13-14). Angels, authorities, and powers are all subject to the ascended Christ (1 Tm 3:16; 1 Pt 3:22).

For the Christian, the ascension of Christ is meaningful in four ways. First, without it there would be no gift of the Holy Spirit, who could not come until Jesus had ascended and sent him (Jn 16:7). Without the Ascension, the church would have Jesus locally in one place, not spiritually present "wherever two or three are gathered" (Mt 18:20; cf. 28:20).

Second, since a truly human Jesus has ascended to heaven, human beings can also ascend there. Jesus went "to prepare a place" for his followers (Jn 14:2). The hope of those who are "in Christ" is that they will eventually ascend to be with him (2 Cor 5:1-10).

Third, the Ascension proves that the sacrifice of Christ is finished and accepted by God. Jesus has passed through the heavens (Heb 4:14) and entered the presence of God (Heb 6:20), which is described as the inner sanctuary of the heavenly temple, the real temple of which the one on earth was a copy (Heb 9:24). Having brought a single, once-for-all sacrifice to God (Heb 9:12), Christ sat down (Heb 1:3; 10:12; 12:2), showing that no repetition of his sacrifice is necessary.

Fourth, the Ascension means that there is a human being in heaven who sympathizes with humanity

and can therefore intercede on humanity's behalf (1 Jn 2:1). Jesus has experienced everything humans experience—birth, growth, temptation, suffering, and death—and therefore he can serve effectively as an intermediary before God in heaven (Heb 2:17; 5:7-10). Christ's ascension assures the church that God understands the human situation and that Christians can therefore approach him boldly in their prayers (Heb 4:14-16).

Thus Christ's ascension is an indispensable aspect of NT teaching. It is the basis for recognition of Christ's exalted status and for the Christian's confidence and hope.

See also Christology; Jesus Christ, Life and Teachings of.

ASCENT OF HERES* Place mentioned in Judges 8:13. *See* Heres #2.

ASCENTS, Song of Superscription of Psalms 120–134. *See* Song of Ascents, Song of Degrees.

ASENATH Joseph's Egyptian wife who became the mother of Manasseh and Ephraim. Asenath was the daughter of the priest Potiphera (Gn 41:45, 50-52; 46:20).

ASER* KJV form of Asher in Luke 2:36 and Revelation 7:6. *See* Asher (Tribe).

ASH* *See* Plants.

ASHAN Town in the southwestern Judean foothills slightly northwest of Beersheba. Ashan first belonged to Judah's tribe (Jos 15:42), then to Simeon's (Jos 19:7), and finally to the Levites as a city of refuge (1 Chr 6:59). David roamed there with his outlaw band (1 Sm 30:30). The city of Ain mentioned in Joshua 21:16 probably refers to Ashan (this should not be confused with Ain in the northeast of Canaan, Nm 34:11). *See* Cities of Refuge.

ASHARELAH* One of Asaph's four sons appointed by David to assist with prophecy and music in the sanctuary (1 Chr 25:2); alternately called Jesharelah in verse 14.

ASHBEA* Name of a family in 1 Chronicles 4:21 (KJV). The NLT is probably correct in translating the name as the family's place of residence. *See* Beth-ashbea.

ASHBEL, ASHBELITE Benjamin's son who emigrated to Egypt with his grandfather Jacob (Gn 46:21; 1 Chr 8:1). The Ashbelites, his descendants, were included in Moses' census in the wilderness (Nm 26:38). Ashbel is elsewhere called Jediael (1 Chr 7:6).

ASHCHENAZ* KJV form of Ashkenaz, Gomer's son, in 1 Chronicles 1:6 and Jeremiah 51:27. *See* Ashkenaz.

ASHDOD, ASHDODITE, ASHDOTHITE* One of the Philistines' five main cities (the "pentapolis") along with Gaza, Ashkelon, Gath, and Ekron (Jos 13:3). Ashdod was located midway between Joppa and Gaza, about three miles (4.8 kilometers) from the coast. The ancient tell has been excavated extensively since 1962. The earliest level found was Canaanite, dating to the 17th century BC. When the Israelites arrived in the Promised Land, the city was inhabited by the giant Anakim (Jos 11:21-22). Though unconquered, it was assigned to Judah's tribe (Jos 15:46-47). Its people were referred to as Ashdodites (Jos 13:4; Neh 4:7). During the 12th century BC the coast of Palestine was invaded by the Sea Peoples, a group of tribes from the Aegean area. Ashdod was destroyed and reoccupied by one of these peoples, the Philistines. Excavations at Ashdod have uncovered three levels of Philistine occupation and have furnished a glimpse of the material culture of these traditional enemies of Israel.

In the days of Eli the priest, the Philistines captured the ark of the covenant and placed it first in the temple of their god Dagon in Ashdod, then in Gath and Ekron (1 Sm 5). A plague broke out wherever the ark went, so the Philistine rulers returned it with an offering of gold (1 Sm 6:1-18). Although David and Solomon controlled Ashdod, it was not until Uzziah came to the throne of the kingdom of Judah (792–740 BC) that Ashdod was actually conquered (2 Chr 26:6). After a while, Judah's military power waned, and the city became independent again. Ashdod resisted Assyrian encroachments until Sargon II attacked and destroyed it in 711 BC, a fact illumined by three fragments of a basalt stele of Sargon found at Ashdod in 1963. Those events led Isaiah to warn Judah against supporting Ashdod or counting on Egypt or Ethiopia to oppose the Assyrians (Is 20). Excavations at Ashdod show evidence of the destruction by both Uzziah and Sargon II.

Ashdod remained under Assyrian control until the Egyptian pharaoh Psamtik I (664–609 BC) took the city after a siege of 29 years (perhaps the longest in history). Later, probably at the time of the fall of Jerusalem (586 BC), Nebuchadnezzar conquered Ashdod and took its king to his court. Jeremiah and Zephaniah had prophesied about the people remaining in Ashdod (Jer 25:20; Zep 2:4). That remnant later opposed Nehemiah's rebuilding of Jerusalem, and its women married Jewish husbands (Neh 4:7; 13:23-24). Earlier, the prophet Zechariah had predicted further desolation for Ashdod (Zec 9:6).

During Maccabean times the city, then called Azotus, was attacked and plundered by both Judas and Jonathan Maccabeus because of its idolatry (1 Macc 4:12-15; 5:68; 10:77-85; 11:4). Freed by Pompey in 63 BC, Ashdod became part of the Roman province of Syria. Later Herod the Great willed the city to his sister Salome. Philip the evangelist preached the message of Christ in Azotus (Acts 8:40). The early Christian historian Eusebius regarded it as an important town in the fourth century AD, and Christian bishops were located there from the fourth through the sixth centuries. During the Middle Ages, Ashdod, or Azotus, began to decline, and now is only a small village called Esdud.

Ashdod was located about three miles (4.8 kilometers) inland and therefore had a port, separated from the city proper, called Ashdod Yam, or Ashdod-on-the-Sea. That coastal town in later years became larger than the inland city. Excavations in the area of the seaport have uncovered remains of Canaanite, Israelite, and Hellenistic occupation. One interesting find was the remains of a Hellenistic dye operation. A purple dye made from the murex shell was used to dye cloth worn by royalty and the wealthy. The site of the port continued to be occupied through the Arabic period, and today Israel has built a port near the site of ancient Ashdod Yam.

ASHDOTH-PISGAH* KJV form of "slopes of Pisgah" (Dt 3:17; Jos 12:3; 13:20), referring to the slopes of Mt Pisgah. *See* Pisgah, Mount.

ASHER (Person) Jacob's son born to Leah's maid Zilpah (Gn 30:12-13). The name Asher, probably meaning "happy," was given to the child by Leah in her delight at his birth. Asher had four sons, Imnah, Ishvah, Ishvi, and Beriah, and a daughter, Serah (Gn 46:17;

1 Chr 7:30). Some have speculated that the tribe of Asher took its name from a locality mentioned in Egyptian texts of the 13th century BC. It is more likely that the tribe bore the name of its ancestor. Asher and his brothers received a special blessing and prediction from Jacob as he was dying (Gn 49:20; cf. Dt 33:24-25, where the dying Moses blessed Asher and the other tribes).

See also Asher (Tribe).

ASHER (Place) Place mentioned in Tobit 1:2, identified as Hazor. *See* Hazor #1.

ASHER (Tribe) Israelite tribe that inhabited the fertile coastal territory when the Promised Land was divided for settlement. Asher's allotment stretched north of Mt Carmel to a point slightly above the city of Sidon. The eastern boundary ran along the western slopes of the hills of Galilee (Jos 19:24-34). The tribes of Zebulun and Naphtali were Asher's eastern neighbors. Due south, the Carmel mountain range was a natural barrier between Asher and the tribe of Manasseh. The land of Asher was agriculturally rich and is still known for its olive groves. Economically, the people of Asher joined in maritime trade with the Phoenicians of the city of Tyre.

As a tribe, Asher fluctuated in size. From the few who entered Egypt with their father, Jacob, the tribe grew to 41,500 adult warriors at Mt Sinai (Nm 1:40-41). At the second census in the wilderness the tribe numbered 53,400 soldiers (Nm 26:47). At the time of King David the number varied from 26,000 to 40,000 warriors (1 Chr 7:40; 12:36). Asher was never more than fifth in size among the tribes of Israel.

The tribe joined the rest of Israel in rejecting the optimistic reports of Caleb and Joshua about the land of Canaan (Nm 13:30–14:10). As a result, that generation perished in the wilderness after 40 years of wandering (Nm 14:22-25).

At the close of the northern campaign in the Promised Land, Joshua gave the remaining seven tribes their own territory (Jos 18:2). The fifth partition went to Asher's descendants. Earlier, Ahihud had been chosen by God to distribute land within the territory given to Asher's tribe (Nm 34:16, 27). Certain Levites, descendants of Gershom, were allocated cities within its borders (Jos 21:6, 30; 1 Chr 6:62, 74).

Like all the Israelite tribes, Asher was never able to possess all of its inheritance. Failure to drive out the inhabitants of Acco, Sidon, Ahlab, Achzib, Helbah, Aphik, and Rehob subjected the tribe to the degradations of pagan culture (Jgs 1:31). The "unpossessed" territory of the Sidonians and the Phoenicians stretched along the coastal region for 200 miles (322 kilometers). Thus "the Asherites dwelt among the Canaanites, the inhabitants of the land; for they did not drive them out" (Jgs 1:32, RSV). It is possible that Asher's tribe, having become a partner in the enterprises of the successful Phoenicians, lost all desire to expel them from their cities.

After the death of the Israelite judge Ehud, Israel fell into the hands of Jabin, king of Canaan. When the judge Deborah stirred up Barak to marshal Israel's forces for battle, God gave their army a great victory and liberated them from their oppressor (Jgs 4). After the victory Deborah complained that "Asher sat unmoved at the seashore, remaining in his harbors" (Jgs 5:17, NLT). Eventually, through amalgamation, the tribe succumbed to Phoenician religious and cultural influences. Foreign invasion and pagan inroads were its downfall.

Little is said in the Bible of the tribe's leadership. At the time of the exodus, when the nation was organized at Mt Sinai, Pagiel the son of Ochran became tribal chief (Nm 1:13; 2:27; 7:72; 10:26). But the Bible is silent from then on about Asher's leaders. None of the judges of Israel came from Asher, and in King David's day the tribes of Asher and Gad were omitted from the list of the nation's chief officers (1 Chr 27:16-22).

Nevertheless, there are some bright spots in Asher's tribal history. The tribe answered the call of Gideon to drive out the Midianite enemy (Jgs 6:1-8, 35; 7:23). They rallied with the rest of the tribes of Israel to defend Saul, their first king (1 Sm 11:7). Later, 40,000 Asherites sided with David to give him Saul's kingdom (1 Chr 12:23-36). After the fall of Samaria in 722 BC, a small remnant came to Jerusalem to observe the first Passover feast in many years (2 Chr 30:5), when King Hezekiah (715–686 BC) invited all the tribes to assemble for the Passover (2 Chr 30:10-11).

In the NT one of Asher's descendants is mentioned, an 84-year-old widow named Anna, a prophetess. She described Jesus as "the redemption of Jerusalem" from the time of his dedication to the Lord in the temple (Lk 2:36-38).

See also Israel, History of.

ASHERAH, ASHERIM*, ASHEROTH*
Singular and plural form of the name of a Canaanite goddess associated with Baal (Jgs 3:7; 1 Kgs 18:19). The words also refer to the wooden poles erected to worship this goddess. *See* Canaanite Deities and Religion; Grove.

ASHES
Fine powder left after something has been thoroughly burned. The burning of sacrificial offerings on the tabernacle or temple altar produced ashes that were disposed of ceremonially (Lv 1:16; 4:12; 6:10-11; cf. Heb 9:13). The ashes on pagan altars figured in several OT accounts (1 Kgs 13:1-5; 2 Kgs 23:4). Ashes thrown into the air by Moses during the contest of God with the Egyptian pharaoh spread like fine dust over all the land of Egypt and caused a plague of boils to break out among both people and animals (Ex 9:8-10).

Ashes are frequently mentioned in the Bible in connection with the ancient custom of putting ashes on oneself as a symbol of extreme grief, penitence, humiliation, or sense of worthlessness. The Bible refers to ashes and dust almost interchangeably in this usage. Examples of such expressions of emotion include Tamar's distress after being sexually assaulted by her half brother (2 Sm 13:19), Mordecai's agony over the Persian king's order of genocide for the Jews of his realm (Est 4:1-3), Daniel's confession and pleading for his captive people (Dn 9:3), and the king of Nineveh's repentance after hearing Jonah's preaching (Jon 3:6; cf. Lk 10:13). Ashes were spoken of as symbols of humility (Gn 18:27), worthlessness or futility (Jb 13:12; 30:19; Is 44:20), and destruction (Ez 28:18; 2 Pt 2:6).

See also Mourning.

ASHHUR
Caleb's son and Tekoa's father (1 Chr 2:24; 4:5), or perhaps the founder of a village named Tekoa (2 Sm 14:1-3; Am 1:1).

ASHIMA
Deity of uncertain origin, worshiped by the inhabitants of Hamath and relocated in Samaria after the fall of Israel in 722 BC (2 Kgs 17:30).

ASHKELON
City dating back to ancient times, also spelled Askelon (KJV). In the Bible, Ashkelon was one of the Philistines' five main cities (the "pentapolis"), along with Gaza, Ashdod, Gath, and Ekron (Jos 13:3).

Ashkelon was located on the Mediterranean coast, 30 miles (48 kilometers) south of modern Tel Aviv, and was always an important port. Often in conflict with Egypt, it was captured by Ramses II (c. 1286 BC) and by Merneptah (c. 1220 BC).

Ashkelon is mentioned as one of the cities conquered by Judah (Jgs 1:18). After the Philistine invasion of Canaan in the 12th century BC, the city became one of the invaders' major centers. When Samson's riddle was answered through the duplicity of his Philistine wife, Samson vented his rage at Ashkelon, killing 30 men (Jgs 14:19). Ashkelon was partially responsible for pushing the tribe of Dan from its allotment; so Samson, a member of that tribe, probably had a long-standing grudge against the city. Ashkelon also figures in the story of the Philistine control of the ark (1 Sm 4–6). On hearing of the deaths of Saul and Jonathan, David lamented the loss of his king and of his friend, exclaiming that their deaths should not be published in Ashkelon (2 Sm 1:20). Various OT prophets refer to Ashkelon (Jer 25:20; 47:5-6; Am 1:8; Zep 2:4-7; Zec 9:5).

In the period of Israel's decline King Pekah of Israel, King Rezin of Damascus, and the king of Ashkelon rebelled against Assyria. Tiglath-pileser III responded with three successive campaigns (734–732 BC), the first of which conquered Ashkelon. Nebuchadnezzar destroyed the city and deported many of its inhabitants to Egypt during his conquest of Palestine (604 BC). Successive invaders then took the city from each other: Scythians, Chaldeans, Persians, Greeks, and Maccabees. Ashkelon was the birthplace of Herod the Great, and ruins of his building projects are to be found there. Ashkelon is not mentioned in the NT but was a battleground in the Jewish rebellion against Rome (AD 66).

Aerial View of Ashkelon

ASHKENAZ Gomer's son and Noah's great-grandson in Japheth's line (Gn 10:1-3; 1 Chr 1:6). Mention of the kingdom of Ashkenaz along with Ararat and Minni (Jer 51:27) suggests that he was the ancestor of the Scythians, a people who resided in the Ararat region in Jeremiah's time. An active, warlike people, the Scythians contributed to the unrest of the Assyrian Empire and to its eventual collapse. The plural term "Ashkenazim" is now used for the Jews who settled in middle and eastern Europe after the Dispersion, in contrast with the Sephardim, those who settled in the Iberian Peninsula (Spain and Portugal).

ASHNAH Name of the two towns that Judah's tribe received after the conquest of Canaan (Jos 15:33, 43). No certain location for either is known, but both were in the lowlands separating Judah and Philistia. Although the Philistines often overran that buffer zone, they never got beyond its eastern border.

ASHPENAZ Official under Nebuchadnezzar in charge of palace personnel (Dn 1:3). Ashpenaz was reluctant to grant the captives from Judah, Daniel and his friends, a reprieve from eating the king's food, but eventually he did so (Dn 1:8-16). (Eating food from the table of Gentiles would have forced Daniel and his friends to violate the law of God.) Three years later, Ashpenaz presented the young men before the king. Nebuchadnezzar found them outstanding in wisdom and good judgment in spite of their vegetarian diet and abstemious lifestyle (Dn 1:18-20).

ASHRIEL* KJV form of Asriel, Manasseh's son, in 1 Chronicles 7:14. *See* Asriel, Asrielite.

ASHTAROTH, ASHTERATHITE* Town of Bashan, named along with Edrei as the home of King Og (Dt 1:4; Jos 9:10; 12:4; 13:12, 31). Ashtaroth is the plural form of Ashtoreth, the name of the Canaanite fertility goddess who was worshiped there. After Og was defeated by the Israelites (Dt 3:1-11), Moses gave Ashtaroth to the half-tribe of Manasseh (Dt 13:12, 31; Dt 3:13). Later, it became a Levitical city inhabited by the Gershonites (1 Chr 6:71). Ashteroth-karnaim (Gn 14:5) is probably the same town as Ashtaroth. Its location is usually identified with Tell Ashtarah, 21 miles (34 kilometers) east of the Sea of Galilee. In 1 Chronicles 11:44 one of David's mighty men, Uzzia, is called an Ashterathite.

ASHTEROTH-KARNAIM City where a coalition of four kings led by Chedorlaomer, king of Elam, defeated the tribe of Rephaim giants (Gn 14:5; cf. Dt 3:11). The area was part of the inheritance given to Abraham and his descendants by the Lord (Gn 15:18-20). It is probably identifiable with Ashtaroth. *See* Ashtaroth, Ashterathite.

ASHTORETH Pagan mother-goddess widely worshiped throughout the ancient Near East (1 Kgs 11:5, 33; 2 Kgs 23:13); also known as Astarte. *See* Canaanite Deities and Religion.

ASHUR* KJV form of Ashhur, Caleb's son, in 1 Chronicles 2:24 and 4:5. *See* Ashhur (Person).

ASHURBANIPAL Esarhaddon's son and the Assyrian ruler (669–633 BC) who reigned in the years during which kings Manasseh, Amon, and Josiah governed the southern kingdom of Judah. The northern kingdom of Israel, whose capital was Samaria, had fallen in 722 BC to another powerful Assyrian ruler, Sargon II.

Throughout his life, Ashurbanipal (also spelled Assurbanipal) had to fight continually to retain, regain, and defend his empire, which included Babylonia, Persia, Syria, and Egypt. Though his chief interests were evidently cultural, he was required to spend most of his time, and almost all the resources of his empire, maintaining the submission of conquered peoples, putting down a civil war fomented under the leadership of his brother, and coping with constant border skirmishes.

Much of what we know about the culture of ancient Mesopotamia—historical facts, religion, legends, and lore—comes from the cuneiform literature collected by Ashurbanipal and deposited in a large library he built in Nineveh, his capital. The remains of this library, discovered about a century ago and now in the British Museum, continue to have impact on biblical knowledge. Without doubt his library has been his most significant memorial.

Ashurbanipal was evidently the Assyrian monarch who sent alien people into Samaria (Ezr 4:10). Deportation of conquered peoples was standard Assyrian policy, which accounts for the assimilation and disappearance of the ten tribes of Israel after its fall to Sargon II. In Ezra 4:10 the Assyrian king is called Osnappar, a transliteration of the Hebrew spelling. The consonantal similarity of the Hebrew word to the Assyrian name Ashurbanipal, plus the list of conquered peoples mentioned in the text, point to Ashurbanipal as the most likely identification.

By 630 BC the Assyrian Empire was experiencing difficulty in maintaining its cohesiveness, and after Ashurbanipal's death it could no longer sustain itself. Innumerable Assyrian soldiers had died on faraway battlefields; mercenaries and captives pressed into the military did not serve well. Moreover, hordes of barbarians from the steppes of Asia battered Assyria from the outside. Vassal Babylon successfully revolted. Though a mere shadow of its former glory, Egypt also slipped from its Assyrian yoke. Ashurbanipal's sons were not equal to the task. Probably no one could have been. In less than 20 years a relatively weak coalition of enemies surrounded Nineveh and in 612 BC razed the city. A spark of resistance continued at nearby Haran, but within months it was snuffed out by Median troops. By the same ruthless, unrestrained cruelty with which it ruled its empire, Assyria perished.

The demise of Assyria gave a new lease on life to the tiny kingdom of Judah. Some scholars place Ashurbanipal's death in King Josiah's eighth year of reign (cf. 2 Chr 34:3-7). As Assyria lost its grip, the resulting vacuum brought back independence by default. Young King Josiah was able to begin and to consummate the most sweeping spiritual revival and political reforms in Judah's history. *See* Assyria, Assyrians; Kings, Books of First and Second.

ASHURITE Probably a variant spelling for Asherite, a member of Asher's tribe. The Ashurites were among those who supported Ishbosheth, Saul's son, instead of David as king over Israel after Saul's death (2 Sm 2:8-9). In Ezekiel 27:6 (KJV) the Hebrew word refers to a kind of wood rather than a group of people.

ASHURNASIRPAL*

1. Ashurnasirpal I (1049?–1031 BC), Assyrian king listed in the synchronistic Assyrian chronicle as the legitimate successor of Shamshi-adad IV (1053?–1050 BC). Ashurnasirpal I ruled during a period of Assyrian weakness following the vigorous reign of Tiglath-pileser I (1115?–1077 BC).

2. Ashurnasirpal II (885–860 BC), Assyrian king, son of Tukulti-ninurta II (890–885 BC). His grandfather, Adad-nirari II (911–891 BC), laid the foundations of the Neo-Assyrian period (900–612 BC). Ashurnasirpal II, its first great monarch, consolidated his position by crushing rebellious middle Euphrates tribes and then conducted campaigns against Syria (877 BC) and Philistia. In his annals he recorded the tribute received from the maritime towns of Philistia: "Gold, silver, tin, copper . . . large and small monkeys, ebony, boxwood, ivory . . . I received." Ashurnasirpal's westward expedition was the first of several Assyrian assaults on Syria, ultimately threatening Israelite forces as well. The expedition also established his reputation as a cruel and merciless opponent, a theme repeated constantly in his annals. A statue of Ashurnasirpal II recovered from Calah depicted him as a stern, egotistical despot. He fashioned the Assyrian army into a military machine that struck terror into the hearts of its opponents.

Ashurnasirpal II was an outstanding example of the way aggressive rulers in the ancient world treated their enemies. In his annals he boasted: "The heads of their warriors I cut off, and I formed them into a pillar over against their city. . . . I flayed all the chief men . . . and I covered the pillar with their skins; some I walled up within the pillar, some I impaled upon the pillar on stakes." Other atrocities included burning captives alive; mutilating prisoners by hacking off hands, noses, or ears; gouging out eyes; disemboweling pregnant women; and leaving prisoners in the desert to die of thirst.

Ashurnasirpal II made Calah (Nimrud) his capital city, employing more than 50,000 prisoners in the work of reconstruction. A. H. Layard, excavating Nimrud in 1845, uncovered the royal palace with its colossal statuary. Ashurnasirpal II was succeeded in 859 BC by his son Shalmaneser III, who reigned for 35 years. *See* Assyria, Assyrians.

ASHVATH Japhlet's son, a great warrior and head of a clan in Asher's tribe (1 Chr 7:33).

ASIA In NT times, the Roman province immediately east of the Aegean Sea. The province was established in 133 BC out of the kingdom left to the Romans in the will of Attalus III, king of Pergamum. Greek geographers generally employed the name Asia to denote the whole eastern continent, but from the second century on, the Romans generally referred to the kings of Pergamum as "kings of Asia." Hence the custom of using "Asia" for the peninsula alone (i.e., Asia Minor) gradually crept into popular usage.

The extent of the province of Asia differed at each stage of its history. Before Roman occupation the word was used to refer to the kingdom of the Seleucid dynasty (founded by Seleucus I; 305–281 BC). The Apocrypha referred thus to Asia (1 Macc 8:6; 11:13; 12:39; 13:32; 2 Macc 3:3), as did the early Jewish historian Josephus in his Antiquities. When the territory was wrested from Seleucid control by the Romans in their war against Antiochus the Great, the Romans gave it to their allies, the Attalids; Attalus III willed it to the Romans. The limits of Roman control were not firmly established until an extensive revolt had been put down. The borders then included Mysia, Lydia, Caria, and Phrygia, and (nearer the Aegean) Aeolis, Ionia, and Troas. The islands off the coast (Lesbos, Chios, Samos, Rhodes, Patmos, etc.) were also included. The mainland now forms part of modern Turkey.

In 116 BC the province was enlarged to include Greater Phrygia. Its geographic limits were then Bithynia to the north, Galatia to the east, Lycia to the south, and the Aegean Sea to the west. Even then, the boundaries were not solidly fixed, for in 25 BC Augustus Caesar augmented Rome's dominion by combining other parts of Phrygia, Lyconia, Pisidia, and possibly Pamphylia into a province called Galatia. Those geographical limits remained until AD 285, when the province was greatly reduced in size and the term Asia became restricted to the coastal areas and lower valleys of the Maeander, Cayster, Hermus, and Caicus Rivers.

During Roman occupation the capital of the province was Pergamum. By the time of Augustus, however, the residence of the Roman proconsul was at Ephesus.

In the NT, Asia generally meant the Roman province of that name. Sometimes the concept was primarily geographical; at other times primarily political. For example, at the Feast of Pentecost in Jerusalem there were Jews who had come from "Asia." These included other provinces governed by Rome, such as Cappadocia, Phrygia, and Pamphylia (Acts 2:9-10). This seems to indicate that Luke, the writer of Acts, used the term to describe the province originally bequeathed to the Romans by Attalus III. Luke used the word again in Acts 6:9, providing tacit evidence of the strength of Jewish communities in Asia Minor as a whole and confirming the use of "Asia" in the restricted sense of the Roman province.

On Paul's second missionary journey, he and Timothy were prevented by the Holy Spirit from preaching in Asia (Acts 16:6-8). Evidently, from the context, Luke again had the old boundaries of the province in mind. On Paul's return from Greece he stopped briefly at Ephesus (Acts 18:19-21). On his third missionary journey, he remained in Ephesus for more than two years, so that from this capital city "all the residents of Asia heard the word of the Lord, both Jews and Greeks" (Acts 19:10, RSV).

Luke further referred to Asia in Acts 19:26-27; 20:4, 16, 18; and 27:2. Paul also made several references to it (Rom 16:5; 1 Cor 1:8; 2 Cor 1:8; 2 Tm 1:15). The apostle Peter likewise used the term (1 Pt 1:1). In the NT the risen Christ was the last to refer to Asia. He instructed the apostle John, then living in exile on the island of Patmos, to write letters to seven specific churches on the mainland of Asia (Rv 1:1-4).

Other cities in this Roman province mentioned in the NT include Laodicea and Hierapolis (Col 4:13), and lesser-known Adramyttium (Acts 27:2), and Assos (Acts 20:13-14).

ASIA MINOR Peninsula synonymous with the Asia of the NT and Anatolia, identifiable with part of modern Turkey. *See* Asia.

ASIARCH* Title of an official of unknown function in the Roman province of Asia. Several such officials were concerned for the safety of Paul during a silversmiths' riot in Ephesus (Acts 19:31). Nothing else is known about their qualifications, periods of tenure, or duties. Why there were a number of such officers in Ephesus at the time of the riot, or why the Asiarchs showed such concern for Paul, is not clear. Perhaps they were deputies of the "Commune of Asia," responsible to promote and protect the imperial cult (the worship practices of Rome and the emperor). The Asiarchs mentioned were evidently not adverse to a religious movement like Christianity, which embarrassed the prevailing pagan cult of Artemis. The long account in Acts 19 repeats one of Luke's themes, that Christianity was not subversive, nor was Paul a political menace. Otherwise the Asiarchs would not have favored him in such a manner.

ASIBIAS Israelite who obeyed Ezra's exhortation to divorce his pagan wife after the exile (1 Esd 9:26). He may be the same person as Hashabiah (Ezr 10:25, KJV "Malchijah").

ASIEL Jehu's great-grandfather. Jehu was a prince of Simeon's tribe (1 Chr 4:35, 38).

ASKELON* KJV alternate form of Ashkelon, a Philistine city, in Judges 1:18; 1 Samuel 6:17; and 2 Samuel 1:20. *See* Ashkelon.

ASMODEUS An evil demon and jealous lover in the story of Tobit (Tb 3:8). In the story, Sarah, only daughter of Raguel of Ecbatana, lost seven husbands to Asmodeus on seven different wedding nights. She remained in a state of deep grief until Tobit's son Tobias married her and, through the advice of the angel Raphael, defeated Asmodeus through a ritualistic burning of the heart and liver of a fish. Generally speaking, Asmodeus was looked on as the king or chief of demons in Hebrew mythology. Possibly he was related to "Aeshma-daeva," a Persian demon of storms, anger, and lust.

See also Tobit, Book of.

ASNAPPER* KJV form of Osnappar, an alternate name for the Assyrian king Ashurbanipal in Ezra 4:10. *See* Ashurbanipal.

ASP* Poisonous snake mentioned in the Bible, probably the Egyptian cobra. *See* Animals.

ASPATHA One of Haman's ten sons, who was killed with his father when Haman's plot to destroy the Jews was foiled (Est 9:7).

ASPEN* *See* Plants.

ASPHALT Brown or black tarlike substance, a variety of bitumen, obtained in ancient times from natural oil seeps and used for mortar and caulking. Mortar, pitch, slime, and tar are other translations of the related terms in Hebrew. *See* Minerals and Metals; Bitumen.

ASPHAR Watering hole in the Tekoa wilderness, perhaps the modern Bir Selhub south of Engedi. Jonathan and Simon Maccabeus camped at Asphar when fleeing from the Syrians under General Bacchides (1 Macc 9:33).

ASRIEL, ASRIELITE Manasseh's son (1 Chr 7:14). His descendants, the Asrielites, were included in Moses' census in the wilderness (Nm 26:31) and were later given a portion of the land allotted to Manasseh's tribe (Jos 17:2).

ASS* Beast of burden used widely in the Near East. *See* Animals.

ASSARION* Coin of small value; a farthing (Mt 10:29). *See* Coins.

ASSHUR Uncertain translation of a Hebrew word, appearing in English translations of the Bible as Assyria, Assyrian, Assyrians, or merely "Asshur." These variants come from the Assyrian word *asshur.*

1. KJV translation of the word for Assyria in Genesis 10:11. It is improperly translated as a person and should be understood as in the NLT: "He [Nimrod]

extended his reign to Assyria." In that country, east of the Tigris River, Nimrod built four cities: Nineveh, Rehoboth-ir, Calah, and Resen.

2. Shem's son (Gn 10:22; 1 Chr 1:17). The reference may be merely a personification of the whole Assyrian people; however, since other names in the account (e.g., Arpachshad, Gn 10:24; 11:12) seem to indicate individual persons, perhaps Asshur should be taken in the same way. If so, this individual may have been the founder of the city Asshur to which he gave his name, the names of a god and nation being further derived from the city. *See* Asshur (Place).

3. Patron god of the city of Asshur.

ASSHUR (Place) Ancient name of a city on the Tigris River whose habitation can be traced back to about 2500 BC. Asshur was not a large city (less than one-tenth the size of Babylon or Nineveh), but it formed the homeland and first capital of the later Assyrian kingdom.

Asshur had become a thriving city by the second millennium BC, trading with the Assyrian colony at Kanish (in modern Turkey). It reached its peak in the old Assyrian Empire under Shamshi-adad I (1813–1781 BC), who stretched his control over most of northern Mesopotamia, including Mari. His empire fell to Hammurabi of Babylon (1792–1750 BC), and Asshur entered a dark period about which little is known. When the Assyrians once again became a major power in the Near East late in the second millennium, the capital was moved away from Asshur; however, it remained the ancient holy city and the home of the Assyrian national god, Asshur.

For centuries the exact location of Asshur was unknown, but during the 19th century it was established that Qalat Shergat in Iraq was the modern location of this ancient Assyrian capital. The Germans excavated the site for a number of years prior to World War I. They uncovered a temple to Anu-adad that contained a large double ziggurat that still dominates the site today. A palace and several other buildings were also excavated. Among the literary discoveries were an Assyrian account of the Babylonian creation epic and a portion of the law code of the Assyrians.

See also Assyria, Assyrians.

ASSHURIM*, ASSHURITES Descendants of Abraham and his second wife, Keturah, through Dedan (Gn 25:3). The Asshurim probably settled in Arabia.

ASSIR

1. Korah's son and a descendant of Levi through Kohath (Ex 6:24; 1 Chr 6:22).

2. Ebiasaph's son and a descendant of #1 above (1 Chr 6:23, 37).

3. Son of Jeconiah (Jehoiachin), king of Judah (1 Chr 3:17, KJV). It has been suggested that the Hebrew word *assir* may here be an adjective (as in NLT) describing Jeconiah and meaning "while captive" (cf. 2 Kgs 24:15). If so, his children were born while he was a captive.

ASSOS Seaport of Mysia in the Roman province of Asia (Minor). The apostle Paul and Luke were reunited in Assos after Paul's journey by land from Troas (Acts 20:13-14). The Roman writer Pliny identified the town as having been founded by the kings of Pergamum and called Apollonia. Assos was located on the top and terraced sides of an inactive volcanic cone 770 feet (234.6 meters) in height. The Greek philosopher Aristotle lived there for several years. It was also the birthplace of Cleanthes, a Stoic poet quoted by Paul (Acts 17:28). Today Assos is known as Behram Kevi.

The Temple of Athena in Assos

ASSUR* KJV transliteration of a Hebrew word usually rendered Assyria (Ezr 4:2; Ps 83:8) by most English versions. *See* Assyria, Assyrians.

ASSURANCE Certainty or confidence about one's beliefs or actions. The "assurance of hope" (Heb 6:11) and the "assurance of faith" (Heb 10:22; 11:1) are mentioned as qualities of wholeness that lead believers to responsible living. Paul spoke of an "assured understanding" of the gospel of Christ, which resulted in love in the community (Col 2:2), and of the "assured blessing" which was his in Christ (Rom 15:29).

GOD'S SOVEREIGNTY AND OUR ASSURANCE
A proper understanding of God's sovereignty should encourage repentant sinners and faltering believers to call upon God for salvation and to walk secure in his love. Jesus said, "All that the Father gives me will come to me; and him who comes to me I will not cast out" (Jn 6:37, RSV).
   Because God has planned and purposed our salvation, we may have assurance that he will accept and forgive those who trust him (Jn 3:16). Christ's sheep hear his voice and follow him; they will never perish or be snatched out of his hand (Jn 10:29).
   Such an attitude of trust in God removes the presumptive pride of the person who trusts his own good works for salvation (Mt 7:21-23; 1 Cor 10:12; Heb 3:12), or the agonizing doubt of the believer who is sensitive to his own sinfulness. Because salvation is by grace (Eph 2:8), the doubting believer may claim the finished and sufficient work of Christ and thus rest secure that God will finish his work in each believer (Phil 1:6).

ASSURBANIPAL* Variant spelling of Ashurbanipal, the Assyrian king. *See* Ashurbanipal.

ASSYRIA, ASSYRIANS Ancient empire considered the symbol of terror and tyranny in the Near East for more than three centuries. Assyria received its name from the

tiny city-state Asshur, on the western bank of the Tigris River in northern Mesopotamia (modern Iraq). The city was the seat of worship of the sun god Asshur (also spelled Ashur). The Hebrew name occurs frequently in the Bible and is translated Assyria (Gn 2:14), Assur (Ezr 4:2; Ps 83:8), or left as Asshur (Gn 10:11, KJV). The form of the name comes originally from the Akkadian language.

   Originally, Assyria was a small district in northern Mesopotamia, lying in a rough triangle between the Tigris River and the Upper Zab, a tributary of the Tigris. Eventually Assyria gained control of northern Syria, securing an outlet to the Mediterranean Sea, and took possession of the fertile Mesopotamian plain, extending Assyrian domain over all of Babylonia to the Persian Gulf.

History

Before the Eighth Century BC By the end of the third millennium BC, the Sumerians were trading with Assyria and influencing its people culturally. Periodically Sumerian kings would claim political control over Assyria. Sargon of Agade (c. 2350 BC) brought Assyria within the sphere of his political and commercial activities, and when the Amorites overthrew the third dynasty of Ur and established their own states, one of them incorporated Assyria into its territory. During the period of Hammurabi, one of the last great kings of the first Babylonian dynasty (c. 2360–1600 BC), the Assyrians supplied building materials and other goods for the Babylonian kingdom.

   Trade between Asshur and the Assyrian colony of Kanish in Anatolia began at a very early time in Assyrian history. Goods were transported by caravans of up to 200 donkeys at a time. The wealth pouring in from such a trade put Assyria in a very strong position economically.

   The early phase of Assyrian commercial development was followed by a long period of decline, culminating in the 15th century BC. At that time Assyria was reduced to a state of vassalage by a non-Semitic people, the Hurrians (biblical Horites) of the state of Mitanni. In the 14th century another non-Semitic people, the Hittites, overthrew the power of Mitanni. Assyria was gradually able to rise again and assume the role of a great power in the ancient Near East, largely through the policies of a shrewd prince, Asshur-uballit. His reign marked the beginning of a long process by which Assyria ultimately rose to supremacy.

Enlil-nirari (1329–1320 BC), son and successor of Asshur-uballit, attacked Babylon and defeated Kurigalzu II, the Kassite king of Babylon (1345–1324 BC). Adad-nirari I (1307–1275 BC) extended Assyria's influence by winning victories over the Kassites in Babylonia. He also added territory to the northwest.

The period of consolidation and expansion in the first Assyrian Empire culminated in the capture of Babylon by Tukulti-ninurta I (1244–1208 BC), which for the first time placed Babylon under Assyrian rule. After that climax, however, Assyrian power declined.

The three centuries from about 1200 to 900 BC were marked by movements of different peoples such as the Greeks, Philistines, Arameans, and Hebrews. Under pressure of people migrating from Europe, the Hittite Empire, which formerly had given political stability to Asia Minor and protected the trade routes, crumbled rapidly. By 1200 BC it fell to attacks by the Sea Peoples from the Greek mainland.

During the tenth century BC, Assyria began to make a slow recovery. In the reign of Adad-nirari II (911–891 BC), Assyria again launched upon a period of conspicuous economic and military expansion. For the next 60 years Assyrian kings followed a consistent policy of consolidating the work of Adad-nirari II. Ashurnasirpal II (885–860 BC) is considered the first great monarch of that new era in Assyrian history. He possessed all the qualities and defects of his successors to the extreme. He had the ambition, energy, courage, vanity, and magnificence of a ruthless, indefatigable empire builder. Ashurnasirpal's first activities were directed to the mountain area to the east, where he extended Assyria's control among the mountain people. In the west he subdued the Arameans with characteristic cruelty and did likewise in Asia Minor.

Shalmaneser III is well known to historians of the biblical world for the battle of Qarqar (853 BC), considered the most fully documented event from the ancient world. He launched an invasion of Syria that was met by a coalition led by Ben-hadad of Damascus and supported by King Ahab of Israel and several other states. Since Shalmaneser was unable to rout the 60,000 troops opposing him, it was many years before the Assyrians were able to conquer Damascus and Samaria. King Jehu of Israel (841–814 BC), who later chose to pay tribute rather than fight, is represented, perhaps by an envoy, on the Black Obelisk of Shalmaneser III, excavated at Shalmaneser's capital city, Calah (now called Nimrud). Jehu is depicted as kissing the ground at the Assyrian monarch's feet and offering a tribute of silver, gold, and lead vessels.

Toward the end of his reign Shalmaneser had to put down a rebellion by some of the principal Assyrian cities. He was succeeded by his heir, Shamshi-adad V (823–811 BC). Shamshi-adad's son Adad-nirari III (810–782 BC) built a new palace at Calah and attacked King Hazael of Damascus (Syria) in 804 BC. Assyrian pressure on the Syrians undoubtedly was a relief to Israel, which had been oppressed by Hazael (2 Kgs 13:22-25).

From the Eighth Century to the Battle of Carchemish (605 BC) Beginning about 800 BC the influence of Urartu (Ararat) began to expand, especially in north Syria, at the expense of Assyria. The next half century saw a drastic decline in Assyria's fortunes. In 746 BC,

during a revolt in the city of Calah, the entire royal family was murdered.

The final phase of Assyrian power was instituted by the usurper Tiglath-pileser III (745–727 BC), known also by his adopted Babylonian throne-name Pul (2 Kgs 15:19; 1 Chr 5:26). His reign began the process by which Assyria recovered and consolidated control of all its territories and established itself firmly as the dominant military and economic power in the Near East. Tiglath-pileser first secured control of the mountain passes in the north in order to eliminate the threat of invasion from that direction. Next he subjected Syria and Palestine in the west and took control of the road to Egypt and the Mediterranean Sea. Finally, through diplomacy, he gained the throne of Babylonia also. Under the name of Pul he governed Babylonia, creating the remarkable situation of two crowns united in one ruler bearing two different names. His political prudence was not usually found in the ruthless Assyrian monarchs.

From the year 743 BC Tiglath-pileser III waged a number of campaigns in Syria and Palestine. King Menahem of Israel (752–742 BC) paid him tribute (2 Kgs 15:19-20), as did Tyre, Byblos, and Damascus. In 738 he subjugated the north central state of Hamath. Responding to an appeal from King Ahaz of Judah (735–715 BC) to help resist the pressures of a proposed anti-Assyrian coalition, Tiglath-pileser conquered Damascus in 732 and Samaria, capital of the northern kingdom of Israel, a decade later. On both occasions deportations of people to Assyria took place. The fall of Samaria in 722 BC marked the end of the kingdom of Israel.

Sargon II (722–705 BC) claimed to be the Assyrian ruler who captured Samaria, but the biblical record attributed the capture to Shalmaneser (2 Kgs 17:2-6). To the policy of deportation, Sargon and his successors added that of colonization. To replace the peoples carried into captivity, these Assyrian kings brought tribes from Babylonia, Elam, Syria, and Arabia and settled them in Samaria and surrounding territory. The new arrivals intermingled with the indigenous people remaining in the land after the deportation and became the Samaritans.

After 10 years of warfare against his enemies to the west in Syria and Asia Minor, and to the north in Urartu, Sargon concentrated his efforts on Babylonia. He chased Merodach-baladan II (721–710 BC; cf. 2 Kgs 20:12-19; Is 39:1) to Elam and made himself king of Babylon in 709. He started building a new capital city for himself, Dur-Sharrukin (Khorsabad) near Nineveh but was killed in battle before it was finished.

Sargon was succeeded by his son Sennacherib (705–681 BC), who was occupied throughout his reign in a series of bitter wars. He is especially known in biblical studies for his campaign against Judah and siege of Jerusalem during the reign of King Hezekiah (715–686 BC) and the ministry of the prophet Isaiah (2 Kgs 18:13–19:37; Is 36–37). It was during that crisis that the celebrated Siloam Tunnel was constructed to bring water into the beleaguered capital from the spring of Gihon, outside the city wall, to the pool of Siloam (2 Kgs 20:20).

Sennacherib was murdered in 681 BC and was succeeded by Esarhaddon, who tried unsuccessfully to establish Assyrian control over Egypt. Esarhaddon was succeeded by Ashurbanipal (669–626? BC), who managed to capture No-amon (Thebes), thereby realizing the greatest victory in Assyrian history (cf. Na 3:3-10). Ashurbanipal established a great library in Nineveh, which was excavated in 1860. Many tablets made of the finest clay and ranging in size from 1 to 15 inches (2.5 to 38 centimeters) were found, containing a vast selection of Akkadian material. Some of the tablets contain historical records; others, astronomical reports, mathematical calculations, and private or public letters. A considerable part of the collection deals with astrology and medicine. Many of the tablets contain prayers, incantations, psalms, and religious texts in general. A copy of the Babylonian account of creation was also found. This library is now one of the principal treasures of the British Museum in London.

Very little is known about Ashurbanipal's reign after 639 BC since his annals do not extend beyond that year. However, some information on events of his last 13 years can be gleaned from allusions in state correspondence, commercial documents, and prayers addressed to the gods. Evidently the situation in Assyria was becoming increasingly serious, and when Ashurbanipal died in 626 his empire declined quickly.

The Medes had entered the Assyrian annals during the reign of Esarhaddon, when they still consisted of a large number of associated but separate tribes. Later those tribes began to be welded into a single kingdom. Herodotus states that Phraortes, their king, attacked Assyria but lost his life on the battlefield and was succeeded by his son Cyaxeres.

The year 626 BC marked several important events in the ancient world. Nabopolassar, a Chaldean prince, became king of Babylon (626–605 BC) toward the end of that year. An alliance between the Medes and Nabopolassar was concluded, and from that time on, the success of Nabopolassar against Assyria was almost inevitable. By the year 617 BC he had cleared Babylonia of all Assyrian garrisons. He then marched up the Euphrates to the Aramean districts that had been part of the Assyrian Empire for two and a half centuries. The plan was for Nabopolassar to attack Nineveh from the west and the Medes to attack it at the same time from the east; however, the combined forces of the Assyrians and Egyptians, now allies, compelled Nabopolassar to withdraw to Babylon.

In 614 BC the Medes carried out a massive attack on Assyria. Although Nineveh was too strong to yield to the attack, the Medes captured some of the neighboring cities, including Asshur, the ancient capital. At that point Nabopolassar arrived with the Babylonian forces. He met Cyaxeres at Asshur, and they established mutual friendship and peace. Their alliance was later confirmed by the marriage of Nebuchadnezzar, Nabopolassar's son, to Amytis, daughter of Cyaxeres. In 612 BC their combined forces launched a final assault against Nineveh, and after three months of siege the mighty city fell (Na 1:8).

Despite the loss of their capital, a weakened Assyrian kingdom survived for three more years. The Assyrian troops who could escape from Nineveh fled westward to Haran, where an Assyrian prince, Asshur-uballit, was made king and sought Egypt's help to restore the kingship of Assyria. Necho II (609–593 BC), known in the Bible as Neco, responded and set off with his Egyptian troops to Haran to fight against the Babylonians, who by now had annihilated Assyria. King Josiah of Judah (640–609 BC), who evidently considered himself a vassal of Assyria's heir, Neo-Babylonia, marched to oppose the Egyptian advance and was mortally wounded by an arrow on the battlefield of Megiddo (2 Kgs 23:29-30; 2 Chr 35:20-24).

When Nabopolassar and his allies attacked Haran in 610 BC, Asshur-uballit did not attempt to defend it but fled southwest to await Necho and his troops. The joint forces of the Egyptians and the Assyrians returned to mount an assault upon Haran with some initial success. But Nabopolassar's army compelled the Assyrian-Egyptian forces to abandon the siege and withdraw to Carchemish (present-day Jarablus). There, under the leadership of Nebuchadnezzar, the Babylonians made a direct attack on the powerful army. The resultant carnage on both sides was graphically depicted by the prophet Jeremiah (46:1-12). Nebuchadnezzar emerged victorious in the battle of Carchemish (605 BC). However, because of the death of his father, he did not pursue his victory but returned to Babylon to assume the throne.

There is a tradition in the Assyrian Christian church that after the collapse of the Assyrian Empire under the onslaught of the Medes and Neo-Babylonians, a remnant of the Assyrian people—chiefly princes, noblemen, and warriors—took refuge in the mountains of Kurdistan. There they built a number of armed fortresses. Alexander the Great (336–323 BC), his successors, and the Roman legions made no attempt to conquer these tribes. Trajan (AD 98–117) marched at the head of the Roman armies through Armenia, touching the northern region of Kurdistan, on his way to Persia. It is asserted that the wise men, or magi, who visited the newly born king in Bethlehem, the baby Jesus, came from Edessa. According to this tradition, the magi, on returning from Bethlehem, proclaimed the amazing things they had heard and seen on their visit to the king. A Christian church was founded among the Assyrians that has survived throughout the centuries.

The region that was Assyria, including all of Mesopotamia, is within present-day Iraq, an Arabic-speaking country predominantly Muslim in religion.

See also Israel, History of; Kings, Books of First and Second; Mesopotamia.

ASTAROTH* KJV form of Ashtaroth, a town known for its pagan worship of the goddess Ashtoreth, in Deuteronomy 1:4. *See* Ashtaroth, Ashterathite.

ASTARTE* Pagan mother-goddess widely worshiped throughout the ancient Near East; also known as Ashtoreth. *See* Canaanite Deities and Religion.

ASTROLOGY Pseudoscience dealing with the supposed influence of the heavenly bodies on human character and destiny. Astrological conclusions are based on the apparent movement of the sun and planets through the zodiac, an arbitrary division of the celestial sphere into 12 segments identified with 12 major constellations. As the sun travels in its path, called the ecliptic, it cuts across the zodiac at various points. The movement of the sun and the planets in relation to the zodiac provides astrologers with patterns or "aspects" from which their interpretative schemes are drawn.

The 12 segments of the zodiac are called "houses." Constellations (e.g., Leo, Virgo, Sagittarius) associated with the respective houses are called "signs." One's date of birth determines the sign under which one is born. Using a rather elaborate procedure, an astrologer attempts to draw up a celestial map or "horoscope." Horoscopes are based on the supposed fact that persons born under a given sign have certain characteristics in common. Positions of the various planets with reference to the signs, or positions of the sun and moon with reference to one another, are regarded as pointing to favorable or unfavorable conditions.

The earliest known account of the use of astrology comes from ancient Sumer, a region in the lower Euphrates River valley. The Sumerian Gudea cylinders contain an account of a dream of King Gudea in which the goddess Nidaba came to him holding a tablet inscribed with a map of the heavens. The dream indicated that it was a propitious time for Gudea to build the Eninnu temple.

Astrology flourished in ancient Babylon under the influence of priests. It was integrally linked with the serious study of celestial phenomena. The superstitious Babylonians were intensely concerned with omens, so it is understandable that they would attempt to find omens in the observable movements of the sun, moon, planets, and stars. To the best of our knowledge the Babylonians originated the zodiac. They also drew up a monthly calendar of days that were propitious and days on which activity should be reduced to a minimum for fear of incurring the anger of one or more deities. This monthly pattern then served for the rest of the year.

Babylonian influence in astronomy and astrology spread to Greece in the fourth century. The Greeks' interest in science and their polytheistic religion, which allowed for the attribution of deity to heavenly bodies, undoubtedly inclined them to take up astrology and to develop it extensively.

The spread of Hellenistic culture brought the practice of astrology to Egypt, where it flourished for a long time. Herodotus, an early Greek historian, stated that the Egyptians were the first to use a person's day of birth to predict character. Herodotus also wrote that the Egyptians kept careful records of unusual phenomena, which they used as a basis for predicting consequences that might follow similar phenomena in the future. The Egyptians contributed a number of refinements to the Greek astrological system, such as division of the sky into 36 sections, each with its own deity. They also divided the day into 24 hours.

The influence of Greek astrology was felt in the Roman world as well. A Roman astrologer named Nigidius, who was strongly influenced by Greek thought, made prognostications that show considerable subtlety—and also considerable vagueness. Not much is known about other Roman astrologers, although astrological belief played an important role in Roman life. A system of lucky and unlucky days was developed. The names of the days of the week were derived from the names of planets (which bore the names of gods). The practice of naming the days of the week for the planets probably goes back to the Hellenistic period. Roman contributions to the calendar system paved the way for an even more widespread use of astrology. For example, astrological computation was made easier for ordinary people by the adoption in 46 BC of the 365-day Julian calendar.

It is often alleged that references to astrological motifs occur in the Bible. The blessings pronounced by Jacob on his 12 sons, for example, have been associated by some with the signs of the zodiac. Apocalyptic imagery of a cosmic nature is frequently regarded as having astrological significance. All such interpretations are highly speculative.

Attempts to predict the future by appeal to false deities, mediums, or objects were forbidden in the OT. The reason was that such attempts ignored God as the true source of revelation. The future was foretold by persons, like Daniel, who could interpret dreams, but the Scriptures make clear that Daniel's ability was given to him by God (Dn 2:17-23).

Specific reference to astrological prognostication is found in Isaiah 47:12-13 in an oracle dealing with the fall of Babylon. In that oracle the prophet Isaiah referred to a number of features that characterized that great empire. He spoke of enchantments practiced in Babylon. In an ironic tone he told the Babylonians to continue with their sorceries—they might bring success. He singled out the astrologers and referred specifically to the division of the heavens, evidently meaning the Babylonian division of the celestial sphere into segments (pos-

sibly the zodiac). He made reference as well to their custom of predicting the future at the time of each new moon. The point of the passage is that destruction will come to Babylon, and even its eminent astrologers will not be able to save it.

The prophet Jeremiah warned the Israelites not to be dismayed by signs in the heavens (Jer 10:1-3). Those signs were evidently unusual celestial phenomena like eclipses, comets, and conjunctions of planets, all of which inspired dread in the hearts of most ancient people. The passage in Jeremiah indicates that it is wrong for God's people to attribute mystical influence to such phenomena or to see in them portents of the future. Prognostication on the basis of such celestial phenomena was considered futile (Jer 10:3, KJV).

The book of Daniel refers to a group of soothsayers, frequently understood to be astrologers (Dn 2:27; 5:11). The meaning of the word, however, is uncertain. It is derived from an Aramaic root meaning "to cut" or "divide" and hence may be a reference to the Babylonian practice of dividing the heavens into zones. The fact that the group is mentioned along with various kinds of diviners makes it quite likely that they were astrologers. The passage in Daniel demonstrates that those who use various "mantic" arts to predict the future are ineffectual.

The magi, who figure prominently in the account of the birth of Christ (Mt 2:1-16), may have been astrologers, although the word "magi" has broader connotations. It is possible that an unusual conjunction of planets at the time of the infancy of Christ was interpreted by them as a sign of the birth of the Jewish king. The magi could have learned about Jewish messianic belief from the book of Daniel or from the many Jewish officials in the Persian Empire. A tradition may have arisen from Numbers 24:17 that a star would be associated with the birth of the messianic king. Any unusual stellar phenomenon in the western sky might have led the magi to follow it to Palestine. The biblical account definitely does not validate astrological principles.

See also Astronomy; Calendars, Ancient and Modern.

ASTRONOMY* Science dealing with the phenomena outside the earth's atmosphere but especially concerned with the observable arrangements, motions, and characteristics of the heavenly bodies. The word "astronomy" is based on two Greek words meaning "the law of the stars."

Astronomy is by no means a modern science. Human beings have always been preoccupied with the heavens. The concern of the earliest civilizations with the universe appears to have been mainly astrological, but intellectual curiosity and the need for navigational orientation were certainly additional factors.

The Bible provides some interesting insights about astronomy. According to Genesis 1:14-19 the sun and moon, along with the stars, have the function of giving light on the earth, determining the seasons, and functioning as "signs." The word "season" may denote festal seasons as well as the annual seasons. The Hebrew calendar was a lunar-solar calendar similar to that of the Babylonians. Hebrew festal seasons were based on the phases of the moon. The function of the heavenly bodies as signs seems to relate to their delineation of the heavens, permitting human beings on earth to orient themselves, navigate, etc.

Although the observed occurrence of an eclipse is never mentioned in the Bible, such a phenomenon is probably behind the numerous references to the darkening of the sun and moon in certain apocalyptic passages (Jl 2:31; Am 8:9; Mt 24:29).

REMARKABLE ASTRONOMICAL EVENTS IN THE BIBLE

Several remarkable astronomical phenomena figure prominently in the Bible, including an apparent long day (Jos 10:12-14), the retrogression of the shadow on a sundial, which was a sign for King Hezekiah (2 Kgs 20:8-11), and the star that led the magi to Bethlehem.

Several explanations of Joshua's long day have been suggested. The opinion is held by some that the rotation of the earth actually ceased. There is no theological difficulty involved in this event, for the Creator may perform miracles within the sphere of the universe by temporarily altering or suspending natural laws. There is a scientific difficulty in the fact that such an interruption of gravitational force probably would have caused great dislocation of everything on the earth's surface. God could have acted within the limitations of natural law to prevent such an upheaval, however.

The long day may have been the result of other changes in the natural phenomena rather than the cessation of the earth's rotation. Some have noted that the Hebrew word translated "stand still" may mean "to be quiet." When applied to the sun, the word would imply a "quieting" of the sun's activity, or a diminution of light. This would be an apt description of the eclipse of the sun. Such an occurrence would cause Israel's enemies to flee in terror. Still others see the account as a highly poetic description of Joshua's victory, not intended to be understood literally because it is a quotation from the book of Jashar. This book was probably a poetic work celebrating the exploits of Israel's heroes.

Examination of the account of the shadow's movement on Ahaz's sundial (as a sign to Hezekiah) shows that the event was purely local, since envoys came from Babylon to learn about it (2 Chr 32:31). It is possible that both the long day and retrogression of the shadow were local phenomena, perhaps caused by abnormal refraction of light. Atmospheric disturbances could have occurred at the time; the account of Joshua's battle specifically mentions hailstones (Jos 10:11).

The star of Bethlehem (Mt 2:1-11) has been identified with various astronomical phenomena such as the conjunction of Mars, Saturn, and Venus in 12 BC. In 2 BC Venus and Jupiter came into close proximity as well. That type of phenomenon does not seem to fit the description of the star, however. The star reportedly went before the magi and hovered over the site of the birth of the Christ child. Of course, the writer may have been using phenomenological language—that is, describing the event as it appeared to the observers. Some think the description points to a nova or supernova, a sudden increase in a star's brightness; supernovas occur in a stellar system about once every 600 years. Although some natural event may serve to explain in whole or in part the star of Bethlehem, many Christians regard it as a miraculous supernatural phenomenon that God used to herald the event of the Incarnation.

These unusual phenomena and others like them accompanied important events in the history of God's dealing with humanity. Not only do they witness to the importance of those events in God's redemptive plan, but they demonstrate God's power as well.

The attempts of some biblical scholars to explain these miracles in terms of natural phenomena is not an attempt to deny the validity of miracles. They only attempt to explain the phenomena within the sphere of observable natural order and the scope of biblical texts. Other scholars understand miracles to be the result of a supernatural alteration of physical laws, believing that the God who created the natural order continues to control that order and may perform miracles by altering the processes of nature to effect his will. In either case the power of God is central to the event, and the Bible faithfully records what took place.

A number of constellations are cited in the OT. It is difficult to determine with certainty, however, which constellations are intended by particular Hebrew words. The Hebrew word translated "Pleiades" (in many versions) means "cluster" or "heap." It is reasonable to suppose that the term applies to the most prominent cluster of stars in the heavens, the Pleiades. That cluster, within the constellation Taurus, is alluded to in Job 9:9; 38:31; and Amos 5:8.

A Hebrew word possibly related to the word "fool" is frequently understood to be the constellation Orion. The connection between that constellation and the word "fool" is unknown. Other constellations are noted as "the constellations of the southern sky" and the "the constellation of the Bear" (Jb 9:9; 38:32, NLT). The Bear is known to most North Americans as the Big Dipper; it can be seen in the northern sky.

The stars are often referred to in Scripture. Their vast number was used as an analogy in God's promise to Abraham (Gn 15:5). The apostle Paul referred to the varying magnitudes of the stars (1 Cor 15:41). The writer of Jude used the concept of wandering stars to describe teachers in the early church who were propounding false doctrine (Jude 1:13). The metaphor is thought by some to be based on the observable movement of the stars around the polestar. It is the fixed polestar, not the stars apparently moving in paths around it, that provides the reference point for navigation. A false teacher, like the

apparently moving stars, would be an unreliable guide. It seems better, however, to understand Jude's metaphor as referring to the planets. The study of astronomy by that time had advanced to the point where the regular apparent movements of the stars around the polestar and the position of constellations and star clusters were all well known. It is unlikely that all stars but the polestar were considered wandering stars. Planets, on the other hand, were regarded by ancient observers as traveling in erratic paths quite different from the fixed rotation of stars around the polestar. Some commentators think wandering stars referred to comets.

See also Astrology.

ASTYAGES Fourth and final king of the Medes (according to an early Greek historian, Herodotus), reigning 35 years until 550 BC. At that time his Persian grandson, Cyrus II, revolted and overthrew Astyages' kingdom. Supposedly Astyages had been forewarned in a dream about the prowess of a future offspring of his daughter Mandane. To protect himself he married her to Cambyses I, a Persian of royal lineage, because the Persians were weak at that time. To make himself even more secure Astyages arranged to have Cyrus, their son, abandoned in the wilds. But Cyrus was allegedly spared and raised by a cowherd until his true identity was discovered, whereupon he was sent to Persia to live with his royal parents.

With the help of Harpagus, a man greatly wronged by Astyages, Cyrus revolted against his Median grandfather and gained the crown for himself. According to Herodotus, Cyrus then allowed Astyages to live in the royal court without further harming him.

Mention of Astyages in an Apocryphal book (Bel 1:1) gives a somewhat different impression, implying that Cyrus received the kingdom upon the death of Astyages. The statement could be merely popular stereotyped expression rather than an attempt to recount actual historical events. Certain cuneiform inscriptions support Herodotus's account.

See also Cyrus the Great.

ASUPPIM* KJV transliteration of a Hebrew word meaning "storehouses," a part of the temple complex, in 1 Chronicles 26:15, 17. *See* Temple.

ASUR One of the temple servants whose descendants were among those who returned with Zerubbabel from the exile (1 Esd 5:31). The name Harhur appears in the parallel lists of Ezra 2:51 and Nehemiah 7:53.

ASWAN *See* Syene.

ASYLUM* Place of refuge where a fugitive from justice is immune to arrest or retribution; also, the protection afforded by such a place. An equivalent term is "sanctuary" (originally meaning "holy place"), from the ancient custom of seeking asylum at an altar or in a temple. Thus Adonijah (1 Kgs 1:50-53) and Joab (1 Kgs 2:28-31) both sought sanctuary from King Solomon at the altar of the tabernacle. In the law of Moses asylum was provided through the establishment of cities of refuge. *See* Cities of Refuge.

ASYNCRITUS One of the Christians in Rome to whom Paul sent greetings (Rom 16:14).

ATAD Site, probably in Canaan, where Jacob's funeral cortege stopped on the way to Hebron. There, at the threshing floor, the household of Joseph and many Egyptians from the pharaoh's house spent seven days mourning the death of the patriarch (Gn 50:10-11). Impressed with their mourning the Canaanites called the place "Abel-mizraim." The first word is a pun, involving the words "meadow" and "mourning," and the second is the Hebrew word for Egypt.

ATARAH Onam's mother and second wife of Jerahmeel (1 Chr 2:26).

ATAROTH
1. Town in the mountainous region east of the Jordan River. Ataroth was rebuilt by Gad's tribe (Nm 32:3, 33-36). It was mentioned on the famous Moabite Stone by King Mesha, who said he brought back the "altar of David" from Ataroth. This Ataroth is probably modern Khirbet Attarus.
2. Town on the southern border of Ephraim's allotment (Jos 16:2), possibly the same as Ataroth-addar (Jos 16:5; 18:13).
3. Town in the Jordan Valley on the northeast border of Ephraim's allotment (Jos 16:7).
4. Town in Judah near Bethlehem belonging to the family of Joab, Salma's son (1 Chr 2:54, KJV).

ATAROTH-ADDAR Town on the boundary between Ephraim's territory and that of Benjamin (Jos 16:5; 18:13), about seven miles (11 kilometers) north of Jerusalem.

ATER
1. Ancestor of a group of people who returned to Judah with Zerubbabel after the exile (Ezr 2:16; Neh 7:21).
2. Ancestor of a family of gatekeepers who also returned to Judah with Zerubbabel (Ezr 2:42; Neh 7:45).
3. Political leader who signed Ezra's covenant of faithfulness to God with Nehemiah and others after the exile (Neh 10:17).

ATHACH City, probably near Ziklag in southern Judah, to which David sent part of his booty after a victory over the Amalekites (1 Sm 30:30).

ATHAIAH Uzziah's son from Judah's tribe, a resident of Jerusalem after the exile (Neh 11:4).

ATHALIAH
1. Wife of King Jehoram of Judah, and daughter of King Ahab of Israel and his wife, Jezebel. Athaliah, Judah's only queen, ruled 841–835 BC (2 Kgs 11; 2 Chr 22–23).

    Like her mother, Jezebel, Athaliah worshiped the Canaanite god Baal and encouraged her husband to do the same. Evidently she had considerable influence over Jehoram. After his death their son Ahaziah was made king (2 Kgs 8:25-27; 2 Chr 22:1). Like Jehoram, Ahaziah was influenced by Athaliah and did "what was evil in the Lord's sight" (2 Kgs 8:27).

    Because the kings of Israel and Judah disobeyed the Lord, Jehu was anointed by God to be the true king of Israel (2 Kgs 9:2-3). Jehu then killed Joram, king of Israel (2 Kgs 9:24), and Ahaziah, king of Judah (2 Kgs 9:27; 2 Chr 22:9). After the death of her son, Athaliah seized the throne of Judah by destroying (so she thought) all the males in the royal family (2 Kgs 11:1; 2 Chr 22:10). But Jehoshabeath, Jehoram's daughter and the wife of Jehoiada the priest, rescued Ahaziah's son Joash and hid him away (2 Kgs 11:2-3, 2 Chr 22:11-12).

    After six years Jehoiada "took courage" and resolved to reveal the young prince Joash to the people, making an agreement with some mercenary army officers who summoned to Jerusalem "the Levites . . . and the heads of fathers' houses of Israel" (2 Chr 23:1-3, RSV). In a secret ceremony in the temple Joash was crowned king. Athaliah heard people rejoicing and blowing trumpets and tried to halt the proceedings by tearing her clothes and yelling, "Treason!" She was immediately taken from the temple area and executed (2 Kgs 11:13-16; 2 Chr 23:12-15). *See* Israel, History of; Kings, Books of First and Second.
2. One of the sons of Jehoram from Benjamin's tribe (1 Chr 8:26).
3. Father of Jeshaiah, the head of the sons of Elam who returned from Babylon with Ezra (Ezr 8:7).

ATHARIM Place, according to the NLT, where the Israelites sought to enter Canaan when attacked by the king of Arad (Nm 21:1). The name means "tracks" and is generally thought to be located near Tamar or Hazazon-tamar several miles south of the Dead Sea. One possible reading of the text makes it identical with Tamar. The KJV, following the Targum and Vulgate, translates it "spies."

ATHBASH* Hebrew cryptograph in which the first letter of the Hebrew alphabet is substituted for the last, the second for the next-to-last, etc., to produce a code. Such a code or cipher was used for the word "Chaldea" in Jeremiah 51:1 (KJV interprets the cipher as meaning "them that rise up against me"). Another athbash was used for

"Babylon" in Jeremiah 25:26 and 51:41 (KJV treats that cipher as a proper name, "Sheshach"). The early Greek translation of the OT, the Septuagint, correctly deciphered these and translated them as "Chaldea" and "Babylon" respectively.

ATHENOBIUS Friend of King Antiochus VII of Syria (1 Macc 15:28-36). When Antiochus besieged the city of Dor the high priest Simon Maccabeus sent him 2,000 soldiers along with gold, silver, and military equipment. Antiochus refused the gift, severed all treaties with Simon, and sent Athenobius to Jerusalem to demand that Simon turn several fortified places over to him or pay heavy tribute, threatening retaliation if Simon refused. When Simon offered to pay only a tenth of the Syrian demands, Athenobius "returned wrath" to Antiochus, who then sent his general, Cendebeus, to attack Judea (1 Macc 15:38-41).

ATHENS Capital of modern Greece and for centuries chief city of the province of Attica. Athens' famous landmark is the Acropolis, a steep flat rock that rises about 200 feet (61 meters) above the plain around it and which still holds several masterpieces of architecture. Walls dating from 1100 BC indicate an advanced community by that time.

Athens began its rise to glory in the sixth century BC, first under the leadership of Solon (d. 559 BC), who established democratic forms of government, and later under Pericles (d. 429 BC), when the magnificent buildings of the Acropolis took form. In this golden age, Athens became the center of philosophy, art, architecture, and drama.

By the time Paul brought the Christian message to Athens (Acts 17:15-34), the city had only a portion of its former glory and prestige. Roman emperors continued to extend patronage by providing for new buildings and the restoration of the Agora (marketplace). Athens continued to be the home of the most prominent university in the Greek world. Both Epicurean and Stoic philosophy had worthy representatives in the city.

The Christian message was first brought to Athens by the apostle Paul on his second missionary journey about AD 50. His only reference to Athens is in 1 Thessalonians 3:1, where he indicated that he and Timothy arrived in the city together but that shortly thereafter he sent Timothy back to Thessalonica while he remained alone in Athens.

Luke has provided a more complete account of Paul's ministry there (Acts 17:16-34). His arrival in a city marked by many statues to the gods, which surpassed anything he had seen in other cities, provoked in him strong feelings against such rampant idolatry. Reared in the strict monotheism of Judaism, Paul apparently viewed Athens as the epitome of sin, and the cultural majesty of the city could not undo this impression.

As did almost all cities of that day, Athens had its community of Jews, and Paul began to speak, according to his custom, with his own kinsmen. Before long he was also in the marketplace, speaking about Jesus to anyone who would listen, including some of the philosophers, who spoke condescendingly of him as peddling "scrap ideas." Paul's preaching of Jesus and the resurrection sounded as though he was proclaiming a new deity,

Aerial View of Athens

which earned him a summons before the Areopagus, a civic body responsible for the religious and moral life of Athens. As such it had to approve any new deity. The name Areopagus came from a small hill just off the Acropolis where the body formerly sat for deliberations. By Paul's time its meetings were commonly held in a portico at one end of the marketplace.

Most of Luke's account consists of Paul's message to the Areopagus, in which he referred to the many gods, even to an "unknown god." Paul declared that he was making known to them the God who was not known. He closed his address with a call to repentance and judgment. His reference to the resurrection brought division, but some individuals wanted to hear more.

Luke says only that a few followed Paul, including Dionysius, a member of the Areopagite council, and a woman named Damaris. Athens seems to be one of the few places where Paul did not succeed in establishing a church, and thus it did not figure prominently in early Christian history.

ATHLAI Bebai's descendant, who obeyed Ezra's exhortation to divorce his pagan wife after the exile (Ezr 10:28).

ATONEMENT In Christian thought, the act by which God and man are brought together in personal relationship. The term is derived from Anglo-Saxon words meaning "making at one," hence "at-one-ment." It presupposes a separation or alienation that needs to be overcome if human beings are to know God and have fellowship with him. As a term expressing relationship, atonement is tied closely to such terms as reconciliation and forgiveness.

In the KJV the word "atonement" occurs many times in the OT but only once in the NT (Rom 5:11). Modern translations generally, and more correctly, render the word "reconciliation." The idea of atonement is ever present in the NT, however, and is one of the fundamental concepts of Scripture. God is seen as taking the initiative in man's salvation; thus atonement is the work of God, who opens the possibility for sinful human beings to receive pardoning grace. For the sinner, who cannot know God, who cannot bridge the gap between himself and God, a "new and living way" is opened up by God.

The need for atonement is bound up with man's thoroughgoing sinfulness. All of Scripture (cited below from the RSV unless otherwise noted) points to the radical nature of that sinfulness. The prophet Isaiah affirmed, "All we like sheep have gone astray" (Is 53:6). According to another prophet, Jeremiah, "The heart is deceitful above all things, and desperately corrupt; who can understand it?" (Jer 17:9). David the psalmist cried, "There is none that does good, no, not one" (Ps 14:3). Paul described the degeneracy of man caused by his disobedience and idolatry (Rom 1:18-32) and summed it up: "All have sinned and fall short of the glory of God" (Rom 3:23). Elsewhere Paul described men as enemies of God (Rom 5:10), as "hostile to God" (Rom 8:7), as "estranged and hostile in mind, doing evil deeds" (Col 1:21). Adam's race is just like Adam: "Therefore as sin came into the world through one man and death through sin, and so death spread to all men because all men sinned" (Rom 5:12).

The problem of the sinfulness of humanity is compounded by the holiness of God, who cannot look upon sin. Isaiah saw the holy God in the temple and drew back because of his own sinfulness (Is 6:1-5). Not only is man terribly sinful, but God is fearfully holy. Consequently man dreads God and can do nothing to change this situation. He is lost, helpless, standing under the

THE SIGNIFICANCE OF ATONEMENT IN THE NEW TESTAMENT

Many terms are employed to express the atoning significance of Christ's death. His death is the "sacrifice to God" (Eph 5:2) and a "single sacrifice for sins" (Heb 10:12; cf. 9:26; 7:27). Paul wrote that God set Christ forth to be a "propitiation" (KJV) or "expiation" (RSV). The NIV helps to clarify the concept by using the term "atoning sacrifice," an expression that includes the ideas of both propitiation and expiation. The death of Christ is seen as the fulfillment of all that was prefigured by the OT sacrificial system.

The sacrificial nature of Christ's death is clearly expressed. He was referred to by Paul as "our paschal lamb" (1 Cor 5:7). The apostle Peter stated that believers are rescued "not with perishable things such as silver or gold, but with the precious blood of Christ, like that of a lamb without blemish or spot" (1 Pt 1:18-19). So also the references in John 1:29, 36 to Jesus as the "Lamb of God" probably had in mind the idea of sacrifice.

If Christ is viewed as our sacrifice, he is also viewed as our representative. That is, he represented us in his death. One of the most difficult phrases to interpret precisely is the common biblical expression "for us" ("for me," etc.). It may mean generally "for my sake" or something more specific. Does Christ represent us? More specifically, is he a substitute for us? Some texts clearly speak of him as our representative. Thus Paul said, "We are convinced that one has died for all; therefore all have died" (2 Cor 5:14). If "substitution" were meant, the last clause would conclude that we will not, or do not, die. Hebrews speaks of Christ as our High Priest before the Father, which is probably what John had in mind when he referred to Christ as our "advocate with the Father" (1 Jn 2:2).

The expression "for us" at times seems to mean much more than representation; it often carries the sense of substitution, an idea prevalent in the OT. So, "For our sake he made him to be sin who knew no sin, so that in him we might become the righteousness of God" (2 Cor 5:21). Two "ransom sayings" also portray substitution: "The Son of man came not to be ministered unto, but to minister, and to give his life a ransom for many" (Mk 10:45, KJV). He "gave himself as a ransom for all" (1 Tm 2:6). He became a "curse for us" (Gal 3:13). The unintended prophecy of Caiaphas the high priest pointed to the same reality: "It is expedient for you that one man should die for the people, and that the whole nation should not perish" (Jn 11:50).

awful judgment of God. He cannot justify himself before God and cannot merit God's concern. The possibility of atonement, then, rests entirely with God. The nature of that atonement, as illustrated in biblical history, affirms simultaneously the nature of both God and man.

The Hebrew term frequently translated "atone" has the basic meaning "to wipe out," "to erase," "to cover," or perhaps more generally "to remove." In the KJV it is translated by such expressions as "to make atonement," "forgive," "appease," "pacify," "pardon," "purge," "put off," and "reconcile."

The most common OT expression of the means of atonement was the sacrifice and offering up of the blood of a victim. In a sacrifice the shedding of blood was the central act. Life was in the blood (Lv 17:11); in the pouring out of the blood, life was given up; that is, death occurred. Elsewhere blood may be a symbol for life, but in the sacrificial motif it symbolized death. Some scholars have argued that in the pouring forth of the blood, life was made available to the people. It was the life *of the flesh*, however, that was in the blood, and the flesh was sacrificed. In the NT it is by virtue of the resurrection that the life of Christ is made available to believers.

Not every OT mention of atonement referred directly to the shedding of blood. On the Day of Atonement one of two goats was slain, but the other was "presented alive before the Lord to make atonement" (Lv 16:10). That "scapegoat" was driven out into the wilderness bearing the sins of the people. Banishment or expulsion took the place of blood as the goat, bearing the sins of the people, suffered the fate of the sinner. The goat was a substitute for the people. Money offered for the temple was also said to make atonement (Ex 30:16). In another text Aaron and Moses prevented the spreading of a plague by carrying incense: "He put on the incense, and made atonement for the people" (Nm 16:47). Those few special expressions do not undo the basic OT theme of atonement through provision of a substitute animal. The NT summarizes that theme by saying that "without the shedding of blood there is no forgiveness of sins" (Heb 9:22).

From atonement for sin in the OT came such terms as "expiation" and "forgiveness." From the idea of atonement for the wrath or judgment of God came "propitiation" and "reconciliation." Hence in modern English translations various terms attempt to express the concept of atonement provided by God.

Throughout the NT it is made clear that the work of Christ, primarily the cross, is what provides atonement. OT language continues to find expression in the NT, especially the term "blood." Thus in the NT we have the "blood of the covenant" (Mt 26:28) and the "new covenant in my blood" (Lk 22:20) as well as the "blood of Christ" (Eph 2:13) and the "blood of his cross" (Col 1:20). Almost equivalent are the frequent references to the cross and the death of Christ. The NT is the "new covenant" of Jesus Christ, sealed by his blood.

See also Propitiation; Expiation; Offerings and Sacrifices; Atonement, Day of; Redeemer, Redemption; Ransom.

ATONEMENT, Day of

Yom Kippur, the most important day in the religious calendar of Israel, falling on the 10th day of Tishri (the Hebrew month corresponding to mid-September through mid-October). On that day the high priest entered the Holy of Holies of the tabernacle (or temple) to atone for the sins of all Israel. The basic idea of atonement is a "covering" of sin; the purpose is to accomplish reconciliation between man and God. In the NT the Day of Atonement was referred to as the "fast" (Acts 27:9). To the rabbis, it was the "Day" or the "Great Day."

Although many additional rites were added over the centuries, the basic description of the original Day of Atonement is Leviticus 16. Complex and detailed ceremonies all focused on the central objective of complete atonement by sacrifice. First, the high priest removed his official garments, made for beauty and glory, and clothed himself in white linen as a symbol of repentance as he went about the duties of the day. Next, he offered a bull calf as a sin offering for the priests and himself. That done, he entered the Holy of Holies with a censer of live coals from the altar of incense, filling the area with incense. He sprinkled the bullock's blood on the mercy seat and on the floor before the ark of the covenant. Then he cast lots over two live goats brought by the peo-

ple. He killed one of the goats as a sin offering for the nation, taking the blood inside the veil and sprinkling it as before, thus atoning even for the Holy Place. He confessed the sins of the nation over the live goat as he placed his hands on its head. Finally he sent the live goat, called the scapegoat (i.e., the escape goat), into the wilderness. Symbolically it carried away the sins of the people. Then the high priest clothed himself in his usual apparel and offered a burnt offering for himself and one for the people with the fat of the sin offering. Outside the camp the flesh of the bull calf and goat was burned.

Other OT references to the Day of Atonement include Exodus 30:10; Leviticus 23:26-32, giving the date in a list of all the annual feasts; Leviticus 25:9-16, stating that each jubilee year began on the Day of Atonement; and Numbers 29:7-11.

The Day of Atonement became so central to Judaism that it survived the destruction of the temple in AD 70 and the end of the sacrificial system. It is the highest holy day of Judaism today. Although nowhere in the books of Moses is there an explanation of "afflicting the soul" required on the Day of Atonement (Lv 23:27-32, KJV), the Jews have continuously interpreted it as referring to fasting (cf. Ps 35:13; Is 58:3-5, 10). In biblical times, celebration of the Day of Atonement showed that Israel believed the cleansing of their sins was accomplished by the rites commanded by God. The forgiveness and grace of God were granted them and were the basis for their continued fellowship with God as his covenant people. Because it was designated as a sabbath of solemn rest (Lv 16:31; 23:32), all work was forbidden on that day as on the weekly observance of the Sabbath.

As with all the prescribed sacrifices throughout the year, the question arises as to the need for a special time for atonement. It is clear that the ritual was meant to avert God's wrath for sins already committed as well as to guarantee the continued presence of God. The sacrifice of the first goat and the sending away of the scapegoat were intended to cleanse the nation, the priesthood, and the sanctuary from sin. The intent of the whole sacrificial system reached its highest expression on that day, called by some the "Good Friday of the OT." The daily, weekly, and monthly sacrifices left something undone, so that the high priest could not enter the holiest place throughout the year. On that one day, however, he was permitted to enter with sacrificial blood as he solemnly represented the nation before the bloodstained mercy seat.

THE DAY OF ATONEMENT AND THE NEW TESTAMENT
In the NT the crucifixion account, many references in Paul's epistles, and the whole book of Hebrews are inseparably connected to the Day of Atonement. The ritual of the day is explained as a "type" of the atonement made by Jesus Christ (Heb 9–10). Christ, the High Priest, shed his blood on Calvary and then, having atoned for the world's sins, appeared in heaven before the Father (Heb 9:11-12). Unlike the annual repetitions of the day in Israel, Christ's atonement is seen in the NT as securing eternal redemption (Heb 9:12; see also Rom 3:25; 5:9-10; 1 Cor 5:7; 2 Cor 5:18-21; Gal 3:13-14; Col 1:14; Ti 2:14; 1 Pt 1:18-19; 1 Jn 2:2; 4:10; Rv 5:9).

The underlying reason for the day was that other offerings for sin could not provide for unknown ("secret") sins. Because of such sins the sanctuary, the land, and the nation remained ritually unclean. The Day of Atonement was instituted by God for the complete atonement of all sin (Lv 16:33). In the person of the high priest the nation was most fully represented by the access of their mediator into the very presence of God. *See* Atonement; Offerings and Sacrifices.

ATROTH-BETH-JOAB Town in Judah near Bethlehem (1 Chr 2:54). Since the Hebrew word *'ataroth* means "crowns," some scholars think that the phrase may not be a town name at all but a reference to Salma's descendants as chiefs of Joab's clan.

ATROTH-SHOPHAN City in Transjordan in Gad's allotment (Nm 32:35). The KJV mistakenly lists this compound name as two cities.

ATTAI
1. Son of Sheshan's daughter and of Jarha, Sheshan's Egyptian slave. Attai was from Judah's tribe (1 Chr 2:35-36).
2. Warrior from Gad's tribe who joined David at Ziklag in his struggle against King Saul (1 Chr 12:11).
3. Son of King Rehoboam of Judah by Maachah, and Solomon's grandson (2 Chr 11:20).

ATTALIA Mediterranean seaport in Asia Minor from which the apostle Paul and Barnabas sailed back to Antioch at the end of Paul's first missionary journey (Acts 14:25). The town was founded by Attalus II Philadelphus, king of the province of Pergamum (159–138 BC), which was taken by the Romans in 779 BC and became a senatorial province in AD 43. In Paul's time Attalia was part of the province of Pamphylia. Today, though its harbor is shallow, it is still an important Turkish seaport (Antalya).

ATTALUS Name or title of several kings of Pergamum. The one who received a "letter of recommendation" for the Jews from the Roman consul Lucius (1 Macc 15:22) was probably Attalus II Philadelphus (reigned 159–138 BC). This Attalus was succeeded by his nephew Philometor Evergetes (reigned 138–133 BC), who bequeathed his kingdom to Rome, ending the history of Pergamum as an independent political entity. Rome, then, organized the kingdom into the province of Asia.

ATTENDANT High-ranking officer in the service of the king. *See* Chamberlain.

ATTHARATES Persian word meaning "governor" (Neh 8:9). "Attharates" is a corrupt form of the title Tirshatha, rendered as a proper name in a parallel verse in the Apocrypha (1 Esd 9:49). *See* Tirshatha.

ATTHARIAS Greek transliteration of the Persian title, Tirshatha, meaning "governor" (1 Esd 5:40; cf. Ezr 2:63).

ATTRIBUTES OF GOD* Virtues, excellencies, and perfections of God. *See* God, Being and Attributes of.

AUGUSTUS CAESAR Roman emperor from 31 BC to AD 14. *See* Caesars, The.

AUGUSTUS'S BAND* Roman military unit mentioned in Acts 27:1 (KJV). Julius, the centurion who had custody of the apostle Paul on the way to Rome, was a member of Augustus's Band. The Greek word translated "band" normally meant a Roman cohort or force of two cohorts. Some scholars, assuming that Julius was in command of that unit, have wondered why an officer normally commanding a century (100 men) should be in charge of 500 to 1,000. Perhaps Julius was not in command of the whole unit, or it was not a regular cohort (tenth part of a Roman legion) but a special courier or guard detachment.
See also Warfare.

AUL* KJV spelling of awl in Exodus 21:6 and Deuteronomy 15:17.

AURANUS Leader chosen by the sacrilegious Lysimachus, brother of the high priest, to put down the angry Jews (2 Macc 4:40). He was demented, and, according to the Syriac version of the Apocrypha, head of a gang of cutthroats.

AUTOGRAPH* One of the original handwritten documents of a book that eventually became part of the Bible. None of the original manuscripts remain but copies called apographs, made by scribes whose occupation was the careful copying of manuscripts, are available. Apographs exist in numbers sufficient to give us confidence that our present Bible accurately preserves the words of the autographs. *See* Bible, Manuscripts and Text of the (both articles).

AVA* KJV spelling of Avva, a Syrian district, in 2 Kings 17:24. *See* Avva.

AVARAN Nickname of Eleazar, brother of Judas Maccabeus (1 Macc 2:5; 6:43). "Awake," "Paleface," and "Piercer" have all been suggested as possible meanings.

AVEN
1. Term used by Ezekiel to describe On (Heliopolis), center of worship of the Egyptian sun god Ra (Ez 30:17). The Hebrew word *aven* ("wickedness") was a play on the name On in a prophecy against the idolatry and wickedness of Egypt. *See* Heliopolis.
2. Epithet for Bethel (Hos 10:8), shortened from Beth-aven, "house of wickedness" (Hos 4:15; 5:8; 10:5). The prophet Hosea was condemning the northern kingdom's idolatry, for which Bethel was one center (1 Kgs 12:28-29). *See* Beth-aven #2.
3. Valley where Syria was to be punished because of its transgression against the Lord (Am 1:5), perhaps an oblique reference to Baalbek, the center of Syria's Baal worship in the Beqa'a valley.

AVENGER OF BLOOD Person who performed the duty of pursuing and ultimately executing the murderer of a close relative (Nm 35). Such a "redeemer" was expected to act in instances of deliberate murder but not of accidental manslaughter. A person guilty of manslaughter could find asylum in any one of six designated cities throughout the land (35:11) so that regular judicial processes could be set in motion. The avenger of blood can be seen in the accounts of Gideon (Jgs 8:18-21), Joab (2 Sm 3:27, 30), the Gibeonites (2 Sm 21), and Amaziah (2 Kgs 14:5-6). During the monarchy the king could evidently thwart the avenger (2 Sm 14:8-11).

The custom was rooted in the ordinance of God that required a life for a life in any case of intentional homicide (Gn 9:6). Unfortunately, the intent of the law—to impress upon humanity the sacredness of human life—has sometimes been greatly distorted, leading to blood feuds and the annihilation of whole families in some societies.
See also Civil Law and Justice.

AVIM* KJV spelling of Avvim, a Benjamite city, in Joshua 18:23. *See* Avvim (Place).

AVIMS*, AVITES* KJV forms of Avvim and Avvites in Deuteronomy 2:23 and Joshua 13:3, respectively. *See* Avvites.

AVITH Capital city for Hadad, Edom's fourth king (Gn 36:35; 1 Chr 1:46).

AVVA District in Syria (the same as Ivvah in 2 Kgs 18:34; 19:13) conquered by Sargon of Assyria in the eighth century BC. After the deportation of the Israelites from Samaria in 722 BC, Shalmaneser, the Assyrian king, sent inhabitants from Avva and other districts to occupy the cities of Samaria (2 Kgs 17:24).
See also Ivvah.

AVVIM* (Persons) *See* Avvites.

AVVIM (Place) City in Benjamin's allotment (Jos 18:23), located south of Bethel.

AVVITES

1. Ancient people who lived in villages near Gaza before they were largely destroyed by a Philistine invasion (Dt 2:23; Jos 13:3).
2. Designation for the inhabitants of the Syrian district of Avva who were relocated by Shalmaneser of Assyria in Samaria after its conquest in 722 BC (2 Kgs 17:31). *See* Avva.

AYYAH Town belonging to Ephraim's tribe (1 Chr 7:28), Gaza, but different from the Philistine Gaza. Some scholars think that Aija (Neh 11:31) refers to Ayyah or to Ai, possibly a neighboring town. Many identify Aiath (Is 10:28) with Ayyah and the town with the modern Khirbet Haiyan.

AZAEL Ezora's son, who obeyed Ezra's exhortation to divorce his pagan wife after the exile (1 Esd 9:34). Azael is omitted in the list of Ezra 10:40-42.

AZAL Unknown place supposedly on the eastern outskirts of Jerusalem (Zec 14:5).

AZALIAH Meshullam's son and the father of Josiah's scribe, Shaphan (2 Kgs 22:3; 2 Chr 34:8).

AZANIAH Jeshua's father. Jeshua was a Levite who signed Ezra's covenant of faithfulness to God with Nehemiah and others after the exile (Neh 10:9).

AZARAEL* KJV form of Azarel in Nehemiah 12:36. *See* Azarel #6.

AZAREEL* KJV form of Azarel. *See* Azarel #1-5.

AZAREL

1. Warrior from Benjamin's tribe who joined David at Ziklag in his struggle against King Saul. Azarel was one of David's ambidextrous archers and slingers (1 Chr 12:2, 6).
2. Levite selected by David to assist in the music of the sanctuary (1 Chr 25:18, NLT "Uzziel").
3. Chief of Dan's tribe appointed by David to be tribal leader during David's ill-fated census (1 Chr 27:22).
4. Israelite of the family of Binnui who obeyed Ezra's exhortation to divorce his pagan wife after the exile (Ezr 10:41).
5. Amashsai's father. Amashsai was a priest of Immer's family who lived in Jerusalem after the exile (Neh 11:13).
6. Priest who blew a trumpet at the dedication of the wall of Jerusalem after the exile (Neh 12:36).

AZARIAH Very common Jewish name. Its numerous occurrences in the priestly genealogies has caused much confusion. The following is one of several possible arrangements:

1. Zadok's son or grandson. According to most translations, Azariah was high priest during Solomon's reign (1 Kgs 4:2). It is possible, however, that his position should be understood as that of a special counselor or keeper of the royal calendar.
2. Nathan's son, a high official in King Solomon's court. He was chief officer over the 12 regional administrators (1 Kgs 4:5).
3. Amaziah's son, king of Judah (2 Kgs 14:21; 15:1-7), more frequently known as Uzziah. *See* Uzziah #1.
4. Ethan's son, a descendant of Judah (1 Chr 2:8).
5. Jehu's son, another descendant of Judah (1 Chr 2:38).
6. Ahimaaz's son and Zadok's grandson (1 Chr 6:9). If Azariah #1 was indeed a high priest, this Azariah could be identified with him.
7. Johanan's son and Amariah's father (1 Chr 6:10-11). He is identical with the Azariah of Ezra 7:3 and 2 Esdras 1:2, whose father (meaning "ancestor") was Meraioth. The parenthetical note about Solomon's temple (1 Chr 6:10) is generally held to go with the Azariah of verse 9 (see #6 above). It is possible, however, that this Azariah served in the temple (built by Solomon) during the reign of Uzziah and is therefore identical with #17 below.
8. Hilkiah's son and Seriah's father (1 Chr 6:13-14; Ezr 7:1; 2 Esd 1:1). Some have identified this Azariah with #10 or #11 below.
9. Zephaniah's son, an ancestor of the singer Heman. Heman sang in the worship ritual instituted by King David (1 Chr 6:36).
10. Hilkiah's son or descendant, one of the first priests to settle in Jerusalem after the exile (1 Chr 9:11; "Seriah," Neh 11:11).
11. Oded's son, a prophet in the days of King Asa of Judah. He encouraged Asa to initiate badly needed reforms in the king's 15th year (2 Chr 15:1-15).
12, 13. Two sons of King Jehoshaphat of Judah. Along with four of their brothers, they were killed for political reasons by Jehoram, heir to the throne (2 Chr 21:1-4).
14. Alternate name of Ahaziah, king of Judah (2 Chr 22:6, KJV). *See* Ahaziah #2.
15. Jehoram's son, one of Judah's military commanders. This Azariah followed Jehoiada the priest in a rebellion that resulted in the execution of Queen Athaliah and the crowning of Joash as king (2 Chr 23:1).
16. Obed's son, another of the five commanders in league with Jehoiada against Athaliah (2 Chr 23:1).
17. High priest in Jerusalem during the reign of King Uzziah (2 Chr 26:16-21). He opposed Uzziah's arrogant attempt to burn incense on the altar. Perhaps the same as #7 above.
18. Johanan's son, a leader of Ephraim's tribe. Azariah and other leaders of the tribe joined the prophet Obed in protesting the capture of Judean prisoners by King Pekah of Israel and in effecting their release (2 Chr 28:12).
19. Descendant of Kohath and the father of a Levite named Joel. Joel participated in the temple cleansing instituted by King Hezekiah of Judah (2 Chr 29:12).
20. Jehallelel's son. This Azariah, a descendant of Merari, also participated in Hezekiah's cleansing of the temple (2 Chr 29:12).

21. Zadok's descendant and high priest during the reign of Hezekiah of Judah (2 Chr 31:10, 13). He participated in Hezekiah's massive religious reforms.
22. Maaseiah's son, a householder in Jerusalem who participated in Nehemiah's rebuilding of the wall (Neh 3:23).
23. Leader who returned to Judah with Zerubbabel after the Babylonian exile (Neh 7:7; "Seraiah," Ezr 2:2).
24. Levitical assistant of Ezra who explained to the people passages from the law read by Ezra (Neh 8:7).
25. Priest who signed Ezra's covenant of faithfulness to God with Nehemiah and others after the exile (Neh 10:2).
26. Participant in the dedication of the rebuilt wall of Jerusalem (Neh 12:33).
27. Alternate form of Jaazaniah, the name of Hoshaiah's son, in Jeremiah 42:1 and 43:2. *See* Jaazaniah #1.
28. One of the three young Jews taken into captivity with Daniel. In Babylon he was renamed Abednego (Dn 1:6-7, 11, 19; 2:17). *See* Shadrach, Meshach, and Abednego.

AZARIAH, Prayer of *See* Daniel, Additions to.

AZARIAS Name or pseudonym taken by the angel Raphael as he accompanied Tobit's son Tobias, in the apocryphal story of Tobias's journey to Media (Tb 5:4, 13; 12:15).

AZAZ Shema's son and Bela's father from Reuben's tribe (1 Chr 5:8).

AZAZEL* Hebrew term of uncertain origin and meaning, occurring in Leviticus 16:8, 10, 26. Since biblical or extrabiblical information is lacking, the meaning of Azazel has been interpreted in at least four ways:

1. Scapegoat. Some have thought the word refers to the scapegoat used in the ceremonies of the Day of Atonement. That interpretation is unlikely because verses 10 and 26 state that the goat was sent *for* and *to* Azazel (RSV).
2. Place to which the goat was sent. This is the view of many Jewish scholars, who attempt to support it by connecting the word "Azazel" with a high and rugged cliff from which the goat was thrown. Others regard the word as meaning "desert places."
3. Abstract "place" or state of being. Some believe Azazel comes from a Hebrew word meaning "depart" or "remove," and thus interpret it as "utter removal," "complete sending away," or "solitude." That the goat "may be sent away into the wilderness to Azazel" (v 10) may be interpreted as "sent into a realm of being (or nonbeing) that is utterly removed." This possibility strengthens the idea of removal of sins: they become "nothing," since they are totally removed. Sending the goat away would then be a symbolic and ritual act through which God annihilates or removes one's past sins.
4. Personal name of a being, most likely a demon, to which the scapegoat was sent. Many modern scholars adopt this interpretation. Some support is found in the noncanonical book of Enoch, where Azazel appears as a ringleader of fallen angels who mislead mankind. Such a being would be an evil spirit to whom the sins of the people belong. Thus one goat is given to the Lord, the other to an evil being. Some have conjectured that that being was Satan himself.

AZAZIAH
1. Levitical musician who played the lyre when King David brought the ark of the covenant into Jerusalem (1 Chr 15:21).
2. Hoshea's father. Hoshea was chief officer over the Ephraimites during King David's rule (1 Chr 27:20).
3. Levite appointed by King Hezekiah of Judah to help oversee the offerings stored in the temple (2 Chr 31:13).

AZBUK Father of the Nehemiah who was ruler of half the Beth-zur district (Neh 3:16). Azbuk's son assisted the more famous Nehemiah, the governor (Neh 10:1), in rebuilding the wall of Jerusalem.

AZEKAH Town in the agricultural plain known as the Shephelah. It existed at least as early as the conquest of Canaan (the Promised Land), since Joshua drove the confederation of Amorite kings to Azekah (Jos 10:10, 22). It is also mentioned in connection with the encounter of David and Goliath (1 Sm 17:1). Archaeological excavations have shown that Azekah was heavily fortified with a system of underground refuge chambers (2 Chr 11:9, 11). Azekah, Lachish, and Jerusalem are mentioned as the only remaining walled cities of the southern kingdom of Judah at the time of Nebuchadnezzar's assault on Jerusalem (Jer 34:7). Azekah was resettled by some who returned from the Babylonian exile (Neh 11:30). Today it is known as Tell Zakariyeh.

AZEL Descendant of Benjamin, Saul, and Jonathan. Azel was the son of Eleasah and the father of six sons (1 Chr 8:37-38; 9:43-44).

AZEM* KJV form of Ezem, a town in the Negev Desert area, in Joshua 15:29 and 19:3. *See* Ezem.

AZGAD
1. Ancestor of a group that returned to Judah with Zerubbabel after the exile (Ezr 2:12; Neh 7:17).
2. Political leader who signed Ezra's covenant of faithfulness to God with Nehemiah and others after the exile (Neh 10:15).

AZIEL Alternative name for Jaaziel, a Levitical musician, in 1 Chronicles 15:20. *See* Jaaziel.

AZIZA Zattu's descendant who obeyed Ezra's exhortation to divorce his pagan wife (Ezr 10:27).

AZMAVETH (Person)
1. Warrior among David's mighty men who were known as "the thirty." Bahurim was his hometown (2 Sm 23:31; 1 Chr 11:33).
2. Jehoaddah's son, a descendant of King Saul through Jonathan (1 Chr 8:36; cf. 9:42, "Jadah's son").
3. Father of Jeziel and Pelet from Benjamin's tribe (1 Chr 12:3). Possibly the same as #1 above.
4. Adiel's son, whom King David put in charge of the palace treasuries (1 Chr 27:25).

AZMAVETH (Place) Town near Anathoth. Forty-two men from the town returned from the Babylonian exile with Zerubbabel (Ezr 2:24; "Beth-azmaveth," Neh 7:28). Later, Azmaveth supplied singers to help celebrate the dedication of the rebuilt wall of Jerusalem (Neh 12:29). It has been identified as Hizmeh, a site five miles (8 kilometers) north of Jerusalem.

AZMON City on the southern border of Judah between Kadesh-barnea and the "brook of Egypt" (Nm 34:4-5; Jos 15:4).

AZNOTH-TABOR Literally the "peaks (or slopes) of Tabor," a location on the southwest border of Naphtali's tribal allotment (Jos 19:34).

AZOR Descendant of Zerubbabel and an ancestor of Jesus (Mt 1:1, 13-14). *See* Genealogy of Jesus Christ.

AZOTUS NT form of Ashdod in Acts 8:40. *See* Ashdod, Ashdodite, Ashdothite.

AZRIEL
1. Family chief in the half-tribe of Manasseh that settled east of the Jordan River. Azriel was taken captive along with others by the king of Assyria (1 Chr 5:23-26).
2. Jeremoth's father. Jeremoth was an official over Naphtali's tribe under King David (1 Chr 27:19).
3. Seraiah's father in the reign of King Jehoiakim. Seraiah was sent by the king to arrest Jeremiah and Baruch for prophesying against the evil ways of Israel and Judah (Jer 36:26).

AZRIKAM
1. One of three sons of Neariah, a descendant of David through Zerubbabel (1 Chr 3:23).

2. One of six sons of Azel, a descendant of Saul (1 Chr 8:38; 9:44).
3. Ancestor of Shemaiah, a Levite who returned to Jerusalem after the exile (1 Chr 9:14; Neh 11:15).
4. Palace officer under King Ahaz of Judah who was killed by Zichri (2 Chr 28:7), possibly the same as #2 above.

AZUBAH
1. Shilhi's daughter and mother of King Jehoshaphat of Judah (1 Kgs 22:42; 2 Chr 20:31).
2. First wife of Caleb and mother of three of his sons (1 Chr 2:18-19).

AZUR* KJV form of Azzur in Jeremiah 28:1 and Ezekiel 11:1. *See* Azzur #2 and #3.

AZZAH* KJV rendering of the Philistine city of Gaza in Deuteronomy 2:23; 1 Kings 4:24; and Jeremiah 25:20. *See* Gaza.

AZZAN Paltiel's father and a member of Issachar's tribe. Paltiel was appointed to help Eleazar and Joshua in apportioning the Promised Land (Nm 34:26).

AZZUR
1. Political leader who signed Ezra's covenant of faithfulness to God with Nehemiah and others after the exile (Neh 10:17).
2. Father of the false prophet Hananiah (Jer 28:1).
3. Father of Jaazaniah, one of the prominent men of Jerusalem whom Ezekiel saw in a vision (Ez 11:1).

B

BAAL (Idol) Name of the most prominent Canaanite deity. As the god of fertility in the Canaanite pantheon (roster of gods), Baal's sphere of influence included agriculture, animal husbandry, and human sexuality. The word Baal occurs in the OT in combination with other terms, such as place-names (Baal-peor, Hos 9:10; Baal-hermon, Jgs 3:3), or with other adjuncts as in Baal-berith (Baal of the covenant, Jgs 8:33). Use of the name in connection with a local place-name may indicate a local cult of Baal worship.

Baal worship became prominent in the northern kingdom of Israel during the days of King Ahab (ninth century BC) when he married Jezebel of Tyre, a city in Phoenicia (1 Kgs 16:29-33; 18:19-40). It later infiltrated the kingdom of Judah when Athaliah, daughter of Ahab and Jezebel, married King Jehoram of Judah (2 Kgs 8:17-18, 24-26). Places for worship of Baal were often high places in the hills consisting of an altar and a sacred tree, stone, or pillar (2 Kgs 23:5). The predominantly urban Phoenicians built temples to Baal; while Athaliah was queen of Judah, even Jerusalem had one (2 Chr 23:12-17).

In the Ugaritic epic material, Baal is pictured as descending into the netherworld, the domain of the god Mot. That descent was evidently part of a cycle intended to coincide with the cycle of seasons. In order to bring Baal up from the realm of Mot and thus ensure initiation of the fertile rainy season, the Canaanites engaged in orgiastic worship that included human sacrifice as well as sexual rites (Jer 7:31; 19:4-6). Sacred prostitutes evidently participated in the autumnal religious ritual. The worship of Baal was strongly condemned in the OT (Jgs 2:12-14; 3:7-8; Jer 19).

See also Canaanite Deities and Religion.

BAAL (Person)
1. Reubenite, the son of Reaiah and the father of Beerah (1 Chr 5:5).
2. Benjaminite and one of the ten sons born to Jeiel, the father of Gibeon, by Maacah his wife. His brother was Kish, the father of Saul (1 Chr 8:30; 9:36).

BAAL* (Place) Alternate name for Baalath-beer, a city defining a portion of the boundary of Simeon's territory, in 1 Chronicles 4:33. *See* Baalath-beer.

BAALAH *See* Balah.

BAALATH
1. Town of Dan that may be the same city as #2 below, although some scholars separate the two (Jos 19:44).
2. Store city built by Solomon, probably west of Gezer in the original territory of Dan (1 Kgs 9:18; 2 Chr 8:6).

See also Baalath-beer.

BAALATH-BEER Place-name meaning "mistress" or "lady of the well." Like the masculine counterpart Baal, Baalath often appears in a compound place-name. It

seems to suggest that the Canaanite goddess Baalath, patron of Byblos, was associated with the particular place or well. Baalath-beer was the name of a town in Simeon's tribe, also identified as Baal or Baalath (1 Chr 4:33), Ramah of the Negev (Jos 19:8), and Ramoth of the Negev (1 Sm 30:27). It may have marked the southern limits of Simeon's inheritance.

BAAL-BERITH Pagan god worshiped in central Canaan around the city of Shechem (Jgs 9:1-4, 44-46). Baal-berith ("lord of the covenant") was probably a local form of Baal, the leading Canaanite fertility god. During the period of the judges, the people of Israel turned from the Lord to worship the idols Baal and Baal-berith (Jgs 8:33). *See* Canaanite Deities and Religion.

BAALE-JUDAH*, BAALE OF JUDAH* Alternate name for Kiriath-jearim, a village on the road from Jerusalem to Tel Aviv (2 Sm 6:2). *See* Kiriath-jearim.

BAAL-GAD Site in the valley of Lebanon at the foot of Mt Hermon marking the northern border of Joshua's conquest of Canaan (Jos 11:17; 12:7; 13:5). *See* Hermon, Mount.

BAAL-HAMON Site of a vineyard owned by Solomon and rented by local farmers (Sg 8:11). The poetic context indicates that the vineyard produced superb grapes.

BAAL-HANAN
1. Acbor's son, a king of Edom (Gn 36:38-39; 1 Chr 1:49-50).
2. Official appointed by King David to be in charge of the royal olive groves and orchards of sycamore-figs in the lowlands bordering Philistine territory (1 Chr 27:28). He came from Geder, a town in the area.

BAAL-HAZOR Mountain home of King David's son Absalom. Two years after Amnon raped Absalom's sister Tamar (Amnon's half sister), Absalom invited Amnon and his other brothers to a feast at Baal-hazor at sheep-shearing time (2 Sm 13:21-30). During the festivities, Absalom got his revenge: he had Amnon killed.

Baal-hazor is not to be confused with the Hazor in Benjamin's territory (Neh 11:33) or the Hazor north of the Sea of Galilee in Naphtali's territory (Jos 11:10-11; 1 Kgs 9:15; 2 Kgs 15:29). Baal-hazor was located in the territory of Ephraim at Jebel el-Asur, northeast of Bethel.

BAAL-HERMON Hivite territory in Transjordan near Mt Hermon, not captured in the Israelite conquest. It was one of the regions God wanted to use to test the younger generation of Israel (Jgs 3:1-6). Baal-hermon may refer to a place on the mountain. It seems to be another name for Baal-gad (Jos 13:5).

See also Hermon, Mount.

BAALI* Hebrew title meaning "my lord" or "my master" (Hos 2:16). The title was rejected by God because of its association with the Canaanite Baal. God chose instead to be addressed with the Hebrew word *'ishi*, "my husband," which has a similar meaning but is untainted by pagan associations. Thus, in a prophetic play on words, God stressed his covenantal love for his people and emphatically rejected any implication that he was for Israel only what Baal was for the Canaanites. *See* Baal (Idol); God, Names of.

BAALIS Ammonite king who arranged for the murder of Gedaliah, governor of the "remnant" left behind after Nebuchadnezzar's capture of Jerusalem and deportation of its inhabitants (Jer 40:14). Although warned by a guerrilla leader, Johanan, Gedaliah refused to take heed and was killed (Jer 41:1-3).

BAAL-MEON City in northern Moab assigned to Reuben's tribe (Nm 32:38; 1 Chr 5:8). It is called Beth-baal-meon in Joshua 13:17, Beth-meon in Jeremiah 48:23, and Beon in Numbers 32:3. About 830 BC it was held by Mesha, king of Moab, and was still in Moabite hands in the sixth century BC (Jer 48:23; Ez 25:9) but may have been in Israelite possession during part of the eighth century BC.

BAAL-PEOR Moabite god worshiped on Mt Peor. It is probable that this god was Chemosh, the national deity of Moab. While camped in Shittim, the Israelites were seduced by Moabite women who persuaded them to worship "Baal of Peor" (Nm 25:3). For that act of idolatry, God struck Israel with a plague that killed 24,000 persons (Nm 25:9; Ps 106:28-31). Baal-peor is also spoken of as the place where Israel worshiped "the Baal of Peor" (Dt 4:3).
See also Moab, Moabites.

BAAL-PERAZIM Location near Jerusalem of a battle in which Israel's newly anointed King David defeated the Philistines (2 Sm 5:20; 1 Chr 14:11). David named the area Baal-perazim to commemorate the Lord's "breaking through" his enemies, since the phrase means the "lord of breaking through." A prophetic reference to a Mt Perazim, where the Lord came "suddenly and in anger," may recall David's battle with the Philistines (Is 28:21).

BAALSAMUS* Levite assistant who explained to the people passages from the law read by Ezra (1 Esd 9:43). In the parallel passage in Nehemiah, the name Maaseiah appears. *See* Maaseiah #11.

BAAL-SHALISHAH Home of a man who brought a sack of fresh grain and 20 barley loaves to Elisha at Gilgal. Elisha had his servant feed 100 young prophets with it and had some left over (2 Kgs 4:42). Baal-shalishah was probably located in a fertile area where early crops were raised.

BAAL-TAMAR Place between Gibeah and Bethel in Benjamin's territory, north of Jerusalem. There the 11 other Israelite tribes rallied their forces in a final victorious battle against the tribe of Benjamin over crimes committed in the city of Gibeah (Jgs 20:33).

BAAL-ZEBUB Pagan god of the Philistine city of Ekron. After King Ahaziah of Israel fell from his upstairs porch (852 BC), he sent messengers to Baal-zebub to ask about his recovery (2 Kgs 1:2). He was severely rebuked for that by the prophet Elijah, who declared that his affront to Israel's God would result in the king's death.
Identification of Baal-zebub (which means "lord of

the flies") is somewhat uncertain. The god may have been thought to give oracles by the flight or buzzing of a fly, or may have protected his worshipers from plagues of flies. Excavations at Philistine sites have uncovered golden images of flies. Most scholars believe that the name is a corruption of Baal-zebul ("Baal the prince"). The distortion was probably a deliberate effort to demean the god.
See also Canaanite Deities and Religion.

CALLING JESUS "BEELZEBUL"
By NT times, the name had changed to Beelzebul (KJV Beelzebub), from the Syriac language meaning "lord of dung." It was a common practice to apply the names of the gods of enemy nations to the devils of one's own religion. Thus, the title was applied by the Jews to the devil, or Satan, the prince of demons (Mt 12:24, 27). In their blasphemous criticism, the Pharisees called Jesus by this title to explain his ability to cast out demons (Mk 3:22; Lk 11:15). In Matthew 10:25 Jesus tells the disciples, "If they have called the master of the house Beelzebul, how much more will they malign those of his household" (RSV). Here Jesus seems to make his point by relying on another possible meaning of the words from rabbinic usage, "lord of the house"—"house" having reference to the temple, the house of the Lord. Thus, in response to the Jewish leaders, a play on words involving contrast may have been employed. They call Jesus "Beelzebul, lord of the dung heap," and Jesus calls himself "Beelzebul, lord of the house." By this, Jesus claims lordship over the house of God.

BAAL-ZEPHON Area opposite the Israelites' encampment just before they crossed the Red Sea (Ex 14:2, 9; Nm 33:7). The exact location of Baal-zephon is unknown but probably was in northeast Egypt. The name means "lord of the north," and a shrine to a Semitic deity was presumably located there. The god Baal-zephon is mentioned in Ugaritic, Egyptian, and Phoenician writings as a sea and storm god.

BAANA
1. Ahilud's son, one of 12 officers appointed to requisition food for King Solomon's household. He served in the district of Taanach and Megiddo (1 Kgs 4:12).
2. Hushai's son, another of King Solomon's supply officers; his district was Asher and Aloth (1 Kgs 4:16).
3. Zadok's father. Zadok helped Nehemiah rebuild the Jerusalem wall (Neh 3:4). He is possibly the same as Baanah (Neh 10:27).

BAANAH
1. Rimmon's son, a member of Benjamin's tribe. Baanah and his brother Rechab were captains under Ishbosheth after Ishbosheth's father, King Saul, died in battle. Ishbosheth, crowned king by Saul's general, Abner, was David's rival to the throne of Israel. Baanah and Rechab murdered Ishbosheth in his sleep and cut off his head (2 Sm 4:2-7). They took the head to David, thinking he would be pleased that they had killed the son of his enemy. But David, who had wept at the death of Saul, God's chosen king (ch 1), was angry instead. He ordered Baanah and Rechab executed. Their hands and feet were cut off and their bodies hanged (4:8-12).
2. Baanah's son, Heled, from the town of Netophah near Bethlehem in Judah's territory, was one of David's 30 "mighty men" (2 Sm 23:29; 1 Chr 11:30).

3. KJV form of Baana, Hushai's son, in 1 Kings 4:16. *See* Baana #2.
4. Leader who returned to Jerusalem with Zerubbabel after the exile (Ezr 2:2; Neh 7:7).
5. Political leader who signed Ezra's covenant of faithfulness to God with Nehemiah and others after the exile (Neh 10:27). He is possibly the same as Baana (Neh 3:4).

BAARA Divorced wife of Shaharaim from Benjamin's tribe (1 Chr 8:8).

BAASEIAH Malchijah's son and ancestor of the temple musician Asaph (1 Chr 6:40). Baaseiah may be a copyist's error for the common name Maaseiah (1 Chr 15:18).

BAASHA Third ruler of the northern kingdom of Israel from 908 to 886 BC and violent founder of the second of its nine dynasties. Baasha was the son of Ahijah of Issachar's tribe, an unknown whom the Lord lifted "out of the dust" to leadership in the army (1 Kgs 16:2). While the Israelite army was besieging Gibbethon (inhabited by Philistines), Baasha assassinated King Nadab and then destroyed all other heirs of the former king, Nadab's father, Jeroboam (15:27-29). For much of his 24-year reign, Baasha warred with Asa, king of Judah (vv 16, 32), over control of the north-south traffic between Israel and Judah. Baasha threatened to cut off trade with Jerusalem and blockaded the northern frontier of Judah by building a fortress at Ramah, just north of Jerusalem (vv 17, 21). Fearing the new encroachment, Asa took all the silver and gold from the temple and his palace treasuries and bribed King Ben-hadad of Syria to break alliance with Baasha (vv 18-20). When Ben-hadad battered several of Israel's northern storage cities and captured land at the headwaters of the Jordan, Baasha lost confidence and withdrew from Judah's borders (vv 20-21).

See also Israel, History of; Kings, Books of First and Second.

GOD'S JUDGMENT ON BAASHA
The Bible's evaluation of Baasha's reign is not favorable. Baasha "did what was evil in the LORD's sight and followed the example of Jeroboam, continuing the sins of idolatry that Jeroboam had led Israel to commit" (1 Kgs 15:34, NLT). He received God's indictment and judgment through the prophet Jehu: since Baasha had led Israel into sin and had angered God, dogs would eat the members of his family who died in the field (16:1-4). Baasha died and was succeeded by his son Elah. Within two years Elah was assassinated, and all the rest of Baasha's heirs were put to death by another usurper, Zimri (vv 8-13).

BABA BATHRA* Tractate, or treatise, in the Talmudic Mishnah (a body of Jewish traditional lore relating to Hebrew law). The Mishnah is divided into six main sections called orders, with each order containing from 7 to 12 tractates. A tractate is divided into chapters, the chapters into sections of legal paragraphs. *Baba Bathra*, which means "last gate," is the third tractate in the fourth order, *Nezikin* ("damages"). It is preceded by *Baba Kamma* ("first gate") and *Baba Metzia* ("middle gate"). The three (originally one tractate) deal with various issues concerning property. Specifically, *Baba Bathra* covers the ownership of real estate and problems relating to it. *See* Mishnah.

BABEL Translation of a Hebrew word in Genesis 10:10 and 11:9. Elsewhere it is translated "Babylonia" or "Babylon" (see 2 Kgs 17:24). The rendering "Babel" in the Genesis passages is intended to relate the name to the early cultural setting reflected by Genesis 11:1-9, especially to the attempt to build a "tower." The translation "Babel" is also intended to associate the Tower of Babel incident with the popular understanding that Babel is derived from a root meaning "to confuse" (v 9).

Archaeological excavations have provided information about the building of towers for temples called ziggurats. The excavation of a number of such towers has made it clear they were structures consisting of several platforms, each of lesser dimensions than the one immediately below it. The top platform served as the location for a small temple dedicated to the particular deity of the builder or of the city in which it was built.

The first ziggurat at Babylon was built by Shar-kali-sharri, king of Akkad in the latter part of the 23d century BC. Archaeologists understand that this ziggurat was destroyed and rebuilt several times across the centuries. It apparently lay in ruins from sometime around 2000 BC to around 1830 BC, at which time a forebear of Hammurabi (1728–1636 BC) founded or rebuilt the city named Bab-ilu, or Babel.

The Babylonian Creation Epic gives details concerning the construction of a "celestial city" as the proper abode of Marduk. It was with this theological understanding that the name Babel, "gate of god," was a significant term. Other terminology associated with the temple built for Marduk and with the ziggurat suggests that Babel, for the early Babylonians, was the on-earth entrance into the heavenly or celestial realm.

Jewish and Arab traditions associate the Tower of Babel of Genesis with a large temple ruin dedicated originally to Nabu in the city of Borsippa, or Birs-Nimrod.

See also Babylon, Babylonia.

BABEL OR BABBLE
The Genesis narrative about the construction of the tower recounts how God intervened and confused the builders so that they could no longer communicate with each other. The word translated "confuse" is *balal*; it means also "to babble." A preposition combined with a form of this root, *ba-bal*, meaning "in confusion" or "in babbling," became the name for the location of the tower-building project. A popular etymology replaced the original meaning of the name.

BABYLON, BABYLONIA Land of southern Mesopotamia. Politically, Babylonia refers to the ancient kingdoms that flourished in southern Mesopotamia, especially in the seventh and sixth centuries BC, whose capital city was Babylon (or *Bab-ilu*, meaning "gate of god"). The term can also be used geographically to designate a whole region (in present-day southeast Iraq). The adjective "Babylonian" has an even looser meaning; it may refer to the land or its inhabitants, to the kingdom or its subjects, or to a dialect of one of the principal ancient Mesopotamian languages.

The two principal features of Babylonia's geography are the Tigris and Euphrates Rivers. Rising in mountainous eastern Turkey, they initially flow in opposite directions but converge near Baghdad and join farther south to flow into the Persian Gulf.

Politically, Babylonia largely corresponded to geographic Babylonia. Its centers, however, were not situated in the fertile alluvial plain between the two rivers, but rather on the banks along the main course and several side branches of the Euphrates. At times the king-dom reached eastward beyond the Tigris, into the flatlands and foothills of the Zagros Mountains, gener-ally along the Tigris's eastern tributaries.

Ancient Babylon

Sumer and Akkad: 3200–2000 BC Babylonia emerged as a culture as the result of Sumerian influence on the diverse peoples who had migrated into the area. The Sumerian civilization began to flourish in Babylonia sometime between 3200 and 2900 BC. (All dates given are approximate.) The two principal languages of the region were Akkadian, a Semitic language, and Sume-rian, whose linguistic affiliation is still unknown. The earliest interpretable inscriptions from Babylonia, dated at 3100 BC, are in Sumerian, which was the written lan-guage throughout Mesopotamia for seven centuries. In fact, cuneiform, the wedge-shaped writing invented by the Sumerians, remained in use for almost 3,000 years.

Eventually the Akkadian way of life began to compete with the Sumerian. Political and cultural leadership was effectively wrested away from the south by Sargon I (*Sharru-kin*, meaning "true king"; 2339–2279 BC), who founded the capital Akkad (or Agade).

The Akkadian Empire, which lasted for nearly two cen-turies under Sargon and his successors (2334–2154 BC), was disrupted by the invasion of the Guti people, moun-taineers from the east, who in turn were defeated by the Sumerian king Utuhegal of the city of Uruk. That event marked a period of revival of Sumerian power and cul-ture in Babylonia, led by a dynasty of kings that estab-lished itself in the once-prominent Sumerian city of Ur.

First Babylonian Kingdom: 1900–1600 BC At the same time, Semitic-speaking people from the west—the Amurru (or Martu), nomads from Syria—were exerting migratory and military pressures on Babylonia.

The Amurru—called by modern researchers "Amorites" after their language—were known in the pre-Sargonid period (before 2340 BC) and were looked upon as barbari-ans by native Babylonians, who scorned their manner of life. During the reign of Shar-kali-sharri (2254–2230 BC), the Amorites began to appear as a menace. A century later, during the early part of the Ur III period, the first major wave of Amorites moved into Babylonia; the second wave came during the reigns of the last two kings of the Ur III dynasty. That second migration coincided with a complex political situation in Babylonia. The undermining of Sumerian political power gave rise to the kingdom of Bab-ylon under Amorite control.

The last Neo-Sumerian king, Ibbi-Sin, was faced with military threats to his kingdom from both east and west. He also had to deal with internal rebellion. Ishbi-Erra, vassal governor of the city of Mari, 500 miles (804.5 kilometers) up the Euphrates, took advantage of the Amorite incursions to revolt against the king and estab-lish a rival kingdom with its capital at Isin, 50 miles (80.5 kilometers) from Ur. At the same time, in Larsa, less than 20 miles (32.2 kilometers) across the Euphrates from Ur, another new dynasty was established by a ruler with an Amorite name.

The founder of the first dynasty of the kingdom of Babylon was Sumuabum (1894–1881 BC). Little is known about him. He and his next four successors, all legitimate descendants—Sumulael (1880–1845 BC), Sabium (1844–1831 BC), Apil-Sin (1830–1813 BC), and Sin-Muballit (1812–1793 BC)—ruled peacefully and uneventfully for a century. They appear to have devoted themselves mainly to religious and defensive construc-tion and to maintenance of an irrigation canal system,

though there is some evidence of conquest and territorial acquisition. Still, the territory of the kingdom of Babylon probably extended no more than 50 miles (80.5 kilome-ters) in any direction from the capital. Hammurabi, the sixth king of that line (1792–1750 BC), enlarged the kingdom toward the dimensions of an empire. At its greatest extent it reached from the Persian Gulf up the Tigris to include some of the cities of Assyria and up the Euphrates to Mari. Babylonia's glory, however, was short-lived; under the reign of Hammurabi's son Samsu-iluna (1749–1712 BC) the realm shriveled. It lasted for another century, but within borders narrower than those established by Sumuabum. Minor dynasties took turns ruling over the area from 1600–900 BC. Then the Assyrians took control.

Assyrian Domination: 900–614 BC The earliest incur-sions of Assyria into Babylonia were by Shalmaneser III. In 851 BC the brother of Marduk-zakir-shumi, reigning king of the eighth dynasty of Babylon, made a bid for the throne with the backing of the Arameans. Marduk-zakir-shumi called on the Assyrians for aid. Shalmaneser defeated the rebels and entered Babylon, treating the ancient city and its inhabitants with great respect. Thereafter, advancing southward, he came to Sumer, inhabited by the Chaldeans, and pressed them back against the gulf. For whatever reasons, Shalmaneser did not annex Babylonia. Marduk-zakir-shumi remained on the throne, though he swore allegiance to the Assyr-ian king.

The final years of Shalmaneser III were darkened by revolts all over the Assyrian Empire. Two strong rulers emerged from the political confusion. In Assyria, Tiglath-pileser III (745–727 BC) usurped the throne. In Babylonia three years earlier a Chaldean, Nabonassar (747–734 BC), took the throne of Babylon as a successor king in the eighth dynasty.

At Nabonassar's death, an Aramean chieftain, Nabu-mukin-zeri (731–729 BC), seized the Babylonian throne and established the ninth dynasty of Babylon. Tiglath-pileser defeated the usurper, ravaged the territory of his tribe, and had himself proclaimed king of Bab-ylon—and thus, of Babylonia—under the name of Pulu (729–727 BC) and as the second king of the ninth dynasty. Little is known of his short-lived successor, Shalmaneser V (727–722 BC). He, too, was proclaimed king of Babylon as well as of Assyria. Under Shalmaneser a siege against the kingdom of Israel began, after its king, Hoshea (732–723 BC), rebelled against Assyria (2 Kgs 17:1-6).

▶**MERODACH-BALADAN** Sargon II (722–705 BC) suc-ceeded Shalmaneser. His rise to power is obscure; he was probably a usurper, which is why he chose the name Sargon ("true king") like his Akkadian namesake 1,500 years earlier. Shortly before Sargon II came to the throne, Elam in the east had begun to take an active part in the affairs of Babylonia by instigating rebellions against Assyria.

After the brilliant successes of his other campaigns, Sargon attacked Babylon again in 710 BC, and this time succeeded in taking it. Although he had himself pro-claimed king of Babylon, he acknowledged Merodach-baladan as king of the Yakin tribe. Merodach-baladan evidently took up residence in Elam at that time. In the year that Sargon's son Sennacherib (705–681 BC) suc-ceeded to the Assyrian throne, Merodach-baladan, assisted by Elamite officers and troops, reappeared. He raised the whole Aramean and Chaldean population of Babylonia against the Assyrians, took Babylon, and had himself proclaimed king again (705 BC).

During that brief period, Merodach-baladan sent an embassy to King Hezekiah of Judah (715–686 BC) "with letters and a present," ostensibly to show sympathy for Hezekiah because of the king's illness (2 Kgs 20:12). More likely, Merodach-baladan's purpose was to secure another ally against Assyrian hegemony; the account of Hezekiah's cordial reception of the Babylonian envoys shows his willingness to join the alliance. Evidently the king's vanity overruled his political sense, and he treated the Babylonians to an extensive tour of his treasury. The proud gesture was rebuked by the prophet Isaiah, who predicted Babylonia's later conquest of Judah, when the king's storehouse would be sacked and his family carried off captive (2 Kgs 20:13-19; Is 39).

Sennacherib was able to quickly dislodge Merodach-baladan from the Babylonian throne, force him into exile, and replace him with a king of his own choice, Bel-ibni.

➤WAR AND PEACE Sennacherib's successor and youngest son, Esarhaddon (681–669 BC), came to the throne of Assyria after a bloody war of succession with his brothers. One of his first acts was to rebuild and enlarge the city of Babylon. Esarhaddon thus won the friendship of many of his Babylonian subjects, who enabled him to enjoy a peaceful reign in that part of his empire. Three years before his death, Esarhaddon named his son Ashurbanipal as his successor (669–627 BC), and another son, Shamash-shum-ukin (668–648 BC), as viceroy in Babylonia.

The empire was not divided by having two sons on two thrones. Ashurbanipal had precedence over his brother, bearing responsibility for the whole empire. Shamash-shum-ukin and his Babylonian subjects, on the other hand, enjoyed sovereignty; as viceroy, he was granted full authority within his realm. That arrangement lasted for 17 years until Shamash-shum-ukin, backed by the Elamites and numerous Arab tribes, rebelled against Ashurbanipal. The revolt was brutally suppressed by 648 BC, and a Chaldean noble, Kandalanu, was appointed Babylonian viceroy. Shortly afterward, Ashurbanipal launched a punitive expedition, devastating Babylonia and completely destroying Elam in the process.

Neo-Babylonian Empire: 614–539 BC Both Ashurbanipal and Kandalanu, his viceroy in Babylon, died in 627 BC. For a year, Babylonia had no recognized ruler. Then the throne was seized by the Chaldean prince Nabopolassar (625–605 BC), who established the 10th dynasty of Babylon, which has come to be called the Chaldean or Neo-Babylonian dynasty.

Aided by Media, the kingdom of the Iranian Plateau, Nabopolassar put an end to the Assyrian Empire. By 612 BC Assyria's chief cities had fallen: Asshur, then the religious center; Nineveh, the administrative center; and Nimrod, the military headquarters. The last light of Assyria was snuffed out by Nabopolassar in 609 BC. Under his son Nebuchadnezzar II (604–562 BC), Babylonia fell heir to the Assyrian Empire. For a moment in history, Babylonia was master of the whole Near East. Nebuchadnezzar brought about the end of the Hebrew kingdom of Judah and the destruction of Jerusalem in 586 BC, deporting part of its population to Babylonia in the event referred to as the exile (2 Kgs 24:1-25:21).

Under Nebuchadnezzar, Babylon became the fabled city of luxury and splendor with which its name is commonly associated. Nebuchadnezzar was succeeded by his son, son-in-law, and grandson within the space of six years. Thereafter, one of his high diplomatic officials, Nabonidus, took the throne (555–539 BC). During his reign, the Medes, formerly allies of the Chaldeans, came under a new ruler, Cyrus II of Persia (559 BC), who over the next 10 years conquered an empire nearly 3,000 miles (4,827 kilometers) in extent, from the Aegean Sea to the Pamirs (mountains in central Asia).

During Cyrus's decade of conquest, Nabonidus was strangely absent from Babylon, residing in Arabia. Although the book of Daniel relates events occurring in the court of Babylon during Nabonidus's reign, his name is never mentioned. Instead, Belshazzar, whom Nabonidus appointed regent in Babylon during his absence, is described as king (Dn 5:1). Perhaps because of his extended absence or perhaps because of his attachment to the moon god Sin and Sin's city, Haran, rather than to the Babylonian national god Marduk and Marduk's city, Babylon, Nabonidus lost the support of the Babylonians. When he finally returned to Babylon, it was on the eve of Cyrus's attack on the city (Dn 5:30-31). Instead of offering resistance, however, the Babylonian army defected to Cyrus and the city gave itself up without a battle (October 539 BC). That surrender ended the Chaldean dynasty and the history of an independent Babylonia.

THE EXCAVATION OF NEBUCHADNEZZAR'S BABYLON Much of Nebuchadnezzar's Babylon was excavated by Robert Koldewey for the German Oriental Society in a series of campaigns beginning in 1899. Koldewey discovered that Nebuchadnezzar's Babylon was the largest city in antiquity, with an area of about 2,500 acres (1,013 hectares). The older part of the city was completely enclosed by two walls made of unbaked mud bricks. The inner and higher wall, which was more than 21 feet (6.4 meters) thick, was separated from the outer wall by a military road 23 feet (7 meters) wide. The outer wall, though thinner, was still more than 12 feet (3.7 meters) thick. Both walls were buttressed by massive fortified towers at intervals of about 65 feet (19.8 meters). Outside the wall was a moat that reached a width of more than 200 feet (61 meters) in places.

One of the most magnificent finds was the Ishtar Gate, a double gateway 40 feet (12.2 meters) high covered with enameled brick reliefs of 575 bulls and dragons in vivid colors. (Ishtar was a goddess of love and fertility.) Through that gate ran the Procession Way, a road covered with limestone slabs 3 feet (.9 meter) square. An inscription credited the road to Nebuchadnezzar. The walls along the Procession Way were overlaid with enameled bricks decorated with 120 lions representing Ishtar. The road led to the temple of Marduk and its adjacent ziggurat.

The Babylon of Nebuchadnezzar's time appears frequently at the end of 2 Kings and 2 Chronicles and in the early part of Daniel. Ezra and Nehemiah record the subsequent return of the remnant of Judah from their Babylonian exile.

Among the prophetic books, Isaiah speaks of Babylon during the period of Assyrian dominance. A century later Jeremiah warns of the threat of Nebuchadnezzar, and Ezekiel and Daniel speak of Babylon from the later viewpoint of those exiled. There are as many references to Babylon in the last half of Jeremiah as in all the rest of the Bible.

See also Postexilic Period; Diaspora of the Jews; Chaldea, Chaldeans; Nebuchadnezzar, Nebuchadrezzar; Daniel, Book of.

BABYLON: A SYMBOL OF THE ENEMY OF GOD'S PEOPLE
Several times in the NT, reference is made to the capital city of Nebuchadnezzar to which the Jews had been deported in 586 BC (Mt 1:11-12, 17); in 1 Peter 5:13 and the book of Revelation, Babylon is used symbolically. "She who is at Babylon" (RSV) was the apostle Peter's way of referring to the church in Rome, a city that had become as immoral and idolatrous as ancient Babylon. Just as that ancient cultural center had oppressed the Judean exiles, so Rome was now persecuting the Christians living there.

In Revelation 14:8; 16:19; 17:5; and 18:2, 10, 21, Babylon was again used as a symbol for first-century AD Rome. It was pictured as the notorious prostitute, who sits upon the many waters. She was gorgeously arrayed like a queen, sitting on a scarlet beast with 7 heads and 10 horns. She was "drunk with the blood of the saints," and on her forehead was written: "Babylon the Great, Mother of all Prostitutes and Obscenities in the World" (17:5, NLT).

An angel helped to interpret the apocalyptic symbolism for John (Rv 17). The "many waters" symbolize nations and peoples. The "seven heads" are seven mountains, which most commentators view as representing the seven hills of Rome. Seven times Babylon is called "the great city" and is described as a dreadfully immoral center of wealth and commerce, ruling over the kings of the earth and especially persecuting the saints of God. The wickedness personified in Babylon clearly symbolizes the historic manifestation of iniquity in first-century Rome.

Revelation 18 completes the picture. "Babylon is fallen—that great city is fallen!" (v 2). God's final judgment upon her will be severe, repaying her a double penalty (v 6). The main reason for her destruction is her immorality and persecution of the saints (19:2). The kings and merchants of the earth will mourn her demise (18:9-19), but the pronouncement is made in order that the saints might rejoice and worship God.

BABYLONIAN CAPTIVITY* Period when many inhabitants of Judah, the southern kingdom, were exiled in Babylonia after Nebuchadnezzar's conquest of Jerusalem (sixth century BC). *See* Babylon, Babylonia; Diaspora of the Jews.

BACA*, Valley of Phrase in Psalm 84:6 often translated "valley of weeping." The Hebrew word *baca* refers to some kind of tree in 2 Samuel 5:23-24 and 1 Chronicles 14:14-15, where it is translated mulberry (KJV), aspen, or balsam. It is not known whether the valley of Baca in Psalm 84 was a literal place or a symbolic expression for grief or difficulty in life. For those who seek to follow in the Lord's steps, the psalmist said, that valley becomes a pool of blessing and refreshment.

Some scholars think the valley was a specific place located near Jerusalem and the valley of Rephaim. If so, it could have been associated with weeping because (1) balsam or other trees in the valley exuded resinous gum, like tears; (2) the path was difficult to follow; or (3) it was a dreary place where waters seeped out of "weeping" rocks.

BACCHIDES Syrian general, governor of the Seleucid territories west of the Euphrates River. The area included Judea, which brought him into contact with five famous men of the intertestamental period: Demetrius I, ruler of the Seleucid kingdom (c. 160–150 BC); Alcimus (Hellenized name of Jakim or Eliakim), puppet high priest (c. 162–158 BC); and Judas, Jonathan, and Simon, the three brothers who ruled Judea in 165–160, 160–143, and 143–135 BC, respectively. Their stories are told in 1 Maccabees.

Bacchides was supported by Demetrius, with whom the story begins. When Antiochus IV Epiphanes died in 163 BC, Demetrius, a hostage in Rome at the time, asked the Roman Senate for permission to claim the throne. When permission was denied, Demetrius fled from Rome, and in a series of successful campaigns (161–160 BC) secured the throne. He then tried to crush the Maccabean secessionists in Judea also. Victorious, he styled himself Demetrius I Soter, meaning "savior."

Alcimus, a descendant of the OT priest Aaron, suggested to Demetrius that the Jews could be united in opposition to Judas Maccabeus if Alcimus were appointed high priest in Jerusalem. Demetrius I agreed and sent his friend Bacchides to install Alcimus in that important office.

Bacchides made three campaigns into Judea in his efforts to carry out his charge. The first campaign (162–161 BC) met with partial success. Some pious Jews, known as the Hasidim, supported a legitimate Aaronic priest until Bacchides and Alcimus treacherously broke their word and slaughtered 60 Hasidim leaders (1 Macc 7:18-20). That act united Judea behind Judas Maccabeus. Not realizing this, however, Bacchides left Alcimus and an army behind and returned to Syria.

Two months later (161 BC) Bacchides returned with 20,000 infantry soldiers and 2,000 cavalrymen, meeting the courageous Judas (who had only 800 men left) in a desperate battle near Elasa (160 BC). In that battle Judas was killed (1 Macc 9:18), and Jonathan and Simon, his brothers, fled into the southern mountains. Bacchides pursued Jonathan, met him in an indecisive battle, and then retreated to Jerusalem. Again, he returned to Syria, leaving an army, the Jewish Hellenists, and Alcimus in charge (1 Macc 9:52-57).

That arrangement lasted two years. Bacchides undertook one final Judean campaign (158 BC). This time disaster dogged him. Alcimus died of a stroke, and Bacchides began to suspect that further support of the Jewish Hellenists was unwise. Sensing his indecision, Jonathan offered a truce and exchange of prisoners. Bacchides accepted that as the most dignified way to withdraw, and returned to Syria, leaving Jonathan in effective control of Judea (1 Macc 9:72).

See also Maccabean Period.

BACENOR One of Judas Maccabeus's officers, according to 2 Maccabees 12:35. The name, however, can be shown to be a corrupt form of "Toubiani," so that the verse should read, "Dositheus, a Toubian, who was on horseback" (see 2 Macc 12:17).

BACHRITE* KJV form of Becherite, a descendant of Becher in Numbers 26:35. *See* Becher, Becherite #2.

BACKSLIDING To wane in religious commitment, to become less arduous in piety or less upright in morals. The principal Hebrew word for backsliding means "turning back" or "turning away." The people of Israel repeatedly turned from God and engaged in the sin and idolatry of their pagan neighbors. In the language of the OT, backsliding Israel lusted after abominations and forsook the Lord and his commandments (Ezr 9:10; Is 1:4; Ez 11:21). They violated the sacred covenant by worshiping idols and practicing harlotry (Ps 78:10; Jer 2:11; Hos 4:10). The people forgot God's mighty works on their behalf, ignored his counsel, and rejected his instruction (Pss 78:11; 107:11; Is 30:9). Hard-hearted and rebellious, they delighted themselves in all sorts of perversions (Jer 3:21). Religious leaders entrusted with the spiritual care of the nation were instrumental in leading the people astray (Is 9:16). The priests proved themselves faithless shepherds (Jer 50:6).

Grieved by the spiritual defection of his chosen people, God declared that "backsliding Israel committed adultery" (Jer 3:8, KJV). Through Hosea, the Lord lamented the fact that "Israel slideth back as a backsliding heifer" (Hos 4:16, KJV). Jeremiah confessed, "Our backslidings are many, we have sinned against thee" (Jer 14:7, RSV).

**THE CONCEPT OF BACKSLIDING
IN THE NEW TESTAMENT**
In the NT, the term "backsliding" does not appear, but the concept is present in a number of ways. It is usually viewed from an individual more than from a group perspective. In a conversation on the Mt of Olives, Jesus observed that toward the end of the age, evil would abound and most people's love would grow cold (Mt 24:12). Steadfastness and perseverance were the only reliable antidotes to backsliding. Paul likewise warned believers of the dangers of falling away. Israel's idolatry in the wilderness and God's judgment upon their waywardness should serve as a stern warning (1 Cor 10:1-11). Paul instructed his converts in Galatia against forsaking their freedom in Christ and an enslaving religion of works. He marveled that the new believers had so quickly been deceived (Gal 3:1) and were abandoning the gospel of Christ (1:6). The new Christians who had begun so well were failing to obey the truth (5:7). In correspondence with Timothy, Paul was grieved to learn that some believers had already turned aside after Satan (1 Tm 5:15). Love of money and philosophical speculation had precipitated their downfall (6:10, 20-21). A Christian by the name of Demas turned back from serving God because he loved the world more than Christ (2 Tm 4:10). Finally, in Revelation, the risen Christ reproached the churches for the spiritual indifference and coldness of their backsliding (Rv 2:4; 3:16).

BADGER Small burrowing mammal with a broad back, thick, short legs, and long claws on the forefeet. *See* Animals.

BAEAN Tribe annihilated by Judas Maccabeus because of its practice of ambushing Jewish travelers (1 Macc 5:4-5). This otherwise unknown tribe was probably located east of the Jordan River.

BAGOAS Steward in charge of the personal affairs of Nebuchadnezzar's general Holofernes (Jdt 12:11). Bagoas discovered the general's body after Judith beheaded Holofernes in his tent (14:14-18). Bagoas may have been a Persian title rather than a proper name.

BAGPIPE* An uncertain term sometimes rendered "bagpipe." The instrument used in King Nebuchadnezzar's court (Dn 3:5, 7, 10, 15) may actually have been a stringed instument. *See* Musical Instruments (Psantrin; Sumponia).

BAHARUM*, BAHARUMITE*, BAHURIM Village in Benjamin's territory on the old road connecting Jericho and Jerusalem, east of the Mt of Olives. Bahurim was located at the site of the present Ras et-Temim. Palti parted from his wife, Michal, there at Abner's command when Michal was being returned to King David (2 Sm 3:16). At Bahurim, Shimei cursed David and threw stones at him and his servants (2 Sm 16:5; 19:16; 1 Kgs 2:8). Jonathan and Ahimaaz, spying for David, were hidden from Absalom's soldiers in a well there (2 Sm 17:18). One of David's mighty men, Azmaveth, came from Bahurim (2 Sm 23:31; 1 Chr 11:33).

BAJITH* Town in Moab (Is 15:2), according to the KJV. But other translations render it as "daughter" or "temple."

BAKBAKKAR Levite who returned to Jerusalem from the Babylonian exile (1 Chr 9:15). His name is missing in a parallel list (Neh 11:17), unless it is the same as Bakbukiah.

BAKBUK Ancestor of a group of temple assistants who returned to Jerusalem with Zerubbabel after the Babylonian exile (Ezr 2:51; Neh 7:53).

BAKBUKIAH
1. Shammua's son, a Levite who assisted Mattaniah at the thanksgiving services in the temple (Neh 11:17).
2. Levite who returned to Jerusalem with Zerubbabel after the exile (Neh 12:9).
3. One of the gatekeepers who had charge of collection centers at the temple gates (Neh 12:25).

It is not clear whether these references refer to one, two, or three persons.

BAKER One who prepares food. In biblical times, the baker operated in the home (Gn 19:3), in the public bakery (Jer 37:21), and in the palaces of kings and nobles (Gn 40:1-22; 41:10, 13; 1 Sm 8:13), preparing bread and cakes from the basic staples of oil and flour. The Israelites fleeing from Egypt baked unleavened bread for their journey (Ex 12:39). The bread and cakes were baked in some kind of pan or oven (Lv 2:4; 26:26). As Israelite society developed, specialized bakers operated and formed guilds. Some have argued that Hosea was a baker because of his knowledge of baking techniques (Hos 7:4-8).
See also Food and Food Preparation.

BALAAM Beor's son, a prophet or soothsayer from northern Mesopotamia who was hired by a Moabite king, Balak, to curse the Israelites who had arrived at the Jordan Valley opposite Jericho after 40 years of wandering in the wilderness. Israel's defeat of the Amorites (Nm 21:21-25) had instilled fear in the heart of the Moabite king (22:3). Because curses and blessings were considered irrevocable (Gn 27:34-38), Balak reasoned that if he could hire a prophet to curse the Israelites in the name of their own God, Yahweh, he could easily defeat them in battle and drive them away from his borders. Balak sent messengers to Pethor, where Balaam lived. The town is believed to be located near Haran along the Habur River, a tributary of the Euphrates. Balak offered Balaam an impressive sum to come down and curse the Israelites.

Balaam, however, was warned by the Lord that he should not go to Moab. The king of Moab would not accept Balaam's refusal and sent his royal messengers back with offers of greater wealth and honor. Balaam revealed an inner lust for wealth and position by returning to the Lord to ask whether he should go. His words to the messengers, however, were very pious: "Though Balak were to give me his house full of silver and gold, I could not go beyond the command of the LORD my God, to do less or more" (Nm 22:18, RSV). Although Balaam would do only what the Lord allowed, he became a prime example of someone who does the right thing for the wrong reason.

Balak had sent along with his messengers "the fees for divination" (Nm 22:7, RSV), which shows that he considered Balaam a diviner of the type pagan nations commonly used. The Israelites were forbidden by the Lord to consult diviners or practice divination (Dt 18:10-11). A true prophet would not have even considered the possibility that serving Balak might be right. God's final permission to let Balaam go, with the stipulation that he say only what God told him, was the Lord's way of frustrating Balak's cause and showing God's care for his chosen people.

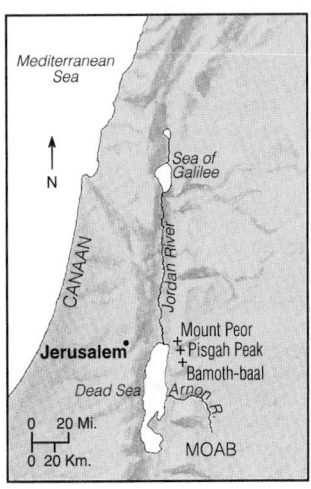

Key Places in the Story of Balaam

At King Balak's request, Balaam traveled nearly 400 miles (643.6 kilometers) to curse Israel. Balak took Balaam to Bamoth-baal ("the high places of Baal"), then to Pisgah Peak, and finally to Mt Peor. Each place looked over the plains of Moab, where the Israelites were camped. But to the king's dismay, Balaam blessed, not cursed, Israel.

Although he gave his permission, God was angry that Balaam went (Nm 22:22). So the Lord placed an angel with a drawn sword in Balaam's path. His donkey could see the angel but Balaam could not. Not knowing why the donkey balked, Balaam beat her, and she was then miraculously given a voice to complain against his cruelty (vv 28-30).

On the surface the story in Numbers 22 presents Balaam as a man who simply did what the Lord allowed him to do. But Deuteronomy 23:5 states that the Lord would not listen to Balaam and turned his intended curse into a blessing. When the Lord opened Balaam's eyes, he saw the angel and fell flat on his face (Nm 22:31). Then he acknowledged his sin and proceeded to say only what the Lord put in his mouth. Balaam's poems in Numbers 23 and 24 are in an archaic form of Hebrew that witnesses to their authenticity. They sometimes describe God's past blessing on his people, and at other points predict his future blessing of Israel in a unique way.

Only blessings on Israel and never a single word of a curse were spoken by Balaam. The infuriated Moabite king took Balaam from one vantage point to another where they could look out over the Jordan Valley and see the Israelite encampment. When Balaam still did not curse them, Balak slapped his hands together in anger and packed the prophet off without any reward at all.

But that was by no means the end of Balak's attempt to weaken Israel.

Numbers 25 tells how the Moabite king almost succeeded in turning the Israelites against the Lord. It describes a scene at Peor where Israelite men engaged in debauchery with Moabite women. That may have meant participation in the common heathen practice of temple prostitution, for according to Numbers 31:14-16, that had been Balaam's advice to Balak and the Moabites on how to weaken Israel. Later Balaam was killed by the Israelites in their campaign against Midian (Nm 31:8; Jos 13:22).

See also Balak.

BLIND BALAAM REBUKED BY A DONKEY
The purpose of this story is to show how spiritually blind Balaam was—no doubt because he had his mind set on the reward he would have if only the Lord would let him curse Israel. In other places in the Bible, Balaam is characterized as a man who "loved to earn money by doing wrong." But Balaam was stopped from his mad course when his donkey rebuked him with a human voice" (2 Pt 2:15-16, NLT). Jude said of certain persons that "like Balaam, they will do anything for money" (Jude 1:11).

BALAC* KJV form of Balak, king of Moab in Moses' time, in Revelation 2:14. *See* Balak.

BALADAN King of Babylon and father of Merodach-baladan. Baladan's son sent letters and a gift to King Hezekiah of Judah after Hezekiah's recovery from a serious illness (2 Kgs 20:12; Is 39:1).

BALAH City in southern Canaan (Jos 19:3), probably identical with Baalah (Jos 15:29) and Bilhah (1 Chr 4:29).

BALAK Zippor's son, king of Moab. Balak became fearful after the Israelites defeated the Amorites, so he attempted to hire a soothsayer named Balaam to pronounce a curse against Israel (Nm 22:1-7). Balak escorted Balaam to three different mountains and offered three different sacrifices, only to have Balaam each time deliver a blessing to the Israelites (chs 22–24). Enraged, Balak sent Balaam away. That event was later remembered as an example of God's special blessing on the Israelites and of the futility of trying to alter God's will (Jos 24:9-10; Jgs 11:25; Mi 6:5; Rv 2:14).

See also Balaam.

BALAMON City near where Judith's husband, Manasseh, was said to be buried (Jdt 8:3).

BALANCE, BALANCES Devices used to weigh an object by opposing it with a known weight. Balances or scales have been used to measure weight since at least the middle of the second millennium BC. Pictures and inscriptions in Egyptian tombs give us an idea of the appearance of the earliest scales. A pair of such balances found in Ugarit dates from about 1400 BC.

Balances usually consisted of four main parts: (1) an upright center standard, (2) a crossbar suspended from it, (3) two pans suspended from each end of the crossbar by cords, and (4) on the more elaborate models, a rod or pointer attached to the center of the crossbar at right angles to it. The rod moved in front of the standard so that when the two pans held equal weights the exact vertical position of the rod would be evident.

Scales or balances were used in the ancient world primarily to measure precious metals such as silver or gold.

The "Story of the Eloquent Peasant," dating from the Middle Kingdom of Egypt, however, mentioned the figurative measuring of a person's heart and tongue.

Balances are mentioned frequently in the OT, with much emphasis on the use of just weights in commerce (Lv 19:36; Prv 11:1; 16:11; 20:23; Ez 45:10; Hos 12:7; Am 8:5; Mi 6:10-12). The weighing of silver with a balance is described (Is 46:6), as when Jeremiah weighed the money that he paid for his nephew's field (Jer 32:8-10). In an acted-out prophecy, Ezekiel was told to cut off all his hair and beard and weigh it in balances to separate it into three equal parts (Ez 5:1-2). Job asked to be "weighed in a just balance," that God might know his integrity (Jb 31:6). Daniel said that Belshazzar had been weighed in the balances (judged) and found wanting (Dn 5:27). One reference to scales or balances is found in the NT, in Revelation 6:5, which speaks of a rider (on a black horse) having a balance in his hand. The prophecy is of severe famine, when some foods can no longer be obtained, when inflation has driven up food prices, and when people check the scales carefully to be sure they are not cheated when buying even the cheapest grains, such as barley (Rv 6:6).

See also Weights and Measures.

BALBAIM Town lying to the south of Dothan, mentioned in the book of Judith (Jdt 7:3); perhaps the same as Belmain, mentioned in the same book (4:4).

BALD LOCUST Variety of locust considered clean and therefore edible (Lv 11:22). *See* Animals (Locust).

BALDNESS Condition of having little or no hair on the scalp. Natural baldness due to age is referred to only indirectly in the Bible, where it is contrasted with baldness due to leprosy (Lv 13:40-42). The Israelites were forbidden to shave their heads or shape their beard in ways that resembled pagan religious practices (Dt 14:1). Such restrictions applied particularly to Israelite priests (Lv 21:5). Shaving off the hair and offering it as a sacrifice to God was a special act prescribed for men or women taking a Nazirite vow (Nm 6:1-5, 18; Acts 18:18).

The Egyptians and other peoples shaved off their hair (and eyebrows) as a sign of respect for the dead. There are many biblical references to the non-Israelite custom of shaving the head as a sign of mourning or anguish (Jer 16:6; 48:37; Ez 27:31; Mi 1:16). Most of these passages speak of God's judgment against pagan cities or nations. Since baldness was associated primarily with leprosy, venereal disease, idolatry, or death, the prediction or threat of baldness sometimes accompanied prophetic warnings (Is 3:16-24).

BALM, BALSAM Resinous plant gum used in medicine, or the plant from which it is derived. *See* Medicine and Medical Practice; Plants.

BALTHASAR* Traditional given name for one of the wise men who brought a gift to Jesus in Matthew 2:1-2. *See* Wise Men.

BAMAH Hebrew word meaning height, ridge, or elevation in the topography of the land (2 Sm 1:19, 25; 22:34); transliterated into English once (Ez 20:29; see NLT). It is a term designating hills or mountains overlooking the Arnon River (Nm 21:28). The plural form (Bamoth) alone or as the first part of a compound is used for the name of towns in Moab (Nm 21:19-20; 22:41; Jos 13:17).

Metaphorically, the word connotes a place of security

(Dt 32:13; Hb 3:19), as well as the high ground that a military commander wished to control in battle. Possession of an enemy's "heights" was synonymous with subjection of that enemy (Dt 33:29; Ez 36:2). The word seems to combine both literal and figurative connotations in several references to Jerusalem, a "high place" in ruin overgrown with scrub vegetation (Mi 3:12; see also Jer 26:18; Ez 36:1-2). "High place" was also a special, or technical, term in Canaanite religion, designating a local shrine on a hill near a town or village, in contrast to the large temples located throughout the land.

See also High Place.

BAMOTH, BAMOTH-BAAL Town in Moab allotted to Reuben's tribe by Joshua (Jos 13:17, called Bamothbaal). It had been one of Israel's last encampments on the route into Canaan, the Promised Land (Nm 21:19-20). Bamoth-baal, a mountain or high place, was probably a shrine to the Canaanite god Baal. King Balak of Moab took the prophet Balaam there to try to get him to curse Balak's enemies, the people of Israel (22:41–23:13).

BAN* Religious practice whereby those hostile to God are devoted to destruction. It is especially associated with Israel's wartime tactics involving the total destruction of the Canaanites because of their wickedness and abominable practices (Ex 34:11-16; Dt 7:2; Jos 6:17).

See also Conquest and Allotment of the Land; Joshua, Book of; Warfare; War, Holy.

BANI

1. Member of Gad's tribe and warrior among David's mighty men who were known as "the thirty" (2 Sm 23:36).
2. Shemer's son and ancestor of Ethan. Ethan was the Levite of Merari's line in charge of the music in the tabernacle during King David's reign (1 Chr 6:46).
3. Member of Judah's tribe and ancestor of Uthai (1 Chr 9:4). Uthai was one of the first to settle again in Jerusalem after the exile. Possibly the same as #4 below.
4. Ancestor of a family that returned to Judah with Zerubbabel after the exile (Ezr 2:10), alternately spelled Binnui in Nehemiah 7:15.
5. Ancestor of a family that returned to Judah with Ezra after the exile (Ezr 8:10; 1 Esd 8:36). Possibly the same as #4 above.
6. Ancestor of some Israelites who were found guilty of marrying foreign women (Ezr 10:29).
7. Ancestor of another group of Israelites who were found guilty of marrying foreign women (Ezr 10:34).
8. Son (descendant) of Bani (#7 above). This Bani was among those found guilty of marrying foreign women (Ezr 10:38, KJV). Because Bani is spelled almost the same as "sons of" in Hebrew, most modern translations render verse 38 "of the sons of Binnui."
9. Rehum's father and a Levite. Rehum repaired a section of the Jerusalem wall after the exile (Neh 3:17).
10. Levitical assistant of Ezra who explained to the people passages from the law read by Ezra (Neh 8:7). He was among those who offered praises to God on the steps of the temple (Neh 9:4-5). He is probably the same as Binnui (Ezr 10:38) and Anniuth (1 Esd 9:48).
11. Another Levitical assistant who explained passages from the law read by Ezra (Neh 9:4b).
12. Levite who signed Ezra's covenant of faithfulness to God after the exile (Neh 10:13). He was a leader of

the people representing the Bani family mentioned under #4 above.

13. Uzzi's father. Uzzi was the head of the Levites in Jerusalem after the exile (Neh 11:22). Possibly the same as #9 or #10 above.

The popularity of this name and its similarity to other Jewish names (e.g., Binnui) has caused much confusion in the genealogical lists. The list above is one of several possible arrangements.

BANISH, BANISHMENT
Exclusion of a person from a country or group as a form of punishment.

"Banishment" or a similar word is used in the Bible to describe God's judgment on Adam and Eve (Gn 3:23-24) and on Cain (4:9-14), Absalom's exile from his father David (2 Sm 13:37-39; 14:13-14), and Israel's exile from the Promised Land (Dt 30:1; Is 11:12; Jer 16:15; Ez 4:13). During the exile, it was included in a list of punishments for those who disobeyed God or the Persian king Artaxerxes (Ezr 7:26).

The Mosaic law specified that an Israelite should be "cut off" from the people of God for various offenses, such as failure to circumcise a male child (Gn 17:12, 14), eating leavened bread during Passover (Ex 12:15), making an unholy animal sacrifice (Lv 17:1-4), eating blood (v 10), sinning deliberately (Nm 15:30-31), or failing to undergo ceremonial cleansing after contact with a dead body (19:11-20). The term "cut off" probably meant exclusion from the social and religious life of the community (cf. Jn 9:18-23, 34). After the exile, when the whole nation of Israel had been "banished," disinheritance and permanent excommunication from God's people were made official punishments (Ezr 10:7-8). The Romans, like other conquerors before them, practiced deportation in various forms. Controversy among the Jews led to the banishment of Jews from Rome under Emperor Claudius (Acts 18:2). The author of Revelation was banished to the island of Patmos during Roman persecution (Rv 1:9). More severe forms of banishment included permanent exclusion from an area, loss of citizenship, and confiscation of all goods and property.

See also Diaspora of the Jews.

BANKER, BANKING
A person who engages in loaning, exchanging, and issuing money. The development of interstate and international trade made it imperative to devise a method of banking to facilitate the transfer of funds. The appearance of coinage in the seventh century BC brought the money changer into being. The royal monopoly in commerce (2 Sm 5:11; 1 Kgs 10:14-29) gave place to a system that resembled modern banking.

In NT times money changers represented one aspect of the banking system. They spent their time converting Roman money into orthodox coinage for the temple half-shekel (Mt 17:24; 21:12; 25:27; Mk 11:15; Lk 19:23; Jn 2:14-15).

Those who lent money (lenders) and those who gave credit in financial transactions (creditors) were protected by a system of guarantees such as pieces of movable property or a pledge of some kind. Interest was theoretically forbidden by Israelite law (Ex 22:25; Dt 15:1-18), although the law was not always observed and exorbitant rates of interest were sometimes charged. Prophets and some national leaders deplored the practice (Neh 5:6-13; Ez 18:8, 13, 17; 22:12). Often, the people of Israel were afraid of their creditors (2 Kgs 4:1; Ps 109:11; Is 24:2; 50:1), who might invade their homes to recover a debt, even carrying off children as slaves (2 Kgs 4:1; Is 50:1). The parable of the creditor and the two debtors in Luke 7:41-42 represents a kindly creditor (cf. Mt 25:14-30; Lk 19:11-27).

See also Money; Money Changer.

BANQUET
Lavish ceremonial meal, usually held in honor of some notable event or person; also a symbol of the feast to be given by Christ in the kingdom of God. Banqueting and feasting were major parts of the social and religious life of biblical times. In addition to the religious feasts prescribed by Mosaic law, banquets and feasts were celebrated on nearly any occasion of joy or solemnity: at the ratification of covenants (Gn 26:30; 31:54; Ex 24:11); at weddings (Gn 29:22; Jgs 14:10); at harvest (Jgs 9:27; Ru 3:1-3); at the shearing of sheep (1 Sm 25:11; 2 Sm 13:23-29); at the arrival of guests (Gn 19:3); at the weaning of a child (21:8); at coronations (1 Kgs 1:9, 19-25); on various state occasions (Est 1:3-9; 2:18; 5:4-8); and for many other reasons.

Many customs associated with banquets in the ancient Near East are portrayed in the Bible and in extrabiblical literature; wall reliefs and carvings from some excavations also depict banquet scenes. The sequence of banquet preparation in Proverbs 9:2-5, Matthew 22:1-14, and Luke 14:15-24 is also known from the legend of King Keret in Ugaritic literature: (1) preparation of the foods, (2) sending messengers with the invitation and announcement that all is ready, and (3) the presentation of food and wine in order. The prophet Amos portrays a lavish feast and shows the main eating customs (Am 6:4-6). Meals were ordinarily taken while reclining on a couch before a table (Est 1:6; Ez 23:41; Am 6:4; Mt 9:10; Lk 7:49; 14:10, 15).

Banquet imagery is prominent in both Testaments with reference to the kingdom of God. Isaiah foresaw the judgment of the nations and the deliverance of Israel followed by the Lord's reign over his people (Is 24:23); inauguration of that reign is accompanied by a huge banquet to which all peoples are invited (Is 25:6-8; cf. Lk 13:29). Meals shared following the sacrifice of animals in the OT prefigure that great feast when there will be no more death, tears, or reproach for the people of God (Is 25:7; cf. Rv 21:4). The banquet of the new covenant likewise directs attention to the future, when the redeemed will drink fine wine (Is 25:6) with Christ in the kingdom of God (Lk 22:14-20). By participating in the Lord's Supper (Communion), all Christians anticipate that great feast.

That future, final banquet in the kingdom of God is also pictured specifically as a wedding feast; all is in readiness, the invitation is issued to many, but few are chosen (Mt 22:1-14). The church looks forward to the marriage feast of the Lamb (Rv 19:7-9).

BAPTISM
Term generally meaning "to dip" or "immerse," but representing a group of words employed to signify a religious rite for ritual cleansing. In the NT it became the rite of initiation into the Christian community, and it was interpreted theologically as a dying and rising with Christ.

PREVIEW
• The Baptism of John
• The Baptism of Jesus
• Jesus' Resurrection Command to Baptize
• Baptism in the Early Church
• The Theology of Baptism in Paul's and Peter's Epistles

The Baptism of John John preached a "baptism of repentance for the forgiveness of sins" (Lk 3:3). The origins of his rite are difficult to trace. Some have claimed that his baptism modeled that practiced by those at Qumran; others have urged that his baptism modeled that practiced by Jews when initiating proselytes to Judaism. The members of the Qumran community viewed themselves as the covenant community of the last days and so dwelt in the desert, living an ascetic life and immersing themselves daily in acts of ceremonial cleansing. At the same time they taught that internal repentance must accompany the external act (1 QS 2:3). Its sacramental nature is seen in the fact that only a full member of the community could practice it, and then only after two probationary years (1 QS 5:6). Converts from pagan religions were admitted to Judaism only after fulfilling certain obligations, which included the study of the Torah, circumcision, and a ritual bath to wash away the impurities of the Gentile background.

John's baptism both parallels and differs with these forms of baptism. The genesis of his baptism may be found in the prophetic acted-out parable, which not only symbolized God's message but also intended to bring it about. John's practice had several theological ramifications: (1) It was intimately connected with radical repentance, not only of the Gentile but astoundingly (to his contemporaries) also of the Jew. (2) It was eschatological at the core, preparing for the Messiah, who would baptize with the Holy Spirit and with fire (Mt 3:11), and therefore looked to the final separation between God's people and the wicked at the eschaton (i.e., "the End," cf. Mt 3:12). (3) It symbolized moral purification and so prepared the people for the coming kingdom (Mt 3:2; Lk 3:7-14). In spite of the obvious connection between John's ceremony and the early church, we cannot posit absolute dependence. In fact, it disappeared from Jesus' ministry. At first, Jesus allowed his disciples to continue the rite (Jn 3:22), but later he seemingly discontinued the practice (Jn 4:1-3), probably for the following reasons: (1) John's message was functional, while Jesus' was personal/ontological. (2) John's was forward-looking, expecting the coming kingdom, while Jesus' was backward-looking, celebrating that event. (3) John's was an interim practice, while Jesus' was sacramental. Jesus' ministry fulfilled John's, so he severed himself from the latter's modus operandi.

The Baptism of Jesus This event has its genesis in a complex interplay of motives, divine and human, within the messianic consciousness of Jesus (see Mk 1:9-11 and parallels). For John it was Jesus' stamp of approval upon his message and ministry. Jesus was in continuity with John's kingdom proclamation. For Jesus, it was also an anointing that signified the inauguration of his messianic ministry. As seen in God's "heavenly voice" of Mark 1:11 and parallels, this has two aspects: (1) The voice alludes to Psalm 2:7, establishing Jesus' unique sonship. (2) It alludes to Isaiah 42:1, establishing him as the messianic "servant of Yahweh." (This is discussed at greater length in the article below.)

Jesus' Resurrection Command to Baptize Here we find the true basis of the church's practice (Mt 28:19). As already stated, the disciples stopped employing it, so it is here that we see the institution reconstituted as an ordinance based on the death and resurrection of Christ. It was no longer a forward-looking phenomenon but had now become a realized activity centering on the gospel message, certified by the risen Christ who is exalted to universal lordship. It also is an essential aspect of the discipling activity, as seen in the use of the participle "baptizing" after the main verb "make disciples." Finally we might note that the act signifies the entrance of the

believer "into" union with (literally "into the name of") the triune Godhead.

Baptism in the Early Church Acts 2:38 shows that baptism was a sacral institution from the very beginning. This takes it back to the earliest days of the church. In the primitive church it was an important part of the salvation process (Acts 2:38, "repent and be baptized") and was accomplished via confession and prayer "in the name of Jesus Christ" (Acts 2:38; 8:16; 10:48; 19:5). Probably there was a question-and-answer period in which the believer confessed his faith and dedicated himself to Christ. The result was reception into and identification with the messianic community of the new covenant, signifying both forgiveness of sins (Acts 2:38; 5:31; 10:43; 13:38; 26:18) and the reception of the Holy Spirit (Lk 3:16; Acts 2:38, 41; 9:17; 10:47-48; 11:16-17; 19:5-7). *See* Baptism of Fire; Baptism of Jesus; Baptism of the Spirit.

Jordan River Jesus was baptized in the Jordan River.

The Theology of Baptism in Paul's and Peter's Epistles Paul's basic statement is found in Galatians 3:27, "baptized into Christ." The rite of baptism is christological at the heart, signifying union with Christ. This is clarified further by Romans 6:3-8, which equates baptism with dying and rising (cf. Col 2:12-13). At the same time baptism is related to the Spirit; 1 Corinthians 12:13 connects "baptism by the one Spirit" with being "given that same Spirit." Many see baptism as the outward confirmation of the inward "seal" by the Spirit (2 Cor 1:21-22; Eph 1:13; 4:30). This leads us to the eschatological dimension of baptism. In its relation to the present work of Christ and the Spirit, it externalizes the outpouring of salvation in the age of fulfillment, because it is the initiatory rite signifying the believer's entrance into the blessings of the new age (Ti 3:5).

There is also a definite link between baptism and the OT covenants. The major connection is with the Abrahamic, especially with the circumcision that characterized it. Paul in Colossians 2:11-12 combines Jewish circumcision with Christian baptism as pictures of the redemptive work of Christ. The debate today centers on the degree of continuity between them—does baptism perform the same function in the New Covenant, i.e., forensic and imputative? Whatever the theological ramifications, Paul at least cannot be made to say this. Rather, he borrows here the Judeo-Christian imagery of the "circumcision of the heart" (Dt 10:16; 30:6; Jer 4:4; Rom 2:28-29; Phil 3:3). Christians experience the fulfillment of that which circumcision merely prefigured, a spiritual, totally efficacious reality.

Baptism is also related to the Noahic covenant in 1 Peter 3:19-21. There Noah's deliverance through the waters is considered a picture of the effects of baptism. The debate centers on the meaning of "baptism now saves you." The answer is connected with the thrust of the ensuing clarification, "an appeal to God for a clear conscience" (RSV, lit. "of a good conscience"). While the developed dialogue between the sacramental and baptist views is considered below, we will simply comment here that the interpretation "appeal *by* a good conscience" best fits the emphatic position of this phrase and the picture in this verse of a pledging convert. Baptism is the seal of the salvation covenant, which itself has been accomplished beforehand by the act of Christ and the faith decision of the individual.

BAPTISM FOR THE DEAD* Custom of uncertain meaning, referred to once in the NT (1 Cor 15:29). Many interpretations have been offered for that much-disputed verse. The important questions are the nature of the practice of baptism for the dead and whether or not the apostle Paul approved of it.

Most interpretations of the phrase "baptized for the dead" fall into one of three categories: metaphoric baptism, normal baptism, or baptism by proxy. In Mark 10:38 and Luke 12:50, baptism is used as a metaphor for suffering or martyrdom. Some scholars, interpreting "baptism for the dead" as a metaphor for martyrdom, would translate it "being baptized with a view to death."

Many prefer to read the phrase in the normal sense of being baptized on one's own behalf. Martin Luther thought it referred to the practice of baptizing over the tombs of the dead. John Calvin believed it had to do with Christians who called for baptism because they were in danger of dying. Others think it referred to converts who were baptized because of the testimony of Christian martyrs or departed loved ones.

The most natural meaning of the words points to a practice of baptism by proxy. The phrase seems to indicate that certain people in Corinth would have themselves baptized vicariously for dead people. The Corinthians may have had a magical view of baptism. That might explain why, to them, Paul belittled his ministry as a baptizer (1 Cor 1:14-17). Comparing the Corinthians' experience with that of Israel in the wilderness (10:1-13), Paul described crossing the Red Sea and gathering manna in terms clearly suggesting baptism and the Lord's Supper. Paul reminded his readers that neither of those dramatic experiences prevented the Israelites from falling into sin. Perhaps the Corinthians regarded the Christian sacraments as rites that guaranteed their salvation. If so, practitioners of baptism by proxy probably believed that the rite had some benefit for the departed.

Did Paul approve of the practice of baptism for the dead? Probably not. It should be noted that in the particular arguments for the resurrection of the dead in 1 Corinthians 15:29-34, Paul separated himself from the practitioners of such baptism. Without implying approval of the practice, Paul used vicarious baptism merely as an illustrative argument: unless *some* Corinthians believed in the actual resurrection of the dead, their practice of baptizing on behalf of the dead would obviously be meaningless.

BAPTISM OF FIRE* Metaphor coined by John the Baptist. John was looking for the coming of One who would "baptize in Spirit and fire" (Mt 3:11; Lk 3:16). The context makes clear that fire in that phrase denotes judgment, a judgment that would presumably purify the penitent (cf. Is 4:4; Mal 3:2-3) as well as destroy the impenitent (Mal 4:1; Mt 3:10,12).

The prophets and apocalyptic writers frequently spoke of a period of tribulation and suffering necessary before the new age could come: "the messianic woes," "the birth pangs of the Messiah," "a river of fire." Parallels to John's phraseology are found in Isaiah 30:27-28 and in the pseudepigraphal 2 Esdras 13:10-11. John the Baptist probably adopted that usage and reexpressed it through a metaphor drawn from his own most characteristic act (baptism). His "baptize in fire" thus probably denoted the purifying judgment that would bring in the new age as well as bring individuals into the new age.

There is no further biblical reference specifically to baptism of fire. Mark and John abbreviate the Baptist's preaching by omitting all mention of judgment. With Pentecost and beyond, John's baptism in water is seen as fulfilled in baptism in the Spirit. But Jesus seemed to echo the Baptist's conviction that a fiery purification was necessary (Mk 9:49). And he clearly picked up the Baptist's prediction, but referred the baptism and presumably the fire to his own death (Lk 12:49-50). His death is understood as suffering the fiery baptism for others. That thought is matched by the apostle Paul in his understanding of baptism into Christ as a baptism into Christ's death (Rom 6:3). So it can be said that John's expectation of a purgative baptism of fire for the penitent is most nearly fulfilled in the believer's being united with Christ in his death and sharing in his sufferings; only in that way does one come to share fully in Christ's risen glory (Rom 6:5; 8:17-23; Phil 3:10-11).

See also Baptism; Baptism of the Spirit.

BAPTISM OF JESUS* Major event in Jesus' life, which marked the beginning of his ministry. The fact that John the Baptist baptized Jesus is disputed by very few scholars today, but the purpose and significance of Jesus' baptism remain controversial.

The Gospel accounts agree that John's baptism was a baptism of repentance (Mt 3:6-10; Mk 1:4-5; Lk 3:3-14). He proclaimed that the kingdom of heaven was at hand and that God's people should prepare for the Lord's coming by a renewal of faith toward God. For John, that meant repentance, confession of sins, and practicing righteousness. That being so, why was Jesus baptized? If Jesus was sinless, as the NT proclaims (2 Cor 5:21; Heb 4:15; 1 Pet 2:22), why did he submit to a baptism of repentance for the forgiveness of sins? The Gospels provide the answers.

The Gospel of Mark Mark presents the baptism of Jesus as a necessary preparation for his period of temptation and ministry. At his baptism Jesus received the Father's approval and the bestowal of the Holy Spirit

(1:9-11). Mark's focus on Jesus' special relation to the Father, "You are my beloved Son, and I am fully pleased with you" (1:11, NLT), brings together two important OT references. Jesus' messiahship is presented in a radically new way, in which the ruling Messiah (Ps 2:7) is also the Suffering Servant of the Lord (Is 42:1). Popular Jewish belief expected a ruling Messiah who would establish the kingdom of God, not a Messiah who would suffer for the people. Mark intended to show that in Jesus alone had God's appointed time for the fulfillment of his purpose come.

The statement that the heavens opened at the baptism of Jesus (Mk 1:10) may proclaim the arrival of the "end times" (the time of fulfillment and the establishment of God's kingdom). A then-current Jewish interpretation of Isaiah 64:1 held that in the last days God would open the heavens and come down to his people. In Jewish thought the rending of the heavens was also associated with hearing God's voice and the bestowal of God's Spirit.

The Gospel of Matthew Matthew's account of Jesus' baptism has more detail than Mark's. It begins by noting John's reluctance to baptize Jesus (3:14). John was persuaded only after Jesus explained to him that the act was "fitting for us to fulfil all righteousness" (3:15, RSV). Although the full meaning of those words is uncertain, they at least suggest that Jesus' baptism was necessary to accomplish God's will. In both the Old and New Testaments (Ps 98:2-3; Rom 1:17) God's righteousness is seen in his salvation for his people. That is why the Messiah can be called "The LORD Is Our Righteousness" (Jer 23:6; cf. Is 11:1-5). Jesus told John that his baptism was necessary to do God's will in bringing about salvation for his people. Thus the Father's declaration at Jesus' baptism is presented in the form of a public announcement, emphasizing that Jesus was God's anointed Servant about to begin his ministry as the bringer of the Lord's salvation.

The Gospel of Luke Luke passes over Jesus' baptism quickly, placing it alongside the baptism of others who came to John (3:21-22). The context in Luke also sheds some light on the purpose of Jesus' baptism. Luke, unlike Matthew, places the genealogy of Jesus after his baptism and just before his ministry begins. The parallel to Moses, whose genealogy occurs just before his primary work begins (Ex 6:14-25), seems more than coincidental. It is probably intended to illustrate Jesus' role in bringing deliverance (salvation) to God's people just as Moses did in the OT. At his baptism, by the descent of the Holy Spirit upon him, Jesus was equipped to do the mission God had called him to do. Following his temptation (Lk 4:1-13), Jesus entered the synagogue and declared to the people that he had been anointed by the Spirit to proclaim good news (4:16-21). That anointing came at Jesus' baptism (cf. Acts 10:37-38).

In his Gospel account, Luke tried to identify Jesus with the common people—for example, in the birth story (with Jesus born in a stable and visited by lowly shepherds, Lk 2:8-20) and through placing the genealogy (stressing Jesus' relation to all of humanity, 3:38) right after the baptism. Thus, Luke saw the baptism as Jesus' first step in identifying himself with those he had come to save.

In the OT the Messiah was always inseparable from the people he represented (see especially Jer 30:21 and Ez 45–46). Although the "servant" in Isaiah is sometimes viewed corporately (Is 44:1) and sometimes individually (53:3), he is always viewed as the representative *of the people* to the Lord (49:5-26), as well as the servant *of the Lord.*

Evidently Luke, along with Mark and Matthew, was trying to show that Jesus, as the divine representative of the people, had identified himself with them in his baptism.

The Gospel of John The fourth Gospel does not say that Jesus was baptized but does say that John the Baptist saw the Spirit descend upon Jesus (Jn 1:32-34). The account emphasizes that Jesus went to John during John's preaching and baptizing ministry; John recognized that Jesus was the Christ, that God's Spirit was upon him, and that he was the Son of God. John also recognized that Jesus, unlike himself, baptized with the Holy Spirit (1:29-36).

John the Baptist described Jesus as the "Lamb of God who takes away the sin of the world" (1:29, NLT). The closest OT parallel to that statement comes from a "servant of the Lord" passage (Is 53:6-7). It is possible that "Lamb of God" could be an alternate translation of the Aramaic term "servant of God."

The sense of Jesus as the one who bears the sins of the people is obviously in view in the fourth Gospel. That Jesus was the promised representative and deliverer of the people was understood by John the Baptist and conveyed by the Gospel writer.

Conclusion In the four Gospels it is clear that the Holy Spirit came upon Jesus at his baptism to enable him to do the work of God. All four Gospel writers saw that Jesus had been anointed by God to accomplish his mission of bringing salvation to the people. Those ideas provide a key to understanding why Jesus was baptized. On that occasion at the beginning of his ministry, God anointed Jesus with the Holy Spirit to do his mediating work between God and the people. At his baptism Jesus was identified as the one who would bear the people's sins; Jesus was baptized to identify himself with sinful people.

See also Jesus Christ.

BAPTISM OF THE SPIRIT* A popularly used phrase, which never occurs as such in the Bible. The NT always uses the verbal phrase "baptize [or baptized] in the Spirit." That gives it a dynamic character that the noun phrase cannot fully convey.

The phrase seems to have been coined by John the Baptist: "I baptize you with water; but he [the One who is to come] will baptize you in the Holy Spirit and in fire" (Mt 3:11; Lk 3:16; but Mk 1:8 and Jn 1:33 omit the words "and fire"). The phrase is clearly a metaphor: it stands in contrast to and as the fulfillment of John's water baptism. It is a metaphor of *judgment,* as the context in Matthew and Luke makes clear. Purification or destruction in a river of fire, by a spirit of cleansing, in the fiery breath of God ("breath" and "spirit" are the same word in Hebrew) was familiar imagery in Jewish thought (Is 4:4; 30:27-28; Dn 7:10). It is also a metaphor of *mercy,* since the purification cleanses; after winnowing, the grain would be gathered into the barn (Mt 3:11-12). And, finally, it is a metaphor of *initiation*— John the Baptist's variation on "the messianic woes," the expectation that the messianic age would be introduced only through suffering and tribulation (e.g., Dn 7:19-22; 12:1; Zec 14:12-15; also the pseudepigraphal 1 Enoch 100:1-3).

In the book of Acts the metaphor retains the initiatory significance given it by John the Baptist. Acts 2:4 fulfills the promise of Acts 1:5. Since the outpouring of the Spirit was seen as *the* mark of "the last days" (Is 44:3;

Ez 39:29; Jl 2:28-29), it was by being thus baptized in Spirit that the disciples *began* to experience the last days for themselves (Acts 2:1-7, 18). Acts 11:17 speaks of Pentecost as the occasion when they came to believe in Jesus Christ as Lord. Similarly the apostle Paul sees the gift of the Spirit as the beginning of Christian experience (2 Cor 1:22; Gal 3:3), so that "having the Spirit of Christ" is the defining mark of the Christian (Rom 8:9). By being baptized in the Spirit, Cornelius and his friends received the forgiveness and salvation that Peter promised them (Acts 10:43-45; 11:13-18). "Baptized in Spirit" is there synonymous with "granted repentance unto life" (11:18) and "cleansed their hearts by faith" (15:8-9). *See* Baptism; Baptism of Fire; Spiritual Gifts.

BAR Term used in the Aramaic language to denote a close familial relationship; for example, Simon Bar-Jona means "Simon, son of John."
See also Ben (Noun).

BARABBAS Criminal who was released instead of Jesus. All four Gospel writers took note of that event (Mt 27:15-26; Mk 15:6-15; Lk 23:18-25; Jn 18:39-40), as did the apostle Peter in his temple sermon (Acts 3:14).
Barabbas was a bandit and/or revolutionary (Jn 18:40) who had been imprisoned for committing murder during an insurrection (Mk 15:7; Lk 23:19). (The word translated "robber" in John 18:40 can denote either a bandit or revolutionary.) He was regarded as a notorious prisoner (Mt 27:16). His insurrection may have been an unusually violent act of robbery or an internal struggle among the Jews, but many scholars view it as a political insurrection against the Roman forces in Jerusalem. It is not unlikely that Barabbas was a member of the Zealots, a Jewish political group that sought to throw off the yoke of Rome by violence.
After examining Jesus, the vacillating Roman procurator, Pilate, recognized that Jesus was innocent and wanted to free him. Yet Pilate also had an interest in pleasing the Jewish leaders in order to protect his own political position. In the face of his dilemma he offered to release a prisoner to the Jews at their Passover feast (Jn 18:39). Given the option of Jesus or Barabbas, Pilate thought that the Jewish crowd would choose to have Jesus set free. Pilate underestimated either the mood of the mob or the influence of the Jewish leaders, or both. Whatever the reason, the throng shouted for Barabbas to be released and for Jesus to be crucified (Mt 27:21-22). Consequently, Jesus was crucified and Barabbas, after being released, disappeared from biblical and secular history.

BARACHEL* Elihu's father, described as a Buzite (Jb 32:2, 6; cf. Gn 22:21; Jer 25:23). Elihu tried to counsel Job after the failed attempts by Job's three older friends.

BARACHIAH, BARACHIAS* Name attributed in the NT to Zechariah's father (Mt 23:35). Zechariah, executed in the temple by order of King Joash, was said to be the son of Jehoiada (2 Chr 24:20-22). "Son of Barachiah" could be a copyist's addition, since in the parallel passage in Luke's Gospel (Lk 11:51) the name does not appear in the most reliable manuscripts. A copyist may have confused the martyred Zechariah with the postexilic prophet Zechariah, whose father was Berechiah (Zec 1:1, 7).

BARAK Son of Abinoam of Kedesh in Naphtali (Jgs 4:6; 5:1) and an associate of the prophetess Deborah. Barak led an army of Israel that defeated the forces of Jabin, king of the Canaanites (Jgs 4). Barak is one of the heroes

of faith listed in the NT (Heb 11:32). *See* Deborah #2; Judges, Book of.

BARAKEL Alternate spelling for Barachel. *See* Barachel.

BARBARIAN* Foreigner, especially a person from a culture regarded as primitive or uncivilized. The Greek word *barbaros*, translated "barbarian" (KJV), originated as a repeated nonsense syllable, "bar-bar," in imitation of the strange sound of a foreign language. The Greeks, viewing themselves as the only truly cultured people in the world, tended to refer to everything non-Greek as barbarian. The Romans adopted Greek culture, considered themselves equals of the Greeks, and regarded other languages, customs, and people as barbarian.
The NT use of the word illustrates its several shades of meaning. The relationship to language is evident in a statement about speaking in tongues through the Holy Spirit (1 Cor 14:11). The apostle Paul said that if a Christian's spiritual language were not understood, the person speaking would be a barbarian to Paul and vice versa. Luke's account of Paul's shipwreck on Malta refers to barbarous people and barbarians (KJV, Acts 28:2-4). Obviously, nothing derogatory was intended, since the kindness of the natives was being described. Elsewhere, Paul used the word in the usual Greek-Roman manner, saying he was indebted both to the Greeks and to the barbarians (Rom 1:14). In a profound statement that the gospel of Jesus Christ is for everyone Paul said, "Here there cannot be Greek and Jew, circumcised and uncircumcised, barbarian, Scythian, slave, free man, but Christ is all, and in all" (Col 3:11, RSV).

BARHUMITE* KJV form for a person from the village of Bahurim in 2 Samuel 23:31. *See* Baharum, Baharumite, Bahurim.

BARIAH Shemaiah's son, a descendant of King David (1 Chr 3:22).

BAR-JESUS Jewish sorcerer, a "false prophet" who worked with the governor of Paphos on the island of Cyprus (Acts 13:6). When the governor, Sergius Paulus, took an interest in the message of Paul and Barnabas, Bar-Jesus tried to influence him against their teachings. Paul confronted Bar-Jesus, denounced him as a "son of the devil," and predicted that a temporary blindness would come upon him as a punishment from God. Bar-Jesus was instantly blinded (Acts 13:7-12), and the governor apparently became a Christian.
The many superstitious people of that day were easy prey for wonder-workers like Bar-Jesus (cf. Acts 8:9-11). The term "sorcerer" applied to him, however, connoted more than just a magician. It often referred to a wise man whose scientific understanding supposedly exceeded that of most others in that society.
Bar-Jesus was also called Elymas, which was his Greek name (Acts 13:8). It was common practice for Jews with contacts in both cultures to adopt a Greek name. According to one view, Elymas is based on an Aramaic word for "strong" and an Arabic word for "wise," which actually means "magician."

BAR-JONA* Aramaic form of Simon Peter's surname, meaning "son of Jonah" (Mt 16:17). Another variant of the name appears in John 1:42 and 21:15-17, where the best Greek texts have "son of John" rather than "son of Jona[s]" (KJV). *See* Simon Peter.

BAR-KOCHBA*, BAR-KOKBA* Hero of the second Jewish revolt against Rome (AD 132-135) during the latter days of the emperor Hadrian's rule. In Jewish sources he is referred to as Bar (or Ben) Koziba; his name means "son of a star." Reasons for the rebellion are not fully known, but they include Hadrian's construction of a pagan city on the site of Jerusalem (destroyed in AD 70), erection of a temple to the Roman god Jupiter on the site of the Jewish temple, and Hadrian's prohibition against circumcision.

Herodium Coins of the Bar-Kochba revolt have been found at the Herodium.

Even allowing for legendary additions to the story of Simeon Ben Koziba, president or prince of Israel, it is clear that he fought fiercely and courageously against the Romans and inspired his men to do likewise. The result was heavy casualties among the Romans and fearsome reprisals by them. Dio Cassius, third-century Roman historian, reported that the Romans destroyed 50 fortresses and 985 Jewish settlements during the war. They killed 580,000 in battle, and left multitudes to die of sickness and starvation. Judea was almost depopulated. Bar-Kochba himself was killed at the end of a long siege of Bethera (Bethar) near Jerusalem in AD 135.

During the terrible struggle, Jews were forced to seek refuge in caves and other hiding places. As a result, discoveries have been made that have raised Bar-Kochba from the level of legend to that of historical certainty. The first Bar-Kochba letters turned up in 1951 in a cave in a canyon called Wadi Murabba'at, 11 miles (17.7 kilometers south of Qumran (site of the Dead Sea Scroll caves), on the Jordanian side of the border in the Judean wilderness. Israelis exploring caves south of En-gedi in the Nahal Hever in 1960–61 found the personal belongings of refugees, letters written by Bar-Kochba, and scores of documents related to his administration. Coins of the Bar-Kochba revolt have also been found at the Herodium near Bethlehem and at Masada, showing that Bar-Kochba's forces used those places as forts.

BARKOS Ancestor of a group of temple servants who returned to Jerusalem with Zerubbabel after the exile (Ezr 2:53; Neh 7:55).

BAR-KOZIBA* Original name of Simeon Bar-Kochba, leader of the Jewish revolt against the Romans in Palestine during the reign of Emperor Hadrian. *See* Bar-Kochba, Bar-Kokba.

BARLEY Important grain and dietary staple in Bible lands. *See* Agriculture; Food and Food Preparation; Plants.

BARNABAS Name given by the apostles to an early convert to Christianity in Jerusalem. Formerly called Joseph, Barnabas probably earned his new name through effective preaching and teaching.

Sources for the life of Barnabas are limited to passages in the book of Acts and Paul's letters. The apocryphal Epistle of Barnabas is almost certainly a mid-second-century composition and therefore not from the hand of Barnabas. The apocryphal Acts of Barnabas is from the fifth century and not useful in establishing reliable information on the person of Barnabas. Tertullian assigned to him the authorship of Hebrews, but internal evidence speaks against this view.

A native of Cyprus, Barnabas was a Jew of the Diaspora. His priestly family background gave him a special interest in Jerusalem. He probably came to live in the Holy City. It is possible that he may even have become acquainted with Jesus in Jerusalem, but his conversion to Christianity probably resulted from the apostles' preaching soon after the resurrection of Christ.

Barnabas first appears as a property owner named Joseph (KJV Joses) in the book of Acts who sold a field and gave the money to the Christian community (Acts 4:36-37). When persecution of Hellenistic Christians broke out in Jerusalem, Barnabas remained in the city though others of similar background fled (8:1-8; 11:19-22). His good reputation in Jerusalem may have influenced the apostles to select him as Paul's companion for missionary work.

As many of the scattered Christians gravitated to Antioch of Syria, the Jerusalem church sent Barnabas to help in the growing work (Acts 11:19-26). The writer of Acts said of Barnabas, "He was a good man, full of the Holy Spirit and of faith" (11:24, RSV). Barnabas recruited Paul, now a Christian, to help in Antioch, and the two men worked in the church for a year, teaching a large company of Christians (11:26). When famine hit Jerusalem, Barnabas and Paul were sent with relief funds. On their return to Antioch, John Mark went with them (12:25).

Barnabas was commissioned with Paul to preach beyond the boundaries of Antioch (Acts 13:2-3). The placing of Barnabas's name before Saul (Paul) may indicate the priority of Barnabas at this time. They went to Cyprus and to several key centers in Asia Minor. At Lystra the citizens identified Barnabas with the mythical god Zeus, and Paul with Hermes (14:8-12).

At a Jerusalem council, Barnabas and Paul reported on their mission to the Gentiles (Acts 15). Following that council, as the two men planned another mission, a serious disagreement arose that led to their separating (vv 36-41). Barnabas wanted to take his cousin John Mark (Col 4:10), but Paul refused on the grounds that Mark had deserted them on the earlier mission (Acts 13:13). Barnabas left for Cyprus with John Mark, and Paul went to Syria and Cilicia with Silas. After that separation the focus shifted from Barnabas to Paul.

See also Apocrypha (Barnabas, Epistle of).

BARODIS* Ancestor of a group of people who returned to Jerusalem with Zerubbabel after the Babylonian exile (1 Esd 5:34). The name Barodis does not appear in parallel lists of returnees (Ezr 2:55-57; Neh 7:57-59).

BARRENNESS Condition of being barren or childless. A closed womb was a personal tragedy in OT times.

God's command to people after the Flood was to be fruitful and increase in number and fill the earth (Gn 9:1); later, Jeremiah offered the same advice (Jer 29:6). A barren wife in a polygamous marriage was subject to ridicule (Gn 16:4) or extreme jealousy (30:1). The social pressure to bear children for her husband was so great that the barren wife sometimes offered her husband a surrogate mother (16:1-2; 30:3). If a husband died without children, it was the responsibility of his brother to have children by his wife for him (38:8).

Barrenness could be a curse (Hos 9:11, 14) or a divine punishment (Gn 20:17-18). It could be removed after earnest prayers (Gn 25:21; 1 Sm 1:16, 20) or by God's prophet (2 Kgs 4:16) or messenger (Gn 18:14). On one occasion, a wife who had stopped having children was able to trade some mandrakes in exchange for sleeping privileges with her husband and had three more children (Gn 30:14-21). God promised Israel no infertility if they obeyed his laws (Dt 7:14). Unique among ancient writings is the concept here that barrenness could be a result of male infertility. Finally, as bad as barrenness was, Jesus told the women of Jerusalem that barrenness and dry breasts would be better than what they were going to go through (Lk 23:29). He was teaching that physical problems are never ultimate; spiritual ones are.

BARSABAS*, BARSABBAS Biblical surname. Barsabas (KJV) means "son of Saba" in Aramaic. Barsabbas, "son of the Sabbath," is the preferred spelling in modern translations. Two people in the NT have this surname: Joseph Barsabbas and Judas Barsabbas (Acts 1:23; 15:22). *See* Joseph #12; Judas #6.

BARTHOLOMEW, The Apostle Disciple of Jesus included in all four lists of the 12 apostles (Mt 10:2-4; Mk 3:16-19; Lk 6:14-16; Acts 1:13), though not otherwise mentioned in the NT. Nothing is told about him in any of the lists. Because the name means "son of Tolmai," it has been speculated that he was known by another name in addition to his "patronymic" name. In the lists in Matthew, Mark, and Luke (the synoptic Gospels), Bartholomew is named immediately after Philip, suggesting the possibility that the Nathanael brought by Philip to Jesus (Jn 1:45-50)—who seems to be linked with some of the disciples (Jn 21:2)—was Bartholomew. It thus seems possible that the apostle Bartholomew is referred to in the fourth Gospel by another name; it is not certain, however, that John's references to Nathanael were intended to identify him as one of the Twelve.

Eusebius, an early church historian, recorded an early tradition that Pantaenus, the first head of the catechetical school in Alexandria (AD 180), went to India and there found Christians who knew of the Gospel of Matthew in Hebrew letters. According to Eusebius, Bartholomew had preached to them and had left the Gospel of Matthew with them. In other traditions, Bartholomew was an evangelistic partner of Philip and Thomas and suffered martyrdom in Armenia.

A number of spurious and apocryphal writings have been ascribed to Bartholomew; none of them is genuine. In the fourth century Jerome mentioned a Gospel of Bartholomew, which is also noted by a few other writers. There are also references to the so-called Questions of Bartholomew (extant in Greek, Latin, and Slavonic fragments) and to a Book of the Resurrection of Jesus Christ by Bartholomew (extant in Coptic). Other references were made to Acts of Bartholomew and Apocalypse of Bartholomew, both otherwise unknown.

See also Apostle, Apostleship; Apocrypha (several titles attributed to Bartholomew).

BARTIMAEUS Timaeus's son, a blind beggar who called out to Jesus as he left Jericho on his final journey to Jerusalem (Mk 10:46-52). Seeing Bartimaeus's faith, Jesus healed his blindness.

BARUCH

1. Neriah's son, secretary of the prophet Jeremiah. In the fourth year of King Jehoiakim of Judah (605/604 BC), Baruch wrote down Jeremiah's prophecy of the evil that God was going to bring upon Judah unless the nation repented (Jer 36:4). God also gave Baruch a special personal message through Jeremiah about humility in service (ch 45).

Baruch read the words of Jeremiah's prophecy to the people and to the princes (Jer 36:9-19). The message finally reached Jehoiakim, who destroyed the scroll and called for Baruch's and Jeremiah's arrest (vv 21-26). In hiding, Baruch again wrote down Jeremiah's prediction of Judah's destruction (vv 27-32).

Baruch was the brother of Seraiah, a close associate of the later King Zedekiah. Seraiah was eventually deported to Babylon with the king by Nebuchadnezzar. With Nebuchadnezzar laying siege to Jerusalem in 587 BC, a year before its final destruction, the imprisoned Jeremiah purchased a field. His act symbolized the eventual restoration of Israel to the land. Baruch was ordered by Jeremiah to keep the evidence of the purchase safe (Jer 32:12-15).

Two months after the destruction of Jerusalem in 586 BC, rebellious Jews murdered Gedaliah, puppet governor of Judah under the Babylonians, and sought to flee to Egypt. Jeremiah advised them to remain in Jerusalem. The rebels blamed Baruch for influencing Jeremiah to give such advice and forced both Baruch and the prophet to accompany them into Egypt (43:1-7).

Scripture does not refer to the final events in Baruch's life. The Jewish historian Josephus recorded that when Nebuchadnezzar invaded Egypt, Baruch was taken to Babylon. The apocryphal book of Baruch begins by noting that the author was in Babylon (1:1-3). Both accounts, however, are historically questionable.

2. Zabbai's son, mentioned in connection with the events surrounding the rebuilding of the Jerusalem wall (about 445 BC) under the supervision of Nehemiah (Neh 3:20).

3. Individual who signed Ezra's covenant of faithfulness to God with Nehemiah and others after the exile (Neh 10:6); perhaps the same as #2 above.

4. Col-hozeh's son, and father of Maaseiah (Neh 11:5).

BARUCH, Book of Deuterocanonical work named after Baruch, who was secretary to the prophet Jeremiah. In antiquity several books were ascribed to Baruch, whose well-known connection with Jeremiah undoubtedly increased their circulation and acceptance. This one emphasizes the righteousness and wisdom of God, at the same time implying that God in his mercy will listen to the supplications of the penitent. It acknowledges that the Jews deserve punishment for their sins from a righteous God. The final passages urge the people of Israel not to be downcast, because a compassionate God will restore them to glory.

The book of Baruch purports to be an account of Jewish exiles in Babylon who fast, weep, and pray over the difficulties of their present position as they remember their past disobedience to God. They formulate a plan to raise a sum of money and send it to the high priest in Jerusalem so that offerings can be made on their behalf. In addition, they send the book of Baruch, which has been read previously to the Jews in Babylon, asking that it be read, particularly on feast days and at "appointed seasons," and be incorporated into the liturgy. They urge the high priest to pray for the well-being of the Babylonian king Nebuchadnezzar and his son so that "the Lord will give us strength, and he will give light to our eyes, and we shall live under the protection of . . . Belshazzar his son, and we shall serve them many days and find favor in their sight" (Bar 1:12, RSV).

A confession that follows the introductory section is in the form of a prayer. The Jews acknowledge that the calamities befalling Israel since the time of Moses are a result of their own sin. They affirm that God is just and they beg his mercy and forgiveness. "Righteousness belongs to the Lord our God, but confusion of face to us and our fathers, as at this day" (Bar 2:6, RSV). The Jews implore God not to punish them for their acts of disobedience and particularly for not having served the king of Babylon as the Lord had decreed. "Hear, O Lord, our prayer and our supplication, and for thy own sake deliver us, and grant us favor in the sight of those who have carried us into exile" (v 14, RSV).

The Jews are then exhorted to adhere strictly to God's law and to rediscover the wisdom that they alone possess, as embodied in the Torah. They are instructed to walk in the ways of God and not to put their trust in gold, silver, or material possessions. The wisdom commended is not the speculative variety occurring in another apocryphal book, the Wisdom of Solomon, but the more practical wisdom found in the canonical OT writings. The intent was evidently to reinforce the conviction that the faithful remnant were still God's special possession and had a future ministry.

The final section comprises a lamentation followed by a brief glimpse of the glory and deliverance that God has in store for a faithful, penitent Israel: "Take off the garment of your sorrow and affliction, O Jerusalem, and put on for ever the beauty of the glory from God. Put on the robe of righteousness from God; put on your head the diadem of the glory of the Everlasting" (Bar 5:1-2, RSV).

After the fifth chapter, according to the Latin Vulgate, is appended "The Letter of Jeremiah." This document, supposedly sent to the Judeans about to be taken captive in Babylonia, is actually a religious tract condemning idolatry.

The book of Baruch was probably the work of several authors and may have been put together by the writer of the introductory section. The confession borrows heavily from the ninth chapter of Daniel. The prayers for forgiveness show strong similarities to biblical prophetic writings. The section of wisdom poetry is quite different in style, resembling Job 28 and 29. The final paragraph suggests Isaiah 40–45 as a source.

Considerable discussion has arisen over the date of the work. It is most likely that the book was originally written in Hebrew and translated into Greek. The translator was very likely the same person who translated the book of Jeremiah for the Septuagint (ancient Greek version of the Old Testament). A date of 582 BC has been proposed on the basis of internal evidence from the first section. A considerably later date is much more likely, possibly in the second century BC.

Although the book circulated widely among dispersed Jews, its influence was greater and lasted longer in the early Christian church. It was highly esteemed and frequently quoted by early theologians. The work was accepted as canonical by the Roman Catholic Church at the Council of Trent (1545–63).

BARZILLAI

1. One of three men who offered hospitality to David and his supporters at Mahanaim during the dangerous time of Absalom's rebellion (2 Sm 17:27). After Absalom was defeated, Barzillai, a Gileadite, came to the Jordan River as David prepared to cross it in a triumphant return to Jerusalem. The 80-year-old Barzillai declined King David's invitation to be his permanent guest in Jerusalem but sent his son Chimham in his place (19:31-40; cf. 1 Kgs 2:7).
2. Adriel's father. Adriel married Saul's daughter Merab (2 Sm 21:8; cf. 1 Sm 18:19). Barzillai was thus the paternal grandfather of five of the seven men hanged in Gibeon in recompense for Saul's guilt in trying to wipe out all Gibeonites (2 Sm 21:1-9).
3. Priest who married the daughter (or descendant) of #1 above and adopted the family name. His descendants returned to Jerusalem in 538 BC with Zerubbabel after the exile. They were refused priestly status because they had lost the genealogies establishing their heritage and priestly descent (Ezr 2:61; Neh 7:63).

BASEMATH

1. Daughter of Elon the Hittite. Basemath was a Canaanite woman whom Esau married against his parents' wishes (Gn 26:34). Basemath may be the same as Elon's daughter Adah, or perhaps was her sister (36:2).
2. Ishmael's daughter, who married Esau (Gn 36:3) and bore Reuel to him (vv 4, 10). This Basemath is probably the same as Ishmael's daughter Mahalath (28:9). Since Ishmael was the son of the patriarch Abraham, this marriage would have been more acceptable to Isaac and Rebekah (36:6-8).

   See also Mahalath (Person) #1.

Identifications of #1 and #2 above are somewhat confused. Most scholars suspect that Esau married Elon's daughter Adah (Gn 36:2-4), who was also called Basemath (26:34). Later, Esau married Ishmael's daughter Mahalath (28:9), who was likewise called Basemath (36:3-4). That two of Esau's wives should be named Basemath could be because Esau chose to give both the same affectionate name, which means "fragrant."

3. King Solomon's daughter who married Ahimaaz, the king's administrator in Naphtali (1 Kgs 4:15).

BASHAN Region east and northeast of the Sea of Galilee. The exact boundaries of Bashan are difficult to determine, but it extended approximately 35 to 40 miles (55 to 64 kilometers) from the foot of Mt Hermon in the north to the Yarmuk River in the south, and stretched some 60 to 70 miles (97 to 113 kilometers) eastward from the Sea of Galilee.

The region ("Hauran," Ez 47:16, 18) is mostly a fertile tableland 1,600 to 2,300 feet (488 to 701 meters) in altitude. Its rich volcanic alluvium is well watered because the low hills of southern Galilee to the west allow the rains to sweep farther inland than in most other places along the Palestinian coast. Today, as in ancient times, it is an agriculturally productive region. In NT times it was a grain-producing area of the Roman Empire. Bashan was known for the quality of its cattle and sheep (Dt 32:14; Ez 39:18; Am 4:1).

In the patriarch Abraham's day, Bashan's inhabitants were giantlike people called Rephaim (Gn 14:5). Og, the last of the Rephaim, was an enemy of the Israelites as they sought to enter Canaan after their Egyptian bondage and wilderness wandering (Dt 29:7). Og was defeated and slain by the Israelites (Nm 21:33-35). Bashan's prosperity at that time is indicated by the fact that one of its provinces, Argob, had 60 great walled cities (Dt 3:4-5). The chief cities of Bashan were Edrei, Ashtaroth, Golan, and Salecah. After Israel conquered the territory east of the Jordan River, Bashan was given to the half-tribe of Manasseh (Jos 13:29-30). Golan and Ashtaroth, two cities in Bashan, were reserved for the Levites (1 Chr 6:71). Ben-geber of Ramoth-gilead administered Argob (a region in Bashan) for King Solomon (1 Kgs 4:13). In the days of Jehu (841–814 BC), King Hazael of Syria conquered the area (2 Kgs 10:33). Tiglath-pileser III incorporated Bashan into the Assyrian Empire in the eighth century BC (15:29). The Nabateans held it in the second century BC, and Herod the Great (37–4 BC) ruled over it at the time of Jesus' birth.

BASHAN-HAVOTH-JAIR* KJV translation in Deuteronomy 3:14 for Havvoth-jair, 60 villages in the region of Bashan. *See* Havoth-jair, Havvoth-jair.

BASHEMATH*
1. KJV form of Basemath, one of Esau's wives, in Genesis 26:34. *See* Basemath #1.
2. KJV form of Basemath, another of Esau's wives in Genesis 36:3, known also as Mahalath. *See* Mahalath (Person) #1.

BASILISK* Word used to translate a particular Hebrew word in two passages of some editions of the KJV (Prv 23:32; Is 14:29). "Basilisk" refers to a kind of lizard and is a mistranslation. It has been corrected to read "adder" or "viper" in later KJV printings and in more recent translations.

BASKAMA Site where Trypho, commander of the Seleucid army, killed his captive, Jonathan Maccabeus. Trypho was holding Jonathan hostage, and when Jonathan was no longer useful, Trypho put him to the sword (1 Macc 12:42–13:23). Exactly where Baskama is located is unknown. The most popular suggestion is Tell el-Jummeizeh ("sycamore tree") near the northeast shore of the Sea of Galilee. That Arabic name is perhaps related to Baskama, which can mean "house of the sycamore." Ancient ruins there might have been a shrine to Jonathan, a great hero. The Jewish historian Josephus calls the spot Basaca.

BASMATH* KJV form of Basemath, King Solomon's daughter, in 1 Kings 4:15. *See* Basemath #3.

BAT Mouselike flying mammal with a furry body and membranous wings, included in the two lists of unclean birds (Lv 11:19; Dt 14:18). *See* Animals.

BATH Unit of liquid measure in the OT (Ez 45:10-11), equal to about six gallons (23 liters). *See* Weights and Measures.

BATHE, BATHING To cleanse as with water; to wash oneself. In the Bible the terms "bathing" and "washing" translate, often interchangeably, a number of different words. One OT passage uses one Hebrew word for cleaning clothes, another for washing other objects, including the body (Lv 15:8-12).

Israel's dry climate and scarcity of water discouraged bathing except where a stream or pool was available (2 Kgs 5:10; Jn 9:7). Yet people still washed babies at birth (Ez 16:4), dead bodies in preparation for burial (Acts 9:37), and sheep for their shearing (Sg 6:6). Frequent bathing of the whole body was probably reserved for the rich (Ex 2:5), but the prevalence of dust made frequent washing of the face, hands, and feet necessary (Gn 18:4; 19:2; 24:32; 43:24; Jgs 19:21; Sg 5:3). Good grooming for the privileged demanded washing of one's body before anointing with oil (Ru 3:3; 2 Sm 12:20; Ez 23:41). A good host provided water for a guest's feet (Gn 18:4; Jgs 19:21; Lk 7:44; Jn

13:4-5). To wash someone's feet was the task of a servant. For anyone else to do so was a sign of humility (1 Sm 25:41; Lk 7:44-47; Jn 13:3-16; 1 Tm 5:10).

Most biblical references to washing or bathing deal with ritual cleansing. Priests and Levites were required to wash their clothes and faces, and sometimes bodies, before approaching the altar and on ceremonial occasions (Ex 29:4; 30:19-21; 40:7, 12, 30-32; Nm 8:21). Before a slain animal was sacrificed, its legs and intestines were washed (Lv 1:9, 13; 8:21; 9:14). Anyone who was once unclean (e.g., a leper who was healed or someone who had experienced a genital discharge) had to wash his or her clothes and bathe to be ritually pure (Lv 14:8-10; 15:5-11, 21-27). Any garment that became polluted had to be ceremonially cleansed (Lv 6:27; 13:54).

"Washing" is also used figuratively for a cleansing from sin (Ps 51:2; Is 1:16; 4:4; Jer 2:22; 4:14; 1 Cor 6:11; Heb 10:22).

BATH-RABBIM, Gate of Gate in the city of Heshbon near which were several pools of clear water. A poetic biblical passage described a young woman's eyes as being like those pools (Sg 7:4).

BATHSHEBA Uriah's wife, with whom David committed adultery and whom he later married. Bathsheba, also spelled Bathshua (1 Chr 3:5), was the daughter of Ammiel or Eliam (2 Sm 11:3) and possibly the granddaughter of Ahithophel, the king's adviser (2 Sm 15:12; 23:34). Her Hittite husband was one of David's top military heroes (2 Sm 23:39).

While Uriah was off fighting under Joab, King David saw a beautiful woman taking her evening bath. Discovering her name and that her husband was away on duty, he sent for Bathsheba and had sexual intercourse with her (2 Sm 11:1-4). When Bathsheba later informed him that she was pregnant, the king ordered Uriah back to Jerusalem, hoping that the husband's return would make Bathsheba's pregnancy appear legitimate. But Uriah considered himself still on active duty and slept with the palace guard, refusing to go home (vv 5-13). Frustrated, David sent him back to the front and ordered Joab to put Uriah in the front lines and then pull back. Consequently, Uriah was killed (vv 14-25).

After Bathsheba's period of mourning, David installed her in the palace as his seventh wife, and she bore the child. The Lord sent the prophet Nathan to pronounce judgment on David's sin through a parable. Nathan prophesied a series of tragedies in David's household, beginning with the death of Bathsheba's infant son (2 Sm 11:26–12:14). David confessed his sin and repented, but the infant became sick and died. The prologue (or superscription) of Psalm 51 describes it as the psalm of repentance David wrote when confronted by Nathan over his adultery with Bathsheba and his murder of Uriah. David comforted Bathsheba, and eventually they had other children (2 Sm 12:15-25).

Of David's 19 sons by his seven wives (1 Chr 3:1-9), the sons born to Bathsheba were Shimea (also spelled Shammua, 2 Sm 5:14; 1 Chr 14:4), Shobab, Nathan, and Solomon. Nathan (Lk 3:31) and Solomon (Mt 1:6) appear in NT genealogies of Jesus Christ. Bathsheba also appears in Matthew's genealogy under the description "she who had been the wife of Uriah." At the very end of David's life, the prophet Nathan told Bathsheba that David's son Adonijah (by his wife Haggith) was conspiring to usurp the throne. Bathsheba and Nathan persuaded David to make Solomon king as he had promised (1 Kgs 1).

See also David.

BATHSHUA

1. Canaanite wife of Judah who bore him three sons: Er, Onan, and Shelah (Gn 38:2-5; 1 Chr 2:3).
2. Alternate spelling of Bathsheba in 1 Chronicles 3:5. See Bathsheba.

BATTERING RAM Ancient military machine with a heavy wooden beam used to batter down gates or walls. Some battering rams had an iron ram's head at the end of the beam. See Armor and Weapons.

BATTLE-AX Heavy ax with a wide blade used as a weapon of war. See Armor and Weapons.

BATTLEMENT Defensive wall, with openings for shooting, on top of a fortress; by extension, a parapet or railing around any flat roof. Houses in the Near East were built with flat roofs, which were used for many different purposes. Rahab hid two Israelite spies on her roof (Jos 2:6). Saul slept on Samuel's roof (1 Sm 9:25). King David from his roof saw Bathsheba taking a bath (2 Sm 11:2). People celebrated on rooftops (Is 22:1-2). Peter prayed on his roof (Acts 10:9). With so much activity on rooftops, it is easy to understand the need for the law "When you build a new house, you shall make a parapet for your roof, that you may not bring the guilt of blood upon your house, if any one fall from it" (Dt 22:8, RSV).

City walls often had battlements at the gates and corners from which the city could be defended from attack. Hebrew words for such fortifications are often translated "towers" (2 Chr 26:15; Zep 1:16).

BAVVAI* Individual who directed the repair of a section of the Jerusalem wall under Nehemiah's supervision (Neh 3:18). Bavvai was Henadad's son and the official of half the district of Keilah, a town 17 miles (27.4 kilometers) southwest of Jerusalem. Binnui (Neh 3:24), also mentioned as Henadad's son (cf. Ezr 3:9), may be a corrupted spelling of Bavvai, or the two may have been brothers. See Binnui #4.

BAY TREE* Tree 40 to 60 feet (12 to 18 meters) high with fragrant, evergreen leaves and native to the Holy Land. See Plants (Laurel or Sweet Bay).

BAZLITH*, BAZLUTH Ancestor of a group of temple assistants returning to Jerusalem with Zerubbabel after the exile (Ezr 2:52, "Bazluth"; Neh 7:54).

BDELLIUM* Substance mentioned twice in the OT, evidently the resinous gum of an Arabian shrub (known scientifically as Commiphora africana). The same genus of Middle Eastern plants includes the shrub from which myrrh is derived and possibly the one from which the biblical "balm" was obtained.

Apart from the Bible, bdellium was described by an English herbalist as an aromatic gum from a tree known in Persia and eastward. In the first century AD the Roman writer Pliny mentioned the same tree and described the gum as waxlike and looking like pearl.

The manna gathered by the Israelites is described in the Bible as having the same color as bdellium (Nm 11:7). Bdellium is also mentioned along with the gold and onyx stone found near the Garden of Eden (Gn 2:12). Because it was included in that list, bdellium was once thought to be pearl or a precious stone.

See also Plants.

BEALIAH Warrior from Benjamin's tribe who joined David at Ziklag in his struggle against King Saul. Bealiah

was one of David's ambidextrous archers and slingers (1 Chr 12:5).

BEALOTH

1. Town along the border of Edom in the Negev Desert area (Jos 15:24).
2. Administrative district in the time of King Solomon governed by Baana, Hushai's son (1 Kgs 4:16).

BEAM

1. Weaver's beam—round wooden roller on which the cloth or carpet was wound during the weaving process in Bible times. The spears of the giant Goliath (1 Sm 17:7; 2 Sm 21:19; 1 Chr 20:5) and an Egyptian killed by Benaiah, one of David's mighty men (1 Chr 11:23), were compared to a weaver's beam.
2. Tree trunk or log that has been squared and used for building purposes. King Solomon used beams and planks of cedar to build the temple (1 Kgs 6:9; 2 Chr 3:7) and his "House of the Forest of Lebanon" (1 Kgs 7:2, 12). Another mention of cedar beams probably refers to their aroma (Sg 1:17).
3. Crossbeam of a Hebrew balance from which the scales were hung by cords.
4. Beam (KJV) or log (RSV) referred to by Jesus (Mt 7:3-5; Lk 6:41-42). Jesus contrasted the beam in an accuser's eye with the mote (KJV) or speck (RSV) in his brother's eye.

BEAN Any of various plants of the legume family, and part of the diet of the peoples of Bible lands. See Agriculture; Plants; Food and Food Preparation.

BEAR (Animal) Large, short-tailed, shaggy animal that feeds on plants as well as small animals. The bear mentioned several times in the Bible is the Syrian brown bear still found in Syria and Turkey but no longer in Israel. See Animals.

BEAR (Astronomy) Constellation of stars (Ursa Major, also known as the Big Dipper) mentioned in Job 9:9 and 38:32. See Astronomy.

BEARD Hair growing on the lower part of a man's face, worn as a sign of maturity among all ancient Semitic peoples, including the Israelites. Among the Israelites, care of the beard took on religious significance (Lv 19:27). Levitical law prohibited priests from shaving their heads or clipping their beards (21:5-6). David's ambassadors to an Ammonite king were humiliated by having one side of their beards shaved off by the Ammonites. That indignity and others led to war (2 Sm 10:1-8). Removal of an Israelite's beard, however, was considered appropriate under certain circumstances. Suspicion of leprosy on the head or face required shaving around the suspected spot to permit better diagnosis (Lv 13:29-37). A shaven head, along with wailing and the wearing of sackcloth, was a way of proclaiming impending or prevailing doom (Is 15:1-3). Ezra dramatized Israel's spiritual disaster by pulling hair out of his head and beard (Ezr 9:3).

BEAST Animal in both the OT and NT, having in some cases a figurative significance. The word has a variety of meanings in the OT. Some of the diversity is due to inconsistent translations of several Hebrew words that can signify "living creature" as well as "beast," but which have sometimes been translated only as "beast." In the OT, therefore, beast can refer to the following:

1. In general, any animal (e.g., Gn 1:24; Ps 36:6), but

often distinguished from fish, birds, and insects (e.g., Gn 6:7; Lv 11:2; Dt 4:17; Jb 12:7; 35:11; Zep 1:3).

2. A domesticated animal (e.g., Ex 19:13; 22:10; Nm 3:13; 31:47; Jgs 20:48; Prv 12:10; Jer 21:6; Zec 8:10).

3. A wild and sometimes carnivorous animal (e.g., Gn 37:20; Ex 23:11; Dt 28:26; 1 Sm 17:44; Ez 14:15).

4. The figurative usage of the word "beast" is most apparent in the books of Daniel and Revelation. In Daniel (especially Dn 7) the beast is a symbol of a world ruler who persecutes and oppresses the people of God. In Revelation the apostle John took over that concept with its vivid imagery to speak of the final persecution of God's people at the end of history. John's beast in its apostasy closely resembles the "antichrist" of his earlier epistles (1 Jn 2:18, 22; 4:3; 2 Jn 1:7) and Paul's "man of lawlessness" (2 Thes 2:3). Many Bible commentators regard the three as designating the same individual. *See* Antichrist; Armageddon; Mark of the Beast; Revelation, Book of.

BEATITUDES*, The Term derived from Latin *beatitudo*; it is not used in the English Bible. Technically it means "blessedness" as described in the OT and NT. "Blessed" is translated from both Hebrew and Greek words to refer to divine favor conveyed to people.

The formal utterance "happy is," or "blessed is," is a common declaration in the book of Psalms (used 26 times) and Proverbs (8 times). It is used 10 times in the other books of the OT and 13 times in the apocryphal books. These beatitudes are pronounced upon the person who is righteous, having faith and hope in God. They are signs of a life lived in proximity to Yahweh, in the experience of forgiveness, and in the love and favor of God. Such life is a totality, so such blessings are expressive of holistic enrichment, harmony, and fecundity, whether in family life, in temple worship, in public life, or in the interior of one's own being. The person so blessed is in touch with the fruitfulness of the Creator himself. Such a one lives a fulfilled life, life as God intended it to be lived before him.

THE BEATITUDES, MATTHEW 5:1-12, NLT
One day as the crowds were gathering, Jesus went up the mountainside with his disciples and sat down to teach them.

² This is what he taught them:

³ "God blesses those who realize their need for him, for the Kingdom of Heaven is given to them.
⁴ God blesses those who mourn, for they will be comforted.
⁵ God blesses those who are gentle and lowly, for the whole earth will belong to them.
⁶ God blesses those who are hungry and thirsty for justice, for they will receive it in full.
⁷ God blesses those who are merciful, for they will be shown mercy.
⁸ God blesses those whose hearts are pure, for they will see God.
⁹ God blesses those who work for peace, for they will be called the children of God.
¹⁰ God blesses those who are persecuted because they live for God, for the Kingdom of Heaven is theirs.

¹¹ "God blesses you when you are mocked and persecuted and lied about because you are my followers. ¹² Be happy about it! Be very glad! For a great reward awaits you in heaven. And remember, the ancient prophets were persecuted, too.

In the NT, references to "blessing" occur seven times in the book of Revelation, three times in the Epistle to the Romans, and once in John's Gospel. The prominence of "blessedness" in Matthew and Luke gives rise to the technical term "Beatitudes." There are interesting contrasts between Luke's "sermon on the plain" (Lk 6:20-23) and Matthew's "sermon on the mount" (Mt 5:3-12). The pronouncement of the blessings in Luke is done immediately after the selection of the 12 disciples (Lk 6:12-16). Yet the sermon is addressed to the crowd generally and speaks of the advent of God's kingdom as the reversal of the social conditions of the human race. So Luke balances four blessings with four woes—changing from the present tense to the future tense—to heighten the contrast of the impending reversal of social conditions.

In Matthew's account, the advent of the kingdom has already commenced, indicated by the use of the present tense. It is addressed to the disciples particularly and is not a general proclamation. The sermon is set within two statements of Jesus: he has not come to destroy but to fulfill the Mosaic law (Mt 5:17); and it is necessary to have a kind of righteousness that exceeds that of the scribes and Pharisees (Mt 5:20). So these Beatitudes are more concerned with the interior life of the disciple, to activate here and now the kind of life Jesus communicates in those who follow him, for Jesus has already inaugurated the kingdom. These eight Beatitudes reflect on the traits of those who belong to that kingdom and who therefore reflect Christ's own life. The people and situations described may seem pitiable by human standards, but because of God's presence in their lives, they are actually blessed and should be congratulated and imitated. *See* Jesus Christ, Life and Teachings of.

BEAUTIFUL GATE Gate of Herod's temple in Jerusalem where a man born lame was miraculously healed through the ministry of Peter and John (Acts 3:2, 10). The location of this gate is uncertain, but it was probably the gate leading from the Court of the Gentiles into the Women's Court, called the Corinthian Gate (for its Corinthian bronze) by the Jewish historian Josephus. According to him, it measured 75 feet (22.9 meters) high by 60 feet (18.3 meters) wide. A burial inscription found on Mt Olivet attributes the building of the gate to an Alexandrian Jew named Nicanor.
See also Temple.

BEAUTY Harmonious combination of qualities pleasant to see. Archaeological materials indicate that the ancient Hebrews were concerned more with usefulness than with beauty. Hebrew pottery, for example, was generally more bulky than Canaanite pottery. Yet such artifacts do not mean that the Hebrews had no aesthetic appreciation.

The OT speaks of God's creation as beautiful (Gn 2:9; Jb 26:13; Ps 19:1-6; Sg 6:10). The land of Canaan is a "pleasant land" (Jer 3:19). Jerusalem is called "beautiful" (Is 52:1; Lam 2:15), as is one of its temple gates (Acts 3:2, 10). The Hebrews admired the wild grandeur of the Lebanon mountain range (Ps 104:16; Is 60:13). The Canaanite city of Tirzah ("beauty"), King Baasha's capital in the northern kingdom (1 Kgs 15:33), was so named for its attractive location.

Although the Hebrews did not exalt the human form as did the ancient Greeks, the OT does idealize physical attractiveness. A bride's beauty is described eloquently by her bridegroom in love lyrics in Song of Songs 4:1-15; 6:4. Such praise of the bride may have been a traditional feature of Israelite weddings. Several women prominent in the OT are described as beautiful (Gn 29:17; 2 Sm

11:2; Est 2:7). But sensual beauty was secondary to industry, resourcefulness, and traditional piety in a woman (Prv 31:10-31). A number of men also were known for their physical attractiveness—for example, David (1 Sm 16:12) and Absalom (2 Sm 14:25). Cosmetics, jewelry, and other accessories were used as female beauty aids in OT times. The prophet Isaiah listed such items (Is 3:18-24), and Ezekiel mentioned cosmetic practices current in his day (Ez 16:10-13). Israelite worship was beautiful, too, with the high priest's elaborate ceremonial robes designed for glory and beauty (Ex 28:2, 40).

The concept of beauty is applied also to God in the OT. The Lord's favor is called his "beauty" (Ps 90:17). Isaiah recorded God's promise to give his people "beauty for ashes" (Is 61:3). The psalmist expressed a desire to spend time in the temple enjoying the Lord's beauty, his "incomparable perfections" (Ps 27:4). Isaiah described God as a "diadem of beauty" to the faithful Israelite remnant (Is 28:5), and the Messiah was spoken of as a beautiful king (33:17). Thus in the OT the concept of beauty had a deeper meaning than simply physical attractiveness. It became a theological concept affirming God's essential glory.

The NT urges Christ's followers to live lives that will "adorn" the teaching of the Savior, making it attractive to nonbelievers (Ti 2:10). Those who preach the gospel of Christ are spoken of as beautiful (Rom 10:15). The apostles Paul and Peter warned women against being satisfied with outward beauty (1 Tm 2:9-10), reminding them that beautiful character is the true adornment of godliness (1 Pt 3:3-5). The beauty of the believer's final home in heaven is reflected in the description of the "new Jerusalem" as a bride and in the symbolism of treasured precious stones of antiquity (see Rv 21–22).

BEBAI (Person)
1. Ancestor of a family that returned to Jerusalem with Zerubbabel after the exile (Ezr 2:11; 8:11; Neh 7:16). Some of the members of that family were guilty of marrying foreign women (Ezr 10:28).
2. Levitical leader of Israel who signed Ezra's covenant of faithfulness to God with Nehemiah and others after the exile (Neh 10:15). This individual was perhaps a member of the family of #1 above.

BEBAI (Place) Unidentified Israelite city mentioned in Judith 15:4.

BECHER*, BECHERITE*
1. Benjamin's second son, who migrated to Egypt with his grandfather Jacob (Gn 46:21; 1 Chr 7:6).
2. Ephraim's second son, from whom the family of Becherites originated (Nm 26:35). He is also called Bered (1 Chr 7:20).

BECORATH Zeror's father, a member of Benjamin's tribe and an ancestor of King Saul (1 Sm 9:1).

BECTILETH Plain mentioned only in the Apocrypha. Nebuchadnezzar's general, Holofernes, camped there on his western conquest (Jdt 2:21-23).

BED See Furniture.

BEDAD Father of Hadad, one of the kings of Edom before the Israelite monarchy (Gn 36:35; 1 Chr 1:46).

BEDAN
1. One of Israel's deliverers, along with Gideon, Jephthah, and Samuel, during the time of the judges

(1 Sm 12:11, KJV; RSV mg). The name Bedan may be either a shortened form of Abdon (Jgs 12:13) or a scribal error for Barak (Jgs 4:6).
2. Ulam's son, a descendant of Manasseh (1 Chr 7:17).

BEDEIAH Bani's son, who obeyed Ezra's exhortation to divorce his pagan wife after the exile (Ezr 10:35).

BEE See Animals.

BEELIADA* Former name of Eliada, one of King David's sons, in 1 Chronicles 14:7. See Eliada #1.

BEELZEBUL* Epithet meaning "lord of the flies" or "lord of the manure pile," referring to Satan. It was used against Jesus by his enemies (Mt 10:25, KJV "Beelzebub"; 12:24; Lk 11:15). See Baal-zebub.

BEER
1. Israelite campsite on their wilderness journey, probably just north of the Arnon River on the Moabite-Amorite border (Nm 21:16). The name means "a well." Water from the well they dug there was commemorated in a song (Nm 21:17-18). A Moabite well that was later called Beer-elim (Is 15:8) may have been the same location. See Wilderness Wanderings.
2. Place to which Gideon's son Jotham escaped after telling a parable against his half brother Abimelech, who had killed all the other sons of Gideon in an attempt to become king of Israel (Jgs 9:21).

BEERA Zophah's son, a warrior in Asher's tribe (1 Chr 7:37).

BEERAH Chief of Reuben's tribe (1 Chr 5:6, 26) taken captive by the Assyrian king Tilgath-pilneser (a later spelling of Tiglath-pileser).

BEER-ELIM One of the cities of Moab that Isaiah predicted would hear wailing at the fall of the Moabite kingdom (Is 15:8); perhaps the same as Beer (Nm 21:16).

BEERI
1. Judith's Hittite (Hethite) father. Judith was one of the wives of Esau (Gn 26:34).
2. Father of Hosea the prophet (Hos 1:1).

BEER-LAHAIROI Well between Kadesh and Bered where Hagar, pregnant with Ishmael, was confronted by the angel of the Lord (Gn 16:7-14). The name given to the site means "the well of the Living One who sees me," referring to God's appearance to Sarai's servant girl. Later, it became a frequent watering place for Isaac on his travels (Gn 24:62; 25:11).

BEEROTH One of four Hivite cities that secured Joshua's promise not to destroy them when the Israelites marched into Canaan (Jos 9:17). Beeroth was later identified as a city in Benjamin's territory (Jos 18:25; 2 Sm 4:2-3). It was the home of Rechab and Baanah, assassins of King Ishbosheth (2 Sm 4:2-9), and of Naharai, Joab's armor bearer (2 Sm 23:37; 1 Chr 11:39). The city was repopulated after the exile (Ezr 2:25; Neh 7:29). El Bireh near Ramallah and Nebi Samwil north of Jerusalem have both been suggested as possible locations for Beeroth.

BEEROTH BENE-JAAKAN* Site where the Israelites camped during their wilderness journey from Egypt, near

Moserah or Moseroth (Dt 10:6; see NLT mg); also called
Bene-jaakan in Numbers 33:31-32. Beeroth Bene-jaakan
means "well of Jaakan's sons." *See* Wilderness Wanderings.

BEEROTHITE* Inhabitant of Beeroth (2 Sm 4:2-9, KJV,
RSV). *See* Beeroth.

BEERSHEBA Scriptural designation for the southern
extremity of the Promised Land, located 28 miles (45.1
kilometers) southwest of Hebron. It was an important
Negev site at an early time. Hagar wandered with
Ishmael in this area, as did Abraham. Later Isaac (Gn
26:23) and Jacob (46:1) both had significant spiritual
experiences there, and later yet it was important in the
lives of numerous other Hebrews.

Beersheba of the Hebrew monarchy period was
located at Tell Beersheba, two miles (3.2 kilometers)
northeast of the modern city. Recent excavations reveal
that the city was founded by the Hebrews in the 12th or
11th century BC and probably was the place where the
sons of Samuel judged the people (1 Sm 8:2).

This city was only about two and a half acres (one
hectare) in size. In its ruins there were the remains of a
horned altar, which when reassembled stood to a height
of about five feet (1.5 meters). This is the same height as
the altar found at Arad, and the two are the only Hebrew
altars yet found that date to the period of the first temple. These altars were the same height as the one in the
tabernacle (Ex 27:1) and probably the same as the original altar in Solomon's temple (2 Chr 6:13). A great water
system was also uncovered similar to those of Megiddo
and Hazor.

BE-ESHTERAH City of the half-tribe of Manasseh
given to the Levitical family of Gershonites in the partitioning of the Promised Land (Jos 21:27). The spelling is
a shortened form for Beth-ashtaroth ("house or place
of Ashtaroth"). It seems to be the same as the city of
Ashtaroth found in a similar passage (1 Chr 6:71). *See*
Ashtaroth, Ashterathite; Levitical Cities.

BEETLE* KJV for cricket in Leviticus 11:22. *See* Animals
(Cricket).

BEGGAR One who asks for charity, especially one who
lives by begging, a mendicant.

Biblical references to begging are limited to such
Hebrew verbs as "to seek" or "to ask," and, as a noun, to
"the poor and needy"; in the NT, Greek terms refer to
being "poor" or "miserable," and to those who "ask for
more." Professional beggars were unknown in Moses'
time, since the law made ample provision for taking care
of the poor.

Earliest legislation (Dt 15:11) mandated the care of
those who were poor. There were regulations such as the
Sabbath year, the year of remission to those indebted (Lv
25). In that year the produce of the land was left to the
poor and destitute (Ex 23:11), and all debts were canceled (Dt 15:1). The duty of lending liberally to the poor
was promoted (vv 7-11), and hired laborers were protected (24:14-15). The purpose was that "there should be
no more poor among you" (15:4). Indeed, in the early
days of Israelite settlement, all Israelites enjoyed a comparable standard of living.

In excavations at Tirsah near Nablus, the size and
arrangements of houses of the tenth century BC are all
about the same. By the eighth century BC, there is a striking
contrast, with houses on the same site clearly divided into
the town's richer and poorer quarters. The social revolu-

tion between those two centuries was associated with the
rise of the Israelite monarchy and growth of a class of officials who gained private profits from their positions. The
prophets condemned the fact that wealth was ill-gotten
and badly distributed in their day (e.g., Is 5:8; Hos 12:8;
Am 8:4-7; Mi 2:2). The prophet Amos denounced creditors who felt no pity for the poor (Am 2:6-8; 8:6). Yet,
throughout the OT, there is essentially no reference to
beggars. During the intertestamental period, however,
almsgiving became an important religious duty.

Aerial View of Tell Beersheba

In the NT, begging seems to be prevalent. In the ministry of Jesus, references are made to a blind beggar (Jn
9:8-9), to blind Bartimaeus (Mk 10:46-52), and to Lazarus, a godly beggar who is contrasted with a rich man (Lk
16:19-31). The apostles Peter and John encountered a
crippled beggar by the "Beautiful," or Nicanor, Gate in
Jerusalem (Acts 3:1-11). Jesus rebuked an ostentatious
show of almsgiving (Mt 6:1-4) but stressed the importance of giving to the poor from right motives (Mt
5:42-48). By the time of Jesus, Jerusalem had become a
center for beggars, probably because almsgiving in the
Holy City was then regarded as particularly meritorious.
Begging in Jerusalem was concentrated around the holy
places. The pool of Beth-zatha was a place of healing,
and the sick, blind, lame, and paralyzed lay there to beg
as well as to get into the waters for healing (Jn 5:2-9).

In the early Christian community, the first organization of officers was made to provide for a fair distribution of funds to the poor (Acts 4:32-35; 6:1-6). On the
first day of each week, some portion of each Christian's
income was to be allotted to the needy (11:27-30; Rom
15:25-27; 1 Cor 16:1-4). Possibly the poverty of Palestine was made worse by heavy Roman taxation; tax gatherers as well as beggars are prominent in the Gospel
narratives. It has also been suggested that the rise of the
Zealots was closely associated with the social factor of
poverty; the revolutionary Zealots were largely comprised of society's "dregs," according to the Jewish historian Josephus. In AD 66 the Zealots burned the Jerusalem
archives, no doubt intending to destroy the records of
their debts kept there. Josephus reports that before the
Roman destruction of Jerusalem, gangs of beggars were
terrorizing the whole city. *See* Alms; Poor, The.

BEHEADING Form of execution practiced in Bible
times. *See* Criminal Law and Punishment.

BEHEMOTH Hebrew word in plural form usually translated "beasts" or "wild animals" (as in Dt 28:26; 32:24; Ps 50:10; Is 18:6; 2 Esd 6:49, 51; Hb 2:17). Most English versions refer only once to "behemoth," where the context seems to refer to a specific animal, large and powerful, believed by many biblical scholars to be the hippopotamus (Jb 40:15). In ancient times, the hippopotamus was well known in Egypt and may have inhabited the Jordan Valley. Job 40:23 may, however, refer to any river swollen like the Jordan in flood season. *See* Animals.

BEHISTUN INSCRIPTION* *See* Inscriptions.

BEKA*, BEKAH* Six-gram weight called "half a shekel, by the shekel of the sanctuary" (Ex 38:26). *See* Weights and Measures.

BEKER, BEKERITE Alternate spelling for Ephraim's second son (Nm 26:35) and his descendants. *See* Becher, Becherite #2.

BEL Title of the state god of Babylon, Marduk, mentioned disdainfully by Isaiah (Is 46:1). Jeremiah speaks of Bel (Jer 50:2; 51:44), and Bel is the idol in the apocryphal Bel and the Dragon. *See* Marduk.

BELA (Person)
1. Beor's son, a king of Edom who ruled before Israel had a king (Gn 36:31-33). Because Balaam, the pagan prophet from north Syria, also had a father named Beor (Nm 22:5), some ancients and a number of modern critical scholars have confused the Edomite Bela with Balaam.
2. Benjamin's oldest son (Gn 46:21; 1 Chr 8:1), whose descendants were called Belaites (Nm 26:38).
3. Azaz's son, a descendant of Reuben who lived in Gilead in Transjordan. So vast were his family's holdings that they pastured their cattle as far east as the Euphrates River (1 Chr 5:8-9). In the reign of Saul, his family successfully held their land against Hagrite opposition.

BELA* (Place) Alternate name for Zoar, a city of the plain, in Genesis 14:2. *See* Cities of the Plain; Zoar.

BELAH*, BELAITE KJV rendering of Bela, Benjamin's oldest son, in 1 Chronicles 8:1. His descendants were called Belaites (Nm 26:38-40; see NLT). *See* Bela (Person) #2.

BEL AND THE DRAGON *See* Daniel, Additions to.

BELIAL*, BELIAR* Common Hebrew noun meaning "baseness," "worthlessness," "wickedness," or "lawlessness." Belial, however, is often rendered as a proper noun. Thus, such translations as "sons of Belial" appear (Jgs 19:22; 1 Sm 2:12, KJV), "daughter of Belial" (1 Sm 1:16), or "children of Belial" (Dt 13:13; Jgs 20:13). Newer translations generally apply the common noun form and give such readings as "worthless rabble" or simply "worthless" and the like (Dt 13:13; Jgs 19:22; 20:13; 1 Sm 1:16; 2:12; 10:27; Prv 6:12). One possible exception to this rule is found in Nahum 1:15, which some scholars think should be rendered as "Belial," a personalized designation of the Assyrian conqueror who had been a threat to the southern kingdom of Judah.

Intertestamental literature often used "Belial" as a proper noun and thus prepared the way for its NT usage. In the NT the term appears once as "Belial" (or Beliar in 2 Cor 6:15) and is identified with Satan, the personification of all that is evil. Noncanonical writings of the NT period commonly used it as a name for Satan or the Antichrist.

BELIEF, BELIEVE Conviction based on testimony that something is true or that someone is reliable. As used in the Bible, to believe in God involves the element of trust, not mere acknowledgment of his existence. *See* Faith.

BELIEVERS Those who believe; in the NT, specifically, those who believe in Jesus as Lord and follow him (Acts 5:14). One would expect the term "believers" (sometimes translated "faithful") to be a title for Christians, since the NT stresses belief in Jesus. Although NT authors emphasized believing, they rarely used the term "believer" as a name for Christians. There are a few clear examples (Acts 4:32; 10:45; 19:18; 1 Tm 4:12), but in other places the term is a description, not a name (Acts 2:44; 15:5; 18:27; 1 Tm 4:3). As a name, "believer" points to the personal commitment of Christians to Jesus. Christians were called not merely to believe something but to give themselves to someone.

BELL Small noisemaker. Bells were intermittently attached between ornamental pomegranates around the lower hem of the high priestly robe (Ex 28:33-34; 39:25-26). *See* Musical Instruments (Pamonim); Music.

BELMAIN Samaritan city that served as a camp for Nebuchadnezzar's invading general, Holofernes, against the Jews (Jdt 4:1-4). Probably the same as Balbaim (7:3), Balamon (8:3), and perhaps Bebai (15:4).

BELOVED DISCIPLE* Designation of one disciple, evidently the author of the Gospel of John (Jn 21:20-24). Five passages in John's Gospel mention the disciple whom Jesus loved: (1) The disciple whom Jesus loved lay close to Jesus' chest during the Last Supper and was beckoned by Peter to ask Jesus who the betrayer would be (13:21-26). (2) The disciple whom Jesus loved stood near the cross, and Mary the mother of Jesus was given to his care (19:25-27). (3) Mary Magdalene came to Peter and the disciple whom Jesus loved, reporting that Jesus' body was missing from the tomb (20:2). (4) The disciple whom Jesus loved was in a fishing boat with Peter and the other disciples and recognized Jesus standing on the shore (21:7). (5) The disciple whom Jesus loved was following Jesus by the lakeshore, and the author reminded his readers that this was the same disciple spoken of at the Last Supper (21:20-23; cf. 13:21-26).

Because the phrase is found only in John's Gospel, could it be the author's way of referring to himself? Several passages make that seem very likely.

A list of names given in John 21:2 indicates that the disciples present at the lakeshore were Peter, Thomas, Nathanael, the sons of Zebedee (James and John), and two others. Evidently the beloved disciple was one of the sons of Zebedee or else one of the two unnamed disciples.

The beloved disciple was almost certainly one of the Twelve, since he was present at the Last Supper, and evidently only the 12 disciples were there with Jesus (Mt 26:20; Mk 14:17-20; Lk 22:14, 30). That eliminates Lazarus and John Mark, who have sometimes been suggested as possibilities for the beloved disciple.

The beloved disciple appeared to be close to Peter (Jn 13:23-24; 20:2; 21:7; see also Acts 3; 8:14; Gal 2:9). Matthew, Mark, and Luke record that Peter, James, and John were constantly selected by Jesus to be with him. Since Peter was mentioned in connection with the disciple whom Jesus loved, and since James was martyred early (Acts 12:2), only John is left as a reasonable possibility—if, as is generally regarded, John's Gospel was written long after James's death.

See also John, The Apostle.

BELSHAZZAR Babylonian king who was co-regent with Nabonidus in the final days of the Babylonian Empire. His name means "Bel protect the king." Daniel identifies him as the son of Nebuchadnezzar (Dn 5:2, 11, 13, 18), though in fact he was the natural son of Nabunaid (Nabonidus). The seeming discrepancy arises from the fact that in Hebrew literature "father" may signify "ancestor" or "predecessor," and "son" may designate "descendant" or "successor in office." Some have concluded that Belshazzar's mother was a daughter of Nebuchadnezzar and that Belshazzar was therefore the grandson of the great Babylonian. Clearly his father, Nabunaid, was the son of a nobleman and the high priestess of the moon god at Haran. Nabunaid had usurped the throne in 555 BC.

A greater difficulty in the biblical text is the fact that Daniel presents Belshazzar as the king of Babylon when it fell to the Persians, whereas secular historical records picture Nabunaid as the last king of the Babylonian Empire. Critical scholars have therefore questioned Daniel's accuracy. Inscriptions have now been found, however, which make it clear that Belshazzar's father entrusted the rule of the capital to him and was out of the city for over 10 years campaigning in Arabia. Religious concerns also took Nabunaid out of Babylon during part of his reign. When Cyrus invaded the Babylonian Empire, Nabunaid marched east to meet him but fled before Cyrus's advancing armies. Later he returned to Babylon and surrendered to the Persians after the city had already fallen to Cyrus. Thus he was out of the city when the Persians overcame the royal forces there under the command of Belshazzar, the crown prince and co-regent.

While Nabunaid's armies were being routed by the Persians, Belshazzar was giving a sensual feast for the leaders of Babylonian society. Half drunk, he called for the gold and silver vessels from the Jerusalem temple to be brought in for use in a deliberate act of sacrilege. Immediately handwriting appeared on the wall, his doom was announced, and Persian armies entered the city without a fight (October 12, 539 BC). They did so by diverting the waters of the Euphrates so the river would no longer serve as a moat around the city and its defenses could be easily breached. *See* Daniel, Book of; Babylon, Babylonia.

BELTESHAZZAR Daniel's Babylonian name (Dn 1:7). Daniel was one of the young men taken captive to Babylon to be trained as counselors for King Nebuchadnezzar (ch 1). *See* Daniel (Person) #3.

BEMA* Greek term for a judgment seat or tribunal of a Roman official. Although the term also means "to step" or "stride," it was used in the first century AD primarily to denote an elevated area or platform (reached by steps) from which political orations or judicial decisions were made. Excavations in the city of Corinth have revealed a large, elaborately decorated *bema* located in the center of the marketplace.

In the NT, Jesus was questioned before the judgment seat of Pilate (Mt 27:19; Jn 19:13). Herod Agrippa I addressed the people of Tyre and Sidon from a *bema* (Acts 12:21). The apostle Paul was brought before the

tribunal of Gallio in Corinth (18:12-17) and again before Festus's tribunal in Caesarea (25:6, 10, 17).

In two passages, Paul used the term to refer to God's judgment seat. In Romans 14:10 he warned those who would arrogantly judge others that all must stand before the tribunal of God. According to 2 Corinthians 5:10, the merits of each person's work will be determined before the judgment seat of Christ (cf. 1 Cor 3:13-15).

See also Judgment; Judgment Seat; Last Judgment.

BEN (Noun) Hebrew word often used as a prefix to describe a relationship. Literally meaning "son," it is found some 4,850 times in the OT. The Aramaic equivalent is *bar* (see Mt 16:17).

See also Bar.

BEN* (Person) Levite musician appointed by King David (1 Chr 15:18, KJV). The Masoretic Text (the OT as annotated by medieval Hebrew scholars) and the KJV include the name Ben, but the Septuagint (ancient Greek translation of the OT) and modern versions omit it because it is missing in verses 20 and 21. Since the Masoretic Text also omits it in the later verses, the inclusion of Ben in verse 18 may be a scribal error.

BEN-ABINADAB One of 12 officers appointed to requisition food for King Solomon's household. His administrative district comprised the area around Naphath-dor, the coastal city south of Mt Carmel (1 Kgs 4:11). The name means "son of Abinadab" and probably indicates that Ben-abinadab was the son of Solomon's uncle Abinadab (1 Sm 16:8; 1 Chr 2:13).

BENAIAH Popular name meaning "the Lord has built," used primarily by Levites.

1. Son of Jehoiada the priest, from the south Judean town of Kabzeel. Benaiah was engaged in military service, and his loyalty gained for him the rank of commander in chief of the army during the reign of Solomon (1 Kgs 2:35; 4:4).

   Before David became king, Benaiah distinguished himself in a number of daring military and protective feats to become one of the mighty men (2 Sm 23:20-22) during David's flight from King Saul. He attained command of "the thirty" (1 Chr 27:6), a group second only to "the three" of highest valor (2 Sm 23:23). He later had a high place in the armed forces when Joab was commander in chief and was placed over King David's elite troops, the Cherethites and Pelethites (8:18). He was also made third commander by David, with 24,000 men under him, and with annual responsibility for priestly service in the temple during the third month of the year (1 Chr 27:5-6).

   Benaiah stayed loyal to David during the rebellion of Absalom (2 Sm 20:23; see 15:18) as well as during the attempt by Adonijah to seize David's throne (1 Kgs 1:8), and therefore had the privilege of assisting in Solomon's coronation at Gihon (vv 32-40). As army commander and chief bodyguard to Solomon he was responsible for executing Adonijah (2:25), Joab (v 34), and Shimei (v 46) by orders of the new king.

2. Warrior from the town of Pirathon who was among David's mighty men known as "the thirty" (2 Sm 23:30; 1 Chr 11:31). Benaiah commanded the 11th division of the army in the rotation system established by David (1 Chr 27:14).

3. Prince in Simeon's tribe who participated in the conquest of Gedor during Hezekiah's reign (1 Chr 4:36).

4. Levitical musician who played the harp when King David brought the ark to Jerusalem (1 Chr 15:18, 20; 16:5, RSV). Afterward, he was appointed to minister daily before the ark under the direction of Asaph (16:5).
5. Priestly musician who blew the trumpet before the ark when King David brought it to Jerusalem (1 Chr 15:24). Afterward he was appointed to play regularly before the ark (16:6).
6. Father of Jehoiada, King David's counselor after the death of Ahithophel (1 Chr 27:34; see also 2 Sm 17:1-14).
7. Levite Asaph's descendant and grandfather of Jahaziel (2 Chr 20:14). Jahaziel delivered an encouraging prophecy to King Jehoshaphat of Judah before his battle against the Moabites and Ammonites (vv 1-29).
8. Levite appointed by King Hezekiah to help oversee the tithes and contributions brought to the temple (2 Chr 31:13).
9. Parosh's son (or descendant), who obeyed Ezra's exhortation to divorce his pagan wife after the Babylonian exile (Ezr 10:25).
10. Pahath-moab's son (or descendant), who also obeyed Ezra's exhortation to divorce his pagan wife after the exile (Ezr 10:30).
11. Bani's son (or descendant), another who divorced his pagan wife after the exile (Ezr 10:35).
12. Nebo's son (or descendant), who also divorced his pagan wife after the exile (Ezr 10:43).
13. Pelatiah's father (Ez 11:1, 13). Pelatiah was a prince of the people of Israel during the time of the prophet Ezekiel.

BEN-AMMI Son born to Lot and his younger daughter. A similar incestuous liaison between Lot and his older daughter produced a son named Moab. The two sons are identified as the ancestral heads of the Ammonite and Moabite peoples (Gn 19:38).

Although the promise made to Abraham could have been enjoyed by Lot (Gn 11:31; 12:1-4), Lot went his own way (13:2-12) and failed to trust the Lord (19:15-23). Lot's relationship to Abraham, however, evoked deferential treatment by the Israelites (Dt 2:8-19) toward these occasionally powerful enemies (2 Chr 20:1-12).

See also Ammon, Ammonites.

BEN-DEKER One of 12 officers appointed to requisition food for King Solomon's household (1 Kgs 4:9, KJV "son of Dekar"). Ben-deker's administrative district comprised an area along the southern border of Dan's tribe near Beth-shemesh.

BENE-BERAK One of the cities of Dan (Jos 19:45). The modern name is Ibn Ibrak, a suburb northwest of Tel Aviv.

BENEDICTION* Pronouncement of God's favor upon an assembled congregation (Gn 27:27-29; Lk 24:50; 2 Cor 13:11, 14). *See* Bless, Blessing.

BENE-JAAKAN Place where Israel camped near Edom's border (Nm 33:31-32). *See* Beeroth Bene-jaakan.

BEN-GEBER Literally, "Geber's son," an official in King Solomon's court who administered the sixth of 12 districts. Ben-geber's area of responsibility began at Ramoth-gilead in northern Transjordan and extended north as far as Argob in Bashan (1 Kgs 4:13). His identification with Geber, son of Uri (v 19), is debatable.

BEN-HADAD Title of two or possibly three kings of Syria, meaning "son of Hadad." Hadad was the Syrian storm god probably identical with Rimmon (2 Kgs 5:18).

1. Ben-hadad I, son of Tabrimmon and grandson of Hezion. In spite of a history of Syrian hostility to Israel, Ben-hadad I entered into an alliance with King Baasha (908–886 BC) of the northern kingdom of Israel (1 Kgs 15:18-20). The pact was broken, however, when continuing hostilities between Israel and the southern kingdom of Judah erupted into a major encounter. Baasha conducted a major campaign against King Asa (910–869 BC) of Judah. In order to cut off infiltration into his kingdom and defection to the southern kingdom, Baasha fortified the city of Ramah, situated north of Jerusalem but uncomfortably close to it. His action extended Israel's territory into Judah.

In the face of that threat, Asa sent his remaining wealth to Ben-hadad I, asking him to break his pact with Baasha (vv 18-19). The Syrian king took advantage of the offer and sent his armies against Israel. He conquered the cities of Ijon, Dan, and Abel-beth-maacah plus the territory of Naphtali (v 20), thus ensuring Syrian control of the main caravan routes through Galilee. Baasha was forced to abandon Ramah and move to Tirzah. Asa then conscripted the population of Judah to dismantle and carry off the fortifications erected by Baasha. Materials taken from Ramah were used to help build Geba in the territory of Benjamin. Asa's victory became the subject of a prophetic protest by Hanani, who berated Asa for his reliance on the king of Syria (16:7).

2. Ben-hadad II. The biblical accounts in 1 Kings and 2 Chronicles do not make a clear differentiation between Ben-hadad I and II. Some scholars have therefore identified them as a single person. This view finds apparent support in the "Melqart Stele," which mentions Ben-hadad and to which a date of about 850 BC has been assigned. It seems better, however, to posit a Ben-hadad II who was the son of Ben-hadad I. If one does not distinguish between the two, Ben-hadad's activity must overlap both the reign of Ahab (874–853 BC) and that of Baasha. In each, a military encounter with Ben-hadad was recorded; one must posit an interval of up to four decades between the encounters if no distinction is made.

Ben-hadad II led a coalition of armies against Samaria during the reign of King Ahab of Israel. In the course of the siege, Ben-hadad demanded that Ahab surrender his wealth, wives, and children to him. Ahab agreed to that demand, but when Ben-hadad added the condition that he be given anything that his aides laid their hands on, Ahab refused on advice of his counselors. His refusal enraged Ben-hadad.

An anonymous prophet predicted that Ahab would defeat the armies of Ben-hadad (1 Kgs 20:13). Ahab's victory came when aides of the district governors killed the soldiers who had come out of the Syrian camp to take them captive. The Syrian forces fled. Ben-hadad was again defeated by the Israelites the next year when he attempted to engage them in battle on the plain rather than in the hill country. His reason was his belief that the "gods" of the Israelites were gods of the hills (v 23). That Syrian defeat was also predicted by a prophet, who declared its cause to be Ben-hadad's misconception of the nature of Israel's God (v 28).

Ben-hadad pleaded for his life, promising to restore all the cities his father had taken from Israel. Ahab agreed, but his action met with prophetic protest (vv 35-43). The pact established by the two kings brought about a cessation of hostilities that lasted only three years. The peace was broken by Ahab, who, at the instigation of King Jehoshaphat of Judah, sought to regain the city of Ramoth-gilead. Guidance was first sought from a group of prophets who predicted victory. Micaiah, however, a true prophet, predicted defeat (22:5-28). Ahab's forces were defeated, and Ahab died in battle (vv 29-36).

Ben-hadad also figured in the life of the prophet Elisha, whom he sought to capture (2 Kgs 6:11-19). The attempt was thwarted when the Syrian army was stricken with blindness.

3. Ben-hadad III, son of King Hazael of Syria. This Ben-hadad was not related to Ben-hadad I or II but adopted the name. Because Jehoahaz (814–798 BC), king of Israel, did not follow the Lord, God allowed Israel to come under the control of Ben-hadad III. Release from the oppression of Ben-hadad III was accomplished by a "savior" (2 Kgs 13:5), probably a reference to Assyrian incursions into Syria.

See also Syria, Syrians; Israel, History of.

BEN-HAIL One of five officials sent out by King Jehoshaphat of the southern kingdom of Judah to teach the people the law of the Lord (2 Chr 17:7).

BEN-HANAN Shimon's son of Judah's tribe (1 Chr 4:20).

BEN-HESED One of the 12 officers appointed to requisition food for King Solomon's household (1 Kgs 4:10, KJV "son of Hesed"). His administrative district comprised an area south and west of Arubboth in the western part of Manasseh's tribe.

BEN-HUR One of 12 officers appointed to requisition food for King Solomon's household (1 Kgs 4:8, KJV "son of Hur"). His district was the hill country of Ephraim.

BENINU Levite who signed Ezra's covenant of faithfulness to God with Nehemiah and others after the exile (Neh 10:13).

BENJAMIN (Person)

1. Youngest of Jacob's 12 sons and full brother to Joseph. Jacob named him Benjamin ("son of my right hand") after his dying mother Rachel had called him Ben-oni ("son of my sorrow," Gn 35:18). After Joseph had been sold into Egypt by his half brothers, their father, Jacob, assumed that Joseph was dead and became very protective of Benjamin. Later, with Joseph controlling the plot, Benjamin was used in the reunion in Egypt of Jacob and his 12 sons (Gn 42–45). When prophesying concerning each of his sons, Jacob spoke of Benjamin's skill as a warrior or prophesied of the military fame of his descendants by saying, "Benjamin is a wolf that prowls. He devours his enemies in the morning, and in the evening he divides the plunder" (49:27, NLT). *See* Benjamin, Tribe of.
2. Bilhan's son and Jacob's great-grandson (1 Chr 7:10).
3. Member of Harim's clan of the postexilic community who married a pagan wife (Ezr 10:32).
4. One who repaired a section of the wall next to his own house (Neh 3:23).
5. One of the company of Jews who participated in the dedication of the wall at Jerusalem (Neh 12:34). He may be the same as #4 above.

BENJAMIN, Gate of One of the gates in Jerusalem's old wall. The Gate of Benjamin was probably at the northeast corner, since the prophet Jeremiah passed through it on his way to Benjamin's territory northeast of Jerusalem (Jer 37:12-13). On at least one occasion King Zedekiah held court there (38:7). It was essentially opposite the west wall's Corner Gate (Zec 14:10). When the walls of Jerusalem were rebuilt at the end of the exile, a new gate known as the Sheep Gate (Neh 3:1, 32) or possibly the Muster Gate (Neh 3:31) may have been at the same site. *See* Jerusalem.

BENJAMIN, Tribe of One of the smallest of the 12 tribes of Israel, made up of descendants of Jacob's youngest son (Nm 1:36). In the OT the tribe is often referred to as simply "Benjamin." Though small, the tribe of Benjamin played an important role in Israelite history, particularly in their conduct as great warriors (Jgs 20:13-16; 1 Chr 12:1-2).

At the Israelite conquest of Canaan, after the tribes of Judah and Ephraim had received their territory, the first lot came to Benjamin. The tribe was allotted territory between Judah and Ephraim, a strip of land between Mt Ephraim and the Judean hills. The southern boundary with Judah was clearly defined: through the valley of Hinnom immediately south of Jerusalem to a point north of the Dead Sea. Its eastern limit was the Jordan, and its northern boundary with Ephraim ran from the Jordan to Bethel to Ataroth-addar south of Lower Beth-horon (Jos 18:11-20).

Benjamin's territory extended about 28 miles (45.1 kilometers) from west to east and 12 miles (19.3 kilometers) north to south. It was hilly country, strategically located to control key passes, but with fertile hill basins. Among its hill settlements were the important towns of Jerusalem, Jericho, Bethel, Gibeon, Gibeah, and Mizpeh (Jos 18:21-28). Not all of its towns were immediately taken from their previous possessors; Jerusalem, for example, was in the hands of the Jebusites until David's time. The environment bred a hardy race of highlanders, well described in Jacob's blessing of Benjamin as "a wolf that prowls" (Gn 49:27).

Ehud of Benjamin was one of the early judges in Canaan, a "deliverer" of the Israelites who killed Eglon, king of Moab (Jgs 3:15). Members of the tribe later helped Deborah and Barak defeat Sisera (5:14). The tribe continued to produce great men: political leaders (1 Chr 27:21), captains in Saul's army (2 Sm 4:2) and David's army (23:29), skilled archers (1 Chr 8:40), and overseers in Solomon's labor force (1 Kgs 4:18).

Less noble traits were also shown by Benjamin's descendants. Palti, a Benjaminite, was one of the scouts making a bad report when the 12 spies returned from the land of Canaan (Nm 13:1-2, 9, 31-33). The tribe as a whole displayed disobedience and lack of consistent courage by failing to clear their inheritance of Canaanites (Jgs 1:21). Following the custom of the day, the whole tribe defended the lewd treatment and murder of a concubine from another tribe by a few of their members (chs 19–20). That act of gross immorality united the other tribes against them, and the tribe of Benjamin was almost decimated. To keep the tribe from dying out, the other tribes allowed the Benjaminites to take captive several hundred women who then became their wives (Jgs 21).

Benjamin's tribe proved to be dependable in various ways. During the exodus from Egypt, it took its place in the organization (Nm 1:11) and the army (2:22) and made its tribal offerings (7:60). It demonstrated remarkable loyalty to the throne, initially to Saul and his family

(2 Sm 2:8-31). Later David received its faithful support, as did his descendants, for Benjamin remained with Judah, loyal to Solomon's son Rehoboam when Jeroboam led a secession (1 Kgs 12:21-24).

Other men of Benjamin (often called Benjaminites) spoken of in the OT include Cush, of whom David sang (Ps 7 superscription); Jeremiah the prophet, who, though a Levite, lived within Benjamin's tribe (Jer 1:1; 32:8); and Mordecai, uncle and adviser to Queen Esther (Est 2:5).

In the NT the apostle Paul made no apologies for his ancestry, twice referring to himself as a Hebrew of Benjamin's tribe (Rom 11:1; Phil 3:5). In his sermon at Antioch of Pisidia, Paul also mentioned Benjamin as the tribe of King Saul, in his brief account of Israel's history (Acts 13:21). In one other NT reference Benjamin is named with the other 11 tribes in John's apocalyptic vision (Rv 7:8). *See* Benjamin (Person) #1.

BENJAMINITE, BENJAMITE* Member of Benjamin's tribe. *See* Benjamin, Tribe of.

BENO Jaaziah's son in a list of Levites assigned to temple duty (1 Chr 24:26-27). It is possible that the Hebrew word is not a proper name; it has sometimes been translated "his son."

BEN-ONI Name Rachel gave to her last son as she died in childbirth (Gn 35:18). His father, Jacob, changed his name from Ben-oni ("son of my sorrow") to Benjamin ("son of my right hand"). *See* Benjamin (Person) #1.

BEN SIRACH*, Jesus Son of Sirach and author of Wisdom of Jesus ben Sirach (also known as Ecclesiasticus). *See* Wisdom of Jesus ben Sirach.

BEN-ZOHETH Ishi's son from Judah's tribe (1 Chr 4:20).

BEON Alternate name for Baal-meon, a city east of the Jordan, in Numbers 32:3. *See* Baal-meon.

BEOR
1. Bela's father (Gn 36:32). Bela was a king of Edom.
2. Balaam's father (Nm 22:5; 2 Pt 2:15, KJV "Bosor"). Balaam was asked by Balak, king of Moab, to curse Israel.

BERA Ruler of Sodom in the days of Abraham and Lot. Bera was one of five Canaanite city kings who unsuccessfully rebelled against King Chedorlaomer of Elam and his three allies (Gn 14:2).

BERACAH Warrior from Benjamin's tribe who joined David at Ziklag in his struggle against King Saul. Beracah was one of David's ambidextrous archers and slingers (1 Chr 12:3).

BERACAH*, Valley of Place where King Jehoshaphat gathered the people of Judah to praise the Lord (2 Chr 20:26). The people were grateful for God's help in defeating the attacking armies of Moab, Ammon, and Mt Seir (2 Chr 20:1-25). It is most often identified with the area Wadi el 'Arrub, not far from Tekoa, where a ruin called Bereikut exists.

BERACHIAH* KJV spelling of Berechiah, Asaph's father, in 1 Chronicles 6:39. *See* Berechiah #2.

BERAIAH One of Shimei's sons from Benjamin's tribe (1 Chr 8:21).

BEREA
1. Place north of Jerusalem where the Syrian army camped before launching an attack that killed Judas Maccabeus in 161 BC (1 Macc 9:4).
2. Ancient city of Macedonia (a region now divided among Greece, Yugoslavia, and Bulgaria), probably founded in the fifth century BC. The city was approximately 25 miles (40.2 kilometers) inland from the Aegean Sea on a scenic and fertile plain 600 feet (182.8 kilometers) high in the foothills north of the Olympian range. Conquered by Rome in 168 BC, Berea (alternately spelled Beroea in older English translations) was one of the most populous Macedonian cities in the time of Christ. Today the city is known as Verria.
   Berea was visited by the apostle Paul on his second missionary journey (Acts 17:10-15) and was the home of Sopater, Paul's companion (Acts 20:4). Paul and Silas left Thessalonica when violent religious and political opposition arose and went to Berea, 50 miles (80.5 kilometers) southwest. There both Jews and Greeks eagerly received the gospel, but Paul had to leave the city when angry Jews arrived from Thessalonica to stir up trouble.

BERECHIAH*
1. Son of Zerubbabel and descendant of King David (1 Chr 3:20).
2. Levite, Gershon's descendant and father of Asaph (1 Chr 6:39; 15:17). Asaph was a famous musician of Israel.
3. Asa's son and head of a family of Levites who returned to Judah after the Babylonian exile (1 Chr 9:16).
4. Levite appointed by King David as gatekeeper for the ark of the covenant (1 Chr 15:23).
5. Meshillemoth's son, a leader of Ephraim's tribe. He was one of three men in Samaria who supported the prophet Obed in sending prisoners of war back to their homes in Judah (2 Chr 28:12).
6. Meshullam's father. Meshullam assisted Nehemiah, the governor, in rebuilding the wall of Jerusalem (Neh 3:4, 30; 6:18).
7. Iddo's son and father of Zechariah the prophet (Zec 1:1, 7).
   See also Barachiah, Barachias.

BERED (Person) Alternate name for Beker, one of Ephraim's sons, in 1 Chronicles 7:20. *See* Beker, Bekerite #2.

BERED (Place) Unknown site in Israel's southern Negev Desert region. God spoke to Sarai's maid, Hagar, at a well between Kadesh and Bered (Gn 16:14).

BEREKIAH Alternate spelling for Berechiah. *See* Berechiah.

BERI Zophah's son, head of a subclan. Beri was a skilled warrior (1 Chr 7:36, 40) listed with Asher's descendants.

BERIAH
1. Asher's son, who migrated to Egypt with his family, relatives, and grandfather Jacob (Gn 46:17; 1 Chr 7:30). His descendants were called Beriites (Nm 26:44).
2. Ephraim's youngest son, born after several of his brothers were killed at Gath for cattle rustling (1 Chr 7:20-23).
3. Elpaal's son, head of a family in Benjamin's tribe. This Beriah lived at Aijalon and helped repel invaders from Gath (1 Chr 8:13).

4. Shimei's son, a Levite of Gershon's clan who served in the temple at Jerusalem. Because neither Beriah nor his brother Jeush had many sons, their families were counted as a single subclan in the Levitical system (1 Chr 23:10-11).

BERIITE Member of a family descended from Beriah, one of Asher's sons (Nm 26:44). *See* Beriah #1.

BERITE* KJV rendering of Bichrite, a descendant of Bichri, in 2 Samuel 20:14. *See* Bichri, Bichrite, Bicri.

BERNICE Eldest daughter of Herod Agrippa I. Bernice was present during the apostle Paul's speech before her brother King Agrippa II (Acts 25:13, 23; 26:30). Bernice (also spelled Berenice) was born around AD 28. At 13 she married Marcus, son of the Jewish official Alexander. After her husband's death, her father betrothed her to his elder brother, Herod of Chalcis. Two sons, Bernicianus and Hyrcanus, were born to them before her second husband's death in AD 48. When the young widow's relationship with her brother, Agrippa II, deepened, there were rumors of incest. In defense, Bernice persuaded Polemo, king of Cilicia, to marry her. But she left him shortly afterward.

In AD 66 Bernice bravely but unsuccessfully appealed to the mad Roman procurator Gessius Florus not to ransack the temple in Jerusalem. She was at her brother's side when he warned the people against war. When war broke out that year, Jewish rebels set fire to her palace as well as to her brother's.

BERODACH-BALADAN* KJV spelling of Merodach-baladan, the king of Babylon during the reign of Judah's King Hezekiah, in 2 Kings 20:12. *See* Merodach-baladan.

BEROEA* *See* Berea #2.

BEROTHAH, BEROTHAI City between Damascus and Hamath mentioned by the prophet Ezekiel as lying on the northern border of the restored Israel (Ez 47:16). Berothah is probably the same as Berothai, a city captured by David (2 Sm 8:8; called Cun in 1 Chr 18:8).

BEROTHITE* KJV form of Beerothite, an inhabitant of Beeroth, in 1 Chronicles 11:39. *See* Beeroth.

BERRY* Fleshy fruit, usually with many seeds and having no stony seed covering. *See* Plants (Bramble; Caper Plant).

BERYL Hard, lustrous mineral of various colors, mentioned in the Bible as a gemstone (Ex 28:20; Rv 21:20). *See* Minerals and Metals; Stones, Precious.

BESAI Ancestor of a group of temple assistants who returned to Jerusalem with Zerubbabel after the Babylonian exile (Ezr 2:49; Neh 7:52).

BESODEIAH Meshullam's father. Along with Joiada, Meshullam helped rebuild a portion of the Jerusalem wall after the exile in Babylonia (Neh 3:6).

BESOM* Old English word meaning "broom" (Is 14:23, KJV). The besom, or broom, of destruction is a Near Eastern metaphor signifying total destruction. It refers to the annihilation or "sweeping away" of Babylon by the Lord.

BESOR, Brook of Brook that David crossed to pursue the Amalekites southward after they had raided Ziklag,

his home base. Exhausted, 200 of David's men remained at the brook while the other 400 overtook and defeated the enemy (1 Sm 30:9-21).

BETAH* Alternate name for Tibhath (1 Chr 18:8), a town in the city-kingdom of Aram-zobah, subjugated by King David, in 2 Samuel 8:8. *See* Tebah (Place).

BETEN City allotted to Asher's tribe for an inheritance, mentioned between Hali and Achshaph (Jos 19:25).

BETHABARA* Village where messengers from the Pharisees questioned John the Baptist (Jn 1:28, KJV). Modern translations have "Bethany" instead of Bethabara in accordance with superior manuscript evidence. John called it Bethany "beyond the Jordan" to distinguish it from the Bethany near Jerusalem. *See* Bethany #2.

BETH-ANATH Town assigned to Naphtali's tribe (Jos 19:38) from which the tribe failed to drive out the original inhabitants (Jgs 1:33). The Israelites, who often made slaves of the remaining Canaanite people, were in many cases eventually corrupted by their pagan religious practices.

BETH-ANOTH Village in the hill country assigned to Judah's tribe after the Israelite conquest of Canaan (Jos 15:59).

BETHANY
1. Village on the eastern slope of the Mt of Olives about a mile and a half (2.4 kilometers) east of Jerusalem. Jesus and his disciples sometimes stayed in Bethany when in Judea, as when they attended temple observances during Passover (Mt 21:17; Mk 11:11). Jesus was eating at the home of Simon the leper in Bethany when a woman came and anointed his head with costly perfume (Mt 26:6-13; Mk 14:3-9). Bethany was also the home of Mary and Martha and their brother Lazarus, where Jesus raised Lazarus from the dead (Jn 11:1, 18). The village was near Bethphage on an approach to Jerusalem (Mk 11:1; Lk 19:29) that Jesus followed in preparation for his triumphal entry into Jerusalem. In Bethany Jesus blessed his disciples after the resurrection and parted from them (Lk 24:50). Today the town is called el-Azariyeh (the place of Lazarus).
2. Village on "the other side of the Jordan" (the east side), where John the Baptist baptized (Jn 1:28).

BETH-ARABAH One of six cities in the wilderness southeast of Jericho on the boundary between the territories of Judah and Benjamin (Jos 15:6, 61; 18:22). The modern Ain Gharbeh in the Wadi el-Quelt may be the site of Beth-arabah.

BETH-ARAM* KJV rendering of Beth-haram, a Gadite town, in Joshua 13:27. *See* Beth-haram, Beth-haran.

BETH-ARBEL Town whose violent destruction at the hands of the Assyrians was compared by the prophet Hosea to Ephraim's forthcoming destruction (Hos 10:14). Beth-arbel is most commonly identified with present-day Irbid in Gilead, located at an important crossroads in northern Transjordan.

BETH-ASHBEA Place where certain families descended from Judah were known for their production of linen (1 Chr 4:21). The KJV renders "Ashbea" as a family name rather than as a place of residence.

BETH-AVEN

1. Town in Benjamin's territory, located west of Michmash on the border of the wilderness, near Ai, to the east of Bethel (Jos 7:2; 18:12; 1 Sm 13:5; 14:23).
2. Term used by Hosea contemptuously to refer to Bethel, an ancient center of worship, because the "House of God" (Bethel) had become a "house of wickedness" (Beth-aven or just Aven; Hos 4:15; 5:8; 10:5). *See* Aven #2.

BETH-AZMAVETH

Alternate name for Azmaveth, a town near Jerusalem, in Nehemiah 7:28. *See* Azmaveth (Place).

BETH-BAAL-MEON

Alternate name for Baal-meon, a city in Reuben's territory, in Joshua 13:17. *See* Baal-meon.

BETH-BARAH

Place where warriors of Ephraim's tribe under Gideon tried to block the retreat of the Midianites over the Jordan River (Jgs 7:24).

BETHBASI

Town in the Judean wilderness where Jonathan and Simon Maccabeus took refuge from General Bacchides and, having fortified it successfully, withstood the onslaught of the Syrian forces (1 Macc 9:62-68). After that defeat Bacchides was forced to make peace with Jonathan (vv 69-73).

BETH-BIRI

Alternate name for Lebaoth, a city in Judah's southern territory (1 Chr 4:31). *See* Lebaoth.

BETH-CAR

Place in Benjamin's territory to which a Philistine army was pursued by the Israelites after the second battle of Ebenezer (1 Sm 7:11).

BETH-DAGON

Shrine of the Philistine and Canaanite god Dagon mentioned in several sources other than the Bible. A fortress called Dagon near Jericho was mentioned by the Jewish historian Josephus, for example. Many Canaanite locations may have been known for their shrines to Dagon:

1. Town in Judah's lowlands (Jos 15:41). This Beth-dagon was mentioned both by Ramses III of Egypt and by Sennacherib of Assyria (701 BC) as having been captured by them.
2. Town on the border of Asher's territory, east of Mt Carmel (Jos 19:27).
3. Temple in Ashdod (1 Sm 5:1-2; called Azotus in 1 Macc 10:83-84).

BETH-DIBLATHAIM

Town in Moab (Jer 48:22), and probably identical with Almon-diblathaim. *See* Almon-diblathaim.

BETH-EDEN

Small Aramean (Syrian) state north of Damascus. Assyria conquered Beth-eden and deported its people to Kir (2 Kgs 16:9), fulfilling the prediction in Amos 1:5 (KJV "house of Eden"). Beth-eden, which means "house of delight," is sometimes equated with the Eden of Ezekiel 27:23, the location of which is unknown. Its inhabitants are referred to as the "children of Eden" in 2 Kings 19:12 (KJV).

BETH-EKED

Place between Jezreel and Samaria where Jehu killed Ahaziah's kinsmen at a pit or cistern (2 Kgs 10:12, 14, KJV "shearing house").

BETHEL (God)

Pagan deity mentioned in ancient texts and thought by some to have biblical reference (Jer 48:13; Am 5:5; Zec 7:2). *See* Canaanite Deities and Religion.

BETHEL (Place), BETHELITE*

1. Important OT city located about 11 miles (17.7 kilometers) north of Jerusalem on the north-south ridge road at the tribal borders of Benjamin and Ephraim (Jos 16:1-2; 18:13). Hiel, a resident of the city, is referred to as a Bethelite in 1 Kings 16:34 (KJV). As a trading center, Bethel attracted merchandise both from the Mediterranean coast and from Transjordan via Jericho. Although the site was located in dry hill country, several springs supplied ample water for its inhabitants (the oldest artifact recovered from the site is a water jar dating from about 3500 BC).

The name of Bethel, meaning "house of El (god)," may have been used as early as the fourth millennium BC by Canaanites in the area. Archaeological excavations at Chalcolithic levels (i.e., between the Stone Age and the Bronze Age) indicate that pagan worship of the Canaanite deity El took place on top of the hill at that early period. The patriarch Jacob named the place Bethel, or gave the old name new significance, after having a dream from God there (Gn 28:10-22). The site was said to be known as Bethel to the patriarch Abraham (12:8); that designation, however, could be a scribal updating of a more ancient local name, since Bethel had earlier been known as Luz (28:19). Possibly the sanctuary was known as Bethel, the nearby settlement as Luz. No doubt the name Bethel was firmly established by the beginning of the intermediate Bronze Age (c. 2200 BC) and remained throughout its history. An OT passage mentioning both names records that a man from Luz founded another city of that name in Hittite territory (Jgs 1:26).

Although Bethel was assigned to Benjamin's tribe, Ephraim's tribe actually captured Bethel from its Canaanite fortress in their own territory (Jgs 1:22-26; 1 Chr 7:28). Under the judges, the ark of the covenant was located at Bethel, where the normal functions of Israelite worship were carried out; the ark was superintended by the high priest Phinehas, son of Eleazar (Jgs 20:18-28; 21:2-4). There is no archaeological evidence of Philistine occupation of Bethel in the time of the judges; in the days of King Saul it was bypassed when other Israelite centers were being attacked (cf. 1 Sm 12–14). Archaeological discoveries indicate that Bethel flourished in the early reign of Saul but declined when he made Gibeah his capital city.

When Israel and Judah became separate entities in the time of Jeroboam I (930–909 BC), Bethel returned to prominence as the capital of the northern kingdom of Israel, thus becoming the counterpart of Judah's capital, Jerusalem. Bethel was one of two northern cities where golden calves were worshiped (1 Kgs 12:28-33); the sanctuary area for that cultic practice has not been discovered. The city was the home of an elderly prophet (13:11) who may have been connected with the prophetic colony existing there in the time of Elijah and Elisha (2 Kgs 2:2-3). During the reign of Judah's King Abijah (913–910 BC), Bethel fell under Judah's control (2 Chr 13:19) but later was returned to Israel. The prophet Amos went to Bethel to deliver scathing denunciations about contemporary social and religious life in Israel, for which the priest Amaziah had him expelled (Am 7:10-13).

There is no archaeological evidence that Bethel was destroyed during the Assyrian conquest of Israel (722 BC). In fact, one of its deported priests was returned to

Bethel to instruct Mesopotamian colonists in the ways of the Lord (2 Kgs 17:28). Under Judah's King Josiah, the pagan shrine was demolished (23:15-20), but no damage was done to the city itself. Under either Nabonidus (555–539 BC) or Darius I (521–486 BC), however, the city was burned, so that by Ezra's time Bethel had reverted to a small village settlement (Ezr 2:28).

2. Alternate name for Bethuel, a town in Judah's territory, in 1 Samuel 30:27. See Bethuel, Bethul (Place).

BETH-EMEK Town on the territorial boundary between the tribes of Asher and Zebulun (Jos 19:27).

BETHER* Hebrew word occurring in the phrase "upon rugged mountains" and regarded as a proper name in the KJV ("mountains of Bether," Sg 2:17). Occurrence of the phrase "mountains of spices" in an almost identical verse (8:14) suggests "spices" or a particular spice (such as cinnamon) as an appropriate translation of *bether*. Bether also occurs as the name of the city Beth-anoth in the hill country of Judah in Joshua 15:59 (but only in the Septuagint). In 1 Chronicles 6:59 the Septuagint reads "Bether" instead of "Beth-shemesh." Some scholars identify this Bether with Khir-bet el-Jehudiyeh, southwest of Bittir, which may preserve the ancient name. It is unlikely that Bether is related to the phrase "mountains of Bether."

In AD 135, Bether became the site of the last Jewish stronghold against the Romans in the Second Revolt (AD 132–135). There Simon Bar-Kochba, the designated "messiah," and the Jewish forces were massacred.

BETHESDA Name of a pool in Jerusalem to which many sick and infirm people came (Jn 5:2). Bethesda is an Aramaic word transliterated into Greek and is the name of a pool in Jerusalem in Jesus' day that was surrounded by five porches or colonnades that gave an arcadelike walkway around the pool. Located near the Sheep Gate, it was the place where the handicapped and ill came with the hope they would be miraculously healed if they could get into the pool at the proper time.

A number of other forms of the name of this pool occur in different manuscripts. These are Bethsaida ("house of fish"), Belzetha, and Bezatha, the latter two apparently variants of Bethzaitha. Another form is Beth-zatha, meaning "house of olives." Recent studies, especially of the Copper Scroll of Qumran Cave Three, suggest that Bethesda is the correct form among the several variations. Further, it is a dual form, which indicates that the site of Bethesda was characterized by two pools. This understanding shows that the older theory that Bethesda meant "house of mercy" is incorrect.

The archaeological activity of the Franciscan Fathers of the Church of St Anne near St Stephen's Gate in the Old City has been a corrective of older views as well as the means of clarifying where the pool actually was. Their research has shown that the pool of Bethesda is not to be identified with Birket Israel, a pool about 360 feet (109.7 meters) by 126 feet (38.4 meters), located between St Anne's and the temple area to the south; or with the large cisterns under the convent of the Sisters of Zion several hundred yards west of St Anne's on the Via Dolorosa; or with the pool adjacent to the Gihon, still farther south than Birket Israel on the slope of Ophel. Rather, the pool of Bethesda is to be identified with the excavated ruin in the St Anne Courtyard, a ruin with two pools of considerable size. Arched pillars originally bordering the two reservoirs were covered intact with 25 to 30 feet (7.5 to 9 meters) of debris. Excavated, these now stand impressively as witness to an astounding architectural achievement.

Architectural style and inscription point to Herodian times, making it one of the many magnificent building projects of Herod the Great. The debris and ruins of several centuries were dumped into the pool area, filling the space around the still-standing colonnades. This debris was later leveled and a Byzantine church constructed on top of it in the fifth century AD. Thus through various literary and archaeological studies, Bethesda is now correctly understood to mean "a place of two pools" located near the Sheep Market of St Stephen's Gate. See Bethsaida; Beth-zatha.

BETH-EZEL One of several small towns, probably in southwest Judah, whose destruction was lamented by the prophet Micah (1:11).

BETH-GADER Town mentioned in connection with its founder, Hareph, a Calebite (1 Chr 2:51).

BETH-GAMUL City of Moab against which Jeremiah prophesied God's judgment for their ill treatment of Israel (Jer 48:23). It has been identified as Khirbet Jumeil, located eight miles (12.9 kilometers) east of Dibon.

BETH-GILGAL Town from which Levitical singers came to Jerusalem to celebrate the rebuilding of the wall under Nehemiah (Neh 12:29). See Gilgal #1.

BETH-HAGGAN Town to which King Ahaziah of Judah fled for his life from Jehu of Israel (2 Kgs 9:27). Beth-haggan was probably the same as En-gannim. It has been identified as modern Jenin.

BETH-HAKKEREM Town in the hilly area between Jerusalem and Bethlehem. The prophet Jeremiah referred to signal fires set at Beth-hakkerem to warn of invasion from the north (Jer 6:1). Malchijah is mentioned as a political leader in Beth-hakkerem in Nehemiah's time (Neh 3:14).

BETH-HARAM, BETH-HARAN Town given to Gad's tribe at the partitioning of Canaan (Jos 13:27). Fortified and used to accommodate sheep herds (Nm 32:36), it is probably the same as Beth-aramphtha, a city mentioned by the Jewish historian Josephus.

BETH-HOGLAH City allotted to Benjamin's tribe (Jos 18:21). It was southeast of Jericho near the mouth of the Jordan River on the boundary line between the territories of Judah and Benjamin (Jos 15:6; 18:19). It is identified with modern Ain Hajlah.

BETH-HORON Canaanite place-name perhaps meaning "the house of Hauron," the god of the underworld. Beth-horon was a dual settlement 10 and 12 miles (16.1 and 19.3 kilometers) northwest of Jerusalem. Located on the boundary between the tribal territories of Ephraim and Benjamin (Jos 16:3, 5), the twin settlements controlled the valley of Aijalon, one of the most important ancient routes between the Mediterranean coast and the interior hill country. The upper town controlled a strategic pass. Ephraim's "Beth-horon with its pasture lands" was assigned to the Levite family of Kohath (Jos 21:22; 1 Chr 6:68).

Many armies marched through the Aijalon Valley. Amorites pursued by Joshua's army fled past Beth-horon after being defeated at Gibeon on "the day the sun stood still" (Jos 10:1-14). A band of Philistines approached it to make war with Saul (1 Sm 13:18). The Egyptian army of Shishak passed by Beth-horon (according to his Karnak inscription). Syrian armies under Seron (1 Macc 3:13-24) and Nicanor (7:39-43) were defeated by Judas Maccabeus at Beth-horon. The Romans under Cestius were nearly annihilated there by the Jews, according to Jewish historian Josephus.

Beth-horon was probably destroyed and rebuilt more than once. Sheerah, Beriah's daughter and Ephraim's granddaughter, is credited with building both lower and upper Beth-horon (1 Chr 7:24). King Solomon fortified both Beth-horons after raids in the vicinity by an Egyptian pharaoh (1 Kgs 9:15-17; 2 Chr 8:5). In the intertestamental period Beth-horon was fortified by the Syrian general Bacchides after a battle with Jonathan Maccabeus (1 Macc 9:50).

BETH-JESHIMOTH City assigned to Reuben's tribe (Jos 13:20), later described as a Moabite town (Ez 25:9). Prior to Israel's conquest of the Promised Land, they made camp along the Jordan from Beth-jeshimoth to Abel-shittim (Nm 33:49). The city is usually identified with Tell el-Azeimeh.

See also Wilderness Wanderings.

BETH-LEAPHRAH Town mentioned by the prophet Micah. Since Beth-leaphrah (KJV "house of Aphrah") means "house of dust," Micah made a sarcastic pun by telling its idolatrous inhabitants to "roll in the dust" (Mi 1:10, NLT).

BETH-LEBAOTH Alternate name for Lebaoth, a city of Simeon in the southern extremity of Judah's tribe, in Joshua 19:6. See Lebaoth.

BETHLEHEM
1. "City of David" and the birthplace of Jesus Christ, five miles (8 kilometers) south of Jerusalem. This city is sometimes called Bethlehem-judah (KJV) or Ephrath (Gn 35:19; Mi 5:2) to distinguish it from the Bethlehem of Zebulun.

As an early Canaanite settlement, it was associated with the patriarchs, for Rachel died and was buried in its vicinity (Gn 35:16, 19; 48:7). The earliest known historical reference to Bethlehem occurs in the Amarna texts (14th century BC) in which battle reports refer to *bitil u-lahama* south of Jerusalem. The name may have meant "house of (the goddess) Lahama." A branch of Caleb's family settled there, and Caleb's son Salma was known as "the father of Bethlehem" (1 Chr 2:51). Bethlehem was the home of a young Levite who served as priest to Micah (Jgs 17:7-8), and of Boaz, Ruth, Obed, and Jesse, the Bethlehemite, David's father (Ru 4:11, 17; 1 Sm 16:18).

Bethlehem was the birthplace of David (1 Sm 17:12) and the home of one of David's mighty men, Elhanan (2 Sm 23:24; 1 Chr 11:26). It was the scene of a daring exploit by three of David's warriors; they broke through the cordon of Philistine marauders occupying Bethlehem to bring David water from the well (or cistern) near the city gate of his hometown (2 Sm 23:14-17). Much later, Bethlehem is mentioned as being adjacent to the village of Geruth-kimham, where Jews fleeing from the Babylonians stayed en route to Egypt (Jer 41:17). People from Bethlehem were among those returning from the Babylonian exile (Ezr 2:21; Neh 7:26; 1 Esd 5:17).

When Jesus was born there, Bethlehem was only a village (Mt 2:1-16; Lk 2:4-6, 15; Jn 7:42). Under the census decree of Caesar Augustus, Joseph had to go to Bethlehem "because he was of the house and lineage of David" (Lk 2:4). The family may still have had property

there. The birth of Jesus possibly took place in a cave in the rocks outside the town. The early Christian writer Justin Martyr thought so, as did Origen some years later. Origen frequently resided in the Holy Land and wrote, "In Bethlehem you are shown the cave where he was born, and within the cave the manger where he was wrapped in swaddling clothes."

Jerome later described the grotto over which the Emperor Constantine had built a basilica. In excavations in 1934–35, evidence indicated a second period of building in the reign of Justinian (AD 527–565), when Constantine's basilica was extended beyond its original proportions. Steps lead down to the grotto, the rectangular shape of which suggests that Constantine's builders reshaped the original. But there is no description of the grotto prior to the construction of Constantine's basilica.

2. Town in Zebulun (Jos 19:15), probably the home of the judge Ibzan (Jgs 12:8-10), an early ruler of Israel. It is identified today with the village of Beit Lahm, some seven miles (11.3 kilometers) northwest of Nazareth.

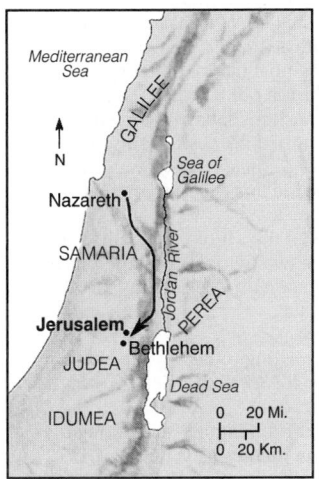

Joseph and Mary's Journey to Bethlehem Caesar's decree for a census of the entire Roman Empire made it necessary for Joseph and Mary to leave their hometown, Nazareth, and journey the 70 miles (112.6 kilometers) to the Judean village of Bethlehem.

BETHLEHEMITE* Inhabitant of Bethlehem of Judah (1 Sm 16:1, 18; 17:58; 2 Sm 21:19). *See* Bethlehem #1.

BETH-MAACAH*, BETH-MAACHAH* Alternate name for Abel-beth-maacah in 2 Samuel 20:14-15. *See* Abel (Place).

BETH-MARCABOTH City in Judah's territory given to the tribe of Simeon (Jos 19:5; 1 Chr 4:31), possibly the same as Madmannah (Jos 15:31). The name Beth-marcaboth means "house of chariots," and consequently some have seen a link to the chariot cities of Solomon (1 Kgs 9:19; 10:26). Its location is unknown unless it can be identified with Madmannah.

BETH-MEON Alternate name for Baal-meon, a town formerly belonging to Reuben's tribe, in Jeremiah 48:23. *See* Baal-meon.

BETH-MILLO House or fortress associated with the city of Shechem mentioned in connection with the crowning of Abimelech (son of Gideon) as king there (Jgs 9:6, 20). Since the term "millo" probably means "mount" or "earthwork," Beth-millo is often identified with the "tower of Shechem" mentioned later in the same chapter (Jgs 9:46-49).

BETH-NIMRAH Moabite city given to and rebuilt by Gad's tribe at the partitioning of Canaan, the Promised Land (Nm 32:3; Jos 13:27). Beth-nimrah has been identified with modern Tell el-Bleibil, eight miles (12.9 kilometers) east of the Jordan River.

BETH-PALET* KJV spelling of Beth-pelet, a city of Judah, in Joshua 15:27. See Beth-pelet.

BETH-PAZZEZ City given to Issachar's tribe at the partitioning of the Promised Land, apparently near Mt Tabor (Jos 19:21).

BETH-PELET City assigned to Judah at the partitioning of the Promised Land (Jos 15:27). Later resettled by the people of Judah after the return from exile in Babylon (Neh 11:26), Beth-pelet was possibly the hometown of David's warrior Helez the Paltite (2 Sm 23:26; 1 Chr 11:27, "Pelonite").

BETH-PEOR Moabite city given to Reuben's tribe in the partitioning of the Promised Land (Jos 13:20). Prior to the Israelites' entrance into the land of Canaan, they made camp in a valley opposite Beth-peor. Here the people assembled to hear Moses' final message after he had viewed the land from the top of Mt Pisgah (Dt 3:29; 4:46). It was here that Moses was buried, having been forbidden to enter the territory promised the descendants of Abraham (Dt 34:6). Baal-peor (or Baal of Peor) was the name of a local deity worshiped in this region (Nm 25:3-5).

BETHPHAGE Village on the Mt of Olives adjacent to Jerusalem. At Bethphage two disciples obtained the donkey colt on which Jesus rode into Jerusalem (Mt 21:1-6; Mk 11:1-6; Lk 19:29-35).

BETH-PHELET* KJV spelling of Beth-pelet, a city of Judah, in Nehemiah 11:26. See Beth-pelet.

BETH-RAPHA Place or clan name listed among the descendants of Eshton in Judah's tribe (1 Chr 4:1, 12).

BETH-REHOB City or district mentioned in Judges 18:28 and 2 Samuel 10:6; probably the northernmost point reached by the 12 Israelite spies when they searched out the land of Canaan. It is probably identifiable with Rehob (Nm 13:21; 2 Sm 10:8). See Rehob (Place).

BETHSAIDA
1. Town northeast of the Sea of Galilee. Bethsaida was the home of three of Jesus' disciples: Andrew, Peter, and Philip (Jn 1:44; 12:21). Jesus announced that calamity would come upon Bethsaida because of its unbelief in spite of the mighty works he had done there (Mt 11:21-22; Lk 10:13). A blind man was healed in Bethsaida (Mk 8:22-26), and nearby over 5,000 people were fed by the miracle of the loaves and fish (Mk 6:34-45; Lk 9:10-17).
   Bethsaida is mentioned in several ancient sources, chiefly the writings of Josephus, a first-century AD Jewish historian. Two Bethsaidas, one on each side of the Sea of Galilee, were once postulated because the reference in Mark mentions the feeding of the 5,000 as happening across the lake from Bethsaida, whereas in Luke it seems to have taken place near Bethsaida. One solution is that the miracle occurred in the district surrounding Bethsaida, but that the quickest way to reach the city itself was to cross part of the lake. Such an interpretation questions the traditional location of the miracle (et-Tabgha on the west shore, nearer to Capernaum)

but is preferable to the proposal of two Bethsaidas so close to each other.
   Bethsaida was merely a fishing village until it was enlarged and beautified by Philip the tetrarch (4 BC–AD 34), son of Herod the Great, after the death of Caesar Augustus. Philip was later buried there, according to Josephus. Bethsaida's name was changed to Julias in honor of Julia, daughter of Augustus. That city was defended by Josephus when he was its military commander during the first Jewish revolt against Rome (AD 66–70).
   Josephus wrote that Bethsaida was "at the lake of Gennesareth" but "near to the Jordan River." He also said that it was in lower Gaulanitis, a district that touched the northeast quarter of the Sea of Galilee. There is, however, no ancient "tell" or ruin fitting the size or description of the city near either the lake or the river. A suggestion that the small harbor of el-'Araj is the site of Bethsaida has little archaeological support, but et-Tell, located about two miles (3.2 kilometers) from the lake, shows evidence of extensive Roman occupation and building activity. At present, et-Tell seems to be the most satisfactory candidate for identification of Bethsaida.
2. A variant name for the pool at Jerusalem, otherwise called Bethesda or Beth-zatha. See Bethesda; Beth-zatha.

BETH-SHAN, BETH-SHEAN* Strategic Palestinian town located in the subtropical Jordan Valley 15 miles (24.1 kilometers) south of the Sea of Galilee and 4 miles (6.4 kilometers) west of the Jordan River. Beth-shan (alternately Beth-shean) stood at the eastern end of the valley of Jezreel, guarding an important Jordan River crossing. It lay at the junction of two trade routes, one leading north toward Galilee and Damascus, the other leading from the mountains of Gilead west through the Jezreel Valley and the hills of Samaria.
   When the Philistines defeated Israel under King Saul at the battle on Mt Gilboa, Beth-shan was a Philistine city. The slain bodies of Saul and his sons were hung in disgrace on the city wall, and Saul's head was displayed in the temple of Dagon, a Philistine deity (1 Sm 31:10-13; 2 Sm 21:12-14; 1 Chr 10:8-10). The city later became a part of David's kingdom.

Aerial View of Beth-shan

   Identification of Beth-shan with Tell el-Husn is confirmed by two Egyptian texts found there that mention its name. The tell, or mound, is 213 feet (64.9 meters) high and about one-half mile (804.5 meters) in circumference at its base. At the time of Israel's conquest of Canaan, the area that included Beth-shan was allotted to Issachar's tribe, but Manasseh's tribe evidently took it over (Jos 17:11). Under King Solomon it was incorporated into the administrative district of Baanah (1 Kgs 4:12). The city is thought to have been destroyed by Shishak (Sheshonk I), pharaoh of Egypt in the 10th century BC. It was insignificant during the remainder of the OT period; occupation during the Babylonian exile and the postexilic Persian period seems to have been sporadic.

In the Hellenistic period Beth-shan received the name Scythopolis, presumably because it was settled by a colony of Scythian mercenaries serving the Egyptian king Ptolemy II. Temples to the Greek deities Dionysus and Zeus were built. Under the Hasmonean dynasty, Beth-shan became an important administrative center. It prospered as a member of the league of Greco-Roman commercial cities called Decapolis (Mt 4:25; Mk 7:31) and was the only league member west of the Jordan.

Aerial View of Beth-shemesh

BETH-SHEMESH

1. Canaanite city on the northern border of Judah's territory (Jos 15:10) and the southern border of Dan's (before that tribe migrated north). Beth-shemesh means "the house of Shamash," the Canaanite sun god. As Ir-shemesh, it was included in the list of cities of Dan (19:41). Beth-shemesh was one of the towns of Judah granted to the Levites (Jos 21:16; 1 Chr 6:59). Its inhabitants were called Beth-shemites (1 Sm 6:14, 18, KJV). When the Philistines decided to dispose of the captured ark of the covenant because plagues were breaking out in their cities, they took it to Beth-shemesh. The area was also the scene of a great victory of King Joash (Jehoash) of Israel over King Amaziah of Judah (2 Chr 25:21-23). About a century later, Beth-shemesh was captured from King Ahaz of Judah by the Philistines (28:16-20). After that, the settlement fell into decline and was finally destroyed by Nebuchadnezzar in 586 BC.
2. Canaanite city allotted to Issachar's tribe (Jos 19:22).
3. Fortified Canaanite city allotted to Naphtali's tribe (Jos 19:38). The inhabitants of this Beth-shemesh were not driven out by the Israelites (Jgs 1:33).
4. KJV reference to the Egyptian city of Heliopolis (or On), where the sun was worshiped (Jer 43:13). See Heliopolis.

BETH-SHEMITE*
Inhabitant of Beth-shemesh (1 Sm 6:14, 18). See Beth-shemesh #1.

BETH-SHITTAH Town between the Jordan River and the valley of Jezreel to which the Midianites fled when defeated by Gideon (Jgs 7:22).

BETH-TAPPUAH Town in the hill country of Judah's territory (Jos 15:53) named "place of fruit trees" because of its high ridge location and many fruitful orchards. Beth-tappuah is identified with modern Taffuh about four miles (6.4 kilometers) northwest of Hebron.

BETH-TOGARMAH Hebrew phrase meaning "house of Togarmah," referring to the nation descended from Gomer's son of this name, and which traded with Tyre (Ez 27:14; 38:6). See Togarmah.

BETHUEL (Person) Youngest son of Abraham's brother Nahor and his wife, Milcah. Bethuel was thus Abraham's nephew (Gn 22:23). He was the father of Rebekah (24:15, 24) and was referred to as an Aramean of Paddan-aram (25:20; 28:5).

BETHUEL, BETHUL (Place) One of the cities allotted to Simeon's tribe within Judah's inheritance (1 Chr 4:30). Bethuel is alternately called Bethul in Joshua 19:4, and is perhaps identifiable with Chesil (Kesil), a city assigned to Judah's tribe (Jos 15:30), and with Bethel in the Negev to which David sent spoils (1 Sm 30:27). See Kesil.

BETHULIA Town described in the book of Judith as being near Dothan on a hill overlooking the plain of Esdraelon (Jdt 4:6; 6:11). Nebuchadnezzar's general, Holofernes, tried to bring Bethulia into submission by controlling its water sources (Jdt 7:6-7).

BETH-ZAITH City where Bacchides, a Syrian general of the Maccabean period, camped after his massacre of 60 Hasidian Jews in Jerusalem (1 Macc 7:19). At Beth-zaith more Jews were slaughtered and thrown into a pit. Beth-zaith is identified with modern Beit Zeita, near Bethlehem.

BETH-ZATHA* Variant name for the pool in Jerusalem. The name is generally believed to mean "house of olives," occurring only in John 5:2. In many translations this is a variant given in the margin for Bethesda. See Bethesda.

BETH-ZECHARIAH Place 10 miles (16.1 kilometers) southwest of Jerusalem where Judas Maccabeus was defeated by a Seleucid ruler, Antiochus V Eupator, son of Antiochus Epiphanes (1 Macc 6:32-47).

BETH-ZUR Hill town of Judah in the mountains north of Hebron (Jos 15:58). Beth-zur was settled by Maon, one of Caleb's descendants (1 Chr 2:45), and was one of the natural strongholds of Judah. It was fortified by King Rehoboam of the southern kingdom in the 10th century BC, even though it had begun to decline in importance (2 Chr 11:7). It served as an administrative center during the time of Nehemiah (Neh 3:16). In the Maccabean period it was known by the Greek name Bethsura. Judas Maccabeus defeated Syrian general Lysias there (1 Macc 4:29, 61) and lost the town a few years later. After recapturing Beth-zur from the Syrians, Simon Maccabeus strengthened it in 140 BC, making it one of the most important fortresses on the border between Judah and Idumea (11:65-66; 14:33).

BETOMASTHAIM, BETOMESTHAIM Unidentified place located near Dothan, mentioned in the book of

Judith. The inhabitants of Betomasthaim and Bethulia were ordered by the high priest to block the advancing Assyrian army that was led by Holofernes. After Holofernes was killed, Betomasthaim was one of the cities asked by Uzziah, the leader of Bethulia, to destroy the remnant of the Assyrian army (Jdt 4:6-7; 15:4).

BETONIM City in the territory assigned to Gad's tribe for an inheritance (Jos 13:26). It has been identified with modern Khirbet Bat-neh, 16 miles (25.7 kilometers) northeast of Jericho.

BETROTHAL* First stage of marriage transaction; engagement. *See* Marriage, Marriage Customs.

BEULAH* Hebrew word used once in the KJV as a proper name for Jerusalem, denoting a promised blessing for the people of God (Is 62:4). The word means "married" and was used symbolically by the prophet Isaiah to describe what God's special relationship would be to his restored people. The same theme recurs in NT references to the "Bride of Christ."
See also Bride of Christ.

BEZAI
1. Ancestor of a group of people who returned to Jerusalem with Zerubbabel after the Babylonian exile (Ezr 2:17; Neh 7:23).
2. Political leader who signed Ezra's covenant of faithfulness to God with Nehemiah and others after the exile (Neh 10:18).

BEZALEEL*, BEZALEL
1. Uri's son and the master craftsman from Judah's tribe who was specially equipped by God to be in charge of the construction and furnishing of the tabernacle (Ex 31:2; 35:30-31; 36:1-2; 37:1; 38:22; 1 Chr 2:20; 2 Chr 1:5) In the KJV the name is Bezaleel.
2. Pahath-moab's son, who obeyed Ezra's exhortation to divorce his pagan wife after the exile (Ezr 10:30). In the KJV the name is Bezaleel.

BEZEK
1. Site of a major victory for the tribes of Simeon and Judah over the Perizzites and Canaanites (Jgs 1:3-7). Adoni-bezek, which means "lord of Bezek," was king of the city at that time. Bezek was perhaps located at Khirbet Bezqa, a few miles northwest of Jerusalem.
2. Place where Saul gathered an army to attack the Ammonites who were troubling Jabesh-gilead (1 Sm 11:8-11). This Bezek is usually located at Khirbet Ibziq, a little south of Mt Gilboa.

BEZER (Person) Zophah's son in Asher's tribe (1 Chr 7:37).

BEZER (Place) City of refuge in Reuben's desert territory east of the Jordan River (Dt 4:43; Jos 20:8), later allotted to the Merari family of Levites (Jos 21:36; 1 Chr 6:78). It is probably a variant spelling of Bozrah in Jeremiah 48:24. According to the Moabite Stone, Bezer was among the cities rebuilt by King Mesha of Moab.
See also Bozrah #2; Cities of Refuge.

BIBLE* Derived from the Greek *biblia* ("books"), which, though plural, came to be used as a singular noun and to stand for the collection of books known as the Scriptures. The idea of a collection of holy writings developed early in Hebrew-Christian thought. Daniel in the sixth century BC spoke of a prophetic writing as "the books"

(Dn 9:2). The writer of 1 Maccabees (second century BC) referred to the OT as "the holy books" (12:9). Jesus referred to the OT books as "the scriptures" (Mt 21:42), and Paul spoke of them as "the holy scriptures" (Rom 1:2).

The Bible is divided into the Old Testament and the New Testament. Of course, there was no OT and NT before the coming of Christ, only one collection of sacred writings. But after the apostles and their associates produced another body of sacred literature, the church began to refer to the OT and the NT. Actually "testament" is the translation of a Greek word that might better be rendered "covenant." It denotes an arrangement made by God for the spiritual guidance and benefit of human beings. The covenant is unalterable: humankind may accept it or reject it but cannot change it. "Covenant" is a common OT word; of several covenants described in the OT, the most prominent was the law given to Moses. While Israel was chafing and failing under the Mosaic covenant, God promised them a "new covenant" (Jer 31:31).

The term "new covenant" appears several times in the NT. Jesus used it when he instituted the Lord's Supper; by it he sought to call attention to the new basis of communion with God he intended to establish by his death (Lk 22:20; 1 Cor 11:25). The apostle Paul also spoke of that new covenant (2 Cor 3:6, 14), as did the writer to the Hebrews (Heb 8:8; 9:11-15). The detailed description of God's new method of dealing with people (on the basis of the finished work of Christ on the cross) is the subject of the 27 books of the NT. God's dealing with people in anticipation of the coming of Messiah (Hebrew equivalent of "Christ," meaning "anointed one") is certainly the major theme of the 39 books of the OT, though they deal with much more than that. Latin church writers used *testamentum* to translate "covenant," and from them the use passed into English; so old and new covenants became OT and NT.

At least the first half of the OT follows a logical and easily understood arrangement. In Genesis through Esther the history of Israel from Abraham to the restoration under Persian auspices appears largely in chronological order. Then follows a group of poetic books and the Major and Minor Prophets ("Major" meaning the books that are relatively long; "Minor" meaning the books that are relatively short).

The NT also follows a generally logical arrangement. It begins with the four Gospels, which describe the birth, life, death, and resurrection of Christ and his training of disciples to carry on his work after his ascension. The book of Acts continues the narrative where the Gospels end and details the founding of the church and its spread through Mediterranean lands. In the latter part of the book the spotlight focuses on the apostle Paul and his church planting activities. Next come letters Paul addressed to churches he founded or to young ministers he tried to encourage. Following the Pauline Epistles come a group commonly called the General Epistles. The last book, Revelation, is an apocalyptic work.

The OT was written almost entirely in Hebrew with a few isolated passages in Aramaic in the latter books. If one accepts the view that Moses wrote the first five books of the OT (the position the Scripture itself takes), the earliest books of the OT were written by about 1400 BC (provided one accepts the early date proposed for the exodus). If the last book written was Malachi (before 400 BC), composition took place during 1,000 years of time. All the writers (some 30 in number) were Jews: prophets, judges, kings, and other leaders in Israel.

The NT was probably written entirely in Greek. If James was the first to write a NT book before the middle of the first century, and if John was the last (composing Revelation about AD 90), the NT was written during a 50-year period in the latter half of the first century. All the writers (probably nine) were Jews, with the exception of Luke (writer of Luke and Acts), and they came from a variety of walks of life: fishermen, doctor, tax collector, and religious leaders.

In spite of great diversity of authorship in the OT and NT, and composition spanning over 1,500 years, there is remarkable unity in the total thrust. Christians believe that God must have been superintending the production of a divine-human book that would properly present his message to humankind.

The OT and NT are component parts of one divine revelation. The OT describes man and woman in the first paradise on the old earth; the NT concludes with a vision of the new heaven and new earth. The OT sees humankind as fallen from a sinless condition and separated from God; the NT views believers as restored to favor through the sacrifice of Christ. The OT predicts a coming Redeemer who will rescue men and women from eternal condemnation; the NT reveals the Christ who brought salvation. In most of the OT the spotlight focuses on a sacrificial system in which the blood of animals provided a temporary handling of the sin problem; in the New, Christ appeared as the one who came to put an end to all sacrifice—to be himself the supreme sacrifice. In the OT, numerous predictions foretold a coming Messiah who would save his people; in the New, scores of passages detail how those prophecies were minutely fulfilled in the person of Jesus Christ: the "son of Abraham" and the "son of David" (Mt 1:1). As Augustine said more than 1,500 years ago, "The New is in the Old contained; the Old is in the New explained."

The Authority of the Bible Judge of men and nations, the self-revealed God wields unlimited authority and power. All creaturely authority and power is derived from that of God. As the sovereign Creator of all, the God of the Bible wills and has the right to be obeyed. The power God bestows is a divine trust, a stewardship. God's creatures are morally accountable for their use or misuse of it. In fallen human society God wills civil government for the promotion of justice and order. He approves an ordering of authoritative and creative relationships in the home by stipulating certain responsibilities of husbands, wives, and children. He wills a pattern of priorities for the church as well: Jesus Christ the head, prophets and apostles through whom redemptive revelation came, and so on. The inspired Scriptures, revealing God's transcendent will in objective written form, are the rule of faith and conduct through which Christ exercises his divine authority in the lives of Christians.

Revolt against particular authorities has in our time widened into a revolt against all transcendent and external authority. The widespread questioning of authority is condoned and promoted in many academic circles. Philosophers with a radically secular outlook have affirmed that God and the supernatural are mythical conceptions, that natural processes and events comprise the only ultimate reality. All existence is said to be temporal and changing, all beliefs and ideals are declared to be relative to the age and culture in which they appear. Biblical religion, therefore, like all other, is asserted to be merely a cultural phenomenon. The Bible's claim to divine authority is dismissed by such thinkers; transcendent revelation, fixed truths, and unchanging commandments are set aside as pious fictions.

In the name of man's supposed "coming of age," radical secularism champions human autonomy and creative

individuality. Man is his own lord and the inventor of his own ideals and values, it is said. He lives in a supposedly purposeless universe that has itself presumably been engendered by a cosmic accident. Therefore, human beings are declared to be wholly free to impose upon nature and history whatever moral criteria they prefer. In such a view, to insist on divinely given truths and values, on transcendent principles, would be to repress self-fulfillment and retard creative personal development. Hence, the radically secular view goes beyond opposing particular external authorities whose claims are considered arbitrary or immoral; radical secularism is aggressively hostile to all external and objective authority, viewing it as intrinsically restrictive of the autonomous human spirit.

Any reader of the Bible recognizes rejection of divine authority and of a definitive revelation of what is right and good as an age-old phenomenon. It is not at all peculiar to contemporary man to "come of age"; it was found already in Eden. Adam and Eve revolted against the will of God in pursuit of individual preference and self-interest. But their revolt was recognized to be sin, not rationalized as philosophical *gnosis* at the frontiers of evolutionary advance.

If one takes a strictly developmental view, which considers all reality contingent and changing, what basis remains for humanity's decisively creative role in the universe? How could a purposeless cosmos cater to individual self-fulfillment? Only the biblical alternative of the Creator-Redeemer God, who fashioned human beings for moral obedience and a high spiritual destiny, truly preserves the permanent, universal dignity of the human species. The Bible does so, however, by a demanding call for personal spiritual decision. The Bible sets forth man's superiority to the animals, his high dignity ("a little lower than God," Ps 8:5, NASB) because of the divine rational and moral image that he bears by creation. In the context of universal human involvement in Adamic sin, the Bible utters a merciful divine call to redemptive renewal through the mediatorial person and work of Christ. Fallen humanity is invited to experience the Holy Spirit's renewing work, to be conformed to the image of Jesus Christ, and to anticipate a final destiny in the eternal presence of the God of justice and justification.

Contemporary rejection of biblical tenets does not rest on any logical demonstration that the case for biblical theism is false; it turns rather on a subjective preference for alternative views of "the good life."

The Bible is not the only significant reminder that human beings stand daily in responsible relationship to the sovereign God. The Creator reveals his authority in the cosmos, in history, and in inner conscience, a disclosure of the living God that penetrates into the mind of every human being (Rom 1:18-20; 2:12-15). Rebellious suppression of that "general divine revelation" does not succeed in wholly suspending a fearsome sense of final divine accountability (1:32). Yet it is the Bible as "special revelation" that most clearly confronts our spiritually rebellious race with the reality and authority of God. In the Scriptures, the character and will of God, the meaning of human existence, the nature of the spiritual realm, and the purposes of God for human beings in all ages are stated in propositionally intelligible form that all can understand. The Bible publishes in objective form the criteria by which God judges individuals and nations, and the means of moral recovery and restoration to personal fellowship with him.

Regard for the Bible is therefore decisive for the course of Western culture and in the long run for human civilization generally. Intelligible divine revelation, the basis for belief in the sovereign authority of the Creator-Redeemer God over all human life, rests on the reliability of what Scripture says about God and his purposes. Modern naturalism impugns the authority of the Bible and assails the claim that the Bible is the Word of God written, that is, a transcendently given revelation of the mind and will of God in objective literary form. Scriptural authority is the storm center both in the controversy over revealed religion and in the modern conflict over civilizational values.

The Bible's View of Itself The intelligible nature of divine revelation—the presupposition that God's will is made known in the form of valid truths—is the central presupposition of the authority of the Bible. Much recent neo-Protestant theology demeaned the traditional evangelical emphasis as doctrinaire and static. It insisted instead that the authority of Scripture is to be experienced internally as a witness to divine grace engendering faith and obedience, thus disowning its objective character as universally valid truth. Somewhat inconsistently, almost all neo-Protestant theologians have appealed to the record to support cognitively whatever fragments of the whole seem to coincide with their divergent views, even though they disavow the Bible as a specially revealed corpus of authoritative divine teaching. If God's revelational disclosure to chosen prophets and apostles is to be considered meaningful and true, it must be given not merely in isolated concepts capable of diverse meanings but in sentences or propositions. A proposition—that is, a subject, predicate, and connecting verb (or "copula")—constitutes the minimal logical unit of intelligible communication. The OT prophetic formula "Thus saith the Lord" characteristically introduced propositionally disclosed truth. Jesus Christ employed the distinctive formula "But I say unto you" to introduce logically formed sentences that he represented as the veritable word or doctrine of God.

The Bible is authoritative because it is divinely authorized; in its own terms, "all Scripture is God-breathed" (2 Tm 3:16, NIV). According to this passage, the whole OT (or any element of it) is divinely inspired. Extension of the same claim to the NT is not expressly stated, but it is not merely implied. The New Testament contains indications that its content was to be viewed, and was in fact viewed, as no less authoritative than the Old. The apostle Paul's writings are catalogued with "other Scriptures" (2 Pt 3:15-16). Under the heading of "Scripture," 1 Timothy 5:18 cites Luke 10:7 alongside Deuteronomy 25:4 (cf. 1 Cor 9:9). The book of Revelation, moreover, claims divine origin (1:1-3) and employs the term "prophecy" in the OT sense (22:9-10, 18). The apostles did not distinguish their spoken and written teaching but expressly declared their inspired proclamation to be the word of God (1 Cor 4:1; 2 Cor 5:20; 1 Thes 2:13).

The Bible remains the most extensively printed, most widely translated, and most frequently read book in the world. Its words have been treasured in the hearts of multitudes like none other's. All who have received its gifts of wisdom and promises of new life and power were at first strangers to its redemptive message, and many were hostile to its teaching and spiritual demands. In all generations its power to challenge persons of all races and lands has been demonstrated. Those who cherish the Book because it sustains future hope, brings meaning and power to the present, and correlates a misused past with the forgiving grace of God would not long experience such inner rewards if

Scripture were not known to them as the authoritative, divinely revealed truth. To the Christian, Scripture is the Word of God given in the objective form of propositional truths through divinely inspired prophets and apostles, and the Holy Spirit is the giver of faith through that word.

PREVIEW
Several other major articles on the Bible follow:
• Bible, Canon of the
• Bible, Inspiration of the
• Bible, Manuscripts and Text of the (Old Testament)
• Bible, Manuscripts and Text of the (New Testament)
• Bible, Quotations of the Old Testament in the New Testament
• Bible, Versions of the (Ancient)
• Bible, Versions of the (English)

BIBLE*, Canon of the Those books in the Jewish and Christian Bible considered to be Scripture and therefore authoritative in matters of faith and doctrine. The term translates both a Greek and a Hebrew word that mean "a rule," or "measuring rod." It is a list to which other books are compared and by which they are measured. After the fourth century AD, the Christian church found itself with only 66 books that constituted its Scripture; 27 of these were the NT and 39 were the OT. Just as Plato, Aristotle, and Homer form a canon of Greek literature, so the NT books became the canon of Christian literature. The criteria for selecting the books in the Jewish canon (the OT) are not known but clearly had to do with their worth in the ongoing life and religion of the worshiping nation. The criteria of the selection of NT books revolved around their "apostolicity," according to early church writers. Like those of the OT, these books were collected and preserved by local churches in the continuing process of their worship and need for authoritative guidance for Christian living. The formation of the canon was a process, rather than an event, that took several hundred years to reach finality in all parts of the Roman Empire. Local canons were the basis for comparison, and out of them eventually emerged the general canon that exists in Christendom today, although some of the Eastern churches have a NT that is slightly smaller than that accepted in the West. Judaism, as well as Christianity as a whole, believes that the Spirit of God was operative in some providential way in the production and preservation of his Word.

Canon of the Old Testament The Old Testament is a name that does not appear in Jewish literature. Jews prefer to call their collection of Scriptures the TANAK—an acronym formed from the first letters of *Torah* (Law), *Nevi'im* (Prophets), and *Kethubim* (Writings). In Luke 24:44 (NIV), these are called the "Law of Moses, the Prophets and the Psalms" (the first book of the Writings in the Hebrew Bible). Christians called their collection of writings the New Testament, or covenant, the latter term being a designation earlier used of the agreement God made with Abraham and the patriarchs, which was repeated by Christ to his apostles (Mt 26:28). Christians in the first century considered their new covenant from Christ (1 Cor 11:25) to be a continuation of the one made earlier with the patriarchs (Eph 2:12), spoken of by the prophets (Jer 31:31-34), and which was therefore called a former covenant (Heb 8:7-13; 9:1, 15-22) or in later centuries the OT. The terms "Old" and "New" do not appear in the apostolic fathers of the first and second century or in the apologists of the early- to mid-second century, but they do appear in the latter half of the second century in Justin Martyr (*Dialogues* 11:2), Irenaeus (*Against Heresies* 4.9.1), and Clement of Alexandria (*Stromata* 1:5). In these authors the expression referred more to the covenant itself than to the books containing it, though the transfer was eventually made. The term "canon" was not used in the OT or NT to refer to the Jewish Scriptures. The idea of limitation inherent in the word was not appropriate to the nature of religious authority in Jewish religion during the thousand years when the OT books were being written. Only the Torah was conceived as incapable of being added to or taken from (Dt 4:2). Jewish religion existed for a millennium, from Moses to Malachi, without a closed canon, i.e., an exclusive list of authoritative books. Never in their history did the people of the OT have the entire 39 books of the OT. When their canon was closed is not known. Although some questions were being asked about religious authority by rabbis at Jamnia 20 years after the fall of Jerusalem in AD 70, we have our first list of 39 books produced by Melito of Sardis around AD 170. That list included no books written after the time of Malachi, unless one is disposed to date Daniel to the second century. The Prophets and the Writings were always considered secondary to the Law. Their composition and collection was a process rather than an event in the life of the people of Israel and functioned largely as a record of the nation's response to the Law, which was so sacred that it was kept (according to rabbinical tradition: Babylonian Talmud, *Baba Bathra* 14a; cf. also *Cairo Damascus Document* 5.2) in the ark of the covenant that stood in the Holy of Holies in the tabernacle. In Deuteronomy 31:26, however, the Levites were commanded by Moses merely to put the Book of the Law beside the ark. Nevertheless, its very presence in the Holy of Holies establishes its uniqueness in relation to other OT books.

THE OLD TESTAMENT CANON

The Jews divide their Scriptures into three sections.

1. **The Law**	2. **The Prophets**	3. **The Writings**
Genesis	*Former Prophets*	Psalms
Exodus	Joshua	Proverbs
Leviticus	Judges	Job
Numbers	Samuel (1 & 2)	Five Scrolls
Deuteronomy	Kings (1 & 2)	Song of Songs
		Ruth
	Latter Prophets	Lamentations
	Isaiah	Ecclesiastes
	Jeremiah	Esther
	Ezekiel	Daniel
	The Twelve	Ezra-Nehemiah
	Hosea	Chronicles (1 & 2)
	Joel	
	Amos	
	Obadiah	
	Jonah	
	Micah	
	Nahum	
	Habbakuk	
	Zephaniah	
	Haggai	
	Zechariah	
	Malachi	

The 39 books of the modern OT were originally divided into only 24, according to the uniform testimony of early Hebrew tradition. The Talmud, rabbinic literature, and probably 4 Esdras testify to this arrangement that included five books of the Law, eight Prophets, and eleven Writings (Greek—Hagiographa). Modern Hebrew Bibles reflect this tripartite arrangement that was used in the first three printed editions (Soncino, 1488; Naples, 1491–1493; Brescia, 1492–1494). The Law contained the Pentateuch in our familiar order, Genesis to Deuteronomy. The eight Prophets were Joshua, Judges, Samuel (1 and 2), Kings (1 and 2), Isaiah, Jeremiah, Ezekiel, and the Minor Prophets (all 12), which were considered as one book and arranged in the same order as our English Bibles. The eleven books of Writings contained three of poetry (Ps, Prv, Jb), the Five Scrolls (Sg, Ru, Lam, Eccl, Est), which were read at the important feasts and arranged in the chronological order of their observance, and three of narrative or historical (Dn, Ezr-Neh, 1 and 2 Chr).

Apart from authentic Jewish tradition, efforts were made to divide the books into 21, combining Ruth with Judges, and Lamentations with Jeremiah. Josephus was the first to do so, in the first century AD, but he was influenced by the Greek OT, the Septuagint. Origen observed in the early third century that this arrangement also corresponded to the number of letters in the Hebrew alphabet, as did Athanasius in the fourth, and others, including Jerome. It was dubiously concluded that the number of books in the Hebrew Bible had been divinely ordained to agree with the number of letters of the Hebrew alphabet! Church fathers added their support to this coincidence, which became providence to them. All such efforts, however, are of Greek origin and have no support in Hebrew tradition.

The oldest extant manuscripts of the complete OT in Hebrew are the Masoretic Texts, which are no earlier than the eighth century AD. Only manuscripts of individual books have been found in the Dead Sea Scrolls. The Masoretic scribes apparently laid down no rules about arrangement of books because there is no uniform order of the Latter Prophets or the Writings in early Hebrew manuscripts. Nor is the situation any different in ancient Greek translations of the Hebrew. Great diversity exists in the order of books in all three of our oldest manuscripts—Codex Alexandrinus, Vaticanus, and Sinaiticus. All the early Christian authors who profess to give the order and contents of the Hebrew Bible but who do not reflect the Hebrew tripartite division are clearly dependent on the Alexandrian order reflected in these Greek editions, rather than on the Hebrew Bible. Modern Protestant Bibles follow the order of the Latin Vulgate and the content of the Hebrew. Both the Vulgate and the Septuagint (Greek translation) contained the Apocrypha, which was never accepted by the Jews. The Roman Catholic Church includes the Apocrypha in its English translations because of the influence of the Vulgate on Catholic tradition. It is considered deuterocanonical.

Even though no uniformity of order was maintained, the Alexandrian order, reflected in the Greek manuscripts, generally arranged books according to their subject matter—narrative, history, poetry, and prophecy, with the apocryphal books appropriately interspersed into these categories. The Hebrew division was totally ignored.

Early Hebrew Bibles divided the text into small paragraphs and larger sections somewhat akin to our paragraphs. These were indicated by spaces left between them—three letters between the small sections and nine letters between the larger ones. The number of sections is not the same in all manuscripts. Jesus probably referred to such sections in his comment concerning the "passage about the bush" (Mk 12:26). Later, liturgical needs led to further divisions of the text for the complete reading of the Law in Babylonian synagogues in one year (54 sections) and in Palestinian synagogues in three years (154 sections). These are reflected in the lectionary cycles marked in some early Hebrew Bibles.

The division of the text into modern chapters, done in the 13th century (c. 1228) for the Latin Vulgate by Stephen Langton, was applied to the Hebrew Bible in 1518 (Bomberg Edition), but the numbers were not given to the chapters until 1571 in the text of Montanus, a Hebrew Bible with Latin interlinear translation. The verses were introduced in Bomberg's Great Bible of 1547–48 in which every fifth verse was designated by a Hebrew numeral 1, 5, 10, and so on. Verses were inserted into the Latin Vulgate in 1555 in the small octavo edition of Stephanus.

Canon of the New Testament The NT was written within the period of half a century, several hundred years after the completion of the OT. Both halves of that statement would be questioned by modern critics, who would extend the time span for completion of both Testaments. The writer of this survey is confident of its truthfulness to historic fact, however, and the approach taken to canonization of both OT and NT is based solidly upon that twofold premise.

In a sense, we possess far higher certification of the OT canon than of the NT canon. We refer to the fact of our Lord's own imprimatur by way of his use of the Hebrew Scriptures as the authoritative Word of God. Yet there is a sense in which Jesus Christ did establish the NT content or canon as well, by way of anticipation. It was he who promised, "The Counselor, the Holy Spirit, whom the Father will send in my name, will teach you all things and will remind you of everything I have said to you" and "he will guide you into all truth" (Jn 14:26; 16:13, NIV).

THE NEW TESTAMENT CANON
Christians divide their Scriptures into three sections.

1. **Gospels and Acts**	2. **Paul's Epistles**	3. **General Epistles and Revelation**
Matthew	Romans	Hebrews
Mark	1 Corinthians	James
Luke	2 Corinthians	1 Peter
John	Galatians	2 Peter
Acts	Ephesians	1 John
	Philippians	2 John
	Colossians	3 John
	1 Thessalonians	Jude
	2 Thessalonians	Revelation
	1 Timothy	
	2 Timothy	
	Titus	
	Philemon	

From this we can derive, in turn, the basic principle of canonicity for the NT. It is identical to that of the OT, since it narrows down to a matter of divine inspiration. Whether we think of the prophets of OT times or the apostles and their God-given associates of the New, the recognition at the very time of their writing that they were authentic spokesmen for God is what determines the intrinsic canonicity of their writing. It is altogether God's Word only if it is God-breathed. We can be assured that the books under question were received by the church of the apostolic age precisely when they had been certified by an apostle as being thus inspired. The apparent variation, relative to geographic area, in acknowledgment of some of the NT epistles may well reflect the simple fact that this attestation was by its very

nature localized at first. Conversely, that all 27 books of the now universally received NT were ultimately agreed upon is evidence that proper attestation was indeed confirmed after rigorous investigation.

Tertullian, an outstanding Christian writer in the first two decades of the third century, was one of the first to call the Christian Scriptures the "New Testament." That title had appeared earlier (c. 190) in a composition against Montanism, the author of which is unknown. This is significant. Its use placed the NT Scripture on a level of inspiration and authority with the OT.

From available information, the gradual process that led to full and formal public recognition of a fixed canon of the 27 books comprising the NT takes us down into the fourth century of our era. This does not necessarily mean that these Scriptures were lacking recognition in their entirety before that time, but that a need for officially defining the canon was not pressing until then.

Though a much shorter period of time was involved in the writing of the NT than the OT, the geographic range of its origin is far wider. This circumstance alone is sufficient to account for a lack of spontaneous or simultaneous recognition of the precise extent of the NT canon. Because of the geographic isolation of the various recipients of portions of the NT, there was bound to be some lag and uncertainty from one region to another in the acknowledgment of some of the books.

In order to appreciate just what did transpire in the process of canonization of the NT books, we must review the facts available to us. This will enable us to analyze *how* and *why* our early Christian forebears settled upon the 27 books in our NT.

The historic process was a gradual and continuous one, but it will help us understand it if we subdivide the nearly three and a half centuries involved into shorter periods of time. Some speak of three major stages toward canonization. This implies, without justification, that there are readily discernible steps along the way. Others simply present a long list of the names of persons and documents involved. Such a list makes it difficult to sense any motion at all. A somewhat arbitrary breakdown into five periods will be made here, with the reminder that the spreading of the knowledge of sacred literature and the deepening consensus as to its authenticity as inspired Scripture continued uninterruptedly. The periods are:

1. First Century
2. First Half of Second Century
3. Second Half of Second Century
4. Third Century
5. Fourth Century

Again, without meaning to imply that these are clear-cut stages, it will be helpful to notice the major trends observable in each of the periods just identified. In the first period, of course, the various books were written, but they also began to be copied and disseminated among the churches. In the second, as they became more widely known and cherished for their contents, they began to be cited as authoritative. By the end of the third period, they held a recognized place alongside the OT as "Scripture," and they began to be both translated into regional languages and made the subject of commentaries. During the third century AD, our fourth period, the collecting of books into a whole "New Testament" was underway, together with a sifting process that was separating them from other Christian literature. The final, or fifth, period finds the church fathers of the fourth century stating that conclusions regarding the canon have been reached that indicate acceptance by the whole church. Thus, in the most strict and formal sense of the word, the canon had become fixed. It remains to list in greater detail the forces and individuals that produced the written sources witnessing to this remarkable process through which, by God's providence, we have inherited our NT.

Period One: First Century The principle determining recognition of the authority of the canonical NT writings was established within the content of those writings themselves. There are repeated exhortations for public reading of the apostolic communications. At the close of his First Letter to the Thessalonians, possibly the first book of the NT to be written, Paul says, "I command you in the name of the Lord to read this letter to all the brothers and sisters" (1 Thes 5:27, NLT). Earlier in the same letter Paul commends their ready acceptance of his spoken word as "the word of God" (2:13), and in 1 Corinthians 14:37 he speaks similarly of his "writings," insisting that his message be recognized as a commandment from the Lord himself. (See also Col 4:16; Rv 1:3.) In 2 Peter 3:15-16 Paul's letters are included with "the other Scriptures." Since Peter's is a general letter, widespread knowledge of Paul's letters is thereby implied. Highly indicative also is Paul's usage in 1 Timothy 5:18. He follows up the formula "the Scriptures say" by a combined quotation about not muzzling an ox (Dt 25:4) and "the worker deserves his wages" (cf. Lk 10:7). Thus, an equivalence is implied between OT Scripture and a NT Gospel.

In AD 95, Clement of Rome wrote to the Christians in Corinth using a free rendering of material from Matthew and Luke. He seems to be strongly influenced by Hebrews and is obviously familiar with Romans and Corinthians. There are also reflections of Ephesians, 1 Timothy, Titus, and 1 Peter.

Period Two: First Half of Second Century One of the earliest NT manuscripts yet discovered, a fragment of John from Egypt known as the John Rylands papyrus, demonstrates how the writings of the apostle John were revered and copied by about AD 125, within 30 to 35 years of his death. There is evidence that within 30 years of the apostle's death all the Gospels and Pauline letters were known and used in all those centers from which any evidence has come down to us. It is true that some of the smaller letters were being questioned as to their authority in some quarters for perhaps another 50 years, but this was due only to uncertainty about their authorship in those particular locales. This demonstrates that acceptance was not being imposed by the actions of councils but was rather happening spontaneously through a normal response on the part of those who had learned the facts about authorship. In those places where the churches were uncertain about the authorship or apostolic approval of certain books, acceptance was slower.

The first three outstanding church fathers, Clement, Polycarp, and Ignatius, used the bulk of the material of the NT in a revealingly casual manner—authenticated Scriptures were being accepted as authoritative without argument. In the writings of these men only Mark (which closely parallels the material of Matthew), 2 Peter, 2 and 3 John, and Jude are not clearly attested.

The Epistles of Ignatius (c. AD 115) have correspondences in several places with the Gospels and seem to incorporate language from a number of the Pauline letters. The Didache (or Teaching of the Twelve), perhaps even earlier, makes references to a written Gospel. Most important is the fact that Clement, Barnabas, and Ignatius all draw a clear distinction between their own and the inspired, authoritative apostolic writings.

It is in the Epistle of Barnabas (c. AD 130) that we first find the formula "it is written" (4:14) used in reference to a NT book (Mt 22:14). But even before this, Polycarp, who had personal acquaintance with eyewitnesses of our Lord's ministry, used a combined OT and NT quotation. Citing Paul's admonition in Ephesians 4:26, where the apostle quotes Psalm 4:4 and makes an addition, Polycarp in his Epistle to the Philippians introduces the reference by "as it is said in these Scriptures" (12:4). Then Papias, bishop of Hierapolis (c. 130–140), in a work preserved for us by Eusebius, mentions by name the Gospels of Matthew and Mark, and his use of them as the basis of exposition indicates his acceptance of them as canonical. Also around AD 140, the recently discovered Gospel of Truth (a Gnostic-oriented work probably authored by Valentinius) makes an important contribution. Its use of canonical NT sources, treating them as authoritative, is comprehensive enough to warrant the conclusion that in Rome at this period there was a NT compilation in existence corresponding very closely to our own. Citations are made from the Gospels, Acts, letters of Paul, Hebrews, and the book of Revelation.

The heretic Marcion, by defining a limited canon of his own (c. 140), in effect hastened the day when the orthodox believers needed to declare themselves on this issue. Rejecting the entire OT, Marcion settled for Luke's Gospel (eliminating chapters 1 and 2 as too Jewish) and Paul's letters (except for the pastoral ones). Interestingly, especially in the light of Colossians 4:16, he substitutes the name "Laodiceans" for Ephesians.

Near the end of this period, Justin Martyr, in describing the worship services of the early church, puts the apostolic writings on a par with those of the OT prophets. He states that the voice which spoke through the apostles of Christ in the NT was the same as that which spoke through the prophets—the voice of God—and the same voice that Abraham heard, responding in faith and obedience. Justin was also free in his use of "it is written" with quotations from NT Scriptures.

Period Three: Second Half of Second Century Irenaeus had been privileged to begin his Christian training under Polycarp, a disciple of apostles. Then, as a presbyter in Lyons, he had association with Bishop Pothinus, whose own background also included contact with first-generation Christians. Irenaeus quotes from almost all the NT on the basis of its authority and asserts that the apostles were endowed with power from on high. They were, he says, "fully informed concerning all things, and had a perfect knowledge . . . having indeed all in equal measure and each one singly the Gospel of God" (*Against Heresies* 3.3). Irenaeus gives reasons why there should be four Gospels. "The word," he says, "gave us the Gospel in a fourfold shape, but held together by one Spirit." In addition to the Gospels, he makes reference also to Acts, all the letters of Paul except Philemon, 1 Peter, 1 John, and the book of Revelation.

Tatian, pupil of Justin Martyr, made a harmony of the four Gospels, the *Diatessaron*, attesting to the equal status they had in the church by AD 170. Other "gospels" had come into existence by then, but he recognized only the four. Also dating from about 170 was the *Muratorian Canon*. An eighth-century copy of this document was discovered and published in 1740 by librarian L. A. Muratori. The manuscript is mutilated at both ends, but the remaining text makes it evident that Matthew and

Mark were included in the now missing part. The fragment begins with Luke and John, cites Acts, 13 Pauline letters, 1 and 2 John, Jude, and Revelation. There follows a statement, "We accept only the Apocalypse of John and Peter, although some of us do not want it [Apocalypse of Peter is 2 Peter?] to be read in the Church." The list goes on to reject by name various heretical leaders and their writings.

Translated versions existed by this period. In the form of Syriac and Old Latin translations we secure, by AD 170, adequate witness from the extreme eastern and western branches of the church, as we might well expect from the other evidence in hand. The NT canon is represented with no additions and the omission of only one book, 2 Peter.

Period Four: Third Century The outstanding Christian name of the third century is that of Origen (AD 185–254). A prodigious scholar and interpreter, he made critical studies of the NT text (alongside his work on the *Hexapla*) and wrote commentaries and homilies on most of the books of the NT, emphasizing their inspiration by God.

Dionysius of Alexandria, pupil of Origen, indicates that while the Western church accepted the book of Revelation from the first, its position in the East was variable. In the case of the Letter to the Hebrews, the situation was reversed. It proved to be more insecure in the West than in the East. When it comes to other contested books (note, incidentally, that all in that category have the hindmost position in our present Bibles—Hebrews to Revelation), among the so-called "Catholic Epistles" Dionysius supports James and 2 and 3 John but not 2 Peter or Jude. In other words, even at the end of the third century there was the same lack of finality about certain books as at its beginning.

Period Five: Fourth Century Early in this period, the picture begins to clarify. Eusebius (AD 270–340, bishop of Caesarea before 315), the great church historian, sets forth his estimate of the canon in his *Ecclesiastical History* (3.3–25). Herein he makes a straightforward statement on the status of the canon in the early part of the fourth century: (1) Universally agreed upon as canonical were the four Gospels, Acts, letters of Paul (including Hebrews, with question about his authorship), 1 Peter, 1 John, and Revelation. (2) Admitted by a majority, including Eusebius himself, but disputed by some were James, 2 Peter (the most strongly contested), 2 and 3 John, and Jude. (3) The Acts of Paul, the Didache, and Shepherd of Hermas were classified "spurious," and still other writings were listed as "heretical and absurd."

It is in the latter half of the fourth century, however, that the NT canon finds full and final declaration. In his *Festal Letter* for Easter, 367, Bishop Athanasius of Alexandria included information designed to eliminate once and for all the use of certain apocryphal books. This letter, with its admonition, "Let no one add to these; let nothing be taken away," gives us the earliest extant document that specifies our 27 books without qualification. At the close of the century, the Council of Carthage (AD 397) decreed that "aside from the canonical Scriptures nothing is to be read in church under the Name of Divine Scriptures." This, too, lists the 27 books of the NT.

The sudden advance of Christianity under Emperor Constantine (Edict of Milan, 313) had a great deal to do with the reception of all the NT books in the East. When he assigned Eusebius the task of preparing "fifty copies of the Divine Scriptures," the historian, fully aware of which were the sacred books for which many believers had been willing to lay down their very lives, in effect established the standard that gave recognition to all of the once-doubtful books. In the West, of course, Jerome and Augustine were the leaders who exercised a determinitive influence. Publication of the 27 books in the Vulgate version virtually settled the matter.

Principles and Factors Determining the Canon By its very nature, Holy Scripture, whether OT or NT, is a production given of God, not the work of human creation. The key to canonicity is divine inspiration. Therefore, the method of determination is not one of selection from a number of possible candidates (there are no other candidates, in actuality) but one of reception of authentic material and its consequent recognition by an ever-widening circle as the facts of its origin become known.

In a sense, the movement of Montanus, which was declared heretical by the church of his day (mid-second century), was an impetus toward the recognition of a closed canon of the written Word of God. He taught that the prophetic gift was permanently granted to the church and that he himself was a prophet. The pressure to deal with Montanism, therefore, intensified the search for a basic authority, and apostolic authorship or approval became recognized as the only sure standard for identifying God's revelation. Even within the Scripture record, first-century prophets were subordinate and subject to apostolic authority (see, for example, 1 Cor 14:29-30; Eph 4:11).

When all things were being reexamined in the Protestant Reformation, some of the Reformers sought means of reassuring themselves and their followers about the canon of Scripture. This was in some ways an unfortunate aspect of Reformation thinking, because once God in his providence had determined for his people the fixed content of Scripture, that became a fact of history and was not a repeatable process. Nevertheless, Luther established a theological test for the books of the Bible (and questioned some of them)—"Do they teach Christ?" Equally subjective, it would seem, was Calvin's insistence that the Spirit of God bears witness to each individual Christian in any age of church history as to what is his Word and what is not.

Actually, even for the initial acceptance of the written Word, it is neither safe nor sound (as far as Scripture or history teaches us) to say that recognition and reception was an intuitive matter. It was rather a matter of simple obedience to the known commands of Christ and his apostles. As we saw at the outset, our Lord promised (Jn 14:26; 16:13) to communicate all things necessary through his agents. The apostles were conscious of this responsibility and agency as they wrote. Paul's explanation in 1 Corinthians 2:13 is apropos: "In telling you about these gifts we have even used the very words given to us by the Holy Spirit, not words that we as men might choose. So we use the Holy Spirit's words to explain the Holy Spirit's facts" (TLB).

Hence, the early church, with closer ties and greater information than is available to us today, examined the testimony of the ancients. They were able to discern which were the authentic and authoritative books by their apostolic origin. Mark's association with Peter, and Luke's with Paul, gave them such apostolic approval, and epistles like Hebrews and Jude were also tied in with the apostolic message and ministry. Incontrovertible consistency of doctrine in all the books, including the sometime contested ones, was perhaps a subordinate test. But historically the procedure was essentially one of acceptance and approval of those books that were vouched for by knowledgeable church leaders. Full acceptance by the original recipients followed by a continued acknowledgment and use is an essential factor in the development of the canon.

The church's concept of canon, derived first of all from the reverence given the OT Scriptures, rested in the conviction that the apostles were uniquely authorized to speak in the name of the one who possessed all authority—the Lord Jesus Christ. The development from there is logical and straightforward. Those who heard Jesus in person were immediately subject to his authority. He personally authenticated his words to the believers. These same believers knew that Jesus authorized his apostles to speak in his name, both during and (more significantly) after his earthly ministry. Apostolic speaking on behalf of Christ was recognized in the church, whether in personal utterance or in written form. Both the spoken word of an apostle and the letter of an apostle constituted the word of Christ.

The generation that followed that of the apostles themselves received the witness of those who knew that the apostles had the right to speak and write in the name of Christ. Consequently, the second and third generation of Christians looked back to apostolic words (writings) as the very words of Christ. This is what is really meant by canonization—recognition of the divinely authenticated Word. Hence, the believers (the church) did not establish the canon but simply bore witness to its extent by recognizing the authority of the word of Christ.

BIBLE*, Inspiration of the

Theological term for the influence God exerted on the writers of Scripture, enabling them to transmit his revelations in writing.

The Bible itself tells us that it is an inspired text. It says, "All scripture is given by inspiration of God" (2 Tm 3:16, KJV). A translation closer to the original language (Greek) would be, "All Scripture is God-breathed" (NIV). This tells us that every word of the Bible was breathed out from God. The words of the Bible came from God and were written by men. The apostle Peter affirmed this when he said that "no prophecy of Scripture came about by the prophet's own interpretation. For prophecy never had its origin in the will of man, but men spoke from God as they were carried along by the Holy Spirit" (2 Pt 1:20-21, NIV).

"Men spoke from God." This short sentence is the key to understanding how the Bible came into being. Thousands of years ago, God chose certain men—such as Moses, David, Isaiah, Jeremiah, Ezekiel, and Daniel—to receive his words and write them down. What they wrote became books, or sections, of the OT. Nearly 2,000 years ago, God chose other men—such as Matthew, Mark, Luke, John, and Paul—to communicate his new message, the message of salvation through Jesus Christ. What they wrote became books, or sections, of the NT.

God gave his words to these men in many different ways. Certain writers of the OT received messages directly from God. Moses was given the Ten Commandments inscribed on a stone when he was in God's presence on Mt Sinai. When David was composing his psalms to God, he received divine inspiration to foretell certain events that would occur 1,000 years later in Jesus Christ's life. God told his prophets—such as Isaiah and Jeremiah—exactly what to say; therefore, when they gave a message, it was God's word, not their own. This is why

many OT prophets often said, "Thus says the Lord." (This statement appears over 2,000 times in the OT.) To other prophets, such as Ezekiel and Daniel, God communicated his message through visions and dreams. They recorded exactly what they saw, whether they understood it or not. And other OT writers, such as Samuel and Ezra, were directed by God to record events in the history of Israel.

ANTILEGOMENA: THE BOOKS THAT DIDN'T MAKE IT

In AD 303, the Roman emperor Diocletian began to direct severe persecution against the church. Orders were given to seek out and burn all Christian literature. In an effort to preserve their most sacred writings, the church leaders (or "fathers") were forced to decide which books were of such importance that they had to be protected at all costs. Other books, of lesser spiritual value, could then be surrendered. In order to make such a distinction, two criteria were generally agreed upon for evaluating the worth of a writing: its association with the early apostolic community and its spiritual value, determined by the degree to which it was used in the church. Despite agreement on those criteria, the fathers were unable to agree on the worth of several books. In 325 Eusebius of Caesarea in his *Ecclesiastical History* summarized the situation by distinguishing three classes of NT writings: the *homologoumena*, writings accepted by all; the *antilegomena*, disputed books; and the *notha*, writings that were completely absurd and unholy.

Eusebius subdivided the *antilegomena* into two groups. The first he called "the generally recognized books," writings of good quality and reputation. In that category Eusebius included James, 2 Peter, 2 and 3 John, and Jude. Those books later came to be completely accepted and along with the *homologoumena* now comprise the NT canon. The second group of *antilegomena* was called the "spurious" writings generally doubted by the fathers. Included among them were the Acts of Paul, Apocalypse of Peter, Shepherd of Hermas, Barnabas, Didache, the Gospel of Hebrews, and the Apocalypse of John (the NT book of Revelation). The fact that John's Apocalypse was numbered among both the *homologoumena* and the spurious *antilegomena* indicates the controversial nature of that work in the early church.

Four hundred years after the last book of the OT (Malachi) was written, God's Son, Jesus Christ, came to earth. In his talks, he affirmed the divine authorship of the OT writings (see Mt 5:17-19; Lk 16:17; Jn 10:35). Furthermore, he often pointed to certain passages in the OT as having predicted certain events in his life (see Lk 24:27, 44). The NT writers also affirmed the divine inspiration of the OT text. It was the apostle Paul who was directed by God to write, "All Scripture is God-inspired." Quite specifically, he was speaking of the OT. And, as was already noted, Peter said that the OT prophets were motivated by the Holy Spirit to speak from God.

The NT is also a God-inspired book. Before Jesus left this earth and returned to his Father, he told the disciples that he would send the Holy Spirit to them. He told them that one of the functions of the Holy Spirit would be to remind them of all the things that Jesus had said and then to guide them into more truth (see Jn 14:26; 15:26; 16:13-15). Those who wrote the Gospels were helped by the Holy Spirit to remember Jesus' exact words, and those who wrote other parts of the NT were guided by the Spirit as they wrote.

The inspiration for writing the Gospels didn't begin when the authors set pen to papyrus; the inspiration began when the disciples Matthew, Peter (for whom Mark wrote), and John were enlightened by their encounters with Jesus Christ, the Son of God. The apostles' experiences with him altered their lives forever, imprinting on their souls unforgettable images of the revealed God-man, Jesus Christ.

This is what John was speaking of in the prologue to his Gospel when he declared, "The Word became flesh and lived among us, and we have seen his glory" (1:14, paraphrased). The "we" refers to those eyewitnesses of Jesus' glory—the apostles who lived with Jesus for over three years. This reminiscence is expanded upon in John's prologue to his first epistle, where he says "we have heard him, touched him, seen him, and looked upon him" (1 Jn 1:1-2, paraphrased). In both the Gospel and the Epistle, the verbs are in the perfect tense, denoting a past action with a present, abiding effect. Those past encounters with Jesus were never forgotten by John; they lived with him and stayed with him as an inspiring spirit until the day—many years later—he wrote of them in his Gospel. The same could be said for Matthew, who wrote an important Gospel, and Peter, who was really the author behind Mark's composition. Luke was not an eyewitness, but he based his Gospel on the accounts of those who were (see Lk 1:1-4).

The inspiration for the writing of the Epistles can also be traced to the writers' encounters with the living Christ. The most prominent epistle writer, Paul, repeatedly claims that his inspiration and subsequent commission came from his encounter with the risen Christ (see, for example, 1 Cor 15:8-10). Peter also claims that his writings were based upon his experiences with the living Christ (see 1 Pt 5:1; 2 Pt 1:16-18). And so does John, who claims to have experienced the God-man visibly, audibly, and palpably (see 1 Jn 1:1-4). James and Jude make no such claim directly, but since they were the brothers of Jesus who became converts when they saw the risen Christ (this is certain for James—see 1 Cor 15:7—and presumed for Jude—see Acts 1:14), they too drew their inspiration from their encounters with the living Christ. Thus, all the epistle writers (with the possible exception of the one who wrote Hebrews, who is unknown) knew the living Christ. This is the relationship that qualified them to write those books that became part of the NT canon. This made them distinct from all others, no matter how good their writings were.

The writers of the NT epistles were inspired by the Spirit when they wrote. Speaking for all the apostles, Paul indicated that the NT apostles were taught by the Holy Spirit what to say. The writers of the NT did not speak with words "taught by human wisdom," but with "words taught by the Holy Spirit" (see 1 Cor 2:10-13). What they wrote was Spirit-taught. For example, when the apostle John saw that Jesus Christ had come to give eternal life to men, the Spirit helped him express this truth in many different ways. Thus, the reader of John's Gospel sees different phrases about Jesus giving life: "in him was life," "a well of living water springing up into eternal life," "the bread of life," "the light of life," "the resurrection and the life," etc. (see Jn 1:4; 4:14; 6:48; 8:12; 11:25; 14:6). When the apostle Paul contemplated the fullness of Christ's deity, he was inspired by the Spirit to use such phrasing as "in him dwells all the fullness of the Godhead

bodily," "in him are hid all the treasures of wisdom and knowledge," and "the unsearchable riches of Christ" (see Col 2:3, 9; Eph 3:8).

As the Spirit taught the writers, they used their own vocabulary and writing style to express the thought of the Spirit. As such, the Scriptures came as the result of divine and human cooperation. The Scriptures were not mechanically inspired—as if God used the men as machines through whom he dictated the divine utterance. Rather, the Scriptures were inspired by God, then written by men. The Bible, therefore, is both fully divine and fully human.

BIBLE*, Manuscripts and Text of the (Old Testament) Copies of the OT books produced by scribes and editions made from these copies. The ancient manuscripts of the OT are the basic working material used to seek out the original text of the Bible with as great a degree of accuracy as possible. This process is called textual criticism, sometimes designated "lower criticism" to distinguish it from "higher criticism," which is analysis of the date, unity, and authorship of the biblical writings.

PREVIEW
• Important Old Testament Manuscripts
• Significant Old Testament Versions
• The Text of the Old Testament

Important Old Testament Manuscripts Most medieval manuscripts of the OT exhibit a fairly standardized form of the Hebrew text. This standardization reflects the work of the medieval scribes known as Masoretes (AD 500–900); the text that resulted from their work is called the Masoretic Text. Most of the important manuscripts dated from the 11th century AD or later all reflect this same basic textual tradition. But since the Masoretic Text did not stabilize until well after AD 500, many questions about its development in the preceding centuries could not be answered. So the primary task for OT textual critics has been to compare earlier witnesses in order to discover how the Masoretic Text came to be, and how it and earlier witnesses of the Hebrew Bible are related. This leads us to the initial task of textual criticism: the collection of all possible records of the biblical writings.

All the primary sources of the Hebrew Scriptures are handwritten manuscripts, usually written on animal skins, papyrus, or sometimes metal. The fact that they are handwritten is the source of many difficulties for the textual critic. Human error and editorial tampering are often to blame for the many variant readings in OT and NT manuscripts. The fact that the ancient manuscripts are written on skins or papyrus is another source of difficulty. Due to natural decay, most of the surviving ancient manuscripts are fragmentary and difficult to read.

There are many secondary witnesses to the ancient OT text, including translations into other languages, quotations used by both friends and enemies of biblical religion, and evidence from early printed texts. Most of the secondary witnesses have suffered in ways similar to the primary ones. They, too, contain numerous variants due to both intentional and accidental scribal errors and are fragmentary as a result of natural decay. Since variant readings do exist in the surviving ancient manuscripts, these must be collected and compared. The task of comparing and listing the variant readings is known as collation.

Manuscripts with the Masoretic Text The textual history of the Masoretic Text is a significant story in its own right. This text of the Hebrew Bible is the most complete in existence. It forms the basis for our modern Hebrew Bibles and is the prototype against which all comparisons are made in OT textual studies. It is called Masoretic because in its present form it is based on the *Masora*, the textual tradition of the Jewish scholars known as the Masoretes of Tiberias. (Tiberias was the location of their community on the Sea of Galilee.) The Masoretes, whose school flourished between AD 500 and 1000, standardized the traditional consonantal text by adding vowel pointing and marginal notes. (The ancient Hebrew alphabet had no vowels.)

The Masoretic Text, as it exists today, owes much to the Ben Asher family. For five or six generations, from the second half of the eighth century to the middle of the tenth century AD, this family played a leading role in the Masoretic work at Tiberias. A faithful record of their work can be found in the oldest existing Masoretic manuscripts, which go back to the final two members of that family. The oldest dated Masoretic manuscript is Codex Cairensis (AD 895), which is attributed to Moses ben Asher. This manuscript contained both the Former Prophets (Joshua, Judges, Samuel, and Kings) and the Latter Prophets (Isaiah, Jeremiah, Ezekiel, and the 12 Minor Prophets). The rest of the OT is missing from this manuscript.

The other major surviving manuscript attributed to the Ben Asher family is the Aleppo Codex. According to the manuscript's concluding note, Aaron ben Moses ben Asher was responsible for writing the Masoretic notes and pointing the text. This manuscript contained the entire OT and dates from the first half of the 10th century AD. It was reportedly destroyed in anti-Jewish riots in 1947, but this proved to be only partly true. A majority of the manuscript survived and will be used as the base for a new critical edition of the Hebrew Bible to be published by the Hebrew University in Jerusalem.

The manuscript known as Codex Leningradensis, presently stored in the Leningrad Public Library, is of special importance as a witness to the Ben Asher text. According to a note on the manuscript, it was copied in AD 1008 from texts written by Aaron ben Moses ben Asher. Since the oldest complete Hebrew text of the OT (the Aleppo Codex) was not available to scholars earlier in this century, Codex Leningradensis was used as the textual base for the popular Hebrew texts of today: *Biblia Hebraica*, edited by R. Kittel, and its revision, *Biblia Hebraica Stuttgartensia*, edited by K. Elliger and W. Rudolf.

There are quite a number of less important manuscript codices that reflect the Masoretic tradition: the Petersburg Codex of the Prophets and the Erfurt Codices. There are also a number of manuscripts that no longer exist but which were used by scholars in the Masoretic period. One of the most prominent is Codex Hillel, traditionally attributed to Rabbi Hillel ben Moses ben Hillel about AD 600. This codex was said to be very accurate and was used for the revision of other manuscripts. Readings of this codex are cited repeatedly by the early medieval Masoretes. Codex Muga, Codex Jericho, and Codex Jerushalmi, also no longer extant, were also cited by the Masoretes. These manuscripts were likely prominent examples of unpointed texts that had become part of a standardizing consensus in the first centuries AD. These laid the groundwork for the work of the Masoretes of Tiberias.

Despite the completeness of the Masoretic manuscripts of the Hebrew Bible, a major problem still remains for OT textual critics. The Masoretic manuscripts, as old as they are, were written between 1,000 and 2,000 years after the original autographs. Earlier witnesses to the ancient Hebrew text were needed to testify to the accuracy of the Masoretic Text.

The Dead Sea Scrolls The most important ancient witnesses to the Hebrew Bible are the texts discovered at Wadi Qumran in the 1940s and 1950s. (*Wadi* is an Arabic word for a riverbed that is dry except in the rainy season.) Before the Qumran discoveries, the oldest existing Hebrew manuscripts of the OT dated from about AD 900. The greatest importance of the Dead Sea Scrolls, therefore, lies in the discovery of biblical manuscripts dating back to only about 300 years after the close of the OT canon. That makes them 1,000 years earlier than the oldest manuscripts previously known to biblical scholars. The texts found at Wadi Qumran were all completed before the Roman conquest of Palestine in AD 70, and many predate this event by quite some time. Among the Dead Sea Scrolls, the Isaiah Scroll has received the most publicity, although the collection contains fragments of all the books in the Hebrew Bible with the exception of Esther.

Because the discovery of the Dead Sea Scrolls is so important for OT textual criticism, a short history and description of these recent discoveries is appropriate. The manuscripts now known as the Dead Sea Scrolls are a collection of biblical and extrabiblical manuscripts from Qumran, an ancient Jewish religious community near the Dead Sea.

Before the Qumran find, few manuscripts had been discovered in the Holy Land. The early church father Origen (third century AD) mentioned using Hebrew and Greek manuscripts that had been stored in jars in caves near Jericho. In the ninth century AD a patriarch of the eastern church, Timothy I, wrote a letter to Sergius, metropolitan (archbishop) of Elam, in which he, too, referred to a large number of Hebrew manuscripts found in a cave near Jericho. For more than 1,000 years since then, however, no other significant manuscript discoveries were forthcoming from caves in that region near the Dead Sea.

Scroll Discoveries at Wadi Qumran The history of the Dead Sea manuscripts, both of their hiding and of their finding, reads like a mystery adventure story. It began with a telephone call on Wednesday afternoon, February 18, 1948, in the troubled city of Jerusalem. Butrus Sowmy, librarian and monk of St Mark's Monastery in the Armenian quarter of the Old City of Jerusalem, was calling John C. Trever, acting director of the American Schools of Oriental Research (ASOR). Sowmy had been preparing a catalog of the monastery's collection of rare books. Among them he found some scrolls in ancient Hebrew that, he said, had been in the monastery for about 40 years. Could ASOR supply him with some information for the catalog?

The following day Sowmy and his brother brought a suitcase containing five scrolls or parts of scrolls wrapped in an Arabic newspaper. Pulling back the end of one of the scrolls Trever discovered that it was written in a clear, square Hebrew script. He copied several lines from that scroll, carefully examined three others, but was unable to unroll the fifth because it was too brittle. After the Syrians left, Trever told the story of the scrolls to William H. Brownlee, an ASOR fellow. Trever further noted in the lines he had copied from the first scroll the double occurrence of an unusual negative construction in Hebrew. In addition, the Hebrew script of the scrolls was more archaic than anything he had ever seen.

Trever then visited St Mark's Monastery. There he was introduced to the Syrian archbishop Athanasius Samuel, who gave him permission to photograph the scrolls. Trever and Brownlee compared the style of handwriting on the scrolls with a photograph of the Nash Papyrus, a scroll inscribed with the Ten Commandments and Deuteronomy 6:4 and dated by scholars in the first or second century BC. The two ASOR scholars concluded that the script on the newly found manuscripts belonged to the same period. When ASOR director Millar Burrows returned to Jerusalem from Baghdad a few days later, he was shown the scrolls, and the three men continued their investigation. Only then did the Syrians reveal that the scrolls had been purchased the year before, in 1947, and had not been in the monastery for 40 years as was first reported.

How had the Syrians come to possess the scrolls? Before that question could be answered, many fragmentary accounts had to be pieced together. Sometime during the winter of 1946–47 three Bedouin were tending their sheep and goats near a spring in the vicinity of Wadi Qumran. One of the herdsmen, throwing a rock through a small opening in the cliff, heard the sound of the rock evidently shattering an earthenware jar inside. Another Bedouin later lowered himself into the cave and found ten tall jars lining the walls. Three manuscripts (one of them in four pieces) stored in two of the jars were removed from the cave and offered to an antiquities dealer in Bethlehem.

Several months later the Bedouin secured four more scrolls (one of them in two pieces) from the cave and sold them to another dealer in Bethlehem. During Holy Week in 1947, St Mark's Syrian Orthodox Monastery in Jerusalem was informed of the four scrolls, and Metropolitan Athanasius Samuel offered to buy them. The sale was not completed, however, until July 1947, when the four scrolls were bought by the monastery. They included a complete Isaiah scroll, a commentary on Habakkuk, a scroll containing a Manual of Discipline of the religious community at Qumran, and the Genesis Apocryphon (originally thought to be the aprocryphal book of Lamech but actually an Aramaic paraphrase of Genesis).

In November and December of 1947 an Armenian antiquities dealer in Jerusalem informed the late E. L. Sukenik, professor of archaeology at Hebrew University in Jerusalem, of the first three scrolls found in the cave by the Bedouin. Sukenik then secured the three scrolls and two jars from the antiquities dealer in Bethlehem. They included an incomplete scroll of Isaiah, the Hymns of Thanksgiving (containing 12 columns of original psalms), and the War Scroll. (That scroll describes a war, actual or spiritual, of the tribes of Levi, Judah, and Benjamin against the Moabites and Edomites. *See* War of the Sons of Light against the Sons of Darkness.)

On April 1, 1948, the first news release appeared in newspapers around the world, followed by another news release on April 26 by Sukenik about the manuscripts he had already acquired at Hebrew University. In 1949 Athanasius Samuel brought the four scrolls from St Mark's Monastery to the United States. They were exhibited in various places and finally were purchased on July 1, 1954, in New York for $250,000 by Sukenik's son for the nation of Israel and sent to Hebrew University in Jerusalem. Today they are on display in the Shrine of the Book museum in West Jerusalem.

Because of the importance of the initial discovery of the Dead Sea Scrolls, both archaeologists and Bedouin continued their search for more manuscripts. Early in 1949, G. Lankester Harding, director of antiquities for the kingdom of Jordan, and Roland G. de Vaux, of the Dominic Ecole Biblique in Jerusalem, excavated the cave (designated Cave One, or 1Q) where the initial discovery was made. Several hundred caves were explored the same year. So far, 11 caves in the Wadi Qumran have yielded treasures. Almost 600 manuscripts have been recovered, about 200 of which are biblical material. The fragments number between 50,000 and 60,000 pieces. About 85 percent of the fragments are leather; the other 15 percent are papyrus. The fact that most of the manuscripts are leather contributed to the problem of their preservation.

Probably the cave next most important to Cave One is Cave Four (4Q), which has yielded about 40,000 fragments of 400 different manuscripts, 100 of which are biblical. Every book of the OT except Esther is represented.

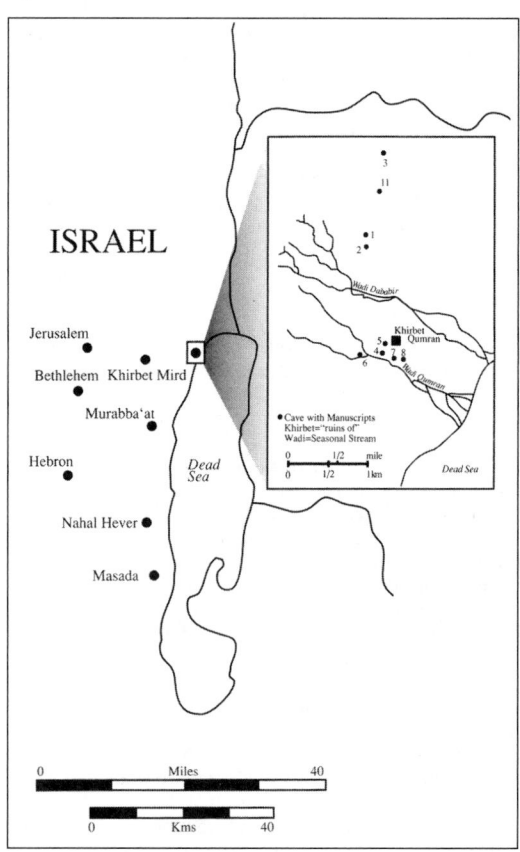

Map of Dead Sea and Qumran Area

In addition to the biblical manuscripts the discoveries have included apocryphal works such as Hebrew and Aramaic fragments of Tobit, Ecclesiasticus, and the Letter of Jeremiah. Fragments were also found of pseudepigraphal books such as 1 Enoch, the book of Jubilees, and the Testament of Levi.

Many sectarian scrolls peculiar to the religious community that lived at Qumran were also found. They furnish historical background on the nature of pre-Christian Judaism and help fill in the gaps of intertestamental history. One of the scrolls, the Damascus

Document, had originally turned up in Cairo, but manuscripts of it have now been found at Qumran. The Manual of Discipline was one of the seven scrolls from Cave One. Fragmentary manuscripts of it have been found in other caves. The document gives the group's entrance requirements, plus regulations governing life in the Qumran community. The Thanksgiving Hymns include some 30 hymns, probably composed by one individual.

There were also many commentaries on different books of the OT. The Habakkuk Commentary was a copy of the first two chapters of Habakkuk in Hebrew accompanied by a verse-by-verse commentary. The commentary gives many details about an apocalyptic figure called the "Teacher of Righteousness" who is persecuted by a wicked priest.

A unique discovery was made in Cave Three (3Q) in 1952. It was a scroll of copper, measuring about eight feet (2.4 meters) long and a foot (30.5 centimeters) wide. Because it was brittle, it was not opened until 1966, and then only by cutting it into strips. It contained an inventory of some 60 locations where treasures of gold, silver, and incense were hidden. Archaeologists have not been able to find any of it. That list of treasures, perhaps from the Jerusalem temple, may have been stored in the cave by Zealots (a revolutionary Jewish political party) during their struggle with the Romans in AD 66–70.

During the Six-Day War in June 1967, Sukenik's son, Yigael Yadin of the Hebrew University, acquired a Qumran document called the Temple Scroll. That tightly rolled scroll measures 28 feet (8.5 meters) and is the longest scroll found so far in the Qumran area. A major portion of it is devoted to statutes of the kings and matters of defense. It also describes sacrificial feasts and rules of cleanliness. Almost half of the scroll gives detailed instructions for building a future temple, supposedly revealed by God to the scroll's author.

Important Dead Sea Scroll Manuscripts Among the hundreds of biblical manuscripts discovered in the 11 caves around the Dead Sea, there are some very significant ones—especially for textual studies. These are listed below. (The first number signifies the cave, Q indicates Qumran, the abbreviation for the biblical book follows, often followed by a superscript letter for successive manuscripts containing the same book.)

►1QISA[a] This is the first Dead Sea Scroll to receive widespread attention. It is dated to c. 100 BC. The text, which includes most of Isaiah, is proto-Masoretic with some significant variants.

►1QISA[b] The text, which includes most of Isaiah, is proto-Masoretic. It is dated to a period from 25 BC to AD 50.

►2QJER This manuscript is dated to a period from 25 BC to AD 50 and has portions of Jeremiah chapters 42–49. It has some readings that follow the Septuagint (LXX), while it follows the order of chapters found in proto-Masoretic texts. For the book of Jeremiah, the Septuagint and Masoretic Text are quite different: the Septuagint is one-eighth shorter and has a different arrangement of chapters.

►4QPALEOEXOD[m] This manuscript, containing most of Exodus, is dated quite early: 200–175 BC. As such, it has provided scholars with some interesting insights into the early history of textual transmission of Exodus and the Pentateuch. The manuscript shows many similarities with the Samaritan Pentateuch.

►4QNUM[b] This manuscript, dated 30 BC–AD 20, contains most of Numbers. The book of Numbers existed in three distinguishable textual traditions: the Masoretic Text, the Samaritan Pentateuch, and the Septuagint. This manuscript, 4QNum[b], shows similarities with the Samaritan Pentateuch and the Septuagint, while having its own unique readings.

Famous Isaiah Manuscript from Qumran The scroll is open to columns 32 and 33, showing Isaiah 38:4–40:28, from 1QIsa[a].

➤4QSAM[a] This manuscript, containing about one tenth of 1 and 2 Samuel, is dated c. 50–25 BC. This manuscript, showing some similarities with the Septuagint, is believed to have several readings that are superior to the Masoretic Text.

➤4QJER[a] This manuscript, containing portions of Jeremiah 7–22, dates c. 200 BC. It generally concurs with the Masoretic Text.

➤4QJER[b] This manuscript, dated c. 150–125 BC, follows the arrangement of the Septuagint, as well as its brevity. The significance of this is that two different texts of Jeremiah were used in the pre-Christian era—one that was proto-Masoretic (as with 4QJer[a]) and one that was like the Septuagint.

➤11QPS[a] This manuscript, dated c. AD 25–50, preserves many psalms. However, these are not in the traditional sequence found in the Hebrew Bible. Furthermore, the manuscript has several other psalms, some of which were known from other ancient versions and others that were unknown until they surfaced in this manuscript.

Scroll Discoveries at Wadi Murabba'at In 1951 Bedouin discovered more manuscripts in caves in the Wadi Murabba'at, which extends southeast from Bethlehem toward the Dead Sea, about 11 miles (17.7 kilometers) south of Qumran. Four caves were excavated there in 1952 under Harding and de Vaux. They yielded biblical documents and important materials, such as letters and coins, from the time of the second Jewish revolt under Bar-Kochba in AD 132–135. Among the biblical manuscripts was a scroll containing a Hebrew text of the Minor Prophets, dating from the second century AD. This manuscript corresponds almost perfectly to the Masoretic Text, hinting that by the second century a standard consonantal text was already taking shape. Also found in Wadi

Murabba'at were fragments of the Pentateuch (the five books of Moses) and Isaiah.

Apart from the Dead Sea Scrolls, ancient witnesses to the Hebrew OT that are actually written in the Hebrew language are almost nonexistent. Because of this, the Dead Sea Scrolls may easily be one of the greatest archaeological finds of all time. They take us 1,000 years deeper into the history of the Hebrew OT, giving us the ability to assess all the other ancient witnesses with greater understanding.

The most frequently represented OT books among the Dead Sea Scrolls are Genesis, Exodus, Deuteronomy, Psalms, and Isaiah. The oldest text is a fragment of Exodus dating from about 250 BC. The Isaiah Scroll dates from about 100 BC. These ancient witnesses only confirm the accuracy of the Masoretic Text and the care with which the Jewish scribes handled the Scriptures. Except for a few instances where spelling and grammar differ between the Dead Sea Scrolls and the Masoretic Text, the two are amazingly similar. The differences do not warrant any major changes in the substance of the OT. Yet these discoveries are helping biblical scholars gain a clearer understanding of the text at an earlier time in its history and development.

Early conclusions about the antiquity of the first Dead Sea Scrolls were not accepted by everyone. Some scholars were convinced that the scrolls were of medieval origin. A series of questions relate to the dating problem. When were the texts at Qumran composed? When were they deposited in the caves? Most scholars believe the manuscripts were placed in the caves by members of the Qumran community when Roman legions were besieging Jewish strongholds. That was shortly before the destruction of Jerusalem in AD 70.

Careful study of the contents of a document sometimes reveals its authorship and the date when it was written. An example of using such internal evidence for

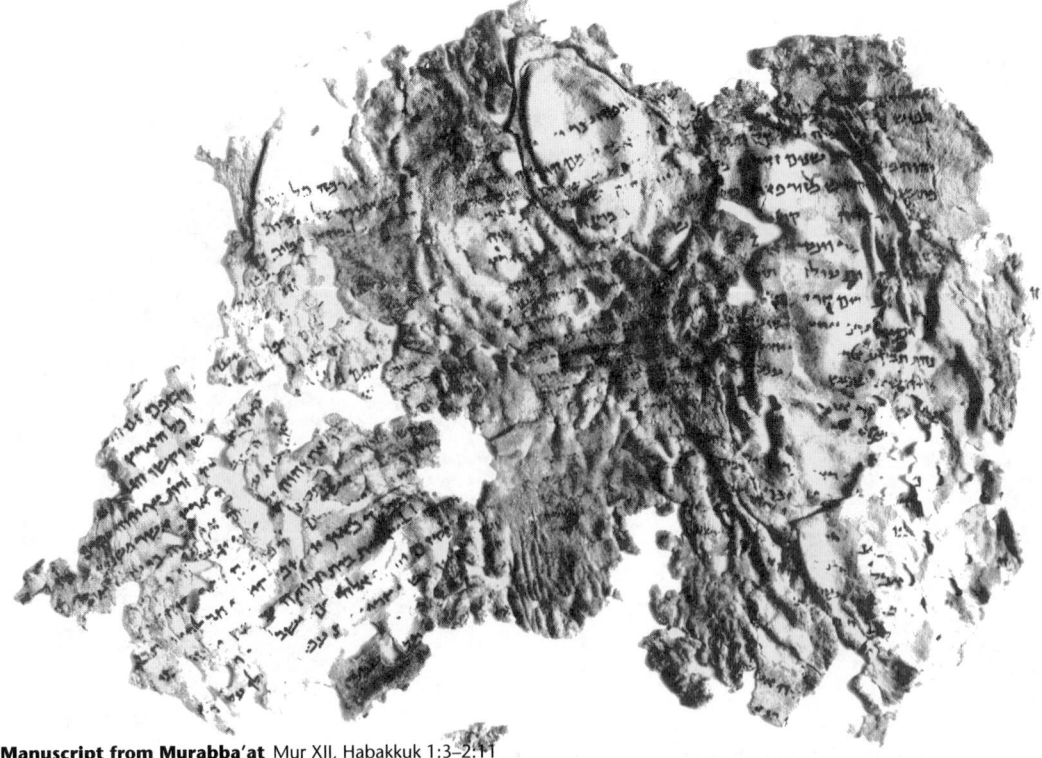

Manuscript from Murabba'at Mur XII, Habakkuk 1:3–2:11

THE SIGNIFICANCE OF THE DEAD SEA SCROLLS

Before the Qumran discoveries, the oldest existing Hebrew manuscripts of the OT dated from about AD 900—with the exception of the Nash Papyrus fragments (see below). The oldest complete manuscript was the Firkowitsch Codex from AD 1010. The greatest importance of the Dead Sea Scrolls, therefore, lies in the discovery of biblical manuscripts dating back to only about 300 years after the close of the OT canon. That makes them 1,000 years earlier than the oldest manuscripts previously known to biblical scholars. The most frequently represented OT books are Genesis, Exodus, Deuteronomy, Psalms, and Isaiah. The oldest text is a fragment of Exodus dating from about 250 BC. The Isaiah Scroll from Cave One dates from about 100 BC.

The Dead Sea Scrolls show that the OT text has been handed down along three main lines of transmission. The first is the Masoretic Text, which was preserved in the oldest Hebrew manuscripts known before the Qumran discoveries. The Masoretes, whose scholarly school flourished between AD 500 and 1000 at the city of Tiberias, standardized the traditional consonantal text by adding vowels and marginal notes (the ancient Hebrew alphabet had no vowels). Some scholars dated the origin of the consonantal Masoretic Text to the editorial activities of Rabbi Akiba and his colleagues in the second century AD. The discoveries at Qumran, however, proved them wrong, by showing that the Masoretic Text went back several more centuries into antiquity and had been accurately copied and transmitted. Although there are some differences in spelling and grammar between the Dead Sea Scrolls and Masoretic Text, the differences have not warranted any major changes in the substance of the OT. Yet they have helped biblical scholars gain a clearer understanding of the text.

A second line of transmission of the OT text has been the Greek translation of the Hebrew OT known as the Septuagint. The majority of OT quotations in the NT are from the Septuagint. That translation was made about 250 BC and ranks second in importance to the Masoretic Text for reconstructing an authentic OT text. Some scholars used to attribute differences between the Septuagint and the Masoretic Text to imprecision, subjectivity, or laxity on the part of the Septuagint's translators. Now it seems that many of those differences resulted from the fact that the translators were following a slightly different Hebrew text. Some Hebrew texts from Qumran correspond to the Septuagint and have proved helpful in solving textual problems. Septuagint manuscripts have also been found among the Dead Sea Scrolls.

A third line of OT transmission has been in the Samaritan preservation of the Hebrew text of the Pentateuch dating from the second century BC. The copies of the Samaritan Pentateuch were written in the same script used in some of the Qumran documents. Some of the Hebrew biblical texts found at Qumran have closer affinities with the Samaritan version than with the one handed down by the Masoretic scholars. All of the manuscripts have shed new light on grammatical forms, spelling, and punctuation.

Whatever differences may have existed between the community at Qumran and the mainstream of Jews from which they separated, it is certain that both used common biblical texts. The discovery of the Dead Sea Scrolls is thus a witness to the antiquity and accurate transmission of the biblical text.

---

dating a nonbiblical work is found in the Habakkuk Commentary. It gives hints about the people and events in the days of the commentary's author, not in the days of the prophet Habakkuk. The commentator described the enemies of God's people as the *Kittim*. Originally that word denoted Cyprus but later came to be more generally the Greek islands and the coasts of the eastern Mediterranean. In Daniel 11:30 the term is used prophetically, and most scholars identify the *Kittim* with the Romans. Thus, the Habakkuk Commentary was probably written about the time of the Roman capture of Palestine under Pompey in 63 BC.

Another important item to consider when dating a manuscript is its copy date. Although the vast majority of manuscripts are undated, it is often possible to determine when a manuscript was written by paleography, the study of ancient handwriting. That was the method initially employed by Trever when he compared the script of the Isaiah Scroll with the Nash Papyrus, thus dating it to the pre-Christian era. His conclusions were confirmed by the late William F. Albright, then the foremost American archaeologist. During the time of the Babylonian captivity, the square script became the normal style of writing in Hebrew (as well as in Aramaic, a cousin of Hebrew). The evidence of paleography clearly dates the majority of the Qumran scrolls in the period between 200 BC and AD 200.

Archaeology provides another kind of external evidence. The pottery discovered at Qumran dates from the late Hellenistic and early Roman periods (200 BC–AD 100). Earthenware articles and ornaments point to the same period. Several hundred coins were found in jars dating from the Graeco-Roman period. A crack in one of the buildings is attributed to an earthquake that, according to Josephus (a Jewish historian who wrote during the

first century AD), occurred in 31 BC. The excavations at Khirbet Qumran indicate that the general period of their occupation was from about 135 BC to AD 68, the year the Zealot revolt was crushed by Rome.

Finally, radiocarbon analysis has contributed to dating the finds. Radiocarbon analysis is a method of dating material from the amount of radioactive carbon remaining in it. The process is also known as carbon-14 dating. Applied to the linen cloth in which the scrolls were wrapped, the analysis gave a date of AD 33 plus or minus 200 years. A later test bracketed the date between 250 BC and AD 50. Although there may be questions concerning the relation of the linen wrappings to the date of the scrolls themselves, the carbon-14 test agrees with the conclusions of both paleography and archaeology. The general period, then, in which the Dead Sea Scrolls can be safely dated is between about 150 BC and AD 68.

The Nash Papyrus Prior to the discovery of the Dead Sea Scrolls, the oldest Hebrew witness to the OT was the Nash Papyrus. This manuscript was acquired in Egypt by W. L. Nash in 1902 and was donated to the Cambridge University Library. This manuscript contains a damaged copy of the Ten Commandments (Ex 20:2-17), part of Deuteronomy 5:6-21, and also the *Shema* (Dt 6:4ff.). This is clearly a collection of devotional and liturgical passages, and has been dated to the same period as the Dead Sea Scrolls, between 150 BC and AD 68.

The Cairo Geniza Fragments Near the end of the 19th century, many fragments from the 6th to the 8th centuries were found in an old synagogue in Cairo, Egypt, which had been St Michael's Church until AD 882. They were found there in a geniza, a storage room where worn or faulty manuscripts were hidden until they could be disposed of properly. This geniza had apparently been walled off and forgotten until its recent discovery. In this small room, as many as 200,000 fragments were preserved, including biblical texts in Hebrew and Aramaic. The fact that the biblical fragments date from the 5th century AD makes them invaluable for shedding light on the development of the Masoretic work prior to the standardization instituted by the great Masoretes of Tiberias.

Significant Old Testament Versions

The Samaritan Pentateuch Exactly when the Samaritan community separated from the larger Jewish community is a matter of dispute. But at some point during the postexilic period (c. 540–100 BC), a clear division between Samaritans and Jews was marked off. At this point, the Samaritans, who accepted only the Pentateuch as canonical, apparently canonized their own particular version of the Scriptures.

A copy of the Samaritan Pentateuch came to the attention of scholars in 1616. Initially, it caused a great deal of excitement, but most of the early assessments of its value to textual criticism were negative. It differed from the Masoretic Text in some 6,000 instances, and many judged this to be the result of sectarian differences between Samaritans and Jews. By some, it was simply viewed as a sectarian revision of the Masoretic Text.

After further assessment, however, it became clear that the Samaritan Pentateuch represented a text of much earlier origin than the Masoretic Text. And although a few of the distinctions of the Samaritan Pentateuch were clearly the result of sectarian concerns, most of the differences were neutral in this respect. Many of them had more to do with popularizing the text, rather than altering its meaning in any way. The fact that the Samaritan Pentateuch had much in common with the Septuagint, some of the Dead Sea Scrolls, and the NT, revealed that most of its differences with the Masoretic Text were not due to sectarian differences. More likely, they were due to the use of a different textual base, which was probably in wide use in the ancient Near East until well after the time of Christ. This realization, though not solving any real problems, did much to illustrate the complexity of the OT textual tradition that existed before the Masoretic standard was completed.

The Septuagint (LXX) The Septuagint is the oldest Greek translation of the OT, its witness being significantly older than that of the Masoretic Text. According to tradition, the Septuagint Pentateuch was translated by a team of 70 scholars in Alexandria, Egypt. (Hence its common designation LXX, the Roman numerals for 70.) The Jewish community in Egypt spoke Greek, not Hebrew, so a Greek translation of the OT was sincerely needed by that community of Jews. The exact date of translation is not known, but evidence indicates that the Septuagint Pentateuch was completed in the third century BC. The rest of the OT was probably translated over a long period of time, as it clearly represents the work of many different scholars.

The value of the Septuagint to textual criticism varies widely from book to book. It might be said that the Septuagint is not a single version but a collection of versions made by various authors, who differed greatly in their methods and their knowledge of Hebrew. The translations of the individual books are in no way uniform. Many books are translated almost literally, while others like Job and Daniel are quite dynamic. So the value of each book for textual criticism must be assessed on a book-by-book basis. The books translated literally are clearly more helpful in making comparisons with the Masoretic Text than the more dynamic ones.

Septuagint Text of Genesis Genesis 16:8-12, papyrus Oxyrynchus 1166, third century

The content of some books is significantly different when comparing the Septuagint and the Masoretic Text. For example, the Septuagint's Jeremiah is missing significant portions found in the Masoretic Text, and the order of the text is significantly different as well. What these differences actually mean is difficult to know with certainty. It has been conjectured that the Septuagint is simply a poor translation and is therefore missing portions of the original Hebrew. But these same differences could also indicate that editorial additions and changes worked their way into the Masoretic Text during its long history of development. It is also possible that there were a number of valid textual traditions at that time, one followed by the Septuagint, and another followed by the Masoretic Text. This illustrates some of the difficulties that arise while doing OT textual criticism.

The Septuagint was the standard OT text used by the early Christian church. The expanding Gentile church needed a translation in the common language of the time—Greek. By the time of Christ, even among the Jews, a majority of the people spoke Aramaic and Greek, not Hebrew. The NT writers evidence their inclination to the Septuagint by using it when quoting the OT.

Other Greek Versions Because of the broad acceptance and use of the Septuagint among Christians, the Jews renounced it in favor of a number of other Greek versions. Aquila, a proselyte and disciple of Rabbi Akiba, produced a new translation around AD 130. In the spirit of his teacher, Aquila wrote an extremely literal translation, often to the point of communicating poorly in Greek. This literal approach, however, gained this version wide acceptance among Jews. Only fragments of this version have survived, but its literal nature reveals much about its Hebrew textual base.

Symmachus produced a new version around AD 170 designed not only for accuracy but also to communicate well in the Greek language. His version has survived only in a few *Hexapla* fragments. A third Greek version came from Theodotion, a Jewish proselyte from the end of the second century AD. His version was apparently a revision of an earlier Greek version, possibly the Septuagint. This version has survived only in a few early Christian quotations, though it was once widely used.

The Christian theologian Origen (c. AD 185–255) arranged the OT with six parallel versions for comparison in his *Hexapla*. In his effort to find the best text of the Septuagint, Origen wrote out six parallel columns containing first the Hebrew, second the Hebrew transliterated into Greek characters, third the text of Aquila, fourth the text of Symmachus, fifth his own corrected Septuagint text, sixth the text of Theodotion. Jerome used this great Bible at Caesarea in his work on the Vulgate (after 382—see below). Almost four centuries after Origen's death, a Mesopotamian bishop, Paul of Tella, also used the *Hexapla* in the library at Caesarea (616–17) to make a translation into Syriac of Origen's fifth column, the corrected Septuagint. Then in 638 the Islamic hordes swept through Caesarea and the *Hexapla* disappeared. Other than a few fragments, only Bishop Paul's Syriac translation of Origen's fifth column remains.

An eighth-century copy of Bishop Paul's Syriac *Hexapla* Septuagint is extant in a Milan museum. Other famous uncial manuscripts of the Septuagint are the codices: Vaticanus, early fourth century, now in the Vatican Library; Sinaiticus, mid-fourth century; and Alexandrinus, probably from the fifth century—both of the latter are in London's British Museum. These copies are intensely studied because they bear a Greek witness to Hebrew texts far earlier than the Masoretic or "received text."

The Aramaic Targums The Aramaic Targums were Aramaic translations of the Hebrew OT. Since the common language of the Jews during the postexilic period was Aramaic and not Hebrew, a need for Aramaic translations of the Hebrew Bible arose. Hebrew remained the language of scholarly religious circles, and translations for the common people were often spurned by the religious leadership. But over time, the reading of the Scriptures and commentaries in Aramaic became an accepted practice in the synagogues.

The purpose of these translations was to get the message across and to edify the people. Thus, the translations were extremely interpretive. The translators paraphrased, added explanatory glosses, and often boldly reinterpreted the text according to the theological biases of their time. They sought to relate the Bible text to contemporary life and political circumstances. Because of the dynamic approach evident in these translations, their use in textual criticism is limited, but they do add to the welter of evidence to be collected and collated in order to reconstruct the text of the OT.

The Syriac Version Another version worthy of note is the Syriac version. This version was in common use in the Syriac (eastern Aramaic) church, which designated it the *Peshitta,* meaning "the simple or plain." What they intended by this designation is difficult to discern. It may indicate that it was intended for popular consumption, or that it avoided adding explanatory glosses and other additions, or perhaps that it was not an annotated text, as was the annotated *Syro-Hexapla* then in use by the same community.

The literary history of the Syriac version is not known, though it is clearly complex. Some have identified it as the recasting of an Aramaic Targum in Syriac, while others claim it has a more independent origin. Some connect it to the conversion of the leaders of Adiabene (east of the Tigris River) to the Jewish faith during the first century AD. Their need for an OT could have brought about the development of a version in their common tongue—Syriac. Still others connect it to Christian origins. Obvious later revisions to the *Peshitta* complicate matters even more. More study needs to be done to assess the nature of this version before it can lend much insight into the history of the Hebrew text.

The Latin Versions Latin was a dominant language in western regions of the Roman Empire from well before the time of Christ. It was in the western regions of southern Gaul and North Africa that the first Latin translations of the Bible appeared. Around AD 160 Tertullian apparently used a Latin version of the Scriptures. Not long after this, the Old Latin text seems to have been in circulation, evidenced by Cyprian's use of it before his death in AD 258. The Old Latin version was translated from the Septuagint. Due to its early date, it is valuable as a witness to the early Septuagint text, before later editors obscured the nature of the original. It also indirectly gives clues to the nature of the Hebrew text at the time of the Septuagint's translation. Complete manuscripts of the Old Latin text have not survived. After the completion of Jerome's Latin version, the Vulgate, the older text fell into disuse. Enough fragmentary manuscripts of this version do exist, however, to lend significant information to the early OT text.

Around the third century AD, Latin began to replace Greek as the language of learning in the larger Roman world. A uniform, reliable text was badly needed for theological and liturgical uses. To fill this need, Pope Damasus I (AD 336–84) commissioned Jerome, an eminent scholar in Latin, Greek, and Hebrew, to undertake the translation. Jerome began this work as a translation from the Greek Septuagint, considered inspired by many church authorities, including Augustine. But later, and at the risk of great criticism, he turned to the Hebrew text being used in Palestine at that time as the base text for his translation. During the years between AD 390 and 405 Jerome wrote his Latin translation of the Hebrew OT. Yet, despite Jerome's return to the original Hebrew, he was heavily dependent on the various Greek versions as aids in translation. As a result the Vulgate reflects the other Greek and Latin translations as much as the underlying Hebrew text. The value of the Vulgate for textual criticism is its pre-Masoretic witness to the Hebrew Bible, though this was compromised to a great extent by the influence of already existing Greek translations.

The Text of the Old Testament The task of the textual critic can be divided into a number of general stages: (1) the collection and collation of existing manuscripts, translations, and quotations; (2) the development of theory and methodology that will enable the critic to use the gathered information to reconstruct the most accurate text of the biblical materials; (3) the reconstruction of the history of the transmission of the text in order to identify the various influences affecting the text; (4) the evaluation of specific variant readings in light of textual evidence, theology, and history.

Both OT and NT textual critics undertake a similar task and face similar obstacles. They both seek to unearth a hypothetical "original" text with limited resources that are at varying degrees of deterioration. But the OT textual critic faces a more complex textual history than does his NT counterpart. The NT was written primarily in the first century AD, and complete NT manuscripts exist that were written only a few hundred years later. The OT, however, is made up of literature written over a 1,000-year period, the oldest parts dating to the 12th century BC, or possibly even earlier. To make matters even more difficult, until recently, the earliest known Hebrew manuscripts of the OT were medieval. This left scholars with little witness as to the OT's textual development from ancient times to the Middle Ages, a period of over 2,000 years.

Until the discovery of the Dead Sea Scrolls in the 1940s and 1950s, secondary Aramaic, Greek, and Latin translations served as the earliest significant witnesses to the early Hebrew Scriptures. Since these are translations, and subject to sectarian and contextual alterations and interpolations, their value to the textual critic, though significant, is limited. The recent discoveries of the Dead Sea Scrolls and other early manuscripts, however, have provided primary witnesses to the Hebrew OT in earlier times. The scholarly assessment of these discoveries is, at present, far from complete, and the discipline of OT textual criticism anxiously awaits a more complete assessment of their significance. In a general sense, however, the Dead Sea Scrolls have affirmed the accuracy of the Masoretic Text that we use today.

Reconstruction of the history of the transmission of the text is an important element in evaluating variant readings. Material from a wide variety of sources must be combined in order to arrive at even a tentative reconstruction of the text. A brief sketch of scholarly opinion follows.

The early history of the OT text as reflected in the Dead Sea Scrolls, the Samaritan Pentateuch, the Septuagint, and the ancient Hebrew text shows a remarkable fluidity and diversity. Evidently the standardizing process did not begin at the earliest stages. For example, the materials from the Qumran community, where the Dead Sea Scrolls were found, do not reflect any frustration with varying texts within that community.

Some scholars have attempted to account for such diversity by theories of local texts. They theorize that various localities in the Near East (e.g., Babylon, Palestine, Egypt) had differing text types that are reflected in the various surviving Hebrew texts and versions. Other scholars account for the diversity by recognizing a precanonical fluidity. They feel that until the process of canonization was complete, accurate reproduction of the manuscripts was not viewed as very important. It should be noted, however, that the basic text that modern scholarship has identified as closest to the original was among the Dead Sea texts (for example, the large Isaiah Scroll).

Destruction of the temple in AD 70 provided an impetus for standardization of the consonantal text. The texts found at Wadi Murabba'at, copied during the first centuries AD, reflect the new stage. The scholars initially reporting on the discovery were disappointed to find in these texts so few variations from the standard Masoretic Text. To scholars, the very early texts from the Dead Sea Scroll discoveries had become the standard consonantal text to the exclusion of other variants. Scholars have now gone so far as to identify the only slightly later Wadi Murabba'at texts as a "proto-Masoretic" standard. This seems to indicate that the Hebrew consonantal text was already approaching a standard in Palestine by the first centuries AD.

Standardization as practiced by the Masoretes meant identifying one text as normative and copying carefully from that text. It also meant correcting existing texts by the normative text. The Hebrew text, of course, was written with consonants alone, not with consonants *and* vowels, as we write English.

The next stage in the transmission of the OT text was standardization of punctuation and vowel patterns. That process, which began fairly early in the NT period, extended over a period of 1,000 years. A long series of Masoretes provided annotations known as *Masora*, which, in Hebrew, means "tradition." Two different motivations are evident in their work. One was their concern for accurate reproduction of the consonantal text. For that purpose a collection of annotations (on irregular forms, abnormal patterns, the number of times a form or word was used, and other matters) was gathered and inserted in the margins or at the end of the text.

A second concern of the Masoretes was to record and standardize the vocalization of the consonantal text for reading purposes. Up until this point, scribes had been prohibited against inserting vowels to make the vocalization of the text clear. Because of this, a proper reading of the text depended on the oral tradition passed down from generation to generation. The origins of vocalization reflect differences between Babylon and Palestine. The Tiberian Masoretes (scholars working in Tiberias in Palestine) provided the most complete and exact system of vocalization. The earliest dated manuscript from that tradition is a codex of the Prophets from the Karaite synagogue of Cairo dated AD 896. Today the standard Hebrew text of the OT, *Biblia Hebraica Stuttgartensia,* an updated version of Kittel's *Biblia Hebraica,* is constructed on the basis of the Tiberian Masoretic tradition.

Standardization of both the consonantal text and vocalization succeeded so well that the manuscripts that have survived display a remarkable agreement. Most of the variants, being minor and attributable to scribal error, do not affect interpretation.

Methodology of Old Testament Textual Criticism The search for an adequate methodology to handle the many variant readings found in manuscripts is inseparably intertwined with our understanding of the history of transmission. The basic issue in textual criticism is the method used to decide the relative value of those variant readings. Many factors must be evaluated in order to arrive at a valid decision.

Modern science has provided a number of aids for deciphering a manuscript. Scientific dating procedures help to determine the age of the writing material. Chemical techniques help clarify writing that has deteriorated. Ultraviolet light enables a scholar to see traces of ink (carbon) in a manuscript even after the surface writing has been effaced.

Each manuscript must be studied as a whole, for each has a "personality." It is important to identify the characteristic errors, characteristic carelessness or carefulness, and other peculiarities of the scribe(s) who copied the material. Then the manuscript must be compared with other manuscripts to identify the "family" tradition with which it agrees. Preservation of common errors or insertions in the text is a clue to relationships. All possible details of date, place of origin, and authorship must be ascertained.

Scribal errors fall into several distinct categories. The first large category is that of *unintentional errors:* (1) Confusion of similar consonants and the transposition of two consonants are frequent errors. (2) Corruptions also resulted from an incorrect division of words (many early manuscripts omitted spaces between words in order to save space). (3) Confusion of sounds occurred particularly when one scribe read to a group of scribes making multiple copies. (4) In the OT, the method of vocalization (addition of vowels to the consonantal text) created some errors. (5) Omissions of a letter, word, or phrase created new readings. (6) Repetition of a letter, word, or even a whole phrase was also common. (7) Omission (called haplography) or repetition (called dittography) could be caused by the eye of a scribe slipping from one word to a similar word or ending. (8) Omissions by *homoioteleuton* (Greek meaning "similar endings") were also quite common. This occurred when two words that were identical, similar, or had identical endings were found close to each other, and the eye of the copyist moved from the first to the second, omitting the words between them. (9) In the OT, errors were at times caused by the use of consonants as vowel letters in some ancient texts. Copyists unaware of this usage of vowel letters would copy them in as aberrant consonants. Normally unintentional errors are fairly easy to identify because they create nonsense readings.

Intentional errors are much more difficult to identify and evaluate. Harmonizations from similar materials occurred with regularity. Difficult readings were subject to "improvement" by a thinking scribe. Objectionable expressions were sometimes eliminated or smoothed out. Occasionally synonyms were employed. Conflation (resolving a discrepancy between two variant readings by including both of them) often appears.

Awareness of these common problems is the first step in detecting and eliminating the more obvious errors and identifying and eliminating the peculiarities of a particular scribe. Then more subtle criteria for identifying the reading most likely to be the original must be employed. Procedures for applying such criteria are similar in both OT and NT work.

General Methodological Principles Through the work of textual critics in the last several centuries, certain basic principles have evolved. The primary principles for the OT can be briefly summarized.

1. The basic text for primary consideration is the Masoretic Text because of the careful standardization it represents. That text is compared with the testimony of the ancient versions. The Septuagint, by reason of age and basic faithfulness to the Hebrew text, carries significant weight in all decisions. The Targums (Aramaic translations) also reflect the Hebrew base but exhibit a tendency to expansion and paraphrase. The Syriac (*Peshitta*), Vulgate (Latin), Old Latin, and Coptic versions add indirect evidence, although translations are not always clear witnesses in technical details. Use of such versions does enable scholars to use comparative philology in textual decisions and thus expose early errors for which the original reading probably has not survived.

2. The reading that best explains the origin of other variants is preferable. Information from reconstruction of the history of transmission often provides additional insight. Knowledge of typical scribal errors enables the critic to make an educated decision on the sequence of variants.

3. The shorter reading is preferable. The scribes frequently added material in order to solve style or syn-

tax problems and seldom abridged or condensed material.

4. The more difficult reading is more likely to be the original one. This principle is closely related to the third. Scribes did not intentionally create more complex readings. Unintentional errors are usually easy to identify. Thus the easier reading is normally suspect as a scribal alteration.

5. Readings that are not harmonized or assimilated to similar passages are preferable. Copyists had a tendency to correct material on the basis of similar material elsewhere (sometimes even unconsciously).

6. When all else fails, the textual critic must resort to conjectural emendation. To make an "educated guess" requires intimate acquaintance with the Hebrew language, familiarity with the author's style, and an understanding of culture, customs, and theology that might color the passage. Use of conjecture must be limited to those passages in which the original reading has definitely not been transmitted to us.

Conclusion It should be remembered that textual criticism operates only when two or more readings are possible for a specific word or phrase. For most of the biblical text, a single reading has been transmitted. Elimination of scribal errors and intentional changes leaves only a small percentage of the text about which any questions occur.

The field of textual criticism is complex, requiring the gathering and skillful use of a wide variety of information. Because it deals with the authoritative source of revelation for all Christians, textual argumentation has often been accompanied by emotion. Yet in spite of controversy, great progress has been made, particularly in the last century. Refinement of methodology has greatly aided our understanding of the accumulated materials. Additional aid has come from accumulations of information in related fields of study such as church history, biblical theology, and the history of Christian thought.

Collection and organization of all variant readings have enabled modern textual critics to give strong assurance that the Word of God has been transmitted in accurate and dependable form. Although variant readings have become obvious through the publication of so many manuscripts, inadequate, inferior, and secondary readings have been largely eliminated. In relatively few places is conjectural emendation necessary. In matters pertaining to the Christian's salvation, clear and unmistakable transmission provides authoritative answers. Christians are thus in debt to the textual critics who have worked, and are working, to provide a dependable biblical text.

BIBLE*, Manuscripts and Text of the (New Testament)
Copies of the NT books produced by scribes and editions made from these copies. In the centuries prior to the simultaneous-multiple production of copies via dictation (wherein many scribes in a scriptorium transcribed a text dictated to them by one reader), all manuscript copies were made singly—each scribe producing a copy from an exemplar.

Prior to the 15th century, when Johannes Gutenberg invented movable type for the printing press, all copies of any work of literature were made by hand (hence, the name "manuscript"). According to a current tabulation, there are 99 papyrus manuscripts, 257 uncial manuscripts, and 2,795 minuscule manuscripts. We can add 2,209 Greek lectionaries to this list. Therefore, we have over 5,350 manuscript copies of the Greek NT or portions thereof. No other work of Greek literature can boast of such numbers.

PREVIEW
- Important Papyrus Manuscripts
- Important Uncial Manuscripts
- The Text of the New Testament

Important Papyrus Manuscripts Papyrus is a tall, aquatic reed, the pith of which is cut into strips, laid in a crosswork pattern and glued together to make a page for writing. The papyrus rolls of Egypt have been used as a writing surface since the early third millennium BC. The Greeks adopted papyrus around 900 BC, and later the Romans adopted its use. However, the oldest extant Greek rolls of papyrus date from the fourth century BC. Unfortunately, papyrus is perishable, requiring a dry climate for its preservation. That is why so many papyri have been discovered in the desert sands of Egypt.

The NT papyrus manuscripts (abbreviated as "P") are generally the earliest manuscripts of the NT. Broadly speaking, the most important ones can be categorized in three groups: the Oxyrhynchus Papyri (from Oxyrhynchus, Egypt), (2) the Beatty Papyri (named after the owner); and (3) the Bodmer Papyri (named after the owner).

The Oxyrhynchus Papyri Beginning in 1898 B. P. Grenfell and A. S. Hunt discovered thousands of papyrus fragments in the ancient rubbish heaps of Oxyrhynchus, Egypt. This site yielded volumes of papyrus fragments containing all sorts of written material (literature, business and legal contracts, letters, etc.) as well as over 40 manuscripts containing portions of the NT. Some of the more noteworthy papyrus manuscripts from Oxyrhynchus are as follows:

➤ P1 (P. OXY. 2) This late second-century manuscript contains Matthew 1:1-9, 12, 14-20. Grenfell and Hunt in the winter of 1896–97 went to Oxyrhynchus (now called El Bahnasa) in search of ancient Christian documents. P1 was discovered on the second day of the dig. At the time of this discovery, this was the earliest extant copy of any NT portion—at least 100 years earlier than Codex Vaticanus. The copyist of P1 seems to have faithfully followed a very reliable exemplar. Where there are major variants, P1 agrees with the best Alexandrian witnesses, especially B (Codex Vaticanus), from which it rarely varies.

➤ P5 (P. OXY. 208 AND 1781) Two separate portions of this third-century manuscript were unearthed from Oxyrhynchus by Grenfell and Hunt, both from the same papyrus manuscript. The first portion contains John 1:23-31, 33-40 on one fragment and John 20:11-17 on another—probably on the first and last quires of a manuscript containing only the Gospel of John. This portion was published in volume II of *Oxyrhynchus Papyri* in 1899; the second portion—containing John 16:14-30—was not published until 1922 in volume XV of *Oxyrhynchus Papyri*.

After examining the first portion, Grenfell and Hunt said, "The text is a good one, and appears to have affinities with that of Codex Sinaiticus, with which the papyrus agrees in several readings not found elsewhere." The papyrus, written in a documentary hand, is marked for its brevity.

➤ P13 (P. OXY. 657 AND PSI 1292) This manuscript, dated between 175 and 225, contains 12 columns from a roll preserving the text of Hebrews 2:14–5:5; 10:8-22; 10:29–11:13; 11:28–12:7. The text of Hebrews was written in a reformed documentary hand on the back of the papyrus containing the new epitome of Livy. For this reason, some scholars think the manuscript was possibly brought to Egypt by a Roman official and left behind when he left his post. P13 very often agrees with B, and it

supplements B where it is lacking—namely, from Hebrews 9:14 to the end of Hebrews. P13 and P46 display nearly the same text. Out of a total of 88 variation-units, there are 71 agreements and only 17 disagreements.

➤ P77 (P. OXY. 2683 + 4405) Dated c. 150–75, this is the earliest manuscript of Matthew (23:30-39). The manuscript is clearly a literary production. It was written in an elegant hand and has what was or became a standard system of chapter division, as well as punctuation and breathing marks. P77 has close textual affinities with Codex Sinaiticus.

➤ P90 (P. OXY. 3523) This second-century manuscript (c. 150–75) contains John 18:36–19:7. The handwriting (an upright, rounded, elegant script) is much like that found in P66. Furthermore, P90 has more affinity with P66 than with any other single manuscript, though it does not concur with P66 in its entirety.

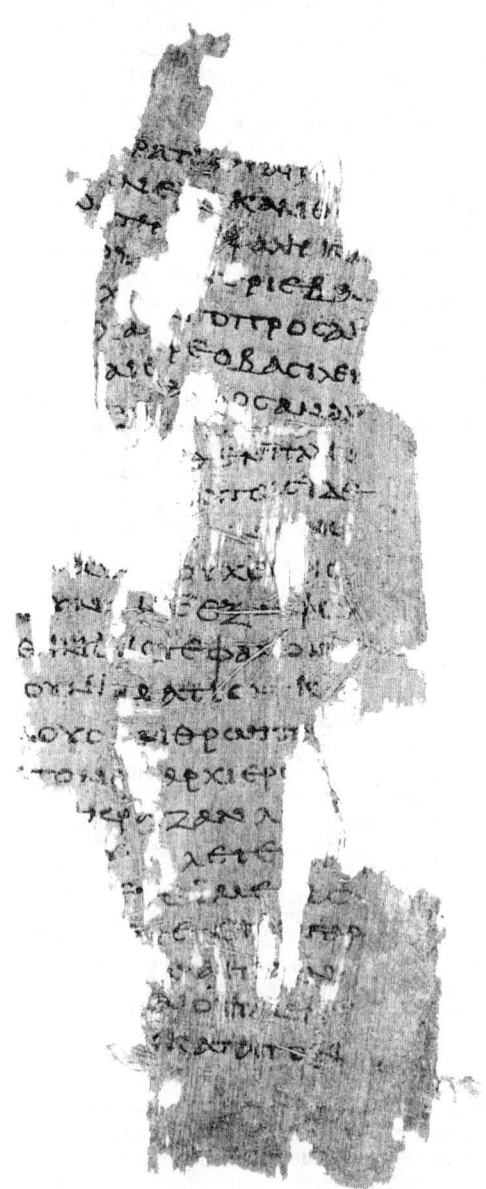

Papyrus Manuscript of John John 18:36–19:7, Papyrus Oxyrhynchus 3523, late second century—P90

➤ **P. OXY. 4404** Containing Matthew 21:34-37, 43, 45, this manuscript could be the earliest extant manuscript of the NT in that the script is early Roman and therefore could be dated to the early second century.

The Chester Beatty Papyri These manuscripts were purchased from a dealer in Egypt during the 1930s by Chester Beatty and by the University of Michigan. The three manuscripts in this collection are very early and contain a large portion of the NT text. P45 (c. 200) contains portions of all four Gospels and Acts; P46 (c. 125) has almost all of Paul's epistles and Hebrews; and P47 (third century) contains Revelation 9–17.

➤ **P45 (CHESTER BEATTY PAPYRUS I)** This codex has the four Gospels and Acts (Mt 20:24-32; 21:13-19; 25:41–26:39; Mk 4:36–9:31; 11:27–12:28; Lk 6:31–7:7; 9:26–14:33; Jn 4:51–5:2, 21-25; 10:7-25; 10:30–11:10, 18-36, 42-57; Acts 4:27–17:17). The order of books in the original intact manuscript was probably as follows: Matthew, John, Luke, Mark, Acts (the so-called Western order). This manuscript was dated by Kenyon to the early third century, a date that was confirmed by the papyrologists W. Schubart and H. I. Bell. This continues to be the date assigned to this manuscript in modern handbooks on textual criticism and critical editions of the Greek NT, but the consistent formation of certain letters suggests an earlier date—maybe sometime in the late second century.

The scribe of P45 worked without any intention of exactly reproducing his source. He wrote with a great amount of freedom—harmonizing, smoothing out, substituting at will. In short, the scribe did not actually copy words. He saw through the language to its idea-content, and copied that in words of his own choosing, or in rearranged order. Thus, in the scribe of P45 we see an exegete and a paraphraser.

➤ **P46 (CHESTER BEATTY PAPYRUS II)** This codex has most of Paul's epistles (excluding the Pastorals) in this order: Romans 5:17–6:14; 8:15-15:9; 15:11–16:27; Hebrews 1:1–13:25; 1 Corinthians 1:1–16:22; 2 Corinthians 1:1–13:13; Ephesians 1:1–6:24; Galatians 1:1–6:18; Philippians 1:1–4:23; Colossians 1:1–4:18; 1 Thessalonians 1:1; 1:9–2:3; 5:5-9, 23-28 (with minor lacunae in each of the books).

The manuscript was originally dated to the early third century. But others, since, have dated the manuscript earlier in the second century. The scribe who produced this manuscript used an early, excellent exemplar. He was a professional scribe because there are stichoi notations at the end of several books (see the conclusion of Romans, 2 Corinthians, Ephesians, Philippians). The stichoi were used by professionals to note how many lines had been copied for commensurate pay. Most likely, the ex officio of the scriptorium (perhaps connected wth a church library) paginated the codex and indicated the stichoi. The scribe himself made a few corrections as he went, and then several other readers made corrections here and there.

The text of P46 shows a strong affinity with B (especially in Ephesians, Colossians, and Hebrews) and next with ℵ (Codex Sinaiticus). P46 agrees much less with the later representatives of the Alexandrian text. In short, P46 is proto-Alexandrian. In Hebrews, P46 and P13 display nearly the same text. Out of a total of 88 variation-units, there are 71 agreements and only 17 disagreements.

➤ **P47 (CHESTER BEATTY PAPYRUS III)** This third-century codex contains Revelation 9:10–17:2. The text of P47 agrees more often with that of Codex Sinaiticus than with

any other manuscript (including Codex Alexandrinus and Codex Ephraemi Rescriptus), though it often shows independence.

The Bodmer Papyri These manuscripts were purchased by M. Martin Bodmer from a dealer in Egypt during the 1950s and 1960s. The three important papyri in this collection are P66 (c. 175, containing almost all of John), P72 (third century, having all of 1 and 2 Peter and Jude), and P75 (c. 200, containing large parts of Luke 3—John 15).

➤ **P66 (PAPYRUS BODMER II)** This manuscript contains most of John's Gospel (1:1–6:11; 6:35–14:26, 29-30; 15:2-26; 16:2-4, 6-7; 16:10–20:20, 22-23; 20:25–21:9). The manuscript does not include the pericope of the adulteress (7:59–8:11), making it the earliest witness to not include this spurious passage. The manuscript is usually dated as c. 200, but the renowned paleographer Herbert Hunger has argued that P66 should be dated to the first half, if not the first quarter, of the second century.

According to recent studies, it seems evident that P66 has preserved the work of three individuals: the original scribe, a thoroughgoing corrector, and a minor corrector. With a practiced calligraphic hand, the original scribe of P66 wrote in larger print as he went along in order to fill out the codex. The large print throughout indicates that it was written to be read aloud to a Christian congregation. The text exhibits the scribe's knowledge of other portions of Scripture (inasmuch as he harmonized John 6:69 to Matthew 16:16 and John 21:6 to Luke 5:5), his use of standard *nomina sacra* (a way of writing divine names), and his special use of *nomina sacra* for the words "cross" and "crucify."

The original scribe was quite free in his interaction with the text; he produced several singular readings that reveal his independent interpretation of the text. While the numerous scribal mistakes would seem to indicate that the scribe was inattentive, many of the singular readings—prior to correction—reveal that he was not detached from the narrative of the text. Rather, he became so absorbed in his reading that he often forgot the exact words he was copying. His task as a copyist was to duplicate the exemplar word for word, but this was frustrated by the fact that he was reading the text in logical semantic chunks and often became a coproducer of a new text. As a result, he continually had to stop his reading and make many in-process corrections. But he left several places uncorrected, which were later fixed by the *diorthotes* (official corrector). The finished product is quite good, presenting a text that is very close to the Alexandrian witnesses.

➤ **P72 (PAPYRUS BODMER VII–VIII)** This manuscript, dated late third century, has an interesting collection of writings in one codex: 1 Peter 1:1–5:14; 2 Peter 1:1–3:18; Jude 1:1-25; the Nativity of Mary, the apocryphal correspondence of Paul to the Corinthians, the eleventh ode of Solomon, Melito's Homily on the Passover, a fragment of a hymn, the Apology of Phileas, and Psalms 33 and 34.

Scholars think that four scribes took part in producing the entire manuscript. First Peter has clear Alexandrian affinities—especially with B. Second Peter and (especially) Jude display more of an uncontrolled type text (usually associated with the "Western" text), with several independent readings.

➤ **P75 (PAPYRUS BODMER XIV–XV)** This codex contains most of Luke and John (Lk 3:18–4:2; 4:34–5:10; 5:37–18:18; 22:4–24:53; Jn 1:1–11:45, 48-57; 12:3–13:1, 8-9; 14:8-30; 15:7-8.) The manuscript does

Papyrus Manuscript of Paul's Epistles
End of Romans, beginning of Hebrews,
Chester Beatty Manuscript II, late second century—P46

Thus, we have a manuscript written by a Christian for other Christians.

There are several indications of the scribe's Alexandrian orientation. First and foremost is his scriptoral acumen. He is the best of all the early Christian scribes, and his manuscript is an extremely accurate copy. P75 is the work of an extremely disciplined scribe who copied with the intention of being careful and accurate. Scholars generally agree that P75 displays the kind of text that was used in making Codex Vaticanus (there is 87 percent agreement between P75 and B). As such, textual scholars have a high regard for P75's textual fidelity.

Other Papyrus Manuscripts

➤P4 + P64 + P67 These three papyrus manuscripts are part of one codex dated AD 150–175. The manuscript was the work of a professional scribe, and the text is extremely accurate.

➤P32 (RYLANDS PAPYRUS 5) This manuscript, preserving Titus 1:11-15; 2:3-8, is dated c. 175, making it the earliest extant copy of any of the Pastoral Epistles. P32 shows agreement with ℵ and with F and G. Since F and G (nearly identical manuscripts) go back to the same archetype, it is possible that P32 could be linked to the same source.

➤P52 (RYLANDS PAPYRUS 457) This fragment, containing John 18:31-34, 37-38, is noteworthy because of its date: c. 110–125. Many scholars (F. Kenyon, H. I. Bell, A. Deissmann, and W. H. P. Hatch) have confirmed this dating. The manuscript came from the Fayum or Oxyrhynchus site. It was acquired in 1920 by Grenfell, but it remained unnoticed among hundreds of papyri until 1934, when C. H. Roberts recognized that this fragment preserves a few verses from John's Gospel.

Important Uncial Manuscripts The manuscripts typically classified as "uncial" are so designated to differentiate them from papyrus manuscripts. In a sense, this is a misnomer because the real difference has to do with the material they are written on—vellum (treated animal hide) as compared to papyrus—not the kind of letters used. Indeed, the papyri are also written in uncials (capital letters), but the term "uncial" typically describes the majuscule lettering that was prominent in fourth-century biblical texts, such as in ℵ, A, B, C.

Codex Sinaiticus (or ℵ) This codex contains the entire OT and the NT in this order: the four Gospels, the Pauline Epistles (including Hebrews), Acts, the General Epistles, Revelation. It also includes the Epistle of Barnabas and the Shepherd of Hermas. The codex cannot be earlier than 340 (the year Eusebius died) because the Eusebian sections of the text are indicated in the margins of the Gospels by a contemporary hand. Most scholars date it 350–375.

This codex was discovered by Constantin von Tischendorf in St Catherine's Monastery (situated at the foot of Mt Sinai). On a visit to the monastery in 1844 he noticed in a wastebasket some parchment leaves that were being used to light the lamps. He was allowed to take this waste paper, which proved to be 43 leaves from various parts of the Greek translation of the OT.

In 1853 he made a second trip to the monastery and found nothing. In 1859, however, on his third trip, he found not only other parts of the OT but also the complete NT. He was finally able to persuade the monastery authorities to present the manuscript to the czar, the great patron of the Greek Catholic Church, who placed it in the Imperial Library in St Petersburg. The czar gave great honors to the monastery and its authorities, and

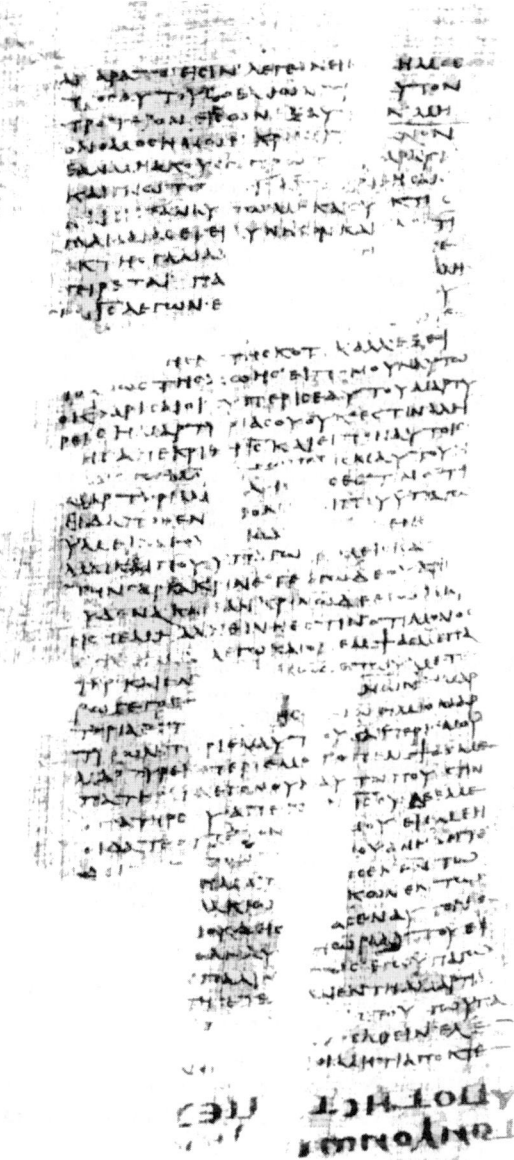

Papyrus Manuscript of Luke and John John 7:49–8:22 (lacking the story of the adulterous woman), Bodmer Manuscript XIV–XV, c. 175—P75

not include the pericope of the adulteress (7:59–8:11). The manuscript can be dated to the late second or early third century.

The copyist of P75 was a literate scribe trained in making books. His craftsmanship shows through in his tight calligraphy and controlled copying. The handwriting displayed in this manuscript is typically called by paleographers the common angular type of the late second to early third century. The scribe's Christianity shows in his abbreviations of the *nomina sacra*, as well as in his abbreviation of the word "cross." These are telltale signs of a scribe who belonged to the Christian community. Furthermore, the large typeface indicates that the manuscript was composed to be read aloud to a Christian congregation. The scribe even added a system of sectional divisions to aid any would-be lector.

everybody seemed well pleased. Later Tischendorf was charged with having stolen the manuscript from its lawful owners, but the better textual scholars do not accept that story.

KΑΙΟΜΟΛΟΓΟΥΜε
ΝωϹΜΕΓΛΕϹΤΙΝ
ΤΟΤΗϹΕΥϹΕΒΕΙΛϹ
ΜΥϹΤΗΡΙΟΝΟϹΕ
ΦΑΝΕΡωΘΕΝϹΑΡ
ΚΙ· ΕΛΙΚΛΙωΘΕΝ
ΠΝΙωΦΘΗΛΤΓΕλοΙϲ
ΕΚΗΡΥΧΘΕΝΕ
ΘΝΕϹΙΝΕΠΙϹΤΕΥ
ΘΗΕΝΚΟϹΜω·
ΛΝΕΛΗΜΦΘΕΝ
ΛΟϟΗ

Codex Sinaiticus This replication shows 1 Timothy 3:16.

The manuscript remained in the Imperial Library until 1933, when it was purchased by the British Museum for the huge sum of £100,000 (about $500,000). Textual criticism made the headlines because one manuscript was bought for this much money, raised largely by public subscription during the Great Depression. The manuscript is now on display in the manuscript room of the museum, where it is considered one of its most prized possessions.

The text of Sinaiticus is very closely related to that of Codex Vaticanus. They agree in presenting the purest type of text, usually called the Alexandrian text type. Tischendorf greatly used the textual evidence of Codex Sinaiticus in preparing his critical editions of the Greek NT. Tischendorf thought four scribes had originally produced the codex, whom he named scribes A, B, C, D. After reinvestigation, H. J. Milne and T. C. Skeat identified only three scribes: A (who wrote the historical and poetical books of the OT, as well as most of the NT), B (who wrote the Prophets and the Shepherd of Hermas), and D (who wrote some Psalms, Tobit, Judith, and 4 Maccabees, and redid small sections of the NT). Milne and Skeat demonstrated that scribe A of Codex Vaticanus was likely the same scribe as scribe D of Codex Sinaiticus. If this true, then ℵ is contemporary with B—perhaps produced in the same scriptorium in Alexandria. Codex Sinaiticus provides a fairly reliable witness to the NT; however, the scribe was not as careful as the scribe of B.

Codex Alexandrinus (A) This is one of the three most important codices containing early copies of the whole Bible in Greek (the other two being the Vaticanus and Sinaiticus codexes). The name Alexandrinus comes from ancient records suggesting that it was copied in Egypt during the early part of the fifth century AD. The early history of this manuscript and its Egyptian provenance is partially revealed by its flyleaves. A note by Cyril of Lucar

(patriarch of Alexandria and then of Constantinople in the 1620s) states that, according to tradition, it was written by Thecla, a noble lady of Egypt shortly after the Council of Nicaea (325) and that her name was originally inscribed at the end of the volume but the last page was lost due to mutilation. An Arabic note of the 13th or 14th century also says that the manuscript was written by "Thecla the martyr." Another Arabic note says that is was presented to the patriarchal cell of Alexandria (c. 1098). Cyril of Lucar took the manuscript from Alexandria to Constantinople in 1621 and then gave it to Charles I of England in 1627, where it became part of the Royal Library, then later the British Museum.

Only 773 of the original 820 or so pages still exist. The rest were lost as the book was passed down through the centuries. The surviving parts of Alexandrinus contain a Greek translation of the whole OT, the Apocrypha (including four books of Maccabees and Psalm 151), most of the NT, and some early Christian writings (of which the First and Second Epistles of Clement to the Corinthians are the most important).

Frederick Kenyon thought the codex was the work of five scribes, to each of whom he designated a Roman numeral. According to Kenyon, scribes I and II copied the OT; scribe III did Matthew, Mark, 1 Corinthians 10:8—Philemon 1:25; scribe IV did Luke—Acts, General Epistles, Romans 1:1—1 Corinthians 10:8; and scribe V did Revelation. Milne and Skeat, however, argued that the whole codex was the work of two copyists (I and II). W. H. P. Hatch noted that many corrections have been made in the manuscript, most of them at an early date. Some of these corrections were introduced by the scribe himself, and others came from later hands.

Evidently, the scribes of this codex used exemplars of varying quality for various sections of the NT. The exemplar used for the Gospels was of poor quality, reflecting a Byzantine text type. Its testimony in the Epistles is much better, and in Revelation it provides the best witness to the original text.

ΠΡΟϹΕΧΕΤΕΕΑΥΤΟΙϹ ΚΑΙΠΑΝ·
ΤωΙΜΝΙωΕΝωΥΜΑϹΤΟΠΠ
ΛΓΙΟΝΕΘΕΤΟΕΠΙϹΚΟΠΟΥϹ
ΠΟΙΜΑΙΝΕΙΝΤΗΝΕΚΚΛΗϹ
ΤΟΥΚ͞ΥΗΝΠΕΡΙΕΠΟΙΗϹΛΤΟΛ
ΤΟΥΛΙΜΑΤΟϹΤΟΥΛΙΟΥ

Codex Alexandrinus This replication shows Acts 20:28.

Codex Vaticanus (B) Codex Vaticanus is the Vatican Manuscript, so named because it is the most famous manuscript in the Vatican Library in Rome. This manuscript has been in the Vatican's library since at least 1475, but it was not made available to scholars, such as Constantin von Tischendorf and Samuel Tregelles, until the middle of the 19th century.

At one time, the codex contained the whole Greek Bible, including most of the books of the Apocrypha, but it has lost many of its leaves. Originally it must have had about 820 leaves (1,640 pp), but now it has 759—617 in the OT and 142 in the NT. The major gaps of the manuscript are Genesis 1:1–46:28; 2 Samuel 2:5-7, 10-13; Psalms 106:27–138:6; Hebrews 9:14–13:25; the Pastoral Epistles; and Revelation. Each leaf measures ten and a half by ten inches (26.7 by 25.4 centimeters). Each page has three columns (two for the poetical books) with 40 to 44 lines to the column. The manuscript was written by two different scribes. It is dated in the early to middle part of the fourth century. It is not known where the manuscript originated, but it has been in the Vatican Library from the time of its earliest catalog in 1475.

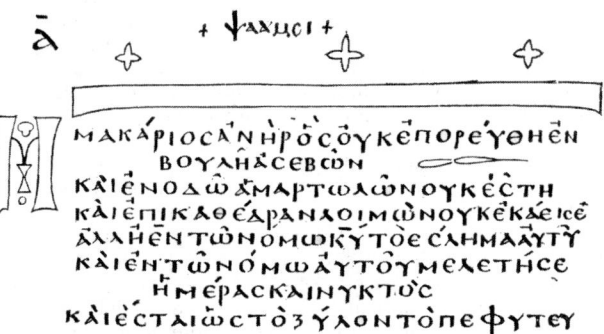

Codex Vaticanus This replication shows Psalm 1:1-3.

When Napoleon conquered Rome, he brought its treasures to Paris, including this manuscript. The scholar Hug identified it and called the attention of other scholars to it. After the downfall of Napoleon, the manuscript was returned to the Vatican Library. Competent textual scholars were not allowed to do careful work on it until a photographic edition was published in 1890. It is now on exhibit in the Vatican Library.

The text of the Vatican Manuscript is much like that of Codex Sinaiticus. These are generally recognized as the two finest examples of the Alexandrian type of Greek text of the NT. The Greek text of the OT is very fine too, but it is not quite so important, as the original language of the OT was Hebrew. Virtually all the textual scholars since the days of Brooke Westcott and Fenton Hort (who brought out their Greek Testament, including their theory of textual criticism, in 1881), recognize this neutral type of text as a very early text and a very pure text, an extremely accurate reproduction of what the original text must have been. Westcott and Hort called it a second-century text accurate in 999 out of 1,000 words so far as any matter of translatable difference was concerned. ℵ and B are the finest examples of this type of text, but it is also found in a few other Greek uncial manuscripts, a few of the early translations, and in the writings of a few of the early church fathers. Since the days of Westcott and Hort, their theory has been confirmed by the discovery of some papyrus manuscripts, notably the Bodmer Papyri, discovered in the 1950s.

Codex Ephraemi Rescriptus (C) This codex is a palimpsest (the original writing was erased and different words written on the same material). It originally contained the entire Bible but now has only parts of six OT books and portions of all NT books except 2 Thessalonians and 2 John. The single-column Bible text, written in the 5th century AD, was erased in the 12th century and replaced by a two-column text of a Greek translation of sermons or treatises by a certain Ephraem, a 4th-century Syrian church leader. Such a practice was common in periods of economic depression or when parchment was scarce. The original writing was scraped from the writing surface and the surface smoothed. Then new compositions could be written on the prepared surface. Using chemicals Tischendorf was able to read much of the erased document.

The manuscript may have been brought from the east to Florence by a learned Greek named Andrew John Las-

car in the time of Lorenzo de'Medici. Since Lascar was known as Rhyndacenus (from the river Rhyndacus), he probably came from the region of Phrygia (site of ancient Laodicea). Where the manuscript was prior to this is not known. The Ephraemi manuscript was brought to Italy in the early sixth century, where it became the property of the Medici family. Catherine de'Medici took it to France, where it remains today.

The text of this manuscript is mixed—it is compounded from all the major text types, agreeing frequently with the later koine of Byzantine type, which most scholars regard as the least valuable type of NT text.

Codex Bezae (D) This is a Greek-Latin diglot containing Matthew—Acts, 3 John, with lacunae. Most scholars date it late fourth or early fifth century (c. 400). Some scholars think the codex was produced in either Egypt or North Africa by a scribe whose mother tongue was Latin. Another scholar (D. C. Parker) has argued that it was copied in Beirut, a center of Latin legal studies during the fifth century, where both Latin and Greek were used. Evidently, it was produced by a scribe who knew Latin better than Greek, and then was corrected by several scribes. In any event, the codex somehow came into the hands of Theodore Beza, French scholar and successor to Calvin. Beza gave it to the Cambridge University Library in 1581.

This codex is probably the most controversial of the NT uncials because of its marked independence. Its many additions, omissions, and alterations (especially in Luke and Acts) are the work of a significant theologian. A few earlier manuscripts (P29, P38, P48, and 0171) appear to be precursors to the type of text found in D, which is considered the principal witness of the Western text-type. Thus, Codex Bezae could be a copy of an earlier revised edition. This reviser must have been a scholar who had a propensity for adding historical, biographical, and geographical details. More than anything, he was intent on filling in gaps in the narrative by adding circumstantial details.

Codex Washingtonianus, or The Freer Gospels (W)
This codex, dated around 400, has the four Gospels and Acts. It is often referred to as the Freer Gospels—named after its owner, Charles Freer. The codex likely came from the ruins of a monastery near Giza. The handwriting is quite similar to that found in a fifth-century fragment of the book of Enoch found at Akhmim in 1886.

Codex W was copied from a parent manuscript (exemplar) that had been pieced together from several different manuscripts. This is obvious because the textual presentation of W is noticeably variegated and even the stratification of the text is matched by similar variations in paragraphing. The scribe who collated the parent manuscript drew upon various sources to put together his Gospel codex. It is likely that the scribe of the parent manuscript used a text that came from North Africa (the "Western" text) for the first part of Mark, and the scribe of W used manuscripts from Antioch for Matthew and the second part of Luke to fill the gaps in the more ancient manuscript he was copying. Detailed textual analysis reveals the variegated textual stratifications of W, as follows: in Matthew the text is Byzantine; in Mark the text is first Western (1:1–5:30), then Caesarean in Mark 5:31–16:20 (akin to P45); in Luke the text is first Alexandrian (1:1–8:12), then Byzantine. John is more complicated because the first part of John (1:1–5:11), which fills a quire, was the work of a seventh-century scribe who must have replaced a damaged quire. (W^s designates the work of this scribe.) This first section has a mixture of Alexandrian and Western readings, as does the rest of John.

Codex 1739 This tenth-century codex has Acts and the Epistles. The manuscript was discovered at Mt Athos in 1879 by E. von der Goltz. The manuscript has strong textual affinities with P46, B, 1739, Coptic Sahidic, Coptic Boharic, Clement, and Origen. The relationship between P46, B, and 1739 is remarkable because 1739 is a tenth-century manuscript that was copied from a fourth-century manuscript of excellent quality. According to a colophon, the scribe of 1739 for the Pauline Epistles followed a manuscript that came from Caesarea in the library of Pamphilus and that contained an Origenian text. The three manuscripts, P46, B, and 1739, form a clear textual line: from P46 (early second century) to B (early fourth century) to 1739 (tenth century based on fourth century).

The Text of the New Testament The original text of the NT is the "published" text—that is, the text as it was in its final edited form and released for circulation in the Christian community. For some books of the NT, there is little difference between the original composition and the published text. After the author wrote or dictated his work, he (or an associate) made the final editorial corrections and then released it for distribution. As is the case for books published in modern times, so in ancient times, the original writing of the author is not always the same as what is published—due to the editorial process. Nonetheless, the author is credited with the final edited text, and the published book is attributed to the author and considered the autograph. This autograph is the original published text. Of course, in this case the autographs do not exist, so scholars have to rely on copies to recover or reconstruct the original wording.

Some scholars think it is impossible to recover the original text of the Greek NT because they have not been able to reconstruct the early history of textual transmission. Other modern scholars are less pessimistic but still quite guarded in affirming the possiblity. And yet others are optimistic because we possess many early manuscripts of excellent quality and because our view of the early period of textual transmission has been getting clearer and clearer.

When we speak of recovering the text of the NT, we are referring to individual books of the NT, not to the entire volume per se, because each book (or group of books— such as the Pauline Epistles) had its own unique history of textual transmission. The earliest extant copy of an entire NT text is the one preserved in Codex Sinaiticus (written about AD 375). (Codex Vaticanus lacks the Pastoral Epistles and Revelation.) Prior to the fourth century, the NT was circulated in its various parts: as a single book or a group of books (such as the four Gospels or the Pauline Epistles). Manuscripts from the late first century to the third century have been found with individual books such as Matthew (P1, P77), Mark (P88), Luke (P69), John (P5, 22, 52, 66), Acts (P91), Revelation (P18, 47), or containing groups of books, such as the four Gospels with Acts (P45), the Pauline Epistles (P30, P46, P92), the Petrine Epistles and Jude (P72). Each of the books of the NT has had its own textual history and has been preserved with varying degrees of accuracy. Nonetheless, all of the books were altered from the original state due to the process of manual copying decade after

decade and century after century. And the text of each of the books needs to be recovered.

The NT text was affected with many variations in its early history. In the late first and early second century, the oral traditions and the written word existed side by side with equal status—especially with respect to the material of the Gospels. Often, the text was changed by scribes attempting to conform the written message to the oral tradition or attempting to conform one Gospel account to another. By the end of the second century and into the third century, many of the significant variant readings entered into the textual stream.

The early period of textual transmission, however, was not completely marred by textual infidelity and scribal liberty. There were those scribes who copied the text faithfully and reverently—that is, they recognized that they were copying a sacred text written by an apostle. The formalization of canonization did not ascribe this sacredness to the text. Canonization came about as the result of common, historical recognition of the sacredness of various NT books. Certain NT books, such as the four Gospels, Acts, and Paul's epistles were considered inspired literature from the onset. As such, certain scribes copied them with reverential fidelity.

Other scribes, however, felt free to make "improvements" in the text—either in the interest of doctrine and harmonization or due to the influence of a competitive oral tradition. The manuscripts produced in such a manner created a kind of "popular text"—i.e., an uncontrolled text. (This text type used to be called the "Western text," but scholars now recognize this as a misnomer.)

During the second century, there were a few men who produced recensions of the NT text. According to Eusebius, Theodotus (and his followers) altered the text for their own purposes. In the middle of the second century, Marcion expunged his copies of the Gospel according to Luke of all references to the Jewish background of Jesus, and Tatian's harmony of the Gospels contains several textual alterations that gave support to ascetic views. And yet another recendor created the D-type text for the Gospels and Acts. This theologically minded redactor, living in the late second or third century, created a text that had short-lived popularity. Three third-century papyri, P29, P38, P48, each containing a portion from the book of Acts, may be precursors to the D-type text in Acts. But there are other papyri containing portions of Acts that provide even earlier testimony to a purer form of Acts—namely, P45 (c. 150) and P91 (c. 200), thereby showing that the D-type text of Acts did not necessarily antedate the purer form.

Besides these endeavors—which are all noted for creating textual impurities—there was no recension of the NT text in the second century. Rather, it was a period in which there were scribes who exercised freedom in copying and those who demonstrated acumen. The manuscripts produced by the latter are those that come closest to preserving the original text. A prime example of an accurate late-second-century manuscript is P75.

It is a well-known fact that the text produced by the scribe of P75 is a very accurate manuscript. It is also well-known that P75 was the kind of manuscript used in formulating Codex Vaticanus—the readings of P75 and B are remarkably similar. Prior to the discovery of P75, certain scholars thought Codex Vaticanus was the work of a fourth-century recension; others (chiefly Hort) thought it must trace back to a very early and accurate copy. Hort said that Codex Vaticanus preserves "not only a very ancient text, but a very pure line of a very ancient text" (Westcott and Hort, *The Introduc-*

tion to the New Testament in the Original Greek, pp 250–51). P75 appears to have shown that Hort was right.

Prior to the discovery of P75, many textual scholars were convinced that the second- and third-century papyri displayed a text in flux, a text characterized only by individual independence. The Chester Beatty Papyrus, P45, and the Bodmer Papyri, P66 and P72 (in 2 Peter and Jude), show this kind of independence. Scholars thought that scribes at Alexandria must have used several such texts to produce a good recension—as is exhibited in Codex Vaticanus. But we now know that Codex Vaticanus was not the result of a scholarly recension, resulting from editorial selection across the various textual histories. Rather, it is now quite clear that Codex Vaticanus was simply a copy (with some modifications) of a manuscript much like P75, not a fourth-century recension.

Some scholars may point out that this does not automatically mean that P75 and B represent the original text. What it does mean, they say, is that we have a second-century manuscript showing great affinity with a fourth-century manuscript whose quality has been highly esteemed. But various scholars have demonstrated that there was no Alexandrian recension before the time of P75 (late second century) and B (early fourth) and that both these manuscripts represent a relatively pure form of preservation of a relatively pure line of descent from the original text.

The current view about the early text is that certain scribes in Alexandria and/or scribes familiar with Alexandrian scriptoral practices (perhaps those in Oxyrhynchus) were probably responsible for maintaining a relatively pure text throughout the second, third, and fourth centuries. The Alexandrian scribes, associated with or actually employed by the scriptorium of the great Alexandrian library and/or members of the scriptorium associated with the catechetical school at Alexandria (called the *Didaskelion*), were trained philologists, grammarians, and textual critics. Their work on the NT was not recensional—that is, it was not an organized emendation of the text. Rather, the work of purification and preservation was probably done here and there by various individuals trained in text criticism. This is apparent in the production of P66, which contains the Gospel of John. This manuscript was probably produced in an Egyptian scriptorium by a novice scribe who made many blunders, which were subsequently corrected by another scribe working in the same scriptorium. The first text produced by the novice could be classified as being very "free," but the corrected text is far more accurate. (See the discussion on this manuscript above.)

What appears to have happened with the copying of the NT text in the early period in Egypt has been poignantly characterized by Zuntz. He said that when a book was immensely popular (such as Homer's *Iliad* and *Odyssey*, or Plato's writings), it was copied with wild enthusiasm by novice and scholar alike. But when grammarians and scribes got ahold of it, they tried to rid it of textual corruption. In the process, however, they may have obliterated some authentic readings, but not many. Thus, the popular text (also known as the "Western text") could have preserved the original wording in some cases. The popular or free kind of text is displayed in several third-century manuscripts: P9, P37, P40, P45, P72, and P78.

In brief, this popular text is usually displayed in any kind of manuscript that was not produced by Alexandrian influences. This text, given to independence, is not as trustworthy as the Alexandrian text type. But because the Alexandrian text is known as a polished text, the popular text sometimes preserved the original wording. When a variant reading has the support of "Western" and Alexandrian texts, it is very likely original; but when the two are divided, the Alexandrian witnesses more often preserve the original wording.

One dilemma still remains for some textual critics. They cannot explain how a P75/B-type text coexisted with a Western-type text in the second century. All that can be said is that the Western text generally appears to be inferior to the P75/B-type text. Of course, this kind of judgment troubles certain scholars, who point out that the esteem given to B and P75 is based on a subjective appreciation of the kind of text they contain (as over against the Western text) rather than on any kind of theoretical reconstruction of the early transmission of the text. This same subjective estimation was at work when Westcott and Hort decided that B was intrinsically superior to D (see their *Introduction*, pp 32–42). Yet the praxis of textual criticism time and again demonstrates that the P75/B-type text is intrinsically superior to the Western text.

In the final analysis, the manuscripts that represent a pure preservation of the original text are usually those called "Alexandrian." Some scholars, such as Bruce Metzger, have called the earlier manuscripts "proto-Alexandrian," for they (or manuscripts like them) are thought of as being used to compose an Alexandrian-type text. However, this is looking at things from the perspective of the fourth century. We should look at things from the second century onward and then compare fourth-century manuscripts to those of the second. The second-century manuscripts could still be called "Alexandrian" in the sense that they were produced under Alexandrian influences. Perhaps a distinguishing terminology could be "early Alexandrian" (pre-Constantine) and "later Alexandrian" (post-Constantine). Manuscripts designated as "early Alexandrian" would generally be purer, less editorialized. Manuscripts designated "later Alexandrian" would display editorialization, as well as the influence of other textual traditions.

The "early Alexandrian" text is reflected in many second- and third-century manuscripts. On the top of the list is P75 (c. 175), the work of a competent and careful scribe. Not far behind in quality is P4+P64+P67 (c. 150), the work of an excellent copyist. Other extremely good copies are P1 (c. 200), P20 (early third century), P23 (c. 200), P27 (third century), P28 (third century), P32 (c. 150), P39 (third century), P46 (c. 125), P65 (third century), P66 (in its corrected form—P66ᶜ; c. 150), P70 (third century), P77 (c. 150), P87 (c. 125), P90 (c. 175), and P91 (c. 200). Several of these manuscripts have been placed in the "strict" category by textual critics Kurt and Barbara Aland—that is, they exhibit "strict" scribal control and therefore are accurate copies of an exemplar, if not the original. These manuscripts are P1, P23, P35, P37, P39, P64/67, P65, P70, and P75.

The "later Alexandrian" text, which displays editorial polishing, is exhibited in a few manuscripts, such as ℵ (fourth century), T (fifth century), ℸ (seventh century), L (eighth century), 33 (ninth century), 1739 (a tenth-century manuscript copied from a fourth-century Alexandrian manuscript much like P46), and 579 (13th century). Beginning in the fifth century, Byzantine-type manuscripts began to make their influence in Egypt. Some manuscripts dated around 400 that came from Egypt clearly reflect this influence; Codex Alexandrinus (A) is probably the best example. Other Egyptian manuscripts of this era, such as Codex Sinaiticus (ℵ) and Codex Washingtonianus (W) display large-scale harmonization, which cannot be directly linked to any kind of recension.

At the end of the third century, another kind of Greek text came into being and then grew in popularity until it became the dominant text-type throughout Christendom.

This is the text-type first instigated by Lucian of Antioch, according to Jerome (in his introduction to his Latin translation of the Gospels). Lucian's text was a definite recension (i.e., a purposely created edition)—as opposed to the Alexandrian text-type that came about as the result of a process wherein the Alexandrian scribes, upon comparing many manuscripts, attempted to preserve the best text—thereby serving more as textual critics than editors. Of course, the Alexandrians did do some editing—such as we would call copy-editing. The Lucianic text is the outgrowth and culmination of the popular text; it is characterized by smoothness of language, which is achieved by the removal of obscurities and awkward grammatical constructions and by the conflation of variant readings. Lucian (and/or his associates) must have used many different kinds of manuscripts of varying qualities to produce a harmonized, edited NT text. The kind of editorial work that went into the Lucianic text is what we would call substantive editing.

Lucian's text was produced prior to the Diocletian persecution (c. 303), during which time many copies of the NT were confiscated and destroyed. Not long after this period of devastation, Constantine came to power and then recognized Christianity as the state religion. There was, of course, a great need for copies of the NT to be made and distributed to churches throughout the Mediterranean world. It was at this time that Lucian's text began to be propagated by bishops going out from the Antiochan school to churches throughout the East, taking the text with them. Lucian's text soon became the standard text of the Eastern church and formed the basis for the Byzantine text—and is thus the ultimate authority for the Textus Receptus.

While Lucian was forming his recension of the NT text, the Alexandrian text was taking on its final shape. As was mentioned earlier, the formation of the Alexandrian text-type was the result of a process (as opposed to a single editorial recension). The formation of the Alexandrian text involved minor textual criticism (i.e., selecting variant readings among various manuscripts) and copy-editing (i.e., producing a readable text). There was far less tampering with the text in the Alexandrian text-type than in the Lucian, and the underlying manuscripts for the Alexandrian text-type were superior to those used by Lucian. Perhaps Hesychius was responsible for giving the Alexandrian text its final shape, and Athanasius of Alexandria may have been the one who made this text the archetypal text for Egypt.

As the years went by, there were fewer and fewer Alexandrian manuscripts produced, and more and more Byzantine manuscripts manufactured. Very few Egyptians continued to read Greek (with the exception of those in St Catherine's Monastery, the site of the discovery of Codex Sinaiticus), and the rest of the Mediterranean world turned to Latin. It was only those in the Greek-speaking churches in Greece and Byzantium that continued to make copies of the Greek text. For century after century—from the 6th to the 14th—the great majority of NT manuscripts were produced in Byzantium, all bearing the same kind of text. When the first Greek NT was printed (c. 1525), it was based on a Greek text that Erasmus had compiled, using a few late Byzantine manuscripts. This printed text, with minor revisions, became the Textus Receptus.

Beginning in the 17th century, earlier manuscripts began to be discovered—manuscripts with a text that differed from that found in the Textus Receptus. Around 1630, Codex Alexandrinus was brought to England. An early fifth-century manuscript, containing the entire NT, it provided a good, early witness to the NT text (it is an

especially good witness to the original text of Revelation). Two hundred years later, a German scholar named Constantin von Tischendorf discovered Codex Sinaiticus in St Catherine's Monastery (located near Mt Sinai). The manuscript, dated around AD 360, is one of the two oldest vellum (treated animal hide) manuscripts of the Greek NT. The earliest vellum manuscript, Codex Vaticanus, had been in the Vatican's library since at least 1481, but it had not been made available to scholars until the middle of the 19th century. This manuscript, dated slightly earlier (AD 350) than Codex Sinaiticus, had both the OT and NT in Greek, excluding the last part of the NT (Hebrews 9:15 to Revelation 22:21 and the Pastoral Epistles). A hundred years of textual criticism has determined that this manuscript is one of the most accurate and reliable witnesses to the original text.

Other early and important manuscripts were discovered in the 19th century. Through the tireless labors of men like Constantin von Tischendorf, Samuel Tregelles, and F. H. A. Scrivener, manuscripts such as Codex Ephraemi Rescriptus, Codex Zacynthius, and Codex Augiensis were deciphered, collated, and published.

As the various manuscripts were discovered and made public, certain scholars labored to compile a Greek text that would more closely represent the original text than did the Textus Receptus. Around 1700 John Mill produced an improved Textus Receptus, and in the 1730s Johannes Albert Bengel (known as the father of modern textual and philological studies in the NT) published a text that deviated from the Textus Receptus according to the evidence of earlier manuscripts.

In the 1800s certain scholars began to abandon the Textus Receptus. Karl Lachman, a classical philologist, produced a fresh text (in 1831) that represented the fourth-century manuscripts. Samuel Tregelles (self-taught in Latin, Hebrew, and Greek), laboring throughout his entire lifetime, concentrated all of his efforts in publishing one Greek text (which came out in six parts, from 1857 to 1872). As is stated in the introduction to this work, Tregelles's goal was "to exhibit the text of the NT in the very words in which it has been transmitted on the evidence of ancient authority." Henry Alford also compiled a Greek text based upon the best and earliest manuscripts. In his preface to *The Greek New Testament* (a multivolume commentary on the Greek NT, published in 1849), Alford said he labored for the "demolition of the unworthy and pedantic reverence for the received text, which stood in the way of all chance of discovering the genuine word of God."

During this same era, Tischendorf was devoting a lifetime of labor to discovering manuscripts and producing accurate editions of the Greek NT. In a letter to his fiancé he wrote, "I am confronted with a sacred task, the struggle to regain the original form of the NT." In fulfillment of his desire, he discovered Codex Sinaiticus, deciphered the palimpsest Codex Ephraemi Rescriptus, collated countless manuscripts, and produced several editions of the Greek NT (the eighth edition is considered the best).

Aided by the work of the previous scholars, two British men, Brooke Westcott and Fenton Hort, worked together for 28 years to produce a volume entitled *The New Testament in the Original Greek* (1881). Along with this publication, they made known their theory (which was chiefly Hort's) that Codex Vaticanus and Codex Sinaiticus (along with a few other early manuscripts) represented a text that most closely replicated the original writing. They called this text the Neutral Text. (According to their studies, the Neutral Text described certain manuscripts that had the least amount of textual corruption.) This is the text that Westcott and Hort relied upon for compiling their volume.

The 19th century was a fruitful era for the recovery of

the Greek NT; the 20th century, no less so. Those living in the 20th century have witnessed the discovery of the Oxyrhynchus Papyri, the Chester Beatty Papyri, and the Bodmer Papyri. To date, there are nearly 100 papyri containing portions of the NT—several of which date from the late first century to the early fourth century. These significant discoveries, providing scholars with many ancient manuscripts, have greatly enhanced the effort to recover the original wording of the NT.

At the beginning of the 20th century, Eberhard Nestle used the best editions of the Greek NT produced in the 19th century to compile a text that represented the majority consensus. The work of making new editions was carried on by his son for several years, and then came under the care of Kurt Aland. The latest edition (the 27th) of Nestle-Aland's *Novum Testamentum Graece* appeared in 1993. The same Greek text appears in another popular volume published by the United Bible Societies, called the *Greek New Testament* (fourth edition). Aland has argued that the Nestle-Aland text, 27th edition (NA[27]), comes closer to the original text of the NT than did Tischendorf or Westcott and Hort. And in several writings he intimates that NA[27] may very well be the original text. Though few, if any, scholars would agree with this, the 27th edition of the Nestle-Aland text is regarded by many as representing the latest and best in textual scholarship.

New Testament Textual Criticism Textual critics working with ancient literature universally acknowledge the supremacy of earlier manuscripts over later ones. Textual critics not working with the NT would love to have the same kind of early witnesses that biblical scholars possess. In fact, many of them work with manuscripts written 1,000 years after the autographs were composed! We all marvel that the Dead Sea Scrolls have provided a text that is nearly 800 years closer to the originals than the Masoretic manuscripts, and yet many of the Dead Sea manuscripts are still over 600 to 800 years removed from the time of original composition. NT textual critics have a great advantage!

The 19th-century NT textual scholars—such as Lachmann, Tregelles, Tischendorf, Westcott and Hort—worked on the basis that the earliest witnesses are the best witnesses. Some textual scholars have continued this line of recovery using the testimony of the earlier witnesses. But many textual scholars since the time of Westcott and Hort have been less inclined to produce editions based on the theory that the earliest reading is the best. Most present-day textual critics are more inclined to endorse the maxim: the reading that is most likely original is the one that best explains the variants.

This maxim (or "canon" as it is sometimes called), as good as it is, produces conflicting results. For example, two scholars, using this same principle to examine the same variant unit, will not agree. One will argue that one variant was produced by a copyist attempting to emulate the author's style; the other will claim the same variant has to be original because it accords with the author's style. One will argue that one variant was produced by an orthodox scribe attempting to rid the text of a reading that could be used to promote heterodoxy or heresy; another will claim that the same variant has to be original because it is orthodox and accords with Christian doctrine (thus a heterodox or heretical scribe must have changed it). Furthermore, this principle allows for the possibility that the reading selected for the text can be taken from any manuscript of any date. This can lead to subjective eclecticism.

Modern textual scholars have attempted to temper the subjectivism by employing a method called "reasoned eclecticism." This kind of eclecticism applies a combination of internal and external considerations, whereby the character of the variants is evaluated in light of the manuscripts' evidence and vice versa. This is supposed to produce a balanced view and serve as a check against purely subjective tendencies.

The Alands favor the same kind of approach, calling it the local-genealogical method, which is defined as follows:

> It is impossible to proceed from the assumption of a manuscript stemma, and on the basis of a full review and analysis of the relationships obtaining among the variety of interrelated branches in the manuscript tradition, to undertake a recension of the data as one would do with other Greek texts. Decisions must be made one by one, instance by instance. This method has been characterized as eclecticism, but wrongly so. After carefully establishing the variety of readings offered in a passage and the possibilities of their interpretation, it must always then be determined afresh on the basis of external and internal criteria which of these readings (and frequently they are quite numerous) is the original, from which the others may be regarded as derivative. From the perspective of our present knowledge, this "local-genealogical" method (if it must be given a name) is the only one which meets the requirements of the NT textual tradition. (Introduction to *Novum Testamentum Graece*, 26th edition)

The "local-genealogical" method assumes that for any given variation unit any manuscript (or manuscripts) may have preserved the original text. Applying this method produces an extremely uneven documentary presentation of the text. Anyone studying the critical apparatus of NA[27] will detect that there is not an even documentary presentation. The eclecticism is dispersed throughout the text.

"Reasoned eclecticism" and/or the "local-genealogical" method tend to give priority to internal evidence over external evidence. But it has to be the other way around if we are going to recover the original text. This was Westcott and Hort's opinion. With respect to their compilation of *The New Testament in the Original Greek*, Hort wrote, "Documentary evidence has been in most cases allowed to confer the place of honour against internal evidence" (*The Introduction to the New Testament in the Original Greek*, p 17).

In this respect, Westcott and Hort need to be revived. Earnest Colwell was of the same mind when he wrote "Hort Redivivus: A Plea and a Program." Colwell decried the growing tendency to rely entirely on the internal evidence of readings, without serious consideration of documentary evidence. He called upon scholars to make an attempt to reconstruct a history of the manuscript tradition. The abundance of manuscripts—several of which are very early—will aid scholars in this ongoing task.

BIBLE*, Quotations of the Old Testament in the New Testament

OT passages cited or alluded to in the NT writings.

One of the most complex problems in interpreting the Bible is in understanding how NT writers quoted the OT. Obviously nothing is so formative and authoritative for the NT writers as Scripture. However, the way that they used OT passages often seems strange to modern readers.

The OT has provided the words and ideas for much of the NT. Unless one has a Bible that prints OT quotations in distinctive print, this may not be easily seen, for the NT writers often weave the OT words into their own without indicating they are borrowing from the OT. There are over 400 passages of the OT that are explicitly cited in the NT. Almost half of these are introduced by a statement like "Scripture says" to draw attention to the fact that the authority and thought of the OT is being implemented. For the others, however, the OT words are woven into the fabric of the author's own statement.

In addition to the over 400 passages cited explicitly, there are well over 1,000 places where there is an allusion to an OT text, event, or person. The difference between a quotation and an allusion is sometimes debated for particular texts, but usually the distinction is that in a quotation the author consciously uses the words of an OT passage, whereas with an allusion he has the texts in mind but is not consciously trying to use the words.

Quotations are easy to identify if there is an introductory formula such as "the Scripture says" (as in Rom 10:11; cf. Is 28:16). Where there is no introductory formula, it is easy to overlook explicit quotations (Rom 10:13; cf. Jl 2:32). The allusions are, of course, harder still to recognize, but they often provide the key to interpretation. For example, John 1:14-18—with its mention of glory, grace and truth, Moses, and the fact that no one has seen God—is much more easily and profoundly understood when read in connection with Exodus 33:17–34:8. In the Exodus passage the glory of God and his grace and truth are revealed to Moses. The author was showing that a much more complete revelation of God was given in Jesus than was given Moses in the account recorded in Exodus.

In addition, significant light is shed on many NT passages from OT passages with similar ideas and words even where the NT author may not have been consciously alluding to those texts (e.g. Mt 16:19; Is 22:22). What was behind the author's thinking is not certain, but in such cases the NT reflects the thinking, the culture, and language of the OT period.

Distribution of Old Testament Quotations The books of the NT that show the most dependence on the OT are Matthew, John, Romans, Hebrews, 1 Peter, and Revelation. Such a statement can be misleading, however, because the writers have different methods.

Matthew quotes or consciously reflects the wording of OT passages about 62 times, almost half of which have an introductory formula. The book of Revelation, on the other hand, never quotes the OT and never has an introductory formula but is probably more dependent on the OT than any other NT book. The book of Hebrews quotes or consciously reflects the OT about 59 times, again half of which have an introductory formula, but the Gospel of John does so only 18 times, nearly always with an introductory formula. However, the allusions to the OT are present on virtually every page of John's Gospel, so much so that some scholars have argued that he has modeled his account on the exodus narrative, the Jewish feasts, or OT persons and images. Paul's Letter to the Romans uses the OT 54 times (about three-fourths of which have introductory formulas), but nowhere else so frequently (e.g., 1 Cor 16 times, Gal 11 times, Phil one time, 1 Thes one time).

In addition to the indication that Philippians and 1 Thessalonians use the OT only once each, some other books make explicit use of the OT rarely or never. Colossians, Titus, Philemon, and the Johannine letters do not use the OT at all; 2 Timothy and Jude use the OT only once; while 2 Peter and 1 Timothy make use of it twice.

The important point is to realize that the OT is used most frequently in circumstances where the audience is familiar with the OT or where the OT is essential for describing the events relating to Christ and the church. The books using the OT most frequently (Mt, Jn, Rom, Heb, 1 Pt, Rv) either stem from or are addressed to a Jewish context or, as in the case of Romans and John, deal specifically with the relation of Jews and Christians. The Gospels make rather extensive use of the OT because the

language of the OT is necessary to convey the identity and importance of Jesus in the purposes of God. Similarly 1 Peter uses the OT frequently because the author is trying to convey to his persecuted audience that they are the people of God and the inheritors of the promises of God.

Difficulties in Interpretation Often when people think of quotations of the OT in the NT they think only in terms of prophecy. Some have been guilty of counting up the OT statements that the NT applies to Christ and the church and then claiming these OT texts as predictions that prove Jesus is the Messiah. Such a procedure is filled with problems because it is too simplistic and does not do justice to either the OT or to the way the NT uses it. Of course, the early church used the OT to show that Jesus fulfilled the promises of God and did God's work, but the use the church made of the OT was quite varied and much of it cannot be classified as predictive prophecy. Prophecy itself is too complex to be limited to predictive thinking.

Some of the most obvious examples of the difficulties appear in Matthew's Gospel, although they are by no means confined there. Matthew 2:15—"Out of Egypt I called my son"—is a quotation of Hosea 11:1, but in Hosea these words do not refer to the Messiah. They refer to the nation of Israel. Similarly Matthew 2:18 quotes Jeremiah 31:15 ("A voice is heard in Ramah, weeping and great mourning, Rachel weeping for her children and refusing to be comforted, because they are no more," NIV) as fulfilled in the slaughter of the innocent babies in Bethlehem, but in Jeremiah the weeping is over the destruction of Jerusalem. John 12:40 views Isaiah 6:10 as fulfilled in Jesus' ministry, but this verse deals with the call of Isaiah and is not a prediction concerning the ministry of the Messiah. The examples could be multiplied but these should be sufficient to illustrate the problem. For this reason the NT writers have often been accused of twisting the Scriptures, but this charge is as simplistic as the thought that all prophecy is predictive and in fact springs from the same error. Therefore, any attempt to understand the use of the OT in the NT will have to deal with the variety of ways in which the OT is used and with the methods employed by the NT writers.

There are other difficulties that are encountered as well. Sometimes the NT writer will indicate that some fact related to Christ is a fulfillment of the OT but the explicit text that he had in mind cannot be identified. For example, John 7:38 introduces the words "Out of his heart shall flow rivers of living water" with the statement "as Scripture has said." No OT text reads this way. Possibly the allusion is to the rock that provided water in the wilderness (Ex 17:1), or to the waters that flowed from the new temple (Zec 14:8) or, more generally, it may be a reference to Isaiah 58:11. Similarly, the difficulty in determining the OT text behind the prophecy that Christ will be called a Nazarene (Mt 2:23) is notorious. Probably the reference is to Isaiah 11:1 and the Hebrew word there translated as "branch," but the connection is not easily made and is not certain. A third example of this kind of difficulty is in 1 Corinthians 14:34, where Paul indicates that women should be in submission just as the Law says, but there is no OT text expressing this idea. His statement in probably to be understood as a summary rather than a quotation or allusion. Similarly on a few occasions an OT text is seemingly attributed to the wrong OT book. In Mark 1:2-3 an OT quotation is attributed to Isaiah but the quotation is really a conflation (or mixing) of Exodus 23:20, Malachi 3:1, and Isaiah 40:3. Matthew 27:9-10 quotes a passage that is said to be from Jeremiah, when really it is dependent on Zechariah 11:13 and might best be described as a summary of Zechariah 11:12-13, with certain words included from Jeremiah 32:6-9. These two examples do not create a major problem, however, for the determination of the origin of the words may be due to their use in collections of quotations from various prophets, in which case the more prominent prophets would be used to designate origin.

The wording of the quotations of the OT text does not always conform to the modern form of the OT. Just as today there are numerous translations of the Bible, when the NT was being written there were various forms of the OT text. With regard to the Hebrew text (for the OT was written mostly in Hebrew), there were different traditions. Such differences in the Hebrew traditions would have been relatively small. Because of the increasing importance of Aramaic after the Babylonian captivity and of Greek after the conquests of Alexander the Great, the OT was also known and used in both these languages when the NT was being written. In fact, the Jews found it necessary in their synagogue services after reading the Hebrew OT to paraphrase the reading in Aramaic so that all could understand. These paraphrases were later written down and are known as Targums. The Greek translation of the OT that stems from the third century BC is known as the Septuagint, but there were also other Greek translations in use. This being the case, the wording of a NT quotation is not identical in every detail to the text of the Hebrew OT.

Added to the fact that there were various forms of the text known in first-century AD Palestine is the complicating factor that NT writers often did not intend to quote the OT exactly. The use of formal quotation marks is a modern device, and ancient writers were not so taken by technical precision. They were more concerned with the intention of a text and consequently might copy or quote it verbatim, quote it from memory, use or adapt part of a verse, or even change certain words as they borrowed the verse to express their points. (The NT writers often use the OT words describing God's actions in the past to explain what he has done in their time.) The importance of any differences between the NT quotation and the OT depends on the use to which the quotation is put and the degree to which the use is dependent on textual differences.

Some examples should illustrate the nature of these difficulties. Ephesians 4:8 quotes Psalm 68:18. Whereas the Hebrew and Septuagint read, "You ascended to the heights, you lead captivity captive, you received gifts among mankind," Ephesians records the verse as "After he ascended into the heights, *he* led captivity captive; he *gave* gifts to men." Paul is stressing that Christ has given grace to people for ministry. He has either adapted the wording of the OT to make his point or he quoted a variant reading, *"he gave* gifts." Some versions do have this reading. In fact, the Targum understands this verse as Moses giving the words of the law to the children of men, and Paul may well be adapting this understanding to the new revelation that has come in Christ.

Matthew 1:23 quotes Isaiah 7:14, but there are distinct differences between the Hebrew text and the wording in Matthew. The Hebrew reads, "Behold the young woman will become pregnant and will bear a son and you will call his name Immanuel," whereas Matthew's text records "Behold, the *virgin* will become pregnant and will bear a son, and *they* will call his name Immanuel." The Septuagint does have the specific word "virgin," like Matthew, but is not the source of Matthew's quotation since other differences exist. Some have argued that the change from "you will call" to "they will call" was made by Matthew when he applied the words to Jesus. However, there are several traditions known for this part of the quotation and partial support for the reading in Matthew is provided by the text of Isaiah found among the Dead Sea Scrolls.

Romans 11:26-27 is a conflation of Isaiah 59:20-21 and part of Isaiah 27:9, but there are important differences. One of these is that the OT has "the redeemer will come to Zion," whereas Romans has "the deliverer will come *from* Zion." The change to "from Zion" could indicate that Paul had a different textual tradition, could be the result of an intentional change by Paul, or more probably, could reflect the wording of Psalm 14:7.

An awareness of the difficulties involved in the quotations of the OT by the NT writers will prohibit a simplistic approach and will prevent hasty conclusions. Care to ask not only which text was used but also which form of the text was used and how is obviously essential in any serious study. In addition it is necessary to allow for the possibility that the NT writers knew forms of a text that are now lost.

The Methods of the New Testament Writers The methods used by the NT writers were not unique to them. Many of these methods were also employed in first-century Judaism. In fact, both the technique used in quoting and the understanding of the OT text itself in many cases are paralleled in Judaism. For example, from the standpoint of technique used in quoting, the same kinds of formula introductions are used in the Dead Sea Scrolls, the rabbinic writings, and elsewhere. The rabbinic technique of "pearl stringing," that is, of applying verses from various parts of the OT (the Law, the Prophets, the Writings) to a subject, can be seen especially in Paul's writings (note Rom 9:12-19 or 11:8-10). Somewhat related is the practice of using quotations that all contain a key word or key words (note 1 Pt 2:6-8, which draws together quotations using the word "stone," or Rom 15:9-12, which joins OT verses referring to the "nations").

The methods used in the NT to interpret an OT text are also displayed in Judaism. Some passages interpret the OT "literally," such as Jesus' replies during temptation (see the quotations of Dt 8:3; 6:16; 6:13; in Mt 4:3-10), his teachings on marriage based on Genesis 2:24 (Mt 19:5), or Paul's use of Habakkuk 2:4 (Rom 1:17) or Genesis 15:6 (Rom 4:3-9). Many such examples could be given. With regard to prophecy, some of these statements are fulfilled in a "literal" or "direct" way in keeping with the intention of the OT (e.g., Mi 5:2, Bethlehem as the birthplace of the Messiah; Mt 2:4-6). Jeremiah 31:31-34, the promise of the new covenant, is viewed as directly fulfilled in Christ (Heb 8:7-13). The prophecy of Joel 2:28-32 concerning the pouring out of the Spirit of the Lord is directly fulfilled in the Pentecost event (Acts 2:17-21), but the changing of the sun to darkness and the moon to blood are certainly not understood literally in connection with this event.

A different method of interpretation is based on the concept of *corporate solidarity*. This technical expression is an attempt to convey the idea that the individuals among God's people are not merely individuals; they are part of a larger whole. Consequently, what is said about the individual can apply to the whole and vice versa. This is the reason the Servant of the Lord in Isaiah is seen both as the nation (44:1) and as an individual (52:13–53:12). Also the king is sometimes viewed as representative of the nation. The easiest places to see the concept of corporate solidarity are in the effect of the sin of Achan on all the people (Jos 7) or the sin of David in numbering the people (1 Chr 21:3-8).

Correspondence in history is not so much a method of interpretation as it is a way of thinking about God. It assumes that the things that happen to God's people are the things that have happened to previous generations and that God is faithful and operates in the present as he has in the past. Consequently, the trials and deliverance of God's people are often expressed with words borrowed from the previous accounts of God's people. Isaiah describes the anticipated deliverance in terms of a second exodus (11:15-16). Ezekiel describes the king set up over the people in terms of a second David (Ez 37:25). In the NT, Revelation 22 describes the new heavens and the new earth in terms of the Garden of Eden (Gn 2–3). Sometimes this technique is described as "typology," but this term has been used for so many questionable interpretations that it is misleading. The most important thing about this concept is that it is a view of God and his working among his people.

With these two concepts, the way that the OT is quoted in the NT can be understood. The conviction that Jesus was the promised deliverer and that the last days had dawned in his ministry are evident everywhere. The quotation of Hosea 11:1 can be used in Matthew 2:15 because of corporate solidarity and correspondence in history. What was said of the nation is true of the one who is its representative, and there is correspondence in their respective histories. Jeremiah 31:15 can be used in Matthew 2:18 because of correspondence in history and especially because Jeremiah looked forward to God's intention for Israel and prophesied a new covenant (31:17, 31-34). Matthew saw not only the correspondence in history but believed that in Jesus this promised salvation had been granted. John 12:40 can quote Isaiah 6:10 of Jesus' ministry, not because he twists the meaning of the OT text, but because he saw that what had happened with God's messenger before happened again and even *ultimately* in Jesus' ministry. The instances of such correspondences in history are numerous.

There are other texts where there seems to be an *actualization* of the OT text. Some quotations seem to be "lived out" in the ministry of Jesus. Because of their conviction about Jesus and his kingdom, the NT writers often saw certain OT texts as appropriated and made alive by Jesus. Psalm 118:22 was not intended as a prophecy of the Messiah, but Jesus saw it as descriptive of his ministry (Mt 21:42), and the early church saw this verse as actualized in his death and resurrection (Acts 4:11). Isaiah 53 is another text that the NT views as actualized in Jesus' ministry (see Acts 8:32-35 and 1 Pt 2:22-25). Some Christians would view Psalm 22 as a prophecy of the crucifixion of Jesus, but it seems instead to be the lament of a righteous OT sufferer. Through correspondence in history, and because Christians saw so much of the psalmist's plight actualized in Jesus' crucifixion, the psalm became the easiest way to describe what once again had happened to God's righteous sufferer. The words of Isaiah 40:3 describe the ministry of John the Baptist (Mt 3:3). Jews had come to see this verse as a prophecy of God's end-time salvation, and the early church saw John the Baptist fulfilling this forerunner's task. Luke made this identification (Lk 3:4-6), but he applied the same role to Jesus' disciples (9:52; 10:1). This seems to be a further example of actualization and correspondence in history. In other places the church has applied to Christians ideas that were previously understood of Christ (e.g., the stone in 1 Pt 2:4-5; the ministry of the Suffering Servant in Acts 13:46-47).

The most convenient term to describe the way the OT is "fulfilled" in Christ is to say that the OT finds its climax in Jesus. Even where actual quotations are not involved, the OT ideas such as prophet, priest, or king are climaxed in him as the ideal and embodiment of all the OT models. He could tell religious authorities that "one greater than Solomon is here" (Mt 12:42) or "one greater than the temple is here" (Mt 12:6). Those passages involving correspondence in history or actualization also lead to the conviction that he is the climax of the OT Scriptures.

The Purposes of the Use of the Old Testament

The variety of methods of interpretation and application of the OT parallels the fact that the OT was used for a variety of purposes. People tend to think only in terms of the use of the OT to show that Jesus was the Messiah, but there are a number of other uses with a variety of goals. Many OT texts are used to show Jesus is the Messiah, the fulfillment of the OT promises (Lk 4:16-21). Without lessening the fulfillment emphasis, however, other verses are applied to Jesus for other purposes: to evangelize (Acts 8:32-25); to demonstrate or convince (Acts 13:33-35); to rebuke (Mk 7:6-7; Rom 11:7-10); and to describe (Rv 1:12-15). On the other hand, many quotations of the OT in the NT are not directly related to the Messiah. OT passages are adapted to provide a word from God on some aspect of life or ethics. For example, Jesus used Genesis 2:24 to substantiate his teaching on divorce as he attempted to deal with the issues raised by the civil regulation of divorce (Dt 24:1; Mt 19:1-12). The stress on the OT commandments shows their importance for Christians (Mt 19:16-22; Rom 13:8-10). Often OT statements deal with specific problems. The problem of pride at Corinth is solved by the quotation of Jeremiah 9:24 ("Let the one boasting, boast in the Lord," 1 Cor 1:31). First Peter 3:10-12 incorporates Psalm 34:12-16 as ethical instructions, and 3:14-15 borrows from Isaiah 8:12-13 to address the fear of suffering. The spiritual armor in Ephesians 6:14-17 is derived largely from OT passages. Such examples are so numerous that there can be no doubt that the OT is used to describe Christian existence. In fact, nearly every subject discussed in the NT is presented somewhere via OT terms and quotations. Frequently OT passages are used to describe the church as God's end-time community. Hosea 2:23 is used to show that those who formerly were not God's people now are (Rom 9:25-26; 1 Pt 2:10). Several OT texts contribute to the description of the church in 1 Peter 2:9. OT texts that speak of the word of God describe the apostles' preaching (Rom 10:8; 1 Pt 1:24-25). OT quotations describe the sinful condition of humanity (Rom 3:10-20). Salvation is explained through OT concepts and symbols and is based on OT statements (Jn 6:31-33; Gal 3:6-13). The words of Daniel describe the Second Coming (7:13-14; cf. Mt 24:30). Even the worship of early Christians was expressed through use of the OT (see Acts 4:24; Rom 11:34-35).

HOW TO UNDERSTAND THE USE OF THE
OLD TESTAMENT IN THE NEW TESTAMENT
The description of the use of the OT in the NT has pointed to the frequency of use, the difficulties encountered, and the variety of methods and purposes employed. A concluding list of suggestions for understanding the use of the OT follows:
(1) Identify, if possible, which OT text is being employed. (2) Compare the wording of the NT and the OT passages. If there are significant differences, assistance may be required from scholarly studies before drawing conclusions. (3) Determine the original intention of the OT text in its context. (4) Determine how the NT used the OT text. Identify both the method by which the OT text is appropriated and the purpose for which it is employed. (5) Identify the teaching of both the OT and the NT texts for Christian understanding.

While the use of the OT in the NT is complex, no subject is more important or rewarding for a faith that speaks of itself and its founder as the fulfillment and climax of God's word in the OT.

BIBLE*, Versions of the (Ancient)

To get a picture of how the Bible has come to different peoples in the world, spread out a map of the eastern hemisphere and imagine Palestine as the center of a pool. Think of God's revelation of himself through the prophets, the Christ, and the apostles as a pebble dropped into the center of that body of water. In your mind's eye watch the advance of the concentric circles out across that world pool from Palestine and call out the languages covered by the fast-spreading ripple: to the south, Coptic, Arabic, Ethiopic; to the west, Greek, Latin, Gothic, English; to the north, Armenian, Georgian, Slavonic; and eastward toward the rising sun, Syriac. The farther the Bible moved from its Hebrew/Aramaic/Greek center in Palestine, the later the date of its translation into yet another language.

That pebble of God's revelation, the Bible, was produced in the Middle East predominantly in two of Palestine's languages. The OT was written in Hebrew with the exception of portions of the books of Daniel and Ezra, which may have been written in Aramaic, the language of the Captivity. Probably the entire NT was written in common Greek (koine), which was the dominant language of the eastern half of Caesar's domain and understood almost everywhere else in the Roman Empire. Therefore every person who did not speak Hebrew or Greek was apt to remain untouched by God's written revelation until someone translated the Bible into his language.

The process of Bible translation began even before the birth of Christ, with translations of the OT being made into Greek and Aramaic. Many of the dispersed Jews who lived prior to the coming of Christ did not know Hebrew and therefore required a translation in Greek or Aramaic. The most popular Greek translation of the OT was the Septuagint. It was used by many Jews, and then by many Christians. In fact, the Septuagint was the "Bible" for all the first-generation Christians, including those who wrote various books of the NT.

The early Christian missionaries carrying a text of the Septuagint (or Hebrew Bible) and the Greek NT (or portions thereof), which they themselves could read, moved ever outward from those early churches at Jerusalem and Antioch about which we read in the book of Acts. They moved out among peoples whose language they learned to speak. Such missionaries orally translated or paraphrased Bible passages necessary for instruction, preaching, and liturgy. Converts were made. New churches sprang up. Feeling an urgent need for the Bible to be put in the language of the new believers, missionaries would soon set about translating the whole Bible into their language. The impulse behind our modern Wycliffe Bible Translators has always been at the heart of missions, and in that way the major Bible versions were born.

Bible translation was thus spontaneous, invariably informal and oral at first, and sharply evangelistic in its motivation. The early church enthusiastically encouraged and undertook translating efforts. Even as late as the birth of the Slavonic version in the mid-ninth century, popes Adrian II (867–72) and John VIII (872–82) endorsed the project. But an amazing change came in the Western church in regard to Bible translation. Latin took over as the dominant language—such that no one read Greek anymore. Then, as learning became the province of only the wealthy nobility and prelates (churchmen of high rank, such as bishops), as the splendors of classical civilization were lost in the ferment of feudalism in Europe, and as the Roman Catholic hierarchy—headed by the pope—claimed a firm grip on Western Christendom, the Bible was removed from the hands of the laity.

Therefore, as long as the priests could read the Latin texts and speak the liturgy in Latin (at least at a minimal level), there was no longer significant motivation for translations into the vernacular.

Latin came to be considered almost a sacred language, and translations of the Bible into the vernacular were viewed with suspicion. Pope Gregory VII (1073–85) gave voice to such suspicions when, only 200 years after Adrian II and John VIII had called for a Slavonic translation, Gregory attempted to stop its circulation. He wrote to King Vratislaus of Bohemia in 1079:

> For it is clear to those who reflect upon it that not without reason has it pleased Almighty God that holy scripture should be a secret in certain places lest, if it were plainly apparent to all men, perchance it would be little esteemed and be subject to disrespect; or it might be falsely understood by those of mediocre learning, and lead to error.

Meanwhile in Palestine and northern Africa, the inexorable march of Islam changed the religious texture of the Mediterranean's eastern and southern littorals. Within 100 years of Muhammad's death (570–632), over 900 churches had been destroyed and the Koran became the "bible" in the great circle from the walls of embattled Byzantium round to the west—to the Spanish end of Europe.

Cramped by official opposition in the West and hindered by Islamic conquest in the Middle East, Bible translations slowed to a trickle for half a millennium. Translation efforts did not regain vitality until the Protestant Reformation of the early 16th century, at which time missionaries took advantage of movable-type printing (invented by Johannes Gutenberg) to produce multiple translations of the Bible. Erasmus expressed the desire of all Bible translators in the preface of his freshly published Greek NT (1516):

> I wish that even the weakest woman should read the Gospel—should read the Epistles of Paul. And I wish these were translated into all languages, so that they might be read and understood, not only by Scots and Irishmen, but also by Turks and Saracens. To make them understood is surely the first step. It may be that they might be ridiculed by many, but some would take them to heart. I long that the husbandman should sing portions of them to himself as he follows the plough, that the weaver should hum them to the tune of his shuttle, that the traveller should beguile with their stories the tedium of his journey.

But what materials were used by the early translators and copyists who worked so painstakingly over their Bible translations? At the time of Christ and through the first two centuries of the church, the most popular writing materials were ink on papyrus. Until the first century, "books" were actually scrolls with long sheets of papyrus paper glued end to end and rolled up on paired spindles. Then, later in the first century, another form of a book was created—called the codex (the precursor to the modern form of a book with folded sheets and stitched spine). Christians were among the first to use this form for books. In AD 332 the first Christian emperor, Constantine I, ordered 50 Bibles for the churches of his new capital city, Constantinople. He ordered those from Eusebius, bishop of Caesarea, and specified that they were not to be scrolls, but codexes (or codices). They were also to be not of papyrus but of vellum, carefully prepared sheep or antelope skins, for it was right about this time, in the late third and early fourth centuries, that codexes and vellum almost universally replaced scrolls and papyrus.

For centuries scribes laboriously copied Bibles all in capital letters; the earliest surviving manuscripts of Bible versions are of that type, called "uncials." In the ninth and tenth centuries it became the fashion to write in lowercase letters; surviving manuscripts of that type are called "minuscules" or "cursives." (There were, however, occasional cursive manuscripts as far back as the second century before Christ.) Minuscules dominate the surviving biblical manuscripts from the 10th through the 16th centuries.

It was in 1454 that Johannes Gutenberg made manuscript writing obsolete by using movable type for the first time. His first printed book appeared in 1456, a splendid Latin Bible.

Our printed Bibles today contain chapter and verse divisions that were a relatively late development. Chapter divisions began in the Latin Vulgate and are variously credited to Lanfranc, archbishop of Canterbury (d. 1089), to Stephen Langton, archbishop of Canterbury (d. 1228), or to Hugo de Sancto Caro of the 13th century. Verse numbers first appeared in the fourth edition of the Greek NT issued at Geneva in 1551 by Robert Estienne (Stephanus) and in the Athias Hebrew OT of 1559–61.

PREVIEW
• Earliest Versions of the Old Testament
• Complete Bible Versions of Christendom
 •Latin Versions
 •Coptic Versions
 •Gothic Version
 •Syriac Versions
 •Armenian Version
 •Georgian Version
 •Ethiopic Version
 •Arabic Versions
 •Slavonic Version

Earliest Versions of the Old Testament The first version to be considered, the Samaritan Pentateuch, cannot rightly be termed a translation because it is a Hebrew version of the first five books of the OT, the books of the Law. These books comprise the total canon of Scripture for the Samaritan community, which still survives and is now centered in modern Nablus in Palestine.

The Samaritan Pentateuch reflects a textual tradition different from that of traditional Judaism, whose Hebrew text goes back through the centuries to the work of the Masoretes. The Masoretes were a body of scribes charged with OT text preservation, beginning about AD 600 and extending to the first half of the 10th century. It was they who devised a pointing system to indicate the vowels missing from consonantal Hebrew. It is this so-called Masoretic Text that forms (as the "received text") the basis for the King James Version OT.

The Samaritan Pentateuch, on the other hand, goes back to the fourth century before Christ. According to textual scholars, the Samaritan Pentateuch differs from the "received" or Masoretic Hebrew text in about 6,000 places. About 1,000 of those differences need to be taken seriously. Where the text of the Samaritan Pentateuch agrees with the Septuagint or one of the other ancient versions against the Hebrew of the Masoretic Text, its witness must be regarded as important. The two oldest manuscripts of the Samaritan Pentateuch outside of Nablus are both codexes. One copy in the John Rylands Library in Manchester, England, bears a date corresponding to AD 1211 or 1212; the other is somewhat older

than 1149 and is presently in the University Library at Cambridge, England. Two minor translations of the Samaritan Pentateuch also exist; one is the Aramaic Samaritan Targum from early Christian times, the other an Arabic translation from about the 11th century.

The second OT version, the Septuagint, is an actual translation from the Hebrew into the Greek. It is the first translation of the OT known. It was the Bible used by the apostles, the version from which most OT quotations in the NT come, and the Bible of the early church as far as the OT was concerned.

The story of its production, from which it draws its name, is told in "The Letter of Aristeas" (written around 150–100 BC). Aristeas purportedly was an official of Egypt's Ptolemy Philadelphus (285–247 BC). Ptolemy was attempting to gather all of the world's books into his great Alexandrian library. The OT was not on hand in translation, the letter says, so Ptolemy sent to the high priest in Jerusalem for texts and scholars to translate. Texts and six elders of each tribe were sent. After being royally entertained by Ptolemy, these 72 elders were cloistered and in exactly 72 days produced the full Greek translation of the OT, called Septuagint ("Seventy") and usually abbreviated LXX in Roman numerals.

The truth of the matter is probably more prosaic. The Septuagint is a translation done for Hellenized Jews of the Diaspora who, no longer understanding Hebrew, wished to hear and teach the Bible in their language. Scholars argue over the date of the translation, placing portions as early as 250 BC and other parts as late as 100 BC. Most concur that it was translated in segments by many translators over a couple of centuries and then was gathered together into one library of scrolls or one codex. The Septuagint follows a different order from English Bibles and usually includes up to 15 apocryphal or noncanonical books.

The third OT version is the Aramaic. Biblical Aramaic, called Chaldee up through the 19th century, was the language of the conquerors that gradually became the household speech of the conquered. When the Jewish exiles began to return to Palestine from Babylon in 536 BC, they brought Aramaic with them. Many scholars believe that when Ezra and the Levites "explained the meaning of the passage" as the Book of the Law was read (Neh. 8:8), they were paraphrasing the Hebrew into Aramaic so all could understand. Aramaic remained as the living language in Palestine up to the Bar-Kochba revolt against the Romans (AD 132–135), and Hebrew became increasingly a religious language for synagogue and temple specialists. As priests and scribes read the Law and Prophets, the custom of following the reading with an Aramaic translation spread. Such translations were called targums.

Rabbinical leadership was very loathe to formalize and write down the targums, but inevitably they were collected and standardized. The earliest standardized Targum was that of the Law done by someone known as Onkelos, sometime in the second or third century AD. Targums on the historical and prophetic books were crystallized in the third and fourth centuries AD, with the most important one called the Targum Jonathan ben Uzziel. Evidently no Targums of the Wisdom Literature (Proverbs, Ecclesiastes, Job, some Psalms) were completed earlier than the fifth century AD. Finally rabbinical Aramaic Targums included all of the OT except Daniel, Ezra, and Nehemiah. Meanwhile, the Islamic conquest of the entire Middle East gave people a new common language, Arabic. Rabbis were apt to find themselves beginning to produce informal oral Arabic targums, and Aramaic faded from the synagogue into religious history.

Complete Bible Versions of Christendom As the church gathered the NT together and added it to the Old, there began the process of Bible translation that has marked the growth of Christianity from Jerusalem through Judea to Samaria and on toward the "uttermost part" of the world.

Latin Versions Like the Aramaic Targums of Jewish worshipers, the Old Latin Bible was an informal growth. In the early days of the Roman Empire and of the church, Greek was the language of Christians. Even the first bishops of Rome wrote and preached in Greek. As empire and church aged, Latin began to win out, especially in the West. It was natural that priests and bishops began informally to translate the Greek NT and Septuagint into Latin. The initial Latin version is called the Old Latin Bible. No complete manuscript of it survives. Much of the OT and most of the New, however, can be reconstructed from quotations of the early church fathers. Scholars believe that an Old Latin Bible was in circulation in Carthage in North Africa as early as AD 250. From the surviving fragments and quotations there seem to have been two types of Old Latin text, the African and the European. The European existed in an Italian revision also. In textual study the major importance of the Old Latin is in comparative study of the Septuagint because the Old Latin was translated from the Septuagint before Origen made his *Hexapla.*

From every quarter, church leaders voiced the need for an authoritative and uniform Latin translation of the whole Bible. Pope Damascus I (366–384) had an exceptionally able and scholarly secretary named Jerome (c. 340–420), whom he commissioned to make a new Latin translation of the Gospels in 382. Jerome completed the Gospels in 383; Acts and the rest of the NT evidently followed. The Gospels were a thorough and painstaking retranslation based on the European Old Latin and an Alexandrian Greek text. The rest of the NT, however, was a much more limited effort with the Old Latin remaining dominant unless the Greek text demanded change. In all probability it was not the work of Jerome himself.

Jerome left Rome in 385, and in 389 he and a follower, Paula, founded two religious houses near Bethlehem. At one of these Jerome presided. There he turned his attention to the OT. He realized that what was needed was a retranslation from the Hebrew, not a revision of the Greek Septuagint. He used Jewish rabbis as consultants and completed work through the books of Kings by 390. Jerome reworked an earlier translation he had made of the Psalms and completed the prophets, Job, Ezra, and Chronicles in 390–96. After a two-year illness, he picked up the task again and translated Proverbs, Ecclesiastes, and Song of Solomon. In 404 he worked through Joshua, Judges, Ruth, and Esther. Soon afterward he did the apocryphal parts of Daniel and Esther and translated the apocryphal Tobit and Judith from Aramaic. He did not touch the Wisdom of Solomon, Ecclesiasticus, Baruch, or the Maccabean literature, so those apocryphal books passed into the official Latin Bible in their Old Latin form. Jerome's work was not uniform in quality, nor did he gather it all together into a unified Bible.

Jerome's work was fiercely criticized, and though he defended it with facile pen and ready temper, he did not live long enough to see it win universal respect. Yet his life's work passed into what is now known as the Vulgate Bible (*vulga* meaning the "vulgar," or everyday, speech of the people). Evidence seems to indicate that the compiling of all of Jerome's work into one book may have been done by Cassiodorus (died c. 580) in his monastery at

Scylacium in Italy. The earliest extant manuscript containing Jerome's Bible in its entirety is the Codex Amiatinus written in the monastery at Jarrow, Northumbria, England, around 715. The old texts of the Vulgate are second only to the Septuagint in importance for Hebrew textual study, for Jerome was working from Hebrew texts that antedated the work of the Jewish Masoretes.

Only very gradually did the Vulgate supplant the Old Latin Bible. It took 1,000 years before the Vulgate was made the official Roman Catholic Bible (by the Council of Trent in 1546). That council also authorized an official, corrected edition, which was first issued by Pope Sixtus V (1585–90) in 1590 in three volumes. It proved unpopular, however, and Pope Clement VIII (1592–1605) recalled it and issued a new official Vulgate in 1592, which has been the standard edition to recent times.

Coptic Versions Coptic was the last stage of the Egyptian language and thus the language of the native populations who lived along the length of the Nile River. It was never supplanted by the Greek of Alexander and his generals or even threatened by the Latin of the Caesars. Its script was composed of 25 Greek uncials and 7 cursives taken over from Egyptian writing to express sounds not in the Greek. Through the centuries it developed at least five main dialects: Akhmimic, sub-Akhmimic (Memphitic), Sahidic, Fayumic, and Bohairic. Fragments of biblical material have been found in the Akhmimic, sub-Akhmimic, and Fayumic. No one knows whether or not the whole Bible ever existed in these dialects. They gradually faded out of use until—by the 11th century—only Bohairic, the language of the Delta, and Sahidic, the language of Upper Egypt, remained. They too, however, had become largely forgotten or strictly religious languages used only in Coptic churches by the 17th century because of the long dominance of Arabic that began with the Islamic conquest of Egypt in 641.

The earliest translation was in Sahidic in Upper Egypt, where Greek was less universally understood. The Sahidic Old and New Testaments were probably completed by around AD 200. Greek was so much more dominant in the Delta that the translation of the Scriptures into Bohairic probably was not completed until somewhat later. Since Bohairic was the language of the Delta, however, it was also the language of the Coptic Patriarch in Alexandria. When the patriarchate moved from Alexandria to Cairo in the 11th century, the Bohairic texts went along. Bohairic gradually became the major religious language of the Coptic church. The Copts had separated from the Roman Empire, or the so-called Great Catholic Church, over doctrinal issues after the Council of Chalcedon in 451 and had then been isolated from Western Christendom by centuries of Islamic rule.

Gothic Version The Gothic language was an East Germanic language. The earliest literary remains known in any Germanic tongue are the fragments of the Bible done by Ulfilas (or Wulfila), who made the translation to bring the gospel to his own people. Ulfilas (c. 311–83), one of the early church's most famous missionaries, was born in Dacia of Roman Christian parents who had been captured by the raiding Goths. He traveled to Constantinople from his tribal area, and he may have been converted there. While in the East, he was ordained as bishop around 340 by the Arian bishop Eusebius of Nicomedia. Ulfilas himself was of the Arian persuasion (believing that Christ was Savior and Lord by divine appointment and by his obedience, but that he was less than God or was subservient to God).

Ulfilas returned to preach to his people, evidently invented an alphabet for them in order to reduce their language to writing, and then translated the Scriptures into that written language. Records from that time say Ulfilas translated all of the Bible except the books of the Kings, which he excluded because he felt they would have an adverse influence on the Goths, who were already too warlike. Scattered fragments of his OT translation survive and only about half of the Gospels are preserved in the Codex Argenteus, a manuscript of Bohemian origin of the fifth or sixth century now at Uppsala in Sweden.

Syriac Versions One of the family of Semitic languages, Syriac was the predominant tongue of the region of Edessa and western Mesopotamia. The version known today as the *Peshitta* Bible (still the official Bible of Christians of the old Assyrian area churches and often lacking 2 Peter, 2 and 3 John, Jude, and Revelation) developed through several stages. One of the most famous and widely used translations in the early church was the Syriac *Diatessaron*, done by Tatian, a man who had been a disciple of Justin Martyr at Rome. The *Diatessaron*, Tatian's harmony of the Gospels translated from the Greek about AD 170, was very popular among Syriac-speaking Christians. Syrian bishops had an uphill battle getting Christians to use "The Gospel of the Separated Ones" (meaning the manuscript in which the four Gospels were separated from one another rather than blended) in their churches.

Other portions of the Bible were also put into Old Syriac. Quotations from the church fathers indicate that some type of second-century Old Syriac text existed along with the *Diatessaron*. In fact, the OT may have been a Jewish translation into Syriac that Syrian Christians made their own, just as Greek Christians had done with the Septuagint. It then underwent a more or less official revision around the end of the fourth century, emerging as the *Peshitta* (meaning "basic" or "simple") text. Tradition indicates that at least the NT portion of that version may have been made at the instigation of Rabbula, bishop of Edessa (411–35).

In the meantime, Syrian-speaking Christians underwent a schism in AD 431 when the Monophysite (or Jacobite) groups split off from the Nestorian believers (the battle was over the view of the Person of Christ). For a time both groups used the *Peshitta*, but the Jacobite groups began to desire a new translation. Working from the Septuagint and Greek NT manuscripts, Bishop Philoxemus (or Mar Zenaia) of Mabbug (485–519) on the Euphrates River did a new Syriac translation that was completed in 508. The importance of that version was that it included for the first time 2 Peter, 2 and 3 John, and Jude, which then made their way into the standard *Peshitta* text.

Though the *Peshitta* has been in continuous use since the fifth century, and reached as far as India and China in its distribution, it has not been nearly so important a source for textual scholars as the Septuagint. That is because it had undergone constant revision through comparison with various Greek texts at Constantinople, Hebrew texts, Origen's *Hexapla* Septuagint, and the Aramaic Targums; therefore, its witness to an early textual source is very difficult to trace. One of the most valuable *Peshitta* manuscripts extant is the Codex Ambrosianus of Milan, which dates from the sixth century and contains the entire OT.

Armenian Version Syrian Christians carried their faith to their Armenian neighbors in eastern Asia Minor. As early as the third century, with the conversion of Tiridates III (reigned 259–314), Armenia became a Christian kingdom—the first such in history. Sometime during the fifth century, an Armenian alphabet was created so that the Bible could be translated into the language of these new believers. The Armenian translation is considered one of the most beautiful and accurate of the ancient versions of the Greek, even though textual evidence indicates it may have been done from the Syriac first and then modified to the Greek. (The Armenian language is allied closely with the Greek in grammar, syntax, and idiom.) An old tradition says that the NT was the work of Mesrop (a bishop in Armenia, 390–439) who is credited with inventing both the Armenian and Georgian alphabets. The book of Revelation was not accepted as part of the canon in Armenian churches until as late as the 12th century.

Old Main Gate of Dura-Europos Only one Greek manuscript of Tatian's *Diatessaron* has been discovered (known as 0312, third century)—at Dura-Europos in Syria.

Georgian Version The same tradition that credits Mesrop with translating the Bible into Armenian also credits an Armenian slave woman with being the missionary through whom Georgian-speaking people became Christian. The earliest manuscripts for the Georgian Scriptures go back only to the eighth century, but behind them is a Georgian translation with Syriac and Armenian traces. Evidently the Gospels first came in the form of the *Diatessaron;* therefore, Georgian fragments are important in the study of that text. There is a whole manuscript copy of the Georgian Bible in two volumes in the Iberian Monastery on Mt Athos.

Along with the Armenians and Georgians, a third Caucasian people, the Albanians, apparently received an alphabet from Mesrop for the purpose of scriptural translation. Their church, however, was wiped out by the Islamic wars and no remains of that version have ever been found.

Ethiopic Version By the middle of the fifth century, a Christian king ruled in Ethiopia (Abyssinia), and until the Islamic conquests close ties were maintained with Egyptian Christianity. The OT was probably translated into Old Ethiopic (called Ge'ez) by the fourth century. That version is of special interest for two reasons. It is the Bible of the Falashas, that remarkable community of African Jews who claim to be descendants of Jews who migrated to Ethiopia in the time of King Solomon and the Queen of Sheba. Further, the Old Ethiopic version of the OT contains several books not in the Hebrew Apocrypha. Most interesting of these is the book of Enoch, which is quoted in Jude 1:14 and was unknown to Bible scholars until James Bruce brought a copy to Europe in 1773. The apocryphal 3 Baruch is known only from the Ethiopic also.

The NT was translated into Old Ethiopic somewhat later than the OT and contains a collection of writings mentioned by Clement of Alexandria, including the Apocalypse of Peter. Both Testaments are extant in Ethiopic manuscripts. None, however, is earlier than the 13th century, and these manuscripts seem to rest rather heavily on the Coptic and the Arabic. Nothing survived the total chaos that reigned in Ethiopia from the 7th to the 13th centuries. Because they are so late, the Ethiopic manuscripts have had little value for textual study.

Arabic Versions Around AD 570 Muhammad was born in Mecca. At the age of 25 he married a wealthy widow, Khadijah. His "call" came at the age of 40. In 622 the "Hegira" to Medina took place. In 632 he died, the undisputed master prophet of Arabia. Within a hundred years, Islamic domains stretched from the Pyrenees through Spain, jumped the Gibraltar Strait, embraced all of North Africa, and captured Egypt and the Bible lands. Thus began a relentless pressure on Byzantium that culminated in the fall of Constantinople in 1453. Eventually, the Islamic conquest extended to lands as far east as India. Arabic became the most universal language the world had seen since Alexander had spread Greek over nine centuries earlier.

There were a number of strong Jewish communities in Arabia in the time of Muhammad, and the vast conquests engulfed hundreds of Christian communities, a few of which stubbornly survived. Yet the Bible in Arabic evidently did not come into existence until the work of Saadya Gaon. Saadya was born in the Fayum in Upper Egypt in 892 and died in Babylon in 942. He translated the Pentateuch from the Hebrew. Other parts of the OT followed—Joshua from the Hebrew; Judges, Samuel, Kings, Chronicles, Job from the *Peshitta*; and the Prophets, Psalms, and Proverbs from the Septuagint—not necessarily the work of Saadya. The resulting version has been used by Arabic-speaking Jews down to this century. The Qara'ites, disapproving of Saadya's rather free work, made rival translations, the most notable that of Japheth ben-Eli-ha-Levi in the tenth century. NT translations into Arabic sprang up from Syriac, Greek, and Coptic sources in the seventh to the ninth centuries. Arab writers say that John I, a Jacobite patriarch of Antioch (631–48), translated the Gospels from Syriac into Arabic. Another John, Bishop of Seville in Spain, is said to have produced Arabic Gospels from the Vulgate around 724. The final form of the Arabic NT rested most heavily on the Coptic Bohairic. Because of their late date and mixed background, Arabic texts have had little importance in textual studies.

Slavonic Version Though the Slavs were one of the great ethnic groups contiguous to the centers of early Christianity, Bible translations into Slavonic cannot be traced earlier than the ninth century. Two brothers, Constantine and Methodius, sons of a Greek nobleman, began by putting church liturgy into Slavonic. With the approval of popes Adrian II and John VIII (as noted above), they translated the Bible. Constantine (who later changed his name to Cyril, 827–69) and Methodius (826–85) worked among the Slavs and Moravians. Constantine (Cyril) invented the alphabet that bears his saint name—Cyrillic—to facilitate the translation. Manuscript portions from the 10th or 11th centuries survive, but the oldest manuscript of the whole Bible is the Codex Gennadius in Moscow, which is dated 1499 and is too late to be of much value for textual study.

BIBLE*, Versions of the (English) Translations of the Bible in the English language.

PREVIEW

Versions Discussed Below:
- Early Translations: Caedmon's, Bede's, Alfred the Great's
- Other Early Versions: Lindisfarne Gospels, Shoreham's Psalms, Rolle's Psalms
- Wycliffe's Version
- Tyndale's Translation
- Coverdale's Version
- Thomas Matthew's Version: The Great Bible
- The Geneva Bible and the Bishops' Bible
- The King James Version
- The English Revised Version and the American Standard Version
- The Twentieth Century New Testament
- *The New Testament in Modern Speech*
- *The New Testament: A New Translation*
- *The Complete Bible: An American Translation*
- The Revised Standard Version
- The *New English Bible*
- The *Good News Bible:* Today's English Version
- *The Living Bible*
- The *New American Standard Bible*
- The New International Version
- *The Jerusalem Bible* and *The New American Bible*
- *The Holy Scriptures according to the Masoretic Text, A New Translation*
- The New King James Version
- The Revised English Bible
- New Revised Standard Version
- New Living Translation

Early Translations: Caedmon's, Bede's, Alfred the Great's As the gospel spread and churches multiplied in the early centuries of the Christian era, Christians in various countries wanted to read the Bible in their own language. As a result, many translations were made in several different languages—as early as the second century. For example, there were translations done in Coptic for the Egyptians, in Syriac for those whose language was Aramaic, in Gothic for the Germanic people called the Goths, and in Latin for the Romans and Carthaginians. The most famous Latin translation was done by Jerome around 400. This translation, known as the Latin Vulgate (*vulgate* meaning "common"—hence, the Latin text for the common man), was used extensively in the Roman Catholic Church for centuries and centuries.

The gospel was brought to England by missionaries from Rome in the sixth century. The Bible they carried with them was the Latin Vulgate. The Christians living in England at that time depended on monks for any kind of instruction from the Bible. The monks read and taught the Latin Bible. After a few centuries, when more monasteries were founded, the need arose for translations of the Bible in English. The earliest English translation, as far as we know, is one done by a seventh-century monk named Caedmon, who made a metrical version of parts of the Old and New Testaments. Another English churchman, named Bede, is said to have translated the Gospels into English. Tradition has it that he was translating the Gospel of John on his deathbed in 735. Another translator was Alfred the Great (reigned 871–99), who was regarded as a very literate king. He included in his laws parts of the Ten Commandments translated into English, and he also translated the Psalms.

Other Early Versions: Lindisfarne Gospels, Shoreham's Psalms, Rolle's Psalms All translations of the English Bible prior to the work of Tyndale (discussed later) were done from the Latin text. Some Latin versions of the Gospels with word-for-word English translations written between the lines, which are called interlinear translations, survive from the 10th century. The most famous translation of this period is called the Lindisfarne Gospels (950). In the late 10th century, Aelfric (c. 955–1020), abbot of Eynsham, made idiomatic translations of various parts of the Bible. Two of these translations still exist. Later, in the 1300s, William of Shoreham translated the Psalms into English and so did Richard Rolle, whose editions of the Psalms included a verse-by-verse commentary. Both of these translations, which were metrical and therefore called Psalters, were popular when John Wycliffe was a young man.

them could have a personal relationship with God through Christ Jesus—apart from any ecclesiastical authority. Wycliffe, with his associates, completed the NT around 1380 and the OT in 1382. Wycliffe concentrated his labors on the NT, while an associate, Nicholas of Hereford, did a major part of the OT. Wycliffe and his coworkers, unfamiliar with the original Hebrew and Greek, translated the Latin text into English.

After Wycliffe finished the translation work, he organized a group of poor parishioners, known as Lollards, to go throughout England preaching Christian truths and reading the Scriptures in their mother tongue to all who would hear God's Word. As a result the Word of God, through Wycliffe's translation, became available to many Englishmen. He was loved and yet hated. His ecclesiastical enemies did not forget his opposition to their power or his successful efforts in making the Scriptures available to all. Several decades after he died, they condemned him for heresy, dug up his body, burned it, and threw his ashes into the Swift River.

One of Wycliffe's close associates, John Purvey (c. 1353–1428), continued Wycliffe's work by producing a revision of his translation in 1388. Purvey was an excellent scholar; his work was very well received by his generation and following generations. Within less than a century, Purvey's revision had replaced the original Wycliffe Bible.

As was stated before, Wycliffe and his associates were the first Englishmen to translate the entire Bible into English from Latin. Therefore, their Bible was a translation of a translation, not a translation of the original languages. With the coming of the Renaissance came the resurgence of the study of the classics—and with it the resurgence of the study of Greek as well as Hebrew. Thus, for the first time in nearly 1,000 years (500–1500—the approximate time when Latin was the dominant language for scholarship, except in the Greek church) scholars began to read the NT in its original language, Greek. By 1500, Greek was being taught at Oxford.

Tyndale's Translation William Tyndale was born in the age of the Renaissance. He graduated in 1515 from Oxford, where he had studied the Scriptures in Greek and in Hebrew. By the time he was 30, Tyndale

---

The Gospell.

that the sepulcre be made sure vntyll the thryd daye: lest paraventure his disciples come, and steale hym awaye and saye vnto the people: he ys rysen from deeth. And then the laste erroure shalbe worsse then the fyrst was. Pilate sayde vnto them: Take watchemen: Go and make ytt as sure as ye can. They went and made the sepulcre sure with watchemen and sealed the stone.

The xxviij. Chapter.

The sabboth daye att eve which dauneth the morowe after the sabboth. Mary magdalene and the other Mary cam to se the sepulcre. And beholde there was a greate erthquake. For the angell of the lorde descended from heven: and cam and rowlled backe the stone ffrom the dore and sate apon it. His countenaunce was lyke lyghtnynge and his raymēt whyte as snowe. For feare of hym the kepers were astonyed: and were as deed men.

The angell answered and sayde to the wemen: Feare ye not. I knowe welle ye seke Iesus which was crucified: he is not here: he is rysen as he sayd. Come and se the place where the lorde was put. And goo quickly and tell his disciples that he is rysen from deeth. And beholde he wyll goo before you into Galile there ye shall se hym. Lo I have tolde you.

And they departed quickly from the sepulcre with feare and greate ioye. And did runne to bringe his disciples worde. And as they went to tell his disciples beholde Iesus mett them sayinge: God spede you. They cam and hyld hym by

Of. S. Mathew. Fo. xliij.

the fete and worshipped hym. Then sayde Iesus vnto them: be not afrayde: Go and tell my bretren that they goo in to galile and there shall they se me. When they were gone, beholde some of the kepers cam in to the citie and shewed vnto the prelates all thinges whych had hapened. And they gaddered them to gedder with the seniours and toke counsell and gave large money vnto the souders sayinge: Saye that his disciples cam be nyght and stole hym awaye whyll ye slept. And yf this come to the rulers eares we wyll pease hym and make you safe. And they toke the money and dyd as they were taught. And this sayinge is noysed amonge the iewes vnto this daye.

Then the xi. disciples went there ware into galile into a mountayne where Iesus had apoynted them. And when they sawe hym they worshipped hym. But some of them douted. Iesus cam and spake vnto them sayinge: All power ys geven vnto me in heven and in erth. Go therfore and teache all nacions baptisynge them in the name of the father and the sonne and the holy goost: Teachinge them to observe all thinges whatsoever I comaunded you. And lo I am with you all wayes even vntyll the ende off the worlde.

Here endeth the Gospell of S. Mathew.

¶ iiij

Tyndale's Version This photo shows the ending of Matthew's Gospel.

Wycliffe's Version John Wycliffe (c. 1329–84), the most eminent Oxford theologian of his day, and his associates were the first to translate the entire Bible from Latin into English. Wycliffe has been called the "Morning Star of the Reformation" because he boldly questioned papal authority, criticized the sale of indulgences (which were supposed to release a person from punishment in purgatory), denied the reality of transubstantiation (the doctrine that the bread and wine are changed into Jesus Christ's body and blood during Communion), and spoke out against church hierarchies. The pope reproved Wycliffe for his "heretical" teachings and asked that Oxford University dismiss him. But Oxford and many government leaders stood with Wycliffe, so he was able to survive the pope's assaults.

Wycliffe believed that the way to prevail in his struggle with the church's abusive authority was to make the Bible available to the people in their own language. Then they could read for themselves about how each one of

had committed his life to translating the Bible from original languages into English. His heart's desire is exemplified in a statement he made to a clergyman when refuting the view that only the clergy were qualified to read and correctly interpret the Scriptures. Tyndale said, "If God spare my life, ere many years, I will cause a boy that driveth the plough to know more of the Scripture than thou dost."

In 1523 Tyndale went to London seeking a place to work on his translation. When the bishop of London would not give him hospitality, he was provided a place by Humphrey Monmouth, a cloth merchant. Then, in 1524, Tyndale left England for Germany because the English church, which was still under the papal authority of Rome, strongly opposed putting the Bible into the hands of the laity. Tyndale first settled in Hamburg, Germany. Quite possibly, he met Luther in Wittenberg soon thereafter. Even if he didn't meet Luther, he was well acquainted with Luther's writings and Luther's German translation of the NT (published in 1522). Throughout his lifetime, Tyndale was harassed for propagating Luther's ideas. Both Luther and Tyndale used the same Greek text (one compiled by Erasmus in 1516) in making their translations.

Tyndale completed his translation of the NT in 1525. Fifteen thousand copies, in six editions, were smuggled into England between the years 1525 and 1530. Church authorities did their best to confiscate copies of Tyndale's translation and burn them, but they couldn't stop the flow of Bibles from Germany into England. Tyndale himself could not return to England because his life was in danger since his translation had been banned. However, he continued to work abroad—correcting, revising, and reissuing his translation until his final revision appeared in 1535. Shortly thereafter, in May of 1535, Tyndale was arrested and carried off to a castle near Brussels. After being in prison for over a year, he was tried and condemned to death. He was strangled and burned at the stake on October 6, 1536. His final words were so very poignant: "Lord, open the king of England's eyes."

After finishing the NT, Tyndale had begun work on a translation of the Hebrew OT, but he did not live long enough to complete his task. He had, however, translated the Pentateuch (the first five books of the OT), Jonah, and some historical books. While Tyndale was in prison, an associate of his named Miles Coverdale (1488–1569) brought to completion an entire Bible in English—based largely on Tyndale's translation of the NT and other OT books. In other words, Coverdale finished what Tyndale had begun.

Coverdale's Version Miles Coverdale was a Cambridge graduate who, like Tyndale, was forced to flee England because he had been strongly influenced by Luther to the extent that he was boldly preaching against Roman Catholic doctrine. While he was abroad, Coverdale met Tyndale and then served as an assistant— especially helping Tyndale translate the Pentateuch. By the time Coverdale produced a complete translation (1537), the king of England, Henry VIII, had broken all ties with the pope and was ready to see the appearance of an English Bible. Perhaps Tyndale's prayer had been answered—with a very ironic twist. The king gave his royal approval to Coverdale's translation, which was based on the work done by Tyndale, the man Henry VIII had earlier condemned.

Thomas Matthew's Version: The Great Bible In the same year that Coverdale's Bible was endorsed by the king (1537), another Bible was published in England. This was the work of one called Thomas Matthew, a pseudonym for John Rogers (c. 1500–55), a friend of Tyndale. Evidently, Rogers used Tyndale's unpublished translation of the OT historical books, other parts of Tyndale's translation, and still other parts of Coverdale's translation, to form an entire Bible. This Bible also received the king's approval. Matthew's Bible was revised in 1538 and printed for distribution in the churches throughout England. This Bible, called the Great Bible because of its size and costliness, became the first English Bible authorized for public use.

Many editions of the Great Bible were printed in the early 1540s. However, its distribution was limited. Furthermore, King Henry's attitude about the new translation changed. As a result, the English Parliament passed a law in 1543 restricting the use of any English translation. It was a crime for any unlicensed person to read or explain the Scriptures in public. Many copies of Tyndale's NT and Coverdale's Bible were burned in London.

Greater repression was to follow. After a short period of leniency (during the reign of Edward VI, 1547–53), severe persecution came from the hands of Queen Mary. She was a Roman Catholic who was determined to restore Catholicism to England and repress Protestantism. Many Protestants were executed, including John Rogers, the Bible translator. Coverdale was arrested, then released. He fled to Geneva, a sanctuary for English Protestants.

The Geneva Bible and the Bishops' Bible The English exiles in Geneva chose William Whittingham (c. 1524–79) to make an English translation of the NT for them. He used Theodore Beza's Latin translation and consulted the Greek text. This Bible became very popular because it was small and moderately priced. The preface to the Bible and its many annotations were affected by a strong evangelical influence, as well as by the teachings of John Calvin. Calvin was one of the greatest thinkers of the Reformation, a renowned biblical commentator, and the principal leader in Geneva during those days.

While the Geneva Bible was popular among many English men and women, it was not acceptable among many leaders in the Church of England because of its Calvinistic notes. These leaders, recognizing that the Great Bible was inferior to the Geneva Bible in style and scholarship, initiated a revision of the Great Bible. This revised Bible, published in 1568, became known as the Bishops' Bible; it continued in use until it was superseded by the King James Version of 1611.

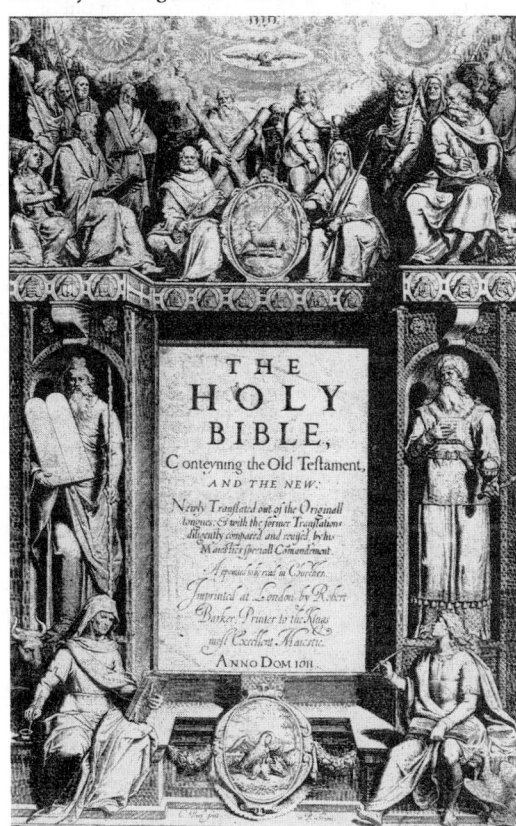

Frontispiece of the Authorized King James Version, 1611

The King James Version After James VI of Scotland became the king of England (known as James I), he invited several clergymen from Puritan and Anglican factions to meet together with the hope that differences could be reconciled. The meeting did not achieve this. However, during the meeting one of the Puritan leaders, John Reynolds, president of Corpus Christi College, Oxford, asked the king to authorize a new translation because he wanted to see a translation that was more accurate than previous translations. King James liked this idea because the Bishops' Bible had not been successful and because he considered the notes in the Geneva Bible to be seditious. The king initiated the work and took an active part in planning the new translation. He suggested that university professors work on the translation to assure the best scholarship, and he strongly urged that they should not have any marginal notes besides those pertaining to literal renderings from the Hebrew and Greek. The absence of interpretive notes would help the translation be accepted by all the churches in England.

More than 50 scholars, trained in Hebrew and Greek, began the work in 1607. The translation went through several committees before it was finalized. The scholars were instructed to follow the Bishops' Bible as the basic version, as long as it adhered to the original text, and to consult the translations of Tyndale, Matthew, and Coverdale, as well as the Great Bible and the Geneva Bible when they appeared to contain more accurate renderings of the original languages. This dependence on other versions is expressed in the preface to the King James Version: "Truly, good Christian reader, we never thought from the beginning that we should need to make a new translation, nor yet to make of a bad one a good one . . . but to make a good one better, or out of many good ones one principal good one."

The King James Version, known in England as the Authorized Version because it was authorized by the king, captured the best of all the preceding English translations and far exceeded all of them. It was the culmination of all the previous English Bible translations; it united high scholarship with Christian devotion and piety. It came into being at a time when the English language was vigorous and beautiful—the age of Elizabethan English and Shakesperean English. This version has justifiably been called "the noblest monument of English prose." Indeed, the King James Version has become an enduring monument of English prose because of its gracious style, majestic language, and poetic rhythms. No other book has had such a tremendous influence on English literature, and no other translation has touched the lives of so many English-speaking people for centuries and centuries, even until the present day.

The 18th and 19th Centuries: New Discoveries of Earlier Manuscripts and Increased Knowledge of the Original Languages The King James Version became the most popular English translation in the 17th and 18th centuries. It acquired the stature of becoming the standard English Bible. But the King James Version had deficiencies that did not go unnoticed by certain scholars. First, knowledge of Hebrew was inadequate in the early 17th century. The Hebrew text they used (i.e., the Masoretic Text) was adequate, but their understanding of the Hebrew vocabulary was insufficient. It would take many more years of linguistic studies to enrich and sharpen understanding of the Hebrew vocabulary. Second, the Greek text underlying the NT of the King James Version was an inferior text. The King James translators basically used a Greek text known as the Textus Receptus (or, the "Received Text"), which came from the work of Erasmus, who compiled the first Greek text to be produced on a printing press. When Erasmus compiled this text, he used five or six very late manuscripts dating from the 10th to the 13th centuries. These manuscripts were far inferior to earlier manuscripts.

The King James translators had done well with the resources that were available to them, but those resources were insufficient, especially with respect to the NT text.

After the King James Version was published, earlier and better manuscripts were discovered. Around 1630, Codex Alexandrinus was brought to England. A fifth-century manuscript containing the entire NT, it provided a fairly good witness to the NT text, especially the original text of Revelation. Two hundred years later, a German scholar named Constantin von Tischendorf discovered Codex Sinaiticus in St Catherine's Monastery. The manuscript, dated around AD 350, is one of the two oldest manuscripts of the Greek NT. The earliest manuscript, Codex Vaticanus, had been in the Vatican's library since at least 1475, but it was not made available to scholars until the middle of the 19th century. This manuscript, dated slightly earlier (AD 325) than Codex Sinaiticus, is one of the most reliable copies of the Greek NT.

As these manuscripts (and others) were discovered and made public, certain scholars labored to compile a Greek text that would more closely represent the original text than did the Textus Receptus. Around 1700 John Mill produced an improved Textus Receptus, and in the 1730s Johannes Albert Bengel, known as the father of modern textual and philological studies in the NT, published a text that deviated from the Textus Receptus according to the evidence of earlier manuscripts.

In the 1800s certain scholars began to abandon the Textus Receptus. Karl Lachman, a classical philologist, produced a fresh text in 1831 that represented the fourth-century manuscripts. Samuel Tregelles, self-taught in Latin, Hebrew, and Greek, laboring throughout his entire lifetime, concentrated all of his efforts in publishing one Greek text, which came out in six parts, from 1857 to 1872. Tischendorf devoted a lifetime of labor to discovering manuscripts and producing accurate editions of the Greek NT. He not only discovered Codex Sinaiticus, he also deciphered the palimpsest Codex Ephraemi Rescriptus, collated countless manuscripts, and produced several editions of the Greek NT (the eighth edition is considered the best). Aided by the work of these scholars, two British men, Brooke Westcott and Fenton Hort, worked together for 28 years to produce a volume entitled *The New Testament in the Original Greek* (1881). This edition of the Greek NT, based largely on Codex Vaticanus, became the standard text that was responsible for dethroning the Textus Receptus.

The English Revised Version and the American Standard Version By the latter part of the 19th century, the Christian community had been given three very good Greek NT texts: Tregelles's, Tischendorf's, and Westcott and Hort's. These texts were very different from the Textus Receptus. And as was mentioned earlier, the scholarly community had accumulated more knowledge about the meaning of various Hebrew words and Greek words. Therefore, there was a great need for a new English translation based upon a better text—and with more accurate renderings of the original languages.

A few individuals attempted to meet this need. In 1871 John Nelson Darby, leader of the Plymouth Brethren movement, produced a translation called the *New Translation*, which was largely based on Codex Vaticanus and Codex Sinaiticus. In 1872 J. B. Rotherham published a translation of Tregelles's text, in which he attempted to reflect the emphasis inherent in the Greek text. This translation is still being published under the title *The Emphasized Bible*. And in 1875 Samuel Davidson produced a NT translation of Tischendorf's text.

The first major corporate effort was initiated in 1870 by the Convocation of Canterbury, which decided to sponsor a major revision of the King James Version. Sixty-five British scholars, working in various committees, made significant changes in the King James Version. The OT scholars corrected mistranslations of Hebrew words and reformatted poetic passages into poetic form. The NT scholars made thousands of changes based upon better textual evidence. Their goal was to make the NT revision reflect not the Textus Receptus but the texts of Tregelles, Tischendorf, and Westcott and Hort. When the complete Revised Version appeared in 1885, it was received with great enthusiasm. Over three million copies sold in the first year of its publication. Unfortunately, its popularity was not long lasting because most people continued to prefer the King James Version over all other translations.

Several American scholars had been invited to join the revision work, with the understanding that any of their suggestions not accepted by the British scholars would appear in an appendix. Furthermore, the American scholars had to agree not to publish their own American revision until after 14 years. When the time came (1901), the American Standard Version was published by several surviving members of the original American committee. This translation, generally regarded as superior to the English Revised Version, is an accurate, literal rendering of very trustworthy texts both in the OT and the New.

The 20th Century: New Discoveries and New Translations
The 19th century was a fruitful era for the Greek NT and subsequent English translations; it was also a century in which Hebrew studies were greatly advanced. The 20th century has also been fruitful—especially for textual studies. Those living in the 20th century have witnessed the discovery of the Dead Sea Scrolls, the Oxyrhynchus Papyri, the Chester Beatty Papyri, and the Bodmer Papyri. These amazing discoveries, providing scholars with hundreds of ancient manuscripts, have greatly enhanced the effort to recover the original wording of the Old and New Testaments. At the same time, other archaeological discoveries have validated the historical accuracy of the Bible and helped Bible scholars understand the meaning of certain ancient words. For example, the Greek word *parousia* (usually translated "coming") was found in many ancient documents dated around the time of Christ; very often the word indicated the visitation of royalty. When this word was used in the NT concerning Christ's second coming, the readers would think of his coming as being the visitation of a king. Another example is that in koine Greek, the expression *entos humon* (literally, "inside of you") often meant "within reach." Thus, Jesus' statement in Luke 17:21 could mean "The kingdom is within reach."

As earlier and better manuscripts of the Bible have emerged, scholars have been engaged in updating the Bible texts. OT scholars have still used the Masoretic Text but have noted significant differences found in the Dead Sea Scrolls. The current edition used by OT scholars is called *Biblia Hebraica Stuttgartensia*. NT scholars, for the most part, have come to rely upon an edition of the Greek NT known as the Nestle-Aland text. Eberhard Nestle used the best editions of the Greek NT produced in the 19th century to compile a text that represented the majority consensus. The work of making new editions was carried on by his son for several years and then came under the care of Kurt Aland. The latest edition (the 27th) of Nestle-Aland's *Novum Testamentum Graece* appeared in 1993. The same Greek text appears in another popular volume published by the United Bible Societies, called the *Greek New Testament* (fourth edition—1983).

Early 20th-Century Translations in the Language of the People
The thousands and thousands of papyri that were discovered in Egypt around the turn of the

century displayed a form of Greek called koine Greek. Koine (meaning "common") Greek was everyman's Greek; it was the common language of almost everybody living in the Graeco-Roman world from the second century BC to the third century AD. In other words, it was the *lingua franca* of the Mediterranean world. Every educated person back then could speak, read, and write in Greek just like every educated person in modern times can speak a little English, read some English, and perhaps write in English. Koine Greek was not literary Greek (i.e., the kind of Greek written by the Greek poets and tragedians); it was the kind of Greek used in personal letters, legal documents, and other nonliterary texts.

NT scholars began to discover that most of the NT was written in koine Greek—the language of the people. As a result, there was a strong prompting to translate the NT into the language of the people. Various translators chose to divorce themselves from the traditional Elizabethan English as found in the King James Version (and even in the English Revised Version and American Standard Version) and produce fresh renderings in the common idiom.

The Twentieth Century New Testament The first of these new translations was *The Twentieth Century New Testament* (1902). The preface to a new edition of this translation provides an excellent description of the work:

> *The Twentieth Century New Testament* is a smooth-flowing, accurate, easy-to-read translation that captivates its readers from start to finish. Born out of a desire to make the Bible readable and understandable, it is the product of the labors of a committee of twenty men and women who worked together over many years to construct, we believe under divine surveillance, this beautifully simple rendition of the word of God. (Preface to the new edition—1961—published by Moody Press)

The New Testament in Modern Speech A year after the publication of *The Twentieth Century New Testament*, Richard Weymouth published *The New Testament in Modern Speech* (1903). Weymouth, who had received the first doctor of literature degree from the University of London, was headmaster of a private school in London. During his life, he spent time producing an edition of the Greek text (published in 1862) that was more accurate than the Textus Receptus, and then he labored to produce an English translation of this Greek text (called *The Resultant Greek Testament*) in a modern speech version. His translation was very well received; it has gone through several editions and many printings.

The New Testament: A New Translation Another new and fresh translation to appear in the early years of this century was one written by James Moffatt, a brilliant Scottish scholar. In 1913 he published his first edition of *The New Testament: A New Translation*. This was actually his second translation of the NT; his first was done in 1901, called *The Historical New Testament*. In his *New Translation* Moffatt's goal was "to translate the NT exactly as one would render any piece of contemporary Hellenistic prose." His work displays brilliance and marked independence from other versions; unfortunately it was based on Hermann von Soden's Greek NT, which, as all scholars now know, is quite defective.

The Complete Bible: An American Translation The earliest American modern speech translation was produced by Edgar J. Goodspeed, a professor of NT at the University of Chicago. He had criticized *The Twentieth*

Century New Testament, Weymouth's version, and Moffatt's translation. As a consequence, he was challenged by some other scholars to do better. He took up the challenge and in 1923 published *The New Testament: An American Translation*. When he made this translation, he said that he wanted to give his "version something of the force and freshness that reside in the original Greek." He said, "I wanted my translation to make on the reader something of the impression the NT must have made on its earliest readers, and to invite the continuous reading of the whole book at a time." His translation was a success. An OT translation followed, produced by J. M. Powis Smith and three other scholars. *The Complete Bible: An American Translation* was published in 1935.

The Revised Standard Version The English Revised Version and the American Standard Version had gained a reputation of being accurate study texts but very "wooden" in their construction. The translators who worked on the Revised Versions attempted to translate words consistently from the original language regardless of their context and sometimes even followed the word order of the Greek. This created a very unidiomatic version and called for a new revision.

The demand for revision was strengthened by the fact that several important biblical manuscripts had been discovered in the 1930s and 1940s—namely, the Dead Sea Scrolls for the OT and the Chester Beatty Papyri for the NT. It was felt that the fresh evidence displayed in these documents should be reflected in a revision. The revision showed some textual changes in the book of Isaiah due to the Isaiah Scroll and several changes in the Pauline Epistles based on the Chester Beatty Papyrus, P46. There were other significant revisions. The story of the woman caught in adultery (John 7:52–8:11) was not included in the text but in the margin because none of the early manuscripts contain this story, and the ending to Mark (16:9-20) was not included in the text because it is not found in the two earliest manuscripts, Codex Vaticanus and Codex Sinaiticus.

The organization that held the copyright to the American Standard Version, called the International Council of Religious Education, authorized a new revision in 1937. The NT translators generally followed the 17th edition of the Nestle Text (1941), while the OT translators followed the Masoretic Text. Both groups, however, adopted readings from other ancient sources when they were considered to be more accurate. The NT was published in 1946, and the entire Bible with the OT in 1952.

The principles of the revision were specified in the preface to the Revised Standard Version:

> The Revised Standard Version is not a new translation in the language of today. It is not a paraphrase which aims at striking idioms. It is a revision which seeks to preserve all that is best in the English Bible as it has been known and used throughout the years.

This revision was well received by many Protestant churches and soon became their "standard" text. The Revised Standard Version was later published with the Apocrypha of the OT (1957), in a Catholic Edition (1965), and in what is called the *Common Bible*, which includes the OT, the NT, the Apocrypha, and the deuterocanonical books, with international endorsements by Protestants, Greek Orthodox, and Roman Catholics. Evangelical and fundamental Christians, however, did not receive the Revised Standard Version very well—primarily because of one verse, Isaiah 7:14, which reads, "Therefore the Lord himself will give you a sign. Look, the young woman is with child and shall bear a son, and shall name him Immanuel." Evangelicals and fundamentalists contend that the text should read "virgin," not "young woman." As a result, the Revised Standard Version was panned, if not banned, by many evangelical and fundamental Christians.

The *New English Bible* In the year that the NT of the Revised Standard Version was published (1946), the Church of Scotland proposed to other churches in Great Britain that it was time for a completely new translation of the Bible to be done. Those who initiated this work asked the translators to produce a fresh translation in modern idiom of the original languages; this was not to be a revision of any foregoing translation, nor was it to be a literal translation. The translators, under the direction of C. H. Dodd, were called upon to translate the meaning of the text into modern English. The preface to the NT (published in 1961), written by C. H. Dodd, explains this more fully:

> The older translators, on the whole, considered that fidelity to the original demanded that they should reproduce, as far as possible, characteristic features of the language in which it was written, such as the syntactical order of words, the structure and division of sentences, and even such irregularities of grammar as were indeed natural enough to authors writing in the easy idiom of popular Hellenistic Greek, but less natural when turned into English. The present translators were enjoined to replace Greek constructions and idioms by those of contemporary English.
>
> This meant a different theory and practice of translation, and one which laid a heavier burden on the translators. Fidelity in translation was not to mean keeping the general framework of the original intact while replacing Greek words by English words more or less equivalent. . . . Thus we have not felt obliged (as did the Revisers of 1881) to make an effort to render the same Greek word everywhere by the same English word. We have in this respect returned to the wholesome practice of King James's men, who (as they expressly state in their preface) recognized no such obligation. We have conceived our task to be that of understanding the original as precisely as we could (using all available aids), and then saying again in our own native idiom what we believed the author to be saying in his.

The entire *New English Bible* was published in 1970; it was well received in Great Britain and in the United States (even though its idiom is extremely British) and was especially praised for its good literary style. The translators were very experimental, producing renderings never before printed in an English version and adopting certain readings from various Hebrew and Greek manuscripts never before adopted. As a result, *The New English Bible* was both highly praised for its ingenuity and severely criticized for its liberty.

The *Good News Bible*: Today's English Version The NT in Today's English Version, also known as *Good News for Modern Man*, was published by the American Bible Society in 1966. The translation was originally done by Robert Bratcher, a research associate of the translations department of the American Bible Society, and then further refined by the American Bible Society. The translation, heavily promoted by several Bible societies and very affordable, sold more than 35 million copies within six years of the time of printing. The NT translation, based upon the first edition of the *Greek New Testament* (the United Bible Societies, 1966), is an idiomatic version in modern and simple English. The translation was greatly influenced by the linguistic theory of dynamic equivalence and was quite successful in providing English readers with a translation that, for the most part, accurately reflects the meaning of the original texts. This is explained in the preface to the NT:

> This translation of the NT has been prepared by the American Bible Society for people who speak English as their mother tongue or as an acquired language. As a distinctly new translation, it does not conform to traditional vocabulary or style, but seeks to express the meaning of the Greek text in words and forms accepted as standard by people everywhere who employ English as a means of communication. Today's English Version of the NT attempts to follow, in this century, the example set by the authors of the NT books, who, for the most part, wrote in the standard, or common, form of the Greek language used throughout the Roman Empire.

Because of the success of the NT, the American Bible Society was asked by other Bible societies to make an OT translation following the same principles used in the NT. The entire Bible was published in 1976, and is known as the *Good News Bible: Today's English Version.*

The Living Bible In 1962 Kenneth Taylor published a paraphrase of the NT epistles in a volume called *Living Letters.* This new dynamic paraphrase, written in common vernacular, became well received and widely acclaimed—especially for its ability to communicate the message of God's Word to the common man. In the beginning its circulation was greatly enhanced by the endorsement of the Billy Graham Evangelistic Association, which did much to publicize the book and distributed thousands of free copies. Taylor continued to paraphrase other portions of the Bible and publish successive volumes: *Living Prophecies* (1965), *Living Gospels* (1966), *Living Psalms* (1967), *Living Lessons of Life and Love* (1968), *Living Books of Moses* (1969), and *Living History of Moses* (1970). The entire Living Bible was published in 1971 (the *Living New Testament* was printed in 1966).

Using the American Standard Version as his working text, Taylor rephrased the Bible into modern speech—such that anyone, even a child, could understand the message of the original writers. In the preface to *The Living Bible,* Taylor explains his view of paraphrasing:

> To paraphrase is to say something in different words than the author used. It is a restatement of the author's thoughts, using different words than he did. This book is a paraphrase of the Old and New Testaments. Its purpose is to say as exactly as possible what the writers of the Scriptures meant, and to say it simply, expanding where necessary for a clear understanding by the modern reader.

Even though many modern readers have greatly appreciated the fact that *The Living Bible* made God's Word clear to them, Taylor's paraphrase has been criticized for being too interpretive. But that is the nature of paraphrases—and the danger as well. Taylor was aware of this when he made the paraphrase. Again, the preface clarifies:

> There are dangers in paraphrases, as well as values. For whenever the author's exact words are not translated from the original languages, there is a possibility that the translator, however honest, may be giving the English reader something that the original writer did not mean to say.

The Living Bible has been very popular among English readers worldwide. More than 40 million copies have been sold by the publishing house Taylor specifically created to publish *The Living Bible.* The company is called Tyndale House Publishers—named after William Tyndale, the father of modern English translations of the Bible.

The *New American Standard Bible* There are two modern translations that are both revisions of (or based on) the American Standard Version (1901): the Revised Standard Version (1952) and the *New American Standard Bible* (1971). The Lockman Foundation, a nonprofit Christian corporation committed to evangelism, promoted this revision of the American Standard Version because "the producers of this translation were imbued with the conviction that interest in the American Standard Version 1901 should be renewed and increased" (from the preface). Indeed, the American Standard Version was a monumental work of scholarship and a very accurate translation. However, its popularity was waning, and it was fast disappearing from the scene. Therefore, the Lockman Foundation organized a team of 32 scholars to prepare a new revision. These scholars, all committed to the inspiration of Scripture, strove to produce a literal translation of the Bible in the belief that such a translation "brings the contemporary reader as close as possible to the actual wording and grammatical structure of the original writers" (ibid.).

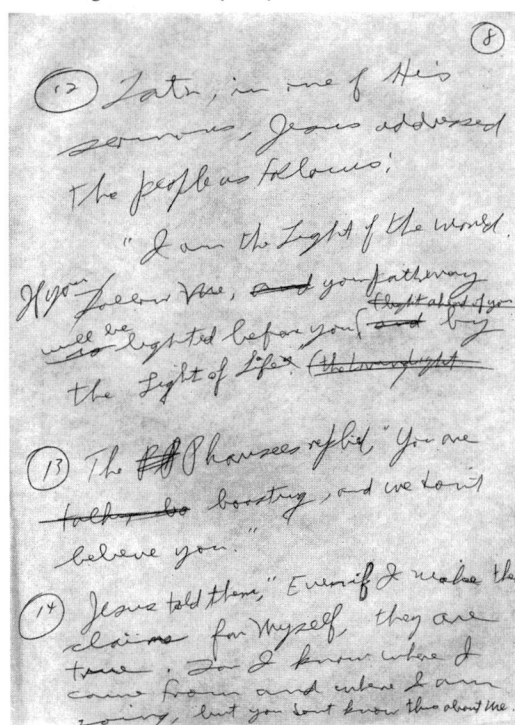

Original Manuscript of *Living Gospels*

The translators of the *New American Standard Bible* were instructed by the Lockman Foundation to adhere to the original languages of the Holy Scriptures as closely as possible and at the same time to obtain a fluent and readable style according to current English usage. After the *New American Standard Bible* was published (1963 for the NT and 1971 for the entire Bible), it received a mixed response. Some critics applauded its literal accuracy, while others sharply criticized its language for hardly being contemporary or modern.

On the whole, the *New American Standard Bible* became respected as a good study Bible that accurately reflects the wording of the original languages yet is not a good translation for Bible reading. Furthermore, it must be said that this translation which was originally supposed to follow the 23d edition of the Nestle text, tends to follow the Textus Receptus, especially in its inclusion of passages considered spurious by most modern scholars.

The New International Version The New International Version is a completely new rendering of the original languages done by an international group of more than 100 scholars. These scholars worked many years and in several committees to produce an excellent thought-for-thought translation in contemporary English for private and public use. The New International Version is called "international" because it was prepared by distinguished scholars from English-speaking countries such as the United States, Canada, Great Britain, Australia, and New Zealand, and because the translators sought to use vocabulary common to the major English-speaking nations of the world.

The translators of the New International Version sought to make a version that was midway between a literal rendering (as in the *New American Standard Bible*) and a free paraphrase (as in *The Living Bible*). Their goal was to convey in English the thought of the original writers. This is succinctly explained in the original preface to the NT:

Certain convictions and aims guided the translators. They are all committed to the full authority and complete trustworthiness of the Scriptures. Therefore, their first concern was the accuracy of the translation and its fidelity to the thought of the New Testament writers. While they weighed the significance of the lexical and grammatical details of the Greek text, they have striven for more than a word-for-word translation. Because thought patterns and syntax differ from language to language, faithful communication of the meaning of the writers of the New Testament demanded frequent modifications in sentence structure and constant regard for the contextual meanings of words.

Concern for clarity of style—that it should be idiomatic without being idiosyncratic, contemporary without being dated—also motivated the translators and their consultants. They have consistently aimed at simplicity of expression, with sensitive attention to the connotation and sound of the chosen word. At the same time, they endeavored to avoid a sameness of style in order to reflect the varied styles and moods of the NT writers.

The NT of the New International Version was published in 1973, and the entire Bible in 1978. This version has been phenomenally successful. Millions and millions of readers have adopted the New International Version as their "Bible." Since 1987 it has outsold the King James Version, the best-seller for centuries—a remarkable indication of its popularity and acceptance in the Christian community. The New International Version, sponsored by the New York Bible Society (now the International Bible Society) and published by Zondervan Publishing House, has become a standard version used for private reading and pulpit reading in many English-speaking countries.

Two Modern Catholic Translations: *The Jerusalem Bible* and *The New American Bible* In 1943 Pope Pius XII issued the famous encyclical encouraging Roman Catholics to read and study the Scriptures. At the same time, the pope recommended that the Scriptures should be translated from the original languages. Previ-

ously, all Catholic translations were based on the Latin Vulgate. This includes Knox's translation, which was begun in 1939 and published in 1944 (the NT) and in 1955 (the whole Bible).

The first complete Catholic Bible to be translated from the original languages is *The Jerusalem Bible*, published in England in 1966. *The Jerusalem Bible* is the English counterpart to a French translation entitled *La Bible de Jerusalem*. The French translation was "the culmination of decades of research and biblical scholarship" (from the preface to *The Jerusalem Bible*), published by the scholars of the Dominican Biblical School of Jerusalem. This Bible, which includes the Apocrypha and deuterocanonical books, contains many study helps—such as introductions to each book of the Bible, extensive notes on various passages, and maps. The study helps are an intricate part of the whole translation because it is the belief of Roman Catholic leadership that laypeople should be given interpretive helps in their reading of the sacred text. The study helps in *The Jerusalem Bible* were translated from the French, whereas the Bible text itself was translated from the original languages with the help of the French translation. The translation of the text produced under the editorship of Alexander Jones is considerably freer than other translations, such as the Revised Standard Version, because the translators sought to capture the meaning of the original writings in a "vigorous, contemporary literary style" (from the preface to *The Jerusalem Bible*).

The first American Catholic Bible to be translated from the original languages is *The New American Bible* (not to be confused with the *New American Standard Bible*). Although this translation was published in 1970, work had begun on this version several decades before. Prior to Pope Pius's encyclical, an American translation of the NT based on the Latin Vulgate was published—known as the Confraternity Version. After the encyclical, the OT was translated from the Hebrew Masoretic Text and the NT redone, based on the 25th edition of the Greek Nestle-Aland text. *The New American Bible* has short introductions to each book of the Bible and textual notes. Kubo and Specht provide a just description of the translation itself:

The translation itself is simple, clear, and straightforward and reads very smoothly. It is good American English, not as pungent and colorful as the N.E.B. [New English Bible]. Its translations are not striking but neither are they clumsy. They seem to be more conservative in the sense that they tend not to stray from the original. That is not to say that this is a literal translation, but it is more faithful. (*So Many Versions?* p 165)

Jewish Translations In the 20th century some very important Jewish translations of the Bible were published. The Jewish Publication Society created a translation of the Hebrew Scriptures called *The Holy Scriptures according to the Masoretic Text, A New Translation* (published in 1917). The preface to this translation explains its purpose:

It aims to combine the spirit of Jewish tradition with the results of biblical scholarship, ancient, medieval and modern. It gives to the Jewish world a translation of the Scriptures done by men imbued with the Jewish consciousness, while the non-Jewish world, it is hoped, will welcome a translation that presents many passages from the Jewish traditional point of view.

In 1955 the Jewish Publication Society appointed a new committee of seven eminent Jewish scholars to make a new Jewish translation of the Hebrew Scriptures. The translation called the New Jewish Version was published in 1962. A second, improved edition was published in 1973. This work is not a revision of *The Holy Scriptures according to the Masoretic Text;* it is a completely new translation in modern English. The translators attempted to produce a version that would carry the same message to modern man as the original did to the world of ancient times.

Revisions of the Late 20th Century In the 1980s several significant revisions appeared: The New King James Version (1982); *The New Jerusalem Bible* (1986); *The New American Bible,* revised NT (1986); and The Revised English Bible (1989), which is a radical revision of *The New English Bible.* Other translations, such as the New International Version and Today's English Version, were also revised in the 1980s but not publicized as such. Two other important revisions in the late 1980s and 1990s are the New Revised Standard Version and the New Living Translation.

One reason for this continual influx of new revisions and translations is the ever-changing consensus regarding the original text of the Bible. Most contemporary translators of the OT use the Masoretic Text of the Hebrew Bible because it is generally considered the most authoritative standard text of the OT. At the same time, they make use of the findings of the Dead Sea Scrolls and a few other important versions, including the Septuagint. The Masoretic Text, with up-to-date textual notes, is published in an edition called *Biblia Hebraica Stuttgartensia* (1967, 1977).

Most translators of the NT use two standard editions of the Greek NT, which are the *Greek New Testament* published by the United Bible Societies (fourth revised edition, 1993) and *Novum Testamentum Graece,* edited by Nestle and Aland (27th edition, 1993). These two volumes, which have the same text but differ in punctuation and textual notes, represent the latest in modern textual scholarship.

Most contemporary translators and revisers also make it their goal to reflect the changes that have occurred in the English language. One of the most obvious recent changes has been in the area of gender-inclusive language. Today's English readers have come to expect that translations will not employ unnecessarily male-dominant language. This creates problems for modern translators of the ancient biblical text, which was originally written in a male-oriented culture. Modern translators must respect both the ancient milieu and the modern audience. Often the original language itself allows a rendering that is gender-inclusive. For example, the Greek word *anthropos,* traditionally rendered "man," really means "human being" or "person." (A different Greek word, *aner,* specifically refers to a male.) Likewise, in Hebrew the word *'adam,* traditionally translated "man," usually means "human being," while *'ish* specifically designates an adult male. There are other occasions where the original language is male-oriented primarily because there is no neutral gender to be used. In these cases, the biblical writers defaulted to the masculine gender. For example, in the Pentateuch most of the laws are stated in language that is replete with masculine pronouns. Since it is clear that the recipients of these laws were both males and females, however, many translators generally use gender-neutral language.

The New King James Version The New King James Version (NKJV), published in 1982, is a revision of the King James Version, which is itself a literal translation. As such, the New King James Version follows the historic precedent of the Authorized Version in maintaining a literal approach to translation. The revisers have called this method of translation "complete equivalence." This means that the revisers sought to provide a complete representation of all the information in the original text with respect to the history of usage and etymology of words in their contexts.

The most distinctive feature of the NKJV is its underlying original text. The revisers of the NKJV NT have chosen to use the Textus Receptus rather than modern critical editions, including the Majority Text and the Nestle-Aland text. By way of concession, they have footnoted any significant textual variation from the Majority Text and modern critical editions. The Majority Text, which is the text supported by the majority of all known NT manuscripts, hardly differs from the Textus Receptus; thus, there are few significant differences noted. There are well over a thousand differences footnoted regarding the Nestle-Aland/United Bible Societies' text. This means that there are at least that many significant differences between the Textus Receptus and these modern critical editions.

Though exhibiting an antiquated text, the language of the NKJV is modern. All the Elizabethan English of the original King James Version has been replaced with contemporary American English. Though much of the sentence structure of the NKJV is still dated and stilted, contemporary readers who favor the spirit of the King James Version but can't understand much of its archaic language will appreciate this revision.

The Revised English Bible The Revised English Bible (1989) is a revision of *The New English Bible* (NEB), which was published in 1971. Because the NEB gained such popularity in British churches and was being regularly used for public reading, several British churches decided there should be a revision of the NEB to keep the language current and the text up-to-date with modern biblical scholarship.

For the OT, the revisers used the Masoretic Text as it appears in *Biblia Hebraica Stuttgartensia* (1967, 1977). They also made use of the Dead Sea Scrolls and a few other important versions, including the Septuagint. The revisers of the NT used Nestle-Aland's *Novum Testamentum Graece* (27th edition, 1993) as their base text. This choice resulted in several textual changes from *The New English Bible* text, which followed a very eclectic text. The Greek text used by the NEB was produced by R. V. G. Tasker *after* the English translation had been published. This Greek text was decided upon by the translation committee on a verse-by-verse basis. The resulting Greek text was very uneven and yet very interesting. The translators of the NEB adopted readings never before put into print by English translators. The scholars working on The Revised English Bible eliminated many of these readings, however, in the interest of providing a more balanced text.

New Revised Standard Version The New Revised Standard Version (NRSV), published in 1989, is an excellent example of the current trend to publish revisions rather than new translations. In the preface to this revision, Bruce Metzger, chair of the original revision committee, wrote:

> The New Revised Standard Version of the Bible is an authorized revision of the Revised Standard Version, published in 1952, which was a revision of the American Standard Version, published in 1901, which, in

turn, embodied earlier revisions of the King James Version, published in 1611.

The need for issuing a revision of the Revised Standard Version of the Bible arises from three circumstances: (a) the acquisition of still older Biblical manuscripts, (b) further investigation of linguistic features of the text, and (c) changes in preferred English usage.

Metzger's three reasons for producing the New Revised Standard Version are essentially the same reasons behind all revisions of Bible translations.

Of all the translations, the NRSV most closely follows the text of NA[26]/UBS[3]. No doubt this is due to Bruce Metzger's involvement in both editorial committees—a leading member of the NA[26]/UBS[3] committee and the chair for the NRSV committee.

Perhaps the most notable feature of the NRSV is its attention to gender-inclusive language. While respecting the historicity of the ancient texts, the NRSV translators attempted to make this new revision more palpable to readers who prefer gender-inclusive language. They did this by avoiding unnecessarily masculine renderings wherever possible. For example, in the NT epistles, the believers are referred to with a word that is traditionally rendered "brothers" (adelphoi), yet it is clear that these epistles were addressed to all the believers—both male and female. Thus, the NRSV translators have used such phrases as "brothers and sisters" or "friends" (always with a footnote saying "Greek, brothers") in order to represent the historical situation while remaining sensitive to modern readers.

Metzger and the other translators were careful, however, not to overemphasize the gender-inclusiveness principle. Some readers had been hoping for a more radical revision regarding gender-inclusiveness. Many of these readers were hoping that the revision would incorporate this principle with language about God, changing phrases such as "God our father" to "God our parent." But the NRSV revisers, under the leadership of Metzger, decided against this approach, considering it an inaccurate reflection of the original text's intended meaning.

New Living Translation With over 40 million copies in print, *The Living Bible* has been a very popular version of the Bible for more than 30 years. But various criticisms spurred the translator of *The Living Bible,* Kenneth Taylor, to produce a revision of his paraphrase. Under the sponsorship of Tyndale House Publishers, Taylor's company, *The Living Bible* underwent a thorough revision. More than 90 evangelical scholars from various theological backgrounds and denominations worked for seven years to produce the New Living Translation (NLT). As a result, the NLT is a version that is exegetically accurate and idiomatically powerful.

The scholars carefully revised the text of *The Living Bible* acccording to the most reliable editions of the Hebrew and Greek texts. For the OT, the revisers used the Masoretic Text as it appears in *Biblia Hebraica Stuttgartensia* (1967, 1977). They also made use of the Dead Sea Scrolls and a few other important versions, including the Septuagint. The revisers of the NT used the text of NA[27]/UBS[4] as their base text.

The translation method behind the NLT has been described as "dynamic equivalence" or "functional equivalence." The goal of this kind of translation is to produce in English the closest natural equivalent of the message of the Hebrew and Greek texts—both in meaning and in style. Such a translation should attempt to have the same impact upon modern readers as the original had upon its audience. To translate the Bible in this manner requires that the text be interpreted accurately and then rendered in understandable, current English. In doing this, the translators attempted to enter into the same thought pattern as the author and present the same idea, connotation, and effect in the receptor language. To guard against personal subjectivism and insure accuracy of message, the NLT was produced by a large group of scholars who were each well studied in his or her particular area. To ensure that the translation would be extremely readable and understandable, a group of stylists adjusted the wording to make it clear and fluent.

A thought-for-thought translation created by a group of capable scholars has the potential to represent the intended meaning of the original text even more accurately than a word-for-word translation. This is illustrated by the various renderings of the Hebrew word *hesed*. This term cannot be adequately translated by any single English word because it can connote love, mercy, grace, kindness, faithfulness, and loyalty. The context—not the lexicon—must determine which English term is selected for translation.

The value of a thought-for-thought translation can be illustrated by comparing 1 Kings 2:10 in the King James Version, the New International Version, and the New Living Translation. "So David slept with his fathers, and was buried in the city of David" (KJV). "Then David rested with his fathers and was buried in the City of David" (NIV). "Then David died and was buried in the City of David" (NLT). Only the New Living Translation clearly translates the intended meaning of the Hebrew idiom "slept with his fathers" into contemporary English (from the introduction to the New Living Translation).

BICHRI*, BICHRITE*, BICRI Sheba's father in Benjamin's tribe. Sheba led a revolt against King David (2 Sm 20:1-22). Bicri's descendants were known as Bicrites (2 Sm 20:14).

BIDKAR Aide of King Jehu of the northern kingdom of Israel. Bidkar fulfilled a prophecy about the fate of Ahab's family by throwing the body of Joram, Ahab's son, into Naboth's field after Jehu had killed Joram (2 Kgs 9:24-26).

BIGAMY* Marriage to a second wife while still legally married to another. *See* Marriage, Marriage Customs.

BIGTHA Eunuch who served King Ahasuerus of Persia. He and six others were in charge of the royal household (Est 1:10). He is perhaps identifiable with Bigthana in Esther 2:21; 6:2.

See also Bigthan, Bigthana.

BIGTHAN*, BIGTHANA Eunuch who served King Ahasuerus of Persia as a palace guard. He and a fellow guard named Teresh planned an assassination attempt on the king's life. When their plot was overheard by Queen Esther's uncle Mordecai, the two conspirators were executed (Est 2:21-23; 6:2, "Bigthana").

See also Bigtha.

BIGVAI
1. Ancestor of a group of people who returned to Jerusalem with Zerubbabel after the Babylonian exile (Ezr 2:2, 14; Neh 7:7, 19). Since his name is Persian, Bigvai may have been born or renamed during the exile.
2. Political leader who signed Ezra's covenant of faithfulness to God with Nehemiah and others after the exile (Neh 10:16); possibly a representative for the family descended from #1 above.

ENGLISH TRANSLATIONS: ANCIENT AND MODERN/JOHN 1:1-5

TYNDALE'S TRANSLATION

In the beginnynge was the worde, and the worde was with God: and the worde was God. The same was in the beginnynge with God. All things were made by it, and with out it, was made nothinge, that was made. In it was lyfe, and the lyfe was the lyghte of men, and the lyghte shyneth in the darckness, but the darckness comprehended it not.

KING JAMES VERSION

[1]In the beginning was the Word, and the Word was with God, and the Word was God.[2]The same was in the beginning with God.[3]All things were made by him; and without him was not any thing made that was made.[4]In him was life; and the life was the light of men.[5]And the light shineth in darkness; and the darkness comprehended it not.

AMERICAN STANDARD VERSION

[1]In the beginning was the Word, and the Word was with God, and the Word was God. [2]The same was in the beginning with God. [3]All things were made through him; and without him was not anything made that hath been made. [4]In him was life; and the life was the light of men. [5]And the light shineth in the darkness; and the darkness apprehended it not.

REVISED STANDARD VERSION

[1]In the beginning was the Word, and the Word was with God, and the Word was God. [2]He was in the beginning with God; [3]all things were made through him; and without him was not anything made that was made. [4]In him was life, and the life was the light of men. [5]The light shines in the darkness, and darkness has not overcome it.

NEW AMERICAN STANDARD BIBLE

[1]In the beginning was the Word, and the Word was with God, and the Word was God. [2]He was in the beginning with God. [3]All things came into being by Him, and apart from Him nothing came into being that has come into being.

[4]In Him was life, and the life was the light of men. [5]And the light shines in the darkness, and the darkness did not comprehend it.

NEW INTERNATIONAL VERSION

[1]In the beginning was the Word, and the Word was with God, and the Word was God. [2]He was with God in the beginning.

[3]Through him all things were made; without him nothing was made that has been made. [4]In him was life, and that life was the light of men. [5]The light shines in the darkness, but the darkness has not understood it.

TODAY'S ENGLISH VERSION

[1]Before the world was created, the Word already existed; he was with God, and he was the same as God. [2]From the very beginning the Word was with God. [3]Through him God made all things; not one thing in all creation was made without him. [4]The Word was the source of life, and this life brought light to mankind. [5]The light shines in the darkness, and the darkness has never put it out.

THE LIVING BIBLE

[1-2]Before anything else existed, there was Christ, with God. He has always been alive and is himself God. [3]He created everything there is—nothing exists that he didn't make. [4]Eternal life is in him, and this life gives light to all mankind. [5]His life is the light that shines through the darkness—and the darkness can never extinguish it.

NEW ENGLISH BIBLE

When all things began, the Word already was. The Word dwelt with God, and what God was, the Word was. The Word, then, was with God at the beginning, and through him all things came to be; no single thing was created without him. All that came to be was alive with his life, and that life was the light of men. The light shines on in the dark, and the darkness has never mastered it.

NEW LIVING TRANSLATION

[1]In the beginning the Word already existed. He was with God, and he was God. [2]He was in the beginning with God. [3]He created everything there is. Nothing exists that he didn't make. [4]Life itself was in him, and this life gives light to everyone. [5]The light shines through the darkness, and the darkness can never extinguish it.

THE NEW JERUSALEM BIBLE

[1]In the beginning was the Word:
    the Word was with God
    and the Word was God.
[2]He was with God in the beginning.
[3]Through him all things came into being,
    not one thing came into being
        except through him.
[4]What has come into being in him
        was life,
    life that was the light of men;
[5]and light shines in darkness,
    and darkness could not overpower it.

THE NEW AMERICAN BIBLE

[1]In the beginning was the Word,
    and the Word was with God,
    and the Word was God.
[2]He was in the beginning with God.
[3]All things came to be through him,
    and without him nothing came to be.
    What came to be [4]through him was
        life,
    and this life was the light of the
        human race;
[5]the light shines in the darkness,
    and the darkness has not overcome it.

NEW REVISED STANDARD VERSION

[1]In the beginning was the Word, and the Word was with God, and the Word was God. [2]He was in the beginning with God. [3]All things came into being through him, and without him not one thing came into being. What has come into being [4]in him was life, and the life was the light of all people. [5]The light shines in the darkness, and the darkness did not overcome it.

BILDAD One of three friends who came to comfort Job in his anguish, identified as a Shuhite (Jb 2:11). That term suggests that he was a descendant of Shuah, son of Abraham and his second wife Keturah (Gn 25:1-2). Bildad spoke to Job on three occasions. In his first speech he asserted that God upholds the just and punishes the wicked (Jb 8). Job must therefore be a hypocrite to say that he is right with God. In his second speech Bildad emphasized the immediate punishment of the wicked in this life (ch 18). Job must therefore be wicked because of his intense suffering. In his third speech Bildad proclaimed the majesty of God and called man a worm by comparison (ch 25). He implied that Job was foolish to claim to be righteous before such a holy God. *See also* Job, Book of.

BILEAM Alternate name for Ibleam, a Levitical city in Manasseh's territory, in 1 Chronicles 6:70. *See* Ibleam.

BILGAH

1. Head of the 15th of 24 divisions of priests whom King David assigned to official duties in the temple (1 Chr 24:14).
2. Priest who returned to Jerusalem under Zerubbabel's leadership after the exile (Neh 12:18). He is perhaps identifiable with Bilgai in Nehemiah 10:8. *See* Bilgai.

BILGAI Priest who signed Ezra's covenant of faithfulness to God with Nehemiah and others after the exile (Neh 10:8); possibly the same person as Bilgah in Nehemiah 12:18. *See* Bilgah #2.

BILHAH (Person) Servant given by Laban to his daughter Rachel when she married Jacob (Gn 29:29). Realizing her own childlessness, Rachel gave Bilhah to her husband as a concubine and accepted their two sons as her own, naming them Dan and Naphtali (30:3-8;

35:25; 46:25). Archaeological investigation has confirmed the custom of a barren wife's providing a concubine to guarantee children to her husband. Such an arrangement is mentioned in marriage contract documents dug up at Nuzi and dated from about the same time as the Genesis 29 events. Jacob's son Reuben was later guilty of incest with Bilhah (35:22).

BILHAH (Place) Town in the territory allotted to Simeon's tribe (1 Chr 4:29), probably identical with Baalah (Jos 15:29) and Balah (19:3).

BILHAN
1. Ezer's firstborn son and a descendant of Seir (Gn 36:27; 1 Chr 1:42).
2. Jediael's son from Benjamin's tribe (1 Chr 7:10).

BILSHAN One, who with Nehemiah and Zerubbabel, led a group of Jews to Jerusalem following the exile (Ezr 2:2; Neh 7:7).

BIMHAL Japhlet's son, a great warrior and head of a clan in Asher's tribe (1 Chr 7:33, 40).

BINDING AND LOOSING* Biblical concept much discussed and debated throughout Christian history. Jesus referred to binding and loosing on two different occasions. After Peter's confession that Jesus was the Messiah, Jesus said to him: "I will give you the keys of the kingdom of heaven, and whatever you bind on earth shall be bound in heaven, and whatever you loose on earth shall be loosed in heaven" (Mt 16:19, RSV). Later, Jesus gave the same authority to bind and loose to all of the disciples (18:18).

Matthew is the only Gospel writer to record those specific words of Jesus. According to the Gospel of John, Jesus addressed similar but not identical words to the disciples after the resurrection: "If you forgive the sins of any, they are forgiven; if you retain the sins of any, they are retained" (Jn 20:23, RSV). A problem arises in identifying both the nature and the extent of the authority Jesus gave.

"Bind" and "loose" translate two Greek words, themselves translations of words in Aramaic, the language spoken by Jesus. Among Jesus' Jewish contemporaries, the two Aramaic words were often used as technical rabbinic terms. They referred to the verdict of a teacher of the Law who, on the basis of his authority as an expert in the interpretation of the Mosaic law, could declare some action "bound" (forbidden) or "loosed" (permitted). (Compare Mt 23:2-3, where Jesus said: "The scribes and Pharisees sit on Moses' seat; so practice and observe whatever they tell you," RSV.) Among the greatest Jewish rabbis, Shammai "bound" many actions that the more liberal teacher Hillel "loosed."

Alongside that scribal use of the terms was their use in judicial contexts. They referred to the imposition or the removal of a ban or judgment. In that context the words meant "to condemn; imprison" and "to absolve; set free." Both sets of meanings have been used to interpret the two texts in Matthew.

The precise meaning of the words in Matthew must be understood on the basis of their use in specific situations and in the light of the general NT understanding of apostolic authority. In Matthew 16:19 Peter's authority to bind and loose is connected with his receiving "the keys of the kingdom of heaven." In the Gospels the "kingdom of heaven" (that is, kingdom of God) is the sphere of God's rule, the "community" of people whom he rules as Lord. In a figurative sense, Peter was entrusted with the

keys to that kingdom, that "building." (See 1 Cor 3:9, 16-17; Eph 2:20-22; 1 Pt 2:4-5 for the idea of the people of God as his building.) The keys symbolize the authority entrusted to Peter as the one who confessed Jesus as Lord (Mt 16:16), and as the one who represents all those disciples who utter the same confession.

According to Matthew 23:13, the scribes were understood as guardians of the kingdom, since the knowledge of God had been entrusted to them (Lk 11:52). But they did not fulfill their trust; they shut the doors of the kingdom. Therefore, their task was transferred to Peter, spokesman for the 12 disciples, who were representatives of a new Israel (see Mt 21:43).

See also Keys of the Kingdom.

INTERPRETATIONS ON BINDING AND LOOSING
The nature of Peter's task and of his authority has been understood in various ways. Within the Roman Catholic tradition, the power of the keys has been taken to mean admission to, or exclusion from, the church. The authority to bind and loose is understood as apostolic authority to forgive sins or to refuse forgiveness. Further, it is understood as the authority to deliver decisions with regard to Christian faith and practice that are binding. Within the Roman Catholic tradition, it is also maintained that such authority belongs exclusively to the apostles and their successors, and most supremely to Peter and his successors, the bishops of Rome. Since those church authorities are seen as Christ's representatives, their decisions on Christian faith and practice are believed to have received divine confirmation: "shall be bound . . . [or] loosed in heaven" (that is, by God).

Within the Reformation tradition, the Roman Catholic interpretation of apostolic authority to bind and loose is rejected on the basis of several considerations. First, Jesus said nothing about successors to Peter and the other disciples. The concept of "apostolic succession" is therefore not grounded in the NT but was the result of historical development. Second, the position and authority of the original apostles was unique and unrepeatable. Jesus, the Christ, who lived on earth at a specific time and place, had a specific group of eyewitnesses who passed on his unique word, and on whose own witness the community of God's people was built.

Thus, the authority to bind and to loose is not a scribal-type authority that forbids or permits certain things; nor is it the authority to refuse or to permit entrance into the kingdom of heaven, the sphere of God's rule. Jesus' disciples were called to be messengers of good news (Mt 10:7; 24:14); it is response to that Good News (the gospel) that binds or looses, which leads to forgiveness or to continuing bondage to sin, which sets persons free or judges them (Mt 10:14; Rom 10:14-17; 1 Cor 1:18; 2 Cor 2:15-16).

BINEA Moza's son from Benjamin's tribe and a descendant of King Saul through Jonathan's line (1 Chr 8:37; 9:43).

BINNUI
1. Noadiah's father. Noadiah was a Levite in charge of weighing temple valuables after the exile (Ezr 8:33). Possibly the same as #4 below.
2. Pahath-moab's son or descendant. He obeyed Ezra's exhortation to divorce his pagan wife after the exile (Ezr 10:30).

3. According to the Apocrypha and the KJV, one of Bani's sons (descendants) who also obeyed Ezra's exhortation to divorce his pagan wife (Ezr 10:38; 1 Esd 9:34). Because the list of Bani's descendants is proportionally very long and because verse 38 in Hebrew can easily be construed "of the sons of Binnui," most modern translations make Binnui an ancestor of a new group rather than a descendant of Bani.

4. Henadad's son who repaired part of Jerusalem's wall after the exile (Neh 3:24). He was among the Levites who signed Ezra's covenant of faithfulness to God (Neh 10:9).

5. Alternate spelling for Bani in Nehemiah 7:15. See Bani #4.

6. Levite who returned to Judah with Zerubbabel after the exile. He was one of several in charge of songs of thanksgiving (Neh 12:8).

The popularity of this name and its similarity to other Jewish names (e.g., Bani and Bavvai) has caused much confusion in the genealogical lists. The above is one of several possible arrangements.

BIRDS Feathered vertebrates of the class Aves. Over 8,000 species of birds are known. Approximately 400 species are found in the Holy Land and about 40 are mentioned in Scripture.

Modern scientists classify organisms on the basis of internal and external structure, but the biblical writers generally classified organisms according to habitat. Thus, in the Bible, bats are listed with birds as creatures of the air (Lv 11:19; Dt 14:18).

Precise identification of biblical birds is often difficult or impossible. The biblical languages were not highly specialized scientific languages. People in biblical times generally knew the difference between similar animals now categorized as separate species. For birds, however, they frequently used poetic, descriptive terms. Biblical scholars attempt to overcome the difficulties in identification by comparing the Hebrew words with similar words in related languages and by attention to the habitat, habits, and characteristics attributed to the birds in Scripture. Nevertheless, different scholars sometimes arrive at different identifications.

PREVIEW

• Bittern	• Owl, Great
• Buzzard	• Owl, Little
• Cormorant	• Owl, Scops
• Crane	• Partridge
• Cuckoo	• Peacock
• Eagle	• Pelican
• Fowl, Domestic	• Pigeon or Dove
• Goatsucker or Night Hawk	• Quail
• Goose	• Raven
• Hawk	• Seagull
• Heron	• Sparrow
• Hoopoe	• Stork
• Ibis	• Swallow
• Kestrel or Falcon	• Swan
• Kite or Glede	• Swift
• Lammergeier	• Vulture
• Ostrich	• Vulture, Black, or Osprey
• Owl	• Vulture, Egyptian
• Owl, Barn or White	• Vulture, Griffon
	• Water Hen

Biblical References to Birds The Bible refers to birds both in literal and figurative senses. The biblical writers were keen observers of nature, their awareness of birds and bird life being reflected in many passages. They asserted that God knows all the birds (Ps 50:11) and cares for them (Mt 10:29). They saw God's covenant with Noah after the flood, his promise never to destroy life again by flood, as extending even to the birds and animals (Gn 9:10).

The Mosaic law declared many birds "unclean," mostly species that were scavengers or predators, or inhabited waste places. Centuries later the early Christians came to regard unclean species as clean by God's decree, revealed in the apostle Peter's vision (Acts 10:12). Other birds, like quail, sustained the Israelites in their wanderings (Ex 16:13). The Law prescribed birds as sacrifices for a firstborn child (Lk 2:24), for a Nazirite vow (Nm 6:10), for cleansing a leper (Lv 14:22), and as a burnt offering and sin offering (12:8).

Birds are easily subject to extinction, especially through human activity. God required the Israelites to practice conservation to prevent any birds from becoming extinct in the Holy Land, both for the birds' sake and so the Israelites would have a continuous source of food. The Law allowed foraging Israelites to take eggs or the young from a bird's nest, but they were not permitted to kill both a mother bird and her young (Dt 22:6).

Biblical writers turned to nature frequently for illustrations of divine principles or human characteristics. Comparisons of humans to birds sometimes carry a sense of lowness, as when King Nebuchadnezzar developed claws like a bird in his madness (Dn 4:33), or when Job remarked that birds did not know the source of wisdom (Jb 28:21). In Jesus' parable of the sower, the birds that ate the seed scattered by the wayside may represent indifference and a lack of spiritual understanding (Mt 13:4).

Scripture also contains sympathetic images of the plight of birds. A lonely man praying was likened to a lonely bird on a housetop (Ps 102:7). If someone was unjustly hunted by his enemies, he would understand a hunted bird's plight (Lam 3:52). Birds were said to be affected by curses on evildoers as they fled from Jerusalem or from the face of the earth (Jer 9:10; Zep 1:3).

In spite of such misfortune visited upon birds, Scripture affirms that, like other creatures, they are cared for and delighted in by God (Ps 50:11; Mt 6:26; 10:29). Both Pharaoh and Nebuchadnezzar were compared to a tree that gives shelter to the birds (Ez 31:6; Dn 4:12; cf. 2:38). Human power, however, fails eventually as when the tree representing Nebuchadnezzar was cut down, forcing the birds to flee (Dn 4:14). God's protection, by contrast, is unfailing. Jesus likened the kingdom of God to a mustard seed, growing to become a shelter for birds (Mt 13:32). God provides a habitation for birds (Ps 104:12), although Jesus, the Son of Man, had nowhere to rest his head (Mt 8:20).

Birds were considered evidence of God's handiwork (Jb 12:7). Bird lore provided examples of good sense in learning from a mistake (Prv 1:17; 6:5) and of bad judgment in failing to avoid the snares of immorality (7:23). Birds and other creatures could be tamed, unlike the wicked human tongue (Jas 3:7). Birds flying without alighting were an image of an undeserved curse (Prv 26:2). Without trust in God, people might be forced by evil to flee like a bird to the mountains (Ps 11:1). Birdsong was said to bring joy (Sg 2:12). The return of God's people to the Promised Land would be like birds returning (Hos 11:11). Jesus expressed his love for Jerusalem by saying that he longed to gather his people to himself as a hen gathers her brood under her wing (Mt 23:37).

Finally, birds were occasionally regarded as ominous signs. For example, Pharaoh's baker learned of impending death because in a dream birds ate the food from a basket on his head (Gn 40:17). Solomon warned against cursing the king, even in private, because "a little bird may tell them what you said" (Eccl 10:20). A vivid biblical image is that of scavenging, carrion-eating birds consuming the bodies of evildoers. To the Israelites, such a desecration of humanity was an image of ultimate horror (Dt 28:26; 1 Sm 17:44; Is 46:11; Jer 7:33; 12:9; Ez 29:5; 39:4; Rv 19:17, 21).

Individual Species

Bittern Long-legged wading bird *(Botaurus stellaris)* similar to the heron, but with shorter legs and a smaller, more compact body. Bitterns inhabit marshes, where it is easy for them to hide with their natural camouflage. A bittern's mottled plumage of barred brown and black so duplicates the color and shape of swamp vegetation that at times the bird seems to disappear before the observer's eyes. The neck is covered with long, soft feathers, making it appear disproportionately heavy. Bitterns are wary and solitary. During mating season the bittern's larynx is modified to produce a mysterious-sounding cry. The body twists in an unusual manner in harmony with the notes. Bitterns nest alone in grassy marshes. Because they are shy, they have become symbols of places of desolation and loneliness.

There is some question as to whether the bittern is actually mentioned in the Bible. The KJV has "bittern" in three places (Is 14:23; 34:11; Zep 2:14). Many biblical scholars believe the Hebrew word in those verses refers not to the bittern but to the hedgehog (Is 14:23; Zep 2:14, RSV) or porcupine (Is 34:11, RSV). The Hebrew word is similar to an Arabic word meaning "porcupine." Other scholars point out that the references suggest a bird rather than a mammal, especially Zephaniah 2:14, which speaks of the creature making its "lodge in her capitals" (i.e., above Nineveh's doorposts). Bitterns are particularly abundant in the swamps of the Tigris River (near Nineveh). The bittern's characteristics may fit the references in the three passages better than do the hedgehog's.

See also Hedgehog; Animals (Porcupine).

Buzzard Hawklike soaring bird *(Buteo vulgaris* or *Buteo ferox)*. It resembles the kite, though its tail is straight and not cleft. It is mentioned in the list of unclean birds (Dt 14:13). But other translations render the word as "glede" (KJV) or "kite" (NASB, NEB). The parallel list in Leviticus 11, however, substitutes "kite" (RSV, NASB, NEB) or "vulture" (KJV) for "buzzard." Thus, it is difficult to determine whether the buzzard is actually mentioned in the Bible, even though it is a common resident of Israel.

Like other great soaring birds, the buzzard is noted for its sharp eyesight, and may be the bird mentioned for that quality in Job 28:7 (variously translated "falcon," "eagle," or "vulture"). It will trail its prey for hours, and has a remarkable ability to see a carcass on which it descends to feed. Somewhat larger than the common buzzard is the long-legged buzzard, found in Israel, western Asia, and Syria.

See also Kestrel; Kite; Vulture (below).

Cormorant Large, black gooselike bird *(Phalacrocorax carbo)*, repeatedly depicted in art from Egypt and the Holy Land. Its length varies from 19 to 40 inches (48.3 to 101.6 centimeters). Its feet have webs between all four toes. The feet, attached far back on the body, serve as propellers when the cormorant dives to catch its meal of fish, crustacea, or amphibia. The long bill is curved at the tip, and under the bill is a sac in which the cormorant keeps the captured fish.

Cormorants live in large companies, making nests of sticks and other vegetation that they carry to trees or to rocky shelves near coasts. Up to four eggs are incubated, and the young are fed by both parents.

The cormorant frequents swamps around the Sea of Galilee, Lake Huleh (the waters of Merom), and the Mediterranean coast. Its Hebrew name originally denoted the "hurling down" of the bird at its prey. Cormorants dive into deep water and sometimes seem to zoom beneath the surface in their hunt for fish. The cormorant's greed is proverbial. It was ceremonially unclean for the Israelites (Lv 11:17; Dt 14:17).

See also Pelican (below).

Crane Tall wading birds *(Grus grus)* resembling storks and herons but with shorter talons. The plumage has a silvery gloss and the tail feathers are wavy. Large flocks of cranes flying in wedge-shaped formations pass over the Holy Land during the daylight hours each fall on their way to Africa from the northern countries of Europe and again in the spring when they return north to breed. Migratory flocks may number as many as 2,000 birds. Jeremiah 8:7 refers to the crane's migratory habits.

The usual call of the crane is best described as a bellow, but during migratory flight they emit a chattering sound that may be referred to in Isaiah 38:14. Cranes have remarkably powerful voices, their calls seeming to carry for miles. Migrating flocks usually have a flock leader who does the calling.

A crane's height may reach 40 to 60 inches (101.6 to 152.4 centimeters). Except for the ostrich, the crane is the tallest bird ever to inhabit the Holy Land. A crane's wingspread may exceed 90 inches (228.6 centimeters). The overall color is steel gray; the head and neck are black with a longitudinal white stripe. The crane feeds on land rather than in shallow water. It feeds primarily on grass and grain yet may devour insects, snakes, small alligators, frogs, and worms, using its long, powerful bill as a sharp hammer for killing such creatures.

The crane usually nests in solitary places, often in shallow water or nearby. Its nest is a mass of vegetation, holding two or three eggs that are light-colored with darker spots.

Cuckoo Small, drab brown bird known for its parasitic habits. The term the KJV used in Leviticus 11:16 and Deuteronomy 14:15 may refer either to the common cuckoo *(Cuculus canorus)* or to the great spotted cuckoo *(Clamator glandarius)*. The bird acts as a brood parasite, laying its eggs in the nest of another species after pushing out one of the eggs of the host species. The young cuckoo hatches before the young of the host species and evicts the other young. The foster parents raise it as their own.

The cuckoo, an insect eater, is considered ritually unclean in Scripture, which might imply that it is a predator or carrion-eater. For that reason some believe the Hebrew word actually refers to the seagull or sea mew rather than the cuckoo. Gulls, terns, and petrels are all common on the seashore and lakes of the Holy Land.

Other scholars believe that the Hebrew word refers not to the cuckoo but to one of the owls, possibly the long-eared owl.

See also Owl; Seagull (below).

Eagle Large bird of prey, genus *Aquila*. Vultures were often confused with eagles, making identification of the biblical birds difficult. Eagles' heads are not bald as are the heads of vultures, but from a distance they appear similar. It is possible that the Hebrew word translated "eagle" (which literally means "to tear with the beak") may have referred to all large birds of prey, eagles and vultures alike. A number of references to the eagle in Scripture are actually references to the griffon vulture (e.g., Hos 8:1; perhaps Mt 24:28). In certain passages, however, the true eagle may be meant.

The Holy Land has several varieties of eagle, including the imperial eagle *(Aquila heliaca)* and the less common golden eagle *(Aquila chrysaetos)*. These birds are powerfully built with strong wings; their movements reveal suppleness and strength. A distinctive hooked beak, which enhances the eagle's dignified and somewhat ferocious appearance, provides it with an effective instrument for tearing and killing prey. Short, powerful legs and prehensile claws enable an eagle to apply an almost unbreakable grip on a struggling victim. The strong talons have sharp points and edges. The eagle hunts by day.

For Jeremiah and other prophets, the eagle was the epitome of swiftness. The golden eagle, which can fly three or four miles (5–7 kilometers) in ten minutes, may have evoked the comparisons in 2 Samuel 1:23; Jeremiah 4:13; 49:22; Lamentations 4:19 (KJV), and Habakkuk 1:8. Moses used a similar comparison to emphasize the sudden striking power of a hostile enemy (Dt 28:49). The author of Proverbs, observing the high altitude to which the eagle soars, applied that image to the human situation (Prv 23:4-5; cf. Rv 12:14).

The eagle's strength and invincibility were mentioned often with reference to powerful nations attacking Israel. The prophet Ezekiel described Nebuchadnezzar as an eagle (Ez 17:3). Both the Babylonians and Assyrians frequently depicted the eagle in their art, especially as a deity with a man's body and an eagle's head. Nebuchadnezzar even had an experience of temporary insanity in which "his hair grew as long as eagles' feathers, and his nails were like birds' claws" (Dn 4:33, RSV).

The eagle builds its nest on inaccessible mountain peaks or at the top of the tallest trees, a fact noted by Jeremiah (Jer 49:16; cf. Jb 39:27-28; Ob 1:4). The brood consists of two or occasionally three eggs. Only the female sits on the nest, but the young eaglets are fed by both parents. Eagles are devoted to their offspring and train them with great care in the art of flying. Some commentators interpret Exodus 19:4 and Deuteronomy 32:11 as evidence of the eagle's practice of catching its young on its wings. There is virtually no evidence from observation, however, that any eagle can perform such a feat. In some versions the wording avoids a direct statement that eagles bear their young on their wings.

Some eagles in captivity have lived to an age of over 100 years. This remarkable longevity caused the psalmist to speak of the eagle whose youth is renewed (Ps 103:5). Confronted by its impressive qualities, biblical authors observed the eagle with awe and wonder (Jb 39:27-30; Prv 30:18-19). Those awesome qualities also contributed to several prophetic visions, including Ezekiel's vision of a creature with an eagle's face (Ez 1:10) and the apostle John's vision of a holy beast like a flying eagle (Rv 4:7).

See also Vulture (below).

Fowl, Domestic Domesticated poultry *(Gallus gallus domesticus)*, probably derived from the red jungle fowl of India. They seem to have been known already in OT times (Prv 30:31). A seal of Jaazaniah (see 2 Kgs 25:23), dating from about 600 BC, bears the image of a fighting cock. A reference to fowls or poultry for Nehemiah's table, however, may be to wild game rather than domestic fowl (Neh 5:18).

Poultry symbolized fertility, and the Jews carried a cock and hen in front of bridal couples at weddings. The motherly concern of hens gathering their broods was familiar to Jesus' hearers (Mt 23:37; Lk 13:34).

Since roosters habitually crow an hour or two before dawn, the third watch of the night, from midnight to 3:00 AM, was known as the cockcrow. According to the Talmud (a commentary on Jewish law), keeping chickens was prohibited in Jerusalem in NT times to prevent the insects and larvae that breed in chicken droppings from contaminating sacrificial flesh. For that reason the cock that Peter heard (Mt 26:34, 74; Lk 22:34, 60-61) probably belonged to Romans living there or to Jews who did not follow Jewish regulations.

Goatsucker or Night Hawk Migratory bird, dark in color and short-legged, similar to the American whippoorwill. The goatsucker (genus *Caprimulgus*) resembles an owl with a flat head, large eyes, soft plumage, and a noiseless flight. It hunts insects at night, catches them on the wing, and during the day rests on branches. Goatsuckers were so named because they were thought by the ancients to milk goats. According to Leviticus 11:16 and Deuteronomy 14:15, they were ritually unclean. Although some scholars believe that an owl is intended, there seems to be good reason to accept the "night hawk" translation.

Goose Long-necked, web-footed water birds with waterproof feathers (genus *Anser*). Domestic geese were known to the Greeks of Homer's day, since they are mentioned in the *Odyssey*. They were domesticated in Egypt perhaps as early as the Old Kingdom (c. 2500 BC) and certainly by the time of the New Kingdom (c. 1500–1100 BC). They were used for food and sacrifice. The breeding of geese was widespread in Canaan in biblical times; ivory carvings of the 13th or 12th century BC showing geese have been found in excavations at Megiddo in Israel.

Many species of geese spend most of their lives on land even though they are waterfowl; some even build their nests in trees. Wild geese tend to inhabit flatlands and prairies rather than mountainous terrain.

Geese may have graced the table of King Solomon. In 1 Kings 4:23 they are referred to as "fatted fowl," a term that may also refer to ducks, swans, guineas, pigeons, or other domestic edible birds.

Hawk Small birds of prey found in the Holy Land. Most references are probably to the sparrow hawk *(Accipter nisus)*. This bird is slightly larger than the kestrel, has a grayish-brown back and a white belly with black and brown bars. It has short feathers, long, curved talons, and broad wings, rounded at the outer ends, which enable it to soar on updrafts. The long tail, acting as a rudder, helps the bird change its course swiftly in flight. It is hence very maneuverable in the air when chasing warblers or other small birds. It does not seize its prey on the ground, as does the kestrel, but hunts and attacks small birds in flight. Hawks hunt in the daytime, unlike owls that are adapted for nighttime hunting. With their eyes located on the side of the head, hawks are very keen-sighted. They usually nest in tall trees and their nests are often occupied by the same pair year after year.

The Egyptians embalmed sparrow hawks and regarded all hawks highly. The god Horus was depicted with the head of a hawk or falcon.

The sparrow hawk was ceremonially unclean to the Israelites (Lv 11:16; Dt 14:15). It was not a permanent resident of Israel but stopped off as it migrated from north to south. Its southward migration is mentioned in Job 39:26. A reference in Isaiah 34:11 to "hawk" ("cormorant," KJV) is uncertain. *See* Kestrel or Falcon; Kite (below).

Heron Wading bird (genus *Ardea*) with a long, thin neck and long legs. It has a characteristic comblike growth on the inner side of the third toe.

Herons are generally white, blue, green, or gray. They nest together in rookeries, and both parents bring in food for the young. Herons feed on fish, small reptiles, and insects, gulping them down in one swallow. Adults and young migrate in the late fall to warm southern climates. The white heron attains a length of more than 3 feet (.9 meter), whereas the dwarf heron is only about 22 inches (55.9 centimeters) long.

At least seven varieties of heron are reported in the Holy Land. The white ibis, or buff-backed heron (*Buphus russatus*), was probably the most common species. The purple heron *(Ardea purpureus)* is a summer breeder found in all parts of the Holy Land where there is standing water.

The blue-gray heron (*Ardea cinerea*) winters in southern Europe and North Africa, migrating to northern Europe in the early spring. In Israel it builds its winter nest near water, in swamps and along riverbanks, where it feeds on fish and frogs. It will stand patiently in the water for hours, and then suddenly its long, pointed beak darts down with lightning speed to catch its prey. Often the blue-gray heron builds its nest in a tall tree to which it may return year after year.

According to Leviticus 11:19 and Deuteronomy 14:18, the heron was ceremonially unclean to the Israelites. Some scholars believe those references are to the cormorant, but most scholars think they refer to one of the herons.

See also Cormorant (above).

Hoopoe One of the Holy Land's most beautiful birds (*Upupa epops*). It has vividly colored plumage, a lovely crown-shaped crest that becomes erect when the bird is alarmed, and a long, slender curved bill. The pinkish-brown hoopoe is about 11 inches (27.9 centimeters) long, with black and white bands on its back, tail, and wings. Hoopoes are basically desert-dwelling birds.

The name "hoopoe" is derived from the sound of the bird's call. To emit the sound, the neck feathers are puffed up and the head snapped in the air. When on the ground, the bird hammers its beak into the earth.

The hoopoe arrives in the Holy Land in February, breeds in the summer, and leaves in September. It was held in religious reverence by the Egyptians. It was listed as ritually unclean (Lv 11:19; Dt 14:18), probably because it searches for grubs and small insects in such unsanitary places as dunghills.

Ibis Wading bird (*Threskiornis aethiopica*) presently unknown in the Holy Land but possibly known there in biblical times. It was well known in ancient Egypt, where it was sacred to the god Thoth. Today it has practically vanished with the disappearance of swamps along the Nile.

There is some question as to whether the ibis is meant in Leviticus 11:17, where it is classified as ceremonially unclean. The same Hebrew word in Deuteronomy 14:16 and Isaiah 34:11 is translated "great owl," a translation preferred by most scholars.

See also Owl, Great (below).

Kestrel or Falcon Small hawk (*Falco tinnunculus*) about a foot (30.5 centimeters) long with brown, black, and yellow feathers on its breast. It was abundant in the Holy Land in villages and in the countryside, nesting on rooftops and among rocks. Like most hawks, the kestrel is able to hover and float in midair and then swoop down

on its prey, seizing it with sharp, hooklike talons. It feeds largely on mice, small reptiles, and insects.

Embalmed kestrels have been found in ancient Egyptian tombs. The Egyptians also embalmed the hunting kestrel *(Falco cherug)*, which can be tamed and trained to hunt rabbits and other small game. Falconry (hunting with hawks of various species) was well known among the ancients and is still practiced today. That the Assyrians were familiar with falconry is seen in the records of Ashurbanipal. Because the kestrel is a predator, it was ceremonially unclean (Lv 11:14). Some translations render the word as "kite" (Lv 11:14, KJV; Dt 14:13, KJV, RSV), an illustration of the difficulty of identifying biblical birds precisely.

See also Kite or Glede (below).

Kite or Glede Large bird of prey (*Milvus milvus*). The average length of the kite is about 19 inches (48.3 centimeters). The upper part is generally dark, and the belly is white. Kites nest high in trees and build nests of vegetation, including sticks. They rarely have more than two or three young, which they feed on snakes, grasshoppers, and so on. Sometimes kites are called snake hawks.

The kite is a migratory bird that stays in Israel during the summer, especially in the mountains of southern Judea, in the trackless wastes west of the Dead Sea, and in the wilderness of Beersheba.

The red kite or glede is a medium-sized bird of prey. The edges of the upper part of the bill overlap with the lower one, forming sharp scissors. The tail is forked or cleft like that of a fish. Its loud cry often includes sharp whistling notes. Other Holy Land species include the black kite *(Milvus migrans)* and the black-winged kite *(Elanus caeruleus)*.

The kite is listed among the unclean birds in Mosaic law (Lv 11:14; Dt 14:13), but the precise identification of the birds mentioned there is disputed by some scholars and translators.

See also Buzzard; Kestrel or Falcon (above).

Lammergeier Largest of the vultures and less common than the other members of the family. It is grayish brown with white streaks and has a black tuft of stiff hairs in the facial area that gives it the name "bearded vulture." Another name for it is "lamb vulture."

The lammergeier *(Gypaetus barbatus)* has a unique way of killing its prey; since its beak is not particularly powerful it carries its victim high in the air and then drops it on rocks.

The lammergeier is especially partial to tortoises and to marrow bone. After jackals and smaller vultures have reduced a carcass to bone, the lammergeier crushes the bones to obtain the marrow, or swallows the pieces intact. Hence it is also known as the ossifrage, from a Latin word meaning "bone crusher." The lammergeier was unclean in Mosaic law (Lv 11:13; Dt 14:13; both translated "vulture" in NLT and "ossifrage" in KJV).

See also Vulture (below).

Ostrich Two-toed, swift-running, flightless bird (*Struthio camelus*) that lives in deserts or in areas covered with stunted bushes.

In biblical times ostriches ranged as far north as Syria and were found over the entire wasteland of the Negev Desert, but they have since become extinct there. Its Hebrew name means "daughter of the desert." It is the largest of all living birds, attaining a height of about 10 feet (3 meters) and a weight of 175 pounds (79.5 kilograms), though some males may weigh as much as 300 pounds (136.4 kilograms). The female is considerably smaller. Powerful thighs and long legs give the ostrich great speed, reported to be as high as 40 MPH (64 KPH).

The ostrich is omnivorous. It eats grass, fruits, small mammals, birds, snakes, and lizards, as well as large pebbles that assist in the breakdown of food in its gizzard. The ostrich is hunted, but its eggs are generally more sought after than the bird itself. The empty shells are traded throughout the Mediterranean area for use as utensils, or when broken up as raw material for beads. The eggs—as many as 25 in one clutch—are laid in a shallow nest of sand, with some left uncovered. They may appear to be neglected by day, but only because they are ordinarily incubated at night. The cock does most of the incubating; the female participates only during cold days. The strong, thick eggshell protects the embryo from the heat of the desert.

Occasionally the ostrich is used for riding or even for pulling small carts. Ostrich feathers are in great demand. Ostrich plumes graced ancient royal courts as fans. An ivory-handled fan of Pharaoh Tutankhamen (King Tut) had lovely ostrich plumes. The plumes are white in the male and brownish gray in the female. The reputation of the ostrich for stupidity comes from its behavior when hunted and cornered; it fails to take evasive action even when doing so would save it. In open country, however, it is very wary and runs at great speed to escape. In contrast to the partridge, an ostrich will run away from its eggs and chicks when pursued.

Most biblical references to ostriches emphasize their negative characteristics. They were regarded as unclean in Jewish law (Lv 11:16; Dt 14:15). Several references associate ostriches with images of wilderness and desolation (Jb 30:29; Is 13:21; 34:13; 43:20; Jer 50:39). Their night cry, which has been compared to an ox's lowing in pain, is referred to in Micah 1:8. Biblical writers also noted the apparent indifference of the ostrich to its brood (Jb 39:13-18; Lam 4:3).

of the Jordan River in Israel. They seldom come near inhabited dwellings.

Owls have excellent night vision, which they use to capture rodents or other animals. Although unusually large, the owl's eyes are almost useless in the daylight because the light dazzles them. The owl is able to swallow its prey whole because of its elastic esophagus. Indigestible hair and bones are regurgitated as pellets. The bill is short but sharply hooked.

Owls may lay up to ten eggs. The young are cared for on the nest by both parents. Both adults and young tend to remain in the area in which they were hatched. Eight species of owls are found in the Holy Land, of which five are plentiful. It is difficult, however, to identify a particular species with any of the four Hebrew words translated "owl" in Scripture. A fifth word translated "owl" (KJV) is more appropriately identified with the ostrich (RSV). Owls appear in the lists of unclean birds (Lv 11:17; Dt 14:16), and although translations differ, they concur that all species of owls, being predators, are unclean.

See also Ostrich (above); Owl, Barn or White; Owl, Great; Owl, Little; Owl, Scops (below).

Owl, Barn or White Large owl *(Tyto alloa)* with a distinct heart-shaped face. It may get its Hebrew name from a snoring sound it makes when breathing in the nest. In flight it emits a frightening screech, and thus is sometimes referred to as the screech owl. Its somewhat sinister features—a large head and wide pop eyes—have led some people to consider it demonic, but they have also inspired another name, the monkey-faced owl. It is a useful bird, however, devouring rodents that raid fields and damage stored grain. Like other owls, it sleeps during the day and hunts at night with a well-developed sense of hearing and sight. Its color is light brownish yellow with a white mask around the eyes and cheeks. The whole leg is covered with feathers that protect it against the bites of struggling victims in its talons.

Osprey (or Fishhawk)

Partridge

Kite

Rock Dove

Owl Nocturnal birds (order Strigiformes) with large heads and large, forward-looking eyes. Their wing and tail feathers are soft as velvet, helping to make their flight noiseless. The owl's body is small and slender, about the size of a pigeon, but it appears bulky because of the thick covering of feathers. Owls have been considered bearers of misfortune and omens of disaster. In the Near East, owls now live in temple ruins and pyramids in Egypt, and in rock-hewn graves, ruins, and caves on both sides

Some modern translations mention the barn or white owl by name (Lv 11:17, NJB; 11:18, NASB; Dt 14:16, NJB, NASB).

See also Owl (above); Owl, Scops (below).

Owl, Great Large owl, standing nearly two feet (60.9 centimeters) tall *(Asio otus)*. The color is mouse gray with gray-brown spots and black stripes. As one of its names indicates, it has tufted "ears" and is sometimes called the great horned owl. It feeds on rodents, such as rats and mice. It winters in Israel among ruins and in groves.

The great owl may be the owl mentioned in the Bible among the birds of desolation that will inhabit devastated Edom (Is 34:11, NASB mg). It is also mentioned by name in some translations of the lists of ritually unclean birds (Lv 11:17, KJV, NASB; Dt 14:16, KJV, NASB, RSV).

Owl, Little Smallest of all nocturnal birds of prey. Chiefly insectivorous, the little owl *(Athene noctua glaux)* also feeds at times on tiny birds. It is the most common owl in the Holy Land, dwelling among ruins, tombstones, rocks, and thickets (perhaps the owl of Ps 102:6). Its voice sounds like that of a dying person. On occasion it may be observed perched on a rock with its large eyes gazing off into the distance, a pose that the ancients considered a sign of wisdom. The Greeks associated the little owl with the goddess Athena. It is mentioned by name in several translations (Lv 11:17, KJV, NASB; Dt 14:16, KJV, NASB, RSV).
See also Owl (above).

Owl, Scops Small owl *(Otus scops)* distinguished by two horn-shaped crests of hairlike feathers on its head. It perches in an inclined posture and hops and dances like a goat. During the hatching period, the male's hooting sounds like a moan. The scops owl feeds on insects, rodents, and birds. During invasions of mice or locusts, these owls have appeared in large flocks and helped to destroy the pests. They have been known to attack humans who intrude on their nests. They are well-known inhabitants of Eurasia and Africa.

Some scholars suggest that the scops is the true screech owl, because of its whistling calls that resound through the night. The screech owl is mentioned only once in Scripture (Is 34:14, KJV), but that translation is the subject of scholarly debate. Following traditional Jewish mythology, some translations use the Hebrew word *(lilith)* as a proper name. In Jewish tradition Lilith was a witch-demon who, before Eve's creation, was Adam's wife. She became the mother of demons and was thought to attack children during the night; thus the name "Lilith" is translated "night hag" (RSV) or "night monster" (NASB). Most scholars favoring the mythical interpretation, however, suggest that Isaiah was using a popular legend to evoke a sense of desolation and did not himself believe in the existence of Lilith. There is little support for "screech owl" as an appropriate translation of the name.
See also Owl; Owl, Barn or White (above).

Partridge Most common game bird in the Holy Land. The partridge resembles a chicken in its basic anatomy but has a less chunky body and a longer tail. Two species of partridge inhabit the Holy Land: the sand partridge *(Ammoperdix heyi)*, found near the Dead Sea, in the Jordan River valley, and in the Sinai Desert; and the chukar partridge *(Alectoris graeca)*. The sand partridge is a medium-sized bird with yellow feet. The male has sandy-buff plumage, upper tail feathers penciled and barred with brown, and a chestnut and white undersurface. The female is a grayish buff. The chukar partridge resembles the common French partridge of Europe, having a body about 16 inches (40.6 centimeters) long. It is covered with beautiful and radiantly colored feathers.

The biblical reference (1 Sm 26:20; probably the sand partridge because of the geographical context) alludes to the common method of catching it by chasing. It was also hunted with snares (cf. Ps 91:3) or by hunters hiding in a blind. The fast-running partridge soon becomes exhausted, which enables hunters to run it to the ground and kill it. Nevertheless, by running and jumping, it can

ascend very steep cliffs. The bird finds refuge among bushes into which its brownish-green feathers blend protectively. If it were not such a prolific breeder, it would probably have become extinct by being hunted for food.

The biblical description of the partridge gathering a brood she did not hatch (Jer 17:11) seems to be based on the fact that the hen lays at least two clutches of eggs, one for herself and one for the cock to incubate.

Peacock Member of the quail, partridge, and pheasant family, the peacock *(Pavo cristatus)* is actually the male peafowl. Its mate is properly known as the peahen. The male attracts attention because of a stately, luxurious appearance enhanced by magnificent feathers. The breast is a brilliant metallic blue, and each tail feather has a brilliant eye near the tip. When lowered, the unusually long tail feathers form a train behind the peacock on the ground, giving it an overall length of up to six feet (1.8 meters). The train can also be raised to form a huge fan adorned with the multicolored eyes. During courtship the feathers are raised and vibrated to make a distinct rustling noise. The rather drab peahen lacks the long train.

Because it is not native to the Holy Land, the peacocks referred to in 1 Kings 10:22 and 2 Chronicles 9:21 are thought by some scholars to be Old World monkeys or baboons brought from east Africa, or guinea hens from the upper Nile River region. There is evidence, however, that the Phoenicians introduced peacocks to the Egyptian pharaoh, perhaps as early as the time of King Solomon. It is possible that Solomon's trade expeditions ranged as far as India, where the peacock is native. The peacock was also well known to the Greeks and Romans. Alexander the Great prized its beauty and forbade his soldiers to kill the bird.

In the early Christian church the peacock became a symbol of the immortality promised in the resurrection of Christ. In addition, the eyes of its tail came to represent the all-seeing eye of God.

Pelican Largest of all aquatic birds, considerably larger even than the swan. The pelican *(Pelecanus onocrotalus)* is generally about 50 inches (127 centimeters) long with a 16-inch (40.6-centimeters) beak, the upper part of which is hooked downward at the end, facilitating fish catching. The lower part of the bill supports a yellow pouch extending down the throat. The pouch may hold up to three gallons (11.4 liters) of food (small fish) and water. The pelican's webbed feet are peculiar in having webs between all four toes. Pelicans are expert swimmers as well as efficient fliers. The pelican's massive body, long neck, and comparatively small head give it proportions that make rising from the water difficult. To take off, a pelican must first flap awkwardly along the surface, pounding at the water with its legs.

Pelicans fly and nest in groups. Both sexes care for the young that hatch from the one to four eggs. Whereas most birds feed their young by placing food into their mouths, the pelican reverses the process; the young pelican sticks its head and most of its body into its mother's throat and plucks partially digested food from the mother's crop. The deep penetration of the young's beak into the mother's gullet led ancients to believe that the young were feeding on the blood of the mother's breast, thus giving rise to wide usage of the pelican as a symbol of Christ's atonement, and of charity in general.

The roseate pelican is white, at times with a faint rose tinge, and has black feathers growing from the wing joint farthest from the body. The legs, pouch, and skin around the eyes are yellow; the hook of the beak is red. This species may grow up to six feet (1.8 meters) long with a wingspread of up to eight feet (2.4 meters). During the breeding season, the coloration of the exposed areas of the roseate pelican's legs and face changes from gray to bright orange or red. At the same time the white feathers acquire a beautiful pink tint originating from an oil-gland secretion. The oil is spread throughout the plumage by the bird as it preens.

Some scholars question whether "pelican" is an appropriate translation of the Hebrew in several verses, believing rather that the word refers to one of the owls, hawks, or vultures. Most translations include the pelican in the lists of ritually unclean birds (Lv 11:18; Dt 14:17). Opinion on the other references is more sharply divided. Some scholars maintain that the desert context of the verses eliminates the possibility of a water bird like the pelican (cf. Ps 102:6, "vulture," RSV; Is 34:11, "cormorant," KJV; "hawk," RSV; Zep 2:14, "cormorant," KJV; "vulture," RSV). On the other hand, the roseate pelican frequents the rivers, lakes, and marshes of the Holy Land. After flying out to sea as far as 20 miles (32.2 kilometers) to swoop down on fish near the surface, the pelican often returns inland to a deserted place to digest its enormous meal. Thus, the pelican may be the lonely wilderness bird of those passages.

Pigeon or Dove Species of the pigeon family (Columbidae). In common usage the names "pigeon" and "dove" are virtually interchangeable. The common domestic pigeon familiar to city dwellers the world over, for example, is actually a descendant of the wild rock dove. Both names are used in English translations of the Bible to translate the same Hebrew word. A second Hebrew word is usually translated "turtledove." Nevertheless, it seems clear that the ancient Hebrews recognized differences among dove species.

At least six species of pigeon or dove reside in modern Israel: the rock, ring, and stock doves (genus *Columba*), and the turtle, collared, and palm doves (genus *Streptopelia*). Of the six, the rock dove (*Columba livia*) and the turtledove (*Streptopelia turtur*) seem to be the two most often referred to in Scripture.

Pigeons vary in size from 6 to over 12 inches (15 to 30 centimeters). The most colorful Israeli species is the rock dove, which can be a beautiful silvery gray with grayish-green iridescent plumage on the wings (noted by David, Ps 68:13). The smaller doves (*Streptopelia*) are less colorful, mostly gray or buff with a blackish or checkered half collar on the back of the neck. Pigeons have short necks and small heads, plump bodies, and short wings controlled by strong muscles that enable them to fly considerable distances. The smaller doves have longer tails.

At present, the wild rock dove is found primarily in the area around the Sea of Galilee and farther to the south in the many ravines leading down to the Dead Sea. Wild rock doves prefer to build their nests on rocks and cliff faces, a fact precisely described in Scripture (Sg 2:14; Jer 48:28). All Israeli doves build fragile nests of scraps of vegetation. Eggs are hatched twice a year. Doves seldom lay more than two eggs. The young are cared for in the nest by both parents, who rove over the fields eating seeds and weeds. The adult's crop contains digested food in a milky condition, called pigeon's milk, which can be regurgitated and fed to the young.

During courtship there is a great deal of rivalry among the male doves. The turtledove's courtship dance is an awesome aerial display. The attention to courtship, the joint care of young, and the solicitude of the parents for each other, noted from earliest times, have made the dove one of the most popular symbols of love and peace (Sg 1:15; 2:14; 4:1; 5:2).

A major distinction between pigeons (ring doves) and turtledoves seems to have been recognized by ancient writers. Pigeons are year-round residents and easily tamed, whereas turtledoves are migratory. Turtledoves were confined in cages singly or in pairs as pets or for sacrifices. Pigeons were probably the first birds to be domesticated, perhaps as early as Noah's time (Gn 8:8-12). They were depicted on the earliest Egyptian monuments, and their edibility was mentioned in early Egyptian texts. Before long, domestic pigeons were regarded as evidence of a household's prosperity. In the more prosperous households they nested in dovecotes of molded pottery clay fashioned in latticelike structures (hence the "windows" of Is 60:8).

In NT times there were many dovecotes in the parks around Herod the Great's palace in Jerusalem. The dove's popularity was due not only to its docility but also to its desirability as food and as an acceptable and relatively inexpensive sacrifice. The turtledove may have been regarded more highly as a sacrifice because of its wildness and consequent lesser availability. The two biblical references to turtledoves not in a sacrificial context refer to their migratory habits and to their arrival in Israel in the spring (Sg 2:12; Jer 8:7; cf. Hos 11:11).

Most of the references to doves and pigeons in the Bible are in statements about sacrificial procedures (Gn 15:7-10; Lv 1:14; 5:7; 12:6; Nm 6:10; Lk 2:24). Other references, however, include a range of observations and symbolic usages of the dove. Its throaty moaning was often observed (Is 38:14; 59:11; Ez 7:16; Na 2:7). Its power of flight was well known (Ps 55:6), as were its beauty (Sg 1:15; 4:1; 5:12), its gentleness and loyalty to its mate (Sg 2:14; 5:2; 6:9), its affection (Ps 74:19), and its innocence (Mt 10:16). The one negative reference to doves is in Hosea 7:11, where they are said to be senseless and foolish, perhaps in reference to their overly trusting nature.

Of NT references, perhaps the most significant is the description of the Holy Spirit at Christ's baptism as a descending dove (Mt 3:16). The dove's loving nature made it natural for early Christians to connect the dove image with the concept of the Comforter. Since then the dove has remained the most popular symbol of the Holy Spirit.

Quail Short, stocky birds with bills and feet similar to those of chickens; hence they are adapted to eating seeds or insects. Quail (*Coturnix coturnix*) are the smallest of the subfamily of poultry that also includes pheasants and partridges. Quail (or "quails," another plural form) are about ten inches (25.4 centimeters) long and have small, rounded wings. They burst from their hiding places in the grass or bushes with a whirring sound. The belly of the quail is white. Up to 18 eggs are laid, and if the mother dies, the male has been known to assume the care of the young. Quail of the Mediterranean region winter in the Sudan and migrate northward in vast flocks in the spring. Quail cannot maintain a long sustained flight but make use of wind currents to keep them aloft.

Enormous flocks of quail twice served as food for the Israelites in the wilderness of Sinai, when the birds were driven down in the desert miraculously by winds (Ex 16:13; Nm 11:31-32; Ps 105:40). The second time they were probably flying along the Gulf of Aqaba and were blown off course by the east wind (Nm 11:31; Ps 78:26-28). Their inability to sustain long flight may account for their low flying level—two cubits, or about 40 inches (101.6 centimeters). When exhausted, they were easily caught by hand (Nm 11:31-32). Quail were considered clean and the most delicate eating of all game birds, and they were preserved by drying in the sun.

Raven Member of the crow family (Corvidae). The Hebrew word for "raven" means "black one." The raven (*Corvus corax*) weighs about three pounds (1.36 kilograms) and varies from 22 to 26 inches (56 to 66 centimeters) in length. Its tail is broader in the middle than at either end. Eight species are found in Israel: three ravens, two jackdaws, one crow, one rook, and one chough. The crow, about 20 inches (50.8 centimeters) long, is smaller than a raven, and its tail is uniform in width. The raven's most conspicuous feature is its glossy black iridescent plumage.

Ravens and crows have survived in spite of the dislike many humans have for them. Excellent fliers, they migrate by day and congregate in great flocks of up to several hundred thousand. During the nesting season, they make nests of sticks in which two to seven eggs are laid. Ravens mate for life. Equipped with strong wings, a strong bill, and strong feet, ravens can live in isolated places from which they range widely for food. That it did not return to the ark was a good sign to Noah, indicating that the raven could find food and possibly a place to rest on dry mountaintops (Gn 8:7).

The raven, essentially a scavenger, was ceremonially unclean (Lv 11:15; Dt 14:14). Yet ravens fed Elijah at God's command (1 Kgs 17:4-6). Job was told that God gave the raven its food (Jb 38:41), as the psalmist and Jesus repeated (Ps 147:9; Lk 12:24). The raven's glistening black plumage inspired the bride's comparison of her beloved's hair (Sg 5:11). They prefer desolate, uninhabited areas as their home territory (Is 34:11). Ravens are crafty, active birds. Some are capable of speaking, solving puzzles, and performing feats of memory. Bold and curious, they sometimes use their talents for theft.

Seagull Robust seabirds, primarily scavengers (family Laridae). Several species of gulls live along the seacoast of the Holy Land. They are usually gray-backed with white heads and underparts and black wing tips. The slender bill ends in a downward curve.

Seagulls may be 8 to 30 inches (20 to 76 centimeters) long. Many species migrate, traveling long distances with their superb flying ability. Gulls can also swim easily because of their webbed feet. Their voice is like a harsh scream or squawk. In nesting season many nest together in any available place, such as a cliff or tree. Both male and female incubate and care for the young.

Because gulls will eat almost anything, they are listed as ritually unclean birds (Lv 11:16; Dt 14:15, ASV has "sea mew," a common European gull). Some commentators believe that those passages refer to an owl or to the cuckoo and not to the seagull.

See also Cuckoo (above).

Sparrow Small bird of the finch family (Fringillidae) or the weaver finch family (Ploceidae), considered to be of little worth. The Hebrew word is a general term for "bird" and refers to any small bird such as a sparrow, finch, thrush, or starling. In translation, however, the word sometimes refers to the common English or house sparrow (*Passer domestica*; Ps 84:3; Prv 26:2).

Dull in color with a black throat, the male house sparrow is a noisy and energetic creature. The nest, when built in open places, has an opening on the side and is made of almost anything available. Sparrows also nest in sheltered places, in dwellings, boxes, or holes in trees. They lay four to seven eggs.

The common or house sparrow was known in ancient Greece and Egypt. There it had a reputation for invading fields in large swarms and picking the seeds from them. It is a permanent resident of the Holy Land.

The sparrow is prolific and lives in close association with humans. It was considered ritually clean. Sparrows brought low prices in countries where they were sold (Mt 10:29; Lk 12:6). Today in Near Eastern marketplaces, boys offer live sparrows for sale. Tied together in groups of four to six by strings attached to one leg, the birds fly about over the boys' heads. Evidently such a sight was common in NT times.

Stork Long-legged, white wading bird (genus *Ciconia*) having large, powerful wings with glossy black primary and secondary feathers. The flapping of its wings produces a loud rushing sound. Connecting membranes between the toes prevent the bird from sinking into the mud. Its red bill is sharp and long, serving to seize and lift its prey out of the water. Storks are mute, lacking a voice box.

Flocks of storks pass through the Holy Land during their September migration on the way to central and southern Africa and likewise in the spring on their return flight to their homes in northern Israel, Syria, and Europe. Storks travel in vast flocks during the day, spreading out against the sky.

The stork's faithful tending of the young is proverbial, as is its habit of returning annually to the same nesting place. Storks have the habit of adding to their nests each year, and it is possible to find nests that are 100 years old and have a height of more than three feet (.9 meter).

Two species of storks frequent the Holy Land. The white stork (*Ciconia alba*) is 40 inches (101.6 centimeters) tall, and its wingspread is six feet (1.8 meters), enabling it to move with a slow, sustained flight or to soar. In folklore the white stork is sometimes considered to be a harbinger of good fortune.

The black stork (*Ciconia nigra*), common around the Dead Sea valley, nests in trees; hence it may be the tree-dwelling species referred to in Psalm 104:17. The Hebrew name for "stork" means literally the "kingly one," or the "loyal one," a reference to the care of the bird for its young. Like the heron, the stork was ceremonially unclean because of its diet of aquatic organisms, refuse, small animals, birds, and reptiles (Lv 11:19; Dt 14:18). Jeremiah mentioned the stork's uncanny and instinctive knowledge of the time of its migration (Jer 8:7). Its impressive wings figured in one of Zechariah's visions (Zec 5:9).

Swallow Small, nearly black, forked-tailed bird with long, tapering wings, noted for its graceful flight (*hirundo rustica*). The small, weak feet are poorly adapted for walking. Swallows resemble swifts in shape and life habits but are somewhat smaller.

The swallow's large mouth enables it to catch insects while in flight. Colors vary from brown and blue to white. Swallows often nest in buildings, a feature noticed by the psalmist, who reported a swallow's home at the temple (Ps 84:3).

Swallows are basically resident in Israel, whereas the swift is a migratory bird noted for the regularity of its migratory schedule. The "swallow" of Isaiah 38:14 probably refers to a swift, as does Jeremiah 8:7, where the dependability of the bird is contrasted with the irregularity of God's people. Proverbs 26:2 may be a reference to either the swallow or the swift.

See also Swift (below).

Swan Large, graceful water birds. Two species of swan (genus *Cygnus*) are found in the Middle East as passing migrants (*Cygnus olor* and *Cygnus musicus*). Swans are known as the best musicians among the birds and were considered sacred to the god Apollo by the Greeks. Their voices sound like flutes and harps.

The references in Leviticus 11:18 and Deuteronomy 14:16 (KJV) are probably not to the swan but to the water hen or the barn owl, since there seems little reason to declare the vegetarian swan an unclean animal.

See also Owl, Barn or White (above); Water Hen (below).

Swift Small, strong flyers (genus *Apus*). Like the swallow, the swift has long, bent wings and a cleft tail, enabling it to obtain great speed as it skims the ground and sweeps through the air. A swift devours a great many harmful insects, catching them in its mouth in flight. Many swifts make their nests in rooftops and in nooks and crannies of city walls. Their nests are built with strong feathers cemented together with saliva. Other swifts live in caves and clefts of rocks.

Common swifts are native to Israel, and in the Jordan Valley they occur in large flocks. Isaiah 38:14 (NIV) seems to be clear reference to the swift's plaintive call, since the swallow's sharp chirp is not a striking simile for a distraught king's cry. The swift has a soft, delicate voice, and its cry could be easily interpreted as melodious wailing.

The migratory swifts arrive on a precise schedule in the Holy Land in late winter, and immense flocks fill the cities with their cries. Thus the reference in Jeremiah 8:7 to swallows, which are largely permanent residents, is probably to swifts.

See also Swallow (above).

Vulture Subfamily (Aegypiinae) of the hawk family (Accipitridae). Each of the four species of Old World vultures is found in the Holy Land: the Egyptian, griffon, black, and bearded vulture (the bearded vulture is also known as the lammergeier). These birds range in size from the 24-inch (61-centimeters) Egyptian vulture to the huge bearded vulture, largest of all flying birds in the Holy Land.

Most vultures are brown or black, having a short neck and a short, hooked bill with which they tear the dead animal flesh of which they are fond. All vultures, except the bearded, have bare or down-covered heads and necks, enabling these scavengers to penetrate deep into a carcass without spoiling the plumage. Excellent eyesight enables a vulture to locate a carcass from a lofty soaring position. Considering the decayed condition of most of its food, a vulture's poor sense of smell may be a fortunate limitation. Vultures nest in any convenient place; both parents care for the young.

The Hebrew word usually translated "eagle" in the OT may have been a general term for all large birds of prey, including vultures. Thus many of the passages about eagles may refer to either the eagle or the vulture (cf. Lv 11:13; Dt 14:12, NASB mg). Such passages include references to nesting habits (Jb 39:27-28; Jer 49:16; Ob 1:4), care for fledglings (Dt 32:11), powers of flight (Ex 19:4; Dt 28:49; Jb 9:26; Lam 4:19), and extremely high soaring altitude (Prv 23:5; 30:19; Is 40:31). Despite variations among translations, the vulture clearly belongs in the list of unclean birds because of its foul diet (Lv 11:13, 18; Dt 14:12, 17).

Several references to the eagle in the KJV have been changed to "vulture" in modern translations. The change seems appropriate in the references to the vulture as a sign of present or impending doom (Lam 4:19; Hos 8:1). Likewise the eye-plucking bird of Proverbs 30:17 is probably a vulture. The phrase "bald as the eagle" (Mi 1:16) clearly should read "bald as the vulture," since there are no bald eagles in Israel and most vultures are bald. Since the vulture, like the eagle, was a symbol of sovereignty and domination in the ancient Near East, some gods were represented as vultures. Thus Ezekiel's comparison of the kings of Babylon and Egypt to eagles may be conceived alternatively as comparisons to vultures (Ez 17:3, 7). Jesus' reference to the eagles congregating around corpses at the end times (Mt 24:28) should also be revised to vultures, since eagles are usually solitary eaters, whereas vultures generally flock together around carrion.

Several KJV references to vultures are usually translated "kite" or "falcon" in modern translations (cf. various versions of Lv 11:14; Dt 14:13; Jb 28:7; Is 34:15).

See also Eagle; Kestrel; Kite; Lammergeier; Vulture, Black, or Osprey; Vulture, Egyptian; Vulture, Griffon.

Vulture, Black, or Osprey Diurnal flesh eater, a little over three feet (.9 meter) long with a wingspread of over three yards (2.7 meters). The feathers of the black or osprey vulture (*Aegypius monachus*) are black and the head and upper part of the neck are bald like those of other carrion eaters. It nests in the Jordan River valley and seems to have been abundant in biblical times. Today it is quite rare. The black vulture is probably the osprey of Leviticus 11:13 and Deuteronomy 14:12.

See also Vulture (above).

Vulture, Egyptian Also known as the gier eagle or as pharaoh's hen. The plumage of the Egyptian vulture (*Neophron percnopterus*) is basically white with a naked head and yellow neck. The Egyptian vulture breaks bones left by other vultures. Its flight is slow and easy, and its voice is a croak. Measuring about 24 inches (61 centimeters) in length, it is the smallest of all the carrion-eating birds found in the Holy Land. It may be referred to in the list of unclean birds (Lv 11:18; Dt 14:17, "gier eagle," KJV; "carrion vulture," RSV, NASB, NLT). *See* Vulture (above).

Vulture, Griffon One of the largest flying birds in the Holy Land (*Gyps fulvus*). Until a generation ago, the griffon vulture was one of the most common birds in the Holy Land. Today it is on the verge of extinction. Many have been killed by eating poisonous bait meant for foxes and jackals. In addition, its reproduction is limited; the female lays only one or two eggs a year.

The griffon vulture measures about four feet (121.9 centimeters) in length and up to ten feet (3 meters) between wing tips. Its beak is extremely strong, and its short toes are fitted with blunt talons. It is a light-brown bird with a pale yellow head and neck that are almost bare, being covered only with a very fine down.

The griffon vulture feeds mostly on carrion, but also on locusts and small tortoises. It is able to go without food for several days with no ill effects, but when it does break its fast, it gorges itself. It is found especially in the region of the Sea of Galilee. Most biblical references to the vulture are likely to be to the griffon vulture.

See also Eagle; Vulture (above).

Water Hen Small water bird of the rail family. The water hen listed among unclean birds (Lv 11:18; Dt 14:16, RSV only) may be the biblical bird most difficult to identify. Several alternatives have been suggested, including the swan (KJV), one of the owls (NASB, NEB), or the marsh hen (TLB). Most scholars rule out the swan, since it is a vegetarian bird and thus should not be considered unclean. An owl remains a possibility.

The marsh hen is a rail, several species of which inhabit Israel. One of those species is the purple gallinule (*Porphyrio porphyrio*). Rails are very thin birds varying from 6 to 20 inches (15 to 51 centimeters) in length. They live in marshes, where they eat a great variety of animal and vegetable matter, thus making them a candidate for inclusion in the Mosaic lists of unclean animals.

See also Animals.

BIRSHA Ruler of Gomorrah in the days of Abraham and Lot. Birsha was one of five Canaanite city-kings who unsuccessfully rebelled against King Chedorlaomer of Elam and his three allies (Gn 14:2).

BIRTH*, New Means of receiving "spiritual life" and entering the kingdom of God (Jn 3:3-7). *See* Regeneration.

BIRTHRIGHT Right or privilege belonging to the first-born son in a Hebrew family. The eldest son ranked highest after the father and in the father's absence had the father's authority and responsibility, as illustrated by Reuben's relationship to his younger brothers (Gn 37:19-22, 28-30). However, because he later committed incest, Reuben forfeited his birthright (Gn 49:1-4). Next in line were Simeon, Levi, and Judah (Gn 29:31-35), but Jacob, their father, passed over Simeon and Levi because of their lack of character (Gn 49:5-7). Although he praised Judah (Gn 49:8-10), Jacob gave the birthright to his favorite son, Joseph (Gn 49:22-26; 1 Chr 5:1-2; cf. Gn 37:2-4).

Tablets recovered from Nuzi in Mesopotamia have shown that the birthright could be exchanged among members of the same family (cf. Gn 25:19-34). The holder of the birthright appears to have been in possession of the "teraphim," or household idols (31:19, 32, 34), which were small terra-cotta images, presumably of the particular deity worshiped locally. These tokens would reinforce the position and authority of the firstborn.

The birthright meant not only the honor of family leadership but also an inheritance of twice the amount received by every other son. In polygamous Israelite society the birthright belonged to the actual firstborn of the father and could not be transferred to the son of a favorite wife without just cause (Dt 21:15-17). However, the birthright did not belong to the firstborn son if his mother was a concubine or slave (Gn 21:9-13; Jgs 11:1-2). The rights of the firstborn son of a king included the right of succession to the throne (2 Chr 21:1-3). When King Rehoboam of Judah violated custom by making his favorite son, Abijah, his successor, he had to pay off his other sons to avoid trouble (11:18-23; 12:16).

In the NT, reference is made to the OT account of Esau, the son of the patriarch Isaac, who impulsively traded his birthright for a bowl of lentil stew (Heb 12:16-17; cf. Gn 25:19-34). Christians are warned not to throw away their inheritance of spiritual blessing from God the way Esau lost his birthright and his father's blessing (Gn 27).

See also Inheritance; Heir; Firstborn.

AN ETERNAL INHERITANCE
Jesus Christ's authority over heaven and earth results from his exalted status as the firstborn Son of the heavenly Father (Rom 8:29; Col 1:17-19; Heb 1:2-6). As the "second Adam," Christ is the firstborn from the dead by virtue of the resurrection (Rom 1:4; 1 Cor 15:20-28, 42-50; Eph 1:22). He has received the kingdom from his Father and rules as Lord of Lords (Acts 2:36; Phil 2:9-11; Rv 5:12-13; 19:16; cf. Dn 7:13-14, 26-27). Believers also share in this kingdom and inheritance and look forward to the consummation, when by virtue of union with Christ they shall receive their inheritance in full (Rom 4:13; Gal 3:29; Eph 1:18; Heb 11:16).

BIRZAITH, BIRZAVITH* Malchiel's son of Asher's tribe (1 Chr 7:31). Since parallel lists fail to mention him (Gn 46:17; Nm 26:44-47), it is possible that Birzaith (KJV "Birzavith") was the name of a city Malchiel

founded. If so, the city may have been northwest of Bethel, near Tyre, and is now called Birzeit.

BISHLAM Resident of the vicinity of Jerusalem who opposed the rebuilding of the city after the exile. He and his associates wrote a letter complaining about the rebuilding to the Persian king Artaxerxes (Ezr 4:7).

BISHOP* Official in the church whose qualifications are listed in 1 Timothy 3:2-7 and Titus 1:6-9. The Greek word from which the English title "bishop" and the adjective "episcopal" are derived is often translated in modern versions as "elder," "overseer," "shepherd," or "guardian," corresponding closely to the current term "pastor." Jesus is called "the Shepherd and Bishop of your souls" (1 Pt 2:25, KJV).

In the NT, "bishop," and "elder" refer to the same office, as shown by the apostle Paul's telling Titus to appoint "elders in every town" and then referring to those same individuals as "bishops" (Ti 1:5, 7). While at Miletus, Paul summoned the elders from the church at Ephesus and then addressed them as "overseers" or "guardians" (Acts 20:17, 28). In his letter to Philippi, Paul greeted the "bishops and deacons" (Phil 1:1). The fact that there were numerous bishops at Philippi, as well as in Ephesus, shows that the episcopal office had not yet developed into what it later became: a single bishop governing one or more churches.

Bishops obviously had positions of authority, but the duties of the office are not clearly defined in the NT. One task was to combat heresy (Ti 1:9) and to teach and expound the Scriptures (1 Tm 3:2). In addition, there is some evidence that a primary concern was with economic matters and the care of the poor, as well as with a general overseeing of the congregation. The lists of qualifications in Paul's letters to Timothy and Titus indicate that a bishop was considered a leader in the congregation and a representative to the non-Christian world. *See* Elder; Pastor; Presbyter.

BITHIAH Mered's wife. Bithiah may have been a princess, or the phrase "daughter of Pharaoh" (KJV) may merely indicate that she was Egyptian (1 Chr 4:17-18). Her name (meaning "daughter of Yah") seems to indicate that she was a Jewish convert.

BITHRON* Term in 2 Samuel 2:29 (KJV; NLT mg) whose meaning is uncertain. Abner, commander of Ishbosheth's army, fled through Bithron after losing a battle to David's army. The Hebrew root has the meaning "to cut into pieces." Three explanations have been suggested: (1) it refers to a valley, perhaps the Jabbok; (2) it is the area "cut off" by a great curve in the Jabbok River; (3) it refers to the first part of the day, "all through the morning" (NLT).

BITHYNIA Roman province located in the northwest corner of Asia Minor. The apostle Paul and Silas wanted to preach the gospel in Bithynia on Paul's second missionary journey but were prevented by the Holy Spirit from doing so (Acts 16:7). The apostle Peter may have ministered in Bithynia and other provinces of Asia Minor, since he addressed his first letter to believers there (1 Pt 1:1). Christianity entered Bithynia somehow, possibly through Peter.

Bithynia was occupied by a Thracian tribe that established a prosperous kingdom there in the third century BC. In 75 BC, when Bithynia's last king, Nicomedes III, willed his kingdom to the Roman people, it became part of the Roman Empire. For administrative purposes, it was generally linked with the province of Pontus to the east.

After NT times, Bithynia figured significantly in church history. Early in the second century, its Roman governor, Pliny the Younger, elicited from the emperor Trajan the earliest stated imperial policy on persecution of Christians. Later, the church councils of Nicaea (AD 325) and Chalcedon (451) were held in two of Bithynia's western cities. The Council of Nicaea declared the full deity of Christ; the Council of Chalcedon made pronouncements on the nature of the person of Christ and the canonicity of the 27 NT books.

The Roman province of Bithynia was bordered on the north by the Black Sea, on the west by the Propontis (modern Sea of Marmara), on the south by the province of Asia, and on the east by Galatia and Pontus. Bithynia was mountainous, with Mt Olympus in the south rising to 7,600 feet (2,315.5 meters), but had districts of great fertility near the seacoast and in its interior valleys. Besides producing fruit and grain, the province had fine marble quarries, good timber, and excellent pasturage. The principal river was the Sangarius (modern Sakarya), which flowed from south to north into the Black Sea. Transportation was largely along the river valleys.

BITTER HERBS Some kind of bitter vegetable(s), perhaps a certain variety of lettuce. The people of Israel were commanded to eat bitter herbs, roast lamb, and unleavened bread on the night when the Lord inflicted the plague of death on all the Egyptian firstborn (Ex 12:8-11).

See also Plants.

THE SIGNIFICANCE OF BITTER HERBS
The significance of the bitter herbs is not explained in the Exodus narrative. In the traditional interpretation, the herbs symbolize the bitterness of the Hebrews' experience of Egyptian bondage. The two other references to bitter herbs (Nm 9:11; Lam 3:15) shed no direct light upon the kind of plant or its significance. The Numbers passage specifies how the Passover commemoration was to be celebrated by persons unable to participate at the normally appointed time (Nm 9:6-12). The Lamentations passage describes the prophet Jeremiah's personal affliction. He pictures himself as suffering at the hands of the Lord who has filled him with bitterness. If the prophet's experience could be symbolized by reference to bitter herbs, it is reasonable that Israel's experience of slavery in Egypt might also have been symbolized in that way. After that night of the Hebrews' deliverance from bondage, the herbs were used annually in a commemorative observance of the Passover.

Today the Samaritans use the leaves of the wild lettuce plant as bitter herbs for their Passover observance. Jews of European origin customarily use red horseradish.

BITTERN* KJV translation for the Hebrew word that may designate some kind of bird (Is 14:23; 34:11). Most modern translations substitute the word "porcupine" in Isaiah 34:11.

See also Birds; Animals (Porcupine).

BITTERNESS OR JEALOUSY*, Water of OT "trial" procedure employed when a husband suspected his wife of adultery but had no evidence to support his suspicion. The ritual, described in Numbers 5:11-31, is thought by some scholars to belong to a class of procedures known as "trials by ordeal." Such an ordeal subjected an accused woman to some physical hazard for the purpose of

determining her guilt or innocence. The effect of the hazard-producing agent on the accused individual determined the verdict. The premise was that a higher power who knew the guilt or innocence of the accused would act to influence the outcome appropriately.

In Israel, as in many other ancient societies, women had few rights. An Israelite husband could resort to the trial procedure when he had no evidence of his wife's unfaithfulness but simply had a "spirit of jealousy" concerning her (Nm 5:11-14). Very likely a pregnant wife would be subjected to the ritual if her husband suspected the unborn child was not his own.

The suspicious husband brought his wife to the priest with a special offering of a coarse barley meal (Nm 5:15; cf. Lv 2; 5:11). The priest would take the woman and "set her before the Lord," mix "holy water" (probably from the tabernacle laver or basin) with dirt from the tabernacle floor, unbind the woman's hair (perhaps as a sign of shame), and place some of the barley meal offering in her hands (Nm 5:16-18). Then the priest made her swear an oath asserting that, if she had been unfaithful, drinking the "water of bitterness" would bring a curse upon her. She gave assent by saying "Amen, Amen" (vv 19-22). Somehow, after writing out the words of the curse, the priest washed them off into the water. After making a ceremonial offering of a handful of barley meal, the priest made the woman drink the water (vv 23-26). The effect of a guilty verdict was evidenced by bitter suffering, causing the woman to become infertile (v 27).

BITUMEN* Asphalt as found in its natural state; pitch, tar. "Bitumen" (KJV "slime") was used for mortar in the Tower of Babel's construction (Gn 11:3) and to seal the reed basket in which baby Moses was concealed (Ex 2:3). In Israel, the valley of Siddim was dotted with numerous bitumen pits into which a number of soldiers fell during Chedorlaomer's war against Sodom and Gomorrah (Gn 14:10).

See also Asphalt; Minerals and Metals.

BIZIOTHIAH, BIZJOTHJAH* Listed in Joshua 15:28 (KJV "Bizjothjah") as a city in the Negev Desert area of Judah. The Greek OT, called the Septuagint, has "and her daughters," which would mean that this was not a specific place but rather the cluster of villages surrounding Hazar-shual and Beersheba. Such a translation is possible with a slight adjustment to the Hebrew text. It is difficult to say how the Hebrew text originally read.

BIZTHA One of the seven eunuchs King Ahasuerus commanded to bring Queen Vashti to his drunken party (Est 1:10).

BLACK *See* Color.

BLACK OBELISK* Shaft of black limestone describing the military successes of Shalmaneser III of Assyria (858–824 BC) during the first 31 years of his reign. Six and a half feet (2 meters) high, smoothed off on its four sides, the obelisk has five rows of bas-reliefs extending around it with inscriptions between them written in cuneiform. The pictures show payment of tribute from five parts of Shalmaneser's Empire.

Of special interest to Bible students is the second row of reliefs, portraying King Jehu of the northern kingdom of Israel (2 Kgs 9–10) bowing before Shalmeneser, who is accompanied by 13 Israelites bearing tribute. The inscription identifies him as Jehu and lists the tribute brought as including silver and gold bowls and vases, tin, and a royal staff. The relief is the only contemporary representation of any Israelite king. Jehu is shown in a long fringed cloak, a pointed soft cap, and a short rounded beard. His payment of tribute dates to 841 BC, but there is no reference to it in the Bible.

BLASPHEMY Profane or contemptuous speech or writing about (or action toward) God. In a general sense, "blasphemy" can refer to any slander, including any word or action that insults or devalues another being. In Greek literature the term was used for insulting or deriding living or dead persons, but it was extended to cover the gods as well, including both doubting the power of and mocking the nature of a god.

In the OT, "blasphemy" always means to insult God, either by attacking him directly or mocking him indirectly. Either way the glory and honor of God are lessened, so blasphemy is the opposite of praise. An Israelite might directly insult the "Name" by cursing God (Lv 24:10-16) or deliberately disobey God's law (Nm 15:30). Either of those blasphemies was punishable by death, as was idolatry, the ultimate blasphemy (Is 66:3). It was thought that Gentiles, who had never experienced the power and majesty of the Lord, were the most likely blasphemers. Thus the king of Assyria blasphemed in equating the Lord with the gods of the nations he had already conquered (2 Kgs 19:4-6, 22). For his arrogance the king was doomed by the word of the prophet Isaiah. God was also mocked when Israel was exiled (Is 52:5), when Edom derided the desolate "mountains of Israel" (Ez 35:12, KJV), and when the enemy scoffed that God had not protected Jerusalem (Ps 74:18; 1 Macc 2:6).

In the NT, blasphemy takes on the wider Greek meaning, for it includes slandering a human being (Mt 15:19; see also Rom 3:8; 1 Cor 10:30; Eph 4:31; Ti 3:2), as well as God. It even includes mocking angelic or demonic powers, which is just as wrong as mocking any other being (2 Pt 2:10-12, Jude 1:8-10). In other words, slander, derision, and mocking of any kind are totally condemned in the NT.

The most common form of blasphemy in the NT is blasphemy against God. One might insult God directly (Rv 13:6; 16:9), mock his word (Ti 2:5), or reject his revelation and its bearer (Acts 6:11). Jesus was accused of blasphemy when he claimed to have a prerogative belonging to God—the power to forgive sins (Mk 2:7). John 10:33-36 reports an attempt to stone Jesus; his accusers said to him, "You, being a man, make yourself God" (v 33). Jesus was condemned by the highest Jewish court, the Sanhedrin, on the charge of blasphemy, because he claimed to be the Son of Man (the Messiah) but in their view had given no evidence that he was such an exalted personage, thus appearing to mock the Messiah and, by extension, to mock God himself (Mk 14:64).

Naturally the early Christians viewed Jesus' trial from another perspective: the guards insulting Jesus (Lk 22:64-65) and the crowds and two dying robbers mocking him on the cross (Mk 15:29-32) were the real blasphemers. Observing how their Lord had been treated, the church was prepared to accept insult as their own lot, both personally (1 Cor 4:13; 1 Tm 1:13; Rv 2:9) and as a response to their message (Acts 13:45; 18:6). On the other hand, the church recognized that even Christians could blaspheme by giving way under persecution (26:11), by teaching false doctrine (2 Pt 2:2), or by behaving in an unbecoming fashion, which would bring others to think less of Christ (Rom 2:24; Ti 2:5).

The Bible makes clear that blasphemy is forgivable (Mt 12:32; Mk 3:28-29), but if a person will not repent, the only remedy is to turn him or her over to Satan to be taught the lesson (1 Tm 1:20).

BLASPHEMY AGAINST THE HOLY SPIRIT
This is a sin mentioned only in Mark 3:28-29 and its parallels, Luke 12:10 and Matthew 12:31. The context in Mark portrays unbelievers reacting to Jesus' sudden popularity and startling power in two ways: (1) his family considered him insane and tried to take him home; and (2) the religious leaders, who had already proclaimed him a blasphemer (Mk 2:1-12), attributed his success to demon-possession. Matthew adds that the religious leaders were Pharisees upset by a particular healing. (Luke includes the saying in a totally different context, one of confessing Christ.) Jesus, pointing out that the charge of demon-possession was illogical, also stated strongly that blasphemy against the Holy Spirit can never be forgiven. Jesus was saying that to slander the Holy Spirit is worse even than insulting or blaspheming the Son of Man or God himself (a crime punishable by death in the OT; see Lv 24:16). Yet Jesus said that those sins are forgivable. Many Jews believed that death forgave all sins, so when Jesus called blasphemy against the Holy Spirit "an eternal sin," he was making it serious indeed.

The religious leaders to whom Jesus spoke had seen clear, public, and compelling evidence of the good hand of God. By calling that power evil or demonic, they were wickedly and consciously rejecting God, his power, and his saving grace. That was willful and high-handed sin by those who had seen the truth but rejected it and slandered it to others. Thus, the "unforgivable sin" is not some serious moral failure nor persistence in a particular sin nor even insulting or rejecting Jesus in blindness or a fit of rebellion. It is conscious rejection of the "good power of God." It represents a perversion of the mind in which God and Satan are *willfully* confused, a free choice of evil rather than good.

How can this sin be unforgivable if God is always willing to forgive? Because it has gone beyond the possibility of recovery on the sinner's part and because God respects the freedom of persons. It is unrepentable because the person, having refused so stubbornly to repent, finally becomes unable to repent; evidence is in, and such a one will still reject the truth while knowing it to be true.

From the definition it is clear that anyone who believes he or she has committed "the unforgivable sin" could *not* have done so; a troubled conscience and that kind of sin could never coexist. The fact that a person feels remorse proves that blasphemy against the Holy Spirit has not yet been committed. On the other hand, Jesus' teaching about it warns all who know the truth of God not to reject that truth or to abandon their faith.

BLASTUS Royal secretary to Herod Agrippa I (Acts 12:20). The cities of Tyre and Sidon were looked down upon by Herod, so when their delegates wanted an appointment with the king when he was in nearby Caesarea, they approached him through Blastus. Herod addressed them and was struck by a fatal illness for accepting their worship (vv 21-23).

BLESS, BLESSING Pronouncement of the favor of God upon an assembled congregation. Worship services, especially observances of Holy Communion in Eastern Orthodox, Roman Catholic, and most Protestant churches, usually end with a blessing spoken by the senior clergyman present. This pronouncement (called "blessing" in the Roman Catholic, Eastern Orthodox, and Anglican churches and "benediction" in most Protestant churches) is based upon the widespread biblical precedent of blessing (Gn 27:27-29; Nm 6:22-27; Lk 24:50; 2 Cor 13:11, 14; Phil 4:7; 2 Thes 2:16-17; Heb 13:20-21).

The practice of benediction or blessing is often regarded merely as a ritual of dismissal, but it is actually a pronouncement of God's gracious favor, to be given only by his ministers on the authority of Holy Scripture to faithful believers. In this action Christians are assured that the grace of God the Father, the love of the Son, and the communion of the Holy Spirit are with them.

The term "blessing" is also applied to thanksgiving for food and drink (Mt 14:19; Mk 8:7; Lk 24:30).

See also Beatitudes, The.

BLINDNESS Condition of lacking the ability to see. Physical blindness was common in the ancient Near East and is still prevalent among the poor and tribal peoples lacking the benefits of modern medicine.

Medical causes of blindness are not specified in the Bible, but poor personal hygiene and unsanitary living conditions were undoubtedly contributing factors. Newborn babies were especially susceptible. Much blindness from birth (Jn 9:1-3) was probably gonorrhea of the eyes. In the birth process germs from the mother passed to the eyes of the infant, where they found an ideal medium for growth. Within three days inflammation, pus and swelling would be evident. In such cases, primitive treatment could not prevent some permanent or even total damage to the eye. Modern medical practice treats all newborn babies with antiseptic eyedrops; but such treatment is not always available to the poor, or is rejected by them in parts of the Middle East today. Babies and young children have also been threatened by infectious ophthalmia. Carried by flies, that disease causes heavy crusting, droopy eyelids, loss of eyelashes, and eventually clouding of the cornea, often leading to total blindness. In parts of the world one may still see a mother (because of folk superstition) permitting flies to swarm continuously on her baby's face even as she holds the infant in her lap. Blindness among adults might be due to side effects from illnesses such as malaria, long exposure to sandstorms and sun glare in the desert, accidents, punishment (as with Samson, Jgs 16:21), or old age (Gn 27:1; 1 Sm 4:15; 1 Kgs 14:4).

The OT demanded special consideration for the blind (Lv 19:14) and imposed punishment for misleading a blind person (Dt 27:18). A blind man, considered defective, was not permitted to serve as a priest (Lv 21:18).

Jesus' healing ministry brought sight to the blind in fulfillment of prophecy (Lk 4:18). His ability to restore vision was one of the proofs given to John the Baptist that Jesus was the Messiah (Mt 11:5). Jesus healed two blind men in Galilee (9:27-30), one blind man in Bethsaida (Mk 8:22-26), a man blind from birth in Jerusalem (Jn 9), and a blind beggar named Bartimaeus and his friend at Jericho (Mk 10:46-52; cf. Mt 20:30-34; Lk 18:35-43). At times Jesus commanded immediate restoration (Mk 10:52). On other occasions he used "means" such as clay and water (Jn 9:6-11) or his own saliva (Mk 8:23). The apostle Paul was blinded at his conversion and received a miraculous cure in the presence of Ananias (Acts 9:1-9, 18). Paul later afflicted a sorcerer, Elymas, with temporary blindness for opposing his ministry on the island of Cyprus (13:11).

See also Medicine and Medical Practice; Disease.

SPIRITUAL BLINDNESS
Spiritual blindness is a figurative way of defining the lost and hopeless condition of sinful humanity. Such blindness includes willful rejection of God's revelation in his creation and in Scripture, and an inability to see the truth of the gospel. Moses spoke of Israel's apostasy as "blindness" (Dt 29:4); Isaiah called it "dim" eyes (see Is 6:10, NASB). Jesus charged the Pharisees with unbelief that made them "blind guides of the blind" (Mt 15:14; 23:16). Spiritual blindness is related to "hardness of heart" (Mk 8:17-18; Eph 4:17-18) and is understood as the judgment of God both upon unbelievers (Rom 1:20-21) and upon Israel (Is 29:10; Rom 11:7-8). According to Paul, it is also the work of Satan, who "has blinded the minds of those who don't believe" (2 Cor 4:4). Healing from spiritual blindness is a special gift of God's grace through the "new birth" (Jn 3:3) and by seeing "the glorious light of the Good News" (2 Cor 4:4, NLT).

BLOOD Fluid that circulates through the body of a person or a vertebrate animal. Aside from reference to the common physical substance, the term "blood" has a number of metaphorical uses in the Bible. At times, it refers to a red color: "the sun will be turned into darkness, and the moon will turn bloodred" (Acts 2:20, NLT). The "blood of the grape" means wine (Dt 32:14, RSV). In the NT the expression "flesh and blood" refers to human life, to "natural" humanity: "Flesh and blood has not revealed this to you, but my Father who is in heaven" (Mt 16:17, RSV; see also 1 Cor 15:50; Gal 1:16; Eph 6:12). After betraying Jesus, Judas recognized that he had "sinned in betraying innocent blood" (Mt 27:4, RSV). In such passages "blood" has reference to life lived at the human level, natural life as opposed to spiritual or divine life.

The term "blood" is also used in the sense of shedding blood, that is, in killing or murder. Psalm 9:12 speaks of one "who avenges blood." Genesis 37:26 refers to the brothers who concealed Joseph's blood, that is, his murder. To be "burdened with the blood of another" (Prv 28:17, RSV) means to be guilty of murder. At the crucifixion Pilate said, "I am innocent of the blood of this man" (Mt 27:24-25). Thus, the idea of violent death is regularly connected with blood.

The logic of such expressions becomes particularly clear when one sees how closely life is associated with blood. Three passages specifically tie the two together. "Only you shall not eat flesh with its life, that is, its blood" (Gn 9:4, RSV). "For the life of the flesh is in the blood" (Lv 17:11, RSV). "The only restriction is never to eat the blood, for the blood is the life" (Dt 12:23, TLB). Because God is the author of all life, any shedding of blood (any killing) is a serious matter. A certain sanctity associated with blood forms the basis for prohibitions against eating it. (Compare what the apostles said in Acts 15:20.) Blood stands for the "life principle" that is from God.

Because of its association with life, blood takes on a special significance in the sacrificial motif. On the Day of Atonement (Lv 16), the blood of a bull and of a goat was sprinkled upon the altar as a "covering" of the people's sin. Life was poured out in death. Animal life was given up on behalf of the life of the people. Judgment and atonement were carried out through a transfer of the sin of the people to the animal sacrifice. Transference is depicted also by the scapegoat in the same ceremony (Lv 16:20-22). In the first Passover (Ex 12:1-13), the blood bore the same meaning. Animal blood posted on each door was a sign that a death had already taken place, so the angel of death passed over.

Further, because life is connected with blood, blood becomes the supreme offering to God. In the ratification of the covenant (Ex 24), Moses poured half the sacrificial blood on the altar; after reading the covenant to the people and receiving their affirmative response, he sprinkled the rest of the blood on them and said, "This blood confirms the covenant the LORD has made with you in giving you these laws" (Ex 24:8, NLT). Sprinkling blood on both the altar and the people bound God and the Israelites together in covenant relationship. In the sacrifices of Israel, blood stood for death and depending on the context, might also stand for judgment, sacrifice, substitution, or redemption. Life with God was made possible by blood.

In the NT, apart from medical references (e.g., Mt 9:20) and references to murder (e.g., Acts 22:20), the primary reference is to the blood of Christ, an allusion to the OT motifs. The synoptic Gospels show that at the Last Supper Jesus spoke of his blood with reference to a new covenant (Mt 26:28; Mk 14:24; Lk 22:20). The language surrounding those sayings reveals the sacrificial motif; Jesus was speaking of his death and its redemptive significance. The fourth Gospel expresses the same theology in different terms and in a different context: "Unless you eat the flesh of the Son of Man and drink his blood, you cannot have eternal life within you" (Jn 6:53, NLT). The believer is said to participate by faith in the death and resurrection of the Lord (see also 1 Cor 10:16).

The apostle Paul's letters likewise associate blood with Christ's death, so much so that the word becomes—like the term "cross"—synonymous with the death of Christ in its saving significance: making peace "by means of his blood on the cross" (Col 1:20, NLT); and in a passage on reconciliation: "though you once were far away from God, now you have been brought near to him because of the blood of Christ" (Eph 2:13, NLT). "Blood" and "cross" both stand for the death of Jesus in reconciling Jew and Gentile to God and in the creation of a new humanity. Paul evidently had in mind the sacrifice of the Day of Atonement when he said that God purposed that Christ be an atoning sacrifice by his blood (Rom 3:25). His vocabulary (from Lv 16) focused on the most important sacrifice of Jewish tradition.

Peter made reference to the blood of the covenant (Ex 24) when he described Christian exiles as having been sprinkled with the blood of Christ (1 Pt 1:2). He reminded his readers that they had been redeemed by that blood (v 19). In calling Christ the "spotless lamb of God," he may have had in mind either the servant of Isaiah 53 or the Passover lamb, both of which had redemptive significance in his readers' minds. Finally, to the writer of Hebrews the whole OT system of sacrifices found its ultimate fulfillment in the blood of Christ, that is, in his sacrificial death (Heb 9:7-28; 13:11-12).

Thus, NT references to the blood of Christ point to the culminating and comprehensive redemption achieved by God in the death of his Son (Heb 10:20). Both justice and justification were thus achieved (Rom 3:26). The blood of Christ is therefore called the "once for all" means of redemption (Heb 9:26). See Atonement; Offerings and Sacrifices.

BLOOD*, Avenger of
Person who sought justice by killing a murderer. The avenger of blood was usually the nearest relative of the one who had been murdered. The Mosaic law regulated this kind of vengeance killing. See Avenger of Blood.

BLOOD, Field of
Name given to the field purchased with the "blood money" Judas accepted to betray Jesus (Mt 27:8; Acts 1:19). The field was purchased by the chief priests as a burial ground for strangers (formerly, the potter's field). Judas hanged himself and his intestines burst open there. This account uses the Aramaic expression Akeldama (KJV "Aceldama"), translated "field of blood." The Akeldama is situated on the southern slope of the valley of Hinnom near the Kidron Valley.

BLOOD*, Flow of
1. Vaginal discharge such as that during menstruation. Leviticus 15 contains social and sanitary laws that God gave to Moses concerning genital discharges. A woman with vaginal bleeding was considered ceremonially unclean during bleeding and for seven days afterward. She could not go to the tabernacle or temple for worship while unclean or mingle with crowds in the street or market. Anyone touching her or her clothes, bed, chair, and the like was also ceremonially unclean (Lv 15:19-28). Sexual intercourse was not allowed while the woman was ceremonially unclean. Seven days after her bleeding stopped, a woman would present to the priest two turtledoves or young pigeons as offerings to atone for the time of her uncleanness (Lv 15:29-30).

Jesus' miraculous healing of a woman who had been hemorrhaging (slowly or intermittently) for 12 years was recorded in three of the four Gospels (Mt 9:20-22; Mk 5:25-34; Lk 8:43-48). If her bleeding was vaginal, the years of ceremonial uncleanness and separation must have been particularly distressing for her. Besides being anxious and uncomfortable, she would also have been unable to bear children. Further, she had "suffered a great deal from many doctors" and "had spent everything she had to pay for them, but she had gotten no better" (Mk 5:26). In despair she ignored the rules about uncleanness and made her way through a crowd to touch Jesus. When she touched him, the bleeding stopped immediately and permanently.

2. Bloody stools. The "bloody flux" (KJV) from which Publius's father suffered was some form of dysentery (Acts 28:8).

See also Medicine and Medical Practice; Hemorrhage.

BLOODGUILT*
Term used in some English Bibles to translate a Hebrew word meaning "blood" or "bloods" (Ex 22:2-3; Lv 17:4; 1 Sm 25:26, 33; Hos 12:14). The translation "bloodguiltiness" occurs only in Psalm 51:14. The plural form almost invariably means the shedding of blood, but the singular can mean blood itself, bloodshed, or the guilt incurred by bloodshed (i.e., by killing). The idea that killing was punishable by death pervades the Bible; killing was generally done by literally shedding another's blood.

The first category of bloodshed resulting in bloodguilt was deliberate homicide, murder "in cold blood," as moderns say, or of "innocent blood," as the OT says (Jon 1:14). Several passages define the shedding of innocent blood and its punishment (Gn 9:6; Dt 19:11-13; 2 Kgs 24:4; Ez 33:6). The Bible prohibits any ransom for a murderer (Nm 35:31).

Another category was accidental homicide (Nm 35:9-28, Dt 19:4-10). After an accidental killing, the "avenger of blood" might retaliate if he caught the offender outside a city of refuge. If the murderer was unknown, the town nearest the discovered corpse assumed the guilt; Deuteronomy 21:1-9 prescribes a ceremony for removing such guilt.

In ancient Israel it was possible to shed the blood of an animal and incur bloodguilt (Lv 17:3-4, 10-11). An animal that was legally guilty of bloodshed was to be stoned (Ex 21:28-29). Exceptions to bloodguilt were made in the case of self-defense (22:2), capital punishment (Lv 20:9-16), and war (1 Kgs 2:5-6). Frequently the prophets would use the Hebrew word for "bloods" or "blood" to speak of the whole nation's guilt (Is 1:15; 4:4; Ez 7:23; 9:9; Hos 1:4; 4:2, KJV; Mi 3:10; Hab 2:8, 12, 17; and many others). Other crimes beside bloodshed could bring on a death sentence (Lv 20:9-16; Ez 18:10-13). Such crimes included honoring pagan deities, worshiping idols, adultery, robbery, oppressing the poor, breach of promise, and usury.

From the beginning (Gn 4:10-12), through the Prophets (Is 26:21; Ez 24:6-9), and into the NT (Rv 6:10), the Bible supports the idea that God will avenge wrongs and punish those guilty of bloodshed.

See also Cities of Refuge; Criminal Law and Punishment.

THE BLOODY-SWEAT PASSAGE
This is the name for Luke 22:43-44, which speaks of Jesus sweating, as it were, drops of blood. But the genuineness of this passage is doubted—at least, as to Lucan authorship. Several important manuscripts do not include the passage: P69, P75, Codex Sinaiticus, Codex Vaticanus, Codex Borgianus, and Codex Washingtonianus—manuscripts dating from the second to the fifth century. Other signs of its doubtfulness appear in manuscripts marking the passage with obeli (symbols), including 0171 (dated around 300) or crossing out the passage (as was done by the first corrector of Codex Sinaiticus). Writing in the fourth century, Epiphanius (*Ancoratus* 31.4-5) indicated that the verses were found in some "uncorrected copies" of Luke. But other early church fathers (Justin, Irenaeus, Hippolytus, Dionysius, Eusebius) acknowledged this portion as part of Luke's Gospel.

The debate about the genuiness of this passage has focused on what view one takes concerning whether or not Jesus needed to have been strengthened by angels during his trial in the Garden of Gethsemane. Some have said that the passage was excised because certain Christians thought that the account of Jesus overwhelmed with human weakness was incompatible with his deity. But it is more likely that the passage was an early (second century) interpolation, added from an oral tradition concerning the life of Jesus. Its transposition to Matthew 26 in some manuscripts and lectionaries indicates that it was a free-floating passage that could be interjected into any of the Passion narratives.

Despite the textual evidence against the passage, most English versions have kept it in the text for the sake of tradition. Therefore, many Christians consider this detail about Jesus' Passion to be authentic. However, it is often interpreted incorrectly to say that Jesus was in such agony that he was sweating blood (technically called hemohydrosis or hematidrosis); that is why the passage is often called "the bloody-sweat" text. But the text says that he was sweating so profusely that it looked like blood dripping from a wound, not that his sweat became dripping blood.

BLOODY SWEAT* Rare medical condition called hemohydrosis, thought to result from hemorrhage of small blood vessels into the sweat glands. It occurs only in extreme emotional stress and is of biblical interest because of the reference to Jesus in the Garden of Gethsemane before his betrayal: "And being in agony He was praying very fervently; and His sweat became like drops of blood, falling down upon the ground" (Lk 22:44, NASB). Although some translations make it appear that Jesus actually sweat blood, the Greek text is clearly making a comparison. That is, sweat poured off of Jesus "as though he were bleeding," an apt analogy for Luke, a physician, to make.

BLUE *See* Color.

BOANERGES* Name meaning "sons of thunder" given by Jesus to James and John, Zebedee's sons (Mk 3:17). Its derivation is uncertain. The name may have referred to the volatile personalities of the two brothers (Lk 9:54), to their possible revolutionary past as Zealots, or even to a "thundering" style of speech.

See also James (Person); John, The Apostle.

BOAR Wild or domesticated animal of the swine family (Ps 80:13). *See* Animals (Pig).

BOAST To speak of deeds, abilities, or characteristics in a manner showing pride or self-satisfaction. In the Bible the word also has a more positive connotation ("to glory in").

In the OT, "boasting" is often used to describe the basic attitude of the ungodly, who depend on their own resources rather than on God (Pss 52:1; 94:3-4). Enemies of Israel boasted of their victories and claimed the glory for themselves (Dt 32:27; Pss 10:3; 35:26; 73:9; Is 3:9). They boasted of their riches (Ps 49:6) and wisdom (Is 19:11). According to the Lord, the rich and wise are to "boast about this: that he understands and knows me, that I am the LORD, who exercises kindness, justice and righteousness on the earth" (Jer 9:24, NIV).

Jesus depicted a proud Pharisee boasting to God in prayer (Lk 18:10-14). Most of the NT usages of the word occur in the apostle Paul's letters. The negative aspect of vaunting one's own accomplishments is contrasted with the positive counterpart of glorying in what the Lord has done (Rom 3:27-28; 2 Cor 10:17; Gal 6:14). Selfrighteousness and bragging are to be avoided (Rom 1:30; 2:17, 23; Eph 2:9; 2 Tm 3:2). Paul associated boasting with the attitude of those Jews who developed a feeling of self-confidence because of having kept the law. For Paul, the only legitimate boasting was to boast (rejoice) in the Lord (Rom 5:11). In Romans 5:3, the rabbinic view of glorying in one's sufferings is contrasted with Paul's view that his present sufferings pointed to God's power and toward Paul's hope for the future.

Paul's boasting was not based upon comparisons with others, in contrast to the boasting of his opponents. Because Christ worked through him (2 Cor 3:2-6) and God commended him (10:18), he could give glory to God. Paul preferred to boast of his own weakness, and of the Lord's power and strength (12:5, 9).

On occasion, the apostle did boast concerning a particular group of Christians (7:4, 14; 8:24; 9:2-3), but with the implication that he was expressing confidence in *them*, not bragging about his own successes. Concerning himself, Paul boasted reluctantly and only as a means of defense against an unsupportive element in the Corinthian church. He said that those who should have commended him had instead compelled him to engage in "foolish" boasting (2 Cor 12:11).

See also Pride.

BOAT Small watercraft. Boats mentioned in the Bible were propelled by oars or sails and used for fishing or travel, or as lifeboats on larger vessels. *See* Travel.

BOAZ (Person) Salmon's son of Judah's tribe (Ru 4:18-22). Boaz lived in Bethlehem in the days of the judges and married Ruth, a Moabite woman. Boaz was an ancestor of Christ (Mt 1:5; Lk 3:32) and a wealthy relative by marriage of Ruth's mother-in-law, Naomi. Ruth attracted the attention of Boaz when she was gleaning in one of his fields (Ru 2). His kindness to Ruth convinced Naomi that Boaz might be willing to redeem some land her husband had owned and at the same time accept the levirate marriage with Ruth that such a transaction required.

See also Ruth, Book of; Marriage, Marriage Customs; Genealogy of Jesus Christ.

BOAZ (Pillar) Name (meaning "strength") given to one of the two pillars erected in front of King Solomon's temple (1 Kgs 7:21; 2 Chr 3:17). *See* Temple; Jachin and Boaz.

BOCHERU* Azel's son, a descendant of King Saul (1 Chr 8:38; 9:44).

BOCHIM* Place near Gilgal mentioned in Judges 2:1-5 where the angel of the Lord confronted the nation of Israel with their failure to drive out the Canaanite inhabitants of the land. For their disobedience, judgment was pronounced. The heathen peoples would become "thorns" in their sides, and their gods, "snares." The people wept, and the place was named "Bochim," meaning "weepers." Many scholars feel Bochim was merely another name for Bethel. This is supported by the Septuagint, which reads Bethel in this passage.

BODILY PRESENCE* Phrase used to describe the relation of Christ's body to the elements of the Lord's Supper. *See* Lord's Supper, The.

BODILY RESURRECTION OF CHRIST* *See* Resurrection.

BODY Term used biblically in several different ways, including certain metaphorical or theological expressions. Many of the biblical references illustrate special features of Hebrew thought about human life.

In the Old Testament The OT writers used a number of Hebrew words translated "body" in English versions, mostly with reference to physical life. The body suffers; it is plagued with illness or is injured. Sometimes it is dead, that is, a corpse or carcass. Reference is even made to the "bodies" of spiritual beings—of the cherubim in Ezekiel's vision (Ez 1:11) and of an angel (Dn 10:6). Jeremiah spoke of the bodies of pagan gods, referring to their images in the form of idols (Jer 10:1-16). Such usages indicate that the Hebrews thought of all beings, whether heavenly or earthly, as embodied.

At times, the word "body" is close to the meaning of "flesh," and frequently the same Hebrew word lies behind both terms. "Body" is man in his total physical experience. "Flesh" is generally used to refer to the sinfulness or creatureliness of man.

Human beings have bodies and a bodily existence; each person also has a spirit and a spiritual dimension in life. But in Scripture the two are not set over against each other or viewed as separate "parts" of man. The body is not seen as a hindrance to the soul (as in much Greek thought). Not until the intertestamental period did Jewish writers begin to speak of the body as evil or as something set over against the soul.

In the New Testament Though "body" is used in the NT in the same ways as in the OT, the concept is given new significance. The body of Jesus (i.e., his corpse) was taken down from the cross (Mk 15:43). A body could experience illness and healing (5:29) and needed to be clothed (Jas 2:16); yet the body (i.e., physical life) is more than clothing (Mt 6:25). Jesus said not to fear those who kill the body but cannot kill the soul; rather, fear those who can destroy both soul and body in hell (10:28).

At the Lord's Supper Jesus said with reference to the bread, "This is my body," and then added—with the cup in his hand—"This is my blood" (Mk 14:22, 24). Those terms from the OT sacrificial system were intended to underscore the sacrificial significance of Jesus' death. Under both the old and new covenants, a real, physical life was offered in death for the sake of the "covenant people."

The apostle Paul made the term "body" a fundamental reference in the understanding of Christian experience. Most of the NT references to "body" are in his letters.

The Sinful Body In Romans 6:6 Paul spoke of the destruction of the "sinful body." The phrase did not mean that the body itself is sinful, as though sin is in some way tied to physical matter. Neither did it refer to some entity, sin, thought to dwell within human nature. Nor did it personify sin. Rather, the phrase referred to the physical life of human beings—life on earth—which is dominated by sin's influence. In Christian conversion Paul saw that familiar pattern of human experience being destroyed. To link sin with the body is only to recognize that human beings in their earthly life ("life in the body") are pervasively sinful. After describing the awful conflict in human experience, Paul cried out, "Who will deliver me from this body of death?" (Rom 7:24, RSV). Human life, "spoiled" by sin and its consequences at every point, requires Christ's redemption (7:25–8:4).

The Body of the Believer In conversion, believers are said by Paul to experience not only the "saving of the soul" but also the transformation of present life. They have died to sin and have been freed from sin's bondage. Paul therefore called for holiness of life "in the flesh." "Let not sin therefore reign in your mortal bodies, to make you obey their passions" (Rom 6:12, RSV). Righteousness, not sin, is to govern a Christian's physical experience. The social and personal lives of believers are to be characterized by holiness. Believers are in the world (Jn 17:11) and are to live for God in the world (i.e., in their bodily existence); they are not to be indifferent to the world.

Physical, earthly life thus takes on new significance. Paul told Christians to present their bodies as a living sacrifice (Rom 12:1). Each individual human life is to be a "living sacrifice" to God. Far from deprecating earthly existence, Paul saw that in Christ it had new potential. The reason is that the Holy Spirit is found there. "Your body is a temple of the Holy Spirit within you, which you have from God" (1 Cor 6:19, RSV). That affirmation is not to be read materialistically, as though the Spirit takes up residence in certain tissues; "body" means one's whole physical, earthly existence.

Paul also anticipated an ultimate transformation of life in the body through Christ. He spoke of the "redemption of our bodies" (Rom 8:23) and of the transformation of "our lowly bodies to be like his glorious body" (Phil 3:21). The Bible, although it has a realistic view of human sin and physical deterioration, does not share the pessimism of worldviews that seek escape from the world.

The Resurrection Body The possible separation of body and soul did not occur to the Hebrew mind. Biblically, life beyond death is not bodiless but an existence for which a "new body" is prepared. Though Paul raised many questions in 1 Corinthians 15:35-57, it is clear that he saw continuity between the earthly body and the resurrection body. "It is sown a physical body, it is raised a spiritual body" (v 44). That expression may be derived in large part from the experience of Jesus, whose dead body was not only brought to life but also transformed so that it was not bound by earth. His resurrection body was derived from the earthly. But Paul was sure that in the promised resurrection, life would return to the body without its present limitations and with new manifestations. Death, said Paul, is thereby "swallowed up in victory" (v 54).

See also Resurrection; Body of Christ; Church; Man.

BODY OF CHRIST Scriptural phrase referring to (1) the physical body of Jesus Christ, (2) his broken body and shed blood viewed symbolically and memorially in the bread and wine of the Lord's Supper, and (3) both the local and universal church viewed metaphorically.

The Physical Body of Jesus Christ The NT declares that the Son (the second person of the Trinity) had a human body prepared for him by God the Father (Heb 10:5). The earthly body was engendered by the conceptive work of the Holy Spirit through the virgin Mary (Mt 1:20); the one thus born, humanly speaking, as a descendant of David (Rom 1:3), was also to be called the Son of God (Lk 1:35). The apostle John emphasized that the body of Christ was really human physically, not something gaseous or ethereal (1 Jn 4:2-3) as some persons in John's day were already beginning to argue. God "became flesh and dwelt among us" (Jn 1:14; cf. Is 53:1-4). Jesus' earthly body possessed ordinary human characteristics and limitations. That is, as a real human being, Jesus Christ experienced sorrow (Jn 11:35; Heb 5:7-8), weariness (Jn 4:6), thirst (19:28), and pain (vv 1-3).

When Jesus gave up his spirit, his physical body died on the cross (Jn 19:30, 33). The NT proclaims that he bore the sins of the world in his body on the cross (1 Pt 2:24; 1 Jn 2:2; cf. Is 53:5-6). His death is described as a perfect sacrifice for sinners (Heb 9:12-14, 26-28), a sacrifice of his body that makes believers in him holy and righteous (2 Cor 5:21; Heb 10:10).

Christ's physical body was prepared in the normal way for burial (Mt 27:59; Mk 15:46; Lk 23:53, 56; 24:1; Jn 19:39-40) and placed in the rock tomb of Joseph of Arimathea (Mt 27:57-60; Jn 19:41). On the third day the body of Christ experienced a real physical resurrection, as he had predicted (Jn 2:19-22). He was seen in his physical resurrection body (Mt 28:9; Lk 24:31, 36; Jn 20:10-19, 26). He was heard, touched, and held onto (Mt 28:9; Lk 24:39; Jn 20:17; 1 Jn 1:1). He offered his body, scarred by his crucifixion, to be touched (Lk 24:39; Jn 20:17). The fact that he ate shows that his resurrection body was a physical one (Lk 24:42-43). In addition, Christ's body was "glorified," that is, it was not restricted

as ordinary bodies are: he entered and left rooms in a remarkable way (Lk 24:31, 36; Jn 20:19, 26). Christ's bodily resurrection is said in Scripture to guarantee that believers in Christ will experience resurrection of their own bodies (1 Cor 15:20-23, 50-57; Phil 3:20-21).

The Body of Christ in the Lord's Supper At the last supper (Mt 26:26-29; Mk 14:22-25; Lk 22:15-20; 1 Cor 11:23-26), which accompanied the Passover supper, Jesus held up a loaf of bread and said, "This is my body"; then he picked up a cup of wine and said, "This is my blood of the covenant" (Mt 26:26, 28). Jesus meant that the bread symbolized his body, which would be broken when he was beaten at his trial and pierced at his crucifixion (Lk 23:33; Jn 19:1-2). The apostle Paul said that Christ, our paschal lamb, was sacrificed for us (1 Cor 5:7), meaning that the Passover lamb in the OT was an object lesson pointing to "the Lamb of God, who takes away the sin of the world!" (Jn 1:29).

For Christians, the body of Christ is viewed symbolically as a broken body (Mt 8:17; 1 Pt 2:24; cf. Is 53:4-5) in the breaking of the bread at the Lord's Supper. The cup is a sign of his blood poured out, viewed as the central factor in God's covenant of grace with his people. Jesus referred to "the new covenant in my blood" (Lk 22:20). The whole ceremony of the Lord's Supper was also to be a memorial (1 Cor 11:25-26). In the ceremony believers are reminded that Christ died for sinners, that is, for the forgiveness of their sins (Mt 26:28). They are also reminded that they are participating in the body of Christ in that they are united with him (Rom 6:1-11; 1 Cor 10:16; Gal 2:20; Phil 3:10).

The Body of Christ, the People of God The phrase "body of Christ" is also used as a metaphor for the whole church, a unity of believers connected with and dependent on Christ. God's people are thus said to be members of Christ's "mystical body" (1 Cor 12:27), in fellowship with Christ and spiritually nourished by him (Eph 5:25, 29). A number of other metaphors are also used for the whole people of God, such as the vine (Ps 80:8), temple of God (1 Cor 3:16-17), building (1 Pt 2:5), chosen people (v 9), and family of God (Eph 3:15). Such metaphors amplify the interrelatedness, communion, and dependence of the "body of Christ" upon the living God.

The term "body of Christ" was often used by Paul to remind a local church that it was a vital part of the larger body. Paul said to the church at Rome, "For as in one body we have many members, and all the members do not have the same function, so we, though many, are one body in Christ, and individually members one of another" (Rom 12:4-5, RSV). Paul taught the Corinthian Christians that they, individually and collectively, were part of the body of Christ (1 Cor 12:27). They and Paul were all baptized by one Spirit into that one body (Eph 5:30).

In a number of passages written by Paul, the church is called the "body" and Christ the "head" (Col 1:18). Christ has been made "head over all things for the church," which "is his body" (Eph 1:22-23). The body grows by "holding fast to the Head" (Col 2:19). As head of the body, Christ is its Savior (Eph 5:23). The head/body metaphor stresses the organic dependence of the church on Christ and his lordship over the church. The church finds its self-understanding in terms of its Head. The relationship is organic in that the life flows from, and is sustained by, the Head. The relationship is immediate, direct, and complete. Apart from Christ, both in his historic atoning sacrifice and in his present position at the right hand of God, the church has no existence.

In the NT the term "body of Christ" is used to mean both the universal church and each local group of believers. In both senses the church is said to be the spiritual body in which believing Jews and Gentiles are united (Eph 2:14-16; 3:6; 4:4). It is the body that Christ redeemed (Eph 5:23), over which he presides (Col 1:18) and sovereignly rules (Eph 1:22-23) and for which he supplies strength and unity (Eph 4:15-16; Col 2:19).

Each member of the body of Christ has been given spiritual gifts with which to serve Christ in the body (Rom 12:6; 1 Cor 12:11). Such gifts are enumerated several times in Scripture, and range from apostleship and pastoring to encouraging and showing mercy (Rom 12:7-8; Eph 4:11). The ministry of serving is to be shared by all Christians, for example, through giving to the physical needs of others (Acts 11:29-30; 1 Cor 16:1-4; 2 Cor 8:1-5) and praying for one another (Eph 1:15-23; 3:14-19; 6:18-20). No one should look down on others or on their gifts, since God has chosen each one to function in his or her place in the body (1 Cor 12:14-26). The gifts are given to equip "the saints, for the work of ministry, for building up the body of Christ, until we all attain to the unity of the faith and of the knowledge of the Son of God, to mature manhood, to the measure of the stature of the fulness of Christ" (Eph 4:12-13, RSV). The goal is "to grow up in every way into him who is the head, into Christ" (vv 15-16, RSV). *See* Body; Church; Lord's Supper, The; Resurrection.

BOHAN, Stone of Stone marking the northeast boundary between the tribes of Judah and Benjamin. Bohan, a descendant of Reuben, is not mentioned elsewhere in the OT (Jos 15:6; 18:17).

BOIL Inflamed localized swelling on the skin. In modern medicine the term "boil" is restricted to a pus-filled swelling caused by infectious germs, usually staphylococci. The pus is a mixture of germs and white blood cells, which are the body's defense against germs. Although painful, boils usually heal naturally after rupturing or being lanced. A more severe boil with several openings is called a carbuncle. If the infection goes deeper and injures internal organs or tissues, it is called an abscess and can even be fatal.

In the Bible the word translated "boil" probably referred to a variety of skin diseases. The sixth plague that God inflicted on Egypt through Moses and Aaron was a plague of boils (Ex 9:9-11; Dt 28:27, 35) or blisters. Boils or skin eruptions of a certain type were described in the Mosaic health and sanitation code as one indication of leprosy (Lv 13:1-8, 18-23). Job's "terrible case of boils from head to foot" (Jb 2:7-8, 12, NLT) were probably too extensive to be boils in the modern sense; he may have had smallpox, psoriasis, tubercular leprosy, or some other disease accompanied by severe itching. King Hezekiah's boil was probably a carbuncle (2 Kgs 20:1-7; Is 38:21). *See* Medicine and Medical Practice; Disease; Plagues upon Egypt.

BOKERU Alternate spelling for Bocheru. *See* Bocheru.

BOKIM Alternate spelling for Bochim. *See* Bochim.

BOND, BONDAGE Anything that fastens or restrains; subjection or slavery. The basic concept in Hebrew and Greek words translated "bond" or "bondage" is "loss of freedom." The concept connotes servitude to another. The OT uses several words for bondage to describe the period of Israelite servitude in Egypt as well as the Babylonian captivity and Persian domination. Some English versions use the word "bond" to denote a state of individual servitude, such as the conditions of indenture permitted under the laws of Moses (Lv 25:39-44, KJV). The archaic term "bondmaid" is used to denote a concubine or secondary wife. The concept is used metaphorically to describe the control that God exercises over the nations of the world (Ps 2:3).

In the NT the bondage metaphor has positive and negative aspects. Negatively, it indicates spiritual subjection to sin or Satan (Heb 2:14-15; 2 Pt 2:19), to the flesh (Rom 8:12-14), or to the Law (Gal 2:4; 5:1). Human beings are enslaved when forces hostile to their well-being control their actions. The term is also used to picture the subjugation of creation to physical decay (Rom 8:21), which itself is the result of human sin.

The positive aspect draws upon the broader use of bondage in the Bible to denote servanthood, especially service to God as an obligation or vow (Nm 30:2-15; Ez 20:37). The term describes the necessity and value of suffering (Heb 10:34; 13:3). Paul especially uses it in a double sense (calling himself a "prisoner of Christ") to associate his physical bonds with his spiritual bondage to Christ (Eph 3:1; Phil 1:7-14; 2 Tm 1:8; 2:9; Phlm 1:9-10, 13).

See also Slave, Slavery.

BONDAGE*, House of Expression used in the OT for Egypt, where Israel was enslaved before the exodus (Ex 13:3; Jos 24:17). *See* Exodus, Book of.

BONDMAID*, BONDMAN*, BONDSERVANT* *See* Servant.

BONE One of the separate parts of the human or animal skeleton. After death, bones retain their form long after the soft tissues have decomposed, so bones are often associated with dead bodies or with death itself. The Israelites were concerned about proper respect for the bodies of the dead (Gn 50:25; 1 Sm 31:11-13; 2 Kgs 23:14-18; Ez 39:14-16; Am 2:1; Heb 11:22).

A valley of "old, dry bones" symbolized the people of Israel, who were without hope until the Spirit of the Lord would put life back into them (Ez 37:1-14). In a living body, however, bones are living tissue, and Ezekiel knew that broken bones could heal (30:21). Intact bones were a requirement for an unblemished lamb for the Passover (Ex 12:46; Nm 9:11-12). Thus, the NT states that when Jesus Christ, the "Lamb of God" (Jn 1:36), was crucified, contrary to Roman practice, his legs were not broken (Ps 34:20; Jn 19:30-37).

Some references to bones in the Bible (Jb 2:5; 19:20; 30:30) carry the connotation of deep feelings, as in the phrase "I feel it in my bones." Other references are metaphorical expressions of close kinship, "flesh and bone" (Gn 2:23; 29:14; Jgs 9:2) being equivalent to the expression "one's own flesh and blood."

BOOK A set of written sheets or a scroll—whether composed of wood, parchment, papyrus, or paper—containing records or a literary composition. With respect to the Bible, each individual composition is called a "book" because that was what the document was before it became part of the biblical collection. As such, the Bible has 66 books—such as Genesis, Isaiah, Matthew, and Revelation.

The most important book to the ancient Hebrews was the Book of the Law (2 Kgs 22:8), because it came from God to Moses (Jos 23:6; Mk 12:26) and contained the record of the Mosaic covenant (e.g., Ex 20). God instructed Joshua to meditate on it day and night (Jos

1:8). The prophets appealed to it constantly, particularly to Deuteronomy. The discovery of the Book of the Law during the renovation of the temple in Josiah's reign led to important religious reforms (2 Kgs 22:8-13).

Some books specifically labeled as biblical source materials are the Book of the Wars of the Lord (Nm 21:14), the Book of Jashar (Jos 10:13; 2 Sm 1:18), the Book of the Acts of Solomon (1 Kgs 11:41), and the Book of the Chronicles of the Kings of Judah (14:29). A number of prophetic works are cited in the books of Chronicles as sources for the material recorded in those books. Some of these are the Chronicles of Samuel the Seer, the Chronicles of Nathan the Prophet, the Chronicles of Gad the Seer (1 Chr 29:29), and the Prophecy of Ahijah the Shilonite (2 Chr 9:29). The fact that prophetic sources were used for Chronicles demonstrates that the Hebrew people regarded their history as the record of God's activity. See Writing.

BOOK OF LIFE Term used to refer to a heavenly record. The phrase appears seven times in the NT: Philippians 4:3; Revelation 3:5; 13:8; 17:8; 20:12, 15; 21:27. The Christian understanding of the phrase, however, is rooted in the OT. Passages such as Exodus 32:32; Psalm 87:6; Daniel 7:10; 12:1; and Malachi 3:16 imply or affirm a record kept by God. God is seen as keeping account of his people's faithfulness and disobedience—and possibly that of other nations as well (e.g., Ps 87:6). Psalm 69:28 uses the phrase "book of the living"; parallel poetic lines refer to physical living.

In Daniel 7:10; 12:1; and Malachi 3:16 references are linked with descriptions of final judgment and events of the end times. Names and deeds from the divine records are evidence set before a judge. Luke 10:20 and Hebrews 12:23 reflect similar thought; no concrete mention of a "book" is made but a heavenly record is assumed. In Philippians 4:3 Paul uses "Book of Life" to encourage his fellow workers in a lively hope for the future.

"Book of Life" in the book of Revelation refers to a heavenly record with the names of persecuted Christians who remain faithful. It is used first in the letter to Sardis (3:5) where the risen Lord, identified as "the Lamb" is keeper of the book (13:8; 21:7). If a person's name is found in the book, admittance is granted to new Jerusalem (20:15; 21:27). If one's name is not written there, the judgment is final destruction. Absolute confidence in God's care for his own is affirmed by the words "written before the foundation of the world" (13:8; 17:8).

See also Book of Remembrance.

BOOK OF REMEMBRANCE* Divine record of the names of those who fear God, referred to once in the OT (Mal 3:16, NLT "scroll"). The prophet Malachi was struggling against moral decline in his day. Arrogant individuals were seemingly justified in their haughtiness, and evildoers were blessed materially rather than being brought to judgment. His reference to a book of remembrance suggests that God in due time would turn things around, so that there would be a proper distinction between the righteous and the wicked. See Book of Life.

BOOK OF THE COVENANT Term occurring in two OT contexts. It describes, first, a document read by Moses to the people of Israel at Mt Sinai (Ex 24:7), and second, a document discovered in the temple by Hilkiah the priest at the time of King Josiah's program of repairing the temple (2 Kgs 23:2, 21; 2 Chr 34:30). The term "covenant" refers to the covenant laws that God made with his people Israel in the time of Moses. The Hebrew term "book" means any written document, whether written on clay or stone tablets or on parchment scrolls.

Ancient covenants were often in written form. The main problem in understanding the two references to "book of the covenant" is in trying to determine the concepts of those particular documents.

The book read at Mt Sinai has been taken to refer either to the Ten Commandments or to the whole section of Exodus 20 to 23, minus the narrative parts. Since the people responded, "All that the Lord has spoken we will do," it was evidently legal in its thrust, but it seems impossible to define its contents more precisely than that. The fact that Moses wrote the book (Ex 24:4) need not exclude the Ten Commandments, which are explicitly stated to have been written by God (32:15-16). Moses could also have written them down, perhaps in a preliminary stage (19:25; 20:1).

The content of the "book of the covenant" read by King Josiah to the people of Judah is uncertain. Some scholars have tried to reconstruct its contents on the basis of Josiah's reforms, concluding that those reforms were similar to principles taught in the book of Deuteronomy. That approach has several weaknesses. First, some of the reforms are nowhere mentioned in the Law (e.g., burning the chariots of the sun—2 Kgs 23:11) and would have to represent inferences Josiah derived from the Law. It becomes unclear how much of his reform was based on explicit passages in the Book of the Covenant and how much on inferences. Second, the account in 2 Chronicles 34:30-33 indicates that much of the reform took place *before* discovery of the Book of the Covenant.

On the other hand, explicit statements in 2 Kings indicate that some of the reforms were based on the Book of the Covenant. Thus the book must have contained instructions on the Passover (2 Kgs 23:21). It probably dealt with mediums, wizards, and other idolatrous practices, unless that reform was an inference suggested by the wording. In addition, the book evidently contained warnings of the destruction God would bring if his words were not followed (22:16-19). Those expressions probably indicate that Josiah's Book of the Covenant was larger than Exodus 21–23. In the older book, the Passover is mentioned only as the Feast of Unleavened Bread (Ex 23:15). Exodus 22:18 might possibly give a basis for Josiah's action against wizards. But in Exodus 21–23 no statement of judgment for disobedience is sufficient to explain the wording of 2 Kings 22:16-19; the closest thing to it is Exodus 23:33.

Finally, the fact that Josiah's Book of the Covenant is also called the Book of the Law (2 Kgs 22:8) suggests that numerous references to the Book of the Law in the OT should also be understood as referring to the Book of the Covenant.

See also Exodus, Book of; Law, Biblical Concept of.

BOOK OF THE DEAD* Modern name (nonbiblical) given to ancient Egyptian funerary (burial) texts. In the broadest sense, it designates all such texts, whether found on pyramid walls, coffins, or papyri. Some scholars use the term in a narrower sense, to mean the later forms of such texts written on papyri.

The purpose of any Book of the Dead was to describe a person's journey from this life to the next as an assured accomplishment. Its ancient Egyptian name was "Chapters of Coming Forth by Day." Such a book would be prepared for any deceased person of importance. In later stages of Egyptian history such texts were mass-produced, spaces being left for the person's name. For influential people the papyrus could be up to 100 feet (30.5 meters) long and lavishly illustrated with scenes depicting the person's experiences after death. There was no standard selection or arrangement of the material.

The ultimate goal of a deceased person was to go to the Other World, the kingdom of Osiris, and ultimately to become a god. In order to get there, the soul had to pass through various gates and be able to give the name of the gatekeeper to be admitted. Thus the texts meticulously informed the deceased of information they might need. One particularly important phase of the journey was judgment at the Hall of Truth. There the person's heart was weighed in the balance over against the feather of truth and justice. The soul would pray for the outcome and make a "negative confession," disclaiming any guilt, particularly with regard to theft and other social relationships. If the heart was as light as the feather, it was declared truthful. Otherwise it was given to destruction. The texts also provided the soul with an ample supply of hymns and prayers to assist it on its journey. Thus more emphasis was placed on magic and ritual than on truly moral character.

BOOK OF THE LAW *See* Book of the Covenant.

BOOTH Small, temporary hut or shelter constructed of branches and sticks when permanent buildings were unavailable. Booths provided shade during the day and protection from the dew and winds during the night (Gn 33:17; Jon 4:5). The word is also used as a figure of speech for something fragile and easily destroyed (Jb 27:18; Is 1:8).

See also Feasts and Festivals of Israel.

BOOTHS*, Feast of One of the three great festivals of Israel, celebrating the completion of the agricultural year. The Jews built booths (temporary shelters) to commemorate their deliverance from Egypt by the hand of God (Lv 23:39-43).

See also Feasts and Festivals of Israel.

BOOZ* KJV form of Boaz in Matthew 1:5 and Luke 3:32. *See* Boaz (Person).

BOR-ASHAN Alternate name for Ashan, a town originally assigned to Judah's tribe, in 1 Samuel 30:30. *See* Ashan.

BORN AGAIN Expression used by Jesus in explaining to Nicodemus how one enters the kingdom of God (Jn 3:3-7). *See* Regeneration.

BORROW, BORROWING Receiving money or goods that one pledges to return. The Mosaic law regulated borrowing and lending (Dt 23:19-20). *See* Banker, Banking.

BOSCATH* KJV form of Bozkath, a city in Judah, in 2 Kings 22:1. *See* Bozkath.

BOSOR* (Person) KJV form of Beor, Balaam's father, in 2 Peter 2:15. *See* Beor #2.

BOSOR (Place) City in Gilead captured by Judas Maccabeus in order to rescue the Jews living there (1 Macc 5:26, 36). Today this city is known as Busr El-Hariri. *See* Bozrah #3.

BOTTOMLESS PIT Phrase used in the Bible to denote the abode of the dead and of demonic forces. The Hebrew word (literally "the deep") is translated "abyss" in many versions of the Bible. In the ancient world, the concept referred to anything so deep as to be unfathomable—for example, wells or fountains. It is used in that way in the OT to describe the primeval sea (Gn 1:2) or the ocean depths (Pss 33:7; 77:16). In Near Eastern cul-

tures, the term was used to signify the inverse of the great vault of heaven; hence, it came to be used metaphorically for the grave, synonymous with Sheol (Ps 71:20). In intertestamental times, it came to be used for the abode of evil spirits (Jubilees 5:6; 1 Enoch 10:4, 11).

In the NT, the term is used in both of these metaphorical ways. The demons pleaded not to be flung into "the abyss" (Lk 8:31), which many connect with later references to a "prison" (2 Pt 2:4; Jude 1:6). The exact meaning of such a prison is difficult to define; recent studies of passages like the above and of 1 Peter 3:19 and 4:6 suggest that the abyss is probably not meant to be synonymous with hades. More likely, it refers to a place where evil spirits are confined. Romans 10:7, on the other hand, uses the term for the grave, contrasting descent into it with ascension into heaven. Paul there freely adapted Deuteronomy 30:12-13.

The major use of the term comes in the book of Revelation. There the "bottomless pit" is the abode of scorpion-like locusts (Rv 9:1-11); of the prince of the underworld, named "Abaddon" or "Destruction" (9:11); and of the "Beast," or Antichrist (11:7; 17:8). It is also the place where Satan is confined for 1,000 years (20:1, 3).

Several characteristics should be noted in a study of the "bottomless pit" concept in Revelation. First, it is under the absolute control of God. The angel "was given the key of the shaft of the bottomless pit" to unlock it (9:1, RSV); the Beast "is to ascend from the bottomless pit and go to perdition" (17:8, RSV). Satan is seized, bound, thrown, and locked in it (20:2-3). Second, from the beginning it is meant for eternal destruction. After it was opened, "from the shaft rose smoke like the smoke of a great furnace" (9:2, RSV). Although the bottomless pit is not the place of torment (i.e., "the lake of fire" in 20:10-15), it will be replaced by eternal punishment after the End (cf. 17:8). Finally, it is the reverse image of heaven, and from it wickedness gushes forth. This is in keeping with the metaphor and the picture throughout Revelation in which the dragon (12:9) and the Beast attempt to duplicate the power and glory reserved for God alone. Just as heaven is the source of all that is worthwhile, the bottomless pit is the source of all that is evil. *See* Revelation, Book of.

BOW *See* Archer, Archery.

BOWELS A portion of the intestines. The word was also used metaphorically in the KJV to connote the place where pity, mercy, and tenderness are felt (see Phil 1:8; 2:1-2).

BOWELS*, Disease of Term used 37 times in Scripture (KJV) but only once in connection with a disease (2 Chr 21:15-19). The evil King Jehoram was punished with an incurable chronic disease of the bowels, which resulted in his painful death two years later. The disease caused prolapse of the intestines (v 19). Either an inflammatory bowel disease or cancer of the colon or rectum could have accounted for these symptoms.

The only fatal intestinal disease recorded in the NT also occurred in a king (Acts 12:21-23). Josephus the historian records that King Herod, aged 54, suffered with severe pains in his abdomen, which lasted until he died five days later. An acute intestinal obstruction, possibly due to roundworm infestation, could account for these symptoms. Roundworms may have been expelled during the illness, or maggots could have been seen on necrotic skin resulting in the observation by Luke that Herod was "eaten of worms and died."

See also Disease; Medicine and Medical Practice.

BOWL *See* Pottery.

THE BRANCH: A SYMBOL FOR THE MESSIAH

In the following key passages, the "branch" is used as a symbol for the Messiah:

1. Isaiah 4:2-6 is the first occurrence of "branch" as a title: "In that day the branch of the LORD shall be beautiful and glorious, and the fruit of the land shall be the pride and glory of the survivors of Israel" (RSV). Many scholars interpret "branch" here to mean the Messiah for several reasons: (a) The whole tenor of the chapter makes it likely that it refers to the Messiah, who provides the harvest, establishes holiness, executes judgment, and creates "glory" in the land. (b) Isaiah 28:5 describes the Lord in similar terms, making a messianic interpretation of Isaiah 4:2 more probable. (c) Jeremiah 23:5 and 33:15, which seem to be commentaries on Isaiah 4:2, interpret it to refer to the Messiah. Mention of a righteous remnant illustrates a concept developing along with the "branch" imagery and amplifying its meaning. The branch will become the "beauty and glory" of the remnant of Israel and will wreak destruction on apostate Israel (Is 4:4).
2. Isaiah 11:1 adds a Davidic element to Isaiah 4:2, since Jesse was David's father. The "shoot" grew out of the "stump of Jesse," that is, the royal line of David. The Davidic line is pictured as a fallen dynasty, a tree cut down (the passage probably mentions Jesse rather than David to stress a lowly origin). The stump remains, however, and there is still life within it. That stump is insignificant in contrast to the mighty forest of Assyria, but the Lord will level that forest (Is 10:15-19, 33-34) and bring forth from Jesse's stump a fruitful shoot who will recover the Israelite remnant (Is 11:4, 11-12), destroy their adversaries, and reign in wisdom through the Spirit of the Lord.
3. Jeremiah 23:5 and 33:15 contrast the righteous reign of the Branch with the evil leadership of King Zedekiah. In both passages a remnant is pictured under the metaphor of a flock gathered back to their fold under caring shepherds (Jer 23:3-4; cf. 33:12-13). The shepherds are ruled by the Branch, who is given the title "The LORD is our righteousness" (33:16). That phrase in Hebrew is a deliberate wordplay on the name "Zedekiah" (meaning "the Lord is my vindication"). Zedekiah was righteous in name but not in reign. The Branch of the Lord, in contrast, will rule justly.
4. Zechariah 3:8 and 6:12 apply the branch metaphor in a different context—that of the postexilic task of rebuilding the temple. Zechariah described Joshua the high priest as a symbol of the future "servant-Branch" to be sent from the Lord. The Branch is seen as performing a priestly function in restoring righteous worship to the land. The royal line would be reinstated and the glories of the priestly line would also be reconstituted in the Branch. The servant of the Branch is probably taken from Isaiah's servant songs, where similar language is used (Is 53:2). Zechariah specifically related the priestly activity to rebuilding the temple. Zerubbabel had earlier been given the task of completing the literal building (Zec 4:7-9), so the allusion must go beyond that to the "spiritual temple" to come. (Since Zerubbabel's name means "shoot of Babylon," the connection seems deliberate). Finally, Zechariah combines the two messianic aspects of the Branch: "He will build the LORD's Temple, and he will receive royal honor and will rule as king from his throne. He will also serve as priest from his throne, and there will be perfect harmony between the two" (6:13, NLT).

"Branch" is never used as a title in the NT. Yet there are hints of that concept's influence, as in the familiar "vine and branches" metaphor (Jn 15:1-8), in the use of palm branches at Jesus' triumphal entry into Jerusalem (12:13; cf. Mk 11:8 and parallels), and possibly in the origin of the titles "Righteous One" (Acts 3:14; 7:52; cf. Jas 5:6) and "Just One" (Acts 22:14). Some have also taken an enigmatic reference to Christ, "He shall be called a Nazarene" as an allusion to the "branch" because in Isaiah 11:1 and other references *netzer* is similar to "Nazarene."

BOWMAN* *See* Archer, Archery.

BOX TREE* KJV translation of a tree of uncertain identity in Isaiah 41:19 and 60:13, called "pine" in the RSV. *See* Plants.

BOZEZ One of a pair of distinctive rocks (Seneh was the other) flanking the road between Michmash and Gaba. Jonathan and his armor bearer scaled one of these crags to take on a Philistine outpost (1 Sm 14:4). The two rocks are still visible in the modern Wadi Suweinet. *See* Seneh.

BOZKATH Town near Lachish and Eglon in Judah's territory (Jos 15:39), home of King Josiah's mother (2 Kgs 22:1).

BOZRAH

1. Well-fortified city in northern Edom (Gn 36:33; 1 Chr 1:44), regarded as impossible to conquer because it was protected by cliffs on three sides. Located 30 miles (48.3 kilometers) north of Petra, at modern Buseirah, it controlled the traffic on the King's Highway. Bozrah was mentioned as one of the strongholds that would fall

when God judged Edom (Is 34:6; 63:1; Jer 49:13; Am 1:12).
2. One of the cities cited by the prophet Jeremiah as collapsing with the Moabite nation (Jer 48:24); probably a variant spelling of Bezer. *See* Bezer (Place).
3. City also called Bosorah captured by Judas Maccabeus in the course of his Gilead campaign (1 Macc 5:26, 28). It is perhaps the same place as #2 above.

BRACELET Ornamental band or chain worn on the wrist or arm in the ancient world.

BRAMBLE Translation of several words designating a shrub with prickly stems and runners, often forming tangled masses of vegetation. *See* Plants.

BRANCH Literally, a shoot or sprout from a tree or bush; figuratively, a messianic or other spiritual metaphor. It is used for the three sets of arms that come off the main shaft of the golden lampstand in the tabernacle (e.g., Ex 25:31-36) and for the palm fronds from which booths were constructed for the ancient Jewish Feast of Tabernacles (Lv 23:40-43).

Metaphorically, the expression is found in passages

where Israel is described as an olive tree (Hos 14:6), a cedar (Ez 17:23), and a vine (Ez 17:6; cf. Ps 80:8-11). "Branch," with its implication of new growth, can signify prosperity (Gn 49:22; Jb 8:16; Ps 80:8-11; Ez 36:8). Branches can be cut or broken off; hence, the word may depict judgment (Jb 18:16; Is 9:14; Jer 11:16). Such passages speak of withering, being cut, or being burned; Jesus combined all three ideas into one metaphor (Jn 15:6). In a similar way, the apostle Paul wrote that the Jews who didn't believe would be broken off (Rom 11:19-21).

The major use of such symbolism refers to the Davidic Messiah. Although that use of "branch" actually stems from the prophetic period, its roots go much farther back. The concept was used with reference to an influential figure, such as a king's personal servant (Gn 40:9-13), the patriarch Joseph (49:22), Job (Jb 29:19), or the Assyrian king Nebuchadnezzar (Dn 4:12). Passages such as 2 Samuel 23:4 and Psalm 132:17 speak of the Davidic line as "growing" or "sprouting forth" (the literal meaning of the Hebrew verbs). Finally, images of agricultural prosperity were used as promised blessings of the messianic age (cf. Lv 26 with the prophetic passages on previous page). It is understandable how the term "branch" could become a technical designation for the Messiah, as is described above.

BRASS* *See* Minerals and Metals.

BRAZEN SERPENT* *See* Bronze Serpent, Bronze Snake.

A Grindstone Used to Crush Grain

BREAD Food made from the dough of flour or meal from grain.

Kinds of Seed Used in Making Bread The Bible tells us that wheat, barley, rye, beans, lentils, millet, and manna were used in making bread.

Wheat Wheat is mentioned frequently in Scripture (about 48 uses of four Hebrew words in the OT; 14 uses of one Greek word in the NT). The hard winter grain *(Triticum aestivuum)* remains the most popular with farmers of Palestine, who still sow in the fall and reap in the following summer.

Barley Barley matures faster and produces more prolifically than wheat. The hail plague in Egypt destroyed the barley crop because it had ripened; at the same time wheat and rye had not matured (Ex 9:31-32). Barley is mentioned 32 times in the OT. Barley produced a crop even in time of famine (Ru 1:22; 2:17, 23; 3:2, 15, 17) and sold cheaper than wheat (2 Kgs 7:1, 16). Poorer people depended on barley. The boy who contributed his lunch to Jesus to feed 5,000 had barley bread (Jn 6:9, 13). Palestinians fed barley to cattle (1 Kgs 4:28). Barley on the stalk carries a larger husk with a long, wiry hair (thus the name in Hebrew means "long hair"), making chaff separation more difficult. The greater likelihood of extraneous matter in the flour, combined with the less-liked flavor, made barley cheaper.

Rye "Rye" translates a Hebrew word appearing in various versions as "vetch," "fitches," or "spelt" (Ex 9:32; Is 28:25; Ez 4:9). A hardy grass, it produces a crop even on poor soil. Rye bread gained popularity in northern Europe and to some degree in Egypt (Ex 9:32). Isaiah 28:24-28 summarizes the farmers' work in growing and threshing various seed crops. Jews occasionally made bread from rye (Ez 4:9), but normally used it for cattle feed.

Other Seeds Beans, lentils, and millet were ground and mixed to make a bread, along with wheat, barley, and spelt (Ez 4:9). The prophet Ezekiel ate this concoction as a sign of the "defiled bread" the Jews would eat in captivity among the Gentiles.

Manna Numbers 11:8 tells us that the people ground the manna in mills or beat it in a mortar and baked it in pans and made loaves of bread. However, in its prime state God called it bread (see Ex 16:4-32). It appeared as coriander seed (Ex 16:31; Nm 11:7); therefore, the dull white grains were smaller than wheat. The Hebrews complained they had not bread, and their souls hated "this light bread" (Nm 21:5, KJV). The psalmist called it "the bread of the angels" (Ps 78:25).

Equipment Used in Making Bread Bas-reliefs in Egyptian mastaba tombs illustrate most of the equipment used in ancient Near Eastern bakeries.

Sieve A wicker strainerlike device helped separate small impurities from the grain.

Grindstones A pair of stones were shaped so that a top stone turned against the bottom stone, crushing grain into flour.

Jars Clay jars contained olive oil, water, and liquid leaven to be mixed with the flour to make dough (Lv 2:4; 1 Kgs 17:12-16).

Bowls Kneading bowls (Ex 8:3; 12:34; Dt 28:5, 17), boards or tables made of wood, provided space for a thorough mixing of ingredients.

Pans The poor used heated flat stones or the inside walls of their ovens as baking pans. Most people used iron griddles, plates, or pans (Lv 2:5; 6:21; 7:9; Nm 11:8; 1 Chr 9:31; 23:29; 2 Chr 35:13; Ez 4:3). These were often flat, with handles up to five feet (1.5 meters) long. The dough placed on the griddle was ready for the heat.

Ovens Sometimes ovens had a chamber separated from the fire, but usually not. A fire of wood, dried grass (Mt 6:30), or dung (Ez 4:12, 15) heated the oven (Lv 2:4; 7:9; 11:35; 26:26; Hos 7:4-7). While the coals and oven walls retained their heat, the plate carrying bread was inserted. Flat, hard unleavened cakes, or small leavened cakes (Mt 14:17; Mk 6:38; Lk 9:13) were done in a few minutes. Large loaves about one foot in diameter would swell to more than three inches (7.6 centimeters) thick, would weigh more than two pounds (.9 kilogram), and required about 45 minutes for baking (1 Sm 17:17; 2 Sm 16:1).

See also Food and Food Preparation; Meals, Significance of; Bread of the Presence; Leaven; Unleavened Bread.

BREAD OF THE PRESENCE
Loaves of bread placed on a special table in the sanctuary or Holy Place of the tabernacle and later in the temple. Two other terms in the OT are used to describe the "bread of the Presence," which means bread that has been set before the Lord's face (Ex 25:23, 30; 35:13; 39:36; 1 Kgs 7:48; 2 Chr 4:19). The term "showbread" (KJV "shewbread") refers to the arrangement of the bread in rows on the table (1 Chr 9:32; 23:29; 28:16; 2 Chr 2:4; 13:11; 29:18).

Although the table of showbread, the altar of incense, and the golden lampstand were not in the Holy of Holies, they were nevertheless considered to be in the presence of God. As an offering placed before the presence of God, the loaves were considered holy and could be eaten only by priests. Later in Israel's history, provision for offering the bread of the Presence as well as other temple services was financed by a tax of one-third shekel upon all citizens (Neh 10:32-33).

The bread of the Presence consisted of 12 very large loaves, each made of one-fifth ephah of fine flour. Since an ephah was just over a bushel, two and a half bushels (30.3 liters) of finely ground wheat were required to make the 12 loaves. They were sprinkled with frankincense, arranged in two rows, the one leaning against the other, and placed on the table of showbread (Lv 24:5-9). Arranged in that way, the bread became an "offering of food" to the Lord. The loaves were changed weekly on the Sabbath day.

The bread of the Presence is featured in one incident recalled in the NT. The tabernacle was at Nob when David was fleeing from the presence of King Saul. David went to Ahimelech, the priest, in search of food (1 Sm 21:1-6). Ahimelech had only the showbread, which he agreed to share with David's men, provided they had been sexually continent for a period of time before their eating. Jesus later referred to the incident as a parallel to his own ministry of supplying the needs of those who followed him (Mt 12:1-8; Mk 2:25-26; Lk 6:1-5). As God's anointed, David and his men were permitted to eat the holy bread. Likewise Jesus, God's anointed one, provided for the needs of others in spite of the Sabbath regulations.

See also Tabernacle; Temple.

BREAKFAST
First meal of the day, "breaking the fast." See Family Life and Relations; Food and Food Preparation.

BREAKING OF BREAD*
Phrase used in the NT in reference to the Lord's Supper. See Lord's Supper, The.

BREASTPIECE*, BREASTPLATE*
1. Part of the ceremonial garment of the high priest (Ex 25:7). See Priests and Levites.

2. Piece of armor worn to protect the chest. The word is used figuratively in several passages. Isaiah 59:17 says that God put on righteousness as a breastplate or body armor as he prepared to take vengeance on his enemies. The apostle Paul exhorted Christians to wear a breastplate of righteousness in order to stand against the devil (Eph 6:14) and a breastplate of faith and love as they await Christ's return (1 Thes 5:8).

See also Armor and Weapons.

BRIAR*
Prickly or thorny bush, frequently mentioned in the Bible. See Plants (Bramble; Thistle, Thorn).

BRIBE, BRIBERY
To give a person in authority something valuable in order to influence that person's decision or action. Bribery was prohibited under OT law (Ex 23:8; Dt 16:19) and condemned by the prophets (Is 1:23; Am 5:12; Mi 3:11). Although Samuel denied that he ever took a bribe (1 Sm 12:3), his sons did not maintain the same standard (8:3).

The distinction between bribery and merely giving gifts was not always clear. Hence, giving something valuable is seen as a way to prevent unwanted conflict (Prv 21:14). Giving a gift is described (with neither approval nor condemnation) as a way to get ahead (18:16).

For the most part, bribery is seen in the Bible as despicable. "The wicked accept secret bribes to pervert justice" (Prv 17:23, NLT). Any system that legitimizes bribery gives the rich an unfair advantage in persuading leaders and judges; the poor find it difficult to get a fair hearing. Innocent people who are poor can be condemned; guilty people who are rich can offer a sizable bribe and go free (Ps 15:5b; Is 5:23). In extreme cases, bribes are said to have been used to hire killers (Dt 27:25; Ez 22:12).

BRICK, BRICK KILN
Oblong block of shaped mud or clay that has been dried either by the sun or by burning in a kiln for use in building or paving, and the furnace in which bricks are burned and hardened. Brick was the most extensively used building material in the ancient biblical world, especially common in Babylonia. The Hebrew word for "brick" is taken from a verb meaning "to be white," referring to the appearance of the clay out of which brick was made.

In Babylonia, stone suitable for building was seldom at hand, so Babylonian architects used it sparingly, usually for lintels, thresholds, and door hinges. Babylonian bricks were made from the mud or clay of marshes and plains, after removing foreign substances such as pebbles. The clay was mixed with chopped straw or grass that, on decaying, released acids that gave the substance greater moldability. The brick maker added water, kneaded the mixture by foot, and molded it into square bricks, each about 8 to 12 inches (20 to 30.5 centimeters) across and 3 to 4 inches (7 to 10 centimeters) thick. The bricks were frequently stamped with a wooden block bearing the name of the reigning king (e.g., Sargon). Some peasant houses found near Babylon today have bricks containing King Nebuchadnezzar's stamp.

Babylonian bricks were commonly burned in brick kilns rather than sun-dried. Sun-dried bricks disintegrated easily in heavy rainfall, whereas bricks burned in a kiln were virtually indestructible. Kiln-burnt bricks were used especially for facings, pavements, and important buildings. Archaeological remains of many brick kilns have been found in Babylonia.

Evidence exists of walls, temples, and storehouses constructed of brick in ancient Egypt, although almost no brick kilns (KJV "brickkiln") have been found. Egyptian bricks were usually sun-dried rather than burned. Clay bricks were sometimes made without straw, but bricks made of mud from the Nile River required straw to keep them from falling apart. Egyptian bricks were rectangular, ranging from about 4 to 20 inches (10 to 51 centimeters) long, about 6 to 9 inches (15 to 23 centimeters) wide, and about 4 to 7 inches (10 to 18 centimeters) thick. Egyptian bricks were also often stamped with an identifying seal.

The Egyptians regarded brick making as a lowly occupation to be imposed upon slaves. Thus, during their bondage in Egypt, the Israelites were forced to make bricks (Ex 1:11-14; 5:6-19). Their suffering was increased by denying them the usual supplement of straw, since they had to take time to locate their own straw while keeping up the required production quota. The Israelites carried the art of brick making back to the Promised Land at the exodus.

See also Architecture; Pottery.

BRIDE AND BRIDEGROOM Terms used for a woman and man about to be married or just married; also used to describe the relation of Christ to his church (Eph 5:25-27). *See* Bride of Christ; Church; Jerusalem, New; Marriage, Marriage Customs.

BRIDECHAMBER* Room in which the marriage ceremonies were held. *See* Marriage, Marriage Customs.

BRIDE OF CHRIST* One of the NT metaphors for the church. In it Christ is pictured as a husband, and the church as his bride.

Addressing the church at Corinth, the apostle Paul referred to himself as the one who gave the church to Christ, presenting her as a pure bride to her one husband (2 Cor 11:2-3). In ancient Near Eastern culture the father gave his daughter in marriage to the bridegroom, assuring him of her purity. To Paul, understanding himself as the church's spiritual father (1 Cor 4:15), the thought of the church as his daughter sprang readily to mind. To be Christ's pure bride requires the church to have pure and simple devotion. Like a concerned father, Paul was worried that the young bride (the church) might commit adultery by her willingness to accept "another Jesus," "another Spirit," or "a different gospel" (2 Cor 11:4). As between marriage partners, the relation between the church and Christ is governed by a covenant of mutual faithfulness. Disloyalty shatters the covenant.

The OT furnished Paul a rich background for that image of the church. God's covenant with Israel was commonly pictured as a marriage pledge, with Israel as God's bride. Through the prophet Jeremiah, the Lord said to Israel: "I remember the devotion of your youth, your love as a bride" (Jer 2:2, RSV). He went on to lament the fact that Israel had been faithless; by going after other gods, she had actually prostituted herself and become an adulteress (Jer 3:6-9, 20).

The theme of Israel's desertion of her lover (God) was explicitly treated in Ezekiel 16 and in Hosea. The terms "harlotry" and "whoredom" were used to connote disloyalty to Yahweh and allegiance to other gods. Thus, adultery and idolatry became synonymous. Through his own struggles with a faithless wife, the prophet Hosea experienced God's agony over his bride Israel and his longing for her to return. Hosea was given a vision of a future day in which God would betroth his people to him forever in steadfast love and faithfulness (Hos 2:19-20). That vision may have enabled Paul to transfer the image of Israel as God's bride to the church as the bride of Christ.

In Ephesians 5:22-33, the relationship between Christ and his church is compared to the relationship between a husband and wife. The image is taken from the common understanding of the husband-wife relationship in that part of the world. The church's submission to Christ is compared with the wife's submission to the husband, but the stress of the passage is on the role of the husband: he is to love her as Christ loved the church and gave himself up for her. Christ relates to the whole church on the basis of self-sacrificial love. Just as a husband is joined to his wife, with a mutual interdependence so intimate that they become one, so Christ and his church become one body. As the man's love for his wife intends her wholeness, so Christ's love of the church intends her completeness.

A variation on the theme is found in John the Baptist's testimony to Jesus (Jn 3:29). John saw himself as "the Bridegroom's friend" who, according to Jewish custom, takes care of the wedding arrangements. The Messiah is identified with the bridegroom to whom the bride (his messianic community) belongs and who comes to claim that bride.

In Revelation 19 and 21 the metaphor of the church as the Messiah's bride is further developed. The vision in Revelation 19:7-8 announces the marriage of the Lamb (Christ) to the bride (church). In Revelation 21 the vision depicts the new Jerusalem coming down from heaven, "prepared as a bride adorned for her husband" (v 2). Then the seer is invited to behold "the Bride, the wife of the Lamb" (v 9) and to see the Holy City "coming down out of heaven from God" (v 10). The new Jerusalem is identified as the people of God, the bride of Christ, among whom and with whom God will be present forever.

See also Church; Jerusalem, New.

BRIER Prickly or thorny bush, frequently mentioned in the Bible. *See* Plants (Bramble; Thistle, Thorn).

BRIMSTONE* Old name for the nonmetallic element sulfur, literally "the stone that burns." Sulfur ignites at a relatively low temperature and burns to produce acrid fumes of sulfur dioxide. Sulfur occurs naturally in volcanic regions such as the valley of the Dead Sea. "Fire and brimstone" are strongly associated in the Bible with divine retribution (Gn 19:24; Dt 29:23; Jb 18:15; Ps 11:6; Ez 38:22; and in KJV, Lk 17:29; Rv 9:17-18; 14:10; 19:20; 20:10; 21:8). The last volcanic eruptions in Israel, which radiocarbon dating indicates took place about 4,000 years ago, probably left an impression on the inhabitants of the area that was passed on for generations. *See* Minerals and Metals.

BROAD WALL, The Section of the outer wall of Jerusalem that Nehemiah rebuilt in the fifth century BC. The Broad Wall was possibly located on the city's northwest side (Neh 3:8; 12:38). *See* Jerusalem.

BRONZE Durable alloy of copper and tin widely used for ornaments, weapons, coins, and other purposes in ancient times. *See* Minerals and Metals.

BRONZE SEA Large tank of water in Solomon's temple yard for the priests' washing (1 Kgs 7:23-44; 2 Kgs 16:17; 25:13; 1 Chr 18:8; 2 Chr 4:2-6, 15; Jer 52:17). Cast from bronze and about three inches (7.6 centimeters) thick (a handbreadth), it was mounted on 12 bronze oxen (three facing in each compass direction) in the courtyard at the southeast corner of the sanctuary. It was five cubits (about 7.5 feet, or over 2 meters) high and ten cubits (15 feet, or 4.6 meters) in diameter, with a capacity of either 2,000 baths (1 Kgs 7:26) or 3,000 (2 Chr 4:5). The discrepancy possibly comes from a scribal error. The bath (originally a vessel large enough to hold a person) was a liquid measure of about 6 gallons (23 liters), so the tank held perhaps 18,000 gallons (68,136 liters) of water.

See also Temple; Laver.

BRONZE SERPENT, BRONZE SNAKE Piece of
sculpture that God commanded Moses to make when the Israelites were being bitten by "fiery serpents" (Nm 21:4-9). The serpents had been sent as a judgment because the people were grumbling against God and against Moses. When the people repented, God ordered the replica made; those who looked at it were healed.

Some connect the theological meaning of the scene with an episode in which Moses' rod became a serpent, swallowed up the serpent-rods of the Pharaoh's magicians, and then became a rod again (Ex 7:8-12; cf. 4:2-5, 28-30). The serpent was a deified figure in both the Egyptian and Canaanite religions. Therefore, the triumph of God's serpent figure typified the superiority of the Lord over the pagan gods. In Numbers 21, however, such a realization must have been secondary. That event was the last of a number of "apostasies" in the wilderness (cf. 1 Cor 10:9), all of which included four elements: complaints against God, judgment, repentance, and forgiveness or deliverance. The major theological theme is not the Lord's superiority but his provision of salvation. The stress was not on a magical formula for healing, but rather on the serpent as a symbol of salvation offered to all who would focus on it.

The bronze serpent appears again in 2 Kings 18:4. In the intervening centuries it had become an idolatrous object, and King Hezekiah (716–686 BC) of the southern kingdom of Judah abolished it in his reform movement. The final reference to it in pre-Christian literature is in the apocryphal book Wisdom of Solomon, which supports the above interpretation: salvation came not through the serpent but through God's provision. "He who turned towards it was healed, not by what he saw, but by you, the Savior of all" (Wisd of Sol 16:7).

Against this background, Christ said that he, like Moses' serpent, must be lifted up (Jn 3:14). The "lifting up" of the "Son of Man" is a definite reference to Christ's death and has two foci. One is a "death as salvation" theme, seen in the Mosaic serpent imagery and the divine imperative "must" (in Jn referring to the necessity of God's ordained plan of salvation). The other is a "death as exaltation" theme, seen in the verb itself (containing the idea of majesty) and in John's stress on the glory of Jesus' earthly ministry and of his resurrected status.

BROOD Term often used in the Bible for young birds,
especially of the domestic fowl. *See* Birds (Fowl, Domestic; Partridge). Also used of snakes or vipers, as a metaphor for "sinners" (Nm 32:14; Mt 3:7; 12:34; Lk 3:7).

BROOK *See* Wadi.

BROOK OF EGYPT Natural border between the Negev
Desert area of Israel and the Sinai Peninsula, about 50 miles (80.5 kilometers) southwest of Gaza. The brook of Egypt, modern Wadi el-Arish, flows only during the rainy season (Nm 34:5; Jos 15:4, 47; 1 Kgs 8:65; 2 Kgs 24:7; 2 Chr 7:8; Is 27:12; Ez 47:19; 48:28). A different Hebrew word, signifying an ever-flowing river, appears in Genesis 15:18, where God spelled out the boundaries

of the Promised Land to the patriarch Abraham. That reference may be to the easternmost branch of the Nile (the Pelusiac), which flows into the Mediterranean Sea near modern Port Said, and to the line of ancient fortifications marking Egypt's border.

BROOK OF THE ARABAH* Unidentifiable brook
presumably draining into the Arabah (Am 6:14). The Arabah is part of the desert rift extending from the Sea of Galilee to East Africa. A wadi (streambed) named Arabah is south of the Salt (Dead) Sea, but in the Bible, Arabah ("desert" or "wilderness") designates portions of the Jordan Valley (Dt 4:48-49; Jos 8:14; 2 Kgs 25:4) as well as the Salt Sea (Dt 3:17). In the Wadi Arabah several springs and occasionally rain-fed streams drain into the Salt Sea.

See also Arabah.

BROOM Palestinian shrub or bush that often grows
quite large, providing shade (1 Kgs 19:4). KJV translates the Hebrew word as "juniper." *See* Plants.

BROTHER Man or boy in his relationship to the other
children of his parents; also a close male friend or fellow member of the same race, creed, profession, organization, and the like; a kinsman.

In the OT the Hebrew word translated "brother" describes the relationship between male children who have at least one parent in common. Joseph and Benjamin were children of Jacob and Rachel (Gn 35:24), but the other sons born to Jacob are also called Joseph's brothers (42:6). The love Joseph had for Benjamin is not always found between brothers. Cain killed his brother Abel (4:8), and Esau hated his brother, Jacob (27:41). A brother may be a bad influence (Dt 13:6-7), but ideally he is one who helps in times of need (Prv 17:17). The law of levirate marriage required that if a man died leaving a childless widow, the man's brother had to raise up children through her to perpetuate the family name (Dt 25:5).

David spoke affectionately of his "brother" Jonathan, although they were not related (2 Sm 1:26). A fellow Israelite could be called brother. The relationship required certain obligations: money could not be loaned to a brother at interest, and a brother could not be enslaved (Lv 25:35-43).

In the NT the Greek word is used to describe natural brothers, such as Andrew and Peter (Jn 1:41). Four brothers of Jesus are named (Mk 6:3). (The Roman Catholic view is that they were really Jesus' cousins, but the Greek language has several words for cousin, and the word "brother" is used here; thus, it refers either to children or foster children of Mary and Joseph.) Jesus' brothers did not believe in him at first (Jn 7:5), but after the resurrection they were meeting with the Christian community (Acts 1:14). Jesus taught that his disciples had one Father (God) and were therefore brothers (Mt 23:8-9), and he graciously identified himself with the disciples as their brother (28:10).

Early in the history of the church it became customary for Christians to address one another as brother (Acts 9:17; Col 1:1); on two occasions the Christian community is called "the brotherhood" (1 Pt 2:17; 5:9, RSV). Specific duties and responsibilities accompany Christian brotherhood. A Christian's love for his brother will be demonstrated in the restraint of sexual passions (1 Thes 4:6), provision of material goods when needed (Jas 2:15-16), and determination not to offend (Rom 14:13). A Christian must not "go to law" against a brother (1 Cor 6:5-6), but brothers must resolve their problems either personally or within the church group (Mt 18:15-17). The relationship between Christians is significant because a Christian cannot offer worship to God if he is out of harmony with his brother (Mt 5:23-24).

See also Family Life and Relations; Brothers (and Sisters).

BROTHERS (and Sisters)
Designation of those in the household of God. Good evidence exists that Jews at the time of Jesus frequently referred to themselves as brothers (Acts 2:29, 37; 7:2; 22:5; 28:21; Rom 9:3). From the beginning it seemed natural for Jewish Christians to call each other "brothers" (that is, "siblings"—the term included both male and female; Acts 1:15-16; 9:30; 11:1). Members of gentile religious communities also called each other brothers, so the name found a home in the gentile churches as well (Acts 17:14; Rom 1:13; 1 Cor 1:1, 10; plus dozens of other places in Paul's letters to gentile churches). In fact, along with "disciple" (in Acts) and "saint" (always plural in the writings of Paul and the book of Revelation), it was one of the most popular names for Christians and the only one used in James and 1 John.

Each Christian was called "brother," and the Christians collectively were "the brothers." The name stressed the intimacy of the Christian community. That is, the relationship of believers to one another was as close as that of blood kin (closer, in fact—Mk 10:23-31). In 1 John and James the name underlines the claim that poorer Christians have upon those better off (Jas 2:15; 1 Jn 3:10-18; 4:20-21). It also points to equality among members of the Christian community.

BROTHERS OF JESUS*
James, Joses (or Joseph), Simon, and Judas, identified in the NT as members of Jesus' own family (Mt 13:55; Mk 6:3). They are described as visiting Jesus with Mary, his mother (Mt 12:47-50; Mk 3:34-35; Lk 8:19-21), and hearing Jesus' statement that all who did the will of God were brother, sister, and mother to him.

They were well enough known in Nazareth that when Jesus returned to preach there, the people said, "Is not this the carpenter, the son of Mary and brother of James and Joses and Judas and Simon, and are not his sisters here with us?" (Mk 6:3, RSV). In Matthew's Gospel the order of the names of the last two brothers is reversed (Mt 13:55). When Jesus and his disciples went to Capernaum, they were accompanied by Mary and his brothers (Jn 2:12). Just before the Feast of Tabernacles the brothers visited Jesus to persuade him to go to Jerusalem for the festival. Although they were skeptical about his miracles, they said he should perform his feats in public to gain recognition (Jn 7:4). Jesus acknowledged opposition from within his family when he said, "A prophet is honored everywhere except in his own hometown and among his own family" (Mt 13:57, NLT). His brothers or other friends from home thought him to be losing touch with reality when crowds were first attracted to him (Mk 3:21).

In spite of their earlier skepticism, however, the brothers became active members of the Jerusalem church during its earliest days. They are mentioned as being frequently at prayer in an upper room with Mary, showing a sharp reversal from their earlier lack of faith (Acts 1:14). One of the resurrection appearances was made to James (1 Cor 15:7). On Paul's return to Jerusalem after his conversion, he met Peter and James, "the Lord's brother," but not the other apostles (Gal 1:19). When the apostle Peter was released from prison, he went to the home of Mary the mother of John Mark,

and despite the excitement of the occasion, he immediately asked the group to "tell this to James and to the brethren" (Acts 12:17, RSV). A number of references in Acts show James as a strong, respected leader of the Jerusalem church (Acts 15:13-21; 21:18). In the council at Jerusalem, he expressed a strong opinion on the acceptance of Gentiles into the church; he was later visited by Paul, who told him about his ministry and the many conversions among the Gentiles. Although James is mentioned more often by name, all the brothers seem to have been well respected at that time. Thus, their actions were used as an example by Paul when he argued that it would be appropriate for him also to have a wife accompany him on his journeys, as Jesus' brothers did (1 Cor 9:5).

The author of the Epistle of James is generally assumed to be the Lord's brother, although he does not identify himself specifically that way (1:1). It seems clear, though, that the author wrote as a recognized leader in the church; hence, to identify him as the Lord's brother seems logical. The author of the Epistle of Jude identifies himself as the brother of James. The reference would most logically be to James, the leader mentioned in Acts and probably the author of the other epistle. The author thus seems to be the Judas named as the brother of the Lord in the Gospels (Mt 13:55; Mk 6:3).

Throughout the NT the group of the 12 apostles is consistently distinguished from the brothers of the Lord. Luke named the apostles and then said, "All these with one accord devoted themselves to prayer, together with the women and Mary the mother of Jesus, and with his brothers" (Acts 1:13-14). The apostle Paul pointed to the brothers of the Lord as a group separate from the apostles (1 Cor 9:5); each mention of them in the Gospels describes them as family members and distinct from the disciples.

See also James (Person) #1; Joseph #7; Jude (Person); Mary #1.

BROTHERS, STEPBROTHERS, OR COUSINS?
Whether the "brothers of Jesus" were half brothers (children of Mary by Joseph), stepbrothers (children of Joseph by a former marriage), or cousins (children of Mary's sister) is a matter of controversy. The Protestant position maintains that the brothers were actual half brothers of Jesus. The Roman Catholic position asserts that the four were cousins of Jesus. The Greek Orthodox position agrees with the Roman Catholic stance that Mary and Joseph had no other children, but assumes that the brothers and sisters were Joseph's by a former wife.

Protestants contend that not only the four brothers but at least two sisters were the children of Mary and Joseph. The plain sense of several passages is in favor of the usual meaning of the word "brother," since no instance of a wider use of that word for actual kinship appears in the NT. Consistent with that understanding of "brother," wherever brothers and sisters of Jesus are mentioned (except Jn 7 and 1 Cor 9), is their appearance in close connection with Jesus and his mother, evidently one family under Mary's care. That closeness could possibly fit their being Mary's stepchildren, but it makes it less likely that they were only cousins of Jesus.

BUCKLER* Small, usually round shield carried in the hand or worn on the arm in battle. *See* Armor and Weapons.

BUILD, BUILDING Construction, usually with wood, masonry, and similar materials. The Bible has many references to the building or rebuilding of altars, temples, houses, and whole cities. The term is sometimes used as a metaphor for God's activity among his people (1 Pt 2:4-8). *See* Architecture.

BUKKI

1. Leader of Dan's tribe who assisted Joshua in dividing up the land of Canaan (Nm 34:22).
2. Ezra's ancestor (1 Chr 6:5, 51; Ezr 7:1, 4-5).

BUKKIAH Heman's eldest son, who served with his father and 13 brothers as a temple musician (1 Chr 25:4, 13).

BUL* Eighth month of the preexilic Canaanite calendar. In this month King Solomon's temple was completed (1 Kgs 6:38). *See* Calendars, Ancient and Modern.

BULL, BULLOCK* Male, adult and young, of any bovine animal, such as oxen, cattle. *See* Animals (Cattle).

BULRUSH Any of a number of reed plants that grow in marshes and beside streams and rivers. *See* Plants (Reed).

BUNAH Jerahmeel's son from Judah's tribe (1 Chr 2:25).

BUNNI

1. Levite who sang praise to God after Ezra's public reading of the law (Neh 9:4).
2. Political leader who signed Ezra's covenant of faithfulness to God with Nehemiah and others after the exile (Neh 10:15).
3. Hashabiah's father (Neh 11:15), a Levite descended from Merari (1 Chr 9:14). Possibly the same as #1 above.

BURIAL, BURIAL CUSTOMS* The Bible makes frequent reference to burial practices. A society's burial customs are a reflection of its views about death and the afterlife. The ancient Egyptians, for example, thought of life after death as a continuation of physical activities in another realm, as evidenced by their elaborately furnished tombs. The ancient Hebrews emphasized a more spiritual concept of union or fellowship of the departed with generations gone on before.

Graves and Tombs Among the Hebrews, location of burial plots was generally determined on a family basis. The OT contains many references to an Israelite's desire to be buried in the family burying place, describing his death as "going to his fathers" (Gn 15:15; 1 Kgs 13:22).

The cave of Machpelah at Hebron was one example of family "cohabitation" of a tomb for a succession of generations. Abraham purchased the site from Ephron the Hittite at the time of Sarah's death (Gn 23). When Abraham died, Isaac and Ishmael laid his body in the same tomb (25:9), and there Jacob in turn buried his parents, Isaac and Rebekah, as well as Jacob's wife Leah (49:31). After his death, Jacob's body was buried with his father's in accord with his own request (49:29; 50:13). Jacob's son Joseph made his kinsmen promise that his remains would be preserved so they could be carried back to the homeland when God enabled his people to return from Egypt (50:25). Samuel is spoken of as being buried in his house at Ramah, evidently referring to a family graveyard plot (1 Sm 25:1). Joab was buried in his own house in the wilderness (1 Kgs 2:34). King Manasseh was buried

in the garden of his palace (2 Kgs 21:18), and Joshua in his own inheritance at Timnath-serah (Jos 24:30). Kings were careful to perpetuate their memory by special burial sites, often in the City of David (the part of Jerusalem on the southeastern ridge first occupied by that great king). King Josiah designated his burial place in advance, most likely an ancestral tomb (2 Kgs 23:30).

Individual burial sites, such as that of Deborah near Bethel (Gn 35:8) and of Rachel on the road to Ephrath (Gn 35:1, 20), were an exception necessitated by sudden death at some distance from the family tomb.

Bodies were buried in tombs, that is, natural caves or rock-hewn sepulchers, such as that belonging to Joseph of Arimathea where the body of Jesus was laid (Mt 27:59-60). They were also buried in shallow graves covered with rock heaps, serving both to mark them and to prevent desecration of the body by animals.

Some graves were marked by a monument erected in love (Gn 35:20) and honor (2 Kgs 23:17), but stones were sometimes heaped on a dishonorable burial place, as in the case of Achan (Jos 7:26) and Absalom (2 Sm 18:17). Tombs were often adorned or embellished, sometimes whitewashed, in part to warn against ceremonial contamination prohibited by Mosaic law. Jesus spoke of such embellishment in a rebuke of the Pharisees (Mt 23:27).

Treatment of the Corpse The assurance given by God to Jacob that "Joseph's hand shall close your eyes" (Gn 46:4, RSV) probably alludes to the custom of a near relative closing the eyes of one who died with a fixed stare. Close relatives might also literally embrace and kiss the body immediately upon expiration. The body was washed and dressed in the deceased one's clothing. Pins and other ornaments found in excavated tombs are evidence that the dead were buried fully clothed. Soldiers were buried in full regalia, with shields covering or cradling the armored bodies, their swords under their heads (Ez 32:27).

Embalming was not a usual practice in Israel. Egyptian treatment for Jacob and Joseph was the exception rather than the rule. According to the Greek historian Herodotus, the Egyptians commenced embalming procedures by removing the brain from the cranium through the nasal apertures, piecemeal, using a long curved hook. When this had been done, the cranial cavity was rinsed out with a mixture of resins and spices. The corpse was eviscerated, and the entrails were placed in four canopic jars. The body was soaked in a solution of natron for a period of from 40 to 80 days, depending on the cost of the burial. At the time of interment, the corpse was wrapped in strips of fine linen cloth from head to foot and put in an anthropoid coffin. The canopic jars were placed in the tomb along with the body, symbolizing the reuniting of the personality and its survival after death.

Cremation of the bodies of Saul and his sons (1 Sm 31:12-13) was also an exception to normal practice. The Roman historian Tacitus wrote that in contrast with Roman custom, Jewish piety required the burying rather than burning of dead bodies. Under Mosaic law such burning was reserved as a sentence of judgment (Lv 21:9; Jos 7:25).

After preparation of the body, it was carried on a bier (a simple frame with carrying poles) without being placed in a coffin. The body was laid either in a prepared niche in the wall of a rock-hewn chamber or directly in a shallow grave dug in a burial plot. Neither bier nor any form of casket entered the pit with the corpse. The spices used as a perfume and temporary deterrent to decay cannot properly be considered an attempt at embalming (Mk 16:1).

As we know from the Gospel record of Jesus' burial, some cave tombs had a seal at the doorway, either a hinged wooden door or a flat stone shaped so it could be rolled into place. Such a stone seal could be reopened only with extreme effort (Mk 15:46; 16:3-4). By NT times the Jews sometimes economized on the use of a family tomb by placing the dry bones of formerly buried relatives in ossuaries. These boxlike receptacles were probably an adaptation of chests used by the Romans for holding ashes after a cremation.

Under Mosaic legislation, ceremonial defilement was contracted either through physical contact with the corpse or by participation in the formalities of mourning. Especially stringent prohibitions applied to the priests of Israel. The high priest himself could have nothing at all to do with mourning. In particular, he "must never defile himself by going near a dead person, even if it is his father or mother. He must not desecrate the sanctuary of his God by leaving it to attend his parents' funeral, because he has been made holy by the anointing oil of his God" (Lv 21:10-12, NLT).

Although the customs and procedures were evidently modified little from OT to NT times, some added details are given in the NT record. For example, it is noted that the corpse was washed (Acts 9:37). The body was then anointed and wrapped in linen cloths with spices enclosed (Mk 16:1; Jn 19:40). Finally, the limbs were tightly bound and the head covered with a separate piece of cloth (Jn 11:44).

See also Mourning; Funeral Customs.

BURNING BUSH Flaming bush on Mt Horeb, where Moses experienced God's presence and received the commission to lead the people of Israel out of Egypt (Ex 3:1-15; Mk 12:26; Lk 20:37; Acts 7:30-34). The enigma of a plant burning without being consumed provided the opportunity for God to reveal his name, "I AM WHO I AM." The burning bush was a theophany, a visible revelation of God's glory. Association of clouds, fire, and smoke with the manifestation of God's glory is a common biblical theme (see Ex 13:21; 19:18; 1 Kgs 8:10-11; 2 Kgs 1;12; 2:11; Is 6:1-6; 2 Thes 1:7; Rv 1:14; 19:12).

The burning bush was also symbolic of God's holiness. Moses was commanded not to approach, but to remove his shoes because the place where he was standing was holy ground (Ex 3:5). Unlike the gods of Egypt, who were pictured as living in gloomy darkness, Israel's God revealed himself as one who lives in unapproachable light (1 Tm 6:16). The burning bush evidently symbolized his intent not to consume or destroy his people, but to be their savior, to lead them out of bondage in Egypt and into the Promised Land.

See also Exodus, Book of; Moses; Theophany; God, Names of.

BURNT OFFERING Form of Israelite sacrifice in which a choice animal offered to make atonement for sin was completely consumed by fire (Lv 1). *See* Offerings and Sacrifices.

BUSH *See* Plants.

BUSHEL
1. Small vessel ("basket," NLT) that could cover a light (Mt 5:15; Mk 4:21; Lk 11:33). *See* Weights and Measures.
2. Unit of measure (Hebrew *ephah*) roughly equal to 19 quarts (18 liters).

BUTLER* Translation of a Hebrew word meaning "cupbearer" or "wine taster" in Genesis 40 and 41. *See* Cup-bearer.

BUZ (Person)
1. Abraham's nephew, and one of Nahor's eight sons (Gn 22:21).
2. Member of Gad's tribe (1 Chr 5:14).

BUZ (Place) Place of uncertain location mentioned along with two Arabian villages or oases, Dedan and Tema (Jer 25:23).

BUZI Father of the prophet Ezekiel (Ez 1:1-3).

BUZITE Resident of Buz. Elihu, one of Job's protagonists, is described as being the son of Barachel the Buzite (Jb 32:2, 6). *See* Buz (Place).

BUZZARD Any of a number of birds of prey declared ritually unclean (Dt 14:13). *See* Birds.

C

CAB* Alternate rendering of kab. *See* Kab.

CABBON Town in the foothills of Judah (Jos 15:40) east of Lachish, identified with Hebra and sometimes equated with Macbenah (1 Chr 2:49).

CABUL

1. Asherite town near Mt Carmel on the border between Israel and Tyre (Jos 19:27).
2. Territory given to Hiram, king of Tyre, by Solomon in exchange for a gift of 120 talents (9,000 pounds, 4 metric tons) of gold for completion of the temple. Hiram, not impressed with this northern Galilean province (1 Kgs 9:13-14), later returned it to Solomon (2 Chr 8:2).

CAESAREA City named in honor of Augustus Caesar, built by Herod the Great from 22 to 10 BC. The 8,000-acre (3,240-hectare) site lies 25 miles (40 kilometers) south of modern Haifa, in the beautiful plain of Sharon on Israel's Mediterranean coast. Known as Caesarea Maritima, it became the administrative center of the country throughout the period of Roman occupation. Three Roman governors of Palestine lived there: Felix (Acts 24), Festus (25:1, 4-6, 13), and Pontius Pilate, who visited Jerusalem on special occasions (as in Jn 19). Archaeologists found Pilate's name carved in stone in the theater at Caesarea.

Caesarea served as the major seaport of Judea in NT times. Since the southern Palestinian coastline lacked a good harbor, Herod created one by building two huge breakwaters that could shelter ships from Mediterranean storms.

A Roman officer named Cornelius was converted to Christianity in Caesarea (Acts 10:1, 24). Later, the apostle Peter visited Philip, a prominent Christian leader who lived there (21:8). Paul spent more than two years in prison in Caesarea (24:27–25:1) and embarked from there on his journey to Rome (ch 27). In AD 70 Roman general Titus returned to Caesarea after conquering Jerusalem, as did Flavius Silva in AD 73 after defeating the fortress cities of Masada and Herodium (both in eastern Judea).

Continuous excavations since 1971 have added to the wealth of information about Caesarea. Herod built a high-level aqueduct to bring freshwater from Mt Carmel to Caesarea; the water originated from springs to the northeast and traveled in an underground aqueduct to Mt Carmel. A smaller aqueduct brought brackish water from a spring north of the city for irrigation. Large sewers (mentioned by the Jewish historian Josephus), flushed by the action of the sea, have been found running under the city. A 30,000-seat hippodrome (racetrack) lay on the east side of the city. It appears to have been built in the second century AD but was destroyed during the Muslim invasion of 640, along with a large archives building on the coast. Excavation of the archives building produced several inscriptions on its mosaic floors, among which were two

Aerial View of Caesarea Maritima

quotations of the Greek text of Romans 13:3. Still lying beneath the ground and visible only in infrared photography is a large amphitheater northwest of the hippodrome.

Excavations in 1976 produced the first evidence of Strato's Tower, the Hellenistic site near which Herod built Caesarea, according to Josephus. A small synagogue was excavated north of a large fort built at the Herodian harbor during the Crusades. The harbor area contained many stone storerooms; although 7 have been entered, as many as 73 may still lie unexcavated. One storeroom was reused by the Roman legions as a Mithraeum (a cultic center dedicated to the Persian god Mithras), the only one ever found in Palestine. The city of Caesarea was not rebuilt after its destruction by Muslims in the 13th century.

CAESAREA PHILIPPI

CAESAREA PHILIPPI City at the northern extremity of Palestine, on the southern slopes of Mt Hermon near the ancient city of Dan. Caesarea Philippi lies in a beautiful area on one of the three sources of the Jordan River, the Wadi Banias.

In the second century BC, the place was called Panion because the Greek god Pan was worshiped in a cave there. It is mentioned by Polybius, a Greek historian, as the place where Syrian king Antiochus III defeated the Ptolemies of Egypt in an important battle about 200 BC. The Jewish historian Josephus (*Antiquities* 15.10.3) wrote that "Panium" was governed by Zenodorus; its cultic site was "a very fine cave in a mountain, under which there is a great cavity in the earth, and the cavern is abrupt, and prodigiously deep, and full of a still water; over it hangs a vast mountain, and under the caverns arise the springs of the river Jordan."

After the death of Zenodorus, Augustus Caesar gave the city to Herod the Great, who, according to Josephus, "adorned this place, which was already a very remarkable one" with a "most beautiful temple of the whitest stone." When Herod died in 4 BC, his son Philip was given the territory surrounding Panion, an area known as Paneas. Josephus (*War* 2.9.1) reported that "Philip built the city Caesarea, at the fountains of Jordan, and in the region of Paneas." Philip made it his capital and named it Caesarea Philippi after the Roman emperor Tiberius Caesar and himself, thus distinguishing it from the larger Caesarea Maritima on the Mediterranean coast. Josephus (*War* 3.9.7) wrote that emperors Vespasian and Titus both "marched from that Caesarea which lay by the seaside, and came to that which is named Caesarea Philippi."

It was in Caesarea Philippi that the apostle Peter confessed Jesus to be "the Christ, the Son of the living God" (Mt 16:13-16; Mk 8:27-29).

About AD 50, Agrippa II enlarged Caesarea Philippi and named it Neronias in honor of the emperor Nero. The modern name, Banias, derives from the Arabic difficulty in pronouncing Paneas.

CAESARS, The

CAESARS, The Succession of Roman emperors. The name Caesar, which has derivatives in the German Kaiser, Dutch Keizer, and Russian Czar, goes back to the family name of Julius Caesar (100–44 BC), which his successors took to themselves. Luke's Gospel mentions Caesar Augustus (Lk 2:1) and Tiberius Caesar (Lk 3:1). In the book of Acts the title "Caesar" is used to refer to Nero (Acts 25:11-12, 21; 26:32; 27:24; 28:19). During NT times, 12 Caesars reigned, 6 of them actually of the Caesarean lineage.

Emperors of Caesar's Lineage

Julius Caesar (100–44 BC) Julius had imperial powers but never held the title of emperor. Rome had been a republic (really an aristocracy) for almost 500 years. Its citizens hated the idea of a monarch, a position Julius Caesar judiciously declined, accepting a republican office but ruling as virtual dictator. The republic was dead in practice if not in principle. Vainly hoping to revive it and fearing Caesar's imperial ambitions, a group of republicans conspired to assassinate him. Caesar was murdered on March 15 (the "ides of March"), 44 BC, as he entered the Roman Senate. Although the conspiracy succeeded, its purpose failed. In the civil war that followed, Caesar's grand-nephew Octavian emerged as victor and in 31 BC became the first Roman emperor.

Augustus (63 BC–AD 14, reigned 31 BC–AD 14) Gaius Octavianus (Octavian) was the grandson of Julia, Julius Caesar's sister. He was 18 and studying in Greece when his great-uncle was assassinated. Caesar's will, which adopted him as son and made him heir, brought him into the resulting power struggle.

Within a year and a half, a trio consisting of Antony, Lepidus, and Octavian was confirmed in power. The following year, in a battle at Philippi (in Macedonia, now Greece), Octavian defeated both Cassius and Brutus, the chief conspirators against Caesar. Antony took command of the eastern provinces (which included Greece and Egypt), Octavian led his forces back to Italy, and Lepidus assumed jurisdiction over Gaul and western North Africa. Lepidus, however, was forced into retirement, and the area he controlled fell to Octavian. Thus Octavian and Antony, who had clashed even before their alliance, became rivals again. In the battle of Actium (31 BC), Octavian defeated Antony to become sole ruler of the Roman world and its first emperor.

Octavian did not possess the military brilliance of his great-uncle, but he had a talent for ending strife and maintaining peace, which immediately gained him the support of the people. During his reign Roman culture enjoyed a golden age, particularly in architecture and literature. Augustus founded the Praetorian Guard, the emperor's private honor corps of 9,000 soldiers. Originally intended to secure the emperor's position, it later became so influential that it could independently depose an emperor or elect a new one without Senate confirmation.

The title Augustus (*Augoustos*), meaning "exalted one," was given to Octavian in 27 BC. The title reflects the practice of emperor worship that had been partly initiated in the reign of Julius Caesar, who declared himself to be "the unconquered god" and "the father of the fatherland." Augustus continued the cult, although at first he declared that he should be worshiped only in association with the goddess Roma. Later, however, Augustus's name became equated with Rome, and the emperor was regarded as the savior of the world. A temple to Augustus was built in Athens, and even Herod the Great built temples in his honor.

When Augustus became emperor, he devoted himself to reorganizing his empire. Because of the chaos that had prevailed in the provinces, he took it upon himself to restructure economic and financial policies.

Though Caesar Augustus is mentioned only once in the NT, he nevertheless is known to every reader of the Bible because of the census he decreed in all the provinces just before the birth of Jesus (Lk 2:1). Little information is available about that census, but Luke wrote that the first census was held when Jesus was born. The second was conducted in AD 6 and resulted in an uprising instigated by Judas of Galilee (Acts 5:37).

During the time of Augustus's reign, Herod the Great gained the emperor's trust and was allowed to rule the Jews without Roman interference. In appreciation Herod rebuilt the old city of Samaria and renamed it Sebaste to honor Augustus. Caesarea on the Mediterranean coast of Palestine was also named in his honor.

Conflicts between Herod and his sons were settled by Augustus in 12 BC. When dispute between father and sons arose again, however, Augustus ordered that it be settled in a Roman court, which ruled in 7 BC that two of them, Alexander and Aristobulus, be executed. In 4 BC, Augustus permitted the execution of Herod's son Antipater.

In Herod's last will and testament, three of his sons (Archelaus, Antipas, and Philip) were appointed to rule his kingdom. Augustus's approval of those appointments was necessary. Archelaus made a personal visit to Rome immediately after the death of his father to request possible changes in his status. Likewise, Antipas journeyed to Rome to see whether Augustus might be willing to grant him royal status as well. While the two of them sought separate audiences with the emperor, a delegation representing the people of Judea appeared before Augustus with the request that the Herodian rule—which was never very popular—be terminated. At the same time riots in Judea had to be suppressed by Roman legions sent from Syria.

Augustus compromised. He converted Herod's old kingdom to a Roman province and refused kingship to all of Herod's sons. Otherwise he kept to the provisions of Herod's testament: Archelaus became ethnarch (overlord) of Judea, Samaria, and Idumea (half of the new province); Antipas became tetrarch of Galilee and Perea (one quarter of the province); Philip became tetrarch of Iturea and Trachonitis (Lk 3:1; an area east of Galilee—the final quarter of the province). Because Archelaus was unable to rule effectively, he was deposed by the emperor in AD 6 and banished to Vienne in southern France.

Augustus died in AD 14 after a brief illness, leaving the empire to his appointed successor, Tiberius.

Tiberius (42 BC–AD 37, reigned AD 14–37) Tiberius Claudius Nero became Octavian's stepson at the age of four, when his mother, Livia, divorced his father to marry the future emperor. Tiberius was made Augustus's co-regent in AD 13 and succeeded him the following year. When he became emperor, he changed his name to Tiberius Caesar Augustus.

Tiberius did not have an easy life. His stepfather had forced an unhappy marriage upon him. The Roman Senate often opposed him. In AD 27 Tiberius left Rome for the island of Capri, leaving the task of governing the empire in the hands of Sejanus, a Roman prefect (high-ranking official). During the next five years, Sejanus secretly tried to depose the emperor and seize power for himself. His conspiracy almost succeeded, but Tiberius eventually had him executed. Despite this, Tiberius's administration was characterized by wisdom, intelligence, prudence, and duty. He continued his predecessor's policy of striving for peace and security.

In AD 26, presumably before going into semi-retirement, Tiberius appointed Pontius Pilate as governor of Judea. Directly responsible to the emperor, Pilate could be immediately removed from office if word of Jewish disturbances or complaints reached Tiberius. Pilate's capitulation to the Jewish authorities during the trial of Jesus can be best understood in view of this. The Jews accused Jesus of claiming to be king, implying a rivalry with the emperor. When Pilate judged Christ innocent of the charge and sought to release him (Jn 18:33-38), the Jews insisted he could not do so and still be a friend of Caesar (19:12). If he released Jesus, they insinuated, he would risk losing the emperor's favor. Because of crimes committed at his command against

the Jews, Pilate knew they might carry out their threat, resulting in his banishment. So, surrendering to their demands, he condemned Jesus to death by crucifixion.

Tiberius Caesar is mentioned only once in the NT. The Gospel of Luke states that John the Baptist began his ministry in the 15th year of Tiberius Caesar's reign, when Pontius Pilate was governor of Judea (Lk 3:1). Whether that date was calculated from Tiberius's actual accession or from the time of his co-regency is difficult to determine.

Tiberius was a strangely humble emperor. At his own request he was never officially recognized as a god (a sort of honorary title that the Senate had given to his predecessors). Interest in emperor worship had waned, and Tiberius intended to confine deity to his two predecessors. He also stopped the practice of naming months of the year after emperors; thus there is a July for Julius, an August for Augustus, but no Tiber for Tiberius. Plagued by domestic and political problems all his life, Tiberius died a tired and dejected old man. In fact, he was an excellent administrator.

Caligula (AD 12–41, reigned AD 37–41) At the death of Tiberius, Gaius Julius Caesar became emperor at the age of 25. He was the son of an influential general, Germanicus; Augustus had forced Tiberius to adopt Gaius and make him his heir. As a child, Gaius had accompanied Germanicus on his military duties along the Rhine River in Germany. The soldiers nicknamed him Caligula ("Little Boot") for his military attire. The name stuck.

To gain popularity with the Romans, Caligula began his reign by pardoning people and recalling exiles. He squandered the money of the Roman treasury, however, and was forced to levy new taxes. His popularity was short-lived.

Six months after assuming office, Caligula suffered a serious illness that left him insane. On one occasion, for example, he appointed his horse as consul (chief magistrate). He insulted many people, banished others on whim, and had others murdered without provocation. When he felt that he had been insulted by the Jews in Jamnia, a Judean town near the Mediterranean coast, he ordered a statue of himself placed in the temple at Jerusalem in revenge. The Jews were outraged, and a full-scale revolt was avoided only by the prudence of the governor of Syria, Petronius, who delayed carrying out the order. Not long afterward the emperor was assassinated by one of the many men he had insulted.

It was Caligula who appointed Herod Agrippa I (Herod in Acts 12) king over a tetrarchy northeast of Galilee—one of the first acts he performed as emperor, according to the Jewish historian Josephus. The two had become close friends before either had come to power, while Agrippa was living in Rome, where even as king he later spent much of his time. But unlike Caligula, Agrippa was a capable and popular ruler. Both king and emperor, in the tradition of many eastern monarchs, fancied themselves gods. Caligula, in fact, revived the notion in Rome of the emperor's deity and madly proclaimed himself equal to Jupiter. The Senate, however, refrained from officially recognizing that status.

Claudius (10 BC–AD 54, reigned AD 41–54) Tiberius Claudius Germanicus was born in Lyon (France). He was Tiberius's nephew and a grandson of Livia, the wife of Augustus. In AD 37 he was appointed consul by Caligula. After Caligula's death Claudius was proclaimed emperor by the Praetorian Guard, and the Senate approved the choice.

When Claudius became emperor, he faced the task of healing the broken relationships caused by Caligula's madness. He ended the persecution of Jews in the city of Alexandria. Josephus recorded an edict that Claudius sent to

Egypt, which read, in part: "Tiberius Claudius Caesar Augustus Germanicus, high priest and tribune of the people, ordains thus. . . . I will, therefore, that the nation of the Jews be not deprived of their rights and privileges on account of the madness of Gaius; but that those rights and privileges that they formerly enjoyed, be preserved to them, and that they may continue in their own customs."

That change of policy reflected the emperor's friendship with Herod Agrippa, who had played an influential role in Claudius's succession as emperor. Claudius, in turn, added Judea and Samaria to Agrippa's kingdom, giving him the dominion that once belonged to his grandfather, Herod the Great. He also promoted him to consular rank. Further, having complete trust in Agrippa's abilities, Claudius removed Judea from Roman provincial rule.

Agrippa's rule, however, was of short duration. In order to please the Jews, he had the apostle James, Zebedee's son, killed. He also had the apostle Peter imprisoned, planning to have him executed after the Passover feast in the spring of AD 44 (Acts 12:1-5). Peter escaped. During the summer of that year, Agrippa, who was wearing a glistening garment made of silver thread, gave a speech from his throne. The people acclaimed him as a god (v 22), and immediately he was struck down by an angel of the Lord. Five days later he died.

The emperor wished to stay on the right side of the Jewish people, yet five years after the death of Agrippa, Claudius issued an edict expelling all Jews from Rome. Luke related that Aquila and Priscilla were among those who had been ordered to leave the imperial city (Acts 18:2). The Roman biographer and historian Suetonius wrote that "because the Jews of Rome were indulging in constant riots at the instigation of Chrestus he [Claudius] expelled them from the city." The writer could easily have been uncertain of the spelling, because Chrestus, a common slave name, was pronounced virtually the same as Christus. It appears that Suetonius sought to convey to his readers that Chrestus was the founder of a movement (presumably Christianity).

Because of mismanagement by Caligula, the supply of grain for food was at an all-time low when Claudius began to reign (cf. Acts 11:28). Josephus related that during Claudius's administration, famine plagued Judea, Samaria, and Galilee. To alleviate the famine in Jerusalem, Helena, mother of the king of Adiabene, bought grain from Egypt and dried figs from Cyprus. That must have taken place in AD 45–46. Various ancient historians, including Tacitus, Suetonius, and Eusebius, reported that on frequent occasions famines prevailed in Rome and elsewhere. Repeatedly, harvests were minimal and distribution of food supplies was poor.

Claudius's family life and reputation were marred by intrigue. His immoral third wife, Messalina, was eventually put to death. Causing a slight scandal, he married his niece Agrippina, who had a son by a former marriage. She wanted her son Nero to be emperor, but Britannicus, Messalina's son, stood first in line. In AD 54, when Claudius decided that Britannicus should succeed him, Agrippina poisoned her husband and made Nero emperor. The Senate officially deified Claudius, making him the third emperor to receive that honor.

Nero (AD 37–68, reigned AD 54–68) Nero was born Lucius Domitius Ahenobarbus. His father was a senator and consul who died when Nero was still a boy. His mother, Agrippina, Germanicus's daughter, was reputed to be one of the wealthiest and most beautiful women in Rome. When she married the emperor, her son received the name Nero Claudius Caesar Germanicus at his adoption by Claudius.

Nero was at first dominated by his proud mother, who wished to reign alongside her son. In those years Rome was a hotbed of political intrigue, murder plots, and assassinations. During the first five years of his reign, Nero had Britannicus and Agrippina eliminated in quick succession. A few years later he banished his wife, Octavia, and had her killed.

Ironically, the church at Rome flourished at that same time. The last chapter of the apostle Paul's Letter to the Romans, written from Corinth in AD 57, contains a long and impressive list of names of personal acquaintances—especially impressive because Paul had never been in Rome.

Nero had reigned more than five years when Paul, imprisoned at Caesarea, appealed to Caesar (Acts 25:11). Motives for the appeal may have been a prison release for Paul and an opportunity to seek legal recognition of Christianity. Paul's appeal to Caesar, however, does not necessarily mean that he was judged by Nero. The emperor had made it known at the beginning of his reign that he would not be a judge. Instead, he appointed prefects of the Praetorian Guard to judge cases for him. In the early part of AD 62, Nero changed that rule and judged a case himself. Therefore, whether Paul stood before Nero or before one of the prefects is difficult to determine. If prosecutors failed to appear, Paul's case may not have come before the judge at all. According to Philippians 1:7-14, Paul was still expecting a trial at the time of his writing that letter.

In AD 62 Nero's adviser Afranius Burrus died. Burrus had been a prefect of the Praetorian Guard and, together with an able senator, Seneca, had ruled the empire effectively while Nero spent his time on pleasure. After Burrus's death (Seneca was forced to commit suicide three years later), Nero began to indulge his whims unchecked. His greedy advisers, who sought self-advancement at the expense of the state, caused a severe financial crisis. Nero was also unbalanced in regarding himself the savior of the world.

In AD 64 a fire broke out at the Circus Maximus in Rome. It spread quickly, devouring everything in its path. Fanned by the wind, it raged for more than five days and devastated a large area of the city before being brought under control. At the time, Nero was at Antium, his birthplace, some 33 miles (53 kilometers) to the south. He rushed to Rome to organize relief work. Because of his evil record, however, people put stock in the rumor that Nero had set the fire himself.

Nero, in turn, found a scapegoat in the Christians, whom he charged with the crime. Many were persecuted. Perhaps the apostle Peter in his first letter was referring to the sufferings of Christians during the last few years of Nero's reign (1 Pt 4:12). Nero may have been influenced by his second wife, Poppaea, to blame the Christians for the devastation of Rome. The church had increased in numbers and had become a movement. Tacitus alluded to the size of the church when he wrote that "a huge crowd was convicted not so much of arson as of hatred of the human race."

It is likely that Peter and Paul were executed during the Neronian persecution. Clement of Rome, an early church father, in his letter to the church at Corinth (written presumably in AD 95), referred to the heroes of faith "who lived nearest to our time," namely Peter and Paul, who suffered martyrdom.

In AD 66 a Jewish revolt broke out in Caesarea. Nero dispatched his general Vespasian to squelch the revolt, taking no interest himself in the affairs of state. He left Rome for a journey to Greece, leaving the responsibility of governing the empire to a Roman prefect, Helius. Because of the inescapable opposition he encountered from leading governors in France, Spain, and Africa on his return, Nero committed suicide in AD 68. He was the last emperor of the Caesarean line by blood or marriage.

Some Later Emperors

Galba (3 BC–AD 69, reigned AD 68–69) After Nero's death, the Praetorian Guard selected Serius Sulpicius Galba to become emperor. Galba was a popular and capable governor at various times in the provinces of France, Germany, Spain, and Africa. He was a less successful emperor and became increasingly unpopular with the army and the people for his frugality and dislike of ceremony. The German legions of the Roman army, who had only reluctantly recognized him as their commander-in-chief, withdrew their support in AD 69, proclaiming Aulus Vitellius emperor.

When Galba failed to appoint one of his chief supporters, Marcus Salvius Otho, as his successor, he in essence signed his own death warrant. Otho gained the support of the Praetorian Guard, was proclaimed emperor, had Galba killed, and was confirmed by the Senate.

Vespasian (AD 9–79, reigned AD 69–79) In the fall of AD 69, Vespasian found Rome ready for a period of stability, peace, and order. The son of a tax collector, he lived frugally, reestablished Rome's finances, reorganized the armies, and reemphasized the outward forms of the old republic. According to Suetonius, no innocent party was ever punished while Vespasian was emperor. He grieved when convicted criminals were executed.

Because of Nero's financial mismanagement, Vespasian had to levy new taxes and increase existing taxes in order to meet his fiscal obligations. As a result he was slandered as avaricious, although he was generous in aiding underprivileged senators and impoverished ex-consuls. Vespasian improved a number of cities in the empire that had been devastated by fire or earthquake, and he promoted the arts and sciences. In Rome he built the Temple of Peace after the destruction of Jerusalem and the defeat of the Jews, erected a forum, restored the Capitol, and began construction of the Colosseum.

During his 10-year reign, Vespasian established peace throughout the empire. His son Titus ended the war in Palestine, and other Roman generals suppressed a revolt in Germany. Public confidence was largely restored with the return to earlier standards of morality. Vespasian appointed his sons Titus and Domitian to succeed him.

Titus (AD 39–81, reigned AD 79–81) Titus Flavius Vespasianus had served efficiently as a colonel in Germany and Britain. When the Jewish revolt broke out, he accompanied his father to Palestine. When Vespasian left for Rome five years later, Titus was appointed general of the Roman forces in Palestine. On September 26, AD 70, the temple in Jerusalem was destroyed by fire, the citadel fell into the hands of the Romans, and countless Jews were killed. Titus returned to Rome with Jewish captives and spoils from the temple to celebrate his victory with his father. The Arch of Titus was erected in Rome, depicting his conquest of Jerusalem.

Until Vespasian's death, Titus was almost a co-ruler with his father. He served as Vespasian's secretary, drafted edicts, and addressed the Senate in session. Titus was a talented person, especially in politics and music. He had fallen in love with Queen Bernice, King Agrippa II's sister (see Acts 25–26) and allegedly had promised to marry her, but moral integrity prevented him when rumor reached him of an incestuous relationship with her brother.

During Titus's brief reign as emperor (AD 79–81), a series of catastrophes occurred: Mt Vesuvius in southern Italy erupted and buried the towns of Pompeii, Stabiae, and Herculaneum (August, AD 79); a fire raged for three days and nights in Rome (AD 80); and a plague spread throughout the imperial city. Suetonius wrote that during those disasters Titus cared for the people with a love resembling the deep love of a father for his children. When Titus died unexpectedly, his death caused universal mourning; he was eulogized by senators and common people alike.

Domitian (AD 51–96, reigned AD 81–96) During Titus's rule, his brother Domitian expressed bitterness at having to take second place, openly coveted power, and conspired to seize command of the armed forces. He secretly rejoiced over Titus's sudden death and tried to slight his older brother's reputation. As it turned out, Domitian proved to be a capable administrator: he restored the fire-gutted Capitol and built a temple to Jupiter, the Flavian Temple, a forum, a stadium, a concert hall, and an artificial lake for sea battles. He instituted the Capitoline Festival, promoted the arts and sciences, and maintained the public libraries.

After the custom of earlier emperors Domitian proclaimed himself divine and had his subjects call him "Lord God." The Senate, however, never officially deified him. Throughout his reign they resented and often opposed the power he exercised by prerogative. Domitian did not hesitate to persecute senators who made their objections known. In order to protect himself, he sought the army's support by periodically increasing their pay. He collected additional taxes and often resorted to extortion. Jewish people were especially affected by his taxation. In the last years of Domitian's reign, religious persecution was revived.

The early Christian writers Irenaeus, Tertullian, and Eusebius mention the persecution of Christians during Domitian's administration. Domitian appears to have been a relentless persecutor, second only to Nero. He even put members of his own family to death; his wife, Domitia, feared for her life because of her alleged affiliation with Christianity. With friends and freedmen, she plotted her husband's assassination.

After ruling the empire for 15 years, Domitian was murdered. Mourned by none, except perhaps his well-paid army, he left in the wake of his reign a bitter memory of oppression.

Trajan (AD 53–117, reigned AD 98–117) Trajan was born Marcus Trajanus of Roman parents in Italica, Spain. His father was a soldier who was promoted to governor of an eastern province in Spain. Trajan, trained to be a military commander, proved himself in campaigns in Spain, Syria, and Germany. In AD 97, Emperor Nerva adopted him as his son and heir. Upon Nerva's death the following year, Trajan was named emperor.

A powerful military leader, Trajan expanded the Roman Empire by many conquests in Dacia (now part of Romania and Hungary), Arabia, and Parthia (now part of Iran). He established new cities, including Thamugadi in what is now Algeria. He also oversaw many building programs, including bridges across the Danube River in Dacia and Tagus River in Spain, and a harbor at the port of Rome. According to the writings of Pliny (see *Letters* 10.96), we know that Trajan instigated persecutions against Christians because their worship of Jesus threatened to exterminate the traditional forms of Roman worship. The Christians' refusal to invoke the Roman gods and make offerings to the emperor's statue was considered a treasonous act because it undermined the empire's security.

Diocletian (AD 245–313, reigned AD 284–305) Born to parents of humble means in Dalmatia (now part of Yugoslavia), Diocles changed his name to Diocletian when he became emperor. As a young man he joined the army and rose in rank, becoming commander of the imperial guard. When the emperor Numerian was murdered, Diocles' troops proclaimed him the new ruler. Numerian's brother, Carinus, was killed by his own troops when he sought the throne, and the way was clear for Diocles to assume control unopposed.

Diocletian, an able organizer and administrator, used his skills to enact many structural reforms in the Roman Empire, including the establishment of the tetrarchy (293), a new imperial system in which four rulers shared power. His other reforms affected military, administrative, and economic areas. As a result of such reorganization, Diocletian created an efficient bureaucracy. Nevertheless, Rome declined as a political power center, and the Senate was further subordinated to the tetrarchy.

A persecution of Christians began during Diocletian's reign in 303, which was aimed at destroying church buildings and copies of the NT Scriptures. Among the tetrarchs, Galerius was the most active in carrying out the persecution. Because persecution continued under Galerius after Diocletian's abdication, some scholars maintain that Diocletian was not responsible for the policy. Diocletian retired to a villa at Split in his native Dalmatia, avoiding public association with the new administration's superstitious and violent policies.

Constantine the Great (AD 272 or 273–337, reigned AD 306–337)

Constantine's parents were Constantius Chlorus, the Western co-emperor of the Roman Empire, and Helena, a concubine. When his father died in England in 306, Constantine was proclaimed emperor by the troops and grudgingly accepted by Galerius, the Eastern emperor. The government of the empire was thrown into turmoil, and within two years five men had claimed to be emperor.

Shortly before his death in 311, Galerius, the senior co-emperor, issued an edict of toleration that ended the persecution of Christians. With Galerius gone, Constantine and Licinius (who had become his co-emperor) allied themselves against Maxentius and Maximin Daia. In 312 Constantine defeated and killed Maxentius in a battle at the Mulvian Bridge near Rome. Maximin Daia fell to Licinius in the next year. An uneasy peace between Constantine and Licinius was maintained until 323, when Constantine crossed into Licinius's territory while chasing out Gothic invaders. Battles at Adrianople and Chrysopolis in the next year decided the matter and left Constantine the sole emperor.

One of his most significant political moves was the founding of the city of Constantinople, dedicated in 330 on the site of Byzantium. Its location on the Strait of Bosporus was ideal from a military standpoint since it gave access to both the Rhine-Danube and Persian fronts. Constantine continued a reorganization of government started by Diocletian (reigned 284-305) and reformed the currency. He also allowed barbarians to settle within the empire in order to use them in the army.

Constantine is most remembered for his religious policies. The nature of his own religious beliefs has been disputed. From the first he was tolerant of Christians in his own realm. His preference for Christianity was demonstrated just before the battle at the Mulvian Bridge. According to one account, in a dream before the battle Constantine saw a vision of a monogram composed of the first two Greek letters of the name of "Christ." The next day he had his soldiers inscribe that monogram on their shields. Another story says that, while marching one day, he and his army saw the image of a cross appear before the sun with the words "In this sign conquer." During the winter of 312–13, he wrote to an officer in North Africa

Constantine's Image

Coin of Constantine Coin commemorating the first official recognition of Christianity

instructing him to supply money to the bishop of Carthage in order to pay expenses of the clergy. When he and Licinius met in Milan in 313, they issued an edict granting all persons the freedom to follow whichever religion they wished. His Christian sentiments also resulted in laws allowing bishops to decide civil lawsuits, banning any branding on the face (because it marred the image of God), closing law courts and workshops on Sunday, and banning gladiatorial games. Though he favored Christianity, Constantine was also tolerant of paganism and, as late as 324, pagan themes were engraved on his coins. With Christians such a minority in the empire, Constantine felt he could not risk offending the pagan majority.

Constantine took an active role in church controversies. When Caecilian was challenged as bishop of Carthage (313) by the Donatists (separatists in the African church), Constantine instructed the bishops of Rome to summon a commission to hear the case. Since the Donatists were not content with the results of that commission, Constantine himself eventually heard the case, and in 316 he declared Caecilian to be the rightful bishop. Constantine also summoned the Council of Nicaea in 325, which ruled against Arianism (a heresy that denied that Christ as the Son of God was coeternal with the Father). It was the emperor's edict that gave legal force to the Nicaean decision.

One serious scandal marred Constantine's reign. In 326 he had his son Crispus and his own wife, Faustus, executed on charges of adultery. Constantine was succeeded by his three other sons (Constans, Constantius, Constantine II), after being baptized a Christian on his deathbed (according to legend).

See also Rome, City of.

CAESAR'S HOUSEHOLD*

Term referring to imperial servants, both slave and free, in Rome and in the provinces of the Roman Empire. The apostle Paul closed his letter to the Philippian Christians with greetings from those "of Caesar's household" (4:22, RSV). The imperial household staff numbered in the hundreds, and the positions carried a certain amount of social importance.

According to the Martyrdom of Paul, written in the second century, when Paul arrived at Rome, he was greeted by people "from Caesar's household." He put himself in communication with the local Jewish leaders and preached and taught unhindered (Acts 28:17, 31). Some men and women were convinced and believed (Acts 28:23-24), no doubt including some in Caesar's household. The message even spread to the whole Praetorian Guard (Phil 1:13). Some scholars trace certain believers mentioned in Romans 16 to members of the imperial household.

See also Caesars, The.

CAIAPHAS

High priest during the life and ministry of Jesus. As official head of the Jewish state, Caiaphas presided over the council, or Sanhedrin—its highest court. Next to the Roman governor, he was the most powerful man in Judea and was responsible to the Romans for the conduct of the nation. Caiaphas was, therefore, especially concerned about the popular enthusiasm and political unrest centering on the ministry of Jesus and about its implications for the revolutionary sentiment of the time. The activities of the Zealots were increasing and were destined to break out soon into open revolt.

A huge stir among the people, caused by the raising of Lazarus (Jn 11), brought matters to a head. Alarmed lest the activities of those seeking a political messiah should lead the Romans to intervene with armed force, Caiaphas advised that Jesus should be put to death (Jn 11:48-50). The Gospel writer John pointed out that, in so doing, Caiaphas unwittingly prophesied concerning the atoning nature of Jesus' death (Jn 11:51-52).

Caiaphas played a chief role in Jesus' arrest and trial. The leaders laid their plans in his palace (Mt 26:3-5); it was there also that part of Jesus' preliminary trial took place with Caiaphas presiding (vv 57-68). That was after Jesus had first been taken before Annas, Caiaphas's father-in-law (Jn 18:13). Matthew, Mark, and Luke omit the visit to Annas, and Mark and Luke do not refer to Caiaphas by name. Upon Jesus' admission that he was "the Christ, the Son of God," Caiaphas tore his robes and charged him with blasphemy (Mt 26:63-66). After Pentecost, he, along with other Jewish leaders, presided over the trial of Peter and John when the council attempted to stop the preaching of the apostles (Acts 4:5-6).

Annas, who had held the office of high priest before Caiaphas, remained influential in the affairs of the nation. That explains why Luke, in his Gospel, set the ministry of John the Baptist "in the high-priesthood of Annas and Caiaphas" (Lk 3:2), and in Acts called Annas the high priest (Acts 4:6). John's account of Jesus' visit to Annas makes plain that Annas was still popularly referred to as "high priest" (Jn 18:22).

The historian Josephus records that Caiaphas was appointed to his office about AD 18 and ruled until he was deposed about AD 36. The high priest held office at the whim of the Romans, so Caiaphas's unusually long term indicates that he was a man of considerable political skill. Caiaphas was removed from his position by the proconsul Vitellus, and nothing more is known of him.

CAIN (Person) First son of Adam and Eve, who became a tiller of the soil while his brother, Abel, was a keeper of sheep. Cain's murder of Abel became proverbial of similarly violent and destructive sins (Jude 1:11). Each of the two brothers had brought a sacrifice to the Lord (Gn 4:3-4). According to Hebrews 11:4, Abel had acted in faith by bringing a more acceptable sacrifice than that of Cain. The latter's anger had flared against the divine rejection. In retaliation, he killed his brother, whose offering had been accepted (Gn 4:5-8). In seeking a reason for Cain's inappropriate violent reaction, biblical commentary simply says that he belonged to the evil one (1 Jn 3:12). The Lord confronted Cain with his guilt, judged him, and pronounced a curse upon him, driving him out to the land of Nod, east of Eden (Gn 4:9-16). When he complained that his punishment was greater than he could bear and that someone would find him and kill him, the Lord placed a mark on Cain and promised to take sevenfold vengeance on anyone who dared to kill him.

In the land of Nod, Cain built a city and named it after his son Enoch (Gn 4:17). Through Enoch, Cain became the progenitor of a large family that during its early gen-

erations became tent-dwelling herdsmen, musicians, and fashioners of metal objects and implements (vv 18-22).

CAIN* (Place) KJV spelling of Kain, the name of a city in the southern hill country of Judah's territory, in Joshua 15:57. *See* Kain (Place).

CAINAN
1. A son of Arphaxad (Lk 3:36; Gn 10:24, LXX; 11:12-13).
2. Adam's great-grandson, also called Kenan (Gn 5:9-14; 1 Chr 1:2; Lk 3:37). *See* Kenan.

CALAH One of the ancient capital cities of Assyria built by Nimrod (Gn 10:11-12). Calah is the ancient name for modern Nimrud, which is located 24 miles (38.6 kilometers) south of Nineveh on the east bank of the Tigris River. It was excavated by Henry Layard from 1845 to 1849 and by the British School of Archaeology in Iraq from 1949 to 1964. The site was occupied from prehistoric times down to the Hellenistic period.

Excavations at Calah revealed a large ziggurat and temples dedicated to Ninurta and Nabu. A large citadel constructed by Shalmaneser I in the 13th century BC and a palace built by Ashurnasirpal II (883–859 BC) were also uncovered there. Palaces of Shalmaneser III (858–824 BC) and Esarhaddon (680–669 BC) were partially cleared. Among other notable discoveries from the city is the black obelisk of Shalmaneser III, which is presently in the British Museum. The monument is important to biblical studies because of its record of tribute paid by King Jehu of Israel to the Assyrians.

Tiglath-pileser III (745–727 BC) and Sargon II (721–705 BC) launched their attacks on Israel and Judah from Calah. Sargon captured Samaria. Tiglath-pileser was involved with Judah when Ahaz formed a coalition with him against Israel and Syria (Is 7:1-17). Calah was eventually destroyed by the Babylonians and Medes in 612 BC.

CALAMUS Variety of sweet-smelling cane (Ex 30:23; Sg 4:14; Ez 27:19). *See* Plants.

CALCOL One of Mahol's three sons and a member of Judah's tribe (1 Kgs 4:31, KJV "Chalcol"; 1 Chr 2:6). He and his brothers were noted for their wisdom and musical abilities.

CALEB
1. Son of Jephunneh the Kenizzite (Nm 32:12; Jos 14:6) and older brother of Kenaz (Jgs 1:13). Caleb was one of the 12 spies sent to scout out the land of Canaan. Although he and Joshua, another spy, recommended an immediate attack, their suggestion was rejected by the Israelite tribes because of other reports of heavily defended fortresses. Consequently, entrance into Canaan, the Promised Land, was delayed for some years as a divine judgment (Nm 14:21-23, 34-35).

When Israel under Joshua's leadership finally occupied Canaan, Caleb, at age 85 (Jos 14:6-7, 10), was assigned Hebron, which he conquered by overcoming its Anakim inhabitants (vv 13-14). Caleb offered his daughter Achsah to whomever would overthrow nearby Debir (Kiriath-sepher). Othniel, Kenaz's son and Achsah's cousin, was able to claim her as his wife by conquering the town (15:16-17).

Hebron later became a Levitical city of refuge (Jos 21:13; 1 Chr 6:55-57). In some portion of Caleb's territory David spent time as an outlaw and met his future wife Abigail, then the wife of Nabal, a Calebite (1 Sm 25:3). Here also his wives were captured by

Amalekite marauders who had raided southern Judah and "the Negev of Caleb" (1 Sm 30:14).

2. Hezron's son and brother of Jerahmeel (1 Chr 2:18, 42), also called Chelubai (v 9). Many scholars, however, believe that this Caleb is the same as #1 above because (1) Achsah is mentioned as the daughter of both (v 49); and (2) the prominent place of an otherwise unknown Caleb in the genealogy would be hard to account for. According to these scholars, Caleb was listed as a son of Hezron (the grandson of Judah) in order to establish his position and inheritance in Judah's tribe. In reality, however, Caleb was a foreigner, son of Jephunneh, a Kenizzite, who had joined himself and his clan to Judah's tribe. Some support this view by arguing that Caleb is a Horite rather than Israelite name.

3. Hur's son, according to the KJV (1 Chr 2:50). Most likely, however, the KJV joins what should be two separate phrases. The NLT correctly renders it, "These were all descendants of Caleb. The sons of Hur . . ."

CALEB-EPHRATHAH

Possibly a Hebrew place-name (1 Chr 2:24, KJV, NLT). A number of modern translations follow the Septuagint (early Greek translation of the OT) in treating Ephrathah as the name of one of Caleb's wives instead of a place.

CALEBITE*

Descendant of Caleb, Jephunneh's son (1 Sm 25:3). *See* Caleb #1.

CALENDARS, Ancient and Modern

Systematic arrangements showing the beginning and length of each year and its division into days, weeks, and months. The modern calendar is usually taken for granted. But without a calendar it would be extremely difficult to establish a uniform chronology (that is, a system for arranging events in the time sequence in which they actually happened). Also, accurate prediction of the coming and going of seasons would be impossible.

Before the calendar took on its modern format, it had to progress through a number of developmental stages.

PREVIEW
• Days and Their Divisions
• Astronomy and the Calendar
• Jewish Calendar
• Jewish Festivals
• Conclusion

Days and Their Divisions

The earliest attempt to mark off time was probably the simple counting of days, followed by the subdivision of each day into what eventually became 24 equal parts called hours. Since the Sumerians seem to have originated the measurement of time by minutes, hours, and days, they obviously also knew the narrower meaning of "day," which for them designated a 12-hour period.

Measurement of time in the days of King Ahaz is illustrated by reference to a sundial (2 Kgs 20:9; Is 38:8). The precise measurement of hours, however, must have been a relatively late practice. Early Europeans, like the ancient Egyptians, placed the beginning of the day at midnight, further dividing the period into two 12-hour segments. In the second century BC the Egyptian astronomer Ptolemy and his disciples devised an astronomically convenient method of calculating each day from high noon, when the sun reached its apex in the heavens. The Roman day began at sunrise, with the second part of the day commencing at sunset.

Astronomy and the Calendar

Ancient peoples constructed their calendars on the basis of their observations of "cycles" of the sun and moon. The solar year is the period of time in which the earth accomplishes a complete revolution in its orbit around the sun.

The life of ancient peoples was closely tied to the changes in temperature and in the relative length of days and nights characteristic of the four seasons. Seasonal changes result from the fact that while the earth is orbiting the sun, it is also rotating on its own axis, tipped at an angle to the plane of its path around the sun. The longest day of the year in the northern hemisphere is called the summer solstice (about June 21 on the modern calendar). At the winter solstice (December 21 or 22) the noonday sun appears lowest (farthest south) and the days are shortest. (In the southern hemisphere summer and winter are reversed by the effect of the earth's tilt.) Halfway between, at the vernal (spring) equinox about March 21, and the autumnal (fall) equinox about September 23, the sun is directly over the equator and there are as many hours of daylight as of darkness. The term "equinox" is from the Latin words for "equal night." A solar year could be measured by ancient peoples as the period between two similar solstices or equinoxes.

The solar calendar marks off days by observing the period between consecutive returns of the sun to a similar position above the earth, such as its rising, setting, or highest point at midday. A "day" thus represents one complete rotation of the earth on its own axis, now divided into 24 hours. Since that rotation is not directly related to the earth's annual orbit around the sun, calendar problems arise because the true solar year does not equal a certain whole number of days but 365 days plus a fraction of a day.

The most significant calendar problems arise when the sun's motion is not the only factor taken into consideration in marking off a year. Considerable difficulties were encountered in ancient attempts to reconcile solar and lunar periods, especially when subdivisions of the year (months) were made to correspond to the more irregular phases of the moon. The fact that while the moon is orbiting the earth, the earth is orbiting the sun (and rotating at the same time) produces many complications.

The lunar calendar measured time by lunations (a lunation is the interval of time, expressed in days, between two successive new moons). Each lunar month, beginning when the thin crescent of the new moon first becomes visible at dusk, averages just over $29\frac{1}{2}$ days. The moon actually orbits the earth in about $27\frac{1}{3}$ days. Because the earth is meanwhile moving around the sun, it takes the moon two extra days to come to the same position between the sun and earth and produce a "new moon."

A lunar year of 12 months was approximately 11 days shorter than the solar year, so additional days were inserted to make up for the difference. The practice of insertion, known as intercalation, was a device common to several lunar calendar systems. The ancient Chinese compensated by adding an intercalary month every 30 years to their calendar, which consisted of 12 months of 29 or 30 days each. The Muslim lunar calendar, still used throughout Islam, also recognized 30 years as a cycle. Beginning with the second year within each cycle, and at subsequent intervals of three years, a "leap year" (a year of abnormal length) is observed. In that framework a leap year comprises 355 days as opposed to the ordinary Muslim year of 354 days. Calculation of the ancient Hebrew year suffered the same problems as other lunar calendars.

THE HEBREW CALENDAR

A Hebrew month began in the middle of a month on our calendar today. Crops were planted in November and December and harvested in March and April.

Month	Today's Calendar	Bible Reference	Israel's Holidays
1 Nisan (Abib)	March–April	Exodus 13:4; 23:15; 34:18; Deuteronomy 16:1	Passover (Leviticus 23:5) Unleavened Bread (Leviticus 23:6) Firstfruits (Leviticus 23:10)
2 Iyyar (Ziv)	April–May	1 Kings 6:1, 37	Second Passover (Numbers 9:10, 11)
3 Sivan	May–June	Esther 8:9	Pentecost (Weeks or Harvest) (Leviticus 23:16)
4 Tammuz	June–July		
5 Ab	July–August		
6 Elul	August–September	Nehemiah 6:15	
7 Tishri (Ethanim)	September–October	1 Kings 8:2	Trumpets (New Year's Day, Rosh Hashanah) (Leviticus 23:24; Numbers 29:1) Day of Atonement (Leviticus 23:27) Tabernacles (Shelters, Booths) (Leviticus 23:34)
8 Marcheshvan (Bul)	October–November	1 Kings 6:38	
9 Kislev	November–December	Nehemiah 1:1	Dedication (Hanukkah) (John 10:22)
10 Tebeth	December–January	Esther 2:16	
11 Shebat	January–February	Zechariah 1:7	
12 Adar	February–March	Esther 3:7	Purim (Esther 9:24-32)

Jewish Calendar It is hard to imagine a people with lives more closely bound to and regulated by the calendar than the people of ancient Israel. The Jewish calendar is dated from what is supposed to have been the Creation: 3,760 years and three months before the Christian era. Accordingly, to find the current year in the Jewish calendar, one must add 3,759 to the date in the Gregorian calendar. The system, however, will not work to the exact month, since the Jewish year (running on the civil calendar) begins in autumn rather than in midwinter.

Months Most of the 12 months of the postexilic calendar have names adapted from the Babylonians. The months do not correspond to but overlap the months of the Roman calendar.

The names of over half the months are mentioned in the OT: Kislev (Neh 1:1; Zec 7:1; RSV "Chislev"), Tebeth (Est 2:16), Shebat (Zec 1:7), Adar (Est 3:7, 8:12), Nisan (Neh 2:1; Est 3:7), Sivan (Est 8:9), and Elul (Neh 6:15).

Since the Jewish month invariably began with the new moon, at intervals of approximately 29½ days, the Jewish year ran 354 days. No exact information is available to explain how the Jews originally adjusted their inaccurate lunar calendar to synchronize with the actual solar year. Late in Israel's history an extra month was inserted between Adar and Nisan. That month, sometimes called Veader ("second Adar"), was added seven times within a 19-year cycle (at which time Adar received an extra half day).

The names for the Jewish months as now known come from the period following the return from Babylonia to Palestine. Before the Babylonian exile at least four other names were in use: Abib (Ex 13:4), Ziv (1 Kgs 6:1, 37), Ethanim (8:2), and Bul (6:38). After the Captivity, they were renamed Nisan, Iyyar, Tishri, and Heshvan (originally Marcheshvan), respectively. The preexilic names carried agricultural connotations. For example, Abib signified the month in which the heads of the grain became ripe; Ziv was the month for desert flowers to bloom. An agricultural orientation is apparent in what is evidently the oldest Hebrew calendar, found at Gezer (southeast of Tel Aviv) in 1908 and dating from the 10th century BC. Probably the work of a Jewish schoolboy, the calendar breaks down the year by agricultural activities such as sowing, reaping, pruning, and storage.

Primarily, however, the months were religiously significant to the Jews and enabled them to commemorate the important events of their history. Each month's beginning was considered holy. To ancient Israel, the moon became a spiritual symbol of the nation itself; the sun eventually became symbolic of the Messiah (Mal 4:2). Since the moon produces no light of its own, the symbolism is especially appropriate: Israel was supposed to reflect the Messiah's light to the world.

The Jewish calendar remained unchanged during the period between the OT and NT (approximately 400 years) despite an attempt by Hellenistic rulers to introduce a modified lunar month system, presumably of Macedonian origin. According to that calendar, five days were added to the final month of the year, with each of the 12 months containing 30 days. Even then, it only approximated the solar year.

Reckoning of Dates We know of no era in which the ancient Hebrews recorded dates by citing a month and day. Rather, dates were computed by reference to some significant event such as the accession year of the reigning king. In NT times the Jews continued the OT method of dating events by synchronizing them with events either in their religious calendar or within the secular sphere of the Roman world. Writers of the NT followed the same principle (Lk 1:5; Jn 12:1; Acts 18:12). Only as the calendar reforms of Julius Caesar became embedded in the culture did people change from that long-standing method to a more standardized system.

Jewish Festivals In addition to keeping the Sabbath, Jews observe seven annual festivals.

1. Passover (14th of Nisan) marks the deliverance from Egypt (the exodus). The first day of Nisan determines the date for Passover. Passover is observed for seven days and encompasses the Feast of Unleavened Bread, an event recalling Israel's hasty preparation for the flight from Egypt (Ex 12:15). The festival for the firstfruits of the barley harvest immediately follows (Lv 23:10, NLT).
2. Pentecost is celebrated 50 days after Passover. A time of joyful celebration for the people, Pentecost is the Feast of Ingathering of the firstfruits of the wheat harvest (Ex 34:22; Lv 23:15-17).
3. Next in order is New Year's Day, the beginning of Tishri. The first of Tishri, according to the rabbis, was the day in which the Lord created the world. It is called Rosh Hashanah, "head of the year."
4. On the 10th of Tishri, Israel's most solemn day, Yom Kippur (the Day of Atonement), is observed. This holiest of days is known as "the Sabbath of Sabbaths," and the complex ritual for its observance is set forth in the Bible (Lv 16).
5. Succoth, the Feast of Tabernacles, occupies the 15th through the 22d of Tishri. A largely agricultural festival, it celebrates the ingathering of the autumn harvest. The apostle John referred to it simply as "the feast" (Jn 7:37). The Feast of Tabernacles, sometimes called the Feast of Booths (Shelters), is also a spiritual commemoration; it recalls God's care over his people throughout Israel's 40 years in the wilderness (Lv 23:39-43).
6. Of later origin is the Festival of Hanukkah, the Feast of Dedication. It commemorates Judas Maccabeus's decisive victory over Antiochus Epiphanes and the Syrians 150 years before Christ. Since Malachi, the last of the OT prophets, had passed from the scene long before that event, tradition alone governs the manner in which the occasion is celebrated. On the 25th of Kislev and the following seven days, joyous activities mark the Jewish calendar.
7. Concluding the sacred festivals for the year is Purim, which falls on the 14th and 15th of Adar. The feast, which finds its origin in ancient Persia, commemorates the deliverance brought through Mordecai and Esther when they frustrated Haman's plot to destroy the Jews (Est 9).

Conclusion As ancient sundials and modern clocks mark the passage of minutes and hours, a calendar marks the passage of days, weeks, months, years, and even centuries. A uniform, understandable way of measuring the longer units of time aids secular enterprises such as agriculture, business, and government; it is essential to historians and brings unity to the celebration of religious rites. Development of the modern (Gregorian) calendar represents an interaction between the science of astronomy and much historical and religious tradition. The religious significance of the calendar for Christians stems partly from the biblical contrast between God's timelessness and human mortality (Ps 90). The psalmist asked God to "teach us to number our days that we may get a heart of wisdom" (Ps 90:12, RSV).

See also Astrology; Astronomy; Day; Feasts and Festivals of Israel; Jubilee Year; Moon; Night; Sun.

CALF *See* Animals (Cattle).

CALF, Golden Calf-shaped idol fashioned at the Israelites' request from their own gold jewelry (Ex 32:1-4). Under Aaron's supervision, the idol was created while Moses was receiving the Ten Commandments on Mt Sinai. Upon seeing the golden calf and the immoral

carousing in which the people were engaged, Moses smashed the tablets containing the commandments. He then ground the calf to powder, scattered it on the water, and made the people drink it (vv 15-20). Some of the transgressors were slaughtered (vv 25-29), while others were punished by God himself with a plague (vv 33-35).

Aaron's golden calf was probably modeled after Apis, an Egyptian bull god. Apis was connected with another Egyptian god, Osiris. Magnificent bulls worshiped in life as Apis were buried at death as Osiris-Apis, a name that became Serapis during the intertestamental period. The notoriety of Aaron's golden calf is underscored by several biblical references to it in historical summaries (Dt 9:16, 21; Neh 9:18, Ps 106:19-20; Acts 7:39-41).

Jeroboam I (930–909 BC), the first king of Israel after the division of the monarchy, set up shrines at Dan in the far north and at Bethel in the south, installing a gold calf in each (1 Kgs 12:26-33; 2 Chr 11:13-15). Israel's prophets knew that such calves were not the one true God (Hos 8:5-6). Hosea called the calf at Bethel ("house of God") the calf of "Beth-aven" ("house of wickedness," Hos 10:5-6). Within two centuries after Jeroboam's time, people had stooped to kissing calves (13:2), and Jeroboam's sinful act was listed as one of the main factors leading to the destruction of Samaria, Israel's capital city, and the northern kingdom's exile in 722 BC (2 Kgs 17:16).

CALIGULA* Roman emperor AD 37–41. *See* Caesars, The.

CALL, CALLING *See* Elect, Election.

CALLISTHENES A Syrian in General Nicanor's army who set fire to the temple gates during the persecution of the Jews by Antiochus Epiphanes (2 Macc 8:33). After Nicanor's defeat in 165 BC, Callisthenes and others responsible for burning the sacred gates were burned to death by the Jews.

CALNEH
1. City in Babylon (Gn 10:10).
2. City identified as Kullani (Kullan Koy), about 20 miles (32.2 kilometers) north of Aleppo in northern Syria. This northern identification is hinted at in Isaiah 10:9, where Calno is associated with Carchemish, some 50 miles (80.5 kilometers) to the northeast, as well as in the context of Amos 6:2 (note the north-to-south progression—Calneh, Hamath, Gath). Canneh in Ezekiel 27:23 seems to refer to the same general location and is perhaps to be linked with Calneh. Kullani was captured by Tiglath-pileser II, king of Assyria, about 741 BC.

CALNO Alternate name for Calneh, a city in northern Syria, in Isaiah 10:9. *See* Calneh #2.

CALVARY* In Luke 23:33, KJV translation of Golgotha ("the skull"), the place of Jesus' crucifixion. *See* Golgotha.

CAMEL Domestic animal used as a means of travel and for carrying goods in the Near East. *See* Animals.

CAMEL'S THORN Low, thorny shrub whose root is used in making a fragrant ointment (Ecclus 24:15).

CAMON* KJV form of Kamon, the burial place of the Israelite judge Jair, in Judges 10:5. *See* Kamon.

CAMPHIRE* KJV name for henna, a shrub with pale-green leaves and clusters of white, pink, or yellow blossoms that emit a delightful fragrance (Sg 1:14; 4:13). *See* Plants (Henna).

CANA
Galilean town that was the scene of Jesus' first miracle: changing water into wine at a wedding feast (Jn 2:1, 11). Jesus was again in Cana when he told a nobleman that his son, who was seriously ill at Capernaum, would live (Jn 4:46). Cana was also the home of Jesus' disciple Nathanael (Jn 21:2).

During the first Jewish rebellion, which resulted in the destruction of Jerusalem in AD 70, Cana was made headquarters for defending Galilee against the Romans. After the destruction of Jerusalem and the temple, the town became the seat of the priestly family of Eliashib. John's Gospel refers to it as "Cana of Galilee," evidently to distinguish it from the Kanah located near the Phoenician city of Tyre (Jos 19:28). The traditional site of Cana, revered as such since Byzantine and medieval times, is Kefar Kana, about four miles (6.4 kilometers) east of Nazareth on the main road from Nazareth to Tiberias. Contemporary scholarship, however, has almost unanimously settled on Khirbet Kana as the site of NT Cana. That ruin is about eight miles (12.9 kilometers) north of Nazareth on the northern edge of the Battuf Plain. The Arabs of the region call it Cana of Galilee to this day. Archaeologists exploring at the site have found pottery from the Hebrew monarchy period (c. 900–600 BC) as well as from Hellenistic, Roman, Arabic, and Crusader times.

CANAAN, CANAANITE
Palestinian territory (the Promised Land) west of the Jordan River, settled by the Israelites at the time of Joshua's leadership. Portions of southern Syria were also frequently considered part of Canaanite territory, the northern borders of which were never clearly defined. The pre-Israelite peoples of western Palestine, excluding northern Syria and such places as Ugarit (Ras Shamra) on the Mediterranean coast of Syria, carried the broad designation of Canaanites.

PREVIEW
- Land and People
- Language
- Literature
- History
- Religion
- Influence on Israel

Land and People In the "table of nations" (Gn 10:15-19), Noah's grandson Canaan was progenitor of 11 groups that lived in the area of Syria and Palestine. The first six evidently occupied territory at or south of Sidon, whereas the others lived farther north. The northerners mostly settled on the edge of the coastal plain; in the south, settlement spread eastward to the upland areas. OT references specifically placed the Canaanites in western Palestine's valleys and coastal areas; the upland country was occupied by Amorites and other peoples (Nm 13:29; Jos 5:1; 7:9; Jgs 1:27-36).

One of the earliest known references to the people of Canaan is in a tablet from Mari (15th century BC), in which a military officer reported his surveillance of "thieves and Canaanites." The Canaanites were listed as a group on the Memphis Stele (inscribed column) of the Egyptian pharaoh Amenophis II (c. 1440 BC). The land of Canaan was mentioned in a 15th-century inscription of Idrimi, king of Aleppo (west of Ugarit), who fled to the Canaanite seaport of Ammiya and then became ruler of Alalakh (north of Ugarit). During the Amarna Age

(15th–14th centuries BC), Palestine was politically dominated by Egypt, according to the Egyptian Amarna tablets.

Just as "Canaan" designated the whole western Palestinian area, so "Canaanite" described its pre-Israelite inhabitants without specifying race. Among the peoples who lived in Palestine, the Amorites first appeared in the second millennium BC as immigrants from Mesopotamia.

Several OT references seem to equate Amorite territory and the land of Canaan (Gn 12:5-6; 15:18-21; 48:22), a tradition reflected in the 18th-century BC Alalakh tablets, which depicted "Amurru" as part of Syria-Palestine. Tablets from Mari from about the same period speak of an Amorite ruler of Hazor in northern Palestine. The Tell el-Amarna texts (14th–13th centuries BC) indicate that the Amurru kingdom of the Lebanon region was monopolizing coastal trade and commerce; therefore, references to the two peoples (Amorites and Canaanites) together in Moses' time and throughout the late Bronze Age (c. 1550–1200 BC) are not surprising.

At the end of that period, the "Sea Peoples" (largely Philistines) destroyed the Hittite Empire, and in the time of Ramses III (c. 1180 BC) occupied western Palestine. The Israelite conquest of Palestine broke the power of many Canaanite and Amorite city-states, while the rise of a Philistine confederacy on the southern Palestinian coast restricted further the range of specifically Canaanite territory. From the beginning of the Iron Age the cultural heirs of the Canaanites were the Phoenicians, centered in the city-states of Tyre and Sidon, who themselves liked to be known as Canaanites (cf. Mt 15:21-22; Mk 7:24-26).

Language The various groups that inhabited western Palestine in the pre-Israelite period probably spoke related dialects of the Northwest Semitic linguistic family. The large territory covered by those peoples and the possible influence of Amorite, Hurrian, and Ugaritic languages complicate modern theories about what is properly meant by "Canaanite" as a language.

Literature As with language, it is difficult to be specific about Canaanite literature. One clear fact is that our own alphabet originated in middle Bronze Age Canaan. Before that time, writing was either pictographic (words or ideas represented by pictures), cuneiform (wedge-shaped impressions in soft clay representing syllables and whole words), or hieroglyphic (Egyptian pictorial writing). Alphabetical writing was passed on through the Hebrews and Phoenicians to the Greeks, who gave our present alphabet its classical form.

Until 1929 little Canaanite literature was known, but with the discoveries at Ugarit a large body of literary material came to light. The discoveries included portions of an epic poem about the god Baal and his consort Anath (possibly from c. 2000 BC), a legend about a royal personage named Aqhat (from c. 1800 BC), the legendary activities of King Keret (written c. 1500 BC), and fragmentary religious, medical, and administrative material.

History Archaeological evidence shows that western Palestine was occupied as far back as the Old Stone Age. Mesolithic, Neolithic, and Chalcolithic deposits have also been found at several sites. It is possible that Semitic-speaking peoples inhabited places such as Jericho, Megiddo, and Byblos around 3000 BC. Discoveries at Tell Mardikh (Ebla) show that a vigorous Canaanite Empire existed in Syria about 2500 BC, and there is no doubt that both Amorite and Canaanite peoples were firmly settled in Syria and Palestine by 2000 BC. The best evidence for Canaanite occupation of western Palestine has come from the middle and late Bronze Age (c. 1950–1200 BC), when the land was dotted with Canaanite and Amorite city-states.

The Egyptians made periodic forays into Palestine during their 5th and 6th dynasties; in the 13th dynasty (second millennium BC) they controlled much of Syria-Palestine both politically and economically.

Canaanite contacts with Mesopotamia from about 2000 BC are indicated in texts discovered at Mari and Ugarit. Evidently Amorites, Hurrians, early Assyrians, and other peoples periodically migrated to Canaan, bringing with them a diversity of political and social forms. By the late 16th century BC, most of the small Canaanite kingdoms were firmly under Egyptian control. Within two centuries the most northerly ones were subject to Hittite political influence.

Canaanite history is further complicated by the activities of the Hyksos people between about 1800 and 1500 BC. Of mixed Asiatic origin, the Hyksos owed much of their political influence to their military use of iron-fitted chariots and the compound Asiatic bow. From Canaanite locations like Hazor and Jericho, they invaded Egypt and established control there from about 1776 to about 1570 BC. When they were expelled at the start of Egypt's New Kingdom (1570–1100 BC), they retreated to fortified sites in southern Canaan.

Egyptian control over western Palestine had disappeared by the time of the Israelite conquest of Canaan; Joshua met predominantly Canaanite and Amorite opposition. The Israelite occupation of Canaan was aided by the state of decay into which the small Palestinian kingdoms had fallen. With the destruction of Hittite culture by the Sea Peoples and their occupation of the northern and coastal regions, the traditional city-states collapsed. From about 1100 BC, Canaanite culture was restricted to Tyre, Sidon, and a few other places.

Religion Before the Ugaritic discoveries, little was known about Canaanite religion apart from OT references to it. From what is now known of Canaanite culture, the head of the Canaanite list of gods was a shadowy personage named El, who was worshiped as the "father of man." His consorts were Athirat, known to the Israelites as Asherah, Astarte, and Baaltis. El had a son, Baal, a fertility god described in myths as the lord of rain and storm. Baal succeeded his father as head of the pantheon (list of gods) and supposedly resided in the distant northern heavens. A monument found at Ugarit represented him carrying a thunderbolt at his left side and a mace in his right hand.

Many small terra-cotta figurines with exaggerated secondary sexual characteristics, representing one or the other of the female deities, have been recovered from middle and late Bronze Age sites in western Palestine. A center devoted to the Anath cult, excavated at Byblos in Phoenicia, was evidently notorious for religious prostitution and sexual fertility rites; many naked female figures were found there. Other Canaanite cult objects included a sacred pillar of some sort *(massebah)* and a wooden image *(asherah)*, probably of the goddess herself.

In the Amarna Age, Canaanite orgiastic religion was especially influential in the Near East; it infiltrated to some extent even the conservative religions of Egypt and Babylonia. Four principal festivals associated with agriculture seem to have been celebrated by the Canaanites, invariably occasions of revelry, drunkenness, and sexual excess. Canaanite religion was evidently the most sexually depraved of any in the ancient world.

Influence on Israel Israelite morality, as defined by the covenant laws of Mt Sinai, was very different from the cultic traditions of Canaanite life. Hebrew ethical

monotheism was in many ways opposite to the depraved polytheistic nature worship of Canaanite religion. It was clear that the two systems could not coexist. Hence the law contained strict instructions that the Canaanites and their ways were to be eliminated from the Promised Land (Ex 23:24; 34:13-16; Dt 7:1-5) and that the Hebrews were to remain separate from Canaanite religion in loyalty to God's covenant. That was far from easy, if only because both peoples spoke closely related dialects and therefore used similar expressions of speech. Further, the invading Israelites under Joshua found that the Canaanites were superior to them in building stone structures and in making metal tools, implements, and weapons. The Hebrews, at a disadvantage, must have faced the prospect of requiring technical help from the Canaanites. In the time of King Solomon, Canaanites from Phoenicia were enlisted to design and construct the temple of the Lord in Jerusalem. A superficial resemblance between some aspects of Canaanite and Hebrew religion, such as peace offerings and certain divine titles, also made it difficult to maintain Israel's cultural distinctiveness.

Except for the "ban" imposed at Jericho, the Israelites were able to use Canaanite equipment captured in battle. Hence their determination to destroy all traces of the Canaanites, including their corrupt religion, was gradually weakened. By the time of King Ahab, when the worship of the Tyrian Baal was firmly entrenched in the northern kingdom of Israel, the Hebrews were in serious danger of losing their spiritual and theological distinctiveness. Their priests, who should have played a major part in maintaining the uniqueness of the covenant faith, often lapsed into Canaanite ways, emulating the immorality of their pagan neighbors and encouraging the Israelite people to do likewise (cf. 1 Sm 2:22).

As a result, Hebrew prophets proclaimed that their nation, which had almost completely succumbed to Canaanite blandishments, would have to be purified by exile before a renewed faith could become a possibility for Israel.

See also Canaanite Deities and Religion; Israel, History of; Palestine.

CANAANITE DEITIES AND RELIGION Study of the polytheistic religion of the Canaanites has contributed much to our understanding of the religion of ancient Israel. The Hebrew theological and religious structures were given by God to a people who were influenced and affected by other religions. To appreciate the Israelites' monotheistic faith fully, one must understand the polytheistic setting that challenged their life and unity as a nation.

Contact among the many religions of the ancient Near East produced not only tension but also much syncretism or borrowing of concepts and practices. The Arameans and Philistines who settled in Canaan adopted the practices of the Canaanites; similarly the Amorites accepted much of the Sumerian religion as their own when they moved into Mesopotamia. Among all those peoples, however, the Hebrews took an independent course. Their God was the unique and cosmic deity who demanded exclusive allegiance. Such a concept ran against the grain of all the religions of the day.

Until the early part of the 20th century, most of what was known about Canaanite religion came from the Bible. In 1928 many clay tablets were found at a site called Ras Shamra, which was the ancient Syrian city of Ugarit. They contained abundant new information about the religious life of Canaan. Most of them were in a cuneiform alphabet and written in a previously unknown

Northwest Semitic language quite similar to Hebrew, Aramaic, and Arabic. The documents are often called the Ugaritic texts or the Ras Shamra tablets.

Discovery of these texts opened doors of understanding that had long been closed. The texts provided scholars with an important mythological literature that gave not only the names and functions of the gods but also much information on Canaanite society.

Canaanite deities had two striking features: an extraordinary fluidity of personality and function, and names whose meanings and sources could be easily traced. These facts, coupled with the nature of the mythology, mark Canaanite religion as relatively primitive.

Dagon, the Fish God

The general Canaanite word for "god" probably meant "the strong, powerful one." The head of the pantheon, or array of gods, was called El ("the mighty one"). El, a remote and shadowy figure, lived far away from Canaan "at the source of the two rivers," hence in paradise. He apparently had three wives who were also his sisters: Astarte, Athirat (Asherah, also called Elat), and Anath. He presided over a divine council of gods who were his children. Although he was brutal enough to slay his own son, he was called Lutpan ("the kindly one") and was described as an old man with white hair and a beard.

Baal, the great storm god, king of the gods, was the central figure in the pantheon and was functionally far more important than El. Baal acted as El's prime minister and eventually dethroned him. "Baal" means simply "lord" and could be applied to different gods. Soon, however, the ancient Semitic storm god Hadad became the "Baal" par excellence. Hadad was considered to be the "lord of heaven," the "one who prevails," the "exalted, lord of the earth." He alone reigned over all else. His kingdom was "eternal to all generations." He was the giver of all fertility. When he died, all vegetation and procreation ceased. He was the god of justice, the terror of evildoers. Baal was called the "son of Dagon." Dagon, meaning "fish," was the chief god of Ashdod (cf. 1 Sm 5:1-7).

The Canaanites explained nature by reference to their gods. Each god represented some force of nature. The moon, sun, important stars, and visible planets were each considered a god or goddess. Baal, seen as god of the thunderstorm, personified the power of all nature.

The Canaanites' personification of the forces of nature accounted for the succession of the seasons. The dry period from April to the end of October repre-

sented the duration of Baal's death after his unsuccessful battle each spring with Mot (or with "the devourers," who at Ras Shamra performed the same general function as Mot). Revival of the rain-and-vegetation deity Baal toward the end of October signaled commencement of the autumn rains, which continued intermittently until the following April. The Canaanites believed that the land regained its fertility because of the annual mating of Baal and Anath. What better form could their own religious activities take than that of imitating the sexual behavior of their chief deities? Hence there was always a pronounced orgiastic element in Canaanite religion.

The three goddesses—Athtarat (Astarte or Ashtaroth in the OT, Dt 1:4, KJV "Astaroth"; Jgs 2:13), Anath (appearing in the OT in the name of the town Anathoth and as Shamgar's progenitor), and Athirat (Asherah in the OT)—presented an intricate set of relationships. Astarte was the same as Ashtar or Venus, the evening star. Anath's original character is uncertain. Athirat was primarily goddess of the sea and the wife of El. She was also called Elat, the feminine form of El. All three goddesses were concerned mainly with sex and war. Their primary function was to have sexual relations with Baal on a continual yearly cycle, yet they never lost their "virginity"; they were "the great goddesses who conceive but do not bear."

Ironically, the goddesses were considered sacred prostitutes and as such were called the "holy ones." Idols representing the goddesses were often nude and sometimes had exaggerated sexual features. In what circumstances early cultic prostitution was practiced is a matter of some debate, but there is no doubt that both male and female temple prostitutes were used in the cult of Canaanite religion.

The fertility deities were also goddesses of war. In the Baal Epic of Ugarit, Anath has a gory thirst for blood. In New Kingdom Egyptian sources, Astarte appears as a nude and ferocious cavalry warrior, sporting shield and lance.

In the KJV the name Asherah was translated "grove," following the Septuagint (third-century BC Greek translation of the OT). She seems to have been represented by some kind of wooden cult object set up in "high places" beside incense altars and stone pillars.

Continual struggle for survival no doubt led the Canaanites to worship things that they felt would benefit them materially. If the gods and goddesses were pleased by the worship, the result would be a plentiful harvest. Canaanite worship centered on a cultic shrine or "high place" where sacrifices were offered. Archaeological evidence indicates that animals of all sizes were offered at great temple-shrines such as Beth-shan. The city received its name from the temple located there: *beth* means "temple," and Shan was patron deity of the city.

As noted, human sacrifice became a part of religious practice in Canaan. Second Kings 3:27 mentions Mesha, king of Moab, who, after defeat at the hands of a confederation of kings, offered up his son as a burnt offering to his god Chemosh.

See also Canaan, Canaanite; Gods and Goddesses; Idols, Idolatry.

CANDACE* Title given to ancient Ethiopian queens. Philip, a leader in the early church, met and baptized an Ethiopian eunuch, who was a minister under Candace, queen of the Ethiopians (Acts 8:27). That Candace, whose name was probably Amanitere, ruled over Nubia (modern Sudan) from AD 25 to 41.

CANDLE*, CANDLESTICK* KJV words more correctly translated as "lamp" and "lampstand." Candles in the modern sense, typically made of wax and containing a wick, were unknown in ancient times. *See* Lamp, Lampstand.

CANE *See* Plants.

CANKER* KJV rendering of "gangrene" or "cancer" in 2 Timothy 2:17. *See* Gangrene.

CANKERWORM* KJV translation of the Hebrew word meaning "locust." *See* Animals (Locust).

CANNEH Alternate name for Calneh, a city in northern Syria, in Ezekiel 27:23. *See* Calneh #2.

CANON OF THE BIBLE* *See* Bible, Canon of the.

CANTICLES* Alternate title for the biblical book Song of Songs, derived from the Latin name of the book, *Canticum Canticorum*. *See* Song of Songs.

CAPERNAUM City of Galilee, mentioned only in the Gospels, which was the headquarters of much of Jesus' ministry. It lay on the northwest side of the Sea of Galilee (or Lake of Gennesaret). Its name means "village of Nahum," but it is impossible to say who this Nahum was, whether the OT writer or someone else. Matthew gives us the following information: Capernaum was located near the Sea of Galilee, in the territory of Zebulun and Naphtali (Mt 4:13). The west shore of the lake was settled by the tribe of Naphtali. Two of the characters described as being in Capernaum help to identify its location as being near the border of the Jordan and the political frontier. The story of the centurion (Mt 8:5; Lk 7:2) points to the small garrison of about 100 men found at such a frontier town. The story of Levi's call to leave the customs post controlling the taxation of the area reflects on the same border character of the town (Mt 9:9; Mk 2:14; Lk 5:27).

Jewish evidence argued for Tell Hum as the site for ancient Capernaum. The Greek *Capharnaum* is rendered by the Hebrew *Kaphar nahum* in Midrash Kohelet 1.8 and 7.26 (c. AD 110), proving that Capernaum still existed in the second century. There is no further mention until 1160, when Benjamin of Tudela refers to "Capharnaum which is Kaphar Nahum." The Franciscans, who acquired the site, have found a considerable number of coins of that period at Tell Hum, and the ruins of the synagogue there may well date from the third century AD. Recent excavations of Tell Hum have revealed that it is unquestionably the site for ancient Capernaum. During the excavations, a private house was uncovered beneath a fourth-century Jewish-Christian place of meeting. As early as the first half of the second century, it had served as an assembly hall for the early Christians. Inscriptions and the reports from early Christian travelers make it likely that it was the home of Peter.

Capernaum was an important settlement, with a Roman garrison, adopted by Jesus as his own city after his rejection by Nazareth (Mt 9:1). Here he was at home (Mk 2:1) and performed many miracles (Mk 1:34): the healing of the centurion's servant (Mt 8:5); the healing of Peter's mother-in-law (Mk 1:31); and the exorcism of the unclean spirit (Mk 1:23; Lk 4:33). Thus highly favored by the ministry of Jesus, there was also a heavy curse imposed on the city because of its unrepentance: "And you, Capernaum, will you be

exalted to heaven? You shall be brought down to Hades" (Mt 11:23, RSV).

CAPER PLANT* Low, spreading plant whose fruit was used as an appetite stimulant. *See* Plants.

CAPHAR-SALAMA Village where a battle was fought between Judas Maccabeus and the Syrian commander Nicanor (1 Macc 7:31). After about 500 of Nicanor's men had been killed, the fugitives took refuge in the "city of David," so Caphar-salama must have been near Jerusalem.

CAPHTOR*, CAPHTORIM*, CAPHTORITES Place-name and the name of the people associated with the place. The Caphtorim among the Hamitic peoples in the "table of nations" are listed as the "sons" of Egypt (Gn 10:13-14; 1 Chr 1:12, KJV "Caphthorim"). The text makes the Casluhim the parent people of the Philistines. However, prophets referred to the Philistines as colonists from Caphtor (Jer 47:4; see Am 9:7). This has been the basis for some translators to transpose the clause of Genesis 10:14 and to translate "Caphtorites, from whom the Philistines were descended" (NEB). Others understand that although the Philistines may originally have been a Casluhian colony, they settled in regions that became known primarily as those of the Caphtorites.

Aerial View of Ancient Synagogue in Capernaum

Caphtor is referred to as *Kaptara* in Accadian, *kptr* in Ugaritic, and *Keftiu* in Egyptian. These references are to be dated from as early as 2200 BC down to about 1200 BC. The Egyptian sources are especially helpful in identifying Caphtor as Crete. On the other hand, there is a Jewish tradition that the Caphtorim were from Cappadocia; the Septuagint reads "Cappadocia" instead of "Caphtor." This has led some to suggest that Caphtor is to be identified with a coastal region of Asia Minor or with the island of Carpathos. Perhaps by the 13th century BC, "Caphtor" was used in a broad sense for the Aegean area from which the Philistines came.

The Caphtorim are mentioned also as a people who invaded the region around Gaza, dispossessed the Avvim, and settled there (Dt 2:23). It appears that the Caphtorim were firmly settled around Gaza before Israel crossed the Jordan at the time of the Conquest. *See* Casluhim, Casluhites.

CAPITAL In architecture, the uppermost part of a pillar, often ornately fashioned. Capitals (KJV "chapter") topped the five pillars of the tabernacle during the wilderness wanderings of the people of Israel (Ex 36:38), as well as the pillars called Boaz and Jachin in King Solomon's temple (1 Kgs 7:16-22, 40-42).

See also Architecture.

CAPITAL PUNISHMENT* *See* Criminal Law and Punishment.

CAPPADOCIA
Plateau region of eastern Asia Minor intersected by mountain ranges. The name Cappadocia does not occur in the Hebrew OT. Passages that mention Caphtor or Caphtorim (Dt 2:23; Am 9:7), however, were rendered "Cappadocia" in the Septuagint (ancient Greek translation of the OT). A few scholars suggest that Cappadocia was the original home of the Philistines.

In the NT, Cappadocia was the homeland of some of the visitors to Jerusalem who were amazed at hearing their own languages spoken on the day of Pentecost (Acts 2:5-13). Cappadocia was later one of the places in Asia Minor where Christians settled, people to whom the apostle Peter addressed his first letter (1 Pt 1:1).

Cappadocia was bordered by Pontus on the north, Syria and Armenia on the east, Cilicia on the south, and Lycaonia on the west. Noted for its wheat, cattle, and horses, it also exported alabaster, mica, silver, and lead. The region was traversed by important trade routes, such as the route through the Cilician Gates northward to Pontus. The area was controlled or dominated in turn by Hittites, Assyrians, Babylonians, Persians, Greeks, Seleucids, and Romans.

Reference to a letter to Ariarathes, Cappadocia's king (1 Macc 15:22), may indicate that a significant Jewish settlement was there at the beginning of the second century BC. Jews from that community were apparently visiting in Jerusalem at the time of Pentecost. Christianity seems to have spread northward into Cappadocia along the road from Tarsus. Cappadocia became a region of strong Christian church leaders by the fourth century AD.

CAPTIVITY, The
Period when many inhabitants of the southern kingdom of Judah were exiled in Babylonia after Nebuchadnezzar's conquest of Jerusalem (sixth century BC). *See* Diaspora of the Jews.

CARAVAN
Traveling group of merchants, pilgrims, or others in Bible times who joined together for mutual protection. Usually travelers used pack animals to carry their wares or personal belongings. To transport goods from one district to another, donkeys were mainly used until about 1100 BC, when the use of camels became more common. Ancient Palestine, situated between the Mediterranean Sea and Egypt on one side and Syria, Mesopotamia, Arabia, and lands farther east on the other, was crisscrossed by trade routes. The nation of Israel was thus intimately acquainted with caravans, many in OT times coming from Transjordan and Arabia. Arabian caravans often transported spices and incense, products that were particularly lucrative. The rulers of Sheba were engaged in that enterprise (1 Kgs 10:2). The size of a caravan depended on the amount of traffic, precariousness of the route, and availability of camels. Perhaps 40 camels might be joined by ropes attached from the saddle of one camel to the nose ring of the trailing camel. Caravans could travel in single file or with three to four camels abreast. In hot weather or on an extensive journey, a camel

could carry about 350 pounds (159 kilograms); on short, cool trips, it could carry much more. Joseph was sold into slavery to a spice caravan going to Egypt (Gn 37:25-28). Raiding expeditions also formed caravans at times (Jgs 6:3-5; 1 Sm 30:1-20).

See also Travel.

CARBON DATING*
In archaeology, a method of dating objects of organic material by using the radioactive isotope carbon-14. *See* Archaeology.

CARBUNCLE*
Red or fiery colored stone such as a garnet or ruby; mentioned as one of the gems in the high priest's breastplate (Ex 28:17). *See* Stones, Precious.

CARCAS
One of King Ahasuerus's seven counselors, in Esther 1:10.

CARCHEMISH
Ancient city commanding an important ford on the west bank of the upper Euphrates River, about 65 miles (104.6 kilometers) northeast of Aleppo. Today part of the ruin is located in Turkey and part in Syria. The word is also written "Charchemish" (2 Chr 35:20, KJV). The meaning of the name is uncertain, although recent discoveries at Ebla suggest "city of Chemosh" (Moabite god).

A north-south trade route (roughly following the river) and an east-west route (connecting Nineveh with the Mediterranean Sea) both passed through Carchemish. Pottery finds indicate that the site was occupied in prehistoric times. The earliest reference to it is in the Ebla tablets (c. 2400 BC). Since Carchemish is about 75 miles (120.7 kilometers) west of Haran, Abraham probably passed through Carchemish on his way to Canaan.

Early in its history Carchemish was allied first to Mari and then to Aleppo. In 1355 BC it fell to the Hittites, became a regional capital of eastern Hatti, and adopted Hittite culture and language. After several centuries of unsuccessful attempts to incorporate Carchemish into their empire, the Assyrians under Sargon II finally conquered the city in 717 BC (Is 10:9) and made it their northwestern stronghold. When Nebuchadnezzar's Neo-Babylonian kingdom succeeded the Assyrian Empire, Carchemish was the last city to fall (605 BC). The Assyrians were aided in their defense by Pharaoh Neco II of Egypt (2 Chr 35:20; Jer 46:2). Thereafter, the city decreased in importance.

Archaeological excavations show that the city had features of both Hittite and Assyrian architecture. It had a casemate wall atop sloping embankments to hinder attackers. Within the city on the highest point stood a citadel surrounded by its own wall, as well as a palace with its own temple and monumental staircase.

CAREAH*
KJV spelling of Kareah, Johanan's father, in 2 Kings 25:23. *See* Kareah.

CARIA
Region in southwest Asia Minor. When Simon was high priest at Jerusalem, Lucius, the Roman consul, sent a letter to King Ptolemy (reigned 145–116 BC) concerning friendly relations between Rome and Simon. Along with other Greek states, Caria is listed as a recipient of the letter (1 Macc 15:23). In his letter Lucius instructed that any miscreants fleeing from Israel to districts of Asia Minor be returned to Simon to be punished according to Jewish law (v 21).

CARMEL

1. Mountainous ridge extending about 20 miles (32.2 kilometers) along the Mediterranean Sea and jutting southeastward into the Jezreel Valley. Its greatest width at the southeast is 13 miles (20.9 kilometers); its highest point, 1,742 feet (530.7 meters). Geologically, the ridge is of the same Cenomanian limestone formation as the central range of Palestine. Mt Carmel forms a headland south of the Bay of Acre. The modern city of Haifa, which rises in tiers on Carmel's northwestern corner, has splendid harbor facilities. Nestled in Mt Carmel's slopes are also several Jewish settlements and two large Druze villages. (Druzes are members of a particular Muslim sect.) The plain of Sharon extends to the south.

Mt Carmel was renowned for its beauty and fertility (Is 33:9; 35:2); in ancient times it was forested with oak trees, olive groves, and vineyards. "Carmel" is a contraction of a Hebrew word meaning "vineyard" or "garden of God." Parts of Carmel were so covered with dense wild vegetation that, with its gorges and caves, the ridge provided refuge for robbers and outcasts (Am 9:3). Carmel is still forested, and large parts of it have been made a nature reserve. The biblical poet of love described his beloved by saying, "Your head is as majestic as Mount Carmel" (Sg 7:5, NLT)—perhaps likening her hair to the thick, luxuriant foliage of Carmel.

Mt Carmel was an obstacle to north-south military and trade routes. Conquerors and traders commonly skirted its base and moved through the Jezreel Valley to the east or the Zebulun Valley to the northeast. Important passes cut through the mountain, however, such as the narrow pass through the lower slopes at its southern end linking the plains of Sharon and Esdraelon. That route was taken by Pharaoh Thutmose III early in the 15th century BC and also by British Lord Allenby when he conquered Palestine in 1918. The tribal territories of Asher, Zebulun, Issachar, and Manasseh met at Mt Carmel, but evidently possession of the heights was never fully settled.

Mt Carmel seems to have had special religious significance. It was the scene of a contest between Elijah and the prophets of Baal (1 Kgs 18); the site was fitting because Carmel was disputed territory between Israel and the Phoenicians, and thus between the Phoenician god Baal and Israel's God. Elijah was not the first to build a Hebrew altar on the mountain; the narrative describes him as repairing a ruined "altar of the LORD" before offering his sacrifice (v 30). The traditional location of that contest is Qeren ha-Carmel at 1,581 (481.7 meters), overlooking the Jezreel Valley. The brook Kishon (v 40) flows through that valley and around to the north of Carmel before emptying into the Bay of Acre.

2. Town in Judah (Jos 15:55) identified with el-Kirmil (Kermel), seven miles (11.3 kilometers) south of Hebron. King Saul set up a memorial to his conquest of the Amalekites there (1 Sm 15:12). Carmel was also the home of Nabal, a churlish man who refused kindness to David (25:2-14). After Nabal's death, his beautiful wife, Abigail, married David. Carmel is mentioned as the home of Hezro, one of David's 30 heroes (2 Sm 23:35).

CARMI

1. One of Reuben's sons; he accompanied his grandfather Jacob into Egypt (Gn 46:9; Ex 6:14; 1 Chr 5:3) and founded the family of Carmites (Nm 26:5-7).

Aerial View of Mt Carmel

2. Achan's father and a member of Judah's tribe (Jos 7:1, 18; 1 Chr 2:7; 4:1).

CARMITE Descendant of Carmi, Reuben's son (Nm 26:6). *See* Carmi #1.

CARNAIM* Important fortress city in Gilead after the Babylonian exile. Judas Maccabeus destroyed Carnaim, including its temple of Atargatis, the Syrian fish goddess (1 Macc 5:26, 43-44; 2 Macc 12:21-23, 26). *See* Ashteroth-karnaim.

CARNELIAN Variety of chalcedony that may vary in color from deep red to almost white; mentioned as one of the foundation jewels in the wall of the new Jerusalem (Rv 21:20). *See* Stones, Precious.

CAROB TREE* Evergreen leguminous tree commonly found throughout the Middle East, yielding edible pealike seeds contained in a pod. *See* Plants.

CARPENTER One who worked with timber, setting up the framework of houses, the roofing, windows, and doors. Often small structures were erected by the householder, but temples and palaces required specialized artisans where carpenters worked alongside stonemasons (2 Kgs 12:11; 22:6; 1 Chr 14:1; 22:15; 2 Chr 24:12; 34:11; Ezr 3:7). Carpentry is seldom referred to in the NT, though it was the profession of Jesus and his father Joseph (Mt 13:55; Mk 6:3).

CARPUS Man with whom the apostle Paul left his cloak at Troas. Paul instructed Timothy to bring it when he came to see him in prison (2 Tm 4:13). Carpus was possibly one of Paul's converts. According to tradition, Carpus became bishop of Berytus at Thrace.

CARRION VULTURE Bird of prey, also called the gier eagle in the KJV (Lv 11:18; Dt 14:17). *See* Birds (Vulture).

CARSHENA One of seven princes who were wise men of Persia and Media, and whom King Ahasuerus (Xerxes) consulted for legal advice (Est 1:14).

CASIPHIA Place to which Ezra sent for Levites when he realized that his company of returnees from the exile lacked persons qualified for temple service (Ezr 8:17). Casiphia was perhaps Ctesiphon on the Tigris River near modern Baghdad.

CASLUHIM*, CASLUHITES Descendants of Noah through his son Ham and grandson Mizraim ("Egypt" in some versions), and ancestors of the Philistines (Gn 10:14; 1 Chr 1:12).

CASPIN A town east of the Jordan River, probably the same place as Chaspho (1 Macc 5:26, 36), although ancient and modern authorities differ on the precise location. The historian Josephus identifies Caspin (2 Macc 12:13) with Maked. In 1 Maccabees 5:24-36, Judas and Jonathan Maccabeus marched into Transjordan. There Judas "took Chaspho, Maked, and Bosor, and the other cities of Gilead" (v 36, RSV).

CASSIA Type of tree that produces a spice resembling cinnamon (Ex 30:24; Ez 27:19). *See* Plants.

CASTANET A small handheld percussion instrument (2 Sm 6:5). *See* Musical Instruments; Music.

CASTOR AND POLLUX* Twin sons of Zeus according to Greek and Roman mythology. The apostle Paul sailed from Malta to Puteoli on a ship whose sign or figurehead was the "Twin Brothers" (Acts 28:11). *See* Dioscuri.

CATERPILLAR Wormlike larva of a butterfly, moth, and some other insects. *See* Animals.

CATHOLIC LETTERS* Traditional name for seven NT books (letters): James; 1 and 2 Peter; 1, 2, and 3 John; and Jude. The term "catholic" has been given various interpretations: (1) These letters express the views of all the apostles. (2) They are canonical or genuine. (3) Thus they were distinguished from contemporaneous heretical works. (4) They are encyclical, that is, addressed to general audiences of believers rather than to specific congregations, as were some of the apostle Paul's letters. Of course, 2 John and 3 John are exceptions to this, for 2 John is addressed to a lady or a local church and 3 John is addressed to an individual.

See also James, Letter of; John, Letters of; Jude, Letter of; Peter, First Letter of; Peter, Second Letter of.

CATTLE Domesticated bovine animals such as cows and oxen, but in the Bible sometimes also sheep and goats. *See* Agriculture; Animals.

CAUDA Small island south of Crete. The ship carrying the apostle Paul to Rome sought temporary refuge at Cauda during a storm (Acts 27:16). In the lee (calmer waters) behind the island the sailors hoisted on board a boat being towed by the ship and made efforts to strengthen the ship's hull. Even after lowering the sails, they were driven past the island and eventually wrecked. Cauda is the modern island of Gaudos (Gozzo). Ancient manuscripts are divided on the spelling of the name, some reading "Cauda" (as in most modern versions) and others, "Clauda" (as in KJV, NASB).

CAULK, CAULKER A waterproofing substance, such as bitumen, and the one who puts it into the seams of a ship's planking to make them watertight (Ez 27:9, KJV "calker").

CAVALRY *See* Warfare.

CEDAR Tree indigenous to Palestine whose wood was used in construction (1 Kgs 6:9). *See* Plants.

CEDRON* KJV name for Kidron, the river valley between Jerusalem and the Mt of Olives, in John 18:1. *See* Kidron.

CENCHREA, CENCHREAE* Seaport city that served the maritime needs of the larger city of Corinth, about eight miles (12.9 kilometers) to the west. Cenchrea is known as early as the fifth century BC in connection with an Athenian attack on Corinth. Before the Corinthian Canal was cut through the isthmus, traffic to Europe from Asia often passed from Cenchrea through Corinth to Lechaion.

Harbor View of Cenchrea

Excavations begun in 1963 have located the harbor mole (breakwater), warehouse remains dating to the early first century, and a large second-century stone building. A fourth-century church testifies to the influence of Christianity in the city. Portions of the ancient road leading southeast from the Cenchrean Gate in Corinth may still be seen among the ruins of that city's *agora* (marketplace).

Cenchrea is mentioned twice in the NT. The apostle Paul took an oath requiring the cutting of his hair before leaving Cenchrea during his third missionary journey (Acts 18:18). In his letter to the church in Rome, Paul commended Phoebe, a deaconess of the church in Cenchrea, well known for her Christian service (Rom 16:1).

CENDEBEUS Commander-in-chief of the seacoast of Syria-Palestine about 138 BC under Antiochus VII (1 Macc 15:38). Cendebeus was ordered to build a fortress at Kedron (probably the Gederah of Jos 15:36), after which he transferred his headquarters to Jamnia and from there made raids into Judea (1 Macc 15:39-40). Simon Maccabeus, unable to fight back because of his old age, dispatched his sons Judas and John Hyrcanus against Cendebeus with 20,000 soldiers and horsemen. Judas was wounded, but the Jews prevailed after slaying about 2,000 men. Cendebeus was pursued back to Kedron, and the Jews returned to Judea (16:1-10).

CENSER Vessel used to burn incense. On the Day of Atonement, the high priest was to burn two handfuls of incense in the censer within the Holy of Holies before the Lord (Lv 16:12). The censers of the tabernacle were made of bronze (Nm 16:39); those used by the angels in the book of Revelation were of gold (Rv 8:3-5).

See also Tabernacle; Temple.

CENSUS Registration and enumeration of a people, usually for purposes of war or taxation. A few censuses are mentioned in the Bible.

The first census was held at Mt Sinai two years after the exodus. In order to assess Israel's military potential, all Israelite males over 20 years old were counted—603,550 in all (Nm 1:1-3, 46). A special census was taken of the Levites, who were expected to serve in the tabernacle in place of military obligations. Every male Levite at least a month old was counted—22,000 in all, although of that number only 8,580 actually qualified for priestly service (3:15, 39; 4:46-48).

A second census, conducted at the close of Israel's 40 years of wandering in the wilderness, is recorded in Numbers 26. It, too, was primarily a military census, part of the strategic calculations made at Shittim in Moab just before the Israelite invasion of the Promised Land. The number of men able to bear arms was 601,730 (Nm 26:51), again excluding the Levites. The 23,000 Levites were counted separately because they were not going to receive an allotment of land (26:62). The rules for registration of the Israelites (given in Ex 30:11-16) included payment of one-half shekel each, about one-fifth ounce (6 grams) of silver.

A third census occurred near the end of King David's reign (2 Sm 24:1-17). The two censuses under Moses had been conducted at God's command; David's census came at a time when God was angry at Israel. The record says that the Lord "incited David against them," without specifying David's own motivations for the census (cf. the later interpretation of 1 Chr 21:1). It may have been for the purpose of conscription or taxation or simply to measure the extent of the king's power by the number of his subjects. At any rate, Joab, David's chief military commander, sensed that something was wrong about taking a census at that time and attempted to dissuade David. After the registration was conducted—there is some ambiguity as to whether it was ever completed (cf. 1 Chr 21:6; 27:23-24)—David realized his mistake and repented. Nevertheless, the census angered God, and as a punishment he gave David the choice of three years of famine, three months of flight before an enemy, or three days of pestilence. David chose the pestilence, in which 70,000 men died. The census identified 800,000 able-bodied men in Israel and 500,000 in Judah (2 Sm 24:9). An alternate account reported a potential militia of 1,100,000 in Israel and 470,000 in Judah (1 Chr 21:5), plus a separate count of 38,000 Levites qualified to serve in the temple (23:3).

Scholars have puzzled over the fact that figures for the third census (despite their variation in the two different records) approximately double the figures for the first two. Many attempts have been made to explain those variations in the strength of the military and in the size of the total population they imply. So far, no explanation is fully satisfying.

A fourth census, recorded in Ezra 2, was taken on the return of the exiles to Jerusalem. The final total included 42,360 males of Israelite descent, 7,337 slaves (male and female), and 200 singers (male and female).

In the NT a census played a role in the circumstances of Jesus' birth: "At that time the Roman emperor, Augustus, decreed that a census should be taken throughout the Roman Empire. (This was the first census taken when Quirinius was governor of Syria.) All returned to their own towns to register for this census" (Lk 2:1-3, NLT).

Josephus, a first-century AD Jewish historian, records that Quirinius completed a census under the emperor's direction soon after his tenure as governor of Syria began in AD 6. Matthew 2, however, places the birth of Jesus during the reign of Herod the Great, who died in 4 BC. There were probably two enrollments or censuses taken during this time. Luke's reference to the "first enrollment" (Lk 2:2) may have been made to distinguish it from the more famous enrollment of AD 6-7. Luke was obviously aware of the later census, which he mentions in a passing reference in Acts 5:37. A series of censuses known to have been made in Egypt about the same time lend credence to the theory of a similar series in Palestine. Thus, the most plausible solution suggests that an earlier census took place during the influential leadership of Quirinius before his full governorship.

Luke's reference to the census under Quirinius serves two purposes in his Gospel. First, it provides a date for the birth of Jesus. Second, it explains why Joseph and Mary were in Bethlehem at that time. The census under Quirinius was probably for purposes of taxation, since the Romans exempted the Jews from military service. The requirement to return to one's hometown, reflecting the patriarchal element in Hebrew religion, probably also reflects the general willingness of Caesar Augustus to let the Jews follow their own customs.

CENTURION*

Commander of 100 men in the Roman army. There were generally six centurions in each cohort and ten cohorts in a legion. Each legion had six tribunes to whom its centurions were subordinate. In Acts 22:26, for example, a centurion appealed to his tribune for a decision concerning the apostle Paul. A centurion's authority was actually quite extensive because he was the working officer who had direct contact with the men. He went to the field with them and made spontaneous decisions according to each situation.

The office of centurion was normally the highest one within reach of the ordinary soldier. Centurions often rose from the ranks because of their experience and knowledge. After one became a centurion, further promotion could come by transfer to positions of increasing responsibility, the highest being senior centurion over the first of ten cohorts in a legion. Thus, a centurion might move about extensively throughout the Roman Empire.

A centurion had many duties besides maintaining discipline among the ranks. He had to oversee executions for capital offenses (Mt 27:54; Mk 15:39, 44-45; Lk 23:47). He was responsible for his troops at all times, whether they were Roman citizens or recruited mercenary soldiers. The position of centurion was prestigious and high-paying; those who reached that rank usually made a career of it.

Six centurions are mentioned in the NT, at least two of whom seem to have become followers of Christ.

1. A centurion at Capernaum pleaded for the life of his dying servant because he believed that diseases would obey Jesus just as his soldiers obeyed him (Mt 8:5-13; Lk 7:2-10). In spite of his high-ranking position, he was a humble man, willing to admit his inadequacy and helplessness. He cared deeply for his servant's welfare. Jesus marveled at that example of faith and healed the sick man.
2. The centurion in charge of the squad that executed Jesus declared, "Truly this man was the Son of God!" (Mk 15:39, RSV) and "Certainly this man was innocent!" (Lk 23:47). The apocryphal Acts of Pilate, probably dating from the fourth century, named the believing centurion as Longinus. He has been regarded as a saint in Roman Catholic tradition. A marble statue depicting his dramatic confession,

sculpted by the 17th-century baroque artist Giovanni Bernini, is located in St Peter's Basilica in Rome.

3. A centurion in Caesarea named Cornelius was converted to Christ through the testimony of the apostle Peter, whose reluctance to share the gospel with Gentiles had been broken down by a vision from God (Acts 10).
4. A centurion in Acts 22:25-26 helped save the apostle Paul from a scourging when he reminded his tribune that the accused was a Roman citizen.
5. Another centurion helped save Paul from a Jewish plot to murder him (Acts 23:17-22).
6. A centurion named Julius was assigned to guard Paul on his journey from Caesarea to Rome (Acts 27:1). When their ship broke up in a storm, Julius prevented the soldiers from killing all the prisoners on board, including Paul (vv 42-43).

See also Warfare.

CEPHAS Aramaic name of Simon Peter the apostle in John 1:42; 1 Corinthians 1:12; and Galatians 1:18. *See* Simon Peter.

CEREAL OFFERING* RSV for "grain offering," one of the several types of offerings to God that reflected consecration and commitment. *See* Offerings and Sacrifices.

CERINTHUS* Gnostic heretic (died c. 100) whose heresy was condemned by the apostle John. Probably born in Egypt and reared a Jew, Cerinthus was leader of a group of Christians who had Gnostic tendencies. He apparently believed that the world was created not by God but by a lesser being (called the Demiurge) or by angels, one of whom gave the law to the Jews. Cerinthus also taught that Jesus was an ordinary man, upon whom "the Christ" descended at his baptism. This divine power revealed the transcendent and unknown God. This "Christ" abandoned Jesus before his crucifixion.

The church father Eusebius (c. 260–340) quotes a story from Irenaeus (who lived in the late second century), who heard it from Polycarp (a disciple of the apostle John). The story says that John heard that Cerinthus had come into an Ephesian bathhouse where he (John) was. John immediately rushed out of the bathhouse shouting, "The building will collapse because the enemy of truth is inside!" Some scholars believe that certain passages in John's writings may have been directed against Cerinthus (see Jn 1:1-3, 14; 1 Jn 4:1-3).

CERTIFICATE OF DIVORCE* Document a man was obligated to give to his wife if he divorced her. *See* Divorce, Certificate of.

CHABRIS Gothoniel's son, and one of three magistrates of Bethulia (Jdt 6:14-15; 10:6). Chabris and his colleagues were rebuked by Judith for putting a time limit on how long they would wait for the Lord to deliver their city from the Assyrians (Jdt 8:9-27).

CHAEREAS Brother of Timothy and governor of Gazara (2 Macc 10:32). Both Chaereas and Timothy were killed along with many others in the assault by the Maccabees on the city (vv 36-37).

CHAFF Loose hulls separated from the edible grains by threshing and winnowing. In Bible times the common sight of winnowed grain remaining when the wind blew away the lighter husks gave rise to the vivid image of good people or nations surviving judgment while the wicked do not. So, for example, sinners "are like worthless chaff scattered by the wind" (Ps 1:4, NLT).

The prophet Isaiah said of the Assyrians, "You conceive chaff, you bring forth stubble; your breath is a fire that will consume you" (Is 33:11, RSV). Likewise, in Nebuchadnezzar's dream, the nations of the world collapse and are like the chaff of the summer threshing floors before the victory of the coming kingdom of God (Dn 2:35).

In the NT it is said that the coming Messiah will "gather his wheat into the granary, but the chaff he will burn with unquenchable fire" (Mt 3:12, RSV).

CHALCEDONY* Kind of quartz, variously colored, usually grayish or milky. *See* Minerals and Metals; Stones, Precious.

CHALCOL* KJV spelling of Calcol, a man of wisdom, in 1 Kings 4:31. *See* Calcol.

CHALDEA*, CHALDEANS Ancient region in Mesopotamia and its inhabitants. The name comes from the Chaldean (or Kaldu) tribes that shared Babylonia in southeastern Mesopotamia with several other peoples, especially the Sumerians and Akkadians. After the old Babylonian Empire was absorbed by the Assyrians, the Chaldeans under Nebuchadnezzar's leadership took control and built a Neo-Babylonian Empire that dominated the Near East for nearly a century. The region called Chaldea is also associated with the patriarch Abraham, whose Mesopotamian home was "Ur of the Chaldeans" (Gn 11:28).

The Land and People Until the end of the eighth century BC, Chaldea referred only to a small territory in southern Babylonia. Within 100 years, following a rapid and successful bid for power, it embraced all of Babylonia. At that time it included the territory from Baghdad on the Tigris River to the Persian Gulf and extended up the Euphrates River as far as the city of Hit. Although Chaldea is usually placed between the Tigris and Euphrates, it reached into the flatlands between the Tigris and the Zagros Mountains to the east and also included some land west of the Euphrates. The Arabian Desert formed its western boundary. Chaldea rarely exceeded 40 miles (64.4 kilometers) in width, having an area of about 8,000 square miles (12,872 square kilometers), approximately the size of New Jersey. On today's map Chaldea falls inside Iraq, with its southwestern tip touching the small kingdom of Kuwait.

History First mention of the Chaldeans is found in the Assyrian annals of Ashurnasirpal II (885–860 BC), leading some authorities to suggest that they entered Babylonia about 1000 BC. They are usually associated (though not identified) with the Semitic Aramean tribes who were constantly pushing their way from the western deserts into Mesopotamia. They settled primarily in the southern tip of Babylonia, at the northern end of the Persian Gulf, perhaps centuries before the Assyrian annals mentioned them.

Job 1:17 mentions three bands of Chaldeans who participated in a raid against Job's camels and servants, probably in the vicinity of Edom or northern Arabia. Their presence in those regions does not necessarily mean they lived nearby, since armies from Babylonia (Sinar) and Elam ranged as far as Palestine centuries earlier (Gn 14:1-2).

Under Assyrian Rule Living by the marshes and lakes of the extreme south, the Chaldeans maintained a high degree of independence, even when Assyrian dominion extended over them. It was difficult for invading armies to maneuver in the Chaldean marshes. As a result, the Chaldeans resisted paying taxes or providing any form of service to the Assyrian government. When the Assyrians sought to limit their freedom, the Chaldeans turned to guerrilla warfare and political intrigue. They were quick to disregard treaties or to switch alliances as circumstances dictated. Under Assyrian rule, whereas the native residents of Babylonian cities were generally content, the Chaldeans became the leaders of a national independence movement. For 250 years the Assyrians had to enforce their dominion against persistent Chaldean attempts to assert their autonomy and influence.

Finally, in 721 BC the Chaldean leader Marduk-apla-iddina II (known as Merodach-baladan in 2 Kgs 20:12 and Is 39:1, who sent an embassy to Hezekiah, king of Judah) entered Babylon and claimed the kingship of Babylonia, a position long appointed by the Assyrian king. Crafty and resourceful, he successfully maintained his claim for 10 years before being driven back into his own southern territory by Assyria's Sargon II. On Sargon's death in 705 BC, he reasserted his claim but was defeated by the new Assyrian king, Sennacherib, who destroyed Babylon as a lesson to the Chaldeans and their allies.

Sennacherib's son and successor, Esarhaddon, pursued a policy of conciliation with the Babylonians and rebuilt their capital city, a gesture that effectively neutralized Chaldean agitation and inaugurated a period of peace that lasted over 30 years. The last unsuccessful revolt occurred under Ashurbanipal's reign and was actually instigated by his brother, whom the Assyrian king had appointed to the Babylonian throne. The Chaldeans gladly joined the rebellion, which was crushed in 648 BC.

The Neo-Babylonian Empire Two decades later, at the time of Ashurbanipal's death, Assyrian power suddenly and dramatically slipped. Nabopolassar, a Chaldean governor, took the opportunity to drive the Assyrians out of Babylonia. He became king of Babylon in 625 BC. Allied with the Medes, the Babylonians went on to destroy the Assyrian Empire, capturing the capital cities of Asshur in 614 and Nineveh in 612. They divided the conquered lands with the Medes and annexed the Assyrian regions west and south of the Tigris, creating a new Babylonian Empire. (The first Babylonian Empire, with which Hammurabi is associated, had flourished over 1,000 years earlier.) Throughout the Near East, Chaldea and Babylonia became synonymous.

During the long and brilliant reign of Nabopolassar's son Nebuchadnezzar (or Nebuchadrezzar) II, the empire reached its zenith. As crown prince, he won a decisive victory in 605 BC over the Egyptians at Carchemish (the battle mentioned in 2 Chr 35:20), which effectively established Babylonian supremacy in the Near East (see 2 Kgs 24:7). That same year the southern kingdom of Judah became a vassal nation to Babylon. Nebuchadnezzar won the submission of King Jehoiachin, carried off the choicest articles from the temple for his own temple in Babylon, and took the outstanding leaders and youth of Judah captive (2 Kgs 24:1; 2 Chr 36:5-7; Dn 1:1-4). When Judah revolted several years later at the instigation of Egypt, the Chaldean army captured Jerusalem in 597 BC. Judah's new king, Jehoiachin, was deposed at that time together with more of its leaders (2 Kgs 24:8-16). A second revolt in 594 BC by the Chaldean-appointed king (Zedekiah) resulted in a third

invasion, the destruction of Jerusalem in 586 BC, and the exile of most of Judah's citizens (2 Kgs 24:20–25:12; 2 Chr 36:11-21). With the booty from that and other conquests, Nebuchadnezzar built Babylon into one of the most dazzling cities in the ancient world. His projects included the Hanging Gardens (one of the seven wonders of the ancient world), the Ishtar Gate, and a 17-mile (27-kilometer) outer wall designed for defense of the city. His pride in such accomplishments eventually brought the judgment of God (Dn 4:30-33).

Nebuchadnezzar was succeeded by his son Amel-marduk (Evil-merodach in 2 Kgs 25:27 and Jer 52:31, remembered there for his special kindness to the exiled king Jehoiachin). After two years he was killed in an armed rebellion led by his brother-in-law, Nergal-shar-usur (Nergal-sharezer of Jer 39:3), who attempted to establish his own dynasty. After a four-year reign Nergal-shar-usur was succeeded by his son, who lasted only a few months before being ousted by a usurper, Nabonidus.

CHALDEANS AS ASTROLOGERS
Long after the Chaldean Empire had ceased to exist, the name "Chaldeans" lingered in Hellenistic Egypt, Greece, and Rome as a term for magicians, astrologers, and diviners. The same usage of the term appears in the book of Daniel, where Chaldeans were linked with soothsayers, conjurers, and sorcerers (Dn 2:2, 10; 4:7; 5:7).

Babylonians had long been renowned for their advanced knowledge of astronomy and for their dependence on the stars to help them predict the future. One Babylonian text from about 700 BC described the zodiacal belt and named 15 constellations. Several of the names are still used by astrologers today: the Bull, the Twins (Gemini), the Scorpion, and Capricorn. In Daniel 2:2 and 4:7 one of the terms linked with the Chaldeans is related to a Babylonian word referring to a class of priests who made use of incantations. Just how important they were for society has been shown in excavated tablets that describe the priests' training. The most outstanding youths of Judah, including Daniel, were selected for a similar educational program (Dn 1:4).

The Fall of Babylon Nabonidus was the last of the Chaldean monarchs. His installation as king was supported by many Babylonian officials. They were watching their former allies, the Medes, gradually become a rival power and saw in Nabonidus a ruler strong enough to meet their threat. Strong or not, his attempts to reform Babylonian religion proved extremely unpopular, and his efforts to strengthen the economy were unsuccessful. Both facts made Babylon an unpleasant residence for Nabonidus; during one extended absence from the capital city, he installed his son Belshazzar as co-regent. (Belshazzar's position explains why he is described as the king of Babylon in the OT book of Daniel and why in Dn 5:7 he could make Daniel only "the third ruler in the kingdom.")

While Belshazzar was handling government affairs, the famous incident of the "writing on the wall" occurred, ominously predicting Babylon's downfall (Dn 5). The Elamites, in fact, were already attacking the empire's eastern flank. Rumors of Persian power in the north brought Nabonidus back to Babylon just in time for an invasion by the Persian king, Cyrus the Great. Cyrus took Babylon without a fight, putting an end both to Chaldean power and to the Neo-Babylonian Empire.

See also Assyria, Assyrians; Astrology; Babylon, Babylonia; Daniel, Book of; Diaspora of the Jews; Nebuchadnezzar, Nebuchadrezzar; Ur (Place).

CHALKSTONE* Literally "stones of chalk," mentioned as illustrative of the destruction of the pagan altars in Judah (Is 27:9). Chalk beds cap many of the Judean hills, and since the substance easily erodes, Isaiah's prophecy is apt.

CHALPHI Father of Judas, one of the two captains of Jonathan Maccabeus's army who stood firm at the battle of Gennesarat (1 Macc 11:67-74) when others fled after being ambushed. Jonathan, Judas, and the other captain, Mattathias, rallied the troops and repulsed the enemy.

CHAMBERLAIN* Originally, a royal official in charge of the private quarters of the king. They sometimes had other significant tasks and had great influence with those in authority (Acts 12:20). The chamberlain Erastus (Rom 16:23, KJV) was actually the city treasurer. Nathan-melech the chamberlain (2 Kgs 23:11) was a court official at the time of Josiah. The Persian kings used eunuchs as chamberlains (Est 1:10, 12, 15; 2:3, 14-15; 4:4-5; 6:2, 14; 7:9).

CHAMBERS OF THE SOUTH* Possibly a constellation of stars, or the vast stretches of southern sky without stars (Jb 9:9, KJV). *See* Astronomy.

CHAMELEON Any of a number of lizards having the ability to change color rapidly, declared ritually unclean (Lv 11:30). *See* Animals.

CHAMOIS* Small, goatlike antelope that lives primarily in the high mountains of Europe. In Deuteronomy 14:5 "chamois" is an inaccurate translation of the Hebrew word that is better rendered "mountain sheep." *See* Animals (Sheep).

CHANAAN* KJV spelling of Canaan in Acts 7:11 and 13:19. *See* Canaan, Canaanite.

CHANNELS OF THE SEA* Valleys or stream beds in the ocean floor. When the Lord delivered David from all his enemies and from King Saul, David praised God's great power, which could expose the ocean floor with a blast of his breath (2 Sm 22:16; Ps 18:15).

CHANT Recitation in song or monotonous voice (Ps 8:1; Ez 32:16). *See* Music.

CHAOS*, Waters of In ancient thought, the primeval seas that were divided. The world was then situated between the "waters above" and "waters below," or "the Deep" (Gn 1:1-2, 6-7).

CHAPHENATHA A section of Jerusalem that Jonathan Maccabeus repaired to protect the city from enemy attack (1 Macc 12:37). Pinpointing the exact location has given rise to much unsettled debate. Some scholars think the word should be emended to Chapheltha, an equivalent of the area called the Mishneh, or Second Quarter (cf. 2 Kgs 22:14, Zep 1:10, etc.). Others say Chaphenatha refers to "the bend of the fountain," i.e., near the pool of Siloam. There is no decisive evidence either way.

CHAPITER* KJV rendering of capital, architecturally the uppermost part of a pillar. *See* Capital.

CHARASHIM* KJV rendering of Ge-harashim, a valley on the plain of Sharon's southern border, in 1 Chronicles 4:14. *See* Ge-harashim.

CHARAX Place, possibly in the land of Tob, through which Judas Maccabeus and his army passed in the pursuit of their Syrian enemies (2 Macc 12:17-19).

CHARCHEMISH* KJV spelling of the city Carchemish in 2 Chronicles 35:20. *See* Carchemish.

CHARIOT

Ancient Assyrian Chariot

Ancient two-wheeled vehicle pulled by animals, usually horses, and normally thought of as an instrument of war. Chariots were also used as a means of transportation for persons of rank or wealth, and for hunting.
See also Travel; Warfare.

CHARISMATA* Abilities the Holy Spirit gives to the church (1 Cor 12; 14). *See* Spiritual Gifts.

CHARM Small object worn around the neck to ward off evil. *See* Amulet; Magic; Sorcery.

CHARMIS Melchiel's son and one of three magistrates of Bethulia (Jdt 6:14-15; 10:6). Charmis and his colleagues were rebuked by Judith for putting a time limit on how long they would wait for the Lord to deliver their city from the Assyrians (8:9-27).

CHARRAN* KJV spelling of Haran, a Mesopotamian city, in Acts 7:2-4. *See* Haran (Place).

CHASPHO Town east of the Sea of Galilee mentioned in 1 and 2 Maccabees. Judas and Jonathan Maccabeus led their army into Transjordan and "took Chaspho, Maked, and Bosor, and the other cities of Gilead" (1 Macc 5:36). Caspin, which appears in a similar passage in 2 Maccabees 12:13, is considered to be the same as Chaspho by most scholars. Chaspho has been identified as el-Muzeirib in the Hauran plain and Tell el-Jamid on the Yarmuk River. But most today locate it at Khisfin, about 10 miles (16.1 kilometers) east of the Sea of Galilee.

CHASTEN, CHASTISEMENT* Correction intended to produce righteousness (Dt 21:18; Jb 5:17; 2 Tm 2:25). *See* Discipline.

CHEBAR* *See* Kebar.

CHEDORLAOMER* *See* Kedorlaomer.

CHEESE Milk product produced by curdling milk, draining the whey, pressing the curds into cakes, and drying them. One of the earliest biblical references to cheese is in Job 10:10: "Didst thou not pour me out like milk and curdle me like cheese?" (RSV). *See* Food and Food Preparation.

CHELAL* Pahath-moab's son, who obeyed Ezra's exhortation to divorce his pagan wife after the exile (Ezr 10:30). Also spelled Kelal.

CHELLEANS People mentioned in the book of Judith. There is little agreement about the identity of the Chelleans, who are listed in connection with a campaign of Holofernes, chief general of Nebuchadnezzar's army (Jdt 2:23). Geographical considerations make it unlikely that they were from the town of Chelous, modern Khalasa. More probable is an identification with ancient Cholle, located between Palmyra (Tadmor) in the Syrian Desert and the Euphrates River. That site, modern el-Khalle, fits well with the other geographic references in Judith 2:21-25.

CHELLUH* KJV rendering of Keluhi, Bani's son, in Ezra 10:35. *See* Keluhi.

CHELOUS According to Judith 1:9, Chelous was one of the cities to which messengers were sent by King Nebuchadnezzar to procure aid for his campaign against Arphaxad. Most scholars think that Chelous is the site known by some ancient geographers as Elusa but which is now called Khalasa. Khalasa is located south of Beersheba on a latitude line running through the southern shore of the Dead Sea. It is situated near an important crossroads.

CHELUB*
1. Shuhah's brother and the father of Mehir from Judah's tribe (1 Chr 4:11).
2. Father of Ezri. Ezri oversaw the tilling of soil in King David's fields (1 Chr 27:26).

CHELUBAI* Hezron's son and the brother of Jerahmeel (1 Chr 2:9); alternately called Caleb in 1 Chronicles 2:18, 42. *See* Caleb #2.

CHEMARIM*, CHEMARIMS* Hebrew term often translated "idolatrous priests" (2 Kgs 23:5; Hos 10:5; Zep 1:4). In the KJV this word appears in Zephaniah 1:4 as a proper name, spelled either Chemarim or Chemarims. The exact meaning of the word is uncertain.

CHEMOSH Name of the national god of Moab (Nm 21:29); also associated with the Ammonites (Jgs 11:24). *See* Canaanite Deities and Religion; Moab, Moabites.

CHENAANAH* *See* Kenaanah.

CHENANI* *See* Kenani.

CHENANIAH* *See* Kenaniah.

CHEPHAR-AMMONI*, CHEPHAR-HAAMMONAI* *See* Kephar-ammoni.

CHEPHIRAH* *See* Kephirah.

CHERAN* *See* Keran.

CHERETHIMS*, CHERETHITES* *See* Kerethites.

CHERITH*, The Brook *See* Kerith, The Brook.

CHERUB* (Place) *See* Kerub.

CHERUB*, CHERUBIM Winged creatures mentioned occasionally in Scripture ("cherubim" is the plural form of the Hebrew "cherub"). They belong to a supernatural created order along with the seraphim and angels. Some scholars have argued that the term "cherub" had its origin in the *karibu* ("intercessor") of Akkadian mythological texts, commonly represented in Mesopotamian art as a griffin (a creature half lion and half eagle) or as a winged human. The sphinx also appears to go back to this concept. The biblical evidence, however, does not seem to support that identification.

The prophet Ezekiel described four "living creatures," each with four faces and four wings (Ez 1:5-24); those creatures corresponded to cherubim (10:2-22). The splendor of Ezekiel's vision was recaptured more modestly in his description of the king of Tyre, who in the midst of his own prosperity seemed to be playing the part of a towering or guardian cherub before being dispossessed (28:13-16). That passage has been interpreted by some as a description of Satan's "fall from grace" after he had once been in the service of God as a ranking member of a high celestial order.

Despite Ezekiel's elaborate visionary descriptions, it is difficult to be certain about the form in which cherubim appeared. Thus, in Ezekiel 41:18 the cherubim that were to decorate Ezekiel's ideal temple had only two faces, a man's and a young lion's, in contrast to the four-faced creatures of the earlier visions. The four faces of Ezekiel 1:10 were those of a man, a lion, an ox, and an eagle, whereas in Ezekiel 10:14 the cherub had its own face ("the face of the cherub"), along with the faces of a man, a lion, and an eagle. If the cherub's face corresponded to that of an ox, that might account for the fact that cherubim in Near Eastern art were represented as four-footed creatures, though frequently different otherwise from biblical cherubim. In addition to their wings, the cherubim of Ezekiel's vision had straight legs and feet with hooves like those of a calf (Ez 1:7).

That complex description has led scholars to try to identify cherubim in the statues and carvings of non-Israelite peoples. The throne of Ahiram, king of Byblos, was flanked by sphinxes, which some have judged to be cherubim. The sphinx, however, seems to have been a popular decorative motif, as evidenced by an ivory box from Megiddo and ivories from Samaria, Nimrud, and elsewhere. Other decorative creatures have various combinations of human and animal bodies, with wings generally prominent. None of them adequately represents the OT descriptions of cherubim.

The four living creatures of the book of Revelation were similar to the cherubim of Ezekiel but lacked their whirling wheels (Rv 4:6-9). Subsequent references to the creatures in Revelation (5:6-14; 6:1-8; 7:1-11; 14:3; 15:7; 19:4) add nothing to the initial description.

The cherubim of Genesis 3:24 acted as guardians or custodians. Supernatural guardians seem to have been common in Near Eastern thought. In Ezekiel 10 the cherubim were also executors of divine judgment, spreading burning coals over a city (Ez 10:2, 7).

In early Israelite thought the cherubim stretched out their wings and provided God with a throne (1 Sm 4:4; 2 Sm 6:2; etc.). God spoke to Moses from such a throne on the cover of the ark of the covenant (Ex 25:22). In Ezekiel's vision (Ez 1:26; 10:1) God was seated in a four-wheeled chariot moved by the cherubim and borne aloft by their wings. In Hebrew poetry God was portrayed as employing clouds for his chariot (Ps 104:3; cf. Is 19:1) or riding on a cherub in flight (2 Sm 22:11;

Ps 18:10). The idea of cherubim furnishing a seat or platform for the invisible deity found expression in Near Eastern art, where the pagan gods stood on the backs of animals.

In Israel cherubim were carved on the covenantal ark (Ex 25:18-20; 37:7-9), and representations of them were also embroidered on the curtains of the tabernacle and the veil that screened the innermost sanctuary in which the ark rested.

The Most Holy Place of Solomon's temple was adorned by two large representations of cherubim, made of olive wood and covered with gold leaf. When placed side by side with outstretched wings, they spanned the entire width of the inner sanctuary. Smaller cherubim and palms were carved on the temple's wooden panels and some of the doors, and were also represented on the sides of the laver stands (1 Kgs 7:29, 36). Cherubim alternating with palm trees formed part of the decor of Ezekiel's visionary temple (Ez 41:17-20).

See also Angel; Seraph, Seraphim.

CHESALON* *See* Kesalon.

CHESED* *See* Kesed.

CHESIL* *See* Kesil.

CHESTNUT* KJV mistranslation for plane tree, a tree indigenous to Palestine (Gn 30:37; Ez 31:8). *See* Plants (Plane Tree).

CHESULLOTH* *See* Kesulloth.

CHEZIB* *See* Kezib.

CHICKEN* Common domestic fowl raised for its edible eggs and flesh. *See* Birds (Fowl, Domestic).

CHIDON* *See* Kidon.

CHIEF PRIEST Highest office in the hierarchy of priests and Levites. It was the chief priest who alone went into the Most Holy Place of the temple once a year to make atonement for the sins of the whole nation of Israel.

See also Priests and Levites.

CHILD *See* Family Life and Relations.

CHILDLESS *See* Barrenness.

CHILDREN*, Song of the Three Addition to Daniel that begins with the "Prayer of Azariah"; the song is also called "Song of the Three Young Men." *See* Daniel, Additions to.

CHILDREN OF EDEN* KJV name for the inhabitants of Beth-eden, an Aramaic city-state conquered by Assyria, in 2 Kings 19:12. *See* Beth-eden.

CHILDREN OF GOD *See* Sons and Daughters of God.

CHILEAB* *See* Kileab.

CHILION* *See* Kilion.

CHILMAD* *See* Kilmad.

CHIMHAM* *See* Kimham.

CHINNERETH*, CHINNEROTH* *See* Kinnereth.

CHIOS* *See* Kios.

CHISLEU*, CHISLEV* *See* Kislev.

CHISLON* *See* Kislon.

CHISLOTH-TABOR* *See* Kisloth-tabor.

CHITLISH* *See* Kitlish.

CHITTIM* *See* Kittim.

CHIUN* KJV form of Kaiwan, an Assyrian astral deity, in Amos 5:26. *See* Kaiwan.

CHLOE Woman whose household members (possibly slaves) informed Paul in Ephesus of arguments in the Corinthian church (1 Cor 1:11). It is not known whether Chloe lived in Corinth or Ephesus, or even whether she herself was a believer.

CHOBA Village mentioned in the book of Judith as being fortified by the Jews when Assyrian commander Holofernes invaded Palestine (Jdt 4:4). The precise location cannot be identified, but it may be el-Makhubbi, three miles (4.8 kilometers) from Besan, or possibly the Hobah of Genesis 14:15. The account indicates that the Jews pursued Holofernes' army to Choba and beyond Damascus (Jdt 15:4-5).

CHOINIX* Dry commodity measure equivalent to a little more than a quart (one liter) (Rv 6:6; see NLT mg). The RSV and NIV read "quart." *See* Weights and Measures.

CHOIR DIRECTOR, CHOIRMASTER* Director of music; referred to in the superscriptions of 55 psalms. *See* Music; Musical Instruments.

CHOOSE *See* Elect, Election.

CHOR-ASHAN* KJV rendering of Bor-ashan in 1 Samuel 30:30. Bor-ashan was an alternate name for Ashan, a town originally in Judah's territory. *See* Ashan.

CHORAZIN* *See* Korazin.

CHOSEN *See* Elect, Election.

CHOZEBA* KJV form of Cozeba in 1 Chronicles 4:22. Cozeba was an alternate name for Achzib, a city in Judah's territory. *See* Cozeba.

CHRIST Official title given to Jesus in the NT. It signifies his office as anointed Savior and alludes to his spiritual qualifications for the task of saving his people. The word derives from Greek *Christos*, which translates Hebrew *Messiah* (Jn 1:41). Both terms come from verbs meaning "to anoint with sacred oil"; hence, as titles they mean "the Anointed One." Applied to Jesus, they express the conviction that he had divine appointment for his office and function.

In the NT the title is used in combination with the given name, as "Jesus Christ" (Mt 1:1; Mk 1:1; Rom 1:4), "Christ Jesus" (NIV Rom 1:1; 1 Cor 1:1), with the article "the" (Rom 7:4), or with another title "Lord" (Rom 16:18). It is also used alone as the one favored substitute name or title for Jesus (Jn 20:31; Rom 15:3; Heb 3:6; 5:5; 1 Pt 1:11, 19).

The Gospels portray Jesus as modestly accepting the title and role of the Messiah. His baptism should be understood as his anointing to the threefold office of prophet, priest, and king. At his baptism by John (the new Elijah, Mt 11:14), Jesus received the outpouring of the Spirit and God's mandate to begin his ministry (Mt 3:16–4:17). John himself denied being the anointed one but tacitly identified Jesus as the Christ (Jn 1:20; Lk 3:14-17). Jesus' first disciples followed him because they knew he was the Messiah (Jn 1:41). The demons recognized him as "the Holy One [anointed] of God" (Mk 1:24; cf. Mt 8:29). The crowds followed him as the Prophet, the new Moses (Jn 6:14, 32), but deserted him when they understood that his kingdom was a spiritual, not a political realm (v 66). The Twelve remained loyal, saying, "We believe . . . you are the Holy One of God" (Jn 6:69, NIV). The confession of the disciples voiced by Peter and approved by Jesus as a divine revelation is "You are the Christ, the Son of the living God" (Mt 16:16, NIV). At his trials the decisive factor in Jesus' condemnation was his claim to be the Christ (Mt 26:63-64, 68; 27:11, 17, 22, 37).

An important feature in the earliest Christian preaching was the proclamation that Jesus is the Christ (Acts 2:36; 3:18-20; 9:22; 28:23, 31). This remains the earliest (Mt 16:16) and most basic article of Christian confession (1 Cor 1:23; 1 Jn 5:1), affirming that Jesus perfectly fulfilled the role of anointed prophet, priest, and king as the servant of God for his people (Lk 7:16, 1 Cor 15:25; Heb 7:22-28; Rv 19:16).

See also Jesus Christ, Life and Teachings of; Messiah.

THREE ANOINTED ONES FORESHADOW THE MESSIAH
Jesus' office and function were foreshadowed by the three groups of OT anointed officials: prophets, priests, and kings. Elisha's anointing by Elijah (1 Kgs 19:16) shows anointing of prophets was practiced, although not required by OT law. Moses was the first OT prophet (Dt 18:18) whose ministry prompted the messianic hope for the coming of the Prophet (Jn 6:14; Heb 1:1). All priests, from Aaron on, were ordained by anointing with oil in required consecration rites (Ex 28:41; 29:7-9; 30:30). The kings of Israel, beginning with Saul and David, were anointed as a sign of divine choice and approval (1 Sm 9:15-17; 10:1; 16:13). Essential to the external ceremony was the pouring of perfumed olive oil upon the person's head (Ex 30:22-33). The internal reality was the gift of the Spirit to the recipient: "from that day on the Spirit of the LORD came upon David in power" (1 Sm 16:13, NIV). The anointed person was not a free agent. As prophet, priest, or king, he spoke, served, or ruled in the name of the Lord and as his representative to the people of God.

CHRISTIAN Name first given to the followers of Jesus Christ (Acts 11:26). When the Christian movement reached Antioch in Syria, the gospel was preached to Gentiles as well as Jews. Such evangelism marked the sect as more than a new type of Judaism; it was a new religion. The Gentiles in Antioch invented a name for the new group. Since members of the group constantly talked about Christ, they were called Christians, meaning the "household" or "partisans" of Christ. Some satire may have been intended in the name. For instance, since the "Augustinians" were an organized group who led the public praise of the emperor Nero Augustus, the citizens of Antioch may have made a comparable Latinized name out of Christ as a joke. Similar groups included Herod's

partisans, the Herodians. "Christ" was an unusual and meaningless name to Gentiles, but Chrestos (meaning "good" or "kind") was a common name; some pagans called the new sect "Chrestians." Thus, Suetonius wrote of the Jews being expelled from Rome in AD 49 on account of "Chrestus."

The Christians themselves apparently did not appreciate the name, but like many other nicknames, "Christian" stuck. It appears only three times in the Greek NT: Acts 11:26 describes its origin; Acts 26:28 records Herod Agrippa II saying satirically to Paul, "In a short time you think to make me a Christian!"; 1 Peter 4:16 instructs believers not to be ashamed if they suffer because the name has been applied to them. No further record of the name appears until the second century, when Ignatius of Antioch became the first Christian to call believers Christians. The Roman governor Pliny (from the area to which 1 Peter was addressed) wrote to the emperor Trajan about people accused in his court of being Christians. From that time on, the nickname became popular among Christians. What better name could there be than one declaring that they belonged to Christ?

CHRISTOLOGY* The study of the person and work of Jesus Christ. The confession that Jesus is the Christ, the Son of the living God, first ventured by Peter at Caesarea Philippi (Mt 16:16), is the heart of the Christian faith. It is this confession that makes one a Christian, and all Christian theology is thinking, in the light of this confession, about the meaning of this confession. The first major theological decision of the church resulting from such believing thought was the affirmation of the essential deity of Jesus as the Son of God. As such he was declared to be of one essence with the Father and the Spirit (the dogma of the Trinity promulgated at Nicaea, AD 325). Since this affirmation was made with reference to the man Jesus of Nazareth, it forced upon the church, inescapably, the further question: How could one and the same person be both God and man? How could he who is infinite become finite; he who is eternal become temporal; he who is God become man?

To answer this question, the church embraced the doctrine of the Incarnation. The statement of the doctrine was arrived at only after much controversy. In the course of the debate the church rejected all efforts, on the one hand, to preserve the deity of the Son at the expense of his humanity (docetism), and on the other, to preserve his humanity at the expense of his deity (adoptionism). In the former category were the doctrines of those who claimed that the Son only *seemed* to have a human body, or (like the Apollinarians) that while he had a true body and soul, the divine Logos took the place of the human spirit. In the latter category was the doctrine of those who claimed that the man Jesus, through the process of moral development, was elevated to divine sonship and so adopted into the Godhead. Some placed great stress on Jesus' endowment with the Spirit at baptism as the moment of his adoption, while others, citing Acts 13:33—"today I have begotten thee"—believed Jesus became the unique Son of God at the resurrection. The church also rejected all attempts to resolve the problem of the Savior's divinity and humanity by suggesting that he was both a divine person and a human person (Nestorianism) or, contrariwise, that the unity of his person implied a fusion of the divine and human in one nature (monophysitism).

The Chalcedonian Creed At the Ecumenical Council of Chalcedon (AD 451), the position was adopted that the Lord Jesus Christ was truly God and truly man (*vere Deo, vere homo*). The creed said:

> [He is] consubstantial with the Father as to his Godhead, and consubstantial also with us as to his manhood; like unto us in all things, yet without sin; as to his Godhead, begotten of the Father before all worlds; but as to his manhood, in these days, born for us men and for our salvation, of the virgin Mary, the mother of God, one and the same Christ, Son, Lord, only-begotten, known in two natures, without confusion, without conversion, without severance, and without division; the distinction of the natures being in no wise abolished by their union, but the peculiarity of each nature being maintained, and both concurring in one person and subsistence. We confess not a Son divided and sundered into two persons, but one and the same Son, and only-begotten, and God-Logos, our Lord Jesus Christ.

This confession was adopted in all its essential features by the Reformers at the time of the Protestant Reformation.

Chalcedonian Christology does not remove the mystery of the Incarnation but rather indicates, as it were, the boundaries of believing thought about the person of the Redeemer, boundaries that have proved significant in the history of Christian thought. As for the key terms in the creed, the following should be noted: the word "nature" (*physis*) as used by the church fathers does not have reference to the physical, material order that is the object of investigation by the "natural" sciences. "Nature" rather refers to being or reality in distinction from appearance. To say that Jesus Christ has a divine nature is to affirm that all the qualities, properties, or attributes by which one describes the divine order of being pertain to him. In short, he is God himself, not *like* God, but just *God*. So also with the affirmation that Christ has a human nature. Christ is not God *appearing* as a man; he *is* a man. He is not *only* a man nor *only* God; he is the God who *became* a man. He did not cease to be God when he became a man; he did not exchange divinity for humanity. Rather, he assumed humanity, so that he is now both divine and human. He is the God-man.

The term "person" (*hypostasis*) was used by the fathers to describe Jesus Christ as a self-conscious, self-determined Subject, one who designates himself by the word "I" over against a "thou." The Mediator between God and man is *a person* who has a divine nature and a human nature. While there can be no "person" where there is no "nature," it does not follow that there is no distinction between the terms, for there can be a "nature," as defined above, where there is no "person." (An object may have the properties of "nature" of a stone: grayness, hardness, roundness, smoothness. But this object, which has the "nature" of a stone, is not a "person"; it is not self-conscious and self-determined.)

The distinction between the "person" and the "nature" of the incarnate Christ speaks of him as being a "person" with a "divine nature" and a "human nature." The fathers were teaching through this that while we must ascribe to Christ all the qualities that belong to the divine order of being and to the human order of being (including bodily, physical, objective being—the Word "became flesh," Jn 1:14), we cannot say that he is "two persons." He is a divine person with a human nature, not a human person as such. All human persons have a first moment. Wheresoever and whensoever we may identify that first moment for a human "I," whether at conception or at fetal quickening in the womb, whether at the moment of birth, or

even as late as the first moment of self-awareness in the young child, no human "I" is aware of himself as a "subject," as an "I," before he is conceived in the womb of his mother. The man Jesus of Nazareth, however, unlike any mere man, could say, "Before Abraham was, I am" (Jn 8:58). This affirmation is neither the late theological invention of Christian fancy nor the claim of a man suffering from delusions of grandeur, but rather the sober truth. This person sitting on a mountainside preaching, this person standing by the sea calling fishermen to be his disciples, is a person who always was a person, even before there were any fishermen by the sea to call or any people to preach to on the mountainside—in fact, before there was any sea or any mountain.

Christ is not the divine Logos, who inspires and uniquely endows the man, Jesus of Nazareth, with moral and religious insights. Rather, this man Jesus is the eternal Son of God, and God's eternal Son has become this man, Jesus. The Son of God did not assume a man's *person* to his own *nature*, but a man's *nature* to his own *person*. He continues to be the same person, though he now assumes our humanity. Hence, he can speak both as a Subject consciously in history and as a Subject consciously transcending history, even in one and the same sentence. "*I have glorified thee on the earth: I* have finished the work which thou gavest me to do. And now, O Father, glorify thou me with thine own self with the glory which *I* had with thee *before the world was*" (Jn 17:4-5, KJV, emphasis added). Here the same person, Jesus, speaks as a person in the world, an "I" who has done certain things in the world, and as a person before there was any world, an "I" who shared his glory with a "thou" whom he calls "Father" before all time. All efforts at rational analysis of this mystery, which the church designates by the word "incarnation," run the risk of losing the truth by explaining it. One arrives at a position in which Christ is a divine being who appears human (docetism) or a human being who either achieves divine status for himself (adoptionism) or divine worth for us (Ritschlianism).

In order to preserve fully both our Lord's deity and his humanity, the creed employs four terms in which we are told what did *not* happen in the Incarnation. The union of the two natures is declared to be "without confusion," "without conversion," "without separation," and "without division." Some have ridiculed these "four bald negatives," but they are by no means wholly without value. Should any of these basic negatives be violated, we would lose what is essential to Christian faith, the "one and the same Son, our Lord Jesus Christ, complete as to his Godhead, and complete as to his manhood."

But the creed contains not only a negative affirmation—what did *not* happen in the Incarnation; it also contains a positive affirmation. The union of the two natures concurs in one Person, who is the eternal Son of the Father. The union, then, of the divine and the human in Christ is a personal one; more specifically, the union is the act of the divine Person who is the Son of God. Here we approach the very heart of the mystery of the Incarnation. No one can say how the infinite God could become a finite man. Naturally, however, theologians have thought a great deal about the matter; Chalcedon does not mark the end of all inquiry.

In theological parlance it has become customary to speak of the union of the divine and the human in the Person of the incarnate Redeemer as the "hypostatic" union (*unio hypostatica*), from the Greek word for "person." It is important to note not only *that* the union is personal, but also *why* it is so. Theologians speak of the union as personal because it is the act of a Person, namely the Son of God, the Word who became flesh. This means that the Person of the incarnate Redeemer is divine, the object of Christian worship. He cannot, then, be a mere human being as other men are mere human beings. To worship one who is a man and only a man would be idolatry. And because this personal union of the divine and the human is truly a *union*, the Redeemer is one Person, not two. If to worship a human person would be idolatry, to worship two persons—one human, one divine—would be an absurdity. This Person, who unites in himself the divine and the human, is often described by theologians as a "theanthropic" person, the God-man. If one does not mean that he is a hybrid—half God, half man—then this mode of speaking is unobjectionable inasmuch as it simply says that this Person, Jesus Christ, is both divine and human, which is what the creed intends.

Christology after Chalcedon Matters become more difficult and unanimity less in evidence, however, when the question is raised as to the personal qualities of Christ's humanity. The formulation most consistent with Chalcedon and generally held by Protestants speaks of the "impersonal humanity" of our Lord. It has also been defended in modern times by the Swiss theologians Karl Barth and Emil Brunner and by G. C. Berkouwer of the Netherlands.

Actually the meaning of the phrase "impersonal humanity" *(impersonalitas)* is not that in the case of the incarnate Son there is no manifestation of the personal at the human level. Rather, it means that this humanity, of itself, has no independent existence apart from the divine Person who assumed this humanity in the act of becoming incarnate. So far as Jesus of Nazareth is concerned, that which is human exists in and through the Word who is God himself. There is a sense in which God is present to *all* created reality (the doctrine of the divine immanence). But howsoever we may conceive of this divine presence of power (providence) and of grace (salvation), there can be no thought of *identity* between God and the creature. Even when the church, following the usage of the NT, speaks of the Christian as "indwelt by the Holy Spirit," there is no identity of *being* affirmed; there is no ontological union of the human and the divine. But in the case of the man Jesus Christ, something absolutely unique is affirmed: this man is declared to be identical with God because he, the Person, is the "Word who was made flesh and dwelt among us." "Therefore," says Barth, "he does not only live through God and with God; he is himself God. Nor is he autonomous and self-existent. His reality, existence and being are wholly and absolutely that of God himself, the God who acts in his Word. His manhood is only the predicate of his Godhead, or better and more concretely, it is only the predicate, assumed in inconceivable condescension, of the Word acting upon us, the Word who is the Lord."

In other words, Jesus our Lord is, as man, so united with God that he exists as man only and insofar as he exists as God. The doctrine of *anhypostasy* states this truth negatively. It affirms that the human nature of our Lord does not possess the mode of its being as personal in and of itself. The doctrine of *enhypostasy* states this truth positively. It affirms that the particular human nature that is our Lord's acquires its personal mode of being by union with the personal Son of God. It is not Jesus of Nazareth who becomes the Son of God (adoptionism) but the Son of God who becomes Jesus of Nazareth. The Incarnation is a unique act of a divine Person, not a unique experience of the divine on the part of a human person. The Subject of the Incarnation is a divine Subject who acts, not a human subject who is acted upon. But inasmuch as the divine Subject, the eternal Son, so acts

as to become this man, Jesus of Nazareth, this man is—not just symbolizes, but *is*—the Son of God as no other man is or ever can be the Son of God.

The scriptural basis of the doctrine of the Incarnation includes, of course, the entire range of data in the Gospels as well as several passages in the Pauline Epistles, especially Philippians 2:6-8, which is, perhaps, the single most important christological passage in the NT. Here Paul, using the words of a primitive Christian confession, speaks of him "who, though he was in the form of God, did not count equality with God a thing to be grasped, but emptied himself, taking the form of a servant, being born in the likeness of men" (RSV).

The Chalcedonian Creed does not resolve the mystery of the Incarnation, and theologians have made many efforts to better understand the mystery. One of the best known is based on an inference drawn from the passage quoted above. It is known as *kenosis*, the theory that when the Son became man, he emptied himself of some aspect of his divinity. The text of Philippians does not say that he emptied himself *of* anything, but only that he emptied *himself*, a striking figure of speech denoting condescension ("made himself of no reputation," KJV). In spite of the exegetical difficulties in this statement, kenotic theory has persisted, in one form or another, especially in British theology. Another effort at understanding suggests that our Lord's humanity was the *incognito* (Kierkegaard's term) that hid his identity as a divine person from all but the eyes of faith. Thus, the Incarnation was a revelation that veils as well as discloses the truth.

See also Ascension of Christ; Christ; Incarnation; Jesus Christ, Life and Teachings of; Kingdom of God, Kingdom of Heaven; Messiah; Parable; Son of God; Son of Man; Virgin Birth of Jesus; Word.

CHRONICLES, Books of First and Second

Two OT books, historical records of King David and his successors in the land of Judah. The books of Chronicles are among the most neglected books in the Bible, partly because most of the material can be found in Samuel, Kings, or elsewhere in the OT. Fourteen chapters (1 Chr 1–9; 23–27) are little more than lists of names; the rest of the material is primarily historical narrative, which some people find almost as boring as lists. Yet the content of Chronicles is not history in a professional or academic sense because the materials used are comparable to the annals compiled by ancient Near Eastern court scribes. Those sources recorded each year's most important events and were frequently more propagandistic than objectively historical. The records in Chronicles, somewhat eclectic in nature and ignoring certain facets of national history while emphasizing others, deal with only a selected portion of the history of the Israelites. A good deal of the criticism that the work is historically unreliable has come from lack of understanding the book's character. Chronicles is not so much a history as a metaphysical interpretation of events in Israelite life in light of covenantal values. It was not sufficient for the Chronicler that kings rose and fell; the events were interpreted from a special religious standpoint.

PREVIEW
• Author
• Date
• Background
• Origin and Purpose
• Content

Author In the Hebrew Bible, 1 and 2 Chronicles form a single book. The Bible does not say who wrote that book

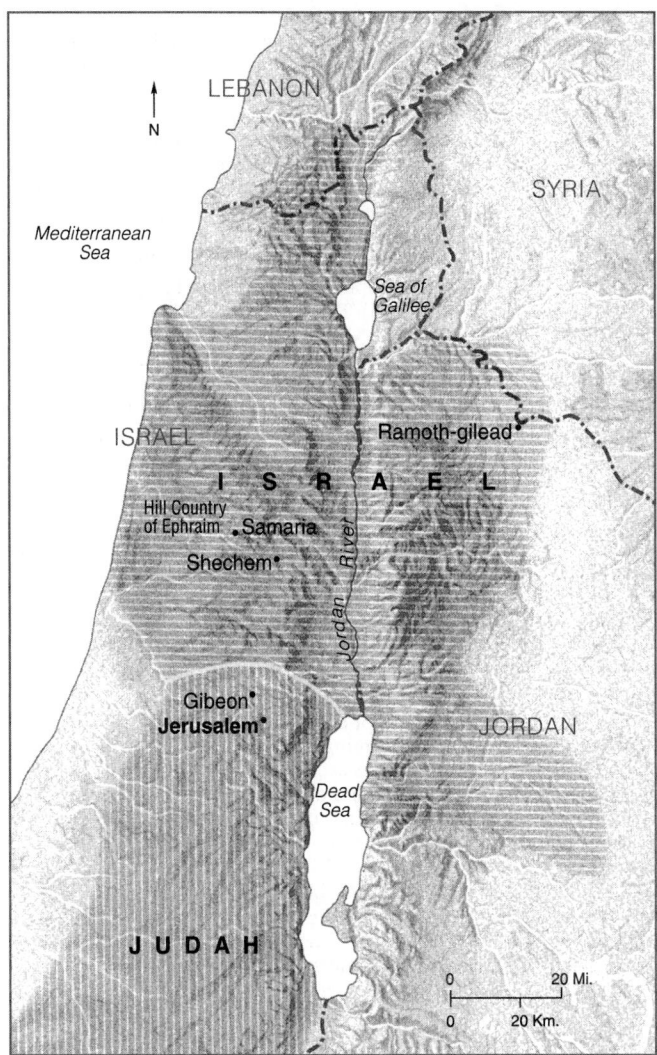

The broken lines (—·—·) indicate modern boundaries.

Key Places in 1 and 2 Chronicles

three books. In the Hebrew Bible, Ezra-Nehemiah is considered one book and stands before Chronicles. Chronicles stands at the very end of the Hebrew Bible.

Date It is not possible to determine precisely when the book of Chronicles was written. The book ends with a reference to the decree of Cyrus, king of Persia, permitting the Jewish captives in Babylon to return to their homeland. Since Cyrus's decree is usually dated about 538 BC, Chronicles could not have been written before that date. But if Ezra-Nehemiah is a part of the same work as Chronicles, the materials could not have been written until Nehemiah returned to Jerusalem in 444 BC.

Genealogies in Chronicles and Ezra-Nehemiah may shed some light on the dating of the books. In 1 Chronicles 3:10-24 the lineage of David and Solomon is traced through the sixth generation after the exile, which would make the date for Anani (the last person in the list) about 400 BC.

The language of Chronicles is definitely that of postexilic Hebrew. The use of the Persian word *daric* (1 Chr 29:7), plus a lack of any Greek words, places Chronicles in the Persian period (538–331 BC). The word *midrash* ("exposition") appears in the OT only in Chronicles (2 Chr 13:22; 24:27) but is very common in postbiblical Hebrew. Around 400 BC is probably the best estimate for the date of Chronicles, based on evidence now available.

Background During the Persian period, some of the Jews returned to Jerusalem from Babylon soon after Cyrus's decree. They rebuilt the temple and waited for the messianic age to come. But with drought, economic hardships, and moral and spiritual laxness, their hopes faded. Judah was stable politically as a part of the large, dominant Persian Empire. There was not the slightest possibility of restoring the Davidic kingdom.

If the kingdom of David could not be restored politically, how was a Jew of the early fourth century BC to understand history and the place of the Jews in God's plan? The Chronicler, living at that time, found the key to history in God's covenant with David. The first 10 chapters of 1 Chronicles lead up to David; chapters 11–29 detail events of David's rule. Moses is mentioned in Chronicles 31 times; David, more than 250 times. David planned the temple and collected money to build it. He appointed Levites, singers, and gatekeepers. He divided the priesthood into its orders. He was responsible for the temple worship, which was tremendously important to the Chronicler and his contemporaries.

The Persian period of Israel's history is largely a silent one, both in other OT materials and in archaeological finds. Of course, all the evidence is not yet in, as archaeologists continue their investigations of the period.

or when it was written. According to the Jewish Talmud, Ezra wrote "his book and Chronicles—the order of all generations down to himself." Although many scholars defend the view that Ezra wrote Chronicles, there is still no general agreement about the date and authorship of the book.

The author is usually called "the Chronicler," a title suggesting that he was a historian. It is possible that he was a scribe, priest, or Levite. Evidently the writer had access to government and temple archives, because repeated references are made to a number of official records of kings (1 Chr 9:1; 27:24; 2 Chr 16:11; 20:34; 25:26; 27:7; 28:26; 32:32; 33:18; 35:27; 36:8) and prophets (1 Chr 29:29; 2 Chr 9:29; 12:15; 13:22; 20:34; 26:22; 32:32; 33:19).

The evidence is suggestive, but not conclusive, that the author of Chronicles also wrote the books of Ezra and Nehemiah. The last two verses of Chronicles are almost the same as the first three verses of Ezra. The language and literary style of all three books are similar. The same theological concerns for the temple and its worship and the same interest in lists and genealogies appear in all

Origin and Purpose The Chronicler must have lived in Jerusalem and written for the Jewish community there. He refers to Jerusalem about 240 times and to

Judah more than 225 times. A negative feeling toward the northern kingdom of Israel can be seen in the almost total lack of references to any northern king. The Chronicler's attitude toward the north is clearly expressed in the two following verses: "The northern tribes of Israel have refused to be ruled by a descendant of David to this day" (2 Chr 10:19, NLT) and "Don't you realize that the LORD, the God of Israel, made an unbreakable covenant with David, giving him and his descendants the throne of Israel forever?" (13:5, NLT).

The Chronicler wanted the Jewish people to see that God was sovereign over all things. For example, he includes David's affirmation: "Yours, O LORD, is the greatness, the power, the glory, the victory, and the majesty. Everything in the heavens and on earth is yours, O LORD, and this is your kingdom. We adore you as the one who is over all things. Riches and honor come from you alone, for you rule over everything. Power and might are in your hand, and it is at your discretion that people are made great and given strength" (1 Chr 29:11-12, NLT).

Compiled in the postexilic period, Chronicles was meant to emphasize the significance of the theocracy seen in light of earlier history. The theocracy was a social configuration God planned for postexilic Judah, a religious rather than secular community. Instead of a king, the Jews had a priesthood of which the Lord approved (as distinct from the corrupt priests who had been to a large extent responsible for the preexilic moral and spiritual collapse of the nation).

The postexilic Judeans were to live as a holy nation, not as people with political and nationalistic ambitions. Therefore, the Chronicler demanded implicit obedience to the Mosaic covenant so that the returning Jews could find prosperity, divine blessing, and grace. The Jews were still the chosen people, purged by the experience of exile, with a new opportunity to fulfill the Sinai covenant.

The Chronicler gave great weight to divine retribution and was insistent that all action be guided by specific moral principles, to reflect God's character clearly in his people. Because the writer saw God's hand in all history, punishing the apostate and being gracious to the penitent, he saw in the chastened remnant of the exile the true spiritual heirs of the house of David. He insisted that the postexilic community adhere rigorously to the morality of Sinai, guarding against preexilic apostasy and ensuring divine blessing.

The writer wanted the Jews to know God's power. He also wanted them to believe in the Lord so that they would be "established." If they believed God's messengers, they would succeed (2 Chr 20:20). He also wanted the people to know that Jerusalem was God's chosen place of worship (2 Chr 5–6), and that the temple, priests, singers, Levites, and gatekeepers had been divinely appointed (1 Chr 28:19). The temple was meant to be a place where all their needs could be met (2 Chr 6:19–7:3).

Content Chronicles can be briefly outlined as follows: 1 Chronicles—genealogies (1–9); the reign of David (10–29); 2 Chronicles—the reign of Solomon (1–9); the kings of Judah (10:1–36:21); epilogue on the exile and return (36:22-23). Since the Chronicler's writings do not have a didactic format, the reader must draw out those ideas and principles that are prominent and basic.

One important idea running through Chronicles is the greatness, power, and uniqueness of God. It is expressed most beautifully and forcefully in 1 Chronicles 29:11-12, which declares that everything in heaven and earth belongs to God and he is head over all. Other passages make a similar claim. When Sennacherib, king of

Assyria, attacked Judah and Jerusalem, King Hezekiah of Judah admonished his people not to fear the king of Assyria.

Several times the Chronicler repeats the idea that Israel's God is unique: there is no other God like the Lord. In 1 Chronicles 16:25-26, Psalm 96:4-5 is quoted: "Great is the LORD! He is most worthy of praise! He is to be revered above all gods. The gods of other nations are merely idols, but the LORD made the heavens!" (NLT). Both David and Solomon are quoted as saying that there is no other God but the Lord (1 Chr 17:20; 2 Chr 6:14).

Chronicles emphasizes that the Lord is "greater than all gods" (2 Chr 2:5). The classic passage that stresses the differences between God and the "god" of a nation is in 2 Chronicles 32. When Sennacherib attacked Jerusalem, he asked the people what they were relying on to withstand the siege in Jerusalem. Sennacherib was saying, in effect, "Don't let Hezekiah deceive you by telling you that your God will deliver you. No god of any nation so far has been able to stand against me. Your God is like the gods of all the other nations. He will not be able to deliver you from me." The Chronicler observes that the Assyrians spoke of the God of Jerusalem as they spoke of the gods of the peoples of the earth. But God did deliver Hezekiah and the inhabitants of Jerusalem from Sennacherib.

Several passages declare that God rules over the nations (1 Chr 17:21; 2 Chr 20:6). In fact, the Chronicler saw the Lord as the one who directs history. The Lord brought Israel out of Egypt and drove the Canaanites out of their land (1 Chr 17:21; 2 Chr 6:5; 20:7). Some seeming quirks of history are explained with such phrases as "it was ordained by God" (2 Chr 22:7, RSV). Over and over in telling the story of the struggles of the kings of Judah with other nations, Chronicles points out that the Lord always decided the battle (1 Chr 10:13-14; 18:6; 2 Chr 12:2; 13:15; 20:15; 21:11-14; 24:18; 28:1, 5-6, 19).

To the Chronicler the Lord was a covenant-keeping God (2 Chr 6:14). He was the God of justice and righteousness (12:6), so human judges must judge honestly and fairly (19:7). The Chronicler made it clear that no individual or nation could succeed by opposing God (24:20); not only would people fail against God, but they were powerless without him (1 Chr 29:14; 2 Chr 20:12).

The Lord is seen not only as a unique, righteous, and powerful God, but also as a wise God. God tests the human heart and knows when he finds integrity (1 Chr 29:17). Solomon prayed for God to "hear thou from heaven thy dwelling place, and forgive, and render unto every man according unto all his ways, whose heart thou knowest; (for thou only knowest the hearts of the children of men)" (2 Chr 6:30, KJV).

Although God knows all about human beings, and has supreme power in heaven and on earth, men and women are still free to obey or disobey the Lord. The stories in Chronicles depict people who chose to obey or disobey God. Those who obeyed succeeded; but to the extent that others, even kings, disobeyed God, they failed. Three of the Chronicler's heroes were Jehoshaphat, Hezekiah, and Josiah. Each was a great reformer, and each was commended for obeying the Lord. But each one sinned near the end of his life and incurred the disfavor of God. Jehoshaphat joined an alliance with a wicked king from the north (2 Chr 20:35-37). Hezekiah sinned in receiving envoys from Babylon and "God left him to himself" (32:31). Josiah did not obey the word of God spoken by Pharaoh Neco and was killed (35:21-24).

The Chronicler believed that all human beings have sinned (2 Chr 6:36), and should repent with all their mind and heart (6:38). One of the greatest passages on repentance in all the Bible is in 2 Chronicles 7:14.

A prominent theme in Chronicles is the importance of the temple as the place to meet God in worship. One could say that almost everything in Chronicles is related to the temple in one way or another. For a person living in Jerusalem in the fourth century BC under the domination of the Persians, temple worship was very significant. The Chronicler expressed the importance of true community and institutional worship.

Worship was the dominant attitude of the Chronicler, whose God was worthy to be praised. A worship service is described in 2 Chronicles 29:20-30. Hezekiah commanded a burnt offering and a sin offering to be made for all Israel. The Levites were stationed in the house of the Lord with cymbals, harps, and lyres. The priests had trumpets. "Then Hezekiah ordered that the burnt offer-

ing be placed on the altar. As the burnt offering was presented, songs of praise to the LORD were begun, accompanied by the trumpets and other instruments of David, king of Israel. The entire assembly worshiped the LORD as the singers sang and the trumpets blew, until all the burnt offerings were finished. Then the king and everyone with him bowed down in worship. King Hezekiah and the officials ordered the Levites to praise the LORD with the psalms of David and Asaph the seer. So they offered joyous praise and bowed down in worship" (2 Chr 29:27-30, NLT).

See also Chronology of the Bible (Old Testament); Israel, History of; King; Kings, Books of First and Second.

CHRONOLOGY OF THE BIBLE* (Old Testament) Branch of biblical studies that attempts to assign

---

QUESTIONING THE AUTHENTICITY OF THE CHRONICLES
The books of Chronicles, referred to as a single book in this article, have received considerable scholarly criticism about the nature of their content and about apparent discrepancies with material in Samuel and Kings. The differences can be classified as numerical, theological, and historical.

As an example of numerical differences, 1 Chronicles 11:11 says that one of David's "mighty men" killed 300 men with his spear at one time, but the parallel account in 2 Samuel 23:8 says he killed 800 at one time. Again, 1 Chronicles 18:3-4 says that after defeating King Hadadezer of Zobah, David took from him 1,000 chariots, 7,000 horsemen, and 20,000 foot soldiers; a parallel account in 2 Samuel 8:3-4 says that David took 1,700 horsemen and 20,000 foot soldiers. Although 2 Chronicles 22:2 says that Ahaziah was 42 years old when he began to reign, 2 Kings 8:26 says he was 22; and so on.

Many numbers in Chronicles seem exceptionally high. In 1 Chronicles 21:5, Israel had just over a million men and Judah had 470,000. In another example of a remarkably high number, the temple's vestibule is said to have been 120 cubits, or approximately 180 feet (54.8 meters), in height (2 Chr 3:4). In 2 Chronicles 13:3, Judah's army had 400,000 men and Israel's army 800,000. Some 500,000 of Israel's army were slain (2 Chr 13:17). In 2 Chronicles 14:9, Zerah the Ethiopian had an army of a million men and 300 chariots.

How should such problems with numbers in Chronicles be understood? First, some of the problems in the text as it now stands may have come about from faulty copying. Also, some excessively high numbers may have been used figuratively to indicate a very large army, or perhaps as estimates. Though not all questions have been answered, scholars have found credible solutions to some of the problems. In the meantime, such matters are seen by evangelical scholars as verifying the human side of the Scriptures without necessarily detracting from their divine origin.

Chronicles also contains some different theological emphases from earlier materials. The best example can be seen by comparing 1 Chronicles 21:1 with 2 Samuel 24:1. In the Samuel account the anger of the Lord was kindled against Israel, and he incited David to harm them by taking a national census. The Chronicler's account is that "Satan stood up against Israel, and incited David to number Israel." In one account God moved David to take the census; in the other Satan was the prime mover.

The authenticity of the Chronicler has also been questioned on historical grounds. Several incidents reported in Samuel-Kings are told in a different manner in Chronicles. In 2 Samuel 8:13 David is said to have slain 18,000 Edomites at the Valley of Salt, whereas the Chronicler reports that Abishai, David's cousin, killed the Edomites (1 Chr 18:12). Again, according to 2 Samuel 21:19, Elhanan slew Goliath the Gittite, whereas the Chronicler says that Elhanan slew Lahmi, the brother of Goliath the Gittite (1 Chr 20:5; most OT scholars today believe that Chronicles preserves the true reading of the original text). A more difficult historical problem is seen by comparing 2 Chronicles 20:35-37 with 1 Kings 22:48-49. The Kings account says that the ships Jehoshaphat, king of Judah, built to bring gold from Ophir were wrecked at Ezion-geber, evidently before they ever left port. When Ahaziah, king of Israel, asked that his servants be allowed to go on the ships with Jehoshaphat's servants, Jehoshaphat refused. The Chronicler's version of what happened is different. There Jehoshaphat joined with the wicked Ahaziah in building ships at Ezion-geber to go to Tarshish, but a prophet prophesied that the Lord would destroy the ships because of the alliance with Ahaziah. Both accounts agree that Jehoshaphat built ships at Ezion-geber and that the ships were destroyed before they left port. On the basis of the present status of the texts, however, one cannot tell whether or not Jehoshaphat joined Ahaziah. Whatever happened, the ships were lost.

In a comparison of Chronicles with Kings, a serious problem arises over the war between Asa of Judah and Baasha of Israel. In 2 Chronicles 16:1 one reads that in Asa's 36th year of reign, Baasha challenged Judah by building a fortress at Ramah. But according to the chronology of 1 Kings 16, Baasha was not even alive in the 36th year of Asa's reign. First Kings 16:6-8 says that Baasha died and his son Elah succeeded him as king in the 26th year of Asa's reign.

At one time scholars were quite skeptical about the authenticity of Chronicles. Now they tend to treat Chronicles with respect and appreciation. In some instances new archaeological evidence has tended to support the historicity of the Chronicler's statement. In other instances reexamination of a discrepancy has shown it to be more apparent than real. If all the facts were known, other problems might also be cleared up to the satisfaction of impartial scholars.

dates and sequences to OT events. Chronology is a science. It deals with evidence, theories, assumptions, and the balance of probabilities. Often it boils down to a matter of choosing among theories that are equally unable to solve all the problems raised by other points of view. OT chronology is an accredited branch of biblical studies primarily because it is essential for understanding the proper historical background of the biblical texts. In general, the chronology of the OT is understood well enough to vindicate the basic accuracy and sequential order of Scripture.

Both biblical and nonbiblical materials are utilized by students of OT chronology. Biblical data include (1) genealogies showing personal and tribal affiliations among various peoples; (2) specific numbers given by biblical authors to indicate a person's longevity, a king's reign, or the duration of a specific event; (3) synchronizing statements that date an event in a specific year of a king's reign or relate it to a natural phenomenon assumed to be common knowledge at the time of writing (e.g., Am 1:1; Zec 14:5).

From the abundance of such chronological passages in the OT, one might conclude that establishment of OT dates and sequences would be a simple procedure. Each of the three kinds of biblical materials, however, exhibits special problems that must be solved first.

Nonbiblical materials that shed light on OT chronology are quite numerous, and more are discovered year by year. They include (1) official records of important affairs such as military campaigns from countries like Egypt or Babylonia; (2) official inscriptions that are dedicatory or commemorate a great victory; (3) annals listing major accomplishments of a ruler year by year; (4) ostraca (inscribed pieces of pottery) containing letters, tax transactions and economic records, military dispatches between field leaders and command headquarters, or other information. Ostraca may be dated archaeologically and are often used to supplement the biblical record.

The chronologist tries to examine the pertinent biblical and nonbiblical information, notes areas of correlation among all the data, and finally establishes a working system into which most facts can be fitted. New evidence uncovered at any time may necessitate shifts in the present working system. Although the basic structure of biblical chronology seems reasonably firm, many details will no doubt be subject to change as new evidence is discovered.

As a general rule, the earlier the period, the less certain one can be of one's dating. In the second millennium BC, for example, many dates can be assigned within a range of about 100 years. By the time of David and Solomon (c. 1000 BC), the margin of error over which scholars debate is a decade or less. The range narrows as one comes toward the present, so that, with the exception of one or two problem eras, dates accurate to within one or two years are possible by roughly the middle of the ninth century BC. Such limitations must be kept in mind in any examination of the major periods of OT history.

PREVIEW
•Prepatriarchal Period
•From Abraham to Moses
•Conquest and Consolidation
•The Monarchy
•Judah after the Fall of Israel
•Beyond 586 BC

Prepatriarchal Period

Biblical Evidence In the first 11 chapters of Genesis are found accounts of the Creation (chs 1–2), the fall (ch 3),

Cain and Abel (ch 4), the Flood (chs 6–9), and the Tower of Babel (ch 11). Those events are set within a certain chronological framework.

According to Genesis 5, a period of 10 generations elapsed between the Creation and the Flood. Although the individuals listed enjoyed a total life span of a hefty 847 years plus, the total time elapsing between Adam and the Flood was only 1,656 years.

According to Genesis 11, another 10 generations elapsed from the time of the Flood until the time of Abraham (at least in the Septuagint, the third-century BC Greek translation of the OT; the Hebrew Masoretic text has 9). In that period the average age attained by individuals in the list is 346 years (using a figure of 460 for Arphaxad's son Cainan, who is included in v 13 of the LXX; cf. Lk 3:36); the total elapsed time from the Flood to Abraham is only 520 years. Taken literally, that would mean that all of Abraham's ancestors as far back as Noah's son Shem were still alive at Abraham's birth, and that a total of only 2,176 years elapsed from the time of Creation to Abraham.

Interpretation of the Biblical Data A literalistic or slavishly mathematical interpretation of the figures, as has appeared in the margin of many KJV Bibles, requires a number of assumptions: that no names are omitted from the genealogies, that all the numbers given are consecutive, and especially that numbers used in an ancient biblical source carry the same meaning as that associated with them in the modern Western mind. Each assumption needs serious examination in the light of other established facts.

A cursory reading of other biblical genealogies, for example, reveals that not all the names of a given family were always included. Even Matthew recorded a total of 28 generations (two sets of 14 each) between David and Jesus, and comparison with OT genealogies reveals that Matthew omitted several names. Luke listed a total of 42 generations for the same interval. Omissions are also obvious when one compares the genealogical lists given in 1 Chronicles 1–8 with those recorded earlier in Genesis, Exodus, Numbers, Joshua, 1 and 2 Samuel, and 1 and 2 Kings.

Further, ancient peoples thought of numbers in a schematic or stylized way. Use of numbers among the ancient Near Eastern nations differed sharply from current Western practice. Examples of that practice are known from both biblical and nonbiblical sources. For example, a list of eight Sumerian kings who ruled in the city of Shurruppak before the "great flood" of the Jemdet Nar era (c. 3000 BC) assigns each man an average reign of more than 30,000 years. Berossus, a Babylonian priest of Marduk living in the third century BC, added two names to the eight found in that earlier list of kings and assigned an average of 43,200 years to each king. Such extraordinarily high numbers provide a perspective for considering the numbers of Genesis.

Therefore, although one can assume that the numbers assigned to the ages of the patriarchs preceding Abraham in Genesis had real meaning for those responsible for their preservation, they should not be employed in a purely literal sense to compute the length of the various generations mentioned in the text. Further, the numbers given in the Septuagint and in the Samaritan Pentateuch, another early version of the Pentateuch, diverge in many details from those of the Hebrew Masoretic Text. That means, among other things, that the Genesis numbers caused problems for even the earliest scholars of Scripture.

Nonbiblical Evidence Archaeology provides no evidence that may be used to date either the Creation or any other account preserved in Genesis 1–11. The Flood is an exam-

SIGNIFICANT OLD TESTAMENT EVENTS AND DATES

Event	Reference Point	Biblical Basis	Date
Nehemiah's wall	20th yr. of Artaxerses I of Persia	Neh 2:1	444 BC
Return decreed	1st yr. of Cyrus II of Persia over Babylon	Ezr 1:1	538
Fall of Jerusalem	19th yr. of Nebuchadnezzar II of Babylon	2 Kgs 25:8	586
Fall of Samaria	Last yr. of Shalmaneser V of Assyria	2 Kgs 17:3	722
Division of Kingdom	77 yrs. before 6th yr. of Shalmaneser III	1 Kgs 11:29-43	930
Temple founded	4th yr. of Solomon	1 Kgs 6:1	966
Exodus from Egypt	480 yrs. before temple's founding	1 Kgs 6:1	1446
Descent into Egypt	Inaugurating a 430 yr. sojourn there (but 397 there, plus 33 in Canaan, for "the sons of Israel," according to Greek).	Ex 12:40	1876
			Gk/Heb Text
Jacob born	130 yrs. before	Gn 47:9	1973 (2006)
Isaac born	60 yrs. before	Gn 25:26	2033 (2066)
Abraham born	100 yrs. before	Gn 26:5	2133 (2166)

ple that illustrates some of the difficulties. Many claims have been made by persons from a wide variety of backgrounds (scientists, explorers, theologians, and others) to the effect that archaeology has proven the Genesis Flood narrative to be true. Yet no city so far excavated in Palestine and Syria (including some of the oldest towns in the world) shows archaeological evidence of the Flood.

Although several cities in Mesopotamia do exhibit evidence of a flood, three factors make it difficult to link that evidence with Genesis 6–9. Each of the flood levels so far discovered dates from a different period. Further, since nearby sites show no evidence of flooding, all of the Mesopotamian flood evidence points to relatively small local floods. Finally, the evidence indicates no great cultural discontinuities of the sort that would result from destruction of an entire population. Thus, it seems that the ancient Mesopotamian floods discovered through archaeological research are of the same kind as the floods that still occur in the Euphrates River valley.

Clearly, certain questions one might ask of the Genesis narratives simply cannot be answered. Many who regard the Bible as the Word of God have concluded that the dating of events found in Genesis 1–11 must be less important than the theological truths of salvation, faith, and obedience that these accounts present.

From Abraham to Moses

The Patriarchal Age The date of Abraham is still a lively topic among biblical scholars who agree that Abraham, Isaac, and Jacob were indeed historical persons. Opinions range from an early-date view that estimates that the patriarchal age extended from 2086 to 1871 BC, to a late-date view placing Abraham at around 1400 BC. Since each position claims to fit the biblical data, a closer look at the two points of view is in order.

Many OT passages seem to support the view that puts Abraham at a comparatively early date. First Kings 6:1 computes 480 years back from the founding of the temple in the fourth year of Solomon's reign (961 BC, according to the early-date view) to the exodus from Egypt, which would then be dated 1441 BC. Counting 430 years as the period of the Israelite sojourn in Egypt (see Gn 15:13; Ex 12:40) takes the date back to 1871 BC. To that date are added the 215 years demanded by the total of (1) Abraham's age upon entering Canaan (75 years according to Gn 12:4); (2) 25 additional years before the birth of Isaac (Gn 21:5); (3) 60 more years to the birth of Jacob (Gn 25:26); and (4) the appearance of Jacob before the pharaoh at age 130 (Gn 47:9). Those 215 years added to the previous total give a date of 2086 BC for the entrance of Abraham into Canaan and a date of 2161 BC for his birth.

Such a calculation does not use all of the chronological evidence presented in the OT; consequently, the date for Abraham is open to challenge. For example, the 480 years between the exodus and Solomon's fourth regnal year represent a period of time into which the wilderness wanderings, the career of Joshua and his immediate successors, the period of the judges, Samuel, Saul, and David must all be placed. Although the OT does not specifically say how long were the careers of Joshua, Samuel, or Saul, even a modest reckoning pushes the total years required by all the biblical data together to approximately 600.

In addition, the length of time to be assigned to the Egyptian sojourn is problematic. The Samaritan Pentateuch and the Septuagint both view the number 430 (in Ex 12:40) as applicable not only to the years in Egypt but to the years of Abraham, Isaac, and Jacob in Canaan as well. Evidently Paul followed the Septuagint tradition when he dated the giving of the law 430 years later than the time of

God's promise to Abraham (see Gal 3:15-18). That means the Septuagint figure cannot be dismissed lightly.

The late dating of Abraham (c. 1400 BC) is based on two propositions: (1) The picture of patriarchal society portrayed in Genesis most closely parallels that reflected in the cuneiform tablets recovered from Nuzi, a town in northeastern Mesopotamia about 175 miles (282 kilometers) north of Baghdad. (2) Because those tablets must be dated in the 15th and 14th centuries BC, the parallel patriarchal age must have fallen within the same general time period.

Those who hold the late-date view are aware that their date for Abraham cannot be equated with the set of numbers on which the early-date view depends. They point to other data, also from the OT. Joseph, who was already a highly placed Egyptian official when Jacob moved to Egypt, lived to be 110 years old (Gn 50:26). Moses was a great-grandson of Levi, Joseph's older brother. Since Joseph lived to see his own great-grandchildren born (who would probably be younger than Moses since their great-grandfather was younger than his), the late-date view concludes that Joseph could have been alive when Moses was born. The four-generation genealogy of Moses (Levi-Kohath-Amram-Moses, in Ex 6:16-20; Nm 3:17-19; 26:58-59; 1 Chr 6:1-3) was evidently thought to be complete according to Genesis 15:16, which predicted that Abraham's descendants would be freed from Egyptian bondage "in the fourth generation."

However, a date of around 1400 BC for Abraham cannot be aligned with certain other biblical data, including the long Egyptian sojourn demanded by Genesis 15:13 and Exodus 12:40 and a 40-year (or "one-generation") wilderness existence. Some normally moderate scholars are forced to reduce the wilderness time to two years in order to maintain their late date for Abraham.

In short, the late-date theory is consistent with part of the biblical evidence (the genealogies of Moses), but the early-date theory conforms to another part (the actual year figures listed in scattered verses from Genesis and Exodus). The late-date theory holds that the genealogies represent more reliable information in Semitic societies generally, whereas the early-date theory computes years given in the biblical account literally throughout its scheme.

Because of problems attached to both positions, a large group of scholars take a middle ground in dating the patriarchal age. Archaeologically, they say, Abraham and his life and times fit perfectly within the early second millennium, but imperfectly within any later period. By placing Abraham roughly between 1800 and 1600 BC, they provide enough latitude for a merging of all the available evidence, biblical and nonbiblical, into a workable chronological scheme. Archaeology provides four major bits of evidence for an early second-millennium patriarchal era.

1. Though the Nuzi tablets furnish a clear parallel to patriarchal social life, other tablets from other towns and an earlier era reflect many of the same customs common to Nuzi and Genesis. Since the Nuzians were Hurrians who came to northeastern Mesopotamia from elsewhere (perhaps Armenia), their social customs originated no doubt much earlier than the time of their tablets now in our possession. Accordingly, the 15th-century BC date of the Nuzi tablets does not preclude an earlier date for Abraham.
2. The names of several of Abraham's ancestors listed in Genesis 11 can now be identified with towns in the northern area of Mesopotamia around Haran, the city from which Abraham migrated to Canaan (Gn 11:31–12:3). Significantly, Haran flourished in the 19th and 18th centuries BC.
3. Shortly after 2000 BC Semitic nomads from the desert invaded the civilized communities of the Fertile Crescent. Those invaders, called Amorites in the OT, established themselves in several cities in northern Syria and Mesopotamia. One of the Amorite cities was Babylon, ruled by Hammurabi sometime around the beginning of the 18th century BC. Although the King Amraphel of Genesis 14:1 is not linguistically identifiable with the Babylonian king Hammurabi, as earlier scholars believed, the picture of the times following the Amorite invasion still accords well with the Genesis narratives generally.
4. Mari, another Amorite town, is now well known because of more than 20,000 tablets recovered from its royal palace and archives. Geographically, Mari is located in the general area of Haran. Chronologically, the tablets recovered come from the 18th century BC. One 18th-century king of Mari, Zimri Lim, carried on extensive correspondence with Hammurabi of Babylon. The tablets from Mari also furnish valuable information about tribal and ethnic groups and their movements in the general region. Of basic importance for dating the Genesis materials are certain documents from Mari that include personal names very similar to Abraham (Abi-ram), Jacob, Laban, and several other West Semitic names.

Archaeological evidence neither proves nor disproves the actual existence of Abraham, Isaac, or Jacob. That is admitted on all sides. What archaeology has done is to provide a framework of probabilities within which the biblical patriarchal narratives appear more and more to be at home.

Date of the Exodus The problem of dating the patriarchal age is closely related to the problem of assigning a date to the exodus of the Israelites from Egypt. Since the evidence does not permit a precise date for Abraham, a precise date for the entry of Joseph or Jacob into Egypt is likewise unobtainable. Further, the biblical evidence does not yield an exact figure for the length of the Israelite sojourn in Egypt.

For many years biblical scholars viewed 1 Kings 6:1 as a foundation upon which to build an unshakable date for the exodus. Because Solomon's fourth year could be unquestionably fixed to within at least a 10-year span (967–958 BC), the exodus too could be dated with the same precision simply by adding 480 years. But other biblical data raise serious questions about that simple procedure. When the Bible deals with all the events between the time of the exodus and the founding of Solomon's temple, that is, from Numbers to 1 Kings 5:18, the precise numbers given total not 480 but closer to 600 years.

Because the evidence is insufficient to allow a precise date for the exodus, scholarly opinion remains divided between two possibilities. A 15th-century exodus is supported by several pieces of evidence. The chronology in 1 Kings 6:1 appears to be independently corroborated by a passage in Judges 11:26. It claims that Israel had occupied the area around Heshbon for 300 years preceding Jephthah's own day. If Jephthah is dated at roughly 1100 BC, one is obviously led back to an exodus in the middle of the 15th century. Also, three successive generations of pharaohs who ruled in the 16th and 15th centuries produced no male offspring, making it more likely that Moses would have become the foster son of a royal princess during that time; all of the 19th-dynasty kings (1306–1200 BC) had legitimate male heirs.

In addition, a 15th-century date makes possible a connection between the Habiru invasion of Canaan (1400–1350 BC)—described in the Amarna letters found at Tell el-Amarna, Egypt—and the invasion of Canaan by the Hebrews described in the OT book of Joshua. Related to that is a reference to "Israel" in the Merneptah Stele, a stone pillar inscribed with the deeds of the Egyptian king, Merneptah, of about 1220 BC. It implies that the people referred to, met by Merneptah in the course of a Canaanite military campaign, had been in existence for some time. Finally, an excavator of Jericho, John Garstang, placed the destruction of that city at around 1400 BC.

Other evidence, however, strongly implies not a 15th- but a 13th-century date for the exodus. Many scholars assign a date between 1290 and 1275 BC on the basis of that evidence. First, the 480 years of 1 Kings 6:1 discussed above may be interpreted as schematically representing 12 generations, as indicated by 1 Chronicles 6:3–8. Thus if 12 generations averaged 25 years instead of 40 years, the reduction of 480 schematized years to 300 actual years would point to an exodus date of around 1266 BC. Second, archaeological evidence exists that dates destruction at the assumed sites of several cities conquered by Joshua (Lachish, Debir, Bethel, and Hazor) to the late 13th century. Third, there is no biblical mention of Egyptian military campaigns (such as Merneptah's 1220 BC incursion); Israelites living in Canaan before the time of the militarily active pharaohs Seti I (1319–1301 BC) and Ramses II (1301–1234 BC) would certainly have been affected by such activity. Fourth, Exodus 1:11 mentions the city of Rameses, the capital built by Ramses II, according to his own inscriptions. A fifth line of argument comes from archaeological conclusions that Transjordan and the Negev Desert were not occupied by sedentary people between 1900 and 1300 BC, whereas the Bible states clearly that the Israelites encountered stiff opposition from groups in that same region. Thus, it is argued, the Israelites must have entered that region after 1300 BC. Sixth, connecting the Habiru with the Israelites of the Conquest lacks weight because many texts besides the Amarna tablets attest to the existence of Habiru groups virtually all over the ancient Near East. "Habiru" seems to be a much broader term, possibly meaning "trespasser," and is probably unrelated etymologically or semantically to "Hebrew." Seventh, and finally, Garstang's work at Jericho has now been revised by archaeologist Kathleen Kenyon, who showed that the fallen walls that Garstang had dated about 1400 BC in reality were destroyed in 1800 BC or earlier.

So far, it has been impossible to decide with precision between the two centuries proposed for the exodus. The majority opinion among OT scholars generally, including a growing number of moderate or conservative scholars, is in favor of the 13th-century option. On the other hand, many other conservative scholars continue to favor the 15th-century date. Dogmatism is unwarranted since problems remain unresolved with either option.

In accordance with the majority opinion, however, a date of about 1290 BC for the exodus will be used in dealing with subsequent problems.

Conquest and Consolidation The chronological task for the period of conquest and consolidation is to fit all the events narrated by the OT, chiefly in Joshua and Judges, between the exodus (c. 1290 BC) and the times of David (c. 1000 BC) and Solomon (d. 930 BC). In other words, one must fit roughly 550 years of biblical events between Moses and David into a 290-year span.

Although assigning an early date for the exodus (c. 1447 BC) would make the task somewhat easier, the mere addition of about 157 years does not by itself solve all the problems. Neither date allows enough time for all the OT events from Joshua to David to take place singly and consecutively. Accordingly, advocates of both dates assume that some of the judges ruled simultaneously rather than consecutively. The difference is one of degree only.

The book of Joshua furnishes most of the OT evidence regarding the conquest of Canaan by the Israelites. Unfortunately, the book of Joshua has no chronological notes that specify the amount of time elapsing during Joshua's career. Further, there are no biblical references to major contemporary events in other parts of the ancient world, the dates of which could be used to fix the chronology. Rather, in what is obviously a telescoped account, the book of Joshua records the fall of Jericho and Ai, followed closely by a southern and then a northern campaign. After those victories, covering much of the total territory of Canaan, various parcels of land were distributed to the tribal groups of Israel; the tribes were expected to complete the task of destroying whatever Canaanite inhabitants remained in their particular region. One seeks in vain, however, for any statements indicating how long those events took.

In the book of Judges a slightly different circumstance prevails. There the OT furnishes a rather complete list of figures to indicate the duration of periods of foreign oppression, judgeships, and ensuing peace. The total number of years described for that period is 410, but that total does not include any time for the many "minor" judges. It seems obvious, therefore, that if not all of the judges were simply local chieftains whose activity was simultaneous with that of other judges, at least for part of their reign. Unfortunately, the book of Judges provides no cross-reference system to indicate which judges were contemporaries of which others. Perhaps the best one can do is to assume general guidelines for the chronology of that period between Moses and David.

Two significant facts should be kept in mind. First, archaeological information seems to demand a Conquest date beginning about 1250 BC rather than 200 years earlier. Assuming concurrent careers for the judges allows one to compress the literal OT figures into the general scheme demanded by other evidence.

Second, the ancient scribes evidently related the chronology of the period to a 40-year or generation-based schema, a practice that lasted until the time of the divided kingdom, when a regular dynastic chronology was introduced. In the face of so many careers being assigned exactly 40 years, the fact remains that the literal totals of such numbers cannot be harmonized with either the biblical or the archaeological evidence for the period. Accordingly, most scholars doubt that the number 40 was ever intended to be an exact mathematical calculation. That view permits enough leeway for cautious fitting of biblical and other evidence into a general timetable.

The Monarchy

Types of Evidence For the period of the Israelite monarchy, chronological evidence is abundant.

The OT itself strives to provide all the information necessary for the chronology of the period, including (1) a complete list of all the kings in Israel and in Judah both before and after the division of the kingdom; (2) the age of each king (except Saul) at his accession; (3) synchronisms of the northern kingdom of Israel and the southern kingdom of Judah showing in what year of his contemporary in the other kingdom each king came to the throne; and (4) precise calculations of the length of each king's reign. In addition some important events are dated by reference to another event; others are coordinated with concurrent events in secular history.

Outside the OT an abundance of material provides evidence for a chronology of the period. By far the most important single source is a collection of Assyrian *limmu* lists. In Assyria a record of each king's reign was kept on a particular kind of annal. Each year of reign was named after an individual of high rank in the court; the first year was named after the king himself, the second after the next highest-ranking official (though that name appears to have been selected by lot originally), and so on, down until the death of the king. The word *limmu* was used to introduce the name of the official after whom the current year was to be named, hence the designation "*limmu* lists."

Assyrian *limmu* lists are tied precisely to the solar year, making the documents highly reliable. Further, in addition to many events in Assyrian history, notable natural phenomena were dated on the basis of the *limmu* in which they occurred. For example, a solar eclipse dated by the Assyrian scribes in the *limmu* year of Bur-Sagale has been computed astronomically as June 15, 763 BC. Beginning with the year 763, then, and working both backward and forward, a complete list of Assyrian *limmu* officials has been obtained for the period between 891 and 648 BC.

With the accuracy of the Assyrian *limmu* lists corroborated by a number of sources, they can be used with confidence in reconstructing the chronology of the corresponding period of biblical history. That is especially true where a biblical writer related an Israelite or a Judahite event to a particular year in the reign of an Assyrian king whose *limmu* list indicates the precise years of his reign.

There are also records from Chaldean (Babylonian) king lists and from later Greek historians. Ptolemy, in the second century AD, for example, gave dates for Babylonian kings from 747 BC and continued with dates for Persian, Greek, and Roman rulers down to AD 161. Finally, useful information is found in inscriptions from monuments, stelae, and other artifacts from Assyria and elsewhere.

Monarchical Chronology The *limmu* list of the Assyrian king Shalmaneser III provides a basis for the first comparison of dates among Assyria, Israel, and Judah. In the *limmu* of Daian-Assur, Shalmaneser's sixth year on the throne, Ahab of Israel was listed as one of the kings who fought against the Assyrians in the battle of Qarqar. Thus the date for that battle may be placed confidently in 853 BC.

Assyrian records also indicate that Shalmaneser III came into contact with an Israelite king 12 years later, in 841 BC. That king was Jehu. Thus two fixed points are available for correlating the biblical information. Following the death of Ahab, which is not dated exactly by reference to the Assyrian records, two of his sons came to power. The first, Ahaziah, reigned two years (1 Kgs 22:51); the second, Joram (also called Jehoram), reigned a total of 12 years (2 Kgs 3:1). Recognizing a nonaccession-year reckoning by the Israelites in that era, the apparent total of 14 years may be reduced to an actual total of 12. Thus it seems evident that Ahab not only fought Shalmaneser III in 853 BC but also died in that year. Ahab was then followed by his two sons for a total of 12 years before the accession of Jehu in time to account for his contact with Shalmaneser II in 841 BC. Further, because Jehu murdered both the king of Israel (Jehoram) and the king of Judah (Ahaziah) at the same time (2 Kgs 9:24-27), a fixed synchronism is provided between the two kingdoms for the year 841 BC.

The first nine kings of Israel ruled an apparent total of 98 years or an actual total (taking into account Israel's nonaccession-year policy) of 90 years. Zimri, who ruled only seven days (1 Kgs 16:15-18), counts as one of the nine but does not insert an extra year in either the actual or apparent totals. The accession of Jeroboam I thus occurred in 930 BC (adding 90 years to 841 BC), and Rehoboam of Judah began to rule in that same year as well. Allowing Solomon the 40-year reign indicated in 1 Kings 11:42 points to the year 970 BC for his accession. The death of David would also be pinpointed in that period, although allowance must be made for the possibility of a short co-regency of David and Solomon before David's death. The reign of Saul then falls approximately in the late 11th century BC.

In Judah the period between the death of Solomon in 930 BC and the murder of Ahaziah by Jehu in 841 BC was occupied by the kingships of six men whose time on the throne totals 95 biblical years. Computation of that era in Judah is not as simple as for the Israelite kings for several reasons. Problems include a change from accession-to nonaccession-year reckoning sometime around 850 BC, at least two co-regencies (Jehoshaphat with Asa and then Jehoram with Jehoshaphat), and the calendar differences between the two kingdoms. It is clear that the 95 apparent years must be reduced, on the basis of the differences in computation and calendar, to 90 actual years in order to bring the Judahite figures into line with the established Assyrian and Israelite synchronisms.

After the year 841, the next biblical event to be certified by nonbiblical materials is the fall of Samaria in 722 BC. That date is furnished by the annals of Sargon II of Assyria (722–705 BC), successor to Shalmaneser V (727–722 BC). Although that date comes just 120 years after the fixed point of 841 BC in Israelite history, the chronological materials for that period are quite difficult to interpret accurately. In the past, scholars resorted to assumptions of extensive co-regencies, to presumed confusion on the part of certain scribes over methods to be followed in computations, or to other theories in attempting to understand the period. In spite of the many difficulties, however, all the biblical and Assyrian dates for the period of the divided monarchy have been harmonized—with the exception of four figures related to the closing years of the Israelite kingdom, all connected in some way with the problematic reign of Hoshea.

Judah after the Fall of Israel Following the fall of Samaria in 722 BC, OT chronology is concerned only with the southern kingdom of Judah until its destruction some 135 years later. Two events in the biblical record important for establishing a chronology for that period are the siege of Jerusalem by Sennacherib of Assyria in the late eighth century and the eventual fall of Jerusalem to the Babylonians in the early sixth century.

Sennacherib's Invasion of Judah The Assyrian invasion (704–681 BC) is recorded in 2 Kings 18:13-16, where verse 13 dates the event to the 14th year of King Hezekiah. Sennacherib's own inscriptions include a lengthier version of the affair. From them the date of 701 BC is established, placing the accession of Hezekiah in 715 BC. That much is simple, but problems still arise. For example, 2 Kings 19:9 reports that Sennacherib was in contact with an Ethiopian king, Tirhakah (c. 690–664 BC), during the course of his campaign, which included a siege of Jerusalem. Obviously, contact with a ruler who came to power in 690 BC at the earliest could not refer to events in 701 BC. It is possible, however, that Sennacherib actually made two invasions of Judah, the first in 701 and the second sometime later. The date of that supposed second invasion is not assured, although 2 Kings 19:35-37 may imply that Sennacherib was murdered only shortly after his withdrawal from Jerusalem. Since Sennacherib was succeeded by his son Esarhaddon in the year 681, the presumed second invasion of Judah would have occurred somewhere in the last half of the same decade.

A number of scholars oppose the assumption of a second invasion of Jerusalem by Sennacherib. They suggest the possibility that Tirhakah, though king only from 690 BC, may have led troops against Sennacherib as early as 701, before acceding to the throne. The reference to King Tirhakah in 2 Kings 19:9 would then be understood as use of his eventual title in an effort to identify him to a later generation of readers.

However the question of the number of invasions is decided, it is certain that Sennacherib invaded Judah in 701 BC, the 14th regnal year of Hezekiah. Such a synchronism establishes Hezekiah's accession year as 715 BC, but that date raises another problem. The fall of Samaria, now established at 722, is dated by 2 Kings 18:10 in the sixth year of Hezekiah's reign. The most likely solution is that Hezekiah began a co-regency with his father, Ahaz, six years before Samaria fell. The possibility for confusion arises from the fact that one verse (2 Kgs 18:13; repeated in Is 36:1) synchronizes Sennacherib's 701 BC invasion with the 14th year of Hezekiah's independent reign; another verse (2 Kgs 18:10) correlates the fall of Samaria with the beginning of Hezekiah's co-regency. Thus from about 728 to 715 BC Hezekiah was co-regent with Ahaz. From 715 to 697 he reigned alone. From 696 to 686 his son Manasseh was co-ruler with him.

According to the chronological information given by a number of verses in 2 Kings, a total of 128 years and six months elapsed between the time of Hezekiah's accession in 715 and the capture of King Jehoiachin in 597, a date to be discussed below. Thus another problem is to explain the more than 10-year excess apparently demanded by the biblical totals. The best solution appears to lie in the assumption that Manasseh first came to power in 697 as co-regent with his father, Hezekiah. Manasseh died in 642, following what 2 Kings 21:1 states was a 55-year reign. Hezekiah, who came to the throne in 715, is said to have reigned 29 years (2 Kgs 18:2), which would mean that he was king until 686, roughly 11 years after the time when Manasseh must have come to the throne in order to have completed a 55-year reign by 642.

Fall of Jerusalem Contemporary Babylonian records are available to shed valuable light on the last few years of Judah's existence. For the years 626–623, 618–595, and 556 BC the Babylonian Chronicle, a formal record of Babylonian affairs of state, has been recovered. From information contained in that chronicle and other cuneiform documents of the period, three dates in Judah's history may be fixed firmly. The first is the death of Josiah in 609; the second is the battle of Carchemish in 605; the third is the end of the reign of Jehoiachin, which is dated by the Babylonian Chronicle to the second month of Adar in the ninth year of Nebuchadnezzar, or March 16, 597.

After Jehoiachin's capture, Zedekiah became puppet king of Judah for 11 years (2 Kgs 24:18). On the tenth day of the tenth month during Zedekiah's ninth regnal year (2 Kgs 25:1), the final siege of Jerusalem was begun by the Babylonian army. That day was January 15, 588.

On the ninth day of the fourth month during the 11th regnal year of Zedekiah, after a siege of almost 18 months, the wall of Jerusalem was broken through (2 Kgs 25:3-4). The temple was burned on day seven of the following (fifth) month.

Beyond 586 BC Following the tragedy of 586 BC, several further developments are given chronological notice in the OT. Jeremiah 52:30 records a third deportation of Jews to Babylonia in the 23d year of King Nebuchadnezzar (582 or 581 BC). Both 2 Kings 25:27 and Jeremiah 52:31 give evidence of the release of King Jehoiachin from prison; the Babylonian Chronicle dates that event at 27 Adar, or March 21, 561 BC.

In 539 BC the Babylonians themselves were destined to learn the meaning of defeat. In that year a Persian ruler, Cyrus the Great, launched a successful campaign against Babylon and its king, Nabonidus. Inheriting control over the exiled Jews and many other groups of people conquered earlier by Babylonia, Cyrus moved quickly to initiate a policy of tolerance toward his new subjects. In the first year of his rule Cyrus issued an edict making it possible for Jews to return to their former land (Ezr 1:1). On the first day of the following year, 1 Tishri (Ezr 3:6), an altar was set up in Jerusalem. In Iyyar of the following year (April/May 536) work was begun on the temple itself (Ezr 3:8).

After a period of frustrating work stoppages of varying lengths, the preaching of Haggai and Zechariah spurred on the Jews to complete the temple. Work resumed in 520 (Ezr 4:24; Hg 1:1, 15) and was finally completed on 3 Adar, or March 12, 515 (Ezr 6:15). The final stages of OT chronology pertain to the careers of Ezra and Nehemiah. The traditional view of their era places Ezra in the seventh year of Artaxerxes I (458 BC) and Nehemiah in the 20th (445 BC).

See also "Date" under each OT book; Conquest and Allotment of the Land; Diaspora of the Jews; Exodus, The; Israel, History of; Patriarchs, Period of the; Postexilic Period; Wilderness Wanderings.

CHRONOLOGY OF THE BIBLE* (New Testament)
Branch of biblical studies that attempts to discover the sequence of NT events and the amount of time that elapsed between them. Chronology is essential to historians, whose task it is to determine the causes and effects of past events. Generally, for a historian's purpose, assigning absolute dates is less important than knowing the sequence of events that may have influenced each other. Very few NT happenings, in fact, can be given exact dates.

SIGNIFICANT NEW TESTAMENT EVENTS AND DATES

6/5 BC	Christ's birth
AD 6/7	Jesus in the temple
26	John the Baptist begins his ministry
26/27	Christ is baptized, begins his ministry
30	Christ is crucified, resurrected, and enthroned
30	Pentecost
34/35	Paul's conversion
44	James, the apostle, is martyred
46-48	Paul's first missionary journey
49/50	Jerusalem Council
50-52	Paul's second missionary journey
53-57	Paul's third missionary journey
59-62	Paul's imprisonment in Rome
67	Paul's second imprisonment
65-67	Peter martyred
68	Paul martyred
70	Jerusalem falls
90-95	John exiled
c.100	John dies

A remarkable testimony to the influence of Christianity is the fact that the entire Western world now divides history into BC (before Christ) and AD (*anno Domini*, "in the year of the Lord"). Before that method of dating became widespread in the Middle Ages, events were dated by their relation to other important events such as the founding of Rome or the beginning of a king's reign. When a monk named Dionysius Exiguus (sixth century) invented our present method of dating, with the birth of Christ dividing history, he made a mistake in his computations. The odd result is the historical anomaly that Jesus himself was born no later than four years "before Christ."

Chronology of Jesus' Life

Birth According to Matthew 2:1 Jesus was born "in the days of Herod the king." A first-century AD historian, Josephus, recorded that Herod died in the spring of the year we identify as 4 BC. Hence, Jesus was born sometime before that, but how much before is uncertain. Luke 2:1-2 records that Jesus' birth occurred when "Caesar Augustus," the Roman emperor, decreed that a census, or enrollment, should be taken throughout the nation. "This was the first census taken when Quirinius was governor of Syria" (NLT). Those statements raise two questions: When was such a census taken, and when was Quirinius governor of Syria? Neither question has received a completely satisfying answer.

Census documents discovered in Egypt, together with earlier references, suggest that such enrollments were held every 14 years. That would put a census roughly in 8 or 9 BC. In view of the time needed to carry out the census (which required a person to travel to his birthplace), the birth of Jesus may have been somewhat later than the actual year of the decree (perhaps 7 BC).

Josephus recorded that Quirinius became governor of Syria in AD 6, rather late as a date for Jesus' birth. But some scholars have argued from ancient inscriptions that Quirinius also served in Syria as a special legate of the emperor Augustus before 6 BC. That could be the period referred to in Luke 2:2. Why did Luke choose to cite Quirinius instead of the regular governor of Syria at that time? Perhaps by so doing he could provide a more exact date for the birth of Jesus, since Quirinius was in authority for a shorter time than the regular governor of Syria.

A reasonable conclusion is that Jesus was born about 7 or 6 BC. That fits with Matthew 2:16, which seems to say that Jesus was born at least two years before Herod's death in 4 BC. No clear evidence exists concerning the day and month of his birth. Celebration of December 25 as Christmas originated in the fourth century, probably as a Christian alternative to the pagan winter solstice festival (Saturnalia).

The Beginning of Public Ministry Luke 3:23 says that Jesus, "when he began his ministry, was about thirty years of age"; since the age given is only approximate, he may have been two or three years older or younger (cf. the pseudepigraphal Testament of Levi 2:2; 12:5). If exactly 30 is added to the suggested date of birth, one gets AD 24. That date cannot be right, because Jesus' ministry began after John the Baptist appears; Luke 3:1-3 dates John's public appearance precisely in "the fifteenth year of the reign of Tiberias Caesar" while Pilate was procurator (governor) over Judea. Pilate governed from AD 26 to 36, and the 15th year of Tiberius was most likely AD 27. Therefore Jesus did not begin his public ministry before AD 27. If only a short time elapsed between the beginning of John's ministry and the beginning of Jesus' ministry, then Jesus probably began in AD 27 or 28 when he was approximately 33 years old.

Jesus' Death All four Gospel records seem to imply that Jesus ate the Last Supper with his disciples on Thursday evening, was crucified on Friday, and rose from the dead early Sunday morning (Mt 28:1; Mk 16:1; Lk 24:1). The claim that Jesus rose on the third day (1 Cor 15:4) comes from the Jewish custom of counting a part of the day as a whole day. According to Matthew (26:19), Mark (14:12), and Luke (22:15), the Last Supper was the Passover meal, a yearly celebration of Israel's escape from Egypt (Ex 12–15). But according to John 13:1 and 19:14, the Passover meal had not yet been eaten on Friday; hence the Last Supper in John was not the Passover meal.

No completely satisfying solution to the apparent discrepancy has been put forward. Some scholars suggest plausibly that the use of two different calendars was responsible. According to that theory, Jesus was following a calendar that placed the Passover meal on Thursday night. Temple officials, on the other hand, followed an alternate calendar that placed the killing of sacrificial victims on the next day. John may have used the second system to emphasize the fact that Christ was offered as the Passover sacrifice (cf. Jn 19:36; 1 Cor 5:7).

To find out how long Jesus' public ministry lasted and thus the year in which he died, one can turn to time references in John's Gospel. John referred to at least three Passovers (2:13; 6:4; 13:1) and possibly four (5:1). Since the Passover was a yearly feast, the ministry of Jesus would have lasted at least two and possibly three years. In Matthew, Mark, and Luke the Friday of Jesus' death occurred on the 15th of the Jewish month Nisan (which overlaps March and April). According to John, Jesus died on 14 Nisan. The question is: In which years from 26 to 36 (when Pilate was procurator in Judea) did 14 or 15 Nisan fall on a Friday? The answer is AD 27, 29, 30, and 33. Of those, the year 27 is too early and 33 is probably too late. Thus Jesus was probably crucified in 29 or 30, his public ministry lasted two or three years, and he was 35 or 36 years old when he died.

Events from AD 30 to 50 Acts is the only NT book that records how much time elapsed between Jesus' death and his ascension: "To them he presented himself alive after his passion by many proofs, appearing to them during forty days, and speaking of the kingdom of God" (Acts 1:3, RSV). The next key event after the ascension of Jesus into heaven was Pentecost (Acts 2:1). Pentecost, the Greek word for "fiftieth," referred to a celebration of the Feast of Weeks/Harvest (cf. Ex 34:22; Dt 16:9-12) 50 days after the Passover. Since Jesus was crucified during the Passover season, the Pentecost of Acts 2:1, during which the disciples were filled with the Holy Spirit, took place in AD 29 or 30, some 50 days after the Crucifixion and about 10 days after the Ascension.

After that, events of the early chapters of Acts are hard to date because no precise statements are made about the amount of time between various events. Therefore, the usual method for dating events of the apostolic age is first to find at least one event that can be dated with relative certainty from sources outside the NT; one then dates events before and after that event by figuring out how much time elapsed between them. Sometimes Acts records how much time passed between two events; usually it does not, so dating can only be approximate.

One pivotal starting point is the great famine prophesied by Agabus, which befell Palestine during the reign of the Roman emperor Claudius (Acts 11:28-29). Josephus, who was alive at the time, gives enough information to locate the famine sometime between the years 46 and 48. We also know from the Mishnah, a collection of Jewish laws, that the autumn of 47 to the autumn of 48 was a sabbatical year, when the Jews let the land rest and harvested nothing (cf. Lv 25:2-7). That could have aggravated and prolonged a famine, but one cannot be sure how early the famine started; some scholars propose 46 and some 47.

At first, it seems peculiar that Luke, the author of Acts, should have recorded that famine (Acts 11:28) before recording the death of Herod Agrippa (12:20-23). From facts reported by Josephus, the death of Herod (a grandson of Herod the Great) can be dated in AD 44, probably in the spring. That means that Herod must have died several years before the famine Luke recorded earlier. Some scholars think that Luke simply got his chronological facts wrong. Others see Acts 12:1-24 as a kind of flashback to bring the history of the church in Jerusalem up to date. Such a practice was common among ancient historians, who often followed one source up to a suitable stopping point before moving on to another source. To charge Luke with inaccurate dating, it is argued, is to misunderstand the techniques of historical writing he was using.

Since Herod Agrippa died in AD 44 (Acts 12:23), the apostle James, whom Herod put to death with the sword (v 2), must have died soon before 44, perhaps during the Passover season of 43 (v 3). The apostle Peter's imprisonment and his miraculous escape (vv 3-17) also belong to that period.

When the Christians of Antioch decided to send relief to the Christians in Jerusalem in the midst of the great famine (Acts 11:29), Barnabas and Paul were appointed to transport the money to Jerusalem. That was Paul's second visit to Jerusalem after his conversion. The first visit is recorded in Acts 9:26-30. The third comes in Acts 15 when Paul and Barnabas were sent to discuss with the apostles and elders whether gentile converts to Christianity had to be circumcised. How one dates the first and third visits to Jerusalem, as well as Paul's conversion, depends on how those Jerusalem visits are related to those reported in Paul's letter to the Galatians.

The basic problem, which still divides NT scholars, is this: In Galatians 1:15–2:10 Paul recounted that his conversion was followed by two visits to Jerusalem, one three years after his conversion (1:18) and one 14 years after that (2:1-10). All scholars agree that the first visit three years after his conversion is the same as the first visit recorded in Acts 9:26-30. Answers differ, however, to the question of whether Galatians 2:1-10 refers to the second (famine) visit to Jerusalem in Acts 11:30 (in which case the third visit of Acts 15 is the one omitted from Galatians) or whether Galatians 2:1-10 refers to the visit in Acts 15 (in which case the famine visit was the one omitted from Galatians).

TWO POSSIBLE RECONSTRUCTIONS

Reconstruction 1	Reconstruction 2
Acts 9:26-30	Acts 9:26-30
Acts 11:30	Acts 11:30
Acts 15:1-29	Acts 15:1-29
Galatians 1:18	Galatians 1:18 omitted
Galatians 2:1-10 omitted	Galatians 2:1-10

Those who favor the first reconstruction offer six arguments: (1) The reason Paul gave such a rigorous account of his comings and goings in Galatians 1:15-24 was to show that he did not get his gospel from men, nor was he taught it (1:12). In other words, his visits to the Jerusalem apostles were not for the purpose of receiving his gospel. If that is so, for Paul to omit the second Jerusalem visit would jeopardize his integrity and his authority with the Galatians. The first reconstruction avoids that difficulty; omission of a third Jerusalem visit from Galatians 2:1-10 could mean that it had not yet happened when Galatians was written. (2) Galatians 2:1-10 pictures a private meeting between Paul and Barnabas on one hand and the "pillar" apostles on the other. But the meeting in Acts 15 was public and before the whole church. Hence Galatians 2:1-10 more likely refers to a private meeting during the visit of Acts 11:30, which Galatians does not record. (3) Paul's eagerness to give to the poor mentioned in Galatians 2:10 connects naturally with the second Jerusalem visit, when he was in fact delivering relief to the poor (Acts 11:30). (4) If Galatians 2 recorded the same trip as Acts 15, one would expect some mention of the decision reached by the Jerusalem Council, especially since that decision related directly to the problem of circumcision that Paul was handling in his Letter to the Galatians. (5) Further, it seems unlikely that the Jerusalem Council preceded the event of Galatians 2:11-21, when Peter was rebuked by Paul for withdrawing from fellowship with gentile believers; that incident could hardly have happened so soon after the issue of gentile status in the church had been settled in Jerusalem. (6) According to Galatians 1:6, the letter was written "quickly" after Paul had established the Galatian churches. That makes sense if Galatians was written soon after the first missionary journey, hence just before the Jerusalem Council of Acts 15; that would make Galatians Paul's first letter.

Scholars who favor the second reconstruction offer four arguments: (1) The main purpose of Paul's visit in Galatians 2:1-10 appears to be the same as that in Acts 15:1-20; both dealt with the issue of whether circumcision should be required of gentile converts (Gal 2:3-5; Acts 15:1, 5). That similarity is obvious, but there is no such explicit similarity between Galatians 2 and Acts 11:30. (2) On the basis of form and content Galatians is similar to Romans and to 1 and 2 Corinthians; it would thus seem to come from the same period—considerably later than the Jerusalem Council. If so, it is likely that Paul would have included a reference to the Jerusalem Council (namely Gal 2:1-10) in his recollections, since its outcome supported his own stance on circumcision set forth in the letter. (3) Acts 11:30 pictures Barnabas as the leader of the Barnabas/Paul team, since his name is given first place (as in Acts 12:25; 13:1-2, 7; cf. 11:25-26). But in the description Paul gives of the visit in Galatians 2, he sees himself as the leader of the team. Since Acts does picture Paul as the leader from the time of the first missionary journey (Acts 13:9, 13, 43, 46, 50), including the third Jerusalem visit (15:2), it is more likely that Galatians 2 records the trip of Acts 15. (4) Finally, in Galatians 2:7-8 Paul was recognized as an apostle to the Gentiles with a standing equal to that of Peter. But if Galatians 2 recorded the events of Acts 11:30 and the first missionary journey had not yet occurred, the "pillar" apostles could hardly have recognized Paul's authority as apostle to the Gentiles. It is more likely that Galatians 2 followed the first missionary journey, just as Acts 15 followed the first missionary journey in Acts, and that both refer to the same event.

The significance of those arguments for chronology is that, according to the first view, Paul's conversion came 17 years before the famine visit of Acts 11:30 (cf. Gal 1:18; 2:1). According to the second view, Paul's conversion took place 17 years before the Jerusalem Council in

Acts 15. The difference amounts to only one year, however.

It is helpful to consider one more date that can be fixed with high probability—namely, Paul's arrival in Corinth on his second missionary journey (Acts 18:1). On the second missionary journey (15:40–18:22), Paul and Silas set out on land through Syria, Cilicia, Phrygia, and Galatia, visiting churches founded on the first missionary journey. They came to Troas, then passed over to Philippi and continued down the coast through Thessalonica and Berea. Paul went on to Athens before arriving at Corinth. From Acts 18:12 we know that Gallio was a proconsul in Corinth while Paul was there. An inscription discovered at nearby Delphi indicates that in all likelihood Gallio's term of office was from mid-51 to mid-52. The incident recorded in Acts 18:12-17 probably occurred at the beginning of Gallio's term, since the Jews hoped to get a ruling against Paul from their new proconsul. Not long after that, Paul left Corinth, probably in the summer or autumn of 52. According to Acts 18:11 Paul had spent 18 months in Corinth; that means that he probably arrived in the early months of 50 or the end of 49. That arrival date is confirmed by Acts 18:2, which says that Aquila and Priscilla had only recently been exiled from Rome when Paul came to Corinth. A fifth-century historian, Orosius, dated the edict of Claudius expelling the Jews from Rome in AD 49. Therefore, Paul and Aquila and Priscilla probably arrived close together late in 49 or early in 50. Early in his 18-month stay Paul wrote his First and Second Letters to the Thessalonians.

The two fixed dates, then, are 46 or 47 for the famine visit (Acts 11:30) and late 49 or early 50 for Paul's arrival in Corinth (Acts 18:1). Taking into account the time gaps mentioned in Galatians 1:18 and 2:1, as well as the supposition that the first missionary journey lasted about a year, the two reconstructions are presented in the following table. Keep in mind that they are approximations and that they reflect the ancient custom of counting a part of a year as a whole year.

Jerusalem (20:6–21:16). Before his Passover visit to Philippi, Paul had spent three months in Greece (20:3). Allowing some time for him to travel through Macedonia and visit the Thessalonians and Bereans, those three months were probably the winter months of 56–57 (Acts 20:3; cf. 1 Cor 16:6). No doubt they were spent in the main church of Greece, Corinth, and were used in part for the writing of the Letter to the Romans.

Between Paul's departure from Corinth on the second missionary journey (Acts 18:18) in the autumn of 51 and his arrival in Corinth on the third missionary journey (20:2) in the late winter of 56 are five years of activities that cannot be given exact dates. Paul said that he worked during three of those years in Ephesus (20:31; cf. 19:1–20:1). With enough time allowed for the travels before and after, that stay at Ephesus probably lasted from 52 or 53 to the summer of 55 or 56 (cf. 1 Cor 16:8). During his long stay in Ephesus, Paul wrote his First Letter to the Corinthians. Then, on his way to Corinth in 56, he wrote 2 Corinthians from Macedonia.

Festus arrived as governor in the summer of 59, after Paul had been in prison in Caesarea for two years. Within a matter of days, Paul was tried before Festus (Acts 25:1-12). Not wanting to be remanded to the Jewish authorities, Paul appealed to Caesar (v 12), which meant that he would go to Rome. The account in Acts gives no hint of a delay, so the voyage most likely began in the summer or fall of 59 (27:2).

Luke reported that when Paul the prisoner got to Fair Havens on the island of Crete, the weather had become dangerous for sea travel "because the fast had already gone by" (Acts 27:8-9). One ancient writer said that sailing became dangerous between mid-September and mid-November, and after that, impossible until spring. The fast referred to was no doubt the one in preparation for the Day of Atonement, which in the year 59 fell on October 5. It is not surprising that, 14 days after leaving Fair Havens, the ship in which Paul was traveling was wrecked on the coast of Malta, south of Sicily (vv 27-44). Three months later Paul set sail for Rome again in a ship

TWO POSSIBLE CHRONOLOGIES

Earlier Dates	Event	Later Dates
31 or 32	Paul's conversion (Acts 9:3-19)	32 or 33
33 or 34	First Jerusalem visit (Acts 9:26-30)	34 or 35
46 or 47	Famine visit (Acts 11:30)	46 or 47
47–48	First missionary journey (Acts 13:4–14:28)	47–48
48	Jerusalem Council (Acts 15:1-29)	48
Late 49 or Early 50	Paul's arrival in Corinth on second missionary journey (Acts 18:1)	Late 49 or Early 50
Autumn 51	Paul's departure from Corinth (Acts 18:18)	Autumn 51

Events from AD 50 to 70 Acts 24:27 describes an event that helps us date events in the rest of the book, namely, Porcius Festus's replacement of Felix as the governor of Judea. A careful analysis of the evidence given by Eusebius, a fourth-century historian, leads to the probable conclusion that Felix was replaced in the summer of 59.

Working backward from that date, Paul's arrest in Jerusalem (Acts 21:33) must have occurred in 57, some two years before the coming of Festus. More precisely, Paul's arrest probably occurred in the late spring or summer of 57; Paul's goal (20:16) was to arrive in Jerusalem by Pentecost of that year, and Pentecost occurred at the end of May. He was not long in the city before he was arrested.

The Passover festival, 50 days before Pentecost, was celebrated by Paul with the church in Philippi (Acts 20:6). That would have been April 7–14, AD 57. Only after the feast did he continue his hurried journey to Caesarea and

that had spent the winter at Malta (28:11). Soon he was welcomed into Rome by Christians who came out to meet him (v 15). Thus Paul arrived in Rome in the early part of AD 60. The book of Acts closes with the remark that "For two whole years Paul stayed there in his own rented house" (v 30, NIV). The NT does not report the outcome of his trial. During that period, according to the traditional view, he wrote Ephesians, Philippians, Colossians, and Philemon.

Eusebius wrote, "Tradition has it that after defending himself the Apostle was again sent on the ministry of preaching, and coming a second time to the same city suffered martyrdom under Nero." Nero, who was the Roman emperor from 54 to 68, put to death a multitude of Christians in Rome soon after a disastrous fire in July of 64, according to the Roman historian Tacitus. A number of early Christian writings (e.g., Clement) seem to indicate that Peter and Paul were both killed in Rome during that savage persecution. If so, and if Eusebius was right, then Paul may have spent the two years from 62 to 64 freely ministering back in the eastern provinces. Many conservative scholars date Paul's First Letter to Timothy and his Letter to Titus from that period. Written from Rome shortly before Paul's martyrdom in 64, 2 Timothy was probably his last letter (2 Tm 2:9; 4:6).

In Jerusalem, within three years after Paul had been carried off to Rome, James the brother of Jesus was stoned to death by the Jewish authorities. According to Josephus, that occurred in 62. Not long afterward, according to Eusebius, the church in Jerusalem received a prophecy warning them to leave that doomed city and settle in Pella, one of the cities of the Decapolis ("ten cities") east of the Jordan. Thus when war broke out between the Jews and the Romans in 66, the Christians for the most part escaped its fury. That war ended in 70 with the destruction of Jerusalem and the temple (cf. Mk 13:2; Lk 21:24).

See also Acts of the Apostles, Book of the; Apostle, Apostleship; Age; "Date" under each NT book; First Jewish Revolt; Genealogy of Jesus Christ; Jesus Christ, Life and Teachings of; Paul, The Apostle.

CHRYSOLITE Magnesium, iron silicate, usually olive green; mentioned in Ezekiel's vision of the four wheels (Ez 1:16) and as one of the gems in the foundation wall of the new Jerusalem (Rv 21:20). *See* Minerals and Metals; Stones, Precious.

CHRYSOPRASE, CHRYSOPRASUS* Light-green variety of chalcedony; mentioned as one of the gems in the foundation wall of the new Jerusalem (Rv 21:20; KJV "chrysoprasus"). *See* Minerals and Metals; Stones, Precious.

CHUB* KJV spelling of Kub, a place in Ezekiel 30:5 identified as Libya. *See* Kub.

CHUN* KJV spelling of Cun, a city from which David took much bronze, in 1 Chronicles 18:8. *See* Cun.

CHURCH A group or assembly of persons called together for a particular purpose. The term appears in only two verses in the Gospels (Mt 16:18; 18:17) but frequently in the book of Acts, most of the letters of Paul, as well as most of the remaining NT writings, especially the Revelation of John.

One way of referring to the body of Israel in the OT was simply "the congregation." Groups claiming to be the true Israel spiritually rather then naturally called themselves "the congregation." The term was used by the writers of the Dead Sea Scrolls as well as by early Christians; it is the actual meaning of the word "church." Christians often referred to themselves simply as the church or the congregation (with "of God" being understood). The term could be applied either to all believers in the world or to any local group of them. It meant the total presence of God's people in a given location. That is why the NT often uses the singular "church" even when many groups of believers are included together (Acts 9:31; 2 Cor 1:1); the term "churches" is rarely found (Acts 15:41; 16:5). Each group or the whole group was the place where God was present (Mt 16:18; 18:17); God had purchased the congregation with the blood of his Son (Acts 20:28). The use of the word "church" in the NT is also somewhat dependent upon the Greek world. In the Greek world the word translated "church" designated an *assembly* of people, a meeting, such as a regularly summoned political body, or

simply a *gathering* of people. The word is used in such a secular way in Acts 19:32, 39, 41.

The specifically Christian usages of this concept vary considerably in the NT. (1) In analogy to the OT, it sometimes refers to a church meeting, as when Paul says to the Christians in Corinth: "When you meet as a church . . ." (1 Cor 11:18). This means that Christians are the people of God especially when they are gathered for worship. (2) In texts such as Matthew 18:17, Acts 5:11, 1 Corinthians 4:17, and Philippians 4:15, "church" refers to the entire group of Christians living in one place. Often, the local character of a Christian congregation is emphasized, as in the phrases, "the church in Jerusalem" (Acts 8:1), "in Corinth" (1 Cor 1:2), "in Thessalonica" (1 Thes 1:1). (3) In other texts, house assemblies of Christians are called churches, such as those who met in the house of Priscilla and Aquila (Rom 16:5; 1 Cor 16:19). (4) Throughout the NT, "the church" designates the universal church, to which all believers belong (see Acts 9:31; 1 Cor 6:4; Eph 1:22; Col 1:18). Jesus' first word about the founding of the Christian movement in Matthew 16:18 has this larger meaning: "I will build my church, and the powers of death shall not prevail against it" (RSV).

The church, both as a universal reality and in its local, concrete expression, is more specifically designated in Paul's writings as "the church of God" (e.g., 1 Cor 1:2; 10:32) or "the churches of Christ" (Rom 16:16). In this way a common, secular Greek term receives its distinctive Christian meaning and sets the Christian assembly/gathering/community apart from all other secular or religious groups.

It is clear from the NT as a whole that the Christian community understood itself as the community of the end time, as the community called into being by God's end-time act of revelation and divine presence in Jesus of Nazareth. So Paul tells the Christians in Corinth that they are those "upon whom the end of the ages has come" (1 Cor 10:11, RSV). That is, God had visited his creation, had called out of both Judaism and the gentile world a new people, empowered by his Spirit to be present in the world, sharing the Good News (gospel) of his radical, unconditional love for his creation (Eph 2:11-22). The Gospels tell us that Jesus chose 12 disciples who became the foundation of this new people. The correspondence to the 12 tribes of Israel is clear, and it shows that the church was understood both as grounded in Judaism and as the fulfillment of God's intention in calling Israel to become "a light to the nations, that my salvation may reach to the end of the earth" (Is 49:6, RSV; Rom 11:1-5). It is this recognition that allows Paul to call this new Gentile-Jewish community, this new creation, "the Israel of God" (Gal 6:15-16). In this new community the traditional barriers of race, social standing, and sex—barriers that divided people from one another and categorized them into inferior and superior classes—are seen to be shattered: "There is neither Jew nor Greek, slave nor free, male nor female, for you are all one in Christ Jesus" (Gal 3:28, NIV). This one entity is called "the body of Christ."

Paul is alone among NT writers in speaking of the church as Christ's body (Rom 12:5; 1 Cor 12:27; Eph 1:22-23; 4:12; see also 1 Cor 10:16-17; 12:12-13), or as "the body" of which Christ is the "head" (Eph 4:15; Col 1:18). The origin of this way of speaking about the church is not clear. Among a number of suggestions, two are particularly revealing about Paul's thought: (1) The Damascus road experience. According to the accounts in Acts (9:3-7; 22:6-11; 26:12-18), Jesus identifies himself with his persecuted disciples. By persecuting these early Christians, Paul was actually fighting against Christ himself. It is possible that later reflection on this experience led Paul to the conviction that the living Christ was so identified with his community that it could be spoken of as his "body," that is, the concrete expression of his real presence. (2) The Hebrew concept of corporate solidarity. Paul was a Hebrew of the Hebrews (Phil 3:5), and his thinking was thoroughly Jewish. In that context, the individual is largely thought of as intimately tied into the nation as a whole; the individual does not have real existence apart from the whole people. At the same time, the entire people can be seen as represented by one individual. Thus, "Israel" is both the name of one individual and the name of a whole people. The "servant" of Isaiah 42–53 can be both an individual (Is 42:1-4) and the nation of Israel (49:1-6). This idea of corporate solidarity (or personality) is the background for the intimate connection Paul makes between "the first Adam" and sinful humanity as well as between "the last (or second) Adam" (Christ) and renewed humanity (1 Cor 15:45-49; see also Rom 5:12-21).

The reality of the intimate relation between Christ and his church is thus expressed by Paul as the organic unity and integration of the physical body (Rom 12:4-8; 1 Cor 12:12-27). For Paul, the Lord's Supper is a specific manifestation of this reality: "The bread which we break, is it not a participation in the body of Christ? Because there is one bread, we who are many are one body, for we all partake of the one bread" (1 Cor 10:16b-17, RSV). Since this is the case, Paul goes on to argue, all the functions of the body have their legitimate and rightful place. Division within the body (i.e., the church) reveals that there is something unhealthy within. It is this image of the church as the "body of Christ" that lies behind Paul's repeated call for and insistence upon unity within the Christian community.

**UNITY WITH CHRIST MEANS
COMMUNITY WITH CHRISTIANS**
The equation of Christ and the church in this image of "body" leads to a very particular understanding of the nature of Christian existence. Paul speaks of the life of faith as life "in Christ." To be "in Christ" is to be a "new creation" (2 Cor 5:17). But for Paul, this is not just an individual experience, a kind of mystical union between the believer and Christ. For in a real sense, to be "in Christ" is at the same time to be in the church. To be "baptized into Christ" (Gal 3:27) is to become one with a community where the traditional barriers of human society are overcome—"for you are all one in Christ Jesus" (3:28). Again, to be "in Christ" is to be "baptized into one body" (1 Cor 12:12-13), for "you are the body of Christ and individually members of it" (12:27, RSV). For Paul, then, there is no such thing as a Christian in isolation, nurturing an individual relationship with Christ. To be a Christian is to be incorporated into a community of persons that is growing toward expressing, in its "body life," the reality of Christ, fleshing out this reality in its common life and work.

CHURCH MEETINGS The assembling together of the believers. In the NT, the Greek word *ecclesia* (usually translated "church") is used primarily in two ways: (1) to describe a meeting or an assembly, and (2) to designate the people who participate in such assembling together—whether they are actually assembled or not. The NT contains a few places that speak of a secular

Greek assembly (Acts 19:32, 41); every other instance speaks of a Christian assembly. Sometimes the word *ecclesia* is used to designate the actual meeting together of Christians. This is certainly what Paul intended in 1 Corinthians 14:19, 28, and 35, in that the expression *en ecclesia* must mean "in a meeting" and not "in the church." To translate this phrase "in the church" (as is done in most modern English versions) is misleading, for most readers will think it means "in the church building." The NT never once names the place of assembly a "church." Aside from the few instances where the word clearly means the actual meeting together of believers, *ecclesia* most often is used as a descriptor for the believers who constitute a local church (such as the church in Corinth, the church in Philippi, and the church in Colosse) or all the believers (past, present, and future) who constitute the universal church, the complete body of Christ.

When reading the NT, Christians need to be aware of the various ways in which the word *ecclesia* ("church") is used. On the most basic level, the *ecclesia* is any gathering of believers. On another level, the *ecclesia* is an organized local entity—comprised of all the believers in any given locality, under one pluralistic eldership. On another level, the *ecclesia* is the universal church whose constituents are all the believers who have ever been, are now existing, and will ever be. The word *ecclesia* was used by the NT writers with these various aspects of meaning, though, at times, it is not possible to differentiate one from the other. Nevertheless, students of the NT could avoid some confusion if they used discrimination in their exegesis of the text. Some interpreters have taught that the smallest unit of the church is the local church, but the NT writers sometimes used the word "church" to indicate a small home gathering. Other interpreters confuse the local church with the universal church. But some things in the NT are addressed to a local church that do not necessarily apply to the whole church, and some great things are spoken of the universal church that could never be attained by any particular local group. The things Paul said about the church in the Epistle to the Ephesians (which was written as an encyclical for several churches and not just for the church in Ephesus) could never be attained by a local church. For example, what local church could attain to the fullness of the stature of Christ?

There is much to be said about how interpreters have confused the local church with the universal church, but this article is devoted to clearing up the confusion about what constitutes the smallest unit of the church—the local church, or what could be called the house church or home gathering.

The NT seems to present the fact that a particular local church (i.e., a church comprising all the believers in a given locality under one eldership) could and did have several *ecclesiai*—"meetings" or "assemblies" (carried on in homes of the local Christians). Thus, the smallest unit to comprise a "church" was one of these home meetings. However, there is no indication in the NT that each of these home meetings had its own eldership or was a distinct entity separate from the other gatherings *(ecclesiai)* in the same locality. According to Acts 14:23 and Titus 1:5, elders were appointed for every local church (compare the expressions "appointed elders in every church" and "appoint elders in every city")—not for every house church. Nevertheless, it appears that every local church of some size had several such *ecclesiai* ("meetings") going on within that locality.

The church in Jerusalem must have had several home meetings (see Acts 2:46; 5:42; 8:3; 12:5, 12), as did the church in Rome (see Rom 16:3-5, 14-15 and comments below). A small local church may have had only one home gathering—as was probably the case with the church at Colosse (see Phlm 1:2 and comments below), but this would have been impossible for large local churches like those in Jerusalem, Rome, and Ephesus, in which there must have been several "house churches" (see 1 Cor 16:19-20 [1 Cor was written from Ephesus] and comments below). An examination of the passages that deal with the issue of the "house church" should affirm this. These passages are Romans 16:3-5, 14-15; 1 Corinthians 16:19-20; Colossians 4:15-16; and Philemon 1:1-2 (all quoted from the RSV).

Romans 16:3-5, 14-15 In the last chapter of Romans, Paul asked the believers in Rome, to whom he had written this epistle, to greet Priscilla and Aquila and the church that met in their home (16:3-5). The entire church in Rome could not have met in Priscilla and Aquila's home, for the church was much too large to have assembled in a single home. Rather, the church in Priscilla and Aquila's home must have been one among several such "house churches" in Rome. The following discussion should substantiate this position.

Paul's Epistle to the Romans was addressed to "all God's beloved in Rome" (1:7), not to "the church in Rome." At the time of writing, Paul had not been to Rome—nor had any other apostle. The church was probably started there by Jewish Romans who had been converted during their visit to Jerusalem during Pentecost (Acts 2:10) and then returned to Rome. Since the church had not been started by an apostle, it could have been that there were no "ordained" elders in the church at Rome and that there were several gatherings of believers in various parts of Rome and its suburbs. Paul knew some of the saints in Rome (whom he addressed by name in the last chapter) and thus addressed an epistle to all the saints in that locality, instead of to the church in that locality—which was his usual practice (see 1 Cor 1:1; 2 Cor 1:1; 1 Thes 1:1; 2 Thes 1:1). Nonetheless, "all the saints in Rome" would comprise "the church in Rome" (cf. Phil 1:1, in which Paul addressed his epistle to all the saints in Philippi).

In the final chapter of Romans, Paul asks all the believers in Rome (which equals the "local" church in Rome) to greet the church in Priscilla and Aquila's house. Later in the chapter, Paul asks the church to greet Asyncritus, Phlegon, Hermas, Patrobas, Hermes, and the brothers with them; and then again he asks the church to greet Philologus, Julia, Nereus and his sister, Olympas, and all the saints with them (16:14-15). Evidently, Paul was identifying two other groups of believers who must have met together. (And perhaps Paul was referring to two more groups in 16:10-11, which in the Greek could mean the ones of Aristobulus's and Narcissus's *households* or the ones of their *fellowships*.) It seems that the church in Rome, like the church in Jerusalem and Ephesus, had several home *ecclesiai* (meetings).

The Epistle to the Romans was written around AD 58. The Neronian persecution began around AD 64. Secular historians such as Tacitus tell us that a vast multitude (*ingens multitudo*) of Christians were tortured and killed during this persecution (*Annals* 15.44). Seutonius (in his book *Nero,* ch 16) said that the rapid increase of the Christians in Rome had made them unpopular. Indeed, at the time Paul penned the Epistle to the Romans he said their faith was known throughout the world (1:8), which indicates that the church in Rome had already made an impact on the Mediterranean world. When Paul came to Rome three years later (AD 61), he came to a city that had a large church there already. From Romans

15:23, we know that the church had been in existence for many years even before Paul wrote his epistle to them. In short, the church in Rome was a large church around the time Paul wrote his epistle to them. The entire church could not have met in the home of Aquila and Priscilla, who would have had only a modest-sized dwelling (for they were tentmakers). Besides, Paul greeted over 25 individuals by name in chapter 16—and he had not yet even been to Rome!

There must have been several *ecclesiai* in Rome, i.e., several home churches all unified as the one local church in Rome. For example, the Christians in Rome apparently worshiped in numerous homes such as Priscilla and Aquila's. Other churches in homes are mentioned in Colossians 4:15 and Philemon 1:2. Groups of Christians met in houses of prominent believers or in other available rooms (cf. Mt 26:16; Acts 12:12; 1 Cor 16:19; Col 4:15; Phlm 1:2). The church in Priscilla and Aquila's house is the first of five groups of believers in Paul's list, but the only one referred to definitely as a church (see Rom 16:5, 10-11, 14-15). Priscilla and Aquila opened their home for Christian meetings. The church mentioned there was obviously only a part of the total number of Christians in Rome. Verses 10-11 and 14-15 seem to refer to two other household churches in Rome. Apparently, there were at least three churches there, and probably more. Each house church could not have been a separate entity with a separate church government; rather, each house church must have been simply one home meeting of some of the saints in the one local church at Rome.

1 Corinthians 16:19-20 In this passage we again see Aquila and Priscilla and again discover that a church met in their house. According to Romans, their house church was, of course, in Rome. According to 1 Corinthians (written from Ephesus), their house church was in Ephesus. Many scholars think Aquila and Priscilla left Rome around AD 49 at the time of Claudius's edict expelling Jews from Rome. They very well could have already been Christians at this time. According to Acts 18, they joined Paul in Corinth (where they all worked together in their craft of tentmaking) and then went on with him to Ephesus, during the time (around AD 51) the church in Ephesus was first established. Paul continued on with his second missionary journey, while Aquila and Priscilla remained in Ephesus. No doubt, the early church there first met in their home. Paul returned to Ephesus a few years later and remained there for two years (around AD 53–54). During this time, Paul's proclamation of the gospel went out from Ephesus (as a center) to all of Asia Minor (see Acts 19:8-10). As this was going on, the church in Ephesus grew (see vv 18-20).

It was during these years that Paul wrote to the Corinthians, in which he sent greetings from the churches in Asia, from Aquila and Priscilla—and the church in their house, and from all the brothers (1 Cor 16:19-20). In giving this kind of greeting, it seems that Paul was sending greetings from (1) all the churches in Asia Minor, (2) the church in Ephesus (equivalent to "all the brothers"), and (3) those believers who gathered with Aquila and Priscilla in their home. It would be hard to imagine that all the saints in Ephesus met at Aquila and Priscilla's home. The church probably began that way, but as it grew, so did the number of home meetings. From other portions of the NT (specifically 1 Timothy, which was written around AD 64 by Paul to Timothy while Timothy was leading the church in Ephesus), we discover that there must have been several home meetings in Ephesus because there were so many saints there (see 1 Timothy 5–6, which reveal that there must have been a large number of saints in Ephesus—young men, young women, older men, widows, and so forth). At any rate, several saints must have hosted an *ecclesia*, a meeting, in their home. (Aquila and Priscilla left Ephesus around AD 56/57 and returned to Rome, where again they hosted a church in their home. Others in Ephesus would have to open their homes.) But each such *ecclesia* did not have its own eldership; rather, all of the church in Ephesus was under one eldership—headed up by Timothy, Paul's coworker.

Colossians 4:15-16 In this portion, we again read about a church existing in the home of one called Nymphas. In his final remarks to the church in Colosse, Paul asked the saints in Colosse to send his greetings to (1) the brothers that are in Laodicea, (2) Nymphas in particular, and (3) the church in Nymphas's house. According to the structure of Colossians 4:15, it seems evident that the first greeting included all the believers in Laodicea (a neighboring church to Colosse), who would comprise the entire church in Laodicea (called "the church of the Laodiceans" in Col 4:16), and that the second and third greetings were to a specific individual (Nymphas) in the church in Laodicea and a church meeting in Nymphas's house. This church meeting in Nymphas's house would probably be one of several home meetings—all part of the one local church in Laodicea.

There is a textual problem in this passage that could have some effect on the interpretation of it. Some manuscripts read "his house"; others read "her house"; still others read "their house." Because it cannot be determined from the Greek text whether Nymphas was male or female, various scribes used different pronouns before "house." Between the readings "her" and "his," it is far more likely that the pronoun "her" was changed to "his" than vice versa. Some scholars say that "their" refers to "the brothers" at Laodicea. But that does not make sense if we understand that "the brothers in Laodicea" is equal to the church in Laodicea. How could the church in Laodicea have the church in their house? Other scholars indicate that the Greek word for "their" *(auton)* refers to the ones with Nymphas—i.e., the members of his household. Whether the reading was "her house" or "their house," a particular group of believers within the church of Laodicea met there. Their meeting could legitimately be called an *ecclesia*—an assembling together.

Philemon 1:1-2 This is the last time in the NT we read about a church in a particular home. Paul wrote a short epistle to Philemon, an elder of the church in Colosse, on behalf of Onesimus, Philemon's runaway slave converted by Paul to Christ. In his introduction to this short epistle, Paul sends his greetings to Philemon, Apphia, Archippus, and the church in Philemon's house. It is important to note that Paul did not send greetings to all the saints in Colosse and then to the church in Philemon's house (as is the pattern in 1 Cor 16:19-20 and Col 4:15); instead, he just sent greetings to Philemon and to the church in his house. Therefore, we can assume that the entire church in Colosse must have met at Philemon's house.

Worship in the Home Meetings and Church Meetings When the church first began in Jerusalem, the believers met in homes for fellowship and worship. Acts 2:42-47 tells us that the early Christians met in homes to hear the apostles' teachings and to celebrate Communion (which is called "the breaking of bread"). During such gatherings, the Christians often shared meals with one another in what was called a love feast (2 Pt 2:13; Jude 1:12). At these meetings, the Christians recited Scripture, sang hymns and psalms, and joyfully praised the Lord (see Eph 5:18-20; Col 3:16-17). Christians also gathered together in homes to pray (Acts 12:12) and read the Word.

Small groups of believers met in homes for worship quite regularly; in a city where there were several such *ecclesiai*, all the believers would gather together for special occasions. Scripture tells us that all the believers would come together to hear an epistle from the apostles read out loud (see Acts 15:30; Col 4:16), and we can surmise from the NT record that all the Christians in a city met together once a week on Sunday, which was called the Lord's Day. First Corinthians provides several insights about how the early Christians worshiped together when all the believers in one city met together. We know that 1 Corinthians pertains to this larger gathering because in 11:20 Paul spoke of all the believers coming together in one place and in 14:23 he spoke of the whole church coming together in one place.

Paul used this epistle to correct the Corinthians' behavior in the celebration of the Lord's Supper (1 Cor 11:17-34) and in the exercising of spiritual gifts during church meetings (ch 14). Paul's adjustments reveal his perceptions of a model Christian meeting, and his preceptions were probably developed from actual experience in other church meetings. Paul urged the Corinthians to celebrate the Lord's Supper together in a manner that reflected Jesus' institution of that meal. They were to remember the Lord and his death for them, and they were to partake of the bread and wine with all seriousness. At the same time, they were to be conscious of the fact that they were members of the same body of Christ—joined to one another, and also to Christ.

According to Paul's presentation in chapter 14, this "body consciousness" should be evident in the way the believers worshiped together. One's personal experience and liberty should not hinder the coordination of the body in worshiping God corporately. Thus, when the believers exercised their spiritual gifts—whether it be prophesying, speaking in tongues, providing interpretations of the tongues, or teaching—it should be done in good order and for the edification of the congregation, not personal edification. When all the church assembled together to worship God, it should be a display of spiritual unity.

See also Church.

CHURCH OFFICERS* *See* Bishop; Deacon, Deaconess; Elder; Pastor; Presbyter; Spiritual Gifts.

CHUSHAN-RISHATHAIM* KJV spelling of Cushanrishathaim, a Mesopotamian king and oppressor of Israel, in Judges 3:8-10. *See* Cushan-rishathaim.

CHUSI Place mentioned near Acraba and beside the brook Mochmur (Jdt 7:18). Chusi is probably south of modern Nablus in Israel.

CHUZA Steward of Herod Antipas, either a manager of Herod's property or a political appointee; a man of influence and prestige. He was married to Joanna, who was healed by Jesus and subsequently accompanied Jesus and his disciples on their travels (Lk 8:3).

CILICIA Province of the Roman Empire, located in southeastern Asia Minor. Its capital was Tarsus, Paul's hometown (Acts 21:39; 22:3), hence permitting Paul Roman citizenship (16:37) even though he was a Jew.

Jewish presence in the area probably dated to the time when Antiochus the Great settled 2,000 Jewish families in the Asia Minor regions of Lydia and Phrygia in the second century BC (Josephus's *Antiquities* 12.3.4).

In antiquity Cilicia (called Kue in OT times) formed a bridge between the country now known as Turkey and Syria, its neighbor to the southeast. Geographically the country was divided between Cilicia Tracheia, the mountainous region in the western half, and Cilicia Pedias, the lovely plains to the east. Entrance into Turkey (ancient Asia Minor) was possible through the Cilician Gates, a narrow pass in the Taurus Mountains. Cilicia Pedias was early attached to the province of Syria (c. 38 BC) and was known in the NT times as Syria and Cilicia (Gal 1:21). The western part, Cilicia Tracheia, was given by Mark Antony to Cleopatra in 36 BC, but by the time of Paul, it was ruled by the Hellenist king Antiochus IV of Commagene (AD 38–72). In AD 72 the two areas were unified into one Roman province, called Cilicia, by the Roman emperor Vespasian.

Jews from Cilicia participated in the persecution of Stephen (Acts 6:9). After his conversion to Christianity, Paul eventually returned to Tarsus, later accompanying Barnabas to Antioch (Acts 11:25-26). Syria and Cilicia thus became the first major center of non-Jewish Christianity, and from this region Christianity spread to the rest of the gentile population of the Roman Empire.

See also Kue.

CINNAMON Spice made from the dried inner bark of several oriental trees. *See* Food and Food Preparation; Plants.

CINNEROTH* KJV spelling of the place-name Kinnereth in 1 Kings 15:20. *See* Kinnereth.

CIRCUMCISION Surgical removal of the foreskin of the male reproductive organ. In Bible times circumcision was the seal of God's covenant with Abraham (Gn 17:1-14). While circumcision originated as an ancient tribal or religious rite, since the early part of this century it has been practiced in Western nations for hygienic purposes. Many physicians believe that circumcision helps prevent genital cancers in both men and their wives, so that this minor operation is performed a few days after birth on nearly all newborn males in North America. Outside of Judaism the procedure no longer carries religious significance.

PREVIEW
• Circumcision in the Ancient World
• Circumcision in the Old Testament
• Circumcision in the New Testament

Circumcision in the Ancient World The rite of circumcision is far older than the Hebrew people. Cave paintings give evidence that it was practiced in prehistoric times. Egyptian temple drawings show that the operation was common in 4000 BC and probably earlier. Peoples practicing circumcision lived on almost every continent. The rite was observed among Central and South American Indians, Polynesians, the peoples of New Guinea, many Australian and African tribes, Egyptians, and pre-Islamic Arabs. The rite is not mentioned in the Koran, but because Muhammad was circumcised, tradition dictates that male Muslims follow the ancient custom. Arab ancestry is traced to Abraham through Ishmael (Gn 17:20), so a common age for Muslim cir-

cumcisions is 13, because Ishmael was circumcised at that age (v 25).

Among the West Semitic people, the Ammonites, Edomites, Midianites, Moabites, and Phoenicians all practiced circumcision (Jer 9:25-26). The Philistines, however, did not (Jgs 14:3; 15:18; 1 Sm 14:6; 17:26, 36; 18:25, 27; 31:4; 2 Sm 1:20; 3:14; 1 Chr 10:4).

Young men were usually circumcised at puberty, evidently in preparation for marriage and entrance into full tribal responsibilities. The Hebrews were the only ancient practitioners of circumcision to observe the rite in infancy, thus freeing it from association with fertility rituals.

Circumcision in the Old Testament In the Bible the practice of circumcision began in Genesis 17 as a sign of the covenant between God and Abraham. God promised Abraham a land and, through a son yet to be conceived, numerous descendants, from whom kings would come. Blessings would come upon Abraham and through him to all nations (Gn 12:1-3). After the covenant was formally inaugurated (ch 15), God sealed it, ordering Abraham to be circumcised along with all the males in his household (17:9-13).

Circumcision was to be an expression of faith that God's promises would be realized. Because Abraham's faith had lapsed (Gn 16) even after he had seen the awesome display of God's majesty (15:9-17), a permanent reminder of God's covenant promises was placed on his body and the bodies of his male descendants (17:11). This sign was so closely related to God's covenant promise that the rite itself could be termed the "covenant" (Gn 17:10; Acts 7:8).

Circumcision was to be performed on the eighth day after birth (Gn 17:12; Lv 12:1-3; see Gn 21:4; Lk 1:59; 2:21; Acts 7:8; Phil 3:5), customarily by the boy's father (Gn 17:23; 21:4; Acts 7:8), at which time a name would be given (Lk 1:59; 2:21). Flint knives were used in the early days (Ex 4:25; Jos 5:2-3). Later, the rite was carried out by a trained practitioner called a *mohel*. Medical research has determined that prothrombin, a substance in the blood that aids in clotting, is present in greater quantity on the eighth day than at any other time in life.

Theological Meaning Circumcision had to do with the fulfillment of God's promise concerning Abraham's descendants (Gn 17:9-12). Because it was applied to the reproductive organ, the sign involved the propagation of the race. Its application to the eight-day-old infant demonstrates the gracious character of God's promise to Abraham's descendants and indicates that God's people are in need of cleansing grace from birth (Lv 12:1-3). The promises of the covenant were reaffirmed to each generation before the recipients were able to respond in either faith or unbelief; nothing in the hearts of the chosen people could either bring about or thwart the ultimate fulfillment of the promises given to Abraham and his posterity.

Circumcision also had to do with the fulfillment of God's promise concerning the land (Gn 17:8). The land was God's holy possession, and the Israelites had to be holy to possess it. When Joseph and his descendants were in Egypt, they continued to circumcise their sons. But following the great sin at Mt Sinai after the exodus, the unbelieving Israelites failed to place the covenant sign upon their children as they wandered in the wilderness. Because the new generation had not been circumcised, the people were unprepared to enter the Promised Land. Therefore, God ordered Joshua to circumcise the men of Israel. The people's obedient response was an act of faith, since the armies of the enemy were camped nearby as the Israelite warriors lay incapacitated by the surgery (Jos 5:2-9).

From the beginning, participation in the covenant promises was open to persons outside Abraham's household (Gn 17:12-13). Exodus 12:43-49 gives non-Israelites the opportunity to participate in the Passover if they are willing to fulfill the same stipulation placed upon the Jews—that of circumcision.

The provision for admission to God's people by reception of the covenant sign was abused by Jacob's sons when circumcision was made a precondition for intermarriage with the Shechemites. While the Shechemites were disabled by their wounds, Simeon and Levi killed them, plundering the city to exact retribution for the rape of their sister Dinah (Gn 34).

The sign of the covenant was not to be treated lightly. The penalty of excommunication rested upon the uncircumcised (Gn 17:14). The strange incident recorded in Exodus 4:24-26 seems to have been God's reminder to Moses of the stipulations of the covenant made with Abraham. Moses had proved an unfaithful servant of the Lord by neglecting to circumcise his son but was rescued from judgment when his wife Zipporah took a flint rock and circumcised the boy, throwing the bloody foreskin at her husband's feet.

THE SPIRITUAL SIGNIFICANCE OF CIRCUMCISION
The hygienic act of circumcision symbolized the need for cleansing if the holy God was to enter into relationship with an unholy people. At first it was God's intention to let the ritual teach its own lesson. In Genesis 17:9-27 the observance merely serves as the covenant seal; Abraham is given little explanation of the significance of the rite itself. Later Moses used the expression "uncircumcised lips" to describe his unskilled speech (Ex 6:12, 30). When Israel entered the Promised Land, the yield of its fruit trees was to be considered "uncircumcised" for the first three years; after that it would be holy to the Lord (Lv 19:23-24).

By the time of the exodus, it became evident that circumcision had to do with ethical as well as physical considerations. In Deuteronomy 10:16 Moses exhorted the people to circumcise the foreskins of their hearts, and in Deuteronomy 30:6 this command assumes the form of a promise: "The LORD your God will circumcise your heart and the heart of your offspring, so that you will love the LORD your God with all your heart and with all your soul" (RSV).

Sin in the lives of the chosen people made their circumcision meaningless before God. Thus Moses told the Israelites to humble their uncircumcised hearts (Lv 26:41). The prophets further develop this teaching. Jeremiah urged the citizens of Judah to remove the foreskins of their hearts to avoid God's wrath because of their evil ways (Jer 4:4), warning that the "uncircumcised ears" of Israel were not sensitive to the word of the Lord (Jer 6:10, RSV mg). Judgment will come upon Egypt, Edom, Ammon, Moab, and Judah, declares God, for "I am going to punish all who are circumcised only in flesh . . . for all these nations, and the whole House of Israel too, are uncircumcised at heart" (Jer 9:24-25, JB). Through Ezekiel the Lord complains that the temple has been profaned by the admission of aliens uncircumcised in heart and flesh (Ez 44:7, 9). Isaiah looks forward to the day when there will be a new Jerusalem into which the uncircumcised and unclean will no longer come.

Circumcision in the New Testament John the Baptist was circumcised, as were Jesus and Paul (Lk 1:59; 2:21; Phil 3:5). Jesus recognized the cleansing significance of circumcision (Jn 7:22-23), contrasting the rite with his healing ministry that made a man completely well and therefore ceremonially "clean." Just before he was stoned, Stephen referred to the covenant of circumcision, charging that his Jewish accusers, like their ancestors, were stiff-necked and uncircumcised in heart and ears, always resisting the Holy Spirit (Acts 7:8, 51).

For a time the first Christians continued to participate in the Jewish rites and customs, even attending the services of the temple (Acts 3:1; 5:21, 42). As Gentiles came to Christ, controversy arose between those who said that participation in the covenant community required circumcision and those who believed the rite was unnecessary. It was argued that since the covenant promise of the Messiah was given to the Jews, Gentiles must first be circumcised and become Jews before they could receive salvation in Christ.

In the time of Christ, many Jews misunderstood the significance of circumcision, believing that the physical act was necessary for and a guarantee of salvation. Thus for Jews the observance became not only a symbol of religious privilege but also a source of racial pride (Phil 3:4-6). These Jews associated the ceremony with the Mosaic law rather than the promise to Abraham (Jn 7:22; Acts 15:1). Because Greeks and Romans did not practice circumcision, Jews had come to be called "the circumcision" (KJV Acts 10:45; 11:2; Rom 15:8; Gal 2:7-9; Eph 2:11; Ti 1:10), and following OT practice (Ez 28:10; 31:18; 32:19-32), Gentiles were termed "the uncircumcision" (KJV Gal 2:7; Eph 2:11).

While visiting Caesarea, Jewish believers were amazed to realize that uncircumcised Gentiles received the purifying gift of the Holy Spirit (Acts 10:44-48). Moses had promised that God would circumcise the hearts of his people to love the Lord with heart and soul (Dt 30:6), and Ezekiel had prophesied that the Lord would sprinkle clean water on his people, giving them a new heart and putting his Spirit within them (Ez 36:25-27). As these Jewish believers saw the prophecy that God would pour out his Spirit upon all flesh (Jl 2:28; Acts 2:17) being fulfilled, they realized that the inward reality symbolized by circumcision could be accomplished without the physical sign. Thus, the gentile believers were immediately baptized.

Not all the Jewish believers were immediately willing to accept Gentiles into the church. When Peter returned to Jerusalem after his visit to Caesarea, "the circumcision party" criticized him. But after telling how the Spirit had fallen upon the Gentiles, Peter declared that he could not stand against God. At this the Jewish believers were silenced and glorified God that repentance unto life had been granted to Gentiles (Acts 11:1-3, 15:8).

Certain "Judaizers" of the Pharisaic party taught the Christians in Antioch that circumcision was necessary for salvation (Acts 15:1, 5). After debating these persons, Paul and Barnabas went to Jerusalem to consult with the other apostles and elders (v 2). Peter argued that God had given the Spirit to Gentiles and "cleansed their hearts by faith," affirming that "we believe that we shall be saved through the grace of the Lord Jesus, just as they will" (vv 8-9, 11, RSV). Therefore, James and the other Jerusalem leaders agreed that circumcision should not be imposed on the Gentiles (vv 13-21).

It was decided that Peter, James, and John would be entrusted with the gospel to "the circumcised," while Paul and Barnabas would preach to "the uncircumcised" (Gal 2:7-9). Because of his evangelistic policy to be "all things to all people" with respect to spiritually indifferent matters of custom (1 Cor 9:19-23), Paul had Timothy circumcised. Timothy was reckoned by Jews as one of their race because his mother was Jewish (Acts 16:1-2). But Paul resisted attempts to have Titus circumcised, since he was a Gentile (Gal 2:3). Paul apparently allowed Jewish believers to circumcise their sons (Acts 21:21).

Yet Paul charged that those who argued that the Galatian Christians must be circumcised and keep the law did not keep it themselves but wanted to boast in the Galatians' flesh and avoid persecution for the cross of Christ (Gal 6:12-13)—persecution Paul was willing to bear (5:11). Granting for the sake of argument the Pharisaic assumption that salvation could be merited by keeping the law, Paul declared that those who received circumcision must obey every other Jewish law (vv 2-3). Christ would be "of no advantage" to those who "would be justified by the law"; this attempt at works righteousness would evidence that the Galatians were "severed from Christ," having "fallen from grace" (vv 2-4). These Christians were being tempted to turn to "a different gospel" (1:6-7).

Because of the serious threat the Judaizers posed to the gospel of free grace, Paul wished that those who unsettled the Galatians would "mutilate themselves" (Gal 5:12). He termed the Judaizers "dogs" and "evil workers" (KJV "concision"), asserting that Christians are "the true circumcision," because they worship God in spirit and glory in Christ Jesus, putting no confidence in human works to merit salvation (Phil 3:2-3).

Paul taught that circumcision was indeed of value to Jews, for it was the sign that to them had been committed the "oracles of God," that is, God's word concerning the promise of salvation (Rom 3:1-3). He reminded the prideful Ephesians that as Gentiles they had once been "strangers to the covenants of promise," not bearing the covenant sign in their flesh (Eph 2:11-12; see Col 2:13). Likewise, Jews had no cause for pride, for disobedience could cause outward circumcision to be counted as uncircumcision (Rom 2:25).

Paul and the other apostles followed Moses and the OT prophets in teaching that true circumcision was a matter of the heart. The teaching of the NT goes further to affirm that a faithful believer, though physically uncircumcised, is regarded by God as circumcised, "for he is not a real Jew who is one outwardly, nor is true circumcision something external and physical" (Rom 2:28, RSV). Both Jews and Gentiles are saved by grace (Acts 15:11), and circumcised and uncircumcised alike are justified on the ground of their faith, apart from works of the law (Rom 3:28-30).

Abraham served as an example of a person whose faith was reckoned to him as righteousness (Rom 4:3; see Gn 15:6). Paul argued that both Gentiles and Jews are justified by faith, because Abraham was accounted righteous before he was circumcised. Abraham did not receive circumcision to obtain righteousness, but as a sign or seal of the righteousness that he had by faith while he was still uncircumcised. Thus, Abraham is the father of all who believe without being circumcised, as well as those who are circumcised but also follow the example of Abraham's faith (Rom 4:9-12; see Gal 3:6-9).

See also Baptism; Cleanness and Uncleanness, Regulations Concerning; Uncircumcision.

CIS* KJV form of Kish, King Saul's father, in Acts 13:21. *See* Kish #1.

CISTERN Place to store water; a man-made catch basin or reservoir. Stone cisterns plastered with lime came into common use in Palestine in the 13th century BC.

Leaky or abandoned cisterns were often used as burial, torture, or prison chambers. For example, the dungeon into which the prophet Jeremiah was lowered was an abandoned muddy cistern (Jer 38:6). Ishmael threw the bodies of 70 murdered men into a large cistern originally constructed by King Asa for a wartime water supply (41:4-9).

Cisterns were vitally important in the arid Near East. King Uzziah of Judah is described as hewing out many cisterns in areas where springs or wells were lacking (2 Chr 26:10). An Assyrian general taunting King Hezekiah and his people promised that, if they would submit, everyone would drink the water of his own cistern (Is 36:16; cf. 2 Kgs 18:31). Much earlier, Moses had assured the Israelites that cisterns already hewn out would be among God's blessing in the Promised Land (Dt 6:11).

FIGURATIVE USE OF "CISTERN"
The word "cistern" is also used figuratively in the Bible. Through the prophet Jeremiah, God rebuked Israel for rejecting him, the "fountain of living waters." Instead, they had "dug for themselves cracked cisterns that can hold no water at all" (Jer 2:13, NLT). Ecclesiastes 12:6 refers to a broken wheel at a cistern as a figurative description of old age.

CITADEL A city's stronghold, tower, or fortification of last resort where people sought safety during an attack. The citadel of Penuel was destroyed by Gideon after he captured two Midianite kings (Jgs 8:17). The citadel of El-berith at Shechem was burned to the ground by Abimelech and his men (9:46-49). Abimelech was killed shortly thereafter when a woman in the citadel at Thebez dropped a millstone on his head and crushed his skull (vv 50-54). David conquered Jerusalem by capturing its citadel (2 Sm 5:7-9; 1 Chr 11:5-8).

During the Maccabees' struggle for independence in the second century BC, the citadel in Jerusalem often aided the party in power (1 Macc 1:29-33; 11:41-42; 13:49-51). The Fortress of Antonia, the Jerusalem citadel in the day of Jesus, fell to the Romans in AD 70.

CITIES OF REFUGE Six cities, three in Canaan and three in Transjordan (area east of the Jordan River), designated as places of safety for persons suspected of manslaughter. The six cities were among the 48 assigned to the Levites (Nm 35:6). The three Transjordanian cities were Bezer, Ramoth, and Golan (Dt 4:43; Jos 20:8). The three cities west of the Jordan were Kedesh, Shechem, and Kiriath-arba (that is, Hebron) in the hill country of Judah (Jos 20:7). They were distributed so that east of the Jordan, Golan was located in the north, Ramoth in the center, and Bezer in the south. West of the Jordan, Kedesh, Shechem, and Hebron were located north, center, and south respectively. That made it possible for an accused manslayer to reach a city of refuge quickly.

In ancient Israel the nearest relative of a murder victim was required to take the life of the murderer (Nm 35:19-21). It was his duty to the widow, other family members, and to society. Murderers were not allowed to live, and there was no way to ransom them (v 31).

Accidental death, however, was another matter. Manslaughter without malice or premeditation had a special provision in the law of Moses. A man who accidentally killed someone could flee to the nearest city of refuge, where the local authorities would grant him asylum

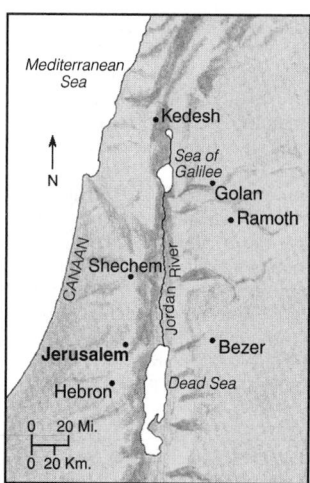

Mediterranean
Sea

Sea of
Galilee

N

•Kedesh

•Golan
•Ramoth

Shechem

Jerusalem•
Hebron•

•Bezer

Dead Sea

0   20 Mi.
0   20 Km.

Cities of Refuge Six cities were designated as cities of refuge. They were spaced throughout the land and protected those who had accidentally committed a crime or who were awaiting trial.

(Dt 19:4-6). When the case came to court, if the man was found guilty of premeditated murder, he was handed over for execution (19:11-12). If the death was deemed accidental, the person was acquitted. Nevertheless, he had to pay a penalty. The manslayer had to stay in the city of refuge as long as the current high priest was in office (Nm 35:22-28). That would be a considerable hardship in some cases. It meant either separation from one's family or the expense and risk of moving from one's ancestral land and trying to make a livelihood in a new city.

See also Asylum; Civil Law and Justice.

CITIES OF THE PLAIN
Group of five cities in the plain or basin of the Jordan River which were also referred to as "cities of the valley." Since the region in which these cities were located was particularly fruitful, it attracted Abraham's nephew Lot when the growing size of the flocks and herds forced a division of these two patriarchal communities (Gn 13:10-12). The cities are enumerated as Sodom, Gomorrah, Admah, Zeboiim, and Bela or Zoar. Evidently each was a city-state with its own king.

These cities entered the biblical narrative in four connections. (1) They provided a region where Lot could settle; he ultimately decided to make his home in Sodom. (2) The five kings of the cities of the plain fought with a superior force led by four kings of lands far to the east. In the struggle they were defeated and their cities ransacked. The plunder was great, as was the number of captives, especially women and children (Gn 14). Since Lot was among those carried off, Abraham felt an obligation to launch a rescue operation. In this he was immensely successful, recovering not only Lot but also the other captives and the booty. (3) The wicked cities of the plain later came in for God's judgment. Their evil was so great that Abraham's intercession on their behalf was to no avail (Gn 18:22-33). Their depravity is illustrated by the account of the homosexual mob at Lot's door in Sodom (ch 19). Soon thereafter, Lot and his family were ordered to flee before the cities were wiped out. Brimstone and fire obliterated the cities, changing the composition of the whole area. (4) References to the destruction of these cities appear in numerous passages in both the OT and NT to serve as a warning of divine punishment for sin (Is 3:9; Jer 50:40; Ez 16:46-56; Mt 10:15; Rom 9:29).

CITIZENSHIP In NT usage (1) designation of belonging to the city or city-state where one was born and reared, and (2) status of sharing in the privileges and responsibilities of the Roman Empire. Thus the apostle Paul claimed to be a citizen of both Tarsus (Acts 21:39) and Rome (22:27-28).

The right of Roman citizenship most commonly was acquired by birth, as was true of Paul. The status of a child whose parents were married was determined by the status of the father at the time of conception. The status of a child born out of wedlock was determined by that of the mother at the child's birth. Slaves automatically became citizens when freed by their masters. Although known as "freedmen," they were often denied the rights of regular freeborn citizens. Greedy magistrates frequently sold the right of citizenship for a high price. The tribune Claudius Lysias received his citizenship in that manner (Acts 22:28). Citizen rights could also be granted by treaty or imperial declaration. Following the Social War (about 90–85 BC), citizenship was granted to all the inhabitants of Italy. Julius Caesar extended the right to colonies in Gaul (France) and provinces in Asia Minor. According to the census of the emperor Augustus (Lk 2:1), there were approximately 4,233,000 Roman citizens at the time of Christ's birth. By the time of Paul's ministry, the number had reached 6,000,000.

> **WHERE ARE THESE CITIES?**
> The question of the location of the cities of the plain has been an intriguing one in biblical study. Today scholars generally conclude that these cities stood at the south end of the Dead Sea. Scripture itself connects them with the valley of Siddim. Either they stood in the valley or else the valley lay adjacent to the plain where they were located. Between the days of Abraham and Moses, the water level of the Dead Sea evidently had risen enough to cover at least part of the valley of Siddim; Genesis 14:3 declares that the valley of Siddim was "the Salt Sea" (in Moses' time). The southern part of the Dead Sea is now only 12 to 15 feet (3.7 to 4.6 meters) deep, whereas the northern part reaches a depth of 1,300 feet (396 meters). Josephus, a first-century AD historian, declared that ruins of the five cities were still to be seen at the south end of the Dead Sea. No trace of these ruins has been discovered in modern times.
> Though much of the region south of the Dead Sea is now burned out and sterile, the area to its southeast is still fertile. Three streams pour down from the mountains of Moab into this area and furnish water for irrigation. W. F. Albright, a 20th-century archaeologist, noted that five streams flow into the south end of the Dead Sea. A town could have stood on each of them.

Roman citizens were often required to give proof of their citizenship. That was usually accomplished by reference to the census archives, where the name of every citizen was recorded. In addition, freeborn citizens possessed a small wooden birth certificate containing information about their status at birth. Military documents and taxation tables also carried the names of registered citizens. Further, every Roman citizen had three names, whereas noncitizens generally had only one.

The rights of Roman citizenship were extensive, including the right to vote; to hold office; to serve in the military; to purchase, possess, sell, and bequeath property; to enter into a legal contract; to have a fair trial; and to appeal to Caesar. Thus Paul, upon mention of his Roman citizenship, received an apology from magistrates at Philippi for having imprisoned him without a trial (Acts 16:38-39). He also avoided a scourging in Jerusalem (22:24-29) and was able to request a trial before Caesar (25:10-12; cf. 26:32).

CITY The Bible does not generally distinguish between city, town, and village. The emphasis upon walls (Lv 25:29-31) and fortifications (Jos 19:35), with repeated references to towers, gates, and sieges, indicates that cities provided the primary security for the surrounding towns and villages.

Origin and Antiquity

Practical Prerequisites The existence of settled communities depended upon a controlled food supply. In contrast to the city dweller, the nomad lived in a portable tent, appropriate for a never-ceasing search for food. The contrast between settled city life and the nomadic experience is illustrated by a NT reference to the seminomadic Abraham: "He looked forward to the city which has foundations, whose builder and maker is God" (Heb 11:10, RSV).

The First Biblical City The first biblical reference to a city is in Genesis 4:17. The Hebrew verb indicates that Cain "was building" the city. Probably he did not complete it, nor did he permanently reside there; he had earlier been condemned to a vagabond's existence (v 12).

The Genesis account, affirming that city life came early in human existence, is internally consistent. The first human offspring, Cain and Abel, were involved in food production (Gn 4:2). Cain was an agriculturist, and Abel tended domesticated flocks. Genesis 4 shows both the prerequisite of food production and the resulting specialization. With Jabal, tentmaking was associated (v 20); with Jubal, music (v 21); and with Tubal-Cain, metalworking (v 22).

Archaeological Evidence The testimony of archaeology generally agrees with an early date for the origin of cities. The oldest city thus far discovered in Canaan was Jericho. Using carbon-14 analysis of wood materials from the site, Kathleen Kenyon assigned a date prior to 7000 BC. Although less than 10 acres (4 hectares), it was a well-developed city with an impressive wall 6 feet (1.8 meters) thick and a round stone tower almost 30 feet (9 meters) high equipped with an inside staircase from top to bottom.

Jericho seems to be 3,000 years older than other Canaanite cities. Most of the great Sumerian cities such as Ur, Ish, Lagah, and Uruk were founded later, in the fourth or early third millennium BC.

Location and Name

Topographical Prerequisites There were four primary considerations in the selection of a site for a city.

1. The topographical situation of the ancient city had to contribute to its defense. A city built on a natural hill tended to be less vulnerable than one in the valley. Substantial advantage was given to the defenders if an enemy was forced to attack up an incline.

The topography of Jerusalem illustrates the factor of security in the selection of a site. Although surrounded by higher mountains (Ps 125:2), Jerusalem originally was established on a limestone ridge protected on the east by the deep Kidron Valley and on the west by the equally formidable Tyropoean Valley. The two valleys met, thus affording Jerusalem protection from the south. To complete the security, walls were constructed around the city, with special emphasis on the northern side, where Jerusalem was otherwise exposed (cf. 2 Sm 5:6).

2. A water source conveniently located was an absolute necessity for a city's existence. The city spring or well became the center of social intercourse, particularly for the women, who were traditionally the water carriers. Biblical examples of socializing at the village well are numerous (Gn 29:1-12; 1 Kgs 1:38-39).

In general, water sources were located in valleys, so the nearest spring to a city was frequently outside the walls. If an attacking enemy seized the water source, a city could be forced to surrender when the water supply stored within the walls ran dry. In Jerusalem, King Hezekiah constructed a water tunnel to neutralize the impending attack of the Assyrian king Sennacherib (2 Kgs 20:20; 2 Chr 32:30). His amazing engineering feat, more than 1,700 feet (518 meters) long and over 2,500 years old, can still be seen by visitors to Jerusalem.

3. Every city needed adequate food for its inhabitants. Ancient agriculturalists lived in a village or city and walked each day to their fields. The existence of a city, therefore, depended upon nearby cultivable fields adequate to meet the needs of the population.

4. To facilitate importation of raw materials and exportation of finished products, proximity to local and international roads was desirable if not imperative. The important cities of the Bible were located along primary arteries of commerce.

The relative importance of these four factors has changed over the centuries. With the appearance of strong nation-states such as Rome, cities could depend upon standing armies and thus give up their inconvenient hilltop sites. Development of plastered cisterns and aqueducts made possible the founding of cities some distance from water sources; for example, Caesarea, built by Herod the Great, was 12 miles (19.3 kilometers) from Mt Carmel's springs. Trade routes shifted with changing international conditions, causing the demise of some cities and the development of others.

See also Archaeology and the Bible.

CITY OF DAVID

1. Southeastern hill (Ophel) in the present-day city of Jerusalem, the site occupied by King David as his royal city; also called Zion (e.g., 1 Kgs 8:1). David captured the Jebusite fortress of Jerusalem and transferred his capital to it from Hebron (2 Sm 5:1-10). *See* Jerusalem.

2. Alternate name for Bethlehem, David's hometown, in the NT (Lk 2:11). *See* Bethlehem.

CITY OF DESTRUCTION* KJV translation in Isaiah 19:18 (NLT "City of the Sun"), generally understood as a reference to the Egyptian city Heliopolis.
See also Heliopolis.

CITY OF PALMS Phrase referring to Jericho, so named for its many palms (Dt 34:3). *See* Jericho.

CITY OF SALT City located near the Dead Sea, assigned to Judah's tribe for an inheritance (Jos 15:62).

CITY OF THE SUN Phrase in Isaiah 19:18, generally taken as a reference to the Egyptian city Heliopolis. *See* Heliopolis.

CIVIL LAW AND JUSTICE* Civil law deals with private disputes between individuals occasioned by debt, divorce, inheritance, or other relationships. In contrast, criminal law deals with crimes such as murder, treason, or theft. In civil cases the guilty party is asked to compensate the victim in an appropriate way.

This distinction between civil and criminal law is quite foreign to biblical thinking. Nearly all offenses were matters for private prosecution. If someone was murdered, his relatives were responsible for killing the murderer or chasing him to the nearest city of refuge, where a trial would be held. All offenses in Israel had a religious dimension: theft or adultery was not merely an offense against one's neighbor but was a sin against God. This meant, in theory, that every Israelite would be shocked by such behavior and would want it punished. If such acts continued, God himself might step in to punish the individual, his family, or even the whole nation. This religious dimension gave an aura of criminality to every offense, even though in most cases prosecution was left in the hands of individuals.

See also Courts and Trials; Criminal Law and Punishment; Dietary Laws; Divorce; Divorce, Certificate of; Hammurabi, Law Code of; Law, Biblical Concept of; Leviticus, Book of; Marriage, Marriage Customs; Commandments, The Ten.

CLAUDA* Ancient name (and variant spelling) of a small island south of Crete, in Acts 27:16. *See* Cauda.

CLAUDIA Christian woman known to the apostle Paul and to Timothy (2 Tm 4:21).

CLAUDIUS Roman emperor from AD 41 to 54, mentioned twice in the NT (Acts 11:28; 18:2). *See* Caesars, The.

CLAUDIUS*, Edict of Marble slab inscription from Nazareth prohibiting grave robbing, dated to Claudius's reign (AD 41–54). *See* Inscriptions.

CLAUDIUS LYSIAS Commander of the Roman garrison in Jerusalem who wrote a letter to the Roman procurator Felix concerning the apostle Paul (Acts 23:26). His title in Greek *(chiliarch)* identifies him as a commander of 1,000 troops. Although Claudius Lysias is unknown outside the NT, some information about him is supplied by the book of Acts. His surname Lysias is Greek. The Roman name Claudius was evidently taken at the time he purchased his Roman citizenship (22:28).

Stationed in the Antonia fortress overlooking the northern sector of the temple area in Jerusalem, he rescued Paul from a Jewish mob that was about to kill him there. He allowed Paul to speak to the Jews from one of the two staircases that led from the Court of the Gentiles in the temple up to the Antonia (Acts 21:40) and prevented Paul from being scourged when he learned of Paul's Roman citizenship (22:22-29). Claudius Lysias sent Paul secretly to Caesarea under heavy guard when Paul's nephew informed the tribune of a Jewish plot to murder the apostle in Jerusalem (23:16-35).

How Luke, the writer of Acts, obtained a copy of the official letter about Paul written by Claudius to Felix the governor is not known, but the document provides an important vindication of Paul's character and conduct in the face of his opponents' accusations.

CLAY *See* Minerals and Metals; Pottery.

CLAY TABLET* *See* Writing.

CLEANNESS AND UNCLEANNESS, Regulations Concerning Aspect of Hebrew religion having physical, ceremonial, moral, and spiritual significance.

Though these senses of clean and unclean can be distinguished with reference to their contexts, they also merge into and illustrate each other; the physical and ceremonial contexts point to a moral state of the worshiper and to a spiritual relationship between God and his people.

The OT vision of a people's relationship with God is along moral and personal lines—God's personal nature being expressed in his giving of the law to Moses. The personal and uniquely consistent character of Israel's Lord made him morally a completely different being from the many gods of pagan cultures. Unlike the Lord, the Baals of the Canaanites were capricious and vicious; nobody expected them to be ethically consistent. Israel's Lord, on the other hand, could be trusted to keep his word (a verbal communication through his chosen prophets). Nobody, not even the high priest or the king, was above the law, which expressed not only God's character but also his sovereign will for the individual and the nation. His moral consistency carried over into his miraculous interventions into history to protect his people, to judge them and their enemies, and to redeem humanity itself.

Cleanness as defined in the book of Leviticus, therefore, was always conditioned by the presence of the personal God who gave the law. As the people sought to approach the Lord, they necessarily did so on his terms and therefore within the framework of the cultic ceremonies he had prescribed. Details of the Levitical ceremonies were designed to illustrate the moral implications of the sinner's approach to God and God's provision for his people to become morally clean in his sight.

The meaning of the Levitical system was stated clearly in the psalmist's words: "Who shall ascend the hill of the LORD? And who shall stand in his holy place? He who has clean hands and a pure heart, who does not lift up his soul to what is false, and does not swear deceitfully" (Ps 24:3-4, RSV). One's state of cleanness depends not only on external actions but also on an internal relationship with God. As a result, the sinner's inability to satisfy the moral demands of a holy God leads to his or her complete dependence on God and on God's provision for satisfying his own demands. That provision was detailed in the law.

PREVIEW
- Early History
- Levitical Prescriptions
- Purification Rites
- New Testament Perspective

Early History

Gentile Religious Background The gentile conscience was no doubt a strong influence on the development of ethnic notions of clean and unclean. The subjective sense of sin's uncleanness is universally encountered in one form or another in the literature of every great religion, whatever explanation is given for it. Many religions have rites of purification based on water and washings. The Hebrews' ritual avoidance of certain objects, some because of their holiness and others because of their unholiness, finds an analogy in the taboos of many primitive religions, including some of those with which the early Hebrews came into contact.

The similarities between the Hebrew and other ancient religions are easily established by superficial comparison. It would be surprising if there were none. Those differences that give biblical religion its distinctive character, however, must be accounted for.

Levitical Prescriptions

Ceremonial and Moral Law The relationship between the external ceremonial details of the Mosaic law and the internally directed moral requirements of such parts of it as the Ten Commandments is one of the fundamental issues of OT theology. It is possible to demonstrate that, throughout the OT, uncleanness and sin are virtually synonymous. In many passages sin is described as uncleanness (e.g., Lv 16:16, 30; the ordeal of the bitter water in Nm 5:11-28; Zec 13:1).

The relationship between ceremonial and moral cleanness can be illustrated from passages mentioning clean hands on the one hand (2 Sm 22:21; Jb 17:9; 22:30) and a clean heart on the other (Pss 24:4; 51:10; 73:13; Prv 20:9). The prophet Isaiah felt convicted of "unclean lips" when he was in God's presence; a purifying coal, perhaps representing forgiveness and atonement, cleansed him (Is 6:5-7). In many passages cleanness represents innocence before God (Jb 11:4; 33:9; Ps 51:7-10; Prv 20:9), and uncleanness is said to come from sin (Ps 51:2; Is 1:16; 64:6).

Causes of Uncleanness From the Mosaic law a number of causes of uncleanness can be derived.

1. Some foods were not to be eaten. Various laws concerning animals make a "distinction between the unclean and the clean and between the living creature that may be eaten and the living creature that may not be eaten" (Lv 11:47, RSV). Permitted food was what was acceptable to God (see also Dt 14:3-21; Acts 15:28-29).

2. Diseases, especially leprosy, produced an unclean state (Lv 13–14). The story of Naaman refers to leprous defilement (2 Kgs 5:1-14). The Gospels refer often to lepers (e.g., Mt 8:1-4; 10:8; 11:5; Lk 4:27). Many swellings, sores, and rashes were included under that heading, including Hansen's disease (modern leprosy). The defilement of disease included all things touched by a diseased person (Lv 14:33-57).

3. Bodily discharges were unclean, and contact with them defiled a person for various periods of time. Emission of semen produced uncleanness until the evening, whether in intercourse (Lv 15:16-18) or inadvertently during the night (Dt 23:10). An unnatural discharge, since it usually indicated disease, made a person unclean for seven days after it had ceased (Lv 15:1-15). Menstruation also produced uncleanness lasting seven days after it ceased (Lv 15:19-24; 2 Sm 11:4). Sexual intercourse during that time made both partners unclean (Lv 15:19-24; 20:18). Contact with the spittle of an unclean person produced uncleanness for a day (15:8).

4. Dead bodies, or even parts of them such as bone, caused uncleanness (Nm 19:16). Persons who touched a dead body were unclean for a month, and only after that period could they celebrate their own Passover if they had missed it (9:6-11). The high priest could not even bury his own parents because of his special ritual responsibilities (Lv 21:10-11; cf. Nm 6:6-7; Hg 2:13; Mt 23:27).

5. Idolatry was the greatest source of spiritual defilement. The entire nation of Israel was defiled because of it (Ps 106:38; Is 30:22; Ez 36:25), as were the Gentiles (Jer 43:12). Consequently, contact with Gentiles was thought to produce defilement. The gospel's universal appeal confronted that conviction (e.g., Jn 4:9; Acts 10:28; cf. Gal 2:11-14). Closely related to the defilement of idolatry was the defilement caused by unclean spirits (Zec 13:2; cf. Mt 10:1; Mk 1:23-27).

Laws about Objects Certain laws illustrate the principle that uncleanness was transmitted much like a contagion. Dead bodies contaminated what they touched, as did dead insects and certain crawling things (Lv 11:29-38). It is interesting that dry grain, running springwater, and water in a cistern were expressly excluded from that law of contamination; perhaps otherwise, starvation would have resulted, dead insects and mice being found in grain and water every day in an agricultural community. Unclean pottery had to be broken, but wooden vessels merely required washing (Lv 15:12). Even uncovered pots in a house where a person had died became unclean (Nm 19:15); everyone who entered the house was unclean.

Because of their idolatrous associations, the possessions of pagans were unclean; therefore, booty taken in war had to be cleansed by fire or washing (Nm 31:21-24). Clothing of wool, linen, or leather could contract unclean "leprosy" from diseased persons and had to be tested. If the leprous spots (greenish or reddish patches) spread after a test period, the garments had to be burned (Lv 13:47-59; 14:33-53).

Laws about Places The land and people of Israel were holy; they could be defiled by the uncleanness of economic oppression or idolatry (Jos 22:17-19; Jer 13:27). Jerusalem was a holy city, but it could be defiled by the sins of its people (Ez 22:2-4; Lam 1:8) or by the blood of its slaughtered inhabitants (Lam 4:15).

The temple could be defiled by unclean persons. It was necessary for Hezekiah to cleanse the temple after Ahaz's idolatrous worship (2 Chr 29:15-19); Nehemiah had to cleanse the rooms in which Tobiah had been living (Neh 13:9). One of the functions of the Day of Atonement was removal of impurities transferred to the temple by the sins of the Israelites during the past year (Lv 16:16-19; 31-33).

An unclean place received the pieces of a leprous house after its demolition (Lv 14:45). The valley of Hinnom became Jerusalem's garbage dump in later years, giving rise to the visions of "Gehenna" as a place of eternal punishment in NT eschatology. Since the Israelite camp was a holy place, care was taken to bury human excrement outside its boundaries (Dt 23:12-14). The value of that simple expedient in preventing disease during military excursions can hardly be exaggerated, since plagues were a great scourge of ancient armies.

Laws about Food Certain kinds of animals were unclean and thus could not be eaten (Lv 11; Dt 14:3-21). Animals that died of old age, disease, or injury, or had been wounded by predators, were unclean. Animals that did not both chew the cud and have a cloven hoof were unclean, a definition that included pigs, camels, badgers, and rabbits among others. Israelites could eat only those fish that had both fins and scales. Birds of prey and scavengers were unclean. All winged insects were unclean except hopping insects (locusts, grasshoppers, and crickets). A large classification of "crawling things" was prohibited, including worms, lizards, snakes, weasels, and mice. In addition to all those was the ancient prohibition against eating blood (Gn 9:4; Lv 17:14-15; Dt 12:16-23; Acts 15:28-29).

Purification Rites

Purification by Lapse of Time Secondary contamination could often be canceled simply by waiting until the evening (Lv 11:24) or for 7, 14, 40, or 80 days. Dead bodies contaminated what they touched for 7 days (Nm 19:11), as did menstruation (Lv 15:19). When a child was born, the mother's unclean condition lasted 7 days for a boy and 14 days for a girl. An additional 33 days for a male child and 66 days for a female were required before the mother could touch any sacred thing.

Purification by Water Contact with unclean things, such as bodily discharges, often required washing of hands and clothing, usually accompanied by the lapse of a day (Lv 15:5-11).

Purification by Ceremonial Substances Ceremonial substances used in purification rites included the ashes of a red heifer mixed with water (Nm 19:1-10), and (in cases of leprosy) cedarwood, scarlet cloth, hyssop, and blood (Lv 14:2-9). When the altar was used in a purification ceremony, only blood was suitable, since the altar was the place of sacrifice for sin (Lv 16:18-19; Ez 43:20).

Purification by Sacrifice Sacrifice was the ultimate source of both ritual and moral purification. All bodily discharges except sexual ones were purified by offerings of doves and pigeons (Lv 15:14-15, 29-30). Childbirth required a lamb and a bird (12:6). Poor people could offer birds in place of an animal (Lv 12:8; 14:21-32; Lk 2:24).

In sacrifice, blood was symbolic of a life given and therefore a death experienced; the uncleanness of disease or sin was thought of as being transferred to the victim, thus removing the uncleanness (Lv 14:7). Sacrificial death, therefore, always had a substitutionary element. Only blood sacrifice could provide the moral cleansing necessary for sin itself; such sacrifice was therefore the basis of all cleansing, including that of disease.

Purification by Fire Some contamination could be removed only by fire, such as contamination of metal pots (Nm 31:22-23). Incest was punishable not only by death but also by burning the bodies (Lv 20:14). Idolatry had to be put away by total destruction of the objects and by burning (Ex 32:20). Cities consecrated to pagan deities were to be burned.

New Testament Perspective The NT did not reject the OT concept of clean and unclean, but rather reinterpreted it in a new context. It stressed in particular the moral sense of the concept as well as the identification of uncleanness with sin.

The Gospels were written in the context of OT law and its Pharisaic and Sadducean accretions. Jesus obeyed the law but was often at odds with the practical casuistry (system) that had grown up around it. Jesus taught that true defilement came from the sinner's heart and not from outside contamination (Mk 7:14-23; Lk 11:39-41). A central element in his teaching was his attack on the ceremonial externalism of the Pharisees. Thus it has been said that Jesus "internalized" the law. It would be more correct to say that he forced attention to the law's demands on people's inner lives.

The intrinsic wickedness of demons is underscored by the use of the term "unclean spirit" throughout the Gospels. In fact, the word "unclean" itself always appears in the Gospels in the context of spirit, a detail that illustrates the NT shift of emphasis from ritual uncleanness to sin and its guilt.

An important episode in the life of the early church came in Acts 10, when God taught the apostle Peter that Gentiles were not unclean in themselves and that Peter was obliged to receive them. The result was Cornelius's conversion.

Jesus' assertion that uncleanness originates in the heart

bore fruit in the apostle Paul's doctrine of Christian freedom. Paul, a Pharisee who could say of himself that he had never broken an external law, came to see that nothing is unclean in itself (Rom 14:14-20). Throughout his epistles, cleanness is the result of obedience of the heart flowing from regeneration; it is based on the cleansing power of the Atonement (see Rom 6:19; 1 Thes 2:3-4, where uncleanness is strictly moral).

Christ's atonement was the final cleansing agent for sin and its moral results (Heb 9:14, 22; 1 Jn 1:7), doing in reality what the blood of bulls and goats only typified. Thus those who are washed in the blood of the Lamb (Rv 7:14) are seen as wearing clean white robes (15:6; 19:8-14). His blood, symbolizing the life given and the death died by the Son at the behest of the Father, satisfies the attributes of personal justice of the triune God. Because the personal character of a righteous Father was vindicated, the personal forgiveness of sinners is morally possible. God can be in history only what he is eternally: he is both just and the justifier of believers in Christ (Rom 3:24-26).

See also Baptism; Circumcision; Uncircumcision; Offerings and Sacrifices; Law, Biblical Concept of; Dietary Laws.

CLEANTHES* Leader of the Athenian Stoic school of philosophy from 269 to 232 BC. Cleanthes' poem "Hymn to Zeus" was adapted in part by another Stoic poet, Aratus, in his own creation "Phaenomena." Centuries later the apostle Paul quoted the fifth line of "Phaenomena" as he spoke to a crowd on the Areopagus in Athens: "We are his offspring" (Acts 17:28, NLT).

CLEMENT Coworker with Paul at Philippi who worked side by side with him in the furtherance of the gospel there (Phil 4:3). Paul includes him in the group of those whose names are written in the Book of Life. Even though some early church fathers identified this Clement with the third bishop of Rome, there is no evidence to substantiate their claims.

CLEMENT*, Epistle of Letter written by Clement of Rome to the church at Corinth around AD 96. This letter is probably the earliest extant Christian epistle outside the NT. Around AD 170, Dionysius of Corinth recorded the earliest claim that Clement was the author of this letter. Origen and Eusebius also identified Clement as the epistle's author.

Clement's epistle to the Corinthians admonishes several younger believers who led a revolt and ousted the leading elders of the Corinthian church. These young men may have wanted a more flexible system of ministry and recognition of their spiritual gifts. They were ascetics and claimed a secret knowledge *(gnosis)* of the faith that was revealed only to the elite.

This letter was sent from the entire Roman church rather than from a single individual. The early churches did not consider themselves to be isolated loners. They knew they were a part of the universal church and were not immune to the events and conditions of their sister congregations. They felt responsible to warn and advise each other.

The Septuagint (the Greek translation of the OT) is cited often in this letter. The heroes of the OT are held up as patterns for Christian conduct, thereby mingling NT and OT themes. The apostle Paul's First Letter to the Corinthians is the pattern for Clement's letter to the same church. Clement closely imitates 1 Corinthians 13 in chapters 49 and 50, and he grounds many of his beliefs in Paul's writings regarding the resurrection and schisms. But Clement's writing is moralistic and ethical and often more akin to Hellenistic Judaism and Stoicism than to Pauline theology. Clement also describes a hierarchical form of ministry and endorses the doctrine of apostolic succession.

Clement quoted extensively from the words of Jesus, using sayings found in Matthew, Mark, and Luke. He also quoted Romans, 1 Corinthians, and Hebrews. Thus, Clement provides important evidence that books that later became part of the NT canon were circulating among the churches by the end of the first century. Clement's letter also provides important evidence for the martyrdom of the apostles Peter and Paul and for Paul's mission to the "western boundary" (Spain?).

CLEMENT OF ROME* A presbyter and bishop in Rome who wrote a letter to the church at Corinth (AD 96), probably the earliest Christian writing outside the NT. Dionysius of Corinth (AD 170) was the first to name Clement as the author of that letter. Origen, an Alexandrian theologian, and Eusebius, the first church historian, identified the writer as the Clement listed in the *Shepherd of Hermas*, a Christian writing from the mid-second century.

See also Clement, Epistle of.

CLEOPAS Follower of Jesus who conversed with him on the way to Emmaus (Lk 24:18). Some identify this Cleopas with the Clopas of John 19:25, but this is unlikely. *See* Clopas.

CLEOPATRA Name of a queen of Egypt and her daughter mentioned in the Apocrypha and in the writings of the Jewish historian Flavius Josephus.

1. Probably the wife of Ptolemy VI Philometor (ruled 181–146 BC). Dositheus, who said that he was a Levite priest and Ptolemy's son, brought the Letter of Purim to Egypt in the fourth year of Ptolemy's reign (Add Est 11:1). This "Letter" probably refers not merely to Mordecai's letter (Est 9:20-22), but to the Greek translation of the book of Esther made by Lysimachus.
2. Probably the daughter of #1 above. Cleopatra was married to Alexander Epiphanes (d. 145 BC) following his conquest of Syria, which he ruled from 150 to 145 BC (1 Macc 10:57-58). Later, as a sign of his anger against Alexander, Cleopatra's father Ptolemy VI Philometor took her from Alexander and gave her to Demetrius Nicantor upon his invasion of Syria (1 Macc 11:8-12). Alexander was killed battling the combined forces of Demetrius and Ptolemy, while Demetrius himself was in captivity in Parthia, so that Cleopatra was married to Demetrius's brother Antiochus VII (Sidetes), who in the absence of his brother had taken the throne of Syria in 137 BC.

CLEOPHAS* KJV form of Clopas, Mary's husband, in John 19:25. *See* Clopas.

CLOAK Translation of several words referring to outer garments. *See* Clothing.

CLOPAS Husband of Mary, one of the women who was present at Jesus' crucifixion (Jn 19:25). From the Greek it cannot be determined if Mary the wife of Clopas was also the sister of Jesus' mother or a different person. One tradition identifies Clopas as the brother of Joseph. Another links him with Cleopas of Luke 24:18, even though "Clopas" is of Hebrew origin and "Cleopas" is Greek. A third possibility is to equate him with

Alphaeus. This is feasible only if James, son of Alphaeus (Mt 10:3; Lk 6:15; Acts 1:13) is the same as James, son of Mary (Mt 27:56; Mk 15:40), and Mary is the same person mentioned in John 19:25. These suggestions are theoretical; it is possible that Clopas, Cleopas, and Alphaeus are all separate individuals.

CLOSED WOMB *See* Barrenness.

CLOTH AND CLOTH MANUFACTURING* Since antiquity, cloth has been made from such natural fibers as flax, wool, cotton, silk, and hair. Linen (spun from flax), wool, and sackcloth (woven from goat's or camel's hair) are the fabrics most frequently mentioned in Scripture. The Bible also refers to silk and cotton.

Fibers for Weaving

Linen Flax was cultivated extensively in the Near East. In Palestine it flourished around the Sea of Galilee. The stalks were gathered into bundles and steeped in water, causing the fibers to separate from the nonfibrous stem. The bundles were then opened and spread out to dry in the sun. Rahab hid Hebrew spies on the roof of her house amid stalks of flax laid out to dry (Jos 2:6). After drying, the stalks were split and combed to separate the fibers for spinning and weaving into linen. Biblical references to flax include Exodus 9:31, Judges 15:14, and Proverbs 31:13.

The type of fabric from which the priestly coats, girdles, and caps (Ex 28:40) were made is not stated, though the mention of linen breeches may imply that most, if not all, of the priestly garments were made of linen. The finest linen, worn by kings and nobles, served as a mark of honor or as a special gift. Joseph was given a garment of fine linen when he was made ruler of Egypt (Gn 41:42). When the Hebrews left Egypt at the time of the exodus, they took with them a high-quality linen and donated it to the tabernacle (Ex 25:4; 35:6). A craftsman who was trained to work in fine linen came from Tyre to work for Solomon on temple hangings (2 Chr 2:14).

Wool Wool was another extremely important fiber in the Near Eastern economy. Wool could come in any shade from creamy yellow to tan or black. Sometimes to obtain pure white wool a sheep was kept wrapped to prevent its fleece from being soiled. Preparation of wool was a home craft in antiquity (Prv 31:13; cf. Ex 35:25). Wool had to be washed thoroughly, dried, and then beaten to detach the fibers and remove the dirt before being carded and spun. Women spun their own yarn and wove garments for their families. Wool was the fabric of seminomadic, sheep-raising people; by contrast, the growing of flax required a more settled lifestyle.

Goat's Hair A thick cloth that was extremely warm as well as waterproof was woven from goat's hair (Ex 35:23, 26). Clothing worn by the poor was often manufactured from goat's or camel's hair. That coarse-haired fabric (sackcloth) on occasions was worn next to the skin as a form of penitence (Neh 9:1; Dn 9:3; Mt 11:21), as a mourning vestment (Gn 37:34; 2 Sm 3:31), or even as a prophetic protest against luxurious living (Rv 11:3).

Cotton, Silk, and Gold Thread The people of Judea would certainly have been aware of cotton during their Persian exile (beginning in 538 BC). Cotton is mentioned once in a description of elaborate hangings in the Persian king's palace (Est 1:6). It is doubtful, however, that cotton was cultivated in ancient Palestine or even found there until after the exile.

Earlier in Israel's history, part of the tabernacle fabric was woven with gold thread, made from thin sheets of beaten gold cut into fine wire strips (Ex 39:3). A wider type of gold wire with a flat surface was used to adorn expensive Palestinian and Syrian garments. An ancient hank of fine gold thread was uncovered during excavations at Dura on the Euphrates River.

Spinning In Bible times a spindle was a slender rounded stick, tapered and notched at one end and weighted at the other end with a "whorl" of clay, stone, glass, or metal to serve as a kind of flywheel. The thread spun at the tapered end was wound on the spindle. Another thin stick, called a distaff, held the fibers to be fed onto the twirling spindle.

Looms and Weaving Weaving is the interlacing of "warp" threads stretched on a loom with threads of "weft" or "woof" passed from side to side over and under the warp. A primitive warp could be stretched around pegs or rods tied to a tree or roof beam and sometimes connected to the weaver's waist.

As weaving technique developed, three types of loom emerged: the horizontal ground loom, the vertical two-beamed loom, and the warp-weighted loom. In a horizontal ground loom the warp was stretched between two wooden beams fastened to the ground by four pegs. Traveling nomads could pull out the pegs and roll up the unfinished weaving on the beams. Delilah wove Samson's hair on a horizontal ground loom (Jgs 16:13-14).

The vertical two-beamed loom had its warp stretched on a rectangular wooden frame. In addition to the two uprights and two warp beams, another beam was often used to maintain the tension of the warp, especially on longer lengths.

The warp-weighted loom, also on a vertical frame, was worked from the top down. The lower edge was weighted with loom weights, often shaped lumps of clay.

The degree of sophistication in weaving techniques in biblical times is seen in the specifications regarding fabrics for the tabernacle and its court. Hangings for the court were to be 50 yards (45.7 meters) long and probably a standard 2 yards (1.8 meters) wide (Ex 27:9-18). The tabernacle veil (26:31) and screen for the entrance (v 36) were to be of "blue and purple and scarlet stuff," probably highlighted or embroidered with linen.

Garments such as the tunic that Jesus wore were woven in one piece with the selvage (edge of the weaving) coming at the neck and hem, the areas of greatest wear. A tunic woven on a narrow loom would be constructed of three pieces.

Cloth Dyes and Dyeing Like the fibers, the dyes used in antiquity were also of animal or plant origin. A red dye was obtained from the body of an insect. Purple came mainly from two kinds of mollusks found in many parts of the eastern Mediterranean seaboard. The purest shade of purple could be obtained from mollusks found on the shore at Tyre, so a large industry developed there (Ez 27:1-3,16). Purple, the most expensive dye, remained the distinguishing color of kings and nobles. The first Christian convert in Europe, Lydia, was a businesswoman who sold the costly purple cloth (Acts 16:14). Yellow was obtained from the petals and flower heads of the safflower. Saffron (orange-yellow) came from the stigmas of the crocus that grew extensively in Syria and Egypt. Green was usually concocted from a mixture of other dyes. In Hellenistic times woad, a plant of the mustard family, was cultivated in Mesopotamia for its blue dye. Indigo was grown in Egypt and Syria. Dyeing in antiquity was often carried out in large vats,

pictures of which have been found in paintings and on pottery. The ruins of structures including vats have been excavated at some Palestinian sites.

See also Dye, Dyeing, Dyer.

CLOTHING Clothing mentioned in the Bible is usually referred to in such general terms as "inner garment," "outer garment," or "tunic." Few descriptions give specific details of costumes or clothing, and it is therefore necessary to rely on paintings, pottery, decorations, statues, and bas-reliefs to show the clothing styles of the period.

Many ancient Near Eastern peoples (including the Israelites) kept flocks of sheep before the discovery of spinning and weaving and used the leather of their hides for clothing. Later, wool plucked from the sheep and from branches on which the fleece had accumulated as the animals brushed past was made into a feltlike fabric. Wool remained one of the most important fabrics for clothing throughout the biblical period.

As the seminomadic Israelite tribes became more sedentary in nature, flax was cultivated. It was woven into linen, which became a commonly used fabric. At the beginning of the middle Bronze Age (c. 2000 BC), fine silks began to be imported from China, and wild silk was produced in some areas of the Near East. Cotton was known in Egypt, but it does not appear to have been produced anywhere in Palestine in the biblical period.

Male Clothing Early in biblical times the loincloth formed an important item of male clothing that was worn by all levels of society. Prior to 2000 BC, a type of loincloth was also the customary piece of clothing for all Egyptians, from the lowliest laborer to the pharaoh. At a later period, however, it appeared only as part of military dress (Ez 23:15). The inner garment (a tunic or shirt) was made of wool or linen. It had openings for the neck and arms, and appears to have had long sleeves, although some styles had half sleeves. It was worn next to the skin and fell either to the knees or, more often, to the ankles, frequently being belted at the waist. The Greek *chiton* ("coat") and the Roman tunic would have been undergarments of a similar character. A man who was wearing nothing except this undergarment was considered "naked." The young man who followed after Jesus at Gethsemane at his arrest was probably attired in this manner (Mk 14:51-52).

Generally speaking, the outer garment, formed out of a square-shaped piece of cloth, was referred to as a cloak or mantle. It had openings for the arms and was draped over one or both shoulders.

A Hebrew man was considered improperly dressed without his cloak, and one was forbidden to demand another's mantle as a loan or pledge. At night, when the other items of clothing were removed, the cloak, which was often made of animal skin or wool, was used as a blanket (Ex 22:26-27; Dt 24:13). Cloaks made of goat's hair or camel's hair, such as John the Baptist wore (Mt 3:4; Mk 1:6), would have been particularly warm at night.

The coat of many colors that Jacob gave to Joseph was probably a striped shirt or tunic made of leather or wool felt. The entire garment may have been bound with a woolen border (Gn 37:3). The garment Hannah made each year for the young Samuel was probably a coat or mantle (1 Sm 2:19).

Cloaks were usually made with a hem; it was this that the woman touched when she came to Jesus for healing (Mt 9:20). The robe that Roman soldiers placed derisively upon Jesus to symbolize his kingship was probably a purple military cloak such as Roman officers commonly wore (Mt 27:28-31; Mk 15:17; Jn 19:2).

The Greeks used the term *himation* for an outer garment, similar to the robe that was placed on the prodigal son (Lk 15:22) when his father celebrated the son's return with his best food, clothing, and jewelry. The cloak that Paul wore (2 Tm 4:13) may well have been a circular style of cape that was popular in the first century AD.

Garments were of different qualities and signified rank or office (Is 3:6). The scribes and prophets wore special mantles symbolic of their professions. Elijah wore a prophet's mantle (1 Kgs 19:13, 19; 2 Kgs 2:8, 13-14). In NT times scribes wore special robes (Mk 12:38; Lk 20:46).

Christ and his disciples probably wore tunics and sandals, and carried moneybags and staffs (Mt 10:9-10; Mk 6:8; Lk 9:3; 10:4). When Roman soldiers divided Jesus' clothing after the Crucifixion (Jn 19:23-24), they cast lots for the inner garment, one woven without any seams and probably made of wool. This was the most valuable of Jesus' items of clothing.

Footwear In Bible times footwear consisted of shoes and sandals, which were an essential part of a person's wardrobe (2 Chr 28:15; Acts 12:8). Occasionally sandals had wooden soles, but usually they were leather. Sometimes they had an enclosed upper front and open back. The upper part was typically made of open strips of leather, and sometimes the sandal merely consisted of a sole with thongs laced around the leg or ankle. A woman's sandals were considered an attractive and fashionable part of her wardrobe (Jdt 10:4; 16:9).

On a long journey through the country, one's sandals might be carried and saved for arrival in the next town, so that they would not be worn out. (Being barefoot in a town or city was a sign of abject poverty.) Since sandals were so open in design, one can easily understand the necessity for the ritual foot washing of a guest.

Shoes were not worn in the temple or on any holy ground (Ex 3:5; Jos 5:15) and were also taken off when a person was in a house. It was customary to remove the sandals at a time of mourning. The shoes that the Israelites wore in their wilderness wanderings did not wear out (Dt 29:5).

See also Cloth and Cloth Manufacturing.

CLOUD, Pillar of Supernatural phenomenon of God's presence that guided the Israelites through the wilderness. *See* Pillar of Fire and Cloud; Shekinah; Wilderness Wanderings.

CNIDUS Port city situated off the southwest corner of Asia Minor, mentioned as a harbor passed by the apostle Paul en route to Italy (Acts 27:7). During the second century BC, it had a Jewish colony (1 Macc 15:23). The island on which Cnidus was built is now joined to the mainland by a sandbar.

COAL Translation of several Hebrew or Greek words in the Bible referring primarily to charcoal (mineral coal is not found in Palestine). The glowing embers from a wood fire were used for heating (Is 47:14; Jn 18:18), cooking (Is 44:19; Jn 21:9), and by blacksmiths (Is 54:16). Coals from the altar were used in religious ritual (Lv 16:12; Is 6:6-7).

Figuratively, the term is used in descriptions of God's infinite brightness and glory (2 Sm 22:9, 13), of his revelation (Ps 18:8), of divine judgment (140:10) and of

creatures associated with God's throne (Ez 1:13; 10:2). In other metaphorical passages, glowing coals stand for life (2 Sm 14:7, RSV), the breath of a huge beast ("leviathan," Jb 41:21), and the risk of being "burned" by sexual sin (Prv 6:28).

COAT Translation of several words referring to various garments. *See* Clothing.

COAT OF MAIL Piece of armor, covering the body from the neck to the girdle, probably made of leather with small interlaced metal places sewn onto it. *See* Armor and Weapons.

COCK* Adult male of the domestic fowl. *See* Birds (Fowl, Domestic).

COCKATRICE* KJV rendering of serpent, adder, and viper in Isaiah 11:8; 14:29; and 59:5, respectively. *See* Animals (Snake).

COCKLE* KJV term for "foul weeds" in Job 31:40. *See* Plants (Thistle, Thorn).

CODEX* Earliest form of the book, consisting of sheets of papyrus or vellum folded and bound together and enclosed between two wooden leaves or tablets. *See* Writing.

COELESYRIA Literally, the term means "hollow Syria." It was used somewhat loosely in referring to parts of the Jordan Valley. This designation is not found in the Bible but is mentioned a number of times in the Apocrypha, by itself in 1 Maccabees 10:69 and together with Phoenicia elsewhere (1 Esd 2:17, 24, 27; 4:48; 6:29; 7:1; 8:67; 2 Macc 3:5, 8; 4:4; 8:8; 10:11). It was the name commonly given to the approximately 100-mile-long (161-kilometer) valley that stretches between the Lebanon and Anti-Lebanon mountains after the time of Alexander the Great, but it is apparent from the use of the term by ancient writers that it did not always indicate the same territory.

COFFIN *See* Burial, Burial Customs.

COINS Pieces of metal used and accepted as a medium of exchange. A coin has a specific weight and bears some type of authentication to make it easily recognizable. The word "coin" originally referred to a wedge-shaped die or stamp used to "strike" the metal blank. The first coins may have been minted in the late eighth century BC.

PREVIEW
• Earliest Coins in Palestine
• Coinage from the Maccabees to Herod Agrippa I
• Roman Coins in New Testament Times

Earliest Coins in Palestine Not until the time of Darius the Great (Darius I of Persia, 521–486 BC) did an official government-sponsored coinage become current in Palestine. Those earliest coins were oval-shaped gold darics, along with some silver coins.

"Dram" is another term for the Persian gold daric. It is mentioned in Ezra 2:68-69 (KJV), where Zerubbabel's caravan offered gold darics amounting to $30,000 toward rebuilding the temple. This passage is the first mention of an actual coin in the Bible.

Almost at the same time that the Persian coins became current in Palestine, the widely popular silver tetradrachmas (four-drachma pieces) of Athens began to find their way to the mercantile centers of the Phoenician, Israelite, and Philistine coasts. Archaeologists have unearthed them in hoards throughout the eastern Mediterranean region. They continued to be used through the Persian period, which lasted until the Persian Empire was conquered by Alexander the Great in 334–330 BC. The coin was thick and heavy in appearance, but being of high-quality silver, it was in great demand for international commerce. Presumably Greek merchants found they could obtain the most desirable Asiatic imports in exchange for that particular form of currency.

The silver didrachma, or half-drachma, in general use in the Greek Empire from the fourth century BC, continued through Roman times. After Alexander's conquests, of course, Greek coins were used throughout the Macedonian Empire from present-day Yugoslavia to Pakistan. They were almost certainly employed for business purposes in Judea, for example.

The shekels of the Phoenician trade centers of Tyre and Sidon, which had contributed substantially to the money supply in the Persian period, continued to be accepted in Judea even after the Alexandrian conquest. Typical of Sidon was a silver shekel portraying the battlements and walls of Sidon's harbor, with a ship lying at anchor and two prancing lions in the foreground. A typical Tyrian shekel showed the god Baal robed and wearing a tiara. He was riding a hippocamp (winged horse with the tail of a fish) on the sea, with a fish or dolphin beneath. The reverse showed an Egyptian-type owl facing right, plus a shepherd's crook and flail, both royal insignia in Egypt. The stater (or tetradrachma) found by the disciple Peter in a fish's mouth and used to pay the temple tax for himself and Jesus may have been a Tyrian coin (Mt 17:27; RSV "shekel").

The talent, which represented a certain weight of gold or silver, was a common medium of exchange before the development of coinage. During the Maccabean period, John Hyrcanus saved the city of Jerusalem from destruction in 133 BC by paying a ransom from a 900-year-old hoard stored in David's sepulcher. Three thousand talents of silver were sent to the Seleucid king Antiochus VII Sidetes in return for his promise to withdraw his troops. Treasure plundered from the temple by the Romans in AD 66 is recorded as amounting to 17 talents. In gold talents that sum would represent the equivalent of the purchase price of about 15 large houses in a modern Western city.

Coinage from the Maccabees to Herod Agrippa I

Even though a native Jewish dynasty assumed the government of the Holy Land, it was many years before any indigenous Jewish coinage was minted. Presumably the inhabitants continued to use the coinage of Tyre and Egypt and of the Seleucid Empire for their commercial transactions. It was formerly supposed that silver shekels bearing images of the chalice and pomegranate cluster dated from the reign of Simon Maccabeus (142–134 BC); more recent archaeological discoveries prove that those coins date from the first Jewish revolt (AD 66–70).

When the time came to issue the first Jewish coins, the die makers faced several problems. No mint was available, and no local people were skilled in design or die sinking. Coins current in the Near East at that time, which showed a high degree of design and craftsmanship, each bore the portrait head of a ruler or a god. For the Jews to make such coins would have meant contravening the second commandment, "You shall not make for yourself a graven image" (Ex 20:4, RSV). Not until well into Roman times was a coin struck in Palestine bearing a portrait head of a Roman emperor.

The earliest coinage of the Hasmonean dynasty (the regnal name of the Maccabees) was the small bronze lepton (plural, lepta) of John Hyrcanus I (134–104 BC), son of Simon Maccabeus. The obverse showed two cornucopias with a pomegranate between them. That image symbolized the fertility that God had granted to the land. The reverse contained an inscription within a wreath, "John the high priest and the community of the Jews." Small bronze lepta from the reign of Alexander Janneus, son of Hyrcanus I, have been found in great numbers. They were evidently much in demand for transactions at the temple, where money changers converted the gentile currency of visiting worshipers into the more acceptable Jewish money. Undoubtedly Hasmonean lepta were the coins Jesus scattered over the pavement of the Court of the Gentiles when he overturned the tables of the money changers (Mt 21:12; Jn 2:15). The lepton, or "mite," of bronze or copper, worth $\frac{1}{400}$ of a shekel, was mentioned by Jesus on another occasion. He praised a widow's gift of two mites to the temple treasury with the comment that the rich "contributed out of their abundance; but she out of her poverty has put in everything she had, her whole living" (Mk 12:44, RSV).

Herod I came to power in Judea under the patronage of Mark Antony and secured the allegiance of the pro-Hasmonean Jews by marrying Mariamne, granddaughter of Hyrcanus II, in 38 BC. Herod was empowered to strike his own bronze coins. Although he had a free hand to introduce innovations, Herod's lepta followed tradition quite faithfully. The lepta carried an anchor with letters meaning "Of King Herod." The reverse bore the double cornucopias with a pomegranate (or poppy) between them. Herod also minted a large bronze coin with what appears to be a Macedonian helmet on the obverse and a slender tripod on the reverse, along with an inscription of Herod's name. Other designs he employed included wheat, eagles, and wreaths. He issued no silver coinage, relying instead on the available supplies of silver coins from Tyre, Syria, Asia Minor, Greece, and Rome.

After Herod's death in 4 BC, his son Herod Archelaus assumed control. Lepta from that period bore a hanging cluster of grapes with a Greek inscription, and on the reverse a two-plumed Macedonian helmet. Grapes were an allusion to Israel as the Lord's vine (Is 5).

When Herod Antipas began his rule, also in 4 BC, he had no authority in Judea or Samaria. That portion of the former Jewish kingdom was placed under the control of Roman governors, or procurators, appointed directly by the emperor himself. Most familiar of the Roman procurators of Judea was Pontius Pilate (AD 26–36). His bronze coinage showed some bold innovations; his designs included representations of instruments used in the Roman religion such as the augur's wand (resembling a shepherd's crook in shape) and a ladle used in connection with broth prepared at sacrifices. The reverse bore a wreath enclosing the regnal date of AD 30–31. The two lepta put into the temple treasury (Lk 21:2) could have been lepta issued by Pilate or his predecessor. More likely, however, they were the Hasmonean lepta of Hyrcanus or Janneus, which were free of any taint of pagan Roman influence.

Herod Agrippa I (AD 37–44), grandson of Herod the Great, continued the family tradition of ingratiating himself with the Roman overlords. Many of Herod Agrippa's lepta have been found, showing a conical tasseled umbrella (perhaps symbolizing his royal protection of the people of Palestine) plus a Greek inscription indicating his reign. The reverse showed a bound cluster of three wheat ears and bore the regnal year as the legend.

Roman Coins in New Testament Times The Roman "as" came into circulation about 348 BC as a bronze coin bearing the figure of an animal. The coin was named after the Roman one-pound weight, equivalent to 12 ounces (340 grams) in our modern system. At the time of Christ's birth, the Roman "as" minted for use in the Asiatic provinces bore the head of the emperor Augustus, with a laurel wreath on the reverse. A smaller bronze quadrans, or quarter "as," was also minted by the Romans.

Another bronze coin found in Greek and Roman currency was the assarion, first minted in the first century BC but still in use in the Christian period. One type was stamped with a winged sphinx, with an amphora on the reverse. It is still debated whether the coin described as a "farthing" in the KJV was in fact a Greek assarion or a Roman "as" or quadrans. The coin is mentioned four times in the NT, most familiarly in the question "Are not two sparrows sold for a farthing?" (see Mt 5:26; 10:29; Mk 12:42; Lk 12:6, RSV "penny"). There is no doubt that the KJV translators decided to make the coin seem more familiar to their readers by using the name of the smallest copper coin in circulation in England at that time.

The word translated "penny" in the KJV is the Greek form of "denarius," the normal daily wage for a laborer in NT times. In the parable of the laborers in the vineyard, for example, the master agreed to pay each man "a penny" for his day's work (Mt 20:2, KJV; RSV "a denarius"). "Two pence" was the amount paid to the innkeeper by the good Samaritan (Lk 10:35, KJV). Because of the influence of the Roman denarius on British currency, the English penny has always been represented by the initial letter of its Roman equivalent.

When the denarius, or "penny," is recognized as a normal day's wage, the astonishment of Jesus' disciples when they were expected to find food for 5,000 people is better understood. They exclaimed that "two hundred pennyworth" of food would not feed such a crowd (Jn 6:7, KJV); that sum represented more than six months' work.

As might be expected, the silver and gold coinage current in Palestine during the time of Christ and for the remainder of the first century AD came primarily from Rome. The larger silver coins, however, that are referred to as tetradrachmas or staters in the NT came from Egypt, Phoenicia, or Antioch. The silver coin most frequently mentioned in the NT was the Roman denarius or the Greek drachma. Since few drachmas have been found in excavations dating from the first century, it is possible that the term was used in popular speech to refer to the denarius (plural, denarii), which was approximately the same size as the average Greek drachma. Actually, few Greek cities were permitted by their Roman overlords to continue minting drachmas.

Caesar Augustus issued a decree for all the Roman world to be enrolled (Lk 2:1-2) in an empire-wide census just about the time that Jesus was born (6 or 5 BC). During his long reign (27 BC–AD 14), Augustus authorized a large variety of denarii. They generally carried his likeness on their obverse with the inscription "Augustus, son of the divine one" (that is, son of Julius Caesar, who had been voted divine honors by the Roman Senate).

In Matthew 22:19 Jesus asked those trying to trick him with a question to show him a coin used to pay the government tax. They handed him a denarius bearing the portrait and inscription of Caesar (Mt 22:21). That coin could have been a denarius of Augustus, who had died some 16 years before, or of Tiberius (AD 14–37), who was then on the throne. The silver denarius of Tiberius read "Tiberius Caesar Augustus, son of the divine Augustus." The reverse showed the high priestess of the vestal order, flaming torch in hand, seated on her throne facing right. The title "pontif(ex) maxim(us)" referred to Tiberius rather than to the priestess.

See also Minerals and Metals; Money; Money Changer.

COL-HOZEH The father of Shallum, who was ruler of the district of Mizpah (Neh 3:15). Col-hozeh, the son of Hazaiah in Nehemiah 11:5, may be another person.

COLOR The OT and NT have no exact word for "color," although the word appears several times in our English Bibles. The words translated "color" have quite different meanings in the original languages.

The word most frequently translated "colour" in the KJV literally means "eye" and suggests "appearance" (Lv 13:55; Nm 11:7; Prv 23:31; Ez 1:4, 7, 16, 22, 27; 8:2; 10:9; Dn 10:6). Only Leviticus 13:55 retains the translation "color" in the RSV. Other words translated as "color" in the RSV refer to facial appearance (Dn 5:6-10; 7:28), fabrics of variegated colors (Prv 7:16; Ez 17:3; 27:24), stones (1 Chr 29:2), and breastplates (Rv 9:17). Joseph's "coat of many colours" (Gn 37:3, KJV) and Tamar's "garment of divers colours" (2 Sm 13:18-19, KJV) were either long-sleeved robes or richly ornamented tunics that served as a mark of preferred status.

In the NT, a word that means "pretense" is used archaically in Acts 27:30 and was interpreted as "colour" by the KJV translators. They also added the word "colour" to Revelation 17:4, evidently to clarify the meaning.

Though many colors are mentioned in the Bible, colors are not particularly singled out for emphasis. Natural colors are seldom mentioned in descriptions. Colors that appear frequently and that are most carefully differentiated are manufactured colors, especially dyes.

Colors Mentioned in the Bible Because the Hebrews perceived color differently than we do in Western culture, it is sometimes difficult to translate precisely the various Hebrew words denoting colors. Thus there is often a wide variation in translations of such words in English Bibles. To provide a base for comparison, this article will follow the RSV except as noted.

Colors mentioned most often in the OT and NT are the following:

"Black" is the translation of five words in the OT and one in the NT, expressing varying degrees of darkness. The words describe the color of lambs (Gn 30:32-33, 35, 40), hair (Lv 13:31, 37; Sg 5:11; Mt 5:36), skin (Jb 30:30), horses (Zec 6:2, 6; Rv 6:5), the sky (1 Kgs 18:45; Is 50:3; Jer 4:28), the day (Jb 3:5; Mi 3:6), the darkened sun (Rv 6:12), and an invading army (Jl 2:2). Job's "blackness" (Jb 30:28) has been understood as disease or sadness.

"Blue" probably refers to a blue-purple dye obtained from Mediterranean mollusks. A popular color, it was considered less desirable in antiquity than "royal" purple. Both dyes were produced in Tyre, which at one time had a monopoly on the manufacture of blue and purple dye (2 Chr 2:7, 14; Ez 27:24). Ships of Tyre had awnings of blue and purple (Ez 27:7). Blue was used in the tabernacle fabrics (Ex 26:1; Nm 4:6-9), the priests' garments (Ex 28:5-6), in Solomon's temple (2 Chr 2:7, 14), and in the Persian court (Est 1:6; 8:15). Blue is not mentioned in the NT.

"Crimson" is the English translation of three different Hebrew words. This red color of varying shades was derived from certain insects. The word describes certain fabrics in Solomon's temple (2 Chr 2:7, 14; 3:14) and was used figuratively to describe sin (Is 1:18). The word translated "crimsoned" to describe garments from Bozrah (63:1) probably means "vivid colors" rather than a specific hue.

"Gray," a color found only in the OT, is used exclusively to describe old age—as in gray hair or gray-headed (Gn 42:38; 44:29-31; Dt 32:25; 1 Sm 12:2; 1 Kgs 2:6, 9; Jb 15:10; Ps 71:18; Prv 20:29; Is 46:4; Hos 7:9). A different word used to describe dappled gray horses (Zec 6:3) probably means "spotted" or "speckled."

"Green" translates seven words in the OT and two in the NT. Most of the words refer to vegetation and are descriptive of the fresh or moist condition of plants rather than their color. The following are described as "green": plants (Gn 1:30), trees (1 Kgs 14:23), branches (Jb 15:32), pastures (Ps 23:2; Jl 2:22), herbs (Ps 37:2), olive trees (Ps 52:8; Jer 11:16), thorns (Ps 58:9), leaves (Jer 17:8), grass (Mk 6:39; Rv 8:7), and wood (Lk 23:31). In addition to various plants, a dove's wing (Ps 68:13), a couch (Sg 1:16), and a righteous person (Ps 92:14) are also described as "green." Idolatrous worship practices took place under "every green tree" (Dt 12:2; 2 Kgs 16:4; Is 57:5; Jer 2:20; Ez 6:13), although the word actually describes the luxurious growth of the leaves rather than their color.

Another word, "greenish," is derived from one of the OT words for "green" and refers to disease (Lv 13:49) and fungus that forms on the walls of houses (14:37).

"Purple" was the most highly valued dye in the ancient world. Encompassing shades varying from actual purple to red, it was obtained from mollusks of the Gastropoda class. The first people to use the dye were perhaps the ancient Phoenicians, whose name may come from a Greek word meaning "bloodred." At any rate, the Phoenicians monopolized the purple industry for many years. Some fabrics were described as being purple: those used in the tabernacle (Ex 25:4; 26:1), in the garments of the priests (28:5-8, 15, 33), in Solomon's temple (2 Chr 2:7), in the upholstery of Solomon's chariot (Sg 3:10), and in decorations of the Persian court (Est 1:6). Purple was customarily worn by wealthy people and royalty (Jgs 8:26; Prv 31:22; Dn 5:7). Mordecai was rewarded with a garment of purple (Est 8:15). Daniel was given a similar garment (Dn 5:29). It was worn by Assyrian soldiers (Ez 23:6). Jeremiah described idols that were robed in blue and purple garments (Jer 10:9). Ships of Tyre had awnings of blue and purple (Ez 27:7), and purple dye was an item of trade between Tyre and the people of Aram (v 16). It is used once to describe the color of hair (Sg 7:5).

References to purple in the NT are fewer than in the OT but affirm the continued economic importance of the dye. Purple clothing denoted wealth (Lk 16:19). Jesus was robed in purple by Roman soldiers (Mk 15:17, 20; Jn 19:2, 5; cf. Mt 27:28, "scarlet"). The purple and scarlet garment of the harlot Babylon symbolized royal rank (Rv 17:4). Lydia of Thyatira was a seller of purple fabrics (Acts 16:14).

"Red" frequently refers to the natural color of certain objects mentioned in the Bible: skin (Gn 25:25), pottage (v 30), the eye (49:12, though the word used here may mean "sparkling" or "dark"), a sacrificial heifer (Nm 19:2), water (2 Kgs 3:22), the face of a weeping person (Jb 16:16), wine (Prv 23:31), the eyes of one drinking wine (v 29), clothing (Is 63:2), a shield (Na 2:3), and horses (Zec 1:8; 6:2). It is used figuratively to describe sin (Is 1:18). A leprous disease (Lv 13:49), a spot on the skin (vv 19, 24, 42-43), and fungus on the wall of a house (14:37) were discolored with a reddish hue. The Red Sea is mentioned frequently in the OT (Ex 10:19; 15:4), but the Hebrew words thus translated actually mean "Sea of Reeds." However, in the NT the Greek word is actually the word "red" (Acts 7:36; Heb 11:29).

In the NT, red is used to describe the color of the sky (Mt 16:2-3), a horse (Rv 6:4), and a dragon (12:3).

"Scarlet," a brilliant red hue derived from certain insects, was used for fabrics and yarns and was highly valued in the ancient world (Rv 18:12). It is difficult to distinguish between "scarlet" and "crimson" in the Bible. A scarlet thread was bound to the hand of Zerah at birth (Gn 38:28, 30). The word describes certain fabrics in the tabernacle (Ex 25:4; 26:1, 31, 36; 27:16), the priests' garments (28:5-8, 15, 33), rope (Jos 2:18, 21), clothing (2 Sm 1:24; Prv 31:21; Jer 4:30), lips (Sg 4:3), and soldiers' uniforms (Na 2:3). Some kind of scarlet material was used during the ratification of the covenant at Sinai (Heb 9:19), for the cleansing of a leper (Lv 14:4-6) and of a house (vv 49-52), for covering the articles on the table of the bread of the Presence (Nm 4:8), and for the ritual of the red heifer (19:6). Matthew described Jesus' robe at his trial as scarlet (Mt 27:28). The woman of Revelation 17:3-4 was dressed in purple and scarlet and seated upon a scarlet beast. The luxury associated with Rome is suggested by the description of clothing of purple and scarlet (Rv 18:16). Scarlet, like crimson and red, is also used figuratively of sins (Is 1:18).

"White" translates a number of words found in the Bible. It is generally the color of natural objects such as goats (Gn 30:35), hair (Lv 13:10; Mt 5:36; Rv 1:14), diseased skin (Ex 4:6; Lv 13:4, 17), manna (Ex 16:31), snow (2 Kgs 5:27), milk and teeth (Gn 49:12), horses (Zec 1:8; 6:3; Rv 6:2; 19:11), a donkey (Jgs 5:10, KJV; RSV "tawny"), wool (Ez 27:18), special stones (Rv 2:17), light (Mt 17:2), clouds (Rv 14:14), and fields ready for harvest (Jn 4:35). It is used to describe the color of curtains (Est 1:6), clothing (Est 8:15; Eccl 9:8; Dn 7:9; Mk 16:5; Rv 3:5, 18; 4:4), the garments of angels (Jn 20:12; Acts 1:10), and a throne (Rv 20:11). It is used figuratively to describe cleansing from sin (Ps 51:7; Is 1:18; Dn 12:10) and the appearance of princes (Lam 4:7).

See also Cloth and Cloth Manufacturing; Dye, Dyeing, Dyer.

SYMBOLIC USES OF COLORS
It is difficult to determine what the different colors symbolized in the ancient world. Some interpreters find no significance at all in the colors found in the Bible, whereas others do. According to Philo, a Greek-speaking Jewish writer who lived at the time of Christ, white represented the earth; purple, the sea; blue, the air; and scarlet, fire—reminiscent of the four basic elements of earthly matter in Aristotle's philosophy. Ancient rabbis thought they could identify nations with the colors of Zechariah's horses (e.g., red stood for Babylon because that empire had shed much blood). The Scofield Reference Bible (1909) interprets the colors in the tabernacle symbolically: gold represented death; silver, redemption; bronze, judgment; blue, heaven; purple, royalty; and scarlet, sacrifice.

It is probably unwise to insist that each color in the tabernacle hangings symbolized something. Only a few colors are given explicit significance in the Bible; further, no rule says that a color given symbolic meaning in one usage will always retain that meaning. The following colors frequently have symbolic meaning in the Bible: red, war and bloodshed (2 Kgs 3:22); black, gloom or mourning (Is 50:3); white, purity or righteousness (Is 1:18); green, prosperity and health (Ps 92:14); purple, royalty or honor (Mk 15:17). Those colors have maintained similar symbolic associations to the present day.

COLOSSAE*, COLOSSE Ancient city in Asia Minor, located in the southwestern part of present-day Turkey, and remembered primarily for the apostle Paul's letter to the church there (Col 1:2). Colosse was near the Lycus River, a tributary of the Meander. The city flourished during the sixth century BC. According to Herodotus, an ancient Greek historian, when the Persian king Xerxes came to Colosse, it was a city of great size. Another Greek historian, Xenophon, related that Cyrus the Great, founder of the Persian Empire, had passed Colosse still earlier on his way to Greece.

Colosse was situated in the region known as Phrygia and was a trading center at a crossroads on the main highway from Ephesus to the east. In Roman times relocation of the road leading north to Pergamum brought about both the growth of Laodicea, a city 10 miles (16 kilometers) away, and Colosse's gradual decline. Colosse and Laodicea shared in the wool trade. Thus, the name Colosse was derived from a Latin name *collossinus,* meaning "purple wool."

In the apostle Paul's time Colosse was a small city with a mixed population of Phrygians, Greeks, and Jews. During his extended stay in Ephesus, Paul may have taught Jews and Greeks who lived in Colosse (Acts 19:10). Epaphras, a Colossian, visited Paul in Rome and informed him about the condition of the church at Colosse (Col 1:7; 4:12), then was later imprisoned with Paul (Phlm 1:23). Others from the Colossian church included Philemon, Apphia, Archippus, and Onesimus, a slave who became a Christian (Phlm 1:16). Subsequent history is silent on the church at Colosse. The city was weakened under Islamic rule and was eventually destroyed in the 12th century.

COLOSSIANS, Letter to the NT epistle, one of four "prison letters" attributed to the apostle Paul. As with Ephesians, Philippians, and Philemon, Paul said he was in prison when he wrote Colossians (Col 4:3, 10; cf. Eph 3:1; 4:1; 6:20; Phil 1:12-14; Phlm 1:9-10). He sent three of the letters to churches in Asia Minor and linked them with his colleague, Tychicus (Col 4:7-9; Eph 6:21-22). That seems to indicate that he wrote them at approximately the same time and that Tychicus delivered them.

PREVIEW
- Author
- Date, Origin, and Destination
- Background
- Purpose and Teaching
- Content

Author Though the tradition that Paul wrote Colossians stands on solid ground, many scholars today debate its authorship. Reasons for their doubts fall into two main categories—theology and style.

First, some scholars question Paul's authorship on theological grounds. Development of certain major theological themes in Colossians differs from the way they are set forth in the undisputed letters of Paul. In Colossians the doctrine of Christ is developed on the basis of a hymn about Christ in 1:15-20. There he is seen as the "firstborn of all creation"; all things owe both their origin and continuing existence to him. In him resides all the fullness of deity. His death is interpreted not as a victory over sin, law, and death, but as a triumph over the cosmic authorities and powers.

To some scholars that suggests that the Christology in Colossians is much more "exalted" than in any of the undisputed letters. Yet Paul characteristically regarded Christ as highly exalted. He declared Christ to be creator

of all things (1 Cor 8:6) and set forth his lordship over the whole cosmic order by citing another hymn (Phil 2:6-11). Further, the kind of statements made about Christ in Colossians was demanded by the situation that had arisen in the city of Colosse. The heresy that had broken into the congregation required such statements.

Colossians also appears to teach doctrines about "the last things" and baptism that are somewhat different from the doctrines in the undisputed letters. In Corinthians, Paul based his teaching about the last things on the Jewish doctrine of the "two ages." Judaism taught that in "this age" the world is under the tyranny of the evil powers, but that in "the age to come" God would set it free. In contrast, Paul's teaching was unique in holding that the age to come had already come in the advent of Christ—though not in its fullness. Paul saw the time between the first and second advents of Christ as a period of conflict. Christ "must reign until he has put all his enemies under his feet" (1 Cor 15:25). Christ by his mission is liberating the present age from the evil powers, but the conflict will not end until his second coming. Therefore Christians live in hope of his future appearing. That future element of hope is not stressed in Colossians (though see 3:1-4); rather, the emphasis is on a hope already present in heaven (1:5).

The doctrine of baptism in Colossians has been influenced by the stress on the realized aspect of hope. In his Letter to the Romans, Paul taught that baptized Christians live by faith in the resurrected Lord and are filled with hope for their future resurrection (Rom 6:1-11). In Colossians he declared that baptized believers have not only died with Christ but have already been raised with him (Col. 2:12-13; 3:1). The hope for the future is not for resurrection but for the manifestation of the life that is already hidden with Christ in God (3:2-3). Further, in Romans Paul stated that in baptism Christians have died to sin, so they no longer need serve it. Colossians, on the other hand, states that in Christ, Christians died to what can literally be translated as the "rudiments of the universe" (2:20). Many interpret that phrase to mean the basic religious teaching of the world. In Colossians, however, a strong case can be made that the phrase means "the elemental spirits of the universe" (RSV). In either case, the emphasis, if not the meaning, differs from Romans.

Such theological matters have led many to believe that Paul could not have written the Letter to the Colossians. Rather, they see the letter as the product of a disciple of Paul who wrote at a later time. It should be noted, however, that the differences are of perspective or emphasis, not differences that result in contradiction.

The second reason for questioning Paul's authorship of Colossians is literary, pertaining to vocabulary and style. The brief letter uses 34 words that occur nowhere else in the NT. Also, common Pauline terms are absent from passages where they might logically be expected. Further, the style of the letter, though similar to Ephesians, is notably different from other undisputed letters of Paul. In those letters the thoughts are usually developed in an argumentative style similar to the discussions of the Jewish scribes. Colossians is marked by stylistic features that one finds in hymns, liturgies, and early Jewish and Christian catechisms. But some obvious differences in theological perspective and literary style do not force one to conclude that someone other than Paul wrote Colossians.

Date, Origin, and Destination The date of Colossians depends on where Paul was imprisoned when he wrote. Traditionally scholars have held that all

Papyrus Manuscript of Colossians Colossians 1:5-13, Chester Beatty Manuscript II, late second century—P46

four "prison letters" came from Rome. If so, Paul would have written them between AD 60 and 62.

The book of Acts indicates three places where Paul was imprisoned: Philippi, Caesarea, and Rome. Paul, writing 2 Corinthians before either of the last two imprisonments, suggested that he had already been in prison many times (2 Cor 11:23). Ephesus is a likely place for one of those imprisonments (cf. Acts 19–20; 1 Cor 15:32; 2 Cor 1:8-10). Consequently, an increasing number of scholars name that city as the probable place where Paul wrote the

prison letters. If that is correct, Paul wrote Colossians sometime between AD 52 and 55. But the general consensus is that all the Prison Epistles were written in Rome, thus leading to AD 60–62 as the date of Colossians.

Background To identify the teaching that endangered the church at Colosse is a difficult task. The problem is not insufficient data but the opposite. Historical research has uncovered a wealth of information about the religious beliefs and practices that proliferated in the first-century Roman world. Asia Minor was a particularly fertile region for religions. Many people even belonged to more than one religious sect, and it was common to select ideas and practices of several religions. Christians were not exempt from those tendencies.

Colossian Heresy Paul gave no formal definition of the Christian heresy in Colosse. Rather, he dealt with a number of issues without precisely identifying them. If one is given only the answers to a number of questions, however, it may be possible to recreate the questions from them. The reader of Colossians must attempt to define the tenets of the false teaching on the basis of Paul's response to them.

Some scholars have concluded that the heresy rose out of the flesh-spirit dualism that became characteristic of later Greek and oriental Gnosticism. The later Gnostics taught that the material order of things is evil, so only what is free from matter is good. Other scholars, noting Paul's injunctions against certain food laws, festivals, sabbaths, and external circumcision, have concluded that the false teaching rose out of Jewish beliefs. Since the tendency to blend a variety of ideas was so prevalent, both theories are probably true.

Paul regarded the heretical teaching as a "philosophy" based on human tradition (2:8). His prayer for the Colossians (1:9-11) and certain other remarks (1:26-28; 2:2-3) suggest that he was countering the notion that for certain people "philosophy" led to some special, perhaps magical, understanding. That philosophy was based on "the rudiments of the universe." This phrase is open to two main lines of interpretation. First, the basic meaning of "rudiments" is "objects that stand in a row or series," such as the letters of the alphabet. It can readily be extended to mean rudimentary principles or basic teaching. Such is the meaning in Hebrews 5:12, where the term refers to the "first principles" of God's Word. Second, the Greeks applied the phrase to the four physical substances they thought made up the world: earth, water, fire, and air.

A first-century BC Greek text, referring to the followers of the philosopher Pythagorus, uses several of the same words that Paul applied to the Colossian heresy. A messenger of the highest gods carries the soul through all the elements of the world, from the lowest of earth and water to the highest. If the soul is pure, it remains in the highest element. If not, it is returned to the lower ones. The required purity is achieved by self-denial and certain cultic observances. The upper air contains the sun, moon, and stars, regarded as gods who control human destinies. In addition, the atmosphere around the earth is filled with spirit powers who are to be revered. In that way, the elements of the world become associated with the gods and spirit-powers who hold all people captive and determine their fate. With the help of magical knowledge and cultic ceremonies, human beings could not only escape from the destiny imposed by the spirit powers but even manipulate them for their own advantage.

To summarize, the phrase "rudiments of the universe" can refer either to basic religious teaching or to the spirit powers of the universe. The statements in Colossians make the latter meaning probable. Through his cross, Christ has triumphed over the rulers and authorities and has publicly exposed them (2:15). They do not rule the world order; he does (1:16-20). The divine "fullness" dwells in Christ, not in a remote deity (1:19; 2:9). The spirit powers are under the authority of Christ (2:10) and owe their existence to him (1:16). The "worshiping of angels" (a practice probably including homage paid to

heavenly powers) is so wrong that it may have disastrous consequences (2:18).

Main Features of the Heresy A major dogma of the Colossian philosophy seems to have asserted that God was remote and inaccessible. Two factors point in that direction. First, the fascination with the angels and spirit-powers just discussed seems to indicate that the remote God was accessible only through a long chain of intermediaries. Christ seems to have been regarded as one of them, perhaps enthroned above them. Second, the philosophy evidently held to a dualism that separated the high God from creation. To approach him, seekers first had to be delivered from the evil influence of the material order.

How could human beings short-circuit or manipulate the angelic star powers who hindered them from reaching the high God? How could they be delivered from the enslaving power of matter? The philosophy evidently offered magical wisdom and insight as the answer. Through worshiping angels and observing special days and cultic practices (2:16-18), seekers could placate or please the intermediaries and get through to the divine "fullness." By voluntary self-abasement, self-denial, and the achievement of visions (2:18, 21-23) they could escape the pull of the material order. The practice of self-denial through abstinence from food and possibly from sexual relations ("touch not" in 2:21) seems to have been limited to special seasons for attaining the "vision" of God. Otherwise, the philosophy seems to have permitted freedom to engage in libertine practices (3:5-11).

Purpose and Teaching A warning in Colossians 2:8 points to the main purpose of the Colossian letter. The readers are admonished against following anyone who "makes a prey of you by philosophy and empty deceit, according to human tradition, according to the elemental spirits of the universe, and not according to Christ" (RSV). A false teaching was settling in and threatening the health of the congregation, so Paul wrote Colossians to counter it.

Paul approached the heresy by contrasting its teachings with the correct teaching his readers had received in the traditions previously delivered to them, probably by Epaphras (1:7; 4:12-13). God through Christ had qualified them to be uniquely his own people, his church (1:12-14). The proponents of the false teaching threatened to disqualify the Colossians from that favored position by persuading them not to hold fast to Christ, the Head of the church (2:18-19). Consequently, the traditions Paul cited mainly teach about Christ or about the church. The former are primarily related to the impressive hymn about Christ (1:15-20; referred to again in 2:9-10, the latter mainly associated with baptism).

Christ In 1:15-20 Christ is celebrated as the preexistent Creator of all and as the divine Redeemer of all. The "all" has cosmic dimensions. It includes the earth and the heavens, the visible and the invisible, the church and the universal powers. All things, including the heavenly powers, owe their existence, sustenance, and destiny to Christ. He is not to be regarded as one of the heavenly mediaries. He is the preeminent one in whom all the fullness of God dwells (1:19; 2:9) and in whom human beings find fulfillment (2:10).

Paul gave special attention to the significance of Christ's death. In the hymn of Colossians 1 he explained the reconciling work of Christ by the phrase "making peace through the blood of his cross" (1:20). He contrasted the past and present experiences of the readers.

Formerly they were alienated from God both in attitude and behavior. Now they are reconciled "in his body of flesh by his death" (1:21-22). As a consequence of that reconciliation, God transforms human character.

The death of Christ not only brings about restored relationships between individuals and God, but it also liberates them from the hostile intentions of the "principalities and powers." Those powers seem to be demonic agents who bring accusations against human beings—accusations grounded on a "certificate of indebtedness" based on ordinances (laws). Paul proclaimed to the Colossians that God had removed the ground of those accusations, nailing it to the cross (2:14), and that in the cross he had publicly exposed and triumphed over the accusers (v 15). Christ's death was not a tragedy but a life-changing, liberating triumph over sin and evil powers.

The Church The church is the "body" of Christ (1:18, 24), over which Christ is the Head and source of life (2:19). It is a community that the Father has qualified to participate in the heavenly inheritance with the saints; he has delivered it from the powers of the evil age and made it participate in the power of the age to come, "the kingdom of his beloved Son" (1:13). The church, therefore, should not live in fear of the "rulers" and "authorities," but should participate in Christ's triumph over those hostile powers.

Content In writing to the Colossians, Paul followed a standard letter form of salutation, thanksgiving, prayer, main body, and concluding remarks. The salutation (1:1-2) carries greetings to the church from himself and Timothy. Then follows a statement of thanksgiving for the good condition of the community (1:3-8) and a prayer that the Colossians may be filled with a knowledge of God's will, which will result in worthy conduct (1:9-11).

The first part of the body of the letter summons the Colossians to praise and then quotes and applies the great hymn about Christ (1:12-23). Specifically, the first part begins with a confessional thanksgiving to the Father for calling them to be his own unique people (1:12-14). A hymn follows, celebrating Christ as the sovereign Creator and Redeemer of all that exists (1:15-20). The Colossians are participants in the results of Christ's reconciling ministry (1:21-23).

The second part of the body of the letter describes Paul's apostolic ministry (1:24–2:5). His was the task of making known the mystery of God concerning Christ to the Gentiles in general (1:24-29) and to the churches of Colosse and Laodicea in particular (2:1-5).

The third part of the body of the letter introduces Paul's primary concern for the Colossian congregation: they are to follow the received tradition about Christ (that is, the teachings about Christ they had first accepted), and not to fall prey to the current false teaching (2:6-23). They are to walk in the light of the received tradition (vv 6-7), and they are warned against the false philosophy (v 8). The hymn of 1:15-20 is again referred to, here stressing Christ's divine lordship (2:9-10) and proclaiming his victory over the principalities and powers (vv 11-15). Because of such a Christ, the Colossians are exhorted not to submit to the regulations and tenets of the false teaching (vv 16-23).

The fourth part of the body of the letter summons the church to a life befitting Christians (3:1–4:6). Those who have been raised with Christ are to seek the things that are above (3:1-4). That means they are to put off the traits and attitudes listed in a catalog of vices (vv 5-11) and to put on the traits and attitudes listed in a catalog of virtues (vv 12-14). In worship they are to conduct themselves in a unified and orderly way (3:15–4:1). The so-called "household code" concerning marriage, children, and slavery (3:18–4:1) appears in a context dealing with worship (3:15-17; 4:2-6). The most pressing admonitions in the code are addressed to wives and slaves, groups that especially would crave the equality promised in the gospel (Gal 3:28; note Col 3:11). So Paul probably used the code to call for order in the public worship service.

Paul concluded his letter by first stating that Tychicus and the recently converted slave, Onesimus, would inform the church about his circumstances (4:7-9), and then added a series of greetings (vv 10-18).

See also Acts of the Apostles, Book of the; Apostle, Apostleship; Colossae, Colosse; Paul, The Apostle.

COMFORTER* KJV translation of the Greek word *parakletos* in John 14:16, 26; 15:26; and 16:7. *See* Paraclete.

COMMAND, COMMANDMENT *See* Commandment, The New; Commandments, The Ten.

COMMANDMENT, The New Christ's commandment for Christians to love each other. The phrase "new commandment" occurs four times in the NT, all in the writings of John (Jn 13:34; 1 Jn 2:7, 8; 2 Jn 1:5). Initially, it was a command given by Jesus to his disciples on the night of his arrest: "I am giving you a new commandment: Love each other. Just as I have loved you, you should love each other" (Jn 13:34, NLT). The same command occurs elsewhere (Jn 15:12, 17; Rom 13:8; 1 Pt 1:22; 1 Jn 3:11, 23; 4:7, 11-12) but is not called "new" in those passages.

Love as a Commandment Jesus had already commanded his disciples to love their enemies (Mt 5:43-45) and to love their neighbors as themselves (Lk 10:25-37). The "new commandment" demanded that Christians love each other. In no sense did it overrule the other two love commands. Jesus' command to love those within the church was intended to produce a compelling testimony to those outside the church. It would offer them demonstrable proof (1) that his followers were Christlike in their love toward one another; (2) that the basis for vital human community could be found "in Christ"; and (3) that, by extension, what Jesus said about himself and his work was really true (Jn 13:35; 17:21-23).

Jesus chose the word used to describe the OT law, giving similar authority to his new commandment. In fact, the law included commands to love (Lv 19:18, 34; Dt 10:19). The apostle Paul thought of love as the "law of Christ" (Gal 6:2), and James called the love command "the royal law" (Jas 2:8) and "the perfect law of liberty" (1:25; 2:12).

The word "commandment" had another meaning as well. Many Jews in Jesus' day wrongly supposed that the commandments were given in order that men, by obeying them, could show themselves worthy of God's blessing (Rom 8:3; Gal 3:2). Jesus made it clear, however, that love was a natural result of God's blessing, not a necessary condition for it. For Jesus, the commandment expressed how one who is already living in the joy of God's blessing should act. Disciples were commanded to love in the same sense that branches were "commanded" to bear fruit: the branch by abiding in the vine, the Christian by abiding in Christ (Jn 15:4).

What Made It New? The character of the new commandment comes from the "new covenant" (Jer 31:31-34; Lk 22:20; 1 Cor 11:25), which Jesus inaugurated at the Last Supper. Under the new covenant, God "writes" his law on the hearts of believers (Heb 10:16). That is, he actively works in them in the person of the Holy Spirit (Ez 36:27; 2 Cor 3:3), and gives them a new willingness to obey him (Rom 8:4; Gal 5:16). The new commandment of love is the all-embracing, single requirement of the new covenant (Rom 13:8, 10; Gal 5:14). Obedience, therefore, is a gift, because "love is from God; and every one who loves is born of God" (1 Jn 4:7, NASB). It is the fruit of faith (3:23) and part of the gospel itself (v 11).

The close relationship between the new covenant and the new commandment may explain partly why the command to love was called "new." Christ's incarnation inaugurated a new age. "The darkness is disappearing," John wrote, "and the true light is already shining" (1 Jn 2:8, NLT). Anticipating his ascension into heaven (Jn 13:33-35), Jesus left one inclusive commandment to preserve his disciples in the new age until its consummation at the Judgment Day (Jn 5:28-29; 1 Jn 4:17). Obedience to the new commandment was supposed to identify them as Jesus' disciples during his absence (Jn 13:35; 17:21-23). The love command was thus new in the sense that it had a special function in the new age.

What made the age new was that Jesus Christ's coming had revealed God the Father with an unprecedented and incomparable clarity (Jn 1:18; 10:30; 17:6-8). No prophet had ever been able to say, "Anyone who has seen me has seen the Father" (14:9, NIV). Therefore Jesus' demand that the disciples love each other "as I have loved you" (13:34) was, by every human standard, new and astonishing. No human had ever loved perfectly like Jesus (v 1). To follow his example of love, then, was a new commandment. The greatness of Jesus' love moved him to "lay down his life for his friends" (15:13, NIV). Accordingly, John drew the conclusion that "we ought to lay down our lives for our brothers" (1 Jn 3:16, NIV). It follows that love means never shutting one's heart against another Christian in need (v 17), but rather rejoicing to sacrifice one's temporal good for another's blessing.

See also Commandments, The Ten; Law, Biblical Concept of.

NEW BUT NOT NEW
Why does 1 John 2:7-8 stress that the new commandment is *not* new but old? The phrase "from the beginning" (also found in 1 Jn 2:24; 3:11; 2 Jn 1:6) no doubt refers to the beginning of the readers' Christian experience, that is, when they first heard the word of the gospel. Thus John meant that he was not teaching anything beyond the original message. His command was the same old "new commandment" that they heard when they first believed. He probably stressed its "oldness" because of false prophets in the churches (1 Jn 4:1) who were leading people into heresy by new and different teaching (2 Jn 1:9). The best protection against that deception was to obey what Jesus taught "of old," including the new commandment (vv 6-7).

COMMANDMENTS, The Ten List of commands given by God to Moses. The Ten Commandments are stated twice in the OT; first in the book of Exodus (20:2-17), in a passage describing God's gift of the commandments to Israel, and second in Deuteronomy (5:6-21), in the context of a covenant renewal ceremony. Moses reminds his people of the substance and meaning of the commandments, as they renew their covenant allegiance to God. In the original language, the com-

mandments are called the "Ten Words" (from which comes the name Decalogue). According to the biblical text, they are "words," or laws, spoken by God, not the result of human legislative process. The commandments are said to have been written on two tablets. This does not mean that five commandments were written on each tablet; rather, all ten were written on each tablet, the first tablet belonging to God the lawgiver, the second tablet belonging to Israel the recipient. The commandments pertain to two basic areas of human living: the first five concern relationships with God, the last five, relationships between human beings. The commandments were given first to Israel in the making of the covenant at Mt Sinai, shortly after the exodus from Egypt. Though the date of the Sinai covenant cannot be fixed with certainty, it was probably around 1290 BC. In order to understand the commandments, it is necessary first to understand the context in which they were given.

PREVIEW
•The Context of the Commandments
•The Meaning of the Commandments
•The Principle of the Commandments

The Context of the Commandments The commandments are inseparable from the covenant. The making of a covenant between God and Israel at Sinai was the formation of a particular relationship. God made certain commitments to Israel and in return imposed certain obligations upon Israel. Although Israel's obligations are expressed in detail in a mass of precise legal material, they are given their most precise and succinct expression in the Ten Commandments. The commandments set down the most fundamental principles of all Hebrew law, and the detailed laws contained in the Pentateuch are for the most part applications of the principles to particular situations. Thus, the role of the Ten Commandments in ancient Israel was to give direction to a relationship. They were not to be obeyed simply for the sake of obedience, as though obedience accumulated some kind of credit. Rather, they were to be obeyed in order to discover the fullness and richness of life in a relationship with God.

The commandments in ancient Israel were not an ethical code or compilation of advice on the fundamentals of morality. The covenant was between God and a nation; the commandments were directed toward the life of that nation and its citizens. Consequently, the initial role of the commandments was similar to that of criminal law in a modern state. Israel was a theocracy, a state whose king was God (Dt 33:5). The commandments provided guidance to the citizens of that state. In addition, to break a commandment was to commit a crime against the state and the ruler of that state, God. Thus, the penalties were severe, for the breaking of the commandments threatened the covenant relationship and the continued existence of the state. This state context is important for understanding the commandments in their initial form.

The Meaning of the Commandments The commandments begin with a preface (Ex 20:2; Dt 5:6) that identifies the lawgiver, God, who gave the commandments to a people with whom he already had a relationship. The lawgiver is the God of the exodus, who redeemed his people from slavery and granted them freedom. The preface is vital, for it indicates that God's gift of law was preceded by an act of love and grace. The commandments were given to a people who had been redeemed; they were not given in order to achieve redemption. There are some variations in the manner of numbering the commandments. According to some systems, the preface is identified with the first commandments. It seems preferable, however, to understand the opening words as a preface to all ten commandments. In the notes on the Ten Commandments that follow, there is first an explanation of the original meaning, then some indication of the contemporary meaning.

First Commandment: Prohibition of Worshiping Gods Other Than the Lord (Ex 20:3; Dt 5:7) The first commandment is in negative form and expressly prohibits the Israelites engaging in the worship of foreign deities. The significance of the commandment lies in the nature of the covenant. The essence of the covenant was a relationship, and the essence of relationship, from the biblical perspective, is faithfulness. God's faithfulness to his people had already been demonstrated in the exodus, as indicated in the preface to the commandments. In turn, God required of his people, more than anything else, a faithfulness in their relationship with him. Thus, though the commandment is stated negatively, it is full of positive implications. And its position as first of the ten is significant, for this commandment establishes a principle that is particularly prominent in the social commandments (six through ten).

The contemporary significance of the commandment is in the context of faithfulness in relationship. At the heart of human life, there must be a relationship with God. Anything in life that disrupts that primary relationship breaks the commandment. Foreign "gods" are thus persons, or even things, that would disrupt the primacy of the relationship with God.

Second Commandment: Prohibition of Making Images (Ex 20:4-6; Dt 5:8-10) The second commandment prohibits the Israelites from making images of the Lord. To make an image of God, in the shape or form of anything in this world, is to reduce the Creator to something less than his creation and to worship the created instead of the Creator. The temptation for Israel to worship God in the form of an image must have been enormous, for images and idols flourished in all the religions of the ancient Near East. But the God of Israel was a transcendent and infinite being, and could not be reduced to the limitations of an image or form within creation. Any such reduction of God would be so radical a misunderstanding that the "god" worshiped would no longer be the God of the universe.

In the modern world, the shape of the temptation has changed. Few are tempted to take power tools and shape from wood an image of God. Nevertheless, the commandment is still applicable, and the danger against which it guards is always present.

Third Commandment: Prohibition of the Improper Use of God's Name (Ex 20:7; Dt 5:11) There is a popular understanding that the third commandment prohibits bad language or blasphemy; however, it is concerned with the use of God's name. God had granted to Israel an extraordinary privilege; he had revealed to them his personal name. The name, in Hebrew, is represented by four letters, YHWH, which are variously rendered in English Bibles as LORD, Yahweh, or Jehovah. The knowledge of the divine name was a privilege, for it meant that Israel did not worship an anonymous and distant deity but a being with a personal name. Yet the privilege was accompanied by the danger that the knowledge of God's personal name could be abused. In ancient Near Eastern religions, magic was a common practice. Magic involved the use of a god's name, which was believed to control a

god's power, in certain kinds of activity designed to harness it for human purposes. Thus, the kind of activity that is prohibited by the third commandment is magic, namely, attempting to control God's power, through his name, for a personal and worthless purpose. God may give, but must not be manipulated or controlled.

Within Christianity, the name of God is equally important. Through God's name is access to God in prayer. The abuse of the privilege of prayer, involving calling upon the name of God for some selfish or worthless purpose or swearing falsely by it, is tantamount to the magic of the ancient world. In both, God's name is abused and the third commandment is broken. Positively, the third commandment is a reminder of the enormous privilege of knowing God's name, a privilege not to be taken lightly or abused.

Fourth Commandment: Requirement to Observe the Sabbath (Ex 20:8-11; Dt 5:12-15) This commandment, once again, has no parallels in ancient Near Eastern religions; furthermore, it is the first of the commandments to be expressed in a positive form. While most of life was characterized by work, the seventh day was to be set aside. Work was to cease and the day was to be kept holy. The holiness of the day is related to the reason for its establishment. Two reasons are given, and though at first they appear different, there is a common theme linking them. In the first version of the commandment (Ex 20:11), the Sabbath is kept in commemoration of Creation; God created in six days and rested on the seventh day. In the second version (Dt 5:15), the Sabbath is observed in commemoration of the exodus from Egypt. The theme linking the two versions is creation: God not only created the world but also "created" his people, Israel, in redeeming them from Egyptian slavery. Thus, every seventh day throughout the passage of time, the Hebrew people were to reflect upon Creation; in so doing, they were reflecting upon the meaning of their existence.

For most of Christianity, the concept of "sabbath" has been moved from the seventh to the first day of the week, namely Sunday. The move is related to a change in Christian thought, which is identified in the resurrection of Jesus Christ on a Sunday morning. The change is appropriate, for Christians now reflect each Sunday, or "Sabbath," on a third act of divine creation, namely the "new creation" that is established in the resurrection of Jesus Christ from the dead.

Fifth Commandment: Requirement to Honor Parents (Ex 20:12; Dt 5:16) The fifth commandment forms a bridge between the first four, concerned primarily with God, and the last five, concerned primarily with human relationships. On first reading, it appears to be concerned with family relationships only: children are to honor their parents. Although the commandment establishes a principle of honor or respect in family relationships, it is probably also related to the responsibility of parents to instruct their children in the faith of the covenant (Dt 6:7), so that the religion could be passed on from one generation to another. But instruction in the faith required an attitude of honor and respect from those who were being instructed. Thus, the fifth commandment is concerned not only with family harmony but also with the transmission of faith in God throughout subsequent generations.

With the fifth commandment, there is little need to convert its meaning into contemporary relevance. At a time in which so much education is undertaken beyond the confines of the family unit, the commandment serves a solemn reminder, not only of the need for harmonious family life, but also of the responsibilities of religious education which rest upon both parents and children.

Sixth Commandment: Prohibition of Murder (Ex 20:13; Dt 5:17).
The wording of this commandment simply prohibits "killing"; the meaning of the word, however, implies the prohibition of murder. The word used in the commandment is not related primarily to killing in warfare or to capital punishment, both of which are dealt with in other portions of the Mosaic law. The word could be used to designate both murder and manslaughter. Since manslaughter involves accidental killing, it cannot be sensibly prohibited; it, too, is dealt with in other legislation (Dt 19:1-13). Thus, the sixth commandment prohibits murder, the taking of another person's life for personal and selfish gain. Stated positively, the sixth commandment preserves for each member of the covenant community the right to live.

In the modern world, a similar statute prohibiting murder exists in almost all legal codes, having become a part of state law, in addition to purely religious or moral law. Jesus, however, pointed to the deeper meaning implicit in the commandment. It is not only the act, but also the sentiment underlying the act, that is evil (Mt 5:21-22).

Seventh Commandment: Prohibition of Adultery (Ex 20:14; Dt 5:18)
The act of adultery is fundamentally an act of unfaithfulness. One or both persons in an adulterous act are being unfaithful to another person or persons. Of all such crimes, the worst is that which signifies unfaithfulness. It is for this reason that adultery is included in the Ten Commandments while other sins or crimes pertaining to sexuality are not included. Thus, the seventh commandment is the social parallel to the first commandment. Just as the first commandment requires absolute faithfulness in the relationship with the one God, so the seventh requires a similar relationship of faithfulness within the covenant of marriage.

The relevance of the commandment is apparent, but again Jesus points to the implications of the commandment for the mental life (Mt 5:27-28).

Eighth Commandment: Prohibition of Theft (Ex 20:15; Dt 5:19)
The eighth commandment establishes a principle within the covenant community concerning possessions and property; a person had a right to certain things, which could not be violated by a fellow citizen for his or her personal advantage. But while the commandment is concerned with property, its most fundamental concern is human liberty. The worst form of theft is "manstealing" (somewhat equivalent to modern kidnapping)—that is, taking a person (presumably by force) and selling him or her into slavery. The crime and the related law are stated more fully in Deuteronomy 24:7. The commandment is thus not only concerned with the preservation of private property but is more fundamentally concerned with the preservation of human liberty, freedom from such things as slavery and exile. It prohibits a person from manipulating or exploiting the lives of others for personal gain.

Just as the sixth commandment prohibits murder, so the eighth prohibits what might be called "social murder," that is, the cutting off of a man or woman from a life of freedom within the community of God's people.

Ninth Commandment: Prohibition of False Witnessing (Ex 20:16; Dt 5:20)
The commandment is not a general prohibition against lies. The wording of the original commandment sets it firmly in the context of Israel's legal system. It prohibits perjury, or the giving of false testimony within the proceedings of the law court. Thus, it establishes a principle of truthfulness and carries implications with respect to false statements in any context. Within any nation, the courts of law must be able to operate on the basis of true information. If law is not based on truth and righteousness, then the very foundations of life and liberty are undermined. If legal testimony is true, there can be no miscarriage of justice; if it is false, the most fundamental of human liberties are lost. Thus, the commandment sought to preserve the integrity of Israel's legal system while guarding against encroachments on personal liberties.

The principle is maintained in most modern legal systems—for example, in the taking of an oath before giving evidence in court. But in the last resort, the commandment points to the essential nature of truthfulness in all interpersonal relationships.

Tenth Commandment: Prohibition of Coveting (Ex 20:17; Dt 5:21)
The tenth commandment is curious in its initial context. It prohibits the coveting, or desiring, of persons or things belonging to a neighbor (that is, a fellow Israelite). To find such a commandment in a code of criminal law is unusual. The first nine commandments prohibited acts, and a criminal act can be followed by prosecution and legal process if detected. But the tenth commandment, in contrast, prohibits desires, or covetous feelings. Under human law, it is not possible to prosecute upon the basis of desire, since proof would be impossible. While the crime involved in the tenth commandment could not be prosecuted within the limitations of the Hebrew system, it was nevertheless known by God, the "Chief Judge." The genius of the commandment lies in its therapeutic nature. It is not enough merely to deal with crime once it has been committed; the law must also attempt to attack the roots of crime.

The root of almost all evil and crime lies within the self, in the desires of the individual. Thus evil desires are prohibited. If covetous desires are gradually eliminated, then natural desires may be directed toward God.

The Principle of the Commandments The relevance of each commandment is understood in the underlying principle of the whole Decalogue. The principle of the whole is the principle of love, the heart of Israel's religion. God loved Israel and called them in love. In return, he imposed one commandment upon Israel that superseded all others: "You shall love the LORD your God with all your heart, and with all your soul, and with all your might" (Dt 6:5, RSV). That is the central commandment of Israel's religion. How to love the invisible, intangible God is partly explained in the Decalogue. For the person who loves God, the Ten Commandments provide guidance; they point to a way of life that, if lived, reflects love for God and leads to a deeper experience of God's love. Therefore, the Ten Commandments continue to be a central part of Christianity. Jesus repeated the commandment to love from Deuteronomy 6:5 and he called it "the first and greatest commandment" (Mt 22:37-38). Consequently, the Ten Commandments still serve as a guide for the Christian community.

See also Civil Law and Justice; Law, Biblical Concept of.

COMMUNICATION
The act of transmitting a message. Fire, light, and smoke signals were probably the earliest methods of communicating over any distance. The Babylonians were the first to employ a primitive heliograph system (reflected sunlight) for signaling over short distances. A classic use of fire beacons was related

by Aeschylus, a Greek dramatist, who described the news of the fall of Troy being relayed to Clytemnestra of Mycenae (c. 1084 BC) by a dozen or more fires lighted on mountaintops. Similarly, the Lachish letters mention the use of fire signals to coordinate Israel's defense against the Babylonians in 587 BC. One letter concludes, "Let my lord know that we are watching for the fire signals of Lachish according to the signs my lord has given, because we do not see Azekah" (see Jer 6:1; 34:7). Later, fire signals were communicated from lighthouses such as the famous one at Alexandria, Egypt.

Projected sounds have been used as a means of communication for thousands of years. Around 550 BC, Cyrus of Persia built a network of towers from which a soldier shouted a message to a soldier in a nearby tower. According to legend, Alexander the Great had a giant megaphone that could carry a voice several miles. The historian Severus said that the Romans had brass speaking tubes to aid in defense along the northern wall in England. The Hebrews used the *shofar*, a ram's horn trumpet, to announce the new moon, the beginning of the Sabbath, and the approach of danger (Jos 6:4; Jgs 7:16; Hos 8:1). Also, drum tattoos were used in communication. Even today Ashanti drummers in Ghana can render high and low tones that correspond to the tonal values of their language.

Archaeological excavations have uncovered thousands of ancient business and family letters written on clay tablets. As early as 2000 BC the Assyrians maintained an informal postal service with eastern Anatolia (Asia Minor), using the caravans that frequently went between them. Later, Assyrian roads used by the army were also traveled by royal messengers of an efficient government mail service. A network of postal officials stationed in key population centers supervised the couriers and the mail. Clay tablets listing the place-names along a given route and the distances between them served as travel guides. Many royal letters of Assyria and other parts of the Middle East now help to reconstruct ancient history.

After the Persians ascended to power, they expanded the Assyrians' postal service. The Persian "royal road" was built for government messengers, but it was open to all. It extended more than 1,600 miles (2,574 kilometers) from Sardis in Asia Minor to Susa, the Persian capital located near the head of the Persian Gulf (Est 3:13; 8:10). Royalty and officials traveling that highway found rest houses and inns about 15 miles (24 kilometers) apart, forts at strategic points, and ferries for river crossings. Ordinary travelers, averaging 18 miles (29 kilometers) a day, would spend three months traveling the full length of the road. The Persian dispatch service, however, relaying messages on fresh mounts between regular stages, probably traversed the same distance in two or three weeks. Describing a Persian messenger, the Greek historian Herodotus in the fifth century BC reported that neither snow nor rain nor heat nor gloom of night prevented the swiftest possible completion of their appointed rounds.

At the same time as the Persians, the Chou dynasty in China had built up an efficient postal system. By the third century BC, the Han dynasty of China and the Ptolemies of Egypt were operating the closest thing to a modern postal system that the ancient world was to know. A system of communication, necessary to rule the large Roman Empire, was devised in the reign of Caesar Augustus (27 BC–AD 14). The idea for the system came after the Romans annexed Egypt in 30 BC. The Roman system did not stress speed or regularity, and although the mail moved speedily over short distances, it could take weeks over long distances or over water. Usually the mail system of the emperors did not benefit the ordinary public; rather, it was an added tax burden. Wealthy families had their own slaves deliver mail, businesses employed letter carriers, and the poor asked traveling friends to carry messages.

A letter written by Christian leaders in Jerusalem to the churches of Asia Minor was delivered by the apostle Paul and Barnabas (Acts 15:22-29). Later, Paul requested Timothy (1 Thes 3:2), Tychicus (Col 4:7, 9), and Epaphroditus (Phil 2:25; 4:18) to serve as messengers.

One means of local communication was the Roman *album* (Latin for "white"), a white-painted public bulletin board displayed in the center of a city on which messages were painted in black.

See also Travel.

COMMUNION*, Holy *See* Lord's Supper, The.

COMPASSION Quality of showing kindness or favor, of being gracious, or of having pity or mercy. In the Bible, God is described as being like a compassionate father to those who revere him (Ps 103:13). Jesus Christ exemplified God's compassion in his preaching and healing (Mt 9:36; 14:14), in his concern for the lostness of humanity (Lk 19:41), and finally in his sacrifice on the cross (Rom 5:8). The church is to demonstrate compassion as one facet of the love Jesus commanded (Mt 5:4-7; Jn 13:34; Jas 2:8-18; 1 Jn 3:18). In scriptural usage compassion is always both a feeling and the appropriate action based on that feeling.

In the OT, compassion describes one aspect of God's covenantal relationship with his people. One of the Hebrew words translated "compassion" is derived from a root word meaning "womb," thus comparing God's love with maternal love. God's compassion, however, went beyond simply feeling the emotion; it was always demonstrated by definite acts that testified to his covenant with Israel. In spite of Israel's rebellions, God still had compassion on his people (2 Kgs 13:23; 2 Chr 36:15; Ps 78:38), as well as on all his creation (Ps 145:9). When Israel was chastised, the nation often feared that God had permanently withdrawn his favor (Ps 77:9; Is 27:11; 63:15; Jer 13:14; 21:7; Hos 13:14). Yet God's compassion would revive, and he would restore his people (Dt 30:3; Ps 135:14; Is 14:1; 49:13; 54:7-8; Jer 12:15; 30:18; Mi 7:19).

In the NT, Jesus Christ, the Son of God, exactly reflected the Father's compassion in his dealings with a fallen humanity. Jesus healed diseases and infirmities, cast out spirits, empowered others, and sent them out to do likewise. He fed hungry people and, in response to a mother's grief, raised her only son from the dead. Following Jesus' example, Christians are to show compassion in dealing with others. Jesus set forth the example in the parables of the Good Samaritan, who had compassion on a wounded traveler (Lk 10:33), and the Prodigal Son, whose father had compassion on him when he returned home (15:20).

The apostle Paul listed a number of qualities that the Colossian church "as God's chosen ones" was to incorporate; the first was compassion (Col 3:12). It was to be an integral part of the concept of Christian community. The Greek word means literally "to be moved in one's bowels." The term points to the very core of one's inner feelings, much as the term "heart" does today. One's intense inner feelings should always lead to outward compassionate acts of mercy and kindness.

CONANIAH

1. Levite and chief officer who supervised tithes, contributions, and the dedicated things given to the temple during the reign of Hezekiah (2 Chr 31:12-13).

2. One of the chief Levites during the time of King Josiah (2 Chr 35:9); perhaps identifiable with Jeconiah in 1 Esdras 1:9.

CONCISION* KJV translation in the text of Philippians 3:2, meaning "mutilation of the flesh."

CONCUBINAGE*, CONCUBINES Practice of a man cohabiting with a woman (concubine) who is regarded only as his sexual partner or as a secondary wife in his household, of lower station than his primary wife. Concubinage was practiced in many ancient cultures, especially in Mesopotamia, where the king maintained a harem and where a private citizen might have one or two concubines in addition to his primary wife. Both types of concubinage are referred to in the Bible. A concubine was often a slave or part of the booty of war (Jgs 5:30).

A man might have a concubine simply as an economical form of marriage, since no dowry, or bride-price, was required. A concubine could add to a man's prestige by giving him two wives and thus an increased capacity for children. Such offspring were normally delivered onto the knees of the legal wife, thus establishing their legitimacy as family members. The concubine was also another servant to add to the man's work force.

In the patriarchal period, concubinage was customary (Gn 22:24; 35:22; 36:12), especially when the primary wife was childless (Gn 16:1-3; 25:5-6; 1 Chr 1:32). A concubine could exercise certain rights and secure recognition and inheritance for her offspring (note Gn 49:1-28, where the sons of Bilhah and Zilpah were included along with the sons of Leah and Rachel; cf. Gn 35:22-26). The custom was not suppressed by the Mosaic law, which must have included concubines in its treatment of multiple wives (Dt 17:17; 21:15-17).

Concubinage continued through the period of the judges. Gideon had a concubine (Jgs 8:31), as did an unnamed man of Levi's tribe (Jgs 19). Abuse of that man's concubine by men from Benjamin's tribe caused a bloody civil war (Jgs 20–21). During the period of Israel's monarchy, the luxury of concubines could be afforded only by kings such as Saul (2 Sm 3:7), David (5:13; 15:16), Solomon (1 Kgs 11:3), and Rehoboam (2 Chr 11:21). Royal harems existed in many other cultures of that time, including Egypt, Persia (Est 2:14), and Babylon (Dn 5:2-3, 23).

Concubines were thus a legitimate part of many ancient cultures, even when a society acknowledged the superiority of monogamous marriage. Concubinage was fostered by a desire for prestige and a large family, but could at times degenerate into a license for sexual freedom (cf. Eccl 2:8). Concubinage was part of the contemporary Greek and Roman cultures, but it was not in keeping with the teachings of Jesus (Mt 19:1-9).

See also Civil Law and Justice; Family Life and Relations; Marriage, Marriage Customs.

CONDUIT* Water tunnel or channel. In the OT the Hebrew word can mean rivulets in the ground made by rain (Jb 38:25, "channel"; Ez 31:4, "stream") or a simple trench such as Elijah dug around the altar in his encounter with the prophets of Baal, a Canaanite fertility god (1 Kgs 18:31-38).

A water tunnel was constructed during King Hezekiah's reign to bring water from the Gihon Spring, once located outside the walls of Jerusalem, to inside the city proper ("pool," 2 Kgs 18:17; 20:20; Neh 2:14; Is 7:3; 22:9-11; 36:2). The mouth of the spring was sealed and its water diverted into the city through the conduit to keep Israel's enemies from using the spring during a siege of the city. That tunnel expanded a tunnel begun by earlier inhabitants of the city, the Jebusites. David and his men may have entered Jerusalem through that first tunnel to overthrow the Jebusites (2 Sm 5:8).

See also Architecture; Siloam, Pool of.

CONEY* Small, rabbitlike animal declared unclean in Leviticus 11:5 and Deuteronomy 14:7 (KJV). *See* Animals (Badger).

CONFECTION*, CONFECTIONARIES* KJV rendering of perfumer in Exodus 30:35 and 1 Samuel 8:13. *See* Perfumer.

CONFESSION Admission, especially of guilt or sin; also, a statement of religious belief. "To confess" can mean to agree, to promise, or to admit something.

Two types of confession occur in the Bible. First, individuals confess that they have sinned and are therefore guilty before God, often confessing a particular sin (Lv 5:5; 1 Jn 1:9). In such confession one agrees or acknowledges that he or she has broken God's law (Ps 119:126), that its penalty is justly deserved (Rom 6:23), and that in some specific way God's standard of holiness has not been met (Lv 19:2; Mt 5:48).

In OT times the high priest would confess the sins of the whole nation (Lv 16:21); the nation of Israel was expected to confess when it had rebelled against the law of God (Lv 26:40; 2 Chr 7:14). Pious Jews were quick to confess; Daniel, Ezra, and Nehemiah confessed their nation's sins, agreeing with God that his punishment of the people (including themselves) was just, yet praying for God's mercy and deliverance (Dn 9:20; Ezr 10:1; Neh 1:6).

Second, individuals confess that God is God and that he rules the world (1 Chr 29:10-13), that he is faithful in showing his love and kindness (Ps 118:2-4), and that he has helped his people (Ps 105:1-6). Such confession or agreement, expressed publicly in worship or song (Ps 100:4), is spoken of in the OT as "blessing the Lord."

The two types of confession are often combined in the Bible, producing many psalms of thanksgiving. In general those psalms contain some or all of the following ideas: (1) I have sinned; (2) I became ill and nearly died; (3) I prayed to God, who delivered me; and (4) now I offer this song of confession, which I promised him (Pss 22; 30; 32; 34; 40; 51; 116). The same Hebrew word means both "praise" and "confession of sin"; the two meanings were part of a single concept. The psalmist began by admitting sin and God's justice, and he ended by confessing God's forgiveness and delivering power.

Both those meanings also occur in the NT. Christians confess (that is, they declare as a matter of conviction and allegiance) that Jesus is the Christ and that they belong to him. "Whosoever therefore shall confess me before men, him will I confess also before my Father which is in heaven" (Mt 10:32, KJV). Not to confess Christ is the same as denying him (Mt 10:33; Lk 12:8; cf. 2 Tm 2:11-13; Rv 3:5). The Christian life therefore begins with a confession of faith, a public declaration before witnesses (Rom 10:9-10; 1 Tm 6:12). An additional dimension of the Christian's confession is provided in 1 John 4:2: one must confess that "Jesus Christ has come in the flesh," that is, acknowledge Jesus' divinity and preexistence as the Son of God (that he "has come"; see also 1 Jn 4:15) as well as Jesus' humanity and incarnation (that he has come "in the flesh"). The Greek word "confession" literally means "saying the same thing." The Christian's "good confession" is modeled after the pattern of Christ's confession (1 Tm 6:12-13).

In only a few passages does the NT discuss confession of sin. Those being baptized by John the Baptist publicly admitted their sins and repented (Mk 1:4-5). All Christians, in fact, must agree with God that they are sinners (1 Jn 1:8-10). James presented a fuller picture: when a Christian is ill, the elders are to visit and give the person opportunity to confess any sins. As in the Psalms, forgiveness and healing (the moral and the physical) are tied to confession. Recalling that principle, James urged Christians to confess their sins to one another.

See also Conversion; Forgiveness; Repentance.

CONFORM*, CONFORMATION*

Spiritual process of molding the believer into the image of Jesus. Paul speaks of this in Romans 8:28-30:

> And we know that in all things God works for the good of those who love him, who have been called according to his purpose. For those God foreknew he also predestined to be conformed to the likeness of his Son, that he might be the firstborn among many brothers. And those he predestined, he also called; and those he called, he also justified; those he justified, he also glorified (NIV).

Since it is God's desire and plan to have many sons and daughters, each believer has to be conformed to the prototype, Jesus. Note how the words "predestined," "called," "justified," and especially "glorified" in Romans 8:29-30 are in the past tense. That is because God, from his eternal perspective, sees this process as having been completed already. From God's perspective, believers have been glorified already because he sees them like his Son. But still, in the reality of time, they must undergo the process of being conformed to the image of God's Son. God is working together all things in the lives of those who love him and are called according to his purpose. His goal is to conform each son and daughter to the image of his beloved Son.

When one continues to read the rest of Romans 8, it is quite evident that the "things" God uses to conform Christians involve various kinds of suffering. Conformity to the image of Jesus Christ necessitates conformity to his death (see Phil 3:10). Whereas transformation involves an inward, life-imparted change in our essential constitution, conformation entails outward pressure that works the image of Christ into his children. If they are to be made like him, they must have both. To know Jesus, as far as Paul was concerned, was to know both the power of his resurrection and the fellowship of his sufferings. No one likes to suffer; no one wants to be a Job. But Job was insightful when he said, "When he has tried me, I shall come forth as gold" (Jb 23:10, RSV). Suffering produces an element in the believer that they do not inherently possess. God uses sufferings to conform them to the image of his Son.

The Lord Jesus left his followers a pattern of suffering that cannot be avoided. This is the path that he, the pioneer of salvation, took. The Father perfected him through suffering (Heb 2:10)—i.e., he, as a man, was made fully qualified to be our leader and even our merciful High Priest because of what he suffered on our behalf. Christians should expect to suffer, at least in part, some of the things Jesus suffered. Of course, this does not mean that any believer can repeat his unique act of suffering on the cross for redemption. Peter says that "Christ also suffered for you, leaving you an example, that you should follow in his steps" (1 Pt 2:21, RSV). The Greek word underlying "example" *(hupogramma)* in common Greek usage designated a tracing tablet that contained the entire Greek alphabet. Students would use this to trace the alphabet.

They would have to learn each letter, from alpha to omega. The life of Jesus, a life of suffering, is just such a tracing tablet. Those who learn to follow Jesus will be those who know what it is to suffer, for suffering is the means by which God conforms us to the image of Jesus.

See also Transformation.

CONGREGATION

Assembly of people, particularly for religious purposes. The Bible describes Israel as the congregation of the Lord because it was a covenant nation. The whole nation was considered to be the people of God (Ex 3:6-8, 15-16; 12:6; Is 1:2-4; 14:1).

As a chosen nation, Israel was to display God's greatness in the midst of other nations (Dt 4:6-14; Is 42:1; 45:4; 65:9, 22). Because of this, the whole nation was called "the assembly of the congregation of the people of Israel" (Nm 14:5, RSV; see also Lv 4:13; Nm 16:3).

The church of the NT owes much to the spiritual heritage transmitted by the OT congregation of God's people. This relationship of the church to the OT people of God is highlighted in several places (Heb 2:10-13; 1 Pt 2:9-10; see also Rom 9:1-8; Gal 6:16).

See also Church.

CONGREGATION*, Mount of the

KJV translation for "mount of assembly," the name of a mountain that figured in Babylonian and Canaanite mythology, in Isaiah 14:13.

CONIAH*

Alternate name for Jehoiachin, king of Judah, in Jeremiah 22:24, 28; 37:1. *See* Jehoiachin.

CONONIAH*

KJV spelling of Conaniah the Levite, in 2 Chronicles 31:12-13. *See* Conaniah #1.

CONQUEST AND ALLOTMENT OF THE LAND

Terms referring to Israel's winning of the Promised Land and the distinctive way in which it was divided among the Israelite tribes.

Conquest The conquest of Canaan by the Israelites is one of the most remarkable events of OT history: a

---

WIPING OUT THE CANAANITES
Many have expressed objection to the apparent cruelty of the Israelites in wiping out the Canaanite people, sometimes calling it barbarism. It should be noted, however, that total annihilation was not practiced everywhere but only in Jericho and Ai and the later punishment of the Amalekites under Saul (1 Sm 15). As in the earlier conquest of the Midianites (Nm 31:17-18), not all the population was killed. In Deuteronomy 20:10-18 and 21:10-14, a distinction is drawn between the treatment of Canaanites (actually a heterogeneous group, see Dt 20:17) and other captive peoples. With the Canaanites, the command to "save alive nothing that breathes" (v 16, RSV) was given "that they may not teach you to do according to all their abominable practices which they have done in the service of their gods, and so to sin against the LORD your God" (v 18, RSV).

In Abraham's time the wickedness of the Amorites was not yet "complete" (Gn 15:16), but by Joshua's time it was. Archaeology has documented the sexual perversions, child sacrifices, idolatry, and cruelty of the Canaanites. The Land of Promise was intended to be swept clean of such abominations so that Israel could live an unhampered life, ordered by the covenant law of their God.

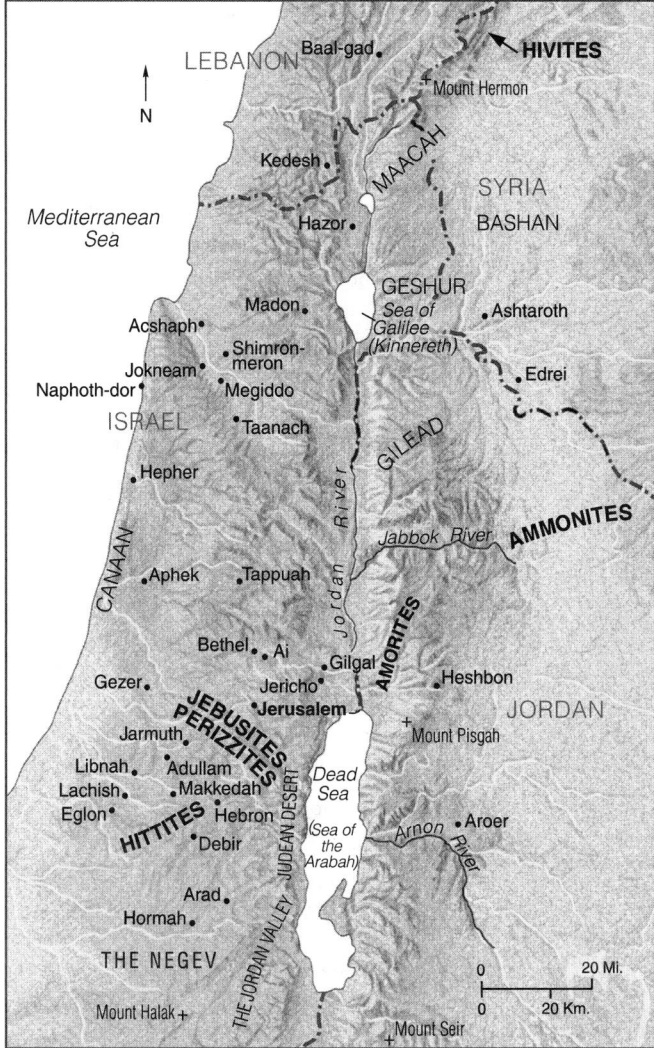

The broken lines (— · — ·) indicate modern boundaries.

The Conquered Land Joshua displayed brilliant military strategy in the way he went about conquering the land of Canaan. He first captured the well-fortified city of Jericho to gain a foothold in Canaan and to demonstrate the awesome might of the God of Israel. Then he gained the hill country around Bethel and Gibeon. From there he subdued towns in the lowlands. Then his army conquered important cities in the north, such as Hazor. In all, Israel conquered land both east and west of the Jordan River, from Mt Hermon in the north to beyond the Negev to Mt Halak in the south.

argued with the king of Ammon about Israelite possession of land east of the Jordan River, he indicated that Israel had occupied this territory 300 years. Saul's accession to kingship about 1020 BC was still some decades off, so the later date proposed for the exodus does not allow sufficient time for the period of the judges. Further, the apostle Paul referred to a period of about 450 years from the exodus to Samuel's day (Acts 13:20).

Joshua's Campaigns A picture of a concentrated period for the Israelite conquest of Canaan is given in the book of Joshua. Yet many scholars insist that an earlier gradual penetration occurred (by Hebrews who supposedly did not accompany Jacob into Egypt), plus an extended mopping-up procedure that continued down to the time of the monarchy. Although the biblical record allows for later acquisitions in some areas (e.g., Megiddo and Beth-shan), there is no valid reason for rejecting the description of the major Conquest given in Joshua 1–12.

The Conquest began on the east side of the Jordan River under Moses. After Moses' death, Joshua led Israel across the river, capturing first the fortified cities of Jericho and Ai. Those strategic victories provided access to the hill country and drove a wedge into the middle of Canaan. Two major campaigns followed—a southern and then a northern—which won for Israel in six years' time the key cities of Canaan, defeating 31 kings and concluding the initial and principal stage of the Conquest.

Numbers 32 records the earlier assignment of territory east of the Jordan (Gilead and Bashan, acquired by the defeat of two kings, Sihon of the Amorites and Og of Bashan) to the tribes of Reuben, Gad, and the half-tribe of Manasseh. Though their land had already been acquired, the men of those tribes were obligated to cross the Jordan with the rest to participate in the military conquest of Canaan itself.

Joshua 2–8 records the unusual events of the destruction of Jericho and Ai in the initial thrust westward. Those victories tended to demoralize the remaining cities of the land. Chapters 9 and 10 describe the southern campaign, including the Gibeonites' procurement of a treaty by deception. Joshua 10, with its account of the remarkable rout of the enemy forces (vv 9-12) and miraculous prolonging of daylight, is the central passage about the southern campaign. In the subsequent battle, an alliance of five Amorite kings was crushed, the kings were killed, and the

loosely organized nomadic people successfully invaded a long-established culture secure in its protected urban centers. That achievement, according to the Scriptures, was the result of a promise God had made to Abraham, Isaac, and Jacob that their descendants would possess the land (Gn 17:8; 26:4; 28:13; Ex 3:15-17). Dispossession of the pagan inhabitants was a divine judgment on false religion and its associated immorality (Dt 7:1-5).

Scholars who attempt to reconstruct the history of the Conquest face certain problems. Critical scholarship has run into conflict with statements in the Bible at three key points: chronology, rate of occupation, and the issue of Israel's military annihilation of portions of the population of the Canaanite city-states.

Date Reference works and scholarly treatments of OT history often suggest a date for the exodus from Egypt in the 13th century BC (1280 BC or later). Several biblical references to that event would seem to call for an earlier date. According to 1 Kings 6:1, construction of Solomon's temple was begun in the fourth year of his reign, 480 years after the exodus. Since Solomon's fourth year was about 960 BC, that would place the exodus at 1440 BC. In Judges 11:26-28, when Jephthah, eighth of the named judges, city-states of the area were destroyed, except for Jerusalem (later captured by David).

In his northern campaign, Joshua confronted a more formidable alliance. Yet even Jabin, the powerful king of Hazor, largest of the Canaanite cities, supported by his local vassals, was no match for Israel's armies. Joshua 11 describes that phase, then sums up the entire Conquest in verses 16-23 and on through chapter 12.

See also Allotment of the Land.

CONSCIENCE Self-awareness that judges whether or not an act one has carried out or plans to carry out is in harmony with one's moral standards. The conscience also functions to make a person aware of actions taken that were wrong.

"LET YOUR CONSCIENCE BE YOUR GUIDE"
Since knowledge of what is good has been distorted by sin, can conscience be a valid moral guide? Many ethicists hold that all moral intuitions are developed entirely through social training; others take a less extreme view. Certainly children's consciences are influenced by reinforcement of approved conduct and by discipline of misbehavior within the framework of family life. From a Christian point of view, although one's conscience is an inner witness to spiritual and moral truth, it cannot be regarded invariably as the voice of God. No one has such a grasp on moral truth that his or her sinful nature may not overwhelm the conscience and render it unreliable.

Nonetheless, the existence of conscience argues strongly for God's existence and reveals something about his nature—namely, that God always does what is right and that he punishes the transgression of his laws. Even unbelievers, simply from recognition of their moral nature, sense that they are ultimately responsible to God (Rom 1:19-20, 32). The 18th-century philosopher Immanuel Kant, for example, posited belief in God, freedom, and immortality on the basis of conscience. The Christian knows that behind conscience is a God who is personal, ethical, self-revealing, and the Creator, Sustainer, and moral Governor of the universe.

In essentially every culture certain kinds of conduct are approved or disapproved. Such evidence suggests that conscience cannot be explained merely on the basis of social convention or the preferences of individuals. Within the Christian community, where considerable diversity also exists, the standard of morality is not provided primarily by a narrow social structure but by a broad allegiance to biblical truth. Maturity comes as Christians recognize themselves as part of a larger body, under the lordship of Christ, fellowship is maintained and a good conscience preserved by walking in the light (1 Jn 1:7). A bad conscience is cleansed by confession of sin and the acceptance of God's forgiveness (v 9).

Both the English word "conscience" and the Greek word translated as "conscience" in the NT literally mean "to be with knowledge." In the OT, Adam and Eve hid themselves from God in shame because their consciences passed moral judgment on their disobedience (Gn 3:8-10). All human beings normally have the power of moral judgment: "The spirit of man is the lamp of the LORD, searching all his innermost parts" (Prv 20:27, RSV). Conscience, then, is a gift of God to provide light in matters of good and evil.

In the New Testament The word "conscience" is found 32 times in the NT (see KJV), especially in the writings of the apostle Paul. Conscience, in Paul's writings, is regarded as passing judgment not only on conduct that has already taken place but also on what ought to be done in the future. The behavior of people who are without God's law shows that the law's requirement is "written on their hearts" (Rom 2:14-15). Paul's statement that every person should "be subject to the higher authorities" to avoid God's judgment and "for the sake of conscience" presupposes that conscience can establish obedience as a moral requirement (13:5).

To approve, or pronounce "not guilty," is a function of conscience just as important as self-condemnation. Paul said, "I am not aware [using the same root word from which 'conscience' is derived] of anything against myself" (1 Cor 4:4, RSV). Yet conscience is neither a final court of appeal nor an all-sufficient guide: Paul went on to say, "I am not thereby acquitted. It is the Lord who judges me." In another passage Paul called on his conscience to verify his truthfulness, linking the verdict of conscience with the Holy Spirit (Rom 9:1; cf. 2 Cor 1:12) without developing the nature of that relationship.

Justifying his ministry to the Corinthians, Paul asked them to judge his conduct in the light of their own consciences (2 Cor 4:1-2). Insisting that God knew the motivation behind his conduct (that is, the "fear of the Lord"), he hoped that the Corinthians' conscience would also recognize it (5:11). When Paul wrote to Timothy, he linked a good conscience with sincere faith (1 Tm 1:5); when people depart from the faith, their consciences can become "seared" or rendered insensitive by their persistence in evil (4:2).

Answering a question about meats offered to idols, Paul spoke of the conscience as exercising judgment on prospective as well as on past behavior (1 Cor 8-10). Some had a conscience that was "weak" due to ignorance (1 Cor 8:7); they failed to understand that everything is clean (Rom 14:20).

CONSECRATION* Separation of persons, utensils, buildings, or places from everyday secular uses for exclusive dedication to holy or sacred use. In the Bible consecration was demonstrated by an appropriate rite or vow. Hebrew expressions imply "separation" (Ex 13:2; Lv 8:10-12; Dt 15:19), "dedication" (Lv 21:12; Nm 6:9), or "ordination" (lit. "filling the hand," Ex 28:41; 1 Kgs 13:33). NT references are fewer, but they frequently connote the idea of holiness (Jn 10:36; 1 Cor 7:14; 1 Tm 4:5).

In church usage, especially among hierarchical denominations, the term describes solemn rites that establish a bishop. It is also used to describe dedication of shrines, reliquaries, cathedrals, elements of the Mass, or buildings set aside for ecclesiastical functions.

Protestant teaching stresses the priesthood of every believer. Thus all Christians are "saints" (from the same root word as "consecration"), that is, devoted to God for life. In Roman Catholic doctrine the church consecrates (canonizes) great Christians as saints after they have died.

Consecration is significant in relation both to God and to the world. The apostle Paul spells out the term's meaning in Romans 12:1-2, stressing that consecration involves a living sacrifice to God. Its importance in relation to people and things is a basic theme of the apostle Peter's first letter. In everyday life each Christian is meant to live out a "holy" and "royal" priesthood for God's glory (1 Pt 2:9). Christians consider the consecration of one's own personality by the work of the Holy Spirit to be an important mark of spiritual maturity.

CONSTELLATION Certain number of stars in the sky, arbitrarily chosen as a group and named for an object, animal, or person that the outline of the group is said to resemble. A number of constellations are mentioned in the Bible.

See also Astronomy.

CONSUL* Title of the two highest civil and military magistrates of Rome in the time of the Republic. The consuls functioned as the heads of state, commanding the army and governing with the Senate. They also had certain judicial functions. Ordinarily a consul was appointed to a one-year term. A letter from the consul Lucius Calpurnius Piso (consul, 140–139 BC) to Ptolemy VII Physcon (reigned 145–116 BC) of Egypt is mentioned in 1 Maccabees 15:16.

CONSUMPTION* Medical term historically referring to pulmonary tuberculosis. The word "consumption" appears twice in the Bible (Lv 26:16; Dt 28:22, RSV). However, it does not specifically mean tuberculosis; rather, it specifies any chronic wasting disease process, perhaps including cancer, diarrhea, malnutrition, malaria, kidney failure, and other disorders. In the biblical references, consumption is listed as one of many medical symptoms threatening those who do not follow the commandments of the Lord.

See also Disease; Medicine and Medical Practice.

CONVERSION Total change in one's direction in life or moral orientation. For Christians this means a change from an orientation that does not take God into account to one in which the person is submitted to Christ. Conversion is the result of repentance.

In the OT conversion is basically a turning or returning from one's former course of life toward the Lord, the God of Israel. Israel often had to return to their God (Dt 4:30), either as individuals (Ps 51) or as a nation (Jer 4:1); foreign nations needed to turn to God for the first time (Ps 22:27). The characteristic feature is that one turns from wickedness (Jer 26:3; 36:3; Ez 18:21, 27; 33:9, 11), from a life of disloyalty to God to a life of obedience to God (Is 10:20-21; 14:2; Jer 34:15; Hos 14:4). Conversion means a change in inward orientation that finds expression in a changed lifestyle.

In the NT John the Baptist begins the call to conversion (Mt 3:2; Mk 1:4; Lk 3:3), giving a prophetic call for people to change their minds (which is the root meaning of the Greek term) in the light of the nearness of God's kingdom. This change of life must include a change in actions to prove its reality (Mt 3:8; Lk 3:8). Jesus preached the same message (Mt 4:17; Mk 1:15), adding that since the kingdom had arrived in his person, obedience to him was part of the good news of conversion. Yet it could also be bad news, for one would be damned if he failed to make this radical change (Mt 11:20; Lk 13:3-5). Conversion is radical but also simple, for it requires the simplicity of a child who commits his whole self, not the calculating self-protectiveness of the adult (Mt 18:3).

Outside the Gospels, "conversion" is not a frequently used term except in the book of Acts, where it forms the call to commitment climaxing evangelistic sermons (2:38; 3:19; 8:22), describes the commitment of new Christians to the Lord (9:35; 11:21), and pictures the change of life as a turning from darkness to light (26:18-20). Later writers look back upon conversion (2 Cor 3:16), worry about Christians converting to paganism or Judaism (Gal 4:9), and call for the reconversion of Christians who have left the faith and are in danger of judgment (Jas 5:19-20; Rv 2:5, 16, 22; 3:19).

As in the OT and in the preaching of John and Jesus, conversion has three factors. First, it is a turning *from* something, which includes specific sins, false gods, or simply a life lived for oneself (1 Thes 1:9; Rv 9:20-21; 16:11). Second, conversion is a product of the will of God and his gracious working in the world (Acts 11:18; Rom 2:4; 2 Cor 7:10; 2 Tm 2:25; 2 Pt 3:9). Third, conversion is a turning *to* someone, a commitment of one's whole life to God in Jesus Christ (Acts 14:15; 1 Thes 1:9; 1 Pt 2:25). It is thus a total reorientation, whether spectacular or undramatic, sudden or gradual, emotional or calm, in which a person transfers his or her total allegiance to God.

See also Faith; Grace; Justification, Justified; Repentance; Sanctification.

CONVOCATION*, Holy Solemn assemblies celebrated in Israel at appointed feasts in order that the people and the temple might be sanctified; the days were specially devoted to rest and sacrifice to God. *See* Feasts and Festivals of Israel; Atonement, Day of; Sabbath.

COOS* KJV spelling of Cos, an Aegean island and city, in Acts 21:1. *See* Cos.

COPPER Reddish-brown, malleable metal found in the ground (Dt 8:9) and fashioned into ornaments, tools, and coins. *See* Minerals and Metals.

COPPERSMITH One who worked in copper and fashioned bronze and copper tools, implements, and ornaments (Ex 26:11, 37; 27:2-10; Jos 6:19, 24; 1 Sm 17:5-6; 2 Sm 8:8). Only in the NT (2 Tm 4:14) is the term "coppersmith" used; however, the occupation was important throughout Bible history.

See also Minerals and Metals.

COR* Large dry measure. *See* Weights and Measures.

CORAL Calcareous skeletal deposits of marine organisms of a low order. The red coral of the Mediterranean was used for jewelry. *See* Animals; Minerals and Metals; Stones, Precious.

CORBAN* Greek transliteration of a Hebrew term *(korban)* that occurs only in Mark 7:11, where Mark provides an editorial explanation: corban is "given," that is, "dedicated or given to God." Hence, corban is an offering.

Jewish law allowed individuals to earmark their service or property as "dedicated to God," thus removing it from profane use and giving it the character of an offering intended for God. To do this was a serious decision (according to the Mishnah, *Nedarim*) and was rarely reversed (*Nedarim* 5), for violation of a corban vow risked the severe consequences of divine judgment. In Mark 7 Jesus chastises the scribes because, theoretically, a son could exclude his parents from gaining any benefit from his estate by declaring his property "corban to them." This in effect nullifies the fifth commandment (see Ex 20:12), setting rabbinic traditions against the law of Moses. Worse still, if the son repented of his vow—arguing that it had been given in haste—a rabbinic tribunal would no doubt forbid a reversal of corban (Mk 7:12; cf Nm 30:1-2).

CORE* KJV spelling of Korah, Izhar's son, in Jude 1:11. *See* Korah #3.

CORIANDER Annual herb native to Palestine. The fragrant seeds of this plant are mentioned twice in the description of manna (Ex 16:31; Nm 11:7).

See also Food and Food Preparation; Plants.

CORINTH Prominent city of Greece, formerly the capital of the ancient province of Achaia, in which the apostle Paul preached. The site of ancient Corinth lies to the west of the isthmus separating the Peloponnesian Peninsula from mainland Greece. The ancient ruins, largely of Roman origin, are situated about four-fifths of a mile (1,285 meters) from present-day Corinth. The area was inhabited from Neolithic times. Corinth is dominated by an outcrop of rock known as Acrocorinth (Upper Corinth). The grandeur of the Greek period is evident in the remains of the temple of Apollo, whose massive columns dominate the site. Entrance to the ancient city is by means of a very broad avenue that lies in a straight line from the city gate. That avenue ends in the marketplace, with roads leading from there to the Acrocorinth. In the apostolic period the city was a bustling commercial and industrial center boasting a population of almost 700,000.

History and Archaeology By the mid-eighth century BC, Corinth, strategically located along east-west trade routes, was a flourishing city-state. From 350–250 BC it was the most prominent city in Greece. Then the Roman military machine began a relentless march to forge a vast empire. In 146 BC Corinth was completely destroyed and lay in ruins for a century. In 46 BC Julius Caesar moved a mixed group of Italians and dispossessed Greeks onto the site, and once more a magnificent city arose, this time as a Roman colony. As in most Roman cities, marble temples dominated the landscape. The city was supplied with water from an underground well. It became a cosmopolitan city attracting tradespeople from all over the world, though its reputation grew simultaneously as a center of luxury, indulgence, and vice. A large colony of displaced Jews (part of the Diaspora) developed in the city, the group that undoubtedly attracted the apostle Paul.

In 1896 the American School of Classical Studies at Athens secured permission to begin excavation of the ancient site. The finds are of special interest for study of the NT Corinthian epistles. An important archaeological find was a doorway lintel bearing a portion of an inscription designating the building as the "Synagogue of the Hebrews." It may have marked the synagogue in which the apostle preached (Acts 18:4). Another discovery was the *bema*, or judgment place (vv 12-17), located in the center of the *agora*, or marketplace. There Paul appeared before Gallio, proconsul of Achaia. The dates of Gallio are well established by other inscriptions. He must not have arrived in Corinth before July, AD 51. Paul appeared before him after having ministered in the city for almost 18 months. That would date Paul's arrival in Corinth as the beginning of AD 50.

Corinth is significant in the history of the church because of the ministry of the apostle Paul in response to

The Corinthian Canal

his Macedonian vision (Acts 16:9-10). He established churches in Philippi, Thessalonica, Berea, and possibly Athens on his way to Corinth. Acts 18 describes Paul's work at Corinth, first with the Jews, who violently opposed him (v 6). At Corinth, Paul engaged in the longest ministry up to that time in either of his first missionary journeys. The Corinthian church, born in such a crucible of paganism, had to go through serious birth pangs. Paul's letters to the group of believers there reflect a large catalog of troubles for Christians in the first century, a list not unlike the problems of Christians today.

Remains of the Temple of Apollo in Corinth

See also Corinthians, First Letter to the; Corinthians, Second Letter to the.

ISTHMIAN GAMES AT CORINTH AND PAUL'S ATHLETIC IMAGERY
Corinth was prominent because of the Isthmian Games, which occurred in the first and third years of the Olympiad (the four-year period between Olympic Games). They were supposedly originated by the mythical king Sisyphus and date from 523 BC. Competition centered on three kinds of events: equestrian, gymnastics, and music. By the NT period, the games were influenced by Roman civilization, so chariot racing and other spectacles were probably added to the Hellenistic competitions. In an allusion to athletic contests, Paul mentioned both running and boxing (1 Cor 9:24-26). The prize for winning the games was a wreath made of myrtle, olive, or pine branches, plus the additional benefits of a stipend from the state, remission of taxes, and special benefits for the champion's children. Winners were national heroes.

CORINTHIANS, First Letter to the

PREVIEW
• Author
• Date and Origin
• Background
• Purpose and Teaching
• Content

Author There is no doubt about who wrote 1 Corinthians, for all scholars agree that the apostle Paul wrote it on his third missionary journey while he was living in Ephesus. By this time Paul was a mature, middle-aged (perhaps 55 years old) missionary, fully seasoned from planting churches around a quarter of the Mediterranean world.

Date and Origin Paul worked in Corinth from about AD 50 to 52. After a brief stay in Jerusalem, he returned to his missionary work, this time at Ephesus (Acts 19), where he ministered for three years (AD 53–55/56). During this period, he wrote at least three letters to Corinth and made a visit as well. His first letter, often called "the previous letter," is referred to in 1 Corinthians 5:9-11. We know from this reference that the letter was misunderstood, but we know little of its content, for it has been lost.

Sometime in AD 55, after hearing reports from Chloe's household (1 Cor 1:11), who were probably members of Chloe's house church, he dictated a second letter to Corinth, our 1 Corinthians. This was probably sent off in the hands of Stephanas, Fortunatus, and Achaicus (16:17). Paul would later write a third letter to Corinth, called "the letter of tears" (2 Cor 2:2-3), and then finally 2 Corinthians.

Background Corinth was a seaport city, destroyed by the Romans in 146 BC and rebuilt in 46 BC by Julius Caesar. After 27 BC, it was the Roman capital of Achaia, where the proconsul had his residence (Acts 18:12). The city itself was really three cities: the port of Cenchrea, about eight miles (13 kilometers) to the east, where ships from the Aegean would unload; the port of Lechaion, about a mile (1.6 kilometers) to the west on the Gulf of Corinth, where the ships would be reloaded, their goods having been transported in wagons over the isthmus and the ships on rollers; and the city itself on the high ground in between.

The acropolis of the city, on top of the steep, high Acrocorinth, contained the temple of Aphrodite, where 1,000 female slaves were dedicated to the service of this goddess of love. This distinctive cult of Corinth was dedicated to the veneration of Aphrodite, goddess of love, beauty, and fertility, who is identified with the Roman Venus. Associated with such religious practices was a general moral degradation. Corinthian morals were notoriously corrupt, even when compared with pagan Rome. Down in the city was the synagogue (Acts 18:4); for while the city as a Roman colony was largely populated by Italians, it had attracted other peoples from the Mediterranean, among whom were the Jews.

Purpose and Teaching The main concern of Paul in 1 Corinthians was the unity of the church. There was a self-centeredness in Corinth that resulted in building cliques within the church, in flaunting knowledge and liberty in the face of others scandalized by it, and in selfish displays in the worship services.

Two other major concerns also surface in the book. First, along with other pagan practices, the lax sexual ethics of Corinth had influenced the church; Paul needed to erect some barriers. Second, there was a problem in accepting the resurrection of the body; Paul realized that this issue had implications for the core of the faith and vigorously affirmed the resurrection.

Both of these latter two areas, as well as aspects of the unity issue (particularly their concern with knowledge), have been identified by some scholars as Gnostic motifs, leading to the conclusion that Paul was opposing a Gnostic party in Corinth. Careful examination reveals, however, that while some of the elements floating in the Corinthian milieu would later contribute to the develop-

ment of Gnosticism, it would be anachronistic to call them gnostic. While recognizing protognostic ideas in the Corinthian situation, it is important to keep interpretation within the first-century context.

Thus, the focus of Paul's concern was the church, its unity and purity. Paul was fighting to keep this church from disintegrating into a number of competing and bickering factions divided over moral and doctrinal issues. Furthermore, he wanted to keep the focus of the church on Jesus, the exalted Lord.

Content

Greeting, 1:1-9 Paul begins with a standard greeting, followed by his usual thanksgiving prayer. Two features stand out. First, the greeting associates Sosthenes with Paul. While we cannot be sure who Sosthenes was, he was surely well known to the Corinthians; probably he was the Sosthenes whom Acts 18:17 identifies as the ruler of the synagogue, following the conversion of Crispus.

Second, Paul stresses the Corinthians' abilities in speech, knowledge, and spiritual gifts. They had all of these, and these were genuine, but it was precisely these good things that they were abusing. Paul's solution is not to suppress these gifts (indeed, he thanks God for them), but to place them in a new context.

Report from Chloe's People, 1:10-4:21 The Corinthians had made Paul, Cephas (Peter), Apollos, and even Christ into party leaders. We are not sure what each of these groups stood for, but one might guess that the Pauline group stressed Paul's slogans of liberty; the Petrine group, the need to hold to Jewish practices; and the Apollos group, the value of philosophical understanding and oratory. Whatever they stood for, Paul is appalled that it breaks their unity. His first response is to argue that his behavior was not calculated to build a following but to point to Christ. That is, he did not insist on personally baptizing converts; who performed these acts did not matter, since they were all baptized into Christ.

Paul immediately moves to the underlying issue, that of various persons wanting to show themselves better or wiser than others who did not have the insights of their party in the church. Their seeking for wisdom contradicts Paul's preaching of the gospel.

First, the message of a crucified Christ (1:18) made no sense within the wisdom and values of either Jews or Greeks. It demanded a whole new way of looking on life—God's way.

Second, God had not chosen them on the basis of their status in society; quite the contrary, he had made their only status the equal status they received from him (1:26-31).

Third, their faith had not been based on Paul's oratory but on the gifts of the Spirit that Paul had manifested (2:4), which had convinced them that God was acting in Paul. Thus, it was not argument that led them to God, but God's Spirit. Therefore it was the Spirit, not human reasoning, that would continue to reveal God to them. Unless they became fools with respect to the world's ways of reasoning, they would never be able to rethink life from the perspective of the Spirit, who gives true wisdom.

Fourth, they were not acting on this spiritual level when they claimed Paul and others as party leaders; this activity demonstrates the evil impulse in human beings ("the flesh" or "fallen human nature") at work since it elevates human servants rather than the God who works equally in each of them.

Fifth, these servants were working together to build

one "temple" for God based on the one foundation in Jesus Christ, that is, the church. God alone will judge how each Christian contributes to the work of building the church. But woe to the person who divides the church, for "if anyone destroys God's temple, God will destroy him" (3:17, RSV). (Note that here the temple imagery is used collectively; the church is the temple. In chapter 6 it will be used individually; each Christian is the temple.)

Finally, he points to their overrealized eschatology, for with their spiritual gifts (which were genuine) and vaunted wisdom (which was worldly) they claimed they were reigning with Christ (4:8-13). Paul, with ironic sarcasm, points out how different this claim is from the lifestyle of the apostles. The apostles lived like Jesus—a life of suffering, expecting exaltation later. The Corinthians were trying to have their exaltation now without crucifixion.

Paul closes this section with an admonition. He softens his words toward some who would be responsive, urging them to copy his lifestyle. The teacher was the message (vv 14-16). Timothy will also faithfully live the truth before them. Then he threatens the "arrogant" (v 18), pointing out that he will not challenge their words but their spiritual power if he comes.

The Report from the Corinthian Messengers, 5:1–6:20
Paul now turns to three issues raised by oral reports from the messengers bearing the Corinthians' letter to him.

The first issue is that of church discipline (5:12-13). Paul cites a case of flagrant immorality—that of incest. This immorality was so clear (even pagans considered it immoral), that it was not a case of ignorance of Christian principles. Further, the church had taken no action but rather boasted in its tolerance, perhaps on the basis of a misunderstanding of Paul's teaching on freedom from the law.

Paul presents three principles in this section: (1) the primary goal of church discipline is the repentance and restoration of the offender; (2) the secondary goal of church discipline is the protection of the church (5:6-8); and (3) the church is not to seek to judge or control the actions of evil persons in the world—they are God's responsibility—but to discipline those within the church (vv 9-13). Paul will use these principles also in the following chapters (cf. 7:12-16).

The second issue is that of lawsuits between Christians (6:1-11). The Corinthian society was as prone to litigation as our own, and Christians did not see anything wrong in suing each other. Paul was troubled. If Christians are to judge the world, they certainly should not bring the world in to judge issues within the church. Rather than put their cases before "those who are least esteemed by the church" (6:4, RSV, i.e., pagan judges), they should decide the cases within the church.

Paul has an even better way than bypassing the pagan courts, and that is to simply suffer the wrong (1 Cor 6:7). Applying the teaching of Jesus quite literally (Mt 5:38-42), Paul argues that it would be best to allow themselves to be defrauded. Instead, the Corinthians are willing to step on their brothers in Christ to get what they feel are their rights. This raises the issue as to whether greed is not still in their hearts (1 Cor 6:9-11). While Paul accepts people who formerly did all sorts of evil (for Jesus has cleansed them), he makes it very clear that anyone presently practicing greed or immorality is not part of the kingdom, whatever their doctrinal commitments may be.

The final issue in this section is that of casual sexual intercourse (6:12-20). In a world where virginity was important if a woman wished to be married and where

slaves in the temple of Aphrodite were available as prostitutes, prostitution was the major form of casual sex. The libertine party used two slogans: "All things are lawful for me," a saying that may well have been derived from Paul's teaching, and "Food is meant for the stomach and the stomach for food"—that is, since the body works this way, it must be the Creator's purpose. Paul qualifies rather than contradicts their slogans. Freedom is subordinate to other goals (6:12, 20). The body is not made to be used as we wish, but is to be dedicated to the Lord, as the doctrine of the resurrection demonstrates (vv 13-14).

Furthermore, sexual intercourse is an act of the whole person, unlike eating (Paul cites Gn 2:24; cf. Jesus in Mt 19:5). Therefore, this act takes a member (i.e., the person) from the body of Christ and makes him a unity with a prostitute (1 Cor 6:15-17). Thus immorality is unlike other sins that are external to the self, for it changes the self and thus defiles the body, the place where the Holy Spirit dwells. It disregards the fact that Christ has redeemed the body, and that the whole of the Christian belongs to God, not to the Christian.

Paul's Answers to the Corinthians, 7:1–16:4
Now Paul turns to the Corinthians' own issues, building on the answers he has already given to questions they did not ask.

The first issue is that of marriage (7:1-24). The slogan of the ascetic party in Corinth (perhaps a reaction against the libertines of ch 6) was "It is good for a man not to touch a woman" (7:1, KJV). The Corinthians applied this slogan to both married and unmarried, arguing that married Christians should abstain from sexual relations. Paul clarified the matter with three points. First, he said that this was totally unrealistic, for total abstinence would lead to immorality (vv 2, 7-9). Second, when people get married they no longer own their own bodies; their bodies belong to each other for their mutual benefit (vv 3-4). Sexual refusal denies a spouse what rightly belongs to him or her. Third, abstinence is allowed for limited periods by mutual agreement as a type of fast to help focus on Christ (v 5).

While Paul will address the issue of the unmarried more fully in 7:25-40, in a side remark he indicates that he is himself content to be unmarried. But since some do not have this gift, full sexual expression in marriage is far better than fighting passion (7:7-9). Once two Christians are married, divorce is unthinkable. A clear word of Christ proves this (Mt 5:31-32; Mk 10:11-12; Lk 16:18 and parallels), so there are no exceptions (Paul either does not know of the exception clause in Mt 19:9 or he understands it as referring to something like premarital unchastity discovered before the wedding, not to adultery after the wedding). Although in some cases a Christian couple must live separately, it is always with a view to reconciliation. The teaching of Jesus does not allow him to think of the marriage as ending (1 Cor 7:10-11).

But what if the spouse is not a Christian? Paul applies his principles to a situation for which Jesus did not leave a clear word. First, since Jesus told Christians not to divorce, even in this situation the Christian may not initiate a divorce (7:12-13). Second, since Christians are not to control or judge non-Christians (6:12-13), the Christian does not need to continue the relationship if the non-Christian insists on a divorce (7:15). Third, far from defiling the Christian (as the relationship in 6:15 does), the Christian will make the relationship holy, with positive results for the children and the possible salvation of the spouse (7:14, 16). While this is no call to remain in situations of physical or sexual abuse, it is a call to remain faithful to a mixed marriage situation.

Paul does not believe that one normally needs to change one's life situation to serve Christ (7:17-24). Therefore, normally each person should remain in that state of life in which he or she was when called to Christ. Paul's examples show that he was thinking in terms of marriage or singleness, Jew (circumcision) or Gentile, slave or free, not in terms of situations that might be immoral in themselves. In the case of slaves, they can accept freedom if it becomes available, but it does not make an essential difference in their real state before God or their ability to serve Christ (vv 21-23).

The second issue is that of the unmarried (7:25-40). Paul argues that single people and widows may marry—it is not wrong. Yet he advises them to remain single. Since all in this age is passing away, it would be good to stay single so as to avoid the extra suffering to which marriage exposes a person (vv 25-31). What is more, marriage always divides one's attention between the Lord and the legitimate needs of the spouse. One must not abandon the spouse or ignore his or her needs in order to serve the Lord, but one can remain single so that the Lord can be the sole focus of life and devotion (vv 32-35). Finally, if one is in a situation in which marriage is expected, the person must make his own decision as to whether he should marry the woman for her sake (and perhaps that of the wider family) or whether he can and should simply care for her as a single person (vv 36-38). Paul closes this section by repeating his general principles (vv 39-40).

The third issue Paul deals with is that of food that has been offered to idols (8:1-11:1). Most meat that was available in the marketplace came either from animals slaughtered as sacrifices in the temples or from groups of animals from which one was offered as a dedicatory sacrifice. To scrupulous Jews, all of this meat would be untouched. Furthermore, pagans invited Christians to feasts in their homes and to private feasts held in the precincts of pagan temples, where trade guilds also held feasts. Paul discusses these issues and uses them to teach wider principles of Christian conduct.

First, love, not knowledge, is the key to correct behavior (8:1-13). Some Corinthians felt superior because they were convinced that idols had no reality (there is only one God), and therefore any food offered to them was still fit to eat. Paul again accepts their slogans, but counters with the statement, "Knowledge puffs up, but love builds up" (v 1, NIV). God is not concerned with what we know or eat, but he is concerned with whether or not we love our fellow Christians. The concern is not that a fellow Christian might become enraged because one indulged, but that he or she might have a vulnerable conscience and indulge himself, even though he believed it wrong and thus in his own eyes apostasizes from the faith (i.e., rebels against Christ). Such leading astray is not love. It would be better never to eat meat than to lead a fellow Christian into sin.

Second, he points out that one should subordinate one's own interests to those of others, especially those of Christ and his gospel (9:1-23). Both the examples of the apostles, who expected the church to support them and their families (cf. Lk 10:5-7), and Scripture prove that Paul had the right to demand support from the Corinthians. This had not been his practice, for he had normally made tents to support his ministry, though he did accept gifts from other churches. Paul did this to prevent people from thinking he was peddling religion for profit (9:12) and for the personal satisfaction of doing more than he had to do (vv 16-17). This was part of Paul's larger pol-

icy of subordinating his own personal preferences and interests to those of Christ and his gospel (vv 19-23).

Third, the bravado of the strong who demonstrate their liberty with disregard of fellow Christians is spiritually dangerous (9:24-10:22). It is not who begins but who completes the Christian life that counts; therefore, it is a life of discipline, not relaxed license (9:24-27). Israel in the wilderness presents an example of failure in this regard. They had "baptism" and "the Lord's Supper" (10:2-4), just like the church, yet most of them did not make it to the Promised Land. The reason God destroyed them was simple: they turned to sin. Likewise, the Christian has to be careful not to be so proud about faith and freedom that he becomes careless about sin and falls from the faith (v 12). On the other hand, Christians need not be fearful, for the temptation is not more powerful than they are; God has provided a way of escape, if they will take it (v 13).

Another link between the Israelites and the Corinthians pertains to partaking of a sacrificial meal (10:14-22). In the Lord's Supper there is a sharing of the blood and body of Christ, just as real as Israel's sacrifices on the altar. Food offered to idols is also a sharing, not with the supposed god, but with the real demon that is behind the idol. To try to share at both tables is to provoke God's jealousy just as Israel did (v 22).

A summary of the discussion draws the three chapters together (10:23-11:1). Since the food is not changed by being offered to idols, and since all food really belongs to God, one may eat anything sold in the market—do not ask any questions (10:25-26). Likewise, the Christian may eat anything served at a dinner in the home of an unbeliever. However, if someone points out that the food was offered to idols, the Christian should pass it by, not because it would hurt him, but because it is an issue with the person who raised the question, and the Christian is concerned about the good of his neighbor (vv 27-30). In other words, follow Paul's example as he patterns himself in turn after Christ, who served others rather than himself. Act so that God's reputation and character shine through even in what one eats (v 31); try to offend no one but to benefit each person in moving him toward salvation (v 32).

The fourth issue Paul deals with is that of order in church meetings (11:2-14:40). The Corinthians' house churches had lively meetings, but rather than showing unity in Christ, they demonstrated selfishness. Paul had no desire to change what they did; he did want to change how they did it.

The first problem in the meetings was the behavior of married women (11:1-16). The sign of marriage in that day was the wearing of a veil or distinctive hairstyle, as a ring is today. Women praying and delivering prophecies in church was no issue for Paul, but the women may have felt that this loosed them from their husbands (cf. Mk 12:25) and therefore was a reason to set aside their veils. Paul argues that husband and wife are intimately joined, just as humans are to God (1 Cor 11:3). Therefore as humans should not shame but glorify God, so the wife should act toward her husband. Thus, while Paul approves of ministry by women, he puts marriage first.

The second problem in the meetings was that of making class distinctions (11:17-34). Until the weekly Lord's Supper began to be turned into the sacrifice of the Mass in the third and fourth centuries, it was a full shared meal. Middle- and upper-class Christians could come earlier to the church gatherings and also provide better food and drink for themselves. Following the customs of pagan clubs, they had no scruples against starting early and feasting as befit their class, so long as at least simple food was provided for the slaves and peasants who could not come as early (v 21). This shamed the poorer Christians and made them feel class distinctions keenly (v 22). This, argues Paul, is not the Lord's Supper but a sham (v 20).

Paul repeats the words of institution to point out that they all are participating in Christ's body and blood (cf. 10:16-17), not their own meal. To do it in an unworthy manner, with divisions and class distinctions among them, is to profane his meal by failing to demonstrate the unity of his body, the church (11:29), and thus invite his judgment, which they were already experiencing. Instead, they should examine their own motives and truly gather as one to eat this common meal.

The third problem in their meetings was the use of spiritual gifts (12:1–14:40). It is possible that some people in these house churches, under the influence of Gnostic ideas in which the spiritual is good and the material evil, and feeling inspired by a spirit, cried out, "Jesus [meaning the human Jesus as opposed to the spiritual Christ] be cursed." It is not the Spirit of God saying this, argues Paul, for the Spirit in us cries the basic Christian confession, "Jesus is Lord."

Others in these churches were exalting their own particular gift, especially the gift of tongues, shouting down others or refusing to give them a turn. There is only one Spirit and he gives all the gifts, Paul argues (12:4-6). The Spirit manifests himself sovereignly in each Christian, not simply for the Christian's own benefit, but for the good of all (v 7). Since it is the Spirit, not a given manifestation, that the Christian has, the gifts manifested could change from meeting to meeting.

That same Spirit has made all Christians into one organic unity in Christ (12:12-13). Thus not only does the one Spirit give all the gifts—all are equally inspired—but all the gifts are equally needed for the proper functioning of the body of Christ (vv 14-26). No one can say that his lack of a given gift makes him less a part of the body; indeed, the less noticeable gifts may well be the more important. Thus, within the body of Christ, there are not only different manifestations of the Spirit through individuals in a given meeting, but different ministries or functions of individuals in the body (vv 27-31).

Therefore, it is not the demonstration of a particular gift that shows one's spirituality, but how one demonstrates it—that is, whether one manifests it with love (13:1-13). Any gift exercised for selfish purposes may be a genuine gift of the Spirit, but it is worthless to the individual (vv 1-3). This is because love is the opposite of selfishness (vv 4-7). In fact, the gifts of the Spirit are only for the period between Jesus' first coming and his second coming, when the kingdom of God will be perfectly revealed and the King will be present in person, and thus the intermediary gifts of the Spirit will be no longer necessary (vv 10, 12). It is not giftedness but faith and hope that will have a reward then, and love, which is the greatest, because it will continue as Christians live in perfect love with each other and with Jesus (v 13).

Applying this to Corinth, Paul argues that while one should desire all the gifts, love dictates that prophecy should be the gift of choice in the church meetings (14:1-25). The Corinthians had evidently been stressing tongues. Tongues without interpretation is of little value to anyone except to the speaker himself. It does not build anyone up; its confusion seems madness to outsiders. Outside the church meetings there is a role for tongues, both as a sign of judgment (v 21) and for private devotion (v 18), but inside, only with interpretation. Prophecy, however, both builds up and convicts, and thus is to be sought in the meetings.

In the church meetings, then, both gifts and order are

to prevail (14:26-40). All types of gifts are allowed expression with a goal of mutual edification, not selfish demonstration (v 26). Tongues speakers must have an interpreter; both they and prophets must speak in turn, with time being taken to evaluate the utterances after every few speakers (vv 27-33). Furthermore, the women, who were perhaps chatting in the service (perhaps due to habits learned in Jewish synagogues, where they were segregated and did not participate) are to cease their chattering, pay attention, and learn, asking questions at home if they do not understand (vv 34-36). In his concluding summary, Paul states that all should be done in an orderly manner (vv 37-40).

The fifth issue Paul deals with is that of the resurrection of the dead (ch 15). Some of the problems mentioned earlier concerning loose morals (chs 5–6), ascetic denial, sexuality (ch 7), or feeling one was resurrected already (ch 11) point to the fact that some Corinthians did not believe in the resurrection of the body, though they apparently believed in the resurrection of Jesus and the immortality of the human soul.

Paul reaffirms that the resurrection of Jesus is an essential part of the gospel message (15:1-19). The unified voice of the church was that Jesus not only died but rose again and appeared to numerous witnesses (vv 3-11). If they were consistent in their antiresurrection argument, Christ could not have been raised. Yet if this were the case, the whole gospel message is false and all their hopes for salvation are in vain (vv 12-19).

Since Christ has been raised, Christians will also be raised because of their solidarity with him (15:20-28). As they had experienced the results of being in Adam, so now they will experience the results of being in Christ. But resurrection does not happen at once. There are progressive stages: (a) Christ was first; (b) Christians will be raised at his coming; (c) Christ must reign until he extends kingdom rule over the whole world, destroying all demonic powers (including death itself); and (d) then he will turn over the perfected kingdom to the Father (vv 23-28).

Resurrection hope also explains Christian practices such as baptizing people on behalf of others who had died (probably people who had turned to Christ but had died before they could be baptized, 15:29), and willingness to risk death for Christ (vv 30-32).

Paul admits that there are intellectual problems involved, but these are solved when one realizes that resurrection includes both continuity and discontinuity (15:35-50). Just as seed and plant are the same and yet different, and just as many types of bodies exist, so it is with the resurrection. What was perishable, dishonorable, weak, and physical (i.e., in Adam) will be raised imperishable, glorious, powerful, and spiritual (i.e., in Christ). Indeed, it is only as Christians thus become like Christ, the heavenly man, that they can become part of God's kingdom.

With excitement Paul shares his real hope, that of transformation (15:51-58). At the coming of Christ the dead will be raised and transformed. But the living will also need transformation, and this will happen in a split second, making all of them impervious to death. Then they will truly know the victory already present in Jesus' resurrection (vv 54-57). A concluding summary draws the practical conclusion that this teaching should give them assurance of a reward for anything done for Christ now (v 58).

The sixth issue Paul deals with is that of the collection for the needy Jerusalem church (16:1-4). Because of famine in Judea in the 40s, the church there had become impoverished. Partly because of the need and partly to further the unity of the church, Paul took up a collection in some of his churches for the Judean church. He answers the Corinthians' practical queries by stating that the collection should be made weekly according to ability, not all at once when Paul arrives (16:2). When he comes, he will send off the money with their own messengers. Paul remains vague about whether or not he will accompany them, allaying suspicions that somehow he plans to profit from it (cf. 2 Cor 8–9).

Final Remarks and Closing, 16:5-24 Having come to the end, Paul discusses his travel plans, including his intention for a lengthy visit whenever he leaves Ephesus (cf. 2 Cor 1). Timothy was either coming with the letter or else would arrive shortly after another mission; they were to respect him and help him return. Paul points out that he urged Apollos to visit Corinth, in case some suspect Paul is against him. A closing formal exhortation to firm faith and love leads into his final customary greetings. He praises the Corinthian messengers who had brought him their letter (16:15-18) and sends greetings from Aquila and Prisca (Priscilla), his comissionaries who had helped him found the church in Corinth (Acts 18:2-3, 18). Referring to the customary greeting in the church, he tells them to greet each other with a kiss on each cheek (16:20). Paul then takes the pen from the scribe, as was normal, and writes the closing exhortation—placing a curse on those who do not love Jesus, the common Aramaic expression used in the church "Come, O Lord" (*Marana tha,* perhaps used to close services), and providing an assurance of his own love for them (vv 21-24).

See also Acts of the Apostles, Book of the; Corinth; Corinthians, Second Letter to the; Paul, The Apostle.

CORINTHIANS, Second Letter to the

PREVIEW
• Author
• Date and Origin
• Background
• Purpose and Teaching
• Content

Author The apostle Paul is the acknowledged author of 2 Corinthians. While some scholars argue that 2 Corinthians 2:14–7:4 and 10–13 are separate letters, only in the case of 6:14–7:1 is Paul's authorship disputed. This section is admittedly a strange digression, but stranger still would be the thought that an editor could have inserted it in such an unusual place. Also the repetition of thought in 7:2 from 6:13 indicates that Paul is aware that he has digressed from his topic and is repeating a phrase to bring his readers back to the subject.

Date and Origin After writing both the "previous letter" (1 Cor 5:9) and 1 Corinthians from Ephesus in AD 55, Paul continued to work there. Sometime during the next year a crisis arose in Corinth. Paul made a quick trip across the Aegean Sea, but he could not resolve the crisis, and due to the personal opposition of a leader in the church (likely an interloper bearing letters of recommendation from Jerusalem), he had to withdraw (2 Cor 2:1, 5). Returning to Ephesus from this "painful visit," Paul dispatched Titus with a blistering "letter of tears," his third letter to that church (2 Cor 2:4; 7:8, 12), which led to the excommunication of the leader and the repentance of the church. This letter has been lost. Meanwhile a situation erupted in Ephesus during which death (probably execution) seemed so certain that Paul despaired of life (see Acts 19:23-41; cf. Rom 16:4; 2 Cor 1:8-9). Paul was not killed, but his escape seemed miraculous.

Leaving Ephesus in early AD 56, Paul traveled north to Troas seeking Titus and news of Corinth. Unable to endure without news, he abandoned a promising mission in Troas and sailed for Philippi. There he met Titus, who explained the change of heart in Corinth. Second Corinthians 1–9 responds to this situation, with chapters 8–9 preparing the Corinthians for an upcoming visit. Later Paul received further news from Corinth that renewed opposition to him was present. In response he penned the self-defense found in 2 Corinthians 10–13. Paul followed up the letter with a visit later in the year (Acts 20:2-3). We do not know the response to 2 Corinthians or the outcome of his final visit, but later the troubled history of the Corinthian church continued, with another Christian leader needing to write a letter at the end of the century (Epistle of Clement).

Background The Corinthian house churches always had great diversity. While those who liked Apollos undoubtedly despised Paul's crude style, others who preferred Peter likely appealed beyond Paul to the more genuine "original" apostles in Jerusalem with their Jewish customs (1 Cor 1). Traveling teachers with letters of commendation from these apostles easily drew a following when they came to Corinth and undermined Paul's authority and even his character. Furthermore, because of this outside influence, the collection for the poor in Jerusalem that Paul had initiated (16:1-4) was left in abeyance, both because it was connected to Paul and because the teachers themselves were taking money from the church. Paul writes to reaffirm his love and to repair the damage caused by the interloper.

Purpose and Teaching In the first section of the letter, Paul has two main purposes. The first is to cement his restored relationship with Corinth, explaining situations, forgiving those who opposed him, and reflecting on the nature of ministry. For Paul, ministry meant both intense suffering and comfort. Physical and emotional suffering came from the situations and people he worked with, but his knowledge of future reward and his experience of the power of God working in him brought profound joy and comfort. Due to his own recent brush with death, Paul also reflects on what happens at death. His expectation is to receive a resurrection body and be in the presence of Jesus at death.

The second purpose of this section is to get the collection for Jerusalem on track again. In this context he gives major teaching on giving and Christian economics: Christians are to follow Christ in giving freely; economic equality is the principle governing who gives to whom.

The second section of the letter is an impassioned self-defense, refuting the interloper's claims to superiority. Neither oratory nor pedigree counts in Christian ministry, but only the call of God.

In both sections one observes Paul's deep desire for the unity of the church, both unity within the local community and unity with leaders appointed by God, such as Paul.

Content

Greeting, 1:1-7 A standard greeting (2 Cor 1:1-2) comes before Paul's usual thanksgiving (vv 3-7). The topic of the thanksgiving—comfort in the midst of suffering—is the topic of chapters 1–7. Paul knows what it is to suffer, but it is in suffering that he has experienced God's comfort, which he passes on to the Corinthians.

Paul's Explanation, 1:8–2:13 Paul informs them of the danger he had suffered in Ephesus, one so great that he did not believe he would survive. His eventual survival seemed like a virtual resurrection, reinforcing his conviction that God, not human strength, is the only Christian refuge (1:8-11). In that and in all situations, Paul's one boast is that of a clear conscience before God (vv 12-14).

Paul had told them of plans for a double visit (cf. 1 Cor 16:5-6), but except for his brief "painful visit," he had not fulfilled his plan (2 Cor 1:15–2:4). He defends himself from charges of either not planning in the Spirit or hypocritical vacillation. He was indeed as good as his word (cf. Jas 5:12), for his life reflected God's fulfilled promise in Jesus, but he had changed plans so as not to repeat the "painful visit" of the previous year. It was love, not fickleness, that motivated the delayed visit.

The Corinthians had responded to Paul's "letter of tears" by excommunicating the person who had opposed Paul (not the same person as in 1 Cor 5). Since the person became repentant, Paul called for his restoration to the community, freely and graciously forgiving the man who had hurt him. Excommunication is for the unrepentant; its purpose is complete once the person repents (2 Cor 2:5-11).

Paul then recounted his journey from Ephesus to Philippi, when he sought news of the response to the "letter of tears" (2:12-13). After telling how he left an opportunity to minister in Troas to go to find Titus in Philippi, he breaks the narrative with a long digression.

Nature of Apostolic Ministry, 2:14–7:4 The apostolic ministry in which Paul took part is like the ministry of Jesus, one of suffering and glory. Even in suffering there is triumph in Christ, for Christians share Christ's triumph. Yet just like the perfumes of a Roman triumph were joy to the victors but meant death for prisoners on their way to execution, so Jesus' triumph is life to the believer and death to the unbeliever (2:14-17).

This triumph may have sounded like a boast, but Paul is not engaging in self-exaltation. Indeed, he has no need of the letters of commendation that the interloper in Corinth carried from Jerusalem, for the Corinthians are themselves the proof of his ministry (3:1-3). His boast is not in himself but in the new covenant in the Spirit, which unlike the old covenant is not fading (here Paul follows one Jewish interpretation of Ex 34:29-35, that Moses put the veil over his face so the people would not see the glory fade), nor does it veil the presence of God. The new covenant is permanent; it reveals God directly in the Spirit. There is no deceit or hiddenness, for the message is not about Paul but about Jesus, who is light itself (2 Cor 3:4–4:6).

Paul the messenger, however, is simply the cheap, breakable pot that contains the priceless treasure, revealing by way of contrast that the only power in the gospel is God's power. This contrast of weakness and power is seen in the sufferings of the apostle, a type of living death modeled after the sufferings of Jesus, out of which the life of Jesus flows to others (4:7-15).

Therefore, despite intense suffering, Paul has courage, for he looks beyond this life to the rewards of the coming life. His whole motivation is one of faith, not sight, for he lives already for unseen realities (4:16-18). When he dies, Paul expects to receive an eternal resurrection body. His hope is not of becoming a disembodied soul ("naked") but of passing immediately into a glorified bodily life, already guaranteed by the presence of the Spirit. This hope was likely the fruit of his near brush with death in Ephesus, when he must have meditated and prayed about what would come at death (5:1-5). Because this future includes Christ's judgment, Paul wanted to make every effort to live in the light of that judgment, which he already saw by faith (vv 6-10).

Far from trying to commend or exalt himself, Paul was simply presenting what he was—a person filled with the love of Christ and convinced that all should live not for themselves but for Christ (5:11-15). No one should be valued from a merely human point of view, not Paul, nor even Christ (for Paul before his conversion had a human opinion of Christ that his conversion had radically changed); everyone should be valued from the point of view of the new creation. Paul's job was simply to announce the reconciliation of the new creation, which God has already effected on his side and which only awaits a person's ratification on the human side (5:16-20).

Paul, then, was a coworker with God, announcing salvation, using every means consistent with God's character to proclaim the message, and suffering everything imaginable to demonstrate the extent of God's love (6:1-10). Therefore, Paul had nothing against the Corinthians. If there was any blockage in their relationship with him, it must be on their side (6:11-13).

Digression on Purity, 6:14–7:1 Perhaps suspecting that the real block in the relationship was their love of the world, or that the Corinthians might not be totally over the problems mentioned in 1 Corinthians, Paul digressed into a discussion about the purity and sanctification of believers. There are two groups, light and darkness, Christ and the devil, believers and unbelievers. Therefore, as Exodus 25:8, Leviticus 26:11-12, Isaiah 52:11, Ezekiel 37:27, and Hosea 1:10 show (phrases from these passages flow into each other in a style of chain quotation familiar to Jews), Christians should not be closely bound to unbelievers in marriage or in business, for it will affect their moral purity.

Return to the Nature of the Apostolic Ministry, 7:2-4 Picking up from 6:13, Paul points out that the Corinthians have nothing substantial against him. He is not criticizing but simply appealing to them in love; even now he is prepared to die for them.

Explanation Concluded, 7:5-16 Having concluded his digression, Paul now returns to his journey, which he left in 2:13. When he met Titus, he received good news about Corinth. He was relieved that his "letter of tears" had been effective, not in simply making them sorry but in bringing them to true repentance that yielded zeal, moral purity, and joy. Furthermore, their behavior toward Titus had been so impressive that Titus's enthusiastic report of his own impressions had further cheered Paul.

Collection for Jerusalem, 8:1–9:15 In the context of restored relationships Paul turns to the sensitive topic of the collection for the church in Jerusalem, which had been impoverished through famines in Judea in the 40s. This collection was both an act of charity (cf. Acts 11:27-30; Gal 2:10) and a symbolic act of unity and fellowship between the Gentile and Jewish branches of the church.

The impoverished and suffering church in Macedonia (Philippi) had given eagerly. Therefore, Titus was coming back to help the Corinthians complete what they had begun the previous year (and probably dropped during the controversy with Paul, 2 Cor 8:1-7). The principles of the collection are (1) the Corinthians should follow the example of Jesus, who became poor for them; (2) they should give freely what they can without regretting that they cannot give more, for God values the eagerness to give expressed in action, not the net amount of the gift; and (3) there should be an economic equality among sections of the church, no one section being enriched at the expense of another (cf. Ex 16:18). This economic equality extends to the relationship between two churches a continent apart (2 Cor 8:8-15).

Titus and two absolutely trustworthy men appointed by the churches for this work will come to supervise the final gathering—Paul would have nothing to do with the money personally—for it is important that not only God but the world be able to see the honesty and integrity of the way the church handles money (8:16-24).

In this section Paul points out that he does not need to argue the reasons for this collection; they were aware of them when they began to gather money the year before. This letter is not an argument for the collection but an encouragement to finish the work, so that when Paul arrives with representatives of other churches carrying their contributions, the Corinthians would not be embarrassed by their relatively wealthy churches not being ready or able to give generously, despite Paul's boasts about their previous eagerness. In saying this, Paul shows himself diplomatic and insightful in motivating human behavior; he makes the best assumptions possible about the present situation (9:1-5).

Paul would not want the Corinthians giving out of guilt, although he, like Jesus (Mt 6:19-20), pointed out that the only real value of money is in giving it to help others. Rather, he wanted them so convinced of God's generosity and ability to provide that they give freely and joyfully. God wanted to enrich them so they could give more. The giving would result in thanksgiving to God by the recipients, who would also pray for those who gave the gift, thereby binding the church together. A closing reminder of the extent of God's own giving finishes the section (2 Cor 9:6-15).

Paul's Self-Defense, 10:1–13:14 There is an abrupt change in tone between 9:15 and 10:1. Now, instead of the tone of conciliation found in 1:1–7:16, there is argument and defense, even threat. Paul's apostleship has been attacked, and he will defend it with vigor.

Paul was indeed a humble person who preferred not to use his authority. Yet when forced, he had something more than authority; he had spiritual power, capable of destroying opposing arguments and bending all to obedience to Jesus. He would use that power in Corinth if he must, though up to that time he had been gentle and had shown this side of his ministry only in letters (10:1-11).

His opponents talked of their qualifications and compared themselves favorably with other ministers. Paul would not enter into this game of comparisons. God had set the sphere of his labors, which was the area in which he founded churches. He was the one who pioneered the church in Corinth, so it is his sphere of ministry, not the interloper's (and such like him). They boasted in having reaped the benefits of his ministry; Paul could point to an original ministry given by God, for it is God's commendation in the end that counts (10:13-18).

Yet the Corinthian rebellion is serious enough to force him into self-defense, ridiculous as such an exercise is. He was shocked by how readily they turned away to every novel doctrine that came along. This tendency strikes fear in Paul's heart (11:1-6).

Paul had been criticized for refusing financial support from Corinth (even though he accepted gifts from other churches; cf. 1 Cor 9). He would continue to refuse such support, for he wanted to undermine the claims of the interloper. If the interloper was really serving God alone, let him work on the same basis as Paul! But since the interloper was false at heart, serving Satan and not God,

he sought money from the church. Paul was astonished that in the Corinthians' vaunted wisdom they did not see through this hypocrisy, yet he hoped that even if he must play the fool in making a self-defense, they would at least accept a fool like Paul. The irony is that his very tender care and concern for the church, his gentleness, was being used against him as a supposed "weakness." Paul, the opponent argued, knew he was false, so therefore did not dare take money from the Corinthians (11:7-21).

Interlopers claimed to come with authority from Jerusalem. They had letters from the apostles; it is unlikely, however, that the apostles would have approved of their activities. Still, they were Jews with respectable authority behind them. Paul felt compelled to state his own credentials. If they were Jews, he was just as pure a Jew. If they served Christ, could their work and sufferings match his? The list of sufferings both gives historical information not found in Acts and points to tireless labor, including days of fasting ("gone without food") and nights spent in prayer ("gone without sleep") (11:21-29).

But this boasting was repulsive to Paul, so he isolated one particular suffering—his escape from Damascus, when he had to hide and slip out of the city in a basket. The story at once shows his effectiveness as an evangelist (in that he was a target of persecution) and shames him, for he could not defend himself and had to slip away under cover of darkness. Yet that weakness was indeed his glory (11:30-33).

His opponents boasted in revelations from God. Paul knew that this boasting was senseless; however, if he must, he would tell them of a revelation superior to theirs, a time when he actually saw the inside of heaven (he is not sure whether it was a vision or an actual bodily experience). This probably happened about AD 42, while Paul was in Tarsus, before Barnabas came for him (Acts 9:30; 11:25). Paul disliked telling about this, for God's power is more easily seen in his weakness. In fact, Paul's opponents were an affliction of Satan that God allowed to keep Paul humble and to demonstrate his power in Paul's weakness. (The image of a "thorn in my flesh" is one of enemies—Nm 33:55; Jos 23:13; Paul also describes what he means more clearly in 2 Cor 12:10). If vulnerability shows God's power, Paul willingly accepts the weakness (12:1-10).

Paul felt ashamed that he had to boast. The opponents boasted in coming from the Jerusalem "superapostles." Paul pointed out that he was their equal, although both are nothing. God had set his mark upon Paul's work. With biting irony he asks forgiveness for not having taken money from the Corinthians (12:11-13).

Yet Paul would come a third time, and he would keep to the same policy of not taking any support from them but giving himself freely to them, just as Jesus had done on earth. Not only he, but all his envoys, kept to the same policy. No one could accuse him of deceit or inconsistency (12:14-18). However, he feared coming to them, for he knew that the community had not just rebelled against him but was also in internal disorder. This disunity and immorality would humble and pain Paul (12:19–13:4).

Therefore, the Corinthians had better examine themselves. Were they really following Jesus or not? If so, they should see that Paul was also following Jesus. Yet Paul's concern was not for his own position—he was content to be rejected ("weak")—but for their following the truth. He hoped for their repentance, not to protect himself, but so that he need not be severe when he came (13:5-10).

Probably taking the pen from the scribe at this point, Paul closes with a final appeal to repent and come to unity as a church. Brief greetings from the church in Macedonia and a formal blessing closes his correspondence with the Corinthians (vv 11-13).

See also Acts of the Apostles, Book of the; Corinth; Corinthians, First Letter to the; Paul, The Apostle.

CORMORANT Large, black web-footed waterfowl, considered ceremonially unclean for the Israelites (Lv 11:17; Dt 14:17). *See* Birds.

CORN Word often used to denote grain, especially wheat. Maize, the plant known in America as corn, was unknown in the Middle East in biblical times. *See* Plants (Barley; Wheat).

CORNELIUS Roman centurion and the first gentile Christian mentioned in the book of Acts.

The story of Cornelius's conversion through the preaching of the apostle Peter is recorded in Acts 10:1–11:18. Before his conversion, Cornelius was well known to the Jews as a person who feared God, prayed continually, and gave alms.

At first the church was composed only of Jews, who were reluctant to preach the gospel to Gentiles because law-abiding Jews never had fellowship with "pagans." Peter, a law-abiding Jew, had scruples about entering a Gentile's house and eating "unclean" food. Through a vision, however, God led Peter to Cornelius's house to preach the gospel to him and his family and close friends. Before Peter had finished speaking, and before baptism or the laying on of hands could be administered, God dramatically demonstrated his acceptance of Gentiles into the fellowship of the church by giving them the gift of the Holy Spirit. Peter remained several days in Cornelius's house, no doubt rejoicing in the centurion's conversion and instructing him in his newfound faith.

Cornelius's conversion represented a significant step in the separation of the early church from Judaism. Cornelius did not have to submit to any of the Jewish practices, such as circumcision or eating only ritually "clean" animals. For the first time a gentile believer was accepted into the church on equal terms with Jewish Christians.

See also Acts of the Apostles, Book of the.

CORNER GATE Gate presumably located in the northwest corner of the Jerusalem wall. After King Jehoash of Israel captured King Amaziah of Judah, he tore down a section of the Jerusalem wall from the Corner Gate to the Ephraim Gate (2 Kgs 14:13; 2 Chr 25:23); later King Uzziah of Judah built towers at this gate (2 Chr 26:9). Jeremiah (Jer 31:38) foretells a time when the Jerusalem wall will be rebuilt from the Tower of Hananel to the Corner Gate. Zechariah (Zec 14:10) also envisions a period of security and prosperity epitomized by the presence of the Jerusalem wall, including the Corner Gate.

See also Jerusalem.

CORNERS OF THE EARTH Figurative term denoting the borders and extremities of the earth (Jb 37:3; Is 11:12; Jer 25:32; 31:8; Ez 7:2; Rv 7:1; 20:8).

CORNERSTONE Term used in the NT to describe the exalted position of Jesus.

Jesus used this term to speak of himself in the parable of the wicked tenants (Mt 21:42; Mk 12:10; Lk 20:17). The setting for this parable was his final ministry in Jerusalem after he had cleansed the temple. The Jewish leaders had questioned him about his actions, and part of his reply was this parable, which symbolically addressed the situation between Jesus and the leaders. The Jewish leaders were represented in the parable as the tenants who were caring for the vineyard, which symbolized God's people. Those tenants wickedly refused to honor the owner, who represented God, ultimately putting his son to death. The parable speaks of the coming death of Jesus in symbolic terms, and Jesus concluded it by referring the Jewish leaders back to their own Scriptures, specifically Psalm 118:22-23 (cf. Is 28:16), which he understood as speaking of his rejection and exaltation. The Jewish leaders rejected Jesus, but God would exalt him as the cornerstone.

Second, the term is used in Acts 4:11, which describes Peter's defense before the Jewish rulers in Jerusalem. Peter explained to them the healing of the lame beggar by the temple gate, stressing that the healing took place by the name of Jesus Christ, the Nazarene whom they had crucified but whom God had raised from the dead (v 10). He then quotes Psalm 118:22 to confirm the events as being according to Scripture. It seems clear that Peter intended the rejection of the stone to refer to Jesus' death and the placing of the stone as the cornerstone to refer to Jesus' resurrection and exaltation. Thus, "cornerstone" designates Jesus in his exalted position with the Father.

The term is also used in 1 Peter 2:6-7. In verse 4 Peter combines the idea of the rejection of the stone in Psalm 118:22 with the idea of the chosen and precious stone in Isaiah 28:16, adding the idea of living from his own experience of Jesus' resurrection. Peter is encouraging his readers to come to Jesus, that they may be built up as a spiritual house to God. This imagery is used to bring out the exalted nature of Jesus. In verse 6 Peter quotes Isaiah 28:16, which speaks of the chosen and precious cornerstone, and related this to believers. In verses 7-8 he quotes Psalm 118:22, referring to the rejection of the stone, and Isaiah 8:14, which speaks of a stone of stumbling, and relates these to unbelievers. Peter's purpose is to set before his readers the exalted position of Jesus and to encourage them to remember him to whom they were called.

It is evident that the OT concept of cornerstone is applied to Jesus to emphasize his exalted position with the Father and so to encourage the believer. In Ephesians 2:20 brief reference is also made to Christ Jesus as the cornerstone upon which the church is built.

CORNET* *See* Musical Instruments (Hatzotzrot); Music.

CORRECTION *See* Discipline.

CORRUPTION, Mount of Southern end of the Mt of Olives, called "corruption" because King Solomon built idols there for his foreign wives (1 Kgs 11:7; 2 Kgs 23:13). The term is possibly an ironic play on the Hebrew word for "anointing." The site may have originally been called the "Mount of Anointing" because oil from the many olive groves on its slopes was used in consecration ceremonies. *See* Olives, Mount of.

COS Island of the Sporades group in the Aegean, containing a city of the same name, located off the coast of Caria in Asia Minor. Cos was the apostle Paul's first stop beyond Ephesus on his voyage to Jerusalem at the end of his third missionary tour (Acts 21:1, KJV "Coos"). In the Apocrypha, Cos and other areas are mentioned as recipients of a decree by the Roman consul Lucius forbidding war against the Jewish population (1 Macc 15:23).

Cos (modern Kos) was a major shipping center,

famous for its wheat, ointments, wines, and silk. It eventually became one of the financial centers of the eastern Mediterranean.

Hippocrates, the "father of medicine," was born and practiced medicine there in the fifth and fourth centuries BC. Under King Herod's rule Cos received perpetual revenues, and a statue was built there to honor his son Herod Antipas.

COSAM Ancestor of Jesus, Addi's father and Elmadam's son, listed only in Luke's genealogy (3:28). *See* Genealogy of Jesus Christ.

COSMETICS* That which is applied to the body to enhance one's appearance.

Eye paint originally served the medical purpose of preventing flies from spreading infection by settling on the eyes, especially of sleeping persons. Substances such as kohl, malachite, and stibium had astringent and antiseptic properties and so were useful medications. These minerals were found and made into a paste by mixing them with gum arabic or water. The paint was compounded in a small bowl and applied either with a spatula or with the finger. Many such bowls dating to 800 BC have been found at various Palestinian sites. Much earlier ones have been recovered from Egypt, where women used green malachite as an eye paint. In the Roman period antimony came into popular use.

When eye makeup became fashionable as a cosmetic procedure, the eyes were outlined in black, using galena or lead sulphide to make them look large, a practice that was followed particularly in Egypt, Palestine, and Mesopotamia. Eyebrows were also darkened by the application of a black paste. Jezebel decorated her eyes with cosmetics just before her dramatic death in about 841 BC (2 Kgs 9:30). In biblical Jewish society, painted eyes were associated with women lacking in virtue (Jer 4:30; Ez 23:40). Henna was used as a paint and was applied to parts of the body, including the hands and feet, as well as the fingernails and toenails.

Oils, often perfumed, were used as a protection for the skin against the sun. Anointing with oil was considered so important that when the troops of the Israelite king Ahaz were repatriated in about 730 BC, they were clothed, fed, and anointed (2 Chr 28:15). Anointing a guest's feet was a normal act of hospitality. The process may also have had hygienic significance. Many persons found it far more convenient to apply perfumes than to wash the body, particularly when water was in short supply.

An alabaster jar of ointment (Lk 7:37) was an extremely expensive gift since it would have to be imported. At the archaeological dig of Lachish an excellent ivory ointment flask from about the 13th century BC was unearthed. A Babylonian inscription described a fragrant ointment made from the root of ginger grass, which was imported from Arabia. In NT times costly ointments most probably came from India.

COTTON Soft, white, fibrous hairs surrounding the seeds in the boll of various plants of the mallow family (genus *Gossypium*), woven into thread and cloth (Is 19:9). *See* Cloth and Cloth Manufacturing; Plants.

COUCH Article of furniture for reclining in sleep or rest. *See* Furniture.

COUNSEL, COUNSELOR Advice; adviser, especially on legal matters (such as a lawyer). In Bible times a counselor in a king's court was like a U.S. cabinet member today. A counselor might at times have been in line to succeed the king. Ahithophel, counselor to David and Absalom, gave advice as sound as the "oracle of God" (2 Sm 16:23). The elders of Israel counseled King Rehoboam (1 Kgs 12:6), as did the friends with whom Rehoboam had grown up (vv 7-8), although his friends gave poor advice. The Bible mentions official counselors in Egypt (Is 19:11) and Babylon (Dn 3:2-3).

A wise person seeks counsel when making plans: "Plans go wrong for lack of advice; many counselors bring success" (Prv 15:22, NLT). One's counselors may be one's parents (1:8), older people (Ez 7:26), prophets (2 Chr 25:16), wise men (Jer 18:18), or friends (Prv 27:9, KJV). Some counselors are evil, giving deceitful advice (Prv 12:5).

According to the Bible, God also counsels. He frustrates the counsel of the nations who oppose him (Ps 33:10), but his own counsel endures for many generations (v 11). No one may counsel the Lord (Is 40:13). His Messiah is called "Wonderful Counselor" (9:6).

According to the NT, the Spirit counsels or comforts believers (Jn 14:16-17). Christ sends the Holy Spirit to his people (16:7), and the Spirit, also called the Spirit of truth, bears witness to Christ (15:26). The ascended Jesus Christ is seen as a counselor in God's heavenly court (1 Jn 2:1, "advocate").

See also Spirit of God.

COURT Area enclosed by buildings or walls and without a roof. The temple had courts for priests, women, and Gentiles. Courts were common in private homes as well. *See* Architecture; Homes and Dwellings; Tabernacle; Temple.

COURTS AND TRIALS Legal disputes were as much a part of life in Bible times as they are today. The ways that courts operated and trials were conducted, however, were quite different. Unless those customs are understood, modern readers of the Bible, thinking of contemporary legal procedures, may misunderstand the judicial accounts contained in the Bible.

Old Testament Legal Procedures

Exodus to Deuteronomy The books of Exodus, Leviticus, Numbers, and Deuteronomy contain most of the law in the OT, plus much other information about courts and legal procedures. Those books reveal how trials were conducted before Israel had kings. Certain changes in the legal system occurring after the establishment of the monarchy (c. 1000 BC) are described in other OT books.

The OT depicts God as supreme lawgiver and judge, with Moses and later the kings as God's deputies. But Moses did not create the law or decide the most difficult cases, which were referred directly to God for the decision (see Lv 24:10-23; Nm 15:32-36; 27:1-11). When disputes arose between Israel's leaders, God intervened, judging the guilty party directly (Nm 16–17). Thus law is seen in the OT as a divine revelation, not a human creation, as it was regarded in ancient Babylon.

Usually it was not necessary to seek God's direct guidance; precedent was sufficient. Elders were appointed in Israel to serve as judges of all but the most serious cases, relieving Moses of the burden of judging all the people himself (Ex 18:13-27). Deuteronomy 16:18 specifies that "judges" be appointed in every town; in other passages those responsible for punishing criminals are called "the elders" (Dt 19:12). The local judges were obviously nonprofessionals selected from the most respected members of each tribe or village. Difficult cases were referred to a central court of justice to be decided by the priests and, in the period of the judges, by the civil and military leader (17:8-12). Deborah and Samuel were both examples of such "judges of Israel." Samuel even conducted a circuit court in a number of different centers (Jgs 4:4-5; 1 Sm 7:15-17).

In Israel, as in other ancient societies, private prosecution was the norm. An individual with a grievance had to bring the case before the court. Only in situations of idolatry or other serious religious crimes were public prosecutions instituted (Dt 13; 17:2-7). Even in murder cases prosecution was left in the hands of the victim's relatives. One relative, called the "avenger of blood," had to pursue the alleged murderer to the nearest city of refuge, where a trial was held (Nm 35:10-34; Dt 19:1-13).

Trials were held in a public place, such as the open space near a city gate (Dt 21:19). During the trial, the judges were seated, but the parties to the dispute and the witnesses stood. At least two witnesses were required to convict (19:15). They had to be eyewitnesses who had caught the accused red-handed. Where such clear-cut evidence was lacking (for example in disputes over ownership), the litigants could take an oath to demonstrate their honesty (Ex 22:8-13). If a husband suspected his wife of infidelity but had no proof, he could require her to undergo an ordeal of drinking "bitter water" to demonstrate her innocence (Nm 5:6-31).

When all the evidence had been presented, the judges gave their verdict. Those who had brought the accusation had the duty of enforcing the court's sentence. Thus, a witness of idolatry had to throw the first stone at the guilty person's execution (Dt 17:7). Certain administrative officials may have had the job of writing down the court's decision and seeing that it was enforced (16:18). At times it may have been difficult for people to uphold their legal rights if their opponent came from a strong and wealthy family.

Other Old Testament Books When Israel became a kingdom, certain changes were made in its judicial system. Most obviously, the king became the supreme judge who dealt with the most difficult cases. Solomon demonstrated his great wisdom in adjudicating between two women who both claimed to be the mother of a particular baby (1 Kgs 3:16-28). Kings, who had all the power necessary to enforce their decisions, were expected to use it to help the weak members of society, such as orphans and widows (Ps 72:12).

In practice, however, Israel's kings did not always live up to that ideal. Absalom sowed the seeds of a revolution by telling those who came to the royal court that his father, King David, did not administer justice well (2 Sm 15:1-6). One notable trial in the OT illustrates how royal judicial powers could be completely misused by unscrupulous rulers. Naboth was put to death on a trumped-up charge of blasphemy so that King Ahab could extend his palace grounds by taking over Naboth's vineyard. Though the charge was false, the trial followed correct legal procedures. Two scoundrels were found to give evidence that they had heard Naboth curse God and the king (1 Kgs 21:10); one witness would have been insufficient to secure conviction. Naboth was tried by the elders of the city in a public place. After being convicted he was taken outside the city and executed (vv 11-13). In other trials the prophet Jeremiah was charged with subversive activities more than once (Jer 26; 37:11–38:28).

The prophets sometimes pictured God as taking Israel to court to answer for the nation's misdeeds. God would list Israel's sins and invite the people to explain their behavior. Sometimes heaven and earth, or the mountains, were called to be witnesses confirming the truth of God's accusations. Finally judgment was pronounced (e.g., Is 1:2-26; 43; Jer 2:4-37; Mi 6).

A theme running through the book of Job is Job's request for a trial. Job thought that if he were given a fair hearing, his innocence would be demonstrated and God would stop causing him so much suffering (cf. Jb 13:23). Eventually God heeded Job's request and a long cross-examination began, finally reducing Job to silence (42:1-6).

New Testament Legal Procedures Numerous trials occur in the NT. Jesus was tried by the Sanhedrin (the supreme Jewish religious court) and also by the Roman governor. The book of Acts mentions various court actions designed to stop the spread of Christianity. Luke, the author of Acts, presents a vivid and accurate description of how courts operated in provinces of the Roman Empire. Acts reaches a climax with Paul traveling to Rome to have his case heard by the Roman emperor Nero. Legal procedures in Roman courts were governed by complicated rules broadly resembling modern judicial technicalities. Serious crime was handled by public prosecutors, and trials were usually conducted by one judge. There were lawyers for the prosecution and lawyers for the defense.

In Judea and other provinces of the empire, the local legal system was not suppressed. Traditional Jewish courts were allowed to try minor and religious offenses (Acts 4; 6:12–7:60) but were not permitted to handle serious cases where the death penalty might be involved. For that reason, when the Sanhedrin found Jesus guilty of blasphemy for claiming to be the Son of God and the Messiah, they had to transfer the case to Pontius Pilate, the Roman procurator (governor) of Judea. The Jews considered blasphemy worthy of death, but as they admitted to Pilate, "It is not lawful for us to put any man to death" (Jn 18:31, RSV). The rule throughout the Roman Empire was that only governors could pronounce the death sentence. Execution of the apostle James by Jewish authorities, mentioned by the Jewish historian Josephus, took place during an interregnum between two governors. The stoning of Stephen was done in haste, without the consent of Pilate (Acts 7).

The Trials of Jesus Jesus was first tried by the Sanhedrin, presided over by the high priest. By later standards of Jewish legal practice, that trial was somewhat irregular. For example, it seems to have been held both at night and on the eve of a festival. Criminal trials were not supposed to take place at such times. It is uncertain that those rules existed in Jesus' day, but even if they did, little can be made of that technicality since the Jewish court had no power to carry out its sentence.

After conviction by the Sanhedrin, Jesus was taken to Pilate, whose Jerusalem residence, the old royal palace called the Praetorium, was on the western side of the city near the modern Jaffa Gate. The Romans were unlikely to sentence anyone to death in a religious matter, so the Jewish authorities presented their charges against Jesus in political language: he violated the law by "forbidding us to give tribute to Caesar, and saying that he himself is Christ a king" (Lk 23:2, RSV). Perhaps sensing something false about those charges (they were actually religious rather than political), Pilate sent Jesus to Herod, the ruler of Galilee, who was in Jerusalem at the time. Pilate, who did not have to send Galileans to Herod for trial, probably saw this as a means of avoiding an uncomfortable decision. Herod, however, pronounced Jesus innocent and returned him to Pilate.

Pilate offered to give Jesus a disciplinary beating traditionally given to troublemakers as a warning to behave themselves in the future (Lk 23:16). But that did not satisfy Jesus' accusers, who pressed the charge of insurrection, threatening to report Pilate to the emperor if he did not convict Jesus. Pilate, who had not been a very successful governor, feared official complaints about his administration, so the threat worked. He sentenced Jesus to be crucified on the charge of being king of the Jews. The heavy scourging that preceded the Crucifixion was never a punishment by itself but was a frequent accompaniment to other punishments. Another feature of Roman legal practice illustrated in the Gospels was the division of Jesus' clothes among the soldiers; executioners were allowed to keep such personal effects as a fringe benefit.

The Trials of the Apostle Paul

Paul's trials recorded in the book of Acts also reflect the division between Jewish and Roman authority in legal matters. When arrested, Paul had a preliminary hearing before the Sanhedrin (Acts 23). He was then transferred to the governor for a formal trial in Caesarea, the governor's usual headquarters. There he was tried before Felix, who adjourned the case for two years until a new governor could be appointed. Luke reported that Felix (another unpopular governor) did that to please the Jews, but it was quite common for governors to leave cases to be dealt with by their successors.

When Festus, the new governor, arrived, he suggested that Paul be tried in Jerusalem. Paul, disliking the prospect of being tried there, exercised his right as a Roman citizen to be tried in Rome before the emperor (Acts 25:1-20). The rest of the book of Acts tells how Paul eventually reached Rome and had to wait another two years before his case was heard. No details of Paul's trial in Rome are known, but Nero, who was emperor when Paul arrived, tried very few cases himself. He appointed judges to handle appeals cases such as Paul's, so it is unlikely that Paul was actually tried by Nero.

The right of appeal to the emperor was not the only legal right possessed by Roman citizens. They were also protected from being beaten without a trial, a right asserted by Paul in Philippi and Jerusalem (Acts 16:37; 22:24-29).

See also Avenger of Blood; Cities of Refuge; Civil Law and Justice; Criminal Law and Punishment; Sanhedrin.

COVENANT Arrangement between two parties involving mutual obligations; especially the arrangement that established the relationship between God and his people, expressed in grace first with Israel and then with the church. Through that covenant God has conveyed to humanity the meaning of human life and salvation. Covenant is one of the central themes of the Bible, where some covenants are between human beings, others between God and human beings.

The covenant theme in the OT is developed from Noah to Abraham and reaches its first climax in the covenant formed between God and Israel at Mt Sinai. After King David's time, the history of the covenant becomes a less prominent theme.

At a low point in covenant history the Bible introduces the prophet Jeremiah's prophecy of a "new covenant" in Israel's future. Christians believe that Jeremiah's prophecy eventually found fulfillment in the person and work of Jesus Christ. It is not accidental that the two volumes of the Christian Bible have been called the Old Covenant and New Covenant (the word commonly translated "testament" means "covenant").

PREVIEW
- The Meaning of Covenant
- Human Covenants
- Divine-Human Covenants
- Beginnings of the Covenant Tradition
- The Sinai Covenant
- The Covenant with David
- The New Covenant Predicted in the Old Testament

The Meaning of Covenant The essence of covenant is to be found in a particular kind of relationship between persons. Mutual obligations characterize that kind of relationship. Thus a covenant relationship is not merely a mutual acquaintance but a commitment to responsibility and action. A key word in Scripture to describe that commitment is "faithfulness," acted out in a context of abiding friendship.

In the OT the word "covenant" was used in an ordinary human sense as well as in a theological sense. An understanding of human covenants provides a starting point for understanding the covenant between God and human beings.

Human Covenants A variety of human relationships, from profoundly personal to distantly political, may be described as covenantal. The deep brotherly love that David and Jonathan shared led to a formal covenant between them (1 Sm 18:3). Their covenant of friendship was more than a token of esteem; it bound them to demonstrate mutual loyalty and loving-kindness in certain tangible ways. Jonathan's covenant faithfulness was typified on an occasion when David was out of favor with the king; Jonathan braved his father's wrath to speak favorably for his friend. Subsequently, he warned David secretly to flee into hiding (1 Sm 19–20).

To appreciate the many OT laws on marriage and divorce, one must understand that marriage itself was a covenant relationship (Mal 2:14). The solemn promises exchanged by a man and woman became their covenant obligations. Faithfulness to those promises brought marital blessing (cf. Ps 128; Prv 18:22); violation brought a curse.

An individual could, at least figuratively, make a covenant or vow with himself or herself (something like a New Year's resolution). Job, arguing his integrity before God, referred to a covenant he had made with his eyes to keep him from looking at women licentiously (Jb 31:1).

Covenants could also have a national or international character. The elders of Israel made a national covenant with King David in Hebron (2 Sm 5:3). Probably it contained explicit promises both from the elders on behalf of the people to submit themselves to the king's authority and from David to rule the nation justly and according to the law of God (Dt 17:15-20). The covenant relationship described mutual obligations between a senior partner (the king) and junior partners (the Israelites). In international relationships OT covenants were similar to modern treaties or alliances. King Solomon entered into such a covenant with Hiram, king of Tyre; that covenant, like many modern international treaties, was a trade agreement between the two nations (1 Kgs 5:12).

Covenant is thus an interpersonal framework of trust, responsibilities, and benefits, with broad application to almost every human relationship from personal friendship to international trade agreements. In Scripture covenant is also the most comprehensive concept covering an individual's relationship to God.

Divine-Human Covenants The same basic characteristics of a strictly human covenant are present in a divine covenant: (1) a relationship between two parties (God and a human being or nation), and (2) mutual obligations between the covenant partners. To the OT believer, religion meant covenant. OT religion was faithfulness to the covenant relationship between God and his chosen people; religious responsibilities for both the faith and practice of Israel were covenant responsibilities.

The concept of a divine-human covenant in the OT was not static. Although the fundamental character of covenant remains the same throughout the Bible, the specific nature and form of the covenant changed and developed in the course of ancient Israel's history. A brief survey of covenant history will further clarify its dimensions.

Beginnings of the Covenant Tradition

Adam Adam and Eve were placed in the Garden. God was their Creator; they were his creatures. The meaning of their lives was to be found in relationship with each other and with God, the giver of the Garden. The fall, however, brought a disruption of the divine relationship, and they were expelled from the Garden.

The fall substantially influenced the nature of subsequent religious covenants. The separation of humankind from God clarifies the nature of the human predicament. Created for a relationship with the Creator, sinning humans are excluded from that relationship and cannot, on their own accord, reestablish it. From that circumstance emerges a distinctive feature of divine-human covenants, namely, that God alone can initiate the relationship of covenant.

Noah The first explicit mention of covenant in Scripture refers to the initiative taken by God to bind himself again to human beings in a covenant, despite human faithlessness. When God warned Noah to build an ark in order to escape the impending Flood, he also promised to establish a covenant with him (Gn 6:18). The corruption and violence of the human race had provoked God's anger, but his grace was shown in his dealings with Noah. The promised covenant provided that God would maintain a relationship with one family, even though other divine-human relationships were being formally severed. Significantly, God's covenant promise to Noah came in a context of demand: God ordered Noah to build an ark (v 14). Noah's receipt of the covenant blessing depended on his obedience to a divine command.

The covenant was elaborated only after the Flood, when Noah had made an offering to God (Gn 8:20-22). The covenant with Noah was in fact a universal covenant with humankind and all living creatures (9:8-10). God promised never to send such a flood again as judgment on the world. The sign of that covenant was the rainbow.

The covenant with Noah affords some perspective for understanding the "covenant God." Although human beings may deserve destruction because of their wickedness, God withholds that destruction. The covenant of Noah did not establish an intimate relationship between God and each living being; nevertheless, it left open the possibility of a more intimate covenant. Human beings, in spite of their evil, are allowed for a time to live in God's world; during those years, they may seek a deeper relationship with that world's Creator.

Abraham The first explicit reference to God's covenant with Abraham is in Genesis 15. When the Lord called the 75-year-old Abram (as he was first called) to leave his home city of Ur and set out on a journey, a relationship already existed between God and Abram. In that relationship, which enabled God to command Abram's obe-

dience, God made certain promises to him: "I will make of you a great nation, and I will bless you, and make your name great, so that you will be a blessing" (Gn 12:2, RSV).

Formal establishment of the covenant with Abram is described in Genesis 15 as a profound religious experience. The initiative lay entirely with God, who approached Abram in a vision and spoke with him. Abram raised a fundamental objection: how could he experience the blessing of God if it was to come to him through a son he did not have? His wife Sarai was past the childbearing age, and he himself was "as good as dead" (Rom 4:19). God assured the old man that he would have a son through whom his descendants would eventually be as numerous as the stars of heaven. Abram's belief at that point introduced the theme of righteousness central to the covenant concept: Abram "believed the LORD, and he reckoned it to him as righteousness" (Gn 15:6, RSV). At the end of that day, Abram knew that his own future and the future of his descendants were firmly in the hands of the covenant God. "On that day the LORD made a covenant with Abram, saying, 'To your descendants I give this land' " (v 18, RSV).

The covenant is more fully expressed in Genesis 17, which probably records a renewal of God's covenant with Abram. The initiative once again lay with God (Gn 17:1). God addressed the 99-year-old Abram in words that made clear that the covenant was not a relationship between equal partners. God was the Almighty; Abram was a human being to whom an extraordinary privilege had been granted.

Yet the details of the covenant in Genesis 17 show that both partners assumed responsibilities. God committed himself voluntarily to Abram and his descendants while requiring certain commitments from Abram. The blessing Abram would receive as a covenant partner became clear from the new name God gave him. "I am changing your name. It will no longer be Abram; now you will be known as Abraham, for you will be the father of many nations" (Gn 17:5, NLT). God would give to Abraham, through his descendants, the land of Canaan as an everlasting gift and would be the personal God of Abraham and his family in perpetuity (vv 7-8).

God's giving required a response of obedience from Abraham: "Live a blameless life" (Gn 17:1, NLT). Those simple words indicate the essence of covenant relationship: to relate to God is to live in his presence; since God is holy, one who knows him is expected to live a life of integrity and blamelessness.

The covenant also had a more formal aspect. Abraham and the male members of his household were to undergo the rite of circumcision as a symbol of covenant commitment. Abraham was an old man when he was circumcised (Gn 17:24), though male children born into the covenant family were to be circumcised when they were eight days old (v 12). Circumcision was not in itself a ritual peculiar to the Hebrews; it was practiced in most societies in the ancient Near East (the Philistines were one exception). The distinctiveness lay in what the act symbolized: among other things, a continuing and faithful relationship with the living God.

God's covenant with Abraham was characterized by both present and future realities. The covenant established a continuing relationship between Abraham and his Creator. Yet its thrust pointed to future blessing—in the children yet to be born, the "chosen people," and in the land that eventually his descendants would call their own.

Another dimension of the covenant lay still further in the future: "All the families of the earth will be blessed through you" (Gn 12:3, NLT). Early in the OT, the idea of election (God's unconditional preference; cf. 2 Thes 2:13) is present. God chose to enter into a covenant relationship with a particular man and his particular descendants. Yet God always elects a person to serve: Adam, to cultivate the Garden; Noah, to build an ark; Abraham, to leave his home for another land and to live blamelessly before God (cf. Eph 2:8-10). Further, the "particularity" of Abraham's election contained within it a universality: through his descendants the blessing of God would be offered to all.

Thus, the future aspects of Abraham's covenant reflect two stages. From Abraham's perspective, in the relatively near future his descendants would possess a land given them by God. But in the more distant future was the prospect of a universal blessing, the culmination of God's work in the world. The initial fulfillment of that distant future is perceived in the NT, but the more immediate fulfillment of God's promise was the Sinai covenant at the time of Moses.

The Sinai Covenant The covenant established between God and Israel at Mt Sinai is the focal point of the covenant tradition in the OT. It was anticipated in the covenant of Abraham and lay behind the covenant of David and the proclamation of the prophets. It was central to OT religion, laying down the foundations of Judaism that continue into the modern world. The Sinai covenant was the formal institution of a relationship between God and his chosen people, Israel.

In order to appreciate the impact of the Sinai covenant, one must understand its historical context. It was preceded by the exodus of the Hebrew people from Egypt under the leadership of Moses. The exodus was an extraordinary act of liberation in which God intervened in the normal course of history to free his people from slavery in Egypt. The exodus is interpreted in the OT as a divine act comparable to Creation, the act through which God "created" the nation of Israel. Examination of the two versions of the fourth commandment (Ex 20:8-11; Dt 5:12-15) shows that the exodus from Egypt directly parallels the creation of the world as a basis for Sabbath observance. Although Israel was created in the exodus, the nation had neither a constitution nor land. The covenant provided the nascent state of Israel with a constitution, making it a theocratic state (a state ruled by God).

The basic account of the Sinai covenant is contained in Exodus 19 and 20. The initiative came from God, who gave instructions through Moses to prepare for the covenant; God spoke the words that contained the covenant offer. There was no doubt that the God of Israel was the senior partner in the relationship made formal at Sinai. The God who had revealed himself through his acts in the exodus then revealed himself in words. Those two aspects—the God who acts and speaks—are central to OT theology. And although the covenant contained law, it was preceded by the exodus, an act of divine grace.

God's offer of covenant carried with it a divine promise: "You will be to me a kingdom of priests, my holy nation" (Ex 19:6, NLT). The promise was one of extraordinary privilege; an entire nation was called upon to represent all other nations before the God of the universe. But the priestly office, though it carried privilege, was also a demanding office. A priest had to be pure and had to know the God whose presence he was required to enter. Thus Israel, the priestly nation, received a law that would provide direction in living, in loving God, and in serving all people. The law given with the covenant expressed the requirements for God's covenant people.

The Covenant Law The covenant law had two principal parts. First, the Ten Commandments expressed God's requirements of Israel in a concise form (Ex 20:2-17). The commandments specified the covenant people's relationship both to God and to other human beings. Although the tendency in the present day is to view the Ten Commandments as a system of ethics or morality, they had a different role in ancient Israel. The covenant law was the foundation or constitution of a new nation, a special "nation of priests." The head of the nation-state was God. Hence, in ancient Israel the status of the Ten Commandments was approximately that of the code of criminal law in a modern nation-state. To break one of those laws was to commit a crime against God, the head of the state. Yet the laws had a positive purpose. They set down a way of life that would result in a full and rich communion with God and community with others.

The second part of the covenant law was a detailed law code covering the activities of everyday life. Examples of such laws are found in Exodus 21–23. These laws were compiled and recorded in the "Book of the Covenant" (Ex 24:7). Although many laws were contained in this book, it was impossible to codify every aspect of human behavior. The diversity of the examples given indicates that for the covenant member no area of human life was beyond the influence of the covenant. Persons who entered into a relationship with God entered into a relationship that impinged on every possible aspect of their lives.

Covenant Renewal The covenant at Sinai was made with a particular group of people under the leadership of Moses but was binding on future generations. Consequently, the covenant was renewed from time to time. Covenant renewals are recorded in the time of Joshua (Jos 8:30-35; 24:1-28) and, much later, during the reign of King Josiah (2 Kgs 23:1-3).

The most important passage in the Bible for understanding covenant renewal and the nature of covenant is the book of Deuteronomy. The entire book describes a particular covenant renewal ceremony that occurred at a critical juncture in Israel's early history. The Sinai covenant was renewed just before Moses' death, before the transition of leadership to Joshua, and before a major military campaign to possess the Promised Land.

The covenant since the time of Abraham had contained a promise of land. Immediately before they entered that land (c. 1250 BC), the covenant vows were renewed with a new generation of Israelites, most of whom had not stood at the foot of Mt Sinai some 40 years earlier. Although covenant renewal is the central theme of Deuteronomy, the writer focused primarily on Moses' sermon rather than on a detailed account of the renewal ceremony.

Many aspects of the ceremony were simply a repetition of what happened at the original ratification of the covenant. The Ten Commandments were repeated (Dt 5:6-21), and the laws of the Book of the Covenant were expounded in greater detail (Dt 12–26). Two points emerging in Deuteronomy are particularly significant for an understanding of covenant: a clear statement of covenant love and a detailed statement of the blessings and curses that accompanied the making and renewing of the covenant.

The Covenant with David The covenant tradition underwent modification during the time of King David (c. 1000 BC). The Sinai covenant had been established between God and Israel, with Moses acting as mediator. In David's time an additional element was added: God entered into a covenant with David as king. That royal covenant was intimated to David through the prophet Nathan (2 Sm 7:8-16), indicating once again the divine initiative. It was to be an everlasting covenant with David's royal lineage (23:5).

THE DOCUMENTARY FORM OF THE COVENANT
Modern biblical scholarship has established that the Sinai covenant and its renewals were formally patterned after a particular type of human covenant, namely the suzerainty treaty of the ancient world (an agreement between a great power and a lesser power). Archaeological discoveries in the 20th century brought to light a number of such international political documents, the most interesting coming from the ancient Hittite Empire and dating from approximately the 14th century BC. Study of those treaty documents has revealed a fairly consistent pattern. Comparison with biblical passages describing the Sinai covenant shows a remarkable parallel.

In Deuteronomy, the Hebrews seem to have adapted the form of international suzerainty treaties to express their own covenant relationship with God. Why did they choose that particular form? Perhaps the Hebrews had been bound to their Egyptian masters by that kind of treaty, so they wanted to dramatize their liberation by making a new treaty, this time with their God at Sinai. Also, the Sinai covenant formed the constitution of a new but small Near Eastern nation. Whereas other small nations commonly depended for their existence on the generosity of a suzerain power (e.g., Egypt), Israel was to be a free nation, owing allegiance only to God. Israel's "treaty" with God meant that it could acknowledge no other master. Its freedom and strength lay in its wholehearted commitment to God alone.

Christians generally interpret the covenant with David as a messianic covenant. For several centuries the dynasty established by David ruled a united Israel, then ruled the remaining southern kingdom of Judah. But in 586 BC Judah was conquered by the Babylonians. At that point a descendant of David was no longer ruling an independent kingdom of God's chosen people. The everlasting nature of the covenant with David was brought out, however, not in the pages of ancient history but in the expectation of a Messiah who would be born of David's descendants. Matthew and Luke both pointed to Jesus' Davidic descent (Mt 1:1; Lk 3:31). The NT thus extends the covenant acts of God into the new age in the person of Jesus.

The New Covenant Predicted in the Old Testament Although David's covenant with God was eternal, in a sense the covenant established with Israel on Mt Sinai was temporal. The Sinai covenant included conditional clauses, stated in the blessings and curses of Deuteronomy. Israel's disobedience of the covenant law would at worst bring exile from the Promised Land, a central covenant theme from Abraham to Moses and beyond.

The Hebrew prophets often perceived the danger of an end to the covenant as a result of Israel's sins. Some of the prophets, especially Hosea and Jeremiah, also perceived a deeper truth; namely, that the covenant was rooted in divine love and that therefore even the curse of God could not be final.

Hosea dramatically expressed that truth through the "living parable" of his marriage (Hos 1–3). He married Gomer at God's command, but later, as a result of her unfaithfulness, the marital covenant was dissolved by divorce. Although Gomer's adulterous acts compelled Hosea to divorce her, he did not cease to love her. God later commanded Hosea to go back to Gomer (Hos 3:1).

Despite her unfaithfulness, the prophet was to take her again into the covenant relationship of marriage. That acted-out parable depicted God's actions with Israel. Israel's sin would inevitably culminate in a divorce from God, but Hosea perceived a new marriage. In the new covenant between God and Israel, Israel would be graciously accepted back into a relationship with God (2:14-18).

The new covenant is given powerful expression in the writings of the prophet Jeremiah, who lived through the end of the seventh and beginning of the sixth centuries BC. In his lifetime Jeremiah saw the kingdom of Judah defeated in war. The nation lost its independence and became a vassal of the Babylonian Empire. In an external sense, that defeat in 586 BC marked the end of the Sinai covenant. Israel could no longer call the Promised Land its own. Yet Jeremiah perceived a truth beyond the contemporary political realities. God's work in the world, like his love for the world, was not over.

Thus Jeremiah spoke of a new covenant that God would bring into effect: "The days are coming, says the LORD, when I will make a new covenant with the house of Israel and the house of Judah" (Jer 31:31, RSV). The new covenant would be marked by an act of God within human hearts, a radical spiritual transformation (Jer 31:34). At the Last Supper Jesus declared to his disciples that "this cup which is poured out for you is the new covenant in my blood" (Lk 22:20, RSV). To the writer of Hebrews, the new covenant was central to a full understanding of the ministry of Jesus Christ (Heb 8:8-12).

Conclusion Covenant is a concept central to the message and the history of the OT. The covenant theme continues into the NT as a way of interpreting the Christian gospel. Meaning in human life is to be found in a covenant relationship with the living God. Yet sinful human beings cannot work their way into such a relationship; God alone can initiate it. According to the NT, God's act in giving his son, Jesus, to die opened up the covenant relationship to all human beings. The forgiveness made available by Jesus' "blood of the new covenant" makes it possible for any individual to enter into a covenant relationship with God. Entry into such a relationship, today as in Abraham's time, hinges upon faith (Gal 3:6-14).

See also Alliance; Covenant, The New; Law, Biblical Concept of; Oath; Vows.

COVENANT, Book of the Phrase used by Moses in reference to the Ten Commandments and the laws and stipulations recorded in Exodus 20:22–23:33. *See* Book of the Covenant.

COVENANT, The New A gracious provision of God given through Jesus Christ for the redemption of fallen humanity—replacing and fulfilling the old covenant, which was expressed primarily through the Mosaic law. The expression "new covenant" is found principally in the NT.

Although the concept of a new covenant is found in several places in the OT (Ez 34:23-31; 37:24-28; Jl 2:12-32), the actual phrase occurs only once (Jer 31:31-34). That passage contrasts the new covenant that the prophet Jeremiah saw God making with Israel "after those days" (vv 32-34) with the covenant God had made with his people in the days of Moses. The contrast is seen, first of all, in the internal nature of the new covenant. Whereas the old covenant was written on tablets of stone (Ex 31:18; 34:27-32; Dt 4:13; 5:22; 9:11; 10:3-4) and in a book (Ex 24:7; cf. the phrase "old written code,"

Rom 7:6, RSV), the new covenant is to be written on the human heart. One result is a clearer revelation of what God demands; another is the enablement of believers to fulfill those demands (see Rom 8:2-4). The interior nature of the new covenant is spoken of in several other passages (Ez 11:19-21; 36:26-27) and made explicit in the prophet Joel of a time when God "will pour out [his] spirit on all flesh" (Jl 2:28-32).

A second contrast is in the way God's people know him under the two covenants. There is no doubt that Israel under the old covenant "knew" God; God had revealed himself, though at times the nation tended to forget this (Jgs 2:10; Hos 4:1, 6). What the prophets envisioned in the new covenant is a unique personal knowledge of God by each individual member of the covenant community.

Finally, the two covenants differ in regard to God's dealing with human sin. Jeremiah promised that God would forgive the iniquity of his people and blot out their sin. Israel already knew that God delighted in mercy and forgiveness (Ex 34:6-7), but Jeremiah was saying that God would never again remember their sin (Jer 31:34). Under the old covenant there was a reminder of sin year after year (Heb 10:3); under the new covenant no remembrance of sin remains (v 14).

A New Covenant The expression "new covenant" is found at least six times in the NT (1 Cor 11:25; 2 Cor 3:6; Heb 8:8, 13; 9:15; 12:24; and probably Lk 22:20, according to some manuscripts). In certain Greek manuscripts the phrase is also found in Matthew 26:28 and Mark 14:24, where "new" seems to have been added by various scribes to "blood of the covenant," in order to make these accounts conform to parallel accounts of the Lord's Supper in 1 Corinthians or possibly in Luke.

Even though the term "new" is not found in the accounts in Matthew and Mark in the best Greek manuscripts, and was therefore probably not part of the original text, it is clear from all four accounts that Jesus saw the Lord's Supper as instituting a different and therefore "new" covenant. The covenant was being sealed by his sacrificial death, that is, by his blood, just as the Mosaic covenant was sealed by the "blood of the covenant" (Ex 24:6-8). The cup of the Lord's Supper symbolizes the blood of Christ's sacrifice, sealing the new covenant God has at last made with his people. The new covenant, ratified by Christ's death, is what the church therefore commemorates each time it celebrates the Lord's Supper.

In his institution of the Lord's Supper, Jesus did not elucidate what the "newness" of the covenant entailed. Elsewhere he mentioned a "baptism with the Holy Spirit" (Acts 1:5; 11:16; cf. Mt 3:11; Mk 1:8; Lk 3:16; and Jn 1:33, where this promise is found on the lips of John the Baptist; cf. also 1 Cor 12:13). Yet both OT prophecies refer to the same new covenant that God would establish in the future, as shown in 2 Corinthians 3:6. There the apostle Paul stated that God "has qualified us to be ministers of a new covenant" (RSV; cf. Jer 31:31), not "in a written code but in the Spirit" (RSV; cf. Jl 2:28-32), for "the written code kills, but the Spirit gives life" (RSV).

Superiority of the New Covenant In 2 Corinthians 3, Paul was showing that in contrast to the old (Mosaic) covenant (v 14), which was a dispensation of death, carved in letters on stone (v 7), the new covenant instituted by Jesus is one of far greater splendor (vv 8-9), written on the human heart by the Spirit of the living God himself (v 3).

The new covenant concept is treated most exhaustively and systematically in the book of Hebrews. In Hebrews 8:8-12 the quotation of Jeremiah 31:31-34 is the longest OT quotation found in the NT. In Hebrews 12:24 a different Greek word for "new" is used, but the meaning remains the same. The theme of the new covenant dominates the book of Hebrews, which was written to encourage faltering Christians by demonstrating the superiority of the Christian faith over their old Jewish beliefs and practices. In Hebrews the new covenant is seen as better than the old "obsolete" covenant in a number of ways.

1. The new covenant has a better priesthood than the old covenant, since there is no longer any need for a continual change of priests due to death (Heb 7:23). One continual priest now lives forever to make intercession before God on behalf of his people (vv 24-25).
2. The new covenant priest is better than those of the old covenant, since Jesus does not have to offer sacrifices continually for his own sins and then for the sins of his people. He has instead made one complete and perfect offering (7:27; 9:25-28; 10:12).
3. The new covenant has a better sacrifice than the old covenant; what the blood of bulls and goats could not do, since the atonement they brought could at best be only partial (10:2-3), the blood of Christ has done once for all (9:11-14; 10:1-10).
4. The new covenant is built on "better promises" than the old (8:6).
5. Whereas the old covenant was imperfect (8:7) and thus became obsolete (8:13), the new covenant is perfect and eternal (13:20).
6. Whereas the old covenant provided a believer with no direct access to God (9:6-8), the new covenant provides a direct access to God that can purify and perfect the believer's conscience (cf. 9:14 with 9:9).
7. The new covenant possesses a better "surety," or guarantee, an oath sworn by God himself (7:20-22).
8. The new covenant assures the presence of the Holy Spirit in the life of each believer. The new covenant community has been touched by the promised Spirit (6:4), who, according to Paul, is both the seal and guarantee of their inheritance (see 2 Cor 1:22; 5:5; Eph 1:13-14).

Conclusion The new covenant and its accompanying new commandment are both fulfillments of what was implicit in the old. The new covenant is written on the heart of each member of the new covenant community by the Holy Spirit. The power of God's Spirit within, enabling the believer to carry out the new commandment (Rom 8:2-4; Gal 5:16-25), is a distinctive feature of the new covenant.

See also Covenant.

COVENANT OF SALT* Biblical phrase for a two-way agreement, the inviolability of which was symbolized by salt. A Middle Eastern saying, "There is bread and salt between us," meant that a relationship had been confirmed by sharing a meal. Salt symbolized the life and enduring nature of the alliance. In the OT salt appears in the relationship between God and Israel (Lv 2:13). As a purifying agent and preservative in the cereal offering, salt symbolized the indissoluble nature of the covenant between God and Israel.

An everlasting "covenant of salt" (Nm 18:19) was made between God and Aaron, who represented the whole priesthood of Israel. Since the Levites received no inheritance in the Promised Land, God himself was to be their special portion forever. God's covenant with King

David and his sons was also called a covenant of salt (2 Chr 13:5).

See also Covenant.

COVERING OF THE HEAD

Issue pertaining to female decor discussed by the apostle Paul in 1 Corinthians 11:2-16. In Paul's day Jewish women always wore veils in public and Greek women generally went veiled—a practice that showed deference to authority and dignified the wearer.

Disagreement arose in the church at Corinth when women prayed publicly with uncovered heads. Since women had traditionally covered their heads out of respect for men (or "husbands"), it seemed shameful for a woman to pray or prophesy unveiled; it was viewed as if her head were shaven (v 5), a sign of dishonor.

Paul responded to that confusion with a brief theological excursus about Creation (v 8). An enigmatic reference to "angels" (v 10) precedes his statement on the interdependence of men and women (vv 11-12). Some interpret the word translated "veil" (v 10) as a symbol of new authority, since in the synagogues women were permitted no part in Jewish worship services. In contrast, a Christian woman could participate in Christian worship provided she wore a veil.

Paul spoke of "nature" as teaching men and women on the subject. Some scholars think he meant that since a woman's long hair was her pride (v 15), she should cover her head. Some think that the phrase referred to hairstyle. Others believe Paul was saying that a veil was not needed since a woman's hair is given to her for a covering (v 15). Paul encouraged freedom but also insisted on order in the churches. He upheld certain customs to avoid offense (see 1 Cor 9:19-23). Yet he challenged other customs for the sake of the gospel's integrity (see Gal 6:12).

In most church traditions, covering the head is considered necessary only in societies where it is considered proper for women to be veiled. Some groups, however, believe that all women should still wear hats or something on their heads in church services. In a few groups women regularly wear small "coverings" in their hair so they will always be able to pray with their heads "covered."

See also Corinthians, First Letter to the.

COVET, COVETOUSNESS*

The desire to have something for oneself that belongs to another—a craving or passionate desire. Three Hebrew words are translated "covet" in the OT (see RSV). In one recital of the Ten Commandments (Dt 5:21) the text reads, "You shall not covet your neighbor's wife." The same Hebrew word occurs in Proverbs 21:26: "All day long the wicked covets." Another word implies dishonest gain (Hb 2:9). In the Exodus listing of the Ten Commandments, a third word is used for craving a neighbor's wife (Ex 20:17). The same word is used of Achan's coveting of the spoils of Ai (Jos 7:21; cf. Mi 2:2). To covet is to desire inordinately, to place the object of desire before love and devotion to God.

That idea is conveyed in the NT by a Greek word literally meaning "inordinate desire to have more." The apostle Paul listed that kind of covetousness among earthly attitudes of which Christians are to rid themselves. "Put to death therefore what is earthly in you: immorality, impurity, passion, evil desire, and covetousness, which is idolatry" (Col 3:5, RSV; cf. Eph 5:3; 1 Cor 6:10).

Covetousness is pictured as a serious sin that leads to a variety of other sins. The love of money is the root of all evils (1 Tm 6:9-10; cf. Prv 15:27). It was the sin of Ananias and Sapphira (Acts 5:1-3; cf. 1 Sm 15:9, 19;

Mt 26:14-15; 2 Pt 2:15; Jude 1:11). Jesus warned: "Take heed, and beware of all covetousness; for a man's life does not consist in the abundance of his possessions" (Lk 12:15, RSV). Another Greek word translated "covet" in the KJV is better translated "earnestly desire" in a positive sense (1 Cor 14:39).

The translators of the OT who produced the Septuagint used still another Greek word for the three Hebrew words rendered "covet" in English versions. In the NT the verb form of that word is used in both a positive and negative sense. It means "to desire or long for," whether food (Lk 15:16), the divine mysteries (Mt 13:17; 1 Pt 1:12), some good thing (Phil 1:23; Heb 6:11), or some evil thing (Mt 5:28; 1 Thes 4:5; 1 Jn 2:17). The noun form of the same word generally reflects an attitude of disobedience to the law of God in which desire has given place to an evil impulse that results in sin (Jn 8:44; Rom 1:24; 6:12; 7:7-8; 13:14; Gal 5:16, 26).

See also Commandments, The Ten.

COW

See Animals (Cattle).

COZ*

KJV spelling of Koz in 1 Chronicles 4:8. *See* Koz #1.

COZBI

Midianite woman with whom a Hebrew named Zimri entered into an illicit relationship. Phinehas, the grandson of Aaron, stopped a plague on Israel by executing Zimri and Cozbi (Nm 25:15-18).

COZEBA

Alternate name of Aczib, a city in Judah's territory, in 1 Chronicles 4:22. *See* Aczib #1.

CRAFTSMEN, Valley of

Place named for a community of craftsmen who lived in a valley on the southern border of the plain of Sharon (1 Chr 4:14; Neh 11:35). *See* Ge-harashim.

CRANE

Translation of a Hebrew word in Isaiah 38:14 and Jeremiah 8:7, the meaning of which is uncertain. *See* Birds.

CRAWLING THINGS*

Translation of various Hebrew words primarily referring to reptiles. *See* Animals (Adder; Asp; Chameleon; Gecko; Lizard; Snake).

CREATION

The divine act of making something out of nothing; the divine act of bringing the world into ordered existence. Human beings unaided by divine revelation cannot arrive at the biblical doctrine of Creation by theological, philosophical, or scientific speculation. According to the Bible, knowledge of Creation must come by God's revelation (cf. Heb 11:3).

PREVIEW
• Understanding Creation
• Creation and Theology
• Creation and Science
• The Issues Surrounding Evolution
• Creation, Science, and Morality

Understanding Creation To start a discussion about Creation with a comparison of the Genesis record and modern science is to begin at the wrong place. One should first ask what the Creation account would have meant to a Hebrew person in Bible times; then one should ask what use the prophets of Israel made of the doctrine of Creation. The following are some points to be noted.

1. Creation was a conquering of chaos. Most creation accounts from the ancient world began with a pri-

meval chaos. The God who could conquer chaos was understood as the true and living God. Genesis 1 is a magnificent account of how the God of Israel brought the chaos of Genesis 1:2 into an ordered cosmos.

2. Creation was prompted by God's good will. It was the free act of God. It is good (Gn 1:4, 10, 12, 18, 21, 25, 31). On the basis of that fact, Christians assert that life is a gift of God. The Christian affirmation stands against all the nihilisms and pessimisms found in religious and philosophical history.

3. Creation is under the shadow of sin (Rom 8:18-25). Scripture teaches that creation today is not seen in its original pristine purity but rather is seen as a world with a large measure of ambiguity.

4. Creation is dependent upon God. The relationship of God to his creation is set out in Ephesians 4:6. God is above all; that is, he is transcendent. God is through all; that is, he works in all things. God is in all; that is, he is divinely present or immanent in the entire creation (Ps 90:1-4; cf. Jn 1:3; 1 Cor 8:6; Col 1:16-17).

5. Creation is by the word of God (Gn 1; Heb 11:3). Students of literature have said that the creation of the world by the "word of God" is one of the most sublime of all human thoughts. Among other things it means creation by a Person. The vast expanse of the universe and the enormous number of stars and galaxies can numb a thoughtful person into a sense of meaninglessness. But when one knows that it was all created by the word of God, one knows that a Person is behind the frigid mask of the stellar spaces (Pss 8; 19; Rom 1:20).

6. Creation as depicted in the Bible stands up to critical examination. Scholars have studied parallel accounts of other peoples of biblical times, and none of them has the majesty and theological purity of the Genesis account.

Creation and Theology The doctrine of Creation is built on the sum of all the biblical teachings on Creation. Examination of that material leads to a number of conclusions.

1. The doctrine of Creation gives us our fundamental understanding of humanity. Men and women are in the image of God (Gn 1:26-27). That means, at least, that a human being is more than an animal, even though both were created from the dust of the earth and have much in common. Many conjectures have been made about the positive meaning of the expression "image of God." If there is a common denominator, it is that human beings find their meaning, their destiny, and their worth in their special relationship to God.

2. Parallel to the statement of humanity's relationship to God is the affirmation that humanity is to be lord of God's creation. Again, human beings are separated from the animal world, and their responsibility before God is specified (Gn 1:28; 2:15; Ps 8).

3. Both male and female are in the image of God. That means that the divine image is borne equally by both sexes. It also means that sexuality in human beings has many more dimensions than sexuality among animals. The sexual life of human beings is therefore vastly richer than that of animals and subject to deeper corruption (Mk 10:2-9; 1 Cor 7:1-5; Eph 5:25-31; cf. Heb 13:4).

4. The doctrine of prayer as "asking and receiving" is grounded in the providence of God, which in turn is grounded in Creation. There is meaning in petitionary prayer only if there is a sovereign Creator who can answer the petitions of his own creatures (Mt 6:5-13; Col 4:2; 1 Pt 5:6-7; Rv 8:3).

5. The history of humanity and of Israel begins with Genesis 1. Creation begins history; it is not merely the premise of history. The God of Creation is the God of Abraham, of Moses, of the prophets, and of Jesus Christ.

6. Creation is a witness to the existence and nature of God (Ps 19; Rom 1:18-19). In theology the expression used is "general revelation." "General" means that it is a revelation witnessed by all people.

7. Creation is a total creation. The Genesis account mentions certain bodies in the skies, certain creatures in the seas, certain plant and animal life on the earth. The number of species runs into the millions. Genesis does not attempt to list them but merely suggests such a list. God has made all that there is (cf. Jn 1:1-2). Therefore, there is never a threat to the believer in the Lord from any part of the universe. There is only one Lord, not many gods and lords, to whom all are called in obedience. The personal meaning is found in Romans 8:38-39, where the apostle Paul searches the entire universe and can find nothing in it, anywhere or at any time, that can separate a believer from the love of God in Christ.

8. The chief theological use of the doctrine of Creation in the OT is to label idolatry for the sin that it is. Idolatry is the primeval lie and it leads to immorality, making a lie of one's life.

9. One of the remarkable doctrines of the NT is the "cosmic Christ"—which means he is the Creator and Sustainer of the universe (Jn 1:1-2; Col 1:16-17; Heb 1:3). The purpose of linking Christ with Creation is to show that he is more than a first-century Jew from Palestine.

Creation and Science Does science prove Creation? Some scientists have thought that the innumerable conditions necessary for life, which do as a matter of fact exist on the earth, is such a proof. That argument has been called "cosmic theology."

Another so-called proof of Creation from science is the "big bang" theory of the origin of the universe. Although that view has forged ahead of its competitors, it is a theory of "first states" and not of the absolute origin of all things. The Christian doctrine of creation from nothing (Latin, ex nihilo) means more than that: it means that the absolute origin, sustaining, and meaning of all things is in the living Lord of Israel and of the church.

Another argument comes from the second law of thermodynamics and the concept of entropy. (Entropy refers to the leveling off of energy or temperature to a state in which no energy is available.) Heat systems cool off. The universe is not infinitely old or it would now be cool. Since there are still stars and suns, the universe must have been created a finite time ago. A related argument is that it was necessary to create a universe that would run down. In so running down, it supplies heat to the earth so that the drama of God and man could unfold.

The Issues Surrounding Evolution When Charles Darwin proposed biological evolution in the middle of the 19th century, many evangelical Christians took exception to it. They objected even more strenuously when books were written about human evolution. Two famous debates resulted from that controversy. In England the issue was debated in 1860 before the British Association at Oxford. That debate pitted Bishop Samuel Wilberforce (against the theory) against T. H. Huxley (for the theory). Although there was no formal decision, sentiment was with Huxley. The second debate was the famous Scopes trial in Dayton, Tennessee, in 1925. William Jennings Bryan defended the law that said that John T. Scopes should be found guilty of teaching evolution in the classroom. Clarence Darrow defended Scopes. Again, the sentiment was with the proponent of evolution, Darrow (although Bryan gave a sturdier defense of his beliefs than is generally acknowledged).

Both orthodox Roman Catholics and evangelical Protestants have taken various views of the controversy, of which only a few can be mentioned.

1. Some argue that evolution is contrary to the teachings of Scripture and is—in the name of science—actually the supreme defiance of Scripture's authority. Thus, no quarter must ever be given in the battle against evolution.
2. Others find a satisfactory resolution in "theistic evolution"—that is, God began the evolutionary process.
3. Many see the parallels between the order of fossil-bearing strata in the so-called "geological column" and the six days of Creation as too close to be accidental. For them there is essential harmony between "Genesis and geology."
4. Many regard evolution as a theory like all other theories, which will be made or broken in the laboratory or in fieldwork. They see the doctrine of Creation as neither for nor against evolution. It is on a different level of explanation: "Science tells how; Scripture tells why."
5. Jesuit paleontologist Teilhard de Chardin attempted to save Christianity from evolution by "christifying" the whole evolutionary process.
6. British author C. S. Lewis, among others, distinguished evolution from what might be called "evolutionism." Lewis said that the validity of evolution as a narrow scientific thesis is for scientists to decide. But the notion of a total, all-encompassing evolutionary myth, as a human pseudodoctrine of Creation, is clearly not scientific.

Creation, Science, and Morality The growth of world population and the spread of industrialization have produced the problem of local and worldwide pollution. The ecological crisis has been said by some scholars to be the fault of Christian faith, which inspired man—as the "lord of creation"—to exploit creation. But that is hardly the meaning of Genesis 1:28, which is an injunction to responsibility. A number of OT texts show clearly that the concern of Scripture is for human responsibility in God's world; hence, Scripture parallels modern ecological concerns.

Science stretches theological understanding by continually revising our knowledge of the universe, but the biblical doctrine of Creation does not retreat as science advances. For the Christian, the world studied by scientists and pondered by philosophers remains God's created world.

See also Creation Myths; God, Being and Attributes of.

CREATION, New *See* New Creation, New Creature.

CREATION MYTHS* Religious stories explaining the origin and order of the universe. Parts of some Mesopotamian creation myths bear a close resemblance to the biblical accounts of Creation and earliest times.

Stories explaining creation were known throughout the ancient Near East. Many were based on stories originating in Sumer, one of the earliest Mesopotamian civilizations. Although now commonly regarded as fanciful and even entertaining explanations for why things were as they were, the myths seem to have fulfilled an impor-

tant social function. Their recital at religious festivals was believed to have magical power to revitalize nature and society. The creation stories assured worshipers that the original state of order created by the gods would continue to overcome the forces of chaos that threatened illness, ruin, sterility, and death.

PREVIEW
• Sumerian Creation Myths
• Akkadian Creation Myths
• Egyptian Creation Myths
• Creation Myths and Genesis

Sumerian Creation Myths The Sumerians flourished in southern Mesopotamia between 4000 and 3000 BC. Although they were non-Semitic, their cosmology influenced the Semites (various peoples inhabiting Palestine, Phoenicia, Assyria, and Arabia), who eventually adopted the Sumerian chief deities. About 5,000 tablets and fragments inscribed with an assortment of Sumerian literary works have been discovered. Although most of those tablets were inscribed in the early post-Sumerian period (c. 1750 BC), the compositions belong to at least the latter half of the third millennium (2500–2000) BC. As yet, no Sumerian account dealing directly with the origin of the universe has been uncovered. What is known about their notions of creation has been gleaned in part from brief passages scattered throughout their literature, especially from the introductions to poems, where Sumerian scribes were accustomed to writing several lines dealing with creation. In addition, nine myths have survived about the gods who organized the universe, created human beings, and established civilization.

The Sumerian religion, like that of all ancient Near Eastern peoples except the Israelites, was a naturalistic polytheism: they worshiped as gods the natural forces governing fertility (rain, wind, clouds, sun, moon, rivers, seas, and so on). Consequently, people understood the origin of the universe (cosmogony) as accompanying the origins of the gods (theogony).

Heaven and Earth In a tablet cataloging the Sumerian gods, the sea goddess Nammu is described as "the mother, who gave birth to heaven and earth." In another text she is described as "the mother, the ancestress, who gave birth to all the gods." Evidently the Sumerians looked upon the primeval sea as the first cause and prime mover of all things, believing that "the heaven and earth" were somehow engendered in that sea. Moreover, in their view the major components of the universe were heaven and earth; their term for universe was a compound word meaning "heaven-earth" (exactly as in the opening verse of the book of Genesis, where "heaven and earth" designate the entire organized universe). Before Enlil, the air god, separated them, heaven-earth was conceived of as a mountain whose base was the earth and whose peak was heaven.

Enlil, called "the king of heaven and earth" or "the king of all the lands," was the most important of the Sumerian gods. His creative work in organizing the earth is celebrated in "The Creation of the Pickax," which describes his fashioning and dedicating that valuable agricultural instrument. In part it reads:

> *Enlil, who brings up the seed of the land from the earth,*
> *Took care to move away heaven from earth,*
> *Took care to move away earth from heaven.*
> *. . . He brought the pickax into existence, the "day" came forth.*
> *He introduced labor, decreed the fate.*
> *Upon the pickax and basket he directs the "power."*

Thus Enlil separated heaven from earth, brought seed to fruition, and fashioned the pickax for agriculture.

Civilization The water god Enki was also god of the abyss and wisdom. Although Enlil drew up "blueprints" for the universe, Enki did most of the work carrying them out. His efforts went beyond fashioning the natural world to initiating the most important aspects of culture and civilization. In "Enki and the World Order," the water god makes his way to the banks of the Tigris and Euphrates, the two rivers that water the sandy Mesopotamian valley, and fills them with life-giving rains and winds. Then, preparing the earth for cultivation, he "turns the hilly ground into fields, . . . directs the plow and . . . yoke, . . . opens the holy furrows, and grows the grain in the cultivated field." Then the god lays the foundations of houses, stables, and sheepfolds, and builds them. He fixes the "borders" and sets up boundary stones. Finally he invents weaving, called "that which is woman's task." Having organized the earth, Enki entrusts each place and element to a special deity.

Sumerian Eden Another myth, "Enki and Ninhursag: A Paradise Myth," bears a remote resemblance to the biblical story of the Garden of Eden. The myth seems to take place before the creation of animals or humans in Dilmun, a land in the east where the gods reside— "pure," "clean," "most bright," and probably without sickness or death. Having filled that land with fruitful fields, Enki successively impregnates three goddesses: Ninhursag, "the mother of the land"; Nimmu, his daughter by that union; and Ninkurra, his granddaughter by Nimmu.

Ninhursag seems to use Enki's semen to make eight new plants. Evidently they are "forbidden fruit," because when Enki eats them, Ninhursag curses him and leaves the garden, adding, "Until he is dead I shall not look upon him with the eye of life." Under the curse, the garden languishes and the gods mourn. Enlil, the king of the gods, seems unable to cope with the situation. Enki lies dying. The fox, evidently already present in Dilmun, saves the day by luring Ninhursag back to Dilmun, where she heals Enki and revives the garden.

The Creation of Humans Regarded as the mother of all gods, Ninhursag may have personified Earth. In "The Creation of Man," she plays an important role along with Enki.

Having come into existence before there was meat or bread for them to eat, the gods face a dilemma:

> *They knew not the eating of bread,*
> *Knew not the dressing of garments,*
> *Ate plants with their mouth like sheep,*
> *Drank water from the ditch.*

To relieve that situation, Enlil and Enki fashion a cattle god and a grain goddess. Cattle and grain suddenly abound, but the gods are unable to utilize them. Something is still needed to tend the animals and make grain into bread. The gods complain to Enki and command him to create servants to take care of their needs.

Coming to their aid, Enki takes "clay that is over the abyss" and with Ninhursag oversees its fashioning into human beings who are pressed into the gods' service, especially to make them bread. At a feast afterward, Enki and Ninhursag get drunk and ineptly make several abnormal human types, including the barren woman and the eunuch. But whole or flawed, man and woman are the clay of the abyss, and are related by nature to chaos.

Akkadian Creation Myths The Babylonian and Assyrian cultures, both Semitic, shared the Akkadian language, which distinguished them from the non-Semitic and linguistically different Sumerians. By far the most familiar creation myth of the ancient Near East is the Babylonian creation epic known as *Enuma Elish* (from its opening words). It deals explicitly with the creation of the universe and contains some parallels to the biblical account. A later Assyrian version of the myth appropriately substituted the national god Asshur for Babylon's god Marduk.

In *Enuma Elish* the human race is made from the blood of Kingu, leader of a rebel horde against the creator god Marduk. Consequently, in the Babylonian myth, man and woman are again related to chaos. In another myth preserved in an Old Babylonian fragment, humankind is made from the blood of a slain god:

> *Let [man] appear!*
> *He who shall serve all the gods,*
> *Let him be formed out of clay,*
> *be animated with blood!*
> *Enki opened his mouth,*
> *saying to the great gods: . . .*
> *Let them slay one god.*
> *With his flesh and his blood . . .*
> *let Ninhursag mingle clay.*

According to another Akkadian myth, the gods created man as a perverse being, presenting him with twisted speech, lies, and untruth.

Egyptian Creation Myths The customary Egyptian myth of creation (found, for example, in the dedication ritual of a royal pyramid or in the *Book of the Dead*) relates that before the creation there was a watery void, accompanied by darkness, formlessness, and invisibility. That watery chaos bore the name Nun, "the great god who came into being by himself . . . the father of the gods." The void subsides, leaving a primordial mound of earth with the creator god Atum ("totality") upon it. Atum brings into being the rest of the universe and assigns places and functions to its parts.

In a detail similar to the Mesopotamian myths, the air god Shu separates heaven-earth by lifting the sky goddess Nut from the earth god Geb and placing himself between the two.

The most significant Egyptian creation myth is the so-called "Memphite Theology" (c. 2700 BC), which sought to move the Egyptian capital to Memphis by claiming it to be the site of the original creation mound. Rather than describing the creation in purely physical terms, that myth conceives of the universe as coming into existence through the mind ("heart") and commanding speech ("tongue") of the creator god. According to that myth, then, an intelligent will controlled the universe.

Creation Myths and Genesis The Genesis account of Creation differs from pagan myths in at least two ways. First, the accounts differ in their purpose. The pagan myths served principally to preserve life and society by magical recitation. Although the biblical account has implications for life and society, it serves primarily to teach a covenant people about God and is devoid of any occult claims or power.

Second, the accounts differ in their quality. The Genesis Creation narrative presents a straightforward theology with a minimum of adornment. Told as a story, it rings true even in an age of scientific discovery, when people are accustomed to mechanistic explorations of natural phenomena. An intelligent, well-informed person can accept Genesis as an authoritative statement of nature's meaning and purpose and on it base a life of devotion to the divine Creator. In contrast, the creation myths present a debased theology and an even more debased morality. The most ancient myths, which may appeal to modern practitioners of "occult sciences" for various reasons, are simply unbelievable as religious truth. The gods of the ancient myths have been buried in the rubble of long-dead civilizations or transmuted into the gods of modern polytheistic religions; the God of the Bible lives on.

The literary form of Genesis 1–3 shows that it is not theology; that is, it does not make analytical statements about God. Yet it presents a view of God distinctively different from the gods of the pagan myths. God is present "in the beginning." He is one; he creates with singleness of purpose, unchallenged. In contrast, the pagan myths portray the beginning as impersonal and chaotic. Chaos evolves into a cosmos, out of which the gods emerge by chance. The subsequent development of heaven and earth is viewed as a cosmic power struggle between rival gods. Again, the Creator in Genesis is different from and "bigger" than the heavens and earth he creates. The pagan gods are material and made up of the same cosmic stuff as the world; the world is bigger than they are.

Biblical and pagan anthropologies are also significantly different. In Genesis man and woman are creatures distinct from the Creator, although bearing his "image." They are created for the purpose of ruling the earth as God's agents and are accordingly assigned clear responsibilities. In pagan mythology human beings come from the same stuff as the gods, though humans are more closely related to chaos than to the gods who fashioned them. The pagan gods made humans as slaves to take care of the gods' material needs, so the gods treat them with either contempt or indifference. The Near Eastern worldview was not only pessimistic but also fatalistic. Human beings, far from being responsible or significant, were assigned at birth an inexorable destiny that they could not overrule.

The best that most Near Eastern inhabitants could

hope for was a relatively prosperous and regular life before their fated end, and for that they thought they had to manipulate their deities through recital and reenactment of the ancient myths. Genesis, on the other hand, as part of the larger OT teaching, sought to bring the human community into a living, personal, covenant relationship with God.

See also Creation.

CREATURE, New *See* New Creation, New Creature.

CREDIT, CREDITOR Acknowledgment of payment on a debt incurred through goods or services sold on trust, and the one who operates the business of selling on credit. The Mosaic law regulated credit and creditors (Dt 23:19-20).

See also Banker, Banking; Debt.

CREEPING THINGS Reference to insects, reptiles, and some other animals that crawl on the belly or creep on four or more feet. *See* Animals.

CRESCENS Coworker of the apostle Paul. Crescens went on to Galatia when Paul was imprisoned in Rome (2 Tm 4:10).

CRETE Fourth largest island in the Mediterranean, lying approximately 60 miles (97 kilometers) southeast of Greece and 110 miles (177 kilometers) southwest of Turkey. It is 160 miles (257.4 kilometers) long from east to west, with a width of approximately 36 miles (58 kilometers), an area of 3,200 square miles (5,149 square kilometers). Through the island stretches a mountain range dominated in the center by the sacred Mt Ida (altitude 9,000 feet or 2,742 meters). These mountains slope down sharply to the southern coast, with the result that most of the inhabitants live on the more gradual northern slopes.

Civilization in ancient Crete reached its climax with the Minoan era (3000–1100 BC). The spectacular remnants of this high civilization may be seen best at Knossos, thanks to the labors of British archaeologist Arthur Evans. About 1950–1900 BC, beautiful pottery

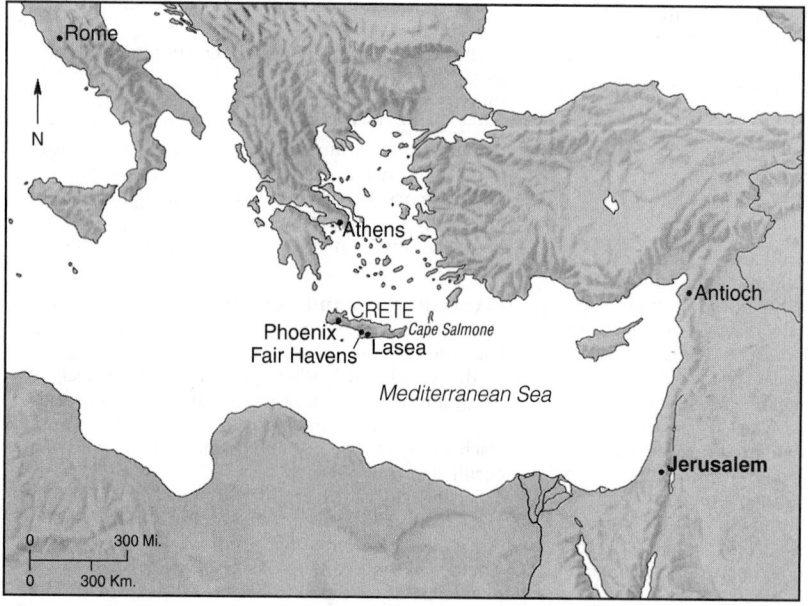

Crete, an Island in the Mediterranean Tradition says that after Paul was released from prison in Rome (before his second and final Roman imprisonment), he and Titus traveled together for a while. They stopped in Crete, and when it was time for Paul to go, he left Titus behind to help the churches there.

was produced and exported. Metallurgy was highly developed, and hieroglyphic writing was introduced. This civilization was suddenly and dramatically destroyed in a mysterious manner about 1700 BC, perhaps by volcanic eruption or earthquake. Following this, the towns and palaces were rebuilt, and the island enjoyed its greatest prosperity. The partially restored palace of Knossos amazes today's visitor with superb frescoes, stairways, and pillars. All this ended in destruction about 1450 BC. Some think it was caused by the volcanic explosion at the nearby island of Santorini.

Crete is important in the history of the Christian church. When Paul went to Rome as a prisoner, the ship sought refuge from a storm at Fair Havens (Acts 27:8). The ship tried in vain to reach the more commodious harbor at Phoenix (v 12) but was blown off course and sought refuge at an island off the southwest coast of Crete, called Cauda (v 16). Paul may have visited Crete after imprisonment in Rome, for in his Letter to Titus, he said, "I left you on the island of Crete" (Ti 1:5, NLT). On the basis of this and other evidence, many scholars conclude that Paul was released and had an extended ministry before his second imprisonment and execution (2 Tm 4:6). Paul had little good to say about the people of Crete, quoting one of their own poets as saying they were "liars, cruel animals, and lazy gluttons" (Ti 1:12). But the gospel must have made quite a difference there, for today the name of Titus is honored in many villages, churches, and monasteries.

Because of its location and its relative fertility, Crete has been a prize of war and of commerce. The island was conquered by Rome in 67 BC and became a separate province. The inhabitants prospered under the Romans and later under the Greek Christians (Byzantines). The Saracens (Muslims) occupied the island for over a century (AD 823–960). After centuries of Christian leadership, it was conquered by the Turkish sultan, and civilization languished (1669–1898). In the 20th century Crete has been a part of Greece, except for a period of German occupancy during World War II.

CRICKET A four-footed winged insect, considered edible by the Israelites (Lv 11:22). *See* Animals.

CRIMINAL LAW AND PUNISHMENT* The science or philosophy of law is called jurisprudence. Although modern jurisprudence bears little resemblance to biblical concepts of law, the Scriptures have played a definite role in its development. Today, criminal law is clearly distinguished from civil law; in Bible times the distinction was much less clear. Today, offenses against civil law (torts) are distinguished from minor crimes (misdemeanors) as well as from serious crimes (felonies). In the Bible, "crimes" included all punishable offenses, even religious offenses such as idolatry (worshiping a false god) or blasphemy (speaking or behaving with contempt toward God).

PREVIEW
• Near Eastern Context
• Hebrew Criminal Law
• Punishment
• Conclusion

Near Eastern Context In ancient societies as in modern ones, laws were considered necessary to regulate individual behavior for the good of the community, state, or nation. Today laws are thought of as made by people for their own protection. In contrast, all ancient Near Eastern law codes were considered to have come directly from

some divine source. Hebrew law, though distinct, followed the general pattern of Near Eastern law codes, as is known from those that have survived—such as the Code of Hammurabi and Assyrian and Hittite laws.

Conclusions about the "origin" of ancient laws should be made cautiously. Although evidence indicates that Hammurabi based his legislation partially on earlier Sumerian codes, he declared that his code had been received from Shamash, god of justice. That declaration must have been intended to convey primarily that his code had the express sanction of Shamash, since at least some people would recognize it as a compilation based largely on earlier laws. Similarly, the clear biblical statements about Moses receiving the law on Mt Sinai (Ex 19–24) do not rule out the possibility that parts of the Decalogue (the Ten Commandments) may have existed in earlier codes. Possibly the Mosaic legislation included some social rules adapted from the period of Israel's sojourn in Egypt.

Hebrew Criminal Law

Laws Governing Offenses against God Since Hebrew law was designed for a group of people for whom religion was of paramount importance and whose faith was endangered by the influence of the beliefs of their pagan neighbors, it is not surprising that so much of Hebrew law dealt with crimes committed against God. The prohibition against worshiping idols is stated and repeated in the Torah, or Pentateuch (first five books of the Bible): "You shall not make for yourself a graven image, or any likeness of anything that is in heaven above, or that is in the earth beneath, or that is in the water under the earth; you shall not bow down to them or serve them" (Ex 20:4-5, RSV). Sacrifice of infants, practiced in some pagan religions, was specifically prohibited in Israel. The penalty for that crime, as for the other forms of murder, was stoning to death (Lv 20:2).

In the book of Leviticus, death by stoning was recorded as the appropriate punishment for blaspheming the name of God (Lv 24:11-16). False prophecy was also a criminal offense; that accusation could apply to a person making a prediction in the name of a god other than the Lord, or implying falsely that one's prophecy resulted from a communication with God. Jeremiah, whose prophecy of Nebuchadnezzar's victory over the southern kingdom of Judah was for a time considered to be false, was almost lynched by a mob (Jer 26:8-9).

The idea of keeping the seventh day holy stemmed from the celebration of God's work in creating the universe in six days and resting on the seventh. Keeping the Sabbath required cessation of manual work for the entire family, including farm animals (Ex 16:23; 20:8-11). People were also required to meet together on the Sabbath for worship, which at a later period in Hebrew history included the reading of Scripture, prayer, and preaching. Anyone breaking the Sabbath could be sentenced to death, as happened to a man caught gathering firewood on the Sabbath (Nm 15:32-36).

Any type of premeditated crime was considered an offense against God, the giver of all law; hence, it was punishable by death (Nm 15:30-31). Hebrew law also insisted on donation of the firstfruits of harvest to the Lord without delay. That requirement was sometimes carried over to include a first child, whose life was dedicated to service in the temple (Ex 22:29-30; Dt 15:19).

Personal Injury Murder, an offense against "God's image," was one of many crimes punishable by death in OT times. The book of Exodus stated unequivocally that "anyone who hits a person hard enough to cause death must be put to death" (Ex 21:12, NLT). A murderer who killed by using a weapon such as a stone, a piece of wood, or iron could be killed in revenge by a relative of the deceased. If the original death happened accidentally, the community would sometimes help to conceal the killer and encourage him to hide in a nearby city of refuge, where he would be safe as long as he remained within its gates. He had to stay in that sanctuary until the death of the high priest then in office, after which he was free to return to his own city (Nm 35:10-28). The sixth commandment enjoined, "You shall not kill" (Ex 20:13). The Hebrew word referred specifically to murder, not to all forms of killing. Killing an enemy in battle and the execution of a murderer were considered necessary and were not prohibited. More than one witness was required for any conviction, particularly in a murder case (Nm 35:30; Dt 17:6; 19:15).

In the Code of Hammurabi a man responsible for an accidental injury to another was required to pay for the services of the physician. If the victim died, a fine was payable according to the victim's rank. In a sense the Hebrews went further by requiring payment for any loss of time suffered by the injured person (Ex 21:18-19).

Kidnapping was punishable by death in the OT. Exodus states that "Kidnappers must be killed, whether they are caught in possession of their victims or have already sold them as slaves" (Ex 21:16, NLT). Joseph's being sold into slavery by his brothers illustrates this kind of kidnapping.

Laws concerning Property The book of Exodus is quite specific about anyone responsible for damage to the property or crops of another. If a field caught fire and the fire spread, damaging crops in other fields, the person who started the fire, or perhaps the owner of the first field to catch fire, was responsible for the damage (Ex 22:6). Hammurabi's code cited a similar instance of a man who neglected to keep a dike in repair and was therefore responsible for flood damage to his neighbor's crops.

Injuries to animals, especially oxen, or injuries to people or property caused by such animals formed an important area of Hebrew law. If an ox that had been previously good-tempered killed a man, the owner would be blameless, although the ox would be put to death—a severe financial penalty for the owner. If an ox with a history of goring killed a man because its owner failed to restrain it adequately, both ox and owner would be put to death. The owner's life could be ransomed by payment of an agreed-upon sum. If the person an ox gored was a servant, the ox was stoned and the owner paid a fine (Ex 21:28-32). The Code of Hammurabi also recommended no punishment for a first offense by an animal, but if the owner knew that the ox was dangerous and had taken no steps to prevent harm, a fine in silver was payable—a very large fine for an upper-class victim, slightly less if the victim was a slave. However bad the circumstances and however vicious the ox, the Code of Hammurabi stopped at a fine for the offense, never imposing a death penalty on either the animal or the owner.

Negligence causing injury to an animal was also punished in Hebrew law. If an ox or a donkey fell into a pit carelessly left uncovered, the owner of the animal was reimbursed for its loss (Ex 21:33-36).

In ancient cultures women were generally considered chattel (personal property), much like animals or slaves. A daughter was considered to be her father's property until her marriage, then the property of her husband. Therefore, any offense against a married woman was regarded as an offense against the property of the husband. According to the Code of Hammurabi, a child could be sold into slavery as a servant or bondsman, usually in payment of the father's debt (cf. Ex 21:2-7; Neh 5:5-8; Is 50:1). Parental authority was so highly regarded in biblical law that a stubborn and rebellious son could be brought before the elders on the grounds of being disobedient and a glutton or a drunkard. He might then be convicted and stoned to death on the spot by the men of the city (Dt 21:18-21). Even that, however, was a protection of the child's rights; some Near Eastern legislation allowed a parent to order the death of his offspring without reference to the elders or to anyone else. With daughters in particular being held in such low esteem, it is perhaps remarkable that a daughter could inherit property if there were no sons (Nm 27:8).

Adultery, prohibited in the Decalogue, was another crime against a man's property, specifically his wife. The book of Deuteronomy goes into considerable detail about cases of adultery—the punishment for both persons being death (Dt 22:22). If a man seduced a young woman who was not betrothed, he was required to pay her father the bride price (50 silver shekels); he could not divorce her but had to keep her as his wife for the rest of his life (Ex 22:16; Dt 22:28-29).

In a situation where a wife was accused of adultery but without evidence, a trial was conducted. The husband would bring his wife to a priest and present a small offering (a tenth of a measure of barley meal, with neither oil nor frankincense on it), indicating the low esteem in which he now held his wife. The woman then stood before the Lord holding an earthen jar of "holy water." Dust from the floor of the tabernacle was mixed with the water, and the cereal offering was placed in her hands. Her hair was loosened by the priest to show not only her grief but also to give an impression of abandonment. She was then required to take an oath. After that, the priest pronounced a curse upon her to the effect that her womb would be fertilized easily, but that she would have many miscarriages. She had to give her consent to that pronouncement. The priest then wrote the curses in a book and symbolically washed them off into the "bitter water." The woman was required to drink the water while the priest waved the cereal offering from her hands before the Lord and burned some of it on the altar. The priest told her that if she was guilty, the water would make her thigh rot and her abdomen swell. If that happened, she would become an outcast; but if she were proved innocent, she would be free. Whatever the result, no blame for false accusation fell upon the husband (Nm 5:12-31).

If a slave was struck by his master in such a manner as to cause instant death, the slave's death had to be avenged. If the slave lingered, possibly for days, he did not need to be avenged, his loss being a sufficient punishment for the owner (Ex 21:20-21). It is unlikely that the Hebrews had much experience with that law, which had no parallels in Hammurabi's code. If an owner injured his slave by causing the loss of an eye or a tooth, Hebrew law required that the slave be set free (vv 26-27). The Code of Hammurabi gave an example of a man injuring another man's slave; the owner had to be paid half the slave's value.

Little emphasis was placed on burglary or larceny in the Hebrew law code. A burglar was presumed to be repentant and ready to make restitution. After return of the stolen property and payment of a small additional fine, a thief could again "approach the Lord" (Lv 6:2-7).

By contrast, the Code of Hammurabi prescribed the death penalty for burglary. In Hebrew law, theft of an animal required restitution to be made in the ratio of at least two to one; if a bull or a cow had been stolen or sold, the thief had to restore the property fivefold. The Code of Hammurabi contained a similar statute: "If a man steal ox or sheep, ass or pig, or goat—if it be from a god or a palace, he shall restore thirtyfold; if it be from a freeman, he shall render tenfold. If the thief have nothing wherewith to pay, he shall be put to death." In Hebrew law goods stolen from a home were simply to be restored without additional penalty. If the thief no longer had the goods and was unable to pay the equivalent value, he might be sold into slavery until restitution was made (Ex 22:1-4).

General Laws The Hebrew code as contained in Exodus and Deuteronomy included many general prohibitions. Some concerned business dealings such as the removal of boundary markers (Dt 19:14). The use of false weights and measures was condemned (Lv 19:35; Dt 25:15; Prv 11:1; 20:23; Mi 6:11). Bribery was strictly forbidden (Ex 23:8), yet no punishment was specified for those who broke that law. In the Code of Hammurabi, if a judge changed his decision and was unable to give a satisfactory explanation, particularly if bribery was suspected, the judge had to pay 12 times the amount of the penalty and lost his seat on the bench. In the Hebrew code, perjury was also dealt with, although again no punishment was specified. The Code of Hammurabi stated that for perjury in cases where the punishment was death, persons giving false testimony were to be sentenced to death themselves (cf. Ex 23:1).

A number of Hebrew laws reflected concern for the poor. For example, poor people were not to be subjected to usury if they were in debt, or left cold at night if their coats were taken as a pledge. Widows, orphans, and strangers were also to be treated with mercy and understanding (Ex 22:21-27; 23:9; Dt 23:19; 24:17).

Some Hebrew laws concerned family behavior, such as those previously mentioned who cursed or disobeyed their parents (Ex 21:17; Lv 20:9; Dt 27:16; cf. Prv 20:20; 30:17). Family responsibilities were strong; an entire family frequently suffered punishment for the crime of one of its individual members (Jos 7:20-26; 2 Sm 3:29; 21:1-9; 2 Kgs 5:27; Lam 5:7). Over a period of time, as individual responsibility came to be recognized, parents were no longer put to death for the crimes of their children, or vice versa (cf. Jer 31:29-30).

Sorcery and witchcraft were forbidden. The book of Exodus stated explicitly, "A sorceress must not be allowed to live" (22:18, NLT). Sexual perversions, such as intercourse with animals, were forbidden under penalty of death. Regulations prohibiting marriage with close relatives were given in detail (Lv 20:17-21).

In Hebrew law no parallel existed for some interesting items in the Code of Hammurabi concerning surgery. That code mentioned veterinary surgery and even operations on the human eye. A Babylonian surgeon had to be wary, for "if a physician makes a deep incision upon a man with his bronze lancet and causes the man's death or operates on the eye socket of a man with his bronze lancet and destroys the man's eye, then they shall cut off his hand." Surgery was virtually unknown among the ancient Israelites except for the ritual practice of circumcision.

Punishment Near Eastern punishments for murder and personal injury were retaliatory and often of the same nature as the offense. Other methods of punishment tended to vary with individual countries or traditions.

Many kinds of punishment were inflicted on people defeated in both a full-scale war or a small insurrection.

Physical Punishment Many forms of punishment stopped short of killing but could nevertheless be quite severe.

1. In the OT beating with rods or switches was the traditional form of discipline for children, fools, and slaves (Ex 21:20; Prv 13:24; 26:3). Scourging (also called flogging) was more severe than beating. The whip employed could be made of several strips of leather fastened at one end or of two interwoven leather strips. A whip nicknamed "scorpion" (because of the barbs in its end) was one of the cruelest instruments of punishment mentioned in the OT (1 Kgs 12:11, 14). The severity of punishment could be increased by inserting pieces of metal or bone into the leather.

   Before a scourging, the victim would be examined for physical fitness. If death resulted from the blows, no blame was attached to the person administering the punishment. The victim was stripped to the waist and tied to a pillar, his hands bound with leather thongs. The severity of a scourging depended on the crime, although the Mosaic law set an upper limit of 40 lashes (Dt 25:1-3). To guard against a miscount, that number was later lowered by one (2 Cor 11:24). Lashes might be administered both on the chest and the back. Under some law codes, scourging could be used as a private punishment; in that case, if the victim died, another life was forfeit.

   In offenses against the law, synagogue authorities administered scourgings (Mt 10:17). A husband might be scourged by the elders of the city for defamation of his wife's character (Dt 22:18). Scourging was also used as a means of interrogating a prisoner—hence, a Roman captain's comment that the apostle Paul should be "examined by scourging" (Acts 22:24).

   The Romans usually reserved scourging for non-Roman citizens, such as slaves or aliens, as well as for those condemned to death. Normally, criminals were scourged after they had been condemned to death; it is therefore unusual to find the scourging of Jesus taking place before his condemnation. Pilate may have hoped to soften the people's hearts by Jesus' suffering so that they would not demand the death penalty (Lk 23:16, 22; Jn 19:1).

   Citizens of the Roman Empire could never be beaten or scourged before sentencing (Acts 22:25). Hence, the magistrates were afraid when they heard that Paul, a Roman citizen, had been beaten under those circumstances (16:37-39).

2. The gouging out of the eyes of prisoners and captives was a common practice in the Near East. The Philistines blinded Samson before imprisoning him (Jgs 16:21). The Babylonians did the same to King Zedekiah in 587 BC before taking him into captivity (2 Kgs 25:7). The Ammonite king Nahash was prepared to accept peace overtures from the men of the city of Jabesh on condition that all their right eyes be gouged out. Nahash's purpose was to disgrace them and prevent them from further active participation in warfare (1 Sm 11:1-4).

3. Several forms of mutilation served as punishments in the Near East. The Israelites considered their own bodies sacred and made in God's image, but that did not prevent them from mutilating their enemies by cutting off their thumbs and large toes.

   The Code of Hammurabi and the Assyrian law code prescribed mutilation of the eye, nose, ear, breast, tongue, lip, hand, and finger as punishments for specific crimes. In Assyria, punishment was often inflicted by the victim of the crime under supervision of court officials. The Code of Hammurabi also contained safeguards so that criminals were not punished in excess of the law's sentence.

4. Stocks are mentioned as a form of punishment in the later OT period. The prophets Hanani (2 Chr 16:10) and Jeremiah (Jer 20:2-3) suffered the indignity of being placed in stocks. Both ankles, and sometimes the wrists and head as well, were placed in holes in two large pieces of wood. In Roman times, stocks were converted to a form of torture, with a prisoner's legs stretched to holes increasingly far apart. In the NT, Paul and Silas had their feet placed in stocks by a Philippian jailer (Acts 16:24). The same Greek word, meaning "confinement," can refer to fetters chaining a prisoner or to an iron collar like that worn by runaway Roman slaves.

Capital Punishment Capital punishment was common in many Near Eastern countries. Several methods were used.

1. Those who offended a king were beheaded with a sword (2 Sm 16:9; 2 Kgs 6:31-32), as were idolaters and murderers (according to the Mishnah, the Jewish commentary on the law). The sword was probably used for private executions as well. Inhabitants of entire cities were sometimes "put to the sword" for their denial of the faith (Ex 32:27; Dt 13:15).

2. Certain sexual offenses were punished with death by burning (Lv 20:14; 21:9). Tamar, Judah's daughter-in-law, was accused of adultery and ordered to be burned to death outside the city (Gn 38:24). The Lord instructed that anyone whose feet touched the holy ground of Mt Sinai was to be shot with arrows or stoned (Ex 19:13).

3. Hanging may have been a form of execution in biblical times. But many scholars think the word translated "hanging" or "hanging on a tree" actually meant impalement (Nm 25:4; Dt 21:22-23; Jos 8:29; 2 Sm 21:6, 9; Est 9:14). A spiked wooden stake was set in the ground and the victim's body was forced onto the spike, the tip of which probably protruded from the chest or mouth. Commonly practiced by the Assyrians, that form of execution was reserved for those guilty of the worst crimes and for prisoners of war or deserters. The Persian king Darius is reputed to have impaled 3,000 men when his army entered Babylon. Impalement was the penalty Darius set for changing his edict concerning the rebuilding of the temple (Ezr 6:11-12). It is not certain whether Haman was hung or impaled (see Est 7:9-10, NLT and mg notes).

Usually "hanging" was a means of exhibiting a corpse as a warning to local inhabitants (Gn 40:19; Jos 8:29; 10:26; 2 Sm 4:12). Corpses were exhibited for only one day and were buried before nightfall. The hanging corpse was considered a defilement of the land that God had given (Dt 21:22-23). According to the Mishnah, the hands were tied together and the body hanged from the arm of a wooden gallows.

4. Crucifixion was a punishment employed by the Syrian king Antiochus IV Epiphanes in 167–166 BC; according to Josephus, a first-century AD Jewish historian, Jews who refused to give up their traditional faith were so executed. During the Maccabean period (167–40 BC), Alexander Janneus crucified 800 rebellious Pharisees in an attempt to reestablish his authority. Crucifixion was a widespread form of execution: it was used in most places in the Roman Empire, including India, North Africa, and Germany. Between 4 BC

and AD 70, on some occasions the number of people crucified at one time reached into the thousands.

Three types of crosses seem to have been used: a cross with the crossbar below the head of the upright bar (Latin cross); a T-shaped cross (St Anthony's cross); and an X-shaped cross (St Andrew's cross). Matthew records that an inscription, "This is Jesus, the King of the Jews," was placed over Jesus' head (Mt 27:37). That indicates that for Jesus' crucifixion a Latin cross was used, as artists have traditionally depicted it. In crucifixions the victim was most likely affixed to the cross while it was still lying flat on the ground. Then the cross was raised into position and dropped into a hole. The hands were either nailed or bound to the cross; it is uncertain whether the feet were nailed with one or two nails. The weight of the body was supported by a piece of wood at the feet and possibly by another that was like a spike between the legs.

5. Stoning was the most common Hebrew death penalty. The first stones were thrown by the prosecution witnesses, who were then joined by spectators. Stoning was the punishment for certain religious offenses (Lv 24:16; Nm 15:32-36; Dt 13:1-10; 17:2-5), adultery (Dt 22:23-24), child sacrifice (Lv 20:2), divination of spirits (Lv 20:27), and rebellion (Dt 21:18-21). Before his conversion, the apostle Paul witnessed and consented to the stoning of Stephen (Acts 7:58-59). Paul himself later survived a stoning at Lystra (14:19). In Roman times, a person would occasionally be stoned as he stood on a gallows.

Conclusion Hebrew law was part of the Torah ("instruction") given by God to make his covenant people holy. At that time the Israelites were a seminomadic band of former slaves. Although there are similarities with the Code of Hammurabi and other laws of settled Near Eastern cultures, there are also many differences. Hebrew law often had a broader view, even in its less sophisticated cultural setting, as though its purpose was more to teach godly behavior than to stabilize society. The simplicity and directness of the Ten Commandments, in particular, continue to influence jurisprudence, even in modern secular society.

The Bible's primary message is God's love for his covenant people, yet it never overlooks the harsh realities of life in a fallen world. Human beings sin and they commit crimes; they suffer estrangement from God because of their sin and are punished for their crimes. Christians are constantly reminded of the realism of God's love by the cross as the symbol of Christian faith. They see the crucifixion of Jesus Christ as the fulfillment of OT prophecy that the Lord put our iniquity on him (Is 53:5-6). The NT conviction is that Christ died for our sins in accordance with the Scriptures (1 Cor 15:3).

See also Civil Law and Justice; Courts and Trials; Hammurabi, Law Code of; Law, Biblical Concept of.

CRIMSON *See* Color.

CRISPUS Synagogue leader at Corinth who (along with all his household) was converted during the apostle Paul's 18-month missionary visit to the city (Acts 18:8, 11). Paul referred to Crispus as one of the few persons he personally baptized in Corinth (1 Cor 1:14).

CROCODILE Large aquatic, flesh-eating reptile with a lizardlike body; long, pointed head; long, powerful tail; and short legs. Although specifically mentioned once (Lv 11:30) in some versions, it is often identified with the Leviathan of Job 41. *See* Animals.

CROOKBACKT* KJV reading for hunchback in Leviticus 21:20. *See* Deformity.

CROSS *See* Crucifixion.

CROWN Headpiece symbolizing honor or high office. In addition to using the word metaphorically, the OT refers to three kinds of crowns. One type of crown was worn by the high priest and Hebrew kings. The high priest's "holy crown" was a gold plate engraved with the words "Holy to the Lord" fastened to the front of a turban (Ex 29:6; 39:30). It symbolized his consecration as the people's representative before God. The Hebrew kings wore a crown light enough to be worn into battle (2 Sm 1:10)—perhaps a narrow band of silk studded with jewels. Like the high priest's, the king's crown also indicated a divinely appointed office (2 Kgs 11:12; Pss 89:39; 132:18). A second type of crown was a massive gold and jeweled symbol of office worn by pagan kings and idols (2 Sm 12:30; Est 1:11). The prophet Zechariah placed such a crown on Joshua the high priest to indicate the union of royal and priestly functions (Zec 6:11, 14). A third type of crown was a wreath of flowers used at a banquet to symbolize joy and celebration (Sg 3:11; Is 28:1; Wisd of Sol 2:8).

The word "crown" is used metaphorically to indicate rule or royalty (Na 3:17, KJV), glory or honor (Jb 19:9; Ps 8:5; Ez 16:12), joy (Ez 23:42), or pride (Jb 31:36; Is 28:3).

In the NT the most common word for "crown" means a laurel wreath worn at banquets or a prize given as a civic or military honor. The apostle Paul alluded to its use as an athletic prize when he urged Christians to be disciplined in striving for a "crown" that would not wither (1 Cor 9:25; 2 Tm 2:5). Paul regarded his converts as his "joy and crown" (Phil 4:1; 1 Thes 2:19).

A victor's wreath symbolizes the eternal life inherited by Christians who have persevered (Jas 1:12; 1 Pt 5:4; Rv 2:10; 3:11). In the book of Revelation the victories of the locusts (9:7), the woman (12:1), and Christ (6:2; 14:14) are symbolized by laurel crowns. A different Greek word, meaning a royal crown, is used for the diadems on the heads of the dragon (12:3), the beast from the sea (13:1), and Christ (19:12).

Jesus' crown of thorns was a circlet formed from a prickly shrub—an ironic parody of a victor's wreath (Mk 15:17-18). Its combination with the robe, scepter (Mt 27:27-29), and satirical inscription on the cross that Jesus was "the King of the Jews" (Mk 15:26), were all meant to mock him as a defeated messianic aspirant.

CRUCIFIXION Form of execution employed in the death of Jesus Christ. Two concepts related to crucifixion occur in Scripture: the "cross," a pagan mode of capital punishment, and the "tree," which was a Jewish form. Jesus' crucifixion was the means by which he procured atonement for humanity. The term "cross" was also used figuratively by Jesus to portray the sacrifice required in discipleship, and it was used by the apostle Paul to symbolize the death of self in the process of transformation.

PREVIEW
•Historical Background
•Christ's Crucifixion
•The Theological Significance of Christ's Crucifixion

Historical Background

The Pagan Mode Literally, the word "cross" in Greek referred to a pointed stake used for various purposes, including an instrument of execution. It could be an upright stake, used to impale a victim, or a vertical stake with a crossbeam either across the top (T) or across the middle (+), used to hang or crucify a criminal, with the added disgrace of public display. Evidently crucifixion was practiced first by the Medes and Persians and later by Alexander the Great (356–323 BC), the Carthaginians, and the Romans. Both Greeks and Romans restricted its use to slaves, considering it too barbaric for citizens. In the imperial era the Romans extended the use to foreigners, but even so it was used mainly for crimes against the state.

Crucifixion was universally recognized as the most horrible type of execution. In the East, in fact, it was used only as a further sign of disgrace for prisoners already executed, usually by decapitation. In the West the condemned criminal was scourged (whipped), usually at the place of execution, and forced to carry the crossbeam to the spot where a stake had already been erected. A tablet stating the crime was often placed around the offender's neck and was fastened to the cross after the execution. The prisoner was commonly tied or sometimes nailed to the crossbeam (with the nails through the wrists, since the bones in the hand could not take the weight). The beam was then raised and fixed to the upright pole. If the executioners wished a particularly slow, agonizing death, they might drive blocks or pins into the stake for a seat or a step to support the feet. Death came about either through loss of blood circulation followed by coronary failure or through the collapse of one's lungs, causing suffocation. That could take days, so often the victim's legs would be broken below the knees with a club, causing massive shock and eliminating any further possibility of easing the pressure on the bound or spiked wrists. Usually a body was left on the cross to rot, but in some instances was given to relatives or friends for burial.

The Jewish Mode A different form of crucifixion is seen in the OT. King Saul's body was decapitated and affixed to a wall by the Philistines (1 Sm 31:9-10). The Persian king Darius made impaling the penalty for altering his decree (Ezr 6:11). According to Deuteronomy 21:22-23, the Eastern form was employed by the Jews with the added proviso that the body must be removed from "the tree" before nightfall, because the victim was "accursed by God" (cf. Gal 3:13) and must not remain to "defile the land." The Roman form of crucifixion was not employed by the Jews. The only exception was a mass crucifixion of 800 rebels by the Jewish ruler Alexander Janneus in 76 BC, reported by the Jewish historian Josephus as being universally condemned by the Jews. Some believe that Jewish courts did practice the Western method of crucifixion after the second century BC.

Christ's Crucifixion The NT (quoted in this article from the RSV) has much to say about Christ's crucifixion because it is the central theme of the Christian faith.

The Predictions The Gospels record three predictions by Christ of his own crucifixion (Mk 8:31; 9:31; 10:33-34 and parallel passages). In addition, John recorded three sayings about the Son of Man being "lifted up" (Jn 3:14; 8:28; 12:32-33), which parallel the synoptic predictions. Several themes are interwoven into those passages: (1) Christ's passion (a term used for his suffering on the cross) was part of God's redemptive purpose (Mk 8:31, "must"). (2) Both Jew and Roman were guilty of "delivering" and of "killing" Jesus. (3) His death would be followed by vindication via the resurrection. (4) His death itself, in a paradoxical way, was seen as a means of his entering into "glory" (seen in the symbolism John attached to "lifted up"). Other sayings that hint at Jesus' fate are his comment about the murder of the prophets (Mt 23:29-30; Lk 13:33), his parables about the death of the prophets and the "son" (the marriage feast, Mt 22:1-14; the wicked tenants, Mk 12:1-10), and his teachings about the coming similar suffering of his disciples (Mt 10:24-28; Mk 8:34-35; Jn 15:18-25).

The Historical Event The crucifixion of Jesus combined Roman and Jewish elements. Although the Gospel writers stressed Jewish guilt for their own polemical purposes, they were careful to distinguish between the leaders and the common people. It was the leaders who initiated Jesus' arrest (Mk 14:43) and his trial by the Sanhedrin (vv 53-64). Though Pilate seemed to vacillate and in the end surrendered weakly to the crowds by "washing his hands" of any guilt (Mt 27:24), Rome was clearly implicated in the Crucifixion. Since the Sanhedrin did not have the power to inflict capital punishment, Pilate's decision was necessary before crucifixion could occur. Further, Romans actually carried out the execution.

At Jesus' crucifixion Roman custom was observed in his scourging, his mock enthronement and stripping, the bearing of his own crossbeam, his being nailed to the cross, and the breaking of the two thieves' legs. The elevated site fits the custom of displaying certain criminals publicly. So does the height of Jesus' cross, probably seven to nine feet (2 to 3 meters). The presence of a tablet bearing the inscription "The King of the Jews" on the cross suggests that the crossbeam was fixed somewhere below the top of the stake. Jewish elements are seen in the wine mixed with myrrh (Mk 15:23), the vinegar on the hyssop reed (v 36), and the removal of the body before sunset and the beginning of the Sabbath (Jn 19:31).

Although the fact of Jesus' crucifixion is seldom challenged historically, the varying details in the four Gospels are sometimes regarded as later additions due to the influence of prophetic "fulfillment," to Christian-Jewish polemics or to cultic considerations. However, one cannot conclude from the differences in the Gospel accounts that the details are not historical. Narrative selectivity on the part of the Gospel writers is in no sense evidence of fabrication.

The Emphasis in Each Gospel The elements found in the individual passion narratives were selected by each writer to present a particular view of the crucifixion scene. It has been realized for some time that the Gospel writers were not only historians but also theologians, selecting scenes and portraying them to show the significance of the events for the Christian faith. Their selection is poignantly evident in the crucifixion narratives.

Mark and Matthew both show the horror of the Messiah being put to death by human beings. The first half of Mark's scene contrasts the taunts of the crowd with the true significance of Jesus' death. The twofold "save yourself" (Mk 15:29-31) repeats Jesus' words about rebuilding the temple in three days—prophetically pointing to the resurrection. The second half of Mark's description stresses the horror of the scene, progressing from a darkness motif to the cry of abandonment to further taunts (vv 33-36).

The Gospel of Matthew extends Mark's imagery in certain important directions, adding that Jesus refused the stupefying drink (a drugged wine to alleviate pain) "when he tasted it" (Mt 27:34), as well as adding "yielded up his spirit" to the death scene (v 50). Matthew thus emphasizes that Jesus voluntarily faced his death fully conscious and in complete control of himself. Matthew's irony and allusion also bring out the disparity between Jesus' suffering and his vindication. Elements of vindication include the ripping of the temple veil (v 51) and the centurion's

testimony (v 54). In the remarkable supernatural scene of Matthew 27:52-53, Jesus' death is followed immediately by an earthquake that opened tombs and revived "many bodies of the saints" who had died. For Matthew those events and others inaugurated the last days, the new age of salvation, when the power of death is broken and life is made available for all.

The account in Luke's Gospel is also quite remarkable. It has two major thrusts. First, Jesus is portrayed as the perfect example of the righteous martyr who forgives his enemies and by his attitude converts some of his opponents. The taunts of the rulers and soldiers are reversed when the crowd returns home "beating their breasts" (Lk 23:48) and the centurion cries, "Certainly this man was innocent!" (v 47). Second, in Luke the entire setting has an atmosphere of reverence and worship. Omitted are the wine and myrrh, the cry of abandonment, and the Elijah taunt. Other episodes are noted instead—in particular, the prayers of Jesus. In Luke alone are related (1) Jesus' prayer that God forgive his executioners, placing it in contrast with the soldiers' mockery; (2) the promise in answer to the prayer of the "believing" criminal; and (3) the commitment of Jesus' spirit to the Father. Luke's presentation makes the Crucifixion a kind of worshipful commemoration.

In the Gospel of John also one finds a change of theological focus. It goes further than Luke in removing shocking details such as the darkness and the taunts. Calm pervades throughout. Stress is laid on Jesus' sovereign control of his situation, as the Crucifixion virtually becomes a coronation procession. John alone states that the inscription on the cross was written in Hebrew, Latin, and Greek—the charge thus becomes a worldwide proclamation of Christ's enthronement. The inscription, "Jesus of Nazareth, King of the Jews," continues Pilate's dialogue on kingship beyond Jesus' trial. John thus adds to Matthew's emphasis: Jesus has not only become king but has been sovereign all along. The king is pictured as performing the priestly function and himself becoming the sacrifice. John alone mentions the hyssop (which had been used to sprinkle the blood of the lamb at the Passover, Ex 12:22) and Jesus' cry, "It is finished" (Jn 19:29-30). Further, the piercing of Jesus' side (vv 31-37), which shows the reality of his death, may also be seen symbolically, along with the "rivers of living water" (7:37-38), as typifying the outpouring of life in the new age.

Thus, each Gospel pictures the meaning of Jesus' death from a different vantage point. To combine their pictures gives new understanding of the significance of the cross. Rather than contradiction, one sees separate parts of a compelling whole.

The Theological Significance of Christ's Crucifixion The cross plays a dual role in Christian theology. Some theologians emphasize the significance of the historical crucifixion of Jesus Christ and what it accomplished for the believer. Others focus on the symbolism of the cross in each believer's life.

The death and resurrection of Jesus of Nazareth are the central events of Christian theology. The cross has meaning because of the significance of the person who was put to death on it and because of what his death accomplished. "The word of the cross" was central in the salvation proclamation of the early church. Above all, the event of the cross was God's principal saving act in history; hence the cross, though a past event, has present significance. Christ crucified and risen is the core of the church's message (Gal 3:1).

The central passage is 1 Corinthians 1:17–2:5. There the "word of the cross" (1:18) is contrasted with "eloquent wisdom" (v 17). Sounding like foolishness, it is offensive to both Greek philosophy and Jewish legalism (cf. Gal 6:12-15), but that very "weakness" in human eyes opens the door for the "power of God" (1 Cor 1:18). The cross in the church's *kerygma* (proclamation) illustrates the pattern of God's action: he forges out of the debilitated things of life both power and wisdom (vv 26-30). Because philosophical speculation replaces God's message with human wisdom and thus empties the cross of its significance, Paul rejected "lofty words" and preached only the "crucified Christ." The "Holy Spirit's power" thus became evident in Paul's "weakness" (2:1-5). The central core of the gospel is God's demonstration of victory emerging from seeming defeat, of power arising out of infirmity.

The cross as the basis of atonement is the principal emphasis in the Epistles (see Eph 2:16; Col 1:20; 2:14), whereas in the book of Acts the resurrection seems more central (see Acts 2:33-36; 3:19-26; 13:37-39). The reason for the different emphasis is found in the different purposes of those writings: the cross tends to be used in didactic (instructional) sections, the resurrection in apologetic (persuasive) or kerygmatic sections, when the basis for salvation is being presented. In actuality they were a single event in salvation history. Jesus "was put to death for our trespasses and raised for our justification" (Rom 4:25).

Paul expressed the significance of the cross in the words "redemption," "propitiation," and "justification." The first two concepts have the "for us" theme traceable to the suffering servant (Is 53:10-12), whose death was for "the sin of many." The idea of redemption in both Testaments is the payment of a price to "ransom" those held captive. That price, the NT explains, was paid on the cross, and humanity was thereby freed from sin (Mk 10:45; Ti 2:14; 1 Pt 1:18). The connection between Jesus' death and the substitutionary preposition "instead of" is also seen in Galatians 3:13, which adds to the curse of Deuteronomy 21:23 the interpretation "for us" (cf. Rom 5:10-11, 18; 1 Cor 11:24; Eph 1:7; 2:13). Similarly, Paul's concept of justification centers on the cross. It is "Christ crucified" who declares humanity righteous and makes freedom from sin possible (Rom 6:6; Gal 2:19-21). Human guilt was transferred to the cross and expiated there, opening up God's forensic (legal) forgiveness of all who avail themselves of its power (1 Pt 1:18-21; 2:24; 3:18). Finally, the result is "reconciliation"—both vertically, between humans and God (Col 1:20), and horizontally, between previously opposed human forces (e.g., in Eph 2:13-16, between Jew and Gentile).

Beyond the theological meaning of the literal cross on which Jesus Christ was put to death in Judea nearly 2,000 years ago is the symbolic significance of the cross for his followers today.

Jesus made "bearing the cross" a condition of discipleship in five passages. There are two major variants: one, found in the material common to Matthew and Luke (Mt 10:38; Lk 14:27), is phrased negatively ("cannot be my disciple"); the other, which is found in all three synoptic Gospels (Mt 16:24; Mk 8:34; Luke 9:23), is phrased positively ("If anyone would come after me"). Two major motifs are found in the sayings. The major motif comes from the imagery of a condemned man carrying his cross to an execution site; a necessary part of discipleship is a daily (Lk 9:23) willingness to sacrifice all and to suffer for the sake of Christ. The central point is not death but disgrace; the disciple must be ready to become an outcast from society.

Paul extended Christ's metaphor to the death of self.

He may have taken the idea from the early catechism, as seen in the baptismal creed of Romans 6:1-8, which identifies baptism as being "buried with him." Paul interpreted the Christian's identification with Christ's death to mean that "our old self was crucified with him so that the sinful body might be destroyed, and we might no longer be enslaved to sin" (Rom 6:6). As further developed in 2 Corinthians 5:14-17, the believer participates in the death and resurrection of Christ, so that the old life has passed away and the new has come (5:17). The same view is found also in Galatians, which contrasts the mystical death of self to the legalistic system of the Judaizers. The believer is "crucified with Christ," with the result that "it is no longer I who live" (Gal 2:20); "the flesh with its passions and desires" is "crucified" (5:24); and "far be it from me to glory except in the cross of our Lord Jesus Christ, by which the world has been crucified to me, and I to the world" (6:14). Believers must experience the cross before they can find the resurrection life.

See also Atonement; Criminal Law and Punishment; Eli, Eli, Lema Sabachthani; Golgotha; Redeemer, Redemption; Seven Last Sayings of Jesus.

CRUSE* Small earthen vessel or flask, about four to six inches (10 to15 centimeters) tall, used for holding liquids (1 Kgs 17:12-16). In the KJV, two other Hebrew words are translated "cruse." However, a bottle or jar is probably in view in 1 Kings 14:3, and an open dish or bowl in 2 Kings 2:20.

See also Pottery.

CRYSTAL Variety of quartz, usually clear or nearly so. Two Hebrew words and two Greek words are translated "crystal." *See* Minerals and Metals; Stones, Precious.

CUB* Name of a place, identified as Libya (RSV mg), in Ezekiel 30:5. *See* Libya, Libyans.

CUBIT* Linear measure, about 18 inches (46 centimeters), the length of a man's forearm from the elbow to the tip of his middle finger. *See* Weights and Measures.

CUCKOW* KJV translation of a Hebrew word better rendered "seagull" in Leviticus 11:16 and Deuteronomy 14:15 (RSV). *See* Birds (Cuckoo).

CUCUMBER Garden vegetable of the gourd family, mentioned as one of the foods desired by the wandering Israelites (Nm 11:5). *See* Food and Food Preparation; Plants.

CUMMIN Herb of the carrot family cultivated for its aromatic seeds, which are used for seasoning food (Is 28:25-27; Mt 23:23). *See* Food and Food Preparation; Plants.

CUN Syrian city belonging to Hadadezer, king of Zobah. David raided Cun, taking away large quantities of bronze (1 Chr 18:8). In a parallel account, Berothai may be the same place (2 Sm 8:8).

See also Berothah, Berothai.

CUNEIFORM* Ancient writing script in which nail or wedge-shaped marks are impressed into a writing material, usually clay, in specific patterns. Each pattern, or "sign," represents a sound or word. The system was employed by the Akkadians, Elamites, Hittites, Hurrians, and Sumerians. Ugaritic is also a cuneiform language script.

See also Writing.

CUP The word may refer either to the vessel itself or to its contents and may be intended literally or figuratively.

1. A small drinking vessel, made of various materials (leather, metal, or pottery), sizes, and designs.
2. A figure of speech to represent one's portion of or participation in something. It is associated with consolation (Jer 16:7), demons (1 Cor 10:21), divination (Gn 44:2, 5), drunkenness (Prv 23:31), immorality (Rv 17:4; 18:6), inheritance (Ps 16:5), judgment (Pss 11:6; 75:8; Is 51:17, 22; Jer 49:12; Ez 23:33; Zec 12:2; Rv 14:10; 16:19; 18:6), the Lord (1 Cor 10:21), prosperity or blessing (Ps 23:5), salvation (Ps 116:13), suffering (Mt 20:22; 26:39; Mk 10:39; 14:36; Lk 22:42; Jn 18:11), and thanksgiving (1 Cor 10:16).

See also Cup of Blessing.

CUP-BEARER Official whose primary duty was to taste the wine served to the king as a precaution against poisoning. Cup-bearers frequented the courts of kings and high officials in antiquity (1 Kgs 10:5). These men were close to those in authority and sometimes exercised considerable influence. Generally several of them served the king with the "chief cup-bearer" (butler) at their head (Gn 40:1-23). Solomon's court included cup-bearers (2 Chr 9:4), and Nehemiah was the king's cup-bearer (Neh 1:11–2:1); Rabshakeh may have been a cup-bearer (2 Kgs 18:13-19; Is 36:2).

CUP OF BLESSING* Theological phrase used in two contexts: (1) in Jewish usage, a cup of wine drunk at the end of a meal and having special Passover significance; (2) in Christian usage, the Communion goblet.

In the Passover feast the cup of blessing is the third of four cups required in the ceremony of the Paschal meal. It derives its name from the prayer offered over the cup: "Blessed art thou, O Lord our God, who givest us the fruit of the vine."

The apostle Paul used the term in reference to the wine of the Lord's Supper (1 Cor 10:16). His words are taken by many interpreters as evidence that the early church saw the Lord's Supper as a transformation and fulfillment of the Passover celebration. To participate in drinking the cup of blessing is to commit oneself to Christ, "our paschal lamb" (5:7), whose death it commemorates, and to enter into "communion" or fellowship with him. The phrase "cup of the Lord" (10:21; 11:27) or simply "the cup" (11:25) is also used. Paul added that true communion with Christ, signified by the cup of blessing, should exclude communion with spiritual forces opposed to Christ, signified by the "cup of demons" (10:21).

See also Lord's Supper, The.

CURSE, CURSED Invocation of evil or injury against one's enemies. As practiced in Bible times, cursing was the opposite of blessing and should not be confused with profanity in the modern sense.

Pagan Beliefs Curses and blessings were linked to the ancient pagan belief that spirits of "the gods" could be invoked to act on behalf of a person who repeated certain incantations or performed certain deeds (such as sacrifices). It was thought that a spoken curse possessed an occult power to work calamity on one's enemies. In some pagan cultures, curses were written on clay jars that were then smashed, symbolically initiating or effecting the intended curse.

Tombs were protected against would-be desecrators by means of curses. Royal inscriptions were protected by maledictions aimed at anyone who might alter, destroy, or defy the written decree (Ezr 6:11-12).

Curses in Old Testament Times Among the Hebrews a curse, valid only within a covenant framework overseen by God, was spoken for the sake of justice. In the OT the curse was an integral part of a covenant relationship— between God and the community, between God and an individual, or among members of the community. To break the terms of a covenant was to merit the covenant curse or curses. A curse invoked under other conditions was powerless. "Like a sparrow in its flitting, like a swallow in its flying, a curse that is causeless does not alight" (Prv 26:2, RSV). A curse could be retracted by pronouncing a blessing (Ex 12:32; Jgs 17:1-2; 2 Sm 21:1-3).

The Mosaic law forbade the cursing of parents (Ex 21:17; cf. Prv 20:20; Mt 15:4), the ruler (Ex 22:28), and the deaf (Lv 19:14). A man who suspected his wife of unfaithfulness could require that she submit to a test administered by the priest that would result in a curse upon her if she was guilty (Nm 5:11-31). Individuals might pronounce a curse upon themselves to show the truthfulness of their assertions or promises (Nm 5:19-22; Jb 31:7-10, 16-22; Ps 137:5-6). In the NT the apostle Peter followed the OT practice when he used a curse to deny that he knew Jesus (Mk 14:71). Certain men who wished to kill the apostle Paul proved their sincerity by such a solemn curse (Acts 23:12, 14, 21). Cursing God was punishable by death (Lv 24:10-16; cf. Ex 22:28; Is 8:21-22).

Curses in Bible history include God's curse on the serpent, Adam, and Eve (Gn 3:14-19); on Cain (4:11-12); on those who might curse the patriarch Abraham and his descendants (12:3); and on those who put their trust in human strength instead of in the Lord (Jer 17:5). When the people of Israel passed through Moab on their way to the Promised Land, Moab's king, Balak, hired Balaam to curse the Israelites; he and Balaam learned, however, that they could not curse those whom God had blessed (Nm 22–24). Joshua cursed anyone who might try to rebuild Jericho (Jos 6:26; fulfilled in 1 Kgs 16:34). King Saul made a curse that almost cost his son Jonathan's life (1 Sm 14:24, 43-45). Many other curses are mentioned in the OT (see, e.g., Gn 9:25; 49:5-7; Jos 9:22-23; Jgs 9:7-21, 57; 2 Sm 16:5-13; 1 Kgs 21:17-24; 2 Kgs 2:24; Mal 2:2; 4:6). The pronouncement of "woe" (NLT "destruction") is also the language of curse (Is 5:8-23; cf. Mt 23:13-33, where "alas" and "woe" can be used synonymously and may be either an exclamation of sorrow or of impending doom and calamity).

Psalm 109 contains a lengthy imprecation against the psalmist's enemies, evidently because they had spoken some words against him falsely (see also Pss 58:6-11; 69:19-28; 143:12). The prophet Jeremiah was not averse to calling on God to punish his tormentors (Jer 11:20; 12:3; 15:15; 17:18; 18:21-22; 20:11-12) or asking God not to forgive them (18:23). Such imprecations against one's enemies are difficult for Christians today to understand because they contrast sharply with the NT commands to "bless those who curse you" (Lk 6:28; cf. Rom 12:14). Jesus' injunction to "love your enemies" (Mt 5:44) may be intended to point beyond the cursing practiced in the OT to a fuller understanding of God's command to love one's neighbor as oneself.

Covenant Curses Protection of a contract or treaty by invoking a curse on the violator was common in OT times. Sometimes a covenant was sealed by cutting up an animal and having the covenanting individuals walk between the severed pieces; the slain animal symbolized the curse to befall the violator. God agreed to submit to such a curse on himself if he broke the covenant he made with the patriarch Abraham (Gn 15:7-21). Later, God accused the leaders and people of Israel of breaking their covenant with him and warned them of the consequences to follow (Jer 34:18-19). An essential part of the covenant God made with Israel at Mt Sinai was the promise of blessings for keeping the covenant and curses for breaking it (Dt 11:26-28; 27:15-26; 28:15-68; 30:19; cf. Lv 26:3-39). Israel suffered those curses in the time of the prophets Jeremiah and Ezekiel; the covenant breakers, including the king, were threatened with a curse (Jer 11:3; Ez 17:11-21).

The Ban on "Devoted Things" A special kind of curse was the ban or anathema. Strictly speaking, it was a vow to devote persons, animals, or objects under such a curse to God. In some cases the priests could use objects that had fallen under the ban (Nm 18:14; Ez 44:29), but that provision did not apply to living beings. All persons or animals under the ban were sacrificed or destroyed (Lv 27:28-29). The ban was commonly used in Israel's wars against its pagan neighbors. Sometimes everything was declared anathema (Jos 6:17-19), but normally only persons and heathen images were destroyed (Dt 2:34; 3:6; 7:2, 25-26—not even the melted gold of images was to be kept). To violate the ban by preserving any part of the cursed things was to come under the ban oneself. Because Achan did not respect the ban placed upon Jericho, the terms of that curse came upon all Israel until Achan confessed and was executed (Jos 7).

After the exile, the Jews did not practice the anathema (or ban) by putting people to death; people who violated a curse were excommunicated and put out of the congregation of Israel (Ezr 10:8). That meant that the person was no longer part of God's people and was considered "dead."

Curses in New Testament Times Jewish synagogues practiced excommunication, or anathema, in the NT period (Lk 6:22; Jn 9:22; 12:42; 16:2). Later, Christians excommunicated persons by declaring them outside of the redeemed community (Mt 18:17) or "delivered to Satan" (1 Cor 5:5; 1 Tm 1:20). Both practices stemmed from the OT ban. Unlike that curse, however, the excommunication could be removed as soon as the person repented.

Since the anathema branded a person as "rejected" or "cursed by God," Saul of Tarsus, before his conversion, tried to compel Christians to renounce Christ by calling him accursed (cf. Acts 26:11). Later, as an apostle, Paul (Saul) warned that no one speaking by the Spirit of God could call Jesus accursed (1 Cor 12:3). Paul pronounced anathema (destined for judgment and perdition) upon anyone who preached another gospel than the one he and the other apostles preached (Gal 1:8-9). Paul said he wished he could be accursed, cut off from salvation and the people of God, if that could lead to the salvation of his fellow Israelites (Rom 9:3). His desire reflected the love of Christ, who accepted the "curse of the law" upon himself in submitting to suffering and death on the cross in order to redeem human beings from that curse (Gal 3:8-14; cf. Dt 21:22-23). The NT promises that a time will come when "there shall no longer be any curse" (Rv 22:3, NASB).

See also War, Holy.

CURTAINS *See* Furniture; Homes and Dwellings; Tabernacle; Temple.

CUSH (Person)
1. Eldest of Ham's four sons (Gn 10:6; 1 Chr 1:8). Because the other three (Egypt, Put, and Canaan) are place-names, it is likely that Cush also is a place. It is

usually identified with Ethiopia. *See* Cush (Place); Ethiopia.
2. Benjamite and presumably David's enemy, mentioned in the title of Psalm 7.

CUSH (Place)
Egyptian, Akkadian, and Hebrew term broadly referring to the countries of the Upper Nile south of Egypt. In a narrower sense Cush consisted of the territory between the second and fourth cataracts of the Nile, roughly the present northern Sudan (equivalent to ancient Nubia). The OT generally uses the term in that sense. The Greeks called it Ethiopia, which eventually gave its name to modern Ethiopia (farther to the south and east).

The meaning of "Cush" in the book of Genesis, however, is problematic. In the Garden of Eden narrative (Gn 2:13), Cush seems to be located in Mesopotamia, the region of the Tigris and Euphrates rivers (v 14). Perhaps the term there should be equated with Kassite (Cossaean), the usual designation of the Babylonian rulers who held sway in Mesopotamia for about half a millennium down to the 12th century BC. The Cush of Genesis 10:6-8, then, could be divided into two locales: Nubia (vv 6-7) and Mesopotamia (vv 9-12). Alternatively, the Cush of Genesis 2:13 and 10:8 could be Kish, the Mesopotamian city that was traditionally the seat of the first Sumerian dynasty after the Flood.

Less uncertainty exists over use of the term "Cushite." With one possible exception (Nm 12:1), Cushite always refers to people from Nubia, the African Cush.

The first messenger whom Joab, King David's commander in chief, sent to announce Absalom's defeat to David was a Cushite (2 Sm 18:21-32). That messenger's foreign origin is reflected in the fact that he was unaware of a shortcut as well as in his insensitivity to the feelings of David when he gave him the message. The KJV transliterates the Hebrew word as a proper name (Cushi), but that rendering is unlikely. Most English versions translate the other occurrences of Cush and Cushite as Ethiopia and Ethiopians.

Moses had a wife who was known as a Cushite (Nm 12:1). In that context it is possible to understand Cushite in several ways: as a person from Nubia—which would make her a second wife, different from Zipporah; as a person from Cushan—making her possibly a Midianite, perhaps identical with Zipporah; or as a reference to her darker skin and foreign origin—possibly but not necessarily a reference to Zipporah.

See also Cushan; Cushi #1; Ethiopia.

CUSHAN
Name of a tribe or place mentioned only once in the Bible (Hb 3:7). Some have identified Cushan with the people and land referred to in the OT as Cush, or Ethiopia in most English versions. The parallel position of "Cushan" to "the land of Midian" in Habakkuk 3:7, however, as well as the location of the other places mentioned in the passage (Teman, Mt Paran) seems to place Cushan in the vicinity of Edom and Midian, south and southeast of the Dead Sea.

See also Cush (Place).

CUSHAN-RISHATHAIM
King of Mesopotamia whom Israel served for eight years. The Lord raised up Othniel, Kenaz's son, to deliver Israel out of his hand; later, Cushan-rishathaim was defeated by Othniel in war (Jgs 3:8-10). His exact identity is uncertain.

CUSHI
1. Joab's messenger sent to David to announce Absalom's defeat (2 Sm 18:21-32). However, the Hebrew

word transliterated "Cushi" should more likely be translated "Cushite." *See* Cush (Place).

2. Jehudi's great-grandfather. Jehudi was a prince in the court of King Jehoiakim of Judah in the time of Jeremiah the prophet (Jer 36:14).

3. Father of the prophet Zephaniah (Zep 1:1).

CUSHITE Person from the African region of Nubia (2 Sm 18:32).

See also Cush (Place).

CUSTODIAN* Servant whose responsibility was to accompany, protect, and sometimes discipline his master's son until the boy reached maturity. These custodians supervised their charges' moral conduct and general behavior. Their methods of persuasion varied from physical punishment to shaming. Paul regarded the Mosaic law as a "schoolmaster" (KJV) or "tutor" (NASB) to lead us to Christ (Gal 3:24-25). To return to the law represented a reversion to childhood.

CUTH*, CUTHAH Town in southern Babylonia (2 Kgs 17:24) from which some people were taken and relocated in Samaria after the Assyrian conquest (722 BC). The name appears also in Assyrian and Babylonian sources. In 1881 Hormuzd Rassam identified Cuthah as an ancient city whose towering ruins are located at modern Tell Ibrahim, about 20 miles (32.2 kilometers) northeast of Babylon. Cuthah was the location of a temple dedicated to Nergal, its patron deity (v 30).

The Cuthans seem to have been a predominant segment of the population of postexilic Samaria, since Jews in later centuries applied that name to Samaritans in general. The religious syncretism of which the Cuthans were a part produced hostilities between Judah and Samaria following the Jews' return from their exile. That animosity between Jews and Samaritans continued across the centuries to Jesus' day (Jn 4:7-9).

CYAMON Site mentioned in the book of Judith as demarcating the camp of Holofernes' army (Jdt 7:3). The name is uncertain: "Cyamon" is found in the Greek text, but the Syriac has "Cadmon." Two later Hebrew manuscripts have "Selmon," another "Hermon." The Latin Vulgate has "Chelmon." Some scholars have connected the site with Jokneam, modern Tell Qeimum (Jos 12:22). The only clue in the book of Judith is that it faced Esdraelon, the western portion of the plain of Jezreel.

CYLINDER SEALS* Inscribed stone cylinders used for identification of ownership, developed by the ancient Sumerians but used primarily by other Mesopotamian peoples between about 3200 BC and the fourth century BC. Occasionally, cylinder seals were used in adjacent regions such as Asia Minor (the Hittite Empire) and Persia. After about 700 BC, they were gradually replaced by stamp seals. In Palestine the stamp seal was commonly used in biblical times.

The earliest cylinder seals were engraved with a distinctive scene that could signify ownership for the one to whom it belonged. A cylinder seal was often less than an inch (2.5 centimeters) in length and normally had a hole drilled through the barrel so it could be hung about the neck or waist. By 2700 BC the seals also carried a cuneiform inscription of the name and title of their owner. During the Akkadian period (2360–2180 BC), professions were also indicated. Early in the second millennium BC the owner usually identified himself as the servant of a particular god. By the mid-second millennium, prayers were commonly added.

In the fourth and third millennia BC, cylinder seals were used primarily to indicate ownership of property, perhaps by rolling a seal across the wet clay of a jar or package. They were also used to identify and seal documents inscribed on clay tablets. At first they were used only by kings and top officials, but during the second millennium BC large numbers of the aristocracy had them. Cylinder seals were buried with their owners; nearly 15,000 have been recovered. They are an important contribution to the study of the art, economy, sociology, and religion of Mesopotamia and neighboring regions.

CYMBAL Percussion instrument consisting of two round, thin, slightly concave, metal plates that are struck together. Cymbals were used in the worship of God (2 Sm 6:5; Ezr 3:10; Ps 150:5).

See also Musical Instruments (Zelzelim); Music.

CYPRESS Evergreen tree with dark foliage and distinctive symmetrical form. Cypress is mentioned as one of the materials in Solomon's temple (1 Kgs 5:8). *See* Plants.

CYPRUS Island country located in the northeastern Mediterranean Sea, 50 miles (80.5 kilometers) south of Turkey (Asia Minor), 70 miles (112.6 kilometers) west of Syria, and 245 miles (394.2 kilometers) north of Egypt. This island, about 110 miles (177 kilometers) long and 50 miles (80.5 kilometers) wide, supports the Kyrenia and Troodas Massif mountain ranges separated by the fertile Mesaoria Plain. A narrow strip of land 40 miles (64.3 kilometers) long and 5 miles (8 kilometers) wide extends from the northeastern part of the island. Cyprus is rimmed with a number of natural harbors. In antiquity these harbors provided a strategic meeting place of sea routes from Asia Minor, Syria, Palestine, and Egypt. The Cypriot copper mines, though now largely depleted, have long been a source of revenue for its inhabitants.

During the Bronze Age (late fourth–second millennia BC), Cyprus experienced an increased growth in population and economic importance among the Mediterranean communities. The island at that time was named Alashiya, as attested in the ancient documents of Ebla (24th century BC), Mari (18th century BC), Ugarit, and Tel el-Amarna (14th century BC). Elishah, an OT name for this island, is perhaps identifiable with the extrabiblical Alashiya (cf. Ez 27:7). Alashiya (Cyprus) established a network of trade with Syria, Palestine, and Egypt and became known for its exports, especially copper, oil, wood, and pottery. Pieces of Alashiyan pottery have been found at over 50 sites in Egypt, 25 sites in Palestine, and 17 sites in Syria. The ancient texts of Ebla, Mari, and Amarna record the business transactions involving Alashiya's treasured copper. Toward the end of the Bronze Age (c. 1270–1190 BC) the Mycenian and Achaian Greeks began to migrate to Cyprus. During this period, the Greek colonies of Salamis and Paphos were founded.

In the ninth and eighth centuries BC, the Phoenicians settled their people and asserted their dominance on Cyprus. King Hiram II of Tyre (741–738 BC) included Cyprus in his royal domain, according to the inscriptions found at Mt Sinoas. Kition, near modern Larnaka, was a Phoenician settlement whose inhabitants were called Kittim. The Hebrews named the whole island Kittim (Nm 24:24, KJV "Chittim") and eventually referred to any maritime country by this name (Jer 2:10; Dn 11:30; 1 Macc 1:1). Isaiah announced that from the ports of Kittim (Cyprus), the reports of Tyre's destruction would be confirmed to its homeward-traveling sailors (Is 23:1, 12).

Assyria, rising as the superior power in the Near East

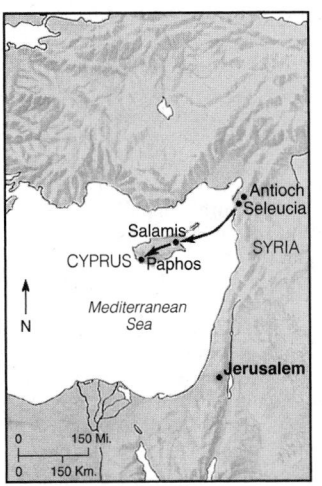

The First Missionary Journey: To Cyprus The leaders of the church in Antioch chose Paul and Barnabas to take the gospel westward. Along with John Mark, they boarded ship at Seleucia and set out across the Mediterranean for Cyprus. They preached in Salamis, the largest city, and went across the island to Paphos.

during the eighth and seventh centuries BC, made Cyprus one of its tributaries. The stele of King Sargon II (721–705 BC) records the tributes received by seven kings of Cyprus. The prism of Esarhaddon (c. 670 BC) registers ten Cypriot kings with their cities. During the Assyrian occupation, Cyprus was called Iadnan. After the dissolution of the Assyrian Empire, Cyprus was governed by Amasis, king of Egypt (569–527 BC), and later by King Cambyses II of Persia (529–522 BC).

After Alexander the Great's decisive defeat of the Persian army at Issus in 333 BC, Cyprus sent 120 ships to help support his siege against Tyre. The Ptolemies of Egypt (a subdivision of the Greek Empire) gained possession of the island after Alexander's death in 323 and retained control of Cyprus from 294–258 BC. This period brought relative peace and prosperity to the island. Cyprus, meaning copper in Greek, was the name assigned to it.

Cyprus was annexed to Rome in 58 BC, and Cicero was appointed its governor in 52. In 22 BC Rome made Cyprus into a senatorial province; Sergius Paulus was selected as its proconsul in AD 46. Later, Hadrian suppressed a violent Jewish revolt in 117, after which he banished all Jews from the island.

In the NT, Cyprus is first mentioned as the birthplace of Barnabas (Acts 4:36). Later, Jewish believers sought refuge at Cyprus from the persecutions that arose in Jerusalem on account of Stephen (11:19-20). On Paul's first missionary journey he and Barnabas set sail from Seleucia, crossing to Cyprus before going on to Asia Minor (c. AD 47). Landing at the eastern seaport of Salamis, they gradually made their way westward across the island until they reached the western harbor town of Paphos. Here they met Bar-Jesus, the false prophet, and converted the Roman proconsul Sergius Paulus. From Paphos, Paul and Barnabas sailed to Asia Minor, docking at Perga in Pamphylia (13:4-13). Paul bypassed Cyprus on his second missionary journey; however, Barnabas with John Mark revisited the island (15:39). On Paul's final trip to Jerusalem, Cyprus was used as a navigational landmark in crossing from Patara to Tyre (21:3). On the journey to Rome, Paul's ship sailed under the lee of Cyprus to avoid rough winds (27:4).

CYRENE, CYRENIANS* City and its people on the coast of North Africa that was the capital of Cyrenaica. It was founded in the seventh century BC by Greeks who engaged primarily in agricultural pursuits. Herodotus comments in his fifth-century BC *Histories* that "the land of Cyrene, the highest of that part of Libya which is inhabited

by Nomads, has the remarkable peculiarity of three separate harvest-seasons . . . making for the fortunate people of Cyrene, a continuous autumn of eight months on end" (4.199). It was conquered by Alexander the Great in 331 BC and later became a part of the Roman Empire. During the period of the NT, the city contained a large Jewish population that had come from Alexandria. One such person, named Simon, was visiting Jerusalem during the Passover feast the year Jesus Christ was crucified and was forced to carry his cross (Mt 27:32). Fifty days later Peter preached to Jews from Cyrene on Pentecost day in Jerusalem (Acts 2:10). Stephen was attacked by Jews associated with a synagogue that included people of Cyrene (6:9), some of whom were later converted and became preachers (11:20). They appear to have traveled as far north as Antioch, where a prominent Christian teacher was Lucius of Cyrene (13:1).

CYRENIUS* KJV rendering of Quirinius, the governor of Syria when Christ was born, in Luke 2:2. *See* Quirinius.

CYRUS CYLINDER* Baked clay barrel nine inches (22.9 centimeters) long inscribed in cuneiform, found by archaeologist Hormuzd Rassam during his excavations at Babylon (1879–82). Now in the British Museum, London, the inscription was written by Cyrus the Great (who founded the Persian Empire and ruled it 539–530 BC) as an effort to describe and justify his policies. The largely intact text is about 1,000 words in translation and dates from about 536 BC.

Cyrus began his text with an attack on Nabonidus (last ruler of the Neo-Babylonian Empire, father of and co-regent with Belshazzar). He described Nabonidus as a "weakling" who had removed the images of the gods from their temples and had forsaken the proper worship of Marduk, chief of the Babylonian family of gods. To make matters worse, Nabonidus had also required his subjects to labor on a variety of public works projects.

Historians now believe that Nabonidus had turned from the worship of Marduk to that of Sin, the moon god with great centers of worship at Ur and Haran. Before the fall of Babylon, Nabonidus had tried to transport many of the gods of the Babylonian cities to the capital. Such tampering with the empire's religion had won Nabonidus the undying hostility of powerful entrenched religious interests and of much of the general populace.

Cyrus continued the cylinder inscription with an observation that Marduk had heard the complaints of the gods and sought for a righteous ruler. His search led him to Cyrus, a man of "good deeds" and "upright heart." The god subjected many lands to Cyrus and ordered him to march against Babylon, "going at his side like a real friend." The result was that Cyrus took the capital without a fight, and Marduk delivered Nabonidus into Cyrus's hands. According to Greek sources, Nabonidus's life was spared. Moreover, the entire populace of Babylonia rejoiced over Cyrus's kingship, delighted that they had been spared damage and disaster.

Next, Cyrus spoke of his lineage in order to show that he was from an established line of kingship in Anshan, a region east of the head of the Persian Gulf. Moreover, the Babylonian gods Bel and Nebo delighted in him. Perhaps Cyrus felt it necessary to make that statement because he had usurped the throne of the Median Empire (of which Anshan was a part) and had taken the Neo-Babylonian Empire by force.

Having spoken of his legitimate right to rule, Cyrus described his reception by the populace, his faithfulness in worshiping Marduk his benefactor, and his beneficent treatment of his subjects. His beneficence included strict control over his troops to prevent acts of terror against the newly conquered subjects, maintenance of peace in the cities of Babylonia, abolition of the hated public works detail, and development of public housing projects. Cyrus saw Marduk as pleased with his deeds and bestowing favor on Cyrus, his son Cambyses, and his troops. Moreover, princes from all over the empire came to Babylon to pay homage and bring tribute.

The next section of the inscription relates to the Jews and to a significant part of biblical history. Cyrus decided to reverse the deportation policy of the Babylonians and of the Assyrians before them. He permitted all the captive peoples who had been uprooted to return to their ancestral homes. He also returned the images of the gods to their former sanctuaries and helped the various groups to rebuild the temples of their gods. Thus it is clear that Ezra's decree permitting the Jews to return to Palestine (Ezr 1) was not a result of Cyrus's conversion to faith in the God of Israel, but only part of a larger public policy. Presumably each of the subjected peoples had its own decree of rehabilitation.

In the last paragraph of his text he asked all the resettled gods to intercede with Bel and Nebo for long life for him and to commend him to Marduk. Cyrus obviously thought that grateful priests and worshipers who were praying for him would be loyal subjects. Thus important sources of disaffection would be removed.

See also Cyrus the Great.

CYRUS THE GREAT* Persian king (559–530 BC) who founded the Achaemenid dynasty and the Persian Empire. Cyrus (II) was the son of Cambyses I (600–599 BC), who ruled the unified territories of Parshumashanshan and Parsa. Cyrus's mother was Mandane, daughter of the Median king Astyages (585?–550 BC). The ancestor of the dynasty was Achaemenes. Cyrus succeeded his father and established himself in Pasargadae about 559 BC. Ambitious and daring, he aligned his kingdom with neighboring peoples and tribes into a solid block of Persian power, then revolted against Astyages of Media. When it became evident that Cyrus would win in the struggle to control Media, the troops of Astyages

mutinied and deserted to Cyrus. When Cyrus conquered the Median kingdom, however, he came into conflict with Babylon, since the two kingdoms claimed much of the same territory.

Cyrus consolidated his power before fighting with Babylon. First, he conquered Asia Minor. Wealthy King Croesus of Lydia and the Lydians submitted to him. Then he overran the northern mountainous region between the Caspian Sea and the northwest corner of India.

By 539 BC, Cyrus was ready to move against Babylon. The Babylonian governor of Elam defected to Cyrus and joined his army. With a minimum of opposition, the armies of Cyrus entered the Babylonian capital in 539 BC. Nabonidus was taken prisoner but was treated with respect and mercy. Sixteen days later Cyrus himself entered the city, to the acclaim of many of its inhabitants. Isaiah's prophecy spoke of Cyrus as the Lord's anointed (Is 45:1). Israel regarded him as called and empowered by their God to free them. Under Cyrus, the Jews were allowed to rebuild Jerusalem and its temple (44:28). Documents preserved in the OT state that in his first year in Babylon, Cyrus issued a decree permitting the reconstruction of the house of God at Jerusalem (2 Chr 36:22-23; Ezr 1:1-3; 6:2-5). He also returned sacred vessels taken from the temple by Nebuchadnezzar. Biblical descriptions of the decree say nothing about rebuilding the city, but that would be in harmony with the king's policy.

During excavations (1879–82) at Babylon, archaeologist Hormuzd Rassam discovered a clay barrel inscription on which Cyrus told of taking the city and of his resulting policies. Isaiah and Chronicles reflect the content of the inscription, which says that captured peoples were allowed to return home and build sanctuaries to their own gods.

Nothing is known about the death of Cyrus. Accounts that have been preserved make it clear that he was killed in battle, but the statements are conflicting. Probably the Greek historian Herodotus is right in indicating that Cyrus died in a terrible disaster that destroyed the Persian army fighting the Massagetae. The tomb of Cyrus can still be seen at Pasargadae in Iran.

See also Cyrus Cylinder; Persia, Persians.

The Cyrus Cylinder

D

DABAREH* KJV spelling of the town Daberath in Joshua 21:28. *See* Daberath.

DABBESHETH Designation for a camel's hump (Is 30:6). The name also refers to a town ("camel's hump hill") situated on the western border of the land allotted to Zebulun's tribe for an inheritance (Jos 19:11).

DABERATH Town in Issachar's territory given to the Levite family of Gershon (Jos 21:28; 1 Chr 6:72). It was located west of Mt Tabor on the Issachar-Zebulun border, and has been identified with the modern Deburiyeh.
   See also Levitical Cities.

DAGGER Short sword. *See* Armor and Weapons.

DAGON Deity worshiped throughout the Mesopotamian world. In the OT, Dagon is the principal god of the Philistines (Jgs 16:23; 1 Sm 5:2-7; 1 Chr 10:10). Shrines to Dagon were found in Israel's territories (Beth-dagon, Jos 15:41; 19:27). *See* Canaanite Deities and Religion.

DALAIAH* KJV spelling of Delaiah, Elioenai's son, in 1 Chronicles 3:24. *See* Delaiah #1.

DALMANUTHA Area on the west side of the Sea of Galilee near the southern end of the plain of Gennesaret. Its exact location is uncertain. Jesus and his disciples stayed there briefly after the incident of the feeding of the 4,000 (Mk 8:10). The Pharisees came to him seeking a sign from heaven in order to test him. After his answer that no sign would be given to this generation (v 12), he departed from there.
   The word "Dalmanutha" is present in the best manuscripts, although other sources record Magadan or Magdala. The parallel passage in Matthew 15:39 cites Magadan. Because of this, the exact name and location have been difficult to pinpoint. Probably the various names are meant to designate the same site or at least two places in the same area.
   See also Magadan; Magdala.

DALMATIA Mountainous region on the eastern shore of the Adriatic Sea, across from Italy. The Dalmatians were an Illyrian (Greek) tribe, or group of tribes banded together, coming from the area around the town of Delmion (or Delminium). Their piracy gave the Romans considerable difficulty until Octavian thoroughly subjugated them in 33 BC.
   At the time of Paul, Dalmatia was the name of the Roman province; its southern boundary was Macedonia, and its northern boundary is not clearly known. There is one reference to the province in the NT: Titus is mentioned as going there in 2 Timothy 4:10. We are not told why he went. It may be that Paul had organized some churches there, or Titus may have been opening up a new mission field.

DALPHON Haman's son killed by the Jews in the aftermath of the plot against Mordecai (Est 9:7).

DAMARIS Woman mentioned (Acts 17:34) as one of the first converts in the city of Athens, following Paul's preaching there. Since Luke singles her out by name, she may have been a person of importance (see Acts 13:50; 17:12).

DAMASCUS Syrian oasis city protected on three sides by mountains and situated on trade routes about 160 miles (257 kilometers) northeast of Jerusalem. The name Damascus can also refer to the surrounding area and to the southern Syrian state. Though close to the desert, the district is rich in almonds, apricots, cotton, flax, grains, hemp, olives, pistachios, pomegranates, tobacco, vineyards, and walnuts. These crops grow well because the land is watered by two rivers: the Nahr Barada, "the Cool" (biblical Abana), which runs from the northwest mountains through a deep ravine to the city; and the Nahr el-A waj, "the Crooked" (biblical Pharpar), which flows west to east. Together the two rivers irrigate 400 square miles (643.6 square kilometers) of land. Their beauty and importance in biblical times is conveyed by the haughty words of Naaman, a resident of the area, who almost refused to wash his leprosy away in the Jordan, as Elisha had prescribed, because it was such a poor river in comparison with the Abana and Pharpar (2 Kgs 5).

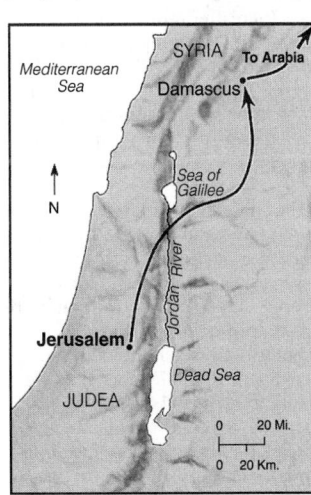

Damascus The apostle Paul had his famous conversion experience on his way to Damascus. Paul (then called Saul) traveled 150 miles (241.4 kilometers) from Jerusalem to Damascus in order to bring Christians back in chains. But as he neared the ancient city, he discovered that God had other plans for him (Acts 9:15).

Of the several trade routes that converged in the area, one led to Tyre and down the Mediterranean coastline, another to Megiddo and eventually to Memphis and Egypt, and a third to the Gulf of Aqaba.
   The first biblical mention of Damascus (Gn 14:15) refers to the city in connection with Abraham's successful attack upon the confederation of kings who kidnapped

Lot and his family. The Bible does not refer to the city again until the time of David (c. 1000 BC).

Israel occupied a strategic position along the trade routes between Mesopotamia and Egypt. Although in the time of Joshua and the judges Israel was in conflict with its immediate neighbors, the Amorites, Moabites, Philistines, Ammonites, and Midianites, there was relatively little opposition from Syria.

By the time of Saul, Zobah, an Aramean kingdom to the north of Damascus, was menacing the Israelites. Damascus was possibly in alliance with Zobah at this time, and the Israelites fought a defensive action (1 Sm 14:47). David subsequently defeated Hadadezer of Zobah and gained control over southern Syria and Damascus, where he garrisoned his troops. David's forces under Joab continued to be successful, and tribute was sent from Damascus to Israel. One of Hadadezer's officers, Rezon, deserted and formed a guerilla band in the Damascus area. Subsequently, in Solomon's reign he eroded even the Israelites' economic control of the region and set himself up as king in Damascus around 940 BC (1 Kgs 11:23-25).

In the reign of Ben-hadad I, about 883–843 BC, soldiers from Damascus besieged Samaria and sent reasonable terms to Ahab, which were accepted swiftly. Damascus was at the height of its power when Ben-hadad was campaigning successfully against the Assyrians. At this time, when Jehoram, Ahab's son, was king of Israel, Naaman the leper, a Syrian captain, was healed by the prophet Elisha when he accepted humbly the prescribed cure.

The strategy of overcoming the kingdom by killing the king had been successful for Ben-hadad in his fight with Ahab, and he continued to follow the same policy. Shortly afterward, in a further effort to subdue Samaria, he sent assassination squads to murder either Jehoram or the prophet Elisha. The Lord preserved the lives of the pursued, and the Syrian attacked without success. Several years later, Elisha, who had gained the respect of the Syrians, entered Damascus boldly and announced that Ben-hadad's illness was not fatal but that his death was imminent. Ben-hadad was thereafter murdered by Hazael, who then succeeded him. Although Damascus was soundly defeated by Assyria about 838 BC, Hazael rebounded quickly, and by 830 BC other predictions of Elisha were fulfilled. Damascene troops then controlled large areas of Palestinian territory, and the temple treasure was used to bribe the Syrians and save Jerusalem (2 Kgs 12:17-18).

Planning to continue the subjection of Israel, Ben-hadad II found himself having to contend instead with resumed attacks from Assyria. In 803 BC Damascus became a tributary of Assyria, but the northern forces were unable to hold the area. After a further campaign in which Assyria again proved dominant, a weakened Damascus was unable to quash an Israelite rebellion in 795 BC. By the time of Jeroboam II, the Damascenes were forced to pay tribute to Samaria (2 Kgs 14:28).

About 738 BC the Syrians, led by their new leader Rezin, joined forces with Pekah, king of Israel, to subjugate Judah. Much land was captured, although their siege of Jerusalem was unsuccessful (2 Kgs 16:5-6; 2 Chr 28:5). At this time of seeming success for Damascus, the city's doom was predicted by Isaiah (Is 8:4; 17:1), Amos (Am 1:3-5), and Jeremiah (Jer 49:23-27). Rejecting God, Ahaz of Judah turned for protection to an alliance with the Assyrians, whom he bribed with the temple treasure. The Assyrian king Tiglath-pileser III ("Pul") agreed and marched against the Syro-Israelite confederation. After defeating Israel, he attacked Damascus, plundered the city, deported the population, and replaced them with foreigners from other captured lands. Damascus was no longer an independent city-state.

Due to its key location, Damascus remained important, and the Assyrians used the city as a provincial capital. Their records mention it in 727, 720, and 694 BC, and also in the days of Ashurbanipal (669–663 BC). Assyrian world dominance succumbed to that of Neo-Babylon, which was later replaced by that of Medo-Persia. During the period of Persian control, Damascus was a noted administrative center. Under the regime of Alexander the Great, the importance of Damascus was diminished by the rise in commercial significance of Antioch.

During intertestamental times, Damascus passed from one ruler to another. Following the death of Alexander, the city was controlled by the Ptolemies of Egypt and the Seleucids of Babylon. Somewhat before 100 BC, Syria was divided, with Damascus becoming the capital of Coele-Syria. Its non-Syrian kings were constantly in trouble at home with the economy and abroad with the Parthians, Hasmoneans, and Nabateans, who under Aretas controlled Damascus from 84 to 72 BC. Subsequently, authority passed to the Hasmoneans, descendants of the Maccabees, and then the Idumeans (the Herods). The area was subjected to Roman dominance after the defeat of Syria by the Romans in 65 BC.

Shortly after the death of Christ, the Nabateans regained control of the area, ruling Damascus from Petra through an ethnarch. It was under the control of an Arab appointee, probably Aretas IV, when Saul of Tarsus sought Jewish authority to purge Damascus of its Christians (2 Cor 11:32). Luke's report in Acts 9, corroborated by Paul's own confession (Acts 22:5-21; 26:11-23), relates Saul's vision, blinding, and subsequent conversion on the road to Damascus. This may have been close to the place where Syrian soldiers were blinded when planning to assassinate Elisha (2 Kgs 6:18-23). After Saul's sight was restored in a house on the street called "Straight," he preached Christianity. Apparently the uproar in the Jewish quarter concerning his preaching was so great that the ethnarch was willing to condone Saul's murder by orthodox Jews. Acts 9:23-25 describes his escape to Jerusalem. Damascus is not mentioned thereafter in biblical history.

See also Syria, Syrians.

DAMNATION *See* Hell; Judgment.

DAN (Person)
Fifth son of the Jewish patriarch Jacob. Dan's mother was Bilhah, maid of Jacob's wife Rachel (Gn 30:1-6). Dan's descendants settled in Israel overlooking the Huleh Plain, in territory actually assigned to Naphtali, Dan's full brother (Gn 30:7-8; 35:25; Jos 19:32-48). The two brothers are mentioned together in a number of references (e.g., Ex 1:4).

Dan's name was given to him not by Bilhah but by Rachel, who considered the child her own. Rachel had long been childless—a shame to women in ancient cultures—and she was jealous of Jacob's other wife, Leah, who had already borne him four sons. Rachel viewed the birth of Bilhah's son as averting her shame and as God's vindication of her status as wife. The name Dan ("he judged") meant that God had judged her and had vindicated her through the child's birth (Gn 30:6).

Evidently Dan had only one son to continue his line, Hushim (Gn 46:23; "Shuham," Nm 26:42-43). In Jacob's patriarchal blessing, Dan was promised the role of "judge" among his people but was also spoken of as one who would be stealthy and dangerous, like a serpent (Gn 49:16-17). How that blessing worked out in the life of his descendants is unknown. The small amount of information given about Dan himself parallels the insignificance of his tribe in later times.

See also Dan (Place); Dan, Tribe of.

DAN (Place)

1. Phoenician city, originally named Leshem (Jos 19:47) or Laish (Jgs 18:7), which was conquered by Dan's tribe when it migrated northward. The city lay a day's journey from Sidon in the valley near Beth-rehob (v 28) at the southern base of Mt Hermon. It was the most northerly point of the ancient Israelite kingdom, and was used as a topographical marker in the phrase "from Dan to Beersheba" (cf. Jgs 20:1; 2 Sm 3:10).

The site of Dan guarded a major trading route running between Damascus and Tyre, and was therefore an important commercial center. The Nahr el-Leddan, one of the principal sources of the Jordan, rose in the area, and this made the Huleh Valley below Dan lush and fertile even in the heat of summer. Consequently, the territory around the city produced grain and vegetable crops in abundance, as well as supplying the needs of flocks and herds adequately.

In the early Iron Age, Dan was a prosperous city, as indicated in Judges 18:7, but by the middle of the 11th century BC, it had been destroyed, evidently as a result of occupation by the Danites. When Jeroboam I became king of the separate northern kingdom of Israel, Dan was one of two shrines where the golden calves were worshiped. The high place at Tell el-Qadi (Tell of Dan), a square masonry platform some 61 by 20 feet (18.6 by 6.1 meters), has been excavated, but no trace of the golden image has been found.

Aerial View of the Tell of Dan

The cultic worship of Baal at Dan survived even Jehu's drastic purge (2 Kgs 10:28-31), but during Ben-hadad's reign, the city fell under Syrian control (cf. v 32). When the Syrians were attempting to ward off Assyrian attacks on their eastern border during the time of Jeroboam II (793–753 BC), Dan was reconquered by the northern kingdom. It did not remain in Israelite hands for long, however, for its inhabitants were deported to Assyria (2 Kgs 17:6) by Tiglath-pileser III (745–727 BC). Nevertheless, the site continued to be inhabited (cf. Jer 4:15; 8:16), and its high place, or acropolis, at the northern extremity of the mound was used for worship. This particular area was enlarged periodically in both Greek and Roman times, and it is from the latter period that a statue of Aphrodite came. In NT times Dan was eclipsed by

Caesarea, which was only a few miles distant. Josephus (*War* 4.1) recorded that Titus crushed a revolt at Dan in AD 67.

See also Dan (Person); Dan, Tribe of.

2. KJV rendering of an obscure Hebrew word (Vedan) in Ezekiel 27:19, alternately translated "wine," a commodity from Uzal, in the RSV.

See also Uzal (Place).

DAN, Tribe of

Israelite tribe named for the patriarch Jacob's fifth son. The tribe of Dan, descended from Dan's only known son, Hushim (cf. "Shuham" in Nm 26:42-43), had little distinction in its early years. Some Danites are mentioned in the wilderness narratives: Oholiab, a craftsman of the tabernacle (Ex 31:6; 35:34; 38:23); another whose mother married an Egyptian and who blasphemed God (Lv 24:11); and Ahiezer, chief prince of Dan during the exodus (Nm 1:12).

Dan was the second largest tribe at the first census taken in the wilderness (62,700 warriors—Nm 1:38-39). They were instructed to encamp on the north side of the Israelites' camp along with Asher and Naphtali (Nm 2:25-31), and were to bring up the rear in the line of march (Nm 2:31; 10:25). At the second census 40 years later, just before entering the Promised Land, they had grown only to 64,400 (26:42-43), still second in size. The tribe does not stand out in the Conquest narratives (Dt 2:16–3:29; Jos 1–24; Jgs 1). Dan is listed among the tribes who reminded Israel of the covenant curses at Mt Ebal (Dt 27:13; cf. Jos 8:30-33). The tribe is called a "lion's whelp" in Moses' blessing (Dt 33:22). Some believe that the reference to "Bashan" in that blessing prefigured the Danites' migration to the northern territory where they eventually settled.

One of the most significant references to Dan's tribe is the account of its northward migration (Jos 19:40-48; Jgs 18). The Danites had been allotted a portion of Canaan between Judah and Ephraim bordering the Mediterranean seacoast (Jos 19:40-46; Jgs 5:17), but were unable to occupy their territory except for the valley at Zorah and Eshtaol (Jgs 13:25; 18:2). As a result, a group of Danites, discouraged with their situation, marched north and captured Laish, located about 25 miles (40 kilometers) north of the Sea of Galilee and just below Israel's northernmost border. Laish was renamed Dan at that time (18:27-29). Their association with that northern territory eventually gave rise to the expression "from Dan to Beersheba" (Jgs 20:1; 2 Sm 3:10) as designating Israel's northern and southern borders.

Southern Dan continued for some time, as illustrated in the exploits of Samson of the tribe of Dan (Jgs 13–16). Evidently the southern Danites gradually merged into the tribe of Judah, and no historical reference to the southern Danite tribe is made in the rest of the OT. The Danites were mentioned in King David's time as mustering a considerable army loyal to David (1 Chr 12:35; 27:22).

The Danites were among the tribes who did not drive the Canaanites from their territory (Jos 13:4-5; cf. Jgs 1:34-35). Joshua had to prod them into the task at the Shiloh assembly (Jos 18:1-4; 19:40-48). Eventually the Danites gave up the effort and sought other lands in the north, where conquest was easier. Their disobedience was further manifested in their open sin of setting up a "graven image" and establishing a rival priesthood, even though their priest was a Levite (Jgs 18:30-31). The result of that idolatry was that, at the division of the Israelite kingdom at the end of King Solomon's reign, King Jeroboam of the northern kingdom of Israel chose the city of Dan as one of the idol shrines in which to set up the golden calves (1 Kgs 12:28-29). The Danites' apostasy, and that of the other northern tribes, continued throughout their history (2 Kgs 10:29), and because of it they were eventually carried captive to Assyria (2 Kgs 17:1-23).

The tribe name is mentioned in the prophet Ezekiel's idealized description of the restored land and Jerusalem (Ez 48:1-2, 32). In the NT, the apostle John omitted the tribe from a list of Israel's tribes (Rv 7:4-8).

See also Israel, History of; Dan (Person); Dan (Place).

DANCE

DANCE Form of artistic expression incorporated into Israel's worship, used especially during times of celebration. *See* Music.

DANIEL (Person)

1. David's second son, the first by his wife Abigail (1 Chr 3:1); also called Kileab (2 Sm 3:3).

   See also Kileab.
2. Priest, descendant of Ithamar. He signed Ezra's covenant of faithfulness to God with Nehemiah and others after the exile (Ezr 8:2; Neh 10:6).
3. Jewish statesman and seer in the Babylonian court whose career is recounted in the book of Daniel. Daniel's early life is cloaked in silence. Nothing is known of his parents or family, though he was probably descended from Jewish nobility (Dn 1:3). If born during the time of King Josiah's reforms (c. 621 BC), Daniel would have been about 16 when he and his three friends—Hananiah, Mishael, and Azariah—were deported from Jerusalem to Babylon by King Nebuchadnezzar. They may have been hostages to assure the cooperation of the royal family in Judah.

   Daniel, renamed Belteshazzar (meaning "may Bel [god] protect his life"), was trained for court service. He quickly established a reputation for intelligence and for absolute fidelity to his God. After three years of instruction, he began a court career that lasted nearly 70 years (Dn 1:21). Daniel had hardly finished his training when he was called on to interpret one of Nebuchadnezzar's dreams, in which a great image collapsed and disintegrated when struck by a stone. God revealed its meaning to Daniel, who explained it to the king. In gratitude Nebuchadnezzar offered him the post of governor of Babylonia, but Daniel requested that the honor be conferred on his three companions in captivity.

   Near the end of Nebuchadnezzar's life, Daniel was able to interpret a second dream (Dn 4). That dream intimated the king's impending insanity. Daniel urged the king to repent (4:27), but he did not, and subsequently for a period of time he became deranged.

   After the death of Nebuchadnezzar in 562 BC, Daniel dropped from public view and evidently occupied an inferior position in the royal court. Although he received visions (Dn 7-8) in the first and third years of the Babylonian regent Belshazzar's reign (555 and 553 BC), it was not until 539 BC that Daniel made another public appearance. During a banquet hosted by Belshazzar, the king profaned the sacred vessels pillaged from the Jerusalem temple. A disembodied hand suddenly appeared and wrote on the palace wall the mysterious words, "Mene, Mene, Tekel, Parsin." Summoned to explain the message, Daniel interpreted it as a forecast of the imminent end of the Babylonian kingdom. That same night Belshazzar was killed by the Persians, who attacked and successfully overtook the capital city (5:30).

   Under Darius the Mede, Daniel became one of three "presidents" (administrators) of the realm (6:2).

Daniel's rank, along with his capable and distinguished management, infuriated his political enemies. They persuaded Darius to pass a decree forbidding petition to any god or man but the king, under penalty of being cast into a lions' den. Daniel's religious integrity forced him to violate the law. Thrown to the lions, he remained miraculously unscathed. Vindicated, he was restored to office (vv 17-28).

The latter part of the book of Daniel describes several visions he received of future events. The visions dealt with four beasts (ch 7), future kingdoms (ch 8), the coming of the Messiah (ch 9), and Syria and Egypt (chs 11–12). The prophet Ezekiel alluded to Daniel's great wisdom (Ez 28:3) and ranked him in righteousness with Noah and Job (14:14, 20).

See also Daniel, Book of; Diaspora of the Jews; Prophet, Prophetess.

DANIEL, Additions to Part of the Deuterocanonical works, consists of three supplementary sections to the book of Daniel. This additional material is in the Greek translation of the OT book of Daniel, but not in the ancient Hebrew-Aramaic texts. One such addition is the Prayer of Azariah and the Song of the Three Young Men inserted between Daniel 3:23 and 3:24. These 68 verses describe the actions and words of Hananiah, Azariah, and Mishael in the fiery furnace. The second addition was the colorful story of Susanna, a maiden whom Daniel saved from execution, brought about by a false accusation of adultery. Susanna's location in the text varies. The Septuagint and the Latin Vulgate place it after Daniel 12. Other ancient versions, such as the Old Latin, Coptic, and Arabic versions place it before chapter 1 because of Daniel's apparent youth. The third addition, Bel and the Dragon, tells how Daniel duped pagan priests and killed a dragon "without sword or club." The Roman Catholic Church accepts this material as canonical.

PREVIEW
• Prayer of Azariah and the Song of the Three Young Men
• Susanna and the Elders
• Bel and the Dragon

Prayer of Azariah and the Song of the Three Young Men Prayer for deliverance and hymn of praise attributed to three young Jews thrown into King Nebuchadnezzar's fiery furnace. Along with Daniel, the three youths had been taken into the court of the Babylonian king during the exile of the kingdom of Judah (Dn 1:1-6). Azariah was given the Babylonian name Abednego (v 7). He and his two friends were condemned to death for refusing to worship the king's gold statue (3:1-23) but were so miraculously preserved from burning that "they didn't even smell of smoke" (vv 24-27). Acknowledging that the God whom they worshiped had saved them, the king commanded that none of his subjects should ever dishonor the God of the Jews (vv 28-30).

The Prayer and Song are among several "Additions to Daniel" found in early Greek and Latin versions but not in the original Hebrew and Aramaic texts. The additions seem to date from the intertestamental period of Jewish history, but the language of their composition is not certain. These two works, possibly composed in Hebrew, appear first in Greek in the Septuagint translation of the OT made in the second or third century BC. They were inserted in a logical place in the biblical narrative, following Daniel 3:23. Thus, the Septuagint version of Daniel contained 68 additional verses between 3:23 and 3:24, the first 22 being the Prayer of Azariah.

In the fourth century AD, when Jerome translated the Bible into Latin, he realized that the Prayer, the Song, and several stories added onto the end of the book of Daniel (Susanna and the Elders; Bel and the Dragon) were not in the original texts, but he left them in place. Altogether, Jerome's Vulgate Bible included 14 or 15 books or portions of books not recognized by Jewish scholars as part of their Scriptures. These writings are now known as the OT Apocrypha, and are usually omitted from Protestant Bibles. When Martin Luther translated the Bible into German in AD 1534, he collected them in a separate section at the end of the OT with a note that the Apocrypha (plural form of a Greek word meaning "hidden") were "useful and good to read" even if not "equal to the sacred Scriptures."

Azariah's prayer is certainly "useful and good" as a model prayer, being very similar to Daniel's prayer (Dn 9:3-19) and to several of the biblical psalms (compare Pss 31 and 51). It contains confession and repentance as well as a plea for deliverance. Azariah admits that God's people deserve his righteous judgment "because of our sins," but he pleads with God to remember his promise to bless the descendants of Abraham, Isaac, and Jacob. He offers as sacrifice "a contrite heart and a humble spirit," dedicating himself and his companions to God.

After Azariah's prayer comes an account of how "the angel of the Lord" came down and "made the midst of the furnace like a moist whistling wind," causing the three rescued youths to praise God "as with one mouth." Their song, like Psalm 148, calls upon all of creation to "bless the Lord."

Susanna and the Elders In the Greek Septuagint and the Latin Vulgate, it follows the canonical conclusion of Daniel. It was probably written by a Jew who lived in Palestine in the middle of the first century before Christ. The setting of the story, however, is in Babylon.

Susanna, daughter of Hilkiah, was a very beautiful woman married to Joakim, a rich man of distinction. Joakim's distinction increased in the community when he opened up his beautiful garden to the Jewish community in exile. It was a proper meeting place for the elders and judges. Trouble arose when two elders recently elected as judges were filled with lust for Susanna. Their office as judge brought them back to Joakim's garden whenever the court was in session. At opportune times the two judges, who knew nothing of each other's desires, feasted their eyes on her beauty. One day they found themselves in a situation wherein they were forced to admit their passions to each other. The impropriety of their thoughts resulted in a plot to seduce Susanna quietly.

Susanna, who was used to bathing herself in the garden pool to cool herself off in the heat of the day, came to the pool with her two maids for the purpose of bathing. The three ladies were unaware of the presence of the two judges, who had hidden themselves. When the two maids left to bring Susanna soap and olive oil, the judges took the occasion to present themselves to Susanna. They admitted to her their sexual desire for her and requested her permission to have relations with her. Their legal minds had devised a trap so that, if Susanna were to refuse them, a case would be presented in court according to which they would claim to have witnessed Susanna's adulterous relation with a young man. Susanna, believing that adultery was a grievous sin against the Lord punishable by death, refused the judges, shouted for help, and hoped to be sustained by the

members of her household. During the resulting tumult, the judges falsely accused Susanna to her servants.

The piety of Susanna was tested in a court that favored the case of the judges. Since they were men of social standing in the community and they were united in their witness against Susanna, she had no chance for a fair trial. The court judged her guilty of adultery and condemned her to death. Her execution was delayed by the counsel of a young man named Daniel. He requested that the trial be reopened on the ground that the witnesses had not been cross-examined. In a separate cross-examination, it was discovered that their testimony did not corroborate. The one had seen Susanna with her young man under a clove tree and the other had seen them together under an oak tree. At the contradiction of the testimony, the assembly admitted the false evidence of the judges and the innocence of Susanna. Instead of Susanna, the two judges were put to death on the ground of having given false witness.

The purpose of the story is threefold. It celebrates the piety and virtue of Susanna and the corruption of the judges, who "no longer prayed to God, but let their thoughts stray from him and forgot" the claims of morality. Second, it challenges the traditional legal method by which two witnesses could falsely accuse a man and their testimony was accepted as true. Naboth, Jesus, and others had been accused by false witnesses and found guilty without any cross-examination. Third, the story introduces the reader to Daniel, who is here pictured as a young, wise man whose wisdom challenges that of the elders.

Bel and the Dragon The book has always been regarded as apocryphal by the Protestant churches but was confirmed as canonical by the Roman Catholic Church at the Council of Trent (1545-63).

The book contains two tales of Daniel, that is, the story of Bel and the story of the Dragon. The setting is in Babylon during the reign of Cyrus. Daniel was highly honored and was living as companion to the king but continued to worship God and to pray. Among the gods worshiped by Cyrus and the Babylonians, one of the greatest was Bel, or Marduk (OT Merodach).

One day the king ordered Daniel to worship Bel because he was a powerful god, a fact supposedly proven by his voracious appetite. The king explained that Bel consumed 12 bushels (432 liters) of flour, 40 sheep, and 50 gallons (189 liters) of wine left for him daily in the temple. To the local people, Bel was obviously a mighty god. Daniel pointed out to the king that an idol made of clay and bronze could not possibly be consuming the food, and Daniel offered to prove it. In anger the king sent for the priests and demanded to know what happened to the food. They assured him that it was indeed eaten by the god.

The next day the food was taken to the temple and placed on the table as usual. Unknown to the priests, Daniel had his servants sprinkle the floor with fine ashes. The temple was then sealed with the signet rings of the king and several of the priests. The next morning the seal was found intact and the group entered the temple. Seeing the table empty, the king rejoiced in the power of Bel. Daniel, however, pointed to many footprints clearly visible in the ashes, revealing to the king the trickery of the priests. They confessed that they had been entering by a secret door and removing the food. Cyrus ordered the 70 priests and their families killed and permitted Daniel to destroy the pagan temple.

The second tale recounts events surrounding the worship of a dragon (possibly a serpent). The Babylonians venerated a dragon that, as the king pointed out to Daniel, was very much alive. Here there was no possibility of trickery, since all had seen the dragon eat and drink. But Daniel again refused the king's request to worship an idol. Further, Daniel asked permission to kill the dragon without using either sword or staff, a seemingly impossible task. Receiving the king's permission to try, Daniel made a concoction of pitch, fat, and hair; boiled it together; formed it into cakes; and fed it to the dragon. After eating the cakes, the dragon burst apart and died immediately. At the death of their dragon-god the king had to face the anger of the Babylonians, who were convinced that he had been converted to Judaism. To turn away their wrath, the king reluctantly delivered Daniel to them to be put to death.

Two persons, usually condemned criminals, were thrown into a den of seven lions every day. This time the lions were not fed, but Daniel was thrown in alive. After six days, however, Daniel was still alive, although both he and the lions were extremely hungry. In a section of the text probably added later, the Lord sent an angel to the prophet Habakkuk, ordering him to take to Daniel a meal he had prepared for his reapers. Habakkuk began to make excuses that he had never been to Babylon and didn't know where the lions' den was. The angel then took him by the hair and deposited him in the lions' den, where Habakkuk told Daniel that the Lord had remembered him. After giving Daniel the food, Habakkuk was returned safely to his own home.

The next day the king arrived on the scene to bewail the death of Daniel, only to find to his amazement that his friend was still alive. Daniel was released from the den and his accusers were thrown in and devoured immediately by the ravenous lions.

Bel and the Dragon exists in two principal Greek and two Syriac texts, almost certainly derived from a lost Hebrew original. The author, place, and date of the original are unknown. It is possible that the story of Bel could have been written as early as the fourth century BC, with the dragon story composed later, possibly by a different author. The most satisfactory date, judging by the content and purpose of the work, would be 150–100 BC, a time of great religious and political difficulty for the Jews.

Bel and the Dragon was written to convey the futility of idol worship and to impress on the Jews the need to continue firm in their faith in times of persecution and hardship. Babylonian gods were ridiculed in both tales. The book may also have been a warning not to trust the friendship of the heathen, who in time of trouble might find it expedient to sacrifice the life of a friend. Despite the fact that Daniel was described as the king's companion, under pressure the king was prepared to hand Daniel over to a mob.

In the contest with Bel (Marduk), Daniel confronted a god who had been the patron of Babylon since 2275 BC. Frequent references to him were made in cuneiform inscriptions. For example, Nebuchadnezzar II had commanded the temple of Bel to be restored to a position of supremacy as one of the finest and most majestic ziggurats (pyramidal towers). The apocryphal writer would have been aware of the destruction of that famous landmark by the Persian king Xerxes I (ruled 486–464 BC), who carried off the seated golden image from the shrine. The temple was described as being in ruins at the time Alexander the Great entered Babylon in 332 BC. The dragon in the second tale had long been venerated in Near Eastern religion and was well known in legends of ancient Sumeria.

DANIEL, Book of Fourth book of the Major Prophets in the OT, characterized by vivid symbolism and reflecting heroic historical events during the Babylonian exile of the Jewish people. Because Daniel is not an easy book to understand, its interpretation requires careful study and reflection. Daniel himself wrote, when reflecting on the meaning of one of his visions, "I was greatly troubled by the vision and could not understand it" (Dn 8:27, NLT).

In the old Jewish division of the OT, Daniel is part of the third section, called the Writings, along with such books as Psalms, Proverbs, and Job. It was not included in the second section of the OT, called the Prophets. Although portions of his book may be interpreted from a prophetic perspective, Daniel is never explicitly identified as a prophet. The book's two major divisions are narratives about Daniel's life (1–6) and Daniel's visions (7–12).

PREVIEW
•Author
•Date
•Language
•Background
•Purpose and Theological Teaching
•Content: Stories about Daniel (1–6)
•Content: Daniel's Visions (7–12)

Author In terms of having a known author, the book of Daniel is anonymous, as are many books coming from the ancient world. The existing text bears only a title, "Daniel," identifying the key subject matter of the book: the man himself.

The first six chapters of the book contain information about Daniel written in the third person; beginning in Daniel 7:2, however, the book purports to contain words written by Daniel in the first person. Although the traditional view within Judaism, later adopted by Christianity, was that Daniel wrote the entire book named for him, there is little confirming evidence. Jesus' words about things "spoken of by the prophet Daniel" (Mt 24:15) do not clarify who wrote the whole book, since the words in question appear in the second half of the book of Daniel, explicitly identified as his words. Thus the problem of who wrote the first part remains.

Whether or not Daniel wrote the entire book, he is definitely the key character. The only source of information about him is the book itself. Daniel was a Hebrew from Judah, probably of royal lineage, born late in the seventh century BC. As a young boy, he was taken from his homeland to Babylon (in what is now southern Iraq) around 605 BC. There, after three years of formal education in language and literature (Dn 1:4-5), he became an official in the royal household. The first six chapters tell of particular incidents in Daniel's life but do not provide a comprehensive biography of his life and times.

Daniel's name means "God is my judge." As a foreign resident in Babylon, he was given another name, Belteshazzar, which may have meant "may Bel (god) protect his life" in the Babylonian language.

Date Uncertainty about the authorship of the book of Daniel naturally contributes to uncertainty about the date of its writing. If Daniel was the author of the whole book, a date in the second half of the sixth century BC is likely. If he was not the author, a later date is possible. The conservative interpretation has usually been that the book was written in the sixth century BC. An alternative position is that the book was written about 165 BC.

Evidence exists to support both the early and late dates of Daniel. Those who argue for a late date and an author

Greek Text of Daniel Daniel 6:14 in Chester Beatty Manuscript X (third century) besides Daniel normally use two lines of argument, one historical and the other linguistic. But those espousing an earlier date have counterarguments, all of which are discussed below.

Historical Argument According to the historical argument, the writer was thoroughly familiar with the history of Near Eastern imperial power from the sixth to the second centuries, but had an incomplete, erroneous view of the historical details in the second half of the sixth century, Daniel's era. Such an imbalance in knowledge implies a late date of writing.

The first part of the historical argument must be conceded by those holding a more conservative view. The book of Daniel does present a remarkable knowledge of Near Eastern history. The critical question is whether that knowledge was normal human knowledge, gained after the events, or special knowledge revealed to Daniel beforehand. That question is answered in different ways by different people, depending on their view of prophecy and other factors.

The second part of the historical argument is technically more complex. Was the writer's knowledge of history in the late sixth century BC really erroneous? The most significant problem is that of the identity of Darius the Mede (Dn 5:30-31). The book of Daniel says that Darius the Mede conquered Babylon and was succeeded at a later date by Cyrus. External historical sources contain no reference to a Darius at the time, but show clearly that it was Cyrus who conquered Babylon. Advocates of a late date consider that strong evidence. Those who advocate an early date have no simple solution to the problem. One proposed solution is that Darius and Cyrus are two names for the same person. A basis for that hypothesis is that Daniel 6:28 can be translated: "Daniel prospered in the reign of Darius, even [that is] the reign of Cyrus the Persian." An analogy appears in the use of the names Pul and Tiglath-pileser in 1 Chronicles 5:26. In summary, the dating of Daniel on the basis of the writer's historical knowledge is difficult, whether one suggests an early or late date.

Linguistic Argument The linguistic arguments for the date of Daniel are also complex, especially for a person not familiar with the original languages of the book (Hebrew and Aramaic). Advocates of a late date use three related arguments: (1) the Aramaic language of the book is typical of late Aramaic (second century BC and later); (2) the presence of Persian loan words is a further indication of the late date of the book's Aramaic; and (3) the presence of Greek loan words in the Aramaic shows that the language must be dated after the time of Alexander the Great's conquest of the Orient (c. 330 BC). For the advocates of a late date for the book's composition, the last argument is most compelling. It would be impossible, they affirm, to find Greek loan words in Aramaic two centuries before Alexander's time.

Although the arguments are at first convincing, on closer examination they are less persuasive to those who hold the conservative view. Each of the three parts of the argument has been answered.

1. Aramaic was in common use in the Near East from about the ninth century BC, being recognized as an official language in Assyria from the eighth century BC. Ninety percent of the Aramaic words in Daniel were used in that older language, in both the Old and Imperial Aramaic dialects. The remaining 10 percent, known only in later texts in the light of present evidence, might indicate a late date, but they could equally be early uses of the words in question.

2. The evidence of Persian loan words in Aramaic can function like a boomerang. It is true that later Aramaic has many Persian loan words (about 19 appear in Daniel), but one can give an alternative explanation for Persian loan words in Daniel at an early date. The story of Daniel is set, in part, in the context of life in a Persian-controlled court. The Persians used Aramaic in their administrative control of the empire, and their own language inevitably penetrated Aramaic. If one assumes an early date for the book of Daniel, then it was being written in precisely the period when Persian would be having its greatest influence on Aramaic.

3. The evidence of Greek words in Daniel's Aramaic (a total of three) is not altogether compelling. Greek (or "Ionian") traders traveled in various parts of the Near East from the eighth century BC onward. Greek mercenaries fought for Near Eastern states in and after the seventh century BC. In Daniel's lifetime King Nebuchadnezzar is known to have employed Greek artisans in the city of Babylon. Thus, it is unnecessary to limit the possibilities of Greek penetration of the Aramaic language to the period after Alexander. The conqueror was by no means the first Greek to set foot in the Orient.

Conclusion The historical and linguistic arguments for the date of Daniel are inconclusive for either an early or late date of writing. To a large extent, dating the book depends on other matters, such as authorship, intention, and the extent to which one takes a "prophetic" interpretation of portions of the book. To postulate that Daniel was the author is consistent with the evidence currently available. Further, evidence provided by some of the Daniel material from the Dead Sea Scrolls at Qumran does not support a late date for the book. All Daniel manuscripts and fragments are second-century BC copies, thus requiring an earlier date for the original. One manuscript, related paleographically to the large Isaiah Scroll, must have come originally from the same period—estimated to be several centuries before the Qumran copy of Isaiah. Other manuscripts from Qumran show that no OT canonical material was composed later than the Persian period. Thus, no manuscript evidence exists for a second-century BC date for Daniel.

Language One of the most interesting features of the book of Daniel is not immediately evident to a reader of the English Bible. The book is bilingual. Daniel 1:1–2:4a and Daniel 8–12 are written in Hebrew, the language of the other OT books. The middle section (Dn 2:4b–7:28), however, is written in Aramaic, a different but related language. Various explanations have been offered for this phenomenon. Some have suggested that an original Aramaic book was expanded by a Hebrew writer, with additions to the original book at the beginning and the end. Others suggest that a portion of the original Hebrew book was lost, so the missing section was replaced from a surviving Aramaic translation. More complex and ingenious suggestions have also been made, but none has been commonly accepted.

Another suggestion is possible. The book of Daniel (whatever date one prefers) may simply reflect the bilingual character of its cultural setting. (As a modern example, consider the many written materials in Canada that appear in both English and French.) Finally, one can regard the bilingual character as another of the mysterious aspects of the book that make its interpretation difficult.

Background The background of the book of Daniel can be examined from two perspectives. It may be viewed from the perspective of the Babylonian exile, of which Daniel was a part (early sixth century BC), or in the light of future historical events (second century BC), toward which the visions in the book's second half seem to point.

The Babylonian Exile Although Daniel himself was exiled about 605 BC, the major phase of the Babylonian exile began in 586 BC, following the defeat of the kingdom of Judah and the destruction of Jerusalem. The account extends through the reigns of Nebuchadnezzar (properly Nebuchadrezzar) and Belshazzar, culminating in the early years of the Persian king Cyrus, who took over the city of Babylon in 539 BC. For the Jews the exile was a time of hardship but also a time of renewed theological understanding. Both aspects are reflected in the book of Daniel.

The Seleucid Period in Palestine Daniel's visions in the latter half of the book appear to refer to the Seleucid period in Palestine, specifically the time when the Jews were ruled by Antiochus Epiphanes, a member of the Seleucid dynasty (175–163 BC). Whether the visions were prophetic anticipations of future events or reflections of contemporary culture, the Seleucid period is important to a full understanding of the book.

Under Antiochus, Palestinian Jews experienced a time of considerable hardship. The ancient faith was severely undermined, the high priesthood in Jerusalem was sold to the highest bidder, and the temple was desecrated in several ways. Pressure was exerted on the Jews to adapt their lives and faith to Hellenistic (Greek-influenced) culture. Although some capitulated, others refused and steadfastly held firm to the old faith. A rebellion against the oppressive measures of Antiochus began in 168 BC. By 164 the rebels had largely succeeded in getting rid of the objectionable practices. But the Seleucid period was generally a bad time for faithful Jews, when all the forces of history seemed to work against the true faith. Part of the book of Daniel's greatness lies in its theological understanding of history, which enabled men and women to continue living in faith through a time of terrible crisis.

Purpose and Theological Teaching The scriptural section of the OT called the Writings served a variety of purposes. The psalms, for example, were used primarily in Israel's worship. The proverbs may have been part of Israel's school curriculum. The book of Job addressed a specific human and theological problem.

The purpose of the book of Daniel is not so easy to determine, since it is essentially a story, a partial biography of Daniel. It is not strictly a prophetic book, nor is it history in the modern sense. Much of it is concerned with dreams and their interpretations.

Nevertheless, the word "history" provides a clue to its purpose. Daniel seeks to provide theological understanding of history. The first six chapters tell about Daniel and his companions, not merely to satisfy historical curiosity but to teach the reader. OT theology insisted that the God of Israel participated in human life and history. To read biblical history, therefore, is to discover God's participation in human affairs and to learn how God and human beings relate to each other. In the opening chapters of Daniel one reads of events in the life of a man of remarkable faith, the kind of history from which one may learn how to live.

The last six chapters focus on Daniel's dreams. Although neither the dreams nor the interpretations are easy to understand, it is possible to see the theme of history emerging again. The emphasis in chapters 7–12 is not

on history as a record of past events but on the meaning of history and the world's future. In the biblical perspective, the movements of human societies in the present and future matter as much as past history. Though Daniel's visions are dominated by nations and superpowers, they have a more basic theme: God's power over human beings and nations. History often appears to be a conglomeration of chaos and human conflict. Yet God ultimately controls history and moves it toward a goal. In spite of ambiguous details at the end of the book, Daniel provides hope for people living in a time of crisis. Even if what is said about the "time of the end" cannot be understood now (Dn 12:9), the end of history is full of hope for those with faith in God (v 13). The purpose of the book of Daniel thus has to do with the meaning of history, both what can be learned from the past and what can be hoped for in the present and future.

The book also contains specific theological statements on such matters as human faith, divine salvation, and the nature of revelation. One theological matter in Daniel deserves particular attention: the doctrine of resurrection.

The NT's clear doctrine of resurrection followed by judgment is not a central theme in the OT. For the most part, the Hebrews' faith was fixed on the realities of earthly life. Hope for life beyond the grave is hinted at in many texts but remains implicit. Only in the later writings of the OT, especially those of Ezekiel and Daniel, does a more explicit doctrine of resurrection develop.

THE KINGDOM WILL COME
Earthly kingdoms dominate Daniel's visions, but Jesus established the kingdom of God. That kingdom, however, has only partially come; it will reach its fullness in Christ's second advent. The message of Daniel speaks within that tension of a kingdom already come and yet still to come in its fullness. The modern world reveals not the universal kingdom of God but the clamorous kingdoms of humanity. They are powerful and often appear to hold the world's future firmly in their hands. Daniel's message is that they do not: God is sovereign, and his kingdom will finally come in its full power.

To say more than that with respect to Daniel's visions is a delicate business. Trying to identify the nations of Daniel's dreams with modern nations misses the intention of the book. If Daniel, even with the help of angelic interpreters, found it difficult to understand his own visions, caution is appropriate for the modern reader. Yet Daniel ended his mysterious book with a note of hope: "As for you, go your way until the end. You will rest, and then at the end of the days, you will rise again to receive the inheritance set aside for you" (12:13, NLT).

The focal point of that doctrine in the book of Daniel is 12:2: "Many of those whose bodies lie dead and buried will rise up, some to everlasting life and some to shame and everlasting contempt" (NLT). The doctrine of personal resurrection provides a basis for individual hope within an understanding of present and future history. Nations move against nations in apparent turmoil. God is believed to be in ultimate control, but what becomes of all the people who die while history is still in motion? The dead shall rise again, says Daniel, and in their resurrection bodies shall be judged according to their deeds. Some will be rewarded with everlasting life, but others will be condemned to shame.

To the readers of the book of Daniel, the doctrine of resurrection provided hope in an otherwise bleak and hopeless world. It was a reminder that the actions of earthly life are important—they form the basis of future judgment. The world has a larger horizon of life beyond the body's death. Ultimately, there will be justice, even though justice is rarely seen in the present existence. Evildoers may live without ever being punished. Yet beyond the death of the body lies a final judgment characterized by God's justice.

So the book of Daniel is about history and hope. Life must be lived now; for that, the book offers in the first six chapters the insight of Daniel's experience. Life is lived in the context of war and international chaos; for that, chapters 7–12 depict God's sovereignty and his purposes in history. Individual life moves toward death; for that, the writer speaks of resurrection and judgment.

Content: Stories about Daniel (1–6)

Daniel and His Companions (1:1-21) Daniel and his companions—Hananiah, Mishael, and Azariah—were exiled to Babylon some 19 years before the main exile following the destruction of Jerusalem. The four healthy young men, selected from among many Jewish exiles, were at the command of King Nebuchadnezzar assigned to a special three-year training program to make them court aides.

As soon as the four Jewish youths entered Babylon's high society, they faced a dietary problem. The king provided them with the best food and wine from the royal kitchens, but a Jew's diet was restricted by the laws of God (see Dt 14). The four asked for a diet of vegetables and water, not to be fussy or ungrateful, but to remain faithful to their God. The story tells how the dietary situation worked out and sees them through their education and Daniel's appointment as a royal counselor.

The first episode thus focuses on a key issue faced by all Jewish exiles: How could one live in a foreign land, with foreign food and customs, yet remain faithful to God and his laws? Daniel provided a model. He was courageous enough not to compromise, but wise enough to seek a solution acceptable to all. His faithfulness was rewarded by God. By the end of the episode, Daniel is seen as a person with special wisdom and gifts from God. The rest of his life was marked by the exercise of those gifts.

Nebuchadnezzar's Dream (2:1-49) The king had a dream and, although he could not remember its substance, it weighed heavily on his mind. When his corps of professional interpreters could do nothing for him, he ordered that they be executed. The king's order included Daniel and his companions, whose training qualified them as interpreters. Daniel obtained a stay of execution by offering to interpret the dream. After prayer, Daniel received from God both the substance of the dream and its interpretation, which he relayed to the king. The grateful Nebuchadnezzar promoted Daniel and his companions to important positions in Babylon.

Although the writer recorded both the king's dream and Daniel's interpretation, the problem for a modern reader is how to interpret the interpretation. The king saw in his dream a statue, with head of gold, chest and arms of silver, belly and thighs of brass, legs of iron, and feet of part iron and part clay. The interpretation identified Nebuchadnezzar as the head of gold. His kingdom would be followed by three other kingdoms, each represented by the statue's parts and substances. At that point modern interpretations begin to diverge.

A common interpretation of the four sequential king-

doms is as follows: Chaldean Empire (gold), Medo-Persian Empire (silver), Greece (brass), Rome (iron and clay). Others suggest an alternative interpretation: Chaldean Empire (gold), Media (silver), Persia (brass), Greece (iron and clay). To focus too much attention on identifying the four kingdoms can result in failure to see the chapter's key feature. From the midst of those human kingdoms, "During the reigns of those kings, the God of heaven will set up a kingdom that will never be destroyed; no one will ever conquer it. It will shatter all these kingdoms into nothingness, but it will stand forever" (2:44, NLT). The Babylonian king's dream anticipated the coming of a greater kingdom, that of Jesus Christ.

The Fiery Furnace (3:1-30) The story continues, focusing on Daniel's three friends and using their Babylonian names—Shadrach, Meshach, and Abednego. King Nebuchadnezzar constructed a massive gold statue, 90 feet (27.4 meters) high. At its dedication ceremony everyone was required to bow down and worship as a band began to play. The three young Hebrews, who refused to worship, were summoned before the king. Their continued firm refusal led to a sentence of execution, and they were thrown into a fiercely burning furnace. Remarkably, they did not burn, and a fourth being appeared with them in the furnace. As they emerged unharmed from the ordeal, the king acknowledged God's power of salvation and rewarded them.

The story illustrates a second dilemma of the Jews in exile. Faithfulness to God's first commandment, "You shall have no other gods before me" (Dt 5:7), could lead to death. The three young men were faithful—not out of confidence that God would rescue them, but whether or not he chose to spare their lives (Dn 3:17-18). As it happened, God delivered them; they were tossed into the furnace bound, but they came out free men. The message was profound: certainly the Jews should believe in a God able to deliver from the flames of persecution, but they should believe and hold fast even if no deliverance could be seen beyond the trial.

Nebuchadnezzar's Second Dream and Madness (4:1-37) On two occasions Nebuchadnezzar had confessed faith in the living God: when Daniel had interpreted his dream of the statue (2:47), and on the release of Daniel's three companions from the furnace (3:28). Nonetheless, the king's faith was shallow. The story in chapter 4 recounts a lapse of faith that brought terrible consequences. After eight years, when those consequences had run their course, the king again acknowledged God (4:37).

The entire story is presented in the form of a proclamation, written by Nebuchadnezzar and widely circulated after the events in the story had transpired. The king dreamed of a tall tree growing in a field to ever greater heights. A divine messenger ordered the tree cut down, with only a stump and roots left in the ground. The stump and roots then took the form of a man, but the man's mind was replaced with that of an animal. For seven years that semihuman creature behaved like a beast.

Daniel showed the king how the dream applied to the king himself. Nebuchadnezzar was the great tree that would be cut down; he would behave like a beast in the field for seven years. One year after the king had been told that interpretation, the judgment came. For seven years he behaved like an animal until his sanity returned.

The moral of the king's story is that his madness was no accident but rather divine judgment. His arrogant belief that he had the power of God led to heavy retribution (4:30). The king was probably afflicted with a rare and peculiar form of mental illness today called "boanthropy." The true meaning of the story lies at a deeper level: to think that one is God, having absolute power and control of one's own life, is madness. That kind of madness can be cured and overcome only with the realization that absolute power and authority belong to God alone.

Belshazzar's Feast (5:1-31) The scene shifts to the reign of a later king in Babylon, Belshazzar. The son of Nabonidus, he was probably co-regent with Nabonidus (555?–539 BC), with special authority in the region of Babylon. The theme of his story is similar to that of chapter 4. Belshazzar, in the course of an enormous feast, called for the sacred vessels captured from the temple in Jerusalem. With the sacred vessels the Babylonians toasted the local gods, a sacrilegious act that invited divine judgment. It came in the form of words written on the wall by a hand, which Daniel interpreted for the king as words of judgment (5:26-28). Although he praised Daniel for the interpretation, the king missed both the true meaning of the words and the lesson taught to Nebuchadnezzar, his predecessor (vv 18-22). Belshazzar was killed that very night when Darius the Mede entered the city and captured it. The theme continues remorselessly: human pride and arrogance do not pass unnoticed by the God of history, who controls and directs human events toward the fulfillment of his purpose.

The Den of Lions (6:1-28) The theme of chapter 6 is similar to that of chapter 3, but with Daniel as the story's central figure. He is portrayed as one unwilling to compromise, fully obedient to Darius as long as that was possible, but unwilling to disobey the law of God. Hence, Daniel knowingly disobeyed a royal decree that prohibited prayer to anyone other than the king himself. Although he was aware of the consequences, Daniel remained faithful to God. The immediate outcome, when his enemies reported him, was an order of execution—Daniel was thrown to the lions. He was delivered from the hungry cats, and the king, relieved of a terrible predicament, had the plotters punished.

A double message emerges from the story. On the one hand, God's servant must be faithful in prayer and worship, regardless of the outcome; God delivers, and in that case did deliver Daniel from disaster. On the other hand, the effect of Daniel's faithfulness was that the king, who had ordered his subjects to worship him, learned about true worship (6:25-27). The effects of faithfulness, like ripples from a pebble tossed in a pool, spread far beyond the one who is faithful.

Content: Daniel's Visions (7–12) With the beginning of chapter 7 the chronological sequence of the book of Daniel changes; Daniel's first vision goes back to the first year of Belshazzar (7:1), but subsequent visions take place as late as the reign of Cyrus, the Persian king (10:1). Chapters 7–12 emphasize the meaning of history and God's sovereignty in history, expressed in the mysterious symbolism of dreams. The whole section can be divided as follows: (1) vision of four beasts (7:1-28); (2) vision of the ram and the goat (8:1-27); (3) Daniel's prayer (9:1-27); (4) vision of the end times (10:1–12:13).

The first vision again takes up the theme of four kingdoms, already seen in Nebuchadnezzar's dream (ch 2). In the second vision the focus is narrowed down to two kingdoms, Persia and Greece. Much of the final vision of the end times deals with events occurring during the reign of Antiochus Epiphanes in the second century BC. All the visions play on the same theme. Although human

kingdoms may exert their might in a chaotic world, the sovereign God acts through history's apparent chaos toward an ultimate goal of salvation.

The primary interpretation of the visions can be perceived in past historical events, but a further messianic dimension can be seen in the light of the NT. That dimension is most evident in chapter 7. In the context of the four kingdoms, a divine court of judgment is established, presided over by the "Ancient of Days"—the almighty God (7:9). Then Daniel sees the arrival of "one like a son of man" (7:13). Though the phrase "son of man" was later perceived to be a messianic title, it did not technically have that meaning in the book of Daniel. Daniel 7:13 is a principal source for the title "Son of Man," which Jesus commonly used to designate himself. His most significant use of that term was at his trial, where he directly associated his title with Daniel 7 (Mt 26:63-64).

See also Daniel (Person) #3; Diaspora of the Jews; Israel, History of; Prophecy; Prophet, Prophetess.

DANITE* Member of Dan's tribe (Jos 19:47; 1 Chr 12:35). See Dan, Tribe of.

DAN-JAAN Geographical landmark denoting the northern limit of David's kingdom (2 Sm 24:6). Joab's census taking stopped here. Some think this is a copyist's error, because no town with a similar name is known to have existed in that area. Others believe that it means "Dan in the wood," referring simply to Dan (see RSV). Still others think it refers to a town within Dan, perhaps Jaan, of which all traces have vanished.

DANNAH Town located in the hill country of Judah between Socoh and Kiriath-sannah (Debir) (Jos 15:49).

DAPHNE A beautiful grove and sanctuary to Apollo located near Antioch in Syria. The Greek ruler Seleucus I lived here and built a huge statue of Apollo in addition to a temple. Here, criminals and political refugees could take asylum, as it was illegal to arrest anyone within Daphne. In 2 Maccabees 4:33 the high priest Onias, who had been true to Yahweh in boldly scolding King Menelaus, hid here. He was, however, brought out by trickery and murdered.

DARA*, DARDA Mahol's son (1 Kgs 4:31), a Judahite of the family of Zerah (1 Chr 2:6). With Ethan the Ezrahite and Heman and Calcol, also sons of Mahol, Darda is mentioned as the proverbial example of wisdom, though he is surpassed by Solomon (1 Kgs 4:31-32). First Chronicles 2:6 sometimes gives the name as Dara, probably the error of a copyist, and includes a fifth man, Zimri. That there are two different fathers (Mahol and Zerah) mentioned in the two passages may be explained by making Mahol the natural father and Zerah the Ezrahite an earlier ancestor.

DARIC* Persian gold coin. See Coins.

DARIUS Name of three emperors in the Persian dynasty of the legendary King Achaemenes. A Darius appears in the biblical books of Ezra, Nehemiah, Haggai, and Zechariah as a Persian king, and in the book of Daniel as a Mede who became king over the Chaldeans (Dn 9:1).

Darius I (521–486 BC) Also known as Darius Hystaspes and Darius the Great, Darius I seized the throne of the Persian Empire after the death of Cambyses II. Although he was an Achaemenid, he was from a different branch of the royal family than

Cyrus and Cambyses, and his authority was not accepted in all the provinces. After Darius quelled several revolts, however, his power was firmly established, and he turned his attention to expanding the empire. His military campaigns extended Persian borders to the Danube River in the west and to the Indus River in the east, making him ruler of the largest empire the world had known. Greco-Persian conflict, which continued until Alexander the Great conquered the empire in 330 BC, began when Darius launched two invasions of Greece after conquering Thrace and Macedonia. The first expedition was destroyed by a storm in the Aegean Sea; the second was defeated by the Athenians in the famous battle of Marathon in 490 BC.

An able administrator, Darius did much to promote trade and commerce. He instituted a uniform system of weights and measures. During his reign, a canal from the Nile River to the Red Sea was completed, and a sea route from the Indus River to Egypt was explored.

During Darius's reign, Persian architecture developed a style that continued until the end of the Achaemenid dynasty. Darius built at Babylon, Ecbatana, and Susa, his capital. A great royal road was constructed from Susa to the Lydian capital of Sardis. His greatest architectural accomplishment was the founding of Persepolis, a new royal city to replace the emperor's residence at Pasargadae. Darius also allowed temples to be built in Egypt and in Jerusalem, continuing Cyrus's policy of respecting the religious customs of his subjects.

Darius I is the Darius, king of Persia, mentioned in the books of Ezra, Haggai, and Zechariah. Ezra 5–6 record that Zerubbabel and Jeshua, with the help of Haggai and Zechariah, finished rebuilding the temple during Darius's reign while Tattenai was governor of the province "Beyond the River" (Syria-Palestine). Zerubbabel and Jeshua had returned to Jerusalem under Cyrus II about 538 BC (Ezr 2:2). They completed the temple in the sixth year of Darius (6:15). That must have been the sixth year of Darius I (516 BC), since the sixth year of Darius II would certainly be too late. That identification was confirmed by discovery of a Babylonian document, dated June 5, 502 BC, which refers to Tattenai as "the governor of Beyond the River."

In chapter 4 of Ezra three Persian rulers are mentioned: Darius (vv 5, 24); Ahasuerus (probably Xerxes I, v 6); and Artaxerxes (probably Artaxerxes I, vv 7-23). The chapter is a brief record of resistance to Jewish efforts to rebuild the city of Jerusalem and the temple. Verse 24 states that work on the temple stopped until "the second year of the reign of Darius," yet the temple was completed in the sixth year of Darius I. Obviously, work on the temple could not have stopped in the second year of Artaxerxes' son Darius II (421 BC) if it had already been finished in 515 BC. Therefore, Ezra 4:24 should be understood not as a chronological continuation of the first 23 verses but as an introduction to the next two chapters, which discuss the building of the temple.

Darius II (423–404 BC) Also known as Ochus (his real name) and Darius Nothus ("Darius the bastard"), Darius II was the son of Artaxerxes I by a Babylonian concubine. Before he became emperor, Ochus was a satrap (governor) of Hyrcania, a region on the southeast coast of the Caspian Sea. In 423 BC his half brother, Sogdianus (or Secydianus), killed Xerxes II. Ochus then seized the throne from Sogdianus, whom he executed, and adopted the name Darius II. His reign was plagued with revolution and corruption. His own full brother, Arsites, revolted soon after Darius seized the throne, and Darius had him executed.

After an alliance with Sparta was formed against Athens, Persia joined the Peloponnesian War. Several successful military campaigns succeeded in recovering the Greek coastal cities of Asia Minor and breaking Athenian power in the Aegean area. Darius II died in Babylon in 404 BC, the year the Peloponnesian War ended.

The Darius mentioned only once in the book of Nehemiah probably is Darius II. The passage states that Jewish priests were recorded "until the reign of Darius the Persian" (Neh 12:22b); descendants of Levi were recorded "until the days of Johanan son of Eliashib" (Neh 12:23). An Aramaic document found in Elephantine, Egypt, refers to Johanan the high priest in Jerusalem. The document was written in 407 BC, thus placing Johanan in the reign of Darius II.

Darius the Mede Unknown in historical documents of the period of the Babylonian and Persian empires, this biblical Darius has been identified with several known figures. The most important efforts have identified Darius the Mede as another name for Cyrus II ("Cyrus the Persian," Dn 6:28); for Cambyses II, Cyrus's son; or for Gubaru, who was governor of Babylon and the province Beyond the River during the reigns of Cyrus II and Cambyses II.

According to the book of Daniel, "Darius the Mede received the kingdom" when Belshazzar, king of Babylon, was slain (Dn 5:30-31). Darius was about 62 years old (v 31) and was "the son of Ahasuerus, by birth a Mede" (9:1). Daniel never suggested that Darius was king of Media or of the whole Persian Empire, only of the Chaldean (Babylonian) kingdom. The Babylonian Empire included Mesopotamia (Babylonia and Assyria) and Syro-Palestine (Syria, Phoenicia, and Palestine). In the Persian Empire, that huge area became known as the province of Babylon (Mesopotamia) and Beyond the River (Syro-Palestine). Daniel also recorded that Darius appointed governors in the kingdom. By the third year of Cyrus the Persian (536 BC), the first year of Darius the Mede had already passed (Dn 10:1–11:1).

According to Nabonidus's Chronicle and the Persian Verse Account of Nabonidus (two cuneiform documents from Nabonidus's reign), Nabonidus was in Tema until Cyrus's invasion of Babylonia. While he was away, he "entrusted the kingship" to his son Belshazzar. On October 12, 539 BC, Babylon fell to Ugbaru, general of Cyrus's army. Cyrus entered Babylon on October 29, 539 BC, and appointed a person named Gubaru governor of Babylon. Gubaru then appointed other governors under him. General Ugbaru died on November 6, 539 BC.

Clearly there is no place for Darius the Mede between the reigns of Nabonidus/Belshazzar and Cyrus II. Thus Darius the Mede must be Cyrus, a subordinate of Cyrus, or Cambyses, crown prince under Cyrus. But Cyrus II is mentioned as a separate person (Dn 6:28; 10:1–11:1), and it seems unlikely that the author would name the same figure both "Cyrus the Persian" and "Darius the Mede." Cambyses II could not have been 62 years old; also, since he was not made king of Babylon until he became king of the empire in 529 BC, Cambyses' first year could not precede Cyrus's third year (536 BC).

Darius the Mede was thus probably a subordinate of Cyrus who was made ruler of "the realm of the Chaldeans" after Belshazzar and who could have been considered a king by his subjects. Accordingly, the reign of Darius (Dn 6:28) should be understood as simultaneous with that of Cyrus, not as a preceding reign. Thus, Gubaru was made governor of Babylon immediately following the reign of Belshazzar, and he appointed governors, as did Darius the Mede. There is no record of Gubaru's age, nationality, or ancestry. He may well have been a 62-year-old Mede whose father was named Ahasuerus. The Ahasuerus of the book of Esther and of Ezra 4:6 should be identified with a later king, probably Xerxes I.

Many Babylonian texts record that Gubaru was governor of Babylon and the province Beyond the River for about 14 years (539–525 BC). The documents attribute much power to him. His name is a final warning to officials who might disobey the laws. In documents that mention Cyrus II or Cambyses II, crimes in Babylon are stated to be sins against Gubaru, not against Cyrus or Cambyses. The province of Babylon and Beyond the River was the richest and most populous in the Persian Empire, encompassing many nations and languages. For a powerful governor of such a region to be called "king" by his subjects seems only natural.

The case for Gubaru is admittedly circumstantial, but it remains the best solution to the problem. Until further evidence comes to light, it is safe to assume that Darius the Mede, "king over the realm of the Chaldeans," was actually Gubaru, the known governor of that realm.

See also Medes, Media, Median; Persia, Persians.

DARKNESS Absence of light or brightness. Although the Bible seldom refers to literal darkness, a number of words translated "darkness" are used in a figurative or metaphorical sense.

When God created the world, there was no light until he commanded that light appear. He then made distinction between light and its opposite, darkness, which he called night (Gn 1:2, 4-5, 18). Literal darkness is also mentioned in the account of the plagues God inflicted on Egypt; the ninth plague was an intense darkness that could be "felt" (Ex 10:21-23). That darkness lasted three days and was selective; wherever Egyptians were, it was dark, but where the Israelites were, there was light. The Israelites left Egypt accompanied by a cloud that separated them from their enemy, evidently giving light to the Israelites but making darkness for the Egyptians (Ex 14:20). The Bible notes that thieves or adulterers are likely to do their evil deeds in the dark or at night (Jb 24:16-17).

In the NT "darkness" is used twice in its literal sense. At the crucifixion of Jesus, for a three-hour period from noon to three o'clock, there was not light (Mt 27:45; Mk 15:33; Lk 23:44). The other reference is to Christ's second coming, when "the sun will be darkened, and the moon will not give its light" (Mt 24:29, RSV).

Several biblical passages speak of a darkness surrounding God, evidently moving from a literal sense of absence of light to a more profound meaning. God spoke to Moses on Mt Sinai in a dense, black cloud (Ex 20:21; Dt 4:11) or from the darkness (Dt 5:23). Darkness is pictured as a shelter or cloak around God (2 Sm 22:12; Pss 18:11; 97:2). God sets a boundary for light and darkness (Jb 26:10), brings darkness (Pss 104:20, 105:28), and creates light and darkness (Is 45:7). God dwells in thick darkness (1 Kgs 8:12; 2 Chr 6:1), and thick darkness is under his feet (2 Sm 22:10; Ps 18:9).

Most figurative references to darkness appear in poetic material, such as Job, Psalms, and Isaiah. Generally, such darkness depicts ignorance about God's will. Knowledge of God is "light"; hence, lack of such knowledge is "darkness" (Jb 12:24-25; Mt 4:16; Jn 1:5; 8:12; 12:35, 46; 1 Jn 1:5; 2:8-9, 11).

Job spoke of darkness as equivalent to nothingness (Jb 3:4-6). In other references darkness stands for death, a land of shadows and gloom, the dwelling place of the dead far from the light of day (Jb 10:21-22; 15:24; 17:12-13; 18:18; Eccl 6:4; 11:8).

Darkness frequently stands for distress and anxiety, or for the confusion and destruction experienced by the wicked (Gn 15:12; Jb 5:14; 12:25; 15:22, 30; 19:8; 22:11; Pss 35:6; 107:10, 14; Eccl 5:17; Is 5:30). Moral depravity is sometimes described as darkness (Prv 2:13; 4:19; Is 5:20; 60:2). In the NT darkness is generally a metaphor of moral depravity and spiritual ignorance (Mt 4:16; 6:23; Lk 1:79; 11:35; 22:53; Rom 2:19; Col 1:13).

A major theme of OT prophets was the Day of the Lord, often associated with darkness (Ez 32:8; Jl 2:2, 31; Am 5:18, 20; Zep 1:15). The NT also links darkness with judgment in connection with Christ's second coming (Mt 8:12; 22:13; 25:30; 2 Pt 2:17; Jude 1:6, 13). Those who come to know God are said to come out of darkness (Is 9:2; 29:18; 42:7); darkness cannot be a hiding place from God (Jb 34:22; Ps 139:11-12; Is 29:15).

See also Light.

DARKON Ancestor of a group of people who returned to Judah with Zerubbabel after the exile (Ezr 2:56; Neh 7:58).

DART Sharp, pointed weapon used as an arrow or light spear for thrusting. *See* Armor and Weapons.

DATE, DATE PALM Fruit and tree mentioned only a few times in the Bible (2 Sm 6:19; 1 Chr 16:3; Sg 7:7). *See* Plants (Palm).

DATHAN Reubenite, son of Eliab and brother of Abiram; one of the leaders of Israel who, with Korah, rebelled against Moses during the wilderness wanderings (Nm 16:1-27; 26:9; Ps 106:17).

DATHEMA A fortress in Bashan where Jews took refuge during the Maccabean revolt (1 Macc 5:9). Here they hid from Timothy until Judas the Maccabee rescued them by defeating the enemy (v 29). The location of Dathema has not been identified by modern archeologists.

DAUGHTER *See* Family Life and Relations.

DAUGHTER-IN-LAW *See* Family Life and Relations.

DAVID Israel's most important king. David's kingdom represented the epitome of Israel's power and influence during the nation's OT history.

The two books in the OT devoted to David's reign are 2 Samuel and 1 Chronicles. His earlier years are recorded in 1 Samuel, beginning at chapter 16. Almost half of the biblical psalms are ascribed to David. His importance extends into the NT, where he is identified as an ancestor of Jesus Christ and forerunner of the messianic king.

PREVIEW
• Early Years
• Preparation for Kingship
• David as King
• David's Lasting Influence

Early Years

Family David was the youngest son in Jesse's family, part of Judah's tribe. The family lived in Bethlehem, about six miles (10 kilometers) south of Jerusalem. His great-grandmother was Ruth, from the land of Moab (Ru 4:18-22). Genealogies in both the OT and the NT trace David's lineage back to Judah, son of the patriarch Jacob (1 Chr 2:3-15; Mt 1:3-6; Lk 3:31-33).

Training and Talents Little is known about David's early life. As a boy, he took care of his father's sheep, risking his life to kill attacking bears and lions. Later, David publicly acknowledged God's help and strength in protecting the flocks under his care (1 Sm 17:34-37).

David was an accomplished musician. He had developed his ability as a harpist so well that, when a musician was needed at the royal court of King Saul, someone immediately recommended David.

In Jesse's family, David was regarded as unimportant. When the nationally known prophet Samuel visited Jesse's home, all the older sons were on hand to meet him; David was tending the sheep. Samuel had been instructed by God to anoint a king from Jesse's family, not knowing beforehand which son to anoint. Sensing divine restraint as seven brothers passed before him, he made further inquiry. When he learned that Jesse had one other son, David was immediately summoned. David was anointed by Samuel and endowed with the Spirit of the Lord (1 Sm 16:1-13). Whatever Jesse and his family understood by that anointing, it seems to have made no immediate change in David's pattern of living. He continued to tend the sheep.

Preparation for Kingship During his youth, David was willing to serve others, even though he had been anointed king. It was his willingness to take supplies to three of his older brothers in the army that gave him his opportunity for national fame.

As a young man, David was also sensitive toward God. While greeting his brothers on the battlefield, he was disturbed by the Philistine Goliath's defiance of God's armies. Although rebuked by his brothers, David accepted the challenge to take on Goliath. He had a reasonable confidence that God, who had helped him encounter a lion and a bear, would aid him against a champion warrior. So, with faith in God and using his ability to sling stones, David killed Goliath (1 Sm 17:12-58).

National Fame Killing Goliath made David a hero to the nation of Israel. It also brought him into close relationship with the royal family of Saul. But success and national acclaim brought on the jealousy of Saul and ultimately resulted in David's expulsion from the land of Israel.

In the Royal Court Saul promised his oldest daughter, Merab, to David in marriage, but then Saul went back on the promise and offered David another daughter, Michal. The dowry of trophies from dead Philistines demanded by Saul was designed to bring about David's death at Philistine hands. But again David was victorious. Women sang praises of his exploits, intensifying Saul's jealousy and further endangering David's life (1 Sm 18:6-30).

In the meantime, David and Saul's son Jonathan developed a deep friendship. When they made a covenant, Jonathan gave David his choicest military equipment (sword, bow, and belt). Although Saul tried to turn Jonathan against David, the friendship deepened. Because Saul was trying to kill him, David had to flee from the court and live as a fugitive.

After Jonathan had warned David of Saul's continuing designs on his life, David went to Ramah to see the prophet Samuel. Together they went to Naioth, near Ramah. After sending several groups of men after David, Saul finally went with them himself. All his attempts to seize David were thwarted by the Spirit of God, who caused Saul and his men to prophesy all night in religious fervor (1 Sm 19).

Conferring again with Jonathan, David realized that Saul's jealousy had developed into hatred. Jonathan, aware that David would be the future king of Israel, requested assurance that his descendants would receive protection under David's rule (1 Sm 20).

Life as a Fugitive Fleeing from Saul, David stopped at Nob. By deceiving Ahimelech, who was officiating as priest there, David obtained food supplies and Goliath's sword (kept as a trophy). An Edomite named Doeg, chief of Saul's herdsmen, saw what happened at Nob. David continued his flight, taking refuge temporarily in Gath with King Achish (1 Sm 21), then finding shelter in the cave of Adullam, located 10 miles (16.1 kilometers) southwest of Bethlehem. There his relatives and about 400 fighting men joined him. He went to Mizpeh in Moab, appealing to the Moabite king for protection, especially for his parents. When the prophet Gad warned him not to stay there, David moved back to Judah to the Hereth woods (1 Sm 22:1-5).

David's freedom of movement enraged Saul, who charged his own people with conspiracy. When Doeg reported what he had witnessed at Nob, Saul executed Ahimelech and 84 other priests, then massacred all of Nob's inhabitants. One priest named Abiathar escaped to report Saul's atrocities to David, who assured him of protection (1 Sm 22:6-23).

The Philistines were always ready to take advantage of any weakness in Israel. David's reprisal after a Philistine raid on Keilah, 12 miles (19.3 kilometers) southwest of Bethlehem, gave Saul an opportunity to attack David, who escaped to the wilderness of Ziph, a desert area near Hebron. David and Jonathan met for the last time in that wilderness. Pursued by Saul's army, David fled still farther south. He was almost encircled in uninhabited country near Maon when Saul had to march his army off to respond to a Philistine attack (1 Sm 23).

At his next place of refuge, En-gedi, on the western shore of the Dead Sea, David was attacked by Saul with 3,000 soldiers. David had an opportunity to kill Saul but refused to harm the "Lord's anointed" king of Israel. Learning of David's loyalty, Saul confessed his sin in seeking David's life (1 Sm 24).

During the years they roamed the wilderness in the Maon/Ziph/En-gedi area, David's band provided protection for Nabal, a rich man living in Maon with large flocks of sheep at Carmel. In exchange for that protection, David proposed that Nabal share some of his wealth. Nabal's scorn angered David, but Nabal's wife, Abigail, appealed to David not to take revenge. When Abigail told Nabal of his narrow escape, he was evidently so shocked that he had a heart seizure. He died ten days later, and Abigail later became David's wife (1 Sm 25).

Once more Saul came with an army of 3,000 men into the Ziph Desert to find David, and David again passed up an opportunity to harm the king. Finally realizing the folly of seeking David's life, Saul abandoned pursuit (1 Sm 26).

Refuge in Philistia David continued to feel unsafe in Saul's kingdom. Returning to Gath in Philistine country, he was welcomed by King Achish. His followers were allotted the city of Ziklag, where they lived for about 16 months, attracting new recruits from Judah and the rest of Israel (1 Sm 27; 1 Chr 12:19-22).

The Philistine army, marching up to the Megiddo Valley to fight Saul's army, was uneasy with David's guerrillas in their rear column, so the commanders put pressure on Achish to dismiss David. When he returned to Ziklag, David found that the city had just been raided by the Amalekites. He pursued the enemy, rescued his people and goods, and divided the spoils with those who had remained behind to guard the supplies (1 Sm 29–30). Meanwhile, the Philistines routed the Israelites at Mt Gilboa, killing Jonathan and two of Saul's other sons in a fierce battle. Saul, badly wounded, killed himself with his own sword (ch 31).

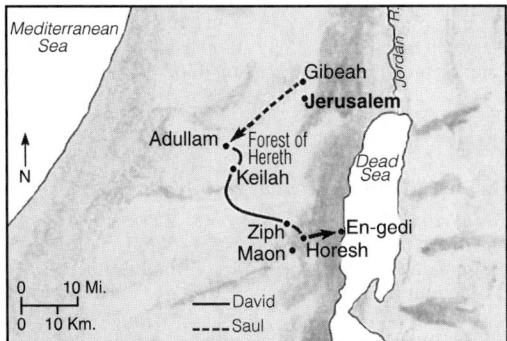

David Flees from Saul David and his men attacked the Philistines at Keilah from the forest of Hereth. Saul came from Gibeah to attack David, but David escaped into the wilderness of Ziph. At Horesh he met Jonathan, who encouraged him. Then he fled into the wilderness of Maon and into the strongholds of En-gedi.

David as King

David ruled over Israel for about 40 years, although the accounts of his reign do not contain enough information for an exact chronology. He began his rule at Hebron and reigned over Judah's territory for seven or eight years. With the death of Saul's successor, Ishbosheth, David was recognized as king by all the tribes and made Jerusalem his capital. During the next decade, he unified Israel through military and economic expansion. Then came approximately 10 years of disruption in the royal family. The last years of David's reign seem to have been devoted to plans for the Jerusalem temple, which was built in the reign of his son Solomon.

The Years in Hebron David was subjected to an unusually rugged period of training for his kingship. Serving under Saul, he gained experience in military exploits against the Philistines. Then, during his fugitive wanderings in the desert area of southern Judah, he ingratiated himself with the landholders and sheep raisers by giving them protection. Being recognized as an outlaw of Israel even enabled him to negotiate diplomatic relations with Moab and Philistia.

David was in Philistine country when news came to him that both Saul and Jonathan had been slain. In a beautiful elegy he paid tribute to his friend Jonathan as well as to King Saul (2 Sm 1).

Sure of God's guidance, David returned to his home, where the leaders of Judah anointed him king at Hebron. He sent a message of commendation to the men of Jabesh for providing a respectable burial for King Saul, probably also bidding for their support.

Confusion probably swept through Israel when Saul was killed, because the Philistines occupied much of the land. Various leaders gathered whatever fighting men they could find, as old tribal loyalties reasserted themselves. David had most of Judah's tribe firmly behind him.

A kind of civil war broke out between the followers of David and those of Saul, with David gaining the alle-

giance of more and more people. Saul's general, Abner, eventually negotiated peace with David, who requested the restoration of Michal as his wife, indicating that he held no animosity toward Saul's dynasty. With the consent of Saul's son Ishbosheth, whom Abner had enthroned as king, Abner went to Hebron and pledged Israel's support for David. But Abner was killed by Joab, one of David's captains, in a family vendetta, and soon afterward Ishbosheth was assassinated. David publicly mourned Abner's death and had Ishbosheth's two murderers executed. Thus, when Saul's dynasty ended, David was seen by the people not so much as a challenger but as a logical successor. Hence, he was recognized as king by all Israel (2 Sm 2–4).

Consolidation in Jerusalem When the Israelites turned to David as king, the Philistines became alarmed and attacked (2 Sm 5; 1 Chr 14:8-17). David was strong enough to defeat them and thus unify the people of Israel.

In search of a more central location for his capital, David turned toward the city of Jerusalem, a Jebusite stronghold. Joab responded to his challenge to conquer the city and was rewarded by being made general of David's army. Jerusalem became known as the "city of David" (1 Chr 11:4-9).

In the same way that he had organized his earliest followers into an effective guerrilla band (1 Chr 11:1–12:22) at Hebron, David began organizing the whole nation (12:23-40). Once established in Jerusalem, he quickly gained recognition from the Phoenicians, contracting for their artisans to build him a magnificent palace in the new capital (14:1-2). He also made sure that Jerusalem would become Israel's religious center (2 Sm 6; 1 Chr 13–16). His abortive attempt to move the ark of the covenant by oxcart (cf. Nm 4) reminded the powerful king that he still had to do things God's way to be successful.

With Jerusalem well established as the nation's capital, David intended to build God a temple. He shared his plan with the prophet Nathan, whose immediate response was positive. That night, however, God sent a message via Nathan that David should not build the temple. David's throne would be established eternally, the prophet said, and unlike Saul, King David would have a son to succeed him and perpetuate the kingdom; that son would build the temple (2 Sm 7; 1 Chr 17).

Prosperity and Supremacy Little is recorded about the expansion of David's rule from the tribal area of Judah to a vast empire stretching from the Nile River of Egypt to regions of the Tigris-Euphrates valley. Nothing in secular history negates the biblical perspective that David had the most powerful kingdom in the heart of that "Fertile Crescent" about 1000 BC.

It is likely that skirmishes with the Philistines to the west were frequent until they finally became subservient to David and paid him tribute. In Saul's day the Philistines had enjoyed a monopoly on the use of iron (1 Sm 13:19-21). The fact that David freely used iron near the end of his reign (1 Chr 22:3) hints at profound economic changes in Israel.

David's kingdom expanded southward as he built military garrisons in Edomite territory. Beyond Edom, he controlled the Moabites and Amalekites, who paid him tribute in silver and gold. To the northeast, Israelite domination was extended over the Ammonites and the Arameans, whose capital was Damascus. David's treatment of both friends and enemies seemed to contribute to the strength of his kingdom (2 Sm 8–10). Although he was a brilliant military strategist who used all the means and resources available to bring Israel success, David was humble enough to glorify God (2 Sm 22; see Ps 18).

Sin in the Royal Family A lengthy section of the book of 2 Samuel (chs 11–20) gives a remarkably frank account of sin, crime, and rebellion in David's family. The king's own imperfections are clearly portrayed; the king of Israel himself could not escape God's judgement when he did wrong.

Although polygamy was then a Near Eastern status symbol, it was forbidden for a king of Israel (Dt 17:17). David practiced polygamy, however; some of his marriages undoubtedly had political implications (such as his marriages to Saul's daughter Michal and to princess Maacah of Geshur). Flagrant sins of incest, murder, and rebellion in his family brought David much suffering and almost cost him the throne.

David's sin of adultery with Bathsheba, committed at the height of his military success and territorial expansion, led him further into evil: he planned a strategy to have Bathsheba's husband, Uriah, killed on the front line of battle. David seems to have excluded God from consideration in that segment of his personal life. Yet when the prophet Nathan confronted the king with his sins, David acknowledged his guilt. He confessed his sin and pleaded with God for forgiveness (as in Pss 32 and 51). God forgave him, but for nearly ten years David endured the consequences of his lack of self-restraint and his failure to exercise discipline in his family. Although unsurpassed in military and diplomatic strategy, David lacked strength of character in his domestic affairs. Evil fermented in his own house; the father's self-indulgence was soon reflected in Amnon's crime of incest, followed by Absalom's murder of his brother.

Having incurred his father's disfavor, Absalom took refuge in Geshur with his mother's people for three years. Joab, David's general, was eventually able to reconcile David with his alienated son. Absalom, however, having taken advantage of his position in the royal family to gain a following, went to Hebron, staged a surprise rebellion, and proclaimed himself king throughout Israel. His strong following posed such a threat that David fled from Jerusalem. David, still a master strategist, gained time through a ruse to organize his forces and put down his son's rebellion. Absalom was killed while trying to flee; his death plunged David into grief.

On his return to Jerusalem, David had to work at undoing the damage caused by Absalom's revolt. His own tribe of Judah, for example, had supported Absalom. Another rebellion, fomented by Sheba of Benjamin's tribe, had to be suppressed by Joab before the nation could settle down.

David's Last Years Although David was not permitted to build the temple in Jerusalem, he made extensive preparations for that project during the last years of his reign. He stockpiled materials and organized the kingdom for efficient use of domestic and foreign labor. He also outlined details for religious worship in the new structure (1 Chr 21–29).

The military and civic organization developed by David was probably patterned after Egyptian practice. The army, rigidly controlled by officers of proven loyalty to the king, included mercenaries. The king also appointed trusted supervisors over farms, livestock, and orchards in various parts of his empire (1 Chr 27:25-31).

David took, or at least began, a census of Israel (2 Sm 24; 1 Chr 21). The incompleteness of the accounts leaves unanswered such questions as the reason for God's punishment. The king overruled Joab's objection and insisted that the census be taken. Since David later seemed keenly aware that he had sinned in taking the census, it may be that he was motivated by pride to ascertain his exact military strength (approx. 1.5 million men). God may also have been judging the people for their support of the rebellions of Absalom and Sheba.

Through the prophet Gad, David was given a choice of punishments for his sin. He chose a three-day pestilence. As David and the elders repented, they saw an angel on the threshing floor of the Jebusite Ornan (Arunah). David offered sacrifice there and prayed for his people. Later he purchased the threshing floor, located just outside the city of Jerusalem, concluding that it should be the site for the temple to be built by his son Solomon (1 Chr 21:28–22:1).

David's Lasting Influence

The Writer of Psalms The OT book of Psalms became one of the most popular books in ancient Israel, and has remained so among countless millions of people throughout the centuries. These words of praise prepared by David were intended for use in the temple worship (2 Chr 29:30). The 73 psalms ascribed to David generally grew out of his own relationship to God and to other persons.

SOME PSALMS FROM DAVID'S EXPERIENCES

Psalm	Historical Reference
59	1 Sm 19:11
56	1 Sm 21:10
34	1 Sm 21:13
142	1 Sm 22:1
52	1 Sm 22:9
54	1 Sm 23:19
57	1 Sm 24:1
7	1 Sm 24:11-12
18	2 Sm 7:1; 22
32	2 Sm 12:13-14
51	2 Sm 12:13-14
3	2 Sm 15:16
63	2 Sm 16:2

David probably compiled Book I of the book of Psalms (1–41) and Book IV (90–106), since most of those psalms were written by David himself. Other psalms of his (Pss 51–71) are in Book II (42–72), which was probably compiled by Solomon. As those psalms were used for worship in later generations, various people added others until the time of Ezra.

David's psalms provided much of the poetry that was set to music for Israel's worship. His organization of the priests and Levites and his provision of instruments for worship (2 Chr 7:6; 8:14) set the pattern for generations to come in the religious life of Israel.

David in the Writings of the Prophets David, recognized as the greatest Israelite king, is often mentioned as a standard of comparison in the writings of the OT prophets. Isaiah (as in Is 7:2, 13; 22:22) and Jeremiah often referred to their contemporary kings as belonging to the "house" or "throne" of David. Contrasting David with some of his descendants who did not honor God, both Isaiah and Jeremiah predicted a messianic ruler who would establish justice and righteousness on the throne of David forever (Is 9:7; Jer 33:15). When Isaiah described the coming ruler, he identified him as being from the lineage of Jesse, David's father (Is 11:1-10). Predicting a period of universal peace, Isaiah saw the capital in "Zion," identified with the city of David (2:1-4).

Ezekiel promised the restoration of David as king in an eschatological and messianic sense (Ez 37:24-25), and of "my servant David" as Israel's shepherd (34:23). Hosea likewise identified the future ruler as King David (Hos 3:5). Amos assured the people that God would restore the "tabernacle" of David (Am 9:11) so that they could again dwell in safety. Zechariah referred five times to the "house of David" (in Zec 12–13, RSV), encouraging the hope of a restoration of David's glorious dynasty. The concept of the eternal throne promised to David during his reign was delineated in the message of the prophets even while they were announcing judgments to come on the rulers and people of their time.

David in the New Testament David is frequently mentioned by the Gospel writers, who established Jesus' identity as the "son of David." The covenant God made with David was that an eternal king would come from David's family (Mt 1:1; 9:27; 12:23; Mk 10:48; 12:35; Lk 18:38-39; 20:41). According to Mark 11:10 and John 7:42, the Jews of Jesus' day expected the Messiah (Christ) to be a descendant of David. While stating that Jesus came from the lineage of David, the Gospels also clearly teach that Jesus was the Son of God (Mt 22:41-45; Mk 12:35-37; Lk 20:41-44).

In the book of Acts, David is recognized as the recipient of God's promises that were fulfilled in Jesus Christ. David is also seen as a prophet whom the Holy Spirit inspired to write the psalms (Acts 1:16; 2:22-36; 4:25; 13:26-39).

In the book of Revelation, Jesus is designated as having the "key of David" (Rv 3:7), and as being "the Lion of the tribe of Judah, the Root of David" (5:5). Jesus is quoted as asserting that "I am the root and the offspring of David, the bright morning star" (22:16).

See also Christology; Chronology of the Bible (Old Testament); Israel, History of; King; Kingdom of God, Kingdom of Heaven; Messiah.

DAVID, A MAN OF GOD
David, one of the most gifted and versatile individuals in the OT, is second only to Moses in Israel's history. He was keenly conscious that God had enabled him to establish a kingdom (Ps 18; cf. 2 Sm 22); it was in that context that he was given the messianic promise of an eternal kingdom.

From David's own suffering, persecution, and nearness to death came prophetic psalms that portrayed the suffering and death of the Messiah (e.g., Pss 2; 22; 110; 118). Even the hope of the resurrection is expressed in Psalm 16, as the apostle Peter noted on the day of Pentecost (Acts 2:25-28).

Awareness of a vital personal relationship with God is expressed more consistently by David than by any of the faithful men and women who preceded him. He knew that it was not legalistic observance of rules or rituals that made him acceptable to God. Offering and sacrifice could not atone for sin if one had no accompanying contrition and humility. Many of David's prayers are as appropriate for Christians as they were for God-fearing people in the OT. David's writings show that "knowing God" was as real in OT times as it was for the apostle Paul, even though the full revelation of God in Jesus Christ was still in the future.

DAVID, City of
1. In the OT, the city of Jerusalem. "City of David" referred originally to the old Jebusite stronghold captured by King David (2 Sm 5:6-9). David, Solomon, and many of their descendants who ruled over Judah were buried in the City of David (1 Kgs 2:10; 11:43). Solomon considered it a holy place because of the presence of the ark of the Lord. Therefore, he moved his pagan wife, Pharaoh's daughter, away from the City of David and built a house for her in another place (2 Chr 8:11).

After Solomon's time, the term "city of David" was also used in a larger sense to describe the entire city of Jerusalem, including the newly built temple area. The old section of Jerusalem below the temple site was still specifically designated as the "city of David," however (Neh 3:15). David's tomb was close to the pool of Siloam and to the stairway that descended from the City of David (Neh 3:15-16). *See* Jerusalem; Zion.

2. In the NT, the town of Bethlehem. Bethlehem was David's birthplace and home until he went to Saul's palace as a musician (1 Sm 16:16-23). When David became Judah's king, he chose Hebron as his capital, as the Lord had instructed him (2 Sm 2:1-11). Bethlehem was the birthplace of Jesus, who was a descendant of David (Mi 5:2-4; Lk 2:11).

See also Bethlehem #1.

DAVID*, Root of Phrase applied to Jesus Christ in the book of Revelation (Rv 5:5; 22:16). Though "root" usually means "source," the metaphor depicts Jesus as David's royal descendant, as indicated by the parallel word "offspring" in Revelation 22:16. That is, Jesus came from King David's family as a branch grows from a rooted tree (cf. Is 11:1).

See also Jesse, Root of.

DAVID, Tower of
1. Fortress built by David, with a thousand shields hung on it, commemorated in Song of Songs 4:4 but otherwise unknown.
2. David's Tower in Jerusalem, near the Jaffa Gate, built in medieval times. *See* Jerusalem.

DAY Most literally, a period of time delimited by the earth's rotation around its axis, such as the period between two consecutive sunrises; also, the portion of that period in which the sun is visible, the other portion being called "night." The word "day" occurs over 2,000 times in the OT, over 350 times in the NT. The Hebrew word for "day" is used in a variety of ways, not merely in the literal sense. The Hebrew day began in the evening and continued until the following evening, a reckoning presumably based on the Torah (cf. Gn 1:14, 19). That kind of literal solar (24-hour) day is known as a civil day. Among other ancient Near Eastern nations the civil day began at different times. Greek custom agreed with that of the Hebrews; the Babylonians started their day at sunrise; the Egyptian and Roman day stretched from one midnight to the next.

Biblical Days and Weeks Commonly recognized units of the visible (12-hour) day were morning, noonday, and evening (Ps 55:17). Those divisions were sometimes defined by terms for dawn (Jb 3:9), the heat of the day (1 Sm 11:11), noon (Gn 43:16), the cool of the day (3:8), and evening (Ru 2:17). The Hebrew phrase "between the two evenings" (Ex 12:6, RSV mg) probably referred to dusk, the dark part of twilight (Ex 16:12). Division of days into consecutive hours did not take place until the time of Christ. The closest OT approximation to such a unit was the division of the day into quarters (Neh 9:3), perhaps a counterpart of the preexilic division of the night into watches.

The ancient Hebrews did not name the days of the week other than the Sabbath. Rather, they referred to them numerically, a practice carried over into NT times (Lk 24:1). Because of the traditional Hebrew emphasis on the Sabbath, it was important for the Jews to know the exact time when the Sabbath began. The Pharisees therefore decided that the appearance of three stars following sunset would determine the Sabbath day's beginning.

Days of Creation Many people believe that the days mentioned in the Genesis Creation narrative were 24-hour periods. The phrase "there was evening, there was morning" is used to support that idea. That expression, however, is actually a Sumerian literary figure that pairs opposites together to describe totality. Thus "evening-morning" means a complete phase of time within the total creative cycle; it emphasizes the completeness or comprehensiveness of the process, not the specific period of time in which that process was accomplished. The totality of Creation, phase by phase, may have been thus depicted without any necessary reference to a defined time period.

Since the Sumerian civil day included only the visible (12-hour) period, a legal day of other nations was actually a "double day" (24 hours). If the early Genesis material reflects Sumerian culture, the use of "evening-morning" would preclude current concepts of a civil day and point instead to a phase or general time period.

Old Testament In the OT, "day" frequently has a figurative meaning—for example, the "day of the Lord" (Jl 1:15; Am 5:18), the "day of trouble" (Ps 20:1), and the "day of God's wrath" (Jb 20:28). The plural form is sometimes used to describe a king's reign (1 Kgs 10:21) or the extent of an individual's life (Gn 5:4; 1 Kgs 3:14; Ps 90:12). God is described in the book of Daniel as the "Ancient of Days" (Dn 7:9, 13).

In addition to the Sabbath (Gn 2:3; Ex 20:8-11), which was reserved for rest and worship, "day" was applied to the Passover celebration each spring (Ex 12:14; Lv 23:5) and the Day of Atonement (Lv 16:29-31) each autumn. As with the Sabbath, no work was performed on those occasions; prescribed religious rituals were observed.

New Testament In the NT the use of "day" followed Semitic usage to some extent, although the four military night watches were of Greek and Roman origin. The 12-hour day of NT times was a legacy of Babylonian astronomy (cf. Jn 11:9).

In addition to the literal usage of "day," NT authors sometimes employed it figuratively, as in such expressions as the "day of salvation" (2 Cor 6:2) and the "day of Jesus Christ" (Phil 1:6). Or they described specified periods of time, as in the "days of his Temple duties" (Lk 1:23, TLB). Special feasts mentioned include the Passover (Jn 12:1), the days of Unleavened Bread (Acts 12:3), and the Day of Pentecost (2:1).

As in the OT, the period of human life is described as days (Jn 9:4). Christians are called "children of the light and of the day" (1 Thes 5:5, NLT). Longer periods or eras are referred to as days (2 Cor 6:2; Eph 5:16; 6:13; Heb 5:7). The ominous note struck by the Hebrew prophets about a day of judgment is matched by NT stress on a day of final divine judgment when the Son of Man (Jesus) will reveal himself as Lord (Lk 17:30; Jn 6:39-44; 1 Cor 5:5; 1 Thes 5:2; 2 Pt 2:9; 3:7, 12; 1 Jn 4:17; Rv

16:14). The "day of eternity" marks that point at which time will become eternity (2 Pt 3:18, RSV). The new Jerusalem, dwelling place of God's people, is described as a place of perpetual day (Rv 21:25).

See also Calendars, Ancient and Modern; Day of the Lord; Eschatology.

DAY OF ATONEMENT *See* Atonement, Day of.

DAY OF CHRIST* Phrase used by the apostle Paul in reference to the second advent of Christ (Phil 1:10; 2:16). *See* Day of the Lord.

DAY OF THE LORD Expression used by OT prophets (as early as the eighth-century BC prophet Amos) to signify a time in which God actively intervenes in history, primarily for judgment. Thus "the day of the Lord" is also called "the day of the LORD's anger" (Zep 2:2).

Sometimes "the day of the Lord" is used in the OT to speak of a past judgment (Lam 2:22). More often, an impending future judgment is in view (Jl 2:1-11). Ultimately, though, the term refers to climactic future judgment of the world (Jl 3:14-21; Mal 4:5). Often, prophecy of a near-future event and an end-time prophecy are merged—the immediate judgment being a preview of the final Day of the Lord. The prophecy of Isaiah against Babylon is an example (Is 13:5-10). Jesus combined events described there with other prophecies to explain his second coming (Mk 13:24-37). Another example is Joel's prophecy of the Day of the Lord (Jl 1:15–2:11). Though the prophet initially spoke of God's judgment on Israel by a locust plague, that judgment prompted further pronouncements about a final Day of the Lord far beyond Joel's time (2:14-17, 31). That Day of the Lord extended even beyond the outpouring of the Holy Spirit at Pentecost predicted by Joel's prophecy (Jl 2:28-32; Acts 2:16-21; Rv 6:12-13). The NT uses the term exclusively to mean the end time.

The final Day of the Lord is characterized in the Bible as a day of gloom, darkness, and judgment. Associated with God's judgment is language depicting changes in nature, especially a darkening of the sun, moon, and stars (Is 13:10; Jl 2:31; 3:15; Mt 24:29; Rv 6:12). Nations will be judged for their rebellion against God's anointed people and king (Jl 3:19; cf. Ps 2). Israel is counseled not to be eager for that day, because it will also include judgment on the chosen nation (Am 5:18-20). But the prophets promise that a believing "remnant" will be saved by looking to the Messiah they once rejected (Jl 2:32; Zec 12:10). Following the judgment, the future Day of the Lord will be a time of prosperity, restoration, and blessing for Israel (Jl 3:18-21).

The more explicit NT expressions—"the day of our Lord Jesus Christ" (1 Cor 1:8), "the day of the Lord Jesus" (1 Cor 5:5; 2 Cor 1:14), and "the day of Christ" (Phil 1:10; 2:16)—are more personal and more positive. They point to final events related to Christian believers, who will not experience the wrath of God (1 Thes 5:9). When the Day of the Lord comes, the earth will be renewed and purified through a judgment of fire (2 Pt 3:10-13). In the book of Revelation the final purging seems to come after the Millennium—that is, the 1,000-year reign of Christ (Rv 21:1).

See also Eschatology; Last Days; Last Judgment.

DAY'S JOURNEY Way of estimating distances in Bible times. A day's journey approximated 20 miles (32.2 kilometers) but depended on such things as mode of travel, the terrain, and the weather. Scripture refers both to a day's journey (Ex 3:18; Nm 11:31; 1 Kgs 19:4; Lk 2:44)

and to a Sabbath day's journey (Acts 1:12). A Sabbath day's journey was probably about 3,500 feet (one kilometer). *See* Sabbath Day's Journey.

DAYSPRING*, DAY STAR*

KJV translations in Job 38:12 ("dawn," RSV), Luke 1:78 ("day," RSV), and 2 Peter 1:19 ("morning star," RSV) referring to Venus, the star that heralds the dawn, or to the first light of dawn itself.

In Isaiah 14:12, "Day Star" is a designation for the haughty king of Babylon ("Lucifer," KJV) who, having aspired so high at the cost of Israel, will surely be brought down by God. *See* Morning Star.

DEACON, DEACONESS*

Terms designating an officer in a local church, derived from a Greek word meaning "servant" or "minister." The term "diaconate" is used for the office itself or for the collective body of deacons and deaconesses. As with many other biblical words used today in a technical sense, the words "deacon" and "deaconess" began as popular, nontechnical terms. Both in secular first-century AD Greek culture and in the NT, they described a variety of services.

Origins of the Concept

Greek Usage References have been found in extrabiblical writings where the Greek word "deacon" meant "waiter," "servant," "steward," or "messenger." In at least two instances it indicated a baker and a cook. In religious usage the word described various attendants in pagan temples. Ancient documents show "deacons" presiding at the dedication of a statue to the Greek god Hermes. Serapis and Isis, Egyptian deities, were served by a college of "deacons" presided over by a priest.

General New Testament Usage The same word was used by biblical writers in a general sense to describe various ministries or services. Not until later in the development of the apostolic church was the term applied to a distinct body of church officers. Among its general usages, "deacon" refers to a waiter at meals (Jn 2:5, 9), a king's attendant (Mt 22:13), a servant of Satan (2 Cor 11:15), a servant of God (6:4), a servant of Christ (11:23), a servant of the church (Col 1:24-25), and a political ruler (Rom 13:4).

The NT presents servanthood in the sense of ministry or service as a mark of the whole church—that is, as normative for all disciples (Mt 20:26-28; Lk 22:26-27). Jesus' teaching on the final judgment equates ministry with feeding the hungry, welcoming strangers, clothing the naked, and visiting the sick and imprisoned (Mt 25:31-46). The entire NT emphasizes compassionate care for individuals' physical and spiritual needs as well as the giving of oneself to meeting those needs. Such service is ultimately a ministry to Christ himself (v 45).

Origin of the Office There is little question that before the end of the first century the general term for service or ministry became a kind of title for a position or office in the church. That development evidently went through several stages.

Some biblical scholars emphasize a relationship between the *hazzan* of the Jewish synagogue and the Christian office of deacon. The *hazzan* opened and closed the synagogue doors, kept it clean, and handed out the books for reading. It was probably to such a person that Jesus handed the scroll of Isaiah after finishing his reading (Lk 4:20).

Other NT scholars give considerable attention to the choosing of the seven (Acts 6:1-6); they see that action as a historical forerunner of a more developed structure (Phil 1:1; 1 Tm 3:8-13—the two specific references to an

"office" of deacon). Luke devoted considerable attention in Acts to the selection of a new set of church leaders. Overworked with a variety of responsibilities, the 12 apostles proposed a division of labor to ensure care for the Hellenist (Greek-speaking) widows in the church's daily distribution of food and alms. Seven men of good repute, full of the Spirit and of wisdom (Acts 6:3), subsequently became prominent in the Jerusalem congregation, doing works of charity and caring for physical needs.

Some scholars caution that the diaconate should not be exclusively linked with charitable works, since the Greek word used in Acts 6:2 is related to the word translated "ministry of the word" in verse 4. Those chosen to oversee the care for physical needs were people of spiritual stature. Stephen, for instance, "full of grace and power, did great wonders and signs" (6:8, RSV). Philip, appointed as one of the seven in Acts 6, "preached good news about the kingdom of God and the name of Jesus Christ" (8:12). Philip also baptized (v 38) and is referred to as an evangelist (21:8).

Deacons in the Early Church Those who cite Acts 6 as a preliminary stage of the office of deacon refer to the spread of the practice from the church in Jerusalem to the gentile congregations sprouting elsewhere. Many churches probably took the appointing of "the Jerusalem seven" as a pattern to follow, some even adopting the number seven. In a letter of the third-century pope Cornelius, for example, the church of Rome was said to have maintained seven for the number of deacons.

By the time the church of Philippi received its instructions from the apostle Paul (c. AD 62) and Timothy had Paul's first letter in hand, "deacon" had become a technical term referring to a specific office in the churches. In Philippians 1:1 Paul addressed the church in general and then added "with bishops and deacons." Some interpreters consider that to be a clear establishment of two distinct groups within the larger church body, though no further description was given. Possibly the deacons of that congregation were responsible for collecting and then dispatching the offerings referred to (Phil 4:14-18).

In 1 Timothy 3:8-13 instructions are given about qualifications for the office of deacon. Although that is the most detailed treatment of the subject in the NT, it is actually quite sketchy. Most of the qualifications, dealing with personal character and behavior, are similar to those for a bishop. For instance, a deacon is to be truthful, monogamous, "not addicted to much wine," and a responsible parent. Verse 11, requiring that "the women likewise must be serious, not slanderers, but temperate, faithful in all things" (RSV), may refer not to deacons' wives but to deaconesses, as several translations note (NIV, NEB). In any event, it is clear that women participated in the work of the diaconate.

In contrast to the office of bishop (1 Tm 3:2), deacons are not described as providing teaching or hospitality. In fact, no mention is made of any functional qualifications to clarify deacons' or deaconesses' roles in the early church. The character qualifications listed are appropriate for those with monetary and administrative responsibilities (as Acts 6:1-6 suggests). Timothy is told that good deacons will not go unrewarded; not only will their faith increase, but also their good standing among those whom they serve (1 Tm 3:13).

The NT writings indicate that to be chosen as a deacon or deaconess is a high compliment and affirmation. Named as "deacons" were Timothy (1 Thes 3:2; 1 Tm 4:6), Tychicus (Col 4:7), Epaphras (1:7), Paul (1 Cor 3:5)—and even Christ (Rom 15:8, "servant"). Biblical "deaconing" is not characterized by power and prominence but by service to others. In imitation of Jesus' life, the deacon or deaconess followed the servant pattern. The Christian diaconate thus contrasted sharply with the prevailing Greek thought of service, which was considered unworthy of the dignity of free men. (The Greek philosopher Plato wrote, "How can man be happy when he has to serve someone?")

The office of deacon differed from the office of elder, which was adapted from a definite Jewish pattern in the OT (see Nm 11:16-17; Dt 29:10). The diaconate, on the other hand, developed from the strong, personal, historical example of Jesus, the servant who compassionately met concrete human needs.

As the office of deacon became more firmly established, its duties could be defined as those of pastoral care. The poor and the sick received their service not only physically but also with instruction and consolation. The homes of church members became familiar territory to a deacon or deaconess. A pattern of visitation was established to discover and then meet the needs of the church body at large. Although that included the administration of funds, it went far beyond it. Those who served as deacons and deaconesses undoubtedly became symbols of loving care for the church in general.

Where the office of deacon fits into the larger pattern of church order within the NT is difficult to determine because of the obvious variety present during the formative years. Some church historians conclude that as ecclesiastical structure developed, elders provided congregational leadership. Deacons assisted them, especially in social services and pastoral care. The late first and early second centuries witnessed a distinctive threefold ministry of deacons, elders (presbyters), and bishops. Bishops or "overseers" began to exercise authority over areas or groups of churches.

Deaconess Where did women fit into the ministry of the early church? Paul's inclusion of references to women in ministry is striking when compared with the role of women in general in the first century. He commended Phoebe for her service in the church at Cenchrea, using the word "deacon" to describe her (Rom 16:1). He praised her as a "helper" (v 2), a word that denotes leadership qualities (cf. Rom 12:8; 1 Tm 3:4-5). Some scholars have used that reference as an example of early development of the office of deaconess. Others have interpreted it in a nontechnical sense, meaning that Phoebe functioned in a generally serving role and thus was worthy of recognition at Rome. Whether "deacon" was used technically or descriptively, ministry for both women and men in the NT was patterned after the example of Jesus, who "came not to be served but to serve" (Mk 10:45). Because of the large number of female converts (Acts 5:14; 17:4), women functioned in such areas of ministry as visitation, instruction in discipleship, and assistance in baptism. Deaconesses are mentioned in third-century documents as administering baptism to female converts.

Considering the rigid separation of the sexes in the Near East at that time, female participation in church ministry stands out in bold relief. A governor of Bithynia, Pliny the Younger (early second century), in his *Correspondence with Trajan* verified women officeholders in the church. Pliny also mentioned two deaconesses who were martyred for the cause of Christ.

See also Bishop; Elder; Pastor; Presbyter.

DEAD, Place of the Term covering a number of descriptive biblical images of the whereabouts of those who have died. Those images include Sheol and "the pit" in the OT, plus hades, Gehenna, paradise, and "Abra-

ham's bosom" in the NT. As their understanding advanced, the Hebrews' idea of what happens at death changed from rather hazy beginnings to a developed concept found in the NT.

In the Old Testament The OT contains meager information about the dead. At death, according to some OT passages, one descends to Sheol (often translated as "grave," "hell," "pit," or simply "the dead"), which at times means merely that one is laid in a grave (Nm 16:30, 33), but more often indicates an underworld. The abode of the dead is pictured as a place beneath the earth to which one "goes down" (Gn 42:38; Prv 15:24; Ez 26:20) and as a place of gloomy darkness (Jb 10:21-22), silence (Pss 94:17; 115:17), and forgetfulness (Ps 88:12). God is not remembered there and his praises are never sung (Pss 6:5; 30:9; 115:17). Even God himself, it was believed, does not remember those who are there (Ps 88:5, 11; Is 38:18). The dead were seen as permanently cut off from contact with the Lord and from participating in his activity in history. Even though the border between life and death was considered fluid (as shown by a resurrection in 2 Kgs 4:32-37 and by Samuel's ghost in 1 Sm 28:7-25), communication with the dead was forbidden to the Jews (Dt 18:11). (Worshiping the dead was a common practice in the nations surrounding Israel.)

Although one's fate in the underworld could not properly be called life, it was a kind of existence, perhaps even in the company of one's countrymen and ancestors (Gn 25:8; Ez 32:17-30). The realm of the dead was not beyond the reach of God's power (Ps 139:8; Am 9:2; Jon 2:2). Although Sheol was pictured as a hungry monster wolfing down the living (Prv 27:20; 30:16), God's power could save one from its grasp (Pss 49:15; 86:13). By the end of the OT period, there was even hope that one would finally be delivered from Sheol (Jb 14:13-22; 19:25-27; Pss 49:15; 73:23-28), although only Daniel expressed that hope clearly (Dn 12:1-2). So although the ancient Hebrews never looked forward to death in the same way that the apostle Paul could in the NT (2 Cor 5:1-8; Phil 1:21-23), nevertheless they did come to understand that death was not a hopeless state.

In the Intertestamental Writings Between the exile and the beginning of the NT period (586 BC–AD 30, overlapping with the end of the OT), contact with the religions of Persia and Greece stimulated the Jews to clarify their ideas about life after death. When the OT was translated into Greek, the Greek name for the underworld, "hades," was used to translate the Hebrew "Sheol." In the NT, hades was carried over to become the common name for the abode of the dead.

Along with new names came new ideas. Many different notions circulated about the place of the dead. A common one appears in the pseudepigraphal 1 Enoch 22, where the dead are said to be kept in hollow places in a great mountain waiting for the final judgment. One relatively pleasant section was reserved for the righteous and one full of torments for the wicked. Other writers continued the OT concept of hades or Sheol as a place of separation from God and from happiness (Ecclus 14:12, 16; 17:27-28).

During that period, the Jews also began to use a new term, "Gehenna" (Hebrew "Hinnom"), the name of a valley south of Jerusalem. The valley was noted in the OT period for the abomination of child sacrifices (2 Kgs 16:3; 21:6; 23:10) and in the NT period for its smoldering garbage. Gehenna became a designation for the final place of the wicked dead, a place of fiery torment (1 Enoch 90:20-27; 2 Esd 7:70). Over against that place of punishment stood "paradise" (a Persian name for a pleasure garden), a place where the righteous would enjoy blessedness.

All those concepts—hades, Gehenna, paradise—were molded by NT writers into forms most appropriate to the revelation of Christ.

In the New Testament Although the NT uses a variety of terms for the abode of the dead, it contains surprisingly few references to it—about 35 verses in all. Those passages are concentrated in the Gospels and the book of Revelation. The apostle Paul said a lot about heaven, but only Jesus and John said much about hell.

The word "hades" is attributed to Jesus only once, in the parable of the rich man and Lazarus (Lk 16:23). In that parable hades is a place of torment where the wicked go at death. The torment is described as a "flame" that afflicts a person physically despite bodily death. All comfort is refused to those in agony.

Although the wicked go to hades as soon as they die, their ultimate destination is Gehenna, a place of fire and worms, both indicating corruption (Mt 5:22, 29-30; 18:9; Mk 9:48, quoting from Is 66:24). Jesus also referred to Gehenna as "the outer darkness" where there will be "weeping and gnashing of teeth" (Mt 8:12; 22:13; 25:30). Evidently, after the final judgment, the wicked are sent there at the command of Christ (Jn 5:22, 27; Acts 10:42; 17:31; 2 Tm 4:1). That place of torment picks up the negative side of the OT concept of Sheol as a place of separation from God.

As a preacher of repentance, Jesus stressed the danger of Gehenna. He had much less to say about the place of the righteous when they die. Ultimately, though, the righteous would enter into "the kingdom," instead of Gehenna, after the last judgment (Mt 25:34). Jesus twice indicated that the righteous enter a blessed state immediately at death. Luke 16:22 refers to the dead Lazarus as being in "Abraham's bosom," a place of comfort and peace. Luke 23:43 calls the same place paradise in a promise that the dying thief would join Jesus there at death. Paul's wording about paradise seems to align it with heaven (2 Cor 12:2-3), and John associates paradise with the new heaven and new earth (Rv 2:7; 21:1-2; 22:1-2).

Paul and other writers of the NT epistles had little to say about the abode of the wicked dead. Paul spoke only in passing of "the abyss"—his term for the pit of Sheol (Rom 10:7). His reference to Christ's descent to the "lower parts of the earth" (Eph 4:9) is probably only his way of saying that Christ, having died, went to the place of the dead. ("The lowest earth" was a term used by Jewish rabbis for Sheol/hades/Gehenna.) Peter spoke of Christ's going in "spirit" after his death to some "prison" where he "preached to the spirits" (1 Pt 3:18-20). Interpretations of that passage differ. Some think that Christ entered hades and preached to the fallen angels of Noah's day ("sons of God," Gn 6:1-4), not that he preached to imprisoned human spirits. In 2 Peter 2:4 the prison for spirits (usually translated "hell") comes from "Tartarus," another Greek name for the underworld.

Paul had much to say about the abode of the righteous dead. In his earliest letters he never mentioned their location, only that they would be resurrected (1 Cor 15; 1 Thes 4:13-17). After facing almost certain death himself (2 Cor 1:8-11), he began to discuss where the dead "went." To die means to be with Christ, Paul said, and thus is better than life (Phil 1:23). To be "away from the body" is to be "at home with the Lord" (2 Cor 5:8). Paul probably meant that the righteous dead went directly to paradise to be with Jesus (cf. 2 Cor 12:2-4, where Paul called paradise "the third heaven"). Death has absolutely no power to separate Christians from Christ (Rom 8:38-39). Instead, it brings them into the presence of God.

The book of Revelation contains much about the abode of the dead, especially the wicked dead. It uses two names for that place: "the abyss," the home or prison of all evil spirits; and "hades," the name for the place of the human dead. From the abyss (or bottomless pit) come the demonic forms that torment humanity (Rv 9:1-11) and the satanic "beast," who kills the two witnesses and carries the "great prostitute" on its back (11:7; 17). There Satan himself will be imprisoned (20:2-3). Jesus described it as a place prepared for the devil and his angels (cf. Mt 25:41). The good news for Christians is that the abyss, or hades, is not an autonomous realm. The book of Revelation begins with Jesus' announcement that he has the keys to hades (Rv 1:18), and in the end he will force it to give up its dead (20:13). Until then, the key to the abyss is not in the hand of Satan, but hangs on a heavenly key ring to be distributed only to the messengers of God (9:1; 20:1). In the end, hades, death, and the wicked will be cast into the lake of fire (Gehenna), where they will suffer eternal torment (19:20; 20:10, 14-15; 21:8).

John, the writer of the Revelation, agreed with Paul that the righteous will not share the fate of the wicked at death. Instead of going to hades, they go to heaven. The martyrs appear under the altar, calling to God to avenge them (Rv 6:9-11). In another image innumerable Christians appear before the throne of God, praising him (7:9-17). Those believers, shepherded by Christ himself, suffer no hunger, thirst, discomfort, or sorrow.

Conclusion In summary, the place of the dead began in the OT as an undifferentiated, hazy idea of a place of separation from life and God. Later writers came to see that instead of one place for all (Sheol), there must be two. According to Christian teaching, the wicked enter the underworld, hades, a place of torment, where they suffer until the time of judgment; ultimately they will be cast into Gehenna, the lake of fire. Christ—not the devil—is in control of hades, as he is of the rest of creation. The righteous do not go to hades, but go directly to paradise ("Abraham's bosom" or heaven). There they are with Christ; faith has become sight, suffering has become blessedness, and prayer has become praise. Christians believe that death, although fearful as the "last enemy," has no torment for them. It has no power to separate them from their Lord. Rather, it brings them face-to-face with the One they love.

This meeting may occur as soon as one dies or as soon as one is resurrected—the intervening time is of no consequence, because it is nothing more than just a time of sleep. In other words, the very next experience after death for the believer will be that of meeting Christ.

Both Old and New Testaments speak of death as sleep. Commonly in the OT, when a person dies, he is said to go to sleep with his fathers (e.g., Dt 31:16; 2 Sm 7:12). Jesus himself spoke of death as sleep (Mt 9:24; Jn 11:11). So did the apostle Paul (1 Cor 11:30; 15:20, 51; 1 Thes 4:14). At least in some of these references it would seem that it is the temporary nature of death that is the reason why it is spoken of as sleep. Even in the OT passage Daniel 12:2, it is said that death is a sleep, until the dead rise up—some to everlasting life and some to shame and everlasting contempt.

See also Gehenna; Hades; Heaven; Hell; Intermediate State; Paradise; Sheol.

DEAD SEA A large saltwater lake into which the river Jordan empties. Since the Greek era, Western civilization has referred to this mysterious body of water as the "Dead Sea." However, the frequent OT term for this sea is the "Salt Sea" (Gn 14:3; Nm 34:3, 12; Dt 3:17; Jos 3:16; 12:3; 15:2, 5; 18:19), the name deriving from that most important and valuable commodity traded in antiquity. It is also designated the Sea of the Arabah (Dt 3:17; 4:49; Jos 3:16; 12:3; 2 Kgs 14:25) and the Eastern Sea (Ez 47:18; Jl 2:20; Zec 14:8). Apocryphal, classical, and Talmudic authors make reference to the Sea of Sodom, Sea of Asphalt, and Sea of Lot. The NT makes no reference at all to the sea.

Aerial View of the Dead Sea

The sea lies in the great trough of the Jordan Valley, known also as the Rift Valley. This valley forms part of the longest and deepest crack in the earth's crust, extending from the Taurus Mountains in southern Turkey, through Syria, Lebanon, Palestine, the Gulf of Aqaba, the Red Sea, and East Africa to Mozambique (there called the Great African Rift Valley). The chasm measures between 2 to 15 miles (3.2 to 24.1 kilometers) wide, and in its deepest spot, along the shoreline of the Dead Sea, it plummets to about 1,300 feet (396 meters) below sea level, marking this as the lowest area on the earth not covered by water. The sea itself is oblong in shape, measuring approximately 53 miles (85 kilometers) from the mouth of the Jordan River in the north to the Sebhka region in the south, and some 10 miles (16 kilometers) in width, enclosed on both sides by steep, rocky cliffs. It is divided into two basins by the eight and a half mile (13.7 kilometer) Lisan Peninsula, which juts out from the eastern shore. The northern basin is larger, and at its deepest point (in the northeast sector), has a water depth

of about 1,300 feet (396 meters). The southern basin is flatter, and its water depth ranges between 3 and 30 feet (1 and 9 meters).

The forces of nature seem to have conspired against the Dead Sea. Fed by the Jordan River, four or five perennial streams, and numerous wadis (an average daily inflow totaling some 7 million tons, or 6.4 million metric tons), the sea possesses no outlet for this water except evaporation. This condition, coupled with aridity (with an average annual precipitation of from 2 to 5 inches, or 5 to 13 centimeters) and enormous heat (with the mercury sometimes soaring as high as 125 degrees Fahrenheit, or 52 degrees Celsius, in the summer), quite often creates an extremely high rate of evaporation and dense haze virtually impenetrable to human eyesight. Most of the streams that feed the Dead Sea are unusually saline, flowing through nitrous soil and sulphurous springs. At the same time, springs under the waters of the sea pump chemicals (especially bromine, magnesium, and calcium) into the sea. And along its shores are extensive sulphur deposits and petroleum springs. In the southeast corner there is a 300-foot-thick (91.4-meter-thick) rock-salt ridge, which is only the tip of an estimated 4,500-foot (1,371-meter) salt plug stretching some 5 miles (8 kilometers). Finally, the bed of the sea contains salt crystals. All these factors combine to produce a total salinity of approximately 26 percent, compared to the average ocean salinity of 3.5 percent. This makes the Dead Sea the earth's most saline water body, completely devoid of marine life, with an ever-increasing solidity.

In ancient times the Dead Sea was valued for its salt and bitumen (a commodity prized for waterproofing properties, consisting of petroleum hardened by evaporation and oxidation). During the NT era, the Dead Sea bitumen trade was apparently controlled by the Nabateans, who also exported the product to Egypt for use in embalming. It has been suggested that Cleopatra's desire to govern the Dead Sea region was stimulated by her desire to regulate the bitumen trade.

The ominous desolation and barrenness of the Dead Sea apparent to the gaze of the modern onlooker is also reflected in the pages of history. The events of Genesis 19, the destruction of Sodom and Gomorrah, transpired in this vicinity. Mt Sedom, the salt plug located at the southeast corner of the sea, obviously reflects the name Sodom. The archaeologist Nelson Glueck affirms that the region surrounding Sedom was occupied by as many as 70 towns dating back to about 3000 BC. The exact nature of the destruction rained upon Sodom and Gomorrah is variously interpreted either as a volcanic eruption or as the spontaneous explosion of subsurface pockets of bituminous soil. Karstic salt pillars, known as "Lot's wife," are a frequent phenomenon in this locality.

The howling wilderness that surrounds the sea provided a suitable refuge for the fugitive David (1 Sm 23:29–24:1ff.), the contemplative company of Qumran Essenes, and the disenfranchised Jewish insurgents of the second Jewish rebellion. On the other hand, Ezekiel envisioned (Ez 47:1-12; cf. Zec 14:8) a time when even the briny waters of the Dead Sea would be recreated afresh and the stark, lifeless character of the sea would issue forth in life.

DEAD SEA SCROLLS* *See* Bible, Manuscripts and Text of the (Old Testament); Qumran.

DEAF, DEAFNESS Inability to hear; term used in Scripture to describe both a literal, physical inability and a figurative, spiritual defect. The spiritually deaf were those who either refused to hear the divine message or were rendered incapable because of their lack of spirituality (Ps 38:13). The prophet Isaiah forcefully addressed both types of deaf persons (the figurative in Is 42:18; 43:8; the literal in Is 29:18; 35:5). In the OT, although the condition was considered the result of God's judgment (Ex 4:11; Mi 7:16), it was wrong to curse a deaf person (Lv 19:14). In the NT the deaf were among those Jesus healed (Mt 11:5; Mk 7:32-37; Lk 7:22). An epileptic boy whom Jesus healed was afflicted with a "dumb and deaf spirit" (Mk 9:25, RSV). Such healings authenticated Jesus' role as Messiah.

See also Medicine and Medical Practice.

DEATH Cessation of life (physical death) or separation from God (spiritual death).

Old Testament View In the OT death was accepted as the natural end of life. The goal of an Israelite was to live a long and full life, produce many descendants, and die in peace with the children and grandchildren gathered about. The OT contains many protests against an early death (e.g., Hezekiah's, 2 Kgs 20:1-11). An early death might appear to be the result of God's judgment; hence, Job saw the need to vindicate his character prior to death (Jb 19:25-26). Only in Ecclesiastes 3:19-20 is outright pessimism expressed in the face of death—and that book probably shows considerable non-Hebraic influence.

Death, although a natural ending to life, was never viewed as pleasant. Death cut one off from human community as well as from the presence and service of God. God may offer comfort in the face of death (Ps 73:23-28), but he is rarely portrayed as present with the dead, and that only in later biblical literature (Ps 139:8). For that reason, death was never viewed as the threshold to a better life.

The relationship of sin to death is seen in the death penalty in the law of Moses. A serious offender was put to death. The punitive phrase "he shall be cut off" implied that although the nation went on living, the criminal was separated from it by death. The Israelites were warned that to disobey God's commandments could bring premature death as a consequence of breaking fellowship with God (Dt 30:15-20; Jer 21:8; Ez 18:21-32).

In the intertestamental period, as Jewish ideas of afterlife and resurrection developed more explicitly, so too did Jewish thinking about death. Death itself, not just a premature death, came to be seen as an evil result of sin (2 Esd 3:7; Ecclus 25:24). Sometimes all death is depicted as the result of the "first sin" (Adam and Eve's disobedience). In other references, everyone dies as a result of his or her own sin. The first clear indication in Scripture of a resurrection of the dead and a final judgment or punishment occurs in the book of Daniel (Dn 12:2), one of the last OT books to be written. That teaching is echoed throughout the intertestamental period (2 Esd 7:31-44). During that time, it was believed that the soul survived death either in some immortal form (Wisd of Sol 3:4; 4:1; 4 Macc 16:13; 17:12) or awaiting the resurrection (1 Enoch 102). Some of those extrabiblical writings incorporated Greek ideas that the body was a burden to be gotten rid of—a notion foreign to Hebrew thought.

The concept of resurrection and a life redeemed from death, however, set the stage for the NT revelation focusing on Christ's resurrection and his conquest of death.

New Testament View In the NT, death is seen more as a theological problem than as a personal event. Death goes beyond the simple ending of physical life, which the authors accept almost without difficulty. Death is seen as affecting every part of a person's life. God alone is immortal, the source of all life in the world (Rom 4:17; 1 Tm 6:16). Only as human beings are properly related to God's life can they live. But it has been unnatural for people to be in personal communion with the divine source of life since sin was introduced into the world (Rom 5:12, 17-18; 1 Cor 15:22). When Adam separated himself from God, that separation brought death. Each human being has followed in Adam's footsteps (Rom 3:23; 5:12), bringing death for everyone as the absolutely necessary result (Rom 6:23; Heb 9:27). Death, then, is not merely something that happens to people at the end of their lives; it is also the living out of their lives apart from fellowship with God.

The extent of death's domination is vast. It affects every aspect of culture. All of human life is lived under the shadow of the fear of death (Rom 8:15; Heb 2:15). Death reigns over all that is "of the flesh" (Rom 8:6). Anyone not living in relationship to Christ lives in a state of death (Jn 3:16-18; 1 Jn 5:12). The devil, who rules the world, is the lord of death (Heb 2:14). Death is sometimes personified as a demonic power at large in the world but finally brought to bay by Christ himself, the only one who could master it (1 Cor 15:26-27; Rv 6:8; 20:13-14).

Christ died, was buried, and rose again on the third day (Rom 4:25; 1 Cor 15:3-4; 1 Thes 4:14). Through that historic event, the power of death was broken. The NT in various ways expresses Christ's subjection to death in payment for sin. He became obedient to death (Phil 2:8); he died as a sacrifice for the sins of all (1 Cor 5:7; 2 Cor 5:15); and he descended into hades, the place of the dead (1 Pt 3:18-19). The major point of all such passages is that he did not remain dead but defeated the devil, took the power (keys) of death, and ascended in victory (Heb 2:14-15; Rv 1:17-18). Jesus Christ worked not for his own benefit but for those who commit themselves to him (Mk 10:45; Rom 5:6-8; 1 Thes 5:9-10). By accepting a death he did not deserve, Christ has broken the power of death for his followers.

The Christian is thus delivered from "this body of death" (Rom 7:24) by the power of Christ. Salvation comes through being baptized into Christ's death (6:3-4), and "dying with Christ" to the world and the law (Rom 7:6; Gal 6:14; Col 2:20). That is, the death of Christ is counted by God as the believer's death. The rebellious world's sin (Rom 6:6) and self-idolatry (living for oneself, 2 Cor 5:14-15) become things of the past. The death of Jesus for his people is the means by which his life is given to them (4:10). The result is that believers are separated from the world just as they were once separated from God. From the world's point of view, they are dead; Christ is their only life (Col 3:3).

The apostle John expressed it somewhat differently. Jesus came into the world to give life to the dead (Jn 5:24). That life-giving will not happen at the resurrection; it is already happening. All who commit themselves to Jesus pass immediately from death to life. Or, to put it another way, those who keep (obey) his words will never see death (8:51-52). The point is that all who are outside Christ are already dead, and those trusting in Christ are already enjoying life. The radical difference between the Christian and the non-Christian is a difference between life and death.

Naturally, the NT writers knew that Christians die; their problem was to find words to explain the difference from non-Christian death. Believers who die physically are said to be "dead in Christ" (1 Thes 4:16). Or they are not dead at all, but merely "asleep" (1 Cor 15:6, 18, 20, 51; 1 Thes 4:13-15; cf. Jesus' words, Jn 11:11-14). Although their bodies are dead, deceased believers are not separated from Christ; that is, they are not really dead. All the powers of death and hell cannot separate believers from Christ (Rom 8:38-39). For them, death is not a loss but a gain; it brings them closer to Christ (2 Cor 5:1-10; Phil 1:20-21). What is more, believers will share in Christ's victory over physical death as well. Because he is the "firstfruits" of those rising from the dead (1 Cor 15:20; Col 1:18), those "in Christ" will rise "on the last day" to be with him, whole and complete.

On the other hand, for those who do not belong to Christ, there is a final, total separation from God. At the last judgment, all whose names are not "written in the Book of Life" are consigned to a lake of fire, in the company of death itself and hades. That final separation from God is the "second death" (Rv 20:14). Christians, however, have been saved from death (Jas 5:20; 1 Jn 3:14). The second death has no power over those who are faithful to Christ (Rv 2:11; 20:6). Instead, they will live with God, in whose presence there can be no death, for he is life itself (21:4).

See also Dead, Place of the; Intermediate State; Wrath of God.

DEATH, The Second Term used in the NT only in the book of Revelation, to describe God's eternal judgment on sin. Originally a rabbinic expression, the second death will be experienced by those whose names are not written in the "Book of Life" (Rv 20:15). The second death is equated with the "lake of fire" (v 14), or the lake that burns with "fire and brimstone" (21:8, KJV), and is described as the lot of "the cowardly, the faithless, the polluted, . . . murderers, fornicators, sorcerers, idolaters, and all liars" (RSV). Those who are victorious in this life have nothing to fear from the second death (2:11).

See also Death; Eschatology; Fall of Man; Last Judgment.

DEATH OF CHRIST *See* Crucifixion; Jesus Christ, Life and Teachings of.

DEBIR (Person) One of the kings of Eglon who became an ally of Adoni-zedek, the king of Jerusalem. Debir was executed by Joshua (Jos 10:22-27).

DEBIR (Place)
1. Canaanite city originally held by the Anakim before being conquered by the Israelites (Jos 11:21; 15:15). There are two accounts of the conquest of Debir (10:38-39; 15:13-17). One of these lists Joshua as the conqueror, and the other lists Othniel as the conqueror (by request of Caleb). It is possible that the Othniel account is simply a further elaboration of the Joshua account, or it is possible that Debir was retaken by the Canaanites and the Othniel-Caleb account tells of the subsequent recapture by the Israelites. The latter explanation, however, does not seem to accord well with the apparent finality of the Joshua account. Thus, it would seem that the former explanation is more probable.

Debir, with its pasturelands, was finally given to the priestly descendants of the Aaronites (Jos 21:15; 1 Chr 6:58). This might seem fitting, since prior to its capture by the Israelites, Debir was known for its pagan temple. Debir was also known as Kiriath-sannah, meaning "city of the scribes" (Jos 15:49), and Kiriath-sepher, meaning "city of the books" (v 15). Its exact location is disputed among scholars, but most likely it was located near Khirbet Rabud in the southern Judean hill country.

2. Gadite town east of the Jordan River near the Sea of Galilee (Jos 13:26). It is possibly the same site as Lo-debar (2 Sm 9:4-5; 17:27; Am 6:13), where Mephibosheth once lived before David summoned him.
3. Town on the northern border of Judah some 10 miles (16 kilometers) northeast of Jerusalem (Jos 15:7).

DEBORAH Name of two OT women. The word in Hebrew means "honeybee" (Ps 118:12; Is 7:18).

1. Rebekah's nurse (Gn 35:8). Deborah died as she was traveling to Bethel with her master Jacob's household. She was buried in a spot remembered as Allon-bacuth ("the oak of weeping"), indicating that she had been well loved. She was probably Rebekah's longtime companion (see 24:59-61).
2. Prophetess and judge (Jgs 4–5). Deborah's position as a prophetess, indicating that her message was from God, is not unique in the Bible, but it was unusual. Other prophetesses included Miriam (Ex 15:20), Huldah (2 Kgs 22:14), and Anna (Lk 2:36). Deborah was unique in that only she is said to have "judged Israel" *before* the major event that marks her narrative (Jgs 4:4). Her husband, Lappidoth, is otherwise unknown.

Deborah, heralded as a "mother in Israel" (Jgs 5:7), remained in one location and the people came to her for guidance. Evidently over 200 years later, when the book of Judges was compiled, a giant palm tree still marked the spot. Though residing within the boundary of Benjamin (Jgs 4:5; cf. Jos 16:2; 18:13), Deborah was probably from the tribe of Ephraim, the most prominent tribe of northern Israel. Some scholars, however, place her in the tribe of Issachar (Jgs 5:14-15). At that early time, the tribes were loosely organized and did not always occupy the territory they had been allotted.

Under Deborah's inspired leadership, the poorly equipped Israelites defeated the Canaanites in the plain of Esdraelon (Jgs 4:15); flooding of the Kishon River evidently interfered with the enemy's impressive chariotry (5:21-22). The Canaanites retreated to the north, perhaps to Taanach near Megiddo (v 19), and never reappeared as an enemy within Israel. The Song of Deborah (ch 5) is a poetic version of the prose narrative in Judges 4.

See also Barak; Deborah, Song of; Judges, Book of.

DEBORAH, Song of Ancient poem found in Judges 5, celebrating an Israelite victory over the Canaanites. Similar to Moses' song (Ex 15:1-18), and paralleling a prose account in Judges 4, the Song of Deborah describes the miraculous defeat of a powerful Canaanite king, Jabin of Hazor, and of Sisera, his general. The song's poetic style and occasional use of archaic Hebrew forms are reflected in slightly differing translations in modern versions of the Bible. The poem's vigorous language suggests that it was composed by an eyewitness of the battle, probably Deborah herself.

Judges 5:2 addresses Israel with an exhortation to praise the Lord. A second exclamation exhorts foreign kings to learn of Israel's God and his exploits. It is not clear whether verses 4-5 describe the present battle or refer to God's previous appearance to Moses at Mt Sinai. Verse 5 could be translated, "The mountains quaked at the presence of the One of Sinai."

Deborah is first introduced in verse 7. Verse 8 could mean either that Canaanite oppression prevented open displays of Israelite weaponry or, more likely, that the

Canaanites had wiped out all weapon-making industry in Israel (cf. 1 Sm 13:19). In an atmosphere of fear, indecision, and isolationism, Deborah, a judge, urged the Israelite tribes to battle. When Deborah appealed to the whole nation for help, some tribes were apathetic, but others gave assistance. The battle took place at Taanach, 15 miles (24.1 kilometers) southwest of Mt Tabor. The Canaanites had mobilized in that vicinity (Jgs 4:13), so the Israelites lost whatever advantage their mountain position would have afforded. Deborah's song, however, implies the Lord's intervention, perhaps through a severe storm. Divine aid is also alluded to in Judges 4:14 ("for the LORD is marching ahead of you," NLT). The stars that fought Sisera and the flooding of the river Kishon represent the forces of nature helping Israel (5:20-21). In addition, any advantage of the Canaanites' chariotry was nullified after Jael, a heroic Hebrew woman, killed Sisera, the chariot leader (vv 24-27). Sisera's death fulfilled Deborah's prophecy to the Israelite commander, Barak, that a woman, not he, would receive glory for that feat (4:9).

Sisera's mother is seen pathetically awaiting his return. In contrast to the sardonic portrayal of that Canaanite woman, the last words of Deborah's song are a fervent prayer for future safety. Although Jael was blessed (Jgs 5:24) and Deborah acclaimed, the God of Israel (vv 1-3) received the glory.

DEBT Something owed to another person, such as goods, property, or money. In the Bible, righteous conduct is something one "owes" to God; hence, in theology, sin is described figuratively as being "in debt."

In Hebrew culture, debt was usually connected with usury (the business of lending money on interest). The Hebrew verbs describing usury picture a painful situation. One word for usury means "to bite," a vivid image for the way high interest "ate up" any kind of business transaction so that borrowers never received the full value of the money. People could be ruined financially by heartless exaction of interest (2 Kgs 4:1-7). Another verb is usually translated as "increase" or "profit" (Lv 25:37), since lenders profited from others' labor. Ancient Near Eastern interest rates on produce and goods might be as much as 30 percent of the loan per year; on money, as much as 20 percent. Clay tablets from Nuzi, an ancient town in northeastern Mesopotamia, indicate interest rates of even 50 percent.

The Law of Moses The Mosaic covenant given to Israel immediately after the exodus sought to eliminate extortionist practices from Hebrew life. Thus God's revelation had many rules and restrictions relating to debt and credit in Israel.

Protection for the Poor Portions of the legislative sections of the Pentateuch (the first five books of the Bible) regulated the practice of lending in a way that protected the poor and secured each person's right to earn a living and support a family. Many popular Hebrew proverbs dealt with that theme. The positive thrust of the biblical laws was to ensure help for the financially needy, without interest. No personal profit was to be made at the expense of the poor (Ex 22:25; Dt 23:19-20); God was their special advocate. Thus, by lending without interest, the Israelites could demonstrate their reverence for God (Lv 25:35-37).

That point was reemphasized 40 years later when Moses renewed the covenant with Israel just before their entrance into the Promised Land. God was the landlord, and his tenants were to respect his word. God promised the Israelites that if they would lend so as to alleviate

human misery, they would be unusually blessed by the Lord (Dt 15:6; 23:19-20; 28:12). Interest could be charged to a foreigner not living under the Mosaic law, which was a condition parallel to commercial treaties prevalent in the ancient Near East.

In ancient Israel, financial ruin was frequently brought about by poor harvests. Often they were taken as an indication that the relationship between God and his people was not right (Lv 26:14, 20). The wealthy were expected to help, not to add more burdens to those who suffered from poor harvests.

Violation of the Law The law was so often violated that eventually exorbitant interest became a social plague, making the situation of debtors hopeless. Many of the fighting men who rallied around David early in his military career were "outlaws" unable to repay their loans and interest (1 Sm 22:2). The prophet Ezekiel called people to task for their failure to observe God's commands about usury (Ez 18:5-18; 22:12). When Nehemiah returned from the exile to rebuild the walls of Jerusalem, he brought charges against the government officials whose interest rates had enslaved the people (Neh 5:6-13).

The Wisdom Literature, which included Job, Proverbs, and Ecclesiastes, added that those who acquired riches by usury would not profit in the long run, because God would give their profits to others who looked after the welfare of the poor (e.g., Prv 28:8). The prophet Amos gave a similar warning to corrupt merchants in Israel: "Because you trample upon the poor and take from him exactions of wheat, . . . you have planted pleasant vineyards, but you shall not drink their wine" (Am 5:11, RSV). In spite of such warnings, the law was often ignored, and burdensome interest charges were laid on borrowers who were already poor.

Pledges and Surety When it was necessary to borrow, the law provided alternatives to the unfair practice of usury. When taking out a loan, a borrower would surrender some movable property as collateral to ensure repayment. That "pledge" represented a tangible sign of the debtor's intention to repay the loan. Certain restrictions applied to such pledges. For example, a creditor could not take a widow's clothes (Dt 24:17). Tools (such as millstones) or animals (such as oxen) necessary for daily life were forbidden as pledges (v 6). Clothing absolutely essential to the borrower (e.g., to keep warm) could be temporarily offered as a pledge, but the temporary token had to be returned before nightfall (Ex 22:26-27; Dt 24:10-13).

In drastic circumstances, where there was no collateral, a debtor could pledge a son, daughter, or slave. The value of the child's or slave's labor could then be credited against both interest and principal. An account in the Bible of a widow's two sons about to go into slavery shows how cruel the custom could be (2 Kgs 4:1-7). Pledging labor or their children's labor was the only way slaves could pay off a debt when they had to borrow.

A borrower could also have a wealthy friend assume responsibility as a cosigner on a loan and thus become the pledge, or surety. The book of Proverbs cautioned against standing surety for others, however, especially for strangers (Prv 6:1-3; 11:15; 17:18; 22:26; 27:13).

Sabbatical and Jubilee Years Two legal provisions to curb the enslavement of people by long-standing debts were the sabbatical year and the jubilee year. The sabbatical year, or "year of release," took place every seventh year. At that time debts were canceled and slates wiped clean (Dt 15:1-12; cf. Ex 21:2; 23:10-11; Lv 25:2-7). The law clearly forbade lenders to withhold loans to those in desperate need during a sixth year. Jewish tradition held strict injunctions against a lender trying to collect on a loan that should have been forgiven in the sabbatical year.

Every 50 years Israel had its Year of Jubilee. In that year land reverted to its original owner if it had not already been redeemed by some relative. That provision prevented the buildup of landed estates by the wealthy few while the many poor suffered in slavery (Lv 25:13-17). Although the Mosaic law could not guarantee economic utopia, it sought to curb the greediness in human nature. It also aimed at providing everyone with an equal opportunity and a fresh start every 50 years.

Debt in the New Testament The NT shows how various cultures handled the matter of loans and debts. There were Jewish people who adhered strictly to the Mosaic law and refused to charge their fellow Jews high interest. Hellenistic and Roman legal practices, however, penetrated parts of Jewish society.

Jesus' Parables Jesus alluded to non-Jewish economic practices in his parable of a servant who jailed a fellow slave for not repaying a loan (Mt 18:23-35). The parable illustrates the ordinary Hellenistic and Roman custom of jailing or restraining such a person as surety. That practice forced a debtor to sell his property, to ask family and friends to cover the loss, or to sell himself into slavery. The parable of the talents (25:14-28) and the parable of the pounds (Lk 19:12-24), speaking allegorically about the kingdom of God, mention earning interest on money invested with bankers.

Economic and Theological Instruction The apostle Paul instructed Christians to "owe nothing to anyone" (Rom 13:8), which means at the very least that Christians should make good on loans promptly. On the other hand, a Christian's economic activity should be characterized by kindness toward those in need, generosity, and willingness to help (Mt 5:42; Lk 6:35).

The NT also presents a number of lessons in doctrine based on a figurative use of "debts" and "debtors." Jesus once referred to sinners (Lk 13:2) with a word literally meaning "debtors" (v 4). In the Lord's Prayer "debts" is paralleled with "sins" (Mt 6:12; Lk 11:4).

Sin is seen as an enslavement (Jn 8:34), and all men and women as debtors to God. Redemption can be made only by God, who "gave his only Son" to set people free (3:16-18). The writer to the Hebrews showed that Jesus was made the surety of the new covenant (Heb 7:22).

The apostle Paul felt indebted to all people because of his own salvation, a debt he could pay by preaching the gospel (Rom 1:14-15). The NT teaches that all who receive the gospel are likewise in debt and therefore should devote themselves to serving others as a way of serving God (cf. 15:26-27).

See also Banker, Banking; Money.

DECALOGUE* Greek term meaning "ten words," referring to the Ten Commandments. *See* Commandments, The Ten.

DECAPOLIS* Group of city-states where Greeks settled following Alexander the Great's conquest of the area in the fourth century BC. They were located to the southeast of the Sea of Galilee, with the exception of Scythopolis, which was west of the Jordan River. About AD 77 Pliny gave what is the earliest known list of the cities: Canatha, Damascus, Dion, Gadara, Gerasa, Hippos, Pella, Philadelphia, Raphana, and Scythopolis.

With the rise of Jewish nationalism in the second century BC, the Jewish king Alexander Janneus seized control of a few of these cities; they remained in the hands of Israel until they were recaptured by the Roman general Pompey in 63 BC. During the lifetime of Jesus, the cities of the Decapolis, which had become moderately prosperous trade centers, were consolidated into a Roman alliance against a possible Jewish uprising.

The Decapolis is mentioned three times in the NT. The first is in Matthew 4:25, where great crowds (mostly Greeks and Canaanites) followed Jesus during his early ministry. As we see in Mark 5:20 the demoniac who was healed by Jesus went and proclaimed Jesus throughout the Decapolis region. Finally, Mark 7:31 says Jesus passed through the Decapolis region on his way from Tyre and Sidon to the Sea of Galilee.

DECISION, Valley of Place mentioned in Joel 3:14, where the Lord will judge the heathen nations gathered against Judah. It is the same as the valley of Jehoshaphat (see Jl 3:2). *See* Jehoshaphat, Valley of.

DECREES OF GOD *See* Foreordination.

DEDAN (Person)
1. Grandson of Cush in the list of Noah's descendants. His father was Raamah, and his brother's name was Sheba (Gn 10:7; 1 Chr 1:9).
2. Grandson of Abraham through Keturah (Gn 25:3). His father was Jokshan, his brother was Sheba, and his descendants were the Asshurim, Letushim, and Leummim.

DEDAN (Place) Region located in the Arabian Peninsula. The Dedanites were listed among those who rejoiced at the downfall of Israel during the time of the Babylonian captivity. Jeremiah and Ezekiel foretold Dedan's approaching destruction (Jer 25:23; 49:8; Ez 25:13; 38:13). Apparently the Dedanites were merchants who traveled by caravan and traded saddlecloths and various garments associated with riding (Is 21:13; Ez 27:20). Dedan is believed to have been located at or near an oasis called El-'ula in the central portion of the Arabian Peninsula. This oasis was part of the ancient trade routes, and undoubtedly played a role in the Dedanites' mercantile way of life.

DEDICATION*, Feast of Designation by the apostle John for the Feast of Lights, or Hanukkah (Jn 10:22). The feast lasts eight days and begins on the 25th day of Kislev (November to December). *See* Feasts and Festivals of Israel.

DEER Hoofed, cud-chewing mammal, considered clean by the law. *See* Animals.

DEFILE To make ethically or ritually unclean. *See* Cleanness and Uncleanness, Regulations Concerning.

DEFORMITY Any obvious physical abnormality. In the OT sacrificial system both the animal to be sacrificed (Lv 1:3; 4:3) and the priest who performed the sacrifice (ch 21) had to be perfect physical specimens, without defect or blemish. By being perfect, they are both OT types of Christ.

Of the 11 defects that would exclude a man from becoming a priest (Lv 21:17-20), seven are in the musculoskeletal system, two are in the eye, one is of the skin, and one is in the reproductive system. The deformity of the "flat nose" (KJV) or "disfigurement" (NIV) in Leviticus 21:18 does not refer to a normal variant, but to a severely diseased nose. There are a large number of genetic syndromes and inherited diseases that feature very deformed noses. Likewise, the acquired infectious diseases of syphilis, tuberculosis, and leprosy can cause destruction of the bone and cartilage support of the nose. With the support gone, the skin of the nose sinks inward. This is referred to today as a "saddle-shaped" deformity of the nose.

Both the OT and the NT describe an instance where a man has a "withered" (KJV) or "shriveled" (NIV) arm or hand. Such a defect occurs when the nerves supplying an extremity are damaged and the muscles atrophy. An injury from a sword striking an arm can cause this (Zec 11:17). From the NT we learn that Jesus had the power to instantly heal a man with a chronically paralyzed hand (Mt 12:10; Mk 3:1; Lk 6:6).

See also Disease; Medicine and Medical Practice.

DEGREES*, Song of
Superscription of Psalms 120–134 (KJV). *See* Song of Ascents, Song of Degrees.

DEHAVITES*
Group of people among those colonized in Samaria by the Assyrian king Ashurbanipal (Ezr 4:9). The Dehavites, whom some scholars associate with the Daoi (a Persian tribe originating near the Caspian Sea), wrote to Artaxerxes to protest the rebuilding of Jerusalem by the returning Jewish exiles. Some interpreters suggest that the word translated "Dehavites" could mean "that is," so that the phrase would read "the men of Susa, that is, the Elamites" (RSV).

DEKAR*
KJV spelling of Deker, one of King Solomon's officials, in 1 Kings 4:9. *See* Ben-deker.

DELAIAH
1. Son of Elioenai who traced his line of descent through Zerubbabel to David (1 Chr 3:24, KJV "Dalaiah").
2. Priest in the time of David (1 Chr 24:18).
3. Head of a postexilic family that returned with Zerubbabel to Judea. The group was unable to prove true Israelite descent (Ezr 2:60; Neh 7:62).
4. Father of a fifth-century BC man named Shemaiah. Shemaiah opposed Nehemiah (Neh 6:10).
5. Counselor in the reign of Jehoiakim (609–598 BC) who urged the king not to destroy Jeremiah's scroll, which Baruch had just read (Jer 36:12, 25).

DELILAH
Samson's mistress, who betrayed him to his Philistine enemies (Jgs 16). Because Philistia held southern Israel in vassalage at the time (c. 1070 BC), Samson was chosen by God to begin the delivery of Israel. His success prompted the five Philistine rulers to offer Delilah a bribe if she would help capture him by discovering the secret of his enormous strength.

REMBRANDT'S SAMSON AND DELILAH
Probably no painting more brutally depicts the theme of betrayal than that of the 17th-century Dutch artist Rembrandt. Delilah is hurrying out of her room, scissors and her lover's streaming hair in hand, while Samson's captors gouge out his eyes. The Bible makes no further mention of Delilah after the betrayal.

Delilah was from the valley of Sorek, in the southeast corner of Dan's territory, only a few miles from Samson's home in Zorah. It is clear from Judges 14:1 that she was a Philistine, although the large reward she accepted (5,500 pieces of silver) implies that her motivations were other than Philistine loyalty. Her unhindered contact with men probably indicates that she was a prostitute.

On her fourth attempt Delilah finally tricked Samson into revealing his secret. His strength was from God; his long hair, which signified that he was under a Nazirite vow (see Nm 6:1-8) and thus "set apart" by God for special service (Jgs 13:5), was never to be cut. Delilah lulled him to sleep, shaved his head, and delivered him (still unsuspecting) into the hands of his enemies.

See also Samson.

DELIVERANCE, DELIVERER
Rescue or redemption and the agent of such a rescue. Scripture teaches that God's ultimate goal in history is to rescue people from the curse of sin, death, Satan, and hell. The OT depicts God as delivering his chosen people from Egyptian slavery, from Babylonian captivity, and from oppression at the hands of various Palestinian tribes. To Christians those deliverances foreshadow the coming of Jesus Christ as supreme deliverer.

The noun "deliverer" occurs a number of times in the OT. Three times the word refers to a human being. Othniel delivered Israel from subjugation to Cushan-rishathaim, king of Mesopotamia (Jgs 3:8-10). Ehud delivered Israel from Eglon, king of Moab (vv 15, 30). Judges 18:27-29 states that "there was no deliverer" to protect Laish from conquest by Dan's tribe. Other uses of "deliverer" refer to God himself as personal deliverer of his people (2 Sm 22:2; Pss 18:2; 40:17; 70:5; 144:2).

The basic OT concept of deliverer is expressed in a Hebrew word for "next of kin." A close relative was responsible to aid an individual in distress and to redeem him or her from slavery. God sent deliverance when his people were in danger, or God himself acted as deliverer, uniquely and forcefully in the exodus from Egypt (Ex 3:7-8).

In the NT, Jesus quoted a messianic passage (Is 61:1-2) as describing his own mission to proclaim release (or, deliverance) to the captives (Lk 4:18). In Acts 7:35 Moses is called a "deliverer" of Israel. In Romans 11:26 the apostle Paul paraphrased Isaiah 59:20, saying "A Deliverer will come from Jerusalem"—referring to Jesus Christ.

See also Messiah; Redeemer, Redemption.

DELUGE*, The
See Flood, The.

DEMAS
One of Paul's associates who was with him during one of his imprisonments. Little is known about Demas beyond the brief information given in the NT. Initially he supported Paul's ministry and was mentioned in the salutations of Paul's letters to the Colossians (Col 4:14) and to Philemon (Phlm 1:24). However, in 2 Timothy 4:10 Paul writes that Demas deserted him because of his love for the present world.

DEMETRIUS
Name ("Son of Demeter") of five persons in biblical times: three Syrian kings and two NT figures.

1. Successor to Antiochus V Eupator. Demetrius I was king (160–151 BC) when the Jewish uprising led by Judas Maccabeus was under way. He attempted several unsuccessful campaigns against the Jews (1 Macc 7:1-10; 2 Macc 14:1-15, 26-28). Toward the end of his reign Demetrius was challenged by Alexander Epiphanes and was killed in battle (1 Macc 10:46-50).
2. Son of Demetrius I. After his father's defeat and death, Demetrius II sought refuge in Crete, then challenged Alexander Epiphanes by invading Syria with an army of foreign mercenaries. Demetrius eventually

concluded a treaty with the Jews and gained the Syrian throne in 145 BC (1 Macc 11:32-37). The Jews also helped Demetrius against another rival, Trypho, until he broke his word to them (vv 54-55). In the subsequent contest between Demetrius and Trypho, the Jews, under Jonathan's brother Simon Maccabeus, achieved independence (13:34-42). Demetrius was captured by Arsaces VI (Mithridates I), king of Parthia, around 138 BC (1 Macc 14:1-3). He returned to the Syrian throne 10 years later and reigned briefly until his assassination (125 BC).

3. Grandson of Demetrius II. Demetrius III ruled Syria (95–88 BC) in the turbulent years of the Seleucid era. One ruling party in Israel, the Pharisees, unsuccessfully enlisted his aid in their contest with the priest-king Alexander Janneus.

4. Pagan silversmith in the city of Ephesus. He provoked a riot against Christian evangelists whose preaching had detrimental effects on his trade (Acts 19:23-41). The city of Ephesus was a center of the worship of Diana (Latin counterpart of the Greek goddess Artemis), the goddess of hunting. A huge temple, one of the seven wonders of the ancient world, had been erected there for her worship. Among the commercial enterprises connected with the cult of Diana was the making of religious images out of various materials, including silver.

Demetrius, speaking for the silversmiths, said that both his business and the worship of Diana were threatened by the preaching of the apostle Paul and his companions. Gathering the other silversmiths together, he denounced Paul. The meeting caused a general uproar, and a mob dragged three of Paul's companions to the amphitheater. Finally the town clerk, who was responsible to the Roman authorities for maintaining civic order, was able to quiet the mob, persuading them to take any grievances they might have to the courts.

5. Christian believer whom the apostle John commended in his third NT letter (3 Jn 1:12). Demetrius may have been the carrier of that letter.

See also John, Letters of.

DEMON Fallen angel who, under the leadership of Satan, rebelled against God. Demonism is the activity of demons, while demonology is the study of demons and their activity for the purpose of knowing the tactics of the enemy (2 Cor 2:11) in order to properly exercise authority over them (Lk 10:19).

Who Demons Are The English word "demon" is derived from the Greek *daimon*, which essentially means "a divinity, a deity" (i.e., a false deity, a demon; cf. 1 Cor 10:20). Any deity other than the one true God is a spirit opposed to him; therefore, such a spirit is an evil spirit, or demon. The word "demon" does not appear in the KJV, which mistranslates *daimon* as "devil." There is only one devil (Greek *diabolos*), who is known by a variety of names, titles, and epithets in the Bible. He is the prince or ruler of all the other demons, who are subject to him.

Often in the Bible the word "spirit" is used for demon, along with a descriptive or identifying phrase; for example, "evil spirit" (Acts 19:12-13), "unclean spirit" (Mt 10:1; Mk 1:23, 26; Acts 5:16), "spirit of infirmity" (Lk 13:11), "dumb and deaf spirit" (Mk 9:25) (all quotes from the RSV). Spirits may be identified by their specific role or function, such as a spirit of murder, suicide, lust, depression, fear, lying, etc., associating them with various sins or attitudes contrary to God.

In the Hebrew OT there is no word for "demon." The term "evil spirit" occurs (Jgs 9:23; 1 Sm 16:14-23; 18:10; 19:9). In the KJV there are references to "a lying spirit" (1 Kgs 22:22-23; 2 Chr 18:20-22), "familiar spirit" (1 Chr 10:13; 2 Chr 33:6), "perverse spirit" (Is 19:14), "spirit of deep sleep" (29:10), and "spirit of whoredoms" (Hos 4:12; 5:4).

A specific powerful demon referred to by title in the OT is "the prince of the kingdom of Persia," who hindered the archangel Gabriel from coming to bring information to Daniel, so that the archangel Michael came to Gabriel's assistance (Dn 10:13).

The number of demons is unknown; it appears that it is a vast number, perhaps incalculable. From Revelation 12:4 it is inferred that one-third of the angels were led astray by Satan. This means that the hosts of heaven outnumber Satan's powers by two to one. Ephesians 6:12 suggests an order or rank of demons: "principalities," "powers," "world rulers of this present darkness," "spiritual hosts of wickedness in the heavenly places" (RSV).

Demons are created beings—personal, immortal, and incapable of reconciliation with God. They have great power as compared with humans, but little power as compared with God. God has given us authority over them, so that in the name of Jesus they must obey God's people, even as they must obey the Lord himself.

What Demons Do Angels were created to worship and praise God, to serve him, and to act as his messengers. The Bible states that they are "spirits sent from God to care for those who will receive salvation" (Heb 1:14, NLT). The fallen angels have a similar function but a different master. Their allegiance is to the devil, whom they serve out of fear and delusion. They desire to work with human beings, but their purpose is to carry out the schemes of Satan and to oppose God. They tempt, deceive, and delude people so as to bring them to eternal damnation. In opposing God they attack, oppress, hinder, and accuse the people of God.

Since Satan is not omnipresent, he uses his demonic hosts to execute his will; for example, in the parable of the sower (Mt 13:3-9; Mk 4:1-20; Lk 8:4-15) they snatch away the word before it can take root (Mk 4:15). By persecution, Satan causes some to fall away before they have made a genuine commitment (v 17). By the cares of the world and the delight in riches and the desire for material things, he chokes the word so that little or no fruit is produced (v 19).

Basically, demons operate according to the pattern set by Satan in his threefold approach with Eve: (1) they deny the truth of the word of God and challenge its statements; (2) they deny the reality of death (typically they substitute something like reincarnation); and (3) they appeal to human vanity and pride by telling men and women that they can become like God or be gods (Gn 3:1-5). These also are the basic methods and teachings underlying most cults and false religions.

The Final Destiny of Demons It is written concerning the angels who sinned that God "cast them into hell and committed them to pits of nether gloom to be kept until the judgment" (2 Pt 2:4, RSV). The Lord spoke of the eternal fire prepared for the devil and his angels, into which the cursed among humans are also to go (Mt 25:41). Eventually Satan and his host will be thrown into the lake of fire (Rv 20:10), which is also the place of eternal torment for all whose names are not written in the Book of Life (vv 12-15).

See also Demon-possession.

DEMON-POSSESSION Demonic occupation of a human being. The term "possession" is misleading and is not the best translation for the Greek word *daimonizomai*, which literally means to be "demonized" and can often best be translated as "to have a demon." The noun form is "demoniac."

Demons can enter the body of a person (Lk 8:30; 22:3), in order to control the individual's thoughts and actions. Sometimes a distinction is made between demonic oppression and demonic possession; this supposedly differentiates an attack from without and control from within. Although a non-Christian may be said to be "possessed" by a demon, the Christian cannot be so possessed, for he belongs to Christ and his human spirit has been sealed by the Holy Spirit (Eph 1:13). Demonic spirits somehow know and acknowledge this seal.

Demons can also enter the bodies of animals, as in the case of the swine in Mark 5:13. Demons are associated with books of magic (Acts 19:19), idols (1 Cor 10:19-21), and fetishes. Demons often cause illness or physical disability; Luke 13:11 tells of a woman who had "been crippled by an evil spirit" for 18 years but was delivered and healed by Jesus. Since evil spirits often attack the mind and the emotions, many symptoms of mental illness may be attributed to their activity. The boy whom Jesus delivered just after the Transfiguration exhibited symptoms of epilepsy. Paranoia may be the work of a spirit of fear. Some individuals suffering from schizophrenia (split or multiple personality) may in reality be demonized by a number of spirits. It is possible for a person to have many demons. Jesus cast seven of them out of Mary Magdalene (Lk 8:2). The spirit in the Gerasene demoniac gave his name as Legion, "for we are many" (Mk 5:9; Lk 8:30). In the time of Augustus a Roman legion consisted of 6,000 foot soldiers, usually accompanied by an equal number of auxiliary troops.

Demonization occurs in various ways. Some people are demonized by a hereditary curse, which may continue to the third or fourth generation (Ex 20:5). The curse against illegitimacy was particularly strong, for the bastard could not enter the congregation of Israel until the tenth generation (Dt 23:2). Curses may also be placed upon someone by spells, incantations, or similar practices such as voodoo or other forms of witchcraft. Galatians 3:13 speaks of redemption from the curse of the law through Christ's having "become a curse" for us. Usually believers are immune from curses made against them, unless they have given grounds to the devil (Eph 4:27). Such grounds may be provided through drugs, illicit sex, the occult, or any other avenue forbidden in the Bible. Involvement with tarot cards, horoscopes, or any other form of fortune-telling may give demons opportunity to enter. Such contacts may seem innocuous, but Satan utilizes the smallest foothold to gain advantage over people.

Manifestation Often demons prefer to hide rather than to make their presence known, for then they can exercise control without hindrance. When they do manifest themselves, often when challenged, all sorts of strange and frightening things may occur. They possess supernatural powers (cf. Rv 16:14), which they exhibit outright or through their victims. The Gerasene demoniac had superhuman physical strength, so that he could not be bound with fetters or chains (Mk 5:4-5); he lived in tombs and went about night and day screaming and injuring himself with stones.

The spirit in the demonized boy in Mark 9 rendered him dumb and deaf, threw him on the ground, and caused him to roll about and to foam at the mouth (9:18-20). The demon caused him to grind his teeth and

become rigid; he had tried to kill the boy by throwing him into the fire and into the water on various occasions (vv 18-22). Before leaving at the command of Jesus, the demon cried out (cf. Mk 1:26), convulsed the boy terribly, and left him lying like a corpse. Jesus took him by the hand and raised him up (9:27). Similar manifestations take place today.

Exorcism Casting out demons, or exorcism, was a regular and frequent part of the ministry of Jesus, and he taught and commanded his followers to do the same. This command has never been abrogated, and the ministry of deliverance should be even more important today, when the forces of evil are so rampant. The following principles are derived from the practice of Jesus, the Scriptures, and personal observation and involvement.

1. Jesus spoke to demons and commanded them to come out (Mk 1:25; 9:25). He cast them out "with a word" (Mt 8:16). Jesus gave his followers authority to use his name in casting them out and used this as a sign of the believer (Mk 16:17). His name is not a magical formula, and its use depends on the relationship between the Lord and the person using his name, as the sons of Sceva found out to their dismay (Acts 19:11-18).

2. Jesus cast out demons by the Spirit of God (Mt 12:28). God anointed Jesus of Nazareth with the Holy Spirit and with power to heal all who were oppressed by the devil (Lk 4:18-19; Acts 10:38).

3. The Lord gave clear teaching about "the binding of the strong man" in deliverance (Mt 12:29; Mk 3:27) and about binding and loosing (Mt 18:18).

4. Prayer is an important weapon in spiritual warfare. When the disciples asked (Mk 9:28) why they could not cast out a demon, Jesus replied that this kind comes out only with prayer.

5. Revelation 12:11 testifies to the power of "the blood of the Lamb" in overcoming Satan. Demons do not like to hear of the blood of Jesus and often become agitated at the mention of it.

6. God has equipped the believer with armor for defense in spiritual battle (Eph 6:10-17).

7. The Lord answered Satan with correctly applied texts from the Bible. We have been given the sword of the Spirit, the Word of God (Eph 6:17; Heb 4:12), as a means of defense and for attack against the enemy.

8. We must come against the hosts of hell from our position in the heavenly places (Eph 2:6), not from our limited earthly station.

9. We must recognize that the ultimate victory has already been won by Jesus, who came to destroy the works of the devil (1 Jn 3:8) and to destroy him who has the power of death (Heb 2:14-16). When Jesus cried out on the cross, "It is finished," he meant that the redemptive work was done; when he arose from the dead, he demonstrated his power over death. We win only as we enter into his victory.

See also Demon.

DEMOPHON Syrian officer and district governor in Palestine, under the command of Antiochus V (about 164 BC). Along with his fellow governors, Timothy, Apollonius, and Hieronymus, he continued to harass the Jews after covenants had been made between Lysias and Judas Maccabeus (2 Macc 12:2).

DENARIUS* Roman silver coin, equivalent to one day's wage. *See* Coins; Money.

DEPUTY

1. Official of superior rank whose authority is normally granted by a king (1 Kgs 22:47; Jer 51:28). *See* Governor.
2. KJV translation for "proconsul," an officer appointed over provinces by the Roman senate, in Acts 13:7-12; 18:12; and 19:38.

   See also Proconsul.

DERBE A city of the Roman province of Asia located in the district of Lycaonia (Acts 14:6) in the province of Galatia. Derbe was the last city on Paul's first missionary journey (v 20), the first city on his second journey (16:1), and likely one city he revisited on his third journey (18:23). Gaius, one of Paul's missionary companions on his third journey, was from Derbe (20:4).

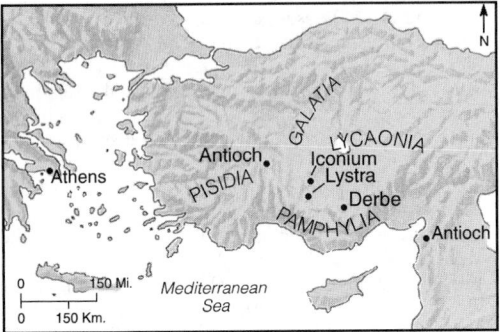

Derbe After Paul was stoned in Lystra, he and Barnabas traveled 40 miles (64.4 kilometers) to Derbe, a frontier town.

DESCENT INTO HELL* Reference to a controversial statement about Christ in the Apostles' Creed. Speaking of Christ, the creed affirms that he "suffered under Pontius Pilate, was crucified, dead, and buried; he descended into hell; the third day he rose from the dead." Interpretation of "he descended into hell" has produced much disagreement. Although the expression appears in creedal formulations as early as the fourth century, opinion remains divided about both its meaning and its relationship to Scripture.

The most natural interpretation in the context of the Apostles' Creed is that descent into hell was one step in the succession of saving deeds accomplished by Jesus Christ in his redemptive career. Since the other steps are presented chronologically in the Apostles' Creed, that descent would have occurred between Christ's death and resurrection. On that almost all orthodox commentators agree.

Several questions remain to be debated. Is the phrase to be interpreted literally? Does it refer to an actual place or state of existence? How did Christ "descend"? In what state? For what purpose?

The word "hell" is itself problematic. The Hebrew word for "grave" acquired in OT times the larger meaning of "abode of the dead." The Greek translation (in the Septuagint and the NT) was *hades*. Both words are rendered "hell" in many English translations, as is the Greek word *Gehenna*, which closely approximates what most people think of as hell, a place of torment for the wicked referred to by Jesus (Mt 5:22, 29-30). The earliest versions of the Apostles' Creed are in Greek, but in the phrase "he descended into hell," none of those words is used. Another expression is used that means "the lowest part." Later Latin versions translated it *ad inferna* ("to the

place beneath"), which in the course of centuries became identified with the place of torment (the inferno).

Literal Descent The traditional view, officially maintained by Roman Catholics and Lutherans, interprets the phrase literally. Christ actually visited the place of the dead *(hades)*. Within the framework of that view, two principal opinions have arisen concerning the purpose of Christ's descent.

To Liberate the Old Testament Faithful In one literal view, believers who had lived and died before Christ's advent (a partial list of whom appears in Heb 11) existed in a part of hades in a state of abeyance, in neither torment nor bliss, awaiting salvation. After Christ had accomplished salvation on the cross, and in the interval between his death and resurrection, he visited (descended into) hades, liberated those souls, and led them to heaven.

That interpretation claims support from Ephesians 4:8-10, a difficult passage that speaks of Christ as "descended to the lower, earthly regions" and also "ascended" on high, leading "captives in his train" (NIV). The "lower, earthly regions" is identified with hades and the "captives" with the throng of OT believers whom Christ released from their waiting stance and triumphantly conducted into full fellowship with God.

To Preach the Gospel to the Impenitent Dead A related passage is 1 Peter 3:18-20, in which Christ went and "preached to the spirits in prison—those who disobeyed God long ago" (NLT) in the time of Noah. That passage seems to conflict with the first view, since those who hear Christ's preaching in 1 Peter are disobedient rather than believing spirits. Therefore, some have suggested a second view, that Christ descended into hades in order to bring a special message of salvation to the dead who were lost in their sins but who had no opportunity during their lifetime to hear the news of redemption. In that view the "hell" of the Apostles' Creed is the place of the doomed dead. The purpose of Christ's descent was to secure the redemption of some or all of them by preaching.

That interpretation also seeks support from Ephesians 4 and 1 Peter 3–4. "Captives" in Ephesians 4 is seen as referring to those who had died in the "bondage" of sin. In 1 Peter 3 "the spirits in prison" refers to those in hades who would be condemned if it were not for the gospel that they heard and responded to in the afterlife. First Peter 4:6 is sometimes quoted in that connection, with the meaning that "the gospel was preached even to the dead" after they had died. On the other hand, 1 Peter 4:6 may refer instead to preaching presented while they were alive to people dead at the time of writing. Many commentators argue that a preaching of the gospel after death, in order for people who did not accept salvation during their lifetime to do so after their death, seems contrary to Scripture's emphasis on the necessity of acceptance now in the present life (Heb 3:7-15), as well as on a judgment based only on what was done on earth.

Figurative Descent Because of difficulties in both literal approaches, many scholars (like John Calvin) have interpreted the passage in the creed figuratively. Instead of viewing "the descent" as an actual event, occurring chronologically between Christ's death and resurrection, they see it as a reference to the intensity of Christ's suffering. "He was crucified, dead and buried" describes his physical suffering; "he descended into hell," the depth of his spiritual suffering. He endured the agony of hell as the substitute guilt-bearer for the human race. That was expressed in his cry of dereliction, "My God, my God, why hast thou forsaken me?" (Mt 27:46, KJV). Hell's worst feature is separation from God (7:23; 25:41)—the very agony Christ as the Lamb of God endured in order to make the atoning sacrifice and vindicate the justice of the triune God.

That interpretation, endorsed by the Heidelberg Catechism (1562), a Calvinist document, fits well with a substitutionary view of the Atonement and represents the immensity of Christ's sufferings as portrayed in Scripture. Yet some question whether that interpretation represents the intended meaning of the Apostles' Creed in its original formulation.

Another figurative interpretation, found in the Westminster Standards, also a Calvinist document, views the descent as a commentary on the preceding passages. The Westminster Larger Catechism paraphrases it like this: "Continuing in the state of the dead and under the power of death till the third day." A serious problem with that interpretation is that the creed is extremely condensed and seems to avoid such repetition.

Because of difficulties in all four points of view, some Christians omit the statement altogether when they recite the creed. In support of their attitude they argue that the phrase has an unclear biblical foundation, is late in origin, found no general acceptance until the fifth century at the earliest, and was never included in the Nicene Creed. Yet the form of the creed agreed on by the ecumenical councils includes the passage.

Aerial View of Sinai Desert

DESERT Empty waste place, often arid, sandy, and incapable of sustaining vegetable life, as for example the Negev of southern Palestine. A desert frequently includes local areas where marginal life is possible. The most common Hebrew term for desert means "wilderness" and is perhaps related to a verb meaning "to drive," as a shepherd drives sheep to pasturage. The Greek word commonly used in the NT and in the Septuagint (ancient Greek translation of the OT) implies an unenclosed, uncultivated area where wild beasts roam (Dt 32:10; Jb 24:5). The wilderness is also sometimes a place of pasturage (Ex 3:1; Ps 65:12; Jer 23:10; Jl 2:22).

The Bible often refers to wilderness regions (e.g., Gn 16:7; 21:20; 1 Sm 17:28; Mt 3:1; Mk 1:13; Lk 15:4). "Wilderness" is usually a place with no settled population (Nm 14:33; Dt 32:10; Jb 38:26; Prv 21:19; Jer 9:2) but is the dwelling place of wildlife: the vulture (Ps 102:6), wild asses (Jb 24:5), jackals (Mal 1:3), and

ostriches (Lam 4:3). The term is also used figuratively (Hos 2:3; Jer 2:31).

Another Hebrew term for desert, from a root meaning "to be arid," refers to an infertile, desolate, bare steppe (Jb 24:5; Is 33:9; Jer 51:43). The plural form of that word describes topographical features of the desert plains of Moab (Nm 22:1; 26:3, 63; Dt 34:1) and of Jericho (Jos 4:13; 5:10; 2 Kgs 25:5). With the definite article, that word (the Arabah) is the plain of the Jordan Valley and of the environs of the Dead Sea. The geography of that region contains sharp contrasts; the Jordan Valley, dense with a junglelike forest sheltering wild beasts (including lions in biblical times), gives way to the steppe lands of the Dead Sea area, which have always been desert.

Two other Hebrew terms, meaning "waste" and "ruin," refer to districts or settlements once inhabited but later devastated (Is 1:7; 5:9; 6:11; Jer 42:18; Ez 35:7). They are also used more generally for any desolate or waste place (Lv 26:31, 33; Jb 3:14; Pss 9:6; 109:10; Is 5:17; 44:26; 51:3; 52:9; Jer 7:34; Ez 5:14). One of them is also used once for the wilderness of the exodus (Is 48:21). Another word meaning "waste" (Ps 78:40; Is 43:19-20), when prefixed with the definite article, is a proper name for Jeshimon, a tract of land west of the Dead Sea (Nm 21:20; 1 Sm 23:24; 26:1).

In the NT the noun for "wilderness" and the adjective "desert" (Mt 3:1; 24:26; Lk 5:16; Jn 6:31; Acts 8:26) come from the same Greek root.

The whole of biblical history has been interpreted as having a desert or wilderness motif. It can be seen in the realm of disobedient human experience outside the Garden of Eden; in the wandering of Israel during the exodus; in the struggle between pure faith in the desert and soft, idolatrous city life. The desert is viewed as a realm of demons and death (Dt 32:17; Is 34:13-14); its demonic wildness resembles the primeval chaos of the Creation (Gn 1:2; Jb 26:7). Several moving passages of Scripture deal with renewal of life in a desert valley (e.g., Ez 37), or with transformation of arid land into a productive garden (Is 41:18-20).

The desert is also a place where God is close to his people (Dt 32:10-12), both watching over them and testing their obedience (Jer 2:2; Hos 2:14-15). Finally, the desert is a place of refuge, cleansing, and consecration. In the Gospels the desert theme of the exodus recurs in the 40 days and nights in which Jesus was tempted in the wilderness (Mk 1:13; cf. Ps 91). The desert fathers of the early church and the hermits of the Middle Ages emulated the prophet Elijah and John the Baptist (1 Kgs 19:4-8; Mt 3:1-6).

See also Negeb, Negev; Palestine; Wilderness.

DESERT OF SIN *See* Wilderness of Sin.

DESIRE To long for, want, or covet; also the object so desired. The word "desire" occurs many times in the KJV. As a noun it translates 12 Hebrew words and 3 Greek words. As a verb it represents about 12 each of Hebrew and Greek verbs. Some of the original words simply mean "ask" or "seek," and are translated that way in modern versions.

Desire is a basic part of life, neither good nor bad in itself. The important moral issue is how one responds to his or her desires. It is possible to let desires control one's conduct, or to control one's desires and use them to serve their God-appointed purposes.

Christians have differed on the appropriate reaction to desire. Ascetics have claimed, for example, that the desire for food and the enjoyment of eating is sinful. But Jesus' examples in the Gospels show that he enjoyed good meals—so much so that his critics called him a glutton

(Lk 7:34). His first miracle in John's Gospel was performed at a wedding in Cana of Galilee, where the feasting probably went on for several days (Jn 2:1-11).

Many think that sexual desire is bad, but it is of itself no more evil than the desire for food. God created people with both desires, and they both must be kept under control, in obedience to God's law.

How does one distinguish between good desire and bad desire? Ultimately there is one basic issue: Is a person's desire self-centered or a desire for God's will? The Bible teaches that the essence of sin is a determination to have one's own way. Although King Saul never committed the dual crimes of adultery and murder that King David did, David was honored and Saul was reproached. The reason given by the Bible is that David was "a man after [God's] heart," who wanted to do God's will (Acts 13:22). But Saul was stubborn and self-willed, and he was rejected for that reason (1 Sm 15:23).

Evil desire, therefore, is not necessarily a desire for something that one might label as wicked. It is essentially the desire to have one's own way. As such, it is idolatry, putting self in place of God. Without desire, nothing is accomplished in life. But one's actions must always be in accord with God's will as it is revealed in his Word. The Bible even promises that if people take delight in the Lord, then God will give them the desires of their heart (Ps 37:4; cf. Ps 145:16, 19; Prv 10:24; Mt 6:33). When God is one's greatest desire, all other desires become properly oriented and can thus mirror God's own desires for his people's well-being.

DESSAU A village in Judea where the Jews led by Judas Maccabeus attacked forces of Nicanor (2 Macc 14:16). Nicanor was a Syrian officer under the command of Lysias.

DESTINY

1. Pagan god (Meni) mentioned in connection with another pagan god (Gad); presumably a deity of good luck or fortune (Is 65:11).
2. Foreordination of the Hebrews as God's elect people (Ex 19:5-6). In the NT eternal destiny depends upon

one's relationship with Christ (Acts 17:30-31; 1 Jn 5:1-5). *See* Elect, Election; Foreordination.

DESTROYER, The

1. Divine agent sent to carry out a sentence of destruction. The destroyer killed Egypt's firstborn, culminating the plagues and releasing the Hebrews from slavery (Ex 12:23; cf. Heb 11:28). The apostle Paul used the term for God's judgment on the rebellious Israelites in the wilderness (1 Cor 10:10; cf. Nm 16:44-50).
2. In plural form, "destroyers" implies destruction carried out by a group of agents, whether angelic or human (Jb 33:22; Jer 22:7).
3. In a broader sense, any agent of destruction (Jb 15:21; Jer 4:7).
4. Samson was called a destroyer by his Philistine captors (Jgs 16:24).

DESTRUCTION*, City of Phrase in Isaiah 19:18 (KJV), generally taken as a reference to Heliopolis. *See* Heliopolis.

DEUEL Eliasaph's father. Eliasaph led the tribe of Gad during the Israelites' wilderness wanderings (Nm 1:14; 7:42, 47; 10:20). In Numbers 2:14 the name is spelled Reuel in most manuscripts and Deuel in some others, due to a confusing similarity between the Hebrew letters for "d" and "r."

DEUTERO-ISAIAH* *See* Isaiah, Book of.

DEUTERONOMY, Book of Fifth book of the OT, and last of the Pentateuch (the five books of the Law). In it Moses restated to the people of Israel various laws and precepts of the covenant that God had revealed to them at Mt Sinai. Thus, the book has become known in Greek and Latin tradition as Deuteronomy ("second law"). That name has led some to misinterpret the significance of its contents as secondary. The book makes an important contribution to God's unfolding revelation of his purpose for the nation of Israel. Moses' reminders of the wilderness wanderings and the Ten Commandments, plus his instructions for life in the

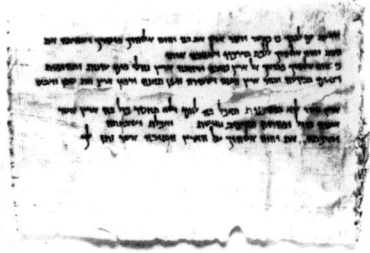

Dead Sea Scroll Text of Deuteronomy 4QDeut[n], c. 30 BC

Promised Land, are a vital part of the OT covenant literature.

PREVIEW
• Date and Authorship
• Historical Setting
• Significance of Deuteronomy
• Deuteronomy and the Law
• Content

Date and Authorship Two basic views (with variations) on the date and authorship of Deuteronomy are advocated by modern biblical scholars. Those who consider Moses the author date the book in the 14th or 13th century BC. Others believe that it was composed by an unknown author in the seventh century BC, when Josiah was king in the southern kingdom of Judah.

The Case for a Seventh-Century Date As early as 1805, W. M. L. de Wette advocated that Deuteronomy was used by Josiah in his seventh-century reforms, and that it was written shortly before that. Biblical critic Julius Wellhausen adopted that view, which has been advocated by many scholars ever since S. R. Driver publicized it in his *Introduction to the Literature of the Old Testament* (1891). According to that view, the book was written late but ascribed to Moses.

Many modern scholars, such as Gerhard von Rad and G. E. Wright, regard Moses as the founder of Israel's faith. They argue that whatever in Deuteronomy is from Moses was transmitted orally until about the seventh century BC. Denying that Moses actually wrote Deuteronomy, they attribute its present form to numerous writers and editors over an extended period of centuries.

The Case for Mosaic Authorship In recent decades, studies of Hittite suzerainty treaties from the second millennium BC have yielded interesting comparisons between those treaty forms and the books of Exodus and Deuteronomy. In 1954 G. Mendenhall suggested that the form of the covenant at Mt Sinai was the same literary form used by Hittites in treaties with Syrian vassal states during the 14th and 13th centuries BC. In 1960 M. G. Kline applied that idea to the book of Deuteronomy, seeing it as a renewal of the Sinaitic covenant and outlining its structure as a literary unit reflecting the pattern of Hittite covenant forms.

The book of Deuteronomy does contain certain parallels to Hittite vassal treaties. As a renewal treaty it appeals to the covenant of God with Israel at Mt Sinai, recorded in the book of Exodus.

1. The "preamble" in ancient Hittite treaties usually identified the suzerain or ruler. In Deuteronomy 1:1-5 (Ex 20:1) Moses as the speaker represents God, the King of Israel. As his death approaches, Moses makes an appeal for the renewal of the covenant.
2. In the "historical prologue" the suzerain usually cited the benefits he had bestowed on his vassal. In Deuteronomy 1:6–4:49 (Ex 20:2) Moses declares what God has done for Israel since his revelation at Mt Sinai. Moses reminds the people of Israel of God's faithfulness even when they had been unfaithful.
3. The "stipulations" were usually stated by the suzerain in the treaty's third division. In Deuteronomy 5–26 Moses outlines the stipulations for Israel in their covenant relationship to God. The basic requirement in Deuteronomy 5–11 (Ex 20:3-17) is exclusive, wholehearted love for God. In the following chapters, Deuteronomy 12–26, the basic principle of exclusive love for God is applied to specific areas of cultic

ceremonial consecration (Dt 12:1–16:17), judicial justice in government (16:18–21:23), the sanctity of God's order (chs 22–25), and public acknowledgment of God as their Redeemer and King (ch 26).
4. "Covenant ratification" usually contained a provision for treaty renewal and a formula for curses and blessings. In Deuteronomy 27 provision is made for Joshua to conclude the renewal of the covenant after the Israelites occupy the land. In addition, the divine threat and promise are expressed in blessings and curses as Israel swears its oath of allegiance on the plains of Moab.
5. "Succession arrangements" were usually the concluding part of suzerainty-vassal treaties. In chapters 31–34 Joshua is designated as Moses' successor. The written text is deposited in the sanctuary with the song of witness and a testamentary blessing by Moses. The book of Deuteronomy thus constitutes the documentary witness of God's covenant as it concludes with the death of Moses.

The fact that the literary structure of Deuteronomy parallels the legal forms characteristic of ancient Hittite treaties supports the traditional viewpoint that Moses is the author of Deuteronomy. When Moses is recognized as the mediator between God and Israel in the Sinaitic covenant, it is significant that the book of Deuteronomy represents Moses' renewal of the covenant in the literary form current in the culture of his day.

Historical Setting Moses led the Israelites from Egypt through the wilderness to the plains of Moab east of the Dead Sea. Exodus 1–19 gives an account of the enslavement of the Israelites in Egypt, the birth and preparation of Moses, his contest with the pharaoh, the miraculous deliverance out of Egypt, and the journey to Mt Sinai (probably also known as Mt Horeb).

In that desert area God's great revelation came to Israel through Moses (Ex 20–40; Lv 1–27; Nm 1–9). At Mt Sinai, God identified himself as the one who had delivered the Israelites. There he established an agreement by which they would be exclusively devoted to him as his holy nation. There the tabernacle was built and the priesthood established. Instructions were given for making sacrifices and offerings, and for observing feasts and seasons, so that Israel's pattern of living would show that they were God's holy people. The tribes were also organized for encampment around the tabernacle and for the march to Canaan, the Promised Land.

Numbers 10–21 is an account of the 38 years the Israelites spent in the wilderness. In 11 days they marched from Mt Horeb to Kadesh-barnea, about 40 miles (64 kilometers) south of Beersheba. From there 12 spies were sent into Canaan. Their report produced a crisis in the form of a revolt against God. Subsequently, Israel wandered in the wilderness for 38 years, during which those who had been at least 20 years old when they left Egypt died. The new generation moved to the plains of Moab, located east of the Dead Sea and north of the Arnon River. Numbers 20–36 tells of the conquest and occupation of the land east of the Jordan River.

The book of Deuteronomy presents Moses' address to the new generation of Israelites. In Exodus and Numbers God frequently speaks to Moses; in Deuteronomy, Moses is speaking at God's command to the Israelites (Dt 1:1-4; 5:1; 29:1). In contrast to the preceding books, Deuteronomy has a style of exhortation in which Moses admonishes the new generation about their responsibility in view of the preceding generation's failures. Whatever repetition occurs in Deuteronomy is carefully selected, with the specific purpose of warning the new generation so that they will not fail to conquer and occupy Canaan. Deuteronomy is not primarily retrospective; its outlook is optimistic about the future, offering hope for fulfilling the promises God made to the Israelites in Egypt.

Significance of Deuteronomy Deuteronomy (with Genesis, Psalms, and Isaiah) is among the most frequently quoted books in the early Christian centuries. More than 80 OT quotations in the NT come from Deuteronomy.

Jesus focused attention on Deuteronomy when he summarized the essence of the entire OT Law and Prophets in the two great commandments of love for God and neighbor (Mt 22:37; see Dt 6:5; 10:19). Jesus also quoted Deuteronomy (6:13, 16; 8:3) in his temptation experience (Mt 4:4-10). Deuteronomy unfolds the essence of what God revealed to Moses at Mt Sinai. In Deuteronomy, Moses shares with the Israelites the core of God's revelation without repeating details of sacrifices, observances, or rituals. He expounds the character of Israel's faith and nationhood. Moses repeatedly emphasizes his concern that they faithfully maintain a good relationship with God. An exclusive devotion to God expressed in everyday life is the key to a lifetime of blessing.

The primary need of love toward God and neighbor eventually became a basic requirement for the followers of Jesus Christ (Lk 10:25-28). The book of Deuteronomy is thus crucially important to the Christian concern to maintain a vital relationship with God.

Deuteronomy and the Law To designate the book of Deuteronomy as a "second law" or a repetition of the law is misleading. Moses' emphasis is not legalistic. Details of worship and ritual are not repeated or delineated to any great extent. Although the Ten Commandments are repeated, emphasis is placed on the first commandment, explicitly requiring exclusive devotion to God. Moses is primarily concerned with Israel's relationship with God and their determination to maintain it in their own and their children's lives.

The NT reveals that a legalistic interpretation of the Mosaic revelation was held by the Jews of the first century AD. Such legalism developed in Judaism especially during the intertestamental era. The Judaistic legalism of NT times has in modern times been ascribed wrongly to Moses. Moses did warn of the necessity of keeping all of God's law (Dt 28:1, 58), but in Deuteronomy his message as a whole makes it clear that he was not exclusively concerned about legalistic observance. Rather, the central theme of Deuteronomy is the unique relationship that had been established by a unique God with a unique people, the Israelites.

Content

Brief Historical Review (1:1–4:43) Moses is identified as the speaker, addressing the Israelites on the plains of Moab during the last year of his life. The Israelites were on the verge of entering the Promised Land of Canaan.

Moses began with a reference to Mt Sinai, scene of the greatest revelation in OT times. He focused attention on God's explicit command for them to move up to Canaan and occupy the land promised to Abraham, Isaac, and Jacob. Their rebellion brought divine judgment, so the conquest of Canaan had been delayed 38 years while an entire disobedient generation died in the wilderness.

Instructed by God not to molest the Edomites or Moabites, Moses had led the Israelites to the Moab plains north of the Arnon River. The Israelites defeated Sihon, the Amorite king of Heshbon, and Og, king of Bashan. The tribes of Reuben and Gad and half the tribe of Manasseh appropriated the territory east of the Jordan River as their land (Nm 32). On the basis of that conquest, Moses encouraged Joshua to believe that God would aid him and the Israelites in the conquest of the land of Canaan west of the Jordan River.

The Israelites should learn from the mistakes of the generation that died in the wilderness (Dt 4:1-40). They should consider the fact that the word of God had been spoken to them. The revelation that had come to them through Moses was unique, and the most important thing was for them to revere the God who had revealed himself. The uniqueness of Israel's God among the nations that worship idols should never be forgotten.

Moses reminded the Israelites that they had entered into a contractual agreement with their unique God. That covenant was mentioned 26 more times by Moses. No nation had ever experienced anything like it. If Israel obeyed, they would enjoy God's blessing and favor.

Exhortations and Applications (4:44–26:19) The circumstances in which Moses addressed the Israelites are reported in a short transitional passage (Dt 4:44-49). From the slopes of Mt Pisgah (or Nebo), with Israel encamped in the valley opposite Beth-peor, Moses made his appeal to the people before they crossed the Jordan River.

Moses' exposition of the "great commandment" is centered in the agreement made between God and Israel. He repeated the Ten Commandments as the essence of God's revelation at Sinai. As Moses explained what God expected of Israel, he elaborated the first commandment: "I am the LORD your God, who brought you out of the land of Egypt, out of the house of bondage" (5:6, RSV). Their relationship with God was of basic importance, since God's wrath will be against those who worship other gods (v 9).

Love is the key word in the relationship between God and Israel. Moses boldly asserted, "Hear, O Israel! The LORD is our God, the LORD alone. And you must love the LORD your God with all your heart, all your soul, and all your strength" (Dt 6:4-5, NLT). All other commandments are significant because they bear on that relationship (as spelled out in chs 5–11).

Exclusive love and devotion to God are essential. In a relationship of wholehearted love, no idols can be recognized or tolerated. Yet Moses wanted Israel to convey its consciousness of God to future generations by many external things: signs on their hands, frontlets (or "phylacteries") on their foreheads, Scripture verses on their doorposts, and so on. By precept and example they should convey to their children that they love God (Dt 6).

The Israelites should never forget that God had chosen them to be his people (Dt 7). They were to execute God's judgment on the Canaanites, who had been spared judgment since Abraham's time (Gn 15:16). Although the Israelites themselves did not merit God's love, in love and mercy he had redeemed them out of Egypt.

Moses appealed to the people to remember what God had done for them (Dt 8). To God's sustaining provisions they should respond with thankfulness, recognizing that the power to achieve anything they had done had been God's gift.

The Israelites had repeatedly failed in their faith and commitment to God (9:1–10:11). Through Moses' intercession they had been spared. It was for no merit of their own that they would enter Canaan; that was God's gracious provision for them. Moses' appeal for a wholehearted commitment is summarized in Deuteronomy

10:12–11:32. It is necessary to display reverence, respect, love, and obedience to God (see also 6:5, 13, 24).

The God whom the Israelites must love sincerely and without reservation is the Lord of the cosmos. He is the righteous judge who rules supreme over all nature and history. God loved their forefathers, the patriarchs. He redeemed the Israelites from Egyptian enslavement and gave them his covenant. He manifested himself in helping the orphans, widows, and strangers. He multiplied Israel to be as numerous as the stars of the heavens.

Moses gave two basic instructions to apply in daily life to maintain their relationship with God as a reality: "circumcise therefore the foreskin of your heart" (Dt 10:16, RSV). He did not refer to physical circumcision, a sign of the covenant between God and Abraham (Gn 17). Circumcision, which was not observed during the years of wilderness wanderings, was reinstituted under Joshua after the Israelites crossed the Jordan River (Jos 5:2-9). Moses referred to "spiritual circumcision" (see Lv 26:40-41; Jer 4:4; 9:25; Rom 2:29). All things that might restrict, interfere with, or negate total devotion to God were to be cut away (circumcised) so that the Israelites would continue to love God with all their heart.

"Love the foreigner" (Dt 10:19) ranks second in importance to wholehearted love for God. Love for the stranger or neighbor is basic to all other human obligations (see Lv 19:9-18). Social obligations issue out of a person's relationship with God. Being recipients of God's love, the Israelites were to love others. They were to remember God's love for them when they were slaves and strangers in Egypt. God loves the stranger, the widow, and the orphan; therefore, if anyone loves God, he or she is under obligation to love other people. God is concerned about justice and righteousness; a person who professes to love God must be concerned about just treatment for other people.

The Israelites were to be known for their concern for people whose social position exposed them to exploitation and oppression. The profound humanitarian spirit of the Mosaic law stands in unique contrast to the Babylonian Code of Hammurabi and the Assyrian and Hittite law codes of that day. In those codes human relationships reflected no vital consciousness of a love relationship with deity.

In the first century AD Jesus Christ came into conflict with Jewish religious leaders who had lost the essence of God's law in a maze of legalism. For Jesus, the greatest commandment was to love God; the second was to love one's neighbor. Those two commandments (which constitute the essence of the entire OT revelation) would, if kept perfectly, provide the basis for eternal life (Mt 22:37-39; Mk 12:29-31; Lk 10:27-28). Christians believe that the climax of God's revelation of love came in Jesus Christ. For them, responding to God's love means to accept Jesus Christ in wholehearted devotion and to love one's neighbor as Jesus exemplified in his life.

In Deuteronomy 12:1–26:19, Moses gave instruction in practical living for a God-related people when they resided in the land God had promised to them. Having once survived on manna supplied directly by God, in Canaan they would enjoy the fruit and produce of the land. They would also encounter a culture permeated by Canaanite religion.

In worshiping God in their new setting, they were cautioned to maintain due sanctity (Dt 12:1–14:21). They were not to worship at pagan shrines. They should bring their offerings to divinely appointed places for fellowship and rejoicing together in the Lord's presence. Idolatry was not to be tolerated in any form. Any prophet who deviated from the law of Moses in advising the worship

of other gods should be stoned. Exclusive devotion to God was to be daily practice.

Canaan's abundant blessings should be shared with neighbors (14:22–15:23). Tithes should be brought to the central sanctuary where Levites assisted the priests in religious ministration. Joy in sharing life's blessings and opportunities was to characterize Israel's pattern of living.

Moses prescribed three annual pilgrimages (16:1-17). The people should remember their deliverance out of Egypt by observing the feasts of Passover and Unleavened Bread. Seven weeks later, when the barley harvest was completed, they should spend time rejoicing before the Lord in a one-day festival called the Feast of Weeks. When the vintage as well as the grain harvest was completed, they were to observe the Feast of Ingathering (or Booths), a time of thanksgiving and sharing with others. Every seven years the law was read at the Feast of Ingathering.

In human relations justice was to prevail among the Israelites (16:18–21:23). The Book of the Law kept at the main sanctuary was their divine authority, providing God's instructions for them. The king was to have a copy of this law and govern his life in accordance with it. Prophets and priests played an important role as religious leaders in the life of Israel. Judicial authority was vested in the priests. In contrast to the brutality of other nations, humanitarian principles were to prevail in Israel's warfare. Fathers were responsible for their own family households.

In domestic and social relationships, the law of love was to prevail (22:1–26:19). Many regulations governed family life. In matters of sustenance, wages, and business dealings, the Israelites were admonished to be compassionate and just. Promises and warnings raised their consciousness about using the resources of land and animals entrusted to them so that their stewardship would please God.

In Deuteronomy 26, Moses instructed the Israelites in two liturgical confessions and a reaffirmation of the covenant. By acknowledging that God was the giver of all they had, and by confessing before God that they shared his gifts with others, they confirmed their covenant with God.

Alternatives: Blessings or Curses (27:1–30:20) Moses set before the Israelites the alternatives of blessings or curses. Under Joshua they were to renew the covenant publicly. At Mt Ebal stones were to be erected for inscribing the law and an altar constructed for offering sacrifice. The curses were to be read from Mt Ebal and the blessings from Mt Gerizim. Conditional self-curses were read regarding offenses against God and other human beings (Dt 27:15-26). Thus they acknowledged their accountability to God. Though their sins might be hidden from people, it was God to whom they were primarily and ultimately accountable. Blessings as a way of life and curses as a way of death were clearly set before the Israelites (ch 28). Setting them in the perspective of history, Moses appealed to the new generation to take advantage of their present opportunity (ch 29). Warning that, should they fail to love God, they would ultimately be subjected to dispersion, Moses admonished them to choose the way of life and good rather than the way of death and evil (ch 30).

Transition: from Moses to Joshua (31:1–34:12) When the life and ministry of Moses were nearing completion, and transfer of leadership was near (Dt 31:1–34:12), Joshua had already been designated by God as Israel's new leader. Moses assured the Israelites that God would

be the same with Joshua in charge. The revelation given through Moses had been put in writing and now was committed to the priests, the custodians of the Book of the Law. Joshua, who had already distinguished himself in responsible leadership, was publicly confirmed at the door of the tabernacle (31:1-29).

The "Song of Moses" is the covenant's document of witness (32:1-47). In it Moses spoke with prophetic understanding as he recounted Israel's past experience. Reiterating the consequences of their attitude toward God, he assured the people of restoration if they failed again. He encouraged them to fix their hearts on what God had revealed to them and to impress it on their children. Keeping the covenant by maintaining a wholehearted love for God would be important for all future generations as well as for those then listening to Moses.

After some final, brief instructions (32:48-52), Moses pronounced his blessings on the Israelites, whom he had led for 40 years (33:1-29). In his final blessing, also called the "Testament of Moses," the greatness of God and his special relationship with Israel are delineated. Israel is unique among all the nations of the world.

The book of Deuteronomy appropriately ends with an account of the death of Moses, the greatest prophet in OT times (34:1-12).

See also Israel, History of; Moses.

DEVIL, The *See* Satan.

DEVOTED THINGS Persons, animals, or objects that God forbade the children of Israel to possess (Lv 27:28-29; Nm 18:14). *See* Curse, Cursed.

DEW Moisture condensed from warm air during a cool night, usually found as small droplets on surfaces the next morning. Dew was an important source of moisture for the people of the ancient Near East, replacing some of the moisture lost during the hot days in that region. It was important to the growth of plants and successful harvests (Hg 1:10). In the Bible dew and rain are spoken of together as of great value (1 Kgs 17:1). During the exodus, dew was a source of sustenance (Ex 16:13-21; Nm 11:9). Figuratively, "dew" was sometimes used as a symbol of blessing; for example, Isaac blessed Jacob by asking that "the dew of heaven" be given to him (Gn 27:28; cf. Dt 33:13; Mi 5:7). Dew was also a symbol of refreshment, renewal, or prosperity (Jb 29:19; Hos 14:5). A king's favor was said to be like dew upon the grass (Prv 19:12). Dew could represent stealth, coming silently by night (2 Sm 17:12); it also depicted circumstances that could change rapidly, since it evaporated so quickly in the morning (Hos 6:4). A passage in one of David's psalms declares that God will renew his strength like the morning dew (Ps 110:3).

DIADEM* *See* Crown.

DIAMOND Precious gem, usually colorless, consisting of crystalized carbon. In the Bible "diamond" seems to indicate the hardness, rather than the actual identification, of the stone. *See* Stones, Precious.

DIANA* Roman name for the mythological Greek goddess Artemis, daughter of Jupiter and Latona and the twin sister of Apollo. She renounced all idea of marriage, supposedly because she was appalled at the birth pains her mother had suffered in bearing her, and remained the unattainable virgin goddess. Although goddess of the moon, Diana was more often portrayed as the huntress with two dogs beside her.

The Temple of Diana at Ephesus was one of the seven wonders of the ancient world. The impressive building was supported on 100 large columns. The local legend was that her statue fell there from the sky (Acts 19:35). This may have been a reference to a meteorite. Pliny described a large stone over the doorway, which, according to tradition, had been put in place by Diana. Ceremonies and services of worship in her honor were conducted by eunuch priests.

Among the statues that have been excavated, some show Diana as a multibreasted female; others show a shrine with the goddess attended by lions. Models of the temple were sold as souvenirs by the silversmiths, who were reluctant to see any slackening of this lucrative trade when Paul began his preaching in Ephesus (Acts 19:23–20:1). The discontent and agitation of the silversmiths led to the riot of the crowd, culminating in the roar "Great is Diana of the Ephesians" (19:28, 34, KJV). Inscriptions in the British Museum refer to the goddess as "Artemis the Great." If the silversmiths are to be believed, she was worshiped throughout the known world. The form of worship is not known for certain, but the worship of the goddess Diana may have been associated with a fertility cult.

DIASPORA OF THE JEWS* Dispersion of Jewish people from Israel to foreign lands. *Diaspora,* a Greek noun meaning a "sowing" or "scattering," is regularly used in the Septuagint to mean "exile" (Jer 25:34; cf. Is 11:12; Ez 20:23; Zep 3:10). The word occurs twice in the NT (Jas 1:1; 1 Pt 1:1), referring to Christian Jews residing outside Palestine as a result of the several dispersions in Israel's history. Diaspora sometimes refers to the exiled people, sometimes to the place of exile.

Major Diasporas From the end of the eighth century BC onward, Jewish history was marked by several major dispersions.

Diaspora of the Northern Kingdom After Solomon's death, his kingdom broke in two. The northern kingdom of Israel sunk deeper into idolatry and immorality (2 Kgs 17:14-18). Jeroboam, the first king of the divided Israel, established a pattern of apostasy ("falling away" from faith). Epitaphs for succeeding kings regularly recorded that the deceased ruler "did not turn from the sins of Jeroboam" (10:31; 13:11; 14:24; 15:9, 18, 24, 28, RSV). Assyria conquered the northern kingdom in 722 BC and took over 27,000 Israelites into exile, as had been predicted (17:23). They were settled in cities along the tributaries of the Euphrates River and in Media. Assyrians from cities around Babylon, in turn, colonized Israel (vv 6, 24).

Diaspora of the Southern Kingdom The southern kingdom of Judah suffered exile to the east in Babylonia and to the south in Egypt. The Babylonian king Nebuchadnezzar captured Judeans in several expeditions from 605 BC to the fall of Jerusalem in 586 BC. The first deportation to Babylon took Jerusalem's treasures from the temple and palace, and "all the princes, and all the mighty men of valor, ten thousand captives, and all the craftsmen and the smiths; none remained, except the poorest people of the land" (2 Kgs 24:12-14, RSV; cf. 2 Chr 36:10; Jer 52:29-30).

A year later a second expedition focused on the rebellious Jewish vassal king Zedekiah and his sons (2 Kgs 25:1, 6-7; Jer 52:4-11). In the 19th year of Nebuchadnezzar's reign, Babylonia struck Judah a third time, destroyed the temple and the king's palace, and broke down the city's walls. All but the very poorest people were carried away captive (2 Kgs 25:8-21; Jer 52:12-16).

Shishak, king of Egypt, deported exiles from Judah as early as the 10th century BC. Judah lost people and also temple gold at that time (1 Kgs 14:25-26; 2 Chr 12:9). About 400 years later, Johanan, a Judean, thought he could escape from Nebuchadnezzar by fleeing to Egypt. Johanan forced Jeremiah and a group of other Jews to go with him; they settled at Migdol, Tahpanhes, and Memphis. Nevertheless, the Babylonians pursued them, took control of Egypt, and executed many of the Jews there (Jer 43:5–44:30). Records of property ownership and artifacts of an altar suggest that the few surviving exiles established permanent colonies in Egypt (Is 19:18-19).

Other Diasporas The Egyptian king Ptolemy I (323–285 BC) captured many Jews and carried them off to Egypt about 300 BC. Those exiles populated Alexandria, a city thereafter noted as a center of both Greek and Jewish scholarship. Elsewhere large colonies of Jews were exported from Babylonia to Phrygia and Lydia by Antiochus III (the Great) of Syria (223–187 BC). The Romans transplanted a sizable group of Jews to Rome. The Roman general Pompey took many there as slaves in the first century BC.

How widely the Jews were scattered is suggested in the NT book of Acts, where Luke listed Jerusalem's visitors: Parthians, Medes, Elamites, people from Mesopotamia, Judea, Cappadocia, Pontus, the province of Asia, Phrygia, Pamphylia, Egypt, and the areas of Libya toward Cyrene, visitors from Rome (both Jews and converts to Judaism), Cretans, and Arabians (Acts 2:9-11). Those Jews of "the Diaspora" were in Jerusalem to celebrate the Feast of Pentecost.

Other Jewish communities were located in the Macedonian cities visited by the apostle Paul on his missionary journeys: Thessalonica, Berea, and Corinth (Acts 17:1, 10; 18:2-4). Around the middle of the first century AD, the Roman emperor Claudius commanded all Jews to leave Rome (18:2). Scholarly estimates of the Jewish population in Palestine at the time of Jesus' birth range from about four to six million. The dispersion population numbered several times that of Palestine; communities with more than a million each flourished in Asia Minor, Mesopotamia, and Alexandria. Today, even with a national homeland, far more Jews still live outside Israel than inside.

In spite of their scatterings, Jews of various diasporas retained a basic unity with Palestinian Jews through several practices. (1) The great national feasts—Passover, Harvest, and Tabernacles (Ex 23:12-17; Dt 16:1-17)—continued to be observed abroad. (2) The temple tax used for the temple's upkeep (Ex 30:11-16) was collected in foreign Jewish communities even after the temple had been destroyed. (3) All Jews everywhere recognized the authority of the Sanhedrin (the Jewish religious council) over them.

Positive Aspects In exile the Jews tended to abandon the idol worship that had in part alienated them from God. Their exile led them to establish synagogues as institutions for prayer and education. Alexandrian Jews translated the OT Scriptures into Greek, at that time the international language. The result, called the Septuagint, was the version often cited by NT writers.

From the Christian point of view, the network of dispersed Jewish communities had a special significance. They provided strategic bases for the spread of Christianity, which quickly broke out of those communities and into the surrounding gentile world. Thus, God used the dispersions to bring the gospel to the Gentiles (Rom 1:11-15; 1 Cor 10:11-12).

Finally, the arts, sciences, and humanities have been greatly enriched by the Jews scattered throughout Western culture. Few other peoples have endured so much ferocious ethnic bigotry as the Jews and yet rewarded that rejection with cultural gifts and graces of such excellence. Although the church of Jesus Christ has become a "new Israel" and a "chosen race" (1 Pt 2:9), the testimony of history and of Scripture indicates that God still has a unique interest in the Jews.

See also Israel, History of; Postexilic Period.

DIBLAH* ASV form of Riblah, the name of the place from which King Nebuchadnezzar directed operations against Jerusalem in 588–586 BC (Ez 6:14; cf. Jer 52:9-27). *See* Riblah.

DIBLAIM Father of Gomer, Hosea's wife (Hos 1:3). The name Diblaim is thought by some to be an allusion to Gomer's harlotry, since the name means "raisin cakes" and raisin cakes were used in ancient fertility-cult rites.

DIBLATH* KJV rendering of Riblah in Ezekiel 6:14. Compare Jeremiah 52:9-27. *See* Riblah.

DIBON

1. City in Moab, east of the Dead Sea and north of the Arnon River. It was located on the King's Highway in Amorite territory and was a camping station for the Israelites during the exodus. Israel asked permission of Sihon, the Amorite king, to pass through his territory, but he refused. Israel then fought and defeated Sihon, thus gaining control of Dibon (Nm 21:30). Following the Hebrew conquest of Palestine and its division among the 12 tribes, Dibon was given to Gad (32:3, 34), being also referred to as Dibon-gad (33:45-46). One biblical reference assigns it to Reuben (Jos 13:17).

During the period of the judges, Moab under King Eglon oppressed Israel and apparently retook Dibon. It was probably recovered under the leadership of Ehud (Jgs 3:12-30). Subsequently, Dibon was ruled by Israel under King David (2 Sm 8:2).

In the preexilic period Dibon was again under Moabite influence (Is 15:2; Jer 48:18, 22). Isaiah condemned Dibon (Dimon) as chief among the wicked cities of Moab (Is 15:9). Dimon is probably a play on words (from the root "blood") predicting Dibon's bloody and disastrous fate.

In 1868 excavations uncovered the famous Moabite Stone at Dibon, erected by Mesha, king of Moab, who built "Qarhah" as his capital. This may have been a new capital city replacing Dibon, or a renaming of Dibon by Mesha. Most likely "Qarhah" referred to the fact that Dibon was built on two elevations. The higher one was Qarhah, the defensive citadel of the city, surrounded by a wall and possessing a water reservoir, several cisterns, the royal palace, and a shrine ("high place," Is 15:2) to Chemosh, the principal god of Moab.

Excavations conducted in 1950–56 at Dibon (modern Dhiban) uncovered remains of the city from a period about 3000 BC. Evidence indicated that it contained only a nomadic population in the period 2100–1300 BC and that it was settled again about 1300 BC. The earliest excavations found five city walls, the oldest dating to about 3000 BC. The heaviest wall was from 7½ to almost 11 feet (2 to 3 meters) thick, built with large, well-squared blocks, and is considered to have been built in Mesha's time.

2. Town in the Negev of Judah inhabited by Babylonian exiles who returned to Palestine during Nehemiah's time (Neh 11:25).

DIBON-GAD Alternate name for Dibon, a Moabite city, in Numbers 33:45-46. *See* Dibon #1.

DIBRI Father of Shelomith from Dan's tribe. Shelomith married an Egyptian man, and her son by this marriage was stoned in the wilderness for blaspheming the name of God (Lv 24:10-11).

DIDACHE* (Teaching) A manual of church discipline, otherwise known as "The Teaching of the Lord to the Gentiles through the Twelve Apostles." Its origin and date are difficult to determine precisely, but scholars generally agree that it was written in Syria or Palestine during the late first century or early second century. The practices described in the manual were established much earlier, however. The Didache (which means "teaching") was compiled from various sources that detail the traditions of well-established church communities.

This handbook contains a number of texts that were intended to instruct new converts in the Christian faith. Chapters 1–6 present the "Two Ways" of life and death, based on Deuteronomy 30:15. This section resembles many Jewish teachings and may find its source in the apocalyptic writings of the Qumran community (where the Dead Sea Scrolls were compiled). The manual also contains several parallels with the Epistle of Barnabas and the Shepherd of Hermas. These first chapters include a distinctly Christian collection of sayings that resemble Jesus' teachings about loving one's neighbor (as recorded by Matthew and Luke).

Chapters 7–10 contain instructions for baptism, fasting, prayer, and the Eucharist. Baptism is to be performed "in the name of the Father, Son, and Holy Spirit"; fasting is to be practiced on Wednesdays and Fridays, in contrast with the Jews who fasted on Mondays and Thursdays; and the Lord's Prayer (with the doxology) is to be recited daily. The prayers in chapters 9 and 10 are based on Jewish table prayers, so it is not clear whether they are meant for the Eucharist or for a common church meal (sometimes called a "love feast"). The prayers contain no references to the words of Jesus at the Last Supper, and they place the blessing of the cup before the blessing of the bread (cf. 1 Cor 10:16). The Didache does note that believers are not required to use these model prayers.

Chapters 11–15 give instructions for church leadership. They discuss the marks of true apostles and prophets, who are referred to as "high priests," and the church's responsibilities toward them. The Didache ends with a prediction of the imminent return of Christ.

The Jewishness of the Didache may reflect the influence of the Jerusalem church's teachings. The description of church leadership, however, seems to be drawn from Paul, who details the roles of apostles, prophets, and teachers in 1 Corinthians. The Didache also stresses the function of the prophets. The teachings of the Didache reflect those of a church in the developmental stages of its institutions and practices. The church still appears to be developing characteristics that clearly distinguish it from Judaism. The Didache was highly regarded by the early church. Eusebius listed it with the orthodox writings that were eventually excluded from the NT canon.

DIDRACHMA* Greek silver coin worth two drachmas and equivalent to the Jewish half-shekel. Every Jew was required to pay this amount as the annual temple tax (Mt 17:24). *See* Coins.

DIDYMUS* Greek for "twin" and another name for the apostle Thomas in John 11:16, 20:24, and 21:2, NLT mg. *See* Thomas, The Apostle.

DIETARY LAWS* Regulations of food preparation and consumption provided by God for his people in OT times. The dietary laws formed part of broader regulations on "cleanness" that were designed to maintain Israel's status as a holy people.

PREVIEW
• Holiness and Dietary Law
• Before Moses
• The Mosaic Law
• After Moses
• Symbolism
• Reactions from the Church

Holiness and Dietary Law Biblical laws concerning diet and cleanness were based on the idea of holiness. The underlying meaning of the Hebrew word for "holiness" is difficult to ascertain but most probably was "to cut," or "to be separate," or "to set apart." The Lord told Israel, "You shall be holy to me; for I the LORD am holy, and have separated you from the peoples, that you should be mine" (Lv 20:26, RSV). God is the supreme example of holiness; he is the one uniquely separate in his character and being (Is 6:3). But God wanted his covenant people to be holy, too. One of the ways that God made the Israelites different from the other peoples of the world was by giving them dietary laws: "I am the LORD your God; consecrate yourselves and be holy, because I am holy" (Lv 11:44, NIV). Keeping the dietary laws did not automatically make the people "holy" (i.e., separated to God); rather, it was one of the ways OT believers could show their gratitude to God for his deliverance.

Before Moses From the Creation, God approved all varieties of fruit and vegetables as legitimate, clean food (Gn 1:29). After the fall of humanity, God distinguished between clean and unclean animals. At the time of Noah, God directed that additional specimens of clean animals be taken aboard the ark (7:2; 8:20). After the Flood, God prohibited the eating of blood because blood represented life (9:4). To commemorate the patriarch Jacob's wrestling with the Angel of the Lord, Jacob's descendants refrained from eating a certain hip muscle (32:32), though that was not a command from God.

The Mosaic Law The primary revelation of the Lord's dietary standards for Israel was given through Moses. Dietary laws are found among the ceremonial regulations received at Mt Sinai (Lv 11). Moses repeated many of those laws 39 years later, shortly before the people entered the Promised Land (Dt 14:3-21). The dietary laws concerned only animal products, except for the prohibition of wine to certain people (Lv 10:9; Nm 6:3-4; cf. Jgs 13:14; Jer 35:6).

Five categories of living things were regulated for food. To be edible an animal had to have cloven (divided) hooves and had to chew its cud. According to Leviticus, that requirement ruled out camels, horses, rabbits, and pigs (Lv 11:2-8). Sea life had to have fins and scales (vv 9-12). Birds were edible if they were not predatory (vv 13-19); Moses went on to list 20 species specifically prohibited because they were birds of prey or scavengers. Winged insects were forbidden (vv 22-23) except for certain types of locusts and grasshoppers (food commonly eaten by desert nomads). Finally, "the animals that move about on the ground," including reptiles and rodents (vv 29-31, NIV), were ruled out.

Further prohibitions were made about food that otherwise would have been considered clean. For example, nothing found already dead (Dt 14:21) or that had been torn by beasts (Lv 17:15) was to be eaten. Food could become defiled by contact with some other thing that was unclean, like a dead mouse that happened to fall into a food container (11:32-34). A young goat was not to be boiled in its mother's milk (Ex 23:19; 34:26; Dt 14:21). When clean animals were slaughtered, their blood was to be drained out (Lv 17:14). All pieces of fat (3:16; 7:23), especially a sheep's fat tail (Ex 29:22; Lv 3:9), were restricted for use in sacrifices to the Lord. Through Moses the Lord reiterated the prohibition against eating blood (Lv 17:10; 19:26; Dt 12:16; 15:23).

Several reasons, stated in or inferred from Scripture, account for the dietary laws and apply to the Bible's cleanness regulations in general. Some seem to be natural reasons; others may be symbolic or relational.

Hygiene Some dietary laws, such as those against eating vermin or decomposing flesh, circumvented obvious health hazards and were given for the people's protection. But hygiene alone cannot account for all the regulations; in fact, some foods that might have been acceptable from a hygienic viewpoint, such as rabbit or clams, were excluded.

Aversion Worms and snakes are generally considered loathsome, whatever their actual food value. Such animals were not *kosher* (proper).

Relationship to Pagan Practice Boiling a young goat in its mother's milk has now been documented as a pagan rite among Moses' contemporaries, the Canaanites. God's people were not to imitate the practices of the peoples around them (Dt 18:9).

After Moses The dietary laws given at Mt Sinai continued to be recognized throughout Israel's history. Before the birth of Samson, the child's mother was warned, "Now see to it that you drink no wine or other fermented drink and that you do not eat anything unclean" (Jgs 13:4, NIV). During the Philistine wars of the next century (c. 1041 BC), King Saul's soldiers sinned by disregarding requirements about the proper draining of blood from animals (1 Sm 14:32-34).

Later, when the Israelites were exiled in heathen lands, they were faced with situations in which the selection of food and its preparation could render it unclean (Ez 4:12-14). Daniel's refusal to be defiled by pagan delicacies at Nebuchadnezzar's Babylonian court (605 BC) illustrated his loyalty to God (Dn 1:8).

From the prophet Isaiah's day (740 BC) onward, the most abhorrent food to the Israelites was the meat of swine (Is 65:4; 66:3, 17). In the Maccabean period the "abomination of desolation," which the Jewish hero Judas Maccabeus and his followers resisted to the death, included sacrifices of pigs on the temple altar in Jerusalem by the pagan ruler Antiochus Epiphanes (1 Macc 1:54, 62-63; 2 Macc 6:5; 7:1).

Symbolism Certain food products were ruled out because of something they symbolized. God said not to eat blood: "Be sure that you do not eat the blood; for the blood is the life, and you shall not eat the life with the flesh" (Dt 12:23, RSV). Blood had a ritual function. It was used to make atonement on God's altar and therefore was not to be eaten (Lv 17:11-12). The NT writers recognized the sacrificial blood of the OT as a "type" or foreshadowing of the blood of Jesus Christ shed on the cross as a sacrifice for sin (Heb 10:1, 4, 12; 1 Pt 1:18-19). A symbolic regard for maternal life may explain why one who came upon a bird's nest was allowed to take the eggs or the young but had to leave the mother bird unharmed (Dt 22:6-7). The need to preserve a fragile desert ecosystem may also have been a factor.

Reactions from the Church At first the early church, with its Jewish background, found it difficult to break away from Hebrew dietary traditions. The apostle Peter was given a vision, repeated three times, about no longer calling either non-Jewish food or the non-Jews who ate it "unclean" (Acts 10:9-16; 11:1-10). Later, a council at Jerusalem officially decided not to retain Moses' ceremonialism in the church, except that gentile Christians should abstain "from food polluted by idols, from sexual immorality, from the meat of strangled animals and from blood" (Acts 15:20, NIV) in order not to offend Jewish Christians. That was an application of the NT teaching of consideration for those with sensitive consciences. "Do not destroy the work of God for the sake of food. All food is clean, but it is wrong for a man to eat anything that causes someone else to stumble. . . . But the man who has doubts is condemned if he eats, because his eating is not from faith; and everything that does not come from faith is sin" (Rom 14:20, 23, NIV).

Jewish dietary laws also have relevance to Christians because of certain OT promises. God promised, first to Abraham and, by reiteration or allusion, throughout the OT, that the Gentiles would be included in his covenant. By preserving the health of the Hebrew people, God was ensuring their continuation as a nation. According to the NT, the salvation of both Jews and Gentiles was achieved by Christ, a Jew. The nation through which Christ came was protected in order that God's promise could be fulfilled. Thus, the dietary laws need not be seen as burdensome restrictions of the law; they were part of God's way of working out his redemptive plan.

See also Cleanness and Uncleanness, Regulations Concerning; Leviticus, Book of.

DIKLAH Son of Joktan in the list of nations descended from Noah's sons (Gn 10:27; 1 Chr 1:21); perhaps the name refers to an Arabian tribe or territory, living in or near a palm-bearing area, as the name suggests (Diklah is a variant of the Hebrew word *dikla*, which means date tree or palm tree).

DILEAN Obscure Judean village near Lachish. It is mentioned only once in the OT (Jos 15:38).

DILL Herb from an annual plant known in Bible times. Dill has been widely used as a seasoning, especially for pickles, and for certain medicinal purposes. The KJV translation of "anise" instead of "dill" is considered incorrect by most scholars.

See also Plants.

DIMNAH Alternate name for Rimmon, a Levitical city in Zebulun's territory, in Joshua 21:35. *See* Rimmon (Place) #2.

DIMON* KJV translation of a Moabite city in Isaiah 15:9, alternately named Dibon in the large Dead Sea Isaiah Scroll. The site of Dimon is identified with Khirbet Dimneh, nearly three miles (5 kilometers) northwest of Rabbah. *See* Dibon #1.

DIMONAH Town mentioned in Joshua 15:22 as being located in the Judean Negev, close to Edomite territory.

It was one of 29 towns in the general area of Beersheba; some scholars have identified it with the Dibon mentioned in Nehemiah 11:25.

DINAH Daughter born to Jacob and Leah (Gn 30:21), whose name means "judgment." Living with her family at Shechem, a Canaanite city (33:18), Dinah went in to visit some neighboring pagan women (34:1). Shechem, the Hivite prince of the area, saw her and, while Dinah's brothers were away in the fields tending their herds, he raped her. Shechem then requested Dinah from Jacob as a wife.

Jacob's sons, enraged at the dishonor done to their sister, plotted revenge. They agreed to the marriage on the terms that all the Hivite males be circumcised. Hamor, Shechem's father, consented. While the Canaanite men were still incapacitated from their surgery, Dinah's brothers Levi and Simeon led a massacre in the city and killed every male. Dinah was retrieved and the city plundered. The brothers excused their action as a just retribution for one of the Canaanites having treated their sister as a harlot (Gn 34:27-31). For their use of weapons of violence (49:5), Simeon and Levi were later cursed by Jacob.

DINAITES* Postexilic group involved in a protest to Artaxerxes about the rebuilding of the Jerusalem temple (Ezr 4:9, KJV). The name is evidently an Aramaic title for "judge" (RSV); such judges are mentioned in fifth-century BC Aramaic administrative papyri.

DINHABAH Capital city of Edom before the time of Israel's monarchy, whose king Bela is mentioned in the Bible (Gn 36:32; 1 Chr 1:43). Its site is unknown.

DION* One of the cities of the Decapolis, built after the death of Alexander the Great by some of his soldiers. The city (not mentioned in the Bible) was culturally Greek, attracting many Greek immigrants; it was also a mercantile center of exchange. Dion was one of only two Decapolis cities having a Macedonian name (the other being Pella). It was located in Palestine east of the Jordan, possibly near the Yarmuk River and the town of Gadara. *See* Decapolis.

DIONYSIUS Prominent citizen of Athens; a member of the Areopagus, the Athenian supreme court, and one of Paul's few converts during his brief ministry at Athens (Acts 17:34).

DIOSCORINTHIUS* Problematic word occurring once in 2 Maccabees 11:21. "Dioscorinthius" formed part of the date in a letter written by Lysias, a Syrian official, to the Jewish people during the Maccabean revolts around 164 BC. Most scholars believe the word indicates the name of a month.

Part of the name may have referred to the Macedonian month Dios, but the significance of the rest is unknown. The early Jewish historian Josephus identified Dioscorinthius with the Jewish period "Marcheshvan" (November-December), but that gives no help in determining the precise meaning. Dioscorinthius has also been connected with Dioscurus, the third month of the Cretan calendar, but again the significance of that connection is unclear. Equally doubtful is the suggestion that Dioscorinthius was a short month inserted into the Jewish calendar to balance the lunar and solar years.

DIOSCURI* Twin sons of Zeus known as Castor and Pollux. In Greek mythology they were the patron deities

of navigation and represented in the constellation Gemini. The Dioscuri (the "Twin Brothers") were the figurehead of the Alexandrian ship on which Paul sailed to Rome (Acts 28:11).

DIOTREPHES A church member whom John reprimanded for his contentious behavior (3 Jn 1:9-10). He spoke against John; had resisted John's authority by refusing to receive an earlier letter; and refused to show Christian hospitality, urging others to do likewise. He may have been an official in the church who abused his position, since he liked to put himself first.

DIPHATH* Alternate spelling of Riphath, Gomer's son, in 1 Chronicles 1:6. *See* Riphath.

DISCERNING OF SPIRITS* *See* Spiritual Gifts.

DISCIPLE Someone who follows another person or another way of life and who submits himself to the discipline (teaching) of that leader or way. In the Bible the term "disciple" is found almost exclusively in the Gospels and the book of Acts, the only exceptions being Isaiah 8:16 and less directly Isaiah 50:4 and 54:13, where the same Hebrew word is translated "learned" and "taught," respectively. Yet clearly wherever there is a teacher and those taught, the idea of discipleship is present.

In the Gospels the immediate followers of Jesus, called by his authority from a wide variety of circumstances, not only the Twelve but all those who were sympathetic to his teaching and committed to him, are called "disciples." The calling of these disciples took place at a time when other teachers had their disciples, most notably the Pharisees (Mk 2:18; Lk 5:33) and John the Baptist (Mt 9:14). It is evident from the practice of John the Baptist that different leaders called for different disciplines from their followers. John's way was considerably more ascetic in character than that of Jesus; however, it too involved not only teaching regarding conduct and manner of life, but also a distinctive pattern of praying (Lk 11:1).

The disciples of Jesus had a unique experience. Not only did they benefit from the immediate teaching of Jesus, his looks and tones of voice (Mk 10:21) as well as his words, but they were also witnesses of the unfolding drama of redemption that had Christ as its center. They followed a teacher who embodied the substance of that teaching. The first disciples could be taught by Christ only little by little, not only because of the need to remove their misconceptions (Mt 16:21), but also

Theater of Dionysius in Athens

because the full significance of what Jesus said and did could not be most fully appreciated until after the events of his death and resurrection (Mt 28:9). It is not surprising that the period of "discipling" covered the time before and after Christ's death and resurrection, and also after Pentecost, when the Holy Spirit taught the disciples about matters that they could not "bear" while Jesus remained on earth (Jn 16:12).

Groups of Jesus' first disciples, both the Twelve and the Seventy (Mt 26:20: Lk 10:1), received his teaching, taught others in turn (Lk 10:1-11), and were given power to heal (Mt 10:1). They were also to proclaim the message of salvation through Christ. Yet the Twelve were given special prominence, and with the exception of Judas Iscariot (whose place was taken by Matthias, Acts 1:26), they became the foundation teachers of the newly emerging Christian church. Their authority in the church, given by Christ (Mt 16:19; 28:16-20), was to be characterized by a unique style of self-giving service (Lk 22:24-30). To this group of disciples, who came to be known as the apostles (though this term is occasionally given to a wider application), Saul of Tarsus was added. At his conversion on the road to Damascus, he saw the risen Lord and was immediately commissioned by Christ (Gal 1:12, 16) as the apostle to the Gentiles (Acts 9:15).

At the time of his ascension Christ commissioned the first disciples to "make disciples of all nations" (Mt 28:19); hence, the term "disciple" is also used in the book of Acts to describe believers, those who confess Christ. Though they have not been directly called by Christ himself, such disciples are called by Christ's Spirit through the message delivered by the first disciples; disciples called later are not in any sense inferior to the first disciples, even though they are less privileged. It was proper for early Christians to be called disciples of Jesus of Nazareth or simply "the disciples" (Acts 6:1-2, 7; 9:36; 11:26) because they were carrying on the teaching of Jesus and living the life he had exemplified. They were thus recognized as a "school" or living community that embodied the teaching of their "master" in practice. The book of 1 John emphasizes that only those who keep Christ's commandments show real love for God (1 Jn 2:3-6; 3:10-11).

DISCIPLINE

DISCIPLINE Learning that molds character and enforces correct behavior—from a Latin word meaning "instruction" or "training." To discipline a person or a group means to put them in a state of good order so that they function in the way intended. Discipline, in spite of a popular misconception, is not inherently stern or harsh. Bible translators chose "disciple" as an appropriate term for one who learns by following.

PREVIEW
• Biblical Teaching
• Self-Discipline
• Parental Discipline
• Church Discipline

Biblical Teaching Although used only once in the KJV (Jb 36:10), the word "discipline," in various noun and verb forms, occurs frequently in modern versions of the Bible. The Hebrew and Greek words commonly rendered "discipline" are sometimes translated as "reproof," "warning," "restraint," "correction," or (especially in KJV) "chastisement." More positive synonyms include "upbringing," "training," "instruction," and "education."

OT usage of "discipline" is noticeably more negative than in the NT, principally because of the legal aspect of God's approach to Israel under the old (Mosaic) cove-

nant. The "new covenant" approach to the church leads to a more positive language of discipline in the NT. Yet both covenants had the same goal: righteousness. Considered in that light, even the OT emphasis on punishment proceeds from a positive motive toward a constructive goal. Where the OT emphasized retaliation, it was to teach offenders the nature of their offense by showing them an effect like the one they had caused. Vindication of a wronged person's rights also vindicated God's righteousness. Vindication was an important way of upholding God's justice. Retribution was also important. Covenant breaking brought on the covenant curse (Dt 27:26) in the form of punitive discipline. Retribution reestablished the authority of God's law and taught respect for his standards of righteousness.

Complementary to punitive discipline, positive discipline can be thought of as reinforcive discipline. God always disciplines; he does so punitively when necessary, but reinforcingly when possible.

Discipline is frequently spoken of as being exercised by God over Israel (Lv 26:23; Dt 4:36; 8:5; Jer 31:18), over the nations (Ps 94:10), or over individuals (Jb 5:17; Ps 94:10, 12; Heb 12:5-11; Rv 3:19). In Israel parental responsibility to discipline children was taken seriously (Dt 21:18). Fathers were solemnly charged to discipline their sons (Prv 13:24; 19:18; 22:15; 23:13; 29:17; cf. Eph 6:4; Heb 12:7-10). In the church, disciplining was a pastoral responsibility (2 Tm 2:25).

It is understandable that people fear discipline from God (Ps 6:1), but it is his wrath that should be feared. His wrath is directed only against those who have proved themselves by their actions to be God's enemies (Dt 11:2-3). God's discipline is different from his wrath and should not be despised (Prv 3:11) or taken for granted (Heb 12:5). Only a fool or wicked person hates it (Ps 50:17; Prv 5:12; Jer 31:18). God disciplines his people as a loving father disciplines a beloved son (Dt 8:5; Prv 3:11-12; Heb 12:5-7). According to Scripture, a wise person should love discipline (Prv 12:1; 13:24; 2 Tm 1:7; Heb 12:5, 9).

The fruit of discipline is knowledge (Prv 12:1) and parents' delight (29:17). One who is disciplined can be spoken of as "blessed" (Jb 5:17; Ps 94:12). Where the purpose of discipline is left unspecified, the discipline is nevertheless understood as good and righteous (Dt 4:36; Jb 36:10; Prv 13:24; Rv 3:19). Specifically, discipline is called "the way of life" (Prv 6:23). It saves one from destruction (19:18) and allows one to escape both folly (22:15) and God's condemnation of the world (1 Cor 11:32). It eventually leads to sharing God's holiness (Heb 12:7), and yields "the peaceful fruit of righteousness" (v 11, RSV). In contrast, the consequences of a lack of discipline are stipulated to be abandonment by God (Lv 26:23-24), death (Prv 5:23), and destruction (19:18).

The book of Proverbs speaks of discipline as necessary to avoid sexual immorality (5:12-23; 6:23-24). Loose or wicked women probably symbolize many kinds of deceptive and enticing situations. To be able to act maturely and responsibly in such situations requires that young people respond to wise and loving parental discipline so that they learn to live disciplined lives. They will then do by "bent of nature" what is right because their nature has been shaped to what it right. Evil can then be shunned, even when it is encountered unexpectedly.

The book of Hebrews also urges its readers to respond to discipline rather than to react against it. In Hebrews two harmful reactions are stipulated and the helpful response is identified. On the one hand, no individual should regard lightly the discipline of the Lord (Heb 12:5). Discipline should be regarded neither as worthless nor as being of little value. On the other hand, one should not lose courage when he is punished by the Lord. That is, preoccupation with the negative aspect of the disciplinary procedure must not obscure its goal or demoralize persons being disciplined. There is a purpose for what happens, which should be sought and realized: "No discipline is enjoyable while it happening—it is painful! But afterward there will be a quiet harvest of right living for those who are trained in this way" (Heb 12:11, NLT). The exhortation is not to reject discipline or be dejected by it, but to accept it and be instructed by it.

Self-Discipline Jesus' ethics of righteousness both fulfill and surpass the stringent code of the old covenant (Mt 5:17-48). Yet Christians are not therefore inherently more legalistic than were the Pharisees. Set free from "the law of sin and death," Christians have "the law of the Spirit of life in Jesus Christ" (Rom 8:1-8) to provide a built-in dynamic to fulfill the will of God. Beyond slavish obedience to the letter of the law, believers are enabled by the indwelling Spirit of God to exercise self-discipline. Spiritual transformation is accompanied by renewal of the mind (Rom 12:2), which brings fresh understanding of oneself, one's motivations, and one's attitudes.

DISCIPLINE IS GOOD FOR US
Over the centuries the church has realized the value of certain "spiritual disciplines" encouraged in the NT. In the Roman Catholic tradition, they formed the basis for the way of life of "the religious" (priests, nuns, monks, etc.). Prayer (cf. Lk 6:12; Acts 6:4; Rom 12:12; 1 Pt 4:7), fasting (Mt 6:16-18), study of Scripture (Acts 17:11; 2 Tm 2:15; 3:16-17), and charity, or almsgiving (Mt 6:1-4; Acts 11:29-30; 2 Cor 9; 1 Tm 6:17-19) have always been included among the spiritual disciplines. Protestants have been less inclined to establish religious orders or communities based on the spiritual disciplines, more often trusting the Holy Spirit to produce self-discipline in individual lives and seeking fellowship and exhortation in the context of the church. Among evangelicals there seems to be a new appreciation of the need for spiritual discipline. A well-ordered, wholesome, liberated life that releases the Christian for service is almost always a self-disciplined life.
Such ideals and the lifestyle they engender run counter to much of the prevalent permissiveness in Western culture. Young people are surrounded by superficial commitments, short-term relationships, instant gratification, the quest for freedom without responsibility, and obsession with self-centered indulgence. Christian parents need to help their children develop the self-discipline to stand against such pressures. Adult self-discipline often has its roots in a biblical pattern of discipline and an appreciation for the desirability of such discipline inculcated in childhood.

Parental Discipline The family constitutes the basic unit of the human community. Within that cell of intimate relationships, parents are entrusted with the responsibility of guiding and correcting their children (Dt 6:7; Prv 22:6). The biblical view is essentially pessimistic about the perfectibility of human nature. Therefore, parents are urged not to leave children at the mercy of their own natural tendencies. Undisciplined children are potential victims of the powerful conditioning exerted by a predominantly pagan culture. To exercise their responsibilities properly, parents must model val-

ues, practices, and attitudes to their children, besides teaching them through instruction and correction.

The parents' educational task is best accomplished through positive means such as advice, exhortation, counseling, family devotions, and Christian training in church and Sunday school. But it also may require negative measures, such as prohibitions and disciplinary action. When verbal admonitions are not heeded by small children, punishment becomes an effective form of persuasion (Prv 13:24). Physical discipline, however, should be administered on the basis of clearly stated and understood principles. Christian parents must avoid punishing out of anger or personal animosity, and must never cause injury to a child. Physical discipline should be viewed as a last resort intended to obtain maximum educational results with minimum outrage to children (Eph 6:4).

Human fallenness (Gn 3) means that self-centeredness infects even children (cf. Ps 51:5). Somehow children must learn respect for themselves and for others. Left on their own and then battered by a fallen society, they can become rebellious social misfits leaving a trail of heartache in their own lives and in the lives of other people. Love for one's children does not preclude the use of negative disciplinary measures. As distasteful as they may seem to both parents and children, genuine love may require them. A family environment regulated by consistent and loving firmness will enhance the chances for children to mature as responsible and considerate individuals.

Church Discipline The church is basically a large family of which each believer is a member. The nature of the church—as a community intended to reflect in the faith, worship, and lives of its members the true character of God—distinguishes it from all other groups.

At the same time, the church is called to be an open community of concern, reaching out in compassion to desperately needy human beings. Christian lifestyles clearly differ from pagan lifestyles. That difference often creates a barrier isolating the "lost" from the very people who could extend to them God's deliverance from loneliness, addictions, disorientation, broken relationships, and so on. The church has a responsibility not to place unscriptural obstacles in the way of its outreach to unbelievers, yet the tension between openness and purity is difficult to resolve. Without a careful balance, a church can easily become unduly restrictive or overly permissive. In either extreme its witness is impaired.

The solution to the dilemma lies in formulating church discipline that is authentically biblical. The Scriptures provide the church with ample guidance for the formulation of standards of conduct (e.g., Ex 20:1-17; 1 Cor 5:11; 6:9-11; Eph 4:25-32; 5:1-21; Col 3:5-11). As those standards are spelled out, however, it is necessary to differentiate between biblical absolutes and cultural norms. For instance, though drunkenness is expressly forbidden in the NT, there is no scriptural prohibition on the drinking of wine. Some churches allow drinking but decry drunkenness, others recommend abstinence to their members, and still others make abstinence from alcoholic beverages a condition of membership. The NT, recognizing that conflict sometimes occurs between Christian liberty and Christian responsibility, gives guidelines for resolving such conflicts (1 Cor 8).

For the sake of scriptural consistency and in order to be credible, church discipline should oppose sins of attitude with the same severity as for "gross sins." The NT condemns immorality, murder, and drunkenness—but along with them envy, jealousy, anger, selfishness, complaining, and criticism. Each of the vices is an impediment to entering the kingdom of God (Gal 5:19-21). Unbelievers are often made to feel unwelcome in the church because of secondary matters such as smoking or drinking. Yet gossiping, complaining, and selfishness among church members are seldom exposed and properly disciplined. A more consistent position would promote the purity of the church and would also enhance its ministry as a supportive, accepting center of Christian love.

In addition to affirming the necessity for discipline within the church, the NT delineates a procedure for carrying out disciplinary action (Mt 18:15-18; 1 Cor 5:3-13; Gal 6:1). Offenders are first to be approached and admonished privately. If they refuse to repent or mend their ways, the case is to be presented before the leadership of the church and then, if necessary, before the whole congregation. Should offenders persist in their error, they are to be ostracized, not out of vindictiveness but with the hope of bringing them to repentance and restoration (2 Thes 3:14-15).

The Bible's emphasis on the necessity for self-discipline, parental discipline, and church discipline seems underscored by the moral decline evident in many areas of modern society. God's love, as depicted in the Bible and exemplified in Jesus Christ, is intended to teach all people how to live. Those who spurn God's "positive reinforcement" encounter the negative aspects of his discipline. Christians who discipline themselves, their children, and each other in a loving way honor Christ and model his way of life, thus helping others to understand God's purposes.

DISEASE Term used in Scripture synonymously with sickness, infirmity, illness, plague, and pestilence. However, plague and pestilence are generally used when there are large numbers of victims, as in epidemics. "Pestilence" literally means "destruction" and usually describes an epidemic with a high mortality rate. "Affliction" and "torment" are other terms that may include disease, but are broader and are not used synonymously with disease.

During the time the Bible was written, people did not have a detailed concept of anatomy or of how the specific organs of the body functioned. Disease was thought of as abnormal, something that limits one's ability to function with strength and vitality. The Hebrew word translated "sickness" as a noun means "to be weak" in its cognate verb form. The sick man by the pool of Bethesda is described as being "impotent" (Jn 5:7, KJV), unable to get around by himself.

Sources of Disease According to the Bible, disease has four sources: (1) God, (2) Satan, (3) sins of ancestors, and (4) breaking of physical, mental/emotional, or moral laws of nature.

God All early peoples attributed events and phenomena to the supernatural, either to various gods or to evil spirits. The Hebrews were different by being strong monotheists, attributing all phenomena to the one true God who had revealed himself to them (Is 45:21). God was responsible for everything, including disease and evil (v 7). This same God could also give material blessings, health, and heal all diseases (Ps 103:3). To the Hebrews, God could give health or sickness, and in either case, he had his purpose or reason.

One purpose of disease was punishment for wrongdoing (2 Sm 24:1, 12-16; 1 Cor 10:8). In the Hebrew mind, even when the immediate cause of the disease and death was obvious—as in many poisonous snakes biting people in the camp—the response was not to kill all the snakes but to pray to God for forgiveness (Nm 21:4-9). Leprosy, which literally means "a smiting," was a devas-

tating disease sent by God to punish individuals who sinned (Nm 12; 2 Kgs 5:27).

God also sent disease to demonstrate his power or to protect his people. The 10 plagues in Egypt illustrate the former; the elimination of Sennacherib's army, the latter (2 Kgs 19:34-36).

Satan Satan and other evil spirits could also be responsible for disease. In the biblical scheme of things, Satan's ability to bring disease is in the permissive will of God. The restriction on Satan's capacity for harm is clearly spelled out in the case of Job (Jb 1:12). The message of the NT is also clear that, despite cases of demon-possession and of people acting under Satan's influence, Satan's time is finite and his ultimate total defeat and destruction are certain.

Sins of Ancestors Sickness could also come about because of the sins of one's ancestors (Ex 20:5; Lv 26:29; 1 Kgs 17:18; Jb 21:19; Lam 5:7). The most striking example of this is the death of David's son as a result of his sin with Bathsheba (2 Sm 12:15). This concept of the origin of disease continued into NT times and was familiar to the disciples of Jesus (Jn 9:2).

Violation of Natural Laws This idea sets the Hebrews apart from the other peoples of their day. With the understanding that disease can follow the violation of fixed physical, mental/emotional, and moral laws comes the idea of personal accountability in obeying these laws and avoiding disease. A person is responsible for his and the community's health and is not merely a passive victim of supernatural forces.

Based on this concept, Moses set up elaborate codes of behavior to maintain personal health and the health of the community. The Mosaic law covers the areas of diet, personal hygiene, Sabbath observance, sanitary regulations in the camp, cleanliness, and sexual relations. In following these natural laws established by God, the Hebrews could expect freedom from disease (Ex 15:26) and long life (Prv 3:1-2). These health laws of Moses make a lot of sense from a public health point of view even today and are far more rational than the approach of any other ancient people.

Another major consequence of understanding that disease can follow the breaking of the laws of nature is the shift away from the priest and toward physicians when looking for cures. As long as diseases were of supernatural origin, there was no basis for attempting to learn about disease processes in the search for cures. The Hebrews were familiar with physicians in Egypt (Gn 50:2), where they seem to have functioned as embalmers. Physicians were practicing in Israel throughout its history, but only gradually developed the capacity to be of much help (2 Chr 16:12; Jer 8:22; Mk 5:26; Col 4:14). While validating the use of physicians for sick people (Mt 9:12) and of drugs for medicinal purposes (Prv 31:6; 1 Tm 5:23), the Scriptures emphasize the role of the Christian community and its elders in ministering to the sick (Jas 5:14).

Jesus Christ and Disease Christ's approach to people with disease was distinctly different than that of the OT. He was nonjudgmental, interacting with them as people of worth, not as social outcasts. He was full of genuine compassion for them as suffering people—touching them, comforting them, healing them, and speaking normally and naturally with them.

Jesus evidently thought of disease as a hindrance that prevented people from being the whole persons they were created to be. When confronted by a woman with a severe back deformity of 18 years duration, he healed her, saying she had been "bound by Satan" (Lk 13:16). His healing of incurable diseases was one of the proofs he offered that he was the Messiah (Lk 7:19-23). His ministry was directed toward releasing men and women to live life more abundantly (Jn 10:10). He did not fully subscribe to the punitive concept of disease (9:3). When a leper mentioned the possibility that it might not be God's will for him to be well, Jesus healed him instantly (Mk 1:40; Lk 5:12-13).

Jesus was always concerned with the person's total health or wholeness, rather than merely the symptoms of disease. He frequently dealt with spiritual issues first, even though the sick person was brought to him for a physical problem. His conversation with the Samaritan woman at the well focused on the basic conflicts in her disturbed personality (Jn 4:5-30). And the Sermon on the Mount, which basically deals with right attitudes and motives for human behavior, would greatly reduce personal and social suffering if it were followed. To Jesus, health is more than the mere absence of physical and mental disease; it is whole persons being all that they were meant to be.

See also Medicine and Medical Practice; Pestilence; Plague.

DISH A vessel, usually made of baked clay or metal, used in everyday life and in religious ceremony. Dishes were used to serve or preserve food (Jgs 5:25; Mt 26:23; Mk 14:20). They had to be wiped and left to dry (2 Kgs 21:13), but later the Pharisees added a ritual cleansing as well (Mt 23:25-26; Lk 11:39). Dishes were used in connection with the meal offering (Nm 7:13) and with the table of showbread for worship in the OT tabernacle and temple (Ex 25:29; 37:16; Nm 4:7).

DISHAN Chieftain in the land of Seir, a mountainous area southwest of the Dead Sea. Dishan's father was Seir the Horite (Gn 36:21; 1 Chr 1:38). The Horites were driven out of their territory by the Edomites (Dt 2:12). Later OT references often use Seir and Edom synonymously.

DISHON
1. Seir's fifth son and a Horite leader in Edom (Gn 36:21; 1 Chr 1:38), whose people were eventually displaced by the Edomites.
2. Grandson of Seir and son of Anah, a Horite leader. This Dishon was also the brother of Oholibamah, Esau's wife (Gn 36:25; 1 Chr 1:41).

DISPERSION OF THE JEWS* *See* Diaspora of the Jews.

DIVES* Traditional name of the rich man in Christ's parable about the beggar Lazarus (Lk 16:19-31). It came from the Latin term *dives*, translating a Greek word for "rich," "wealthy." Though the rich man was not named in the parable, this name was already well accepted in the church by the third century. A second-century Egyptian scribe gave him the name "Neves," meaning "nothing." *See* Lazarus #1.

DIVINATION *See* Magic.

DIVINE PRESENCE* *See* God, Being and Attributes of; Presence of God, The.

DIVINERS' OAK Place apparently near Shechem (Jgs 9:37); mistakenly called "the plain of Meonenim" in

the KJV. The Diviners' Oak may have been associated with those who practiced divination, hence the name.

DIVISION OF THE LAND Assignment of portions of the Promised Land to the 12 tribes of Israel following the Conquest. *See* Conquest and Allotment of the Land.

DIVORCE Biblical provisions regulating divorce are closely bound up with the various definitions given to marriage within the successive phases of God's progressive revelation in history.

In the Genesis Creation account, marriage is defined as the "one flesh" union established by God in the context of a sinless environment (Gn 2:24). Given such conditions, the dissolution of the marriage relationship was inconceivable. During his ministry, Jesus affirmed this aspect of God's original design for marriage. He described the implications of the "one flesh" relationship as the abrogation of the separateness of the spouses and the creation of an inviolable union (Mt 19:6).

The Old Testament's View on Divorce The disruptions brought about by the fall had grievous consequences for the male/female relationship. Having allowed sin to sever their primary dependency on God, man and woman became respectively subject to the elements from which they had been originally made. Man became subject to the dust of the ground whence he had come (Gn 2:7; 3:19), and woman became subject to the man from whom she had been formed (2:22; 3:16). Prior to the fall, man and woman had enjoyed a relationship of equality as cosharers in the divine image (1:27) and as partners in the divine mandate to exercise dominion over creation (v 28). After the fall man became ruler over woman, and woman became subject to man (3:16).

As a result of these new conditions, man assumed rights of disposition over woman that he did not possess prior to the fall. The "one flesh" relation was violated when the right of rulership opened the way for the male ruler to multiply the number of his female subjects. This disparity between male and female resulted in the practice of polygamy (Gn 4:19; 16:3; 29:30) and of serial monogamy, which required the termination of each successive marriage by an act of divorce (Dt 24:1-4). Thus, the emergence of the practice of divorce appeared as the inevitable consequence of the principle of male rulership. Neither rulership nor divorce was part of God's original design for the marriage relationship. The Mosaic regulation on divorce was a concession made by God to the fallen condition of mankind (Mt 19:8). Characteristically, the option of divorce was a right available only to the male rulers. As subjects of their male rulers, wives became the victims of divorce. Men could divorce their wives; women could not divorce their husbands.

As unfair as it may seem, the Deuteronomic provisions for divorce were actually intended to offer a modicum of protection for its female victims. A husband had to justify a divorce action against his wife by citing something indecent about her. He was to give his divorced wife a bill of divorce that accounted for her marriage to him (Dt 24:1). Moreover, a divorced husband was forbidden to remarry his ex-wife after her subsequent marriage, since his original divorce was viewed as a defilement of her (v 4).

Although the Mosaic dispositions on divorce were granted as a divine concession to Israel's hardness of heart, the OT emphatically states that God hates divorce (Mal 2:16). The right of divorce was grudgingly granted as an accommodation to the principle of male rulership that had resulted from the fall. But God's original design, reflected in the "one flesh" marital relation, remained the standard for the union of man and woman in marriage.

Jesus' Teaching on Divorce Inasmuch as Christ's ministry of redemption signaled a return to God's original purposes in Creation, the old covenant regulations on divorce were abrogated in the Christian community. In order to justify the inviolability of the marriage bond among his followers, Jesus directed them to the creational model. Referring negatively to the intervening Mosaic allowance for divorce, Jesus upheld God's original creation order by stating that "from the beginning it was not so" (Mt 19:8). Christ repudiated the fall and affirmed the Creation design.

In Matthew 5:31-32 Jesus explicitly abrogated the Mosaic legislation that allowed men to divorce their wives. He viewed the practice as a violation of the integrity of women. Adulterous men who divorce their wives reduce them to the status of whores, using them as commodities to be passed around through the expediency of easy divorce. By divorcing their wives, men treat them as adulteresses. By marrying a woman discarded from a previous marriage, a man perpetuates the demeaning process and becomes guilty of adultery.

Jesus deliberately withdrew from men the ruler's right of discarding a wife at will and reinstated the creational pattern of the lifelong "one flesh" union. His disciples understood his intent accurately. But the principle of male privilege was so deeply ingrained in their mentality that they declared the freedom available in celibacy preferable to a commitment to lifelong monogamous marriage (Mt 19:10).

Not only did Jesus reaffirm the validity of the "one flesh" union for the community of redemption, but the NT reinforced the inviolability of the marriage bond by defining it as an earthly copy of the relationship between Christ and the church (Eph 5:25).

Despite such strong sanctions for the permanency of the marriage bond, the NT permits divorce as an exception intended to protect the innocent spouse in the case of immorality and desertion. Jesus made exceptions that established the right of a spouse wronged by an unfaithful mate to press for divorce (Mt 5:32; 19:9). Obviously, the wronged spouse has the option of maintaining the marriage bond despite the breach of commitment by the unfaithful mate. But in view of the exception allowed by Scripture, the obligation to maintain or reinstate the disrupted marriage may not be imposed upon the innocent spouse.

The other exception that justifies divorce, according to the NT, is desertion. Although the provisions of 1 Corinthians 7:15 refer primarily to desertion by an unbelieving spouse, it should be noted that a believer guilty of desertion is to be treated as an unbeliever (1 Tm 5:8). Behavior equivalent to the abandonment of the marriage relationship constitutes a breach of conjugal commitment and becomes subject to the provision stated in 1 Corinthians 7:15.

In either case, adultery or desertion, the aggrieved party has the right to seek divorce from the offending spouse and, having obtained it, becomes again a single person. Should repentance and reconciliation fail to restore the violated union, the aggrieved spouse is not bound to the marriage. According to Scripture, a person who is not bound is free to remarry, but only "in the Lord," meaning to another Christian (1 Cor 7:39). The injunction for a single person who does not have the gift of celibacy to marry (v 9) applies to a person formerly married but who has become single by a scripturally legitimate divorce. In keeping with Christ's teaching in Mark 10:11-12 and Luke 16:18, the remarriage of believers may not be approved when the divorce has been used as a means of changing mates, since such intent makes the divorce adulterous.

Many factors usually combine to destroy a marriage; therefore, the church must deal with each case of divorce and remarriage on an individual basis, taking into account God's inexhaustible capacity to forgive sin and to restore broken lives. Obviously, the scriptural restrictions on divorce do not apply to believers whose broken marriages predate their conversion, since God's forgiveness wipes clean the sin of their pre-Christian past and makes them new creatures in Christ.

See also Adultery; Civil Law and Justice; Marriage, Marriage Customs; Sex, Sexuality.

DIVORCE*, Certificate of A document declaring the separation of a husband and wife, mandated by Mosaic law (Dt 24:1-4; see Mt 5:31; 19:7; Mk 10:4). The certificate of divorce protected the woman's rights, providing evidence of her freedom and ensuring that her husband could not claim her dowry. An example of the wording of such a document is Hosea 2:2: "She is no longer my wife, and I am no longer her husband" (NLT). The OT prophets used this statement figuratively to portray God's desire to separate himself from his rebellious people (Is 50:1; Jer 3:8).

See also Civil Law and Justice; Divorce; Marriage, Marriage Customs.

DI-ZAHAB Name, listed along with Paran, Tophel, Laban, and Hazeroth, meant to designate the locale of Moses' final address to Israel (Dt 1:1).

DOCTOR OF THE LAW* Translation in the KJV for "teacher of the law" in Luke 5:17, and Acts 5:34. *See* Pharisees; Teacher.

DODAI Ahohi's descendant and a commander of one of Israel's 12 contingents of soldiers (24,000 men each) during David's reign (1 Chr 27:4). Dodai is perhaps alternately called Dodo, Eleazar's father, in 2 Samuel 23:9 and 1 Chronicles 11:12. *See* Dodo #2.

DODANIM* Descendants of Noah's son Japheth (Gn 10:4). The name is emended to Rodanim in 1 Chronicles 1:7. *See* Rodanim.

DODAVAH*, DODAVAHU Inhabitant of Mareshah and father of Eliezer the prophet. Eliezer spoke against King Jehoshaphat of Judah because of his alliance with King Ahaziah of Israel (2 Chr 20:37, KJV "Dodavah").

DODO

1. Grandfather of Tola, a minor judge who judged Israel from his native city, Shamir (Jgs 10:1).
2. Father of Eleazar, one of David's mighty men known as "the Thirty" (2 Sm 23:9; 1 Chr 11:12). Dodo is perhaps identifiable with Dodai the Ahohite in 1 Chronicles 27:4. *See* Dodai.
3. Father of Elhanan, one of David's mighty men known as "the Thirty" (2 Sm 23:24; 1 Chr 11:26). Dodo lived at Bethlehem.

DOE Female deer (Prv 5:19). *See* Animals (Deer).

DOEG Official of Saul who was commanded to kill the innocent priests at Nob (1 Sm 21–22). An Edomite, he was either a proselyte or a prominent Edomite chieftain captured by Saul (14:47). He was subsequently given supervision over Saul's flocks (21:7; cf. 1 Chr 27:30, where David had a foreign head over his herd). The reason for his presence at the sanctuary at Nob (1 Sm 21:7) is not clear, though he had some religious purpose in being there, maybe being detained while in a purification process (e.g., a Nazirite vow, Nm 6:13). Possibly he secretly hid there as a spy for Saul. Whatever the case, it is evident that he saw an opportunity to gain favor with Saul when he observed David hospitably treated by the priests, who even supplied him with a weapon—the sword of Goliath (1 Sm 21:9). Shortly thereafter, he had occasion to report this to Saul (22:9-10; Ps 52 title), hoping thereby to demonstrate his loyalty. His brutal killing of the priests and the inhabitants of the city of Nob (1 Sm 22:18-19) shows his ruthless character and intimates further that he was not an Israelite.

DOG *See* Animals.

DOLEFUL CREATURE* Designation for animal of uncertain identity in Isaiah 13:21 (KJV), better rendered "howling creature" (NLT). The context implies such beasts are unclean; hence, suggested creatures include the horned owl, hyena, jackal, and leopard. *See* Animals; Birds.

DOMITIAN* Roman emperor (AD 81–96) who persecuted both Jews and Christians. Tradition says that under Domitian the apostle John was banished to Patmos, where he wrote the book of Revelation (Rv 1:9). *See* Caesars, The.

DONKEY Domesticated ass. *See* Animals (Ass).

DOORKEEPER *See* Gatekeepers.

DOPHKAH Name of an area near the wilderness of Sin where the Israelites camped on their way to Mt Sinai (Nm 33:12-13). Its site is perhaps identical with Serabit el-Khadem, an Egyptian turquoise mining center. *See* Wilderness Wanderings.

DOR Fortified Palestinian city (modern el-Burj) situated along the Mediterranean coast, south of Mt Carmel and eight miles (12.9 kilometers) north of Caesarea. It is mentioned occasionally in connection with events in the period of the judges and the united monarchy (Jos 17:11; Jgs 1:27; 1 Chr 7:29). Dor is probably the same city as Naphath-dor (Jos 12:23; 1 Kgs 4:11) and Naphoth-dor (Jos 11:2). During the days of the Conquest, the king of Dor joined Jabin's confederacy against Joshua (Jos 11:2), but was defeated (12:23). The city was assigned to Manasseh's tribe, but the tribe failed to dispossess its inhabitants (Jgs 1:27).

DORCAS Christian woman in Joppa of Judea, noted for her acts of charity (Acts 9:36-41). Dorcas is called a disciple in Acts 9:36, which is the only instance where the feminine form of the word is used in the Greek NT. Her ethnic origins are not known, since Dorcas, her Greek name, was in common use among both Jews and Greeks. The Aramaic equivalent, Tabitha, meant "gazelle."

When Dorcas died, the apostle Peter was nearby at Lydda. In response to news of his healing ministry there, two men were sent to bring Peter to Joppa. When he arrived, the body had been prepared for burial and placed in an upper room. Peter sent the mourners from the room, knelt to pray, and raised Dorcas back to life. Her restoration was the first of such miracles performed by an apostle.

DOSITHEUS

1. A Jew representing himself as a priest and Levite. He delivered a letter from Mordecai concerning the Feast of Purim (possibly containing the book of Esther) to Ptolemy and Cleopatra in the fourth year of their reign (Add Est 11:1).
2. One of Judas Maccabeus's captains. With Sosipater he captured and destroyed a stronghold of 10,000 soldiers left behind by Timothy, one of Antiochus IV Epiphanes' governors (2 Macc 12:19).
3. One of Bacenor's men. This Dositheus was a horseman with great strength. His attempt to capture Gorgias (one of Ptolemy's generals) was unsuccessful (2 Macc 12:35).
4. Drimylus's son and an apostate. A general of the Seleucids, he prevented the assassination of Ptolemy (ruler of the Seleucid Empire) by Theodotus (3 Macc 1:3).

DOTHAN Ancient city located about 60 miles (97 kilometers) north of Jerusalem, 13 miles (21 kilometers) north of the city of Samaria, and about 5 miles (8 kilometers) southeast of Megiddo. The two cities of Engannim (modern Jenin) and Ibleam guarded a narrow pass on the road leading to Dothan and on to the coastal plain.

The mound of Tell Dotha, site of Dothan, rises 200 feet (61 meters) above the surrounding plain to a height of 1,200 feet (365.6 meters) above sea level. The top of the mound comprises some 10 acres (4 hectares). From there one can look out upon fertile land boasting good crops. Flocks pasture here as they did in biblical times, drawn to the area in part by the adequate water supplied by its springs.

Dothan was the place where Joseph's brothers sold him to a caravan of Ishmaelites (Gn 37). A millennium later the city was surrounded by Syrian forces in an attempt to capture Elisha, who lived there and who was thought to be betraying the Syrian plans to the Israelite king (2 Kgs 6:8-14). Dothan was mentioned also in the lists of places conquered by Pharaoh Thutmose III and, in the intertestamental period, in connection with the military campaigns of Holofernes.

DOVE Small pigeon. *See* Birds (Pigeon or Dove).

Aerial View of Dor Plain

Aerial View of Dothan Plain

DOVE'S DUNG Source of food eaten when Samaria was besieged by Ben-hadad, king of Syria (2 Kgs 6:25). Taken literally as pigeon excrement, the reference would indicate how desperate conditions were in the famished city.

Some scholars suggest that dove's dung refers to the small, edible bulb of the star of Bethlehem plant, also known as bird's milk or bird's dung. The bulb could be boiled or roasted to make flour for bread. The "kab" in verse 25 is a unit of measure approximating 1.3 quarts (1.2 liters).

DOWRY Gift of property or goods from the bride's family to the bride or groom prior to marriage. *See* Marriage, Marriage Customs.

DRACHMA* Greek coin made of silver, roughly equivalent to the Roman denarius. *See* Coins.

DRAGON Term indicating a number of monstrous land or sea creatures. *See* Animals.

DRAGON'S WELL* *See* Jackal's Well.

DRAM* KJV for daric, a Persian gold coin, in 1 Chronicles 29:7, Ezra 2:69, 8:27, and Nehemiah 7:70-72. *See* Coins.

DREAMS Thoughts, images, or emotions occurring during sleep. Dreams have always fascinated people; the events experienced in dreams are too vivid and real to be ignored.

Ancient Understanding From the earliest times people viewed dreams as a mystery, provoking speculation

about another actual sphere of existence in which the person lived and acted while the body slept. Dreams, especially those of emperors and kings, were held to be messages from the gods.

Ancient recorded dreams focused on three main areas: religion, politics, and personal destiny. Religious dreams called for piety and devotion to the gods. Political dreams supposedly forecast the outcome of battles and the future destiny of nations. Personal dreams guided family decisions and presaged serious crises.

Sometimes the god took the initiative and forewarned the person about something unexpected. Sometimes the ruler or general would go to a pagan temple or holy place and sleep there, hoping to bring on a dream that would help him cope with some serious problem. In some dreams the message was clear; more often it had to be discovered by individuals who specialized in dream interpretation. Records were kept concerning specific dreams and the subsequent events.

Old Testament Use Dreams played an important part in the lives of God's people. Of the nearly 120 references to dreams in the OT, 52 come in Genesis during the early patriarchal period and 29 in the book of Daniel. In reality, however, only 14 specific dreams are recorded in the OT. Most of them are in Genesis and reflect God's direct revelation to the patriarchs. Even Daniel tells about only two of Nebuchadnezzar's dreams—the large, manlike image and the gigantic tree chopped down—and his own dream about the four beasts and the Ancient of Days.

The OT understanding of dreams had several significant features. Like the rest of the ancient world, people of God believed that God communicated in dreams. Yet there is in the OT accounts a reserve that is lacking in the perverse and obscene scenes often described in pagan dream records. Another distinction is that God is the initiator; he gives the revelatory dreams when, where, and to whom he pleases—a truth painfully learned by Saul (1 Sm 28:6, 15). More significantly, the secular approach to interpretation was specifically rejected. Understanding of dream symbols came not by research in dream books or by natural human ability. When Joseph interpreted the dreams of his two Egyptian fellow prisoners and later of the pharaoh himself, he insisted on giving full credit to God (Gn 40:8; 41:7, 25, 28, 39). Similarly, Daniel informed Nebuchadnezzar that the God in heaven who reveals secrets would make known the king's dream and its meaning, in which task professional dream interpreters had failed (Dn 2:27-28).

Unlike their neighbors, the OT saints knew that a dream was a "vision of the night" (Jb 33:15), and figuratively represented the spiritual realm (Jb 20:8; Pss 73:20; 126:1; Is 29:7-8).

God used dreams in OT days to protect his servants (Gn 20), to reveal himself to people in a special way (28:12), to provide guidance in specific circumstances (31:10-13), and to forewarn about personal future events (37:5-20). Dreams were also used to predict the history of nations (chs 40–41) and to foretell the four great successive world empires that would be replaced by God's eternal kingdom (Dn 4:19-27).

During the approximately 1,000 years between Joseph and Daniel, only two dreams are recorded. One assured Gideon that God would defeat the Midianites (Jgs 7:13-15); the other concerns how Solomon became so wise after his humble, unselfish request for "an understanding heart" (1 Kgs 3:9, 15) thoroughly pleased God.

In the final OT dreams, God gave Nebuchadnezzar an overview of future world history (Dn 2:31-45) and a prediction of the king's temporary insanity (4:19-27). Daniel's dream of the four beasts was similar to the king's first dreams, but with added details concerning future international relations (7:13-14).

Dreams were seen as one means by which God would speak to prophets (Nm 12:6). But how could the people of God distinguish a true prophet from an imposter? God gave two tests: the ability to predict the immediate future (Dt 18:22) and the consistency of the message with previously revealed truth (13:1-4). False prophets were put to death (v 5). False prophecy was a serious problem in the days of Jeremiah (Jer 23:25-32) and Zechariah (Zec 10:2). Despite repeated warnings by Jeremiah (Jer 23:32; 27:9-10; 29:8-9), the people preferred to listen to the false prophets with their empty messages of hope. Dreams were also a part of Israel's prophetic hope (Jl 2:28).

New Testament Use The few specific dreams in the NT all come from Matthew, five of these in the first two chapters. They emphasize the divine care and protection of the baby Jesus. First, there was God's provision that Jesus would grow up in a home with a father and mother and thus would avoid the cruelty and shame of being unjustly called an illegitimate child (Mt 1:19-23). Then the wise men were instructed in a dream not to tell Herod where Jesus was living (2:12). Jesus was further protected from jealous King Herod by the dream that told Joseph to flee to Egypt with Mary and the child (v 13). On Herod's death, Joseph was divinely advised in a dream to return home from Egypt (v 20). Finally, God warned Joseph to avoid Judea, where Herod's evil son Archelaus reigned, and to settle in Galilee instead (v 22).

The only other specific dream mentioned in the NT prompted Pilate's wife to warn her husband, "Don't have anything to do with that innocent man" (Mt 27:19, NIV).

See also Prophecy; Visions.

DRINK OFFERING *See* Offerings and Sacrifices.

DROMEDARY* Swift-footed camel of the Arabian species. *See* Animals (Camel).

DROPSY* Old medical term for excessive accumulation of watery fluid in any tissue or space of the body. Dropsy, mentioned in Luke 14:2, is a symptom of several serious disorders such as heart, kidney, or liver disease; Jesus healed a man "who had dropsy" but whose underlying illness is not described. The word "dropsy" has generally been replaced with more specific medical terms: excessive abdominal fluid is now referred to as ascites, cutaneous or subcutaneous dropsy as edema, and pleural dropsy as hydrothorax. Dropsy is not mentioned directly in the OT. A reference to swollen feet (Dt 8:4) could refer to pedal edema or simply to the formation of blisters.

See also Medicine and Medical Practice.

DRUSILLA Third and youngest daughter of Herod Agrippa, king of Judea. A Jewess, Drusilla was born about AD 38 and had two sisters, Bernice and Mariamne. She became engaged to Epiphanes, prince of Commogene, but the engagement was broken as a result of his refusal to convert to Judaism.

Drusilla's brother Agrippa II, then arranged for her to marry Azizus, king of Emesa, who agreed to be circumcised. Soon after her marriage, Felix, a gentile governor of Judea, fell in love with the 16-year-old Drusilla. Around AD 54 he persuaded her to break the Jewish law and leave her husband to marry him.

Drusilla and Felix heard the apostle Paul's proclamation of the gospel, while Paul was held in custody at Caesarea (Acts 24:24). Their son, Agrippa, perished when the Italian volcano Vesuvius erupted in AD 79.

DULCIMER* KJV translation of "pipe" in Daniel 3:5, 10, 15. *See* Musical Instruments (Psantrin); Music.

DUMAH (Person) Ishmael's son, who founded an Arab tribe (Gn 25:14; 1 Chr 1:30).

DUMAH (Place)
1. Region of the 12 tribes of Ishmael (Gn 25:14; 1 Chr 1:30) where there were a number of oases; identified with el-Jof, modern Dumat el-Jendel. This place was located about three-fourths of the way from Damascus to Medina.
2. Town in the highlands allotted to Judah's tribe for an inheritance (Jos 15:52). Its site is probably identifiable with ed-Domeh, 10 miles (16.1 kilometers) southwest of Hebron.
3. Hebrew term referring to the land of silence or death; that is, the place of graves (Pss 94:17; 115:17).
4. Perhaps a designation for Edom or Idumea in Isaiah 21:11.

DUMBNESS *See* Muteness.

DUNG GATE One of the 11 gates in the Jerusalem wall in Nehemiah's time (Neh 2:13; 3:14). It was located near the southwest corner of the city and led to the valley of Hinnom, where rubbish and refuse were dumped. This particular gate had been reconstructed by Malkijah, son of Recab (Neh 3:14), and was situated between the Fountain Gate and the Valley Gate. When the restored walls of Jerusalem were completed, the ceremony of dedication took place near this gate. Josephus knew it as the Essene Gate.

See also Jerusalem.

DURA, Plain of Location in the province of Babylon where Nebuchadnezzar set up the great image of gold, which all his subjects were ordered to worship (Dn 3:1). Its exact location is uncertain. It may be situated to the southeast of Babylon, or perhaps even located within the great outer wall of the city itself. The image was doubtless in a prominent place, probably in an open area used for public gatherings. Since *dur* means "rampart," the phrase should probably be read as "the plain of the rampart" (within Babylon).

DYE, DYEING, DYER Method of coloring textiles practiced in the Near East with natural materials even before the time of the patriarch Abraham. The Bible mentions four colors of dyes: purple, blue (actually a shade of violet), crimson, and scarlet. The purple and blue dyes were extracted from small murex shellfish found along the Phoenician coast. The dye, a glandular secretion of the mollusk, changed color on exposure to air from whitish-yellow to red, violet, or purple, depending on how it was treated. Because that dye was costly to produce, only the rich could afford purple clothing; purple, therefore, became a symbol of royalty and luxury. The dye was commonly known as "Tyrian purple" because the Phoenician cities of Tyre and Sidon were the major suppliers (Ez 27:16).

Crimson and scarlet were among several shades of bright red obtained from the kermes insect, a grub that feeds on a species of oak growing in southern Europe and Asia Minor. Some Syrian dyers still use the kermes in spite of the availability of artificial European dyes. The "tanned rams' skins" mentioned in Exodus 25:5 are still made in Syria. The tanned skin is rubbed with dye made by boiling the kermes in water. When dry, the skin is oiled, polished, and used for Bedouin slippers and other beautiful leather articles.

The "purple goods" sold by Lydia of Thyatira (Acts 16:14) were actually a dull red, now sometimes called "Turkey red." It was produced from the root of the madder plant, both for export to Europe and for local use in dyeing cotton and wool for rugs and clothing. Cultivation of madder was a major industry in Cyprus and Syria. A father customarily planted a new madder field for each son born, which would eventually be that son's inheritance. Thyatira had a dyers' guild.

See also Cloth and Cloth Manufacturing.

DYSENTERY Diarrhea caused by parasitic bacteria, protozoa (amoeba), or worms in contaminated food or drink. Dysentery is accompanied by intestinal spasms and ulceration, with the appearance of blood and pus in the excrement. On the island of Malta the apostle Paul miraculously cured a person of dysentery (Greek *dysenteria,* Acts 28:8). As the verse indicates, high fever accompanies acute dysentery, epidemics of which still plague Malta. A disease described in the OT was probably amoebic dysentery, in which intestinal tissue can be sloughed off day by day (2 Chr 21:14-19). A sporadic form of dysentery occurs when the body is able to tolerate the disruptive organism for the most part.

See also Medicine and Medical Practice.

DYSMAS* Name given to the repentant thief on the cross in apocryphal narratives based on Luke 23:39-43. Sources such as the Arabic Gospel of the Infancy and the Acts of Pilate contain fanciful accounts of earlier dealings between Christ and Dysmas. Patristic writers often commended the repentance of the "good thief," and the Latin church ultimately canonized him as a saint.

E

EAGLE Large, carnivorous bird of the falcon family noted for its strength, keen eyesight, and graceful flight. *See* Birds.

EARRING *See* Jewelry, Jewels.

EARTH Term used for our inhabited planet; the world, as distinguished from heaven and hell; land; soil; and in several other ways. Biblical usage is as broad as modern usage.

One Hebrew word translated "earth" is also used generically for "man," or Adam (Gn 2:7, 19). That word refers to reddish soil from which Adam's body was made. Another Hebrew word translated "earth" or "land" can refer to a country (21:21). A word translated "dust" can mean simply earth or dry ground (3:19). In the NT one Greek word translated "earth" can refer to a land or country (Mt 27:45). The Greek word from which "ecumenical" is derived refers to the whole inhabited earth (Lk 21:26) or the Roman Empire of those days (2:1).

In the beginning "God called the dry land Earth, and the waters that were gathered together he called Seas. . . . And God said, 'Let the earth put forth vegetation' " (Gn 1:10-11, RSV). In some passages "the earth" is used in essentially the modern sense for the whole planet (Jb 1:7), hanging in empty space (26:7). References to the earth's four corners (Is 11:12; Ez 7:2) allude to the points of a compass, not to the earth's shape. The circle of the earth probably refers to the circumference of the horizon (Is 40:22; cf. Jb 38:13). The earth is sometimes pictured as supported on pillars (Jb 9:6; Ps 75:3) or foundations (Ps 104:5; Prv 8:29; Is 24:18; Jer 31:37). Since many of the biblical usages are found in figurative passages of poetry or prophecy, they reveal little about the Hebrews' cosmological understanding.

"Earth" sometimes refers to the soil or ground that a farmer works (cf. 2 Kgs 5:17). According to the Bible, the original condition of the earth (Gn 2:6) was affected by the curse of human sinfulness (3:17-19). (Modern ecologists seem to agree that the earth suffers because of human greed and arrogance.) After Abel's blood was spilled on the ground, Cain's difficulty in making the soil produce for him was a constant reminder that he had murdered his brother (4:8-12).

The Israelites were instructed to let the land rest every seventh year (Ex 23:10-12; Lv 25:4-5), allowing the soil to replenish nutrients used up by crops. After seven such "sabbath years," in the 50th "jubilee year" the land reverted back to original family holdings (Lv 25:10-17). That provision not only reminded the people of God's ultimate ownership but kept potential "land barons" from amassing huge estates.

The Mosaic law instructed the Israelites that the land's condition would be a spiritual barometer of their relationship with God. Drought or lack of productivity was a sign that the relationship had been broken (Lv 26; Dt 28). Israel was warned that their wickedness could become so great that the Lord would evict them from his land (cf. Lv 26:37; Dt 28:64). Even if that happened, however, God would eventually restore his people so they could again be "wedded" to the land (Is 62:4).

Many passages point to a "coming age," when the earth will be set free from its "bondage to decay," a deliverance for which the whole creation is said to be "groaning" in anticipation (Rom 8:19-23). The Bible pictures a period of prodigious renewal of the earth's fertility (Ez 47; Jl 3:18; Am 9:13-15; Zec 14:6-9). One day, however, "the heavens will pass away with a loud noise, and the elements will be dissolved with fire, and the earth and the works that are upon it will be burned up" (2 Pt 3:10, RSV). Yet in the apostle John's apocalyptic vision, he saw "a new heaven and a new earth, for the old heaven and the old earth had disappeared" (Rv 21:1, NLT).

See also New Heavens and New Earth.

EARTH, New *See* New Heavens and New Earth.

EARTHENWARE* *See* Pottery.

EARTHQUAKE Shaking or trembling of the earth originated by volcanic or tectonic activity. Earthquakes occur frequently in Palestine due mostly to the volcanic nature of the regions around the Dead Sea and the Sea of Galilee. The primary centers of earthquakes in Palestine are upper Galilee, the Samaritan country near Shechem, and the western edge of the Judean Mountains near Lydda.

The Hebrew word for "earthquake" indicates a great noise or a tremendous roaring, suggesting that the Israelites were impressed with the rumbling connected with earthquakes.

REPORTS OF ANCIENT EARTHQUAKES
The Jewish historian Josephus described a quake that occurred during the battle of Actium in which many animals and more than 30,000 people were killed. The earthquake in AD 79 at Vesuvius was reported throughout the Roman world. Among many others, Agrippa was killed in this earthquake. Eusebius recorded the destruction of Caesarea and Emmaus by an earthquake during the reign of Hadrian. In spite of much ancient and modern earthquake activity in Palestine, Jerusalem has remained relatively undamaged.

Instances of earthquakes are (1) at Mt Sinai, in connection with God's giving the law to Moses (Ex 19:18); (2) during the wilderness wandering of the Israelites, when Korah and his followers rebelled against Moses and were destroyed as punishment for their rebellion (Nm 16:31-33); (3) among the Philistines on the occasion when Jonathan and his armor bearer fought a garrison of Philistines (1 Sm 14:15); (4) after Elijah killed the prophets of Baal and, fleeing Jezebel's wrath, sat under a juniper tree feeling sorry for himself (1 Kgs 19:7-9, 11); (5) in the reign of King Uzziah (Am 1:1); (6) at the death of Jesus on Calvary (Mt 27:51-54); (7) at the resurrection of Jesus (Mt 28:2); and (8) at Philippi while Paul and Silas were in jail (Acts 16:26). Earthquakes are also mentioned as one of the phenomena in connection with the "Day of the Lord" (Zec 14:4-5) and the consummation of this age (Rv 6:12-24; 11:19; 16:18).

EAST*, Children of the Phrase used in reference to those nations that were east of Israel (e.g., Jgs 6:3, NLT "people of the east"). *See* People of the East.

EASTERN SEA* Alternate name for the Salt Sea, or Dead Sea, derived from the sea's location on the eastern boundary of the land of Israel (Ez 47:18; Jl 2:20; Zec 14:8). *See* Dead Sea.

EAST GATE Gate in the walled city of Jerusalem (Neh 3:29). "East gate" also refers to the gate of the temple mentioned in Ezekiel 10:19; 11:1; and 43:1. *See* Jerusalem.

EAST SEA* KJV name for the "eastern sea," an alternate name for the Dead Sea, in Ezekiel 47:18. *See* Dead Sea.

EAST WIND Wind coming mostly in May, September, and October. This scorching wind, also called a sirocco, destroyed vegetation (Gn 41:6; Ez 17:10; Jon 4:8), withered flowers (Ps 103:15-16), and dried up fountains and springs (Hos 13:15). The Lord used an east wind to drive back the waters of the Red Sea for the Israelites to cross (Ex 14:21). The east wind also depicts God's judgment (Is 27:8; Jer 4:11; 18:17). An east or northeast wind drove the apostle Paul's ship off course (Acts 27:14, KJV "Euroclydon"). That wind, which is frequent in the western Mediterranean, is called a "levanter."

EBAL
1. Shobal's son and descendant of Seir the Horite (Gn 36:23; 1 Chr 1:40).
2. Joktan's son and descendant of Shem (1 Chr 1:22). He is called Obal in Genesis 10:28.

EBAL, Mount Mountain just over 3,000 feet (914.4 meters) high in the central hill country of Israel. Mt Gerizim is usually mentioned with it (Dt 11:29; 27:13; Jos 8:33). There is no certain known meaning to the word. It is quite unlikely that it was connected in any way with a son of Shobal, whose name is spelled the same as the mountain (Gn 36:23; 1 Chr 1:40; cf. 1 Chr 1:22, where Ebal is a variant of the spelling Obal of Gn 10:28).

Years before the entrance into the Promised Land, God, through Moses, designated the twin mountains Ebal and Gerizim as the place for the recitation of the curses and blessings of Deuteronomy 27–28. According to Deuteronomy 27:12, six tribes of Israel were to stand on Gerizim and shout the blessings. These were Simeon, Levi, Judah, Issachar, Joseph, and Benjamin. "Joseph" here would mean the tribes of Ephraim and Manasseh in whose territory these two mountains belonged. The other six tribes—Reuben, Gad, Asher, Zebulun, Dan, and Naphtali—were to recite the curses from Mt Ebal. It is interesting that Ebal is north of the east-west valley that separates the two mountains and it is the more northerly tribes that stand on it.

The fulfillment of the divine directive is recorded in Joshua 8:33. Joshua also obeyed in another matter—that of building on Mt Ebal an altar of unhewn stones (Jos 8:30) as Moses had commanded (Dt 27:4).

EBED
1. Gaal's father (Jgs 9:26-35). Gaal led the men of Shechem in an unsuccessful revolt against Abimelech, judge of Israel.
2. Adin's descendant and son of Jonathan. Ebed was the head of a family that returned to Judah with Ezra after the exile (Ezr 8:6).

EBED-MELECH Ethiopian eunuch in King Zedekiah's court. He secured the king's permission to rescue the prophet Jeremiah out of a cistern where he had been thrown to die (Jer 38:6-13). For this righteous act, Ebed-melech was promised God's safety at the fall of Jerusalem (39:16).

EBENEZER
1. Site where the Israelite army encamped before a battle with the Philistines (1 Sm 4:1-11). It is thought to have been near Aphek, where the Philistines were encamped. The Israelite army was badly defeated in the battle, and 4,000 of its men were slain on the field. The elders of Israel tried to change their fortunes by bringing the ark of the covenant into their camp, but Israel was again defeated with a loss of 30,000 foot soldiers, and the ark of God was captured (1 Sm 4:3-11; 5:1).
2. Site near Mizpah, where God gave Israel a great victory over the Philistines. To commemorate the victory Samuel set up a stone between Mizpah and Jeshanah and called its name Ebenezer, meaning "the stone of help," for the Lord had helped them get the victory (1 Sm 7:12).

EBER
1. Abraham's ancestor (Gn 10:21-25; 11:14-17; 1 Chr 1:18-25; Lk 3:35) from whom the word "Hebrew" may be derived. Eber lived 464 years and was the ancestor of the "sons of Eber," a phrase possibly equal to the "Hebrews," as "sons of Heth" equals the "Hittites" (Gn 23:10, NASB). However, the term "Hebrew" may be an indication of social class rather than of descent from Eber. Eber had a son in whose time the earth was divided, a division possibly into nomadic and sedentary groups.
2. Gadite leader registered during the reigns of Jothan, king of Judah (950–932 BC), and Jeroboam II, king of Israel (993–953 BC; 1 Chr 5:13, KJV "Heber").
3. Benjamite and Elpaal's descendant (1 Chr 8:12).
4. Benjamite and Shashak's descendant (1 Chr 8:22).
5. Head of Amok's priestly family during the days of the high priest Joiakim (Neh 12:20).

Mount Ebal and Mount Gerizim

EBEZ City in the plain of Esdraelon, allotted to Issachar's tribe for an inheritance (Jos 19:20).

EBIASAPH* Kohathite Levite, Elkanah's son and the father of Assir (1 Chr 6:23, 37; 9:19); alternately called Abiasaph in Exodus 6:24.

EBLA TABLETS* Tablets, dating c. 2220–2240 BC, discovered in the ancient Syrian city-state of Ebla, now identified with the site of Tell Mardikh.

Ebla was a commercial center, manufacturing items of textiles, wood, ceramics, gold, silver, and other metals. A large number of the clay tablets unearthed are economic documents, recording transactions with many other cities, stretching from Asia Minor to Egypt and from Cyprus to Iran (Persia). Thousands of cities are named in these documents. Included are many familiar biblical names, such as Hazor, Megiddo, Dor, Joppa, Gaza, and Urusalim (Jerusalem, or possibly "city of Salem"). In one text we also see Sodom, Gomorrah, and Zoar. Zoar is described as "in the territory of Bela" (cf. Gn 14:2). According to the biblical account, Sodom and Gomorrah were destroyed in the days of Abraham (Gn 19:24-29); hence, the details recorded in Genesis 14 and 19 could not have been reconstructed at a later date unless there was a living tradition recording the events.

Many personal names appear in the tablets from Tell Mardikh that have biblical equivalents, e.g., Abram (*ab-ra-mu*), Israel (*ish-ra-ilu*), Saul (*sha-u-lu*), and David (*da-u-du*). To some, this fact raises questions, while others find it to be a confirmation of the biblical record. For example, it might be asked how the name "Israel" could be found four or more centuries before God gave the name to Jacob. The Bible does not suggest that the name was new. Names in those days were often composed of the name of a deity plus a verbal form (e.g., Isaiah = "Yah is salvation"). It is entirely conceivable that parents named their children *ish-ra-ilu*, "El [God] has prevailed," before the days of Jacob. What was new in the biblical experience was the personal encounter with God and the blessing that it brought on Jacob.

A number of the names from Ebla seem to appear in two forms, one compounded with -*ilu* (El), the other with -*ya* (Yah). Thus the names *mi-ka-ya* (Micaiah, Micah) and *mi-ka-il* (Michael) are reported by Pettinato, along with other theophoric (God-bearing) names. The appearance of the ending -*ya*, if it has been properly interpreted as a divine name (Yah, the Lord), raises an important question. According to Exodus 6:3, God told Moses that he appeared to Abraham, to Isaac, and to Jacob as El Shaddai, "but by my name Yahweh I did not make myself known to them." This seems to say that the name Yahweh was not known prior to the revelation to Moses at Sinai. On the other hand, the name Yahweh is found many times in Genesis, not only in narrative portions (where a later author or editor might have inserted a name, such as was done with certain place-names), but also in oaths taken in the name of Yahweh and in quotations that imply that the name of Yahweh was actually in use. This problem has long been recognized, and biblical scholars have divided into two groups: those who held that the name was *not* known prior to the time of Moses, and those who held that the name *was* known but that it took on a new meaning in the light of the Sinai-exodus event. If the interpretation of the Eblean materials proves to be correct—namely, that -*ya* is a divine-name element in personal names—then we shall have to conclude that the name Yah(weh) was known in patriarchal times but that its true significance, that Yahweh is the ever-living

and life-giving God, only began to be fully revealed in his deliverance of his people from Egyptian bondage.

The Eblean materials have certainly opened a new door to a rich storehouse of knowledge. It will be many years before all the implications of this discovery are fully realized. But certain facts are already clear, and among these is this very important truth: the patriarchal stories in Genesis 11–35 can no longer be ascribed to authors of the eighth or seventh centuries BC. To assume that such an author could have included hundreds of names of places and persons, items of trade, and the many details that are found in these chapters, and then to suggest that it is mere coincidence that has brought to light the same names, places, trade relationships, and countless other details through modern archaeological discoveries, is simply unreasonable. Ebla has delivered the coup de grâce to such theories.

See also Inscriptions.

DO THE EBLA TABLETS PROVE THE BIBLE?
The discoveries at Tell Mardikh, astounding as they are, do not "prove" the Bible, for it does not need the proof of archaeology or of any other human skill. The Bible is God's Word. Any attempt to "prove" it only exhibits our doubts. As other archaeological discoveries have done, the discoveries at Ebla will help us to see what kind of men and women God was dealing with, what kind of world they were living in, and how much he must have loved them to want to deliver them from the ways of the world to walk in his way. We still have much to learn, and Ebla will supply some of the background for that learning process.

EBONY Black wood, highly prized in antiquity for use in home furnishings. *See* Plants.

EBRON* Town belonging to Asher's tribe, in Joshua 19:28, according to some Hebrew manuscripts. Other manuscripts read Abdon. It was a Levitical city located about 15 miles (24.1 kilometers) south of Tyre and inland from Aczib on the Mediterranean coast.

EBRONAH* KJV form of Abronah, an Israelite stopping place in the wilderness, in Numbers 33:34-35. *See* Abronah.

ECBATANA Greek name for the capital of the ancient Median Empire, later one of the capital cities of the Persian and Parthian empires. It is often spelled Achmetha (Ezr 6:2, KJV), approximating its Aramaic name. The Old Persian name, Hangmatana, may have meant "place of assembly." Modern Hamadan covers most of the ruins of the ancient city.

The city is at 6,300 feet (1,920.1 meters) on the eastern slopes of Mt Oronte (Alvand), a granite peak reaching to a height of 12,000 feet (3,657.4 meters) above sea level, part of an impassable range broken only by the pass leading to Ecbatana. Major trade routes converged on this pass and gave Ecbatana its strategic importance.

The altitude of the city also accounted for its popularity as the summer residence of Persian and Parthian kings. In the winter, blizzards pile snow several feet deep and temperatures plummet below zero, but the summer climate is cool and comfortable; mountains shade the afternoon sun, while melting snows bring ample water. Greek general Xenophon reported that the Persian king Cyrus annually spent three months of spring in Susa, seven months of winter in Babylon, "and in the height of summer two months in Ecbatana."

The Greek historian Herodotus recorded that the city was established by Deioces, founder of the Median dynasty, early in the seventh century BC. In 550 BC Cyrus captured the city from a Median king, Astyages. It was from Ecbatana that Cyrus issued his 538 BC decree that all Jews throughout his kingdom might return to Jerusalem to rebuild the temple of the Lord (Ezr 1:2-4). Later, an Aramaic memorandum regarding this decree was found in the records of Ecbatana after a fruitless search of the archives in Babylon (6:1-12). After Darius I (521–486 BC) quelled a revolt in securing the throne, he had the famous Behistun inscription carved in the side of Mt Orontes high above the city. The city was taken and pillaged by Alexander the Great in 330 BC.

Although Ezra 6:2 is the only explicit biblical reference to the city, Ecbatana could have been one of the Median cities receiving exiles from the northern kingdom (722 BC), if the city were in existence before fortification by Deioces (2 Kgs 17:6). The book of Tobit places Jewish exiles in Ecbatana in the seventh century (3:7; 7:1; 14:14), though that is of questionable historical worth. The book of Judith records a battle between a Median king, Arphaxad, and an Assyrian king, Nebuchadnezzar, in which the Assyrians capture Ecbatana (1:1-2, 14), but the account is dubious because the identity of those kings is unknown. Antiochus Epiphanes may have died there in 164 BC (2 Macc 9:1-3, 19-28).

Ecbatana is the only one of the three Persian capitals that has yet to be completely excavated, since it lies partly within the modern city of Hamadan, Iran. Ancient Greek authors gave elaborate descriptions of the city and its wealth. Polybius, for example, reported that it "greatly exceeded all the other cities in wealth and the magnificence of its buildings." Incidental archaeological discoveries of two foundation inscriptions in silver and gold from the time of Darius I and column bases from Artaxerxes II suggest the great promise of excavations there. Excavations have been forestalled, however, because extensive demolition of modern Hamadan would be necessary for access to much of the ancient city below.

See also Persia, Persians.

ECCLESIASTES, Book of

OT book of Wisdom Literature. Ecclesiastes is philosophical in character, posing deep questions about the meaning and nature of human existence.

"Ecclesiastes" is the Greek title for the book and has come into English from the Septuagint (Greek translation of the OT). In keeping with an early Jewish practice of adopting the first few words of a book as the title, the Hebrew title of Ecclesiastes is "The Words of Koheleth, the Son of David, King in Jerusalem." It is also known simply as "Koheleth."

The term "Koheleth" is the author's title for himself throughout the book (Eccl 1:1-2, 12; 7:27; 12:8-10). It is the Hebrew participial form of a verb meaning "to assemble," and thus it seems to designate one who speaks in an assembly. The word has often been translated "the Preacher" in English. Because of the philosophical nature of the book, however, the title possibly indicates the author's function or station as a leader in the community of wise men.

PREVIEW
• Author
• Date
• Purpose and Theological Teaching
• Content

Author The authorship of Ecclesiastes presents complex questions, on which biblical scholars disagree. Early Jew-

ish tradition was divided over the issue, ascribing the book to King Hezekiah and his school, as well as to King Solomon.

Internal evidence is often appealed to for support of Solomon as the author of Ecclesiastes. The first verse ascribes the authorship of the book to "the son of David." Other passages (e.g., 1:16-17; 2:6-7) also seem to refer to Solomon, who succeeded David as king of the united kingdom of Israel. Those who reject Solomonic authorship interpret such references as literary devices, written by a later unknown author in order to use Solomon's devotion to wisdom as a context for his own ideas about life's purpose and meaning.

A number of passages in the book have been appealed to in support of non-Solomonic authorship. Some scholars allege that if the book had been written by Solomon, he would not have used the past tense about his reign "over Israel in Jerusalem" (1:12). Proponents of Solomonic authorship point out, however, that the Hebrew verb "was" can also mean "became," thus stating that Solomon had become king in Jerusalem.

It is also alleged that 1:16 supports a date of writing by an author who lived much later than Solomon. They say that Solomon could not have said that he was wiser than "all who were over Jerusalem before me," for that would point to a long succession of kings before him. But the author may have meant prominent wise men rather than kings (see 1 Kgs 4:31).

One of the chief difficulties with Solomonic authorship is the fact that OT history does not record a period of spiritual revival in Solomon's life as a context for the book of Ecclesiastes. That is not a conclusive argument, however, for the thoughts recorded in the book are intensely personal in nature. The historical books of the OT deal primarily with historical developments, mentioning personal aspects of human life only where they bear upon God's purposes as reflected in the national history. It would, in fact, be surprising if the extremely personal struggles recorded in Ecclesiastes were cited by the historical writers.

The question of authorship is a difficult one, but there seems to be no conclusive evidence against Solomon as the author of Ecclesiastes.

Date The majority of scholars who hold to the Solomonic authorship of Ecclesiastes date the book in Solomon's final years as king (c. 940 BC). The book would then have been written in the golden era of Israelite wisdom, by one of the foremost proponents of wisdom teaching.

Those who deny Solomonic authorship disagree among themselves as to when the book was written, but most date it in the postexilic period. A Maccabean date (c. 165 BC) is difficult to maintain, because fragments of the book, dated in the second century BC, have been found at the Dead Sea site of Qumran. Also, the apocryphal book of Ecclesiasticus, probably written in the early second century BC, was heavily influenced by Ecclesiastes. Such factors would allow little time for the writing and circulation of the book in the Maccabean period.

A number of conservative scholars, such as Franz Delitzsch and E. J. Young, have assigned a fifth-century BC date to the book. Many others consider it a third-century BC document.

Internal Evidence Attempts have been made to determine the date of the book of Ecclesiastes from alleged historical allusions. But the somewhat gloomy observations found in such passages as 1:2-11 and 3:1-15 need be nothing more than the author's conclusions about the emptiness of life. They do not necessarily indicate that the book was written in a time of national decline or social decay within Israel, a time that would not fit with the reign of Solomon.

It is also alleged that the book contains allusions to Greek philosophical concepts. That would indicate that it was written sometime after the Hellenization of the Syro-Palestinian world effected by the conquests of Alexander the Great (356–323 BC).

One of those philosophical concepts is the "golden mean" propounded by Aristotle. The golden mean calls for avoiding extremes in the pursuit of satisfaction in life, and it is reflected in Ecclesiastes 7:14-18. The same concept is found in Egyptian wisdom literature (*Instruction of Amen-em-opet* 9.14), as well as in Aramaic wisdom literature. In one of the finest examples of Aramaic wisdom, *The Words of Ahiqar*, the golden mean is expressed in the words "Be not (too) sweet, lest they [swallow you]; be not (too) bitter [*lest they spit you out*]." But the golden mean concept need not indicate one particular period of thought; it may simply represent a basic kind of wisdom shared by people of all times and all ethnic backgrounds.

Linguistic Considerations The most critical issue in dating Ecclesiastes is the nature of the book's language. The Hebrew of Ecclesiastes is unique, differing stylistically and linguistically from such fifth-century OT books as Ezra, Nehemiah, and Zechariah.

Some scholars maintain that the language of Ecclesiastes was heavily influenced by Aramaic, and thus the book was written at a time when the Aramaic language was influential in the Hebrew-speaking world. Others have argued that the peculiarities of the Hebrew should be understood as affinities with Canaanite-Phoenician dialects.

It is often asserted that the Hebrew of the book is similar to later Mishnaic Hebrew, particularly in its use of the relative pronoun. Yet the language of Ecclesiastes is dissimilar to the Mishnah in other ways.

The linguistic evidence could point to a late date for the book, but it is also possible that Solomon wrote in a literary style that was heavily influenced by Phoenician literature. Such a style may have become a standard for the literary genre into which Ecclesiastes falls. During the reign of Solomon, contacts between Palestine and Phoenicia were quite common.

Purpose and Theological Teaching The book of Ecclesiastes demonstrates the meaninglessness of a worldview that does not press beyond the limits of human experience to include God. It seeks to show that meaningful satisfaction may be attained in a universe that seems to be nothing more than a succession of wearying cycles—a universe into which people are locked with no apparent means of escape. According to Koheleth, freedom can be achieved by fearing God and believing that God will ultimately judge everything fairly. Thus, life has a goal and purpose that it will reach, although in the course of history and the processes of the physical world, it may not look that way.

The book's chief theological tenet is that God is not disinterested in the course of human events with its gross injustices. He will judge every deed. Life, therefore, has a purpose, and human deeds have meaning.

Koheleth is often accused of having a pessimistic view of life. One cannot read such passages as 1:12-14, 18 and 2:1-9, 18-23 without feeling his helplessness as he viewed what seemed an empty existence. But Koheleth's pessimism had to do with life apart from God. To him such a life had no meaning.

A positive good emerges from the book, however, even though it is often overlooked. Koheleth speaks in terms of absolutes as he spins his argument. There is an absolute good for people as they live in a seemingly meaningless world. That good is the enjoyment of God's gifts to his people. Thus Koheleth is not an utter pessimist. When he lifts the horizons of his worldview to include the hand of God at work in the world, he becomes an optimist. But when he looks at life without God, he is pessimistic, for such a view offers only despair.

Koheleth's "theology of contentment" is clear in such passages as 2:24-25, 3:10-13, and 3:22. The first passage seems to express a hedonistic view of life, making eating and drinking the main purpose. The expression "eat and drink" is a Semitic idiom that seems to express the everyday routines of life (cf. Jer 22:15; Lk 17:27-28). Koheleth's use of the phrase, then, simply means that one should enjoy God's providence. Life is meant to be enjoyed, not endured.

In 3:10-13 Koheleth sets forth the great enigma of humankind: God has put the knowledge of eternity in the human mind. That is, he has made the mind able to go beyond the limits of physical existence. Yet even that ability to conceptualize the eternal does not explain all of God's purposes. Therefore, it is good for a person simply to accept human limitation and enjoy whatever knowledge God gives.

Ecclesiastes 3:16–4:3 is a difficult section of the book. There Koheleth observes the inequities of life and concludes that God allows such things for the purpose of "sifting" people to show them that they are no more than animals. The same principle appears in 8:11, where Koheleth observes that when evil goes unpunished, the wicked are encouraged to continue to do evil. In 3:18 he asserts that injustice is present in the world to distinguish the good from the wicked. The Hebrew in that assertion should be translated "in and of themselves." That is, viewed alone, apart from God, humankind is no better than animals. If one adopts a worldview that omits God, there can be no way of knowing what lies beyond the grave (3:21). The inequities that Koheleth observes will be corrected only in the Day of Judgment. Thus, it is best for a person to be content with God's providence and not to be anxious about tomorrow (3:22).

The key to understanding the book of Ecclesiastes is the recurring phrase "under the sun." That phrase defines Koheleth's perspective. He is not judging all human experience as vain. Rather, he is observing life "under the sun," or apart from God, as vain. The apostle Paul rendered the same verdict on the created world in Romans 8:20-23, but he went on to say that God uses all things in his world to work out good results for his people (Rom 8:28). Koheleth's viewpoint is similarly helpful.

Koheleth has often been interpreted as expressing an Epicurean view of life, that eating and drinking are humanity's highest good. In 2:1-8, however, he tests pleasure and finds it futile. He concludes that pleasure is not an absolute good. The passages that speak of eating and drinking refer only to the enjoyment of those good and necessary things that come from God's hand.

Content

The Vanity of the Cycle of History and Nature (1:1-11)

Koheleth begins his recital of the vanity of life by observing its emptiness and the apparent lack of purpose in the processes of nature. Human toil is fruitless (1:3), and the endless cycle of life and history is meaningless (1:4-11).

The Vanity of Koheleth's Own Experience (1:12–2:26)
In this dramatic section Koheleth looks back to observe the futility of aspects of his life that some might have regarded as possessing great value. He recalls his search for wisdom, but pronounces human philosophy futile (1:12-18). His search for pleasure (2:1-11) also ended in futility. In the light of this conclusion, Koheleth hardly sets forth the attainment of pleasure as life's highest good. The search for valid philosophical verities is wearisome and futile in its outcome (vv 12-17). Human toil is also vain (vv 18-23), because one can never be sure who will inherit the reward of one's toil (v 21). Koheleth concludes that the greatest good is to accept God's providence joyfully (vv 24-26), an optimistic note in his message.

The Plight of Humanity apart from God (3:1-22)
Koheleth's familiar statement that everything in life has its time (3:1-9) has often been interpreted as crassly fatalistic. But those verses more probably set forth the unalterability of life's circumstances. Humankind is locked into a continuum from which there is no escape, yet people are able to think in terms that go beyond the physical (v 11). That is the enigma of humankind. Viewed apart from God, people really are no better than animals (vv 19-20).

Conclusions Resulting from Koheleth's Observations (4:1-16)
The author begins with a gloomy outlook on life (4:1-3) but goes on to draw conclusions of permanent value. He points out, for example, that life's difficulties are better faced with a partner than alone (vv 9-12).

The Vanity of Living Only for Oneself (5:1–6:12)
Koheleth gives a powerful denunciation of a self-seeking life by focusing on God (5:1-2, 4-6). His condemnation of the misuse of riches and his concern for the poor (5:8–6:9) are themes later emphasized in the NT.

Wisdom for Living (7:1–8:17)
This fine example of OT Wisdom Literature uses a proverbial pattern (7:1-13) and personal references (vv 23-29) to give insight into how one may find true satisfaction. The whole passage upholds the virtue of godly wisdom. Koheleth's theology of contentment underlies his observation that God is the source of adversity as well as prosperity (v 14). He affirms that one should accept both as coming from God. Applying wisdom to governmental authority (8:2-9), Koheleth counsels the reader to obey the authorities. The apostle Paul gave the same advice in Romans 13. Koheleth strikes an optimistic note (Eccl 8:13), exalting the fear of God. The author is not totally pessimistic, for he shows that fearing God leads to genuine satisfaction.

Observations on Life's Seeming Injustices (9:1-18)
"Under the sun," that is, apart from God, there are no apparent differences among human beings (9:1-6, 11-12). Great deeds often go unnoticed and unthanked (vv 13-16). A person should nonetheless be content, for life does offer certain benefits (vv 7-10).

Wisdom and Folly (10:1-20)
Wisdom in the OT basically means knowing God, and folly is rejection of God. Koheleth shows how wisdom can lead to honor and satisfaction, and folly can lead to ruin.

Koheleth's Conclusion—Fear God (11:1–12:14)
The book of Ecclesiastes began with a pronouncement of vanity on all creation, and it ends with Koheleth looking beyond his gloomy vistas to see God. Chapter 11 begins with a statement of human inability to understand the ways of God. Though people are meant to enjoy life,

they must remember that the future will bring God's judgment (11:9-10). After giving a beautiful description of old age (12:1-8) and encouraging the reader to fear God in youth, Koheleth states his conclusion. A person's whole duty is to fear God (vv 13-14). The pleasure of youth will burst like a bubble and, without God, one will finally have nothing. Satisfaction can come only as one fears God. Life without God is the ultimate vanity.

See also Solomon (Person); Wisdom; Wisdom Literature.

ECCLESIASTICUS *See* Wisdom of Jesus ben Sirach.

ECLIPSE*
Total or partial obscuration of the sun as a result of the passing of the moon between the sun and the earth; thus, a possible explanation for certain unusual astronomical events in the Bible. *See* Astronomy.

EDAR*
KJV spelling of Eder in Genesis 35:21. *See* Eder (Place) #1.

EDEN
1. Place where Adam and Eve lived until they sinned against God and were banished (Gn 2:8, 15; 3:23-24). *See* Garden of Eden.
2. Alternate form of Beth-eden in Ezekiel 27:23. *See* Beth-eden.

EDER (Person)
1. Member of Benjamin's tribe and the son of Beriah, a leader in the town of Aijalon (1 Chr 8:15).
2. Levite of Merari's clan and the son of Mushi (1 Chr 23:23; 24:30).

EDER (Place)
1. First camping place of Jacob between Ephrath (Bethlehem) and Hebron, following Rachel's death. The tower of Eder, meaning "the tower of the flock," was perhaps a watchtower constructed for shepherds to guard their flocks (Gn 35:21). It was located a short distance from Bethlehem.
2. One of the 29 cities located near the border of Edom in the southern extremity of the land allotted to Judah's tribe for an inheritance. It is listed between Kabzeel and Jagur in Joshua 15:21. Its site is unknown.

EDH*
Hebrew name of an altar built in God's honor by the Reubenites, Gadites, and the half-tribe of Manasseh (Jos 22:10, 34, NLT mg) when these tribes took possession of Gilead. The name means "witness." The Hebrew Masoretic Text and the Greek Septuagint do not contain the word, but it has the authority of a few ancient manuscripts.

EDNA
Raguel's wife and mother of Sarah (Tb 7:2; 10:12; 11:1). Sarah married Tobias, son of Tobit (7:13).

EDOM, EDOMITES
Land and its inhabitants found on the high plateau to the south and southeast of the Dead Sea. The biblical term Edom, meaning "red," denotes either the name of the land or the name of Esau, in remembrance of the red pottage or stew for which he exchanged his birthright (Gn 25:30; 36:1, 8, 19). The country of Edom was also known as Seir (Gn 32:3; 36:30; Nm 24:18).

Geography The northern boundary of Edom was the Wadi Zered, the "Brook of the Willows" (Is 15:7). In ancient geological times the area was thrust up to a considerable height, and dark-red sandstone cliffs were exposed along the western side where the land falls steeply into the Arabah, the southern extension of the deep depression in which the Dead Sea and the Jordan Valley lie. The Edom Plateau rises to over 5,000 feet (1,523.9 meters), reaching over 5,600 feet (1,706.8 meters) in places. The area divides into two unequal parts. The region of Punon forms something of a valley between the smaller northern part and the longer southern part. The northern section is not quite so high, though in a limited area near Radhadiyeh it reaches 5,300 feet (1,615.4 meters). The southern section is longer and generally higher, being over 5,000 feet (1,523.9 meters) throughout the central ridge and touching 5,687 feet (1,733.3 meters) at one point. To the east, the escarpment does not fall below 4,000 feet (1,219.1 meters), except in the north. The desert lies beyond and limits expansion eastward. To the west, the land falls away rather steeply into the Arabah. The extent of Edom to the west varied from time to time. It was comparatively easy to gain access to the Negev of southern Judah in this area, and Edomite encroachments were made from time to time. The southern frontier was marked by an extensive limestone scarp at the southern edge of the plateau. This ran eastward from Ain Gharandal in the Arabah. Beyond this barrier to the south lay rocky, uninhabitable desert, through which merchants must have journeyed to the port at Ezion-geber for trade.

The land of Edom was, on the whole, inhospitable, though there were areas where farming could be undertaken, particularly to the northeast. Here herds of animals could be grazed. Edom's wealth, however, came largely from the caravan trade that came up from the south and brought goods from India and South Arabia to the Mediterranean coast and Egypt. The important King's Highway (Nm 21:22) passed through Edom on its way north.

History Biblically, the name Edom does not appear in the genealogy in Genesis 10. It first appears in the story of Esau in Genesis 25:30. Esau was called Edom from the red color of the pottage for which he sold his birthright to his brother, Jacob. In Genesis 36 there is reference to an Edomite kingdom at a time well before the appearance of an Israelite kingdom, though it is possible that the "chiefs" of Edom were tribal chieftains or nondynastic leaders like the Israelite judges.

The earliest nonbiblical references come from Egypt and seem to confirm this. Amarna Letter 288 (early 14th century BC) refers to the "lands of Seir," and the crossing of the Shashu tribes of Edom into Egypt is mentioned by Seti II (1214–1208 BC) and Ramses III (1198–1166 BC). There are no Egyptian references to towns or rulers, only to tribal Bedouin from Seir-Edom. There is some evidence that Ramses II was in Transjordan about 1280–1270 BC, but there is no clear evidence that there was a centralized government before the 13th century BC. Rather, the land was occupied mainly by seminomadic people. From then on, permanent settlements began to appear, a fact that has relevance for the date of the exodus. The Song of Moses in Exodus 15 refers to the "chiefs of Edom." By the time of the exodus, there appears to have been a kingdom of Edom (Nm 20:14, 18, 20-23; 33:37; 34:3). The Israelites skirted Edom on their journey to the Promised Land (Jgs 5:4; 11:17-18).

At the time of the rise of the Israelite monarchy, Saul fought successfully against Edom (1 Sm 14:47). Doeg the Edomite was the chief of Saul's herdsmen (21:7; 22:9, 18-22). At the beginning of the 10th century BC, David defeated Edom in the Valley of Salt and killed many Edomites (2 Sm 8:13; 1 Chr 18:12). Thereafter, David placed garrisons in Edom, and the Edomites became his subjects (2 Sm 8:14). It is not clear whether David saw in these people a military threat or whether he was interested in the supply of copper from their land and the potential wealth that would flow from the caravan traffic passing through Edom. David's successes resulted in the flight of a certain Hadad, who was "of the royal house of Edom" to Egypt (1 Kgs 11:14-17), where he married a member of the Egyptian royal family (vv 18-20). On David's death, Hadad returned to Edom, where he became king. It would seem that a monarchical form of government had developed by David's time. Solomon continued to exert influence in Edom. He had access to the port of Ezion-geber (9:26).

The biblical records provide no information about Edom from the end of Solomon's reign until the days of Jehoshaphat of Judah (872–848 BC). Jehoshaphat was able to occupy the port of Ezion-geber, although his ships were wrecked there, possibly by the Edomites (1 Kgs 22:48; 2 Chr 20:36-37). Israel combined with Judah and Edom in an unsuccessful campaign against King Mesha of Moab (2 Kgs 3:4-27). Edom was able to throw off Judah's authority under King Jehoram (853–841 BC) and set up a king of its own (8:20-22). It remained independent until the days of King Amaziah of Judah (796–767 BC), who conquered Edom as far south as Sela, defeating a large army of the Edomites in the Valley of Salt (2 Kgs 14:7; 2 Chr 25:11-13). This gave Judah control of the copper mines in the Punon area. King Uzziah of Judah (792–740 BC) was able to push his control south to Elath (near Ezion-geber; 2 Kgs 14:22; 2 Chr 26:1-2). Before the end of the eighth century BC, in the days of Ahaz (735–715 BC), Edom defeated Judah and recovered Elath (2 Kgs 16:6). Thereafter, Judah lost control over Edom.

During the eighth century BC, the Assyrians began to move into Transjordan. About 800 BC Adad-nirari III (810–782 BC) claimed to have conquered several of these western states and to have imposed the payment of tribute. Then Tiglath-pileser III (745–727 BC) received tribute from Qaus-malaku of Edom. Sargon II (722–705 BC) spoke of an unnamed ruler of Edom who was involved in the rebellion of Ashdod in 713 BC. Sennacherib (705–681 BC) spoke of a certain Aiarammu, who brought gifts from Edom. Esarhaddon (681–669 BC) referred to Qaus-gabri, king of Edom, who came to Nineveh with 22 vassals to swear allegiance. Under Ashurbanipal (669–627 BC), Edom appears on Assyrian records. Thereafter, Assyria itself was defeated by the Babylonians. Under the Babylonians, Edom seems to have remained a subservient vassal, although in 594 it joined other small nations in discussing rebellion (Jer 27). When Nebuchadnezzar attacked these, however, Moab and Edom were not involved. In the overthrow of Jerusalem in 586, Edom remained neutral and even allowed some refugees from Judah to shelter there for a time (40:11). The prophet Obadiah castigated Edom for not assisting Judah at the time of the Babylonian invasion (Ob 1:11). Instead, they raided Judah, handed over captives to Babylon, and possessed lands in the Negev area to the south (Ez 35).

A long history of enmity existed between Judah and Edom, and several prophets spoke unfavorably about Edom (Is 11:14; 34:5-17; Ez 32:29; Am 1:11-12; Mal 1:2-4). In the sixth century BC, Edom entered a period of decline. Several cities were abandoned. At the same time Edomite colonies west of the Arabah in the southern hill country of Judah emerged, and by Roman times there was a province of Idumea, which was the descendant of the Persian province of Edom, with its administrative center at Lachish. In the old Edomite homeland, Arab groups began to move in. Finally, ancient Edom became the home of the Nabateans.

EDREI

1. City of residence for Og, king of Bashan (Dt 1:4; 3:10; Jos 12:4; 13:12). It was located on the southern branch of the Harmuk River, which was the southern border of Bashan. At this strategic point Og could look over the neighboring region for invaders from the south or from the east, where the land turned into a desert. At Edrei, Moses was able to defeat Og before destroying the city (Nm 21:33-35; Dt 3:1-6). The territory was allotted to the Machirites, the eastern clan of the tribe of Manasseh (Jos 13:31). The modern site for Edrei seems to be Derba, a town of 5,000 in Syria. Many important remains from antiquity survive in this town, including shops, cisterns, streets, and underground caves.
2. Fortified city allotted to Naphtali (Jos 19:37). It was near Kedesh, and may possibly be identified with the modern Tell Khureibeh.

EDUCATION The act or process of educating or being educated. The original purpose of Jewish education was to teach children to know and understand their special relationship with God, to teach them to serve him, and to educate them in holiness. Later Jewish education included character development and the history of God's people (particularly through rehearsing his acts of deliverance). Because of that education, the Jews knew the Mosaic law and their own history, and so, during periods of subjection to foreign powers, they were able to maintain their national pride. In modern times they have reestablished themselves as a nation (1948).

PREVIEW
•Education in the Home
•Religious Education
•Formal Education
•Literacy among the Jews
•Education in Surrounding Cultures

Education in the Home The priority given to education stemmed from the value of children in the Jewish family. Children were a great joy and reward (Ps 127:3-5). Education in the home began soon after a child could talk, and certainly by the age of three. Parents taught prayers and songs, which children learned by repetition, just as children today learn nursery rhymes.

At home, children became aware of certain religious items and symbols. They were encouraged to ask about the meaning of the annual Passover ritual (Ex 12:26), which served throughout Hebrew history as a fundamental means of instruction about the nature and significance of God's power in human life. Children undoubtedly had questions about objects they encountered, whether sacred vessels, ornaments, or clothing used in the tabernacle or temple worship, or more mundane things of everyday life.

Parental responsibility for education was clearly defined. A father was expected to give his son instruction in religion and in the history of the Hebrew people. He was also specifically required to teach his son a trade, often his own, since a boy without a trade was thought to have been trained for life as a thief. A father's other responsibilities included finding his son a wife and teaching him to swim.

Rabbis held that women could not study the Law because they were "of light mind." Nonetheless, influen-tial women in the Bible include Deborah (Jgs 4:4-5), Jael (vv 18-24), the wise woman of Tekoa (2 Sm 14:2-20), the wise woman of Abel (20:16-22), Lois, Eunice, and Priscilla (Acts 18:2; Rom 16:3; 1 Cor 16:19; 2 Tm 1:5).

The Jewish mother played a considerable role in a child's education, particularly in the earliest years. A mother was expected to assist in teaching her sons, but her major responsibility was to train her daughters. Since daughters were less highly esteemed than sons, a girl's education took place entirely in the home. The mother was responsible for educating her daughters to be successful homemakers: obedient, capable, and virtuous wives. Girls learned the skills of cooking, spinning, weaving, dyeing, caring for children, and managing slaves. They learned how to grind grain and at times helped with the harvest. Occasionally they were expected to help guard the vineyard or, if they had no brothers, to help care for the flocks.

Girls probably learned music and dancing and were expected to have good manners and high moral standards. They were taught to read, and some learned to write and reckon weights and measures. In exceptional circumstances a girl might receive an advanced education privately at home from a tutor.

Even when education was entirely home-centered, it is probable that most wealthy and especially royal children were instructed by a tutor, following a tradition established by other Near Eastern peoples.

Religious Education At an early age children accompanied their parents to religious services. At the great festivals they were introduced to important episodes in Jewish history. The Jews, an agricultural people, believed that agricultural knowledge had been revealed by God and that tending the ground was a basic human responsibility. Like some other Near Eastern nations, they believed that the land belonged to God. They were merely tenants. If a crop failed, it was because God withheld rain, but he would do that only if the people were sinful.

The celebrations of the Passover, Pentecost, and the Feast of Tabernacles were associated with the harvest. Throughout the biblical period, those festivals remained closely identified with the growing season. Such occasions became educational opportunities for children. They learned that the Passover commemorated the deliverance of their ancestors from slavery in Egypt. At Pentecost the Jewish people remembered God giving the law to Moses on Mt Sinai. The Feast of Tabernacles, with its green booths made from tree branches, commemorated God's faithfulness to the Jews on their seemingly endless journey to the Promised Land.

An example of a ceremony used as a teaching tool is the Passover ritual, which, of the three great festivals, was the least directly connected in origin with the harvest. That feast, which was immediately followed by a seven-day period known as the Feast of Unleavened Bread (Lv 23:6), was associated with the beginning of the barley harvest in April. (The exodus from Egypt had taken place at that time of year.)

In the Passover ceremony the priest would take one of the first sheaves of the barley harvest and wave it before the Lord (Lv 23:9-11). Before that, the men would choose a barley field at random and bind some of the best sheaves, leaving them standing. The following evening three men would go out to that field with sickles and baskets to reap those specifically prepared sheaves. As onlookers (including the children) gathered to observe the ceremony, the reapers would ask the crowd certain traditional questions. Year by year the children saw that ritual and heard the answers. The barley was cut and taken to the temple court, where it was threshed and winnowed. Some of it was mixed with oil and incense and used as an offering. The remainder went to the priests.

Formal Education Jewish education during the biblical period helped Jews to know of the Law, study the history of the Jewish people, and become proficient in reading, writing, and a certain amount of arithmetic. To that, incidental information such as the medicinal value of certain herbs (see 1 Kgs 4:33) might sometimes be added.

Teachers Priests instructed the people in the knowledge of God. As officers of the synagogue, the Levites also performed a teaching role (cf. Dt 33:10; 2 Chr 35:3). Before the exile, the prophets assumed the role of instructors, teaching the historical heritage of the people and acting as critics of injustice and improper social behavior. Their responsibility was to interpret the law for contemporary society. By the fourth century BC, the prophets' role as instructors had passed to the scribes and to others designated as teachers.

In the centuries before Christ, scribes not only transcribed and preserved the traditions in written form but were students and interpreters of the law. The scribes were known as "doctors of the law" (Lk 5:17, KJV), lawyers (Mt 22:35), and rabbis (23:8). All higher education was in their hands, and they developed a complex system of instruction known as "the tradition of the elders" (15:2-6). Although the scribes needed leisure for their scholarly pursuits, they did not despise laborers. Most of them, in fact, practiced a trade as a means of support when necessary.

Although the scribes were influential in the time of Christ (Mt 23:1-2), they undoubtedly found, like the prophets before them, that their words were not always heeded. The scribes, who exercised an important influence over contemporary life and morals, were notable for their fierce opposition to Jesus (Mk 2:6) and to the early church (Acts 4:5; 6:12).

By the NT era, the entire community was expected to establish and maintain elementary schools. The community was also responsible for financing the education of poor or orphaned children. Out of high regard for earlier priests, prophets, and scribes, and because of the eminent position given to education, teachers were highly esteemed by the Jewish people. Because God had given them the law, it was of greatest importance. One who worked as God's servant expounding the law was therefore the most important person in the community. To be a teacher was life's highest privilege and the most significant task a man could perform.

Teachers were expected to demonstrate exceptional character along with their academic qualifications. They were expected to keep children from having contact with anything harmful. They were not to show bitterness or give preference to one child over another. Rather than threatening, they were to explain right and wrong and the harmfulness of sin. Teachers were expected to keep promises to children lest the students grow accustomed to broken words and lies. Teachers were to be even-tempered, never impatient or lacking in understanding, always prepared to repeat explanations. It was said that children should be treated like young heifers, with their burdens increased daily. Yet any teacher who was too severe was dismissed.

Subject Matter Early education consisted of learning the law through listening and oral repetition, along with the study of the written text. The content of the law covered three main areas: ceremonial, civil, and criminal. Stu-

dents needed to master these, preparing themselves to take responsibility for observing the law as adults.

The Scriptures contained such a variety of writings that pupils learned about religion, history, law, morals, and manners, plus reading, writing, and arithmetic. They studied from great literature; along with the Law, they used the books of Psalms, Proverbs, and Ecclesiastes extensively as texts. The Dead Sea Scrolls have shown that some classical Hebrew was still being spoken in NT times. Students who commonly spoke Aramaic or Greek were faced with a difficult situation when learning the Hebrew of the OT. The problem was especially complex because the Hebrew was written without any vowel sounds. Those had to be memorized in association with the consonants of the text.

Since the ancient Hebrews were generally regarded as the most proficient musicians and singers in the Near East, it is probable that basic instruction in singing and playing instruments, such as the pipe and harp, was received at home. Although no Hebrew hymns have survived in musical form, temple singers would almost certainly have been familiar with the kind of music theory known among the Canaanites. (A musical text recovered from Ugarit [Ras Shamra] consisted of a ballad or a hymn inscribed on clay with curious musical symbols that long defied identification. Dating to perhaps 1800 BC, that Canaanite text has been described as the "oldest sheet music in the world.")

During the exile especially, great emphasis was placed on recording and preserving ancient customs and ceremonies in order to maintain the distinctiveness of Hebrew culture. The captives recognized the importance of keeping alive their national heritage and the Law during the years they were living in an alien culture.

The synagogue developed during the exile as a place for the study of religion and for prayer, becoming the center of instruction in the Jewish faith. Previously, the temple at Jerusalem had been the only place for sacrifice. Because that ritual could not be performed in Babylon, it was natural for the synagogue to increase in importance in worship as well as in education.

The exile brought about fundamental changes in Jewish life in areas other than the purely religious. Education received considerable stimulation from the Jewish exiles' contact with the more sophisticated culture of the Babylonians. The Babylonian law code was a precise and well-established feature of life. Schools and libraries in Babylonia had been in existence for many centuries. Mesopotamian knowledge of medicine, astronomy, mathematics, architecture, and engineering was far superior to that of the Jews. In that intellectual environment the literature of the Jews took on new meaning; it was from that period that the books of Ezekiel and Daniel emerged.

In the postexilic period, teaching was based extensively on Proverbs and the apocryphal books of Ecclesiasticus and the Wisdom of Solomon. From those works the Jews received practical training for a successful life. The scribes taught that wisdom came from God and that those who obeyed the commandments would bring joy and honor to others.

Under Persian rule in the sixth century BC, the Jews had been encouraged to return to Jerusalem and rebuild the temple. After 332 BC, when Alexander the Great defeated the Persian king Darius, strong efforts were made to Hellenize the conquered peoples. The Greek language was introduced along with Greek religion, political procedures, and educational methods. The drive for Hellenization continued under the rule of the Ptolemies (a Macedonian family line that ruled Egypt) and the Seleucids (a Syrian dynasty). Coincident with the establishment of foreign rule came the dominance of the Jewish priesthood in Judean political matters. Greek influence was seen in the enriched aesthetic appreciation typical of certain Jewish rulers.

Although Greek philosophy and sports remained outside the realm of Jewish education, there was a noticeable decline in Jewish religious and moral standards in the Hellenistic period. Some Jews were eager to obtain advancement from the foreign masters by adopting the Greek culture. Others fought desperately to preserve their Jewish heritage. During Roman times, the foreign influence was again ignored by faithful Jews whenever possible.

Teaching Methods Teaching methods, developed from memorizing the Law, stressed the importance of retention and recollection. Children were taught to memorize as soon as they could talk, and they were trained to repeat the exact words so that no nuance of meaning would be altered. The alphabet was taught and memorized by being repeatedly written and drilled. Students copied and recopied passages from the written Law in precise, neat handwriting. Any piece of writing containing a mistake was considered dangerous, since it might imprint the wrong word or spelling on the learner's mind. Reading aloud was recommended as an aid to memorization.

To aid learning, each boy was also given a personal text beginning with the first letter of his name and ending with the last. As soon as he demonstrated his ability to read, he received a scroll that contained the first words of Deuteronomy 6:4: "Hear, O Israel: The LORD our God is one LORD" (RSV). That was recited every morning and evening in postexilic times, along with the Hallel (or psalm of praise), the story of Creation, and the main part of the Law contained in Leviticus.

Teachings also came in the form of proverbs or parables, a device later used by Jesus (Mk 4:1-2). An open sharing of knowledge occurred in question-and-answer periods (for example, the visit of the 12-year-old Jesus to the temple in Jerusalem, Lk 2:46-47).

Very little information is available on education in the early Christian era. We know that Jesus could read and expound the Scriptures and was knowledgeable enough to discuss theology with the learned men in the temple. He probably learned at home and received the elementary education common to most Jewish boys at that period.

Discipline Discipline, almost always an important element in education, was important to the ancient Hebrews. A system of reward and punishment was used in which corporal chastisement was normal. Punishment was considered to be an outward symbol of God's love and concern for the instruction of his people (Ps 94:8-13), although the Jews as a people did not always learn from those corrections (Jer 5:3; Am 4:6-13). A child was thought to need "breaking" like a horse: "A horse that is untamed turns out to be stubborn, and a son unrestrained turns out to be wilful" (Ecclus 30:8, RSV).

Adult Education When Ezra the scribe returned from Babylon with a copy of the Book of the Law, he taught it to the Levites and to the people. That material, together with the book of Proverbs and literature from the preexilic and exilic periods, became basic in Jewish education. In the postexilic period, priests traveled to the towns, addressing people in the synagogue on the Sabbath and in the square on market days, when a large crowd would be gathered. Some individuals may have extended their learning through discussion with the elders (cf. Ez 8:1).

For those who continued their education, the next phase was probably instruction by scribes. The scribes, leaders of a Jewish sect called Pharisees, had developed Ezra's principles into strict rules on tithing, ritual purity, and synagogue worship. As a young man, Saul of Tarsus came to Jerusalem to study with Gamaliel, an honored rabbi (Acts 22:3). At that time the curriculum was an advanced study of theological law, both written and oral, along with the rites and ceremonies of Jewish culture.

School Buildings By NT times, some schools operated in special buildings and others in the teachers' own houses, but most were attached to the synagogue. When a separate building was designed, it was considered inadvisable to construct it in a crowded area. In a large town the community was expected to provide two schools, especially if a river divided the town. A school did not operate in the heat of the day (between 10 AM and 3 PM), and would meet only four hours a day in July and August. Class size was expected to be 25, with a teacher and an assistant for 40 students and two teachers for 50. At school the boys sat on the ground at the teacher's feet and learned from the Scriptures. Thus, the school became known as the "House of the Book."

Literacy among the Jews The extent of literacy among Jews over the centuries is difficult to determine, but indications can be found from specific examples. The book of Joshua describes three men chosen from each tribe who had to prepare a written report about the land of Canaan (Jos 18:4-9). Later, Gideon captured a youth who was able to make a written list of the important men of the city (Jgs 8:14). Writing was probably a common skill since the Israelites were exhorted to use it frequently (Dt 6:9; 27:2-8). Simple mathematical terms could be written and understood by boys, and there are indications of familiarity with the geometrical relationship of a circle's radius and circumference (the concept of pi; see 2 Chr 4:2). The development of cursive script implies widespread use of writing from at least the eighth century BC. It is noteworthy that a synagogue service could be performed by any ten men in the congregation, which presupposes that there were more than 10 men in any synagogue who were literate enough to fulfill that duty.

When fears of Hellenism were strong and the existence of Judaism was threatened in the first century BC, it was decreed that every Jewish boy should attend elementary school. Since such a system probably already existed, that decree merely made attendance compulsory for all males up to 16 or 17 years of age. No doubt the reason was that thorough knowledge and careful observance of the Law were vital to the survival of the Jewish heritage.

Joshua ben-Gamala (high priest AD 63–65) is considered the founder of universal education. His instructions for setting up schools in towns and villages were precise, requiring attendance of boys from the age of six or seven years. The community was responsible for setting up a school and maintaining a teacher in any town where there were at least ten Jewish families. Fathers were required to see that their sons attended school. When a family lived in an isolated area, a teacher often lived with the family. Teachers were probably paid either by the family or from a community tax, although scribes were not paid directly for the instruction they gave. It is difficult to know if the goal of universal elementary education was attained.

Education in Surrounding Cultures The theological emphasis of Hebrew education contrasted sharply with the aims of education in Greece and Rome. Those societies, however, were also concerned with developing a particular type of character.

In Sparta the purpose of educational training was to develop young men to be fighters who would subject themselves to the welfare of the state. Character development was achieved by eliminating luxuries and by systematically disciplining mind and body through physical activity. Survival techniques encouraged resourcefulness and initiative. Girls received the same education, since it was considered important to develop women who could give birth to strong warriors.

In Athens education was deemed essential to life. Because transmission of culture would enable boys to become perfect citizens, they were taught letters, music, morals and manners, mathematics, and gymnastics (development of a healthy body). Education was ideally a noble pursuit—a training of the mind, the birthright of every citizen—but in practice it was restricted to a small section of the aristocracy. The educated despised earning a living as a way of life suitable only for slaves. Women received no education. The teacher in elementary schools was a lowly individual.

Roman education prepared a boy mentally and physically for farm, battlefield, or wherever his services were required by the state. Education was a family responsibility—the boy learning first from his mother, then from his father. Basic reading, writing, arithmetic, language, structure, and debating skills were taught, sometimes by private tutors. When schools were developed, they seem to have been noisy, storefront activities operated by poorly paid teachers. Girls were taught housekeeping skills at home.

Egyptian boys attended the "House of the Books" for their studies and learned reading and elementary arithmetic. Writing in hieroglyphs on papyrus was the most difficult task. Like students in other cultures, boys were subject to corporal punishment. Egyptian teachers considered that "a boy's ears are in his back," following up that conviction with frequent use of a cane.

EDUTH* Hebrew word usually translated "testimony," "witness," or "commandment." It is used with reference to the tabernacle (Nm 17:7-8; 18:2; 2 Chr 24:6), the ark (Ex 25:16), the Ten Commandments (Ex 31:18), and the law of God in general (Ps 19:8). The transliterated form appears only in the title of Psalm 60 in the Hebrew phrase *Shushan Eduth*. The phrase means "Lily of Testimony."

See also Music.

EGLAH One of King David's wives and mother of Ithream (2 Sm 3:5; 1 Chr 3:3). Born while David was still in Hebron, Ithream was the sixth son.

EGLAIM Town mentioned in Isaiah 15:8. It cannot be located with certainty, but it was probably in southern Moab. A village called Aigaleim was mentioned by Eusebius and another called Agalla by Josephus (*Antiquities* 14.1.4). However, their identification with Eglaim is uncertain.

EGLATH-SHELISHIYAH Place in Moab mentioned in Isaiah 15:5 and Jeremiah 48:34 in pronouncements of judgment. The name means literally "the third Eglath." It was probably near Zoar at the southern end of the Dead Sea, but its exact location is uncertain.

EGLON (Person) Moabite king who captured Jericho and held it for 18 years, exacting a tribute from Israel.

Ehud, an Israelite judge pretending to bring tribute, killed Eglon (Jgs 3:12-30). *See* Moab, Moabites.

EGLON (Place) Town situated seven miles (11.3 kilometers) southwest of Lachish, assigned to Judah's tribe for an inheritance (Jos 15:39). It is generally identified with the modern Tell el-Hesi.

EGYPT, Brook of *See* Brook of Egypt.

EGYPT, EGYPTIAN Egypt figured significantly as a stage on which the biblical narrative was enacted. Here Abraham lived in time of famine. Joseph, his great-grandson, was sold into slavery in Egypt and rose to a position equivalent to that of prime minister. Through Joseph's intercession, Jacob and the rest of the Hebrew patriarchal family living in Palestine came to reside in the eastern delta region of Goshen—again as a result of famine. Initially treated favorably, they were later reduced to bondage; crying to God, ultimately they were released through the 10 plagues. Thereafter, for 40 years, they wandered in the Egyptian Sinai, where they received the law, specifications for building the tabernacle, and instructions for the priestly and sacrificial systems.

After the destruction of Jerusalem in 586 BC, a group of Jews forced Jeremiah to go with them to Egypt (Jer 43:6-7), where they became numerous during the intertestamental period and gradually forgot their Hebrew. At Alexandria, Jews translated the OT into Greek (the Septuagint) between about 250 and 150 BC. This became the Bible of the early church, especially of those Christians outside Palestine.

When the NT period opened, Egypt served as a refuge for Joseph, Mary, and Jesus as they fled to escape the assassination attempts of Herod the Great (Mt 2:13-23). At several other points, Hebrew and Egyptian history intersected—for example, when Shishak I invaded Palestine in the days of Rehoboam (1 Kgs 14:25-28).

PREVIEW
• Geography
• History
• Social Life
• Religion
• Learning and Culture

Geography Egypt is the gift of the Nile, without which it could not exist. From time immemorial the Nile has deposited a thin layer of rich silt each year as it overflowed its banks. This ribbon of loam along its course contrasts vividly with the sterile sands that stretch from the river valley often as far as one can see. Then, having deposited this soil, the Nile provides water for its irrigation. This is necessary in a land that receives only six to eight inches (15 to 20 centimeters) of rainfall per year along the Mediterranean, two inches (5.1 centimeters) or less per year at Cairo, and less than that farther south.

The Nile Valley is a tube, shut in on either side by cliffs and corked up at the southern end by cataracts, six places where the river has failed to cut a clear channel and where rocks are piled in irregular masses in the streambed. From cliff to cliff the Nile Valley ranges from about 10 to 31 miles (16 to 50 kilometers) in width between Cairo and Aswan. But the cultivated area along this stretch is only about six to ten miles (10 to 16 kilometers) wide, and narrows to one or two miles (1.5 to 3 kilometers) in width around Aswan. This cultivated tract is only about 5,000 square miles (8,045 square kilometers) in total.

But Egypt is more than the valley. It is also the delta, a

pie-shaped area north of Cairo also deposited by the Nile over the millennia. The delta measures some 125 miles (201.1 kilometers) north and south, and 115 miles (185 kilometers) east and west. Its more heavily populated southern region provided ancient Egyptians with some 5,000 square miles (8,045 square kilometers) of farmland, making the total of valley and delta about 10,000 square miles (16,090 square kilometers), roughly equal to the state of Maryland.

Boats on the Nile River

West of the Nile extends a chain of oases, the largest of which is the Fayum, about 70 miles (112.6 kilometers) southwest of Cairo. In the center of the Fayum is Lake Qarun, which today covers 90 square miles (144.8 square kilometers) and is about 17 feet (5.2 meters) deep. It is surrounded by about a half million acres of good farmland.

Ancient Egypt extended some 125 miles (201.1 kilometers) from the Mediterranean to Cairo (Lower Egypt) and another 600 miles (965.4 kilometers) from Cairo to Aswan (Upper Egypt). At the height of its power, Egypt also controlled the valley from the first cataract at Aswan south to the fourth cataract (Nubia). Thus its domain extended a total of some 1,100 miles (1,769.9 kilometers) south from the Mediterranean.

Egypt's most important resource was the rich loam along the Nile. On it, in antiquity, farmers raised grains, such as barley, emmer, and wheat. Onions, leeks, beans, and lentils were common vegetables. Dates, figs, and grapes were the most widely grown fruits. Oil came from castor oil plants and sesame rather than from the olive, as in other Mediterranean lands. Flax provided linen for clothing. Domesticated animals included oxen, cattle, sheep, goats, pigs, donkeys, and horses.

Another important resource was an abundant supply of stone. Granite mountains rise between the Nile and the Red Sea, and deposits of alabaster and other fine stone are found in the same region. South of Aswan stand the granite mountains of Nubia. The quarries of Syene at Aswan are famous for their extremely hard and durable red granite. Gold was reasonably plentiful in the Nubian Mountains, and gold-bearing quartz veins were found in the mountains east of the Nile. Egyptians controlled the copper and turquoise mines of the Sinai during much of their important historical periods. In early antiquity some timber was available in Nubia for building the barges that carried the huge loads of stone for construction of pyramids, temples, and other magnificent structures.

The Nile itself was an all-weather highway. One could float northward with the current and sail southward against the weak current (3 miles, or 5 kilometers, per hour) by means of the prevailing northerly winds. In fact, the Nile was the road of ancient Egypt. Land routes

normally conducted traffic only to the river's edge. In addition to the massive north-south commerce, ferry boats regularly moved from shore to shore.

Along the river grew papyrus reeds, from which writing material could be made. And along the Nile, clay was deposited from which could be made pottery and sun-dried bricks for the houses of the poor.

The ancient Egyptians lived in comparative isolation and peace in their valley home. The cataracts on the south, the deserts on east and west, and the harborless coast of the Mediterranean protected them from invasion and left them free to develop a homogeneous culture. Outside influences could sift in chiefly at the two northern corners of the delta. There were Semitic incursions from the east, and Libyans (possibly of European origin) from the west. Defenses were erected to protect against both. The security of their valley home and the regular provision of the sun and the Nile gave the Egyptians a sense of confidence and well-being that was not the lot of other peoples of the ancient Near East.

History It is wrong to think of the contemporary rulers of Egypt as descendants of the pharaohs or the present inhabitants of the land as Egyptians in any but a geographic sense. Egypt as an area of distinctive civilization ended with the Arab conquest in the seventh century AD and was greatly diluted during the several preceding centuries by Greco-Roman influences.

Origins Though the origins of the ancient Egyptians are imperfectly understood, physically they show affinities to Hamites, Semites, and Mediterraneans. Hamites with negroid characteristics moved north from Nubia. Asiatics migrated across the Isthmus of Suez into the delta, and the small, brown, finely boned Mediterranean people dominated the Nile Valley from early times. However diverse their origins may have been, Egyptians of the ancient period were conscious of themselves as a nation, a distinctive people. Men stood about five feet six inches (1.7 meters) in height and women about five feet (1.5 meters). They were slight but strong-boned, with round heads and oval faces. The men had little face or body hair, and throughout antiquity they were commonly smooth-shaven, while Semites were bearded.

Archaeologists list a series of successive predynastic cultures—Fayumic, Meridian, Tasian, Badarian, Amratian, Gerzean, and Semainean—who mastered basic techniques and learned how to build a civilization with minimal resources. Of course, they developed an irrigation system for the maintenance of an effective agricultural program. At a very early time they discovered how to turn flax into linen and thus to produce clothing. Boats were made from papyrus reeds and trees that grew along some of the streambeds in the south. Sun-baked bricks provided building material, and clay was available for pottery. The latter was made by hand; the pottery wheel did not appear until dynastic times.

Writing appeared in Egypt about the end of the predynastic period. Their hieroglyphs, or sacred signs, were called "the words of God" and were believed to be of divine origin. By 2700 BC, they had learned how to make "paper" by crisscrossing strips cut from the pith of the papyrus plant and forming them into sheets. About the same time they developed techniques for cutting stone from the quarry. Commonly they cut a groove along a line where a block was to be split off. There they drove in wedges of dry wood and wetted them to swell the wood and split the block off. Sometimes they lit a fire along the groove to heat the stone and then poured water over it to split it away from the main rock.

Unification of Egypt In the period just before about 3100 BC, Egypt consisted of the two separate kingdoms: Lower Egypt and Upper Egypt. Then the king of Upper Egypt conquered Lower Egypt and unified the two lands under his sole rule. But the division was never quite forgotten, and Egypt was referred to as the "Two Lands" throughout its history. The pharaohs wore a double crown, a combination of the low red crown of Lower Egypt and the white crown of Upper Egypt. The king's palace was called the "double palace," and even the royal granary was double. The Hebrews recognized this duality, for throughout the OT they called Egypt *Mitzrayim*— a word with a dual ending.

The pharaoh who was credited in the ancient sources with the unification of Egypt was sometimes called Narmer and sometimes Menes; presumably these were different names for the same person. Narmer-Menes began the first dynasty of united Egypt. Though the ancient Egyptians did not reckon in dynasties, modern historians follow the practice of Manetho, an Egyptian priest of the mid-third century BC, who compiled a list of kings down to the Persian period and divided it into 30 dynasties; later others added a 31st dynasty. The ancients did not use such terms as "Old Kingdom" and "Middle Kingdom" either, but modern scholars find them a convenient way of organizing Egyptian history.

Early Dynastic Period (3100–2700 BC) Kings of the first two dynasties ruled at This, or Thinis, some 300 miles (482.7 kilometers) south of Cairo, but they built Memphis as another administrative center. They consolidated their hold over the land and developed the theory that the king was divine. Contacts with the outside world were considerable, and there are many indications in Egypt of influences from Mesopotamia at this time.

Old Kingdom (2700–2200 BC; Dynasties 3–6) The Old Kingdom is especially remembered for its building operations. The pyramids were erected at that time. The capital was located at Memphis (biblical Noph), southwest of modern Cairo. Contacts with Phoenicia were numerous, and some believe Egyptians were so heavily involved there and elsewhere that it is proper to speak of the "Old Empire." Artistic standards were being developed, and literary and medical beginnings were significant. Egypt was an absolute monarchy. The divine king was served by an army of officials; the whole population might be regimented during his lifetime to prepare his tomb.

The first king of the third dynasty was Djoser, who built the step pyramid at Saqqara. The earliest great stone structure in the world, it consists of six layers, or steps, rising to a height of 204 feet (62.2 meters). The architect was Imhotep, his vizier or prime minister, who later was deified and credited with the beginnings of architecture, literature, and medicine, and identified by the Greeks with the god of medicine, Asklepios.

The fourth-dynasty pharaohs were the great pyramid builders. They were responsible for erecting the three great pyramids at Giza between about 2600 and 2500 BC. The greatest of these, attributed to Khufu, covers 13 acres, originally rose to a height of 481 feet (146.6 meters), and contains about 2.3 million blocks of limestone averaging two and a half tons each. The second pyramid stands 447½ feet (136.4 meters) high and is accompanied by the sphinx, a couchant lion with the face of the king. The third pyramid is 204 feet (62.2 meters) high. These pyramids are not isolated examples. Several more small pyramids were built at Giza, and there were nine pyramid fields in all, scattered along the western bank of the Nile south of Memphis. During the fifth and sixth dynasties, there appeared the pyramid texts, carved and painted inscriptions, magical spells, and hymns that were supposed to aid the deceased in the afterlife.

The artistic standards of Egypt were established during the Old Kingdom. The king and the gods were portrayed in a stylized form. Art tended to be conceptual rather than perceptual; that is, instead of reproducing what he saw, the artist painted what he knew to be there. For example, a school of fish became individual fish painted whole instead of being pictured naturally with one fish obscuring part of the fish next to it. In a similar manner the saddlebags on a donkey were shown with the one facing the viewer reproduced in a natural way; the other one, known to be behind the donkey's back, was flipped up in the air above the donkey's back.

The importance of an individual determined his size in a pictorial representation. In a battle scene the pharaoh would be the largest figure, his commanding officers next in size, the common soldiers smaller yet, and enemy troops smallest of all.

Egyptian art was intended to tell a story: much of it was more like a motion picture than a snapshot. A wine-making scene might include picking the grapes, treading out the juice (normally done by stomping with bare feet), and storing the juice in jars.

Evidently Egyptian medical knowledge was also developing during the Old Kingdom. Though the sources for knowledge of Egyptian medicine are the great papyri of the Middle Kingdom, there is some indication that medical knowledge claims far greater antiquity. Numerous archaic expressions appear in the texts. Perhaps Egyptians knew something of the circulation of the blood; they talked about feeling the "voice of the heart." Egyptian medical practice combined a hodgepodge of home remedies, charms and incantations, and scientific expertise. The Edwin Smith Surgical Papyrus is a remarkable study dealing especially with the treatment of broken bones.

During the sixth dynasty, the Old Kingdom began to break up as a result of poor rulers, aggressive nobles, fiscal difficulties, Nubian incursions in the south, and Asiatic attacks in the northeast.

First Intermediate Period (2200–2050 BC; Dynasties 7–11) During the Old Kingdom, there was political stability and prosperity. The Nile flood came predictably and not devastatingly. There was enough for all to eat. If one behaved himself and worked hard and studied diligently in school, he could count on the proper promotions and general success in life. Familiar social, political, economic, and religious institutions remained constant and could be counted on to assume their regular place in the rhythm of life. Now the old aristocracy had fallen. The central government had broken down; nobles ruled many districts and took the title of kings. It was no longer true that if one did certain things he could count on success. The collapse of the whole philosophy of life of the Old Kingdom brought a spiritual upset and spawned attempts at reevaluation of life. Some of the literature of the time advocates the hedonistic approach of drowning one's problems in pleasure, and some recommended a stoical approach—to steel oneself against the hardships of life.

Middle Kingdom (2050–1780 BC; 12th Dynasty) Late in the 11th dynasty, princes of Thebes (440 miles, or 708 kilometers, south of Memphis) struggled to restore order and royal control and were partially successful. The Middle Kingdom was the period of the 12th dynasty, native Thebans who made their capital at Lisht in the Fayum. The six rulers of this dynasty took the names of Amenemhet and Sesostris. Each of them ruled some 30 years, and most of them took their sons to the throne as co-regents before death, eliminating the danger of a usurper. Since these kings did not dare to deprive the nobles of their largely independent power, a feudal condition existed during much of the period.

Unable to function as absolute kings, these pharaohs had to rule by persuasion and the development of goodwill. Their rendering of *ma'at* (social justice) was constantly emphasized, and if a person could not obtain *ma'at* at the hands of the nobles, he was promised it at the hands of the king. Their propaganda program also portrayed the pharaoh as concerned with responsible leadership instead of merely exercising authority. The pharaoh was the shepherd of his people.

Middle Kingdom pharaohs were wise enough not to exhaust the treasury on great pyramids; instead, they undertook public works, such as a massive effort to increase cultivable acreage in the Fayum, construction of a defensive wall across the isthmus of Suez, and systematic working of the Sinai copper mines. Trade was extensive with Crete, Lebanon, Syria, and Punt.

The Middle Kingdom was a time when Amon began to emerge as the great god of Egypt. He was grafted onto the sun god Re as Amon-Re and came to supersede the gods who had formerly stood for Thebes. As god of the nation, he was to become the great imperial god under the empire and thus to assume a universal quality. Religious texts, which had graced the walls of the pyramids during the Old Kingdom, now were inscribed on coffins instead, and their use was available to nobles as well as kings.

A literary flowering occurred during the Middle Kingdom. Scientific literature is represented by such outstanding works as the Rhind Mathematical Papyrus and the Smith Surgical and Ebers Medical papyri. The "Instructions of Merikare" portrays something of the wisdom literature of the period, and the "Tale of Sinuhe" introduces the genre of entertainment literature.

If one holds to the early date of the exodus (c. 1446 BC) and adds 430 years for the period of Israelite sojourn in Egypt (Ex 12:40), he will conclude that the Israelites entered Egypt about 1876 BC. This would be early in the reign of Sesostris III (of Senwosret, or Sen-Usert; 1878–1840 BC). Sesostris was a vigorous king who extended Egyptian control south to the second cataract and campaigned up into Syria. He was also able to reverse the feudalistic conditions of the earlier period; he took away the power of the nobles and appointed royal officials in their stead. Possibly this achievement was somehow related to famine in Joseph's day and Joseph's use of that famine to fasten royal control on all the populace of the land (Gn 47:13-26).

Second Intermediate Period (1780–1570 BC; Dynasties 13–17)

With the passing of the strong 12th dynasty, Egypt relapsed once more into a period of disintegration. The Hyksos ("rulers of foreign lands"), Semites from Syria and Palestine, gradually infiltrated into the delta region and took control there about 1730 BC, maintaining their capital at Tanis, or Avaris, in the eastern delta. Meanwhile, Theban princes ruled weakly in the south and were commonly vassals to the Hyksos.

Apparently as a result of Egyptian hatred of the Hyksos and stringent efforts to obliterate their memory, the Hyksos are a very shadowy people. Little remains on which to base a reconstruction of their history. Presumably they were responsible for introducing new kinds of bronze swords and daggers, the powerful compound bow, and above all the horse and chariot. The Egyptians adopted these with good success and used them to overthrow Hyksos power and then to build an empire in Palestine and Syria. The struggle of Theban princes to gain release from Hyksos control was prolonged and apparently fierce at times. The effort began late in the 16th century BC and was completed by Ahmose I (1570–1546 BC).

The Empire Period (1570–1090 BC; Dynasties 18–20)

Ahmose launched the 18th dynasty, and may be viewed as initiating the empire, or New Kingdom, period as well. After defeating the Hyksos in Egypt, he carried on successful campaigns against Nubia and Sharuhen in southern Palestine. Subsequently he was forced to subdue nobles who had managed to gain independence from the central government during the Hyksos era. Amenhotep I (1546–1525 BC) was also forced to fight the Nubians in the south and Libyans in the northwest.

Dying without a son to succeed him, Amenhotep was followed on the throne by his sister Ahmose, who married a Thutmose (Thutmose I, 1525–1508 BC), probably a relative. Thutmose had to resubjugate rebellious Nubians during the first year of his reign and in subsequent campaigns considerably expanded Egypt's Nubian holdings. Between those two Nubian attacks, he mounted an offensive in Syria; thus he could claim an empire that stretched from the Euphrates to the third cataract of the Nile. Moses may have been born early in his reign. Thutmose began the practice of carving out royal tombs in the Valley of the Kings west of Thebes.

Evidently the only surviving child of the union of Thutmose and Ahmose was a daughter, Hatshepsut, who was married to Thutmose II (1508–1504 BC), a son of Thutmose I by a secondary princess. Thutmose II had to quell rebellious Nubians, but little else is known of his reign. Since his marriage to Hatshepsut produced two daughters but no sons, he decided to marry his daughter Marytre to a son by a minor wife (Thutmose III, 1504–1450 BC).

Hatshepsut continued to rule during the minority of Thutmose III and refused to step aside when he came of age. She dominated Egypt from 1504–1482 BC. During her reign, Egypt enjoyed economic prosperity. Her building activities were considerable; not the least of her achievements was the erection of two great obelisks at the temple of Karnak at Luxor. The one remaining shaft stands $97\frac{1}{2}$ feet (29.7 meters) high and weighs about 700,000 pounds (317,800 kilograms). She also conducted trade expeditions to the land of Punt. Hatshepsut is sometimes identified as the pharaoh's daughter who rescued Moses from the Nile (Ex 2:5).

Finally, in 1482 BC, Hatshepsut met an untimely end, probably at the hands of Thutmose III as he burst his bonds and assumed rule over the realm. Within 75 days he had assembled an army and was leading it north into Palestine-Syria to subjugate rebellious princes there. A great initial victory at Megiddo and a sack of the city after a seventh-month siege cowed northern Palestinians but did not break their will to resist. Thutmose found himself campaigning in Palestine or Nubia almost annually for the next two decades.

What started out as an Egyptian impulse to punish the Hyksos turned into a spirit of imperialism, which enjoyed a sense of power in victory. As the frontiers expanded, there was almost always a peril to attend to somewhere during subsequent generations; some of them were real and some remote. Thus the sense of security that Egyptians had enjoyed during earlier centuries when they were shut up in their valley home gave way to a feeling of insecurity. And as the god Amon-Re smiled on Egyptian military efforts, he was rewarded with quantities of booty and handsome gifts. In time the temples gained so much wealth and power that they came to exercise great clout in political and economic circles. Especially great was the power of the priesthood of Amon at the temple of Karnak.

Thutmose III was one of the greatest of Egypt's ancient pharaohs. A conqueror and empire builder, he is often called the Napoleon of ancient Egypt. There was hardly a city of any size in the kingdom where he did not engage in building activities. With him began an effort to glorify the pharaoh as sportsman, athlete, and warrior that was to last for several generations; he had the powers of a god in conducting the affairs of men. If one accepts the early date of the exodus, Thutmose III is often considered to have been the pharaoh of the great oppression of the Hebrews.

Thutmose was succeeded by his son Amenhotep II (1452–1425 BC), who may have been the pharaoh of the exodus. Serving briefly as co-regent with his father, he enjoyed an easy transition to sole rule over the empire. Though forced to conduct two campaigns into Syria and Palestine to subdue rebellious towns, he seems generally to have enjoyed a peaceful reign. Like his father, he sought to be known for his prowess as a sportsman and his ruthlessness as a warrior.

After the little-known reign of Thutmose IV (1425–1412 BC), Amenhotep III (1412–1375 BC) ascended to the throne of Egypt. Frequently called "the magnificent," he reveled in the wealth that poured in from the empire. Once, in the brief space of only 14 days, he had excavated for his wife a lake 6,400 feet (1,950.6 meters) long and 1,200 feet (365.7 meters) wide. Here on the west bank of the Nile at Thebes a royal barge could float about while musicians aboard provided entertainment for the king and queen. Amenhotep built several temples, including a mortuary temple at Thebes, to which were attached the famous colossi of Memnon, seated statues of the king about 70 feet (21.3 meters) high. Though artists dutifully represented him as a great conqueror on temple walls, he seems to have engaged in stifling only one uprising in Nubia and probably never set foot in Palestine or Syria.

Just as Amenhotep III made no effort to maintain the empire, neither did his son Amenhotep IV (1387–1366 BC). Because of ill health, Amenhotep III made his son co-regent in 1387 BC, but the son paid little attention to the affairs of state. Of a mystical bent, he devoted himself to the establishment of the cult of the sun god Aton at a new capital named Amarna. Aton worship was almost monotheistic (the king being worshiped along with the god) and thus constituted a virtual religious revolution, but it had few adherents outside the court. Religious changes, political changes connected with the move of the capital, and artistic changes were three of the main elements of the so-called "Amarna Revolution." The loose naturalism in art, almost bordering on caricature, was not new, however, since it had been accepted as early as the reign of Thutmose IV. Amenhotep IV took the name Akhnaton ("spirit of Aton").

Akhnaton paid no attention to numerous appeals (the Amarna letters) from royal princes of Palestine and Syria for help to repel invaders, and the empire disintegrated. Acceptance of the early date of the exodus would place the Hebrew conquest and the subsequent settling-in process during the reigns of Amenhotep III and IV, precisely when Egyptian power over Palestine disappeared. However, the Habiru, which some of these appeals name as attackers, should not be identified as Hebrews. Much of what is said about them could not have been true of Hebrews.

When Amenhotep IV died, Tutankhamen (1366–1357 BC) succeeded to the throne. A young boy of eight or nine, he was associated with Eye, a favorite of Akhnaton, as co-regent. When Tutankhamen died nine years later, Eye continued to rule until 1353 BC. Because of the discovery of his magnificently furnished, unrifled tomb in 1922, Tutankhamen has received attention out of proportion to his significance in antiquity. The thousands of objects from his tomb illustrate the wealth, grandeur, and artistic achievements of ancient Egypt and help to demonstrate what it meant for Moses to turn his back on the riches of Egypt (Heb 11:26).

When Eye died, Harmhab, commander-in-chief of the army, succeeded to the throne (1353–1319 BC). He reorganized the state and reestablished a strong government. Dying childless, Harmhab designated as his successor Ramses I, commander of the army and vizier, or prime minister. Ramses (1319–1318 BC) and Seti I (1318–1299 BC) made valiant attempts to restore the Asiatic empire lost by Akhnaton. In connection with their efforts, the capital was moved to Tanis in the delta, from which military campaigns could be more effectively launched.

Ramses II (1299–1232 BC) continued the effort to restore Egyptian control in Palestine. In the fifth year of his reign, he met the Hittites in battle at Kadesh on the Orontes in Syria and narrowly missed destruction of his forces. Subsequently, he fought battles all the way from southern Palestine to northern Syria. If the Hebrews were then in the land, as an early date of the exodus requires, they probably never made contact with the Egyptians because they were shepherds and vinedressers in the hills of Palestine, and Ramses moved along the coastal road. Finally, in his 21st regnal year, Ramses made a peace treaty with the Hittites and kept it to the end of his days. He built massively all over Egypt, notably at his capital of Tanis, at Thebes, at Abu Simbel (south of Aswan), and at Memphis. Many of those who accept a later date for the exodus believe he was the pharaoh of the exodus.

Ramses' 13th son, Merneptah (1232–1222 BC), was the only Egyptian king who claimed to have defeated the Hebrews in battle. But some scholars argue that he never invaded Asia and that this statement is to be interpreted as a customary claim of victory over the king's opponents in surrounding lands, whether or not he ever met them in battle.

Ramses III (1198–1164 BC) also fought off a Libyan invasion of the delta in his 5th and 11th regnal years, and in his eighth year he repulsed an invasion of Sea Peoples, among whom were Philistines. He was the last ruler of the empire period to maintain outposts in Palestine and Syria. In his later years the Egyptian economy deteriorated, and inflation and breakdown of the government's ability to meet the public payroll brought great suffering. Hunger marches resulted.

During the reigns of Ramses IV–XI (1167–1085 BC), there was a steady decline of the state. Graft and inflation increased. During the reign of Ramses IX (1138–1119 BC) unpaid mercenary troops seem to have roamed as marauders in the delta, and tomb robbery reached epidemic proportions. Finally Herihor, viceroy of Nubia and commander of military forces in the south, seized control of Upper Egypt and made himself high priest of Amon in Thebes. The empire had come to an end.

The Postempire Period In the postempire period, Egypt came under the rule of Libyan kings (945–712 BC) and Ethiopian kings (712–670 BC). After a brief period of Assyrian domination (670–663 BC), a native dynasty asserted itself (663–525 BC). Then the Persians conquered and held the land until Alexander the Great marched through in 331. Thereafter, the Ptolemies ruled Egypt until the death of Cleopatra in 30 BC. At that point the Romans took over. They controlled the land when Mary and Joseph fled there after the birth of Jesus. During the Greco-Roman period, Hellenistic culture dominated Egypt.

During the early postempire period, when Egyptian culture was still dominant, several kings figured in biblical history. During the fifth year of Rehoboam, king of Judah (probably 926 BC), Shishak I of Egypt invaded Judah and wrought great havoc there (1 Kgs 14:25-26). He even marched into the territory of Israel, as archaeological discoveries show. About 700 BC, in the days of King Hezekiah and the prophet Isaiah, Tirhakah of Ethiopia led an army into Palestine to help the Jews against invading Assyrians (2 Kgs 19:9). Near the end of the seventh century BC, Pharaoh Neco led an army through Judah to come to the aid of weakened Assyria. When King Josiah tried to stop him, the Hebrew monarch lost his life (2 Kgs 23:28-30). During the last days of the kingdom of Judah, while Nebuchadnezzar was besieging Jerusalem (588–586 BC), Pharaoh Hophra invaded Palestine in a vain effort to aid the Hebrews and defeat the Babylonians. Jeremiah predicted the Egyptians' destruction (Jer 44:30).

Social Life

Social Classes In theory and in practice, the king owned all the land of Egypt. He was divine, and the gods had assigned to him the deeds to all the land. Of course, he made gifts—to the gods for the support of the temples, to his most loyal supporters, and for the maintenance of his own worship cult after his death. Thus, large parts of the kingdom slipped from his hands, but much remained as the possession of the crown. Although by the beginning of the Middle Kingdom, nobles held great tracts of land, the king managed to sweep aside their power and repossess a considerable amount of acreage. During the Empire, the king made large grants to the temples, especially the temple of Amon at Thebes. This generosity enhanced the power of the priesthood at the expense of the crown.

As increasing amounts of land passed out of the control of the crown, and as social and economic life became more complex, a complicated class structure developed. The major division in Egyptian society was between the educated elite and the uneducated masses, but such an observation is too simplistic. At the top were the royal family and the great nobles. Below them was a group of lesser nobles and officials. Lower yet was a class of craftsmen who served both upper classes. Then, at least during the Empire, there were farmers who owned small plots which they worked themselves. At the bottom of the social structure were free serfs and slaves. Slavery became common only under the Empire, when slaves were obtained as prisoners of war, primarily in Palestine and Syria to the north and Nubia to the south. Some slaves found their way into domestic service at the palaces and on the large estates, but most of them worked on the land and some served in the mines. Slavery was never as important in Egypt as in other Near Eastern countries.

Family Life Egyptians apparently married in early adolescence. Children were weaned at three. Boys were circumcised between the ages of 6 and 12. Although education was designed for boys of the upper classes, girls—especially of royal families—frequently received some formal education. Egyptian women evidently enjoyed much greater freedom and prestige than women of other Near Eastern countries. They went about rather freely; they accompanied their husbands in the conduct of business and even at social events. The family might even accompany the husband and father on an outing when he went fishing or hunting, though they did not take part in the action. Egyptians normally were not monogamous, the size of the harem being dictated by economic considerations. But the status of the chief wife was protected, and her first son was her husband's heir. Professions open to women included the priesthood, midwifery, mourning, dancing, and perhaps scribal activity (there was a feminine word for scribe).

Furniture was meager in an Egyptian house. Beds, chairs, stools, footstools, and stands for water jugs seem to have been the main items. Dining tables do not appear to have been used; there were stands on which trays of food might be placed. The poor simply sat on the floor, slept on mats on the floor, and spread out their meals on the floor.

Houses were normally built of mud brick. Those of the wealthy were set amid gardens and frequently had decorative pools. Rooms might be color-washed on the inside and even decorated with frescoes. Roofs were flat and provided a second bedroom in the hottest months. Houses sometimes had a second story. Though remains of two or three villages of workmen on government projects have been found, virtually nothing is known of the layout or size of the important cities of ancient Egypt.

Dress Women wore long linen garments extending from the armpits to the ankles and held up by straps over the shoulder. During the Empire period, the skirt was made fuller and pleated. Men wore loincloths fastened with a belt and extending to the knee. The upper classes often wore it pleated in front. During the Middle Kingdom and the latter part of the Empire, the loincloth was extended to midcalf, and men sometimes also wore a short-sleeved tunic. As a result of Asian influence, Egyptians of the upper classes frequently wore colored clothing during the Empire, instead of the prevailing white of other periods.

Egyptian Wall Paintings This Egyptian artwork represents typical Egyptian dress.

Men were clean-shaven, but the king and a few top officials wore false beards for ceremonial purposes. Both men and women wore wigs, and both men and women used eye paint for medicinal and decorative purposes. Women wore lipstick and rouge and applied henna to their nails, the palms of their hands, and the soles of their feet. Men and women of the upper classes wore a variety of jewelry. People of all classes applied oils and fats to their skin to protect them in the hot, dry climate. The use of perfume was also universal.

Entertainment There were no organized games in ancient Egypt. Sportsmen went out alone or with their families. They might hunt in the desert with bows and arrows and dogs, go fishing, try to knock down birds with a boomerang in a marsh, or go driving in a chariot. Boys and young men among the peasants especially enjoyed wrestling. Soldiers participated in war dances, which were a sort of physical drill. A game like checkers was the chief indoor game of men and women alike.

Law and Punishment The king was viewed as the source of all law, and apparently there was no written code to which all could appeal. Courts followed precedent set in past cases, and periodically the king modified the legal system by new edicts. Procedure in the courts involved administering an oath to tell the truth, speeches by accuser and accused, judgment of the court, and note taking by a court recorder. In some cases torture was used to extract a confession.

Treason, murder, and perjury were among the capital crimes. The latter was so serious because the court oath was taken "by the life of Pharaoh"; thus, swearing falsely meant injury to the king. Other serious crimes were punishable by mutilation (cutting off nose or ears) or hard labor in the mines and quarries (a living death). A person convicted of theft might be sentenced to repay double or triple what he had taken. Beating was the usual punishment for minor offenses. During the Empire, Egypt had a kind of police force with a contingent in each town.

Religion All of Egyptian life was bound up with religious considerations. As the "gift of the Nile," Egypt worshiped the great river as Hapi. The sun, which gave life to all things, was deified under such names as Amon-Re and Aton. The king was the offspring of the gods and was in some sense god incarnate. The 10 plagues in Moses' day were an attack on the gods of the Egyptians. Turning the Nile into blood, bringing intense darkness on the land, and smiting the firstborn of the divine pharaoh involved a discrediting of Egyptian gods, as did the other plagues in various ways.

The greatest concern of all individuals was immortality and the blessing of the gods upon them in the next life. Egyptians were not morbid in that they were preoccupied with death; they sought to project or continue as many of the pleasant aspects of this life as possible into the next life.

Ancient Egyptians, unlike modern Western peoples, had no concept of an inanimate world. All natural phenomena were personalized and acted as friendly or unfriendly beings whenever they affected human activity. The gods were looked on as patrons of various activities or functions. Thus, Bes, a bandy-legged dwarf, was the patron of music and conception, and the goddess Taurt (a combination of hippopotamus, lioness, and crocodile) was associated with childbirth. Charms of both were made in abundance, and these two seem to have been more widely regarded among the masses than the chief gods of Egypt.

Most important of all the gods was Re, or Ra, the sun god. The pharaoh was his physical son and earthly embodiment. When he died, he rejoined his divine father in the sky. Re generated the god Shu, personification of air, and the goddess Tefnut, personification of moisture. These gave birth to two children, Geb the earth god and Nut the sky goddess. The legends present different stories of how mankind came into being. One legend has Re generating them with his tears; another has Khnum forming them on his potter's wheel. During the Empire, the god of Thebes, Amon, was identified with Re, and the sun god henceforth became known as Amon-Re. The great triad of Thebes was Amon, his consort Mut, and their son Khonsu (the moon god).

Rivaling Amon-Re in importance was Osiris, god (king) of the dead. Legend has it that the benevolent ruler Osiris was murdered by his brother and brought back to life by his wife, Isis, through various magical devices; thereafter, he ruled in the west as king of the blessed dead. Eventually the experience of Osiris became that of every human being. Through magical formulas of the sort used by Isis, the individual could come to Osiris and even in some sense become Osiris. In addition to the knowledge and pronouncement of such formulas, the individual had to appear at a judgment for the weighing of his heart in the balance of righteousness. If declared innocent of wrongdoing, he was allowed to enter the kingdom of Osiris and enjoy a blessed hereafter.

Some of these notions about exiting to the next life began to appear on the walls of pyramid tombs in the Old Kingdom ("pyramid texts"). During the Middle Kingdom, they were recorded on coffins ("coffin texts"). During the Empire, they were compiled as the "Book of the Dead." Portions continued to be inscribed on the walls of tombs from the Empire period to about AD 300.

Learning and Culture

Language and Writing Ancient Egyptian was related to both Semitic and Hamitic languages. By about 311 BC, both hieroglyphics (pictorial characters used in inscriptions and more formal writing) and hieratic (a more running hand) were in use. Hieroglyphs may stand for a letter, a syllable, a sound, a word, or an idea. Francois Champollion cracked the decipherment of the hieroglyphs in 1822, primarily with the help of the Rosetta Stone. About 700 BC, a more rapid script called demotic came into being and continued to be written until early Christian times. Thereafter, Coptic, the ancient Egyptian language, came to be written down in a Greek script with a few extra letters.

Education Egyptian education, available almost exclusively to upper-class boys, was designed to provide trained personnel for the priesthood, government offices, or the professions. Few had a chance to obtain any education at all. Boys began their training at an early age, commonly about four. Classes started early in the morning and normally ended about noon, in order to avoid the heat of the day. Reading, writing, and arithmetic were the standard fare. Good handwriting and the ability to compose letters were essential for all leaders in society. Eloquence was also valued. Learning by imitation was achieved through copying handwriting samples and model letters. Pieces of stone and potsherds provided inexpensive writing tablets, with papyrus being reserved for final drafts of important compositions. Knowledge of arithmetic was especially important for workers in government offices where taxes were collected in kind.

The highest form of education was priestly training, and a prince might enroll in a school for priests. But often he was educated by tutors in classes held at the palace. Such classes normally were designed for children of the harem; princesses and nonroyal children might also attend them.

After lower school, a boy might attend a "House of Life," a kind of academy or senior college. There outstanding persons might lecture on a variety of subjects (including medicine). Presumably resembling Plato's academy in Athens, such "Houses" did not have a prescribed curriculum or regular examinations. They were equipped with libraries.

Science The ancient Egyptians excelled in applied mathematics, astronomy, and medicine. The annual flood of the Nile required an early development of the ability to resurvey the land rapidly after waters receded. Engineering skills were necessary to produce the irrigation system on which all Egyptian life depended. Moreover, their massive building projects necessitated a knowledge of mathematics. Egyptians could add and subtract but had cumbersome procedures for multiplication and division. They could calculate the area of a square, a triangle, a rectangle, and a circle and could do simple exercises in geometry. It is thought that experience rather than mathematical reasoning ability was responsible for most of their mathematical successes. They understood that the calendar must have 365¼ days in it, and they divided the year into 12 months and the months into three 10-day weeks. As early as 2000 BC, they had invented an adequate water clock.

With their elaborate practice of embalming, one would expect their knowledge of anatomy to be superior. They distinguished between injuries and diseases and performed some amazing surgery. Treatment was, however, a curious combination of scientific and superstitious efforts. Egyptian scientists, with a practical rather than theoretical motivation, amassed a vast collection of facts about astronomy, chemistry, geography, medicine, surgery, mathematics, and natural history.

Architecture As the ancient Egyptians built their great temples, they were most concerned with stability and enduring qualities. They were built to last forever. Thus they were made of stone (commonly limestone or sandstone) and roofed with great stone slabs supported on massive columns. The capitals generally were lotus, papyrus, or palm leaf in design. Great statues of a king were placed inside these temples; as mere architectural decoration, these sculptures appear stiff and formal. Light entered the temple through windows in the side of the raised central hall; the side aisles were lower. Though the roofs of these temples were flat, Egyptians knew how to construct a round arch by at least 2700 BC. Greatest of the remaining temples is the temple of Karnak at Luxor. The hypostyle hall there, built by Ramses II, has a forest of 134 sandstone columns, the central avenue of which has 12 columns that soar to a height of 70 feet (21.3 meters), the tallest columns in the ancient world.

Egyptian Pyramid

Pharaohs of the Old Kingdom built great pyramids as burial places along the west bank of the Nile south of Memphis. Pharaohs of the Middle Kingdom constructed smaller pyramids in the Fayum area. During the empire period, they carved tombs out of the cliffs west of Thebes. Pharaohs as divine beings covered the walls of their tombs at Thebes with religious scenes. The nobles had their tombs decorated with scenes of everyday life—a life that they wished to perpetuate beyond the grave.

Houses were constructed of sun-dried brick; a few remain at Amarna and in a couple of abandoned workers' camps.

Music All that is known of Egyptian music must be gleaned from musical instruments found in tombs or representations of musical instruments painted on tomb walls. Three instruments used in religious exercises were the sistrum, tambourine, and castanets. The sistrum was a metal loop fastened to a handle. Holes were cut in the sides of the loop so that three metal rods could be loosely fastened in it. When the sistrum was shaken, the rods would rattle. This is the instrument referred to in 2 Samuel 6:5. Miriam used the Egyptian timbrel, or tambourine, in the celebration after crossing the Red Sea (Ex 15:20).

Stringed instruments in ancient Egypt included the harp, lyre, lute, and a kind of guitar. Wind instruments included the single and double flute and the trumpet, the latter apparently used only for military purposes. At first, instruments were used singly to accompany a singer or dancer. Orchestras existed during the Empire period, when Israel escaped from Egyptian bondage.

See also Exodus, The; Pharaoh; Plagues upon Egypt.

EGYPTIAN, The Unidentified antagonist of Rome who led a revolt into the wilderness with a host of barbarous assassins (the Sicarii). After an uproar at the Jerusalem temple, the tribune Claudius Lysias challenged the apostle Paul, asking if he were the Egyptian insurrectionist (Acts 21:38). According to Josephus, the Egyptian led a Jewish rebellion that was suppressed by the procurator Felix. Accounts vary as to the number of assassins involved, but all point to a revolt led by an Egyptian who apparently escaped.

EHI Benjamin's son (Gn 46:21); perhaps a scribal error for Ahiram. *See* Ahiram, Ahiramite.

EHUD

1. Judge of Israel from Benjamin's tribe who delivered Israel from Eglon, king of the Moabites (Jgs 3:12-30). He was notable because he was left-handed (Hebrew "hindered in the right hand"). Before taking Israelite tribute to Eglon, he made an iron dagger, with which he assassinated the unsuspecting Eglon during a private audience. He then rallied the Israelites west of the Jordan to encircle the Moabite troops before they could return south to Moab. When the 18-year rule of Eglon over the Israelites ended, an 80-year period of peace began.
2. Bilhan's son, a member of Benjamin's tribe (1 Chr 7:10; 8:6).

EKER Jerahmeelite and the son of Ram from Judah's tribe (1 Chr 2:27).

EKREBEL Mentioned in Judith 7:18 as a place "located near Chusi in the vicinity of the brook Mochmur." It is possibly modern Akrabeh, which is about 25 miles (40.2 kilometers) north of Jerusalem near the city of Shechem.

EKRON, EKRONITES* Most northerly city among the major Philistine settlements. During the Hebrew conquest of Palestine, Ekron was not taken by Joshua (Jos 13:3). When the land was divided among the 12 tribes, Ekron was given first to Judah and then to Dan (15:11, 45-46; 19:43). It was eventually taken by Judah (Jgs 1:18), but it subsequently fell back to the Philistines.

Ekron played a prominent role in the story of the capture of the ark of the covenant. After the ark brought disaster to Ashdod and Gath, it was taken to Ekron (1 Sm 5:1-10). The Ekronites did not want the ark, so they consulted with the "lords of the Philistines" and proposed that the ark be sent back to Israel (v 11).

After David killed Goliath, the Israelites pursued the Philistines to the gates of Ekron, which at that time apparently was the nearest walled city in which fugitives could take refuge (1 Sm 17:52).

Ekron was apparently the center of the worship of the god Baal-zebub. When Ahaziah injured himself and lay ill, he preferred to consult with Baal-zebub rather than with God. Elijah was sent by God to denounce Ahaziah and tell him that he would die (2 Kgs 1:2-18). Baal worship may have been increasing in Israel at this time. Ekron is included in the denunciations of several prophets: Jeremiah (25:20), Amos (1:8), Zephaniah (2:4), and Zechariah (9:5-7).

Assyrian records inform us that Ekron revolted against Sennacherib in 701 BC. The rebels deposed Padi, the ruler of Ekron, who was loyal to Assyria, and handed him over to Hezekiah in Jerusalem for imprisonment. Sennacherib moved against Ekron, and Ekron called for aid from the king of Mutsri (either Egypt or a district of northwestern Arabia). Sennacherib lifted his siege of Ekron long enough to defeat the army of Mutsri, and then returned to take Ekron. He executed the rebels, made captives of their followers, forced Hezekiah to release Padi, and restored Padi as ruler of the city. Padi also received some territory taken from Judah. Padi's successor, Ikausu, was not so fortunate. He, along with Manasseh of Judah, was forced to pay heavy tribute to both Esarhaddon and Ashurbanipal.

In 147 BC the king of Syria, Alexander Epiphanes, gave Ekron to Jonathan Maccabeus as a reward for his loyalty (1 Macc 10:89). In the fourth century AD it still had a large Jewish population.

See also Philistia, Philistines.

EL* Ancient Semitic name for deity, perhaps meaning "power" (cf. Gn 17:1); used by the Hebrews generally in a poetic sense to denote the true God of Israel. The same word was used for the senior Canaanite god and the god in Ugaritic mythology. The "Il" or "El" of ancient Canaanite mythology (before 3500 BC in the region of Syria) was not as active as the god Baal, who struggled with Death and triumphed over Chaos. But Il was the father god of the Canaanite pantheon. OT critics have suggested that the Hebrews adopted the clan gods of the Canaanites, including Il. Yet Phoenician and Ugaritic literature use Il in the feminine form for the names of goddesses. The Hebrew avoids such usage. El is combined with other adjectives to describe the numerous attributes of God; for example, God Most High (Gn 14:18-24), the seeing God (16:13), the jealous God (Ex 20:5), the forgiving God (Neh 9:17), and the gracious God (v 31).

See also Canaanite Deities and Religion; God, Names of.

ELA Father of Shimei, one of the 12 officers appointed to requisition food for King Solomon's household (1 Kgs 4:18).

ELADAH* KJV form of Eleadah, Ephraim's descendant, in 1 Chronicles 7:20. *See* Eleadah.

ELAH

1. Esau's descendant and a chief of Edom (Gn 36:41; 1 Chr 1:52).
2. KJV rendering of Ela, Shimei's father, in 1 Kings 4:18. *See* Ela.
3. Baasha's son and fourth king of Israel. Elah reigned for only two years (886–885 BC). While in a drunken stupor, he was murdered by one of his generals (1 Kgs 16:8-14).
4. Father of Hoshea, the last king of the northern kingdom of Israel (2 Kgs 15:30; 17:1; 18:1, 9).
5. Caleb's second son and father of Kenaz (1 Chr 4:15).
6. Uzzi's son, descendant of Benjamin (1 Chr 9:8). Elah was among the first to resettle in Jerusalem after the Babylonian exile. He is not mentioned in the parallel list of Nehemiah 11.

ELAH, Valley of Southernmost valley in the Shephelah, starting at Hebron and descending in a northerly direction before turning west. At the Wadi al-Sant it comes together with other valleys, and at this juncture there is a wide, level valley about one-half mile (.8 kilometer) wide. It was here that the great struggle between David and Goliath took place, with the Philistine army camped on the southern hills and Saul's army on the north or northeast (1 Sm 17:2, 19; 21:9).

ELAM (Person)

1. Firstborn son of Shem and a grandson of Noah (Gn 10:22; 1 Chr 1:17).
2. Benjamite and the son of Shashak (1 Chr 8:24).
3. Korahite Levite and the fifth son of Kore from the house of Asaph (1 Chr 26:3).
4. Forefather of 1,254 descendants who returned with Zerubbabel to Judah following the exile (Ezr 2:7; Neh 7:12). Later, 71 members of Elam's house accompanied Ezra back to Palestine during the reign of King Artaxerxes I of Persia (464–424 BC; Ezr 8:7). In postexilic Judah, Shecaniah, Elam's descendant, urged Ezra to command the sons of Israel to divorce their foreign wives (10:2); a number from Elam's house eventually did so (v 26).
5. Another forefather of 1,254 descendants who returned with Zerubbabel to Judah (Ezr 2:31; Neh 7:34).
6. One of the chiefs of Israel who set his seal on Ezra's covenant (Neh 10:14).
7. One of the priestly musicians who performed at the dedication of the Jerusalem wall (Neh 12:42).

ELAM (Place), ELAMITES Occupying an area roughly the size of Denmark, Elam was located in southwest Asia, east of Babylonia and north of the Persian Gulf, on a plain known to the Iranians since the Middle Ages as Khuzistan. The region today corresponds to southwest Iran. Mountainous areas to the north and east, known as the Anshan range, formed a peripheral part of Elam. The land's fertility was linked to several waterways, the most significant of which—the Karkheh—forms Elam's western boundary.

A people with a culture and history spanning more than 2,000 years, the Elamites seem to have lived in constant strife with the Sumerians, Babylonians, Assyrians, and finally the Persians, by whom they were absorbed. As a race, the Elamites were a mixture of dark-skinned aboriginals of questionable origin and Semites who had spilled over into the land from Mesopotamia.

Western civilization would know virtually nothing of

Elam were it not for the biblical witness. Elam is mentioned in conjunction with Shem's progeny (Gn 10:22), and in the book of Acts it is reported that among the Israelites present in Jerusalem for the Feast of Pentecost were some from the old area of Elam (Acts 2:9). Isaiah prophesied that the Jews carried away in the Babylonian exile would return from such places as Elam (Is 11:11); however, these were most likely Aramaic-speaking Jews who had decided not to return to their homeland following the repatriation edict of Cyrus of Persia (Ezr 1:1-4). The name Kedorlaomer, king of Elam (Gn 14:1), is demonstrably an authentic Elamite name, thereby lending additional support to the accuracy of the historical narrative in Genesis. Daniel's vision at Shushan in the province of Elam (Dn 8:2) reveals precise knowledge of the geography of the area and its waterways. In such accounts the Bible shows itself to be a valuable adjunct to extrabiblical literature for the history of the ancient Near East.

In the eighth century BC, Isaiah summoned Elam to participate in the shattering of Babylon as an act of the Lord's judgment (Is 21:2); there is little information, however, about Elam's role in the overthrow of Babylon in 540 BC. Elam, with other rebellious nations, would eventually experience the cup of God's wrath (Jer 25:15-26). Even its world-renowned archers would prove no match for the Lord of hosts (Is 22:6-12; Jer 49:35; Ez 32:24). Ezekiel's dirge over Elam dramatically illustrates the horror of a godless grave (Ez 32:24-25). Jeremiah warns the Elamites that they cannot escape the judgment of God, made certain by the presence of his throne among them (Jer 49:38). Yet Elam's destruction, though politically complete in Persia's conquest, would not be altogether irremediable (v 39). Though its dislocation would rival those of its contemporaries, Jeremiah spoke of a time when God would extend mercy to descendants of the Elamites. Such an expectance, following the phrase, "in the latter days," may point to the messianic age. The prophet may well have envisioned that momentous Day of Pentecost, when many from Elam would be among those in Jerusalem upon whom the Spirit of the Lord fell.

ELASAH

1. Priest of Pashhur's clan who obeyed Ezra's exhortation to divorce his pagan wife after the exile (Ezr 10:22).
2. Shaphan's son and King Zedekiah's envoy to King Nebuchadnezzar of Babylon. On his trip to Babylon, Elasah also carried a letter of encouragement from the prophet Jeremiah to the Jewish exiles there (Jer 29:3).

ELATH Edomite city (also spelled Eloth) at the head of the Gulf of Aqaba (Dt 2:8; 1 Kgs 9:26), on the eastern border of the wilderness of Paran (Gn 14:6, where it is alternately called El-paran). It probably owed its named (which means "grove of trees") to the many palm trees in the area and may have been located in a grove of sacred trees. Elath was strategically located along a primary trade route running from southern Arabia and Egypt to Phoenicia, making it a valuable city to possess.

Elath was taken by Kedorlaomer from the Horites (Gn 14:5-6). Later it was regarded as the southern limit of the territory of Edom (Dt 2:8). David probably captured it when he conquered Edom (2 Sm 8:14). During the reign of Joram, Jehoshaphat's son, revolt restored it to the Edomites (2 Kgs 8:20-22). A few years later it was recaptured and rebuilt by Judah's King Uzziah (2 Kgs 14:22). It remained under Judah's rule until the time of Ahaz, when it was taken by Rezin of Syria and occupied by Syrians (2 Kgs 16:6). From about 753 BC onward, it

remained an Edomite city until it was abandoned sometime between the sixth and fourth centuries BC. Then the Nabateans, who controlled the area, built a city a little farther east of the original site and renamed it Aila.

See also El-paran.

EL-BERITH* Local god worshiped at Shechem (Jgs 9:46). He is usually identified with the god Baal-berith (8:33; 9:4).

EL-BETHEL Name Jacob gave to the place at Luz (Bethel) where he built an altar after he returned from Haran with his family (Gn 35:7). *See* Bethel (Place), Bethelite.

ELCHASAI*, The Book of Lost Jewish work composed in Aramaic by Elchasai during the reign of Emperor Trajan (AD 98–117). It was intended for his followers, the Elchasaites (or Sabai), but was read by both Jews and Jewish Christian groups. Portions of the book are quoted by early church fathers Hippolytus, Epiphanius, and Origen (quoted in Eusebius).

The book is a syncretism of Jewish, Christian, gnostic, and pagan ideas. Baptism is linked to forgiveness of sins and is a way a person can be healed. It prescribes a form of Jewish legalism but rejects the need for sacrifices and a priesthood.

ELDAAH Midian's fifth son and a descendant of Abraham and his wife Keturah (Gn 25:4; 1 Chr 1:33).

ELDAD One of the 70 elders of Israel who were commissioned to assist Moses in governing the people (Nm 11:26-27). Though Eldad and another elder, Medad, were not among the 68 elders who had gathered around the tabernacle at Moses' command, they too received the Spirit and prophesied. When Joshua, out of concern for Moses' authority, asked Moses to stop them, Moses showed great humility and sensitivity to God's will by answering, "I wish that all the LORD's people were prophets" (Nm 11:29, NIV).

ELDER Person who, by virtue of position in the family, clan, or tribe; or by reason of personality, prowess, stature, or influence; or through a process of appointment and ordination, exercised leadership and judicial functions in both religious and secular spheres in the ancient world, both among biblical and nonbiblical peoples. The roots of the development of the presbytery (group of elders) in the NT and postapostolic church originate in Judaism and the OT, though the figure of the elder or groups of elders can also be found in the world surrounding ancient Israel and in the Greco-Roman world of the NT period.

In the Old Testament The elder, or the institution of elders, is closely linked with the tribal system. Tribes were composed of clans, and clans of large, extended family units. By virtue of age and function in a patriarchal society, the father of a family ruled. This fact of age, as well as the wisdom and maturity invested in older persons, is undoubtedly the origin of the authority that these elders exercised. A clan was ruled by the heads of the families constituting it, forming a council of elders. In time of war, each clan furnished a contingent; these were led by a chief, probably chosen from the ranks of the elders.

In Israel's premonarchy period, local administration and judicial action was largely in the hands of those elders. In the exodus narrative, it was the elders of Israel (heads of families) who were instructed by Moses concerning the first Passover meal (Ex 12:21-22). It was these elders who, in Exodus 18:12, met with Jethro, Moses' father-in-law, and from whose ranks were chosen worthy representatives to assist Moses in the interpretation of the law of God and the administration of justice (18:13-23). Similarly, according to Numbers 11:16-17, Moses was instructed by God to select 70 men from among the elders of Israel to assist him in leadership of the people. In this latter account, the elders were marked by a special endowment of God's Spirit. In the former the elders—chosen as coadministrators with Moses—were those known to be trustworthy.

A central function of elders was the administration of justice. They were the "judges," who sat "in the gate," the traditional courtroom of ancient villages and towns. Here disputes and trials were settled by the elders, and community affairs were discussed and decisions made (Gn 23:10, 18; Jb 29:7; Prv 24:7; 31:23). The preservation and application of the law was clearly in the hands of elders who sat at the gate of the town (Dt 19:12; 21:19; 22:15; 25:7-10). Ruth 4:1-12 provides an excellent description of such a process.

During the period of the monarchy, local administration and judicial authority continued to be invested in councils of elders. At the end of Saul's reign, David sent messages and gifts to the elders of the towns of Judah (1 Sm 30:26), obviously recognizing that his efficient rule would depend on their goodwill and allegiance. In the time of Jehu (2 Kgs 10:5), we hear of elders in Samaria, side by side with a governor and master of the palace. To facilitate her plot against Naboth, Jezebel wrote instructions to the elders and nobles of Jezreel (1 Kgs 21:8-11). Again, Josiah convened the elders of Judah and Jerusalem to hear the reading of the law and to enter with him into a new covenant of obedience (2 Kgs 23:1). It is clear that the elders of Israel were now responsible for the application of the law within their jurisdictions. Besides administrative and judicial functions, elders also assumed cultic roles (Ex 24:1, 9; Lv 4:14-15).

The institution of the elders survived the collapse of the royal institutions. Elders were present during the exile (Ez 8:1; 14:1; 20:1-3) as well as after the return (e.g., Ezr 10:16).

In Judaism of the New Testament Period While use of the title "elder" to designate officers of various Greek cult associations and village magistrates may have influenced the development of community structure in the gentile churches, the Christian office (or function) of elder stems from a very similar institution within Judaism. In the first three Gospels and in Acts there are numerous references to elders as functionaries within the communal and religious life of Judaism. Generally they are mentioned together with one or more other groups of functionaries (quoting the RSV): "elders and chief priests and scribes" (Mt 16:21); "chief priests and elders of the people" (21:23; 26:3, 47); "scribes and elders" (26:41, 57); "chief priests and elders" (27:1, 3, 12, 20); "rulers and elders and scribes" (Acts 4:5); "rulers of the people and elders" (v 8). From these NT passages we cannot determine what exactly their functions were, or how they differed from rulers or scribes. However, the duties of Jewish elders are clearly described in the tractate *Sanhedrin* in the Mishnah, as well as in the community rule books of the Qumran ascetics, discovered among the Dead Sea Scrolls.

Each Jewish community had its council of elders, who had general administrative oversight and represented the community in relations with Roman authorities. Their primary duty was judicial. They were custodians of the law and its traditional interpretations (see Mt 15:2), and they were charged with both its enforcement and the punishment of offenders. The most important of these councils of elders was the Sanhedrin in Jerusalem, a group of 71 men who acted as the final court for the entire nation.

In the Christian Community Since the primitive church eventually regarded itself as the new Israel (Mt 21:43; Gal 6:16), it is easy to see why it should gradually adopt the institution of elders. Though it is difficult to make out the order that prevailed in the first Christian communities, because it apparently varied according to place and time in both form and extent, the presence and functioning of elders was part of the reality of early church life.

In Luke's account of the origin and spread of Christianity, the elders are already present in the church at Jerusalem. In Acts we see Christians at Antioch sending famine relief "to the elders [of the Judean churches] by Barnabas and Saul" (Acts 11:30). On their first missionary journey, Paul and Barnabas "appointed elders in every church" (14:23). Later, Paul and Barnabas were sent from Antioch to Jerusalem "to the apostles and elders" about the question of circumcision of gentile Christians (15:2), and were "welcomed by the church, and the apostles, and the elders" (v 4), who gathered to hear the case and resolve the issue (vv 6-23).

Who these elders were, and how they were chosen, we are not told. It seems possible to argue, on the basis of Jewish precedent, that age and prominence gave them the privilege of rendering special service within the community. Veneration for age was a deeply rooted sentiment among Jews, and the name "presbyter" (elder) was derived from Jewish usage. It is also possible that, like the appointment of "the seven" for special service by the laying on of hands (6:1-6), the first elders in the Jerusalem church were appointed by the apostles. Apparently they functioned in the Christian community in ways comparable to the elders in the Jewish communities and the Sanhedrin (11:30; 15:2-6, 22-23; 16:4; 21:18).

Paul apparently continued the practice among the gentile churches, though elders are not mentioned in the earliest Pauline writings. They are mentioned only in the Pastoral Epistles (1 Tm 5:17, 19; Ti 1:5). On his last journey to Jerusalem, Paul summoned the elders of the church at Ephesus to Miletus (Acts 20:17) to bid them farewell, and to instruct them to be faithful in their task of overseeing and caring for the Christian flock, the church of God (20:28).

Although elders are not explicitly mentioned in Paul's early letters, they may have been among the leaders who presided over the congregations (Rom 12:8; 1 Thes 5:12-13). Philippians 1:1 certainly reveals a definite stratification of leadership ("overseers and deacons") within a young Pauline congregation. And 1 Timothy 5:17, reflecting what is often considered a later phase in the development of church government, attributes the functions of preaching and teaching to the ruling elders. Further, that Christian elders exercised pastoral functions may be inferred from 1 Peter 5:1-5 and James 5:14.

There is one passage where we find a possible identification of an apostle (Peter) as also being an elder: "I exhort the elders among you, as a fellow elder and a witness of the sufferings of Christ" (1 Pt 5:1a, RSV). This text may indicate that elders were appointed and functioned as extensions of apostolic servanthood. Paul's practice of appointing elders in the churches before his departure may support such a suggestion. The fact that in the tradition of the later church the "elder" of 2 and 3 John was identified as the apostle John points in a similar direction. Though such an identification is implicit, the apostles could function as elders but not the other way around.

The elders had several functions. For example, 1 Timothy 5:17 speaks of elders as involved in preaching and teaching; James 5:14 sees them involved in a healing ministry; 1 Peter 5:2 exhorts them to tend the flock. Thus, the prophets and teachers who led the church at Antioch (according to Acts 13:1-3) may well have been the elders of this community.

The diaconate, too, whose roots are to be seen in the selection of "the seven" for service to those in need (Acts 6:1-3), was not restricted to purely external service. Two of these men, whom Luke introduces to us as deacons, appear at the same time as evangelists who were particularly effective as preachers of the Word, performers of miracles, expounders of the Scriptures (Stephen, Acts 6:8-10; Philip, Acts 8:4-13, 26-40).

Whereas in the later church bishops and elders were clearly distinguished, the NT reflects an early period when these offices were virtually synonymous. In Paul's farewell speech at Miletus (Acts 20), addressed specifically to the Ephesian church elders (v 17), he tells them that the Holy Spirit has made them "overseers, to care for the church of God" (v 28). Whether "overseer" is used here in the later technical sense of bishop or the more general sense of guardian is not clear. However, in Titus 1:5-7, the elders of verse 5 are clearly the same persons as the bishops of verse 7. Again, the bishops of Philippians 1:1 are likely to be understood as the elders appointed by Paul upon his leaving this mission station.

It is clear that church government in the NT period was still relatively fluid, but the seeds for the later structures were surely planted. The institution of the elders, on the basis of Jewish precedent, was central. The episcopate (overseers/bishops) probably emerged out of the presbyterian (elders), one elder being appointed as overseer by the entire council of elders.

See also Bishop; Deacon, Deaconess; Pastor; Presbyter; Spiritual Gifts.

ELEAD Ephraim's descendant who was killed in a raid against the Philistine city of Gath (1 Chr 7:21).

ELEADAH Ephraim's descendant (1 Chr 7:20, KJV "Eladah").

ELEALEH Town in the Transjordan northeast of Heshbon conquered by Reuben and Gad (Nm 32:3, 37). It was taken back by the Moabites and is associated with Heshbon in the prophetic denunciations of Moab (Is 15:4; 16:9; Jer 48:34).

Eusebius refers to it in the fourth century AD as a large village. It is identified with the modern el-'Al, a village 2,986 feet (910.1 meters) above sea level in a region rich in vineyards. The remains of walls from the prepatriarchal period have been uncovered by archaeologists.

ELEASAH

1. Helez's son and member of Judah's tribe (1 Chr 2:39-40).
2. Raphah's son and descendant of King Saul (1 Chr 8:37; 9:43).

ELEAZAR

1. Third of Aaron's four sons (Ex 6:23). Eleazar ("God has helped") was consecrated as a priest with his

brothers and Aaron in the Sinai (Ex 28:1; Lv 8:2, 13). When his brothers Nadab and Abihu were killed by God as they offered "unholy fire" to the Lord (Lv 10:1-7), Eleazar and Ithamar took leading positions as Aaron's sons (Nm 3:1-4).

Eleazar is described as "chief of the leaders of the Levites" (Nm 3:32). Under his supervision were the sanctuary and its vessels (4:16; 16:37-39; 19:3-4). Eleazar was installed as high priest by Moses when Aaron died on Mt Hor (Nm 20:25-28; Dt 10:6). He was then considered Moses' assistant (Nm 26:1-3, 63; 27:2, 21). Joshua was commissioned by Moses in the presence of Eleazar (27:18-23). In the conquest of Canaan, Joshua and Eleazar served together as leaders. It was Eleazar's function as Joshua's counselor to inquire of the Lord (v 21). He also had his share in the census taking at Shittim. He took part in the partitioning of Canaan, the east bank (34:17), and the west bank (Jos 14:1; 17:4; 19:51; 21:1).

When Eleazar died, he was highly regarded and memorialized in the land of Ephraim (Jos 24:33); his son Phinehas followed him as high priest.

In the oversight of the priests, 16 divisions were assigned to Eleazar's descendants and eight to Ithamar's (1 Chr 24). The ancestry of the prominent priests Zadok and Ezra is traced to Eleazar (1 Chr 6:3-15, 50-53; 24:3; Ezr 7:1-5). In King Solomon's time the priests of Zadok replaced Abiathar, a descendant of Ithamar (1 Kgs 2:26-27, 35). The descendants of Eleazar would be the only ones permitted to minister in Ezekiel's ideal temple (Ez 44:15).

See also Aaron.

2. Abinadab's son, charged with caring for the ark by the people of Kiriath-jearim, when it was brought from Beth-shemesh and placed in the "house of Abinadab on the hill" (1 Sm 7:1).
3. Dodo's son, one of the three mighty men whose exploits against the Philistines gained him great fame (2 Sm 23:9; 1 Chr 11:12).
4. Merarite Levite, son of Mahli. Eleazar died without sons, so his daughters were married to their first cousins (1 Chr 23:21-22; 24:28).
5. Priest descended from Phinehas. This Eleazar helped inventory the temple treasure on returning from the exile with Ezra (Ezr 8:33).
6. Parosh's son, listed with others who divorced their foreign wives in the reform under Ezra (Ezr 10:25).
7. Priest in attendance at the dedication of the rebuilt walls of Jerusalem following the exile (Neh 12:42).
8. Person in the lineage of Joseph, husband of Mary (Mt 1:15). *See* Genealogy of Jesus Christ.

ELECT, ELECTION In modern English, terms referring to the selection of a leader or representative by a group of people. An element of choice is involved, since usually there are several candidates out of whom one must be chosen.

When the verb "elect" is used theologically in the Bible, it usually has God as its subject. In the OT it is used for God's choice of Israel to be his people (cf. Acts 13:17). Israel became God's people, not because they decided to belong to him, but because he took the initiative and chose them. Nor did God's choice rest on any particular virtues that his people exemplified, but rather on his promise to their forefather Abraham (Dt 7:7-8). God also chose their leaders, such as Saul and David (1 Sm 10:24; 2 Sm 6:21), apart from any popular vote by the people. The word thus indicates God's prerogative in deciding what shall happen, independent of human choice.

THE MYSTERY OF ELECTION

In the teaching of Augustine and Calvin, the doctrine of election is of fundamental importance. They taught that God had chosen before the creation of the world to save a number of specific individuals from sin and judgment and to give them eternal life. Those whom he chose did nothing to deserve it; their merits are no better than the rest of humankind who will be judged for their sins. But in his mercy God decided to save some; therefore, he chose them and sent Jesus to be their Savior. The Holy Spirit regenerates and brings to faith through an "effectual calling" those whom God has elected. God's Spirit effectively persuades each of them to submit to the gospel, so they are guaranteed recipients of eternal life.

This choice by God to save some selectively may seem unjust. But God is not obliged to show mercy to anybody; he is free to show mercy as he pleases. People cannot protest that because they were not the elect, they never had a chance of being saved. They never deserved that chance anyway. But anybody who hears the gospel and responds to it with faith can know that he is one of the elect. Whoever rejects the gospel has only his own sinfulness to blame.

Many Christians reject that explanation of God's election. They maintain that, although it appears to be logically consistent with Scripture, it makes God the prisoner of his own plan. His predestination of certain individuals to salvation commits him personally to a detailed, predetermined, unilateral course of action that reduces human action to a charade and renders it insignificant. God ceases to be a person dealing with persons.

The Augustinian and Calvinist view of election, according to its critics, also makes God out to be arbitrary in his choice of the elect. In effect, chance becomes the arbiter of human destiny rather than a holy and loving God. Those difficulties arise because, they say, the teaching of Scripture has been pressed into an artificial logical system that distorts it.

Some Christians avoid the difficulties by saying that God elects "those whom he foreknew" (Rom 8:29), that is, those whom he knew beforehand would respond to the gospel in faith. Augustine briefly held that view but eventually rejected it. Many believe that the "solution" produces even greater logical problems and undermines the sovereignty of God.

Karl Barth proposed an alternative solution. Instead of teaching that God has chosen to save some of humankind and has passed by the others or chosen to reject them, Barth has noted how Jesus is spoken of in Scripture as "the Elect One." Jesus is the object both of God's rejection and of his election. In him the human race was rejected and endured judgment for its sins, Barth argued, but in him also the race is chosen and appointed to salvation. It is thus in Jesus Christ that we are chosen by God (Eph 1:4). Barth's interpretation could conceivably lead to universalism (that is, the view that all humanity will be saved), but Barth explicitly rejected that as a necessary conclusion. He insisted that a person may reject his or her calling and election. Nevertheless, difficulties remain. It has been argued that Barth's view places too much weight on one text and also that it confuses God's election of Jesus for service with his election to salvation of the whole human race.

The teaching of Scripture should not be overly systematized. In the words of the Westminster Confession, election is a "high mystery . . . to be handled with special prudence and care, that men attending the will of God revealed in his word, and yielding obedience thereunto, may, from the certainty of their effectual vocation, be assured of their eternal salvation" (3:8).

The same thoughts are found in the NT. God's people are described as his "elect" or "chosen ones," a term used by Jesus when speaking of the future time when the Son of Man will come and gather together God's people (Mk 13:20, 27). He will vindicate them for their sufferings and for their patience in waiting for his coming (Lk 18:7). In 1 Peter 2:9, God's people are called a "chosen [elect] nation." This phrase was originally used of the people of Israel (Is 43:20), and it brings out the fact that the people of God in the OT and the Christian church in the NT stand in continuity with each other; the promises addressed to Israel now find fulfillment in the church.

In Romans 9–11 Paul discusses the problem of why the people of Israel as a nation have rejected the gospel, while the Gentiles have accepted it. He states that in the present time there is a "remnant" of Israel as a result of God's gracious choice of them. This group is "the elect." They are the chosen people who have obtained what was meant for Israel as a whole, while the greater mass of the people have failed to obtain it because they were "hardened" as a result of their sin (Rom 11:5-7).

Nevertheless, God's choice of Israel to be his people has not been canceled. Most Jewish people have aligned themselves against the gospel, so that the Gentiles may come in and receive God's blessings in their place; however, they still are loved by God, and God will not go back on his original calling of them (Rom 11:28). Con-sequently, Paul is confident that in due time there will be a general return to God by the people of Israel.

The word translated "elect" is generally found in the plural and refers either to the members of God's people as a whole or to those in a particular local church (Rom 8:33; Col 3:12; 1 Thes 1:4; 2 Tm 2:10; Ti 1:1; 1 Pt 1:1-2; 2 Pt 1:10; Rv 17:14; cf. Rom 16:13 and 2 Jn 1:13, which have the singular form). The use of the plural may partly be explained by the fact that most of the NT letters are addressed to groups of people rather than to individuals. More probably, however, the point is that God's election is concerned with the creation of a collective people rather than the calling of isolated individuals.

The word "election" emphasizes that membership of God's people is due to God's initiative, prior to all human response, made before time began (Eph 1:4; cf. Jn 15:16, 19). It is God who has called men and women to be his people, and those who respond are elect. God's call does not depend on any virtues or merits of humankind. Indeed, he chooses the foolish things by worldly standards to shame the wise, the weak to confound the strong, and the lowly and insignificant to bring to nothing those who think that they are something (1 Cor 1:27-28). The effect of election is to leave no grounds whatever for human boasting in achievement and position. Whatever the elect are, they owe it entirely to God, and they cannot boast or compare themselves with other people.

God's elect are a privileged people. Since they now have God to uphold them, no one can bring any accusation against them that might lead to God's condemnation (Rom 8:33). They constitute a royal priesthood; they are God's servants with the right of access to him (1 Pt 2:9). It is for their sake that the apostles endured hardship and suffering, so that they might enjoy future salvation and eternal glory (2 Tm 2:10).

The elect are distinguished by their faith in God (Ti 1:1), and they are called to show the character that befits God's people (Col 3:12). They must make their calling and election sure; that is, they must show that they belong to God by the quality of their lives (2 Pt 1:10). They must continue being faithful to the One who called them (Rv 17:14).

The relationship between God's call and human response is explained in Matthew 22:14: "For many are called, but few are chosen." Although God calls many through the gospel, only some of those respond to the call and become his elect people. The text sheds no light on the mystery of why only some become God's people. Certainly, when a person does respond to God's call, it is because the gospel comes to him or her "in power and in the Holy Spirit and with full conviction" (1 Thes 1:4-5). When men and women refuse the gospel, it is because they have become hardened as a result of sin and their trust in their own works. Scripture does not go beyond that point in explanation, and neither should Christians.

"Election" can also be used of God's choice of people to serve him. Jesus chose the 12 disciples out of the larger company of those who followed him (Lk 6:13; Acts 1:2). The same thought reappears in John's Gospel; Jesus commented that although he chose the Twelve, one of them turned out to be a devil (Jn 6:70; 13:18). When a replacement was needed for Judas, the church prayed to Jesus and asked him to show them which of the two available candidates he would choose to fill the gap in the Twelve (Acts 1:24). Peter attributes his evangelism among the Gentiles to God's election of him for that purpose (15:7). Similarly, Paul was an elected instrument for God's mission to the Gentiles (9:15). The initiative in Christian mission rests with God, who elects people to serve him in particular ways.

See also Foreknowledge; Foreordination.

ELECT LADY* Greeting found in 2 John 1:1. The phrase has been interpreted two ways.

Some interpreters regard 2 John as addressed to a particular woman. Ancient Greek manuscripts show that the word *kuria* (translated as "lady" or "mistress") was used by letter writers as a personal term for family members or close friends of either sex. Thus, the phrase could be translated, "to my dear friend, Eklete." Some scholars associate the elect lady with Martha of Bethany (whose name in Aramaic also means "mistress").

Other interpreters regard the phrase as signifying a local congregation. John possibly portrayed this Christian community as a mother, the members as her children, and other congregations as sisters (2 Jn 1:13; cf. 1 Pt 5:13). The phrase could thus be translated, "the lady elect."

See also John, Letters of.

EL-ELOHE-ISRAEL Name of an altar built by Jacob on land he purchased from the sons of Hamor, near Shechem (Gn 33:20). Jacob used the Canaanite deity's name, El, as a designation for Israel's God.

Some scholars, thinking this a strange name for an altar, have suggested that the combination of names reflects later scribal emendations of the scriptural texts. They argue that the Septuagint corrects the difficulty by saying that Jacob had called "upon" the God of Israel. Others speculate that Jacob built a pillar, not an altar (cf. Gn 35:14, 20).

See also God, Names of.

EL-ELYON* Hebrew for "God Most High" (Gn 14:18). *See* God, Names of.

ELEMENTAL SPIRITS*, ELEMENTS Alternative translations of a Greek word used in the NT, "elemental spirits" being spiritual forces at work in the world, and "elements" being either the basic constituents of the physical world or of human life or the basic principles of a system of thought. In three passages the meaning is clear (Heb 5:12; 2 Pt 3:10, 12). The other four passages, however, have caused considerable debate. The difficult phrase "the elements of the world" appears in three of the four passages (Gal 4:3; Col 2:8, 20). The meanings of "elements" in the fourth passage (Gal 4:9) is probably the same as in the other three because of its similar context.

Range of Meanings The principal meaning of the Greek word is "basic or fundamental component." The word, however, occurs frequently in ancient Greek literature and takes on a variety of connotations in the different contexts in which it appears. Most frequently it was used literally to refer to the physical elements of the world: earth, air, water, and fire. This is probably the meaning of the term in 2 Peter 3:10-12, which states that the world's elements, the physical matter, will be destroyed by fire.

In antiquity the word also commonly referred to the letters in a word, notes in music, the "elementary" rules of politics, or the foundations or basic principles in science, art, or teaching (particularly logical propositions basic to the proof of other propositions). The last is clearly the meaning of the word in the Epistle to the Hebrews (5:12), which describes people's need to have someone teach them the basic principles or elementary truths of God's Word.

In the third century AD another meaning of "elements"—elemental spiritual beings—became current. The development of this meaning has led to the current debate over its suitability in Paul's context.

Elementary Spirits A difficulty with Paul's use of "elements" is that any of three possible meanings makes sense. One can understand "elements" to mean spiritual beings and view Paul's reference as similar to his mention of the principalities and powers (e.g., in Eph 6:12). Translating Galatians 4:3 according to this view (as in the RSV), Paul would have been saying that before conversion a person is enslaved to spiritual forces who rule this world. In 4:9, he asks how the Galatians could wish to be enslaved to these forces again. The references to "beings that by nature are no gods" (v 8) and to angels through whom the law was mediated (3:19) are both used to substantiate the meaning "elemental spirits."

Similarly, Colossians 2:8 would be warning Christians against being led away captive through the philosophical speculations and empty deceit that are perpetrated by human traditions and the elemental spirits. Only two verses later Paul declares that Christ is the head of every principality and power (Col 2:10). Many commentators now believe that Paul intended "principalities and powers" to refer to demons who temporarily ruled various spheres of life in the world. Paul announces that Christ has conquered them and displayed them publicly as captive in his triumphal procession (v 15). Thus, Colossians 2:20 might mean that Christians have "died" to those elemental spirits as elsewhere Paul wrote of "dying" to sin (Rom 6:2).

However, despite the fact that Paul spoke of the principalities and powers as spiritual forces, and despite the ease with which this meaning fits Paul's use of "elements of the world," many scholars regard this interpretation as the least likely of the three possibilities. The earliest certain evidence for the use of "elements" to mean spirits is from the third century AD, which is far too late to reflect common usage in Paul's day. In addition, nowhere else did Paul speak of Christians being in bondage to angels or having died to demonic powers.

Elementary Principles Some scholars understand "the elements of the world" to refer to elementary religious teaching (as in Heb 5:12). Paul may have been appealing to the "ABCs of religion," perhaps the elementary character of the law (cf. Gal 3:24; 4:1-4) or pagan religious teaching (4:8). The "weak and beggarly elements" (KJV) may be explained by the fact that the Galatians were legalistically observing special days, months, seasons, and years as if their righteousness before God depended on it.

Similarly, in Colossians the elements of the world seem to be parallel to human traditions (Col 2:8). The problem again is the same as in Galatians, legalism (vv 16, 20-23). In both contexts the bondage warned against is bondage to elementary religious thinking that comes merely from humans and would be equivalent to contrasting a kindergarten level of thought with the advanced teaching that comes in Christ. Some scholars believe that this interpretation has more in its favor than the meaning "elemental spirits," but others argue that it is not precise enough.

Elementary Existence By far, the most frequent use of "elements" in ancient literature is literal, referring to the physical elements of the world, which were usually considered to be earth, air, water, and fire. The third interpretation, which many scholars prefer, draws on this understanding of "elements of the world." The meaning of the phrase "of the world" determines how the passages in question are to be interpreted. In the NT writings "world" was not merely physical. Frequently, "world" was viewed in an ethical sense, standing for human life apart from God or even lived in opposition to God and Christ. The world often represented unregenerate humanity with its culture, customs, worldview, and ethics—the part of creation that had not yet been redeemed and was helpless to save itself. Thus, the ele-

ments of the world, in this view, are the "basics" of a merely human existence. According to this interpretation, Paul warned the Colossian Christians against being led away captive by philosophical speculation and empty deceit that were in accord with human traditions and with the basics of a merely human existence and not in accord with what they had in Christ (Col 2:8). They had died from the basics of a merely human life (v 20), and being no longer bound to that level of existence, they possessed a life that came from Christ (3:1-4).

This interpretation still leaves the precise meaning of Galatians 4:1-3 uncertain. Was Paul addressing both Jews and Gentiles or only Jews (the "we" in Gal 4:3)? No doubt Paul viewed both Jews and Gentiles as being in bondage to a merely human existence. Even though the Jews possessed God's law, it was ineffectual for salvation. Christ's coming broke that bondage and brought the Holy Spirit, who would give Christians a completely new quality of human life. Therefore, Paul warned against becoming enslaved again to such weak and poverty-stricken basics of a merely human existence (v 9).

In this view, then, the elements of the world are the "basics" of existence before and outside of Christ. Paul nowhere recorded specifically what he included in those basics. The contexts of both Galatians and Colossians, however, seem to imply that the basics at least included the law and "the flesh" (that is, life lived ethically apart from God). Such a view of "elements" accords well with the wider context of these passages and with other passages (especially Rom 6–8; Gal 3:2-3, 23-25; 4:1-10).

ELEPH* KJV translation for the town Haeleph in Joshua 18:28. *See* Haeleph.

ELEPHANTINE PAPYRI* Aramaic documents from the fifth century BC discovered at Elephantine, an island in the Nile River. At the time of the documents' writing, Elephantine was a Persian military outpost, manned in part by a group of Jewish mercenaries with their families. The documents, numbering over 100, belong primarily to three archives—two familial and one communal. The archives contained many complete scrolls that were still tied and sealed at the time of their discovery, along with numerous broken papyri and fragments.

The manuscripts are of considerable archaeological importance. Several centuries older than most of the Dead Sea Scrolls, they portray the social, political, and religious life of a Jewish community outside Palestine. Several points of contact are made with the books of Ezra and Nehemiah.

Since most of the documents are legal texts, they are an important link in the history of law in the ancient Near East. The texts also provide valuable information about the Aramaic spoken in the period and illustrate the daily life of a Persian frontier military colony.

Ancient Elephantine Elephantine was located on the southern tip of a small island in the Nile River a few kilometers north of the first cataract, opposite its twin city, ancient Syene (modern Aswan). The Bible probably includes the twin cities of Elephantine and Syene in two occurrences of the phrase "from Migdol to Syene" (Ez 29:10; 30:6), that is, from Egypt's northern border to its southern border. The city's name was an Aramaic version of an Egyptian name meaning "city of ivories" and was translated into Greek as *Elephantine*. Because of its strategic importance on Egypt's southern boundary with Nubia, it was probably fortified as early as the third dynasty (27th century BC) and figured repeatedly in Egypt's military history.

Elephantine Island on the Nile River

Elephantine was also a major commercial center. Since the first cataract was just upstream from Elephantine/Syene, the twin towns were the terminal ports for deep water navigation. Both towns had wharves and were fortified with garrisons to protect the trade in ivory, animal skins, spices, minerals, slaves, and food. Also a religious center, Elephantine was the temple city of Khnum, the Egyptian god of the cataract region, who presided over the flood cycles of the Nile.

Discovery of the Papyri Elephantine came into archaeological prominence with the discoveries of the papyri. The discoveries were made in three stages. The first group to be published (in 1906) had been gathered by purchases from antiquities dealers and was housed in the Cairo Museum. That first publication stimulated German and French excavations at Elephantine in the hope of discovering more papyri. The Berlin Museum was rewarded for its efforts with a second group of papyri, published in 1911. Ironically, a group of papyri discovered in the late 19th century was the last to be studied and published. American scholar C. E. Wilbour purchased papyri in 1893 from some Arab women at Aswan. In storage until Wilbour's daughter bequeathed them to the Brooklyn Museum, they were finally published in 1953. Since 1912, other excavations have been mounted by the pontifical Biblical Institute of Rome and the Egyptian government, but no further papyri were found.

Jewish Colony At the time the papyri were written, the Jews were already well established in Elephantine. The legal documents among the excavated papyri give a clear picture of life in the military colony at Elephantine. In addition to the Jewish mercenaries ("men of the regiment"), Jewish civilians ("men of the town") were also present. The soldiers were organized into military units, which also appear to have had socioeconomic functions. Though subject to military discipline, the soldiers enjoyed considerable personal freedom. They led normal family lives, engaged in all types of commerce, and bequeathed their properties to their children. Marriage at Elephantine required the consent of the bride as well as the father, and could be dissolved by either party through a public declaration that he or she "hates" the other.

The Elephantine Jews worshiped in their own temple, which was dedicated to the Hebrew God, whom they called Yahu (a variation on Yahweh). Political and religious leaders at Elephantine were in correspondence with officials in Jerusalem and Samaria.

There is no conclusive evidence regarding when the Jewish presence at Elephantine began. Jews could have entered Egypt on any of several occasions from the eighth to the early sixth centuries BC. One document from Elephantine claims that the Jewish temple there was built during a period of native Egyptian rule before the Persian conquest under Cambyses (reigned 529–522 BC). That would give a date for the construction of the Elephantine temple by the mid-sixth century at the latest.

Elephantine Judaism In spite of the law of a single sanctuary (Dt 12:1-11), and in spite of the recent reforms of kings Hezekiah and Josiah in the seventh and eighth centuries BC that centralized worship in Jerusalem, the Elephantine Jews seem to have felt no wrong in having a temple in Egypt. Neither the German, French, Italian, nor Egyptian excavations located the Jewish temple, but the documents record that the temple was oriented toward Jerusalem.

The Elephantine Jews may have recognized Jerusalem's primacy in religious affairs. When the temple at Elephantine was destroyed by priests of the Khnum temple in 410

BC, an appeal was sent to Johanan the high priest (cf. Neh 12:22; 13:28) and Bagoas the governor of Judah, seeking their permission and influence for its restoration. The appeal produced no response, perhaps because of the Jerusalem leadership's disapproval of the temple in Egypt. A second appeal, sent three years later to Bagoas, governor of Judah, and to Delaiah and Shelemiah, sons of Sanballat, governor of Samaria, produced an oral reply, recorded in a memorandum. The reply ordered the temple's rebuilding and the resumption of meal and incense offerings. Permission to reinstitute the burnt offering, however, was not given, perhaps as a concession to Egyptian or Persian religious convictions. A deed for a piece of property, dated 402 BC, mentions the temple of Yahu, implying that it was in fact rebuilt.

The Elephantine Jews probably brought with them to Egypt the popular religion that was so strongly denounced by the prophets before the destruction of the Jerusalem temple. God was central in their faith, but they also worshiped other gods, even if only in a subsidiary fashion. Evidence of departure from orthodox worship of God comes from a list of offerings that mentions two Aramean deities, Eshembethel and Anathbethel. Oaths at Elephantine were sworn almost exclusively in the name of Yahu, but they were also sworn occasionally in the names of an Egyptian goddess, Sati, and another Aramean deity, Herembethel. Salutations in letters invoked the blessings of a variety of deities. Moreover, intermarriage with surrounding peoples, forbidden in the OT because it would lead to religious apostasy (Ex 34:11-16; Dt 7:1-5), had become a common practice at Elephantine. It was a contemporary problem in Israel as well under Ezra and Nehemiah (Ezr 9:1–10:44; Neh 13:23-28). Children of mixed marriages in Elephantine often had Egyptian names.

Nevertheless, the archives also show that the Elephantine Jews continued to observe the Jewish feasts. An order from King Darius II in 419 BC commanded the Jews at Elephantine to observe the Feast of Unleavened Bread. The text, broken immediately before this reference, presumably also contained instructions to observe the Passover. Four ostraca (potsherds) also refer to the Sabbath but provide few clues regarding Sabbath observance at Elephantine.

Language of the Papyri Except for slight differences, the Aramaic of the Elephantine papyri is the same as biblical Aramaic. Both are a part of a dialect known as Imperial Aramaic, the international and commercial language of the Persian Empire. The personal names continued to be Hebrew, but there is no direct evidence that Hebrew was used by the community. Aramaic was the daily language, and there is no suggestion of controversy over whether or not Hebrew should be used in Jewish homes, as was the case with Nehemiah in Jerusalem (Neh 13:23-25).

ELEUTHERUS A small river mentioned in 1 Maccabees 11:7 and 12:30 and almost certainly to be identified with the Nahr-el-Kebir, which begins in the northeast base of Lebanon and flows into the Mediterranean about 18 miles (29 kilometers) north of Tripoli. It marked the limits of Jonathan's expeditions.

ELEVEN, The Designation for the disciples after the resurrection of Jesus (Mk 16:14; Lk 24:9, 33), and at Pentecost (Acts 2:14), Judas Iscariot having committed suicide. See Apostle, Apostleship.

ELHANAN

1. Hebrew soldier who distinguished himself by killing a Philistine giant. In one passage he is named as the son

of Jaare-oregim of Bethlehem, and is said to have killed Goliath the Gittite (2 Sm 21:19). In another passage he is named as the son of Jair, and is said to have killed Lahmi, the brother of Goliath (1 Chr 20:5).

2. Dodo's son and warrior among King David's mighty men (2 Sm 23:24; 1 Chr 11:26).

ELI Priest in the sanctuary of the Lord at Shiloh in the period of the judges (1 Sm 1:3, 9). Shiloh, about 10 miles (16 kilometers) north of Jerusalem, was the central shrine of the Israelite tribal confederation. Eli had two sons who were priests, Hophni and Phinehas (which are Egyptian names). No lineage is recorded for Eli, but there are two possible suggestions: he is a descendant of Ithamar, Aaron's younger son (1 Sm 22:20; 1 Kgs 2:27; 1 Chr 24:3); or he comes from the house of Eleazar (Ex 6:23-25; 2 Esd 1:2-3). In 1 Samuel 1, Eli blessed the childless Hannah, Elkanah's wife, after learning of her prayer for a son. Subsequently, Samuel was born, and when he was weaned, he was brought by his mother to Eli for service and training in the sanctuary, according to her promise to the Lord.

Hophni and Phinehas were corrupting the Israelites despite Eli's protests, and for this sin God promised judgment upon Eli's family (1 Sm 2:27, 36). The sons of Eli were to die on the same day (v 34), and the fulfillment came in a battle with the Philistines at Aphek (4:11, 17). Eli, too, died when he heard of the defeat and the loss of the ark of the covenant to the Philistines. At his death he was 98 years old, and besides being priest, he also had judged Israel for 40 years (vv 15-18). Eli's daughter-in-law, Phinehas's wife, died in childbirth, brokenhearted over the loss of her husband and the ark. She named her son Ichabod because she felt that there was no more hope (vv 19-22).

Eli was not characterized by a firm personality. He was no doubt sincere and devout, but he was also weak and indulgent.

ELI, ELI, LAMA SABACHTHANI?* One of Jesus'
cries from the cross, properly translated "My God, my God, why have you forsaken me?" (The NLT uses an alternate spelling, "lema," for the third word in the expression.) This form of the "cry of dereliction" (Mt 27:46) is slightly different from its other recorded form, "Eloi, eloi, lama sabachthani?" (Mk 15:34). Both versions are adaptations of Psalm 22:1 in the Aramaic, the common language of first-century AD Palestine. The only difference in the two accounts is that Mark's version is completely Aramaic, whereas Matthew retains the Hebrew word for God (which was not uncommon for Aramaic-speaking Jews). The fact that some of Jesus' hearers thought he was calling Elijah indicates that Matthew's version is probably the original. Elias (Elijah) could have been confused with "Eli" more easily than with "Eloi" (Mt 27:47; Mk 15:35).

The textual variants that exist suggest the difficulties copyists and interpreters have had with Jesus' words. After meditating on the passage, Martin Luther exclaimed, "God forsaken of God! Who can understand it?" Luther's statement of the major theological problem, that Jesus was forsaken by God, is not the only possible understanding of the text. Debate has focused on two questions: whether in fact abandonment by God was expressed by Jesus' use of the psalmist's words, and why the onlookers spoke of Elijah.

Meaning of the Cry At one extreme, many have been struck by the starkness of Jesus' words. Some have even seen in them a realization on the cross that he had failed and that all hope was lost for the coming of God's kingdom. From that perspective Jesus' words were a cry of

despair over a lost cause. However, such a view hardly fits the rest of the NT presentation of Jesus.

At the opposite extreme, some interpret the words as neither stark nor negative in any sense. They view the cry as an affirmation of Jesus' faith in committing himself to God (Lk 23:46). To such interpreters, the fact that Jesus began his question with "My God, my God" and used a biblical quotation indicates religious reverence and continued faith. In Jewish practice sometimes the first line of a psalm or song would be quoted to refer to the whole work. Hence Jesus might have been quoting Psalm 22:1 as a way of referring to the whole psalm. Psalm 22 is clearly the lament of a righteous sufferer. Psalms of lament always expressed a prayer of confidence in God and praise to God as well as a prayer for help from God. Thus, from a certain point of view, the cry from the cross can be seen as a confident prayer.

Many biblical scholars find the second view as unconvincing as the first. The Gospel writers did not clarify the meaning of the cry. Yet if the words were an expression of confidence or praise, some indication would be expected in the text. As they stand, the words are hardly an expression of religious reverence. The words themselves and the fact they were expressed in a loud cry do not suggest a prayer of confidence or praise.

Another approach views the words as expressing Jesus' feeling of isolation in a moment of extreme anguish but rejects the notion that he was actually forsaken by God.

But the interpretation that has become "traditional" is that Jesus *was* forsaken by God. In that view the context of the Garden of Gethsemane (Mt 26:36-46; Mk 14:32-42; Lk 22:39-46) indicates the kind of conflict expressed in Jesus' cry on the cross. Jesus' identification with sinners was so real that taking on their sin broke the closeness of his communion with the Father. Thus, Jesus' abandonment by God is seen as an important aspect of the atonement. Although stressing that Jesus was actually forsaken, the traditional view goes on to stress that the unity of the Trinity remained unbroken.

The explanation of such a paradox is not easy. Some view it as a divine mystery and make no attempt to explain it at all. Others attempt to make some kind of distinction between what happened on the cross and the reality of God's being. For example, in the early centuries of the church the view was expressed that only Jesus' humanity was affected by the separation, so that his deity remained intact with God. Others argue that Jesus was separated from the Father "functionally" in the work of salvation but not "really" with respect to his existence.

The refusal of the Gospel writers to explain Jesus' cry should make scholars hesitate to give precise or dogmatic explanations. At the least, one can confidently state that (1) the cry reflects the reality of Jesus' humanity in the face of death, (2) the particular kind of death ("even death on a cross," Phil 2:8) was especially scandalous, and (3) Christ's identification with sinners was a horribly painful experience. Thus, although the cry is somehow related to the Atonement, the biblical texts do not discuss whether Jesus was absolutely abandoned. Further, they do not explain how God could recoil from sin at the same time that "in Christ God was reconciling the world to himself" (2 Cor 5:19). In doing justice to the depth of emotion expressed in the cry, one should be cautious not to force the text to say something the author did not intend.

Elijah and the Cry Various possibilities of connections between the cry and Elijah have been offered. If the cry refers to the whole of Psalm 22, mention of Elijah by the bystanders would show that they understood Jesus' words as expressing confidence in salvation. A salvation mediated by Elijah would have seemed natural to the Jews, who often saw Elijah as a deliverer of the righteous oppressed. Others claim that the bystanders were willfully and maliciously distorting Jesus' words in order to mock him. Still others view the mention of Elijah as an honest misunderstanding because of the similarity of the words. The view that one adopts will depend to some extent on how Jesus' cry is understood.

See also Crucifixion; Seven Last Sayings of Jesus.

ELIAB

1. Helon's son and leader of Zebulun's tribe when the Israelites were roaming in the Sinai wilderness after their escape from Egypt (Nm 1:9; 2:7; 10:16). As leader, he presented his tribe's offering at the consecration of the tabernacle (7:24, 29).
2. Member of Reuben's tribe and son of Pallu. Eliab was the father of Nemuel, Dathan, and Abiram. Dathan and Abiram rebelled against Moses and Aaron in the wilderness (Nm 16:1, 12; 26:8-9; Dt 11:6).
3. Jesse's eldest son and brother of King David. An impressive person physically, he was rejected by God for the kingship in favor of David (1 Sm 16:6; 1 Chr 2:13). Eliab served King Saul when Goliath defied Saul's army (1 Sm 17:13, 28). He was appointed leader of Judah's tribe during David's reign (1 Chr 27:18). His granddaughter Mahalath married King Rehoboam of Judah (2 Chr 11:18).
4. Variant name for Elihu in 1 Chronicles 6:27. *See* Elihu #1.
5. Warrior from Gad's tribe who joined David at Ziklag in his struggle against King Saul (1 Chr 12:9). Eliab was an expert with the shield and spear (v 8).
6. Levite musician assigned to play the harp in the procession when King David brought the ark to Jerusalem (1 Chr 15:18). He was assigned permanently to service in the tabernacle (16:5).

ELIADA

1. One of King David's sons, born in Jerusalem (2 Sm 5:16; 1 Chr 3:8). He is also called Beeliada in 1 Chronicles 14:7.
2. Father of Rezon, the king of Damascus and an adversary of Solomon (1 Kgs 11:23).
3. General under King Jehoshaphat. Eliada and the 200,000 warriors he commanded were from Benjamin's tribe (2 Chr 17:17).

ELIADAH* KJV spelling of Eliada, Rezon's father, in 1 Kings 11:23. *See* Eliada #2.

ELIAH* KJV form of the name Elijah in 1 Chronicles 8:27 and Ezra 10:26. *See* Elijah #2, #4.

ELIAHBA Warrior among David's mighty men who were known as "the thirty" (2 Sm 23:32; 1 Chr 11:33).

ELIAKIM

1. Hilkiah's son and a royal officer in the household and court of King Hezekiah (2 Kgs 18:18, 26, 37). His position had increased in importance since Solomon's reign (1 Kgs 4:2-6) until he was second only to the king. As such, Eliakim had absolute authority as the king's representative.

When Sennacherib of Assyria moved against Jerusalem in 701 BC, Eliakim was one of the diplomatic emissaries who conferred with the Assyrian officers on behalf of Hezekiah (2 Kgs 18:18, 26). He was also sent by Hezekiah in sackcloth to Isaiah to ask for prayer on Jerusalem's behalf (2 Kgs 19:1-5).

2. King Josiah's second son. When Eliakim was made king of Judah by Pharaoh Neco, his name was changed to Jehoiakim (2 Kgs 23:34; 2 Chr 36:4). *See* Jehoiakim.
3. One of the priests who assisted at the dedication of the Jerusalem wall after it was rebuilt by Zerubbabel (Neh 12:41).
4. Abiud's son in Matthew's genealogy of Jesus (Mt 1:13). *See* Genealogy of Jesus Christ.
5. Melea's son in Luke's genealogy of Jesus (Lk 3:30). *See* Genealogy of Jesus Christ.

ELIAM

1. Alternate name for Ammiel, Bathsheba's father, in 2 Samuel 11:3. *See* Ammiel #3.
2. Alternate name for Ahijah the Pelonite in 2 Samuel 23:34. *See* Ahijah #7.

ELIAS* KJV rendering of the prophet Elijah's name in the NT. *See* Elijah #1.

ELIASAPH

1. Leader of Gad's tribe appointed by Moses. He was the son of Deuel (Reuel) (Nm 1:14; 2:14; 7:42, 47; 10:20).
2. Gershonite Levite and the son of Lael. His responsibility in the tribe was to take charge of the tabernacle coverings, the curtains of the court and of the main altar (Nm 3:24-25).

ELIASHIB

1. Elioenai's son and a descendant of Zerubbabel in the royal lineage of David (1 Chr 3:24).
2. Aaron's descendant chosen by David to head the 11th of the 24 courses of priests taking turns in the sanctuary services (1 Chr 24:12).
3. High priest in the second succession from Jeshua (Neh 12:10). Eliashib assigned a chamber of the temple to Tobiah the Ammonite, a relative by marriage. When Nehemiah returned from exile, he had Tobiah removed from his temple lodging (Ezr 10:6; Neh 3:1, 20; 13:4, 7-8, 28).
4. Levite and temple singer. He pledged to put away his foreign wife at Ezra's command (Ezr 10:24).
5, 6. Two men, a son of Zattu and a son of Bani, similarly persuaded by Ezra to put away their foreign wives (Ezr 10:27, 36).

ELIATHAH Son of Heman appointed to assist in the temple service during David's reign (1 Chr 25:4, 27).

ELIDAD Benjamite, of the sons of Kislon, appointed to work under Eleazar and Joshua in allotting Canaanite territory west of the Jordan to the 10 tribes (Nm 34:21).

ELIEHOENAI

1. Korahite Levite who, with his six brothers and his father, Meshelemiah, served as a temple doorkeeper during David's reign (1 Chr 26:3).
2. Zerahiah's son, who came to Jerusalem with Ezra, bringing his family and others from Babylon (Ezr 8:4).

ELIEL

1. Warrior and head of a family of the half-tribe of Manasseh that lived east of the Jordan River (1 Chr 5:24).
2. Tola's son, a Kohathite who was one of the Levitical singers in the time of David (1 Chr 6:34); possibly the same as Eliab (1 Chr 6:27).

3. Shimei's son and a chief of Benjamin's tribe (1 Chr 8:20).

4. Shashak's son and a chief of Benjamin's tribe (1 Chr 8:22).

5. Warrior among David's mighty men (1 Chr 11:46), called a Mahavite.

6. Another warrior among David's mighty men (1 Chr 11:47).

7. Warrior from the Gadites who joined David at Ziklag in his struggle against King Saul. Eliel was one of those experts with a shield and spear. Whether the Eliel of 1 Chronicles 12:11 should be equated with either of the two Eliels of 1 Chronicles 11:46-47 is impossible to say.

8. Levite and chief of the family of Hebron, who was involved in bringing the ark to Jerusalem in David's time (1 Chr 15:9).

9. Priest who assisted in bringing the ark to Jerusalem (1 Chr 15:11); possibly the same as #8 above.

10. Levite who assisted Conaniah in the administration of the tithes, contributions, and dedicated things given to the temple during Hezekiah's reign (2 Chr 31:13).

ELIENAI Benjamite and the son of Shimei (1 Chr 8:20). His name may be a contraction of Eliehoenai (see 1 Chr 26:3).

ELIEZER

1. Native of Damascus and Abraham's servant, who according to custom was the adopted heir before Ishmael and Isaac were born (Gn 15:2).

2. Moses and Zipporah's second son (Ex 18:4; 1 Chr 23:15-17).

3. Benjamite and Becher's son (1 Chr 7:8).

4. One of the seven priests who blew a trumpet before the ark of the covenant when David moved it to Jerusalem (1 Chr 15:24).

5. Zichri's son and a chief officer in Reuben's tribe (1 Chr 27:16).

6. Son of Dodavahu of Mareshah, who prophesied against King Jehoshaphat of Judah because of his alliance with Ahaziah, king of Israel (2 Chr 20:37).

7. One of the leaders sent by Ezra to Iddo at Casiphia to request Levites for the house of God (Ezr 8:16).

8, 9, 10. Three men of Israel—a priest, Levite, and Israelite—who were encouraged by Ezra to divorce their foreign wives during the postexilic era (Ezr 10:18, 23, 31).

11. Ancestor of Christ (Lk 3:29). See Genealogy of Jesus Christ.

ELIHOENAI* KJV spelling of Eliehoenai, Zerahiah's son, in Ezra 8:4. See Eliehoenai #2.

ELIHOREPH Prominent official in the time of Solomon (1 Kgs 4:3) who, with his brother Ahijah, was a royal secretary. Attempts to regard Elihoreph as the title of an official and not a personal name find no support in the Hebrew text.

ELIHU

1. Ephraimite, Tohu's son and an ancestor of Samuel the prophet (1 Sm 1:1); perhaps also called Eliab and Eliel in 1 Chronicles 6:27, 34, respectively.

2. One of the soldiers of Manasseh's tribe who joined up with David's army at Ziklag (1 Chr 12:20).

3. Korahite Levite and a gatekeeper of the tabernacle during David's reign (1 Chr 26:7).

4. Alternate name for Eliab, David's eldest brother, in 1 Chronicles 27:18. See Eliab #3.

5. One of Job's friends, a Buzite, the son of Barachel (Jb 32:2). He spoke about suffering as a form of discipline after three of Job's friends failed to answer Job's arguments (chs 32–37).

ELIJAH

1. Ninth-century BC prophet of Israel. Elijah's name means "my God is the Lord"—appropriate for a stalwart opponent of Baal worship. The Scriptures give no information regarding his family background except that he was a Tishbite who probably came from the land of Gilead on the east bank of the Jordan River. He lived primarily during the reigns of kings Ahab (874–853 BC) and Ahaziah (853–852 BC) of Israel. The biblical account of Elijah runs from 1 Kings 17 to 2 Kings 2.

Elijah was called by God at a critical period in Israel's life. Economically and politically the northern kingdom was in its strongest position since its separation from the southern kingdom. Omri (885–874 BC) had initiated a policy of trade and friendly relations with the Phoenicians. To show his good faith, Omri gave his son Ahab in marriage to Jezebel, the daughter of Ethbaal, king of Tyre. She brought Baal worship with her to Israel, a false religion whose rapid spread soon threatened the kingdom's very existence. Elijah was sent to turn the nation and its leaders back to the Lord through his prophetic message and miracles.

Warning of Drought Elijah began his recorded ministry by telling Ahab that the nation would suffer a drought until the prophet himself announced its end (1 Kgs 17:1). He thus repeated Moses' warning (Lv 26:14-39; Dt 28:15-68) of the consequences of turning away from God.

Elijah then hid himself in a ravine on the east bank of the Jordan River by the brook Cherith (possibly the valley of the Yarmuk River in north Gilead). There he had sufficient water for his needs, and ravens brought him food twice daily. When the brook dried up, Elijah was directed to move to the Phoenician village of Zarephath near Sidon. A widow took care of him from her scanty supplies, and her obedience to Elijah was rewarded by a miraculous supply of meal and oil that was not depleted until the drought ended.

While Elijah was staying with the widow, her son became ill and died. By the power of prayer, the child was restored to life and good health.

In the drought's third year the Lord told Elijah to inform Ahab that God would soon provide rain for Israel. On his return, Elijah first encountered Ahab's officer, Obadiah, who was searching for water for the king's livestock. Elijah sent Obadiah to arrange a meeting with Ahab. At first Obadiah refused. For three years Ahab had searched Israel and the neighboring kingdoms in vain for the prophet, no doubt in order to force him to end the drought. Obadiah was certain that while he went to bring Ahab, Israel's most wanted "outlaw" would elude them again, thus enraging the king. When Elijah promised him that he would stay until he returned, the officer arranged for Ahab to meet the prophet.

In the subsequent meeting Elijah rejected the king's allegation that he was the "troubler of Israel" (1 Kgs 18:17-18). He was only obeying God, he insisted, in pointing out Ahab's idolatry. Ahab had even permitted Jezebel to subsidize a school of Baal and Asherah prophets. Elijah then requested a public gathering on Mt Carmel as a contest between the prophets of Baal and the prophets of the Lord to determine who was the true God.

Confrontation on Carmel One of the highlights of Elijah's ministry was the contest on Mt Carmel. Ahab assembled all Israel along with 850 prophets of Baal and Asherah. The famous challenge was issued: "How long are you going to waver between two opinions? If the LORD is God, follow him! But if Baal is God, then follow him!" (1 Kgs 18:21, NLT). Sacrificial animals were to be placed on two altars, one for Baal and one for the Lord, and the prophets representing each were to ask for fire from their God.

All day long the pagan prophets called in vain on Baal. They danced a whirling, frenzied dance, cutting themselves with knives until their blood gushed. But there was no answer. Finally, Elijah's turn came. He repaired the demolished altar of the Lord and prepared the sacrifice. For dramatic effect, he built a trench around the altar and poured water over the sacrifice until the trench overflowed. Then he said a brief prayer, and immediately fire fell from heaven and consumed the burnt offering, the wood, the stones, and the dust, and licked up the water that was in the trench (1 Kgs 18:38).

When the people saw it, they fell on their faces in repentance, chanting, "The LORD is God! The LORD is God!" (1 Kgs 18:39). At Elijah's command the people seized the prophets of Baal and killed them by the brook Kishon. Then Elijah, at the top of Carmel, began to pray fervently for rain. Dramatically, the sky became black with clouds and rain began to pour, ending the long drought. Ahab rode back in his chariot to Jezreel, 20 miles (32.2 kilometers) to the east. God's Spirit enabled Elijah to outrun Ahab, and he arrived in Jezreel first.

Jezebel, furious over the massacre of the Baal prophets, sent a message to Elijah: "May the gods also kill me if by this time tomorrow I have failed to take your life like those whom you killed" (1 Kgs 19:2, NLT). When Elijah received her message, he panicked and fled to Beersheba.

Experience at Horeb Elijah left his servant in Beersheba, going another day's journey into the desert alone. There he lay down under a broom tree and, in despair and exhaustion, asked God to take his life. Instead, an angel appeared, nourishing him twice with bread and water. After he had slept, Elijah continued on his way.

Elijah Flees from Jezebel After killing Baal's prophets, Elijah fled from Jezebel to Beersheba, then to the wilderness, and then to Mt Horeb (Sinai).

After 40 days, Elijah arrived at Mt Horeb, where he found shelter in a cave. There the Lord spoke to him, asking what he was doing there. The prophet

explained that he was the only prophet of God left in Israel, and now even his life was threatened. In response, the mighty forces of nature—a great wind, an earthquake, and fire—were displayed before Elijah to show him that the omnipotent God could intercede on his behalf with a powerful hand. Finally God encouraged Elijah in a "still, small voice." The Lord had further tasks for him to accomplish. God also told Elijah that he was not the only faithful person in Israel; 7,000 others remained true to the Lord.

Since Elijah had faithfully delivered God's message to Ahab, the Lord commissioned him to deliver another message, one of judgment on Israel's continuing failure to listen to God. The instruments of retribution were to be Hazael, who would become king in Syria (c. 893–796 BC), and Jehu, who would become king of Israel (841–814 BC). Elijah was instructed to anoint both of them. He was also told to anoint his successor, Elisha, to be his understudy until it was time for Elisha's full ministry to begin.

Confrontation concerning Naboth After his return to Israel, one of Elijah's boldest confrontations with King Ahab was over Naboth's vineyard. Although Ahab wanted Naboth's property, he was sensitive to the law regarding ownership of land. Further, Ahab never completely abandoned the faith of his fathers (1 Kgs 21:27-29). Jezebel, however, had no regard for the Mosaic law and conspired to have Naboth put to death on a false charge.

When Ahab then took possession of the vineyard, Elijah branded him as a murderer and a robber. He predicted divine judgment—the fall of Ahab's dynasty and Jezebel's horrible death (1 Kgs 21:17-24). Ahab repented, however, and the judgment was postponed.

Ahaziah's Folly The Lord's judgment on Ahab was finally executed when the king was killed in a battle with Syria in 853 BC. The dogs licked up Ahab's blood, as the prophet had predicted (1 Kgs 21:19). Shortly after Ahaziah had succeeded his father as king, he suffered a crippling fall. While lying ill, he sent messengers to ask Baal-zebub, the god of Ekron, whether he would recover. The Lord sent Elijah to intercept them and give them a message for the king: a rebuke for ignoring the God of Israel and a warning of the king's impending death.

Ahaziah angrily sent a captain with 50 soldiers to arrest Elijah. They were consumed by fire from heaven at Elijah's words. A second captain and another 50 soldiers were sent but met the same fate. The third captain who came begged the prophet to spare his and his soldiers' lives. Elijah went with this captain and delivered God's message to the king personally. The king would not recover but would die because he had inquired from pagan gods rather than from the true God.

Warning to Jehoram Elijah had been called primarily to minister to Israel, but he also delivered God's word of warning to Jehoram, king of Judah, rebuking him for following Israel in its idolatry and for not walking in the godly ways of his father and grandfather (2 Chr 21:12-15).

Elijah's Ascent into Heaven When the end of Elijah's ministry drew near, Elisha refused to leave him. After a journey that took them to schools of the prophets at Bethel and Jericho, the two crossed the Jordan River miraculously; Elijah struck the waters with his mantle and they parted. Elisha requested a double portion (the firstborn's share, cf. Dt 21:17) of his master's spirit, for he desired to be Elijah's full successor. Elisha knew his request was granted because he saw Elijah pass into the heavens in a whirlwind bearing a chariot and horses of fire. The young prophets who had accompanied Elisha searched in vain for Elijah in the mountains and valleys around the Jordan; God had taken his faithful prophet home. Elijah thus joined Enoch as the only other man in the Bible who did not experience death.

Elijah's Message and Miracles As the Baal worship of Tyre made inroads into Israel through Jezebel, Elijah was sent to check its spread by emphasizing again that Israel's God was the only God of the whole earth. He began a vital work that was continued by Jehu, who slaughtered many of the Baal worshipers among Israel's leaders (2 Kgs 10:18-28). Elijah's specific mission was to destroy heathen worship in order to spare Israel, thus preparing the way for the prophets who were to follow in his spirit.

Miracles were prominent in Elijah's ministry, given as a sign to confirm him as God's spokesman and to turn Israel's kings back to God. Some scholars have rejected these miracles or tried to explain them away. The OT, however, clearly testifies to their validity, and the NT affirms them.

Elijah and the New Testament Malachi named Elijah as the forerunner of the "great and terrible day of the LORD" who will "turn the hearts of fathers to their children and the hearts of children to their fathers" (Mal 4:5-6). Jewish writers have often taken up the same theme in their literature: Elijah will "restore the tribes of Jacob" (Ecclus 48:10); he is mentioned in the Qumran *Manual of Discipline* of the Dead Sea Scrolls; he is the central sign of the resurrection of the dead according to the Mishnah, the collection of Jewish oral law; and he is the subject of songs sung at the close of the Sabbath.

In the NT, Malachi's prophecy was interpreted in the angelic annunciation to Zechariah as pointing to John the Baptist, who was to do the work of another Elijah (Lk 1:17, KJV "Elias") and was confirmed by Jesus himself (Mt 11:14; 17:10-13).

Jesus also alluded to Elijah's sojourn in the land of Sidon (Lk 4:25-26), and the apostle Paul referred to the prophet's experience at Mt Horeb (Rom 11:2). The apostle James used Elijah to illustrate what it means to be a righteous man and a man of prayer (Jas 5:17).

Elijah appeared again on the Mt of Transfiguration with Moses as they discussed Jesus' approaching death (Mt 17:1-13; Lk 9:28-36). Some Bible scholars believe that Elijah will return as one of the two witnesses of the end times (Rv 11:3-12), in fulfillment of Malachi's prophecy that he is to come before the dreadful judgment day of God.

2. Chief of Benjamin's tribe (1 Chr 8:27, KJV "Eliah").
3. Priest who married a gentile wife (Ezr 10:21).
4. Layman who also married a foreign wife (Ezr 10:26).

ELIKA Harodite, listed as one of David's mighty men (2 Sm 23:25). His name is not included in a similar list in 1 Chronicles 11:27.

ELIM Early encampment of the Israelites after their passage through the Red Sea (Ex 15:27; 16:1). Elim was situated between Marah and the desert of Sin. It had 12 springs of water and 70 palm trees (Nm 33:9-10).

Most scholars identify Elim with Wadi Gharandel, 63 miles (101.4 kilometers) from Suez. At this wadi the vegetation consists of palm trees, tamarisks, and acacias. But if Mt Sinai is to be located somewhere in Arabia, Elim would be much closer to the Gulf of Aqaba.

ELIMELECH Man from Bethlehem who took his wife, Naomi, and his sons, Mahlon and Chilion, to sojourn in Moab because of famine in Judah (Ru 1:2-3). While in Moab, he died; then his sons also died; and Naomi decided to return to Judah. One daughter-in-law, Orpah, preferred to remain in Moab; the other, Ruth, chose to accompany Naomi. Boaz, a kinsman of Elimelech, bought Elimelech's land and married Ruth (4:9-10). From this union came a great-grandson, David, and the royal line in which the Messiah would eventually be born. *See* Ruth, Book of.

ELIOENAI
1. Postexilic descendant of Solomon and the father of Hodaviah and Eliashib (1 Chr 3:23-24).
2. Simeonite chieftain (1 Chr 4:36).
3. Head of a Benjamite family (1 Chr 7:8).
4. KJV spelling of the Levite Eliehoenai in 1 Chronicles 26:3. *See* Eliehoenai #1.
5. Man of the priestly family of Pashhur who divorced his foreign wife in Ezra's day (Ezr 10:22).
6. Zattu's son, who was encouraged by Ezra to divorce his foreign wife during the postexilic era (Ezr 10:27).
7. Postexilic priest who assisted in the dedication of the rebuilt Jerusalem wall (Neh 12:41).

ELIPHAL Ur's son and one of David's mighty men (1 Chr 11:35); alternately called Eliphelet, son of Ahasbai, in 2 Samuel 23:34. *See* Eliphelet #2.

ELIPHALET* KJV spelling of Eliphelet, David's son, in 2 Samuel 5:16 and 1 Chronicles 14:7. *See* Eliphelet #1.

ELIPHAZ
1. Oldest son of Esau and his wife Adah (Gn 36:4-16; 1 Chr 1:35-36). He was the ancestor of a number of Edomite clans.
2. One of Job's friends, called the Temanite (see Jer 49:7). Teman was traditionally associated with wisdom; hence Eliphaz's speech depicts the orthodox view of sin and punishment. His three addresses (Jb 4, 15, 22) failed to grapple with the essence of Job's problem because he assumed previous major sin in Job's life.
   See also Job, Book of.

ELIPHELEHU Levitical musician who played the lyre (harp) when the ark was brought to Jerusalem in David's time (1 Chr 15:18, 21).

ELIPHELET
1. One of David's 13 sons born in Jerusalem (2 Sm 5:16; 1 Chr 3:8; 14:7).
2. Ahasbai's son and one of David's mighty men (2 Sm 23:34); perhaps the same as Eliphal, Ur's son, in 1 Chronicles 11:35. *See* Eliphal.
3. Another of David's sons born at Jerusalem but perhaps earlier than #1 above (1 Chr 3:6; 14:5).
4. Eshek's son and a descendant of Saul and Jonathan (1 Chr 8:39).
5. One of Adonikam's three sons who returned with Ezra from Babylon (Ezr 8:13).
6. Hashum's son whom Ezra persuaded to divorce his foreign wife during the postexilic era (Ezr 10:33).

ELISABETH* KJV spelling of Elizabeth, John the Baptist's mother. *See* Elizabeth.

ELISHA Prophet in Israel during the ninth century BC.

Background and Call Elisha is first mentioned in 1 Kings 19:16, where he is described as the son of Shaphat, who lived at Abel-meholah. That place has been tentatively identified with the modern Tel Abu Sifri, west of the river Jordan, though many scholars place it to the river's east. The prophet Elijah had been ordered by God to anoint Elisha as his successor, but the narrative does not make it clear whether Elisha was already one of Elijah's disciples. When the two met, Elisha was busy plowing a field, and he does not seem to have greeted Elijah with the respect that a disciple would normally show to his teacher.

Elisha's use of 12 yokes of oxen in his agricultural work has been taken as a sign that he was wealthy, for normally two yoked oxen would be handled by one person. When Elijah passed by and placed his cloak on Elisha's shoulder, the latter man knew it was a sign that he should inherit the great prophet's mission. The nation needed a prophet, for it was increasingly indulging in Canaanite idolatry with the encouragement of King Ahab and his Phoenician wife, Jezebel.

After Elijah commissioned him symbolically and strode away, Elisha hurried after the prophet to request a brief interval of time to announce his new vocation to his parents before leaving home. The prophet's reply, "Go back again; for what have I done to you?" (1 Kgs 19:20, RSV), helped Elisha to make up his mind immediately. Delay in implementing his vocation would almost certainly have been fatal for Elisha (cf. Mt 8:21-22; Lk 9:61-62).

To mark the change in his way of life, Elisha made a great feast for his neighbors, roasting two oxen. This is another hint that he came from a wealthy family. From that time, he was no longer a farmer; by associating with Elijah, he began to prepare for his own ministry. There is no record of Elisha being anointed to the prophetic office, but the transfer of prophetic authority by means of the cloak would leave no doubt in anyone's mind that Elisha was the next official prophet in Israel.

"Sons of the Prophets" That there could have been some question of Elisha's authority is implied by the existence of groups of people known as "sons of the prophets." The phrase meant that those persons were heirs of the prophetic teachings and traditions, though apparently none of them was a major prophet. The prophet Amos even denied any connection with such groups, which seem to have died out in the eighth century BC (Am 7:14). In the time of Elisha, the "sons of the prophets" were located in Gilgal, Bethel, and Jericho, and seem to have exercised a primarily local ministry. They may have gone out under the instructions of Elijah and Elisha to teach people God's law and to pronounce divine revelations, as in the days of Saul (cf. 1 Sm 10:5, 10).

Just before Elijah was taken to heaven, he and Elisha visited such prophetic groups, and Elijah tried in vain to persuade Elisha to stay behind at Gilgal and at Bethel (2 Kgs 2:1-4). The prophetic group at Bethel may have been warned by God that Elijah would be taken from them, for they questioned Elisha about the matter and ascertained that he also was aware of the situation.

Successor to Elijah After miraculously parting the waters of Jordan, Elijah asked his successor what he might do for him (2 Kgs 2:9). Elisha requested a "double share" of his spirit as they parted, the share of an inheritance normally given to a firstborn son (Dt 21:17). His request was granted when Elisha saw his master taken up to heaven in a fiery chariot, and it took immediate effect when Elisha parted the Jordan's waters and crossed over (2 Kgs 2:14).

His prophetic authority now recognized, Elisha began his ministry to Israel at approximately the end of King Ahab's reign (c. 853 BC). His work lasted for half a century, and in contrast with the harried, austere, and sometimes dramatic ministry of Elijah, the activities of Elisha were mostly quieter and took place among the ordinary people of Israel. But he also addressed the royal court, though not in conflicts with Canaanite priests, such as Elijah had experienced.

Miracles The miraculous element was prominent in Elisha's ministry. When the people of Jericho reported that the local springwater was brackish, Elisha purified it (2 Kgs 2:19-22). To this day, it is the only significant freshwater spring in the area (Tell es-Sultan).

As the prophet left for Bethel, he encountered a group of youths who mocked his baldness (2 Kgs 2:23-24). He cursed them in the name of the Lord, and two bears came from the woods and mauled the offenders. What at first sight seems to be an immoral act on God's part was actually full of foreboding for the nation. The youths at Bethel were a generation of Israelites who had so absorbed the immoral, pagan culture of their city that they rejected both the person and the message of God's prophets. They were not merely irreligious but also unbelievably discourteous, according to ancient Near Eastern standards, in ridiculing a bald man instead of respecting his seniority.

The curses Elisha pronounced "in the name of the LORD" were not his own reactions to the treatment he had received, but instead were covenant curses (Dt 28:15-68) that would come upon all who rejected the Sinaitic laws and went back on their promises to God (see Ex 24:3-8). The two bears were also symbolic of Assyria and Babylonia, which would tear apart the nation at different times. One small incident was thus a somber forecast of what the future held for a wicked and disobedient people.

In one of his contacts with royalty Elisha gave a message (although unwillingly) from God to King Jehoram of Israel (853–841 BC). The king had allied with King Jehoshaphat of Judah (872–848 BC) and the Edomite ruler against Mesha, king of Moab. The allied forces were deep in Edomite territory when they ran out of water, and in despair they turned to Elisha, the local prophet. He refused to say anything at first, but finally predicted ample supplies of water and victory for the coalition. Both occurred on the following day (2 Kgs 3:1-27).

Miracles of Charity The kind of work for which Elisha was justly renowned was usually performed for people who could not help themselves. Such a person was a poor widow who had almost pledged her two children to a creditor. Her only asset was a jar of oil. Elisha instructed her to borrow empty jars from her neighbors and fill them with the oil from her own jar. In a miraculous manner every jar was filled. Elisha then told her to sell the oil, pay her debts, and use the balance of the money for living expenses (2 Kgs 4:1-7).

A similar act of charity was performed for a Shunammite woman, who had persuaded her husband to provide a room where the prophet could stay when in the area. In return for her kindness Elisha predicted that the woman, previously childless, would have her own son. About a year later it happened (2 Kgs 4:8-17). The boy later contracted a severe ailment, perhaps meningitis, and died suddenly. His mother laid the body on Elisha's bed while she hurried to Mt Carmel to seek the prophet. Elisha was apparently unaware of the situation until the distraught mother informed him of the boy's death. As an emergency measure Elisha dispatched his servant Gehazi to put the prophet's staff on the child's face. That did not revive the child, but when Elisha arrived and lay down on the body, the boy was healed and returned to his parents (vv 18-37).

Another beneficial incident was the correction of a potentially disastrous situation. When some poisonous gourds were accidentally cooked and served, Elisha rendered the mixture harmless by adding meal to the contents of the cooking pot (2 Kgs 4:38-41). A miracle similar to Christ's multiplying of the bread loaves (see Mt 14:16-21; 15:32-38) occurred when someone brought the prophet several loaves of bread and fresh ears of corn. Elisha instructed his servant to set the food out for 100 people, and when that was done, the people ate and had food left (2 Kgs 4:42-44).

The healing of Naaman, a Syrian commander, came through the influence of a Hebrew maid in the man's household, who persuaded Naaman's wife that Elisha could heal her husband. The Assyrian king sent his general to the Israelite ruler with instructions for Naaman to be healed. The afflicted man was sent to Elisha, who ordered him to wash in the Jordan River. Reluctant at first, Naaman finally obeyed and was cured of his affliction. In gratitude the Syrian leader acknowledged the power of Israel's God (2 Kgs 5:1-19).

Encounters with Royalty When Syria attacked Israel, Elisha revealed the movements of the Syrians to the Israelite king. Syrians tried to capture the prophet at Dothan, but God blinded them and Elisha led them to the Israelite capital of Samaria. Their sight returned, and Elisha advised the Israelite king to spare the captives, feed them well, and send them home. Because their evil was rewarded with good, the Syrians did not attack Israel for a while (2 Kgs 6:8-23).

When the Syrian king Ben-hadad besieged Samaria years later, famine conditions there became so severe that the king threatened to execute Elisha. In response, the prophet promised an abundance of food the following day. The Syrians fled from their camp for some unspecified reason, and the prophecy was fulfilled (2 Kgs 6:24–7:20). In an unusual encounter with the ailing king of Syria, Elisha was visited by Hazael, servant of Ben-hadad, who had been sent to ask about the prospects for his master's improvement. Elisha sent back a reassuring reply, but at the same time said that Hazael would shortly succeed Ben-hadad (8:7-13). On another occasion Elisha sent a prophet to Ramoth-gilead to anoint Jehu, son of Jehoshaphat, as king of Israel to replace Joram, whom Jehu proceeded to kill in battle (9:1-28).

Elisha's final contact with Israelite rulers came at the time of his own death, when Joash the king visited him to lament the prophet's illness. On that occasion, by the symbolic handling of arrows, the dying prophet promised Joash that he would defeat the Syrians in battle but would not exterminate them (2 Kgs 13:14-19).

The prophet also intervened a second time on behalf of the Shunammite woman whose son he had healed, instructing her to move her household into Philistine territory during a seven-year famine in Israel. When she came back, her house and property had apparently been occupied by others, so she appealed to the king for help in recovering it. Elisha's servant Gehazi told the ruler about her, and on interviewing her himself, the king ordered all her property to be returned (2 Kgs 8:1-6).

Continuing Influence Elisha's final miracle occurred after his death, when a corpse that was tossed hurriedly into the prophet's tomb came abruptly to life (2 Kgs 13:21). Jesus mentioned Elisha once in connection with the healing of Naaman; Jesus declared that God's mercy was not restricted to the Israelites (Lk 4:27).

See also Elijah; Israel, History of; Prophecy; Prophet, Prophetess.

ELISHAH Javan's son (Gn 10:4; 1 Chr 1:7). The Hebrew term for Greece is Javan; hence, Elishah could be the term for the western Aegean islands or coastlands (cf. Gn 10:5) that supplied dye stuffs to the inhabitants of Tyre (Ez 27:7). The Jewish historian Josephus identified Elishah with the Aeolians; other suggestions are Carthage in North Africa, Hellas, Italy, and Elis. A Mediterranean site seems probable from the context of Ezekiel 27:6-7, perhaps an area of Cyprus that exported copper.

ELISHAMA
1. Ammihud's son and leader of the Ephraimites at the beginning of the journey in the wilderness (Nm 1:10; 2:18; 7:48, 53). His was the ninth tribe in line during the wilderness march (10:22). Elishama was the father of Nun and grandfather of Joshua (1 Chr 7:26).
2. One of David's 13 sons born in Jerusalem to a legitimate wife (2 Sm 5:16; 1 Chr 3:8; 14:7).
3. Ishmael's ancestor. Ishmael killed Gedaliah, the governor of Israel appointed by Nebuchadnezzar (2 Kgs 25:25; Jer 41:1).
4. Man of Judah descended through Jerahmeel and Sheshan (1 Chr 2:41).
5. Another of David's sons (1 Chr 3:6); alternately called Elishua in 2 Samuel 5:15 and 1 Chronicles 14:5. *See* Elishua.
6. Priest sent by Jehoshaphat to instruct the Judeans in the law of God (2 Chr 17:8).
7. Prince and scribe in Jeremiah's time (Jer 36:12). He heard Baruch read the words of God, and later the scroll of the Lord remained in Elishama's chamber until the king requested it to be read (vv 20-21).

ELISHAPHAT Military commander in Judah who supported Jehoiada the priest in overthrowing Queen Athaliah and making the young Joash king (2 Chr 23:1).

ELISHEBA Wife of Aaron (Ex 6:23), who bore him Nadab, Abihu, Eleazar, and Ithamar. Her father was Amminadab and her brother was Nahshon, the leader of Judah (Nm 1:7; 2:3), the tribe to which Elisheba also belonged. After Aaron died (Nm 20:28), Moses invested Eleazar, Elisheba's third son, with the office of chief priest.

ELISHUA One of the 13 children fathered by David during his reign in Jerusalem (2 Sm 5:15; 1 Chr 14:5). In the parallel passage of 1 Chronicles 3:6, the name Elishama appears in Elishua's place in most Hebrew manuscripts.

ELIUD Achim's son, Eleazar's father, and an ancestor of Jesus Christ according to Matthew's genealogy (Mt 1:14-15). *See* Genealogy of Jesus Christ.

ELIZABETH Woman of priestly descent (Lk 1:5) and mother of John the Baptist, she was a relative of Mary, mother of Jesus (v 36). The name Elizabeth, which derives from the same Hebrew word as Elisheba, wife of Aaron (Ex 6:23), means "my God is an oath." Only Luke's Gospel, which characteristically focuses greater attention upon the role of women, mentions Elizabeth and her husband, Zechariah.

Luke emphasized Elizabeth and Zechariah's godly character and blameless conduct (Lk 1:6) before stating that the elderly couple had not been favored with children. Although in Jewish culture childlessness was regarded as a reproach (Gn 30:22-23; Lk 1:25), the devout pair continued to steadfastly worship and serve God. Unexpectedly, an angel of the Lord appeared to Zechariah with the announcement that Elizabeth would conceive and bear a son, who would be the forerunner of the promised Messiah (Lk 1:13-17). When Elizabeth conceived, she withdrew from public life for five months, during which time her kinswoman Mary visited her.

See also John the Baptist.

ELIZAPHAN

1. Kohathite Levite and Uzziel's son (Nm 3:29-30), who assisted in removing the bodies of Nadab and Abihu from the camp (Lv 10:4). Elizaphan's descendants were responsible for caring for the ark, the table, the lampstand, and vessels of the sanctuary (cf. 1 Chr 15:8; 2 Chr 29:13). His name is alternately spelled Elzaphan (Ex 6:22; Lv 10:4).
2. Parnach's son and a leader from Zebulun's tribe, who helped Eleazar and Joshua divide the Canaanite territory west of the Jordan among the 9½ tribes (Nm 34:25).

ELIZUR Shedeur's son and leader of Reuben's tribe at the start of Israel's wilderness journey (Nm 1:5; 2:10; 7:30-35; 10:18).

ELKANAH

1. Levite of Korah's family (Ex 6:24) from the house of Izhar (v 21). He was Assir's son, and fathered Ebiasaph (1 Chr 6:23).
2. Father of the prophet Samuel (1 Sm 1:19). He was the son of Jeroham of Ephraim, from Ramathaim-zophim (v 1). Elkanah had two wives, Hannah and Peninnah, the former being barren (v 2). Hannah begged God repeatedly for a son whom she would give to the Lord's service. Samuel was subsequently born, and after his weaning, he was brought to the aged priest Eli for training. Elkanah had other sons and daughters by Hannah (2:21), and became the forefather of Heman, a singer in David's time.
3, 4. Name of two Kohathite Levites descended from Korah's line and ancestors of Heman the singer (1 Chr 6:26, 35).
5. Levite who dwelt in the village of the Netophathites and later lived in Jerusalem in the postexilic era (1 Chr 9:16).
6. Benjamite warrior who joined David's mighty men at Ziklag (1 Chr 12:6).
7. Gatekeeper (guard) for the ark of the covenant during David's reign (1 Chr 15:23). He is perhaps the same as #6 above.
8. One who held an authoritative post in King Ahaz's court. Elkanah was slain by Zichri, an Ephraimite, for having forsaken the Lord (2 Chr 28:7).

ELKIAH Ananias's son and father of Oziel, an ancestor of Judith (Jdt 8:1).

ELKOSH Home or birthplace of the prophet Nahum (Na 1:1). Three sites have been suggested: (1) Hilkeesei, a village in Galilee, perhaps corresponding to modern el-Kauzeh; (2) Capernaum near the Sea of Galilee, where Jesus frequently taught; and (3) Bein Jebrin in southern Judea.

ELLASAR Place in Babylonia; a few scholars have suggested that Arioch was its king. He joined a coalition that included Kedorlaomer, king of Elam, and together they raided the Jordan Valley during the time of Abraham (Gn 14:1, 9).

ELM* KJV mistranslation for terebinth, a large Palestinian tree, in Hosea 4:13. *See* Plants (Terebinth).

ELMADAM, ELMODAM* Ancestor of Jesus Christ, according to Luke's genealogy (Lk 3:28, KJV "Elmodam"). *See* Genealogy of Jesus Christ.

ELNAAM Father of two mighty warriors in David's army, Jeribai and Joshaviah (1 Chr 11:46).

ELNATHAN

1. Grandfather of King Jehoiachin. His daughter, Jehoiachin's mother, was Nehushta (2 Kgs 24:8).
2, 3, 4. Three Jewish leaders whom Ezra sent to Iddo at Casiphia to obtain Levites and temple servants for the caravan of Jews returning to Palestine from Babylonia (Ezr 8:16).
5. Acbor's son, who was ordered by King Jehoiakim to bring back Uriah from Egypt to be executed for prophesying against the king (Jer 26:22-23). Elnathan was present with other princes when Baruch read the Lord's words of warning written at Jeremiah's dictation on a scroll (36:12); he tried unsuccessfully to prevent Jehoiakim from burning the scroll (v 25).

ELOAH* Hebrew name for God stressing that he alone is deserving of worship. *See* God, Names of.

ELOHIM* General name for God in the OT. The etymology of *Elohim* is uncertain, but it is generally agreed that it is based on a root that means "might" or "power." The word is plural in form, but when applied to the true God, it is used in a singular sense and most frequently with verbal elements. The most common explanation for the plural form of *Elohim* as applied to God is that it is "plural of majesty," that is, all the majesty of deity is encompassed by him.

Elohim also occurs as a designation of deity in other languages, such as Assyrian and Ugaritic; it is used of other nations' gods, thus demonstrating its more general sense. It seems to be used in a general sense in the OT, particularly the Pentateuch (the five books of Moses), denoting God's transcendence and capacity as creator of the universe. It is thus somewhat different from the designation *Yahweh*, which usually connotes God in his personal relationships to people.

Elohim is used as a designation of Israel's rulers and judges (Ps 82:1, 6), perhaps denoting their function as God's earthly representatives (Ex 21:6). That meaning of the word was used by Christ (Jn 10:34-36) in a defense against his detractors.

The word is also used of angelic beings (Ps 8:5, KJV; cf. Heb 2:7), and in the expression "sons of God" (Jb 1:6).

See also God, Names of.

ELOI, ELOI, LAMA SABACHTHANI? One of Jesus' cries from the cross (Mk 15:34). *See* Eli, Eli, Lama Sabachthani.

ELON (Person)

1. Hittite who was the father of Basemath (perhaps also called Adah, Gn 36:2), one of Esau's wives (26:34).
2. Second of Zebulun's three sons (Gn 46:14) and the founder of the Elonite family (Nm 26:26).
3. Judge from Zebulun who judged Israel for 10 years. He was buried in Aijalon (Jgs 12:11-12).

ELON (Place) Village near Timnah, the home of Samson's first wife. Elon was included in the inheritance allotted to Dan's tribe in Joshua's distribution of the

Promised Land (Jos 19:43; cf. 14:1-2). It is generally identified with Khirbet Wadi 'Alinm near 'Ain Shems.

ELON-BETHHANAN Administrative district in Dan during the reign of Solomon (1 Kgs 4:9). It is perhaps identifiable with the Danite town of Elon.

ELONITE Descendant of Elon, Zebulun's son (Nm 26:26). See Elon (Person) #2.

ELOTH* Alternate spelling of the Edomite town Elath, in 1 Kings 9:26; 2 Chronicles 8:17; and 26:2. See Elath.

ELPAAL Benjamite and one of Shaharaim's sons (1 Chr 8:11-12, 18).

ELPALET* KJV spelling of Elpelet, an alternate name for David's son Eliphelet in 1 Chronicles 14:5. See Eliphelet #3.

EL-PARAN Place located on the edge of the wilderness of Paran, probably at the southern tip of the mountains of Seir in the Sinai Peninsula, present-day Arabia. It was the farthest point south to which King Kedorlaomer and his allies pushed their punitive raid against the rebellious kings of Sodom and Gomorrah (Gn 14:5-6). See Elath.

ELPELET Alternative name of David's son Eliphelet in 1 Chronicles 14:5. See Eliphelet #3.

ELASA Mentioned in 1 Maccabees 9:5 as the place where Judas Maccabeus pitched his tents when Bacchides engaged him in battle and Judas was killed (9:18). It is usually identified with Il'asa near Beth-horon.

EL SHADDAI* Hebrew for "God Almighty" (Ps 68:14). See God, Names of.

ELTEKEH City allotted to Dan's tribe for an inheritance (Jos 19:44); it was later assigned to the Kohathite Levites (21:23). An important battle was fought near Eltekeh between King Sennacherib of Assyria and the Egyptians. The Egyptians were subsequently routed, and the city was captured by the Assyrians. From here Sennacherib went on to invade Judah (2 Kgs 18:13). Eltekeh was located north of Ekron and west of Timnah, but its exact site is uncertain.

ELTEKON Town located in the hill country of Judah. It was assigned by Joshua to Judah's tribe (Jos 15:59), and may be the modern Khirbet ed-Deir, west of Bethlehem.

ELTOLAD Town assigned to Simeon's tribe in the southern portion of Judah's inheritance (Jos 15:30; 19:4). It is alternately called Tolad in 1 Chronicles 4:29.

ELUL* Hebrew month generally corresponding to mid-August to mid-September (Neh 6:15, NLT mg). See Calendars, Ancient and Modern.

ELUZAI One of the men of Benjamin who came to join David in Ziklag (1 Chr 12:5). Eluzai was an ambidextrous slinger and bowman.

ELYMAIS Formerly thought to be a city in Persia, greatly renowned for riches, silver, and gold (1 Macc 6:1), but now generally regarded as a district of Persia. Josephus (*Antiquities* 12.9.1), following 1 Maccabees, alludes to it as a city, but it is otherwise unknown.

ELYMAS Another name for Bar-Jesus, a Jewish magician and false prophet, in Acts 13:8. See Bar-Jesus.

ELYON* Hebrew name for God meaning "Most High." See God, Names of.

ELZABAD
1. Military leader from Gad's tribe who joined David at Ziklag (1 Chr 12:12).
2. Korahite Levite from Obed-edom's family, and a gatekeeper of the sanctuary (1 Chr 26:7).

ELZAPHAN Alternate spelling of Elizaphan, a Levite chief, in Exodus 6:22 and Leviticus 10:4. See Elizaphan #1.

EMBALM See Burial, Burial Customs.

EMBROIDERER, EMBROIDERY The art of making decorative designs on clothing. This was an art practiced both in the home and as a profession; it was done on a loom or with a needle. Delicate fabrics in the tabernacle and temple (Ex 26:1, 31) and the garments of priests (28:6, 8; 39:2) were beautifully embroidered. The art was practiced in Canaan (Jgs 5:30), Egypt (Ez 27:7), Syria (v 16), Babylonia (Jos 7:21), Assyria, and Persia (Est 1:6).
See also Cloth and Cloth Manufacturing.

EMEK-KEZIZ City allotted to Benjamin's tribe for an inheritance; it was mentioned between Beth-hoglah and Beth-arabah (Jos 18:21).

EMERALD Rich green variety of beryl, regarded as a precious stone. See Stones, Precious.

EMEROD*
1. KJV rendering of ulcer in Deuteronomy 28:27. See Sore.
2. KJV rendering of tumor in 1 Samuel 5:6-12 and 6:4-17. See Tumor.

EMIM*, EMITES Name given to the original inhabitants of Moab (Gn 14:5) by the Moabites who ousted them from their land. They were a tall people, known also as Rephaim (Dt 2:10-11), and were compared with the Zuzites, Anakim, and Horites for their size. This phenomenon is evidently an indication of genetic isolation. See Giants.

EMMANUEL* Alternate spelling of Immanuel in Matthew 1:23. See Immanuel.

EMMAUS Town in Judea that appears in Luke (see 24:13) and also in 1 Maccabees (3:40, 57). It was the destination of two disciples to whom Jesus appeared after the Crucifixion. Following the resurrection, Cleopas and a friend were going to Emmaus when they encountered another traveler. They walked the road and talked together, but the disciples did not recognize that the stranger was Jesus. Jesus asked them the nature of their conversation, and he was told of the Crucifixion, the empty tomb, and their discouragement that things had not worked out as they hoped. Jesus then rebuked them, and "beginning with Moses and all the prophets, he interpreted to them in all the scriptures the things concerning himself" (Lk 24:27, RSV). When they reached their destination, Jesus accepted an invitation to spend the night. As they ate the evening meal, he blessed the bread, broke it, and gave it to them to eat. At that moment they recognized him. After Jesus vanished from their sight, they returned to Jerusalem to report the event to the apostles.

Though Emmaus, which means "warm wells," was near Jerusalem, its exact location has never been determined. Several locations have been suggested:

1. Colonia (Qaloniyeh), about four miles (6.5 kilometers) west of Jerusalem on the main road to Joppa.
2. El-Qubeibeh, about seven miles (11.3 kilometers) northwest of Jerusalem on a Roman road passing by Nebi Samwil. Its identification with Emmaus dates back to AD 1099, when the Crusaders found a Roman fort there named Castellum Emmaus.
3. Abu Ghosh, about nine miles (14.5 kilometers) west of Jerusalem. Identified with the OT Kiriath-jearim, it is also known as Kiryat el-Enab, where a Crusader church was built over a Roman fort. This site appears to be too far from Jerusalem to be the biblical Emmaus.
4. Amwas, also known as Nicopolis, about 20 miles (32.2 kilometers) west of Jerusalem on the Jaffa road. This is the Emmaus of 1 Maccabees 3:40, 57. This site has the earliest claim to being Emmaus and also has two "warm wells." Eusebius and Jerome accepted it as the site. The primary objection to its being the NT Emmaus is its distance from Jerusalem, which exceeds the distance stated by Luke, as given in several manuscripts.

No conclusive evidence has been offered to substantiate the claim for any of these sites as being Emmaus; hence its location remains unknown.

EMMOR* KJV rendering of Hamor, Shechem's father, in Acts 7:16. *See* Hamor.

EMPEROR Official designation of the Roman sovereign beginning in 27 BC with the reign of Caesar Augustus; a derivation of imperator, an honorary title of supreme command conferred by the Roman Senate upon one of its victorious generals. *See* Caesars, The.

ENAN Ahira's father. Ahira was appointed by Moses as the commander of the tribe of Naphtali during the first census of Israel in the desert of Sinai (Nm 1:15; 2:29; 7:78, 83; 10:27). The name is apparently preserved in the name Hazar-enan (-enon), a town somewhere between Damascus and Hauran (Nm 34:9; Ez 47:17; 48:1).

ENCHANTMENT Act of casting charms or incantations to influence others or to obtain knowledge. Balaam could place no enchantment against Israel but could only bless them (Nm 23:23). Enchanters were present among the wise men of Nebuchadnezzar's court; however, Daniel and his three friends were found to be ten times wiser than they (Dn 1:20). The enchanters were unable to recall King Nebuchadnezzar's forgotten dream (2:2-27) or to interpret his second one (4:7); later, under Belshazzar, they could not read or interpret the handwriting on the palace wall (5:7-15). According to the prophet Isaiah, even the great powers of Babylon's enchantments would not save it from eventual destruction (Is 47:9, 12). In a more figurative sense, the psalmist writes: wickedness "does not hear the voice . . . of the cunning enchanter" (Ps 58:5, RSV).

See also Magic; Sorcery.

END OF THE WORLD *See* Day of the Lord; Eschatology; Last Judgment.

ENDOR Ancient Canaanite city, four miles (6.5 kilometers) south of Mt Tabor, assigned to the tribe of Manasseh, though never fully taken by them (Jos 17:11).

EMPEROR WORSHIP
Emperor worship had its origins in the Near Eastern practice of considering the king divine. The Egyptian pharaoh was considered a descendant of the sun god Ra (Re), and Mesopotamian legends speak of kingship "descending from heaven." Alexander the Great and other Greek heroes were worshiped after their deaths. The idea of a ruler's divinity was encouraged by the central place of the king in pagan cults. Israel was directly affected by such worship during the Babylonian exile (see Dn 3).

Such a background set the pattern for the Seleucid king Antiochus IV Epiphanes, who believed himself to be an incarnation of the Greek god Zeus. He desecrated the temple in Jerusalem by setting up an altar to Zeus in it (167 BC). That event, which the Jews never forgot, triggered the Maccabean war for the liberation of Palestine.

Roman generals and emperors likewise assumed godhood as soon as they penetrated Asia Minor, especially after Augustus Caesar came to full power (27 BC). Augustus saw his reign as the inauguration of a new age of peace for Rome and the world. Although the Romans acclaimed him as "savior," he claimed for himself only the high priesthood. In the eastern provinces coins were minted with a double temple for Rome and Augustus. In Antioch coins depicted Augustus as the incarnate Zeus or "worship-worthy Son of God," and altars were erected in his honor. Augustus encouraged the cult as a unifying element in his diverse empire and as a type of patriotism. After his death, temples were built in his honor and the symbols of divinity were transferred to succeeding emperors. For decades all new temples were for the imperial cult. (In Mk 12:13-17 and parallel passages about paying taxes, the coin was probably inscribed "Tiberius Caesar . . . Son of the Divine Augustus.")

Gaius Caesar, nicknamed Caligula (AD 37–41), was the first emperor to be worshiped in Rome during his own lifetime. On hearing of a dispute between Jews and Gentiles over worshiping him in Jamnia, he ordered a statue of himself to be placed in the temple in Jerusalem. His plan, which would surely have caused a general revolt, was averted only by the intercession of Herod Agrippa I. Under the succeeding emperors, Claudius (AD 41–54) and Nero (AD 54–68), the cult reached ridiculous extremes. Later emperors varied in how seriously they took the imperial cult, but it remained a test of loyalty to the empire, similar to loyalty oaths or pledging allegiance to the flag. For the sake of the empire's unity, other religions had to accommodate emperor worship one way or another.

Emperor worship naturally caused problems for Christians, since the titles given to the emperor ("lord," "prince of peace," "son of god," "savior") were the same as those used for Christ. The confession "Jesus is Lord" (Rom 10:9) was bound to conflict with the claim "Caesar is lord." Christians who would not sacrifice to the emperor were charged with treason. The conflict between emperor worship and Christianity remained a focal point for the persecution of the church until the time of Constantine (AD 306–37).

The city witnessed the defeat of Jabin and Sisera by Barak (Ps 83:9-10). Endor is best known as the dwelling place of the witch who was called upon by King Saul (1 Sm 28:7). On that occasion, Saul disguised himself because his journey to Endor took him near the Philistine army encamped at Shunem.

EN-EGLAIM Place mentioned in Ezekiel 47:10 where, in a description of the millennial age, it is said that "fishermen will stand beside the sea; from En-gedi to En-eglaim it will be a place for the spreading of nets; its fish will be of very many kinds, like the fish of the Great Sea" (RSV). This condition will be in sharp contrast to the present lack of marine life in the Dead Sea. The location is on the shore of the Dead Sea, probably south of Khirbet Qumran, perhaps 'Ain Feshkha.

ENGAGEMENT Act of commiting oneself to another by a pledge to marry. *See* Marriage, Marriage Customs.

EN-GANNIM
1. Village in the lowland of Judah near Beth-shemesh (Jos 15:34). Some identify it with the modern Beit Jemal, but this is doubtful.
2. Town on the boundary of Issachar (Jos 19:21). It was a Levitical city of the Gershonites (21:29) and the Anem of 1 Chronicles 6:73, which may be a copyist's mistake. It seems to be the Ginaea of Josephus (*Antiquities* 20.6.1). Its site is the modern Jenin, a village on the southern edge of the plain of Esdraelon, five miles (8.1 kilometers) northeast of Dothan and about 68 miles (109.4 kilometers) north of Jerusalem.
   See also Levitical Cities.

EN-GEDI A vital oasis on the west side of the Dead Sea about 35 miles (56.3 kilometers) southeast of Jerusalem. Allotted to Judah's tribe for an inheritance (Jos 15:62), En-gedi contained a hot water spring coming from the side of a limestone cliff, producing semitropical vegetation. The area became known for its palms, vineyards, and balsam (Sg 1:14; Josephus's *Antiquities* 20.1.2). The ancient site was southeast of the oasis at Tell el-Jarn near modern 'Ain Jidi.

En-gedi was called Hazazon-tamar in 2 Chronicles 20:2, and figured in several OT events. There Kedorlaomer conquered the Amorites (Gn 14:7); David sought refuge from Saul (1 Sm 23:29); and in Ezekiel's vision of Israel's restoration, fishermen would catch fish from the Dead Sea from En-gedi to En-eglaim (Ez 47:10).

ENGRAVER, ENGRAVING *See* Stonecutter.

EN-HADDAH City allotted to Issachar's tribe for an inheritance, mentioned between En-gannim and Beth-pazzez (Jos 19:21).

EN-HAKKORE* Spring of water that burst forth when Samson cried to the Lord after he had slaughtered the Philistines (Jgs 15:19, NLT mg).

EN-HAZOR Fortified city of the OT (Jos 19:37). One of several Hazors in the OT, En-hazor was probably located in Galilee.

EN-MISHPAT Early name for Kadesh, mentioned in the account of Kedorlaomer's battles (Gn 14:7). *See* Kadesh, Kadesh-barnea.

ENOCH (Person)
1. Cain's son and grandson of Adam (Gn 4:17, 19).
2. Jared's son among the descendants of Seth; Methuselah's father (Gn 5:18-24; 1 Chr 1:3). He lived in such close relationship to God that he was taken to heaven without having died.

ENOCH (Place) City that Cain named for his first son, Enoch (Gn 4:17).

ENOSH Seth's son and the grandson of Adam (Gn 4:26; 1 Chr 1:1). He became the father of Kenan at 90 years of age, after which he fathered other sons and daughters, dying at the age of 905 (Gn 5:6-11). He is mentioned as Jesus' ancestor in Luke's genealogy (Lk 3:38; KJV, RSV "Enos"). *See* Genealogy of Jesus Christ.

EN-RIMMON Town assigned first to Judah and then to Simeon (Jos 15:32; 19:7; 1 Chr 4:32). These verses refer to two places, Ain and Rimmon, but this was probably a scribal error for the one town, En-rimmon (see Jos 19:7). It was resettled after the exile (Neh 11:29), and is perhaps the Rimmon south of Jerusalem mentioned in Zechariah 14:10. En-rimmon is thought to be the modern Khirbet Umm er-Rumamin, nine miles (14.5 kilometers) north of Beersheba.

EN-ROGEL Spring that was an important landmark identifying the boundary line between the tribes of Judah and Benjamin (Jos 15:7; 18:16). Jonathan and Ahimaaz hid at En-rogel when they were spying on Absalom's troops for King David (2 Sm 17:17), and from there a maidservant delivered their messages to the king. Here also Adonijah sacrificed sheep, oxen, and goats when he anticipated David's death and wished to set himself up as king (1 Kgs 1:9).

Of the two suggested locations for En-rogel, the older suggestion identifies it with a spring in a cave near Siloam, on the west side of the Kidron Valley, known as the Virgin's Fount. There is strong evidence, however, that this is actually the Gihon Spring (1 Kgs 1:33), which is mentioned as distinct from En-rogel. A more likely suggestion is another spring south of Jerusalem known as the Well of Job.

ENROLLMENT Registration of people according to tribe, family, and position. *See* Census.

EN-SHEMESH Place mentioned only in Joshua 15:7 and 18:17 as a boundary marker between Judah's northern border and Benjamin's southern border. The usual identification is with 'Ain el-Hod, about three miles (4.8 kilometers) east of Jerusalem on the road to Jericho. On the basis of a tradition that the apostles drank there, it is sometimes referred to as the Spring of the Apostles.

EN-TAPPUAH* Canaanite town located on the border between Ephraim's and Manasseh's territory (Jos 17:7). It is usually identified with the modern Sheikh Abu-Zarad, about eight miles (12.9 kilometers) south of Shechem. *See* Tappuah (Place) #2.

ENUMA ELISH* Title of the Babylonian creation epic found during excavations at Nineveh (1848–76). The words *enuma elish* mean "when on high" and are the first two words of the epic, introducing the reader to a time when the heavens "on high" had not been named and the earth did not yet exist. The cuneiform tablets containing the epic were found in the library ruins of the Assyrian king Ashurbanipal. The epic was probably composed in the time of the Babylonian king Hammurabi (c. 1791–1750 BC). One of the chief purposes of the epic is to show the sovereignty of the Babylonian god Marduk.

See also Ashurbanipal; Creation; Creation Myths.

EPAPHRAS Coworker with the apostle Paul. Epaphras, a native of Colosse, was responsible for the city's evangelization, as well as that of Laodicea and Hierapolis. Through him Paul learned of the progress of the Colossian church and thus wrote his letter to the Colossians. Paul's high regard for Epaphras was evidenced by his use of such terms as "beloved fellow servant," "faithful minister of Christ" (Col 1:7), and "servant of Christ" (4:12), a title of esteem Paul bestowed only on one other person—Timothy (Phil 1:1). Epaphras was in prison with Paul at the time the letter to Philemon was written (Phlm 1:23).

See also Colossians, Letter to the.

EPAPHRODITUS Leader in the Philippian church. Epaphroditus was sent to the apostle Paul during Paul's first Roman imprisonment; his mission was to deliver gifts (Phil 4:18) and to assist the apostle in his work (2:25). While in Rome, Epaphroditus became seriously ill and nearly died. After a period of convalescence, he returned to Philippi with Paul's letter instructing the church to receive him (v 29). Epaphroditus's devoted service endeared him to the Philippian believers and to Paul, who termed him "brother and fellow worker and fellow soldier" (v 25, RSV).

See also Philippians, Letter to the.

EPENETUS Believer greeted by Paul in Romans 16:5 as "my dear friend" and "the very first person to become a Christian in the province of Asia" (NLT). It is not known if Epenetus was a personal convert of Paul. Mention of his name has been used to promote the hypothesis that the letter was written for the Ephesians, but this is not sufficient grounds for making this identification.

EPHAH (Measurement) Measure of grain, about half a bushel (18 liters). *See* Weights and Measures.

EPHAH (Person)
1. Son of Midian, an offspring of Abraham through his concubine Keturah (Gn 25:4; 1 Chr 1:33). Isaiah mentions him as a gold trader (Is 60:6). Some manuscripts mention two sons of Midian with the same name, Ephah, but that is an error of misspelling.
2. Caleb's concubine, who bore him three sons (1 Chr 2:46).
3. Jahdai's son from Judah's tribe (1 Chr 2:47).

EPHAI Netophathite (resident of the town Netophah, near Bethlehem) whose sons fought against the Babylonian army (Jer 40:8). They, with others, approached Gedaliah, the governor of Judah appointed by Babylon, and requested his protection. They died, along with Gedaliah, in an uprising led by Ishmael, the son of Nethaniah (41:3).

EPHER
1. Son of Midian and grandson of Abraham through his concubine Keturah, whose tribe was sent to the east. Some were supportive of Abraham's descendants and others became enemies (Gn 25:4; 1 Chr 1:33).
2. Son of Ezrah from Judah's tribe (1 Chr 4:17).
3. Head of a household and a great warrior in the half-tribe of Manasseh. He lived between Bashan and Mt Hermon (1 Chr 5:24).

EPHES-DAMMIM Location between Socoh and Azekah in Judah (1 Sm 17:1) where the Philistines encamped. It was called Pas-dammim in 1 Chronicles 11:13. The reference to blood (dammim) in the name probably has to do with the number of battles fought there, or it may refer to the red earth of the area. Tradi-

tionally identified with the ruins of Damun, about four miles (6.5 kilometers) northeast of Socoh, the exact location of the site is unknown.

EPHESIANS, Letter to the Letter to the Christians in Ephesus and the surrouding churches written with a magnificence that both instructs and inspires the reader. It provides a sweeping view of the role of the church as history moves toward the ultimate recognition of the universal headship of Christ.

PREVIEW
•Author
•Destination
•Date and Origin
•Background
•Purpose and Theological Teaching
•Content

Author The writer of the letter identifies himself as the apostle Paul (Eph 1:1; 3:1). He also describes his own ministry in terms that reflect what we know of Paul (3:7, 13; 4:1; 6:19-20). This claim is confirmed by the testimonies of Irenaeus, Origen, Polycarp, Tertullian, and Ignatius, who in his own espistle to the Ephesians alludes to the frequent and affectionate mention made by Paul of the Christian state, privileges, and persons of the Ephesians.

There are some characteristics of the letter, however, that have caused many scholars to question its clear claim to Pauline authorship. Some of these characteristics would be a problem only if the letter were intended exclusively for people in Ephesus, but such was probably not the case. Otherwise, it would be hard to understand why, after establishing the church there over a three-year period, Paul would write as though author and recipients had only a secondhand knowledge of each other. It would also be strange that the warm personal words of greeting to various individuals that are found in other Pauline letters are missing here. There is instead only a general greeting to "the brothers" (6:23). But all this can be easily explained once it is understood that the epistle was an encyclical for several churches.

Destination This epistle was addressed, most probably, to several churches in the district around Ephesus—namely, Asia. The Epistle to the Ephesians, so-called, was not really intended to be only for the church at Ephesus. Most modern scholars are convinced that it was an encyclical that went to several churches in Asia, including Ephesus. There are several reasons to affirm this. First, the earliest manuscripts (the Chester Beatty Papyrus—P46, Codex Sinaiticus, Codex Vaticanus) do not contain the words "in Ephesus" in Ephesians 1:1. It appears that Paul purposely left the name of the locality out, so as to be filled in later as the letter circulated to each locality. (The Greek construction in 1:1 calls for a prepositional phrase designating a locality to be present in the sentence.) Since Ephesus was the leading city of Asia, it was quite natural for scribes to assign this epistle to the church at Ephesus. Second, the Epistle to the Ephesians has all the marks of being a general treatise rather than an epistle to a specific local church. Paul had lived with the believers at Ephesus for three years (Acts 20:31). He knew them intimately, yet in this epistle there are no personal greetings or specific exhortations. When we consider Paul's manner in many of his other epistles, it would be quite unlike him to have excluded these personal expressions. Quite the contrary, Paul speaks to the saints whom he has only heard about and who have

Papyrus Manuscript of Ephesians Opening page of Ephesians
Chester Beatty Manuscript II, late second century—P46

only heard about him (see Eph 1:15; 3:1). It is possible that this epistle was the one sent to Laodicea.

In all fairness it must be said that the encyclical theory has been opposed by some scholars. For example, Henry Alford makes the following objections to this theory: (1) It is at variance with the spirit of the epistle, which is clearly addressed to one set of persons throughout, coexisting in one place and as one body and under the same circumstances. (2) It is improbable that the apostle, who in two of his epistles (2 Corinthians and Galatians) has so plainly specified their encyclical character, should have here omitted such specification. (3) The absence of personal greetings is not an argument for either of the two theories, for similarly there are none in Galatians, Philippians, 1 and 2 Thessalonians, and 1 Timothy. The better he knows the parties addressed, and the more general and solemn the subject, the less he seems to give of these individual notices.

Date and Origin Ephesians 3:1, 4:1, and 6:20 indicate that the letter was written while Paul was a prisoner. Since he was imprisoned several times, it is necessary to narrow the options. The first major imprisonment may have been at Ephesus itself, but this is obviously not in consideration. The second was at Caesarea for two years (Acts 24:27; cf. 23:23-24, 33). It is possible that Paul wrote some letters at that time, but most scholars think that Ephesians (along with Colossians, Philemon, and probably Philippians) was written during Paul's imprisonment at Rome (28:16, 30). This probably took place sometime between AD 59 and 63 and lasted for two years. This period of time, following about 25 years of spiritual growth and 12 years or so of missionary experience, gave Paul a splendid opportunity for reflection and writing.

Background Ephesus was the most important city in Asia Minor, located on the Cayster River, with a harbor on the Aegean Sea. With this location it became a center for commercial travel, and major trade routes led to it from several directions. A great pagan temple dedicated to the goddess Artemis (Diana) was located in Ephesus. Paul made the city a center of evangelistic and church-building ministry (Acts 19), spending three years there (20:31). It was natural, therefore, for a letter intended for a wide readership in that part of Asia Minor to have Ephesus as its main destination.

Paul's first visit to Ephesus (on the seacoast of Lydia, near the river Cayster) is related in Acts 18:19-21. The work, begun by his disputations with the Jews in his short visit, was carried on by Apollos (vv 24-26) and Aquila and Priscilla (18:26). At his second visit, after his journey to Jerusalem, and thence to the east regions of Asia Minor, he remained at Ephesus "three years" (19:10—the "two years" in this verse are only *part* of the time—and 20:31); therefore, the founding and rearing of this church occupied an unusually large portion of the apostle's time and care. The language in the epistle shows a warmth of feeling and a free outpouring of thought, and a union in spiritual privileges and hope between him and them, such as are natural from one so long and so intimately associated with those whom he addresses. On his last journey to Jerusalem, he sailed by Ephesus and summoned the elders of the Ephesian church to meet him at Miletus, where he delivered his remarkable farewell charge (20:18-35).

Purpose and Theological Teaching It may be said that the purpose of Ephesians is "doxological"; that is, it

---

THE RELATIONSHIP BETWEEN EPHESIANS AND COLOSSIANS

Written at approximately the same time as Colossians, Ephesians displays both striking similarities and significant differences in comparison with that letter. By studying these, some knowledge can be gained about the composition of Ephesians.

Many words and phrases appear in almost identical form in the two letters. This is often more obvious in the Greek text than in modern translations. One example is found in Ephesians 1:4 and Colossians 1:22, where at the end of each verse Paul states that God will not charge the believer with any fault. There are also longer passages that are parallel to one another. These include teachings on adopting a new way of life (e.g., Eph 4:22-24; Col 3:8-10), singing praise (Eph 5:19-20; Col 3:16-17), and living together in harmony (Eph 5:22–6:9; Col 3:18–4:1).

These similarities are not absolute, however. In the passages just cited on human relationships, Ephesians has a detailed section on husbands and wives that is lacking in Colossians. Also, in Ephesians some unique sections are interspersed that are thought to have a liturgical character (Eph 1:3; 3:20-21; 4:5-6; 5:14). Others sound as though they were intended for public exhortation, some think at a baptism or for renewal of dedication (4:17–5:2; 5:3-21).

Further, some verses in Ephesians seem to be conflations of verses from various parts of Colossians. For example, Ephesians 1:7 seems to combine thoughts found in Colossians 1:14 and 20. The ideas of Colossians 1:3-4 and 9 seem to be brought together in Ephesians 1:15-16. A similar instance is Ephesians 2:1-5, which combines two widely separated verses, Colossians 2:13 and 3:6.

Theories abound to account for such similarities and differences. A few have proposed that Ephesians was written first; most, however, grant priority to Colossians. Some think that a preliminary version of one was used in the other, and was then expanded into its present form. According to one popular theory, which assumes that Paul is not the author, Ephesians was written by a later Christian who prepared it as an introduction to a collection of Paul's genuine writings, drawing material from Colossians and other Pauline letters.

The most satisfying reconstruction is that Paul wrote Colossians to meet the specific needs of the church at Colosse, planning to ask his friend Tychicus to take the letter there (Col 4:7). Meanwhile, Paul was reflecting on several of the themes touched on in Colossians. He thought also about the ultimate goals of his missionary endeavors. God had revealed to Paul his comprehensive plan for the church and the universal headship of Christ. Paul wrote Ephesians by drawing on some of the phrases and sentences that were fresh in his mind from Colossians.

This reconstruction also explains why some of the terms are used in a somewhat different way than they are in Colossians. Paul's purposes were different. Colossians is polemical, dealing with the problem of false teachers and teaching. Ephesians is reflective, dealing with the general subject of the church. There are other topics that are distinct in Ephesians but barely touched on in Colossians.

It is then clear why the term "mystery" is applied differently (see article). In Colossians, where the issue revolves largely around the person of Christ, the "mystery" is applied to the Lord himself. In Ephesians, with its emphasis on the church, the term is applied to the unity of Jews and Gentiles in the church. Neither usage exhausts the comprehensive meaning of the term.

should cause the readers to glorify God, both in grateful praise and in manner of life. This is seen in the opening section, which is like a hymn in style: "Praise God, the Father of our Lord Jesus Christ" (Eph 1:3; cf. the Doxology often sung in church). Paul says three times in the first chapter that the result of God's blessings should be praise (vv 6, 12, 14).

While the letter contains much doctrinal and moral instruction (with the latter solidly based on the former), its purpose is not only teaching or exhortation, important as these are. It is rather to lift up its readers to a new vantage point that will help them to identify with the risen, ascended Christ and to share his perspective on the church and its role in the world.

In this connection a significant term occurs in 1:3 and elsewhere. It is perhaps best translated "heavenly realms." It is different in form from the usual word for "heaven" and seems to have a special significance in Ephesians as the realm of Jesus' victorious reign in the present age. This is seen in 1:20, read in the context of verses 19-23. Whatever beings there may be, Christ is above them all. The believer, although obviously on earth physically, "sits with Christ" in the heavenly realms (2:6) and is "blessed" (1:3), drawing on the unlimited resources of heaven for his daily life. It is also in this realm that the spiritual conflict takes place (6:12).

Paul thus makes it clear that Christians are not to have a limited or merely earthly viewpoint. Those who do, mistakenly think that their enemies are people (6:12) and our resources human (2 Cor 10:3-4). With this orientation to the heavenly world of the Lord's present exaltation, the reader is prepared to understand that the church does not function merely to carry out routine activities here, but that it displays the wisdom of God to beings who exist in the heavenly realms (Eph 3:10). Even the function of church leaders is discussed in terms of the gifts of the Christ who has ascended to the heavens (4:8-10).

There is a strong sense of ultimate purpose in Ephesians. The first chapter contains a number of different expressions of purpose. The great goal of history is expressed in 1:10. The sense of purpose is never lost. The church is even seen, in chapter 3, as the expression of God's eternal, secret plan. There is also a movement throughout the letter, from (1) reconciliation of individuals to God, to (2) their reconciliation to each other, to (3) their life together in the church. There is no arguing of points along the way, such as one finds in most of the letters, but rather a connected series of affirmations, each leading the reader on to the next.

Paul discusses a number of topics from this heavenly perspective and the sense of purpose this provides. These topics will be discussed below in such a way as to show their interconnection, rather than necessarily in the order of their importance or prominence in Ephesians.

The Church Paul employs a number of figures of speech to describe the church, including a household, a temple, and a body (1:22-23; 2:19-22). Actually, it may be insufficient to call the word "body" a figure of speech, because it seems to be more than that. There is a sense in which Christ and the church have an actual organic relationship, in which he functions as the head and believers as parts of his body.

The church is the result of the reconciling work of Christ, whose death has made peace between mutually hostile Jews and Gentiles (2:11-18). The ensuing unity was long planned by God (3:2-6), and is furthered by a proper attitude and mutual ministry (ch 4).

An especially remarkable feature of Ephesians is the parallel drawn between the relationship between a husband and wife and that between Christ and the church (5:22-33). In this comparison the prior reality is not marriage, with the relationship of Christ and the church only providing an illustration. Rather, the essential reality is Christ and the church.

The Headship of Christ Not only is Christ the head of the church, but he is head over all things to the church's benefit (1:22). The meaning of 1:10 is that the presently disparate parts and beings of the universe will be brought into order under the headship of Christ. This universal headship is anticipated in the ascension and present exaltation of Christ. The expression of universal domination—"God has put all things under his feet" (1:22, from Ps 8:6)—fortifies this expectation.

The "Mystery" or "Secret Plan" The Greek word "mystery" has a special meaning in early Jewish and Christian literature. It refers to the private eternal decisions of God concerning his saving work and his ultimate purposes in history, which are revealed stage by stage. The term is used in connection with the kingdom in the Gospels (Mt 13:11), with the preaching of the gospel in 1 Corinthians 1:18-2:16, with the destiny of Israel in Romans 11:25, and elsewhere with differing applications. Finally, Revelation 10:6-7 declares that there will be no more delay, but that God's "mystery," initially announced by the prophets, will reach its completion.

The aspect of God's plan that Paul presents in Ephesians 3:3-6 is not only the inclusion of Gentiles among God's people but their complete integration with Jews in the church. The extent of this was not revealed prior to the time of Paul's ministry.

Content

The Divine Purpose: The Glory and Headship of Christ (1:1-14) This whole section constitutes a "doxology." Paul reminds readers, by expressing his own prayer of praise, of all the blessings God has given believers. These include being chosen to live in God's presence without guilt (v 4), being given the destiny of full sonship (v 5), and being forgiven because Christ died for them.

But Paul is not only giving a recitation of what God has done; he interweaves a number of words and phrases indicating *why* God has acted, that is, what God's *purposes* are. Various translations use different English words to represent Greek expressions of purpose, such as "chose," "predestined," "plan," "will," "secret reason," "good pleasure," "purpose" (vv 4-10). Perhaps the most comprehensive statement is in verses 11-12.

It is clear from this that the ultimate purpose of God's saving work is not merely the happiness of believers but the glory of God through the Lord Jesus Christ. The Spirit is given to guarantee not only the believer's security but also God's investment, so to speak, in the believer.

Prayer That Christians May Realize God's Purpose and Power (1:15-23) Paul's prayer issues from his opening section, constituting a request that believers may appropriate all that is contained in that statement. It is here that the fact of Jesus' death, resurrection, and ascension is cited as the basis for the believer's present vantage point and power.

Steps toward the Fulfillment of God's Purpose (2:1-3:21) The first step was the death of Christ in order to save individuals from sin and death (2:1-10). Since this was at God's initiative, not man's, and since man was spiritually "dead" and helpless, salvation can only be by grace.

The second step was the reconciliation of people not

only to God but to each other (2:11-18). Paul thus moves from the individual to the corporate aspect of salvation. This was particularly significant for Gentiles, who previously did not have even a formal relationship with God. One of the key words in this section is "peace" (vv 14-17).

Step three goes beyond reconciliation to the actual uniting of Jews and Gentiles in one "household" (2:19-22). God has not only brought people individually to himself, and to each other as individuals, but has formed a new corporate entity, a new society that is described both in political and family terms. Ultimately, believers together form a corporate body in whom God is exalted.

This third step is amplified in a fourth step, the revelation of God's eternal purpose in the formation of this one body, the church (3:1-13). Using the biblical concept of the "mystery," Paul shows how the church displays the wisdom of God to all who may be looking on throughout the universe. This immediately gives the believer a new awareness of the reason for his salvation and participation in the church. Self-centeredness and boredom with the routine of church activity give way to a sense of meaning and purpose.

These steps are now summarized in a second prayer (3:14-21). An exalted series of petitions culminate in another "doxology." This expresses Paul's awe over the infinite power of God to accomplish all that he has described in the epistle thus far, and his desire that this will indeed result in great glory to God both in the church and in Christ.

Practical Ways to Fulfill God's Purpose in the Church (4:1–6:20)
Doctrine and life are never separated in Paul's thinking, but in Ephesians the connection is even more vital than usual. The believer's life is to be lived in a manner worthy of the great purposes of God. The believer's "calling" is not merely to be saved or eternally happy, but to participate with the entire body, the church, in bringing glory to God. This contributes to the realization of the prayer in 3:20-21.

The first way to fulfill God's purpose is to maintain the unity he established in the church. This is accomplished by recognizing the strong basis for unity ("one Lord, one faith," etc., 4:5-6). Then believers must acknowledge diversity in that unity, remembering that God has given each one special abilities (vv 7-8). These abilities are to be used to bring the church both individually and corporately to maturity. This diversity in unity constitutes the second way in which God's purpose is fulfilled. Christian maturity enables the individual members of the church to relate to each other in love (v 16).

The third way to accomplish the purposes of God is by renewal of personal life (4:17–5:21). Paul emphasizes the kind of lifestyle that is expected of a Christian by contrasting the behavior patterns that had characterized the believers before their conversion. But the new life of the believer is not simply structured as a reaction against the old. Rather, the Lord has given both his teachings and the example of his own sacrificial love (4:20-21, 32; 5:1-2). The believer should cast off his old way of life, his old self or character. (The actual term is "old man" in Paul's wording, not, as is often thought, "old nature.") He should at the same time put on the "new man," which, in Paul's words in verse 24, is "created according to God" (NIV "created to be like God"). The section closes with the important exhortation to be filled with the Spirit (5:18).

The expression of the new character in interpersonal relations is the fourth way in which believers can forward the purposes of God in the church. Unity is either

achieved or broken in accordance with the presence or absence of the proper submission described in 5:22–6:9. The basic principle of submission is first expressed by verse 21 as a result of the Spirit's full control.

Marriage then provides the first example of mutual submission. The wife submits to the husband, and this in turn is an expression of her submission, along with that of the whole church, to the Lord. The husband loves his wife as Christ loved the church. While the husband's love is not described as submission, in effect, love does cost the lover his freedom. Jesus thus expressed his love for the church by his death (5:25). Further, husband and wife are bound together in a unity, just as God intended at the time of creation (Gn 2:24, quoted here in 5:31). This unity portrays that spiritual unity that exists between Christ and the church.

It should be noted that this list of examples is similar to a pattern used elsewhere in the NT (e.g., Col 3:18–4:1; 1 Pt 3:1-7). Thus, following the example of marriage, Paul turns to the relationship that should exist between parent and child. The child obeys the father; the father refrains from excessive reactions (6:1-4). The last example is that of slaves and masters.

THE CHURCH DISPLAYS GOD'S MANIFOLD WISDOM
The Epistle to the Ephesians is Paul's treatise on the universal church, the body of Christ. As such, it is not encumbered with local problems. It soars high above any mundane affairs and takes us into heaven, where we are presented with a heavenly view of the church as it fits into God's eternal plan. In this epistle Paul paints the church with multifarious splendor. He depicts her as God's inheritance (1:11); Christ's body, his fullness (vv 22-23), God's masterpiece (2:10); the one new person (v 15); the household of God (v 19); the habitation of God (vv 21-22); the joint body comprised of Jewish and Gentile believers (3:6); the vessel for God to display his manifold wisdom (v 10); the body equaling Christ's full stature (4:12-13); the full-grown, perfect person (v 13); the body growing into a building (v 16); the bride of Christ (5:23-32); the object of Christ's love (v 25); the very members of Christ's body (v 30); and God's warrior against Satan (6:11-18).

Paul's presentation of the church reached its pinnacle in this epistle. The church he pictured with words was the church in ideal perfection, the church as seen from heaven but not yet manifested on earth in fullness. There have been real expressions of this church throughout history, but most would agree that the church has not yet reached the measure of the stature of the fullness of Christ. Nor is it yet the glorious church without spot or blemish. But there is the expectation that the church will grow and grow until its manifestation matches the ideal image.

The final way in which believers forward God's great purposes is to carry on the spiritual conflict by depending on spiritual resources (Eph 6:10-20). Drawing on imagery both from the OT and from contemporary Roman warfare, Paul shows that the heavenly perspective is essential for victory. This includes dependence on God as expressed in prayer (vv 18-20). He acknowledges his own need in this respect.

The conclusion to the letter (6:21-24) is a word of encouragement and an explanation of Paul's decision to send the letter in the good hands of Tychicus. One of the concluding words is "grace," a word that underlies the entire divine process described in Ephesians.

See also Colossians, Letter to the; Ephesus; Paul, The Apostle.

EPHESUS Most important city of the Roman province of Asia, located on the western shore of Asia Minor (modern Turkey). Ephesus was built on a natural harbor whose waves, according to the Roman writer Pliny the Elder, "used to wash up to the temple of Diana." Ephesus was described by Strabo, an early Greek geographer, as the largest commercial center west of the Taurus Mountains. It was also well known as the "guardian" of the temple of Artemis, or as the Romans called her, Diana (Acts 19:34).

Christianity's threat to that pagan temple and to the commerce it produced for the makers of idols almost cost the apostle Paul his life (Acts 19:24, 30-31). Priscilla and Aquila were associated with the early preaching in Ephesus (18:18-19), as were Timothy (1 Tm 1:3) and Erastus (Acts 19:22). According to Irenaeus, an early Christian writer, the apostle John, after his exile on the island of Patmos (Rv 1:9), returned to live in Ephesus until the time of the emperor Trajan (AD 98–117). The commendable practices of the Christian community described in the letter to the Ephesians had been largely abandoned by the time John wrote the book of Revelation (Rv 2:4).

Aerial View of Ephesus

Ephesus was founded by Ionian Greeks at a location where the Cayster River emptied into a gulf of the Aegean Sea. It had been a city for about 1,000 years when Paul arrived there on his third missionary journey. The worship of Artemis in Ephesus was as ancient as the city itself. The temple, built in the middle of the sixth century BC, was the largest edifice in the Hellenistic world and the first of monumental size ever to be constructed entirely of marble. Two excavated images of Artemis, magnificently sculpted in marble, date to the period of the emperors Domitian and Hadrian (the lifetime of the apostle John). The temple of Diana, "mother of the gods," was considered one of the seven wonders of the ancient world. Although persistent effort by British archaeologist J. T. Wood resulted in the temple's discovery in 1869, its great altar was not found until recently. Excavation has shown the altar to be larger than the later altar of Zeus at Pergamum. The original temple was partially destroyed in 356 BC but was later rebuilt on its original plan.

Excavations have also uncovered the theater mentioned in Acts 19:29. Situated next to the main shopping area (Greek *agora*), it is known to have seated 24,000 people in three tiers. The theater was 495 feet (151 meters) in diameter with two doors opening to the most impressive street in Ephesus. That street, leading to the harbor, was about 35 feet (10.5 meters) wide and was flanked by tall columns. It passed through a magnificent monumental gateway on its western end. In the other direction the road continued around the theater and marketplace, making its way southeast between Mt Koressos and Mt Pion. It became narrower and was bordered by lovely fountains, civic buildings, houses, shops, a library, baths, and a small theater, which probably doubled as a council chamber for city officials.

Ephesus was a wealthy city. The multistoried residences of its upper-middle-class society rested on the north terraces of Mt Koressos. Some homes had mosaic floors and marble walls. Two were found with heated bathrooms. Many had running water. The moral status of the city can be partially ascertained from a centrally located house of prostitution and gambling tables; fertility motifs are evident in the exaggerated sexual features of the Diana statues.

The impact of Christianity was felt in Ephesus for centuries. The third ecumenical council was held there in AD 431 (in the Church of Mary northwest of the theater), a council that established Mary's place as the "Mother of God" in Western Catholic theology. By that time Diana, whose temple had been burned by the Goths in AD 262, was no longer influential among the Ephesians. The truth of Paul's message that "gods made with hands are not gods" (Acts 19:26) had to some extent been realized.

See also Ephesians, Letter to the.

EPHLAL Jerahmeel's descendant, who could trace his ancestry through Perez to Judah (1 Chr 2:37).

EPHOD (Garment) Upper garment worn during religious services associated with the tabernacle or temple. "Ephod" generally referred to the ornamented vest that the high priest wore over a blue robe (Ex 28:31). Included with the ephod were the Urim and Thummim, the sacred lots. Sometimes "ephod" meant the complete dress of the high priest (1 Sm 2:28; 23:6, 9; 30:7) or similar garments worn by lesser priests.

Made of dyed material and fine linen, the garment was embroidered in blue, purple, scarlet, and gold. At the upper end were attached two shoulder straps, each having an onyx stone inscribed with the names of Israel's 12 tribes. The breastplate, also containing the tribal names, was bound to the ephod by an elaborate series of cords and chains (Ex 28:22-29).

Jewish writers suggest various appearances for the ephod: (1) apronlike, covering the body from the chest to the heels; (2) enveloping the body only from the waist down, the upper body being covered by the breastplate; or (3) sleeved and jacketlike, with the middle of the breast uncovered so the breastplate could be inserted easily.

Prior to the Babylonian exile, the ephod served as a means of revelation from God, especially concerning military operations. Abiathar the priest brought the ephod into David's camp on one occasion for consulting the Lord (1 Sm 23:6-9; 30:7). It is uncertain whether the priest donned or held the ephod whole, seeking counsel from the Lord by means of the Urim and Thummim.

During the period of the judges, the ephod was often misused, as by Gideon (Jgs 8:27), Micah (17:5), and Jonathan, grandson of Moses (18:30; cf. vv 14, 17, 20). Either the garment itself or an image that represented

God, on which the garment was placed, was worshiped as the people sought revelation in a manner condemned by God. Household idols (teraphim) were also associated with this ungodly practice (17:5; Hos 3:4).

Besides the high priest, other priests wore an ephod for certain religious services (1 Sm 22:18), and even Samuel (2:18) and David (2 Sm 6:14) wore one. By the postexilic period, and perhaps as early as Solomon, the ephod was no longer consulted (Ezr 2:63; Neh 7:65). There was no need for ephod or Urim revelation once there was the more complete revelation of the prophetic ministry promised by Moses (Dt 18:15-22). However, the high priest continued to wear this vestment until the destruction of Jerusalem in AD 70.

See also Priests and Levites.

EPHOD (Person) Father of Hanniel, the prince of the children of Joseph (Nm 34:23). Hanniel was responsible for distributing Canaanite territory among the Israelite tribes.

EPHPHATHA* Transliteration in the imperative voice of the Aramaic expression "be opened," used by Jesus in the healing of a deaf mute (Mk 7:34, NLT mg). No attempt at establishing a magical word formula was intended; Mark simply preserved Jesus' actual wording.

EPHRAEMI SYRI*, Codex See Bible, Manuscripts and Text of the (New Testament).

EPHRAIM (Person) Joseph's younger son, born of Joseph and Asenath before the seven years of famine in Egypt (Gn 41:52). He was the ancestor of an Israelite tribe, and his name came to designate the northern kingdom of Israel (Is 7:5, 8; Jer 31:18-20; Hos 5:3-5). Ephraim's boyhood overlapped the last 17 years of his grandfather, the patriarch Jacob, who migrated to Egypt during the years of famine. Thus Ephraim could learn of God's promises and blessings directly from Jacob. After Jacob exacted an oath from Joseph to bury him in Canaan he adopted his grandsons Ephraim and Manasseh. That adoption gave the two brothers the position and legal rights equal to Jacob's eldest sons, Reuben and Simeon (Gn 48:5).

See also Ephraim, Tribe of.

EPHRAIM (Place)
1. Area allotted to Ephraim's tribe for an inheritance (Jos 16:5-8; 17:7-11). Ephraim and Manasseh originally were recognized as "the people of Joseph" (Jos 16:4). Together they occupied the central highlands area between Jerusalem and the plain of Esdraelon. Ephraim's territory lay to the south of Manasseh. The area was relatively high, and the expression "the hill country of Ephraim" (1 Sm 1:1) was an apt description. In places the hard rocks form steep and difficult slopes, and the valleys leading to the west are steep. Roads followed the spurs between the valleys rather than the valleys themselves. Movement between Ephraim and the coastal plain along the edge of the rocky Sarida Valley was not easy, but it was possible. Another road followed by the Philistine invaders (1 Sm 4) led up from Aphek. The expression in Joshua 16:9, "the towns which were set apart for the Ephraimites within the inheritance of the Manassites" (RSV), suggests that there had once been a disputed boundary; however, Ephraim was evidently able to strengthen itself and to emerge as a dominant force in Israel. Indeed, the name Ephraim is sometimes used as the equivalent of Israel (Hos 4:17; 5:3, 11-14; 6:4, 10).

The extent of the tribal area of Ephraim is given in Joshua 16:5-8 and 17:1-11. It would appear from the abundant detail given in these passages that the main topographical features of Ephraim's boundaries would be easy to determine. Yet the precise identification of a number of the places mentioned is uncertain. The eastern boundary began at Micmethah, tentatively identified with Khirbet en-Nabi. It continued south through Taanath-shiloh, Janoah, Ataroth, and Naarah to a point near Jericho. The southern boundary seems to have passed westward toward Bethel, Beth-horon, and Gezer to the Mediterranean Sea. The western boundary is not defined and probably encroached on Canaanite areas in early times. The northern boundary separating Ephraim from Manasseh went from Micmethah, which was "before Shechem," toward Tappuah and then ran along the Wadi Qana to the Mediterranean Sea north of Joppa. But it must be stressed that the precise definition of the boundaries is by no means clear. Immediately to the south of Ephraim lay the tribal area of Benjamin.

The rainfall in the hill country of Ephraim is greater than that in Judea, which lay further south, and the soil is reddish in color, rich and fertile. Because of this, Ephraim was very productive. Today the country is dotted with orchards, and olive trees are abundant. The description in Deuteronomy 33:14-17 of an area which yielded "the choicest fruits of the sun, and the rich yield of the months, with the finest produce of the ancient mountains, and the abundance of the everlasting hills, with the best gifts of the earth" (RSV) gives an excellent picture of the general nature of the region.
2. Town near Baal-hazor to which Absalom invited his half brother Amnon in order to have him put to death (2 Sm 13:23-29) for incest with Absalom's sister Tamar. The town lay to the north of Jerusalem and was possibly identical with Ephron (2 Chr 13:19). It was no doubt the same town near the wilderness to which Jesus retired after raising Lazarus from the tomb (Jn 11:54). It is generally identified with et-Taiyibeh, 13 miles (20.9 kilometers) northeast of Jerusalem and four miles (6.5 kilometers) northeast of Bethel.

EPHRAIM, Forest of Rocky, wooded stretch of country east of the Jordan in the area of Mahanaim. It was here that David's army defeated Absalom (2 Sm 18:6). The connection of this location with the territory of Ephraim is difficult. The most probable explanation is that Ephraim once extended farther to the east but that this area was lost by the tribe after its defeat by Jephthah and the Gileadites near Zaphon (Jgs 12:1-6). The name may have been used while the Ephraimites held the land, or perhaps been given at a later date as a reminder of Ephraim's defeat. Some speculate that Ephraimites once established a colony in the area (Jos 17:14-18).

EPHRAIM, Gate of Gate in the Jerusalem wall positioned about 600 feet (182.9 meters) east of the Corner Gate (2 Kgs 14:13; 2 Chr 25:23). It was rebuilt in Nehemiah's day (Neh 12:39) and was situated close to the Water Gate and courts of the temple.

See also Jerusalem.

EPHRAIM*, Mount KJV expression referring to the hill country in central Palestine where Ephraim's tribe was located (Jos 20:7; Jgs 19:1, 16, 18; 1 Sm 1:1). The area was one of the most productive in Palestine.

See also Ephraim (Place) #1.

EPHRAIM, Tribe of Tribe descended from the patriarch Joseph's second son. Both Ephraim and his brother

Manasseh were regarded as sons also by their grandfather Jacob and became his heirs.

Many Bible commentators think that in naming his son Ephraim (Gn 41:52), Joseph was making a play on words based on a Hebrew root meaning "to be fruitful." In support of this theory they note that the hill country later assigned to Ephraim's tribe was one of the most fertile areas in Palestine, and at present is still planted with vines and fruit trees, such as olive, pomegranate, and carob. Prior to Israelite settlement, the area was wooded (Jos 17:18). During the monarchy, wild animals still roamed there (2 Kgs 2:24).

It is difficult to determine the exact limits of Ephraim's territory, since it is often mentioned with Manasseh's tribe. Ephraim was allotted land in the heart of Canaan, the Promised Land, between the Jordan River and the Mediterranean Sea. One half of Manasseh's allotment formed Ephraim's northern boundary (Jos 16:5-9).

Ephraim became a great tribe, and its members often held prominent positions. The first census taken in the wilderness lists the total of Ephraimite soldiers as 40,500 (Nm 1:33). After the wilderness wanderings, the number of warriors dropped to 32,500 (26:37). In Israel's encampment around the tabernacle, Ephraim was the leader of the western camp, supported by the tribes of Manasseh and Benjamin (2:18-24).

Joshua the son of Nun, one of the 12 spies, was descended from Ephraim (Nm 13:8, "Hoshea"). Under Joshua's leadership, Ephraim and the other tribes conquered Canaan and received their promised inheritance (Jos 16).

In the days of the judges, the Ephraimites felt slighted when they were not called upon to assist others in their battles. They quarreled with Gideon because of his belated invitation to help against the Midianites (Jgs 8:1-6), as well as with Jephthah of Gilead, who defeated the Ammonites (12:1-6). The judge Abdon came from Ephraim's tribe (v 13). The idolatrous Micah (17:1), as well as the prophet Samuel, lived in Ephraim (1 Sm 1:1). The military and political importance of the Ephraimites is reflected in the Song of Deborah (Jgs 5:14), an ancient biblical poem.

Judah was Ephraim's main rival, and even under David, that animosity was evident (2 Sm 18; 19:41-20:22). Discontent in the north with Solomon's rule (1 Kgs 11:26-40), combined with a foolish decision by Rehoboam, Solomon's son, brought about the division of the kingdom. The 10 northern tribes (Israel) were then ruled by Jeroboam I.

After the northern tribes seceded, the capitals of the northern kingdom—Shechem, Tirzah, and Samaria— were situated in Ephraim. The establishment of Samaria by King Omri of Israel gave the Ephraimites more direct access to the great north-south trunk road (Via Maris) through the western plain. This contact with trade routes gave the northern kingdom greater world consciousness and brought greater temptation to depart from God and his commands.

The prophets proclaimed that Ephraim and the other northern tribes would one day be reunited with the southern kingdom of Judah in the messianic kingdom (Hos 1:11). The division introduced by Jeroboam I would be healed when a king descended from David would rule over Judah, Ephraim, and all the tribes of Israel (Ez 37).

See also Ephraim (Person); Ephraim (Place) #1; Israel, History of.

EPHRAIMITE Name given to a person from the tribal area of Ephraim. *See* Ephraim (Place) #1.

EPHRAIN* KJV form of Ephron, a town near Bethel, in 2 Chronicles 13:19. *See* Ephron (Place) #2.

EPHRATH (Person) Mother of Hur and Caleb's second wife (1 Chr 2:19, 50).

EPHRATH (Place)
1. Town in the Judean hill country later named Bethlehem. It was on the road to Ephrath that Rachel died while giving birth to Benjamin (Gn 35:16-19). This town was the home of Naomi's family, who identified themselves as Ephrathites (Ru 1:2). Ephrath was the dwelling place of Ruth and Boaz (Ru 4:11), the childhood home of David (1 Sm 17:12), and the announced birthplace of the Messiah (Mi 5:2).
   See also Bethlehem #1.
2. District in which the city of Kiriath-jearim was situated and where the ark of the covenant was kept (Ps 132:6).

EPHRATHITE Inhabitant of the town of Ephrath (Bethlehem) in Judah (1 Sm 17:12). *See* Ephrath (Place) #1.

EPHRON (Person) Hittite from whom Abraham purchased the cave of Machpelah with its adjoining field for 400 shekels of silver (Gn 23:8-17). Sarah was buried there, as was Abraham (25:9) and Jacob (50:13).

EPHRON (Place)
1. Mountainous district on the northern edge of Judah (Jos 15:9).
2. City near Bethel, captured by Abijah (2 Chr 13:19); perhaps the Ophrah of Joshua 18:23.

EPICUREANS Those who followed the teachings of the Greek philosopher Epicurus (342–270 BC). Paul encountered some of them while in Athens (Acts 17:18).

Epicurus spent his childhood on the island of Samos, near the western coast of what is today Turkey. In his late teens he moved to Athens for military service. After his tour of duty, he devoted his time to the study and teaching of philosophy. This work took him from Athens, but he returned in 307 BC to found a school. He attracted a considerable following, and his disciples spread his message throughout the civilized world. The fact that Paul met Epicureans over three centuries after the death of Epicurus shows both the attractiveness of his teachings and the commitment of his disciples. In the first century BC these teachings found expression in the writing of the Roman poet Lucretius. His *On the Nature of Things* is a helpful guide to understanding Epicurus, especially since only fragments of Epicurus's own writings remain.

The Epicureans were empiricists; they relied upon sense experience for knowledge. This put them in opposition to those who chose to make statements about the world on the basis of reason alone, distrusting or rejecting the data of the senses. Epicureans were concerned with natural evidence and with practicalities, thus showing a somewhat scientific character. They were unenthusiastic about mathematics because of what they took to be its abstract quality, having little to do with the important matters of living. Ethics, the study of right behavior, was their focus.

The Epicurean judged the value of an action or thing in terms of the pleasure or pain it brought—a position called hedonism. It was egoistic hedonism because the person sought his own pleasure rather than the pleasure of others. This description can bring to mind the image of an irresponsible glutton or lover of wild parties, but this image, encouraged by the modern sense of the word "epicurean," is misleading. Epicurus rejected just such behavior. He realized that momentary pleasure can lead to enduring pain and that some pain can be beneficial. He viewed pleasure more as a quality of life than a series of thrills. What he sought is better called happiness. Basing his counsel on experience, he urged moderation, calm, friendship, a simple life. He avoided feasting, sexual passion, and strife. In fact, he avoided pain more than he sought pleasure. The pleasure of tranquillity, of peace, could be found in the absence of pain, and this was his aim. To ensure tranquillity, a man must tend to his stomach, but he must also attend to his mind, directing it toward wisdom.

Epicurus saw belief in gods as a serious threat to tranquillity. Gods were generally viewed as meddling and powerful beings who terrified ordinary mortals—sources of insecurity, not peace and happiness. Epicurus taught that the gods were not, in fact, like this but were tranquil hedonists who stayed away from men. They avoided the strife involved in contact with people on earth. In short, they were nothing to fear.

Epicurus taught that we, and everything in our world, are made up of atoms of different qualities. For example, the atoms of the human soul are smooth and round. Although atomic theories often lead to the conviction that all human actions are determined by the laws that rule the motion of atoms, Epicurus's theory did not. He allowed for human freedom by claiming that some atoms spontaneously leave their straight paths, thus setting off an unpredictable chain of collisions. Man's behavior is then free and not machinelike.

In spite of his freedom, man is still a collection of atoms, and when the atoms separate, the man ceases to exist; he is not immortal. Epicurus saw this as reason no longer to fear death. For after death, all experience ceases. There will be no pain, and so there is no cause for anxiety.

Epicurean themes can be found in the Bible—for example, moderation (Phil 4:5) and the peace that comes from the exercise of wisdom (Prv 3:13-18). But the differences are clear. The Bible reveals a God who is intimately involved in the world; the immortality of man's soul; and the truth that genuine happiness depends upon communion with and service to God (Phil 4:6-7).

See also Philosophy.

EPIGRAPHY* The study of ancient inscriptions. *See* Inscriptions (Alphabet).

EPILEPSY*, EPILEPTIC Disease of the central nervous system, and one afflicted with the disease, characterized by unconsciousness and convulsions. Seizures can be either petit mal (twitching of the face or hands, brief but sharp abdominal pain, and possible momentary unconsciousness) or grand mal (convulsions, foaming at the mouth, and unconsciousness lasting from 5 to 20 minutes). Although the causes of epilepsy are still not known, drugs are available to prevent or control the seizures.

In biblical times, epilepsy (known as the "falling sickness") could not be treated effectively. Jesus healed a boy evidently suffering from that affliction (Mt 17:14-18; Mk 9:17-27; Lk 9:37-42). The KJV description of the boy as a "lunatic" (from Latin *luna*, "moon") is an incorrect usage. The Greek word in Matthew (literally "moonstruck") reflected ancient belief in a connection between certain diseases and the lunar phases. According to the biblical account, the youth was healed when Jesus called

forth a demon, or "unclean spirit," from him. *See* Medicine and Medical Practice.

EPIPHANES Name taken by Antiochus IV, meaning the "Manifest God." Alexander Balas also used the name Epiphanes in his claim to the kingship. *See* Antiochus IV; Alexander Epiphanes.

EPISTLE* *See* Letter Writing, Ancient.

EPISTLE OF THE APOSTLES* *See* Apocrypha (Apostles, Epistle of the).

EPISTLES*, Apocryphal Writings in epistolary form and apocryphal in nature. *See* Apocrypha (Apocryphal Epistles).

ER
1. Eldest son of Judah and Bathshua, a Canaanite woman (Gn 38:3). The Lord killed him before he and his wife, Tamar, could have any children (Gn 38:7; 46:12; 1 Chr 2:3).
2. Grandson of Judah and father of Lecah (1 Chr 4:21); a nephew of #1 above.
3. Joshua's son and an ancestor of Joseph, the husband of Mary (Lk 3:28). *See* Genealogy of Jesus Christ.

ERAN Grandson of Ephraim and the oldest son of Shuthelah (Nm 26:36), from whom came the Eranite family. In 1 Chronicles 7:20, Eran was replaced by Eleadah, which may be a copyist's error.

ERASTUS Name mentioned three times in the NT. Whether only one individual is being referred to cannot be ascertained, although in each case Erastus is an associate of Paul's. The three instances are (1) a helper of Paul sent with Timothy into Macedonia (Acts 19:22); (2) the city treasurer of Corinth (a steward of financial affairs, possibly a slave or freedman of some wealth and an important man in the Corinthian community), who sends greetings with Paul to the church in Rome (Rom 16:23); and (3) a friend of Paul's who stayed at Corinth (2 Tm 4:20).

ERECH Important Sumerian city, located at what is now called Warka near the Euphrates River, 40 miles (64.4 kilometers) northwest of Ur and 160 miles (257.4 kilometers) south of Baghdad. Genesis 10:10 refers to Erech as the second of four cities founded by Nimrod. Partial excavations have uncovered the city walls (6 miles, or 9.7 kilometers, in circumference), canals, and the remains of elegant buildings with fluted walls decorated with colored cones and inscriptions. Two ziggurats are among the oldest ever discovered, and several temples date back to the late fourth or early third millennium BC. The use of clay cylinder seals began in Erech, and from the same period have come hundreds of pictographic inscriptions.

Ancient inscriptions indicate that Erech and its surroundings were regarded as extremely beautiful and fertile. Its religious pantheon centered on the aggressive goddess of love, Inanna, who was supposed to have brought to Erech the "divine laws" to which it owed its greatness. She helped Erech to subjugate its enemies and married King Dumuzi to ensure the fertility and prosperity of Sumer. Dumuzi, in turn, was identified with Tammuz, the fertility god widely worshiped in Mesopotamia and Palestine.

Among Erech's rulers in the third millennium was Gilgamesh, hero of the great Akkadian epic. From the time of Hammurabi, Erech became part of Babylonia, and it continued to flourish until after 300 BC. Ezra 4:9 refers to "Archevites" (KJV), or men of Arku, the Assyrian name from which the Hebrew "Erech" is derived. Strabo, Ptolemy, and Pliny mention its renown as a center of learning, chiefly astronomical.

ERI Gad's fifth son (Gn 46:16) and founder of the Erite family (Nm 26:16).

ESAIAS* KJV form of Isaiah the prophet, in the NT. *See* Isaiah (Person).

ESARHADDON King of Assyria (681–669 BC). Though probably not the eldest son of Sennacherib, he was the eldest surviving son following several interfamily murders. Sennacherib was assassinated by his sons Adrammelech and Sharezer, and civil war ensued between their supporters and those who accepted the youthful, newly proclaimed king, Esarhaddon. As the threat from the brothers was eliminated by death or exile, Esarhaddon solidified his position. He ruled from Nineveh and proclaimed his twin sons, Ashurbanipal and Samas-sum-ukin, crown princes of Assyria and Babylonia but his attempt thus to ensure a smooth changeover of rule at his own death was frustrated.

Esarhaddon's immediate task was to settle the rebellious border areas, which he did by launching military campaigns. He installed governors he could rely on, and he increased substantially the level of tribute required. Some kings were replaced and others subsequently restored. Of the latter, Manasseh (2 Chr 33:11), taken in chains to Babylon, later continued to reign in Jerusalem, although this incident may not have taken place until the reign of Ashurbanipal. Of the strong cities, Sidon was finally subdued, but Esarhaddon was forced to come to terms with Baslu, king of Tyre.

In 675 BC, Esarhaddon invaded Egypt and destroyed the royal city of Memphis, together with many other towns and cities. Prince Taharqa, who had fled to Nubia on the initial invasion, continued to rule over Egypt and subsequently led a rebellion against Esarhaddon. During his second Egyptian campaign, Esarhaddon succumbed to a fatal sickness.

Esarhaddon was a strong, cruel, and fearless ruler who was proud of his achievements. He maintained dominion over a vast area, claiming control not only of Babylonia and Syria but also of Egypt and Ethiopia, the lands bordering on Assyria, and some of the islands of the eastern Mediterranean. He built a palace at Karesarhaddon near Nineveh and restored the fabled temple of Ashur originally constructed by Shalmaneser I about 1250 BC. He commemorated the deeds of his reign on numerous stelae and prisms. Esarhaddon is mentioned in 2 Kings 19:37, Ezra 4:2, and Isaiah 37:38.

See also Assyria, Assyrians.

ESAU Isaac's son, and the older twin brother of Jacob (Gn 25:24-26), who was given this name because of the hair on his body at birth. The reddish color of the baby, together with the color appearing in the episode of the lentil soup (v 30), led to the use of the term Edom, or "red." The Edomites claimed to be descended from Esau, and naming their land Seir may have been an attempt to retain an association with the word *sair*, meaning "hairy."

A proficient hunter, Esau brought tasty wild meat to his father, who enjoyed its stronger flavor much more than that of the mild meat provided from the family flocks by Jacob. On a certain day Esau returned home from an unsuccessful hunting expedition; he was very hungry. Esau was persuaded by Jacob to surrender his birthright in return for food (Gn 25:29-34).

Archaeological information from Nuzi shows that giving up the birthright to another member of the family was not unknown. Esau's marriage to two local women who were not descendants of Abraham made life extremely difficult for his parents (Gn 26:34-35). This may have been the reason why his mother, Rebekah, decided to coach Jacob to obtain the patriarchal blessing that normally belonged to his elder brother Esau (ch 27). Esau's anger on discovering the deception of his brother prompted Jacob to leave for Haran, though 20 years later, through the generous forgiveness of Esau, the brothers were reunited (33:4-16).

At birth Jacob had come into the world grasping the heel of Esau, an omen that was interpreted to show that the Edomite descendants of Esau would be subject to the offspring of Jacob. The subservient relationship between the Edomites and the Israelites in the time of David (2 Sm 8:11-15; 1 Chr 18:13) continued until the time of Jehoram (2 Kgs 8:20-22; 2 Chr 21:8-10). Following a rebellion in 845 BC, the Edomites gained their independence for a while but were reconquered by Amaziah (796–767 BC). Regaining their freedom in 735 BC, they subsequently remained independent of Judah. *See* Edom, Edomites.

ESCHATOLOGY* Branch of theology concerned with the study of the last things, or end times, whether in relation to the individual or the world.

Topics of Eschatology

Death The Bible teaches that all humans will die (Heb 9:27). The only exceptions will be those who are still alive when Christ returns (1 Thes 4:17). Physical death, or the "first death," is the separation of the soul from the body. Because of the presence of sin in the world, everyone must die (Rom 5:12).

The Intermediate State This refers to the condition of the person between the time of death and the resurrection. The traditional orthodox view is that believers experience a state of conscious bliss in the presence of the Lord, while unbelievers are tormented by separation from the presence of God. This, however, is a relatively incomplete state when compared with the final destiny of each. Some groups, such as Seventh-Day Adventists, have held a belief in a type of "soul sleep," or unconsciousness, between death and resurrection. Still others, notably Roman Catholics, believe in a place of purging in preparation for the future life.

The Second Coming Scripture teaches that at the end of time Christ will return in a personal, bodily form (Acts 1:11). No one knows exactly when this will occur, and it will consequently catch some by surprise, coming as a thief in the night (Lk 12:39-40). Although the time is not known, the fact that it will occur is very definite. Many of Jesus' parables (especially in Mt 24–25) refer to this fact and to the appropriateness of alert, faithful, and intensive activity.

The Resurrection All who have died will come to life. This will be a bodily resurrection, a resumption of the bodily existence of each person. For believers, this will take place in connection with the second coming of Christ and will involve the transformation of the body of this present flesh into a new, perfected body (1 Cor 15:35-56). The Bible also indicates a resurrection of unbelievers, unto eternal death (Jn 5:28-29).

The Judgment There will be a time of judgment in which the Lord will determine the spiritual condition of all who have lived, based on their relationship to him. On these grounds some will be sent off to everlasting reward and others to eternal punishment. Some theologians distinguish between the times when believers and unbelievers will be judged. Some see as many as seven different judgments occurring.

The Final States The Bible teaches the existence of heaven, a place of eternal joy, where Christians are in the presence of God. The Bible also speaks of hell (specifically Gehenna, or the lake of fire), a state of anguished separation of unbelievers from the presence of God. These are fixed states, determined by decisions made within this life.

The Millennium Many Christians believe there will be an earthly reign of Jesus Christ, called the Millennium, immediately preceding the final judgment. This belief is based on Revelation 20:4-7. Those who hold that Christ will return personally to inaugurate this period are called premillennialists. Others, who teach that the kingdom will be established through the progressive successful preaching of the gospel, are termed postmillennialists. Still others, called amillennialists, do not believe that there will be any earthly reign of Christ at all, interpreting the 1,000 years of Revelation 20 symbolically.

WATCH OUT

Sometimes eschatology has been a divisive force within Christian circles because believers have quarreled over minor points. In some cases denominations in which there was agreement on the major doctrines of eschatology have split over a minor point, such as the tribulational views. Another danger to be avoided is date setting. While we are to be alert to the "signs of the times," we must remember that God has not revealed the exact time of our Lord's return to any human being, or even to the angels (Mt 24:36). Some have believed that they could determine the exact time of the Lord's return. When their calculations proved incorrect, these believers had their faith jeopardized as a result.

Properly understood and applied, eschatology has a powerful positive significance for Christians. It is to be a source of comfort (1 Thes 4:18) and encouragement (1 Cor 15:58); it challenges Christians to watchfulness and faithful service (Mt 25:14-30). Because the time is limited, Christians are to use faithfully the opportunities that are theirs. Because of the certainty of our Lord's return, we are to be filled with hope and courage.

The Great Tribulation The Bible speaks of a time of great anguish or tribulation, which will come upon the earth, exceeding anything that has ever occurred before. Some, identifying this with the 70th week of Daniel 9:24-27, believe it will be of seven years duration. Some believe the church will be present to experience this because the Lord will not return until the end of the period. These are termed posttribulationists. Others, known as pretribulationists, believe that the Lord's second coming will be in two stages, or phases: (1) Christ will come for his church to take the believers away before the great Tribulation; (2) Christ will then make an open display of his glory before the whole world. Still others, known as midtribulationists, believe that the church will be present for the first half of the seven years

but will be removed before the severe part of the Tribulation begins.

See also Apocalyptic; Day of the Lord; Death; Eternal Life; Heaven; Hell; Intermediate State; Judgment; Last Days; Last Judgment; Millennium; Resurrection; Second Coming of Christ; Daniel, Book of; Tribulation; Wrath of God.

ESDRAS, First Book of Book that is largely a compilation of material from 2 Chronicles, Ezra, and Nehemiah.

PREVIEW
• Author and Date
• Background
• Content

Author and Date The author or compiler of 1 Esdras is unknown, and scholars disagree about its origin. Three theories seem to summarize the critical debate. Some think that 1 Esdras might be the original Septuagint (ancient Greek Old Testament) version, and that canonical Ezra and Nehemiah reflect the translation and editing of Theodotion, a second-century AD reviser of the Septuagint. Others speculate that 1 Esdras goes back to a now-lost Hebrew text outside the Masoretic Hebrew Text tradition. Most scholars, however, think that 1 Esdras is probably an edited compilation taken from the Septuagint translation of 2 Chronicles, Ezra, and Nehemiah.

Esdras (or Ezra, the spelling most familiar to American Protestants) was a descendant of Aaron's priestly line and one of those (like Nehemiah and Zerubbabel) who led parties of exiled Jews back to Judea from Babylon. His ministry of leadership, and preservation and promulgation of the law, probably can be dated to the latter part of Persian king Artaxerxes I Longimanus's reign (465–424 BC).

It is certain that 1 Esdras was written before AD 90 because first-century Jewish historian Josephus quoted from it. The best date for 1 Esdras is probably around 150–100 BC.

Background There are four books about Ezra and the history of the postexilic restoration of the Jews in Judea. Two of those books, titled Ezra and Nehemiah in Protestant versions of the Bible, are accepted as canonical by Jews, Roman Catholics, and Protestants alike. The other two books, 1 Esdras and 2 Esdras, were not included in the Hebrew canon of the OT by Jews or by Protestants, who followed Hebrew tradition in identifying the books of the OT. The two Esdras books were included in the Latin Vulgate Bible (a translation from the Hebrew by biblical scholar Jerome completed in AD 404), and when the Roman Catholic Council of Trent (1545–1663) defined the apocryphal books that would be recognized by Catholics as part of the OT Scriptures, 1 and 2 Esdras were included. In the Vulgate, 1 Esdras is called 3 Esdras; Ezra and Nehemiah there are named 1 Esdras and 2 Esdras, respectively.

Content First Esdras is a history of the Jews from the reign of King Josiah in Jerusalem (640–609 BC) through the postexilic ministry of Ezra, accentuating the career of Ezra and deletes all mention of Nehemiah. Originally written in idiomatic Greek, 1 Esdras retells the material found in 2 Chronicles 35:1–36:23, Ezra 1:1–10:44 (excluding 4:6 and placing 4:7-24 before 2:1), and Nehemiah 7:73–8:12. Esdras contains two sections of material, one minor (1:23-24) and the other major, not found in the canonical records. The major addition (3:1–4:63) is a story about three youths who are bodyguards or pages of Darius I of Persia (522–486 BC). They engage in a contest to determine whether wine, royal power, or women are the strongest. The third youth, Zerubbabel, argues for women but adds "truth" as part of his argument, and thereby wins the verbal contest. For his reward he requests permission to rebuild the temple in Jerusalem, which Darius grants. The story concludes with the preparations for Zerubbabel's temple-building expedition. Thus, 1 Esdras differs from canonical Ezra and Nehemiah by placing Zerubbabel's return under Darius I rather than under Cyrus (559–530 BC).

ESDRAS, Second Book of
Composite Jewish and Christian writing included in some canons of the Bible (see discussion above under 1 Esdras).

PREVIEW
• Author
• Date
• Background
• Purpose and Theological Teaching

Author The core of 2 Esdras (chs 3–14) possibly was written by a Palestinian Jew. Two additions (chs 1–2 and 15–16) were written by later, unknown Christian authors. Some students of the text think it may originally have been written in Hebrew, though the extant manuscripts consist only of Greek and Coptic fragments and full Syriac, Ethiopic, Arabic, Armenian, Georgian, and Latin versions.

Date Most textual critics date the Jewish portions of the book to around AD 95–100. Chapters 1 and 2 are thought to have been written about AD 200 or later. Chapters 15 and 16 are variously dated from AD 120 to 300 because they seem to reflect Christian persecution conditions.

Background Second Esdras was written in an apocalyptic style. Jewish or Christian apocalypses, often produced during periods of persecution, portray a certain prophetic viewpoint about God's ultimate purpose in history, with highly descriptive and symbolic language. Such writings were prevalent between 200 BC and AD 350, dates that embraced the persecution of Jews in the Maccabean period, the armed conflict between zealot Judaism and Rome, and persecution of Christians in the Roman Empire. A common thread among Jewish apocalypses was the destiny of Israel or Judaism. Second Esdras 14 mentions a restoration of the "sacred books" to Ezra through a series of visions as he prepared to die. Along with 24 OT books, 70 esoteric apocalypses are alluded to, indicating that to the author and his readers the apocalypse was a popular phenomenon. Jews at that time thought that prophecy had come to an end, so the author used a standard apocalyptic device of putting supposed revelations in the mouth of an earlier prophetic figure. Here the author is supposedly Ezra writing 30 years after the destruction of Jerusalem by the Babylonians.

The Jewish core of the apocalypse (chs 3–14) was evidently titled "Ezra the Prophet," or "The Apocalypse of Ezra." It became known as 4 Esdras from the Latin Vulgate Bible (a translation from the Hebrew by biblical scholar Jerome completed in AD 404) and is known as 3 Esdras in the Septuagint (the ancient Greek OT). The book is called 2 Esdras in Protestant versions. The Christian additions were sometimes circulated separately. Chapters 1 and 2 were called 5 Esdras, and chapters 15 and 16 were titled 6 Esdras. The so-called "Confession of Ezra" (8:20-36) also circulated separately, adding to the confusion of manuscripts, texts, and editions.

Purpose and Theological Teaching The occasion for the writing of 2 Esdras was the destruction of Jerusalem and the temple by the Romans in AD 70. The book attempts to provide a brighter hope for the Jews' future.

The Jewish portion of the book grapples with some basic theological questions. Why does God not reward the piety of the faithful instead of letting them suffer under pagan rule? Why does God allow humans to have evil in their hearts? When God gave his law, why did he not remove people's evil inclination so they could keep the law? Why are humans given understanding but denied answers to these questions? No final answers are given, and Ezra is reminded that God's ways are inscrutably higher than man's. Such problems will be solved only in the end-of-the-age occurrences themselves: the manifestation of God's justice in a 400-year rule by the Messiah, the resurrection, the judgment, and eternal reward in heaven or punishment in Gehenna (hell). Ezra is told that God does rejoice in the righteous few, however, and Ezra and those like him are assured of their salvation.

Second Esdras is considered to be one of the best and most profound of the Jewish apocalypses. Its perceptive theological concern and daring analysis gave it broad appeal in the revelation of things to come. The fourth vision is of a mourning woman who is transformed into the heavenly Jerusalem, typifying Zion's eventual redemption. In vision five an eagle with 12 wings and three heads—usually thought to be Rome's Flavian emperors Vespasian (69–79), Titus (79–81), and Domitian (81–96)—is equated with the fourth beast in the book of Daniel (Dn 7). Ezra witnesses the eagle's destruction by a lion, symbolizing the Messiah. A man rising from the sea and attacked by "an innumerable multitude," which he destroys, comprises vision six and again speaks of the Messiah's victories. In the last vision Ezra dictates the contents of 94 sacred books to five specially chosen scribes, and prepares for his assumption into heaven.

Chapters 15 and 16 threaten judgment on heathen nations for their unbelief and comfort God's people who are suffering persecution.

ESDRIS Mentioned in 2 Maccabees 12:36 as an army officer under Judas Maccabeus. Some Greek texts and the KJV read Gorgias, which may be either a place or a person.

ESEK* Name Isaac gave to a well dug by his servants in the valley of Gerar (Gn 26:20; see NLT mg). The name means "argument." When the herdsmen of Gerar claimed it belonged to them, Isaac relinquished Esek and another well, called Sitnah, to induce the men of Gerar to allow him to live peacefully in the land.

ESHAN Town in the hill country of the territory allotted to Judah's tribe for an inheritance (Jos 15:52).

ESHBAAL King Saul's fourth son, who became Israel's king after his father's death. Eshbaal literally means "man of Baal," or "Baal exists" (1 Chr 8:33; 9:39). During the period of the judges and the early monarchy, many Hebrew names were compounded with "baal," a word that can mean "master" or "possessor." Later generations were reluctant to speak the name "baal," so "bosheth" (shame) was substituted (cf. Hos 2:16-17). Thus, Eshbaal was altered to Ishbosheth (2 Sm 2:8), which means "man of shame." Perhaps later copyists changed the name in the book of Samuel because it was read aloud in synagogue services, whereas Chronicles was not.

After the death of Saul and his older sons, Abner, commander of Saul's army, installed Ishbosheth as Israel's king (2 Sm 2:8-9). Judah's tribe, however, followed King David, who struggled with Ishbosheth for leadership of all the tribes. The conflict lasted a long time, but the house of David gradually overwhelmed the house of Saul (3:1). Abner deserted Ishbosheth and was murdered by Joab, one of David's men (v 27), thus removing an important leader of Israel and causing the people to despair (4:1). Soon afterward Ishbosheth was murdered by two of his captains (v 7). Although David disapproved of the deaths of Abner and Ishbosheth, the last obstacles to his kingship over all the tribes had been removed.

See also David; Israel, History of; Saul #2.

ESHBAN Dishon's second son and grandson of Seir the Horite (Gn 36:26; 1 Chr 1:41).

ESHCOL (Person) Amorite who, with his brothers Mamre and Aner, helped the patriarch Abraham defeat the forces of Kedorlaomer and rescue Lot and his family (Gn 14:13, 24).

ESHCOL (Place) Valley near Hebron from which the spies sent by Moses brought back pomegranates, figs, and a large cluster of grapes (Nm 13:23-24; 32:9; Dt 1:24). This site may be identifiable with 'Ain Eshkali, just north of Hebron.

ESHEAN* KJV spelling of the town Eshan in Joshua 15:52. *See* Eshan.

ESHEK Descendant of Jonathan, Saul's son. Eshek's grandsons were mighty men of valor in the tribe of Benjamin (1 Chr 8:38-40).

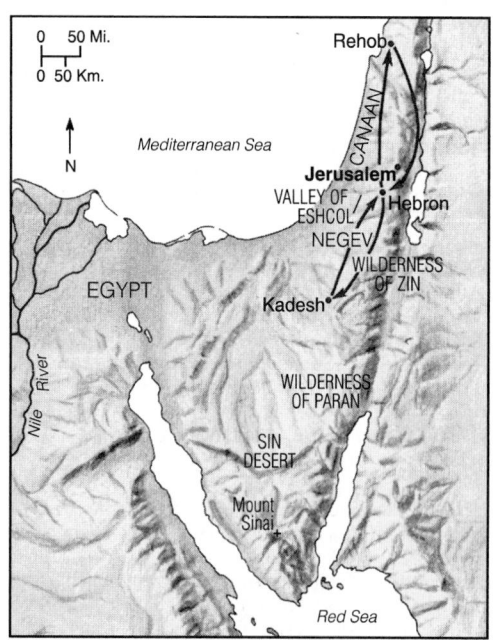

Valley of Eshcol The spies traveled from Kadesh-barnea, through the valley of Eshcol, to Rehob, and back again—a total of 500 miles (804.5 kilometers).

ESHKALONITE* Inhabitant of the Philistine city Ashkelon (Jos 13:3, KJV). *See* Ashkelon.

ESHTAOL Lowland town on the border between Judah and Dan (Jos 15:33; 19:41), always mentioned along with nearby Zorah. In this area the young Samson began to be moved by the Spirit of the Lord (Jgs 13:25), and here he was later buried (16:31). Dan's tribe sent out five brave men from Zorah and Eshtaol to seek additional land for tribal expansion. When they reported the vulnerability of the city of Laish, 600 men from Zorah and Eshtaol attacked it, opening the area for occupation by the Danites (ch 18).

ESHTEMOA (Person)
1. Ishbah's son from Judah's tribe (1 Chr 4:17).
2. Maacathite from Judah's tribe (1 Chr 4:19).

ESHTEMOA, ESHTEMOH (Place) City south of Jerusalem allotted to Judah when Palestine was divided among the 12 tribes (Jos 15:50). Eshtemoa was assigned to the Levites (Jos 21:14; 1 Chr 6:57). After an Amalekite victory, David sent booty to his allies in Eshtemoa (1 Sm 30:26-31). The site may be modern al-Samu'a, eight miles (13 kilometers) south of Hebron.

See also Levitical Cities.

ESHTON Mehir's son and the grandson of Chelub from Judah's tribe (1 Chr 4:11-12).

ESLI Nahum's father and ancestor of Jesus, according to Luke's genealogy (3:25). *See* Genealogy of Jesus Christ.

ESPOUSAL* *See* Marriage, Marriage Customs.

ESROM* KJV rendering of Hezron, Perez's son, in Matthew 1:3 and Luke 3:33. *See* Hezron (Person) #2.

ESSENES* Jewish sect or community in Palestine in the last century BC and the first century AD.

PREVIEW
•The Name
•Sources of Information
•Origin and History
•Admission to the Sect
•Community Life
•Religious Beliefs
•The Essenes and the Qumran Community

The Name The sect is called *Esseni, Osseni, Ossaei, Essaeans,* and other variations; sometimes two different forms are found in the same author. No satisfactory explanation of the name has been given, but a number of scholars tend to prefer "healers," which hardly seems likely since the term describes the Therapeutae ("Healers"), a sect that was only distantly related to the Essenes, if at all.

Sources of Information The principal sources of information about the Essenes are (1) Philo of Alexandria, a Jew who lived in Egypt from about 30 BC to sometime after AD 40, in his works *Let Every Good Man Be Free* and *Apology for the Jews;* (2) Flavius Josephus, a Jew of Palestine and later of Rome, who lived from AD 37 to about AD 100, in his works *War of the Jews* and *Jewish Antiquities*—our most extensive sources; (3) Pliny the Elder, a Roman who died in AD 79 and who may have been in Palestine with Titus during the Jewish War, in his *Natural History;* and (4) Hippolytus of Rome, in his work

A Refutation of All Heresies, written about AD 230 and largely dependent on Josephus.

Josephus tells us that he determined to know the three Jewish "sects" intimately, so he joined the Essenes when he was 16. But since he was a Pharisee by the time he was 19, and since it took at least three years for the initiatory rites of the Essenes, we must conclude that he did not have time or opportunity to learn much about the inner life of the Essenes.

Origin and History The first mention of the Essenes, as well as that of the Pharisees and the Sadducees, is in the time of Jonathan (160–143 BC), successor of Judas Maccabeus (see Josephus's *Antiquities* 13.5.9). Josephus calls these groups "sects" (Greek *haireseis*), a term that sometimes connotes heretical movements, but this is a later meaning of the word. Luke uses the very same term for Pharisees (Acts 15:5; 26:5), Sadducees (5:17), and Christians (24:5, 14; 28:22).

The Maccabean revolt began in 167 BC. The background of the uprising had been a struggle between the Seleucid Greeks and the Ptolemaic Greeks, with Palestine as the object of the struggle. The Seleucids won in 198 BC, but there were pro-Syrian and pro-Egyptian parties in Judea. Moreover, Hellenism, which was strongly promoted by the Seleucids, had taken a deep hold on many Jews. In order to participate in the athletic games, some Jews even resorted to operations to obliterate the sign of circumcision (1 Macc 1:15). In 168 the Seleucid king Antiochus IV Epiphanes sold the Jewish high priesthood to the highest bidder, Menelaus. When this was rejected by the Jewish populace, violent persecution broke out. Somewhere along the line a group of pious Jews came into existence, and they joined the Maccabees in the revolt. We know them as the Hasidim (or Hasideans, Assideans, "pious ones"; cf. 1 Macc 2:42).

Because of numerous similarities in doctrine, it is generally accepted that the Pharisees are either the direct descendants of the Hasidim or one of two or more groups of descendants. It is further generally accepted that the Essenes are a group that split either from the Pharisees or from the Hasidim. Qumran (the community of the Dead Sea Scrolls) is looked upon either as a branch of the Essenes or as another closely related group of separatists whose origin was at approximately the same point in time.

Josephus speaks of only three Jewish sects: Pharisees, Sadducees, and Essenes (*Antiquities* 18.1.2). Therefore, it is often concluded that these were the only Jewish sects at that time. This is a false conclusion. We know of at least seven Jewish sects, and perhaps as many as twelve. There is probably some overlap, and it is not always clear whether a particular group should be described as a religious party (e.g., the Zealots). But we can argue against Josephus's number of sects by other data he supplies. According to Josephus, there were 6,000 Pharisees (*Antiquities* 17.2.4) and 4,000 Essenes (*Antiquities* 18.1.5; cf. Philo's *Every Good Man* 76), and the Sadducees were fewer in number than the Pharisees (cf. *Wars* 2.8.14). This would account for, at most, 16,000 persons, and the population of Judea was well beyond that figure. Moreover, Josephus himself speaks of a "fourth philosophy" (*Antiquities* 18.1.6), which some scholars identify with the Zealots, although Josephus never does so. We can only conclude that in Josephus's view there were three principal sects or groups of Jews.

The Essenes left the cities of Palestine and lived in the towns and villages. Pliny locates them west of the Dead Sea and says, "Below them was En-gedi" (*Natural History* 5.15.73), a statement that could mean either that

En-gedi was at a lower elevation or that it was to the south. Scholars are not unanimous in the interpretation of this statement.

Admission to the Sect Admission to the Essenes was a long, complicated process, consisting of one year as a postulant and two additional years of limited participation in the community. The novice took solemn oaths, which included his relationship to God and to his fellow members. He swore to hate the wicked and to love truth, to conceal nothing from the community and to reveal nothing to outsiders, and to transmit doctrines exactly as he received them. Until he took these oaths, he could not touch the food of the community.

Community Life When a new member joined the Essenes, he turned over all property to the community. The individual members were without goods, property, or homes. They lived frugally, having only what was necessary for life. They despised riches, had no slaves, and did not engage in commerce. They worked in fields or at crafts that contributed to peace, and would not make instruments of war. They dwelt in brotherhoods, ate together, held property in common, had a common purse and a common store of clothing. They always wore white clothing.

Evidence is somewhat confusing about their views on marriage. They either banned it entirely or disdained it, counting continence as one of their virtues. There were Essenes who did marry, but these looked upon the marriage relationship as existing only for the purpose of raising children so that the race might continue.

There is also mixed evidence concerning children. According to Philo, they had no children, no adolescents, not even young men. Josephus, on the other hand, tells us that they adopted children, and the Essenes who married raised children of their own.

The Essenes were divided into four lots or ranks and would do nothing unless ordered by superiors, except for works of mercy. They obeyed their elders. Justice was dispensed at an assembly of 100 members or more. For serious offenses the penalty was expulsion from the community, and the expelled member usually starved to death because of the tremendous oaths he had taken.

A Typical Day Josephus describes a typical day in the life of the Essenes. They rose before dawn and recited prayers to the rising sun (which probably is not to be interpreted as sun worship). Then each man worked at his craft until the fifth hour (11 AM). At that time the community assembled, put on linen loincloths, bathed in cold water, and then went to the building that was restricted to members, to a dining hall that was further restricted to those who were pure. Each Essene received bread and one bowlful of food. The priest said a prayer before anyone was permitted to touch the food, and another prayer after the meal. Then the members laid aside their sacred garments and resumed their work until evening. The evening meal was in the same manner as the noon meal. They ate quietly and spoke only in turn, eating and drinking only what they needed to satisfy them.

Religious Beliefs It is somewhat risky to attempt to reconstruct Essene theology from Josephus and Philo, for both of these writers thought in philosophical rather than theological forms.

The Essenes were not concerned with logic or natural philosophy, but rather devoted themselves to ethics. Josephus likens them to the Greek Pythagoreans (*Antiquities* 15.10.4), but he does not explain this further. The Essenes were concerned with purity and holy minds. They rejected oaths (apparently excepting the tremendous oath they took upon entering the sect), and considered their word sufficient. They observed the seventh day, going to synagogues and sitting according to age. One would read and another explain, making use of symbols and the triple use of definitions (which may be a reference to the rabbinic method of exegesis). They would do no work on the Sabbath. There is confusion concerning the matter of sacrifices; either they did not offer sacrifices (Philo's *Every Good Man*) or they sacrificed among themselves and did not send sacrifices to the temple (Josephus's *Antiquities* 18.1.5). They did send offerings to the temple, according to this same passage in Josephus. The name of the lawgiver (Moses? or God himself?) was an object of great veneration.

The Essenes studied holy books and were skilled at predicting the future. Josephus tells of one Essene, Menahem, who foretold that Herod would be king (*Antiquities* 15.10.5). They also studied the works of the ancients (which appears to mean works other than the Scriptures), and became proficient in the knowledge of healing, of roots, and of stones. The Essenes believed that their souls were immortal; however, as Josephus seems to have understood this doctrine, the body was "corruptible and its constituent matter impermament" (*War* 2.8.11), which may imply a denial of the resurrection.

The material available to us is hardly satisfactory for reconstructing Essene theology. It is clear, however, that they were Jews, devoted to the law, but with certain emphases or aberrations that set them apart from both the Pharisees and the Sadducees. They were ascetic, although some of them married, and they were pacifists, although Josephus tells of an Essene named John who was a general in the army (*War* 2.20.4). Above all, they were exclusivistic, withdrawing from other Jews and living a communal or communistic type of life.

The Essenes and the Qumran Community There are many similarities between the Essenes and the people of the Dead Sea Scrolls. Both were Jewish sects. Both were communal groups that had withdrawn from the common stream of Judaism. Both were located west of the Dead Sea. Both had long and rigid processes for admission of new members. Both had an oath of admission. Both hated the wicked and loved the members of the community. Both required the handing over of all property to the sect. Both kept their secrets within their own group. The daily life—prayers, ritual bathing, common meals, the study and interpretation of the Bible, and concern with purity—is markedly similar. Scrupulous observance of the Sabbath, the division into ranks or lots, and the authority of elders and superiors are features of each group. Both had a minimum group of ten required for assembly. Both had laws of expulsion for serious offenses.

The differences are also noteworthy and not as often pointed out. Obviously the Qumran community could not have constituted all of the Essenes but were at most a small fraction (perhaps 200) of the 4,000 Essenes. Moreover, they were at best only one of the towns and villages of the Essenes. If Qumranians worked at crafts, we know nothing of it either from their texts or from the archaeology of Qumran. Similarly, we know nothing of their attitude toward war or the implements of war. But we do know from the War Scroll (1QM) that they had an elaborate concept of the final war, with an army, weapons, maneuvers, and the like, and they do not sound like pacifists (cf. 1QS 9:16, 22-23; 10:18; 1QSa 1:19-21). It appears that the Qumranians did engage in commerce (CD 13:14-15). We have no information about any common store of clothing at Qumran. From the Dead Sea literature we know that there were provisions for marriage, for young children, adolescents, and young men. Of course, the Qumranians may have been the marrying Essenes to whom Josephus refers. Admission to the Qumran group was a two-year process; to the Essenes, it was three years.

We know nothing of Qumran prayers to the sun or of daily bathing, although some of the "cisterns" were probably immersion pools. Unlike the Essenes, the Qumranians did use oaths, and there are extended sections on oaths in their literature (CD 9:8-12; 15:1-10; 16:6-18). The Qumran attitude toward sacrifices is not entirely clear, but there is provision for sending sacrifices to the temple. We know of no aversion to oil among the Qumranians, such as is described for the Essenes.

THE ESSENES AND CHRISTIANITY
Some scholars have compared certain sayings of Jesus in the Gospels, certain passages in Acts, and certain statements in Paul's epistles, and constructed a fantasy Christianity that is ascetic, communal, and legalistic. In short, they have painted early Christianity to be an Essene community. Point by point we could demonstrate parallels with Essene beliefs and practices, but such techniques are a denial of true scholarship. Taken as a whole, the teachings of Jesus exalt marriage and the family, and place the rights and proper use of property in the conscience of the owner, while legalism is strongly rejected. The same can certainly be said for the early church as portrayed in Acts and for the teaching of Paul in his epistles. By no proper use of the materials can Christianity be equated with Essenism, or for that matter, with Qumranism.

This is not to deny, however, that there are elements of Essenism that can be compared with elements of Christianity. We should not object to the theory that some Essenes may have heard the gospel and become Christians. Nor is there any sufficient reason to reject the notion that certain Essene ideas could have been influential in the early church. A careful study of the NT will show that there were many currents and crosscurrents in the early church. The differences between Peter and Paul provide only one example out of many. If the ultimate redemptive purpose of God is to remove the divisions that man has erected and to unify those who have been divided (cf. Eph 2:14), then we may properly conclude that the church on earth must be the mixing bowl where all kinds of ingredients are brought together, to be sifted, blended, and purified by God's Spirit.

There is no evidence that the Qumranians used triple definitions in their biblical interpretation. There is a minimum use of symbols in their writings. There is no evidence that they studied the knowledge of healing, roots, or stones. If they were experts at predicting the future, we have no record of it.

The seating arrangement at Qumran was by rank and not by age, as among the Essenes. Rank was altered by an annual examination at Qumran. There is no indication that justice at Qumran was handled by 100 men; rather, it seems to have been administered by a council of 15 (1QS 8:1) or 10 (CD 9:4-5).

In view of the similarities, we must conclude that there was some kind of relationship between the Essenes and the Qumran community. In view of the differences, we are forced to the conclusion that they were not exactly the same. There are several possible explanations: (1) The

Essenes and the Qumranians may have started out as the same split-off from the Hasidim, and then later split again. In fact, the Dead Sea Scrolls, particularly the Damascus Document (CD), hint at some kind of split in the earlier period of the group. (2) The Essenes of Josephus and Philo are about a century later than the literature of the Qumranians, and may have altered somewhat during that period of time. (3) The Essenes were located in a number of towns and villages and they may have developed significant local variations, so that Josephus may have drawn his description from one location, Philo and Pliny from others, while the Qumran group represents yet another local variant form. There is little to guide a preference for any one of these explanations.

See also Dead Sea Scrolls; Judaism; Pharisees; Qumran.

ESTHER (Person)
One of two names borne by the Jewish queen of Persia. Hadassah (Hebrew "Myrtle") apparently was her Jewish name (Est 2:7), and Esther (Persian "Star") her name as queen of Persia. Some scholars speculate about a connection with the Babylonian goddess Ishtar, since exiled Jews were occasionally given pagan names (see Dn 1:7).

Esther was an orphan from the tribe of Benjamin who lived with the Jewish exiles in Persia. She was reared by her cousin Mordecai, a minor government official and covert leader of the Jewish community (see Est 3:5-6) in Susa, capital of the Persian kingdom. Esther became queen after King Ahasuerus (Xerxes) became displeased with Queen Vashti when she refused to obey his command to attend a banquet (1:11-12).

After Esther's coronation, she discreetly won Xerxes' confidence by informing him of an assassination plot (Est 2:21-23). The favor she won in the king's eyes enabled her to deliver her family and her people from a massacre by Haman, a high official to the king.

The Feast of Purim was instituted to celebrate God's deliverance of his people through Esther and Mordecai. This festival is still observed annually by Jews.

See also Esther, Book of.

ESTHER, Additions to
Six passages of about 105 verses added to the Hebrew text of Esther. The Additions to Esther was apparently the work of a Jewish writer eager to supply a spiritual and universal note that was thought to be lacking in the book. Some scholars assert that the additions were originally written in Greek, while others maintain they were translated from Hebrew or possibly Aramaic. The date cannot be determined with certainty, although 100 BC is generally suggested, which would place them considerably later than the canonical Esther.

A summary of the additions is as follows:

1. 11:2–12:6: Mordecai's dream, including the plot against the king's life. This passage preceded Esther 1:1.
2. 13:1-7: The edict of Artaxerxes. This addition follows Esther 3:13, where the king is called Ahasuerus.
3. 13:8–14:19: The prayers of Mordecai and Esther. This passage was to be inserted after Esther 4:17.
4. 15:1-16: The king's anger at Esther's appearance, and his subsequent change of attitude. This was to be inserted before Esther 5:3, since it is an expansion of Esther 5:1-2.
5. 16:1-24: The edict of Ahasuerus relating to the Jews. This section was to follow 8:12.
6. 10:4–11:1: The interpretation of Mordecai's dream. This addition follows 10:3.

The additions contain discrepancies that make it clear they were never part of the original Esther. These can be seen as follows:

1:19 and 8:8 compare 16:17
2:15-18 compare 14:15
2:16-19 compare 11:3–12:1
2:21-23 and 6:3-4 compare 12:5
3:1 compare 16:10
3:5 compare 12:6
5:4-8 compare 14:7
7:10 compare 16:18
9:20-32 compare 16:22

The Septuagint (Greek translation of the OT) and Old Latin texts contained the additions in the text of Esther at the places indicated. Jerome, a fourth-century Christian scholar, put the additions as an appendix in the Vulgate, his Latin translation of the Bible.

ESTHER, Book of
Old Testament book telling the story of a Jewish woman's protection of her people after her marriage to a gentile king.

PREVIEW
• Author
• Date, Origin, and Purpose
• Canonicity
• Background
• Content

Author The book of Esther is an anonymous composition. The reference in 9:20 that Mordecai "recorded these things" implies that part, if not all, of the book was written by him. The absence of God's name in the book of Esther may be due to the fact that the author intended the book to become part of the official Persian court record. The use of God's name might have prevented that from happening.

The author of the book had considerable knowledge of Persian court life and customs. Thus, Mordecai might be identified with a Morduka mentioned as a Persian court official in the reign of Darius I (521–486 BC) and Xerxes (486–464 BC).

Date, Origin, and Purpose Immediate impressions favor a date for the book of Esther shortly after 465 BC, if Ahasuerus is identified with Xerxes, who died that year. Many contemporary scholars, however, favor a later date. The apocryphal book of Ecclesiasticus, written about 180 BC, refers to that period. Jewish heroes are mentioned there, but Esther and Mordecai are not included. Some also suggest the period of the Maccabees as the time of the book's writing. Others have identified it with a cultic story from ancient Babylon, associating Esther with the goddess Ishtar and Mordecai with the god Marduk. The earliest postbiblical reference to the Feast of Purim is 2 Maccabees 15:36, probably written about 75 BC.

The book of Esther claims to record events in Persia sometime during the fifth century BC, surrounding the selection of Esther as queen. If a later date is preferred, the book can be viewed as written to encourage Jews during a time of persecution. One definite purpose of the book of Esther is to explain the origin of the Jewish Feast of Purim (Est 9:16-28). The term "purim" is probably related to the Assyrian word *puru*, meaning a small stone used for casting lots.

Canonicity The major theological problem with the book of Esther is the absence of any mention of God and the lack of even an intimation of divine providence. As a result, some scholars in both Jewish and Christian circles question its canonicity. But closer observation reveals an obvious providential dimension in the book. The reference to fasting in 4:16, for example, implies prayer as well as abstinence from food. Esther's being in the right place at the right time is no accident. The fall of Haman is also not accidental. On the negative side, the extreme measures taken in hanging Haman's sons reflects a collective view of guilt that is not acceptable today (9:13-14). Implicit, too, is the theme of God's protection of his covenant people even in times of persecution. That fact has made the book of Esther a favorite of Jews throughout history.

Its practical implications, however, have not kept some from questioning the book's genuineness as a part of the Bible. The book of Esther appears in the third part of the Jewish canon, as part of the five scrolls known as the Megilloth; its companions there are Ruth, Song of Songs, Ecclesiastes, and Lamentations. The Septuagint (Greek version of the OT) contains 107 extra verses in the book of Esther. These additions form part of the Apocrypha in English versions of the Bible. Even as late as the Reformation era, Esther's canonicity was being debated, and some contemporary evangelicals have raised doubts about its value. Its canonicity is favored by (1) its history of acceptance in both Judaism and the Christian church, and (2) its illustrative value for teaching God's providential care of the Jewish people (see Rom 9–11; Rv 7, 14).

Background A number of historical problems have been noted: (1) Xerxes' known wife was named Amestris, according to the historian Herodotus. But it is likely that the king had more than one wife. (2) The implication that Mordecai went into exile in 597 BC would have made him about 120 years old during the reign of Xerxes. But the text of 2:5-6 might mean that Mordecai's great-grandfather was the original exile rather than Mordecai. (3) Various details seem fanciful to some modern readers: a banquet lasting 180 days; Esther's 12-month beauty treatment; a gallows 83 feet (25.3 meters) tall; the Jews killing 75,000 of Xerxes' subjects (see 1:4; 2:7, 12; 7:9; 9:16). But what appears mythological sometimes turns out to be historical.

Several elements in the book of Esther point to a genuinely historical setting for the book. Ahasuerus is usually identified with Xerxes. Xerxes' father was Darius, from whom have come some notable inscriptions and relief sculptures, one of them showing Darius seated on his throne with Xerxes standing behind him. Xerxes is believed to have been a weak-willed man in domestic affairs, easily influenced by flattering and scheming courtiers. On the field of battle, however, he was a vigorous leader who ferociously pursued his objectives. His energetic suppression of a revolt in Egypt was a prelude to mustering a navy to attack Athens. Only the skill and daring of the Greek forces at the naval battle of Salamis (480 BC) saved Greece from complete Persian occupation. Xerxes eventually lost the war and retired to his elegant palaces at Persepolis and Susa. He rejected the traditional gods of Egypt and Babylon and became a devotee of Ahuramazda, the Persian spirit of good.

Content The book of Esther portrays the reign of King Ahasuerus, whose empire stretched from India to Ethiopia (1:1-9). The center of his empire was in Susa (Shushan), in Persia. Because Queen Vashti disgraced the king by refusing his order to appear in court, she was removed, and a search began for a new queen (1:10-22). A young Jewish woman named Hadassah, without parents and living with her kinsman Mordecai, was selected to replace Queen Vashti (2:1-18). Early in her reign Esther and Mordecai helped to save the king's life (vv 19-23). A man named Haman, who was promoted to an influential position in the palace court, plotted to kill the Jews because he hated Mordecai (ch 3). Mordecai intervened through Queen Esther, and the queen called on the Jews in Susa to fast for deliverance (ch 4). Esther's intervention with the king led to a sleepless night for Ahasuerus (5:1–6:1). He reviewed the records of "memorable deeds," and discovered that Mordecai's earlier help had gone unrewarded. When Haman arrived to initiate his plot against the Jews, the king ordered him to honor Mordecai (ch 6). When Haman's plot was then discovered, the schemer was hanged (ch 7). The king honored Mordecai and sent out an edict protecting the Jews from harm (ch 8). The Jews, by the king's permission, killed the soldiers who would earlier have killed them in Haman's plot (9:1-16). To celebrate their national deliverance, the Jews planned a great celebration (9:17–10:3). That celebration became the Festival of Purim—a time of feasting and distribution of gifts to all, especially to the poor.

See also Esther (Person); Persia, Persians.

ETAM

1. Rocky area in western Judah where Samson hid from his pursuers (Jgs 15:8, 11).
2. Unknown site located in Simeonite territory (1 Chr 4:32).
3. Town in the Judean uplands near Bethlehem fortified by Rehoboam of Judah after the division of the kingdom (2 Chr 11:6). It is identified with Khirbet el-Khokh, just southwest of Bethlehem. The spring at Etam supplied Jerusalem with additional water in the Greek and Roman periods.

ETERNAL LIFE Mode of existence referred to in Scripture characterized by either timelessness or immortality; kind of life attributed to God and distributed to believers. The perspective of the biblical writers flowed from an understanding of a living God who existed prior to the world's creation and who will continue to exist when the end of time arrives. God's gift to those who are obedient and responsible to him is designated as "eternal life" or some such synonym. John's Gospel provides the most definitive material on eternal life.

The phrase "eternal life" occurs only once in the Greek version of the OT (Dn 12:2, with the basic meaning of "the life of the age," designating the life of the age beyond the resurrection from the dead). The primary meaning of "life" in the OT, however, is the quality of well-being in earthly existence.

In the intertestamental period, the rabbinic distinction between "this age" and "the age which is to come" emphasized that the concept of life in the new age consists of a qualitative, rather than simply a quantitative, distinction from the present age.

The Greek word translated "eternal" is derived from the word for "age" or "eon." The setting of the NT within the context of Judaism, with its concept of a living God and the consequent promise of "the age which is to come," gives depth and color to the meaning of the adjective "eternal." Jesus Christ's coming as God's definitive revelation brings the possibility of the qualities of life in the future messianic age into present reality.

The rich young ruler came to Jesus and asked for directions on how to inherit eternal life (Mk 10:17). He was obviously thinking of resurrection in the age to come. Jesus answered in the same terms (v 30).

In his response to the rich young ruler, Jesus equated

the reception of eternal life with entrance into the kingdom of God (Mk 10:23-25). The kingdom of God is not simply a future event but is already inaugurated in Jesus' life, ministry, and teachings. The kingdom is a gift of life available while the follower still lives within the present age. Many of Jesus' parables emphasize this point (e.g., those in Mt 13). The Beatitudes in the Sermon on the Mount (5:3-12) reinforce the concept of a present blessedness that includes salvation, forgiveness, and righteousness. Thus eternal life is a present blessing available to those who submit to God's reign and are enjoying the blessing of this new era of salvation before the final consummation at the present age's end.

The definitive discussion of eternal life comes from John's Gospel. John's purpose delineates the crucial significance of the concept: "But these are written that you may believe that Jesus is the Christ, the Son of God, and that believing you may have life in his name" (Jn 20:31, RSV). The earliest Johannine reference to eternal life is found in John 3:15.

John clearly shared in the Jewish expectation of the age to come with its anticipated blessings (e.g., Jn 3:36; 4:14; 5:29, 39; 6:27; 12:25). Eternal life is defined by the special gifts of the messianic age when it arrives at consummation. Lazarus's resurrection (ch 11) was a living parable demonstrating the future life available to those who trust in Christ. Martha, before her brother's actual resurrection, asserted her belief that Lazarus would be raised on the last day (v 24). Jesus responded that he himself is the resurrection and the life, and that those who believe in him will never die, even if they die physically (vv 25-26).

The central emphasis of John's Gospel, however, does not lie in the anticipated future but in the present experience of that future life. The life of the age to come is already available in Christ to the believer. The metaphors with which Jesus defined his own mission emphasize the present new life: living water that is a spring of water welling up to eternal life (Jn 4:10-14); living bread that satisfies the world's spiritual hunger (6:35-40); the light of the world who leads his followers into the light of life (8:12); the good shepherd who brings abundant life (10:10); the life giver who raises the dead (11:25); the way, the truth, and the life (14:6); and the genuine vine who sustains those who abide in him (15:5).

Jesus was very careful to note that the accomplishment of his mission did not rest in his own nature and ability but in the Father who sent him. Jesus' submission to the Father highlights again the fact that life is a gift of God. Those who believe in the Son of God are recipients of the life that God alone gives—eternal life. Thus the promise of resurrection for all believers, made explicit in Lazarus's resurrection and guaranteed in Christ's resurrection as the "firstfruits" (in Pauline terminology, KJV 1 Cor 15:23), is the natural consequence of God's gift (Jn 5:26-29).

Jesus added further content to the concept of eternal life by connecting it with knowing the true God (Jn 17:3). In Greek thought, knowledge referred to the result of either contemplation or mystical ecstasy. In the OT, however, knowledge meant experience, relationship, fellowship, and concern (cf. Jer 31:34). This connotation of knowledge as intimate relationship is underlined by the usage of the verb form to designate sexual relations between male and female (cf. Gn 4:1). Jesus stated, "I am the good shepherd; I know my own and my own know me, as the Father knows me and I know the Father" (Jn 10:14-15, RSV). The intimate and mutual relationship of Father and Son is the model for the relationship of the Son and his disciples. This knowledge does not come by education or manipulation of the mind but by revelation through the Son (1:18; cf. 14:7).

A brief survey of the primary elements in the concept of eternal life clearly shows that it is not simply an endless or everlasting life. Although there are no final boundaries to eternal life, the Bible's primary emphasis is on the quality of life, especially its divine elements. Eternal life is the importation of the qualities of the age to come into the present through the revelation of a faithful God in Christ, and it brings knowledge of God's relationship with him.

See also Life; New Creation, New Creature; Regeneration.

ETERNAL PUNISHMENT *See* Hell.

ETERNITY Duration of time that cannot be measured.

The OT does not have a single word corresponding to our English word "eternity." The concept grows out of such expressions as "from generation to generation" and "from age to age." The understanding of God as the Creator and controller of history led to the understanding of his endless life span. Thus, God himself is designated by the adjective "eternal" (cf. Gn 21:33; Is 26:4; 40:28). The Hebrews simply understood that God is the God of the past and the God who will always be—in stark contrast to humans whose days on earth are limited.

The NT picked up these concepts from Judaism and the OT. In Greek the same root word is used to describe the ages of time and God's agelessness. For example, the word "eternal" used in Romans 16:26 comes from the Greek root transliterated into English as "eon." The God who rules the ages or eons is himself the ageless one who brings continuity and stability into the human life so severely bounded by this age. The clear understanding that time will come to an end, provided by NT revelation, added to the OT's vivid understanding of creation, serves to underline and clarify the concept of an eternal God. God's preexistence and postexistence is yet another way of expressing his eternal being.

The NT regularly spoke of the temporal sequences of God's revelation in Christ in much the same way as the OT spoke of God's self-revelation to Israel. The NT usage of prepositions with "eon" is particularly instructive: for example (translated literally) "out of the age" (Jn 9:32), "from the age" (Lk 1:70; Acts 3:21), "into the age" (Jude 1:13), "into the ages" (Jn 4:14). The first two phrases reflect an indefinite time preceding the present moment, and the last two point to a future indefinable time (often translated as "forever").

The biblical concept of eternity stands in contrast to that of other cultures of the time, which often thought in cyclical terms. The Greek world particularly thought of time in the analogy of a circle—an ever-recurring sequence of events. Salvation was to find an exit from that vicious cycle, thus being freed from time in order to experience timelessness. The biblical concept pictures time as a line with beginning and end guaranteed by the eternal God. Thus, in the biblical view, salvation could not occur within a designated sequence; it only occurs in the experience of the individual and moves on to the historical consummation directed by the eternal God.

The contrast between Greek and biblical ways of viewing time raises the question of the exact nature of eternity. Is it to be understood as merely unlimited time or, in direct contrast to present time, as timelessness? The biblical view seems to be that eternity is not timelessness and does not stand in contrast to present time as its opposite, since present time and eternity share basic qualities.

The NT (following Judaism) uses "eon" or "age" to divide time into "this present eon" and "the eon that is about to be" or "the coming eon." The contrast is not simply between time and timelessness, for the "eon that is about to be" is future and shares a specific and identifiable character. The biblical picture of the start of the "coming age" is dramatically painted with broad sequential brush strokes. The new age is not simply a restoration to the primitive and naive innocence of the earliest stage, but a consummation according to the purposes of him who is and who was and who is to come (Rv 1:4). Thus, it is designated as the new creation.

The NT clearly teaches that the "age that is to be" has now begun in the life and ministry of Christ, although there is a definite overlap in the two ages. The frequency of such terms as "the firstfruits," "the earnest of the Spirit," and "the last days," reflects this understanding (e.g., Heb 6:5: "and have tasted . . . the powers of the age to come"). The believer enjoys the blessings of the future age imported into the present through Christ's redemptive work.

The concept of eternity, then, does not stand in opposition and contrast to time as timelessness. Eternity is the unlimited and incalculable space of time bounded at its beginning by the introduction of the kingdom of God in Christ and stretching out into the unlimited future. Both time ("the present evil age," Gal 1:4) and eternity are governed by God as the Lord of all time, the one who gives content and meaning to both.

See also Age; God, Being and Attributes of.

ETHAM First encampment of the Hebrews after leaving Succoth (Ex 13:20), perhaps located on the border of the wilderness of Shur (Ex 15:22; Nm 33:6-8). The suggestion that it was an Egyptian fortress is improbable.

ETHAN
1. Wise man comparable to Solomon (1 Kgs 4:31) and probably the author of Psalm 89. It is uncertain whether he was a contemporary of Solomon.
2. Descendant of Judah and son of Zerah (1 Chr 2:6), perhaps the same as #1 above. However, they are ascribed different fathers in the two passages.
3. Son of Zimmah, a descendant of Gershon, Levi's oldest son (1 Chr 6:42).
4. Descendant of Levi through his son Merari, and the son of Kishi (1 Chr 6:44) or Kushaiah (15:17). He was one of three outstanding musicians, along with Heman and Asaph, appointed by David (vv 16-19). It was probably this Ethan whose name is ascribed in the title to Psalm 39 (as "Jeduthun," which he is called in 1 Chr 16:41; 25:1) as "chief musician"; it is likely that he composed the music for the psalm.

ETHANIM* Early name for the seventh month in the Jewish calendar (1 Kgs 8:2, NLT mg). *See* Calendars, Ancient and Modern.

ETHBAAL King of Sidon whose daughter Jezebel entered into a political marriage with Ahab of Israel (1 Kgs 16:31). Ethbaal was credited with building Botrys in Phoenicia and founding the colony of Auza in Libya. He also established commercial relations with Damascus.

ETHER
1. A town in Judah in the Shephelah region (Jos 15:42). The modern town of Khirbet el-Ater is the probable site.
2. A village in Simeon (Jos 19:7), paralleled in 1 Chronicles 4:32 by "Token."

ETHIOPIA In the OT, Ethiopia was generally referred to as Cush (Gn 10:6; 1 Chr 1:8; Is 11:11, KJV), which is a transliteration of the only Hebrew word used to describe the land lying to the south of Egypt. The Greek version, however, spoke of this territory as Ethiopia and kept the name Cush for the lists of peoples in Genesis 10:6-8 and 1 Chronicles 1:8-10. English translations have generally followed the Greek, except in cases where Cushi appears as a personal name (2 Sm 18:21-23, 31-32).

Location The Hebrew name *Cush* is actually an old Egyptian loanword that came into use in the early Middle Kingdom period. At that time it was used of a small area between the second and third cataracts of the Nile. Later on, in the New Kingdom period (c. 1570–1160 BC), it was applied to a larger area that extended some distance to the south. This broader designation corresponds geographically to the modern lands of Nubia and northern Sudan. It is misleading to think that the Ethiopia of Scripture is the same territory as the Ethiopia of modern times, which in an earlier period was called Abyssinia. The name Ethiopia was of Greek origin, and according to some interpreters means "burnt-faced" (cf. Acts 8:27). This tradition has been perpetuated by the Arabic name Beled es Sudan, or "land of the blacks," from which the designation Sudan comes.

The use of Cush by the OT writers seems to have paralleled the Egyptian geographical terminology in naming an arid land stretching south to Aswan, the Syene of Ezekiel 29:10. The borders of Ethiopia were never clearly defined, even by the Egyptians, so the territory may be regarded as extending to some indeterminate point in the Sudan beyond Meroé.

Ethiopia consisted predominantly of desert lying east of the Nile, and the topography of the region made travel hazardous. Even the river itself presented obstacles to navigation in the form of cataracts. Outcroppings of hard stone forced the Nile down narrow channels and produced rough water that swamped boats easily. Such forbidding natural obstacles protected Egypt against invasion from the south but also gave an inhospitable character to Ethiopia. Almost all the land suitable for farming in Egyptian Nubia and part of northern Sudan was inundated, and the Nubians were compelled to move below Aswan to Kom Ombo.

Since the area covered by Nubia is predominantly desert, it is hardly surprising that the rainfall is minimal, except for the upstream areas. The territory around Meroé, which was the capital during the Meroitic period, experiences seasonal rains; an area bordered on the west and north by the Nile and the Atbara, the so-called "island of Meroé," was apparently quite fertile in antiquity and may have been heavily forested.

Biblical References In Esther 1:1 and 8:9, Ethiopia is described as the most distant southwesterly province in the Persian Empire. Its "rivers" were presumably the Nile and the Atbara (cf. Is 18:1; Zep 3:10). The products of Cush were referred to in Job 28:19 and Isaiah 45:14, which according to Egyptian lists included semiprecious stones, animals, and agricultural products. Some prophets expected exiled Jews in Ethiopia to return (Ps 87:4;

Is 11:11), while others foresaw divine judgment coming upon the land (Is 20:3; Ez 30:4; Zep 2:12). But since Cush was under God's sovereignty, it could hope for divine blessing as well as punishment—hence, the expectation in Psalm 68:31, Isaiah 45:14, and Zephaniah 3:10 that its peoples would be converted to the Hebrew faith. The Ethiopia of Acts 8:27 was the kingdom of Candace ("queen"), who ruled from Meroé, where the capital of Cush had been moved about 300 BC.

See also Cush (Place).

ETH-KAZIN One of the towns marking the eastern boundary of Zebulun's tribe (Jos 19:13).

ETHNAN Member of Helah's family from Judah's tribe (1 Chr 4:7).

ETHNARCH Title given to one who rules by the authority of another country. Ethnarch was a position below a king but above a tetrarch or governor. Three ethnarchs who ruled in Palestine were Simon, during the Maccabean period (1 Macc 14:47), Archelaus in the time of Jesus (Mt 2:22), and one in Damascus during the life of the apostle Paul (2 Cor 11:32, NASB).

ETHNI Alternate name for Jeatherai, Zerah's son, in 1 Chronicles 6:41. *See* Jeaterai, Jeatherai.

EUBULUS Roman believer who sent greetings to Timothy during Paul's second Roman imprisonment (2 Tm 4:21). His Greek name indicates his probable gentile origin.

EUCHARIST* *See* Lord's Supper, The.

EUERGETES* Title of honor belonging to two Ptolemaic rulers. From the Greek word meaning "Benefactor," the title was ascribed to rulers known for their benevolent actions. *See* Ptolemaic Empire.

EUMENES The designation of a king of Pergamum, Eumenes II (197–158 BC) mentioned in 1 Maccabees 8:8 in connection with an alliance that Judas Maccabeus made with the Romans during their war with Antiochus the Great.

EUNICE Timothy's mother, daughter of Lois (2 Tm 1:5), and the wife of a pagan Greek. She was a Jewish Christian (Acts 16:1). She apparently taught her son the OT Scriptures "from childhood" (2 Tm 3:15) and was converted to Christianity during Paul's first trip to her home in Lystra, previous to his visit mentioned in Acts 16:1.

EUNUCH Officer or chamberlain in the court or household of a ruler, often assigned to the women's quarters. Many of these men were emasculated, though not always (cf. Gn 39:1, NEB). Eunuchs were public officials in Israel (1 Sm 8:15, NEB; 1 Chr 28:1, NEB), Persia (Est 2:3), Ethiopia (Jer 38:7; Acts 8:27), and Babylon (Dn 1:3). Eunuchs were not included in public worship in Israel (Dt 23:1), but the prophet Isaiah referred to their restoration in the messianic kingdom (Is 56:3-5; see Acts 8).

The Ethiopian eunuch of Acts 8:27-39 was probably minister of the treasury and has been credited with founding Christianity in Ethiopia.

Jesus mentioned three classes of eunuchs (Mt 19:12), including those who made themselves eunuchs for the sake of the kingdom. This is generally understood in a metaphorical sense of voluntarily forgoing marriage in order to serve the kingdom (e.g., John the Baptist, Jesus, and the apostle Paul).

EUODIA, EUODIAS* Prominent woman in the Philippian church whom Paul asked to resolve her differences with Syntyche (Phil 4:2). The nature of their disagreement is not known, but it was of enough severity to reach Paul in Rome. Both women had labored with him in the work of the gospel (4:3).

EUPATOR Surname of Antiochus V, the Seleucid king. The name means "son of a noble father." *See* Antiochus V.

EUPHRATES RIVER Largest river in western Asia, formed by the union of two rivers in Asia Minor, the Kara-Su and the Murat-Suyu. Its source is in central Armenia. The river flows generally in a southeasterly direction for some 1,800 miles (2,896.2 kilometers) until it reaches the Persian Gulf. At Korna, about 100 miles (160.9 kilometers) from the gulf, it joins with the Tigris River. The Euphrates is shallow until it combines with the Tigris and can be navigated for about 1,200 miles (1,930.8 kilometers) by small boats only. After the union of the Tigris and Euphrates, ocean liners can proceed as far as Basra. Melting snows at the source cause the river to rise from about the middle of March until about June. Control and storage of water in flood canals during the overflow of the river made possible abundant harvests that sustained large populations in antiquity.

The Euphrates was one of four branches issuing from the river that watered the Garden of Eden (Gn 2:14). In the promises made to Abraham, the northern boundary of the land of Israel was to be the upper division of the river (Gn 15:18; Dt 1:7; 11:24). These boundaries were approximately reached during the period of kings David and Solomon (2 Sm 8:3; 10:16; 1 Kgs 4:24). The Euphrates is called "the river" (Nm 22:5; Dt 11:24; Jos 24:3, 14) or "the great river" (Jos 1:4). People living east of the Euphrates referred to Israel and its surrounding territories to the west as "beyond the river" (Ezr 4:10; Neh 2:7-9). It was to this river that Jeremiah sent Seraiah with a book of prophecies relating to the destruction of Babylon. After reading them, Seraiah was told to throw the book into the Euphrates as a symbol of the way Babylon would sink to rise no more (Jer 51:63).

Two NT references to the Euphrates appear in the book of Revelation (Rv 9:14; 16:12).

See also Babylon, Babylonia; Mesopotamia.

EUPOLEMUS A Jewish ambassador sent by Judas Maccabeus to Rome along with Jason, the son of Eleazar, to establish an alliance. He is identified in 1 Maccabees 8:17 as the son of John, the son of Accos.

EUROCLYDON* KJV transliteration of the Greek word for the northeasterly wind mentioned in Paul's journey to Rome in Acts 27:14. *See* Northeaster.

EUTYCHUS Common slave name, mentioned only in Acts 20:9. It was Eutychus's misfortune to become sleepy while sitting on a windowsill listening to the apostle Paul preach at Troas. He sank into a deep sleep and fell from the ledge, which was in the third loft. The apostle Paul revived him from the dead (vv 7-12).

EVANGELIST NT term referring to one who proclaims the gospel of Jesus Christ. There are only three occurrences of the word in the NT. The apostle Paul exhorted the Ephesian church to walk worthy of their calling

(Eph 4:1-12). The exhortation stressed the gifts given to each within the unity of the Spirit. Paul explained that the ascended Christ has given "some as apostles, and some as prophets, and some as evangelists, and some as pastors and teachers" (v 11, NASB). Paul was saying that Christ calls persons to these ministries and gives them to the church. The evangelist is one of Christ's gifts to the church. The meaning of the term indicates that the task of such a person is to function as a spokesperson for the church in proclaiming the gospel to the world. An evangelist is similar to an apostle in function, except that being an apostle involved a personal relationship to Jesus during his earthly ministry (Acts 1:21-22). The evangelist stands in contrast to the pastor/teacher. The former makes the initial proclamation, and the latter provides continuing follow-up ministry that develops maturity in the believer. The reference to Philip the evangelist (21:8) supports the idea of evangelism as a gifted ministry to which Christ calls some in the church.

More than one gift or ministry may be performed by the same person. Paul charged Timothy with his responsibilities as a pastor and teacher, and also exhorted him to "do the work of an evangelist" (2 Tm 4:5). Therefore, "evangelist" can refer to a person called to that distinct ministry, and also to a function that may be performed by others.

See also Spiritual Gifts.

EVE First woman, "the mother of all living" (Gn 3:20). The book of Genesis recounts that after God had finished his creation of Adam, he saw that it was not good for Adam to be alone. He decided to create "a helper fit for him" (2:18). The woman is called *ezer* (in Hebrew lit. "help"), a word that appears elsewhere in the OT in reference to God as Israel's help. Causing Adam to fall into a deep sleep, God took one of his ribs and used it to fashion Eve (vv 21-25).

Eve was given two names by Adam. The first was "woman," a generic designation with theological connotations that denote her relationship to man (Gn 2:23). The second, Eve ("life"), was given after the fall and refers to her role in the procreation of the human race (3:20).

Adam and Eve are pictured as living in Eden, serving God and fulfilling each other's needs. Then evil entered when Eve was tempted by the serpent to disobey God's command, which forbade their eating the fruit of the tree of the knowledge of good and evil (Gn 2:17; 3:3). Tricked by the serpent's subtle persuasion, Eve transgressed God's will by eating the fruit. Adam did the same when she brought some to him, although he was not deceived as she had been. Both then recognized their nakedness and made garments of fig leaves.

When God came to commune with them, they hid from him. When he demanded an account, Adam blamed Eve, and Eve blamed the serpent. God told Eve that as a result of their sin, childbirth would be a painful experience and her husband would rule over her (Gn 3:16). Eve later became the mother of Cain, Abel, Seth, and other children (4:1-2, 25; 5:4).

Eve is mentioned twice in the NT. In his letter to Timothy, the apostle Paul referred to her when discussing whether or not women could teach (1 Tm 2:13). He said that a woman could not teach or have authority over a man because of man's priority in creation and Eve's responsibility for the original transgression (see 2 Cor 11:3).

See also Adam (Person); Garden of Eden.

EVENING *See* Day.

EVENING SACRIFICE *See* Offerings and Sacrifices.

EVERLASTING LIFE *See* Eternal Life.

EVI One of five Midianite kings killed in a battle against Israel under the leadership of Moses (Nm 31:8). Apparently, God directed Moses to go to battle against Midian because the Midianites had led the Israelites into pagan religious practices. In Joshua 13:21, Evi is called a prince of Sihon, the Midianite king.

EVIL *See* Sin.

EVIL-MERODACH Son and successor of Nebuchadnezzar as king of Babylon, who reigned for two years (561–560 BC). During his reign, he released Jehoiachin, former king of Judah, from imprisonment (2 Kgs 25:27-30; Jer 52:31-34). Aside from this fact, little is known about his reign. He was killed by his brother-in-law Neriglissar, who succeeded him to the throne. *See* Babylon, Babylonia.

EVIL ONE NT designation for Satan. *See* Satan.

EVIL SPIRIT Another name for demon. *See* Demon; Demon-possession.

EWE Female sheep. *See* Animals (Sheep).

EXALTATION OF CHRIST* The glory and dominion which Jesus attained subsequent to the completion of his earthly work of suffering and death. It is at one and the same time the consummation of his redemptive sacrifice and the reward of his full obedience to the will of the Father. The exaltation thus includes the biblical doctrines of Jesus' resurrection, ascension, and heavenly enthronement.

During his earthly ministry, Jesus predicted not only that he would suffer, die, and be buried (Mt 20:28; Jn 3:14; 6:51; 10:11; etc.) but also that he would thereafter be exalted by the power of the Father to heavenly dominion and glory (Lk 24:26; Jn 17:5). This humiliation-exaltation pattern was plainly indicated by Jesus on the occasion of his encounter with a delegation of proselytes who sought to meet with the Lord (Jn 12:20-36). Jesus far exceeded the expectations of these Greeks by declaring that fellowship with his Father would be extended to the Gentiles in consequence of his imminent passion and resurrection. By affirming, "The hour has come for the Son of man to be glorified" (Jn 12:23, RSV), Jesus indicated that he would be endowed with honor and splendor at his exaltation to the presence of the Father in heaven. Jesus' teaching in respect to his exaltation to heaven provided the foundation for the church's more explicit teaching on the subject.

The resurrection, the initial event in the exaltation of Jesus, is one of the central affirmations of NT teaching (Acts 2:24, 32; 3:15; 4:10; Rom 1:4; 1 Cor 15:4). From apostolic times Christians have consistently affirmed that at a particular moment in time and in a given place its founder literally passed from a state of death to a state of endless life. The absolute uniqueness of Christ's exaltation via bodily resurrection from the dead sets Christianity in a class by itself among the religions of the world. A reading of the NT plainly indicates that Jesus openly predicted that death was unable to defeat him. To the skeptical Jews who demanded from Jesus a sign of the authority by which he purged the temple, the Lord answered: "Destroy this temple, and in three days I will raise it up" (Jn 2:19, RSV). After Peter's crucial confession of Christ's divine sonship at Caesarea Philippi, Jesus gave to his followers a more detailed account of the divine plan whereby he would be raised from the dead on the third day (Mt 16:21). To the disciples who assembled in Galilee shortly after his transfiguration, Jesus spoke plainly of his forthcoming exaltation: "The Son of man is to be delivered into the hands of men, and they will kill him, and he will be raised on the third day" (17:22-23, RSV). In the NT, the apostolic teaching about Christ's death is almost always accompanied by an emphasis upon the certainty of his physical resurrection after three days.

Furthermore, the NT writers were careful to spell out the profound theological significance of Christ's exaltation in resurrection: (1) it demonstrates Christ's certain power over death and the grave (Acts 2:24; 1 Cor 15:54-56); (2) it confirms the validity of Christ's teachings, particularly his claims to divine Sonship (Acts 2:36; Rom 1:4); (3) it represents God's ultimate vindication of his obedient, suffering servant (Phil 2:8-9); (4) it is the means of the justification (Rom 4:25) and regeneration (1 Pt 1:3) of the believer; and (5) it is the guarantee of the future resurrection of the Christian (Rom 6:5; 1 Cor 15:22-24). The effective cause of Christ's resurrection is declared to be, on one hand, God (Ps 16:10; Acts 2:32; Eph 1:19-20) and, on the other hand, our Lord himself (Jn 2:19; 10:17-18).

The ascension represents the second phase of the exaltation of Christ. According to the two NT historical accounts (Lk 24:50-51; Acts 1:9-11), 40 days after his death Jesus left his disciples for the last time and ascended into heaven. Jesus, who several times in John's Gospel specifically refers to his ascension (Jn 3:13; 6:62; 14:12; 20:17), regarded the place to which he would depart as an actual locality in the heavenly realm (14:2). In his reflection upon this second stage of the exaltation intimated by Psalm 68:18, the apostle Paul associates the ascension with Christ's triumph over his foes and the bestowal of spiritual gifts to the church (Eph 4:8). The victor triumphantly returned to his Father's throne in order to bless his people. In what may be part of an early Christian hymn, Paul explicates what he regards as the supreme "mystery" of the Christian faith, namely, that Christ Jesus who "was manifested in the flesh" was at the close of his life "taken up into glory" (1 Tm 3:16).

Alone among the writings of the NT, the Epistle to the Hebrews associates Christ's ascension with his high priestly ministry in the heavenly sanctuary. He who steadfastly withstood every earthly trial, having "passed through the heavens," is fully able to empathize with his people and impart grace to the tempted and distraught (Heb 4:14 ff.). Employing the symbolism of the ancient Hebrew sanctuary, the writer conceptualizes the Ascension as the event whereby Christ enters into the inner shrine behind the curtain (6:19), bringing with him his own blood (9:12), to the end that he might appear in the presence of God on our behalf (v 24).

The NT thus attributes considerable theological significance to this phase of Christ's exaltation. By virtue of his exaltation to the Father, Christ (1) demonstrated his defeat of every earthly enemy (Eph 4:8); (2) sent the promised Holy Spirit (Jn 16:7; Acts 2:33), which awaited his glorification (Jn 7:39); and (3) formally undertook his heavenly priestly ministry (Heb 6:20).

The third stage of Christ's exaltation is his heavenly enthronement at the right hand of the Father. Following his passion, death, resurrection, and ascension to the heavenly realm, Christ is represented in Scripture as having taken his seat at the Father's right hand. The biblical phrase "right hand of God" (Acts 7:55-56), which has been preserved in many later Christian creeds and con-

fessions, is an anthropomorphism that figuratively describes Christ's universal dominion, authority, and power in the presence of the Father. This aspect of Christ's exaltation represents the fulfillment of his prayer recorded in John 17:5: "Now, Father, glorify me in your own presence with the glory I had with you before the world was made."

In the OT the description of God seated on the throne of the universe is a sign of his sovereignty (1 Kgs 22:19; Ps 99:1), majesty (Is 6:1-4) and holiness (Ps 47:8). That one should be invited to take a seat on the right hand of the sovereign in Eastern cultures was a token of extraordinary honor and authority (1 Kgs 2:19). The fact that the exalted Christ would be accorded this particular privilege was anticipated in the Scriptures of the OT (see Ps 8:5, quoted in Heb 2:8; and see Ps 110:1).

The Epistle to the Hebrews, which shows unusual interest in the doctrine of Christ's exaltation, represents Christ's heavenly enthronement both as the sequel to his completed earthly sacrifice and as the commencement of his High Priestly ministration in the sanctuary on high. Affirming the superiority of Christ as High Priest of the new covenant, Hebrews 8:1-2 portrays Christ as seated at the right hand of the throne of the Majesty in heaven, a minister in the heavenlies. Christ's enthronement affirms not only the finality of his earthly work of self-sacrifice but also his newly acquired status as mediator of the new and better covenant. Hebrews 10:11-18 pointedly contrasts the ineffectual sacrifices of the legal priests who *stand* in the performance of their ritual sacrifices with the effectual single sacrifice of Christ, who is now *seated* at the right hand of God as intercessor for the saints.

EXECRATION TEXTS* Certain Egyptian Middle Kingdom texts containing curses (execrations) directed against the pharaoh's enemies. Such texts have been found on 20th- to 19th-century BC bowls from Thebes, and on 19th- to 18th-century figurines from Saqqara. The bowls or figurines, inscribed with names of rulers, cities, or persons and accompanied by a curse, were ceremonially smashed and given a ritual burial, symbolizing the curse intended for damage would be done to those named in the inscription.

This form of magic was aimed at both nations and individuals who constituted a threat to the kingdom. Egypt's neighbor Libya is mentioned infrequently in the texts, but there were evidently more powerful enemies in the Sudan. Eight Egyptian individuals who were presumably part of a harem conspiracy were execrated. But the greatest threat loomed in the area of Palestine and Syria; over 60 towns or regions were singled out for execration. The list of place-names includes such well-known towns as Byblos, Ashkelon, Tyre, Jerusalem, and Beth-shan, and it provides an important source for the study of the historical geography of ancient Palestine.

EXECUTION *See* Criminal Law and Punishment.

EXHORTATION* Translation of a Greek word literally meaning "a calling of someone alongside to help." Its primary meaning in the NT is the urging of someone to do something—particularly some ethical course of action. In some contexts, the same Greek word may also include the idea of comforting and consoling. The given context will determine which meaning to use.

A passage that most clearly illustrates "exhortation" in the sense of inciting or spurring people on to action is Luke 3:7-18. John the Baptist exhorts his Jewish hearers to bring forth fruits in keeping with repentance, to stop resting on descent from Abraham as protection from punishment for sin, and to share clothing and food. He exhorted tax gatherers to collect no more money than they had a right to take, and soldiers not to take money from anyone by force, not to accuse anyone falsely, and to be content with their wages.

The ability to exhort is said to be a spiritual gift that God has given to some in the church for the benefit of the whole (Rom 12:8). In addition, exhortation is one of the results of a proper use of the gift of prophecy, as seen in 1 Corinthians 14:3, 31. It was also one of the responsibilities that Paul commanded of Timothy: "Give attention to the public reading of Scripture, to exhortation and teaching" (1 Tm 4:13, NASB). The writer to the Hebrews also refers to an exhortation addressed to the readers lest they regard lightly the discipline of the Lord or "faint" when they are reproved (Heb 12:5, KJV).

In 2 Corinthians 1:3-7 the Greek word for exhortation is used in the sense of consolation or encouragement. The context is one in which serious suffering for Christ is evident. Paul said that God encourages us in our times of testing so that we may be able to do the same for those experiencing similar trials. Acts 15:31 refers to the encouragement and consolation that came to the church at Antioch when the decree of the Jerusalem Council was read in their hearing. They had been fearful that the Judaizers might have their way and that Christians would be required to become circumcised in order to be saved. Another clear illustration of this word meaning "comfort" is in 1 Thessalonians 4:18, where Paul instructs the believers that those who die in Christ will not miss out on the blessings of the day of Christ; he then exhorts them to "comfort one another with these words." *See* Spiritual Gifts.

EXILE *See* Diaspora of the Jews.

EXODUS, Book of Second book of the Bible, containing the story of God's liberation of the people of Israel from slavery in Egypt. Few books of the OT are as important historically and theologically as the book of Exodus.

Historically, the exodus event was the birth of Israel as a nation. At Mt Sinai a group of tribes who were descendants of Abraham became a nation ruled by God. The book of Exodus explains how the Israelites were able to resettle the land God had promised to Abraham and gives the basis for this religious, political, and social life.

Theologically, the book of Exodus is so frequently referred to in the OT and NT that theologians speak of an "exodus motif." In Psalm 68, for example, David received assurance in remembering that his God was the same one who rescued Israel from Egypt. The prophet Jeremiah compared the future regathering of Israel to their exodus from Egypt as an even more miraculous event (Jer 16:14-15). The return of Jesus and his parents from Egypt is associated with the exodus in Matthew 2:13-15. The deliverance of the Jewish people from Egypt was interpreted as a prototype for God's freeing of all his people, both Israel and the church. Thus, the message of the book of Exodus is foundational to understanding God's plan of salvation throughout the Bible.

The English title "Exodus" comes from the Septuagint, a pre-Christian translation of the OT into Greek. The word means "a way out" or "departure" and refers to Israel's rescue from Egypt. The Hebrew title is *Shemoth* ("these are the names"), from the book's opening words, referring to the names of the sons of Jacob who joined Joseph in Egypt.

PREVIEW
• Author
• Date
• Background
• Purpose and Theological Teaching
• Content

Author According to tradition, Exodus and the entire Pentateuch (first five books of the Bible) were written by Moses. Exodus was probably written at Mt Sinai or shortly after the events there, according to this view. There is much to support that claim: (1) The book states that Moses wrote God's words in at least one book (Ex 17:14; 24:2, 7; 34:27-28). According to Deuteronomy 31:9, 24, Moses recorded God's law in a book that was deposited beside the ark of the covenant as a witness for God. (2) Many OT writers referred to portions of Exodus as the "law of Moses" (1 Kgs 2:3; 2 Chr 34:14; Neh 8:1; 13:1). The NT, including the testimony of Jesus, calls Moses the author (Mk 7:10; 12:26; Jn 1:45; 7:19).

Various other theories about the origin of Exodus have been proposed. Some scholars credit Moses with writing nearly the entire book. One writer claims that Moses was an unknown desert sheikh who never even met the Israelites. Some critics think they detect in the book several documents from various periods in Israel's history that were finally put together by an editor centuries after Moses' death. Others have isolated various literary forms, such as the "Song of Moses" (Ex 15), and traced their development. Another interpretation says that the exodus story was passed on by word of mouth for many generations before being written.

Although such theories are held by biblical scholars, they deny what the text of the book repeatedly affirms: that Moses wrote Exodus. The book of Exodus contains evidence of being written by an eyewitness. Only such a person would recall, for example, that there were 12 fountains and 70 palm trees at Elim (Ex 15:27). The author shows a thorough knowledge of Egyptian court life, customs, and language. Some of the materials used to construct the tabernacle, such as acacia wood for its furniture (25:10) and rams' skins for the outer covering (v 5), are found in Egypt and the Sinai Peninsula but not in Palestine. The book thus seems to have had a desert setting.

Moses was not only commissioned by God to write the book of Exodus, but he was also well qualified. He was "instructed in all the wisdom of the Egyptians, and he was mighty in his words and deeds" (Acts 7:22, RSV). In addition, the 40 years spent in the wilderness of Midian and Sinai gave him a thorough knowledge of the geography and wildlife of the regions through which the Israelites traveled. The events of the exodus—deliverance from the Egyptians and God's giving of the law—were so central to the history of Israel that Moses took special care to preserve the record so it could be passed on to following generations.

Date If one accepts the traditional view that Moses wrote Exodus, then the book is to be dated in the time of Moses. Two dates are generally suggested for the exodus from Egypt.

The "Late Date" View This view says that the pharaoh who oppressed the Israelites was Seti I (Sethos, c. 1304–1290 BC) and the pharaoh of the exodus was Ramses II (c. 1290–1224 BC). The exodus would thus have occurred in 1290, and the conquest of Canaan would have begun in 1250. There are two principal

Ancient Hebrew Manuscript of Exodus Dead Sea Scroll manuscript 4QpaleoExod^m, c. 200 BC

arguments for this view: (1) According to Exodus 1:11, the Israelites were forced to build the store city of Rameses; therefore, Ramses II must have been ruling at the time. But the city of Rameses could have existed earlier under a different name and then been renamed after Ramses II when he rebuilt it. Or there could have been an earlier monarch named Ramses who commissioned its construction. (2) There is archaeological evidence of movements of people and widespread destruction in Canaan around 1250 BC. If this destruction was caused by the Hebrew conquest under Joshua, this would place the exodus around 1290. But it could just as easily have been the result of social turbulence and anarchy in the period of the Israelite judges, or of the military activities of neighboring peoples.

The "Early Date" View This view says that the pharaoh of the oppression was Thutmose III (c. 1504–1450 BC) and the pharaoh of the exodus was Amenhotep II (c. 1450–1424 BC). Thus, the exodus would have occurred about 1440, and the conquest would have begun around 1400. Three chief arguments support that view: (1) If the fourth year of King Solomon was 966 BC, then the 480 years of 1 Kings 6:1 would place the exodus at 1446. (2) If the time of Jephthah was 1100 BC, then the 300 years of Judges 11:26 would date the conquest at 1400. (3) The late date would not leave enough time for the period of the judges, which most chronologies indicate lasted between 300 and 400 years. On the basis of such biblical references to the date of the exodus, the early date appears preferable.

Background Some events in Egypt during the period covered by the book of Exodus shed additional light on the biblical record. Exodus 12:40 records that the Israelites lived in Egypt for 430 years. That would place the settling of Jacob and his family in Goshen (Gn 47:4, 11) at about 1870 BC, during the powerful 12th dynasty of Egypt's Middle Kingdom. Around the turn of the century, two weaker dynasties followed. Semite invaders from Asia began to infiltrate northern (or Lower) Egypt. Those outsiders, known as the Hyksos, were able to displace the native dynasty with their own king around 1730. That was the "new king" who "did not know Joseph" (Ex 1:8). Being foreigners themselves, they were naturally concerned about the Israelites, who were too many and too mighty for them (v 9). Enslavement was the easiest solution to the problem of the Israelites. The Hyksos kings could use the new source of labor to enlarge Rameses, at that time the capital of Lower Egypt.

Not until about 1580 BC were the Egyptians, led by Ahmose, able to drive out the Hyksos and reestablish an Egyptian line of kings. Because the Israelites were still multiplying, despite their hard labor, the pharaohs of the 18th dynasty continued their bondage and decreed that all male children must be killed. When Moses was born (c. 1560 BC), that edict was still in effect. Thutmose I (1539–1514), the great empire builder and third of that dynasty, was pharaoh.

Thutmose I's only surviving legal heir was a daughter, Hatshepsut. Her husband assumed the name Thutmose II (1514–1504). When he died, another of the pharaoh's descendants was named the successor—Thutmose III (1504–1450), who was ten years old at the time. Hatshepsut took the kingdom from the young ruler and controlled it for 22 years (1503–1482). Such a strong-willed woman could have the nerve to disobey her father's command by saving the life of a Hebrew baby and raising him in the palace at Thebes.

Hatshepsut, who continued to rule despite Thutmose III's coronation, possibly intended for Moses to have the throne, or at least a high position in the realm. Thutmose III, once he had full power after Hatshepsut's death, would have been eager to do away with Moses. Moses' hurried flight into the wilderness after killing the overseer fits well with such historical possibilities. Thutmose III's death in 1450 BC opened the way for Moses to return and confront Pharaoh Amenhotep II with God's command, "Let my people go."

INSCRIPTION ON THE GREAT SPHINX
An interesting inscription has been found on a granite column between the paws of the great Sphinx of Giza. The god Horus is said to have promised the throne of Egypt to Thutmose IV (1424–1417), Amenhotep II's successor. Thus, Thutmose IV was possibly not the rightful heir to the throne. If so, then the biblical account that the pharaoh's eldest son died in the tenth and final plague is verified (Ex 12:29).

Purpose and Theological Teaching The purpose of the book of Exodus is to show how God's promise to Abraham (Gn 15:12-16) was fulfilled when the Lord rescued the Israelite descendants of Abraham from Egyptian bondage. It also explains the origin of the Passover festival, the beginning of the nation by God's establishment of a covenant with Israel, and the giving of the law on Mt Sinai.

The book of Exodus tells the moving story of a mighty God, creator of the universe, beyond all limitations of time and space, who intervenes in history on behalf of a helpless group of slaves. God defeats the ruler of the greatest empire on earth and then leads his oppressed people from that land to freedom. Exodus is the story of a single family that providentially grows into a multitude. Through God's covenant a nation is formed, and through his law the nation is given stability and set apart from all its neighbors. The book of Exodus tells of an unusual man, whose 80 years of preparation are equally divided between the palace of a king and the pasture of a nomadic priest. Moses is a reluctant leader, but he defies the pharaoh, speaks with God face-to-face, and writes nearly one-fourth of the Hebrew Scriptures.

The God of Exodus is faithful. He makes promises and keeps them. Genesis 15:13-16 records an amazing prophecy: "Then the LORD said to Abram, 'Know of a surety that your descendants will be sojourners in a land that is not theirs, and will be slaves there, and they will be oppressed for four hundred years; but I will bring judgment on the nation which they serve, and afterward they shall come out with great possessions. . . . And they shall come back here in the fourth generation' " (RSV). In response to this promise, Joseph, "at the end of his life, made mention of the exodus of the Israelites and gave directions concerning his burial" (Heb 11:22, RSV).

That promise provides a background for the drama of redemption on which the book of Exodus focuses. Redemption can be defined as "deliverance from the power of an alien dominion, and enjoyment of the resulting freedom." It speaks of a deliverer and what he does to achieve deliverance. The book of Exodus is full of the vocabulary of redemption. It tells of the God who "remembers" his promise to the Hebrew patriarchs (Ex 2:24; 6:5). God "comes down to deliver" the Israelites (3:8), or "save" them (14:30; 15:2), in order to "bring them" out of the land of Egypt (3:10-12). Redemption involves these aspects:

1. The Lord is the author of redemption. In Exodus 6:1-8, as God answered Moses' prayer to deliver his people, he used the pronoun "I" 18 times to empha-

size that he was the one initiating the action. The Hebrew descendants of Abraham had known God primarily by the Hebrew name "El," a common title in the ancient Near East for the supreme deity. But in Exodus, Israel learned that God is "Jehovah" or "Yahweh." That is his personal name, a reminder that he is the God of the covenant who personally cares for his people's welfare. In Exodus 3:14, God told Moses, "I am who I am" or "I will be who I will be." Some scholars think that statement shows that the name Yahweh comes from the Hebrew verb "to be." In any case, the concept of "name" in the Hebrew culture is synonymous with "character." To know the name of God is to know something of his character. Israel knew God as the one who is eternally self-existent yet present with them wherever they would go, acting on their behalf (Ex 3:12; 33:14-16).

2. The reason for redemption was God's promise to the forefathers of the Israelites. When God heard the groaning of the people of Israel, he remembered his covenant with Abraham, with Isaac, and with Jacob (Ex 2:24; cf. 6:5). In response to their need, he selected an agent of redemption, the unwilling Moses. Moses exhausted every possible excuse, but God would not take no for an answer. Moses is a vivid example of how God prepares, empowers, and sustains his chosen servants, using them to accomplish his purpose.

3. The motive of redemption was God's grace and love (Ex 15:13; 20:6; 34:6-7). The purpose of redemption was that Israel and the Egyptians might know God (6:7; 7:5; 8:10; 14:18). The Lord worked so that all who were involved—Moses, the Israelites, Pharaoh, and the Egyptians—would be sure that he alone is God. The Hebrew understanding of knowledge is not primarily intellectual but experience-oriented. The desired response to God's action is not mere mental assent but also faith and obedience.

4. Redemption is achieved in Exodus by miracles (4:21)—all natural processes controlled supernaturally by God. They are variously described as signs and wonders (7:3), great acts of judgment (6:6; 7:4), and "the finger of God" (8:19). Such miracles were not frivolous fireworks but purposeful works of God. Some of the miracles prove that Moses was sent by God. The miraculous plagues proved that God is supreme, for each of them was a direct challenge to one of the gods of Egypt: Osiris the river god, Yeqt the frog god, Ra (Re) the sun god, Athor the cattle god. The miracles in the wilderness proved that God fulfills all the needs of his people.

5. The pharaoh was the villain—a picture of rebellious humanity confronted by God's command (Ex 4:21-23). Ten times the pharaoh hardened his heart. Yet, in a sense, it was God who hardened the pharaoh's heart, effecting the king's decision to defy him.

6. The Passover marked the purchase of redemption (Ex 12:23-27; 15:16). It was a clear example of salvation by substitution. When the death angel saw the blood on the doorposts and lintels, he passed by.

7. The recipients of God's redemption in Exodus were the Israelites. God took them as his own special people (6:7), and they were no longer free to do as they pleased. Even before the exodus he had claimed them, telling Pharaoh, "Israel is my first-born son, and I say to you, 'Let my son go that he may serve me' " (4:22-23, RSV).

8. The demand of redemption was obedience. On the basis of his deliverance of the Israelites from bondage, God set forth the Ten Commandments (20:1-17) and the rest of the law for them to obey. The people, though quick to pledge their obedience (19:8; 24:3), were even quicker to disobey (32:8). Because the Lord is holy and wants his people to be holy and wholehearted in devotion (34:14), he must punish iniquity. But being compassionate, he also forgives. Throughout the centuries of Israel's history, God pleaded with his people through the prophets to remember the exodus and repent (see Mi 6:3-4). The faithful responded in gratitude with Moses' "song of redemption" (Ex 15; cf. Rv 15:3-4).

Content The book of Exodus can be divided into four sections, each describing one aspect of God's dealings with the Israelites during the 15th century BC.

God's Unveiling (Ex 1–6) The book of Exodus begins with the 70 descendants of Jacob who joined Joseph in Egypt for the duration of a famine that was afflicting their land (cf. Gn 46–50). After more than a century of prosperity for the Israelites in the land of Goshen, a new dynasty is established in Egypt whose leaders are not friendly toward Israel. In order to stem the rapid growth of the Hebrew people, the Egyptians force them to do hard labor, building storage cities for the pharaoh.

A further command requires all Israelite male children to be killed at birth. The superintendents of the midwives do not comply, however, and God rewards them—not to show his approval of their lie but because they fear and obey God rather than the pharaoh. A new command calls for all male Israelite babies to be drowned in the Nile River. One special child, who escapes when Pharaoh's daughter has his basket fished out of the Nile, is Moses. Ironically, Moses' mother is paid by the princess to raise her own child, who grows up in the palace as the princess's adopted son.

As an adult, Moses chooses to identify with his Hebrew kin, a tribute to the early instruction given him by his godly parents (see Heb 11:24-26). He sets out to liberate Israel from the Egyptians, one man at a time. But he has to flee to Midian, at the eastern edge of the Sinai Peninsula or in Arabia beyond the northern top of the Gulf of Aqaba. Moses marries into the household of Jethro, also named Reuel. Reuel ("friend of God") is probably the man's personal name, and Jethro ("excellence") his title. Because he is called a "priest of Midian" (Ex 2:16), some scholars have maintained a "Kenite hypothesis," suggesting that Moses adopted the religion of his father-in-law and taught it to the Israelites. But the Bible states that Moses received his religion by a direct revelation from God. Jethro seems to believe only after he sees that God has rescued Israel from the Egyptians (18:10-11).

While their future deliverer is in Midian, the Israelites continue to be oppressed and cry out to God in their misery (2:23-25). God responds by descending to his people. He came down to rescue Israel (3:8). He appears to Moses in a burning bush and identifies himself as the same God who promised the patriarchs a land "flowing with milk and honey" (3:17). Moses will lead the Israelites there, assisted by his brother, Aaron.

Assured that God's presence and miraculous signs will accompany him, Moses takes his wife Zipporah and his two sons and departs for Egypt. On the way, the Lord meets him and seeks to put him to death (4:24). That is probably the Hebrew way of saying that God strikes him with a mortal illness. Moses, who is going to deliver God's people, has neglected the sign of the covenant in failing to circumcise one of his sons (Gn 17:14). Moses recovers after the rite is performed and continues on to

Egypt, meeting Aaron at Mt Sinai. Their reception by the Israelites is more cordial than that of Pharaoh, who refuses to honor the God who sent Moses. Instead of releasing the Israelites to offer sacrifices to their God in the wilderness, he increases their burdens. The people complain to Moses, and Moses complains to God. God appears again to Moses (Ex 6), reassuring him that Israel will be delivered by divine power. God's plan is not a failure—he is just beginning to put it into action.

God's Deliverance (Ex 7–19) Chapters 7–12 record ten plagues with which God afflicts the Egyptians. Even before the first of them, the pharaoh has hardened his heart to defy God (7:13). There are three cycles of three plagues each:

Announced in the morning	Announced before Pharaoh	Unannounced
1st cycle	2nd cycle	3rd cycle
blood	flies	hail
frogs	cattle	locusts
gnats	boils	darkness

The first three plagues affect both the Egyptians and the Israelites; the Israelites are protected from the final six. The Egyptian magicians are able to duplicate the first two plagues, but when the third strikes, they admit, "This is the finger of God" (8:19). After the plague of flies covers the land, the pharaoh offers Moses the first of four compromises, but Moses refuses all of them (8:25-29; 10:8-11, 24-29). The first plagues are merely unpleasant, but the final ones are destructive and inflict much suffering. Since all of the plagues are common to that area, they themselves are not miraculous. The miracle is how the phenomena are multiplied and limited to the land of Egypt.

The nine plagues serve to harden the pharaoh's heart even more, so God prepares one final stroke. The death of every firstborn male, among both animals and humans, will be the fatal blow. God warns the Israelites to get ready to leave. To avert the death angel, they must put blood from an unblemished yearling male sheep or goat on their doorways. While they are eating the Passover meal, the death angel begins moving through the land of Egypt. In anguish the pharaoh drives the Israelites from the land; the slaves are free at last. Just as he has promised, the Lord goes before the children of Israel in a pillar of cloud by day and of fire by night.

But once again the pharaoh's heart is hardened and he gives pursuit. God parts the waters of the sea with a great wind. The literal meaning of the name given that body of water is "sea of reeds." It could refer to any shoreline where the water is sufficiently shallow for such plants to grow (see 1 Kgs 9:26, where the same term refers to the Gulf of Aqaba near Eloth). Whatever the location, there God hands the Egyptians their final defeat. The rescue is complete.

Moses and the Israelites respond with renewed faith in the Lord and with a song of victory and praise (Ex 14:31–15:21). Soon, however, thanksgiving turns into grumbling because of bitter water (15:22-26), lack of meat and bread (16:1-15), and lack of water (17:1-7). In each situation God provides for their need. He also gives them victory over the Amalekites (vv 8-16). As the Israelites approach Mt Sinai, Moses' family rejoins him, accompanied by Jethro. Jethro now confesses his faith in the God of the Israelites and shares in a fellowship meal with the leaders. He also assists Moses in reorganizing the judicial system, then returns to Midian (ch 18).

The Israelites arrive at Mt Sinai, also called Horeb (3:1), and prepare to meet the Lord who has rescued

them in fulfillment of his promise to Moses (v 12). The Lord establishes his covenant with Israel, taking them as his own possession, "a kingdom of priests, my holy nation." They quickly respond, "We will certainly do everything the LORD asks of us" (19:5-8, NLT).

God's Instruction (Ex 20–24) The God who redeems a people, who literally "buys them back from slavery," has a right to make certain demands of them. The commandments God gives to Israel at Sinai are not burdensome requirements but protective guidelines for living as God's people (20:2-3).

The Law (or Torah, meaning "instruction") revealed at Sinai consists of three parts:

1. The Ten Commandments (ch 20), addressing a person's relationship to God and other people. Based on God's nature (and therefore permanent), the Ten Commandments are unique in the history of the nations.
2. The judgments (chs 21–23), social regulations for governing the people as a theocracy, similar in many ways to the law codes of Israel's neighbors.
3. Ordinances (chs 24–31) regulating religious ceremonies.

All of the laws are given to Moses during the weeks he spends with God on the mountain.

The Ten Commandments form the basis of all other laws in Israel (20:1-17). The first five deal with honoring the Lord, the second five with respecting one's neighbor. The last commandment deals with one's thoughts and intentions rather than with specific actions. It thus forms a safeguard against all sins not included in the first nine.

The judgments recorded in chapters 21–23 deal with master-slave relationships (21:1-11), offenses punishable by death (vv 12-17), compensation for injury to persons or damage to property (21:18–22:15), various interpersonal relationships (22:16–23:9), and Sabbaths, feasts, and the offering of firstfruits (23:10-19). Many of the judgments would not take effect until Israel settled in the Promised Land. Accordingly, that section of the Law closes with a solemn warning against being rebellious and adopting pagan ways. It also contains a bright promise that God will drive out Israel's enemies, protect his people from sickness, and grant them prosperity, if they obey the Lord's commands (23:22).

Exodus 24 records a reaffirmation of the covenant between God and Israel, as Moses seals it with the blood of a sacrifice. In response, God appears to the leaders of the people, giving them a glimpse of his splendor. Then Moses ascends the mountain one more time to receive the stone tablets containing the commandments, as well as further instructions regarding the meeting tent (tabernacle), the priesthood, and worship.

God's Presence with his People (Ex 25–40) After the Lord redeemed the Israelites, he told Moses, "I will make you my own special people, and I will be your God. And you will know that I am the LORD your God who has rescued you from your slavery in Egypt" (6:7, NLT). Moses had seen that wonderful promise fulfilled, yet one further step remained: "I want the people of Israel to build me a sacred residence where I can live among them" (25:8). God's dwelling among his people is possible because God had descended to deliver the people and because they had pledged to meet his demands. God calls for a contribution from all whose hearts were willing to give, and he shows Moses a detailed pattern of the tabernacle and its furniture. Aaron and his sons are set apart to serve in the tent. Stipulations for the various offerings, including the Day of Atonement, are given.

God tells Moses that he has chosen Bezalel and Oholiab to build the tabernacle and to craft its furnishings, having filled them with his Spirit.

In the meantime the Israelites, who so recently promised total obedience, grow impatient as Moses lingers for 40 days on the mountain. They demand that Aaron make an idol for them. Under pressure, Aaron complies and forms a molten calf, a representation of a pagan deity (32:4).

The Lord informs Moses of the people's idolatry, revelry, and immorality and says that he is angry enough to destroy all of them and start again with Moses' offspring. Moses pleads for Israel until the Lord relents, then descends from the mountain to punish the people. Moses pleads again for forgiveness for Israel, and God in mercy pardons their terrible sin (34:8-10).

Once more God offers to make a covenant with the people (34:10). Moses spends another 40 days with the Lord, writing the commandments on tablets to replace those smashed when he saw the golden calf. When he returns to the people, his face shines from being in God's presence, and he must keep it veiled.

Now that Israel has been restored to God's favor, the construction of the tabernacle can begin. The contributions are so generous that Moses must restrain the people from bringing any more. Finally, all is ready. Moses examines the tabernacle, and it is erected on the first day of the first month, nearly a year after the first Passover. The priests are consecrated, the lamps are lit, and the first burnt sacrifice is offered. A cloud descends, filling the tabernacle with the glory of the Lord. God dwells among his people, the goal of redemption has been attained, and the drama of the book of Exodus has come to an end.

See also Chronology of the Bible (Old Testament); Egypt, Egyptian; Exodus, The; Feasts and Festivals of Israel; Israel, History of; Moses; Plagues upon Egypt; Tabernacle; Temple; Commandments, The Ten.

EXODUS, The Departure of Israel from Egypt led by Moses. The exodus was one of the most significant events in the history of the Hebrews. It was a unique demonstration of God's power on behalf of his people, who were working under conditions of forced labor for the Egyptians. So dramatic were the circumstances in which the exodus occurred that they were mentioned frequently in subsequent OT periods. When the Hebrews were oppressed, they looked back to that great historical event and trusted God for future liberation.

The historicity of the exodus from Egypt is, beyond question, one of the pivotal historical and religious points of the Jewish tradition. It is quite another matter, however, to assign a firm date to the event, partly because certain scriptural references can be interpreted in various ways, and partly because little archaeological evidence from Egypt exists that bears on the question. Since the Egyptians regularly ignored defects in their records and defaced inscriptions belonging to unpopular fellow countrymen, it is improbable that anything approaching an Egyptian literary record of the exodus will ever be obtained. Much of the information regarding the date of the exodus is therefore inferential in character, and that presents biblical historians with one of the most complex problems of chronology.

Date of the Exodus Determining the date of the exodus has long been a problem for biblical scholars. At the beginning of the 20th century many scholars, both liberal and conservative, placed the date toward the end of the 13th century BC. Not all of them agreed that the exodus was a single event, however. Some believed that the

Hebrews entered Palestine twice at widely separated times. But such a view disregards the biblical account.

According to Exodus 12:40, the length of time that Jacob's descendants resided in the land of Egypt was 430 years. God had already predicted that interval of time to Abram (Gn 15:13). The Genesis prophecy, however, did not indicate when that occupation would begin.

The Septuagint (the first Greek translation of the OT), in its version of Exodus 12:40, reduced the period of occupation in Egypt to 215 years. That may mean that two traditions of exodus history existed. A stay of four centuries may have been reckoned from the period when an Asiatic people known as the Hyksos invaded Egypt (c. 1720 BC) and governed it for about a century and a half. The period of 215 years preserved in the Septuagint may be the interval of time between the expulsion of the Hyksos and the exodus itself.

More specific information from Israel's early monarch, however, has a bearing on the time when the Hebrews escaped from Egypt. First Kings 6:1 indicates that Solomon constructed the temple in Jerusalem 480 years after the Israelites were led out of Egypt by Moses. Taking that figure at face value, and allowing a date of 961 BC for the reference to Solomon, the exodus would have occurred about 1441 BC. On the basis of such biblical data, some scholars argue for a 15th-century BC date for the exodus, connecting it with the reign of Pharaoh Amenhotep II (c. 1450–1425 BC) as the time of Israel's oppression. Other scholars feel equally persuaded that the exodus occurred in the 13th century BC.

Route of the Exodus The biblical data concerning the route of the exodus placed the beginning of the flight at Rameses (Ex 12:37). This place was identified with Tanis by early investigators, but more recent work suggests Qantir, about 17 miles (27.4 kilometers) southwest of Tanis, as the preferred site. It now seems certain that the monuments at Tanis apparently erected by Ramses have been misunderstood. None of those monuments seems to have originated at Tanis but were brought there by later kings who reused them. Thus the primary evidence for identifying Tanis with Ramses has proved to be misleading. Excavations at Qantir, on the other hand, have revealed indications of palaces, temples, and houses, all of which were local in origin. Such evidence suggests that Qantir, not Tanis, was the Rameses from which the exodus commenced. In addition, Rameses, unlike Tanis, was located beside a body of water (the "Waters of Re" mentioned in Egyptian sources), which again conforms to the biblical account.

Key Places in the Exodus The Israelites left Succoth and camped first at Etham before going toward Baal-zephon to camp by the sea (14:2). God miraculously brought them across the sea, into the Shur Desert (15:22). After stopping at the oasis of Elim, the people moved into the Sin Desert (16:1).

From Rameses the Israelites moved to Succoth (Nm 33:5), generally identified with Tell el-Maskhuta, a fortification in the eastern area of the Wadi Tumeilat, west of the Bitter Lakes. From Succoth they journeyed to Etham (Ex 13:20), which was on the frontier of the wilderness of Shur. The Hebrews were then instructed to return northwestward so that the stage might be set for the events of the exodus proper. Accordingly, they encamped between Migdol and the "sea," close to two sites called Pi-hahiroth and Baal-zephon. Pi-hahiroth may have been a lake, the "Hi-waters," mentioned in Egyptian documents. Baal-zephon has been identified with the later Tahpanhes (Tell Defenneh) near Qantara. Both identifications lack certainty, but these places were probably located in the northeast part of the Nile River delta area near Lake Menzaleh. The "sea" was a lake of papyrus reeds, described in Exodus 15:22 as the "reed sea," the English equivalent of an Egyptian phrase meaning "papyrus marshes." In most English translations from the time of the KJV onward, the Hebrew for "reed sea" was rendered as "Red Sea."

Sources from the 13th century BC mention the existence of a large papyrus marsh in the area of Rameses that could be the one referred to in Scripture. Other suggestions equate the "reed sea" with the southeast extension of Lake Menzaleh, or with some body of water just to the south, perhaps Lake Ballah, all of which are reasonably close to each other. The topography can never be determined with complete accuracy, since the construction of the Suez Canal drained a series of lakes and swamps, of which the "reed sea" was possibly one.

At the camp at Migdol, the Hebrews were overtaken by the pursuing Egyptians and appeared to be trapped hopelessly. Then the Lord worked one of the greatest miracles of history. He first prevented the Egyptians from encountering the Hebrews that night by means of a pillar of cloud (Ex 14:19-20). Moses raised his rod over the reed sea, and a strong east wind blew on the water all night. By morning a strip of the sea bottom had been exposed and dried out, enabling the Israelites to flee across it. When the Egyptians pursued their former slaves, Moses again raised his rod, the wind ceased, and the waters returned to normal levels, trapping the Egyptian chariots and soldiers and causing heavy losses. A victory song (Ex 15:1-21), typical of ancient Near Eastern customs in warfare, was the liberated captives' immediate response to God.

The parting of the waters is a phenomenon that has been observed periodically in various parts of the world. It always occurs in the same manner and involves a strong wind displacing a body of water. Shallow lakes, rivers, or marshes are parted readily under such conditions. The scriptural reference to the east wind indicates that God miraculously employed that natural phenomenon to rescue his people.

Having escaped successfully from the Egyptians, the Hebrews journeyed to the wilderness of Shur, three traveling days away from the bitter waters of Marah (Ex 15:22-25). In Numbers 33:8 the wilderness of Shur is identified with Etham, which the Israelites had already left. Thus it appears that they had moved north from Migdol, after which they moved south again to the wilderness in the area of Etham. The Israelites were not able to go into the Sinai Peninsula along the normal routes, which were guarded by Egyptian fortresses. In addition, they had been instructed not to travel along the northward road going to the "way of the land of the Philistines" (Ex 13:17) into Canaan. Consequently, the best means of satisfying both conditions was to move southeastward to Sinai as unobtrusively as possible, taking care to avoid the access routes to Serabit el-Khadem in the central peninsula region, where the Egyptians mined turquoise and copper. The narratives of Numbers 33:9-15 show that the Israelite camps were located in an area south of the "reed sea," proving that the refugees had not taken the northerly, or "Philistine," route.

The Exodus Theme in Scripture

Old Testament The motif of deliverance from captivity in Egypt became etched indelibly upon the Hebrew mind, particularly since it was reinforced each year by the celebration of the Passover meal (Ex 12:12-14). At each celebration thereafter the Hebrews were made aware that they had once been captives, but by the provision and power of God they were now free people—an elect nation and holy priesthood (Dt 26:19).

In later periods psalms were written recounting Israel's history in the light of the great liberating event of the exodus (Pss 105; 106; 114; 136). Those compositions resound with triumph and thanksgiving. Hebrew accounts of the bondage in Egypt depict the rigorous life, the oppression, and the hard labor. It is now known that there were a number of foreign groups in Egypt at the time, and that the corporal punishment suffered by the Hebrews was a normal feature of everyday Egyptian life. In short, there was no discrimination against the Hebrews as a group; instead, they enjoyed the dubious distinction of being treated like ordinary Egyptian workers. Ever after, when they were oppressed, the Hebrews could look back to the great miracle of the exodus and believe that what God had done once he could do again. That was of great consolation to the faithful exiles weeping by the waters of Babylon (Ps 137:1) as they looked forward to another exodus when God would lead them in triumph from a destroyed Babylon (v 8) back to Palestine.

New Testament God's mighty work at the time of the exodus was recalled on a few occasions by NT writers, even though Christ had been sacrificed as "our Passover lamb" (1 Cor 5:7, NIV) by that time. In his speech before the Jerusalem Council, Stephen gave a traditional recital of OT history, mentioning the event of the Red Sea (Acts 7:36) as part of a demonstration of God's power to change human affairs. The apostle Paul used the experience of the exodus to remind his hearers that many who were delivered from oppression at that time never reached the Promised Land (1 Cor 10:1-5). Instead of committing themselves wholly to God in trust and obedience, the Israelites fell victim to temptations of various kinds in the wilderness. Thus, Paul stressed that since it is possible for Christians to become castaways (9:27), they should cling to Christ the Rock and take their spiritual responsibilities seriously. In Hebrews 11:27-29 another historical recital lists the heroes of faith, mentioning especially Moses and his role at the exodus.

See also Exodus, Book of.

EXORCISM*, EXORCIST* Art of expelling demons and evil spirits, and the practitioner of this art.

The ability to expel or control demons was claimed by many in the ancient Near East. Aside from the miracles of Jesus recorded in the Gospels, only in Acts 19:13 is there a biblical reference to exorcism among the Jews. However in 1 Samuel 16:14-23 David functioned as an exorcist by playing a lyre to cast out an evil spirit from Saul.

See also Demon; Demon-possession.

EXPIATION* Atonement, purification, or removal of sin or its guilt. The term occurs in some English translations (such as ASV, ERV) for "reconciliation" (Heb 2:17) or

"propitiation" (Rom 3:25; 1 Jn 2:2; 4:10). "Expiation" also appears in some English translations of some OT passages (Nm 35:33; Dt 32:43; 1 Sm 3:14; Is 27:9). The word does not appear in modern Bible translations.

The Hebrew family of words translated by "expiation" speaks fundamentally of a solution for sin, and the most common association is with the idea of atonement. Expiation has to do with removing the blot of sin, and hence the term is related to such words as "forgive," "purge," "cleanse," or "atone."

All NT references to expiation have to do with the sacrifice of Christ for human sin. In the Bible both expiation and propitiation are part of God's atoning work. Christ's sacrifice both propitiates (turns away) the wrath of God and expiates (covers) human sin. God's redemptive work is both personal, or relational, and objective. When a biblical context concentrates on God's wrath, propitiation is involved; when human sin is the focus, then redemption provides expiation.

See also Atonement; Offerings and Sacrifices; Propitiation.

EYE PAINT *See* Cosmetics.

EZAR* KJV spelling of Ezer, Seir's son, in 1 Chronicles 1:38. *See* Ezer #1.

EZBAI Father of Naarai, one of David's elite force known as "the thirty" (1 Chr 11:37). In 2 Samuel 23:35 he is called Paarai the Arbite. This has led some interpreters to suggest that "the son of Ezbai" in the 1 Chronicles passage is a corruption of "the Arbite" and that the correct reading of his name should be Naarai the Arbite.

EZBON
1. Gad's son (Gn 46:16), called Ozni in Numbers 26:16; perhaps an eponym of a Gadite family.
2. Benjamin's grandson (1 Chr 7:7). It has been proposed that 1 Chronicles 7:6-11 is a genealogy of Zebulun assigned to Benjamin by error, and that Ezbon suggests Ibzan (Jgs 12:8-10), a minor judge of Bethlehem.

EZEKIAS* KJV spelling of Hezekiah, Judah's king, in Matthew 1:9-10. *See* Hezekiah #1.

EZEKIEL (Person) Priest and prophet during Israel's Babylonian exile. Ezekiel was a descendant of the influential priestly family of Zadok (Ez 1:3). He was probably reared in Jerusalem and was familiar with the temple ritual; it is unknown whether he served as a priest there. All that is known of his personal life is obtained from the OT book of Ezekiel.

Ezekiel was married (24:16-18) and lived at Tel-abib in Babylonia (3:15), in his own house (3:24; 8:1). Most of the Judean captives had settled by the Kebar Canal (1:3), which went from Babylon by Nippur to Erech. The elders of Israel there sought out Ezekiel for counsel (8:1; 14:1; 20:1). In the fifth year of the exile, when Ezekiel was between 25 and 30 years old, he received God's call to the prophetic office (1:1–3:11). His wife died suddenly during the exile, but he was forbidden to mourn for her in public (24:16-18). Her sudden death was meant to convey a striking and solemn warning of what would occur in the captives' homeland (vv 15-27).

The time of Ezekiel's ministry was unusual in many ways. It was a period of great prophetic activity. With the prophets Jeremiah and Daniel, Ezekiel spoke to the nation's needs at the time of the Babylonian captivity. It was an era of upheaval and uprooting for the southern

kingdom of Judah, and a time of persistent apostasy, idolatry, and general disobedience to the Mosaic law. It was also a period of international conflict and shifting power balances throughout the Near East.

Ezekiel's ministry seems to have extended from 592 BC to at least the 27th year of the exile (29:17). It falls into two main periods. During the first period (592–587 BC), his messages were repeated warnings—in prose discourse and symbolic acts—intended to lead the exiles to repentance and faith in God. During the second period (586–570 BC), after Nebuchadnezzar's destruction of Jerusalem and the temple, the prophet comforted the exiles and encouraged them to look to the future in hope (chs 33–48). There were 13 years in which no prophetic utterances were delivered, namely 585 BC (32:1, 17; 33:21) to 572 BC (40:1). The prophet learned of the fall of Jerusalem while in Babylon (33:21-22).

The burden of Ezekiel's message was that Judah was ripe for judgment. His preparation for speaking God's message is given in the picture of his eating the written prophecies (2:8–3:3). At first the messages were not accepted, but later his prophecies were vindicated as they began to come true and as the nation was purged of its idolatry. Ezekiel has been called "the father of Judaism" because of his supposed influence on Israel's later worship. His greatest contribution to postexilic Jewish worship consisted in establishing the basis of the synagogue. He stressed the teaching of personal immortality, resurrection, and the ritual law.

Ezekiel carried out his messages with vivid and dramatic acts of symbolism (e.g., 4:1-8; 5:1-17). His style has been characterized as heavy and repetitious, but it was designed with the themes of apostasy and subsequent judgment in view.

The place and circumstances of his death are unknown, and Ezekiel is not mentioned elsewhere in the OT.

See also Diaspora of the Jews; Ezekiel, Book of; Prophet, Prophetess.

EZEKIEL, Book of Prophetic book of the OT, originating in the time of the Babylonian exile.

PREVIEW
•Author
•Date and Background
•Content

Author Ezekiel was the son of Buzi (1:3), a member of a priestly family. It is unclear whether he actually served in the temple as a priest, but such was his training. His writings show that he knew the regulations for sacrifices, the rituals, and the people's expectations of a priest. In exile Ezekiel the priest spoke God's word about the future of the temple to his fellow exiles. Settled at Tel-abib, on the canal of Kebar, the thousands of deportees eked out a meager existence. They hoped for a speedy return to Judah and a change for the better in the international situation. Their hope was enflamed by the spirited preaching of false prophets, likened to jackals among the ruins (13:4). They piously said, "The Lord declares . . . ," but they were actually self-commissioned (v 6). They deceived the people with a message of peace at a time when God's judgment was about to be poured out on his people (v 10). They had led the people to distrust prophecy to such an extent that a proverb circulated among the people that "the days grow long, and every vision comes to nought" (12:22). Much time had passed since visions of God's judgment had been given to the people, and nothing could be interpreted as a fulfillment of those visions. Ezekiel was called to serve his community by symbolic acts, visions, and verbal messages in order to convince the people that God's judgment was imminent (v 23).

Date and Background The ministry of the prophet Ezekiel can be understood best against the backdrop of his time. If, as the church father Origen believed, the vague reference "in the thirtieth year" (1:1) marks the prophet's age at the time of his first vision, Ezekiel was born during the rule of King Josiah of Judah (c. 640–609 BC). Josiah was the grandson of King Manasseh, whose sacrilegious acts had brought God's judgment on the kingdom of Judah (2 Kgs 21:10-15).

Though Judah's political situation was perilous, Josiah led the nation in a radical reformation that began with the finding of the "Book of the Law" (2 Kgs 22) in the year that Ezekiel was born (c. 621 BC). Idolatry was done away with and the people turned back to God, but God's judgment on Judah was unchangeable (23:26-27). Josiah erred in trying to make Judah a kingdom with which other states had to reckon. He was threatened when the Egyptian pharaoh Neco passed through Judah on his way to aid the weakened Assyrian kingdom. Josiah marched to meet the Egyptian forces, but his troops were unable to stand against the Egyptians, and he died in battle (v 29). Egypt took control of Judah, and Pharaoh Neco placed Jehoiakim in power over Jerusalem. Egyptian control did not last long, however, for in 605 BC Egypt and Assyria were defeated by Babylonia's king Nebuchadnezzar at Carchemish. The Babylonians then pushed south to Jerusalem, and the first deportation of Judean leaders (among them the prophet Daniel) took place.

Jehoiakim was permitted to continue ruling over Judah as a vassal king of Nebuchadnezzar. But his dealings with Egypt brought the emperor's wrath down upon him. Before the Babylonians could address the Judean situation, Jehoiakim died and his son Jehoiachin was crowned. When the Babylonian forces arrived at the gates of Jerusalem, Jehoiachin and thousands of the aristocracy were taken to Babylon (2 Kgs 24:10-17). Among those deportees was Ezekiel, then about 25 years old.

Although the book says otherwise, many scholars think that Ezekiel lived and taught in Judah for the duration of the siege and the fall of Jerusalem (586 BC). They conclude this from Ezekiel's familiarity with idolatry in the temple and his vivid descriptions of Jerusalem's last days (Ez 8:11). Others believe that Ezekiel ministered both to the exiled community and to the Judeans living in Judah. Neither interpretation does full justice to the claims of the book itself. Ezekiel was exiled in 597 BC. He was called to bring God's word to the deportees at Tel-abib; he was granted a vision of the horrible practices in the temple court; and he was familiar with Jerusalem and Judah from having lived there and from reports on affairs in Jerusalem coming to the exiles through messengers. Jeremiah, Ezekiel's contemporary, was prophesying in Jerusalem, but there is no evidence that Jeremiah and Ezekiel knew of each other's ministry. If Ezekiel had brought God's word to Jerusalem during the siege, some reference to Jeremiah might appear in his writings. If Jeremiah was supported by Ezekiel's ministry in Jerusalem, he probably would have included a positive word for his colleague in his book. The book of Ezekiel plainly says that Ezekiel lived and preached in exile (see 1:1-3; 11:24-25).

Content The prophecy of Ezekiel is easily outlined by subject matter and chronology. The chronology of the period permits a division before and after 586 BC (the fall of Jerusalem). Chapters 1–24 cover the pre-586 ministry of Ezekiel, whereas chapters 33–48 represent his post-586 ministry. Chapters 25–32 (oracles against the foreign nations) function as a transition between the book's two major divisions.

The book's outline according to subject matter divides into four parts: Ezekiel's call (1:1–3:21); prophecies of judgment against Israel (3:22–24:27); oracles against the nations (25:1–32:32); and proclamation of hope (33:1–48:35).

Ezekiel's Call (1:1–3:21) The prophet's call in one sense was similar to that of Isaiah and Jeremiah. Isaiah received his mission in a vision of God's glory in the temple (Is 6). Jeremiah was called unexpectedly in his youth, and received signs that solemnly set forth the nature of his mission (Jer 1:11-15). The call of Ezekiel combined those two elements. Revelation of God's glory to the prophet at the same time revealed the nature of the prophet's mission. Ezekiel's call contained a full description of God's glory. Isaiah briefly stated that he saw the Lord enthroned in the temple, and he concentrated on the seraphim representing and magnifying God's glory. Ezekiel elaborated on the revelation of the Lord's glory as well as on the ministering angels who went before the Lord as part of his royal entourage. The vision of God's glory, though difficult to understand, is the key to the book of Ezekiel.

Ezekiel, as a priest, was concerned about the future of the temple. That sacred place had been ordained by God as his home among his people. The glory, presence, and holiness of God were symbolized in the temple (see 1 Kgs 8:10-11). In exile Ezekiel could not serve his people as a priest, for they were far from Jerusalem, the city God had chosen. Against all expectations the Lord revealed himself to Ezekiel in the land of Babylon. In calling Ezekiel to a prophetic ministry, God assured his servant that he had not forsaken his people, even though they had been banished from the Promised Land.

The prophet's vision began with a storm. As a large cloud approached from the north, Ezekiel saw a brightness surrounding the cloud, four creatures, and four wheels. The combination of creatures and wheels suggests that the Lord appeared in a chariot. God's chariot is a familiar OT representation of his coming in judgment (see Is 66:15-16). The wheels within wheels and the position of the four living creatures may signify God's total control over the whole earth, so he could move his "chariot of judgment" in any direction. It is also possible that the living creatures with their four faces, and the wheels full of eyes, may be separate symbols showing that God sees all that happens and thereby knows the plight of the exiles. In the vision the prophet's attention was drawn to a throne above the heads of the creatures. On the throne was "the appearance of the likeness of the glory of the LORD" (1:28). In his vision of God's coming in judgment, Ezekiel received his call to the prophetic ministry: "Son of man, I send you to the people of Israel, to a nation of rebels who have rebelled against me" (2:3, RSV). During a dark hour of Israel's history, Ezekiel had to prophesy, rebuke his fellow exiles (3:11), and be responsible as a watchman over the house of Israel (3:17; cf. 33:1-9). Symbolic of his mission was a scroll filled with lamentations and woe (2:9-10), which when eaten became sweet as honey (3:1-3). Difficult as the mission was, God's presence and the certain fulfillment of the prophecies sweetened Ezekiel's task. Such encouragement was intended to take away any fear of the rebellious Israelites (2:6-7). Instead of being elated with his mission, however, Ezekiel became despondent.

A week later, the word of the Lord came to Ezekiel to remind him of his important role as a watchman

(3:16-17). Ezekiel became responsible for Israel as a nation, not just for individuals. His witness to Israel had the express aim of national repentance (vv 18-19).

Ezekiel was confined to his house by God (3:24-25). The house ministry was to be carried on only with those Israelites who sought God's will, for the Lord had abandoned those who continued in their apostasy. The prophetic word would not help the apostates (v 26). The principle of Ezekiel's ministry is found in 3:27: "Whenever I give you a message, I will loosen your tongue and let you speak. Then you will say to them, 'This is what the Sovereign LORD says!' Some of them will listen, but some will ignore you, for they are rebels" (NLT; cf. Mt 11:15; 13:43).

Prophecies of Judgment against Israel (3:22–24:27)

Symbolism figures prominently in Ezekiel's writing. His priestly background and preparation probably suited him to receive and communicate God's word in symbolic acts and speech. Chapters 4 and 5 contain four symbolic acts: (1) Jerusalem's siege is portrayed on a brick (Ez 4:1-3); (2) Israel's iniquity is represented by Ezekiel's lying on his sides (vv 4-8); (3) Jerusalem's grief and horror in the last days of the siege are represented by Ezekiel's food and drink (vv 9-17); (4) Jerusalem's fate is represented by the prophet's hair being cut off (5:1-4).

Ezekiel's instructions were further illuminated by God's explanation of Israel's apostasy (5:6-7) and his judgment on Israel (vv 8-12). The judgment will last until the Israelites admit that in covenant faithfulness their Lord has inflicted righteous judgment on them (v 13).

God would direct his judgment first against the people and the city of Jerusalem. Next in line were the mountains of Israel (ch 6) and the land (ch 7). God's wrath included the cities and cultic sites in the hill country of Judah, leaving no protection for the people (6:3-6). Abominations that were practiced throughout the land caused God's judgment to fall on the land as well as on the people (7:2-3, 10-11, 23). But because God is righteous, he judged the people according to their ways of life, desiring that they would once more acknowledge him as their God (7:27).

The prophet then (chs 8–11) focused on the abominations practiced in Jerusalem, particularly idolatry in the temple courts, which caused the judgment announced in chapters 1–7. An idol had been erected in the inner court (8:3-5). By the wall of the court, elders of the city were paying homage to the idols that surrounded the court (vv 11-12). Closer to the temple, women were weeping for the god Tammuz (v 14), and men were worshiping the sun (v 16). In preparation for the ultimate judgment on the land, the prophet placed a mark on the foreheads of the few faithful Israelites so that they would survive (9:4-6). Then (ch 10), the glory of God, which had filled the temple from the time of Solomon, gradually left: "Then the glory of the LORD went up from the city and stopped above the mountain to the east" (11:23, NLT). The people, now without divine protection, were being handed over to the Babylonians (v 9).

The message of doom for Jerusalem contains four elements of hope: restoration of the people (11:17), restoration of the land (v 17), purification of the people (v 18), and renewed fellowship between God and his people (vv 19-20). The prophet develops those four themes in chapters 33–48.

The visions of chapters 10 and 11 made clear that when God removed his presence from Jerusalem, the exile was approaching. Those who were already in Babylon were unwilling to believe that such an extensive devastation of Jerusalem would happen or that the people would all be exiled and the land become desolate.

Ezekiel acted out the certainty of God's word of judgment by packing his bags and showing the baggage to his fellow exiles. First, he placed the bags in the courtyard outside his modest home. Next, he went out by making a hole through the wall. Finally, the prophet walked about the settlement with his bags in full view. Skeptical observers did not understand Ezekiel and probably thought he was crazy. The believers who saw him understood. His strange actions dramatized how the king's aides would do all they could to help King Zedekiah escape just before the fall of Jerusalem. Second Kings 25 tells how the king and his soldiers left Jerusalem for the wilderness, to be overtaken by the Babylonians at Jericho and brought before Nebuchadnezzar at Riblah. As a captive, Zedekiah witnessed the murder of his sons; then his eyes were put out, and he was sent into exile with the other Judeans (cf. Ez 12:13). The prophet's explanation concluded with a word of comfort. Because of his covenant with Abraham, God promised not to destroy the people completely. A remnant who overcame the sword, famine, and pestilence would live to tell the story of God's judgment (vv 15-16).

Ezekiel further illustrated the nation's plight by eating as though full of fear, depicting the great trauma that all of Judah's inhabitants would soon undergo.

Both symbolic acts, packing his belongings and eating, emphasized the truthfulness of God's word. The people needed to face the nature of their God: He is magnificent, and when he speaks, his words are powerful and come to pass. Thus, the devastation of the land and the people's exile were a fulfillment of God's word through the prophets. The judgment was meant to produce a recognition of the Lord, repentance, and a return to God. Some in Judah doubted the efficacy of God's prophecies, saying, "Time passes, making a liar of every prophet" (12:22). Others thought God's word would come true in the distant future (v 27). The prevailing attitude of distrust in God's word had been stimulated by the popular preaching of false prophets (ch 13). Never commissioned by the Lord, they deceived God's people by lying and misdirecting them with messages of peace (vv 8-10). Wickedness, lying, and deceit were encouraged among the people by such false prophets (v 22). The magnitude of their sin and their great responsibility for Judah's fall would be matched by the Lord's heavy judgment. Yet God would save his people from such evil and will prepare a righteous nation with whom to maintain his covenant (v 23).

The certainty of the judgment has been connected with the truthfulness of God's word. Ezekiel's difficult task of affirming the doom of Jerusalem to stubborn hearers was intensified by the people's idolatry. Their whole way of life denied the existence of God. They practiced idolatry in their worship, and they had set up idols in their hearts (14:3). Before the covenant with God could be restored, they had to be purified from their idolatry. Even so, repentance would not guarantee immunity from judgment. Sword, famine, wild beasts, and plagues would ravage the population (v 21). After the execution of his judgment, God would take back those survivors who had turned to him for mercy. God would surely accomplish all that he intended for his people's good (v 23).

In chapters 15–17 Ezekiel uses three parables to set forth the apostasy, present uselessness, and judgment of Israel. Jerusalem and Judah are compared to a piece of charred wood, an adulterous woman, and a vine.

Chapter 15 reviews Jerusalem's case. Jerusalem is compared to a piece of wood, both ends of which have been charred with fire, so that the wood is of no value. As the whole piece of wood is burned instead of being saved, so Jerusalem would undergo complete devastation (15:7-8).

Chapter 16 presents God's case against Jerusalem from a different perspective, stressing his care for Jerusalem in the past. The beginnings of her history are compared to the birth of a female child, left abandoned by her mother (16:3-5). God adopted the child and washed and clothed her (vv 6-7). He made a covenant with her (v 8), making her his own possession. He generously gave her all the fine things of life (vv 9-13). In the height of her development, Jerusalem's fame spread to the nations (v 14). Her self-reliance made her a spiritual prostitute as she took up the religious practices and way of life of the nations (vv 15-34). The cities of Sodom (Gn 19) and Samaria (2 Kgs 17:6), known for their immorality, are called Jerusalem's sisters (Ez 16:46). They had been judged by God, but the corruption of those cities was little compared to the lewdness of Jerusalem (vv 48-51). Thus, Jerusalem also would surely fall and become desolate. Yet Ezekiel anticipates the judgment's final outcome; Jerusalem will be restored to covenantal blessing (vv 62-63) after her repentance.

The third parable (ch 17) focuses on God's sovereignty over political developments. Assyria was no longer a power to be reckoned with. Babylon and Egypt both exercised dominion, although the balance of power was veering in favor of Babylon. Their extension of power is likened to an eagle. Nebuchadnezzar, pictured as "a great eagle with broad wings full of many-colored feathers," took control over the affairs of Judah by removing Jehoiachin, "the highest branch of a cedar tree," from office and by exiling him with young leaders of the Judean state (17:3-4). Ezekiel was among them. Nebuchadnezzar let the Judeans control their own affairs under Zedekiah but expected them to be subject to Babylon and not to any other power. But Judah (likened to a vine) tried to ally itself with Pharaoh Hophra of Egypt, "another great eagle with broad wings and full plumage" (v 7), against Nebuchadnezzar. Zedekiah's folly in turning to Egypt would cause Nebuchadnezzar to pull up the vine by its roots and make it wither (vv 9-10). In explaining the parable, God told the exiles that Judah's fall was a result of its unfaithfulness to King Nebuchadnezzar, to whom Judah owed allegiance by covenant (vv 13-18). Judah's unfaithfulness thus extended to all of its relationships: religious, cultural, and political. After the exile, God promised, he would restore his people to their land under a Messiah, "a tender shoot" (v 22). The messianic rule is signified by the young twig, which when planted in the land will become a magnificent cedar, giving shade and protection to the birds. Chapter 17 is an inspiring affirmation of the sovereignty of God in human affairs ("All the trees will know that it is I, the LORD, who cuts down the tall tree and helps the short tree to grow tall. It is I who makes the green tree wither and gives new life to the dead tree"—17:24, NLT).

Chapters 18–22 contain Ezekiel's oracles to Judah, its leaders, and the exiles. First, he enunciates God's standard of righteousness: "The person who sins will be the one who dies" (18:4, NLT). The people are charging God with injustice, for they believe themselves to be under God's judgment for the sins of their ancestors (vv 25-29). Although the Ten Commandments do say that God may punish "the sins of their parents to the third and the fourth generations" (Ex 20:5, NLT), the prophet vindicates God's justice, telling the people that they are not being punished merely for their ancestors' sin. Each person must be directly accountable to God; the sinner will die in wickedness, and the righteous will live by righteousness. A life of faithfulness to God's moral and civil law will be rewarded (Ez 18:5-9). Even if one's father was a sinner, the father's sin is not transferable (vv 14-18).

God is ready to forgive any sinner who repents (v 27). The prophet's vindication of God's justice becomes a call to repentance. The sinners in Judah and in exile were thus warned of the consequences of their evil, and were exhorted to return to their God and his standard of right and wrong (vv 31-32).

Chapter 19 contains two parables in the form of a lamentation. The first portrays a lioness and her two cubs. The lioness is Hamutal, the wife of King Josiah (2 Kgs 23:31), who bore two sons: Jehoahaz and Zedekiah. Jehoahaz is referred to in Ezekiel 19:3-4 as a cub who grew up and was taken to Egypt (by Pharaoh Neco in 608 BC; see 2 Kgs 23:31-34). Zedekiah succeeded to the throne ten years later. In the lamentation the prophet imaginatively represents Zedekiah as a young cub who is ultimately taken to Babylon as a rebellious ruler (Ez 19:7-9). The second parable changes the imagery to a vine, representing Israel (v 10). In its early days God blessed Israel with strong rulers, but now the vine was wilting as Zedekiah irresponsibly led Judah to its last days. Ezekiel's lamentation stresses the lack of a good candidate for the throne and the lack of life in the vine (vv 13-14).

In chapter 20 the prophet concludes God's argument against his people. He reviews the history of Israel's past, starting with God's self-revelation in Egypt (20:5-6). He took to himself a stubborn nation, tied to idolatry (v 8) and prone to apostasy (vv 13, 21). Israel wanted to be one of the great nations (v 32) instead of a sanctified people (v 12). As a result of its spiritual hardness, Israel is dispersed to live among the nations (v 35). Yet God had a solemn covenant with Israel, made by oath to the patriarchs Abraham, Isaac, and Jacob. On the basis of that covenant, God will reach out with compassion to those who repent of their sinful ways (vv 37-44). In Israel's judgment and restoration the nations will see the holiness of God, which does not tolerate unfaithfulness in Israel (v 41).

Ezekiel's prophecies alternate between God's judgment on Israel's sin and his restoration of Israel, spanning the bridge between Israel's past and future. In view of the people's doubts of the coming judgment on Jerusalem, he stresses the necessity of judgment and the need for repentance. Still, the future restoration of a remnant is touched upon here and there as the counterpart of his message of judgment. After announcing the fall of Jerusalem, the prophet shifts from a message of judgment to one of hope.

The prophet returns to the proclamation of judgment in four oracles (20:45–21:32). He speaks against the Negev Desert area (20:45-49), Jerusalem and the land of Israel (21:2-17, 20-27), and against the Ammonites (vv 28-32). God permitted the sword of Nebuchadnezzar to be his instrument of judgment upon the Judeans (v 19). He would see to the judgment on the Ammonites. The Judeans would recover their previous glory, but the memory of the Ammonites would perish (vv 27, 32). The oracle against the Ammonites anticipates a larger treatise on Israel's other neighbors: Moab, Edom, Philistia, Tyre, Sidon, and Egypt (chs 25–29).

Chapters 22–24 contain a renewed series of indictments against Jerusalem. Jerusalem's religious and civil leadership (the prophets, priests, and princes) are corrupt, and the people have followed their example (22:25-30). The parable of the two sisters, Oholah and Oholibah, is a variation of the parable of adulterous Jerusalem (ch 23; cf. ch 16). It differs in that the comparison drawn between Jerusalem, soon to be exiled, and Samaria, already in exile, is more explicit in the parable of Oholah and Oholibah. In chapter 16 Jerusalem was charged with greater sins than Sodom and Samaria, but was promised restoration. Only the adulterous nature of the two sisters and God's judgment on them is emphasized in chapter 23, with no word of restoration. This parable is a fitting introduction to that of the boiling pot (ch 24), in which Jerusalem is compared to a rusty pot boiling with water. The Jerusalemites, likened to pieces of meat in the boiling pot, will die in the city. The parable was pronounced on the starting day of Nebuchadnezzar's siege of Jerusalem. Thus, the exiles were divinely forewarned of God's intent to destroy the temple (24:21) and were prepared for messengers bringing the bad news of Jerusalem's fall.

Those oracles and parables conclude the first division of the book. Ezekiel has stated God's case against the rebellious house of Judah in many ways. His metaphors have likened Judah to a burnt piece of wood, to an uprooted vine, to a baby who grew up to be an adulteress, and to Oholibah, the adulterous woman. He has countered arguments against the fulfillment of God's word and against the justice of God. He has reassured the exiles that God will not leave the righteous and that the future of Israel begins with a righteous remnant. The pendulum of Ezekiel's writing has swung from judgment to restoration, while the clock was bringing Judah closer to the hour of its fall.

Oracles against the Nations (25:1–32:32) Ammon, Moab, and Edom were Israel's neighbors to the east. Because they were ethnically related to Israel, they were not attacked by the Israelites on their march to the Promised Land. Ammon and Moab were descendants of Lot, Abraham's nephew, and the Edomites descended from Esau, the brother of Jacob. Although God forbade war with them, relations between Israel and its eastern neighbors were always tense. Israel had been overrun by the Ammonites for a time, and Israel was never successful in controlling the Edomites' competitive trade relations. Those neighboring nations joined the Babylonian attack against Jerusalem and rejoiced when Jerusalem fell and the temple was devastated (Ez 25:3-12). They were ready to take over and loot Judah's cities, and to instigate trouble in a time when Jerusalem was distressed. Therefore, says Ezekiel, God's judgment will also extend to Ammon, Moab, and Edom (vv 4-14).

The Philistines had been Israel's enemy to the southwest. During the period of the judges and the united monarchy, the Philistines had controlled much of Israel's territory. King David successfully limited the Philistine threat by confining them to their own territory. But in Ezekiel's day they were still considered Israel's "everlasting" enemy (25:15), possibly intensified by Philistine support of the Babylonian invasion of Judah.

The city of Tyre had received reports of the overthrow of Jerusalem and was ready to exploit the opportunity for its own advantage (26:2). Tyre's trade position was unrivaled; its ships crossed the seas to exchange goods with many distant lands (Ez 27). But Tyre would soon be broken by the Babylonians, its wealth dried up with the destruction of the fleet and the murder of its sailors (27:26).

The prince of Tyre is singled out in chapter 28, but verse 12 refers to the "king" of Tyre. Interpreters disagree whether they are one person or two. Those who distinguish between the two understand the prince of Tyre to be the ruler of that city, but they consider the "king" of Tyre to represent Satan (28:13-15). The Garden of Eden with all its splendor is an appropriate setting for the original glory of an angelic Satan before his fall. But there is no reason within the context to distinguish between the prince and the king of Tyre. Each is said to have exalted himself, and both took authority over men as if they were gods and enjoyed all the splendor and royalty that belong to God. And both prince and king fall from their high position.

The passage is a magnificent example of Ezekiel's literary ability. He draws a glorious picture of the Garden of Eden, reworking the same theme as he depicts the glory and fall of the king of Tyre. Ezekiel presents him as a cherub, in accordance with the local belief that the king was divine. He wore the finest clothing, with nine kinds of precious stones (v 13). Though God had elevated him to the royal throne (vv 13-14), the king's heart turned to materialism and to religious and judicial corruption (vv 16-18). In a sense the king (prince) represents the people of Tyre. They were all guilty of corruption, injustice, and violence. If God judged his covenant people for their perversion of justice and for their sins, his judgment would surely come also on the city of Tyre (vv 18-19). When the Babylonians marched on Tyre, they laboriously built a jetty from the mainland to the city. At the same time Tyrian ships loaded with goods and treasures sailed out across the Mediterranean, so that when Nebuchadnezzar's troops finally breached the walls, little loot could be taken (29:18).

The city of Sidon also cheered Jerusalem's destruction. Sidon was a port city in Phoenicia, to the north of Tyre. By pestilence and war, the inhabitants of Sidon would learn the justice of Israel's God.

Six nations (Ammon, Moab, Edom, Philistia, Tyre, and Sidon) scorned Israel at the fall of Jerusalem. Because God had invested his holiness in the temple of Jerusalem and in his people, the temple's destruction and the people's exile signified to the nations that Israel's God was impotent. They did not realize that the reason for Israel's fate was God's intolerance of his people's sin. God's holiness required the punishment of sin, and it also required vindication for his name (28:22-23). God was still concerned for his people, that Israel might know he had removed the scorn of their neighbors (v 24). In the restoration of Israel the Lord would further manifest his holiness before the nations. Israel would receive back the land, vineyards, and houses, and would enjoy the bounty of the Lord in peace (vv 25-26).

Egypt had convinced the people of Israel and Judah that with its help the Assyrians and the Babylonians could not stand their ground in Palestine. In 722 BC the Assyrian troops took the northern capital of Samaria, and in 586 the Babylonians conquered Jerusalem, while Egypt remained passive. The Egyptians had desired control over Palestine for economic reasons, but not at the expense of their own welfare. Egypt, too, would lose its leadership under God's judgment (29:9-16). Reduced to dependence on foreign powers, Egypt would no longer be a stumbling block for Israel. First, Babylonia was permitted to break Egypt's power (23:1–32:21); later, the Persians, Greeks, and Romans would incorporate Egypt as a province. The fall of Egypt coincided with the fall of several great and small kingdoms: Assyria (32:22-23), Elam (vv 24-25), Meshech and Tubal (vv 26-28), Edom (v 29), and Sidon (v 30).

Proclamation of Hope (33:1–48:35) After the visions of God's judgment on the surrounding nations, Ezekiel returns to the future hope of Israel. In the first major section of his book he dealt with the reasons for Judah's exile and the destruction of the temple, alluding often to the future of Israel. But the prophet's organization of his material included, between prophecies of Israel's judgment and restoration, the oracles of God's judgment on Israel's neighbors who had encouraged and rejoiced in its fall. Throughout its history Israel had allowed foreign nations to influence its religion, culture, and form of government. The reduction of their powers meant Israel, restored to the Promised Land, would be more free for faithfulness to God. Before taking up the theme of the restoration,

Ezekiel reviews the emphases of chapters 1–24: (1) He was called to be a watchman over Israel (33:1-9; cf. 1:1–3:21). (2) Israel had sinned against the Lord and had to receive a righteous judgment (33:10). (3) Jerusalem was to be taken by the Babylonians (v 21). (4) Israel's repentance is necessary for restoration (vv 11-16).

Thus far, his ministry had not met with success. The exiles who had heard his messages were full of appreciation for Ezekiel's rhetorical and literary abilities (33:32). They readily accepted Ezekiel as a watchman who warned the people of the impending catastrophe at Jerusalem, and they may have admitted that their sin was the reason for God's judgment on Israel and Jerusalem. But they were slow in applying the prophetic word to their own lives. God was ready to forgive their sins if they repented, acknowledged him, and demonstrated their renewed spirit by practicing the law of God (v 32). Now that the news of Jerusalem had been reported to the exiles (v 21), the necessity for the people to act responsibly was even more urgent. The Lord had demonstrated that Ezekiel was a true prophet (v 33).

The success of Ezekiel's ministry was not measured in numbers. He faithfully declared the word of God in word, sign, and parable. The exiles had followed the false hopes proclaimed by false "shepherds" who had fattened themselves at the expense of the flock (34:2-3). They did not take care of those in need (v 4), and they allowed the flock to be scattered (vv 5-6). God promised his people that he would be the faithful shepherd, bring the sheep together, feed them, and care for them (34:11-15; cf. Ps 23). God would also distinguish between the sheep and the goats, to find out whose hearts were right with him, so that the true sheep could be restored to God's flock (Ez 34:20-22). God's promise included the restoration of the land and the restoration of the divinely appointed Davidic dynasty (v 24). The renewed fellowship between the Lord and Israel under the messianic ruler would be sealed with a new covenant, the "covenant of peace." That covenant assured the people of God's blessing on their labor, bringing them abundant harvests (vv 26-27). The people would not be forced to fight against nature in their pursuits (vv 25-28). They would not have to struggle against other peoples who might try to share in their blessings by force (vv 27-29). The prophetic vision telescoped the events of the restoration of Israel after the exile, the coming of Jesus the Messiah (cf. Jn 10), and the full restoration of the sin-cursed world.

Chapter 34 is the key to the messages of restoration. The emphases include the outworking of the frequently repeated verse "They will truly be my people, and I will be their God" (11:20; cf. 34:30; 36:28). The most significant aspects of the restoration theme include: (1) God's gracious restoration of his people to covenant blessing (36:20-36; 37:23-26; 39:25); (2) God's restoration of the nation of Israel to the land (36:1-15, 24; 37:14-23; 39:27); (3) God's new covenant, giving his Spirit to his people (36:25-27; 37:14; 39:29), and his blessing on his people (36:8-12, 29-38; 39:9-10, 26), assuring them of victory over their enemies (35:1-15; 36:36; 37:28; 38:1–39:24); (4) God's appointment of a Davidic king, the Messiah, over his people (37:24-25); and (5) God's temple restored among his people (37:26-27).

➤THE PEOPLE OF GOD The rejection of the exiles did not last forever. Based on the Abrahamic covenant, the Lord promised to bless the faithful remnant and to make of them a new people. The imagery of a valley of dry bones is particularly fitting. The dry bones represent God's people without hope (37:11). Ezekiel proclaims to them the good news that God will renew and restore them (v 12).

The Lord's purpose for his people is that all the nations may honor his holy name through his people (39:7, 25-27).

➤THE LAND The promise also extends to the land, originally given to Abraham and his descendants. The Abrahamic covenant included a messianic element, for through the family of Abraham living in the Promised Land all nations would receive God's blessing (Gn 12:3). In a vision Ezekiel saw the boundaries and described the division of the land (Ez 47–48). The royal city of Jerusalem is the central symbol of God's presence among his people; its name will be "The Lord is there" (48:8-35).

➤THE NEW COVENANT The Abrahamic covenant is renewed, a gracious covenant that expresses the restored relationship. "Covenant of peace" fittingly describes its nature and benefits. The restless people of God are promised rest from their searching, their enemies, and their toil. The change in relationship is further emphasized by God's sending of his Spirit, who will add a new dimension to the lifestyle of his people. Obedience to God will no longer be constrained, for God's Spirit helps his people to do his will. A new heart, controlled by the Spirit of God, is given to the Lord's people (36:26-27). The presence of the Spirit also signifies a new life for the people (37:14; see Jn 3:8, 16; Acts 2:38; Rom 8:2-4, 15).

➤THE MESSIAH The OT hope of a messianic king is crystallized in Ezekiel's message. His rule will be everlasting (Ez 37:25), over all God's people who have new hearts (vv 15-25).

➤THE TEMPLE As a priest, Ezekiel remained keenly interested in the temple, priesthood, sacrificial regulations, and festivals. A large section of the prophecy's last division describes the temple's revived worship (40:1–46:24). His vision of the glory of God, so important in the messages of God's judgment on Jerusalem (chs 1, 10–11), now assures the remnant that God did not forsake his people (43:2-5). He will dwell among them, for the temple is a symbol of God's presence (37:27). Some interpreters believe that the temple, with its ritual as described in Ezekiel 40–46, will be restored in the messianic era before the last judgment. Others believe the promises about the temple provide a positive symbolic answer to Ezekiel's greatest concern: whether God will return to be with his people (48:35; see Jn 2:21; Rv 21:22).

Ezekiel's Temple

There are various interpretations of chapters 34–48. As a watchman to Israel, Ezekiel had a message for the exiled Jewish community. Thus the prophecy's fulfillment must have begun with the decree of Cyrus I (538 BC) permitting the Jews to return to their land (Ezr 1:1-3). Two rival schools of interpretation exist on how the prophecy is fulfilled beyond Israel's restoration to the land. Those who interpret Israel as simply the nation view the modern return of Jewish people to the land of Israel as a continuation of God's prophetic promise. They believe that God's plan for Israel is being fulfilled along with, and in addition to, his plan for the Christian church. The fulfillment of those prophecies will be inaugurated by the coming of the messianic king, who will give earthly peace to the Jewish people. The temple worship (Ez 40–48) will be restored in some way during the period of the messianic kingdom. The church will enjoy a small share in all the events centered on the Jews. The promises of Ezekiel's vision are thus limited to the nation of Israel and must be fulfilled before the coming of a new heaven and earth.

Other interpreters believe that Ezekiel wrote for the benefit of spiritual descendants of Abraham who believe, as Abraham did, in God's promises (Gn 15:6; cf. Rom 4:11-13; Gal 3:6-9, 29). All who have faith like Abraham, whether Jews or Gentiles, are regarded as Abraham's offspring (Gal 3:28-29). Ezekiel's message thus would include all of God's gracious work among Christian Gentiles, who have become the recipients of God's promises and benefits. It is possible, on the basis of 1 Peter 1:10-11, to interpret Ezekiel's language as a prophetic expression of how God's grace would come to all those who become reconciled to God through faith in the gospel.

See also Diaspora of the Jews; Ezekiel (Person); Prophecy.

EZEL* Hebrew word designating a stone where Jonathan and David met prior to David's departure from the court of Saul (1 Sm 20:19, NLT mg).

EZEM City allotted to Judah's tribe (Jos 15:29), then later to Simeon's tribe, for an inheritance (Jos 19:3; 1 Chr 4:29). Joshua 15 locates the city in the extreme southern part of Canaan.

EZER
1. Chieftain of a Horite tribe (Gn 36:21; 1 Chr 1:38).
2. Descendant and probably the son of Ephraim. He was killed while making a raid on the cattle of the Philistines (1 Chr 7:21).
3. Man of Judah, descended from Hur (1 Chr 4:4).
4. Gadite who joined David at Ziklag (1 Chr 12:9).
5. Jeshua's son, who ruled Mizpah and repaired the Jerusalem wall (Neh 3:19).
6. Priest who took part in the ceremony at the dedication of the Jerusalem wall (Neh 12:42).

EZION-GEBER Important port near some significant ruins at the head of the Gulf of Aqaba. Ezion-geber was one of the stations where the Israelites encamped while on their way to the plains of Moab (Nm 33:35-36; Dt 2:8). The city is not mentioned again until Solomon's time. From this port Solomon and Hiram, king of Tyre, carried on a profitable commercial venture. Solomon's products included copper (mined in the Arabah at Timna, 15 miles, or 24.1 kilometers, north of Ezion-geber), olive oil, and possibly products bought from Egypt, such as linen, and chariots (1 Kgs 10:28-29). The "ships of Tarshish," with the ships of Hiram, made a round trip of three years from Ezion-geber to many ports along the

coasts of Africa and Arabia and possibly even as far as India (1 Kgs 10:22). In exchange the fleet brought back gold from Ophir, along with precious stones, almug wood (vv 11-12), silver, ivory, apes, and peacocks (v 22). Solomon's alliance with the Phoenicians of Tyre gave him a port on the Mediterranean (which he himself did not have). The alliance also gave Hiram and the Phoenicians an outlet at Ezion-geber for trading in the Indian Ocean.

With the division of the kingdom after Solomon, the port was under Judah's control. It was burned and destroyed by Shishak of Egypt in his invasion of Judah in Rehoboam's fifth year (925 BC). A second city was built on the ruins, but there is no mention of a navy. Jehoshaphat was able to restore the fleet to sail once again, but some storm or other disaster wrecked the ships (1 Kgs 22:48). In subsequent Judean history, Judah was able to use the port when it was strong, but in its times of weakness, other nations did (e.g., Edom, 2 Kgs 8:20-22; 16:6). *See* Exodus, The; Wilderness Wanderings.

EZNITE* KJV designation for the preeminent leader of David's mighty men in 2 Samuel 23:8. Most consider Adino the Eznite a later scribal alteration of the Hebrew text and prefer the reading "Jashobeam the Hacmonite."

EZRA (Person)
1. Religious reformer following Israel's return from exile. Ezra's genealogy (Ezr 7:1-5; cf. 1 Chr 6:3-15) places him in the high priestly Aaron-Zadok family line, which accounts for the importance of his scribal and priestly activities. He is called "priest" (Ezr 10:10, 16; Neh 8:2), "scribe" (Ezr 7:6; Neh 12:36), and "priest and scribe" (Ezr 7:11-12; Neh 8:9; 12:26). The OT scribe was not a mere copyist, as in Christ's time, but a profound student of God's laws and commandments (Ezr 7:11-12; Jer 8:8). In the commission of the Persian king Artaxerxes to Ezra, the king described him as "priest" and "scribe" (Ezr 7:6-11). It was Ezra who began the traditional view of the scribe as a religious leader, a "bookman"; the view lasted until 200 BC. Scribes were qualified to teach and preach the Scriptures as well as interpret them, but by the first century AD, the scribe's function was more specialized.

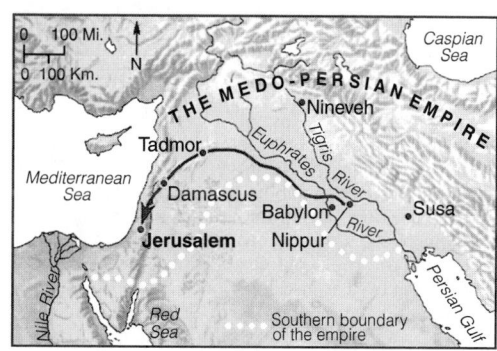

Ezra's Journey to Jerusalem Ezra led a second group of exiles back to Judah and Jerusalem about 80 years after the first group. He traveled the dangerous route without military escort (Ezr 8:22), but the people prayed and, under Ezra's godly leardership, arrived safely in Jerusalem after several months.

As "Secretary of State for Jewish Affairs" in the Persian Empire, Ezra visited Jerusalem about 458 BC, and on his return reported his findings. Little was done, however, until Nehemiah went to Jerusalem in 445. Once the city walls had been rebuilt, Ezra instituted a religious reformation in which the ancient Torah (the Law) was made the norm for Jewish life. He also demanded that Jews who had married foreigners must divorce them to maintain the Jewish purity the Torah required. Ezra set an example of piety and dedication through prayer and fasting, and this placed his reforming zeal in proper spiritual perspective. He set the pattern for life in the postexilic Jewish commonwealth, making God's Word and worship central features. The date and place of his death are unknown.

See also Ezra, Book of; Postexilic Period.

2. KJV rendering of Ezrah in 1 Chronicles 4:17. *See* Ezrah.

EZRA, Book of One of the historical books of the OT, associated with 2 Chronicles and Nehemiah.

PREVIEW
•Name
•Background
•Sources
•Date
•Languages, Texts, and Versions
•Purpose and Content

Name In the Talmud tractate *Baba Bathra* 15a, the rabbis and scribes regarded Ezra and Nehemiah as one book. Josephus (*Apion* 1.8) also considered the two books to be one when the number of OT books was given as 22. Some church fathers, such as Melito of Sardis and Jerome, thought of them as one book. The Septuagint (Greek translation of the OT) also grouped the two books as one, referring to them as 2 Ezra to distinguish them from an apocryphal book known as 1 Ezra. The Latin Vulgate, however, called Ezra "1 Ezra" and Nehemiah "2 Ezra."

Background The Jewish people came under the rule of the Persian Empire when Cyrus conquered Babylon in 539 BC. From then until Ezra's time, the Persian kings were Cyrus (539–530 BC), who allowed the Jewish people and other captives to return to their homeland (Ezr 1); Cambyses (529–522 BC); Gaumata, a usurper of the throne (522 BC); Darius I (521–486 BC; Ezr 5:6); Xerxes I (OT Ahasuerus, 486–465 BC; Ezr 4:6); and Artaxerxes I (465–424 BC; Ezr 4:7-23; 7:1–10:44). Both Ezra's and Nehemiah's work fall within the period between Cyrus and Artaxerxes I. Some scholars, however, place Ezra during the reign of Artaxerxes II (404–359 BC).

Sources By tradition, the Jewish leader Ezra researched and put together the material that forms his book. Chapters 7–10 are written in the first person singular, and Ezra may have used the autobiographical passages as the core of this book, adding information from other sources. That the book contains portions written in Aramaic has been used as justification for assigning a date later than Ezra's time. But the Aramaic of Ezra bears a remarkable similarity to fifth-century BC Aramaic papyri from the Jewish community at Elephantine in Egypt.

The book is largely a compilation, using autobiography, official documents, edicts, and other material. The present book of Ezra contains four identifiable strata of source material.

Memoirs of Ezra Certain sections appear in the first person singular (7:27–9:15), located between third-person narratives (7:1-26; 10). The memoirs were probably part of Ezra's own official reports.

Aramaic Documents Aramaic was the diplomatic language of the Persian Empire, and a number of docu-

ments appear in the book of Ezra. A letter of complaint was written to Artaxerxes I about the rebuilding of the city walls, for example, and Ezra also included the official reply (Ezr 4:8-23). There is also a letter of Darius I and the king's reply (5:1–6:18). An official authorization by the Persian court of Artaxerxes permitted Ezra to return, and this included a description of material entrusted into his keeping (7:12-26). Since all of those sections were official correspondence, the record naturally is written in Aramaic.

Hebrew Lists Ezra included Hebrew documents listing people's names for a number of purposes. One such document indicated the Persian government's permission for Jewish immigrants to return to the land of Israel (Ezr 1:2-4). It was a Jewish version of Cyrus's general edict expressing concern for all his subjects. The edict in Aramaic is repeated by Ezra in 6:3-5, and that version is probably taken from an original memorandum of a royal decision. Ezra included lists of the immigrants who returned to begin the second commonwealth of Israel (ch 2, repeated in Neh 7). The book also contains a list of immigrants who returned with Ezra by permission of Artaxerxes I (Ezr 8:1-14). Lists of those who had married pagan wives are provided as well (10:18-43).

Narrative The rest of the book comprises narrative by Ezra himself. For the period of the first return prior to his own time, he probably drew upon existing sources, either oral or documentary. Material in the book that was contemporary with the scribe would be his personal account about his own work.

Date Traditionally, the Artaxerxes in Ezra 7:1 has been identified with Artaxerxes I Longimanus. Ezra's arrival in Jerusalem would thus have been in 458 BC (see NLT mg for 7:8). Therefore, Ezra's work at Jerusalem started before that of Nehemiah, who came in 445 BC.

But the traditional dates are questioned from a number of sources. One alternative is to place Nehemiah during the reign of Artaxerxes I (464–424 BC) and Ezra at a later date, in the reign of Artaxerxes II Mnemon (404–359 BC). Such a suggestion creates a difficulty with Nehemiah 8:2, because there Ezra is named as Nehemiah's contemporary and coworker.

In addition, the Elephantine papyri (407–400 BC) mention the high priest Johanan in Jerusalem, and Sanballat as governor of Samaria. Johanan is considered a grandson of Eliashib, but Nehemiah was a contemporary of Eliashib (Neh 3:1, 20). The biblical material that speaks of Nehemiah going to Jerusalem in the 20th year of Artaxerxes (Neh 2:1, 445 BC) and again during the 32d year (Neh 13:6, 433 BC) refers to Eliashib's contemporary high priesthood with Ezra. The traditional position thus furnishes a reasonable date for the book of Ezra. If the scribe were placed during the reign of Artaxerxes II (c. 397 BC), his ministry would be too late for the high priesthood of Johanan.

Languages, Texts, and Versions The primary language of the book of Ezra is Hebrew; the exceptions are 4:7, 6:18, and 7:12-26, which are written in Aramaic. The Hebrew portion appears to resemble the language of Daniel, Haggai, and 2 Chronicles much more than later Hebrew, such as that of Ecclesiasticus. As indicated, the Aramaic portions resemble the Elephantine papyri, dated about 407–400 BC. In addition, Persian personal and family names and Persian words and expressions occur in the book, such as Bigvai, Mithredath, and Elam. All of these evidences serve to place the book in about the fifth century BC.

The Hebrew Masoretic Text of Ezra seems well preserved. The Septuagint version is a bit shorter than the Masoretic Text. Only parts of Ezra 4 and 5 have been found among the Dead Sea Scrolls.

Purpose and Content The book of Ezra is a straightforward account of one of the most important events in Jewish history. From a priestly point of view, it is an account of the restoration of Jewish people to their homeland following the Babylonian dispersion. The record tells of two distinct returns, one under the leadership of Zerubbabel (chs 1–6; 538 BC), and 80 years later, the second return led by Ezra (chs 7–10; 458 BC). The book emphasizes Ezra's leadership and the reestablishment of the people on their land, both of which were to have important future consequences.

Little is known about the political activity of Ezra in the Persian court. He appears to have been a man of considerable influence, however, and could well be described as an official who held a position corresponding to that of "Secretary of State for Jewish Affairs." To what extent that function applied to the Persian Empire as a whole is uncertain, since Ezra's recorded activities took place only in the area known to the Persians as the province "Beyond the River," that is, the territory lying to the west of the Euphrates. The importance of Ezra's position in the Persian Empire is indicated by the fact that King Artaxerxes gave him full authority to do whatever he thought necessary for the welfare of his people and the empire (7:21-26). Ezra's genealogy is given in 7:1-5, and he is consistently spoken of as a scribe learned in the Mosaic law. As a descendant of Zadok the priest, he would have the authority to instruct others in the Torah.

Chapter 4 speaks of the opposition to rebuilding the temple and the walls. We should recognize that Ezra's approach in this chapter is topical rather than chronological where, in the middle of describing the earlier opposition to building the temple (5:1-5), he complained that the same kind of opposition was being repeated in his day concerning the attempt to rebuild the city walls and repair the fortifications of Jerusalem (5:7-23). Internal evidence suggests that a long historical interval ensued during the reign of Ahasuerus, or Xerxes, and the early part of Artaxerxes' regime. During this period, complaints were made to the Persian authorities that the returned Judeans were rebuilding the city wall of Jerusalem, and as a result the work was halted for some time. It readily can be seen that Ezra was dealing with the evil intentions of Judah's enemies and that the opposition of Rehum and Shimshai did not appear in the 520s (when the temple was being built) because they lived in the 460s, early in the reign of Artaxerxes I.

But the initial passage is actually a history of opposition to rebuilding the ruined temple. It narrates the frustrations experienced by the Judean community from the time of return to their homeland during Cyrus's rule (4:1-5) up to the time of King Darius (v 24). The prophet Haggai (520 BC) aroused the people with his message and persuaded them to lay the foundations of the new temple.

Ezra resumes the theme of the book in chapter 5. He points out the problems, frustrations, and hindrances the Jewish people had with the construction of the temple. It was not until a diligent search had been made in the archives by the Persian authorities that the original edict granting permission to build the temple was found (5:7–6:5).

See also Ezra (Person) #1; Postexilic Period.

EZRAH Father of four sons from Judah's tribe (1 Chr 4:17).

EZRAHITE Word occurring only three times in the OT. Twice it is used as a title for Ethan (1 Kgs 4:31; Ps 89 title) and once as a name given to Heman (Ps 88 title). It is no longer thought to be a family name, but instead signifies a member of a pre-Israelite family.

EZRI Son of Kelub and one of the men who supervised the tilling of David's lands (1 Chr 27:26).

F

FAIR HAVENS Small harbor, identifiable with modern Limenes Kali, positioned along Crete's southern coast about five miles (8.1 kilometers) east of Cape Matala near the city of Lasea. Here Paul's ship sought shelter from contrary winds on his voyage to Rome (Acts 27:8).

FAITH Belief in that which has no tangible proof; trust in God.

Definition of Faith In the OT and NT, "faith" carries several meanings. It may mean simple trust in God or in the Word of God, and at other times faith almost becomes equivalent to active obedience. It may also find expression in the affirmation of a creedal statement. Thus, it also comes to mean the entire body of received Christian teaching or truth—"the truth." In Colossians 2:7, the term suggests something to be accepted as a whole and embodied in personal life. In 2 Timothy 4:7, Paul witnesses to having "kept the faith."

Faith in the Old Testament The OT also strongly emphasizes faith as confidence in God's covenant or in the covenant God made with Abraham and his descendants. The call of Abraham and the promise that his descendants would be used in the history of redemption became the basis of the narratives of the OT, being seen as the working out of that covenant. Once the nation Israel was brought into being, God sustained and protected it. The exodus from Egypt is a prominent indication that God was at work restoring his people to the Promised Land. The obedience of the people of God as the proper expression of faith is seen clearly in the OT. Without seeing God, his people believed and obeyed him. Abraham left his native land to go into unknown territory. The people of Israel left Egypt following the leadership of God to a land they could not see. The promise of God gave them courage to possess the land promised to them. After the exodus, the covenant of Abraham was confirmed with the people of Israel by the sprinkling of blood (Ex 24:6-7). There was to be strict obedience to God's commands as an expression of faith. This response of human faith to the Lord's faithfulness was national and collective. There also were commands to, and instances of, personal faith.

Not only the narrative and legal portions of the OT but also the poetic and prophetic writings emphasize faith. The Psalms abound in expressions of personal confidence in the Lord even in dark times. Habakkuk points out that "the righteous shall live by his faith" (Hb 2:4). From such instances it is clear that, as the Lord's education of Israel proceeded, the matter of faith in God's faithfulness became more and more a matter of individual and personal response, and it is in the Prophets that several ingredients—such as trust, obedience, fear, and certainty—blend into the understanding of such personal faith.

Faith in the New Testament As over against the OT, where the accent is on the faithfulness of God, in the NT the emphasis is placed on the active, responding faith of the hearer to the promised, final revelation in the Mes-

siah, Jesus. Both verb and noun regularly describe the adequate response of people to Jesus' word and to the gospel.

The Synoptic Gospels The most striking feature of the synoptic Gospels (quoted below from the RSV) is the use of faith without identifying its object: "If you have faith as a grain of mustard seed" (Mt 17:20); "When Jesus saw their faith" (Mk 2:5); "Your faith has saved you" (Lk 7:50). Jesus is portrayed as one who by his work and word opens the door to faith and makes faith possible. The question is not whether the faith is in Jesus or in the Father; the implication is undoubtedly both, but as with every true bearer of the Word of God, the eye of faith is turned to the One who sends.

On more than one occasion, Jesus denies the request for a miracle to substantiate his words (Mt 12:38-39; 16:1-4). Faith is response to the Word alone without any supporting props. No sign is to be given but the sign of Jonah. In the story of the rich man and Lazarus (Lk 16:19-31), Jesus denies the request for the spectacular and insists that the hearer must respond to the word given to him (cf. Jn 20:29). The Word demands self-surrender and commitment. Hence, the very nature of the Word and of faith becomes an obstacle to the proud and the powerful.

Faith is the medium by which the power of God is made visible. It moves mountains, heals the sick, and is the means of entrance into the kingdom. It may be mingled with doubt, as with the father who sought healing for his son ("I believe; help my unbelief!" [Mk 9:24]), or as with John the Baptist in prison, who, even with his doubts, was confirmed by Jesus as the greatest of the offspring of woman (Mt 11:2-15). Peter's (and the other disciples') perception was faulty, but Jesus affirms Peter's confession as the foundation stone of the church. The synoptic Gospels portray the early faith of the disciples in all its limitations and weaknesses, yet it is still faith in that it is their positive response to Jesus' word and work.

The Fourth Gospel Faith is an especially significant concept in the Gospel of John (quoted below from the RSV), though the word (in the Greek) occurs only as a verb. Quite often the reference has to do with the acceptance that something is true, that is, simple credence, or belief: "Believe me that I am in the Father and the Father in me" (Jn 14:11); "If you believed Moses, you would believe me" (Jn 5:46).

Even more significant is the special expression "to believe into" in the sense of putting one's trust into another. The particular form of the expression is without parallel before the fourth Gospel and may well express the strong sense of personal trust in the eternal Word made flesh. In John 3:16, whoever puts trust in him has eternal life. Those who put their trust in him are given power to become sons of God—to be born of God (Jn 1:12). They will never thirst (6:35); they will live, even though they die (11:25).

In other places, John speaks of trust or faith in an

absolute sense, that is, without referring to the one in whom trust is placed. In John 11:15 Jesus arrives after the death of Lazarus and is glad "in order that you might believe." The outcome is going to be faith. Similarly, in the prologue (1:7), John the Baptist bears witness in order that through him all might believe. As Jesus satisfies the doubt of Thomas concerning the resurrection, he says, "Have you believed because you have seen me? Blessed are those who have not seen and yet believe" (20:29). In these and other passages the fundamental outcome of Jesus' witness to himself is trust.

Faith and knowledge are closely related. In John 6:69 Peter says, "We have believed, and have come to know, that you are the Holy One of God." In his priestly prayer Jesus says that eternal life is to "know you, the only true God, and Jesus Christ whom you have sent" (Jn 17:3). Also, God is seen through the eyes of faith. No one has ever seen God, but the Only Begotten has revealed him (1:18). He who has seen Jesus has seen the Father (14:9).

To believe is also expressed in the verb "receive." Those who receive Christ are given power to become the sons of God (Jn 1:12). Trust is that form of knowing or seeing by which the glory of God (1:14; 17:4) is made present.

Paul's Writings In Paul's letters (quoted below from the RSV), he writes about faith from a number of angles. He sets faith over against "works of the law" as the only and true basis for righteousness (Rom 1–4; Gal 1–4) and appeals to Abraham to prove his point: "Abraham believed God and it was reckoned to him for righteousness" (Gn 15:6; cf. Rom 4:5; Gal 3:6). This is entirely apart from the law (Rom 3:21); righteousness is the gift of God through faith in Christ, specifically in his atoning work. Behind Paul's conviction lies his awareness of the radical and pervasive sinfulness of humans that renders each one helpless. Humanity is dead in sin but is made alive by faith in the word and work of Jesus mediated through the gospel.

Faith, then, is faith in Jesus Christ. The number of metaphors Paul employs to describe the consequences of faith is staggering. It is by faith that believers are justified (Rom 5:1), reconciled (2 Cor 5:18), redeemed (Eph 1:7), made alive (2:5), adopted into the family of God (Rom 8:15-16), re-created (2 Cor 5:17), transported into a new kingdom (Col 1:13), and set free (Gal 5:1). Faith is, for Paul, the *sine qua non* of every aspect of salvation, from the grace that convicts to the receiving of the full inheritance at the coming of the Lord.

In Paul's letters, faith is bound up with love so that the great exponent of justification by faith becomes also the articulate exponent of distinctive Christian love. To say that faith is indispensable to salvation is only part of the truth, for faith expresses itself through love: "For in Christ Jesus neither circumcision nor uncircumcision is of any avail, but faith working through love" (Gal 5:6); "If I have all faith, so as to remove mountains, but have not love, I am nothing" (1 Cor 13:2). Love is both the genesis and the ultimate expression of faith. Hence, even for Paul there can be no *total* separation between faith and works. This love of which Paul speaks is the essential fruit of the Spirit through whom the life of faith is lived. Only by virtue of the indwelling Spirit does faith find expression in love.

General Epistles James speaks of faith as being completed by works (Jas 2:22). He opposed that concept of faith that thinks primarily of creedal assent, of believing that something is true without acting upon it. James, like Paul, assumes the primacy of faith, but he is warning against those who would draw wrong conclusions. Faith

apart from works is not faith; it is barren (v 20). The practical dimension of faith is the burden of much of this epistle.

The writer of Hebrews recognizes that faith has always been characteristic of the people of God and their specially called leaders. Faith makes substantial what is otherwise nebulous and uncertain; it makes evidential what is not visible. By faith the people of God have a more certain ground for their lives and their actions than the world is able to discern (Heb 11:1). The great cloud of witnesses (12:1) bear testimony by their faith to the faithfulness of God.

Faith is opened up by the Word of God, finds expression through the Holy Spirit who is given, and bears witness to the lordship of Jesus Christ.

FAITHFULNESS Maintaining faith or allegiance; showing a strong sense of duty or conscientiousness. In biblical Hebrew, "faith" and "faithfulness" are grammatically related. Although both concepts are important in the OT, there is no English word exactly equivalent to the Hebrew terms. The most relevant Hebrew verbal root (related to our word "amen") carries such meanings as "strengthen," "support," or "hold up." In a physical sense it is used of pillars that provide support for doors (2 Kgs 18:16). Moses used the word when he disclaimed any role as supporter of the Israelites (Nm 11:12). God, however, is an eternally firm support for his people (Dt 7:9; Is 49:7).

With that notion of firm support as the bedrock for faith, words such as "firmness," "constancy," or "trustworthiness" best convey the related concept of faithfulness. Trustworthiness, or steadfastness of character, is ascribed to the object of one's trust. To be unfaithful is to be unworthy of confidence or belief. In the OT a synonym for "faithfulness" is "truth." Since God is consistently true, he is the logical object of human trust (Ps 71:22; Is 61:8). When used of God in the OT, the word "faithfulness" frequently refers to his unwavering commitment to his promises.

God's Faithfulness In spite of Israel's faithlessness (Dt 32:20; cf. Rom 3:3), God showed himself to be absolutely reliable. His faithfulness is great (Lam 3:23). He is loyal to his covenant and will always manifest his steadfast love to his people (Ps 136).

The pinnacle of faithfulness in the Bible is seen in the work of Jesus Christ, who showed himself faithful to his Father (Heb 3:2) and in his witness (Rv 1:5). God calls men and women to be faithful by following Christ, relying on him for all things (Hb 2:4; cf. Rom 1:17).

Human Faithfulness Faith and faithfulness are logically and linguistically united in the OT and NT. That is, the major words for faith in both Testaments also connote the concept of faithfulness. This indicates that faith is more than momentary assent to the truth of God. It is commitment to that truth, and it manifests itself in continued obedience. Abraham's life in this regard is instructive. He assented to, relied upon, and acted in conformity to the revealed word of God. He received God's revelation as true (i.e., demonstrating faith), and his subsequent actions proved his faithfulness. He left home and country, settled in a strange land, and offered up his son Isaac as God commanded. His willingness to sacrifice his only son is an unparalleled expression of faithfulness in the OT. It is no surprise, therefore, that Abraham is commended for his steadfastness and is set forth in the NT as one whose behavior should be imitated by Christians (Gal 3:6-9; Heb 11:8-10). Faithfulness, then, must not be viewed as an isolated act. Rather, it is an attitude that should characterize the entire life of those who say they have faith in God.

FALCON Bird of prey noted for keen eyesight, and declared unclean in the OT (Lv 11:14; Jb 28:7). *See* Birds (Kestrel or Falcon).

FALL OF MAN* Transition from a condition of moral innocence and favor with God to a condition of being condemned to death, which occurred in the history of humankind with Adam's eating of the forbidden fruit.

Biblical Evidence The narrative of Creation in Genesis 1 and 2 affirms the distinctiveness of both man's nature and task. Man (used in this article as a generic term for male and female human beings) was created in the image of God for the purpose of communion and fellowship with God. As God's representative, he was given dominion on the earth to cultivate and use its resources for the glory of God.

In addition to the cultural mandate, man also received a specific command. He was authorized to use the vegetation of the Garden of Eden for food, but he was expressly forbidden to eat of the tree of the knowledge of good and evil. The purpose of this command was to introduce into the human consciousness the radical antithesis between good and evil and to confirm man in the service of the Creator. As a faithful and loyal servant, man was to enjoy all the blessings bestowed by his Father in heaven and at last be led into the fullness of eternal life with God.

Man was made a living creature, as were the animals, but the core of his life was to be union and communion with God. Fellowship with God was to become Adam's conscious possession, in contrast to the animals that know neither the possibility of sin nor conscious communion with God. In full awareness of the evil of the alternative, man was to serve God willingly and lovingly. His life before God was therefore to be religious rather than instinctive.

The purpose of God in giving the command not to eat the fruit of the knowledge of good and evil was to establish humans in the ways of righteousness and faith, but Satan used the command as an occasion to tempt man to rebel against God. Although there was no evil for man in being tempted, it was evil for Satan to tempt man to sin. This means that there was evil in the universe prior to the fall of man. It was the apparent purpose of Satan to subject man to himself, and through man to extend his kingdom of darkness over the earth. The fall of man and the subsequent program of redemption must be understood in the context of the cosmic conflict between God and Satan, in which the ultimate triumph of God is assured. Satan approached Adam by way of Eve, using the serpent as his instrument to entice them to eat of the tree of the knowledge of good and evil.

The difference between good and evil was not concealed from man prior to the fall, though man's experiential knowledge was only of the good. Adam was to receive instruction concerning the nature of this distinction and the consequences of eating or not eating only from God. As he had received life in the beginning from his Creator, so now he was to live in obedience to every word that proceeded from the mouth of God. The purpose of the temptation was to urge independence from God. Satan called into question the truth of God and challenged his authority. He led man to think that he could determine for himself the difference between good and evil and that he could control the consequences to his own advantage. It was the temptation for man to be a god to himself.

Adam fell when he yielded to the temptation of Satan and, together with his wife, ate of the forbidden fruit. The act of rebellion was an act of disobedience, disloyalty, faithlessness, and unbelief. As the command not to eat summarized and brought to a focus all that was involved in righteousness before God, so the transgression epitomized radical apostasy from God. Undivided obedience to God gave way to whole-souled rebellion and complete revolt: the authority of God was repudiated; the goodness of God was doubted; the wisdom of God was disputed; and the truth of God was contradicted. A whole new complex of affections and emotions took possession of the heart and mind of man.

Effects of the Fall The immediate effects of the fall are visible in the loss of boldness and joy in the presence of God and the emergence of fear and shame. They are visible also in the alienation of Adam and Eve from God. This is exemplified in the curse in relation to man, but more pointedly in the expulsion of Adam and Eve from the Garden. The Garden was the dwelling place of righteousness, the sphere of union and communion between man and God. Expulsion was inevitable once the communion was severed by unrighteousness. As God had warned, the consequence of sin was death. Since death intervenes at every point where there is life, it works itself out also in the dissolution of the body in the grave.

The consequences of the fall are not limited to Adam and Eve but extend to all those descended from the first

---

CONTEMPORARY UNDERSTANDING OF THE FALL
Within contemporary theology of all confessional varieties, there is widespread denial of the historicity of the biblical account of the fall. It may be granted that the Genesis account is told as history continuous with subsequent history and that within the worldview of the writers of the Bible the account is alluded to as history. But it is argued that moderns can receive the story of the fall only as myth. This view has its source in the development of an evolutionary view of human origins coupled with a negatively critical evaluation of the literary history of the Genesis account.

Although the historicity of Adam is often abandoned, there is usually an attempt to appreciate the "truth" conveyed by the myth. For example, it is said that every person is Adam, and that everyone living is a sinner as far back as he or she can remember. Others see in the myth not a fall but an ascent to conscious and independent responsibility. Sin is thought of as necessary to religious maturity in the same way that exposure to competition from opponents strengthens the prowess of an athlete.

Because of the way the Bible parallels Adam and Christ (Rom 5:12-19; 1 Cor 15:22), a mythological understanding of Adam leads to a mythological understanding of Christ. As Adam becomes a symbol for the universality of sin and death, so Christ becomes simply a symbol for the inherent righteousness and redemption of all men.

The modern isolation of the message from the history of Genesis 1–3 violates the integrity of the account without offering a valid explanation for the universality of sin and death. Christian doctrine holds that sin entered the world through a specific man, Adam, and was overcome by Jesus Christ, another man, by his death and resurrection.

pair by natural generation, because there is a unique relation of solidarity existing between Adam and the rest of the race. Some theologians accent the generic connection between Adam and his descendants, while others focus on the covenant relationship of Adam as the head and representative of his posterity. The consequences of Adam's transgression for the human race are the imputation of his sin to all his descendants, their consequent liability to death, and their inheritance of a depraved nature.

The results of the fall are also manifest in the cosmos as the curse works itself out in the resistance offered to the accomplishment of the original cultural mandate. Only with the pain and danger attendant upon childbirth is the world populated, and only with arduous, toilsome labor are the food, clothing, and shelter necessary to sustain life provided.

However, the fact that death does not descend *immediately* upon man after the fall as *final* judgment is indicative of God's saving purpose for man. Adam does not hear the curse of death pronounced until he has heard the promise of a Savior (Gn 3:15).

After Genesis 3, the Bible only infrequently refers to the fall of man, but this historical event is the indispensable presupposition of all that follows. The thrust of the Bible is toward the future—the widening effects of sin and the unfolding of God's remedy.

See also Adam (Person); Death; Sin.

FALLOW DEER* KJV translation of roebuck, a ruminant and member of the deer family, in Deuteronomy 14:5. *See* Animals (Deer; Gazelle).

FALSE CHRISTS*, FALSE MESSIAHS Those who falsely claim to be the Christ or Messiah. False christs are mentioned only in the eschatological discourse of Jesus recorded by Matthew (24:24) and Mark (13:22).

In that discourse Jesus instructed his disciples about the future. He prophesied the destruction of the temple in Jerusalem and warned about the deception and persecution that would confront the disciples. He especially warned his disciples that during the terrible days surrounding the destruction of the temple they were not to be deceived by false christs and false prophets (Mk 13:21-23). In this particular form of deception, some would claim that the Christ was in a particular location (v 21). Those deceivers would perform signs and wonders to try to deceive the elect. But Jesus prepared his disciples by instructing them that there will be cosmic signs preceding his return as the Son of Man (vv 24-25) and that his coming will be with great power and glory visible to all.

From history we know that Jesus' instruction enabled Christians to flee the destruction of Jerusalem and the temple in AD 70, and to withstand the deception of false christs. The church still awaits Jesus' return as the glorious Son of Man.

See also Antichrist.

FALSE PROPHETS *See* Prophets, False.

FAMILY LIFE AND RELATIONS In Bible times, the family comprised members of a household, including not only parents and children, along with other relatives and concubines, but also servants, travelers, aliens, and anyone else who happened to be within the house and was therefore under the protection of the head of the family. The family of Jacob, for example, comprised three generations (Gn 46:8-26). Biblically, the term "family" is interchangeable with "house," and "founding a house" can refer to setting up a separate dwelling as

well as establishing a family. In the broader sense, "house" may refer to an entire nation ("house of Israel"). The heads of families returning from Babylon in the postexilic period controlled sometimes several hundred family members (Ezr 8:1-14). The family was a smaller part of a clan and tribe. In nomadic times the responsibilities and allegiances centered on the larger family group.

Those who belonged to the clan knew that they had to work for common interests and accept responsibility for the whole group. All members of the family were to be protected and assisted in time of need.

As the life of the Israelites became more settled, families (in the wider sense of the term) lived in villages surrounded by fields of wheat, barley, and flax, with areas of grazing land for sheep and goats. Each group of villages consisted of an intermarried, interdependent family group, such as that of the Danites of Zorah and Eshtaol (Jgs 18:11). The hard life of those days demanded a sharing of work and the loyal cooperation of the entire family for survival.

As crafts and trades developed, along with a more sedentary lifestyle, sons learned their fathers' skills and continued the family trade. Consequently, the whole village might follow a particular craft (1 Chr 4:14; Neh 11:35). By specializing in such trades, however, the villagers became less self-sufficient, depending more on farmers for food and on other specialized villages for the production of cloth or pottery (1 Chr 4:21-23).

With the growth of cities, related groups lived together in specific areas. Many members of the tribes of Benjamin and Judah were listed in the census of Jerusalem by Nehemiah (Neh 11:4-8), and by the writer of Chronicles (1 Chr 9:3-9). One consequence of life in the cities was the fragmentation of the family group. As the bonds of the wider family were loosened, the unit consisted increasingly of a husband and wife with their children, living in one house. The size of houses that have been excavated precludes the idea of any larger family unit as the norm in OT societies.

During the kingdom period, King David's sons Amnon and Absalom set up their own separate houses (2 Sm 13:7-8, 20). At that time there were few slaves in Hebrew society, but they also were considered members of the family. As bonds of the wider family loosened, and the master of the household lost a degree of authority, the society became one in which the king was sovereign and all the people were his subjects.

The early kings of Israel promoted such a change in order to establish a central ruling authority for the entire country. The king's subjects fell broadly into the categories of employers and employees, corresponding to the rich and poor of society. By the eighth century BC, members of the wider family no longer worked for the communal good under the authority of the clan's head; rather, individuals worked primarily for the good of their own immediate family. Hence one's labor and devotion were focused more narrowly, and the greatest beneficiary was the king, the personal symbol of the nation.

Emphasis on the smaller family unit increased, and old duties that had been willingly accepted by the wider groups in former times came to be neglected. People did not always help relatives in times of need, and they frequently had to be reminded of their obligations, particularly toward widows and orphans (Is 1:17; Jer 7:6). Family feuds also declined because members no longer felt responsible to take vengeance as a way to uphold the honor of the clan (2 Sm 3:27; 16:8; 2 Kgs 9:26). Nevertheless, Nehemiah expected Israelites to fight for their family honor (Neh 4:14). In NT times, the family was such a unit that it could be sold for a debt incurred by one of its members (Mt 18:25).

The Hebrew religion's emphasis on family participation in certain celebrations strengthened the small unit. The Passover, for example, was always celebrated as a family thanksgiving meal (Ex 12:3-4, 46). The prophet Samuel's parents made a traditional annual pilgrimage to the shrine at Shiloh (1 Sm 2:19). In modern times, a young Jewish boy's arrival at the threshold of manhood is celebrated with the Bar Mitzvah ceremony. Being so honored in the midst of a religious family preserves the ancient Hebrew tradition of family participation in religious ceremonies.

In his preaching Jesus used the family as a symbol for the relationship of God to his people (Mt 19:14; 23:9; Lk 8:21). From the cross he handed over responsibility for the care of his mother to his disciple John (Jn 19:27).

In NT times, the communion meals in the Jerusalem church took place by households (Acts 2:46). Early Christian meetings were held in the homes of believers because of opposition by the authorities. The book of Acts contains examples of entire families being converted to Christianity (Acts 10:24, 44-48; 16:15, 31-32). Timothy learned the gospel from his grandmother and mother (2 Tm 1:5).

PREVIEW
• Status of Family Members
• Marital Security
• Position of Children
• The Rights of Children
• Daily Life of the Hebrew Family
• In New Testament Times

Status of Family Members From nomadic times, a father's authority held the family group together in their encampment, and he became the symbol of their security. In ancient patriarchal societies, the father was an absolute master who had the power of life and death over family members, ruling with unchallenged authority. Although he had extensive responsibilities for those under his care, his power was awesome and his status unquestioned.

A man's possessions included his wife, servants, slaves, and animals (Ex 20:17; Dt 5:21). In fact, the phrase "to marry a wife" comes from a Hebrew root meaning "to become the master of a wife." A husband was as much the master of his wife as he was of his home or his fields. Consequently, the wife addressed him in a subservient manner, as a slave would address a master (Gn 18:12; Jgs 19:26). This low status for a woman extended to a daughter's position in the ancient household. Females were always under the authority of a male relative: first, the father; then a husband. If a woman became a widow, she was subject to her husband's nearest male relative, who became her "redeemer." The bride price (Gn 29:18, 27; Ex 22:16-17; 1 Sm 18:25; 2 Sm 3:14) paid by her husband was not exactly a purchase of the woman from her father, but the exchange of money did stigmatize her. The amount of a bride price depended on the father's status (Gn 34:12). The usual price was probably 20 to 30 shekels of silver. The bride received gifts of jewelry, ornaments, and clothing from her future husband, and she occasionally enjoyed some sort of financial or material return from the bride price for her own use (Jos 15:19; Jgs 1:15). When her father or husband died, the money frequently reverted to her.

An engaged woman was considered her fiancé's property just as much as if she were already married to him (Dt 22:23-27). The woman left her own family at marriage, to live with and become part of her new husband's family. Normally, any succeeding marriages would be with members of that family.

Despite the low legal status of the mother of the family, her life was not as bad as one might suppose. She was the legal wife, not an unpaid servant, and she frequently took a strong role as adviser to her husband in family affairs. Her most important function, aside from childbearing, was organization of the household, of which she was generally the respected manager. Even though the wife might have been acquired through capture in war (Dt 21:10-14), she could not be sold as a slave or daughter could (Ex 21:7; Neh 5:5).

Nevertheless, her position was precarious, in that she could be disowned or divorced by her husband as the result of a simple renunciation: "She is no longer my wife, and I am no longer her husband." Perhaps he had found fault with her culinary skills, or possibly he was casting his eyes on another woman. In any event, a husband knew that if his wife did not obey even a signal or a glance, he was within his rights to obtain a divorce (cf. Ecclus 25:26). The wife, however, obtained a certain degree of protection in the letter of repudiation, by which her freedom was formally restored. Under Jewish tradition, a wife could not divorce her husband.

In matters of domestic protocol, the Hebrew wife was not introduced to her husband's guests, a tradition that subsequently led to considerable embarrassment for Abraham's wife, Sarah, and for Rebekah (Gn 20:16). A woman normally remained veiled in public (24:65; 38:14; Is 47:2).

The imagery in Proverbs 19:13 and 27:15 draws a vigorous comparison between a contentious woman and water dripping from a leaky roof. The OT leaves little doubt about the type of behavior expected from a woman. She was expected to be charming, soft-spoken, discreet, and calm (Prv 9:13; 11:16, 22; 21:9). She was also to be responsible, well-organized, intelligent, thoughtful, reverent, and a good manager of both the household and the family purse (31:10-31). A woman should also be pious and beautiful, and in NT tradition, submissive to her husband, as befitted a woman adorned with the priceless jewel of a gentle and quiet spirit (Ti 2:4-5; 1 Pt 3:1-6).

The actions of a few women whose roles in life do not seem to fit the pattern of the meek, passive female pictured above, are recorded in the Bible and the Apocrypha. The books of Judith and Esther recount heroic tales of how national fortunes were saved by women. Deborah and Jael were renowned heroines (Jgs 4–5), and the kingdom of Judah was ruled by a vicious woman, Athaliah, for several years (2 Kgs 11). The women who stepped to the forefront of public life were exceptional and few in number. Judith was a rich widow, an unusual thing in Israel.

Marital Security The security of a wife's position improved considerably when she produced her first child, particularly if it was a son. A woman's primary duty to her husband and his family was procreation (Gn 1:28; 9:1), and until she gave birth to a son, she feared displacement by a second wife or a concubine. Polygamous marriages were by no means rare, especially in wealthy families. They resulted in two ill-defined family groups, controlled by the mothers but under the overall authority of fathers; there were inevitable jealousies and frictions.

The legal status of a woman was consistently poor in

Bible times. With no evidence at all, a husband could accuse his wife of adultery, and she was compelled to face a trial by ordeal. She had to abase herself by taking an oath, eating dust and a cereal offering, and drinking bitter water. A priest, meanwhile, made pronouncements regarding the dire results that would come to her if she were guilty: she would become an outcast with no hope of survival. But if she maintained her serenity, and if her thigh did not rot nor her abdomen swell, she was considered to have "proved" her innocence. In such an event she would go free, and her husband bore no blame whatsoever for his false accusation (Nm 5:12-31).

If a woman took a vow, it was legal only as long as her father or husband approved it. If she became a widow, the vow still remained in force and could be used against her (Nm 30:3-15).

A woman in Israel was always under the protection of a male, be it her father, grandfather, great-grandfather, brother, husband, or some other member of her husband's family. She had few legal rights and, in contrast to Babylonian traditions, could not inherit at her husband's death. It is small wonder that widows were classed with orphans and the poor. A childless widow could on occasion return to her father's family (Gn 38:11; Lv 22:13; Ru 1:8), thus becoming subject again to the authority of her father. A Hebrew widow could also remain with her late husband's family. She would then come under the protection of her "redeemer," a male relative of her husband's family who assumed responsibility for her. If a husband died leaving a woman childless, it was the responsibility of the husband's brother to marry her. The first son born of such a union was then regarded as the heir of the first husband.

It was normal for a brother to accept the obligation for such a marriage (levirate). It could be refused on various grounds, but such refusal was considered dishonorable, for it was a man's duty to perpetuate his brother's name and to safeguard the family fortune.

A redeemer's responsibilities were considerable. In addition to the marriage, he was perhaps involved in avenging the family reputation, and he had to ensure that family property increased and remained within family control.

If an Israelite fell into debt and was forced to sell himself into slavery, he would normally be "redeemed" by one of his relatives (Lv 25:47-49). If in his penury an Israelite had to sell his land or his house, the redeemer had the right of first refusal over all other prospective purchasers. It was as much his duty as his right to prevent family property from passing into the hands of strangers (v 25). The prophet Jeremiah bought his cousin Hanamel's field under similar circumstances (Jer 32:6-15).

The most familiar OT story of a childless widow, her "redeemer," and their levirate marriage is recorded in the book of Ruth. One of Naomi's two sons married Ruth. When Ruth was widowed, her impoverished mother-in-law, Naomi, left her home in Moab and returned to Bethlehem to sell some of the family property. Although a close relative was prepared to buy the land and keep it in the family, he was not ready to marry Ruth as well (Ru 3:12; 4:4). He knew that a son of that union would be deemed a son of the deceased, bearing the dead husband's name, and thus ultimately inheriting the land (4:4-6). The next relative in order of kinship was Boaz, who became Ruth's "redeemer." He was prepared to accept the double obligation of purchasing the land and marrying Ruth (4:9-10).

Position of Children Children were generally well loved, but their childhood was short and they were often regarded as laborers for the house or fields. According to the law of primogeniture, the eldest son received a double portion of the estate as his birthright (Dt 21:17). Thus, he was assured of the position of family head. Even during his father's lifetime, the eldest son took precedence over his brothers and sisters (Gn 43:33). Where twins were born, the first to emerge from the womb was considered the elder, with all the attendant privileges (25:24-26; 38:27-30).

For a serious offense, the eldest son could lose the right of primogeniture (Gn 35:22; 49:3-4; 1 Chr 5:1), or it could be surrendered voluntarily, as Esau did by selling his birthright to his brother Jacob (Gn 25:29-34). There was a law protecting the eldest son from his father's favoritism for a younger brother (Dt 21:15-17). Nevertheless, King David gave his kingdom to Solomon, his youngest son (1 Kgs 2:15).

In a family with no sons, a daughter could inherit property (Nm 27:8). Frequently, parents consulted neither sons nor daughters when marriage partners were arranged for them. Marriage was often an alliance or contract between two families, and thus the wishes and concerns of individuals were considered unimportant. Love matches were few, although occasionally a son would marry in defiance of his parents, as Esau did (Gn 26:34-35). Although it was rare for young people to express their feelings and preferences about marriage in an open fashion, Saul's daughter, Michal, made known her love for David (1 Sm 18:20).

There is no record of legal adoption among the Hebrews, but it was practiced from ancient times in Mesopotamia. It was especially useful as a means of ensuring a childless couple that their land would be tilled and that they would be cared for in their old age. All examples of adoption mentioned in the OT took place outside the land of Israel (Ex 2:10; 1 Kgs 11:20; Est 2:7, 15) and are not examples of true adoption as a lifetime member of a family.

The Rights of Children The nature of patriarchal society made for unfortunate distinctions between male and female children. The position of a daughter, who could be sold into slavery or sold to be the concubine of a man and then possibly sold again (Ex 21:7-11), was certainly inferior to that of a son. In the patriarchal period, however, both a son and a daughter could be put to death for disobeying the head of the family. One's children could also be sacrificed in worship rituals (see Gn 22; Jgs 11). It is probable that infant sacrifice was practiced by nations neighboring Israel, including Canaan and Ammon.

The rights of children were improved considerably with the promulgation of the code of Mosaic law. A father was no longer permitted to put his child to death without referring the case to the elders (Dt 21:18-21). Both sons and daughters could be brought before such authorities and accused of being disobedient, gluttonous, or drunkards. A father's absolute authority even extended to his married son and family if they were living under his roof. The law also prohibited children from being held responsible for the crimes of their parents (Dt 24:16). In King David's time a person convicted by the community had the right of appeal to the king (2 Sm 14:4-11).

In Hebrew families both parents were held in high respect. Honor had to be given to both mother and father (Ex 20:12), and the law condemned offenses against either parent (21:17; Lv 20:9; Dt 21:18; 27:16). Respect due to the mother is a recurrent theme in the Wisdom Literature (Prv 19:26; 20:20; cf. Ecclus 3:1-16).

Daily Life of the Hebrew Family In the everyday affairs of a Hebrew household, it was the father's responsibility to maintain the family fortune and to be the provider. He might work in the fields, most probably with crops of flax, barley, or wheat. Or he would work at a trade, possibly as a weaver, builder, potter, dyer, fuller, or a worker in copper or bronze. If he lived near the shore, he might be a fisherman.

The father was also responsible for the religious well-being of the family. It was his duty to take over his sons' education from the mother at an early age, teaching them the tenets of Hebrew religion (Ex 10:2; 12:26; Dt 4:9; 6:7). He also explained all the facets of the law and the interwoven history of the nation.

The father was the disciplinarian of the family, with the rod being used to drive home the lessons taught (Prv 13:24; 22:15; 29:15-17). Though children were loved and valued, they were not pampered (Ecclus 30:9-12). In postexilic times education also took place within the precincts of the synagogue, and shortly before the time of Christ, a general elementary education was introduced. It was also imperative that a father teach his sons a trade, normally his own, for a man without a trade either starved or became a thief. Another important paternal responsibility was to provide wives for male offspring in the household.

The mother was responsible for her sons' and daughters' early education (Prv 1:8; 6:20), teaching them religious songs and prayers as soon as they could talk. A father took over the education of his sons, but the mother continued with the daughters, training them to spin, weave, cook, clean, trim the lamps, and generally to become competent in all the household duties (31:13-31).

With little furniture, keeping a house clean meant sweeping the floors to keep them free from dust and dirt. Cooking was at once simple and difficult. It was simple in that much of the food was cooked in the form of a soup or stew, or else made into a cake and cooked on a griddle. It was difficult in that the corn had to be ground by hand and bread was baked daily.

A mother was expected to take wool, card it, spin it, and often weave and make clothes for her family. In addition, she would help her husband in the fields at harvesttime. Because many families had one or more olive trees, a few grapevines, and fig trees, the mother would also assist in picking the fruit. She would sometimes work at the press when the olives or grapes were being processed. Frequently the treading of grapes in the family vat would be done together by husband and wife. Drawing water from the well was considered a menial task and was generally the wife's responsibility, although sometimes it was assigned to the children (Gn 24:15-16).

As in all societies, there was a time when children laughed and played together (Zec 8:5; Mt 11:16), although childhood and adolescence were not recognized as specific stages of development. Children were considered as sucklings if under three, but were regarded as boys or girls when they were able to take care of themselves. A small child sat on his mother's lap and was played with (Is 66:12). There is no evidence of organized sports for children. Toys, including whistles, rattles, dolls, and miniature cooking utensils, have been excavated at Palestinian sites.

As soon as a boy was old enough, he took his place in the family and accepted his appointed task. Among other things, children were expected to gather fuel (Jer 7:18). Young boys and girls tended the flocks. The sheep had to be protected from marauding wild beasts, guarded against their own folly when they wandered near crevices, steered toward good pasture and water, and carried home when sick or injured (Gn 29:6; Ex 2:16). The care of cattle was also the responsibility of children (1 Sm 16:11). Of necessity, boys were trained in the various arts of war.

Children sometimes joined their fathers in the fields, and their presence was always welcome. From earliest times, boys in particular would watch their fathers until they too picked up a tool or implement to try their skill; girls watched and learned from their mothers. Young children frequently listened to the talk of the elders at the city gates or in the villages. A visit to a sanctuary at festival time was a family affair, furnishing an ideal learning experience. As a child, Jesus accompanied his parents, Mary and Joseph, to the temple in Jerusalem (Lk 2:42-47).

Young girls were surprisingly free to go about their appointed tasks. They were not secluded or veiled and could visit uninhibited with friends and neighbors (Gn 34:1). They were also able to converse with men without embarrassment (24:15-25; 29:11-12; 1 Sm 9:11-13).

Mealtimes were strictly family times. It is doubtful whether a meal comparable to a breakfast was eaten, and a farmer would probably have a light lunch in the fields. The main meal of the day was prepared by the mother, and it would be eaten in the early evening. Although the variety of food available was limited, its preparation was time-consuming.

Feast times were periods of great religious significance and were also the days when family members participated in the symbolic rituals of their faith. Among the Israelites several kinds of food were fundamental to their religious ritual. Family unity and the national religion were molded together by special meals in the home.

Daylight played an important part in the daily habits of the people in antiquity. Although oil lamps were readily available in later periods, it was customary to rise with the sun and go to bed relatively soon after dark. The wife would probably be up before sunrise and might continue her labor after dark.

In New Testament Times By NT times, for those who followed the Greek and Roman style, life became more elegant. Despite that, the status of many family members did not change substantially. Wealthier families had more slaves, and the children were more likely to have formal education, sometimes spending less effort on family chores. Even in Roman times, however, the father still had a legal right to accept or reject his child.

The status of the woman had definitely improved by the NT period. A Roman matron was highly respected and exerted a strong influence over her husband. She was not sequestered in a particular section of the house, as a Greek woman was, but managed and supervised tasks in any part of her home. She helped her husband in business, had her own place in theaters, games, and religious festivals, and sometimes managed her own property. Palestinian women began to enjoy a new status and dignity as the result of Jesus' attitude toward women and its influence on the early Christian church.

See also Education; Marriage, Marriage Customs; Sex, Sexuality; Widow; Woman.

FAMINE Prolonged and extreme lack of food. Famine, along with other disasters (such as war and disease), has always been part of the human experience. Sometimes there was enough rainfall, properly timed, but occasionally rainfall was too early or late or insufficient (Lv 26:19;

Am 4:7-8). The Hebrews and other people in the Near East viewed famine as judgment from God. Since God is the Creator and Sustainer, he has power over the natural world. He could use his created order as he chose; it was no accident when there was famine. Whether a famine occurred through lack of rainfall, hailstorms, or any other event, God was the agent.

The most prevalent cause of famine in the ancient world was lack of rain. Such famines occurred in the time of Abraham (Gn 12:10) and Isaac (26:1). Joseph was greatly concerned about overcoming the famines in Egypt (chs 41–47). The Nile River usually provided the Egyptians with enough water for their crops; a failure to receive adequate water supplies from upland regions meant famine for Egypt.

Besides lack of rainfall, famine could result from other causes, such as hail and thunderstorms (Ex 9:28; 1 Sm 12:17). Sieges on crops by locusts and other pests sometimes caused famine (Ex 10:15; Am 4:9). Invasion by foreign armies also brought on famine (Dt 28:53; 2 Kgs 6:25; 25:3; Lam 4:9-10). Disease often accompanied famine (1 Kgs 8:37; Jer 14:12; 21:9).

Famine brought changes to the lives of Naomi and Ruth (Ru 1:1). God raised Joseph to a position of power in famine conditions. Famine also affected the lives of King David (2 Sm 21:1), Elijah (1 Kgs 17), Elisha (2 Kgs 4:38; 6:25), and Zedekiah (25:2-3).

Famine was used by God to warn (1 Kgs 17:1), correct (2 Sm 21:1), and punish his people or the heathen (Jer 14:12, 15). The famines predicted by Jesus and the writer of the book of Revelation were signs of judgment (Mk 13:8; Rv 18:8).

FARMER, FARMING *See* Agriculture.

FARTHING*

1. KJV translation for penny, a copper coin equivalent to one-sixteenth of the silver denarius (Mt 10:29; Lk 12:6).
2. KJV translation for another word translated "penny" (RSV), a coin equivalent to one-fourth of #1 above, or one-sixty-fourth of the denarius (Mt 5:26; Mk 12:42).

See also Coins; Money.

FAST, FASTING Eating sparingly or abstaining from food altogether, either from necessity or desire. In medical terms, fasting is the detoxification of the body through the restriction of food.

Spiritual fasting entails setting aside activities as well as reducing the intake of food and replacing these activities with the exercise of prayer and preoccupation with spiritual concerns. The NT word that is translated "fasting" literally means one who has not eaten, one who is empty.

Three types of fast are generally recognized: *normal,* in which there is no intake of food for a prescribed period of time, though there may be an intake of liquids; *partial,* in which the diet is limited, though some food is allowed; and *absolute,* in which there is a total abstinence from food and liquids in all forms.

In the OT the fast was regarded as an act of self-renunciation designed to mollify God's wrath and move him to act in gracious disposition. In times of emergency, the people fasted to persuade God to spare them from impending calamity (Jgs 20:26; 1 Sm 7:6; 1 Kgs 21:9; 2 Chr 20:3; Jer 36:6, 9). Individuals fasted in the hope that God would liberate them from trouble (2 Sm 12:16-20; 1 Kgs 21:27; Pss 35:13; 69:10). Fasting was accompanied by prayer (Ezr 8:21; Neh 1:4; Jer 14:12).

Regular fasts were usually for one day, morning to evening, with food permitted at night (Jgs 20:26; 1 Sm 14:24; 2 Sm 1:12), although there are reports of longer fasts, such as Mordecai's call for a three-day fast (night and day specified—Est 4:16) and the seven-day fast at Saul's death (1 Sm 31:13; 2 Sm 3:35). Among special fasts were Moses' 40 days on Mt Sinai (Ex 34:28) and Daniel's three-week fast prior to receiving visions (Dn 9:3; 10:3, 12).

In general, in the OT, fasting was abused. Instead of a sincere act of self-renunciation and submission to God, fasting became externalized as an empty ritual in which a pretense of piety was presented as a public image. Hence, the prophets cry out against the callousness of such hypocrisy. Jeremiah records the Lord as saying, "Though they fast, I will not hear their cry" (Jer 14:12, RSV; see Is 58:1-10).

The setting for the NT understanding of fasting lies in the development of the rabbinic tradition that grew out of the period between the Testaments, during which fasting became the distinguishing mark of the pious Jew, even though it was largely still ritualistic. Vows were confirmed by fasting (Tb 7:12), remorse and penitence were accompanied by fasting (4 Esd 10:4), and prayer was supported by fasting (1 Macc 3:47). Special fast days were observed, some voluntarily imposed (2 Macc 13:12; 4 Esd 5:13).

This developed into a rabbinic tradition in which fasting was viewed as meritorious and therefore became the primary act of demonstrating piety. It was, however, a false piety consisting mostly in the externals of fastidious observance of fast days, both public and private. With the exception of ascetic groups such as the disciples of John the Baptist, the prevailing mood of fasting when Jesus appeared on the scene was one of mournful sadness, an obligatory necessity, a self-imposed requirement to produce the discipline of self-denial.

Jesus' understanding of fasting is significant in that it represents a shift in the role of fasting. His initial attitude undoubtedly reflected the fact that he grew up participating in the regular fasts and therefore shared the prevailing teachings of his day. Yet his mature teaching about fasting breaks with the rabbinic tradition. Two accounts relating to Jesus and fasting are important: his fast as a part of his temptation in the wilderness (Mt 4:2; Lk 4:2), and his teaching about fasting in the Sermon on the Mount (Mt 6:16-18).

His temptation was born out of the context of struggle. Immediately after his baptism, he was cast out into the wilderness by the Spirit to face the temptation of Satan. In the midst of his temptation, he fasted and prayed, thereby showing his dependence upon God.

Jesus' words about fasting in the Sermon on the Mount constitute a radically different approach to voluntary fasting. In condemning the type of fasting that seeks favor with men by an ostentatious display of outward piety, Jesus taught instead a robust faith that sought genuineness of relation to God through a pure heart. Jesus does not condemn fasting as such, nor does he forbid it. He does, however, give it a new meaning. Fasting is service to God.

This new understanding of fasting is set within the context of the dawning of the time of salvation. The Bridegroom is here. It is a time of joy, not of sorrow. Consequently, the prevailing mood of fasting as mournful stress and pretended piety is inconsistent with the mood of the new age that has begun.

Jesus' teachings may be summarized: Fasting is transcended by the beginning of the eschatological times. The rule of the Messiah has broken the power of the evil age. Fasting would appear to be no longer consistent with the spirit of thanksgiving and joy that marks the framework of the new age, since the Christian life is not to be dominated by tragedy but by joy and happiness.

Yet the kingdom is not fully realized. There is a place for fasting, properly understood. Fasting must be done within the context of the joyful thanksgiving of the new life in Christ. The context of fasting is prayer. It should conform to the same conditions as prayer: unostentatious quietness before God, arising out of gratitude, expressing thanksgiving, grounded in faith, as a means of spiritual growth.

See also Prayer.

FATHER, God As *See* God, Names of; Trinity.

FATHER, Human *See* Family Life and Relations.

FATHER-IN-LAW *See* Family Life and Relations.

FATHOM* Unit of measure equivalent to about six feet (1.8 meters) (Acts 27:28, NLT mg). *See* Weights and Measures.

FAWN Designation for a young animal, usually a deer. *See* Animals (Deer).

FAYUM Egypt's largest oasis, about 70 miles (112.6 kilometers) southwest of Cairo. In the center is Lake Qarun, Egypt's only large inland lake, which today covers 90 square miles (144.8 square kilometers), is about 17 feet (5.2 meters) deep, and has a surface 147 feet (44.8 meters) below the level of the Mediterranean Sea. Lake Qarun is surrounded by about a half million acres of farmland. In ancient times Qarun evidently was much larger than it is today.

Many ancient writers, following fifth-century BC Greek historian Herodotus, believed that the lake, which made the Fayum possible, was an artificial construction. But modern investigations have concluded that it was spring-fed. Sometime after 2000 BC, during the Middle Kingdom period of Egypt, a canal was dug with sluice gates to connect Lake Qarun and the Nile River. Rulers during that period also constructed an irrigation system and brought much of the area under cultivation.

Ancient Towns of the Fayum

Prosperity of the Fayum declined when Ramses II and others used buildings of the area for stone quarries. The Ptolemies restored its prosperity during the third and second centuries BC, when many Greek colonists arrived. In addition to exploration of the monuments of the Fayum, archaeologists have unearthed quantities of papyrus literature written in Greek. These papyri have helped to clarify the meaning of some words used in the NT.

FEAR Emotional foreboding or dread of impending distress or misfortune. Often spoken of as the cause of people wanting religion. Yet fear alone can never account for true religion, since men are impelled to draw near unto God, the object of their worship. One does not desire to come close to the being one fears.

The biblical conception of fear embraces a much wider dimension than does our common English word, which simply denotes dread or terror. While this meaning forms an essential part of the scriptural picture, it is by no means the primary significance, especially when the fear of God—an awe-inspiring reverence—is referred to.

There is, of course, a legitimate place for the fear of God in the lower, anxious sense. We are told, "It is a fearful thing to fall into the hands of the living God" (Heb 10:31, RSV). Jesus taught that we should fear God because he has the power to punish sin and consign people to utter destruction (Lk 12:4-5). Fear has a constructive role to play in enabling men to realize both the degeneracy of their souls and their need of divine forgiveness. The first occurrence of such fear may be found in Genesis 3, where Adam and Eve recoiled from the presence of the holy God whose commandment they had blatantly spurned. Their fear was entirely reasonable because they had been sternly warned that disobedience would incur a grave judgment. Fear is quite naturally the logical consequence of sin (Gn 3:10; 4:13-14; Prv 28:1). The Bible presents an array of people who are plagued with deep-reaching anxiety (e.g., Cain, Saul, Ahaz, and Pilate). Anxious fear seizes the wicked (Jb 15:24), surprises the hypocrite (Is 33:14), and consumes evildoers (Ps 73:19), whose faithless lives are characterized by fear (Rv 21:8). Pharaoh's mighty host was virtually paralyzed by fear as God moved against them (Ex 15:16), and Job's associate Bildad spoke of men driven to their knees by the judgments of God (Jb 18:11).

Fear has a tendency to either immobilize people or seriously affect their activity. This is especially true of the spiritually uncommitted. Saul's fear of the people caused him to transgress the commandment of God (1 Sm 15:24). The parents whose blind son was miraculously healed by Jesus were afraid to support Christ because they feared the Jews (Jn 9:22). In the parable of the talents Jesus told of a man whose fear prevented him from doing his reasonable duty (Mt 25:25).

Jesus Christ, by his atoning death, resurrection, and heavenly intercession for believers, is the unique liberator from fear. The apostle Paul encouraged the Romans (Rom 8:15) by informing them that in their conversion to Christ they received the Holy Spirit, not as a spirit of fear and bondage, but as the spirit of adoption, whereby they could address God as "Abba" (the Aramaic word commonly used by Jewish children to address their fathers). This is the word by which our Lord Jesus addressed his heavenly Father and which Christians, by virtue of their adoption into the family of God, may also use in speaking to God (Gal 4:6). Recipients of God's love have received a dynamic force for casting out their anxieties (1 Jn 4:18).

Unwarranted fear may harm the efforts of the people of God. Jeremiah was warned by God not to fear the faces of his opponents (Jer 1:8) lest God allow calamity to befall him (v 17). Similar calls to courage were given to Jeremiah's contemporary, Ezekiel, and to a great many others (Jos 1:7-9; Ez 2:6). We realize that even godly people are tempted to fear and may be temporarily overwhelmed (Ps 55:5). Therefore, God repeatedly counsels his people not to succumb to that temptation (Is 8:12; Jn 14:1, 27). He tells them to heap their anxieties upon the God of their redemption, whose care for his sheep is infinitely great (1 Pt 5:7). Faith, then, is the indispensable antecedent of fearlessness as seen in the words of Isaiah: "Thou wilt keep him in perfect peace, whose mind is stayed on thee: because he trusteth in thee" (Is 26:3, KJV). The psalmists repeatedly stress the role of faith in conquering fear (Pss 37:1; 46:2; 112:7).

Genuine faith is expressed in, and animated by, a reverential awe, and this is the basic meaning of the biblical idea of the fear of God. Unless there is personal awareness of the awesome and majestic sovereignty of God, it is impossible to have a meaningful faith existing in one's

FEASTS AND FESTIVALS OF ISRAEL
Occasions of public or private rejoicing to commemorate some significant event or personage. The element of celebration has a special meaning in the cycle of religious occasions and the rites and ceremonies associated with these particular days. While the idea of a feast commonly implies a banquet with plenteous food and drink, this element is not indispensable. Sometimes there is only a token amount, as in the celebration of Holy Communion.

In contemporary usage "festival" usually refers to activities extending over a period of time, while "feast" indicates one part of the celebration, often a meal. However, in religious usage, both ancient and modern, the two words are used interchangeably. The ancient Hebrews employed the words *mo'ed* ("seasons") and *hag* for their great public celebrations, while feasts of a more private nature were commonly described by the term *mishteh*. The majority of English translations of Scripture do not differentiate between these words.

ANNUAL FEASTS AND FESTIVALS OF ISRAEL (Beginning with Nisan [Abib], the first month in the calendar of Israel)

Feasts and Festivals	Day(s) and Post- (Pre-) exilic Month	Gregorian Month	Major References
Passover	14th of Nisan (Abib)	March/April	Ex 12:1-30; Lv 23:5; Nm 9:1-5; 28:16; Dt 16:1-8
Unleavened Bread	15th–21st of Nisan (Abib)	March/April	Ex 34:18-21; Lv 23:6-8; Nm 28:17-25; Dt 16:1-8, 16-17
Firstfruits	22d of Nisan (Abib)	March/April	Lv 23:9-14
Pentecost (Shavout, Harvest, Weeks)	6th of Sivan	May/June	Ex 34:22; Lv 23:15-21; Nm 28:26-31; Dt 16:9-12, 16-17
Trumpets (Rosh Hashanah)	1st of Tishri (Ethanim)	September/October	Lv 23:23-25; Nm 29:1-6
Day of Atonement (Yom Kippur)	10th of Tishri (Ethanim)	September/October	Lv 16:29-34; 23:26-32; Nm 29:7-11
Tabernacles (Shelters Succoth, Booths, Ingathering)	15th–22d of Tishri (Ethanim)	September/October	Ex 34:22; Lv 23:33-43; Nm 29:12-38; Dt 16:13-17
Dedication (Lights, Hanukkah)	25th of Kislev	November/December	1 Macc 4:41-59; 2 Macc 10:6-8; Jn 10:22
Nicanor (Fast of Esther)	13th of Adar	February/March	1 Macc 7:33-49
Purim (Lots)	14th of Adar	February/March	Est 9:21, 27-28

heart (Pss 5:7; 89:7). Though Christians are to be liberated from the fear of men (Heb 13:6), death (2:15), and life in general (2 Tm 1:6-7), they must never lose their sense of the awesomeness of God. Such awareness not only leads to true wisdom (Ps 111:10) but also provides direction for the child of God throughout life (Eph 5:21; Phil 2:12). Those who love God learn of wholesome fear by searching the Scriptures (Prv 2:3-5), the Word of God, which the ancient Israelites were commanded to cleave to and obey as evidence of their reverence for God (Dt 6:2). In Acts 10:2 Cornelius and his family were called "God-fearers" because of their high regard for the God of Israel and because they stood in awe of his person. True reverence for God must invariably express itself in good works and holy living (2 Cor 7:1). This holy fear is actually a source of joy (Ps 2:11) and a veritable fountain of life (Prv 14:27). The fear of the Lord is more valuable than the greatest material riches (15:16) because the Lord takes pleasure in those who hold him in such high regard (Ps 147:11).

FEAST OF LIGHTS*
Alternate name for Hanukkah, one of Israel's festivals celebrating the rededication of the temple in 164 BC. *See* Feasts and Festivals of Israel.

Feasts and Their Functions Each festival places great emphasis on community participation and on the continuity of social or religious tradition, especially where the celebrations are elements of a regular civil or religious calendar. Without community backing, even in a family celebration, no festival can be successful. When there is communal participation, a festival can reinforce the individual and community memory of specific occasions, and can perpetuate that store of recollection over years and generations. Such shared memory has a cohesive effect upon a cooperating community, large or small, and serves to establish the traditions by which the group lives. If the festival commemorates a particular event or celebrates some lofty ideal, that theme becomes more firmly embedded in the minds of the participants by being associated repeatedly with the rites and ceremonies performed. The feasts of the ancient Hebrews had this positive function. The great festivals of their religious calendar commemorated specific occasions when God had reached out in power to intervene for his people or had provided for them in their distress. By celebrating these feasts on a regular basis, the Hebrews continually affirmed that their God had directed their destiny. Their repeated rehearsal of God's help and love for them reminded them that he was still able to sustain them. Especially in times of hardship, it pointed to the reality of God's presence and activity among them. Faith sustained by this means furnished an invaluable spiritual dimension to the life of the nation and provided a sense of continuity under divine provision and guidance. Only when corrupt or pagan elements were introduced into festive occasions did this important ingredient of national life begin to lose its vitality.

Old Testament Festivals

General Festivals These occasions were surprisingly numerous in Israel, considering the rather austere mode of life reflected in much of the OT. No doubt such celebrations offset or compensated for the hardships and insecurities of existence in the ancient Near East, and the Israelites made the most of every opportunity. A wedding was one of the most obvious occasions for celebration, and it is not surprising that a feast was prepared for the marriage of Rachel and Jacob (Gn 29:22) in which the whole neighborhood participated. Just how long this particular feast lasted is unknown, but some marriage festivals continued for a week, as in the case of the marriage between Samson and the woman of Timnah (Jgs 14:17). Wine that makes glad man's heart (Ps 104:15) was consumed freely on such occasions.

Birthdays were often observed in a festive spirit, especially where a royal person was concerned (Gn 40:20). Solomon's dream was commemorated with a feast provided for his servants (1 Kgs 3:15), and when the temple was dedicated, the occasion was celebrated for a full week (8:65). Kings and queens held feasts periodically to mark certain occasions or to express goodwill (cf. Est 1:3; 2:18; 5:4, 14; 7:2, 7; Dn 5:1). Herdsmen traditionally made a feast for the shearing of the first sheep (Dt 18:4).

Preexilic Festivals In addition to the general festivals, which were frequently of a secular nature, communal feasts were prescribed for the Israelites that had a specifically spiritual significance. They were meant to emphasize the activity of God on behalf of his people and to remind them that continued divine blessing depended upon their obedience to his will. The catalog of festivals in Leviticus 23:2 began with an injunction to observe the Sabbath. The seventh day, in which God ceased from creating (Gn 2:3), was holy, though it is difficult to determine the extent to which it was kept until the time of Moses (Ex 20:8-11). From that time on, Sabbath observance stressed refraining from all work so as to commemorate properly God's own rest from creative activity (31:17) and his deliverance of his people from bondage in Egypt (Dt 5:12-15). Sabbath celebration was the sign of a special relationship between God and the Israelites. During this 24-hour period, even trivial tasks like making a fire (Ex 35:3) or gathering wood (Nm 15:32-33) were prohibited on pain of death. Journeys of any distance also came under the Sabbath ban (Ex 16:29). Special offerings were part of the observance (Nm 28:9-10), and the bread of the Presence was replaced in the tabernacle (Lv 24:5-8). Despite the restrictions on activity, the Sabbath was meant to symbolize a time of happiness and security in the presence of God (cf. Is 58:13-14), since its observance would bring blessing to the individual and to the whole land.

➤ FESTIVAL OF THE NEW MOON The new moon was a monthly celebration based on the lunar calendar. It was especially appropriate for an agricultural people, since everyone could tell when the moon was new. Special offerings were prescribed for this festival, consisting of a burnt sacrifice, a grain offering, and a drink offering (Nm 28:11-15). In addition, a male goat was sacrificed to God as a sin offering, and trumpet blasts were sounded over the sacrificial offerings as a memorial before God (10:10). The sacrifices prescribed for the new moon festival were significantly greater than those required in Numbers 28:9-10 for the weekly Sabbath.

This lunar feast was popular throughout Israelite history. During the monarchy, the Levites were required to assist the Aaronic priests at the new moon festival, as well as on the Sabbath (1 Chr 23:29-31). The preexilic prophets may well have taken advantage of the large gatherings to give guidance to the people or proclaim prophetic oracles (cf. 2 Kgs 4:23), though to what extent this was done is uncertain. Not everyone found the period of rest and celebration valuable, however, and Amos (Am 8:5) complained about those avaricious Israelites who felt that such observances interfered with the business of making a living. The feast could not be observed when the Judeans were in exile in Babylonia (cf. Hos 2:11), but under Ezra and Nehemiah, its observance was restored (Neh 10:33). In Isaiah 66:22-23 it was related to Israel's final destiny and was an accepted part of the ordinances for Ezekiel's ideal temple (Ez 45:17).

The purpose of the festival was to enhance the unity of national life by reminding the Israelites that God's covenant with their ancestors was permanent and still binding upon the nation. It also stressed the loving nature and providence of a God who could begin such a relationship and carry out his promises with complete faithfulness (cf. Ps 104:19).

➤ THE FESTIVAL OF TRUMPETS The Festival of Trumpets was celebrated on the first day of the seventh new moon. This month, subsequently named Tishri, was especially holy, and for this reason was governed by certain regulations different from those of ordinary new moon festivals. The trumpets were blown on the first day (Lv 23:24) as the animal and cereal sacrifices were offered. From Numbers 29:2-6 it appears that the offerings required for this particular feast exceeded those prescribed for normal Sabbath sacrifice, but were somewhat less than those required for the regular new moon festival (cf. Nm 28:11). This feast was to be observed as a day of solemn rest and as a holy convocation, and the trumpets were sounded as a triumphant memorial to God's great provision for his people through the Sinai covenant.

The seventh month was particularly sacred, partly because of its place in the hallowed cycle of sevens, but also because the Day of Atonement (or Yom Kippur) and the Feast of Tabernacles, or Booths (Shelters), occurred during this period. The latter feast followed the Day of Atonement by some five days (Lv 23:33), and its joyful character served to offset somewhat the solemnity of the annual penitential occasion when the nation confessed its collective sins and saw them banished symbolically into the wilderness as the scapegoat was driven from the congregation.

➤ THE SABBATICAL YEAR Another festival closely connected with the institution of the Sabbath was the sabbatical year. At the end of each cycle of six years, the following 12 months were observed as a "sabbath of rest for the land." During this interval, the ground was to lie fallow (Ex 23:11) without any form of cultivation, and whatever sprouted and grew from it naturally was assigned to the poor and needy (Lv 25:6). This provision for the land itself constituted one of the most important ecological principles of Scripture. Like God's people, the land was holy, and just as they needed to have regular intervals of rest from daily work in order to regain their energy and spiritual vitality through worship, so the ground needed to rest and recuperate from the strain of constant cultivation. The festival reminded the Israelites that the land on which they lived had been given to them by God in fulfillment of his covenant undertaking to provide richly for their physical needs (cf. Dt 8:7-10). To keep the Israelites from experiencing any shortages or other hardships during the Year of Sabbath, God promised that in the year immediately preceding the sabbatical period, the land would bear fruit to suffice for the next three years (Lv 25:21). This assurance was based upon the experience of the wilderness wanderings, when on the sixth day of the week sufficient manna appeared to last through the Sabbath (Ex 16:5).

In this festival period, God's absolute claim over the land was reaffirmed (cf. Lv 25:23), and the faith of the nation in God's ability to provide for future needs was reinforced. The provisions that freed the land for a year from agricultural bondage were paralleled in the seventh year of rest by those requiring liberation of slaves and debtors. These underprivileged members of society were to be released from their obligations of servitude. As a result, men and women who had become slaves for one reason or another were given personal liberty (Ex 21:2-6), and under proclamation of the Lord's release, the provisions applying to debt were rescinded (Dt 15:1-6). The sabbatical year seems to have been a regular part of preexilic Israelite life, although some abuses were noted in Jeremiah 34:8-22. There the prophet took advantage of the opportunity presented to instruct the people in the nature and purpose of the sabbatical year ordinance. He also warned the wayward Judeans that because they had disobeyed the commands of God in denying proper liberty to their slaves, they would have their own freedom taken away in a far more serious manner by being carried captive to Babylonia after seeing their land destroyed. The lesson was not lost upon those who returned from exile, for under the administration of Nehemiah, the Jews bound themselves by a covenant to observe the principle of the sabbatical year (Neh 10:31). This undertaking evidently took its impetus from the reading of the law of Moses at the Feast of Booths (Shelters), which coincidentally occurred at the beginning of the sabbatical year (Neh 8:13-18).

➤JUBILEE Still another feast based on the principle of the sabbath was the Year of Jubilee, or Pentecostal year (Lv 25:8-55; 27:17-24). As the sabbatical year was related to the concept of the seventh day, so the Pentecostal (50th) year marked the completion of a cycle of seven sabbatical years. The commencement of a jubilee year was proclaimed on the Day of Atonement throughout the land by means of trumpet blasts (Lv 25:9). The activities that took place during the Pentecostal year were similar to those prescribed for the sabbatical year. A special feature was that land that had been sold during the preceding 49 years was returned to its original owners, a procedure that sometimes involved financial adjustments. To prevent abuse of the process through opportunism or speculation, the Hebrews were instructed to deal fairly and honestly with one another in the fear of God, who was the real owner of the land (Lv 25:14-17). As with the sabbatical year, God promised to make provision before the jubilee year so that no one would suffer hardship. It was during the Year of Jubilee that those who were slaves in Hebrew households were given their liberty, so that everyone in the land would commence a new cycle of sabbatical years on the same footing, as free persons under God.

Seasonal Festivals Three annual festivals that followed the seasons of the year rather than phases of the moon furnished important occasions for commemorating God's power and provision in national life. These festivals were designated by the term *hag,* indicating a festival usually observed by some sort of pilgrimage. These three festivals were prescribed in Exodus 23:14-17 and Deuteronomy 16:16, and consisted of the Feast of Passover and Unleavened Bread, the Feast of Weeks (Pentecost), and the Festival of Booths (Tabernacles). On these occasions, all the males of Israel were commanded to make pilgrimage to the sanctuary and celebrate these festivals (Ex 12:14). The Passover and the Feast of Unleavened Bread were originally separate ordinances, but since the latter always followed immediately upon the Passover rite, they naturally blended into a single festival.

➤PASSOVER The Passover was of supreme theological significance for the Israelites, since it marked one of the most momentous acts of divine intervention in their history, the beginning of their deliverance from bondage in Egypt when, in the final plague, God destroyed the firstborn of the Egyptians but spared those Israelites whose homes had blood smeared on the doorposts (Ex 12:11-30). God commanded that the day was to be observed as a memorial feast (v 14), and the next Passover celebration occurred in the Sinai Desert (Nm 9:1-5). In the Hebrew calendar the Passover festival came in the first month, called Abib in Deuteronomy 16:1, but known after the exile as Nisan (cf. Neh 2:1). The Passover rite took place the 14th evening (Lv 23:5), and this was followed by a seven-day period during which nothing leavened was to be eaten. The principle for removing all leaven from bread was similar to that underlying the draining of blood from animal flesh. Both leaven and blood had quickening power and were to be kept separate as an offering to God. The first and seventh days of this period were marked by a holy assembly, during which the only work permitted was the preparation of food (Ex 12:16). This period when unleavened bread was eaten was described as a festival because it opened the seven-week period of grain harvest (Dt 16:9). During this feast, special burnt sacrifices were offered, followed with a sheaf of newly harvested barley at the Feast of Firstfruits. By NT times the festivals of Passover and Unleavened Bread were well-attended celebrations and were known as the "days of unleavened bread" (Lk 22:1; Acts 12:3). The theme of Israel's deliverance from the power of Egypt by divine intervention assured the Israelites that God was always ready to act on behalf of a faithful and obedient covenant people. It also reminded them that they had once been slaves (Dt 16:12). In Israelite life the early Passover and Unleavened Bread observances were comparatively simple in character, but during the monarchy more elaborate Passover rituals came into use (cf. 2 Kgs 23:21-23; 2 Chr 35:1-19).

➤PENTECOST The second great festival, Pentecost (or Weeks) lasted one day only and was observed on the 50th day after the newly harvested barley sheaf had been waved before the Lord at the end of the Feast of Unleavened Bread (Dt 16:9-12). The festival marked the end of the barley harvest and the beginning of the wheat harvest, the beginning of the period when firstfruits could be offered (cf. Ex 23:16; 34:22; Nm 28:26). The feast day was marked by the presentation of two wheat-flour loaves along with sacrifices of seven lambs, two rams, and a bull (Lv 23:15-20). Freewill gifts to God were presented to reflect gratitude for his blessings, and the entire occasion was one of communal rejoicing (Dt 16:10-11). Since Pentecost was essentially a harvest festival (Ex 23:16), the Israelites were called on to recognize that they depended entirely upon God for their material prosperity. In Deuteronomy 26, specific instructions were given for the ritual of presenting firstfruits from the harvest. It comprised a great confession of faith set within the framework of Israel's history, and it recounted God's deliverance of the nation from Egyptian oppression and his provision of a land that could amply supply the needs of his people.

➤ **FESTIVAL OF TABERNACLES** This festival, known variously as the Feast of Booths, Tabernacles, Shelters (Lv 23:34; Dt 16:13), or Ingathering (Ex 34:22), was the third great occasion that all Hebrew males were required to observe annually. It began on the 15th day of the seventh month (Tishri), shortly after the observance of the Day of Atonement, which fell on the 10th day. The Feast of Booths lasted for one week and involved pilgrimage. It was associated initially with the end of the year (Ex 34:22), when the agricultural work had been completed. The first day was marked by a symbolic cessation from all activity, after which burnt offerings were presented to the Lord. The eighth day was also one on which the congregation of Israel abstained from manual work and again offered burnt sacrifices. Leviticus 23:39-43 furnished details for the rituals that gave the festival its special name of booths or shelters or tabernacles. The fruit of "goodly trees" was to be gathered on the first day of the feast, along with palm fronds, willow branches, and boughs from trees in full leaf. From these, rough shelters or booths were to be constructed in which the people lived for the week of the feast. Every seventh year the observances were marked by a public recital of the covenant provisions to which the Israelites under Moses had committed themselves, a procedure designed to keep fresh in their minds the obligations as well as the blessings of the covenant relationship. A particularly significant observance of the Feast of Tabernacles took place in the time of Ezra, when the Judean community returned from Babylon—a celebration of a kind unknown for centuries (Neh 8:13-18). From the context it appears that observance of the feast had lapsed during the monarchy. The feast at Shiloh where Hannah was mistaken for a drunken woman and the feast referred to in Judges 21:19 were evidently the Feast of Booths. In a prophetic vision in which he saw all nations coming to Jerusalem to observe the Festival of Booths, Zechariah warned that those who did not continue this tradition could expect hardship and shortages of food (Zec 14:16-19).

Postexilic Festivals There are a few minor festivals that were created in the period after the Jews returned from exile; some of these festivals had their origin in specific historical occasions.

➤ **THE FESTIVAL OF PURIM** The Festival of Purim, also known as the Festival of Lots, was a joyful occasion occurring on the 14th day of the 12th month (Adar). It celebrated the way in which Esther and Mordecai were used by God to deliver his people in the Persian Empire from extermination by Haman (Est 9:21, 24-28). The feast was observed on the 14th day of Adar by those living in villages, and on the 15th by the inhabitants of walled towns and cities. The explanation of the name of the festival is given in Esther 9:24-26, and its observance reminded the Hebrews of God's ability to save them during a time of anti-Semitic activity in Persia. The deliverance memorialized in this festival has consoled the Jews on other occasions when they have suffered persecution. Traditionally the scroll of Esther was read aloud in the synagogue on the evening before the feast, and there was a great outcry, especially among the children present, whenever the names of the hated Haman and his sons were mentioned.

➤ **FESTIVAL OF THE DEDICATION OF THE TEMPLE** Another joyous festival that lasted for eight days was the Feast of the Dedication of the Temple (1 Macc 4:52-59; 2 Macc 10:6-8), familiar to modern readers as Hanukkah, or the Festival of Lights. The specific dedication that prompted the feast occurred in 164 BC, when Judas Maccabeus reconsecrated the temple in Jerusalem after it had been defiled by Antiochus IV Epiphanes. The celebrations commenced on the 25th day of the ninth month (Kislev) and were marked at night by blazing lights and lanterns. The stories of brave opposition by the Maccabees to the crushing forces of paganism were recounted, and the feast was one of praise to God for his marvelous deliverance of the Jews during the Maccabean period.

New Testament Festivals In Christ's time the Sabbath was observed rigorously and was the occasion for synagogue worship (cf. Lk 4:16; Acts 13:14; 18:4). Pharisaic law prohibited all work, and Jesus came into conflict with the authorities periodically for breaches of the Sabbath regulations (cf. Mt 12:1-4; Mk 3:1-5; Lk 13:10-17). In the primitive church, worship occurred on "the first day of the week" (i.e., Sunday) to commemorate Christ's resurrection. The early Christians initially participated in Jewish ceremonies (cf. Acts 20:16; 1 Cor 16:8). It was during the Feast of Pentecost, after Christ's resurrection and ascension, that the Spirit was poured out (Acts 2:1-4), fulfilling Joel 2:28-32 and commencing the history of the Christian church as such.

The Passover and Feast of Unleavened Bread were of great significance in the life of Christ (cf. Jn 4:45; 5:1; 6:4; 12:1-26), for the occasion was a very popular one in NT times (cf. 12:20). On the Passover, Pilate had instituted the custom of clemency to a prisoner nominated by the populace (Mt 27:15; Mk 15:6). Jesus participated actively in the Passover rituals (cf. Lk 2:42; Jn 2:13; 6:4). The Last Supper with his disciples occurred just prior to the Passover (Jn 13:1), when Judas Iscariot betrayed Jesus to the Pharisees (Lk 22:4-6). The breaking of bread and the drinking of wine at that Passover celebration (Mk 14:22-25) were related directly to Christ's forthcoming death on the cross in a sacramental manner. Christ's disciples were instructed to observe this rite as a memorial of his suffering and death for human sin (1 Cor 11:24-26) and as a proclamation of the power of the cross until the Lord returns in glory. Some scholars have suggested that Christ was actually hanging on the cross when the Passover lamb was being slaughtered, and if that chronology is correct, it would represent Jesus graphically as the "Lamb of God, who takes away the sin of the world" (Jn 1:29, RSV). Jesus was also present once when the Feast of Tabernacles was celebrated (7:10). In his day water was carried in procession from the pool of Siloam as an offering to God, and the ceremony most probably prompted Christ's discourse on living water and eternal life (vv 37-39). On at least one occasion Jesus was in Jerusalem when the Festival of Lights occurred (Jn 10:22) and narrowly missed death by stoning.

Jesus was entertained occasionally at private feasts (cf. Lk 5:29), and once remedied an emergency situation when the wine ran out at a wedding ceremony (Jn 2:8-10). He was critical of the Pharisees for securing the chief seats at feasts (Mt 23:6; Mk 12:39; Lk 20:46) and taught that festivals ought to benefit the poor (Lk 14:13).

Symbolism of Feasts Many aspects of the ancient Hebrew feasts were interpreted symbolically in the early church. Paul regarded the earliest Hebrew Christians as the firstfruits of the Israel of God (Rom 11:16). In Romans 8:23, the Holy Spirit as possessed by Christians was regarded as only a token of what was to come, and as such was the firstfruit of the Spirit. Christians themselves were described in James 1:18 as the firstfruits of God's creatures who were brought forth by the Word of Truth. The resurrection of Jesus was considered by Paul to be the firstfruits of those who slept (1 Cor 15:20, 23). In an allusion to OT festivals, Paul spoke of the Sabbaths, new moons, and feasts as merely being a shadow of good things to come (Col 2:16-17). The Passover was used figuratively to emphasize that Christ our Passover Lamb had been sacrificed for us. Believers were urged to keep the feast with the unleavened bread of sincerity and truth, and not with the old leaven of malice and evil (1 Cor 5:7-8).

See also Calendars, Ancient and Modern; Offerings and Sacrifices; Tabernacle; Temple.

FELIX, Antonius

FELIX, Antonius Roman procurator (governor) of Judea (AD 52–60) succeeding Cumanus, appointed by Claudius and succeeded by Festus Porcius. Felix's brother, Pallas, a prominent, more influential Roman, interceded on his behalf after he was recalled from his procuratorship by Nero. During his oppressive rule, Felix utilized the aid of robbers to have Jonathan, the high priest, murdered. His tyranny has been cited as the cause for the Jewish revolt that broke out six years after he was recalled. Felix had three wives: one unknown, another the granddaughter of Mark Antony and Cleopatra, and another the Jewish sister of Agrippa II, whose name was Drusilla. At the age of 16 Drusilla left her husband, King Azizus of Emesa, to marry Felix. She later bore him a son, Agrippa.

Felix was serving as governor when the apostle Paul was brought before him in Caesarea to answer charges against him after the riot in Jerusalem (Acts 23:24–24:27). After a five-day delay, Tertullus, spokesman for the Jews, and others arrived to state their charges. Felix put off a decision until he could hear from Lysias, the tribune. In the meantime Paul was placed in limited custody. Felix hoped to obtain bribe money for his release. As a result, Paul was detained for two years, during which time he and Felix often conversed. The apostle's message of "justice, self-control, and future judgment" alarmed Felix greatly (24:25). Record of his life after being recalled by Nero is not available.

FELLOWSHIP

FELLOWSHIP Communion with God, which results in common participation with other believers in the Spirit of God and God's blessings.

In the beginning Adam was placed in the Garden to enjoy friendship and communion with God. When Adam and Eve chose to assert their own autonomy rather than live under the Creator's gracious care, the fellowship was broken. As a result, Adam and Eve hid themselves from the Lord's presence (Gn 3:8). Yet God immediately sought them out and revealed his plan for the ultimate restoration of sinners through the work of the Redeemer (v 15).

The OT tells how God began to draw a special people into fellowship with himself. Enoch is described as a man who walked with God (Gn 5:22, 24). Noah, likewise, walked in communion with the Lord (6:9). And Abraham, the father of Israel, is called "the friend of God" (Jas 2:23). No OT person had deeper fellowship with God than did Moses during his 40-day encounter with the Lord on Mt Sinai (Ex 24). Later in Israel's history, David wrote psalms that reflect a heart vitally in tune with the living God (Pss 16, 34, 40, 63).

As a result of Christ's finished work on the cross, God now makes his permanent abode in each believer's heart (Jn 14:23). As a result, the fellowship that now prevails

under the new covenant is nothing less than the vital, spiritual union of the believer with Christ (vv 20-21). Fellowship with God is the goal of the Christian life (1 Jn 1:3), and this relationship will be perfected forever when we see our Savior "face to face" (1 Cor 13:12), when God dwells with his people in eternity (Rv 21:3).

The gospel restores fellowship not only with God but also among believers. Jesus' Last Supper with his disciples illustrates the relationship between the vertical and horizontal dimensions of fellowship (Mk 14:22-25). In the upper room, Jesus shared with his disciples a sacred love feast. The hearts of the Lord and his followers were knit together by a deep sense of love and commitment. Later, the disciples discovered that their own hearts were strongly united out of their common loyalty to Jesus. Following the cross and the outpouring of the Spirit, the church was born—that new society of people in fellowship with God and with one another.

The depth of camaraderie among the first Christians is portrayed in the early chapters of Acts. The believers met together in house groups for teaching, fellowship, the Lord's Supper, and prayer (Acts 2:42, 46). So profound was their sense of togetherness that the Christians pooled their possessions and distributed them to brothers and sisters in need (2:44-45; 4:32-35). Perhaps the dominant characteristic of this early Christian fellowship was the love among the believers (1 Thes 4:9; 1 Pt 1:22).

Motivated by love, Paul organized among the gentile churches a collection for poor believers in Jerusalem. In Romans 15:26, which speaks of the gifts of the churches in Macedonia and Achaia, the word translated "contribution" is the common Greek word for "fellowship." Similarly, the fellowship that the Philippian church shared with Paul assumed the form of gifts to support the apostle's ministry (Phil 1:5; 4:14-15).

Scripture uses several images to describe the spirit of togetherness that characterized the early church. The first is "the household of God" (Eph 2:19; 1 Tm 3:15), or "the household of faith" (Gal 6:10). In God's household, love and hospitality are to be the rule (Heb 13:1-2). Further, the church is depicted as the family of God on earth (Eph 3:15). God is the Father, and believers are his faithful sons and daughters. The life of God's family is to be governed by love, tenderness, compassion, and humility (Phil 2:1-4). Finally, the Christian fellowship is represented as the "one new man" or the "one body" (Eph 2:15-16). In spite of great natural diversity in the body, the Holy Spirit binds believers together into a single organism (4:4-6). In this fellowship of love, no believer is insignificant. Each member has been endowed with gifts for the spiritual edification of the entire body.

Scripture lays down the basis of fellowship in 1 John 1:7: "If we walk in the light, as he is in the light, we have fellowship with one another" (RSV). Jesus Christ, then, is the source and fount of all spiritual communion. Only when rightly related to the Lord do we experience true fellowship with another Christian. Just as light and darkness are incompatible, so a believer can have no real fellowship with an unbeliever. Neither can the Christian be in fellowship with one who walks contrary to the teaching of Christ (2 Jn 1:9-11), or a professing brother who is immoral, idolatrous, a drunkard, or a thief (1 Cor 5:11).

Scripture lays down several guidelines for enhancing the communion of believers in the body: (1) Love one another with the same compassion that Christ displayed to his own (Jn 13:34-35; 15:12). The law of the fellowship should be the rule of love (Heb 13:1). (2) Cultivate that spirit of humility that seeks the other person's honor (Phil 2:3-5). (3) Lighten fellow believers' loads by bearing one another's burdens (Gal 6:2). (4) Share material blessings with brothers and sisters in need (2 Cor 9:13). (5) Tenderly correct a sinner while helping to find solutions to the problems (Gal 6:1). (6) Succor a fellow believer in times of suffering (1 Cor 12:26). (7) Pray for one another in the Spirit without ceasing (Eph 6:18). The Christian will want to seriously regard the saying of an anonymous saint, "You cannot draw nigh to God if you are at a distance from your brother."

FERRET* KJV translation for gecko, a kind of reptile, in Leviticus 11:30. *See* Animals (Gecko; Lizard).

FERTILITY CULTS* *See* Canaanite Deities and Religion.

FESTIVAL *See* Feasts and Festivals of Israel.

FESTUS, Porcius Roman procurator (governor) of Judea, who succeeded Felix Antonius and who was succeeded by Albinus. The precise date of Porcius Festus's accession to power is debatable but has been narrowed to sometime between AD 55 and 60. The only sources mentioning Festus are the book of Acts and the writings of Josephus, a Jewish historian who lived in Rome in the first century AD (*Antiquities* 20.8.9-11; 9.1).

Josephus wrote that Festus ruled wisely and justly, in contrast to Felix and Albinus. Sicarii bandits (named after the small swords they carried) who had terrorized the Palestinian countryside were eliminated under Festus's rule. In spite of this, he could not reverse the damage incurred by his predecessor, Felix, who had aggravated the conflict between pagans and Jews.

The NT recounts that the new procurator Festus traveled from Caesarea (where Paul was in custody) to Jerusalem (Acts 25:1). The Jewish leaders confronted him there and brought charges against Paul. Upon returning to Caesarea, Festus heard Paul's defense (v 6). He granted the apostle's appeal to be heard by Caesar (the right of any Roman accused of a capital offense) in an effort to avoid further religious disputes in his jurisdiction (vv 11-12). When King Agrippa arrived a few days later, Festus was in a quandary, unable to understand the Jews' charges against Paul (vv 25-27). After Paul's address before the king, Festus loudly declared him to be mad (26:24), though still agreeing that Paul had done nothing to deserve death or imprisonment (v 31).

FIELD OF BLOOD *See* Blood, Field of.

FIERY SERPENT* Bronze symbol of a snake made by Moses on God's instruction to save the Israelites.

Deadly snakes were sent by God to punish the Israelites for their rebellious grumblings, many of whom died from the poisonous bites (Nm 21:4-9). Recognizing their sin, they cried out to God for deliverance, and he instructed Moses to make a fiery (bronze) serpent and set it on a pole. Healing was granted to those who gazed at the uplifted figure.

Jesus Christ referred to the bronze serpent incident as a symbol of the saving power of his crucifixion. A person who looks in faith to the uplifted Christ will receive deliverance from sin and have eternal life (Jn 3:14-15). The apostle Paul also drew upon the OT event as a warning to those who might arrogantly test God (1 Cor 10:9).

See also Bronze Serpent, Bronze Snake.

FIG, FIG TREE *See* Plants.

FINANCE *See* Money; Banker, Banking.

FINGER* (Measure) Linear measure equivalent to the width of a finger (Jer 52:21). *See* Weights and Measures.

FIRE, Lake of *See* Lake of Fire.

FIRE, Pillar of Supernatural phenomenon of God's presence that guided the Israelites in the wilderness. *See* Pillar of Fire and Cloud; Wilderness Wanderings.

FIRKIN* Measure of about 10 gallons (37.9 liters). In John 2:6, firkin is the KJV translation for the name of a Greek liquid measure. *See* Weights and Measures.

FIRMAMENT* Bible word for the atmosphere about the earth. The original meaning of this word refers to space that is stretched out or expanded. The Hebrews probably considered the "firmament" as voidlike sky where the clouds, sun, and moon were.

During the second day of Creation, God created the atmosphere, or firmament, above the earth. He did this to divide the waters under it from the waters above it. God called the firmament heaven (Gn 1:6-8). The atmospheric firmament serves as a supportive area in which the heavenly bodies exist and function according to the purposes for which God made them. On the fourth day of Creation, God created the lights in the firmament. They were to distinguish night and day as well as be signs of the different seasons. The greater light in the firmament, the sun, controlled the days, whereas the lesser light, the moon, controlled the nights (vv 14-19).

The term "firmament" is mentioned twice in the Psalms as the place of God's handiwork (Pss 19:1; 150:1). Also occurring in the books of Ezekiel (Ez 1:22-26; 10:1) and Daniel (Dn 12:3), the firmament is always related to Creation.

FIRSTBORN Term used in the Bible to describe a family's oldest son or daughter (Gn 22:21; 29:26). Israel was called God's firstborn because of that nation's miraculous beginning and special deliverance out of Egypt (Gn 17:5, 15-16; Ex 4:22). As God's firstborn, Israel had unique privileges over all other nations. Gentiles were "blessed" only in relation to their kindness to Israel (Gn 12:3; Ex 19:6; Dt 4:5-8). The prophet Isaiah foresaw a day when Israel would have a double portion of inheritance (Is 61:7). Thus, being firstborn implies priority or preeminence, as well as an inheritance.

The expression "first-born of the poor," (Is 14:30, RSV) means one who is supremely poor, the poorest of the poor. Another figurative expression, "first-born of death" (Jb 18:13, RSV), implied that Job's disease was fatal.

Because God delivered Israel's firstborn sons from death in Egypt, he expected each firstborn to be sanctified to him (Ex 11:4-7; 13:12). The first male child was a representative of the entire offspring (Gn 49:3; Ex 22:29; Nm 3:13). The firstborn of all animals used in sacrifice was to be sanctified to the Lord (Ex 13:2, 15).

Firstborn and Redemption The firstborn of every tribe except Levi's was to be redeemed by a sum not to exceed five shekels (Nm 18:15-16). Redemption implied a previous bondage and was to remind Israel of their redemption from bondage in Egypt (Ex 13:2-8).

The firstborn of ritually clean animals was devoted to the Lord. It was brought to the tabernacle (or later, the temple) within a year from the eighth day after birth. This animal was then sacrificed and its blood sprinkled on the altar. The meat of the sacrificed animal was for the priests (Ex 13:13; 22:30; cf. Nm 18:17). The firstborn of unclean animals could be redeemed with an addition of one-fifth of the value as determined by the priest. If not redeemed, these animals were sold, exchanged, or destroyed by the priests (Lv 27:27). The colt of an ass was to be redeemed with a lamb (Ex 13:13). If not redeemed, it was to be killed. Meat from unclean animals was not eaten.

Firstborn and Birthright The firstborn acted as priest of the family in the father's absence or death. Esau and Reuben are both examples (Gn 27:19, 32; 1 Chr 5:1-2). This position of the firstborn ceased when the priesthood was committed to Levi's tribe (Nm 3:12-13). All the firstborn of succeeding generations had to be redeemed. The redemption money became part of the Levites' yearly income (8:17; 18:16).

A double portion of the family inheritance was the right of the firstborn. This protected the firstborn when there was a polygamous marriage. The son of a favorite wife could not take the place of the first son born of the household (Dt 21:17).

The title "firstborn" is applied to Christ (Lk 2:7; Rom 8:29; Col 1:15, 18; Heb 1:6; Rv 1:5). It stresses Christ's preeminence over all because he was the first to rise from the dead. As firstborn, Christ is heir of all things (Heb 1:2) and the head of the church (Eph 1:20-23; Col 1:18, 24; Heb 2:10-12).

See also Birthright; Heir; Inheritance; Primogeniture.

FIRST DAY OF THE WEEK Sunday. *See* Lord's Day, The.

FIRSTFRUITS Firstborn child or animal or first parts of any crop that, in Hebrew thought, were considered as holy and therefore belonged to the Lord. The firstfruits, as a foretaste of more to come, were offered to God in thanksgiving for his goodness in providing them.

Firstfruit offerings could include produce either in its natural state or prepared or processed in some way, such as dough, bread, wine, olive oil, and wool. The firstborn son and the firstborn of the animals that one owned were to be treated as belonging to God. The firstborn children and the firstborn of the unclean animals were "redeemed" (paid for) with money by the offerer, and the firstborn of the cows, sheep, and goats were offered in sacrifice to God (Nm 18:14-17).

Firstfruits of any kind were reserved for those whom God designated, namely, the priests. At least three times "the first of the firstfruits" is mentioned in the OT. This may be a reference to the first ripened of the firstfruits, or it may refer to the choicest of them. These offerings were especially designated for the priests and could be eaten by any of them who was ritually clean (Nm 18:12-13). For other references to the firstfruits, see Exodus 23:15-19; 34:22, 26; Leviticus 2:14; 23:10-17; Numbers 15:20-21; 28:26-31; and Deuteronomy 26:1-11.

The firstfruits were presented to God by bringing the offering to the priest at the tabernacle and, in later times, at the temple (Dt 26:2). The priest took the offering, and on the first day of the week, with arms outstretched, waved it before the Lord. On the same day, the person presenting the firstfruits offered a male lamb as a burnt offering to the Lord, a grain offering of fine flour mixed with olive oil, and a drink offering of wine. Fifty days later another grain offering was to be made. Each family was to give two loaves of bread to the Lord as a special gift. These were also given with appropriate animal, grain, and drink offerings (Lv 23:9-22).

In the NT the apostle Paul referred to Jesus Christ's resurrection as the firstfruits of the resurrection of believers that will occur at Jesus' return (1 Cor 15:20, 23). The Holy Spirit, who indwells all believers (Rom 8:9), is also said to be the firstfruits of the full redemption that is yet to come. "Firstfruits" is sometimes used of the first believers in a geographical area (Rom 16:5; 1 Cor 16:15). They were a kind of promise of a spiritual harvest to follow in that particular locality.

Christian believers are said to be firstfruits, referring to their being a unique and sacred possession of God out of all he has created (Jas 1:18). Similarly, in the book of Revelation the 144,000 are said to have been redeemed from humanity as firstfruits belonging to God and to the Lamb, Jesus Christ (Rv 14:4).

See also Feasts and Festivals of Israel; Offerings and Sacrifices.

FIRST JEWISH REVOLT* Uprising in AD 66–70, which occurred as the result of a series of ineffective Roman governors in Judea. After the last Jewish king, Agrippa I (the Herod of Acts 12), died in AD 44, the next 20 years were filled with persecution and humiliation for the Jews in Palestine. The unrest needed only a spark to flame into open revolt; the spark was provided by Florus, the Roman governor appointed in AD 64. His demand for money from the temple treasury, and the slaughter and pillage by Roman soldiers, provoked the Jews into an uprising in the year 66.

Rebellion quickly spread throughout Palestine, accompanied by a general struggle between Jews and pagans in several eastern Mediterranean cities. The revolt in Palestine was led by the Zealots, a Jewish group that had long wanted the Romans to leave Palestine. After an initial Jewish victory at the pass of Beth-horon, the emperor Nero dispatched his most able general, Vespasian, to direct the operation of punishing the rebels. By the autumn of AD 67, all of Galilee and other northern lands were back in Roman hands. In 67 and 68 further operations in Samaria and Judea left only four strongholds in Jewish control. At this point the Roman campaign slackened. Nero committed suicide in AD 68, and after three short-lived emperors, General Vespasian gained control of the empire in AD 69. His son Titus took command of the forces in Palestine and laid siege to Jerusalem in AD 70.

The Jews in the capital might have been better prepared had they taken advantage of the turmoil in Rome to consolidate their own position and resolve disputes among warring Jewish factions. As it was, the arrival of Titus with 80,000 soldiers forced them to unify for a last defense of the city.

The siege of the city lasted for five months. Jerusalem held out heroically against the advancing Romans, forcing a step-by-step conquest of the city. A tragic moment in Jewish history came early in August of AD 70 when for the first time in centuries the morning and evening sacrifices were not offered at the temple. About 29 August, under circumstances still not clear, the sanctuary was put to the torch and the temple destroyed, thereby fulfilling Jesus' prophecy (Mt 24:1-2; Mk 13:1-2; Lk 19:43-44; 21:5-7). For another month some resistance continued, but by the end of September, the conflict was over in the desolated city. In all, perhaps one million Jews were killed and 900,000 taken captive during the course of the revolt.

See also Israel, History of; Jerusalem; Judaism.

FIR TREE Translation of several Hebrew words in the OT that possibly designate a conifer. Positive identification is not possible. *See* Plants.

FISH *See* Animals.

FISHERMEN Those who caught fish for a living. Fishing was carried on by fishermen in the Holy Land from early times and is referred to in both the OT (Is 19:8; Jer 16:16; Ez 47:10) and the NT (Mt 4:18-19; Mk 1:16-17; Lk 5:2; Jn 21:7). Fishermen formed a distinct class in society. Jesus included several fishermen among his disciples (Mt 4:18-22; Mk 1:16-20; cf. Lk 5:2-11). Their work was strenuous (Lk 5:2-5) and not always rewarding (Lk 5:5; Jn 21:3). Jesus used the metaphor "fishers of men" of his disciples to denote how they would "catch" people for the kingdom (Mt 4:19; Mk 1:17; Lk 5:10).

A modern fishing boat in the Holy Lands

FISH GATE Gate probably located in the north wall of the city of Jerusalem. The Fish Gate was built in David's time and later formed part of Manasseh's fortifications (2 Chr 33:14). After the Babylonian exile, it was restored under Nehemiah (Neh 3:3; 12:39); it is mentioned along with the Mishneh or Second Quarter (Zep 1:10). The gate was probably so named either because fish were brought into the city from the north, or because it was located near the city's fish market.
See also Jerusalem.

FITCH* KJV translation of two Hebrew words. "Fitch" is actually an older form of the word "vetch," the name of many species of leguminous plants. The "fitch" of Isaiah 28:25-27 (NLT "dill") is the nutmeg flower, the seeds of which are used as a condiment. The "fitch" of Ezekiel 4:9 (NLT "spelt") is probably emmer, an inferior kind of wheat.
See also Plants (Nutmeg Flower; Spelt).

FLAG* KJV rendering of an uncertain marshland plant in Job 8:11. *See* Plants (Papyrus; Reed; Rush).

FLAX Cultivated plant providing one of the oldest textile fibers. The term may also refer to the fiber itself, thread spun from it, or the woven linen cloth. *See* Cloth and Cloth Manufacturing; Plants.

FLEA Small, wingless insect with strong legs for jumping. The flea is mentioned only in 1 Samuel 24:14 and 26:20, where David refers to himself as a flea. *See* Animals.

FLESH The body; the physical being of humans; the human person and human existence; the carnal nature of humans.

In the Old Testament Term commonly used to designate the material stuff of the body, whether of people (Gn 40:19) or of animals (Lv 6:27). However, "flesh" is used in the OT with a variety of meanings. Sometimes it is used as equivalent for the whole body (Prv 14:30), and the meaning is extended to designate the whole person ("my flesh also shall rest in hope," Ps 16:9, KJV). This idea leads to the union of two different persons, man

and wife as "one flesh" (Gn 2:24), and a man can say of his relatives, "I am your bone and your flesh" (Jgs 9:2). The idea of flesh as the whole person leads to the expression "all flesh," denoting the totality of humankind, sometimes including also the animal world.

Perhaps the most distinctive use of "flesh" in the OT is found in those passages where it designates human weakness and frailty over against God. "My spirit shall not abide in man for ever, for he is flesh" (Gn 6:3, RSV). In Psalm 78:39, God attributes sin to the fact that men are but flesh. In 2 Chronicles 32:8 the arm of flesh of the king of Assyria (i.e., his weakness) is contrasted with the all-powerful God. The one who puts trust in God need not fear what "flesh" can do (Ps 56:4), but the one who puts trust in human flesh instead of in God is under a curse (Jer 17:5). In Isaiah 31:3 flesh is contrasted with spirit, as weakness is with strength.

However, nowhere in the OT is flesh viewed as sinful. Flesh is conceived as being created by God of the dust of the earth (Gn 2:7), and as God's creation, it is good.

In the New Testament Paul ascribes many—often unique—definitions to the word "flesh" (Greek *sarx*).

Flesh as the Stuff of the Body "Flesh" is frequently used to describe the tissues that constitute the body. There are different kinds of flesh—"of men," "of animals," "of birds," "of fish" (1 Cor 15:39). Pain and suffering may be experienced in the flesh (2 Cor 12:7). Circumcision is done in the flesh (Rom 2:28). While "flesh" in such references is not sinful, it is corruptible and cannot inherit the kingdom of God (1 Cor 15:50). Jesus' body was also a body of flesh (Col 1:22).

Flesh as the Body Itself By a natural transition, the part is used for the whole, and in many places "flesh" is synonymous with the body as a whole rather than designating the fleshy part of the body. Paul may thus speak either of being absent in the body (1 Cor 5:3) or in the flesh (Col 2:5). Paul can say that the life of Jesus may be manifested in our body or in our mortal flesh (2 Cor 4:10-11). "He who joins himself to a prostitute becomes one body with her. For, as it is written, 'The two shall become one flesh' " (1 Cor 6:16, RSV).

Flesh as Person with Reference to Origin Following OT usage, "flesh" was used by Paul to refer not merely to the stuff of the body or to the body itself, but concretely to the person as constituted by flesh. In this usage the word may refer to the person's human relationship, the physical origin and the natural ties that bind one to other humans. Paul speaks of his kinsmen "according to the flesh," his fellow Jews (Rom 9:3, KJV), and even uses "my flesh" (11:14, KJV) as a synonym for these kinsmen. The "children of the flesh" (9:8) are those born by natural generation in contrast to those born as a result of divine intervention. Christ was descended from David according to the flesh (1:3). The phrase does not designate the source merely of his bodily life but of his entire human existence, including both his body and his human spirit.

Flesh as Human Existence Another use of "flesh" simply designates human existence. As long as a person lives in the body, that one is "in the flesh." Thus, Paul can speak of the life that he lives "in the flesh" as lived by faith in the Son of God (Gal 2:20, RSV). Referring to Jesus' earthly ministry, Paul says that he abolished "in the flesh" the enmity between Jew and Gentile (Eph 2:15). Peter has the same meaning when he speaks of Jesus having been put to death "in the flesh" (1 Pt 3:18). So also John: "Jesus Christ is come in the flesh" (1 Jn 4:2). This usage is reflected most notably in the Johannine saying "The Word became flesh and dwelt among us" (Jn 1:14).

Flesh as Human Existence in Terms of Outward Presentation "Flesh" also extends beyond humans in their bodily life to include other factors crucial to human existence. Thus, "confidence in the flesh" (Phil 3:3, RSV) does not mean confidence in the body but confidence in the whole complex of the outward realm of human existence. It includes Paul's Jewish ancestry, his strict religious training, his zeal, and his prominence in Jewish religious circles. The phrase to "glory after the flesh" (2 Cor 11:18, KJV) is rendered "boast about their human achievements" in the NLT. A good showing "in the flesh" is practically synonymous with worldly prominence (Gal 6:11-14). The Judaizers insisted upon circumcision to promote a sense of prideful attainment in the religious life so that they might have a ground of glorying. But these external distinctions and grounds for glorying no longer appealed to Paul, because the world had been crucified to him and he to the world.

"Flesh" is also used of outward relationships, as when describing the social ties existing between slave and master (Eph 6:5; Col 3:22; Phlm 1:16). "In the flesh" also describes the realm of marital relationships, which entails certain troublesome problems (1 Cor 7:28).

This usage illuminates an otherwise difficult saying, "Henceforth know we no man after the flesh; yea, though we have known Christ after the flesh, yet now henceforth know we him no more" (2 Cor 5:16, KJV). The RSV correctly renders the phrase "from a human point of view." The verse does not mean that Paul had heard and seen Jesus in Jerusalem at some previous time and had gained some acquaintance with Christ "after the flesh." "After the flesh" modifies the verb "to know," not the noun "Christ." Before his conversion, Paul knew all people "after the flesh"; that is, he judged them by worldly, human standards. To know Christ "after the flesh" means to look at him through merely human eyes. As a Jew, Paul had felt that Jesus was a deluded messianic pretender. According to the Jewish understanding, the Messiah was to reign over the earth as a Davidic king, save his people Israel, and punish the hated Gentiles. But Paul surrendered this false human view and came to know Christ as he really is—the incarnate Son of God, the Savior of all who believe. As a Christian, Paul no longer judged others according to the flesh.

Flesh as Fallen Humanity When Paul says that "flesh and blood cannot inherit the kingdom of God" (1 Cor 15:50, RSV), he does not mean that humans cannot inherit the kingdom of God but rather that human fallenness cannot; as the next clause shows, "neither does corruption inherit incorruption." The weak, fallen, corruptible body cannot inherit the kingdom of God; there must be a change; the "corruptible must put on incorruption, and this mortal must put on immortality" (1 Cor 15:53, KJV). This is not the salvation of the soul or spirit but the exchange of one kind of body for another that is suited to the final glorious kingdom of God.

When Peter confessed the messiahship of Jesus, Jesus replied, "Flesh and blood has not revealed this to you, but my Father who is in heaven" (Mt 16:17, RSV). The meaning of this verse is obvious. This knowledge of Jesus' messiahship was not a human deduction; it could be achieved only by divine revelation.

Flesh as Sinful Humanity There remains a group of ethical references that are distinctly Pauline. The most important feature of this usage is that man is seen not only as fallen and weak before God, but as fallen and sinful. Flesh is contrasted with human spirit regenerated by the divine Spirit, and without the aid of the Spirit, one cannot please God. The most vivid passage is the first part of Romans 8, where Paul sharply contrasts those who are "in the flesh" with those who are "in the Spirit." To be "in the Spirit" in this sense does not mean to be in a state of ecstasy but to be living one's life in that spiritual realm that is controlled by the Spirit of God. Those who are "in the flesh," that is, unregenerate, cannot please God. There are two contrasting and mutually exclusive realms: "in the flesh" and "in the Spirit." To be "in the Spirit" means to be indwelt by God's Holy Spirit, that is, to be a regenerate person.

In Romans 7–8 Paul makes it clear that the unregenerate person cannot please God by loving and serving him as God requires. Thus, the Law was unable to make mankind truly righteous, because the flesh is weak (8:2). To live after the flesh is death; to live after the Spirit is life (8:6). Elsewhere Paul says, "For I know that in me (that is, in my flesh,) dwelleth no good thing" (7:18, KJV). Flesh here cannot be the physical flesh, for the body of flesh is the temple of the Spirit (1 Cor 6:19) and a member of Christ (6:15) and is to be the means of glorifying God (6:20). Paul, therefore, means that in his unregenerate nature there dwells none of the goodness that God demands.

While Paul makes a sharp and absolute contrast between being "in the flesh" (unregenerate) and "in the Spirit" (regenerate), when one becomes regenerate and comes to be "in the Spirit," that person is no longer in the flesh, but the flesh is still in him. In fact, there remains in the believer a struggle between the flesh and the Spirit. Writing to people who are "in the Spirit," Paul says, "For the flesh lusteth [strives] against the Spirit, and the Spirit against the flesh: and these are contrary the one to the other: so that ye cannot do the things that ye would" (Gal 5:17, KJV). Because the Christian life is the battleground of these two opposing principles, it is impossible to be the perfect person that one would wish to be.

The same situation is reflected in 1 Corinthians 2:14–3:3 where Paul describes three classes of people: the "natural" (2:14, KJV); the "carnal," that is, fleshly man (3:1, 3, KJV); and the "spiritual man" (3:1, KJV). The "natural man" is unregenerate. Those who are "in the flesh" (Rom 8:9) have devoted the whole of their life to the human level and hence are unable to know the things of God. "Spiritual man" refers to those whose life is ruled by the Spirit of God, so that the fruits of the Spirit (Gal 5:22-23) are evident in their life. Between these two there is a third class—those who are "fleshly" yet who are babes in Christ. Therefore, they must be "in the Spirit," yet they do not walk "according to the Spirit." Because they are "babes in Christ," the Spirit of God dwells in them, yet the Holy Spirit is not allowed to have full control over them, and they are still walking "like men" (1 Cor 3:3), manifesting the works of the flesh in jealousy and strife.

Works of the Flesh In Galatians 5:19-23 Paul contrasts the life in the flesh and the life in the Spirit: "Now the works of the flesh are manifest, which are these: adultery, fornication, uncleanness, lasciviousness, idolatry, witchcraft, hatred, variance, emulations, wrath, strife, seditions, heresies, envyings, murders, drunkenness, revellings, and such like" (Gal 5:19-21, KJV). The important thing to note about this list is that while some of these are sins of bodily and sexual appetite, others are religious sins—idolatry, witchcraft—and several are sins "of the spirit," that is, of the disposition—hatred, variance, emulations, wrath, strife. The words "seditions" and "heresies" refer not to theological heresies but to a factious, divisive spirit. This proves conclusively that for

Paul the "flesh" is not synonymous with the body but includes the whole person, with all the inner attitudes and disposition.

Victory over the Flesh While a struggle remains in the Christian between the Spirit and the flesh, Paul knows of a way of victory for the Spirit. The flesh of the body comes within the sphere of sanctification (1 Thes 5:23), but the flesh as the unregenerate human nature can only be put to death.

This is called the tension between the objective and the subjective. Because certain things have happened in Christ (objective), certain inevitable results should accrue (subjective). In Paul's view, the flesh has already been put to death in the death of Christ. Those who belong to Christ have already crucified the flesh with its passions and desires (Gal 5:24). Paul elsewhere says, "I have been crucified with Christ" (2:20) and "our old self was crucified with him" (Rom 6:6). Such references make it clear that "flesh" and the "self" are in some ways to be identified. This identity is further supported in the teaching about crucifixion, for Paul means the same thing by the crucifixion of the flesh that he means when he says, "How shall we, that are dead to sin, live any longer therein? We were baptized into his death. We are buried with him by baptism into death" (vv 1-4). It is I myself who have died with Christ.

This crucifixion and death of the flesh does not, however, work automatically. It is an event that must be appropriated by faith. This involves two aspects. First, believers are to recognize that the flesh has been crucified with Christ. "Reckon ye also yourselves to be dead indeed unto sin, but alive unto God through Jesus Christ our Lord" (Rom 6:11, KJV). One cannot consider the self dead with Christ to sin unless that person has actually died and been crucified with Christ, but because this has already happened at the moment of saving faith, it can be put into daily practice. Those who have died with Christ are to "mortify [put to death] the deeds of the body" (8:13, KJV). "Body" is here used as a vehicle for the works of the "flesh"—the sensual life of the unregenerate nature. Those who have been brought from death into life are to yield their members to God as instruments of righteousness (6:13). One who has died with Christ is to "mortify" (KJV), that is, put to death what is earthly—fornication, uncleanness, covetousness (Col 3:5). Having already put off the old nature and put on the new, the believer is to put on compassion, kindness, lowliness and the like.

Victory over the flesh is sometimes described as walking in the Spirit. "Walk by the Spirit, and do not gratify the desires of the flesh" (Gal 5:16, RSV; cf. Rom 8:4). Walking in the Spirit means to live each moment under the control of the Holy Spirit.

See also Body; Sin.

FLINT Dark, fine-grained, hard silica (rock) used for blades of tools. Flint when struck against other hard surfaces produces sparks and so was used for lighting fires. *See* Minerals and Metals.

FLOGGING Beating a person with a whip or other instrument, sometimes used as a legislated punishment. *See* Criminal Law and Punishment.

FLOOD, The Rising and overflowing of water to cover the land, specifically the flood of Noah.

Biblical Account The narrative of Noah's flood, found in Genesis 6–9, is referred to frequently elsewhere in the Bible, in each case being mentioned as a historical event

(Gn 10:1, 32; 11:10; Mt 24:38-39; Lk 17:27; 2 Pt 2:5). According to the biblical account, God brought about the Flood because of human society's increasing deterioration, which finally reached a point where "the wickedness of man was great in the earth" (Gn 6:5, RSV). God determined to destroy the race and to begin again with a new people who would obey him (cf. Gn 1:26-28). Of all the people on earth, only Noah, his sons, and their wives remained faithful to the Lord. They became God's means of repopulating the earth following its watery destruction. After a period of 120 years' preparation, during which Noah built a great ship and preached God's coming judgment (Gn 6:3; cf. Heb 11:7; 1 Pt 3:20; 2 Pt 2:5), the Flood came in the form of heavy rain, giving rise to subterranean waters (Gn 7:11). Only the selected pairs of land animals brought aboard the vessel were saved from the onslaught. For more than a year the waters prevailed, until finally the waters receded and the earth was dry and habitable again (Gn 7:6-12, 24; 8:3-6, 10-14). When Noah and his family left the ark, they offered sacrifices to God in thanksgiving. God then promised that he would never again destroy the earth by a flood.

Extent of the Flood Scholars who view the flood account as history are divided as to its geographical extent. An objective reading of the story would seem to indicate that the whole earth was flooded, even to the height of the highest mountains (Gn 7:17-20; 8:4). Some have argued that waters high enough to cover "all the high mountains under the whole heaven" (7:19, RSV) would extend over the entire earth. Some advocates of a local flood respond that the narrative uses the language of appearance (that is, to Noah it *appeared* that all the earth was flooded). Thus a universal flood was unnecessary, for God wished to destroy only the human race, which at that time may have lived only in Mesopotamia. Others point out translation difficulties in the use of the word "earth." In Genesis 1:1, it is part of an ancient idiomatic expression denoting totality ("heaven and earth" means "cosmos"). Sometimes "earth" describes a person's country (Gn 47:13), the soil itself (23:15), and so on. Thus, one should not necessarily assume that the use of the word in the Genesis flood story implies the complete inundation of the world.

Some advocates of a universal flood use the presence of marine fossils on the tops of the world's highest mountains in support of their arguments. But others disagree, saying that since all the mountains originally emerged from the seas, they would be expected to preserve traces of their marine ancestry on their summits. One's view on the matter must be determined in the final analysis on theological considerations as well as interpretive factors. *See* "Scientific Evidence for the Flood?" on page 490.

See also Gilgamesh Epic; Noah #1.

FLOOD MYTHS* *See* Gilgamesh Epic.

FLOUR Fine, powdery substance produced by grinding the inner kernels of wheat. Flour was used in baking and also for cereal offerings (Lv 2). *See* Food and Food Preparation.

FLOWER *See* Plants.

FLUTE Translation of several Hebrew words designating various kinds of wind instruments played by blowing across or through a hole. *See* Musical Instruments (Halil).

SCIENTIFIC EVIDENCE FOR THE FLOOD?

With the beginning of modern archaeology in Mesopotamia, it became popular to associate evidence of flood destruction in sites such as Kish, Ur, and Shuruppak with the biblical Flood. Those places, however, were destroyed by different floods at different times. Their floods were also much too limited in scope to suit any interpretation of the Genesis account. More recently a "catastrophism" movement has developed within conservative circles, interpreting the world's great geologic upheavals as chaotic remnants of the destruction caused by Noah's Flood. That view suggests, among other things, that such geological formations may have taken shape in a short time (during the Flood) and in a relatively recent era (the time of Noah). Though that theory satisfies many, its opponents point out that some means of dating show the formations to be much earlier than the time of Noah.

Geologists exploring the Mt Ararat region have discovered on the mountain what is called "pillow lava," volcanic rock formed under water. Such lava structures have been located up to the mountain's ice cap at 13,500 feet (4,114.6 meters), so water evidently reached that height at one period. That phenomenon has been taken by some as a confirmation of worldwide scope for the Genesis Flood, but it does not prove that the lava was formed on Mt Ararat in the time of Noah. All it really indicates is that the structures originated under water, just as all land masses did.

The presence of "conglomerates" on Mt Ararat is cited as yet another proof of a universal deluge. Such rocks, varying in size from pebbles to boulders, resulted from a process of fusion in which eruptions of lava interacted with a violent disturbance of water. But again, the presence of such material at the 13,000-foot (3,962.2 meter) level merely indicates that Mt Ararat was born in precisely the same manner as modern islands and that the highest levels involved an eruption of volcanic rock in the ocean. Nor can such geological structures be used to imply that Mt Ararat was in the process of growth even while the Flood occurred. The Genesis account says nothing about the mountain erupting during Noah's deluge. In any event, the material deposit would have been silt, not lava.

Interest in the nature of the Genesis Flood has been stimulated periodically since 1856, for some 200 persons have claimed to have seen Noah's ark on Mt Ararat in 23 separate sightings. At least one report was a hoax, but many of them agree on the general nature of the object that has been sighted. Despite such apparent evidence, all concerned must admit that no conclusive proof exists that Noah's ark is located on Mt Ararat. From a crevasse near the top of the mountain, Fernand Navarra in 1955 recovered a five-foot (1.5 meter) piece of wood, which was hand-tooled and originated at some distance from the mountain. Carbon-14 dating techniques, however, produced widely differing dates for the artifact. It has so far been impossible to locate what many have thought to be remains of the ark, despite the use of sophisticated photographic techniques.

The nature of the Genesis Flood will continue to be a matter of debate among interested parties, but it seems unlikely that the issue will be resolved unless some new archaeological or compelling scientific evidence is forthcoming. That there was a flood of enormous proportions is hardly to be doubted in the light of the Genesis account and other ancient traditions. However, the precise nature and extent of the biblical deluge must remain a matter of interpretation and speculation until incontrovertible evidence settles the issue.

FLY Two-winged insect. In Scripture, several species are in view, including the common housefly (Eccl 10:1) and the horsefly (Is 7:18). *See* Animals.

FOLLOWERS OF THE WAY Designation for Christians in the book of Acts (Acts 9:2; 19:9, 23; 22:4; 24:22). In its early years, Christianity was called "the Way." *See* Way, The.

FOOD AND FOOD PREPARATION Substances required by the body to sustain life, and the methods of making them edible. Food consumed in Bible times included bread, milk products, fruit, meat, and fish. Food was also offered sacrificially or given as gifts. The availability of food was a perpetual concern because of the recurrent scarcity: droughts were frequent (2 Kgs 4:38; Jer 14:1, 4-6; Hg 1:11), hailstorms wrought devastation among crops (Hg 2:17), farming was frequently interrupted by warfare with neighboring nations (2 Kgs 6:25), and intermittent plagues of locusts ravaged large areas.

Food was more plentiful in Palestine (described as a "land flowing with milk and honey") than in many other parts of the Near East. Shallow cultivation of the soil, however, made crops highly reliant on regular rainfall. Egyptian crops were far less susceptible to weather variations, because the Nile provided a dependable source of water.

Food shortages were considered warnings or punishment from God (Lam 4:9, 11; Am 4:6-9) to teach the Hebrews that life is more than food and that faith must continue despite scarcity, famine, or even death (Dt 8:3; Hb 3:17-18).

The staples of nomadic Hebrews were milk, curds, and cheese. As the people became more stationary, they grew grains and vegetables and planted orchards and vineyards. Grain would sometimes be grown for a season, and then after the harvest, the tribes would move their flocks to other pastures and find other arable land. Religious sacrifices and festivals were times not only of solemnity but also of rejoicing and great feasting. Victories were also celebrated with banquets and feasting on the food obtained from the camp of the vanquished enemy.

PREVIEW
- Dairy Products
- Grain Crops
- Animal Products
- Insects and Their Food Products
- Vegetables and Seasoning
- Fruits, Nuts, and Wine

Dairy Products Milk and its by-products formed a vital part of the Hebrew diet (see Jgs 4:19). Goat's milk was most frequently used, although milk from camels, cows, and sheep was also available (Gn 32:15; Dt 32:14; Prv 27:27).

Since fresh milk could not be preserved in Palestine's hot climate, it was processed into buttermilk, curds, and cheese. Milk was poured into goatskins, where it soured and thickened because of the nonsterile condition of the previously used skins and the movement as it was transported. That movement of the pouch (often made from a cow's stomach, containing the enzyme rennin used in cheese making) produced curds. Curds are first mentioned in the Bible as part of the meal that Abraham provided for his extraordinary guests (Gn 18:8).

The Hebrew word for curds *(chena)* is also translated "butter" (Jb 10:10). This butter would be similar in consistency to yogurt from which the water has been squeezed out. When pressed and rolled into small balls, it kept indefinitely, despite the climate. Thus, compressed curds were particularly valuable for journeys in arid regions where food was scarce.

Grain Crops The most frequently mentioned food in the Bible is bread. The term refers in a general sense to all foods but more particularly to food prepared from grain. In biblical times bread was prepared from several grains. Wheat, barley, and spelt were grown in Egypt (Ex 9:31-32).

An Egyptian physician named Sinuhe, living in the mid-20th century BC, recorded that bread was baked daily in Palestine and Syria, and it is probable that it was served with every meal. This bread was probably a wafer or flat cake made from barley or emmer (an inferior form of wheat), since these were the two grain crops that Sinuhe mentioned seeing. Wheat was the most expensive grain. Fine wheat flour was a luxury only the rich could afford (Gn 18:6; Ez 16:13, 19). In later periods wheat became a valuable export crop that was shipped from Tyre to other ports in the Mediterranean.

Because barley could grow in less productive soil and was more tolerant of drought conditions, it became a popular grain crop in the ancient Near East. Barley could also be harvested several weeks earlier than wheat. Barley bread (Jgs 7:13; 2 Kgs 4:42) and barley cakes (Ez 4:12) were eaten by the average laborer. Jesus miraculously multiplied a young boy's five barley loaves and two fishes and fed five thousand (Jn 6:9-13).

Millet, a cereal with a small grain head growing on a stalk less than two feet (.6 meter) high, and spelt, a type of wheat, were also used in times of need as a border around the edges of fields.

The most primitive way of processing grain was to rub the ears between the hands to separate the kernels, as Jesus and his disciples did (Lk 6:1). To perform this act on the Sabbath (the day of rest) was considered the equivalent of reaping and was therefore forbidden.

Parching (roasting the grain lightly in a pan) was another simple method of preparation (Jos 5:11; 1 Sm 17:17). It formed a quick and easy meal for laborers or kings (Ru 2:14; 1 Sm 25:18; 2 Sm 17:28). Parched corn was ideal for taking on journeys.

Bread making was a strenuous task. Mortars, pestles, and simple mills with upper and lower stones were used for grinding flour in ancient Egypt around 2900 BC. These primitive mills were normally placed on the ground, and one was compelled to kneel in order to do the backbreaking work. The resulting meal was coarse and filled with small pieces of husk.

When the flour had been prepared, water was added and the mixture was kneaded in a special trough. The dough could then be made immediately into cakes, pancakes, or unleavened bread (Gn 19:3). These flat cakes or wafers were often baked on previously heated stones, on the inner walls of small conical ovens, or in larger communal ovens. Leaven was added to make a lighter dough. The leaven was normally a piece of dough left over from an earlier mixing and allowed to ferment before being used. The flour meal was also mixed with a porridge made of lentil beans in order to stretch the food supply.

Animal Products The introduction of meat as part of the diet seems to have coincided with the time when Noah and his family left the ark (Gn 9:3). After this time, however, the animals normally eaten for food were so valuable that only the wealthy could afford to slaughter them. So in biblical times the peasant had a simple, somewhat monotonous diet, while the rich feasted on meat, delicacies, and imported commodities. As a result, meat was a luxury item that the poor would rarely enjoy except on such occasions as the Passover celebration or sacrifices in which the worshiper ate part of the offering (Ex 12:8). Although it was clearly uneconomic to slaughter an animal that produced such staples as milk, curds, and cheese, the rules of hospitality in the Near East dictated that an animal should be killed to entertain an honored guest (2 Sm 12:2-4).

Domestic sheep, goats, and oxen provided the main source of meat, although venison was popular with the upper classes. When the blind Isaac was deceived by his son Jacob, the father was offered the luxury of both kid's meat and wild game (Gn 27:3, 9, 19). The ox kept in a stall or the fatted calf were reserved for occasions of great festivity (Mt 22:4).

The use of meat for sacrifice was given definitive form in the provisions of Leviticus and Deuteronomy. The Law forbade anyone to slaughter an animal and its offspring on the same day (Lv 22:28). Another prohibition, perhaps directed at pagan Canaanite sacrificial rituals, would not allow a kid to be stewed or poached in its mother's milk (Dt 14:21). Mosaic law was emphatic in prohibiting the consumption of blood in any form. Animal blood was considered the source of the animal's life and was offered by priests as a sacrifice to God to atone for human sin (Lv 17:11). In the Mosaic law, pigs, camels, badgers, and rabbits were considered unclean and were therefore forbidden for food, principally on hygienic grounds (11:4-8).

In the ancient world, meat was usually boiled or stewed. Roasting an ox or a kid would usually occur only as part of a special feast or sacrificial ritual. Animals might also be roasted for members of the royal palace or for a king's special guests.

Despite the fact that hunting was enjoyed by all who were able to participate, wild game provided only a minor part of the diet. Among the game found in Palestine and mentioned in the Bible are gazelle, roebuck, wild goat, and deer (Dt 14:5; 1 Kgs 4:23). It is probable that pheasants were available, and there were certainly turtledoves, pigeons, quails, and partridges, although the precise quantities of food that these birds provided is not certain (Gn 15:9; Ex 16:13). Goose was the most popular dish in Egypt, and marsh ducks were also highly esteemed as game. After the Persian period, chickens were eaten (2 Esd 1:30), and eggs and omelettes were popular in Rome in early Christian times. The eggs mentioned in Deuteronomy are probably wild birds' eggs (Dt 22:6-7; cf. Is 10:14).

Thirty varieties of fish were available in the Jordan, and an extensive fishing industry existed on the shores of the Sea of Galilee at the time of Christ. Supplies of fish were readily available from the Mediterranean coast during the Roman period, but at an earlier time the fish supply depended to a large extent upon whichever nation had control of the coastline. In the postexilic period the people of Tyre supplied the city of Jerusalem with fish, which were sold near the Fish Gate (Neh 3:3). In the regulations concerning the types of fish suitable for food, only those that had fins and scales were acceptable (Lv 11:9-12).

In NT times many of the distinctions concerning food were eliminated. In the Gospel of Mark, Jesus, challenging the Pharisees' hypocrisy, upset the Jewish food laws by saying that evil thoughts, not certain foods, make a person unclean (Mk 7:19). As Christianity spread into gentile areas, there was, however, a continuing concern about eating meat that had been offered to idols. The question came to a head in Corinth. The apostle Paul maintained that though the meat was acceptable, one should take care not to cause spiritual damage to another Christian with a more sensitive conscience.

Insects and Their Food Products Wild honey was found in Palestine, but there is no evidence of bee-keeping. Egyptians, however, did practice beekeeping at that time.

The honeycomb is mentioned specifically in 1 Samuel 14:27 and Song of Solomon 5:1; liquid honey is referred to in 1 Kings 14:3. Honey was to be found in crevices of rocks and on trees (Dt 32:13). It was the primary sweetener in cooking. Although it could not be used in a sacrifice to the Lord (Lv 2:11), honey was prized as a delicacy. In the 15th century BC, when Thutmose III was campaigning in Syria and Palestine, he brought back vast quantities of honey as tribute from his newly conquered lands.

Locusts were probably first eaten in desperation after they had devastated crops. They are one of the few insects mentioned as a permissible source of food (Lv 11:22). Locusts were fried in flour or honey, or were preserved by being dried. Locusts and wild honey formed John the Baptist's basic diet in the wilderness (Mt 3:4; Mk 1:6). Although locusts contain little protein, they are rich in fat and have some mineral content.

Vegetables and Seasoning The Hebrew people wandering in the Sinai wilderness bemoaned the loss of the flavorful vegetables they had become accustomed to during their Egyptian captivity. In particular, they expressed a longing for cucumbers, melons (possibly watermelons), leeks, onions, and garlic (Nm 11:5). Many of these vegetables were later grown in Palestine (particularly in the Gaza). When cucumbers were first cultivated, they were regarded as luxury items and had to be protected by guards who lived in shacks overlooking the gardens (Is 1:8). Beans, lentils, and parched grain were among the items brought to David and his soldiers at Mahanaim (2 Sm 17:28). Lentils were known in Egypt from at least the 13th century BC and were used extensively both then and in later times by the Israelites. Lentil soup is mentioned in Genesis 25:34.

In times of hunger the husks of the carob tree, normally fed to cattle, could be used for food. These would have been most acceptable to the prodigal son (Lk 15:16). There were many kinds of green herbs that could provide a meal for the poor in time of need (Prv 15:17). In cases of extreme hunger, some kinds of mallow and juniper roots could also be used as food. In Elisha's time a group of prophets at Gilgal prepared a stew of wild vegetables, to which they mistakenly added poisonous wild gourds. Elisha rectified the situation by adding meal to the pot (2 Kgs 4:38-41). While there is no actual record of the kinds of bitter herbs used as part of the Passover offering (Ex 12:8; Nm 9:11), mint and cummin were most probably included. Dill, cummin, rue, and mint were common garden herbs (Mt 23:23; Lk 11:42).

Seasonings were welcome additives to the rather bland character of typical Israelite fare. Salt came mainly from the Dead Sea area and was essential as a seasoning and preserving agent. Salt was so important in the diet that it became part of the vocabulary of moral obligation. The sharing of salt with a person at a meal sealed a covenant or pact (Nm 18:19). In the Levitical sacrificial ritual, salt was part of meat and cereal offerings, since it signified the sealing of God's covenant with Israel (Lv 2:13; Ez 43:24).

The mustard tree, which was probably grown for its oil content, grew from a minute seed to the height of 15 feet (4.5 meters) (Mt 13:31-32). Anise, coriander, and cinnamon were also available (Ex 16:31; Nm 11:7). Perhaps the most popular and widely used spice, apart from salt, was garlic. Vinegar was also probably used as a flavoring agent and a preservative. From the number of seeds and plants found in Egyptian tombs from the 18th dynasty, it is obvious that the use of seasoning was widespread in antiquity.

Fruits, Nuts, and Wine Olive trees grew abundantly in Palestine and were an excellent source of food and oil. Even in poor soil, one tree could sufficiently supply a family for a whole year. Some green olives were pickled in brine and eaten with bread, but the olive was most important as a source of oil. Olive oil was used in baking bread and cakes and in frying foods. The best quality olive oil was used in the temple sacrifices.

Oil was extracted from olives by a simple process: for the finest quality oil, olives were picked before fully ripe and then crushed by hand with a stone mortar and pestle. Usually, however, pickers beat the olives from trees with long poles and collected them in baskets. The oil was then trodden out, probably in the same vat used for grapes (Mi 6:15), which were harvested approximately four weeks later.

An oil mill was developed subsequently, and the heavy upper grinding stone was turned by two people. As the oil dripped through, it was collected in another stone vat and was allowed to settle and purify. When refined, the oil was stored in skins or jars.

Fig trees grew in all areas of Palestine. They required little attention and provided two or three crops per year. The most abundant of these was the second, which ripened in late summer. The first figs of the season were considered a great delicacy (Is 28:4; Mi 7:1). The prophet Hosea suggested that the Israelites were like the firstfruits of the fig tree (Hos 9:10). Another prophet, Jeremiah, spoke of those who had gone into exile as being like the first figs, while those who were left behind were the bad figs, fit only for destruction (Jer 24:1-10).

Figs were usually eaten fresh from the trees, but some were pressed into cakes to use when traveling (1 Sm 25:18; 30:12; 1 Chr 12:40). Figs were also valuable for medicinal purposes, since effective poultices could be made from them (2 Kgs 20:7; Is 38:21). Sycamore trees produced small, figlike fruit eaten primarily by the poor. A short time before harvest, the fruit was slightly incised, making it swell and ripen more quickly. The prophet Amos notched sycamore fruit before he was called by God (Am 7:14).

Fruit from the date palm could also have been pressed into flat cakes for travelers, as figs were. The Bible, however, makes no specific reference to its fruit as food (see Jgs 4:5; Ps 92:12; Jl 1:12; Jn 12:13).

Another popular Near Eastern fruit was the red pomegranate. It was eaten whole, or the seeds were pressed to provide a refreshing drink. The pomegranate is mentioned in temple ritual as one of the fruits brought back from Canaan to Moses by his spies (Ex 28:33) and as an exotic drink (Sg 8:2). The "apple" mentioned in Scripture (Prv 25:11; Sg 2:5) was most likely a type of apricot or quince, not an apple as we know it today. Nuts were used for additional flavor in cooking. Almonds and pistachio nuts were among the gifts sent by Jacob to ransom his sons (Gn 43:11).

Grapes were popular and plentiful from the early Bronze Age. In addition to being eaten fresh from the vine, grapes were dried as raisins (Nm 6:3; 1 Sm 25:18) or pressed, their juice drunk either as new wine or fermented into an alcoholic drink. One of the duties of the cup-bearer in ancient royal courts was to provide grape juice or wine for the king, his family, and guests (Gn 40:9-13).

The juice of grapes also provided vinegar when wine deteriorated. Vinegar was used as a flavoring agent in cooking and as a preservative. When diluted with water, it supplied a refreshing drink for workers in the fields. A type of jelly was made in the Near East by boiling grapes until they assumed the consistency of molasses. This syrup could also be used as a sweetening agent in cooking.

Wine was the universal drink in antiquity. It could be diluted with water or mixed with spices or honey to make a mulled wine (Sg 8:2; Is 5:22). The Hebrew word for "banquet" or "feast" literally means "drinking," which reveals much of the character of such occasions. A certain amount of merriment was considered proper at a festival or banquet (Gn 43:34; Jgs 9:13; Lk 5:34).

Wine making was similar in many respects to the production of olive oil. Clusters of grapes were cut from the vine with a sickle, collected in baskets, and taken to the winepress, where they were trodden by men and women. The juice ran into a lower vat, where, under the hot sun, fermentation began almost immediately. The wine was left to settle so that any twigs or skins would form a sediment; after that the wine could be strained off. In about six weeks the wine was ready to drink or store in earthenware jars or wineskins.

See also Animals; Bread; Family Life and Relations; Leaven; Meals, Significance of; Plants; Unleavened Bread.

FOOTSTOOL
Low stool used to support one's feet. Part of King Solomon's great revenue of gold was used to fashion a footstool for his ivory throne (2 Chr 9:18). The word is frequently used metaphorically. Both the ark of the covenant and the temple are referred to as God's footstool because they were places where God rested (his glory resided there) and reigned (1 Chr 28:2; Pss 99:5; 132:7; Lam 2:1; cf. Is 60:13). The enemies of the Messiah were to become his footstool; that is, they would be fully subjected to him by the power of God (Ps 110:1). Many of the NT references to a footstool (lit. "something under the foot") parallel the OT expectation of the final conquest of Messiah's enemies (Mt 22:44; Mk 12:36; Lk 20:43; Acts 2:35; Heb 1:13; 10:13).

FORDS OF THE JORDAN
Shallow places where people and animals could wade through the Jordan River. Many OT personalities crossed over the Jordan at its two main fords: these people include Jacob (Gn 32:10), Gideon (Jgs 8:4), David (2 Sm 10:17; 17:22), Absalom (17:24), Abner and his men (2:29). Joshua led his followers across the Jordan on dry land during a flood, truly a God-given miracle (Jos 3:15-16). Jesus crossed the Jordan on several occasions on his trips between Galilee and Jerusalem.

The two main fords of the Jordan were at Jericho (Jos 2:7; Jgs 3:28; 2 Sm 19:15) and at Bethabara, where John baptized (Jn 1:28, KJV). In certain places and at certain times the Jordan was not fordable: after the melting of the snows in the Lebanon Mountains, and near the Dead Sea, where the Jordan is about 100 feet (30.5 meters) wide and from 5 to 10 feet (1.5 to 3 meters) deep (Jos 3:15).

See also Jordan River.

FOREIGNER
Noncitizen or alien, temporary guest, sojourner, or stranger.

The Hebrew word meaning "foreigner" is rendered correctly on all occasions in the RSV, but the KJV uses it in its truest sense on only two occasions (Dt 15:3; Ob 1:11). In most cases the KJV translates the word as "alien" (Dt 14:21; Jb 19:15; Ps 69:8; Lam 5:2) or "stranger" (Gn 15:13; Ex 2:22; Lv 25:35). Another Hebrew word means "dweller" (Lv 25:35; 1 Chr 29:15; Ps 39:12) or "settler." For the most part, however, it is rendered "foreigner."

A temporary guest or sojourner was usually someone who wanted to take up temporary residence or had moved from one tribe of people to another, and then attempted to obtain certain privileges or rights belonging to the natives. A whole tribe might be sojourners in Israel. This was the case with the Gibeonites (Jos 9) and the Beerothites (2 Sm 4:3; cf. 2 Chr 2:17). The Israelites themselves were sojourners in the land of Egypt (Gn 15:13; 23:4; 26:3; 47:4; Ex 2:22; 23:9) and in other lands (Ru 1:1).

Foreigners or sojourners had certain rights but also certain limitations while in Israel. They could offer sacrifices (Lv 17:8; 22:18) but could not enter the sanctuary unless circumcised (Ez 44:9). They were allowed to participate in the three great Jewish festivals (Dt 16:11, 14) but could not eat the Passover meal unless circumcised (Ex 12:43, 48). Foreigners were not obliged to follow the Israelite religion, but they shared in some of its benefits (Dt 14:29). They were not to work on the Sabbath or the Day of Atonement (Ex 20:10; 23:12; Lv 16:29; Dt 5:14) and could be stoned for reviling or blaspheming God's name (Lv 24:16; Nm 15:30). Foreigners were forbidden to eat blood (Lv 17:10-12) but could eat animals that had died a natural death (Dt 14:21). Israel's code of sexual morality also applied to the foreigner (Lv 18:26). There were prohibitions against Israelites intermarrying with foreigners, but it was nevertheless a common occurrence (Gn 34:14; Ex 34:12, 16; Dt 7:3-4; Jos 23:12).

Civil rights were provided for foreigners by the law of Moses (Ex 12:49; Lv 24:22), and they came under the same legal processes and penalties (Lv 20:2; 24:16, 22; Dt 1:16). They were to be treated politely (Ex 22:21; 23:9), loved as those under the love of God (Lv 19:34; Dt 10:18-19), and treated generously (Lv 19:10; 23:22; Dt 24:19-22). They could receive asylum in times of trouble (Nm 35:15; Jos 20:9). Foreign servants were to receive treatment equal to Hebrew servants (Dt 24:14). A foreigner could not take part in tribal deliberations or become a king (17:15). The prophet Ezekiel looked forward to the messianic age when the foreigner would share all the blessings of the land with God's own people (Ez 47:22-23).

In the NT, "foreigner" is often used metaphorically. On the one hand, the work of Christ allowed all foreigners (i.e., those alienated from Christ) to become members of God's household (Eph 2:11-19). On the other hand, Christians should consider themselves foreigners in this world (Heb 11:13; 1 Pt 2:11).

See also Barbarian; Neighbor.

FOREKNOWLEDGE*
Knowledge of things or events before they exist or happen.

In the NT the Greek equivalent of "foreknowledge" appears only seven times. It refers to the Christian's advance warning about false teachers (2 Pt 3:17); the Jews' previous knowledge of Paul's early life (Acts 26:4-5); God's previous knowledge of the death of Christ (Acts 2:23; 1 Pt 1:18-20); and knowledge of his people (Rom 11:2) and of the church (Rom 8:28-30; 1 Pt 1:1-2). The concept of foreknowledge does, however, appear throughout the Bible in other ways. First, the all-inclusiveness of the knowledge of God is clearly taught. God's understanding is unlimited (Ps 147:5). He knows every heart and thought (1 Chr 28:9). Psalm 139 provides an extended poetic description of God's knowledge of all human thoughts, words, and actions. This knowledge extends to the flight of a sparrow and the number of hairs on the head (Mt 10:29-30). From such limitless knowledge, it may be inferred that God also knows the future events of human history.

In addition, Scripture directly teaches that God is aware of events before they happen. This sets him apart from heathen idols, who lack the ability to foresee the future (Is 44:6-8; 45:21). It is God's foreknowledge that provides the basis for the predictions of the prophets. God announced to Adam and Eve that the seed of the woman would certainly defeat the serpent and his seed (Gn 3:15). Promises of future blessing were given to Abraham (12:3). God said to Moses, "I know that the king of Egypt will not let you go" (Ex 3:19, RSV). The coming glory of the Messiah was declared by the OT prophets (see, e.g., Is 9:1-7; Jer 23:5-6; Ez 34:20-31; Hos 3:4-5). In Daniel 7, God revealed the rise and fall of future world empires and the establishment of the kingdom of God (see also Dn 2:31-45). In many places the NT sees Christ's ministry and the establishment of the Christian church as fulfillment of predictions made beforehand by the OT prophets (Mt 1:22; 4:14; 8:17; Jn 12:38-41; Acts 2:17-21; 3:22-25; Gal 3:8; Heb 5:6; 1 Pt 1:10-12).

For many of the early Greek philosophers, fate rigidly controlled all future events, including not only the events of human history but also the fortunes of the gods. Occasionally, a future event might be known by the gods and revealed to people, and such foreseen events could in no way be altered. This view is, of course, far different from the biblical view of the personal Creator who knows the future and guides history according to his own purpose.

Nevertheless, the question of the relationship between God's foreknowledge and human freedom has occupied the attention of theologians and philosophers over the centuries. It is sometimes argued that if God knows what will happen in the future, then it must happen. Therefore, it makes no difference at all what choice a person makes, since it could not have been otherwise.

The theologians of the early church emphatically denied that foreknowledge implies any predetermination of events. Justin Martyr, for example, said, "What we say about future events being foretold, we do not say it as though they come about by fatal necessity." In other words, this means that just because God knows what is going to happen before it happens does not necessarily mean that he has *caused* it to happen.

Other theologians, fearing that foreknowledge destroys human freedom and responsibility, insist that God does not know future events either certainly or completely. Modern process theology, for example, conceives of God as growing and developing along with nature and man. This God, it is argued, can at most know only those events that have already taken place. Hence the future remains open and uncertain for God as well as for man. An older theologian, Adam Clarke, suggested that although God can know all future events, he chooses not to know some events beforehand.

Augustine denied foreknowledge for a different reason. He argued that God lives in eternity where all things are present. For God, then, there is no past or future. Hence he would not know things before they happened, since he would see all events from the vantage point of an eternal "now." Augustine, of course, did not deny God's knowledge of all things, even of things that are still in the future as far as we are concerned.

Because of the clear biblical teaching regarding God's foreknowledge, evangelical theologians have generally held that God has complete knowledge of all future events. There is a further distinction, however. The followers of Calvin insist that God knows all events precisely because he sovereignly determines what is to happen in human history right down to the tiniest detail. Here foreknowledge is closely tied to, if not identified with, foreordination. At the same time, most Calvinistic theologians assert that human beings are nonetheless responsible for their choices—not victims of a blind fate. It is also generally held that God is not the author of sin. Rather, sin is the result of the rebellion of angels and men against a holy and righteous God.

Evangelicals in the Arminian tradition, on the other hand, distinguish foreknowledge from the foreordination of events. While salvation of the world, and human history in broad outline, are predetermined by God, it is argued that individual response to God is not so predetermined. Hence, God can foreknow an event without directly decreeing that event to take place.

While evangelical Christians differ in their descriptions of the relationship between the eternal all-knowing God and the events of human history, it should be kept in mind that Scripture teaches both God's foreknowledge of all things and the responsibility of humans for their choices.

See also Elect, Election; Foreordination.

FOREORDINATION*

Activity of God by which he establishes events and outcomes before they occur. In common usage, "foreordination" and the term "predestination" are synonymous. "Predestination" and "election," however, specifically refer to the destiny of persons.

Foreordination was referred to by many early church fathers and was a major emphasis in the theology of Augustine of Hippo (354–430). Augustine greatly influenced the Reformers, particularly John Calvin. Reformed theologians begin the study of the doctrine of foreordination with the eternal decree of God, as indicated by creeds such as the Westminster Confession of Faith. The decree of God is one, but for purposes of discussion and explanation it is usually referred to as "the decrees of God." Martin Luther believed in foreordination but did not stress it as much as Calvin. Luther's theology is generally silent on foreordination, primarily discussing predestination, or election. Contemporary Lutheran thought stresses conditional, rather than absolute election, that is, election or predestination based on foreseen faith.

Foreordination underlies the whole plan of God: his decision to create the universe, to care for it (providence), and to determine its destiny "according to the counsel of his will" (Eph 1:11, RSV). The Westminster Shorter Catechism states the teaching in this way: God has decreed "his eternal purpose according to the counsel of his will, whereby, for his own glory, he hath foreordained whatsoever comes to pass." Foreordination, then, is at the foundation of all Christian teaching, for it concerns the history and destiny of the whole world, the universe, and all that it contains.

The apostle Paul spoke of God's plan for the fulfillment of all creation: "For the creation waits with eager longing for the revealing of the sons of God; for the creation was subjected to futility, not of its own will but by the will of him who subjected it in hope; because the crea-ation itself will be set free from its bondage to decay and obtain the glorious liberty of the children of God" (Rom 8:19-21, RSV). Scripture gives only a glimpse of the redemption of the whole creation. It speaks of new heavens and a new earth in which righteousness dwells (2 Pt 3:13). Those things that mar human existence and demonstrate human fallenness and sinfulness (i.e., depravity) will all pass away. God will make "all things new" (Rv 21:1-5), so the destiny of everything rests with God himself.

Foreordination creates problems for theology and commonsense thinking, particularly in relation to human freedom and responsibility and that aspect of foreordination concerned with salvation. How can people be held responsible for their actions and decisions if those actions have been predetermined? To remove that difficulty, some have denied God's foreordination as it relates to human freedom. In creating free beings, they argue, God must have limited his determination of things that "must" come to pass. Otherwise, free and responsible human activity has no meaning. Calvinism rejects such an argument, insisting that free activity is possible even though it is foreordained and foreknown.

Denial of the doctrine of foreordination implies that God does not control his creation. If that were true, the existence and happenings in the universe, including human activity, would be determined either by something above or beyond God, or by occurrences whose ultimate causes are unknown. God's providence and care revealed in the Bible and human experience make such a view untenable. Christian thought generally states that God foreordains and controls his creation and that humans are able to act freely and responsibly within that larger control. The apparent contradiction or paradox remains unresolved because there is a limit to human understanding.

Foreordination in Scripture There are many references to foreordination (including predestination, or election) and the related idea of foreknowledge in the Bible. Foreordination can be thought of as logically prior to foreknowledge, but there is no actual priority since both activities are eternal in God.

Speaking of judgment to come upon Babylon, God said, "This is the purpose that is purposed concerning the whole earth; and this is the hand that is stretched out over all the nations. For the LORD of hosts has purposed, and who will annul it? His hand is stretched out, and who will turn it back?" (Is 14:26-27, RSV). God also declared that he has determined the end from the beginning. "My counsel shall stand, and I will accomplish all my purpose" (Is 46:10, RSV). Paul stated that the purpose of God is carried out "according to the counsel of his will" (Eph 1:11, RSV; cf. Ps. 119:89-91; Dn 4:35).

With respect to human affairs, it is said that one's life span is determined (Jb 14:5), that God's concern extends to his creatures (Ps 104:14-30; Mt 10:29), and even the hairs on our heads are numbered (Mt 10:30). Furthermore, God's plan extends to peoples and nations, for "he made from one every nation of men to live on all the face of the earth, having determined allotted periods and the boundaries of their habitation" (Acts 17:26, RSV).

God knows and even uses people's evil acts for his own ends. For example, although Joseph's brothers sinned by selling him into slavery, Joseph later said, "As for you, you meant evil against me; but God meant it for good, to bring it about that many people should be kept alive, as they are today" (Gn 50:20, RSV). Judas Iscariot betrayed Jesus, but God used that sinful intent. Jesus said, "For the Son of man goes as it has been determined; but woe to that man by whom he is betrayed!" (Lk 22:22, RSV). On the day of Pentecost the apostle Peter said, "This Jesus, delivered up according to the definite plan and foreknowledge of God, you crucified and killed by the hands of lawless men" (Acts 2:23, RSV; cf. 4:27-28). Paul refers to God's determining authority over Pharaoh's acts (Rom 9:17). Revelation 17:17 says, "God has put it into their hearts to carry out his purpose" (RSV). God, then, foreordains the events of nature and history, and even evil acts are subject to his control and are made to fulfill his purposes.

Election of sinners to salvation through Christ is also included in God's foreordination (Rom 8:28-39; cf. Acts 13:48; Phil 2:12-13; 1 Pt 2:9). God's plan of salvation is grounded in his eternal love and good pleasure (Eph 1:3-14; Rom 5:6-11). The Christian is the recipient of God's grace in that the believer knows God and is known (i.e., loved) by God (Gal 4:9). Both election and believers' faith are part of the salvation process.

Foreordination and Providence The doctrine of foreordination is implied in the doctrine of providence or God's care. Providence is the working out of God's plan for the world. God's care and control of the whole creation point to his plan of redemption for man and woman made in his image. God sovereignly controls the events that take place in the world, but God is not responsible for sin. He created human beings who may say no to God as well as yes. That does not mean that God's plan can be thwarted; it goes on in spite of opposition. God's ultimate plan is being realized through all the events of human history, evil and good. Yet his sovereignty is not imposed arbitrarily. God is not a tyrant but rather is holy, loving, and righteous. His plan is carried out according to his nature, which is expressed in care and concern for the whole creation and in steadfast love for undeserving sinners.

"Natural law" refers to the rules God has laid down (foreordained) to control the universe. What about destructive forces of nature, such as earthquakes, tornadoes, and hurricanes? Why are such apparent evils necessary in a world made and controlled by a loving God? It is no answer to suggest that God is unable to act or control nature fully. If life's total meaning resided in the temporal, physical world, there might be reason for complaint. But considering the whole plan of God and his ultimate redemptive purpose, the answer takes on a different dimension. God's ultimate purpose transcends the present life and centers in the fullness of the redemptive kingdom yet to be revealed (Rv 11:15; 21:1-4). The doctrine of foreordination is a great mystery, but it should be a source of joy and comfort to believers whose loving Lord has brought them to a knowledge of his great plan.

See also Elect, Election; Foreknowledge.

FORERUNNER* Scout sent in advance of troops, or a herald who precedes a high official to announce his coming. The term is used to describe the man who ran ahead of Joseph when he was vice-regent of Egypt (Gn 41:43), and to refer to the first grapes of the season in the land of Canaan (Nm 13:20). In the Apocrypha, hornets are said to be sent as forerunners of the Israelite army, who were to bring judgment on the people of Canaan (Wisd of Sol 12:8).

Although John the Baptist is commonly viewed as the forerunner of Jesus Christ, the term is not used in the Bible with reference to him. The word occurs only once in the NT, where Christ himself is described as our forerunner (Heb 6:20). Under the old covenant, the people never accompanied the high priest into the most sacred place of the temple. The book of Hebrews, in discussing the new covenant, describes Jesus as a high priest who has entered heaven—the Holy Place—ahead of those who believe in him (cf. 2:17–3:2; 5:1-9).

FORGETFULNESS, Land of Euphemism for the abode of the dead. Once in the land of forgetfulness, the dead are thought to be forgotten by God (Ps 88:12) and people (Eccl 9:5-6) alike. Job 14:21-22, suggests, however, that the deceased retain some self-consciousness in Sheol.

See also Sheol.

FORGIVENESS Pardon, involving restoration of broken relationships; ceasing to feel resentment for wrongs and offenses. Primarily, forgiveness is an act of God, releasing sinners from judgment and freeing them from the divine penalty of their sin. Since only God is holy, only God can forgive sin (Mk 2:7; Lk 5:21). Forgiveness is also a human act extended toward one's neighbor—a manifestation of one's realization and appropriation of God's forgiveness. Hence, forgiveness is a uniquely Christian doctrine.

In other religions, forgiveness does not have the same force. In animism, there is no awareness of a personal relationship with God. In Hinduism, all have to pay the inexorable consequences of karma in the wheel of reincarnations. Buddhism likewise knows nothing of a forgiving God. The idea is present in Islam, but there is no personal God and Father. Even in Judaism, forgiveness remains a limited experience, though forgiveness as developed in the NT adds dimension to the teaching of the OT.

Expressions of Forgiveness in the Old Testament The idea of forgiveness is expressed in various metaphors. The command is *nasa*, to "send away," as the scapegoat was sent away into the wilderness to bear the sins of the Israelites. It is also rendered "to be merciful" (Lv 4:20; 1 Kgs 8:30, 34; Pss 86:5; 103:3). The Hebrew word *kapar* is commonly used of atonement, meaning "to cover up," as the sacrifice was offered to cover the deficiency of the worshiper (Ex 29:36; Dt 21:8; Jer 18:23; Ez 43:20; 45:20). Cognates of *salah* always refer to God's act of forgiveness (Nm 30:5, 8, 12; Pss 86:5; 130:4; Dn 9:9). God lets go of the transgression; he removes it. Another expression is *maha*, to "wipe away" (Ps 51:1, 7; Is 43:25; 44:22).

The OT teaches that God is a forgiving God (Ex 34:6-7; Neh 9:17; Dn 9:9), yet he is just and punishes sin. Many incidents are also given where God refuses to forgive when the proper conditions are not met, or when certain serious offenses are committed (Dt 29:20; 2 Kgs 24:4; Jer 5:7). Forgiveness is rooted in the character of God, but his forgiveness is never indiscriminate, for people must also be penitent. The OT (cited here in the RSV) uses vivid imagery to indicate the magnitude of God's forgiveness. Sin is cast "into the depths of the sea" (Mi 7:19), removed "as far as the east is from the west" (Ps 103:12), hid behind God's back (Is 38:17), "remembered no more" (Jer 31:34). The stain and soil of sin is bleached white (Is 1:18). Sin, which burdens like a weight, is forever lifted and remitted.

The dynamic of forgiveness in the OT is thus releasing one from the past. The past acts and deeds of sin are not denied, but there is no longer any bondage. Forgiveness brings freedom.

Forgiveness in the New Testament In the NT, the concept of the unmerited forgiveness of God is intensi-

fied by the fact that God forgave our sins when Christ died for us. Each human is an insolvent debtor (Mt 18:23-35) who has no hope of repayment. Sinners all, we cannot keep the law or save ourselves (Mk 10:26-27). This highlights the NT teaching that it is in the person of Christ himself that there is forgiveness. He alone has the power to forgive sins (2:5-10). It is his death that is redemptive (Mt 26:28; Mk 10:45) and his blood that is the basis of a new covenant (1 Cor 11:25). It is through him that one can enter into the living experience of forgiveness (Heb 9:15, 22). So forgiveness is inseparable from the proclamation of Jesus Christ (Acts 13:38; Eph 1:7; Col 1:14; 1 Jn 2:12).

THE CHRISTIAN EXPERIENCE OF FORGIVENESS
The Christian understanding of forgiveness has broad implications:

1. **It reflects the character of God as one who pardons and enters into a meaningful relationship with his creature, producing a change in human relationship with him. This has been done in the costly anguish of the cross of Christ.**
2. **It expresses the efficacy of divine atonement in the reconciliation of man with God. Those who truly realize their condition as sinners know that God can remove sin and redeem sinners. This must be experienced, not just comprehended intellectually. In Christ's death, sin is condemned and absolutely judged, and yet Christ bears the penalty on our behalf by his sacrifice.**
3. **For the apostle Paul, the bare concept of forgiveness does not convey deeply enough the full consequences. Instead, he speaks of being justified. To be "treated as righteous" is a rich consequence of forgiveness (Rom 4:5), a gift of God's grace (3:24), a present experience (1 Cor 4:4) for those who have a faith relationship with Christ (Rom 3:26). Thus, justification is the positive relationship that forgiveness provides.**
4. **Forgiveness implies that God has reconciled man to himself (Eph 2:14-17). The outcome is peace with God (Phil 4:7; Col 3:15), a reconciliation accomplished by the cross (Col 1:20). This is the implication of all the references in Romans 5 to being justified, reconciled, and trusting.**
5. **Forgiveness includes the theme of fellowship with God the Father (1 Thes 1:3), Son (1 Cor 1:9), and Holy Spirit (2 Cor 13:14). It is expressed in the Pauline phrase "in Christ" or "in the Lord" (used some 164 times), indicating a profound relationship of communion and union with God. Forgiveness as reconciliation and restoration to fellowship with God comprehends, in effect, the whole nature of the Christian life. Sanctification is its fruit, and glorification is its objective. In forgiveness, God ultimately remains God, and the erring sinner is brought home to the Father who has eternally loved him.**

There are other distinctively NT concepts of forgiveness. The Greek word *charizomai*, meaning "to forgive sins," is distinctively developed by Paul in terms of God's gracious pardon (2 Cor 2:7; 12:13; Eph 4:32; Col 2:13; 3:13). Sin is considered as a debt, and *aphesis* denotes the discharge of a debt ("putting it away"—see Lk 6:37). Forgiveness is also treated as remission, *paresis* ("passing over"). God has not executed the full retribution called for by sin (Acts 14:16; 17:30); instead, he has shown mercy.

Yet the NT speaks of two limitations to forgiveness. One is the unpardonable sin (Mt 12:31-32; Mk 3:28-30; Lk 12:10). In this regard Christ speaks of those who, like the Pharisees, are so warped in their moral judgments that they cannot distinguish between acts of Satan and the good deeds of Christ. There is also "the sin against the Holy Spirit" that is "sin unto death" (1 Jn 5:16). This sin is not specifically defined, but its essence seems to be consistent rejection of the grace of God.

The ethics of forgiveness in the NT insists not only on penitence as a condition for forgiveness (2 Cor 7:10), but also on the need to forgive others (Mt 6:14-15). If in the midst of receiving forgiveness one does not forgive others, it is a clear sign that repentance is not complete. Several times in his parables the Lord insists that the readiness to forgive others is a sign of true repentance (Mt 18:23-35; Lk 6:37). So Christ taught that to forgive is a duty, and no limits can be set on it. It must be granted without reserve, even to 70 times 7 (Mt 18:21-22). Forgiveness is part of the mutual relationship of believers: since all are dependent upon God's forgiveness, all are required to forgive one another. "As the Lord has forgiven you, so you also must forgive" (Col 3:13).

See also Confession; Repentance.

FORMER RAIN* KJV term for important rainfall that begins the agricultural year in Palestine, usually in October (Dt 11:14; Jer 5:24; Jas 5:7). *See* Palestine.

FORNICATION* Unchastity, sexual immorality. The word "fornication" is used in the Scriptures to mean several different things.

Its general meaning refers to every kind of illegal sexual intercourse, that is, any intercourse except that between a husband and wife. For example, in 1 Corinthians 5:1 (KJV) the word is used twice to refer to a sin that was being tolerated by the church: a man apparently was cohabitating with his stepmother. In a list of terrible sins in Romans 1:29, the apostle Paul included fornication, apparently intending the term to mean all acts of sexual immorality (KJV). In 1 Corinthians the context suggests that Paul used the word in reference to all sorts of illicit sexual activity (6:13, 18). In 1 Corinthians 7:2 (KJV) Paul used the plural Greek word for "fornications" to imply the various ways in which the sin may manifest itself. He thus gave a reason why people in Corinth should marry and live together properly. One of the sins included in the word's general sense is adultery.

"Fornication" also has a more limited sense of immoral sexual activity between unmarried people. Such a meaning is implied in those biblical lists where both fornication and adultery come together. Jesus' list of the defiling sins that proceed out of a person's heart includes "fornication" and "adultery" (Mt 15:19; Mk 7:21). Paul's list of those sinners who will not inherit the kingdom of God also contains both fornicators and adulterers (1 Cor 6:9, KJV).

"Fornication" in Matthew 5:32 and 19:9 (as translated by the KJV) is usually taken by biblical students today to refer specifically to adultery (see NLT). The translation of *porneia* has to do with interpretation rather than translation. Scholars disagree as to whether Jesus' exceptive phrase relative to divorce has to do with fornication in a general or limited sense. He might have meant adultery alone, or he might have been including it generally with other sexual sins.

A figurative use of the word "fornication" appears in both the OT and NT. Originating in descriptions of Israel and the church as the Lord's wife or the bride, apostasy from God and idolatry are called fornication (see, e.g., Jer 2). Ezekiel 16 uses unfaithfulness to marriage vows as a symbol of Jerusalem's wayward relationship with God. Jerusalem had become an "unfaithful wife" to him. The first three chapters of Hosea use the relationship of the prophet Hosea and his unfaithful wife, Gomer, as an illustration of how the nation of Israel had become guilty of fornication against its "husband," the Lord, by going after other gods. In the book of Revelation the figurative use of "fornication" and "impure passion" is ascribed to Babylon the great, the mother of harlots (Rv 14:8; 17:2-4; 18:3; 19:2).

See also Adultery.

FORT, FORTIFICATION Walls, citadels, and sometimes moats protecting most cities in the ancient world. Fortifications followed the natural contour of the area encircling a city. Early city defenses consisted of simple banks of earth tossed against the walls and outer structures to make it difficult for hostile forces to approach and enter the city. Wherever possible, the site chosen for the location of a city would be a naturally favorable topographical situation, such as a steep elevation in an isolated place or a hill that afforded natural protection. Some sites were chosen because of their ample water supply, good navigation, or central location at a crossroads of traveled highways, even if they had no natural defenses. The difficulty and cost of fortifications were then obviously much more serious.

In general, whatever materials were available were used for construction of fortifications, including debris, rubble, and beaten earth. Those materials were faced with hard-packed clay or lime plaster to prevent an enemy from knowing the quality of the underlying filling. Commonly a ditch or moat was dug or cut out of solid rock in front of the walls. This hindered an enemy's advance and made any attempt to tunnel under the walls and into the city more difficult.

Towers were built for added strength and protection at potentially weak spots, such as corners, gateways, or openings for water supplies. Towers had inner access stairways and chambers for use by soldiers who manned the structures and for use by watchmen who announced the approach of danger. Gateways were provided with massive piers and bronze or iron bars and bolts. Gates were hung on pivots driven into the pavement below and into the lintel above and had to be strongly fortified and carefully protected. Often they consisted of a series of entrances, one inside the other, with guardrooms between them.

Excavations of ancient forts reveal the development of fortifications from primitive beginnings to NT times. Earliest strongholds were constructed with crude brick and rough stone work. Masonry was irregular, and large stones of various sizes and shapes were roughly trimmed and crudely placed into the wall structures. Stone facings and wall joints were packed with pebbles or limestone chippings. During later times, carefully prepared mortar was used to cover the walls to give greater strength and support to the fortifications. Not until late in the Hebrew period were stones with ornamentation and skilled drafting used.

Scripture uses the imagery of a fortress or high tower to picture the confidence that believers can have in God's strength and protection. The prophets realized that the strength and defense of the nation lay not in fortifications of brick and stone but in God, and they urged the people to put their trust in him as a secure refuge (2 Sm 22:2-3, 33; Prv 10:29; Is 25:4; Jer 16:19; Hos 8:14; Jl 3:16; Na 1:7).

See also Warfare; City; Watchtower.

FORTUNATUS Member of the church at Corinth. Fortunatus is a Roman proper name written in Greek and found only once in the NT (1 Cor 16:17). Paul rejoiced that he, along with Stephanas and Achaicus, had come to be with him in Ephesus. The Textus Receptus has a subscript naming these three men as the carriers of Paul's letter to the Corinthians.

FORUM Open area in Roman cities used for commerce, political affairs, and judicial matters. The forum was usually on level ground, rectangular in shape, and surrounded by temples, law courts, colonnades, and other public buildings.

The forum of Appius was a traveler's stop on the Appian Way, 43 miles (69.2 kilometers) south of Rome, where Paul was met by Christians from Rome on his way to the capital under guard (Acts 28:15).

The most important of the forums were those located in the city of Rome. These were built at different times in its history, and existing forums were changed through continued building. The Rome to which Paul went for his trial had several forums, including those of Julius Caesar (begun by him but actually completed by Augustus Caesar) and of Augustus Caesar. Most important was the Roman Forum, center of the world in Paul's day. It lay between the two central hills of the seven hills on which the city was built. It contained many columns, statues, works of art, and buildings important in the political and religious life of the empire.

If Paul was brought directly into the city by the centurion who had charge of him, he would have passed the triumphal arch of Augustus, the temple of Castor and Pollux, and the temples dedicated to Julius and Augustus for emperor worship. Arriving at the Roman Forum proper, he would have noticed on the northwest the famous ideal center of the city (and thus of the empire), and on the southwest the gilded milestone, giving distances to places as far away as London to the west and Jerusalem to the east. In the background was the temple to Jupiter, chief god in the Roman pantheon. On the south side was a large public building, the Basilica Julia, completed in AD 12, the probable site of the pronouncement of Paul's death sentence. On the north side was the Basilica Aemilia, a building from which marble columns were taken and used in the building of a church over the traditional site of Paul's tomb. That church was completed in AD 398 and stood for 1,400 years.

See also Appius, Forum of.

FOUNDATION GATE Structure mentioned in 2 Chronicles 23:5, in the narrative about Queen Athaliah's execution. The parallel passage in 2 Kings 11:6 reads "Sur Gate," while the Septuagint has "gate of the ways," indicating some difficulties within the Hebrew text.

FOWL KJV common translation for bird. In modern usage and the RSV, the term is reserved for domestic birds or wild fowl that are eaten. *See* Birds.

FOWLER* One who traps or shoots wild birds. The catching of birds for pets, food, and sacrifices was the business of the fowler. This was done by the use of a bow and arrow, a sling, or a net (Prv 1:17; Ez 12:13; 17:20; Hos 7:12; 9:8). Other methods included the use of bird lime, a sticky substance to which birds adhere, and a throw stick that broke the birds' legs. Fowlers lay in wait near their trap, placing the captured birds in a basket (Jer 5:26-27). The term "fowler" appears also as a metaphor for wicked men who trap other men (Pss 91:3; 124:7; Jer 5:26; Hos 9:8).

See also Hunting.

FOX Small, wild, carnivorous, doglike mammal, several species of which existed in Palestine in the biblical period. *See* Animals.

FRANKINCENSE Fragrant gum resin that can be ground into powder and burned to produce a balsamlike odor. It was often associated with myrrh (Sg 3:6; 4:6; Mt 2:11). Frankincense is obtained from balsam trees of the genus *Boswellia*, specifically the species *B. carterii, B. papyrifera,* and *B. thurifera.* These trees, which are related to turpentine trees, have star-shaped flowers that are pure white or green, tipped with rose. To obtain the resin, a deep incision is cut into the trunk, yielding an amber-colored gum. Since these trees were native only to Saba (Sheba) in southern Arabia (Is 60:6; Jer 6:20) and Somaliland, the resin was a costly item transported into Palestine by caravan. The so-called frankincense tree growing in Palestine (Ecclus 50:8) was probably *Commiphora opobalsamum* whose resin was used to produce perfume.

Frankincense was used alone or with other materials for incense. It was one of the ingredients of the holy incense used for worship in the tabernacle (Ex 30:34). It was placed on the bread of the Presence (Lv 24:7) and mixed with oil on the cereal offerings (Lv 2:1-2, 14-16; 6:15), but it was excluded from the sin offering (5:11). A supply of frankincense was maintained in the Jerusalem temple (Neh 13:5, 9). It was later used in cosmetics and perfume (Sg 3:6). Both the costly value and its use for worship made the presentation of frankincense to the infant Jesus an appropriate gift (Mt 2:11). *See* Plants.

FREEDMEN* Members of a Jewish synagogue in Jerusalem (Acts 6:9), descended from Jews who had been captured and taken to Rome by the general Pompey (106–48 BC), then later released. Pompey found that the Jews adhered so strictly to their religious and national customs that they were worthless as slaves.

Not all the freedmen returned to Jerusalem; some stayed in Rome. In the time of the Roman writer Pliny, a freedman was described as a "mean commoner." The freedmen (or "Freed Slaves," NLT) derived their name from a Latin term for one manumitted, or the son of such a former slave. *See* Libertines.

FREEDOM *See* Liberty.

FREED SLAVES NLT rendering of Freedmen in Acts 6:9. *See* Freedmen.

FREEWILL OFFERING Voluntary peace offering (Lv 7:16; Dt 12:6). *See* Offerings and Sacrifices.

FRIENDS Term used to indicate close acquaintances. Since Jesus called his disciples friends (Lk 12:4; Jn 15:14-15), it would have been natural for Christians to refer to themselves as "the friends of Christ," especially since such terminology was used for members of philosophical groups in the Greek world. But no such terminology emerged.

FRINGE The border of a garment, or a "tassel," four of which were worn on the upper garments of Jewish men according to the Lord's commandment (Dt 22:12). Those tassels were to be reminders of God's laws.

FROG Aquatic, tailless, smooth-skinned amphibian, mentioned in connection with the second plague in Egypt (Ex 8; Pss 78:45; 105:30; Rv 16:13). *See* Animals.

FRONTLET* Translation of a Hebrew word referring to anything bound on the forehead (Ex 13:16; Dt 6:8; 11:18). The phylacteries of Jesus' day (Mt 23:5) were worn daily at morning prayer by every male Israelite over the age of 13. They consisted of four Scripture passages (Ex 13:1-10; 13:11-16; Dt 6:4-9; 11:13-21) written on parchment and placed in small leather boxes tied to the forehead and the left arm. Whether the phylacteries were the parchments or the leather boxes is debated. There is no evidence that the Israelites in Moses' day made such phylacteries. It is probable that the commands were to be understood figuratively, portraying the memorial value of the Feast of Unleavened Bread and the importance of the Law in the people's lives. For the Pharisees, the outward observance had replaced the obligation to apply the power of God's Word to the heart (Mt 23:5).
See also Phylactery; Amulet.

FROST Frozen water vapor or dew (Pss 78:47; 147:16; 148:8; Jer 36:30; Zec 14:6).

FRUIT *See* Food and Food Preparation; Plants.

FRUIT OF THE SPIRIT* Expression taken from Galatians 5:22-23. As listed there, this fruit is the evidence one may expect from a life in which the Spirit of God is living and reigning. The fruit of the Spirit, as listed in Galatians 5, is love, joy, peace, patience, kindness, goodness, faithfulness, gentleness, and self-control. "Love" is that outgoing, self-giving kind of action, not necessarily emotion, that characterized God himself when he loved the world so much that he *gave* his only Son (Jn 3:16). "Goodness" is the translation of a Greek word that includes the idea of generosity. The word "faith" refers usually to trust or confidence in someone or something. However, the word can also refer to that which causes trust and faith, namely faithfulness and reliability. Both meanings are in the use of the word here as another evidence of the Spirit-controlled life. Another fruit, translated "temperance" by the KJV, is the Greek word for self-control, that ability to hold oneself in, to keep oneself in check. It is significant that the Spirit is said to be the one responsible for this fruit. Since these qualities are the fruit of the Spirit, it is self-evident that legalism and obedience to law cannot originate or produce them.

This fruit appears in a context within Galatians where Paul is emphasizing Christian freedom from obedience to the law as a meritorious means of being justified before God. He warns the Galatian Christians, who were in danger of returning to the law, that physical circumcision is an outward sign of a return to legalistic means of justification and that to attempt to obtain it this way is impossible (Gal 5:3). However, lest the Galatians overemphasize their freedom in Christ, Paul cautions that this liberty does not mean license to sin, an opportunity for gratifying the desires of the flesh, but rather an opportunity to continue as loving bondservants belonging to one another (v 13). Life in the Spirit means that one will not fulfill the lusts or desires of the flesh (v 16). Then Paul identifies both the works of the flesh and the fruit of the Spirit. A person who is abstaining from the works of the flesh and is demonstrating the fruit of the Spirit in his life will be loving, joyful, peaceful, patient, kind, good, dependable, gentle, and self-controlled. These are not said to be gifts of the Spirit, however, but graces that will adorn the life that is under the Holy Spirit's control.

FULLER* One who cleans, shrinks, thickens, or dyes cloth or newly shorn wool. It was the fuller's job to prepare fibers used for weaving by cleansing them of oil and other impurities. The cleansing materials the fuller used were white clay, urine, and ashes of special plants. The fuller's plant lay outside the town because of offensive odors and because space was needed for spreading the fibers to dry, as was the case of the Fuller's Field outside Jerusalem in Isaiah's day (2 Kgs 18:17; Is 7:3; 36:2).

FULLER'S FIELD* Place outside Jerusalem that was linked to a spring or pool by a causeway or aquaduct (2 Kgs 18:17; Is 7:3; 36:2). It has been generally identified with an area near En-rogel ("spring of the fuller"). The spring was south of Jerusalem in the Kidron Valley. It was originally the tribal boundary between Judah and Benjamin (Jos 15:7; 18:16). When Absalom rebelled and King David fled from Jerusalem, two of David's men stayed at En-rogel to gather information about the rebellion (2 Sm 17:17).

En-rogel has been identified with the modern Bir Attub, or "Job's Well," on the left bank of Wadi en-Nar. The well sinks deep into the rock, reaches an underground stream, and gushes forth following rainfalls.
See also Jerusalem.

FULLNESS Common translation of the Greek term *pleroma*. The word carries various shades of meaning that must be determined by observing its use in context.

General Usage In Greek usage outside the NT, the word means "that which fills." It is found in reference to the cargo or crew that fills a ship, the people that make up a crowd, and the years that fill a person's life. The philosopher Aristotle used the term to denote the population that fills a city. That sense is used in Matthew's and Mark's Gospels of a patch that fills up a hole in an old garment (Mt 9:16; Mk 2:21), and in Mark of the pieces of fish that fill a basket (Mk 6:43; 8:20).

"Earth" Expressions In several instances in the KJV the term is found in the phrase "the earth and its fullness" (Pss 24:1; 50:12; 89:11; 1 Cor 10:26) or "the sea and its fullness" (1 Chr 16:32; Ps 96:11-12), meaning "contents." Beyond its obvious quantitative sense, the meaning in these expressions may reflect a qualitative character: the contents of the earth are good and special. The Hebrew mind viewed the created order as a reflection of the Creator (Pss 8:5-6; 19:1-6; Jer 23:24). Accordingly, whenever people entered into relationship with anything God had created, whether in work or meals or relationships, they also entered objectively into relationship with God, who had given those things. Thus, the Jews heard with horror the prophetic announcement of God's intention to bring destruction upon "the land and all that fills it" (Jer 8:16; 47:2; Ez 12:19; 19:7; 30:12).

The Apostle Paul's Usage The origin of Paul's understanding and use of "fullness" as a significant theological term has been debated. It is held by some that the word was a technical term used by the Gnostics in reference to a realm of spiritual beings that bridged the space between the true God and an "evil" earth. Subsequently, false teachers came to view Christ as one among many deities who lived in that "fullness." In order to correct the misunderstanding, Paul borrowed the term from his opponents and applied it to Christ. Jesus is not just one of the beings between God and humanity, Paul taught; rather, he is all there is ("the fullness") between God and humanity (Col 1:15-20).

Against that view it is argued that Paul used the term in several contexts where that interpretation is obviously inadequate (Rom 13:10; Eph 1:22-23). In addition, it is likely that Paul, with his Pharisaic Jewish background, would understand the term in light of its OT usage. Thus, Paul's use of the term may be better understood as not borrowed from his opponents.

Paul used the term four times in the book of Romans. It can be rendered "full inclusion" in reference to the total number of Jews (Rom 11:12) or Gentiles (v 25) who will come to God. In verse 12, however, the term is set in opposition to the "failure" and "trespass" of the Jews, who feel that righteousness is a matter of their Jewish heritage rather than faith. It may be that Paul used the term in reference to "complete obedience to God's will." Thus, in essence Paul said, "If their disobedience means this much good for the world, think of what their obedience will mean." It is in this active sense that "fullness" is used in Romans 13:10. Love brings to realization all that the law intends. Similarly, Paul desires that his own life be a full expression of the gospel of Christ (15:29).

In the book of Ephesians, the church is referred to as the "fullness of Christ" (Eph 1:22-23; 4:13), and "the fullness of God" (3:19). A variety of interpretations have been offered for this phrase: the church is filled, made complete or whole by Christ; the church possesses the attributes of Christ; the church is the agent through which Christ does all his work. The church is full of Christ in that it is the complete, continuing expression of his words and works (compare Col 2:10). In the book of Colossians, Paul used the term in reference to Christ; in him dwells the "fullness of God" (1:19; 2:9). These passages are often interpreted as proclaiming the equality of Christ with God. All of God's attributes are contained in Christ. All that God is, Christ is.

The Apostle John's Usage The prologue to John's Gospel states that the "fullness of Christ" is received by all believers (1:16). The exact nature of this fullness is defined in verse 14: "And the Word became flesh and dwelt among us, full of grace and truth." The Greek word for "fullness" here indicates plenitude and totality. The Gnostics used the word to describe the totality of all deities. John, as with Paul, used the word to describe Christ as the fullness, the plenitude of God, for all the fullness of the Godhead dwells in him bodily (see Col 1:19; 2:9).

Since all of God's fullness dwells in Christ, every spiritual reality is found in Christ. In Christ, believers lack nothing. Of course, no single believer could receive all that Christ is; it takes the body of Christ to appropriate Christ's fullness and to express it (Eph 1:23). Nevertheless, each believer receives in measure the same content of that fullness. Christ is continually full; he never is depleted. No matter how much the believers receive of him, he keeps on giving. Believers do not need to seek any other source but Christ.

FULLNESS OF TIME* Expression meaning "when the time was ripe," occurring in English translations of Galatians 4:4 and Ephesians 1:10. In Galatians the refer-

ence is to the time when "God sent forth his Son." The apostle Paul used the image of a child coming of age to say that Jesus came at a point in human history when the time was ripe and released humanity from bondage to the law.

Traditionally, theologians have seen indications of the ripeness of the time of Jesus' birth in the historical circumstances of his day. Rome's conquests had produced "Roman peace," so that travel was both safe and easy. That political unity was built on the earlier victories of Alexander the Great, whose expansion from Greece to Egypt to India left in its wake the Greek language and culture, which later made the spread of the gospel easier. Greek-speaking Jews lived in every city of the Roman Empire. Their religion was protected by Roman law, and that law protected Christianity for its first half century. Many Gentiles who were interested in the monotheism and morality of Judaism went to the Jewish synagogues. Thus, the synagogue was a natural starting point for the church's early outreach to Gentiles.

In Palestine the Jews were longing for a Messiah (deliverer) since they were politically subject to the Herods and the Romans. Messianic rebellion simmered constantly, and even repeatedly broke out in open battle. Socially, peasants were oppressed by large landholders, who used every opportunity and legal loophole to expand their properties. Many of those oppressors were from the chief priestly families, whose greed was well known to all. Throughout Palestine, messianic speculation was at a high point. The Pharisees talked about what would happen when the Messiah came, and the scribes at Qumran (the Dead Sea Scrolls community) wrote books about it. The time was ripe for Jesus' coming, as he himself indicated (Mt 13:11, 16-17; Mk 1:15).

In Ephesians 1:10, Paul used a slightly different Greek expression, which covers the whole of the time between Jesus' first coming and his future return to complete God's plan in history. Jesus revealed this plan (or "mystery," as Paul called it—Rom 16:25-26; Eph 1:9; 3:4-5; Col 1:26), which works out in the church as people repent and are joined to him. In the ultimate sense, the full "ripeness" will come when God's plan or purpose ("dispensation," KJV) is completed and Christ becomes head over all things. Paul knew that this completion was in progress, but he awaited its total realization in what he hoped would be the near future.

FUNERAL CUSTOMS Practices and rites that encompass the dying and death of human beings. Funerary rites have been practiced by all social groups from their very beginnings.

Most anthropologists believe that funeral customs fulfill certain important social functions for the living. However, the general meaning these customs provide for any given culture is a matter of longstanding dispute. On the one hand, some behavioral scientists believe that funeral rites alleviate the sudden anxiety that death

Ancient Jewish Funeral Procession

brings for the grieving. On the other hand, some believe that the purpose of death customs is not to dispel anxiety but rather to foster the feelings of religious awe or group solidarity. In varying degrees both of these factors probably underlie most funeral rites. Funerary customs remind the participants that death must be taken seriously, while at the same time they provide a comforting interpretation of death.

Belief patterns have profoundly influenced funeral customs. A conception of immortality is one of the more commonly held beliefs. The discovery of artifacts such as tools, ornaments, and even food in the oldest known human graves may be evidence of the pervasive conviction that human beings continue to exist in some form after death. Proper funeral rites were believed to assist the dead in reaching their final habitat, which usually included a journey fraught with various perils, such as crossing mythical rivers or wide chasms. The rites also assured the living that the spirits of the dead would not harm them.

Disposing of the Corpse A common form of disposing of a corpse has been burial in the earth (inhumation). This practice may have emerged because of the belief that the abode of the dead was located under the ground. Often the grave was considered the entrance to the underworld, although some groups considered the habitation of the dead to be in the sky. Above-ground disposal has also been practiced by many. Some communities place the corpse on a rack to be devoured by birds or other animals. A few groups have been known to eat the corpse, believing that the good qualities of the deceased could be ingested. Many Asian societies have traditionally practiced cremation, or the burning of the corpse. In the past, it was not uncommon for the wife and slaves of a deceased man to throw themselves on the burning pyre. Cremation is becoming popular in the West and may become more widely practiced because of the increasing scarcity of land for grave sites.

Nearly every society observes special mourning customs during the disposal of the body. These include the wearing of special clothing, emotional outbursts, seclusion, and food taboos. Most societies mark the experience by a ceremony that may include purification rites and the sharing of special meals by the friends and relatives of the dead. In almost every cultural group, status symbols infiltrate the funeral customs and rituals. For instance, if the deceased were of a high social standing, then the funeral ceremonies would be more elaborate.

Funeral Customs and the Bible While the Bible does not provide a detailed picture of burial procedures, it does allude to the common burial practices of the Hebrew people and contains some scattered prohibitions relating to death. Placing the corpse in the ground or in a cave was the principal method for disposing of the dead. One of the worst indignities was to be left unburied or become food for predators (Dt 28:26; 1 Kgs 11:15). If possible, the deceased were to be buried on the day of death (Dt 21:23). While embalming was not practiced, the corpse was dressed in special burial clothes and sprinkled with various perfumes (Mk 15:46; Jn 11:44).

Intense weeping surrounded funerary rites during biblical times. This mourning did not simply result from spontaneous grief but was part of the funeral ritual (Mt 11:17). In ancient Israel, groups of paid mourners emerged who could wail on ritual cue. Much of the funeral service centered on these professional mourners who sang psalms and delivered elaborate eulogies for the dead (2 Chr 35:25; Jer 9:17-22). The emphasis upon mourning resulted from the Hebrew appreciation of human life and health, which was considered one of God's greatest gifts (Ps 91:16), and also from a view of human nature that affirmed embodied existence (16:9-11). This latter belief may have contributed to the OT's lack of a full-fledged doctrine of immortality, even though it implies that the dead partake in the "shadowy existence" of Sheol and will someday be resurrected (Jb 14:13; Ez 37).

The early Christian church affirmed the Jewish belief in embodied existence but highlighted a belief in existence after death. Unlike the Greek dualists, who asserted the immortality of only the soul, the NT writers, following the OT, emphasized a belief in eternal life that entailed not only the soul but also the body. This view became the fulcrum for the belief in the bodily resurrection, which undergirded Christian funeral customs. Nearly every practice symbolized a belief in the resurrection and eternal life. Thus, the emphasis upon lamentation gave way to joyful singing of psalms. The body was washed, anointed with perfumes and spices, wrapped in linen, and surrounded by candles, all of which represented eternal life. Friends and relatives usually held a vigil at the home of the deceased, and scriptural passages dealing with the resurrection and eternal life were read. Whenever possible, the Lord's Supper was observed, symbolizing the sacrifice of Christ. At the church or at the grave site, a funeral oration was delivered both to eulogize the dead and to comfort the living. Many of these practices are still observed by Christians today.

See also Burial, Burial Customs; Mourning.

FURLONG* Linear measure of about 202 yards (184.6 meters). *See* Weights and Measures.

FURNACE Brick or stone structure varying in size and shape, depending on whether it was to be used domestically or commercially. A typical furnace consisted of a firebox, a flue, a chamber for the material to be heated, and an opening to give the refiner access from the outside. Common uses of the furnace were to smelt ore, melt ore for casting, heat ore for forging, fire ceramic materials, fire bricks, and make lime.

Various types of furnaces are mentioned in Scripture. The potter's kiln was used to make lime and to fire and glaze pottery (Gn 19:28; Ex 9:8, 10; 19:18). It was commonly made of limestone, was dome-shaped, had a chimney for smoke to escape, and a hole at the bottom for fuel. Such a furnace emitted a thick, dark column of smoke.

Larger furnaces used for smelting ore were seldom employed by the Hebrews, except possibly in the time of King Solomon. The Hebrews, however, knew of this type of furnace, probably from its extensive use in Lebanon. Most OT references to such furnaces are figurative (Dt 4:20; 1 Kgs 8:51; Prv 17:3; 27:21; Is 48:10; Jer 11:4; Ez 22:18-22). This kind of large, ore-smelting furnace is central in the story of Shadrach, Meshach, and Abednego, the three Jewish men whom King Nebuchadnezzar threw into the fiery furnace for refusing to bow down and worship his golden idol (Dn 3).

The most common use of "furnace" in the Bible is to provide a figurative description of God's discipline or punishment and his refining of character (Dt 4:20; 1 Kgs 8:51; Is 48:10; Jer 6:27-30; Ez 22:18-22). In the NT "furnace" is used as a symbol for hell (Mt 13:42, 50; Rv 9:2). The refining image is used to refer to the trials of life that prepare a person for life after death (Jas 1:12; 1 Pt 1:7). In John's vision, the one who is like the Son of Man has "feet like unto fine brass, as if they burned in a furnace" (Rv 1:15, KJV). This reference to refined brass, an extremely hard metal, is symbolic of Christ's power to conquer his enemies.

FURNACES*, Tower of the KJV rendering of Tower of the Ovens in Nehemiah 3:11 and 12:38. *See* Ovens, Tower of the.

FURNITURE Items of material culture used in homes, palaces, and temples. Because of its close geographical proximity to other nations, Israel had extensive contact with neighboring cultures. Historical surveys document parallels between the furniture of Israel and that of other tribes and countries.

Palestine in Old Testament Times OT passages supply most of the information about furniture in ancient Palestine, although there are also significant archaeological data. There are many references to beds in the OT, using at least three Hebrew nouns. Jacob is pictured as sitting up in bed (Gn 48:2) and as dying on his bed (49:33). Moses threatened that frogs would invade the bedroom and bed of the Egyptian pharaoh (Ex 8:3). Michal, Saul's daughter, placed an effigy in David's bed (1 Sm 19:11-17) when Saul sent messengers to capture him there. King David condemned the practice of killing a defenseless person sleeping in bed (2 Sm 4:7, 11). The prophet Elijah laid a dead boy on his bed and revived him (1 Kgs 17:19).

King Ahab sulked on his bed (1 Kgs 21:4), and King Ahaziah lay on his sick bed (2 Kgs 1:4-6, 16). The prophet Amos criticized the rich who lay on beds of ivory and stretched out on their couches (Am 6:4). The prophet Ezekiel spoke symbolically of disobedient Jerusalem as a prostitute sitting on a stately couch with the Lord's incense and oil on a table nearby (Ez 23:41). Isaiah promised that the righteous would rest in their beds (Is 57:2) and also spoke of the unrighteous setting their beds among false worshipers (vv 7-8). The psalmist flooded his bed with tears (Ps 6:6), and Proverbs refers to a sluggard on his bed (Prv 26:14).

"Table" in the OT refers both to the temple table for the bread of the Presence and to the table used in the palace or home for meals or banquets. King Adoni-bezek had his captives scrambling for scraps under his table (Jgs 1:7). Jonathan's disabled son Mephibosheth was allowed to sit at David's table (2 Sm 9:7, 10-13; 19:28). Solomon's table is described several times (1 Kgs 2:7; 4:27). The queen of Sheba was particularly impressed by the food and table service in Solomon's palace (10:5). The prophets frequently refer to tables (Is 21:5; 28:8; 65:11; Ez 40:39-43). The few references to chairs describe people reclining at meals and indicate couches rather than actual chairs (Am 6:4).

There are numerous mentions of thrones, including those of the pharaoh (Gn 41:40; Ex 11:5), David (2 Sm 3:10; 7:13), Solomon (1 Kgs 10:18), the kings of Israel and Judah (1 Kgs 22:10), and God (1 Kgs 22:19; Pss 9:4, 7; 11:4; 93:2). The OT writers sometimes indicate thrones decorated with ivory (1 Kgs 10:18).

The exact character of furniture in Palestine is difficult to determine. Bas-reliefs and wall paintings are more common among Israel's neighbors. Excavations in Jericho, however, have unearthed some valuable archaeological clues. Tombs of the middle Bronze Age produced reasonably well-preserved tables, stools, and boxes, making possible a study of ancient joinery methods. A variety of small trinket boxes show evidence of bone inlay and incised decoration. Some large slabs of timber may have been beds. Although primarily Canaanite styles, the furniture reflects the household furniture used in Israel in the centuries to follow.

Greek and Roman Historians are quite informed about Greek furniture because of the abundance of decorated vases, bas-reliefs, bronze and terra-cotta statuettes, and literary descriptions. That archaeological evidence indicates that Greek furniture was influenced by preceding civilizations. The picture is generally one of comparative simplicity, far removed from the cluttered and crowded rooms of later civilizations.

The Greeks made several types of seats: (1) the throne, often with a back, legs of various shapes, and armrests; (2) the lighter curved-back chair with arm supports; (3) the four-legged stool; (4) the folding stool with crossed legs traceable to Egyptian models; and (5) the bench. Representations that regularly appear on monuments dating from the eighth to the second century BC link Greek chairs to Egyptian and Assyrian prototypes.

Greeks used couches for sleeping and for reclining at meals. Footstools were used to rest the feet or as a step up to higher couches. Like chair legs, couch legs varied in style. Some were carved in the shape of animal legs, some were turned, some were rectangular. From about the sixth century BC, the legs projected above the frame. Such projections later became headboards and footboards. In Hellenistic times these headrests and footrests were carved and carried bronze medallions in high relief depicting children, satyrs, and animals. Turned legs replaced the rectangular ones. Couches were normally in wood, although bronze and marble couches are known.

Tables were used during meals to hold dishes and food and were removed after the meal. They were made of wood, bronze, and marble and normally had four legs, but three-legged tables were occasionally used. Chests, large and small, served to store clothes, jewelry, and other articles. They were normally of wood, although some were bronze.

Rome Roman furniture continued many Greek patterns. The eruption of the volcano Vesuvius in AD 79 preserved actual pieces of Roman furniture in its lava flow.

Chairs with backs were heavier than their Greek counterparts and widely used. There were several types of stools: the folding stool, mostly wooden, though sometimes metal; and a newly developed decorative stool, often of bronze, that was supported by four curved legs ornamented with scrolls.

A variety of couches were in use. Some followed Greek models, but others were of Roman invention. Excellent examples of bronze bed frames have been preserved. Presumably, interlaced strips of leather or cords were stretched crisscross on the frame. Gold, silver, tortoise-shell, bone, and ivory decoration were used along with veneer work in rare timber. Later, couches in Italy and in other lands had high backs and sides. The Romans seem to have used tables more widely than Greeks. They appear often as permanent supports for vases and other possessions. Tables were normally rectangular with four legs, but table makers also constructed some with three legs, or even resting on a single support. Round tabletops and legs of animals became popular from the fourth century BC on. Plain, undecorated wooden tables and benches were used in kitchens and workshops. Outdoor tables were usually of marble with carved animal legs or decorative figures of animals and monsters.

There were various chests and boxes in daily use. Shelves and cupboards became much more popular than in Greek times.

Palestine in New Testament Times The nature of furniture in the NT is probably best understood in relation to contemporaneous Roman models. The NT refers to beds in several passages. People brought a paralytic lying on his bed to Jesus (Mt 9:2, 6; Lk 5:18). When the apostles went into Solomon's portico, people brought the sick to them on beds (Acts 5:15). A Syro-Phoenician woman's sick child lay on a bed (Mk 7:30). Jesus spoke of setting a lamp on a stand and not placing it under a bed (Mk 4:21; Lk 8:16), and described what would happen to people in bed when the Day of the Lord came (Lk 17:34). In another parable Jesus spoke of a needy person begging for bread at midnight from a friend who was already in bed with his family (Lk 11:7). Beds of the poor and sick were probably only pallets or mattresses (Mk 6:55; Jn 5:8). When people reclined at meals, they would have been lying on a couch (Jn 13:23).

There are numerous NT references to tables. Jesus mentioned crumbs falling from a rich man's table (Mt 15:27; Mk 7:28; Lk 16:21). Jesus overthrew the money changers' tables in the temple (Mt 21:12; Mk 11:15). Jesus sat with his disciples at a table for the Passover meal (Lk 22:21) and promised his disciples that they would sit at his table in God's kingdom. The apostles were relieved of serving tables in order to preach (Acts 6:2).

The household lamp is referred to a number of times (Mt 25:1; Mk 4:21). Terra-cotta domestic lamps have been found in abundance in excavations.

FUTILITY Frustration, vexation, uselessness, and meaninglessness.

In Ecclesiastes (1:2, 14; 2:1, 11, 15, 17; etc.) the expression appears again and again in a haunting refrain that is difficult to render in an English translation because the Hebrew term *hevel* has so many connotations. The traditional rendering, "vanity of vanities," found in many older translations, has been replaced in newer versions with more creative attempts at capturing the meaning. In some translations the idea is "meaninglessness" (see NIV, NLT); in others, "emptiness" (see NEB); in still others, "uselessness" (see TEV). One of the best renderings is found in the REB: "Futility, utter futility, says the Speaker, everything is futile" (Eccl 1:2). Koheleth points to the futility of all human endeavors that seek to bring lasting satisfaction in and of themselves. One might as well try to "catch the wind." A person can find permanent meaning and lasting contentment only in God with whom there is no meaninglessness.

In Paul's writings there are two Greek words, often used synonymously, that convey the idea of futility: *kenos* and *mataiotes*. The two words are frequently used together in the Septuagint (e.g., Jb 20:18; Is 37:7; Hos 12:1), in classical Greek, and in Hellenistic Greek. *Mataiotes* is the word used in the Septuagint. *Kenos* is used by Paul to signify that which is empty and hollow—hence, pointless and futile. *Mataiotes* is employed by Paul to signify that which is vain and useless—hence, ineffective and futile.

In Paul's writings *kenos* expresses the emptiness of all that is not filled with spiritual substance; it speaks of the "zeroness" of human words and human endeavors that lack divine content. Nothing comes from this nothingness; it is futility. Paul used *kenos* to describe the hollow utterances (see 1 Tm 6:20) spoken by Judaizers and/or Gnostics trying to entice the believers with philosophy and empty deceit (see Col 2:8; cf. Eph 5:6). In contrast, Paul claimed that his preaching was not "futile" but purposeful and effective (1 Cor 15:14). He made the same claim for his labor among the believers (1 Thes 2:1). Paul made sure that his labor had not been for nothing (Gal 2:2; 1 Thes 3:5), for he had not been a recipient of God's grace "to no effect" (1 Cor 15:10). His preaching and labor were not futile but purposeful because the One he had proclaimed and labored for, the risen Lord Jesus, had filled Paul with divine life and substance (v 14).

Paul's use of *mataiotes* was likely informed by the Septuagint, especially Ecclesiastes. Although the adjective *mataios* was regularly employed in Greek literature to describe that which is vain or empty, *mataiotes* is almost strictly a biblical term used often in the Septuagint to depict uselessness, worthlessness, and futility.

Nowhere in the NT is the kind of futility described in Ecclesiastes so characterized as in Romans 8:20. When Paul speaks of the creation being subjected to futility, he is focusing on the inability of creation to function as it was originally designed to do. When people fell into sin, God subjected the earth to a curse for their sake. Since then, all of the creation's attempts to express God are doomed to failure until it is released from its bondage. Redeemed humanity must take the lead, then creation—joining in the final redemption—will also be liberated from *mataiotes*.

In other portions, Paul used *mataiotes* to depict the futility that has its source in the thought life of fallen man. He characterizes the "thoughts of the wise" as being futile (1 Cor 3:20), and he describes the Gentiles as those living "in the futility of their minds" because "they are darkened in their understanding, alienated from the life of God because of their ignorance and hardness of heart" (Eph 4:17-18, NRSV). The thought life of the unregenerate is futile and aimless because it lacks divine substance and spiritual insight; it produces a life of purposelessness and ineffectiveness. Salvation from *mataiotes* for now comes from the indwelling Spirit of Christ (see Rom 8:10-11, 26-27) and in the future will be given when Christ returns and the believers (along with all creation) receive their full redemption (see Rom 8:22-25).

G

GAAL Ebed's son, who persuaded the men of Shechem to revolt against Abimelech, the judge of Israel. The revolt, however, was quickly crushed and Shechem was destroyed (Jgs 9:26-41).

GAASH
1. Mountain about 20 miles (32.2 kilometers) southwest of Shechem. Joshua was buried at Timnath-serah (Timnath-heres) in the hill country of Ephraim, near Mt Gaash (Jos 24:30; Jgs 2:9).
2. Stream in the vicinity of the mountain, mentioned as the home of Hiddai (alternately Hurai), one of King David's mighty soldiers (2 Sm 23:30; 1 Chr 11:32).

GABA* KJV spelling of the Benjamite city, Geba, in Joshua 18:24, Ezra 2:26, and Nehemiah 7:30. *See* Geba.

GABAEL
1. Ancestor of Tobit and a member of the tribe of Naphtali (Tb 1:1).
2. Brother or son of Gabrias and resident of Rages, a city in Media, with whom Tobit left in trust 10 talents of silver (Tb 1:14). Tobit later told his son Tobias about the money, and Tobias was led by the angel Raphael to Gabael (4:1, 20; 5:6; 6:9; 10:2).

GABATHA* Alternate name for Bigthan, one of Ahasuerus's eunuchs (Add Est 12:1). *See* Bigthan, Bigthana.

GABBAI Head of a family that returned to Jerusalem with Zerubbabel after the Babylonian exile (Neh 11:8).

GABBATHA Transliteration of an uncertain Aramaic expression, which is rendered in Greek as "paved with stones" and refers to the raised area before the palace in Jerusalem where formal sentencing by the governor occurred. Pilate seated himself on the elevated judgment seat here in order to preside over the trial of Jesus (Jn 19:13).

GABRI, GABRIAS* Brother or father of Gabael. The genitive case of the original does not make the exact relationship certain; it simply specifies that there is a relationship (Tb 1:14; 4:20).
See also Gabael #2.

GABRIEL One of the two angels mentioned by name in the Bible (the other is Michael). Gabriel appeared in human form to Daniel to reveal to him the meaning of a vision, to show what would transpire on the Day of Judgment, and to give Daniel wisdom and understanding (Dn 8:16; 9:21-22). In the NT Gabriel appeared to Zechariah the priest as he served in the temple, to announce the birth of Zechariah's son, John the Baptist (Lk 1:11-20). Six months later Gabriel appeared to Mary to announce that she would become the mother of Jesus, the long-awaited Messiah (Lk 1:26-33). Gabriel is com-

monly called an archangel but is not referred to as such in the Bible.

There is an abundance of material about Gabriel in the noncanonical writings of the Jews. In the books of Enoch he is pictured as one of the four chief angels, along with Michael, Raphael, and Uriel (1 Enoch 40:3, 6). He is one of the holy angels (20:7) who looks down from heaven and is a principal intercessor (1 Enoch 9:1; 40:6; 2 Enoch 21:3). He is to destroy the wicked (1 Enoch 9:9-10) and cast them into the furnace (54:6) and is set over all powers (40:9). Michael sits at God's right hand, and Gabriel sits on the left (2 Enoch 24:1). Michael, as guardian angel of Israel (cf. Dn 12:1) and a high priest of heaven, is more occupied with affairs in heaven, but Gabriel is God's messenger who goes from heaven to execute God's will on earth.
See also Angel.

GAD (Person)
1. One of the 12 sons of Jacob (Gn 35:26; 1 Chr 2:2). He was the first of the two sons born to Jacob by Zilpah, Leah's maid. Delighted with giving Jacob another son, Leah named the boy Gad, meaning "good fortune" (Gn 30:11). Later, Gad moved his family with Jacob to Egypt (Ex 1:4). When Jacob blessed his sons, he predicted that Gad would constantly be troubled by foreign invaders but would successfully withstand them and put them to flight (see Gn 49:19 and discussion below under Gad, Tribe of). Gad became the father of seven sons (Gn 46:16) and the founder of the Gadites (Dt 3:12, 16), one of the 12 tribes of Israel (Nm 2:14).
See also Gad, Tribe of.
2. Prophet and seer during the reign of David. He counseled David to leave Mizpeh of Moab and return to the land of Judah (1 Sm 22:5). Gad communicated David's punishment for numbering the fighting men of Israel (2 Sm 24:11-14, 18-19; 1 Chr 21:9-19), assisted David and Nathan in setting up the order of worship in the sanctuary (2 Chr 29:25) and later wrote an account of David's life (1 Chr 29:29).

GAD* (Idol) Canaanite god of fortune or fate whom the Israelites worshiped (Is 65:11).
See also Canaanite Deities and Religion.

GAD, Tribe of Descendants of Jacob's seventh son Gad (Gn 30:11; Nm 1:24-25), and eighth largest of the 12 tribes that came out of Egypt with Moses (according to the number of warriors in Nm 1:1-3, 24-25). They raised livestock and had a reputation for being fierce in battle (Nm 32:1; Dt 33:20).

During the wilderness period, they were led by Eliasaph's son Deuel (Nm 1:14; 2:14; 7:42; 10:20). When Israel encamped, Gad was located south of the tabernacle behind the tribes of Reuben and Simeon (2:14-15). They are mentioned at the tribal offering to the tabernacle, and after the plague, which God brought upon Israel (7:42-47; 26:15, 18). Maki's son Geuel represented the tribe as one of the 12 spies sent by Moses into Canaan (13:15).

At the close of the wilderness period, Gad, Reuben, and half of Manasseh's tribe requested permission to settle east of the Jordan, for it had good pastureland (Nm 32:1-2). This was permitted on the condition that they would help in the conquest of Canaan (Nm 32:20-22; Jos 1:12-18).

During the Conquest under Joshua, Gad is mentioned only at the battle of Jericho (Jos 4:12). After the end of the conflict, Gad, Reuben, and half of Manasseh settled their land east of the Jordan (cf. Nm 34:13-14; Jos 12:6; 13:8).

Gad's inheritance was between Manasseh's tribe to the north and Reuben's to the south. The Arabian Desert formed its eastern border and the Jordan River its western. There seem to have been no fixed borders between the two and a half tribes, and the whole area was often referred to as Gilead and Bashan (2 Kgs 10:33). Its land ran north to the Sea of Chinnereth (Galilee), but among the mountains it seems to have run eastward only as far as the Jabbok River. To the south, the cities of Aroer and Heshbon mark their southern limits (Dt 3:12-13; Jos 12:1-6; 13:24-28).

The history of Gad from its settlement to the Captivity was closely tied with the two neighboring Hebrew tribes. Shortly after returning to their lands, these two and a half tribes almost started a civil war by erecting a large altar (Jos 22:10-34). During the time of the judges, Gilead (including Gad) was threatened, if not occupied, by the Ammonites until they were defeated by Jephthah (Jgs 11). Some Gadites joined David at Ziklag during his exile (1 Chr 12:14, 37). In the 14th year of David's reign the two and a half tribes were formally brought together under an overseer named Jerijah (and his brothers, 26:30-32).

During the time of the divided kingdom, the tribes east of the Jordan were constantly under attack. During Jehu's reign (841–814 BC), Hazael annexed all the land east of the Jordan, and they were later carried off into captivity by Tiglath-pileser, king of Assyria (2 Kgs 15:29; 1 Chr 5:26-27). Subsequently, the Ammonites occupied Gad's land (Jer 49:1).

In the postexilic period Gad is mentioned only once—in Ezekiel's vision of the restoration of Israel (Ez 48:1, 27-28, 34). In the NT, Gad is mentioned only in the book of Revelation, in the list of the tribes sealed by God (Rv 7:5).

See also Israel, History of; Gad (Person) #1.

GAD*, Valley of

Translation of a Hebrew phrase in 2 Samuel 24:5, meaning literally "the river or streambed of Gad." It is rendered "in the midst of the river of Gad" (KJV), "in the middle of the valley, toward Gad" (RSV), "the valley of Gad" (ASV) and "in the direction of Gad" (NLT). The valley of Gad was the beginning point for David's census, and the "river" or "valley" is undoubtedly the Arnon.

GADARA*, GADARENES

City of the Decapolis and its inhabitants, mentioned only once in the better manuscripts of the NT. Jesus had crossed to the eastern side of the Sea of Galilee and healed the demoniac named Legion, whom he encountered in "the country of the Gadarenes" (Mt 8:28). Mark's account in 5:1 and Luke's in 8:26, 37 read "Gerasenes." (The KJV, following the Textus Receptus, has variant names here; in Matthew 8:28 it reads "Gergesenes," and in Mark and Luke it reads "Gadarenes.") The variant names among the Gospel writers may be due to the fact that Gerasa was the wider

geographical area of which Gadara was a chief city. Geographers conclude that the most likely location for the leap of the swine into the sea would have been a strip of steep coastline near Gergesa, a smaller, less important town of the area. This would fit another suggestion that Matthew was a native of the region and so he pinpointed the precise place, while Mark and Luke intended to point out the general location for their Greek and Roman readers, since Gergesa was small and relatively unknown, while Gadara was a Greek city of some importance.

The name Gadara indicates that the city was of Semitic origin. It was located five to six miles (8 to 10 kilometers) southeast of the Sea of Galilee, and its territory included the hot springs of el Hamme, north of the Yarmuk River. The first reference to it in history was when it was captured by Antiochus III (218 BC). Later, it was taken by the Jews under Alexander Janneus (103 BC), and the inhabitants were enslaved and forced to receive the law of Moses. The city was demolished by the Jews, but when the area was reconquered by Pompey, it was rebuilt (63 BC). It became a free city under Pompey and joined the federation of Greek cities in the Transjordan known as the Decapolis. Augustus Caesar added Gadara to the territory of Herod the Great (30 BC), and at Herod's death it was annexed to Syria (4 BC). During the Jewish rebellion (AD 66–70), Vespasian took the city, and it continued to flourish for many years. It was the seat of a Christian bishopric from AD 325 until the Muslim conquest. *See* Decapolis; Gerasa, Gerasenes; Gergesa, Gergesenes.

GADDI

Man from Manasseh's tribe sent by Moses to search out the land of Canaan (Nm 13:11).

GADDIEL

Sodi's son from Zebulun's tribe, sent by Moses to search out the land of Canaan (Nm 13:10).

GADFLY

Any of a number of large flies, including the horsefly and botfly, that irritate livestock. King Nebuchadnezzar is called a gadfly in the only biblical reference to this insect (Jer 46:20). *See* Animals (Fly).

GADI

Father of Menahem. Menahem revolted and killed Shallum, king of Israel, placing himself on the throne as king (2 Kgs 15:14, 17).

GADITE

Member of Gad's tribe (Dt 3:12, 16). *See* Gad (Person) #1; Gad, Tribe of.

GAHAM

Son of Nahor, Abraham's brother, and his concubine Reumah (Gn 22:24).

GAHAR

Ancestor of a group of temple assistants that returned to Jerusalem with Zerubbabel after the exile (Ezr 2:47; Neh 7:49).

GAIUS

1. Native of Macedonia and traveling companion of Paul during the apostle's third missionary journey. He and Aristarchus were both seized at Ephesus during the riot caused by Demetrius the silversmith (Acts 19:29).
2. Native of Derbe in Lycaonia, who traveled with Paul from Ephesus to Macedonia (Acts 20:4). Some have identified him with #1 above.
3. Prominent believer in Corinth and host to Paul and the whole church there (Rom 16:23). Since Romans was written in Corinth, the Gaius mentioned in 1 Corinthians 1:14 was probably the same person. If so, he was baptized by Paul.

4. Man to whom John addressed his third letter (3 Jn 1:1).

GALAL

1. Levite and Mica's son, who returned from exile in Babylon (1 Chr 9:15).
2. Levite and forefather of Obadiah (Abda). Obadiah returned from exile in Babylon (1 Chr 9:16; Neh 11:17).

GALATIA Ancient kingdom resulting from migrations of Gallic people from the west and settlement on the central plain of Asia Minor. An earlier migratory movement resulted in the sack of Rome by the Gauls (or Celts) in 390 BC, but in a later attempt to overrun Greece the Gallic invaders were repulsed. That unsuccessful invasion into Greece led the Gauls to turn their attention to Asia Minor. They penetrated the larger part of the area but were defeated by Attalus I in 230 BC. As a result, they became restricted to that part of Asia later known as Galatia. By that time, the Gauls consisted of three tribes, the Trocmi, Tolistobogii, and Tectosages, which settled into the towns of Tavium, Pessinus, and Ancyra, respectively. In 189 BC these Galatians were subdued by the Romans but were allowed to govern themselves.

After the death of Amyntas in 25 BC, Galatia became a Roman province. Within its boundaries were the ethnic areas of Galatia proper, Lycaonia, Isauria, and parts of Phrygia and Pisidia. The new province, therefore, included the towns of Derbe, Lystra, Iconium, and Pisidian Antioch, all of which the apostle Paul visited on his first missionary journey. The term "Galatia" was used in two different ways, one to describe the area occupied by the Gauls in the north, and the other to describe the whole Roman province, including the southern towns. That ambiguity has given rise to a problem over the destination of Paul's letter to the Galatians.

The original inhabitants of north Galatia were Phrygians, many of whom still remained in the first century AD, together with some Greeks and a fairly large community of Jews. Although the area was cosmopolitan, the Celtic element predominated. These people were known for their sturdy independence as well as for their drunkenness and revelings. In religious matters there is evidence that they were highly superstitious and were especially attracted to the wild rites of the goddess Cybele.

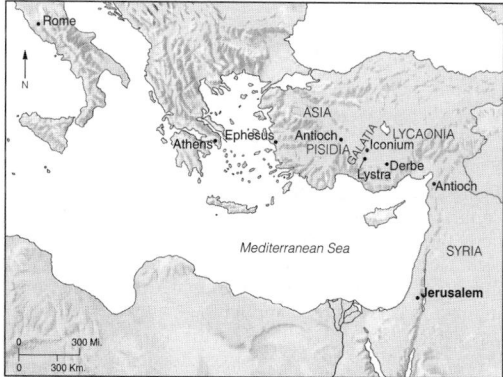

Galatia and the Surrounding Regions Paul and Barnabas, thrown out of Antioch in Pisidia, descended the mountains, going east into Lycaonia. They went first to Iconium, a commercial center on the road between Asia and Syria. After preaching there, they had to flee to Lystra, 25 miles (40.2 kilometers) south. Paul was stoned in Lystra, but he and Barnabas traveled the 50 miles (80.4 kilometers) to Derbe, a border town. The pair then boldly retraced their steps.

In towns of the southern region, Greek influence was more pronounced, especially among the more educated members of the communities. But the Phrygian element was still strong among the humbler inhabitants. They, too, were predominately devotees of Cybele, although there the cult had become modified by Greek influences. In Pisidian Antioch, for instance, the goddess was known as the Genius of Antioch, while in Iconium she was known as Athena Polias.

Geographically the northern towns, situated on a well-watered plateau and served by a major road from the Aegean shores to the west, became prosperous centers of commerce. But access from north to south was difficult and communication poor because of the mountainous terrain leading up to the plateau. The southern towns were situated on the route between Syria and Asia. Their strategic location explains why churches were established in those towns on Paul's first missionary journey (cf. Acts 13–14).

Galatia, linked with Phrygia, is mentioned in Acts 16:6 and 18:23, but it is not clear whether Paul ever visited or established churches in the northern area. The only other references to Galatia in the NT are probably to the southern towns (1 Cor 16:1; 2 Tm 4:10; 1 Pt 1:1). *See* Galatians, Letter to the.

GALATIANS, Letter to the This letter has an important place in the NT. It reveals much of Paul's character and sheds light on his teaching. It has appropriately been called the charter of Christian liberty.

PREVIEW

• Author
• Destination and Date
• Purpose and Theological Teaching
• Content

Author The author of the epistle is explicitly stated to be Paul the apostle (Gal 1:1). The letter gives some brief but telling glimpses of his experience before he became a Christian. He mentions his former life in Judaism (v 13). The fact that he had been a thoroughly devout Jew has an important bearing on what he writes in this letter. He remembered his passionate devotion to his former faith, in whose cause he had violently persecuted the church of God. He reminded the Galatians about this, for the Jewish traditions had meant a great deal to him. There is no doubt that he had once regarded his violent opposition to the church as a religious act of the highest order. Indeed, his strong devotion to Judaism sets in clear relief the remarkable transformation that occurred when he became a Christian. A revelation from God, he was convinced, gave him special authority to write the way he did.

In this epistle he mentioned two features of his conversion experience that had a profound effect on him. One is the purpose of God for his life, which he recognized as reaching back even before he was born (v 15). He did not go into detail, but he never tired of talking about the grace of God. He had turned his back on the idea of earning merit through his own efforts. The second aspect of his conversion that deeply impressed him was the recognition that his call to preach could be traced to that occasion. When he preached to the Galatians, he did so with divine authority because he was conscious of having received a divine commission. The apostles and elders of the church did not decide it would be a good thing for him to preach the gospel; it was God who planned it. Moreover, Paul was equally convinced that the gospel he preached was not of his own making. He had received it through a revelation of Jesus Christ (v 12).

Paul went to some lengths to demonstrate that he had received his apostleship from God (1:1). He was conscious not only of a call to preach but also of a call to exercise apostolic authority on an equal footing with the Jerusalem apostles. He certainly seemed to be on the defensive, but this was prompted by the special situation that had arisen among the Galatians and that caused this letter to be written.

Paul gives one biographical detail in this letter that is not mentioned in his other letters. He states that after his conversion he went away into Arabia (1:17). The apostle does not tell us what he did there, but probably he was quietly reorienting his thoughts. According to the book of Acts, when he returned to Damascus he powerfully proved that Jesus was the Messiah (Acts 9:22). He also refers to traveling in Syria and Cilicia (Gal 1:21), which must have been prior to his first missionary journey.

Destination and Date It is impossible to determine the date of this letter before discussing its destination.

Destination Paul addresses his letter to the Galatians. But there has been much debate over where they lived, because the term Galatia was used in two different senses. It was used of the province that stretched from the borders of Pamphylia in the southern part of Asia Minor to the border of Pontus toward the northern seacoast. The term was also used of a part of the province in the north where a group of people from Gaul had settled and given their name to the whole area. Hence "Galatia" could mean either the geographical area in the north or the whole province. It is not easy to decide what the term meant when used by Paul. The debate is between the view that the term was used geographically, in which case some churches in the north are in mind (North Galatian Theory), or politically, in which case Paul may be referring to the churches in southern Galatia founded on his first missionary journey (South Galatian Theory). It may at first sight seem a quite unimportant issue, but since the decision affects the date of the letter and to some extent its occasion and purpose, a review of the positions must be made.

Until the beginning of the 20th century, no one seems to have questioned that Paul was writing to the inhabitants of the geographical district in the northern part of the province. This view agrees with the oldest use of the term, since the provinces did not come into existence until 25 BC, whereas there were Galatians in the north some time before this. It is reasonable to suppose that the southerners would not have taken too kindly to being addressed as "Galatians." It may be argued that most people in those days would have thought of the northern peoples when hearing the name.

Luke's habit when writing Acts was to use geographical rather than political descriptions of places. He refers, for instance, to Lystra and Derbe as cities of Lycaonia, not as cities of Galatia. It is reasonable, therefore, that when he refers to Phrygia and Galatia in Acts 16:6 and 18:23, he means that Paul went through the northern area. There were three main towns in that district—Ancyra, Tavium, and Pessinus—and it would therefore follow that Paul must have established churches there.

The traditional North Galatian view has, however, been challenged. It is pointed out that although Luke prefers geographical descriptions, Paul prefers political ones for grouping his churches. In this letter he mentions the churches of Christ in Judea (1:22). Elsewhere he mentions the "churches of Asia" (1 Cor 16:19). Several times Paul refers to the believers in Macedonia (e.g.,

2 Cor 8:1; 9:2; 1 Thes 4:10) and in Achaia (1 Cor 16:15; 2 Cor 1:1), while both are mentioned together in Romans 15:26, 2 Corinthians 9:2, and 1 Thessalonians 1:7. This seems to be Paul's normal habit, in which case a letter addressed to the Galatians would be circulated to all the existing churches in the province of Galatia.

South Galatian supporters do not agree that the southern people would have resented the name Galatians, maintaining that there would have been no other name available with which to describe them. One fairly positive piece of evidence is found in Paul's statement that it was because of a bodily ailment that he first preached to the Galatians (Gal 4:13). But a glance at the map, particularly a relief map, would show that the route to the northern area was over mountainous terrain, and it is difficult to think that a sick man would have attempted it. Under the southern theory, the journey would have been much shorter and less arduous.

Another argument in support of the South Galatian Theory assumes that Acts 20:4, which mentions the names of those who accompanied Paul to Jerusalem, is referring to delegates appointed by the churches in support of the collection to aid the poor churches of Judea. If this assumption is right, it is noticeable that no representative is included from the northern area, although both Gaius and Timothy were from the south. This would be more weighty if Acts had actually mentioned the collection. One last point is that Barnabas is mentioned three times (Gal 2:1, 9, 13) suggesting that he is known to the readers. Yet according to Acts, he accompanied Paul only on the first missionary journey.

It is difficult to reach a conclusion, but it seems that the arguments for a South Galatian Theory have more weight than those for the older theory.

Date Under the North Galatian Theory, it is claimed that the letter was written after the events mentioned in Acts 18:23—that is, during the course of the third missionary journey (c. AD 56), possibly while Paul was at Ephesus or soon after.

On the other hand, if the letter was addressed to the south Galatian churches founded on the first missionary journey, any date after that journey is possible, including during the third journey, as mentioned above. But a further possibility opens up since a much earlier date might more readily fit into the background of the letter. Thus, it is possible that this letter is among the earliest that Paul wrote.

The main problem with assigning a date is that in Galatians 1–2 Paul mentions two visits to Jerusalem (1:18; 2:1), whereas Acts mentions (or implies) three visits (Acts 9:26; 11:29-30; 15:2). It has traditionally been supposed that the second visit (2:1) can be identified with the events of Acts 15. This would mean that Paul was giving his own account of the decisions of the so-called Council of Jerusalem. There is much to be said for this view. There are similarities between the two passages. In both, Barnabas is mentioned. In both, questions are asked about the circumcision of the Gentiles. And in both, Paul and Barnabas give a report about the matter to the Jerusalem leaders. The main difficulty is that Paul's wording in Galatians 2:1 suggests that this event took place on his *second* visit to Jerusalem, whereas Acts 15 relates his *third* visit. It is traditionally explained that on the second visit Paul and Barnabas had no contact with the apostles but simply handed over the collection from the Antioch church to the Jerusalem elders (cf. Acts 11:30). A difficulty with this view is that Galatians 2 speaks only of conversations with the three leading apostles at Jerusalem and does not mention the whole church (as Acts 15 clearly does). Paul does not refer to the decision reached by the church, but only to his agreement with those he calls the "pillar" apostles. It could, of course, be that before the general meeting of Acts 15 (which occured in AD 50), Paul and Barnabas had a behind-the-scenes meeting with the leaders and preferred to mention the decision reached with them rather than quote an ecclesiastical edict. This may also explain another difficulty—the lack of any mention of the prohibitions that the Jerusalem church imposed on the Gentiles (Acts 15:20). Paul simply mentions the need to remember the poor (Gal 2:10). Yet another difficulty with the traditional view is that Paul mentions his dispute with Peter over the question of Gentile-Jewish fellowship (vv 11-14) *after* his account of the agreement reached with the Jerusalem apostles. This places Peter in a compromising position. It is difficult to explain his inconsistency. He may have agreed that Gentiles should not be circumcised, but then vacillated over the question of fellowship.

An alternative view suggests that when Paul and Barnabas went to Jerusalem with the collection they also had private talks with the leading apostles. Acts 11:29-30 is set in a period of political activity against the apostles (Acts 12 records the martyrdom of James and the arrest of Peter), and this may explain the private nature of the meeting. This interpretation would explain why Paul makes no mention of the church's decision—because the meeting happened before the Jerusalem Council. It would also make it easier to explain Peter's actions at Antioch, if this behavior occurred before the church as a whole had discussed and resolved the matter. According to this view, Paul's Letter to the Galatians may be the earliest of his letters (pre–AD 50).

There are, however, some difficulties with this view. Acts 11:30 mentions no apostles as meeting Paul and Barnabas. Nor is there any reference to Titus, whom Paul says they took with them (Gal 2:1). Further, Paul's references to preaching among the Gentiles (v 2) would seem to require a date after the first missionary journey, unless he was thinking of his work in Antioch, a Jewish-Gentile church.

It is difficult to decide between these two views. Chronological considerations (based on Paul's mention of 14 years in 2:1) slightly favor a later date, while the relationship of the content of this epistle to the Jerusalem Council (AD 50) points to an early date.

Purpose and Theological Teaching Difficulties had arisen in the Galatian churches because a group of people had been insisting that Gentiles must be circumcised. These people must have been Judaizers, that is, Christian Jews who could see no hope for Gentiles unless they accepted circumcision as an initiatory rite. Linked with this was a criticism of Paul's apostolic status. The opponents were claiming the support of the Jerusalem apostles, whom they regarded as superior to Paul. This would explain why Paul saw the issue so clearly as a challenge to the gospel he preached. His letter strongly expressed his understanding of the seriousness of the situation.

Interpretation will vary slightly according to which date one assigns to the letter. If it was written before the Jerusalem Council (Acts 15), the circumcision issue had not yet been thrashed out and the Galatian situation would be the first major crisis over it. But if the Jerusalem Council had already happened, the south Galatian churches would already have received those decisions (16:4), and apparently had allowed themselves to be affected by Judaizers who took a harder line than the Jerusalem apostles had. If the northern churches are indi-

cated, there is no direct evidence to show that they had received the decrees.

We may conclude that the apostle's aim in this letter is twofold—to maintain the validity of his apostleship, and to uphold the character of the gospel he preached. In the first part of the letter he is concerned to show his relationship with the Jerusalem "pillar" apostles in order to demonstrate his equality with them, while at the same time claiming his independence of them. Moreover, he asserts that there is only one gospel, which suggests that his opponents were charging him with preaching a different gospel. But he claims to have received his gospel from God, not from men.

In the course of his letter, Paul expressed some important theological truths. The main body of the letter issues a strong warning against a form of legalism that is applicable not only to the situation Paul confronted in the Galatian churches but wherever dependence on legal observances is considered essential for salvation. If a Gentile could not become a Christian without being circumcised, it would not only make an external rite a condition for Christian salvation but in addition would imply a commitment to keep the whole Jewish law. When Paul argued against justification by works of the law, he showed the superiority of justification by faith or lawkeeping. The whole letter extols the doctrine of grace.

Nevertheless, in contesting the doctrine of works, the ' apostle gave no support to spiritual license. He posited that the alternative to legalism is not the absence of all restraint. Although Christ has secured freedom for the believer, that freedom must not be used to indulge the flesh (Gal 5:13). Indeed, Paul's exposition of the Christian life in this letter is of a high moral order. He sets the standard himself by declaring that he has been crucified with Christ (2:20). Not only is this letter a charter for Christian liberty, but it is also a charter for Christian living.

Content

Introduction (1:1-5) The opening to this letter is more abrupt than those in Paul's other letters. He omits the usual thanksgiving and expands the usual greeting. In the first words he strongly affirms the divine origin of his apostleship.

The Opponents (1:6-10) Paul is astonished that the Galatians have allowed themselves to be influenced so quickly by those who were perverting the gospel. He expresses an anathema against any who preach another gospel.

A Defense of His Apostleship (1:11–2:14) There are several stages in Paul's argument about his own position. He states that his teaching has come from God, not from men, showing his awareness that God has not only called him to be an apostle but has also sanctioned his gospel. It is important for him to make clear that he is not dependent on others for his position, although he proceeds to show that there is no difference between him and the leading apostles (1:11-12). He next contrasts his former zeal in Judaism with his calling to preach the gospel, again emphasizing the divine nature of his call (vv 13-17).

He then proceeds to mention that he has on two occasions had meetings with the Jerusalem apostles. As a result, he has been offered the right hand of fellowship—a way of showing that there is no disagreement between them. It was agreed that Paul should be entrusted with the gospel for the uncircumcised, and that Peter should go to the circumcised. There was no questioning of Paul's apostleship. They all agreed on the Christian responsibility to remember the poor (1:18–2:10).

In order to give a tangible example of his apostolic position, Paul mentions the occasion of his public rebuke of Peter. Peter had acted inconsistently for fear of certain men who had come from James in Jerusalem, and who were representatives of the circumcision party. Paul's challenge to Peter sets the scene for the introduction of the doctrinal part of the letter (2:11-14).

A *Defense of the Gospel* (2:15–4:31) Paul introduces the issue of justification by works of the law and contrasts it with justification by faith. He sees the whole situation as a choice between Christ and the law (2:15-21).

His aim is to show the superiority of Christianity over Judaism in the matter of salvation. He notes first that the Galatians had become Christians through the Spirit and wonders what is possessing them to return to the works of the law, which Paul then equates with the "flesh" (3:1-5).

Abraham is brought into the discussion presumably because the opponents were maintaining that only Abraham's seed would receive the inheritance, and circumcision was regarded as an indispensable sign of a son of the covenant. But Paul points out that even Abraham was justified by faith, not by the law (3:6-9).

Indeed, the law could only bring a curse on those who disobeyed. This leads Paul to show how Christ has become a curse for us. Hence, he claims that in Christ we may still inherit the blessing promised to Abraham (3:10-14).

Paul anticipates that some may say it is invalid to appeal to the promise to Abraham to counteract justification by works of the law. He shows that the promise preceded the law by four centuries and cannot be invalidated by it (3:15-18).

This leads the apostle to reflect on the function of the law. He points out that it served to prepare the way for Christ by showing mankind's need and by revealing its own inability to give life. Paul calls the law our custodian, whose function (in ancient times) was to guard and guide a son until he reached the age of independence (3:19-29).

The contrast between those under a guardian versus fully independent sons causes Paul to reflect on the superior position of sons. The Spirit of God has enabled believers to call God "Abba" (Father), something the law could not do (4:1-7).

The apostle has made his point, but he supports it with a personal appeal. He reminds his readers of their state of bondage before they became Christians and deplores that they have returned to such a state in wanting to observe ritual feast days after the Jewish manner. He also reminds them of the former affectionate relationship they had with him when they first became Christians. He is deeply affected by their present attitude (4:8-20). Finally, Paul appeals to a scriptural allegory in support of his argument. He sees Isaac and Ishmael, both sons of Abraham, as representing the distinction between sonship and slavery, which he has already mentioned (vv 21-31).

Practical Advice (5:1–6:10) Paul proceeds to draw out the practical consequences of his doctrinal arguments. He sets out the way in which those who are liberated in Christ should live. They should not commit themselves to Judaism by submitting to circumcision (5:1-6). Paul again attacks those who were leading the Galatians astray (vv 7-12). The new principle that must replace legalism is love. Love is possible only by living in the Spirit. This

will lead not only to a rejection of the works of the flesh but also to the development of the fruit of the Spirit (5:13-26). The spiritual man will have a concern for the burdened and will seek to help others, particularly fellow Christians (6:1-10).

Conclusion (6:11-18) Paul now takes the pen and writes his final word with his own hand. He sees fit to contrast his own aim in glorying in the cross of Christ with his opponents' aim to glory in the flesh. There are no greetings at the end of this letter, only a request that no one should bother him further.

See also Galatia; Judaizers; Law, Biblical Concept of; Paul, The Apostle.

GALBANUM One of the ingredients used to make a special perfume for the tabernacle (Ex 30:34). Galbanum comes from a waxy, brownish gum excreted from the lower part of a plant that is a member of the carrot or parsley family and is native to Syria and Persia. It is a tall herb that bears small, greenish-white flowers and fruit at the stem tip in bunches or clusters. Its leaves are compound and divided into many fine parts like the leaves of parsley or carrots. An incision made in the stem a few inches above soil level yields a milky sap that hardens. Galbanum is presently used in the manufacture of varnish.

Galbanum is mentioned in the apocryphal book of Ecclesiasticus as having a pleasant odor (24:15). Although galbanum is not an agreeable perfume when used alone, it was evidently mixed with other substances to yield a fragrant ointment.

See also Plants.

GALEED Name meaning literally "a heap of witness." Jacob gave this name to a pile of stones erected as a witness to the pact of friendship made between himself and his father-in-law, Laban, who named the cairn Jegarsahadutha (Gn 31:47-48). Its location is unknown. The name Galeed is not to be confused with the name Gilead, designation of the territory east of the Jordan.

GALILEE Area in northern Palestine that, in Israel's earlier history, had boundaries that were not clearly defined but that became more precisely defined in the period of Roman rule. The English name Galilee comes from two Hebrew words meaning "circuit" or "district."

Historical Background In OT times Galilee was not significant in Israelite life, but in NT times it was a prominent Jewish population center. Galilee is first mentioned in the Bible as the location of Kedesh, a city of refuge in the hill country of Naphtali (Jos 20:7; cf. 21:32; 1 Chr 6:76).

Galilee originally designated the area occupied by the tribes of Naphtali, Zebulun (Is 9:1), and possibly Asher (if Cabul in Jos 19:27 is the same city as in 1 Kgs 9:11-13). None of those tribes was able to completely expel the original Canaanite inhabitants (Jgs 1:30-33; 2:1-4), and as a result, Galilee tended to be racially mixed. The cities that King Solomon gave to Hiram, gentile king of Tyre, were within Galilee (1 Kgs 9:11), and the gentile intermixture in that area may have influenced Solomon's choice of those cities for a gift. This racially mixed condition is also the probable basis for the designation in Isaiah 9:1, "Galilee of the nations" (cf. Mt 4:15; 1 Macc 5:15).

During the monarchy, Galilee was a buffer zone between Israel and Syria, and it bore the brunt of Syrian invasions against Israel. This fact is cited by the prophet Isaiah (Is 9:1), but he saw it as the prelude to a brighter day when the messianic king would reign. Galilee was conquered by Syrian King Ben-hadad (1 Kgs 15:20) and was probably recovered by Israel's King Ahab. Galilee was later subjugated by the Arameans under Hazael (2 Kgs 10:32; 12:18; 13:22) and regained by Jeroboam II (2 Kgs 14:23-25). As a result of Assyrian conquests in the area of Damascus and Galilee in 732 BC by Tiglath-pileser III (2 Kgs 15:29), more Gentiles were imported into the area while many of the Jewish inhabitants were deported. This naturally led to greater gentile influence and domination in Galilee. Under the successive influence of Babylonia, Persia, Greece, and Syria, Galilee was constantly experiencing infiltration and migration. From the time of the Assyrian conquest of Israel to about the end of the second century BC, Galilee's population was dominated by Gentiles, with only a few Jews.

The Jews remaining in Galilee were brought to Judea by Simon Maccabeus in 164 BC (1 Macc 5:21-23). Galilee was conquered by Aristobulus I (104–103 BC), who forced the inhabitants to be circumcised and to submit to Jewish laws, a work that probably already had been initiated by John Hyrcanus (134–104 BC).

Sea of Galilee

Herod the Great (ruler under Rome, 37–4 BC) affixed Galilee to his kingdom, and more Jews were attracted there. Josephus recorded that Galilee had 240 cities and villages and 100,000 men available to fight against the Romans. After the death of Herod the Great, Galilee was included in the tetrarchy of Herod Antipas (4 BC–AD 39). With the banishment of Herod Antipas in AD 39, Galilee was added to the territory of Herod Agrippa I, who ruled it until he died in AD 44. Rome directly administered Galilee until it was put under the rule of Herod Agrippa II. By siding with the Romans during the Jewish revolts, he was able to retain his position until AD 100. In spite of the Galileans' attempt to gain independence, the revolutionary faction was brought under subjection by Vespasian in AD 67. After Herod Agrippa II's death, Galilee became part of the Roman province of Syria.

Following the fall of Jerusalem in AD 70, the Sanhedrin and many other Jews of southern Palestine flocked to Galilee. As a result, such cities as Tiberias and Sepphoris became Jewish, and the dispersed Jews came to think of Galilee as their center. Tiberias became a center for Jewish learning, and it was there that such major contributions as the Tiberian system of vowel pointing the Hebrew consonantal text were made, as well as the formulation of the Mishnah and the Palestinian Talmud.

From about AD 451 until the Muslim rule over Galilee began in the seventh century, Galilee was governed by the Christian patriarchate of Jerusalem, set up by the Council of Chalcedon in AD 451. Muslim rule from the seventh century on was continuous except for the intervals caused by the twelfth-century Crusades and World War I. All of Galilee has been included in the modern state of Israel since its establishment in 1948.

Boundaries Galilee was bounded on the east by the upper Jordan River and the Sea of Galilee and on the south by the plain of Esdraelon, which served as a natural boundary between Galilee and Samaria. At times the plain was included in Galilee, as it was during the intertestamental period (1 Macc 10:30; 12:47-49). While the northern boundary was uncertain and variable during Galilee's history, in NT times it reached to Lake Huleh. The western boundary followed the Mediterranean Sea to Mt Carmel.

From the time of the divided kingdom until the Assyrian conquest of Galilee (734 BC), it was the northernmost part of the kingdom of Israel. The area was divided into upper Galilee and lower Galilee by the plain of Ramah, which ran between Capernaum and Ptolemais (cf. Jdt 1:8; 1 Macc 12:49; Josephus's *War* 3.3.1). In the Mishnah (compilation of early rabbinical interpretation of the Law), Galilee is divided into three parts corresponding to the natural divisions of plain, hill country, and mountain. Under Roman rule, Galilee was about 25 to 30 miles (40 to 50 kilometers) from east to west and about 35 to 40 miles (55 to 65 kilometers) from north to south.

Geography The attractive Galilean landscape is made up of volcanic limestone hills and fertile alluvial plains. Its climate is cooler than that of any other part of Palestine, and its beauty and fertility contrast sharply with the barren, sun-baked hills of southern Palestine.

The physical features range from the high mountains in the north to the plain of Esdraelon in the south. Mt Tabor is prominent on the east, while Mt Carmel stands out on the west. Much of upper Galilee is 3,000 feet (914.4 meters) above sea level, and in NT times it was largely forested and less densely inhabited than lower Galilee. Lower Galilee starts at 1,500 to 2,000 feet (450 to 600 meters) above sea level and descends sharply to the Sea of Galilee, more than 600 feet (182.9 meters) below sea level.

Besides the average annual rainfall of 25 inches (63.5 centimeters), Galilee is watered by the streams that flow from springs in the hills and are the main sources of the beautiful Kishon River at Janin, and the headwaters of the Jordan River, the largest river in Palestine. The ground is also moistened by heavy dews resulting from climatic conditions created by the Lebanon mountain range to the north.

Cities Among the more notable cities in Galilee's early history were Kedesh in Naphtali, a city of refuge (Jos 20:7; 21:32; 1 Chr 6:76), and Hazor, about 10 miles (16.1 kilometers) north of the Sea of Galilee (Jos 11:10; 1 Kgs 9:15). During the time of Christ, Chorazin (Mt 11:21) and Capernaum (4:13; 11:23) were prominent cities located in the northeast near the Sea of Galilee. Capernaum seems to have been a center for Jesus' ministry in the area (Mt 4:13; Mk 2:1; 9:33; etc.). Nazareth is especially significant as the city of Christ's childhood (Mt 2:22-23; Lk 2:39; 4:16; etc.). Nain (Lk 7:11-17), located on the northern edge of the mountain now called Little Hermon, and Cana of Galilee (Jn 2:1-11) also figured prominently in Christ's ministry. Sepphoris and Tiberias were important cities during Roman administration.

Roads and Travel Many roads traversed Galilee, and those in NT times were superior due to Roman construction and maintenance.

Among the best-known trade routes was the Via Maris (the Way of the Sea), which ran through Galilee on its way from Damascus to Egypt. Another main road ran from Tiberias, near the Sea of Galilee, to Acco (Ptolemais), a port on the Phoenician coast. Major caravan routes also connected Galilee with the markets of the East. The area was tied together by a network of spurs and connecting roads that branched from the main highways.

Inhabitants The occupants of Galilee (Galileans) were basically Jewish in religious and patriotic orientation, but they were composed of various ethnic elements. The influence of this mixture was sufficient to cause recognizable differences in speech from that of southern Palestine (cf. Mt 26:69, 73). The Galileans absorbed more Greek and Roman influences than did the Judean Jews. The racial mixture, differences in speech, and location caused Judean Jews to view Galilee and its inhabitants with contempt (Jn 1:46; 7:41, 52).

Lower Galilee was densely settled with villages, and in NT times the population was probably about three million. The fertility of the soil and resultant fruitfulness of the country produced a prosperous Jewish populace, particularly in the centuries immediately after the time of Christ.

Government Galilee was under the Roman rule of emperors Augustus and Tiberius during the time of Christ. Roman fortifications throughout Galilee were a constant reminder of the presence and influence of the Roman Empire. During Christ's ministry, Rome installed the tetrarch Herod Antipas (Mt 14:1; Lk 23:5-7) to rule the territory. He was appointed to office when 17 years old. Sepphoris was his first capital; in about AD 22 he built Tiberias on the shore of the Sea of Galilee as his new capital, in honor of the emperor.

Products Abundant crops enabled Galilee to provide produce for the neighboring Phoenician cities of Tyre and Sidon around the middle of the first century AD. Main crops included grapes, pomegranates, olives, and grains. Fishing in the Sea of Galilee was a prominent business in NT times (Mk 1:14-20).

Jesus and Galilee Jesus was raised in Galilee (Lk 4:16), and 11 of his 12 disciples were from there (Judas Iscariot was the only Judean).

The culture, commerce, farming, and fishing business of the area formed the background for much of Jesus' ministry, as his parables show (Mt 20:1-8; 21:33; Mk 4:3; Lk 13:6-9). The first three Gospels are largely occupied with Christ's ministry in Galilee, with much of it being spent around the Sea of Galilee. Most of his parables (19 of 32) were spoken here, and the vast majority of his miracles (25 of 33) were performed in Galilee. Jesus received his greatest response in this region. The Sermon on the Mount was spoken in Galilee, and one of its mountains was the scene of the Lord's transfiguration. Many of the women who followed Christ and ministered to him also came from there (Mt 27:55). Two of Christ's most significant postresurrection appearances took place in Galilee (Mt 28:16-20; Jn 21:1-23), and one of Christ's own titles, Jesus of Nazareth (Jn 1:45), identified him as a Galilean.

Galileans Since Jesus and most of the 12 disciples were from Galilee, it was natural for the term to be applied to all of his followers, especially since it implied that the movement was not as pure as Judean Judaism. Some interpreters believe that Luke 22:59 is an example of the use of "Galilean" as a title; in Acts 1:11 and 2:7 it is merely a geographical reference. One sure reference to

Christians by that title appears in the work of the pagan philosopher Epictetus (AD 50?–135?), who was impressed with how Christians died for their faith. It is not clear how common the title of Galilean was, but it had obviously spread from Judea to Rome, where Epictetus lived.

See also Palestine; Sea of Galilee.

GALILEE, Sea of *See* Sea of Galilee.

GALL
1. Yellowish-brown bitter secretion of the liver (Jb 16:13) or the organ containing the gall (20:25).
2. Very bitter, poisonous herb that cannot be identified with certainty, although the hemlock, colocynth, and poppy have been suggested. The Hebrew word occurs periodically in the OT and refers to (1) "gall" in Deuteronomy 29:18 (KJV); (2) the "poison" of a venomous snake in Job 20:14, 16; (3) "gall" or "poison" given to a person for food in Psalm 69:21; (4) divine punishment upon Israel as "water of gall" (Jer 8:14; 9:15; 23:15, KJV; or "poison," RSV); (5) Israel's bitter experience of divine judgment (Lam 3:5, 19); (6) divine judgment upon Israel sprouting up like "hemlock" in the furrows of the field (Hos 10:4, KJV; or "poisonous weeds," RSV); and (7) Israel's perversion of justice by turning "judgment into gall" (Am 6:12, KJV).
3. "Substance of an unpleasant taste" in the NT. Matthew 27:34 mentions the gall mixed with wine that was offered to Christ on the cross. Mark 15:23 speaks of "myrrh," which may be a more specific identification of the liquid mixed with the wine. In Acts 8:23 Peter described the spiritual state of Simon the magician as being "in the gall of bitterness."

See also Plants (Gourd, Wild).

GALLIM Village near Gibeah of Saul and Anathoth in Benjamin, north of Jerusalem and close to Bahurim (1 Sm 25:44; Is 10:30); probably present-day Khirbet Kakul.

GALLIO Marcus Annaeus Seneca's son, and brother of the philosopher Seneca, who lived from 3 BC to AD 65. Born in Cordoba, Spain, Gallio came to Rome during Tiberius's reign. His given name was Marcus Annaeus Novatus, but he assumed the name Gallio after his adoption by the rhetorician Lucius Junius Gallio. The wealthy Lucius trained him for his career in administration and government.

Gallio served as Roman proconsul of Achaia sometime between AD 51 and 53. During the apostle Paul's first visit to Corinth, the Jews brought the apostle before the proconsul, accusing him of having persuaded people to practice religion in an unlawful manner (Acts 18:12-17). Gallio abruptly dismissed the charge since it dealt with Jewish and not Roman law. His action reflected the characteristic behavior of Roman governors toward religious disputes.

Forced to leave Achaia because of illness, Gallio returned to Rome as consul suffectus under Nero. His involvement in a conspiracy against Nero resulted in temporary pardon but eventual obligatory suicide.

GALLIO INSCRIPTION* Dated Greek inscription found in Delphi, Greece, mentioning Gallio as proconsul, and establishing the time of Paul's initial visit to Corinth (cf. Acts 18:12-17). *See* Chronology of the Bible (New Testament); Inscriptions.

GALLOWS Upright frame with a crossbeam and a rope for hanging criminals. In the book of Esther, a gibbet is mentioned, upon which men were impaled and left to hang in scorn. *See* Criminal Law and Punishment.

GAMALIEL

1. Pedahzur's son and captain or prince of Manasseh's tribe (Nm 10:23). Gamaliel was chosen by Moses to help take the census in the wilderness near Mt Sinai (1:10) and to organize the tribe for the journey to the Promised Land (2:20). He participated in the special 12-day ceremonial offering by the princes at the dedication of the altar following completion of the tabernacle (7:54, 59).
2. Jewish scholar. This man lived in the first century AD and died 18 years before the destruction of Jerusalem in AD 70 by Titus, the Roman general.

When Peter and the other apostles were brought before the enraged and threatening council in Jerusalem, Gamaliel, who was highly respected by the council, offered cautionary advice that probably saved the apostles' lives in that situation (Acts 5:27-40).

Gamaliel is also mentioned in Acts 22:3 as the rabbi with whom the apostle Paul studied as a youth in Jerusalem. During that period in Israel, a number of rabbinical schools evolved. Two of the most influential were the rival Pharisaic schools of Hillel and Shammai. Both of those teachers had vast influence on Jewish thinking. Hillel's school emphasized tradition even above the law. Shammai's school preserved the teaching of the law over the authority of tradition. Hillel's school was the more influential, and its decisions have been held by a great number of later rabbis.

Traditionally, Gamaliel is considered to be the grandson of Hillel, and he was thoroughly schooled in the philosophy and theology of his grandfather's teaching. Gamaliel was a member of the Sanhedrin, the high council of Jews in Jerusalem, and he served as president of the Sanhedrin during the reigns of the Roman emperors Tiberius, Caligula, and Claudius. Unlike other Jewish teachers, he had no antipathy toward Greek learning.

The learning of Gamaliel was so eminent and his influence so great that he is one of only seven Jewish scholars who have been honored by the title Rabban. He was called the "Beauty of the Law." The Talmud even says that "since Rabban Gamaliel died, the glory of the Law has ceased."

GAMMAD Home of mercenaries who served in the army of Tyre, according to Ezekiel's prophecy (Ez 27:11). Gammad may have been located in Syria and is identified as Kumidi in the Tell el-Amarna letters.

GAMMADIMS* KJV form of "men of Gamad" (RSV) in Ezekiel 27:11. *See* Gammad.

GAMUL Priest assigned to temple duty in David's time (1 Chr 24:17).

GANGRENE* Death of tissue due to loss of the vital blood supply to that part of the body. Often the most distal tip of an extremity, such as fingertips or toes, will turn black and surgeons will amputate the dead part to prevent extension and harm to more of the limb or to life itself.

The term "gangrene" occurs only once in Scripture (2 Tm 2:17). Paul warns Timothy that godless talk will encourage more godlessness, just like gangrene tends to spread to surrounding tissues.

Although not identified by name, Asa's disease of the feet (2 Chr 16:12) could have been gangrene. Miriam's leprosy was likened to the flesh of a macerated, gangrenous stillborn's body (Nm 12:12).

See also Medicine and Medical Practice.

GARDEN HOUSE* KJV translation of Beth-haggan in 2 Kings 9:27. *See* Beth-haggan.

GARDEN OF EDEN Location in the east of Eden (Gn 2:8) in the Tigris-Euphrates area of Mesopotamia, referred to 14 times in the OT. The information in Genesis 2:8-10 indicates that it was in the Shinar Plain area, and that four "heads" or branches were formed from the one river flowing through Eden to water the Garden. The heads were the Tigris and Euphrates (both of which are familiar modern rivers) and two rivers that have disappeared—the Pishon and Gihon. The latter were most probably natural water channels, later used as irrigation canals, since in cuneiform there is no separate word for "river" and "irrigation canal." If Pishon and Gihon were in fact irrigation canals, then Genesis places Adamic man in an actual geographical setting and therefore obviates the notion that Eden was a myth. If the above identification is correct, Cush referred to the land of the ancient Kassites, while Havilah may have indicated Arabia.

Eden was the testing ground of man's fidelity to God's commands, and through disobedience, the Garden was lost. It will be regained in the form of the new paradise (Rv 22:14).

See also Adam (Person); Eve; Fall of Man; Tree of Knowledge of Good and Evil; Tree of Life.

GAREB (Person) Warrior among David's mighty soldiers (2 Sm 23:38; 1 Chr 11:40).

GAREB (Place) Hill near Jerusalem mentioned in Jeremiah 31:39 as a future boundary of the city, perhaps on the south or west side.

GARLIC Bulbous herb cultivated for use in cooking (Nm 11:5) *See* Food and Food Preparation; Plants (Onion).

GARMITE Designation for Keilah in 1 Chronicles 4:19. The word, which means "bony," seems to denote strength (the same Hebrew word is used in Jb 40:18 and Prv 25:15).

GASHMU* KJV spelling of Geshem the Arab in Nehemiah 6:6. *See* Geshem.

GASPAR* Traditional name for one of the wise men who brought a gift to Jesus in Matthew 2:1-2. *See* Wise Men.

GATAM Esau's grandson, the fourth son of Eliphaz and an Edomite chief (Gn 36:11, 16; 1 Chr 1:36).

GATE *See* Architecture; City.

GATE BETWEEN THE TWO WALLS Entrance in the southeast part of the city of Jerusalem, possibly the same as the Fountain Gate (2 Kgs 25:4; Jer 39:4). *See* Jerusalem.

GATEKEEPERS Those who guarded gates of the cities and doors of palaces, temples, and other large buildings. Their task was to admit or reject visitors (2 Kgs 7:10-11; 11:4-9). In the Bible these men are variously named as gatekeepers, porters, doorkeepers, and guards.

GATH Walled city (2 Chr 26:6) and one of the five chief cities of the Philistines, which also included Gaza, Ashdod, Ashkelon, and Ekron (Jos 13:3; 1 Sm 6:17), all situated on or near the southern coast of Palestine. Although frequently involved in conflict with the Israelites, the city was apparently not subdued until David's time (1 Chr 18:1). It was a Canaanite city, the home of the giant Goliath (1 Sm 17:4) and other men of great height (2 Sm 21:18-22). A remnant of the Anakim was left, even after the extensive campaigns of Joshua (Jos 10:36-39; 11:21-22).

When the Philistines captured the ark of God, they carried it from Ebenezer to Ashdod, from there to Gath (1 Sm 5:8), and then to Ekron. After many of the Philistines died or were stricken with tumors, the ark was returned to Israel, first to Beth-shemesh and then to Kiriath-jearim (6:14; 7:1). When David fled from Saul, he came to Gath and feigned madness before Achish, the king of the city (21:10-15). During the rebellion of Absalom, 600 Gittites served among David's mercenaries (2 Sm 15:18). According to 2 Chronicles 11:8, Rehoboam fortified the city of Gath, and 2 Kings 12:17 relates that it was taken by Hazael, king of Syria, in the ninth century. But it was apparently again in Philistine control when Uzziah broke down its walls (2 Chr 26:6). The city disappeared after being besieged and conquered by Sargon II in the eighth century BC (Am 6:2).

See also Philistia, Philistines.

GATH-HEPHER Town in Galilee, in Zebulun's territory, which was the birthplace of Jonah (Jos 19:13; 2 Kgs 14:25). Modern el-Meshad occupies the site of Gath-hepher.

GATH-RIMMON
1. City located in the land allotted to Dan's tribe for an inheritance (Jos 19:45). It was assigned as one of the four Levitical cities for the Kohathites in Dan (21:24). Lost to the Canaanites, Gath-rimmon was later regained by Ephraim and included as one of its cities for the sons of Levi (1 Chr 6:69). Its site is identifiable with the modern Tell el-Jerisheh.
    See also Levitical Cities.
2. One of two cities given to the Levites in Manasseh west of the Jordan River (Jos 21:25), suggesting a possible transcription mistake, which is better read as Bileam (cf. 1 Chr 6:70).

GAULANITIS* Small province east of the Sea of Galilee, situated between Mt Hermon and the Yarmuk River and extending perhaps to the Jordan River. It took its name from the ancient town of Golan. Archaeologists have discovered extensive ruins 17 miles (27 kilometers) east of the Sea of Galilee, which they consider to be the remains of Golan. Moses named Golan as a city of refuge for Manasseh's half-tribe east of the Jordan (Dt 4:41, 43), and Joshua assigned it to the Gershonite Levites (Jos 20:8; 21:27; 1 Chr 6:71). According to Josephus, Alexander Janneus suffered a heavy defeat in this place and later destroyed the town (*Antiquities* 8.2.3). Josephus also identified a Judas who led a tax revolt as being from Gaulanitis (18.1.1), whereas Luke called him a Galilean (Acts 5:37). Later, Josephus called him a Galilean as well (*Antiquities* 20.5.2; *War* 2.8.1). It is quite possible that this Judas lived in these places at different times.

After Herod's death in 4 BC, Philip inherited Gaulanitis, making his capital Bethsaida Julias, which he had rebuilt and named after Augustus Caesar's daughter. Jesus traveled in this area (Mk 6:45; 8:22), and it remained under firm Roman control until AD 66, when

the Jewish war broke out. Jewish revolutionaries subsequently hid in its heights and the Romans fought several campaigns here.

See also Golan; Herod, Herodian Family.

GAZA City near the Palestinian coast, about 50 miles (80.5 kilometers) west-southwest of Jerusalem. It has been occupied almost continuously since ancient times; modern Gaza has played an important part in the conflict between Arabs and Israelis. Gazite and Gazathite are biblical names for the residents of the town.

Set about midpoint of the length of the plain of Philistia, Gaza was a rich agricultural area where wheat and similar grains flourished. Situated some three miles (4.8 kilometers) from the Mediterranean, Gaza's position as the greatest trading center of ancient Palestine did not come from the sea but from the highways, which brought caravans from all parts of the Fertile Crescent. This accessibility was also a handicap, for the roadways along the coast were the easiest route for the armies of Egypt, Assyria, Babylonia, Persia, Greece, and Rome. Often Gaza was the victim of their passage.

Aerial View of Gaza

In the records of secular history, Gaza first shows up in the annals of Thutmose III in the temple of Karnak. Thutmose wisely scheduled his Asiatic campaigns just after the Egyptian harvest and in time to seize the harvest of Palestine.

In Amarna Letter 289, Abdu-Heba of Jerusalem acknowledged that Gaza was loyal to the king of Egypt but complained that Addaya, the Egyptian ruler of Palestine whose residence was at Gaza, had taken the garrison the pharaoh had sent for Jerusalem. From the late 13th century BC, there is a satirical letter that was composed as an exercise for training scribes. In this letter, written from one scribe to belittle another, various itineraries are traced, including one from the frontier of Egypt to Gaza.

Pharaoh Neco (610–595 BC) captured and chastised Gaza and Ashkelon in the reign of Josiah and Judah (cf. Jer 47:1, 5).

Tiglath-pileser III (745–727 BC) refers to Hanno of Gaza, who fled to Egypt just prior to the capture of Gaza by the Assyrians. On the Oriental Institute Prism and the Taylor Prism, Sennacherib (705–681 BC) tells of his invasion of Palestine and of how he shut up Hezekiah "like a bird in a cage." He captured 46 of Hezekiah's fortified cities and gave them to three minor kings, including Sillibel of Gaza, who is also mentioned by Esarhaddon (681–669 BC) and Ashurbanipal (669–633 BC). Reference to "the king of Gaza" also appears in the records of Nebuchadnezzar II of Babylon (604–562 BC).

In 332 BC Gaza was captured and punished by Alexander the Great. He was angered because it had held out against him for two months, so he killed all of the men and sold the women and children into slavery. During the Maccabean period, it was taken by Alexander Janneus, who slaughtered its inhabitants.

In the Bible, Gaza is first mentioned in Genesis 10:19, where it is said that the territory of the Canaanites extended from Sidon to Gaza. In a summary of the conquests of Joshua, one of the dimensions of the conquered area is "from Kadesh-barnea to Gaza" (Jos 10:41). Joshua destroyed all the Anakim in the land, but some remained in Gaza and other Philistine cities (11:22). Another ancient people, the Avvim, "who lived in villages as far as Gaza," were annihilated and replaced by the Caphtorim from Caphtor, or Crete (Dt 2:23). Gaza, along with its towns and villages, was listed among the tribal inheritance of Judah (Jos 15:47). At the time of Joshua's advanced age, Gaza and the other four cities of the Philistine Pentapolis are said to be among the territories not yet taken (13:3); in Judges 1:18-19, however, it is reported that Judah took it.

During the time of the judges, Midianite raiders swept through Israel, looting and destroying, even as far as Gaza (Jgs 6:4). In this period the main biblical interest in Gaza centers in the life and exploits of Samson. Philistine women were Samson's weakness. He went to Gaza and found a prostitute with whom he had relations (16:1). The people of Gaza learned that he was there and determined to kill him in the morning, but Samson arose at midnight and went to the gate of the city, took the doors, posts, and the bar of the gate and carried them to the top of a hill facing Hebron.

His involvement with another Philistine woman, Delilah, resulted in his capture by the Philistines, who gouged out his eyes and took him to Gaza (Jgs 16:21), where he was bound and forced to grind at a mill in the prison. On a festival day in the temple of Dagon, the reveling worshipers called for Samson to be brought so they could make sport of him. His strength was returning, and God answered his prayer for vengeance. Samson dislodged the two pillars that were the support of the stone slab roof of the pagan temple, so Samson died, along with a great number of Gazites.

Gaza is named as the southern boundary of Israel during the time of Solomon, who ruled over "all the region west of the Euphrates from Tiphsah to Gaza" (1 Kgs 4:24). Hezekiah defeated the Philistines as far as Gaza (2 Kgs 18:8). When he rebelled against Assyria, Sennacherib came and took 46 of Hezekiah's cities and gave them to the king of Gaza and two other kings.

Jeremiah 47 records a prophecy against the Philistines, which the Lord gave to the prophet before Pharaoh attacked Gaza (v 1; cf. v 5; see Neco above). Amos gives specific prophecies of judgment against Gaza (Am 1:6-7). Zephaniah also states that Gaza would be deserted (Zep 2:4). Zechariah 9 gives an oracle of judgment in which it is said that Gaza will suffer and that its king shall perish.

In the NT there is only one reference to Gaza (Acts 8:26). Philip, who was preaching in Samaria, was told by an angel to go south to "the road that goes from Jerusalem to Gaza." Here he met the treasurer of Cush, who was reading Isaiah 53 as he rode in his chariot. Philip preached the gospel to this man and baptized him.

See also Philistia, Philistines.

GAZARA Alternate name for the city of Gezer in 1 and 2 Maccabees. *See* Gezer.

GAZATHITES* KJV alternate spelling for residents of Gaza (Jos 13:3). *See* Gaza; Gazites.

GAZELLE Medium-sized Asian or African antelope. *See* Animals.

GAZER* KJV alternate spelling of the town Gezer in 2 Samuel 5:25 and 1 Chronicles 14:16. *See* Gezer.

GAZEZ

1. Caleb's son by his concubine Ephah, and the brother of Haran (1 Chr 2:46).
2. Son of Haran and the nephew of #1 above (1 Chr 2:46).

GAZITES* Residents of Gaza (Jgs 16:2). *See* Gaza; Gazathites.

GAZZAM Ancestor of a group of temple assistants who returned to Jerusalem with Zerubbabel after the exile (Ezr 2:48; Neh 7:51).

GEBA Levitical city in the territory of Benjamin (Jos 18:24; 21:17), about seven miles (11.3 kilometers) northeast of Jerusalem and south of Michmash (1 Sm 14:5; Is 10:29). It is easily confused with Gibeah, the hometown of Saul, which is also in Benjamin, to the southwest of Geba. Both names mean "hill." The phrase "from Geba to Beersheba" indicated the northern and southern extremities of Judah's tribe (2 Kgs 23:8).

In the time of Saul the Philistines had a garrison at Geba (1 Sm 10:5; 13:3). Jonathan defeated this outpost and stirred up the Philistines, who swarmed into Israel with an army vastly outnumbering the forces of Saul. Saul and his men were at Geba (13:16) and later approached Gibeah (14:2). The Philistines had set up a garrison at Michmash, just opposite Geba. Jonathan proposed to his armor bearer that they go over to this outpost and suggested that if the Philistines called to them to come over, that would be a sign that the Lord had given their enemy into their hand. The Philistines did just that, so the two Israelites approached and killed some 20 of the Philistines, putting the garrison and the entire army to rout. During the reign of David, another horde of Philistine invaders was struck down by him "from Geba to Gezer" (2 Sm 5:25).

Men from Geba are mentioned among the Jews who returned from the Babylonian exile (Ezr 2:26, KJV "Gaba"; Neh 11:31). At the dedication of the rebuilt Jerusalem wall, singers from the area of Geba participated (Neh 12:29).

GEBAL

1. One of the earliest villages in Phoenicia and Syria (along with Ras Shamra and Tell Judeideh); also called Byblos ("books") by the Greeks. It was situated on the Mediterranean about 20 miles (32.2 kilometers) north of modern Beirut and was an important commercial center and outlet for the hardwoods of Lebanon in the period when it was an Egyptian colony and when the diplomatic and commercial interests of Egypt reached all over Syria. It was a city-kingdom according to the Amarna letters (c. 1400–1350 BC), and seal impressions found there from a very early period suggest that it was on a major exchange route through Palestine and Syria. Its inhabitants were called Gebalites (Jos 13:5). While it was a great commercial center, a more important achievement of the

Gebalites was the development of a syllabic script modeled on the Egyptian. Passed on from Phoenicia to Greece, it became the ancestor of our own alphabet.

2. Territory southeast of the Dead Sea, associated with Ammon and Amalek as hostile to Israel (Ps 83:7).

GEBALITE Inhabitant of Gebal (Jos 13:5). *See* Gebal #1.

GEBER

1. Alternate name for Ben-geber, one of Solomon's commissariat officers, in 1 Kings 4:13. *See* Ben-geber.
2. Uri's son, who was responsible for providing food for Solomon's household. His territory was probably south of Ramoth-gilead (1 Kgs 4:19). Perhaps #1 and #2 were related.

GEBIM Small town just north of Jerusalem. Isaiah 10:31 prophesied that its inhabitants would flee when the Assyrian army came to invade. Its exact location is unknown.

GECKO Small lizard, incorrectly identified with the ferret by the KJV translators in Leviticus 11:30. *See* Animals.

GEDALIAH

1. Ahikam's son, and grandson of Shaphan (King Josiah's royal scribe). In 586 BC Nebuchadnezzar, the Babylonian king, appointed Gedaliah as governor over the Jews remaining in Israel to work the fields, vineyards, and orchards (2 Kgs 25:12, 22).

   Gedaliah established his headquarters at Mizpah, where he was joined by the prophet Jeremiah and the Jewish commanders and their guerrilla forces who had escaped capture during the fall of Jerusalem (Jer 40:6-8). Gedaliah assured them that if they would settle down and live in peaceful subjection to Babylon, all would be well (2 Kgs 25:23-24; Jer 40:9-10). On the basis of that assurance, many of the Jews who were dispersed in the Transjordan and other countries returned to Israel to work the land into great productivity (Jer 40:11-12).

   Though warned about a plot against him by Ishmael, Gedaliah entertained the schemer at a meal and was killed (2 Kgs 25:25; Jer 40:11-12; 41:1-3). Along with some pilgrims visiting the temple, Ishmael fled with hostages to Ammon, escaping the vengeance of Johanan (Jer 41:10-15).
2. Temple musician in the time of King David (1 Chr 25:3, 9).
3. Jeshua's son and one called to divorce his foreign wife during Ezra's reforms (Ezr 10:18).
4. Pashhur's son and one of the Jerusalem officials who urged King Zedekiah to put the prophet Jeremiah to death for his pro-Babylonian prophetic pronouncements (Jer 38:1).
5. Amariah's son, grandson of King Hezekiah, and grandfather of the prophet Zephaniah (Zep 1:1).

GEDDALTI *See* Giddalti.

GEDEON* KJV spelling of Gideon, Joash's son and judge of Israel, in Hebrews 11:32. *See* Gideon.

GEDER One of the 31 royal cities in Canaan, whose kings were defeated by Joshua (Jos 12:13). Geder is perhaps identifiable with Gedor in the mountains of Judah (15:58) or with Beth-gader (1 Chr 2:51).

GEDERAH, GEDERATHITES* Town and its inhabitants situated in the Shephelah (lowland hills) of the ter-

ritory allotted to Judah's tribe for an inheritance (Jos 15:36). It was a place where potters lived (1 Chr 4:23). A man from Gederah, Jozabad the Gederathite, is mentioned in 1 Chronicles 12:4.

GEDEROTH Town (modern Qatra) in the Shephelah (lowland hills) assigned to Judah's tribe for an inheritance (Jos 15:41) and later captured by the Philistines from King Ahaz (2 Chr 28:18).

GEDEROTHAIM Village in the Judean Shephelah (Jos 15:36) of unknown location. The Hebrew list contains 14 cities without Gederothaim (vv 33-36), while the Greek version reads, "Gederah and her sheepfolds" (v 36). Gederothaim probably reflects a later scribal error where the copyist accidentally made the term "sheepfold" into a 15th city.

GEDOR (Person) Jeiel's son, who was an ancestor of King Saul. Gedor's family lived in Gibeon (1 Chr 8:31; 9:37).

GEDOR (Place)

1. City in the Shephelah (hill country) allotted to Judah's tribe (Jos 15:58) named with Halhul, Beth-zur, Maarath, Beth-anoth, and Eltekon. It has been identified with Khirbet Gedur north of Hebron near Bethlehem.
2. Place founded by Penuel, one of the families of Judah (1 Chr 4:4).
3. Settlement established by Jered of Judah (1 Chr 4:18).
4. City and its valley settled by the Simeonites (1 Chr 4:39).
5. Town in the territory of Benjamin and the home of Joelah and Zebadiah, the sons of Jeroham (1 Chr 12:7); perhaps the same as #1 above.

GE-HARASHIM* Name for a richly wooded valley near Lod and Ono, settled by Joab from Judah's tribe, whose posterity called the valley Ge-harashim, meaning "valley of craftsmen," after their own trade (1 Chr 4:14, NLT mg). In the fifth century BC the area was resettled by people from Benjamin's tribe (Neh 11:35, "valley of craftsmen").

GEHAZI Servant of Elisha (2 Kgs 5:25) who instructed the prophet how best to recompense the generous Shunammite woman for her kindness to him (4:11-17). Gehazi took Elisha's staff to use in reviving the woman's dead son, but he was unsuccessful (v 31), and the prophet himself had to revive the child (vv 32-37). His greed in securing from Naaman presents declined by Elisha resulted in his contracting Naaman's leprosy (5:20-23, 27). In 2 Kings 8:1-6 Gehazi again encountered the Shunammite woman as she was petitioning the king of Israel.

GEHENNA* English transliteration of the Greek form of an Aramaic word, which is derived from the Hebrew phrase "the Valley of [the son(s) of] Hinnom." The name properly designates a deep valley delimiting the territories of the tribes of Benjamin and Judah (Jos 15:8; 18:16). It is commonly identified with Wadi el-Rababi that runs from beneath the western wall of the Old City, forming a deep ravine south of Jerusalem.

The place became notorious because of the idolatrous practices that were carried out there in the days of Judah's kings Ahaz and Manasseh, especially involving the heinous crime of infant sacrifices associated with the Molech ceremonies (2 Kgs 16:3; 21:6; 2 Chr 28:3; 33:6; Jer 19:6; 32:35). The spiritual reformation of King Josiah brought an end to these sinister proceedings (2 Kgs

23:10). The prophet Jeremiah referred to the valley in picturing God's judgment upon his people (Jer 2:23; 7:30-32; 19:5-6).

Subsequently, the valley appears to have been used for the burning of the city's refuse and the dead bodies of criminals. Interestingly, a well-established tradition locates the scene of Judas's suicide and the consequent purchase of the Potter's Field on the south side of this valley.

The ravine's reputation for extreme wickedness gave rise, especially during the intertestamental period, to use of its name as a term for the place of final punishment for the wicked (1 Enoch 18:11-16; 27:1-3; 54:1ff.; 56:3-4; 90:26; 2 Esd 7:36; cf. Is 30:33; 66:24; Dn 7:10). Jesus himself utilizes the term to designate the final abode of the unrepentant wicked (Mt 5:22; 10:28; 18:9). Since Gehenna is a fiery abyss (Mk 9:43), it is also the lake of fire (Mt 13:42, 50; Rv 20:14-15) to which all the godless will ultimately be consigned (Mt 23:15, 33), together with Satan and his devils (Mt 25:41; Rv 19:20; 20:10).

Gehenna must be carefully differentiated from other terms relative to the afterlife or final state. Whereas the OT "Sheol" and NT "hades" uniformly designate the temporary abode of the dead (before the last Day of Judgment), "Gehenna" specifies the final place where the wicked will suffer everlasting punishment (cf. Ps 49:14-15 with Mt 10:28). The Greek form "Tartarus" occurs only in 2 Peter 2:4 and identifies the particular abode of the angels who fell in the primeval satanic revolt.

See also Dead, Place of the; Death; Hades; Hell; Sheol.

GELILOTH
Place mentioned in the boundary line of Benjamin (Jos 18:17), usually identified with Gilgal. *See* Gilgal #4.

GEMALLI
Father of Ammiel, one of the 12 spies sent by Moses to explore the land of Canaan (Nm 13:12).

GEMARA*
Summary of the important points of rabbinic discussion on the Mishnah (the oral tradition). The Gemara and Mishnah together form the Talmud (which many Jews consider authoritative for their faith). In Aramaic, *Gemara* means "acquired learning." That meaning reflects the teaching method of the rabbis, who passed on the Gemara by committing it to memory rather than writing it down. The word's Hebrew root means "to complete." Since the Gemara takes the form of a running commentary on the Mishnah, it serves to supplement and complete it.

Pages of the Talmud are arranged with the Mishnah in the middle and the Gemara in blocks of print on the side. The Gemara does not necessarily quote the same sources twice when dealing with similar passages from the Mishnah on the same problem, nor does it always contain commentary on the Mishnah. The Gemara also includes folklore, astronomy, astrology, medicine, homiletic parables, and examples from great rabbis' lives.

See also Mishnah; Talmud.

GEMARIAH
1. Hilkiah's son and emissary to Nebuchadnezzar from King Zedekiah. He carried Jeremiah's letter to the exiles in Babylon (Jer 29:3).
2. Son of Shaphan the scribe. In the temple chamber of Gemariah, Baruch read Jeremiah's scroll (Jer 36:10-12, 25).

GEMATRIA*
One of the rabbinic hermeneutic rules for interpreting the OT. It consisted of explaining a word or group of words according to the numerical value of the letters or by substituting and rearranging certain letters according to a set system. By that rule of interpretation, for example, some rabbis have argued that Eliezer (Gn 15:2) was worth all the servants of Abraham put together, for Abraham had 318 servants and Eliezer's name equaled 318 (Gn 14:14). The name Babylon is arrived at in Jeremiah 25:26 and 51:41 by substituting the last letter of the Hebrew word for the first letter of the same word.

The pseudepigraphal Epistle of Barnabas interprets the 318 servants of Abraham (Gn 14:14) as pointing to Jesus' death on the cross, because 300 is the numerical value of the Greek letter "t," which is cross-shaped, and 18 the value of the first two letters of the Greek word for Jesus. In the book of Revelation the number of the beast is 666 (Rv 13:18). If the number seven is considered to be the perfect number in the Bible, and if three sevens represent complete perfection, then the number 666 falls completely short of perfection.

GENEALOGY
Record or study of descent involving a tracing backward or forward of the ancestry of a nation, tribe, family, or individual. The Hebrews were not the only people in the ancient world to take an interest in maintaining genealogical records. The Sumerian king list of the third millennium BC contains records of the early rulers of Mesopotamia. In Babylonian records the word "son" was frequently used in the sense of "descendant of." King Tirhakah of Egypt (c. 685 BC) referred to his "father," Sesostris III, who lived some 1,200 years before him. Greeks and Romans also kept genealogical records. However, the biblical genealogies, especially those in Genesis and 1 Chronicles 1–9, are unique in the literature of the ancient Near East. Only at the beginning of the Islamic age are such broad genealogical records found. Even today among tribal Semites, such as Arab nomads, there is an intense interest in genealogy, and it is not unusual for an Arab to be able to recite accurately the names of his ancestors for 10 or 15 generations back, covering a period of several hundred years.

Terms Used The word "genealogy" occurs only once as a noun in the Hebrew OT (Neh 7:5), where it refers to a register of those who returned to Jerusalem with Zerubbabel at the end of the exile. The verbal form of the same word is found a total of 20 times in 1—2 Chronicles, Ezra, and Nehemiah. The terms "generations" and "book of the generations," used in Genesis and elsewhere in the OT, convey the same idea. The equivalent NT terms are found in 1 Timothy 1:4 and Titus 3:9 ("genealogies") and Matthew 1:1, which refers to the "book of the genealogy" of Jesus Christ.

Purpose of Genealogical Records The keeping of genealogical records in ancient Israel was an important activity and served a number of useful purposes. God's promise of a land to Abraham and his descendants made such records necessary to establish and preserve the allotment of the land; a genealogical record served as evidence of a legitimate title to the ancestral property. Genealogies were essential for the preservation of the exclusive priesthood that had been established by the Mosaic law. In the time of Josephus every priest was supposed to be able to prove his descent.

One of the most important reasons for keeping genealogical records was to establish and maintain the right of royal succession in Judah through the family of David. The belief that the Messiah would come from the Davidic house made such records even more important.

Other purposes served by these family records included the imposition of military duty according to families (Nm 1:2-3). Position in camp and on the march from Egypt was determined by tribes and families (2:2, 17; 10:1-28). Also, God's blessings were passed from one member of the family to his descendants (Gn 27). The stress placed on the purity of the congregation (Dt 7:1-4; 23:1-8) required complete family records, particularly in the postexilic period. With the insistence of Ezra and Nehemiah upon racial purity, and with the purging of foreign elements from among the people (Ezr 2:59-63; 10:9-44; Neh 13:23-28), written evidence of purity of descent became essential; interest in the compilation of genealogies became intense after the exile.

Lineage was ordinarily traced through the male members of the family, with females being mentioned only rarely (e.g., Gn 11:29, Sarah and Milcah; 22:23, Rebekah; and Nm 26:33–27:11, where the property inheritance of the daughters of Zelophehad was involved). Matthew mentions three women: Tamar, Rahab, and Ruth; and in the second group alludes to Bathsheba (see discussion below).

Principal Genealogical Lists in the Bible The principal sources of genealogical material in the OT are found in Genesis, Numbers, 2 Samuel, 1 Kings, 1—2 Chronicles (which contain the greatest amount of genealogical material in the Bible), Ezra, and Nehemiah. The genealogies of Jesus Christ in Matthew 1 and Luke 3 are the only NT records. Together they contain a genealogical record from Adam to Christ.

Grouped together by historical periods, the following are the principal genealogical lists found in the Bible:

Before the Flood Three lists are from this period. The first, found in Genesis 4:17-22, traces the descendants of Cain through seven generations and explains the hereditary origin of certain occupations and crafts. The second, Genesis 4:25-26, begins the account of the descendants of Seth, the posterity of Adam whose faithfulness to God is contrasted with the ungodly posterity of Cain. The third list, Genesis 5:1-32 (cf. 1 Chr 1:1-4), traces the descendants of Adam through Seth down to Noah and his sons at the time of the Flood.

From Noah to Abraham Genesis 10:1-32 (cf. 1 Chr 1:4-23), frequently called the "table of nations," contains a list of the nations descended from the sons of Noah (Shem, Ham, and Japheth). Genesis 11:10-26 (cf. 1 Chr 1:24-27) traces the descendants of Shem to the time of Abraham, and Genesis 11:27-30 (see also Gn 22:20-24) lists the descendants of Nahor, Abraham's brother.

From Abraham to the Descent into Egypt The descendants of Abraham by Hagar, Sarah, and Keturah are found in Genesis 16:15, 21:1-3, and 25:1-4 (introducing the Arabs as descendants of Abraham; cf. 1 Chr 1:28-34). Genesis 19:37-38 links the Moabites and Ammonites to Abraham through his nephew Lot. A very important genealogical list during this period is that of the descendants of Jacob, giving the account of the parentage, birth, and naming of the founders of the 12 tribes of Israel (Gn 29:31–30:24; 35:16-26). Esau is acknowledged as the ancestor of the Edomites; his Edomite descendants are traced through his three wives (Gn 26:34; 36:1-43; 1 Chr 1:35-54). The list of Jacob's family at the time he entered Egypt, numbering 70, is found in Genesis 46:1-27 (cf. Ex 6:14-16; Nm 26:1-51; 1 Chr 2–8). A partial list of the heads of the fathers' houses of Reuben, Simeon, and Levi is found in Exodus 6:14-25; the chief purpose of this genealogy is to establish Aaron and Moses as members of Levi's tribe.

From the Exodus to the Conquest of Canaan While the tribes were still in the desert after leaving Egypt, a census was taken to determine the total number of Israelites (Nm 1:4-54; 2:2-33). During this same period, a genealogy of the family of Aaron was compiled, and a separate census was taken of the Levites (3:1-39). A list of the 12 spies who searched out the land and the tribes they represented is given in Numbers 13:4-16; the most important names on this list are Caleb and Joshua. Near the end of the wilderness wanderings, another census of the people was ordered; the total number was approximately the same as that of the first census almost 40 years earlier (26:4-51, 57-62). As the tribes neared the Promised Land, a list was prepared of the tribal representatives who would take part in the division of the land (34:16-29).

Period of the Kings During the entire period of the monarchy, over 400 years, the only genealogical records of any consequence are those that pertain to David. His descendants are traced through 20 rulers who sat upon the throne of Judah until the nation fell to the Babylonians in 586 BC (1—2 Kgs; cf. 1 Chr 11:1—2 Chr 36:21). A list of David's children is found in 2 Samuel 3:2-5 and 5:14-16 (cf. 1 Chr 3:1-9; 14:4-7). His mighty men, an elite group of soldiers, are named in 2 Samuel 23:8-39 (cf. 1 Chr 11:10-47). His recruits at Ziklag are recorded in 1 Chronicles 12:1-22. Those who were his musicians and doorkeepers when the ark was brought to Jerusalem are named in 1 Chronicles 15:1-24 (cf. 1 Chr 16:5-6, 37-43). David's political and religious organization of the kingdom—including the Levites, priests, singers, porters and other administrative officials, and military officers—is found in 1 Chronicles 23–27. In spite of the literary activity associated with the reign of Solomon, the only genealogical record preserved from this period is that of Solomon's princes and 12 officers (1 Kgs 4:1-19). The genealogy of one prophet is traced back four generations (Zep 1:1).

The Postexilic Period During the postexilic period, the keeping of genealogical records probably received its greatest impetus through the activity of Ezra and Nehemiah, primarily because of their insistence upon racial purity and the purging of foreign elements from the community. A list of the exiles who returned with Zerubbabel is found in Ezra 2:1-70 (cf. Neh 7:6-73, where the same list is found). A list of those who returned with Ezra is included in 8:1-20. Ezra's own genealogy is also recorded (Ezr 7:5). There is a list of the Jews who married foreign women that included priests, Levites, singers, porters, and other Israelites (Ezr 10:18-44). Nehemiah 8:4-7 names the Levites and others who assisted Ezra when he read the law publicly. Nehemiah also contains a list of those who participated in the ceremony of sealing the covenant (Neh 10:1-27) and a list of those who lived in Jerusalem and other cities (11:3-36). His interest in the priesthood is reflected in the list of priests and Levites who returned with Zerubbabel (12:1-9), of the high priests from Jeshua to Jaddua (vv 10-11), of the heads of the priestly families (vv 12-21), of the Levites and porters who served under the high priest (vv 22-26), and of the princes and priests who were present at the dedication of the rebuilt wall of Jerusalem (vv 31-42).

The final genealogical record that must be mentioned is the genealogy from Adam to Saul (1 Chr 1–8), the longest section of genealogical material in the Bible. It is properly included with the genealogies compiled during the postexilic period, as the unknown chronicler (some think he was Ezra) prepared this list around 400 BC from extant records and documents available to him. His purpose seems to have been to conserve the purity of blood in the restored nation and to insist that the nation's well-being depended on its faithfulness to God's law.

The New Testament Period The only genealogies of consequence in the NT are those concerning Jesus Christ in Matthew 1:1-17 and Luke 3:23-38. *See* Genealogy of Jesus Christ.

GENEALOGY OF JESUS CHRIST Account of Jesus'
human descent. The NT records Jesus' genealogy twice in great detail: in Matthew 1:1-17 and in Luke 3:23-38.

PREVIEW
• Matthew's Genealogy
• Luke's Genealogy
• The Relationship between the Two Records

Matthew's Genealogy (1:1-17) Matthew 1:1 presents Jesus Christ as "the son of David, the son of Abraham." By those two names, Matthew highlights Jesus' earthly relationship to the Abrahamic (Gn 17:1-8) and Davidic (2 Sm 7:12-16) covenants of promise. Then beginning with the patriarch Abraham, Matthew traces Jesus' human ancestry through King David to Joseph, "the husband of Mary, of whom Jesus was born, who is called Christ" (Mt 1:16). Matthew summarizes his account: "So all the generations from Abraham to David were fourteen generations, and from David to the deportation to Babylon fourteen generations, and from the deportation to Babylon to the Christ fourteen generations" (v 17, RSV).

An examination of Matthew's handling of this genealogical material discloses several interesting peculiarities:

The Genealogy of Jesus Christ
Matthew 1:1-17 (that of Joseph?)
Abraham ➤ Isaac ➤ Jacob ➤ Judah ➤ Perez ➤ Hezron ➤ Ram ➤ Amminadab ➤ Nahshon ➤ Salmon ➤ Boaz ➤ Obed ➤ Jesse ➤ David ➤ Solomon ➤ Rehoboam ➤ Abijah ➤ Asa ➤ Jehoshaphat ➤ Joram ➤ Uzziah ➤ Jotham ➤ Ahaz ➤ Hezekiah ➤ Manasseh ➤ Amos ➤ Josiah ➤ Jeconiah ➤ Shealtiel ➤ Zerubbabel ➤ Abiud ➤ Eliakim ➤ Azor ➤ Zadok ➤ Achim ➤ Eliud ➤ Eleazer ➤ Matthan ➤ Jacob ➤ Joseph ➤ (Jesus)

Luke 3:23-38 (that of Mary?)
God ➤ Adam ➤ Seth ➤ Enos ➤ Cainan ➤ Mahalaleel ➤ Jared ➤ Enoch ➤ Methuselah ➤ Lamech ➤ Noah ➤ Shem ➤ Arphaxad ➤ Cainan ➤ Shelah ➤ Eber ➤ Peleg ➤ Reu ➤ Serug ➤ Nahor ➤ Terah ➤ Abraham ➤ Isaac ➤ Jacob ➤ Judah ➤ Perez ➤ Hezron ➤ Arni ➤ Admin ➤ Amminadab ➤ Nahshon ➤ Sala ➤ Boaz ➤ Obed ➤ Jesse ➤ David ➤ Nathan ➤ Mattatha ➤ Menna ➤ Melea ➤ Eliakim ➤ Jonam ➤ Joseph ➤ Judah ➤ Simeon ➤ Levi ➤ Matthat ➤ Jorim ➤ Eliezer ➤ Joshua ➤ Er ➤ Elmadam ➤ Cosam ➤ Addi ➤ Melki ➤ Neri ➤ Shealtiel ➤ Zerubbabel ➤ Rhesa ➤ Joanan ➤ Joda ➤ Josech ➤ Semein ➤ Mattathias ➤ Maath ➤ Naggai ➤ Esli ➤ Nahum ➤ Amos ➤ Mattathias ➤ Joseph ➤ Jannai ➤ Melki ➤ Levi ➤ Matthat ➤ Heli ➤ Joseph ➤ (Jesus)

Both Gospels are careful to not connect Joseph to Jesus in a physical father-son relationship.

---

1. The arrangement of the names into three groups of 14 seems to be an artificial device.
2. To have 14 names in the second group, Matthew omits three kings—Ahaziah, Joash, and Amaziah—between Joram and Uzziah (v 8), and one, Jehoiakim, between Josiah and Jeconiah (v 11).
3. In the first group Matthew mentions three women—Tamar, Rahab, and Ruth; and in the second group, he alludes to Bathsheba. This is an uncommon practice in

genealogies, and all the more strange when it is noted that these four represent what could be regarded as moral blemishes in the history of the Davidic dynasty—Tamar, a victim of incest; Rahab, a prostitute; Ruth, a Moabitess; and Bathsheba, an adulteress.
4. In the first group Matthew mentions Judah's brothers and Zerah, Perez's brother. In the second group he refers to Jeconiah's brothers.
5. In verse 6 David is called "the king."

From these data, it is obvious that Matthew does not intend to present a strict genealogy; the arrangement is contrived, and extraneous material is included, probably for some other purpose than merely to present Jesus' forebears. Matthew's arrangement of the names into groups of 14, probably guided by an interest in portraying Jesus to Jews as the promised king of Israel and rightful heir to the Davidic throne, gives a definite historical movement to the genealogy by dividing it into three periods of time. These respectively highlight the origin, rise to power, and decay of the Davidic house, the last point represented by the lowly birth of the promised heir to a carpenter of Nazareth.

The 14 names in each group may be an effort to call attention to the thrice-royal character of Mary's son by focusing on the numerical value 14 of the Hebrew letters in David's name (d=4, v=6, d=4). This number also happens to be twice the sacred number seven, so that the whole list is composed of three sets of two sevens each. It may be, however, that the contrived groupings were merely intended to aid in memorization.

With respect to the second peculiarity—the "missing name" in the third group—one must conclude that either David or Jeconiah is to be counted twice, these being the pivotal names separating the three groups, or that a name was mistakenly dropped out in a copy of Matthew's original Gospel.

The third peculiarity presents no difficulty at all. Numerous genealogies in Scripture omit some names. Ancient Near Eastern writers often used the phrase "the son of," or the word "begat," quite flexibly, relating grandsons or great-grandsons, for instance, to earlier forebears without indicating every intervening ancestor. The modern mind should not require a precision in ancient records that ancient writers themselves did not insist on.

The women listed in the genealogy—the fourth peculiarity—may have been intended to disarm Jewish criticism about Jesus' birth (1:18-25) by showing that irregular unions were not disqualifications for the Messiah's legal ancestry.

The reason for including several brothers in the genealogy at three points—the fifth peculiarity—is not readily discernible. The mention of "Judah and his brothers" (1:2) may simply be following an established practice of speaking of the 12 patriarchs together.

Finally, David's description as "the king" (1:6) underscores the Davidic or royal character of the list.

The sources employed in compiling the first group in the genealogy drew upon records preserved in 1 Chronicles 1:27–2:15 and in Ruth 4:18-22. The second group followed the records found in 1—2 Kings and 2 Chronicles. The third group relied mainly on public or private records from the intertestamental period; the nine names from Abiud to Jacob are not mentioned elsewhere in Scripture.

On the basis of this genealogy, if there had been a Davidic throne in Joseph's day, the lowly carpenter would have been the legal heir to it, and Jesus stood after him as the next in line to inherit the royal seat.

It has been argued against this understanding of Matthew's genealogy that the presence of Jeconiah in the list (Mt 1:11) jeopardizes, if not completely negates, the legal claim to the Davidic throne of everyone descending directly from him. That is because the Lord declared of him: "Write this man down as childless, . . . for none of his offspring shall succeed in sitting on the throne of David, and ruling again in Judah" (Jer 22:30, rsv). Therefore, it is said, it could not have been Matthew's intention to represent the men from Shealtiel to Joseph as legal heirs to the throne.

This is a point that admittedly could dispose of the view that the list presents David's descendants if it were not for the fact that Shealtiel, who in Matthew's record is represented as the son of Jeconiah, appears also in Luke's genealogy as the son of Neri (Lk 3:27). Neri's name is unique to Luke's Gospel, so it is impossible to check its use elsewhere to discover the actual parentage of Shealtiel. But it is not surprising in the light of Jeremiah 22:30 to find him listed in both accounts with different parents. Neri most likely was Shealtiel's real father, and while it is impossible to determine Neri's precise relationship to Jeconiah, it may be that those responsible for determining and keeping the record of the legal heirs to the Davidic throne looked to the collateral line of Neri and selected Shealtiel as the man to be legally adopted into the line and the one through whom the line would continue. Shealtiel may well have died without a male descendant, which made it necessary to look to Zerubbabel, the son of Pedaiah, Shealtiel's brother by adoption, as the legal heir to the Davidic throne. By this pair of adoptions, the curse upon Jeconiah was fulfilled while an actual grandson of Jeconiah continued the line, inasmuch as the grandson was legally the son of Shealtiel, who in turn was the actual son of Neri. Jeconiah's presence in the genealogy is a strength, rather than a weakness, for the interpretation that Matthew's Gospel intended to present the legal heirs of the Davidic throne, since only a writer conscious of the problems surrounding Jeconiah's lineage, but also aware of an explanation, would present such an ancestry to a Jewish audience he was seeking to convince that Jesus was indeed the royal Messiah.

Luke's Genealogy (3:23-38) Luke's genealogy also has peculiarities.

1. Some expositors have thought it significant that Luke's genealogy appears not at the beginning of the Gospel but at the beginning of Jesus' ministry.
2. Luke's account, in contrast to Matthew's, begins with Jesus and traces his lineage back through OT history. This seems irregular, for most genealogies follow the order of succession.
3. Luke's account, furthermore, does not end with Abraham but goes all the way back to "Adam, the son of God" (Lk 3:38).

Some have seen the first peculiarity as a result of Luke's desire to bring a period of sacred history to its close, and to signal the beginning of another with the person and especially the ministry of Jesus. The genealogy, located as it is, sets off the work of Christ from the accounts of his birth and preparation.

Many have suggested that the regressive order in the genealogy is probably Luke's instrument to focus attention on Jesus. The fact that Luke traced Jesus' ancestry back to Adam, "the son of God," was probably due to the fact that he wrote for Romans and Greeks. By tracing Jesus' ancestry back to Adam, he shows Jesus to be related to the whole human race. In Luke's genealogy Jesus and Adam are both "sons of God"; Jesus, of course,

is the son of God by nature; Adam, the son of God by having been created in God's image.

As to his sources, it is rather certain that Luke used the Septuagint version (ancient Greek version of the OT) of Genesis 11:12, which inserts the name Cainan between Shelah and Arphaxad (Lk 3:36), and the records of 1 Chronicles 1–3 for the history down to David. For the period from David to Jesus, most expositors agree that Luke relied upon information probably received directly from Mary or from persons close to her. It was a common practice among the Jewish people for genealogical records to be maintained both publicly and privately. There was special concern in families of Davidic descent to preserve their ancestral records because of OT prophecies that Messiah would be born in the house of David.

Luke no doubt intended to accomplish more by his list than merely a presentation of a number of Jesus' ancestors. Since Luke did not highlight David in his list, it may be assumed that he was not zealous to present a list of legal heirs to the Davidic throne—not that the issue is of no concern to him (cf. Lk 1:27, 32, 69; 2:4, 11). Rather, a concern throughout Luke's Gospel is this emphasis—that of portraying the Christ as the Savior of Romans and Greeks—indeed, of the world. Therefore, though Luke traced Jesus' ancestry through Joseph's ancestral line to David, he continued beyond David to Adam. Jesus is a member of the race to which all people belong.

The Relationship between the Two Records Even a cursory examination of the two genealogies of Jesus will show several differences. For example, Matthew's genealogy comprises 41 generations, while Luke lists 76. Luke includes the period between Adam and Abraham; Matthew does not. While the two lists are practically identical from Abraham to David, they diverge for the period from David to Jesus, Matthew tracing Jesus' lineage from David through Solomon in 27 generations, whereas Luke traces Jesus' lineage from David through Nathan, another son, in 42 generations. Furthermore, at only one point do the lines converge during this period: at the names of Shealtiel and Zerubbabel, who are doubtless the same men in both lists. Finally, Matthew represents Joseph as the son of Jacob (Mt 1:16), whereas in Luke's account he is the son of Heli (Lk 3:23).

How are these differences to be explained? The differences between these lists stem from the purposes for which they were compiled and the meanings they were intended to convey.

A widely held explanation is that Matthew gives Jesus' ancestry through Joseph and that Luke gives his ancestry through Mary. On this interpretation Jacob was Joseph's real father, and Heli (probably Mary's father) became Joseph's foster father, that is, Joseph was Heli's "son," or heir, by his marriage to Mary, assuming that Heli had no sons (cf. Nm 27:1-11; 36:1-12). This view is certainly a possibility and should not be rejected out of hand. If Mary was a direct descendant of David, it could be literally said of any son of hers, "He is the seed of David."

On the other hand, many scholars prefer to regard Luke's genealogy as that of Joseph rather than Mary, since it is to Joseph's ancestry that Luke calls the reader's attention (Lk 1:27; 2:4). Furthermore, nowhere in Scripture is Mary said to be of Davidic descent. If the fact that Joseph was not the actual father of Jesus nullifies any value that Joseph's lineage might otherwise possess for a real son, why does Luke point to Joseph's lineage twice, and to Mary's not at all?

A major difficulty for the view that regards both genealogies as Joseph's is related to Joseph's two fathers. One solution is that Matthew gives the legal descendants of David but Luke gives the actual descendants of David in the line to which Joseph belonged. This would mean that Heli was Joseph's real father and that Jacob was his legal foster father. How this could be is readily explainable. Assuming that Jacob's father, Matthan (Mt 1:15), and Heli's father, Matthat (Lk 3:24), are the same person, then Jacob (the elder) may have died without a male descendant so that his nephew, the son of his brother Heli, would have become his heir.

If Matthan and Matthat are not the same person, one might postulate that Jacob, the legal heir to the throne, died without a descendant and that Joseph, son of Heli, became the legal heir immediately upon the death of Heli and was counted as Jacob's son in a list of legal heirs to the throne. Possibly Heli, a relative, married Jacob's widow, thereby making Joseph, the son of that union, Heli's son and Jacob's son by levirate marriage. In other words, there are a number of possible explanations of this divergence.

One other major objection to the view that regards both genealogies as Joseph's is that, because of the virgin birth of Jesus, one may in no sense speak of Jesus as being literally the seed of David—a proposition that Scripture seems to insist upon. This objection has been adequately countered: (1) because of the realistic manner in which the Jews looked upon adoptive fatherhood; and (2) because the relationship in which Jesus stood to Joseph was much closer than a case of ordinary adoption, there being no earthly father to dispute Joseph's paternal relation to Jesus. Jesus could and would have been regarded as Joseph's son and heir with complete propriety, satisfying every scriptural demand that he be the "seed of David." The question, therefore, whether Mary as well as Joseph was a descendant of David does not need to be answered one way or the other by one who desires to defend Jesus' Davidic descent.

It is beyond human reach to discover for certain the full solution to the divergences between the two genealogies of Jesus, or the actual relationship of Jesus to them. Enough has been said to demonstrate that they are reconcilable, and the purposes of each, suggested here, indicate that either of the ways outlined above does full justice to the Davidic descent of Jesus, as rightful heir to his ancestor's covenanted throne, and also to his virgin birth by Mary.

See also Genealogy; Incarnation; Jesus Christ, Life and Teachings of; Virgin Birth of Jesus.

GENESIS, Book of First book of the Bible.

PREVIEW
•Name
•Author
•Date
•Purpose
•Structure
•Content

Name The name Genesis comes into English as a transliteration of the Greek word meaning "origin" or "beginning." This name was given to the book in the Greek translation of the Hebrew Scriptures, known as the Septuagint. Genesis reflects both the content of the book and the Hebrew name for it, which is taken from its first word, *bere'shith*, "in the beginning."

Author The authorship of Genesis is closely related to the authorship of the entire Pentateuch (lit. "five-volumed," the first five books of the Bible, which in Hebrew are called the Torah). It is clear that the Bible regards the human author of these books as Moses. On several occasions the Lord commanded Moses to write down various things: "in a book" (Ex 17:14) "write these words" (34:27). The Pentateuch reports that "Moses wrote all the words of the LORD" (24:4); he wrote the itinerary of the exodus wanderings (Nm 33:2); "Moses wrote this law" (Dt 31:9). (Here it is not certain that all five books are meant, but it must refer to at least the greater part of Deuteronomy.) In Exodus 24:7 it is said that Moses read the Book of the Covenant, which he must have just completed.

The rest of the OT bears witness to the writing of the Pentateuch by Moses. David referred to "the law of Moses" (1 Kgs 2:3). In the time of Josiah, there was found in the temple the "Book of the Law of the LORD . . . given through Moses" (2 Chr 34:14, NLT). Day by day Ezra read from "the Book of the Law of God" (Neh 8:18, NLT).

In the NT, Jesus refers to "the book of Moses" (Mk 12:26; Lk 20:37) and otherwise mentions the commands or statements of Moses (Mt 8:4; 19:8; Mk 7:10; cf. Lk 16:31; 24:44). The Jews also quoted from the Torah as coming from Moses, and Jesus did not contradict them.

Of Genesis in particular, it may be said that Moses had the opportunity and ability to write the book. He could have written it during his years in Egypt or while exiled with the Kenites. As the recognized leader of the Israelites, he would have had access to, or perhaps even custody of, the records that Jacob brought from Canaan. He was "instructed in all the wisdom of the Egyptians" (Acts 7:22) and probably could have written in several languages and in several scripts (hieroglyphic, cuneiform, Old Hebrew). Although Moses was admirably fitted for the task of writing, one must remember that he was not putting together a human composition but was writing under the inspiration of God (2 Pt 1:21). We may with confidence conclude that Moses was the human author of Genesis.

The liberal view of the authorship of Genesis is that the book is an editorial composite—a view first put forward by a French physician, Jean Astruc, who suggested that the different names for God indicated different documents or sources for the writing of the book. The German higher critics expanded the view of the use of documents in the writing of Genesis and developed it into the Graf-Wellhausen-Kuenen, or Documentary, Hypothesis, which may also be called the JEDP theory of the authorship of the book. This view holds that there were four basic documents: (1) J, which uses the name YHWH (Jehovah or Yahweh) for God, dates from about the ninth century BC and comes from Judah; (2) E uses the name Elohim, dates from the eighth century, and comes from the northern kingdom; (3) D is Deuteronomy and is supposed to come from the time of Josiah, about 621 BC; and (4) P is the priestly element, which deals with matters of the priesthood and ritual, dating to the fifth century BC or later. Some may date portions of Genesis as late as the Hellenistic period. According to this theory, the various documents were blended together by editors, so that there was a JE, JED, and so on.

The science of archaeology discredited many of the extreme postulations of these critics, and the work of W. F. Albright and his followers did much to restore confidence in the historicity of Genesis. Within the last several decades, the patriarchal narratives and the account of Joseph have again come under strong attack, but these views are extreme, and much of the evidence adduced by Albright and earlier scholars like R. D. Wilson, W. H. Green, and others still has validity.

Date The date of the book is also a matter of debate. Even among those who accept Mosaic authorship there is debate as to when Moses lived. Based on the biblical data, Moses should have lived in the 15th century BC (cf. Jgs 11:26; 1 Kgs 6:1), but many scholars incline toward a 13th-century date. As outlined above, the liberal view of the date of Genesis would be from the ninth to the fifth centuries BC, with the final editing coming around the fifth century or perhaps even later.

Purpose Genesis sketches the origin of many things: the universe, the earth, plants, animals, and mankind. It gives the beginnings of human institutions, professions, and crafts. It describes the origin of sin and death, and illustrates the insidious working of Satan in human life. Above all, Genesis relates the beginning of the history of redemption with the announcement of a Redeemer who was to come (Gn 3:15). It names the early progenitors in the lineage of the Messiah and the beginning of the Hebrew people through whom the Bible and the Savior came. Genesis also gives a selective history of people and events as viewed from the perspective of the purposes of God.

Structure The book is divided into 11 parts of uneven length, each set off by the expression "these are the generations [descendants, history] of" (2:4; 5:1; 6:9; 10:1; 11:10, 27; 25:12, 19; 36:1; 37:2). Only three times does the formula coincide with the first verse of a chapter. Usually called a heading or superscription, the expression serves as a kind of link between what precedes and what follows.

Content

The Creation (1:1–2:25) These two chapters have been a scientific-theological battleground for many years, as researchers and students have tried to probe the origins of the universe and of life. Much of the evidence is not subject to scientific scrutiny, for science by definition requires that the evidence must be reproducible by experiment.

The statement of Genesis 1:1 remains the grandest, most precise, and most accurate statement of origins: "In the beginning God created the heavens and the earth." He did this *ex nihilo* ("out of nothing") by his word (Heb 11:3); he spoke the word of command and it was done (Gn 1:3, 6, 9, 11, 14, 20; Ps 33:6, 9).

The date of the beginning is unknown. Uniformitarian cosmogonists (students of the origins of the universe who believe that natural events have always followed a uniform pattern; cf. 2 Pt 3:3-7) have speculated that the beginning of the universe was billions of years ago. But some creationists posit a world thousands of years old.

To accommodate geological ages and the existence of extinct animals, some interpreters have proposed a gap between Genesis 1:1 and 1:2, with Genesis 1:2–2:3 representing a second or new creation. But this is conjecture. So is the idea that each day represents a geological age.

As the text stands, there is a correlation between the first three days and the second three days. Day one saw the creation of light; day four, the light bearers. Day two was the time of the creation of the firmament (better, "expanse"), which divided the waters; day five, birds and swarming water creatures. On day three, God made the dry land and plants; on day six he created the land animals and man. He made man in the image of God (Gn 1:26), "a little less than God" (Ps 8:5), and gave him dominion over the earth. He made everything "according to their kinds," so that each kind is distinct and unique. The perfection of his work is affirmed in that "God saw that it was good" (Gn 1:4, 10, 12, 18, 21; "very good," v 31). The seventh day was a time of cessation from the activity of creating and served as a type for mankind's day of rest (2:1-3).

Critical scholarship eyes 2:4-25 as a doublet in conflict

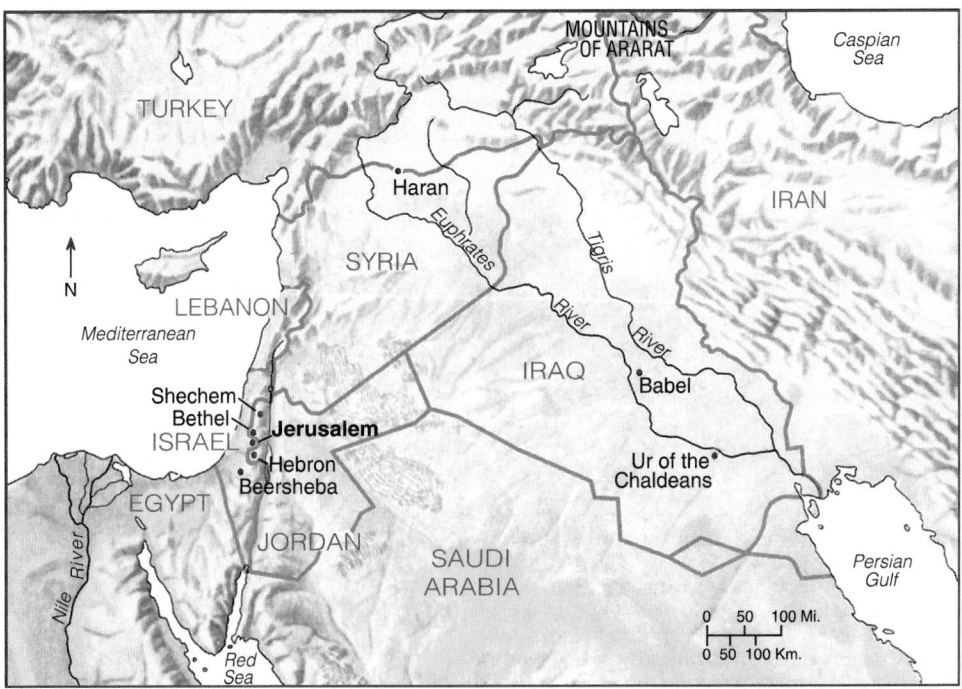

Modern names and boundaries are shown in gray.

Key Places in Genesis God created the universe and the earth. Then he made man and woman, giving them a home in a beautiful garden. Unfortunately, Adam and Eve disobeyed God and were banished from the Garden (3:23).

with Genesis 1:1–2:3. To conservative scholars, the second chapter is the same account from a different perspective. Chapter 1 gives the Creation from the standpoint of sequence; chapter 2 shows it in view of the centrality of mankind in God's creative work.

Chapter 2 gives details of the creation of man of "dust from the ground" (v 7) and woman from a rib of the man (vv 21-22). She was created to be "a companion who will help him" (vv 18-20). They were created as mature adults, with the gift of speech and with great intelligence. Adam had imagination and vocabulary sufficient for naming all of the animal species (v 19).

The location of the Garden of Eden is given (vv 10-14). Two of the four rivers, the Tigris and the Euphrates, can be identified with certainty. So man lived in this beautiful garden in the bliss of innocence.

The History of Humankind from Eden to Babel (3:1–11:26)

➤THE FALL The loss of Eden and the break in fellowship with God is the saddest chapter in human history. The serpent, the devil, approached Eve with the same philosophy he always uses: doubt of God's word (Gn 3:1), denial of death (v 4), and the suggestion of equality with God (v 5). He gained access to her will by deceiving her with the promise that the fruit would make her as wise as God is (Gn 3:5; cf. 1 Jn 2:16). Eve was deceived, but when she offered the fruit to Adam, he took it willingly, knowing what he was doing (Gn 3:6; cf. 1 Tm 2:14). Later, he tried to blame God for giving him the wife who gave him the fruit (Gn 3:12). Fellowship with God was broken (v 8), yet God came seeking Adam and found him.

With sin came judgment, and the Lord pronounced righteous judgment on the serpent, the woman, and the man. The earth was also "subjected to frustration" and now groans as it awaits renewal (Rom 8:21-22). God gave hope to man and a promise of a Redeemer (Gn 3:15), who was to bruise the serpent's head. Adam and Eve were forced out of the Garden, and it was made inaccessible to them.

The impatience of humankind is shown in Eve's expectation that her son Cain was the promised Deliverer. Instead, he developed a wrong-hearted attitude toward God and became so jealous of his younger brother that he murdered him. Apprehended by God and confronted with his crime, Cain showed only self-pity and went east from Eden, where he built a city (4:1-16). Chapter 4 closes with another contrast: the brazen Lamech, who called for vengeance, while others began to call upon the name of the Lord.

➤THE GENERATIONS OF ADAM This genealogical table (5:1-32) brings humankind to the time of Noah and the Flood. The longevity of the antediluvian patriarchs seems very striking to us, but one must remember that the earth had not yet been subjected to pollution and that the effects of sin on the human race were still nominal. The refrain "and he died" reminds us of man's mortality. For Enoch, however, there was something better: "He enjoyed a close relationship with God throughout his life. Then, suddenly, he disappeared because God took him" (5:24, NLT).

➤THE FLOOD With increased population came an eruption of sin (6:1-5). As men multiplied, so did their corruption. The universal condemnation of verse 5 shows a world ripe for judgment. Noah, however, "found favor with the LORD," for he was a righteous and blameless man who walked with God (6:8-9).

The Lord planned to annihilate the human race, but he determined to save Noah and his family. Intending to flood the earth, God instructed Noah to build an ark. Noah was directed to take animals aboard the ark, two by two, male and female, for the preservation of each

species. When all was in readiness, the Flood came: "the underground waters burst forth on the earth, and the rain fell in mighty torrents from the sky" (7:11, NLT). It rained for 40 days and 40 nights. The highest mountains were covered, and life outside the ark perished. "But God remembered Noah" and sent a wind to evaporate the waters (8:1). Eventually the ark came to rest on the mountains of Ararat (v 4). Noah made a sacrifice to the Lord, and the Lord determined that he would never again bring such destruction upon the earth.

The Flood is another of God's acts that has been much debated. Many have argued for a local flood, which affected only part of Mesopotamia. Archaeologists have pointed to various flood strata in the excavation of Mesopotamian city-mounds as evidence for the account of the flood and have cited the various flood stories from that area as the source of the Genesis record. The epic of Gilgamesh gives an interesting tale of this hero, who went on a mission to visit Utnapishtim, the cuneiform Noah, in quest of eternal life. The flood story told by Utnapishtim has many parallels to Genesis, but there are greater contrasts, which demonstrate that the Bible preserves the true account.

Both the Genesis account and the references to it in the NT (cf. 2 Pt 3:6) favor the view that the deluge was not a minor episode in the Tigris-Euphrates area but was an unprecedented worldwide catastrophe. Christian geologists affirm that the Flood had far-reaching effects on the earth itself. Flood stories are almost universally known, lending support to the conclusion that the Flood covered the whole earth. Following the Flood, God blessed Noah and his sons, Ham, Shem, and Japheth. God made a covenant with Noah, promising that he would never again send a worldwide flood. As a sign of this, he established the rainbow.

Noah was the first tiller of the soil, and he planted a vineyard (9:20). Noah became drunk from wine he made and lay uncovered in his tent. Ham saw him and reported this to his brothers, who discreetly covered him. Ham and his son Canaan were cursed; Shem and Japheth were blessed.

➤THE HISTORY OF THE NATIONS "This is the history of the families of Shem, Ham, and Japheth, the three sons of Noah. Many children were born to them after the Flood" (10:1, NLT). This chapter lists the descendants of Noah's three sons, in the order of Japheth (vv 2-5), Ham (vv 6-20), and Shem (vv 21-31). Many of the names of their descendants are preserved in tribes and nations of the world.

➤THE TOWER OF BABEL The building of the Tower of Babel ("Gate of God") illustrates man's perversity and his tendency to want independence from God. The desire of man to displace God follows the fateful example of Lucifer and is a basic tenet of many cults. God thwarted the designs of the builders of Babel by confusing their languages, so that the project came to a halt (11:1-9). The site of this tower is not known with certainty. Some associate it with Birs Nimrud, not far from the ruins of the city of Babylon. Genesis 11:10-25 picks up the line of Shem and carries it down to Terah, the father of Abram.

The History of Abraham (11:27–25:10) and Isaac (21:1–28:5)

Abram came from Ur of the Chaldees, a prosperous city. The city had an imposing ziggurat (temple-tower), with many temples, storehouses, and residences. Abram and Sarai, his half sister and wife, went with his father to Haran in Syria, which like Ur was a center of the worship of the moon god, Sin (or Annar).

➤**ABRAM'S CALL** The call of God came to Abram directing him to leave his relatives and move to a land that the Lord would show him (12:1; cf. Acts 7:2-3). Abram obeyed. At the age of 75, he, Sarai, and his nephew Lot left Haran and went to Shechem, where the Lord appeared to him and promised that land to his descendants.

Famine drove Abram down to Egypt (Gn 12:10-20). Because of Sarai's beauty, he feared that someone might kill him to get her, so he passed her off as his sister. She was taken into the pharaoh's harem. When the Lord plagued Pharaoh because of this, Abram's lie was discovered and Sarai was returned to him.

➤**ABRAM AND LOT** Abram and Lot returned to Canaan, where strife broke out between Abram's herdsmen and those of Lot. Abram suggested that they should separate, and he gave Lot the choice of territory. Lot chose the well-watered Jordan Valley and the cities of the plain, Sodom and Gomorrah (ch 13).

➤**THE INVASION OF THE FOUR KINGS FROM THE EAST** The four kings who invaded along the King's Highway in Transjordan cannot be identified with certainty. Those kings were successful in their attack against the five cities of the plain, and they moved off with much booty and many captives, including Lot. Abram took 318 retainers, born in his household, and set off after them. By surprise attack, Abram recovered both Lot and the loot. On his return he was met by Melchizedek, king of Jerusalem, to whom Abram paid tithes (ch 14).

➤**THE COVENANT** The Lord promised Abram a son as heir, and in an impressive nighttime ceremony, God made a covenant with Abram and promised him the land from the River of Egypt (Wadi el Arish) to the Euphrates (ch 15). Because of her own barrenness, Sarai gave her Egyptian maid, Hagar, to Abram. Hagar gave birth to Ishmael, the progenitor of the Arab peoples. When trouble arose between the women, Sarai sent Hagar away, which was her right according to Near Eastern customs (as illustrated by the Nuzi tablets). God showed mercy to Hagar and promised that she would have a great posterity (ch 16).

God repeated his promise to Abram concerning his descendants and changed the names of Abram ("exalted father") and Sarai to Abraham ("father of many") and Sarah ("princess"). A covenant sign of circumcision was given to Abraham (ch 17). This operation had already been practiced among the Egyptians for several centuries.

➤**THE DESTRUCTION OF THE CITIES OF THE PLAIN** The Lord and two angels appeared to Abraham and announced the birth of the promised heir within a year, as well as proclaimed the impending destruction of Sodom and Gomorrah, concerning which Abraham bargained with God (18:22-33). Lot and his immediate family were rescued from Sodom, and the cities were destroyed by God with brimstone and fire (19:24-25). Lot's two daughters, wishing to preserve their family line, got their father drunk and had sexual relations with him. Moab and Ammon, enemies of Israel in later times, were the result.

In Genesis 20:1-18, Abraham again represented Sarah as his sister and got into trouble with Abimelech, king of Gerar.

➤**ISAAC** When Isaac was born (21:1-3), trouble again broke out between Sarah and Hagar. Hagar was driven out a second time, and once more was befriended by the Lord.

A disagreement arose between Abraham and Abimelech concerning a well, but they made a covenant of peace at Beersheba (21:25-34).

God tested Abraham's faith by asking him to sacrifice Isaac on Mt Moriah, which probably is the same site David later bought from Araunah the Jebusite (2 Sm 24:16-25), the place where the temple was to stand. As Abraham was about to use the knife, God called to him and showed him a ram caught in a thicket. Isaac was freed and the animal was sacrificed in his stead.

Sarah died at Hebron, and Abraham purchased the cave of Machpelah as a burial place from Ephron the Hittite (ch 23), in a transaction typical of Near Eastern business dealings. To find a wife for Isaac, Abraham sent his servant Eliezer back to the area of Haran, and the Lord directed Eliezer to Rebekah (ch 24).

Chapter 25 records the marriage of Abraham to Keturah, who bore him a number of children. Abraham died at the age of 175 years and was buried in the cave of Machpelah by his two sons, Isaac and Ishmael.

The History of Jacob and Esau (25:19–37:1) Rebekah gave birth to twin sons, Esau and Jacob. When the boys were grown, Esau sold his birthright to Jacob for a meal of red pottage (25:27-34).

When famine came to the land, Isaac went to Gerar, as his father had done (ch 20), and repeated his father's lie by calling his wife his sister (26:1-11). Trouble arose with the Philistines over wells, but Isaac was a peaceable man and preferred digging new wells rather than fighting over old ones (vv 17-33).

In Isaac's old age, when his sight had failed, Rebekah connived with Jacob to trick Isaac into giving to Jacob the blessing of the firstborn, which was rightfully Esau's. This oral blessing had legal validity and was irrevocable, according to the ancient Nuzi tablets. Fearing for Jacob's life at the hands of Esau, Rebekah arranged to send Jacob to Haran to find a wife from among her own people. At Bethel, God appeared to Jacob in a dream of a ladder leading up to heaven; God renewed with Jacob the promise made to Abraham and Isaac (28:10-22).

Jacob reached Haran, found his uncle Laban, and was employed by him (ch 29). His wages for seven years of labor were to be Laban's younger daughter, Rachel, as his wife. But Laban substituted Leah, so that Jacob had to work another seven years for Rachel. The Lord prospered Jacob, but he continually had difficulties with Laban. The Lord directed Jacob back to Canaan (31:3), so he left secretly with his wives, children, and property. Laban pursued them because his household gods were missing (possession of these "gods" made the holder heir to the owner's estate, according to Nuzi custom). Rachel had taken them but successfully concealed them from her father, and Laban went back to Haran.

Fearing a meeting with Esau as they passed through Edom, Jacob sent gifts to his brother and divided his own party into two camps for security. On this return journey, Jacob had an unexpected wrestling bout with the Angel of the Lord, and he was left with a limp and a new name, Israel (ch 32).

The meeting with Esau was friendly, and Jacob went on to Shechem (ch 33), where his sons killed the male Shechemites because of the rape of their sister Dinah (ch 34). God told Jacob to go to Bethel and build an altar to the Lord. All idols of foreign gods were buried (35:1-4). At Bethel, God reaffirmed his promise of a posterity and the land (vv 9-15). Rachel died on the way to Bethlehem, while giving birth to Benjamin, Jacob's 12th and last son. Isaac died at Hebron at age 180 and was buried in the cave of Machpelah by Esau and Jacob.

Genesis 36 records "the generations of Esau" (v 1). Here Esau is also named Edom ("Red"; cf. 25:30).

The History of Joseph (37:2–50:26) Joseph was Jacob's favorite son and thus incurred the jealousy of his brothers. This was heightened by Joseph's dreams of lordship over them. Their resentment of Joseph came to a climax when Jacob gave Joseph a beautiful coat. The brothers determined to kill Joseph, but they compromised by selling him to a caravan of merchants, who took him to Egypt and sold him as a slave to Potiphar, an Egyptian captain of the guard (37:36; 39:1).

Chapter 38 relates a historic case of levirate marriage. Judah failed to give his widowed daughter-in-law to his third son. She deceived him into fathering twin sons and forced him to acknowledge his faults. The elder son, Perez, is named in Luke's genealogy of Jesus (Lk 3:33).

The Lord blessed Joseph, who soon was put in charge of Potiphar's household (Gn 39). The young man attracted the attention of Potiphar's wife, who, after many attempts to seduce him, at last accused him of attempted rape. Sentenced on this charge, Joseph met with favor in prison, where he had opportunity to interpret dreams for two of the pharaoh's servants (ch 40). When the king had dreams that his magicians and wise men could not interpret, Joseph was summoned from jail. Joseph told Pharaoh that the dreams meant seven years of plenty, followed by seven years of famine. Joseph was then exalted to the office of vizier, or prime minister, second only to the king, and put in charge of the administration of the land (41:37-44).

When the famine came to Palestine, Jacob sent his sons to Egypt to purchase grain. Joseph recognized his brothers but did not reveal his identity to them. Joseph put them to the test by accusing them of being spies (42:9), by keeping one of the brothers (Simeon) hostage (v 19), and by demanding that if they came to Egypt again, they must bring their youngest brother with them (42:20; 43:3). The famine became so severe in Canaan (43:1) that Jacob at last allowed Benjamin to go with his brothers to Egypt. The brothers were again set up by Joseph, who had his silver cup put into Benjamin's grain sack and then had him apprehended as a thief (ch 44).

At this point Joseph revealed his identity to his brothers (45:4-15) and there was much rejoicing. Joseph pointed out that it was God who had sent him to Egypt (vv 7-8), in order to preserve the lives of all the family. Jacob was then sent for (46:1), and Joseph met him in the land of Goshen (46:28-29). The Israelites were assigned land in the region of Goshen, where they prospered (47:27).

In Jacob's final illness, Joseph brought his two sons, Manasseh and Ephraim, to his father for his blessing. Jacob gave the primary blessing to the second-born, Ephraim (48:13-20). Jacob blessed each of his own sons and then died at the age of at least 130 years. Joseph arranged for Jacob's body to be prepared for burial according to Egyptian custom (50:2-3). After the burial of their father in the cave of Machpelah at Hebron, Joseph's brothers worried about vengeance, but Joseph declared, "As far as I am concerned, God turned into good what you meant for evil. He brought me to the high position I have today so I could save the lives of many people" (v 20, NLT). Joseph died at age 110 with the prophetic request that when the Israelites went up from Egypt they would take his bones with them (50:25; cf. Ex 13:19; Jos 24:32).

See also Abraham; Adam (Person); Covenant; Creation; Eve; Fall of Man; Flood, The; Isaac; Jacob #1; Joseph #1; Nations; Noah #1; Patriarchs, Period of the.

GENEVA BIBLE* Translation of the Bible into English in 1560 in the city of Geneva, Switzerland. *See* Bible, Versions of the (English).

GENNAEUS*, GENNEUS Apollonius's father (2 Macc 12:2). Since Gennaeus means "noble" or "highborn," it may be an epithet rather than a name.

GENNESARET Area on the northwest shore of the Sea of Galilee between Capernaum and Magdala, where many of Jesus' healing miracles took place (Mt 14:34; Mk 6:53).

The plain of Gennesaret, as the region was called, curves along a distance of about four miles (6.5 kilometers) with an average width from sea to mountains of approximately one mile (1.6 kilometers). The topography is generally level, with the land rising slowly as it nears the bordering mountains. The unusually fertile soil is laced with flowing streams and rivers and noted for its productivity. Temperatures ranging from hot to mild allow for a long growing season and abundant crops. The fruits of Gennesaret were so exceptional that the rabbis did not allow them in Jerusalem during feast observances, fearing many would attend only to enjoy their succulence. Rabbis termed this area the Garden of God. During Jesus' lifetime, the area was considered the garden spot of Palestine. Trees such as the walnut, palm, olive, and fig, which require a wide diversity of growing conditions, all flourished here. Rich harvests of grapes, walnuts, rice, wheat, vegetables, and melons, as well as wild trees and flowers, were common. Later, centuries of neglect caused the plain to be largely overgrown with thornbushes, although in more recent years, certain areas have been cleared and productivity restored.

In Luke 5:1, the Sea of Galilee is referred to as the Lake of Gennesaret. The alternate name undoubtedly derived its origin from the bordering plain.

Gennesaret (more accurately termed Gennesar) was also the later name of the town Chinneroth (Jos 11:2), an ancient city that had long since fallen into ruin by Jesus' day.

GENNESARET*, Lake of Alternate name for the Sea of Galilee in Luke 5:1. *See* Sea of Galilee.

GENTILES The non-Jewish nations, known as *goyim* in Hebrew and *ethnoi* in Greek. According to the OT perspective, there are but two categories of people, the Jews (God's elect) and the nations. According to the NT perspective, salvation is offered to Jew and Gentile alike. Both Peter and Paul took the lead in bringing the gospel to the Gentiles. Paul spent his entire ministry trying to unite Jewish and Gentile Christians into one body, the church. *See* Nations; Paul, The Apostle.

GENTILES*, Court of the Large outer portion of King Herod's temple complex. The court was of irregular oblong shape, somewhat broader at the north than the south. In that court, which was open to Gentiles as well as Jews, sacrificial animals were sold and money was exchanged. A warning was posted on a partition wall instructing Gentiles not to stray into the temple's inner courts. Jesus' cleansing of the temple probably occurred in the Court of the Gentiles (Mt 21:12-13; Mk 11:15-18; Jn 2:14-16). *See also* Temple.

GENTLENESS In the OT an attitude of humility or bending low (2 Sm 22:36, KJV; cf. Ps 18:35, KJV). Its adjectival and adverbial forms ("gentle," "gently") can mean courteous and unpretentious (Prv 15:4), quiet and tender (Dt 32:2; Is 8:6), or unharsh (2 Sm 18:5; Jb 15:11).

In the NT several words are translated "gentleness," "gentle," or "gently." Shades of meaning include (1) mildness, meekness, forbearance (Mt 11:29; 1 Cor 4:21; 2 Cor 10:1; Gal 5:23; 1 Tm 6:11; 1 Pt 3:4, 15), or a courteous and unassuming attitude (2 Tm 2:25); (2) kindness expressed toward others (1 Thes 2:7; 2 Tm 2:24, KJV); and (3) fitting, fair, or seemly (1 Tm 3:3; Ti 3:2; 1 Pt 2:18). Church leaders and other believers are instructed to deal gently with those who stumble (Gal

6:1), oppose the faith (2 Tm 2:25), or are ignorant and wayward (Heb 5:2).

GENUBATH Son of Hadad, the Edomite prince who, as a young lad, was taken to Egypt to escape Joab's slaughter. There Hadad married a sister of Queen Tahpenes. She bore Genubath, who was raised by the queen as a son of Pharaoh (1 Kgs 11:20).

GERA

1. One of Benjamin's sons (Gn 46:21). The name, however, does not appear in a similar list in Numbers 26:38-41.
2. Father of the judge Ehud (Jgs 3:15).
3. Shimei's father. Shimei cursed and threw stones at David during Absalom's rebellion; later, he sought David's pardon (2 Sm 16:5; 19:16-18; 1 Kgs 2:8).
4. Bela's son from Benjamin's tribe (1 Chr 8:3, 5); alternately called Heglam in verse 7.

GERAH Measure of weight defined as one-twentieth of a shekel, the latter being the basic weight among Semitic peoples. *See* Weights and Measures.

GERAR City located in the western Negev. It was used as a geographical landmark defining the western boundary of the Canaanite territory from Sidon to Gaza (Gn 10:19). Abraham resided temporarily in this city, at which time he deceived Abimelech the king by giving him the impression that Sarah was his sister (20:1-2). Later, Isaac settled in this city and also disguised his marriage to Rebekah for fear of reprisals from the men of the city. Isaac eventually left the town, moving to the nearby valley of Gerar on account of his conflicts with the Philistines. Here the herdsmen of Gerar quarreled with Isaac's servants over a newly dug well, and Abimelech, king of the Philistines, made a covenant with Isaac (26:1-26). It is doubtful that King Abimelech of Gerar (20:2) was the same person as Abimelech, king of the Philistines (26:8). Abimelech was probably a surname or an official title.

During the patriarchal period, Gerar appeared as a dominant Canaanite city in the Negev; however, in Joshua's recounting of the Conquest, this town was not named among the Philistine cities yet to be conquered (Jos 13:2-3) or in the list of cities already defeated (15:21-22). Later, in the period of the kings, Gerar was mentioned as the southernmost city to which the Ethiopian army fled before it was completely destroyed by King Asa of Judah (910–869 BC) and his army (2 Chr 14:13-14). Perhaps the fertile valley of Gedor (1 Chr 4:39; cf. Gn 26:17), formerly inhabited by the sons of Ham (cf. Gn 10:19), was identical with the valley of Gerar. Gedor was possibly a later scribal error where the copyist confused the Hebrew letter *r* for a *d*.

The site of Gerar is identifiable with Tell Abu Hureireh along the northwestern bank of the Wadi esh-Sheri'ah, 15 miles (24.1 kilometers) northwest of Beersheba and 12 miles (19.3 kilometers) southeast of Gaza.

GERASA*, GERASENES City and district in the Decapolis. Gerasa was a well-known Roman city situated in the hills of the Transjordan about 35 miles (56 kilometers) southeast of the Sea of Galilee and 19 miles (31 kilometers) east of the Jordan River. It was originally established as a Greek city by Alexander the Great around 333 BC. In 85 BC the Jewish monarch Alexander Janneus conquered the city. Gerasa remained in Jewish hands until Pompey brought it under Roman control in 63 BC, at which time it was incorporated into the province of Syria and later included in the Decapolis. The site of Gerasa is identical with the modern Jerash.

Although the city is not named in the NT, Mark 5:1 and Luke 8:26-37 mention the "country of the Gerasenes" (RSV) as the place where Jesus healed the demoniac and the swine drowned in the Sea of Galilee. The parallel account in Matthew 8:28 reads the "country of the Gadarenes" (RSV).

The reading of "Gerasenes" in Mark and Luke is found in the better manuscripts of the NT over the later scribal alterations of "Gadarenes" and "Gergesenes." Gadara was an important city of the Decapolis whose political jurisdiction extended to the eastern shores of the Sea of Galilee. It was added perhaps by later copyists to harmonize Mark's and Luke's accounts with Matthew's Gospel. Gergesa was a city along the eastern coastline of the Sea of Galilee and the name was probably inserted in the texts of Mark and Luke to make better geographical sense of Jesus' miracle. Nonetheless, "the district of the Gerasenes" has the best textual support and should be understood as the intended site of Mark and Luke for Jesus' exorcism and miracle. To the non-Palestinian Roman and Greek readers of Mark and Luke's Gospels, the small regional district of Gadara would be unknown; however, the affluent Roman city of Gerasa would be widely known and suitable as a geographical designation for Jesus' miracle at the Sea of Galilee.

See also Decapolis; Gadara, Gadarenes; Girgashites.

GERGESA*, GERGESENES* City on the eastern shore of the Sea of Galilee. Gergesa is near Gadara, probable site of Jesus' miracle of healing a demon-possessed man and casting the demons into a nearby herd of swine. Though the account of this miracle in Matthew 8:28 refers to the "country of the Gergesenes" (KJV), it is most likely that Matthew used the reference to Gergesa as a regional identifier rather than a specific location. *See* Gadara, Gadaranes; Gerasa, Gerasenes.

GERIZIM, Mount Mountain (modern Jebel et-Tor) from which the blessings were to be pronounced, just as the cursings were to come from Mt Ebal (Dt 11:29). The two mountains designated by God were opposite each other, and the setting was a memorable one with six tribes positioned on Mt Gerizim and six on Mt Ebal, the Levites standing in the valley between—reciting the blessings and the cursings (Dt 27:11–28:68; Jos 8:33-35). The mountain is near Shechem, about 10 miles (16.1 kilometers) southeast of the city of Samaria, and it is referred to by the woman of Samaria in John 4:20-23 as the mountain where "our fathers worshiped." Abraham, indeed, had built an altar in this area (Gn 12:6-7; 33:18-20), and it had been the revered site for Samaritan worship for centu-

Mount Ebal and Mount Gerizim

ries. Jesus responds to the woman by pointing out that the physical locality of worship (whether Gerizim or Jerusalem) is not important—the spirtual reality is. One must worship in spirit and in truth.

It was in this area that the bones of Joseph were buried (Jos 24:32) and that Joshua called upon the people to renew their allegiance to the God of their fathers (vv 25-27). Josephus records in his *Antiquities* (11.8.2-4) Sanballat's promise to Manasseh to preserve for him the honor of the priesthood and also to build a temple on Mt Gerizim like that at Jerusalem. It was apparently destroyed later by the Maccabean forces under Hyrcanus (*Antiquities* 13.9.1). The Samaritans still worship at Nablus, which lies at the foot of Mt Gerizim, but are a diminishing community precariously held together.

GERON* Athenian senator who compelled the Jews to forsake the laws of their fathers and their God during the time of Antiochus IV Epiphanes (2 Macc 6:1, RSV mg).

GERSHOM
1. Moses' son by Zipporah, born in Midian during Moses' exile from Egypt (Ex 2:22; 18:3; 1 Chr 23:15-16).
2. Jonathan's father. He and his sons were priests to Dan's tribe. The Danites set up a graven image to worship and appointed Jonathan to be their priest (Jgs 18:30).
3. Alternate spelling of Gershon, Levi's oldest son (1 Chr 6:1, 16-17, 20, 43; 23:6-7). *See* Gershon, Gershonites.
4. Ancestor of Shebuel, the chief officer over the temple treasury during David's reign (1 Chr 26:24).
5. Phinehas's son who returned with Ezra after the exile (Ezr 8:2).

GERSHON, GERSHONITES Levi's oldest son (also spelled Gershom) who went into Egypt with Israel (Gn 46:11; Nm 3:17; 1 Chr 6:1) and was ancestor of a division of Levites (Gershonites) who came out of Egypt with Moses (Ex 6:16-17; Nm 3:18, 21).

In the list of the allotment of Levitical cities, the Gershonites were listed as one of the largest Levitical groups in Israel (Jos 21:1-7). Some passages indicate that they were at times dominant among the functioning Levitical groups (Gn 46:11; Ex 6:16; Nm 3:17; 26:57; 1 Chr 6:1, 16; 23:6).

According to the book of Numbers, the Gershonites were encamped behind the tabernacle to the west during the wilderness wanderings (Nm 3:23). Early in the second year after the exodus from Egypt, the Gershonite males numbered about 7,500 (v 22). Only those between the ages of 30 and 50 could serve in the tabernacle, which at the time of that early census totaled 2,630 men (4:39-40). They were responsible for the care and transportation of the external furnishings of the tabernacle (3:25-26; 4:24, 27-28) and were given two wagons and four oxen for the purpose, being supervised by Aaron and his sons (4:27).

After the initial settlement of Canaan, the Gershonites were allotted 13 cities among the tribes of Issachar, Asher, Naphtali, and Manasseh in the northern part of Palestine (Jos 21:6).

During the time of King David, they were listed among the Levites appointed to service in the temple (1 Chr 23:6-11). The Gershonite families of Ladan and Jehieli were in charge of the treasury of the house of God (26:20-22). At David's request, music in the temple was directed in part by Asaph and his family, who were Gershonites (25:1-2). In the reign of King Hezekiah the Gershonites are mentioned among the Levites who cleansed the temple (2 Chr 29:1-6, 12). In the postexilic period the descendants of Asaph celebrated the laying of

the temple foundation (Ezr 3:10) and the dedication of the city walls (Neh 12:31-36) with music.

See also Levi, Tribe of; Priests and Levites.

GERUTH-KIMHAM Plot of land (meaning "the lodging place of Kimham") near Bethlehem. Geruth-kimham possibly was given to Kimham for the service that his father, Barzillai the Gileadite, had rendered to King David (2 Sm 19:31-40; 1 Kgs 2:7). After the fall of Jerusalem (586 BC), Geruth-kimham was the camp of Johanan son of Kareah and his men as they prepared to flee to Egypt (Jer 41:17). *See* Kimham.

GESHAN Jahdai's son and a descendant of Judah through Caleb's line (1 Chr 2:47).

GESHEM Arab opponent of Nehemiah who derided those seeking to rebuild the walls of Jerusalem (Neh 2:19; 6:1-6). He was likely an inhabitant of the north Arabian Desert and has been identified with Gashmu son of Shahr in a Dedanite Arabian inscription. Like Sanballat and Tobiah, his economic interests were threatened by the rebuilding of Jerusalem.

GESHUR, GESHURITES
1. District and its inhabitants east of the Jordan River, in the tribal allotment of the half-tribe of Manasseh (Jos 13:11). Most Bible geographers place it near Bashan, on the northeast shore of the Sea of Galilee. In their conquest of the land, the Israelites defeated Og, king of Bashan, and Jair of Manasseh took Bashan as far as the border of the Geshurites and Maacathites (Dt 3:14). Though the land of the Geshurites was given to the Transjordanian tribes (Jos 13:11), Israel did not drive them out (v 13). Later, Geshur and Aram took at least 60 towns from the Israelites in Transjordan (1 Chr 2:23).

   David married Maacah, daughter of Talmai, king of Geshur, and she bore Absalom (2 Sm 3:3; 1 Chr 3:2). After the vengeful murder of Amnon, Absalom fled to Geshur for refuge with his grandfather, Talmai (2 Sm 13:37) and stayed there three years.

   See also Syria, Syrians.
2. Name of an area and its people south of Philistia. Among the lands not yet taken at the time of Joshua's advanced old age are listed "all the regions of the Philistines and Geshurites: from the Shihor River on the east of Egypt to the territory of Ekron on the north" (Jos 13:2-3, NIV). When David lived at Ziklag, in the territory of Achish, king of Gath, David made raids upon the Geshurites and others "as far as Shur, to the land of Egypt" (1 Sm 27:8).

GETHER Aram's son and the grandson of Shem (Gn 10:23). In 1 Chronicles 1:17 he is listed as one of the sons of Shem.

GETHSEMANE Place to which Jesus and his disciples walked after their Last Supper together in the upper room. In Gethsemane, Jesus underwent a great inner struggle, as he realized the hour of his betrayal was at hand (Mt 26:36-56; Mk 14:32-50; Lk 22:39-53).

The name Gethsemane, used only in the Gospels of Matthew (26:36) and Mark (14:32), means "oil press," suggesting the presence of an olive grove. The use of the Greek word "place" in the Gospel accounts indicates that Gethsemane was an enclosed piece of ground. It may be that the grove was privately owned and that Jesus and his disciples had special permission to enter.

Though the Gospels of Luke and John do not mention

the word Gethsemane, they both record Jesus' agony before his betrayal. Luke says the location was on the "Mount of Olives" (Lk 22:39). John describes the area as "across the Kidron Valley" (Jn 18:1); John's is the only Gospel to call the spot a garden. From those accounts it is also evident that Jesus and his disciples gathered in Gethsemane often for fellowship and prayer (Lk 22:39; Jn 18:2). The Gospel narratives indicate that the garden was large enough for the group to separate into different parts of it.

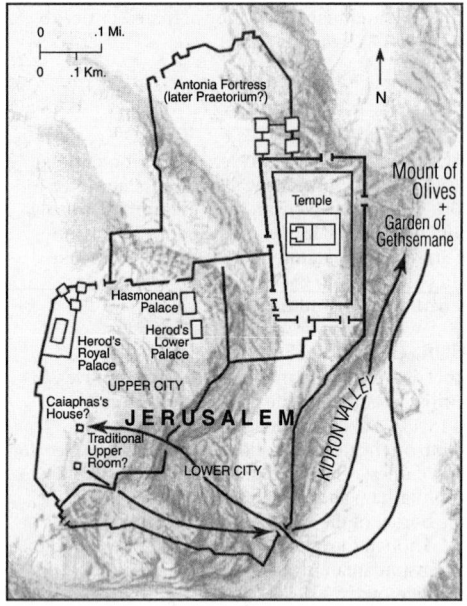

The Garden of Gethsemane After the Last Supper, Jesus went to Gethsemane, where he was arrested and taken to Caiaphas's house.

GEUEL Maki's son from Gad's tribe, and one of the 12 spies appointed by Moses to search out the Promised Land of Canaan (Nm 13:15).

GEZER Modern Tell Jezer (also known as Tell Abu Shusha), and an important ancient city in a strategic position in the north Shephelah hills. The city of the third millennium BC was protected by a brick wall, which was replaced by a 13-foot- (4-meter-) thick stone wall. The Canaanite city reached its zenith during the 20th to 14th centuries BC. The so-called outer wall was 14 feet (4.3 meters) thick and enclosed an area of 27 acres. There was a Canaanite high place (c. 1600 BC) with 10 pillars or standing stones (up to 10 feet, or 3 meters, high) and a stone altar or basin. A 216-foot (65.8-meter) tunnel with steps led down to a spring in a cave, so that there was safe and ready access to water in time of siege, as at Gibeon and other Palestinian sites. Objects found indicate cultural and commercial contacts with Egypt. The Gezer Calendar, a stone tablet with a Hebrew inscription that gives the months of the year in terms of agricultural activities, has been dated to the 10th century BC.

Horam, the king of Gezer, was defeated by the Israelites under Joshua (Jos 10:33). Gezer was a Levitical city in the tribal territory of Ephraim (16:3; 21:21), but Ephraim was unable to drive out the Canaanites (Jgs 1:29). Merneptah (c. 1225–1215 BC) of Egyptian dynasty 19 lists Gezer, along with Ashkelon and Yanoam, on the Israel Stele, which gives an account of his conquests.

During the reign of David, the Philistines invaded the plain of Rephaim, but the Lord instructed David in a successful ambush and David struck down the Philistines "from Geba to Gezer" (2 Sm 5:25).

After Solomon's marriage to the daughter of the king of Egypt, the pharaoh, whose identity is uncertain, captured and burned Gezer and gave it as a dowry to his daughter (1 Kgs 9:16). Solomon rebuilt Gezer, along with a number of other cities that served as store-cities or chariot-cities (cf. vv 15-19). He fortified Gezer and made a strong gate with four sets of piers, like those at Hazor and Megiddo.

In the fifth year of Rehoboam's reign, Shishak (Sheshonk), king of Egypt, invaded Israel (1 Kgs 14:25). Gezer is included in the list of captured cities inscribed on the wall of the temple of Karnak.

The capture of Gezer by the Assyrian king Tiglathpileser III (745–727 BC) was shown in reliefs on the walls of his palace at Nimrud (biblical Calah). The Assyrians brought to Gezer conquered people from other areas, as they did at Samaria (2 Kgs 17:24). Cuneiform tablets of contracts testify to their presence.

See also Levitical Cities.

GEZRITE* KJV spelling of Girzite in 1 Samuel 27:8. The Girzites were raided by David's men while he was at Ziklag. *See* Girzites.

GHOST*, Holy *See* Holy Spirit.

GIAH Unidentified place along the descent from Gibeon to the Arabah to which Joab and Abishai pursued Abner (2 Sm 2:24).

GIANTS English translation of four different Hebrew words. One of these words occurs in Job 16:14, where the Hebrew word is translated "warrior" in the RSV, and "giant" in the KJV. Another Hebrew word is translated "giants" in the NLT and "Nephilim" (a transliteration of the Hebrew) in the RSV (Gn 6:4; Nm 13:33). The original meaning of this Hebrew term is unknown, but it seems to be used of a group or race of people. Since none of the terms translated "giants" has that actual meaning, we cannot be sure that the Nephilim were of unusual physical stature.

In several passages the KJV translates "giants" and the RSV translates "Rephaim" (e.g., Dt 2:20; 3:11; Jos 12:4). That word, usually in plural form, refers to several tribes of people who inhabited Palestine and who may have been unusually large in physical size. They included the Anakim of Judah's coastal area and hill country around Hebron (Dt 2:11), the Emim of Moab (v 10), the Zamzummim of Ammon (v 20), and the inhabitants of Bashan (3:11). The word also appears in Joshua (Jos 12:4; 13:12; 15:8; 17:15; 18:16). Some interpreters have suggested that these people were the original inhabitants of Palestine who were distinct tribes of tall people and who were eventually conquered and absorbed by the Canaanites, Philistines, Hebrews, and other invading peoples. Other interpreters contend that they were not distinct racial tribes but were individuals of great stature, perhaps the result of disease, who were found among the various races and tribes of Palestine. Neither contention can be established with certainty. Another Hebrew term is translated "giant" in both the KJV and NLT (2 Sm 21:16-22; 1 Chr 20:4-8).

Perhaps the most famous giant in biblical literature is Goliath of Gath, the Philistine soldier who challenged King Saul's army at the valley of Elah and caused them to be dismayed and afraid (1 Sm 17). He is said to have been six cubits and a span tall, which has been variously interpreted as being between seven and a half and nine and a half feet (2.3 to 2.9 meters). David's defeat of Goliath brought the youth prominence in Israel (18:5-7). Goliath is not referred to in the text as a "giant," but his height marks him as one of gigantic size. King Og of Bashan was another unusually tall person (Dt 3:11).

See also Nephilim.

GIANTS*, Valley of the
KJV translation for "valley of Rephaim" in Joshua 15:8 and 18:16. See Rephaim, Valley of.

GIBBAR
Forefather of a family that returned to Jerusalem with Zerubbabel (Ezr 2:20). The parallel list in Nehemiah 7:25 reads "sons of Gibeon," suggesting that "Gibbar" may be a textual corruption. Some support for this view lies in the fact that Ezra 2:21 begins listing descendants by their home city rather than by family.

GIBBETHON
City in the western part of central Palestine. It was located in the territory of Dan (Jos 19:44) and allotted to the Levite clan of Kohath (21:23). Baasha killed King Nadab at Gibbethon when Israel was taking the city from the Philistines (1 Kgs 15:27). About 26 years later, Omri was proclaimed king at Gibbethon (16:17).

See also Levitical Cities.

GIBEA
Caleb's grandson from Judah's tribe (1 Chr 2:49).

GIBEAH
1. Town in the hill country of Judah (Jos 15:57). Its exact location is uncertain. Gibeah is listed as being among other towns located in the section of Judah southeast of Hebron and probably was in the fertile plateau containing Maon, Ziph, and Carmel.
2. Town in the province of Benjamin, also called "Gibeah of Saul" (1 Sm 11:4; 15:34; Is 10:29), and its inhabitants are called Gibeathites (1 Chr 12:3). It is first mentioned in the description of the territory assigned to Benjamin (Jos 18:28, KJV "Gibeath") and comes to prominence in the biblical narrative as a result of the atrocity recounted in Judges 19–21 of the Levite and his concubine.

Gibeah was also noted as the home of Saul (1 Sm 10:26). After his anointing as king of Israel, Saul returned to Gibeah, which probably remained his home and his capital (10:26; 22:6; 23:19).

The site of ancient Gibeah has been generally identified as the modern Tell el-Ful. The OT references place Gibeah north of Jerusalem, between Jerusalem and Ramah, and situated near the primary south-north road through the hill country (Jgs 19:11-19). Tell el-Ful is about three and a half miles (5.6 kilometers) north of Jerusalem and is situated on one of the highest areas in that mountain range. Excavations reveal that an early Israelite village was there about the 12th century BC and was destroyed by fire. Probably during the 11th century a stone fortress was built, and its corner tower is still evident. It probably was the citadel of Saul and his royal residence. A second fortress was built about 1000 BC but fell into disuse when David established the Israelite capital at Jerusalem. It then served as an outpost for the capital city. The tower was alternately destroyed and rebuilt through the centuries until its final destruction in the war between Antiochus III and Ptolemy V. Josephus wrote that a village existed at the site of Gibeah during the

Roman period, but it finally ceased to exist with the Roman destruction of Jerusalem (AD 70).

3. Town in the hills of Ephraim that was given to Phinehas, son of Eleazar. It was the burial site of Eleazar (Jos 24:33). An addition to the Septuagint indicates that Phinehas was also buried here. Its exact location is unknown, and several sites have been suggested: Nibi Saleh, about six miles (9.7 kilometers) northwest of Jifna; Jibia, four miles (6.5 kilometers) northwest of Jifna; et-Tell, northeast of Jifna and south of Sinjil; and Awertah, near Shechem.
4. Gibeath-elohim (1 Sm 10:5, RSV; KJV "hill of God"; NLT "Gibeah of God"). At this site Samuel, following Saul's anointing as king, predicted that Saul would meet a company of prophets and would prophesy with them. This was to be a sign of God's selection of Saul as Israel's king. Some have suggested that this is the same place as Gibeah of Benjamin, the home of Saul, but the context suggests that Saul reached this place before he arrived at his home.
5. Hill near Kiriath-jearim, where the ark of the covenant was housed by Abinadab after its return from the Philistines and until it was moved by David to the house of Obed-edom (2 Sm 6:1-4).

GIBEATH*
KJV spelling of the town Gibeah in Joshua 18:28. See Gibeah #2.

GIBEATH-ELOHIM*
Place where Samuel foretold an event that would confirm Saul as Israel's king (1 Sm 10:5, RSV; NLT mg). See Gibeah #4.

GIBEATH-HAARALOTH
Place located between the Jordan River and Jericho, in the vicinity of Gilgal, where Joshua conducted the circumcision of the Hebrew males born in the wilderness during the 40 years of wandering. (Jos 5:3, NLT; KJV "hill of the foreskins").

GIBEATHITE*
Inhabitant of the Benjamite town of Gibeah (1 Chr 12:3). See Gibeah #2.

GIBEON, GIBEONITES
Place and its inhabitants figuring prominently in the OT from the days of Joshua to the days of Nehemiah, though both were in existence outside these time limits. The site may be identified with confidence as el-Jib some five and a half miles (8.9 kilometers) north of Jerusalem. This identification was proposed as early as 1838 by Edward Robinson. Since the excavation of this site in the years 1956, 1957, 1959, 1960, and 1962, and the discovery of 31 jar handles bearing the name of Gibeon, the identification is placed beyond doubt. Certain geographical and chronological considerations also support this. The location of Gibeon, north of Jerusalem and accessible to that city in the days of David, Solomon, and Jeremiah, as well as its location southwest of Ai combine geographically to support this identification. Further, the periods of occupation at el-Jib revealed by excavation are parallel to historical data supplied by the OT.

The first mention of Gibeon and its inhabitants comes in Joshua 9 and 10 in the days of Joshua, perhaps about 1200 BC. Hearing of the success of the people of Israel at Jericho and Ai, the people of Gibeon, Kephirah, Beeroth, and Kiriath-jearim plotted to obtain a covenant of peace from them. By pretending that they had come from afar and displaying worn-out clothing and footwear as well as dried bread, they were able to deceive Joshua into making a treaty with them. When their deception was discovered, they were sentenced to chop wood and carry water for the Israelites (Jos 9:21-27). Neighboring groups of people from Jerusalem, Hebron, Jarmuth, Lachish, and Eglon, led by Adoni-zedek king of Jerusalem, launched an attack on Gibeon because of its defection to Joshua. The Gibeonites appealed to Joshua, and the Israelites made a forced march from Gilgal to assist them. The enemies of Gibeon were driven down the road to Beth-horon. Their rout was completed with the assistance of hailstones. In that day the sun stood still over Gibeon (10:9-13). Only Gibeon made peace with the incoming Israelites (11:19). In due course the town became part of Benjamin's territory (18:25; 21:17).

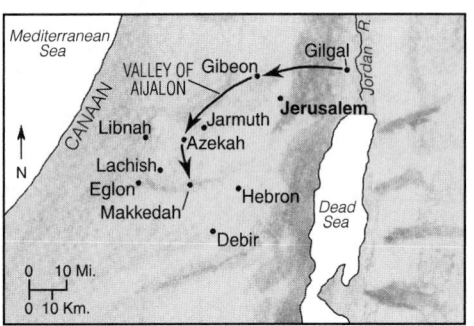

The Battle for Gibeon Israel attacked the Amorite kings outside of Gibeon and chased them as far as Makkedah.

In the days before David was king, Saul's general encountered some of David's men at Gibeon and engaged in an unusual contest at the pool of Gibeon. Twelve men from each side fought and were all thrust through by the swords of their opponents (2 Sm 2:12-17). This encounter was followed by a further skirmish in which David's men were successful (vv 18-32). Later, David's nephew Amasa, captain of the rebel army of Absalom, was attacked by Joab at the "great stone which is in Gibeon" (20:8) and left to die in the highway in his blood. In David's time also, seven sons of Saul were executed "at Gibeon on the mountain of the Lord" (21:1-9) in retribution for Saul's violation of the ancient covenant between Gibeon and Israel when he slew men of Gibeon (vv 1-6).

There was an important high place still operating at Gibeon in David's time. The tabernacle of the Lord rested there, and an altar of burnt offering as well (1 Chr 16:39; 21:29). It was at Gibeon, according to 1 Kings 3:3-9, that Solomon had a dream in which Solomon asked for wisdom to govern Israel well (cf. 2 Chr 1:2-13). A second time God appeared to Solomon at Gibeon to assure him that his prayer had been heard and to urge him to walk in God's ways (1 Kgs 9:2-9). Gibeon was among the cities taken by Pharaoh Shishak in the second half of the 10th century BC. Presumably Gibeon remained an important center during the days of the kings. There was a prophet in Gibeon in the days of Jeremiah, although he prophesied falsely (Jer 28:1-4).

Some of the Gibeonites went into exile in Babylon and a small group returned (Neh 7:25) and assisted Nehemiah in repairing the Jerusalem wall (3:7-8). Later still, Josephus relates that Cestius pitched his camp at Gibeon on his march to Jerusalem in AD 66 (*War* 2.515-516). Biblical references cover a period from about 1200 BC to about 445 BC, in archaeological terms from the beginning of the Iron I period, through the Iron II period, and into the Persian or Iron III period. We would expect, therefore, to find evidence for at least these periods in an excavation.

See also Conquest and Allotment of the Land; Gibbar.

GIBLITE* KJV rendering of Gebalite, an inhabitant of Gebal, in Joshua 13:5. *See* Gebal #1.

GIDDALTI* Heman's son and a temple singer appointed by David to serve under the direction of his father (1 Chr 25:4). The 22d of the 24 divisions of service was appointed to Giddalti (1 Chr 25:29, NLT mg).

GIDDEL
1. Ancestor of a group of temple assistants who returned to Jerusalem with Zerubbabel after the exile (Ezr 2:47; Neh 7:49).
2. Ancestor of a group of King Solomon's servants who returned with Zerubbabel after the Babylonian exile (Ezr 2:56; Neh 7:58).

GIDEON Judge of Israel, son of Joash, of the clan of Abiezer and the tribe of Manasseh. Of the 12 judges of Israel, more verses are devoted to Gideon than any other—Samson running a close second. The narrative in which he is the central character antedates the Christian era by roughly 11 centuries.

Following seven years of cruel oppression by the Midianites, Israel cried out to the Lord for relief (Jgs 6:6). An unknown prophet informs the Israelites that their miserable conditions stem from their forgetting to give exclusive devotion to the one true God. God sends his angel to Gideon. A touch of humor earmarks the angel's greeting, for the "mighty warrior" (v 12) is threshing wheat secretly for fear of the Midianites. Yet God addresses Gideon in realization of what his mighty power is able to accomplish in him (vv 14-16, 34). Conscious of his own weakness and the formidable task before him, Gideon is an ideal vehicle for God's tremendous work of deliverance (cf. 1 Cor 1:27; 2 Cor 12:10).

Gideon's Battle Gideon routed thousands of Midianites, chasing them to Zererah and Abel-meholah.

Gideon's first task is to tear down his father's altar to Baal and the adjacent one to Asherah, Baal's female consort (cf. Is 42:8). Knowing that the people would resist such an act, Gideon and his servants destroy these images of debased Canaanite religion at night. The following day the men of Ophrah confront Gideon and seek his life in retaliation for the act. Joash pleads the cause of his son, inviting Baal, if he indeed is deity, to contend for himself. Out of this confrontation the name Jerubbaal ("let Baal contend") is ascribed to Gideon (Jgs 6:32).

Yet Gideon is a man of inconstant faith, and his desire of further assurance is not rebuked as God graciously and patiently accedes to his requests concerning the dew and the fleece (Jgs 6:36-40). Subsequently Gideon is informed that mere numbers will not assure victory. Moreover, there must be no doubt whatever as to the true source of Israel's liberation (7:2). From 32,000, Gideon's troops are trimmed down to only 300 by an unusual method of reduction (vv 3-7). A secret reconnaissance mission to the outskirts of the oppositions' camp enables Gideon to receive further strengthening as he and his servant Purah overhear a Midianite soldier reveal his dream indicating Israel's imminent victory (vv 13-14). In response to this additional encouragement, he worships the Lord (Jgs 7:15; cf. 6:24).

Divided into three companies, Gideon's army stations itself at night outside the Midianite stronghold. At Gideon's signal each man blows a trumpet (made from an animal's horn) and smashes an empty jar containing a torch, shouting, "A sword for the LORD and for Gideon!" (Jgs 7:20). The effect of the clamor is overwhelming. Thinking themselves outnumbered, the confused and disheartened Midianites flee eastward across the Jordan. In hot pursuit, Gideon's men are joined by Israelites from Naphtali, Asher, and Manasseh, who follow the enemy into the Transjordan area. The men of Ephraim, whose efforts are now called upon for the first time, capture and kill two of the Midianite leaders. Angry with Gideon for failing to enlist their services earlier, the Ephraimites are nonetheless appeased by Gideon's tactful response to their queries (8:1-3).

Gideon's unselfishness shines in response to the people's desire to make him king, but he declines (Jgs 8:22-23). He does, however, receive an immense personal fortune from the spoils of war (vv 24-26). The unfortunate conclusion of Gideon's story relates to his making an ephod from the gold won in battle. Perhaps a garment patterned after the high priest's or a free-standing image, the object ensnares the people, and they worship it at Ophrah (v 27). In 2 Samuel 11:21 Gideon's alternate name, Jerubbaal, becomes Jerubbesheth, "Baal" being replaced with the Hebrew word for "shame" (*besheth*).

Gideon has been singled out in the Letter to the Hebrews as a hero of the faith whose trust in God

brought glory to the Lord (Heb 11:32, KJV "Gedeon"). As far back as the time of Isaiah, "the day of Midian" had become proverbial for deliverance accomplished by the hand of God apart from human strength (Is 9:4).

See also Judges, Book of.

GIDEONI Abidan's father and leader of Benjamin's tribe when the Israelites were roaming in the Sinai wilderness after their escape from Egypt (Nm 1:11; 2:22; 10:24). As leader, Gideoni presented his tribe's offering at the consecration of the tabernacle (7:60-65).

GIDOM Place to which the Benjamite army was driven during a civil war between Benjamin and the rest of Israel (Jgs 20:45).

GIER EAGLE* KJV translation for carrion vulture in Leviticus 11:18 and Deuteronomy 14:17. *See* Birds (Vulture, Egyptian).

GIFTS, Spiritual *See* Spiritual Gifts.

GIHON, Spring of Site in Jerusalem where Solomon was anointed as king (1 Kgs 1:33, 38, 45). There are two sources of running water in Jerusalem: The first is the Ain Umm el Daraj' (also known as the spring of the Mother of Steps, in the OT as Gihon, and to Christians as the Virgin's Fountain), which lies at the eastern ridge. The second is Bir 'Ayub, or the well of Job. The importance of the spring of Gihon for the defense of Jerusalem in time of siege is emphasized by Hezekiah's measures to deny his enemies access to the water supply and provide access for those who defended the city (2 Kgs 20:20; 2 Chr 32:30; cf. 2 Kgs 25:4; 2 Chr 32:3-4; Is 7:3). Hezekiah's tunnel brought the waters from the spring of Gihon in the Kidron Valley (eastern) into the central valley where the present-day pool of Siloam is located. The spring was unable to supply all of Jerusalem's needs after the exile, and in the Roman period aqueducts were built to bring additional water.

See also Siloam, Pool of.

GILALAI Musician present at the dedication of the Jerusalem wall, rebuilt during Ezra's time (Neh 12:36).

GILBOA, Mount Mountain on the east side of the plain of Esdraelon between Galilee on the north and Samaria on the south (modern Jebel Fuqu'ah). Mt Gilboa towers over the valley of Jezreel. It is a weathered limestone ridge reaching to a height of 1,700 feet (518.1 meters) above sea level.

Many battles were fought in the area, including Deborah's defeat of Sisera. At that time the flooding of the Kishon, which rose in Gilboa, greatly helped in the victory (Jgs 5:21). This region was the probable location of Gideon's camp when he attacked the Midianites (6:33). Gilboa is mentioned by name only in connection with Saul's defense of the area against the Philistines. Here his sons were killed, and here he himself committed suicide (1 Sm 31:1, 8; 2 Sm 1:6, 21; 21:12; 1 Chr 10:1, 8).

See also Saul #2.

Aerial View of Mount Gilboa

GILEAD (Person)

1. Makir's son from Manasseh's tribe (Nm 26:29-33) and head of the clan of his descendants (26:29; 27:1) during the time of Moses (36:1).
2. Father of Jephthah during the period of the judges (Jgs 11:1-2). Jephthah was the head of the Gileadites and judge over Israel.

3. Michael's son from Gad's tribe, who lived in Bashan during the initial settlement of Palestine (1 Chr 5:14).

GILEAD (Place)

1. Region east of the Jordan River. Generally used to designate the territory occupied by all the Transjordanian Israelite tribes (Jgs 20:1; 2 Kgs 10:33; Jer 50:19; Zec 10:10). Specifically, Gilead is the area of the Transjordan lying between the Yarmuk and Arnon Rivers and divided by the Jabbok River.

The so-called Dome of Gilead is an extension of the central hill country of Judah, rising to heights of more than 3,000 feet (914.4 meters) above the Jordan Valley. The valleys and hills were well watered by numerous rivers and tributaries, making flatter portions of the countryside well suited for agriculture, especially olive trees, grapevines, and grains (cf. Jer 8:22; 46:11; Hos 2:8). The densely forested and rugged hills were sometimes compared to those of Lebanon (Jer 22:6; Zec 10:10) and made the land a refuge for those in flight, since the terrain prohibited ready pursuit by enemies (cf. Gn 31:21; 1 Sm 13:7).

Originally the region of Gilead was allotted to the tribes of Reuben, Gad, and Manasseh (Nm 32). The period of the judges saw Israelite security there assailed by the Midianites and Amalekites, only to be checked by the military exploits of Gideon (Jgs 6–7). Half a century later, Jephthah was recalled from his banishment to rescue Gilead from oppressive Ammonite rule (chs 10–11). During the united monarchy, Saul delivered Jabesh-gilead from Ammonite dominance (1 Sm 11:1-11; 31:8-13; 2 Sm 2:1-7). Abner installed Ish-bosheth as a rival to David in Gilead (2 Sm 2:8-9). David conquered the Ammonites controlling Gilead as he extended the borders of Israel (8:11-12; 10:1-19). He fled there for refuge in the face of Absalom's rebellion (chs 15–17) and was finally restored to the throne when Absalom was slain in the forest of Ephraim (chs 18–19). Gilead remained a battleground during the divided monarchy, as first the Israelites warred with the Syrians (Arameans; 1 Kgs 20:23-43; 22:1-4, 29-40; 2 Kgs 13:22; Am 1:3) and then with the Assyrians, who wrested the territory from Pekah in 733 BC and deported the Israelite population, thus severing Gilead's tie to the northern kingdom (2 Kgs 15:27-31).

2. A city condemned for its evil (Hos 6:8), possibly an abbreviated name for Jabesh-gilead or Ramoth-gilead. This may be the same Gilead that was identified with Mizpah #5. (cf. Jgs 10:17-18).

GILEAD*, Balm of Substance of uncertain identification and one of several resins used in the Near East for medicinal purposes. It did not grow in Gilead, but it may have received its name from being exported to Egypt and Phoenicia from Gilead (Gn 37:25; Ez 27:17). The substance supposedly had astringent, antiseptic, and other therapeutic qualities.

See also Medicine and Medical Practice; Plants (Balm).

GILEADITE Name given to Israelites from the two and a half Transjordanian tribes. See Gilead (Place) #1; Gilead (Person) #1, #2.

GILGAL

1. Town near Jericho. Gilgal was assigned to Benjamin's tribe when Canaan was divided among the tribes of Israel. For many years it was a center of religious, political, and military importance, especially during the periods of the conquest of Canaan and the early monarchy under Saul.

Gilgal was the first place where Israel encamped in Palestine after the miraculous crossing of the Jordan River (Jos 4:19). No doubt the tabernacle was set up here, since Israel occupied Gilgal for some time and used it as the center of the commonwealth. Several significant religious events occurred at Gilgal: the circumcision of all Hebrew males born in the wilderness during the 40 years of wandering (5:2-9), the celebration of the Passover (v 10), the cessation of the manna (v 12), and a divine manifestation to Joshua by the "commander of the army of the LORD" (vv 13-15).

Militarily, Gilgal was Israel's first foothold in Canaan and the base of operations for the Conquest. From here Joshua led Israel to the conquest of Jericho (Jos 6) and Ai (8:3), formed a treaty with the Gibeonites (9:3-15), attacked the five Amorite kings (10:6-43), and launched his northern campaign (ch 11). At Gilgal, Judah, Manasseh, and Ephraim were assigned their portions of Palestine (chs 15–17).

After the relocation of the tabernacle at Shiloh, Gilgal retained its importance to Israel. It was one of the towns visited regularly by Samuel in his annual circuit as judge (1 Sm 7:16) and was one of the primary places for offering sacrifices (10:8; 13:9-10; 15:21). At Gilgal, Saul, a Benjamite, was crowned king (11:14-15), and later rejected (13:4-15; 15:17-31). Here the men of Judah met David returning to Palestine after Absalom's rebellion (2 Sm 19:15). That Gilgal was still a religious center of some importance as late as the eighth century BC is indicated in the denunciation by Hosea and Amos of the sanctuary and sacrificial cult located there (Hos 4:15; 9:15; 12:11; Am 4:4; 5:5).

The exact location of Gilgal is disputed among archaeologists. Some locate it at Khirbet en-Nitleh about two miles (3.2 kilometers) east of modern Jericho. Others prefer Khirbet Mefjir, a mound about one mile (1.6 kilometers) from ancient Jericho (Tell es-Sultan). Joshua 4:19 places it on the eastern border of Jericho, and Josephus gives the distance from the Jordan fording place to Gilgal as 50 stadia (5.8 miles, or 9.3 kilometers), with Gilgal being about 10 stadia from Jericho (Antiquities 5.6.4). These distances fit best with Khirbet Mefjir.

2. Place perhaps near Jericho (Dt 11:30); however, the language of the passage implies that it is located in the neighborhood of Mt Ebal and Mt Gerizim.

3. KJV rendering of "Goiim in Galilee" in Joshua 12:23. Although its location is uncertain, the context places it in northern Palestine in the area of Galilee. See Goiim #2.

4. Place describing the northern border of Judah (Jos 15:7). It was near Adummim and was perhaps identifiable with Geliloth in Joshua 18:17.

5. Place mentioned in connection with Elijah and Elisha (2 Kgs 2:1; 4:38). It was apparently a town farther from the Jordan River than #1 above. In the story of Elijah's translation into heaven, he and Elisha were going from Gilgal to Bethel to Jericho. Since the account places Bethel between Gilgal and Jericho, it could not have been the first Gilgal. It may refer to the modern Jiljiliah, a town on top of a hill in central Palestine, about seven miles (11.3 kilometers) north of Bethel.

GILGAMESH EPIC* Popular legendary composition about a Sumerian hero's life of adventure and acquisition of wisdom. Gilgamesh was king of Uruk, or Erech (Tell Obeid; modern Warka), at the end of the fourth millennium BC. The legend, which emerged from the first Babylonian dynasty (about 1830–1530 BC), was discovered in the palace library of Ashurbanipal (669–627 BC) at Nineveh.

Written on 12 tablets, the Gilgamesh Epic tells how a strong ruler, Gilgamesh, became friends with Enkidu, a hunter the gods had created to overthrow him. Together the two killed the monster Huwawa. Ishtar, the goddess of love, made advances to Gilgamesh. In resisting her, he killed the sacred heavenly bull. Enkidu died as a punishment for that crime. Gilgamesh, overcome by grief, traveled the world seeking the source of immortality, finally arriving at the homeland of Utnapishtim. In Tablet XI Utnapishtim describes a devastating flood that drowned a large area of Mesopotamia. Through his piety Utnapishtim was saved and given immortality by the gods. The final tablet contains an expression of sadness over Gilgamesh's mortality.

Biblical scholars have compared the epic's flood narrative with the one in the book of Genesis. Both accounts concern a flood, a person or persons to be delivered, the sending out of birds, and a sacrifice made by the hero. There are, however, several differences. The biblical account gives a moral reason for the Flood; the Gilgamesh Epic has a more frivolous one: the gods were irritated by human noise. The types of birds, names of heroes, dimensions of the ark, and duration of the flood all differ. The Genesis account clearly does not depend on the epic. Both may go back to a common tradition. It is also possible that the two accounts are independent descriptions of the same devastating flood.

See also Flood, The; Noah #1.

GILO*, GILOH, GILONITE* Village, and the inhabitants, in the mountains of southern Judah (Jos 15:51). David's counselor Ahithophel was a Gilonite (2 Sm 15:12; 23:34). It has been identified with modern Khirbet Jala just northeast of Hebron.

GIMZO Town of Judah captured by the Philistines during King Ahaz's reign (2 Chr 28:18). It is modern Jimzu, located southeast of Ludd (Lydda).

GINATH Tibni's father. Tibni unsuccessfully attempted to gain the throne of Israel; Omri became king instead (1 Kgs 16:21-22).

GINNETHON
1. Priest who set his seal on Ezra's covenant during the postexilic period (Neh 10:6).
2. Priest and head of Meshullam's household during the postexilic days of Joiakim the high priest (Neh 12:16).

GIRDLE* One of various articles of clothing worn about the waist.

GIRGASHITES Canaanite tribe (Gn 10:16; 1 Chr 1:14) whose land was promised to Abraham (Gn 15:21; Dt 7:1; Jos 3:10) and was ultimately acquired (Jos 24:11; Neh 9:8). The tribe's location is unknown, though they may have lived in Karkisha, a city mentioned in Hittite texts, or in Kirkishati, an area east of the Tigris. The name *Gresh* appeared in 13th century BC Ugaritic texts and might indicate a tribe. In Matthew 8:28; Mark 5:1; and Luke 8:26, a name variously translated as "Gergesenes" (KJV), "Gerasenes," and "Gadarenes" may preserve the tradition of Girgashite occupation of Palestine.

GIRZITES People living in southwest Canaan who were raided by David when at Ziklag (1 Sm 27:8, KJV "Gezrites"). The Hebrew text has *girzi*, while the marginal variant transposes two consonants to read *gizri*, "Gezrites." The Greek version follows the Hebrew marginal variant. The confusion of the name is obviously early. If "Gerzites"

is the original, they could have been a Canaanite tribe living in the Mt Gerizim area. If it was "Gezrites" originally, the people could have migrated from Gezer. They are otherwise unmentioned in the OT.

GISHPA, GISPA* Overseer of the temple servants in Nehemiah's time (Neh 11:21, KJV "Gispa"); perhaps alternately called Hasupha in Ezra 2:43 and Nehemiah 7:46. *See* Hasupha.

GITTAH-HEPHER* KJV form of the town Gath-hepher, in Joshua 19:13. *See* Gath-hepher.

GITTAIM Town in Benjamin to which the inhabitants of Beeroth fled, where they remained under civil protection (2 Sm 4:3). Nehemiah 11:33 lists Gittaim as one of the places where the returned exiles later settled. The two references may indicate two different places. If so, the second Gittaim may be located northwest of Jerusalem. Some scholars, however, believe that there is only one Gittaim, the one near Beeroth.

GITTITE Inhabitant of Gath, the Philistine city (2 Sm 6:10-11; 1 Chr 13:13). *See* Gath.

GITTITH* Obscure Hebrew term in the superscriptions of Psalms 8, 81, and 84 (NLT mg); perhaps a musical instrument or a musical cue, signaling a mood, to which the psalms were to be performed. *See* Music; Musical Instruments.

GIZON, GIZONITE* Designation for Hashem (Jashen, NLT), one of David's mighty men (1 Chr 11:34). Gizon may have been an ancient Canaanite settlement. Some scholars have emended the text to read "Gunite" (cf. 1 Chr 5:15; 7:13) or "from Gimzo" (cf. 2 Chr 28:18).

GLASS Translation for "mirror" in Isaiah 3:23, 1 Corinthians 13:12, and James 1:23 (KJV). Since mirrors of Bible times were polished metal sheets, "glass" is incorrect. *See* Mirror.

GLEAN, GLEANING Practice of allowing the poor to follow reapers in a field to pick up missed spears of grain (cf. Lv 19:9; 23:22; Dt 24:19; Ru 2:2-23). Vineyards, as well as fields of grain, were to be available for gleaning (Lv 19:10; Dt 24:20-21). Olive trees, however, were not to be gone over a second time (cf. Jgs 8:2; Is 17:6; 24:13; Jer 6:9; Mi 7:1). The word "gleaned" is also used to describe the killing of men who fled from a battle (Jgs 20:45, KJV).

GLEDE* KJV translation for "buzzard" in Deuteronomy 14:13. *See* Birds (Kite or Glede).

GLORIFICATION The expression of God's glory and splendor. The Hebrew word for "glory" originally meant "weighty, heavy, or important." From there it moved to the idea of an influential, rich, or prominent person. In ancient cultures the wealthy and the powerful were marked by the finery of their dress and jewels. Hence, a person's glory meant the ostentatious signs of wealth and power. Glory also suggested beauty, since fine clothes and jewels were items of beauty. The concept was then extended to God.

Glory of God In the OT the glory of God means something obvious about God. The book of Exodus is rich with references to God's glory. There was the fiery pillar and the glory that entered into the Holy of Holies in the tabernacle (cf. 40:34-38).

In the making of the tabernacle (Ex 25–27), the concepts of glory and beauty are joined. There is evidence that the "goodness" of the Lord that Moses saw (Ex 33:19) could also be translated as "beauty." Hence, God's glory is his beauty.

The NT continues the thought of the OT that God is a God of glory (cf. the vision of God in his glory in Rv 4). But the primary message in the NT centers on the glory of Christ. The transfiguration of Christ was a breaking out into the open of his glory (Mt 17:1-8). The apostle Paul called Jesus the Lord of glory (1 Cor 2:8) and wrote that the glory of God radiated from his face (2 Cor 3:18). John's Gospel is uniquely the Gospel of glory. In the Incarnation, the Son of God showed the glory that was his as the only begotten of the Father (Jn 1:14). The raising of Lazarus was a manifestation of the glory of God in Christ (11:40). Jesus' prayer in John 17 is filled with comments on the glory of Christ, including the affirmation that the disciples of the Lord would share in that glory.

Glorification of the Believer In 2 Corinthians 3:18 spiritual transformation is described as a changing from glory to glory. Glorification is implied as the last event in the change from glory to glory. In the process of salvation Paul lists glorification as the last and final event (Rom 8:28-30). The verb used in verse 30 is in the past tense, which some have taken to mean the certainty and finality of glorification. Glorification is the completion, the consummation, the perfection, the full realization of salvation.

Glorification is the perfection of sanctification as it pertains to one's inner character. No one passage treats this theme extensively, but Ephesians 5:27 may be taken for all. In that passage Paul wrote of presenting the church to Christ, but what he says of the church is true of each Christian. Jesus will present the church to himself in "splendor, without spot or wrinkle or any such thing, that she [the church] might be holy and without blemish." Or in the language of 2 Timothy 2:10, "Therefore I endure everything for the sake of the elect, that they also may obtain salvation in Christ Jesus with its eternal glory" (RSV).

Just as the inner person undergoes glorification, so does the believer's body. Paul calls the resurrection of the body the redemption of the body (Rom 8:23). In Philippians 3:21 Paul speaks of the transformation of bodies of humiliation (i.e., humiliated by sin and mortality) into bodies of glory identical to that of Christ. The power that shall do this is the power of God by which he subjects all things to his reign.

The most extensive treatment on the glorification of the body is found in 1 Corinthians 15, with some additional details in 2 Corinthians 5. Paul's theme in 1 Corinthians 15 is that as Christians have borne the image of the mortal clay of Adam, they shall bear the image of the immortal Son of God. Paul contrasts the two bodies. The present body is perishable; the resurrection body will be imperishable. This body is one of dishonor; the resurrection body will be one of glory. This body is one of weakness; the resurrection body is one of power. This body is of the current physical order; the resurrection body will be of the future, spiritual, eternal order.

Salvation involves justification, regeneration, and sanctification in this life. In the life to come it means the glorification of the inner person and the resurrection of the body in glory. But such a glorified person must live in a glorified environment. Hence, Scripture must logically end the course of salvation with a glorious new heaven, new earth, and a new Jerusalem.

See also Glory; Resurrection.

GLORY The singular splendor of God and the consequences for humanity.

The Glory of God The glory of God can be described in two senses: (1) as a general category or attribute, and (2) as a specific category referring to particular historical manifestations of his presence.

As an Attribute God's glory refers primarily to his majestic beauty and splendor; it also refers to the expression of God's character (Rom 3:23). The Scriptures record praise to his glorious name (Neh 9:5), describe him as the glorious Father (Eph 1:17) and the King of glory (Ps 24); he is exalted above the heavens, and his glory is over all the earth (Pss 57:5, 11; 108:5; 113:4). He is the God of glory who appeared to the patriarchs of the OT (Acts 7:2). He is jealous to maintain his glory and unwilling that it be given to another (Is 42:8); he acts to bring glory to himself (Ps 79:9; Is 48:11).

The glory of God is proclaimed by the Creation (Pss 19:1; 97:6; Rom 1:20). It is revealed by his mighty acts of salvation and deliverance (1 Chr 16:24; Pss 72:18-19; 96:3; 145:10-12; Jn 11:4, 40). His glory is the theme of the praise (1 Chr 16:24-29; Pss 29:1-2, 9; 66:1-2; 96:7-8; 115:1; Is 42:12; Rom 4:20; Phil 2:9-11).

As His Presence References to the glory of the Lord are often to particular historical manifestations of his presence; images of light and fire are prominently associated with these occurrences. The foremost example is what is known in rabbinical literature as the shekinah glory, a phrase meaning the "dwelling glory." It refers primarily to the presence of God in the pillar of cloud and fire in the OT.

The first explicit reference to the glory cloud is found in Exodus 13:21-22. At the time of the exodus, the glory of God appeared in the pillar of cloud and fire to lead the people through the sea and wilderness (Neh 9:11-12, 19). At Sinai, with Israel encamped around the mountain, the glory of God comes in the cloud and fire to speak with Moses in the sight of the people (Ex 19:9, 16-18; 24:15-18; Dt 5:5, 22-24). When Moses is given a glimpse of that glory unconcealed by the cloud and fire, his own face becomes radiant and must be veiled because of the people's fear (Ex 33:18-23; 34:29-35; 2 Cor 3:7-18).

The picture of Israel encamped around the glory of God on Sinai portrays God dwelling in the midst of his people. When the tabernacle is completed and the people set out on their march, the glory cloud of God's presence dwells above them throughout their journey (Ex 40:34-38; Nm 10:11-12). When they encamp, the tribes encircle the tabernacle (Nm 1:50–2:2), and the cloud reminds them of his presence in their midst. Later, the same glory filled the new temple that Solomon builds (2 Chr 5:13–6:1; 7:1-3). The psalmists celebrated Jerusalem and the temple as the place where his glory dwelt (Pss 26:8; 63:2; 85:9); God was in their midst.

Later in Israel's history they denied God's glorious presence (Is 3:8) and exchanged the glory of the Lord for idols made by human hands (Ps 106:20; Jer 2:10-11; cf. Rom 1:23). Because of their disobedience, judgment came against Jerusalem; the penalties of covenant violation were enforced. God would no longer be the God of a disobedient people (Hos 1:9). God's presence in the glory cloud left the temple (Ez 10:4, 18-19; 11:22), and Israel went into exile (12:1-15).

Yet out of this judgment God determined to bring a remnant to rebuild the city and the temple. In his visions Ezekiel saw the glory of the Lord return to dwell in the temple again (Ez 43:2-9), a time when the glory would return to a purified people and dwell among them forever. When the exile was over and the second temple was under construction, Haggai and Zechariah urged the people on with the promise of the return of the glory of God to fill the temple as it had done in the first temple and to "be glory in their midst" (Hg 2:3-9; Zec 2:5, 10-11).

The Glory of God in Jesus Christ We are not told if the shekinah glory returned to the second temple. But we are told that God's glory was seen again on earth in the person of Jesus Christ. John 1:14 says, "The Word became flesh and *dwelt* among us, and we beheld his *glory, glory* as of the only Son" (italics added). As such, Jesus was the new tabernacle for God's abiding glory. In Jesus, God dwelt among people. Since Christ was (and is) the very image of God, to see the light of his face was to know the glory of God (2 Cor 4:4-6). To see Jesus was to see a "light to the Gentiles and the glory of Israel" (Lk 2:30-32). The disciples who witnessed the Transfiguration (Mt 17:1-8) saw his glory in a marvelous way (2 Pt 1:16-17), for it was a glory that burst out of his human body. This outburst of glory prefigured the glorification Christ experienced in resurrection and ascension (see Jn 17:5; Phil 2:5-11).

Because Jesus humbled himself and was obedient to the point of death, God highly exalted him (Phil 2:8-9). After he suffered death on the cross, he entered into his glory (Lk 24:26) with a new and glorious body (1 Cor 15:39-43; Phil 3:21). The glorified Christ appeared to his servants. Stephen saw his glory (Acts 7:55), and Saul was blinded by his splendor (9:3). That same Christ is predicted to return in glory. He will sit on his throne in judgment (Mt 25:31); evil will be punished (16:27; 24:30; Mk 13:26; Lk 21:27; 2 Thes 2:9-10). Those who have professed him before men need not fear his glorious appearing (Mk 8:38).

At the consummation, the whole earth will be filled with his glory (Ps 72:19; Is 6:3; Hb 2:14). No longer will a glory cloud rest above a temple to mark the Holy Place, for there will be a new heaven and a new earth (Rv 21:1). The Holy City will have the radiance of the glory of God (vv 10-11).

Glory and the People of God The people of God have experienced the glory of the presence of God. The glory cloud of the OT was *their* glory (Ps 106:20; Jer 2:11). Christ came as the embodiment of the glory of God; God was in the midst of his people. When Christ ascended, he sent his Spirit to the believers (Jn 16:7-14) so that God could live in the midst of his people. The Spirit of glory rests on those who suffer for the name of Christ (1 Pt 4:14); that Spirit is the guarantee of the glorious inheritance of the saints (Rom 8:16-17).

God has given to his people the hope of glory (Rom 5:2; Phil 3:21; Col 1:27; Jude 1:24-25). Those whom he has chosen he will also glorify (Rom 8:30; 9:23); they will share in the glory of Christ (Col 3:4; 2 Thes 2:14; 2 Tm 2:10). The sufferings of this age do not compare with the glory that will be revealed (Rom 8:18; 2 Cor 4:17). The whole of creation longs to see the glorious freedom of the children of God (Rom 8:21). This hope of glory is so certain that Peter can speak of participating in it even now (1 Pt 5:1) while looking forward to that eternal glory (v 10). As partakers in the glory of Christ, the church is called to glorify God. Because of the hope that is in them, they purify themselves (1 Jn 3:3).

See also Boast; God, Being and Attributes of; Pillar of Fire and Cloud; Shekinah; Theophany; Wealth.

GLOSSOLALIA* Transliteration of a Greek expression meaning "speaking in tongues." *See* Tongues, Speaking in.

GNAT Small flying insect. The word as found in Matthew 23:24 is a general word for a small fly. *See* Animals.

GNOSTICISM* Religious thought distinguished by claims to obscure and mystical knowledge, and emphasizing knowledge rather than faith. Until the mid-20th century, Gnosticism was regarded as a Christian heresy that developed through the interweaving of Christian experience and thought with Greek philosophy. More recently, many scholars define the Gnostics more broadly as devotees of a religious view that borrowed ideas from many religious traditions. The meanings of these borrowed terms and practices were shaped into mythological expressions of experiential salvation.

Gnosticism as a Heresy During the 20th century, many discoveries of Gnostic documents have enabled scholars to define Gnosticism more accurately. Prior to the 20th century, most of the information available concerning the Gnostics came from early Christian writers (heresiologs) who penned treatises against heretics, and in the process described some of their beliefs and practices. These heresiologs, such as Irenaeus, Tertullian, and Hippolytus, viewed the Gnostics as distorters of Christianity. The Gnostics developed many misinterpretations of the Bible, especially of the creation account and the Gospel of John. Indeed, the Gnostic writers Heracleon and Ptolemais are the first known commentators on the fourth Gospel. The anger of the Christian apologists is well summarized by Irenaeus when he likens the Gnostic interpreter to one who tears apart a beautiful picture of a king and then restructures it into a picture of a fox.

Apparently a number of Gnostics continued as members of local churches and some served in high offices. Indeed, there is speculation that Valentinus may have been considered as a possible candidate for bishop at Rome. Moreover, Marcion, the fabled Christian heretic, reinterpreted Paul in such a way that the OT God became the god of evil and Christ became the messenger of the good God of grace. Many Gnostic heretical tendencies have been associated with Marcion, who developed his own censored canon of the NT and thereby forced the Christians to counter by clarifying their own canon. The early Christian historian Eusebius (d. AD 339), who excerpted some of the early lost works of heresiologs like Hegesippus, also provides insight into the hostility of Christians against various Gnostics like Marcion, Basilides, Tatian, Satornil, Dositheus, and the so-called father of all heresy, Simon the sorcerer.

Types of Gnostics
1. The Iranian type of Gnostic myth that arose in Mesopotamia is an adaption of Zoroastrianism. The myths are constructed with a horizontal dualism in which the opposing powers of good (light) and evil (darkness) are regarded as fairly equal in strength. In the first stage of the myth, a segment of the light is captured by the jealous darkness when the light transcends itself and reaches into the realm occupied by the darkness. The capture of the light has been viewed by some scholars as the Iranian cosmic "fall." Since the Gnostics themselves are usually identified with the captured light particles, a major task of their myths is to describe the process by which the light particles (encapsulated within the bodies of Gnostics) are released. The body, or "flesh" in the Greek sense, is merely a worthless covering or tomb, while the spirit—the spark in man linked to the divine—is the part that seeks release and return to the heavenly bliss. In the Iranian system the light forces regroup and

make a partially successful counterattack on the forces of darkness. Then, primarily through the work of an alien messenger of strength who has gained a foothold in the world, the good forces are able to challenge the work of the evil captors and supply advice (*gnosis*) to their devotees. This *gnosis* leads to salvation or release.

2. The Syrian type of Gnostic myth, which arose primarily in Syria, Palestine, and Egypt, is more complex and involves a vertical dualism. In this system there is only one ultimate being or group of divinities (not two as in the horizontal system). Their dualism is usually explained as the result of a flaw, or error, in the good. The error in good, for example, is frequently attributed to the least member in the good pantheon. The guilty deity is usually designated as Sophia (the Greek term for "wisdom," which indicates the Gnostic's low opinion of the Greek philosopher's quest for wisdom). This Gnostic myth details how, instead of being satisfied with her station in life, Wisdom lusts for the Ultimate Depth. Since this ultimate god cannot tolerate distortion and weakness in the godhead, he must exclude Wisdom's lust from the heavenly realm. This lust is exiled to a lower heaven, is personalized as the Lower Wisdom (sometimes called the demiurge), and becomes the creator of the world. As lesser deities, the creator and subordinate gods (often called fates) are unable to perceive the upper heavenly realm and falsely consider themselves to be ultimate. The upper godhead deviously maneuvers the Lower Wisdom in creating human beings and giving life to them through the process of passing on the breath of life. Unknowingly, in the act of creation, the Lower Wisdom not only gives life to human beings but also passes on the divine light particles. Thus, with the help of a savior—an alien messenger of knowledge sent by the upper godhead and often designated as Jesus—humanity is enabled to perceive even more than the creator and to conquer the spiritual stupor that has come upon him when his spirit was encased by the creator in an earthly body.

As a result of the split within the deity in this system, the biblical Garden of Eden story becomes radically reinterpreted. The creator provides a tree of life (which is a misnomer) and actually offers humanity bondage instead. The lower god also forbids access to the tree of knowledge (*gnosis*), which appears in his creation without his authorization, being provided by the upper godhead for the purpose of awakening Gnostics to the state from which they have come.

Because only those people who have light particles are capable of being saved, the process of salvation in most Gnostic myths is deterministic. Moreover, salvation really occurs at the end of the Gnostic's life when he seeks to escape from the created world. Concurrent with the escape, the Gnostic strips off the created elements of the body from his spirit and climbs through the fates to the heavenly realm.

With respect to both systems of Gnosticism, recent discoveries have clarified our understanding of the myths. New primary sources for the Iranian type of Gnosticism became available during the first half of the 20th century and include the publication of a Manichean psalter (1938) and a Manichean book of homilies (1934). New primary sources for the Syrian type of Gnosticism were made available through the publication of the Berlin manuscript in 1955, but more significantly, our knowledge has recently increased through the discovered codices usually designated as the Nag Hammadi manuscripts.

Understanding the Gnostic Purpose Perhaps one of the greatest problems for the uninitiated readers of Gnosticism is understanding the purpose of the Gnostic myths. The myths often seem so strange that the readers are tempted to scratch their heads and wonder how anyone with any intelligence could believe such wild stories. One must realize, however, that the myth writers were seeking to communicate elements of the unexplained relationships between the human and the divine.

The bondage of evil in the world and its relationship to a good God has stretched the minds of the greatest theologians and philosophers of history. The Gnostics devised their answer to the problem of evil by shifting the blame from this world back to either God himself or to divisions within the divine realm. By compartmentalizing good and evil, it was possible to decide one's destiny by the alignments one made.

But the role of evil was seen as so strong in this world that the Gnostics, like the Greek philosophers before them, concluded the world was a hopeless context for the victory of the good. Accordingly, they abandoned the world to the evil god and developed a theology that focused on salvation as the process of escape from the world. Their theory also provided a salvation while on earth: Since the Gnostics contained divine light particles, they were in fact immortal, and their spirits, though existing in an evil context, would not ultimately be contaminated. The body and all its lust and lower animal desires would be shed from the spirit as it rose through the realms of the lower godhead to be reunited with the divine spiritual realm after death. Some Gnostics, indeed, carried the idea of noncontamination to ridiculous lengths and devised systems whereby sexual relations with various persons represented divine-human encounters—the more, the better! Others tended to affirm more ascetic tendencies whereby they sought to conform the miserable body to the lifestyle of the incorruptible spirit.

One of the realities the Gnostic interpreters encountered was the fact that not everyone accepted their theories. Accordingly, they devised mythical methods to distinguish between various types of people. Using ideas suggested by Paul in 1 Corinthians 2 and Romans 8, the Gnostics developed a highly sophisticated categorization of people. The pneumatic, or spiritual (i.e., Gnostic), persons were divine in origin, being from light particles. The sarkic, or fleshly, persons were formed totally from the substances made by the creator and could never inherit the divine realm. The Christians whom they saw as struggling to be obedient to the biblical message, however, were a kind of mixture. They needed desperately to work out their salvation, and if they were obedient as psychic people, they might gain some form of acceptance. This elitism of the Gnostics and their distortion of the Christian message clarifies the hostility of the Christians against the Gnostics.

The myths were the methodological formulations the Gnostics used to express their theological constructs. To understand them the reader needs the key of *gnosis*, or knowledge. Interpretation of the myths was in fact an early type of demythologizing, not unlike the process Rudolf Bultmann, an early-twentieth-century theologian and NT scholar, employed in interpreting the Bible. The Gnostic writers were among the brightest minds of their day. Their creativity is to be admired. Their theology, however, is to be rejected as a distortion of the biblical message. *See* Nag Hammadi Manuscripts.

GOAD Pointed rod, sometimes tipped with metal, used for driving or guiding cattle, especially oxen in plowing.

GOAH Location mentioned in connection with the hill of Gareb, to which the restored city of Jerusalem will extend. Goah is situated south of Gareb (Jer 31:39, KJV "Goath").

GOAT *See* Animals.

GOATH* KJV spelling of Goah in Jeremiah 31:39. *See* Goah.

GOB Location where David and his men twice encountered the Philistines in battle (2 Sm 21:18-19). In the parallel description of 1 Chronicles 20:4, Gezer is mentioned as the place of war instead of Gob.

GOD, Being and Attributes of Inherent characteristics of God revealed in Scripture and displayed in God's actions in biblical history. They are characteristics equally of the Father, the Son, and the Holy Spirit. God's attributes are revealed in progressively richer and fuller ways within the history of redemption.

According to the Bible, the entire creation shows God's deity and eternal power (Ps 19:1-6; Rom 1:20). God's providence also reveals certain of his attributes (Mt 5:45; Lk 6:35; Acts 14:16-17; 17:22-31). The fullest revelation of God's attributes is seen in his work of redemption through Jesus Christ.

How does Scripture express the characteristics of God? First, in the divine names by which God revealed himself (Gn 1:1; 2:4; 17:1; Ex 3:6, 14-15; 6:2-5). Some of God's attributes are revealed implicitly in the biblical accounts of Creation, fall, Flood, Babel, and the exodus, and more fully in the various covenants God made with his people. To Israel, he identified himself as the God of Abraham, Isaac, and Jacob (Ex 3:15). To the pharaoh, he identified himself as the "God of Israel" or the "God of the Hebrews" (5:1-3).

By the time the people of Israel had reached Mt Sinai, the revelation of God's attributes in the biblical narrative had become more explicit: "The LORD, the LORD, a God merciful and gracious, slow to anger, and abounding in steadfast love and faithfulness, keeping steadfast love for thousands, forgiving iniquity and transgression and sin, but who will by no means clear the guilty, visiting the iniquity of the fathers upon the children and the children's children, to the third and the fourth generation" (Ex 34:6-7, RSV). This summary is repeated elsewhere with slight variations (Nm 14:18; Neh 9:17; Ps 103:8; Jer 32:18; Jon 4:2).

PREVIEW
•The Attributes of God
•Incommunicable Attributes
•Communicable Attributes

The Attributes of God The historic Christian confessions refer to various characteristics of God without calling them attributes or classifying them. The Westminster Shorter Catechism (1647) shows a tendency toward classification, describing God as "a Spirit, infinite, eternal, and unchangeable in his being, wisdom, power, holiness, justice, goodness and truth." The first four attributes qualify the others.

Several ways of classifying the attributes have been suggested. Generally such schemes divide the divine attributes into pairs: negative and positive, natural and moral, absolute and relative, immanent and eminent, intransitive and transitive, quiescent and operative, antithetical and synthetical, or incommunicable and communicable. Roman Catholics prefer the distinction of negative and positive, or natural and moral. Lutherans generally favor the distinction between quiescent and operative attributes. Reformed and evangelical scholars usually distinguish incommunicable and communicable attributes. Karl Barth grouped the attributes under freedom and love, and then proposed pairs of attributes that reflect freedom-love or love-freedom. In spite of the diversity of labels given the groups of attributes, surprising agreement exists in the attributes listed under each group.

This article will make a distinction between incommunicable and communicable attributes without considering the classification itself as significant. No classification of God's attributes is fully satisfactory. The *incommunicable* attributes emphasize the absolute distinctness of God, his transcendent greatness and exalted nature. Such attributes have little or no analogy in God's creatures. The *communicable* attributes find some reflection or analogy in human beings created in God's image. They indicate the immanence of God in relation to creatures. Yet all the attributes are God's attributes; the distinction between God and man, between Creator and creature, is always basic.

Incommunicable Attributes Acknowledging some diversity of theological opinion, the following attributes will be considered incommunicable: unity, spirituality, independence, immutability, eternity, and immensity. In addition, the incomprehensibility of God must be mentioned.

God's *incomprehensibility* is sometimes included in lists of his attributes. It seems preferable to regard it as a description of human inability to understand God fully. Incomprehensibility is therefore not an attribute, although it is a given in every discussion of God. Through his revelation God is truly known by faith, yet no creature will ever comprehend God the Creator. Likewise, no one will ever fully understand any one of God's attributes. Acknowledgment of God's incomprehensibility should contribute to a spirit of humility in every consideration of God and his attributes (Pss 139:6; 145:3; Is 40:28; 55:8-9; Mt 11:25-27; Rom 11:33-36; 1 Cor 2:6-16; 13:8-13).

God's *unity* is an expression of monotheism—the fact that the God of Scripture is the only, living, true God (Dt 6:4; Mk 12:29; Jn 17:3). All other gods are idols and figments of human imagination. This attribute is reflected in the first commandment: "You shall have no other gods before me" (Ex 20:3).

God's *spirituality* indicates that God is not physical and is invisible. Positively it means that God is personal, living, self-conscious, and self-determining. The invisible God cannot be seen by human eyes (Ex 33:20), so the second commandment forbids every visible representation of God (20:4). Because God is Spirit, he must be worshiped in spirit and in truth (Jn 4:24).

God's *independence* or self-existence indicates that he is not dependent upon anything outside himself. He is self-sufficient in his existence, in his decrees, and in all his works. God has "life in himself" (Jn 5:26) and "he himself gives life and breath and everything" (Acts 17:25). To Israel, he revealed himself as the "I AM" (Ex 3:14), and he made Israel a covenant people for his own possession. God continues to work out his will in the world, and even though he uses various means, his independence remains intact. Thus, he enters into fellowship with his covenant people, and he publishes the gospel through human agents.

God's *immutability* or constancy expresses his changelessness and his faithfulness to himself, to his decrees, promises, and works. He remains forever the same true God who undergoes no change from within or from anything outside himself. And so in James 1:17 we read: "Every good endowment and every perfect gift is from above, coming down from the Father of lights with whom there is no variation or shadow due to change" (RSV). God's oath to Abraham expressed his immutability so that his covenant people could be sure of the "unchangeable character of his purpose" (Heb 6:17). Samuel told King Saul that the Lord would not "change his mind; for he is not a man" (1 Sm 15:29, NIV; cf. Nm 23:19). "For I the LORD do not change" (Mal 3:6). That was God's explanation for not destroying sinful Judah; he shows mercy and keeps his covenant. Because "Jesus Christ is the same yesterday and today and forever," Christians are warned not to be "led by diverse and strange teachings" (Heb 13:8-9).

God's immutability or constancy does not imply that he is static or immobile. He is a dynamic, living God who is constantly working (Jn 5:17). Sometimes God is described as being sorry, repenting, or changing his mind (Gn 6:6-7; 1 Sm 15:11; Jon 3:10). In their contexts, such figurative expressions show the constancy of a God who, in holiness and righteousness, always abhors sin and reacts against it. In his grace and mercy, he forgives the penitent, and he carries out his promises without fail (Ps 110:4; Is 46:10; Jer 18:7-10; Eph 1:11). Thus, the constancy of God is significant in all human relationships with him, including petitions offered in prayer.

God's *eternity* indicates his transcendence over time. He is timeless and everlasting. He has no beginning or end; he does not undergo growth, development, or maturation. He existed before the creation of the world; he dwells now in eternity; he will continue as the eternal God even when history ends. Scripture speaks of God as "eternal" (Dt 33:27), "the King" (1 Tm 1:17), "the beginning and the end" (Rv 22:13). He "inhabits eternity" (Is 57:15) and his "years have no end" (Ps 102:27; cf. 2 Pt 3:8). Although God is above time and is timeless, time is his creation and history is the arena of his work. "When the time had fully come God sent forth his Son" (Gal 4:4); Jesus Christ died on a Friday and rose on the third day.

God's *immensity* and *omnipresence* express his transcendence over space. God fills heaven and earth (Jer 23:23-24). Heaven is his throne, and the earth his footstool, so he is not restricted to a temple building (Is 66:1; Acts 17:24). Yet God is immanent in this world and is actively at work in it to establish his kingdom. No one can hide from the omnipresent God (Ps 139:6-12). Jesus promised, "I am with you always, to the close of the age" (Mt 28:20). Since Pentecost (Acts 2), the Holy Spirit is said actually to dwell within the bodies of believers (1 Cor 6:19).

Communicable Attributes Many attributes of God can be classified under this heading, although it is sometimes difficult to say which biblical references to God should be regarded as attributes. A rich diversity of terminology is found in Scripture, with many synonyms. For convenience, the communicable attributes are often classified as intellectual, moral, and volitional.

Intellectual Attributes God's *knowledge* indicates that in a unique way God knows himself and all things possible and actual. *Omniscience* means that "he knows everything" (1 Jn 3:20). "Even before a word is on my tongue, lo, O LORD, thou knowest it altogether" (Ps 139:4), including the secret thoughts of a person's heart. God's righteous judgment is rooted in the fact that he "knows the thoughts of man" (Ps 94:11). Acknowledging that God's omniscience is incomprehensible, the psalmist

finds it a source of comfort (139:1-5). All the "treasures of wisdom and knowledge" are hidden in Christ (Col 2:3); therefore, the Christian is told to bring every thought captive to obey Christ (2 Cor 10:5). Christian sanctification includes renewal in knowledge to become more like Christ (Col 3:10).

God's *wisdom* indicates that he uses his knowledge in the best possible manner to achieve his goals. God's works are varied, but they are all done in wisdom (Ps 104:24). "The LORD by wisdom founded the earth" (Prv 3:19); his providence also displays his wisdom (Gn 50:20). Redemption through Jesus Christ reveals God's wisdom (1 Cor 1:24) and awakens awe and praise (Rom 11:33-36). Human beings should seek wisdom (Prv 3:21)—wisdom rooted in the fear of God (Jb 28:28; Ps 111:10; Prv 9:10). Christians are said to be "wise in Christ" (1 Cor 4:10), and Christ charges them to act wisely (Mt 10:16), thus emulating the wisdom of God.

God's *veracity* expresses his truthfulness and faithfulness. He is the truth and he is faithful to himself, to his Word, and to his promises (2 Tm 2:13). "God is light and in him is no darkness at all" (1 Jn 1:5); therefore, his followers are to walk in the light (vv 6-7). Jesus is "the way, and the truth, and the life" (Jn 14:6); hence, Christians are to walk in the truth and show faithfulness in their lives.

Moral Attributes The most comprehensive description of God's moral character is his *goodness*. God deals bountifully and kindly with all his creatures. He is "good to all" (Ps 145:9). Jesus insisted that "no one is good but God alone" (Mk 10:18; Lk 18:19). The redeemed praise God for his goodness (1 Chr 16:34; 2 Chr 5:13; Pss 106:1; 107:1; 118:1; 136:1; Jer 33:11) and are called upon to emulate this divine characteristic (Mt 5:45; Lk 6:27-36).

God's *love* is the heartbeat of the gospel. Perfect love flows among the Persons of the Trinity (Jn 3:35; 17:24). At Sinai God revealed himself as abounding in steadfast love and faithfulness (Ex 34:6-7), and all his covenantal relations with Abraham's descendants showed his steadfast love. The chief manifestation of God's love was the sending of his Son, Jesus Christ (Jn 3:16). The apostle John, who declared that "God is love," pointed to the cross to indicate what that love really meant: "he loved us and sent his Son to be the expiation for our sins" (1 Jn 4:8, 10).

God's love shown to undeserving sinners is called *grace* (Eph 1:6-8; 2:7-9; Ti 3:4). *Mercy* is God's love (sometimes his goodness) shown to those in misery and distress. God is *longsuffering* or patient in his love; he gives time for repentance.

God's *holiness* depicts the moral purity and excellence of God. The description of Jesus' holiness is applicable to each of the Persons of the Trinity: "holy, blameless, unstained, separated from sinners, exalted above the heavens" (Heb 7:26). The root idea of holiness is to be separate or set apart. Because of his inherent holiness, God is distinct from everything impure or unholy. God alone is holy; his name is holy, and he bears the name the "Holy One" (Pss 78:41; 89:18; 99:3, 9; 111:9; Is 12:6; Jer 51:5; Rv 15:4). Angels praise God's holiness (Is 6:3; Rv 4:8). Objects, places, and people are called holy when set apart for the worship of God. Because God is holy, his people are called to holiness (Lv 11:44-45; 19:2; 1 Pt 1:14-15). God's discipline of his people is aimed at making them share his holiness (Heb 12:10). The holiness of God is so prominent in Scripture that some have (mistakenly) regarded it as God's chief attribute.

Volitional Attributes God's *sovereignty* indicates the divine authority with which he rules the entire creation and in his sovereign good pleasure does whatever he wills. God is King over the entire creation, and he rules the destiny of human beings and nations. He restores his kingdom through Jesus Christ; the risen Lord revealed that all authority in heaven and on earth was given to him (Mt 28:18). Election to salvation in Christ is "according to the purpose of him who accomplishes all things according to the counsel of his will" (Eph 1:11, RSV). God's sovereign will, though free, is not arbitrary; it is righteous and holy. He created the world and gave his law as the rule for his people's lives; he covenants, blesses, and judges. God is the "King of kings and Lord of lords" (1 Tm 6:15); he calls all his subjects to obedient love (Dt 6:4-5; Mt 22:37-40; 1 Jn 5:3).

God's *sovereign power* means that he is without bounds or limit in ability; he is *omnipotent* or almighty (Rv 4:8). By his powerful word, he created all things, and upholds "the universe by his word of power" (Heb 1:3). There is nothing too hard for the Lord God Almighty (Gn 18:14; Jer 32:27; Mt 19:26); he keeps his gracious covenant and fulfills all his promises (Lk 1:37; 2 Tm 2:13; Heb 6:18). The gospel is "the power of God for salvation" (Rom 1:16), for Christ is "the power of God" to save (1 Cor 1:24). Hence, believers must come to know "the immeasurable greatness of his power in us who believe, according to the working of his great might which he accomplished in Christ when he raised him from the dead and made him sit at his right hand in the heavenly places" (Eph 1:19-20, RSV).

God's Glory All the attributes of God are summarized in Scripture's references to the *glory* of God. The majesty, splendor, beauty, and brilliance of God who dwells in unapproachable light are expressed by this indefinable term. The God of glory appeared to our father Abraham (Acts 7:2); God showed his glory to Moses (Ex 33:18-19; 34:6-7). The God of the Lord Jesus Christ is the Father of glory (Eph 1:17). The heavens declare the glory of God (Ps 19:1); the majesty and glory of God fill heaven and earth (8:1). When finally every tongue shall confess Jesus as Lord, it will be for the glory of God the Father (Phil 2:11). Human beings were created for God's glory, and Christian believers are instructed to do everything for the glory of God (1 Cor 10:31), thus reflecting in themselves his inherent glory.

GOD, Names of God's self-identifications expressing various aspects of his being.

PREVIEW
• The Biblical Idea of Name
• The Names of God in the Old Testament
• The Names of God in the New Testament

The Biblical Idea of Name In the Scriptures the name and person of God are inseparably related. This is in keeping with the biblical conception of what a name signifies.

In the Hebrew language, the term for "name" most probably meant "sign" or "distinctive mark." In the Greek language, "name" *(onoma)* is derived from a verb that means "to know." A name, therefore, indicates that by which a person or object is to be known. But the idea of name is not to be taken in the sense of a label or an arbitrary means of identifying or specifying a person, place, or object. "Name" in biblical usage correctly describes the person, place, or object and indicates the essential character of that to which the name is given. Adam named the animals according to their nature (Gn 2:19-20); Noah means "one who brings relief and com-

fort" (5:29); Jesus means "savior" (Mt 1:21). When a person was given a new position or a radical change took place in his life, a new name was given to indicate that new aspect—for example, Abraham ("father of many," Gn 17:5), and Israel ("one who strives with God" or "God strives," 32:28). The name of a person or people expressed what the person or people thought the proper description or statement of character was.

With regard to the names of God, there are considerable differences, and these are most clearly seen when biblical scholars and theologians confront the question of whether the names of God are ascriptions given by God concerning himself or they are ascriptions given to God by people who observed his acts and reflected on his character as discerned through a study of divine deeds. Here are some examples of various kinds of divine names:

1. Proper names: El, Yahweh, Adonai, Theos (God), Kurios (Lord).
2. Personal names: Father, Abba, Son, Jesus, Holy Spirit.
3. Titles: Creator, Messiah/Christ, Paraclete/Comforter.
4. Essential names: Light, Love, Spirit.
5. Descriptive names: Rock, Ba'al, Master, Rabboni, Shepherd.

The Names of God in the Old Testament

El and Related Names The name *'El* is found over 200 times in the Hebrew Bible. It is best translated as "God." The term *'el* has a number of possible meanings. The root is thought by some to be *'ul*, which means "to be first" or "to be strong." Others suggest the root is *'alah*, which means "to precede" and suggests "leader" or "commander." It can also mean "to be afraid." Thus God as *'alah*, as the strong one, is to be feared. Still others suggest the preposition *'el* ("to, toward") as the root; the idea then is of "one giving self to others" or of "one to whom others go for help." Some scholars suggest that the word *'alim*, meaning "to bind," should be considered as a root also—that is, "the strong one binds and holds firm control." Common to these four suggested root meanings is the idea of strength, power, and of supreme excellence and greatness.

'El in the OT is used particularly in the earlier books, where it describes God's exercising dynamic power as distinguished from authority. *'El* speaks of God as the great doer and producer. He is the One who exercises such power that whatever is made, done, kept, or destroyed is his doing (cf. Ex 15). *'El* is also used to express the idea that God is not to be identified as part of creation but as the One who is above, behind, and beyond creation (Ps 19:1).

'Elohim is also commonly used as the name of God, occurring over 2,500 times in the OT. There are differences of opinion concerning the exact origin and meaning of this plural name. Some have suggested that *'Elohim* is the plural form of *'El*, but it seems more likely that it is a plural of *'Eloah*, which appears in the poetical writings. Some critical writers have suggested that this plural form is borrowed from pagan polytheistic sources, but no such plural form is found among pagans as the name of a deity. Others have suggested that the plural form is used to indicate the triune nature of God, and support for this has been seen in the use of a singular verb with this plural noun. The biblical doctrine of the Trinity, as it is developed throughout the Scriptures, does not appear to be based on the use of this plural form of God's name, even though the two positions are not contradictory.

The plural form, *'Elohim*, is best understood as expressing intensity. God makes himself known by this name as the Lord of intense and extensive glory and richness as he exercises his preeminence and power in the created cosmos. Hence, when the Scripture speaks of creation, it states, "In the beginning Elohim created the heavens and the earth" (Gn 1:1). This name is repeated 35 times in Genesis 1 and 2 in connection with God's power as revealed in Creation. In the book of Deuteronomy the name *Elohim* is used repeatedly to stress the majestic power of God that was shown in Israel's release from bondage in Egypt, preservation in the wilderness, and preparation for entrance into the Promised Land. In this context, God *(Elohim)* is also recognized as the Lawgiver who will powerfully execute judgment on covenant breakers. The psalmists also used this named repeatedly as they acknowledged and praised God the majestic ruler who had demonstrated his omnipotence in many dimensions of life (see Ps 68, in which *Elohim* appears 26 times.)

Some scholars point to the use of *Elohim* when God spoke to Abraham and said he would be *Elohim* to the patriarch and his seed; that is, God would be in a covenant relationship to them (Gn 17:1-8). Included in this relationship is the idea that God is ever ready to use his power on behalf of those who are in covenant with him. Thus, *Elohim* also expresses the concept of God's faithfulness in regard to the covenant and the promises and blessings involved in it.

The name *Eloah* occurs mainly in the poetical writings, no fewer than 41 times in Job. Isaiah used it to express the incomparable character of God (Is 44:8). In like manner David asked, "Who is God [*Eloah*], but the LORD?" (2 Sm 22:32). Moses was the first to use the name *Eloah* in his song (Dt 32:15-17), referring to Israel's God in the context of the "no-gods," which had been chosen in place of the Rock of salvation and the incomparable One. This name was probably used to stress the fact that God is the only true and living One, the One to be adored and worshiped; he is to be revered with a holy fear.

Another closely related name is *'Elah*, found in Ezra and Daniel. Some think *'Elah* is a Chaldee or Aramaic form of *'Eloah*. Its root is said to be *'alah*, which means "to fear" or "to be perplexed." God as *'Elah* is the God to be feared and worshiped accordingly. In view of this meaning, it can be understood why, in the time of Israel's exile and immediately after their return, this name was commonly used.

Three other names of God include the term *'El*:

'El 'Elyon is the name used to designate the God of Melchizedek (Gn 14:18-22) as God Most High. In Psalms 57:2 and 78:56 the Hebrew reads *'Elohim 'Elyon*. It is believed that the term *Elyon* is derived from the verb *'alah*, meaning "go up, be elevated, to be exalted." There are a number of instances where the term *'Elyon* is used alone, but the context indicates that it is then used as a synonym for God (e.g., Nm 24:16; Ps 83:18; Is 14:14). The term *'elyon* is used quite frequently as an adjective; it is then translated as "high, highest, upper, uppermost." The basic ascription given to God when this name is employed is to One who is above all things as the maker, possessor, and ruler. He is incomparable in every way; he is subject to no one and no thing; he is the Exalted One.

'El Shaddai is used in the longer form seven times in the Scriptures (Gn 17:1; 28:3; 35:11; 43:14; 48:3; Ex 6:3; Ez 10:5). In the shorter form *(Shaddai)*, it appears more frequently: in Job 30 times; in Psalms 19:1 and 68:14; once in Ruth (1:21), Isaiah (13:6), Ezekiel (1:24), and Joel (1:15). In these passages the combined ideas of God as the all-powerful, all-sufficient, transcendent, sovereign ruler and disposer are present. This meaning is generally accepted, but there are differences as to the exact meaning of the term *Shaddai*. Some have begun with *shad* as

the first concept to be considered; its meaning is "breast, pap, or teat," and it is considered a "precious metaphor" of the God who nourishes, supplies, and satisfies. The root of *shad (shadah)*, in Semitic usage, is to moisten. This meaning is not the preferred one in the context of which *'El Shaddai* appears; nor is *shed* (demon), which some scholars have sought to use because it appears in Deuteronomy 32:17 and Psalm 106:37 speaking of Israel's idolatry. In addition to the fact that *shed* is spelled differently, the connection between the concept of demon and God as all-powerful is difficult to establish. More acceptable is the suggestion that *Shaddai* is a composite term of *sha* ("the one who") and *dai* ("is sufficient"). The later Greek versions have adopted this meaning. The most preferred explanation is that *Shaddai* is derived from the verb *shadad* ("to overpower, to deal violently, or to devastate"). A clear connection between *shadad* and *Shaddai* is said to be found in Isaiah 13:6 and Joel 1:15. God as *'El Shaddai* is presented as the all-powerful One, totally self-sufficient, absolute ruler, and the One who can and does make final disposition. The Septuagint has adapted this meaning; it translates *'El Shaddai* as *Pantokrator*, the "All-Ruler" or "Sovereign One."

'El 'Olam is used to refer to God as the everlasting or eternal One, a clear instance where the name of God and an attribute of God are combined. The term *'olam* has a wide range of uses. It is usually defined in lexicons as meaning "long duration, antiquity, and indefinite futurity." It is used to speak of God's existence, of God's covenant and promises, and of the Messiah's reign. Speaking to God, the psalmist said, "You are from *'olam* (everlasting) to *'olam* (everlasting)" (Ps 90:2), and the prophet Isaiah spoke of God as the everlasting Creator (Is 40:28) and as everlasting strength (26:4), and Jeremiah spoke of God as everlasting King (Jer 10:10). God's everlastingness or eternity speaks of his infinity in relation to time. *'Olam*, as ascribed to God, should not be thought of as duration prolonged indefinitely backward and forward. Rather, the word speaks to God's transcending all temporal limits; in addition, *'olam* refers to the quality of God that differs essentially from time. The Scriptures speak of *'El 'Olam* in contexts where the believer's assurance of well-being, security, and hope are presented as prized possessions.

'El Gibbor is a name that speaks of God's power and might. *Gibbor* alone is used in reference to mighty and heroic men. The two terms together always refer to God, and in some instances *Haggadol* ("the greatest") is added (Dt 10:17; Jer 32:18) to emphasize the greatness and awesome majesty of God. *'El Gibbor* is also used to describe the Messiah in Isaiah 9:6 (cf. Ps 45:4).

'El Ro'i is used once to describe God as the seeing One. Hagar described the Lord this way when she was found in the wilderness (Gn 16:13). Psalm 139:1-2 expresses this concept of God as the all-seeing One from whose eye nothing is hidden (cf. Ps 33:18).

Yahweh is a distinctly proper name of God. It is never used to refer to any pagan gods; neither is it used in regard to men. It appears 6,823 times in the OT, occurring first in Genesis 2:4, where it is joined with *Elohim*. *Yahweh* is used 164 times in Genesis, and it appears 1,800 times in Exodus through Joshua. It never appears in a declined form in the Hebrew language, and it never occurs in the plural form or with suffixes. It is abbreviated as *Yah* and *Yahu* (cf. Ex 15:2; Ps 68:4; Is 12:2; etc.).

The exact meaning of the name *Yahweh* is difficult to determine. Some have sought the root in the verb *hayah* ("to be") or in an ancient form of that same verb, *hawah*. There is no agreement as to whether the *qal* or *hiphil*

God's Name, YHWH, in Ancient Hebrew Letters A manuscript called 1QPHab; column 10; lines 7 and 14, show the ancient letters.

form of the verb should be considered as the root. Those who opt for the *hiphil* form read *Yahweh* to mean "cause to be"; thus Exodus 3:14 would read, "I will cause to be what has come to be." Others look to the *qal* form and then translate the name as "I Am" or "I Shall Be." Still others are inclined to disassociate the name from the verb *hayah* and regard it as an original and independent term, expressing the uniqueness of Israel's gracious God.

Translators of the OT have not agreed upon the correct translation of the name *Yahweh*. Since it is translated into the Greek as *kurios*, which means "Lord," many have rendered *Yahweh* as "Lord." But *'Adonai*, which is best rendered "Lord," appears with *Yahweh* in various instances. The KJV, for example, translates *Yahweh* as "God," and *'Adonai* as "Lord." Some modern translators have chosen to use *Yahweh* (see JB and NJB).

The name Jehovah, as used in the ASV (1901), has been judged unacceptable. This name arose due to the Jewish practice of not pronouncing *Yahweh* because of Leviticus 24:16, "He that blasphemes the name of *Yahweh* shall surely be put to death." This warning against a vain or blasphemous use of the name was taken in an absolute sense, especially after Israel's deportation (cf. Am 6:10). Hence, when reading the OT the Jews substituted either *'Elohim* or *'Adonai* for *Yahweh*. From this, the practice of adding the vowels of *'Adonai* to YHWH (JeHoWaH) became established.

The interpretation of Exodus 6:2-3 has caused much debate. "And God said to Moses, 'I am *Yahweh*; I appeared to Abraham, to Isaac, and to Jacob, as *El Shaddai*, but by my name *Yahweh* I did not make myself known to them.' " This passage has been understood to mean that the name *Yahweh* was not known or used prior to the time of Moses. But that is not what the passage states; rather, it speaks of the patriarchs not knowing God as *Yahweh*. They knew him as *'El Shaddai* in actual revelatory historical deeds. They had not come to know God according to his unique character, that is, as *Yahweh*. In other words, God had always been *Yahweh*; he is saying to Moses that the descendants of the patriarchs would come to know the full, rich meaning of the name by the way God dealt with them.

This name *Yahweh* reveals God's nature in the highest and fullest sense possible. It includes, or presupposes, the meaning of the other names. *Yahweh* particularly stresses the absolute faithfulness of God. God had promised the patriarchs that he would be their God, that he would be with them and deliver and bless them, keep them, and give them a land as a place of service and inheritance. Moses is told by God that Israel is about to behold and experience the unchangeableness of God as he steadfastly and wondrously remembers his word and executes it to the fullest degree. God would prove to be a faithful, redeeming, upholding, restoring God. In working out this redemption, God would demonstrate that he is all that his name implies: merciful, gracious, patient, full of loving-kindness, truthful, faithful, forgiving, just, and righteous (Ex 34:5-6). Truly, Jacob had received an insight into the meaning of the name when he exclaimed, "I wait for thy salvation, O *Yahweh*" (Gn 49:18).

Yahweh, then, is the name par excellence of Israel's God. As *Yahweh*, he is a faithful covenant God who, having given his word of love and life, keeps that word by bestowing love and life abundantly on his own.

In view of the richness of the name *Yahweh*, it can be understood why there were stringent rules regarding its proper use (Lv 24:11, 16). It also explains why thankful, rejoicing, worshiping Israelites used the abbreviated form of *Yahweh* in song when they sang Hallelujah: "Praise Yah" (Pss 104:35; 106:1; 149:1; 150:1).

Yahweh is used in a number of phrases that are considered names of or ascriptions of God. The most common of these compound names is *Yahweh Tseba'oth* ("hosts"). The word "hosts" is used frequently in the Pentateuch to refer to the armies of Israel (cf. Nm 10:14-28). This is because the word is derived from the verb *saba*, which means "to wage" war. It also means "to serve" in some contexts; for example, Numbers 8:24 clearly has reference to the service performed in the tabernacle. The noun *tseba'oth* first occurs in Genesis 2:1, where it refers to the many components of the earth and heaven. Some would limit the reference in these contexts to the stars. Still others would suggest that the *sabaoth* refers to the angels, appealing to Psalm 33:6 for confirmation.

The compound name *Yahweh Tseba'oth* first appears in 1 Samuel 1:3. In view of the frequent use of *tseba'oth* in 1—2 Samuel to refer to armies (1 Sm 12:9; 14:50; 17:55; 2 Sm 2:8; 8:16; 10:16), it is thought that the compound name refers to *Yahweh* as the God of armies, that is, God has his armies to serve him. These are considered to be armies of angels who are ministering servants to God. It has been correctly pointed out that the compound name *Yahweh Tseba'oth* is used most frequently by the prophets (Jeremiah, 88 times; Zechariah, 55 times; Malachi, 25 times; Haggai, 14 times) at times when God's people had either suffered defeat at the hands of enemy armies or were threatened by defeat. Therefore, the compound name was used to remind them that their covenant God had great hosts to fight and work for him on behalf of his people. Thus, though Israel's armies failed, their cov-

enant God was sufficient for every possible circumstance. And it was to this *Yahweh Tseba'oth* that Israel's commanders were to give allegiance (Jos 5:14-15), and in whose name Israel was blessed (2 Sm 6:18).

Several other compound names occur infrequently: *Yahweh-Nissi* (*nissi*, "my banner") is the name that Moses called on when he built an altar celebrating Israel's God-given victory over the Amalekites (Ex 17:15). Isaiah uses the term *nissi* when speaking of the coming Messiah who is to be the conqueror (Is 11:10).

Yahweh-Rapha (*rapha'*, "healer") appears in Exodus 15:26, when Israel is assured that God, their healer, will prevent the diseases of Egypt from affecting Israel. Although the name is only used once, God was often called upon and praised as the healing One (e.g., Ps 103:3; Is 30:26; Jer 6:14).

Yahweh-Rohi (*ro'i*, "my shepherd") appears in Psalm 23:1. The concept of *Yahweh* as shepherd is explicated in Ezekiel 34. "I myself will be the Shepherd of my sheep" (v 15). Jesus demonstrated this concept's full meaning when as a shepherd he gave his life for his sheep.

Yahweh-Jireh (*yir'eh*, "to see ahead or to provide") appears in Genesis 22:14. Abraham gave this name to the place where God provided a substitute for his son Isaac, whom Abraham was to offer as a sacrifice to God. *Yahweh-Shalom* (*shalom*, "peace") is the name Gideon gave to the altar he built when the angel of the Lord came to give him orders to fight the Midianites (Jgs 6:24).

Yahweh appears with a few forms of the term *tsadaq*, "righteousness." *Yahweh* is spoken of as our righteousness in Jeremiah 23:6; the thought evidently is that David's Righteous Branch (the Messiah) will attribute God's righteousness to those who are incorporated in the new covenant. This concept is expressed in the Pentateuch a number of times when it is said that God has provided a way for living righteously; that is, God provides a way of sanctification (cf. Lv 20:8; 22:9).

'Adonai as a name for God appears about 360 times in the OT, though it is not uniformly used. It is first found in Genesis 15:2 and 8, when Abram requests more definite information concerning a son and the Promised Land. It appears only 14 times after that in the Pentateuch. It appears repeatedly in the Psalms (over 50 times), and certain of the prophets use it frequently (Isaiah, 47 times; Jeremiah, 29 times; Ezekiel, over 150 times; and Amos, 27 times).

The word *'adan*, meaning "master, ruler, owner, lord," is thought to be the root of the noun *'adon*, which is frequently used of men. For example, in Genesis and 1—2 Samuel the term is used often for men who own slaves or are in positions of authority. *'Adonai* is correctly described as the name of personal communication between the believer and God. In such communication the worshiper acknowledged God's intense majesty and greatness and also the sense of belonging to this God. *'Adonai*, coming from human lips, expressed honor for God and humble submission on the part of the believing person. *'Adonai*, thus, is the name that expresses faith, assurance, security, ready service, and thanksgiving (Pss 16:2; 57:9-10).

Old Testament Name Combinations In the OT the names of God appear in various combinations. For example *'Elohim-Yahweh*, *'Elohim-Yahweh-'Adonai*, and *'Elohim-'Adonai* are very common. These combinations were an effort to express the fullness of God's being and character as these had been revealed. Names of God in combination with "Israel" occur also as, for example, with *Yahweh*-God-Israel (Jgs 5:3; Is 17:6). God is also invoked in relation to Israel without the mention of one of his names—for example, *Qedosh Yisrael* ("Holy One of Israel," Is 43:14) and *'Abir Yisrael* ("Mighty One of Israel," Gn 49:24; Ps 132:2; Is 49:26). By means of these phrases, the covenantal relationship between God and his people was expressed and God's unchanging character was positively acknowledged.

Old Testament Personal Names The personal names of God are Father, Son, and Holy Spirit and variations of these.

The term *'Abh* ("father") appears more frequently in Genesis than in any other book, and in the Pentateuch more than in any other division of the OT. But it is not used there of God but rather of one who has generated children (i.e., the male parent), the progenitor—head, chief, and ruler of the family group or clan. It is used often in the sense of the responsible one through whom God has spoken, with whom God has dealt, and through whom he has given a rich heritage to the children and descendants of the patriarchs.

In the poetical books, God is referred to as Father but is not directly named as such. Job is asked, "Has the rain a father?" (Jb 38:28). The reference is to God as the maker, source, and controller of rain. In Psalm 68:5 God in his holy dwelling place is the "Father of the fatherless"; the parallel phrase, "protector of widows," indicates the sense. Psalm 89:26 says that David will cry to God, "Thou art my Father," and the parallels use the terms "God" and "Rock of my salvation." The idea here is of God as Creator and Savior who raised up, delivered, and protected David. In Psalm 103:13, "Father" is used analogously, "As a father pities his children."

Isaiah uses the term "Father" in relation to God four times. Three times it refers to the One who has made, saved, formed, kept, and directed Israel (Is 63:16; 64:8). Isaiah says the promised child is to be named Everlasting Father (9:6). Used in this sense, the term establishes the Son's equality with the Father in stature, function, ability, and responsibility. Jeremiah also refers to God as Father in Jeremiah 3:4, 19, meaning the origin, keeper, and friend of his people Israel. Malachi 1:6 and 2:10 speak of God as the parent who deserves honor from his children and as the origin and ruler of all people.

The term "son" is one of the most-used terms in the OT; it commonly occurs in the sense of offspring and descendant. It also appears in the sense of follower or successor. There are a few indirect references to the second person of the Trinity.

The messianic Psalm 2 has such a reference: "You are my son" (v 7). It is stated in the context of the king speaking to one who rules and is to rule with and under the sovereign. The immediate reference may be to the theocratic king; however, the reference is revealed in the NT to be the second person of the Trinity (Acts 13:33). Thus, the term "son" is applied to the promised Messiah who is set forth as the divine sovereign ruler and judge of the nations. The Son is perceived to be equal with the Father in deity and function. Not all biblical scholars accept this interpretation, but support is found in such NT passages as Hebrews 1:8 which quotes Psalm 45:6. As stated above, Isaiah speaks of the son to be given (Is 9:6), the One born of the virgin (7:14), who is Immanuel, Mighty God, Everlasting Father, Prince of Peace.

The name "Holy Spirit" occurs only a few times in the OT. The Spirit is referred to frequently by terms and phrases such as "the Spirit of God" (Gn 1:2), "the Spirit of the Lord God" (Is 61:1), "the Spirit of the Lord" (Ez 37:1), "the Spirit" (Nm 11:17; 27:18), "my Spirit" (Gn 6:3), and "your Spirit" (Ps 51:11). Though the character of the Spirit is not developed as clearly in the OT as in the NT, it can be safely stated that the relationship posited between God and the Spirit is such that there is no doubt that the OT teaches the deity of the Spirit. The character and function of the Spirit is referred to especially in relation to the work of creation (Gn 1:2; Ps 33:6; etc.) and the equipping of servants for the service of God—for example, craftsmanship (Ex 35:31), leadership (Nm 11:17; 27:18), and prophecy (1 Sm 10:6; 2 Sm 23:2; 2 Chr 15:1; Ez 11:5).

The Names of God in the New Testament

Proper Names of God *Theos* is the NT equivalent of the OT names *'El* and *'Elohim; 'Elyon* appears in the NT as *Hupsistos,* the Highest (Mk 5:7; Lk 1:32, 76). *Pantokrator* (*'El Shaddai*) appears with *Theos* (2 Cor 6:18; Rv 16:7). This name was used not only to express God's transcendency, power, sovereignty, and lordship, but also to express that God is one who has a close relationship with his people. This fact is established by the very frequent use of personal pronouns with *Theos.* The name *Theos* appears over 1,000 times in the NT.

Kurios, "Lord," is used to express the OT names *Yahweh* and *'Adonai* in the Septuagint, and the NT follows it. *Kurios* means "power," so the meaning is not the same as with *Yahweh;* yet the NT does give *Kurios* the full weight of meaning that the OT gave to *Yahweh,* espe- cially when used of Jesus Christ (cf. Acts 2:36; Phil 2:9-11; etc.)

Despotes is used five times of God or Jesus in the NT (Lk 2:29; Acts 4:24; 2 Pt 2:11; Jude 1:4; Rv 6:10). It expresses the idea of authority. The idea of brutality conveyed by the modern concept "despot" is absent from the NT usage even when applied to men, where its central thought is ownership (2 Tm 2:21).

Personal Names of God In the baptismal formula, which is part of the Great Commission (Mt 28:19-20), the three personal names of God appear: Father, Son, and Holy Spirit. These names carry the OT meaning, but since the relationship of the three Persons is explicated, the NT meaning of the names is enriched.

"Jesus" is the personal name of the Son, the second person of the triune Godhead. It means "savior" (Mt 1:21). The root of this name "to save" gave rise to names such as Joshua, Hoshea, and Hosea. The basic meaning of the OT root is "to bring into a safe, wide-open place." Joshua, bringing Israel into Canaan, personally did what his name meant. The NT explanation ("save from sin") is not contrary to the OT meaning. To be saved from sin is to be restored to fellowship with God and to enter into the paradise of the heavenly kingdom.

See also Christology; God, Being and Attributes of; Holy Spirit; Jesus Christ, Life and Teachings of; Messiah; Names, Significance of.

GOD-FEARER One who fears God. This can be a term of reverence, an emotional reaction of terror, or a dread of God's vengeance.

Phrases describing the God-fearer in the OT are frequently coupled with such terms as "stood in awe" and "held in awe" (1 Chr 16:25; Ps 22:23). Reverence for the Lord is used less frequently, but it is used with this meaning when Obadiah hid the prophets in a cave to save them from being assassinated by Jezebel (1 Kgs 18:3-4, 12). A man could expect to receive justice from a God-fearing ruler (2 Sm 23:3; 2 Chr 19:7), and long life was a reward for those who feared the Lord (Prv 10:27; 14:27; 19:23). A God-fearing family would rely on the Lord for practical help in time of trouble (2 Kgs 4:1;

Prv 14:26). The fear of the Lord was effective in driving away sin and was itself the beginning of wisdom (Wisd of Sol 10:13).

In the NT fear of God is frequently used in conjunction with admonitions to love and serve the Lord (Col 3:22; 1 Pt 2:17). In the Magnificat, Mary's statement "His mercy is on those who fear him" is used in the sense of revere and obey (Lk 1:50). In Acts, the term "God-fearer" is given a specific interpretation, being used with reference to Gentiles who attended the synagogue. Paul mentions them separately when introducing his address: "Men of Israel, and you that fear God" (Acts 13:16, RSV). Cornelius was an honest, generous, and God-fearing Roman centurion who, although not a Jew, was recognized as leading a life acceptable to the Lord (10:2, 35).

The fear of God was also used in both the OT and the NT to denote dread or terror of the mighty power and judgment of the Lord (Gn 3:10; Dt 9:19; Jb 6:4; 9:28-29; Ps 76:8; Mt 17:7; 28:10; Lk 5:10; 12:5; Acts 5:5, 11; 1 Tm 5:20).

See also Fear; Proselyte.

GODS AND GODDESSES
Male and female deities worshiped by pagans. Although the Bible teaches that there is only one God (Is 45:18, 21-22; Mk 12:32), heathen people in ancient times quickly developed a belief in large numbers of so-called gods (Jer 10:11) and goddesses. Eventually each nation created and worshiped its own deities, usually more than one. Many of these "foreign gods" (1 Sm 7:3) are named in the Bible, and in most cases we are told to what nation each belonged. The list from Mesopotamia, a center of idol worship, is the longest: Adrammelech and Anammelech (2 Kgs 17:31), Bel (also known as Marduk, Is 46:1; Jer 50:2; 51:44), Kaiwan (Am 5:26), Nebo or Nabu (Is 46:1), Nergal (2 Kgs 17:30), Nisroch (19:37; Is 37:38), Rephan (Acts 7:43), Sakkuth (Am 5:26), Succoth-benoth (2 Kgs 17:30), Tammuz (Ez 8:14), and Tartak (2 Kgs 17:31). The Syrians were devoted to Ashima (v 30) and Rimmon (5:18), who was also worshiped under the compound name Hadad-rimmon (Zec 12:11). Israel's eastern neighbors, Ammon and Moab, worshiped Milcom or Molech (1 Kgs 11:5-7, 33; 2 Kgs 23:13) and Chemosh, respectively, although the Moabites also worshiped a local manifestation of Baal (Nm 25:3-5). The Philistine gods were Dagon and Baal-zebub (2 Kgs 1:2-3, 6, 16), who is the equivalent of the NT Beelzebul (Mt 12:24; Lk 11:15). One Canaanite god, Baal, and two Canaanite goddesses, Asherah and Ashtoreth, are mentioned frequently in the OT; Ashtoreth was the same as the Mesopotamian Ishtar, also known as the "Queen of Heaven" (Jer 7:18; 44:17-19, 25). The gods of Egypt are represented by only two names in the Bible: Amon (Jer 46:25) and Apis (v 15). Nibhaz (2 Kgs 17:31) was probably an Elamite god.

At least three Greco-Roman deities are mentioned in the NT: the Greek goddess Artemis (Acts 19:24-28, 34-35), known as Diana by the Romans, and the Greek gods Zeus and Hermes (Acts 14:12-13), known as Jupiter and Mercury, respectively, by the Romans.

The Bible clearly teaches that the gods of the nations have no objective reality (Jer 2:11), even though their worshipers sincerely believe that they actually exist (v 28). But the Lord proclaims that "they are no gods," (Jer 2:11; 16:20) or "gods that are not gods" (5:7, NIV). The NT further declares of idols that "an idol has no real existence" (1 Cor 8:4) and that "gods made with hands are not gods" (Acts 19:26). It is not surprising, then, that when the Israelites began to encounter other nations in significant ways—that is, as early as the time of the exo-

dus—they were told repeatedly that the Lord is greater than all other gods (Ex 15:11; 18:11; Dt 10:17; 1 Chr 16:25; 2 Chr 2:5; Pss 86:8; 95:3; 96:4-5; 97:7-9; 135:5, 136:2; Dn 2:47; Zep 2:11).

Such so-called gods were not worthy of Israel's attention or veneration. Since there is only one God, other gods could not claim and did not deserve Israel's worship (Ex 20:3; Dt 5:7). The Hebrew language did not even have a word for "goddess" and therefore had to use its word for "god" to express that concept (see 1 Kgs 11:5, 33). The Israelites were to make no images (Ex 20:4, 23; Lv 19:4; Dt 5:8) or mention (Ex 23:13; Jos 23:7) of the gods and goddesses of their heathen neighbors.

Yet despite all God's warnings, idolatry was Israel's besetting sin from the earliest times. During the patriarchal period, God's people were attracted to the "household idols" (Gn 31:32) of their relatives, and they continued to worship other gods throughout most of their history (Ex 32:1-4, 8, 23, 31; 34:15; Hos 11:2). Idolatry eventually led to the destruction of the northern kingdom (2 Kgs 17:7-18) in 722 BC and of the southern kingdom (2 Kgs 22:17; cf. Dt 29:25-28) in 586 BC. During their time of exile in Babylonia, the Jewish people saw idolatry at its worst and turned away from it, but their ancestors could have avoided untold agony if they had simply followed the example of Joshua: "As for me and my house, we will serve the LORD" (Jos 24:15).

See also Canaanite Deities and Religion; Idols, Idolatry; High Place.

GOG
1. Reubenite, Shemaiah's son (1 Chr 5:4).
2. Individual described as the prince of Meshech who ruled over the land of Magog (Ez 38:2-21; 39:1-16). Magog was evidently a territory located far from Palestine whose inhabitants would attack Jerusalem in a final attempt to overthrow God's people. The Lord, through Ezekiel, promised Gog a catastrophic defeat.

Attempts to identify Gog with some historical ruler have not been convincing. Gyges of Lydia, who drove out Cimmerian invaders, has been suggested; equally probable are Gaga, mentioned in the Amarna tablets, and Gagi, king of the city-state of Sabi. Some have maintained a mythological interpretation, in which Gog is a symbol of evil actively opposing good. Certainly Gog—connected in Scripture with godless nations such as Gomer, Put, Persia, Sheba, and Tarshish—is depicted as leading an alliance of world powers in opposition to God. Gog also appears in Revelation (20:7-9), where Satan mobilizes Gog and Magog (i.e., the nations of the world) against God's saints in a final battle. A literal view contemplates an attack on Jerusalem by hostile forces (cf. Zec 14), while a symbolic interpretation envisions a climactic conflict between good and evil.

GOIIM
1. People or region mentioned in Genesis 14:1, 9 as ruled by a king named Tidal. The word is variously translated "nations" (KJV) and "Goiim" (RSV, NLT). Tidal, together with three other kings—Amraphel of Shinar, Arioch of Ellasar, and Kedorlaomer of Elam—attacked several cities in the valley of Siddim near the Dead Sea (Gn 14:3). They defeated the five kings of the valley region, looted their towns, and captured Lot, Abraham's nephew, who lived in Sodom (v 12). When Abraham heard of this, he gathered his soldiers, pursued the victorious kings, defeated them, and rescued Lot (vv 13-16).
2. People mentioned in connection with Joshua's victory

over an unknown king of Goiim (Jos 12:23). The location of these people is uncertain, since the verse reads "Gilgal" in the Hebrew text and "Galilee" in the Septuagint.

GOLAN City and a district in the territory given to Manasseh in Bashan. It was the northernmost city of refuge east of the Jordan River (Dt 4:43; Jos 20:8), given to the Levite family of Gershon (Jos 21:27; 1 Chr 6:71). Of uncertain identification, it was known to Josephus as a fertile area, and to Eusebius as a village. The best current suggestion places it at Sehem el-Jolan, east of the river el-'Allan.

See also Cities of Refuge; Levitical Cities.

Ancient Burial Mounds in the Golan Heights

GOLD Soft, yellow metallic element. *See* Coins; Minerals and Metals; Money.

GOLDEN CALF *See* Calf, Golden.

GOLDSMITH Artisan who specialized in fine gold work. They fashioned costly and elegant idols for pagan worship (Is 40:19; 41:7; 46:6; Jer 10:9, 14; 51:17) and prepared items and gold plating for the tabernacle (Ex 31:4; 35:32) and Solomon's temple (1 Kgs 6:20-35). They formed a guild in postexilic times and assisted in the restoration and repair of the temple (Neh 3:8, 31-32).

See also Minerals and Metals.

GOLGOTHA Place where Jesus and two thieves were crucified, in the vicinity of Jerusalem. The term appears in the NT only in the accounts of the Crucifixion. Three of the Gospels use the Hebrew-Aramaic term, "Golgotha" (Mt 27:33; Mk 15:22; Jn 19:17), while one uses the Latin equivalent, "Calvary," meaning "skull or cranium" (Lk 23:33).

The reason why this place was called "the skull" is unknown, although several explanations have been offered. An early tradition, apparently originating with Jerome (AD 346–420), asserted that it was a common place of execution and that the skulls of many who had been executed were strewn around the site. No first-century evidence has been found to substantiate this viewpoint. Some suggest that it was a place of execution and that "skull" was used figuratively, simply as a symbol of death. Origen (AD 185–253) mentioned an early, pre-Christian tradition that the skull of Adam was buried in that place. This is probably the oldest explanation of the name, and is referred to by several writers after Origen. Others have said that the name resulted from the fact that the place of the Crucifixion was a hill that had the natural shape of a skull. No early evidence from any sources has been found to substantiate this

view, and the NT accounts do not refer to the place as a hill.

The location of the site is disputed. The biblical references give us only general indications. It was outside the city proper (Jn 19:20; Heb 13:12). It may have been on an elevated site, since it could be seen from a distance (Mk 15:40). It was perhaps near a road since "passersby" are mentioned (Mt 27:39; Mk 15:29). John's account places it near a garden that contained the tomb in which Jesus was buried (Jn 19:41). The use of the definite article, *"the* place of the skull," would indicate that it was a well-known place.

There seems to have been little interest in the site of Golgotha until the early part of the fourth century. Eusebius, who lived in Jerusalem for several years, said that Constantine the emperor instructed Bishop Macarius to find the site of the Crucifixion and burial. Later accounts said that the bishop was guided to the site by a vision of the Queen Mother Helena. The site that he settled on contained a Hadrianic temple of Aphrodite, which Constantine destroyed. There, tradition says, he found fragments of the cross of Christ. On that site he built two churches, and this is the site of the modern Church of the Holy Sepulcher. Although destroyed and rebuilt several times, this has remained a fixed site since the time of Constantine.

In 1842 Otto Thenius contended that Golgotha was a rocky hill about 250 yards (228.5 meters) northeast of the Damascus Gate. He based his contention on the assertions that it had been a Jewish place of stoning, lay outside the city wall, and was shaped like a skull. Later General Charles Gordon also advocated this spot, and it has come to be known as "Gordon's Calvary."

See also Crucifixion.

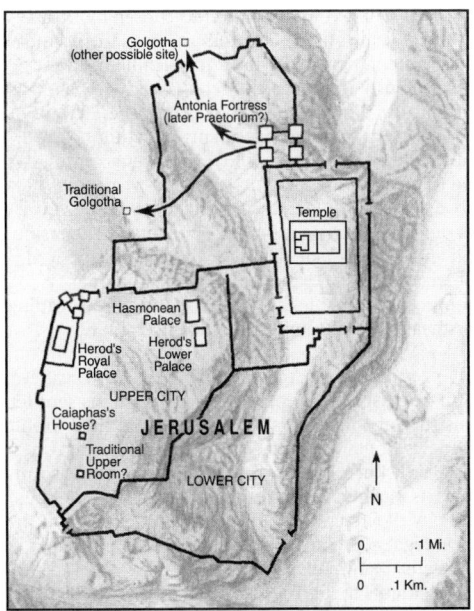

Two Possible Sites for Golgotha This map shows the boundaries of Jerusalem in Jesus' day. Two possible sites for Golgotha (meaning "the place of the skull") are shown—one to the north of the city, outside the Fish Gate; and one to the west of the city, nearer to Herod's palace.

GOLIATH Eleventh-century BC Philistine warrior from Gath, who challenged Israel to battle (1 Sm 17). He was subsequently felled and decapitated by the youthful David. Goliath was over nine feet (2.7 meters) tall, wore armor weighing about 125 pounds (56.8 kilograms), and carried a spear of 15 pounds (6.8 kilograms) weight. His sword, kept at Nob, was later given to David (1 Sm 21:9; 22:10). He may have descended from the Anakim (see Jos 11:22), but his height could have resulted from an anterior pituitary tumor. In 2 Samuel 21:19 his death is attributed to Elhanan, who in 1 Chronicles 20:5 is credited with killing Goliath's brother.

GOMER

1. Son of Japheth, who was a son of Noah (Gn 10:2; cf. 1 Chr 1:5). He had three sons: Ashkenaz, Riphath, and Togarmah (Gn 10:3; 1 Chr 1:6). He is the progenitor of the ancient Cimmerians, who according to Ezekiel's prophecy would join with Gog, the leader of the Magogites, in an effort to stamp out Israel (Ez 38:6).
2. Diblaim's daughter, a prostitute, who then became the wife of Hosea by divine command. Having borne Hosea children, she lapsed into immorality but was redeemed. Her behavior served as an illustration of Israel's infidelity to God (Hos 1–3).
   See also Hosea (Person).

GOMORRAH One of the "cities of the valley" destroyed by God because of its wickedness (Gn 19). *See* Cities of the Plain; Sodom and Gomorrah.

GOOSE* *See* Birds.

GOPHER WOOD* Material Noah used to build the ark (Gn 6:14). *See* Plants (Cypress).

GORGIAS One of the three generals chosen by Lysias, who was "governor of the kingdom, as far as the bounds of Egypt, and of the Lower Asia, and reaching from the river Euphrates," according to Josephus, early Jewish historian. The three, Ptolemy the son of Dorymenes, Nicanor, and Gorgias, are described as "mighty men among the friends of the king" (1 Macc 3:38). They were commissioned to go into Judah and destroy it but were completely defeated, although they greatly outnumbered the forces of Judas Maccabeus (4:1-22). On another occasion Joseph and Azariah were defeated when they disobeyed the orders of Judas and attacked Gorgias at Jamnia (5:56-60). It is probable that Jamnia is the correct reading for Idumea, which is found in 2 Maccabees 12:32.

GORTYNA A city of Crete mentioned in 1 Maccabees 15:23 in the list of places to which the Romans sent letters instructing the kings and countries that they should do the Jews no harm (1 Macc 15:19). In classical times it allied with Knossos to control Crete, but it was soon fighting its partner. Under the Romans, it became the capital city of Crete. Excavations in 1884 recovered the Gortyna legal code of the fifth century BC. Being near Fair Havens, Paul may have preached the gospel to the Jewish residents there on his voyage to Rome (Acts 27:8-9).

GOSHEN

1. Geographical region in Egypt occupied by the Israelites during their sojourn in Egypt from the time of Joseph to the exodus. Genesis 46–47 gives us several pieces of information concerning Goshen: (a) It was a definite part of Egypt. (b) It was the place where Joseph met his father after their years of separation, when Jacob moved his family to Egypt. (c) It was an

area good for grazing flocks. Goshen has been associated with Egyptian bull cults and was important for animal husbandry. At one period the princes of Thebes sent their cattle to the Delta for pasture, even though it was controlled by the Hyksos. Sacred cattle were probably pastured there by Egyptians also. (d) It is called "the best of the land" in two different verses (Gn 47:6, 11) and is identified as the "land of Rameses." (e) It probably had a military outpost on its eastern border and may not have been heavily inhabited by Egyptians.

The name Goshen is not of Egyptian origin but is Semitic and attests to the occupation of the region by Semites before the New Kingdom of Egypt. The Septuagint reads "Gesem of Arabia" instead of "land of Goshen" in Genesis 45:10 and 46:34. Ptolemy the geographer said that Arabia was an Egyptian name for the eastern border of the Nile Delta, and this would account for the terminology of the Septuagint.

Goshen was a region of about 900 square miles (1,448.1 square kilometers), consisting of the two districts. The western half ran from Zoan to Bubastis, a distance of about 35 miles (56.3 kilometers) from north to south. This district was an irrigated plain containing some of the most fertile land in Egypt. It is about 15 miles (24.1 kilometers) wide at the Mediterranean Sea and narrows to about 10 miles (16.1 kilometers) between Zagazig and Tell el-Kebir on the south. The eastern sector contains a large desert area between the Nile Plain and the Suez. As it stretches to the south from Daphnai to the Wadi Tumilat, it increases in width to about 40 miles (64.4 kilometers) from east to west. South of this section more desert area stretches to the Suez on the south and from the Bitter Lakes on the east to Heliopolis on the west. The physical arrangement of Goshen is important in determining the route of the exodus. Given the above description, the Wadi Tumilat would have been the most logical route to the Red Sea for people who were driving flocks and herds. The route would have led from the south side of the field of Zoan near Bubastis, east of the edge of the wilderness and the head of the Bitter Lakes.

2. Area in the territory conquered and occupied by the Israelites under Joshua (Jos 10:41, country of Goshen; Jos 11:16, land of Goshen). It was probably in the hill country of Judah between Hebron and the Negev.
3. Town in the territory of Judah (Jos 15:51). It may have been the central city of the district discussed in #2 above, but this is uncertain.

GOSPEL Word derived from the Anglo-Saxon *godspell* denoting "glad tidings" or "good news."

PREVIEW
•The Gospel Message of Isaiah
•The Gospel in the New Testament
•The Good News of Christ's Coming
•The Gospel according to Jesus
•The Gospel after Jesus' Resurrection

The Gospel Message of Isaiah Of all the passages cited, those of Isaiah provide the most important background for the gospel in the NT. According to Isaiah's gospel, it is God alone who saves, and there is no explanation for his saving action except in his own nature. Israel's deliverance is undeserved; she is no more worthy of the divine love now than when she went into captivity. In whatever measure she has paid the just due for her past sins (Is 40:2), she remains a sinful people (42:25;

46:12-13; 48:1). It is only by God's grace that she is saved (55:1-7). By God's design, Israel's salvation depends not upon her own righteousness but upon his (41:10; 45:24; 46:13; 51:5-6). There being no righteousness to reward, the Lord acts to *create* righteousness in Israel (45:8; 61:3, 10-11). Yet as these references indicate, salvation is not accomplished at the expense of justice. The penalty for Israel's sins is to be paid in full. God's mercy is not hereby called into question. On the contrary, it is precisely here that his mercy is most poignantly expressed, for the penalty is exacted not from his people but from the Servant appointed to stand in their place (53:4-12). Through the Servant's work, many shall be justified (53:11). The coming of the Evangelist—the preacher of the good news—is predicted in Isaiah 61. He is called the anointed One (v 1) who proclaims the year of the Lord's favor (v 2). God will be glorified through his preaching (v 3).

The Gospel in the New Testament

In only two places (Gal 3:8; Heb 4:2, 6) does the NT speak of the proclamation of the gospel prior to the Christian era. This is quite remarkable, given (1) the unmistakable presence of the gospel in the OT, (2) the extent of gospel terminology in the NT (in the Greek the noun appears 76 times; and the verb, 54), and (3) the fact that the NT presents Christ as the fulfillment of the OT and draws heavily on the OT to interpret his person and work. Not only is it remarkable; it is very significant. It indicates that the NT usage depends not only upon the *character* of the message (truth about salvation) but also upon *historical events*. Almost without exception, the NT restricts its application of gospel terminology to proclamations made during the time of fulfillment—the age in which the salvation promised in the OT is actually accomplished. The NT is preoccupied, not with promises of salvation, but with news of salvation. According to Mark 1:1-4, the gospel "begins" not in the OT but with John the Baptist, in whose work OT prophecy is fulfilled. In Romans 1:1-5 the gospel is represented as a blessing promised in the OT but not actually given until Jesus comes (see also Acts 13:32-33).

The Good News of Christ's Coming

The promised birth of John the Baptist is good news (Lk 1:19), not only for his parents (vv 7, 24-25) but for all the people: John is sent to prepare them for Messiah's coming (vv 14-17, 67-79). John's own preaching is gospel (3:18) for the same reason. The Messiah would be coming to execute judgment, a process that involves both condemnation and salvation (vv 3-17). John's message is gospel for sinners in that they are warned of impending doom and urged to repent before the ax falls (vv 7-9); it is gospel for the repentant in that they are promised forgiveness (v 3) and membership in Messiah's community (v 17). The birth of the Savior himself is announced as good news bringing great joy (2:10-11).

The Gospel according to Jesus

The Coming of the Kingdom of God Jesus was authorized by God and anointed by the Spirit to proclaim the gospel (Mk 1:14; Lk 4:18). At the heart of his preaching stands the announcement "The time is fulfilled, and the kingdom of God is at hand; repent, and believe in the gospel" (Mk 1:15). (For further references to this gospel, see Mt 4:23; 9:35; 24:14; 26:13; Mk 8:35; 10:29; 13:10; 14:9; Lk 4:43; 8:1; 16:16.) The message is good news for several reasons: (1) The kingdom is coming. The God whom Jesus proclaims is sovereign over all he has made. Yet paradoxically his rule is incomplete: his will is not done on earth as it is in heaven; wrong, not

right, prevails. But these conditions are not final, according to Jesus. With the coming of the kingdom, God's rule will be completed; wrong will be judged, righteousness established, and his people blessed. (2) The kingdom is *now* being inaugurated. "The time is fulfilled," declares Jesus (Mk 1:15a). The time appointed for the fulfillment of the OT promises has arrived. (3) The consummation of the kingdom is therefore no longer a distant prospect; the full realization of God's rule is "at hand" (Mk 1:15b). (4) God is establishing his rule for a saving purpose. This is implied in Jesus' call to repentance (Mk 1:15c). It is especially clear in the passages to which we now turn.

The Salvation of the Poor Invited to read the Scripture in the synagogue at Nazareth, Jesus turns to Isaiah 61: "The Spirit of the Lord is upon me, because he has anointed me to preach good news to the poor. He has sent me to proclaim release to the captives and recovering of sight to the blind, to set at liberty those who are oppressed, to proclaim the acceptable year of the Lord" (Lk 4:18-19, RSV). Having read the prophecy, Jesus announces its fulfillment in his own ministry (v 21). Included among those whom Jesus has come to free are the physically infirm, such as the blind (v 18) and the leprous (v 27) (cf. the references to healing miracles in vv 23, 33-41; the close connection between evangelizing and healing in Mt 4:23; 9:35; 11:5; Lk 7:21-22; 9:6; and the description in Mt 12:22-29; Lk 13:11-16, of the physically afflicted as captives of Satan now liberated by Jesus). Also included are the materially poor—people like the widow helped by Elijah during the famine (Lk 4:25-26). It is the literally poor and hungry whom Jesus pronounces "blessed" in Luke 6:20-21. Yet it is primarily "spiritual" poverty that is in view. Still applying Isaiah 61, Jesus speaks in Matthew 5:3 of the "poor in spirit." These are people broken and grieved by misery and poverty, oppression and injustice, suffering and death, national apostasy and personal sin—people who in their extremity turn to God and longingly wait for him to bring forth justice, bestow his mercy, and establish his kingdom. It is to just such people that Jesus brings good news (Mt 5:3-10). God sent him to usher in the kingdom, to rescue the lost, to liberate the enslaved, to cure the afflicted, to bind up hearts that are broken, and to forgive the guilty (Mk 2:5, 10, 17; 10:45; Lk 4:18-21; 7:48-49; 15:1-32; 19:10).

The Gift of Grace The coming of the kingdom is not the effect or the reward of human effort but God's answer to the human predicament—the gift of his favor (Lk 12:32). Correspondingly, the explanation for the salvation of the poor lies nowhere but in God's own character. As the prodigal himself recognized, he hardly deserved to be his father's servant, much less his son. Nothing he did, not even his repentance, accounted for the father's love (15:11-32). In the parable of Matthew 20:1-16, it is owing entirely to the goodness of the employer that the last workers to be hired receive a full day's wages. The first debtor in the story of Matthew 18:23-35 earned nothing but the right to be sold into slavery; instead, the king canceled his enormous debt. The publican, who had nothing to offer God but a confession of sin and plea for mercy, went home justified (Lk 18:13-14). The same holds true for the more virtuous among the poor, such as the persons described in Matthew 5:7-10. Their virtue is real, not imagined. Yet in keeping God's commands, they do not put him in their debt; they are simply doing their duty (Lk 17:7-10). Furthermore, even the most merciful need divine mercy (Mt 5:7). For even those most zealous to obey God's law are unable to fulfill all its requirements (cf. 11:28-30). The first servant in Matthew 18:23-35 owes far more money than someone in such a situation could possibly pay—which serves to magnify the generosity of the king. Grace depends for its exercise upon the inability of its objects (Lk 14:12-14).

The Call to Salvation The Israelites are without exception a sinful people, all of them needing the salvation that Jesus brings (Mt 1:21; Lk 1:77). In demonstration of God's grace, Jesus proclaimed his gospel to the entire nation (Mt 4:23; 9:35; 15:24; Lk 4:43; 9:6; 20:1). From the most respectable to the least, all are summoned to submit to God's rule, all are invited to come and partake freely of the banquet he has spread (Lk 14:16-24). But the gift of salvation must be received if it is to be experienced (Mk 10:15). And while it is indeed a gift that costs nothing, it is also a priceless treasure for which a wise person will freely sacrifice everything else (Mt 13:44-46), a sacrifice exceeded only by the cost of rejecting the gospel (Mt 11:20-24; Mk 8:34-39; Lk 14:24, 33). "Repent and believe in the gospel," Jesus commands (Mk 1:15). The self-righteous and the self-sufficient must be jolted out of their false sense of security and humbly recognize their need for God (Lk 6:24-26). Only then will Jesus' message to the poor be seen as gospel. An announcement of liberation (4:18-19) is good news only to people who are enslaved and know they are. The command applies also to the destitute and the afflicted. Those among them who bemoan their lot must repent of their sins. But something further is needed for the response to be complete: a person cannot believe Jesus' gospel without a commitment to the *Person* of Christ (Jn 3:16). Even those who are already "poor in spirit," in the sense defined earlier, are not really "blessed" until they acknowledge the truth of Jesus' claims (Mt 11:6) and commit themselves to a life of obedience on his terms (7:21-27). This prepares us for the next point.

Summary Throughout Jesus' earthly ministry, the theme of his gospel remains the dawning of God's kingdom (Mt 4:23; 24:14; Lk 4:43; 16:16), a message that is preached almost exclusively to Jews (Mt 10:5-6; 15:24). Yet Jesus also provides glimpses into what the gospel was to become once his work on earth was accomplished: (1) In Mark 8:35 and 10:29 Jesus speaks of individuals who needed to make great sacrifices "for my sake and for the gospel." While distinguished from each other, the person of Jesus and the gospel are here associated in the closest possible way. The time was approaching when the Proclaimer of the gospel would become the Proclaimed. (2) In Mark 13:10 and Matthew 24:14 (and the textually doubtful Mk 16:15) Jesus foretells the preaching of the gospel of the kingdom to the gentile nations. (3) In Mark 14, having interpreted a woman's action (v 3) as an anointing of his body beforehand for burial (v 8), Jesus declares, "And truly, I say to you, wherever the gospel is preached in the whole world, what she has done will be told in memory of her" (v 9, RSV; cf. Mt 26:13). This statement strongly implies that both the person of Jesus and the event of his death will figure prominently in the message that is to be proclaimed; otherwise, it is strange that the gospel and this particular act should be so solemnly bound together. Thus, here in the text already is an indication of how crucial Jesus' death is both for the provision of the salvation announced in his gospel (cf. Mk 14:22-24) and for the launching of the evangelistic mission to the Gentiles (Mt 20:28 is vital for explaining the shift from Mt 15:24 to 28:18-20).

The Gospel after Jesus' Resurrection After the resurrection of Jesus, the gospel was proclaimed by his eyewitnesses. The contents of this gospel are recorded in the book of Acts and in Paul's letters. Of the 43 instances of *euangelizomai* ("evangelize") beyond the Gospels, 15 occur in Acts and 21 in Paul's writings; of the 64 instances of *euangelion* ("gospel"), 2 occur in Acts and no fewer than 60 in Paul.

The Gospel of Christ Having risen from the dead, Jesus Christ again evangelizes (Eph 2:16-17), doing so now through his appointed representatives (Rom 15:16-18; 1 Cor 1:17; 9:12-18; Gal 4:13-14; Eph 4:11; 2 Tm 1:9-11). More than that, Christ has become the central theme of the gospel; the Proclaimer is now the Proclaimed. This is repeatedly affirmed in Acts (5:42; 8:4-5, 35; 11:20; 17:18) and in Paul's writings (Rom 1:1-4; 10:8-17; 15:19-20; 2 Cor 4:4-6; 11:4; Gal 1:16; Eph 3:8; Phil 1:15-18; 2 Tm 2:8). The NT always speaks of *the gospel*—never the gospels—of Christ. A second gospel is as inconceivable and as unnecessary as a second Christ. This is the one gospel that God authorizes (e.g., Rom 1:1-17) and proclaims (e.g., 2 Thes 2:13-14). Galatians 2:7-9 speaks not of two gospels but of two mission fields. Paul (the apostle to the uncircumcised) and Peter (the apostle to the circumcised) are both entrusted with "the gospel of Christ" (Gal 1:7; cf. 1 Cor 15:1-11), the message that God has ordained for the salvation of Jews and Gentiles alike (Rom 1:16). The "different gospel" that Paul denounces in Galatians 1:6-9 and 2 Corinthians 11:4 is not another gospel about Jesus but a message about "another Jesus"—not the real one, but one who exists only in the minds and the messages of those who proclaim him. To preach the true Christ is to preach the true gospel, however questionable one's motives (Phil 1:15-18, 27), and to respond rightly to the gospel is to turn to Christ (Acts 11:20-21; Rom 10:8-17; Gal 2:14-16).

The Gospel as a Witness to Saving Events The gospel bears witness to every aspect of Christ's saving work, from his birth (Rom 1:3; 2 Tm 2:8) and public ministry (Mk 1:1; Acts 10:36-38) to his second coming (Col 1:5, 23; cf. 3:1-4; 1 Thes 1:5-10) and the last judgment (Rom 2:16). But it is the death and the resurrection of Christ that are most crucial for the accomplishment of salvation, and that are therefore most prominent in the gospel's witness. These are the events with which Mark's proclamation climaxes (chs 15–16), and for which everything else prepares (8:31; 9:31; 10:33-34; 12:6-8); special stress is placed upon Jesus' death as the means of salvation from sin (10:45; 14:3-9, 22-24). In Paul's gospel, too, the death and resurrection of Jesus are central (Rom 4:25; 1 Cor 15:1-4), with the cross occupying the very center (1 Cor 1:17–2:5). Had Christ not risen from the dead, Paul argues, the preaching of the cross would be a waste of time (1 Cor 15:14, 17; cf. Rom 6:3-11). However, now that Christ has risen, his death deserves special emphasis as the place where God provides atonement for sins (Rom 3:21-26; 5:6-11; 2 Cor 5:14-21; Eph 1:7). The gospel according to Acts proclaims Jesus' death (Acts 8:25; 20:24, 28; cf. 10:36-43) and preeminently his resurrection, the event by which he conquered death and was exalted as Lord and coming Judge (10:36-43; 13:32-33; 17:18, 31). According to 1 Peter, the bearers of the gospel (1 Pt 1:12) concentrated, as had the OT prophets, on "the sufferings of Christ and the subsequent glory" (1:11; cf. 1:18-19; 2:21-24; 3:18-22).

The Gospel as a Power for Salvation The gospel is much more than a report of past events and an exposition of doctrine. Paul declares in 1 Corinthians 1:17-18 and again in Romans 1:16 that the gospel is "the power of God"—not merely a witness to his power but an *expression* of his power. Thus, it cannot be fettered (2 Tm 2:8-9). "Our gospel came to you not only in word, but also in power," Paul writes in 1 Thessalonians 1:5. His point is not that the gospel was accompanied by mighty works (though this happened; cf. Rom 15:18-19), but that the gospel itself is a mighty work. God makes it so through his Holy Spirit (Rom 15:18-19; 1 Cor 2:1-5; 1 Thes 1:6). Furthermore, God's singular purpose in exercising his power is to change people's lives, to liberate them from sin and death, and to reconcile them to himself—in short, to save them. The gospel has power to effect the salvation it announces and to impart the life it promises (e.g., Rom 1:16; 10:8-17; 1 Cor 1:17-18; 15:1-2; Eph 1:13; 2 Thes 2:13-14; 2 Tm 1:8-11; 1 Pt 1:23-25). If people are to experience salvation, they must hear and believe the gospel. It is precisely in and through this message that the saving power manifested in the person and work of Christ (especially in his death and resurrection) is conveyed to men and made effective in their lives. Similarly it is in association with the gospel, or as a direct result of the reception of the gospel, that the Holy Spirit is imparted to believers (Acts 10:36-44; 15:7-8; 2 Cor 11:4; Gal 3:1-2). In short, the gospel is the decisive place of encounter between the sinner and God the Savior.

The Gospel of Grace According to Peter's testimony at the Jerusalem Council (Acts 15:7-11), an essential part of the gospel—for Gentiles and Jews alike—is salvation "through the grace of the Lord Jesus." Toward the close of his missionary career, Paul states that his basic concern has been "to testify to the gospel of the grace of God" (Acts 20:24, RSV). This statement can be understood only in relation to Paul's concept of the righteousness of God, particularly as set forth in Romans. Paul is here not merely expounding a divine attribute. Rather, he is dramatizing a divine activity—the manifestation of God's righteousness now, "in the present time" (Rom 3:26), in the new age inaugurated by the coming of Jesus. The manifestation is twofold. Viewing the two aspects together, and doing so in the light of the gospel declared by Isaiah and by Jesus (both of whom strongly influenced Paul), respectively, will help us to understand why Paul speaks of "the gospel of the grace of God."

First, the gospel is a *witness* to God's grace. In offering his Son as a sacrifice for sins (Rom 3:25a), God demonstrates his righteousness (vv 25b-26). That is, in the death of Jesus sins formerly "passed over" (v 25c) become the object of God's wrath (cf. 1:18) and judgment. Yet in the very place where God deals justly and decisively with sins, he shows his grace to sinners. For the judgment against sin is focused not upon the sinners themselves but upon the One appointed to act on their behalf and to stand in their place (Rom 4:25; 5:6, 11; cf. 2 Cor 5:21; Gal 3:13). On this basis, sinners are freely pardoned (Rom 3:24). "The grace of the Lord Jesus" (Acts 15:11) toward the sinful is also in evidence, for he willingly bears their iniquities and suffers the consequences of their wrongdoing (Gal 2:20; cf. 2 Cor 8:9; Phil 2:6-8).

Second, the gospel is a *channel* of God's grace. "The righteousness of God is revealed" in the gospel, says Paul (Rom 1:17). By this he means, not that the gospel talks about the righteousness of God (though it does), but that God's righteousness is actively at work in the gospel. This activity in turn explains how the gospel becomes "the power of God for salvation" (v 16). And just how does God demonstrate his righteousness at this stage? In short, by bestowing it as a free gift on sinful human beings. It remains the righteousness of God, but by God's grace, it is a righteousness in which humans may share. Furthermore, partaking of God's righteousness depends on being personally united with Jesus Christ. In Paul's view the saved person is one who has been acquitted, justified, "declared righteous" by God the judge. The basis for the verdict is not that I in myself am righteous (God justifies the ungodly, Rom 4:5). Nor does God treat me as though I were righteous. According to Paul I am declared righteous because I really *am* righteous—not in myself but in Christ (1 Cor 1:30; 2 Cor 5:21; Phil 3:9). This union is established through the revelation—and the free offer—of God's righteousness in the gospel (Rom 1:16-17).

Responding to the Gospel The gospel calls for a three-fold response:

1. *Believing.* The gospel, says Paul, is "the power of God for salvation to every one who has faith" (Rom 1:16). For Paul, faith is the abandonment of all reliance upon "works of law" for justification (3:28) and utter dependence upon the grace of God as demonstrated in the work of Christ, especially his death (v 25). Accordingly, the "different gospel" of Galatians 1:6 and 2 Corinthians 11:4 is spurious, for it preaches salvation by personal merit rather than (or together with) the work of Christ (cf. Gal 2:16). Ultimately faith rests upon God (Rom 4:24; 1 Thes 1:8-9) and upon Christ (Rom 3:22, 26; Gal 2:16, 20). Yet it is imperative that one believe the gospel also (Acts 8:12; 11:20-21; 15:7; Rom 1:16; 10:8-17; 1 Cor 1:17-24; Phil 1:27; Heb 4:2), for it is just by this means that God's salvation is made known and mediated. Moreover, believing the gospel entails repentance (Acts 14:15; 20:21, 24; 1 Thes 1:5-10) and obedience (Rom 1:5; 15:16-18; Heb 4:6). Those who refuse to obey the gospel are imperiling their lives (2 Thes 1:5-10; 1 Pt 4:17).

2. *Growing.* The Gospel is more than a message to be received—it is also a place in which to stand (1 Cor 15:1-2). It is sustainer of life as well as giver of life. One grows as a Christian not by turning from the gospel to other things (to turn away from the gospel is to abandon God and Christ, Gal 1:6), but by going ever more deeply into the gospel. In Romans 1:15 Paul expresses his eagerness to proclaim the gospel to the Christians in Rome. In the following chapters, anticipating his visit, he offers one of his most profound expositions of the gospel—one whose truth has never been fathomed and whose power has never been exhausted.

3. *Hoping.* "The hope of the gospel" (Col 1:23) includes not only the return of Christ and the glory of heaven (Col 1:5; 3:1-4; 2 Thes 2:14-16) but the final judgment as well. For those who embrace the gospel, the last judgment holds no terrors, because the Judge is the very one who rescues them from the wrath to come (1 Thes 1:10). Those who are united to him need not dread condemnation now or at the end (Rom 8:1). Instead, the last judgment will mark their final vindication (1 Cor 4:5; Gal 5:5). Accordingly, this theme is not just a corollary but an integral part of the Good News (Rom 2:16). Those who have died since believing the gospel (1 Pt 4:6) may seem to have suffered a fate common to all people, or even the condemnation reserved for the lawless; in fact, their response to the gospel assures them of approval by the coming Lord (4:5-6; 5:4) and of a share in the imperishable inheritance of heaven (1:4).

GOSPELS*, Apocryphal *See* Apocrypha (Apocryphal Gospels).

GOUGING Common practice among the Philistines, Amorites, Babylonians, and other nations surrounding Israel (Jgs 16:21; 2 Kgs 25:7) of forcibly removing the eyes. The practice was intended not only to disable but also to bring extreme disgrace upon the person (1 Sm 11:2). Although the Israelites seem to have known about it from their sojourn in Egypt (Nm 16:14), there is no evidence that it was a common practice in Israel.

See also Criminal Law and Punishment.

GOURD Trailing or climbing plant. *See* Plants (Castor Oil Plant; Gourd, Wild).

GOVERNOR Biblical term translated from at least ten different Hebrew root words and five Greek roots. English versions do not render these words consistently; they use a variety of titles, such as "overseer," "officer," "leader," "judge," and "deputy," to translate the same Hebrew word. The situation is similar in the Septuagint (Greek OT).

A governor was someone of superior rank who exercised authority over persons, territory, or both. Sometimes rank and power were his by virtue of the office; other times accession to office was based on noble lineage, wealth, and public attainment. A governor normally received authority from a king; therefore, he was a deputy in the territory he governed. Such was the case with Joseph (Gn 42:6), Gedaliah (Jer 40:5), Daniel (Dn 2:48), and Zerubbabel (Hg 1:1). One Hebrew term for "governor," however, could mean "absolute ruler" (Jos 12:2) as well as a person who acted under authority.

The term most frequently used in the OT is evidently from an Akkadian expression meaning "lord of a district." Such governors normally relied on military power to maintain their rule (2 Kgs 18:24; Neh 2:7; Jer 51:23, 28). The satrap of the Persian and Greek periods was most probably a civil governor. The leader of a city-state was often known as "governor" in the preexilic period (1 Kgs 22:26; 2 Chr 34:8). The writer of Psalm 22:28 used that title to describe God as the ruler of his people. A temple official who imprisoned the prophet Jeremiah in the stocks (Jer 20:1) was described as a "governor" (RSV "officer"). One who governed an army probably commanded one or more military units. What appears to be a special title is rendered "governor" in Ezra 2:63 and Nehemiah 7:65.

Translation problems from the Greek are also numerous. Different levels and functions in leadership were obviously intended by the various words used. This is most clearly indicated by the use of such terms as *ethnarch* (1 Macc 14:47, RSV; 2 Cor 11:32, NASB), one who governed as a deputy of a king, and by another word referring to Roman provincial officials. Such governors were mentioned in NT writings (cf. Mt 10:18; Lk 2:2; 3:1; Acts 23:24; 1 Pt 2:14) and were responsible for maintaining law and order in their assigned territory. In NT times Judea was under the control of the governor of Syria. Archaic uses of "governor" occasionally appear in the KJV. The "governor" mentioned in James 3:4 (KJV) is the ship's pilot.

GOYIM Alternate rendering for people defeated by Joshua west of the Jordan (Jos 12:23). *See* Goiim #2.

GOZAN City and district near the Euphrates River. The Habor River (modern Khabur) flowed through it. The Assyrians conquered it sometime before Sennacherib's invasion of Judah (701 BC). This fact is mentioned by Sennacherib, king of Assyria, in a blasphemous letter sent to Hezekiah, king of Judah (2 Kgs 19:12; Is 37:12). Later it became one of the places in Assyria where conquered Israelites were deported.

GRACE The gift of God as expressed in his actions of extending mercy, loving-kindness, and salvation to people.

Grace is the dimension of divine activity that enables God to confront human indifference and rebellion with an inexhaustible capacity to forgive and to bless. God is gracious in action. The doctrine of divine grace underlies the thought of both the OT and NT. However, the OT merely anticipates and prepares for the full expression of grace that becomes manifest in the NT.

Grace in the Old Testament Early in the narrative of the OT, God reveals himself as a "God merciful and gracious, slow to anger, and abounding in steadfast love and faithfulness" (Ex 34:6, RSV). As a result, it becomes possible for undeserving humans to approach him with the prayer, "If now I have found favor [or grace] in thy sight, O Lord, . . ." (Ex 34:9, RSV). Through divine initiative, human alienation from God is turned by him into a state of unmerited acceptance that opens the way for reconciliation and redemptive usefulness.

Divine grace was already operative in the Garden of Eden when God responded to the debacle of the fall with the promise of redemption (Gn 3:15) and solicitous care rather than with abandonment or retributive annihilation. The call to Abraham was an extension of grace, not only to him as an individual, but through him as a means of universal outreach. As an inseparable part of God's promise of individual blessing to Abraham and of a national blessing to his descendants, the indication was given that the individual and the national blessings would be instrumental in bringing about a universal blessing to "all the families of the earth" (Gn 12:2-3). Consequently, both the election of Abraham and the promise of universal blessing find expression in a God-given covenant, the object of which is to extend God's grace to the whole human race. In a solemn confirmation of the promise to Abraham, God affirmed, "My covenant is with you, and you shall be the father of a multitude of nations. . . . And I will establish my covenant between me and you and your descendants after you throughout their generations for an everlasting covenant" (Gn 17:4, 7, RSV). This promise was to be understood as finding fulfillment on the basis of grace, not of race, so that it would become applicable to all Abraham's offspring—not only to Jewish believers, his racial descendants, but also to his spiritual descendants, believers from all nations who profess a faith like Abraham's (Rom 4:16). Thus, from the perspective of divine grace, the election of Abraham and of national Israel was not an end in itself. It was God's plan for extending his redemptive designs to all believers, from all nations. In extending his grace to Abraham, God was establishing the beginnings of the church, the community of grace.

The divine particularism evidenced in the election of Abraham and in his becoming the recipient of God's grace provides a model for the selection of all the individuals used by God in the history of redemption. Beyond the benefits of grace accorded to individuals such as Abraham, David, the prophets, and later the apostles, by virtue of their call, loomed the potential of their contributions to the fulfillment of the covenant of God on behalf of the community of those who share the faith of Abraham—the church. In the gracious dealings of God with Israel, with its patriarchs and its leaders, God was laying the basis for his outreach of grace to the church universal. God's gracious interventions in the old covenant were intended to manifest the ultimacy of the church in his redemptive purposes. In the exercise of their ministries, the prophets of the old covenant knew that they were serving not themselves but the church (1 Pt 1:10-12).

As a transitional, mediatory expression of divine grace, the institutions of the old covenant possessed only a temporary validity that has been superseded by the ultimate manifestations of God's grace in the new covenant (Heb 8:6-7). Consequently, the old covenant was to become obsolete and replaced by a new covenant that would display the full manifestation of God's grace. The proverbial tension between law and grace becomes intelligible in this perspective. Like the election of racial Israel, the law (as one of the most visible institutions of the old covenant) was a temporary measure of divine grace accorded to anticipate and prepare the covenant of justification through grace by faith in Jesus Christ (Gal 3:23-29; Heb 10:1).

Grace in the New Testament The concept of grace defined as God's active involvement on behalf of his people receives a sharper focus in the NT. Divine grace becomes embodied in the person of Jesus Christ, who demonstrates visibly the dynamic nature of God's grace and fulfills in his ministry of redemption the old covenant promises relative to God's gracious dealings with humanity (Jn 1:14, 17).

God's grace manifested in Jesus Christ makes it possible for God to forgive sinners and to gather them in the church, the new covenant community. During his ministry, Jesus repeatedly pronounced the words of forgiveness on a great number of sinners and ministered God's benevolent succor to a variety of desperate human needs. Through teachings such as the father's forgiveness of the prodigal son and the search for the lost sheep, Jesus made it clear that he had come to seek and save those who were lost. But ultimately it was his redemptive death on the cross that opened wide the gate of salvation for repentant sinners to find access to God's forgiving and restorative grace. This simple truth is formulated in the doctrine of justification by faith through grace (Rom 3:23; Ti 3:7). According to this teaching, God's gracious provision of the substitutionary death of Christ enables him to pronounce a verdict of "just" or "not guilty" on repentant sinners and to include them in his eternal purposes. As a result, they enter into the realm of God's gracious activity, which enables them to implement the process of individual sanctification in cooperation with the Holy Spirit.

God's grace manifested in Jesus Christ also makes it possible for God to bestow on believers undeserved benefits that enrich their lives and unite them together in the church, the body of Christ. Their acceptance on the basis of grace endows them with a new status as children of God, members of the household of God, so that they relate to him as to their heavenly Father (Gal 4:4-6). Consequently, they become members of a community where race, class, and sex distinctions are irrelevant, since they all became equal inheritors of God's age-long promise to Abraham of universal blessing (3:28-29). In order to enrich their individual lives and to assure the usefulness of their participation in the life of the new community, the Holy Spirit graciously energizes believers with a variety of gifts for the performance of ministries designed to benefit the church (Rom 12:6-8). Foremost among those ministries is that of apostle, itself closely linked to God's gracious provision (1:5; 15:15-16) since it combines with the ministry of the prophets of old to provide the foundational structure of the church (Eph 2:20). Because the riches of divine grace are freely lavished upon believers in their community life upon earth (1:7-8), the church translated into eternity will demonstrate, by its very existence, the immeasurable riches of God's grace in Jesus Christ (2:6).

Finally, God's grace manifested in Jesus Christ makes it possible for God to cause believers to reflect his grace in their character and relationships. The irreducible condition for receiving God's grace is humility (Jas 4:6; 1 Pt 5:5). Such humility in relation to God enables believers to practice humility in regard to other people. From a position of grace, they can set aside selfishness and conceit in order to treat others with deference (Phil 2:3-4) in an attitude of mutual servanthood (Eph 5:21), and in a spirit of mutual forgiveness (Mt 18:23-35) so that even their communication can exhibit divine grace (Col 4:6). Since the grace of Jesus Christ constitutes the existential context of the lives and relationships of believers, they are exhorted not to pervert the grace of God into ungodly practice (Jude 1:4) but instead to grow in the grace of the Lord (2 Pt 3:18).

The essential meaning of grace in the Bible refers to God's disposition to exercise goodwill toward his creatures. This favorable disposition of God finds its supreme expression in Jesus Christ. By its very definition, this grace is rendered fully accessible to all humans with no other precondition than a repentant desire to receive it (Ti 2:11-12). As a result, the human condition of alienation from God and from his purposes becomes replaced with access to the otherwise unapproachable majesty of God represented by a throne, so that his grace may become available to meet human need (Heb 4:16). The tragic alternative to receiving God's grace is to remain in hopeless alienation or to pursue sterile attempts to merit God's favor through human efforts doomed to futility (Rom 1:21). God's unconditional acceptance of sinners may be conditioned only by their rejection of his acceptance.

Because Christ represents the fulfillment, the embodiment, and the dispenser of divine grace, the early Christians freely referred to God's grace as "the grace of our Lord Jesus Christ." This grace was conceived as being so basic and so pervasive to their individual lives and to the existence of their communities of faith that they naturally coupled the traditional greeting of *shalom* ("peace") with a reference to the grace of Jesus Christ. This is the reason for the ubiquitous repetition of numerous variations on the basic greeting formula found in almost every book of the NT, "The grace of our Lord Jesus Christ be with you all" (2 Thes 3:18).

See also God, Being and Attributes of; Love; Mercy.

GRAIN *See* Agriculture; Plants (Barley; Millet; Spelt; Wheat).

GRANARY *See* Agriculture.

GRAPE Smooth-skinned, juicy berry that grows in clusters on woody vines. Grapes are eaten fresh or dried, and are fermented for wine. *See* Agriculture; Plants (Vine); Vines, Vineyard; Wine.

GRASSHOPPER Plant-eating insect equipped with long hind legs for leaping. *See* Animals.

GRATE, GRATING Network of bronze surrounding the lower half of the altar of burnt offering in the tabernacle (Ex 27:4).
See also Altar.

GRATITUDE Natural expression of thanks in response to blessings, protection, or love. In the Judeo-Christian tradition, gratitude is not a tool used to manipulate the will of God. It is never coerced or fabricated in one's mind; rather, gratitude is a joyful commitment of one's personality to God.

In the OT, gratitude to God was the only condition in which life could be enjoyed. For Jews, every aspect of creation provided evidence of God's lordship over all life. The Hebrew people thanked him for the magnificence of the universe (Pss 19:1-4; 33:6-9; 104:1-24). When they received good news, they thanked God for his goodness and great deeds (1 Chr 16:8-12). When they received bad news, they also gave thanks, trusting that he was a just God (Jb 1:21).

These same sentiments are found in later Jewish writings such as the Talmud. The people of Israel thanked God for his faithfulness to covenant promises: (1) for deliverance from enemies (Pss 18:17; 30:1; 44:1-8) and from death (Ps 30:8-12; Is 38:18-20; (2) for forgiveness of sin (Pss 32:5; 99:8; 103:3; Is 12:1); (3) for answers to prayer (Pss 28:6; 66:19); (4) for compassion toward the afflicted and oppressed (Pss 34:2; 72:12); (5) for executing justice (Dt 32:4; Ps 99:4); and (6) for continuing guidance (Ps 32:8; Is 30:20-21).

Gratitude was such a vital part of Israel's religion that it pervaded most ceremonies and customs. Thank offerings acknowledged blessings from God (Lv 7:12-13; 22:29; Ps 50:14). Shouts of joy (Ps 42:4), songs of praise (Pss 145:7; 149:1), and music and dance (Ps 150:3-5) all added to the spirit of thanksgiving in worship. Feasts and festivals were celebrated in remembrance of God's steadfast love throughout their history (Dt 16:9-15; 2 Chr 30:21-22). King David appointed Levitical priests to offer God thanks (1 Chr 16:4). This custom was carried on by the kings Solomon (2 Chr 5:12-13) and Hezekiah (2 Chr 31:2) and by those who returned from the exile (Neh 11:17; 12:24, 27).

In the NT, the object of thanksgiving is the love of God expressed in the redemptive work of Christ. The apostle Paul thanked God for that gift of grace (1 Cor 1:4; 2 Cor 9:15) and the ability to preach the gospel (2 Cor 2:14; 1 Tm 1:12). Paul thankfully participated in the spiritual gifts (1 Cor 14:18). Gratitude for love and faith among believers pervades his letters (Rom 6:17; Eph 1:15-16; Phil 1:3-5; Col 1:3-4; 1 Thes 1:2-3).

Because the expression of gratitude is tied so closely to the response of faith, Paul encouraged believers to give thanks in all things (Rom 14:6; 1 Thes 5:18). He commanded Christians to pray with thanksgiving (Phil 4:6; Col 4:2) in the name of Christ, who has made all thanksgiving possible (Eph 5:20). In his teaching on how to celebrate the Lord's Supper, Paul specified that Christians should give thanks, just as the Lord "had given thanks" (1 Cor 11:24).

GRAVE *See* Burial, Burial Customs.

GRAVECLOTHES *See* Burial, Burial Customs.

GRAVEN IMAGE* Image or representation of a deity made of wood, stone, or metal. *See* Idols, Idolatry.

GREAT LIZARD One of the reptiles that the Jewish law listed as ceremonially unclean (Lv 11:29). *See* Animals (Lizard).

GREAT OWL Name of one of the great horned or eagle owls (Dt 14:16). *See* Birds (Owl; Owl, Great).

GREAT SEA*, The Alternate name for the Mediterranean Sea. It was given this name by the ancient Near Eastern peoples because of its great size in comparison to the other seas they knew (Nm 34:6; Jos 1:4). *See* Mediterranean Sea.

GREAVES* Protective piece of armor worn over the shank of the leg (1 Sm 17:6).
   See also Armor and Weapons.

GREECE, GREEK The biblical references to Greece and the Greek people are often ambiguous. In the OT some references have been understood to mean Greece or the Greeks. Javan, the fourth son of Japheth in the "table of nations" (Gn 10), seems to fit a Greek identification (1 Chr 1:5, 7; Is 66:19; Ez 27:13). The name Greece occurs clearly in Daniel 8:21; 10:20; 11:2; and Zechariah 9:13, and Greeks are mentioned in Joel 3:6. In the NT the term "Greek" appears to have the special sense of Hellenist, that is, Jews living in Hellenistic cities (Acts 6:1; 9:29; 11:20). The term in John 12:20, Acts 14:1, and 16:1-3 seems to refer to Greeks specifically. But often in the NT the term "Greek" was used for non-Jews because the Jews recognized only Jews and non-Jews. Hence the term was virtually synonymous with Gentiles (Rom 1:16; 10:12; 1 Cor 1:22, 24; Gal 2:3; 3:28). Sometimes the term "Greek" refers to the language (Jn 19:20; Acts 21:37; Rv 9:11). The use of the term "Greek" for the Syrophoenician woman (Mk 7:26) may be a cultural term. In Acts, references are made to Greeks in the synagogues as observers. These may have been Greeks as such, although certainty is not possible (Acts 14:1; 17:4; 18:4).

Geography The ancient Greek homeland comprised the southern end of the Balkan Peninsula. But at times Greek speakers were to be found in the islands of the Aegean Sea, western Asia Minor, south Italy, and Sicily.

The Emergence of Greek Culture After the Persian Wars ended (497 BC), Athens entered into a remarkable period of greatness. Athens was rebuilt and its port of Piraeus was fortified. When the Athenian citizens embarked on a course of unbridled democracy, chaos seemed to threaten, but Pericles, a brilliant leader, restored the equilibrium of the state and Athens soon regained her glory. Vast buildings were erected on the Acropolis, notably the Parthenon (dedicated to Athena, the goddess of Athens). Athens became wealthy, partly from the contributions to the Delian League. Athenian sea power grew. There were present in Athens an abundance of slaves, artisans, craftsmen, foreign traders, artists, poets, philosophers, teachers, actors, athletes, scientists, physicians, historians, religious teachers, and experts in military and naval affairs. The great writers of the fifth and early fourth centuries BC included dramatists like Aeschylus, Sophocles, and Euripedes, historians like Thucydides and Herodotus, and philosophers like Socrates, Plato, and Aristotle. There occurred a flowering of art and architecture. It was a golden age of spectacular achievement in art, thought, literature, and architecture.

Ancient Amphitheater in Delphi

The Age of Hellenism The great glory of Athens withered before the fourth century BC was over. Philip of Macedon, with ambitions of empire, drove west, and by 338 BC Athens and Thebes were overwhelmed—Greece became united into a Macedonian Empire. Philip was assassinated in 366 BC, but Alexander, his son, educated in the Athenian tradition, took up his father's work and before his own death in 323 BC had conquered Persia and reached to the Punjab in India. In the end he exerted his control from the Caucusus to the Libyan Desert and the borders of Ethiopia as well. On the death of Alexander, his vast territories were divided among four generals. After some adjustments three divisions emerged—Egypt under Ptolemy; Asia Minor, Syria, and the East under Seleucus; and Macedonia under Antigonus.

Finally the whole of the Greek area came under the control of the Romans, who moved into Greek areas in 198 BC and over the years established a number of Roman provinces, such as Achaia (Acts 18:12). It was into the world of Hellenism, now under Rome, that the Christians moved with the message of the gospel in the first century AD.

The Greeks in Palestine Excavations have shown that there was contact between Palestine and the Aegean areas over many centuries. From the middle Bronze period (the patriarchal age), middle Minoan II pottery has been found at a number of sites. The Philistines, who formed part of the Sea Peoples in the 13th century BC, settled in areas of coastal Palestine and developed their own culture there, leaving a great deal of their distinctive pottery. During the period around 1370–1200 BC, various peoples from the Aegean and western Asia Minor found their way to Palestine. Mycenaean pottery has been found in a number of sites. From a later period still, numerous examples of Attic black-figure ware from the sixth century BC, and Attic red-figure ware from the period around 530–300 BC, have been found in excavations. Silver coins struck in imitation of Attic drachmas come from the same period. With the rise of Hellenism and the occupation of Palestine by the Ptolemaic and Seleucid rulers, Greek influence increased greatly. The presence of Greek pottery, like Rhodian jars, and the influence of Greek architectural features in buildings emphasize the significance of the Greek influence in Palestine as well as throughout the Levant region and the hinterland. With the coming of the Romans, these influences continued. Greek was the language of commerce. Indeed, the NT was written in the Greek of ordinary people, and a wide variety of Greek inscriptions has come to light from Roman times.

See also Alexander #1; Alexandria; Hellenism; Hellenists; Judaism.

GREEK LANGUAGE Language of the Greek people.

The Greek language is a beautiful, rich, and well-tuned instrument of communication. It is a fitting tool both for vigorous thought and for religious devotion. During its classical period, Greek was the language of one of the world's greatest cultures. During that cultural period, language, literature, and art flourished more than war. The Greek mind was preoccupied with ideals of beauty. The Greek language reflected artistry in its philosophical dialogues, its poetry, and its stately orations.

The Greek language was also characterized by strength and vigor. It was capable of variety and striking effects. Greek was a language of argument, with a vocabulary and style that could penetrate and clarify phenomena rather than simply tell stories. Classical Greek elaborately developed many forms from a few word roots. Its complex syntax allowed intricate word arrangements to express fine nuances of meaning.

Ancient History Although the antecedents of Greek are obscure, the first traces of what could be called antecedents of ancient Greek appear in Mycenaean and Minoan documents (1400–1200 BC) that use three different scripts: Minoan hieroglyphic (the earliest), linear A, and linear B (the latest). Linear B, generally considered "pre-Greek," is written in a syllabic script found on clay tablets discovered on the island of Crete and on the Greek mainland.

Egnatian Way The major route through Greece—traveled by Paul many times.

The Mycenaean civilization and script ended suddenly with the Dorian invasions (1200 BC), and writing seems to have disappeared for several centuries. Later, about the eighth century BC, Greek writing appeared in a different script. That script was based on an alphabet presumably borrowed from the Phoenicians and then adapted to the Greek speech sound system and direction of writing. Greek was first written from right to left, like the West Semitic languages, then in a back-and-forth pattern, finally from left to right. Several dialects appeared during the archaic period (8th to 6th centuries BC): Dorian, Eonian, Achaean, and Aeolic.

During the classical period (5th to 4th centuries BC), Greek culture reached its literary and artistic zenith. Classical (or Attic) Greek was characterized by subtlety of syntax and an expressive use of particles (short, uninflected parts of speech, often untranslatable). As the city of Athens attained cultural and political control, the Attic dialect also gained in prestige. With the Macedonian conquests, Attic Greek, combined with influences from other dialects (especially Ionic), became the international language of the eastern Mediterranean area.

Hellenism and the Koine Dialect The conquests of Alexander the Great encouraged the spread of Greek language and culture. Regional dialects were largely replaced by "Hellenistic" or "koine" (common) Greek. Koine Greek is a dialect preserved and known through thousands of inscriptions reflecting all aspects of daily life. The koine dialect added many vernacular expressions to

Attic Greek, thus making it more cosmopolitan. Simplifying the grammar also better adapted it to a worldwide culture. The new language, reflecting simple, popular speech, became the common language of commerce and diplomacy. The Greek language lost much of its elegance and finely shaded nuance as a result of its evolution from classic to koine. Nevertheless, it retained its distinguishing characteristics of strength, beauty, clarity, and logical rhetorical power.

It is significant that the apostle Paul wrote his letter to Christians in Rome in the Greek language rather than in Latin. The Roman Empire of that time was culturally a Greek world, except for governmental transactions.

The Septuagint During the centuries immediately before Christ, the eastern Mediterranean had been undergoing not only Hellenization but also Semitization. Both influences can be observed in the Greek translation of the OT.

Translation of the Hebrew Scriptures into Greek was an epochal event. The Septuagint (the earliest Greek translation of the OT) later had a strong influence on Christian thought. A necessary consequence of Hebrew writers using the Greek language was that a Greek spirit and Greek forms of thought influenced Jewish culture. The Jews soon appropriated from the rich and refined Greek vocabulary some expressions for ideas that were beyond the scope of Hebrew terminology. Also, old Greek expressions acquired new and extended meanings in this translation of the OT by Greek-speaking Jews.

The Greek OT has been very significant in the development of Christian thought. Often the usage of a Greek word in the Septuagint provides a key to its meaning in the NT. The OT dialect of "Jewish Greek" is at times seen in NT passages translated very literally; at other times, the NT translation of OT texts is very loose.

New Testament Greek Although most NT authors were Jewish, they wrote in Greek, the universal language of their time. In addition, the apostle John seems to have been acquainted with some Greek philosophy, which influenced his style. John used "word" (Greek *logos*) in reference to Christ (Jn 1:1), and several other abstract expressions. John may have been influenced by the Egyptian center of Alexandria, where Greek philosophy and Hebrew learning had merged in a unique way.

The apostle Paul also was acquainted with Greek authors (Acts 17:28; 1 Cor 15:33; Ti 1:12). Thus, Greek orators and philosophers influenced Paul's language as well as Hebrew prophets and scholars.

Exactly which dialect of Hebrew or Aramaic Jesus spoke is debated. It is certainly possible that Jesus also spoke Greek. The fact remains that the Gospels were originally written as Greek texts. The records in Greek of Jesus' teachings and accomplishments prepared the way for the gospel to spread throughout a Greek-speaking culture.

The dignity and restraint of koine Greek used by Christian writers was neither so artificial and pedantic as some classical writings nor so trivial and vulgar as spoken koine.

Greek words took on richer, more spiritual meaning in the context of Scripture. Influenced by the simplicity and rich vividness of Semitic style, the NT was not written in a peculiar "Holy Ghost" language (as some medieval scholars believed) but in koine (common) Greek, largely by Semitic-thinking authors. Tens of thousands of papyri unearthed in Egypt in the early 20th century furnish lexical and grammatical parallels to biblical language, revealing that it was part of the linguistic warp and woof of that era. Yet NT Greek was nevertheless "free," often creating its own idiom. Christian writers influenced

Greek thought by introducing new expressions in order to convey their message about Jesus Christ.

Semitic Influence Because NT Greek combines the directness of Hebrew thought with the precision of Greek expression, Greek's subtle delicacy often interprets Hebrew concepts. The Semitic influence is strongest in the Gospels, the book of Revelation, and the Letter of James. Books like Luke and Hebrews exhibit a more typically Greek style. The NT epistles blend the wisdom of Hebrew and the dialectic philosophy of Greek. Sermons recorded in the NT combine the Hebrew prophetic message with Greek oratorical force.

In addition to direct quotes and allusions from the Septuagint, a pervasive Semitic influence on NT Greek has been noted in many areas. For example, the syntax of NT Greek contains many examples of Semitic style.

Vocabulary The Greek NT vocabulary is abundant and sufficient to convey just the shade of meaning the author desires. For example, the NT uses two different words for "love" (for two kinds of love), two words for "another" (another of the same, or another of a different kind), and several words for various kinds of knowledge. Significantly, some words are omitted, such as *eros* (a third kind of love) and other words commonly employed in the Hellenistic culture of that time.

Moreover, Greek words often took on new meanings in the context of the gospel, arising from a combination of new teachings with an exalted morality. The writers did not hesitate to use such words as "life," "death," "glory," and "wrath" in new ways to express new thoughts. Sometimes the literal meaning of a word almost disappears, as when the authors use "water," "washing," and "baptism" for Christ's spiritually purifying power. NT vocabulary also contains words found elsewhere only in the Greek OT, such as "circumcision," "idolatry," "anathema," "diaspora," and "Pentecost." Loan words from Hebrew or Aramaic include *alleluia* and *amen* (Hebrew), and *abba*, *mammon*, and *corban* (Aramaic).

For understanding the meaning of a NT word, then, a lexicon of classical Greek is helpful but not sufficient. One must also know how the word is used in the Greek OT, in Hellenistic writings, and in the inscriptions and documents representing the language of everyday life. Papyrus documents provide many illustrations of the meaning of NT words. For example, the Greek word for "contribution" (1 Cor 16:1), at one time thought to be limited to the NT, is commonly used with the same meaning in the papyri. Many Greek words once defined on the basis of classical Greek have been given sharper meaning in the light of their use in the papyri.

Grammar As in other Indo-European languages, the meaning of Greek words is affected by the addition and

---

THE GREEK ALPHABET

Α Β Γ Δ Ε Ζ
Η Θ Ι Κ Λ Μ
Ν Ξ Ο Π Ρ Σ
Τ Υ Φ Χ Ψ Ω

alteration of various prefixes and suffixes (the process known as inflection). Although its system of inflection is simplified compared to classical Greek, NT Greek is more inflected than are many languages. Greek meaning is thus much less susceptible to ambiguity than English.

In contrast to Hebrew, Greek has a neuter gender as well as masculine and feminine. The many and precise Greek prepositions are subtle, having various meanings depending on their context. NT Greek uses only about half of the particles used in classical Greek.

The Greek verb system, much more complicated than that of Hebrew, is capable of nuances of meaning difficult to express even in English. Each Greek verb has five aspects, which grammarians call tense, mood, voice, person, and number.

Tense Greek verb tense deals primarily with *kind of action* rather than *time of action* as in English. In Greek there are three basic kinds of action: *durative,* expressed by the present, imperfect, and (sometimes) future tenses; *simple* or punctiliar, expressed by the aorist and (often) future tenses; and *completed,* expressed by the perfect tense (results of past action continue into the present) and pluperfect tense (results are confined to the past).

Greek tenses are often hard to translate into English; the time of action as well as the verb stem's basic meaning (such as whether it takes an object) must be subtly blended with the kind of action into a single idea.

Mood The mood shows how a verb's action should be understood. Is the action real? (Use the indicative mood.) Is the action demanded by someone? (Use the imperative mood.) Does the action depend on other conditions? (Use the subjunctive or optative mood.) Is the action basically descriptive of another substantive? (Use a participle.) Is the action basically substantive? (Use an infinitive.) In grammar, a substantive is a word or group of words functioning as a noun; the last two examples are not strictly moods, but they are used that way by grammarians. The moods give a Greek writer a rich choice of verbal expression.

Voice A verb's voice describes whether action is directed outward (active), inward (middle), or back upon the sentence's subject (passive).

Person The person of a verb tells who is doing the acting, whether I (first person), you (second person), or another (third person).

Number Verb number shows whether the action is performed by one person (singular) or more than one person (plural).

Style The NT contains a variety of writing styles in its use of Greek. The Gospels especially exhibit Semitic features. Matthew uses a style less picturesque than Mark's and in some respects close to the style of Luke, Acts, Hebrews, James, and 1 Peter. Luke's style varies from that of both Mark and Matthew; it is elegant. The rather simple style of John contains many Semitisms.

Among the apostle Paul's letters, differences of style have been noted. The least literary and most direct in expression are his Letters to the Thessalonians. The Pastorals (1—2 Timothy, Titus) have a style nearer to the koine than most of the other epistles—not so Jewish, and not so much influenced by the Septuagint as his other letters.

The Letter to the Hebrews combines elegance with Jewish-Greek style. James's letter, though high in cultural quality, is not as sensitive in style as Hebrews. Less elegant is 1 Peter, which is strongly influenced by the Septuagint and thus reflects Semitic style.

The Letter of Jude contains elevated, somewhat ponderous diction, and shows the influence of Jewish style. Second Peter, resembling Jude in its high style, is even more influenced by the Septuagint.

The book of Revelation has a generally simple style but shows considerable Semitic influence in its use of parallelism and redundancy. Linguistic scholars have identified a number of apparent grammatical mistakes in the Greek of Revelation.

GREYHOUND* KJV mistranslation in Proverbs 30:31 (NLT "strutting rooster"). *See* Birds (Fowl, Domestic).

GRIEF Emotional suffering brought on by bereavement, mishap, or disaster. To grieve is either to cause or feel sorrow or distress. The concept is found in the Scriptures under a variety of circumstances. Isaac and Rebekah experienced grief when their son Esau married a Hittite woman (Gn 26:35). God mourned the misery of Israel brought upon them by disobedience (Jgs 10:16). Because she had no son, Hannah was sad—so much so that she appeared to be drunk while praying (1 Sm 1:16). Similarly, Samuel, distraught at King Saul's disobedience, prayed all night. Job was exceedingly sorrowful over his personal loss (Jb 2:13; cf. 6:2; 16:6), and the psalmist poetically demonstrated distress and sorrow (Pss 6:7; 31:9-10; 69:26; 73:21; 95:10; 112:10). The book of Lamentations is devoted to the expression of grief, and the prophets in general speak of judgment because Israel had grieved a holy God.

Jesus experienced sorrow and distress (Mk 3:5; Jn 11:33), including crying over the death of a friend (Jn 11:35). The Jews are said to have been grieved as the apostles taught about Christ (Acts 4:2). The apostle Paul instructed believers not to grieve one another (Rom 14:15) and did not want to cause any sorrow himself (2 Cor 2:1-5). Most of all, the believer is not to grieve the Holy Spirit (Eph 4:30). A believer may, of course, experience grief and suffering in an alien world (1 Pt 2:19). In Bible times grief was given particular expression at a time of death by means of shrieks, wails, and laments (Jer 9:17-18; Am 5:16; Mk 5:38).

See also Mourning.

GROVE* Mistaken KJV translation of a Hebrew word that was the name of a Canaanite goddess, Asherah. Often sacred trees were designated as symbols of that fertility goddess; sometimes wooden poles were erected. God commanded the Israelites to destroy those symbols (called "Asherim," "Asheroth") by cutting them down (Ex 34:13) and burning them (Dt 12:3). Because the poles were wooden, archaeologists have been unable to find any clear remains. In an early sanctuary at Ai, however, a large piece of carbonized wood was discovered lying between incense burners. It may have been a tree trunk from which the branches had been trimmed. Some researchers suggest it was an Asherah pole.

God strictly forbade the Israelites to worship Asherah or to erect sacred symbols in her honor. From time to time Israel disobeyed God and engaged in false worship. One account of the downfall of the northern kingdom attributes its failure to the existence of groves and the worship of the pagan goddess and her male counterpart, Baal (2 Kgs 17:7-18). Jezebel, a priestess of the Tyrian Baal, promoted the spread of such idolatry. The "grove" of Genesis 21:33 (KJV) was actually a tamarisk tree.

See also Canaanite Deities and Religions; Gods and Goddesses; High Place; Idols, Idolatry.

GUARD, Courtyard of the Perhaps an emergency detention area in seventh-century BC Jerusalem, when the city was under Babylonian attack. Although the prophet Jeremiah was placed under arrest there, he was still able to maintain his normal activities, indicating that the area was probably a small courtyard (Jer 32:2-12; 33:1; 37:21; 38:6-28; 39:14-15; KJV "court of the prison").

GUARD, Gate of the Gate located in the north or northwest part of Jerusalem (Neh 12:38-39, KJV "prison gate"), although unrelated to the courtyard of the guard (3:25), which was connected to the palace. Perhaps it was the same as the Muster Gate. *See* Jerusalem.

GUARDIAN *See* Custodian.

GUARDIAN ANGEL* *See* Angel.

GUDGODAH Alternate name for Hor-haggidgad, one of the stopping places in the wilderness wanderings of the Israelites (Dt 10:7). *See* Hor-haggidgad.

GUILT OFFERING *See* Offerings and Sacrifices.

GULL* Any of a number of birds from the family Laridae. The NLT "seagull" (KJV "cuckow") in Leviticus 11:16 and Deuteronomy 14:15 is uncertain. *See* Birds (Seagull).

GUM* General name for tragacanth, used in trade and obtained from the sap of shrubs of the *Astragalus* genus (Gn 43:11). These shrubs grew widely in the Near East. Gum from the *Astragalus tragacantha* is still used commercially. *See* Plants (Aloe; Balm; Myrrh).

GUNI
1. Naphtali's son and the grandson of Jacob (Gn 46:24; 1 Chr 7:13).
2. Abdiel's father from Gad's tribe (1 Chr 5:15).

GUNITE Descendant of Guni, Naphtali's son (Nm 26:48). *See* Guni #1.

GUR, Ascent of Elevated place near Ibleam where Ahaziah, king of Judah, was smitten by the soldiers of Jehu of the northern kingdom. From Gur, Ahaziah fled to Megiddo, where he died (2 Kgs 9:27). Though its location is uncertain, some identify it with the Akkadian Gurra, about one-half mile (800 meters) south of Jenin.

GURBAAL* Town in the Negev occupied by Arabs, possibly in the neighborhood of Edom, which Uzziah of Judah conquered (2 Chr 26:7, NLT mg).

GYMNASIUM* Ancient Greek institution devoted to physical education and intellectual development. By the Hellenistic period, gymnasiums had become centers for the propagation of Greek culture. Students received not only physical training but intellectual and social training also. Gymnasiums were privately owned and organized for children of wealthy families. Attendance was mandatory for Greek youths who wanted to gain citizenship in a particular city.

While under the control of the Ptolemies, a Macedonian dynasty, the city of Jerusalem did not have a gymnasium. At the time of the Seleucids, a Syrian dynasty concerned to Hellenize their subjects, the high priest bribed the ruler, Antiochus IV, in order to receive permission to build a gymnasium in Jerusalem (1 Macc 1:13-15; 2 Macc 4:9, NLT mg).

The activities and practices of the gymnasium were abhorrent to conservative Jews because Jewish children educated there began to think and dress according to Hellenistic norms. The Greek practice of participating in athletic events in the nude was particularly upsetting to devout Jews. Many youths were removing the sign of their circumcision to enter the games (1 Macc 1:13-15).

Alexandrian Jews were not so opposed to the gymnasium as Jews in Jerusalem, but the Greek population there was disturbed by the attendance of non-Greeks such as Egyptians and Jews. Roman policy made the graduates of the gymnasium Greek citizens, enabling them to participate in local government.

The apostle Paul and most early Christians seemingly did not have the same resentment toward gymnasiums as did the Jews in Jerusalem. Paul often described the Christian life in the language of athletic events that took place there (1 Cor 9:24-27; Gal 2:2; 5:7; Phil 1:30; 2:16).

H

HAAHASHTARI Naarah's son from Judah's tribe (1 Chr 4:6).

HABAIAH* Alternate spelling of Hobaiah in Nehemiah 7:63. *See* Hobaiah.

HABAKKUK (Person) Author of the eighth book of the Minor Prophets. The meaning of Habakkuk's name is uncertain. It was probably derived from a Hebrew word meaning "to embrace."

Nothing is known about Habakkuk apart from what can be inferred from his book. Several legends purporting to give accounts of his life are generally regarded as untrustworthy. The apocryphal book Bel and the Dragon describes a miraculous transporting of Habakkuk to Daniel while Daniel was in the den of lions. A Jewish legend makes Habakkuk the son of the Shunammite woman mentioned in 2 Kings 4:8-37. That legend apparently is based on the tradition that she would "embrace" a son. Chronological difficulties make both accounts unlikely.

Habakkuk lived in the period during the rise of the Chaldeans (Hb 1:6), that is, during the reigns of the Judean kings Josiah and Jehoiakim. The dates 612–589 BC delineate the probable period of his prophetic activity.

The book of Habakkuk reveals a man of great sensitivity. His deep concern about injustice and his prayer (Hb 3) show that Habakkuk was characterized by profound religious conviction and social awareness.

See also Habakkuk, Book of; Prophet, Prophetess.

HABAKKUK, Book of Eighth book of the Minor Prophets in the OT.

PREVIEW
•Author
•Date
•Background
•Purpose and Theological Teaching
•Content

Author Little is known about the prophet Habakkuk apart from information that may be gained from the book of Habakkuk itself. In 1:1 and 3:1 he is called a prophet, a spokesman for God to his fellow Israelites.

The prayer of chapter 3 contains several musical designations (Hb 3:1, 3, 9, 13, 19). Such technical notations suggest that the author had some responsibility for the temple music. If that is so, he may have been a member of one of the Levitical families. The apocryphal book Bel and the Dragon contains a reference to Habakkuk as "the son of Jesus of the tribe of Levi," possibly reflecting such a tradition.

The book portrays Habakkuk as a man of deep moral sensitivity who rebelled at the injustice that characterized the society of his day.

Date Although it is difficult to date the prophecy of Habakkuk precisely, several clues to its date appear in the text. In 1:5-6 the prophet refers to the Chaldeans whom God is "rousing." The Chaldeans were originally a group of loosely organized tribes who occupied a large portion of the Assyrian Empire. They were a constant source of trouble to their Assyrian lords. Eventually, the Chaldeans successfully rebelled against the Assyrian power, placing Nabopolassar on the throne (625–605 BC). The Chaldeans then ruled all of Babylonia, establishing the Babylonian Empire and inaugurating a period of extensive expansion. Because the Chaldeans came to power about 625 BC, many scholars think that the prophecy of Habakkuk was written shortly before that time. The book would have been written, then, within the reign of Josiah (640–609 BC). Habakkuk 1:6 does not necessarily refer to the initial rise of the Chaldeans. Their reputation was already established as warlike and cruel, for the prophet described them as cruel and violent; they are said to march across the world and conquer it (1:6-8). Their reputation for military prowess seems to fit best with a time after the battle of Carchemish (605 BC), when Nebuchadnezzar II defeated the Egyptians and established the Babylonians as an important world power, but it is also possible that their reputation was gained from the Babylonian conquest of Nineveh in 612 BC.

The social conditions in Habakkuk's day seem to fit with a time toward the end of the reign of Judah's King Josiah. Although Josiah's reign was characterized by far-reaching religious reforms, initiated by the discovery of the Book of the Law during renovations in the temple (2 Kgs 22:8), Habakkuk describes society as filled with "destruction and violence" (Hb 1:3). An unfair judicial system led to oppression of the righteous (v 4). Because it is also possible that he was referring to the world at large, it seems best to date Habakkuk's ministry as starting between 612 and 605 BC, and continuing during the reign of Jehoiakim (609–598 BC).

Background The historical period inaugurated by King Josiah's death was one of the most bitter in the history of the kingdom of Judah. In 612 BC the Babylonians destroyed the Assyrian city of Nineveh, and in two years they eliminated the last vestiges of formal Assyrian rule in Mesopotamia. The Egyptians, who had been allies of the Assyrians, sought to solidify their hold on the western portion of the former Assyrian Empire. They marched to Carchemish, an important city on the Euphrates River, where they were opposed by Josiah, who died in the battle there.

The Egyptians placed Jehoiakim on the throne in place of Jehoahaz, the rightful successor of Josiah. Jehoiakim was an Egyptian vassal, and the land of Judah was forced to pay heavy tribute. The faith of many people might understandably have begun to falter in that time. The religious reforms under Josiah had resulted not in national blessing but in the loss of their freedom. The tenor of society had changed from one of relative stability to one of oppression and violence (see Jer 22:17).

In 604 BC the Babylonians advanced into the Syro-Palestinian area, encountering only weak resistance. At

Ancient Greek Translation of Habakkuk Manuscript from Nahal Hever, 8Hev grXII, showing Habakkuk 2:4-8 (dated first century BC to first century AD)

that time Jehoiakim transferred his allegiance to Nebuchadnezzar, who continued his advance to the south. When Pharaoh Neco's army challenged the invaders, both sides suffered heavy losses and Nebuchadnezzar retreated to Babylon. The vacillating Jehoiakim then transferred his loyalty to Egypt. In 598 BC the Babylonians again advanced into Syro-Palestine, beginning a campaign that led to the fall of Jerusalem in 586 BC.

Purpose and Theological Teaching The main purpose of Habakkuk's prophecy is to explain what a godly person's attitude should be toward the presence of evil in the world. It also addresses the nature of God's justice in punishing moral evil.

The teaching of the book is set forth in an interesting pattern of crucial questions by the prophet about God's activity in history. His questions may reflect deep doubts and concerns, or they may be a literary device for reflecting the questions that people in his society were asking. In the psalm at the end of the book, the prophet shows that he has reached an understanding of God's purposes, and he rests in utter submission to God. One of the prophet's chief problems was the seeming inactivity of God, as evil continued unpunished. God's answer was that he does punish evil in his own time and with his chosen instruments. The world is not an arena in which evil continually triumphs. History testifies to the fall of tyrants and wicked nations. The godly person thus interprets history in terms of faith—trusting God and affirming God's righteous rule in the world.

The book of Habakkuk does not explain why God has allowed evil in the world. It does affirm that a righteous person will see God's activity in history through the eyes of faith. Chapter 3 eloquently expresses that theme as Habakkuk looks at history and recounts God's gracious activity on behalf of his people.

One of the most important theological concepts in the book is that of God's sovereign activity in history. Habakkuk affirms God's control of all history and demonstrates that even the godless nations are subject to his control. Their rise and fall is determined not by the fortuitous course of events but by God.

Content

The First Complaint and Its Response (1:1-11) The prophecy of Habakkuk begins with a series of questions reflecting the prophet's deep feelings over the wrongs rampant in his society. He begins by asking how long he will have to cry to God, who does not seem to hear. Many have asked that question as they see evil present in a world governed by the sovereign God.

The answer that the prophet received was unusual. The Lord was surely doing something about the evil in his society; he was raising up the Chaldeans as an instrument of his wrath to punish the people of Judah.

The description of the Chaldeans in 1:6-11 is filled with bold metaphors that depict them as an awesome force pillaging as they advance in their conquests. One might well wonder, as the prophet did, why God would use such a tool to accomplish his purposes.

The prophet's first complaint reflects a number of perplexing problems. Why does God not do something about evil? Why does he allow it to continue? God does not always seems to respond when people want him to.

Furthermore, when God did answer, he said he would punish the evil in Judah by using the Babylonians. The prophet's prayer was answered, but in a way he did not expect. God would use a hated and wicked nation to punish the wrongs of his own people. Habakkuk must have been perplexed at this, but he could take comfort in one fact: God was still in control of history (Hb 1:5-6). God governed the rise and fall of nations, using even wicked ones to accomplish his will.

The Second Complaint and Its Response (1:12–2:5) The answer to the first complaint was not enough for Habakkuk. He acknowledged that God had "decreed the rise of these Babylonians to punish and correct us for our terrible sins" (1:12, NLT). But he goes on to say, "You are perfectly just in this. But will you, who cannot allow sin in any form, stand idly by while they swallow us up? Should you be silent while the wicked destroy people who are more righteous than they?" (v 13, NLT). He implies that God observes the wicked Chaldeans but does not punish them for their wrongs. Habakkuk still cannot understand how God can use a wicked nation to punish his own people.

But Habakkuk did learn something from God's first response. He began his second complaint with the affirmation "O LORD my God, my Holy One, you who are eternal—is your plan in all of this to wipe us out? Surely not!" (1:12, NLT). The prophet probably had in mind the previous verse, which declared that the god of the Chaldeans was their own military might. In contrast, Judah's God is eternal and not transitory like the fleeting strength of armies and nations.

Habakkuk's problem was still not resolved, for he next described the rapacious nature of the Chaldeans, wondering how God could use them to punish Judah. The Chaldeans were like fishermen, catching people in their nets and then worshiping their nets (1:15-16). Habakkuk asked God if the Chaldeans would continue emptying their nets and slaying the nations (v 17).

Having posed his questions, the prophet waited to see what God's response would be (2:1). The Lord replied that his answer should be written in large, clear letters, for it was certain (v 2), but it would not be fulfilled immediately (v 3).

What follows is one of the greatest verses about faith in the whole OT (2:4). The words "the righteous will live by their faith" became the touchstone of Paul's message and of the Protestant Reformation. The apostle Paul appealed to Habakkuk 2:4 in his exposition of the doctrine of justification by faith (Rom 1:17; Gal 3:11). This passage was also important in the NT book of Hebrews (Heb 10:38-39).

The word "faith" in the OT basically means "firmness" or "strength." The root of the word is used to describe the supporting posts of a door (2 Kgs 18:16) and firm support for a peg (Is 22:23). When used of God, the word has the sense of faithfulness or of unwavering commitment to his promises. Referring specifically to human faith, it means unwavering trust in the God who promised. Faith in the OT is not an abstract concept but rather is commitment to God. It is not characterized by works but by an attitude of wholehearted trust in God.

God affirms in Habakkuk 2:4 that a truly righteous person will live by unwavering trust in God, trust that remains firm in spite of trials. Jesus taught the same thing in the parable of the sower (Mt 13:21), and it is also expressed in James 1:12.

God's answer to Habakkuk's complaint was that he does punish evil, but in his time and his way. A truly righteous person will not lose faith because evil is not immediately eliminated or the wicked quickly punished. Faith trusts in the sovereignty of God's righteous rule in this world.

A Taunt-Song Celebrating the Fall of the Chaldeans (2:6-20) After hinting at the fall of the Chaldeans, the prophet composes a taunt-song in which he depicts the gloomy future of that nation. When the Babylonian Empire fell to a coalition of Medes and Persians, the prophetic elements in Habakkuk's poem became historical reality.

The prophet affirms that Babylon's "debtors" will arise against her (Hb 2:7). This expression implies that some nations would suddenly arise to bring about Babylon's downfall.

The reason for the destruction of Babylon is cited in 2:8: "You have plundered many nations; now they will plunder you" (NLT). The OT principle of retributive justice teaches that God's moral law extends not only to believers but to unbelievers as well.

The great building efforts of the Babylonian king Nebuchadnezzar seem to be implied in 2:9-11. The prophet says that even the stones and beams of his cities will cry out, as though protesting the fact that the city was built with blood (vv 11-12).

Habakkuk condemns the Chaldeans, not only for their inhuman cruelty, but also for the shameful way in which they treated their captive peoples. The prophet pictures this degrading treatment in a vivid metaphor, saying it is like making others drunk in order to gaze on their shame (2:15).

Habakkuk concludes his taunt-song with a denunciation of Chaldean idolatry, pointing out the folly of those who make gods from wood and stone (2:18-19). The Chaldeans, like other pagan peoples, attributed their success to their idols. The prophet implies that because such trust is groundless—their idols are powerless to help them—Babylon will fall.

Habakkuk goes on to make a striking contrast between the Lord and the idols created by people: "The LORD is in his holy Temple. Let all the earth be silent before him" (2:20, NLT). God is real and he is sovereign. The prophet's word is that the earth should wait in hushed silence for the judgment that will surely come.

The Prayer of Habakkuk (3:1-19) The prophecy of Habakkuk closes with a prayer, reminiscent of some of the OT psalms. It contains a superscription (3:1) and several musical notations.

Some have argued that this chapter is not originally Habakkuk's, because it does not fit the narrative flow of the book. They regard the chapter as originating in the postexilic period.

However, the psalm could have been written by the prophet and added to his prophetic oracles, either by himself or by a secretary. The musical notations do not necessarily point to a later period, because many psalms have such musical directions, and their preexilic date has been substantiated by linguistic and historical studies.

The prayer is similar to the message of Habakkuk. In it he affirms that God will judge his enemies (3:16), and he praises God's sovereignty (v 3). Both themes are prominent in the prophetic oracles of chapters 1 and 2.

The prayer is filled with assurances of God's power and justice. It forms a fitting conclusion to the body of the book, in which the prophet questioned divine providence. It demonstrates that the prophet had come to a place of unshakeable faith as he observed God's activity in history.

See also Habakkuk (Person); Israel, History of; Prophecy; Prophet, Prophetess.

HABAZZINIAH Jaazaniah's grandfather. Jaazaniah was a leader of the Recabites, warriors tested by Jeremiah with regard to their forefather's command not to drink wine (Jer 35:3). They remained loyal to the command, and Jeremiah used their loyalty in an appeal to Judah to be faithful to God.

HABERGEON* KJV translation for coat of mail, part of a soldier's defensive armor (2 Chr 26:14; Neh 4:16; Jb 41:26, NLT "javelin"). *See* Armor and Weapons.

HABOR Modern Habur (Chaboras) River. The Habor River runs from the mountains in north-central Assyria, in Gozan, into the Euphrates River at a junction about 250 miles (402 kilometers) south and west of Nineveh. Numerous tributaries feed the Habor farther to the north. The OT names the river as the site to which King Shalmaneser carried the captive Israelites (2 Kgs 17:6; 18:11; 1 Chr 5:26).

HACALIAH Nehemiah's father (Neh 1:1; 10:1).

HACHILAH* Unidentified site in Horesh, near Hebron, to which David fled when Saul attempted to kill him (1 Sm 23:19; 26:1, 3).

HACHMONI*, HACHMONITE* *See* Hacmoni; Hacmonite.

HACMONI Name of Jehiel's family. Jehiel was David's servant (1 Chr 27:32), apparently a companion or tutor of David's sons.

HACMONITE Designation for Jashobeam (also named Josheb-basshebeth in 2 Sm 23:8), one of David's personal guards (1 Chr 11:11). He is alternately called a Tahkemonite in 2 Samuel 23:8 (NLT mg), but this is probably a textual error.

HADAD
1. Eighth of the 12 sons of Ishmael, and thus a grandson of Abraham (Gn 25:15; 1 Chr 1:30). The KJV reads "Hadar" in Genesis 25:15 and "Hadad" in 1 Chronicles 1:30, whereas RSV and NLT read "Hadad" in both passages.
2. Edomite ruler, son of Bedad, who reigned before the Hebrew captivity in Egypt and who won an important victory over the Midianites in the plain of Moab (Gn 36:35-36; 1 Chr 1:46-47).
3. Another king of Edom, one of the few whose wife, Mehetabel, was mentioned by name. His capital city was Pau (Gn 36:39; 1 Chr 1:50-51).
4. Prince of the royal house of Edom who fled to Egypt after David and Joab conquered Edom and occupied the land. He grew up in Egypt and gained favor with the pharaoh, who gave him his sister-in-law as a wife. Later, when David was dead, he desired to return to Edom and lead a revolt against Solomon (1 Kgs 11:14-25). Some scholars have identified him with #3 above.

HADADEZER King of Zobah in Syria during David's reign in Israel. He apparently ruled a region from Ammon in the south to the Euphrates in the east. According to 2 Samuel 8:3-12 (see also 1 Chr 18:3-10, KJV "Hadarezer"), Hadadezer attempted to restore his power. David engaged him in battle at the river Euphra-

tes and defeated him. When the Syrians came to his aid, David defeated them and occupied Damascus. In 2 Samuel 10 David sent servants to comfort Hanun when his father—Nahash, king of Ammon—died. The servants were mistreated and humiliated (v 4). So David sent Joab against Ammon after Ammon allied with Syria as protection against Israel (v 6). Joab defeated the combined armies (vv 15-19; see also 1 Chr 19:16, 19). After Joab's victory, Hadadezer sent more troops from "beyond the river." The armies met at Helam, David was victorious, and Hadadezer begged for peace, thereby becoming a tributary to Israel.

See also Israel, History of; Syria, Syrians.

HADAD-RIMMON Combination of two storm deities, Hadad (mentioned in the Ugaritic texts) and Rimmon (Babylonian storm god). Hadad-rimmon was formerly thought to be a place. The Ras Shamra material equated Hadad with the vegetation god Baal, who was worshiped in an effort to ensure agricultural productivity. Canaanite fertility rituals included periodic mourning for the deceased Baal by the goddess Anat, his consort. It is to that rite that Zechariah 12:11 alludes. The messianic reference in the previous verse likens the grief in Jerusalem to the lamentation for Hadad-rimmon at the rites near Megiddo.

See also Canaanite Deities and Religion.

HADAR*
1. KJV spelling of Hadad, Ishmael's son, in Genesis 25:15. *See* Hadad #1.
2. Alternate spelling of Hadad, king of Edom, in Genesis 36:39. *See* Hadad #3.

HADAREZER* KJV alternate spelling of Hadadezer, king of Zobah. *See* Hadadezer.

HADASHAH Town in the lowlands of Judah, near Gath, in the vicinity of Zenan and Migdal-gad (Jos 15:37).

HADASSAH Original name of Esther (2:7). *See* Esther (Person).

HADATTAH* Name of a city (KJV) incorrectly derived from the name of the town Hazor-hadattah in Joshua 15:25. *See* Hazor-hadattah.

HADES* Abode of the dead. In Greek mythology Hades was originally the god of the underworld (also named Pluto), a brother of Zeus. He was the abductor of Persephone and thus the cause of winter. His realm, which was called by his name (and also called Tartarus), was the dark land where the dead existed. Odysseus entered that realm and fed the ghosts with blood to get directions back home (Homer's *Odyssey* 4.834). Originally the Greeks thought of hades as simply the grave—a shadowy, ghostlike existence that happened to all who died, good and evil alike. Gradually they and the Romans came to see it as a place of reward and punishment, an elaborately organized and guarded realm where the good were rewarded in the Elysian Fields and the evil were punished (so described by the Roman poet Virgil, 70–19 BC).

"Hades" became important to the Jews as the typical term used by the translators of the Septuagint to render the Hebrew name "Sheol" into Greek. This was a very suitable translation for the Hebrew term, for both words can signify the physical grave or death (Gn 37:35; Prv 5:5; 7:27), and both originally referred to a dark underworld (Jb 10:21-22) where existence was at best shadowy (Jb 38:17; Is 14:9). Sheol is described as under the ocean

(Jb 26:5-6; Jon 2:2-3) and as having bars and gates (Jb 17:16). All people go there whether they are good or evil (Ps 89:48). In the earlier literature there is no hope of release from Sheol/hades. C. S. Lewis describes this concept well in *The Silver Chair:* "Many sink down, and few return to the sunlit lands." Of course, all these descriptions are in poetic literature; how literally the Hebrews (or the Greeks, for that matter) took their descriptions of hades/Sheol is hard to say. They may have simply used the older picture-language of Greek poetry to describe that for which prose words were inadequate.

Jew and Greek alike came in contact with Persia—the Jews at the time the postexilic writers were composing their books (e.g., Malachi, Daniel, and some psalms), and the Greeks somewhat later (they fought the Persians 520–479 BC and conquered them 334–330 BC). Whether because of Persian influence on these groups or not, during this period, the idea of reward and punishment after death developed, and Sheol/hades changed from a shadow land to a differentiated place of reward and punishment for both Greeks (and Romans) and Jews. Josephus records that the Pharisees believed in reward and punishment at death (*Antiquities* 18.1.3), and a similar idea appears in 1 Enoch 22. In these and many other cases in Jewish literature, hades stands for the one place of the dead, which has two or more compartments. In other Jewish literature, hades is the place of torment for the wicked, while the righteous enter paradise (Pss of Sol 14; Wisd of Sol 2:1; 3:1). Thus, by the beginning of the NT period, hades has three meanings: (1) death, (2) the place of all the dead, and (3) the place of the wicked dead only. Context determines which meaning an author intends in a given passage.

All these meanings appear in the NT. In Matthew 11:23 and Luke 10:15, Jesus speaks of Capernaum's descending to hades (NLT mg). Most likely he simply means that the city will "die" or be destroyed. "Hades" means "death" in this context, as "heaven" means "exaltation." Revelation 6:8 also exemplifies this: Death comes on a horse, and hades (a symbol of death) comes close behind. This personification of hades probably comes from the OT, where hades/Sheol is viewed as a monster that devours people (Prv 1:12; 27:20; 30:16; Is 5:14; 28:15, 18; Hb 2:5).

Matthew 16:18 is a more difficult use of hades. The church will be built upon a rock and the gates of hades will not prevail against it. Here the place of the dead (complete with gates and bars) is a symbol for death: Christians may in fact be killed, but death (the gates of hades) will no more hold them than it held Christ. He who burst out of hades will bring his people out as well. This is also the meaning of Acts 2:27 (quoting Ps 16:10): Christ did not stay dead; his life did not remain in hades; unlike David, he rose from the dead. It is uncertain in either of these cases whether hades is simply a symbol for death or whether it means that Christ and the Christian actually went to a place of the dead called hades; probably the former is intended. Whatever the case, since Christ did rise, he has conquered death and hades. He appears in Revelation 1:18 as the one holding the keys (the control) to both.

Two NT passages refer to hades as the place where the dead exist: Revelation 20:13-14 and Luke 16:23. In Revelation 20 hades is emptied of all who are in it (either all dead or the wicked dead, depending on one's eschatology)—the resurrection is complete. When the wicked are judged and cast into the lake of fire (Gehenna), hades is also thrown in. Luke 16:23, however, clearly refers to hades as the place of the wicked dead. There the rich man is tormented in a flame, while the poor man, Lazarus, goes to paradise (Abraham's bosom).

Hades, then, means three things in the NT, as it did in Jewish literature: (1) Death and its power is the most frequent meaning, especially in metaphorical uses. (2) It also means the place of the dead in general, when a writer wants to lump all the dead together. (3) It means, finally, the place where the wicked dead are tormented before the final judgment. This is its narrowest meaning, occurring only once in the NT (Lk 16:23). The Bible does not dwell on this torment—Dante's picture in *The Inferno* draws on later speculation and Greco-Roman conceptions of hades more than on the Bible.

See also Dead, Place of the; Gehenna; Hell; Sheol.

HADID City in Benjamin (Neh 11:31-35) mentioned with Lod and Ono (Ezr 2:33; Neh 7:37) as the home of over 720 Benjamites returning from the Babylonian captivity (Neh 11:34). In 1 Maccabees 12:38 and 13:13 the place is identified with Adida, which was fortified by Simon Maccabeus and later by Vespasian. A more likely suggestion identifies it with the modern site of el-Haditheth, about three to four miles (4.8 to 6.4 kilometers) northeast of Lydda.

HADLAI Amasa's father from Ephraim's tribe (2 Chr 28:12). Amasa opposed the taking of prisoners from Judah's tribe after a battle.

HADORAM
1. Joktan's fifth son; Hadoram and his brothers were the sixth generation from Noah (Gn 10:27; 1 Chr 1:21).
2. Alternate spelling of Joram in 1 Chronicles 18:10 (KJV). *See* Joram #1.
3. Alternate spelling of Adoniram in 2 Chronicles 10:18 (KJV). *See* Adoniram.

HADRACH* Settlement in northwest Lebanon mentioned only in association with Tyre, Sidon, Hamath, and Damascus (Zec 9:1, see NLT mg). The last two cities were listed in Assyrian records with Hatarivia, with which Hadrach is now identified.

HAELEPH City given to Benjamin's tribe for an inheritance after the initial conquest of Canaan (Jos 18:28).

HAGAB Ancestor of a family of temple servants returning with Zerubbabel to Palestine following the exile (Ezr 2:46).

HAGABA*, HAGABAH Forefather of a family of temple servants who returned to Jerusalem with Zerubbabel after the Babylonian exile (Neh 7:48; spelled "Hagabah" in Ezr 2:45).

HAGAR Egyptian handmaid of Sarai, the wife of Abram. At Sarai's insistence, Abram took Hagar as his concubine, and she became the mother of his son Ishmael (Gn 16:1-16; 21:9-21).

When God commanded Abram to leave Mesopotamia, he promised to make a great nation of him and to give the new land to his seed (Gn 12:2, 7). After ten years in Canaan and still childless, Sarai suggested to Abram that he take Hagar as his concubine and have children by her. It was the custom in northeast Mesopotamia that, when a wife failed to produce an heir for her husband, she could give him a slave for that purpose. Any son born of the union of husband and concubine was considered the child of the wife (cf. 30:1-6).

During her pregnancy, Hagar became disrespectful to Sarai. Sarai dealt so harshly with Hagar that she fled to the desert. An angel of God appeared to her at a well in the desert and told her to return to Abram's house, promising that she would have a son, Ishmael ("God hears"), who would be a wild and quarrelsome man. Hagar then named the place Beer-lahairoi, meaning "the well of one who sees and lives."

Ishmael was born when Abram was 86 years old, and 14 years later God gave Abraham and Sarah the promised son, Isaac. At the time of Isaac's weaning (at approximately three years of age), a feast was held. At the weaning feast Ishmael mocked Isaac (Gn 21:9), and Sarah in anger asked Abraham to send Hagar and Ishmael away. Abraham hesitated until God spoke to him and told him to do so (v 12).

Hagar and Ishmael left to wander in the wilderness of Beersheba. When their water was exhausted, God miraculously rescued Hagar and Ishmael from death and assured Hagar that Ishmael would be the father of a great nation (Gn 21:17-19). Ishmael lived in the wilderness of Paran, became a hunter, married an Egyptian, and became the father of the Ishmaelites.

In an allegory developed by Paul (Gal 4:22-31), Hagar represents the old covenant of Sinai. As Ishmael was Abraham's son by human arrangement, the Judaizing Christians who would bind all Christians to the law of Moses are like Hagar's children born in slavery. Sarah, the freewoman, represents the new covenant of Christ. As Isaac was Abraham's son by faith in the divine promise, Christians who are free of the fleshly ordinances of the law are spiritual children of Sarah. The contrast is between salvation by works, which is bondage to the law, and salvation by grace and faith, which is freedom.

See also Abraham; Sarah #1.

HAGARENE*, HAGARITE*, HAGERITE*

KJV alternate forms of Hagrite, the name of a member of an Arabian tribe descended from Hagar living east of Palestine; spelled Hagerite in 1 Chronicles 27:31. *See* Hagrite.

HAGGADAH*

Method of Jewish interpretation that is homiletical in character. Haggadah is usually defined negatively, that is, as that part of rabbinic teaching that is *not* Halakah. Haggadah and Halakah complement each other; the latter is interpretation that gives the rule, statute, or religious law Jews are to follow, while Haggadah aims at edification, inspiration, inner piety, and religious devotion, covering the entire field of religion and ethics. Halakah states the fact; Haggadah stirs one to action. "Halakah" means literally "walking," thus showing the devout Jew how to walk in the way of the Lord. "Haggadah" means literally "narrative" or "storytelling," which includes proverbs, parables, and sermons. Within these artistic forms of instruction are contained moral and ethical principles intended to show one how to live correctly. Among the two types of interpretation, Haggadah is the more "popular," having a wider appeal. Its way of storytelling is designed to touch the human heart "so that one should recognize him who created the world, and so cling to his ways" (Sifrei-Deuteronomy 49). As one Jewish scholar has said, its purpose is "to bring Heaven down to earth and to elevate man to Heaven." Because Haggadah is not Halakah, but rather interpretation, it also contains other material, such as metaphysical speculations, historical and legendary tales of Israel's past, visions of its future, and remarks on scientific subjects, such as astronomy and medicine.

See also Halakah; Talmud.

HAGGAI (Person)

Prophet whose book is the 10th in a series of 12 brief prophetic books concluding the OT. Haggai's name probably came from a word for "festival." We have no information concerning his family or social background. He is referred to merely as Haggai the prophet (Hg 1:1; Ezr 5:1; 6:14). His place in the postexilic community seems to have been a conspicuous one, and according to Jewish tradition, he was known as a prophet in Babylon during the exile. The major concern of his prophetic ministry was to encourage the people to rebuild the temple, which had been destroyed during the earlier years of the exile.

See also Haggai, Book of; Prophet, Prophetess.

HAGGAI, Book of

Tenth of the 12 short prophetic books at the end of the OT.

PREVIEW
• Author and Date
• Purpose
• Teaching
• Content

Author and Date Haggai was among the Jewish colonists at Jerusalem in the year 520 BC when his prophetic words were recorded (Ezr 5:1-2; 6:14). The four messages the Lord gave to Haggai were to be directed to specific individuals. The first was to Zerubbabel the governor and Joshua the high priest (Hg 1:1). The second was to Zerubbabel, Joshua, and the remnant of the people (2:2). The third was a word to the priests (v 11). The final message was limited to Zerubbabel (v 21).

Purpose The key phrase of Haggai's prophecies is "Consider your ways" or "Consider" (1:5, 7; 2:15, 18). The purpose of God's messages to the Judean leadership and people, therefore, was to awaken them to their spiritual responsibilities. Two different classes of Judeans had to be turned from their indifference. The true believers needed to be reminded that God was merciful. The situation could be remedied, even though they thought the sins committed by their fathers were unforgivable. The hypocrites among the Judeans had only sought the promised blessings. They had only exchanged one form of idolatry for another. When the blessings did not materialize, they were disappointed.

The unifying message was that today gives no key to what God will do tomorrow. God's fulfillment of his promises cannot be judged by appearances. Haggai's message was twofold: reproof and encouragement. The colonists needed to be chastised for their indifference and consoled in the midst of their troubles.

Teaching Haggai is a practical book, dealing with the believer's service to God. Procrastination and indifference have been debilitating sins among God's people throughout all ages. Concern and a sense of urgency are always pleasing to God (Rom 13:11-14).

The presence of God is the primary motivation for boldness and the means of banishing discouragement (Mt 28:19-20; Eph 3:8-21; Heb 13:5-6).

Separation from contaminating influences and sin is demanded of all believers (2 Cor 6:14–7:1). Without this quality of life, the believer cannot expect to be found fit for God's service (2 Tm 2:19-26). The disobedient child of God can expect removal of blessing and chastisement from God (Heb 12:3-13; Jas 4:1-3).

The message concerning God's judgment of sin and the establishment of the messianic kingdom is a message of hope to the NT believer as well as the Jews of Haggai's day (Rom 15:4-13; 2 Pt 3:10-18).

The key phrase of Haggai ("consider your ways") has echoes in 1 Corinthians 11:28 and 2 Corinthians 13:5, as do his writings about the effects of sin and the blessings of God (Jude 1:1-25).

The God of Haggai is given the title "Lord of hosts" ("Lord Almighty") 14 times in the book. This title is characteristic of the postexilic prophetic books, Haggai, Zechariah, and Malachi, where it is found more than 80 times. It teaches that God is all-powerful and is Master of all spirit beings in heaven and all created beings on the earth.

Haggai also testifies to the God-breathed quality of the Word of God and its divine authority. Over and over the prophet announces ways that God has spoken to him and is the author of these messages (at least 25 times in the space of 28 verses).

Content

First Message The first message Haggai was to deliver to the Judeans was given to him "on the first day of the month" (Hg 1:1). Upon the first day of each month, the Jews were to bring special offerings to the sanctuary (Nm 28:11-15). God chose this special time to reveal the sin of the people with regard to the unfinished sanctuary.

The leaders of the Judeans were singled out for the first message from the Lord (Hg 1:1). Zerubbabel was the civil leader or governor, and Joshua was the spiritual leader or high priest. Together, they were responsible for the activity (or inactivity) of God's people.

The word of the Lord revealed the procrastination of the people (1:2). God's temple had not been completed because his people had determined for themselves that "the time is not come." The energies and finances of God's people had been channeled selfishly into their own homes (v 4).

"Now" (1:5, RSV) focused the attention of the Jews upon the present requirement of God in the light of their sinful indifference. They were to give attention to their own condition spiritually and materially: "Consider how you have fared." This key phrase of Haggai's prophecies is literally "Set your heart on your ways" or "Lay your ways to your heart." Self-examination would reveal that their procrastination had robbed them of more than just 16 years.

Verse 6 reveals the poverty in which the Jews were living as a result of God's chastisement for their sin. The blessings of God had been withdrawn in accord with his covenant (see Dt 28:15–29:1).

Following another exhortation to "consider" their ways (Hg 1:7), the Lord revealed the remedy for the Jews' cursed condition: "rebuild my house" (v 8). The disobedience with regard to the completion of the temple was the reason for their poverty (vv 9-11).

The response of the leaders and the people was encouraging. The resumption of the construction of the temple was a definite manifestation of belief in the word of God (1:12). Immediate obedience also testified to the acceptance of the ministry of Haggai, who was "the Lord's messenger" delivering "the Lord's message" (v 13).

Second Message Approximately one month later Haggai was summoned again by the Lord (2:1). The second message continued the note of encouragement with which the first message closed. Perhaps the builders had begun to feel the pressures of their service. Perhaps the old doubts and discouragements had plagued their faith again. The adversaries had reappeared to hinder them (Ezr 5:3–6:12). Haggai's second message was similar to Ezra's claim that "the eye of their God was upon the elders of the Jews" (Ezr 5:5, RSV). The Lord not only sees his servants' needs but also sends relief and encouragement.

The day of this second message was the last day of the Feast of Tabernacles (Lv 23:33-43). Perhaps this reminder of God's glorious presence with their ancestors in the wilderness made their present situation all the more discouraging. Therefore, the Lord spoke to all the people rather than just to their leaders (Hg 2:2). Was there any survivor of the preexilic days who had personally beheld the glory of God as it resided in the Solomonic temple (cf. 1 Kgs 8:1-11; Ez 9:1–11:23)? Was the present temple "as nothing" in comparison (Hg 2:3)? The Babylonian Talmud listed five things that were absent in the new temple that had been present in the Solomonic temple: (1) the ark of the covenant, (2) the sacred fire, (3) the shekinah glory, (4) the Holy Spirit, and (5) the Urim and Thummim.

Again, "now" calls attention to God's remedy. Three times the command "take courage" is proclaimed (2:4). Each time the command is given, one of the recipients of God's message is addressed (cf. v 2). The concluding command was "work." The reason for the strength and the activity was God's presence. The Holy Spirit might seem to be absent from the temple, but he would remain among the people "according to the word" of God (v 5).

To encourage the workers further, God revealed the future glory of his house (2:6-9). That glory would come to pass after a time of judgment (vv 6-7a), when the treasures of all nations come in (v 7b). The exact meaning of this verse has been variously interpreted. The views center around two different translations: "the desire of all nations shall come" (KJV) and "and the treasures of all the nations will come to this Temple" (NLT).

The arguments for the messianic interpretation based on the first translation may be summarized as follows: (1) The vast majority of both Christian and Jewish interpreters took this phrase as a reference to the Messiah. (2) The abstract noun "desire" may have the concrete concept of the one who is desirable. (3) Though the verb in the Hebrew is plural, it is grammatically possible for the agreement of subject and predicate to be based upon the second noun ("nations") in a genitive relationship. (4) The time element is suitable since God has just judged the nations and the hour of Christ's coming would be at hand. (5) An alternate translation is available that meets the grammatical difficulties but retains the messianic import: "They [the nations] have come to the desire of all the nations."

In spite of the weight of the arguments for this first view, it seems better to accept the second translation and corresponding view. The arguments are as follows: (1) The vast majority of early Christian and Jewish interpreters base their view on the Latin Vulgate translation (c. AD 400), while the second translation is in agreement with an older version, the Greek Septuagint (c. 300 BC). (2) The singular "desire" may be taken as a collective noun referring to "features" or "wealth." (3) The principle of Hebrew grammar that allows the noun "nations" to be the one with which the verb agrees is a rare occurrence in poetic books for such constructions as this. It is unlikely that such phraseology would be used without Haggai's declaring the exact meaning in the immediate context. (4) The immediate context does solve the difficulty by the plain declaration that the silver and the gold belong to the Lord (2:8). (5) The kingdom context of these verses accords well with such parallel passages as Isaiah 60:5, 11 and Revelation 21:24.

The conclusion to this message of encouragement is that the future glory of the temple (cf. Hg 2:3) will be greater than in the days of the Solomonic temple (v 9), because the shekinah glory will return (Hg 2:7; Ez 43:1-5) and the building will have great beauty (cf. Hg 2:8; Is 60:13, 17). God will also grant peace (Hg 2:9) in his kingdom at the time of this future glorious temple (see Is 9:6-7; 66:12; Zec 6:13).

Third Message About two months later Haggai received a third message from God (Hg 2:10). This time exhortation would be the theme, and the message was directed to the priests alone (v 11). Haggai used questions concerning the law of Moses to instruct the priests in the polluting character of sin. Something clean or holy cannot transfer its sanctity to something else (v 12). But that which is unholy *can* transfer *its* character to something clean, defiling it (Hg 2:13; cf. Lv 22:4-6; Nm 19:11).

The application of this principle to the Judeans was clear: the offerings they brought during their years of disobedience were unacceptable to God because of Judah's uncleanness (Hg 2:14).

By reviving the memory of past disobedience and chastisement, God was exhorting the Jews to constantly "consider" (2:15, 18) the consequences of disobedience. Such consideration should prevent future spiritual indifference. The conclusion of the message was a reminder of the blessing of God upon the obedient (v 19).

Fourth Message On the same day Haggai received another message from God (2:20). This message was to be directed toward Zerubbabel (v 21), who was to be encouraged by the permanency of his inherited Davidic office (cf. Hg 1:1; 2 Sm 7:4-17; 1 Chr 3:1, 5, 10, 17-20). The gentile nations would be judged and the kingdoms of the world overthrown (Hg 2:6-7, 21-22). This would be but the preparation for God's rule (cf. Rv 11:15-18).

The promise to Zerubbabel in Haggai 2:23 was God's means of confirming that his promises to David were still operative even after the 70-year Babylonian captivity and the 16-year stagnation among the Judeans who had returned to Jerusalem. Zerubbabel was appointed "as a signet ring" by God. A signet was a personal cylinder or ring seal and a sign of the authenticity of their signature. Kings used them for identifying their decrees (Est 3:10; 8:8-10) and for confirming the authority of their deputies (Gn 41:42). God's appointment of Zerubbabel "as a signet ring," therefore, meant that Zerubbabel would be God's seal of authority on the continuation of the Davidic line from which the Messiah should come and reign (cf. Mt 1:12; Lk 3:27).

See also Haggai (Person); Israel, History of; Postexilic Period; Prophecy; Prophet, Prophetess.

HAGGEDOLIM Father of Zabdiel, overseer of 128 "mighty men of valor" (RSV) who lived in Jerusalem in Nehemiah's day (Neh 11:14).

HAGGERI* KJV rendering of Hagri, Mibhar's father, in 1 Chronicles 11:38. *See* Hagri.

HAGGI Gad's son and founder of the family of Haggites (Gn 46:16; Nm 26:15).

HAGGIAH Merarite Levite, Shimea's son and the father of Asaiah (1 Chr 6:30).

HAGGITE Descendant of Haggi (Nm 26:15). *See* Haggi.

HAGGITH One of David's wives and the mother of Adonijah (2 Sm 3:4; 1 Kgs 1:5, 11; 2:13; 1 Chr 3:2). She gave birth to Adonijah in Hebron while David maintained his capital there. In 2 Samuel she and her son are fourth in the list of David's wives and sons.

HAGRI Mibhar's father, according to 1 Chronicles 11:38. The parallel list in 2 Samuel 23:36, however, has "Bani, the Gadite" instead of "Mibhar, son of Hagri." Due to some textual difficulties in the 1 Chronicles passage, the 2 Samuel reading is preferred.

HAGRITE Arabian tribe descended from Hagar, Abraham's concubine. Being nomads, the Hagrites roamed the desert east of Gilead. Relations between Israel and the Hagrites were usually hostile. During Saul's reign, Reuben's tribe fought them and were defeated (1 Chr 5:10). Later, however, with the help of Gad and the half-tribe of Manasseh, Reuben was able to take their land and hold it until the exile (1 Chr 5:19-20). In the light of that hostility, it is easy to understand Asaph's prayer against them in Psalm 83:6. David, on the other hand, made a Hagrite, Jaziz, the steward of all his flocks (1 Chr 27:31).

HAHIROTH* Alternate form of Pi-hahiroth in Numbers 33:8. *See* Pi-hahiroth.

HAI* KJV form for the Canaanite city Ai in Genesis 12:8 and 13:3. *See* Ai.

HAIRSTYLES AND BEARDS In Palestine and throughout the Near East, women's hairstyles were long. In NT times a woman who cut her hair might be mistaken for a pagan priestess and thus be disgraced (see 1 Cor 11:15). The apostle Peter warned Christian women against preoccupation with elaborate styles of hair (1 Pt 3:3). When a woman married, it was customary to change her hairstyle slightly, in favor of a more mature appearance. Curling tongs and hair oils were used by some married women.

Dark hair is mentioned frequently in the Bible, although gray hair represented maturity and was respected. Some persons preferred to make use of popular black and red hair dyes. According to tradition, Herod the Great dyed his graying hair with henna.

Beard and hair trimming was performed in a specialized manner in Jewish culture. An Israelite man was instructed not to cut the hair on his temples or trim the corners of his beard (Lv 19:27). This was done to maintain a contrast in every way between the Israelites and the members of idolatrous cults in Canaan and elsewhere (Dt 12:29-30). Beards distinguished Hebrews from Egyptians, who were clean-shaven, although they sometimes wore false beards on ceremonial occasions. Shaving or cutting off the beard of enemy captives was considered the gravest humiliation that the victor could impose. A shaved head, however, was also a recognized symbol of purification at the termination of a vow (Lv 14:8-9; Acts 18:18). Shaving a beard was the usual sign of mourning (Is 15:2). It could also symbolize the approach of doom (Is 7:20; Jer 41:5; 48:37).

HAKILAH *See* Hachilah.

HAKKATAN Member of Azgad's family, the father of Johanan, and one of the exiles who returned to Jerusalem with Ezra (Ezr 8:12).

HAKKOZ Name borne by a priestly family during the monarchy (1 Chr 24:10). In Ezra's time, the family pedigree could not be documented properly; consequently, the privilege of priestly service was withdrawn (Ezr 2:61; Neh 3:4, 21; 7:63; KJV "Koz").

HAKUPHA Forefather of a family of temple assistants who returned to Jerusalem with Zerubbabel after the exile (Ezr 2:51; Neh 7:53).

HALAH Place in Assyria where the inhabitants of Samaria were taken after its fall in 722 BC (2 Kgs 17:6; 18:11; cf. 1 Chr 5:26).

HALAK, Mount Mountain listed as marking the southern boundary of Joshua's conquests (Jos 11:17; 12:7). It is located in the western Arabah and is probably identical with Jebel Halaq on the northwest side of the Wadi Marra.

HALAKAH* Overall term for Jewish law. Halakah, which means literally "walking," gives the authoritative Jewish way of life as contained in the Mishnah. It shows Jews how they are to walk (i.e., live life) and what they must do (see Ex 18:20).

First of all, Halakah rests upon the biblical laws and commandments found in the written Law (the Pentateuch, the first five books of the Bible) and the oral law (according to Jewish tradition, the unwritten law supposedly given to Moses on Mt Sinai and passed down through generations, finally to be recorded in the Talmud). In the Pentateuch, then, Halakah is given as law; for example, we are told not to work on the Sabbath. But what, in this context, does "work" mean? The written Law gives us no help, but in the Talmud we have Halakah, which is interpretation of the written Law, and in the Talmud we learn what "work" means.

Second, Halakah rests upon all the rabbinic legislation and decisions handed down through the ages by great Jewish scholars. All these things, taken together, provide the basis for making religious-legal decisions in the orthodox Jewish community. All these things, the written and oral law plus the history of Jewish legal scholarship, provide us with Halakah.

Halakah is intended to be all-encompassing, to handle every situation in life. One's eating habits, sex life, business ethics, social activities, entertainment—these and much more are dealt with by Halakah. For this reason it has been called "the Jewish way"; it is the Jewish legal and practical guide to living.

See also Haggadah; Talmud.

HALF-SHEKEL TAX* Tax on all adult Jews throughout the world, begun during intertestamental times for the support of the temple, and continued by Vespasian for its Roman replacement; the temple tax of Mt 17:24-25.

HALHUL City assigned to Judah's tribe for an inheritance after the initial conquest of Canaan. It was located between Beth-zur and Beth-anoth, four miles (6.4 kilometers) north of Hebron (Jos 15:58).

HALI Town mentioned among those that formed the border of Asher's tribe (Jos 19:25). Hali may have been located west of Mt Carmel, but this is uncertain.

HALICARNASSUS An important commercial city of Caria in Asia Minor, beautifully situated on a bay about 15 miles (24 kilometers) from the island of Cos. Its excellent natural harbor and the fertile soil in the surrounding area, which produced abundant crops of fruits and nuts, made it a prominent trading center. The tomb of one of the most famous kings of Caria (Mausolus, 377–353 BC) at Halicarnassus was considered one of the wonders of the ancient world. It was also the birthplace of Herodotus and Dionysius. The city was burned by Alexander the Great when he was not able to take the acropolis. From 1 Maccabees 15:23 it appears that it had a substantial Jewish population because a letter written by the Roman Senate asked that no harm should be done to them (1 Macc 15:19). Josephus notes that the city granted the Jews the right to "celebrate their Sabbaths, and perform their holy offices, according to the Jewish laws; and may make their *proseuchae* (places of prayer) at the sea-side, according to the customs of their forefathers" (*Antiquities* 14.10.23). The modern town of Bodrum covers a part of the site of the ancient city.

HALLEL* Hebrew term describing a song of praise to God. It was later used in the Talmud and in rabbinical writings to refer to several groups of psalms of praise to God. Psalms 113–118 were known as the Egyptian Hallel, and first-century AD Jewish tradition assigned them to Moses. During the temple period, this Hallel was recited on 18 days in the year, but only once at night, on the Passover. For that occasion it was recited in parts. Psalms 113–114 preceded the meal, prior to drinking the second cup, and Psalms 115–118 were recited after the last cup was filled. This is probably the song that is meant in the reference to the Last Supper of Jesus and his disciples, when they sang a "hymn" (Mt 26:30; Mk 14:26). This Hallel was also used for the feasts of Unleavened Bread, Pentecost, Tabernacles, and Dedication.

The Great Hallel consisted of Psalm 136 but sometimes included Psalms 120–136. Psalms 146–148 were also considered a single Hallel. These were used in the daily morning service of the synagogue.

See also Hallelujah; Talmud.

HALLELUJAH Important Christian acclamation used extensively in the church's worship and liturgy from early times. "Hallelujah" is a transliteration into Greek, and thence into English, of two Hebrew words that mean "Praise the Lord." This combination of the two Hebrew words forms the characteristic call to praise. Jews living in the Dispersion in pre-Christian times were already using the transliteration in their synagogue worship. "Hallelujah," according to ancient Hebrew tradition, is to be written as one word, except in Psalm 135:3. It occurs nowhere in the OT but in the Psalter, where it occurs 23 times, and for the first time in Psalm 104:35. Each of Psalms 111 to 113 begins with "Hallelujah"; each of Psalms 115 to 117 ends with the word; and each of Psalms 146 to 150 begins and ends with it.

In the Septuagint version of Psalms 113–118, all the individual psalms are headed "Allelujah." Through the Vulgate, this form of the word "Hallelujah" has come into use in the church. Like another famous Hebrew liturgical term, "Amen," "Hallelujah" has passed from the OT to the NT, and thence to the Christian church. But in the KJV and ERV the phrase is rendered "Praise ye the LORD," and similarly, in the RSV and NLT, it is rendered "Praise the LORD."

In Hebrew liturgical usage the Hallel, or Hymn of Praise, Psalms 113–118, is sung at the three great religious festivals of Passover, Pentecost, and Tabernacles. At the domestic celebration of Passover, Psalms 113 and 114 are sung before the meal and Psalms 115–118 are sung after it. Matthew 26:30 and Mark 14:26 refer to the singing of 115–118 as the "hymn" sung by the Lord and

Calligraphy by Timothy R. Botts

his disciples after their celebration of the Passover and before they left the upper room.

"Hallelujah" does not appear anywhere in the NT except in Revelation 19:1-6. There it is a chant of the saints in heaven. It was taken over into the liturgy and hymnody of the church at an early date. It became the characteristic expression of joy and was therefore sung especially at Eastertide, as is witnessed by Augustine. The choice by the Christian church of Psalms 113, 114, and 118 from the Hebrew Hallel as the psalms to be sung on Easter day marks the liturgical connection of Easter with Passover.

See also Hallel.

HALLOHESH, HALOHESH* Shallum's father (Neh 3:12) and one who set his seal on Ezra's covenant (10:24).

HAM (Person) Second son of Noah (Gn 5:32; 6:10; 7:13; 9:18, 22; 10:1, 6, 20). Ham had four sons whose names were Cush, Mizraim (Hebrew for Egypt), Put, and Canaan (Gn 10:6; 1 Chr 1:8). Ham, then, is seen as the ancestor of the Egyptians (though a mixed race apparently occurs later), as well as of peoples in Africa, Arabia, and Canaan.

After the Flood, Noah began cultivating vineyards, and on one occasion exposed himself while drunk (Gn 9:20-24). Ham saw his father lying naked and related the incident to Shem and Japheth, who covered Noah up discreetly. When Noah awoke and learned what "his youngest son" (seen by some as Ham) had done, he cursed Ham's son Canaan, saying his brothers (Cush, Mizraim, and Put) and Shem and Japheth would rule over him. But if Ham is the one referred to in 9:24 as offending Noah, why should the curse fall on his son Canaan? The most likely answer is that Ham is not being referred to in verse 24. The expression is "his youngest son" (the "younger" of the KJV is hardly possible in Hebrew), whereas Ham is repeatedly seen as the second of the brothers, not the youngest (5:32; 6:10; 7:13; 9:18; 10:1), the explicit order of the sons indicating age. Instead, "his youngest son" refers to Canaan, and to some base deed not being recorded, on whom the curse falls. "Son" used for "grandson" is common Semitic material, and it seems to have been used here in this way since Canaan is the "youngest" of the (grand)sons. The curse, then, as the text clearly says, is on Canaan rather

than Ham. Canaan (and his posterity) is to be subjugated by Japheth and Shem with the Canaanites, finally disappearing by NT times.

See also Nations; Noah #1.

HAM (Place) Place where Chedorlaomer and his cohorts defeated the Zuzim (Gn 14:5). The name is probably preserved by Tell Ham, near the modern village on the Wadi er-Rejeilah. Bronze and Iron Age settlements have been unearthed there.

HAMAN Son of Hammedatha the Agagite, a high official under King Ahasuerus (Xerxes) in Persia during the time of Esther. Haman became angry with Mordecai, the uncle of Esther the queen, because Mordecai would not bow down to him as all others did. In anger he planned to exterminate all the Jews in Persia (Est 3:8). While he was plotting Mordecai's hanging, the king was reading about Mordecai's valuable services. Haman's plot to kill all Jews was revealed, and he went to the gallows made for Mordecai. Haman's ten sons were killed shortly after, and their bodies were strung up as well. In the Hebrew Bible the sons' names are written in a perpendicular manner, supposedly to show their relative positions on the gallows. The carnival atmosphere of the Feast of Purim sometimes resulted in Haman being hanged in effigy, or his name being written on the soles of shoes to express contempt.

See also Esther, Book of.

HAMATH

1. City and district located about 125 miles (201 kilometers) north of Damascus (Syria), on the Orontes River. The early residents apparently were of the Hamitic race from the descendants of Canaan (Gn 10:18), but later inhabitants were Semitic. It was to be the northern boundary of the nation of Israel, described as the "entrance of Hamath" (Nm 34:7-8; Jos 13:5; Hebrew, *Lebo Hamath*), but actually it was such only in the early monarchy and under Jeroboam II (793–753 BC). The location is uncertain but was between the Lebanon and Anti-Lebanon Mountains. Some scholars have thought of it as an actual place-name, Lebo-hamath, and have identified it with modern Lebweh on the Orontes. Others have located it elsewhere in Syria.

Hamath was established during the Neolithic period and destroyed about 1750 BC, perhaps by the

Hyksos. It was later rebuilt and conquered by Thutmose III (1502–1448 BC), and while Egypt controlled Syria, Hamath prospered. Several Hittite inscriptions have been discovered that disclose that Hamath had become the capital of a small Hittite kingdom prior to 900 BC.

When David fought Hadadezer, king of Zobah, and defeated him, then Toi, king of Hamath, sent his son to congratulate David (2 Sm 8:9-10). Since Solomon built store-cities in the region of Hamath (2 Chr 8:4), it has been suggested that Hamath had become a tributary kingdom to Israel. During the reign of Ahab of Israel, the Assyrian royal inscriptions state that Irhulini, king of Hamath, allied with Damascus, Israel, and the 12 kings of the coast to resist the advances of Shalmaneser III (860–825 BC). The league halted Shalmaneser, although he continued to harass Syria, and about 846 BC he conquered the Syrian league, when Hamath became subject to Assyria. In 730 BC Eni-Ilus, then king of Hamath, paid tribute to Tiglath-pileser III. About 720 BC Sargon II colonized Hamath with 4,300 Assyrians and moved many people from different areas of his kingdom, including Hamath, to Samaria (2 Kgs 17:24). Israelites also were apparently colonized in Hamath (Is 11:11). Other OT references to the Assyrian conquest of Hamath include 2 Kings 18:34, 19:13, Isaiah 10:9, 36:19, 37:13, and Amos 6:2. Later the city seems to have been subject to Damascus (Jer 49:23). Some of the prophets predicted that Israel would eventually extend its boundaries once again to Hamath (Ez 47:16-17; 48:1; Zec 9:2).

During the Maccabee period, Jonathan Maccabeus and his army met the army of Demetrius at Hamath (1 Macc 12:25). According to Josephus, Antiochus Epiphanes changed its name to Epiphania (*Antiquities* 1.4.2), the name by which it was known to the Greeks and Romans.
See also Hamath, Entrance of.

2. Hamath-zobah is mentioned in 2 Chronicles 8:3 as a town conquered by Solomon. Some have suggested that it was the same city as the Hamath above, while others suggest that it was a different town in the district of Zobah.
See also Hamath-zobah.

HAMATH*, Entrance of
Place of uncertain identification, marking the northern border of the Canaanite territory promised to Israel by God (Nm 34:8), but only attained by the time of the monarchy (1 Kgs 8:65; 1 Chr 13:5; 2 Chr 7:8).

After the death of Solomon, the kingdom was divided and the northern boundary shrank. It was not until the reign of Jeroboam II, son of Joash (793–753 BC), king of the northern kingdom (called Israel), that the northern boundaries extended again to the entrance of Hamath (2 Kgs 14:23-25).

Both Amos and Ezekiel refer to the entrance of Hamath in their prophecies concerning Israel (Am 6:14; Ez 47:15-20; 48:1). Some authorities regard the place as the ancient town Lebo-hamath, identified with modern Lebweh. See Hamath #1; Lebo-hamath.

HAMATHITE
Resident of Hamath (Gn 10:18; 1 Chr 1:16). See Hamath #1.

HAMATH-ZOBAH
City captured by King Solomon of Israel (2 Chr 8:3-4). Its identity is uncertain. It occurs only once in the Bible and is not mentioned in any of the cuneiform inscriptions from that period. Some schol-ars have suggested that there were two Hamaths and that "Zobah" was added to distinguish it from the better-known city (cf. Ez 47:17). The city is mentioned with Hamath and Tadmor and was perhaps located in north-eastern Syria.

HAMMATH (Person)
Ancestor of the house of Rechab (1 Chr 2:55), about whom nothing else is known.

HAMMATH (Place)
Fortified outpost identified with the modern Hamman Tabariyeh (Jos 19:35). This place is located among hot springs on the western shore of Galilee and is probably identifiable with Hammon (1 Chr 6:76), Hammoth-dor (Jos 21:32), and perhaps the Emmaus of Josephus (*Antiquities* 18.2.3).

HAMMEDATHA
Father of Haman, a chief adviser to the Persian king Ahasuerus and a sworn enemy of the Jews, according to the book of Esther (3:1, 10; 8:5; 9:10, 24).

HAMMELECH*
Hebrew word meaning "the king," taken to be a personal name by the KJV, but more correctly translated as "the king" by other versions (Jer 36:26; 38:6).

HAMMOLECHETH*, HAMMOLEKETH
Machir's daughter and Gilead's sister (1 Chr 7:18).

HAMMON
1. One of the cities of Asher mentioned in Joshua 19:28. It was somewhere south of Tyre on the western border of Asher.
2. Alternate name for Hammath in 1 Chronicles 6:76. See Hammath (Place).

HAMMOTH-DOR
Alternate name for the Levitical town Hammath in Joshua 21:32.

HAMMUEL
Member of Mishma's family from Simeon's tribe (1 Chr 4:26).

HAMMURABI*, Law Code of
Law code devised by Hammurabi, the last great king of the first Babylonian dynasty (c. 1790–1750 BC), to safeguard the rights and define the responsibilities of Babylonian citizens. The laws were inscribed on stelae, which were usually erected in marketplaces or near temples for all to see. The most complete example discovered so far dates from the latter part of his reign. The black diorite stele was found at Susa in 1901 by French archaeologists. It stood eight feet (2.4 meters) high and showed a bas-relief of Hammurabi receiving the symbols of kingship and law from the god Shamash. Beneath this was a poetic introduction, followed by the 282 articles of the code, and an epilogue in an equally poetic style extolling the virtues of Hammurabi, his concern for his people, and the way in which he had followed the wishes of the great god Marduk and the god of justice, Shamash. The gods are called upon to curse any who defy the stele.

It had been carried to Susa as a battle trophy by the Elamites in 1160 BC, and it is now in the Louvre in Paris. The code is a collection of laws based on Sumerian and early Semitic laws. Similarities between the code of Hammurabi and those of the Assyrians, Hittites, and Hebrews are numerous.

Hammurabi began his code by setting out punishments for the most obvious crimes, such as kidnapping, theft, receiving stolen property, breaking and entering, looting, perjury, false accusation, and harboring a fugitive. All these could be punished by death, especially where robbery involved the theft of temple or state property, and where perjury was committed by a witness giving testimony in a case involving a capital offense.

All valid transactions took place before witnesses, and it was essential that their testimony was trustworthy in disputed cases. Summary justice was meted out to the man found guilty of breaking and entering: "If a man made a breach in a house, they shall put him to death in front of that breach and wall him in" (section 21), and to the looter at a fire: "If a fire broke out in a man's house, and a man, who went to extinguish [it] cast his eye on the goods of the owner of the house and has appropriated the goods of the owner of the house, that man shall be thrown into that fire" (section 25).

The protection of feudal rights and responsibilities are outlined in the next section. The officer was responsible for soldiers under his command in the same way that the soldier was required to fulfill his duty to the state. The law also protected his property while he was in the army. A tenant was under obligation to use his rented property carefully and advantageously. If a tenant rented land that became flooded before the harvest, the law protected him from having to pay rent for that year. He also had to be thoughtful toward his neighbors' crops and ensure that he didn't inundate their fields by his own overzealous irrigation (sections 30–56).

The detail in which contracts and commercial laws are discussed indicates the extent and variety of such transactions. If money was borrowed from a merchant who foreclosed and the borrower was unable to repay the loan, he had to make payment in kind, for example, in dates from his own crop. The permissible interest rate was approximately 20 percent. The borrower was also protected by law from the practice of the lender's using a small weight of grain or money and insisting on the return with interest at a large weight. Anyone caught doing this forfeited whatever he had lent. Female wine sellers were also cautioned against selling with short weight (section 108). High interest rates were prescribed for obtaining wine on credit, and it is unlikely that many took advantage of this early form of credit.

To ensure an equal division in the breaking up of a partnership, the transaction was performed in the presence "of God," presumably in the temple. A trader borrowing money at interest was expected to make a profit. If he did, he repaid the principal and the interest. If he did not, it was presumed that he was a poor trader, and he was penalized by having to repay the merchant double the amount that he had borrowed. If the money was loaned as a favor, however, and the trader then suffered a loss, the principal only was repayable without interest. A trader who was robbed by bandits was not required to make payment. Sealed receipts were used as a safeguard of fair trading practices. In disputes between a merchant and a trader over a loan, if the merchant proved his case, the trader had to return three times the amount of the money originally borrowed. Where the merchant disputed with a trader who then proved his case, the merchant paid the trader six times the amount of the principal involved (sections 98–107).

A creditor could not come and take a debtor's money or grain without his permission. If he did so, he had to return what he had taken and forfeit the loan. In several instances a person could be held as a pledge. If he died of natural causes during that period, no claim could be made, but if he died as a result of maltreatment, compensation was payable according to rank. If the pledge was a slave (the lowest level of Mesopotamian society),

the amount payable was one-third of a mina of silver and the loan was forgiven. If the pledge was a man's son, the creditor's son was put to death as a recompense. Where a wife, son, or daughter was bound over for service to pay a debt, the maximum period of servitude was three years (sections 113–117).

A man was responsible for the security of anything left with him for safekeeping. If the property was lost through robbery because the building was not secure, restitution had to be made to the owner of the property. Anyone claiming falsely that his property was lost had to pay the city council double the amount of his claim.

There were also extensive laws related to sex and marriage (sections 127–162). Like most transactions, marriage was not valid without a contract. Adultery was frequently punished by death, but a man might plead to have his wife's life spared. The victim of rape was not punished. (According to Mosaic law, such a person was equally guilty if the act took place within the city, as she was expected to scream for help. If it occurred outside the city walls, however, she was not held responsible, on the theory that her screams could not have been heard.) Hammurabi's code shows concern for the woman who was deserted or whose husband was taken captive. She was permitted to live with another man if she had insufficient means to be self-supporting.

A woman's dowry was returned when she was divorced, or if there had been no dowry, a payment of one mina of silver was made to her, or one-third of a mina of silver if her husband was a peasant. If a woman neglected her household duties to set herself up in business, her husband might divorce her without payment or he might remarry without divorcing her, thus forcing her to live on in the house as a servant.

A slave who had borne her master's child could not be sold. If a man married a woman who was sick, and he then decided to marry another, the sick wife might continue to live in the house and her husband had to support her for the rest of her life. A woman who killed her husband for her lover was impaled on stakes (section 153). Incest was punishable by death or banishment. Breach of promise cases usually resulted in the repayment of double the value of the dowry. When a wife died, her dowry became part of her inheritance for her children, but if she died childless and her father returned her marriage price, her husband might not lay claim to her dowry, which had to be returned to her father (sections 162–163). The rights of a younger unmarried son were protected, as were those of the children of a master and his slave. A son was protected against being disinherited by his father unless he had committed some serious offense. A widow was protected against the overzealous financial demands of her children. If a free woman married a slave, their children were free. If the slave died, his widow retained her dowry and half the goods acquired since the marriage, the slave owner being entitled to the remainder. Women temple personnel were also protected by law.

Under Hebrew law, it was a father's duty to teach his son the means of earning a livelihood. Hammurabi's code prescribed that an adopted son had to be similarly trained, and if in any way he was not reared as a natural child within the family, he might return to his own home.

If a man subsequently had a family of his own and the foster child was sent away, he had the right to take with him one-third of the man's goods, although none of his land or his house, since these were the inheritance of the natural children. If a child died in a nurse's care and she took another assignment without informing the new employers of the previous death, her breast was cut off.

The most famous section of Hammurabi's law code concerns assault: "If a [man] has destroyed the eye of a member of the aristocracy, they shall destroy his eye." Similarly, if he broke a man's bone or knocked out a tooth, he would suffer the same fate (sections 196–197). If the injured person was a commoner, however, a fine of one mina of silver was charged for destroying an eye or breaking a bone. When the injured man was a slave, payment of half his value had to be made. Punishments for simple assault depended upon the rank of the two protagonists. Where a man swore that the blow was not deliberate, he might simply pay the physician's bill. Other penalties were set out for instances where the blow was fatal or caused a woman to miscarry (sections 209–214).

Surgeons' fees were also specified. For saving a life or for eye surgery, the fee was ten shekels of silver when the patient was an aristocrat, but only five for a commoner, and two for a slave. If an aristocratic patient died under the surgeon's bronze knife, or lost an eye, the surgeon could have his hand cut off (section 218). If a slave died during surgery, the surgeon had to replace the slave with another. For setting a broken bone or healing a sprained tendon, the physician charged five, three, or two shekels, depending on the patient's status (sections 221–223).

The final section of laws concerns the protection of people from the poor workmanship of house and boat builders, rules and regulations for those who rent animals or hire people, theft of agricultural implements, rates for hiring and paying wages, and rules for the purchase and sale of slaves (sections 228–282).

A man who fraudulently let out his master's oxen for hire rather than using them on his own fields would be required to pay the normal rental of grain for the field. If he was unable to do so, he was to be dragged through that field by the oxen.

Because of similarities in culture, it is hardly surprising that there should be areas of correspondence between Hammurabi's code and the Mosaic law. Thus both bodies of legislation prescribed the death penalty for adultery (Hammurabi section 129; Lv 20:10; Dt 22:22) and for the kidnapping and selling of an individual (Hammurabi section 114; Ex 21:16). The *lex talionis*, or principle of retaliation, in Exodus 21:23-25 and Deuteronomy 19:21 is reflected widely in Hammurabi's laws, including sections 197, 210, and 230. The differences, however, are equally significant. Whereas Hammurabi's legislation allowed women equal rights of divorce (section 142), these were denied under the Mosaic law by simply not being included (cf. Dt 24:1-4). Hammurabi's code was basically pragmatic in nature, and although promulgated under the authority of Shamash, god of justice, the legislation took little notice of ethical and spiritual principles.

See also Civil Law and Justice; Criminal Law and Punishment; Law, Biblical Concept of.

HAMONAH Name of site meaning "horde" in the Transjordan where the marauding armies of Gog will be destroyed by the Israelites (Ez 39:16).

See also Gog #2.

HAMON-GOG* Valley in the Transjordan where the dead of the armies of Gog (Gog's "hordes") will be buried (Ez 39:11, 15).

HAMOR Hivite or Horite prince of the country about Shechem (Gn 34:2), from whom Jacob bought land when returning with his family from Paddan-aram. At this time Hamor's son Shechem committed fornication

with Dinah, the daughter of Jacob. At his son's request Hamor asked Jacob for a marriage alliance between Shechem and Dinah, offering a dowry. Simeon and Levi, in pretended friendship, persuaded the males of the city to be circumcised, but then attacked and killed them before they were healed, taking revenge for their sister's humiliation.

"Hamor" is the Hebrew word that Jacob uses to denote Issachar in blessing his sons (Gn 49:14) and is the usual word for "ass" in the OT (e.g., Gn 42:26; Ex 20:17; Jgs 15:15; Is 1:3; Zec 9:9).

HAMRAN* Alternate name for Hemdan, Dishon's oldest son in 1 Chronicles 1:41 (see NLT mg). *See* Hemdan.

HAMUEL* KJV spelling of Hammuel, the Simeonite, in 1 Chronicles 4:26. *See* Hammuel.

HAMUL, HAMULITE Perez's younger son (Gn 46:12; 1 Chr 2:5) and founder of the Hamulite family (Nm 26:21).

HAMUTAL Daughter of Jeremiah of Libnah, one of King Josiah's wives, and the mother of two kings: Jehoahaz and Zedekiah (2 Kgs 23:31; 24:18; Jer 52:1).

HANAMEL Shallum's son, from whom Jeremiah bought a field in Anathoth (Jer 32:7-12). This purchase signified that God would restore the nation and that possession of the land would again be possible.

HANAN
1. Shashak's son and one of the chief men of Benjamin (1 Chr 8:23).
2. Azel's son from Benjamin's tribe (1 Chr 8:38; 9:44).
3. Warrior among David's mighty men, who were known as "the thirty" (1 Chr 11:43).
4. Ancestor of a group of temple assistants who returned to Jerusalem with Zerubbabel after the exile (Ezr 2:46; Neh 7:49).
5. Levitical assistant who explained to the people passages from the law read by Ezra (Neh 8:7).
6. Levite who signed Ezra's covenant of faithfulness to God with Nehemiah and others after the exile (Neh 10:10).
7, 8. Two political leaders who signed Ezra's covenant of faithfulness to God with Nehemiah and others after the exile (Neh 10:22, 26).
9. One of the Levites whom Nehemiah appointed as treasurer over the storehouses (Neh 13:13).
10. Igdaliah's son and head of a prophetic guild occupying the room in the temple where Jeremiah offered the Rechabites wine to drink (Jer 35:4).

HANANEL, Tower of Tower on the north wall of Jerusalem, located near the Sheep Gate (Neh 3:1; 12:39; KJV "Hananeel"). Later in Israel's history John Hyrcanus erected a Maccabean fortress on this spot, which Pompey destroyed in 63 BC. Still later, Herod the Great built the Tower of Antonia here to oversee the temple area. Two prophecies refer to the Tower of Hananel as a boundary point in the rebuilding of Jerusalem (Jer 31:38; Zec 14:10).

HANANI
1. Seer who rebuked King Asa for giving treasure to Ben-hadad of Syria to persuade him to attack Israel. Hanani was imprisoned for his preaching (2 Chr 16:1-10). Hanani was the father of the prophet Jehu, who made protests against Baasha, king of Israel

(1 Kgs 16:1-7), and Jehoshaphat, king of Judah (2 Chr 19:2).

2. Heman's son, David's seer, and a musician in the temple (1 Chr 25:4, 25).

3. Priest who obeyed Ezra's exhortation to divorce his pagan wife after returning from exile (Ezr 10:20).

4. Brother of Nehemiah who induced him to act on behalf of the Jews when he reported the state of Jerusalem and Judah (Neh 1:2). Hanani was later given responsibility for the city of Jerusalem (7:2).

5. Priest and musician who participated in the dedication of the rebuilt walls of Jerusalem (Neh 12:36).

HANANIAH

1. Zerubbabel's son and a descendant of David (1 Chr 3:19, 21).

2. Benjamite and the son of Shashak (1 Chr 8:24).

3. Heman's son and the leader of the 16th of 24 divisions of musicians trained for service in the house of the Lord (1 Chr 25:4, 23).

4. One of the commanders of King Uzziah's army (2 Chr 26:11).

5. Bebai's son, who returned with the exiles from Babylon and was later encouraged by Ezra to divorce his foreign wife (Ezr 10:28).

6. Perfumer who helped Nehemiah rebuild the Jerusalem wall (Neh 3:8).

7. Shelemiah's son, who with Hanun repaired a section of the Jerusalem wall during the days of Nehemiah (Neh 3:30). He is perhaps identical with #6 above.

8. Commander of the citadel of Jerusalem who was assigned by Nehemiah to rule the city jointly with Hanani, Nehemiah's brother. Hananiah, described as a faithful and God-fearing man, was appointed the task of seeing that the city walls and gates were regularly guarded (Neh 7:2-3).

9. One of the leaders of the people who set his seal on the covenant of Ezra (Neh 10:23).

10. Head of the priestly family of Jeremiah during the days of Joiakim, the high priest, in postexilic Jerusalem (Neh 12:12).

11. One of the priests who blew a trumpet at the dedication of the Jerusalem wall during the days of Nehemiah (Neh 12:41).

12. Gibeonite and the son of Azzur. Hananiah prophesied during the fourth year of King Zedekiah of Judah's reign (597–586 BC). He openly declared in the temple that in two years the Lord would break the yoke of Nebuchadnezzar, king of Babylon (605–562 BC), from the neck of Judah and return its exiles and sacred possessions to Palestine. Told by the Lord that Hananiah's prophecy was false, Jeremiah reproached Hananiah for lying and foretold his imminent death. Hananiah died two months later (Jer 28).

13. Father of Zedekiah, an official of King Jehoiakim of Judah (609–598 BC; Jer 36:12).

14. Grandfather of Irijah, the captain of the guards, who arrested Jeremiah at Jerusalem's Gate of Benjamin for apparently deserting to the Babylonians (Jer 37:13).

15. One of the three Jewish friends of Daniel exiled in Babylon. He was assigned the Babylonian name Shadrach (Dn 1:6-19; 2:17).
    See also Shadrach, Meshach, and Abednego.

HAND
The terminal part of the forelimb that has the ability to grasp. "Hand" is used hundreds of times in the Bible to describe a physical part of one's body. It is also used frequently in metaphors or figurative language.

Figuratively, the hand meant power (Dt 2:15; Ps 31:5;

Mk 14:62). Indeed, in Joshua 8:20 "hand to flee" is translated "power to flee" (see Ps 76:5). Conversely, limp hands symbolized irresoluteness and weakness (Is 35:3). Clasping the hands signified friendship (2 Kgs 10:15). To seat someone on one's right hand denoted favor (Pss 16:11; 77:10; 110:1). Clean hands symbolized innocence (Ps 26:6), while striking hands sealed a bargain (Prv 6:1, KJV). Lifting the hand symbolized violence (1 Kgs 11:26, RSV). The hands were used in supplicatory prayer (Ex 17:11; Lv 9:22; Is 1:15; 1 Tm 2:8) and in making vows (Gn 14:22, KJV; 24:2).

Other idiomatic uses of the hands expressed jeopardizing one's life (Jgs 12:3), gladness (2 Kgs 11:12), generosity (Dt 15:11), grief (2 Sm 13:19), humility (Prv 30:32), and undertaking a duty (Lk 9:62). Manual labor is an expression of man's dignity and duty (Eph 4:28; 1 Thes 4:11), the marks of which Paul was not ashamed to display (Acts 20:34; 1 Cor 4:12). Ritual hand washing was obligatory for the priests before fulfilling their office (Ex 30:19-21; 40:30-32). The scribes and Pharisees so misapplied this that Jesus ignored ceremonial hand washing (Mt 15:1-20; Lk 11:38). Pilate's hand washing (Mt 27:24) disclaimed responsibility for, or professed innocence concerning, a wrong that, however, could not be done without his consent.

When Israel went out of Egypt "with an high hand" (Ex 14:8, KJV), the reference is to the hand or help of the Lord. The hand of the Lord represented God's resistless power (Dt 2:15), judgment (Acts 13:11; Heb 10:31), divine inspiration (Ez 8:1; 37:1), and providential care (Ezr 7:6; Jn 10:28-29).

The laying on of hands had a profound significance and occurs frequently in the Bible. Before making a blood sacrifice, the person making the offering, not the priest, laid hands on the victim. The act signified the transference of guilt to, or self-identification with, the victim (Lv 1:4). Laying on of hands signified appointment to an office, as when Moses commissioned Joshua (Nm 27:12-23), the apostles made seven disciples their associates or deputies in the ministry (Acts 6:5-6), and Paul and Barnabas were appointed missionaries and representatives of the church in Antioch (13:3). By laying on of hands, a person was made an associate with the holder of an office and was admitted to the status of that office (1 Tm 4:14; 2 Tm 1:6). The act was accompanied by prayer and was, in itself, a form of prayer. As Augustine remarks: "What else is the laying on of hands but a prayer over one?"

The laying on of hands accompanied healing in the ministry of the Lord (Mk 6:5; Lk 4:40; 13:11-13) and of the disciples (Mk 16:18; Acts 9:12, 17; 28:8). This expressed the self-identification and sympathy of the healer with and for the sufferer, as well as reinforced the patient's faith and God's imparting health to him in answer to prayer.

See also Right Hand.

HANDBREADTH*
Linear measure equivalent to one-sixth of a cubit or just under three inches (7.6 centimeters) in length. The fingers, up to four (Jer 52:21), made a handbreadth; three handbreadths made a handstretch or span (Ex 28:16). See Weights and Measures.

HANDMAID, HANDMAIDEN*
Female servants. They were familiar members among many households in biblical days. The handmaid cared for the women and children of a family and served as the woman's personal attendant. She enjoyed the protection of the law (Lv 25:6; Dt 5:14; 15:12-15), and as a free wife's maid, sometimes became a concubine where there was a childless marriage (Gn 30:3).

HANDS, Washing of *See* Hand.

HANES City in Egypt included with Zoan (or Tanis) in Isaiah 30:4 as a center of Egyptian government to which ambassadors would be sent. This indicates that it was one of the dynastic centers. It has been identified with Heracleopolis Magna, south of Memphis, the capital of northern Egypt in Roman times, and also with Heracleopolis Parva in the eastern delta region.

HANGING *See* Criminal Law and Punishment; Impalement.

HANIEL* KJV spelling of Hanniel, Ulla's son, in 1 Chronicles 7:39. *See* Hanniel #2.

HANNAH Wife of Elkanah from Ephraim's tribe and the mother of the prophet Samuel. The childless Hannah prayed annually at Shiloh for a son, whom she vowed to dedicate to the Lord.

The Lord answered her prayer, and she called her son Samuel. When he was weaned (probably about age three), she dedicated him at Shiloh to the service of the Lord in the sanctuary. Henceforth, Samuel lived with Eli the priest and was visited by his parents on their annual pilgrimages. Hannah had three more sons and two daughters (1 Sm 1:1–2:21). Her prophetic psalm (1 Sm 2:1-10) anticipates Mary's song of praise, the "Magnificat" (Lk 1:46-55).

HANNATHON Northern border town of Zebulun (Jos 19:14), mentioned in the Amarna tablets (c. 1370 BC) and in the annals of Tiglath-pileser III (745–727 BC). Not yet precisely located, it has been identified with Kefr 'Anau near Rimmon and with Tell el-Bedeiwiyah, north of Nazareth.

HANNIEL
1. Ephod's son and leader of Manasseh's tribe who represented his tribe in apportioning land to Israel under Moses (Nm 34:23).
2. Ulla's son and warrior in the tribe of Asher (1 Chr 7:39).

HANOCH
1. Midian's third son, and grandson of Abraham by Keturah (Gn 25:4; 1 Chr 1:33).
2. Reuben's first son (Gn 46:9; Ex 6:14; 1 Chr 5:3) and ancestor of the Hanochites (Nm 26:5).

HANOCHITE Descendant of Hanoch, Reuben's first-born son (Nm 26:5). *See* Hanoch #2.

HANUKKAH *See* Feasts and Festivals of Israel; Judaism.

HANUN
1. Nahash's son and successor to the Ammonite throne. When King Nahash died, King David of Israel sent messengers to console Hanun and to express his continued friendship. But Hanun insulted David by humiliating his messengers and accusing them of spying. This action led to war and the defeat of Ammon (2 Sm 10:1-14; 11:1; 12:26-31; 1 Chr 19:1–20:3).
2. One who helped repair Jerusalem's Valley Gate during the time of Nehemiah (Neh 3:13).
3. Zalaph's son who repaired a section of the Jerusalem wall during the time of Nehemiah (Neh 3:30); perhaps the same as #2 above.

HAPHARAIM Town included in the territory allotted to Issachar's tribe for an inheritance (Jos 19:19). Some scholars have identified it with et-Taiyibeh, about ten miles (16 kilometers) northwest of Beth-shan.

HAPPIZZEZ Head of a division of priests whom David assigned to official duties in the temple (1 Chr 24:15).

HARA Place where Tiglath-pileser of Assyria exiled Reuben, Gad, and the half-tribe of Manasseh (1 Chr 5:26). A possible miscopying of 2 Kings 17:6 and 18:11 may have substituted Hara for "cities of Media." The Greek version reads "mountains of Media," indicating an area east of the Tigris Valley. A district rather than a single site seems to be indicated.

HARADAH Twentieth wilderness encampment of the children of Israel, and the ninth from Sinai; listed between Mt Shepher and Makheloth. Its location is unknown (Nm 33:24-25).

HARAN (Person)
1. Terah's son, brother of Abraham, and the father of Lot (Gn 11:26-31).
2. Caleb's son by his concubine Ephah, a member of Judah's tribe and the father of Gazez (1 Chr 2:46).
3. Shimei's son, a member of the Gershonite division of Levi's tribe (1 Chr 23:9).

HARAN (Place) City of northern Mesopotamia, first mentioned in Genesis 11:31 as the destination of Terah, Abraham's father, in migrating from Ur of the Chaldees, and his home until his death. At age 75, Abraham was commanded by God to move to a land that God had for him (Gn 12:1-4). There were relatives who remained in Haran, however, to whom Jacob, Abraham's grandson, fled in fear of Esau (27:42-43). Jacob stayed in Haran many years while serving his Uncle Laban and acquiring Leah and Rachel as wives, as well as many sheep and goats, servants, camels, and donkeys (30:43).

This "city of Nahor" (Gn 11:27-29; 24:10; 27:43) was established in the third millennium BC, and its location on a branch of the Euphrates soon made it an important commercial center. Perhaps the ancient trade route that linked Damascus, Nineveh, and Carchemish passed by Haran. Ezekiel mentions trade between Haran and Tyre (Ez 27:23). Haran was an Aramean city and was famous for its worship of the lunar Sin and Nikkal. This system was an offspring of the cult found in Sumerian Ur. Sin and his consort Nikkal were revered not only here but throughout Canaan and even in Egypt. The cult persisted past NT times, its temple finally being destroyed by Mongols in the 13th century AD. It is little wonder that God commanded Abraham to leave this seat of idolatry. Modern Harran preserves the ancient cuneiform spelling of the name (cf. KJV "Charran," Acts 7:2, 4).

HARAR, HARARITE* Terms applied to several names that appear in the accounts of King David's "mighty men." Shammah, one of David's mightiest men, and Jonathan's father (a different Jonathan than Saul's son and David's friend) is called a Hararite (2 Sm 23:11, 33; 1 Chr 11:34 has "Shagee"), as is Agee, Shammah's father (2 Sm 23:11). Sharar, Ahiam's father, is also so named (2 Sm 23:33; 1 Chr 11:35 has "Sachar"). The meaning of the terms are uncertain; possibly "mountain" from the location of a village (Harar) or "mountaineer."

HARBONA One of King Ahasuerus's seven personal attendants. They were ordered by Ahasuerus to parade Queen Vashti before a drunken banquet to satisfy his vanity (Est 1:10). Harbona later suggested that Haman be hanged on the gallows he had built for Mordecai (7:9).

HARDNESS OF HEART* A phrase signifying spiritual obstinacy.

The first references to the hardening of the heart exemplify the fundamental features of this doctrine in Scripture. The number of times it is referred to is surprising; there are at least 20 references to the hardening of Pharaoh's heart in the OT alone, as well as Paul's exposition of its significance in Romans 9:17-24.

The first reference is Exodus 4:21, where God promises Moses that he will harden Pharaoh's heart that he might not allow the Israelites to go. This promise is repeated (see Ex 7:3; 14:4, 17) and rapidly comes to pass (7:13-14), as revelation and miracle follow one another before the eyes of Pharaoh, followed by the actual occurrence of the events God warned about, including all the judgments of the 10 plagues.

No doubt is left in the mind of the reader, either in the exodus account itself or later, that Pharaoh's obstinacy was an act of divine judgment on God's part for his own external ends and purposes (Ex 9:16; Jos 11:20; cf. Rom 9:17-18). Nevertheless, it is also stated that Pharaoh hardened his own heart (Ex 8:15, 32; 9:34; 13:15), showing that the hardening process is a deliberate product of personal rebellion against revealed truth. This is a crucial aspect of the scriptural presentation of the matter; judicial hardening of the heart is not only an act of God upon the sinner's nature but also a willful turning from the truth. The sinner is therefore responsible to God for his hardness of heart.

The process of judicial hardening is described by Paul in Romans 1:18-32. All humans have an innate God-consciousness from which they deliberately turn away. They change the truth into a lie and suppress what truth they have. As a result, hardness of heart takes over. Paul's expression for this is that "their foolish heart was darkened" because "God gave them up" to the results of their own sin. The results are both intellectual ("God gave them over to a reprobate mind") and moral, as well as social or cultural. Paul uses the term "hardness of heart" in Romans 2:5 to describe the general result. It is important to note that it is not against God's wrath or against the results of sin that the wicked are in revolt but against "truth" and against their own conscience (2:14-16).

God often warns his people not to harden their hearts, for Scripture associates hardening with unbelief (Dt 15:7; Heb 3:8, 15; 4:7). Jesus was grieved at the callousness of his hearers' hearts (Mk 3:5; 16:14). He referred to allowances God had made to the Jews concerning divorce because of the hardness of their hearts (Mt 19:8).

On at least two occasions in the Gospels, judicial blindness is ascribed directly to God, and its purpose stated (Mt 13:13-15; Jn 12:39-41). Hardness of heart is therefore an aspect of the development of the fallen character, manifesting the root of rebellion (Ps 95:8; Jn 12:40; Heb 3:8, 15; 4:7). Throughout Scripture, Jewish apostasy is so described (2 Kgs 17:14; Neh 9:16-17; Heb 3:8).

See also Blindness; Judgment; Regeneration.

HARE Small, swift, long-eared mammal similar to the rabbit (Lv 11:6; Dt 14:7). *See* Animals.

HAREPH Caleb's descendant from Judah's tribe and founder (or perhaps father) of Beth-gader (1 Chr 2:51).

HARETH* KJV spelling of Hereth in 1 Samuel 22:5. *See* Hereth.

HARHAIAH Father of Uzziel, a goldsmith who worked to rebuild the wall of Jerusalem in Nehemiah's time (Neh 3:8).

HARHAS Shallum's grandfather. Shallum's wife was Huldah the prophetess (2 Kgs 22:14; spelled "Hasrah" in 2 Chr 34:22), who delivered an oracle for Josiah after the discovery of the Book of the Law by the high priest Hilkiah.

HAR-HERES* Mountain in Aijalon of Dan's territory (Jgs 1:35). *See* Heres #1.

HARHUR Ancestor of a group of temple assistants who returned to Jerusalem with Zerubbabel after the exile (Ezr 2:51; Neh 7:53).

HARIM
1. Priest whom King David appointed to official duties in the temple (1 Chr 24:8).
2. Ancestor of a Jewish family who returned from the Babylonian exile with Zerubbabel (Ezr 2:32; Neh 10:5). Members of this family were guilty of marrying foreign women (Ezr 10:31), but they divorced their wives and a representative of the clan signed Ezra's covenant (Neh 10:27).
3. Ancestor of a family of priests who returned from the exile with Zerubbabel (Ezr 2:39; Neh 7:42). Some identify him with #1 above. Members of this family were guilty of marrying foreign women.
4. Ancestor of Malkijah. Malkijah repaired a section of the Jerusalem wall during Nehemiah's time (Neh 3:11). This Harim could be the same as #2 above.
5. Priest who returned from the exile with Zerubbabel (Neh 12:3; Hebrew "Rehum," see NLT mg). His son (or grandson) Adna is listed as a leading priest during the high priesthood of Joiakim (12:15). Later, under Ezra, a representative of the family (probably related to #3 above) signed the covenant of faithfulness to God (10:5).

HARIPH Ancestor of a family who returned to Jerusalem with Zerubbabel after the exile (Neh 7:24). The name Jorah appears in the parallel list of Ezra 2:18. A representative of this family signed Ezra's covenant of faithfulness to God with Nehemiah and others (Neh 10:19).

HARLOT* *See* Prostitute, Prostitution.

HARMON* Place mentioned by the prophet Amos to which the inhabitants of Bashan would be exiled (Am 4:3, NLT mg). Harmon occurs only once in the Bible, and there is no known place with such a name. There are problems with the text and numerous emendations have been proposed. Some Hebrew manuscripts render it as a common noun, meaning "palace" (KJV), rather than a proper name. The Septuagint renders it "the mountain of Rimmon," perhaps referring to a hill east of Rimmon (see Jgs 20:45-47; cf. Jos 15:32; 19:13).

HARNEPHER Zophah's son from Asher's tribe (1 Chr 7:36).

HAROD
1. Spring beside which Gideon and his army camped before their encounter with the Midianites (Jgs 7:1). Perhaps this is the same spring by which Saul and his army pitched their tents prior to their battle with the Philistines (1 Sm 29:1). The spring of Harod is at 'Ain Jalud by the northern side of Mt Gilboa, about two miles (3.2 kilometers) southeast of Zerin.
2. Home of Shammah and Elika, two of David's valiant warriors (2 Sm 23:25). In the parallel passage (1 Chr 11:27), Elika's name is omitted and Shammah (Shammoth) is listed as a Harorite instead of a

Harodite. "Harorite" reflects a later scribal error where the copyist mistook the Hebrew letter "d" for an "r."

HARODITE* Designation for Shammah and Elika, two of David's mighty men (2 Sm 23:25). *See* Harod #2.

HAROEH Alternate name of Reaiah, Shobal's son, in 1 Chronicles 2:52. *See* Reaiah #1.

HARORITE* Alternate description of one of David's mighty men (1 Chr 11:27). *See* Harod #2.

HAROSHETH-HAGGOYIM Town in Canaan that was the home of Sisera. This Canaanite general led his forces from Harosheth against Deborah and Barak (Jgs 4:2-13, KJV "Harosheth of the Gentiles"). After his soldiers panicked, they fled back to Harosheth where they were defeated (v 16).

HARP Stringed instrument. *See* Musical Instruments (Nebel).

HARROW* Agricultural term for implement or procedure, though no implement corresponding to the modern harrow is known from Palestine or Egypt. Job 39:10 speaks of an ox performing the harrowing, while Isaiah 28:24 notes that plowed ground was leveled as part of the process. Like the foregoing references, Hosea 10:11 speaks of harrowing in connection with plowing. Most probably harrowing consisted of branches being pulled behind an animal or plow to smooth the land and before seeding. *See* Agriculture.

HARSHA Ancestor of a group of temple assistants who returned to Jerusalem with Zerubbabel after the exile (Ezr 2:52; Neh 7:54).

HART* Adult male red deer. *See* Animals (Deer).

HARUM Aharhel's father from Judah's tribe (1 Chr 4:8).

HARUMAPH Jedaiah's father. Jedaiah helped repair the wall of Jerusalem during the time of Nehemiah (Neh 3:10).

HARUPH, HARUPHITE* Name applied to Shephatiah, one of David's ambidextrous warriors from Benjamin's tribe who joined him at Ziklag (1 Chr 12:5). Whether the name refers to a family or a place is uncertain.

HARUZ Maternal grandfather of Amon, king of Judah (2 Kgs 21:19).

HARVEST The gathering in of a crop, especially for food. There was no single harvesttime in ancient Israel. Olives were harvested in September–November, flax in March–April, barley in April–May, and wheat in May–June. Fruits such as figs and grapes were harvested at the end of the summer, in August or September. The Israelites' calendar revolved around the harvest periods (cf. Jgs 15:1; Ru 1:22).

In the OT, Pentecost (a harvest festival) was one of the three major festivals that the Israelites were required by the Lord to keep annually (Ex 23:16). In doing so they would remember that the rich land into which they had been brought from Egypt (Dt 8:7-10) was the gift of God. In offering the firstfruits of the harvest (Lv 23:10-11), the Israelites showed gratitude and acknowledged their dependence on the Lord. Moreover, as the harvest was a gift, they were not to be selfish in enjoying it but to leave some for the underprivileged (19:9-10; 23:22).

NT references to harvest are largely figurative. In one parable (Mt 13:24-30) harvest represents the final judgment and the reapers are angels, gathering in the righteous and excluding the wicked from the kingdom (vv 36-43). In another, the harvest refers to those who have not yet heard the gospel, and the "laborers" are those who bring it to them (Mt 9:37-38).

See also Agriculture; Feasts and Festivals of Israel; Vines, Vineyard.

HASADIAH One of Zerubbabel's sons (1 Chr 3:20).

HASENUAH* KJV rendering of Hassenuah in 1 Chronicles 9:7. *See* Hassenuah.

HASHABIAH
1. Ancestor of Ethan, a Levite and descendant of Merari. Ethan was a musician in the temple during the reign of David (1 Chr 6:45).
2. Ancestor of a group of Levites who helped rebuild the temple after the Babylonian exile (1 Chr 9:14; Neh 11:15).
3. Jeduthun's son, a Levite and musician in the temple during the time of David (1 Chr 25:3, 19).
4. Head of a group of Hebronites who was given the position of overseer of Israel west of the Jordan. He was in charge of both political and religious activities (1 Chr 26:30).
5. Kemuel's son, a Levite and head of a household during the reign of David (1 Chr 27:17).
6. Chief of the Levites who participated in the Passover kept by King Josiah in the kingdom of Judah (640–609 BC; 2 Chr 35:9).
7. Merarite Levite who returned to Jerusalem from Babylon with Ezra (Ezr 8:19).
8. Priest who returned to Jerusalem from Babylon with Ezra (Ezr 8:24); perhaps the same person as #7 above.
9. Parosh's son, who obeyed Ezra's exhortation to divorce his pagan wife after the exile (Ezr 10:25); possibly the same as Asibias (1 Esd 9:26).
10. Ruler over half the district of Keilah (a city of Judah in the Shephelah district of Libnah-mareshah) who participated in rebuilding the Jerusalem wall for his district after the exile (Neh 3:17).
11. Levite who signed Ezra's covenant of faithfulness to God (Neh 10:11).
12. Ancestor of Uzzi, an overseer of Levites in Jerusalem after the exile (Neh 11:22).
13. Priest and head of a household in Palestine after the exile during the time of the high priest Joiakim (Neh 12:21).
14. Chief of the Levites and a temple musician after the exile during the time of Joiakim the high priest (Neh 12:24); perhaps the same person as #11 above.

HASHABNAH One of the leaders who signed Ezra's covenant of faithfulness to God with Nehemiah and others after the exile (Neh 10:25).

HASHABNEIAH, HASHABNIAH*
1. Hattush's father. Hattush assisted in rebuilding the walls of Jerusalem during Nehemiah's day (Neh 3:10).
2. Levite who joined with others in an invocation at the covenant-signing ceremony (Neh 9:5).

HASHBADDANAH Man, possibly of Levite origin, who stood on Ezra's left when Ezra read the law to the people (Neh 8:4).

HASHEM* Warrior among David's mighty men (1 Chr 11:34, NLT mg); alternately called Jashen in 2 Samuel 23:32. *See* Jashen.

HASHMONAH One of the places where the Israelites stopped during the 40 years they wandered in the wilderness (Nm 33:29-30). *See* Wilderness Wanderings.

HASHUB* KJV alternate spelling of Hasshub. *See* Hasshub.

HASHUBAH One of Zerubbabel's sons (1 Chr 3:20).

HASHUM
1. Ancestor of a family who returned from Babylon with Zerubbabel after the exile (Ezr 2:19; 10:33; Neh 7:22).
2. Israelite who stood to Ezra's left at the reading of the law (Neh 8:4).
3. Leader who signed Ezra's covenant of faithfulness to God with Nehemiah and others after the exile (Neh 10:18).

HASHUPHA* KJV alternate spelling of Hasupha in Nehemiah 7:46. *See* Hasupha.

HASIDEANS, HASIDIM* Transliterations of a Hebrew word meaning "the pious." The influence of Greek customs and ways threatened the preservation of Jewish patterns of life in the third and fourth centuries BC. Jews were required to employ the Greek language in their daily lives, and with the language came the influence of Greek culture. This process was quite apparent in Palestine during the second century BC, and the Jewish people responded in two antagonistic ways: one party was friendly to the Greeks; the other party set as their goal strict adherence to the principles of Judaism. The latter group, known as "the pious," or Hasideans, cherished the ideals of responsible covenant observance (Dt 7:9), and in the Maccabean period became militants in their efforts to worship God according to the Mosaic law. Both the Pharisees and the Essenes may have had early roots in the Hasidim movement.
　See also Essenes; Judaism; Pharisees.

HASMONEAN* Family name of the Jews who instigated the Jewish revolt against the Greeks in 167 BC. *See* Judaism.

HASRAH* Variant spelling of Harhas, Shallum's grandfather, in 2 Chronicles 34:22 (NLT mg). *See* Harhas.

HASSENAAH Alternate name for Senaah in Nehemiah 3:3. *See* Senaah.

HASSENUAH Ancestor of a Benjamite family that returned to Judah with Zerubbabel after the exile (1 Chr 9:7; Neh 11:9, KJV "Senuah"); perhaps alternately called Senaah (Ezr 2:35; Neh 7:38), and Hassenaah (Neh 3:3). *See* Senaah.

HASSHUB
1. Merari clan leader of Levi's tribe. Hasshub was the father of Shemaiah, a settler in Jerusalem after the return from captivity (1 Chr 9:14; Neh 11:15).
2. Pahath-moab's son, who repaired a section of the Jerusalem wall and the Tower of the Ovens during the time of Nehemiah (Neh 3:11).
3. Another Hasshub who repaired the Jerusalem wall opposite his house (Neh 3:23).
4. Leader who signed Ezra's covenant of faithfulness to God with Nehemiah and others after the exile (Neh 10:23).

HASSOPHERETH* Ancestor of a family of temple assistants who returned to Jerusalem with Zerubbabel after the exile (Ezr 2:55, NLT mg). He is perhaps identifiable with Sophereth in Nehemiah 7:57.

HASUPHA Ancestor of a group of temple assistants who returned to Jerusalem with Zerubbabel after the exile (Ezr 2:43; Neh 7:46). He is perhaps the same person as Gishpa in Nehemiah 11:21. *See* Gishpa, Gispa.

HAT* *See* Head Covering.

HATACH*, HATHACH Eunuch appointed by the Persian king Ahasuerus to wait on Esther. Hathach brought Esther messages from Mordecai. In this way Esther learned of Haman's plot against the Jews (Est 4:5-10).

HATHATH Othniel's son and the grandson of Kenaz (1 Chr 4:13).

HATIPHA Ancestor of a family of temple servants who returned to Jerusalem with Zerubbabel after the captivity (Ezr 2:54; Neh 7:56).

HATITA Ancestor of a family of gatekeepers who returned to Jerusalem with Zerubbabel after the exile (Ezr 2:42; Neh 7:45).

HATRED Intense feeling of aversion or enmity, which could prompt a person to loathe someone or something, or even to seek revenge for having been wronged. The Scriptures forbid people to hate others (Lv 19:17-18) because it leads to sin. Indeed, hatred itself is considered murder (1 Jn 3:15). We are called upon to let God, the holy one, avenge all wrongs (Prv 20:22), and we are commanded by Jesus to love our enemies (Mt 5:43-44).
　Not all aspects of hatred are sinful. The Scriptures tell us that God hates evil (Prv 6:16-19) and evil people (Ps 5:5). The Scripture also has expressions such as "Jacob have I loved; Esau have I hated" (Mal 1:2-3). This means that God elected Jacob and not Esau to be the progenitor of the chosen Jewish race. In similar fashion, would-be Christians are challenged by Jesus to hate their lives and earthly relationships if they want to follow him (Lk 14:26). This means that they must choose Jesus above all else.

HATTIL Forefather of a family of King Soloman's servants who returned to Jerusalem with Zerubbabel after the exile (Ezr 2:57; Neh 7:59).

HATTUSH
1. Shemaiah's son and a descendant of David (1 Chr 3:22). Hattush returned from the Babylonian exile with Ezra (Ezr 8:3).
2. Son of Hashabneiah, who helped Nehemiah rebuild the walls of Jerusalem (Neh 3:10).
3. Priest who returned from Babylon with Zerubbabel (Neh 12:2). One of his descendants signed Ezra's covenant of faithfulness to God (Neh 10:4). His name is omitted from Nehemiah 12:14 through scribal error.

HAURAN Region in northeastern Transjordan mentioned in Ezekiel's description of the borders of the land (Ez 47:16-18). In biblical times it corresponded to the modern Jebel ed-Druze of the Leja. This area is mentioned as early as the reign of Shalmaneser III of Assyria in his description of a military campaign in 841 BC. His army marched to Mt Khauranu after a siege of Damascus and before crossing Galilee to Mt Carmel.
　In 733–732 BC Tiglath-pileser III of Assyria conquered

Damascus and its surrounding region and organized it into provinces, one of which was Khaurina, or Hauran. The same province is mentioned in the Annals of Ashurbanipal during his campaign against the Arabians (639–637 BC).

HAVILAH (Person)
1. Descendant of Cush (Gn 10:7; 1 Chr 1:9).
2. Descendant of Shem through Joktan (Gn 10:29; 1 Chr 1:23).

HAVILAH (Place)
Land in the neighborhood of Eden, now unknown but said to be watered by the river Pishon and containing supplies of gold, bdellium, and onyx stone (Gn 2:11-12). The location of Havilah has been a matter of much dispute. It cannot have any connection with the Havilah of 1 Samuel 15:7, where Saul fought against certain Amalekites, because the locale of the Eden narratives is Mesopotamian and not Palestinian. On the same basis, any attempt to locate Havilah in southern Arabia, Somaliland, or India would be mistaken. The "river" Pishon may have been an irrigation canal, since Akkadian does not have a separate word for these two different bodies of water, and the Mesopotamian custom was to name large irrigation canals as if they were rivers. This would help to account for the survival of the name "Pishon" long after the canal had disappeared. The Pishon was one of four branches that the river formed once it left Eden; hence, Havilah must have been to the north, since the narrative assumes an upstream perspective. Probably Havilah was in the general area of the Shinar plain and was watered by a major irrigation canal. Both Havilah and the canal have long disappeared.

HAVOTH-JAIR*, HAVVOTH-JAIR*
Series of settlements on the edge of Bashan across the Jordan captured by Jair, according to Numbers 32:41 (NLT mg). Because of their location, they fell into the allotment of the half-tribe of Manasseh. The number of these villages is given in Joshua 13:29-30 as 60, and they are probably included in the cities and towns of 1 Chronicles 2:22-23, although only 23 cities are specified as belonging to Jair. The KJV rendering as "Bashan-havoth-jair" (Dt 3:14) makes the location as specific as in the Hebrew. In Judges 10:4, a judge named Jair had 30 sons who controlled 30 cities named Havvoth-jair. But he is obviously different from the Jair of Numbers 32:41. If his sons controlled only 30 settlements, he himself probably governed the remaining 30. In 1 Chronicles 2:21-24, which reflects a relationship between Judah and Manasseh, Jair was said to have 23 cities in Gilead when Geshur and Aram captured 60 towns from the tent settlements of Jair and Kenath and its dependencies. While the variant numbers present difficulties, the narrative itself may be the Chronicler's way of indicating Judah's sense of sovereignty over Gilead.

HAWK
See Birds.

HAY
Dried grass used as animal fodder.

HAZAEL
King of Syria (843?–796? BC) who came to power by assassinating his ruler, Ben-hadad (2 Kgs 8:7-15), and establishing a new dynasty. An inscription of Shalmaneser speaks of Hazael as a "son of a nobody," and mentions that he had "seized the throne." The Hebrew prophet Elijah was told to anoint Hazael as the next king of Syria (1 Kgs 19:15).

Upon becoming king, Hazael continued the policy of Ben-hadad in resisting the Assyrian military influence in Palestine. Although most of Palestine came under Assyrian control in 841 BC, Hazael was able to retain independence by withstanding the siege of Damascus. Failing in a final attempt to subdue Damascus in 837 BC, the Assyrians withdrew. This allowed Hazael the freedom to begin a series of attacks against Israel that resulted in Syrian domination of most of Palestine.

Toward the end of Jehu's reign in Israel, Hazael occupied Israelite territory in the hills of Galilee and east of the Jordan (2 Kgs 10:32). After Jehu's death, the Syrian king continually harassed Israel, captured much of Philistia, and spared Jerusalem only because Joash, king of Judah, asked for peace and was willing to pay heavy tribute (12:17-18). The Syrian oppression continued during the reign of Hazael's son until Adad-nirari III, king of Assyria, marched into Syria, causing Damascus to submit and pay heavy tribute. This took the pressure off Israel and provided opportunity for her to regain territory taken by Hazael (13:24-25).

Archaeologists found the remains of a bed at Arslan Tash (Hadathah) that may have been included in the tribute taken from Damascus. Part of the inscription on a piece of ivory inlay from the bed reads "to our Lord Hazael." Evidently there was a high level of culture in Damascus under Hazael. According to Josephus, Hazael was long remembered for his part in building temples in Damascus.

See also Syria, Syrians.

HAZAIAH
Maaseiah's descendant from Judah's tribe, who was one of the leaders in Jerusalem after the exile (Neh 11:5).

HAZAR-ADDAR
Town that, with Azmon, defined the southern border of Judah (Nm 34:4), usually identified with Khirbet el-Qudeirat near Kadesh-barnea. The parallel passage in Joshua 15:3-4 lists four places—Hezron, Addar, Karka, and Azmon—instead of two. Some have suggested that Hazar-addar and Addar are the same place; others, that it was renamed Hezron to distinguish it from Addar.

HAZAR-ENAN, HAZAR-ENON*
Place describing the northeast corner of Israel's border (Nm 34:9-10); alternately spelled Hazar-enon in Ezekiel 47:17-18 and 48:1 (RSV). It is identified with modern Hadr at the base of Mt Hermon.

HAZAR-GADDAH
City in the southern extremity of the land assigned to Judah's tribe for an inheritance (Jos 15:27).

HAZAR-HATTICON*
KJV spelling of the place Hazer-hatticon in Ezekiel 47:16. *See* Hazer-hatticon.

HAZARMAVETH
Descendant of Shem through Joktan (Gn 10:26; 1 Chr 1:20) whose progeny lived in southern Arabia (Gn 10:30) in the Wadi Hadhramaut. Excavations there revealed a flourishing economy in the fifth century BC, based on frankincense trade. This trade, revived in the second century BC, made the area prosperous and influential.

HAZAR-SHUAL
Simeonite city located in the southern section of Judah (Jos 15:28; 19:3; 1 Chr 4:28). It is also listed among those cities occupied by the Jews who returned from captivity (Neh 11:27).

HAZAR-SUSAH, HAZAR-SUSIM
City assigned to Simeon within the territory allotted to Judah for an inheritance (Jos 19:5); alternately called Hazar-susim

(1 Chr 4:31). Solomon probably used it as a transfer point for horses brought from Egypt for sale to the Hittites and Syrians, as suggested by its name, meaning "horse station." Hazar-susah has been identified with Sbalat Abu Susein, east of the Wadi Far'ah.

HAZAZON-TAMAR City identifiable with En-gedi in 2 Chronicles 20:2. During the time of Abraham, it was inhabited by Amorites who were subdued by Kedor-laomer as he and other eastern kings swept through the area (Gn 14:7). It has been suggested that it may be the Tamar that Solomon fortified (1 Kgs 9:18), placed by Ezekiel southeast of Israel (Ez 47:18-19; 48:28). Wadi Hasasa has apparently been named after the ancient site.

HAZEL* KJV mistranslation for almond in Genesis 30:37. *See* Plants (Almond).

HAZELELPONI* KJV spelling of Hazzelelponi, Etam's daughter, in 1 Chronicles 4:3. *See* Hazzelelponi.

HAZER-HATTICON Boundary marker along Israel's northern perimeter (Ez 47:16). In conjunction with the use of Hazar-enan in this context, and in comparison with Numbers 34:9-10, it appears that Hazer-hatticon may represent a scribal error for Hazar-enan.

HAZERIM* KJV transliteration of the corresponding Hebrew word in Deuteronomy 2:23. Instead of the proper name for a city, it may be a generic term for "villages," a rendering favored by the NLT.

HAZEROTH Camp of the Israelites during their wanderings in the desert. It was the third camp from Mt Sinai (Nm 11:35; 12:16; 33:17-18; Dt 1:1). Here Miriam and Aaron spoke against Moses for marrying a Cushite woman and questioned whether God spoke only through Moses (Nm 12:1-2). The site is probably modern 'Ain Khadra, about 30 miles (48 kilometers) northeast of Jebel Musa.
See also Wilderness Wanderings.

HAZEZON-TAMAR* KJV spelling of the city Hazazon-tamar in Genesis 14:7. *See* Hazazon-tamar.

HAZIEL Levite and son of Shimei during David's time (1 Chr 23:9).

HAZO Nahor's fifth son (Gn 22:22); probably used as the name for a Nahorite clan. It has been identified with the name Hazu, which designated a mountainous region in northern Arabia mentioned in an inscription telling of Esarhaddon's Arabian campaign.

HAZOR

1. City in northern Palestine in the territory of Naphtali, called "the capital of the federation of all these kingdoms [of Canaan]" in Joshua 11:10. Located five miles (8 kilometers) southwest of Lake Huleh and ten miles (16 kilometers) north of the Sea of Galilee, it is known as Tell el-Qedah (or Tell Waggas) today. At its peak it numbered 40,000 inhabitants and was by far the largest Canaanite city in area and population. It was a great commercial center on the trade routes between Egypt and Babylon.

Hazor is first mentioned in the 19th-century BC Egyptian Execration Texts. It is given prominence in the archives of Mari (18th century BC), being the only Palestinian city to be mentioned in these documents.

It is frequently mentioned in Egyptian documents from the time of Thutmose III to Ramses II, including the Tell el-Amarna correspondence.

The OT mentions Hazor a number of times. The first time concerns the conquests of Joshua in which Hazor was completely destroyed (Jos 11:1-15; 12:19). At that time, Hazor was a Canaanite royal city whose king, Jabin, headed a northern Canaanite federation against the invading Israelites. Hazor figures in the revolt led by Deborah and Barak against another Jabin that resulted in a rout of Jabin's forces under Sisera (Jgs 4–5). Hazor was fortified by Solomon (1 Kgs 9:15); the remains of Solomon's Hazor are clearly preserved. King Ahab (874–853 BC) also added to the fortifications; the elaborate water system Ahab constructed when he rebuilt the whole upper city and fortified it to withstand long siege has been found. The city was destroyed by the Assyrian Tiglath-pileser III about 732 BC, thus bringing to an end its use as a fortified Israelite city (2 Kgs 15:29). Fortresses of the Assyrian, Persian, and Hellenistic periods have been found in various strata of the city. Hazor is not mentioned again in the OT, but 1 Maccabees 11:67 says Jonathan encamped near the plain of Hazor where he fought against Demetrius (147 BC). The last mention of Hazor in ancient sources was by Josephus.

Hazor has been of particular interest for the light it sheds on the conquest of Palestine described in Joshua. Excavations clearly show that the great city was destroyed by fire in the last half of the 13th century BC and was never rebuilt. Archaeological finds support the biblical picture of a violent conquest under Joshua. The meager Israelite occupation in the 12th and 11th century BC was replaced by a well-fortified city during the Solomonic era.

2. Town in southern Judah (Jos 15:23). It is perhaps el-Jebariyeh, on the Wadi Umm Ethnan near Bir Hafir, about nine miles (14.5 kilometers) southeast of el-'Auja.

Aerial View of Hazor

3. Another town in southern Judah, called Hazor-hadattah (Jos 15:25). The KJV translates as separate cities, "Hazor, Hadattah." *See* Hazor-hadattah.
4. Alternate name for Kerioth-hezron (Jos 15:25), probably situated in southern Judah. The KJV translates as separate cities, "Kerioth, and Hezron." *See* Kerioth #1.
5. Town north of Jerusalem occupied by Benjamites after their return from exile (Neh 11:33). The name has been preserved in modern Khirbet Hazzur, west of Beit Hanina.
6. Place somewhere in the Arabian Desert east of Palestine. Jeremiah refers to its kingdoms in his oracle of judgment against Kedar and Hazor (Jer 49:28-33).

HAZOR-HADATTAH One of the cities located in the southern extremity of Judah, near the border of Edom (Jos 15:25). The KJV translates the term as two different cities, "Hazor and Hadattah." The Aramaic adjective "Hadattah" indicates this as a settlement from Hazor, but this is unsure.

HAZZELELPONI Etam's daughter from Judah's tribe (1 Chr 4:3).

HEAD The uppermost portion of the body, containing the brain, major sense organs, and the mouth. It appears many times in the Bible as a physical description. The Hebrew term for *head* is also used figuratively in the Old Testament. Frequently, it designates prominence or authority.

To raise one's head was considered an act of pride (Ps 140:9) or honor (Gn 40:20; Pss 3:3; 27:6). Bowing the head signified humility (Is 58:5) or sadness (Lam 2:10). The Hebrew word is used metaphorically of mountain peaks (Gn 8:5), the tops of buildings (Gn 11:4) or trees (2 Sm 5:24), and river sources (Gn 2:10). The term was commonly used to designate positions of political, military, or familiar authority. In this sense the "head" exercised control over all those subjected to him (Jgs 10:18; 1 Sm 15:17; Ps 18:43; Is 7:8-9; Jer 31:7; Hos 1:11). David was called the "keeper of mine head" (KJV) when he served as the bodyguard of Achish (1 Sm 28:2; cf. Jgs 9:53; Ps 68:21).

Greek philosophers used the image of the body to represent the universe. The head of this body—called Zeus or Reason—was considered responsible for the creation and sustenance of the remaining members (celestial beings, humans, animals, plants, and inanimate objects). The universe, or "body," owed its existence to the "head."

Between 460 BC (the date usually ascribed to the first writings of Hippocrates) and AD 200 (the death of Galen, who developed Hippocrates' findings), Greek medical science came to understand the head as the seat of intelligence. The body was able to operate efficiently only because the brain was capable of interpreting data received from the body (eyes, ears, skin, and so on), and because it was able to send out appropriate impulses to the various members of the body, based upon the data received. The ability of the brain to interpret and direct made the existence of the body completely dependent upon it.

In the NT, the term refers to the actual human head (Mt 5:36; 6:17; 14:8; 26:7; Mk 6:27; 14:3; Lk 7:46; Jn 13:9; 20:7), to apocalyptic beings (Rv 1:14; 4:4; 12:1), and to animals (Rv 9:7, 17, 19; 12:3). Furthermore, it appears in such expressions as "to heap coals of fire upon the head," meaning to return good for evil (Rom 12:20; cf. Mt 5:44); to "shear" or "anoint the head" expressing a vow (Acts 21:24); and "to lay down the head," meaning to sleep (Mt 8:20; Lk 9:58).

The apostle Paul drew from the OT metaphorical understanding of the term to express the headship of God over Christ, Christ over man, and man over woman (1 Cor 11:3-16; cf. Eph 5:23). In the light of these relationships, Paul encouraged women at Corinth to wear veils in worship. The veil gave a woman the authority to worship as an equal with men before God. The term is used again with the meaning "authority" to express the lordship of Christ over the universe (Eph 1:21-22; Col 2:10).

Paul used the image of the head and body to express the relationship between Christ and his church (Eph 4:15; 5:23; cf. 1 Cor 12:12-27). In addition to the OT sense, the contributions of medical science in Paul's day may provide insight into this image, for Christ is not only the dominant ruler over the church but also the dynamic force that provides its direction and unity. The ability of the church to exist and the focal point of its activity are rooted in the work of its "head," Jesus Christ. In this light, various modern exegetes have argued that headship does not mean "authority" as much as it means "source," as in the term "fountainhead." Thus, he who is the head is the source, the supplier. These interpreters see God as being Christ's supplier, and Christ being the church's supplier, and man being woman's supplier.

HEAD COVERING Something used to cover one's head either for protection or for religious reasons.

Men wore a cap, turban, or head scarf for protection against the sun. The cap was similar to a skullcap (a cap without a brim) and was sometimes worn by the poor. The turban (Is 3:23) was made of thick linen wound around the head with the ends tucked inside the folds. The priest's turban had a plate strapped to it bearing the inscription "Holy to the LORD" (Ex 28:36). The head scarf was made from a square yard (.8 square meter) of cloth, folded in half to form a triangle. The sides fell over the shoulders and the V-point down the back, and it was held in place by a headband made of cord. About the second century BC, male Jews began to wear phylacteries on their foreheads, small leather boxes containing special Scripture passages, at morning prayers and at festivals, but not on the Sabbath.

Women were often veiled in public, although this custom changed over the centuries. In NT times, women usually wore veils (1 Cor 11:5-6). Women also wore a cloth similar to the head scarf, but the fabric was different in quality and color from that worn by men. It was often pinned over a stiff hat and set with ornaments. If a woman was married, these and other important coins covered the front of the hat and constituted her dowry (cf. Lk 15:8-10). Women also adorned their heads with an elaborate plaiting of their hair, prompting Peter to warn Christian women about too much concern with external beauty (1 Pt 3:3-4).

HEAL, HEALING To make well. The OT provides the proper background for a Christian understanding of the concept of healing. In the OT the basic point is made that God is the healer of his people. In Exodus 15:22-26, after God has delivered his people from Egypt, led them through the sea, and sweetened the water at Marah, he speaks of himself as their "healer." This refers primarily to physical sustenance, but it points to the more encompassing concept of God sustaining his people in an eternal relationship with himself. In a similar manner, Deuteronomy 32:39 speaks of God as the one who heals. The context in Deuteronomy implies that this healing power derives from the fact that God is God. This concept of God as the healer is echoed throughout the OT by the psalmists (Pss 6:2; 41:4; 103:3) and prophets (Is 19:22; Jer 17:14; Hos 7:1; Zec 11:16).

Jesus the Healer: Accounts in the Gospels The NT significantly emphasizes Jesus as the healer. Mark portrays him as a teacher and healer in his opening account of Jesus' ministry in Capernaum with the healing of the demoniac, Peter's mother-in-law, the sick brought to him in the evening, and the leper (Mk 1:21-45). Indeed, healing sickness and casting out demons characterize Jesus' ministry. Mark presents in rapid succession Jesus' healing of the paralytic (2:1-12), the man with the withered hand (3:1-6), the multitudes by the sea (vv 7-12), the Gerasene demoniac (5:1-20), the woman with a hemorrhage, and Jairus's daughter (vv 21-43). Jesus then commissioned the Twelve to proclaim repentance, to cast out demons, and to heal the sick (6:7-13). He himself continued with healings at Gennesaret (vv 53-56), casting out the unclean spirit from the daughter of the Syrophoenician woman (7:24-30), healing the deaf and mute man (vv 31-37), the blind man of Bethsaida (8:22-26), the boy possessed with an evil spirit (9:14-20), and blind Bartimaeus (10:46-52).

Certainly healing is an important aspect of Jesus' ministry. The healings expressed not only his compassion for those suffering but also constituted a revelation of his person. This is brought out by the climactic statement of Jesus in healing the paralytic: "that you may know that the Son of man has authority on earth to forgive sins" (Mk 2:10, RSV). It also seems that Mark intended his readers to understand that the healing of the deaf and mute man (7:31-37) and the blind man of Bethsaida (8:22-26) symbolize the awakening of spiritual understanding in the disciples of who Jesus is. It is also significant that Mark has placed the healing of Bartimaeus (10:46-52) immediately after Jesus' third announcement of his own coming death (vv 32-34) and the disciples' third failure to understand that his being the Messiah entailed the necessity of suffering (vv 35-45).

Matthew also portrays Jesus as teaching, preaching, and healing (Mt 4:23-25), and parallels the accounts in Mark, except for the healing of the demoniac in the synagogue (Mk 1:23-28) and the blind man of Bethsaida (8:22-26). However, according to his special purpose and structure, Matthew has placed many of Jesus' healings together in a "mighty works" section (Mt 8–9), complementing the "great words" ("sermon") section (chs 5–7). Matthew views Jesus' healings as directly fulfilling the OT, as he states in 8:17. The unique way in which the healings of 8:16 are spoken of as fulfilling Isaiah 53:4 seems to indicate that Jesus' power over sickness derives in some way from his death for sin, which was to be accomplished at the end of his ministry.

It is also interesting that Matthew, in relating Jesus' healing of the multitudes by the sea (Mt 12:15-21; cf. Mk 3:7-12), cites Isaiah 42:1-4. This OT passage speaks of God's servant anointed with the Spirit to proclaim justice to the nations. As used by Matthew, the quotation explains why Jesus commanded those healed not to make him known. Jesus did not want too much publicity about himself to thwart God's plan for him as the Suffering Servant who was to bring salvation to the nations. This action demonstrates that Jesus' healings are revelations of his person. Again another quotation from Isaiah (6:9-10) in Matthew 13:14-15 brings out the fact that healing is understood primarily in the spiritual sense of hearing Jesus' proclamation of the kingdom of God.

Luke, like Matthew and Mark, portrays Jesus preaching and healing. After the account of the birth of John and Jesus and the ministry of John the Baptist, Luke presents Jesus preaching in Nazareth (Lk 4:16-30). Here, in the synagogue of his hometown, Jesus himself, using a quotation from Isaiah 61:1-2, affirms that the Spirit has anointed him to proclaim good news and to announce release for the captives and a recovery of sight for the blind (Lk 4:18). The healing aspect of Jesus' ministry occupies an important place in the rest of the book of Luke. Indeed, Luke has all the healing incidents noted by Mark, except for those in Mark 6:45–8:26. However, Luke's opening scene in Nazareth seems to underscore that Jesus' healing is to be understood, not as merely expressing Jesus' compassion for the needy, but primarily as a sign of the arrival of the kingdom of God as promised in the Scriptures.

This emphasis may be seen in the distinctively Lukan account of the commissioning of the 72 disciples (Lk 10:1-12), where Jesus instructs them to heal the sick in any city they enter and announce to the people there that the kingdom of God has come near to them (vv 8-9).

The first three Gospels take up the OT understanding of God as the healer of his people and see this as fulfilled in Jesus. This fulfillment signifies the presence of God's reign in the ministry of Jesus and points to him as the one through whom God is at work in the midst of his people.

John's Gospel has only four healing incidents: the official's son (Jn 4:46-54), the man ill for 38 years (5:1-18), the man born blind (ch 9), and the climactic raising of Lazarus (11:1-44). The special purpose and structure of this Gospel indicate that these incidents are carefully related to the accompanying discourses and are clearly intended as signs revealing the person of Jesus. The heightened emphasis on healings as revelatory signs in this Gospel confirms the similar intention in the first three Gospels.

Healings Done by the Apostles The Acts of the Apostles tells of the continuation of Jesus' ministry through the Spirit at work in his disciples. The primary focus in Acts is on proclamation, as 1:8 indicates. However, the healing of the lame beggar in Jerusalem indicates that the disciples were able to exercise the power of healing in the name of Jesus (3:1-16; 4:8-16). The healing is clearly intended to point to and glorify the person of Jesus and lead to faith in him (3:12-26). The balanced, twofold ministry of the disciples may be seen in the prayer of 4:29-30: "O Lord, hear their threats, and give your servants great boldness in their preaching. Send your healing power; may miraculous signs and wonders be done through the name of your holy servant Jesus" (NLT).

The ministry of Philip in Samaria was devoted to proclaiming Christ (Acts 8:5) and healing the sick and those with unclean spirits (v 7). Peter heals Aeneas and raises Tabitha (9:34, 40), and in each case the effects are that many believe in the Lord (vv 35, 42). Paul is also described as preaching the gospel (17:2-3), healing (14:8-11; 28:8), casting out spirits (16:18), and raising a dead man (20:9-10).

Healings in the Church Age The letters of the NT say little about healing. First Corinthians speaks of the gifts of healing (1 Cor 12:9, 28). The implication is that such gifts are intended to be part of the ministry of the church, but the context indicates that not all are given such gifts (v 30) and that it is God who sovereignly distributes gifts for the good of the body. James indicates that a believer who is ill should request the church to pray for his healing (Jas 5:14-16; cf. Heb 12:13). The clear implication is that God is willing and able to minister to his people for healing today.

HEALING, Gift of *See* Spiritual Gifts.

HEART Vital bodily organ; emotional center of one's
being.

In Hebrew and Greek, as in modern English, "heart"
is used to designate a physical organ as well as the emotional center of one's being. "Heart" (Hebrew *leb*; Greek
kardia) occurs approximately 1,000 times in the Bible,
though it is often disguised in translation. The range of
meaning is great.

Physical Heart That the beating heart indicates life
seems implied in 1 Samuel 25:37-39 (see NLT mg),
despite the delay in Nabal's death. Physical food and
wine affect the heart (Jgs 19:5; Ps 104:15; Acts 14:17),
and the heart can "faint" and "tremble." The heart's position in the body yields an obvious metaphor for "the
center" (Mt 12:40).

Pyschological Heart The heart attends intellectually
(e.g., Jer 12:11); it also perceives (Jn 12:40), understands
(1 Kgs 3:9), debates (Mk 2:6), reflects (Lk 2:19), remembers (Lk 2:51), thinks (Dt 8:17), imagines (Lk 1:51), is
wise (Eccl 1:17, KJV), has technical skill (Ex 28:3, KJV),
and much more.

Emotionally, the heart experiences intoxicated merriment (1 Sm 25:36), gladness (Is 30:29), joy (Jn 16:22),
sorrow (Neh 2:2), anguish (Rom 9:2), bitterness (Prv
14:10), anxiety (1 Sm 4:13), despair (Eccl 2:20), love
(2 Sm 14:1), trust (Ps 112:7), affection (2 Cor 7:3), lust
(Mt 5:28), callousness (Mk 3:5), hatred (Lv 19:17), fear
(Gn 42:28), jealousy (Jas 3:14), desire (Rom 10:1), discouragement (Nm 32:9), sympathy (Ex 23:9), anger (Dt
19:6, KJV), irresolution (2 Chr 13:7, KJV), and much more.

Volitionally, the heart can purpose (1 Cor 4:5), incline
to (1 Sm 14:7), prompt (2 Kgs 12:4; cf. Prv 4:23), be
steadfast (Acts 11:23), be willing (Ex 35:22), contrive
evil (Acts 5:4), or follow its "treasure" (Mt 6:21).

Morally, the heart can be gentle, lowly (Mt 11:29),
holy (1 Thes 3:13), faithful (Neh 9:8), upright (Ps
97:11), pure, single-minded (Jas 4:8), clean (Acts 15:8),
loving toward God (Mk 12:30) and others (1 Pt 1:22),
hardened, or sensitive (Ez 11:19). Scripture's emphasis
falls upon the heart's evil (Gn 6:5 and throughout), as
self-deceiving (Jas 1:26), deceitful (Jer 17:9), avaricious
(Mt 6:19-21), lustful (Mt 5:28), arrogant (Is 9:9), impious (Acts 7:51), perverse (Ps 101:4), and impenitent
(Rom 2:5). Nothing defiles a man worse than his own
heart (Mk 7:18-19).

Yet out of the heart can come good (Lk 6:45; 8:15).
Even when frustrated by circumstances or by fear, the
heart's good intention remains good; its evil intent, bad
(1 Kgs 8:18; Mt 5:28).

Being so complex, a person's heart is sadly divided,
and Scripture often extols a perfect, whole, true (i.e.,
united) heart (Gn 20:5; Ps 86:11; Acts 8:37). The "heart"
signifies the total inner self, a person's hidden core of
being (1 Pt 3:4), with which one communes, which one
"pours out" in prayer, words, and deeds (Ps 62:8; Mt
15:18-19). It is the genuine self, distinguished from
appearance, public position, and physical presence
(1 Sm 16:7; 2 Cor 5:12; 1 Thes 2:17). And this "heart-
self" has its own nature, character, and disposition
(Dn 4:16; 7:4, KJV; cf. Mt 12:33-37).

The Spiritual Heart The heart is especially important
in biblical religion. The mystery of the hidden self is
fully known to God and to Christ (Jer 17:10; Lk 9:47;
Rom 8:27), and the heart is the seat of our knowledge of
God (2 Cor 4:6). The state of heart governs the vision of
God (Mt 5:8); from the heart one speaks to God (Ps
27:8); the heart is the locus of divine indwelling (2 Cor
1:22; Gal 4:6; Eph 3:17).

On the other hand, moral evil in the heart is seen in
biblical perspective as sin against God. Senseless hearts
are darkened, often secretly idolatrous, far from God,
"not right" before God (Dt 29:18-19; Mt 15:8; Acts 8:21;
Rom 1:21). Yet the Lord will not despise a broken, contrite heart (Ps 51:17). When one's heart is turned toward
God, he promises to make it sensitive to divine things,
renewed and purified (Dt 4:29; 2 Kgs 23:25; Ps 51:10;
Jl 2:13; Ez 36:25-27). God's law shall then be written on
the heart as the inward guide and incentive (Jer 31:33;
Heb 8:10; cf. 2 Cor 3:2-3).

In Christian terms, such transformation involves
believing the gospel from the "honest and good heart"
that provides fruitful soil for the Word of God (Lk 8:15;
Rom 10:9). The true heart draws near to God, loves him
with all its intellect, feeling, and will (Lk 10:27; Heb
10:22). Then God gives strength, reward, renewal, grace,
peace, and joy to the heart (Ps 73:26; Is 57:15; Acts 2:46;
Phil 4:7; Heb 13:9). So the ancient ideal becomes possible again, that of being "a man after God's own heart"
(1 Sm 13:14; Acts 13:22).

HEARTH *See* Homes and Dwellings.

HEATH* Type of evergreen shrub; KJV mistranslation
for shrub or bush in Jeremiah 17:6 and 48:6. *See* Plants
(Juniper).

HEAVEN Realm (or realms) designated by a Hebrew
term used to represent the sky and air and also heaven.
The form of the word in Hebrew is dual (implying two
of something). Although this dual form may only represent an ancient device for expressing the plural, it is supposed by some to imply the existence of a lower and an
upper heaven—a physical and a spiritual heaven.

In the Old Testament The OT writers viewed the
physical heavens as a "firmament" appearing as a great
arch supported on foundations and pillars (2 Sm 22:8)
and spread out above the earth, with rain descending
through its doors (Ps 78:23). The keynote of the OT
revelation about the physical heavens is set forth in
Psalms 8 and 19:1-6. Elsewhere the OT speaks of the
atmospheric heavens as the region of the clouds (Ps
147:8), winds (Zec 2:6), rain (Dt 11:11), thunder (1 Sm
2:10), dew (Dt 33:13), frost (Jb 38:29), and the abode
of birds (Gn 1:26, 30). It is also the locale of such
destructive forces as hail (Jos 10:11), fire, and brimstone (Gn 19:24). In the NT this notion of the vaulted
expanse of the sky as the region in which the elements,
clouds, and tempests gather (Mt 16:2; Lk 4:25) and
birds fly (Lk 9:58) is continued.

In addition to the atmospheric regions, the Hebrew idea
of the physical heavens includes stellar space, which ultimately embraces the universe. The heavenly bodies of the
stellar heavens were viewed by the Hebrews as inexpress-
ibly glorious manifestations of God's handiwork without
having any power or vitality of their own. These include
the sun, moon, planets, and stars, which were but lights in
the firmament of the heavens (Gn 1:14; 15:5). As such,
they were regarded as unworthy of worship because God
had, by his own will and grace, made humans superior to
them. In fact, the Hebrews were expressly forbidden to
worship the stellar bodies (Ex 20:4), the gods and goddesses who represented them (Jer 44:17-25), or to participate in astrological speculation (Is 47:13). Hence, this
unique theological ordinance differentiated the Hebrews,
who viewed the heavenly bodies as made and moved by

the will of God, from the superstitious heathen, who worshiped them.

The term "heaven of heavens" (Dt 10:14; see also KJV 1 Kgs 8:27; Pss 68:33; 148:4) is the literal English rendition of the Hebrew idiom for the superlative "the highest heaven." Some have thought this the counterpart to Paul's expression "the third heaven" (2 Cor 12:2), which parallels the classical Greek conception of three heavens. This notion was subsequently adopted by the Roman Catholic medieval church and in the Latin form of *Coelum Aqueum, Coelum Sidereum,* and *Coelum Empyreum.* The basic concept followed the Greek view, and it coincides with the OT view of the physical and spiritual heavens as indicated earlier. Those who follow this approach tend to regard this third heaven as the place reached by the souls of the blessed as they pass through the two lower regions of the atmosphere and outer space containing the celestial bodies, and enter into the uttermost reaches of the universe.

In the New Testament The Lord Jesus indicated that heaven is the dwelling place of God (Mt 6:9). Jesus, during his earthly ministry, repeatedly claimed that he had come from heaven (Jn 3:13; 6:33-51); and on at least three occasions utterances from heaven confirmed these claims (Mt 3:16-17; 17:5; Jn 12:28). There is where the true tabernacle stands, of which the earthly tabernacle was merely a shadow (cf. Heb 8:1-5). That abode of God was in view when the apostle Paul wrote of "the third heaven" (2 Cor 12:2). As such, it is often seen as a synonym for God himself (cf. Mt 23:22; Lk 15:18).

After Jesus' ascension, recorded in Acts 1:6-11, two angels reminded the disciples that Jesus would return again from heaven. This was later confirmed by the apostle Paul (1 Cor 15:1-11; Eph 4:7-16; 1 Tm 3:16) and reiterated in the summary of the teachings of the NT known as the Apostles' Creed. In all, the relationship of Jesus Christ to the heavenly abode of God is inextricably interwoven in the NT and is inseparable from the gospel message itself. Indeed, it is from the "right hand of God" that Christ forever lives to make intercession for those who have come to him by faith (Heb 7:25; cf. Mk 14:62).

Paul asserts that the believer's body will be made conformable to the glorious body of Jesus Christ when Christ returns from heaven (Phil 3:20-21). The believers need such a heavenly body to match their heavenly citizenship. The term "citizenship" (KJV) or "commonwealth" (RSV) implies a colony of individuals who live in a foreign country while observing the laws of their homeland instead of the land in which they reside (cf. Acts 22:28). The implication for believers is quite clear: They are to live according to the moral and ethical principles of God as revealed from heaven regardless of the standards proclaimed by the world. They have been raised together with Christ and have been instructed to "seek the things that are above, where Christ is, seated at the right hand of God" (Col 3:1). From there Christ has blessed his followers "with every spiritual blessing in the heavenly places" (Eph 1:3). The expression "in the heavenly places" is peculiar to Ephesians (see 1:3, 20; 2:6; 3:10; 6:12), suggesting that the blessings of the spiritual world are not relegated to some remote future time or place but can be perceived by faith here and now. That is why believers are said to have been made partakers already in the heavenly calling (Heb 3:1; 6:4).

In the meanwhile, believers look forward to a new heaven and a new earth with the new Jerusalem. There will be no tears, sorrow, pain, death, and night there because the Son of God will be there (Rv 21:1-4, 27; 22:1-5), and in the resurrected state there will be no marrying or giving in marriage (Lk 20:27-38). At least two OT saints, Enoch (Gn 5:22-24; Heb 11:5) and Elijah (2 Kgs 2:11), were translated directly into the presence of God—into heaven. In addition to Paul's statement about the third heaven, John was called into heaven (Rv 4:1), a heaven that is intended to be populated (cf. 19:1). All believers will ultimately dwell in heaven in their resurrection bodies, which they will receive when the Lord comes for them from heaven (1 Thes 4:16-17; Rv 19:1-4). The Lord will also give treasures and rewards at that time (Mt 5:12; 1 Cor 9:25; 2 Cor 5:1; 2 Tm 4:8; Jas 1:12; 1 Pt 1:4; 5:4; Rv 2:10; 4:10).

See also "Abraham's Bosom," page 7; New Heavens and New Earth; Paradise.

HEAVENLIES*, The Term unique to Paul's Letter to the Ephesians, also translated "heavenly places" or "realms," and referring to the super earthly upper regions of the air. Since the term "in the heavenlies" carried with it associations from pagan cultic vocabulary, it was perhaps used by the apostle in an apologetic manner.

"The heavenly places" indicates the sphere where the risen Christ has been seated at the right hand of God in a position of authority, power, and dominion, reigning as conqueror and ruler high above the heavenly world (Eph 1:20-21). Other usage points to the idea of the realized hope of those who are in Christ, in that believers have already been blessed with "every spiritual blessing in the heavenlies" (v 3) and are raised with Christ, seated with him in the heavenlies (2:6). The church will make known the wisdom of God to the principalities and powers in the heavenlies (3:10). She will thus participate in the victory over the spiritual hosts of wickedness, also present in the heavenly places (6:12).

See also Heaven; Principalities and Powers.

HEAVENS, New *See* New Heavens and New Earth.

HEAVE OFFERING* Portions of the sacrifices and offerings set aside for the Lord and for the priests. *See* Offerings and Sacrifices (Fellowship Offerings).

HEBER

1. Descendant of Jacob through Asher and Beriah (Gn 46:17) and father of the family of Heberites (Nm 26:45; 1 Chr 7:31-32).
2. Husband of Jael, the woman who deceptively killed Sisera, known as Heber the Kenite (Jgs 4:11-21; 5:24).
3. Judahite, Mered's son and the father of Soco (1 Chr 4:18).
4. Elpaal's son from Judah's tribe (1 Chr 8:17).
5. KJV spelling for Eber in 1 Chronicles 5:13; 8:22; and Luke 3:35. *See* Eber #1, #2, #4.

HEBERITES Descendants of Heber in the family of Jacob (Nm 26:45). *See* Heber #1.

HEBREW LANGUAGE Language of the Jewish people. The name Hebrew is not applied by the OT to its own language, although the NT does use the name that way. In the OT, "Hebrew" means the individual or people who used the language. The language itself is called "the language of Canaan" (Is 19:18, NLT mg) or "the language of Judah" (Neh 13:24).

Origin and History In the Middle Ages a common view was that Hebrew was the primitive language of humankind. Even in colonial America, Hebrew was still referred to as "the mother of all languages." Linguistic scholarship has now made this theory untenable.

Hebrew is actually one of several Canaanite dialects that included Phoenician, Ugaritic, and Moabite. Other Canaanite dialects (for example, Ammonite) existed but have left insufficient inscriptions for scholarly investigation. Such dialects were already present in the land of Canaan before its conquest by the Israelites.

Until about 1974, the oldest witnesses to Canaanite language were found in the Ugarit and Amarna records dating from the 14th and 15th centuries BC. A few Canaanite words and expressions appeared in earlier Egyptian records, but the origin of Canaanite has been uncertain. Between 1974 and 1976, however, nearly 17,000 tablets were dug up at Tell Mardikh (ancient Ebla) in northern Syria, written in a previously unknown Semitic dialect. Because they possibly date back to 2400 BC (perhaps even earlier), many scholars think that language may be the "Old Canaanite" that gave rise to Hebrew. By 1977, when another 1,000 tablets were unearthed, only about 100 inscriptions from Ebla had been reported on. Languages change over a long period of time. For example, the English used in the time of Alfred the Great (ninth century AD) seems almost like a foreign language to contemporary English speakers. Although Hebrew was no exception to the general principle, like other Semitic languages it remained remarkably stable over many centuries. Poems such as the Song of Deborah (Jgs 5) tended to preserve the language's oldest form. Changes that took place later in the long history of the language are shown in the presence of archaic words (often preserved in poetic language) and a general difference in style. For example, the book of Job reflects a more archaic style than the book of Esther.

Various Hebrew dialects apparently existed side by side in OT times, as reflected in the episode involving the pronunciation of the Hebrew word "shibboleth/sibboleth" (Jgs 12:4-6). It seems that the Israelites east of the Jordan pronounced the initial letter with a strong "sh" sound, while those in Canaan gave it the simple "s" sound. Scholars have also identified features of Hebrew that could be described as reflecting the northern or southern parts of the country.

Family of Languages Hebrew belongs to the Semitic family of languages; these languages were used from the Mediterranean Sea to the mountains east of the Euphrates River valley, and from Armenia (Turkey) in the north to the southern extremity of the Arabian peninsula. Semitic languages are classified as Southern (Arabic and Ethiopic), Eastern (Akkadian), and Northwestern (Aramaic, Syriac, and Canaanite—Hebrew, Phoenician, Ugaritic, and Moabite).

Character Hebrew, like the other early Semitic languages, concentrates on observation more than reflection. That is, things are generally observed according to their appearance as phenomena, not analyzed as to their inward being or essence. Effects are observed but not traced through a series of causes.

Hebrew's vividness, conciseness, and simplicity make the language difficult to translate fully. It is amazingly concise and direct. For example, Psalm 23 contains 55 words; most translations require about twice that many to translate it. The first two lines, with slashes separating the individual Hebrew words in the original, read:

> *The Lord/[is] my shepherd/*
> *I shall want/not*

Thus eight English words are required to translate four Hebrew words.

Hebrew does not use separate, distinct expressions for every shade of thought. Someone has said, "The Semites have been the quarries whose great rough blocks the Greeks have trimmed, polished, and fitted together. The former gave religion; the latter philosophy."

Hebrew is a pictorial language in which the past is not merely described but verbally painted. Not just a landscape is presented but a moving panorama. The course of events is reenacted in the mind's sight. (Note the frequent use of "behold," a Hebraism carried over to the NT.) Such common Hebraic expressions as "he arose and went," "he opened his lips and spoke," "he lifted up his eyes and saw," and "he lifted up his voice and wept" illustrate the pictorial strength of the language.

Many profound theological expressions of the OT are tightly bound up with Hebrew language and grammar. Even the most sacred name of God himself, "the LORD" (Yahweh), is directly related to the Hebrew verb "to be" (or perhaps "to cause to be"). Many other names of persons and places in the OT can best be understood only with a working knowledge of Hebrew.

Hebrew Script and Grammar

Alphabet and Script The Hebrew alphabet consists of 22 consonants; signs for vowels were devised and added late in the language's history. The origin of the alphabet is unknown. The oldest examples of a Canaanite alphabet were preserved in the Ugaritic cuneiform alphabet of the 14th century BC.

The old style of writing the letters is called the Phoenician or paleo-Hebrew script. It is the predecessor of the Greek and other Western alphabets. The script used in modern Hebrew Bibles (Aramaic or square script) came into vogue after Israel's exile into Babylon (sixth century BC). The older style was still used sporadically in the early Christian era on coins and for writing God's name (as in the Dead Sea Scrolls). Hebrew has always been written right to left.

א = '	ד = *d*	י = *y*	ס = *s*	ר = *r*
ב = *b*	ה = *h*	כ = *k*	ע = '	שׂ = *ś*
ב = *b*	ו = *w*	ך כ = *k*	פ = *p*	שׁ = *š*
ג = *g*	ז = *z*	ל = *l*	ף פ = *p*	ת = *t*
ג = *g*	ח = *h*	ם מ = *m*	ץ צ = *s*	ת = *t*
ד = *d*	ט = *t*	ן נ = *n*	ק = *q*	

' = *ê*	= *ā*	= *a*	= *a*	
' = *î*	= *ē*	= *e*	= *e*	
ו = *ô*	= *ō*	= *i*	= *e* *(if vocal)*	
ו = *û*		= *o*	= *o*	
		= *u*		

The Hebrew Alphabet

Consonants The Canaanite alphabet of the Phoenician and Moabite languages had 22 consonants. The older Canaanite language reflected in Ugaritic had more consonants. Arabic also preserves some Old Canaanite consonants found in Ugaritic but missing in Hebrew.

Vowels In the original consonantal Hebrew script, vowels were simply understood by the writer or reader. On the basis of tradition and context, the reader would supply whatever vowels were needed, much as is done in English abbreviations ("bldg." for "building"; "blvd." for "boulevard"). After the collapse of the nation in AD 70, the dispersion of the Jews and the destruction of Jerusalem led to Hebrew's becoming a "dead language," no longer widely spoken. Loss of traditional pronunciation and understanding then became more of a possibility, so Jewish scribes felt a need for permanently establishing the vowel sounds.

First, vowel letters called "mothers of reading" *(matres lectionis)* were added. These were consonants used especially to indicate long vowels. These were added before the Christian era, as the Dead Sea Scrolls reveal.

Later (about the fifth century AD), the scribes called Masoretes added vowel signs to indicate short vowels. At least three different systems of vowel signs were employed at different times and places. The text used today represents the system devised by Masoretic scribes who worked in the city of Tiberias. The vowels, each of which may be long or short, are indicated by dots or dashes placed above or below the consonants. Certain combinations of dots and dashes represent very short vowel sounds, or "half-vowels."

Linkage Hebrew joins together many words that in Western languages would be written separately. Some prepositions *(be-,* "in"; *le-,* "to"; *ke-,* "like") are prefixed directly to the noun or verb that they introduce, as are the definite article *ha-,* "the" and the conjunction *wa-,* "and." Suffixes are used for pronouns, either in the possessive or accusative relationship. The same word may simultaneously have both a prefix and a suffix.

Nouns Hebrew has no neuter gender; everything is masculine or feminine. Inanimate objects may be either masculine or feminine, depending on the formation or character of the word. Usually, abstract ideas or words indicating a group are feminine. Nouns are derived from roots and are formed in various ways, either by vowel modification or by adding prefixes or suffixes to the root. Contrary to Greek and many Western languages, compound nouns are not characteristic of Hebrew.

The Hebrew plural is formed by adding *-im* for masculine nouns *(seraphim, cherubim)* and *-oth* for feminine nouns.

Three original case endings indicating nominative, genitive, and accusative have dropped away during the evolution of Hebrew. To compensate for the lack of case endings, Hebrew resorts to various indicators. Indirect objects are indicated by the preposition *le-,* "to"; direct objects by the objective sign *eth;* the genitive relationship by putting the word before the genitive in the "construct state," or shortened form.

Adjectives Hebrew is deficient in adjectives. "A double heart" is indicated in the original Hebrew by "a heart and a heart" (Ps 12:2), and "two differing weights" is actually "a stone and a stone" (Dt 25:13); "the whole royal family" is "the seed of the kingdom" (2 Kgs 11:1).

Adjectives that do exist in Hebrew have no comparative or superlative forms. Relationship is indicated by the preposition "from." "Better than you" is expressed literally in Hebrew "good from you." "The serpent was more subtle than any other beast" is literally "the serpent was subtle from every beast" (Gn 3:1). The superlative is expressed by several different constructions. The idea "very deep" is literally "deep, deep" (Eccl 7:24); the "best song" is literally "song of songs" (compare "king of kings"); "holiest" is literally "holy, holy, holy" (Is 6:3).

Verbs Hebrew verbs are formed from a root usually consisting of three letters. From such roots, verbal forms are developed by a change of vowels or by adding prefixes or suffixes. The root consonants provide the semantic backbone of the language and give a stability of meaning not characteristic of Western languages. The vowels are quite flexible, giving Hebrew considerable elasticity.

Hebrew verb usage is not characterized by precise definition of tenses. Hebrew tenses, especially in poetry, are largely determined by context. The two tense formations are the perfect (completed action) and imperfect (incomplete action). The imperfect is ambiguous. It represents the indicative mood (present, past, future) but may also represent such moods as the imperative, optative, and jussive or cohortative. A distinctive usage of the perfect tense is the "prophetic perfect," where the perfect form represents a future event considered so sure that it is expressed as past (e.g., see Is 5:13, KJV).

Style

Vocabulary Most Hebrew roots originally expressed some physical action or denoted some natural object. The verb "to decide" originally meant "to cut"; "to be true" originally meant "to be firmly fixed"; "to be right" meant "to be straight"; "to be honorable" meant "to be heavy."

Abstract terms are alien to the character of Hebrew; for example, biblical Hebrew has no specific words for "theology," "philosophy," or "religion." Intellectual or theological concepts are expressed by concrete terms. The abstract idea of sin is represented by such words as "to miss the mark" or "crooked" or "rebellion" or "trespass" ("to cross over"). Mind or intellect is expressed by "heart" or "kidneys," and emotion or compassion by "bowels" (see Is 63:15, KJV). Other concrete terms in Hebrew are "horn" for strength or vigor, "bones" for self, and "seed" for descendants. A mental quality is often depicted by the part of the body thought of as its most appropriate embodiment. Strength can be represented by "arm" or "hand," anger by "nostril," displeasure by "falling face," acceptance by "shining face," thinking by "say."

Some translators have attempted to represent a Hebrew word always by the same English word, but that leads to serious problems. Sometimes there is considerable disagreement on the exact shade of meaning of a Hebrew word in a given passage. A single root frequently represents a variety of meanings, depending on usage and context. The word for "bless" can also mean "curse, greet, favor, praise." The word for "judgment" is used also for "justice, verdict, penalty, ordinance, duty, custom, manner." The word for "strength" or "power" also means "army, virtue, worth, courage."

Further ambiguity arises from the fact that some Hebrew consonants stand for two different original consonants that have merged in the evolution of the language. Two words that on the surface appear to be identical may be traced back to two different roots. For an example of this phenomenon in English, compare "bass" (a fish) with "bass" (a vocalist).

Syntax Hebrew syntax is relatively uncomplicated. Few subordinating conjunctions ("if," "when," "because," etc.) are used; sentences are usually coordinated by using the simple conjunction "and." English translations of biblical texts generally try to show the logical connection between successive sentences, even though it is not always clear. In Genesis 1:2–3:1, all but three of the 56 verses begin with "and," yet the NLT translates that conjunction variously as "then" (1:3), "so" (v 27), "so" (2:1), "but" (v 6), and "now" (3:1).

Hebrew style is enlivened by use of direct discourse. The narrator does not simply state that "such and such a person said that . . ." (indirect discourse). Instead, the parties speak for themselves (direct discourse), creating a freshness that remains even after repeated reading.

Poetry Hebrew poetry uses a variety of rhetorical devices. Some of them—such as assonance, alliteration, and acrostics—can be appreciated only in the original Hebrew. But parallelism, the most important characteristic of Hebrew poetry, is evident even in English translation. Among the many forms of parallelism possible, four common categories exist: (1) synonymous, a repeating style in which parallel lines say the same thing in different words; (2) antithetic, a contrasting style in which contrary thoughts are expressed; (3) completive, with a completing parallel line filling out the thought of the first; (4) climactic, in which an ascending parallel line picks up something from the first line and repeats it. Numerous other forms of parallelism enrich Hebrew poetry. The possible variations of parallelism are almost endless.

Figures of Speech Hebrew abounds in expressive figures of speech based on the Hebrew people's character and way of life. Certain odd but well-known expressions found in English literature come from the Hebrew style, like "apple of his eye" (Dt 32:10; Ps 17:8; Prv 7:2; Zec 2:8) and "skin of my teeth" (Job 19:20). Some of the more striking Hebrew modes of expression are hard to transfer into English, such as "to uncover the ear," meaning "to disclose, reveal." Others are more familiar, like "to stiffen the neck" for "to be stubborn, rebellious"; "to bend or incline the ear" for "to listen closely."

Legacy English and a number of other modern languages have been enriched by Hebrew. English even contains a number of Hebrew "loan words." Some of these have had wide influence ("amen," "hallelujah," "jubilee"). Many Hebrew proper nouns are used in modern languages for persons and places, such as David, Jonathan/John, Miriam/Mary, Bethlehem (the name of several towns and cities in the United States).

Many common Hebrew expressions have been unconsciously accepted into English figures of speech, as in "mouth of the cave" and "face of the earth." Some figures, such as "east of Eden," have been used as titles for books and films.

HEBREWS, Letter to the
One of the most profound and enigmatic books in the NT. The identity of its author, the time of its writing, and the people and place to which it was sent are all shrouded in mystery. Yet, in spite of the uncertainty, Hebrews remains one of the most timely and relevant books in the Bible. Some 300 years ago John Owen, the English Puritan, appropriately remarked: "No doubt the Epistle next in importance to Romans is this to the Hebrews." The letter is both doctrinal and practical, theological and pastoral. In short, it builds a compelling case for the superiority of Christianity. Hebrews also reflects the impassioned concern of a pastor's heart. Those who have experienced God's ultimate work of grace in Christ are urged to hold fast to God's final word of revelation in his Son.

Unlike most other NT epistles, Hebrews does not begin like a letter. There is no introductory salutation, the writer is not identified, and no mention is made of those to whom the document is addressed. The author characterizes the work as a "word of exhortation" (13:22, RSV), which suggests a sermon or oral homily (cf. Acts 13:15). Nonetheless, its conclusion is that of a conventional letter (Heb 13:22-25). Some have detected a gradual transition in the document from an essay to a more specifically epistolary form (cf. 2:1; 4:1; 13:22-25). The evidence thus suggests that the author may have cast the original homiletic "word of exhortation" into letter form when the need to communicate in writing with his Christian friends became urgent.

PREVIEW
• Author
• Background
• Date
• Origin and Destination
• Purpose
• Content

Author Who wrote the book is not directly stated in the letter. Since the late second century, various authorities have linked the document with the apostle Paul. Clement of Alexandria (d. 220) theorized that Paul wrote the letter in Hebrew for Jews and that Luke translated it into Greek. However, this suggestion has not been widely received by modern scholars. Clement's pupil Origen (d. 254) stated more generally that the thoughts of the letter are Pauline but that the style is unlike that of the known writings of the apostle. Other early authorities, such as Jerome (d. 419) and Augustine (d. 430), persuaded that canonicity demanded apostolic authorship, likewise affirmed that Paul was the author.

Yet a number of factors argue against the Pauline authorship of Hebrews. The anonymity of the letter is contrary to the consistent pattern of Paul's introduction in the opening salutation of his letters. Moreover, Hebrews 2:3 indicates the writer was discipled by eyewitnesses of the Lord. Yet Paul insists that his knowledge of Christ was gained from a firsthand encounter with the risen Christ (cf. Gal 1:12). F. F. Bruce evaluates the authorship of Hebrews as follows: "We may say with certainty that the thought of the epistle is not Paul's, the language is not Paul's, and the technique of OT quotations is not Paul's."

Early Christian tradition suggests that Barnabas may have written Hebrews. According to Tertullian (d. 220), many early authorities believed that Barnabas was responsible for the letter. Acts 4:36 (ASV) speaks of him as a "son of exhortation" (cf. Heb 13:22). Furthermore, as a Levite, Barnabas would have been familiar with the Jewish sacrificial ritual so prominent in the letter.

Luther was the first to suggest that Hebrews may have been penned by Apollos, "an excellent man of learning, who had been a disciple of the apostles and learned much from them, and who was very well versed in Scripture." As a native of Alexandria (Acts 18:24), Apollos would have been familiar with the typological interpretation evident in Hebrews. Clearly Apollos was the sort of man who was qualified to write Hebrews.

Other names have been suggested as possible authors. Calvin surmised that either Luke or Clement of Rome was responsible for the letter. It is noted that the Greek of Hebrews resembles the language and style of the third Gospel and Acts. Others theorize that Hebrews may have been written by Silas, a Jewish Christian from Jerusalem who would have been thoroughly familiar with the Levitical ritual. Silas is described as one of "the church leaders" (Acts 15:22). He was a coworker with Paul in

Ancient Papyrus Manuscript of the Book of Hebrews
Hebrews 1:7–2:3, from Chester Beatty Papyrus Manuscript II, late second century—P46

the gentile mission, and apparently was known in Rome as well as in Jerusalem (1 Pt 5:12-13).

In conclusion, it is probable that the author of Hebrews was a second-generation Jewish Christian, a master of classical Greek whose Bible was the Septuagint, conversant with first-century Alexandrian philosophy, and a creative apologist for the Christian faith. As to the identity of that author, we can affirm no more than

Origin in the third century: "But as to who actually wrote the Letter, God alone knows."

Background The very early title of the letter, "To Hebrews," suggests that the book concerns Jewish Christians living in the Dispersion. The letter itself offers a few hints of the historical circumstances surrounding its composition. Not long after becoming Christians, the readers of the letter were exposed to severe persecution (Heb 10:32-36). During their trial, the new believers endured imprisonment, confiscation of personal property, and public ridicule. Yet the persecution had not been fatal; they had not yet been called upon to lay down their lives in martyrdom (12:4). Amid the excitement of their newfound faith in Christ, they had demonstrated practical concern and love by ministering to fellow believers in need (6:10) and comforting others who had been harassed for their faith (10:34).

But since the time of those earlier trials, the readers had made little progress in Christian maturity (5:11-13). Moreover, in the face of a new wave of persecution, and despondent over an apparent delay in the Lord's coming, the believers had begun to waver and abandon hope. Indeed, they threatened to renounce Jesus Christ and to revert back to the security of the Jewish religion that enjoyed the protection of Roman law.

Thus we read that because of the strange, new teachings of certain Judaizers who sought to draw them back to their former religion (13:9), the wavering believers had neglected to assemble together (10:25) and had lost confidence in their spiritual leaders (13:17). Faced with the possibility that these Jewish Christians might abandon their faith altogether, the writer sternly warns them of the tragic consequences of renouncing the Son (6:4-6; 10:26-31; 13:12-19) and urges them to renew their commitment to Christ, God's foremost and final revelation.

Date Lacking firm information as to the author and recipients of the letter, no certainty exists as to the date of the writing. We have noted that the author of Hebrews, and probably his readers as well, had been discipled by those who were personally acquainted with Jesus (2:3). Further evidence in the letter suggests that Paul probably was not alive. Timothy, Paul's younger associate, was still living (13:23).

The absence of any mention in Hebrews of the destruction of the Jerusalem temple is significant for dating the letter. In terms of his argument that the old covenant had passed away and the legal priesthood had been superseded, the writer would scarcely have omitted mention of the temple's destruction had he written the letter later than AD 70. Hebrews 9:6-10 and 10:1-4, 11-14 plainly suggest that the Jewish sacrifices were still being offered. Hence, it may be supposed with some degree of certainty that the letter was written prior to AD 70. If it was written after Paul's death, that would put it after AD 67, the traditional date of his execution. Thus, Hebrews may have been written in the period AD 67–70.

Origin and Destination The place from which Hebrews was written is also uncertain. Some manuscripts of the letter bear the subscription "written from Rome" or "written from Italy." Such notations are educated deductions drawn from the statement "The Christians from Italy send you their greetings" (13:24). Most probably this indicates that the writer is extending greetings to a church in Italy on behalf of Italian Christians associated with him in another land, possibly Asia. Nevertheless, we cannot locate the point of origin with any certainty.

It has been suggested that the letter was written to a group of Jewish converts to Christianity. Yet the precise community to which it was sent is a matter of debate. Opinions vary from Judea to Spain. Tradition has it that Hebrews was directed to Jewish Christians living in Palestine. But against a Palestinian destination it may be argued: (1) the readers had had no personal contact with Jesus (2:3), an unlikely event for mid-first-century residents of Palestine; (2) the statement in 12:4 that his readers had not yet given their lives could hardly be said of Palestinian Christians of the period; (3) the generosity of the believers (10:34; 13:16) was inconsistent with the poverty of the Jerusalem church; and (4) the general tone of the letter is Hellenistic rather than rabbinical.

Other proposals for the destination of Hebrews include (1) Caesarea, on the supposition of Lukan authorship; (2) Syrian Antioch or Cyprus, assuming Barnabas wrote the letter; (3) Ephesus, in the light of the conversion of many Jews during Paul's ministry in that city; (4) Colosse, noting certain similarities between the Colossian heresy and the false beliefs of the "Hebrews"; and (5) Alexandria, because of the apparent influence of the philosopher Philo Judaeus in the letter.

The thesis that Hebrews was directed to a group of Jewish Christians in Rome has found favor with a number of scholars. Arguments in support of a Roman destination include the following facts: (1) The letter was first known in Rome no later than AD 96. (2) Romans 11:13, 18 suggests that the church at Rome consisted of a Jewish-Christian minority. (3) References to persecution and suffering endured by the readers (Heb 10:32-33; 12:4) are consistent with known repressive measures exacted by the Roman authorities. (4) There is a good possibility that saints who "come from Italy" would convey greetings to their brethren in Rome. (5) The Jewish community in Rome preserved certain features of nonconformist or sectarian Judaism that would explain several notable similarities between the theology and praxis of the Qumran community and that expressed in Hebrews.

It is likely that the letter was addressed to a small subgroup within a local church. The exhortation in 5:12 (RSV)—"by this time you ought to be teachers"—hardly would have been relevant to an entire congregation. Hebrews 13:7, 24 lends further support to the theory that the letter was sent to a small group, perhaps to a "house church" within a larger assembly.

Tentatively, one might conclude that the addressees were converts from Judaism who dwelt in the Dispersion. Hence they were familiar with OT Judaism and were acquainted with the religious philosophy of the Greek world. Possibly the readers comprised a house fellowship that tended to disassociate itself from the parent group (10:25). The existence of such house churches in Rome is confirmed by Romans 16:5, 14-15.

Purpose In response to the threat that his Jewish-Christian friends might renounce Christianity and revert to Judaism, the writer by a "word of exhortation" (13:22) communicated to them the finality of the Christian revelation. He sought also to inform his despondent, vacillating readers that Christ, the object of God's final revelation, is vastly superior to the greatest of Judaism's heroes. The author, in addition, affirmed the heavenly and eternal character of the salvation secured by Christ. Whereas the legal sacrificial system was powerless to effect the remission of sin, Christ the eternal High Priest "is able, once and forever, to save everyone who comes to God through him" (7:25, NLT).

In short, the writer commended to his readers the need for patient endurance amid the persecution and sufferings to which the heirs of eternal salvation are inevitably exposed. Just as Jesus, the forerunner of our faith, suffered and patiently endured in anticipation of eternal reward, so ought harassed, oppressed believers "take a new grip with your tired hands and stand firm on your shaky legs" (12:12, NLT) in anticipation of their reception in that eternal "kingdom that cannot be destroyed" (12:28, NLT).

The author's final purpose for writing was to proclaim the fearful judgment that awaits those who repudiate Jesus Christ. Since "our God is a consuming fire" (12:29, NLT), "what makes us think that we can escape if we are indifferent to this great salvation" (2:3, NLT)?

Content Next to Romans, Hebrews is the most doctrinal book in the NT. The writer develops a series of weighty arguments to demonstrate the superiority of the gospel of Christ to the religion of Judaism. Since Jesus is final both as to his person and his work, Christianity is the ultimate and normative faith. The book's particularism runs counter to the spirit of the modern world.

The Superiority of the Son to Former Revelation
(1:1-4) The writer acknowledges that God revealed himself to the prophets of old in many ways—through dreams, visions, audible speech, and mighty acts. But "in these last days" (the advent of the end times, cf. 9:26) God spoke finally and definitively through his own Son (1:2). Central to the argument is the fact that in one way or another the prophets received an eternal word from God. Yet given the intimate relation of the Son to the Father, God's latest revelation has come forth from the very depths of his own being.

Identification of the Son as the pinnacle of divine revelation leads to a concise but profound statement of Christ's person and his cosmic work. The Son reflects the glory of God in that the sum of the divine attributes brilliantly shine through his person. Moreover, he bears the very image and stamp of God's nature (1:3), as the wax bears the impress of the seal. Jesus as God's final word of revelation is truly the divine and eternal Son of God. Christ's excellence is further displayed in the fact that he is the mighty agent through whom the universe was created (v 2) and by whom the cosmic order is sustained (v 3). In the moral realm he has wrought the purification of sins and now sits enthroned on God's right hand (cf. 8:1). God's pleasure toward the Son is seen in that he has appointed Christ heir and head of all (1:2). His name is surpassed by none save God the Father (v 4).

The Superiority of the Son to Angels (1:5–2:18)
Angels enjoyed an exalted status in biblical and postbiblical Judaism. Traditionally the Jews believed that angels praised God upon his throne, mediated God's revelation to men, attended to God's will, and gave succor to the people of God. Angels were far superior to men in power and knowledge. According to the Jewish Apocrypha, angels ruled the stars and were responsible for the rise and fall of civilizations. In Qumran thought, angelic beings would engage in a final cosmic struggle with Belial and the forces of evil at the end of the age.

Against this background the writer of Hebrews argues that the Son is vastly superior to the angels. To prove his point, the author assembles a string of well-known OT texts and applies them directly to the Son. God never said of any angel, "Today I have become your Father" (Ps 2:7, NLT). Yet just such a claim was made on behalf of the Son (Heb 1:5). When the Son incarnated himself in the world, he received the obedient worship of angels (v 6). His is the sovereignty and the eternality and the majesty at God's right hand (vv 8, 11-12). By contrast, angels are "only servants" (v 14) that rank below the Son in dignity and might.

In Hebrews 2:1-4 the writer parenthetically warns his wavering congregation of the danger of drifting away from the truth of God. If disobedience to the law mediated by angels resulted in stern punishment, how much more severe would be God's judgment on those who trampled under foot the revelation delivered by the Son? If God's saving grace in Christ is neglected, retribution will surely follow (2:3).

The mention of angels turns the writer's mind to Jesus' humiliation and exaltation (2:5-18). Psalm 8, a song about the smallness and yet the significance of man, is applied to the experience of Jesus. In assuming human flesh and blood, Jesus was made "for a little while . . . lower than the angels" (Heb 2:7, NLT). But subsequent to the completion of his earthly work, he was elevated above the angels and crowned with the glory and honor of heaven (v 9). The theological implications of Christ's descent and ascent are carefully spelled out: Christ descended to earth (1) to bring many children to glory (v 10), (2) to destroy the devil (v 14), (3) to deliver his people from the bondage of death (v 15), and (4) to make an offering on the cross for the sins of the people (v 17). He ascended to heaven (1) to intercede on our behalf as a faithful High Priest (v 17), and (2) to succor those who are sorely tempted (v 18). The perfect summary of Christ's person and work is given in Hebrews 2:9: "What we do see is Jesus, who 'for a little while was made lower than the angels' and now is 'crowned with glory and honor' because he suffered death for us. Yes, by God's grace, Jesus tasted death for everyone in all the world" (NLT).

The Superiority of the Son to Moses and Joshua
(3:1–4:13) Jewish Christians contemplating reversion to Judaism surely believed that Moses was one of the greatest figures in Israel's history. So esteemed was the one who led Israel out of Egypt through the wilderness and who gave them the Law that there was no one in Israel's history so honored as Moses. Yet the author of Hebrews argues that Moses, though faithful to his calling, was but a servant in the house of God. Jesus, by contrast, was not a servant but a Son; he was not a mere dweller in the house but the very builder of the structure. Jesus, therefore, far transcends the revered figure of Moses.

Practical implications are drawn from Jesus' superiority to Moses. From Psalm 95:7-11 the writer rehearses the tragic experience of Israel under Moses during the desert wanderings (Heb 3:7-19). Throughout the 40-year wilderness experience the people hardened their hearts and rebelled against God. In turn God was provoked by their stubbornness and swore that those who sinned would never enter the rest he was going to provide (vv 10-11, 18). The writer thus argues that if disobedience to God under Moses had serious consequences, forsaking Christ will be much more perilous. Hence the wavering Christians are urged to watch lest due to an evil, unbelieving heart they should fall away from the living God (v 12). Nothing short of steadfast persistence will lead to the attainment of the heavenly goal (v 14).

Joshua, likewise, was regarded as a great leader of Israel. Yet because of disobedience, the people under Joshua's leadership failed to enter the rest that God had planned. That rest spoken of corresponds to the Sabbath rest of God (4:3-4), and is a concept closely related to salvation. It is a spiritual reality that is achieved by turning from our own empty works and trusting in the finished work of Christ (v 10). The author reminds the readers that "there is a special rest [a Sabbath rest] still waiting for the people of God" (v 9, NLT), one that only Christ can provide. Christians not only benefit from this Sabbath rest in the present age but anticipate its full realization in the age to come. One of the chief means of ensuring entry into the Sabbath rest of salvation is the Word of God (v 12). The living and powerful Word penetrates the innermost depths of the soul, reveals our impoverished condition, and strengthens the trusting heart.

The Superiority of the Priesthood of the Son
(4:14–7:28) Almost half of Hebrews is devoted to the priesthood of Jesus Christ. The writer goes to great lengths to demonstrate that the revered Aaronic priestly system has been superseded by the High Priest "in the line of Melchizedek" (5:6; 6:20; 7:11). This central theme had been anticipated earlier when Christ was referred to as "our merciful and faithful High Priest before God" who has made atonement for sins (2:17, NLT).

Hebrews makes the claim that Jesus' priesthood is the ultimate ground of the believers' confidence (4:14-16). On three counts Jesus surpasses the old legal priestly order. First, he is an *exalted* high priest (v 14). The Jewish high priest climbed the mount to enter the temple sanctuary. But Jesus, our great high priest, has ascended to heaven itself and entered the sanctuary on high. He ministers in no earthly tabernacle but in the very presence of God. Second, Jesus is an *empathetic* high priest (v 15a). Fully God and fully man, Jesus suffers along with his people in their trials and afflictions. From heaven's perspective he knows fully what his people are called upon to endure. He "feels" our hurts, and he does so perfectly. Finally, Jesus is a *sinless* high priest (v 15b). Day in and day out (7:27), year in and year out, the Levitical priests were required to bring sacrifices for their own sins. Yet Jesus had no sin that needed cleansing, for "he is holy and blameless, unstained by sin" (v 26, NLT). In view of Jesus' priestly perfections, sorely tempted Christians are urged to come to the throne of grace to receive mercy and find grace to help in time of need (4:16).

For those not convinced that Jesus was indeed a legitimate priest, two prerequisites for priesthood are detailed. First, if the high priest is to represent humanity before God, he must be taken from among men (5:1-2). And second, he must be called by God to high priestly office, as was Aaron (v 4). Christ has fully satisfied these qualifications. From Psalms 2:7 and 110:4 it is shown that Jesus did not take this office upon himself but was appointed by God (Heb 5:5-6). Moreover, from the obedience that he had to learn (v 8) and from the agony of the Gethsemane experience (v 7) it is clear that Jesus was in every way a man. Nevertheless, Hebrews makes it perfectly clear that Jesus was not a priest after the order of Aaron but a high priest in the line of Melchizedek (v 10).

After introducing the theme of Christ as a Melchizedekian high priest, the writer recalls that his readers were not ready for such advanced teaching. Although not new converts (5:12), his friends had remained spiritually immature and sluggish. Hence the writer issues the challenge to press on to Christian maturity, to be ready for the solid food of advanced teaching.

In his digression the writer warns not only against spiritual immaturity but also against "apostasy." The question now arises whether the author's apostasy teaching in Hebrews 6:4-8 and 10:26-31 contradicts the NT doctrine of the perseverance of the saints. Undoubtedly it does not. Some authorities hold that those addressed were not true Christians, hence the issue is not one of apostasy. It is possible, like Judas Iscariot or Simon Magus (Acts 8:9-24), to possess considerable knowledge

of the gospel and fall short of personal commitment. But the writer makes it quite clear that in the case of his addressees he is persuaded otherwise (Heb 6:9). The most reasonable view is that in these two hortatory passages the writer advances a hypothetical argument warning his friends of the utter seriousness of reverting back to Judaism. That is, if a falling away were to occur, renewal would be impossible unless Christ were to die a second time. The writer sums up the point of these difficult passages with the words "It is a terrible thing to fall into the hands of the living God" (10:31, NLT). Nevertheless, followers of Christ may confidently lay hold of God's promises, confirmed by solemn oath, to see them through their trials (6:13-18). God may be trusted to hold the believer fast.

Hebrews 7 contains an intricate argument for the superiority of Christ's priesthood over the old legal order. Melchizedek, the ancient priest-king of Salem (Gn 14:18-20), is regarded as a primordial type of Christ. He is "king of righteousness" and "king of peace" (Heb 7:2). The solemn priest from Salem has figuratively what Christ possesses actually: neither mother nor father, neither beginning nor end of life (v 3). Melchizedek is shown to be superior to Abraham on three counts: (1) Melchizedek blessed the patriarch (vv 1, 7); (2) he accepted tithes from Abraham (vv 2-6); and (3) Melchizedek lives on since the OT nowhere mentions his death (v 8). It follows that since Levi was in the loins of Abraham as seed (v 10), Melchizedek is superior to the Levitical priests. And inasmuch as Christ is a priest in the likeness of Melchizedek (v 15), it follows that the Son of God is more excellent than the old legal priesthood.

The result is that the old Levitical priesthood has been superseded by the priesthood of Christ. The demise of the old order was inevitable, for its repetitive animal sacrifices could never effect spiritual perfection (7:11). It was a system characterized by weakness and uselessness (v 18). By contrast, Christ's priesthood is indestructible, eternal, uninterrupted, efficacious, final, and perfect (vv 16, 21, 24-27). Forgiveness and reconciliation is possible only through Christ, our great High Priest.

The Superiority of the Priestly Work of the Son
(8:1–10:39) Since Christ's priestly office far excels the old order, it follows that his priestly ministration is superior to all that has gone before. The theme of Christ as high priest in a better sanctuary is introduced (8:1-5). The writer utilizes Plato's distinction between the ideal form in heaven and the imperfect copy on earth to argue that the Levitical sanctuary and sacrifices are mere shadows of the heavenly realities: (1) Christ ministers in the true tent that is the heavenly sanctuary (vv 2, 5); (2) he discharges his high priestly service in the very presence of the Father, which results in a far more effective ministry (vv 1, 6); and (3) his oblation on the cross was the ultimate sacrifice (v 3). How unreasonable it is that his Christian readers should go back to the old Jewish priestly system!

Christ is the minister of a new and better covenant (8:6-13). The old covenant established by God with the nation's fathers was not to be despised; nevertheless, it had become ineffectual and obsolete (v 13). Indeed, the prophet Jeremiah (Jer 31:31-34) foresaw the new covenant that God would inaugurate with his people. This new covenant sealed by Christ involves (1) the immediate work of the Holy Spirit on the mind and heart (Heb 8:10); (2) a personal and intimate knowledge of God (v 11); and (3) the full absolution of sins (v 12). This new and better covenant has been established on the work of Christ, the great High Priest.

Chapter 9 gives a detailed comparison of the efficacy of priestly service under the old and new covenants. The Levitical priests ministered in a material sanctuary on earth (vv 1-5). Features of the tabernacle and its furnishings are described to highlight their obsolescence. More important, however, is the character of the sacrificial ritual conducted in the earthly sanctuary. The Jewish priests in their daily service were not permitted to enter the Holy of Holies, which contained the ark of the covenant and the mercy seat—the place of propitiation of sins (v 6). The high priest alone could enter the Holy of Holies, and then but once a year on the Day of Atonement, and only after sacrificing for his own sins (v 7). The inaccessibility of the Holy of Holies signified that access to the presence of God had not been opened. The presence of the curtain symbolized that the people had no way to the throne of God, the priests had no way, and the high priest had a limited way and only once a year. Moreover, the sacrifices brought by the Jewish priests could not purify the conscience but merely dealt with external ritual cleansing (vv 9-10). A truly effectual sacrifice must await "the time of reformation" (v 10).

Christ's priestly ministration is shown to be far more efficacious. First, the Christian's High Priest has brought a better sacrifice (9:11-14), and here we arrive at the heart of the message of Hebrews. Employing the imagery of the tabernacle, the author demonstrates that Christ our High Priest has accomplished what the Jewish priests failed to do. He entered the heavenly Holy of Holies, not repeatedly, but *once* for all, thereby effecting a completed redemption (v 12). Christ brought to the altar, not the blood of bulls and goats, but his own life's blood. The Lord did not merely lay down a material body, but he presented himself to God through the eternal Spirit (v 14). Christ's better sacrifice thus goes beyond cleansing of the flesh to the purification of the defiled conscience.

Second, Christ through his death has instituted a better covenant (9:15-23). The teaching of Hebrews 8:6-13 is developed further. The old covenant was sealed with the blood of calves and goats (9:19). But the new covenant was ratified with the blood of Christ, God's own Son. The new covenant thus could accomplish what the old covenant merely foreshadowed—forgiveness and cleansing of sins (v 22).

Third, Christ ministers in a better tabernacle (9:24-28). Our Lord entered, not into a merely earthly sanctuary, but into the holy place of heaven, there to represent us (v 24). Access to the throne is not limited to one day per year, for he is continually in the presence of the Father. Nor is it necessary that repeated sacrifices be made. Christ's single sacrifice on the cross has conquered sin once and for all (v 26). In sum, as regards the sanctuary, the covenant, and the sacrifices, the Christian's High Priest is vastly superior to the old Jewish order.

In order to drive home these crucial points, the writer in chapter 10 expands on the theme of the absolute finality of Christ's high priestly work. The earlier argument concerning the futile character of the Levitical sacrifices (9:6-14) is repeated for emphasis (10:1-4). The Mosaic ceremonial legislation called for repetitive sacrifices, which could never perfect the worshiper (v 1). Instead of purifying one's life, they served only as a yearly reminder of sin (v 3) until Christ should come.

The writer discovers in Psalm 40:6-8 a prediction that the eternal Christ would become man for the purpose of offering himself as the ultimate sacrifice for sin (Heb 10:5-10). Once again the sanctifying power of Christ's single self-oblation is emphasized (v 10). The vivid contrast is again drawn between the ineffective ministry of the Jewish priests who stand during the daily ritual

(v 11), and the effectual single sacrifice of Christ, who is now seated at the right hand of God (v 12). Since Jesus "by that one offering . . . perfected forever all those whom he is making holy" (v 14, NLT), nothing can be added to what the seated Sovereign has accomplished (v 18).

In view of the manifest superiority of Christ's priestly office and work, the struggling Christians are exhorted to appropriate the means of grace at their disposal (10:19-39). In the midst of trials and persecution they should remember that Christ has effectively opened the way to God (vv 19-20). They are summoned to come to God in faith with hearts cleansed by Christ's sacrifice (v 22). Those tempted to revert to legal religion should hold fast and support one another in love (vv 23-24). The means of grace afforded by corporate worship should not be neglected (v 25). In short, the wavering Jewish Christians are summoned to renewed endurance and fidelity to their Lord (vv 26-31). What God has promised to his people he will surely make good.

The Superiority of the Life of Faith (11:1–12:29) The discussion of faith and endurance as the solution to despondency (10:36-38) prompts a fuller consideration of the faith theme. Faith is a prominent concept in the book of Hebrews, as attested by the fact that the word occurs some 35 times in the letter. The Pauline idea of faith as the means of legal justification is adapted to the particular circumstances of the threatened Jewish Christians. The concept of faith is broader in this book than the strictly saving faith discussed by Paul, in that it leads to spiritual salvation (11:39-40). Faith is the power by which heaven's unseen realities are laid hold of to satisfy the soul. Faith enables the Christian disciple to view the world and interpret the flow of history from the divine perspective. Faith is the means of victory over the world of sin and woe. Through faith the believer approaches the throne of grace (4:16) with the confidence and assurance that God will enable him to overcome.

The victory faith affords is amply illustrated from the history of God's OT people. Abel, Enoch, and Noah in the primal history; Abraham, the father of faith; Moses, the leader of the young nation; and many valiant prophets and martyrs serve as living memorials to faith's overcoming power. And yet God has something better in store for his sanctified people, the church (11:40): the reality of the living Christ.

Yet the greatest model of steadfast endurance in suffering is Jesus, "the Originator and Perfecter of our faith" (12:2, NLT mg). When surrounded with trials, the Christian needs to recall Christ, who in anticipation of the heavenly crown endured the cross and its shame. The Christian's trials are trivial compared with what Jesus Christ was called upon to suffer (v 3). Moreover, for the people of God, suffering and persecution prove to be disguised blessings. The rod of discipline confirms our status as children of the living God (vv 5-10). But beyond this, the sovereign God is able to transform the Christian's suffering into inestimable blessing (v 11). Hence the wavering saints should strive for spiritual wholeness and maturity, taking care lest they be overtaken by bitterness and resentment (v 15).

Final Exhortations and Benediction (13:1-25) The writer in his closing words challenges his Christian friends to be faithful to the tasks that lie at hand. They are to show continued love to the brethren, to extend hospitality to strangers, to uphold the sanctity of marriage, to be content with what they now possess, and to be obedient to their spiritual leaders (13:1-7).

The readers are warned against the trickery of the Judaizers, who would lead them astray from Jesus Christ, the one who remains "the same yesterday, today, and forever" (13:8). Spiritual determination is strengthened by recalling the example of Christ, who "suffered outside the city gates" for their salvation (v 12). As the people of God, they are challenged to follow Christ "outside the camp," bearing abuse for him (v 13). Patient endurance is possible when the Christian realizes that he has no enduring city here (v 14). His goal is the heavenly Jerusalem, the eternal city of God.

The anonymous letter to the unknown "Hebrews" closes with a glorious benediction. The Christian's God is described as the great "God of peace" (13:20), and Jesus is "the great Shepherd of the sheep," who established a new and eternal covenant and then rose triumphant from the dead. And the promise is made to the trusting soul that the triune God would "equip you with all you need for doing his will" (v 21, NLT).

The letter to the Hebrews is rich in doctrinal teaching. It discloses more about the historical Jesus than any other NT letter. It alone explains the atoning work of Christ under the rubric of the Melchizedekian priest. The letter's discussion of repentance, justification, sanctification, and perseverance makes it a mine of salvation teaching. Its explication of old and new covenants, impending judgment, and the world to come make a significant contribution to Christian theology. And the letter's teaching on faith, endurance, and the practical Christian combine to make Hebrews one of the most important documents God has given to the church.

HEBRON (Person)

1. Third of Kohath's four sons, Hebron was a descendant of Levi (Ex 6:18; Nm 3:19; 1 Chr 6:2, 18; 23:12). Hebron's sons were Jeriah, Amariah, Jahaziel, and Jekameam (1 Chr 23:19). Hebron's descendants were called the Hebronites. They are mentioned in a census taken in the plains of Moab (Nm 26:58). The Hebronites are mentioned in connection with the transfer of the ark to Jerusalem in David's time (1 Chr 15:9; 26:23, 30-31).

2. Mareshah's son and Korah's father (1 Chr 2:42-43).

Hebron: Burial Site for the Patriarchs This building commemorates the traditional site of the cave of Mamre in Hebron, burial location for Abraham, Isaac, and Jacob.

HEBRON (Place)

1. City of antiquity still standing today. It was built on the southern end of the highlands that run north to south through the length of Palestine. In patriarchal times it was known as Kiriath-arba (Gn 23:2) and stood on the hill known as El Arbain. The modern city straddles both ridges of the mountain range.

Hebron is situated 25 miles (40 kilometers) southwest of Jerusalem and less than two miles (3.2 kilometers) from Mamre, where Abraham spent much of his life. It is 3,000 feet (914 meters) above sea level and marks the southern end of the Judean highlands. From this elevation the land slopes down rapidly to the east, but gradually to the west and south. The soil is relatively fertile, and a variety of fruits (apples, plums, figs, pomegranates, apricots), nuts, and vegetables are grown easily. To the south is the Negev, where the grazing land is excellent. A large number of springs and wells dot the landscape and assure residents of an abundance of water.

In OT times Hebron included Mamre, the place where Abraham built an altar to the Lord after parting from Lot (Gn 13:18). It was here, too, that he learned of the capture of his nephew Lot (14:12-16); and here that, years later, he entertained three angels and was told of the judgment soon to fall on Sodom and Gomorrah (ch 18).

Sarah died in Hebron, and Abraham purchased the cave of Machpelah from Ephron the Hittite (Gn 23:8-9, 17; 25:9-10; 49:29-32; 50:12-13) in which to bury her. This cave is now within the walls of the modern city, and the famous mosque of Haram el-Khalil was built over it.

At the time of the exodus of the Israelites from Egypt, spies were sent into the land. They began in the south and traversed the central highlands of Palestine from Kadesh-barnea through Hebron to Rehob (Nm 13:17-21). On their return they brought back evidence of the productivity of the land (vv 23-24). From Numbers 13:33 we know that giants ("sons of Anak") lived in Hebron. The sight of these men filled ten of the spies with fear. Only Caleb and Joshua proved equal to the occasion. Because of their faith, they were promised a possession in the land, and Caleb was given Hebron (Jos 14:9, 13). The unfaithful spies died in a plague in the presence of the Lord (Nm 14:36-37).

During the period of the judges, Hebron is mentioned in connection with Samson. When trapped inside the city of Gaza, he carried off the gates and left them at Hebron (Jgs 16:3). Following the death of Saul, the first king of Israel, David was crowned king of the tribes of Judah and Benjamin in Hebron (2 Sm 2:1). He made this city his capital, for it was more centrally located than Benjamin, and its position at the southern end of the mountain range removed it as far as possible from the 10 northern tribes that followed Ishbosheth, the son of Saul. It was far enough from the Philistines to the west and the Amalekites to the south to avoid notice, and it was also easily defensible. Hebron also lay at the junction of several important trade routes, and this ensured its prominence. Later, however, when David was made king over all Israel, he moved his capital to Jerusalem—an act that must have displeased the people of Hebron.

When Absalom wished to obtain support for his claim to the throne, he initiated his revolt from Hebron (2 Sm 15:7-12). Following the death of Solomon, David's son, the kingdom was divided. Rehoboam, fearing an attack by the Egyptians on his southern border, fortified Hebron (2 Chr 11:1-12). From this time onward the city disappears from the OT record.

2. KJV translation of the town of Ebron, in Joshua 19:28. *See* Ebron.

HEBRONITE Descendant of Hebron from Levi's tribe (Nm 3:27; 26:58; 1 Chr 26:23, 30-31). *See* Hebron (Person) #1.

HEDGEHOG* Small, insect-eating mammal with a coat of short spines and similar to the porcupine (Is 14:23; Zep 2:14). *See* Animals (Porcupine).

HEGAI, HEGE* Chamberlain of Ahasuerus and keeper of his harem when Esther was chosen as queen (Est 2:3).

HEGEMONIDES Principal Syrian officer appointed by Antiochus, king of Syria, to govern the territory from Ptolemais to Gerar (2 Macc 13:24).

HEGLAM* Alternate name for Gera, Bela's son, in 1 Chronicles 8:7. *See* Gera #4.

HEIFER Young cow. *See* Animals (Cattle).

HEIR One who inherits something or who is entitled to a future inheritance; the one who receives the property of a deceased person, particularly on the basis of law and usually by means of a will. In both the OT and NT, the Hebrew and the Greek words encompass these ideas.

In Genesis 15, after God had reiterated his special promise to Abraham, Abraham wondered how the fulfillment of the promise might occur. At the time, only his steward, Eliezer of Damascus, was "the son of his house," that is, the one of his large household who would inherit. There was no natural-born son of Abraham within the family (see Gn 15:3-4). Without a son in patriarchal times, a man's chief steward could be his heir as a substitute. Later, after the birth of Ishmael (Abraham's son by Hagar, Sarah's maidservant) and of Isaac (his son by Sarah, his wife), trouble erupted between the women, and Sarah demanded that Abraham send Hagar and her son away, because Sarah did not want Ishmael to be an heir with her own son, Isaac (Gn 21:10).

A wise woman, at Joab's instigation, told David a story about herself and her two sons. She said that one son killed the other, and that her family now wanted to kill the remaining son for the murder. If this happened, she claimed, the heir of her deceased husband would be destroyed and the family would be left with no inheritance (2 Sm 14:7).

Another biblical illustration of this normal use of the word "heir" is seen in a parable told by Jesus. The workers in the vineyard, who saw the son of their master coming, said among themselves, "This is the heir; come, let us kill him and have his inheritance" (Mt 21:33-43, RSV; cf. Mk 12:7; Lk 20:14).

In a number of references in the NT, the word "heir" is used to refer to the believer in Christ, who has an inheritance coming because of being a child of God the Father and consequently a joint heir with Christ (Rom 8:16-17). The inheritance of salvation is variously referred to in different sections of the NT. In Hebrews 6:17, Christians are called "heirs of the promise." This promise occurred when God said to Abraham, "I will certainly bless you richly, and I will multiply your descendants into countless millions" (Heb 6:14, NLT). In Hebrews 11:7, Noah is described as "an heir of the righteousness which comes by faith" (RSV). In James 2:5, the poor in the world who are rich in faith are said to be "heirs of the kingdom which he has promised to those who love him" (RSV). Paul writes that those who are jus-

tified by God's grace are made heirs according to the hope of eternal life (Ti 3:7).

In Hebrews 1:2, the word "heir" is used with a singular reference to God's Son, who is said to have been appointed "heir of all things" by his Father. Here is an instance where someone has been designated to receive an inheritance but will actually enter into full possession of it much later.

In biblical times the right of primogeniture—that is, the right of the eldest son in the family to be the primary heir in the household—prevailed. In OT times, the firstborn son possessed the birthright, which included inheriting a double portion of his father's possessions and headship of the family (Dt 21:15-17). The other sons shared the remainder equally. If there were no sons to inherit, the daughters became the heirs (Nm 27:8; 36:1-12), although there was a stipulation that the daughters could not marry outside their tribe. This was to preserve the tribal territory intact. If there were no daughters, then the dead man's brothers inherited; if no brothers, then his uncles; and if no uncles, then the nearest relative (27:9-11). Because the matter of tribal possession was so important, it is easy to understand why there was such a concern for genealogical records among the Hebrew people.

See also Firstborn; Inheritance; Birthright.

HELAH One of Ashhur's wives who bore him Zereth, Izhar, and Ethnan from Judah's tribe (1 Chr 4:5-7).

HELAM Place east of the Jordan where David defeated the armies of Hadadezer, king of Syria (2 Sm 10:16-17).

HELBAH One of the Canaanite strongholds that was not conquered by the tribe of Asher after they took possession of the land (Jgs 1:31).

HELBON District north of Damascus, which produced choice wine (Ez 27:18); perhaps identifiable with modern Halbun, where the vine is still cultivated.

HELDAI

1. Baanah's son, described as a Netophathite in the line of Othniel. He appears first as one of David's mighty men (2 Sm 23:29; 1 Chr 11:30, "Heled"). In 1 Chronicles 27:15, he is called a commander of an army division of 24,000 that served during the 12th month of the year.
2. One of the exiles returning from Babylon from whom the prophet Zechariah took gold and silver to make a crown for Joshua, the high priest (Zec 6:10).

HELEB* Alternative name for Heldai, Baanah's son, in 2 Samuel 23:29. *See* Heldai #1.

HELECH Term mentioned in Ezekiel's prophecy against the city of Tyre (Ez 27:11), perhaps referring to Cilicia or to mercenaries from Cilicia, which was southeast of Asia Minor. Assyrian texts indicate that Cilicia was once called Hilakku, but little is known about the people. They are first mentioned by Shalmaneser III, king of Assyria (854–824 BC), in his conquest of Asia Minor. Their history under the Assyrians was quite violent. Sargon, Sennacherib, and Esarhaddon had to put down revolts from the Hilakku. Later, they gave tribute to Ashurbanipal.

HELED Alternate name for Heldai, Baanah's son, in 1 Chronicles 11:30. *See* Heldai #1.

HELEK, HELEKITE Gilead's son from Manasseh's tribe (Jos 17:2) and founder of the Helekite family (Nm 26:30).

HELEM

1. Member of Asher's tribe (1 Chr 7:35), called Hotham in verse 32.
2. KJV rendering for Heldai in Zechariah 6:14. *See* Heldai #2.

HELEPH Village on Naphtali's southern border (Jos 19:33), northeast of Mt Tabor. Its site may be modern Khirbet 'Arbathah.

HELEZ

1. One of David's valiant warriors, called a Paltite in 2 Samuel 23:26 and a Pelonite in 1 Chronicles 11:27. The former is probably correct and refers to a person from Bethpelet. Most scholars think he is the same man as the officer in charge of the seventh course during David's reign (1 Chr 27:10).
2. Jerahmeel's descendant from Judah's tribe (1 Chr 2:39).

HELI Ancestor of Joseph in Luke's genealogy of Christ (Lk 3:23). *See* Genealogy of Jesus Christ.

HELIODORUS There is an inscription in the temple of Apollo at Delos that indicates that Heliodorus was prominent in the court of the Seleucid king Seleucus IV Philopator, who reigned from 187 to 175 BC. In his *Syrian Wars* (45) Appian says that Heliodorus was a close friend of this king. According to 2 Maccabees, he is the object of divine vengeance because Seleucus IV sent him to Jerusalem to remove the temple treasury (2 Macc 3:7ff.). Heliodorus was arriving at the treasury when he was attacked and wounded by a horse with a rider wearing golden armor and two young men of surpassing strength and glorious beauty (vv 25-26). Heliodorus was deprived by this divine act of all hope of recovery (v 29). The Jewish high priest, Onias III, offered a sacrifice for the restoration of Heliodorus. When this occurred, the Syrian offered a sacrifice to the Lord, returned to his king, and gave witness of the miracles of the supreme God (v 36).

HELIOPOLIS Ancient Egyptian city famed as a center for worship of the sun god Re. Heliopolis ("city of the sun") was located in the Nile River delta region of Lower Egypt, a few miles northeast of modern Cairo. Heliopolis became important from about 2400 BC, with the emergence of Atum-Re as the cult deity. Many pharaohs embellished the city's temples and put up various public monuments, especially in the New Kingdom period (1570–1150 BC).

Since the temples contained the royal archives, the priests became the official historians of Egypt. Herodotus, a Greek historian of the fifth century BC, said the priests at Heliopolis were famous for their knowledge of Egyptian history. There were also training schools for priests and a medical school in the city.

Other Egyptian sun worship centers existed at various times, but Heliopolis maintained its popularity for some 2,000 years. Though the city was of little importance politically, it was of primary religious influence. Among Egyptian religious buildings, the temple of Re at Heliopolis was second in size only to the temple of Amon at Thebes.

In the OT, Heliopolis is called On. When Joseph was a member of the Egyptian official class, he married Asenath, the daughter of Potiphera the priest of On (Gn 41:45, 50; 46:20). The prophet Ezekiel warned of coming destruction in Egypt by the Babylonian king Nebuchadnezzar, citing Heliopolis (On) as one of the cities to be destroyed (Ez 30:17). In Amos 1:5, the RSV (mg) has an alternative rendering, "On," for "Valley of Aven," and the same reading in Ezekiel 30:17 for the NLT "Heliopolis." The prophet Jeremiah also predicted the destruction of the obelisks (sacred pillars) of Heliopolis (Jer 43:13, KJV "Beth-shemesh"). Isaiah 19:18 is probably also a reference to Heliopolis (see NLT).

The city lost its prominence in the fourth and third centuries BC, partly because of the library founded at Alexandria early in the third century BC. Alexandria replaced Heliopolis as the leading intellectual center in Egypt.

Little remains today from the ancient city of the sun, but an obelisk erected by Sesostris I (1971–1928 BC) can still be seen at the site of Heliopolis. Several obelisks from Heliopolis, erected by Thutmose III (1490–1436 BC), have been moved to various parts of the world in modern times.

HELKAI Head of Meraioth's priestly house in the time of Joiakim the high priest (Neh 12:15).

HELKATH First of 22 cities mentioned in the territory allotted to Asher's tribe for an inheritance (Jos 19:25). Helkath was one of four cities in Asher given to the Levitical Gershonite families (21:31). It is alternately spelled Hukok in 1 Chronicles 6:75. Its ancient site is perhaps located at the modern Tell el-Harbaj.

HELKATH-HAZZURIM* Area near the pool of Gibeon, where 12 champions from Joab's army and 12 from Abner's battled. All 24 died in the fight, each fighter killing his opponent (2 Sm 2:16). Some scholars think the name may mean "field of the crafty," that is, "field of ambush" or "field of the adversaries." The NLT renders it "the Field of Swords" (mg).

HELL Place of future punishment for the lost, unrepentant, wicked dead.

PREVIEW
• Definition and Description
• Biblical Terms
• The Justice of Eternal Punishment

Definition and Description Hell is the final destiny of unbelievers and is variously described by the figures of a furnace of fire, eternal fire, eternal punishment (Mt 13:42, 50; 25:41, 46); outer darkness, the place of weeping and torment (8:12); the lake of fire, the second death (Rv 21:8); a place for the devil and his demons (Mt 25:41). Evidently, those in hell experience everlasting separation from the Lord, never to see the glory of his power (2 Thes 1:9). Those who worshiped the beast will be subject to continuous torment (Rv 14:10-11).

Other expressions that indicate that the final state of the wicked is eternal are these: "burn with unquenchable fire" (Mt 3:12); "to the unquenchable fire . . . where their worm does not die, and the fire is not quenched" (Mk 9:43, 48); there is sin that "will not be forgiven, either in this age or in the age to come" (Mt 12:32, RSV). When Scripture is understood properly, there is no hint anywhere of the termination of the terrible state of unbelievers in hell. Their doom is unending; there is a solemn finality about their miserable condition. (It is significant that the most descriptive and conclusive utterances about hell come from the lips of Jesus.)

A summary of all Scripture that speaks of hell indicates that there is the loss and absence of all good, and the misery and torment of an evil conscience. The most terrifying aspect is the complete and deserved separation from God and from all that is pure, holy, and beautiful. In addition, there is the awareness of being under the wrath of God and of enduring the curse of a righteous sentence because of one's sins that were consciously and voluntarily committed.

Although the biblical descriptions of hell are stated in very physical and literal terms, the essential character of hell should not be conceived in or limited to designations such as the worm that devours, the stripes that are inflicted, the burning or being consumed by fire. This affirmation does not detract from the horror or the gravity of the situation in hell, because nothing could possibly be worse than separation from God and the torment of an evil conscience. Hell is hell for those who are there essentially because they are completely alienated from God, and wherever there is alienation from God, there is always estrangement from one's fellows. This is the worst possible punishment to which anyone could be subject: to be totally and irrevocably cut off from God and to be at enmity with all those who are around oneself. Another painful consequence of such a condition is to be at odds with oneself—torn apart from within by an accusing sense of guilt and shame. This condition is one of total conflict: with God, one's neighbors, and oneself. This is hell! If the descriptions of hell are figurative or symbolic, the conditions they represent are more intense and real than the figures of speech in which they are expressed.

Punishment for sin is a persistent teaching of the Bible. The doctrine of judgment is as extensive as the Canon itself. Typical of such passages are Genesis 2:17; 3:17-19; 4:13; Leviticus 26:27-33; Psalm 149:7; Isaiah 3:11; Ezekiel 14:10; Amos 1:2–2:16; Zechariah 14:19; Matthew 25:41, 46; Luke 16:23-24; Romans 2:5-12; Galatians 6:7-8; Hebrews 10:29-31; and Revelation 20:11-15.

Biblical Terms The Hebrew word "Sheol" in the OT is predominantly used for "the grave, the pit, the place of the departed dead" (Gn 37:35; Jb 7:9; 14:13; 17:13-16; Pss 6:5; 16:10; 55:15; Prv 9:18; Eccl 9:10; Is 14:11; 38:10-12, 18). There does not seem to be a very clear distinction in the OT between the final destiny of the good and the evil. They all alike go to the grave, to the world below, a world of gloom, weariness, darkness, decay, and forgetfulness, where one is remote from God (Jb 10:20-22; Ps 88:3-6), yet accessible to him (Jb 26:6; Ps 138:8; Am 9:2). It is a place characterized by silence (Pss 94:17; 115:17) and rest (Jb 3:17). Other texts, however, seem to suggest some aspect of consciousness, hope, and communication in Sheol (Jb 14:13-15; 19:25-27; Pss 16:10; 49:15; Is 14:9-10; Ez 32:21). A few texts seem to suggest the threat of divine judgment after death (Pss 9:17; 55:15). On the whole, Sheol was regarded with dismay and foreboding (Dt 32:22; Is 38:18).

It was not until the time of the postcanonical Jewish literature, the writings that were developed between the close of the OT and the beginning of NT times, that clear distinctions were made between the final destinies of the righteous and the unrighteous. The idea of separate divisions within Sheol for the good and the evil was developed. It is unmistakable that there was in Jewish thought, as reflected throughout the OT, a belief in a future and continued existence beyond death, however shadowy and indefinite the concept.

The Greek word "hades" in the NT is used very similarly to "Sheol" in the OT. It was, in fact, used by the translators of the Septuagint, the Greek version of the OT, for Sheol. It designated in general the place or state of the dead, the grave, or death itself. In some versions the word is not translated at all but is transliterated simply as "hades." The NT is not always very explicit about the meaning of hades, other than what has just been described. Use of the word often does not reveal much about the specific condition of the dead. There are some passages, however, that indicate a distinct advance over the use of Sheol in the OT. One NT passage definitely describes hades as a place of evil and punishment of the wicked, and may appropriately be translated "hell" (Lk 16:23). In all other instances, hades indicates nothing more than the place of the dead.

The Greek word "Gehenna" is used in a number of NT texts to designate the fiery place for punishment of sinners and is often translated "hell" or "the fires of hell" (Mt 5:22, 29-30; 10:28; 18:9; 23:15, 33; Mk 9:43, 45, 47; Jas 3:6). It is usually used in connection with the final judgment and often has the suggestion that the punishment spoken of is eternal. Gehenna is derived by transliteration from the Hebrew of the OT "valley of Hinnom" or the "valley of the son of Hinnom," a ravine on the south side of Jerusalem. This valley was the center of idolatrous worship in which children were burned by fire as an offering to the heathen god Molech (2 Chr 28:3; 33:6). In the time of Josiah it became a place of abomination, polluted by dead men's bones and rubbish (2 Kgs 23:10-14) and by the garbage and filth of Jerusalem dumped there. A fire burned continuously in this valley. It thus became a symbol of the unending fires of hell where the lost are consumed in torment. It was a symbol of judgment to be imposed on the idolatrous and disobedient (Jer 7:31-34; 32:35).

Another Greek word used to designate hell or "the lower regions" is "Tartarus" (2 Pt 2:4), a classical word for the place of eternal punishment. The apostle Peter uses it for the fallen angels who were thrown into hell, "committed . . . to pits of nether gloom to be kept until the judgment" (RSV).

As noted above, there are, in addition to these terms, the very explicit and vivid phrases that clearly teach the doctrine of hell, as developed at the beginning of this article. The biblical doctrine is determined much more by these decisive phrases than by the somewhat indecisive but frequently used terms "Sheol" and "hades."

HADES AS HELL: A PROBLEM IN TRANSLATION
The KJV translators caused much confusion by translating two different Greek words (*hades* and *Gehenna*) with the same English word, "hell." Hades almost always denotes the grave or the place of the dead. Gehenna, a much rarer expression in the NT, denotes the eternal fires. Thus, hell, as most people think about it, is really Gehenna, not hades. Unfortunately, this was not distinguished in the KJV. Modern translators have tried to correct the problem, but the popular misconception persists.

The Justice of Eternal Punishment It is difficult for us to understand the righteous judgment of a holy God who, on one hand, hates all evil, yet, on the other hand, loves the evildoers enough to sacrifice his only Son for their salvation from sin. Divine wrath is the necessary reaction of a holy God who hates all that is contrary to his righteous nature. When the only remedy for human sin is rejected and all appeals of a loving, seeking God for the reconciliation of rebellious sinners are refused, there is no other course of action that God himself can pursue but to leave the sinner to his self-chosen destiny. Punishment for sin is then the inevitable and inescapable response of holiness to that which is morally opposite, and it must continue as long as the sinful condition requiring it continues. There is no indication anywhere in Scripture that lost sinners in hell are capable of repentance and faith. If in this life they did not turn away from sin and receive Christ as Savior with all the favorable circumstances and opportunities afforded them on earth, it is unreasonable to think they will do so in the life to come. Punishment cannot come to an end until guilt and sin come to an end. When the sinner ultimately resists and rejects the work of the Holy Spirit whereby he is convicted of sin, there remains no more possibility of repentance or salvation. He has committed an eternal sin (Mk 3:29; Rv 22:11), which deserves eternal punishment.

The impossibility of faith and repentance in hell is seen also from the tragic reality of the depraved will, conditioned and determined by its repeated rebellion against God. Sin reproduces itself in the will, and character tends to become irrevocably fixed. God responds to endless sinning with the necessary counterpart of endless punishment.

If the question is raised, How can a loving God send people to an everlasting hell? it must be replied that God does not choose this destination for people; they freely choose it for themselves. God simply concurs in their self-chosen way and reveals the full consequences of their evil choice. It must always be remembered that God is not only loving; he is also holy and righteous. There must be some adequate reckoning with justice in the universe where a revolt against God has brought evil consequences of enormous proportions.

While the duration of punishment in hell is eternal for all who have chosen that destiny for themselves, there are degrees of punishment proportional to the degrees of guilt of each individual. Only God is able to determine what those degrees are, and he will assign the consequences with perfect justice according to the responsibility of each one. Evidence of such gradations in future punishment is found in Scripture (Mt 11:20-24; Lk 12:47-48; Rv 20:12-13; cf. Ez 16:48-61). An obvious comparison is made in these texts between the differing intensities of punishment that are involved in the contrasting privileges, knowledge, and opportunities.

From all that has been said, it should be obvious that a variety of nonbiblical views must be ruled out, however attractively they may be presented by their advocates and however popular they may be from time to time. Among these views are the erroneous, but sometimes persuasive, doctrines of universalism, annihilationism, and second probation. Universalism promotes the concept that God will save everyone in the end. Annihilationism teaches that hell is not a place of conscious suffering but of final extermination. And second probation is a notion that people can be delivered from hell. It must always be remembered that the Bible is our rule of faith for the doctrine of hell, however difficult the doctrine may seem for natural reason or for human sentiment. Scripture leaves no doubt about the terrible nature and the eternal duration of hell. Rejection or neglect of this doctrine will have dire effects upon the mission of the church.

See also "Abraham's Bosom," page 7; Dead, Place of the; Death; Gehenna; Hades; Intermediate State; Sheol; Wrath of God.

HELLENISM*

That unique blend of Greek cultural, philosophical, and ethical ideals that had a profound effect on the development of culture throughout the Mediterranean world. While the antecedents of the movement occurred long before, the Hellenistic Age is seen by most to have begun in 323 BC, with the death of Alexander, and to have continued until either 30 BC, when Rome conquered Egypt, or (more likely) AD 300. Rome itself was culturally conquered by Hellenism.

PREVIEW
•Hellenistic Age
•Hellenism and Judaism
•Hellenism and Christianity

Hellenistic Age Alexander the Great was more than a military conqueror. He made Hellenistic culture the norm throughout his realm. He taught conquered people the Greek language and customs, and he built new Greek cities (34 in all), like Alexandria in Egypt, which became bastions of Hellenism. His major accomplishment was not so much territorial as cultural; after him, Hellenism controlled the Western world for centuries. It was Alexander who spearheaded the triumph of the Attic *koine* (common) dialect over the other Greek dialects, and this became the primary force in the Hellenization of the East. The *koine* dialect was to be the basis for the acceptance of Hellenism by subject peoples. The first period after his death would be characterized by the dissolution of Alexander's empire and an emerging balance of power among the forces of Ptolemy, who controlled Egypt and Palestine; Seleucus, who ruled Babylon and Asia Minor; and Antipater (followed by Antigonus), who reigned over Macedonia and the Hellespont.

In the East the next century was typified by intermittent skirmishes between the Ptolemies and Seleucids, with the result that Palestine became a buffer state between the two. An important difference is that the Ptolemies had a unified kingdom and so were not interested in change; under their rule, Palestine was autonomous both culturally and religiously. However, the Seleucids controlled many different groups and so tried to unite them by forcing Hellenization on them. This finally led to the successful revolt of the Jews under the Maccabees and the disintegration of both empires. In the West, Rome became progressively involved in Greek affairs and by 149 BC controlled the Greek lands politically, while they themselves were overtaken by Greek ideals culturally.

During this period, there was a growing middle class, which was brought about partly because Alexander's conquests led to a vast dispersion of Greeks into the conquered lands. The redistribution of wealth this engendered was based upon a Greek education and an acceptance of Hellenistic ideals. The term "civilized" came to be identified with the Greek way of life. Education was controlled by the idea of sound rhetoric, so that style triumphed over truth. Greek drama turned to comedy, which stressed realism in human emotions, and Hellenistic art grew even more naturalistic than in the classical period.

Philosophy also developed, with at least three schools arising to dominate Greek thought for the next few centuries. Interestingly, all three centered on practical ethics rather than the classical quest for truth and knowledge. The Cynics, founded by Diogenes, stressed a total self-sufficiency that left the individual in a social vacuum but taught him how to deal with human misery. The two most influential schools were the Epicureans and the Stoics. Epicurus sought freedom from anxiety or fear and taught that peace of the soul could only be derived from a disciplined, moderate experience of pleasures. The result was a retreat from society into one's own selfhood. Stoicism, founded by Zeno and named after the *stoa* (porch) in Athens where he taught, was similar to cynicism in its emphasis on self-sufficiency, but it combined this with a stress on the brotherhood of man. Every person was to strive after virtue and live above the vicissitudes of life. This last philosophy had become the center of Hellenism by the time of Christ.

Hellenism and Judaism Judaism was virtually the only culture that resisted the encroachment of Hellenism. Therefore, the power of this movement can be seen in the degree to which it permeated Judaism.

The pull of Hellenism was always felt primarily by the upper-class nobility, and it was strongest in Jewish communities of the Dispersion. However, under the Seleucids, the temple priesthood was pro-Hellenist, so this added a religious dimension to the economic pressure upon the wealthy. From the beginning Palestine was split into two factions: the urban nobility, who tried to make Jerusalem another *polis*, or Hellenistic city-state, by adding such things as gymnasia and Greek drama; and the agricultural, poor peasants, who saw in Hellenism a threat to the very existence of the Mosaic system.

Jews had to learn *koine* Greek to make business transactions and participate in legal matters. Archaeology shows that almost all inscriptions in Palestine from the third century BC were in Greek, and the translation of the Torah into Greek in the Septuagint shows the permeation of the language in the Jewish communities outside of Palestine (diaspora communities). The gymnasium was the school in Hellenistic cities, and Greek education was the key to citizenship. Alexandria, Egypt, in this regard became the intellectual center of the Greek world, and its influence on the strong Jewish community in that city was considerable. Well-to-do Jews in lands of the Dispersion and in Jerusalem itself were expected to procure a gymnasium education. Many followed the Greek practice of participating naked in sports, as can be seen from the literature of the intertestamental period, which is strongly antagonistic a century later (due to Jewish aversion to such public display). Jewish synagogue schools, as a result of competition with the gymnasia, adopted Greek ways. In fact, the development of the scribal tradition is partly due to this interaction; the movement was away from the oligarchical system of the temple era and toward a democratic instruction of the whole people.

Jewish literature and philosophy became permeated by Hellenistic patterns. This is seen in 1 and 2 Maccabees, which reflect Greek historiography. And Hellenistic influence can be seen in virtually every Jewish work of this period. The major exponent, of course, was Philo of Alexandria, whose allegorical interpretation of the OT was designed to make Jewish teachings palatable to the Hellenistic world and vice versa. This attitude was quite common. The symbolism of Jewish apocalyptic writing was influenced by a combination of Hellenistic and Oriental (primarily Persian) themes, and even the hyperconservative Essene movement used thought forms that had been molded via Judaism's penetration by Hellenistic and Persian ideas. The stress on "eternal knowledge" and "revealed mystery" and the dualistic combination of salvation history and anthropology are evidence of this. Of course, the influence was not all one way. The development of Greek philosophy was strongly influenced by Semitic forms, especially Phoenician; and the strong Jewish piety was very attractive to the Greek mind.

It is accurate to say that even the Judaism of Palestine in the first century BC was a Hellenistic Judaism. The universality of the *koine* Greek, the infiltration of Greek learning and thought patterns, the presence of Jewish literature in Greek, and the permeation of Hellenistic rhetorical devices, even into the very literature of the opposition movement, shows the power of Hellenism in Palestine.

Hellenism and Christianity Some scholars have attempted to stratify early Christianity into periods typified by Palestinian, Hellenistic-Jewish, and Hellenistic outlooks. However, as the evidence above has shown, this is by no means an easy task, since even Judea was penetrated by Greek thought patterns. To be sure, the reactionary stance against Hellenism in Judaism is paralleled by the Hellenist-Hebrew conflict of Acts 6 and the gentile mission. However, from the very earliest stages, the influence of Hellenism on the church can be traced. Moreover, it becomes virtually impossible to know whether a phrase is drawn from Palestinian or from Hellenistic sources, due to the mutual penetration of both into Palestine itself, and to the bilingual nature of the church from the beginning.

This does not mean that there were no differences at all. The Hellenistic background of Stephen allowed him to see the logical implications of the land and the temple typifying Christ (cf. Acts 6–7), while the more conservative Jerusalem church did not. Also, a study of the speeches in Acts shows that the kerygma (preaching) developed differently for Jewish and gentile audiences. The first centered on OT fulfillment and the second on the active penetration of history by the one true God, who, unlike dead idols, involved himself in the affairs of man.

The fact that the NT was written in *koine* Greek makes the influence very direct. Strongly Jewish-oriented works, such as Hebrews or James, are written in polished Greek, and even the Gospels, which record the life of Jesus in a Jewish setting, reflect Hellenistic historiography (e.g., an interest in the theological meaning of the historical events). Most obviously Hellenistic, of course, are ideas found in the Epistles stemming from the gentile mission. Early hymns like Colossians 1:15-22 use terminology from the Hellenistic environs to describe the incomparable superiority of Jesus over pagan ideals. The stress on the universal mission, while based on the teachings of Jesus, developed during the gentile mission; the primitive church interpreted it in keeping with Jewish proselyte theology, which was that the Gentiles became Christians after becoming Jews.

See also Epicureans; Gnosticism; Greece, Greek; Hellenists; Judaism; Stoics, Stoicism.

HELLENISTS* Name used in Acts 6:1, 9:29, and possibly 11:20 for a distinct branch of the early church that was characterized by Greek modes of thinking. Their actual identification is disputed, and the following possibilities have been propounded: (1) Greek-speaking Jews rather than Aramaic-speaking Jews (but "Hebrews," as in 6:1, was seldom used in a linguistic sense); (2) proselytes of "Greeks" as opposed to true Jews (the list of deacons in 6:5 makes this doubtful, for it is unlikely that they were all proselytes); (3) diaspora Jews living in Palestine (fits 6:1-6 but not the other passages); (4) pro-Hellenist sect within Judaism (this does not fit the whole tenor of the passages); (5) Gentiles who joined the church at an early date (this does not really fit the context of all three passages); (6) a general, not specific, term simply referring to one who either speaks Greek or follows Greek customs (or both). This is the best answer, as a study of the context illustrates.

In 6:1 the group was probably made up of Hellenistic Jews then living in Palestine. This is seen in the deacons chosen in 6:5. Luke used Greek names for all of them, probably not because they were Greek but to symbolize the desire of the apostles to unify the separate groups. Most Jews in the ancient world had three names—a Jewish, a Greek, and a Roman name—and used one or the other depending on the occasion. The diversity is even more apparent in 6:9. Hellenistic Jews differed sufficiently in their background and worship habits, especially in the use of Greek in the service, that there would be separate synagogues for them (there were seven such in Jerusalem alone). This created a potentially divisive situation for the early church, and the schism here was the result. The "Hebrews" would naturally tend to allocate the common pool to those they knew, and so the separation between the groups would add to the problem.

In 9:29 the "Hellenists" are members of the same group. Paul, a diasporate Jew himself, would naturally go to his old compatriots on his first visit to Jerusalem after his conversion. In 11:20 the manuscript evidence is equally divided between "Hellenists" and "Greeks." As "Hellenist" is used in 11:20, it designates the Greek-speaking populace of Antioch and therefore Gentiles in general. This is different from the usages in 6:1 and 9:29.

See also Acts of the Apostles, Book of the; Hellenism; Judaism.

HELMET *See* Armor and Weapons.

HELON Father of Eliab, prince of Zebulun's tribe at the taking of the first census (Nm 1:9; 2:7; 7:24, 29; 10:16).

HELPS*, Gift of *See* Spiritual Gifts.

HEMAM* KJV spelling of Heman, Lotan's son, in Genesis 36:22. *See* Heman #1.

HEMAN
1. Lotan's son, the brother of Hori and a descendant of Seir the Horite (Gn 36:22); alternately spelled Homam in 1 Chronicles 1:39, reflecting a later scribal error.
2. Mahol's son, descendant of Zerah from Judah's tribe and one of the sages whose wisdom was surpassed by King Solomon's (1 Kgs 4:31; 1 Chr 2:6). He is perhaps the Ezrahite and author of Psalm 88.
3. Kohathite Levite, Joel's son and one appointed, along with Asaph and Ethan (also called Jeduthun), by David to lead the musicians in the sanctuary (1 Chr 6:33; 15:17; 16:41). During the transport of the ark from Obed-edom's house to Jerusalem, he was responsible for sounding the bronze cymbals (1 Chr 15:19; 2 Chr 5:12). Heman fathered 14 sons and 3 daughters, all of whom served as musicians in the Lord's house (1 Chr 25:1-6). Later, his descendants participated in the cleansing of the temple during King Hezekiah's reign (715–686 BC; 2 Chr 29:14) and assisted with the Passover celebration initiated by King Josiah (640–609 BC; 2 Chr 35:15).

HEMATH* KJV form of Hammath, the Rechabite, in 1 Chronicles 2:55. *See* Hammath (Person).

HEMDAN Dishon's son and a descendant of Seir the Horite (Gn 36:26). He is also called Hamran in 1 Chronicles 1:41 (KJV "Amram").

HEMLOCK* KJV mistranslation for poisonous weeds and for wormwood in Hosea 10:4 and Amos 6:12, respectively. *See* Plants (Wormwood).

HEMORRHAGE Issue of blood, coming from any cut or nosebleed (Prv 30:33). However, in Scripture it almost always refers to vaginal bleeding. Laws concerning normal and abnormal menstruation are given in Leviticus 15:19-30. A woman with normal menstruation was considered unclean for seven days, along with anything that came into contact with her. A woman who bled longer than seven days was unclean as long as she was bleeding plus seven additional days.

All the Gospels except John give an account of the miraculous healing by Jesus of the woman who had a hemorrhage for 12 years (Mt 9:20-22; Mk 5:25-34; Lk 8:43-48). By touching Jesus' garment, the woman was actually violating the OT laws concerning menstruation and making Jesus' garment unclean (Lv 15). Her courageous act of faith in Jesus healed her.

See also Medicine and Medical Practice.

HEN *See* Birds (Fowl, Domestic).

HEN* (Person) KJV alternate name for Josiah, Zephaniah's son, in Zechariah 6:14. *See* Josiah #2.

HENA One of the six cities that the rabshakeh boasted fell before the armies of Sennacherib, in spite of their gods (2 Kgs 18:34). Rabshakeh hoped the example of these cities would strike fear in King Hezekiah's heart and make him doubt the Lord's deliverance as the same hordes surrounded Jerusalem. The kings of the five other cities are mentioned along with Hena again in 2 Kings 19:13 and Isaiah 37:13.

HENADAD Head of a Levite family that participated in the rebuilding of the temple (Ezr 3:9). Members of this family also helped to build the Jerusalem wall (Neh 3:18, 24), and signed Ezra's covenant of faithfulness to God together with Nehemiah (10:9).

HENNA* Fragrant, flowering shrub mentioned in Song of Solomon 1:14 and 4:13. *See* Plants.

HENOCH*
1. KJV form of Enoch, Jared's son, in 1 Chronicles 1:3. *See* Enoch (Person) #2.
2. KJV form of Hanoch, Midian's son, in 1 Chronicles 1:33. *See* Hanoch #1.

HEPHER (Person)
1. Manassite and founder of the Hepherite family (Nm 26:32).
2. Ashhur's son from Judah's tribe (1 Chr 4:6).
3. One of David's valiant warriors (1 Chr 11:36).

HEPHER (Place) Canaanite city located northwest of Jerusalem. It was captured by Joshua (Jos 12:17) and later used as an administrative district under Solomon (1 Kgs 4:10).

HEPHERITE Descendant of Hepher from Manasseh's tribe (Nm 26:32). *See* Hepher (Person) #1.

HEPHZIBAH
1. Mother of Manasseh, king of Judah (2 Kgs 21:1).
2. Symbolic name (KJV) for the restored city of Jerusalem, meaning "my delight is in her" (Is 62:4).

HERB Plant valued for its culinary, medicinal, or aromatic properties. *See* Plants (Cummin; Dill; Mint; Nard); Bitter Herbs.

HERCULES A Greek god, the son of Zeus, renowned for strength. Second Maccabees 4 records the Hellenizing fervor of Antiochus Epiphanes (175–164 BC), who succeeded Seleucus IV Philopator, as he "founded a gymnasium right under the citadel" (2 Macc 4:12). At the quadrennial games in Tyre when the king was present, Jason the brother of Onias, who had obtained the high priesthood by corruption, "sent envoys, chosen as being Antiochian citizens from Jerusalem, to carry three hundred silver drachmas for the sacrifice to Hercules" (v 19, RSV). Those who were sent with the money thought it inappropriate to use it for the sacrifice, so they applied it to the construction of ships instead (vv 19-20), which indicates some resistance to the pattern of Hellenization.

See also Gods and Goddesses.

HERDSMEN Men who cared for domestic animals, such as cattle, sheep and goats (Gn 13:7-8; 26:20; 1 Sm 21:7). They also included shepherds. In the NT shepherds were well known. The metaphor of the shepherd and his sheep was used by Jesus (Jn 10:1-16). Some herdsmen kept pigs (Mt 8:33; Mk 5:14; Lk 8:34).

HERES
1. Region from which the Amorites were not expelled by the Israelites, known as Mt Heres (Jgs 1:34-35, RSV "Har-heres"). In Joshua 19:41-42, Mt Heres is synonymous with the town of Ir-shemesh (Beth-shemesh).
2. Ascent of Heres (Jgs 8:13, RSV; NLT "Heres Pass"). Though the text and the exact nature of the terrain is unclear, it was the place on the Jordan River from which Gideon returned after his victory over Zebah and Zalmunna.

HERESH Levite who returned to Jerusalem following the exile (1 Chr 9:15).

HERESY A sectarian group or teaching that deviates from the norm. The Greek word (*hairesis*), literally meaning "choice," designates a sect or faction. For example, the Sadducees were a sect within Judaism (Acts 5:17), as were the Pharisees (15:5). When many Jews first believed that Jesus of Nazareth was the Messiah, they were known as "the sect of the Nazarenes" (24:5). In each of these verses, the word *hairesis* denotes nothing more than a sect. After the church grew and developed, any factious group within a local church was called *hairesis*—that is, it was a sect that held certain opinions contrary to the truths established by the apostles. In view of this, Paul told the Corinthian church that factious sects would develop among them as a way of separating the false from the true (1 Cor 11:19). Eventually, the word "heresy" came to connote the particular teaching that caused certain ones to break away from orthodoxy. Thus, Peter warned Christians about various false teachers who would try to deceive believers with their heretical teachings (2 Pt 2:1). In the modern era, this is how the word "heresy" is usually understood; it is unorthodox and/or false teaching that damages the faith of certain believers and also causes divisive factions within the church.

HERETH Section of forested land in the territory of Judah where David and his men hid for a time as they fled from King Saul (1 Sm 22:5).

HERMAS
1. Christian to whom Paul sent greetings in his letter to the Romans (Rom 16:14).
2. Christian who wrote the apocryphal book called The Shepherd (referring to the work's central shepherd figure). In The Shepherd, Hermas states that he was originally a slave, gained his freedom, married and started a business, lost nearly everything material, saw his children lapse, and finally brought his family together by acts of repentance. Hermas indicates also that he knew Clement of Rome, late-first-century bishop of Rome. From internal evidences, it is impossible to tell if this biography is fictional or not. As to external facts, references to Hermas are contradictory. Some authorities, most eminently the Muratorian Canon, a late-second-century document, make Hermas a brother of Pius, bishop of Rome about 150. In the third century, Origen thought Hermas was the individual Paul named in Romans 16:14, an identification upholding Hermas's own statements. Modern scholarly commentators lean much toward the first opinion.

See also Shepherd of Hermas.

HERMES
1. Greek god and the son of Zeus by Maia. He was identified with Mercury in the Roman pantheon of deities. In Greek mythology, Hermes was the messenger of the gods and the escort of the dead to hades. He was the god of fertility, the patron of music, the guardian of travelers, and the god of eloquent speech.

Hermes (or Mercury)

While ministering at Lystra, Paul was acclaimed by its people to be Hermes because of his miraculous work and role as chief speaker. The Lystrans thought Paul was a god visiting them in bodily form (Acts 14:11-12, KJV "Mercurius").
2. Christian to whom Paul sent greetings in his letter to Rome (Rom 16:14).

HERMOGENES Prominent Asian believer who "turned away" from Paul (2 Tm 1:15). His actions may have been the result of doctrinal disagreement but more likely involved his unwillingness to come to Paul's defense during the apostle's second Roman imprisonment for fear of suffering the same fate himself.

HERMON, Mount Mountain often mentioned as the northern extremity of the territory conquered by Joshua and Moses in Transjordan; it is also the northern boundary of the inheritance of the half-tribe of Manasseh as well as of Israel in general (Dt 3:8; 4:48; Jos 11:17; 12:1, 5; 13:11; 1 Chr 5:23). Hermon is said to tower over the valley of Lebanon (Jos 11:17; 13:5) and over the land of Mizpah in the valley of Mizpah, to which Joshua pursued the kings of Canaan after his victory over them at the waters of Merom (Jos 11:3, 8). Biblical poetry praises Hermon for its height and for causing dew on Zion (Ps 133:3), and it was famed for its wildlife (Sg 4:8). It also appears in tandem with Mt Tabor (Ps 89:12) and with the Jordan (Ps 42:6). The mountain itself is about 13 miles (21 kilometers) long and rises to a height of 9,166 feet (2.8 kilometers).

Aerial View of Mount Hermon

HERMONITE* KJV mistranslation for Hermon (Mount) in Psalm 42:6. Mt Hermon, a sacred site since antiquity, lies on the northernmost boundary of Joshua's conquest (Jos 12:5; 13:11). *See* Hermon, Mount.

HEROD, HERODIAN FAMILY* Political rulers during the lifetime of Christ. Christ was born when Herod the Great was ruling. Herod's son Herod Antipas was the ruler of Galilee and Perea, the territories in which Jesus and John the Baptist carried out most of their ministries. It was this ruler who beheaded John the Baptist and tried Christ just before his death. Herod Agrippa I is the persecutor of the church in Acts 12, and Herod Agrippa II heard Paul's testimony (Acts 26) just before he went to Rome to be tried by Caesar. Without a knowledge of the Herodian family, one can hardly have a proper understanding of the times of Christ.

PREVIEW
•The Herodian Dynasty
•Herod the Great
•Archelaus
•Antipas
•Philip the Tetrarch
•Agrippa I
•Agrippa II

The Herodian Dynasty (67–47 BC) The Herodian dynasty became prominent during the confusion that resulted in the decay of the Hasmonean dynasty, the transference of Syria and Palestine to Roman rule, and the civil wars that marked the decay of the nation. Much of what we

know about the Herods comes from the historian Josephus's writings: *Antiquities of the Jews* and *The Jewish War*.

Herod the Great (47–4 BC)

As Governor of Galilee (47–37 BC) Herod the Great became governor of Galilee at 25 years of age. Although he gained the respect of both the Romans and the Galilean Jews for quickly capturing and executing the bandit leader Ezekias, some in Hyrcanus's court thought that he was becoming too powerful and arranged to have him brought to trial. He was acquitted and released and thereafter fled to Sextus Caesar at Damascus. Sextus Caesar, governor of Syria, appointed Herod governor of Coele-Syria, and thus he became involved with Roman affairs in Syria. He remained in this position under a series of rulers and was successful in collecting taxes and suppressing various revolts. Thus, in 41 BC when Antony came to power under Octavius Caesar, after asking the advice of Hyrcanus II, Sextus appointed Herod and Phasael as tetrarchs of Judea.

As King (37–4 BC) The reign of Herod is divided by most scholars into three periods: (1) consolidation from 37 to 25 BC; (2) prosperity from 25 to 13 BC; and (3) domestic troubles from 13 to 4 BC.

The period of consolidation extended from his accession as king in 37 BC to the death of the sons of Babas, the last male representatives of the Hasmonean family. During this period, he had to contend with many powerful adversaries.

The first adversaries, the people and the Pharisees, objected to his being an Idumean, a half Jew, and a friend of the Romans. Those who opposed him were punished, and those who took his side were rewarded with favors and honors.

The second adversaries were those of the aristocracy who sided with Antigonus. Herod had executed 45 of the wealthiest and had confiscated their properties to replenish his own coffers.

The third group of adversaries was the Hasmonean family. Herod's chief problem was his mother-in-law, Alexandra. She was upset that he had not appointed another Hasmonean to the high priesthood to replace Hyrcanus, specifically her son Aristobulus. She wrote to Cleopatra, asking her to influence Antony to force Herod to remove the appointed high priest, Ananel, and replace him with Aristobulus. Finally, Herod gave way to the pressure. In the end, after a celebration of the Feast of Tabernacles, Herod had Aristobulus drowned, making it look like an accident. Herod put Alexandra in chains and

Herod Agrippa I This coin bears the Greek inscription meaning "King Agrippa the Great, Lover of Caesar."

placed her under guard to keep her from causing him more trouble.

Herod's fourth adversary was Cleopatra. When civil war broke out between Antony and Octavius, Herod wanted to help Antony. But Cleopatra persuaded Antony to set Herod in battle against the Arabian king Malchus, who had failed to pay tribute to her. When she saw Herod winning, she ordered her troops to help Malchus, hoping to weaken both parties to the breaking point so that she could absorb them both. After a catastrophic earthquake in his domain in 31 BC, Herod defeated the Arabs and returned home. Soon after, on September 2, 31 BC, Octavius defeated Antony in the Battle of Actium, resulting in the suicides of Antony and Cleopatra.

The second period of Herod's reign was one of prosperity (25–14 BC). It was a period of splendor and enjoyment interrupted by occasional disturbances. According to Josephus, the most noble of all Herod's achievements was the rebuilding of the temple in Jerusalem, begun in 20/19 BC (*Antiquities* 15.8.1). Rabbinic literature claims, "He who has not seen the Temple of Herod has never seen a beautiful building" (Babylonian Talmud: *Baba Batha* 4a). Prior to this, he had built theaters, amphitheaters, and racecourses for both men and horses. In 24 BC Herod built himself a royal palace and built or rebuilt many fortresses and gentile temples, including Strato's Tower, later renamed Caesarea.

During this time, he became very interested in culture and gathered around him men accomplished in Greek literature and art. Greek rhetoricians were appointed to the highest offices of the state. One of these was Nicolas of Damascus, Herod's instructor and adviser in philosophy, rhetoric, and history. In late 24 BC he married Mariamne, daughter of Simon, a well-known priest in Jerusalem (she will be referred to as Mariamne II).

During this period, Herod's rule was favorably accepted by the people. They were annoyed, however, by two things. First, he violated Jewish law by his introduction of the quinquennial games in honor of Caesar; and second, he built theaters and racecourses. He demanded a loyalty oath from his subjects, except for a privileged few. Also, he would not allow them to congregate freely for fear of a revolt. Despite these things, he had good control of the people and twice favored them by lowering taxes (in 14 BC he reduced taxes by one-fourth).

The third period of Herod's rule was clearly marked by domestic troubles (13–4 BC). By now he had married ten wives. His first wife, Doris, had only one son, Antipater. He repudiated Doris and Antipater when he married Mariamne I, allowing them to visit Jerusalem only during the festivals. He married Mariamne I in 37 BC. She was the granddaughter of Hyrcanus and had five children, two daughters and three sons. The youngest son died while in Rome, and the remaining two sons were to play an important role in this part of Herod's reign. In late 24 BC he married his third wife, Mariamne II, to whom one child was born, Herod (Philip). Malthace, his fourth wife, was a Samaritan and mother of two sons, Archelaus and Antipas. His fifth wife, Cleopatra of Jerusalem, was the mother of Philip the tetrarch. Of the remaining five wives, only Pallas, Phaedra, and Elpsis are known by name, and none played a significant part in the events of this period.

Alexander and Aristobulus, the sons of Mariamne I, were his favorites. Immediately following their own marriages, troubles began within the Herodian household. Salome, Herod's sister and mother of Berenice (wife of Aristobulus), hated these two sons, mainly because she wanted the position and favor they enjoyed for her own son. Herod decided to recall his exiled son Antipater to

show Alexander and Aristobulus there was another heir to the throne. Antipater took full advantage of the situation and used every conceivable means to acquire the coveted throne. Finally, a man of bad character, Eurycles from Lacedaemon, took it upon himself to inflame the father against his two sons and vice versa. Soon other mischief makers joined Eurycles, and Herod's patience became exhausted. He put Alexander and Aristobulus in prison and named Antipater heir.

In his impatience to gain the throne, Antipater attempted to poison Herod. This plot failed when Pheroras, Herod's brother, drank the poison by mistake. Herod put Antipater in prison and reported the matter to the emperor (c. 5 BC). At this time Herod became very ill with an incurable disease. He drew up a new will that bypassed his older sons, Archelaus and Philip, because Antipater had poisoned his mind against them also. He chose his youngest son, Antipas, as his sole successor.

It was during this time that the wise men arrived in Judea, searching for the newborn king of the Jews. Herod instructed them to report to him the whereabouts of this child as soon as they found him. Being warned in a dream, they did not do so, but rather returned to their homes by another route. God warned Joseph (husband of the mother of Jesus) to flee to Egypt because of Herod's intention to kill Jesus. Joseph took his family and left Bethlehem. Shortly after, Herod killed all the male children in Bethlehem who were two years old and under.

Herod's disease grew increasingly worse. Permission came from Rome to execute Antipater, which he promptly did. He again altered his will, making Archelaus king of Judea, Idumea, and Samaria; Antipas tetrarch of Galilee and Perea, and Philip tetrarch of territories east of Galilee. On the fifth day after Antipater's execution, Herod died at Jericho in the spring of 4 BC. The people acclaimed Archelaus as their king.

Archelaus (4 BC–AD 6) Archelaus was the son of Herod the Great and Malthace (a Samaritan) and was born around 22 BC. Archelaus was faced with a multitude of problems. He had killed 3,000 people in putting down a revolution led by people avenging the blood of those killed by his father, Herod. Thus his rule got off to a bad start. At Pentecost in 4 BC, another revolt broke out, which lasted about two and a half months and during which the temple porticoes were burned and the treasury was pillaged by the Romans. This unrest spread to the countryside of Judea and to Galilee and Perea.

Archelaus treated both the Jews and the Samaritans brutally (*War* 2.7.3), a fact borne out by the Gospels. When Joseph returned from his flight to Egypt and learned that Archelaus was ruling Judea, he was afraid to go there and was warned against it by God; he took the infant Jesus to Galilee instead (Mt 2:22).

Archelaus's tyranny finally caused the Jews and Samaritans to send a delegation to Rome and complain formally to Augustus. The fact that such bitter enemies as the Jews and Samaritans could cooperate in this matter indicates the serious nature of the complaint. Antipas and Philip also went to Rome to complain about him. Presumably they resented his neglect as their Roman representative for Palestine. Thus in AD 6 Archelaus was deposed and exiled to Vienna in Gaul (modern Vienne on the Rhône, south of Lyons). Antipas and Philip were allowed to continue their respective rules, and Archelaus's territories were reduced to a province ruled by prefects or procurators.

Antipas (4 BC–AD 39) Antipas was the younger brother of Archelaus, born around 20 BC. Of all the

Herodians, he is mentioned most in the NT because he ruled over Galilee and Perea, where both Jesus and John the Baptist concentrated their ministries.

Antipas's domain was in turmoil caused by the rebellion begun at Pentecost in 4 BC. He immediately set out to restore order and rebuild what had been destroyed. Following the example of his father, Herod the Great, Antipas founded cities. Sepphoris was his first project; it was the largest city in Galilee and his capital city until he built Tiberias. Since Nazareth was only four miles (6.4 kilometers) south-southeast of Sepphoris, it is quite possible that Joseph, Mary's husband, was employed as a carpenter (Mt 13:55; Mk 6:3) to help rebuild that city.

Of the 12 cities built by the Herodian family, Tiberias is the most important. It was the first city in Jewish history to be founded with the municipal framework of a Greek *polis*. It was built in honor of the reigning emperor, Tiberius. Due to the fact that a cemetery was destroyed in the process of building, Tiberias was considered unclean by the Jews. Antipas offered free houses, land and tax exemptions for the first few years to anyone who would move into the city. He completed the city in AD 23 and made it his capital.

In the Christian world the incident for which Antipas is most remembered is his beheading of John the Baptist (Mt 14:3-12; Mk 6:17-29; Lk 3:19-20; *Antiquities* 18.5.2.116-119). There was a tangle of family events leading up to the death of John the Baptist. Antipas had married the daughter of Aretas IV (the daughter's name is unknown). Aretas IV was the Nabatean king, and Augustus may have encouraged this marriage since he favored intermarriages between various rulers to promote peace in his empire.

Around AD 29 Antipas took a trip to Rome, and on the way he paid a visit to his half brother Herod Philip, who must have lived in a coastal city in Palestine. Antipas fell in love with Herodias, Philip's wife, who was also Antipas's niece. The idea of becoming the wife of a tetrarch appealed to her, and she agreed to marry him when he returned from Rome if he would oust Aretas's daughter. Antipas agreed to the plan, and when Aretas's daughter heard of it, she fled to her father. This was a breach of political alliance as well as a personal insult, which led to retaliation by Aretas.

The marriage of Antipas and Herodias was in violation of the Mosaic law that forbade marriage to a brother's wife (Lv 18:16; 20:21) except in order to raise children for a deceased childless brother by a levirate marriage (Dt 25:5; Mk 12:19). In this case, Philip not only had a child, Salome, but he was still alive. This is the situation that John the Baptist spoke so boldly against, and Antipas threw him in prison. Herodias's hatred of John the Baptist was too great merely to settle for his incarceration. At an appropriate time, possibly Antipas's birthday, she planned a banquet at Machaerus in Perea. Her daughter, Salome, danced for the king, and in an impulsive moment Antipas promised her under oath that he would give her anything, up to half of his kingdom. Following her mother's advice, she asked for John the Baptist's head on a platter. Immediately Antipas was sorry for his rash promise, but in order to save face in the presence of his underlords, he granted the request. Thus, John's ministry ended around AD 31 or 32.

There are three specific times when Antipas and Jesus are mentioned together in the Gospels.

Early in Jesus' ministry Antipas heard of him and commented, perhaps with irony, that Jesus was John the Baptist resurrected (Mt 14:1-2; Mk 6:14-16; Lk 9:7-9). It was obvious to Antipas that Jesus' ministry was even more remarkable than John's, but he was reluctant to use force

to bring about the meeting for fear of once more arousing the people against him. Eventually, Jesus withdrew from Antipas's territories without the two meeting.

Later, as Jesus became more popular, Antipas saw a potential threat to his own power and threatened to kill Jesus. Thus it was that on Jesus' final trip to Jerusalem he was warned by some of the Pharisees that he should leave Antipas's territories for his own safety (Lk 13:31-33). Jesus sent as answer to "that fox" that he would continue his ministry of healing and casting out demons for a little longer, and when he had finished, he would then go to Jerusalem to die. The lion and fox were often contrasted in ancient literature. The Lion of Judah, Jesus Christ, was not going to be coerced by the crafty coward, Antipas.

The final encounter between the two occurred when Jesus was tried by Antipas in AD 33 (Lk 23:6-12). Since this event is mentioned only by Luke, some scholars consider it legendary. It must be remembered, however, that Luke's addressee was Theophilus, probably a Roman officer, who would be especially interested in the reconciliation between Pilate and Antipas mentioned in this passage.

According to Luke's account, when Pilate could find no fault in Jesus, he sent him to Antipas (who was celebrating the Passover in Jerusalem). Pilate thus freed himself from an awkward situation. A more subtle reason may have been to reconcile himself to Antipas. Their relationship had been rather strained since the Galilean massacre (Lk 13:1), and because Pilate brought votive shields into Jerusalem, arousing the anger of the Jews (Philo's *Legatio ad Gaium* 299-304). When Jesus was brought before Antipas, the ruler only mocked him and sent him back to Pilate. The main political accomplishment of the incident was Antipas and Pilate's reconciliation.

Philip the Tetrarch (4 BC–AD 34)

Philip the tetrarch was the son of Herod the Great and Cleopatra of Jerusalem and was born around 22 BC. When Herod's will was resolved, Philip was made tetrarch over Gaulanitis, Auranitis, Batanea, Trachonitis, and Iturea, all in the northern part of Herod the Great's domain (Lk 3:1). His subjects were mainly Syrian and Greek. Thus he was the first and only Herodian to have his image on his coins.

He built two cities. First, he rebuilt and enlarged Paneas and renamed it Caesarea Philippi. Here Peter made his confession of faith to Jesus and was given the revelation of the church (Mt 16:13-20; Mk 8:27-30). Next, he rebuilt and enlarged Bethsaida and renamed it Julias. Here Jesus healed the blind man (Mk 8:22-26), and in a nearby desert place he fed the 5,000 (Lk 9:10-17).

Philip was not as politically ambitious as his brothers. His rule was marked by tranquility and the loyalty of his subjects. When Philip died in AD 34, Tiberius annexed his territories to Syria. After Caligula became emperor in AD 37, he gave the territories to Agrippa I, brother of Herodias.

Agrippa I (AD 37–44)

Agrippa I was the son of Aristobulus (son of Herod the Great and Mariamne I) and Berenice. He was born in 10 BC and was the brother of Herodias.

Agrippa I might be considered the black sheep of the Herodian family. While at school in Rome, he lived a wanton life, incurring many debts. In Rome he became a friend of Gaius Caligula and at one point stated that he wished Caligula were king rather than Tiberius. This was overheard and reported to Tiberius, who imprisoned him. He remained in prison until Tiberius's death six months later.

Upon Caligula's accession to the throne, he released Agrippa and gave him Philip the tetrarch's territories and the northern part of Lysanias's territory as well as the title of king. The title of king aroused the jealousy of his sister Herodias, and that eventually led to her husband, Antipas's, downfall. At that time (AD 39) Agrippa acquired all of Antipas's territories and property.

When Caligula died in AD 41, Agrippa curried the favor of the new emperor Claudius, whereupon Claudius added Judea and Samaria to Agrippa's territory. This territory was once ruled by Agrippa's grandfather, Herod the Great.

Agrippa I is mentioned in the NT for his persecution of the early church in order to gain favor with the Jews (Acts 12:1-19). He killed James, the son of Zebedee, and imprisoned Peter. When Peter was released by an angel, Agrippa put the sentries to death.

Agrippa died in AD 44 in Caesarea. Accounts of this incident are recorded both by Josephus (*Antiquities* 19.9.1.274–275; *War* 2.11.5.214–215) and the Scriptures. The incident occurred at Caesarea; he was wearing a sparkling silver robe, and when the people flattered him by calling him a god, he was suddenly struck with a mortal illness and died a horrible death. He was survived by his daughters, Bernice, Mariamne, and Drusilla, and by a son, Agrippa, who was 17 at the time. Because of Agrippa II's youth, his father's territories were temporarily made a province.

Agrippa II (AD 50–100) Agrippa II was the son of Agrippa I and Cypros. In AD 50, six years after his father's death, Claudius made him king of Chalcis.

Agrippa II was in control of the temple treasury and the vestments of the high priest and thus could appoint the high priest. The Romans consulted him on religious matters, which is probably why Festus asked him to hear the apostle Paul at Caesarea (AD 59), where he was accompanied by his sister Bernice (Acts 25–26).

In May AD 66 the Palestinian revolution began (*War* 2.14.4.284). When Agrippa's attempt to quell the revolt failed, he became a staunch ally of the Romans throughout the entire war (AD 66–70). During this time, Nero committed suicide, the new emperor Galba was murdered, and Vespasian became the emperor. After pledging his allegiance to the new emperor, Agrippa remained with Titus, Vespasian's son, who was in charge of the war (Tacitus's *History* 5.81). After the fall of Jerusalem (August 6, AD 70), Agrippa was probably present to celebrate the destruction of his own people.

Following this, Vespasian added new territories to Agrippa's kingdom, though just which ones is not known. In AD 79 Vespasian died and Titus became emperor. Little is known of Agrippa's rule after this, except that he wrote to the historian Josephus praising him for *The Jewish War*, and he purchased a copy of it (Josephus's *Life* 65.361–367; *Apion* 1.9.47–52).

Although the Talmud implies that Agrippa II had two wives (Babylonian Talmud: *Sukkah* 27a), Josephus gives no indication that he had any wives or children. Rather, he was known for his incestuous relationship with his sister Bernice. He died around AD 100. His death marked the end of the Herodian dynasty.

See also Herodians; Judaism.

HERODIANS* Jewish party mentioned three times in the Gospels in connection with two incidents (one in Galilee and one in Jerusalem) and associated with the Pharisees in their opposition to Christ. In Mark 3:6, after the healing of the man with the withered hand, the Pharisees went out and took counsel with the Herodians, plotting to destroy Jesus. In Matthew 22:16 and Mark 12:13, the Pharisees and Herodians allied against Christ to entrap him with their question as to the lawfulness of paying taxes to Caesar. The Herodians are never mentioned in either Luke or John.

The real problem comes in Mark 8:15, where it speaks of the "leaven of Herod." Another reading is the "leaven of the Herodians." However, the parallel passage in Matthew 16:6 speaks of the "leaven of the Sadducees." Are the Sadducees and the Herodians the same?

Matthew tends to label the religious leaders as Jesus' opponents, whereas Mark emphasizes that Jesus' opponents were both religious and political. What then is the significance of Matthew's use of "the leaven of the Sadducees" in place of Mark's "leaven of Herod" or "leaven of the Herodians"? Some have speculated that the Herodians were a political party composed principally of Sadducees. Some have identified them with the Sadducees, and others with the Boethusians, whose name more often than not was used interchangeably with that of the Sadducees. The Boethusians and the Sadducees were indistinguishable theologically, but the Sadducees were loyal to the Hasmonean dynasty, whereas the Boethusians were attached to the Herodian house and consequently were called the Herodians. Thus the Herodians had political affiliations with the Herodian house and religious affiliations with the Sadducees. Along with the Sadducees, the Herodians were men of influence—the aristocrats of Palestine.

Nevertheless, during Jesus' time the political differences between the Herodians and the Sadducees were not as distinct because of the marriage of the Herodian Herod Antipas to the Hasmonean Herodias. The Herodians and the Sadducees would have been on the same side politically against the Pharisees, the former being pro-government, while the Pharisees were both anti-Hasmonean and anti-Herodian. Congruent with this, Matthew 16:12 and Mark 8:15 represent the Pharisees and the Sadducees/Herodians as contrary parties opposing Jesus.

In summary, the Herodians were also known as the Boethusians. Theologically they were in agreement with the Sadducees, but politically they were more pro-Herodian than the Sadducees. While the Pharisees looked for a cataclysmic messianic kingdom to remove the present Herodian rule, the Herodians worked to keep Herod's dynasty in power.

See also Herod, Herodian Family.

HERODIAS Daughter of Aristobulus, the son of Herod the Great, and Berenice. Born between 9 and 7 BC, her older brother was Herod Agrippa I. In 6 BC, while still in her infancy, she was betrothed by her grandfather, Herod the Great, to his son by Mariamne II named Herod Philip. Herodias was the mother of Salome, born between AD 15 and 19.

Herodias and Herod Philip lived on the seacoast of Judea, possibly at Azotus or Caesarea. In AD 29 Herod Antipas visited Herodias's (his niece) residence on his way to Rome. They were attracted to each other and Herodias agreed to marry him provided he would divorce his present wife, the daughter of Aretas IV, the Nebatean king of Petra. Herodias, being a Hasmonean, did not want to share the house with an Arab—longtime foes of the Hasmonean dynasty. When Aretas's daughter got word of this plot, she secretly escaped to her father, and Herodias and Antipas were married. This incident was the beginning of hostilities between Antipas and Aretas, which eventually led to Aretas's war against and defeat of Antipas in AD 36.

John the Baptist openly denounced this marriage (Mt 14:3-12; Mk 6:17-29; Lk 3:19-20) because Jewish law forbade marriage with one's brother's wife (Lv 18:16; 20:21), except in order to raise children for a deceased childless brother by a levirate marriage (Dt 25:5; Mk 12:19). In this case the brother, Herod Philip, was still alive and had a child, Salome. The bold denunciation by John the Baptist led to Antipas's imprisoning him around AD 30 or 31. Herodias wanted more than this. She arranged, possibly at Herod Antipas's birthday, to have her daughter dance before him and his magistrates. In appreciation, Herod Antipas promised Salome up to half of his kingdom. At her mother's bidding, she asked for John the Baptist's head on a platter.

Herodias last appears in history involved in an intrigue between her brother, Agrippa I, who had been designated king by the emperor Caligula, and her husband Antipas, who had long wanted such a title. Antipas, at his wife's insistence, went to Rome to plead his case, but he lost and was banished. Herodias, however, did remain faithful and followed him into exile, even though Caligula would not have punished her because she was Agrippa's sister.

See also Herod, Herodian Family.

HERODION Christian of Jewish ancestry to whom Paul sent greetings at the conclusion of his Epistle to the Romans (Rom 16:11).

HERON Long-necked wading bird, considered unclean under Jewish law (Lv 11:19; Dt 14:18). *See* Birds.

HESED* Part of the name Ben-hesed (1 Kgs 4:10). *See* Ben-hesed.

HESHBON Important Transjordanian city about 50 miles (80 kilometers) due east of Jerusalem. It had originally been Moabite but was conquered by Sihon, the Amorite king, and became the capital of his kingdom (Nm 21:25-30). The city was captured when Israel advanced into Canaan, and this portion of the Amorite territory was placed under Reubenite control (Nm 32:37; Jos 13:17). However, its position on the boundary between Reuben and Gad (Jos 13:26) resulted in its being occupied by the tribe of Gad. The Moabites soon contested Israel's claim to the territory, and in the period of the judges it changed hands at least once (Jgs 3:12; 1 Sm 12:9-11). Israel controlled Heshbon until around 853 BC, when it was occupied by Mesha, king of Moab. Subsequently, it was mentioned in preexilic prophetic censures of the Moabites (cf. Is 15:4; 16:8-9; Jer 48:2, 33-34). Jeremiah 49:3 seems to indicate that Heshbon was finally occupied by the neighboring Ammonites.

It was an important Nabatean city in the Greek period, and it was conquered by the Jews in the campaigns of Alexander Janneus (103–76 BC). In the Roman period it was incorporated into the province of Syria.

HESHMON Town mentioned only in Joshua 15:27. It was located near Beth-pelet in southern Judah. The notion that the Hasmoneans originated there is unsubstantiated.

HETH* Progenitor of the Hittite people and a descendant of Canaan, in Ham's line (Gn 10:15; 1 Chr 1:13). *See* Hittites.

HETHLON Site mentioned by Ezekiel (Ez 47:15; 48:1) describing part of the northern boundary of the restored kingdom of Israel.

HEXATEUCH* Name meaning "the sixfold book," given to a grouping of the first six books of the Bible. Biblical

critics added Joshua to the Pentateuch, the fivefold book (Genesis through Deuteronomy), because the contents and style of Joshua connected it intimately with the literary elements of the Pentateuch, thus creating the Hexateuch.

HEZEKI* KJV spelling of Hizki, Elpaal's son, in 1 Chronicles 8:17. *See* Hizki.

HEZEKIAH

1. King of Judah from 715–686 BC. The account of Hezekiah's reign is in 2 Kings 18:1–20:21, 2 Chronicles 29:1–32:33, and Isaiah 36:1–39:8.

Chronology Hezekiah succeeded to Judah's throne at 25 and ruled for 29 years (2 Kgs 18:2; 2 Chr 29:1). His mother was Abi (2 Kgs 18:2; 2 Chr 29:1; "Abijah," a longer form), a daughter of Zechariah. The chronology of Hezekiah's reign is difficult to establish with certainty. The Bible says the Assyrian siege of Samaria, capital of the northern kingdom of Israel, began in the fourth year of his reign and that Samaria fell in the sixth year (2 Kgs 18:9-10), which would make his reign begin about 728 BC and end about 699 BC. Assyrian king Sennacherib besieged the fortified Judean cities during Hezekiah's 14th year (2 Kgs 18:13), which would have been 714 BC. Assyrian records, however, indicate that Sennacherib came to the Assyrian throne in 705 BC and that his Judean campaign took place in 701 BC. The most generally accepted solution to the discrepancy is that Hezekiah came to the throne in 715 BC, probably after a co-regency with his father, Ahaz, that began in 728 BC. That solution harmonizes with the statement that Sennacherib's siege took place in the 14th year of Hezekiah's reign, or 701 BC.

Hezekiah's Religious Reforms Hezekiah came to the throne at a critical juncture in Judah's history. Sargon II had taken Samaria in 722 BC, and Judah was militarily weakened from wars and raids by surrounding nations during the reign of Ahaz. Perhaps motivated by warnings to the northern kingdom delivered by the prophets Amos and Hosea that punishment would come if Israel did not turn back to God, Hezekiah began his religious reforms soon after becoming king.

In the first month of his reign, Hezekiah opened the temple doors and repaired them. He brought the Levites together and ordered them to sanctify themselves and the temple and to reinstate the religious ceremonies that had long been neglected. Hezekiah brought sacrifices, and the priestly temple service was restored (2 Chr 29).

Hezekiah then sent invitations throughout Judah and Israel for the Passover celebration in Jerusalem (held a month later than the prescribed time because the priests and people could not be ready earlier). It was hoped that religious unification would be a prelude to political reunification of the northern kingdom of Israel and the southern kingdom of Judah. However, most of the northern tribes mocked the Judean messengers who brought the invitations, and only a few persons from the tribes of Asher, Manasseh, and Zebulun went to Jerusalem for the celebration (2 Chr 30).

After the Passover observance, the worshipers set about destroying the high places and altars. They broke the pillars and cut down the Asherim throughout Judah and Benjamin, and also went into Ephraim and Manasseh (2 Chr 31:1). Hezekiah even smashed the bronze serpent that Moses had made (Nm 21:6-9), for it had become an object of worship and was identified with a serpent deity, Nehushtan (2 Kgs 18:4). Because of his sweeping reforms, later generations said of Hezekiah,

"There was never another king like him in the land of Judah, either before or after his time" (2 Kgs 18:5, NLT).

The Assyrian Threat Hezekiah knew that Assyria's growing international dominance was a serious threat to his kingdom, but following his father's policy of submission, Hezekiah did not attempt any resistance at first.

The inscriptions of the Assyrian king Sargon II record his victorious campaign in 711 BC against a revolt by Aziru, king of Ashdod, who requested help from Egypt and Judah. Perhaps a prophecy received by Isaiah warned Hezekiah not to interfere with the Ashdod siege (Is 20), and so no punitive action was taken against Judah by Assyria. Sargon died in 705, and his son Sennacherib came to the throne. This triggered widespread rebellion throughout the Assyrian provinces. Hezekiah withheld tribute from the new Assyrian ruler and, taking advantage of the confused situation, made raids against the Philistines (2 Kgs 18:8). After subduing rebellious elements in the East, Sennacherib began his campaign against the "land of Hatti" (the Assyrian name for the western countries) in 701 BC. In preparation Hezekiah repaired Jerusalem's city wall, raised towers on it, built another wall outside it, and strengthened the Millo in the City of David. He also stockpiled abundant quantities of weapons and shields (2 Chr 32:5). Knowing the necessity of an adequate water supply for a city under siege, Hezekiah had a 1,777-foot (542-meter) tunnel cut through solid rock from the spring of Gihon to the Siloam Pool to bring water into the city and to prevent the Assyrians from gaining access to the spring water outside the city (2 Kgs 20:20; 2 Chr 32:3-4). The Siloam inscription, carved inside the tunnel itself, records the completion of that remarkable conduit and is one of the oldest preserved examples of the Hebrew language.

Sennacherib invaded Palestine and, after an extensive campaign, put down the rebellion there. That campaign is well documented in Assyrian records, including a description of his siege on Jerusalem in 701, and this documentation is supplemented by the biblical account (2 Kgs 18:13–19:37; 2 Chr 32:1-22; Is 36–37). Sidon, the cities of Phoenicia, and the immediate neighbors of Judah (including Byblos, Arnon, Moab, Edom, and Ashdod) submitted to the Assyrians. Resistant Philistine cities were also taken. Sennacherib laid siege against Ekron, whose king, Padi (a loyal subject of Sennacherib), had been taken prisoner by his own subjects and turned over in chains to Hezekiah. A large Egyptian and Ethiopian army failed to relieve the Ekronites, who were defeated by the Assyrians in the vicinity of Eltekah. Ekron was captured, and Padi was recalled to his throne by Sennacherib.

Sennacherib then turned his attention to the fortified cities of Judah and took them one by one (2 Kgs 18:13). Assyrian records claim that he captured 46 walled cities and countless villages, including Lachish and Debir (southwest of Jerusalem), 200,150 people, homes, cattle, and flocks without number. While Lachish was still under siege, Hezekiah saw that it was hopeless to resist and sent word to Sennacherib offering to surrender and pay whatever tribute he would impose. The Assyrian ruler demanded an enormous tribute of 300 talents of silver (800 talents according to Assyrian records, either an exaggerated figure or computed by a different standard) and 30 talents of gold. In order to pay that tribute, Hezekiah took all the silver in the temple and the royal treasuries, and stripped the gold from the temple doors and doorposts (2 Kgs 18:14-16). This treasure was sent to Sennacherib along with other gifts that, according to

the Assyrian account, included some of Hezekiah's own daughters as concubines.

The account in 2 Kings 18:17–19:37 raises the question of whether there was another invasion of Judah at a later date, or whether this passage gives additional details about the invasion of 701. Although Hezekiah had already submitted and paid tribute, these verses describe further Assyrian demands. Those who believe it was a single invasion suggest that this is an account of the Assyrian deputation sent by Sennacherib to demand Jerusalem's surrender while Lachish was still under siege. The deputation included the Tartan, Rabsaris, and Rabshakeh (titles of court officials rather than personal names). They warned the citizens that their God was no more able to save them than the gods of other cities defeated by the Assyrians. In distress Hezekiah sent word to the prophet Isaiah, who assured the king that Sennacherib would hear a rumor and return to his own land and there die by the sword (2 Kgs 19:1-7). Shortly afterward Sennacherib received word of Babylon's revolt in his eastern provinces, so he departed at once without taking Jerusalem. Assyrian records do not claim that Jerusalem was taken but only say that Hezekiah was "shut up in Jerusalem like a bird in a cage." Judah's surrounding neighbors celebrated their deliverance and brought gifts of gratitude to Hezekiah (2 Chr 32:23).

Later, the Assyrian king heard that Tirhakah, king of Ethiopia, was advancing against him, so he sent another threatening message to Hezekiah, probably to warn him against making an alliance with Tirhakah. Hezekiah took the matter before the Lord and received word from Isaiah that the Assyrian king would return the same way he came and that Jerusalem would be untouched. Soon afterward, in a miraculous intervention by God, 185,000 Assyrian troops were killed, and the Assyrian monarch abandoned his plans to conquer Hezekiah. That embarrassing calamity understandably is not mentioned by the Assyrian records. In 681 Sennacherib was killed by two of his sons as Isaiah had predicted (2 Kgs 19:7, 37).

Sometime prior to 701, Hezekiah became seriously ill, and Isaiah told him to prepare for death. The king earnestly prayed for an extension of life, and God promised him 15 more years as well as deliverance from the Assyrians. Hezekiah asked Isaiah for a sign that he would be healed, and a shadow cast by the sun moved backward 10 steps contrary to its normal direction (2 Kgs 20:1-11).

Sometime after his recovery Hezekiah received a delegation with presents from Merodach-baladan of Babylon, ostensibly to congratulate Hezekiah on his return to health. The real object of the visit was probably to enlist Hezekiah as an ally in a conspiracy being formed against Assyria. The king showed the Babylonian envoys all the gold, silver, and other valuables he possessed. This act brought a warning from Isaiah that the day would come when all those treasures would be carried away to Babylon (2 Kgs 20:12-19).

Hezekiah lived the remainder of his life in peace and prosperity. It may have been during this time that he encouraged literary efforts in Judah, which included copying some of Solomon's proverbs (Prv 25–29). Upon his death in 686, he was succeeded by his son Manasseh, who probably had become co-regent 10 years earlier.

See also Chronology of the Bible (Old Testament); Israel, History of; King.

2. KJV form of Hizkiah, Neariah's son, in 1 Chronicles 3:23. *See* Hizkiah #1.

3. Head of a family of exiles (the sons of Ater), 98 of whose descendants returned from the Babylonian exile with Zerubbabel (Ezr 2:16; Neh 7:21; 10:17).

4. Ancestor of the prophet Zephaniah, possibly King
Hezekiah himself (Zep 1:1).

HEZEKIAH'S TUNNEL* *See* Siloam, Pool of.

HEZION Tabrimmon's father and the grandfather of
Ben-hadad, king of Syria. Ben-hadad formed an alliance
with King Asa of Judah (910–869 BC) and opposed
Israel's King Baasha (908–886 BC; 1 Kgs 15:18).

HEZIR
1. Levite and head of the 17th of 24 divisions of priests
   for sanctuary service formed during David's reign
   (1 Chr 24:15).
2. Israelite leader who set his seal on Ezra's covenant
   during the postexilic era (Neh 10:20).

HEZRAI*, HEZRO One of David's mighty warriors
(2 Sm 23:35; 1 Chr 11:37), a Carmelite by birth.

HEZRON (Person)
1. Reuben's son (Gn 46:9; Ex 6:14; 1 Chr 5:3) and
   founder of the Hezronite family in Reuben's tribe
   (Nm 26:6).
2. Perez's son (Gn 46:12; Ru 4:18-19; 1 Chr 2:5-25; 4:1),
   founder of the Hezronite family in Judah's tribe (Nm
   26:21), and an ancestor of Jesus Christ (Mt 1:3; Lk 3:33).
   See also Genealogy of Jesus Christ.

HEZRON (Place) Town on Judah's border (Jos 15:3).
In Numbers 34:4 it probably forms part of the name
Hazar-addar.

HIDDAI* Name of one of King David's mighty men
(2 Sm 23:30, NLT mg).
   See also Gaash #2.

HIDDEKEL* Hebrew name for the Tigris River (Gn
2:14; Dn 10:4, KJV). *See* Tigris River.

HIEL Bethelite in the days of King Ahab who fulfilled
Joshua's curse upon the city of Jericho (Jos 6:26; 1 Kgs
16:34). Joshua had said centuries before that anyone
attempting to rebuild the city would suffer the loss of his
oldest and youngest sons. It is unclear whether Hiel's sons
died a natural death or were killed in a punitive ritual.

HIERAPOLIS City of southwest Phrygia, strategically
located between Colosse to the east and Laodicea to the

Amphitheater at Hierapolis

south. The founding of the city is credited to Eumenes II
of Pergamum (197–160 BC). Hierapolis, because of its
mineral springs and deep cave known as the Plutonium,
came to be a cultic center for the worship of Phrygian
gods. Lethal vapors issued from the cave, which was
thought to be an entrance to the underworld. Residents
believed that a priest was seated deep inside the cave and
that on certain occasions prophecies would be uttered
for those seeking them. The mineral baths attracted visitors, and gradually the city developed into a leading
commercial center. As Roman rule enveloped the city,
Hierapolis became part of the province of Asia.

Under Paul's influence, Christianity took hold there
during his stay in Ephesus. Paul mentions Hierapolis in
connection with the believer Epaphras, who worked diligently for the inhabitants as well as those in Laodicea
and Colosse (Col 4:13). Even though several early Christians were martyred there, the church continued to grow.
In the fourth century, Christians closed off the Plutonium with stones.

Egyptian Hieroglyphics

HIEROGLYPHICS* Early form of writing by using
pictorial signs. The Egyptian, Hittite, Mayan, and Cretan
civilizations—each one independently of the others—
developed hieroglyphics. The hieroglyphics with which we
are most familiar are Egyptian. They began as pictures of
the objects they represent, so that a circle with rays emanating from the circumference would indicate the sun.
This type of script began to be used in Egypt about 3000
BC. It was usually carved in stone but sometimes was written on papyrus with a reed pen. As papyrus began to be
used more often, the symbols employed for the stone
engravings became much more awkward to use on papyrus. The scribes and bookkeepers who used these symbols
developed a cursive form of hieroglyphics called hieratic.
This was later refined to a shorthand script called demotic.

As the script changed, so did the meaning of the signs.
These signs began as picture-symbols, but they came to
represent the sounds of the symbol. Thus we might use a
ham pictorially for the verb "meet" because a ham is a
type of meat, a word that sounds like "meet." The Egyptians did not convert these signs into an alphabet as did
many of their neighbors.

The use of hieroglyphics in Egypt lasted until the fifth
century AD, when it was finally replaced by the alphabetic scripts of Latin and Greek. During the Middle Ages,
there was little interest in or knowledge of hieroglyphics.
During the Renaissance, interest revived, but scholars
were unable to interpret the script. Its meaning remained
a mystery until members of Napoleon's expedition
to Egypt in 1779 discovered the Rosetta Stone with

inscriptions in Greek, demotic, and hieroglyphic. Twenty-five years later the Frenchman Jean-Francois Champollion deciphered the stone.

HIERONYMUS Hellenistic ruler in intertestamental period. Hostile toward Palestinian Jews who refused to accept Greek ways, Antiochus Eupator sent his vice-regent Lysias with 80,000 troops to solicit compliance. Maccabeus and his band, led by an angel, wrecked Lysias's expedition and evoked a settlement that permitted Jews to maintain their ancestral customs. However, Hieronymus and fellow district governors Timothy, Apollonius, and Demophon would not allow the Jews to live in peace and quiet (2 Macc 12:2).

HIGGAION* Musical notation in text of Psalm 9:16, presumably cueing the instrumental accompaniment to play softly. *See* Music.

HIGH COUNCIL *See* Sanhedrin.

HIGH PLACE Phrase commonly translated from the Hebrew *bamah*, which apparently derived from a word originally meaning "the back (or ridge) of an animal." Thus it came to refer to a height or hill or a stone burial cairn. Usually it was an elevated worship center, such as the ones referred to in Numbers 33:51-52, 1 Samuel 9:13-14, 2 Kings 12:3, 2 Chronicles 21:11, and Ezekiel 36:1-2. But sometimes (as in 2 Kgs 23:8) it was a *bamah* of the gate, a sanctuary with no special reference to height, located at the city gate as in Dan and Beersheba. It might even have been placed in a declivity (Jer 7:31).

That a *bamah* might simply be a burial place with commemorative stelae or memorial stones is clear from such a passage as Ezekiel 43:7. An illustration of such a *bamah* is the so-called Gezer high place. This Bronze Age center with its 10 huge pillars is now interpreted as a mortuary shrine instead of a sanctuary in the strict sense of the term.

A second word translated "high place" is *ramah* (elevation), from the Hebrew meaning "to be high." Ezekiel used this term to refer to illicit worship centers (16:24-25, 31-39) that evidently had no necessary connection with height.

One of the best-known and best-preserved of all high places in the vicinity of Palestine is the great high place at Petra, discovered by George L. Robinson in 1900. Located on a ridge west of the Khazneh, or treasury, it consists of a large rectangular court and adjacent altars. The court is about 47 feet (14.3 meters) long and 21 feet (6.4 meters) wide and is cut into the rock platform to a depth of 18 inches (45.7 centimeters). West of the court stand a square and a round altar, each hewn from the solid rock. South of the court is a pool measuring about eight and a half by nine and a half feet (2.6 by 2.9 meters) and cut four feet (1.2 meters) into the rock. South of the pool stand two sacred obelisks or pillars, also cut out of the solid rock. This whole complex is reached from a lower terrace by two flights of stairs. At this center the ancient Nabatean inhabitants of Petra evidently engaged in feasts and sacrifices to honor their gods. Though the worship center in its present form does not date before the first century BC, it preserves an ancient tradition of Transjordan and illustrates the pagan and Israelite high places of OT times.

The pagan high place was usually located on a physical height, where one could feel closer to the god. Its first essential was an altar, which might be a heap of earth, unhewn stones, or a unit cut out of the solid rock. Second, there was a stone pillar (Dt 12:3) or obelisk *(matsebah)* representing the male deity and having phallic associations; third, a tree or pole *(asherah)* representing the female deity (a fertility goddess); and fourth, a laver for ceremonial washings. A sanctuary with an image of the deity also required a building of some sort to protect it (2 Kgs 17:29).

At these pagan high places sacrifices of animals and sometimes of human beings took place, and religious prostitution or homosexual acts were common. It is natural that such practices should develop in a context of sympathetic magic, where promiscuity and breeding among human beings was supposed to influence animals and crops.

The Hebrews had legitimate high places between the time of the destruction of the tabernacle at Shiloh and construction of the temple, though there was little similarity to pagan accoutrements or practices, apart from the presence of an altar and the offering of sacrifices. At one high place the people ate a sacrificial meal before Samuel anointed Saul king (1 Sm 9:12–10:1). The tabernacle was located at the high place of Gibeon during the reign of David (1 Chr 16:39; 21:29). Solomon offered sacrifices at several high places (1 Kgs 3:2-3), and at the high place of Gibeon he met God and was granted the gift of wisdom for his administration (vv 4-15). Once Solomon's temple was completed, high places were eliminated and were off-limits for the Hebrews.

When the Hebrews entered Canaan, they encountered pagan peoples who had long worshiped at high places. God commanded the Israelites to destroy those sanctuaries (Nm 33:51-52) to avoid contamination by them, but the warning went largely unheeded. At the height of the Hebrew kingdom, after Solomon had completed the temple, he built high places for the god Chemosh of Moab, Molech of Ammon, and other gods of his pagan wives. For this sin God determined to split the Hebrew kingdom (1 Kgs 11:7-11).

After the division of the kingdom, Jeroboam established high places at Dan and Bethel, and Ahab and others proliferated their construction. Judgment was prophesied (1 Kgs 13:2-3; 2 Kgs 17:7-18), and ultimately the kingdom of Israel went into captivity to Assyria for her idolatry.

Rehoboam, the first king of the southern kingdom, spread high places all over his domain (1 Kgs 14:23-24). Though King Asa launched a revival of true religion, he did not remove the high places (15:12-14). Jehoshaphat also initiated revival, but again the high places remained (22:43). On the other hand, his son Jehoram and his wife, Athaliah, encouraged their construction (2 Chr 21:11). Joash, during his revival, did not eliminate the high places (2 Kgs 12:3), nor did the good king Uzziah in similar efforts (15:3-4). Ahaz made no pretense of faithfulness to God, and actively encouraged the idolatry of the pagan sanctuaries (16:3-4). Finally, Hezekiah launched a campaign against the high places (2 Chr 31:1), but his policies were reversed during the reign of his wicked son Manasseh (2 Kgs 21:2-9). Josiah led the last Judean revival and again attacked the high places (23:5, 8).

The prophets Isaiah (Is 15:2; 16:12), Jeremiah (Jer 48:35), Ezekiel (Ez 6:3), Hosea (Hos 10:8), and Amos (Am 7:9) roundly condemned these centers of idolatry. *See* Canaanite Deities and Religion; Gods and Goddesses; Grove; Idols, Idolatry.

HIGH PRIEST *See* Priests and Levites.

HIGHWAY*, King's *See* King's Highway.

HILEN* Alternate name for Holon, a city assigned to Levites, in 1 Chronicles 6:58. *See* Holon #1.

HILKIAH

1. Father of Eliakim, an overseer in King Hezekiah's household (2 Kgs 18:18, 26; Is 22:20; 36:3, 22).
2. High priest and Shallum's son in the reign of King Josiah who, during the repair of the temple, found the Book of the Law (2 Kgs 22:3-14; 1 Chr 6:13; 9:11; 2 Chr 34:14-22). According to Ezra 7:1 (cf. 1 Esd 8:1), he was also an ancestor of Ezra. He is an important figure in the events surrounding Josiah's religious reform, not only because he found the Book of the Law, but also because he led the king's messengers to consult Huldah the prophetess regarding God's Word (2 Kgs 22:14) and later presided over the purification of the temple (23:4).
3. Merarite Levite, the son of Amzi and Amaziah's father (1 Chr 6:45).
4. Merarite Levite and Hosah's son, who was appointed as a gatekeeper in the temple by David (1 Chr 26:11).
5. Companion of Ezra at the public reading of the law (Neh 8:4). Scholars disagree as to whether he was a layman or a priest.
6. Priest among the returned exiles (Neh 12:7).
7. Anathoth priest who was the father of Jeremiah (Jer 1:1).
8. Father of Gemariah whom King Zedekiah sent to Babylon with a letter of assurance from Jeremiah (Jer 29:3).

HILLEL

1. Father of Abdon, one of the judges (Jgs 12:13-15).
2. Jewish teacher and scholar (c. 60 BC–AD 20) who helped to develop the oral law and may have founded rabbinic Judaism. Hillel was called "the Elder," a title that indicates a person holding a position of honor, generally given to those who stood at the head of the community. Born in Babylonia, he moved to Palestine for more advanced studies under two outstanding scholars, Shemaiah and Abtalyon. He first gained recognition when the sons of Bathyra, the chief interpreters of the Law at the time, could not decide on an answer to an important legal problem, namely, whether or not the offering of the paschal lamb overrode the Sabbath prohibitions. Having heard that there was a man living in Jerusalem who had studied under Shemaiah and Abtalyon, they sent for Hillel and told him the problem. Hillel's answer was that the paschal offering took precedence over the Sabbath, and he argued his point so successfully that his ruling was accepted. He was then appointed to replace the sons of Bathyra. It has been argued, however, that Hillel's appointment can hardly be attributed solely to this one incident.

   Hillel was one of the first persons to apply advanced principles of interpretation in determining practical law and action. Thus he is especially important for the development of the Talmud and the oral law. These rules provided the basis for later rabbinic interpretation.

   There are many stories describing Hillel's character, picturing him as a man of great humility and extreme patience, pursuing peace even at the expense of truth. He is usually contrasted with his colleague Shammai, who is portrayed as impatient and ill-tempered. The most famous tale tells of a heathen who came to Shammai to be converted on the condition that he teach him the entire Law while he stood on one foot. Shammai snubbed him, and so the heathen went to Hillel. Hillel replied, "What is hateful to you do not do to your neighbor; this is the entire Law, all the rest is commentary. Now go and learn it." Hillel thus became a model for Jews throughout history.
   See also Judaism; Shammai #4; Talmud.

HIN* Liquid measure equal to one-sixth of a bath, or about one gallon (3.8 liters). *See* Weights and Measures.

HIND* Adult female red deer. *See* Animals (Deer).

HINNOM, Valley of Deep, narrow ravine running south of Jerusalem that marked the boundary between Judah's and Benjamin's territories. *See* Gehenna.

HIPPOPOTAMUS *See* Animals.

HIPPOS* One of the cities of the Decapolis (a loose confederation of 10 Greek cities) established in Palestine after the death of Alexander the Great (323 BC; also called Susitha); not mentioned in the Bible. Its location is in doubt, but most likely it was eight miles (12.8 kilometers) north of Gadara and four miles (6.4 kilometers) east of the Sea of Galilee near the road to Damascus. Its position was of strategic military importance in the defense of Jerusalem, while its location was also ideal for trading, from which it exported not only its merchandise but also Greek culture.
   See also Decapolis.

HIRAH Adullamite and friend of Judah to whose house Judah went after he and his brothers sold Joseph (Gn 38:1). He accompanied Judah to the sheepshearing after Judah's wife died (v 12), and he served as the messenger to carry a kid from Judah to Tamar (v 20).

HIRAM

1. King of Tyre during the time of David and Solomon. After David had conquered Jerusalem and moved his capital there, Hiram sent cedarwood, masons, and carpenters to build David's palace (2 Sm 5:11; 1 Chr 14:1). Hiram remained David's friend throughout his life (1 Kgs 5:1), and after David's death, he sought to continue that friendship with Solomon. When Solomon was ready to build the temple, Hiram provided wood from the forests of Lebanon, gold, and skilled craftsmen to help build and furnish the temple; Solomon, in return, gave Hiram wheat and oil for his household. Moreover, Solomon gave Hiram 20 cities in Galilee, although Scripture indicates that Hiram was not pleased with them (1 Kgs 5:1-11; 9:10-14).

   Although the Israelites were not a maritime people, Solomon did maintain a fleet of ships at Ezion-geber (1 Kgs 9:26-28). Hiram gave his assistance to Solomon by supplying sailors and perhaps ships to make

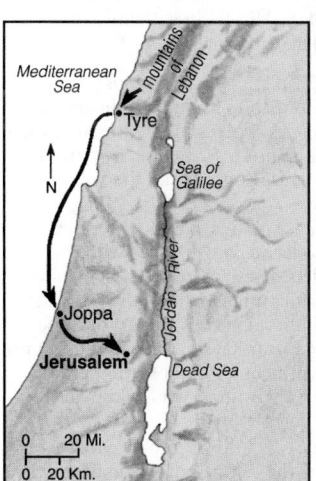

King Hiram Supplies Solomon with Building Materials for the Temple Cedar logs were cut in Lebanon, floated by sea to Joppa, and then transported to Jerusalem.

Solomon's fleet operable. The Phoenicians were noted sailors, who sailed the Mediterranean Sea as far west as Tarshish in Spain.

Hiram was probably the son of Abibal. Hiram reigned in Tyre for 34 years and died at the age of 53. Phoenician historians record that Solomon married the daughter of Hiram.
2. Craftsman from Tyre who worked on Solomon's temple. He was said to be the son of a man of Tyre and a woman from the tribe of Naphtali (1 Kgs 7:13-14), although 2 Chronicles 2:14 says that his mother was from "the daughters of Dan." (Possibly her ancestors were from Dan's tribe; cf. Ex 38:23.) He was responsible for the creation of various furnishings in the temple: 2 bronze pillars, the capitals that adorned the pillars, the molten sea and the 12 oxen on which it stood, the 10 lavers with their bases, as well as shovels, pots, and basins.

His name is also spelled Huram in 2 Chronicles 4:11. He is called Huram-abi (abi meaning "master") in 2 Chronicles 2:13 and 4:16.

HITTITES Biblical people who figure largely in the promises of a land for the descendants of Abram and the children of Israel. Once unknown to secular history and thought to be a mythical people by some critics of Bible history, information about the Hittites has been uncovered by archaeologists and historians, and they now are known to have had an empire centered in Asia Minor. They were of sufficient military strength to challenge the armies of Egypt under the vainglorious Ramses II and fought him to a standstill at Kadesh on the Orontes.

For the most part, the biblical references do not suggest that the Hittites were more than a minor group, but the association of Hittite kings and Egypt with Solomon's trade in horses and their involvement in the conflicts of Syria and Israel in the divided monarchy indicate that the Hittites were a people of great consequence.

Geography The Hittite Empire had its center in Anatolia (Asia Minor, modern Turkey), with its capital at Hattusas (modern Baghazkoy) at the bend of the Halys River (present Kizil Irmak). The empire at times extended over a much larger area without definite boundaries since it included city-states that were dependencies of the Anatolian kingdom, related to it by treaties but otherwise not a part of it. Because of their presence in Palestine-Syria, the Hittites made their influence felt in Egypt and are well known from the art and inscriptions of that country. The presence of Hittites in Palestine is widely attested in the Bible, and the power of the Hittites in Palestinian cities like Hebron is indicated in patriarchal times.

History The Hittites (also known as Hattians) were one of several groups of peoples, thought to be neither Semitic nor Indo-European, who occupied the Anatolian plateau in the third millennium BC. In the late part of this millennium Indo-Europeans overran the area and assumed political power.

History in the true sense, that is, based on written records, begins in Anatolia around 1900 BC with the arrival of Assyrian traders. These merchants established themselves in various cities and corresponded with their homeland using cuneiform tablets. Numbers of these records have been found near Kayseri. These mention the struggle among Hittite principalities for supremacy in Anatolia and refer to a King Anittas, who is known from Hittite sources of later date.

During the 15th century BC, the dominance of the Hurrians was broken by the campaigns of the Egyptian king Thutmose III, but another Hurrian kingdom,

Mitanni, soon became prominent in western Asia. Mitanni presented a threat to the Hittites, but with the arrival of an ambitious and energetic monarch, Suppiluliuma I (c. 1380–1340 BC), there came a resurgence of Hittite vitality and the strength of the empire. This was the time of the writing of the Amarna letters, with their testimony of the confused situation in Palestine-Syria.

Suppululiuma carried out a brilliant military expedition against Mitanni and then, by combining force with diplomatic genius, forged for himself a buffer zone of vassal city-states, which were bound to him by treaties, copies of which were found in the Hittite archives.

During the first half of the 14th century, the languor of Amenhotep III and the religious preoccupation of Akhenaten had allowed the Asiatic empire of Egypt to dwindle away into a memory. But with the beginning of the 19th dynasty, the Egyptians became concerned about regaining what was lost. The contest for Palestine-Syria reached its climax with the famous battle at Kadesh on the Orontes, where the initial advantage was won by Hittite chariots. Ramses II celebrated the battle as a victory, although he barely escaped with his life. The Hittite king, Muwatallis, also claimed a triumph, but in political terms the battle was inconclusive. The next Hittite king after him, Hattusilis III, signed a treaty with Ramses II in the 21st year of the reign of the Egyptian king; the pact was confirmed by the marriage of the daughter of Hattusilis to Ramses II.

Around the middle of the 13th century BC, the Hittites were threatened from the west by the Ahhiyawa, possibly to be associated with the Achaeans and the Sea Peoples (see Philistia, Philistines). It was a wave of the Sea Peoples that brought the Hittite Empire to an end around 1190 BC and surged along the eastern Mediterranean coast until it was finally stopped in the Nile Delta by Ramses III.

In northern Syria, independent city-states continued to be ruled by kings who bore Hittite names and erected monuments inscribed with Hittite hieroglyphs. The Assyrians continued to refer to the area as the Land of Hatti, and the OT speaks of these rulers of principalities as "kings of the Hittites." These little kingdoms were soon placed under Assyrian tribute and became Assyrian provinces in the reigns of Shalmaneser V and Sargon II, the rulers who also put an end to the northern kingdom of Israel by conquering Samaria in 721 BC.

Languages and Literature In the texts found at Boghazkoy, eight different languages were employed. Of these, only two, Hittite and Akkadian, were used for official royal records. Akkadian was the lingua franca of the empire and was also the main language of the Amarna tablets. Hurrian is the only other language in which complete texts were written. The other languages occur mostly in short passages in Hittite religious documents, and one is identified only by some technical terms.

There were eight languages: (1) Hittite, also called Nesite, was recognized by B. Hrozny as having affinities with Indo-European. This proposal met with skepticism among scholars for a while, but it has been proved beyond question. (2) Hattic (Hattian), the language of the aboriginal people of Anatolia, is used for speeches of the priests in the performance of the cultic ritual relating to the Hittite pantheon. (3) Luwian is another Indo-European language, closely related to Hittite. (4) Palaic, a little-known language, is also Indo-European. (5) Hurrian appears in many ritual texts. Fragments of a Hurrian translation of the Epic of Gilgamesh were found. One of the Amarna tablets, written by Tushratta, king of Mitanni, to Amenhotep III, was in Hurrian. Also represented are

(6) the Aryan language of the Mitanni rulers, (7) Akkadian, and (8) Sumerian. In addition to the cuneiform script, the Hittites used hieroglyphs, which have been found inscribed on stone and lead.

The Hittite archives contained texts of official documents, such as treaties, laws, instructions, annals of the kings, letters, and other historical records. There was much religious literature, including myths, legends, epics, incantations, rituals, omens, prayers, and descriptions of festivals and their celebration.

The People The diversity of language characteristic of Hittite civilization is paralleled by the great mixture of ethnic backgrounds, particularly over the geographic range covered by the empire. The physical appearance of the Hittites is known from their own reliefs and from representation on Egyptian monuments. Their own depictions show the Hittites with unattractive faces, heavy coats, tall pointed caps, and shoes with turned-up toes.

Religion The Hittites had a pantheon of deities, known by name from the inscriptions and by appearance from the reliefs. Gods may be identified by a weapon or tool carried in the right hand, a symbol in the left hand, wings or similar appurtenances, or the sacred animal on which a divinity may stand.

A principal god was the weather god, whose sacred animal was the bull. Out of the multiplicity of local cults, there arose an official pantheon, headed by the sun goddess, Arinna, who was the supreme deity of the state and of the king. The treaties of the Hittites typically have a long list of divinities who served as witnesses to the treaty and oath.

Hittites and the Bible The name "Hittite(s)" occurs nearly 50 times in the OT but does not appear in the NT. If one includes the occurrences of the name of Heth, the father of the Hittites, there are more than 60 citations in the Bible. Most have to do with the presence of Hittites in Canaan. Their progenitor and eponym, Heth, is listed second among the sons of Canaan in the "table of nations" (Gn 10:15; cf. 1 Chr 1:13). Most of the references to the "sons of Heth" appear in the narrative of the purchase of the cave of Machpelah by Abraham (Gn 23).

The OT references to Hittites include Genesis 26:34; 27:46 (Hittite women); 49:29-32; 50:13 (Ephron); Exodus 33:2; Numbers 13:29; Deuteronomy 7:1; 20:17 (their destruction); Joshua 11:3; 12:8 (occupants of Canaan); 1 Samuel 26:6; 2 Samuel 11–12 (Uriah, a warrior under David); 1 Kings 9:20; 10:29 (laborers or traders under Solomon); 11:1 (wife of Solomon); Ezra 9:1 (foreigners); Ezekiel 16:3, 45 (Jerusalem's ancestors).

HIVITES Name of a pre-Israelite group living in Canaan. Though not yet discovered/rated archaeologically or from secular history as a people, they were regarded as emerging from a son of Canaan (Gn 10:17) and as inhabiting areas of the Lebanon Mountains (Jgs 3:3) and Mt Hermon (Jos 11:3). They are referred to frequently as a group dispossessed by Israel (Jos 12:8; 24:11; 1 Kgs 9:20) but who managed to survive into the kingdom period (2 Sm 24:7) and lived at that time near Tyre as well as in other possible areas. Some scholars think that an error in copying, involving the changing of the letters *r* (resh) to *w* (waw) was responsible for the origin of the name Hivite from Horite.

Others have suggested a scribal confusion of names, since Zibeon is called a Hivite in Genesis 36:2 and a Horite in verses 20 and 29. In several cases the Septuagint gives "Horite" in place of the Masoretic Text "Hivite"

(Gn 34:2; Jos 9:7). Other passages in the Septuagint read "Hittite" rather than "Hivite" (Jos 11:3; Jgs 3:3).

The overlapping or equivalence of Hivite and Horite in Genesis 36 probably indicates some relationship between the two peoples (cf. Ishmaelites and Midianites in Gn 37:27-28, 36). Perhaps both Horites and Hivites are related to the Hurrians, who are well attested archaeologically.

The fact that there are some 25 occurrences of the name "Hivite(s)" in the OT, nearly one-third of which come in Joshua, makes it probable that they were a distinct people. Aside from Hivites in Palestine, they also appeared in Edomite territory (Gn 36:2). OT references to Hivites include Hamor (Gn 34:2), the men of Gibeon (Jos 9:7), the northern Hivites (Jgs 3:3-8), and those who lived near Tyre (2 Sm 24:7). During the reign of Solomon, the Hivites and other foreign inhabitants of the land were made slaves; that is, they were put under forced labor (1 Kgs 9:20-21; 2 Chr 8:7).

HIZKI Elpaal's son from Benjamin's tribe (1 Chr 8:17).

HIZKIAH
1. Neariah's son and a descendant of David through Rehoboam's line (1 Chr 3:23). *See* Hezekiah #2.
2. KJV spelling of Hezekiah, Zephaniah's forefather, in Zephaniah 1:1. *See* Hezekiah #4.

HIZKIJAH* KJV form of Hezekiah, Ater's descendant, in Nehemiah 10:17. *See* Hezekiah #3.

HOBAB Name associated with Moses' father-in-law (Nm 10:29; Jgs 4:11, NLT mg), who was a priest of Midian (Ex 18:1) and ancestor of the Kenites (Jgs 4:11). He is usually called Jethro (Ex 3:1; 4:18; 18:1-12), but also Reuel (Ex 2:18).

The confusion surrounding the name Hobab has never been satisfactorily resolved. Judges 4:11 seems to identify Hobab with Jethro; there is some manuscript evidence for adding "Hobab" to "the Kenite, Moses' father-in-law" in Judges 1:16, and to the mention of Reuel in Exodus 2:18. But Hobab could be Jethro's son, on one reading of Numbers 10:29a: "Hobab the son of Reuel the Midianite, Moses' father-in-law." In this passage Moses requests that Hobab accompany Israel as guide and adviser in the wilderness.

See also Jethro.

HOBAH Town to which Abraham pursued the armies under Chedorlaomer (Gn 14:15). Its location is uncertain, but various suggestions have been made. Some equate it with the Hobah about 50 miles (80 kilometers) northwest of Damascus; others, with the territory called Ube in the Amarna letters; and still others, with Tell el-Salihite, 10 miles (16 kilometers) east of Damascus.

HOBAIAH Head of a priestly family who returned to Palestine with Zerubbabel after the exile. He was unable to prove his priestly genealogy and so was not allowed to do priestly service (Ezr 2:61; Neh 7:63).

HOD Zophah's son from Asher's tribe (1 Chr 7:37).

HODAIAH* KJV spelling of Hodaviah, David's descendant, in 1 Chronicles 3:24. *See* Hodaviah #1.

HODAVIAH
1. Postexilic descendant of David (1 Chr 3:24).
2. Chieftain of Manasseh's half-tribe east of the Jordan (1 Chr 5:24).

3. Hassenuah's son and the father of Meshullam from Benjamin's tribe (1 Chr 9:7).
4. Progenitor of a family of Levites who returned with the exiles from Babylon (Ezr 2:40); alternately called Judah in Ezra 3:9 and Hodevah in Nehemiah 7:43.

HODESH Name given to Shaharaim's wife from Benjamin's tribe in 1 Chronicles 8:9 (a textually corrupt passage).

HODEVAH* Alternate spelling of Hodaviah in Nehemiah 7:43 (see NLT mg). *See* Hodaviah #4.

HODIAH, HODIJAH*
1. A man of Judah mentioned in 1 Chronicles 4:19.
2, 3, 4. Three of the men who signed the covenant of Ezra (Neh 10:10, 13, 18) bear this name; two of them are perhaps among those who interpreted the covenant to the people at Ezra's public reading of the law (8:7) and stood upon the stairs of the Levites during the service of covenant renewal (9:5).

HOGLAH One of Zelophehad's five daughters (Nm 26:33; 27:1; Jos 17:3). Zelophehad, who was of Manasseh's tribe, had no sons, so that his inheritance passed to his daughters. They married within their own tribe according to God's command, so that their land remained in the tribe of the family of their father (Nm 36:11-12).

HOHAM Amorite king of Hebron, confederate with four other kings in reprisals against Gibeon for making peace with Joshua (Jos 10:3). They were defeated and put to death at the cave of Makkedah (vv 16-27).

HOLINESS Chief attribute of God and a quality to be developed in his people. "Holiness" and the adjective "holy" occur more than 900 times in the Bible. The primary OT word for holiness means "to cut" or "to separate." Fundamentally, holiness is a cutting off or separation from what is unclean and a consecration to what is pure.

In the OT, holiness as applied to God signifies his transcendence over creation and the moral perfection of his character. God is holy in that he is utterly distinct from his creation and exercises sovereign majesty and power over it. His holiness is especially prominent in the Psalms (47:8) and the Prophets (Ez 39:7), where "holiness" emerges as a synonym for Israel's God. Thus, Scripture ascribes to God the title "Holy" (Is 57:15), "Holy One" (Jb 6:10; Is 43:15), and "Holy One of Israel" (Ps 89:18; Is 60:14; Jer 50:29).

In the OT God's holiness denotes that the Lord is separate from all that is evil and defiled (cf. Jb 34:10). His holy character is the standard of absolute moral perfection (Is 5:16). God's holiness—his transcendent majesty and the purity of his character—are skillfully balanced in Psalm 99. Verses 1 through 3 portray God's distance from the finite and earthbound, whereas verses 4 and 5 emphasize his separation from sin and evil.

In the OT God demanded holiness in the lives of his people. Through Moses, God said to the congregation of Israel, "You shall be holy; for I the LORD your God am holy" (Lv 19:2, RSV). The holiness enjoined by the OT was twofold: (1) external, or ceremonial; and (2) internal, or moral and spiritual. OT ceremonial holiness, prescribed in the Pentateuch (the first five books of the OT) included ritual consecration to God's service. Thus priests and Levites were sanctified by a complex process of ritual consecration (Ex 29), as were the Hebrew

Nazirites, which means "separated ones" (Nm 6:1-21). Prophets like Elisha (2 Kgs 4:9) and Jeremiah (Jer 1:5) were also sanctified for a special prophetic ministry in Israel.

But the OT also draws attention to the inner, moral, and spiritual aspects of holiness. Men and women, created in the image of God, are called to cultivate the holiness of God's own character in their lives (Lv 19:2; Nm 15:40). In the NT the ceremonial holiness prominent in the Pentateuch recedes to the background. Whereas much of Judaism in Jesus' time sought a ceremonial holiness by works (Mk 7:1-5), the NT stresses the ethical rather than the formal dimension of holiness (vv 6-12). With the coming of the Holy Spirit, the early church perceived that holiness of life was a profound internal reality that should govern an individual's thought and attitudes in relation to persons and objects in the external world.

The NT Greek equivalent of the common Hebrew word for holiness signifies an inner state of freedom from moral fault and a relative harmony with the moral perfection of God. The word "godlikeness" or "godliness" captures the sense of the primary Greek word for holiness. Another Greek word approximates the dominant OT concept of holiness as external separation from the profane and dedication to the service of the Lord.

Because the NT writers assumed the OT portrait of deity, holiness is ascribed to God in relatively few apostolic texts. Jesus affirmed the ethical nature of God when he enjoined his disciples to pray that the Father's name might be esteemed for what it is: "Hallowed be thy name" (Mt 6:9, KJV). In the book of Revelation the Father's moral perfection is extolled with the threefold ascription of holiness borrowed from Isaiah: "Holy, holy, holy, is the Lord God Almighty, who was and is and is to come" (Rv 4:8, RSV; cf. Is 6:3). Luke, however, contemplated God's holiness in terms of the dominant OT concept of his transcendence and majesty (Lk 1:49).

Similarly the holiness of Jesus Christ is asserted in the NT. Luke (Lk 1:35; 4:34), Peter (Acts 3:14; 4:27-30), the writer of Hebrews (Heb 7:26), and John (Rv 3:7) ascribe holiness to both the Father and the Son.

Since the Spirit comes from God, discloses his holy character, and is the instrument of God's holy purposes in the world, he also is absolutely holy (Mt 1:18; 3:16; 28:19; Lk 1:15; 4:14). The common title "Holy Spirit" underscores the ethical perfection of the third person of the Godhead (Jn 3:5-8; 14:16-17, 26).

In the NT, holiness also characterizes Christ's church. The apostle Paul taught that Christ loved the church and died for it "that he might sanctify her, having cleansed her by the washing of water with the word" (Eph 5:26, RSV). Peter addressed the church as a holy people in language borrowed from the OT. Separated from the unbelieving nations and consecrated to the Lord, the church is "a holy nation" (1 Pt 2:9; cf. Ex 19:6).

But the NT more often discusses holiness in relation to individual Christians. Believers in Christ are frequently designated as "saints," literally meaning "holy ones," since through faith God justifies sinners, pronouncing them "holy" in his sight. A justified sinner is by no means morally perfect, but God does declare believers to be guiltless. Thus, although Christians at Corinth, for example, were plagued with numerous sins, Paul could address his erring friends as those who were "sanctified in Christ Jesus, called to be saints" (1 Cor 1:2, RSV). Despite their problems, the Corinthian believers were "holy ones" in Christ.

The NT, however, places great stress upon the reality of practical holiness in the Christian's daily experience. The

God who freely declares a person righteous through faith in Christ commands that the believer progress in holiness of life. In God's plan, a growth in holiness should accompany believing. God graciously provides the spiritual resources to enable Christians to be "partakers of the divine nature" (2 Pt 1:4).

See also God, Being and Attributes of.

HOLM TREE* Tree mentioned in Isaiah 44:14 (KJV "ash") whose wood was used for fuel and idol construction; its identity is uncertain. *See* Plants (Cypress; Oak; Ash).

HOLOFERNES According to the book of Judith, the chief Assyrian general under King Nebuchadnezzar (Jdt 2:4) who was ordered by the king to "go and attack the whole west country" (v 6). He ravaged the nations one after another (vv 21-27) and his huge army spread terror wherever it went (v 28). He destroyed "all the gods of the land, so that all nations should worship Nebuchadnezzar only, and all their tongues and tribes should call upon him as god" (3:8). When Holofernes made a determined effort to seize Bethulia (7:1ff.), the forces of Israel rallied and took up their weapons. The desperate Jews were about to surrender when the beautiful widow Judith asked permission of the leaders of the Jews to go to Holofernes (8:32-34). The permission was given and Judith called upon God to deliver her people (9:2-14). She "made herself very beautiful" (10:4) and went to meet Holofernes "to give him a true report" (v 13). Holofernes came under the spell of the beautiful Judith, and on the fourth day of her visit he made a banquet and Judith was invited (12:10-11). Holofernes became drunk, and when all the servants had left, Judith took his sword and severed his head from his body and carried it back to Bethulia in a bag and showed it to the leaders of Israel. Jubilant Israelites attacked the leaderless Assyrians, who fled in panic. Led by Judith, the Jews joined in celebration and praise and offered thanksgiving in Jerusalem. This story of defeated pride has been a favorite theme of artists, including Donatello and Dante.

HOLON
1. Town in the uplands of Judah's inheritance (Jos 15:51) given to the Levites (21:15). In 1 Chronicles 6:58, the town is called Hilen. Holon may be Khirbet 'Alin, northwest of Hebron. *See* Levitical Cities.
2. City near Heshbon, located in the plain of Moab (Jer 48:21).

HOLY GHOST* KJV rendering of Holy Spirit. *See* Spirit of God.

HOLY OF HOLIES* Inner room of the tabernacle and temple in which the ark of the covenant was kept. *See* Tabernacle; Temple.

HOLY ONE OF ISRAEL *See* God, Names of.

HOLY PLACE *See* Tabernacle; Temple.

HOLY SPIRIT *See* Spirit of God.

HOLY WAR* *See* War, Holy.

HOMAM* Alternate spelling of Heman, Lotan's son, in 1 Chronicles 1:39 (NLT mg). *See* Heman #1.

HOMER Dry measure of capacity estimated to be anywhere from four to six and a half bushels. *See* Weights and Measures.

HOMES AND DWELLINGS

PREVIEW
• Middle Bronze Age Houses
• Late Bronze Age Houses
• Israelite Houses of the Iron Age
• Houses in New Testament Times

Middle Bronze Age Houses (c. 1800–1500 BC)
Israel's early ancestors lived mostly in tents or temporary dwellings, but the Canaanites of the middle Bronze Age (into whose land the Israelites came) lived in substantial houses of several rooms built around a courtyard.

The simplest form of this new type of house had a courtyard with a single room on one side, generally on the west of the courtyard, to avoid having the prevailing westerly winds blow smoke into the room. Silos for storing grain were normally in the room rather than in the courtyard. Good examples of such one-roomed houses were found at Tell Nagila, northwest of Beersheba, dating to about 1700 BC. Three such houses had a room 10 by 7 feet (3 by 2.1 meters) and a courtyard 10 by 16 feet (3 by 4.9 meters). Partitions sometimes divided the room. The walls were made of rough stone and mud bricks covered by mud plaster and were hardly thick enough to carry a second story. Houses were set close together to take advantage of a common back wall with entrances to the court on roughly parallel streets. Each house contained a stone and clay bench along the walls.

Sometimes several rooms were built off one side of the courtyard. The grandest of these yet found comes from Tell Beit Mirsim, dating from about 1600 BC, probably the house of a local governor or patrician. There were no less than six rooms on the western side of the courtyard, which was some 35 by 19 feet (10.7 by 5.8 meters) in size. The roofed living space, including both the ground and second floors, was about 1,500 square feet (139 square meters); a second floor is assumed from the thickness of the walls all around. The ground floor may have been multifunctional with two stable rooms and two storage areas. Other less imposing variants of the courtyard house with rooms on one side only come from this same tell in Stratum E (c. 1700 BC).

The second type of house in the middle Bronze Age had a roofed hall with rooms on one or two sides. A good example of such a house with rooms on one side comes from Tell Beit Mirsim, dating from about 1800 BC. The large, roofed, rectangular hall contained three large, flat stones set along the long axis to serve as foundations for the wooden roof supports. Rafters of wood and a roof of reeds covered with mud were found in the debris. Each of the three rooms on the west was entered from the hall. The stone foundations and mud brick walls were substantial enough to support a second story that could be reached by an exterior wooden staircase or ladder. The floor of earth, ashes, and straw was carefully smoothed over.

A third type of house consisted of an open courtyard with rooms on two adjacent sides of the court. A good example comes from Tell Beit Mirsim, built on the ruins of the house with the roofed hall. The roofed hall became the court. A house at Tell Taanach from the middle Bronze IIB period (c. 1700 BC) was of very strong construction with walls over three feet (.9 meter) thick laid in mortar. The courtyard contained a cistern, and an oven was found in a room on the east side of the house. The ground floors were plastered and covered 2,300 square feet (214 square meters). An interior staircase led to a second story.

In some houses, rooms were placed at opposite sides of the courtyard. Good examples come from Beth Shemesh (Tell er-Rumeilah) and Megiddo. At Beth Shemesh the city wall formed the south wall of the house, and rooms lay east and west of the courtyard. Entrance was from the street into one of the rooms. The other rooms were entered by crossing the courtyard. The outer walls were over three feet (91.4 centimeters) thick and interior walls a foot and a half (45.7 centimeters) thick. Mud and lime plaster coated the walls.

At Megiddo houses were built against the north city wall. In level XII (c. 1750–1700 BC) three well-preserved houses of this kind have been found. The houses were separated by walls at right angles to the city wall. Entrance to each house was through one door on the street, through a room, and into a courtyard paved with small stones and pebbles. The courtyards housed the ovens, and one house had a cistern.

A fourth type of middle Bronze Age house had rooms on three sides of the courtyard. These rooms varied greatly in size and use. A good example dating to about 1600 BC comes from Megiddo, level IX. The house was 42 by 39 feet (12.8 by 11.9 meters) in size and contained nine rooms of varying sizes. The courtyard was plastered with lime and had a large oven in the center. A second oven was found in an eastern room. Each room had a door to the courtyard. This house, like others of the middle Bronze Age, had burials under the floors (cf. 1 Sm 25:1; 1 Kgs 2:34 for biblical references in the Iron Age).

The wide variety of Palestinian houses during the middle Bronze Age points to a level of prosperity much higher than that of the early Bronze Age. Both houses and tombs yielded quantities of graceful and well-made household utensils.

Late Bronze Age Houses (c. 1550–1200 BC) Information is limited for this period, due partly to the accidents of excavation and partly to the severe destruction of many sites at the close of the age from the hands of Israelites, Sea Peoples, Egyptians, and others.

Israelite Houses of the Iron Age (c. 1200–600 BC) Many examples of domestic buildings come from this period. The Israelite structures were at first rather crude, but the quality improved. Thus at Tell Qasil in the 12th century there were poor homes with a courtyard and single room on one side. At contemporary Beth-shemesh one larger house had a foundation of large uncut stones, a courtyard some 34 by 20 feet (10.4 by 6.1 meters), and three rooms on one side 11 by 10 ½ feet (3.4 by 3.2 meters). There was rough stone paving in the court and in two of the rooms. At Hazor a house was discovered that had a courtyard and rooms on one side dating to about 900 BC. Half of the courtyard was covered, the roof being supported on stone pillars. These stone pillars are very characteristic of the Iron Age houses in Palestine and have been found in sites all over the country.

The most common type of house in the days of the kings of Judah and Israel was one in which rooms were built on three sides of a courtyard. This type of house has sometimes been called the "four-room house." A long room was built across the short axis of the courtyard, and two other rooms, one on each side of the court, were constructed on the long axis. The courtyard was divided into three by two rows of pillars that extended down the long axis of the court. These pillars supported the roof and gave support for walls, either half height or full height. Entrance to the house was from the street into the courtyard, where ovens and silos were normally placed, although this varied. Such a framework could be expanded by adding a row of rooms outside the existing

rooms on the long axis of the court. There were many ways to divide long rooms into smaller ones. In some cases where the walls were strong enough, a second story was added. An excellent example of a four-room house that was later enlarged was found at Shechem and dated to the period around 748–724 BC. The courtyard contained a storage bin, a large open hearth, a quern (hand mill), stone grinders, and the bases of pottery jars resting in stone pedestals. In the rooms that had been added there was a device for catching water from the roof and delivering it to an underground water system. A large silo in one room was connected to a kitchen.

There is evidence that larger Iron Age houses served as industrial or commercial buildings. Certain houses at Tell Beit Mirsim contained dye vats and loom weights. In other places the large number of querns suggests a wheat-grinding industry. There is evidence also of wine vats, or potters' equipment, and of shops. Some houses had rooms set apart for religious purposes and contained incense stands, figurines, small altars, and the like.

The excavations of Kathleen Kenyon at Jerusalem brought to light houses from the last days of Judah. They were rather small and irregularly planned but of the same general design as those in the hill country sites of Judah—a courtyard divided by a row of stone pillars that supported the roof.

The contrast between big houses and small houses in some towns probably indicates the social inequality referred to in the prophets. In the 10th and 9th centuries BC there was a fairly uniform picture of many small houses and a few large ones. By the 8th century BC, at a town like Tirzah, there were three or four large houses and a great many flimsy structures.

Houses in New Testament Times There are references in the NT to houses, roofs, doors, foundations, an upper room, and lamps. One of Jesus' parables refers to good and bad foundations (Mt 7:25). In one incident friends took a paralyzed man up to the roof, which they took apart to lower him into the room where Jesus was (Mk 2:4). Jesus referred to proclamations made from the housetops (Mt 10:27; Lk 12:3), and Peter went up on the roof to pray (Acts 10:9). Houses were swept to find lost objects (Lk 15:8) and illuminated by lamps (Mt 5:15). There are several references to houses of specific individuals (Mk 8:3; Lk 10:5; 16:4; 19:9; Jn 11:20; Acts 4:34; 9:11; 10:32). Some houses had upper rooms on the roof reached by an outside staircase. The Passover meal was prepared in such a large upstairs room (Mk 14:12-15). The disciples lodged in a similar room after the death and resurrection of Jesus (Acts 1:13). In such houses there were sometimes servants (10:7), and some had a guest room (Mk 14:14). We conclude from the NT data that there was a variety in the size and elegance of the houses of Jesus' day. A typical street in Judea or Galilee would have houses ranging from the small house (25 to 30 square feet or 2.3 to 2.8 square meters) to the mansion of the upper classes, which could be two or more stories high embellished by rows of pillars and architectural adornment.

For the precise character of these houses, we have to turn to archaeological and literary evidence. The writings of the rabbis and Josephus fill in many details. Excavation in sites of the early Roman (Herodian) period (37 BC–AD 70) have provided more tangible evidence. A rich source of information is the excavation in the old Jewish quarter in Jerusalem. One large house of some 209 square yards in size had a central courtyard where three cooking ovens and a water cistern were found. Large niches set in some of the walls contained broken pottery and must have been cupboards. Traces of mosaic floors and plastered walls give an idea of the beauty of this house. There were several rooms off the courtyard, perhaps as many as ten. The remains of other fine houses of the late second temple period have been found further west, notably in the area of the Armenian cemetery on Mt Zion, in which beautiful frescoes were preserved exhibiting a unique representation of birds. Other houses have yielded mosaic pavements with purely geometric patterns, thus adhering to the injunction against depicting animal forms.

See also Architecture.

HOMOSEXUALITY *See* Sex, Sexuality.

HONEY Sweet syrup produced by bees (Jgs 14:8), either wild (1 Sm 14:25-26) or domesticated (apparently so in 2 Chr 31:5). Sometimes, however, it may refer to thick grape syrup (as in Arabic) or date syrup (as described by Josephus). Honey was considered one of life's necessities (Ecclus 39:26); one must not, however, eat too much (Prv 25:16, 27). It was part of the diet of John the Baptist (Mk 1:6) and of Immanuel (Is 7:15). Its exclusion, along with leaven, from grain offerings (Lv 2:11) is undoubtedly because it is susceptible to fermentation. Its sweetness became a familiar metaphor (Jgs 14:18; Ps 19:10; Rv 10:9-10).

See also Food and Food Preparation.

HONOR Good reputation, respect, purity, integrity.

To the ancient world, the concept of honor was frequently linked to one's tangible possessions. The honor of Odysseus was bound up with the restoration of his material goods; Achilles' honor was dependent upon the gifts given him. Later, the word acquired the strong ethical nature we now associate with it. Plato was among the earliest to establish the personal moral element of honor, what he called "inward honor." The distinctions accorded a man by the world—"outward honors"—were not of the same value as a virtuous person's inner worth. The Romans as well as the Greeks placed great emphasis on the indispensable role of honor in an individual's life.

Only in the Bible, however, do we gain a true perspective on honor. The OT required children to honor their parents (Ex 20:12), a command that reappears in the ethic of the NT (Eph 6:1-2). Undergirding such action is an even more basic obligation: the giving of honor to God, who worthily merits our devoted obedience (Rv 4:11). Proverbs 3:9 presents the law's requirement that one should honor the Lord with his gifts and with the firstfruits of his entire harvest. Honoring God, then, is expressed in the commitment of both life and possessions to the Lord's service.

That people do not honor God as they should is a lamentable truth of Scripture. In all of history only Jesus Christ truly honored the Father by submitting himself totally to the divine will. His submission led him to the cross, the means whereby Christ is now extremely exalted (Is 52:13–53:12). God the Father raised Christ to his permanent position as our great High Priest, an honor of incalculable significance (Heb 5:4-5). Jesus taught that the one who serves him would also be honored by his Father (Jn 12:26); conversely, those who reject him also reject God the Father (15:23).

Christians are called upon to honor one another—that is, each is to consider his fellow believer more worthy of esteem than himself (Rom 12:10). This orientation receives impetus from the affirmation of 1 Peter 1:7, where Christians are said to possess honor. Showing honor to others should affect one's entire lifestyle. Hus-

bands are to give honor to their wives by showing loving regard for them (1 Pt 3:7). Christian servants are expected to show honor to their masters so as to affirm the cause of Christ (1 Tm 6:1). Beyond the immediate community of the redeemed, too, honor must be appropriately displayed by all those who revere the teaching of Scripture (Rom 13:7; 1 Pt 2:17).

HOOPOE Any of a number of Old World singing birds; considered unclean (Lv 11:19; Dt 14:18). *See* Birds.

HOPE An expectation or belief in the fulfillment of something desired. Present hurts and uncertainty over what the future holds create the constant need for hope. Worldwide poverty, hunger, disease, and human potential to generate terror and destruction create a longing for something better. Historically, people have looked to the future with a mixture of longing and fear. Many have concluded that there is no reasonable basis for hope and therefore that to hope is to live with an illusion. Scripture tells us that those who do not have God do not have hope (Eph 2:12).

The modern world has sought hope in human effort and a belief in the inevitability of progress that assumed everything would naturally get better and better. The threat and reality of war in the 20th century challenged that optimism and left growing despair in its wake. Though many still find little reason to hope, others have returned to a humanistic basis for hope. It is held that because people are the source of the world's problems, they can also be the solution. This position can be called into question on the basis of present and historical evidence to the contrary.

Christianity has often been considered in discussions concerning hope. Unfortunately, Christianity has not always received "good press" in this regard. In the early centuries of church history, stress on the disparity between this world and the next seemed to create an attitude of escapism, futility, or indifference toward the problems and pains of human existence. In the 19th century Prussian philosopher Frederick Nietzsche (1844–1900) claimed that Christianity made people cowards because it taught that whatever happened was God's will, thus discouraging efforts to change the world. Karl Marx (1818–83) said that Christianity or religion was the "opiate of the people." For Marx, religion kept people from rising against those who oppressed them.

The tendency for Christianity to be viewed as otherworldly was opposed by Jürgen Moltmann in what has been called "the theology of hope." That theology was the product of the pessimism and despair of post-World War II Europe. Moltmann's theology of hope says that the future is the basis for changing the present, and that Christian service should be an attempt to make otherworldly hopes a present reality. The resurrection is said to bring hope amid present suffering by becoming the catalyst for human effort to overcome that suffering. But trust in human effort to change the future could lead to a humanistic notion that the resurrection is merely a hopeful symbol that will spur people into action, and not necessarily a reality of God's historical action in the world through Jesus Christ. Another concern is that the discussion of hope for this world by a transformation of political and social structures could neglect the need for personal transformation of people's lives through conversion and repentance. While critical questions have been raised about the theology of hope, on the positive side that theology has led to examination or reexamination of the biblical doctrine of hope.

Biblical hope is hope in what God will do in the future. At the heart of Christian hope is the resurrection of Jesus. Paul discussed the nature, certainty, and importance of the resurrection (1 Cor 15:12-28). That Paul is certain that Christian hope points to the future can be seen by his statement "If we have hope in Christ only for this life, we are the most miserable people in the world" (v 19, NLT). The significance of Christ's resurrection is that it not only points to his victory over death but also extends that victory to those who are his: "Christ was raised first; then when Christ comes back, all his people will be raised" (v 23). The apostle Peter said, "All honor to the God and Father of our Lord Jesus Christ, for it is by his boundless mercy that God has given us the privilege of being born again. Now we live with a wonderful expectation because Jesus Christ rose again from the dead" (1 Pt 1:3, NLT). In that passage, Peter attributes living hope to the resurrection of Christ and points to God's future blessing upon those who belong to Christ. That future hope empowers the Christian to live without despair through the struggle and suffering of the present (cf. Rom 8:18; 2 Cor 4:16-18).

Christian hope is securely based upon the words and actions of God. The promises of God have proven to be dependable. The resurrection of Jesus becomes the ultimate basis for hope. Since God has already overcome death through Christ, the Christian can live with confidence in the present. No matter how dark the present age seems, the Christian has seen the light to come. People need to hope, and hope placed in the personal promise of God is secure. This secure hope is full of social significance, however, freeing one from bondage to materialism and its natural selfishness. Christian hope offers security for the future and loving involvement in sharing for the present.

HOPHNI Brother of Phinehas, with whom he served as a priest at Shiloh (1 Sm 1:3). He was an evil man who flouted the sacrificial rituals (2:12-17) and behaved immorally (v 22). Condemned by God, Hophni died during a Philistine attack on Shiloh and its sanctuary (4:11).

HOPHRA Son of Psammis, ruler over Egypt from 589–570 BC during the 26th dynasty. Called Pharaoh Hophra in Jeremiah 44:30, although he is alluded to several other times during the divided kingdom period (Jer 37:5; 43:8-13; Ez 29:1-3; 31:1-18).

He came to power after the death of his father, and in 589 BC marched into Judah against Nebuchadnezzar and the Babylonians in order to assist Zedekiah. Apparently he retreated before superior forces, Jerusalem was overthrown in 586 (Jer 37:5-8), and Hophra was killed as prophesied (Jer 44:30). This occurred in 566 BC, at the hands of Amasis (Ahmose II), who had usurped the throne of Egypt in 569 BC. Both Jeremiah (Jer 43:9-13; 46:13-26) and Ezekiel (Ez 29–30) foretold this defeat.

HOPPING LOCUST Type of locust (KJV "cankerworm") mentioned in Joel 1:4. See Animals (Locust).

HOR, Mount
1. Mountain located at the border of the land of Edom (Nm 20:23; 33:37). Mt Hor was the first place to which the Israelites came (Nm 20:22) after wandering nearly 40 years (Dt 2:14). Moses' brother, Aaron, would not be permitted to enter Canaan because he had refused to carry out the Lord's instructions at Meribah (Nm 20:7-13, 24). Stripped of his priestly garments, which were then put on his son Eleazar, Aaron died on the top of Mt Hor (Nm 20:25-29) at the age of 123. A similar punishment was later meted

out to Moses, whose death on Mt Nebo is compared to Aaron's death on Mt Hor (Dt 32:49-51). According to Deuteronomy 10:6, Aaron died and was buried at Moserah (probably the Moseroth of Nm 33:30-31), a place that must have been very close to (or perhaps a part of) Mt Hor.

The location of Mt Hor remains uncertain. The traditional site, Jebel Nebi Harun (which means "the mountain of the prophet Aaron") is almost 4,800 feet (1.5 kilometers) high and is the tallest mountain in Edom. The Muslims claim that a small building on its summit is the tomb of Aaron. But Jebel Nebi Harun is located near Petra—in the middle of Edom—and too far east of Kadesh. A more likely location is Jebel Madeira, situated on the northwest border of Edom about 15 miles (24 kilometers) northeast of Kadesh. In any event, the Hebrew word *hor* probably means "mount" (as in Gn 49:26), so that "Mt Hor" perhaps means simply "mountain of mountains" or "high mountain" rather than being a proper name.
2. Another mountain located in the far north (Nm 34:7-8). Generally identified as either Mt Hermon or Jebel Akkar, it too was perhaps simply an unusually high mountain.

HORAM King of Gezer who, while coming to the aid of Lachish, was defeated and killed by Joshua (Jos 10:33).

HOREB*, Mount Alternate name for Mt Sinai. *See* Sina, Sinai.

HOREM Town set up for defense purposes in the uplands of Naphtali's territory (Jos 19:38). Though its exact site is unknown, it must have been in northern Galilee.

HORESH Hebrew word translated as a place-name in 1 Samuel 23:15-19 (part of the wilderness of Ziph). David hid from Saul there, and met secretly with Jonathan. The word is translated simply as "wooded areas" in 2 Chronicles 27:4 (NLT). Authorities differ on whether the place-name in 1 Samuel is warranted.

HOR-HAGGIDGAD Camping place of the Israelites during their wilderness wanderings (Nm 33:32-33). It may be the Gudgodah of Deuteronomy 10:7, and has been identified with Wadi Ghadaghed.
See also Wilderness Wanderings.

HORI
1. Lotan's first son. Lotan was the founder of a Horite subclan in Edom (Gn 36:22; 1 Chr 1:39).
2. Shaphat's father and a member of Simeon's tribe. Shaphat was one of the 12 spies (Nm 13:5).

HORITES Cave dwellers of Mt Seir, according to tradition. These pre-Edomites were called the children of Seir (Gn 36:20). In the Bible they were defeated by Kedorlaomer and his allies (14:6). They were governed by chieftains (36:29-30), and eventually destroyed by the descendants of Esau (Dt 2:12, 22).

The popular and biblical etymology of "Horite" has been disputed since the discovery of the Hurrians (Khurians) as ethnic predecessors of many Near Eastern tribes. The Hurrians were a non-Semite people from the mountains. About the second millennium BC, they migrated into north and northeast Mesopotamia, and later moved into the regions of Syria and Palestine. Since the Hurrian language was prevalent in the western Jordan area, and since phonetically "Horite" is the OT

Hebrew equivalent of the extrabiblical "Hurrian," several scholars and translators have substituted "Hurrian" for "Horite." Many have equated the Hivites, who were part of the Hurrian language and cultural group, with the Horites. These critics assumed an early textual corruption of the *r(esh)* in Horite to *w(aw)* in Hivite. A certain Zibeon is called a Horite in Genesis 36:20-30, whereas in verse 2 the man is called a Hivite. The Septuagint of Joshua 9:7 and Genesis 34:2 reads "Horite" instead of "Hivite" as in the Masoretic Text. Some manuscripts of the Septuagint read "Hittite" for the Masoretic Text's "Hivite" (Jos 11:3, Jgs 3:3). In Genesis 36:2, the extant Hebrew manuscripts erroneously read "Hivite" for "Horite." It appears that the OT references do not fit the Hurrians, nor do the personal names of the Horites correspond to Hurrian examples (Gn 36:20-30). They seem instead to be Semitic. The Horites were from Transjordan and were the predecessors of the Edomites (14:6). Later references to Horites may be to western Horites, who were perhaps Hurrians (Is 17:9) and non-Semitic, but quite distinct from the predecessors of the Edomites, the eastern Horites. The Hebrew of Genesis 34:2 and Joshua 9:7 may be from a different family of manuscripts than those used by the Septuagint translators, preserving its own ethnic traditions. It seems best to think of both Hivites and Horites as ethnic groups connected with the Hurrians by language and culture.

See also Hurrians; Hivites.

HORMAH Town near Beersheba in the Negev and on the border of the tribes of Judah and Simeon. Originally a Canaanite settlement, it became Judah's according to Joshua 15:30 and then Simeon's according to Joshua 19:4, 9. Judah dominated it again by the time of the early monarchy (1 Sm 30:30). The change of the Canaanite name Zephath to Hormah when the Hebrews first conquered it is noted in Judges 1:17. Hormah took David's side during his running feud with King Saul and David rewarded the town by sending it some of the spoils of Ziklag (1 Sm 30). Joshua 15:30 describes it as being in the south near Kesil and Ziklag, but its precise location remains unknown. From the reference in Numbers 14:45, it could well be south of Kadesh-barnea, where the Israelites spent much of the wilderness period.

HORN

1. Musical instrument frequently made from a ram's horn. *See* Musical Instruments (Hatzotzrot).
2. Figuratively, a symbol of power (1 Kgs 22:11) expressing dominance over the weak (Ez 34:21), forces of destruction (Zec 1:18-21), and deliverance from oppression (1 Kgs 22:11; 2 Chr 18:10). Thus, the horn has two connotations: rescue and force (2 Sm 22:3; Ps 18:2). The sprouting of the horn referred to in Psalm 132:17 could mean the continuation of the kingly line. Psalm 75:10 declares that the horns of the wicked shall be cut off but those of the righteous exalted. The symbolic imagery in Daniel and Revelation reinforces the use of the horn to represent power and authority (Dn 7–8; Rv 13, 17).
3. A container. The ram's horn, goat's horn, and horn of a wild ox were used as containers for liquid. They were also ceremonial receptacles for oil (1 Sm 16:1, 13; 1 Kgs 1:39). Cows' horns were forbidden for any religious or ceremonial use.
4. Four horn-shaped projections jutting from the four corners of the tabernacle and temple altars (Ex 27:2; 30:2-3). These altar horns were coated with sacrificial

blood and denoted an area of sanctuary (Ex 29:12; Lv 4:7, 18; 1 Kgs 1:50-51).

HORNET Large wasp. *See* Animals (Wasp).

HORONAIM Moabite settlement of uncertain location, listed in prophetic oracles against Moab (Is 15:5; Jer 48:3-5, 34). It fell to Alexander Janneus, but the Hasmonean rule was subsequently returned to King Aretas by John Hyrcanus (Josephus's *Antiquities* 13.15.4; 14.1.4).

HORONITE Reference to either the residence or birthplace of Sanballat, who opposed Nehemiah's restoration program (Neh 2:10, 19; 13:28). The name probably derives from the two cities of Upper and Lower Beth-horon.

HORSE *See* Animals.

HORSE GATE Gate near the palace in Jerusalem (Jer 31:40), in the southeast part of the city wall. Here Queen Athaliah was put to death (2 Kgs 11:16; 2 Chr 23:15). The gate was restored under Nehemiah (Neh 3:28).
See also Jerusalem.

HORUS* *See* Egypt, Egyptian (Religion).

HOSAH (Person) Merarite Levite who guarded the gate of the tent where the sacred ark was kept (1 Chr 16:38) when David brought it to Jerusalem. His gatekeeping responsibilities were shared by his sons (26:10-16).

HOSAH (Place) City south of Tyre on Asher's border (Jos 19:29).

HOSANNA* Hebrew expression meaning "Save us, LORD," taken from Psalm 118:25.

Psalm 118 is a declaration of confidence in the Lord's salvation, made in a time of need. The psalm as a whole was part of a longer hymn (the Hallel) that was sung on great occasions. Verse 25 in particular was used in the Jewish Feast of Tabernacles. At the point in the worship when this verse was read, the people would wave branches of myrtle, willow, and palm. Branches may have been waved at other times also as a general expression of jubilation. This happens in 2 Maccabees 10:6-7, at a ceremony for the rededication of the temple after it had been defiled.

The crowd welcomed Jesus to Jerusalem with the cry of "Hosanna" (Mt 21:9; Mk 11:9-10; Jn 12:13), followed by a proclamation, "Blessed be he who enters in the name of the LORD" (Ps 118:26, RSV). This means the crowd was greeting Jesus as Messiah. Already before Jesus' time the phrase "blessed is he who comes in the name of the Lord" was taken to refer to the Messiah. And it is possible that the word "Hosanna" by itself had messianic significance. Other expressions in the report of Jesus' entry into Jerusalem support this. In Matthew 21:9 Jesus is called the "Son of David"; in Mark 11:10 there is reference to "the coming kingdom of our father David"; in John 12:13, Jesus is called "the King of Israel." All of these have messianic overtones.

We need not suppose that in shouting "Hosanna" the people had a political deliverance in mind. They probably did not know in what way Jesus would be a deliverer. The most one can say is they believed Jesus was one sent by God for their salvation. Had there not been something in their response to him that Jesus could recognize as proper worship, he would hardly have accepted their praise. It would only appear later, in his death and resurrection, what his messiahship really meant.

See also Hallel; Hallelujah; Messiah.

HOSEA (Person) Prophet of ancient Israel whose sphere of activity was the northern kingdom. Little is known of him outside of the prophetic book that bears his name. His prophetic ministry is best placed in the third quarter of the eighth century BC. His name means "help" or "helper," and is based on the Hebrew word for salvation.

The evidence for placing Hosea in the northern kingdom is basically internal. The book is concerned mainly with the northern tribes, whom he frequently identifies as "Ephraim," a common appellation for the northern kingdom. And the dialect of Hebrew in which the book was written seems to be of a northern cast.

The circumstances surrounding the marriage of Hosea form the catalyst for his prophetic message. He was commanded by God to marry Gomer, who apparently was a harlot; his marriage provided an analogy with Israel, who was guilty of spiritual adultery.

Scholars differ as to the interpretation of this controversial account but there is little reason for doubting that it was a literal event. The act of sacrifice involved in Hosea's obedience to God forms a marvelous picture of God's sacrificial love for man.

See also Hosea, Book of; Prophet, Prophetess.

HOSEA, Book of First of the 12 minor prophets in the traditional arrangements of the OT books. It was written in the last part of the eighth century BC. Hosea's prophecies were proclaimed to the northern kingdom of Israel in the final years of its existence. Hosea was the only prophet to reside in the northern kingdom and also to preach there. God commissioned Hosea to reveal the widespread apostasy and corruption in the northern kingdom and to exhort his fellow countrymen to repent and return to God. Hosea had the unique privilege of illustrating—in his own life—the steadfast covenant love that God had for Israel.

PREVIEW
•Author
•Authenticity
•Background
•Date
•Origin and Destination
•Purpose
•Content
•Message

Author Hosea's ministry extended over a period of at least 38 years (c. 753–715 BC), and he appears as a knowledgeable individual, whether he was a peasant or a member of the wealthier class in Israel.

Hosea's marriage to the prostitute Gomer may have been controversial in his own day, and it has certainly caused a great deal of controversy among Bible students and commentators. It seems best to recognize that Gomer was a publicly known harlot whom Hosea was commanded to marry for the purpose of illustrating Israel's apostasy and God's steadfast covenant love.

Authenticity The authenticity and unity of Hosea is not seriously questioned, even by higher criticism. But two areas of controversy are (1) passages that refer to Judah (e.g., 1:1, 7, 11; 4:15; 5:5, 10-14; 6:4, 11; 8:14; 11:12;

12:2), and (2) those sections that refer to future blessing or national deliverance (e.g., 11:8-11; 14:2-9).

Hosea's references to Judah, however, could be expected from a man of God chagrined by the separation of Israel from the legitimate Davidic line. The northern kingdom, with its ungodly kings, was on the verge of judgment from God. Hosea evidently had received divine revelation concerning his dealings with Judah as well as Israel.

The references to the future blessings and deliverance of Israel do not neutralize the condemnation of the sins of Israel, any more than Hosea's constant love for and reconciliation with adulterous Gomer neutralizes her sin. Restoration and forgiveness need not ignore guilt.

Background Hosea lived during the prosperous days of the northern kingdom of Israel under Jeroboam II (793–753 BC). He also saw its defeat and the deportation of its people after the invasion by the Assyrians (722 BC).

In Hosea 1:1 the following kings are named: from the southern kingdom of Judah—Uzziah, Jotham, Ahaz, and Hezekiah; and from the northern kingdom of Israel—Joash and Jeroboam. Uzziah was a contemporary of both Joash and Jeroboam. Ahaz was king of Judah when Israel was taken captive by Assyria. Hezekiah may have been a co-regent with Ahaz at the time of the Assyrian captivity.

Jeroboam reigned over Israel for 41 years and followed the evil example of his father, Nebat (2 Kgs 14:23-24). Though Israel was prosperous and successful during Jeroboam's reign, the corruption in the government and the degeneracy in the spiritual lives of the people set the stage for more tumultuous times in the days of subsequent kings and paved the way for the fall of Israel. The rich landowners (including the king) oppressed the peasants and caused the lower-class landowners to migrate from the farms to the cities. The social repercussions were soon to engulf Israel in a wave of corruption. Anarchy was a product of those times (Hos 4:1-2; 7:1-7; 8:3-4; 9:15).

Date Hosea's prophetic ministry commenced with the reign of Jeroboam II (793–753 BC) and extended to that of Hezekiah of Judah (715–686 BC).

Several factors indicate that Hosea continued prophesying under Hoshea of Israel (732–722 BC): (1) "Shalman" (Hos 10:14) may be Shalmaneser of Assyria, who invaded Israel early in the reign of Hoshea (2 Kgs 17:3). (2) "Jareb" (Hos 5:13; 10:6, both KJV) may be Sargon II (722–705 BC). (3) Predictions of the Assyrian invasion appear to refer to an imminent event (10:5-6; 13:15-16). (4) Mention of Egypt and Israel's dependence on that nation seem to fit the reign of Hoshea (7:11; 11:11). These factors confirm that the compilation of Hosea's messages may have taken place very near to the time of Israel's fall (722 BC).

Origin and Destination Hosea prophesied while residing in Israel. He refers to the king in Samaria as "our king" (Hos 7:5). His descriptions of Israel show that he was familiar with the geography of the northern kingdom. Gilead is mentioned by Hosea as though he knew that area from personal observation (6:8; 12:11). Hosea was probably the only prophet to the northern kingdom who actually lived there throughout his ministry.

Purpose Hosea proclaimed to Israel the need to repent and return to God. He presented the God of Israel as a patient and loving God who remained faithful to his covenant promises. This emphasis is characteristic of Hosea (cf. 2:19).

"Loving-kindness" is the word that best represents the

covenant faithfulness and love of Yahweh, and Hosea's family life was a living illustration of that lovingkindness.

Content The major divisions and topics of the book of Hosea may be outlined as follows.

The first three chapters of Hosea are concerned with the example of Hosea's life, stressing Hosea's faithfulness and love for his unfaithful wife.

God commanded Hosea to marry the harlot Gomer and to have children by her (1:2–3:5). This command has caused difficulties for some commentators, since priests and prophets in Israel simply did not marry prostitutes. Medieval Jewish writers, therefore, regarded the material as symbolic but unhistorical. Some later scholars drew a distinction between chapters 1 and 3, regarding the latter as an intimate description by Hosea of his marriage; the first chapter was held to contain rather general recollections of his early days as a prophet. Other commentators regarded both chapters as literal fact, while certain scholars thought that chapter 1 was historical whereas chapter 3 represented an allegorical interpretation of the marriage by Hosea himself.

Needless to say, the sexual activities of Gomer have also been discussed widely. Two views predominate. (1) Gomer was a faithful wife to Hosea in their early years of marriage. "A wife of harlotry" (1:2, RSV), which is not the common term for "prostitute," had reference to her sinful and wayward nature, which God later caused to be exposed as an illustration of Israel's idolatry. (2) Gomer was a publicly known harlot whom Hosea was commanded to marry in order to illustrate Israel's idolatry and God's faithful and steadfast love. This latter view seems to have the greatest appeal to evangelical scholars, and is the simplest interpretation within a literal, grammatical, and historical framework of Bible interpretation.

Why it was necessary for her to be ransomed by Hosea is not evident, nor is it known why part of the price was paid in grain and the remainder in money. Perhaps the entire transaction was meant to symbolize God's deliverance of Israel from future exile, although as far as it is known, the 10 northern tribes did not return from exile in Assyria. Such an interpretation could hardly apply to Judah, since Hosea's message was not directed at the southern kingdom, although Judah did receive a warning (6:11).

The children born to Hosea and Gomer were given symbolic names. The first child was a son named Jezreel (1:4a), signifying God's judgment on the house of Jehu for Jehu's slaughter of the house of Ahab in the valley of Jezreel (2 Kgs 10:1-11, 30).

Lo-ruhamah was the second child (Hos 1:6a), whose name means "not compassioned or pitied." The judgment of Israel was thus symbolized. The spiritual corruption of the northern kingdom had run its course, and it would be defeated and taken away into captivity (1:6b).

Lo-ammi was the third child, a second son, whose name means "not my people" (1:8-9). This rejection of Israel as God's covenanted people was to be temporary (1:10–2:1). God's covenant promises to Abraham (cf. 1:10; Gn 22:17) and to Moses (Ex 19:1-7) would be fulfilled in spite of the disobedience of any particular generation.

Not satisfied with her relationship to her husband, Gomer sought other lovers. Israel pursued the same elusive satisfaction in her flirtation and adultery with heathen deities. The good that their merciful God had bestowed upon them they attributed to pagan gods (Hos 2:8, 12). Repentant Israelites would return to their

first love after discovering that there was no lasting satisfaction in their season of sin.

Hosea's declaration of divorce from Gomer for her adultery depicts Yahweh's divorce from Israel for her adultery (Hos 2:2; cf. Jer 3:1–4:2). Their children represent the individual members of the nation of Israel in Hosea's day (Hos 2:2-5).

The illustration of restoration in chapter 3 highlights a concise summary of Israel's history. Israel's bondage to sin and Satan (cf. Heb 2:14-15) is symbolized by the price paid by Hosea for Gomer (Hos 3:2). The price was that of a female slave, since Gomer had become the slave of her adultery (cf. Ex 21:32). The days of Gomer's isolation, like the days of Israel's exile, were established for cleansing (Hos 3:3; cf. Dt 21:13; 30:2).

After the exile period ("afterward"), and "in the latter days," Israel will return to her husband to enjoy the blessings of the renewed relationship. In a messianic reference, David "their king" will be resurrected to lead Israel to the Lord (Hos 3:5).

The last major section of Hosea deals in detail with what has already been illustrated and briefly explained in chapters 1–3. Israel's apostasy (4:1–7:16), punishment (8:1–10:15), and restoration (11:1–14:9) are prophesied by Hosea.

Israel was totally given over to ungodly activities and had separated itself from God (4:1-2; cf. Ex 20:1-17). The people had rejected the word of God through their own indifference and the deception of the priests (Hos 4:6-9; cf. Is 5:13; Am 8:11-12; Zep 1:6). Israel followed the example of corrupt spiritual leaders in the same way her kings followed the corrupt leadership of their predecessors (Hos 4:9). In place of God's word, Israel turned to idolatry and divination for guidance (vv 12-13). Finally, Israel lost its priestly character (4:6; cf. Ex 19:6) because the priests were chiefly responsible for national apostasy (Hos 5:1).

Upon revealing his case against the northern kingdom, God then issues a caution (5:8-14). The trumpet will be raised in the hills of Benjamin (v 8), the buffer zone between Israel and Judah. The alarm in that region will indicate that Israel is being overrun and Judah is endangered (vv 9-12). The northern kingdom had depended upon the commandment of man, not God (v 11). Israel had turned to Assyria for aid but received treachery and defeat at its hands (v 13). In this prophecy of the fall of Israel to the Assyrians (722 BC), Hosea depicts God as the ultimate chastiser (v 14).

God's call for repentance comes hard upon the heels of the revelation of chastisement (5:15–6:3). (The division of chapters at this point is unfortunate. Hosea 6:1-3 belongs with 5:15.) The exhortation to return to Yahweh could have been Hosea's own heart response to the revelation he had received. However, it is best to take 6:1-3 as the words employed by the future returning remnant. Assyria did not offer healing, nor would any other nation, but God will heal Israel spiritually, politically, and physically (6:1; cf. Ex 15:26; Dt 32:39; Is 53:5; Ez 37:1-14; Mal 4:2).

After the call to repentance, God returns to his concern for Israel (Hos 6:4-11; cf. 4:15). Israel has turned from its Creator and has disobeyed his message (6:7). Gilead is but one example of the murderous character of Israel (v 8). Even the priests are known for their violence (6:9; cf. 1 Sm 2:12-17; Jer 5:31). The sin of Israel is "horrible" (Hos 6:10).

Chapter 7 presents God's conclusion concerning Israel. Every attempt of God to bring Israel to repentance only reveals more fully the extent of their sin (7:1). They believe they can sin without God taking account

(Hos 7:2; cf. Ps 90:8; Mt 12:36-37). Their leaders rejoice that the people are as wicked as the king and the princes themselves (Hos 7:3). All Israel is characterized by habitual adultery (v 4). Israel has not separated itself from the heathen (Hos 7:8; cf. Ex 34:12-16; 2 Cor 6:14–7:1). Like "a cake not turned" (Hos 7:8), Israel is not well balanced spiritually or politically but has one side done to a turn and the other side raw.

In the area of foreign affairs, Israel has flitted about from Egypt to Assyria and back again "like a silly dove" without understanding (Hos 7:11). They did not seek the Lord's counsel in their time of need but depended upon worldly powers. The lack of faith in Yahweh and the lack of separation from sin will bring chastisement from God (Hos 7:12; cf. 1 Cor 11:32; Heb 12:5-15).

Chapter 8 deals with Israel's reaping of judgment (cf. Hos 8:7). An alarm is sounded to warn the people of the approach of the Assyrians (Hos 8:1; cf. Ez 17:2-21). They would come against Israel (Hos 8:1) because of their transgression of the Sinai covenant (cf. Dt 27:9–29:29) and disobedience to the law of Moses. Crying falsely to God for deliverance from his rod of punishment (cf. Is 10:5), Israel will receive no answer and Assyria will continue to pursue the 10 tribes (Hos 8:2-3). Other reasons for God's judgment include setting up kings without God's direction (v 4a) and idolatry (vv 4b-6). Israel's sacrifices were unacceptable because of the nation's disobedience (cf. 1 Sm 15:22; Is 1:11-15). Thus they would go into exile just like the earlier exile in Egypt (Hos 8:13).

The theme of exile is continued in chapter 9 of Hosea. There is no joy for Israel (v 1). The produce of the land will not sustain her because she will no longer dwell in the land (vv 2-3). Some Israelites will flee to Egypt in exile, while others will be taken captive to Assyria. All the sacrifices will cease and the sacrificial wines and meats will be drunk and eaten to satisfy their own needs (vv 4-5). Those Israelites who flee to Egypt will be slain by the Egyptians (v 6).

The recompense of Israel's evil is further described in chapter 10. Israel is like a luxuriant vine (10:1), but its bounty is misappropriated, being poured out as sacrifice on heathen altars. They are guilty before God, and he is about to destroy their altars and take away their king (vv 2-3). Gibeah is mentioned again (cf. 9:9), reminding Israel that apostasy is not only infectious, it is also indelible (10:9). The "two crimes" (NJB) of verse 10 may refer to the two calf idols in Bethel and Dan that brought chastisement from God. The punishment will be a sentence of hard labor under a heavy yoke (v 11).

Chapters 11 through 14 close the prophecies of Hosea with a message concerning the restoration of Israel at a future time. The steadfast love of the Father is first given as the ground of future restoration (11:1-12). Israel, as a nation, had been called out of Egypt as a son of Yahweh (Hos 11:1; cf. Ex 4:22-23). Yet Israel did not return the Father's love, but sought pagan alliances (Hos 11:5) that would only bring judgment upon them (vv 5-7). The words of Yahweh reveal his irreversible judgment in his absolute holiness and righteousness (12:1–13:16). The sins of Israel can only be responded to with just recompense (12:1-2). The responsibility for the destruction of the northern kingdom rests upon Israel herself. In spite of Israel's sin, God can yet be her help (13:9).

Israel should have repented quickly, but she did not (13:13). Yet the mercy of Yahweh would ultimately bring about the death of death itself so that Israel might live—spiritually, politically, and perhaps physically (Hos 13:14; cf. Ez 37:1-14; Dn 12:1-2, 13).

Chapter 14 of Hosea sets forth the Father's loving invitation for Israel to repent and return to him in confession, prayer, and praise (Hos 14:2). "Calves of our lips" (v 2, KJV) refers to the thank offering, which normally included young bulls (Ex 24:5; Lv 7:11-15; cf. Pss 51:17-19; 69:30-31; Heb 13:15-16). Part of Israel's confession will involve recognizing that there is no salvation in either Assyria (political alliance) or idols (Hos 14:3).

God repeatedly promises blessing to Israel in their restoration (note "I will," 14:4-5). Yahweh will heal Israel spiritually, love them freely, prosper them completely, and protect them fully (vv 4-7). Israel will be as beautiful as the lily, durable as the cedar, and fruitful as the olive tree.

Message The primary emphasis of Hosea is summarized in the last verse (14:9). The wise will live godly lives, and the foolish will live ungodly lives. The godly will have restoration, victory over death (13:14), and blessing (14:4-7).

Idolatry is essentially anything that usurps the sole place of God in the human heart. In place of Yahweh's counsel, aid, blessing, and salvation, Israel had substituted heathen deities (4:12-19), national pride (5:5), religious ceremony (6:6), political expediency (7:3), political alliances (7:11), civil government (8:4), building projects (8:14), selfish affluence (10:1), and idolatry (13:2). Only in God could they find true blessing and security (13:4, 9; 14:4-7).

Apostasy is presented by Hosea as infectious. The cycle of apostasy may begin with the spiritual leaders or with the people and spread from one to the other (4:9). Apostasy is punished according to the degree of responsibility (5:1; 13:9; 14:4).

See also Hosea (Person); Israel, History of; Prophecy; Prophet, Prophetess.

HOSHAIAH

1. Prince of Judah who led a contingent of princes in procession at the dedication of the walls of Jerusalem after they were rebuilt (Neh 12:32).
2. Father of Azariah (Jer 42:1; 43:2). Azariah was a leader of the people of Judah after the fall of Jerusalem.

HOSHAMA Jeconiah's descendant (1 Chr 3:18).

HOSHEA

1. Original name of Joshua, the son of Nun and Moses' successor, before his name was changed by Moses (Nm 13:8, 16). See Joshua (Person) #1.
2. Son of Elah and the last of the 20 kings of the northern kingdom of Israel (2 Kgs 17:1-6). He reigned for nine years (732–723 BC) before being taken captive by the Assyrians. In the later years of the northern kingdom, Assyria (under the rule of Tiglath-pileser III) had gained control of most of the Middle East and had reduced the scope of the northern kingdom to Ephraim, Issachar, and the half of Manasseh west of the Jordan.

Earlier, the northern kingdom, under Pekah (740–732 BC), entered into an alliance with Rezin of Damascus (Syria) and attempted to coerce King Ahaz of Judah (735–715 BC) to join them in action against Tiglath-pileser (2 Kgs 16:5; Is 7:1-6). Assyria came to Judah's aid, and at this point Hoshea was one of a group of conspirators who assassinated Pekah (2 Kgs 15:30). Tiglath-pileser rewarded Hoshea by making him king over the remnant of the northern kingdom. Hoshea ruled only as a vassal of Assyria and paid heavy tribute, remaining loyal to Assyria until the death of Tiglath-pileser in 727 BC. When Shalmaneser V succeeded to the throne of Assyria, he did not trust Hoshea's loyalty and marched against him, thereby continuing the forced annual tribute (2 Kgs 17:3). In a short time Hoshea attempted to assert independence. He withheld tribute and entered into negotiations with So, king of Egypt (v 4), finding a favorable response, because Egypt would be in a precarious position if Assyria were to control Palestine. Therefore, Egypt was quite willing to support Hoshea in his resistance to Assyria in the hope that Samaria would remain a buffer between Egypt and Assyria. Soon, Shalmaneser directed his army against Samaria (724 BC), and Hoshea discovered that the alliance with Egypt was of little value. Hoshea was taken prisoner, and Assyria apparently besieged Samaria for three years. The city fell in 722 BC, and Sargon II, who had succeeded Shalmaneser about 726 BC, deported many Israelites to various places in Assyria, thus ending the northern kingdom.

3. Son of Azaziah and one of King David's officers set over the Ephraimites (1 Chr 27:20).
4. One who set his seal on Ezra's covenant (Neh 10:23).
5. Eighth-century prophet of Israel better known as Hosea. See Hosea (Person); Hosea, Book of.

HOSPITALITY Biblical concept often used with the terms "guest," "stranger," and "sojourner." It is useful to limit the meaning of "hospitality" to benevolence done to those outside one's normal circle of friends, as is implied in the literal meaning of the Greek word meaning "love of strangers." Although the concept is thoroughly endorsed in the Bible, it is clearly found in nonbiblical cultures as well, especially among the nomadic peoples, where definite obligations to provide food, shelter, and protection are recognized.

The normal exercise of hospitality in the OT can be seen in the examples of Abraham and the three visitors (Gn 18:2-8, 16), Laban's reception of Abraham's servant (24:15-61), and Manoah's treatment of the angel (Jgs 13:15). But there are also cases in which the host felt compelled to take extreme steps to protect his guest, even to the harm of his own family (Gn 19:1-8; Jgs 19:14-24). The hospitality of the Shunammite family is also noteworthy, although Elisha was no stranger to them (2 Kgs 4:10).

According to the NT, Jesus relied on the general practice of hospitality in sending out the disciples (Lk 10:7), as well as in his own travels. As the gospel was spread by traveling missionaries, Christians were commended for entertaining them in their homes (Heb 13:2; 1 Pt 4:9; 3 Jn 1:5-8). Church leaders must not exempt themselves from this ministry (1 Tm 3:2; Ti 1:8); to do so is grounds for judgment (Mt 25:43-46).

See also Foreigner.

HOST, HOST OF HEAVEN* Hebrew expressions found frequently in the OT and literally meaning "army" and "army of the skies." "Host" is basically a military term, occurring nearly 500 times in the OT, and can mean "army" (2 Kgs 18:17), "angels," "heavenly bodies," or "creation."

The phrase "host of heaven" has various applications in the Bible. Ancient writers sometimes referred symbolically to the sun, moon, and stars as an army (Dt 4:19; Jgs 5:20). In the astrological cults of antiquity, it was believed that celestial bodies were animated by spirits and thus constituted a living army that controlled heavenly destiny. The worship of the host of heaven was one of the earliest forms of idolatry, and was common among the Israelites in their times of regression from serving God (Jer 19:13; Acts 7:42). Although warned

against such pagan beliefs (Dt 4:19; 17:3), the Israelites fell into the practice of worshiping heavenly bodies, particularly during the Assyrian and Babylonian periods (2 Kgs 17:16; 21:3-5; 2 Chr 33:3-5; Jer 8:2; Zep 1:5). The corrective to this pagan practice is belief in the Lord as the Creator of heaven and earth, the Almighty, the one who marshaled the heavenly bodies at his command and ordained them to perform a special function (Gn 1:14-19; 2:1; Neh 9:6; Pss 33:6; 103:21; 148:2; Is 40:26; 45:12).

God is frequently called "the Lord God of hosts," that is, of the celestial armies (Jer 5:14; 38:17; 44:7; Hos 12:5). The heavenly host includes angels or messengers who are associated with the Lord's work in heaven and on earth. God presides over a heavenly council composed of angels or "sons of God" (Gn 1:26; 1 Kgs 22:19; Jb 1:6; Ps 82; Is 6) whose messengers are sent from the Lord's council to accomplish his purpose (Gn 28:12-15; Lk 2:13).

Though the hosts are sometimes understood as the stars or angels, the tribes of Israel are also called "the host of the Lord." The "host of heaven" in Daniel 8:10-11 appears to be figurative language referring to Israel, "the holy people," and God, the King of Israel, is called "the Prince of the host."

The Greek words translated "host" occur only twice in the NT (Lk 2:13; Acts 7:42). "Lord of hosts" is used by Paul and James (Rom 9:29; Jas 5:4) as a title for the Lord. The term expresses God's sovereign might and majesty in history, but the precise identification of the "hosts" that stand at his command is uncertain.

See also Hosts, Lord of.

HOSTS*, Lord of Old Testament name for God found mostly in the prophets. The hosts are the heavenly powers and angels that act at the Lord's command. See God, Names of; Host, Host of Heaven.

HOTHAM
1. Variant form of Helem in 1 Chronicles 7:32. See Helem #1.
2. Shama and Jeiel's father. Shama and Jeiel were two of David's mighty men (1 Chr 11:44).

HOTHAN* KJV spelling of Hotham in 1 Chronicles 11:44. See Hotham #2.

HOTHIR Levite and the head of the 21st of 24 divisions of priests for sanctuary service, formed during David's reign (1 Chr 25:4, 28).

HOUR See Day.

HOUSE See Homes and Dwellings.

HOUSEHOLD Persons who live in the same place and compose a family or extended family. In biblical times a household included father, mother(s), children, grandparents, servants, concubines, and sojourners. Jacob's household, for example, included 66 people, not counting the wives of his sons (Gn 46:26). Households were seen as corporately responsible for the honor of the family (2 Sm 3:27 gives an example of revenge by a household). Male members of the entire household were circumcised as a sign of the covenant (Gn 17:23). In the NT era, some entire households were baptized (Acts 11:14).

See also Family Life and Relations.

HOUSE OF GOD Common phrase used in the ancient Near Eastern world for a structure used to accommodate a deity or his servants. In the OT it referred to the tabernacle

(Dt 23:18; 1 Chr 6:31-32), Solomon's temple (1 Kgs 8:11-20; 12:27; Jer 20:1), national shrines, or pagan temples (Jgs 9:4; 2 Kgs 10:21).

In NT times the OT custom of referring to the temple as the "house of God" was still employed (Mt 12:4; Mk 2:26; 11:17; Lk 6:4; Jn 2:16-17), but with some significant changes. After Christ's ascension, the church viewed itself as the house of God (1 Cor 3:9; Heb 3:6; 1 Pt 2:5; 4:17). God no longer dwelt in buildings made by human hands but in the lives of those who confess Jesus as Lord.

See also Tabernacle; Temple.

HOUSE OF THE ARCHIVES*
Building used for storage of records, annals, and decrees; a common structure in Near Eastern nations in the second millennium BC (Ezr 5:17–6:1). In the archives at Ecbatana, a summer resort for Persian kings, King Darius (521–486 BC) found an edict of Cyrus (559–530 BC) that entitled the Jews to begin reconstruction of the Jerusalem temple following the exile (Ezr 6:2). On the basis of that edict, Darius gave his support to renewed reconstruction efforts, which had been halted for 16 years due to local opposition (cf. Hg 1:1; Zec 1:1).

HOUSE OF THE FOREST OF LEBANON*
See Palace of the Forest of Lebanon.

HOZAI*
Author of annals describing the life of Manasseh, king of Judah, and included in the "Chronicles of the Seers" (2 Chr 33:18-19). The Septuagint renders Hozai as "seers," which is preferred by many commentators and the NLT (see 2 Chr 33:19 mg).

HUBBAH
Alternative spelling for Shomer's son from Asher's tribe (1 Chr 7:34).

HUKKOK
Town near Naphtali and Zebulun's boundary, listed next to Aznoth-tabor (Jos 19:34). It has been identified with Yaquaq, northwest of Gennesaret.

HUKOK
Alternate form of the Asherite town Helkath in 1 Chronicles 6:75. *See* Helkath.

HUL
Son of Aram and grandson of Shem (Gn 10:23; 1 Chr 1:17).

HULDAH
Prophetess living in Jerusalem; a contemporary of the prophets Jeremiah and Zephaniah. Huldah is introduced as the wife of Shallum, the wardrobe keeper in King Josiah's court (2 Kgs 22:14; 2 Chr 34:22). Josiah sent his officers to ask Huldah's counsel concerning the book of the Mosaic law that had been found during the temple repair. She prophesied that disaster would strike the nation (2 Kgs 22:16), but that Josiah would be spared because he was penitent and had humbled himself before the Lord (vv 18-19). She declared the destruction would come after his death and that he would be buried in peace (v 20). Although Josiah later died in battle, he was properly entombed (23:30), avoiding the indignity of becoming prey for carrion feeders. It was after receiving Huldah's advice that Josiah carried out his religious reform (2 Chr 35:1-25).

HUMILITY
A condition of lowliness or affliction in which one experiences a loss of power and prestige. Outside of biblical faith, humility in this sense would not usually be considered a virtue. Within the context of the Judeo-Christian tradition, however, humility is considered the proper attitude of human beings toward their Creator. Humility is a grateful and spontaneous awareness that life is a gift, and it is manifested as an ungrudging and unhypocritical acknowledgment of absolute dependence upon God.

In biblical literature there is not a clear distinction between humility and meekness or patience. In early stages of Israel's history, the humble were identified as the poor, the afflicted, and the powerless. The Lord delivers the humble but brings down the proud (1 Sm 2:7; 2 Sm 22:28). Before the power and glory of God, the patriarch Abraham confessed that he was but dust and ashes (Gn 18:27). Israel began as a nation subjected to slavery and knew themselves as a people chosen not because of numerical strength or material wealth but because of God's love (Dt 7:7-8). By attributing the source of all wealth and power to the Lord, those two major sources of human pride and arrogance are brought under control (cf. Jer 9:23-24).

The humble poor are the constant concern of the Lord (Ex 23:6, 11; Dt 15:4, 7). Consequently, the humility of the poor became the symbol of the righteous God-fearer (Nm 12:3). In the development of the concept of humility in the OT, humility is nearly equated with righteousness and is identified, along with justice and mercy, as the requirement of God (Mi 6:8). In the Psalms particularly, "the afflicted" is almost a technical term for the righteous (Pss 22:26; 25:9; 147:6).

In addition, humility is the appropriate response of the sinner in the presence of the holiness of God. The prophet Isaiah, confronted by the glory of God in the temple, cried, "My destruction is sealed, for I am a sinful man" (Is 6:5). Thus humility became more of a character trait than a term that reflected a state of material poverty or affliction. It became a concept reflective of the essence of piety and godliness expected of all people who have God as their Lord.

Only rarely in the NT does humility refer to an objective condition of poverty, affliction, or oppression. The humility motif is developed in connection with Jesus as Messiah. The religious ideal of humility that the OT attributed to the coming King certainly applied to Jesus (Zec 9:9; cf. Mt 21:4-5). As Son of God, Jesus took no thought for himself but lived a life of obedience and trust in God the Father. The apostle Paul attributed to the incarnate Son of God a self-emptying by which he "humbled himself" and took on the form of a servant (Phil 2:5-8). Jesus' character exhibited no pride or arrogance.

Though bold in the face of hypocrisy and unflinching in his repudiation of pretentious religion, Jesus was "gentle and humble in heart" (Mt 11:29). He could, therefore, issue a severe warning against desire for status and openly rebuke the Pharisees for their violence against the poor and oppressed (Lk 14:11; Mt 23:12). At the same time, he was humble before those whose servant and helper he had become (Lk 22:27; Mk 10:45; Mt 20:28). The highest dignity of Jesus and his willingness to accept the cross in submission to the Father's will are one. So his teaching on poverty of spirit rang true as a testimony of his own life. He ascribed all glory to his Father and lived in total dependence upon him (Jn 5:19; 6:38; 7:15; 8:28, 50; 14:10, 24). By washing his disciples' feet, he assumed the role of servant with no loss of dignity or self-worth. And he set forth such service as a model of a life that finds happiness in preferring others over one's self (Jn 13:1-20; Phil 2:1-4).

Consequently, disciples of Jesus are also summoned to a life of humility. Turning their backs on status, security, and success, Christians seek an opportunity to gain themselves in serving others. Humility, thus, is the all-embracing life principle by which love seeks the good of others, and thus fulfills the law (cf. Rom 12:10; 13:8-10).

HUMTAH Settlement in the Judean uplands near Hebron, according to Joshua 15:54.

HUNCHBACK* *See* Deformity.

HUNDRED, Tower of the Tower at the northernmost part of the Jerusalem wall (near where the wall crosses over the Tyropeon Valley). It stood west of the Sheep Gate near the Tower of Hananel (Neh 3:1; 12:39; KJV "tower of Meah").

See also Jerusalem.

HUNDRED-WEIGHT* Measure equal to about 1 talent or 75 pounds (34 kilograms), mentioned only in Revelation 16:21. *See* Weights and Measures.

HUNTING Practice of tracking and pursuing animals for food, animal products, or sport—a practice as old as man. In Bible times hunting was practiced all over the biblical world. Genesis 10:9 refers to a certain Nimrod who was "a mighty hunter in the LORD's sight" (NLT); this was long before the patriarchs. In earliest human history hunting was an essential means of obtaining food, clothing, and tools, and even when civilization developed, hunting provided supplemental food for an agricultural diet.

In lands surrounding Israel, hunting is well represented in paintings and bas-reliefs. In ancient Egypt, hunting became a sport, and Egyptians hunted for game and birds often with the help of dogs and cats. Wild game was driven by dogs or humans into enclosures or toward pits and traps. Similarly, in Mesopotamia, hunting was widely practiced, as is evident from many bas-reliefs depicting stags and deer caught in nets. In Assyria wild animals, like lions, were commonly hunted. The bas-reliefs of Nineveh provide many fine pictures of the hunter's skill.

were "clean" are provided in Deuteronomy 14:4-6. An interesting variety of animals was available to the people of Israel; many were domestic, but there was a variety of wild animals to test the ingenuity of the hunter: the goat, the hare, the gazelle, the roebuck (cf. 1 Kgs 4:23), the wild goat, the ibex, the antelope, and the mountain sheep. In every case the blood of the animal had to be poured out. There was a proverb current in Israel about a slothful man who caught no prey—or if he catches it, doesn't cook it (Prv 12:27).

Some passages in the OT record the killing of animals in self-protection (Jgs 14:6; 1 Sm 17:34-37; 2 Sm 23:20). Shepherds normally carried a club and a sling to protect their flocks from marauding beasts (1 Sm 17:40; Ps 23:4).

A variety of birds was hunted, as for example, the partridge referred to in 1 Samuel 26:20 (cf. Dt 14:11-18). There are references also to some of the devices used in hunting: bows and arrows (Gn 27:3), clubs (Jb 41:29), sling stones (1 Sm 17:40), nets (Jb 19:6), fowlers' snares (Ps 91:3), camouflaged pits (Pss 7:15; 35:7; Prv 22:14; 26:27; Is 24:17-18). Of the traps mentioned in the Bible one seems to have been an automatic device (Am 3:5) that would spring up from the ground when an animal touched it (cf. Ps 69:22; Hos 9:8) or when the fowler pulled a cord (Ps 140:5; Jer 5:26). The method of driving animals into a trap seems to be referred to in Jeremiah 16:16 and Ezekiel 19:8.

HUPHAM, HUPHAMITE Benjamite and the founder of the Huphamite family (Nm 26:39); he is perhaps identifiable with Huppim (Gn 46:21; 1 Chr 7:12, 15) and Huram (1 Chr 8:5).

See also Huppim; Huram #1.

HUPPAH One of the chief men appointed in charge of the 13th division of priests in the time of David and Solomon (1 Chr 24:13).

Hunting and Fishing in Ancient Egypt Ancient Egyptians fishing with a dragnet

Palestine was a land where hunting was practiced very early. This is clear from the bones of hunted animals found in the excavation of early sites. Certainly by the middle Bronze Age (c. 1800–1500 BC), which approximates the patriarchal age, hunting was widely practiced. The reference to Esau as a skillful hunter (Gn 25:27) would be typical of a time when both agricultural and hunting pursuits were followed. The Egyptian "Tale of Sinuhe", from the 20th century BC, mentions hunting with hounds.

The Bible text gives a number of glimpses into the kinds of birds and animals that were hunted. Lists of animals that

HUPPIM Perhaps the son of Ir (Iri) and a descendant of Benjamin through Bela's line (Gn 46:21; 1 Chr 7:12, 15). Huppim is probably an alternate spelling of Hupham, the father of the Huphamite family from Benjamin's tribe (Nm 26:39). His precise lineage is difficult to determine.

HUR

1. Aaron's assistant in supporting Moses' hands until the Amalekites were defeated at Rephidim (Ex 17:8-13). He is mentioned again as assisting Aaron in overseeing

Israel while Moses was on Mt Sinai (24:14). According to Josephus, Hur was the husband of Miriam, the sister of Moses (*Antiquities* 3.2.4).

2. Fourth of the five kings of Midian who was killed with Balaam by the Israelites under Moses (Nm 31:8). He is also referred to as one of the "princes of Midian" and "Sihon" (Jos 13:21).
3. Father of one of the 12 officers whom Solomon appointed to provide food for the king's household (1 Kgs 4:8, KJV; NLT "Ben-hur").
4. Son of Caleb and Ephrath and the grandfather of Bezalel (1 Chr 2:19-20; cf. Ex 31:2; 38:22). Although some interpreters regard the Hur discussed in #1 as the grandfather of Bezalel, others think that the Hur who assisted Moses and the Hur who was Bezalel's grandfather were different men.
5. Father (or perhaps family name) of Rephaiah, a postexilic leader who assisted Nehemiah in rebuilding the Jerusalem wall (Neh 3:9).

HURAI Alternate form of Hiddai in 1 Chronicles 11:32. *See* Hiddai.

HURAM
1. Bela's son from Benjamin's tribe (1 Chr 8:5); perhaps the same person as Hupham (Nm 26:39).
2. Alternate spelling of Hiram, the Phoenician king of Tyre who was an ally of David and Solomon and who supplied materials for the building of the temple (2 Chr 2:3, 11-12; 8:2, 18; 9:10, 21). *See* Hiram #1.
3. Alternate spelling of Hiram, a craftsman from Tyre who worked on Solomon's temple (2 Chr 4:11, NLT "Huram-abi"). *See* Hiram #2.

HURAM-ABI Alternate name for Hiram, Solomon's temple craftsman, in 2 Chronicles 2:13 and 4:16. *See* Hiram #2.

HURI Abihail's father from Gad's tribe who inhabited Gilead in Bashan (1 Chr 5:14).

HURRIANS* People (also called Mitannians) who spoke a language different from Semitic and Indo-European and yet played a significant cultural role in the Near East during the second millennium BC, particularly in transmitting the culture of Sumer and Babylon to western Asia and to the Hittites. That the Hurrians were in an area can be inferred from the presence of Hurrian texts, the presence of people with Hurrian names (or Indo-Iranian as explained below), and from statements in other ancient literature, including the OT.

At the beginning of the second millennium, and even somewhat before, Hurrians are found in the northern-most parts of Mesopotamia, having come there presumably from still farther north. They are found in the 18th century BC at Mari and Alalakh, and in the 15th and 14th centuries BC at Nuzi, Ugarit, Alalakh, a few cities in Palestine, and especially in their political center of Mitanni. During this latter period, their rulers were actually an aristocracy of Indo-Iranian extraction, who often retained their Indo-Iranian names, but who in other respects had adopted Hurrian language, religion, and general culture, and so were for all practical purposes Hurrians.

The main question concerning Hurrian presence is the extent to which they were influential in Palestine, and here the evidence is not clear. The Amarna letters, written by the Mitannian/Hurrian kings and by petty kings of Palestine to the Egyptian pharaohs during the 14th century BC, refer to a few Palestinian kings with Hurrian

(some Indo-Iranian) names such as Abdikhepa of Jerusalem. However, the letters, written in Akkadian by the scribes of these Palestinian kings, betray a local Canaanite rather than Hurrian speech. Interestingly, the Egyptians referred to Palestine as the land of the Hurrians, and indeed one pharaoh claimed to have captured 36,000 Hurrians there, but this could mean inhabitants of Palestine rather than ethnic Hurrians. In view of the evidence of the Amarna letters, it is likely that Palestine was only nominally Hurrian.

See also Hittites; Hivites; Horites.

HUSBAND *See* Family Life and Relations.

HUSBANDMAN*, HUSBANDRY* Occupation and practice of farming and animal production; KJV rendering of farmer, tenant farmer, plowman, tiller, and vinedresser. *See* Agriculture.

HUSHAH, HUSHATHITES* Ezer's son (1 Chr 4:4) or perhaps a town that Ezer founded. The warriors Sibbecai (2 Sm 21:18; 1 Chr 11:29; 20:4; 27:11) and Mebunnai (2 Sm 23:27) were described as Hushathites. Whether this designates genealogical ancestry or geographical locality (or perhaps both) is uncertain.

HUSHAI Friend and adviser who remained faithful to David when his other adviser, Ahithophel, defected to join the rebelling Absalom. According to David's instructions, Hushai pretended loyalty to Absalom and slipped information to David regarding Absalom's plans. Ahithophel urged Absalom to attack the fleeing David before he had a chance to strengthen his forces, but Absalom followed Hushai's advice, which gave David time to escape over the Jordan and ultimately to defeat Absalom's party. When his counsel was not followed, Ahithophel hanged himself, probably anticipating the disastrous outcome (2 Sm 15:32-37; 16:15–17:23). Hushai belonged to the Archite family from Ataroth, a town on Ephraim and Benjamin's border (Jos 16:2, 7).

HUSHAM Temanite who succeeded Jobab as king of Edom (Gn 36:34-35; 1 Chr 1:45-46).

HUSHIM
1. Dan's son (Gn 46:23), alternately called Shuham in Numbers 26:42, where he is mentioned as the founder of the Shuhamite family.
2. Benjamite descendant of Aher (1 Chr 7:12).
3. One of the Benjamite Shaharaim's three wives (1 Chr 8:8-11).

HUZ* KJV rendering of Uz, Nahor's son, in Genesis 22:21. *See* Uz (Person) #2.

HUZZAB* Obscure Hebrew word found only in Nahum 2:7 (KJV). Scholars are uncertain whether the word is a verb meaning "it is decreed," a noun personifying Nineveh, or a reference to an Assyrian queen. The problem is perhaps due to textual error, but thus far neither textual scholarship nor archaeology has been able to resolve the question.

HYACINTH* Plant indigenous to the Holy Land yielding blue fragrant flowers. *See* Plants.

HYENA *See* Animals.

HYKSOS* Term used by Egyptian historian Manetho (c. 280 BC) to designate the foreign rulers of the 15th and

16th dynasties in Egypt (1730?–1570? BC). Once called the shepherd kings, that expression is now thought to have come from a misrendering of an Egyptian text.

The Hyksos were Semites, probably entering Egypt from Syria and Palestine, though their exact origin is unknown. They gradually infiltrated Egypt during the 18th century BC, and it is possible that some intermarriage took place. This infiltration was aided by a weakening of Egyptian power as a result of internal dynastic rivalries. Some of the Hyksos may have held Egyptian administrative posts before the actual Hyksos takeover, which was probably more of a swift political maneuver than a great military conquest.

The Hyksos capital was probably established at Qantir in the delta region of northeastern Egypt. From there they could maintain ties with their cultural base in Palestine and Syria. Qantir was close to Goshen, the Egyptian territory inhabited by the Israelites during their sojourn in Egypt.

The Hyksos introduced the war chariot into Egypt, a military device later used to drive the Hyksos aliens out of Egypt. Horse and chariot warfare became the norm in the following centuries. The Hyksos presence also forced the Egyptians to acknowledge the surrounding Middle Eastern world. Previously Egyptians generally had viewed other peoples as barbarians and themselves as the cultural center of the world. When the Hyksos were evicted by Ahmose in 1570(?) BC, Egypt embarked on a course of conquests initiating its empire period (16th–12th centuries BC). No monuments from the Hyksos era have been found, and whatever monuments did exist were probably destroyed when Egyptian rule was reestablished.

The relation of the Hyksos to Israel's history is debated and depends on a correct interpretation of Exodus 1:8: "Now there arose a new king over Egypt, who did not know Joseph." If Joseph died just before 1800 BC, and if the Hyksos takeover in Egypt was about 1730 BC, then the "new king" was a Hyksos ruler who did not know of Joseph, or perhaps had no reason to respect Joseph's descendants even if he had known Joseph. The new rigor of servitude described in Exodus 1:9-14 would, according to that interpretation, have been introduced by the Hyksos. If so, it may be that the Hyksos were fewer in number than the Hebrews and feared some kind of uprising (v 9), or the Hyksos may have feared an alliance between the Hebrews and the Egyptians, which also might have led to the Hyksos being deposed (v 10). In this view, the pharaoh who ordered the Hebrew midwives to kill newborn Hebrew boys (v 15) ruled Egypt after the Hyksos had been overthrown. Thus there would be a gap of at least 150 years between verse 14 and 15.

The other interpretation places Joseph's arrival in Egypt sometime during the Hyksos rule, not prior to it. Here it is assumed that a Semitic people such as the Hyksos would not be averse to having another Semite in their government, nor would they oppose the settlement of Jacob's family in Egypt. Further, the location of Jacob's family and descendants in Goshen fits with the known fact that the Hyksos had their center of control in that region. This view might also explain why Egyptian records do not mention Joseph—his name would have been offensive to later Egyptian national feeling, and therefore removed from any records. If this line of reasoning were accepted, then the king "who did not know Joseph" came to the throne after the Hyksos had been overthrown. With the Hyksos eliminated by the revived Egyptian dynasty, it follows that the Hebrews, another Semitic group, would be brought into subjection also.

In either case, it is clear that the Hyksos and the Hebrews were not in agreement on religious matters. The Hyksos worshiped the Canaanite gods, especially Baal, in their own lands, and they combined that worship with Egyptian sun-god worship when they ruled in Egypt.

HYMENAEUS Believer, probably of Ephesus, cited by Paul as one who "rejected conscience" (1 Tm 1:19-20) and "swerved from the truth" (2 Tm 2:18). In the first instance, Hymenaeus (mentioned with Alexander) is viewed as having rejected correct beliefs and made a shipwreck of his faith. The seriousness of his offense is evident, as Paul sternly relates that he has delivered him over to Satan. The meaning of this phrase is uncertain, although it might have involved physical affliction, as well as severance from the body of other Christians. The harsh action was meant to bring about, not ultimate destruction, but eventual and lasting benefit to Hymenaeus so he might learn not to blaspheme (cf. 1 Cor 5:5). Apparently, this censure was not successful. In 2 Timothy 2:17-18, Hymenaeus appears as one who is "upsetting the faith." He (along with Philetus) was teaching that the resurrection had already taken place. Most probably, he was teaching that the resurrection takes place at the time of spiritual rebirth and baptism, based on a faulty interpretation of Romans 6:1-11 and Colossians 3:1. Hymenaeus thus sought to teach a spiritualized resurrection taking place as the soul awakens from sin.

HYMN, HYMNODY* *See* Music; Poetry, Biblical.

HYPOCRISY The act of pretending to be what one is not, especially the false appearance of being religious or virtuous. Our modern understanding of the word "hypocrisy" is determined by its use in the NT, especially by Jesus. In both the NT and subsequent understandings the term most often meant deceit, misrepresenting the truth, or claiming virtues or qualities one does not possess.

In contrast to its consistently negative meaning in the Bible, hypocrisy as first used by the Greeks was a neutral word. In its verb form it meant "to explain, to interpret, or to expound." Although the noun "hypocrisy" could mean "answer," the other noun form, "hypocrite," almost always meant "actor" and probably came from the verb meaning "to expound."

Originally, a hypocrite could be a speaker or actor who interpreted the words of a poet or the music of a composer. The actor, or hypocrite, tried to make intelligible for his audience what the poet or composer had written. On a larger scale the hypocrite could be one actor among others in a drama performed on a stage. A good hypocrite faithfully interpreted his assigned role, while an undesirable hypocrite interpreted his role poorly. Because of the word's essential neutrality, accompanying words were necessary to set its direction.

In Hellenistic times (c. 325–125 BC), the world was commonly viewed as a stage and all human conduct as the art of acting. One's role and script were written for him by his familial, cultural, and religious environment and could be performed either successfully or poorly. When used in this sense, hypocrisy did not carry the idea of pretense or sham. Nevertheless, there are instances where the term "hypocrite" was used to describe a person who performed life's role deceptively. The image presented to the public was only a mask behind which the true and different self lay hidden.

The Gospels often use the terms "hypocrisy" (Mt 23:28; Mk 12:15b; Lk 12:1) and "hypocrite" (Mt 7:5; 24:51; Lk 6:42; 13:15) to record the conflict between Jesus and his opponents. With respect to the Pharisees and Sadducees, Jesus detected a blatant contrast between their outward forms of righteousness and their failure to embrace the more substantive aspects of righteousness: mercy, justice, humility, forgiveness, and love toward the unlovely (Lk 11:38, 42). They hid their failure in this matter behind pious pretense (Mk 7:1-13). Inwardly they were full of greed and wickedness (Lk 11:39). Hypocrisy defines the one who presents an outward appearance of righteousness but who is inwardly marked by wickedness (Mt 23:28).

Jesus condemned hypocrisy because it distorts God's righteous command. Rather than pursue an authentic inward holiness, the hypocrites distorted righteousness into a rigid mold whose chief usefulness was exhibition before people (Mt 23:2-7). Their idea of righteousness revealed a warped conception of God and a perverse understanding of how he reconciles sinners to himself (Lk 16:15). The hypocrites, who claimed to interpret God to humans, actually misrepresented him. Consequently, their falsification led sinners away from God rather than toward reconciliation with him (Lk 11:52). Hypocrites not only keep others from entering the kingdom of God, they refrain from going in themselves (Mt 23:13).

HYRCANUS

1. John Hyrcanus, Hasmonean ruler. *See* Hasmoneans.
2. Tobias's son who had a large amount of money deposited in the temple during the time of Heliodorus (2 Macc 3:11).

HYSSOP Syrian or Egyptian marjoram plant (Ex 12:22; Lv 14:4). *See* Plants.

I

"I AM" SAYINGS Self-proclamations made by Jesus in the Gospel of John.

One of the distinctive elements of the teaching of Jesus is the way Jesus expresses important truths in terms of his own personal character and mission. These statements begin with the words "I am" and then continue to express a deep theological thought in terms of metaphorical statement. This method of teaching is preserved for us in the Gospel of John alone. While Matthew, Mark, and Luke emphasize Jesus' mode of teaching in the form of the parable, John pictures Jesus as teaching in discourses. These discourses often find an "I am" statement as the key expression of the central thought.

The "I am" statements found in the Gospel of John are the bread of life or the living bread (6:35, 48, 51), the light of the world (8:12; see also 9:5), the gate (10:7, 9), the good shepherd (10:11, 14), the resurrection and the life (11:25), the way, the truth and the life (14:6), and the vine (15:1, 5).

Each of these statements follows a basic pattern. They are written as metaphors in which one of the key elements is to be the Christ expressed as "I am." The meaning of the metaphor is to be drawn chiefly from the explanatory statement connected with it. Thus when Jesus says, "I am the light of the world," the explanatory statement follows, "So if you follow me, you won't be stumbling through the darkness, for living light will flood your path" (TLB). This latter statement is intended to help a person interpret the metaphor. Most statements have such interpretive elements joined to them.

These metaphorical statements often complement Jesus' miracles. The statement and a miracle each contribute to the understanding of the other. Thus when Jesus proclaims that he is the light of the world, he proceeds to bring sight to the blind man. The controversy that follows between the blind man and the Pharisees shows that the man has received spiritual sight as well as physical. Before Jesus raises Lazarus from the dead, he tells Martha that he is the resurrection and the life. The raising of Lazarus is intended to show Jesus' power to give life now and to demonstrate his power to do what he proclaimed he was able to do. After Jesus had fed the 5,000, he declared that he was the living bread that had come from heaven. Each of these miracles is interpreted by the metaphorical "I am" statement. Each statement is intended to give the miracle meaning for the ministry of Jesus. They show us that Jesus' miracles were not just acts of power or mercy but actions demonstrating the meaning of his ministry and teaching.

Many theologians consider the "I am" formula to reflect an identification of deity found in the OT (see God, Names of). When Moses was called, he asked God to identify himself in such a way that Moses might gain acceptance from the Hebrew people. God revealed himself to Moses as the great "I AM." Moses was to tell the Israelites that "I AM sent me to you" (Ex 3:13-14). From this "I AM" the name Yahweh is derived. Many believe that Jesus used this same formula from the OT to relate his deity. The "I am" statements in John's Gospel help the reader identify Jesus as divine, as God.

IBEX Species of wild goat, declared ceremonially clean in the Law (Dt 14:5). *See* Animals (Goat).

IBHAR Son born to David during his reign in Jerusalem (2 Sm 5:15; 1 Chr 3:6; 14:5).

IBIS* Wading bird with a long, slender bill, declared unclean in Leviticus 11:17. *See* Birds.

IBLEAM City in Manasseh's territory (Jos 17:11; Jgs 1:27; 2 Kgs 9:27), perhaps identifiable with Bileam, a Levitical city west of the Jordan River between Samaria and Jezreel (1 Chr 6:70). *See* Levitical Cities.

IBNEIAH Jeroham's son from Benjamin's tribe (1 Chr 9:8).

IBNIJAH Forefather of Meshullam from Benjamin's tribe (1 Chr 9:8).

IBRI Merarite Levite and Jaaziah's son, who lived during David's time (1 Chr 24:27).

IBSAM Tola's son from Issachar's tribe (1 Chr 7:2).

IBZAN Judge who ruled over Israel, or part of it, for seven years (Jgs 12:8-10). Ibzan was a native of Bethlehem, probably of Zebulun, and was buried in his place of birth. Jewish tradition identified Ibzan with Boaz and consequently understood his native city to be Bethlehem in Judah. Ibzan had 30 sons and 30 daughters and was a man of wealth and high social standing.

See also Judges, Book of.

ICHABOD Name given to Phinehas's son (Eli's grandson) to commemorate the glory that had departed from Israel, after the ark of God was taken by the Philistines (1 Sm 4:19-22; 14:3).

Phinehas was killed in the battle of Aphek, at the same time the Philistines had captured the ark. When Phinehas's wife heard of the tragedy, she went immediately into labor, and when the child was born, she named him Ichabod (meaning "no glory") to express her despair.

ICONIUM City in the southwest part of central Asia Minor located about 95 miles (153 kilometers) from the Mediterranean coast. It is known today as Konya, a Turkish city, and capital of the province bearing the same name.

Iconium was an agricultural center famous for its wheat fields and orchards of apricots and plums. Its ideal location and climate helped establish its place as a major link in the trade routes between Syria, Ephesus, and Rome.

Little is known about the origin of the city. Its

beginnings may be traced to a group of immigrant tribes from northern Greece—the Phrygians. Xenophon, a Greek historian (c. 428–354 BC), mentions it as a Phrygian city visited by Cyrus. Since the Phrygian language was spoken in Iconium, it is likely that the inhabitants considered themselves of this extraction. Although the name Iconium was originally Phrygian, a myth was later created to infuse it with Greek meaning. According to this legend, a great flood destroys mankind. Life is restored when Prometheus and Athena breathe life into human images made from mud left by subsiding waters. The Greek word for "image" is *eikon*, from which comes the name Iconium, according to the legend.

In the third century BC, Iconium was governed by the Seleucid kings of Syria. As proponents of Greek culture, the Seleucids soon turned Iconium into a Hellenistic city. The Greek language was spoken and the people were ruled by two magistrates appointed annually. Despite later domination by the Gauls and Pontic kings (c. 165–63 BC), Iconium retained its Hellenistic character until NT times. In 36 BC Mark Antony gave the city to Antymas. Upon his death in 25 BC, Iconium joined the neighboring cities of Lystra, Derbe, and Pisidian Antioch as a part of the province of Galatia and so became incorporated into the Roman Empire.

The apostle Paul visited Iconium on his first missionary journey. Having been forced to leave Pisidian Antioch (Acts 13:51), Paul came to the synagogue in Iconium. His preaching initially won the approval of both the Jews and Greeks, but unbelieving Jews soon incited a riot against him (14:1-7). Paul fled to Lystra, but he was followed by the Iconian Jews, who stoned him and left him for dead (v 19; cf. 2 Tm 3:11). Cared for by friends, Paul was able to join Barnabas in Derbe, where they made many disciples then later returned to Iconium to strengthen the Christians there (Acts 14:20-23). During the second missionary journey, Timothy was recommended to Paul and Silas by the Christians at Iconium (16:1-2).

IDALAH Town assigned to Zebulun's tribe for an inheritance (Jos 19:15). It is generally identified with Khirbet el-Hawarah, northwest of Nazareth.

IDBASH One of the descendants of Etam from Judah's tribe (1 Chr 4:3).

IDDO

1. Father of Ahinadab, Solomon's official at Mahanaim, who provisioned the royal household (1 Kgs 4:14).
2. Gershonite Levite, descendant of Joah and forefather of Zerah (1 Chr 6:21); perhaps alternately called Adaiah in verse 41. *See* Adaiah #2.
3. Zechariah's son and the chief officer of Manasseh's half-tribe in Gilead during David's reign (1 Chr 27:21).
4. Prophet and seer who recorded the events of Solomon's reign concerning Jeroboam, Nebat's son in a book of visions (2 Chr 9:29), Rehoboam's acts in his genealogical records (12:15), and Abijah's life as part of a commentary (13:22).
5. Grandfather of Zechariah the prophet (Zec 1:1, 7). Iddo was a well-known priest who returned to Jerusalem from exile in 538 BC, and whose household was headed by Zechariah during Joiakim's reign as high priest during the postexilic era (Neh 12:16). According to Ezra 5:1 and 6:14, Zechariah, and not Berechiah his father, was considered Iddo's successor. *See* Zechariah (Person) #20.
6. Leading Levite at Casiphia in Babylonia to whom Ezra sent a delegation of men requesting priests and temple servants to join Ezra's caravan returning to Palestine for service in the Jerusalem temple (Ezr 8:17).

IDOLS, IDOLATRY Man-made images or natural representations worshiped as deities; anything receiving worship other than the one true God. Idolatry is the spiritual worship of an idol. Many idolaters literally serve idols: in ancient Egypt statues of gods were regularly and ritually clothed and fed. Some concept of the worship of a false god, Baal, is given in the account of the contest on Mt Carmel: the priests of Baal cried aloud, they "limped" (RSV) around the altar, they cut themselves with swords and lances (1 Kgs 18:26-29). Baal worship was widely followed by Israel during the period of the monarchy.

In the Old Testament Abraham's ancestors were worshipers of idols in Mesopotamia (Jos 24:2). Archaeological excavations in that area have revealed the images of numerous deities, and Mesopotamian religious literature reveals the gross polytheism out of which Abraham came. The tendency of the Israelites toward idolatry was in part the expression of the universal human longing for a god one can see and know through the physical senses.

Most of the idolatry of the Israelites was borrowed from their neighbors. During the more than 400 years that the descendants of Jacob spent in Egypt, they were exposed to polytheistic idolatry, which influenced their religious mind-set. At Sinai, while Moses was receiving the Ten Commandments from the Lord, the people were demanding that Aaron make gods for them (Ex 32:1-6). He fashioned a golden calf, following an Egyptian form, for the whole bovine family was worshiped in Egypt—the Apis bull, the Hathor cow, and the Mnevis calf.

It was after his stay in Egypt (1 Kgs 11:40) that Jeroboam became king of Israel and set up golden calves, one at Bethel and one at Dan (12:26-33), an action that earned him the label as being the one who made Israel sin (2 Kgs 3:3).

Already in patriarchal times there are references to the teraphim, or household gods. Examples of these idols have been found at Ur of the Chaldees, Nuzi, and other sites, and are referred to in the cuneiform tablets. The teraphim that Rachel stole from Laban could be hidden in her camel's saddlebag (Gn 31:34). It seems, however, that in the time of David such idols were larger, for when Saul's men came to kill David, Michal, David's wife and the daughter of Saul, helped David to escape and then took such an image and placed it in a bed to make the men think that David was sick (1 Sm 19:11-16).

The prohibition of idolatry is explicitly stated in the second commandment (Ex 20:4-5, NLT): "Do not make idols of any kind, whether in the shape of birds or animals or fish. You must never worship or bow down to them, for I, the LORD your God, am a jealous God who will not share your affection with any other god!" (cf. Ex 34:17; Lv 19:4; 26:1, Dt 4:15-19; 27:1-5). This commandment is an extension or auxiliary of the first, for it seeks to preserve God's uniqueness and to protect his glory. The definition of idolatry was broadened during the time of Samuel, who confronted King Saul with the charge that stubbornness is the same as idolatry (1 Sm 15:23).

Previous to the conquest of Canaan, the Lord kept warning Israel against marrying members of the native populace, which he had ordered Israel to annihilate. This measure was intended to prevent the weakening of moral life in Israel (Ex 34:16; Dt 7:3-4). This principle is again expanded in the NT (cf. 1 Cor 15:33; 2 Cor 6:14). The history of Israel demonstrated the practicality of the prohibition against such marriages, for they inevitably led to apostasy. Perhaps the saddest example is Solomon (1 Kgs 11:1-8). When Solomon was old, his wives turned his heart to other gods, so that he was not wholly true to the Lord his God (v 4).

In the time of the judges there was an infamous case of idol worship (Jgs 17:1–18:31). The mother of an Ephraimite named Micah took 200 pieces of silver and had a silversmith make them into a graven image for her son. He also had a shrine, an ephod, and teraphim. He hired a wandering Levite to be his priest, but men from the tribe of Dan came along and took the Levite, the image, and all the accoutrements and set up this idol at Dan and used it as an object of their worship (18:30-31).

In Scripture the kings of Israel are evaluated on the basis of what they did with respect to the "high places" and idols. Asa removed all the idols his ancestors had made (1 Kgs 15:12) and would not let Maacah be queen mother because she had an abominable image made for Asherah. He cut down and burned the image (v 13). The Israelite king Ahab, however, was an idolater (1 Kgs 21:26; cf. 16:30-33).

Hezekiah destroyed the high places, broke down the pillars, and cut down the Asherim (2 Kgs 18:4; 2 Chr 31:1). He also put an end to a strange cult that illustrates the insidious nature of idolatry. The bronze serpent that Moses lifted up on a pole to save the Israelites from death by snakebite (Nm 21:9; cf. Jn 3:14) had been preserved until the time of Hezekiah. It had been given the name Nehushtan, and people venerated it and burned incense to it. Hezekiah destroyed it (2 Kgs 18:4) because what had been an instrument for good had become a thing of evil.

The prophet Isaiah described the making of an idol in human form (Is 40:19-20; 44:9-17). Images were cast in a mold using molten metal (40:19; 44:10). Statues were forged by smiths (44:12), carved from wood (44:13-17), and overlaid with precious metal (40:19). Small clay images and plaques were also molded and fired in a kiln, and statues were sculptured from stone. The psalmist spoke out against idols and images (Pss 96:5; 97:7; 106:34-39) and the helplessness of idols is described in Psalms 115:4-8 and 135:15-18.

The northern and southern kingdoms of Israel went into captivity because they forsook God and served idols. The Jews were well aware that idolatry had brought them into captivity, and during their time in Babylon, they developed an abhorrence to idols that has characterized Judaism to this very day.

In the New Testament The fullest discussion in the NT on idolatry (*eidōlolatreia*) and the idolworshiper (*eidōlolatres*) is found in Paul's First Epistle to the Corinthians. In an earlier (no longer extant) epistle, Paul had told the Corinthians not to associate with those who called themselves believers but were still idol worshipers (1 Cor 5:9-11). After that letter the Corinthians must have asked Paul for clarification on this matter. Thus, in this epistle Paul provides a response to their question; the "idol worshiper" is mentioned in 5:10-11, 6:9, 10:7, and "idolatry" is spoken of in 10:14.

The terms, "idolatry" and "idol worshiper," are related to two other expressions: (1) "idol" (*eidōlon*), found in 1 Corinthians 8:4; 10:19; 12:2; and (2) "food sacrificed to idols" (*eidōlothutos*), found in 1 Corinthians 8:1, 4, 7; 10:19. The kind of idolatry that Paul condemns is that which involved Christians offering sacrifices to idols and then partaking of the food that had been sacrificed to them. The participants are called idol worshipers because their involvement in idolatrous sacrifices was perceived as having fellowship with demons. Paul strictly prohib-

ited the eating of sacrificial food at the popular temples in the presence of idol-demons. As such, he shared the same view about idols as most Jews in his day. For the Jews, idols and heathen deities were identical. (See 1 Thes 1:9, where Paul contrasts "idols" with "the living and *true* God.") To Paul, idols in and of themselves were nothing (1 Cor 8:4); behind the idol, however, was a demon (10:20).

The eating of sacrificial food at the cultic meals in pagan temples was censured by Paul because it was understood that the participants thereby became united to demons (see 1 Cor 10:19-21). However, Paul had no problem with those who purchased food that had been left over from these events and that was later sold in the marketplace. In his judgment, if they ate it at home, they were not participating in idolatry. They could eat this food with a good conscience—unless, of course, in doing so they would be the means of destroying a weaker believer. For the sake of such believers, one should abstain. This was a matter of conscience (10:25-29). But going to pagan festivities and eating meals offered to idols was not permitted in any form.

The Corinthians had participated in these meals regularly before they became Christians and apparently had continued to do so after their conversion. In Corinth such meals were the regular practice both at national festivals and private celebrations. The "gods" (whom Paul considered "demons") were thought to be present at these events because the sacrifices were made to them. Thus, to participate in these events was to join oneself to demons and thereby become an idol worshiper. The ancient Israelites had been carried away into idolatry by their pagan neighbors on several occasions when they were enticed to participate in these pagan celebrations (e.g., Nm 25; cf. Ex 32:6). The festivities involved all sorts of licentiousness. In 1 Corinthians 10, Paul referred to this apostasy of the Israelites and used it as a negative example. Because the Israelites became involved in pagan festivities, they were carried away into idolatry and fornication, which incited God's wrath and brought destruction.

In other Pauline Epistles, idolatry is mentioned but not with the kind of definition and extended discussion that is found in 1 Corinthians. Nonetheless, Paul speaks out against actual idolatry and what we might call figurative idolatry (i.e., idolatry in the sense of desiring something above God).

In Romans 1:18-32 sexual licentiousness and other sins are ultimately traced to idolatry. The Gentiles, who should have known that God existed, as evidenced in creation and conscience, abandoned the immortal, invisible God in exchange for mortal, visible images (i.e., idols). Because of this abandonment, God gave them over to do the filthy things their hearts desired (Rom 1:24). Thus, idolatry is included in Paul's list of what he calls "the works of the flesh" (see Gal 5:19-20). And those who are idol worshipers are included in the catalog of all those evil people who will not inherit the kingdom of God (see 1 Cor 6:9).

In Ephesians 5:5 Paul again includes idolaters among those who will not inherit the kingdom of God. However, such idolaters are not just those who go to pagan temples and worship idols; they are those who are greedy or covetous. According to superior manuscript evidence, the verse reads, "No fornicator or impure person or greedy person, which is the same as an idolater, has any inheritance in the kingdom of Christ and of God." The point seems to be that the greedy, covetous person who makes his desires his god is much the same as an idolater. Thus, covetousness and idolatry are made synonymous. The parallel passage, Colossians 3:5, makes this explicit, which literally says covetousness is idolatry.

See also Canaanite Deities and Religion; Gods and Goddesses; Grove; High Place.

IDUMAEA*, IDUMEA, IDUMEANS Term derived from the Greek form of Edom ("red"). The change from Edomite to Idumean resulted from the conquests of Alexander the Great, which made Greek the common language of the area. The name was applied to the former country of the Edomites and to the portion of south Judah occupied by the descendants of Esau after the Jews had been deported to Babylon following the conquest by Nebuchadnezzar in 586 BC. The country known as Idumea in the intertestamental period had its northern boundary at Bet-sur (Beth-zur), a few miles north of Hebron, and included some of the Shephelah (low country) extending down into the former Philistine country (1 Macc 4:15, 22, 61; 5:65).

First known as Edomites, then as Nabateans, and finally as Idumeans, the ancestors of the Idumeans trace their lineage to the elder brother of Jacob, Esau, who was cheated out of both his birthright and his blessing (Gn 27:1-45). This led to conflict between the children of Israel and the descendants of Esau throughout the entire biblical period.

It is not surprising, therefore, that the Edomites rejoiced when the Babylonians conquered Israel. The Edomites then occupied the territory vacated by the Israelites following the subjugation of the kingdom by the Babylonians after 586 BC.

About 300 BC Arabian tribes invaded and took the Edomite capital Petra, forcing the remaining Edomites into the area south of Judah, which then became included in what was known as Idumea. The invaders, known as Nabateans, made Sela or Petra the center of their caravan trade both from east to west and north to south. These desert tradesmen, influenced now by Greek ideas, fashioned the bowl-like "crater" at Petra into a fantastic city with a concentration of rock-hewn temples, tombs, and buildings made from the colorful red sandstone of the area. In addition to creating the world's most unique city, the Nabateans were excellent traders and farmers. As Josephus says, they were not warlike but skilled in commerce, art, and agriculture. The Nabateans created the strategic desert stronghold of Avedat, which, with Petra, commanded the caravan routes. The Nabateans flourished from about 100 BC to AD 100, when the Romans gradually caused their demise by changing the caravan routes from south of the Dead Sea to the area around Damascus and Palmyra.

During the intertestamental period the returning Jews had border skirmishes with the Idumeans. Hebron was captured by Judas Maccabeus (1 Macc 5:65). John Hyrcanus compelled the Idumeans to become Jews and submit to circumcision. The governor of Idumea, Antipater, who had been made procurator of Judea by Julius Caesar, was an Idumean. Antipater assigned his son Herod as governor of Galilee. This paved the way for Herod to become king of Judea, under the title of Herod the Great. With the conquest of Judea by the Romans, first in AD 70, and later in AD 135, Idumea disappears from history. Only in recent years have archaeologists begun to uncover some of the secrets of the Idumeans and of the Nabateans, their conquerors.

See also Edom, Edomites; Judaism.

IEZER, IEZERITES Contractions of Abiezer and Abiezrite, the names of Gilead's son and that son's descendants (Nm 26:30). *See* Abiezer #1.

IGAL

1. Joseph's son from Issachar's tribe and one of the 12 spies sent by Moses to search out Canaan (Nm 13:7).
2. Nathan's son and one of David's mighty men (2 Sm 23:36). In 1 Chronicles 11:38 he is called Joel, Nathan's brother (in Hebrew, only one letter different from Igal).
3. Shemaiah's son and a descendant of King David through King Jehoiachin (1 Chr 3:22).

IGDALIAH Hanan's father. Hanan's sons had a room adjacent to the temple during Jehoiakim's reign (Jer 35:4).

IGEAL* KJV spelling of Igal, Shemaiah's son, in 1 Chronicles 3:22. *See* Igal #3.

IGNATIUS AND HIS EPISTLES* Bishop of Antioch in Syria in the late first century, whose writings were very close to the thought of the NT writers. He wrote seven letters while en route under armed guard to Rome to suffer martyrdom (probably AD 107). The letters were to churches in cities through which he passed, Philadelphia and Smyrna, and to churches that sent delegations to visit him during this final journey—namely, Ephesus, Tralles, and Magnesia. He sent a letter ahead to the church in Rome to prevent their intervention with the Roman authorities in delivering him into martyrdom. He also wrote a letter to Polycarp, the bishop of Smyrna. Similar to the NT epistles, these writings reveal a strong commitment to Christ and to the physical facts of his birth, death, and resurrection. The Epistles of Ignatius parallel the Gospels in several places and appropriate language from a number of the Pauline letters.

The letters of Ignatius are evidence for the rapid development of the episcopal structure in the early church of Asia Minor and Syria. In the NT, the local church was governed by a body of equal officers called elders or bishops, but in these letters there is reference to a single ruling bishop in each city except Rome. Ignatius is the first writer to use the term "catholic" (universal) to describe the church. His use of the term implied a connectional church with a unity in faith toward Christ and with delegations to express concerns between the churches.

He opposed the Ebionite heresy, which demanded the keeping of the Jewish regulations as the way of salvation. According to Ignatius, in order to affirm Christ the believer must reject Jewish practices. The Christian must worship on the Lord's Day, the day of his resurrection, rather than observe the Jewish sabbaths. Yet he did view the church as the continuation of the OT people of God and the prophets as disciples who looked forward to Christ.

Ignatius also attacked Docetism, which held that Christ only appeared to have real birth, death, and resurrection. In reciting the facts of Christ's life, Igantius was the first one outside the NT writers to speak of the virgin birth of Jesus. Ignatius also emphasized the fact that the apostles touched the body of their risen Lord. Ignatius said it was the real suffering of Jesus Christ on the cross and his physical resurrection that made it possible for him to face martyrdom.

IIM

1. KJV rendering of Iyim, a shortened form of Iye-abarim, in Numbers 33:45. *See* Iye-abarim, Iyim.
2. Town near Edom in the southern portion of the land assigned to Judah's tribe for an inheritance (Jos 15:29).

IJE-ABARIM* KJV spelling of Iye-abarim, one of Israel's stopping places in the wilderness, in Numbers 21:11 and 33:44. *See* Iye-abarim, Iyim.

IJON Town assigned to Naphtali's tribe in the extreme north of Palestine. Some identify it with Tell ed-Dibbon between the Litani River and Mt Hermon, but this is disputed. Ijon was one of the towns taken by Ben-hadad of Damascus during Baasha's reign (c. 900 BC; 1 Kgs 15:20; 2 Chr 16:4). Tiglath-pileser III of Assyria captured the town and deported its people during Pekah's reign (c. 733 BC; 2 Kgs 15:29).

IKKESH Man from Tekoa whose son Ira was one of David's mighty men (2 Sm 23:26; 1 Chr 11:28), and head of a division of 24,000 men during the sixth month of the year (1 Chr 27:9).

ILAI* Alternate name for Zalmon, a renowned warrior, in 1 Chronicles 11:29 (see NLT mg). *See* Zalmon (Person).

ILLNESS *See* Disease; Medicine and Medical Practice.

ILLYRICUM Roman province northwest of Macedonia. During the height of the Roman Empire (c. AD 117), when it included Dalmatia, Illyricum was bounded by the Adriatic Sea on the west and by the provinces of Pannonia on the north, Upper Moesia on the east, and Macedonia on the south. Today Slovenia, Croatia, Bosnia, and Yugoslavia occupy that territory.

Throughout the fourth century BC, the people of Illyricum warred with the Macedonians, until the Macedonian ruler Philip II defeated them in 359 BC. During the third century BC, their acts of piracy against Greek and Roman ships led to a war with Rome that continued on and off for 60 years (229–168 BC). After a series of revolts and sporadic Roman rule, Illyricum was officially made part of the empire in 11 BC and renamed Dalmatia. It took another 20 years for the people to be fully integrated into Roman culture.

from Jerusalem to as far as Illyricum (Rom 15:19). Although Acts does not document a ministry in that region, Paul may have visited Illyricum during his visit to Macedonia and Achaia just before returning to Jerusalem (Acts 20:1-2). Paul expressed a desire to continue his ministry in Spain, a totally Latin environment (Rom 15:28); in Illyricum he would have had his first experience in a culture that was more Latin than Greek.

See also Dalmatia.

IMAGE OF GOD Likeness to God, the most basic affirmation to be made concerning the nature of human beings from a Christian perspective. Humans are unique among the creatures in that they are like God and therefore able to have communion and fellowship with God.

Genesis 1:26-27 teaches that God determined to create man and woman in his own "image" and "likeness" and that they would have dominion over the animal creation. The two terms used in the creation account and found also in the NT convey closely related shades of meaning, but the difference between them is no longer thought to be theologically significant.

Because Genesis 2:7 states unambiguously that *man* became a living being, the Bible does not present the view that a previously living creature developed into a human, nor does it suggest that the image of God evolved from a lower form of life. The moment the man and woman became living creatures, they were the image of God. Both male and female share this likeness to God (Gn 1:27).

Other passages that speak of people being created in the image of God are Genesis 5:1, 9:6, 1 Corinthians 11:7, and James 3:9. Ephesians 4:24 and Colossians 3:10 refer to humanity's redemptive re-creation, but the passages are generally regarded as directly relevant for an understanding of mankind's original likeness to God. Although explicit references to humans as expressing the

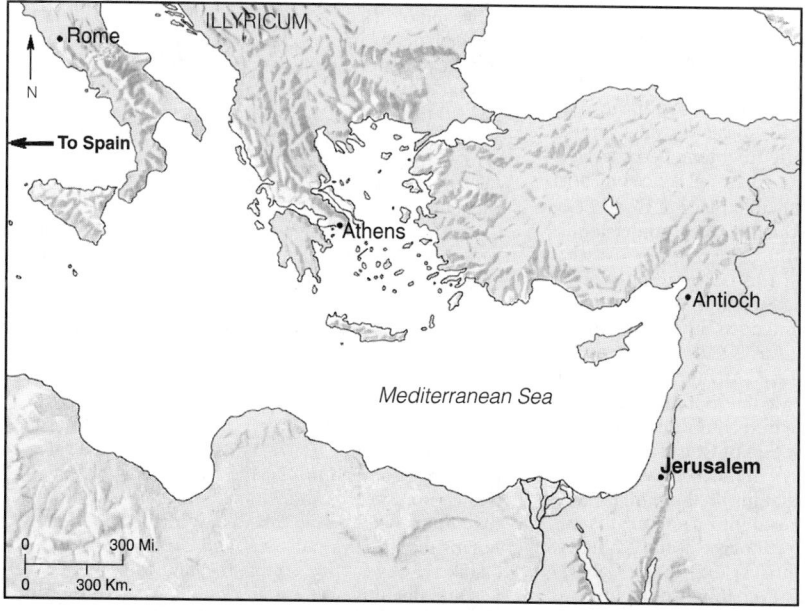

Illyricum According to Romans 15:19, Paul had preached the gospel from Jerusalem to Illyricum, but at the time of writing, he had not yet gone to Rome.

In 229 BC the Roman historian Polybius stated that "the Illyrians were not the enemies of this people or that, but were the common enemies of all." Later Strabo, a first-century Greek geographer, was still describing the people of Illyricum as savage and rapacious.

The sole NT reference to Illyricum is found in the apostle Paul's statement that he had preached the gospel

image of God are comparatively infrequent in the Bible, the truth itself underlies the whole relation between God and humans and is therefore the presupposition of the entire biblical account.

The affirmation in Genesis 1 that man and woman were made in the image of God is not made of any of the other living creatures. The animals, the fish, and the birds do not share this privilege. It is disputed whether the angels are in the image of God, but certain theologians so view them because they find the image to reside in moral righteousness. However, there is no explicit biblical statement to this effect.

By virtue of his creation from the dust of the ground, mankind has an obvious kinship with the earth. It is not strange, therefore, that the body, both in its constitution and its functions, shows similarities with other earthly creatures. But humans are unique in every aspect of their existence; not some part of a human or some faculty of a human, but a human in his or her wholeness is the image of God. The biblical concept is not that the image is *in* man and woman, but that man and woman *are* the image of God.

However, as man's kinship with the earth is most clearly visible in his body, so the image of God is best seen when humans are viewed from the perspective of their spirituality. Theologians have sought at this point to enumerate those aspects of spirituality that define humans and set them apart from the animal creation. The image of God is then found to reside in some attribute or combination of attributes, such as rationality, will, freedom, responsibility, or the like. Contemporary theologians prefer not to enumerate attributes, and the Bible does not set forth the image of God in this way. Nevertheless, it is the personality of humans that separates them from the animals and is a reflection of the personality of God. The animals have their existence *from* God, but humans have their being *in* God, and they are his offspring (Acts 17:28-29).

Another major aspect of the image of God doctrine is developed from Ephesians 4:24 and Colossians 3:10. These verses describe the re-creation of the believers in the likeness of God—in righteousness, holiness of the truth, and true knowledge. In other words, Paul declares that the redeemed are re-created into the image of God as they are transformed into the image of Christ, who bears the untainted image of God. Just as the fall into sin was not without its effect on the image of God, so also redemption from sin affects humans as the image of God. Ephesians and Colossians speak of renewal in the image of God the Creator, but other texts become even more specific in view of the mediatorial office of Christ.

Jesus Christ is preeminently the image of God (2 Cor 4:4; Col 1:15; Heb 1:3). Frequently this is understood exclusively as a reference to the deity of Christ. To see Christ is to see the Father (Jn 14:9). However, in the passages cited, it is the incarnate Mediator, the last Adam, who is at least all that God intended the first Adam to be. Incarnation means that Jesus is truly human, and because he is truly human, he is truly the image of God.

As the last Adam and the Mediator of the new covenant, Jesus brings his people into conformity with his own image, the image of the Son of God (Rom 8:29). He who became like his brethren, in the likeness of sinful flesh, destroys sin in order that his brethren might reflect his own glory. They are changed into the same image from glory to glory by the Spirit of the Lord (2 Cor 3:18). The believer is to "put on Christ" (Rom 13:14; Gal 3:27; cf. Eph 4:24; Col 3:10, "the new nature" in the image of God), an action also described as the formation of Christ in the believer (Gal 4:19).

Conformity to the image of Jesus Christ is achieved through the process of sanctification that is ultimately completed at the resurrection. Only then is the body changed until it is fashioned like unto the glorious body of Christ (Phil 3:21). Restoration in the image of Christ carries beyond creation in the image of God, for the image of the earthly is then exchanged for the image of the heavenly (1 Cor 15:49).

See also Man; Woman.

IMALKUE An Arab chieftain who was in charge of Antiochus, the son of Alexander. Trypho, who had once supported Alexander, sought the aid of Imalkue to have Antiochus crowned king instead of Demetrius. Trypho succeeded and Antiochus became King Antiochus VI. Demetrius's troops supported the new king and routed Demetrius (1 Macc 11:39-55).

IMLAH Father of Michaiah, a prophet during King Ahab's reign, whom the king despised for speaking the truth (1 Kgs 22:8-9; 2 Chr 18:7-8).

IMMANUEL Hebrew masculine name that means "God with us." It appears only twice in the OT (Is 7:14; 8:8) and once in the NT (Mt 1:23), where it is sometimes transliterated "Emmanuel." In the OT the name was given to a child born in the time of Ahaz as a sign to the king that Judah would receive relief from attacks by Israel and Syria. The name symbolized the fact that God would demonstrate his presence with his people in this deliverance. The greater application is that this is a prophecy of the birth of the incarnate God, Jesus the Messiah, as shown in Matthew.

The Prophecy in Isaiah's Day In focusing on the birth of Jesus as Immanuel, there has been some neglect of the historical fulfillment that occurred in the time of Ahaz. Ahaz was the son of a good king, Jotham and the grandson of another godly ruler, Uzziah, but his reign was marked by apostasy and idolatry. He made "molten images" for the Baals, offered incense in the Hinnom Valley, and even burned his sons as an offering (2 Chr 28:2-4). Because of this, the Lord gave him into the hand of Rezin, king of Syria, and of Pekah, king of Israel. The Edomites also invaded Judah, and the Philistines attacked the Shephelah and the Negev and took several cities (vv 17-18).

Ahaz appealed to Tiglath-pileser III of Assyria (745–727 BC) for help against Israel and Syria. Tiglath-pileser accepted tribute from Ahaz, but attacked him instead of helping him (2 Chr 28:20-21). When he went to Damascus to meet the Assyrian king, Ahaz saw an altar, upon which he made offerings to the gods of Syria (v 23). He had a replica of this made and placed in the temple of Jerusalem (2 Kgs 16:10-12). The prophet Isaiah was directed to accost Ahaz at the end of the conduit of the upper pool. God's message to the king was to "take heart," for the attacking kings would fall (Is 7:7-9). Isaiah directed Ahaz to ask the Lord for a sign of this, but the king demurred, having a sudden attack of piety (v 12).

Upon this refusal, the Lord gave to Ahaz a sign: a young woman would conceive and bear a son and call his name Immanuel (Is 7:14). That son would be able to distinguish good from evil by the time he was old enough to eat curds and wild honey, but even before that, the two kings would be removed and the king of Assyria would devastate their lands. The people would be taken away captive, so that the land would lie desolate and uncultivated. A man would have a cow to provide milk for curds, and wild honey would be gathered from the tangle of brush in the untended land.

The identity of this woman and child in Isaiah's time is uncertain. It has been proposed that the woman was Abijah, the wife of Ahaz, and that their son, Hezekiah, was this Immanuel. This is not demonstrable, and it seems inappropriate that a man like Ahaz should be the father of Immanuel.

It has also been suggested that the wife of Isaiah was the mother of Immanuel. Isaiah 7:14 tells of the prospective birth of Immanuel; 8:3 tells of the conception and birth of Isaiah's son, whose name, Maher-shalal-hash-baz ("swift to plunder and quick to spoil") is related to the prediction of the fall of Judah's enemies, for before the child would learn to talk, the lands of Syria and Israel would be taken by the king of Assyria (Is 8:4). Isaiah's statement that he and his children were "signs and portents in Israel from the LORD" (v 18, RSV) enhances the view that it was his son who was also named Immanuel.

The Lord then directed a message to Immanuel (Is 8:5-10). Because the people had refused the gracious invitation of the Lord, the Assyrians would scourge and fill the land of Immanuel. The plotting and plans of the people would come to nothing, for "God is with us" (*'immanu'el*). This is a play on words, using the name Immanuel to express the truth of the Lord's presence.

The Prophecy Fulfilled in Jesus In the fullness of time God sent forth his son; more than 700 years after Ahaz, Jesus was born and here all ambiguities fade away. His mother was a virgin from Nazareth named Mary (Miriam), betrothed to a solid citizen named Joseph. Matthew 1:23 cites Isaiah 7:14 as being fulfilled in the birth of Jesus. The Scripture is very explicit in stating that Mary had no sexual contact with her husband prior to the birth of Jesus (Mt 1:25). The same precision is seen in the Gospel of Luke. When the announcement of this child's conception was made to Mary, she asked, "How can this be, since I have no husband?" (Lk 1:34, RSV). The angelic messenger explained that this conception would be brought about by the coming of the Holy Spirit upon her and by the overshadowing power of the Most High (v 35). For this reason the child would be not only Jesus and Immanuel but he would be called holy, the Son of God, God manifest in the flesh (Jn 1:18); the child would be unique, being both God and man.

There were great distinctions between the Immanuel of Isaiah's day and Immanuel the son of Mary. The first was a type; the other, the antitype. The first was the shadow; the other, the reality. The one symbolized deliverance from foreign oppression; the second was the Deliverer from the oppressor. The first represented God's presence for but a few years; the second Immanuel is the son who lives forever.

The concept of "God with us" was often reiterated by Jesus. He told his disciples that where two or three gathered in his name he would be present (Mt 18:20). Before his ascension, he assured them that he would be with them until the end of the age (28:20).

He spoke also of the promise of the Holy Spirit, who "lives with you now and later will be in you" (Jn 14:17, NLT), who will abide with them forever (v 16). The "God with us" indwelling is spoken of in Colossians 1:27: "Christ lives in you." In the consummation of all things, as shown to the apostle John, the Lord said: "Look, the home of God is now among his people! He will live with them, and they will be his people. God himself will be with them" (Rv 21:3, NLT).

See also God, Names of; Messiah.

IMMER (Person) Priest in the time of David. He became the ancestral head of a house of priests: Pashhur, the priest who had Jeremiah arrested and placed in stocks, was a descendant of Immer (Jer 20:1). There were 1,052 priests of the subclan of Immer who returned from the exile (1 Chr 9:12; Ezr 2:37; Neh 7:40). A descendant of Immer helped rebuild the Jerusalem wall (Neh 3:29) and

128 priests under Amashsai (also a descendant) helped resettle the city and tend the temple (Neh 11:13-14).

IMMER (Place) Place in Babylon. The Jews who returned from Immer had lost the record of their ancestry and could not prove their Jewish lineage (Ezr 2:59; Neh 7:61).

IMMERSION* Method of baptism whereby the believer is submersed under water. *See* Baptism.

IMNA Helem's son from Asher's tribe (1 Chr 7:35).

IMNAH
1. Asher's son (Gn 46:17; 1 Chr 7:30) and founder of the Imnite family (Nm 26:44).
2. Levite and Kore's father. Kore was a temple assistant during King Hezekiah's reign (2 Chr 31:14).

IMNITE Descendant of Imnah from Asher's tribe (Nm 26:44). *See* Imnah #1.

IMPALEMENT Driving of a pointed stake into a human body. It was apparently practiced in ancient Egypt, Assyria, Babylonia, Persia, and possibly also in Israel. There are, however, many problems in understanding the exact nature of impalement and what it means in individual OT passages.

It is not always clear from documents written in Greek whether impalement or crucifixion is being described, since the same Greek word could refer to either procedure. (In crucifixion the body is fastened to a stake rather than being punctured by it.) Nor is it always clear whether the impalement is done to a living body or to a corpse. Probably both types of impalement were employed—the former as a method of execution, the latter as a means of exposing the corpse to the elements, beasts, and general disgrace. Furthermore, it is not clear to what extent "hanging" in the OT refers to impalement. Perhaps the fact that it is typically used with the preposition "on" (rather than "from") indicates that impalement of some kind is intended.

Some light is shed on the nature of impalement through Mesopotamian sources, where it was apparently a means of execution, in one case for a woman who had caused her husband's death because of another man (*Code of Hammurabi* 153), in another for a woman performing an abortion on herself (*Middle Assyrian Laws* 53). The latter law makes it clear that the woman should be impaled whether or not she lived through the abortion. The claim of Assyrian kings to have hung captives of war on stakes correlates with the portrayal in Assyrian art of battle scenes where impaled bodies can be seen. The stake could be pushed up into the chest, with the body resting facedown, or between the legs, with the body upright.

Darius's provision in Ezra 6:11 for the punishment of violators of his decree that the temple in Jerusalem be rebuilt may refer to impalement. If the expression "hang on a tree [stake]" (Gn 40:19; Dt 21:22; Jos 8:29; 10:26; Est 2:23) refers to impalement, at least sometimes it is clear that it was a corpse being impaled (Jos 10:26). This interpretation also applies to Deuteronomy 21:22, in which the victim is first put to death and then "hung." The point of similarity to the crucifixion of Christ (Gal 3:13) is the disgrace involved and not the precise form of treatment. Other possible examples of impalement are found in 2 Samuel 4:12 and 21:6-13.

See also Criminal Law and Punishment.

IMPRECATORY PSALMS* Psalms that contain curses (imprecations, maledictions) against enemies. These elements do not make up an entire psalm, but verses of this nature appear in approximately 20 psalms (e.g., Pss 5, 17, 28, 35, 40, 55, 59, 70, 71, 74, 79, 80, 94, 109, 129, 137, 139, 140). A number of other psalms express the same ideas as future or accomplished acts of the Lord. Usually these expressions are couched in the form of a prayer or a wish. They voice the desire that evil may come upon an enemy as judgment or retribution.

To the casual reader, such statements may appear to be at variance with much of the rest of Scripture, especially with the teaching of Jesus. The clear injunction of Leviticus 19:17-18 states, "Do not nurse hatred in your heart for any of your relatives. Confront your neighbors directly so you will not be held guilty for their crimes. Never seek revenge or bear a grudge against anyone, but love your neighbor as yourself" (NLT). Jesus expanded the concept of neighbor to include even the despised Samaritan (Lk 10:29-37). In the Sermon on the Mount, Jesus declared, "Love your enemies and pray for those who persecute you" (Mt 5:44, RSV; cf. vv 38-48). This is in harmony with the teaching of the OT, which instructs one to feed a hungry enemy and give water to a thirsty one (Prv 25:21-22; cf. Rom 12:20).

Psalm 109 is often singled out as contradicting Jesus' teachings, for it has the greatest imprecatory content, and its statements are stronger than other psalms of this character. Some have suggested that the maledictions of this psalm are unworthy of Scripture and are expressions of wicked human emotions that should not be included in the Bible. However, it needs to be seen that this psalm has been regarded as both prophetic and messianic. This was the view of Chrysostom, Jerome, Augustine, and others. This was also the interpretation of Horne, who in his commentary translates the imperfect tenses of this psalm as futures, not the subjunctives of our English versions. He took his cue for this prophetic interpretation from Peter's quotation of verse 8 upon the occasion of choosing a successor for Judas (Acts 1:20). The psalm can then fit the experiences of the life and passion of Jesus, which changes its tenor completely and in large measure removes it from being imprecatory and makes it predictive.

Another passage that has been abhorrent to many occurs in Psalm 137:8-9, which speaks of the joy of those who dash Babylonian children on a rock. Horne took this as predictive of what took place when the armies of the Medes and Persians conquered the city of Babylon in 539 BC.

If one predicates that the expressions in the psalms are curses or desires for retribution, they are not out of keeping with the rest of Scripture. The prayer of Jeremiah for vengeance on his persecutors (Jer 11:20) received direct affirmative response from the Lord (vv 21-23). The plea of the righteous for justice and vindication will be answered speedily (Lk 18:1-8). In Revelation those who had been slain for the Word of God and for their testimony cry out, "O Sovereign Lord, holy and true, how long will it be before you judge the people who belong to this world for what they have done to us?" (Rv 6:10, NLT), and they were heard. David, to whom Psalm 109 is attributed, was given victory and vengeance over his enemies, as he realized that those who were his enemies were also the enemies of God. Evidently the enemies against whom the psalmist prayed had reached the place where they should receive judgment, and the imprecations of the writer coincided with the judgment of God.

See also Judgment; Psalms, Book of; Wrath of God.

IMPUTATION* Charging to an account, used in the Bible with legal reference to sin and salvation being recorded by God. The biblical teaching on imputation represents one of the principal doctrines of the Christian faith. Although the noun form is not found in Scripture, the verb "to impute" occurs frequently in both the OT and NT. The basic meaning of the biblical word "impute" is "to set down in a record or a ledger." In relation to the doctrine of salvation, the word is consistently used in a legal sense. Philemon 1:18, which affirms that the apostle Paul assumed the debt of Onesimus, aptly illustrates the predominant theological usage of the word: "if he . . . owes you anything, charge that to my account."

When Scripture speaks of the imputation of good or evil, it does not suggest that any change of moral character is involved. Scripture does affirm that, from God's perspective, righteousness or sin is charged to an individual's account. In the broadest sense, Scripture teaches that God participates in the process of imputing (Ps 32:2) as do people (1 Sm 22:15). Good deeds were commonly imputed for reward (Ps 106:30-31), and evil deeds were imputed for punishment (Lv 17:3-4).

The Bible sets forth the theological concept of imputation in three distinct yet related ways. First, Scripture affirms the imputation of Adam's original sin to the entire human race. In the sovereign plan of God, the first man's initial act of disobedience was set to the account of every member of the human family. Every person thus participates in the guilt and penalty of that original sin. Second, the sin and guilt of the human race was imputed to Christ, so that although the Savior was not a sinner, he nevertheless bore the penalty arising from sin. Finally, the Bible teaches that, as a result of his atoning work, Christ's righteousness is set to the believer's account. Although not yet perfectly holy or morally righteous, believers nevertheless are justified before the law of God, and they are "clothed" with the imputed righteousness of Christ.

The apostle Paul developed at length the theme that Christ on the cross bore the punishment for believers' sins. Thus he wrote that God "made him to be sin who knew no sin" (2 Cor 5:21, RSV; cf. Heb 9:28). Similarly, he depicted Christ as bearing the curse of the Mosaic law (Gal 3:13). Finally, reflecting on Isaiah 53, the apostle Peter affirmed that Christ "personally carried away our sins in his own body on the cross" (1 Pt 2:24, NLT). The idea that the guilt of the entire world was charged to the account of the sinless Savior largely explains Christ's impassioned cry on the cross, "My God, my God, why have you forsaken me?" (Mt 27:46, NLT).

The imputation motif is also employed, in the sense of Christ's righteousness being credited to believers. An incident in the life of the patriarch Abraham illustrates the imputation of righteousness on the basis of faith. After God had promised material and spiritual blessing to Abraham, Genesis 15:6 states that he "believed the LORD; and he [God] reckoned it to him as righteousness" (RSV). The Bible teaches that no person naturally possesses the standard of righteousness demanded by God (Ps 130:3; Is 64:6; Rom 3:10). Yet, in his gracious plan of salvation, God himself supplies the righteousness to satisfy his holy character (Is 45:24; 54:17; Hos 10:12). That is, as a person accepts by faith the work of Christ in satisfying the demands of God's law, God imputes or reckons Christ's righteousness to the believer.

The imputation of divine righteousness to the believer constitutes a major theme of Paul's Letter to the Romans (Rom 3:21–5:21). Thus the apostle speaks of the happiness of an undeserving sinner who is declared to be righteous (4:6). Moreover, the imputation of Christ's righteousness results in justification before God's law court (5:18). The merits of Christ's death imputed to the sinner are the basis for acquittal by the holy God. Thus the Bible teaches that the ruinous effects of the imputation of Adam's sin are effectively reversed for those who believe in Christ. The imputation of human sin to Christ makes possible the imputation of his righteousness to believers.

See also Adam (Person); Christology; Fall of Man; Sin.

IMRAH Zophah's son, a chief of Asher's tribe (1 Chr 7:36, 40).

IMRI

1. Ancestor of Uthai, one of the postexilic Jews of Judah's tribe (1 Chr 9:4). In the genealogy of Nehemiah 11:4, Imri and Amariah are probably the same person.
2. Father of Zaccur, a rebuilder of the Jerusalem wall (Neh 3:2).

INCANTATION Chant used in magic. See Magic.

INCARNATION* Literally, "in flesh"; theologically, the doctrine that in Jesus of Nazareth God took on human flesh and became the God-man. Historically, the doctrine of incarnation was central in the christological debates of patristic times and has recently come to the fore again in academic circles. Biblically, it expresses the mystery of Jesus' identity.

New Testament Testimony

The Synoptic Gospels The Gospel of Mark has no account of the Incarnation and stresses Jesus' messiahship more than his deity. As a result, some believe that it represents an earlier stage in the development of the church's theology, before the doctrine of incarnation had evolved. That is doubtful for two reasons: Incarnation passages like the Philippians hymn (Phil 2:6-11) probably antedate Mark's Gospel, and Mark has a well-developed theology of the two natures of Christ. Although he stresses Jesus' humanity, Mark accents it with an emphasis on divinity. Jesus was called the "beloved Son" by a heavenly voice at his baptism and transfiguration (Mk 1:11; 9:7); demons called him divine (3:11; 5:7), as did a Roman centurion (15:39). Jesus' "Abba" prayers (14:36; cf. Mt 26:39; Lk 22:42) indicate his sense of divine identity, and at his trial he was charged with claiming the title "Son of the Blessed" (14:61-62). Thus, though the Incarnation is nowhere explicitly stated in Mark, it is implicitly affirmed.

Matthew and Luke express the Incarnation. The birth narratives, of course, stress the event itself, with Matthew emphasizing Jesus' royal messiahship, and Luke, the divine witness of the Holy Spirit. Matthew's Gospel is Christ-centered; Luke concentrates on Christ as Savior, or more precisely, on salvation-history. Although Matthew presents Jesus' humanity, he emphasizes his lordship (Mt 23:6-10) and divine sonship. The Incarnation thus becomes the means whereby the divine becomes human in a universal sense (1:23; 18:20; 24:14; 28:18-20). Luke shows the greatest interest of the three in Jesus' earthly life. Nevertheless, his Gospel does not stress the human side of Jesus as much as Mark's. Luke portrays Jesus primarily as the divine Savior within history (Lk 2:11; 4:16-30). He combines Jesus' messianic office and divine nature, showing that the incarnate Son of God suffered and was exalted in order to bring people to God.

John's Writings The apostle John's doctrine of incarnation is more explicit than any of the others, teaching not only Jesus' God-man status but also his preexistent "glory" (Jn 1:1-18). Central in this presentation is the oneness between Jesus and God the Father

(10:29-30; 14:8-11; 1 Jn 2:23). The "I am" (the expressed Christ, taken from the OT title for the one true God and probably signifying God's personal name, Yahweh) came to reveal God to his people (Jn 1:4-5, 14, 18). Yet John also has the most balanced presentation of the Incarnation. The divine Logos or Word (1:1-18) is the exemplar of perfect humanity; he "became flesh" (v 14) to enlighten people (vv 5, 9) and generate in them "eternal life" (3:14-18; 1 Jn 1:1-3; 4:9).

Paul's Epistles The apostle Paul presented the Incarnation as Jesus' path to suffering and redemption. In Galatians 4:4-5 the Incarnation ("born of woman") came "in the fullness of time" or at the apex of salvation-history, to "redeem those who were under the law." In the Philippians hymn (Phil 2:6-11, quotes from NASB), the Incarnation is seen in terms of preexistence ("though he was in the form of God"), humiliation ("emptied . . . humbled"), and obedience ("becoming obedient to the point of death"). The goal of the Incarnation was the cross ("even death on a cross"), and its result was Christ's exaltation. The hymn is perhaps the supreme theological statement on the Incarnation in the NT. Jesus' human life was an "emptying," a refusal to seize the prerogatives of his deity ("did not regard equality with God a thing to be grasped").

Paul described Christ as a second Adam (Rom 5:12-19; 1 Cor 15:45-47), who brought humanity a new possibility to attain what Adam had forsaken. Through assuming the form of a man, Christ became the Redeemer who reconciles people to God (Rom 3:25; 2 Cor 5:19; 1 Tm 1:15). Paul stressed even more, however, that the exalted Christ provides newness of life (Rom 6:4-6; 2 Cor 3:17-18; Col 3:1-4). A hymn in the Letter to the Colossians (1:15-20) employs ideas from Jewish wisdom speculation, and possibly Greek themes, to show Christ as the "firstborn" and the "fullness of God." The one who always existed as God, through his sacrificial death, became the exalted Lord and brought humankind to God (see also the "flesh-spirit" theme in Rom 1:3-4; 1 Tm 3:16).

Hebrews The Letter to the Hebrews strongly speaks of the Incarnation. The opening hymn (Heb 1:1-3) accents Christ's exalted status as "the very stamp" of God's image and the radiance of his glory. Christ is superior to the angels (1:4-9), yet he became a man in order to suffer for human salvation (2:9; 5:7-9). The Incarnation is aligned with sinful humankind's need for a Savior. The purpose of Hebrews is to show Christ's incomparable superiority to the OT sacrifices, and at the same time to stress his work of salvation. His real temptation (2:18; 4:15) combined with his sinlessness (4:15; 5:9; 7:26) is the human remedy for human sin. The Incarnation was Christ's path to final, once-for-all atonement and victory over sin (7:28; 9:26).

Historical Development The first group to challenge the traditional doctrine of incarnation was the Gnostics, who in the late first century denied that Jesus was truly human. Their Greek belief that the physical creation was evil led them to deny the Incarnation. They believed Christ to be a quasi-spiritual being who merely appeared human. The theologian Marcion (d. c. 160), trained by Gnostic teachers, also accepted a docetic interpretation of Christ (his humanity was only apparent). Marcion taught his doctrine as an antidote to the OT or Jewish-oriented Christianity in his day. After his excommunication in AD 144, Marcion founded his own church, and his views were widely disseminated in the next two centuries. Partly in reaction to Marcion's christological heresy, the orthodox churches unified their doctrine.

The next challenge to the orthodox view came through

the Arian, Apollinarian, and Nestorian controversies in the third and fourth centuries. Arianism held that the Incarnation was total, so that Christ the Logos was no longer fully God. At the same time, he was not fully human, so Christ was someone between two natures. The Council of Nicaea (AD 325) affirmed that Jesus was indeed both God and man. A further question soon arose, however, as to the relation between his two natures. Apollinarius (310?–390?) taught that only the body of Jesus was human; his soul was absorbed completely into the divine Logos. Nestorius (c. 381–451) taught that the two natures must always remain distinct in the person of Christ; they functioned together but were separate in his being. The Council of Chalcedon (AD 451) affirmed the unity of the two natures in Jesus. Many opponents of Chalcedon arose, called Monophysites, who believed in one divine nature in Jesus, who was only in a sense human. That movement caused serious political and religious divisions, and the Council of Constantinople (680–81) reaffirmed Chalcedon and established the orthodox incarnation theology.

In the eighth century, Spain and France were centers of the "adoptionist" controversy. Adoptionism taught that at birth Jesus was human, but at his baptism he underwent a "second birth" and was "adopted" as Son of God. It was condemned in a series of synods and never gained many adherents until modern times. During the scholastic age, Peter Lombard (1095?–1160) advocated what became known as "nihilism." The Incarnation supposedly caused no fundamental change in Jesus' deity, but his human nature was both insubstantial and unessential. That view likewise was condemned by Pope Alexander III (1159–81). Another debate at that time centered on the relationship between the fall and the Incarnation. Thomas Aquinas (1224–74) concluded that there was a cause-effect connection; the Incarnation was necessitated by sin rather than predestined apart from the fall.

The Roman Catholic Church and the Protestant Reformers follow basically the same orthodox teaching about the Incarnation. The conflict in the Reformation centered more on soteriology (the doctrine of salvation). Several aberrant antitrinitarian movements took advantage of the breakdown in ecclesiastical authority, however. Michael Servetus (1511–53) taught a pantheistic view of the Incarnation, focused on the divine Spirit becoming manifest in the human form of Jesus. Thus the Logos is not a distinct person in the Godhead, nor is it fundamentally different from a "divine spark" in every person. At the same time Laelius Socinus (1525–62) and his nephew, Faustus Socinus (1539–1604), taught a unitarian system. The Incarnation was not a transferral of the divine essence but a communication of divine authority and revelation. Christ thus did not die as an atonement but as a moral example. Both Servetus and Socinianism were condemned by Catholics and Protestants alike.

In the 17th and 18th centuries "kenoticism" (from Greek for "empty") taught that in the Incarnation the Logos totally "emptied himself" (Phil 2:7) of the divine attributes. That doctrine represented the final phase of a dialogue from the scholastic period about the exact communication between Jesus' two natures. Was his human nature omnipotent? If not, how did the man Jesus exercise the divine attributes? The kenotic school believed that Jesus was fully human and that his divine nature was quiescent until after the Ascension. His miraculous powers were external, given by the Spirit. Against that view, the majority of theologians argued that Jesus was at all times both God and man, and that in Philippians 2:6-8 Jesus did not lay aside the attributes of deity (he still exhibited the "form of God") but rather the majesty associated with deity.

The 19th and 20th centuries have given rise to a view that the Incarnation was a "myth," a pictorial way of describing how God spoke through Jesus. The virgin birth was not historical, nor did any of the supernatural events of the Gospels ever take place. Rather, the stories in the Gospels were concoctions of the later church, efforts to portray Jesus' impact on the movement. The Gospels, however, have too strong a flavor of accurate history for such a view to prevail (see Lk 1:1-5; Jn 19:35; 21:24).

Conclusion The NT teaching on the Incarnation balances the humanity and divinity of Christ. Those two facts must harmonize in any theological system, for both are absolutely necessary parts of God's redemptive plan. In the Incarnation, Jesus became a perfect human being. As God in human flesh, he suffered the divine penalty for sin as an innocent substitute. Being both God and man, Jesus simultaneously revealed God's will for human life and reconciled sinful people to God through his own perfect life and death. Because of the Incarnation, therefore, those who believe in Christ have peace with God and new life from God.

See also Christology; Jesus Christ, Life and Teachings of; Genealogy of Jesus Christ; Virgin Birth of Jesus.

MODERN VIEWS ON THE INCARNATION
Recent incarnational theology has sometimes had difficulty balancing its understanding of Christ's humanity and deity. Some theologians have given too much emphasis to his manhood, with the result that his atoning work is neglected. He then becomes an example of God's gracious dealing with humanity. Such theological imbalance appears in those who have reacted too strongly to the "demythologizing" movement, stressing the Jesus of history to the extent that he has become little more than an object of rational thought.

On the other hand, some modern theology focuses only on Christ's divinity. The Bultmannian (after Rudolf Bultmann) school has separated the "Christ of faith" from the "Jesus of history," making him a hero in the Greek style. Some evangelicals make a similar error by removing Jesus' teachings from the real world of history and placing them in a subjective realm of religious experience. Jesus thus becomes a vague object of religious devotion having no contact with the real world.

Another group has interpreted the biblical image of the church as the "body of Christ" to mean that the church somehow continues the Incarnation on earth. The NT does not teach that idea explicitly. Moreover, such an application of the theme can mislead the church to assume more divine authority for itself than it actually possesses.

INCENSE Fragrant spices and oils or sacrifice that sends up perfumed smoke to God in order to please him.

People of every age have loved fragrant odors. In ancient times, sacrifices included sweet smells to make the deity happy. The aroma was a crucial factor in whether the god would accept the offering. Therefore, aromatic plants and exotic perfumes were precious for both secular and religious purposes.

Spices and precious oils were valued along with silver and gold. The queen of Sheba brought spices to Solomon as a gift (1 Kgs 10:2). Incense was kept in the royal treasury (2 Kgs 20:13). The price of spices and oils was extremely inflated because of the difficult work of extracting the juices, transportation costs to import them from faraway places, and high profits for merchants who sold the perfumes.

Consequently, lovers sometimes compared their beloved to "myrrh," a "mountain of myrrh" and a "hill of frankincense" (Sg 1:13; 4:6). The fragrance of incense set the right mood (1:12). Every spice known to a merchant burned beside the couch of Solomon (3:6). A bridegroom delighted in the perfumes of his beloved. She was his own private garden of incense (4:10-14). Even a prostitute burned incense beside her bed (Ez 23:41). No wonder wise men said that "fragrant oil" makes the heart glad and the "sweetness of friendship" comforts the soul (e.g., Prv 27:9).

Types of Incense Frankincense is mentioned most often in the Bible. It was imported from India, Somaliland, and Arabia Felix. Myrrh also came from Arabia Felix. Cinnamon was another important fragrance from Ceylon and China. Galbanum, tragacanth (gum), and laudanum all were grown in the mountains of Asia Minor. Galbanum was the most popular of these three, for it was also found in Turkestan, Persia, Syria, and Crete. Henna, saffron, and balsam came from aromatic plants native to Israel. In postexilic times other plants were introduced to Palestine and cultivated there: the rose, narcissus, and jasmine. Onycha seems to have been produced from the local fauna, and musk (muskin) may have been extracted from a gland of the musk deer.

Incense itself came in many forms. It might be used as granules placed in a bag hung around the neck (Sg 1:13). In the main, however, perfumes were in a liquid form, dissolved in olive oil. A good example of this is the "holy anointing oil" (Ex 30:31). Such oils were used to anoint the priests and kings of Israel. Only priests were allowed to prepare and administer them. The incense contained raw spices beaten into a fine consistency and seasoned with salt to make them holy. Stacte, onycha, galbanum, and pure frankincense were mixed in equal proportions, all according to the art of the perfumer (Ex 30:34-37). The spices and incense for the sanctuary were donated as gifts (Nm 7:14-86; Jer 17:26; 41:5) and kept in the temple (Neh 13:5, 9). Josephus described the incense of his day as a much more complicated compound. He listed 13 ingredients in the best incense of the Herodian era.

Incense Offering Archaeology has demonstrated that incense offerings were common throughout the ancient Near East from the earliest times of organized worship. Egyptian paintings and reliefs from the New Kingdom occasionally show a man holding a censer of burning incense. Incense seems to have been used as well in the rituals of Assyria, Babylonia, and Arabia. Canaanite altars found at Megiddo and Tell Beit Mirsim have horned limestone altars (10th century BC) that may have been designed to hold a bowl of incense. Hence, it is safe to assume that incense offerings also played some part in the worship of Israel from the beginning.

Incense offerings seem to have served a multitude of purposes. They may have been used to drive away evil spirits and thereby sanctify all the utensils of the place of worship (Ex 30:26-29). Undoubtedly, the sweet smell of incense provided an antidote to the putrid odor of the animal sacrifices. Therefore, if God was to receive a sweet savor and thereby be pleased with an offering, incense

was necessary to compensate for the smell of the sacrifices. However, spices were never added to the flesh of the animals or birds.

In some instances, incense itself became a sacrifice. As a supplement to other sacrifices, frankincense alone was burned. To alleviate a plague, Aaron performed a ritual of burning incense (Nm 16:46-47). On the Day of Atonement, the high priest carried burning incense and hot coals on a pan (censer) into the Holy of Holies (Lv 16:12-13). The burning incense was thought to protect the life of the high priest, perhaps because the smoke kept him from seeing the full glory of God.

Frankincense was added to grain for offerings on the altar of burnt offering (Lv 2:1, 15-16; 6:15). It also accompanied the bread of the Presence (24:7) in two dishes. The bronze serpent destroyed by Hezekiah in his reform had become a profane object to which incense was burned (2 Kgs 18:4).

Except on the Day of Atonement, the incense was offered on a special altar (Lv 4:7; cf. Ex 30:9), where it burned morning and evening and came to be called "perpetual incense" (Ex 30:7-8). Probably the altar of gold in Solomon's temple (1 Kgs 6:20-22) was the incense altar.

Offering incense was a holy ritual, and persons who offered it with disrespect for procedures were condemned (Lv 10:1-2; Nm 16:6-50). Uzziah, the king of Judah, became a leper because he dared to offer incense (2 Chr 26:16-21). The burning of incense at "high places" is often criticized (e.g., 1 Kgs 22:43), either because the sanctuaries were idolatrous or because their priests did not take proper care as did the priesthood in Jerusalem. Prophets who criticized the offering of incense (Is 1:13; 66:3; Jer 6:20) did so to condemn a formalism that was void of devotion to the God of Israel.

Meaning of Incense Since incense was such a precious commodity, incense was a fitting offering to God (Mal 1:11). Incense offerings also provided a tangible sense of God's holiness in which the people could experience atonement for sin (Nm 16:46-47). The smoke rising to the sky symbolized the prayers of the people (Ps 141:2; Lk 1:10; Rv 5:8; 8:3-4). At the same time, the smoke in the temple symbolized the presence of God as it had been portrayed in the cloud in the wilderness (Ex 19:18; 33:9-10; Nm 11:25). Together with the rising sun, the smoke provided a powerful symbol for the glory of the Lord (Is 6:1-7).

The significance of incense is further enhanced by NT allusions. The Christian's testimony about Christ is paralleled with the offering of incense (2 Cor 2:14-15). The sweet smell of the gospel is contrasted with the smell of death that leads to doom. Likewise, money from the Philippian Christians came to Paul in the spirit of an incense sacrifice (Phil 4:18), a costly expression of love and devotion. Finally, incense seems to sanctify and accompany the prayers of the saints into the presence of God (Rv 5:8; 8:3-4). None of the NT references call upon the Christian to offer incense, but rather to learn the devotion and dedication to holiness signified by the burning of this precious substance.

See also Plants (Aloe; Balm; Calamus; Cinnamon; Frankincense; Galbanum; Henna; Hyssop; Myrrh; Nard; Storax Tree); Perfume; Tabernacle; Temple.

INCEST* Sexual relations between close relatives.

Prohibitions against incest are prominent in Leviticus 18. Leviticus 20 also addresses the matter and attaches the death penalty to certain kinds of incest. The assignment of severe penalty and the judgments of dishonor and perversion clearly mark incest as a grave offense.

Actual cases in the Bible show incest to be the fruit of a flawed character. Lot's daughters slept with their drunken father and both became pregnant (Gn 19:30-38). And in 2 Samuel 13:1-22, the deceitful Amnon showed no shame in forcing himself upon his half sister Tamar. Paul's strong rebuke in 1 Corinthians 5:1-5 demonstrates that neither the act nor its wickedness is limited to OT times.

Blood relationship, or consanguinity, is one ground for declaring sexual contact unlawful. This applies, for example, to brothers and sisters, parents and children, grandparents and grandchildren, as well as some aunts, uncles, nieces, and nephews.

The relationships denounced in Leviticus 18 are not, however, all based upon blood kinship. A number of them are matters of kinship through marriage, matters of affinity. In this connection, sexual relations with in-laws and certain aunts and uncles are declared incestuous. It should be noted that the in-law rule could be relaxed in ancient Israel when a widowed sister-in-law was left without a son (Dt 25:5-10).

While there are good genetic reasons to shun incest among blood relations, the fundamental problem with incest is that it strikes at the soundness of the family. And since the family is central to God's purposes and work on earth, his judgment on this practice is fierce. Families simply cannot survive sexual intrigue among their members.

INDIA Eastern land of uncertain geographical boundaries in Bible times. The only specific reference to the land of India in the Bible occurs in Esther 1:1 and 8:9, where the boundaries of the empire of Ahasuerus are said to have stretched from Hoddu to Kush. The term "Hoddu" seems to have derived from an Old Persian word *Hindush*, which was itself related to a Sanskrit word *Sindhu*, meaning "stream," that is, the Indus River. Inscriptions from Persia indicate that India was a province of the Achaemenid Empire (559–330 BC), and thus support the biblical statements. Even the Greek historian Herodotus in the fifth century BC seems to have been poorly informed about India (*Persian Wars* 3.94-106; 4.40, 44). There are Hebrew legends and traditions that place Jews in India in the days of King Solomon. Some interpreters have suggested that the river Pishon in Genesis 2:11 in the land of Havilah may refer to India. Others have proposed that goods brought from Ophir, such as sandalwood ("almug wood," 1 Kgs 10:11; 2 Chr 2:8), ivory, and apes, were Indian in origin. Also, some of the items carried by merchants to Tyre, such as ivory tusks and ebony (Ez 27:15), may have originated in India.

There are no references to India in the NT, but there are a number of general references to the land in intertestamental literature and in the later Jewish writings (e.g., the Targums on Esther, the Midrashim, and the Talmud). It was only after the days of Alexander the Great (d. 323 BC) that the literary world of Palestine and Europe begin to record information about India. From 1 Maccabees 6:37, it would appear that Seleucid armies used war elephants (possibly Indian), mounted by Indian drivers in the second century BC, and the reference in 8:8 indicates that the Romans compelled Antiochus III (223–187 BC) to surrender. India is of uncertain value because of textual problems. There is no other evidence that the Seleucid domains stretched as far as India. It is known, however, that the Romans had considerable trading activity in India via Egypt and the Red Sea, and this makes the lack of references in the NT strange. As the Christian centuries passed, references do appear in both Jewish and early Christian literature, and it is certain that early in the Christian era settlements of Jews and monophysite Christians were found in India. According to legend, it was the apostle Thomas who took the gospel to India and founded the Mar Thoma Church.

INFIRMITY* *See* Disease; Medicine and Medical Practice.

INGATHERING*, Feast of One of the three great festivals of Israel, also called the Feast of Booths, or Tabernacles, which celebrated the completion of the agricultural year (Lv 23:39-43). *See* Feasts and Festivals of Israel.

INHERITANCE Legacy or bequest. Inheritance plays an unusually significant role in the Scriptures when it is used to convey theological truths. As we might expect, these theological applications reflect legal customs in force during OT and NT times.

Legal and Historical Aspect

The Patriarchs We learn something of early-second-millennium BC practices from the patriarchal stories in Genesis. For example, the narrative indicates that the firstborn could normally expect to receive the birthright. Yet exceptions abound. Ishmael (Gn 16:15; 17:15-21), Esau (25:23), and Reuben (49:3-4) did not receive the birthright. Another item of special interest is Abraham's suggestion that, in the absence of a son, his servant Eliezer might be regarded as the heir (15:2-5); scholars have found confirmation of this practice in Hurrian legal documents of the second millennium.

The Hebrew Nation According to Deuteronomy 21:15-17, Hebrew firstborns were legally entitled to a double portion of the inheritance. Israelite law also made provision for widows through the practice of levirate marriage (Dt 25:5; see Gn 38:8; Ru 4:5).

According to Numbers 27:1-11, the daughters of Zelophehad argued that they should receive the inheritance since their father had died without sons. Consequently, God decreed that if a man died without sons, the inheritance should be transferred to his daughter; if he had no daughter, to his brothers; if he had no brothers, to his nearest relatives. This particular incident also illustrates the importance of preserving tribal possessions: the daughters of Zelophehad were not allowed to marry outside the tribe of Manasseh, for this would mean transferral of the property to another tribe (Nm 36).

How highly the Israelites valued their family's inherited possessions may be gathered from Leviticus 25:25-28. If an individual sold his land for financial reasons, provision must be made for a relative to redeem it; if he had no near relative, he could still purchase it back at a later time, and even if he could not afford to do so, the land automatically reverted to him in the Year of Jubilee, when all debts were canceled (note also Lv 27:14-25).

In the New Testament Apart from the reference to levirate marriage in Matthew 22:23-33 (Mk 12:18-27; Lk 20:27-40), the NT has little to say about principles of property transferral during Roman times.

In the parable of the prodigal son, the younger son in the family requested his share of the inheritance (Lk 15:12). One should also note that the elder son, who with false piety looked down on his brother's behavior, had not protested when his brother asked for the inheritance; on the contrary, the elder brother too, without complaining, received his share—presumably a double portion.

In another significant passage (Gal 4:1-2) Paul, seeking to illustrate a theological point, refers to secular practices. An heir, he tells us, is subject to guardians and managers during his childhood, up to the time he actually inherits. The point Paul wants to establish is clear enough, but the illustration does not coincide with what we know of Roman law and unfortunately scholars have been unable to identify the precise social custom in view. It may be that Paul was making reference, in general rather than strict legal terms, to some practice with which he and the Galatians were familiar.

Theological Aspect

Canaan as Israel's Inheritance The conviction that God gave Palestine to the Israelites for their inheritance serves as a bridge between the historical and the theological data. The historical element lies in the obvious fact that the Promised Land, a physical entity, was certainly occupied by the Hebrews and distributed among their tribes. Theologically, however, the Scriptures speak of this occupation as a divine gift; in effect, even the method of distribution was based on the concept that the land belongs to God (Lv 25:23; see Ex 15:17; Jos 22:27; Ez 38:16; Jl 1:6).

The theme goes back to Genesis 12:1-3. God, in choosing Abraham, instructed him to move to a new country and promised to make him a great and blessed nation (Heb 11:8). The significance of the land in this Abrahamic promise is made more explicit later, when we are told that God promised to give Canaan to Abraham's descendants after four centuries of Egyptian bondage (Gn 15:12-21; see Acts 7:5).

Since Canaan was occupied by wicked inhabitants, the land was to be taken by force; to inherit the land therefore really means *to take possession* of it. Israel must trust God, whose land it is, to give them the victory (Jos 1:1-9; 21:43-45; Jgs 7:2; Ps 44:1-3; Acts 13:19). Once they conquered the land, it was apportioned among the tribes according to their size (following the instructions in Nm 26:52-54). God further commanded the people to divide the land by lot (vv 55-56). Thus, from the initial promise to Abraham, to the actual apportionment of the land and even with reference to the future (Is 60:21; Ez 45:1-8; 47:13–48:29), the people were made fully aware that their inheritance lay in the hands of a sovereign Lord.

The Believer's Inheritance In the OT we find the concept of inheritance transferred from the purely physical to the spiritual. The tribe of Levi, which constituted the priestly clan, received no inheritance, because "the Lord is their inheritance" (Dt 18:1-2; see Nm 18:8-24). The Levites, in other words, received no land apportionment, but in their service to God they could begin to enjoy the fuller blessings to which the land inheritance pointed.

That this truth could not be restricted to Levites is hinted at in Exodus 19:6, where the whole nation is called "a kingdom of priests" (see 1 Pt 2:9). Psalm 16 makes it clear that no one understood more clearly than David what those words entailed. Even if he were deprived of Israel's physical inheritance, he had received by lot a more beautiful heritage, the Lord himself, in whose presence he found full joy and everlasting pleasures (Ps 16:5-6, 11; see also Pss 73:25-26; 142:5; Is 58:14; Lam 3:24).

In later Judaism, during and after the intertestamental period, the figure was extended considerably. For example, the rabbis began to speak of the law as the inheritance of the faithful. Further, they might give the idea a negative turn, as when the wicked are said to inherit hell (cf. Jb 27:13). Neither of these figures is found in the NT.

We also read in Jewish literature statements about inheriting the age to come, the kingdom, eternal life; these ideas occur frequently in the NT (Mt 19:29; 25:34; Lk 10:25; 18:18; 1 Cor 6:9-10; 15:50; Gal 5:21; Eph 5:5; Ti 3:7; Jas 2:5). Such an inheritance, however, belongs only to those who are sanctified by God's word (Acts 20:32; 26:18; Col 1:12; note also Jn 17:17; Col 3:23-24). These future blessings do not exclude the physical (Mt 5:5; note Ps 37:11, 29; Is 60:21; Rom 4:13; 2 Pt 3:13), but they certainly exclude human frailty, for God's inheritance is imperishable (1 Cor 15:50). In short, our heritage is nothing less than full salvation (Heb 1:14; 11:7), which God carefully guards for us in heaven (1 Pt 1:4).

Doubtless, the most significant feature in the NT is its emphasis that, as a result of the work of Christ, his people begin even *now* to receive the promised inheritance. The Gospel of John frequently stresses the present reality of eternal life, as does the Letter to the Hebrews (cf. 6:12-17 with 9:15 and 11:13, 39-40).

Paul treats this whole matter thoroughly in Galatians 3:7–4:7. In response to the Judaizers, who claim that the Abrahamic inheritance is restricted to those who become Jews through circumcision, Paul argues vigorously that Abraham's true children are those who believe, whether Jew or Gentile (3:7; see Acts 26:16-18; Eph 3:6). They become heirs of God's promise, for they receive the Spirit (Gal 3:14). The principle of inheritance is promise, not the Law (v 18). Those who believe are brought into union with Christ (vv 27-29); but then they are not merely Abraham's children but God's (v 26), for Christ is the Son of God and God has determined to send the Spirit of his Son to believers so that they too may call God *Father* (Gal 4:4-7; see also Rom 8:15-16).

Indeed, Christ himself as the Son is the true heir (Mt 21:38; Mk 12:7; Lk 20:14); he has inherited a name above every name (Phil 2:9; Heb 1:4) and has been appointed heir of all things (Heb 1:2; see Ps 2:7-8; Mt 28:18). But by his grace, all who become his through faith are counted joint heirs with him (Rom 8:17).

God's Inheritance With a bold shift in the metaphor, the Scriptures speak of believers as God's inheritance. In the beautiful "Song of Moses" the author speaks of God as the Israelites' Father (Dt 32:6), who has taken special interest in their inheritance (v 8). Then we are told why God cares: "For the LORD's portion is his people, Jacob his allotted inheritance" (Dt 32:9, NIV). This theme becomes very prominent throughout the OT (e.g., Dt 9:26-29; 1 Kgs 8:51-53; Pss 28:9; 33:12; 74:2; Is 19:25; Jer 10:16; Zec 2:12). Elsewhere, Israel is spoken of as God's special possession (e.g., Ex 19:5; Dt 7:6).

In Ephesians 1:14 "the redemption of the possession" refers to the final salvation of believers, who are God's treasure. Further, "we have obtained an inheritance" (Eph 1:11) may well be translated, "we have been made an inheritance," that is, been "chosen as God's portion," a view supported by verse 18. No more fundamental idea than this can be found in Scripture, and its essence is expressed by the words of the One who sits on the throne: "He who conquers shall have this heritage, and I will be his God and he shall be my son" (Rv 21:7, RSV; see Lv 26:11-12; 2 Sm 7:14).

See also Adoption; Birthright; Firstborn; Heir.

INIQUITY *See* Sin.

INK, INKHORN* *See* Writing.

INN Place of lodging for travelers.

In the OT, the word "inn" occurs three times (KJV): twice in reference to overnight rests of Joseph's brothers during their journeys between Egypt and Canaan (Gn 42:27;

43:21), and once in a similar situation when Moses was returning to Egypt from Midian to lead the children of Israel (Ex 4:24). The RSV translates each of these instances as "lodging place" because in the time of the patriarchs and Moses the Near East had nothing to correspond to the inn as a public place with accommodations for hire to travelers. In a settled country a traveler could ordinarily expect hospitality from the inhabitants. Throughout the Near East, hospitality was viewed as a serious social responsibility (see Gn 19:1-3; Jgs 19:15-21). In deserted areas travelers would provide for their own shelter (e.g., Gn 28:11) and sustenance (e.g., Jos 9:11-13).

The beginning of real inns in Palestine is obscure. It has been argued that they had a foreign origin, since the rabbinic words for "inn" are borrowed from Greek and Latin. References to Rahab (Jos 2:1) as innkeeper in the Targum and in Josephus (*Antiquities* 5.1.12) may be anachronistic, and they provide no reliable witness to the existence of inns during the time of Joshua, though there are parallels in the Near East of women keeping an establishment providing both lodging and sexual activity for travelers. Certainly there is evidence for Greek inns as early as the fifth century BC, and they became common in the Hellenized Mediterranean. They were typically uncomfortable and dangerous.

Such an "inn" with an "innkeeper" sheltered the victim of robbers whom the Good Samaritan befriended (Lk 10:34-35). This inn was probably much like the khan or caravansary, which has been common along the trade and pilgrimage routes of Syria since ancient times. It was built in the form of a square enclosing an open court where water and shelter were available, but the traveler typically supplied his own food and sometimes his own bedding. The Good Samaritan clearly expected the host to provide full care for the wounded man; it is difficult to tell whether this was customary or simply an accommodation to the emergency. The inn of Jesus' story has long been identified with the Khan Hathrur, halfway between Jerusalem and Jericho, though the present structure is probably only one of many built in the same place.

Two other well-known passages in the NT allude, not to a real inn, but to other social customs and arrangements. First, Christians from the church at Rome met the prisoner Paul at Three Taverns, a stopping place 33 miles (53 kilometers) from Rome at the intersection of the Appian Way with the road from Antium (Acts 28:15). Second, there is the "inn" from which Joseph and Mary were excluded (Lk 2:7). The word is elsewhere translated "guestchamber" (KJV) and "guest room" (Mk 14:14; Lk 22:11, NLT). The Jews of Jerusalem took pride in having enough such guest rooms to accommodate the huge influx of pilgrims keeping Passover in the city (cf. Acts 2:6-11 on the crowd at Pentecost); evidently Joseph and Mary expected such accommodation in Bethlehem for the census, but found their place already taken.

See also Travel.

INNER MAN* The inner, invisible being of a human. This Pauline phrase resembles the "hidden man" (KJV) of 1 Peter 3:4 (cf. Rom 2:29), where outward appearance is contrasted with inward reality. It assumes the current Jewish conception of man as a unitary being having both observable and invisible aspects, a physical body including a "psychological" heart. Paul says his members submit to sin's rule even while his "inmost self" (RSV) delights in divine law (Rom 7:22). In Romans 8:13, he speaks of setting the mind on things of the flesh versus things of the Spirit, describing this same conflict between the inner and outer man.

This inner core of personality is already the locus where the Spirit's strength is instilled and where Christ dwells in the Christian. So another contrast is between the mortal and already decaying outward man, weakened by age and by sharing the dying of Christ, and the daily renewed inner man, as the life of the risen Jesus is manifested in mortal flesh (2 Cor 4:10-16). Taken with Romans 8:11, this may possibly echo a speculation of intertestamental Judaism that a spiritual counterpart to the present body is already being prepared by the quickening of divine life in the devout inner man.

See also Man.

INNOCENTS*, Slaughter of the Herod the Great's massacre of all the boys under two years old in Bethlehem and its vicinity (Mt 2:16-18). Herod slaughtered "the holy innocents" in an effort to destroy the child about whom the Magi had told him.

Although Matthew does not specify Herod's motive, secular historians record ample evidence of Herod's jealousy for his throne. He feared his own family as rivals of his power to such an extent that he put his wife and several of his sons to death. His kingdom, rife with messianic hopes and speculations, did produce some claimants. Herod himself made that association with the Magi's quest for one born "King of the Jews" (Mt 2:2). Adding to his instability, a painful form of arteriosclerosis made the king subject to fits of delirium and rage.

Matthew probably had several reasons for including the story in his Gospel. For one thing, its use follows Matthew's pattern of citing OT prophecies (in this case, Jer 31:15). Also, the incident accounts for the sojourn of Jesus' family to Egypt and their subsequent settling in Nazareth (Mt 2:13-15, 19-23).

INSCRIPTIONS Term used to refer to writing in the ancient world that was done on a material of a permanent nature, such as stone or clay, rather than on ordinary and impermanent substances, such as papyri or parchment.

PREVIEW
•Introduction
•Inscriptions on Monuments
•Historical Records
•Official Announcements
•Dedications
•Correspondence
•Mosaic Floor Decorations

Introduction There are occasional references to inscriptions in the Bible; for example, the Ten Commandments were inscribed on stone (Ex 31:18) and given to Moses, and later written by Joshua on stone and set up at Mt Ebal near Shechem (Jos 8:32). In the excavations at Shechem, G. E. Wright found a large stone prepared to receive an inscription that he dated to the time of Joshua on stratigraphic grounds. It may still be seen at the site. A message from the hand of God to the Babylonian king Belshazzar was inscribed on the walls of his palace (Dn 5:5, 24). Paul observed an altar with the inscription "To an unknown god" in the marketplace of Athens (Acts 17:23). The book of Revelation speaks of the names of the 12 tribes of the sons of Israel being inscribed on the gates of the heavenly city (Rv 21:12).

Inscriptions in the ancient world can be found in almost any language and from any period of history: Egyptian, Babylonian, Persian, Greek, Latin, Hebrew, Aramaic, Nabatean, Moabite, and so on. It was once popular to argue that Moses could not have written the Pentateuch because writing had not been invented that early. Inscriptions found at the turquoise mines of Serabit el-Khadim dating to the 15th century BC have disproven this allegation. In addition, it might be noted that clay tablets found at Ras Shamra by Claude Schaeffer and dated to about 1400 BC demonstrate a considerable period of literary activity, as do the tablets at Ebla from approximately 1,000 years earlier.

Inscriptions may be found in almost any position or place, but the most common locations are in the floors of synagogues, church buildings, and mosques; the pavements of forums; the walls of public buildings; dedicatory stones and statues; stelae and monumental plaques; tombs and sarcophagi; and Roman milestones. An exhaustive list is impossible, but a few representative samples will illustrate the various kinds of extant inscriptional material.

Inscriptions on Monuments The Egyptian pharaoh Merneptah commemorated his victory over the Sea Peoples in the 13th century BC by inscribing a black granite stele with a record of his victory. It contains the earliest known reference to Israel outside the land of Palestine: "Israel lies desolate."

The Israelite king Omri (1 Kgs 16:16-30) is referred to in a text carved in the Moabite language on a stone dating near the end of the reign of the Moabite king Mesha, about 830 BC. It was found at Diban (OT Dibon) in 1868 and contains a record of the successful rebellion of the king against Israelite oppression.

Another monumental inscription was found in Persia carved into the steep slope of Mt Behistun. It is a trilingual (Old Persian, Elamite, Akkadian) record of the exploits of Darius I, providing the key to unlocking the mystery of the cuneiform script in which several of these ancient languages were written.

The Assyrian king Shalmaneser III left a record of his first six campaigns of conquest inscribed on a monolith found in 1861 at Kurkh on the Tigris. The stone is carved front and back in cuneiform that is written over a bas-relief of the king. This same king left a black stone obelisk, six and a half feet (2 meters) high, depicting his triumphs over several other kings, among whom is Jehu, king of Israel, depicted in the second panel from the top, prostrating himself before the Assyrian monarch. This is the earliest picture available of an Israelite and the only known representation of an Israelite king by a contemporary. The inscription above the picture reads, "The tribute of Jehu, son [descendant] of Omri . . ." It dates to the mid-ninth century BC.

Historical Records Frequently in the region of Mesopotamia, ancient kings recorded important events or proclamations in stone or clay. A notable example is the clay prism containing the final edition of Sennacherib's Annals dated to 691 BC. It is hexagonal, 15 inches (38.1 centimeters) high and 6 inches (15.2 centimeters) wide, and written on all sides in cuneiform script. The inscription speaks of "Hezekiah the Jew (king of Judah), who did not submit to my yoke. . . . Like a caged bird, I shut him up in Jerusalem, his royal city" (cf. 2 Kgs 18; Is 36–39).

Even though no annals comparable to those produced by the Assyrian kings have survived among the Babylonians, we do have some chronicles written on clay tablets covering the years from 626 BC to the fall of Babylon to Cyrus in 539. One of these, the Babylonian Chronicle, provides an exact date of March 16, 597 BC, for the fall of Jerusalem to the Babylonian king Nebuchadnezzar (cf. 2 Kgs 24:10-17).

Babylon itself fell to Cyrus the Mede, king of Persia, in 539. The event is not only referred to in the Bible (Ezr 1:1-3) but is also described on a clay barrel-shaped cylinder nine inches (22.9 centimeters) in length, written in cuneiform script, during the reign of Cyrus. It refers to his policy that allowed captive nations to rebuild their cities and temples. This provides an explanation of his encouragement and financial help to the Jews in returning to Jerusalem to rebuild the temple of Solomon that Nebuchadnezzar had destroyed (Ezr 1:2-4).

Egyptian pharaohs were fond of publishing records of their exploits in hieroglyphic script on the walls of temples and tombs. These were usually incised into the stone and then painted. One of the most interesting is Shishak's description of his invasion of the land of Israel incised on the southern wall of a court of the temple of Amon at Karnak. The inclusion of Megiddo, as well as other cities in Israel, among the more than 75 cities whose names can still be read adds historical interest to the biblical account of Shishak's invasion and conquest of Jerusalem and "Judah's fortified cities" (1 Kgs 14:25-26; 2 Chr 12:2-10). Archaeological finds confirm a destruction and burning of the city at this time.

Official Announcements When an ancient monarch or public official wanted to publish an announcement with some degree of permanency, it would be carved in stone or set in mosaic. An inscription on a marble slab dating to the reign of Claudius (AD 41–54) was found in 1878, originating in the city of Nazareth. It contains a warning against grave robbing or any other desecration of cemeteries. The penalty for such violation was declared to be death. The inscription may reflect some of the troubles Claudius had in Rome over the person of Christ (Suetonius, *Claudius* 25) which led to the expulsion of Jews from the capital city (Acts 18). At issue must have been the resurrection of Christ as proclaimed in Rome.

Announcements were placed even in temples. Josephus referred to a small wall surrounding the Jewish temple in Jerusalem that contained slabs of stone at regular intervals giving warning in Greek and Latin to Gentiles entering the temple (*War* 5.193-34; 6.125-26; *Antiquities* 15.417). Two fragmentary examples have been found. One discovered by Clermont-Ganneau in 1871 reads: "No foreigner is to enter within the balustrade and embankment around the sanctuary. Whoever is caught will have himself to blame for his death which follows." The Romans allowed the Jews to put anyone to death, even a Roman, who went beyond this barrier (*War* 6.126).

An important inscription commissioned by the emperor Claudius, was found at the beginning of the 20th century in Delphi, Greece. It was written in Greek and mentions Gallio as proconsul with a date that can be established as AD 51–52 for his term of office. This Gallio is the proconsul before whom Paul was brought by the Jews of Corinth (Acts 18:12-17). It is therefore extremely important for establishing the date of Paul's 18-month stay in Corinth, and an important pivotal date for Pauline chronology in general. The inscription is an imperial announcement to the citizens of Delphi regarding the need for increasing the population of the city with eminent people.

The name Pontius Pilate has appeared in a Latin inscription carved into a stone found in the Roman theater at Caesarea Maritima on the coast of Israel. It refers to him, in partially mutilated words, as prefect and contains the name Tiberium, which designates a structure built in honor of the emperor Tiberius.

Dedications Inscriptions were commonly placed on walls or floors of buildings or attached to some other structure dedicating the completed edifice. An inscription was cut into the wall of a long tunnel built by the

Jewish king Hezekiah in Jerusalem when the tunnel was finished (2 Kgs 20:20). It is in Hebrew and is now in the Istanbul museum. One of the oldest inscriptions we have in that language, it describes the construction of the Siloam tunnel.

In the city of Corinth in Greece there is a dedicatory inscription cut into the pavement of a plaza on the north side of the large theater. The abbreviated Latin inscription reads: *Erastus pro aedilitate sua pecunia stravit* ("Erastus, in return for his aedileship, laid the pavement at his own expense"). The bronze has long since been removed from the letters deeply cut into the gray Acrocorinthian limestone. This is probably the same "Erastus, the city treasurer" mentioned by Paul in Romans 16:23. A similar inscription from the Corinthian agora of Paul's day reads: "Gnaeus Babbius Philinus, aedile and pontifex, had this monument erected at his own expense, and he approved it in his official capacity as duovir."

A monumental dedicatory inscription in Greek was found in Jerusalem during excavations in 1913–14, which once stood on the wall of a first-century AD synagogue on Mt Ophel. It refers to a Theodotus, the son of a ruler of the synagogue named Vettenos, who built the synagogue. Since the name Vettenos is Roman, it may be that Theodotus was a Jewish slave who had been freed and given the Roman name of his master. If so, this inscription may have hung on the "synagogue of the Freedmen" in Jerusalem (Acts 6:9).

The British Museum contains a portion of a broken arch that stood over an entrance into the Greek city of Thessalonica from the first century AD until 1867, when it was torn down to provide stone for the repair of the vast city wall. The inscription begins: "In the time of the politarchs . . ." This is a rare word referring to Roman officials and is used in the book of Acts (Acts 17:6) in reference to city authorities of Thessalonica. This word is found nowhere else in Greek literature.

Correspondence In the second millennium before Christ, it was common practice to write correspondence on small clay tablets. More than half a million have been found in Mari, Nuzi, Nineveh, Ebla, and elsewhere. Interesting examples of such correspondence may be found in a great number of clay tablets found at Tell el-Amarna in Upper Egypt. They were written in the Babylonian language using the cuneiform script during the time when Akhenaton was captivated with his reformation of Egyptian art and religion at his new capital Tell el-Amarna (Akhetaten), and Palestine and Syria were left to the mercy of marauders called Habiru in the documents. Many of these are written from cities in Canaan under attack and ask for help from the pharaoh, whose vassals they are at this time (late 14th century BC). Some think that these Habiru were the ancient Hebrews who invaded the land under the direction of Joshua.

Sometimes correspondence was written in ink on broken pieces of ceramic pottery (potsherds) called ostraca. In 1935, 18 of these were found in the excavations at Lachish in southern Israel. They are written in Hebrew and provide examples of the kind of script used by the Judeans in the time of Jeremiah. The language is essentially identical with the Hebrew of the OT. The letters were sent by Hosha'yahu, an officer in charge of a nearby town, to Ya'osh, the military governor of Lachish, during the invasion of Judea by the Babylonians, which ended in the destruction of the temple in Jerusalem in 586 BC.

Eleven such potsherds were found in Masada, on the western shore of the Dead Sea, in excavations conducted by Yigael Yadin from 1963 to 1965. Masada was destroyed by the Roman army under the command of Flavius Silva in AD 73. Nine hundred and sixty men, women, and children committed suicide rather than surrender to the Romans. Ten men were chosen to cut the throats of those who remained. They drew lots for the heartbreaking task, according to Josephus (*War* 7.395), and Professor Yadin thinks the ostraca he found were the ones used in the drawing. One of them contained the name of Ben Yair, who was probably Eleazer ben Yair, the commander of the fortress.

Mosaic Floor Decorations In the Roman and Byzantine periods it was popular to decorate the floors of basilicas, baths, synagogues, churches, and other public buildings with elaborate tesselation containing inscriptions and artwork. Excavation in 1972 disclosed a building in Caesarea Maritima with mosaic inscriptions in six floors throughout the structure. Two of them are the Greek text of Romans 13:3 set in a circular border. Another is a blessing on the one who enters and exits the room: "May the Lord bless your entry and your exit." Two of them invoke the aid of Christ for people associated with the function and construction of the building. These were a part of a building that was destroyed in the seventh century AD.

The floors of the synagogues at Tiberias-hamath, Beth Shan, Beth Alpha, Eshtemoa, Susiya, Hamath-gader, En-gedi, and others in Israel have inscriptions in Greek and Aramaic that usually refer to benefactors of the synagogue. A synagogue floor has been found in Naro, Tunisia, which contains a Latin inscription. In the Tiberias synagogue, Hebrew was used only for defining the astrological symbols that appear in the zodiac. Aramaic was used primarily for Halakah (religious rule or law), and Greek was principally used in honoring donors.

One of the best-known mosaic floor inscriptions in churches was in Madaba, Jordan, where the oldest known map of Israel and Jordan was set into the floor in the sixth century AD. The place-names of cities, geographical features, and passages of Scripture are given in Greek. Church floors typically contain dated or undated dedications, blessings, and Scripture quotations that appear in Aramaic, Coptic, Syriac, Latin, and Greek. Symbolism often accompanies the inscriptions, but in AD 427 an edict was issued forbidding the use of crosses and other religious symbols on pavements so that they might not be stepped on. It is not clear how widespread this prohibition was.

See also Archaeology and the Bible; Pottery.

INSECT Small invertebrates generally characterized by a segmented body (head, thorax, abdomen) and three pairs of legs. *See* Animals (Ant; Bee; Cricket; Flea; Fly; Gnat; Grasshopper; Locust; Moth; Wasp).

INSPIRATION *See* Bible, Inspiration of the.

INSTALLATION OFFERING* *See* Offerings and Sacrifices.

INSTRUCT, INSTRUCTOR* *See* Teacher.

INSTRUMENTS, Musical *See* Musical Instruments.

INTERCEDE, INTERCESSION* *See* Prayer.

INTERCESSION OF CHRIST* Theological term for Christ's activity of petitioning God the Father to save, help, and sustain people on earth.

The Hebrew word meaning "to make intercession" is from a root meaning "to strike"; hence it means "to assail or encounter with a request." That word is used prophetically of the ministry of the "servant of the Lord": "He bore the sin of many, and made intercession for the transgressors" (Is 53:12, RSV). The principal Greek verb meant in secular usage to "meet," "approach," or "make an appeal." In intertestamental literature that word was employed in the sense of personally petitioning an official to gain a favor (e.g., 2 Macc 4:8). The noun form of the word is translated in the NT both as "intercession" (1 Tm 2:1) and as "prayer" (4:5).

Theologians generally see intercession as the second phase of Christ's "high priestly work," after he first made satisfaction for sin through his suffering and death on the cross (1 Tm 2:5-6). In the OT one of the priest's functions was to petition God on the people's behalf. In particular, on the annual Day of Atonement the high priest carried the blood of the sin offering into the Holy of Holies, sanctified the sacred place by means of incense, and sprinkled the sacrificial blood on and about the "mercy seat" (Lv 16:11-19). Correspondingly, after Christ offered himself on the cross as the sacrifice for sins, he ascended to the Father and entered the heavenly sanctuary where he now represents his people (Heb 7:25).

Christ's Intercession on Earth Before his life of intercession in heaven, Jesus Christ exercised such a ministry on earth, consistent with his own teaching that the disciples should always pray and not get discouraged (Lk 18:1). Scripture often points to Jesus in prayer. For example, Jesus interceded at the grave of his friend Lazarus (Jn 11:41-42). Jesus prayed all night on a mountain before selecting the 12 apostles (Lk 6:12-13). After warning his disciple Peter that Satan had designs on him, Jesus said to Peter, "I have prayed for you that your faith may not fail" (Lk 22:32, RSV). Jesus' first words on the cross were a prayer for those who had persecuted him (23:34).

The "high priestly prayer" recorded in John 17 provides the most complete account in Scripture of an intercessory prayer by Jesus. The ground, or basis, of his impassioned petition was his intimate relationship with his heavenly Father (Jn 17:5, 8). The objects of his prayer were (1) himself, that he might glorify the Father and complete the work he had been sent to accomplish (Jn 17:1-5); (2) his disciples, who were chosen to spread the gospel after his departure (vv 8-9); and (3) the entire family of believers (v 20). The goals of his intercession included (1) the unity of God's people (vv 11, 21), (2) their joy in spite of hardships and discouragement (v 13), (3) their preservation from evil (v 15), (4) their sanctification by the Word of God (v 17), and (5) their eternal fellowship with Christ (v 24).

Christ's Intercession in Heaven Christ's intercession for his people, begun on earth, is continued in heaven. The Epistle to the Hebrews depicts Christ as a priest, placing considerable emphasis on his continuing ministry of intercession. Christ's heavenly intercession is a sequel to his earthly sacrifice accomplished "once for all" (Heb 10:10-18). Jesus himself said, "Every one who acknowledges me before men, I also will acknowledge before my Father who is in heaven" (Mt 10:32, RSV). His continuing intercession is recognized in such NT phrases as "through Jesus Christ" (Rom 1:8; 16:27; 1 Pt 2:5), "through him" (Col 3:17; Heb 13:15), and "in the name of our Lord Jesus Christ" (Eph 5:20).

The doctrine of Christ's heavenly intercession is explicitly affirmed in four NT texts. The apostle Paul spoke of Christ "at the right hand of God, who indeed intercedes

for us" (Rom 8:34, RSV). The writer of Hebrews affirmed that Christ "is able for all time to save those who draw near to God through him, since he always lives to make intercession for them" (Heb 7:25, RSV). Further, Christ has entered "into heaven itself, now to appear in the presence of God on our behalf" (9:24). The apostle John also described that ministry: "If any one does sin, we have an advocate with the Father, Jesus Christ the righteous" (1 Jn 2:1). The Greek word for "advocate" meant a legal counselor who appeared before a magistrate to plead a client's cause. John thus pictured the ascended Lord as appearing before God on behalf of his people, presenting his own obedience and suffering as the ground for the believer's acquittal.

The Way Intercession Works Christ's heavenly intercession has both a static aspect (his redemptive work has been completed) and a dynamic aspect (he continues to care for God's people). Thus Christ's intercession is seen as including (1) his presence with the Father as the ground of each believer's justification (Heb 9:24); (2) his thwarting of Satan's accusations against each believer (Rom 8:33; Rv 12:10); (3) his claim for each believer's right of access to the divine presence (Heb 4:14-16); and (4) his mediation of the prayers of each believer. The heavenly Father's response is to impart the full range of spiritual blessings on believers. In the words of the Puritan John Owen (1616–83), "The intercession of Christ . . . is his continual appearance for us in the presence of God, representing the efficacy of his oblation, accompanied with tender care, love and desires for the welfare, supply, deliverance and salvation of the church."

Those for whom Christ intercedes in heaven are described in Scripture both broadly and narrowly. Christ is said to pray for all people everywhere (Is 53:12; cf. Mt 26:28). More specifically, and perhaps more profoundly, he prays for his own redeemed community, the church (Jn 14:16; 17:9, 20; Heb 4:15-16). Nevertheless, Christ's prayers are also centered on the specific needs of individual believers (Lk 22:31-32; 1 Jn 2:1).

INTEREST *See* Debt; Banker, Banking; Money.

INTERMEDIATE STATE* State of the human person after death and before the final resurrection. Such teaching is more developed in the NT than in the OT, though it is a mistake to think that reference to it is totally absent in the OT (Jb 19:25). According to Christ, the intermediate state is deducible from such texts as Exodus 3:6 (Mt 22:32). Even in the NT, an account of the intermediate state is not given explicitly but may be inferred from teaching about the physical death and resurrection of all people, but especially of believers. This is taught by Christ himself (Mt 22:30-32) and by the apostles, particularly Paul (1 Cor 15). In addition, the biblical teaching that the human being is a unity of soul and body and not simply a soul that happens to be embodied (Gn 2:7) has implications for a person's state after death. From such data two conclusions regarding the intermediate state may be drawn. The first is that physical death is not the total cessation of the life of the individual but that the person lives on, not merely in the memories of those who survive, but as a distinct personality, and in the case of believers with awareness of the loving presence of God (Phil 1:23). The second conclusion is that such an existence is not a fully human existence but is incomplete or anomalous, since being embodied is essential for an individual to be in God's image. The individual, surviving death, awaits the resurrection of the body when, in the case of a Christian, he or she will experience complete redemption, a state of complete emancipation from sin in the presence of Christ (1 Cor 15:50-58). The biblical data regarding the character of the intermediate state of those who are outside Christ is less clear, including as it does the difficult reference to Christ's preaching to the "imprisoned" spirits (1 Pt 3:19-20).

Scripture is restrained in its portrayal of what life in the intermediate state is like. Paul says of himself that after his death he will be "with Christ, which is far better" (Phil 1:23) but he gives no details. Nor is it wise to look for such details in such biblical incidents as that of Saul and the medium at Endor (1 Sm 28:7), which is subject to a number of different interpretations. Even Christ's parable of the rich man and Lazarus (Lk 16:19-31), because of its obviously symbolic character and its avowed purpose of teaching about the importance of the present life for a person's eternal destiny, must be treated with caution. Perhaps the most that can be said is that the dead in Christ are "immediately with God" and that they rest in his loving presence until the resurrection, while the unsaved are in a comfortless condition awaiting their resurrection to judgment (Jn 5:29).

Discussion of the intermediate state in the history of Christian thought has focused upon three separate aspects that may help to clarify the biblical data further. First, under the influence of Greek philosophical ideas, there has been a recurring Platonic influence in Christian theology in which the Pauline contrast between the flesh and the spirit has been misinterpreted and the soul has been emphasized at the expense of the body, with the result that the prospective resurrection of the dead and its eschatological setting has either been played down or eliminated altogether because of its allegedly physical (and therefore unspiritual) aspect. The doctrine of the immortality of the disembodied soul is sometimes substituted for the idea of an intermediate state prior to resurrection, but without any warrant from Scripture. In modern theology a tendency to discount the historical has tended to displace the earlier discounting of the physical, but with much the same effect, at best a spiritualizing of postmortem existence, at worst a denial of any such existence. But it is clear from Scripture that the intermediate state is a state between two phases of embodiment, the present state of physical embodiment and that of "spiritual embodiment" (1 Cor 15:44), which is to occur at Christ's second coming (v 23).

Second, during the Reformation, a controversy arose between John Calvin and some of the Anabaptists over "soul sleep." Calvin vehemently maintained that the intermediate state is one of conscious awareness of God's presence—something his opponents denied. For Calvin such a denial was equivalent to holding that the soul is annihilated at death and to denying that Christ exercises rule over the dead before they are resurrected. Calvin's view is supported by Paul's affirmation that nothing separates the believer from the love of God—not even death (Rom 8:35-39). The biblical teaching that upon death the believer "sleeps" (1 Thes 4:14) is interpreted to mean that the dead no longer communicate with the living on earth and no longer engage in labor, but are in repose. To "fall asleep in Jesus" is thus to enjoy the presence of Jesus in a disembodied state, the nearest analogy of which in present experience may be found in dreaming when the awareness of the dreamer does not depend upon the functioning of any of the bodily senses.

A third focus for Christian thought has been on whether or not a person's eternal state is fixed at the time of death, or whether repentance and spiritual growth and purgation are possible or inevitable after death. It is the teaching of the Roman Catholic Church that death is fol-

lowed by purgatory for all who are imperfect. In purgatory the soul is freed from the remnants of sin, and the period of purgation may be lessened by the gifts, prayers, and masses of those who survive the deceased. Such a view is rejected by most Protestants as being inconsistent with the biblical teaching on the complete and finished work of Christ (Heb 9:28), on the impossibility of one human being meriting or otherwise gaining grace for another (Lk 17:10), and on the biblical teaching that the eternal state of the soul is determined by its condition at death (Heb 9:27).

See also Dead, Place of the; Hades; Heaven; Hell; Paradise; Sheol.

INTERPRETER One who facilitates communication between people who speak different languages, or one who explains the meaning of dreams. Joseph pretended to need an interpreter to speak to his brothers (Gn 42:23). Also, dreams needed to be interpreted (Gn 40:8; 41:15-16; Dn 2; 4:6-9, 18-24; 5:7-8, 12-17; 7:16). The interpreter was sometimes one who acted as an intermediary (Jb 33:23). Ezra and Nehemiah functioned as interpreters or translators of the law of Moses when it was read to the Jews who had returned from exile (Neh 8:8-9) and who must not have known Hebrew. In NT times the interpreter explained the utterances of those who spoke in tongues (1 Cor 14:28), translated foreign languages (Acts 2:6), or expounded the Scriptures (Lk 24:27).

INTERTESTAMENTAL PERIOD* Portion of time extending from the close of OT history to the beginning of NT history. Much of this period is covered in the books of 1 and 2 Maccabees. *See* Maccabees, 1 and 2.

IOB* Alternate name for Jashub, Issachar's son, in Genesis 46:13. *See* Jashub #1.

IPHDEIAH Shashak's son from Benjamin's tribe (1 Chr 8:25).

IPHTAH City of the Shephelah assigned to Judah's tribe for an inheritance, listed between Ashan and Ashnah (Jos 15:43).

IPHTAH-EL Valley on Asher and Zebulun's border (Jos 19:14, 27), possibly the modern Sahl el-Battof.

IR Benjamite father of Shuppim and Huppim (1 Chr 7:12), perhaps identical with Iri (v 7). In Numbers 24:19, the name is translated "the city" (KJV, NIV; cf. NLT).

IRA
1. David's priest or chief official in service at the time of Sheba's revolt (2 Sm 20:26).
2. Warrior among David's mighty men, known as "the thirty" (2 Sm 23:26). He was the son of Ikkesh of Tekoa (1 Chr 11:28; 27:9) and became commander of the sixth division of David's militia.
3. Warrior among David's mighty men, "the thirty," identified as an Ithrite (2 Sm 23:38; 1 Chr 11:40; NLT "from Jattir").

IRAD Enoch's son, a member of Cain's line (Gn 4:18).

IRAM Chieftain in Edom (Gn 36:43; 1 Chr 1:54).

IRI Bela's son from Benjamin's tribe (1 Chr 7:7).

IRIJAH Benjamite guard who apprehended Jeremiah as he left Jerusalem to see property that was his by redemption (Jer 32:6-7) and charged him before the princes with deserting to the Chaldeans; as a consequence, Jeremiah was beaten and imprisoned (37:13-14).

IR-NAHASH Son of Tehinnah, Eshton's son from Judah's tribe (1 Chr 4:12). Some translations note the alternate rendering, "city of Nahash" (mg NIV, KJV).

IRON Malleable, metallic element. *See* Minerals and Metals.

IRON* (Place) KJV form of Yiron, a city in Naphtali's territory (Jos 19:38). *See* Yiron.

IRONSMITH* An artisan who normally worked in iron (Is 44:12); a blacksmith. The first worker in iron recorded in the Bible is Tubal-cain (Gn 4:22). In Israel iron became widely known and used about the 11th century BC (Dt 3:11; Jos 6:19, 24; 17:16; Jgs 1:19; 4:3, 13). *See* Minerals and Metals.

IRPEEL City of inheritance allotted to Benjamin's tribe (Jos 18:27), perhaps situated in the hill country several miles northwest of Jerusalem, near Gibeon.

IRRIGATION Watering by artificial means. *See* Agriculture.

IR-SHEMESH City allotted to Dan's tribe for an inheritance (Jos 19:41), probably identical with Beth-shemesh.

IRU Caleb's son from Judah's tribe (1 Chr 4:15).

ISAAC Son of Abraham and Sarah, father of Jacob and Esau, one of the patriarchs of Israel.

The name Isaac has an interesting etymology. It is the Anglicized form of the Hebrew *Yitshaq*, in Greek *Isaak*. If taken as an imperfect form, it means "he laughs"; as a perfect form, it means "he laughed." Scholars have debated this problem and also the absence of an antecedent subject. If God is implied, the name could indicate divine amusement at an aged couple ridiculing the prospect of having a child (Gn 17:17; 18:12) and then suddenly becoming parents, as God had promised.

Isaac's pedigree is also interesting, for Sarah was not only the wife of Abraham but also his half sister (Gn 20:12), and this fact alone may have interfered with conception in their earlier years. Because of this relationship, Isaac belonged to both sides of Terah's family. According to prevailing custom, the son of the legal wife took precedence over the male offspring of concubines, so that Isaac had priority of inheritance over Ishmael. The gifts that Abraham subsequently gave to the sons of his concubines (25:6) were without prejudice to the inheritance of Isaac.

Following God's instructions (Gn 17:10-14), Isaac was circumcised on the eighth day as a member of the covenant community. The next ceremony came when he was old enough for weaning, probably around three years old. In eastern countries where this procedure is still observed, the child's transition from milk to solid protein and carbohydrates is normally celebrated in the context of a feast. During the celebration the mother chews a mouthful of solid food and then pushes it into the baby's mouth with her tongue. The infant is often so shocked by this treatment that it promptly expels the food, whereupon the mother repeats the process. For an observer the procedure can be hilarious, and Ishmael may have been laughing at such a spectacle when he incurred Sarah's wrath (21:8-10).

During the years of Isaac's adolescence, Abraham was living in Philistine territory (Gn 21:34). The supreme test of the father's faith and obedience came in this period. Having watched this son of God's promise grow up into a healthy young man, Abraham is asked by God to offer him as a sacrifice. Isaac was familiar with sacrificial rituals and helped with the preparations, though probably not without some misgivings, for he was also familiar with the patriarchal traditions that gave the head of the family power of life or death over everyone and everything in the family. If he voiced any protest as he lay bound on the sacrificial altar, it is not recorded. When Abraham's faith did not waver, God intervened at the crucial moment and provided another offering in the form of a ram. Because of his obedience, God promised Abraham great blessing, blessing in which Isaac also participated (Gn 22; 25:11). It was this act of faith and obedience that Paul honored centuries later by calling Abraham the forefather of the Christian church (Rom 4).

After Sarah's death (Gn 23), Abraham set about securing a bride for Isaac, as it was the custom for parents to arrange marriages for their children. Rather than have Isaac marry a local pagan woman, Abraham sent his household steward to Nahor in Mesopotamia to seek a bride for his son from among his relatives. In an account that emphasizes faith, perseverance, and divine blessing, Genesis 24 describes how the servant met Rebekah and betrothed her to Isaac even before he had met the rest of her family. Bethuel, her father, and Laban, her brother, assented to this arrangement, and she left with the family's blessing to take up her new responsibilities in Palestine as Isaac's wife.

When Abraham died at a ripe old age, Isaac and Ishmael buried him in the cave of Machpelah (Gn 25:8-9). Isaac was now patriarch of the family. He pleaded with God that his wife, Rebekah, might bear children, and as a result, she bore twin sons, Esau ("the hairy one") and Jacob ("supplanter"). Esau became a hunter, and Isaac favored him, while Jacob was more of a settler and agriculturalist and was favored by his mother. Jacob was also crafty and took advantage of Esau's extreme hunger one day, bargaining with his older brother to exchange his birthright for some lentil stew. Possession of the birthright secured for Jacob a double portion of the inheritance (Dt 21:17).

When famine gripped the land, God instructed Isaac not to visit Egypt (Gn 26:2), but to stay in Palestine, where he would enjoy great prosperity. When the men of the area asked about Rebekah, Isaac became fearful and said she was his sister. When the deception was uncovered, Abimelech the king rebuked Isaac and forbade anyone to interfere with him. Isaac prospered so greatly that Abimelech finally asked him to relocate, so he moved to Beersheba, where there was sufficient water for his flocks, and his fortune increased.

Although Esau was Isaac's favorite son, he displeased his father by marrying two Hittite women. When Isaac felt that the end of his life was approaching, he wanted to bless his firstborn in the traditional patriarchal manner (Gn 27). Rebekah overheard his instructions to Esau, and she encouraged Jacob to deceive the blind old man by disguising himself as Esau and taking his brother's blessing. The deception succeeded, and Isaac gave Jacob the blessing of the firstborn. When Esau appeared to receive his blessing he was too late, and he was very bitter against Jacob because of what had happened. Rebekah sent Jacob away to her brother Laban in Mesopotamia, to escape Esau's anger and also to obtain a wife. Esau did receive a blessing from Isaac, but a lesser one. Two decades later a rich and prosperous Jacob returned with his family. He made peace with Esau before Isaac died, and the brothers buried Isaac in Hebron (Gn 35:27-29).

Isaac is given less prominence in the patriarchal narratives than Abraham or Jacob, but his importance for covenantal faith was recognized in such NT passages as Acts 7:8, Romans 9:7, Galatians 4:21-31, and Hebrews 11:9-20.

See also Israel, History of; Patriarchs, Period of the.

ISAIAH (Person) Eighth-century BC prophet during the reigns of the Judean kings Uzziah, Jotham, Ahaz, and Hezekiah; author of the biblical book of Isaiah. Isaiah was the son of Amoz (Is 1:1) and may have been a relative of King Amaziah. Growing up in Jerusalem, Isaiah received the best education the capital could supply. He was also deeply knowledgeable about people, and he became the political and religious counselor of the nation. He had easy access to the monarchs and seems to have been the historiographer at the Judean court for several reigns (2 Chr 26:22; 32:32).

Isaiah's wife is referred to as a prophetess (Is 8:3) and they had at least two sons, Shear-jashub (7:3) and Maher-shalal-hash-baz (8:3). Isaiah's customary attire was a prophet's clothing, that is, sandals and a garment of goat's hair or sackcloth. At one point during his ministry, the Lord commanded Isaiah to go naked and barefoot for a period of three years, (wearing only a loincloth) (20:2-6). This must have been humiliating in a society that measured status by meticulous dress codes.

Isaiah worked to reform social and political wrongs. Even the highest members of society did not escape his censure. He berated soothsayers and denounced wealthy, influential people who ignored the responsibilities of their position. He exhorted the masses to be obedient rather than indifferent to God's covenant. He rebuked kings for their willfulness and lack of concern.

Isaiah's writings express a deep awareness of God's majesty and holiness. The prophet denounced not only Canaanite idolatry but also the religious observances of his own people that were external ceremonies only and lacking sincerity (1:10-17; 29:13). He preached impending judgment on the idolatrous Judeans, declaring that only a righteous remnant would survive (6:13).

Isaiah foretold the coming of the Messiah, the "peaceful prince," and the ruler of God's kingdom (11:1-11; cf. 9:6-7). He also depicted this Messiah as a suffering, obedient servant (53:3-12). Isaiah was preeminent among the prophets for the variety and grandeur of his imagery. His imagination produced forceful, brilliant figures of speech.

Isaiah prophesied during the last three decades of the northern kingdom of Israel but because he lived in Jerusalem, in Judah, he made little direct reference to Israel. However, when that kingdom fell, Judah lay open to conquest by Assyria. Isaiah advised King Ahaz to avoid foreign entanglements and depend on God to protect his people. Ignoring that advice, Ahaz made an alliance with Assyria.

It was Hezekiah, Ahaz's pious son, who sought to remove Judah from this dangerous situation. When the Assyrians under Sennacherib approached Jerusalem, Isaiah inspired Hezekiah and the Judeans to rely on the Lord for the city's defense, and "the angel of the Lord" destroyed Sennacherib's army (37:36-38), securing a short period of peace for Hezekiah and the Judeans.

Hebrew prophecy reached its pinnacle with Isaiah, who was greatly esteemed in both OT and NT times. One indication of that esteem is the collection of apocryphal literature associated with his name.

See also Isaiah, Book of; Israel, History of; Prophecy; Prophet, Prophetess.

ISAIAH, Book of

PREVIEW
- Author
- Date
- Background
- Literary Unity
- Theological Teaching
- Content

Author The prophet Isaiah, whose name means "the Lord saves," lived and ministered in Jerusalem. Because of his repeated contact with the kings of Judah, some scholars believed that Isaiah was related to the royal family, but this is not certain. According to chapters 7 and 8, Isaiah was married and had at least two sons, Shear-jashub and Maher-shalal-hash-baz, whose symbolic names illustrated God's dealings with the nation as a whole. The "disciples" mentioned in 8:16 probably assisted Isaiah in his ministry and may have helped him record the book that bears his name.

When Isaiah saw the Lord in the famous temple vision described in chapter 6, he was willing to go wherever God sent him, even though he would face strong opposition (6:9-10). King Ahaz proved to be particularly resistant to Isaiah's advice (7:4-17), and the people in general ridiculed his preaching (5:10-12; 28:9-10). During the reign of the godly Hezekiah, however, Isaiah's ministry was much appreciated, and the king consulted him eagerly during times of crisis (37:1-7, 21-35).

Isaiah is usually regarded as the greatest of the writing prophets. Some of the chapters in his book display an unparalleled literary beauty and make use of poetic devices and a rich variety of symbols. Chapters 40–66 contain many powerful passages that underscore the grandeur of the book. It is ironic, then, that many scholars attribute these chapters to a "second" or "third" Isaiah, unknown authors who wrote much later than Isaiah in connection with the Babylonian exile. Yet elsewhere in the OT, the names of all who wrote the prophetic books are preserved, and it would be most unusual for the Jews not to know who wrote such magnificent prophecy as chapters 40–66.

Date Since many of the events recorded in chapters 1–39 took place during the ministry of Isaiah, most of these chapters were probably written by about 700 BC or shortly thereafter. The destruction of the Assyrian army in 701 BC represents the climax of the first half of the book, fulfilling the prophecy of 10:16, 24-34 and 30:31-33. In 37:38 Isaiah refers to the death of King Sennacherib, which did not occur until 681 BC. This means that some of the earlier chapters, along with 40–66, were probably written later, during Isaiah's retirement years. A gap of several decades could help account for the change in subject matter that is found in the last half of the book. In these chapters Isaiah projects into the future as he addresses the Jews who would be in exile in Babylon about 550 BC.

Background Isaiah's public ministry occurred primarily from 740–700 BC, a period marked by the rapid expansion of the nation of Assyria. Under King Tiglath-pileser III (745–727 BC), the Assyrians moved to the west and south, and by 738 BC the Assyrian monarch was demanding tribute from Damascus and Israel. About 734 BC Rezin of Damascus (Syria) and Pekah of Israel organized a coali-

Isaiah Scroll Manuscript from the Dead Sea area of Qumran, 1QIsa[b], showing Isaiah 46:3–47:14

tion to rebel against Assyria, and they tried to enlist the support of King Ahaz of Judah. But Ahaz refused to join, and when the kings of Damascus and Israel invaded Judah (see 7:1), Ahaz appealed directly to Tiglath-pileser for help (cf. 2 Kgs 16:7-9). With little hesitation the Assyrians returned to capture Damascus and to turn the northern kingdom of Israel into an Assyrian province.

The puppet king Hoshea ruled over Israel from 732–723 BC but was imprisoned when he joined a revolt against Shalmaneser V, the new Assyrian king. Shalmaneser besieged the capital city of Samaria, which finally fell in 722 BC, spelling the end of the northern kingdom. Sargon succeeded Shalmaneser in 722 and had to quell a number of revolts. In 711 BC Sargon captured the Philistine city of Ashdod in a campaign that became the occasion of Isaiah's prophecy of chapter 20.

Even more important was the widespread rebellion that broke out with the accession of Sennacherib in 705 BC. King Hezekiah of Judah withheld his normal tribute payment, and by 701 BC Sennacherib had invaded Palestine to punish the rebels. The details of this campaign are given in Isaiah 36–37 and tell how city after city was captured by the Assyrians before the invaders stood at the gates of Jerusalem and demanded total surrender. With almost no hope of survival, Hezekiah nevertheless was encouraged by Isaiah to trust God, and in one night the angel of the Lord struck down 185,000 Assyrian soldiers, virtually wiping out Sennacherib's army (Is 37:36-37).

In an effort to befriend the enemies of Assyria, Hezekiah showed his treasures to envoys of the king of Babylon (39:1-4). Isaiah warned that someday the Babylonian armies would conquer Jerusalem and carry off those very treasures, along with the residents of the city (vv 5-7). Not only did Isaiah predict the Babylonian captivity of

586–539 BC (cf. 6:11-12), but he also foretold that Israel would be released from Babylon (48:20). The Chaldean kingdom led by Nebuchadnezzar would be God's instrument of judgment upon Judah, but they too would suffer defeat. One of Isaiah's most remarkable prophecies was the naming of Cyrus, king of Persia, the ruler who would conquer the Babylonians in 539 BC and release Israel from exile (cf. 44:28). Along with the Medes (cf. 13:17), Cyrus won several important victories before sending his troops against Babylon. Isaiah hailed him as one anointed by the Lord to bring deliverance for Israel (45:1-5).

Literary Unity Largely because of the references to the later kingdoms of Babylon and Persia, the unity of Isaiah has been called into question. Chapters 40–66 move abruptly into the exilic period of 550 BC, almost 150 years after Isaiah lived. Moreover, the Servant of the Lord plays a prominent role in these chapters and the messianic king fades into the background. Brilliant poetic passages are found in chapters 40, 53, 55, and 60, demonstrating remarkable depth and power.

Although these factors are sometimes cited as a sign of disunity, there are actually strong indications for unity in the book. For example, the historical interlude (chs 36–39) forms a hinge or bridge that links chapters 1–35 and 40–66. Chapters 36–37 complete the Assyrian section, and chapters 38–39 introduce the Babylonian material. Most of the linking chapters are written in prose, while the others (in some translations) are largely poetry. From the standpoint of verbal or stylistic unity, one can point to Isaiah's favorite title for God, "the Holy One of Israel." This title appears 12 times in chapters 1–39, and 14 times in chapters 40–66, but only seven times in the rest of the OT. A study of the famous Servant Songs of 52:13–53:12

reveals several ties with earlier passages, especially in chapters 1–6. The servant who is smitten and wounded (53:4-5) receives the same punishment as the beaten and injured nation of 1:5-6 (also cf. 52:13 with 2:12 and 6:1).

DEUTERO-ISAIAH:
A SECOND AUTHOR OF THE BOOK OF ISAIAH?
Since the 18th century, certain Bible critics have questioned the unity of the book of Isaiah. Late in the 19th century a theory emerged that ascribed chapters 40–66 to an unknown prophet—a deutero ("second") Isaiah presumably living among the exiles in Babylon. Some scholars have even posited the existence of a third author (trito-Isaiah), limiting the extent of deutero-Isaiah to chapters 40–54.

The theory was first prompted not by problems of stylistic unity but by the issue of whether OT prophets could really foretell future events, especially with Isaiah's amazing accuracy. Rationalist critics doubted that Isaiah could have possibly foretold the fall of Jerusalem, the later restoration of Palestine, and especially the name of the Persian king (Cyrus; see Is 45:1) who would permit the Jews to return to their homeland from exile—events that did not occur until well over 100 years after the prophet had died.

Most conservative biblical scholars, however, affirm the unity of the book, its single authorship, and the supernatural origin of its prophetic passages.

Theological Teaching Isaiah is to the OT as the book of Romans is to the NT—a book filled with rich theological truth. Like Romans, Isaiah unveils the sinfulness of God's rebellious people and his gracious provision of salvation. Because God is the Holy One of Israel (1:4; 6:3), he cannot ignore sin but must punish those who are guilty. Both Israel (5:30; 42:25) and the other nations (2:11, 17, 20) experience a time of judgment known as the Day of the Lord. In anger God raises his hand against his people (cf. 5:25), but ultimately his wrath is poured out upon Babylon and the nations (cf. 13:3-5; 34:2).

With the fall of Assyria and Babylon, the Day of the Lord becomes a day of joyous victory (10:27; 61:2). According to Isaiah 63:4, it is the year of the Lord's redemption. Earlier, Israel had been redeemed from slavery in Egypt; now the return from the Babylonian captivity brings equal joy (52:9; 61:1). The ultimate redemption is to be accomplished through the death of Christ, and Isaiah 53 describes our Lord's suffering and death in graphic terms. His ministry as the Suffering Servant is also introduced in 49:4 and 50:6-7; meanwhile, 49:6 states that the servant will be "a light for the Gentiles." Looking ahead to the Second Coming, Isaiah predicts a messianic age of peace and righteousness. Nations will "beat their swords into plowshares" (2:4) and the "Prince of Peace" will rule forever (9:6-7).

Throughout the book God is pictured as the all-powerful Creator (48:13)—the sovereign One seated on a throne, high and exalted; the King, the Lord Almighty (6:1, 5). He controls the armies of the earth (13:4) and removes rulers as he wills (40:23-24). Before him, nations "are but a drop in the bucket" (40:15, NLT), and compared with him all idols are worthless and without power (41:29; 44:6). This is the God who shows his fury to his foes and his love to his servants (66:14).

Content

Messages of Judgment and Hope (1–12) In the opening chapter Isaiah characterizes Israel (including Judah) as "a sinful nation" that has rebelled against God. Although the people regularly bring offerings to him, their worship is hypocritical, an attempt to mask their oppression of the poor and helpless. The Lord encourages the nation to repent of their sin or face the fires of judgment. After this introduction, Isaiah turns to describe the peace of the messianic age in 2:1-4. The day will come when all nations will obey God's word and live at peace. "The mountain of the LORD"—Jerusalem—will be raised up "and all the nations shall flow to it" (2:2-3, RSV). In the meantime, however, both Israel and the nations have exalted themselves against the Lord, and he will judge them in an awesome display of power. For Israel, God's judgment will bring great upheaval, including the loss of its leaders. Defiant and ruthless, the rulers will face either death or deportation. Chapter 3 ends by denouncing the pride and vanity of the women of Zion; they, too, will suffer disgrace. After Jerusalem is cleansed of its sin, the remnant will enjoy the rule of "the branch of the LORD," who will protect and shield his people (4:2-6).

In 5:1-7 Isaiah presents a short song about Israel as God's vineyard. The Lord did everything possible to ensure a yield of good grapes, but the vineyard produced nothing but bad fruit and had to be destroyed. Isaiah then pronounces six woes against Israel, and announces that the Assyrian army will invade the land. Against the backdrop of Israel's sin, Isaiah (ch 6) gives an account of the vision through which he was called as a prophet. Overwhelmed by the holiness of God and by his own sinfulness, Isaiah thought he was ruined, but when he was assured that his sins were forgiven, he responded positively to God's call in spite of the stubbornness of the nation to which he was sent.

One of the most stubborn individuals in all the nation was King Ahaz of Judah, and chapter 7 describes Isaiah's encounter with this godless ruler. When Ahaz was threatened by Damascus and the northern kingdom, he refused to believe Isaiah's promise that God would protect him. This was the occasion on which Isaiah gave Ahaz the sign of Immanuel (7:14). The "virgin" refers ultimately to Mary and "Immanuel" to Christ (Mt 1:23), but in the near fulfillment the child could be Isaiah's own son Maher-shalal-hash-baz (Is 8:3). (*See* four interpretations of this passage in Virgin Birth of Jesus.) This name (meaning "swift to plunder and quick to spoil," v 1, NLT mg) would be a sign that soon Judah's enemies would fall; "Immanuel" signified that God would be with Judah (v 10, NLT mg). However, if Ahaz appealed for help to the king of Assyria, Isaiah warned him, Assyria's powerful armies would one day invade Judah also (cf. 7:17-25; 8:6-8). The destruction brought by Assyria would plunge Judah into a time of famine and distress (8:21-22).

Nevertheless, the gloom and darkness associated with the Assyrian invasion would not last indefinitely, and 9:1-5 speaks of a time of peace and joy. Verses 6-7 introduce a child who would become a righteous King and would rule forever. This "Prince of Peace" is the Messiah, the "Mighty God" whose kingdom is described in 2:2-4.

For the immediate future, however, both Israel and Judah will suffer the agony of war as punishment for their sins. God is angry with his people because they are proud and arrogant, and their leaders disregard the pleas of the poor and needy. Civil war and foreign invasion will crush the hapless nation (9:8–10:4). But once Israel has been judged, God will turn his hand against Assyria, the instrument he has used to judge other nations. Because of her string of victories, Assyria is filled with pride and is eager for more triumph. Yet even at the moment when Jerusalem is about to succumb, God will cut down the Assyrian army like a cedar in Lebanon and spare his people (10:26-34).

After Assyria's defeat, Isaiah describes the restoration

of Israel and the powerful rule of the Messiah (ch 11). Both Jews and Gentiles will be attracted to Jerusalem to enjoy an era of peace and justice. Like David, the Messiah will have the Spirit of God resting upon him as he judges the wicked and protects the needy. To conclude these opening messages, Isaiah offers two short songs of praise that celebrate God's past deliverance and his promise of future blessing (ch 12).

Oracles against the Nations (13–23) Although Babylon is not the major power of the day, Isaiah begins his announcements of judgment with two chapters about the destruction of Assyria's neighbor to the south. Babylon will eventually conquer Jerusalem (between 605 and 586 BC), but the Medes (13:17) along with the Elamites will capture Babylon (539 BC). In spite of the glory to be achieved by future kings of Babylon, God will bring their pomp down to the grave (14:9-10). The chapter ends with short prophecies against Assyria and the Philistines.

One of Israel's oldest enemies was the nation of Moab, situated east of the Dead Sea. Even though it was a small country, Isaiah devotes two chapters to these descendants of Lot. Chapter 15 describes the extensive mourning that will overwhelm their cities. After a brief interlude urging the Moabites to submit to Israel and to her God (16:1-5), Isaiah notes that pride will lead to Moab's downfall. Sounds of weeping fill the land as the vines and fields wither and are trampled.

In chapter 17 the fourth oracle is directed against Damascus and Ephraim (the northern kingdom of Israel), probably reflecting their alliance against Judah about 734 BC. Both nations will face ruin, and Ephraim is condemned for abandoning the Lord, her "Savior" and "Rock" (17:10).

In chapters 18 and 19 Isaiah turns to the south and addresses Ethiopia and Egypt, countries that had strong links from 715–633 BC, when an Ethiopian named Shabako became pharaoh in Egypt. But Egypt is plagued with disunity and suffers greatly at the hands of Assyrian kings. In spite of the supposed wisdom of her leaders, Egypt faces economic and political ruin (19:5-15). Yet the time is coming when the Egyptians will be restored and will worship the God of Israel. Along with Assyria and Israel, Egypt will become a blessing (19:24). Some interpreters think this is a prophecy of the salvation of Gentiles during the church age, but others relate this day to the peace of the millennial age (cf. 2:2-4; 11:6-9). For the immediate future, however, Isaiah announces that Assyria will take many Egyptians and Ethiopians into captivity (ch 20).

A second oracle about Babylon (cf. 13:1–14:23) is contained in chapter 21, and Isaiah is staggered as he considers the impact of Babylon's fall (21:3-4). When Babylon collapses, the world will know that her gods were powerless (21:9; cf. Rv 14:8; 18:2).

Although it seems out of place among these oracles against the nations, chapter 22 condemns the city of Jerusalem. Like the nations, Jerusalem is full of revelry (22:2) but will soon experience the terrors of a siege. Since the people no longer rely on the Lord (v 11), he will hand them over to the enemy. Jerusalem's unfaithfulness is exemplified by Shebna, a high official guilty of pride and materialism whose position will be taken by the godly Eliakim (vv 15-23).

The last oracle (ch 23) is directed against the city of Tyre, which resisted capture until Alexander the Great conquered the island fortress in 332 BC. When Tyre fell, the economy of the entire Mediterranean world was shaken, for her ships had carried the goods of the nations far and wide.

Final Judgment and Blessing (24–27) This section functions as a grand finale to chapters 13–23 in that it anticipates God's judgment upon the nations and the inauguration of the kingdom of God. A defiled earth must bear its punishment (24:5-6) and even the forces of Satan face judgment (vv 21-22).

In chapter 25 Isaiah rejoices over God's great triumph and looks ahead to a day when death will be swallowed up and tears will be wiped from all faces (25:8). Israel's longtime enemies, symbolized by Moab, will be laid low (vv 10-12), but Jerusalem will be a stronghold for the righteous (26:1-3). In 26:7-19 the nation prays that these promises will become a reality. Verses 20-21 indicate that the Lord will indeed respond, pouring out his wrath upon a sin-cursed earth and upon Satan himself (27:1). When that takes place, Israel will be a fruitful vineyard, a blessing to the whole world (27:2-6; contrast 5:1-7). First, however, Israel will have to endure war and exile, and then the remnant will return to Jerusalem.

A Series of Woes (28–33) Returning to his own historical period, Isaiah pronounces a series of woes upon both the northern and southern kingdoms, as well as one upon Assyria (ch 33). Chapter 28 begins with a description of the fading power of Samaria, the capital of the northern kingdom. Verses 7-10 portray the leaders of Judah in the same light; they have disregarded Isaiah's message and are out of touch with God. Judgment is on the way, and their false preparation (vv 15, 18) will be of no avail. God will fight against Israel (vv 21-22), and even Jerusalem will be put under siege until God in his mercy intervenes (29:1-8). Because of their hypocritical worship, the people deserve to be punished, but in the future Israel will again acknowledge the Lord and be made physically and spiritually whole (29:17-24).

Chapters 30 and 31 denounce Judah's proposed alliance with Egypt in the effort to thwart Assyria. God wants his people to trust him, not their unreliable neighbors to the south. The Lord promises to protect Jerusalem (30:18; 31:5) and defeat the invading Assyrian army (30:31-33; 31:8-9). None can stand before his mighty sword.

Continuing on this positive note, Isaiah goes on to emphasize the righteous rule of the messianic king in chapters 32 and 33. Zion will enjoy peace and security at last (32:2, 17-18; 33:6), a great change from Isaiah's own time. In eighth-century BC Judah the women might feel secure (32:9), but the Assyrian troops will devastate the crops and precipitate widespread mourning. However, the lamenting will soon end, as the prophet pronounces woe upon Assyria in 33:1. After Isaiah prays for the destruction of Assyria (33:2-9), God promises to take action (vv 10-12). Gone will be the enemy soldiers and officials, for the Lord will save his people and bring them justice and security.

More Judgment and Blessing (34–35) This section forms a climax to chapters 28–33. Once more, cataclysmic judgment precedes a time of blessing and restoration. In chapter 34 Isaiah depicts a judgment of cosmic dimensions as he moves to a consideration of the last days. Heaven and earth endure the wrath of God that is poured out upon the nations, and verse 4 provides the basis for John's description of the great tribulation in Revelation 6:13-14. Edom (like Moab; see Is 25:10-12) represents a world judged by the sword of the Lord in his day of vengeance.

Chapter 35, on the other hand, speaks of joy and restoration in a passage that pulsates with life. A blooming desert corresponds to the physical and spiritual age when God will come to redeem his people. Both the return of the Israelites from the Babylonian captivity and the second coming of Christ fit this glorious scene.

Historical Interlude (36–39) These chapters form the hinge that connects the two halves of the book. Chapters 36 and 37 contain the fulfillment of Isaiah's prophecies about Assyria's collapse, and chapters 38 and 39 introduce the Babylonian captivity that forms the backdrop for chapters 40–66. In 701 BC King Sennacherib of Assyria demands the unconditional surrender of Jerusalem. He sends his field commander to address the people and try to gain their submission. With persuasive words, the commander tries to convince the city that surrender is the best policy. Amazingly the people do not panic, and King Hezekiah asks Isaiah to pray for the beleaguered city. The prophet does so and announces that the proud Assyrians will not triumph. Instead, they suffer a terrible disaster as the angel of the Lord strikes down 185,000 men.

Chapters 38 and 39 relate another crisis in Hezekiah's life when he becomes desperately ill. Miraculously, God heals him, and Hezekiah praises the Lord for his gracious intervention. When the king of Babylon sends envoys to congratulate Hezekiah on his recovery, Hezekiah foolishly shows these messengers his royal treasures. Isaiah solemnly announces that someday the armies of Babylon will capture Jerusalem, plunder the land, and take away these treasures.

The Return from Babylon (40–48) The Babylonian captivity eventually comes, but Isaiah promises that it will end. God, the incomparably powerful Creator, is far greater than any king, nation, or god, and he will bring his people back to Jerusalem. To accomplish this return from exile, God raises up Cyrus, the king of Persia (41:2, 25). The Lord does not forget his people, and he encourages them to take heart and to rejoice.

In chapter 42 we are introduced to a person even more significant than Cyrus the Persian. Verses 1-7 (the first of four Servant Songs) describe the servant of the Lord, who will bring justice to the nations and will be "a light for the Gentiles" (42:6). This is the Messiah, and the redemption he will accomplish on Calvary (cf. ch 53) is greater than the release from Babylon. In light of the good news associated with the servant, Isaiah praises the Lord for punishing the wicked and rescuing his wayward people. Chapter 43 declares that nothing will stand in the way of Israel's return, and the Lord will remember their sins no more. In fact, he will pour out his Spirit on their descendants (44:3).

A God so great is far more powerful than any idol. In 44:6-20 Isaiah makes use of satire to show the worthlessness of man-made images. God alone has the power to create and to restore, and he will bring Cyrus on the scene to effect the release of the exiles and to begin the rebuilding of Jerusalem. Chapters 46 and 47 contrast the God of Israel and the idols of Babylon. When God raises up Cyrus, Babylon's idols will be unable to save their nation, and the queen of kingdoms (47:5) will collapse along with her sorcerers and astrologers. The final chapter in this section (ch 48) restates God's purpose of gaining release of the Israelites from Babylon through his chosen ally, Cyrus of Persia.

Salvation through the Servant of the Lord (49–57) Chapters 49–53 contain the final three Servant Songs (cf. also 42:1-7), culminating in the death of the servant for the sins of the world (52:13–53:12). In the second Servant Song (49:1-7), Isaiah describes the call and ministry of the servant, noting that he will face strong opposition as he accomplishes salvation for Israel and the nations. The rest of chapter 49 deals primarily with the way God will bring Israel back from exile. Soon the land will be filled with a mighty throng (vv 19-21), and the Gentiles will acknowledge Israel and her God (vv 22-23).

Although Israel has fully deserved the exile because of her sins (50:1-3), the suffering endured by the servant (vv 4-11; the third Servant Song) is wholly undeserved. The beating and mocking of verse 6 are prophetic of Christ's experience (cf. Mt 27:26, 30; Mk 15:19). In verses 10-11 of Isaiah 50 the whole nation is challenged to trust in the Lord, as the servant did. There is, in fact, a believing remnant who obey the Lord (51:1-8), and the Lord promises that he will restore them to their homeland. Israel has drunk the cup of God's wrath (vv 17, 22), but the good news of release from exile causes even the ruins of Jerusalem to burst into songs of joy (52:7-10).

Yet the best news of all is salvation from sin; the final Servant Song (52:13–53:12) tells how Christ wins freedom for those held in bondage to sin. In this brief passage we learn how Christ suffers rejection (53:3) and even disfigurement (52:14). Led like a lamb to the slaughter (53:7), he carries our sins in his body as he dies in ignominy. The people think he is suffering for his own sins (v 4), but he is "pierced" and "crushed for our iniquities" (v 5). The first and last paragraphs of this section (52:13-15; 53:10-12) state that through his suffering the servant is highly exalted. What seems like a terrible defeat is actually victory over death and Satan and brings salvation for many.

As a direct result of the servant's death, great joy comes to all people. In chapter 54 this joy is reflected in Jerusalem's new status as the Lord's wife. Her descendants will be numerous and eager to learn from the Lord. For the first time the plural "servants of the LORD" appears (54:17), apparently including all believers, whether Jew or Gentile (cf. 65:8-9, 13-15). Joy and prosperity also characterize chapter 55, an invitation to a great spiritual banquet. All people are urged to turn to the Lord who keeps his promises to Israel. In 56:1-8, foreigners are invited to come to God's "holy mountain" in Jerusalem, for the temple will be a house of prayer for all the nations (56:7; cf. Mt 21:13).

Believing Gentiles are contrasted sharply with unbelieving Jews, and in 56:9–57:13 Isaiah returns again to the theme of judgment. Israel suffers because her leaders are wicked and because the people are guilty of idolatry. Spiritual healing is available, but unless individuals repent, they cannot be part of the remnant who will return from exile and enjoy peace in the Promised Land.

Ultimate Blessing and Final Judgment (58–66) The last nine chapters of Isaiah emphasize redemption and glory, but the reality of judgment is also very much in evidence. In fact, chapters 58 and 59 bemoan the sins of Israel. The people are hypocritical in their worship; they are selfish and fail to keep the Sabbath. Lying, oppression, and murder separate the people from God. When Isaiah openly confesses these sins (59:12-13), the Lord suddenly takes action on behalf of his people. Like a mighty warrior, he rescues the believing remnant from Babylon and brings them back to Jerusalem.

In chapter 60 the glory and wealth of Jerusalem reach new heights. Both the city and the sanctuary are adorned with splendor, matching the prosperity of Solomon's reign. Just as the nations treated Solomon with honor, so earth's leaders will assist and strengthen the returning exiles. While it is true that the Persian government did help the Jews repeatedly, the conditions described here will have their ultimate fulfillment during the Millennium and in connection with the new Jerusalem (cf. Rv 21:23; 22:5). The ancient ruins will be rebuilt (Is 61:4), and the Lord will fulfill the covenant made with Abraham and David (Is 61:8; cf. Gn 12:1-3; Is 55:3). Jerusalem will be the city of the holy people, the redeemed of the Lord (Is 62:12), and the Lord will take delight in her (v 4).

In order to accomplish salvation for his people, God will have to judge the ungodly first. The great trampling of the winepress (63:2-3) graphically portrays the judgment process and is linked with the Day of the Lord (cf. 13:3; 34:2). Since God has promised to intervene on behalf of his people, Isaiah prays for the realization of that promise (63:7–64:12). He recalls God's faithfulness in the past and pleads that he will again have mercy upon his suffering people.

The answer to Isaiah's prayer is found in chapter 65. God does promise to give the Holy Land back to his servants, to those who worship him and obey him. But for that segment of the nation that continues in its obstinacy, God promises anguish and destruction. The ultimate joy of God's servants is contained in a description of new heavens and a new earth (65:17-25). Peace, long life, and prosperity will be among the blessings enjoyed in an era that seems to combine features of the Millennium and the eternal state (cf. ch 60).

In a fitting summary, chapter 66 ties together the themes of salvation and judgment. God will comfort Jerusalem and abundantly bless her, but sinners are the objects of his wrath. Those who honor him will endure forever, but those who rebel will suffer everlasting rejection.

See also Isaiah (Person); Israel, History of; Messiah; Prophecy; Prophet, Prophetess; Servant of the Lord; Virgin Birth of Jesus.

ISCAH Haran's daughter and Milcah's sister (Gn 11:29).

ISCARIOT *See* Judas #1.

ISHBAH Mered's son by Bithiah, the daughter of the pharaoh (1 Chr 4:17).

ISHBAK One of the sons of Abraham by Keturah (Gn 25:2; 1 Chr 1:32).

ISHBI-BENOB Giant who nearly killed David. During one of his many battles with the Philistines, David grew faint and was nearly killed by Ishbi-benob. Abishai killed the giant, saving David's life (2 Sm 21:16).

ISHBOSHETH Alternate name for Eshbaal, Saul's son and successor to Israel's throne (2 Sm 2–4). *See* Eshbaal.

ISHHOD Hammoleketh's son from Manasseh's tribe (1 Chr 7:18).

ISHI
1. Appaim's son, the father of Sheshan and a descendant of Judah through Jerahmeel's line (1 Chr 2:31).
2. Man from Judah's tribe whose descendants were Zoheth and Ben-zoheth (1 Chr 4:20).
3. Simeonite whose four sons led 500 men to Mt Seir, where they destroyed the remnant Amalekites and settled their own people (1 Chr 4:42).
4. One of the leaders of the half-tribe of Manasseh east of the Jordan (1 Chr 5:24).
5. Name of God, meaning "my husband," by which Israel will one day address him (Hos 2:16).
   See also God, Names of.

ISHIAH* KJV spelling of Isshiah, Izrahiah's son, in 1 Chronicles 7:3. *See* Isshiah #1.

ISHIJAH Harim's son, who obeyed Ezra's exhortation to divorce his pagan wife (Ezr 10:31).

ISHMA Etam's son from Judah's tribe (1 Chr 4:3).

ISHMAEL

1. Abraham's first son, born of Hagar, Sarah's Egyptian handmaid, at the instigation of Sarah herself. God promised to make a great nation of the childless Abraham (Gn 12:2), assuring him that his son would be his heir (15:4). But when Sarah was past 75 years old and still barren, she invoked the custom whereby a childless wife gave her maid to her husband as concubine and laid claim to the offspring of their union (16:1-2). When Hagar conceived, the reproach attendant on barrenness prompted the maid to behave contemptuously toward her mistress, and with Abraham's consent Sarah dealt harshly with her and she fled. An angel sent Hagar back to submit to her mistress and promised her a son to be named Ishmael meaning "God hears" (16:9-11). The boy was born near Hebron when Abraham was 86 years old (13:18; 16:16).

Abraham and Sarah received him as the son of God's promise, as attested by their disbelief when the forthcoming birth of Isaac was announced (17:17; 18:12), and by Abraham's subsequent wish that Ishmael should be accepted of God (17:18). At age 13 he participated in the institution of circumcision as a witness of God's covenant with Abraham (17:9-14, 22-27), and the Lord promised to make Ishmael the father of 12 princes, from which would come a great nation, though the covenant was to be established with Isaac (17:20-21).

There is no evidence that Ishmael was out of favor until Isaac's weaning at about three years of age. When Sarah saw Ishmael "making fun" of her son Isaac, she determined that the son of a slave woman should not be heir with her son Isaac, and she demanded that Ishmael and Hagar be banished. Although vexed, Abraham received reassurance from the Lord and sent them away with some provisions. It was then clear to Abraham that Isaac, not Ishmael, was the son of God's promise.

Hagar survived in the wilderness with the guidance of an angel, and Ishmael became a hunter of wild animals. He settled in the wilderness of Paran and married an Egyptian woman (21:20-21). Little else is recorded of him, except that he lived to assist in the burial of Abraham (25:9-10), gave his daughter Mahalath in marriage (28:9), and died at the age of 137 (25:17). The names of his 12 sons and their settlements are recorded in Genesis 25:13-16. In subsequent history, a caravan of Ishmaelite traders (also called Midianites, cf. Jgs 8:22-24) bought Joseph from his brothers and sold him in Egypt (Gn 37:25-28; 39:1).

Though Isaac, rather than Ishmael, inherited the covenantal blessings, it is clear that the covenant was not the only means whereby divine favor could be bestowed. Abraham and Sarah overestimated the importance of Ishmael in God's plan by mistaking him for the heir of covenant promises, but they also underrated God's intentions for him by excluding him altogether from inheritance with Isaac.

In the NT, Paul alludes to Ishmael while urging the Galatians not to see the law as a yoke (Gal 4:22). He states that those who trust the law instead of putting their faith in God's promises do not inherit the kingdom, just as the son of the slave woman did not receive inheritance with the son of the free woman (v 30).

2. Son of Nethaniah, son of Elishama, of the royal family of Zedekiah (2 Kgs 25:25). He was prompted by Baalis, king of the Ammonites, to assassinate Gedaliah, Judean governor of the puppet regime, which Nebuchadnezzar left behind at Mizpah at the time of the Babylonian exile. Gedaliah ignored advance warning of the plot and refused to allow Johanan to assassinate Ishmael first

(Jer 40:14-16). While sharing a meal with Gedaliah, Ishmael and ten companions killed him, along with the Babylonian troops accompanying him. The next day he persuaded a group of 80 pilgrims passing from the north to the temple at Jerusalem to enter Mizpah, where he killed all but 10 who ransomed their lives with stores of food. Hiding all the bodies in a cistern, Ishmael took captive the rest of the population of Mizpah, including Jeremiah and women of the royal family, and set out to join the Ammonites. But Johanan, with an armed force, overtook Ishmael at Gibeon and rescued the captives, whereupon Ishmael fled to Ammonite territory (Jer 41).
3. Son of Azel, a Benjamite of the family of Saul (1 Chr 8:38; 9:44).
4. Father of Zebadiah, the governor of the house of Judah under Jehoshaphat (2 Chr 19:11).
5. Son of Jehohanan, and one of the commanders who allied with Jehoiada the priest to enthrone the child Joash and thus end the reign of Athaliah (2 Chr 23:1).
6. Son of Pashhur, and one of the priests who put away foreign wives during Ezra's reforms (Ezr 10:22).

ISHMAELITE Descendant of Ishmael, Abraham's son by Hagar. *See* Ishmael #1.

ISHMAIAH
1. Warrior from Benjamin's tribe who joined David at Ziklag in his struggle against King Saul. Ishmaiah was one of David's ambidextrous archers and slingers (1 Chr 12:4).
2. Obadiah's son, a chief officer in Zebulun's tribe in David's time (1 Chr 27:19).

ISHMEELITE* KJV spelling for Ishmaelite (Gn 37:25-28; 39:1). *See* Ishmaelite.

ISHMERAI Elpaal's son and a chief in Benjamin's tribe (1 Chr 8:18).

ISHOD* KJV spelling of Ishhod, Hammoleketh's son (1 Chr 7:18). *See* Ishhod.

ISHPAH Beriah's son from Benjamin's tribe (1 Chr 8:16).

ISHPAN Shashak's son and a leader in Benjamin's tribe (1 Chr 8:22).

ISHTAR* Ancient Babylonian fertility goddess. *See* Gilgamesh Epic.

ISH-TOB* KJV translation for "men of Tob" in 2 Samuel 10:6-8. *See* Tob.

ISHUAH* KJV spelling of Ishvah, Asher's son, in Genesis 46:17. *See* Ishvah.

ISHUAI* KJV spelling of Ishvi, Asher's son, in 1 Chronicles 7:30. *See* Ishvi #1.

ISHUI* KJV spelling of Ishvi, Saul's son, in 1 Samuel 14:49. *See* Ishvi #2.

ISHVAH Asher's son (Gn 46:17; 1 Chr 7:30).

ISHVI
1. Asher's third son (Gn 46:17; 1 Chr 7:30) and founder of the Ishvite family (Nm 26:44).
2. A variant form of Ishbosheth, one of King Saul's sons (1 Sm 14:49).

ISHVITE Descendant of Ishvi, Asher's son (Nm 26:44). *See* Ishvi #1.

ISIS* Legendary wife of Osiris. *See* Egypt, Egyptian (Religion).

ISMAIAH* KJV spelling of Ishmaiah, a warrior from Benjamin's tribe who joined David at Ziklag in 1 Chronicles 12:4. *See* Ishmaiah #1.

ISMAKIAH Levite overseer of things dedicated at the temple during Hezekiah's reform (2 Chr 31:13).

ISPAH* KJV spelling of Ishpah, Beriah's son, 1 Chronicles 8:16. *See* Ishpah.

ISRAEL (Person) Name meaning "one who struggles with God" or "God struggles" (Gn 32:28, NLT mg). It was given to Isaac's son Jacob and to his descendants (35:9-12; cf. Dt 6:1-4). *See* Jacob #1; Israel, History of.

ISRAEL (Place) *See* Palestine; Caanan, Caananite.

ISRAEL, History of An account of God's sovereign purpose in calling a people out of paganism and establishing them as witnesses for the true faith among the nations, of God's sovereign power in protecting them from extinction, of his sovereign justice in dealing with their departure from his ways of holiness, of God's sovereign grace in forgiving their sins and restoring them to fellowship with himself by providing through them a Savior for the entire world.

PREVIEW
• Patriarchal Age
• Sojourn in Egypt
• The Exodus
• Wilderness Wanderings
• The Conquest
• The Judges
• The United Monarchy
• The Divided Kingdom
• The Restoration
• The Intertestamental Period
• The Roman Period

Patriarchal Age The story of Israel begins with Abraham, whom God called first at Ur, and perhaps later at Haran (Acts 7:2-4), to leave Mesopotamia and go into a land to which God would direct the way. In calling Abraham, God made with him a covenant (Gn 12:1-3) that promised him a land, special divine favor ("I will bless those who bless you, and the one who curses you I will curse," NASB), and the privilege of being a channel of blessing to the entire world ("In you all the families of the earth shall be blessed," NASB). In Genesis 12:4-8 God confirmed this unconditional covenant, promising Abraham this new land forever, along with innumerable descendants. Subsequently, in Genesis 15:1-21, God again confirmed the covenant but added the significant prediction that the guarantee of holding Canaan in perpetuity did not mean occupation of the land in every generation. God also spelled out the limits of the Promised Land (from the river of Egypt to the Euphrates, some 500 to 600 miles or 804 to 965 kilometers in extent). A final confirmation of the covenant to Abraham appears in Genesis 17:6-8. It guaranteed the land of Canaan to Abraham's posterity and added that kings (an anticipation of the Davidic dynasty) would arise in his line. The covenant was confirmed to Abraham's son Isaac (Gn 26:3-5) and his grandson Jacob (ch 28).

This period is known as the patriarchal age in Hebrew history. The patriarchs were Abraham, Isaac, and Jacob. They were called patriarchs because they were fathers, not only to their immediate families, but also to the extended family of Hebrews, over which they exercised a fatherly control. They served as political, legal, and spiritual heads of their migratory community, looking after their interests and leading them in worship. Periodically they built altars on which they offered sacrifices. That the patriarchal community was very large can be seen from Genesis 14:14, which says that Abraham had 318 armed men in his camp. If one assumes that most of the men were married and had one or more children each, the total extended family may have numbered in excess of 1,000.

Additional developments in the life of Abraham and Jacob were particularly important for world history. Abraham, frustrated at not having an heir, accepted Sarah's suggestion to obtain an heir by the slave girl Hagar. (This was also the custom of the land.) The son born was named Ishmael, progenitor of the Arabs. Thus Abraham is revered by Arabs and Muslims as well as by Jews and Christians. He is the father of the Jews through his son Isaac, child of promise. He holds a special place in Christianity as an example of Christ, through whom all Christians obtain their salvation.

Jacob, a scheming scoundrel in his earlier years, wound up in exile in northern Mesopotamia for 20 years in the home of his uncle Laban. There he married Leah and Rachel and fathered the sons who became the progenitors of the 12 tribes of Israel. On his return to Palestine he met God along the banks of the Jabbok River (Gn 32), and God changed his name to Israel ("a prince of God," KJV mg).

The patriarchal period in Canaan lasted for 215 years. One estimate places Abraham's entry into Canaan at about 2085 BC, when he was 75 years of age. Jacob and his sons migrated to Egypt to escape a severe famine in Canaan in about 1870 BC. During much of the patriarchal period, Palestine experienced a decline in population and was occupied largely by nomadic or seminomadic tribes. It was relatively easy for the Hebrews to enter such a situation. After 1900 Palestine began to enjoy more settled conditions. Shortly thereafter, the Hebrews made the trek into Egypt.

Sojourn in Egypt If Jacob and his sons entered Egypt about 1870 BC, it was the period of the Middle Kingdom. And by that time other migrants from Asia were coming in increasing numbers. The Hebrews settled in Goshen, in the eastern delta region, under the protecting care of Joseph, who held a position at the Egyptian court roughly equivalent to that of prime minister. As more and more Asiatic Hyksos came into Egypt, they began to take over the country—northern Egypt at least. During this same time the Hebrews became increasingly numerous. Some who hold to a different chronology believe the Hebrews were welcomed into Egypt during the days of Hyksos domination (after 1750 BC). At any rate, by about 1580 BC native Egyptian princes regained control of the country and expelled many of the Asiatics.

In process of time there arose a king over Egypt who "knew not Joseph" (Ex 1:8, KJV). Very possibly this meant that a native Egyptian dynasty had arisen in Egypt and they were apprehensive over the fact that the growing numbers and wealth of the Hebrews might jeopardize their own supremacy. But Egyptian measures to subjugate the Hebrews and reduce their birthrate had a reverse effect (Ex 1:12). Finally, the Egyptians ordered the killing of all male Hebrew infants at birth. Among those who disobeyed were the parents of Moses, who set him afloat in a waterproof basket made of reeds. Found by a daughter of Pharaoh, he

was brought up in the Egyptian court, was given a first-class education, and became a high official of the realm.

At the age of 40, Moses identified himself with his own people. He killed an Egyptian in defense of a fellow Hebrew, and immediately fled to the land of Midian in the northeastern part of the Sinai Peninsula. He married and lived there for 40 years, becoming thoroughly familiar with the geography and the ways of the wilderness through which he would later lead the Hebrews. The Egyptians continued to oppress the Hebrew people severely until they cried urgently to God for deliverance. In response, God confronted Moses in the famous burning bush experience and called on him to return to Egypt and lead the people back into the land of Canaan (Ex 3–4). He was to have the help of his brother, Aaron.

The Exodus Understandably the pharaoh of Egypt was reluctant to permit the Hebrews to leave permanently. The value of this great labor force was incalculable. But finally, after suffering a series of ten plagues, lasting perhaps a year, the Egyptians were persuaded to let the Hebrews go (Ex 7–12).

The plagues had a theological as well as a practical purpose. They discredited the gods of Egypt and exalted the most high God of heaven (Ex 12:12). The plagues clearly discredited specific gods of Egypt (e.g., the Nile was worshiped as Hapi, plague one; the frog, worshiped as Heqt, plague two; the bull, worshiped as Ptah, plague five; the sun, worshiped as Amon-Re/Aton, plague nine). Taken together, they struck a direct blow at the Egyptian pantheon.

Just before the last plague, which was the night in which the death angel invaded the homes of the Egyptians, the Israelites made the Passover sacrifice according to divine instructions. This involved killing a lamb for each household (unless the household was too small; in that event, households could combine). Anyone who was careless about applying the blood to the doorpost or who rejected this divine provision came under the judgment of God. After the death of the firstborn throughout the land, the Egyptians begged the Hebrews to leave. Their company numbered 600,000 men over 20 years of age, plus women and children, for a total of over 2,500,000. In addition they took their flocks and herds and personal belongings.

The date they left Egypt is a matter of continuing debate. Traditionally a date of about 1446 BC is given for the exodus (cf. 1 Kgs 6:1, which places the exodus 480 years before construction of the temple started in 966 BC) and 1406 BC for the Conquest under Joshua, and there do not seem to be any compelling arguments for rejecting that position. But a great many scholars prefer 1275 BC for a variety of reasons.

The early date of the exodus would place the later years of the wilderness wanderings and the subsequent conquest of Palestine during the reigns of Amenhotep III and IV (1412–1366), a time when the pharaohs allowed Egyptian control of Palestine to disintegrate. When the Egyptians did reassert their power, about 1300, they restricted their movements largely to the coastal area, and thus did not come in contact with the Hebrews who were living in the hill country of Judea, Samaria, and Galilee.

Wilderness Wanderings The wilderness wanderings were an important interlude in the history of Israel. During those years, significant and basic institutions came into existence at God's command. At Sinai, Moses delivered to Israel the law, the pattern of the tabernacle (which later became the model for the temple) and orders for its operation, as well as detailed instructions for the priesthood and sacrificial system of worship.

The period of the wanderings was truly a remarkable

time. The presence of God was evidenced by a pillar of cloud that hovered over the people by day and a pillar of fire by night. God provided food in the form of manna, periodically provided water by miraculous means, and made sure that clothes did not wear out. In spite of all that, the people murmured and complained continually.

At Sinai, God gave the law (Ex 19:2–24:18), and the people promptly made a commitment to keep it (24:3). Then God gave the pattern for the tabernacle and its furniture (chs 25–27, 30–31, 35–40) and established the priesthood (chs 28–29). While Moses was on the mountain receiving God's revelation, the people grew restless and clamored for gods they could see. Even Aaron was carried away with the idolatrous wave and supervised the casting of a golden calf and building of an altar before it. The fact that they turned to Egyptian cattle worship so readily indicates that paganism must have made deep inroads among them while in captivity (chs 32–34). Moses' intercessory response to God's announcement that he would destroy Israel because of her idolatry led to a divine determination to execute judgment on only the worst offenders (32:9-14).

Subsequently, God revealed the legal and priestly order (Lv 1:1–27:34). Among the divinely appointed institutions described or alluded to in Leviticus are several special days or feasts, including the Sabbath, Passover, Feast of Unleavened Bread, Firstfruits, Pentecost or Feast of Weeks, Feast of Trumpets, Day of Atonement, Feast of Tabernacles, the Year of Sabbath, and the Year of Jubilee.

After camping at Sinai for about a year, the Israelites got their orders to go forward (Nm 10:11-12). Miriam (Moses' sister) and Aaron criticized Moses' leadership and suffered divine punishment as a consequence (ch 12). When the people arrived at Kadesh-barnea, the gate to southern Palestine, they were frightened by the report of most of the spies who had been reconnoitering in Canaan and decided that they should not advance into Canaan. They called for a new leader to bring them back to Egypt. God declared that the entire generation would wander in the wilderness until the adults had died. Only Joshua and Caleb (the two spies in favor of invading immediately) would enter the Promised Land (14:26-30). Near the end of the period of wandering, Moses also lost the privilege of entering the land by an act of disobedience.

The Conquest The latter part of the book of Numbers describes how Moses led the Israelites to victory over the peoples living east of the Jordan River. Reuben, Gad, and the half-tribe of Manasseh requested permission to settle there and reluctantly were allowed to do so on the condition that they would join the rest of the Israelites in conquering Canaan before settling down. Prior to victories in Transjordan, a new census of adult males was taken in order to determine the military capabilities of Israel and to provide a basis for equitable division of the land they were about to enter. The number of males above 20 years of age was 601,730 (Nm 26:51). The book of Deuteronomy consists primarily of a series of speeches delivered by Moses in a covenant renewal ceremony on the plains of Moab just before his death and the appointment of Joshua as leader.

Joshua lost no time in moving forward. Spies sent across the Jordan to Jericho to reconnoiter reported a situation quite different from what the Hebrews had experienced at Kadesh-barnea a generation earlier. Now the people of Canaan were terrified because they had heard of the numerical strength and victories of the Hebrews. Apparently the day after the spies returned, Joshua moved the people to the edge of the Jordan and prepared to cross over. The waters parted for them here as the Red Sea had parted earlier.

The narrative of conquest that appears in the book of Joshua is not a detailed battle account. It describes a thrust into the middle of Palestine around Jericho and Ai, a southerly drive to defeat the Amorite league, and a northern campaign against Hazor and other towns. The history of Joshua is extremely telescoped, for Joshua's major military action must have required about six years. Joshua's friend Caleb was 79 when the Conquest began and 85 after the last great battle with Jabin, king of Hazor (Jos 14:7-10).

When the war was over, major strongholds (e.g., Jerusalem) still remained in enemy hands, but the land west of the Jordan was allocated to the nine and a half Hebrew tribes. The task of reducing enemy towns was left to the individual tribes in whose land they were located. The Joshua account was not so much a narrative of Israelite battle prowess as of God's faithfulness and intervention on behalf of his people. For example, at Jericho they did not attack but merely followed divine orders and watched the defenses collapse; at Gibeon hailstones killed more Amorites than Israelite soldiers did (Jos 10:7-11).

The Judges Joshua died some 30 years after he had led the Hebrews into Canaan, and he was followed by a series of divinely appointed leaders who ruled sometimes over the whole of Israel as a loose confederacy and sometimes over one or more tribes. They were judges, civil functionaries, and military leaders all at the same time.

The book of Judges pictures a series of recurring cycles: apostasy from God, punishment in the form of oppression by neighboring tribes, cries to God for relief, release from bondage under the leadership of a judge, and a period of rest from oppression.

Establishment of the chronology of the judges is one of the thorniest problems of Scripture. Adding up all years of oppression and rest mentioned in the book gives a total of 410. The book of Acts gives a total of 450 years from the days of Joshua to Samuel (Acts 13:19). The difference in Acts may be accounted for by the addition of 40 years of Eli's ministry (1 Sm 4:18). Allowing 410 years for the period of the judges, about 30 for the Conquest to the judges, and 40 for the wilderness wanderings, means 480 years from 1050 BC, the date for Saul's kingship, and would give a date of about 1530 for the exodus. This is about 100 years more than even the early date for the exodus. The most probable explanation is that there is some overlap in oppressions and judgeships. For instance, the activities of Jephthah were centered on the eastern frontier, those of Samson in the Philistine plain to the southwest, and those of Deborah and Barak in the north.

The United Monarchy Because of the weakness of Israel resulting from political disunity and the ineptness and corruption of both Eli's and Samuel's sons, the people of Israel called for a king to rule over them. This demand was in reality a rejection of the divine plan of theocracy—the rule of God. God granted the Hebrews' wish but warned them of the disadvantages of monarchy (1 Sm 8:9-21). The concept of kingship was not new to Israel. It had been hinted at in Genesis 49:10 and Numbers 24:17, and Moses had made some very clear statements about it in Deuteronomy 17:14-20.

The first stage of Hebrew monarchy is commonly called the united monarchy because all Israel was ruled by a single king. This period lasted for 120 years—encompassing the 40-year reigns of Saul (Acts 13:21), David (2 Sm 5:5), and Solomon (1 Kgs 11:42).

The people asked for a king, and God granted them one, but not one like those of the surrounding nations. The Hebrew king was to be a man who followed God's dictates in his public and private life, who did not intrude into the affairs of the priesthood, and who did not fall into idolatry, but exerted all his influence to keep the people faithful to God. If he failed in any of these respects, he ran the risk of being deposed by God, of having his line brought to an end, or even of having the people fall into captivity to a foreign power. All this must be kept in mind when evaluating the reigns of Saul, David, Solomon, and the kings of the divided monarchy.

Saul began well. He won a great victory over the Ammonites at Jabesh-gilead and showed considerable wisdom in administrative matters. But after about two years he intruded into the priest's office to offer sacrifice, bringing the divine prediction that his kingdom would be taken from him (1 Sm 13:8-14). He would go on to enjoy great military victory and ability as a ruler until about the middle of his reign.

After Saul's disobedience to God's command to totally destroy the Amalekites, the Lord repudiated Saul and instructed Samuel to anoint David privately as future king of Israel. David's rise to prominence was spurred by his victory over Goliath and the accompanying defeat of the Philistines. Saul later made David commander of the army, and the young man soon earned a reputation greater than that of the king himself. Saul, who had become increasingly mentally disturbed after his relationship with God was broken, began to make attempts on David's life, and for the last years of Saul's reign David lived as a fugitive. Meanwhile, the Philistines got completely out of control and finally killed Saul and most of his sons in the great battle of Mt Gilboa, which gave the Philistines control over much of Palestine west of the Jordan (1 Sm 31:1-7).

Soon David became king in Judah with his capital in Hebron. A son of Saul, Ishbosheth, established himself at Mahanaim, east of the Jordan. For seven years the two tiny kingdoms existed side by side (2 Sm 2:2-11). But after the Israelite king and his army commander were assassinated, David became ruler of a united Hebrew kingdom.

Not long after the beginning of his reign (1010–970 BC) David completely defeated and subjugated the Philistines. Soon thereafter he captured Jerusalem, making it the capital of the united kingdom. During succeeding years, David built up an empire (2 Sm 8:10; 1 Chr 18–19), conquering Moab, Edom, Damascus, Zobah, and Ammon, so he controlled territory from the Gulf of Aqaba (a branch of the Red Sea) and the Sinai in the south almost to the Euphrates in the north. Moreover, he established good relations, if not an alliance, with Tyre. The establishment of David's empire was possible because of a power vacuum in the Middle East. The Egyptians, Mycenaeans, Hittites, and Assyrians were either decadent or removed from the stage of history. The Phoenicians, a peaceful commercial people, were also free to expand their trade, and they were happy to sell cedar to David for his palace and the temple.

Without doubt, David was Israel's greatest king. Jerusalem came to be known as the city of David. When the king wanted to build the temple as God's house, God replied that his son should do it instead. But God would in a very real sense build David's house; he made a covenant with David, promising him that his house (dynasty, kingdom, throne) would be established forever (2 Sm 7). Christ, the infinite One who came from the line of David, alone was capable of fulfilling this divine promise (see Lk 1:31-33; Acts 2:29-36; 13:32-39; 15:14-17).

Like other Oriental monarchs, David fell into the practice of keeping a harem. Scripture names 8 wives and 21 children and refers to other wives and concubines. Such a situation opened the door to family rivalries and questions about succession to the throne. Two sons, Absalom and Adonijah, made a try for the throne, but both efforts were squelched. Solomon, son of David's favorite wife, Bathsheba, became the next king.

Solomon (970–930 BC) was a man of peace and a builder of palaces, cities, fortifications, and the temple. He fortified cities all over his realm and outfitted cities for his chariot corps and cavalry units. With the help of the Phoenicians, he built a seaport and kept a fleet at Ezion-geber, near modern Eilat on the Gulf of Aqaba. He greatly enlarged Jerusalem by enclosing the temple area to the north of David's city and the southwestern hill now known as Zion. His best-known project was the temple, which took seven years to build. Twice the size of the tabernacle, it was built on the same basic plan; it measured 90 feet (27.4 meters) long and 30 feet (9.1 meters) wide and had magnificent appointments. But he also constructed a palace complex that took 13 years to complete. This included an armory, a throne room, the king's private residence, and a house for the daughter of pharaoh.

Apparently much influenced by the spiritual testimony of David and desiring God's blessing on his rule, Solomon made a great sacrifice to God at Gibeon near the beginning of his reign. God met him there and offered to grant whatever he might request. Solomon asked for understanding and wisdom to govern God's people (1 Kgs 3:9). His God-given wisdom is apparent in many administrative decisions and official policies and building plans.

Unfortunately, Solomon did not show such wisdom in maintaining a harem of 700 wives and 300 concubines or in excessive expenditures that left the state in serious financial straits. He even erected places of worship for his foreign wives, thus subsidizing their idolatries and incurring the wrath of God. In fact, foreign wives and their idolatry proved to be his downfall; before Solomon died, God informed him that for this reason he would divide the kingdom at his death and give most of it to someone other than Solomon's son. But for David's sake, God would keep Judah and Jerusalem in the hands of the Davidic line (1 Kgs 11:9-13).

The Divided Kingdom After the death of Solomon, the Near East was destined to become a very different place. Israel was no longer in a power vacuum. The Assyrian Empire rose in Mesopotamia, to be followed by the Neo-Babylonian and the Medo-Persian Empires in turn. Egypt was temporarily powerful in the south, but it would later come under control of Assyria and Medo-Persia. These empires exerted great pressure on Israel and dominated one or both of the two Hebrew kingdoms.

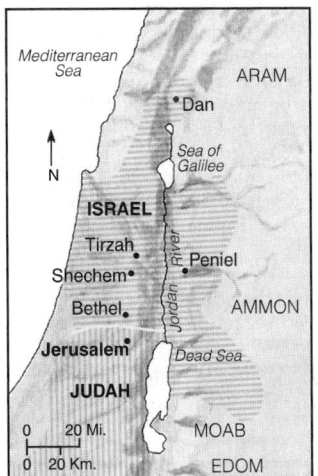

The Divided Kingdom Rehoboam's threat of heavier burdens caused a rebellion and divided the nation. Rehoboam ruled the southern kingdom; Jeroboam ruled the northern kingdom. Jeroboam set up idols in Dan and Bethel to discourage worship in Jerusalem. At the same time, Aram, Ammon, Moab, and Edom claimed independence from the divided nation.

When Solomon died, his son Rehoboam took the throne and was forced to deal with a rising tide of resentment over the high taxes and economic stagnation of Solomon's last years. When Rehoboam refused to give relief, all the northern tribes broke away and formed the northern kingdom, Israel, under the leadership of Jeroboam. The southern kingdom, Judah, was left with only the territory of Judah and Benjamin. A total of 20 kings ruled in each of the separate kingdoms. While the north had several dynasties and the reigns of kings were generally short, in the south the dynasty of David continued to rule and the reigns were longer.

The Northern Kingdom The northern kingdom lasted from the division in 930 BC until its conquest by Assyria in 722. Jeroboam, fearing that he would lose the loyalty of the people if they continued to go to Jerusalem to worship, set up a new religion of his own. Instituting calf worship, he built shrines at Dan in the north and Bethel in the south. This idolatry drew the condemnation of God and fulfilled the prediction that Jeroboam's line would be wiped out. All his successors are said to have followed in his idolatrous steps. Israel found itself at war during much of its history—with Judah, Syria, or Assyria. Jeroboam established his capital first at Shechem and later at Tirzah.

Four other kings of the north require special comment: Omri, Ahab, Jehu, and Jeroboam II. Omri (885–874 BC) must have been an impressive ruler. Generations later, Assyrians still spoke of Israel as the land of Omri. After he had established himself on the throne, he located the permanent capital of the kingdom at Samaria and began the palace complex there. Early in his reign he was successful in conquering Moab, and later he reestablished the good relations with Tyre that existed in the days of David and Solomon. Apparently he established a full alliance and cemented it with the marriage of his son Ahab to Jezebel, a princess of Tyre.

Ahab (874–853 BC) was one of the most significant of Israel's kings. He and his wife, Jezebel, promoted the vile idolatry of Baal worship with its religious prostitution, arousing the powerful opposition of the prophet Elijah. Ahab was a formidable military man, defeating the Syrians in major campaigns and participating in a coalition that fought the Assyrians to a virtual standstill. He also built extensively at Samaria, Hazor, Megiddo, and other towns, as excavations show.

Jehu (841–814 BC) was God's agent for punishing the house of Omri and destroying Baal worship in Israel. He did eradicate Baal worship and liquidated literally scores of relatives and court officials of Ahab. But he was so ruthless that he killed off the people who knew how to run the government; subsequently, it did not work well. Jehu also was forced to become a vassal to Assyria.

Jeroboam II ruled during most of the first half of the eighth century (793–753 BC) and brought the kingdom to its greatest extent and prosperity. He, with his contemporary Uzziah in the south, ruled most of the land David had once controlled. This was possible because the Assyrians were in a period of decline during most of the first half of the century.

Prophets who were active during the history of the northern kingdom include the nonwriting prophets Elijah and Elisha and the writing prophets Jonah, Amos, and Hosea.

The Southern Kingdom The history of the southern kingdom of Judah was quite different from that of the northern kingdom. The temple was there and so were large numbers of Levites, many of whom came south after the division of the kingdom to protest the idolatry of the north. In addition to this spiritual strength, there was greater political stability and unity, promoted by the fact that only two tribes—Judah and Benjamin—shared power, and all the kings were of the Davidic dynasty. Moreover, eight of the kings were good monarchs. There were also periodic religious revivals. God granted the southern kingdom about 100 more years of existence than the north. But Judah, too, fell into idolatry and went into captivity for her sins.

Rehoboam, the first king in the south, is especially remembered because he refused to listen to wise counsel about fiscal matters and perpetrated the division of the kingdom. He is also remembered for his religious policies. After a good beginning, he allowed apostasy to get out of control and brought the judgment of God in the form of an invasion in his fifth year (926 BC) by Shishak I of Egypt, resulting in extensive plunder and payment of tribute. Thereafter, he launched an extensive program to fortify the realm. Shishak's invasion did have the effect of producing a partial and temporary spiritual reform, but the general trend of Rehoboam's reign was downward.

Conditions during the reign of his son, Abijam, were worse, but Asa (910–869 BC) initiated a religious reform that was effective for most of his reign. When threatened by the northern kingdom during his latter years, however, Asa turned to Syria for help instead of to God, and he seems to have defied the prophets of God to his dying day.

Asa's son Jehoshaphat (872–848 BC) was apparently influenced by his father's early religious devotion, and his reign was characterized by faithfulness, winning the favor of God. However, he seems to have made a full alliance with Ahab of Israel, which resulted in the marriage of his son Jehoram to Ahab's daughter Athaliah. This alliance involved Jehoshaphat in almost ruinous joint ventures with Ahab, and later with two of his sons when they became kings of Israel. It also opened the door for the introduction of Baal worship into Judah when Jehoram came to the throne in the southern kingdom. For his sin Jehoram (853–841 BC) suffered internal revolt, invasion, and death from a horrible disease.

After his death, his last remaining son, Ahaziah, ruled less than a year, following the wicked ways of his father. When Ahaziah died in battle, the queen mother, Athaliah, decided to seize the throne for herself and to secure her power by killing off all those in line to the throne. But she missed Ahaziah's infant son Joash, who was kept hidden in the temple for six years.

When Joash was seven, Jehoiada the high priest arranged his coronation and also the execution of the murderous and idolatrous Athaliah. During his early years when Joash was influenced by good counsel, he did well. But after the middle of his reign (835–796 BC), he began to listen to the princes who wanted to restore idolatry, and conditions deteriorated. Military reversals brought on economic decline and ultimately the king's assassination.

His son Amaziah (796–767 BC) started well with victory over Edom and faithfulness to God. But he, too, fell into idolatry and was totally defeated by the northern kingdom, being held prisoner there. At that point his son Uzziah took over (c. 792 BC) and began a long and generally successful reign. During the several decades that followed, Assyria was in decline, and Uzziah and his contemporary in the north, Jeroboam II, were able to expand Hebrew holdings so that between them they controlled most of the territory Solomon had ruled.

Uzziah (792–740 BC) was able to restore the power of Judah rather quickly after his father's defeat by Israel.

Then he subjugated the Philistines in the southwest and the Ammonites across the Jordan; he strengthened his hold on the Edomites. All during his reign economic conditions improved. But at the height of his power Uzziah foolishly violated the high priest's prerogatives and offered sacrifice in the temple. For this he was smitten with leprosy; his son Jotham was co-regent during the years 750–740 BC, going on to rule alone for about five more years. Meanwhile, Assyrian power became resurgent.

By and large, Jotham merely carried on the policies of Uzziah. But the administration of his son Ahaz (735–715 BC) was very much affected by the Assyrian threat. Israel and Syria wanted him to join in war against Assyria, but he refused, being pro-Assyrian in sympathy. When Israel and Syria invaded Judah, King Ahaz sent tribute to Assyria and became her vassal in return for protection. This rash course of action was vainly opposed by Isaiah, who was prophet at court (c. 740–700 BC). Contemporaneously, the prophet Micah ministered to the common people of Judah. The pro-Assyrian policy of Ahaz was accompanied by a renewed sympathy for idolatry, and this brought the judgment of God in the form of invasion by Edomites and Philistines and trouble with Assyria. In fact, during this period, Assyria had annexed the northern kingdom (722 BC) and removed many of her people into captivity.

The next king of Judah, Hezekiah (715–686 BC), was greatly sobered by the fall of Israel because of her sins, and he determined to launch a reform in his realm. He was anti-Assyrian too, but he did not dare to discontinue tribute payments and strike for independence until after Sennacherib came to the throne in Nineveh in 705 BC. At first Sennacherib was too preoccupied to attend to Judah, but finally in 701 he invaded. Despite tremendous initial success, he was stopped by a divinely sent plague (Is 36–39). Isaiah stood by the king to reassure and sustain him during this emergency.

Hezekiah's son Manasseh (697–642 BC) ruled longer than any other king of Israel or Judah. Unfortunately, he turned his back on his father's example and caused the people to fall into gross idolatry (2 Kgs 21:9). Carried away captive by the Assyrians late in his reign, he repented of his evil and God restored him to his throne; thereafter, he led some reforms. But the land was too steeped in iniquity to be rescued. His son Amon (642–640 BC) reverted to the idolatry he knew in his youth.

The situation was different with Josiah (640–609 BC), however. Throughout his reign he dedicated himself to reform. He sought to root out idolatry and to restore the temple and its worship. In 622 BC the Book of the Law was found during repair of the temple, and its demands—which had been forgotten—made a great impression on king and people alike. It is certain that Jeremiah and Zephaniah ministered during Josiah's reign, as did Nahum and Habakkuk (in all probability).

International conditions were now changing rapidly. Assyria was declining, and Nineveh fell to Babylon and the Medes in 612 BC. Three years later Pharaoh Neco of Egypt marched north to aid his Assyrian ally. When Josiah tried to stop him, he was killed in battle.

From this point everything was downhill for Judah. None of the rest of the kings was devout, and political power and economic health rapidly declined. The people put one of Josiah's sons, Jehoahaz, on the throne. He lasted three months. Pharaoh Neco replaced him with Jehoiakim (609–598 BC), another son of Josiah. In 605 Nebuchadnezzar of Babylon defeated Neco, invaded Judah, and took tribute and hostages from Jehoiakim, including Daniel and his friends (Dn 1:1). Jehoiakim revolted in 600 BC, but Nebuchadnezzar did not come to

deal with him personally until 597 BC. He died before the Babylonians arrived, and his son Jehoiachin came to the throne in 598 BC to rule for only three months before the Babylonians carried him away into exile. Ezekiel was among the many captives taken on that occasion.

The Babylonians then put Zedekiah, youngest son of Josiah, on the throne in 597 BC. When he rebelled, Nebuchadnezzar laid siege to Jerusalem and took the city (587 BC), destroying it and the temple and carrying off large numbers of people. The judgment of God had finally fallen on the Jews for their idolatrous ways.

The Restoration In judgment God remembered mercy. This is evident in individual lives, when faithful ones like Daniel, Esther, or Nehemiah rose to a position of importance in political life, or as numerous other persons became prosperous in the foreign environment. It is evident on the community level as God moved to protect Hebrew enclaves scattered abroad and to restore an organized society in Palestine.

Among the exiles, Judaism as a way of life separated from its own political system or cultic center and began to emerge. Jews finally turned their backs on idolatry. And without a temple, priesthood, king, or land, they turned to the divine Scriptures as their rallying point and the foundation of their community. During this period they developed the synagogue as a place for fellowship, prayer, and study.

God's restoration of an organized community to Palestine involved particularly the fortunes of his "anointed" Cyrus (Is 44:28; 45:1). Cyrus was a Persian prince who in 559 BC revolted against the dominant dynasty controlling the Median Empire. After consolidating his hold on the throne, he proceeded to conquer Asia Minor and the Chaldean or Neo-Babylonian Empire. As a humane man and a wise administrator, he permitted the captive peoples to return to their homes and rebuild their communities. Cyrus's decree to the Jews appears in Ezra 1 and dates probably to 538 BC. A total of almost 50,000 went back to Judah as a result of this edict (Ezr 2:64-65).

Under the stresses and strains of reestablishment, the people built their houses but got no further than laying the foundation of a new temple. Finally, the prophets Haggai and Zechariah stirred the people to build the house of God (Ezr 5:1). They began in the second year of Darius I, the Great (520 BC; Hg 1:1; Zec 1:1), and completed the work in his sixth year (515 BC; Ezr 6:15).

During the reign of Darius's son Xerxes (486–465 BC), a plot was hatched to exterminate all the Jews in the Persian Empire, which at that time controlled the lands where Jews lived. Fortunately, Xerxes (Ahasuerus in the book of Esther), in his third year (483 BC; Est 1:3), went searching for a new queen and chose Esther, who managed to preserve her people.

Xerxes' son Artaxerxes I (465–424 BC) also figured significantly in Jewish history. In his seventh year (458 BC; Ezr 7:7), under the leadership of Ezra, a second contingent of Jews returned to Jerusalem. And in Artaxerxes' 20th year (445 BC; Neh 2:1), Nehemiah went to Jerusalem to supervise the rebuilding of the walls of the city. Malachi probably wrote his prophecy to the Jews in Jerusalem during the latter part of Artaxerxes' reign.

After the fall of Samaria and the captivity of Judah, the Hebrews remaining in the land intermarried with various pagan groups in the area. Their offspring became the Samaritans, a religious and racial admixture. These people had moved into the vacuum left by the destruction of Judah, and naturally they looked with disfavor on an intrusion of Babylonian Jews into an area they had come to call their own. They did all they could to frustrate the efforts of Nehemiah to rebuild the walls. It took all the courage, tact, energy, and persuasiveness Ezra and Nehemiah could muster to prevent the returning Jews from intermarrying with racially mixed people of the land. Such intermarriage would have meant the ultimate absorption and destruction of the Jewish people.

A Samaritan temple was later built on Mt Gerizim (probably during the fifth century BC), and it became the center of the Samaritan worship. The hostility between Samaritans and Jews continued on into the NT period (Jn 4) and exists to the present.

The Intertestamental Period Alexander the Great conquered the Persian Empire with lightning speed. When the people of Jerusalem threw open their gates in 332 BC and capitulated without a fight, Alexander treated them well. After his death in 323 BC, Palestine passed back and forth among his successors until Ptolemy I of Egypt managed to establish control in 301 BC. Thereafter the area remained in Egyptian hands until 198 BC. The Ptolemies were tolerant and granted the Jews considerable autonomy, allowing them to develop their unique culture undisturbed as long as they paid their taxes and remained submissive. Many Jews settled in Alexandria and gradually forgot their Hebrew in the Hellenistic environment. As a result, a translation of the OT into Greek (the Septuagint) was produced there. While the Ptolemies did not force Hellenism on the Jews of either Alexandria or Palestine, many were influenced by Hellenistic ideas.

When Ptolemy V came to the throne as a minor in 203 BC, Antiochus III of Syria took advantage of the weakened Egypt and conquered Palestine (198 BC). Apparently the Jews hoped to gain something from the change and welcomed the Syrians. But their hope was ill-founded. Antiochus III suffered disastrous defeat at the hands of Rome at Magnesia in 190 BC. Syria not only lost much territory but also was forced to pay a huge indemnity. Thereafter, the Jews suffered under great financial burdens, along with other peoples of the empire. The next Syrian king, Antiochus IV Epiphanes (175–164 BC), decided to launch an effort to achieve greater internal strength and unity within the empire by forcing, among other things, a greater acceptance of Greek culture and the cult of the divine ruler. Naturally this idolatrous requirement weighed heavily on the monotheistic Jews and incited revolution.

But this does not completely explain the Maccabean revolt against Syria. In 168 BC armed conflict broke out between Jewish factions in Jerusalem. Antiochus IV chose to interpret this as open rebellion and sent an army against the city. His forces demolished part of the city wall and many houses. After this Antiochus decided to suppress Judaism completely, and he dedicated the temple to Zeus and sacrificed swine on the altar. Circumcision, Sabbath observance, and other religious festivals were no longer permitted, and public worship of heathen gods became compulsory.

Some Jews capitulated to Antiochus's orders or only resisted passively, but a few decided to resist openly. Chief among them were Mattathias and his five sons. After the early death of Mattathias, his son Judas Maccabeus led his forces to victory over the Syrians, regaining the right to restore Jewish worship. The rededication of the temple on December 25, 164 BC, inaugurated the Festival of Hanukkah (1 Macc 4:36-59). Subsequently, Jonathan and Simon (other sons of Mattathias) continued the struggle until independence was gained in 142 BC; this was possible in large part because they saw how to take advantage of the increasing weakness of Syrian rulers and the competition for the royal office.

Simon ruled the Jewish state until his assassination in 134 BC, when his son John Hyrcanus (134–104 BC) took over. John Hyrcanus fought successfully in the east, north, and south, gaining land in Transjordan, capturing Shechem and the Samaritan temple on Mt Gerizim, and subjugating the Idumeans in the south, forcing them to adopt Judaism. His son Aristobulus ruled for only about a year (104–103 BC), but he added a portion of Galilee to the kingdom. When he died, his widow married his brother Alexander Janneus (103–76 BC). Janneus carried on almost incessant military action during his reign, and by the time of his death had almost recovered the kingdom of Solomon.

When Janneus died, Alexandra, widow of two kings, took the throne (76–67 BC) and her eldest son, Hyrcanus II, became high priest. Her reign was peaceful and prosperous, but when she died, her sons fell to squabbling. Their appeals to Pompey, who was campaigning in the eastern Mediterranean area, were responsible for Roman interference in the region and conquest of Palestine in 63 BC.

The Roman Period After the Romans took over Palestine, Hyrcanus II was confirmed as high priest and was also appointed as ethnarch or political ruler (63–40 BC). But Antipater, father of Herod the Great, was the real power behind the throne, and during many of those years Hyrcanus was virtually unable to function because of the confusion of the Roman civil wars. Antipater was loyal to Rome and saw that Roman policies were carried out; he won Julius Caesar's favor toward Jews of both Palestine and in the Dispersion.

With the support of Mark Antony, Herod managed to get himself appointed king of Judea by the Roman senate in 40 BC. But a Parthian invasion of Syria and Jewish hatred for the Romans made it possible for Antigonus II, last king of the Maccabean family, to rule for three years (40–37 BC). Finally, Herod ascended his throne in 37 and ruled until 4 BC. As an allied king, Herod proved to be an excellent ruler from the Roman point of view and earned the title of "Great." He brought some order to regions east of the Jordan and made possible organization of the Roman province of Arabia. He also furthered the cultural plans of Augustus for development of a Greco-Roman civilization throughout the whole empire.

Herod admired Greek culture and contributed to building projects in Rhodes, Antioch, Damascus, Athens, and elsewhere outside Palestine. Within Palestine he rebuilt Samaria and named it Sebaste in honor of Augustus (Sebastos is Greek for "Augustus") and also constructed the great port of Caesarea. Probably about as large as Manhattan Island, it became the capital of Roman Palestine. Among his many other building projects, remodeling the temple in Jerusalem was the most famous. Begun in 20 BC, it was not completed until just a few years before its destruction in AD 70.

The material splendor of Herod's reign did not win the affection or support of the Jews, however. Nor did he achieve peace and harmony in his family, among whom there were periodic eruptions of treason, unfaithfulness, and murder. He worried about any threat to his rule and cracked down hard to destroy such threats, as is evident from his slaughter of the infants in Bethlehem after the birth of Christ.

Ultimately, Herod controlled Idumea, Judea, Samaria, Galilee, Perea, and the area northeast of the Sea of Galilee. By his last will, his son Archelaus was to rule Idumea, Judea, and Samaria; Antipas, Galilee and Perea; and

Philip, the region northeast of the Sea of Galilee. Archelaus was deposed in AD 6, and his territory became a Roman province (AD 6–41) to be ruled by direct appointees of Rome. The best-known of these was Pontius Pilate (AD 26–36), who ordered the crucifixion of Jesus. Antipas was more successful and built a new capital at Tiberias, but he ran afoul of the emperor's good pleasure in AD 39 and was deposed. Philip was the most effective of the three and ruled until his death in AD 34. Philip's lands were later given to Herod Agrippa I in AD 37; the holdings of Antipas were then added in AD 39; and in 41 Agrippa also received Samaria, Judea, and Idumea.

Herod Agrippa I (AD 37–44) was the heir of the Maccabees (through his grandmother Mariamne, first wife of Herod the Great), and for this reason had the support of patriotic Jews and of the Pharisees for his observance of divine ordinances. But when he built a new north wall for Jerusalem and dabbled in foreign affairs, he aroused the suspicions of the Romans; when he died in AD 44, they turned the kingdom into a Roman province.

As is clear from the Gospels, several sects had arisen in Palestine by Roman times and were active during the first century. The Zealots opposed Roman rule and advocated armed rebellion. Herodians supported the Herodian family and Roman power. The Pharisees were fanatically devoted to the law and were supernaturalists in theological orientation. They were somewhat content to support Rome if given religious freedom, and they dominated the synagogues of the land. The Sadducees were antisupernaturalists, tended to collaborate with the ruling regime, and were dominant in the temple. Generally speaking, the literature of the intertestamental period and the popular mentality of the time tended to view the Messiah as a political deliverer who would free his people from foreign domination and set up a new independent kingdom.

Roman prefects ruled Palestine from AD 44–66. They had a knack for offending the religious scruples of the Jews and alienating them in other ways. With Felix (AD 52–60) there began a constant tension between Jews and Romans that led to the first Jewish revolt (AD 66–70). While Paul was imprisoned in Caesarea (Acts 23:23–24:27) about AD 58–60, riots broke out there between Jews and Gentiles. Festus (AD 60–62; Acts 25) was an able administrator, but the situation was almost out of hand. After he died in office, there was virtual anarchy until his successor, Albinus, arrived (AD 62–64). Totally incompetent and dishonest, Albinus was recalled in 64 and replaced by Florus (AD 64–66). Florus was even worse, resorting to open robbery and bribery until there was no safety or justice in the land. Finally, the Jews could take no more.

The spark that ignited the fires of rebellion was an anti-Semitic act by the Hellenistic population of Caesarea in AD 66. Soon riots spread to numerous cities, and Roman garrisons were massacred in several places. But the Jews were not united, and in Jerusalem armed bands of Jews fought with each other for mastery. Vespasian was chosen to command the Roman army of some 60,000 to deal with the insurrection. He had subjugated most of Palestine by the time he was elevated to the imperial chair in AD 69 (after the death of Nero), and he left his son Titus in charge of completing the operations. In August of AD 70 the walls of Jerusalem were breached, many of the people butchered, and the city and the temple leveled. Masada held out until AD 73. Palestine had been flattened by Roman might. Loss of life and property had been incalculable and indescribable.

On two more occasions the Jews were destined to fight disastrously against the Romans. Under Trajan's rule a rebellion of Jews broke out in Cyrenaica in AD 115 and spread rapidly to Cyprus, Egypt, Palestine, and Mesopotamia. In the beginning it was an outgrowth of agitation between the Jews and their Hellenistic neighbors, but it developed into a challenge to Roman authority. This was particularly true after the successes of Parthia on Rome's eastern frontier when there seemed to be some hope of success in throwing off the Roman yoke. Wherever Jews got the upper hand, they perpetrated massacres, and the non-Semitic population retaliated in kind. Trajan ruthlessly suppressed the rebels and restored order everywhere except Egypt; his successor, Hadrian, was left to accomplish that.

But Hadrian faced a new rebellion of his own, brought on by his law forbidding circumcision (which he considered to be inhumane) and his decision in AD 130 to rebuild Jerusalem as Aelia Capitolina and erect a temple to Jupiter on the site of the temple of Yahweh. The latter would not only profane the temple site but also would preclude any rebuilding of the Jewish temple.

Leader of this second Jewish revolt was Simeon, prince of Israel, called Bar-Kochba ("Son of the Star"). Both sides fought with such great ferocity for over three years (AD 132–135) that the population of Judea was almost exterminated. Jerusalem was rebuilt as a Roman colony, and Jews were forbidden to enter on pain of death. Even as late as the fourth century they were permitted to enter only once a year, on the anniversary of the destruction of the temple by Nebuchadnezzar. After the Bar-Kochba revolt, Judaism retreated increasingly within the citadel of the written and oral law, thus separating itself from the Gentiles.

See also Abraham; Chronology of the Bible (Old Testament); Conquest and Allotment of the Land; David; Diaspora of the Jews; Exodus, The; First Jewish Revolt; Jew; Judaism; Moses; Patriarchs, Period of the; Saul #2; Solomon; Postexilic Period; Wilderness Wanderings.

ISRAELITE Descendant of the 12 sons of Israel (the name God gave to Jacob, Gn 32:28). As the sons of Abraham, they are distinguished from the Ishmaelites (descended from Abraham by Hagar his concubine), and as sons of Isaac, from the Edomites (descendants of Esau), by having Jacob as their ancestor. They lived in Egypt from the time of Joseph until the exodus, when God led them into Canaan to fulfill his promise to Abraham (17:8).

God led the Israelites out of Egypt, through the wilderness, and into the land of Canaan that he had promised them. They were ruled by judges, kings, and conquerors from other countries. In 722 BC the northern kingdom was conquered by Assyria and became incorporated into that empire. After this time, "Israel" refers to members of the southern tribes, Judah and Benjamin. An "Israelite" was one who, religiously as well as politically, belonged to the remnant of the covenant nation of Israel.

See also Israel, History of; Jew; Judaism.

ISSACHAR (Person)

1. Jacob's ninth son, the fifth by his wife Leah (Gn 30:17-18); his name perhaps means "reward." Jacob, in his final message to his 12 sons says, "Issachar is a strong donkey, lying down between the sheepfolds" (49:14, NASB); the picture suggested is a loaded donkey who refuses to move his burden, a lazy man who is unwilling to do his share of the work. Little is known about Issachar except what he did along with the other sons of Israel. He had four sons (46:13), who headed clans in the tribe (1 Chr 7:1-5). His family went with

Jacob to Egypt, where they died (although Issachar's remains were subsequently moved to Shechem with the other 12 patriarchs—Acts 7:16).

The descendants of Issachar numbered 54,400 at the first census (Nm 1:29), increased to 64,300 at the second (26:25), and to 87,000 during David's reign (1 Chr 7:5). Issachar was the main tribe involved in the fighting led by Deborah, herself a member of the tribe (Jgs 5:15). During the time of David, there were men of the tribe of Issachar who had understanding of what Israel ought to do in warfare (1 Chr 12:32). These men supported David as king to replace Saul.

Issachar was assigned the fourth lot of land after the ark was taken to Shiloh (Jos 19:17). This included the cities of Jezreel, Shunem, and En-gannim, and it lay between the mountains of Gilboa and Tabor. Their allotment was bordered on the south and west by the tribe of Manasseh, on the north by Zebulun and Naphtali, and on the east by the river Jordan. This territory was largely a fertile plain and was often threatened by the Canaanites nearby as well as by foreign invaders.
2. Obed-edom's son, who was a Levite gatekeeper during David's reign (1 Chr 26:5).

ISSACHAR, Tribe of Tribal inheritance of Issachar. The territory is defined in Joshua 19:17-23; detailed boundary descriptions are not included. On the east its boundary ends at the Jordan. The area can be located by the list of towns encompassed by the inheritance of which Jezreel, Chesulloth, Shunem, Anaharath, Kishion, Remeth, and En-gannim have identifications of varying degrees of certainty. Jezreel and En-gannim are in the southeast corner of the valley of Jezreel; Chesulloth is just west of Mt Tabor; and Shunem is at the foot of the hill of Moreh. The northern border can be deduced from the southern boundaries of Zebulun and Naphtali (Jos 19:10-12, 33-34). All three areas, that of Issachar, Naphtali, and Zebulun, met at Mt Tabor. On the south side, there were some major towns not conquered in Joshua's time (Jgs 1:27) that were taken from Issachar and given to Manasseh (Jos 17:11); these included important centers such as Beth-shan, Ibleam, and Tanaach.

In the same territory, there were disturbances among the local tribes (recorded on a stele of Seti I at Beth-shan); the area is called "Mt Yarunta," after Yarmuth (Jos 21:29, Jarmuth = Remeth). Issachar was located on the rich plateau stretching east of Mt Tabor and the hill of Moreh and north of the Beth-shan Valley.

See also Issachar (Person) #1.

ISSHIAH
1. Izrahiah's son from Issachar's tribe (1 Chr 7:3).
2. Warrior from Benjamin's tribe who joined David in his struggle against King Saul. Isshiah was one of David's ambidextrous archers and slingers (1 Chr 12:6).
3. Uzziel's son from Levi's tribe (1 Chr 23:20; 24:25).
4. Rehabiah's son from Levi's tribe and a descendant of Moses (1 Chr 24:21).

ISSHIJAH* Alternate rendering of Ishijah, Harim's son in Ezra 10:31. *See* Ishijah.

ISSUE OF BLOOD* KJV rendering of "hemorrhage" in Matthew 9:20 and Mark 5:25. *See* Hemorrhage.

ISUAH* KJV spelling of Ishvah, Asher's son, in 1 Chronicles 7:30. *See* Ishvah.

ISUI* KJV rendering of Ishvi, Asher's son, in Genesis 46:17. *See* Ishvi #1.

ITALIAN BAND*, ITALIAN COHORT*, ITALIAN REGIMENT Roman military unit to which the centurion Cornelius belonged. The single biblical reference to a regiment (NASB "cohort"; KJV " band") is in Acts 10:1.

The Roman army included auxiliary regiments, most of which seem to have comprised provincial subjects apart from Jews (who were exempted). Such units were sometimes referred to by distinctive names like "Italian" or "Augustan" (Imperial) (Acts 27:1). The Italian Regiment was evidently composed mainly of those who not only were Roman citizens but had been born in Rome. The regiments were made up of six centuries of 100 men, each century commanded by a centurion (in this instance, Cornelius). Ten regiments constituted a legion (6,000 men).

Inscriptions indicate that such an Italian regiment had indeed been stationed in Syria during AD 69–157. This does not rule out an earlier presence in the province; military records are simply not available.

ITALY Boot-shaped peninsula located between the Tyrrhenian and the Adriatic seas. Uplands and two major mountain ranges—the Alps, which form a northern boundary, and the Apennines, which form the backbone of the peninsula—occupy 77 percent of the land. The plains, which are limited to the Po River valley, cover the remaining 23 percent.

The earliest history of the region is found in the artifacts of the Abbevillian and Neanderthal cultures discovered in many areas, including the site at Rome. With the advent of agriculture (6000 BC), the population increased rapidly. By 3000 BC, large groups of farmers had located in southern Italy along the Mediterranean coast and in northern Italy along the Po Valley. During the third millennium BC, a major culture developed in the central part of the peninsula, influenced by Minoan and Mycenaean civilizations and characterized by agriculture, animal husbandry, and bronzeworking.

During the second millennium BC, an invasion of Indo-European tribes reshaped the culture of the peninsula. Each area came to be known by the name of the tribe that inhabited it. Among the most important of these tribes were the Latins, who settled in the valley of the Tiber River—an area that came to be known as Latium. According to the historian Antiochus of Syracuse (fifth century BC), it was also during this time (1300 BC) that King Italos ruled the southwest part of the peninsula. This region came to take his name, which, over the next millennium, was extended northward until, in the time of Augustus (27 BC–AD 14), the entire peninsula was called "Italy."

Toward the end of the eighth century BC, the Etruscans, immigrants from Asia Minor, invaded the peninsula and organized the less-civilized Italic tribes into Etruscan-dominated city-states. The result was political chaos. Wars with Greek colonies, wars to throw off Etruscan domination, and wars between city-states dominated the next five centuries. The city-state that benefited the most from this unrest was Rome. By 220 BC, Rome had conquered the entire peninsula and had united all Italy south of the Po Valley under one rule. After a great revolt (90–88 BC), Italians throughout the peninsula obtained the rights of Roman citizenship, and in 49 BC Julius Caesar extended these rights to the inhabitants of the Po Valley. Thus, by NT times, Italy had essentially come to have its present form.

"Italy" appears three times in the NT. Paul has the opportunity to meet Priscilla and Aquila, recently come from Italy because Claudius had expelled the Jews from Rome (Acts 18:2). Italy is mentioned as Paul's destination following his appeal to Caesar (27:1, 6). The writer of Hebrews sends greetings to his readers from "those who come from Italy" (Heb 13:24).

See also Caesars, The; Rome, City of.

ITHAI Alternate spelling of Ittai, a Benjamite warrior, in 1 Chronicles 11:31. *See* Ittai #2.

ITHAMAR Aaron's fourth and youngest son, who served as a priest to the tribes of Israel during the wilderness period (Ex 6:23; Nm 3:2-4; 26:60; 1 Chr 6:3; 24:2). After the death of two of his brothers, he was given the special duty of overseeing the moving of the tabernacle (Nm 4:28, 33; 7:8). During David's reign, the descendants of Ithamar and Eleazar were organized as the formal temple priesthood (1 Chr 24:3-6). Later, some of his descendants returned with Ezra from Babylon (Ezr 8:2).

ITHIEL
1. Ancestor of Sallu, a Benjamite who lived in Jerusalem after the Babylonian exile (Neh 11:7).
2. One of the two persons to whom Agur spoke his proverbs (Prv 30:1, NLT mg).

ITHLAH City given to Dan's tribe for an inheritance, after the initial conquest of Palestine by Joshua (Jos 19:42).

ITHMAH Warrior of Moabite origin and one of David's mighty men (1 Chr 11:46).

ITHNAN Town in southern Judah (Jos 15:23).

ITHRA* Father of Amasa by Abigail, Zeruiah's sister (2 Sm 17:25, NLT mg). He is called Jether in 1 Kings 2:5, 32 and 1 Chronicles 2:17.

ITHRAN
1. Dishon's son, who was a Horite chief (Gn 36:26; 1 Chr 1:41).
2. One of Zophah's sons (1 Chr 7:37). He is probably the same as Jether mentioned in 1 Chronicles 7:38.

ITHREAM David's sixth son, borne by his wife Eglah at Hebron (2 Sm 3:5; 1 Chr 3:3).

ITHRITE Family or clan that lived at Kiriath-jearim (1 Chr 2:53). Ira and Gareb, two of David's mighty men, were Ithrites (2 Sm 23:38; 1 Chr 11:40; NLT "from Jattir"). Ithnite is a derivation of Jattir or Jether.

ITTAH-KAZIN* KJV form of the town Eth-kazin in Joshua 19:13. *See* Eth-kazin.

ITTAI
1. Philistine from Gath who, with 600 other Gittites, remained loyal to David and accompanied him on his flight from Absalom (2 Sm 15:18-22). Ittai commanded a third of David's army in the battle against Absalom's forces (18:2, 5).
2. Benjamite warrior among David's mighty men (2 Sm 23:29; 1 Chr 11:31, "Ithai").

ITURAEA*, ITUREA, ITUREANS* Small province mentioned with Trachonitis as forming the tetrarchy of Philip, brother of Herod the Great, during the reign of Tiberius Caesar (Lk 3:1). A reasonable assumption places Iturea northeast of the Sea of Galilee and in the area of Mt Hermon, but its location and boundaries have been much disputed. The name almost certainly comes from Jetur, a son of Ishmael (Gn 25:15), whose descendants were among those conquered by the Israelites east of the

Jordan (1 Chr 5:19-20). Thereafter, the Itureans virtually drop from sight until Josephus records another defeat inflicted on them by Aristobulus in 105–104 BC, at which time many of them were faced with a choice between circumcision and exile.

There are frequent mentions by classical writers of Itureans, sometimes described as Syrians or Arabians—skilled bowmen with the predatory tendencies often associated with groups unable or unwilling to settle for long in any one area. In view of this, it is not surprising that we know more about Itureans than we do about Iturea.

Strabo speaks of them as inhabitants of a mountainous country; Dio Cassius a little later tells us that they had a king. Any attempt to understand their history is complicated by divisions in the Roman Empire that affected them, but by the end of the first century AD, many Itureans were to be found under the provincial rule of Syria.

It is easier, then, to discuss the people than the place. Some scholars, indeed, hold that Luke could not have used the noun "Iturea," for this was a form unknown until three centuries later, and that the adjectival form better fits the case. This prompts another question: Was this Iturean territory within Philip's tetrarchy? Could Luke have made a slip and anticipated a later regional regrouping? Josephus at one point lists the constituent parts of Philip's tetrarchy without including Iturea.

Three facts are clear: (1) there is a certain flexibility and overlapping in descriptions of territorial demarcation; (2) the data we have is insufficient for exact conclusions about Iturea; and (3) the evidence is clear from other parts of Scripture that Luke is a careful and reliable writer.

IVAH* KJV spelling of Ivvah. *See* Ivvah.

IVORY Opaque dentine substance, often mentioned along with precious metals and gems in the Bible and ancient Near Eastern writings. As such, ivory was used for combs, small boxes, jars, and other cosmetic articles; for figurines and amulets; for games; and for the adornment of articles of furniture, buildings, and perhaps even ships (Ez 27:6). It is frequently mentioned in Egyptian and Assyrian annals of conquest as part of the spoils of war. Some excellent examples of work with ivory can be found in the famed collection of Tutankhamen.

In the Bible ivory is spoken of as the adornment of Solomon's throne (1 Kgs 10:18; 2 Chr 9:17) and of beds in the time of Amos (Am 6:4). Both references are probably to ivory inlay. The ivory palaces of 1 Kings 22:39, Psalm 45:8, and Amos 3:15, however, may refer to forms of decoration other than inlay. Whether Ezekiel 27:6 actually implies that ships were decorated with ivory is debatable, since that passage forms part of the whole picture of Tyre as an extravagant ship. The articles of ivory that earth's merchants can no longer sell to Babylon (Rv 18:12) include smaller objects of the kind found at various archaeological sites (Megiddo, Samaria, Nimrud).

Originally ivory was available in northern Syria, where Assyrian monarchs hunted elephants. By Solomon's time, however, it was imported (1 Kgs 10:22; 2 Chr 9:21), probably from the east (India) or south (Africa), while the ships of Tarshish may represent the seagoing capability of the ships rather than the source of the ivory. Tyre received its ivory in trade from the "coastlands" (Ez 27:15).

IVVAH City that had already fallen along with others to the Assyrians (2 Kgs 18:34; 19:13; Is 37:13). Sennacherib's representative mocked Hezekiah's belief that God would save Jerusalem. Ivvah was probably in Syria.

See also Avva.

IYE-ABARIM, IYIM* Israelite camping place on the southeast border of Moab during the wilderness wanderings (Nm 33:44). In verse 45 the town is called Iyim, which is a shortened form of Iye-abarim.

IZEHAR*, IZEHARITES* KJV spelling of Izhar, Kohath's son, and his descendants (Nm 3:19, 27). *See* Izhar #1.

IZHAR

1. One of Kohath's sons from Levi's tribe (Ex 6:18, 21; Nm 3:19; 16:1; 1 Chr 6:2, 18, 38; 23:12, 18), and father of the Izharite family (Nm 3:27; 1 Chr 24:22; 26:23, 29); alternately called Amminadab in 1 Chronicles 6:22. One of Izhar's sons was Korah, who led the rebellion against Moses and Aaron (Nm 16:1-11).
2. Helah's son from Judah's tribe (1 Chr 4:7).

IZHARITE Descendant of Izhar from Levi's tribe (Nm 3:27; 1 Chr 24:22; 26:23, 29). *See* Izhar #1.

IZLIAH Elpaal's son from Benjamin's tribe (1 Chr 8:18).

IZRAHIAH Uzzi's son and a leading member of Issachar's tribe (1 Chr 7:3).

IZRAHITE Designation given to Shamhuth, one of David's 12 monthly captains, meaning a man of a family or town called Izra (1 Chr 27:8). The word "Izrahite" is perhaps a corruption of "Zerahite," a descendant of Zerah of Judah (1 Chr 27:11).

IZRI* Temple musician and head of the 4th of the 24 divisions of priests for service as musicians in the sanctuary (1 Chr 25:11, NLT mg). He is called Zeri in 1 Chronicles 25:3.

IZZIAH Parosh's son, who was encouraged by Ezra to divorce the foreign woman he married during the postexilic period (Ezr 10:25).

J

JAAKAN Esau's descendant and a son of Ezer the Horite (1 Chr 1:42, NLT mg); alternately called Akan in Genesis 36:27. *See* Beeroth Bene-jaakan.

JAAKOBAH Leader in Simeon's tribe (1 Chr 4:36).

JAALAH Servant of King Solomon and head of a family who returned to Jerusalem with Zerubbabel after the Babylonian exile (Ezr 2:56; Neh 7:58).

JAALAM* KJV form of Jalam, Esau's son, in Genesis 36:5, 14, 18 and 1 Chronicles 1:35. *See* Jalam.

JAANAI* KJV form of Janai, a Gadite, in 1 Chronicles 5:12. *See* Janai.

JAAR Most common word in Hebrew for "forest." It refers to forests generally (Is 10:18) and to specific forests, such as the "forest of Ephraim" (2 Sm 18:6) and the "forest of Hereth" (1 Sm 22:5), both associated with King David. It also occurs as the name of one of Solomon's buildings, "the Palace of the Forest of Lebanon" (1 Kgs 7:2), apparently because of its extensive use of cedar. Only one occurrence of "Jaar" seems to be a proper name. Psalm 132:6 alludes to the transfer of the ark from Kiriath-jearim to Jerusalem. Here it is called the field of Jaar (or "the wood," KJV), perhaps a poetic abbreviation.

JAARE-OREGIM* Textual corruption of Jair in 2 Samuel 21:19. *See* Jair #3.

JAARESHIAH Jeroham's son, a Benjamite leader who lived in Jerusalem (1 Chr 8:27).

JAASAU* KJV spelling of Jaasu, Bani's son, in Ezra 10:37. *See* Jaasu.

JAASIEL
1. Warrior among David's mighty men. He is called "the Mezobaite" (1 Chr 11:47).
2. Abner's son and the leader of Benjamin's tribe during David's reign (1 Chr 27:21).

JAASU Bani's son, who obeyed Ezra's exhortation to divorce his pagan wife after the exile (Ezr 10:37).

JAAZANIAH
1. Son of Hoshaiah, who was a Maacathite and a leader in the armies of Judah at the beginning of the exile. These troops received assurance of safety in return for loyalty to the Babylonians (2 Kgs 25:23). Jaazaniah is alternately called Jezaniah in Jeremiah 40:8 and Azariah in Jeremiah 42:1 (NLT mg) and 43:2.
2. Son of Jeremiah (not the prophet), who was taken by Jeremiah the prophet into the Lord's house, where he refused to drink wine because of the command of his ancestor Jonadab the Recabite (Jer 35:3-11).

3. Shaphan's son, who led a group of elders in worshiping idols in the temple (Ez 8:11).
4. Azzur's son and one of a group of 25 men seen by Ezekiel in a vision who gave bad counsel and plotted evil in Jerusalem near the time of the exile (Ez 11:1).

JAAZER* KJV alternate form of Jazer, an Amorite city in Gilead, in Numbers 21:32 and 32:35. *See* Jazer.

JAAZIAH Descendant of Merari in a list of family leaders among Levites assigned to temple duty in David's reign (1 Chr 24:26-27).

JAAZIEL One of the eight men appointed to play harps or lyres when the ark was brought up to Jerusalem by David (1 Chr 15:18-20; and probably 16:5a, "Jeiel," which is most likely a copyist's error). He is called Aziel in verse 20.

JABAL Descendant of Cain and the first son of Lamech and Adah. He was the father of a nomadic people who dwelt in tents (Gn 4:20).

JABBOK Eastern tributary of the Jordan, the modern Nahr ez-Zerqa or Blue River. Its source is a spring near Amman, capital of modern Jordan (the Decapolis town of Philadelphia in Hellenistic times). From its source the Jabbok loops northeast before swinging west and cutting a valley that, characteristic of the east Jordan tributary streams, deepens into a canyon. It emerges from this ravine near Tell Deir Alla, which may be the ancient Succoth, quiets its flow, and joins the Jordan at ed-Damiyeh, the ancient Adam, some 15 miles (24 kilometers) north of the Dead Sea. The Jabbok ranks next to the Yarmuk, its more northerly companion stream, in the extent of its watershed, a region of well-watered territory blessed with an average rainfall of some 30 inches (76 centimeters) per year. The Jabbok has a fast, strong, perennial flow; over a large portion of its 60-mile (96.5-kilometer) course, the stream averages an 80-foot (24.4-meter) drop over each mile. The loop of the river north of Amman (biblical Rabbah) was an Ammonite frontier (Nm 21:24). The river separated the kingdoms of Sihon and Og (Jgs 11:19-22; cf. Dt. 3:1-2, 8-10), land in Gilead that was later divided among the tribes of Gad, Reuben, and the half-tribe of Manasseh (Dt 3:12, 16; Jos 12:2-6).
See also Jordan River.

JABESH (Person) Shallum's father. Shallum assassinated Zechariah, king of Israel (2 Kgs 15:10-14).

JABESH, JABESH-GILEAD (Place) Town appearing in the closing chapters of the book of Judges (chs 19–21). This is a sad record of the division and degradation of the land, which tells of a base atrocity committed by the men of Gibeah against a Levite's concubine, a sanguinary war against Benjamin in consequence, and savage reprisals against Jabesh-gilead, whose community had sent no contingent to the battle. Such is the first mention of the town.

The town was repopulated by neighboring Gileadites and next appears in 1 Samuel 11. East of the Jordan River, Jabesh was exposed to Ammonite attack, and Nahash of Ammon forced Jabesh-gilead to seek terms of surrender. The condition imposed by the barbarous Nahash was the loss of the right eye for all the inhabitants, a mutilation intended to humiliate Israel and destroy the military potential of a border fortress. The sequel was Saul's forced march, a fine piece of military prowess, and a tremendous boost for the new king's prestige. Saul gained in one swift blow the support of the Transjordanian tribes and the reduction of the frontier threat that a militarily powerful Ammon would undoubtedly offer. The men of Jabesh-gilead repaid their deep debt to Saul when the king, now unbalanced and rejected, died on Mt Gilboa with his son Jonathan in a last attempt to blunt the Philistine drive to the north. The bodies of Saul and Jonathan, hung headless over the walls of Beth-shan, were cut down and rescued by a commando force from Jabesh-gilead, who made a forced march of nine miles (14.5 kilometers) each way to honor their onetime benefactor (1 Sm 31:8-13; 1 Chr 10:8-12). When David became king, he repaid the men of Jabesh-gilead with gratitude.

The name Jabesh is preserved in that of the Wadi el-Yabis that runs into the Jordan directly south of the southern end of the Sea of Galilee. The town itself, according to Eusebius's generally reliable topography, was about six miles (9.7 kilometers) south of Pella on the road to Gerasa. The twin tells of Tell el-Maqereh and Tell Abu Kharaz on the Wadi el-Yabis correspond with Eusebius's location much better than the other site suggested: Tell el-Maqlub. Tell el-Meqereh and Tell Abu Kharaz are on the eastern rim of the Jordan Valley and fit the details of the historical record—Saul's forced march from Bezek, and the route of the Jabesh-gilead raiding party to Beth-shan.

JABEZ (Person) Member of Judah's tribe who was noted for his godliness. He prayed for God's protection, and his prayer was answered (1 Chr 4:9-10).

JABEZ (Place) City that was probably located in Judah and was inhabited by scribes (1 Chr 2:55).

JABIN

1. King of Hazor who led a coalition against Joshua at Merom. Jabin and his allies were destroyed in the battle, and Hazor was burned to the ground (Jos 11:1-14).
2. King of Hazor during the period of the judges (Jgs 4). God allowed him to oppress Israel for 20 years because of their wickedness. His army included 900 chariots of iron. Eventually, God delivered Israel through the prophetess Deborah and her captain, Barak, who defeated Sisera, the captain of Jabin's army. While resting after his flight from battle, Sisera himself was killed by a woman. Jabin was no longer a threat after Sisera's death and was soon killed (Jgs 4:24; Ps 83:9).

JABNEEL

1. Alternate name for the town Jabneh in Judah's tribe (Jos 15:11). See Jabneh.
2. Town of Galilee near Tiberias, on Naphtali's southern border (Jos 19:33). It was located south of modern Jabneel.

JABNEH Biblical city on the coastal plain between Joppa (modern Jaffa) and Ashdod, first mentioned as Jabneel, on the northern border of the tribe of Judah (Jos 15:11). It is mentioned together with the Philistine cities Gath and Ashdod, whose walls were breached by Uzziah, king of Judah (2 Chr 26:6). In the middle Bronze Age a harbor was established at Jabneh-yam, which is probably mentioned by Thutmose III in his list of conquered cities and in the Tell el-Amarna letters (Jabni-ilu). The remains of the harbor show evidence of all periods—from early Bronze Age down to the Byzantine period. In Hellenistic times Jabneh was called Jamnia and was used as a base by foreign armies for subsequent attacks against the Judean territory of the Maccabeans. After the destruction of Jerusalem in AD 70, a small community of learned refugees was located in Jabneh. Their leader was Johanan ben Zakkai, a former member of the Sanhedrin, the supreme court of the Jews in Jerusalem. He founded a school there. His successor was Gamaliel II. Here the canon of the OT was defined. During the second Jewish war (Bar-Kochba Revolt, AD 132–135), Jabneh was deserted. The spiritual center of the Jewish life was removed to Galilee. The refugees settled down first in Zippori and later in Tiberias, where the Jerusalem Talmud was codified and the Masoretic Text of the OT was produced.

JACAN, JACHAN* Member of Gad's tribe who lived in Bashan during the reign of Jotham, king of Judah (1 Chr 5:13).

JACHIN*

1. Son of Simeon and leader of the Jachinites, who immigrated to Egypt with his grandfather Jacob (Gn 46:10; Ex 6:15; Nm 26:12). He is called Jarib in 1 Chronicles 4:24.
2. Priest who lived in Jerusalem after the exile (1 Chr 9:10; Neh 11:10). The name Jachin may possibly designate a family of priests of which Jachin was the head.
3. Descendant of Aaron and head of the 21st course of priests assigned to temple duty in David's reign (1 Chr 24:17).

JACHIN AND BOAZ* Names of two pillars Solomon set up before the temple vestibule. He named the south pillar Jachin and the north pillar Boaz (1 Kgs 7:21; 2 Chr 3:17). These hollow pillars were cast of bronze and measured about 27 feet (8.2 meters) in height and about 18 feet (5.5 meters) in circumference (nearly 6 feet, or 1.8 meters, in diameter). They were crowned with a capital (ornate cap or top) about 7½ feet (2.3 meters) high that consisted of cast lily work, chains, and 200 pomegranates each (1 Kgs 7:15-20; 2 Chr 3:15-16; 4:13).

JACHINITE* Descendant of Jachin, Simeon's son (Nm 26:12). See Jachin #1.

JACINTH Precious stone mentioned in Revelation 21:20 as a foundation stone in the new Jerusalem. See Stones, Precious.

JACKAL Wolflike mammal known for its distinctive wail (Mi 1:8). See Animals.

JACKAL'S WELL Unknown location along the Jerusalem wall between the Valley Gate and the Dung Gate visited by Nehemiah during his night inspection of the wall (Neh 2:13). It is also called Dragon's Well or Serpent's Well.

JACOB

1. Younger of twin sons born to Isaac and Rebekah (Gn 25:24-26). Isaac had prayed for his barren wife, Rebekah, and she conceived the twins, who jostled

each other in the womb. When she asked the Lord about this, he told her that she was carrying two nations and that the older son would serve the younger (v 23). Esau was hairy and red (later he was called Edom, "red," 25:30; 36:1), but Jacob was born holding the heel of his brother, so that he was named Jacob, "he takes by the heel" (cf. Hos 12:3), with the derived meaning "to supplant, deceive, attack from the rear."

Personal History Esau and Jacob were very different from each other. Esau was an outdoorsman, the favorite of his father, while Jacob stayed around the tents and was loved by his mother.

One day when Jacob was preparing red pottage, Esau came in famished and asked Jacob for some food. Jacob offered to sell Esau some stew in exchange for his birthright as firstborn, and Esau agreed, thus repudiating his birthright (cf. Heb 12:16). The significance of this episode of the red pottage is demonstrated by its association with Esau's second name, Edom ("red") (Gn 25:30).

Isaac became old and blind. One day he asked Esau to take his weapons and get some wild game, of which Isaac was very fond (Gn 27:6-7; cf 25:28), so that he could eat and then confer his blessing upon Esau. Rebekah overheard this, so she called Jacob and told him to go to the flock and select two good kids. She would prepare a dish that would pass for the game while Esau was out hunting. Jacob feared that Isaac would detect the deception, for Esau was very hairy, but Rebekah had everything planned. She placed the skins of the kids on Jacob's hands and neck to give the impression of hairiness (27:16) and clothed him in Esau's best garments, which had the smell of the outdoors on them. Although Isaac recognized the voice of Jacob, his other senses failed him, and he was deceived by the feel of the skins and the smell of the garments. He proceeded to give the blessing to Jacob (vv 27-29).

No sooner had Jacob left than Esau arrived with the game he had cooked. Jacob's ruse was discovered, but the deed could not be undone (Gn 27:33), for, as the Nuzi tablets show, an oral blessing had legal validity and could not be revoked. Esau was heartbroken (cf. Heb 12:17). Isaac gave him a blessing inferior to the one given to Jacob (Gn 27:39-40).

The animosity between the brothers deepened, and Esau plotted to kill Jacob after the death of their father. Rebekah learned of this, so she instructed Jacob to flee to her brother Laban in Haran (Gn 27:42-45). Esau's Hittite wives, meanwhile, had been making life miserable for Rebekah; she complained to Isaac, who called Jacob and sent him to Laban to marry one of his uncle's daughters (27:46-28:4).

Jacob set out for Haran. Using a stone for a pillow, he dreamed one night of a ladder reaching up to heaven, with the angels of God ascending and descending on it. God spoke to Jacob and gave to him the promise he had given to Abraham and Isaac concerning the land and descendants. The next morning Jacob took his stone pillow and set it up as a pillar, anointing it with oil. He named the place Bethel ("house of God") and made a vow that if the Lord would be with him and provide for him, he would give a tithe to the Lord (Gn 28:10-22).

When Jacob reached the area of Haran, he met shepherds who knew Laban. Rachel, Laban's younger daughter, arrived with her father's flock, and Jacob rolled the large stone from the mouth of the well and watered the sheep for her (Gn 29:1-10). When Rachel learned that Jacob was from their own family, she ran to tell her father, who greeted Jacob warmly. After staying with them for a month, Jacob was hired to tend Laban's flocks. When wages were discussed, Jacob proposed to work seven years to earn Rachel as his wife (vv 15-20).

At the end of seven years Jacob was set to claim his wages, but on the night of the wedding feast, Laban gave his older daughter, Leah, to Jacob; Jacob did not discover the substitution until morning. He felt cheated and protested to Laban, but Laban insisted that according to custom the older daughter must marry first and proposed that Jacob work another seven years for Rachel. Jacob agreed to this and put in his time (Gn 29:21-30).

Genesis 29 and 30 relate the births of most of Jacob's children. Leah bore Jacob four sons: Reuben, Simeon, Levi, and Judah (Gn 29:31-35). She named her first son Reuben ("see, a son") since she felt that her husband would love her because she bore a son. Simeon is derived from the root "hear," since Leah thought that God had given her this son because he had heard that she was hated. Levi is related to the verb "join," for Leah thought that her husband would be joined to her because of this third son. Judah means "praise," for she praised the Lord at the birth of her fourth son.

Rachel had not conceived any children, so she gave her maid Bilhah to Jacob. She bore him Dan and Naphtali (Gn 30:1-8). Rachel named the first son Dan ("he judged") because God had judged, that is, vindicated her. Naphtali means "my struggle, my wrestling," for Rachel said she had wrestled with and overcome her sister.

Thereupon Leah gave her maid Zilpah to Jacob as a wife; she brought forth Gad and Asher (Gn 30:11). Gad means "fortune"; Leah said, "Good fortune," when he was born. Asher ("happy") was so named because Leah said, "Now the women will call me happy."

Reuben found some mandrakes in the field, and Leah traded them to Rachel for Jacob's services. Leah then bore sons five and six, Issachar and Zebulun, followed by a daughter, whom she named Dinah (Gn 30:14-21). Issachar perhaps means "reward," for Leah said that God had rewarded her for giving her maidservant to her husband. Zebulun probably means "honor"; Leah thought that now her husband would honor her.

At last Rachel herself conceived and bore her first child, a son whom she named Joseph. "Joseph" means "he will add" or "may he add," for Rachel wanted God to add another son to her.

Jacob wanted to leave and go back to Canaan, but Laban wanted him to stay, for through divination he had learned that the Lord had blessed him because of Jacob (Gn 30:27). They discussed the matter of wages, and Jacob proposed that every speckled and spotted sheep and goat and every black lamb become his (vv 32-33). Laban agreed to this, but he quickly removed all the animals marked in that fashion and put them under the care of his sons, some three days' distance from the rest of the flocks (vv 35-36).

Jacob also contrived to gain an advantage; he tried to influence the genetics of the animals by putting speckled and streaked wooden rods by the water troughs when the best animals were breeding. The Lord blessed Jacob and he became rich in flocks and herds (Gn 30:37-43).

The sons of Laban became very bitter toward Jacob, and Laban's attitude toward him changed also. Jacob noticed this, and now the Lord spoke to Jacob and told him to return to Canaan (Gn 31:3-16). Jacob held a family council with his two wives and told them how God had blessed him, even though their father had cheated him and had changed his wages ten times. Jacob organized his caravan while Laban was away shearing sheep. Rachel stole her father's household gods, for their possession would make the holder heir to Laban's estate (see Nuzi Tablets). The party took off, crossed the Euphrates, and headed for Gilead. Laban and his relatives pursued them, but God spoke to Laban in a dream, warning him not to say anything to Jacob.

When Laban caught up with Jacob, he upbraided him for sneaking away and inquired about his household gods. Jacob did not know what Rachel had done, so he said that the one found with the gods should be put to death (Gn 31:32). Rachel had hidden them in a camel saddle and was sitting on the saddle when her father searched the tent. Laban did not find the idols. After this, Jacob became angry and complained that he had served Laban for 20 years and that Laban had reduced his wages ten times.

Laban suggested a covenant of peace, so the two men gathered stones to make a monument and called it "heap of witness." Early the next morning Laban said his farewells and returned home.

As Jacob and his household journeyed on, he was met by the angels of God ("God's camp," Gn 32:2), so he named that place Mahanaim, "the two camps." Jacob sent messengers ahead to inform Esau of his return. They came back with the news that Esau was approaching with 400 men. Jacob was afraid and sought the Lord's protection. To win Esau's favor, Jacob sent ahead gifts of animals, and that night he sent his family and possessions across the ford of the Jabbok River. Jacob was left alone, and "a man" wrestled with him throughout the night. Toward dawn the man touched Jacob's thigh, and his hip was dislocated, but Jacob would not give up until the "man" blessed him. Here the Lord changed Jacob's name to Israel ("he strives with God"), and Jacob named the place Peniel ("face of God") because he had seen God face to face and lived (Gn 32:30).

Esau was getting near, so Jacob arranged his family and went forward, bowing low before his brother. But Esau was gracious and forgiving and the meeting was a happy one (Gn 33:4). Esau was surprised at Jacob's large family and property and made every gesture of friendship. Esau returned to Seir, and Jacob moved on to Shechem, where he bought a piece of land from Hamor, the father of Shechem. Jacob built an altar there and named it El-Elohe-Israel, "God, the God of Israel" (v 20).

Acting on the Lord's instructions, Jacob moved to Bethel and expelled the foreign gods from his household. At Luz (Bethel) the Lord again met him and reaffirmed his new name, renewing his promise of land and descendants (Gn 35:9-15). As they journeyed south, Rachel died while giving birth to her second son (vv 16-20). She named him Ben-oni ("son of my sorrow"), but Jacob changed his name to Benjamin ("son of the right hand"). Jacob went on to Hebron and found that Isaac was still living. Isaac died at age 180 and was buried by Esau and Jacob.

Although the story of Jacob continues in the book of Genesis, the central figure of chapters 37–50 is Joseph, Jacob's favorite son, the firstborn of Rachel.

Jacob showed this favoritism so openly that the other sons became jealous of Joseph. They plotted to kill Joseph but instead sold him to a caravan of traders on their way to Egypt (Gn 37:9-28). They took Joseph's coat, dipped it into the blood of a goat, and took it to their father, telling him that they had found the robe. Jacob recognized the coat he had given his son and concluded that he was dead. Jacob was heartbroken and would not be comforted.

When a famine hit Canaan, Jacob sent his sons to Egypt to buy grain (Gn 42:1-5), keeping Benjamin at home. When the brothers returned to Canaan, they reported to Jacob that the governor (who was really Joseph) had kept Simeon as a hostage and demanded that they bring Benjamin with them when they came again for grain. The famine continued, and Jacob again sent his sons to Egypt for grain. Very reluctantly, he permitted Benjamin to go with them, also sending a gift for the Egyptian governor (43:11-14).

The next news Jacob received was that Joseph was alive in Egypt and wanted his father and all his family to join him (Gn 45:21-28). Jacob went first to Beersheba and made offerings to the Lord. The Lord spoke to Jacob, telling him to go down to Egypt and confirming once more the promises he had previously made. Jacob and his descendants who were in Egypt numbered 70, including the two sons of Joseph.

When Jacob reached Goshen, Joseph came to meet him, and there was a joyous reunion (Gn 46:28-30). Joseph reported the arrival of his father and brothers to the pharaoh (47:1) and took five of the brothers and his father to meet the ruler. Israel settled in the area of Goshen and prospered there. Jacob spent 17 years in Egypt and reached the age of 147.

When Jacob sensed his death was near, he called Joseph and made him swear that he would bury him with his forebears in Canaan. Joseph took his two sons, Manasseh and Ephraim, to his father for the patriarchal blessing. He presented the boys so that Manasseh, the firstborn, would be on Jacob's right and Ephraim on his left. Jacob, however crossed his hands and gave the younger son the greater blessing (48:13-20). Jacob prophesied that his people would return to Canaan, and he gave Joseph a double portion of the land. Then Jacob called for all his sons and gave to each of them a blessing (49:1-28). Judah received the place of preeminence, and it is he who appears in the genealogies of Jesus (vv 8-12). The blessing of Joseph shows the mark of special favor (vv 22-26). Jacob also charged his sons to bury him in the cave of Machpelah near Hebron, then he drew his feet up on the bed and died.

Joseph summoned the physicians to embalm his father according to Egyptian practice; there were 40 days for embalming and 70 days for the period of mourning (Gn 50:1-3). Arrangements were made to go to Canaan to bury Jacob as Joseph had promised, and a large funeral procession, including many Egyptian officials as well as the family of Jacob, went up from Egypt. The company mourned for seven days at the threshing floor of Atad; then the sons of Jacob buried him in the cave of Machpelah as he had requested. The entire group returned to Egypt, and Joseph assured his brothers that he had no intention of avenging the wrong they had done him. God had meant the whole episode for good (vv 15-21).

Jacob as the Nation Israel God made the same promises concerning the land and the nation to Abraham, Isaac, and Jacob, but it is by Jacob's God-given name, Israel, that the nation is known.

The name Jacob is used for the nation about 100 times (e.g., Nm 24:5, 19; Dt 32:9; Ps 59:13). It is often found as a parallel to Israel (e.g., Nm 23:7; Dt 33:10; Is 14:1). "Jacob" is also used specifically of the northern kingdom of Israel (Am 7:2, 5). In Isaiah 41:21 "the King of Jacob" refers to God himself.

See also Genesis, Book of; Israel, History of; Patriarchs, Period of the.
2. Father of Joseph, the husband of Mary and earthly father of Jesus according to Matthew's genealogy (Mt 1:16). Luke, however, names Heli as Joseph's father (Lk 3:24). *See* Genealogy of Jesus Christ (The Relationship between the Two Records).

JACOB'S LADDER* When Jacob left home after deceiving his father, Isaac, into giving him the blessing that Isaac had intended for Esau (Gn 27:6-40), he was not only desirous of finding a wife from among the daughters of his mother's brother, but he was also literally fleeing for his life, because Esau had determined to kill him (v 41). When he stopped to rest for the night in the open countryside, the Lord appeared to him in a dream and blessed him (28:10-22). In the vision Jacob saw a ladder reaching from the earth to heaven with angels ascending and descending upon it. At the top of the ladder stood the Lord himself, who confirmed to Jacob the promise previously given to Abraham (12:2-3, 7), and repeated to Isaac (26:3-5). In the context it seems clear that the ladder with the ascending and descending angels depicts God reaching out to Jacob and making a way for Jacob to have a relationship with him. The communion that was to exist between God and Jacob is symbolized in the ladder and the movement of the angels. This communication between heaven and earth appears to be the same point that is made in John 1:50 when Jesus says to Nathanael and his other disciples, "You will all see heaven open and the angels of God going up and down upon the Son of Man" (NLT). Jacob was so overwhelmed by God's grace in revealing himself to him in this way that he named the place at which this took place Bethel—the House of God.

JACOB'S WELL Place mentioned only in John's Gospel (Jn 4:5-29). It was here that Jesus sat and talked with the unnamed woman of Samaria, who readily accepted Jesus' words. This well is located in a plot of ground acquired by the patriarch Jacob, about 300 yards (274 meters) southeast of the traditional tomb of Joseph (Gn 33:19; Jos 24:32; Jn 4:5-6). The site is about two miles (3.2 kilometers) southeast of modern Nablus, 600 yards (549 meters) southeast of the site of ancient Shechem (modern Balata), and 1,000 yards (914 meters) south of Sychar (modern Askar). Towering over the site on the northwest is Mt Ebal (at the foot of which lies Askar), and on the southwest Mt Gerizim, mountains of cursing and blessing, respectively (Dt 27:12-13; Jos 8:30-33). Near here Abraham built his first altar, and Jacob his second (Gn 12:6-7; 33:18-20). Thus the site is one of the most ancient and sacred in the Holy Land.

The well is about 100 feet (30.5 meters) in depth and one yard (.9 meter) in diameter, cut through limestone. Fed by subterranean streams from the adjacent mountain slopes, the water is pure and plentiful, the pride of the villagers. A church has existed on the site from at least AD 380. The Greek Orthodox Church acquired the site in 1885 and built a structure on the site. Access to the well is by steps leading from either side of the church altar to the well curb below.

JADA *See* Jade.

JADAH Variant of Jehoaddah (1 Chr 8:36) and Jarah (1 Chr 9:42). *See* Jehoadah, Jehoaddah.

JADDAI Nebo's descendant, who was encouraged by Ezra to divorce his foreign wife during the postexilic era (Ezr 10:43).

JADDUA
1. Leader who set his seal on Ezra's covenant during the postexilic era (Neh 10:21).
2. Eliashib's descendant and a contemporary of Nehemiah (Neh 12:11, 22). Jaddua's father, Jonathan (v 11), is mentioned in the Elephantine papyri as Johanan (see also v 22).

JADE* Onam's son from Judah's tribe (1 Chr 2:28, 32).

JADON Workman on the Jerusalem wall after the return from exile. Jadon worked on the section near the Old Gate of the city with men from Gibeon and Mizpah. He was a Meronothite (Neh 3:7).

JAEL Wife of Heber. Though her husband was from the Kenite tribe, a longtime ally of Israel, he had chosen to side with Jabin, the Canaanite king. Jael demonstrated her loyalty to Israel, Jabin's enemy, however, by inviting Sisera, Jabin's general, into her tent, giving him milk instead of water, providing him a place to sleep, and then driving a tent peg into his temple (Jgs 4:17-18, 21-22). Deborah, the inspired poetess, reflecting on the God-given victory over the Canaanites, praises Jael for this deed (5:6, 24-31).

JAGUR Place in the extreme southern part of Israel, near Edom, inherited by Judah's tribe soon after the Conquest (Jos 15:21).

JAH* Abbreviation of the covenant name of God, YHWH or Yahweh ("Jehovah," KJV; "LORD," most modern translations). The fragment is often used in words and names (e.g., Hallelu*jah*, *Jah*aziel). *See* God, Names of.

JAHATH
1. Reaiah's son and the father of Ahumai and Lahad, Zorathites from Judah's tribe (1 Chr 4:2).
2. Gershonite Levite (1 Chr 6:20), whose descendant Asaph was appointed by King David to serve as a musician in the temple (v 43).
3. A descendant of Shimei, who was a descendant of Gershon from Levi's tribe (1 Chr 23:10-11).
4. Shelomith's son from Levi's tribe (1 Chr 24:22).
5. Merarite Levite, who was one of the supervisors of the temple repairs under Josiah (2 Chr 34:12).

JAHAZ Town east of the Dead Sea (in modern Jordan) where the Israelites defeated Sihon, king of the Amorites, when he refused to permit them to pass through his land (Nm 21:23; Dt 2:32; Jgs 11:20). According to Joshua 13:18, Moses gave the town to Reuben's tribe as part of its allotment. The town with its surrounding pasturelands was given to the Merarite Levites (Jos 21:36; 1 Chr 6:78).

In later times, in prophetic oracles by both Isaiah (Is 15:4) and Jeremiah (Jer 48:21), it is referred to as a city in the land of Moab. This may indicate that it was taken from Israel by Moab (to whom it apparently belonged before Sihon conquered it). The town is mentioned on the Moabite Stone (known as the Dibon Stele and dating to c. 845 BC) as the place where Mesha, king of Moab, had lived while at war with Israel. According to Mesha, he took Jahaz from Israel and added it to his own territory.

JAHAZA*, JAHAZAH* KJV spellings of Jahaz. *See* Jahaz.

JAHAZIAH* KJV rendering of Jahzeiah, Tikvah's son, in Ezra 10:15. *See* Jahzeiah.

JAHAZIEL
1. Warrior from Benjamin's tribe who joined David at Ziklag in his struggle against King Saul. Jahaziel was one of David's ambidextrous archers and slingers (1 Chr 12:4).
2. One of the two priests David appointed to blow trumpets before the ark as it was brought into the tent in Jerusalem, where it remained until the completion of the temple by Solomon (1 Chr 16:6).
3. Levite belonging to the Kohathite division appointed by David to temple duties (1 Chr 23:19; 24:23).
4. Levite of the sons of Asaph who encouraged Jehoshaphat and the army of Judah not to be dismayed by the size of Moabite and Ammonite armies coming against them but to stand still and see the victory of the Lord (2 Chr 20:14). Jehoshaphat's response exemplified a godly king encouraging his people to have faith in the Lord their God (vv 18-21).
5. Shecaniah's father. Shecaniah returned to Jerusalem with Ezra after the exile (Ezr 8:5).

JAHDAI Caleb's descendant from Judah's tribe (1 Chr 2:47).

JAHDIEL One of the family heads of Manasseh's tribe dwelling east of the Jordan following the allotment of the land (1 Chr 5:24). He was noted as one of the mighty warriors in his tribe.

JAHDO Gadite, son of Buz and a forefather of a number of valiant men who were registered during the reigns of King Jeroboam of Israel (793–753 BC) and King Jotham of Judah (750–735 BC; 1 Chr 5:14).

JAHLEEL, JAHLEELITE Zebulun's son (Gn 46:14) and the founder of the Jahleelite family (Nm 26:26).

JAHMAI Tola's son from Issachar's tribe (1 Chr 7:2).

JAHZAH* Alternate form of Jahaz, a town east of the Dead Sea, in 1 Chronicles 6:78 (NLT mg) and Jeremiah 48:21 (NLT mg). *See* Jahaz.

JAHZEEL, JAHZEELITE Naphtali's son (Gn 46:24; 1 Chr 7:13) and founder of the Jahzeelite family (Nm 26:48).

JAHZEIAH Tikvah's son and one of the persons named in connection with the divorce proceedings between the Israelites and their foreign wives (Ezr 10:15). Opinions differ as to whether he was for or against the proceedings. While the Hebrew text can be justifiably read either way, the grammar favors the interpretation that Jahzeiah opposed the proceedings (see NLT).

JAHZERAH Ancestor of a priest who returned to Judah after the Babylonian exile (1 Chr 9:12). He is called Ahzai in Nehemiah 11:13. Little else is known about him except that he was a great-grandson of a priest named Immer who lived in Jerusalem before the exile. *See also* Ahzai.

JAHZIEL* Alternate spelling of Jahzeel, Naphtali's son, in 1 Chronicles 7:13 (NLT mg). *See* Jahzeel, Jahzeelite.

JAIR
1. Descendant of Manasseh (Nm 32:41), who at the time of the Conquest took several villages in the Argob region of Bashan and Gilead and called them after his own name, Havvoth-jair, meaning "Towns of Jair" (Dt 3:14; cf. Jos 13:30; 1 Kgs 4:13; 1 Chr 2:23). *See also* Havoth-jair, Havvoth-jair.
2. One of the judges of Israel. He judged Israel 22 years. His being a Gileadite makes it probable that he was a descendant of #1 above (Jgs 10:3-5).
3. Father of Elhanan, who killed Lahmi, Goliath's brother (1 Chr 20:5). In 2 Samuel 21:19 he is called Jaare-oregim.
4. Father of Mordecai (Est 2:5). Because of the time lapse from the capture of Jeconiah, king of Judah (597 BC), to the beginning of the reign of Xerxes, king of Persia (486 BC), Jair was either the one taken captive with Jeconiah or his father, Shimei, was, in which case Jair would have been born during the Captivity.

JAIRITE Descendant of Jair from Manasseh's tribe (2 Sm 20:26). *See* Jair #1.

JAIRUS Leader of the synagogue, perhaps at Capernaum. Jairus sought Jesus among the crowds and petitioned him to come and heal his critically ill daughter. While delayed by another healing, Jesus learned that Jairus's daughter had died. Encouraging Jairus not to fear but to believe, Jesus went on to the leader's house, dismissed the mourners, and brought the child back to life (Mk 5:22, 35-42; Lk 8:41, 49-55).

JAKAN* KJV spelling of Jaakan, Esau's descendant, in 1 Chronicles 1:42. *See* Jaakan.

JAKEH Agur's father. Agur authored a series of proverbs addressed to Ithiel and Ucal (Prv 30:1).

JAKIM
1. Shimei's descendant from Benjamin's tribe (1 Chr 8:19).
2. Family leader of the 12th group of Aaron's descendants assigned to temple duty in David's time (1 Chr 24:12).

JAKIN *See* Jachin.

JAKIN AND BOAZ *See* Jachin and Boaz.

JAKINITE *See* Jachinite.

JALAM Esau's son and chief of an Edomite clan (Gn 36:5, 14, 18; 1 Chr 1:35).

JALON Ezrah's son from Judah's tribe (1 Chr 4:17).

JAMBRES Enemy of Moses, who, along with Jannes, is used by Paul as an example of the type of person to avoid (2 Tm 3:8-9). *See* Jannes and Jambres.

JAMBRI Ancestor of an Arab tribe. During the Hasmonean (Maccabean) wars when Jonathan was ruler, the Jambrites captured a baggage train of the Jews when it was being sent to the Nabateans for safekeeping (1 Macc 9:36).

JAMES (Person)
1. James, brother of Jesus; leading elder in the church at Jerusalem; author of the epistle bearing his name.
The only two references to James in the Gospels

mention him with his brothers Joseph (Greek Joses), Simon, and Judas (Mt 13:55; Mk 6:3). This James may have been, after Jesus, the oldest of the brothers. The question has been raised about whether these were indeed full brothers of Jesus by Mary, for such a situation has created difficulty for those who cannot square it with their views on the perpetual virginity of Mary. But there seems to be no good reason to challenge the fact from Scripture. As with the other brothers, James apparently did not accept Jesus' authority during his earthly life (Jn 7:5).

There is no specific mention of James's conversion; it may have dated from Jesus' appearance to him and the others after Jesus' resurrection (1 Cor 15:7). He became head of the church at Jerusalem (Acts 12:17; 21:18; Gal 2:9). Although Jesus had always taught the relative subordination of family ties (Mt 12:48-50; Mk 3:33-35; Lk 8:21), it is hard to believe that James's authority was not somehow enhanced because of his relationship to the Master.

James was regarded as an apostle (Gal 1:19), although he was not one of the Twelve. Some suggest he was a replacement for the martyred son of Zebedee; others infer his apostleship by widening the scope of that term to embrace both "the Twelve" and "all the apostles" (see the two separate categories cited in 1 Cor 15:5, 7).

Tradition stated that James was appointed the first bishop of Jerusalem by the Lord himself as well as the apostles. What is certain is that he presided over the first Council of Jerusalem, called to consider the terms for admission of Gentiles into the Christian church, and he may have formulated the decree that met with the approval of all his colleagues and was sent to the churches of Antioch, Syria, and Cilicia (Acts 15:19-20). James evidently regarded his own special ministry as being to the Jews, and his was a mediating role in the controversy that arose in the young church around the place of the law for those who had become Christians, from both Gentile and Jewish origins.

That he continued to have strong Jewish-Christian sympathies is apparent from the request made to Paul when the latter visited Jerusalem for the last time (Acts 21:18-25). This was also the last mention in Acts of James's career. His name also occurs in the NT as the traditional author of the Epistle of James, where he describes himself as "a slave of God and of the Lord Jesus Christ" (Jas 1:1).

According to Hegesippus (c. 180), James's faithful adherence to the Jewish law and his austere lifestyle led to the designation "the Just." It seems clear that James suffered martyrdom. Josephus places it in the year 61, when there was a Jewish uprising after the death of Festus the procurator and before his successor had been appointed.

2. James, son of Alphaeus; one of the 12 apostles.

James, son of Alphaeus, is always listed as one of the 12 apostles (Mt 10:3; Mk 3:18; Lk 6:15; Acts 1:13), but nothing is known for certain about him. Levi (also known as Matthew) is also described as the son of Alphaeus (Mk 2:14), but it is improbable that he and James were brothers. Many scholars have identified him with the one called "James the less" or "James the smaller." The description "the less" seems to have been given to distinguish him from the son of Zebedee, and it may signify that he was either smaller or younger than Zebedee's son (the Greek word can cover both interpretations).

3. James, son of Zebedee. One of the 12 apostles; the first of them to be martyred (AD 44).

James was a Galilean fisherman whose circumstances we can suppose to have been comfortable (Mk 1:19-20) and who was called to be one of the disciples at the same time as his brother John (Mt 4:21; Mk 1:19-20). It is reasonable to assume that he was older than John, both because he is nearly always mentioned first and because John is sometimes identified as "the brother of James" (Mt 10:2; 17:1; Mk 3:17; 5:37).

James, John, and Simon Peter, who were part of a fishing partnership that included Andrew, Simon's brother (Lk 5:10), were a trio who attained in some sense a place of primacy among the disciples. They are found at the center of things—for example, when Jairus's daughter was raised (Mk 5:37; Lk 8:51), at the Transfiguration (Mt 17:1; Mk 9:2; Lk 9:28), on the Mount of Olives (Mk 13:3), and in the Garden of Gethsemane (Mt 26:37; Mk 14:33). It was James and John, moreover, who had earlier accompanied Jesus to the home of Simon and Andrew (Mk 1:29).

James and John were given by Jesus the nickname Boanerges, or "sons of thunder" (Mk 3:17), when they were rebuked by the Lord for impetuous speech and for having totally misconceived the purpose of his coming. This may have been the consequence of the suggestion made by them that they should pray for the destruction of the Samaritan village, the inhabitants of which had rejected the Lord's messengers (Lk 9:54; cf. Mk 9:38; Lk 9:49).

The presumptuous and ill-considered thinking of the two brothers was obvious also when, after asking with his brother for a place of honor in the kingdom, James was corecipient of the prophecy that they would drink the cup their Master was to drink (Mk 10:35-40; cf. Mt 20:20-23). The two sons of Zebedee are also assumed to have been present with the other disciples when the risen Christ appeared by the Sea of Galilee (Jn 21:1), though curiously James's name is nowhere mentioned in the fourth Gospel.

We know nothing about James's career subsequently until about the year 44, when Jesus' prophecy was fulfilled: James was killed "by the sword" by Herod Agrippa I, and thus became the first of the Twelve whose martyrdom was referred to in the NT (Acts 12:1-2).

The wife of Zebedee was Salome (Mt 27:56; Mk 15:40), who may have been a sister of the Lord's mother (Jn 19:25). If this were so, it would mean that James and John were first cousins of Jesus and that they may have considered themselves to have been in a privileged position.

JAMES, Letter of First letter of the General Epistles.

PREVIEW
•Author
•Date, Origin, and Destination
•Purpose of Writing and Theological Teaching
•Content

Author According to the salutation, this letter was written by "James, a slave of God and of the Lord Jesus Christ" (Jas 1:1, NLT). But who was this James? Of the several mentioned in the NT, only two have ever been proposed as the author of this letter—James the son of Zebedee, and James the Lord's brother.

The James who wrote this epistle was probably not James the son of Zebedee, for he was martyred too early (AD 44) to have written it (see Acts 12:1-2). Most scholars have identified this James as Jesus' brother (Mk 6:3;

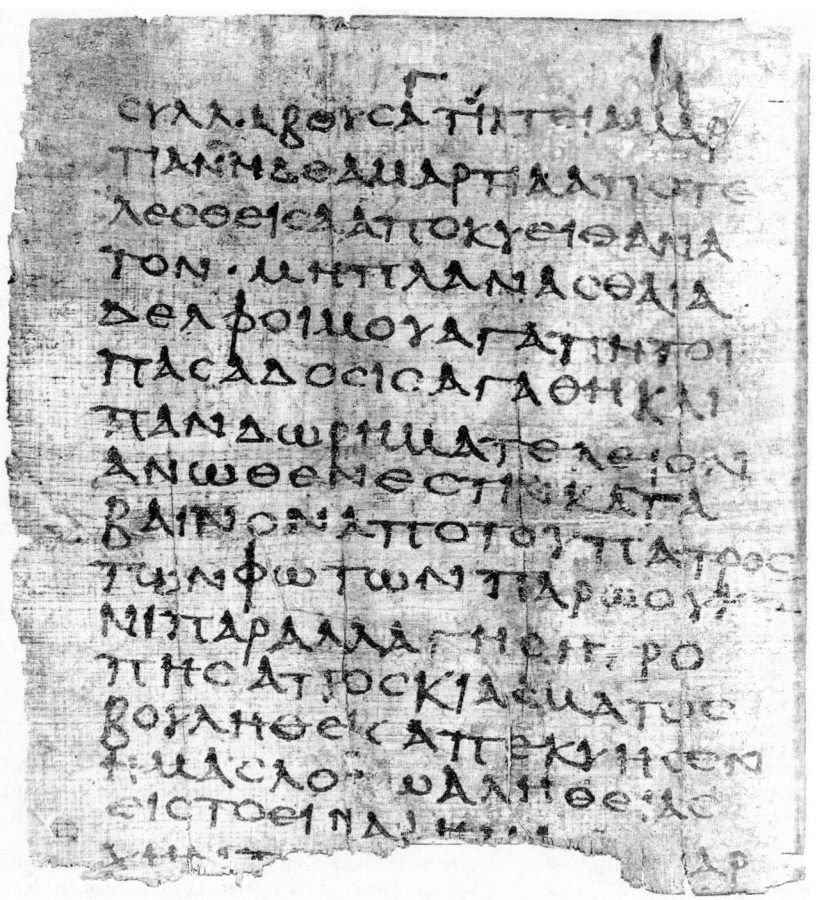

**Ancient Papyrus
Manuscript of James**
James 1:15-18 from
Papyrus Oxyrhynchus 1229
(c. 200)—P23

Gal 1:19), the prominent elder of the church in Jerusalem (Acts 15:13, 19; 21:17-25; Gal 2:12). The whole character of the epistle coincides with what we know of this James's legalism and Jewishness.

As an elder of Jerusalem writing to the 12 tribes of the dispersion (which came as a result of the persecution noted in Acts 11:19), James set forth the gospel in its relation to the law, which the Jews revered. As Paul's epistles are a commentary on the doctrines flowing from the death and resurrection of Christ, so James's epistle has a close connection with Christ's teaching during his life on earth, especially his Sermon on the Mount. In both the Sermon on the Mount and the Epistle of James, the law is represented as fulfilled in love, and the very language is remarkably similar (cf. Jas 1:2 with Mt 5:12; Jas 1:4 with Mt 5:48; Jas 1:5 and 5:14-15 with Mt 7:7-11; Jas 2:13 with Mt 5:7 and 6:14-15; Jas 2:10 with Mt 5:19; Jas 4:4 with Mt 6:24; Jas 4:11 with Mt 7:1-2; Jas 5:2 with Mt 6:19). The whole spirit of this epistle breathes the same gospel-righteousness that the Sermon on the Mount inculcates as the highest realization of the law. James's own character as "the Just" suited this coincidence (cf. Jas 1:20; 2:10; 3:18 with Mt 5:20). It also fitted him for presiding over a church still zealous for the law (Acts 21:18-24; Gal 2:12). If any could win the Jews to the gospel, he was the most likely one because he presented a pattern of OT righteousness, combined with evangelical faith (cf. also Jas 2:8 with Mt 5:44, 48).

Date, Origin, and Destination Many scholars confirm an early date for James's epistle, even as early as AD 45–49, because the whole orientation of the epistle fits

the early history of the church, an era in which many Jewish Christians had not made a complete severance from Judaism. Thus, James uses the terms "the twelve tribes" (Jas 1:1) and "the synagogue" (2:2, Greek); he speaks as an OT prophet (5:1ff.) and as one fond of OT proverbs (cf. Jas 1:5 with Prv 2:6; Jas 1:19 with Prv 29:20; Jas 3:18 with Prv 11:30; Jas 4:13-16 with Prv 27:1; and Jas 5:20 with Prv 10:12). James's message, as was noted earlier, closely follows Jesus' sermons. His message does not deal with the Jewish/Gentile problems that arose in the 50s and 60s. Moreover, he, unlike Peter, Jude, and John (in their epistles), did not deal with false teachings. All these facts point to an early date. This date is probably before AD 50, when the first Jerusalem Council assembled to discuss the Jewish/Gentile problem (Acts 15:1ff.). Also, the date is probably after AD 44, the time of the persecution instigated by Herod Agrippa (12:1). This persecution would have caused many Jewish Christians to leave Jerusalem and thereby be "the dispersed" (Jas 1:1). Thus, James should be dated AD 45–49. As such, the Epistle of James was the first NT book to be written. If these dates are not accurate, then we are, at least, sure that it was written before AD 61 or 62, the time of James's martyrdom, according to Josephus.

Although a number of suggestions have been made from time to time about the origin of the book, there can be little doubt that the letter was written in Palestine. The author makes allusions that are Near Eastern generally and Palestinian particularly (cf. "the early and late rain," 5:7; the spring of brackish water, 3:11; the fig, olive, and vine, 3:12; and the "scorching heat," 1:11).

The contents of the letter indicate clearly that James was writing to Jewish Christians. They are called "the twelve tribes," a title of Israel (1:1); their Christianity is assumed in 2:1; their place of meeting is called a synagogue (2:2); and they are told about the compassion of "the Lord Almighty" (5:4)—a name for God used in the OT. In the shorter, disconnected passages of the letter, it is impossible to discover anything about the readers' circumstances. Most of these exhortations are general and relate to social and spiritual conditions one might find among any group of Christians in any age. The more extended passages that deal with social conditions (2:1-12; 5:1-11) do provide information about the readers' situation. James is addressing poor Christians who are employed as farm laborers by wealthy landowners. A few rich may be included among his Jewish Christian readers (cf. 4:13-17), but James is primarily concerned with the poor. His statements denouncing the rich are reminiscent of the OT prophets, especially Amos.

Purpose of Writing and Theological Teaching

The letter of James was written (1) to strengthen Jewish Christians undergoing trial (Jas 1:2-4, 13-15; 5:7-11); (2) to correct a misunderstanding of the Pauline doctrine of justification by faith (2:14-26); and (3) to pass down to first-generation Christians a wealth of practical wisdom.

James's theology is not dogmatic; it omits the great theological themes that dominate Paul's writings and play such an important role in the rest of the books of the NT. James makes no mention of the Incarnation, and the name of Christ appears only twice (1:1; 2:1). No mention is made of Christ's sufferings, death, or resurrection.

James's theology is practical and has a decided Jewish flavor. The distinctive Christian features, of course, are there. James has simply mingled the two to produce a Jewish-Christian document.

The outstanding theological themes of the letter are as follows:

Temptations and Trials The typically Jewish teachings—joy in trials and the use of trials for the building and perfecting of character—are both found in the letter (1:2-4). James also discusses the origin of temptation (vv 13-15). Here the author comes into conflict with contemporary Jewish theology. The rabbinical solution to the problem of the origin of sin was that there was an evil tendency in man that enticed man to sin. The rabbis reasoned that since God is the Creator of all things, including the evil impulse in people, they are not responsible for their sins. No, says James. "And remember, no one who wants to do wrong should ever say, 'God is tempting me.' God is never tempted to do wrong, and he never tempts anyone else either. Temptation comes from the lure of our own evil desires" (vv 13-14, NLT).

Law The entire letter is concerned with ethical teaching; there is no mention of the central gospel truths of Christ's death and resurrection. James presupposes the gospel and presents the ethical side of Christianity as a perfect law. He seems to be reassuring his Jewish-Christian readers that for them there is still law (the priceless possession of every Jew).

The law (ethical teaching of Christianity) is a perfect law (1:25) because it was perfected by Jesus Christ. It is also a law of freedom—that is, a law that applies to those who have freedom, not from law, but from sin and self through the "word of truth." Thus "law" is a Palestinian-Christian Jew's way of describing the ethical teaching of the Christian faith, the standard of conduct for the believer in Jesus Christ.

This tendency to describe Christian ethical teaching as law is found in 2:8-13, a passage that arises out of a rebuke against the favoritism that James's readers were showing toward the rich. This favoritism was being condoned by an appeal to the law of love to one's neighbor. So James writes, "It is good when you truly obey our Lord's royal command" (2:8, NLT). The "royal command" is for those who are of God's kingdom; it is the rule of faith for those who have willingly subjected themselves to God's rule. The identification of law with the ethical side of Christianity runs through the entire letter.

Faith and Works Faith plays an important role in the theology of James. The basic element of piety (1:3; cf. 2:5) is belief in God—not merely belief in his existence but belief in his character as being good and benevolent in his dealings with mankind (1:6). Faith includes belief in the power of God and in his ability to perform miraculous acts; it is closely associated with prayer (5:15-16; cf. 1:6). James has a dynamic concept of faith and clearly goes beyond Judaism when he speaks of faith directed toward the Lord Jesus Christ (2:1).

Similarities exist between the concept of faith in James and that concept in the teachings of Jesus. For the Lord Jesus, also, faith meant gaining access to the divine power and is often associated with healing (cf. Mt 21:22; Mk 5:34; 11:24).

The best-known passage in which faith is mentioned is James 2:14-26, where it is contrasted with works. From a close study of this passage, it can be determined that James is not contradicting Paul. For both James and Paul, faith is directed toward the Lord Jesus Christ; such faith will always produce good works. The faith of which James speaks is not faith in the Hebraic sense of trust in God that results in moral action. This is not recognized as *true* faith by James (cf. "if a man says he has faith," 2:14), and Paul would agree with him.

James's use of the word "works" differs significantly from Paul's. For James, "works" are works of faith, the ethical outworking of true spirituality and include especially the "work of love" (2:8). (Paul would probably call such works "the fruit of the Spirit.") When Paul uses the word "works," he usually has in mind the works of the law whereby people attempt to establish their own righteousness before God. It is against such theological heresy that Paul's strongest polemics are addressed in the letters to the Galatians and Romans.

Wisdom James's concept of wisdom also reveals the Jewish background of the letter. Wisdom is primarily practical, not philosophical. It is not to be identified with reasoning power or the ability to apprehend intellectual problems; it has nothing to do with the questions *how* or *why*. It is to be sought by earnest prayer and is a gift from God (Jas 1:5). Both of these ideas find their roots in the Wisdom Literature of the Jews (cf. Prv 2:6; Wisd of Sol 7:7; Ecclus 1:1). The wise man demonstrates his wisdom by his good life (Jas 3:13), whereas the wisdom that produces jealousy and selfishness is not God's kind of wisdom (vv 15-16).

Doctrine of the End Time Three important end-time themes are touched upon in the letter.

➤THE KINGDOM OF GOD Mention of the kingdom of God grows out of a discussion of favoritism in the first half of chapter 2. No favoritism is to be shown to the rich, for James asks, "Hasn't God chosen the poor in this world to be rich in faith? Aren't they the ones who will inherit the kingdom God promised to those who love him?" (2:5, NLT). This echoes our Lord's teaching in Luke 6:20: "God blesses you who are poor, for the Kingdom of God is given to you" (NLT). The kingdom is the reign of God partially realized in this life but fully realized in the life to come (cf. "promised," Jas 2:5).

➤JUDGMENT This is a dominant end-time theme of the letter. In 2:12, the readers are admonished to speak and act, remembering that they will be judged under the law of liberty, and they are reminded that judgment is without mercy to one who has shown no mercy. In other words, judgment will be administered according to "works of love." In 3:1, James addresses teachers and reminds them that privilege is another basis on which God judges.

The theme of judgment again appears in 5:1-6, and here the author reaches prophetic heights. God's judgment will fall on the wealthy landowners who have lived self-indulgent, irresponsible lives. Not only have they cheated their poor tenant farmers; they have even "condemned and killed good people who had no power to defend themselves against you [the landowners]" (5:6, NLT). All this has made them ripe for judgment ("your hearts are nice and fat, ready for the slaughter"—v 5, NLT).

The final passage on judgment (5:9) is addressed to those who are exploited or suffering. James's word of exhortation is that they are not to grumble against each other. Judging is God's business, and the Judge is close at hand.

➤THE SECOND COMING The hope of Christ's coming is presented as the great stimulus for Christian living. Every kind of suffering and trial must be endured because the coming of Christ is at hand (5:8). This expectancy is powerful and immediate—like that found in the Thessalonian letters.

Content In the true spirit of Wisdom Literature, James touches upon many subjects. His short, abrupt paragraphs have been likened to a string of pearls—each is an entity in itself. Some transitions exist, but they are often difficult to find and James moves quickly from one subject to another.

The author begins by identifying himself as the "slave of God and of the Lord Jesus Christ," and his readers as the "twelve tribes in the dispersion" (see NLT mg)—that is, the Jewish Christians who left Jerusalem and Israel due to persecution.

His first word is one of encouragement. Trials are to be counted as joy because they are God's way of testing the believer, and they produce spiritual maturity. If the reason for a trial is not clear, God can and will give the answer. He is a lavish giver of wisdom to those who really want it (1:5-8).

A poor Christian should be proud of his exalted position in Jesus Christ, and a rich Christian should be glad that he has discovered there are more important things than wealth. Riches are transitory, like quickly wilting flowers under the hot Palestine sun (1:9-11).

God promises life to those who endure trials. One must not blame God for temptation, for it is contrary to his very nature either to be tempted or to tempt people. Temptation has its origin in people's selfish desire—a desire that, when brought to full fruition, produces death (1:12-15). God is not the origin of temptation but the source of all good. He has given people his best gift, the gift of new life, and this has come through the gospel (vv 16-18).

The proper attitude toward the Word of Truth is receptivity, not anger, and effective listening to that word involves spiritual preparation of heart and mind. Such a reception of the word brings salvation (1:19-21). The word is to be acted upon, not merely listened to. To be a

passive hearer is to be like a man who sees himself in a mirror, and because he takes such a fleeting glance, forgets what he sees. An active hearer, one who takes a long look in the mirror of God's Word, will become a doer, and God will bring great blessing into his life (vv 22-25).

True religion is an intensely practical thing. It involves such things as controlling one's tongue, looking after the needs of orphans and widows, and adopting a nonworldly lifestyle (1:26-27).

Favoritism and faith in Jesus Christ do not go together. It is wrong to show favoritism to a rich man when he comes into the assembly and to ignore a poor man. God has chosen poor people to be heirs of his kingdom. Furthermore, to show favoritism to the rich does not make sense, since they are the very ones who drag Christians into court and blaspheme the name of Christ (2:1-7). If, by showing deference to the rich, the royal law—to love one's neighbor as oneself —is fulfilled, well and good. But to show favoritism is sin, and such sin will be judged by God. In order to be a lawbreaker one has only to break a single law (vv 8-13).

Can a faith that does not produce works save a person? What good is a faith that does not respond to human need? Such a faith is dead. Someone will object by saying that there are "faith Christians" and there are "works Christians." But this is not so. True faith is always demonstrated by works. It is not enough to have orthodox beliefs. Even the demons are theologically orthodox! Abraham, by offering up Isaac, is an example of how true faith and works go together. Even Rahab the prostitute demonstrated her faith by protecting the spies at Jericho. So faith and works are inseparable (2:14-26).

Not many people should become spiritual teachers, because of the awesome responsibility involved. All of us are subject to mistakes, especially mistakes of the tongue, because the tongue is almost impossible to control. It is like a destructive blaze set by hell itself. The tongue is also inconsistent; it is used both to praise God and to curse men. Such inconsistency ought not to be (3:1-12).

True wisdom will always evidence itself in ethical living, whereas false wisdom produces jealousy and selfish ambition (3:13-18).

Strife and conflict arise out of illegitimate desires. Failure to have what one wants arises either from not asking God for it or from asking for the wrong thing. To be a friend of the world is to be an enemy of God, for God is a jealous God and will brook no rivals. He also opposes the proud but offers abundant grace to the humble (4:1-10).

To speak against a brother or sister, or to judge them, is to speak against God's law and to judge it. The Christian's proper role is to be a doer of the law, not a judge. The role of judge belongs to God alone (4:11-12).

Life is uncertain. Therefore, plans for traveling or doing business should be made with the realization that all are subject to the will of God. To do otherwise is to be boastful and arrogant. When what is right is clearly known and one fails to do it, that is sin (4:13-17).

Judgment is coming to the rich because they are hoarding their wealth instead of using it for good purposes. God is not unmindful of the cries of the poor whom the rich have cheated and unjustly condemned. He is preparing the selfish, unscrupulous rich for a day of awful judgment (5:1-6).

In the midst of suffering and injustice, the poor are to be patient for Christ's coming, as the farmer must be patient as he waits for God to send the rains to cause his crops to grow and ripen. The return of Christ is at hand and therefore complaining and judging one another must cease. Job is a good example of patience and endurance in suffering. One need not use oaths to guarantee the truthfulness of his statements. A single yes or no is sufficient (5:7-12).

Suffering should elicit prayer, cheerfulness, and praise. When believers are sick, they should call the elders of the church to pray for them and anoint them with oil. God has promised to answer such prayers. If the sickness is due to personal sin, and if that sin is confessed, God will forgive. Elijah is a classic example of how the prayer of a righteous man has powerful results (5:13-18).

If a Christian sees that another Christian has strayed from the truth and is able to bring him or her back into fellowship with Christ and his church, the consequences will be (1) that the sinner will be saved from death, and (2) that God will forgive the erring Christian (5:19-20).

See also Brothers of Jesus; James (Person).

JAMIN
1. Simeon's son (Gn 46:10; Ex 6:15; 1 Chr 4:24) and founder of the Jaminite family (Nm 26:12).
2. Ram's son from Judah's tribe (1 Chr 2:27).
3. One of the men (perhaps a Levite) who taught and explained the law to the people following Ezra's public reading (Neh 8:7).

JAMINITE Descendant of Jamin from Simeon's tribe (Nm 26:12). *See* Jamin #1.

JAMLECH Leader in Simeon's tribe (1 Chr 4:34).

JAMNIA Alternate name for Jabneh in Judith 2:28. *See* Jabneh.

JANAI Gadite chief who settled, along with his kinsmen, in the land of Bashan (1 Chr 5:12).

JANIM City in the hill country of the territory assigned to Judah's tribe for an inheritance (Jos 15:53). Its location is presumably southwest of Hebron.

JANNAI Ancestor of Jesus recorded in Luke's genealogy (Lk 3:24). *See* Genealogy of Jesus Christ.

JANNES AND JAMBRES Two of Pharaoh's magicians, who opposed Moses and tried to show that they were as effective as he at working miracles (Ex 7–9). Jewish legend regarded Jannes and Jambres (somewhat improbably) as sons of Balaam, the Midianite prophet of Numbers 22–24. Curiously, the Exodus chapters do not identify them by name. The only biblical reference to them appears in the NT. The apostle Paul saw similarity between Jannes and Jambres and the false teachers of debased intellect who were enemies of the truth in his day (2 Tm 3:6-8).

Much speculation has arisen about the two names. They are apparently Semitic, but their precise derivation is unclear. They are referred to in the Qumran documents and in late Jewish, pagan, and early Christian literature. Variations include "Yohanneh and his brother" (Qumran), "Yohane and Mamre" (Babylonian Talmud), and "Mambres" (the translation in most Latin and some Greek manuscripts of 2 Tm 3:8). The names appear also in the writings of Pliny (first century AD) and of Apuleius and Numenius (both second century), though both names are not always cited.

Origen, an Alexandrian church father, twice referred to an apocryphal work entitled The Book of Jannes and Jambres, suggesting that it was the source of Paul's words in 2 Timothy. A Latin church document called the Gelasian Decree (fifth or sixth century?) mentions Penitence of Jannes and Jambres, possibly the work mentioned by Origen.

JANOAH
1. City defining the eastern border of Ephraim's territory, located southeast of Shechem and northeast of Shiloh (Jos 16:6-7). It has been identified with modern Khirbet Yanun.
2. Town (modern Yanuh) of Naphtali's tribe captured by Tiglath-pileser, king of Assyria, during the reign of King Pekah of Israel in 732 BC (2 Kgs 15:29).

JANOHAH* KJV spelling of Janoah, a town in Ephraim's territory, in Joshua 16:6-7. *See* Janoah #1.

JANUM* KJV spelling of Janim, a town in Judah's territory, in Joshua 15:53. *See* Janim.

JAPHETH One of Noah's three sons (Gn 5:32; 7:13; 9:18, 23, 27; 10:1-5; 1 Chr 1:4-5) who, along with his wife, was among the eight human survivors of the great Flood. Because Japheth and his brother Shem acted with respect and modesty in covering their father's nakedness while he was in a drunken condition (Gn 9:20-23), they were both blessed in Noah's prophetic pronouncement of Genesis 9:26-27. Of Japheth, Noah said, "God enlarge Japheth, and let him dwell in the tents of Shem; and let Canaan be his slave" (RSV). There are two interpretations of the meaning of this prophecy. Some understand the enlargement of Japheth to be a reference to a great increase in numbers of descendants. "To dwell in the tents of Shem" is understood as Japheth's sharing in the blessing of Shem. According to this view, there is to be a time when God will work primarily with Shem (the people of Israel), but then, at a later time, Japheth will be brought into connection with the faith of Israel and share in its promises. In this view fulfillment is found in the opening of the gospel to the Gentiles at the inception of the NT church. Others understand the "enlargement of Japheth" to refer to territorial enlargement, and the "dwelling in the tents of Shem" as the conquest of Shemite territory by Japhethites. In this view, fulfillment is found in the Greek and Roman conquests of Palestine.

In the "table of nations" in Genesis 10:2, Japheth is listed as the father of Gomer, Magog, Madai, Javan, Tubal, Meshech, and Tiras. These are the ancestors of peoples who lived to the north and west of Israel and who spoke what today are classified as Indo-European languages.

See also Nations; Noah #1.

JAPHIA (Person)
1. King of Lachish who joined an alliance of four other Amorite kings to punish Gibeon for its treaty with the Jews. Joshua dealt a total defeat to the Amorites at the battle of Beth-horon (aided by hailstones and the sun standing still). Japhia and the four kings hid in a cave at Makkedah but were discovered and hung by Joshua (Jos 10:3-27).
2. Son born to David while he was king in Jerusalem (2 Sm 5:15; 1 Chr 3:7; 14:6).

JAPHIA (Place) Town described as part of the southern border of Zebulun's territory (Jos 19:12). It has been identified with modern Yafa, about two miles (3.2 kilometers) southwest of Nazareth.

JAPHLET Heber's son and chief in Asher's tribe (1 Chr 7:32-33).

JAPHLETITES People occupying an area that marked part of the southern border of Ephraim's territory in the vicinity of Beth-horon (Jos 16:3).

JAPHO* KJV form of Joppa in Joshua 19:46. *See* Joppa.

JAR *See* Pottery.

JARAH* Descendant of King Saul (1 Chr 9:42, NLT mg).

JAREB* Name used by Hosea to designate an Assyrian king (Hos 5:13). Because no such name is to be found in the Assyrian king lists, some have conjectured that it designated Sargon, but this is mere speculation. In all probability Hosea chose this name (which in Hebrew means "contentious") to describe the opposition that Ephraim and Judah would encounter from a contentious king in Assyria because of Israel's sin (10:6).

JARED Mahalalel's son and a descendant of Seth. He was the father of Enoch (Gn 5:15-20; 1 Chr 1:2; Lk 3:37). *See* Genealogy of Jesus Christ.

JARESIAH* KJV rendering of Jaareshiah, Jeroham's son, in 1 Chronicles 8:27. *See* Jaareshiah.

JARHA Egyptian servant of Sheshan, Jerahmeel's descendant, who was given his master's daughter in marriage. Sheshan did this because he had no sons (1 Chr 2:34-35).

JARIB
1. Alternate name for Jachin, Simeon's son, in 1 Chronicles 4:24. *See* Jachin #1.
2. Man who assisted Ezra in securing temple servants before the return to Palestine from exile (Ezr 8:16).
3. From Jeshua's family, a priest who obeyed Ezra's exhortation to divorce his pagan wife after the exile (Ezr 10:18).

JARMUTH
1. Fortified city in the northern part of the Shephelah given to Judah's tribe for an inheritance (Jos 15:35). It was one of five Amorite cities that banded together to attack Gibeon after they had made peace with Joshua and Israel (10:3-5). Jarmuth was reinhabited after the exile by people of Judah (Neh 11:29), and possibly maintained a population throughout the Dispersion. It is identified with Khirbet Yarmuk, 18 miles (29 kilometers) southwest of Jerusalem. Archaeological evidence suggests that the area of the Bronze Age city was six to eight acres (2.4 to 3.2 hectares) and had a population of about 1,500 to 2,000 people. It is mentioned in the Amarna letters as receiving aid from Lachish.
2. One of four cities of Issachar given to the Levites for their inheritance (Jos 21:28-29). It is apparently identifiable with Ramoth in 1 Chronicles 6:73 and Remeth in Joshua 19:21. A stele of Pharaoh Seti I was found at Beth-shan, referring to the whole area as Mt Jarmuth. *See also* Levitical Cities.

JAROAH Gilead's son from Gad's tribe (1 Chr 5:14).

JASHAR, Book of This was an ancient Hebrew writing that is no longer extant. It was probably a national songbook containing songs praising the exploits of Hebrew heroes. It is mentioned in the OT account of Joshua's command to the sun and moon to stand still during the battle with the five kings (Jos 10:13) and in the account of David's lament over Saul and Jonathan (2 Sm 1:17-27). It is also possible that Solomon's words of dedication of the temple (1 Kgs 8:12-13) were included. According to the Septuagint (Greek translation of the OT), the writer of that passage uses the same language as in Joshua 10:12-13 and asks rhetorically if Solomon's statement were written in the book of "Song." Some scholars believe that this question may have accidentally dropped out of the Hebrew text since the whole quotation appears in the Septuagint following Solomon's prayer of 1 Kings 8:14-53. It is also likely that some Hebrew letters may have been transposed so that the Septuagint reads "Song" instead of "Jashar." If one accepts these assumptions, then 1 Kings 8:12-13 would have been part of the Book of Jashar.

It is also possible that the Septuagint rendering, "Book of Song," is the more correct title. All of the quotations are poetry; the term "Jashar" has never been explained satisfactorily; and "Jashar" has similarities to various Hebrew root forms meaning "to sing." Hence, some scholars believe that "Book of Song" is a more correct title.

The nature of the book cannot be determined with certainty except to say that it probably contained a wide variety of songs. This is evident as one considers the types of materials contained in the three passages mentioned above. One is an appeal for the prolonging of daylight in order for Israel to complete a military victory; one is an example of David's literary skill and an expression of the national importance and close friendship of the persons involved; and one is an exclamation extolling God's supremacy over ritual and nature.

The origin of the Book of Jashar is more clouded in obscurity than is its content. Some believe that it was a written collection of songs dating to the days before the monarchy. Some think that it was an oral tradition dating approximately from the time of Solomon. Others suggest that it was a vital instrument in the establishment of literary archives during the monarchy to preserve the notable events of Israelites. This has led to the suggestion that the Song of Miriam (Ex 15:21) and the Song of Deborah (Jgs 5) may have been part of the collection.

The book has long interested many people, and this interest has led to various false imitations, false identifications, and false reproductions of it.

JASHEN One of David's 30 mighty men (2 Sm 23:32). The Hebrew text reads "the sons of Jashen," and 1 Chronicles 11:34 reads "the sons of Hashem the Gizonite." Scholars are generally agreed that the phrase "the sons of" is dittographic and repeats the last three letters of the preceding word. The reading in the original text probably was either "Jashen the Gizonite" or "Hashem the Gizonite," making him, and not his son, the mighty man of David's army.

JASHOBEAM
1. Zabdiel's son who was put in charge of David's "Three" mightiest men (1 Chr 11:11) and also appointed chief of a division (24,000 soldiers) on duty in the first month of the year (1 Chr 27:2). He is the same person as Josheb-basshebeth, the Tahkemonite (2 Sm 23:8, NLT mg). Jashobeam gained renown by killing 300 men, according to 1 Chronicles 11:11, or 800, according to 2 Samuel 23:8.
2. One of the ambidextrous warriors who joined David at Ziklag (1 Chr 12:6).

JASHUB
1. Issachar's third son (1 Chr 7:1; alternately called Iob in Gn 46:13), and founder of the Jashubite family (Nm 26:24).
2. Bani's descendant, who obeyed Ezra's exhortation to divorce his pagan wife after the exile (Ezr 10:29).

JASHUBI-LEHEM Mentioned along with Moab in 1 Chronicles 4:22.

JASHUBITE Descendant of Jashub, Issachar's third son (Nm 26:24). *See* Jashub #1.

JASIEL* KJV form of Jaasiel the Mezobaite in 1 Chronicles 11:47. *See* Jaasiel #1.

JASON
1. Jewish high priest (174–171 BC) who brought about the decline of the priesthood by Hellenizing Jerusalem, making her inhabitants "citizens of Antioch" (2 Macc 4:9ff.). He was deposed by his cousin Onias Menelaus, but when a false report told of the death of Antiochus Epiphanes, Jason attacked Jerusalem without mercy for his own people. Antiochus, returning from an aborted attack on Egypt, retook Jerusalem and Jason was forced to flee to Transjordan and thence from city to city. Second Maccabees reports that at his death, "[Jason] who had cast out many to lie unburied had no one to mourn for him; he had no funeral of any sort and no place in the tomb of his fathers" (5:10, RSV).
2. Jewish Christian at Thessalonica who hosted Paul and Silas (Acts 17:1, 5-9). He and others were called before the city officials on charges of harboring seditionists. He was released when he put up bail.
3. Christian at Corinth who, along with Paul, sent greetings to the church at Rome (Rom 16:21).

JASPER Variety of green quartz. *See* Stones, Precious.

JATHAN* One of the sons of Shemaiah, who had accompanied Tobit to Jerusalem to worship (Tb 5:14, NLT mg).

JATHNIEL Fourth son of Meshelemiah the Korahite and doorkeeper of the temple in David's time (1 Chr 26:2).

JATTIR Town in the hill country of Judah given to the Levites (Jos 15:48; 21:14; 1 Chr 6:57). David sent spoils from his victory over the Amalekites to Jattir (1 Sm 30:27). It is identified with modern Khirbet 'Attir, 13 miles (21 kilometers) southeast of Hebron.

JAVAN (Person) Japheth's son whose seafaring descendants migrated to the north and west of Canaan (Gn 10:2-4; 1 Chr 1:5-7).

JAVAN* (Place) Location commonly identified with Greece. The name is linguistically associated with Ionia, a region in westernmost Asia Minor that was colonized by Greeks. By extension, Javan came to be applied to Greece itself. In most occurrences in the Greek translation of the Bible, Javan appears as "Hellas," Greece.

Some hints as to its location are given as early as the "table of nations," where Javan appears as the fourth son of Japheth (Gn 10:2; cf. 1 Chr 1:5); moving west from Gomer, this tends to place it in Europe. Japheth is also said to be the father of Elishah, Tarshish, Kittim, and Dodanim or Rodanim (Gn 10:4; 1 Chr 1:7). The connections of these areas or peoples is well known.

Most of the references to Ionia (Greece) are in the prophetic books. In Isaiah 66:19 Javan is named along with Tarshish, Put, Lud, and Tubal as places to which the glory of the Lord will be declared. These are taken as a representative of the distant nations.

In a lengthy prophecy against Tyre, Ezekiel refers to Javan, Tubal, and Meshech as those who traded slaves and bronze vessels for the merchandise of Tyre (Ez 27:13), while in Joel 3:6 Tyre is condemned for having sold the people of Judah and Jerusalem to the Greeks. In Ezekiel 27:19 the Hebrew text reads "Vedan and Javan from Uzal." This is translated as "Greeks from Uzal" in the NLT (see also mg). The NASB states, "Vedan and Javan paid for your wares from Uzal"; the KJV reads "Dan also and Javan." The RSV (see also mg) follows the Greek translation: "wine from Uzal."

The references to Javan in Daniel clearly mean Greece. The he-goat who represents the king of Greece (Dn 8:21) is Alexander the Great, whose empire was divided among his four generals upon his death. The prince of Greece in Daniel 10:20 is parallel to the prince of Persia in Daniel 10:13, 20. It has been suggested that "prince" means guardian angel, but the prince of Persia's opposition to the archangel Michael makes it evident that "prince" is a demonic spirit of high rank (cf. Eph 6:12). Conflict between Persia and Greece is predicted in Daniel 11:2, while the following verse tells of the success of Alexander the Great and the breakup of his empire.

See also Greece, Greek.

JAVELIN Light, short, spearlike weapon. *See* Armor and Weapons.

JAZER Town east of the Jordan River in southern Gilead, taken with its surrounding villages by the Israelites under Moses (Nm 21:32). The tribes of Gad and Reuben asked for the lands of Jazer and Gilead. They had large flocks and herds and saw that the east side of the Jordan was fertile and best suited for livestock grazing (32:1-5). They promised to build protection for their women and children, then go with the other tribes to fight in Canaan (vv 6-27). Jazer became a border point marking the inheritance of Gad (Jos 13:25) and was given to the Levites (Jos 21:39; 1 Chr 6:81). When Joab was sent to number the people, he reached the city of Jazer in Gad (2 Sm 24:5). This town was later recognized during a search for "capable men" under King David (1 Chr 26:31). Just over 200 years later, however, it was occupied by Moab (Is 16:6-9; Jer 48:32).

JAZIZ One of David's royal stewards in charge of the flocks (1 Chr 27:30-31).

JEALOUSY*, Ordeal of Numbers 5:11-28 contains a provision by which a man who suspected his wife of adultery could bring her to the priest to determine her guilt or innocence. She had to appear with a grain offering, take an oath, and then drink "bitter" water mixed with dust taken from the tabernacle floor. As the woman drank the water, the priest offered the jealousy offering. If she were guilty, "her abdomen [would] swell and her thigh [would] waste away" (Nm 5:27, NLT mg), and she would be a curse among the people. If she were innocent, no ill effects would result. *See* Bitterness or Jealousy, Water of.

JEARIM, Mount Mountain on the northwest border of Judah's territory between Beth-shemesh and Kiriathjearim. Kesalon was located on its northern slope (Jos 15:10). It is associated with Mt Seir and Mt Ephron.

See also Kesalon.

JEATERAI*, JEATHERAI Zerah's son, a Gershonite Levite (1 Chr 6:21), called Ethni in 1 Chronicles 6:41.

JEBERECHIAH*, JEBEREKIAH Father of Zechariah the scribe. Zechariah, with Uriah the priest, witnessed Isaiah's prophecy of the Assyrian conquest of Israel (Is 8:2).

JEBUS, JEBUSITE Walled city, lying on the boundary between Judah and Benjamin, conquered by David; thereafter, it was known as the "city of David," or ancient Jerusalem. Its occupants were Jebusites (Jos 18:16). They were one of the several clans or tribes collectively known as Canaanites (Gn 10:15-16). Their land, along with that of their neighbors, was repeatedly promised to the Israelites (Ex 3:8; 13:5; 23:23; 33:2; 34:11; Nm 13:29; Dt 7:1; 20:17). This promise was partially fulfilled early in the campaign under Joshua (Jos 3:10; 12:8; 18:16; cf. 24:11). It is said that the men of Judah fought against Jerusalem and took it (18:28). "The Benjamites, however, failed to dislodge the Jebusites, who were living in Jerusalem; to this day the Jebusites live there with the Benjamites" (Jgs 1:21, NIV). Apparently the city was captured by the men of Judah, but its inhabitants were not destroyed and they later reoccupied the site.

Jebus, the Ancient City of David The ancient city, Jebus, was just south of the ancient Old City, Jerusalem.

Jebus (or Jerusalem) lay on the borderline between two tribes, and this may account for its survival until the time of David. The borders of Judah and Benjamin are thus defined: "The boundary then passed through the valley of the son of Hinnom, along the southern slopes of the Jebusites, where the city of Jerusalem is located. Then it went west to the top of the mountain above the valley of Hinnom, and on up to the northern end of the valley of Rephaim" (Jos 15:8, NLT); "it then goes down the valley of Hinnom, south of the shoulder of the Jebusites, and downward to En-rogel" (Jos 18:16, RSV). The two accounts agree: the survey of Judah follows a westerly direction; the survey of Benjamin moves eastward; both indicate that Jebus lay on the southern slope of the "mountain" north of the valley of Hinnom, the site of East Jerusalem today.

The city's survival was assured by a constant supply of water, the spring of Gihon, and by strong natural defenses. It was easily defended by steep valleys on three sides: the Kidron on the east, the Hinnom on the south and west. The Jebusites therefore considered their city impregnable. This gave them a certain arrogance and

complacency. After the death of Saul, when David was seeking to consolidate the kingdom, the Jebusites scornfully challenged David to capture their stronghold (2 Sm 5:6; cf. 1 Chr 11:5). As the last remaining Canaanite stronghold in the area, it presented a unique challenge. Joab apparently led the attack up the water shaft and succeeded where previous attempts had failed (2 Sm 5:8).

For political as well as strategic reasons, David decided to move his capital from Hebron to Jebus. Politically, it lay in neutral territory between Judah and Benjamin and thus aroused no jealousy. Strategically, it was easily defended and more centrally located. The choice proved a wise one. In spite of the fact that Jebus-Jerusalem lies on no waterway or major highway, it has become through the centuries the spiritual capital of the world. Under David and Solomon, it became Israel's religious center, and today it is of prime importance to the three major monotheistic religions of mankind.

See also Jerusalem.

JECAMIAH* KJV spelling of Jekamiah, King Jehoiachin's son, in 1 Chronicles 3:18. *See* Jekamiah #2.

JECHOLIAH* KJV spelling of Jecoliah, King Azariah's mother, in 2 Kings 15:2. *See* Jecoliah.

JECHONIAH* Alternate form of Jehoiachin, a Judean king, in Matthew 1:11-12. *See* Jehoiachin.

JECHONIAS* KJV form of Jechoniah, an alternate name of Jehoiachin, king of Judah, in Matthew 1:11-12. *See* Jehoiachin.

JECOLIAH Mother of King Azariah, or Uzziah (2 Kgs 15:2; 2 Chr 26:3).

JECONIAH* Alternate name for King Jehoiachin of Judah, who was carried into Babylonian exile (1 Chr 3:16-17; Jer 24:1). *See* Jehoiachin.

JEDAIAH
1. Shimri's son and the father of Allon. He is listed in the genealogical tables of the Simeonites who settled in the valley of Gedor in Hezekiah's time (1 Chr 4:37).
2. Harumaph's son, who helped repair the Jerusalem wall after the exile (Neh 3:10).
3. Aaron's descendant and head of the second of the 24 priestly divisions for temple service in David's time (1 Chr 24:7). His descendants are listed among the returned exiles (1 Chr 9:10; Ezr 2:36; Neh 7:39). The individuals and families listed below are probably a part of this priestly line, but their exact relationships are difficult to determine.
4. Provincial priest who agreed to resettle in postexilic Jerusalem (Neh 11:10; cf. v 2).
5. Priest who returned with Zerubbabel after the exile (Neh 12:6-7). In the next generation this was the name of a family (v 21).
6. One of the exiles taken by Zechariah as witness to the symbolic crowning of Joshua (NLT "Jeshua"). He may be the same as #4 or #5 above. He came back from captivity bringing gifts for the temple in the days of the high priest Joshua (Zec 6:10-14).

JEDIAEL
1. Benjamin's son (1 Chr 7:6, 10-11), whose descendants were warriors, numbering 17,200 by David's time. Some suggest that he is identifiable with Ashbel, also Benjamin's son (Gn 46:21).
See also Ashbel, Ashbelite.

2. Shimri's son, listed among David's mighty men (1 Chr 11:45).
3. One who deserted Saul to join David at Ziklag (1 Chr 12:20). He may be the same as #2 above.
4. Member of the Levitical family of Korah, appointed a doorkeeper of the temple during David's reign (1 Chr 26:2).

JEDIDAH Adaiah's daughter, the wife of King Amon of Judah and the mother of King Josiah (2 Kgs 22:1).

JEDIDIAH Name meaning "beloved of the LORD [Yahweh]." God told Nathan the prophet to give Solomon, David's second son by Bathsheba, this name soon after his birth (2 Sm 12:24-25).

JEDUTHUN Member of the Levitical family of Merar who, along with Asaph and Heman, presided over the music in the sanctuary in David's reign (1 Chr 25:1; 2 Chr 5:12; called "Ethan" in 1 Chr 6:44; 15:17). Jeduthun is mentioned in the titles of Psalms 39, 62, and 77. Some of his sons were set apart to prophesy with lyres, harps, and cymbals (1 Chr 25:1-3), apparently following the example of their father, who was called "the king's seer" (2 Chr 35:15). In 1 Chronicles 16:38 and 42, he is listed as Obed-edom's father.

JEEZER*, JEEZERITE* KJV forms of Iezer and Iezerite, contractions of Abiezer and Abiezerite, the names of Gilead's son and his descendants (Nm 26:30). *See* Abiezer #1.

JEGAR-SAHADUTHA Aramaic name given by Laban to the heap of stones that he and Jacob piled up as a memorial to their covenant; Jacob called it "Galeed" (Gn 31:47). The name means "heap of witness."
See also Galeed.

JEHALLELEL
1. Descendant of Judah who had four sons (1 Chr 4:16).
2. Levite of the family of Merari whose son Azariah participated in the cleansing of the temple in Hezekiah's time (2 Chr 29:12).

JEHDEIAH
1. Shubael's son, a Levite in David's time (1 Chr 24:20).
2. Royal steward from Meronoth who was in charge of David's donkeys (1 Chr 27:30).

JEHEZKEL Levite assigned to temple duty in David's time; leader of the 20th division (1 Chr 24:16).

JEHIAH Levite who, along with Obed-edom, was appointed as doorkeeper for the ark when David brought it to Jerusalem (1 Chr 15:24).

JEHIEL
1. KJV spelling of Jeiel, King Saul's ancestor, in 1 Chronicles 9:35. *See* Jeiel #2.
2. KJV spelling of Jeiel, Hotham's son, in 1 Chronicles 11:44. *See* Jeiel #3.
3. A Levite musician who, along with other Levites appointed by David, played a psaltery at the removal of the ark to Jerusalem (1 Chr 15:18-20). Afterward, he was appointed to a permanent ministry of music in the sanctuary (1 Chr 16:5).
4. Levite of the family of Gershon; a chief of the house of Ladan (1 Chr 23:8, NLT mg). He was in charge of the temple treasury during David's reign—an office that seems to have continued in the family (29:8)—and founder

of a priestly family called Jehieli or Jehielites (26:21-22).
5. Hacmoni's son who, with David's uncle Jonathan (a counselor and a scribe), was appointed to take care of the king's sons as a tutor and adviser (1 Chr 27:32).
6. Son of King Jehoshaphat of Judah, placed by his father over one of the fortified cities of Judah (2 Chr 21:2). He and five brothers were slain by Jehoram when Jehoram became king.
7. One of the Kohathite Levites from the family of Heman who assisted in King Hezekiah's reforms (2 Chr 29:14, RSV "Jehuel"). He may be the same Levite who was assigned to oversee the reception and distribution of the sacred offerings (2 Chr 31:13).
8. One of the chief officers of the temple at the time of Josiah's religious reformation (2 Chr 35:8); he contributed many sacrifices for the great Passover service.
9. Father of Obadiah from Joab's house; he returned with Ezra from Babylon (Ezr 8:9).
10. One of the sons of Elam and father of Shecaniah. He was associated with Ezra's marriage reforms (Ezr 10:2) and was perhaps the same Jehiel who was among those who divorced their foreign wives (v 26).
11. Priest who was among those Ezra persuaded to divorce their foreign wives (Ezr 10:21).

JEHIELI*, JEHIELITE* Alternate spelling of Jehiel, a Levite and founder of the Jehielite family, in 1 Chronicles 26:21-22. *See* Jehiel #4.

JEHIZKIAH Shallum's son and a chief of Ephraim during the reign of Ahaz in Judah. He opposed the enslavement of the men of Judah by victorious Israel (2 Chr 28:12).

JEHOADAH*, JEHOADDAH* Ahaz's son and a descendant of King Saul through Jonathan's line (1 Chr 8:36); alternately called Jarah in 1 Chronicles 9:42.

JEHOADDAN*, JEHOADDIN Mother of Amaziah, king of Judah (2 Kgs 14:2; 2 Chr 25:1).

JEHOAHAZ
1. Twelfth king of Israel, succeeding his father, Jehu, and ruling from 814 BC to 798 BC. Because he was an evil king, God punished Israel by subjecting them to the Aramean kings Hazael and his son Ben-hadad. The military force in Israel was reduced to 50 cavalrymen, 10 chariots, and 10,000 infantrymen. The oppression became so severe that Jehoahaz prayed to God, who listened to him and delivered Israel from the Arameans, but not until the reign of Joash (Jehoash) (2 Kgs 13:2-7, 25). During Jehoahaz's reign, relations between Judah and Israel seem to have been fairly good, since Jehoahaz (14:1, "Joahaz") named his son Joash after his contemporary, Joash king of Judah (2 Kgs 13:1, 9; 14:1).
2. Seventeenth king of Judah, ruling three months in 609 BC. The people chose him to succeed his father, Josiah, who was killed in the battle of Megiddo. His mother's name was Hamutal. Jehoahaz was 23 years old at his coronation. He is also called Shallum (1 Chr 3:15), and Jehoahaz may well be a throne name. He is characterized as an evil king before God. His rule ended when Pharaoh Neco imprisoned him at Riblah in Hamath. Later he was taken to Egypt, where he died (2 Kgs 23:30-34). Jeremiah prophesied that Jehoahaz

would never return to Israel but would die in the land of his captivity (Jer 22:11-12).

3. Another form of the name of Ahaziah, the sixth king of Judah, who ruled in 841 BC (2 Chr 21:17; cf. 22:1). Both forms of the name have the same meaning. The difference is the placement of the divine name. In Jehoahaz it comes first, "Jeho-" and in Ahaziah it comes last, "-iah" (-yah). *See* Ahaziah #2.

4. Full name of Ahaz, the 12th king of Judah, according to an inscription of Assyrian king Tiglath-pileser III. *See* Ahaz #1.

See also Israel, History of.

JEHOASH Name of two OT kings, occurring only in the book of 2 Kings. The name means "the LORD is strong" or "the LORD hath bestowed." Joash, the shorter form of the name, frequently appears in the Kings and Chronicles narratives.

1. Son of Ahaziah and seventh king of Judah (835–796 BC). Jehoash ascended the throne after the wicked Athaliah had been killed at the command of Jehoiada the priest. As an infant, he was hidden by his aunt Jehosheba in the temple and thus survived the slaughter of the king's household by Athaliah (2 Kgs 11:1-3; 2 Chr 23:10-12). After remaining six years within the temple precinct, Jehoash was declared king at the age of seven and ruled for 40 years (11:21–12:1; 2 Chr 24:1-3).

His major activity during his reign was the renovation of the temple (2 Kgs 12:4-5; 2 Chr 24:4-5). When, by his 23d year, little progress had been made (2 Kgs 12:6), he revised the taxation schedule, commanded the people of Judah to bring their contributions directly to the Jerusalem temple, and soon restored the Lord's house to its proper condition (2 Chr 24:13).

After the death of the priest Jehoiada, Jehoash and Judah forsook the Lord and served the Asherim and the idols (2 Chr 24:15-18). Not heeding the prophetic warning of divine judgment (v 20), Jehoash and his people were conquered by the Arameans. Though Jehoash had once been able to avert a siege of Judah by paying tribute to Hazael (2 Kgs 12:17-18), the same strategy did not work a second time. The Arameans plundered Judah and Jerusalem, sending the spoil to Hazael in Damascus (2 Chr 24:23-24). Jehoash was assassinated by his servants Jozacar (Jozabad/Zabad) and Jehozabad while recuperating from wounds incurred in battle with the Arameans (2 Kgs 12:20-21; 2 Chr 24:25-26).

2. Son of Jehoahaz and 13th king of Israel (798–782 BC). Jehoash enjoyed a measure of military success that had eluded his father. No longer subject to punitive military exploits from Hazael of Aram, he was able to establish political stability in the northern kingdom. In fact, he subjugated the southern kingdom of Judah while Amaziah was king in Jerusalem (796–767 BC). The conflict between Amaziah and Jehoash was precipitated mainly by Amaziah. Overconfident with his victories in Edom, Amaziah initiated a military conflict with Israel (2 Chr 25:17-19). The battle was fought near Beth-shemesh in the Judean Shephelah. King Jehoash routed the army of Judah, captured Amaziah, and moved on to Jerusalem. Destroying the outer wall from the Ephraim Gate to the Corner Gate, he entered the capital city and plundered the treasures of both the palace and the temple (vv 21-24). He was apparently used as an instrument of the Lord to subdue Judah (v 20).

A contemporary of Jehoash was Elisha the prophet. In spite of the pervasive wickedness in Israel and the apostasy of the king himself (2 Kgs 13:10-11), Jehoash still sought the counsel of this prophet of the Lord. While Elisha was on his deathbed, Jehoash sought the prophet's blessing (v 14). Elisha assured the king that the Arameans would be defeated by Israel at Aphek and that Israel would enjoy three decisive victories over this same enemy (vv 15-19). During his 16-year reign, Jehoash achieved political stability in the northern kingdom. Though considered an evil king, he was used as an instrument of judgment against Amaziah of Judah and enjoyed the blessing of Yahweh against Aram.

See also Israel, History of.

JEHOHANAN

1. Korahite Levite who was a gatekeeper of the sanctuary during David's reign (1 Chr 26:3).
2. Commander of thousands in King Jehoshaphat's army (2 Chr 17:15).
3. Father of Ishmael, commander of a unit of soldiers who helped the priest Jehoiada overthrow the wicked queen Athaliah of Judah (2 Chr 23:1).
4. Eliashib's descendant who owned a chamber into which Ezra retired to pray, fast, and mourn for his people (Ezr 10:6). He is possibly the same as Johanan, a grandson of Eliashib the high priest (Neh 12:22-23, NLT), and Jonathan (a textual variant), Joiada's son, in Nehemiah 12:11.
5. One of Bebai's four sons, who was exhorted by Ezra to divorce his foreign wife (Ezr 10:28).
6. Son of the Ammonite official Tobiah and a contemporary of Nehemiah. He married a Jewish woman whose father, Meshullam, had helped repair the Jerusalem wall (Neh 6:18; KJV "Johanan").
7. Priest and family leader in postexilic Jerusalem during the time Joiakim was high priest (Neh 12:13).
8. One of the priests who participated as a singer in the dedication of the rebuilt Jerusalem wall (Neh 12:42).

JEHOIACHIN King of Judah for a very brief time (598–597 BC). He was the son of Jehoiakim and Nehushta, the daughter of Elnathan of Jerusalem (possibly the Elnathan mentioned by Jeremiah, cf. Jer 26:22; 36:12, 25). The name Jehoiachin means "Yahweh will uphold," and variations include Coniah (Jer 22:24, 28; 37:1), Jeconiah (1 Chr 3:16-17; Est 2:6; Jer 24:1; 27:20; 28:4; 29:2), and Jechoniah (Mt 1:11-12; KJV "Jechonias"). Jehoiachin was 18 years old when he was installed as king upon his father's death, and he ruled for only three months and ten days in Jerusalem (2 Kgs 24:8; cf. 2 Chr 36:9, NLT mg). He inherited a vassal kingdom in revolt. Besieged by the armies of the Babylonian overlord Nebuchadnezzar, Jehoiachin had little choice but to capitulate in the face of insurmountable odds. According to the Babylonian Chronicle, records based on the official annals of the Babylonian kings, Nebuchadnezzar entered Syro-Palestine in December of 598 BC and took Jerusalem on March 16, 597. The Babylonians plundered the palace and temple treasuries. Along with Jehoiachin, his family, prominent military leaders, royal officials, and artisans were taken prisoner and led away to exile in Babylon. Before returning to Babylon, the victorious king placed Jehoiachin's uncle Mattaniah, now named Zedekiah, on the throne in Jerusalem (2 Kgs 24:12-17; cf. 2 Chr 36:10).

According to Jeremiah, the trauma caused by the Babylonian invasion of Judah, and the consequent political upheaval prompted by a succession of three kings in four months, had little impact on the people spiritually (Jer 37–38). This same prophet of God forecast Jehoiachin's exile and predicted he would have no descendants succeeding him on the throne (22:24-30). In contrast, the false prophet Hananiah prophesied Jehoiachin would be restored to the throne of Judah within two years (28:3-4, 11; cf. vv 12-17).

Jehoiachin's continuing royal status as the legitimate claimant to the Judahite kingship was reflected in the fact that Ezekiel's oracles are dated to the year of Jehoiachin's exile, not Zedekiah's reign (Ez 1:2; 8:1; 20:1; etc.). Babylonian records confirm this recognition of Jehoiachin's former position; he retained his title of king and received favorable treatment from the Babylonians. He is certainly the "Yaukin, king of the land of Yahuda" listed in one of the cuneiform tablets; this tablet contains inventories of rations of oil and barley for the king and his five sons and implies they were not imprisoned but living a fairly normal life in Babylonia. At some point Jehoiachin must have been imprisoned, however, because later, during the reign of Evil-merodach, he was released from prison and granted dining privileges with the Babylonian king (c. 562 BC; cf. 2 Kgs 25:27-30; Jer 52:31-34). Whether he was imprisoned for attempting to escape or because of Judah's rebellion against Babylon under Zedekiah is unclear.

Jehoiachin's name appears in Matthew's genealogy of Jesus Christ (Mt 1:11-12), and some contend that this contradicts Jeremiah's oracle of judgment against the king's descendants (Jer 22:30). Yet it is possible to understand Haggai's blessing of Zerubbabel (Hg 2:20-23) as a reversal of Jeremiah's curse and the reinstatement of Jehoiachin's line on the Davidic—and ultimately messianic—throne (cf. Is 56:3-5).

See also Chronology of the Bible (Old Testament); Diaspora of the Jews; Israel, History of.

JEHOIADA

1. Father of Benaiah, a high military officer during the reigns of David and Solomon. Jehoiada was a priest (1 Chr 27:5) who joined forces with David at Hebron and was identified with the house of Aaron (12:27). *See* Benaiah #1.
2. High priest in Jerusalem who organized and led the coup that overthrew Queen Athaliah of Judah, together with the Baal cult she supported, and established his nephew Joash (Jehoash) on the throne (2 Kgs 11:4-21; 2 Chr 23:1-15). As long as he lived, Jehoiada kept the king true to the Lord (2 Kgs 12:1-16; 2 Chr 23:16–24:14). He died at the age of 130 and was buried in the city of David among the kings.
3. Benaiah's son, who succeeded Ahithophel as King David's counselor (1 Chr 27:33-34); he was probably a grandson of #1 above, although some believe these to be the same.
4. KJV spelling of Joiada, Paseah's son, in Nehemiah 3:6. *See* Joiada #1.
5. Alternate name for Joiada, son of Eliashib the high priest, in Nehemiah 13:28. *See* Joiada #2.
6. Priest during the time of Jeremiah who was succeeded by Zephaniah as overseer of the temple (Jer 29:26).

JEHOIAKIM

Second son of Josiah by Zebidah (2 Kgs 23:36; 1 Chr 3:15; 2 Chr 36:4) who became king of Judah in 609 BC. He replaced his younger brother Jehoahaz as king when he was deposed and exiled by Pharaoh Neco after a three-month reign (2 Kgs 23:31-35). Jehoiakim was installed as king at age 25, and he ruled for 11 years in Jerusalem. His given name,

Eliakim, means "God will establish." Upon enthroning him, Neco changed his name to Jehoiakim, meaning "Yahweh will establish" (2 Kgs 23:34), perhaps seeking to claim Yahweh's support for his action.

Neco laid a heavy tribute on Judah, which Jehoiakim raised by levying a tax on the whole land (2 Kgs 23:35; cf. Jer 22:13-17, where the woe oracle against Jehoiakim implies that he appropriated some of these funds for personal use). Jehoiakim remained subservient to the Egyptians until the battle of Carchemish in 605 BC, when Nebuchadnezzar and the Neo-Babylonians routed Neco. Judah then became a vassal state of Babylon for three years (2 Kgs 24:1-2). After Nebuchadnezzar's failure to completely subdue Neco in a second fierce battle in 601 BC, Jehoiakim seized the opportunity to throw off the Babylonian yoke when the Babylonian king returned home to reorganize his army. This ill-advised decision proved costly, as Nebuchadnezzar invaded Judah in 598 BC to punish the rebellious vassal king (2 Kgs 24:3-7). The expected help from Egypt never came, and the Babylonians destroyed the important Judahite cities of Debir and Lachish, seized control of the Negev, and deported several thousand of Judah's ablest citizens. This no doubt crippled the economy and left Judah virtually leaderless. Jehoiakim died during the Babylonian siege (probably late in 598 BC). His son Jehoiachin was placed on the throne.

Although the details of Jehoiakim's death are not reported, the biblical historian does pass judgment on this reign as one that perpetuated the evils of his fathers (see 2 Kgs 23:37; 2 Chr 36:5, 8; cf. Jer 22:18-19 and 36:27-32, which predicted that Jehoiakim's dead body would be cast on the ground outside of Jerusalem without proper burial and he would have no descendants upon the throne). Presumably the reference to "fathers" is to his predecessors Manasseh, Amon, and Jehoahaz. Jeremiah specifies the evils that characterized Jehoiakim's rule, including idolatry, social injustice, robbery of the wage earner, greed, murder, oppression, extortion, and forsaking of the covenant of the Lord (Jer 22:1-17). Despite Jeremiah's extensive activity during his reign (chs 25–26, 36), Jehoiakim remained disobedient, unrepentant, smug, and self-sufficient in his ill-gotten prosperity (22:18-23).

See also Chronology of the Bible (Old Testament); Diaspora of the Jews; Israel, History of.

JEHOIARIB

1. Alternate form of Joiarib, a priestly family in Jerusalem, in 1 Chronicles 9:10. *See* Joiarib #1.
2. Priest in the time of King David, assigned to head the first of 24 divisions of priests for annual temple duty (1 Chr 24:7).

JEHONADAB Alternate name for Jonadab, Recab's son. *See* Jonadab #2.

JEHONATHAN

1. KJV spelling of Jonathan, Uzziah's son, in 1 Chronicles 27:25. *See* Jonathan #7.
2. One of the Levites appointed by Jehoshaphat to travel about Judah teaching the law to the people as part of his national religious reform (2 Chr 17:8).
3. Head of Shemaiah's priestly house in postexilic Jerusalem during the days of Joiakim the high priest (Neh 12:18).

JEHORAM

1. Jehoshaphat's son and Judah's fifth king (853–841 BC; also called Joram). Prior to the rule of the Omride

dynasty in the northern kingdom of Israel (885–841 BC), the relationship between Judah and Israel had been strained. The political influence and economic stability of the united monarchy had long since vanished. Power and wealth had been diminished by Egyptian overlordship under Shishak (2 Chr 12) and by civil war: the unsuccessful Shechem conference (ch 10); Rehoboam of Judah versus Jeroboam of Israel (12:15); Abijah of Judah versus Jeroboam of Israel (13:1-22); and Asa of Judah versus Baasha of Israel (16:1-4). The Omride dynasty in the mid-ninth century BC, however, cast aside familial rivalry and sought to forge a new alliance between the two nations.

The two kingdoms of Judah and Israel were increasingly threatened by the surrounding peoples—the Ammonites, Moabites, Edomites, Syrians, Philistines, Arabs, and Assyrians. In response to this threat Ahab, the second king of the Omride dynasty, secured diplomatic relations with Phoenicia (1 Kgs 16:31) and Judah (22:4). During this time, joint military expeditions by Israel and Judah were not infrequent (1 Kgs 22; 2 Kgs 3; 8:28), though these political alliances were not without their liabilities. The intrusion of the worship of Baal and Asherah led to religious apostasy in Judah and Israel (1 Kgs 16:31-33; 2 Kgs 3:2; 2 Chr 21:11). It was within this political-religious context that Jehoram reigned over Judah.

Though he may have served as co-regent as early as 853 BC, Jehoram was the sole ruler for eight years (848–841 BC). His reign was marked by unnecessary internecine fighting and religious apostasy. His father had generously provided for his six brothers, a decision that Jehoram quickly reversed once he had secured the throne (2 Chr 21:2-3). He executed not only his brothers but also several Israelite princes, thereby removing any political threat to himself (v 4). In addition, he reverted to the idolatrous practices that his father had tried to eliminate by restoring forbidden worship sites, "the high places" (v 11). Jehoram had apparently fallen under the influence of his wife, Athaliah, the daughter of Jezebel (2 Kgs 8:18). As her mother had done in Israel, Athaliah imported Baal worship into Judah. As a result, Elijah the prophet pronounced judgment on Jehoram and the people of Judah—a curse that brought a great plague upon Jehoram's people, children, wives, and possessions, and a gross intestinal disorder upon the king himself. In spite of this pervasive wickedness in Judah, the Lord did not destroy the southern kingdom, because of his promise to David (2 Kgs 8:19; cf. 2 Sm 7:12-16).

Politically, Judah was vulnerable, having lost its control of Edom (2 Chr 21:9) and having sustained attacks by the Philistines and the Arabs. Jehoram was left bereft of possessions, wives, and sons except for Jehoahaz (Ahaziah), his youngest (vv 16-17). At his death Jehoram was not honored and was deprived of burial in the tomb of the kings within the city of David (vv 19-20).

See also Chronology of the Bible (Old Testament); Israel, History of.

2. Ahab and Jezebel's son, and Israel's tenth king (852–841 BC; also called Joram). He succeeded his brother Ahaziah, whose premature death led to Jehoram's ascension to the throne in Samaria (2 Kgs 1:2, 17); he was a contemporary of the Judean kings Jehoshaphat, Jehoram, and Ahaziah.

Jehoram was preoccupied with the political resurgence of the two neighboring kingdoms of Moab and Syria. When Moab withheld its annual tribute to Israel, he sought assistance from both Jehoshaphat and Judah's vassal kingdom, Edom. Jehoram and Jehoshaphat joined forces with the king of Edom but were halted in their attack on Moab when they encountered a serious lack of water. Hesitant to advance with their troops, they summoned Elisha the prophet and asked him to inquire of the Lord's will regarding the expedition. Because of the high regard that Elisha held for Jehoshaphat, the prophet sought the Lord on their behalf, gaining both the Lord's blessing and an abundance of water. The account of the battle records the slaughter of the Moabites as well as the horrible incident of a human sacrifice by the Moabite king. Having won the battle, Israel withdrew (2 Kgs 3:4-27).

Jehoram's conflict with Syria was less successful because the Israelite king sustained a battle wound. Retreating from Ramoth-gilead in Transjordan to his palace in Jezreel (2 Kgs 8:29), he found his problems compounded when one of his generals, Jehu, led an insurrection against him. Commissioned by the Lord and declared to be king of Israel, Jehu confronted Jehoram and his nephew, Ahaziah, king of Judah. The incident culminated in the death of the two reigning monarchs of Israel and Judah (2 Kgs 9:14-24, 27). While Ahaziah was buried in the tomb of the kings in Jerusalem (v 28), Jehoram's corpse was cast into Naboth's field outside the city of Jezreel. His end was the appropriate judgment against the last king of the wicked Omride dynasty (vv 25-26).

3. Levite member of a traveling group of scholars who taught the people from the Book of the Law during the reign of Jehoshaphat (2 Chr 17:7-9).

See also Chronology of the Bible (Old Testament); Israel, History of.

JEHOSHABEATH* Alternate name for Jehosheba, daughter of Judah's King Jehoram, in 2 Chronicles 22:11. *See* Jehosheba.

JEHOSHAPHAT (Person)

1. The fourth king of Judah (872–848 BC), son and successor of Asa (910–869 BC).

Jehoshaphat was 35 years of age when he began his reign; he ruled 25 years, during which time he maintained the stability of the Davidic dynasty (1 Kgs 22:41-42). He was contemporary with King Ahab of Israel (874–853 BC), since his first year on the throne corresponds with the fourth year of the reign of Ahab (v 41). He was also contemporary with Ahaziah (853–852 BC), son of Ahab, and his brother Jehoram (852–841 BC), who succeeded Ahaziah when he died childless (2 Kgs 1:17).

Jehoshaphat is held in high esteem by the Chronicler, along with Hezekiah and Josiah. His successful rule was due to his religious policy. He continued the religious reformation initiated by his father; therefore, the Lord firmly established the kingdom under his control. Everyone in Judah brought tribute to Jehoshaphat, so that he had great riches and honor (2 Chr 17:1-5). The Chronicler praised Jehoshaphat's courageous heart, evidenced in his removing the high places and the Asherim from Judah (v 6). Jehoshaphat is also reported to have closed all the temples of prostitution (1 Kgs 22:46).

The biblical record informs us that Jehoshaphat reversed his father's foreign policy. During his reign, Asa warred against Baasha of Israel (908–886 BC), who exterminated the house of Jeroboam I (930–909 BC) and usurped the throne for himself, keeping it for nearly a quarter of a century. The two kingdoms engaged in warfare over the boundaries between the kingdoms. Jehoshaphat, however, discontinued this war and made peace with the king of Israel (1 Kgs 22:2). To confirm this state of peace, he made an alliance with Ahab and married his son and successor, Jehoram, to Ahab's daughter Athaliah (2 Kgs 8:18; 2 Chr 18:1-2). In accordance with this alliance Jehoshaphat fought on the side of Ahab in his battle against Aram, which took place at Ramoth-gilead (1 Kgs 22; 2 Chr 18). He also was an ally of Jehoram, the younger son of Ahab, against Mesha the king of Moab (2 Kgs 3:4-27).

In his domestic reforms Jehoshaphat sent Ben-hail, Obadiah, Zechariah, Nethanel, and Micaiah to teach the law in the cities of Judah (2 Chr 17:7-9). He is also reported to have organized the use of tribute paid to Judah. The surrounding nations, observing the strength of Jehoshaphat and recognizing the presence of the Lord with him, not only refrained from attacking Judah but even brought tribute to him. He used this tribute to fortify the cities of Judah (vv 10-13). Jehoshaphat also reorganized the army and made arrangements for the defense of the kingdom. He had a standing army in the capital as well as garrisons in the fortified cities. It is evident that the organization centered about the tribal association of Judah and Benjamin (vv 14-19).

A prophet by the name of Jehu rebuked Jehoshaphat for his alliances with Ahab (2 Chr 19:1-3). Evidently, Jehoshaphat took this rebuke to heart and ruled Judah wisely. He swept most of the Asherim from the land and determined in his mind to seek God. He is reported to have gone regularly among the people from Beersheba to Mt Ephraim to convert them to the Lord. He appointed judges in each of the fortified cities of Judah and admonished them to judge as the Lord's representatives. He also appointed Levites, priests, and family heads to handle cases pertaining to the worship of the Lord and to make decisions in disputes arising among citizens (vv 4-11).

In addition to the fortified cities in Judah, Jehoshaphat placed military forces in the cities of Ephraim that his father, Asa, had taken (2 Chr 17:1-2). Though his alliances with Phoenicia and Israel were not approved by the prophets and proved dangerous in the long run, they still brought relative peace and temporary prosperity to his realm. He was held in high esteem by the neighboring Philistines and the Arabs (vv 10-13), and it is also evident that Edom submitted to him. He won victory over the Moabites, Ammonites, and Meunites at En-gedi (20:1-30). Wishing to emulate Solomon, he constructed ships at Ezion-geber to go to Tarshish, but this did not prove a successful venture (vv 35-37).

Jehoshaphat died when he was about 60 years of age and was buried with his fathers in the city of David. His son Jehoram became king in his place (2 Chr 21:1). His name is listed in Matthew's genealogy of Jesus Christ (Mt 1:8).

See also Israel, History of.

2. Son of Ahilud who held the position of "recorder" (the Hebrew word may imply an official historian or a spokesman for the king) in the days of David and Solomon (2 Sm 8:16; 20:24; 1 Kgs 4:3; 1 Chr 18:15).

3. Son of Paruah and one of Solomon's 12 administrative officials who requisitioned food from the people for the king's household. Each of them arranged provisions for one month of the year. Jehoshaphat was the officer assigned for the tribe of Issachar (1 Kgs 4:7, 17).

4. Son of Nimshi and the father of Jehu, who extermi-

nated the dynasty of Omri and became king of Samaria around 842–815 BC (2 Kgs 9:2, 14).

5. KJV spelling of Joshaphat in 1 Chronicles 15:24, a priest during David's reign. *See #2* (above).

JEHOSHAPHAT, Valley of Valley mentioned in prophecy as the place of future judgment (Jl 3:2, 12), sometimes called the valley of decision (v 14). Its exact location is disputed. Some (notably Jerome) identify it with the Kidron Valley, east of Jerusalem, pointing to early Christian tradition; others prefer the valley of Hinnom, south of Jerusalem. This tradition may be traced back through Eusebius to the book of 1 Enoch (1 Enoch 53:1). Still others say the name is symbolic and refers only to coming judgment, not to a specific place.

JEHOSHEBA Daughter of King Jehoram of Judah (853–841 BC) and Queen Athaliah, sister of King Ahaziah (841 BC), and wife of Jehoiada the high priest. Upon Ahaziah's death, Athaliah attempted to kill all the remaining royal heirs to the throne; Jehosheba, however, hid young Joash, Ahaziah's son, in a temple bedroom for the duration of Athaliah's reign (841–835 BC; 2 Kgs 11:2). Jehosheba is alternately spelled Jehoshabeath in 2 Chronicles 22:11.

JEHOSHUA*, JEHOSHUAH* Alternate KJV names for Joshua, son of Nun, in Numbers 13:16 and 1 Chronicles 7:27, respectively. *See* Joshua (Person) #1.

JEHOVAH* Name for God formed by adding the vowels of the Hebrew word *Adonai* to the consonants of the Hebrew divine name, *YHWH*. Out of their respect for God and their fear of defiling his name, the postexilic Jews refused to pronounce the divine name when reading Scripture. Instead, they substituted *Adonai,* a word meaning "my Lord." Prior to the sixth century AD, the Hebrew text had no vowels. These were supplied during the reading of the Scripture by one who was familiar with the language. When vowel points were added to the text (AD 660–700), the vowels of *Adonai* were placed below the consonants of *YHWH* to indicate that *Adonai* should be read.

It is thought that about AD 1520 Petrus Galatinus conceived the idea of combining the two names, thus creating the new form *YeHoWaH,* from which the English term Jehovah comes. Although this form was foreign to the Hebrew language, it gained wide acceptance and was included as the translation for God's name in various verses in the KJV and ASV. Biblical scholars now agree that the original pronunciation of the divine name was *Yahweh* or *Jahveh.*

See also God, Names of.

JEHOVAH-TSIDKENU* Name of the righteous king of David's line who God promised would rule over his people (Jer 23:5-6). The name means "The LORD (Yahweh or Jehovah) is our righteousness." It was also applied to the king's subjects, who will profit by his reign (33:16). To Christians, God's promise finds its fulfillment in Christ, who is Lord of all and the believer's righteousness.

JEHOZABAD

1. Shomer's son, who was a servant of King Joash and later, with another assailant, murdered the king at Millo (2 Kgs 12:21). In a parallel passage, Jehozabad is called the son of Shimrith the Moabitess (2 Chr 24:26). King Amaziah, Joash's son, eventually executed Jehozabad for the murder (25:3).

2. Obed-edom's second son and a member of a Levitical

Korahite family appointed by King David to be gate-keepers in the temple (1 Chr 26:4).
3. Benjamite military commander who served under King Jehoshaphat of Judah and commanded 180,000 men in his army (2 Chr 17:18).

JEHOZADAK Alternate name for Jozadak, Seraiah's son. *See* Jozadak.

JEHU
1. Prophet and son of the "seer" Hanani (2 Chr 16:7), who denounced Baasha for following in the ways of Jeroboam (1 Kgs 16:1-7). In addition to continuing the heretical worship of the golden calves at Bethel and Dan, Baasha also assassinated Nadab, the son of Jeroboam (15:25-32).
  Jehu later rebuked Jehoshaphat, king of Judah, for helping Ahab the king of Israel in his wars against the Arameans (2 Chr 19:1-2). The writings of this prophet were included in one of the records of the reign of Jehoshaphat, *The Book of the Kings of Israel* (2 Chr 20:34).
2. Important army officer during the reigns of Ahab and Jehoram (2 Kgs 9:25), who in reaction to the economic and religious abuses of the house of Omri was anointed as king of the northern kingdom of Israel (1 Kgs 19:16-17). In the following revolution he exterminated the royal house of Israel, the king of Judah, and a royal party from the south (2 Kgs 9–10). He executed the worshipers of Baal in order to revive true worship in Israel. As king, he ruled in Samaria 28 years (841–814 BC) and began a dynasty that lasted some 100 years.
  In the time of Jehu the prophets were engaged in a religious equivalent of war with the adherents of the Tyrian Baal. Elijah met and defeated the Canaanite priests on Mt Carmel (1 Kgs 18:17-40). Later he and then Elisha were commissioned to anoint Jehu as king. The prophets waited until the time was right (2 Kgs 9:1-10), at which time Elisha sent a "son of the prophets" to Ramoth-gilead to designate Jehu as the monarch.
  Jehu left his siege of Ramoth-gilead in northern Transjordan to meet the king of Israel in Jezreel. There he killed King Jehoram and Ahaziah, the king of Judah (2 Kgs 9:17-28). His bloody ways continued as he extinguished the royal house of Ahab (10:1-17) and 42 ambassadors of goodwill from Judah (apparently without provocation, vv 12-14). Israel's bloodbath finally ended in Samaria. There Jehu cunningly vowed to serve Baal with a zeal greater than that of Ahab. Unsuspecting devotees of Baal gathered in great numbers to join in a festival sacrifice. Instead, the devotees themselves became the sacrifice, and the house of Baal in Samaria was destroyed and desecrated by turning its ruins into a latrine (vv 18-27).
  Political and economic problems also contributed to the unrest. Under the reign of Ahab and Jezebel, justice was corrupted. The poor lost their land in the drought and their property rights were ignored (1 Kgs 18:5-6). Jehu threw the body of Jehoram into the field of Naboth the Jezreelite (2 Kgs 9:25-26) as justice for the crime of Ahab and Jezebel (1 Kgs 21:19; cf. v 13). But religious passions dominated the cause. Jehu called his slaughter of the house of Omri his "zeal for the Lord." Jehonadab, a Recabite, joined Jehu as he traveled toward Samaria (2 Kgs 10:15-17). Recabites opposed social and economic developments that took place in the northern kingdom under Ahab. They followed a strict moral code and lived a simple life (Jer 35). Since

Recabites represented the most conservative elements of Yahwism, they became natural allies for the reform of Jehu.
  Jehu's revolution seriously weakened the worship of Baal. Although not all of the adherents were eliminated, Baalism no longer remained the official religion of the state (2 Kgs 10:28). Rather, Baalism united with Yahwism to form the sinister syncretistic religion that was denounced by Hosea.
  Politically, the revolt of Jehu was disastrous. The triple alliance between Tyre, Israel, and Judah was shattered by the atrocities. Israel, now isolated, became easy prey for Assyria and Syria. Jehu attempted to buy some help from Assyria by paying tribute to Shalmaneser III. That event is pictured on the Black Obelisk in a relief from the campaign of 841 BC. An inscription names "Jehu, son of Omri," as the one kneeling before Shalmaneser.
  After the Assyrian threat dissipated in 838 BC, Hazael, king of Aram-Damascus, conquered all of Israelite Transjordan as far as the Arnon (2 Kgs 10:32-33). In a second campaign in 815 BC, Hazael moved across the Jordan River, through the Jezreel plain, and down the coast, conquering the land as far as Gath in the northern Shephelah. There the son of Jehu, Jehoahaz, paid tribute to Hazael (12:18). The revolution weakened Israel both politically and economically.
  Later generations spoke of the massacre of the house of Omri with horror (Hos 1:4). Jehu did not destroy the golden calves of Jeroboam, and so continued the syncretistic worship at Bethel and Dan. In the final analysis the revolution, which was meant to purge Israel of oppression and false religion, succeeded in doing neither.
3. Member of Judah's tribe, the son of Obed and Azariah's father (1 Chr 2:38).
4. Prince of Simeon's tribe, and the son of Joshibiah, who, along with others, migrated from the approaches to the valley of Gedor eastward in search of good pasture (1 Chr 4:35).
5. One of the skilled warriors who joined David at Ziklag. Interestingly, he was of Saul's tribe, Benjamin, and from Anathoth, to which Abiathar of the priests of Eli was later banished (1 Chr 12:3).
  See also Chronology of the Bible (Old Testament); Israel, History of.

JEHUBBAH* Shemer's son from Asher's tribe (1 Chr 7:34).

JEHUCAL Son of Shelemiah who was sent by King Zedekiah to request Jeremiah's prayers for Judah (Jer 37:3; 38:1). Later he tried to kill Jeremiah, who continued to prophesy the invasion of Jerusalem by the Babylonians, thereby undermining the confidence of the people and the army (38:1-6).

JEHUD One of the towns given to Dan's tribe after the Conquest (Jos 19:45). It has been variously identified with the village of el-Yehudiyeh, about seven miles (11.3 kilometers) southeast of Joppa, and with Yazur, about five miles (8 kilometers) southeast of Joppa.

JEHUDI Son of Nethaniah and a messenger of King Jehoiakim of Judah. He was sent by a number of princes to summon Baruch to read Jeremiah's scroll privately to them. Later, Jehoiakim ordered Jehudi to read the same scroll publicly before him and all the court, after which the writing was burned (Jer 36:14-23).

JEHUDIJAH* Not a proper name; KJV mistranslation for "Jewish," a descriptive term distinguishing Mered's Jewish wife from his other wife, who was an Egyptian princess (1 Chr 4:18).

JEHUSH* KJV spelling of Jeush, Eshek's son, in 1 Chronicles 8:39. *See* Jeush #3.

JEIEL
1. Chief in Reuben's tribe (1 Chr 5:7).
2. Benjamite who lived at Gibeon and an ancestor of Israel's first king, Saul (1 Chr 8:29; 9:35).
3. One of David's mighty men (1 Chr 11:44). He is perhaps identical with #1 above.
4. Levite gatekeeper in the sanctuary. He seems to have served as a musician also (1 Chr 15:18, 21; 16:5b). The Jeiel of 1 Chronicles 16:5a is probably a different musician.
5. Levite descended from Asaph and an ancestor of a prophet named Jahaziel (2 Chr 20:14).
6. Secretary for King Uzziah's army, who kept or made military "rolls" or "musters" of the king's troops (2 Chr 26:11).
7. KJV and NLT spelling of Jeuel, Elizaphan's descendant, in 2 Chronicles 29:13. *See* Jeuel #2.
8. Levite leader who contributed Passover offerings during King Josiah's reign (2 Chr 35:9).
9. KJV spelling of Jeuel, Adonikam's descendant, in Ezra 8:13. *See* Jeuel #3.
10. Nebo's descendant who was encouraged to divorce his foreign wife during the postexilic era (Ezr 10:43).

JEKABZEEL Alternate name for Kabzeel, a city in southern Judah, in Nehemiah 11:25. *See* Kabzeel.

JEKAMEAM Hebron's son from the Kohathite division of Levi's tribe (1 Chr 23:19; 24:23).

JEKAMIAH
1. Shallum's son from Judah's tribe (1 Chr 2:41).
2. One of King Jehoiachin's sons (1 Chr 3:18).

JEKUTHIEL Zanoah's father from Judah's tribe (1 Chr 4:18).

JEMIMAH First of the three daughters born to Job when he was restored after his affliction (Jb 42:14).

JEMUEL Simeon's first son (Gn 46:10; Ex 6:15). He is called Nemuel in 1 Chronicles 4:24 and is the founder of the Nemuelite family (Nm 26:12).

JEPHTHAH Illegitimate son of Gilead (Jgs 11:1) and a leader in the period of the judges. The son of a harlot, Jephthah was dispossessed by his father's other sons and refused a share in their father's home. He moved to the land of Tob, a small Aramean state east of the Jordan River (Jgs 11:3-5), and became leader of a band of malcontents and adventurers who went raiding with him.

When war broke out between the Israelites and the Ammonites, the leaders of Gilead begged Jephthah to return and lead their army. At first he refused because of their previous mistreatment of him. When they promised to make him Gilead's ruler, he accepted and became commander in chief and ruler (Jgs 11:4-10). The agreement was ratified before the Lord at a general assembly of the people at Mizpah (v 11) in Gilead, probably just south of the Jabbok River.

After diplomatic negotiations with the king of Ammon failed, Jephthah waged war against the Ammonites. Before the fighting started, he vowed to the Lord that if he was vic-

torious, on his return home he would sacrifice to God whoever met him at the door of his house. Then he successfully led his army against the Ammonites, destroying them with a terrible slaughter (Jgs 11:29-33).

When Jephthah returned home, he was shocked to find that the first person to meet him was his only child, his daughter, playing a tambourine and dancing for joy. When he saw her, he tore his clothes and said, "Alas, my daughter! you have brought me very low, and you have become the cause of great trouble to me; for I have opened my mouth to the LORD, and I cannot take back my vow" (Jgs 11:35, RSV). She submitted to her destiny but begged that it might be postponed for two months so that she and her companions could retreat to the mountains and lament that she must die a virgin (vv 34-38). A woman in ancient Israel could suffer no greater disgrace than to die unmarried and childless. When she returned, her father fulfilled his vow (vv 38-39).

DID JEPHTHAH OFFER HIS DAUGHTER AS A HUMAN SACRIFICE?
We know that human sacrifice was practiced at that time, though it was abhorred by the Hebrews and prohibited in the Mosaic law (Lv 18:21; cf. Ex 13:13). Did Jephthah, however, have his daughter killed? The text points to this sad reality. Indeed, the father's cry seems conclusive proof that her life was to be forfeited as a sacrifice, and the language and tone of the Hebrew text bears this out. The theory that she was spared to become the founder of a sisterhood of perpetual virgins is of very late, medieval origin. The daughter exhibited extraordinary self-denial in her understanding of and respect for her father's commitment. Such a sacrifice was by no means infrequent in Israel, and common in other cultures, however repugnant it seems to us today. For other evidences of its practice, see 2 Kings 16:3, 17:17, 21:6, Jeremiah 7:31, and Micah 6:7. That this took place illustrates how deeply ingrained Canaanite religious practice was in Israel during this dark age.

We should not think that God was pleased with this sacrifice. In fact, God had provided a way out for anyone who had made a rash vow. Those who made rash vows were commanded to confess their sins and then make an offering for sin, whether it be a sheep, a bird, or even fine flour (see Lv 5:4-13).

Jephthah also led Gilead against the Ephraimites, who were resentful that they had not been included in the fight against Ammon. They had been given a previous chance to ally with Gilead but refused. Jephthah captured the fords of the Jordan behind the Ephraimites and prevented their escape by an ingenious strategy. Gileadite guards put fugitives to a test, demanding that they say "Shibboleth." If they could not pronounce the "sh," they were revealed as Ephraimites and killed. The account says that 42,000 Ephraimites died at that time (Jgs 12:1-6).

Jephthah was judge over Gilead for six years (Jgs 12:7), and when he died, he was buried in one of the cities of Gilead. In the Letter to the Hebrews, Jephthah is named with Gideon, Barak, and others as a hero of faith (Heb 11:32).

See also Judges, Book of.

JEPHUNNEH
1. Father of Caleb, one of the 12 spies sent by Moses to search out the land of Canaan (Nm 13:6; 14:6; 26:65; 1 Chr 4:15; 6:56). He is identified variously as a Judahite and a Kenizzite (Jos 14:6).
2. Jether's son from Asher's tribe (1 Chr 7:38).

JERAH Son of Joktan and nephew of Peleg, during whose lifetime the earth was divided, probably a reference to the dispersion following Babel. Jerah is likely also the name of an Arabian tribe or district (Gn 10:25-26; 1 Chr 1:20).

JERAHMEEL

1. Firstborn of Hezron's three sons, the father of six sons and a descendant of Judah through Perez's line (1 Chr 2:9-42). He was the founder of the family of Jerahmeelites, who in David's time lived in the Negev region and occupied a number of cities (1 Sm 27:10; 30:29).
2. Kish's son and a Levite family leader who served in the sanctuary during David's reign (1 Chr 24:29).
3. Son of King Jehoiakim of Judah and one who, with Shelemiah and Seraiah, was ordered by the king to seize Baruch and Jeremiah (Jer 36:26).

JERAHMEELITE

Jerahmeel's descendant from Judah's tribe (1 Sm 27:10; 30:29). *See* Jerahmeel #1.

JERED

1. KJV spelling of Jared in 1 Chronicles 1:2. *See* Jared.
2. Ezrah's son from Judah's tribe (1 Chr 4:18).

JEREMAI

Hashum's son who obeyed Ezra's exhortation to divorce his foreign wife after the exile (Ezr 10:33).

JEREMIAH (Person)

1. Prophet to Judah before its fall in 586 BC; his name is also spelled "Jeremias" (Mt 16:14) and "Jeremy" (Mt 2:17; 27:9) in the KJV.

Jeremiah was born in the village of Anathoth, about three miles (4.8 kilometers) northeast of Jerusalem. His father's name was Hilkiah, and he belonged to the tribe of Benjamin. His call came in the 13th year of King Josiah (640–609 BC). He refers to himself as "a child" when called (Jer 1:6), but the Hebrew word is not the same as used in Jeremiah 30:6 and 31:8 and cannot be limited to preadolescence. He was probably referring to his inexperience rather than to his age. Jeremiah was born about 657 BC during the reign of the wicked king Manasseh, while the great Ashurbanipal, who had shaken the world by sacking the ancient Egyptian city of Thebes in 663 BC, ruled a world empire from Assyria.

God informed Jeremiah that he had consecrated and appointed him before birth (Jer 1:4-5). Jeremiah first shrank with a sense of inadequacy and fear: "O Sovereign LORD, . . . I can't speak for you! I'm too young!" (v 6, NLT). God would not allow Jeremiah to excuse himself. He was assured that words would be given him to speak, and guidance given for the way (v 7). He was promised protection (v 18) and deliverance (v 8) despite opposition (v 19). God touched his mouth, signifying divine inspiration of his words, and gave the sign of a branch from an almond tree, explaining that the Lord is watching (see NLT mg). The third sign was the boiling pot (v 13) facing from the north, picturing the source and fury of impending disaster.

Thus the tone of Jeremiah's life ministry was set: judgment, disaster, danger, defeat, and impending death for the nation.

Early Ministry The messages given by Jeremiah during his first five years of ministry may have been instrumental in the great revival of 622 BC. Those cooperating with King Josiah in the reformation and friendly with Jeremiah included Ahikam and his father, Shaphan (Jer 26:24); Gedaliah, Ahikam's son

(39:14), who later became governor; Acbor, son of Micaiah, also called Abdon, whose son Elnathan joined the opposition (26:22) but later repented (36:25); and Asaiah (2 Chr 34:20). The prophets Nahum and Zephaniah also influenced the reform movement, which must have climaxed under the preaching of Habakkuk and Jeremiah, the priestly ministry of Hilkiah, and the prophecies of Huldah the prophetess. During the reign of King Josiah, Jeremiah spoke without the fear of persecution that plagued his later ministry. Though the content of the book of Jeremiah sometimes appears to be fragmentary, most of chapters 1–19 date to the time of Josiah.

The finding of the lost Book of the Covenant in the temple debris may be the reason for the words in Jeremiah 15:16: "Your words are what sustain me. They bring me great joy and are my heart's delight" (NLT). The words "So be it, LORD" (Jer 11:5) in a context recalling the words of Moses in the Torah may be Jeremiah's response after hearing King Josiah read the newly found book.

Small towns and rural areas, including his hometown, heard Jeremiah's denunciation of high places and idolatry. They sought to kill the young prophet, or at least to intimidate him (11:21). Instead of being silent, Jeremiah asserted that his motivation was for their good and condemned their resistance to the truth as their greatest danger.

Shortly after Jeremiah began his ministry, a number of world-changing events took place. Ashurbanipal died and the Assyrian Empire rapidly declined. Nabopolassar began a 21-year reign in Babylon, leading an expansion that culminated in his son Nebuchadnezzar's subjugation of the known world. As the world news filtered in, Jeremiah turned more toward Jerusalem. His first temple speeches (chs 7–10) may have been uttered at this time.

Nabopolassar felt his strength sufficient to launch an attack against Assyrian territory in 616 BC, but he advanced cautiously because Psamtik I (Psammetichus) of Egypt appeared ready to aid Assyria. Cyaxares of Media pounced on Assyria when Babylon hesitated and took its most sacred city, Asshur, in 614 BC. Babylon joined Media, along with Scythia, and waged an assault against Nineveh, which fell late in the summer of 612 BC. The Assyrian Empire had shriveled to two small holdings, Haran and Carchemish.

Nabopolassar took Haran in 610, and Ashuruballit, having escaped, appealed to Egypt for help at Carchemish. Neco, who had become pharaoh within the year, responded immediately. He marched through Judah without giving Josiah prior notice and asked that the Jews not bother him in view of his haste to go northward (2 Chr 35:21). Ignoring the request, Josiah pursued them to Megiddo and was wounded in the ensuing battle; he died in Jerusalem.

Ministry during the Reign of Jehoiakim In place of Jehoahaz, Josiah's fourth son, who reigned only three months, Pharaoh Neco enthroned Jehoiakim (Eliakim). Neco demanded heavy indemnity payments from Judah and took Jehoahaz prisoner as collateral to assure payment (2 Kgs 23:31-33).

Early in the reign of Jehoiakim, Jeremiah, moved by God's Spirit, delivered his third temple speech (Jer 26) on the occasion of one of the annual Jewish feasts. He called for the people to repent and to act on the basis of the revelation they had heard repeatedly from the Book of the Law. The barb of the sermon came in the warning: "This is what the LORD says: If you will not listen to me and obey the law I have given you, and if you will not listen to my servants, the prophets—for I sent them again and again to warn you, but you would not listen to them—then I will destroy this Temple as I destroyed Shiloh, the place where the Tabernacle was located. And I will make Jerusalem an object of cursing in every nation on earth" (26:4-6, NLT). Shiloh had been the heart of Jewish worship from Joshua to Samuel, but after being destroyed by the Philistines, it never revived. It served as an example of complete desolation following God's judgment in the days of Eli.

Crowds gathered rapidly and reacted angrily against Jeremiah. Priests and princes hurried to the New Gate, where a court was established to bring order and to control violence. Jehoiakim would be no help to Jeremiah, for he had refused to listen to God's messages (Jer 22:21). The priests and false prophets spoke against Jeremiah, calling him a traitor. Then some of the elders spoke to the people about Uriah, who had prophesied the same message. Rather than risk disaster, Ahikam persuaded the court to spare Jeremiah.

Egypt controlled Palestine and Syria after the decay of the Assyrian Empire. In 606 BC Egypt succeeded in annihilating a garrison city of Babylonian soldiers south of Carchemish and then reoccupied Carchemish to await the return blow from Babylon. This Egyptian victory meant persecution for Jeremiah, who was often accused of false prophecy (cf. Jer 20).

Jeremiah never had confidence in Egypt. Each time a Jewish leader would call for a new alliance with Egypt, Jeremiah repeated God's message against it. Whenever a Jewish group fled to Egypt for security, Jeremiah warned of worse things in that land of false refuge (see Jer 44:26-27). Jeremiah's ode and prophecy in chapter 46 poetically describe Egypt's defeat at Carchemish, when Nabopolassar sent his son Nebuchadnezzar to destroy them (605 BC). After smashing the Egyptian army at Carchemish, Nebuchadnezzar pursued the enemy through Judah. "Not a single man escaped to his own country," reads the exaggerated Babylonian record. His father's death, however, prevented him from invading Egypt, and he returned to Babylon to assume the throne. The following year Nebuchadnezzar, now king of Babylonia, returned to accept the homage of the rulers of Judah, Syria, and Phoenicia. On this occasion God gave Jeremiah his great 70-year prophecy (Jer 25:11-12), which became the basis of Daniel 9:2, 24-27.

A year after the decisive battle at Carchemish, Baruch, Jeremiah's scribe, finished recording all the dictated words of Jeremiah and was reading from this scroll at the temple. A report reached the king, who sent Jehudi, a servant, to fetch the scroll and read it to him. When this was done, Jehoiakim burned the scroll in spite of his counselors, who pleaded that the king not do it (Jer 36:23-25). God's message, soon rewritten, added a promise of fearful judgment on Jehoiakim (vv 27-31).

Ambitious young Nebuchadnezzar determined to add Egypt to his dominion. In 601 BC he led his forces through Judah again, but Neco had advance warning and was prepared for the onslaught. In the desert of Shur, Nebuchadnezzar suffered defeat. Encouraged by this display of Egyptian defensive strength, the pro-Egyptian parties in Judah asserted themselves, persuading Jehoiakim to lead them to freedom from Babylon by making an alliance with Egypt (2 Kgs 24:1). But help from Egypt did not come (v 7).

In 599 BC, Nebuchadnezzar armed those surrounding the rebel Jewish kingdom to harass the Jews, which they willingly did (2 Kgs 24:2). Evidently Jehoiakim lost his life in one of these raids. Since the people despised him, his body was thrown out without honorable burial, as Jeremiah had predicted (Jer 22:19).

Ministry during the Reign of Zedekiah Nebuchadnezzar's siege of Jerusalem in 598 BC lasted only a short time because the new king, Jehoiachin, crowned at age 18, knew resistance was useless. He gave himself up, with all his family and court, in March of 597 BC, after serving as king about three months. The Babylonian Chronicle reads: "He [Nebuchadnezzar] seized the city and captured the king."

Jehoiachin was carried to Babylon along with 8,000 (2 Kgs 24:16; cf. v 14) officers, artisans, and executives (Ezekiel among them) and much booty. In his place Nebuchadnezzar appointed Zedekiah, Jehoiachin's uncle, to rule. Zedekiah proceeded to organize his government with the less capable and inexperienced help left after the deportation.

Jeremiah took up his thankless ministry, calling on the Jews to believe God, obey the laws of Babylon, and reject false hopes in Egypt. Zedekiah turned a deaf ear to these appeals, listening rather to the unwise advice of his counselors (Jer 37:1-2). During the first year of Zedekiah's rule, Jeremiah received the vision of the two baskets of figs. The Jews carried to Babylon were like good figs, while Zedekiah and those who trusted in Egypt were like rotten figs (24:1-8). The reason for this reproachful description was that the Jews began plotting rebellion against Babylon along with Edom, Moab, Ammon, Tyre, and Sidon from the beginning of the reign of Zedekiah (27:1-3), thus breaking their oath of loyalty to Nebuchadnezzar and repudiating God's message through Jeremiah.

In Egypt the pharaoh began to renew plans to organize dissidents within the Babylonian Empire to revolt. He hired Jewish soldiers to aid him in protecting his southern border. The Jewish soldiers settled on a Nile island called Elephantine, or Yeb (593–410 BC). Jeremiah addressed an oracle to these Jews (ch 44). The treaty for Jews to help in Egypt evidently also assumed that Egyptians would aid Israel. When the Babylonians besieged Jerusalem in 589, Pharaoh Hophra came to the aid of Zedekiah. Nebuchadnezzar, ruling from Riblah, commanded that the siege against Jerusalem be lifted in order to make a surprise attack on Hophra (37:5). The release gave Jeremiah an opportunity to journey to Anathoth to secure some family property (v 12). However, Irijah, captain of the guard, arrested Jeremiah in the Gate of Benjamin for defecting to the enemy, and he was beaten and flung into a dungeon. King Zedekiah brought him out after many days to obtain a prognostication. With characteristic boldness, Jeremiah told the king he would shortly become a captive. At the same time, Jeremiah requested relief from injustice for himself. He gained part of his request but continued as prisoner in the court of the guard.

The Babylonian army chased Pharaoh Hophra back to Egypt and returned to crush Jerusalem without further mercy. The siege, which began in 589 BC, was restored with rigor in January of 588, Zedekiah's ninth year (39:1). During this time, the Lord gave Jeremiah foreknowledge of a visit from a cousin who wished to sell a field near Anathoth (32:7-9; cf. 37:12). Jeremiah bought the field as an object lesson to verify the message of restoration after a captivity of 70 years (29:10).

The armies of Babylon cut off all supplies from Jerusalem and were able to destroy the last two outlying Jewish fortresses of Lachish and Azekah (34:7). Food became scarce. Disease spread. Undisposed-of sewage and impure cistern water caused pestilence.

With increased distress came Jeremiah's increased appeal for the city to surrender.

Jeremiah remained in the prison court until the Babylonians breached the city wall in July of 586 BC. The king escaped by night and succeeded in reaching the plains of Jericho but was captured there and taken to Riblah. Zedekiah's family and counselors were killed; he himself was blinded and taken in chains to Babylon, where he died soon after (39:6-7).

Back in Jerusalem, Nebuzaradan, the Babylonian general, sent most of the Jews into captivity. Jeremiah, however, was granted special consideration; after being released from prison, he was placed under the care of Gedaliah, son of Ahikam.

After the Fall of Jerusalem A month after the fall of Jerusalem, the city was burned and the walls broken down. Gedaliah was appointed governor of the remaining agricultural community, with headquarters at Mizpah. Jeremiah returned to Jerusalem, where, according to tradition, he took up his abode in a grotto near what is now known as Gordon's Calvary. There he wrote the book of Lamentations.

The Ammonite king Baalis, plotting rebellion against Babylon, instigated the murder of Gedaliah (40:13). In the reaction that followed, the remaining people followed the leader Johanan ben Kareah to a camp near Bethlehem, intending to go to Egypt. They asked Jeremiah, at Jerusalem, to give guidance from the Lord, promising obedience. Jeremiah's message required that they remain in Israel and not go to Egypt. Disobedience was complete and immediate. Fearing Babylon, they departed from Judah, taking Jeremiah with them, and entered Egypt (41:16–43:7).

Jeremiah did not stop his ministry in Egypt. His message at Tahpanhes (43:8-12) assured a victorious conquest of the land by Nebuchadnezzar, which took place in 568–567 BC.

Jews from all parts of Egypt gathered to discuss their future as exiles. Jeremiah took the opportunity to denounce their idolatry. Jewish women as well as men argued that they had enjoyed prosperity while serving idols but had suffered since stopping. Jeremiah condemned their obdurate blindness to reality and gave God's indictment. For a verifying sign, Jeremiah predicted that Pharaoh Hophra of Egypt would be assassinated (44:30), which happened in 466 BC. No later record of Jeremiah's acts exists in the Bible. Tradition says Jeremiah was stoned to death by the people of the Jewish exile settlement in Tahpanhes.

Though Jeremiah suffered continued rejection during his life, he has been honored by numerous apocryphal and traditional embellishments to his history. Jesus could well have had Jeremiah in mind when he said, "You build tombs for the prophets your ancestors killed and decorate the graves of the godly people your ancestors destroyed. . . . [You are] the descendants of those who murdered the prophets" (Mt 23:29-31, NLT). *See* Israel, History of; Jeremiah, Book of; Prophet, Prophetess.

2. Family head in the Transjordan portion of Manasseh whom Tiglath-pileser took captive (1 Chr 5:23-26; cf. 2 Kgs 15:29).

3. Father of Hamutal, a wife of King Josiah (2 Kgs 23:31; 24:18).

4. Ambidextrous Benjamite bowman and slinger who joined David at Ziklag (1 Chr 12:4).

Ancient Greek Text of Jeremiah Jeremiah 5:9-13 in Chester Beatty Papyrus VIII (c. 200)

5, 6. Two Gadite soldiers who joined David's army (1 Chr 12:10, 13).

7. Postexilic priest who with Nehemiah set his seal to the covenant, renewing the people's promise to obey God's laws (Neh 10:2). He is mentioned again (12:34) as part of the procession for the dedication of the new wall of Jerusalem.

8. Priest who returned from exile with Zerubbabel (Neh 12:1) and became head of a family of priests (v 12).

9. Father of Jaazaniah, a Recabite who refused to drink wine (Jer 35:3).

JEREMIAH, Book of OT prophetic book, second in the canonical order of the Prophets.

PREVIEW
• Author
• Authenticity
• The Book of Jeremiah and the Septuagint
• Background
• Date
• Origin and Destination
• Purpose
• Teaching
• Outline and Content

Author Few doubt that the prophet from Anathoth wrote the book of Jeremiah, yet questions persist concerning some parts, particularly chapter 52. The use of the third person cannot be used to discredit Jeremiah's authorship, for Jeremiah used the first and third person, and even the second person, in the same context. For example, 32:6-7 reads: "Jeremiah said [third person], 'The word of the LORD came to me: [first person] . . . your uncle will come to you [second person]' " (RSV).

The problem of the passage of time provides the strongest argument against the Jeremian authorship of chapter 52. Jeremiah was born about 657 BC. Evil-merodoch released Jehoiachin (52:31) about 95 years later. Jeremiah 52:33 summarizes the continuation of events beyond this time. The problem of location also argues against Jeremian authorship, for Jeremiah took up residence in Egypt (43:6-7) while Jehoiachin dwelt in Babylon. Note also that Jeremiah concludes his writing with chapter 51, making chapter 52 a true editorial appendix. Since chapter 52 parallels 2 Kings 24:18–25:30, it may be that other portions of Jeremiah that parallel sections of 2 Kings may have been written by someone other than Jeremiah.

The following table shows such portions and includes harmonic passages in 2 Chronicles. The first column shows historical (chronological) sequence. The last column provides a brief condensation of content.

Baruch served as the secretary for Jeremiah. The rela-

tionship between the two men apparently lasted many years; the prophet gave a word of encouragement as he blessed his helper (45:5). According to the custom of the people, it would have been legitimate for the scribe to write some of the prophet's messages in his own words. This would not deny inspiration.

Authenticity That Jeremiah lived and actually wrote the major part of the book bearing his name is authenticated by numerous references in both biblical and nonbiblical sources (e.g., Dn 9; Ecclus 49; Josephus's *Antiquities* 10; Talmud: *Baba Bathra*). The veracity of the historical sections of Jeremiah have abundant confirmation in contemporary biblical books and in the secular histories preserved in Babylon, Egypt, and Persia.

Higher critics sought to discredit the portions of Jeremiah that were omitted by the Septuagint, or to credit passages to a later writer because of style differences (e.g., chs 30–33) or spelling differences (as found in chs 27–29) or linguistic problems (as in 10:11, written in Aramaic, but this may be a gloss). Another reason for discrediting Jeremiah's authorship is that critics dated some prophecies later than indicated in the context. This results from their requiring that predictive writing follow the record of its fulfillment. None of these reasons is sufficient cause for doubting authenticity. The Hebrew text deserves priority over the Septuagint. Aramaic contact with the Jews became commonplace during this period (cf. Ezr 4–7; Dn 2–7) and therefore explains the presence of Aramaic. Different styles may be expected from the same writer due to differing circumstances and differing purposes. Baruch may have been inspired to write parts of this book and/or edited what Jeremiah wrote. Prediction preceding fulfillment presents no problem for believers.

The Book of Jeremiah and the Septuagint The special problems of the Septuagint translation of Jeremiah demand attention. The Septuagint translators evidently made an inaccurate translation. About 2,300 Hebrew words are omitted from the Septuagint. After chapter 23, the mistranslation, omissions, and mixed chronological order indicate confusion. However, the Dead Sea Scrolls display texts with both the Hebrew and the Septuagint order, indicating the antiquity of both editions. Both have suffered corruption at the hands of scribes and the ravages of the ages. The Septuagint evidently veers much further from the original, yet it has invaluable clues to help suggest answers to some textual problems. The most evident major shift in the Septuagint consists of the removal of chapters 46–51 from the Hebrew order, and the placement of them in the spot from which 25:13b-14 was removed. These chapters are renumbered 26–31 but are mixed and changed considerably from the order of the Hebrew Masoretic Text.

JEREMIAH'S PARALLELS WITH 2 KINGS AND 2 CHRONICLES

This chart follows the order of passages as they occur in Jeremiah.

Order	Jeremiah	2 Kings	2 Chronicles	Content
1	37:1-2	24:17-19	36:10-12	Zedekiah made king
2	39:1-8	25:1-10	36:17-19	Zedekiah rebels; siege begins
7	39:10 and 40:5b	25:12 and 25:22b		Gedaliah made governor
8	40:7-9	25:23-24		Gedaliah urges fidelity to Babylon
9	41:1-3	25:25		Gedaliah assassinated
10	43:5-7	25:26		Jews flee to Egypt
1	52:1-2 (cf. 37:1-2)	24:17-19	36:10-12	Zedekiah made king
2	52:3-5 (cf. 39:1-3)	24:20 and 25:1-2	36:13-16	Zedekiah rebels; siege begins
3	52:6-14	25:3-10	36:17-19	Zedekiah captured; Jerusalem destroyed
6	52:15	25:11	36:20	People deported
5	52:17-23	25:13-17	36:18	Booty taken
4	52:24-27	25:18-21		Nobles slain
11	52:31-34	25:27-30		Later events

Background This is fully discussed in the previous entry. *See* Jeremiah (Person) #1.

ARCHAEOLOGICAL EVIDENCE SHEDS LIGHT ON JEREMIAH'S WRITINGS

A dramatic correspondence illustrating Jeremiah 34:7 came to light with the discovery of 21 inscribed potsherds at Lachish by the Wellcome Expedition between 1932 and 1938. Some of these letters refer to "the prophet" (Letter 16 includes the last letters of the name, -*iah*). The letters were written by Hoshaiah (Jer 42:1; 43:2). The latest letters indicate that fire signals had ceased from Azekah (note the reference to such signals in Jer 6:1). The expected support from Egypt was not available to save either Lachish or Jerusalem.

At Tell Beit Mirsim two jar handles from Jeremiah's time were inscribed with "Eliakim, steward of Jehoiachin." A similar jar handle was discovered at Beth-shemesh. Evidently Jehoiachin was considered as the true king even after he was carried to Babylon, and he maintained his royal holding by the steward in charge of his estate.

The seal of Gedaliah found at Lachish in 1935 evidently gives a direct contact with the governor of Judah appointed by Nebuchadnezzar after the fall of Jerusalem (Jer 40:5-12). The seal of Jaazaniah discovered at Tell en-Nasbeh dates to the time of Jeremiah, and probably belonged to the person named in 2 Kings 25:23, though a man of the same name and time is mentioned in Jeremiah 35:3. The Shallum seal found at Lachish may refer to the youngest son of Josiah (22:11), to the Shallum mentioned in the Lachish letters, or to a person mentioned in Jeremiah 32:7 or 35:4. The phrase "son of Mas" on the seal probably does not denote family relationship. The Hilkiah seal also reads "son of Mas." Since the date of origin for this seal also fits Jeremiah's time, the owner of the seal may have been the father of Jeremiah (1:1) or the high priest or some other person.

One positive identification comes from the excavation near the Ishtar Gate of Nebuchadnezzar's Babylon, where a cuneiform tablet dating about 585 BC lists "Yaukin [Jehoiachin], king of the land of Yahud [Judah]" as one of the resident captives. The Babylonian record even mentions the five sons (cf. 1 Chr 3:17-18) who were under the care of a certain Kenaiah. Another identification comes from the recent discovery of Baruch's seal—Baruch was Jeremiah's secretary.

Date The chronological sequence of the messages of Jeremiah constitutes a major problem that cannot be wholly solved. Nonetheless, the book was written during Jeremiah's ministry (c. 627–586 BC).

Origin and Destination After beginning his ministry in Anathoth, Jeremiah moved to Jerusalem, where he remained until he was forced to join the disobedient refugees who arrived in Egypt about 584 BC. Until the deportation of Jehoiachin (597 BC), Jeremiah addressed his messages to the king and the people residing in Judah. Later messages addressed the same group, plus the captives in Babylon (e.g., ch 29). After the departure to Egypt, he addressed Jews in that land.

Purpose Part of God's commission to Jeremiah stated the purpose of Jeremiah's ministry: "Today I appoint you to stand up against nations and kingdoms. You are to uproot some and tear them down, to destroy and over-

throw them. You are to build others up and plant them" (1:10, NLT). The first four parts of the commission required that Jeremiah, appointed as a "chief governor" over nations, should wreck the existing religious and social structures by his preaching against moral and spiritual sin. Doubtless, the physical destruction caused by the Egyptians, Assyrians, and Babylonians was the accoutrement for the truth uttered by the prophet. Jeremiah is consistent in his blasts at moral and religious wickedness, his call to submit to the punishment that God gives through Babylon, and his assurance that such submission will lead to blessing. When Zedekiah asks advice (38:14), we know what Jeremiah will say. When the captains of the refugees ask if they should go to Egypt, we already know the answer (42:3). We may also anticipate the obdurate rejection of God's message on the part of the inquiring people, who apparently want to know God's will but have no desire to obey it.

Nevertheless, part of Jeremiah's purpose focuses on the most distant future when the new covenant will supplant the old (31:31-37), and a transformed people bent on obedience rather than sin will receive God's promised kingdom.

Teaching National sin brings national punishment. No truth blazes so clearly as this. Gentiles as well as Jews stand under the same judgment, for God is not the God of Israel only.

Individuals are not overlooked in divine judgments on nations. God sets before each the way of life and the way of death (21:8) and appeals to each to choose life (27:13).

Jeremiah illustrates human depravity by questioning if people can change their skin color or leopards their spots (13:23). The depths of depravity reach beyond man's ability to measure (17:9-10). People even love falsehood (5:30-31). Yet God promises to transform willing subjects who call on him (33:3) by giving them a "new heart" (24:7; 32:38-41) as the climactic provision of the new covenant (31:33-35). The Messiah, who accomplishes the saving work, is called the Lord our Righteousness, the King, the righteous Branch, the Branch of David (23:5-6; 33:15-16).

A future nation will be made up of individuals who accept this salvation. Passing through the night of tribulation as of travail (30:6-7), the Jews will understand the true identity of their Messiah, will believe and receive him with repentant sorrow, will be cleansed (33:8), and will be regathered from all countries (32:37) by the omnipotent God (v 27).

Outline and Content Though many see no logical order, a careful reading of Jeremiah will reveal a grouping on the basis of content, as suggested by the following outline:

I. Introduction (1)
II. Oracles against the Jews (2–25)
III. History—Signs and Sufferings of Jeremiah before the Siege (26–29)
IV. The Book of Hope written during the Siege (30–33)
V. History—Signs and Sufferings of Jeremiah after the Siege (34–45)
VI. Oracles against the Nations (46–51)
VII. Conclusion (52)

The prophet opens his ministry with a series of utterances against the sins of Jerusalem (2:1–3:5), followed by similar messages (through ch 4), concluding with words of judgment (chs 5–6). The message in the temple gate (chs 7–10) leads into the proclamation against covenant breakers (chs 11–13). The lamentation over the drought (ch 14) and subsequent miseries (ch 15) compares with many similar expressions of grief. Jeremiah did not differ from other prophets in his use of object lessons. The rotted linen waistband (ch 13), the broken jug (ch 19), figs (ch 24), and ox yoke (chs 27–28) may be supplemented by human object lessons (ch 35), and even the prophet himself, whose celibacy (16:1-4), resistance to sympathetic consolation (16:5-7), and withdrawal from feasts (16:8-9) all served to illustrate and confirm his message.

Places where Jeremiah proclaimed his messages helped bear home his point. He stood in the public gate, where kings came and went, to proclaim that judgment (fire) would come through the gate (17:19, 27; 39:3). Then he went to the potter's house (ch 18), and then to Hinnom or Topath, which would be called the Valley of Slaughter (ch 19).

The persecution suffered by Jeremiah first hinted at (1:8), then predicted (v 19), expresses its venom privately from his home village (11:19-23). The prophet's kindred join the opposition (12:6). Public opposition brings beatings and the stocks (20:2-3). Jeremiah prefers to keep silent rather than to speak and suffer (v 9), but he cannot withhold the word that is as fire in his bones. The result: all his familiars reproached, derided, terrorized, and denounced him, then sought his death (vv 7-18). Jeremiah escaped death at the hands of priests, prophets, and people only because he had a few faithful friends (26:8-24). When his prophecies began to materialize, hatred mounted. He was beaten and put into a dungeon for many days (37:14-17) on a false charge. Temporary relief at the guardhouse (v 21) lasted only a few days. Officials clamored again for his death (38:4) and put him into a cistern, where he sank in the mire (v 6). His rescue (v 10) preserved his life, but his imprisonment at the guardhouse continued (v 28). His writings were cut up and burned (36:23); his words were denied and rejected (43:1-7; 44:16).

The "Book of Hope" (chs 30–33) does contain some words of judgment (32:28-35), and other sections of the prophecy have a few bright spots (3:11-18; 16:14-16; 23:2-8; 29:10-14), but in a volume otherwise dark, these four chapters bring pleasant relief. The climax of hope, as indicated also in the longest NT quotation from Jeremiah (see Heb 8:8-12), predicts a new covenant (31:31-40). Other prophecies also describe the end of the Mosaic law and sacrament (e.g., 3:16), and the new covenant (32:40; 33:19-26).

Little is known of Jeremiah's activity or messages from c. 594–589 BC. Zedekiah's counselors made clandestine plans for throwing off Babylon's yoke by alliances with neighbor nations. A traitor may have reported the conspiracy to Babylon (perhaps Edom). After Babylon attacked, Zedekiah sought a hopeful report from Jeremiah but did not get it.

The Recabite faithfulness to the Nazarite vow (ch 35) dates to the days of Jehoiakim but as an object lesson fits the siege context. Recabites received a human command that they obeyed; Jews received a divine command that they rejected. Recabites will be blessed (35:18-19); Judah, judged (vv 15-17). The reading of the scroll to Jehoiakim and his scornful rejection of it (ch 36) illustrates the prophetic assertion (35:15) that destruction follows the rejection of God's message given through the prophets.

The siege comes into focus in chapter 37 with another inquiry from Zedekiah (the nonchronological chs 35–36 serve as an illustrative parenthesis). Jeremiah 37:11 moves forward to the time of the lifting of the siege of 589 BC when Nebuchadnezzar drove Pharaoh Hophra's army back to Egypt. During the reprieve, Jeremiah sought to attend a meeting of relatives to settle family matters at or near Anathoth. Perhaps the trip involved initiating the purchase that would be made two years later (32:6-15). However, as he was leaving the city, he was arrested for desertion to the Babylonians and jailed in a dungeon cell until Zedekiah granted him privileged prisoner status.

The king's officers had ample cause for the accusation of sedition: Jeremiah had encouraged desertion (21:9; 38:2). Traitors deserved death, and this was their verdict against Jeremiah (38:4-5). The violence of the time encouraged the officers to select a cruel method of execution: let Jeremiah starve and bury himself in the mire at the bottom of an abandoned cistern. A sympathetic Ethiopian, Ebed-melech, made the rescue. Immediately, the unadulterated prophecies of judgment came forth again from Jeremiah's lips, including a message to the king that reflected Jeremiah's own recent experience: "[Your friends] have betrayed and misled you. When your feet sank in the mud, they left you to your fate" (38:22, NLT).

Jeremiah 39:1–43:7 records history from the fall of Jerusalem in 586 BC to the flight into Egypt, including the liberation of Jeremiah (ch 39), appointment and assassination of Gedaliah (chs 40–41), a warning from God against going to Egypt (ch 42), and the obdurate disobedience of the people (43:1-7).

The latest writings of Jeremiah are found in chapter 44. The audience consisted of idolatrous Jews (44:4-6) gathered from various parts of Egypt as far as Aswan (Pathros). Jeremiah repeated the appeal of former prophets to reject false gods in favor of Jehovah, but to no avail (44:15-16).

The message to Baruch (ch 45), written about 605 BC, is placed here to round out the main part of the book, which begins with the commission to "break down" and "pluck up" (1:10) and concludes with the same Hebrew words (45:4). If Baruch had ambition to obtain status in the Judean court like his brother Seraiah (51:59), he was advised that it would be useless because disaster would come, as the preceding chapters indicate.

The oracles against the nations (46–51), introduced by a title superscription (46:1), constitute a distinct stylistic division similar to Isaiah 13–23, Ezekiel 25–32, and Amos 1:3–2:16.

Some of the prophecies against foreign nations in Jeremiah carry dates that show that they were written at different points during his ministry but were collected together for the book.

The prophecy against Egypt opens with a colorful description of Egypt's expulsion from Carchemish (605 BC) after a short occupancy (Jer 46:1-12). The second message (vv 13-26) may picture the attack on Egypt in 601 BC when Neco stopped Nebuchadnezzar at the border; the attack in 589 BC when Hophra lost in his attempt to aid Zedekiah; or (most probably) the invasion of Egypt by Nebuchadnezzar in 568 BC, when Babylon took advantage of the weakness of Egypt to occupy it. At that time Nebuchadnezzar set up his judgment throne as predicted (43:10) and meted out death sentences to all rebels, including those Jews who might have been implicated in anti-Babylonian conspiracies. The conclusion of the Egypt oracle repeats part of the Book of Hope (46:27-28, cf. 30:10-11).

Messages against Edom, Arabia, Phoenician cities, and Ammon generally condemn pride, cruelty, and idolatry. The oracle against Elam is unique. No other prophet speaks judgment against this people, whose dwelling east of Babylon meant rare contact with Judah. Jeremiah predicted that Elam would be doomed, then restored. Ezekiel counts Elamites among the inhabitants of Sheol (Ez 32:24).

The final judgment indicates the unbiased attitude of the prophet. His messages placed him in an advantageous position with the Babylonians, who treated him with respect and kindness, in contrast to their cruelty to other Jews. But when God spoke against Babylon, Jeremiah uttered God's words without respect to his own comfort, just as he had spoken against Egypt when silence would have been logical for self-preservation.

Chapter 51 concludes "the words of Jeremiah."

Chapter 52 repeats historical facts previously stated prophetically by Jeremiah, and partially recorded also as history in chapter 39 (cf. 2 Kgs 25 and 2 Chr 36). The editor of Jeremiah evidently desired to climax the book with a historical confirmation of Jeremiah's prophecy, but he included facts beyond those contained elsewhere.

See also Israel, History of; Jeremiah (Person) #1; Prophecy; Prophet, Prophetess.

JEREMIAH, Letter of *See* Letter of Jeremiah.

JEREMIAS* KJV spelling of Jeremiah in Matthew 16:14. *See* Jeremiah (Person) #1.

JEREMOTH

1. One of Beker's nine sons and a leader in Benjamin's tribe (1 Chr 7:8). His name is rendered Jerimoth in some versions.
2. Benjamite, the son of Beriah and head of his family living in Jerusalem (1 Chr 8:14).
3. Levite of the family at Merari and one of Mushi's three sons registered during David's reign (1 Chr 23:23). His name is alternately spelled Jerimoth here and in 1 Chronicles 24:30.
4. Heman's son and the leader of the 15th of 24 divisions of musicians trained for service in the house of the Lord (1 Chr 25:22, NLT mg). Here and also in 1 Chronicles 25:4 his name is spelled Jerimoth.
5. Azriel's son and the chief official of Naphtali's tribe during David's reign (1 Chr 27:19). His name is spelled Jerimoth in some texts.
6. One of Elam's descendants who was encouraged by Ezra to divorce his foreign wife during the postexilic period (Ezr 10:26).
7. One of Zattu's descendants who was encouraged by Ezra to divorce his foreign wife (Ezr 10:27).
8. One of Bani's descendants who was encouraged by Ezra to divorce his foreign wife (Ezr 10:29). He is named "Ramoth" in the KJV.

JEREMY* KJV spelling of Jeremiah in Matthew 2:17 and 27:9. *See* Jeremiah (Person) #1.

JERIAH Levite of the family of Kohath and head of Hebron's house (1 Chr 23:19; 24:23). David organized Jeriah and other Levites to manage the religious and civil affairs of the kingdom (26:31).

JERIBAI Elnaam's son and one of David's mighty men (1 Chr 11:46).

JERICHO Ancient city on the west side of the Jordan River. The name Jericho may be connected to the ancient name of the Canaanite moon god. The Hebrew words for moon, month, new moon, and Jericho are very similar. Others associate it with the word for spirit or smell, assuming that the pleasant fragrances of the fruits and spices that grew in this oasis occasioned the name of the place. The OT occasionally calls it "the city of palm trees" (e.g., Dt 34:3; 2 Chr 28:15).

Jericho was located on the west side of the Jordan

River about five miles (8 kilometers) from the southernmost fords and about ten miles (16 kilometers) northwest of the Dead Sea. Being in the broad part of the plain of the Jordan, it lies nearly 1,000 feet (305 meters) below sea level and about 3,500 feet (1,067 meters) below Jerusalem, which was a mere 17 miles (27 kilometers) away. This simple topographical fact explains the incidental words in Jesus' parable of the good Samaritan, "down from Jerusalem to Jericho" (Lk 10:30).

History

Prebiblical Record Jericho was a large and thriving city for centuries, even millennia, before the Bible first mentions it in connection with the exodus from Egypt. In fact, Jericho is one of the oldest cities in the world, with remains dating to and before the Neolithic Age 10,000 years ago.

For three reasons primitive people would have chosen this site, first as a settlement and eventually as a key city: (1) It has a copious spring, now called Elisha's Fountain (cf. 2 Kgs 2:18-22). (2) It has a warm climate in the winter, although "hot" describes it in the summer. (3) It is strategically located at a Jordan ford and at the base of several routes leading westward to the foothills.

The comings and goings of various populations can be reconstructed only sketchily from noninscriptional archaeological data. The civilizations grew more complex over the years, going from a simple food-gathering economy at first to the relatively complex urban society, complete with king, soldiers, and guest houses, that Joshua encountered. The first certain identification of its inhabitants occurs in Numbers 13:29: "The Hittites, the Jebusites, and the Amorites dwell in the hill country; and the Canaanites dwell by the sea, and along the Jordan" (RSV).

Aerial View of Jericho

In the Old Testament The Jericho of the OT is best known as the first city taken by the invading Israelites through the miracle of the falling walls. Having spent some time on the east bank of the Jordan in the plains of Moab (Nm 22:1; 26:3, 63), the Israelites targeted it as the first military objective in the Conquest. Joshua sent spies to reconnoiter the land and the city. Rahab the harlot took them in and later engineered their escape. For her cooperation, she and her family were spared when Israel destroyed the city (Jos 2, 6). The fall of the city itself occurred after the Israelites had marched around it in silence, except for the continual blowing of trumpets, once a day for six days and then seven times on the seventh day. Then, as the priests blew the trumpets, the people shouted and the walls collapsed.

Joshua laid a curse on anyone who might rebuild Jericho (Jos 6:26). The curse was fulfilled about 500 years later when Hiel rebuilt the city at the cost of two of his sons (1 Kgs 16:34).

Jericho was in the territory of Benjamin but right on the border with the territory of Ephraim to the north (Jos 16:1, 7; 18:12, 21) and appears in scattered incidents throughout the rest of the OT. In 2 Samuel 10:5 (see also 1 Chr 19:5) David had his humiliated ambassadors wait there until their beards grew back. It served as a kind of headquarters for Elisha and apparently was where a "company of the prophets" lived (2 Kgs 2:5; cf. 1 Sm 10:5). During the time of Ahaz, a return of prisoners took place there (2 Chr 28:15). When Jerusalem fell in 586 BC, the reigning king, Zedekiah, fled to near Jericho but was caught by the Babylonians, who later put out his eyes at Riblah in Syria (2 Kgs 25:5; Jer 39:5; 52:8). The last OT references to Jericho are in the census lists of Ezra (Ezr 2:34) and Nehemiah (Neh 7:36). Men from Jericho also helped rebuild the Jerusalem wall (3:2).

In the New Testament First, it must be understood that the Jericho of NT times was built by Herod more than a mile to the south of the OT site, at the mouth of the Wadi Qilt. It is possible to sort out the healing of the blind men episodes in the synoptic Gospels by understanding that Jesus was passing from the site of ancient Jericho (Mt 20:29; Mk 10:46) and approaching Herodian Jericho (Lk 18:35). The modern city of Jericho includes both these sites. As Jesus passed through Jericho (19:1) he met and ate with Zacchaeus, the wealthy chief tax collector of the new Roman Jericho. The city also figures in the parable of the Good Samaritan (10:30-37).

Postbiblical Record While ancient Jericho was of small consequence after its destruction under Joshua, the Jericho of Herod was a city of beauty and importance. But even this city fell into decay with the decline of Roman influence in the Middle East. Most of what we know of the city until modern times comes from the writings of pilgrims to the Holy Land. They usually report seeing certain things of biblical significance, such as the tree that Zacchaeus climbed, but they also report that Jericho was a squalid, wretched Muslim village. And such it has been until relatively recent times, when it grew in size and importance as a major West Bank city.

ARCHAEOLOGY AT JERICHO
Jericho was excavated first by Charles Warren in 1868, then by Ernst Sellin and Carl Watzinger in 1907–11, and then by John Garstang in 1930–36. Garstang thought he had found the wall that fell before the Israelites, but the more thorough, scientific, and widely accepted results of the investigations by Kathleen Kenyon in 1952–56 showed that the topmost level of ruins was already too early to tell anything of the city of Joshua's day. To her goes the credit for uncovering and interpreting the many layers of civilizations that date back to 8000 BC at Jericho.

JERIEL Tola's son from Issachar's tribe (1 Chr 7:2).

JERIJAH* Alternate spelling of Jeriah, a Kohathite Levite, in 1 Chronicles 26:31 (NLT mg). *See* Jeriah.

JERIMOTH
1. One of Bela's five sons and a leader in the tribe of Benjamin (1 Chr 7:7).
2. Alternate spelling of Jeremoth, Beker's son, in 1 Chronicles 7:8. *See* Jeremoth #1.
3. Benjamite and one of the ambidextrous warriors who came to David's support at Ziklag (1 Chr 12:5).
4. Alternate spelling of Jeremoth, Mushi's son, in 1 Chronicles 23:23 and 24:30. *See* Jeremoth #3.
5. Alternate spelling of Jeremoth, Heman's son, in 1 Chronicles 25:4 and 25:22. *See* Jeremoth #4.
6. Alternate spelling of Jeremoth, Azriel's son, in 1 Chronicles 27:19. *See* Jeremoth #5.
7. David's son and Mahalath's father. Mahalath was married to King Rehoboam of Judah (2 Chr 11:18).
8. One of the Levites who assisted with the administration of the temple contributions during King Hezekiah's reign (2 Chr 31:13).

JERIOTH One of Caleb's wives, according to 1 Chronicles 2:18.

JEROBOAM Name of two kings who reigned in the northern kingdom of Israel: Jeroboam I (930–909 BC), the originator and first monarch of the 10 tribes of Israel, and Jeroboam II (793–753 BC), the 14th king of the northern kingdom.

1. Jeroboam I was the son of Nebat from Ephraim's tribe. He also served King Solomon (1 Kgs 11:26) and his efforts had been rewarded by his placement as the supervisor of an Ephraimite work force. Jeroboam, therefore, helped rebuild an important section of the defenses of Jerusalem (vv 27-28). This efficient and energetic young man did not remain in the employ of Solomon for long, however. Jeroboam's background, his tribe's pride, and the oppression of Solomon had produced a young rebel. Ahijah, the prophet of Shiloh, met Jeroboam outside Jerusalem one day and did a startling thing—he tore a new garment he was wearing into 12 pieces and gave 10 of them to Jeroboam (1 Kgs 11:29-30). Ahijah had symbolically shown Jeroboam that God would give him 10 tribes and would leave the Davidic line intact (vv 31-39). Solomon's idolatry had brought this judgment upon the Davidic line (v 33). Although precise details of a revolt are not given (v 7), Jeroboam fled to Egypt in order to save his life (v 40).

After Solomon's death, Jeroboam returned to Palestine and approached Rehoboam, Solomon's son, with a request that his program of oppression cease (1 Kgs 12:1-4). Rehoboam asked for three days to consult with his advisers before answering (vv 5-11). The counsel of the older advisers was toward clemency, but younger hotheads prevailed with their counsel of increased taxation and forced labor (vv 12-14).

The Israelites responded by rejecting Rehoboam. Jeroboam was quickly elected king of the northern tribes (1 Kgs 12:20), and an uneasy cease-fire temporarily stabilized relationships between the two kingdoms at their division (930 BC).

Being ambitious and skillful, Jeroboam built two capital cities, one at Shechem (cf. Gn 12:6-8; Jos 8:30-35), in the territory west of the Jordan, and one at Penuel (cf. Gn 32:30; Jgs 8:17), east of the Jordan (1 Kgs 12:25). He reinstituted the cult of the golden calves, substituting an ancient religion for the worship of Jehovah. He changed the centers of worship, the object of worship, the priesthood, and the time of worship. The new centers became Bethel and Dan (v 29); Bethel was a place of patriarchal worship

(Gn 28:10-22; 31:13; 35:1-7), and Dan was the site of a renegade Levitical worship established for the tribe of Dan in the days of the judges (Jgs 18).

The object of worship became the idol calf (1 Kgs 12:28). The worship was based upon Aaron's participation in the first instance of this idolatry in Israel. Aaron had presented the golden calf at Sinai as a visible representation of the invisible Yahweh who had brought Israel out of Egypt (Ex 32:4-5). This compromise religion would yet have an appeal to Yahweh worshipers. Aaron's prior establishment of this worship added to the appeal for those who were reluctant to separate from Levitical methodology. The Levites in Dan would also add to the authentication of the calf worship.

Doubtless, the Egyptian sojourn of Jeroboam contributed to this turn of events. The Egyptians' worship of Amon-Re, the sun god, included his representation as a bull. The bull in Egyptian worship was intended to visibly represent an invisible deity. This concept could have easily been transferred by the Israelites to their worship of the invisible Yahweh.

Jeroboam's idolatry would result in the ultimate destruction of his line (1 Kgs 13:33-34). An immediate result was the death of his son Abijah (14:1-18). Jeroboam's plan to deceive the prophet Ahijah failed and became the means of pronouncing judgment upon the house of Jeroboam and the northern kingdom (vv 7-16). One manifestation of the gradual decline of Israel was the defeat Jeroboam suffered at the hand of Abijah of Judah (2 Chr 13:1-20).

Jeroboam I died after reigning 22 years over Israel (1 Kgs 14:19-20). His remaining son, Nadab, ruled for only two years before he was assassinated by Baasha of the tribe of Issachar (1 Kgs 14:20; 15:25-31). The whole household of Jeroboam was then killed by Baasha, fulfilling the prophecy of Ahijah concerning the end of the dynasty of Jeroboam. Yet even Baasha walked in the footsteps of Jeroboam's apostasy (1 Kgs 15:34).

2. Jeroboam II, the son of Joash (or Jehoash, 798–782 BC), reigned over Israel longer than any other northern king even though he followed the evil example of his ancestral namesake, Jeroboam I (2 Kgs 14:23-24). His reign of 41 years included an 11-year co-regency with his father. Evidently, Joash had taken steps to ensure the stability of his kingdom before meeting Amaziah of Judah in battle (2 Kgs 14:8-14; 2 Chr 25:5-24).

Jeroboam II ruled in the city of Samaria (2 Kgs 14:23). The archaeological evidence at Samaria indicates a reconstruction program in the royal palace during the prosperous reigns of Joash and Jeroboam II. In 1910 excavators found over 60 inscribed potsherds that were invoices or labels for oil and wine sent to the royal stores for use in the king's service. The limited number of place-names (27) on the potsherds indicates that the shipments of these commodities were not a nationwide levy of taxes but were probably all from properties belonging to the royal house. These illustrate the extensive holdings and opulence of the royal house in Israel during the reign of Jeroboam II.

Large numbers of carved decorative plaques and panels of ivory were also found in the ruins of Samaria, a reminder of the wealth of the northern kingdom in its latter days. The influence of the pagan societies of Syria, Assyria, and Egypt can be seen by the various figures of deities on the ivories.

The prophet Jonah, son of Amittai, had prophesied the acquisition of power by Jeroboam II (2 Kgs 14:25). Although Jeroboam's reign was late in the history of the northern kingdom, God still desired to exhibit his long-suffering and faithful covenant-keeping love, offering Israel repentance (vv 26-28).

The northern kingdom reached its greatest extension since the time of Solomon as the result of God's care for Israel during Jeroboam's reign. The boundaries stretched from Hamath on the Orontes River in the north to the Gulf of Aqaba, with its cities of Elath and Ezion-geber, in the south. Prosperity did not suffice to deliver Israel from internal and external problems, however. The extensive corruption in government and the degenerate spiritual state of the people propelled Israel into the tumultuous days that would end in the utter destruction of the northern kingdom. Jeroboam's own life must have been in danger from conspirators. Amaziah, a priest at Bethel, even accused the prophet Amos of conspiring to assassinate Jeroboam (Am 7:8-17). Amos had actually prophesied the captivity of Israel and the fall of Jeroboam's dynasty. The word of God had become a threat to Jeroboam because of the hardness of the hearts of all in Israel, including the king.

Economic depression, moral deterioration, political weakness, and governmental corruption served to hasten the fall of Israel. The rich landowners, including Jeroboam II, had oppressed the less wealthy citizens and had forced small landowners to migrate from their farms to the cities.

Within six months of the death of Jeroboam II, the prophecy concerning the end of the dynasty of Jehu (Jeroboam was the fourth king of that line) was fulfilled (2 Kgs 14:29; 15:8-12; cf. 10:12-31). As the son of Jeroboam I, Nadab, was assassinated, so the son of Jeroboam II, Zechariah, was assassinated. Thirty-one years after the death of Jeroboam II, the prophecies concerning the captivity of Israel were fulfilled (722 BC; 2 Kgs 17:5-41).

See also Chronology of the Bible (Old Testament); Israel, History of.

JEROHAM

1. Levite of the family of Kohath, father of Elkanah and a forefather of the prophet Samuel and Heman the singer. Heman was a musician in the sanctuary during David's reign (1 Sm 1:1; 1 Chr 6:27, 34).
2. Benjamite whose sons lived in Jerusalem and were leaders among their people (1 Chr 8:27). He is perhaps identical with #3 below.
3. Benjamite and Ibneiah's father. Ibneiah, head of his family, returned to Jerusalem from exile in Babylon (1 Chr 9:8).
4. Descendant of Pashhur and the father of Adaiah the priest. Adaiah returned to Jerusalem after the exile (1 Chr 9:12; Neh 11:12).
5. Benjamite from Gedor whose two sons, Joelah and Zebadiah, came to David's support at Ziklag (1 Chr 12:7).
6. Father of Azarel, the chief official of the Danites during David's reign (1 Chr 27:22).
7. Father of Azariah, one of the commanders who was instrumental in removing Queen Athaliah from Judah's throne to make way for Joash (Jehoash), the rightful claimant (2 Chr 23:1).

JERUBBAAL Name given to Gideon after he destroyed an altar to Baal (Jgs 6:32). The name means "let Baal contend against him." *See* Gideon.

JERUBBESHETH* An alternate name for Gideon (2 Sm 11:21) *See* Gideon.

JERUEL Wilderness lying southeast of Tekoa near En-gedi, just above and west of the cliff of Ziz (2 Chr 20:16). Some identify it with el-Hasasah.

JERUSALEM Historic city sacred to Christians, Jews, and Muslims; the chief city of ancient Palestine and of the modern state of Israel.

PREVIEW
• Meaning of the Name
• Geographical Situation
• History

Meaning of the Name

Egyptian Meaning The earliest mention of the name occurs in the Egyptian Execration Texts of the 19th and 18th centuries BC in the form probably transliterated *Urusalimum.*

Semitic Meaning In the 14th century BC the name appears in the Abdi-Hepa correspondence from Tell el-Amarna, written *Urusalim.* Later it is found in the inscription of the Assyrian monarch Sennacherib, written *Ursalimmu.* The two transparently Semitic elements, *uru* (city) and *salim* (a divine name), have produced the hyphenated composite meaning "the city of [the god] Salim." Hyphenating geographic names to incorporate divine elements was a common practice in the ancient Near Eastern world, and the deity Salim, or Shalem (Akkadian, Shulmanu; cf. Solomon), was a member of the Amorite pantheon (cf. Ez 16:3). Since the oldest textual evidence—Egyptian, West Semitic, and Akkadian—supports only *urusalim,* and since the OT itself attests that Jerusalem was not originally a Hebrew city, it is probable that the Semitic etymological origin of this name produced the meaning "the city of [the god] Salim."

Hebrew/Aramaic Meaning In the Hebrew OT, Jerusalem is written *yerushalayim,* and in the Aramaic portions the name is rendered *yerushalem.* Containing the elements *yarah* ("to found," cf. Jb 38:6) and *shalem* (a divine name), it yields the meaning "the foundation of [the god] Shalem," the *sh* of the Hebrew/Aramaic to be taken as the phonemic equivalent of the Akkadian *s.*

Greek Meaning In the NT, Jerusalem translates the two Greek words *Ierousalem* and *Hierosoluma.* The former is simply the Greek transliteration of the OT Aramaic form; the latter reflects the word *hieros* (holy), representing a Hellenized paronomasia, corresponding neither with the Semitic root of the name nor with the city's historical reality.

Geographical Situation Jerusalem is situated 31° 46' 45" north latitude and 35° 13' 25" east longitude. The city rises to just over 2,500 feet (762 meters) above sea level and rests some 14 miles (22.5 kilometers) west of the northern end of the Dead Sea and approximately 33 miles (53 kilometers) east of the Mediterranean coast.

A Mediterranean climate pervades Jerusalem. From October to May, the city experiences its rainy season, with an annual accumulation of about 25 inches (63.5 centimeters). Throughout January and February the rains are often driven by winds, and the mercury drops to near freezing (cf. Ezr 10:9); the coldest weather coincides with the days of heaviest rainfall. Snow falls two years out of three. There is no rain between May and September, and a high percentage of solar radiation produces oppressive heat.

Like Rome, Jerusalem is a city set on hills. A cluster of five hills comprise the denuded quadrilateral landmass roughly one mile (1.6 kilometers) long and one-half mile (.8 kilometer) wide, bordered on all sides, except the north, by deep ravines. Stationed astride the crest of Palestine's central plateau and located at the crossroad of the watershed route connecting Hebron, Bethlehem, Shechem (Nablus), and points north with the longitudinal route from the Jordan Valley and the several arteries to the Mediterranean, Jerusalem is commercially central to the country. The lateral highway through the Judean mountains and eastward could not pass south of Jerusalem, being blocked by the Dead Sea and its sheer cliffs. Because it lacked significant water supply, the city's strategic commercial location was probably the deciding criterion for its original occupation.

Water, a lifeline of civilization, has always been in meager supply at Jerusalem. The only natural source of permanent water was the spring at Gihon, today sometimes called the Virgin's Fountain, located in the Kidron Valley immediately east of the ancient fortress conquered by David. Tunnels were burrowed to provide access to

Aerial View of Jerusalem

the Gihon when Jerusalem was besieged. Later, the Siloam Tunnel was cut through nearly 1,800 feet (548.6 meters) of limestone, allowing the waters of the Gihon to pass through the hill of Zion to the pool of Siloam.

Farther south, where the Kidron and Hinnom Valleys converge, there was another spring, called En-rogel in the Bible (modern Bir Eyyub). Owing to the lowering of the water table, this source of water ceased to percolate and was subsequently converted into a well.

These two sources were clearly insufficient to sustain a sizable population, and both were too deep in the Kidron to be employed for irrigation. Hence, a vast network of cisterns, reservoirs, and water conduits for supplemental supply has been devised since ancient times.

History

The Pre-Israelite Period Paleolithic and Mesolithic flint implements of an Acheulian type found in the plain of the Rephaim constitute the earliest evidence of the existence of human beings in the area of Jerusalem. Near the beginning of the fourth millennium BC, the southeastern hill was first occupied by a sedentary group, a fact evinced from the artifactual remains recovered from three graves and the pottery type discovered on bedrock. By 1800 BC, the crest of the southeastern hill was walled in rudimentary form.

From the Bible one learns that Abraham paid tithes to Melchizedek, king of Salem (Gn 14:17-20). Again (ch 22) the great patriarch visited an area later incorporated into Jerusalem, Mt Moriah, the site where Isaac was nearly sacrificed. Second Chronicles 3:1 identifies Mt Moriah as the temple hill. In the 15th century BC or thereabouts the Hurrians (possibly the biblical Horites) penetrated into Palestine. About the same time at Jerusalem, extensive building activities were initiated and improved fortification methods were introduced. Accordingly, most writers attribute these projects at Jerusalem to the Hurrian infiltration.

Conquest and Settlement Period Upon learning of Gibeon's placation of Joshua's army (Jos 9), Adoni-zedek, king of Jerusalem, formed a coalition with the kings of Hebron, Jarmuth, Lachish, and Eglon and attacked Gibeon. In response, Joshua marshaled his forces and defeated the coalition, killing all five monarchs at Makkedah (Jos 10:16-27). It appears that the tribe of Judah temporarily took control of Jerusalem and burned it in the wake of this victory (Jgs 1:8). However, the Jebusites reoccupied the site (Jos 15:63; 1 Chr 11:4-5). Apparently, the Jebusites more or less maintained control of Jerusalem until the time of David.

The city appears again as a boundary separating the tribal inheritances of Judah and Benjamin, becoming the southern border of the latter's domain. The identification of the "shoulder of the Jebusite" (RSV Jos 15:8; 18:16) with Jerusalem is usually explained as a reference to the southwestern hill, probably held also by the Jebusites at this time.

David's Jerusalem Following the Philistine victory atop Mt Gilboa, where Saul and Jonathan were killed in battle (1 Sm 31), David reigned over the tribe of Judah from Hebron, while a surviving son of Saul, Ishbosheth, ruled over the northern tribes from Mahanaim. During the two-year struggle that ensued, the house of David grew stronger while the forces of Ishbosheth shrunk considerably (2 Sm 3:1). This struggle culminated in the death and decapitation of Ishbosheth and the dispersion of his

forces. David became the undisputed monarch of all the tribes of Israel.

But the new monarch recognized that a consolidated

EXPLORATIONS AND EXCAVATIONS

Edward Robinson inaugurated the first important exploratory work. This American scholar made a series of topographical surveys of profound significance even today, and his activities mark the beginning of a flood of literature. Robinson's chief contribution lay in his method. He dared to challenge the axiom that ecclesiastical traditions provide the primary source for reconstructing a city's history. Instead, he sought to reconstruct Jerusalem's history on the basis of the "unsuspected evidence of the stones," thereby signaling for the holy city the advent of the archaeological method.

A second creative venture commenced in 1864 when, through the philanthropic contribution of Lady Burdett-Coutts of London, who wished to improve the sanitary conditions and water supply of the city, the Palestine Exploration Fund launched its first archaeological enterprise, under the direction of Charles Wilson. This nascent venture was enlarged between 1867 and 1870 as Charles Warren carried out extensive excavations around the temple area, on the southeastern hill, and in the Tyropean Valley, employing a system of underground shafts and tunnels. Of special interest is his unearthing of a section of the ancient city wall located near the southeastern sector of the temple. This find led him to postulate that the southeastern hill was the site of original occupation.

In the wake of the much-publicized discoveries of Wilson and Warren came the quests of Conder, Maudsley, and Clermont-Ganneau. In 1881 Guthe conducted additional excavations on the southeastern hill and at the pool of Siloam, while Schick reported the discovery of the now-famous Siloam Inscription. Schick also excavated a number of tombs just off the Nablus Road. At the same time Bliss and Dickie undertook elaborate excavations of the southern wall.

With the work of Raymond Weill, one enters a third creative period. While the territory on the southeastern hill actually excavated by Weill was proportionately small, it was he who first employed the stratigraphic excavation method at Jerusalem.

Following World War I, the southeastern hill was the object of a second campaign by Weill, of a team under the direction of Macalister and Duncan, and of an expedition led by Crowfoot and Fitzgerald. From 1925 to 1927, Sukenik, Mayer, and Fisher explored north of the city, discovering sections of the third (northern) wall (i.e., Herod Agrippa's wall).

An important new period in archaeological research began with the protracted expedition under the leadership of Kathleen Kenyon. From 1961 to 1967, the British School of Archaeology project explored several regions of Jerusalem.

Since 1968 the Hebrew University Museum, under the direction of Amiran and Eitan, has intermittently conducted archaeological research in and near the city. The Israel Department of Antiquities and Museums engaged in isolated excavations of what was known prior to the 1967 war as the Jewish Quarter.

national capital acceptable to both the north and the south would have to be created. Jerusalem had remained neutral in the conflict, being the site of a Jebusite enclave. It also represented a location that was militarily desirable, and by being commercially central to the fledgling nation, it was ideally suited.

In the course of David's 33-year reign at Jerusalem he made the city into the center of an empire that stretched from Egypt to the Euphrates River. He engaged in considerable building and expansion of the city. He fortified the Canaanite walls and prepared an extension of the city, possibly along the east slope of Zion.

David also constructed a royal residence, receiving the technology and many materials from Hiram, king of Tyre (2 Sm 5:11). Nehemiah 12:37 suggests that this palace also may have been near the east side of the southeastern hill. It was from a window of this house that Michal saw David dancing in an undignified manner—according to her perception (2 Sm 6:16-23). From the roof of this palace David gazed upon Bathsheba as she bathed (11:2-5), and from this residence he plotted the murder of her husband, Uriah (vv 14-25).

By bringing the ark of the covenant to Jerusalem (2 Sm 6:1-15)—implying that Yahweh would reside there—David displayed his most profound leadership. For in this perceptive act he merged for the first time in Israel's history its political and religious capitals. Jerusalem took on the unique character of a holy city *and* a royal city. As a result, the city would be known as the "city of David" (5:7) as well as the "city of God" (Ps 46:4). Adult male Jews would make their pilgrimages to Jerusalem to take part in the feasts and offerings. It only remained for David to make this arrangement permanent, to enshrine Yahweh at Jerusalem forever by building him a temple. David aspired to do so (2 Sm 7), but God responded that such an undertaking was to be reserved for a son of the king.

The First Temple Period A growing national realization of the extent and impact of the Davidic empire was employed by Solomon to full advantage. Himself an innovative and dynamic administrator, Solomon turned Jerusalem into a cosmopolitan center. The revenues of caravans from Egypt to Babylonia as well as the Phoenician trade with Elath, the Red Sea, and Ophir passed through his royal capital. Solomon's own naval fleet traveled as far as Tarshish, most likely located on an island along the western coast of Spain. These expeditions returned every three years with such exotic commodities as apes, peacocks, silver, iron, tin, ivory, and gold. The capital swelled with residents and visitors, and the monarch's fame became proverbial (1 Kgs 10).

Solomon was the great OT builder of Jerusalem. His most significant building enterprise was undoubtedly the first temple. Erected on the summit of the temple hill, this edifice required seven years to construct, from April/May 966 (1 Kgs 6:1) to October/November 959 (v 38). Hiram again provided both the technology and the cedar beams.

One may find in 1 Kings 10:27 a succinct encapsulation of the economic wealth lavished upon Jerusalem by Solomon: silver became as abundant as stone, and cedar was as common as sycamore. It is estimated that the annual revenues that coursed into Jerusalem were as high as $17 million. Ironically, it was the fiscal factor that became the burden of Solomon's monarchy. Overextending himself financially, his economic and political programs soon required the levying of heavy taxes (1 Kgs 4:7-19) and the drafting of Israelites into forced labor

(1 Kgs 5:13-18; cf. 9:20-23). These were the primary factors that prompted the schism in Israel's political structure after the death of Solomon and resulted in a divided monarchy by 930 BC.

When the Babylonian army laid final siege to Jerusalem (588 BC), capturing it after many months, the city was completely decimated. The temple and Solomon's palace were destroyed with fire; the city walls were demolished. The temple treasures were completely plundered, and the citizens were deported in large numbers.

The Second Temple Period Jerusalem's doom and 70-year captivity had been spelled out by Jeremiah (Jer 25:11; 29:10; cf. 2 Chr 36:21; Dn 9:2). In 538 BC, after the fall of Babylon, Cyrus, king of Persia, issued his famous proclamation (2 Chr 36:22-23; Ezr 1:1-4; cf. Is 44:28; 45:1). Thereupon, a humble group of Jews returned to Jerusalem with Sheshbazzar, a prince of Judah (Ezr 1:8-11) and Zerubbabel (2:2). In 515 BC, the doors of the second temple were opened officially, and the Passover feast was again observed from Jerusalem (6:15-18).

Ezra came to Jerusalem in the seventh year of Artaxerxes (Ezr 7:7). Assuming this is a reference to Artaxerxes I, the date of Ezra's return would have been 458 BC. Again, it was only a meager remnant who felt the compelling urge to make that difficult journey (cf. Josephus's *Antiquities* 11.1.3).

Moved by reports of troubled conditions (Neh 1:3-4), Nehemiah, in the 20th year of Artaxerxes (445 BC), was able to leave his post as cup-bearer to the king and to go to Jerusalem. If the concern of the earlier returnees focused upon the temple, Nehemiah's was upon the city walls. His is the most comprehensive description of Jerusalem's postexilic city walls and topography (Neh 2:11-16). Spurred on by his energetic enthusiasm, the people completed the task of rebuilding the walls in 52 days (6:15).

The Wailing Wall in Jerusalem

The Roman Period In 40 BC, with the aid of the Parthians, Antigonus attacked and seized Jerusalem, forcing Herod to escape by night. He journeyed to Rome, where the Senate appointed him as "king of the Jews" (cf. Mt 2:1). Armed with this new authority, Herod marshaled two Roman legions, and in 37 BC, he succeeded in forever expelling the Parthians. So began the long and infamous rule of Herod, who reigned at Jerusalem for 33 years (37–4 BC).

It cannot be denied that Jerusalem enjoyed prosperous and peaceful years during his reign. Herod transformed the external aspect of Jerusalem. He transferred the seat of government to the southwestern hill. Here he erected a lavish palace, an arena for athletic contests, a theater, and a vast aqueduct network.

Other building projects concerned the temple hill. Herod transformed the old Maccabean fortress into a much larger structure and named it Antonia, in honor of Mark Antony. In the temple area proper he enlarged the esplanade on both the north and south sides, giving it a rectangular shape. Herod's reconstruction of the temple was undertaken in 20 BC, and it was not completed until around AD 64, just six years prior to its destruction by Titus (cf. Jn 2:20).

See also Israel, History of; Jerusalem, New; Judaism; Zion; Zion, Daughter of.

JERUSALEM, New Phrase appearing only twice in the Bible, once near the beginning and once near the end of the book of Revelation (Rv 3:12; 21:2). In the first of the great visions of that book, the risen Christ speaks to his people in the midst of their conflict in this world. Among his promises to those who conquer is that they will one day be citizens of the new Jerusalem. The last of the book's visions shows the fulfillment of this promise. There we see not only the victorious people of God but also the city that is to be their home in a new world.

This does not, of course, answer the question "What is the new Jerusalem?" A description of what it is like would be relatively simple. An explanation of what it *is* would be more complicated.

Description of the City An angel takes John to a mountaintop to show him the new Jerusalem. In the account that follows (Rv 21:10–22:5), the first thing John notes is the light, like a great jewel-like lamp, that lights the city ("the glory of God," 21:11). Then he describes its walls and gates (21:12-14). The 12 gates bear the names of the tribes of Israel, and the wall between each gate and the next forms a single "foundation," or block, bearing the name of one of the 12 apostles of Christ. Next, the measurements of the city are given (vv 15-17). It is 1,400 miles (2,220 kilometers) each way—not only in breadth and in length but also in height—and its wall is 216 feet (65.8 meters) thick (or high?). By working out these equivalents in miles and feet, however, we miss what John would probably have thought much more important. According to the biblical units of measurement, the city is 12,000 stadia broad and its wall is 144 cubits thick. These numbers are symbolic; as multiples of 12, they signify perfection, as do other occurrences of 12 in Revelation (e.g., 7:4-8).

After this, John describes the materials of which the new Jerusalem is built (21:18-21). The wall is of jasper; its foundation layers are encrusted with other precious stones; its gates are pearls; and the streets and buildings within are made of "transparent gold." As for the city itself, John notes a series of things that it does *not* have (vv 22-27)—no temple, no sun or moon, no night, no closing of its gates, and no evil. Finally, there are the three wonderful things that it *does* have (22:1-5)—the river of the water of life, the tree of life, and the throne and presence of God himself.

Such is the new Jerusalem as John describes it. But he wants us not so much to picture what the city looks like as to understand what it means.

Background of the City OT history presents the city of David, old Jerusalem, as the place where God's rule over his people and his presence among them was centered. In that Jerusalem stood both the temple, where the priests served, and the throne of the kings who governed as God's deputies. It was the metropolis, or "mother city," of Israel, the people of God. But the whole Bible is about God's redeeming a people for himself, out of all nations, in all ages—a greater Israel of which OT Israel is only the vanguard. So it is natural that the last revelation the Bible gives should be a vision of that greater people—home at last in the true mother city, a new and greater Jerusalem.

The OT prophets witnessed the decline of old Jerusalem. They watched with grief and anger as it disappointed the hope that it would live up to its high destiny. As it became infected with sin and folly, and as its kings and priests increasingly betrayed their calling, two of these prophets in particular began to look forward to a Jerusalem that one day would be what it was meant to be. Ezekiel (chs 40–48) foresaw the city and its temple reconstructed in detail; Isaiah (chs 52, 60–66) described this latter-day Jerusalem in even more glowing terms. The vision of both prophets tie in closely with the vision John records in Revelation 21–22.

In the period between the OT and NT, Jewish writers became yet more disillusioned with the way things were going, and they encouraged their readers not so much with hopes of the renewal of the earthly Jerusalem as with imaginative descriptions of the heavenly one. This, they reckoned, existed already; at the end of the age it would come down from God out of heaven, the metropolis of his people, populous and beautiful, the place of his temple and throne. In fact, what was imagined by these apocalyptic writers is in many respects very like what would in due course actually be seen by John.

Jesus develops all these lines of thought in quite a remarkable way. It is not simply that he foretells the final destruction of Jerusalem and its temple (Mk 13; Lk 19:41-44). If that were all, it would leave a great question unanswered. For old Jerusalem existed for a purpose, as we have seen; and if it is to be destroyed, how can that purpose then be fulfilled? Where will God's people then find his throne and his temple?

Jesus' answer is that, since the Incarnation, God's rule and God's presence are to be found *in him* (Mt 28:18; Jn 14:9). He himself is the "new Jerusalem"—an entirely new kind of Jerusalem. This is borne out by the word for "new" that John uses in Revelation. There are two distinct Greek words translated in English Bibles as "new." Sometime after the destruction of Jerusalem in AD 70, the emperor Hadrian built a "new" Jerusalem; that was the kind of "new" that simply meant the latest in a series of cities on the same site. But John's vision is of a Jerusalem that is "new" in the sense of being fresh, clean, and different. The NT speaks in the same way of the new covenant and the new commandment (Jn 13:34; Heb 8:8), the new creation and the new man (2 Cor 5:17; Eph 2:15). John's vision brings out the same truth by telling of seven things that will exist "no more" in the new heaven and earth: no more sea, death, sorrow, crying, pain, curse, or night (Rv 21:1, 4; 22:3-5). In these respects all will be new and different.

There are five passages elsewhere in the NT that help to fill in the background to Revelation 21. In Galatians 4:26 Paul speaks of "Jerusalem above," the mother city of all who receive salvation by faith, as opposed to the old Jerusalem, where those belong who seek to please God by trying to obey the law (v 25). In Ephesians 5:25-32 he speaks of the bride of Christ, by which he means the church; in John's vision the "bride" is the "city" (Rv 21:9-10). In Philippians 3:20 we are told that the heavenly city is not simply the future home of believers but also the place of their present "citizenship."

Hebrews 12:22 makes the same point: those who believe have arrived already at the "heavenly Jerusalem." In other words, *this* Jerusalem is the home of all God's believing people, Jew and Gentile, from OT and NT times, and it seems not only to be future but also to exist already, in some sense, in the present. What, then, are we to make of John's vision?

Meaning of the City Some of those who expect a future Millennium (1,000-year earthly reign of Christ, between his second coming and final defeat of Satan) believe that the new Jerusalem belongs to the Millennium, because of certain indications that they think suit that period better than the eternal state that will follow it (Rv 21:24-26; 22:2). They visualize it as a literal, material city. It will presumably, then, be in the shape of a cube, or perhaps a pyramid, and some even picture it hovering like an immense spaceship above the surface of the earth.

Most millennarians, however, and also many who do not believe in a millennium in the sense just mentioned, think that John is describing the city as it will be in eternity. They, too, may take it literally, or they think that giving the literal details in these chapters—the city's measurements, materials, and so on—is the only way in which John could describe something that is in fact indescribable (though nonetheless real).

In line with the message of the entire book of Revelation, many take the new Jerusalem to be the ideal city of God, which belongs not only to the future but also to the present. It exists here and now because it is a spiritual truth, not a material one. It is always "coming down . . . out of heaven" precisely because it comes to men "from God" (21:2). The fact remains, of course, that everything John records in the last two chapters of Revelation belongs to a world that will only appear after the first heaven and the first earth have passed away—a world that is (to us, at any rate) still future.

Taking into account all these Scriptures, we may come closest to understanding the new Jerusalem if we see it as the community of Christ and his people, which will appear in its perfection only when this age has come to an end. Yet, in another sense, Christians belong to it already, and it gives them both an ideal to strive for in this world and a hope to anticipate in the next.

See also Bride of Christ; Church; Jerusalem.

JERUSALEM COUNCIL* Meeting described in Acts 15:6-29, held about AD 50. Acts records that the conference was held to deal with the question of the requirement for gentile salvation raised by Jews first in Antioch (14:26–15:1) and later in Jerusalem (15:3-5). The matter was subjected to lengthy consideration by the apostles and the elders (v 6), with Peter (vv 7-11), Paul and Barnabas (vv 12, 22-26), and James the brother of Jesus (vv 13-21), who seems to have been the moderator.

The major points agreed upon by the council were the following: (1) God makes no distinction between believers, Jewish or Gentile (15:9); (2) salvation is by grace through faith (vv 9-11); (3) God confirmed his acceptance of Gentiles through signs and wonders (vv 8, 12); (4) inclusion of the Gentiles among his people was part of the divine intention revealed in the OT (vv 15-18; quoting Am 9:11-12). The assembly also issued a list (sometimes called "the decree") instructing gentile Christians to abstain from (1) idolatry, (2) fornication, (3) eating animals that had been strangled, and (4) consuming blood. (The last two items pertained to dietary matters that greatly separated Jews from Gentiles.) The decision was circulated by letter to churches in Antioch, Syria, and Cilicia (Acts 15:23; cf. 16:4).

The account, when viewed within its place in the book of Acts as a whole, forms the culmination of the struggle by the early church to understand itself. The Judaism from which Christianity arose was a legalistic religion wherein people sought to earn God's favor by observing ceremonies and keeping laws. It also held to an exclusive nationalistic outlook that regarded Israel alone as "the people of God" and that required non-Jews desiring to be identified with God to submit to circumcision and the Mosaic law as well as offer prescribed sacrifices. The earliest Christians in Jerusalem seem to have held at least some of these views even after recognizing Jesus as the Messiah.

Acts portrays a series of events through which the fallacy of the Jewish legalistic and exclusivistic attitudes were exposed. Stephen questioned the narrow religious view that restricted God's presence, activity, and concern to Jerusalem (ch 7). Philip led Samaritans and an Ethiopian official, representatives of groups with only loose traditional connections to Judaism, to faith in Jesus (ch 8). At the direct command of God, Peter proclaimed Jesus as Messiah and Lord to Cornelius, a good God-fearing but uncircumcised Gentile (ch 10). Through this incident Peter came to recognize that God does not discriminate between peoples (10:34-35). The undeniable coming of the Holy Spirit upon Cornelius and his household (v 44) provided surprising proof of God's acceptance of the Gentiles, which could not be doubted even by members of the scrupulously Jewish, pro-circumcision group who witnessed the event (vv 45-48) or to whom it was later reported (11:1-18). The conversion of Cornelius became a precedent later cited by Peter at the council (15:7-11).

God's acceptance of Cornelius might have been regarded as an exceptional case by strict Jewish Christians. This was made impossible by the conversion of Greeks at Antioch (11:20, NLT mg), the establishment of a racially and culturally mixed church in that city (as implied by the diverse backgrounds of the leaders mentioned in Acts 13:1), and the large number of Gentiles converted during Paul's missionary journey into south-central Asia Minor (chs 13–14).

Acts records that at this juncture Jewish Christians from Jerusalem came to Antioch and precipitated the crisis that made necessary the convening of the council. Their insistence that gentile believers be circumcised and submit to the Mosaic law was tantamount to requiring them to become Jews nationally, socially, and religiously in order to become Christians. The early church was thus faced with the necessity of clarifying its relation to Judaism (was it a part of or separate from it?) and the nature of the salvation it proclaimed (nationalistic and legalistic or by grace through faith?).

The Jerusalem Council established the truth that salvation is a free gift to be received by faith; it rejected human effort as a means of or contributor to salvation. By implication it also dissociated Christianity from any attempt to restrict it to a particular racial, national, cultural, or social group. The council affirmed Christians to be free from the obligation to earn salvation through ceremonies or law-keeping. At the same time it recognized the practical necessity of responsible and appropriate conduct, which takes into account the moral nature of God and the sensitivities and concerns of other Christians.

See also Acts of the Apostles, Book of the; Galatians, Letter to the; Judaizers; Paul, The Apostle.

JERUSHA, JERUSHAH* Zadok's daughter, wife of King Uzziah of Judah and mother of King Jotham (2 Kgs 15:33; 2 Chr 27:1, alternately spelled "Jerushah").

JESHAIAH

1. Hananiah's son; the father of Rephaiah and a descendant of David through Zerubbabel's line, who lived in postexilic Palestine (1 Chr 3:21).
2. Jeduthun's son and the leader of the eighth of 24 divisions of musicians trained for service in the sanctuary during David's reign (1 Chr 25:3, 15).
3. Rehabiah's son and one of the Levites in charge of the temple treasury during David's reign (1 Chr 26:25).
4. Son of Athaliah from the house of Elam, who returned with Ezra to Judah following the Babylonian captivity (Ezr 8:7).
5. Levite of the family of Merari, who returned with Ezra to Jerusalem after the exile (Ezr 8:19).
6. Benjamite, Ithiel's father, and an ancestor of Sallu. Sallu resettled in Jerusalem during the postexilic era (Neh 11:7).

JESHANAH Border city in the hill country of Ephraim that King Abijah of Judah (913–910 BC) seized from King Jeroboam I (930–909 BC) and the northern kingdom during a civil war (2 Chr 13:19). The Greek and Syriac reading of "Jeshanah" as one of the towns between which Samuel erected the Ebenezer stone may be preferred to the Hebrew "Shen" in 1 Samuel 7:12. Its location is perhaps near Burj el-Isaneh, four miles (6.4 kilometers) north of Bethel.

JESHARELAH* A variant for Asharelah or Asarelah, the name of a Levite musician, in 1 Chronicles 25:14 (KJV; NIV "Jesarelah"). *See* Asharelah.

JESHEBEAB Levite family leader assigned to temple duty during David's reign (1 Chr 24:13).

JESHER Caleb's son from Judah's tribe (1 Chr 2:18).

JESHIMON

1. Desolate wilderness at the end of the Dead Sea, not far from Pisgah and Peor (Nm 21:20; 23:28). In both passages the NLT renders it "wasteland" in the text but has "Jeshimon" in the margin, allowing it to be translated as a specific area. The RSV uses "desert."
2. Wilderness to the north of the hill of Hakilah and of Maon (1 Sm 23:19, 24; 26:1-3); this location was probably just a few miles south of Hebron.

JESHISHAI Descendant of Gad in the days of Jotham, king of Judah (1 Chr 5:14).

JESHOHAIAH One of the 13 Simeonite princes in the days of Hezekiah who participated in the invasion of the valley of Gedor; they killed the inhabitants of the territory and took the land for the pasture of their sheep (1 Chr 4:36).

JESHUA (Person)

1. Levite and head of the ninth of 24 divisions of priests formed during David's reign (1 Chr 24:11). He was perhaps the forefather of 973 descendants who returned with Zerubbabel to Judah following the exile (Ezr 2:36; Neh 7:39).
2. One of the Levites assisting Kore in the distribution of the offerings among his fellow priests living in the priestly cities of Judah during the days of King Hezekiah (2 Chr 31:15).
3. Son of Jozadak (alternately "Jehozadak") the high priest. Jozadak was deported by Nebuchadnezzar to Babylon (1 Chr 6:14-15). Jeshua, Jozadak's successor as high priest, returned with Zerubbabel to Jerusalem after the exile (Ezr 2:2; Neh 7:7; 12:1). Upon arrival, he led his fellow priests in making the altar of God (Ezr 3:2; 5:2) and eventually headed up a construction program to rebuild the temple (3:8). Confirmed as God's leader by Haggai and Zechariah (Hg 1:1-14; 2:2, 4; Zec 3:1-9; 6:11), Jeshua (alternately "Joshua" in these passages) resolutely resisted attempts by adversaries to infiltrate his people and hinder the work on the temple (Ezr 4:3). Joiakim was Jeshua's son and successor as high priest, serving in the days of Nehemiah and Ezra (Neh 12:12, 26).
4. Descendant of Pahath-moab and the forefather of a family of Jews who returned with Zerubbabel to Judah following the Babylonian captivity (Ezr 2:6; Neh 7:11).
5. Father of a family of Levites who returned to Jerusalem with Zerubbabel (Ezr 2:40; Neh 7:43; 12:8). He and his sons were responsible for overseeing the workmen building the temple (Ezr 3:9; this Jeshua may be identical with #3 above).
6. Levite and Jozabad's father. Jozabad assisted Meremoth, Eleazar, and Noadiah with taking inventory of the temple's precious metals and vessels during the days of Ezra (Ezr 8:33).
7. Ezer's father. Ezer was ruler of Mizpah, who repaired a section of the Jerusalem wall during the days of Nehemiah (Neh 3:19).
8. Azaniah's son and a leader of the Levites in the days of Ezra and Nehemiah. Jeshua assisted Ezra with teaching the people the law (Neh 8:7) and later set his seal on Ezra's covenant (10:9).
9. Alternate spelling of Joshua, the son of Nun, in Nehemiah 8:17. *See* Joshua (Person) #1.

JESHUA (Place) Town in the Negev listed before Moladah among the towns where Judeans returned after exile (Neh 11:26; cf. v 20). It may be identical with the Shema mentioned next to Moladah in Joshua 15:26. The name is perhaps preserved in Tell es-Sa'weh, northeast of Beersheba.

JESHUAH* KJV spelling of Jeshua, a priest during David's time, in 1 Chronicles 24:11. *See* Jeshua (Person) #1.

JESHURUN* Poetic name for Israel, possibly derived from the Hebrew root meaning "upright," but according to many scholars a diminutive of Israel. The name Jeshurun is mentioned in Deuteronomy 32:15 and 33:5, 26 (see NLT mg). In the Septuagint, the word is not translated as a proper name but as an adjective, "beloved." In Isaiah 44:2 Jacob is described as "Israel, my chosen one" (with mg note saying "Jeshurun," see NLT), thus linking the name with the idea of election. In Deuteronomy 33:5 Israel is reminded that "the LORD became king in Jeshurun" (RSV), and in verse 26 it is told that there is none like God. If we follow the Septuagint, there is a link with the term "beloved" used of Christ (Mt 3:17; Mk 1:11; Eph 1:6) and of the church (Col 3:12; 1 Thes 1:4; 2 Thes 2:13; Jude 1:1).

JESIAH*

1. KJV rendering of Isshiah, one of David's ambidextrous archers, in 1 Chronicles 12:6. *See* Isshiah #2.
2. KJV rendering of Isshiah, Uzziel's son, in 1 Chronicles 23:20. *See* Isshiah #3.

JESIMIEL One of the 13 Simeonite princes who participated in the invasion of the valley of Gedor in King

Hezekiah's day, killing the inhabitants and taking the land for the pasture of their sheep (1 Chr 4:36).

JESSE (Person) Son of Obed and grandson of Ruth and Boaz (Ru 4:17, 22). Jesse was a shepherd from Bethlehem. He had eight sons, of whom David was the youngest. He had at least two daughters, Zeruiah and Abigail, who became mothers of famous warriors.

When Samuel went to Jesse's home to search for and anoint a king, Jesse did not at first feel it worthwhile to call David for examination (1 Sm 16:11). Later he sent David to play the lyre for Saul (vv 19-21). After David became a fugitive from Saul, Jesse and others of the family came to David in the cave of Adullam. David then brought his father and mother to Mizpah in Moab (22:3). Nothing further is heard of Jesse.

After Saul broke with David, he commonly spoke of David derisively as a "son of Jesse" to underscore his humble origins (1 Sm 20:31; 22:7). This same emphasis on Jesse's modest station in life is found in such messianic references as Isaiah 11:1 and 10, which speak of the "shoot from the stump of Jesse" and "the root of Jesse" (RSV).

See also David; Jesse, Root of.

JESSE*, Root of Figure of speech used by Isaiah (Is 11:10) to express the hope of a messianic king from the line of David. The "root" of a family is its progenitor. Jesse, David's father, is listed as an ancestor of the Messiah (Is 11:1, 10; Mt 1:5-6; Lk 3:32; Acts 13:22-23). Isaiah pictures God's judgment upon Assyria as the cutting down of a forest (Is 10:33-34); Judah likewise will be felled and the proud tree of David's sovereignty hewn down, but a remnant will remain, described by Isaiah as a shoot from a stump (6:13). The messianic shoot will come forth from the stump of Jesse as a branch from his roots. The Spirit of the Lord will rest upon this one who stands as an ensign to the people, so that the nations will seek him in the glory of his dwelling place (Is 11:1-10; see Is 53:2; Jer 23:5; 33:15; Ez 17:22-23; Zec 3:8; 6:12).

The apostle Paul, quoting Isaiah's prophecy, identified Jesus as "the root of Jesse" in whom the Gentiles hope (Rom 15:12). Christ is not only "a shoot from the stump of Jesse" (Is 11:1) but is himself the "root of Jesse" (Is 11:10; Rom 15:12; see Rv 5:5; 22:16, "root of David"). This means that Jesus not only came from Jesse's line but that Jesse (and David) came from Jesus. In other words, the image points to Jesus' divinity. While Jesus was the son of David, Jesus was also David's "Lord." This is the point Jesus made in his debate with the religious leaders of his day who recognized only that the Messiah was a human descendant of David. Matthew 22:42-45 reads: " 'What do you think about the Messiah? Whose son is he?' They replied, 'He is the son of David.' Jesus responded, 'Then why does David, speaking under the inspiration of the Holy Spirit, call him Lord? For David said, "The LORD said to my Lord, sit in honor at my right hand until I humble your enemies beneath your feet." Since David called him Lord, how can he be his son at the same time?' "

See also Christology; David; Genealogy of Jesus Christ; Jesse (Person); Jesus Christ, Teachings of.

JESUI*, JESUITE* KJV forms of Ishvi and Ishvite, one of Asher's descendants and his family, in Numbers 26:44. *See* Ishvi #1.

JESURUN* KJV spelling of Jeshurun, a poetical name for Israel, in Isaiah 44:2. *See* Jeshurun.

JESUS
1. Name meaning "savior" or "Jehovah [Yahweh] is salvation" given to the Messiah. *See* Jesus Christ.
2. KJV translation of Joshua, son of Nun, in Acts 7:45 and Hebrews 4:8. *See* Joshua (Person) #1.
3. Jewish Christian, surnamed Justus, who sent his greetings to the believers at Colosse in the salutation of Paul's Letter to the Colossians (Col 4:11).

JESUS CHRIST Messiah, Savior, and founder of the Christian church.

In providing a biography of Jesus Christ it must be borne in mind that each of the Gospels has its own distinctive purpose. Matthew, for instance, presents Jesus as the messianic King, whereas the emphasis in Mark is more on Jesus as the servant of all. Luke tends to present Jesus in a softer light, showing particularly his amazing compassion to the less fortunate, whereas John plunges the reader into a deeper and more spiritual understanding of Jesus. These different aims caused the four Evangelists to select and arrange the events of Jesus' life differently, resulting in a fourfold portrait of the same man. It was undoubtedly for this reason that the Christian church preserved four Gospels instead of only one.

The following sections present the main events in what may be regarded as the chief stages of the life of Jesus. These stages show a definite progression from Christ's incarnation to his cross. The amount of space devoted to each stage in each of the Gospels is dictated by theological rather than biographical interest. The whole presentation of Christ's life centers on the cross and the subsequent triumphant resurrection and is more an account of God's message to humanity than a plain historic account of the life of Jesus.

PREVIEW
• The Incarnation
• The Birth of Jesus
• Life in Nazareth
• Preparatory Events
• The Early Ministry of Jesus in Judea and Samaria
• The Period of the Galilean Ministry
• On the Way to Jerusalem
• The Final Days in Jerusalem
• The Betrayal and Arrest
• The Trial
• The Crucifixion
• The Burial, Resurrection, and Ascension

The Incarnation The major event of this initial stage was the Incarnation. Only Matthew and Luke give accounts of Jesus' birth. John goes back and reflects on what preceded the birth.

It may seem strange that John began his Gospel with a reference to the Word (Jn 1:1), but it is in this way that he delivers to the reader an exalted view of Jesus. John saw Jesus as existing even before the creation of the world (v 2). In fact, he saw him as having a part in the act of creation (v 3). Therefore, when Jesus was born, it was both an act of humiliation and an act of illumination. The light shone, but the world preferred to remain in darkness (vv 4-5, 10). Therefore, anyone coming to John's records of the life of Jesus would know at once, before even being introduced to the man named Jesus, that here was the record of no ordinary man. The account of his life and teachings that followed could not be properly understood except against this background of his preexistence.

The Birth of Jesus John simply wrote that the Word became flesh and dwelt among us. Matthew and Luke fill in some of the details of how this happened. There is little in common between the two accounts. Each approaches the subject from a different point of view, but the supernatural is evident in both. The coming of Jesus is announced beforehand, through dreams to Joseph in Matthew's account (Mt 1:20-21) and through an angel to Mary in Luke's account (Lk 1:26-33). Matthew leaves his readers in no doubt that the one to be born had a mission to accomplish—to save people from their sins (Mt 1:21). Luke sets his story of Jesus' coming in an atmosphere of great rejoicing. This is seen in the inclusion of some exquisite songs, which have formed part of the church's worship ever since (Lk 1:46-55, 68-79). The homage of the wise men in Matthew 2:1-12 is significant because it sets the scene for a universalistic emphasis that links the beginning of the Gospel to its ending (cf. Mt 28:19-20). A similar emphasis is introduced in the angel's announcement to the shepherds in Luke 2:14 and in Simeon's song (Lk 2:32), where he predicts that Jesus would be a light for Gentiles as well as a glory for Israel. The flight into Egypt for safety (Mt 2:13-15) shows the contribution of a gentile nation in providing protection for a Jewish child.

One feature of the birth stories in Matthew and Luke is that they are both linked to genealogies. It is difficult to harmonize these genealogies since they appear to be drawn from different sources, but the purpose in both cases is to show that Jesus was descended from Abraham and David. The latter fact gave rise to Jesus' title Son of David.

Luke was the only Gospel writer who attempted to link the coming of Jesus with events in secular history. Although problems arise over the dating of the census of Quirinius (Lk 2:1-2), the firm setting of the contemporary scene is highly significant because the Christian faith is a historic faith centered on a historic person.

Life in Nazareth The years of Jesus Christ's human development are given only a few lines in the Gospels. Details are given of only one incident belonging to the period of childhood, the discussion of the 12-year-old Jesus with the Jewish teachers in the temple (Lk 2:41-50). This event is a pointer to one of the most characteristic features of Jesus' later ministry: his display of irrefutable wisdom in dialogue with his Jewish contemporaries. It also reveals that at an early age Jesus was acutely aware of a divine mission. Nevertheless, Luke notes that in Jesus' formative years he was obedient to his parents (v 51). It is assumed that during 30 years at Nazareth Jesus learned the carpenter's trade from Joseph and became the village carpenter after Joseph's death. However, there is no account of this period in the Gospels. This has led to many fantastic imaginings about Jesus' childhood. Many of these fables are recorded in apocryphal gospels, but Luke's account is unembellished. Its remarkable reserve is a strong indication of its historical reliability.

Preparatory Events All four Gospels refer to a brief preparatory period that immediately preceded the commencement of Christ's public ministry. This period focused on three important events.

The Preaching of John the Baptist John the Baptist appeared in the wilderness and caused an immediate stir in Judea, particularly as a result of his call to repentance and to baptism (Mt 3:1-6). John was like one of the OT prophets, but he disclaimed any importance in his own office except as the herald of a greater person to come. His stern appearance and uncompromising moral challenge effectively prepared the way for the public appearance of Jesus (Lk 3:4-6). It is important to note that John the Baptist's announcement of the imminent coming of the kingdom (Mt 3:2) was the same theme with which Jesus began his own ministry (4:17). This shows that John the Baptist's work was an integral part of the preparation for the public ministry of Jesus. The same may be said of the rite of baptism, although John recognized that Jesus would add a new dimension in that he would baptize with the Holy Spirit and with fire (3:11). As the forerunner of Jesus Christ, John proclaimed that the one to follow would not only be greater than he but would also come with high standards of judgment (v 12). The stage was therefore set in stern terms for the initial public act of Jesus—his willingness to be baptized (Mt 3:13-15; Lk 3:21).

The Baptism of Jesus John's baptism was a baptism of repentance. Since Jesus submitted to this, are we to suppose that Jesus himself needed to repent? If this were the case, it would involve the assumption that Jesus had sinned. This is contrary to other evidence in the NT. But if Jesus did not need to repent, what was the point of his requesting baptism at the hands of John? Jesus had come on a mission to others, and it is possible that he deliberately submitted to John's baptism in order to show that he was prepared to take the place of others. This explanation is in line with Paul's later understanding of the work of Jesus Christ (2 Cor 5:21). Matthew is the one Evangelist who records John's hesitation to baptize Jesus (Mt 3:14-15).

The most important part of the baptism of Jesus was the heavenly voice, which declared pleasure in the beloved Son (Mt 3:17). This announcement by God was the real starting point of the public ministry of Jesus. It revealed that the ministry was no accident or sudden inspiration on the part of Jesus. He went into his work with the full approval of the Father. A further important feature is the part played by the Holy Spirit in this scene. The dovelike description is full of symbolic meaning (v 16). It was not just an inner experience that Jesus had. The activity of the Spirit in the ministry of Jesus, although not much emphasized in the Gospels, is nevertheless sufficiently evident to be indispensable to a true understanding of Jesus Christ.

The Temptation of Jesus Jesus' baptism showed the nature of his mission. The temptation showed the nature of the environment in which he was to minister (Mt 4:1; Lk 4:1-2). Confrontation with adverse spiritual forces characterized Jesus' whole ministry. Only Matthew and Luke record details of the temptations to which Jesus was subjected by the devil. All these temptations present shortcuts that, if pursued, would have deflected Jesus from his vocation. The record leaves us in no doubt that Jesus gained the victory. Both Gospels show that he accomplished this by appealing to Scripture. Jesus is also seen in this event as a genuine human who, like all other humans, was subject to temptation. The writer of the Letter to the Hebrews notes that this fact qualified Jesus to act as High Priest and to intercede on behalf of his people (Heb 2:18; 4:15).

The Early Ministry of Jesus in Judea and Samaria

Only John's Gospel tells of the work of Jesus in Judea following his baptism. It first describes his calling of two disciples, John and Andrew (Jn 1:35-39). This event is set against the background of John the Baptist's announcement of Jesus as the Lamb of God who was to take away the sin of the world (v 29). These first two disciples were soon joined by three others: Peter, Philip, and Nathanael (vv 41-51). These five formed part of the nucleus of

Jesus' followers who came to be known as the Twelve. One feature of John's account is the early recognition by the disciples of Jesus as Messiah (Jn 1:41) and Son of God (v 49).

Soon after Jesus began his ministry in Jerusalem, John relates an incident at Cana in Galilee in which water was turned into wine (Jn 2:1-10). This event is important in John's account because it is the first of the signs that he records (v 11). He saw Jesus' miracles as "signs" of the truth of the gospel rather than as mere wonders.

John sets two incidents at Jerusalem in this initial period. The first is the cleansing of the temple (Jn 2:13-16). Matthew, Mark, and Luke all place this event just before Jesus' trial, but John places it at this early stage. The moral intention of Jesus' work is seen in his driving out the money changers who were profiting from worshipers more than was appropriate. This was apparently acceptable to Judaism but was unacceptable to Jesus. The other Evangelists imply that this authoritative act was the event that sparked the final hostility of his opponents. John tells the story for a theological reason; to him, the cleansing of the temple was a parable telling of what Jesus had come to do.

The other incident in Jerusalem is the meeting between Jesus and Nicodemus (Jn 3). Nicodemus was closely associated with Judaism, yet he was also searching for truth. He was unable to understand, however, the spiritual truth about being born again through the Spirit.

John's story then moves from Judea to Samaria and the story of the Samaritan woman at the well (Jn 4:1-42). Jesus used her physical thirst to point to her deeper spiritual thirst. She realized that Jesus had something to offer her that she had not previously known. As a result of this woman's experience and testimony, many of the Samaritan people came to believe in Jesus as the Savior of the world (v 42). In this case John intends that his readers should appreciate the fuller significance of the words of Jesus by viewing them in the light of the resurrection.

The Period of the Galilean Ministry Almost all the information on this period is found in the synoptic

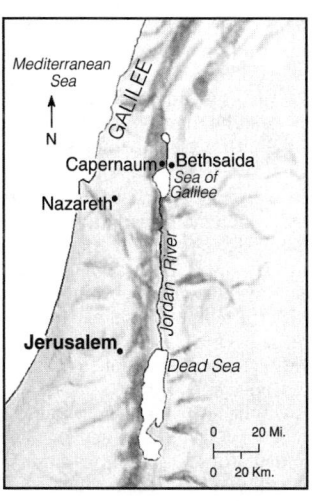

Mediterranean Sea

N

GALILEE

Capernaum • Bethsaida
    Sea of Galilee
Nazareth •

Jerusalem •

Jordan River

Dead Sea

0   20 Mi.

0   20 Km.

Important Places in Jesus' Ministry in Galilee After returning to his hometown, Nazareth, from Capernaum, Jesus preached in the villages of Galilee and sent his disciples out to preach as well. After meeting back in Capernaum, they left by boat to rest, only to be met by the crowds who followed the boat along the shore.

Gospels (Matthew, Mark, and Luke.) It may be conveniently divided into three sections. The first briefly outlines the events leading up to the choosing of the Twelve; the second deals with Jesus' withdrawal from northern Galilee; and the third deals with his departure for Jerusa-

lem. While the synoptic Gospels concentrate exclusively on the events in Galilee, John's account indicates that there were some visits by Jesus to Jerusalem during this period. Also, John records another incident at Cana, where the son of a Capernaum official was healed. This is noted as the second of Jesus' signs (Jn 4:54). It is chiefly important because of the extraordinary faith of the father, who was prepared to take Jesus at his word.

The Calling of the Disciples In the synoptic Gospels there is an account of the initial call to four of the disciples to leave their fishing boats and to become fishers of men (Mt 4:18-22; Mk 1:16-20; Lk 5:1-11). They had already met Jesus and must have had some idea what was involved in following him. Jesus did not at this time appoint them to be apostles, but this call was an indispensable step toward the establishment of the Twelve as a group. Setting apart a particular number of disciples formed an important part of the ministry of Jesus. The miraculous catch of fish, which preceded the call of the disciples in Luke's account, served to highlight the superiority of the spiritual task of catching people rather than fish.

Another significant call came to Levi, otherwise known as Matthew (Mt 9:9; Mk 2:13-14; Lk 5:27-28). As a tax collector, he was of a different type from most of the other disciples. He would certainly have been despised by his Jewish contemporaries because of his profession. But his inclusion in the special circle of Jesus' disciples shows the broad basis on which these men were chosen. One of the others, Simon the Zealot, may have belonged to a group of revolutionaries who were religious as well as political. Even a man like Judas Iscariot was numbered among the Twelve, and he would later betray Jesus to his enemies for a small sum of money. Jesus accepted them as they were and molded them into men who later came to learn how to be totally dependent on God and the power of his Spirit.

Sermon on the Mount The Gospel of Matthew presents a substantial sample of Jesus' teachings commonly called the Sermon on the Mount (Mt 5:1-7:29). Some of the same material occurs in Luke in a different context and different arrangement. It is possible that Jesus often repeated his teachings on different occasions and with different combinations. Matthew's record of the Sermon on the Mount presents an impressive body of teaching, mainly of an ethical character. In it Jesus upholds the Mosaic law and at the same time goes beyond it. The beginning of this sermon has been called the Beatitudes (5:3-12). It commends moral and spiritual values. The teachings recorded in this section were radical, but not in a political sense. The Sermon on the Mount may be taken as a fair sample of the kind of discourses that must have abounded in the ministry of Jesus.

Jesus as Healer Throughout the Gospels there are records of miracles involving Jesus healing people. There are more of these miracles than any other type. In a section in Matthew devoted to a sequence of healings (Mt 8:1-9:34), a leper, a centurion's servant, Peter's mother-in-law, a demoniac, a paralytic, a woman with a hemorrhage, blind men, and a man who was mute—all were healed. In addition, Jairus's daughter was raised from the dead. This concentration of healings focuses on Jesus as a miracle worker, but throughout the Gospels there is no suggestion that Jesus healed by magical means. In some cases an individual's faith was acknowledged (8:10; 9:22). In at least one incident, the healing was accompanied by an announcement of the forgiveness of the sins of the one healed (Mt 9:2; Mk 2:5). This shows that Jesus considered spiritual needs to be of greater consequence than the physical problems.

In view of the widespread belief in the powerful influence of evil spirits over human lives, it is of great significance that Jesus is seen exercising his power of exorcism over demons. Jesus' ministry was set in an atmosphere of spiritual conflict, so the confrontations between the forces of darkness and the Light of the World were to be expected. Those who explain away these cases of demon-possession in psychiatric terms miss this key feature of Jesus' ministry. Each time he exorcised a demon, he was demonstrating victory, which reached its most dramatic expression in his victory over death at his resurrection.

In addition to the healing miracles in this early section, one nature miracle is recorded, that of the stilling of the storm (Mt 8:23-27; Mk 4:35-41; Lk 8:22-25). This miracle focused both on the lack of faith in the disciples and the mysterious power of the presence of Jesus.

The Reaction to Jesus by His Contemporaries In the early stages of his ministry, Jesus was very popular with the ordinary people. There are several notices to this effect (Mt 4:23-25; Mk 3:7-8). This popularity showed no appreciation of the spiritual purpose of Jesus' mission (Lk 13:17). Nevertheless, it stands in stark contrast to the nit-picking opposition of the religious leaders, who even plotted to kill Jesus in the early period of his ministry (Mk 3:6).

Jesus and the religious leaders often clashed over the observance of the Sabbath (Mt 12:1-14; Lk 13:10-17; Jn 5:9-18). Jesus adopted a more liberal view than the rigid and often illogical interpretation of some of his religious contemporaries—as in the instances when he was criticized for healing on the Sabbath even though the Jewish law allowed the rescuing of trapped animals on the Sabbath (Mt 12:11; Lk 13:15). To the Pharisaic mind, Jesus was a lawbreaker. The Pharisees feared that it would undermine their authority if his teaching were permitted to permeate popular opinion.

Preparing the Twelve The synoptic Gospels supply lists of the names of the 12 apostles (Mt 10:2-4; Mk 3:16-19; Lk 6:14-16). Both Matthew and Mark name them in the context of their exercising authority over evil spirits, thereby showing that these men were being called to enter the same spiritual conflict as Jesus.

The synoptic Gospels also give details of the instructions Jesus gave to these disciples before sending them to minister in Israel (Mt 10:5-42; Mk 6:7-13; Lk 9:1-6). Matthew included material in his discourse that appears in a different context in Mark and Luke, but the discourse still shows the concern of Jesus to prepare his disciples for their future work. They were to proclaim the kingdom as he had done, but they were not to suppose that all would respond to it. They were warned about coming hostility and even persecution. It is important to note that Jesus warned his disciples against encumbering themselves with material possessions. Although the instructions given related immediately to a ministry tour, he was laying the foundation for the future work of the church.

The Relationship between Jesus and John the Baptist For a while there were parallel preaching and parallel baptisms by John the Baptist with his followers and Jesus with his disciples (Jn 4:1-2). After John the Baptist was imprisoned by Herod because of his uncompromising condemnation of Herod's marriage to Herodias, his brother's wife (Mt 14:3-4), John began to have doubts about Jesus (Mt 11:1-19; Lk 7:18-35). He may have been expecting Jesus, if he really was the Messiah, to

come to his rescue. When John sent his disciples to Jesus to express his doubts, Jesus took the opportunity to tell the crowds of the greatness of John the Baptist. He said there was none born of women who was greater than John.

Various Controversies Jesus did not hesitate to confront his contemporaries on issues that involved moral or religious questions. The controversy recorded in John's Gospel concerning the keeping of the Sabbath that arose when a lame man was healed on that day (Jn 5:1-18) shows once again that ritual observance of the Sabbath was regarded as of greater importance than a compassionate concern for the physical welfare of the lame man. This was typical of the Jewish approach and led at once to a persecuting attitude toward Jesus, particularly because he claimed to be doing the work of God.

A similar conflict arose after Jesus' disciples had plucked grain in the fields on the Sabbath day (Mt 12:1-8). The Pharisees assumed that this act constituted work and saw it as a sufficient reason to plot how to destroy Jesus. After this event, he healed a paralytic on the same Sabbath day (vv 9-14). The Jewish leaders clearly regarded him as a direct threat to their position among the people.

The rising opposition did not deter Jesus from further healings (Mt 12:15-32), which Matthew depicts as the fulfillment of Scripture. But when Jesus healed a blind and mute demoniac, the Pharisees charged him with casting out demons by Beelzebub, the prince of the demons. Jesus told them that to blaspheme the Holy Spirit was an unforgivable sin. This incident not only brings out the perversity of the religious leaders but also shows that the ministry of Jesus was under the direct control of the Spirit. Other notable miracles were the healing of the centurion's servant, as recorded by Luke (Lk 7:1-10), and the raising from the dead of the widow's son at Nain (vv 11-17). The former of these is notable because of the remarkable faith of a Gentile.

Another example of the Pharisees' criticism was when Jesus attended a meal in Simon the Pharisee's house (Lk 7:36-50). His host had not provided for the usual courtesies toward guests and yet was critical of Jesus for allowing an immoral woman to wash his feet with tears, dry them with her hair, and anoint them with ointment. There is no doubt that most of Simon's colleagues would have shared his reaction, but Jesus did not stop the woman because he knew that the motive impelling her to do it was love. He told Simon a parable to press home his point.

John records two visits by Jesus to Jerusalem. These are difficult to date, but they probably occurred during the early period of the ministry. He attended the Feast of Tabernacles (Jn 7:2) and the Feast of Dedication (10:22). At these times Jesus taught in the temple area and entered into dialogue with the religious leaders. The chief priests became alarmed at his presence and sent officers to arrest him (7:32). They were unable to do so; instead, they themselves were captivated by his teachings. More discussions with the Jewish leaders followed. They charged Jesus with being demon-possessed (8:48). Both in this case and in the event of the healing of the blind man (ch 9), the hostility of the Jewish leaders to Jesus surfaces. When Jesus spoke of himself as the Shepherd, his teaching again raised the anger of his Jewish hearers, who took up stones to kill him (10:31).

Teaching in Parables Matthew's Gospel gives a sample of a continuous discourse by Jesus (Mt 5:1–7:29), but Jesus more often spoke in parables. Matthew collected into a group some of the parables that concern the theme of the kingdom (ch 13). Luke tends to preserve parables of a different kind that are not specially linked to the kingdom. Mark has the least number of parables among the synoptic Gospels, but his writing shows little interest in Jesus as a teacher. John does not relate any parables, although he does preserve two allegories—the Sheepfold and the Vine—which could be regarded as extended parables. The parable was a form of teaching particularly characteristic of Jesus. In addition, Jesus interspersed even his discourses with metaphors akin to the parabolic form. The parable was valuable because it could stimulate thought and challenge the hearer. This is because the form of the parable is easy to retain in the mind. Jesus did not speak in parables in order to obscure his meaning. This would be contrary to all that he aimed to do through his work and teaching.

Significant Events in Galilee In Nazareth there was a striking instance of the unwillingness to respond to the ministry of Jesus. The people of his hometown proved so hostile that he could perform very few miracles there (Mt 13:53-58; Mk 6:1-6). This incident is important because it shows that faith was especially necessary for people to receive his healing miracles.

The one miracle performed by Jesus that all four Evangelists describe is the feeding of the 5,000 (Mt 14:13-21; Mk 6:30-44; Lk 9:10-17; Jn 6:1-15). This occasion shows the great popularity of Jesus at this stage of his ministry. It also reveals that he was not unmindful of the physical needs of people. After this miracle, some wanted to make Jesus king. This casts considerable light on their real motives. They were more concerned with material and political expediency than with spiritual truth. This is why Jesus immediately withdrew from them. When the people found him the next day, he proceeded to instruct them about the spiritual bread that comes from heaven (Jn 6:25-40).

At this point in John's Gospel, Jesus is often seen in dialogue with his opponents. This style of teaching is different from the synoptic parables but familiar in Jewish-style debate. Many of the people found the spiritual themes in the teaching of Jesus too difficult to accept and consequently ceased to be his disciples (Jn 6:51-52, 60, 66). This incident demonstrates the unique challenge presented by Jesus and his teaching. Another miracle closely linked with this is when Jesus walked on the water, demonstrating his power in the natural world. Many have sought to rationalize the event by supposing that Jesus was really walking on the shore, and that the disciples did not realize this in the haze. But this miracle is no more extraordinary than the massive multiplication of loaves and fishes, nor is it inconceivable if the miracle worker was all that he claimed to be.

Leaving Northern Galilee Jesus spent a brief time in the region of Tyre and Sidon, where he performed further healings and made it clear that his main mission was to the house of Israel (Mt 15:21-28). He then moved on to Caesarea Philippi; this was the turning point of his ministry (Mt 16:13-20; Mk 8:27-38; Lk 9:18-27). It was there that Jesus asked his disciples: "Who do people say the Son of Man is?" This caused Peter to confess: "You are the Christ, the Son of the living God." This impressive confession led Jesus to promise that he would build his church on "this rock." There has been much discussion about the meaning of this saying. It is open to some doubt whether Jesus intended to build his church on Peter, on his confession, or on Peter making the confession. Historically, Peter was the instrument God used for

the entrance into the church of both Jews and Gentiles (Acts 2, 10). There is no doubt about Jesus' intention to found a church, since the word occurs again in Matthew 18:17. Despite the glorious revelation of Jesus on this occasion, he took it as an opportunity to begin to inform his disciples of his death and resurrection (Mt 16:21-23).

This revelation of Jesus is considerably reinforced by the event known as the Transfiguration, when Jesus was transformed in the presence of three of his disciples (Mt 17:1-8). It was natural for them to want to keep this glorious vision of Jesus for themselves, but the vision vanished as rapidly as it came. Its purpose was evidently to show the three leading disciples something of the nature of Jesus, which was obscured by his normal human form. A further feature of the vision was the appearance with Jesus of Moses and Elijah, representatives of the Law and the Prophets.

After the Transfiguration, Jesus made two predictions concerning his approaching death. These announcements were a total perplexity to the disciples. In Matthew 16, when Jesus mentioned his death, Peter attempted to rebuke Jesus and was rebuked by Jesus in kind. When Jesus mentioned his death again in chapter 17, Matthew noted that the disciples were greatly distressed (Mt 17:23), while Mark and Luke mentioned the disciples' lack of understanding (Mk 9:32; Lk 9:45). Jesus was approaching the cross with no support from those closest to him. It is not surprising that when the hour arrived they all forsook him.

After the Transfiguration revealed that Jesus was greater than Moses and Elijah and in fact was the beloved Son of God, he was asked to pay the temple tax (Mt 17:24-27). This incident illustrates the attitude of Jesus toward the authorities and practical responsibilities. He paid the tax, although he did not acknowledge any obligation to do so. The method of payment was extraordinary, for it involved the miracle of the coin in the fish. But the greater importance of the incident is the light it throws on Jesus' independence from the Jewish law.

Luke devotes more than half his Gospel to the period that begins with Jesus leaving Galilee and ends with his death and resurrection in Jerusalem. In this section of his Gospel, Luke introduces a great deal of material that does not occur elsewhere. We can do no more than summarize some of the more striking items that throw light on the life of Jesus.

In addition to the mission of the Twelve, Luke records the mission of the Seventy (or Seventy-two—see Lk 10:17-20). Special parables are recorded by Luke in this section—the Good Samaritan (vv 29-37), the lost sheep (15:3-7), the lost coin (vv 8-10), and the prodigal son (vv 11-32). As Jesus moved toward Jerusalem, he was concerned with developing the spiritual life of his disciples. He was mindful of the fact that he would not be with them long and wished to prepare them for the future. He taught them about prayer (11:1-13), the Father's care for them (12:13-34), and preparation for the coming of the Son of Man (vv 35-56).

On the Way to Jerusalem On the approach to Jerusalem, Jesus visited both Jericho and Bethany. At Jericho he healed Bartimaeus (Lk 18:35-43) and had a fruitful encounter with Zacchaeus, who reformed his ways as a tax collector (19:1-10). Bethany was the home of Mary, Martha, and their brother, Lazarus, whom Jesus had raised from the dead (Jn 11). Jesus spent his remaining days in Jerusalem but returned each night to stay at Simon the Leper's house in Bethany in the presence of those who loved him (Mt 26:6). It was there that a woman anointed his body with costly ointment. This

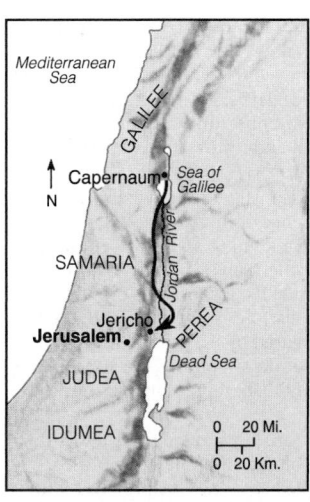

Mediterranean
Sea

GALILEE

Capernaum Sea of
Galilee

N

Jordan River

SAMARIA

Jericho
Jerusalem.

PEREA

Dead Sea

JUDEA

IDUMEA

0   20 Mi.

0   20 Km.

Jesus Travels toward Jerusalem Jesus left Galilee for the last time, heading toward Jerusalem and death. He again crossed the Jordan, spending some time in Perea before going on to Jericho.

was a controversial and prophetic act preparing Jesus for his burial and enhancing the gospel with loving consecration (vv 6-13).

The Final Days in Jerusalem All four Gospels relate the entry of Jesus into Jerusalem (Mt 21:1-11; Mk 11:1-10; Lk 19:29-38; Jn 12:12-15). At this time multitudes greeted Jesus with praises acclaiming him as their king. This welcome stands in stark contrast with the crowd's later cry for his crucifixion. In fact, it was the second crowd that was doing God's bidding, since Jesus had not come to Jerusalem to reign but to die.

The synoptic Gospels place the cleansing of the temple as the first main event following Jesus' entry into the city (Mt 21:12-13; Mk 11:15-17; Lk 19:45-46). The clouds of opposition had been thickening, but the audacity of Jesus in clearing out the money changers from the temple area was too much for the authorities (Mk 11:18; Lk 19:47). The die was cast and the Crucifixion loomed closer.

It was during this period that further controversies developed between Jesus and the Pharisees and Sadducees (Mt 21:23–22:45). In several cases trick questions were posed in order to trap Jesus, but with consummate skill he turned their questions against them. His opposers eventually reached the point where they dared not ask him any more questions (22:46).

Nearing his final hour, Jesus took the opportunity to instruct his disciples about future events, especially the end of the world. He reiterated the certainty of his return and mentioned various signs that would precede that coming (Mt 24–25; Mk 13; Lk 21). The purpose of this teaching was to provide a challenge to the disciples to be watchful (Mt 25:13) and diligent (vv 14-30). This section prepares the way for the events of the arrest, the trial, the scourging, and the cross carrying and crucifixion that followed soon after. But first we must note the importance of the Last Supper.

When Jesus sat at the table with his disciples on the night before he died, he wished to give them a simple means by which the significance of his death could be grasped (Mt 26:26-30; Mk 14:22-25; Lk 22:19-20; 1 Cor 11:23-26). The use of the bread and wine for this purpose was a happy choice because they were basic elements in everyday life. Through this symbolic significance Jesus gave an interpretation of his approaching death—his body broken and his blood poured out for others. It was necessary for Jesus to provide this reminder that his sacrificial death would seal a completely new covenant. It was to be an authentic memo-

rial to prevent the church from losing sight of the centrality of the cross.

John's Gospel does not relate the institution of the Last Supper. Nevertheless, it does record a significant act in which Jesus washed the feet of the disciples as an example of humility (Jn 13:1-20). He impressed on the disciples the principle of service to others. John follows this display of humility with a series of teachings Jesus gave on the eve of the Passion (chs 14–16). The most important feature of this teaching was the promise of the coming of the Holy Spirit to the disciples after Jesus had gone. Even with his mind occupied by thoughts of approaching death, Jesus showed himself more concerned about his disciples than about himself. This is evident in the prayer of Jesus in John 17. All the Evangelists refer in advance to the betrayal by Judas (Mt 26:21-25; Mk 14:18-21; Lk 22:21-23; Jn 13:21-30), which prepares readers for the final stages of the way of Jesus to the cross.

The Betrayal and Arrest There is a sense in which the whole gospel story has been working up to a climax of rejection. The various outbursts of popular support were soon over and the determined opposition emerged as seemingly in control. In John's Gospel the sense of approaching climax is expressed in terms of "his hour" (Jn 13:1). When this at length comes, the betrayal and arrest are seen as part of a larger plan. From the upper room where the Last Supper was eaten, Jesus went straight to the Garden of Gethsemane (Mt 26:36-46; Mk 14:32-42; Lk 22:40-46), where he prayed to his Father with deep intensity and agony. In this we see part of what it cost Jesus to identify himself with man's need. He prayed for the cup of suffering to pass from him but at the same time submitted to the Father's will. The three disciples he took with him all fell asleep, while one of his other disciples, having betrayed his master, appeared at the gates at the head of the group who had come to arrest him. At the moment of confrontation with Judas, Jesus exhibits an amazing dignity when he addressed the betrayer as his "friend" (Mt 26:50). He offered no resistance when he was arrested and chided the crowd of people for their swords and clubs (v 55).

The Trial Jesus was first taken to the house of Annas, one of the high priests, for a preliminary examination (Jn 18:13). During his trial, he was scorned by his enemies, and one of his disciples, Peter, denied him three times (Mt 26:69-75, Mk 14:66-72; Lk 22:54-62; Jn 18:15-27), as Jesus predicted he would (Mt 26:34; Mk 14:30; Jn 13:38). The official trial before the Sanhedrin was presided over by Caiaphas, who was nonplussed when Jesus at first refused to speak. At length Jesus predicted that the Son of Man would come on the clouds of heaven; this was enough to make the high priest charge him with blasphemy (Mk 14:62-64). Although he was spat upon and his face was struck, Jesus remained calm and dignified. He showed how much greater he was than those who were treating him with contempt.

The further examinations before Pilate (Mt 27:1-2; Mk 15:1; Lk 23:1; Jn 18:28) and Herod (Lk 23:7-12) were no better examples of impartial justice. Again Jesus did not answer when asked about the charges before either Pilate (Mt 27:14) or Herod (Lk 23:9). He remained majestically silent, except to make a comment to Pilate about the true nature of his kingship (Jn 18:33-38). The pathetic governor declared Jesus innocent, offered the crowds the release of either Jesus or Barabbas, and then publicly disclaimed responsibility by washing his hands. Pilate then cruelly scourged Jesus and handed him over to be crucified. This judge has ever since been judged by the prisoner.

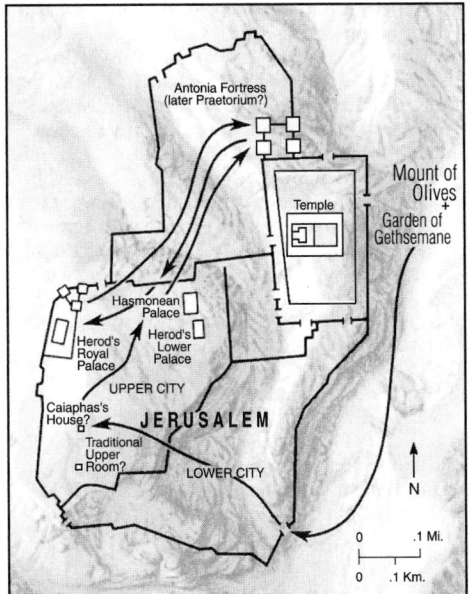

Antonia Fortress
(later Praetorium?)

Mount of
Olives
Temple
Garden of
Gethsemane

Hasmonean
Palace

Herod's
Royal
Palace

Herod's
Lower
Palace

UPPER CITY

Caiaphas's
House?   JERUSALEM

Traditional
Upper
Room?

LOWER CITY

N

0   .1 Mi.

0   .1 Km.

The Last Evening After Judas singled Jesus out for arrest, the mob took Jesus first to Annas and then to Caiaphas, the high priest. This trial, a mockery of justice, convened at daybreak and ended with their decision to kill him, but the Jews needed Rome's permission for the death sentence. Jesus was taken to Pilate (who was probably in the Praetorium), then to Herod (Lk 23:5-12), and back to Pilate, who sentenced him to die.

The Crucifixion The reader of this scene cannot help but see man's inhumanity to man—even the man of all men, Jesus Christ. The soldiers' ribald mockery of Jesus (Mt 27:27-30), mixing a royal robe with a hurtful crown of thorns (Mk 15:17), compelling a passerby to carry the cross (Lk 23:26), the cruel procedure of nailing Jesus to the cross, the callous casting of lots for his garment (Jn 19:23-24), and the scornful challenge to him to use his power to escape (Mt 27:40-44)—all expose the cruelty of Jesus opponents. But against this is Jesus' concern about the repentant criminal who was crucified with him (Lk 23:39-43), his concern for his mother (Jn 19:25-27), his prayer for forgiveness for those responsible for the Crucifixion (Lk 23:34), and his final triumphant cry (Mk 15:37)—all of which show a nobility of mind that contrasted strongly with the meanness of those about him. A few observers showed a better appreciation, like the centurion who was convinced of Jesus' innocence (Mk 15:39) and the women who followed him and stood at a distance (Mt 27:55-56). There was one dark moment, as far as Jesus was concerned— his forsaken cry, which quickly passed (Mk 15:34). There was an accompanying darkness and an earthquake, as if nature itself were acknowledging the significance of the event. Even the temple veil was torn in two, as if it had no longer any right to bar the way into the Holy of Holies (Mt 27:51).

The Burial, Resurrection, and Ascension Jesus' body was placed in a tomb that belonged to Joseph of Arimathea, who was assisted by Nicodemus in laying the body to rest (Mt 27:57-60; Jn 19:39). But the tomb played only an incidental part in the resurrection. The Evangelists concentrate on the appearances of Jesus not only on the day of resurrection but also subsequently. The disciples were convinced that Jesus was alive. Some, like Thomas, had doubts to overcome (Jn 20:24-29).

Others, like John, were more ready to believe when they saw the empty tomb (vv 2-10). It is not without significance that the first to see the risen Lord was a woman, Mary Magdalene (Mt 27:61; 28:1, 5-9), whose presence at the cross put to shame those disciples who had run away (Mt 26:56; Jn 19:25).

We may note that in his glorified, risen state Jesus was in a human form, although he was not at once recognized (Jn 20:15-16). There was a definite continuity with the Jesus the disciples had known. The appearances were occasions of both joy and instruction (cf. Lk 24:44 and Acts 1:3). The resurrection, in fact, had transformed the Crucifixion from a tragedy into a triumph. Forty days after his resurrection, Jesus ascended into heaven to join his Father in glory (Lk 24:51; Jn 20:17; Acts 1:9-11).

JESUS CHRIST, Teachings of Because of the wide variety of forms in which the teachings of Jesus have been preserved, it is difficult to bring out the essence of that teaching in a systematic way. Jesus did not present us with a theological system. His words were essentially practical in intent. Yet from all the variety of sayings it is possible to extract a clear idea of what Jesus thought about a number of important issues. What was his teaching about God? What did he think about himself? What did he mean when he spoke about the kingdom? What light does his teaching throw on the meaning of his death? What did he say about the Holy Spirit? How did he describe human beings and their needs? Did he anticipate the Christian church? Did he teach anything about the end of the world? What were the main features of his moral teaching? The following sections will seek to answer these important questions.

PREVIEW
• Teachings about God
• Teachings about Himself
• Teachings about the Kingdom of God
• Teachings about His Own Death
• Teachings about the Holy Spirit
• Teachings about Humanity
• Teachings about the Church
• Teachings about the Future
• Teachings about Moral Issues

Teachings about God Anyone who comes to the teachings of Jesus after reading the OT will at once recognize that much of his teaching about God is the same. Since Jesus, as all orthodox Jews of his day, accepted the testimony of the OT as inspired, it is not surprising that his approach to God was similar. This is especially true of his assumption that God was Creator. He taught a special providential care over the created order and affirmed that God watched over such small creatures as the sparrow (Mt 10:29). There is no support in the teachings of Jesus for the view that God is uninterested in the world he made.

One of the most characteristic titles Jesus used for God was Father. This was not new, for the idea occurs in the OT, where God is seen as Father of his people Israel. This kind of fatherhood was national rather than personal. In the intertestamental period the Jews came to regard God as so holy that he was removed from direct contact with human affairs. There had to be mediators between God and people. This exalted notion of God was not conducive to the idea of God as Father, and it is against this background that the uniqueness of the personal fatherhood of God in the teaching of Jesus must be seen. There is some evidence in Judaism that prayer to God as "Our Father" was known, but what distinguishes Jesus' teachings from that of his contemporaries is that the fatherhood of God was central to what he taught.

The father-son relationship is particularly vivid in John's Gospel, where Jesus as Son is seen to be in close communion with God as Father. This comes out strongly in Jesus' prayer in John 17 and in the frequent assertions that the Father had sent the Son and that the Son was doing the will of the Father. It is this strong relationship between God and Jesus in terms of fatherhood and sonship that led Jesus to teach men to approach God in the same way. The Lord's Prayer at once recognizes this in its opening words. It is particularly important to note that "Our Father" precedes "hallowed be thy name," for the more intimate idea prepares the way for the more remote. Jesus never taught men to approach God with terror.

Although there is a connection between the way in which Jesus addressed God as Father and the way in which he taught his disciples to approach God, there is also a distinction. Jesus spoke of "my Father and your Father" when he appeared to Mary Magdalene after his resurrection (Jn 20:17), but he did not say "our Father." His sonship was unique, for he claimed that he and the Father were one (Jn 10:30).

In the Sermon on the Mount, Jesus assured his followers that their heavenly Father knows about their needs (Mt 6:32; Lk 12:30), on the strength of which they are exhorted not to be anxious. This gives some insight into the way in which Jesus' teachings about God has a bearing on practical issues.

Teachings about Himself What Jesus said about himself is of great importance, for this undoubtedly formed the basis of what the early church came to teach about him.

Jesus used certain titles of himself or accepted them as descriptions of himself when they were used by others. The most widely used is Son of Man. This title was used by Jesus to refer to himself but was not used by anyone else. It was used, moreover, in several different kinds of sayings. Sometimes the sayings related directly to the public ministry of Jesus, like the saying that the Son of Man was Lord of the Sabbath (Mk 2:28), or that the Son of Man had authority to forgive sins (v 10). Sometimes the sayings had a direct bearing on the Passion, as when Jesus said that the Son of Man must suffer many things (Mk 8:31; note that Mt 16:21 has "he" instead of "Son of Man"). At other times the reference is to a future appearance, as when Jesus declared to the high priest that he would see the Son of Man sitting at the right hand of Power and coming on the clouds of heaven (Mk 14:62). What did Jesus mean by the title, and why did he use it?

The title "Son of Man" had been used before. The phrase occurs in Psalm 8:4, where it refers to man or humans. Again, the expression is used many times in Ezekiel as a mode of address to the prophet, but here also it means man. A rather different use occurs in Daniel 7:13, where one like a son of man comes with the clouds before the Ancient of Days. There is a strong similarity between this passage and the words of Jesus in Mark 14:62. But an important difference is that whereas Son of Man becomes a title in Mark, it is not so in Daniel. There is some evidence for the title in Jewish apocalyptic literature (e.g., in the Similitudes of Enoch), where it represents a preexistent being who will come to judge and overthrow the enemies of God. It seems evident from this that Jesus' use of Son of Man as a title is unique.

The Son of Man sayings are distributed throughout the four Gospels, and there are no appreciable differences in their uses. What is at first astonishing is that though the title is so widespread in the Gospels on the lips of Jesus, it never became a name by which Jesus was known by the early Christians. In fact, only in Acts 7:56 does the title appear, in this case used by Stephen. It is clear, therefore, that it had a special meaning for Jesus that it did not have for others. There is no doubt that he was referring to himself and not to someone else, as a careful study of all the Son of Man sayings shows. Those who think that Jesus was referring to someone else arrive at this conclusion only after first dispensing with some of the sayings. The most probable reason why he used the title Son of Man was because he wanted to avoid a term like Messiah, which carried with it too many political overtones. But what did Son of Man mean to Jesus? It is rich with the idea of humanness, possibly allusions to Daniel's "son of man," and perhaps a touch of the Suffering Servant idea from Isaiah 53. It is most likely that Jesus saw it in terms of his mission in a way that his hearers could not fully appreciate. It is also probable that the early church preferred Messiah because this title carried the meaning of a royal deliverer; also, after the death of Jesus, there would be no further fear of political misunderstanding.

The term Messiah, or Christ, does not belong strictly to the teachings of Jesus, since he himself never used it. The most striking instance where he accepted the ascription of Messiah was in Peter's confession at Caesarea Philippi. All the synoptic Gospels record the confession "You are the Christ," while Matthew adds the significant comment by Jesus that flesh and blood had not revealed it but "my Father who is in heaven" (Mt 16:17). He certainly accepted the confession and regarded it as revelation. One other case in the Synoptics where he does not specifically refute messiahship is his answer to the high priest's question "Are you the Messiah?" (Mk 14:61). In John's Gospel, Andrew tells Peter that he had found the Messiah (Jn 1:41); the woman at Samaria talks to Jesus, and he reveals that he is the Messiah (4:25-26). There was a widespread expectation among the Jews that a deliverer would come to overthrow their political enemies, the Romans. There were various ideas about his origin (a military leader or a heavenly warrior) and his methods (the Zealots believed that deliverance could come only through armed revolution). The reticence of Jesus concerning messiahship is therefore readily understandable.

Another title of utmost importance is Son of God, although it occurs mainly in John's Gospel. That both Mark and John regarded Jesus in this light is clear from explicit statements in their Gospels (cf. Mk 1:1; Jn 20:30-31). There are certainly passages where Messiah is linked with Son of God and where Jesus rejects neither title (cf. Mt 16:16). But in the teachings of Jesus one passage makes abundantly clear the special relationship that Jesus had with God as Son—namely, Matthew 11:27 (also Lk 10:22, a parallel passage), where Jesus implies that he is the Son of the Father.

Many similar passages in John's Gospel are, however, more explicit. The Son is unquestionably preexistent, because he knows he came from the Father and returns to the Father. It is not possible from the many references to sonship in John's Gospel to come to any other conclusion than that Jesus regarded himself as divine. It is particularly important to note that it is also in this Gospel that Jesus is portrayed most clearly in his human nature with its attendant weaknesses. Nowhere in the teachings of Jesus did he explain how God could become man, but he assumed this as a fact. He taught with the authority of God.

Teachings about the Kingdom of God No one can read the synoptic Gospels without being impressed with the frequency with which the expression "kingdom of God" (or of heaven) occurs. It was clearly an important theme in the whole teaching of Jesus. It is less evident in John's Gospel but is nevertheless still present. Many of the parables of Jesus are specifically called parables of the kingdom. Jesus' concept of the kingdom provided a foundational idea to the Christian gospel.

The main idea is the rule of God over people rather than a realm that belongs to God. In other words, the emphasis is on the active reigning of the King. This is important because it means that the kingdom is inextricably affected by relationships between the members and the King. It also means the kingdom will not be expressed in institutional terms.

There is one problem with the kingdom teachings that must be faced: its timing. Some sayings imply that it is already present, while others suggest that it will not come until the future. Some scholars disavow the idea that present and future can be held together; therefore, they reject one and concentrate on the other. Those who maintain a present understanding of the kingdom developed the idea of a social gospel, since Christianity was defined as the establishment of the kingdom of God on earth. According to this view, there is no place for a future arrival of the kingdom. On the other hand, some have denied altogether the present aspect and concentrate on the future. In this case, it is difficult to see in what sense the kingdom teachings are relevant.

Yet others have insisted that since both present and future aspects are found in the Gospel records, no explanation is satisfying that denies one at the expense of the other. One possible solution is to regard the present aspects as applying to this age but as not reaching their fulfillment until the future establishment of the kingdom. A similar solution, expressed differently, is to maintain that the reality is a future kingdom but that it has spilled over into the present. Jesus intentionally included both present and future aspects.

That the kingdom was a theme of common interest is clear from Luke 17:20-21, where the Pharisees asked Jesus when it was coming. His answer, that it was among them, shows unmistakably a present idea. This is equally true of the statement that in the exorcism of evil spirits the kingdom had arrived (Mt 12:28; Lk 11:20). Moreover, Jesus mentioned that the kingdom has been forcefully advancing (Mt 11:12), by which he did not mean by revolutionary methods, although he clearly implied that something dynamic was already happening. This idea of dynamic power is one of the most characteristic features of the kingdom. Jesus spoke of binding the strong, armed man (Lk 11:21-22), which shows that in his ministry he expected to give a powerful demonstration against the forces of darkness.

It is evident that the kingdom Jesus proclaimed was a kingdom in which God was supreme. It was inseparably linked with his redemptive mission, in which God was bringing spiritual deliverance to his people. Moreover, the kingdom teachings of Jesus cannot be regarded in isolation. It is part of the total message; no part of that message can be divorced from any other part without distorting the whole.

The clearest teachings on the future aspect of the kingdom are to be found in some of the parables (Mt 13) and in the discourse on the Mt of Olives (Mt 24–25; Mk 13; Lk 21). In the latter, Jesus spoke of the future using imagery drawn from Jewish literature, like the references to clouds, to glory, and to angels in relation to the coming of the Son of Man (Mk 13:26-27). In Matthew's account there is reference to a trumpet call, another familiar feature (Mt 24:31).

Various features from the kingdom parables give the clearest idea of the nature of the kingdom. Membership in the kingdom is not considered to be universal, for in the parable of the sower not all the soils are productive. The same separation is seen in the parable of the tares and the parable of the dragnet. The tares are destroyed and only the wheat is harvested, while the bad fish are discarded. The members of the kingdom are those who hear and understand the word of the kingdom (Mt 13:23). It is clear, therefore, that a response is necessary if the benefits of the kingdom are to be enjoyed.

There is an emphasis on growth in the parable of the mustard seed, where rapid development occurs from small beginnings. The parables of the treasure and the pearl are intended to underline the value of the kingdom. The universal character of the kingdom comes out sharply in the parable of the vineyard, where the kingdom is said to be taken away from the Jews and given to another "nation," presumably an allusion to the Gentiles (Mt 21:43). This is in line with the great commission Jesus gave to his disciples to preach to all nations (28:19). A universal kingdom would certainly be entirely different from the messianic kingdom idea of Judaism, in which Israel was to be the central unit. It is not easy to appreciate how revolutionary the idea was of a worldwide kingdom with Gentiles and Jews on the same footing.

Teachings about His Own Death The announcement of the kingdom must be linked with Jesus' approach to his own death. Did Jesus see his death as an integral part of his mission? Some have maintained that he ended his life in disillusionment, but a brief survey of his teaching about his own destiny is sufficient to dispel such a theory. To the further question, "What meaning did Jesus attach to his forthcoming death?" he gave a series of passing indications that, when taken together, supply us with a basis on which to reconstruct some idea of the place of his death within the entire range of his mission.

It is important to note that many times Jesus showed his awareness that details of his life were a fulfillment of Scripture (cf. Mt 26:24, 56; Mk 9:12; Lk 18:31; 24:25-27, 44-45). In all the instances cited, the suffering of Jesus is referred to as the subject of OT prophecy. This must mean that he had reflected on OT predictions and recognized that they could be fulfilled only through his own sufferings. In this case the Passion must be regarded as an indispensable part of Jesus' consciousness of his own mission.

This emphasis on fulfillment of Scripture is also seen in John's Gospel. His statement that the Son of Man must be lifted up even as Moses lifted up the serpent (Jn 3:14) illustrates this point. Most of the passages where fulfillment of Scripture is mentioned are the comments of the Evangelist, John. But there can be no doubt that the fulfillment motive played a vital part both in Jesus' own understanding of his mission and in the early Christians' understanding of his death. In this connection, some hold that John puts more stress on the Incarnation as a means of salvation in that he sees it as an illumination of the mind. But this is only part of the truth, for there is more on the meaning of the death of Jesus in John's Gospel than in the others.

The Gospels emphasize the divine necessity of the death of Jesus. In addition to the fulfillment motive, the idea of necessity is strong in the first prediction by Jesus of his approaching death. In John's Gospel Jesus speaks of his "hour" several times in the earlier stages of his ministry as "not yet," but in the later stages as having arrived. There is a sense of definite movement toward a climax, the hour undoubtedly being the hour of the

Passion (cf. Jn 17:1). There is not room for any disillusionment here. Jesus knew that only through the hour of death could the Father be glorified. The climax was according to an orderly plan.

Jesus evidently regarded his death as in some ways a sacrifice. The clearest indication of this is in the words of institution at the Last Supper. The cup is connected with the blood of the new covenant, which is said to be for the "remission of sins" (Mt 26:26-28). No explanation is given of the way in which the coming death, signified by the broken bread and poured-out wine, would bring about forgiveness of sins. But the immediate realization by the early church that Christ died for our sins (cf. 1 Cor 15:3) shows that the importance of what Jesus said had been clearly grasped. The new covenant idea is parallel to the old covenant, which according to Exodus 24 was sealed with sacrificial blood; there can be little doubt that Jesus had this in mind when he spoke the words about the new covenant. It was also akin to the ideas expressed in Jeremiah 31, referring to a covenant written on the heart rather than graven in stone.

Another aspect of the death of Christ seen especially in John's Gospel is the sense of completion that went with it. In Jesus' prayer in John 17, as he faces the cross, he declares that he has finished the work that the Father had given him to do (Jn 17:4). This is reinforced by the cry from the cross, "It is finished," which only John records (19:30). This sense of accomplishment gives an air of triumph to what might otherwise have been considered a disaster.

Teachings about the Holy Spirit At several of the major events in the life of Jesus, the Evangelists note the activity of the Spirit (e.g., the Virgin Birth, the Baptism, the Temptation). It is to be expected, therefore, that Jesus would have instructed his disciples about the Spirit. However, there is surprisingly little in the synoptic Gospels on this theme. Most of the teachings come from John's Gospel.

When Jesus began his preaching ministry in Nazareth, according to Luke, he read the statement in Isaiah 61:1-2 about the Spirit of God and applied it to himself. He saw his ministry as being inaugurated by the Spirit. This becomes clear in the way in which he responded to the charge that he cast out demons by means of Beelzebub, prince of the demons. He identified the reality of the coming of the kingdom by the fact that he was casting out evil spirits by the Spirit of God (Mt 12:28). He was, moreover, sensitive to the seriousness of blaspheming the Spirit, which he implies his accusers were in danger of doing. Whatever he did in his ministry he saw as an activity of the Spirit, and this was especially so in the contest with evil spirits.

While warning his disciples that they would meet with opposition, Jesus assured them of the Spirit's support when they were forced to appear before kings or governors (Mt 10:19-20; Mk 13:11). Indeed, he told them that the Spirit would speak through them, thus emphasizing that he expected a continuation of the Spirit's activity in the future. Luke records one instance in which Jesus comments on what fathers will do for their children and asks whether God will not give the Holy Spirit to those who ask (Lk 11:13). The assumption is that God regards the Holy Spirit as the best gift to give his children. On yet another occasion, Jesus recognized that David was inspired by the Holy Spirit when he wrote Psalm 110 (Mk 12:36), reflecting Jesus' belief in the Spirit's agency in the production of Scripture.

The Gospel of John provides a more detailed development of what Jesus taught about the Spirit. Teachings about the Spirit are usually linked to Jesus' teachings about giving eternal life to those who believe in him and receive him. At the same time he spoke of the new birth and eternal life to Nicodemus, Jesus also spoke of the Spirit (Jn 3:3-8, 15-16). When he spoke of water of life to the Samaritan woman, he also spoke of the Spirit (4:14, 23-24). The same holds true for the discourses on the bread of life (6:48-63) and river of life (7:37-39). Throughout the Gospel, Jesus declares to various people that he can give them eternal life if they would believe in him. He promises them the water of life, the bread of life, and the light of life, but no one could really partake of these until after the Lord was resurrected. As a foretaste, as a sample, they could receive a certain measure of life via the Lord's words, because his words were themselves spirit and life (6:63), but it was not until the Spirit would become available that the believers could actually become the recipients of the divine, eternal life.

After the Lord's discourse in John 6 (a discourse that was very troubling and offensive to most of his disciples), Jesus said, "It is the Spirit who gives eternal life" (6:63). When the Spirit became available, they could have life. Again, Jesus offered the water of life—even life flowing like rivers of living water—to the Jews assembled at the Feast of Tabernacles. He told them to come and drink of him. But no one could, then and there, come and drink of him. So John added a note: "This He spoke of the Spirit, . . . for the Spirit was not yet given, because Jesus was not yet glorified" (7:39, NASB). Once Jesus would be glorified through resurrection, the Spirit of the glorified Jesus would be available for men to drink. In John 6, Jesus offered himself as the bread of life to be eaten by men; and in John 7, he offered himself as the water of life to refresh men. But no one could eat of him or drink of him until the Spirit of the glorified Jesus was made available, as was intimated in John 6:63 and then stated plainly in John 7:39.

In John 14:16-18, Jesus went one step further in identifying himself with the Spirit. He told the disciples that he would give them another Comforter. Then he told them that they should know who this Comforter was because he was, then and there, abiding with them and would, in the near future, be in them. Who else but Jesus was abiding with them at that time? Then after telling the disciples that the Comforter would come to them, he said, "I am coming to you." First he said that the Comforter would come to them and abide in them, and then in the same breath he said that he would come to them and abide in them (see 14:20). In short, the coming of the Comforter to the disciples was one and the same as the coming of Jesus to the disciples. The Comforter who was dwelling with the disciples that night was the Spirit in Christ; the Comforter who would be in the disciples (after the resurrection) would be Christ in the Spirit.

On the evening of the resurrection, the Lord Jesus appeared to the disciples and then breathed into them the Holy Spirit. This inbreathing, reminiscent of God's breathing into Adam the breath of life (Gn 2:7), became the fulfillment of all that had been promised and anticipated earlier in John's Gospel. Through this impartation, the disciples were regenerated and indwelt by the Spirit of Jesus Christ. This historical event marked the genesis of the new creation. Jesus could now be realized as the bread of life, the water of life, and the light of life. The believers now possessed his divine, eternal, risen life. From that time forward, Christ as Spirit indwelt his believers. Thus, in his first epistle John could say, "We know he lives in us because the Holy Spirit lives in us" (1 Jn 3:24).

The indwelling Spirit helped the disciples remember

Jesus' words and actions (Jn 14:26) so that they could teach and write about them with acumen. This means that Jesus did not intend that the preservation of his teachings should be left to chance. All too often theories attempting to explain the way in which the traditions about Jesus and his teachings were transmitted in the period before there were any written Gospels are suggested without any reference to the Holy Spirit. It is not acceptable to concentrate on so-called laws of oral tradition and pay no attention to the unique factor in this case—the Holy Spirit. It is part of the Spirit's mission to preserve and transmit the teaching of Jesus. What Jesus says in this passage about the Spirit has far-reaching significance for the formation of the Gospels.

Another important function is the activity of the Spirit in the world. Jesus made it clear that the Spirit would convict of sin, of righteousness, and of judgment (Jn 16:8). Without the activity of the Spirit, there would be no possibility of the disciples making any impact on the world. Nevertheless, Jesus warned that the world could not receive the Spirit because it did not know him (14:17). The mystery of the Spirit is that he dwells in every believer. This indwelling aspect is of great importance and was particularly developed in the writings of Paul.

Teachings about Humanity Jesus taught about God's providential care over all human beings. A person's hairs are all numbered (Mt 10:30), which is a vivid way of saying that God is concerned about the details of human life. But God is far more concerned with the eternal soul. Jesus made it clear that it would be unprofitable for anyone to gain the world and to lose his or her soul (Mt 16:26; Mk 8:36; Lk 9:25). The focus falls on what a person is and not what he or she has. Jesus even said that a maimed body was preferable to a forfeited life (Mk 9:43-47). One's total fulfillment depends more on one's spiritual condition than on one's environment or physical well-being. He was not, of course, unconcerned about people's physical state, as his many healings show, but his major concern was with people's relationship with God.

Jesus never viewed humans as isolated individuals. Within God's community people were expected to have responsibility toward one another. The Sermon on the Mount illustrated this social emphasis in the teaching of Jesus. Those who are merciful to others will obtain mercy (Mt 5:7). There is special commendation for peacemakers (v 9). The disciples of Jesus are expected to bring light to others (v 16). They are expected to give more than expected (v 40). Jesus is clearly saying that people have responsibility beyond themselves.

The relation of people to God is one of dependence. Jesus taught men and women to pray to God for daily bread (Mt 6:11) as a reminder that they cannot be wholly self-sufficient. He allowed no place in his teaching for humans to boast in their own achievements.

Jesus had some specific things to say about home life. He accepted the sanctity of the marriage contract (Mt 5:31-32; cf. 19:3-9) and therefore showed a high regard for the honor and rights of the wife. It was more in his actions and attitudes rather than his specific teachings that Jesus showed his regard for the status of women. When he spoke of men, he often used the term in the sense of people, including both men and women. There is no suggestion that in matters of faith women were in the least inferior to men. Moreover, Luke points out how many women supported Jesus and his disciples in their travels.

Jesus had a high view of the human potential but also acknowledged their present condition. The stress on

repentance (Mt 4:17) shows a sinfulness of which people need to repent. This sense of need is implicit in the instances where Jesus pronounces forgiveness (e.g., to the paralytic, Mt 9:1-8; and to the woman who anointed him, Lk 7:47-48). In the Lord's Prayer, Jesus instructs his disciples to pray for forgiveness (Mt 6:12; Lk 11:4). He takes for granted that they need it and desire to obtain it.

Jesus gives no support to any self-righteousness in men or women. This is the burden of his criticism of the religious leaders in various sayings, but particularly in Matthew 23. He was critical of Jewish teachers because they placed so much importance on works of merit as contributing to salvation. His whole approach depended on humans casting themselves on the mercy of God. This is vividly illustrated in the parable about the Pharisee and the tax collector at prayer (Lk 18:10-14). It was the latter who threw himself on the mercy of God and who was commended by Jesus.

Undoubtedly, Jesus regarded sin as universal. He never suggested that there was anyone who was exempt from it. The major concept of sin in his teachings was alienation from God. This comes out clearly in John's Gospel, with its strong antithesis between light and darkness, life and death (cf. Jn 5:24). Indeed, the "world" in John's Gospel represents the system that takes no account of God. But sin is also seen as enslavement to Satan. The life and teachings of Jesus are seen against the background of spiritual conflict. Jesus can even say to his opponents, "You are of your father the devil" (Jn 8:44). He assumes throughout that there are hostile forces bringing man into subjection.

In the parable of the prodigal son, sin against God is linked with sin before the father. In other words, it is regarded in terms of rebellion and revolt (Lk 15:21). This is a different assessment of the son's offense than the one arrived at by the elder brother, who could see it only in terms of property. The view that humans are essentially in a state of rebellion against God is a basic tenet of Paul's theological position, and it is important to note that it finds its root in the teachings of Jesus.

There is no question that Jesus had much to say about condemnation. Those who did not believe and were therefore outside the provision of salvation that Jesus had made are declared to be already condemned (Jn 3:18). At various times Jesus mentioned judgment to come, which shows that a person's destiny is related to his or her present spiritual condition. Against this background of humanity's spiritual need, the whole mission of Jesus must be seen. A person, if left to himself or herself, would be totally unable to achieve salvation, but Jesus came to offer eternal life to those who believe in him (Jn 3:16).

Teachings about the Church Some have supposed that Jesus did not predict that there would be a church. But on two occasions he used the word "church," which means a people called out by God. On one of the occasions—at Caesarea Philippi—Jesus told Peter that he would build his church upon the rock (Mt 16:16-19). It seems most probable that "rock" was intended to link the foundation of the church to Peter's particular confession about Jesus. It is certain that the later church was a community that affirmed that Jesus was the Christ, the Son of the living God. It is important to note that it is Christ himself who is the builder of the church. He assured his disciples that it would be impregnable (the gates of hades would not overcome it). Moreover, one of the functions of the church was to proclaim forgiveness of sins, and this is implied in what Jesus said to Peter. That the words were not intended to refer exclusively to him is clear from Matthew 18:18, where similar words were addressed to all the disciples. The church, according to Matthew 18:17, was to be a community that could settle disputes between believers.

In addition to these specific references to the church, Jesus assumed that his followers would meet together in his name (Mt 18:19-20). In his final words in Matthew's account, he commissioned them to teach what he had taught them and to baptize new disciples (Mt 28:19-20). He promised his presence would be with them. The command to baptize was reinforced by Jesus' own example in submitting to John's baptism. One other special rite that Jesus expected his disciples to observe was the Lord's Supper. His instructions about this presuppose a later community that could observe it. Since the form of words used in the institution point to the meaning of the death of Christ, it is clear that Jesus intended the future community to be frequently reminded of the center of the faith. The Christian church was to be a group of people who knew that through Christ they had entered into a new relationship with God.

Although there are no references to the church in John's Gospel, there are certainly hints that support the community idea. Jesus introduced himself as the Shepherd and spoke of his followers as forming a flock (Jn 10:16). The sheep imagery occurs again in this Gospel when Peter is instructed three times by the risen Lord to feed the sheep (Jn 21:15-17). Another figure of speech that Jesus used to bring out the group idea is that of the many branches that draw their life from the vine, and therefore belong to each other because of their common life in the vine.

Jesus recognized that the future community would need the aid of the Spirit. His teachings on this subject laid the foundation for the evident dependence of the early church on the Spirit, as seen in the book of Acts. Finally, it should be noted that there is a close connection between the church and the kingdom, although they are not identical. The kingdom is more comprehensive than the church, which is included within it.

Teachings about the Future Jesus thought of the kingdom in terms of both present realization and future hope. The future aspect is related to the end of the age. Although he did not spell it out in specific terms, Jesus did not leave his disciples without any knowledge of how the present age would end. He gave firm assurance that he would return at some time in the future.

He told the disciples that the Son of Man would come with his angels in his Father's glory (Mt 16:27). In the discourse in which he answers the disciples' question about the end of the world, he speaks again of the Son of Man coming in clouds with power and glory (Mk 13:26), probably drawn from the familiar language of Daniel 7. Jesus described various signs that would precede his own coming. He spoke of wars, conflicts, earthquakes, famines, and disturbances in the heavens. The gospel was to be preached to all nations. At the same time many false Christs would arise.

Jesus gave such details about his return to encourage his disciples in the face of persecution. The future hope had a definitely practical purpose. The disciples were urged to watch. The coming would happen as unexpectedly as a thief in the night. Jesus said that even he himself did not know when the coming would take place (Mk 13:32).

Another important theme affecting the future is emphasized in Jesus' teachings about resurrection. The Sadducees did not believe in the resurrection of the body. They attempted to trap Jesus with a question about a woman who had been married seven times. They wanted to know whose husband she would be at the resurrection (Mk 12:18-27). Jesus pointed out that there would be no marriage when the dead rise. The Sadducees' idea about resurrection was clearly wrong. Jesus' teaching was that the resurrected would be like the angels. There is no doubt about the resurrection of the dead, although no information is given about the resurrection body. Jesus told a story about a rich man and a poor man who both died (Lk 16:19-31). In the afterlife the rich man cries out in torment, while the poor man enjoys a state of blessedness. What is most clear from this is the certainty of the afterlife and the fact of a distinction between the two men, although we are not told on what grounds the distinction is made. Elsewhere in his teachings, Jesus suggested that the most vital requirement is faith in himself. The conversation between Jesus and the dying thief on the cross suggests that paradise for the latter consisted in an awareness of the presence of Jesus (Lk 23:42-43).

The theme of rewards and punishment occurs in many passages. In Matthew 16:27 Jesus says that the Son of Man will reward everyone according to what he or she has done. Those who are worthless are promised punishment in darkness (Mt 25:30). Moreover, Jesus spoke of a day of judgment on which men and women must give an account, even of all their careless words (12:36-37). In the parable of the sheep and the goats, he spoke of a separation that the Son of Man will make when he comes. Those commended are those who have shown concern for the believers (25:31-46).

Among Jesus' most solemn statements are those that speak of hell. There is no way of getting around his teachings about eternal punishment for the unrighteous (as in Mt 25:41, 46), which is opposite to the eternal life promised to the righteous. He taught that his disciples would have a place prepared for them in heaven (Jn 14:2), and spoke of a Book of Life in which the names of his disciples were written (Lk 10:20).

Teachings about Moral Issues Much of the teaching of Jesus is concerned with moral issues—so much so that some scholars have concluded that this was the main burden of his teaching. But the moral teachings cannot be considered apart from the many facets of his teachings outlined above. It has been said that there are close parallels between the teachings of Jesus and the moral teachings of Judaism. What is distinctive about Jesus' teachings about morality is that the motive and power behind moral conduct is not conceived in terms of laws that must be obeyed. Right conduct is seen to be the result of a right relationship with God.

Jesus was himself the pattern for moral behavior. He made clear that his aim was to fulfill the will of God. There is no sense of legalism in his approach to ethical decisions. When—in the Sermon on the Mount—he compared his own teaching with that of Moses, he showed the importance of penetrating to the inner meaning (cf. Mt 5:21-22, 27-28, 31-32). On the face of it, Jesus made more rigorous demands than the Mosaic law, because he was concerned with probing the motives as well as the actions. Many have dismissed the teaching of the Sermon on the Mount as entirely impractical, but Jesus never intended that his teaching would be easy; he set as a target nothing less than the perfection of God himself (Mt 5:48). Nevertheless, he called his yoke easy and his burden light (11:29-30), which suggests that he was not setting out an impossible ethical pattern. It must be remembered that he was not producing a manifesto for society. His concern was that each individual should have powerful motives for right decisions on matters of conduct. His reaction against a rigid application of Sabbath observance at the expense of the welfare of a needy person illustrates this point. Concern for others was rated higher than ritual correctness.

Conclusion No account of the life and teachings of Jesus would be complete without some indication of the place that Jesus Christ gained in the developing church. Such a quest naturally takes us outside the scope of the Gospels into the testimony of the book of Acts and Paul's letters. There we can see whether the predictions of Jesus were fulfilled and whether in fact the early Christians took his teaching seriously. Although there can be no question that Jesus Christ became central to the faith of the early Christians, he was regarded from many points of view. He was seen as Messiah in the sense of a spiritual deliverer, as Lord in the sense of being sovereign over his people, as Servant in the sense of his obedience to suffering, as Son in his relation to his Father. In many ways the full understanding of what and who he was could not have occurred until after the resurrection. Therefore, we find that many facets of his teachings about himself were more fully developed in the reflections of his people. This is true in a special sense of the writings of the apostle Paul.

Many have found a problem in linking the Gospels with their detailed presentation of the acts and teachings of Jesus with the Christ who is so central in Paul's beliefs. The problem arises because the apostle does not refer to any specific incident in the life of Jesus and does not reflect in his epistles any acquaintance with the large amount of teaching material in the Gospels. Does this suggest that Paul had no interest in the historical Jesus? Or could it be maintained that he knew nothing about him? Those who have driven a wedge between Paul and Jesus have not given sufficient weight to those incidental indications that Paul knew a great deal more about the historical Jesus than he states in his letters. He writes, for instance, about the meekness and gentleness of Christ (2 Cor 10:1), suggesting that he knew that Jesus had said of himself that he was meek and lowly of heart (Mt 11:29). Moreover, Paul speaks of the poverty of Christ (2 Cor 8:9) and must have known that the Son of Man had nowhere to lay his head. He certainly knows the details of how Jesus instituted the Lord's Supper (1 Cor 11:23-26), and he knows of his death by crucifixion. It seems reasonable to conclude that Paul assumes that his readers will be acquainted with the Gospel material.

It is perhaps useful in this connection to inquire whether the life and teachings of Jesus played a significant part in the early Christian proclamation. One passage that is valuable in this respect is Acts 10:36-38. In Peter's address to Cornelius, he spoke of God's having anointed Jesus of Nazareth, and of Jesus' having gone about doing good and healing all who were under the power of the devil. It is clear that some account of the acts of Jesus was included in the early preaching, and there is no reason to suppose that this was not a regular procedure.

There is no doubt that the example of Jesus was a powerful motive for promoting right behavior. Peter appeals to it in encouraging Christians who were suffering for their faith (1 Pt 2:21). Paul also knows the value of imitation (1 Cor 11:1; 1 Thes 1:6). Since Jesus was recognized as being a man who did not sin (cf. 2 Cor 5:21), his behavior patterns would have proved invaluable for those who needed a new standard for moral action. While this idea of example is unquestionably present in the Epistles, it would be quite wrong to suppose that it formed a major part of Christian doctrine.

There are a few references to the teachings of Jesus in the non-Gospel portion of the NT. In the Letter of James, which is almost wholly practical, there are more allusions to the teachings of Jesus than anywhere else in the NT. This is especially true in echoes of the Sermon on the Mount, and it shows the strong contribution that the moral teaching of Jesus had on the ethical values of the early Christians. Most of the expositions of doctrine in the Epistles find their basis in some aspect of the teachings of Jesus. These teachings have an ongoing significance for the development of the church.

To what extent is knowledge of the life and teachings of Jesus relevant to the 21st century? Existential theologians have driven such a wedge between the Christ of faith and the Jesus of history that the latter has ceased to have any importance for them. Christians today, no less than their first-century predecessors, need to know that the object of their faith is the same one who lived and taught in Galilee and Judea.

See also Ascension of Christ; Christ; Christology; Genealogy of Jesus Christ; Incarnation; Jesus Christ; Kingdom of God, Kingdom of Heaven; Messiah; Parable; Savior; Son of God; Son of Man; Virgin Birth of Jesus.

JESUS JUSTUS Jewish Christian. *See* Jesus #3.

JETHER
1. Firstborn son of Gideon who, because of his youth, was afraid to execute the Midianite kings Zebah and Zalmunna at his father's request (Jgs 8:20).
2. Ishmaelite and the father of Amasa (1 Kgs 2:5, 32; 1 Chr 2:17). He is alternately called Ithra in 2 Samuel 17:25. *See* Ithra.
3. Firstborn son of Jada, the brother of Jonathan, and a descendant of Judah through Hezron's line. He fathered no children (1 Chr 2:32).
4. Judahite and the firstborn of Ezrah's four sons (1 Chr 4:17).
5. Asherite, the father of three sons (1 Chr 7:38) and probably identical with Ithran, Zophah's son, in 1 Chronicles 7:37.

JETHETH Chief of Edom (Gn 36:40; 1 Chr 1:51).

JETHLAH* KJV form of the Danite city Ithlah in Joshua 19:42. *See* Ithlah.

JETHRO Father-in-law of Moses. Zipporah, Jethro's daughter, became Moses' wife while he was a fugitive in the wilderness (Ex 2:21). When Moses departed for Egypt, he took Zipporah and his sons with him (4:20), but he must have sent them back. Jethro brought them to Moses after the Israelites arrived in Sinai (18:1-7). Through this familial relationship with Moses, Jethro became involved with Israel.

Jethro's relationship with Israel has been variously interpreted. Jethro was a priest of Midian (Ex 2:16; 3:1). It is not definitely known what the religion of the Midianites was, but some scholars have suggested that the Kenites, who were a tribe included in the nation of Midianites (Jgs 1:16), had a tribal god named Yahweh whom Jethro served as priest. Scholars who have suggested that Jethro's tribal god, Yahweh, was introduced to Israel by Moses have not been able to establish their case. Biblical evidence does not support this interpretation. That Jethro was a god-fearing and god-serving man is quite clear. The biblical record could be understood to teach that Jethro knew of Israel's God because he was a descendant of Abraham (Gn 25:2). Having heard of Yahweh's deliverance of his people from Egypt, Jethro acknowledged him as God, greatest of all gods. He also brought a burnt offering and sacrifices, thereby worshiping Yahweh and identifying with Israel (Ex 18:11). This action has been interpreted as Jethro's acceptance of a covenant with Israel, but the interpretation rests upon a faulty reading of what Jethro actually did and the meaning of sacrifice and a fellowship meal. Upon receiving Jethro's good counsel concerning procedures for judging disputes among the people, Moses appointed able men as heads and judges over the people (vv 13-27). Jethro departed to his own land and seems to have had no further interaction with Israel, but his son (Nm 10:29-33) and other descendants later became a part of Israel (Jgs 1:16; 4:11).

Jethro is referred to by other names, both in the Scriptures and later. The Talmud records that his name was Jether originally, but after his conversion it became Jethro; there is no definite evidence to support this. He is called Reuel, the father of seven daughters whom Moses met at a well (Ex 2:16-18; Nm 10:29). He is also referred to by the name Hobab (Jgs 4:11); and he is said to be the son of Reuel (Nm 10:29). The Scriptures do not explain the use of the different names. Suggestions include the following: (1) each Midianite tribe he served as a priest knew him by a different name; (2) Reuel was a tribal name, not personal; (3) Hobab, the son's name, was used to refer to the father; (4) a gloss appears in the text at Exodus 2:18 and Judges 4:11. It can be quite clearly established, however, that Jethro had a son named Hobab.

See also Midian, Midianite; Moses.

JETUR, JETURITES Son of Ishmael and his descendants (Gn 25:15; 1 Chr 1:31); the Israelite tribes who settled east of the Jordan had to fight them (1 Chr 5:19). Also called Itureans, they survived into NT times, giving their name to Iturea, an area northeast of Galilee (Lk 3:1). *See* Ituraea, Iturea, Itureans.

JEUEL

1. Descendant of Judah residing in postexilic Jerusalem (1 Chr 9:6).
2. Levite who took part in Hezekiah's reforms (2 Chr 29:13).
3. Head of a family who returned to Jerusalem with Ezra after the exile (Ezr 8:13).

JEUSH

1. Eldest of three sons born to Esau by Oholibamah, daughter of the Canaanite Anah, and a chief among Esau's descendants in Edom (Gn 36:5-18; 1 Chr 1:35).
2. Bilhan's son from Jediael's house and a leader in Benjamin's tribe (1 Chr 7:10).
3. Benjamite, Eshek's son and a descendant of Saul (1 Chr 8:39).
4. Levite from the family of Gershon and the third of Shimei's four sons. Since he and his youngest brother, Beriah, had few sons, they were together considered one house during David's reign (1 Chr 23:10-11).
5. Eldest of three sons born to King Rehoboam by Mahalath, Eliab's granddaughter (2 Chr 11:19).

JEUZ From Benjamin's tribe, Shaharaim's son by his wife Hodesh (1 Chr 8:10).

JEW Judean, belonging to Judah. The short form of the English word was developed from the French. The underlying Hebrew word is used first in 2 Kings 16:6 as a national term, meaning citizens of Judah. It came into general use in the period of Jeremiah just before the exile

(late sixth century BC; see Jer 32:12). It reflects a growing sense of national identity among foreign nations in an international world. In Jeremiah 34:9, a statement concerning the national principle that an individual citizen had the right to freedom from slavery uses the term "Jew." In Jeremiah 52:28 it is poignantly used in giving the number of deported citizens.

Once the people were in exile, the term's national meaning was expanded with a religious one. The Jews were different from surrounding peoples in that they preserved a living religious tradition of one true God. A Jewish-Gentile polarization developed. Thus in Daniel 3:8-12 certain Jews are accused of deviating from otherwise acceptable Babylonian religious practices. The book of Esther is concerned with the problem of Jewish identity and survival in a hostile alien environment. Esther 8:17 speaks of Gentiles declaring themselves Jews in the religious sense of becoming proselytes.

After the exile, the strongly religious meaning of "Jew" is expressed in the prophecy of Zechariah 8:23 that the Jew would be courted by Gentiles because God was with him. In Ezra 4:12 the term "Jews" is the national designation of the returned exiles, as it is in the book of Nehemiah (e.g., Neh 1:2; 4:2). In Nehemiah 13:24 there is a consciousness of the social exclusiveness of the Jews: on religious grounds, marriage to foreigners is deplored.

In the NT "Jew" continues to have the same national and/or religious meaning. Culturally, Jews have religious and other customs that NT documents addressed to Gentiles find it necessary to explain (Mk 7:3; Jn 5:1; 19:40). Jews are contrasted with Gentiles (Acts 11:19), Samaritans (Jn 4:9, 22), and proselytes (Acts 2:10). Jewish Christians can be called "Jews" (Gal 2:13), but there is an increasing stress on the religious distinctions between Jew and Christian. In Romans 2:17-29 Paul gives an interesting theological analysis of the term "Jew." He is at pains to emphasize that the true meaning of the word lies not in outward religious profession but in an inward attitude to God. Paul was doubtless thinking of the inadequacy of his own life as a Jew before he was converted to the Christian faith (cf. Phil 3:3-6). His mention of "praise" in Romans 2:29 is the climax of the passage. It is a forceful play on words: in Hebrew, Judah means praise (Gn 29:35; cf. 49:8).

The apostle Paul is here moving in the direction of regarding Christianity as the true heir of the faith of the OT. Revelation 2:9 and 3:9 express similar sentiments: to be truly a Jew is much more than a matter of birth and synagogue observance. Underlying these passages in both Revelation and Romans is obviously the issue of the messianic claims of Jesus (cf. Rom 9:3-5; 10:1-4). The NT bears sad testimony to the opposition of Jews to the Christian message. The gospel proved a cause of offense to the Jews (1 Cor 1:23). Paul himself, despite his claim of impeccable Jewish credentials (Acts 26:4-7), found himself the object of bitter Jewish attacks (21:11; 23:12, 27). Revelation 2:9 and 3:9 describe the Jews' opposition as satanic: they were carrying out the work of God's adversary, Satan.

These negative overtones are especially attached to the use of the word "Jew" in John's Gospel. It is found some 70 times, versus about five or six instances in each of the synoptic Gospels. Some passages, such as those already cited, have no associations of hostility. But in most cases the fourth Gospel uses "Jews" in the sense of the religious authorities, especially those in Jerusalem, who were hostile to Jesus (see, e.g., Jn 5:18; 9:18; 11:8; 18:36). It is noteworthy that in 9:22 the parents of the blind man, clearly Jews themselves, are said, literally, to fear the investigating Jews. In 18:14 "Jews" stands for the chief priests and Pharisees of 18:3. It must be emphasized that the author, who was obviously a Jew himself, was not expressing an anti-Semitic viewpoint as such. He condemned not race or people but those who opposed Jesus. He gladly acknowledged that some Jews put their faith in Jesus (8:31; 11:45; 12:11). Nathanael is featured as a type of the Christian Jew, a true Israelite "in whom is no guile" (1:47; cf. v 31; see Gn 27:35; 32:28).

See also Diaspora of the Jews; Israel, History of; Judaism; Judaizers; Pharisees; Postexilic Period.

JEWELRY, JEWELS Decorated adornments. In the Bible, jewelry was used by both men and women (Ex 11:2; Is 3:18-21). Items of jewelry were given as presents (Gn 24:22, 53) and were regularly seized as spoil in war (2 Chr 20:25). Before coinage came into use, jewels were associated with gold and silver as a measure of wealth (21:3) or as a standard of value (Jb 28:16; Prv 3:15).

In the OT a wide variety of jewelry is mentioned—arm bracelets (Gn 24:22, 30, 47; Ez 16:11), ankle ornaments (Is 3:18-20), necklaces (Gn 41:42), crowns (Zec 9:16), earrings (Gn 24:22), nose rings (Is 3:21), and finger rings (Gn 41:42; Est 3:10). In each case a gold or silver mounting was used to hold the precious stones. It would seem that the modern art of faceting was not used but the precious stone was rounded, polished, and sometimes engraved. Many of the precious stones valued in antiquity would hardly be classed as precious today, though they might be classified as semiprecious.

Semiprecious stones were frequently incorporated into necklaces and other pieces of jewelry. Royal headdresses from the graves at Ur near the Persian Gulf give an indication of the skill of jewelers around 2700 BC. Hairbands and pins were necessary parts of hair adornment and have been recovered from numerous Near Eastern archaeological sites. Rings, often with delicately carved stones, were extremely popular, and nose rings were also in use by the middle Bronze Age (see Gn 24:47). Fine gold chains were frequently worn. A signet ring and a heavy gold chain were decorative symbols of office (41:42). Bracelets and amulets were worn around the wrist, the upper arm, and the neck. Decorative pins, similar in design and intent to the modern safety pin, were often used to hold clothing together.

An excellent description of women's clothing and jewelry is found in Isaiah 3:18-23 (NLT), where the prophet warns: "The Lord will strip away their artful beauty—their ornaments, headbands, and crescent necklaces; their earrings, bracelets, and veils of shimmering gauze. Gone will be their scarves, ankle chains, sashes, perfumes, and charms; their rings, jewels, party clothes, gowns, capes, and purses; their mirrors, linen garments, head ornaments, and shawls."

See Minerals and Metals; Stones, Precious.

JEWISH LITERATURE*, Extrabiblical *See* Mishnah; Talmud; Targum.

JEZANIAH Alternate form of Jaazaniah, one of the Judean captains in Jerusalem during the exile (Jer 40:8 NLT mg; 42:1) *See* Jaazaniah #1.

JEZEBEL Daughter of Ethbaal, king of Sidon (1 Kgs 16:31). She became the wife of Ahab, king of the northern kingdom of Israel. The marriage was probably a continuation of the friendly relations between Israel and Phoenicia begun by Omri; it confirmed a political alliance between the two nations. Jezebel exerted a strong influence over the life of Israel, as she insisted on establishing the worship of Baal and demanded the absolute

rights of the monarchy. So strong was her pagan influence that Scripture attributes the apostasy of Ahab directly to Jezebel (vv 30-33).

Jezebel's efforts to establish Baal worship in Israel began with Ahab's acceptance of Baal following the marriage (1 Kgs 16:31). Ahab followed Jezebel's practices by building a house of worship and altar for Baal in Samaria, and by setting up a pole for worship of the Asherah. A campaign was then conducted to exterminate the prophets of God (18:4), while Jezebel organized and supported large groups of Baal prophets, housing and feeding large numbers of them in the royal palace (v 19). To meet this challenge, God sent Elijah to prophesy a drought that lasted three years (17:1; 18:1).

Elijah's confrontation with Jezebel and Ahab culminated on Mt Carmel, where Elijah demanded that the prophets of Baal meet him (1 Kgs 18:19-40). As they and the people of Israel gathered, Elijah issued the challenge to Israel to follow the true God. To demonstrate who was the true God, Baal's prophets and Elijah each took a bull for sacrifice. The prophets of Baal then prepared the sacrifice and called on their god to send fire to consume it. But no answer came. Elijah prepared his sacrifice and had it drenched in water. After his prayer, God sent fire that consumed the sacrifice, the wood, the stones of the altar, the dust, and the water in the trench. Following this, the Israelites fell down in tribute to God. Then Elijah directed the people to take the prophets of Baal to the brook Kishon, and he slaughtered all of them. When Jezebel heard of this, she flew into a rage and threatened Elijah with the same fate. In fear, Elijah fled for his life to the wilderness.

Jezebel's unscrupulous nature is revealed in the account of Ahab's desire for Naboth's vineyard (1 Kgs 21:1-16). Although Ahab desired the vineyard, he recognized Naboth's right to retain the family property. Jezebel recognized no such right in view of a monarch's wishes. She arranged to have Naboth falsely accused of blaspheming God and consequently executed, leaving the vineyard for Ahab to seize. For this heinous crime, Elijah pronounced a violent death for Ahab and Jezebel (21:20-24), a prophecy which was ultimately fulfilled (1 Kgs 22:29-40; 2 Kgs 9:1-37).

The corrupt influence of Jezebel spread to the southern kingdom of Judah through her daughter Athaliah, who married Jehoram, king of Judah. Thus the idolatry of Phoenicia infected both kingdoms of the Hebrews through this evil Sidonian princess.

In Revelation 2:20 the name of Jezebel is used (probably symbolically) to refer to a prophetess who seduced the Christians of Thyatira to fornication and to eating things sacrificed to idols.

See also Ahab #1; Elijah; Sidon (Place), Sidonian.

JEZER Naphtali's third son and the founder of the family of Jezerites (Gn 46:24; Nm 26:49; 1 Chr 7:13).

JEZIAH* KJV form of Izziah, Parosh's descendant, in Ezra 10:25. *See* Izziah.

JEZIEL Warrior from Benjamin's tribe who joined David at Ziklag in his struggle against King Saul. Jeziel was one of David's ambidextrous archers and slingers (1 Chr 12:3).

JEZLIAH* KJV form of Izliah, Elpaal's son, in 1 Chronicles 8:18. *See* Izliah.

JEZOAR* KJV rendering of Izhar, Helah's son, in 1 Chronicles 4:7. *See* Izhar #2.

JEZRAHIAH Leader of the temple singers who participated in the dedication of the rebuilt Jerusalem wall (Neh 12:42).

JEZREEL (Person)

1. Descendant of Etam from the tribe of Judah (1 Chr 4:3). Another possible reading suggests that Jezreel was one of the founding fathers of the town of Etam. Due to numerous scribal alterations within the Hebrew text, it is difficult to discern the original intent of the author.
2. Firstborn son of the prophet Hosea and his wife, Gomer. Jezreel's name, meaning "God sows," prefigured the outpouring of God's wrath on the disobedient kingdom of Israel under Jehu (Hos 1:4-5) and ultimate restoration (2:21-22).

JEZREEL (Place)

1. Town originally founded by the tribe of Issachar to the south of Shunem, a site that was abandoned in the el-Amarna period by earlier settlers (Jos 19:18). The city became associated with a number of important events in the history of Israel.

It probably gained some of its importance from the decline of the ancient town of Beth-shan during the Iron Age. Jezreel became the center of an important district in Saul's kingdom (2 Sm 2:9), and a nearby spring served as the rallying point for Saul's army before they met the Philistines in the battle of Mt Gilboa (1 Sm 29:1). After Saul's death, the town was, for a short time, part of Ishbosheth's kingdom (2 Sm 2:8-11). In Solomon's day it was assigned to the tenth district of Issachar and was excluded from the main Jezreel Valley. It was administered by Jehoshaphat, son of Paruah (1 Kgs 4:17).

In the days of Omri (885–874 BC) it was chosen as the site of the king's winter capital, and the four kings of his dynasty down to Joram (852–841 BC) all resided there. It was to this place that Joram retired to recover from wounds received in battle (2 Kgs 8:29). Jezreel was a walled city with a gate and a tower from which the countryside could be surveyed (9:17), and it was administered by a council of elders and nobles (10:1). The royal palace was adjacent to the vineyard owned by Naboth, the Jezreelite, which was seized illegally by King Ahab (1 Kgs 21). For this dastardly deed the dynasty of Ahab received severe retribution. Jezebel, Ahab's Phoenician wife, was thrown to the dogs through an upper window at the time of Jehu's usurpation of the throne. King Joram, wounded in battle, was slain by Jehu along with his courtiers and his body cast into the field of Naboth (2 Kgs 9:24-26). The remnant of Ahab's household were killed at the same time (10:1-11).

After the downfall of Omri's dynasty, the town declined in importance, although it is mentioned as a village by a number of writers in the Christian era. Eusebius (AD 260–340), for example, refers to it as a village between Scythopolis (Beth-shan) and Legio (*Onomasticon* 108:13ff.). The Crusaders called it "le Petit Gerim" to distinguish it from "le Grand Gerim."

Today Jezreel is identified with Zer'in, the site of an Israeli kibbutz about 55 miles (88.5 kilometers) north of Jerusalem. Archaeological remains found in the area point to an occupation in the Iron Age and the Roman period.

2. Town in the mountains of Judah (Jos 15:56). It was the hometown of Ahinoam, one of David's wives (1 Sm 25:43), but nothing is known about the site today.

JEZREEL VALLEY Largest and richest valley in the land of Israel. It was named after Jezreel, and it was apparently the only town on the plain where the Israelites had gained a foothold in the early stages of their conquest (cf. Jgs 1:27-30). The form of the name in later Greek sources is Esdraelon (Jdt 1:8); some scholars have wrongly applied the latter term to the great western plain and the former to the narrow valley leading eastward to Beth-shan. Comparison of Joshua 17:16 with Judges 1:27-28 and Joshua 17:11 shows that the Beth-shan area was considered as a separate entity from the valley of Jezreel, which included the cities of Taanach and Megiddo among others (cf. also Hos 1:5).

The Midianites camped there, between the hill of Moreh and Mt Tabor (Jgs 6:33; 7:1); Barak defeated the army of Sisera and Jabin there, near Endor (Ps 83:9-10), and later the Philistines gathered there to oppose Saul (1 Sm 29:1, 11; 2 Sm 4:4). Under the monarchy, the valley was an administrative district (2 Sm 2:9; 1 Kgs 4:12). Another name, perhaps applicable only to the southern half of the valley, is the plain of Megiddo (2 Chr 35:22; Zec 12:11).

Aerial View of Jezreel

The valley figures in the wars of Thutmose III and Amenhotep II, and the towns there, especially Megiddo, were under Egyptian control in the late Bronze Age. The southwestern side was famous as a military assembly ground, probably called Harosheth-haggoyim (Jgs 4:2, 13-16).

See also Palestine.

JEZREELITE* Inhabitant of one of two cities named Jezreel. Two such persons are specifically named:

1. Naboth, who lived in the Jezreel in Issachar's territory (1 Kgs 21:1-16; 2 Kgs 9:21, 25). See Jezreel (Place) #1.
2. David's wife Ahinoam, who was a native of the Jezreel in Judah's territory (1 Chr 3:1). See Jezreel (Place) #2.

JIBSAM* KJV form of Ibsam, Tola's son, in 1 Chronicles 7:2. See Ibsam.

JIDLAPH Seventh son of Nahor and Milcah (Gn 22:22).

JIMNA*, JIMNAH*, JIMNITE* KJV forms of Imnah and Imnite, Asher's son and his family, in Genesis 46:17 and Numbers 26:44. See Imnah #1.

JIPHTAH* KJV rendering of Iphtah, a village in Judah, in Joshua 15:43. See Iphtah.

JIPHTHAH-EL* KJV rendering of Iphtah-el, a valley on Zebulun's border, in Joshua 19:14, 27. *See* Iphtah-el.

JOAB

1. Son of Zeruiah, the half sister of David (1 Chr 2:16), who, along with his brothers Abishai and Asahel, was well known for his military valor in Judah (2 Sm 2:18; cf. 1 Sm 26:6). According to 2 Samuel, Joab rose to prominence and distinguished himself at the battle of Gibeon when Saul's troops under Abner were vanquished (2 Sm 2:8-32). Because Abner had slain Joab's brother Asahel (v 23), Joab later killed Abner in revenge (3:26-30), despite Abner's new loyalty to David (vv 12-19). Possibly Joab sensed that Abner would be his rival. Nevertheless, David praised the slain commander as a prince and a great man (vv 31-39) and set a curse on the house of Joab for his insubordination (vv 26-29, 39). This incident illumines Joab's sometimes unscrupulous and ruthless behavior.

  Joab spearheaded David's siege of the Jebusite city of Jerusalem, and when David consolidated his reign there, Joab became the commander of the king's army (2 Sm 8:16; 11:1; cf. 1 Chr 11:6-8; 18:15). He suppressed a rebellion among the Syrians and Ammonites (2 Sm 10:7-14; 1 Chr 19:8-15). At Rabbah he not only conquered the city (2 Sm 11–12) but arranged for the death of Uriah the Hittite so that David could take Uriah's wife, Bathsheba.

  Joab's loyalties to David and shrewd control of the army are seen during Absalom's rebellion (2 Sm 15). Joab suppressed the conspiracy (ch 18), but ignoring a direct order from David not to kill his son (18:5), brutally killed him anyway (vv 10-17). When David mourned, Joab rebuked the king, urging that a crisis with the army was imminent (19:5-7). This insubordination led David to replace Joab with Amasa as commander (v 13), but later, at Gibeon, Joab also killed him dishonorably (20:8-10). Joab's influence in the army must have been great, since he regained his former role as military commander (2 Sm 20:23, 24:2; 1 Kgs 1:19).

  At the end of David's reign, Joab supported the conspiracy of Adonijah and Abiathar against the throne (1 Kgs 1:7). David's distrust of him led the king to warn Solomon specifically about Joab's repeated treacheries (2:5-9). Solomon had to resolve the problem of an untrustworthy army. Therefore, upon his father's death, Solomon pursued the conspirators Adonijah (v 23), Abiathar (v 26), and Joab (v 28). Solomon's officer Benaiah found Joab at the altar seeking refuge and killed him there (vv 28-35), thus cleansing Solomon's reign from the wrongdoing of Joab.

2. KJV translation ("Ataroth, the house of Joab") of Atroth-beth-joab in 1 Chronicles 2:54. *See* Atroth-beth-joab.

3. Judahite, Seraiah's son from the house of Kenaz and forefather of the residents of the valley of craftsmen (1 Chr 4:14).

4. Forefather of a clan of Jews who returned to Palestine with Zerubbabel following the exile (Ezr 2:6; Neh 7:11).

5. Forefather of a family of which 219 members returned with Ezra to Palestine following the exile (Ezr 8:9). He is perhaps identifiable with #4 above.

JOAH

1. Asaph's son and a court official under King Hezekiah (2 Kgs 18:18, 26; Is 36:3, 11, 22). He was one of the officers sent by Hezekiah to deal with the Assyrians during the siege of Jerusalem.

2. Zimmah's son from Levi's tribe (1 Chr 6:21).

3. Levite, Obed-edom's son and a gatekeeper of the sanctuary in David's time (1 Chr 26:4).

4. Joahaz's son and a recorder under King Josiah; he was one of the deputies overseeing the temple repairs (2 Chr 34:8).

JOAHAZ

1. Variant spelling or contraction of Jehoahaz, Jehu's son, in 2 Kings 14:1. *See* Jehoahaz #1.

2. Joah's father. Joah was King Josiah's recorder (2 Chr 34:8).

JOANAN Ancestor of Jesus mentioned in Luke's genealogy (Lk 3:27). *See* Genealogy of Jesus Christ.

JOANNA

1. KJV form of Joanan in Luke 3:27. *See* Joanan.

2. Wife of Chuza, a steward of Herod the tetrarch. She was among those healed of evil spirits and sickness by Jesus, and contributed to his support (Lk 8:2-3). She probably witnessed the Crucifixion and prepared spices for the body; later she found Jesus' tomb empty (23:55–24:10).

JOARIB Ancestor of Mattathias (1 Macc 2:1; 14:29), and according to 1 Chronicles 24:7 (there spelled Jehoiarib), head of the first of the 24 courses of priests in David's time.

JOASH

1. Abiezrite who lived at Ophrah and the father of Gideon. Joash built an altar to Baal and an image of Asherah, which Gideon later destroyed (Jgs 6:11-31; 7:14; 8:13, 29-32).

2. Son of King Ahab of Israel (1 Kgs 22:26; 2 Chr 18:25).

3. Alternate name for Jehoash, Ahaziah's son and king of Judah (835–796 BC), in 2 Kings 11:2-3 and 1 Chronicles 3:11. *See* Jehoash #1.

4. Alternate name for Jehoash, Jehoahaz's son and king of Israel (798–782 BC), in 2 Kings 13:10-13. *See* Jehoash #2.

5. Judahite from the house of Shelah (1 Chr 4:22).

6. Second of Beker's nine sons and a leader in Benjamin's tribe (1 Chr 7:8).

7. Benjamite warrior who supported David at Ziklag (1 Chr 12:3).

8. One of David's officials (1 Chr 27:28).

JOATHAM* KJV spelling of Jotham, king of Judah (750–735 BC), in Matthew 1:9. *See* Jotham #2.

JOB (Person)

1. KJV rendering of Iob, an alternate form of Jashub, Issachar's third son, in Genesis 46:13. *See* Jashub #1.

2. Central character of the book of Job. The intense suffering endured by Job provides the framework for the main theme of the book, which deals with the role of suffering in the life of a child of God.

  The etymology of the name is difficult. Some have seen it as a derivative of a Hebrew word meaning "to be hostile" and have suggested that it reflects Job's adamancy in refusing to bow to God's will. The name occurs in several West Semitic texts as a proper name, however, and it seems best to understand it simply as a common name. The meaning of the name in West Semitic is either "no father" or "where is my father?"

The lack of certainty surrounding the authorship and geographical provenance of the book makes it difficult to place Job in history. The occurrence of Job's name in Ezekiel 14:14, 20 seems to support the possibility that he was a personage of great antiquity.

See also Job, Book of.

JOB, Book of
Old Testament book belonging to the scriptural category called the Writings.

PREVIEW
• Author
• Date
• Background
• Purpose and Theological Teaching
• Content

before he began to speak (2:11-13), did Job find those deep inner questions that the book deals with. Job's high moral character is quite evident in the dialogues, for throughout, even though he cannot comprehend God, he speaks the truth before him.

Other portions alleged to be additions to the book are the speeches of Elihu (32–37), the discourse of God (38–41), and the discourse on wisdom in chapter 28. Some scholars think the author of the final version borrowed these existing works to provide a literary structure for his own work.

The main structure of the book, consisting of prologue, dialogues, and an epilogue, need not necessarily be regarded as the result of a complex process of editing. The Code of Hammurabi, for example, has a similar structure, as does an ancient Egyptian work called *A Dispute over Suicide.*

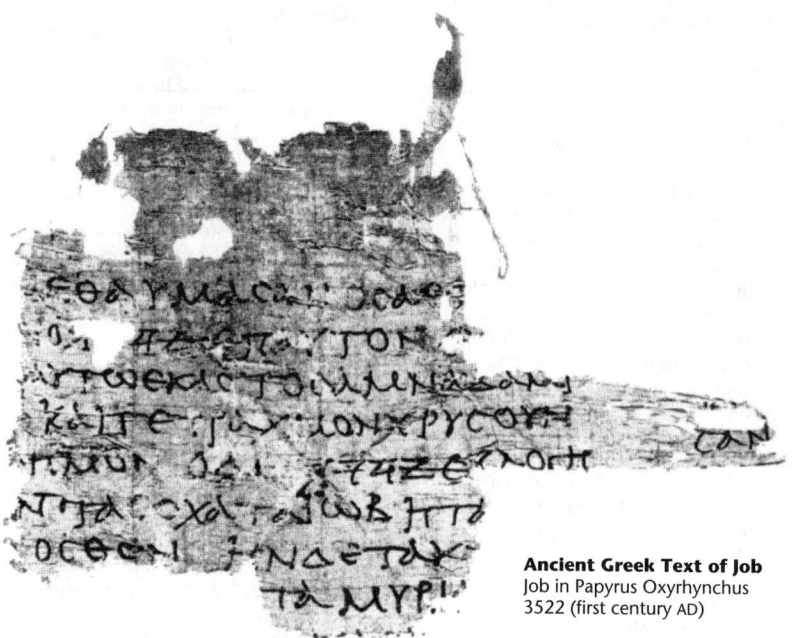

Ancient Greek Text of Job
Job in Papyrus Oxyrhynchus 3522 (first century AD)

Author The question of the authorship of the book of Job is a difficult one. The difficulty is compounded not only by the lack of ascription of authorship to any individual but also by the structure of the book which, according to some scholars, is a composite consisting of several literary works.

Some scholars who think the book is a composite work base their views on alleged incongruities existing among the various sections. The prologue (chs 1–2) and the epilogue (42:7-17), for example, are seen as separate from the body of the book because they seem to present Job as a man of perfect moral character. The dialogues, however, picture a somewhat more human Job whose utterances about God are at times brash and shocking.

It is true that Job is depicted as a man of perfect moral character in the prologue. But it should be noted that while he refuses his wife's suggestion to curse God, an account recorded in the prologue (2:9-10), he does not curse God in the dialogues either. The very point of the book seems to be that even one of the highest moral character must struggle with the ways of God in this world. Only after the series of misfortunes recorded in chapters 1 and 2, and the period of inner struggle that no doubt transpired during the seven days and seven nights

With regard to the problem of authorship, it seems best to acknowledge that the author is anonymous. His theology is certainly Yahwistic; thus, he was probably a Hebrew. His literary skills were remarkable, for he has produced one of the finest works known through the ages.

Date Since the authorship of the book is in question, so is the date of the book. Most modern scholars place the book in the postexilic period, around the fifth century BC. However, some place it toward the end of the exile. Others put it in the Solomonic era, while still others place it in the period of the patriarchs.

The internal evidence points to a very early setting for the book. There are no Levitical institutions cited. Job sacrifices for his family as in the period before the priesthood (1:5). The wealth of Job, given in terms of livestock, seems to reflect the patriarchal milieu (v 3).

The language of the book may also point to an early date. Certain linguistic elements indicate more archaic forms of Hebrew, as preserved in the epic material from Ugarit. It may be that Job himself lived in the second millennium BC. If the book—or part of it—was written then, it may represent the first written material to find its way into the biblical canon. The book may have come into its final form in the Solomonic era, when so much of the Hebrew Wisdom Literature was produced.

Background The book of Job belongs to the body of OT materials known as the Wisdom Literature. This literature deals with the basic issues of human life. The Israelites were not the only ancient people to produce Wisdom Literature. This type of material came out of pagan cultures as well, and often represents efforts to explain the course of human events within the structure of pagan religion.

Several ancient works similar to the OT book of Job are known from ancient cultures. A Sumerian book exists that does not compare with the biblical book, either in literary scope or depth of feeling. It depicts the plight of a young man whose sorrow was turned to joy as a result of extended pleading to his personal deity. According to Sumerian thought, the gods were responsible for evil as well as good. Only placation of some kind could prevent the evil they might do. There is no attempt to philosophize or expound the problem of the presence of evil in the world.

A Babylonian book, commonly titled *I Will Praise the Lord of Wisdom*, is philosophically similar to the Sumerian *Job*. In the work the writer describes his suffering in vivid terminology. No one can help him. He wonders whether the ritual obligations of his pagan religion really are pleasing to a god. An emissary of the god Marduk appears to him in a dream and relieves his suffering. The work ends with a section of praise to Marduk in which occurs the affirmation that the offerings he gave the gods served to gladden the hearts of the gods.

Another work, "A Dialogue about Human Misery," is also similar to the biblical book of Job. It struggles with the fact that worship of the deities seems to make no difference in the quality of one's life. A figure in this work reminds the sufferer that the ways of the gods are difficult to understand, and man is naturally perverse. The sufferer appeals to the gods, but the dialogue ends at that point with no resolution to the problem.

These literary works are not comparable to the OT book of Job theologically or philosophically. They offer only a fatalistic outlook on life and understand life to be governed by the capricious will of the gods. However, these documents, which date variously between the second and first millennia BC, may provide us with the literary ground from which the book of Job sprang. That is, the book of Job may present the inspired answer to the deep questions that were being considered at this time in history. Thus, this type of literature may argue for an early date for the book of Job.

Purpose and Theological Teaching The question of the central purpose of the book of Job has been a serious one in biblical scholarship for ages. It is difficult to assert that the purpose of the book is to present the solution to the problem of evil, for at the very point where an answer is expected, God asks questions instead of giving answers.

Some have suggested that the central purpose is to answer the question "Why do the righteous suffer?" It is true that the book has much to do with this question, but it too presents various problems. When one comes to the end of the book, he or she has only the words of the comforters and the statements of Elihu relating to that question—not a great deal at all. Then one may wonder why we were given the long dialogues with their record of Job's internal struggles. When God speaks from the whirlwind, we find no concern to explain why the

righteous suffer. Job is simply led to accept his place in the universe.

It seems best to adopt another approach to the book. In attempting to find the central theme of any literary work, one should look to the prologue and the epilogue. In the prologue one can see what the author intends to do, and in the epilogue the reader will find the author's understanding of what the author actually has done.

In the prologue of Job, the author deftly establishes an atmosphere of suspense. We are told of Job's perfect moral character. Then Satan taunts, "Take away everything he has, and he will surely curse you to your face!" (1:11, NLT). We wonder whether Job will curse God and thus deny his faith, but then we hear his great affirmation of trust: "The LORD gave me everything I had, and the LORD has taken it away. Praise the name of the LORD!" (v 21).

The writer then sets up another suspenseful situation when Satan proposes to afflict Job. To this trial is added the discouraging words of Job's wife: "Curse God and die." Again we wonder whether this trial will destroy Job's faith. The suspense is broken when we read that "in all this, Job said nothing wrong" (2:10).

The writer then introduces Job's friends into the narrative. We are told that they remained silent for seven days. We wonder what is going on in Job's mind. Is he still the man of staunch faith, or is his trust being eroded as the disease eats at his flesh? When Job speaks and curses the day of his birth, the suspense becomes intense. The writer has raised a question in our minds: Will Job's faith remain secure?

At times we think it will. Job makes several great affirmations of faith. He states that God will vindicate him. One of the greatest affirmations of the book occurs in 19:25-27 (NLT): "But as for me, I know that my Redeemer lives, and that he will stand upon the earth at last. And after my body has decayed, yet in my body I will see God! I will see him for myself. Yes, I will see him with my own eyes. I am overwhelmed at the thought!" At other times Job expresses deep doubts about God's orderly control of the universe. The suspense continues. Throughout the dialogues we trace the pattern of Job's struggle. It is an emotional struggle in which Job speaks from the depths of despair and the heights of triumphant faith.

In the epilogue the suspense is resolved. Job's trials have not destroyed or even eroded his faith. He emerges triumphant, with a humble faith. He can finally say to God, "I know that you can do anything, and no one can stop you. You ask, 'Who is this that questions my wisdom with such ignorance?' It is I. And I was talking about things I did not understand, things far too wonderful for me" (42:2-3, NLT).

The purpose of the writer is clear. At the outset he has raised the question "Will Job's faith endure in spite of trial?" The dialogues have heightened the suspense, and the epilogue resolves it. Job has remained faithful to God in the midst of his suffering. We learn that Job's faith is genuine.

The book of Job, therefore, is a treatise on faith and the role that suffering plays in faith. The book of Job teaches that the truly righteous person will remain faithful to God in spite of the seeming delay of God's justice. He may not be able to comprehend all that God does in history, but his faith in God's good plan and wise providence will remain secure. This aspect of faith is one facet of the total spectrum of faith in the Bible. It does not allow for works but is totally dependent on God.

The same relationship between faith and suffering may be found in the NT as well. In James 1:12 trials and faithfulness are woven together in the word "Blessed is the man who endures trial, for when he has stood the test he will receive the crown of life which God has promised to those who love him" (RSV; see also 1 Pt 1:3-7). According to these passages, trials provide the test of faith and thus reveal whether one's faith is true or false. Faith that is not true will not stand the test of suffering (Mt 13:20-21). The book of Job connects faith and trials; it portrays the nature of a genuine faith, a faith unbroken by suffering.

There are other principles in this rich book. It teaches that sin brings punishment. There is truth in the words of the comforters that is corroborated by Scripture. Yet this is but a small part of the role of suffering in life. The book also teaches that suffering has a didactic function, for it is chastening from the Almighty. In the section in which God speaks from the whirlwind, we learn that suffering is part of the structure of things and that we must submit to the wisdom of the Creator. In this section God reveals himself personally. Job could say, "I had heard about you before, but now I have seen you with my own eyes" (42:5, NLT). When we experience trials, we need a God who is near much more than a philosophical treatise on the problem of evil. Another emphasis is the role of suffering in producing true righteousness. While Job was depicted as a righteous man at the beginning of the book, his righteousness lacked what suffering could give it. At the end of the book, Job is a more humble man, one who sees his role in the universe and who has submitted to the wisdom of God.

Content

The Prologue (1:1–2:13) This section of the book describes the events that led to the suffering of Job. He is pictured at the outset as a man of wealth with a family for whom he cared deeply.

In a dramatic scene set in heaven, Satan appears and is asked by the Lord, "Have you noticed my servant Job? He is the finest man in all the earth—a man of complete integrity. He fears God and will have nothing to do with evil" (1:8, NLT). Satan's reply is "But take away everything he has, and he will surely curse you to your face!" (v 11). There follows the first of Job's great calamities, the loss of his family and his possessions.

Another encounter between the Lord and Satan leads to the physical suffering of Job. It is this loathsome disease that provides the context for the dialogues that follow. In all of this the writer is careful to tell us that Job did not sin. He has resisted his wife's plea to curse God. He has resisted the temptation to forsake God because of the loss of his children. But suddenly the placid picture ends with dialogues as we listen to Job's complaints. We wonder, has Job given up his faith in God?

Three of Job's friends have come to comfort him. They sit silent in his presence for seven days, reluctant to speak. After the period of silence they begin their dialogues with Job.

The Dialogues (3:1–31:40)

➤THE FIRST CYCLE (3:1–14:22) Job's complaint, recorded in chapter 3, questions the wisdom of God in allowing him to be born. He wonders why life was given to one whose lot in life is to suffer.

Eliphaz is the first of Job's friends to speak. A polite man on the surface, he is heartless underneath. His answer is that Job must have sinned—why else would he be suffering so (4:7-11)? Eliphaz clearly believes that Job's questioning represents a negative attitude toward God. He appeals to Job to trust in the Lord (4:8) and

give up his vexation toward God, since his anger will lead only to ruin (5:2). He sees a positive element in suffering, for he affirms that it is chastening from the Almighty (v 17).

Job responds by pointing out that his vexation is warranted in view of the terrible suffering he is enduring (6:1-7). He also complains that Eliphaz is in the wrong in not showing him kindness, likening him to a wadi in the desert that offers no water in the hot, dry season (vv 14-23).

The next comforter, Bildad, is even more heartless than Eliphaz. He, too, repeats the accusation that Job has sinned. His pitiless attitude is evident in his reference to Job's children, blaming their deaths on probable sin in their lives (8:4).

Bildad, like Eliphaz, appeals to Job to turn to God (8:5), assuring him that God will surely respond (v 6). He pictures Job's misfortunes as the result of turning from God (vv 11-19) but assures him that God will not reject a blameless man (v 20).

Job's response to Bildad begins with a poignant question: "How can a person be declared innocent in the eyes of God?" (9:2, NLT). This question is followed by an eloquent statement in which Job pictures the magnitude of God's power as seen in the universe (vv 3-12). Job stands before the mighty God completely helpless to withstand his power. He protests that he cannot contend with such a God, nor protest his innocence before him, for he is too powerful to oppose.

Job also complains that he cannot gain a fair hearing from God because God believes him guilty. The fact that God has punished him with his affliction proves that he does not regard him as innocent (9:14-24). Job continues his response and again questions God's wisdom in bringing him into existence (10:18-22).

The next to speak is Zophar. He also accuses Job of sin (11:4-6). In an insulting statement he says that God "knows those who are false, and he takes note of all their sins. An empty-headed person won't become wise any more than a wild donkey can bear human offspring" (vv 11-12, NLT).

Job's anger is kindled by Zophar's insulting accusations (12:2-3), and he calls on God to withdraw his hand from him and demands that God speak (13:20-28).

➤THE SECOND CYCLE (15:1–21:34) The second cycle of discourses continues in the same pattern as the first. Eliphaz, Bildad, and Zophar continue their accusations, attributing Job's misfortune to sin in his life. But as the narrative continues, the speakers begin to become more involved in their own assertions, and they no longer answer each other's arguments as directly as they did in the first series of dialogues.

➤THE THIRD CYCLE (22:1–31:40) In the third series of dialogues only Eliphaz and Bildad speak. The accusations of sin in Job become even more pointed and cruel. Eliphaz says, "It [your suffering] is because of your wickedness! Your guilt has no limit!" (22:5, NLT). This third dialogue is unusual in that Job speaks more than he does in the others. While Bildad's argument extends for only six verses, Job's reply goes on for six chapters (chs 26–31).

Chapter 31 is an important one. In it Job protests his innocence. It is a chapter in which Job's sincerity cannot be doubted. He affirms that he has been morally pure (vv 1-4), he has not been deceitful (vv 5-8), he has not been guilty of adultery (vv 9-12), he has concern for others (vv 13-23), he has not trusted in wealth (vv 24-28). He concludes with a general affirmation of his innocence (vv 29-40).

A pattern begins to develop. Job gradually moves away from his friends in the discussion. They become more insistent on sin as the cause of his misfortunes, and Job more firmly asserts his innocence. The writer of the book deftly weaves the account so that the reader can find little that is unorthodox in the statements of the friends. Yet while we may agree with their words, we cannot approve their attitudes. It is true that sin brings punishment, but the friends emphasize only that. The next friend, Elihu, will point out another function of suffering.

We hear the ring of truth in Job's protestations of innocence. But if we believe Job and also believe the comforters, we have the same dilemma as Job. We do not know where the truth lies. We do not know why Job is suffering.

The Speech of Elihu (32:1–37:24) Elihu is a young man who listens to Job and to his fellow comforters with growing impatience (32:3). He is overly sensitive about his youth (vv 6-22), but when he speaks, he reveals an understanding of suffering that is more mature than that of his companions.

Elihu emphasizes the fact that God speaks in many ways and that suffering is chastening (33:19), which reveals the goodness of God (vv 29-33). While this thought was found in Eliphaz's first speech (5:17), it is given greater prominence by Elihu, who emphasizes a dimension of suffering that reveals the love of God. But still one feels that the whole answer has not been given. Another dimension follows in the words of God.

The Voice from the Whirlwind and Job's Response (38:1–42:6) God speaks in this section. He poses one question after another to Job, all having to do with some aspect of the Creation. God asks, "Where were you when I laid the foundations of the earth?" Then, in a note of sarcasm, he adds, "Tell me, if you know so much" (38:4, NLT).

God refers to the seas and asks Job who made the ocean basins (38:8-11). He pictures the rising dawn and asks Job, "Have you ever commanded the morning to appear and caused the dawn to rise in the east?" (v 12, NLT). Further questions relate to light (vv 19-21), snow (vv 22-24), rain (vv 25-30), the constellations (vv 31-33), storms (vv 34-38), and animals (38:39–39:30). Job is made to realize the vastness of God's power as revealed in the Creation. Job must have felt rather small and insignificant as he contemplated God's might.

But the questions are meant to accomplish more than to make Job feel small. They are meant to make him feel ashamed of his presumption as well. The sarcasm in this section is particularly biting, and one can imagine Job sinking deeper into the ash heap with each question. In the section dealing with light (38:19-21, NLT), the questions "Where does the light come from, and where does the darkness go? Can you take it to its home? Do you know how to get there?" are followed by "But of course you know all this! For you were born before it was all created, and you are so very experienced!" And in the section dealing with the constellations God asks Job, "Can you hold back the movements of the stars? Are you able to restrain the Pleiades or Orion?" (v 31).

Job has been somewhat brash in his statements to God in the dialogues. He has demanded that God speak to him (13:22), and has accused God of injustice (19:6-7; 24:1; 27:2). Now, as he is reminded of the power of the Almighty, Job begins to recognize his proper place in the universe.

The crucial questions in this long series are those in 40:15–41:34. Here, in an unusual sequence, God draws Job's attention to behemoth (40:15) and leviathan (41:1). While some scholars see these as mythical figures, it is most probable that these, like the others cited throughout this section, are literary depictions of ordinary animals known for their great size and strength. It is suggested by many scholars that behemoth is the hippopotamus and leviathan the crocodile. The contexts in which these animals are described seem to support this. These references to two powerful animals end the section in which the voice of God speaks from the whirlwind. It is a section filled with suspense. At the end of it, the reader finds that Job has learned his lesson (42:1-3).

There is an important reason for these questions that came to Job with such insistent force. Job has been led to see that he does not control the universe—God does. Job is forced to face the power of God and learn that he is only part of this vast structure that reflects God's almighty power. By demanding that God speak to him, Job was attempting to control God. By implying that God was unjust, he was making a judgment on God, thus making himself equal, if not superior, to God. God demands that Job face the power displayed in the universe and repeat his petulant words. Job wanted a God he could control; God demands submission. Job wanted a world run his way; God created a world to be run his way. Job had manufactured an illusory God, one who should obey his own whims. By recognizing God's sovereign control in this world, he is led to see that suffering has a purpose. Job may not recognize that purpose, but it is part of the creation of the Almighty. It is no wonder that Job begins to enter into a settled peace and acknowledge God's sovereignty (42:5-6).

This section of questions is followed by a poignant response from Job. He confesses God's might (42:2). He admits that he did not fully understand things too wonderful for him (v 3), and he repents in dust and ashes (v 6).

The Epilogue (42:7-17) The final part of the book begins with a denunciation of Job's comforters. They are condemned because they did not speak that which was right (42:7). This seemed most unusual, since their words have seemed quite orthodox. Yet, in the final analysis, they did not say what was right because their answer to the problem of suffering was only a partial answer, and because it was partial, it was dangerous. It caricatured God as an austere being who used suffering only to punish sin. It did not allow room for the loving hand of God in suffering, as did Elihu's answer to the problem.

While Job said some things about God that were harsh, he was not berated. In fact, the text says that Job spoke of God that which was right (42:8). This evidently refers to Job's concluding words in 42:1-6, where, purified by suffering, he humbly yielded himself to God's sovereign will.

See also Job (Person) #2; Wisdom; Wisdom Literature.

JOBAB

1. Joktan's son in Eber's line (Gn 10:29; 1 Chr 1:23).
2. Early Edomite king. He was the son of Zerah of Bozrah (Gn 36:33-34; 1 Chr 1:44-45).
3. King of Madon who, along with other Canaanite kings, joined Jabin of Hazor in a northern confederacy to stop the Israelites from taking over the northern section of Canaan. He was killed in battle at the waters of Merom (Jos 11:1; 12:19).
4. Shaharaim's son by his wife Hodesh, a member of Benjamin's tribe (1 Chr 8:9).
5. Elpaal's son from Benjamin's tribe (1 Chr 8:18).

JOCHEBED Amram's wife and the mother of Moses, Aaron, and Miriam (Ex 6:20; Nm 26:59).

JODA Joanan's son, the father of Josech, and a forefather of Jesus Christ living in Palestine during the postexilic era (Lk 3:26). *See* Genealogy of Jesus Christ.

JOED Descendant of Benjamin living in Jerusalem during the days of Nehemiah (Neh 11:7). His name, meaning "Yahweh is witness," does not appear in a parallel list in 1 Chronicles 9:7.

JOEL (Person)

1. Levite from the family of Kohath. He was Azariah's son and an ancestor of Elkanah, the father of Samuel the prophet (1 Sm 1:1; 1 Chr 6:36).
2. Oldest son of Samuel the prophet. He and his brother Abijah so corrupted the office of judge that the elders increased their demands for a king (1 Sm 8:2-5). He was the father of Heman the singer (1 Chr 6:33; 15:17). His name has been mistakenly translated "Vashni" in the KJV in 1 Chronicles 6:28.
3. Prince from one of the Simeonite families that emigrated to the valley of Gedor (1 Chr 4:35).
4. Member of Reuben's tribe (1 Chr 5:4, 8).
5. Chief of Gad's tribe residing in Bashan (1 Chr 5:12).
6. Third of Izrahiah's four sons and a chief of Issachar's tribe in David's time (1 Chr 7:3).
7. Nathan's brother and one of David's mighty men (1 Chr 11:38). He is alternately called Igal the son of Nathan in 2 Samuel 23:36. *See* Igal #2.
8. Levite from the family of Gershon who participated in the royal procession that brought the ark of God to Jerusalem during David's reign (1 Chr 15:7-11). He may have administered the treasuries of the temple in Jerusalem (1 Chr 26:22).
9. Pedaiah's son, who acted as tribal chieftain over the west half of Manasseh's tribe during David's reign (1 Chr 27:20)
10. Levite from the family of Kohath who assisted in King Hezekiah's reform of the temple in Jerusalem (2 Chr 29:12).
11. Nebo's son, who was encouraged by Ezra to divorce his foreign wife during the postexilic period (Ezr 10:43).
12. Zicri's son and the supervisor of 128 Benjaminites who moved to postexilic Jerusalem (Neh 11:9).
13. Prophet who wrote the second book of the Minor Prophets. Little is known about him except that he was Pethuel's son (Jl 1:1; Acts 2:16). *See* Joel, Book of.

JOEL, Book of Old Testament book; second of the Minor Prophets.

PREVIEW
•Author
•Date
•Content
•Message

Author In the first verse the contents of the book of Joel are described as the "message" of the Lord that "came to Joel, the son of Pethuel." We are told nothing more in Scripture about Joel or Pethuel. The name Joel was common; there are 13 different Joels in the OT. From what is said in the book, it would seem that Joel was not a priest but was closely associated with the priests of the temple, and in all probability a man of Jerusalem. More than that we cannot say.

Date Many different views of the date of Joel have been taken by those who have studied this book carefully; thus it is difficult to be dogmatic. The book may be dated to a time after the return to Jerusalem of the Jewish exiles who had been in Babylon—more precisely, to a time after Nehemiah's work of rebuilding the walls of Jerusalem (c. 400 BC). Reasons given in support of this are as follows:

1. Joel 3:2 says that the people of Judah and Jerusalem had been scattered among the nations and their land divided up, but they have been brought back, and their city once again has its walls (2:9).
2. When a call is issued to prayer and fasting, the priests and elders are to take the lead (1:13; 2:16-17). There is no mention of a king at any point in the book. There were kings until the time of the exile, but not for 400 years after it.
3. The preexilic prophets—Amos, Hosea, Isaiah, Micah, and Jeremiah—were often critical of the people for offering sacrifices while they departed from the ways of the Lord in their daily lives. Postexilic prophets like Haggai and Malachi offer encouragement and deep concern for the offering of sacrifices. In the preexilic prophets there was constant rebuke of the people for their worship of idols; this was not a problem with the people after the exile. In both these concerns Joel seems to fit better the postexilic than the preexilic scene.
4. There is no reference to the northern kingdom of Israel in this book. Much is said of Judah and Jerusalem; when "Israel" is spoken of, the reference seems to be to the same people (2:27; 3:16). We would expect to find a different way of speaking before the fall of the northern kingdom to the Assyrians in 722 BC.
5. The other kingdoms referred to are Edom, Tyre and Sidon, the Philistines, and the Greeks. There is no mention of Syria, Assyria, and Babylonia, the inveterate enemies from whom the people suffered so much in preexilic days. Those mentioned were certainly significant to the people in postexilic times, and only then are the Greeks of importance on the Palestinian scene.

Some scholars think there is no great strength in these arguments and that everything in the book can be made to fit a much earlier date. It has sometimes been argued that the book is deliberately placed in the Hebrew Scriptures alongside the two eighth-century BC prophets Hosea and Amos. But the order of the books in the prophetic canon does not determine their date. The postexilic Obadiah stands between the eighth-century BC prophets Amos and Micah, and in fact in the Greek OT Joel was placed in a different position from its place in the Hebrew Bible. Most likely Joel and Amos stand together, as Amos 1:2 has the same words found at the close of the book of Joel (Jl 3:16). Some of those who favor a preexilic date for the book place it in the ninth century, in the early period of the reign of Joash when the king was too young to actually function as ruler of the land. Others place it sometime shortly before the death of Josiah in 609 BC because of the reference to enemy coming from the north (as in Jeremiah) and because of the appeal to the people (like Jeremiah's appeal) to return to the Lord with all their hearts (2:12).

Content

1:1-12 A plague of locusts more devastating than any that past generations had experienced had come on the land (vv 2-4). Drinkers were summoned to see the grapevines devastated and the fig trees stripped (vv 5-7). People were called to mourn at the sight of fields laid waste—especially the priests, as they would no longer be able to bring cereal and drink offerings to the Lord (vv 8-10). Farmers must grieve over the ruin of their harvest, in anguish at the loss of the fruits of the land (vv 11-12).

1:13-20 Because of what had happened, the people were called to prayer and fasting; the priests were to come before the Lord in sackcloth, grieving that no offerings could be brought (v 13). Elders and people alike must come to the temple to pray (v 14). Such a time of crisis, with the crops lost and the sheep and cattle having no pasture, was to be seen as foreshadowing the great coming Day of the Lord, for which everyone should be prepared (vv 15-18). The prophet himself could only cry out to God when he saw the devastation of the land (vv 19-20).

LOCUST PLAGUES
Much in this chapter and the next seems descriptive of the kind of locust plagues that are still common in lands of the Middle East and North and Central Africa. Millions of locusts may cover hundreds of square miles of land. In flight they are like a cloud above the ground, and the sound they make has been described as "less like the whirring of wings than the rattle of hail or the crackling of bush on fire." Nothing can resist their progress as they devastate field after field, stripping everything that is green, even branches of trees. It is thought that some passages in Joel 1 may speak of drought as well as the plague of locusts, but the devastation described may simply be due to the locusts.

2:1-11 In this section the prophet speaks of a time when God's judgment threatens the whole land. It is a time for the alarm to be sounded, when a great and powerful "people" come up on the land, a more threatening foe than any known before. Further, it is a warning of the coming "Day of the Lord," "a day of darkness and gloom" (vv 1-2). The land is devastated as by fire; what was like the Garden of Eden becomes a wilderness (v 3). This invasion is like that of cavalry and the sound of the insurgents like "the rumbling of chariots." Everyone is in anguish at their advance. They march like warriors, burst through the weapons, scale the walls of the city, and come into the houses like thieves (vv 4-9).

Some have taken this description to be a picture of armies of nations who are the foes of Israel, used by the Lord in judgment on his own people. But in that they are described as horses in battle, their noise like "the rumbling of chariots," their advance "like a mighty army moving into battle," it seems that the locust plague is still in mind. Yet the dark cloud of the locusts in the sky and their terrible effect on the land foreshadows the great day when the Lord will speak and act in judgment on all peoples. Then heaven and earth will tremble; sun, moon, and stars will be darkened (vv 10-11).

2:12-17 The prophet repeatedly calls the people to the Lord in humility and penitence so that his mercy and grace may be found. Then it will be possible "to offer grain and wine to the LORD your God as before" (v 14, NLT). A fast is to be appointed, a solemn assembly of young and old called. Even the newlyweds are to come. The priests must lead the people in prayer to God to spare his people (vv 14-17).

2:18-27 According to this passage, it seems that the people did turn to God as the prophet required; in response, the Lord had compassion on them and assured them of renewing their grain, wine, and oil, and removing their reproach (vv 18-19). The "armies from the north" would retreat, and God would restore the pastures of the land, its fruit trees, and its vines (vv 20-22). The people would rejoice, and with the blessing of the early and late rains the land would again be abundantly productive. The losses from the locust plague would be made good (vv 23-25). People would eat food in plenty and praise God. They would know that the one great living God was among them, and they would not be put to shame anymore (vv 26-27).

2:28-32 The prophet also saw that the blessing experienced in this renewal after the plague of locusts foreshadowed greater blessings to come, just as the judgment experienced brought the warning of the great and terrible Day of the Lord to come. God would do greater things for his people in the future; in particular, he would pour out his Spirit on men and women, young and old, slave and free (vv 28-29). There would be awe-inspiring signs in heaven and on earth (vv 30-31). All who called on the name of the Lord would know his salvation (v 32).

3:1-15 The meaning of the Day of the Lord for Israel as a nation and its significance for all nations must be realized. God's people would find restoration by turning to him; those who had scattered them, taken their land, and sold them as slaves would come under his judgment (vv 1-3). Tyre and Sidon and the Philistines especially would have to give account for what they had done, taking the Lord's silver and gold, removing his people from their land, and selling them as slaves to the Greeks. The sons and daughters of these slave traders would in turn be sold as slaves (vv 4-8). So the nations must be prepared for war—to melt their plowshares into swords and to beat pruning hooks into spears—but not for a battle between human armies. Those who have fought against the living God must reckon with him as a mighty warrior (vv 9-11). This mighty warrior is coming to execute judgment. The scene changes from a battleground to a court of justice; great crowds will stand before the Lord "in the valley of decision" on the Day of the Lord, which is a day of dread darkness for those who have made themselves enemies of the Almighty (vv 12-15).

3:16-21 After men have spoken and done their worst, God will speak and act. He will show himself to be his people's "refuge and strength" (v 16). Their city will then be kept from invasion by strangers (v 17). Their land will be wonderfully productive (v 18). Because of what Egypt and Edom have done in violence to Judah, they will be desolate (v 19). Israel will be avenged and restored, and to all it will be clear that the Lord's home is in Jerusalem with his people (vv 20-21).

This account of the contents of the book is based on the view that Joel experienced a plague of locusts in his day and that he saw this as a warning of a greater judgment of God to come. At the same time, he also spoke of a greater restoration and blessing when the people turned back to God with prayer and fasting. Others see the enemies throughout the book as human foes, at least in chapter 2. Some think of the whole book as prophetic of battles to come, and in particular of a final battle of the Lord against those who have made themselves his enemies. Some think of two prophets, or two parts of the book written at different times. But the view of the book taken above seems exposed to the fewest difficulties and makes good sense and meaning of the whole.

Message What can be said finally of the abiding significance of the message of Joel? His, like that of most of the OT prophets, was a message of mercy and judgment.

Such a catastrophe as a plague of locusts was a warning of God's judgment of all men and nations, within history and ultimately at the great Day of the Lord at the consummation of history, when all will be gathered before him. The message of Joel, with its challenge to repentance arising from the events of his time, can be set alongside the words of Jesus himself when he was asked about those who had suffered in the catastrophic events of his time. When asked whether they were worse sinners than others, he answered in the negative, but with the warning, "Unless you repent, you will all of you come to the same end" (Lk 13:5, NEB). The word of God through Joel called people to turn back to him to find his mercy; then to the assurance of mercy was added the hope of the greater things that God in his goodness would do. He would pour out his Spirit freely on all. These words of promise (Jl 2:28) were made more significant than any others in the book of Joel by their quotation in the NT in Peter's sermon on the day of Pentecost (Acts 2:16-21). They stand true for the Christian church ever since that beginning of their fulfilment, and with them stands Joel's great assurance that God makes his home in the midst of his people and that those who turn to him will never be ashamed.

See also Israel, History of; Prophecy; Prophet, Prophetess.

JOELAH Warrior who joined David at Ziklag in his struggle against King Saul. Joelah was one of David's ambidextrous archers and slingers (1 Chr 12:7).

JOEZER Warrior who joined David at Ziklag in his struggle against King Saul. He was one of David's ambidextrous archers and slingers (1 Chr 12:6). He was called a Korahite, which probably refers to his place of origin.

JOGBEHAH City in Gilead (Transjordan) built and fortified by Gad's tribe (Nm 32:35). During the period of the judges, Gideon, in his pursuit of the Midianites, circled to the east of Jogbehah in order to attack the unsuspecting camp of Midian at Karkor (Jgs 8:11). This ancient city is now identified with Khirbet el-Ajbeihat, seven miles (11.3 kilometers) northwest of Amman.

JOGLI Father of Bukki, a Danite leader who helped oversee the distribution of the Promised Land west of the Jordan River (Nm 34:22).

JOHA
1. Benjamite and one of Beriah's nine sons (1 Chr 8:16).
2. Tizite, the brother of Jediael and one of David's mighty men (1 Chr 11:45).

JOHANAN Name meaning "Yahweh has been gracious." It occurs also in the alternate form of Jehohanan. The name John is derived from these names. Several men of this name appear in the OT.

1. Son of Kareah (2 Kgs 25:23). Johanan was a Jewish leader, a contemporary of Jeremiah, and supportive of Gedaliah, the governor of Judah after the fall of Jerusalem (Jer 40:8, 13). He forewarned Gedaliah of Ishmael's plan to assassinate him (vv 13-16). When the warning was ignored and Johanan was refused permission to execute the would-be assassin, Gedaliah was murdered. Johanan took vengeance against Ishmael and rescued those who had been captured (41:14-18), but he was unable to pursue Ishmael. In fear of a Babylonian reprisal, he made plans to seek asylum in Egypt. Jeremiah, whom he consulted, gave God's word against this move (42:1-22), but Johanan was unwilling to take counsel (43:2-3). He led the Judeans, including Jeremiah and Baruch, to Egypt (vv 5-7).
2. Eldest son of Josiah, king of Judah (1 Chr 3:15). Possibly he died young, for he did not succeed his father on the throne, even though he was the firstborn.
3. Son of Elioenai (1 Chr 3:24), a descendant of Jehoiachin, one of the last kings of Judah.
4. Grandson of Ahimaaz. He was the father of Azariah, who served as high priest in the temple of Solomon (1 Chr 6:9-10).
5. Warrior from Benjamin's tribe. He joined David's special forces of 30 men at Ziklag (1 Chr 12:4). The special forces could shoot arrows and sling stones with either hand (v 2).
6. Gadite who joined David in the wilderness (1 Chr 12:8-12). He was also specially trained for war, in that he could handle both shield and spear, could endure hardship, and was quick on his feet.
7. Ephraimite whose son was a leader in the northern Kingdom during the regime of Pekah and protested against the enslavement of 200,000 Judeans (2 Chr 28:12; NLT "Jehohanan"), who were subsequently freed.
8. Son of Hakkatan ("the younger" or "the smaller"). The designation may be read as "Johanan the younger." He was head of a family who claimed their descent from Azgad (Ezr 8:12). He joined Ezra with 110 men in traveling from Babylonia to Judah.
9. Priest under Joiakim. He was one of the priests during whose ministry the Levites and priests formally registered (Neh 12:22). He is alternately called Jehohanan in Ezra 10:6 and Jonathan in Neh 12:11. *See* Jehohanan #4.
10. KJV spelling of Jehohanan, Tobiah's son, in Nehemiah 6:18. *See* Jehohanan #6.

JOHANAN BEN ZAKKAI* Leading Jewish sage at the end of the second temple period. His place of birth is not known; he went to Jerusalem to study, and after 18 years there spent some time in Galilee. Later, he returned to Jerusalem and taught "in the shadow of the temple." He encouraged the Pharisees among the priesthood rather than the Sadducees. During the siege of Jerusalem, he managed to leave, in a coffin according to one version. He was a prisoner of Vespasian, probably in AD 68, who gave him permission to settle in Jamnia. There he began quietly to lay the groundwork for the survival of Judaism without its temple.

See also Judaism; Pharisees.

JOHN (Person)
1. Father of Simon Peter and Andrew (Jn 1:40-42; 21:15-17). According to Matthew 16:17, Peter's father was named Jona (Jonas, Jonah). Either Jona was an alternate form of the name John or, more probably, two independent traditions existed regarding his name.
2. Member of the high priestly family who, along with Annas, Caiaphas, and Alexander, questioned Peter and John after the two apostles had healed a lame man (Acts 4:6).
3. According to the early church bishop Papias, a member of the larger group of Jesus' disciples outside the Twelve (cf. Lk 10:1). Known as "John the elder" (the presbyter), he is often credited with the authorship of 2 and 3 John (2 Jn 1:1; 3 Jn 1:1), although the term "elder" there more likely refers to John the apostle.
4. The apostle. *See* John, The Apostle.

5. The Baptist. *See* John the Baptist.
6. An early disciple known as John Mark, author of the second Gospel. *See* Mark, John.

JOHN, The Apostle

The apostle known as "the disciple whom Jesus loved"; author of the fourth Gospel, three epistles, and probably Revelation.

The apostle John has a high reputation among Christian people, and his influence has been felt throughout the centuries. Despite this, he is a surprisingly shadowy figure. When he appears in the pages of the NT, it is almost always in company with Peter or James, and if there is speaking to be done, it is usually his companion Peter who does it; thus, there is not a great deal on which to base a biography.

John's father's name was Zebedee, and John had a brother called James (Mt 4:21). Among the women at the cross, Matthew names Mary Magdalene, Mary the mother of James and Joseph, and "the mother of Zebedee's children" (27:56). Mark names the two Marys and adds Salome (Mk 15:40). This indicates that Salome may be the name of John's mother. If Matthew and Mark are naming the same women as does John, then Salome was Jesus' "mother's sister" (Jn 19:25). This would make John a cousin of Jesus. We cannot be certain of this, for there were many women there (Mt 27:55) and there is no way of being sure that Matthew, Mark, and John all name the same three. Many accept the identification, but we can scarcely say more.

John was among those whom Jesus called by the Sea of Galilee (Mt 4:21-22; Mk 1:19-20). This makes him one of the first disciples. It is also possible that he was the unnamed companion of Andrew when that apostle first followed Jesus (Jn 1:35-37). John was important in the little group around Jesus since he was one of three who were especially close to the Master. These disciples were selected to be with Jesus on many great occasions. John, along with his brother James and Peter, was present at the Transfiguration (Mt 17:1-2; Mk 9:2; Lk 9:28-29). Jesus also took just these three into the house of Jairus when he brought that man's daughter back to life (Mk 5:37; Lk 8:51). Before Jesus' arrest, it was this trio that he took to pray with him in the Garden of Gethsemane (Mt 26:37; Mk 14:33). Though the three were admonished for sleeping instead of watching in prayer, we must not overlook the fact that in that time of great difficulty, when Jesus faced the prospect of death on a cross, it was to these three that he looked for support.

There are other occasions when John is mentioned in the Gospels. Luke tells us of John's surprise when the miraculous catch of fish took place (Lk 5:9-10). This is especially noteworthy since John was a fisherman. Toward the close of Jesus' ministry, we find John coming to Jesus with Peter, James, and Andrew to ask when the end would come and what would be the sign when all things come to their climax (Mk 13:3-4). And on the last evening, Jesus sent Peter and John to prepare the Passover meal (Lk 22:8).

Passages like these show that John was highly esteemed among the apostles and that he stood especially close to Jesus. But there are indications that at first John was far from appreciating what Jesus stood for. When Mark gives his list of the Twelve, he tells us that Jesus gave to James and John the name "Boanerges," which means "sons of thunder" (Mk 3:17). Some in the early church understood this name as a compliment, thinking it meant that James's and John's witness to Jesus would be as strong as thunder. But most see it as pointing to their tempestuousness of character. We see this, for example, when John encounters a man who was casting out demons in Jesus' name. John instructs him not to, "for he isn't one of our group" (Mk 9:38; Lk 9:49).

Mark also tells us of an occasion when the sons of Zebedee asked Jesus for the two chief places in his kingdom, one to be on his right and the other on his left (Mk 10:35-40). Matthew adds the point that the words were spoken by the men's mother, but he leaves us no doubt that James and John were in on it (Mt 20:20-22). Jesus proceeded to ask them whether they could drink the cup he would drink and be baptized with the baptism he would receive. (Clearly, these are metaphors for the suffering Jesus would in due course undergo.) James and John affirmed that they could, and Jesus assured them that they would indeed do this. However, he gave them no assurance about their places in the Father's kingdom. (But it is plain that James and John would suffer for Christ.) At that time they also failed to understand the loving spirit that moved their Master and was required of them as well.

Another incident that shows the same tempestuous spirit is one involving Samaritan villagers who refused to receive the little band as they traveled. When James and John heard of it, they asked Jesus whether he wanted them to call down fire from heaven to consume the villagers (Lk 9:54). They were clearly at variance with Jesus, and indeed he rebuked them. But we should not miss the zeal they displayed for their Lord, nor their conviction that if they did call down fire it would come. They were sure that God would not fail to answer the prayer of those who asked for vengeance on the opponents of Jesus. There is zeal here and faith, though also a spirit of lovelessness.

The synoptic Gospels thus show us John as a zealous and loyal follower of Jesus. He is not depicted as gentle and considerate. At this time, he knew little of the love that should characterize a follower of Jesus, but he did have faith and a passionate conviction that God would prosper Jesus and those who served him.

John is not mentioned by name in the fourth Gospel, but there are passages that speak about "the disciple whom Jesus loved" (Jn 13:23; 19:26; 20:2; 21:7, 20). We are not told who this was, but the evidence seems to indicate that it was the apostle John. For example, there is an account of a fishing trip in chapter 21, with a listing of those who went fishing. It includes Peter, who must be ruled out as "the disciple whom Jesus loved" because he is often mentioned along with the beloved disciple. Thomas and Nathanael were there, but there seems to be no reason for seeing either as a likely candidate. Two unnamed men and the sons of Zebedee make up the remainder of the party. James is excluded as being the author because of his early death—around AD 44 (Acts 12:2). This leaves us with John or one of the unnamed men. John is favored by the fact that the beloved disciple is linked with Peter on a number of occasions (Jn 13:23-24; 20:2; 21:7). We know from the other Gospels that Peter and John (together with James) were especially close (see also Acts 3; 8:14; Gal 2:9). Of course, one of the unnamed disciples may have been the beloved disciple, but we have no reason to assume this. Further, such a supposition faces the problem of the omission of the name of John the apostle throughout the entire fourth Gospel. If John wrote this book, we can understand his not mentioning himself. But if it was written by someone else, why would that person omit all mention of a man as prominent in the apostolic band as the other Gospels show John to have been? In addition, if John is the author, it would explain why John the Baptist is called simply "John."

It is argued that "the disciple whom Jesus loved" is not the kind of title a man would naturally use of himself, but it must be said also that it is not the kind of title a man would naturally use of someone else, either. And it may be that John uses it in a modest fashion—partly because he did not want to draw attention to himself by using his name, and partly because he wanted to emphasize the truth that it was the fact that Jesus loved him that made him what he was.

If this identification may be accepted, we learn more about the apostle. We should not, of course, read the words "the disciple whom Jesus loved" as though they meant that Jesus did not love the other disciples. He loved them all. But as applied to John, they mean that he was indeed beloved, probably also that he recognized that he owed all he had and all he was to that love. That he was specially close to Jesus is indicated by the fact that he leaned on Jesus' breast at the Last Supper (Jn 13:23). It also tells us something of his relationship to the Master that he was at the cross when Christ was crucified and that it was to him that Jesus gave the charge to look after his mother (19:26-27). One would have expected that Jesus would have selected one of his family for this responsibility. But his brothers did not believe in him, whereas both John and Mary did. This event certainly shows that a close relationship existed between Jesus and the disciple he loved.

On the first Easter morning, John raced with Peter to the tomb when Mary Magdalene told them it was empty. He won the race but stood outside the tomb until Peter came. Peter, the leader of men, went right in, and John followed. We read that he "saw and believed" (Jn 20:8). Then in chapter 21 we read of the beloved disciple fishing with the others. Significantly, it was he who recognized that it was Jesus who stood on the shore and told them where to cast the net (21:7).

There is not much to add to this picture when we turn to Acts. At the beginning, John's name occurs in a list of the Twelve (Acts 1:13); and later, when we are told of James's death, it is noted that he was John's brother (12:2). In every other reference to John, he is in the company of Peter. These two were the instruments God used in bringing healing to a lame man (ch 3). At that time, they were going to the temple at the hour of prayer. This says something about their habits of devotion. Prayer at the ninth hour apparently refers to the Jewish service of prayer that was held at the same time as the evening offering (i.e., at about three o'clock in the afternoon). Evidently, Peter and John were continuing the devotional habits of pious Jews with an interest in the temple and all its doings. On another occasion, these two were arrested and jailed on account of their preaching about Jesus' resurrection (4:1-3). They were brought before the council, where Peter spoke for them. The council saw that these two men were "uneducated, common men" (v 13). This means that they had never had the normal rabbinic education. By the standards of the council, they were uneducated. The council forbade them to speak about Jesus, but the apostles' reply displays John's typical boldness: "Whether it is right in the sight of God to listen to you rather than to God, you must judge; for we cannot but speak of what we have seen and heard" (vv 19-20, RSV).

John was associated with Peter again when the gospel was first preached in Samaria. Philip was the evangelist to the Samaritans, but the apostles in Jerusalem decided to send Peter and John to Samaria when they heard how the people had accepted the gospel message. "As soon as they arrived, they began praying for these new Christians to receive the Holy Spirit" (Acts 8:15, TLB), a revealing illustration of apostolic priorities. In due course, they laid their hands on the new believers and they received the Holy Spirit (8:17). John is not specifically men-

tioned, but he no doubt was included in "the apostles" who were arrested and jailed because of the jealousy of prominent Jews (5:17-18). But that imprisonment did not last long, for an angel released them at night, so that they resumed their preaching in the early morning (v 21). John is mentioned by name in Galatians 2:9, where he is joined with Peter and James and the three are called "the pillars of the church."

This appears to be the extent of the NT's record of the apostle John. Clearly he was an important figure in the little band of early Christians. On almost every occasion when he comes before us in the record, he is in the company of someone else and normally the speaking is done by his companion, not by John. But we may justly conclude that he stood very close to Jesus. Perhaps he had entered into the mind of Jesus more than any of the others. The best evidence of this is the Gospel of John. Clearly the man who wrote this had great spiritual insight. John may have been more the thinker than a man of action and leader of men.

We have seen that there is good reason to think that the fourth Gospel was written by the apostle John. The epistles of John probably came from him also (though, as they stand, they are anonymous). All the Johannine writings probably emanated from the province of Asia. The heretics alluded to in 1 John resemble the Cerinthians (followers of the heretic Cerinthus), who were in Asia Minor at the end of the first century, and tradition connects the author of 1 John with Ephesus. It is certain that the same person wrote all three letters, and reasonably certain that this author also wrote the Gospel of John; the Gospel and the letters certainly represent the same mind at work in different situations.

An author named John wrote the book of Revelation (Rv 1:1), though it is not clear whether this is the apostle or another John. Tradition has identified the John of Revelation (see Rv 1:1, 9; 22:8) with John the apostle, the author of the Gospel of John and the three letters of John. This view was held by Justin Martyr as early as 140. The main objection to this view is that the original Greek is unlike that of the other Johannine writings, showing scant respect for the rules of the language. Some have suggested that a different John wrote Revelation, others that John's disciples wrote the Gospel and letters and that John himself wrote Revelation. But it is still plausible that the apostle John (or one of his close disciples) wrote the Gospel and the letters.

Assuming John the apostle wrote Revelation, he was exiled to Patmos (Rv 1:9). But the date of this is uncertain. Some probably unreliable evidence from the late fifth century suggests that John was martyred at about the same time as his brother James (c. 44; see also Acts 12:2). Jesus' prophecy in Mk 10:39 need not imply that both met with a simultaneous and violent end. Much stronger is the tradition reflected by Polycrates, bishop of Ephesus (c. 190), that John died a natural death in Ephesus, and by Irenaeus (c. 175–195) that John lingered on in Ephesus until the time of the emperor Trajan (ruled c. 97–117).

JOHN, Gospel of The fourth Gospel.

PREVIEW
•Author
•Date, Origin, and Destination
•Background
•Purpose and Theological Teaching
•Content

Author At the end of this Gospel we are told that it was written by "the disciple whom Jesus loved" (Jn 21:20,

Anicient Greek Manuscript of John Opening page of an entire codex Bodmer Papyrus II (late second century)—P66

24), but unfortunately the book nowhere tells us who this disciple was. Evidence shows that the most probable identification is with the apostle John. He fills the place we would have expected John to fill from what we know from the other Gospels. (See discussion above on John, the Apostle.)

The Gospel appears to have been written by one who knew the Jews and the Palestine of Jesus' day well. He was familiar with Jewish messianic expectations (e.g., Jn 1:20-21; 4:25; 7:40-42; 12:34). He knew of the hostility between Jews and Samaritans (4:9) and the contempt the Pharisees had for "the people of the land" (7:49). He knew of the importance attached to the religious schools (v 15). He knew the way the Sabbath was observed and was aware of the provision that the obligation to circumcise on the eighth day overrides the Sabbath regulations (vv 22-23). Throughout the Gospel he moved with certainty in the vast range of Jewish ideas and customs.

It is the same with topography. The writer mentioned many places, and his place-names all seem to be used correctly. He referred to Cana, a village not mentioned in any earlier literature known to us, which means that the reference almost certainly came from someone who actually knew the place. He located Bethany with some precision as about 15 stadia from Jerusalem (about 2 miles, or 3.2 kilometers, 11:18). He had several references to places in or near Jerusalem, such as Bethesda (5:2), Siloam (9:7), and the Kidron Valley (18:1). Of course, this does not rule out some contemporary of John's, but it makes it difficult to think of the author as a much later individual writing at a distance from Palestine. The evidence as we have it indicates that the writer was a Jew in the Palestine of Jesus' day.

To many careful readers, it seems that the Gospel bears the stamp of an eyewitness. For example, Jesus was teaching "in the treasury" (8:20). Nothing is made of the point; the incident could easily have been told without it. It looks like a reminiscence of someone who sees the scene in his mind's eye as he writes. The fact that the house was filled with fragrance when the woman broke the perfume jar (12:3) does not materially affect the account but is the kind of detail that one who was there would remember. The author noted that the loaves used in the feeding of the multitude were barley loaves (6:9) and that Jesus' tunic was seamless, woven in one piece from the top to bottom (19:23). He told us that the branches with which Jesus was greeted were palm branches (12:13), and that it was night when Judas went out (13:30). Such touches are found throughout the Gospel, and it seems unjustified to treat them as no more than an attempt to create verisimilitude. They seem much more like indications that the author was writing about events in which he had himself taken part.

The early church accepted Johannine authorship without question. Irenaeus, Clement of Alexandria, and Tertullian all see the apostle as the author. The first to quote this Gospel by name was Theophilus of Antioch, about AD 180.

Those who object to Johannine authorship emphasize the differences between this Gospel and the Synoptics. The argument is that if Jesus was anything like the Christ portrayed by Matthew, Mark, and Luke, he could not be like the Christ of the fourth Gospel. This is a completely subjective argument, ignoring the fact that any great man will appear differently to different people. The judgment of the church throughout the centuries has been that Jesus was large enough to inspire both portraits. To put the same point another way, we have no reason for holding that the first three Evangelists tell us all there is to know about Jesus. There is no contradiction. John simply brings out other aspects of Jesus' life and teachings.

While we cannot prove beyond all doubt that John the apostle was the author, we can say that there is more reason for holding to this view than to any other.

Date, Origin, and Destination It has been usual for conservatives and liberals alike to date this writing in the last decade of the first century or early in the second. Some liberal scholars have put it well into the second century, but this is not common, and it is remarkable that there has been such a considerable measure of agreement.

It is said that this Gospel is dependent on the Synoptics, which means that it must be dated sometime after them. But this argument has been widely abandoned in recent times. There is so much in John that is without parallel in the other three Gospels, and conversely so much in the other three that John might have used had he known it, that it is very difficult indeed to hold that this writer had any of the other Gospels before him when he wrote, or even that he had read them. Such resemblances as there are seem better explained by common use of oral tradition.

It is also argued that there is a very developed theology in John and that we must allow time for its development. Granted, the theology of this Gospel is profound, but this does not require that we must wait for it until the end of the first century. The theology of the Letter to the Romans is also profound, and there is no reason for dating that writing later than the 50s. On the ground of development, then, there is no reason for putting John later than Romans. Development is a slippery argument at best, for it usually takes place at uneven rates, and we have no means of knowing how fast it took place in the area where the author lived.

Other arguments for a late date are no more conclusive. For example, it is urged that the ecclesiastical system presupposed by the Gospel is too late for the time of the apostle John, and that the sacramental system of chapters 3 and 6 must have taken time to develop. But John does not mention any sacrament. It is true that many scholars think these chapters refer to baptism and the Lord's Supper, but the fact is that John mentions neither.

It is not surprising in view of the way the traditional arguments have crumbled away that many in recent times are arguing that John must have been written before the fall of Jerusalem in AD 70. If it were later, why does not John have some reference to it? Some of his language appears to be earlier. In 5:2 he says there "is" (not "was") a pool called Bethesda. And he often refers to the Twelve as Jesus' disciples, or "his" disciples, or the like. In later times Christians usually said "the" disciples, for they saw no need to say whose the disciples were. But in the early days, when Christians were in contact with rabbis (each of whom had his disciples), it was important to show that Jesus' disciples were in mind. It is important also that John makes no reference to any of the synoptic Gospels. The simplest explanation is that he had not seen them. They were not yet widely circulated.

None of this enables us to date this Gospel with precision. But the weight of evidence points to an early date (before AD 70).

The author was John the apostle, a Jew. However, the writing gives evidence of contact with Greek thought, for example, in the reference to Christ as "the Word" in chapter 1 and the translation of words like "rabbi" (1:38). It is almost universally held that such considerations compel us to see the work as originating in a center of Greek culture, and Ephesus has traditionally been favored. Before the end of the second century we have Irenaeus writing that John published the Gospel during his residence at Ephesus.

Some scholars point to similarities between John and the Odes of Solomon, which they think came from Syria. As there are also some resemblances in the language of Ignatius, bishop of Antioch in the early second century, this is held to show that John was written in Syria, probably at Antioch. Others again think that Egypt was the place, and they support this by pointing out that the oldest fragment of a manuscript of this Gospel was found there. There is no real evidence, and we are left with probabilities. There is much to be said for accepting the evidence of Irenaeus and seeing Ephesus as the place of origin, but we can scarcely say more.

There is no real indication of the intended destination. From 20:31 we learn that the book was written that the readers might believe that Jesus is the Messiah, God's Son, and that by believing they might have life. The Gospel, then, has an evangelistic aim. But it is also possible that "believe" means "keep on believing"—"go on in faith," rather than "begin to believe." That is to say, the book may have been meant from the beginning to build people up in the faith. Probably we should not distinguish between these aims too sharply. Both may well be in mind.

Background Several possible backgrounds to the Gospel have been suggested. The Greek interest is obvious, and this writing has sometimes been called the Gospel of the Hellenists. The suggestion is that we should look to Greek writings, perhaps the works of the philosophers or Philo of Alexandria, to find the right background against which to understand what John has written. This approach may be seen in the work of Rudolf Bultmann, who thought specifically of Gnosticism. Indeed, for Bultmann one of the sources of this Gospel was a discourse source that he thought was taken from non-

Christian Gnosticism. Not many have been prepared to follow Bultmann, but a number of recent commentators have discerned some form of Gnosticism as the backdrop to John.

While such views are put forward seriously, there are some substantial objections. One is that, despite the confident assertions of some scholars, Gnosticism has never been shown to be earlier than Christianity. In the form in which it comes before us in history, it is a Christian heresy, and of course, the Christian faith must appear before a Christian heresy is possible. Another objection is that there is a basic difference between the two systems. Gnosticism is concerned with knowledge (the very word is derived from the Greek word *gnosis,* "knowledge"). Its "redeemer" is one who comes from heaven with knowledge. But John does not subscribe to the view that man is saved by knowledge. The Redeemer comes to take away the sin of the world (1:29). Gnosticism tells people that life is an upward struggle; Christianity tells of a Savior who came down to raise them up. It is not easy to see any form of Gnosticism as the essential background to Christianity.

Much more significant is John's Semitic background. Especially important here is the OT, accepted as sacred Scripture by Jew and Christian alike. It lies constantly behind John's statements, and it must be studied carefully if John is to be understood. It is plain that John knew and loved the Septuagint, the translation into Greek of the Hebrew OT. Again and again, the Septuagint can be shown to lie behind what John says.

In modern times important discoveries have been made at Qumran, in the vicinity of the Dead Sea. Among the scrolls unearthed in the caves of this area are several that have affinities with John. Indeed, one of the interesting facts about the scrolls is that they have more parallels with John than with any other part of the NT, a fact difficult to explain if John was written late and at a distance from Palestine. The resemblances to the Qumran writings must be viewed with care, for there is often a linguistic resemblance where the thinking is quite different. For example, both use the unusual expression "the Spirit of truth." But where John means one of the persons of the Trinity, the scrolls speak of "a spirit of truth" and "a spirit of error" striving in the souls of people. The connection is real, but John is clearly not dependent on the scrolls for his thinking. The contribution of the Dead Sea Scrolls is that they afford additional evidence that this Gospel is basically Palestinian and must be understood against a background of first-century Palestine.

Other backgrounds have been suggested, such as the Hermetic literature. This is a group of writings attributed to Hermes Trismegistus ("Hermes Thrice-greatest"), a designation of the Egyptian god Thoth. There are indeed some points of contact with John, but they are few in comparison with those of writings rooted in Palestine. It is difficult to take such suggestions seriously. John is essentially Palestinian.

Purpose and Theological Teaching

The writer told us that Jesus did many "signs" (or miracles) that he had not recorded, but "these are written so that you may believe that Jesus is the Messiah, the Son of God, and that by believing in him you will have life" (Jn 20:31, NLT). John wrote to show that Jesus is the Messiah. But he did not do this simply with a view to conveying interesting information. He wanted his readers to see this knowledge as a challenge to faith; when they believe, they will have life. John sought to bring men and women to Christ; he had an evangelistic aim. That does not exhaust what he was trying to do, for his words have meaning for believers.

It is important that believers have a right knowledge of Jesus and that they continue to believe.

The main theological teaching of this Gospel, then, is that God has sent his Messiah, Jesus. He is the very Son of God, and he comes to bring life (3:16). Though Jesus told the woman at the well that he was the Messiah, this is not often said so specifically. The avoidance of the term might well be because of the political overtones it had acquired among the Jews at large. They looked for a Messiah who would fight the Romans. He would defeat them and set up a mighty world empire with its capital in Jerusalem. Jesus was not aiming at anything like that, and it was important that he avoid the kind of language that would give that impression. But though the conventional messianic terminology is avoided, John left no doubt that Jesus was God's chosen one. Again and again he depicted Jesus as fulfilling messianic functions. For example, in the long discourse in chapter 6 we see Jesus as the bread from heaven, fulfilling the expectation that when Messiah came, he would renew the manna; and in the giving of sight to the blind man (ch 9) we have another messianic function (cf. Is 35:5).

With this greatness of Jesus, John also combined teaching about his lowliness. A continuing, though unobtrusive, strand of Johannine teaching is that Jesus depends on the Father for everything. Apart from the Father, Jesus said, he could do nothing (Jn 5:30). His very food is to do the Father's will (4:34). He lives through the Father (6:57). It is the Father who gives him his disciples (6:37, 44; 17:6). It is the Father who bears witness to him (5:32, 37). John insists that Jesus is in no sense independent of the Father. In the mission of Jesus, John sees the working out of the purpose of the Father.

Content

Prologue and Chapter 1 John begins with a prologue (1:1-18) that is unlike anything in any of the other Gospels. In it he refers to Jesus as "the Word," a term that has points of contact with both Greek and Hebrew thinking. As John uses it, it conveys the thought that Jesus is the expression of the mind of the Father. John speaks of the Word as God (1:1), sees him as active in creation (1:3-5), goes on to the witness borne to him by John the Baptist (1:6-8), speaks of the coming of the Word into the world (1:9-14), and finishes with a section on the greatness of the Word (1:15-18). In this prologue he briefly introduces some of the great themes that will be developed throughout the Gospel. It is a majestic introduction to the whole.

Next we have the beginnings of Jesus' public ministry (1:19-51). Jesus' work was preceded by that of John the Baptist, and the Evangelist tells us first about the kind of witness that the Baptist gave to Jesus. Witness is one of his important concepts, and witness is all that John the Baptist does in this Gospel. From this witness we move to the way the first disciples came to Jesus. We learn something of how Andrew and Peter came to know the Lord. We read also of Philip and Nathanael, of whom we learn little or nothing in the other Gospels.

The Signs and Discourses (2:1–12:50) The public ministry of Jesus is described in a very distinctive way in this Gospel. John has a long section (chs 2–12) in which he tells of a number of miracles Jesus did, interweaving into his account a series of discourses. Sometimes these are addresses given to groups of people, and sometimes they are talks with individuals. Some scholars call this section of the Gospel the Book of Signs, thus emphasizing the prominent place given to seven miracles. For John they are not simply wonders. They are meaningful; in the literal sense of the term they are *significant*.

The first of them is the turning of the water into wine at a marriage in Cana of Galilee (2:1-11). The water in question is connected with Jewish rites of purification (v 6), and the story is surely to teach us that Jesus transforms life. He changes the water of the law into the wine of the gospel. As a result of this "sign," his disciples believed in him (v 11). John went on to tell how Jesus went up to Jerusalem and drove the traders out of the temple. They were selling animals for sacrifice and changing money. But their business was being done in the Court of the Gentiles, the only place in the temple where a Gentile could come to meditate and pray.

The first discourse is on the new birth (3:1-21). Jesus talked with Nicodemus, a leading Pharisee, about the necessity for radical renewal if one is to enter the kingdom. Jesus was speaking of God's regenerating activity, not some human reformation. Following this, John records a dispute between some of John's disciples with a Jew on the subject of purification. This opens the way for a section that shows the superiority of Jesus over John the Baptist—by the Baptist's own confession (3:22-36).

The second discourse is really a long conversation Jesus had with the woman of Samaria, whom he met by a well (4:1-42). It turns on "the water of life," a term that is not fully explained in this chapter but which we later find points to the life-giving Spirit (7:38-39). This leads to the story of the second sign, the healing of the nobleman's son (4:46-54), notable for the fact that Jesus healed at a distance.

The third sign is the healing of the lame man by the pool of Bethesda (5:1-18). This man had spent many years waiting for healing at the moving of the water. Jesus told him to get up and walk, and he did. Because it was done on a Sabbath, the Pharisees objected. This leads to Jesus' third discourse, that on the divine Son (5:19-47). Here the closeness of the relationship of Jesus to the Father is stressed, and his place in the judgment is brought out. There is emphasis also on the variety of witness who encountered Jesus, which shows how reasonable it is to accept him as God's own Son.

John's fourth sign is the one miracle (apart from the resurrection) found in all four Gospels: the feeding of the 5,000 (6:1-15). It is followed by Jesus' walking on water (vv 16-21), which seems to be meant as the fifth sign (though some scholars think not; if they are right, there are only six signs). Then comes the fourth discourse, the great sermon on the bread of life (vv 22-59). Jesus is this bread, which he gives to all men and women who believe in him. There are references to eating his flesh and drinking his blood (vv 50-58), which point to his death. Some have seen in them a reference to Communion, but it is hard to see why Jesus should refer in this way to an as-yet-nonexistent sacrament. Moreover, much the same effect is attributed in the same discourse to believing (vv 35, 47). It seems best to understand Jesus as meaning that people must believe in him as the one who would die for them in order for them to have life.

There is a section detailing Peter's affirmation of loyalty in the face of some who drifted away from the Master (6:67-71). Then we come to the fifth discourse, on the life-giving Spirit (7:1-52). John has an important explanatory point of his own when he tells us that at the time the Spirit had not been given because Jesus had not yet been glorified (v 39). The fullness of the Spirit depends on the completion of the work of Christ in his death and resurrection.

The sixth discourse tells of the light of the world (8:12-59). This aspect of Jesus' person and ministry is dramatically brought out in the sixth sign, the healing of the man born blind (ch 9). It is a lively narrative, as the healed man conducts a spirited defense against the Pharisees who belittled Jesus.

One of the most beautiful of all the illustrations of Jesus' relations to his people is that on which he dwells in the seventh discourse, where he speaks of himself as the good shepherd (ch 10). There is the obvious truth that sheep depend entirely on their shepherd, but Jesus says something else. Whereas earthly shepherds live to meet the needs of their sheep, Jesus laid down his life for his sheep.

The final sign is the raising of Lazarus (11:1-44), a man who had been dead for four days. The story graphically brings out Jesus' power over death and his readiness to confer the gift of life. Jesus speaks of himself as "the resurrection and the life" (v 25); death cannot defeat him. He brings life to the dead, to the spiritually dead as well as to physically dead Lazarus. John goes on to note the reaction to this miracle: some believed, but some opposed Jesus (vv 45-57). He includes a notable saying of Caiaphas, the high priest, that one man should die for the people (vv 50-52). Caiaphas was speaking as a cynical politician (better one dead, however innocent, than the whole nation be troubled). But John saw in the words the deeper meaning that Jesus' death would bring salvation to many.

John rounds off his account of the ministry with the story of the anointing of Jesus by a woman in Bethany, the triumphal entry into Jerusalem, the coming of some Greeks to Jesus, and his final summary of what he had taught (ch 12).

The Last Supper The account of what went on in the upper room on the night before the Crucifixion is the fullest of all the four Gospels. Curiously, John says nothing about the institution of Communion, a fact that has never been satisfactorily explained. But he tells us how Jesus washed the feet of the disciples (13:1-17), an action splendidly exemplifying the spirit of lowly service so soon to be shown on the cross. Then comes the prophecy of the betrayal, an action that set in motion the events that would lead to the cross (vv 18-30).

In the long discourse that follows, Jesus dealt with some questions posed by his followers and went on to teach them some important truths, for example, that he is the way, the truth, and the life (14:6). He develops the thought that he is the true vine, the disciples being vitally joined to him as branches to the vine. It is important for the branches to remain in the vine if they are to have life (15:1-16). Then come some words about suffering that would be of help to them in times of persecution (vv 17-25). Jesus goes on to speak about the Holy Spirit (15:26–16:15). This is a very important passage, for it contains much more about the Spirit than we find elsewhere in Jesus' words. Jesus calls the Spirit the "Paraclete," a title not easy to understand. It is in origin a legal term, and at least we can say that it indicates that the Spirit brings friendship, encouragement, and help. Jesus went on to speak of his approaching departure from the disciples and to prepare them for the trying time ahead (16:16-33). This part of the Gospel concludes with Jesus' great High Priestly prayer. He prayed for the disciples to be one, as he commended them to the care of the heavenly Father (ch 17).

The Cross and Resurrection When the soldiers came to arrest Jesus, he went forward to meet them and they fell to the ground (18:1-11). He gave himself over to them; they did not take him over. At the outset of his passion narrative, John was making the point that Jesus is sovereign. He was not being defeated by the march of events but was sovereignly doing the will of the Father. John is the only one to tell us that Jesus was taken before Annas, father-in-law to Caiaphas, the reigning high priest (18:12-14, 19-24). He tells also of Peter's three denials of Jesus (vv 15-27). He did not spend much time on the Jewish trial, but he was much more explicit than the other Evangelists in his account of the Roman trial. Clearly, he had some special knowledge of what went on before Pilate. He presents a magnificent picture of Jesus talking with Pilate about kingship—the Son of God discussing with the representative of Caesar the meaning of sovereignty (vv 33-40).

In his account of the Crucifixion John has a number of touches of his own, notably the way Jesus commended Mary to the care of the beloved disciple (19:26-27), the fact that the cry Jesus uttered as he died was "It is finished" (v 30), and the piercing of his side by a soldier's spear (vv 31-37).

John proceeds to the narrative of the burial (vv 38-42) and of the empty tomb (20:1-10). He speaks of appearances of the risen Lord to Mary Magdalene (vv 11-18), and to the disciples—both without (vv 19-23) and with Thomas (vv 24-29).

The final chapter, an epilogue, tells of a miraculous catch of fish (21:1-14) and goes on to the moving account of Peter's threefold declaration of love to Jesus and his restoration.

See also John, The Apostle.

JOHN, Letters of

Three brief epistles ascribed to John. Their brevity is deceiving, for they deal with profound and critical questions about the basic nature of Christian spiritual experience. The Johannine letters also provide interesting insight into the condition of the church at the end of the first century. Heresy is rearing its ugly head. Autonomy and church organization are reflected. The genuine nature of a committed and obedient relationship to God through Christ is powerfully and warmly portrayed and commanded.

PREVIEW
• The First Letter of John
• The Second Letter of John
• The Third Letter of John

The First Letter of John

Occasion and Purpose First John is a simple yet profound response to a heresy threatening the church. The methodology used is a careful and clear delineation of the truth as it is found in Christ. The two different positions—the correct and the incorrect—are clearly contrasted. The lines of demarcation are definitely drawn.

The letter, however, also has a positive purpose. The author wants his "children" to know the truth and respond in relationship to God, who was revealed in Christ: "We are writing these things so that our joy will be complete. This is the message he has given us to announce to you: God is light and there is no darkness in him at all" (1 Jn 1:4-5, NLT). The positive purpose is further designated in 5:20 (NLT): "And we know that the Son of God has come, and he has given us understanding so that we can know the true God. And now we are in God because we are in his Son, Jesus Christ. He is the only true God, and he is eternal life." The clear understanding of Christ—as being both God and man—is of highest importance to the author. The believers need to know this and remain in this truth, so that they can continue to abide in the Son of God and not be taken away from him by heretical teachings.

The Nature of the Opposition Assuming that the letter is written to contest the claims of the heretics provides interesting insights into their identity. According to 2:19, the opponents had been members of the Christian community but later had withdrawn to propagate their own beliefs.

The major christological error of the heretics was a denial of the humanity of Jesus, with the implication that he was not the Messiah. The false prophets in the world can be identified by their confession of Jesus: "This is the way to find out if they have the Spirit of God: If a prophet acknowledges that Jesus Christ became a human being, that person has the Spirit of God" (4:2, NLT). The opening verse of the letter sharply contests the denial of Jesus' humanity. The liar is identified in 2:22 (NLT) as the one "who says that Jesus is not the Christ. Such people are antichrists, for they have denied the Father and the Son."

The practical outcome of these positions was a moral irresponsibility that advocated a life of sin and disregard for others. John, therefore, needs to call these apostates back to a life of ethics and brotherly love in Christ.

The opposition has been identified in various ways. The emphasis on secret and esoteric knowledge points toward a Gnostic-type heresy. The denial of the humanity of Jesus points toward the docetic heresy. Cerinthus of Asia Minor (mentioned by Irenaeus) has often been associated with the opposition in 1 John.

Author Careful comparison of 1 John with the fourth Gospel reveals a marked resemblance in vocabulary, style, and thought. Characteristic words used by both works include "love," "life," "truth," "light," "Son," "Spirit," "advocate," "manifest," "sin," "world," "flesh," "abide," "know," "walk," and "commandments." Combinations of words such as "Spirit of truth," "born of God," "children of God," and "overcome the world" also point to a single author. There are also similarities in grammatical usage and patterns of expression. There are marked similarities in theological outlook as well.

It is difficult to deny the close relationship of the two writings. Those who have attempted to distinguish between the two have had to admit that the variations in style and theological method must have come from one who was closely related and deeply influenced by the writer of the other.

The traditional position on authorship has been that the apostle John was the author of both the Gospel and the letter. The opening words of 1 John point clearly in that direction: "The one who existed from the beginning is the one we have heard and seen. We saw him with our own eyes and touched him with our own hands. He is Jesus Christ, the Word of life" (1:1, NLT). This is clearly intended to let the readers know that the author was an eyewitness of the events.

The traditional position has been questioned on the basis of a quotation from Papias, who was bishop of Hierapolis in Asia Minor (AD 100–140). His comment, transmitted through Eusebius via Irenaeus, is "If anywhere one came my way who had been a follower of the elders, I would inquire about the words of the elders—what Andrew and Peter had said, or what Thomas or James or John or Matthew or any other of the Lord's disciples; and I would inquire about the things which Aristion and the elder John, the Lord's disciples, say." A number of significant commentators have argued for the existence of an elder or presbyter John in Asia Minor as distinct from the apostle John. Irenaeus, in *Against Heresies*, and the Muratorian Fragment (both from the end of the second century), however, assign 1 John to the apostle John.

His claim to be an eyewitness and his air of authority definitely point toward the apostle John as the author of the first letter. Tradition speaks of the advanced age of the apostle as he taught at Ephesus, and of his emphasis upon love among Christians to the very end of his life. First John reflects just such a situation.

Date The date for the composition of 1 John is usually placed near the end of the first century. This date is confirmed by the nature of the heresy condemned and by the references to it in Polycarp and Irenaeus. Greater precision in fixing the date is not possible with the evidence available.

Text The text of 1 John has been preserved rather well. The simplicity of the terminology and the clarity of its thought have contributed to this preservation. Three passages deserve mention in the discussion of text.

The words "all things" (2:20) are found in the nominative case in some manuscripts and in the accusative or objective case in others. The KJV translates the verse: "Ye know all things." Use of the nominative case, which then modifies "you"—"You all know"—is perhaps a better rendering. The emphasis is on the breadth of the distribution of knowledge and not on the completeness of it.

In 4:19 there is no object for the verb "love" in the earliest manuscripts. Some later manuscripts have inserted either "him" or "God" in this sentence (see NLT mg), and the KJV is dependent upon these manuscripts.

The most famous variant in 1 John is found in 5:7-8. "These three agree in heaven: the Father, the Word, and the Holy Spirit . . ." is clearly an interpolation added to the text at a fairly late date. The earliest reference comes from the Spanish heretic Priscillian, who died in AD 385. At a later date it was accepted into the Vulgate. Erasmus, who edited the first Greek Testament ever published, did not include the words on the basis of their absence in Greek manuscripts. The only two Greek manuscripts that contain the words were produced since that date. Thus modern translations have eliminated this verse.

Content Commentators are unable to agree on the specific plan and structure of the first letter. The simple terminology, the narrow range of vocabulary, the repetition of ideas, and the almost monotonous grammatical construction defy logical analysis in terms of outline and structure. Commentators have characterized the argument of the epistle as "spiral." The picture is that of a venerable and respected elder in the community sharing his wisdom without attempting to provide a closely reasoned argument.

Although chapter designations were not introduced into the text of the NT until AD 1228 and are often misleading divisions of thought, they do provide a convenient method for surveying the content of the letter. It should be noted that the letter also departs from the common letter style of the first century so vividly represented in the Pauline letters.

The first chapter is composed of an introduction and a discussion of walking in the light. The nature of God and man in relationship comes into sharp focus.

The introduction stands in the noble tradition of the prologue to the fourth Gospel and the prologue to the Letter to the Hebrews. With majestic profundity the basic dependability of the gospel message is declared. The author claims his status as an eyewitness of the one through whom the Father manifested himself. He claims that he is simply proclaiming the events in which he

himself participated. The emphasis on hearing, seeing, and touching (the frequent use of the perfect tense emphasizes the continuing results) takes the manifestation out of the ethereal and speculative realm and places it directly in the world of experience.

The purpose of the proclamation is fellowship (the Greek word is *koinonia*). This fellowship operates both on the horizontal plane between believers and on the vertical plane between believers and both Father and Son (1:3). The second element of purpose is "to make our joy complete" (v 4).

In the body of the letter the author moves immediately (1:5-10) to the definitive nature of God as light. God's nature as light has a number of significant implications. First, darkness has no place in God at all (v 5). Second, those who walk (live, conduct themselves) in darkness cannot be in fellowship with God (v 6). Third, a relationship with God (walking in the light) results in fellowship with other believers and cleansing from all sin by Jesus, his Son (v 7). Fourth, all have sinned, and denial of that fact does not change the truth (v 8). Fifth, acknowledgment of sin brings forgiveness and cleansing from the faithful and righteous God (v 9). Finally, denial of ever having sinned is a reflection upon God and proves that his word is not present (v 10).

Joy and fellowship are available only to those who walk in the light of God's presence. God—who is light through his Son, Jesus Christ (we are reminded of the prologue of the fourth Gospel, that the Word manifested light to all men)—solves the problem of sin and unrighteousness through forgiveness and cleansing.

The second chapter continues the thought of the final paragraph of chapter 1—the solution to the problem of sin—and then turns to a discussion of the new commandment and the threat of the antichrist.

In 2:1-6 the solution to the problem of sin in the presence of a pure God is expanded. Jesus Christ not only forgives sin and cleanses unrighteousness but also he is our advocate (the same word used in Jn 14–16 and transliterated "Paraclete") before God. Jesus had satisfied the requirements for complete reconciliation between God and humanity.

In response the believer is to keep his commandments. The third verse is the first of a number of verses that respond to one question: How can the believer know that all of this is true? The first test is that of obedience. The implications of the test of obedience is stated positively in verses 3 and 5 and negatively in verse 4. Verse 6 clearly points out that the model for the lifestyle of the believer is to be found in Jesus.

The second test of believing ("abiding in him") is outlined in verses 7-17. The second authentication is love for the brothers and sisters in the Christian community. The author clearly states that it is impossible to walk in the light of God and hate your Christian brother or sister at the same time. This is an expansion on the idea of fellowship in the light found in the opening verses.

After encouraging three different age groups (2:12-14—the reference may well be to stages in the Christian life rather than to chronological age groups), he warns them of the folly of loving the world (vv 15-17). The world consists of transient lusts and pride and is not a part of the Father, who is light. The only one who survives is the one who is obedient to the total will of God.

Then the author turns to the problem of the end times with its manifestation of the antichrist (2:18-27). The antichrists (note the use of the plural) once were members of the fellowship (v 19). Anyone who denies that Jesus is the Messiah falls into that category. The author further declares that it is impossible to deny Christ and embrace God (v 23). Those who are born of God have an anointing from him that enables them to recognize the lies of the antichrist (v 27).

The whole epistle to this point has revolved around the implications of walking with God, who is light. God's revelation of himself in Jesus provides clear direction and understanding to recognize the true and identify the false.

The last two verses of chapter 2 introduce the new topic for chapter 3, being "born of God" (2:29). The children of God do not fear the final revelation of God at the Second Coming. Instead, they anticipate it, for the full quality of their new birth will be made visible (3:2). The author pauses to revel in the function of God's love in our lives as his children (v 1).

The author quickly comes back from the joy of contemplating our status as children of God to the stark realities of the world in which we must live. The world about us is characterized by sin, which is now defined as lawlessness (3:4). Sin finds its origin in the devil, who "has been sinning from the beginning" (v 8). The children of the devil reveal their essential nature by living lawless lives—Cain is used as a model (vv 10-12).

Jesus, whose second appearance is noted in the opening verses, came the first time to take away sins (3:5) and destroy the works of the devil (v 8). Those who live in Jesus should live according to the pattern of their Father, who is righteous (v 7). The righteous lifestyle is characterized by purity (v 3) and cessation of sin (vv 7-9). The contrast between the two lifestyles is obvious (v 10).

The last half of chapter 3 turns to one of the expressions of righteousness—love for others in the Christian community. The negative was already introduced in verse 12 (Cain). Hatred of the brother is equivalent to murder (3:15). Indifference to the need of a brother or sister is also condemned (vv 17-18). The model for the love of the brother is Jesus, who laid down his life for us (v 16). The positive note is that love for one's brothers and sisters is evidence of being born of God—of passing from death into life (v 14). Again, the contrast between the children of God and the children of the devil is obvious.

The last half of chapter 3 highlights one of John's favorite emphases. "We know" is repeated in verses 14, 16, 19, and 24. In a world of uncertainties, John recognizes the great need for assurance. He thus outlines a variety of tests to establish and maintain assurance for the children of God.

The transition to chapter 4 occurs at the end of chapter 3: "We know he lives in us because the Holy Spirit lives in us" (v 24, NLT). Those who have the Holy Spirit need to distinguish between the Spirit of truth and the spirit of error. The doctrinal test is then outlined. Those who have the Spirit of God recognize that Jesus is God come in the flesh (4:2-3). False prophets who deny this have the spirit of the antichrist (v 3). Obedience to God enables the children of God to recognize and respond to the language of God (vv 4-6).

In verses 7-12 John speaks of the origin of love as coming from God who is love (4:8). That love was demonstrated unmistakably in Jesus (vv 9-10) in order to solve the problem of sin. The natural response of the children of God, then, is to love one another (v 11), to the end that God's love may be perfected (reach its designated goal) in us (v 12). In this paragraph being born of God, loving God, and knowing God are inextricably intertwined.

Verse 13 picks up the assurance note of verse 1: "God has given us his Spirit as proof that we live in him and he in us" (NLT). Futher assurance is given to those who recognize that Jesus is the Son of God and the Savior of the world, which leads us to know the love of God. The love of God flows through us to others and is an evidence of our relationship to God (4:14-21). The present assurance is so clear that even the fear of Judgment Day is obviated (vv 17-18).

In the final chapter, John turns to the interrelationship between love and righteousness. Those who are born of God do not find the commandments of God to be burdensome (5:3). The faith of the children of God enables them to find victory over the world that would hinder the fulfillment of commands (v 4). That faith rests in Jesus as the Son of God (v 5). Again, correct belief enters the picture: Jesus was fully human (v 6), and the Spirit bears witness to the reality of Jesus (vv 7-8). The result is a great inner certitude that God "has given us eternal life, and this life is in his Son" (v 11, NLT). Again, the line of demarcation between the one who has life and the one who does not is made crystal clear (v 12).

Verses 13-16 move from the possession of eternal life to certainty in prayer. A solid confidence in God brings answers to prayer (vv 14-15). Confidence also extends to prayer on behalf of others who are committing sin (now John defines sin as unrighteousness rather than the sin that leads to death, v 12); God will honor that prayer by giving life to the sinner (v 16).

The final verses are a reiteration of the major themes of the letter. The victory of the one who is born of God through the true God who has come to us in Jesus clearly differentiates the child of God from the life of the world under the power of the evil one. The shining note of assurance continues to the very end of the letter.

The Second Letter of John

Author, Setting, and Date Second John was written in a setting similar to that of 1 John. The author identifies himself as "the elder" and designates his audience as "the elect lady and her children" (2 Jn 1:1). The "elect lady" is probably a church and the "children" are the members of it. The closing greeting from "your elect sister" (v 13) confirms this analysis. This church was

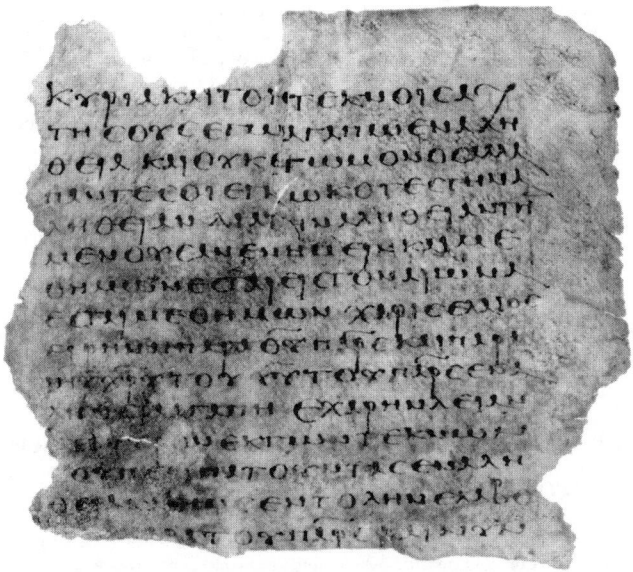

Ancient Greek Text of 2 John 2 John 1:1-5 in Manuscript 0232

harassed by the same heresies that were attacked in 1 John. The heresies are denounced, and the church is warned not to entertain the messengers of the heresy.

The grammar, style, and vocabulary of 2 John compare very closely to 1 John. Eight of the 13 verses of the second letter are almost identical with verses in 1 John.

Information concerning date of writing is inadequate to make any decision. The similarity to 1 John suggests a similar era.

The Message The message of the letter is twofold. In the first place, the members of the Christian community were urged to love one another (v 5). The nature of love is then defined as following his commandments (v 6). The second, and more compelling, element is the warning against the deceivers who refuse to acknowledge Christ and persuade others to do the same. Love indeed has its limits when it comes to even housing those who refuse to acknowledge Christ (vv 8-11). The deceivers are probably the same heretics identified in the first letter.

The letter closes with a promise of further communication in person. The purpose of the visit will be to complete one another's joy (cf. 1 Jn 1:4).

The Third Letter of John

Author, Setting, and Date Third John is also written in a similar setting. The occasion, however, is not the threat of heresy. The problem now is a certain Diotrephes, who is repudiating the authority of "the elder" and trying to frustrate his leadership. The letter is addressed to Gaius, who is still loyal to the elder. The elder asks Gaius to provide for the genuine missionaries who are passing through. In the thanksgiving section Gaius is commended for his faithfulness to the truth, especially as a "child" of the elder.

Again, we have insufficient information to establish date or additional setting. The familiar terminology and writing style tie it closely to the other two letters; as such, the author was probably John the apostle.

Message The burden of the letter is also twofold. The first paragraph (3 Jn 1:5-8) commends Gaius for his hospitality to the itinerant missionaries who are traveling "for the sake of the Name" (v 7), i.e., the Lord Jesus Christ. The missionaries have spoken well of Gaius's love for the church.

The main body of the letter warns against the insubordination of a certain Diotrephes. His love of power and authority has led him not only to defy the authority of the elder but also to convince others to follow his defiance or be excommunicated. He has refused to entertain the genuine itinerant preachers. Gaius is warned not to be influenced by Diotrephes' example.

The conclusion reflects the anticipation of an immediate personal visit. Normal greetings conclude the little letter.

See also John, the Apostle.

JOHN, The Revelation of *See* Revelation, Book of.

JOHN HYRCANUS* Hasmonean ruler of the Jewish people from 135 to 105 BC. *See* Hasmonean.

JOHN MARK *See* Mark, John.

JOHN OF GISCHALA* Leader in the first Jewish revolt, from Gischala (Gush-halab) in Galilee. He was a rival of Josephus Flavius, who had been appointed commander of Galilee by the Jews. When Vespasian sent his son Titus against Gischala in AD 67, John fled to Jerusalem and took part in the defense of the city. Eventually,

he surrendered to the Romans and was imprisoned in Italy. *See* First Jewish Revolt.

JOHN THE BAPTIST Forerunner of the Messiah who prepared the people for Jesus' coming, proclaimed the need for forgiveness of sins, and offered a baptism symbolizing repentance. His ministry included the baptism of Jesus in the Jordan River, where he testified to Jesus being the Expected One from God. John was arrested and beheaded by Herod Antipas in approximately AD 29, while Jesus was still ministering.

PREVIEW
• Birth, Infancy, and Boyhood
• Appearance and Identity
• John's Proclamation
• John's Baptism
• John's View of Jesus
• Jesus' View of John
• Arrest, Imprisonment, and Martyrdom
• The Disciples of John

Birth, Infancy, and Boyhood Luke's Gospel is our only source of information concerning the birth and boyhood of John. The Gospel writer states that John was born in the hill country of Judah (Lk 1:39) of priestly descent, being the son of Zechariah, a priest of the order of Abijah, and Elizabeth, a descendant of Aaron (v 5). Both parents were righteous in the sight of God, following all the commandments closely (v 6). Like the birth of Jesus, only to a much lesser degree, the birth of John the Baptist is described in Luke as extraordinary. The angel Gabriel announced the coming birth to Zechariah in the temple; to the older, barren Elizabeth it came as an answer to prayer (vv 8-13). John's name is announced to Zechariah by the angel, even as his purpose as forerunner is revealed before birth (vv 13-17). Such a consecration from birth is reminiscent of the call of the OT prophet Jeremiah (cf. Jer 1:5).

There existed some familial relationship between the families of John and Jesus. Elizabeth is described as a relative of Mary (Lk 1:36), which may connote cousin or aunt, or may only mean being from the same tribe.

John's childhood, as that of Jesus, is left quite vague in the Gospel account. All that is said is that "John grew up and became strong in spirit. Then he lived out in the wilderness until he began his public ministry to Israel" (Lk 1:80, NLT). Some scholars have suggested that John might have been adopted as a boy by the Essenes (as was their practice) at Qumran and reared in their wilderness community, adjacent to the Dead Sea and near the Jordan River. There are some similarities between the activities of the Qumran sect, known through the Dead Sea Scrolls, and the later ministry of John the Baptist. Both practiced a type of asceticism and removed themselves from the life of Jerusalem. Both practiced baptism and associated this rite with initiation and repentance. Finally, John and the Qumran group were both eschatologically minded, awaiting God's final end-time activity in history. Nevertheless, many significant differences exist between John and the Qumran sect.

Appearance and Identity Mark's Gospel begins with an account of John the Baptist's appearance: "John the Baptist . . . lived in the wilderness and was preaching that people should be baptized to show that they had turned from their sins and turned to God to be forgiven" (Mk 1:4, NLT). A rich OT background lies behind John's association with the wilderness, in this case the wilderness of Judea. It was in the wilderness that God revealed himself to Moses (Ex 3), gave the law, and entered into the covenant with Israel (ch 19). It was also the site of refuge for David (1 Sm 23–26; Ps 63) and Elijah (1 Kgs 19), and in this light became the anticipated site of God's future deliverance (Is 40:3-5; Ez 47:1-12; Hos 2:14-15).

The unusual dress of John the Baptist—"clothing made of camel's hair, with a leather belt around his waist" (Mk 1:6, NIV)—may have suggested to his audience an association with Elijah in particular (2 Kgs 1:8) or with the prophets in general (Zec 13:4). His diet, "locusts and wild honey" (Mk 1:6), was Levitically clean, reflecting one who lived off the desert (such food was also eaten at Qumran) and formed part of the broader asceticism practiced by John and his disciples (Mt 9:14; 11:18).

Who did John understand himself to be? In answer to questions by the multitude whether he was the Messiah, Elijah, or the expected prophet (Jn 1:20-23), John only identified himself as "a voice crying in the wilderness, 'Prepare the way of the Lord' " (Is 40:3). The background for the question lies at the end of the OT period. Prophecy, on the one hand, was considered to have ceased (Zec 13:2-6); yet, on the other hand, it was expected to appear again before the coming of the messianic kingdom (see Jl 2:28-29; Mal 3:1-4). Some anticipated this final prophet to be one who was like Moses (Dt 18:15), others a returning Elijah as foretold in Malachi 4:5-6. While John personally refrained from identifying himself with these specific expectations (Jn 1:20-23), it is clear that his dress, lifestyle, and message caused the people to identify him with this end-time prophet (Mt 14:5; Mk 11:32). Jesus also saw John as this final "Elijah-like" prophet (Mt 11:7-15), who from Malachi's prophecy was to be a forerunner to the coming of the Lord (Mal 3:1-4; 4:5-6).

John's Proclamation John's proclamation involved three elements: a warning of imminent judgment at the hands of the Coming One, a call for repentance in light of the coming kingdom of heaven, and a demand to express this repentance in concrete ethical terms. Many Jews looked forward confidently to the messianic judgment as a time of blessing for themselves and destruction for the gentile oppressors. John, however, warned that Jewish ancestry was false security in the coming judgment (Lk 3:8); true repentance was the only means of escaping destruction (Mt 3:2). John anticipated this judgment at the hands of the Coming One, who would baptize the nation with "the Holy Spirit and with fire" (Lk 3:16). Fire represented the OT means of destruction in the end time (Mal 4:1) as well as purification (Mal 3:1-4), while the outpouring of the Holy Spirit in the end time connoted blessing (Is 32:15; Ez 39:29; Jl 2:28) and purification (Is 4:2-4). The judgment anticipated by John was therefore twofold: destruction for the unrepentant, and blessing for the penitent and righteous (Mt 3:12).

In light of this imminent event John called for repentance on the part of his listeners (Mt 3:2), a true "turning back" or "turning toward" God in obedience that would bring forgiveness of sin. Such a turnabout in an individual's relation with God should be lived out in one's everyday dealings: fairness on the part of tax collectors (Lk 3:12-13) and soldiers (v 14), and the general requirement of compassion for the poor (vv 10-11).

John's Baptism The Gospels record that John baptized those repentant of their sins at several locations: the Jordan River (Mk 1:5), Bethany beyond the Jordan (Jn 1:28), and Aenon near Salim (Jn 3:23). This practice was an integral part of John's call for repentance, given in light of the approaching judgment and the appearance of the Coming One. The baptism of the penitent symbolized desire for forgiveness of sin, a renunciation of past life, and a desire to be included in the coming messianic kingdom.

What was the background for John's practice of baptism? From the OT we know of ceremonial lustrations or washings that guaranteed ritual purity (Lv 14–15; Nm 19). Unlike John's baptism, these washings were repetitive in nature and referred predominantly to ritual rather than moral cleansing. The prophets, however, urged a moral purification associated with the washing of water (Is 1:16-18; Jer 4:14). More significantly, the prophets anticipated a cleansing by God in the end times preceding the Day of Judgment (Ez 36:25; Zec 13:1; cf. Is 44:3), an eschatological element that John may have assumed was being fulfilled in his water baptism.

Another precedent for John's practice may have been proselyte baptism, a rite (along with circumcision and the offering of sacrifices) that constituted the conversion of a Gentile to Judaism. Common to both proselyte baptism and John's baptism were the emphasis on an ethical break with the past, a once-for-all character, and the similarity of immersion. Notable differences were that John's baptism was for Jews, not Gentile converts, and that it had a marked eschatological character as a preparation for the new age. Unless John, in light of the imminence of the messianic age, consciously treated all Jews as "pagan" in need of a baptism of repentance (cf. Mt 3:7-10), it is doubtful that proselyte baptism formed the primary background for John's baptismal ministry.

If John's baptism had a clear association with the forgiveness of sin, the question naturally arises as to why Jesus, the Son of God, sought baptism from John. John himself asks this very question of Jesus (Mt 3:14), to which Jesus responds, "It must be done, because we must do everything that is right" (v 15, NLT). First, it is clear that Jesus' baptism represented an act of obedience on his part to God's will as he saw it. Second, by submitting to the baptism of John, Jesus was clearly validating the ministry and message of John. The imminent coming of the kingdom and its Messiah, and the need for repentance in anticipation of this event that John proclaimed, were affirmed by Jesus through baptism. Third, by being baptized, Jesus condemned the self-righteous for their lack of repentance and took a stand with the penitent publicans and sinners awaiting the kingdom of God (Lk 7:29-30). Fourth, Jesus stepped forward for baptism not as an individual in need of forgiveness but as one who represented the people of God. His baptism, therefore, demonstrated solidarity with the people in their need of deliverance, even as he is judged in their place on the cross. Finally, the voice from heaven (Mk 1:11) and the descent of the Spirit (Lk 3:21-22) signify the inauguration of Jesus' own ministry through his baptism by John.

John's View of Jesus Throughout his ministry John pointed beyond himself to one "who is far greater than I am—so much greater that I am not even worthy to be his slave" (Mk 1:7, NLT). His self-understanding apparently sprang from the application of Isaiah 40:3 to himself, that he was the preparer or forerunner for God's coming activity through the Messiah (Lk 3:4-6). When asked by curious spectators, John firmly denied that he was the Messiah, and according to the Gospel accounts, subordinated himself to the Coming One (Mk 1:7-8; Jn 1:26-28; 3:28-31). The coming of Jesus to baptism seems to represent the first time John identified these expectations with Jesus himself (Jn 1:35-36). His recognition of Jesus as the Messiah prior to baptism (Mt 3:14) was confirmed by the descent of the Holy Spirit as a dove and the voice from heaven quoting a phrase from an OT messianic psalm (Mk 1:11a, from Ps 2:7), together with a phrase from a Suffering Servant song of Isaiah (Mk 1:11b, from Is 42:1). In the fourth Gospel, John the Baptist goes even further in acknowledging Jesus to be the "Lamb of God" (Jn 1:29), in anticipation of Jesus' sacrificial role on the cross. And John recognized him as "God's Chosen One" (v 34, NEB—another term for the Messiah; Ps 2:7, see Mk 1:11).

In light of John's strong affirmation, it is at first difficult to understand his questioning of Jesus while imprisoned: "Are you he who is to come, or shall we look for another?" (Mt 11:3, RSV). Some have suggested that John was merely asking for the sake of his disciples, or that the question reflected John's despondency with being imprisoned. It is more likely, however, that the question represents John's own confusion with the activity expected of the Messiah. John had proclaimed a Coming One who would bring a baptism of fire and judgment upon the wicked (Lk 3:16). It may have been difficult for him to understand Jesus' different emphases on forgiveness and acceptance of sinners (Mt 9:9-13) and his healing of the sick (Mt 8–9). When John's disciples brought their master's question to Jesus, asking whether or not he was the Messiah, Jesus responded by quoting Isaiah 35:5-6 (see also Is 61:1). This text proclaims the activities of healing and proclaiming salvation to the poor to be fulfillments of the Messiah's role, even though they may not have been what John or countless other Jews expected.

Jesus' View of John That Jesus highly regarded John the Baptist is indicated by his baptism by John. It is also explicitly stated on several occasions. Jesus called him the greatest man to have ever lived (Lk 7:28). (Of course, he was not as great as Jesus, the God-man.) Jesus also said that John was a burning and shining lamp (Jn 5:33-35) and that he practiced a baptism divinely ordained (Lk 20:1-8).

John's uniqueness, however, lies in the fact that he stood at the turning of the ages. He was the last of the old era, the period of the law and the prophets (Lk 16:16), which was to precede the coming of the messianic age (the kingdom of God). John was the last of the prophets, the greatest of them, the Elijah figure who would prepare the way for the judgment of God (Mt 11:13-15; Lk 1:17). Because John belonged to the era of the law and the prophets, however, he was not as great as the "least" already in the kingdom of God (Mt 11:11)—that is, those who belonged to the era of the kingdom's appearance in Jesus.

Arrest, Imprisonment, and Martyrdom To understand why John was arrested and beheaded by Herod Antipas, one has to grasp the messianic excitement caused by John's appearance and message (Lk 3:15-18). Herod and other secular rulers were obviously suspicious of anyone who might stir up the crowds with predictions of a coming messianic ruler. Other messianic movements had arisen before John, which resulted in outbreaks of violence against the Roman-Herodian rulership. Moreover, Herod Antipas was under heavy criticism for his marriage with Herodias, the ex-wife of his brother Philip. His first marriage, with the daughter of Aretus II, constituted a political alliance between the Herodian family and the Nabatean kingdom of Perea. His new relationship with Herodias was perceived as a breach of the political alliance and led to friction between the two families. John's denunciation of Herod's new marriage (Mt 14:3-12) could thus have been interpreted by Herod as a subversive rousing of sentiment against his authority. The Jewish historian Josephus states that Herod did, in fact, arrest John because he feared John's influence over the crowds. According to Josephus, John was imprisoned at the fortress Machaerus on the eastern side of the Dead Sea. That he was not killed immediately was due to Herod's personal fear of the righteous John (Mk 6:2) and of the people's reaction (Mt 14:5). On a point about which Josephus is silent, the Gospels record that it was Herodias's feelings against John (Mk 6:17) and her plot, through the dancing of her daughter, which brought about the beheading of John (vv 21-29). John was beheaded at Herodias's request in approximately AD 29 or 30.

The Disciples of John While it is clear that a band of disciples formed around John in his lifetime (Jn 1:35), to suggest that he intended to begin a continuing movement is contradicted by his message on the imminent Day of Judgment. Apparently, John's disciples consisted of a small group of those who had been baptized by him and were awaiting the coming Messiah. Some transferred their loyalty to Jesus after John had identified Jesus as the Coming One (Jn 1:37). Others, however, apparently stayed on with their teacher, communicating with the imprisoned John concerning the activities of Jesus (Lk 7:18-23) and, after his death, taking the body for burial (Mk 6:29).

We know little about the activities and practices of the band of disciples clustered around John. We do know, however, that fasting was one practice specifically associated with the group, and one that marked them as similar to the Pharisees (Mt 9:14). In this practice they no doubt followed the example of John himself (Lk 7:33). Prayer and fasting were often linked in late Judaism. The disciples of John were also known for the prayers taught by their master (11:1). Seeing this practice, the disciples of Jesus asked the Lord to teach them to pray, to which Jesus responded with the Lord's Prayer (vv 2-4).

After his death it is likely that other disciples of John joined the followers of Jesus (see Lk 7:29-30). Not all did so, however, as disciples of John were encountered by Paul and other Christians approximately 25 years later in Ephesus (Acts 18:24–29:7). Upon hearing witness to Jesus, these followers of John proclaimed Jesus as Messiah. When Paul baptized them in the name of Jesus they received the Holy Spirit (19:4-7). Even so, it is apparent from later documents that various groups continued to honor John, even considering him the Messiah, centuries after the NT period.

JOIADA

1. Paseah's son who, with Meshullam, repaired the Old Gate in the Jerusalem wall during the days of Nehemiah (Neh 3:6).
2. Levite and high priest in Jerusalem during the postexilic era, the great-grandson of Jeshua, son of Eliashib, and father of Jonathan ("Johanan" or "Jehohanan," Neh 12:10-11, 22). He is alternately called Jehoiada in Nehemiah 13:28, where we read that one of his sons was expelled from the priesthood for marrying a daughter of Sanballat, governor of Samaria.

JOIAKIM
Levite high priest in a family of high priests. Jeshua's son and the father of Eliashib the high priest, a contemporary of Nehemiah (Neh 12:10-12, 26).

JOIARIB

1. One of the Jewish leaders whom Ezra sent to Iddo at Casiphia to gather Levites and temple servants for the caravan of Jews returning to Palestine from Babylon

(Ezr 8:16). He is alternately called Jehoiarib in 1 Chronicles 9:10.

2. Zechariah's son, the father of Adaiah, and an ancestor of a Judahite family that resettled in Jerusalem during the postexilic era under Nehemiah (Neh 11:5).
3. Father of Jedaiah, a priest who served in the temple during the days of Nehemiah (Neh 11:10). Perhaps Joiarib's forefather was Jehoiarib, who was the head of the first course of priests ministering in the sanctuary during David's reign (1 Chr 24:7; cf. 9:10).
4. One of the leaders of the priests who returned with Zerubbabel and Jeshua to Judah after the exile (Neh 12:6). His family in the next generation was headed by Mattenai (v 19).

JOKDEAM One of the cities located in the hill country allotted to Judah's tribe for an inheritance, mentioned between Jezreel and Zanoah (Jos 15:56).

JOKIM Descendant of Judah through Shelah's line (1 Chr 4:22).

JOKMEAM
1. City mentioned in 1 Kings 4:12 (KJV "Jokneam"); seemingly close in proximity and perhaps the same as Jokneam. See Jokneam.
2. City given to the Kohathite Levites out of Ephraim's inheritance (1 Chr 6:68). A parallel passage in Joshua 21:22 lists the city as Kibzaim. See Kibzaim.

JOKNEAM Royal Canaanite city belonging to Carmel (Jos 12:22), mentioned also by Thutmose III as "the Well of Q." The border of Zebulun touched on the stream near Jokneam (19:11); the town became a Levitical city in Zebulun (21:34). Some think that Jokmeam of 1 Kings 4:12 should be amended to Jokneam, but this is not certain. Eusebius placed it six miles (9.7 kilometers) from Legio (beside Megiddo) on the way to Ptolemais. This is Tell Qaimun, at the mouth of Wadi Milh on the edge of the Jezreel Valley.
See also Levitical Cities.

JOKSHAN Son of Abraham and Keturah, and the father of Sheba and Dedan (Gn 25:2-3; 1 Chr 1:32).

JOKTAN Eber's son and younger brother of Peleg. A number of Arabian groups descended from him (Gn 10:25-29; 1 Chr 1:19-23).

JOKTHEEL
1. Town in the Shephelah of Judah near Lachish (Jos 15:38).
2. Ancient Edomite stronghold originally named Sela. Amaziah changed its name to Joktheel after defeating the Edomites (2 Kgs 14:7).

JONA* KJV form of John, father of Simon Peter and Andrew, in John 1:42. See John (Person) #1.

JONADAB
1. King David's nephew, the son of David's brother Shimeah. As a friend to David's son Amnon, he devised a scheme by which Amnon seduced his half sister Tamar (2 Sm 13:3-5). Absalom, Tamar's brother, sought revenge, eventually killing Amnon.
2. Recab's son; descendant of the Kenites (1 Chr 2:55; NLT "Jehonadab"). He founded the religious order of Recabites, who maintained a nomadic tradition. He encouraged Jehu in his bloody reform of the house of Ahab (2 Kgs 10:15, 23).

JONAH (Person) Prophet of Israel; Amittai's son (Jon 1:1) of the Zebulunite city of Gath-hepher (2 Kgs 14:25). The historian who wrote 2 Kings recorded that Jonah had a major prophetic role in the reign of King Jeroboam II (793–753 BC). Jonah had conveyed a message encouraging expansion to the king of Israel, whose reign was marked by prosperity, expansion, and unfortunately, moral decline.

In the midst of all the political corruption of Israel, Jonah remained a zealous patriot. His reluctance to go to Nineveh probably stemmed partially from his knowledge that the Assyrians would be used as God's instrument for punishing Israel. The prophet, who had been sent to Jeroboam to assure him that his kingdom would prosper, was the same prophet God chose to send to Nineveh to forestall that city's (and thus that nation's) destruction until Assyria could be used to punish Israel in 722 BC. It is no wonder that the prophet reacted emotionally to his commission.

No other prophet was so strongly Jewish (cf. his classic confession, Jon 1:9), yet no other prophet's ministry was so strongly directed to a non-Jewish nation. Jonah's writing is also unusual among the prophets. The book is primarily historical narrative. His actual preaching is recorded in only five words in the Hebrew—eight words in most English translations (Jon 3:4b).

See also Israel, History of; Jeroboam #2; Jonah, Book of; Prophet, Prophetess.

JONAH, Book of Fifth book of the 12 Minor Prophets in the traditional arrangement of the books of the OT. It is a literary narrative rather than a series of prophetic oracles, and it gives the account of Jonah's experiences after he disobeyed a command from the Lord directing him to preach to the people of Nineveh. Several extraordinary events recorded in the book have made it the center of much controversy as to its interpretation.

PREVIEW
• Author
• Authenticity
• Date
• Purpose
• Content

Author The book of Jonah has been traditionally ascribed to Jonah the son of Amittai, a prophet of great influence, who ministered during the reign of Jeroboam II of Israel (2 Kgs 14:25).

The content of the book describes Jonah as an intensely patriotic person, but his misguided patriotism caused him to rebel at the possibility of Israel's former enemies receiving forgiveness from God. One of the most important lessons of the book emerges when God rebukes Jonah's exclusivistic attitude (Jon 4:6-11).

Jesus used two of the experiences of Jonah as signs to his generation. The three days and nights spent by Jonah in the great fish served as an analogy of Jesus' death and resurrection (Mt 12:38-41). Also, the positive response of the Ninevites to Jonah's preaching was used by Jesus as a condemnation of the failure of many in his generation to believe in him (Lk 11:32).

Authenticity The unusual elements in the book of Jonah have led to widely varying views of its nature. Not only has the account of Jonah being swallowed by the fish led some to think the book to be of a fabulous nature, but the account of the repentance of the people of Nineveh (Jon 3:5) also has been regarded as highly unlikely.

The historicity of the book has been championed by outstanding biblical scholars. The basic approach of these scholars has been to counter the arguments of those who deny its historicity and to point to what is regarded as positive evidence for the historicity of the book in Jesus' allusions to the prophecy and in early Jewish tradition.

Opponents of the authenticity of Jonah point to the following difficulties: (1) The use of the expression "king of Nineveh" (3:6) appears to be an inaccuracy because Nineveh was the capital of Assyria. A contemporary would have referred to the king as the king of Assyria. (2) The use of the past tense to describe the city of Nineveh (v 3) seems to point to a much later date than the traditional view of the authorship of the book would permit. (3) The size of the city of Nineveh is described in greatly exaggerated terms (v 3). (4) The mass repentance of the Ninevites lacks historical support. (5) It is unlikely that a human being could exist within a fish for an extended period of time.

With regard to the use of "king of Nineveh," it should be noted that similar expressions may be found in the OT. Ahab, the king of Israel, is called "king of Samaria" (1 Kgs 21:1), and Ben-hadad, the king of Syria, is designated "king of Damascus" (2 Chr 24:23). The designation "king of Nineveh" is therefore not anomalous.

The use of the past tense to describe the city of Nineveh may be regarded as nothing more than a simple narrative past tense describing the size of the city at the time that Jonah prophesied there.

The description of the size of the city ("three days' journey") may be an indication of the length of time that it would take one to go through the suburbs included in the administrative district of Nineveh.

The repentance of the Ninevites is not to be understood as a mass conversion to Yahweh, the God of Israel. The book of Jonah describes their response as repentance in view of the impending destruction threatened by Jonah (Jon 3:4). While secular history does not record such an event, there is evidence that such a response was possible. In less than a decade (765–759 BC) the city of Nineveh had experienced a total eclipse of the sun and two serious plagues. One can understand how the citizens of Nineveh may have been prepared for the preaching of this prophet who came to them in such an unusual way.

It should also be noted that one of the kings of Assyria, Adad-nirari III, limited his worship to the god Nebo. If the prophetic ministry of Jonah was active during the time of his reign (810–783 BC), it is possible that the Jewish monotheism represented by Jonah may have found a more favorable climate than one would normally expect in a pagan society.

The participation of the animals in the national penitence that followed Jonah's preaching (3:7-8) is not unknown from history. The historian Herodotus records a similar event in the Persian Empire.

The event that creates the greatest difficulty, however, is the experience of Jonah in the fish. It has often been pointed out that the gullets of most whales are not large enough to admit an object the size of a man. But the book does not say that it was a whale that swallowed Jonah, but simply a great fish (1:17). Even so, it is possible for a sperm whale to swallow an object as large as a man.

Numerous examples of individuals being swallowed by whales have been cited in the past. While many of these accounts may be disregarded as fancy, it would be wrong to uncritically reject all of them. (An interesting account of one of these experiences may be found in the

Princeton Theological Review 25, 1927, p. 636.) The experience of Jonah in the great fish need not be regarded as an absolute impossibility. The activities of God in history have often been accompanied by unusual or miraculous events.

The difficulties of the book of Jonah have led many to regard the book as a prophetic parable rather than a record of historical fact. The most common interpretation is that the book is an expression of the universal concerns of God. As such, it inveighs against the exclusive nationalism of the Jews. This narrow-minded attitude, some suggest, fits best into the postexilic period, when the hatred of Israel for its former captors was still very bitter.

There are several difficulties with this view. While there are a number of parables in the OT, none is as extensive as the book of Jonah. Also, since the major elements of a parable symbolize persons, objects, or concepts that contribute to the main teaching of the parable, the proponents of this view are hard pressed to show how the account of Jonah's experience in the fish contributes to the central lesson of the parable.

Another approach to the book is to regard it as an extended allegory. An allegory is a literary form, the basic elements of which are intended to symbolize or explain aspects of real life to which they are analogous. The intended meaning is usually evident or explained by the author. In the OT, allegories are short literary forms used to lend force to a pronouncement. The book of Jonah does not seem to fit this category. It is a narrative account with no evident meaning given to the various persons, objects, and events cited.

There seems to be no convincing reason for rejecting the historicity of the book of Jonah on the basis of the arguments generally given. Jesus referred to the account of Jonah in a way that seems to imply his acceptance of its validity.

Date If Jonah was the son of Amittai cited in 2 Kings 14:25, the prophecy would have to be dated in the reign of Jeroboam II of Israel (793–753 BC). Jonah would then be one of the great eighth-century prophets who ministered during the Silver Age of Israel.

Those who understand the book to have been written by an author other than Jonah place the writing at various times, from the period following the fall of Nineveh to well into the postexilic period.

Background Archaeological excavations at the site of ancient Nineveh have yielded many artifacts and literary works indicating that it was a cultural center for a great part of its history. In the Middle Assyrian period, the city of Nineveh was greatly enlarged and became an administrative center. Some of the most powerful Assyrian kings ruled from Nineveh.

The city of Calah, to the south of Nineveh, had an area much smaller than Nineveh but housed almost 70,000 persons. The description of the vast population of Nineveh in the prophecy of Jonah seems to fit with this.

Purpose The purpose of the book of Jonah is to teach that God's grace was not limited to the Hebrew people. This lesson is taught in the dramatic climax of the book. Jonah, filled with self-pity, laments the loss of the plant that gave him shade. God shows Jonah's concern for the plant in stark contrast to his own concern for the thousands of people of Nineveh.

The book clearly sets forth the fact that God's mercy was not the sole possession of the Hebrew people of Jonah's time but was available to all through repentance. Even Israel's enemies could experience God's mercy.

Content The book of Jonah begins with a command from the Lord to the prophet directing him to preach to the people of Nineveh. Jonah was reluctant to go to Nineveh because he knew that the Ninevites would repent. He would therefore find himself in the dubious position of proclaiming God's mercy to the hated Assyrians. Therefore, he fled from Joppa by ship in a futile attempt to flee from the presence of God. He boarded a ship bound for Tarshish, a Phoenician colony in southern Spain. It was as far west as Jonah could flee within the scope of the ancient Mediterranean world (1:1-3).

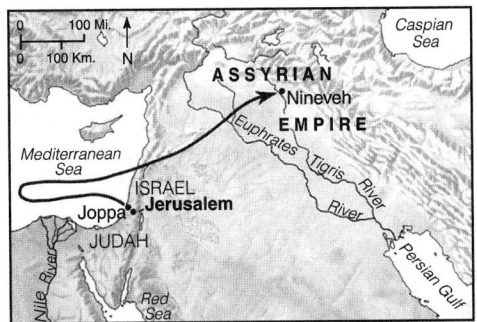

Jonah's Roundabout Journey When Jonah was called to go to Nineveh, he ran from God by boarding a ship in Joppa headed for Tarshish in Spain. Eventually, Jonah could not hide from God; he went to Nineveh.

God would not allow his servant to disobey without chastisement, however (1:4-16). God's love demanded Jonah's discipline. The program of discipline commenced with a divinely originated storm (v 4). In the midst of the terrifying rage of this storm, the sailors busied themselves with supplications to their individual pagan deities and with casting excess cargo overboard (v 5). Through all the commotion Jonah was asleep in the hold of the ship.

The sailors were as yet unaware that Jonah was the real problem. The captain of the ship aroused Jonah and told him to pray to his god for deliverance from the tempest (v 6).

Receiving no response to their supplications, the sailors proceeded to cast lots in an attempt to determine who on board was the cause of the wrath of the god who had brought the storm upon them (1:7); the lot indicated that Jonah was to blame. The sailors then wanted to know what god was responsible for the storm and why. Jonah's testimony was simple and to the point: he was a Hebrew who worshiped the Lord who created both land and sea (v 9).

The sailors asked Jonah what they should do to him since the storm was increasing in its fury (1:11). The captain had previously told Jonah to pray or perish. Now Jonah revealed that praying would not accomplish what his perishing could (v 12). He asked them to throw him into the sea.

Before yielding to Jonah's request, the sailors struggled to save the ship (1:13). Failing in their attempt, they cast him into the sea (v 15). Imagine the impression made on these sailors when the storm ceased as soon as Jonah's body was in the sea. Their experience caused the ship's crew to fear the Lord, and they offered a sacrifice and made vows to him (v 16).

But God was not through with Jonah, for he prepared a great fish to swallow him (1:17). Jonah was in the belly of the fish for three days and nights (cf. Mt 12:38-41).

From within the fish Jonah prayed to God (Jon 2:1), and thanked him for hearing his prayer and saving him from death in the sea (vv 7-8). Jonah's deliverance brought him to the point of renewed devotion to God (v 9). It is significant that his prayer reflected a deep personal acquaintance with the Psalms (cf. Pss 3:8; 5:7; 18:4-19; 30:2-3; 31:6, 22; 39:9; 42:6-7; 59:17; 69:1-2; 120:1; 142:3; 144:2).

The ultimate answer to Jonah's prayers came when God provided him with the opportunity of obeying his commission and keeping his vows. The sea creature spit Jonah out upon the shore (Jon 2:10).

The writer now turns his attention to God's dealing with the city of Nineveh (chs 3–4). Jonah repented of his disobedience and manifested that repentance by going to Nineveh to declare God's message (3:1-3). Upon his arrival in Nineveh, he proceeded to proclaim God's message. The inhabitants of the city were told they had 40 days (v 4), but they evidently responded immediately.

The people and their king repented in sackcloth and with fasting (3:5-6). Having repented privately, the king made a public proclamation to reinforce the response to God's message (vv 7-9).

God's acceptance of Nineveh's repentance (3:10) caused Jonah's grudging attitude to return and he complained (4:1-3). His recently uttered psalm of prayerful praise to God (2:1-9) now turned to bitter grumbling. Jonah prayed again to God (4:2), revealing his reason for refusing to obey the first commission. He had personal knowledge of God's loving and forgiving nature, and he resented that love and forgiveness being extended to the enemies of his country. In foolish abandon, Jonah asked to die rather than to see God's work among the Ninevites (v 3).

God's compassion had been manifested to Nineveh, but he was also to show compassion again to Jonah by illustration and instruction (4:4-11). God's quiet question, "Is it right for you to be angry about this?" must have probed Jonah's innermost being (v 4). But the prophet preferred to put in a temporary shelter on the east side of Nineveh (v 5) waiting to see if anything would happen.

God added a plant (something with large leaves) to the number of nature's objects that he used in his dealings with Jonah (4:6). This provision for Jonah's comfort brought him joy. But the plant was destroyed by a worm sent by God (v 7). Then God sent the hot sirocco wind to dry out the air, increase the heat, and add to Jonah's misery (v 8). Again, Jonah begged to die.

For the second time God questioned Jonah, "Is it right for you to be angry because the plant died?" (4:9, NLT). The point of the illustration was being driven home to the insensitive prophet. Jonah, however, responded with more bitterness (v 9). Jonah was greatly agitated because the loss of the plant affected him personally, even though he had nothing to do with its creation (v 10). The Lord Yahweh had created man. The Lord was concerned for the welfare of the Ninevites. Did not the great Creator have the right to be agitated over the destruction of Nineveh with its 120,000 children and all its animals (v 11)? As Jonah had desired the preservation of the plant, so God had desired even more exceedingly the preservation of Nineveh.

See also Jonah (Person); Prophecy; Prophet, Prophetess.

JONAM, JONAN* Ancestor of Jesus mentioned in Luke's genealogy (Lk 3:30). *See* Genealogy of Jesus Christ.

JONAS*

1. KJV form of Jonah in Matthew 12:39-41 and Luke 11:29-32. *See* Jonah (Person).
2. KJV form of John, Simon Peter's father, in John 21:15, 17. *See* John (Person) #1.

JONATHAN

1. Levite from Bethlehem in Judah, a descendant of Gershom, son of Moses (cf. 1 Chr 23:14-15); he was a priest first to Micah in Ephraim and later to Dan's tribe during the period of the judges (Jgs 17:7-10; 18:30).
2. Benjamite, the firstborn son of Saul and the father of Meribbaal (1 Sm 14:49; 1 Chr 8:33-34). Jonathan was a valiant warrior (1 Sm 13:2-4; 14:1-15; 2 Sm 1:22) and a devoted friend to David (1 Sm 18:1-5; 19:1-7). He was eventually killed, along with his brothers, by the Philistines at Mt Gilboa (1 Sm 31:2; 1 Chr 10:2).
3. Son of the high priest Abiathar and one of David's loyal servants (2 Sm 15:27, 36; 17:17, 20; 1 Kgs 1:42-43).
4. Shimei's son and the nephew of David (2 Sm 21:21; 1 Chr 20:7).
5. Son of Shagee the Hararite and one of David's mighty warriors (2 Sm 23:33; 1 Chr 11:34).
6. Judahite, Jada's son, the brother of Jether, and the father of Peleth and Zaza (1 Chr 2:32-33).
7. Son of Uzziah and one of David's treasurers (1 Chr 27:25).
8. David's relative who served as counselor and scribe in the royal household (1 Chr 27:32).
9. Ebed's father. Ebed returned with Ezra to Judah following the Babylonian captivity (Ezr 8:6).
10. Asahel's son, who, with Jahzeiah, opposed Ezra's suggestion that the sons of Israel should divorce the foreign woman they had married since returning to Palestine from exile (Ezr 10:15).
11. Levite, the son of Joiada, the father of Jaddua, and a descendant of Jeshua, the high priest (Neh 12:11). He is perhaps the same man as Jehohanan (or Johanan), Eliashib's grandson, in Ezra 10:6 (cf. Neh 12:23, NLT). *See* Jehohanan #4.
12. Priest and the head of Malluch's house during the days of Joiakim the high priest (Neh 12:14).
13. Priest, father of Zechariah, and a descendant of Asaph (Neh 12:35).
14. Secretary in whose house Jeremiah was at one point imprisoned during the reign of King Zedekiah of Judah (Jer 37:15, 20; 38:26).
15. Kareah's son who sought protection under Gedaliah (Jer 40:8).
16. Youngest son of Mattathias and brother of Judas Maccabeus. When Judas Maccabeus was killed in battle with Bacchides (1 Macc 9:18), his brother Jonathan became his successor (vv 28-31). Jonathan continued the struggle against Syria for three years with a small band of guerrillas. But the Syrians were busy with an internal struggle for political power, and so, in 157 BC, made peace with him. The political machinations in Syria worked to Jonathan's advantage, and five years later he became high priest in Jerusalem and administrator of Judea (10:1-11). Under his management, Jewish territory and power increased. This occurred partly because Jonathan was able to play the Syrian political rivals against one another. One of these was Tryphon, a pretender to the Syrian throne who saw that his influence was threatened by Jonathan's power. So in 143 BC he decided to overthrow the Jewish leader. Jonathan was taken prisoner by Tryphon through treachery and eventually killed, leaving his brother Simon to lead the Jews (1 Macc 12–13).

JONATH-ELEM-RECHOKIM* Hebrew phrase in the title of Psalm 56 (KJV), translated "To be sung to the tune, 'Dove on Distant Oaks' " (NLT); perhaps a familiar ancient melody to which the psalm was performed.
See also Music.

JOPPA City about 35 miles (56.3 kilometers) northwest of Jerusalem that served as Jerusalem's seaport. Joppa was built on a rocky hill about 116 feet (35.4 meters) high, with a cape projecting beyond the coastline into the sea, and was the only natural harbor on the Mediterranean coast between Egypt and the OT town of Acco. Some 300 to 400 feet (91.4 to 121.9 meters) offshore a series of reefs formed a breakwater so that entrance into the harbor was gained from the north. It is possible that the harbor was larger and better protected in ancient times than it is today. The biblical city was well supplied with water, and the land surrounding it was quite fertile.

Aerial View of Joppa

Joppa first appears in ancient records in the Egyptian list of Palestinian cities captured by Thutmose III (1490–1432 BC). During the Amarna period, it was ruled by a local prince in alliance with Jerusalem. One source from this period describes its beautiful gardens and the craftsmanship of its workers in metal, leather, and wood. When Palestine was divided among the 12 tribes, Joppa was assigned to Dan (Jos 19:46; KJV "Japho"). It was soon taken by the Philistines, who made it one of their seaports. David's conquest of the Philistines restored Joppa to Israel, and during Solomon's reign, it became a major port serving Jerusalem. Cedar logs were floated from Lebanon to Joppa and then transported to Jerusalem for use in building the temple (2 Chr 2:16).

Joppa was the seaport to which Jonah fled in an attempt to avoid preaching to Nineveh (Jon 1:3); there, hoping to escape his responsibility, he boarded a ship bound for Tarshish. When Tiglath-pileser III invaded Philistia in 743 BC, Joppa probably was one of the Philistine cities that fell to him. Sennacherib, in his campaign of 701 BC, lists Joppa as one of the cities he occupied. Subsequent to that, little is known of it until the time of Ezra, when once again cedar logs from Lebanon were floated to Joppa and taken to Jerusalem for the rebuilding of the temple (Ezr 3:7). During the fourth century BC, Eshmunazar of Sidon controlled the city. When Sidon revolted against Persia and was destroyed by Artaxerxes III, Joppa apparently became a free city.

Alexander the Great changed its name from Japho (its OT name) to Joppa and established a mint there, making it a city of some importance in the Greek Empire. Following Alexander's death, his successors fought over the city several times. It was ruled by Egypt from 301 BC until 197 BC, when Antiochus III made it a part of the Seleucid kingdom.

During the Maccabean period, Joppa had varied experiences. When Antiochus IV Epiphanes moved toward Jerusalem in 168 BC to enforce his program of Hellenization, he landed his troops at Joppa. In 164 BC, because of the success of Judas Maccabeus against the Seleucids, non-Jewish citizens drowned about 200 Jews. Judas retaliated by burning the harbor installations and the boats anchored there but was unable to conquer the city itself (2 Macc 12:3-9). In 147 BC Jonathan and Simon defeated Appollonius Taos, the Syrian general, and occupied Joppa for Alexander I Epiphanes, a contender for the Syrian throne (1 Macc 10:74-86). Through a series of political moves in the next few years Simon was able to fortify the city, expel the Greek inhabitants, and firmly establish Joppa as a Jewish city. During Pompey's Roman occupation, Joppa was declared a free city; it was returned to the Jews by Julius Caesar (47 BC); and it was captured by Herod the Great in 37 BC. Hated by the residents of Joppa, Herod built a new port at Caesarea, about 40 miles (64.4 kilometers) north of Joppa. By the time of Jesus' birth, Joppa was under the rule of Caesarea in the province of Syria (Josephus's *Antiquities* 17.13.2-4).

A Christian congregation appeared quite early in Joppa. Among the disciples living there were Dorcas, whom Peter raised from death (Acts 9:36-41), and Simon the tanner (v 43). From Joppa, Peter was called to Caesarea to present the gospel to the Roman centurion Cornelius (10:1-48).

Joppa was a primary center of revolt against the Romans. It was destroyed by Vespasian in AD 68 and replaced with a Roman army camp. It was later rebuilt, and is known today as Jaffa, a suburb of Tel Aviv.

JORAH Alternate name for Hariph in Ezra 2:18 and Nehemiah 7:24. *See* Hariph.

JORAI Member of Gad's tribe (1 Chr 5:13).

JORAM
1. Toi's son and king of Hamath. He was sent by Toi to offer congratulations to David when David won a victory over Hadadezer of Zobah (2 Sm 8:9-12). He is also called Hadoram in 1 Chronicles 18:10.

Headwaters of the Jordan River

2. Alternate name for Jehoram, king of Judah (853–841 BC). *See* Jehoram #1.
3. Alternate name for Jehoram, king of Israel (852–841 BC). *See* Jehoram #2.
4. Jeshaiah's son from Levi's tribe (1 Chr 26:25).

JORDAN RIVER River lying in the bottom of a great canyon called the Jordan Rift, an elongated depression stretching from lower southwest Asia Minor (Syria) to the Gulf of Aqaba. The rift was once filled by the Lisan Lake, but significant geologic activity caused it to recede, and the result was the formation of three separate aqueous bodies: the Huleh Lake, the Sea of Galilee, and the Dead Sea. To this day each of these are fed by the Jordan River, the stream whose name in Hebrew means "the descender."

Sources Originating at the northern end of the Huleh Basin, the river comprises four separate streams: Nahr Bereighith, Nahr Hasbani, Nahr el-Liddani, and Nahr Baniyas. In the northwest corner of the Huleh Valley the Bereighith emerges within the area of Merj Ayoun, flowing from a spring located on a modest knoll west of Mt Hermon. Slightly to the east is the Hasbani, a stream that descends from a spring 1,700 feet (518.2 meters) above sea level and follows a course of about 24 miles (38.6 kilometers). These two smaller streams merge less than a mile above their confluence with the el-Liddani and the Baniyas. The el-Liddani, lying between the Nahr Hasbani and the Nahr Baniyas, is located near Tel el-Qadi (the biblical city of Dan). The most powerful stream of the four; it is fed by 'Ain Leddan, a spring that is nestled among thick underbrush and is fed by the melting snows off Mt Hermon. Flowing quickly and briefly, the el-Liddani rushes to meet the Nahr Baniyas, the last of the four streams. In the northeast corner of the Huleh Valley, at the NT site of Caesarea Philippi, the Baniyas originates from a cave approximately 1,100 feet (335 meters) above sea level and follows a steep descent to its confluence with the others. These four streams, making up the Jordan River, then flow together along a southerly course of 10 miles (16 kilometers) before entering Huleh Lake.

Course and Character of the River The course of the Jordan follows a north-south route through the Great Rift, descending gradually from the Huleh Lake (7 feet, or 2 meters, above sea level) to the Dead Sea (1,274 feet, or 388 meters, below sea level). From the Huleh Lake the river follows a 20-mile (32.2-kilometer) course, passing through the basaltic lip that forms the southern dam of the Huleh Basin (Rosh Pinnah Sill) and descends quickly to the Sea of Galilee (685 feet, or 209 meters, below sea level). To the south lies the Dead Sea at a distance of approximately 65 miles (105 kilometers). The river that connects these two seas, however, travels a circuitous route of 200 miles (322 kilometers), following a snakelike riverbed cut through the Ghor, the canyon floor.

The Jordan has many tributaries, not all of which are perennial. If there is no consistent water source, such as a spring at the head of the riverbed, then these V-shaped watercourses remain dry until a seasonal deluge. When the rain comes, these dry, narrow courses are filled with fast-paced streams that flow off the sides of the canyon into the Jordan River. North of the Sea of Galilee four major systems feed the fluvial system in the Huleh Basin: Nahr Dishon and Nahr Hazor on the west, and Nahr Shuah and Nahr Gilbon on the east. Between the Sea of Galilee and the Dead Sea are the following major tributary systems: on the east—Yarmuq, 'Arab, Tayibeh,

Ziqlab, Jurm, Yabis, Kufrinjia, Rajib, Zarqa, Nimrin, Abu Gharuba; on the west—Fejjas, Bireh, Jalub, Malih, Far'ah, Aujah, el-Qelt.

The character of the Ghor varies from north to south as the canyon floor drops farther below sea level. Just south of the Sea of Galilee arable fields may be cultivated without irrigation, which permits occupation and settlement. South of this and farther below sea level, beyond the narrowest constriction of the canyon at Ghor el-Wahadina, the terrain and climate change. Since the floor now consistently approaches 1,000 feet (305 meters) below sea level, the climatic conditions approximate that of the desert. In this dry and desolate region, the river and its immediate environs now assume a more prominent role, becoming a lifeline to the flora and the fauna that hug its banks. Its course and character are more easily discerned as it has become a veritable stream in the desert. The dense foliage on the banks of the Jordan is still today a wildlife haunt as it was in antiquity, the low-lying shrubs and the tamarisk alike providing thick ground cover. This lower section of the canyon, called the Zor, is 150 feet (45.7 meters) below the Ghor and separated by the *qattara* (a sedimentary deposit of grayish-white marls and clays that form precipitous and barren slopes) from the canyon floor above. Generally inaccessible and extremely dangerous, the Zor and *qattara* form a natural barrier between Cis-Jordan (west) and Transjordan (east). Thus, trade, settlement, and travel were necessarily affected by the various topographical features that characterize this area.

Biblical Events The OT Israelites passed across the Jordan upon entry into the Promised Land (Jos 3:14-17). The fords of the Jordan were the sites of conflict in the war of Jephthah and the Gileadites against the Ephraimites (Jgs 12:1-6). The prophet Elijah sought refuge from Ahab and Israel by the brook of Kerith east of the Jordan (1 Kgs 17:1-5). Elijah was translated up to heaven in a whirlwind after having crossed the Jordan with Elisha on dry ground (2 Kgs 2:6-12). Naaman, the Syrian general, bathed in the Jordan at the command of Elisha and his leprosy was healed (5:8-14). Elisha made the ax head float here (2 Kgs 6:1-7). In the NT, Jesus was baptized by John the Baptist in the Jordan (Mt 3:13-17). Peter confessed that Jesus was the "Christ, the Son of the living God" at Caesarea Philippi—located on one of the sources of the Jordan, Nahr Baniyas (16:13-20). Jesus healed two blind men at Jericho, which is near the Jordan (20:29-34) and visited with Zacchaeus in that same city (Lk 19:1-10).

JORIM Ancestor of Jesus listed in Luke's genealogy (Lk 3:29). *See* Genealogy of Jesus Christ.

JORKEAM, JORKOAM* Identified with Raham, a descendant of Judah through Caleb's line (1 Chr 2:44; KJV "Jorkoam"), the name should perhaps be understood as a place-name and be identified with Jokdeam (Jos 15:56).

JOSABAD* KJV spelling of Jozabad, a Benjamite warrior, in 1 Chronicles 12:4. *See* Jozabad #1.

JOSAPHAT* KJV spelling of Jehoshaphat, Asa's son, in Matthew 1:8. *See* Jehoshaphat (Person) #1.

JOSE* KJV spelling of Joshua, Eliezer's son, in Luke 3:29. *See* Joshua (Person) #5.

Mouth of the Jordan River

JOSECH Ancestor of Jesus mentioned only in Luke's genealogy (Lk 3:26). *See* Genealogy of Jesus Christ.

JOSEDECH* KJV spelling of Jozadak, Joshua's father, in Haggai 1:1, 12, 14; 2:2, 4; and Zechariah 6:11. *See* Jozadak.

JOSEPH

1. Jacob's 11th son and the firstborn son of Rachel. Rachel named the boy Joseph, meaning "may he add," expressing her desire that God would give her another son (Gn 30:24).

   Nothing more is said about Joseph until, at the age of 17, he is seen tending his father's flocks with his brothers (Gn 37:2). Joseph was the favorite of his father, since he was the son of his old age (v 3) and the firstborn son of his favorite wife. Because of this, his brothers hated Joseph. This envy was magnified when Jacob gave Joseph a ground-length, long-sleeved, multicolored robe (vv 3-4). (This type of garment is illustrated by the paintings in the Asiatic tombs of Khnumhotep II at Beni Hasan and of the nobles at Gurneh, near Luxor.) The animosity of his brothers increased still more when Joseph revealed to them his dreams of dominion over them (vv 5-11). Subsequently, when Joseph was sent to check on his brothers and the flocks near Shechem, his brothers sold him to a caravan of traders going down to Egypt (vv 25-28). His brothers then took his robe, dipped it in goat's blood, and brought it to Jacob, who concluded that Joseph had been killed by wild animals (vv 31-33); Jacob was overwhelmed with grief (vv 34-35).

   In Egypt, Joseph was sold to Potiphar, an Egyptian officer of the guard (Gn 37:36; 39:1), who eventually put Joseph in charge of his entire household. However, trouble arose from Potiphar's wife, who was attracted to the young Hebrew and tried to seduce him (39:6-10). He steadfastly resisted her advances, protesting that to comply with her wishes would be a disservice to his master and a sin against God (v 9). One day she seized his garment, but he left the garment behind and fled. Potiphar's wife accused Joseph of attempted rape; her report was believed, and Joseph was incarcerated in the king's prison (v 20), where Pharaoh's butler and baker were also confined. While in prison, Joseph, with the Lord's help, interpreted these men's troublesome dreams. As Joseph had foretold, the baker was executed and the butler was restored to royal favor (ch 40).

Two years later Pharaoh had two dreams that his magicians and wise men could not interpret. The butler, remembering Joseph, had him summoned from prison. God revealed to Joseph that the dreams foretold seven years of abundance, followed by seven years of famine (Gn 41:25-36). Pharaoh, impressed with Joseph's interpretation, made him ruler of Egypt, second only to himself (vv 39-44). Joseph was given a new name, Zaphenath-paneah, and a wife, Asenath, the daughter of Potiphera (v 45).

Joseph was 30 years old when he became ruler of Egypt. During the seven years of prosperity, he gathered the good supplies for the seven years of famine to come (Gn 41:53-56). When the famine eventually became severe in Palestine, Jacob sent all his sons, except Benjamin, his youngest son, to Egypt to purchase grain. Appearing before Joseph in Egypt, they did not recognize him. But he knew them and remembered his dreams of years before (42:8-9). After listening to the report of their family, he accused them of being spies (vv 9-14) and insisted that they leave one of their brothers as hostage and return with Benjamin to verify the truthfulness of their report (vv 19-20). Thus Simeon was bound and left in Egypt (v 24).

After the famine worsened in Palestine, Jacob asked his sons to go back to Egypt to buy more grain (Gn 43:1-2); reluctantly agreeing to the conditions that the Egyptian administrator had placed on them, Jacob allowed Benjamin to go with them (vv 11-13). When they arrived in Egypt, they were taken to Joseph's house, where Simeon was restored to them (v 23) and a meal was prepared for them (v 33). Joseph at last disclosed his identity and declared that God had sent him before them to preserve their lives (45:4-8). Arrangements were then made to send for Jacob; wagons were provided, along with provisions for the journey (v 21). When Jacob came to Goshen in the Nile Delta, Joseph went out to meet him, and another great reunion took place (46:28-29). He also presented his father and brothers to Pharaoh, who let them live in the land of Goshen (47:6).

Upon learning that his father was ill, Joseph took his two sons, Manasseh and Ephraim, to him for his blessing. He presented the sons so that the older would be at Jacob's right hand and the younger at his left in order that Manasseh would receive the blessing of the firstborn. Jacob, however, crossed his hands and with his right hand on Ephraim gave him the greater blessing (Gn 48:14-20). He also gave to Joseph the land that he had taken from the Amorites (v 22). At Jacob's death, Joseph made the funeral arrangements; and after the customary funerary practices were carried out, a great funeral procession went to Canaan, where Jacob was buried by his sons in the cave of Machpelah near Hebron (50:1-12).

When Joseph was 110 years old, he called his brothers and told them that he was about to die. He made them take an oath that when they returned to Canaan they would take his bones with them. So he died, was embalmed, and was placed in a coffin in Egypt (Gn 50:26). Many years later, during the exodus, Moses took the bones of Joseph with him from Egypt (Ex 13:19). Joseph's remains were eventually interred at Shechem in the parcel of land that Jacob had bought from Hamor, the father of Shechem (Gn 33:18-20; Jos 24:32). See Israel, History of; Patriarchs, Period of the.

2. Igal's father from Issachar's tribe. Igal was one of the 12 spies sent by Moses to search out the land of Canaan (Nm 13:7).

3. Asaph's second son and the leader of the first course of priests serving in the sanctuary during David's reign (1 Chr 25:2, 9).

4. One of Binnui's descendants who was encouraged by Ezra to divorce his foreign wife during the postexilic era (Ezr 10:42).

5. Priest and family leader from Shebaniah's line during the days of Joiakim, the high priest (Neh 12:14).

6. Descendant of David (Mt 1:16; Lk 3:23) and the husband of Mary, the mother of Jesus. Joseph was betrothed to Mary, a young woman of the city of Nazareth. Mary had learned from the angel Gabriel that she was to bear the Son of God, whom she was to name Jesus (Lk 1:31) and that this conception was to be a work of the Holy Spirit (v 35). Joseph was not aware of this, so when he learned that Mary was pregnant, he decided to divorce her quietly, for he was a just man and did not want to humiliate her publicly (Mt 1:19). An angel subsequently appeared to him in a dream to tell him what was happening (Mt 1:21; cf. Is 7:14). The text of Matthew makes it clear that there was no sexual union between Joseph and Mary until after Jesus was born (Mt 1:18, 25; see also Lk 1:34-37).

When Caesar Augustus issued a decree that everyone had to register in his native city for purposes of taxation, Joseph and Mary returned to Bethlehem, where Jesus was subsequently born (Lk 2:1-6). Later, Joseph and Mary took the infant Jesus to the temple to present him to the Lord (vv 22, 33). After the visit of the wise men, an angel appeared to Joseph in a dream and instructed him to take Jesus and Mary to Egypt to protect the child from King Herod (Mt 2:13). Upon the death of Herod, an angel similarly advised him to return to Israel, so the family went to live in Nazareth. The last recorded event that involves Joseph is the incident of Jesus at the temple at age 12 (Lk 2:41-51). Joseph is not mentioned by name, but Mary told Jesus that she and his father had been looking for him anxiously.

Jesus was identified by people around Nazareth as "Joseph's son" (Lk 4:22; Jn 1:45; 6:42). It is only through references identifying Jesus that we learn of Joseph's trade. Twice Jesus is referred to as "the carpenter's son" (Mt 13:55; Mk 6:3). Joseph was not a carpenter in our sense of the word, for houses were built mostly of stone and earth. He was a woodworker or artificer in wood, and probably most of his work was with furniture and agricultural implements.

During the ministry of Jesus, it was his mother and his brothers who came to look for him (Mt 12:46-50; Mk 3:31-35), so it is assumed that by this time Joseph was dead. Joseph was most likely the father of James, Joseph, Simon, Judas, and unnamed sisters (Mt 13:55; Mk 6:3).

See also Brothers of Jesus; Genealogy of Jesus Christ.

7. Joseph and Mary's son and the brother of Jesus (Mt 13:55); alternately called Joses in Mark 6:3. See Brothers of Jesus.

8. Native of Arimathea and the follower of Jesus who provided for his burial. He was a rich man from the town of Arimathea and a respected member of the Sanhedrin, or council (Mk 15:43). He was a good and righteous man and did not go along with the decision to crucify Jesus (Lk 23:50-51). Joseph had been a secret follower of Jesus because he was afraid of the Jews (Jn 19:38), but after the Crucifixion he took courage and went to Pilate to ask for Jesus' body. He and

Nicodemus took the body, treated it with spices, and wrapped it in linen cloths, according to the Jewish burial customs. In a nearby garden was Joseph's own new rock-cut tomb in which no one had ever been buried. Here they placed Jesus and sealed the tomb with a large stone.

9. Mattathias's son and an ancestor of Jesus (Lk 3:25). *See* Genealogy of Jesus Christ.
10. KJV rendering of Josech, an ancestor of Jesus, in Luke 3:26. *See* Josech.
11. Jonam's son and an ancestor of Jesus (Lk 3:30). *See* Genealogy of Jesus Christ.
12. Disciple of Jesus who was "called Barsabbas" and "surnamed Justus" (Acts 1:23). Joseph was one of the candidates put forward by the 11 apostles to replace Judas Iscariot. It was Matthias, however, who was chosen.
13. Cypriot Levite who sold a field and gave the proceeds to the apostles. He was surnamed "Barnabas," meaning "son of encouragement," by the apostles (Acts 4:36). *See* Barnabas.

JOSEPH BARSABBAS *See* Joseph #12.

JOSEPH OF ARIMATHEA *See* Joseph #8.

JOSEPHUS*, Flavius Jewish military officer and historian (AD 37–c. 100).

Josephus was born into an aristocratic priestly family in Jerusalem. Through his mother he was related to the Hasmoneans. In his youth he was noted for his memory and ease in learning. As a teenager he attached himself to a member of an ascetic sect. Then he became a Pharisee.

In AD 64 Josephus was a member of an official party sent to Rome to secure the release of some priests. The empire's capital made an indelible impression on him. After his return to Jerusalem, the first Jewish revolt erupted (AD 66). The Sanhedrin (the Jewish governing council) appointed Josephus commander of Galilee. He organized the province well but incurred the opposition of John of Gischala, Galilee's former leader. Conflict between the two men's forces continued until the arrival of the Roman general Vespasian in the spring of 67.

Josephus and the Galileans entrenched themselves at Jotapata. After a siege of six weeks, the Roman army captured and destroyed the city, but Josephus and 40 soldiers escaped to a cave. Josephus, whose life was assured by the Romans through a friend's intervention, persuaded his fellow soldiers to kill each other rather than be captured. When only he and one other remained alive, he surrendered to the Romans.

When Josephus appeared before Vespasian and prophesied that Vespasian would become emperor, his life was spared. Nonetheless, Josephus was held prisoner. Vespasian was proclaimed emperor in the year 69 and Josephus was set free. He then adopted Vespasian's family name, Flavius. In 70, when Vespasian's son Titus marched on Jerusalem, Josephus accompanied him. Several times Josephus tried unsuccessfully to persuade the Jews to surrender.

After Titus's destruction of Jerusalem, Josephus went to Rome, where Vespasian favored him with Roman citizenship and a pension. Free to write, Josephus produced a number of books of considerable historical value. In *The Jewish War* (AD 77–78) Josephus described the Roman-Jewish conflict from the time of Antiochus Ephiphanes to slightly beyond the fall of Jerusalem. Perhaps Josephus's greatest work was *Antiquities of the Jews* (c. 94). A 20-volume work designed to glorify the Jews and eliminate gentile hostility, it traces Jewish history from the Creation to the outbreak of war with Rome in 66. His autobiography, *Life,* was primarily a vindication of his activities as governor of Galilee. Josephus wrote *Against Apion* to counteract claims of anti-Semites; in this work he used logical arguments as well as derision.

As a historian, Josephus sometimes distorted facts in favor of his patrons. However, he was witness to many of the events about which he wrote. His works illumine the period in which the church came into existence, especially concerning the religion, politics, geography, and prominent persons of the early Christian era. Of particular interest to Christians are his references to John the Baptist, Jesus, and James the Just (Jesus' brother).

> **JOSEPHUS'S WORDS ABOUT JESUS**
> In his volume *Antiquities of the Jews* (18.2), Josephus said this about Jesus:
>
> Now, there was about this time Jesus, a wise man, if it be lawful to call him a man, for he was a doer of wonderful works—a teacher of such men as receive the truth with pleasure. He drew over to him both many of the Jews and many of the Gentiles. He was Christ; and when Pilate, at the suggestion of the principal men among us, had condemned him to the cross, those that loved him at the first did not forsake him, for he appeared to them alive again the third day, as the divine prophets had foretold these and ten thousand other wonderful things concerning him; and the tribe of Christians, so named from him, are not extinct at this day.

JOSES*
1. Alternate spelling for Joseph, Mary's son, in Mark 6:3 (NLT mg). *See* Joseph #7.
2. KJV spelling for Joseph, surnamed Barnabas, in Acts 4:36. *See* Barnabas.

JOSHAH Prince in Simeon's tribe (1 Chr 4:34).

JOSHAPHAT
1. Mithnite (NLT "from Mithna") and one of David's mighty men (1 Chr 11:43).
2. One of the seven priests assigned to blow a trumpet before the ark of God in the procession led by David when the ark was brought to Jerusalem (1 Chr 15:24).

JOSHAVIAH Elnaam's son, the brother of Jeribai and one of David's 30 valiant warriors (1 Chr 11:46).

JOSHBEKASHAH Heman's son and head of the 17th of 24 divisions of priestly musicians for ministry in the sanctuary during David's reign (1 Chr 25:4, 24).

JOSHEB-BASSHEBETH* Alternate spelling of Jashobeam, commander of David's mighty men, in 2 Samuel 23:8 (NLT mg). *See* Jashobeam #1.

JOSHIBIAH Simeonite prince, Seraiah's son, and the father of Jehu (1 Chr 4:35).

JOSHUA (Person)
1. Son of Nun, Moses' assistant and successor, and the military leader whom God chose to lead the Israelites in the conquest of Canaan (Nm 13:16, KJV "Jehoshua";

also spelled "Jehoshuah" in 1 Chr 7:27 and "Jeshua" in Neh 8:17).

Early in the exodus, Joshua was sent by Moses to fight against the Amalekites (Ex 17:8-15). Joshua defeated Amalek, and Moses wrote of the event and built an altar that he called "The LORD Is My Banner" (v 15).

When Moses sent 12 men from Kadesh-barnea to spy out the land of Canaan, Joshua represented the tribe of Ephraim (Nm 13:8). At that time Joshua was called Hoshea, but Moses changed his name to Joshua (vv 8, 16). Joshua and Caleb were the only two spies to bring back an affirmative report concerning an Israelite invasion of the land (14:6-9). Consequently, of all the adult Israelite males to leave Egypt in the exodus, only these two crossed the Jordan River and entered the Promised Land (v 30).

When the Lord announced to Moses his impending death, Moses asked about his successor, and the Lord appointed Joshua to that position (Nm 27:12-23). After the death of Moses on Mt Nebo, Joshua's leadership was confirmed (34:17), and the Lord told Joshua to go over the Jordan and take the land (Jos 1:1-2).

From the Transjordan, Joshua sent two men across the river to reconnoiter Jericho (ch 2). In Jericho they were concealed by Rahab and later safely made their way back to Joshua to report that the people of the land were fainthearted because of the Israelites (vv 23-24).

When Israel had crossed the river, the Lord instructed Joshua to set up a circle of 12 stones at Gilgal to commemorate this passage (Jos 4:1-7). The Lord then commanded all of the males who had been born during the exodus to be circumcised (5:2-9).

While camped at Gilgal, near Jericho, Joshua was confronted by a man with a drawn sword. When Joshua challenged the man, he learned that it was the Lord, who told him to remove his shoes, for the ground was holy (Jos 5:13-15). The Lord gave Joshua directions for the destruction of Jericho; these were followed explicitly and the city fell (ch 6). The attack on Ai ended in temporary defeat, until the matter of Achan's sin was discovered and judged (7:10-26). Then Ai was taken and destroyed.

Joshua built an altar on Mt Ebal (Jos 8:30-32), and the blessings and curses were read, as commanded by God through Moses (Jos 8:33-35; cf. Dt 27–28).

Because the Israelites failed to ask direction from the Lord (Jos 9:14), Joshua was tricked into making a covenant of peace with the Hivites of Gibeon. Joshua then reduced them to doing menial tasks in Israel (vv 21-27).

The kings of the various Canaanite cities allied themselves against the Israelite threat (Jos 9:1-2) and a league of five Amorite cities (Jerusalem, Hebron, Jarmuth, Lachish, and Eglon) attacked Gibeon (10:1-5). The Gibeonites appealed to Joshua for help; he responded quickly against this Amorite confederation and routed the Amorite forces. It was on this occasion that Joshua commanded the sun and the moon to stand still so that Israel could have more time to defeat these adversaries (vv 12-14). This victory was followed by a series of successful attacks on enemy towns (vv 28-43).

A northern alliance headed by Jabin, king of Hazor, was the next opposition (Jos 11:1-5). The Lord assured Joshua of success, and the city of Hazor was taken and destroyed by fire (vv 6-15). Joshua 11:23 summarizes the conquest of the land, and chapter 12 enumerates the kings who were conquered.

Joshua was now old, and the Lord told him that much land remained to be possessed. These territories are listed, but the Lord directed Joshua to proceed with the division of the land among the nine and a half tribes (Jos 13:7; cf. 13:8–18:28). Joshua himself was given the city he asked for, Timnath-serah, in the hill country of Ephraim, which he rebuilt and settled (19:49-50).

The Lord told Joshua to appoint cities of refuge to which a person guilty of manslaughter could flee to escape the avenger of blood (Jos 20). Then the Levites came to Eleazar the priest and Joshua to request that they be given their cities, as the Lord had commanded through Moses (21:1-42).

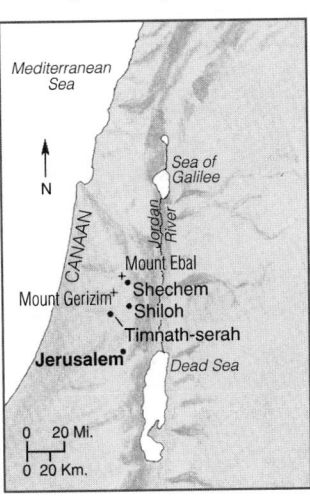

Joshua's Final Days
Joshua gave his final speech at Shechem, then went to his hometown, Timnath-serah, where he died.

In his advanced years Joshua summoned all Israel and solemnly charged them to continue in faithfulness to the Lord (Jos 23). Finally, he called all Israel to Shechem, where he gave them his farewell message. He summed up the Lord's dealings with them from the time of Abraham and again challenged them to serve the Lord, putting before them the well-known choice and decision: "Choose today whom you will serve. . . . As for me and my family, we will serve the LORD" (24:15, NLT).

Joshua died at the age of 110 years and was buried in the land of his inheritance at Timnath-serah (Jos 24:29-30; the parallel account in Jgs 2:8-9 reads "Timnath-heres," NLT mg). Israel served the Lord during all the days of Joshua and the elders who outlived him (Jos 24:31; Jgs 2:7).

See also Conquest and Allotment of the Land; Israel, History of; Joshua, Book of.

2. Inhabitant of Beth-shemesh. It was his grainfield into which the cart carrying the ark sent by the Philistines came. It stopped by a large stone which was then used to commemorate this event (1 Sm 6:14, 18).
3. Governor of Jerusalem during King Josiah's reign (2 Kgs 23:8).
4. Jozadak's son and high priest during the days of Zerubbabel in postexilic Jerusalem (Hg 1:1-14; 2:2-4; Zec 3:1-9; 6:11; NLT "Jeshua"). Joshua is alternately called Jeshua in Ezra and Nehemiah. *See* Jeshua (Person) #3.
5. Eliezer's son and an ancestor of Jesus Christ (Lk 3:29). *See* Genealogy of Jesus Christ.

JOSHUA, Book of First of the historical books in the English Bible and the first of the Former Prophets (including Judges, the books of Samuel, and the books of Kings) in the Hebrew Bible. It begins with the Lord's commission of Joshua (Jos 1:1-9) and concludes with the burial of Joshua, Eleazar, and the bones of Joseph (24:29-33). The purpose of the book is to show how Joshua continued in the footsteps of Moses, how the Lord gave the land to Israel, and how Israel might prosper in the land.

PREVIEW
•Author and Date
•Problems of Interpretation
•Purpose
•Content

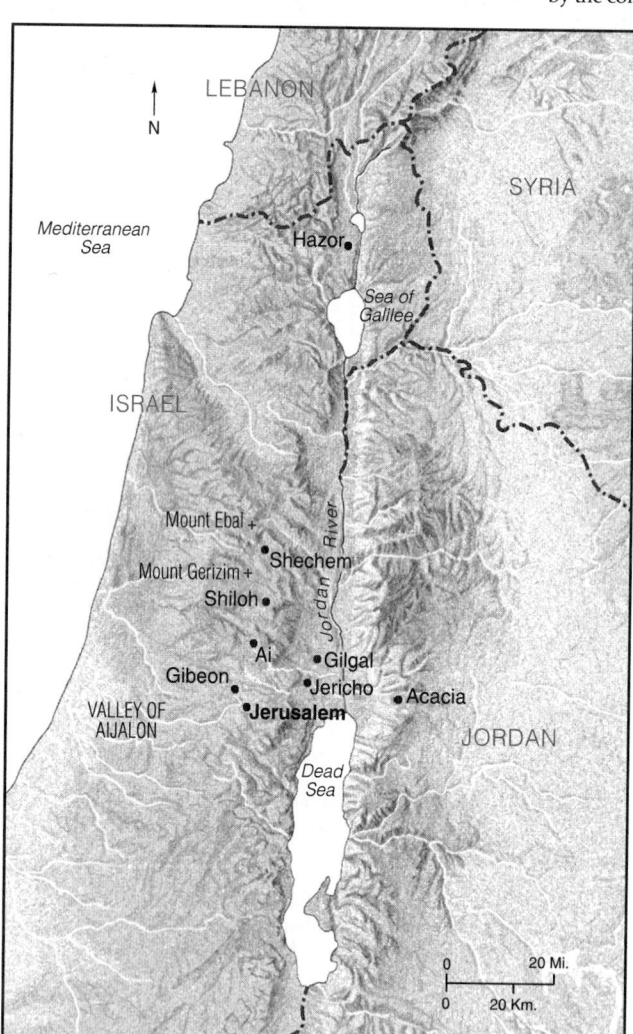

The broken lines (–·–·) indicate modern boundaries.

Key Places in the Book of Joshua

Author and Date According to the Talmud, Joshua wrote the book. This ancient tradition is possibly based on the brief statement that Joshua "recorded these things in the Book of the Law of God" (24:26, NLT). However, this applies only to the renewal of the covenant (ch 24). The issue of authorship is tied up with the dating of the book. Since the book has no unambiguous markers on date and authorship, neither critics nor conservative scholars have been able to come to any agreement on

these issues. According to a conservative analysis of Joshua, the book was written between 1375 BC and 1045 BC (premonarchic). The argument is based on the references to the migration of Dan (19:47; cf. Jgs 18:27-31), to Jerusalem as a Jebusite city (Jos 15:8, 63; 18:16, 28), to Sidon rather than Tyre as the prominent Phoenician city (11:8; 13:4-6; 19:28), and also on the eyewitness style (5:1, 6—in the MT). But critical scholars have raised issues that they considered could best be resolved by positing a seventh-century BC or even an exilic date.

Problems of Interpretation

Holy War The morality of the Conquest may be explained by the concept of holy war. The holy war motif would explain why Israel was to destroy the indigenous population (Dt 7:16; 20:16-18; Jos 6:21; 8:24-26; 10:10, 28-30, 35-42; 11:11). The justification may lie in the concept that Israel was God's instrument of judgment on the Canaanite nations. This argument is related to the mention of the wickedness of the Canaanites (Gn 15:16; Dt 7:2-5, 25-26; 12:30-31; Jos 23:7; Jgs 2:11). However, the canonical narrative of the progression of the Conquest puts the responsibility on the Canaanites. They marched and fought against Israel (Nm 21:21-35; Jos 7:4-5; 8:5, 16-17; 9:1-2; 10:1-6; 11:1-5; 24:11). Therefore, it could be argued that in the process of war a sincere invitation to make peace was given to the kings (cf. Nm 21:21-22; Dt 20:10-11) but was refused. Instead, the kings took the initiative in battle. The responsibility for the destruction of the native population thus lay with the leadership. Yet all this was evidence of God's working in human affairs, which the Bible simply states, "For it was the LORD himself who hardened their hearts to wage war against Israel, so that he might destroy them totally, exterminating them without mercy, as the LORD had commanded Moses" (Jos 11:20, NIV). Even as Pharaoh, whose heart the Lord hardened, was responsible for the plagues in Egypt, so the Canaanite rulers were responsible for the extermination of their populations. The biblical account of the Conquest affirms the mystery of human responsibility and divine sovereignty without explaining it.

Nature of the Conquest Various explanations of the nature of the Conquest have been given. The traditional view of a blitzkrieg type of conquest, which resulted in a complete occupation of the whole land (cf. Jos 10:40; 11:1-3, 16-19), does not fit within the whole picture of the book. The book presents a realistic description of the areas that still had to be conquered (13:1-7) and of the military strength of the indigenous population (cf. 13:13; 15:63; 16:10; 17:12-18; 19:47). Moreover, Joshua promised that the Lord would continue to help Israel to occupy the land, as its population and needs developed (23:5). The occupation of Canaan was in two stages: conquest and gradual occupation (cf. Ex 23:29-30; Dt 7:22).

Purpose The role of the final (canonical) form of the book is to present Joshua's obedience to the law of Moses. Victory and defeat are illustrations of obedience and disobedience. Of course, there is tension in this because the descriptions of the Conquest are complete and yet incomplete. The tension is a dynamic device to show that the Conquest and enjoyment of the land depend wholly on obedience. The period of Joshua is viewed as a paradigm of obedient Israel. Thus, a holistic reading of the book presents an appeal to covenant loyalty directed to future generations.

Content

Conquest of the Land, 1:1–12:24

►THE LORD'S COMMISSION OF JOSHUA, 1:1-9 With the death of Moses (Jos 1:1), the Lord himself confirms Moses' ordination of Joshua (Dt 34:9). He charges him with leadership in the conquest of Canaan (Jos 1:2-3), defines the geographical boundaries of the land (v 4), encourages him with his continued presence (vv 5, 9), and expects him to devoutly follow in "the law of Moses" (i.e., the law given in Dt; cf. Dt 31:9, 24-26; Jos 23:6), so that he may succeed in his mission (1:7-8). The original mission, as well as the ministry of Moses, find their continuity in Joshua.

►CROSSING THE JORDAN, 1:10–5:12 The first stage calls for the preparation of Israel. As their leader, Joshua must demonstrate to the people that he follows in the footsteps of Moses. He does this by reminding the Transjordan tribes to demonstrate loyalty to the command of Moses by joining with the other tribes in the conquest of Canaan (1:13-15; cf. Nm 32:20-27). They submitted to Joshua's authority as to Moses' (Jos 1:16-18). He demonstrates his military leadership in sending the two spies to Jericho (ch 2). His authority is accepted by priests (3:6; 4:10) and people (3:5-9) as they cross the Jordan. The crossing of the Jordan marks the public recognition of Joshua as a leader like Moses (4:14).

The account of the crossing marks an important transition from the era of the exodus/wilderness to the era of the Conquest. On the one hand, the story of Rahab illustrates how the Canaanites had heard about the Lord's mighty acts (2:10-11) and reacted with great fear (cf. Ex 15:15; 23:27-28; Dt 2:25; 7:23; 11:25; 32:30). Rahab's expression of faith in Israel's God (2:11) anticipates the inclusion of the Gentiles in the covenant community as promised to the patriarchs (Gn 12:3). By faith Rahab was included in the covenant and was richly rewarded by the inclusion of her name in the lineage of Jesus (Mt 1:5).

The Israelites crossed the Jordan with the knowledge that the fear of God had come on the Canaanites (Jos 2:24). However, they were also instructed to show their reverence for the Lord by keeping a safe distance between themselves and the ark of the covenant (3:4) and by consecrating themselves (v 5). The "living God" was among them and required holiness and reverence from his people (v 10). He, in turn, would demonstrate his loyalty in the marvelous passage through the Jordan River (v 13) and in the conquest of the land (3:10). After the tribes had crossed the river (4:1), each leader of the 12 tribes took up a stone out of the dried-up riverbed and set up a memorial at Gilgal (vv 1-9, 20). Thus, Israel was to remember that the stones, taken from the place where the priests who carried the ark had stood, were reminders of the majestic presence of God. Future generations who were to hear this report (vv 21-24) were hereby encouraged because the fear of God would fall on all the peoples of the land (v 24).

The consecration before the conquest of Jericho is also symbolized by the act of circumcision (5:1-9) and by the celebration of the Passover (vv 10-12). The events are not necessarily chronologically related but were selected as examples of Israel's responsiveness to Joshua's ministry. Moses' appeal to the new generation had its effect (cf. Dt

4:4-14; 6:1-5). The new generation served the Lord as long as Joshua and the elders were alive (Jos 24:31). Physical circumcision, neglected during the wilderness journey (5:5) due to unbelief, was a sign of spiritual responsiveness. The responsive nation received the external sign of the covenant with the anticipation that the Lord of the covenant would bless his people in giving them victory and the fruit of the land. Their reproach was rolled away (v 9). The covenant continuity is also brought out in the brief mention of the Passover celebration. The newness is their eating the fruit of the land. With the taste of the food of Canaan, the manna stopped. The desert experience was over. A new era was ushered in with their presence in the Promised Land (vv 11-12).

►CONQUEST OF JERICHO, 5:13–6:27 The victory is the Lord's. This is the message with which the battle of Jericho begins. The holy God who appeared to Moses in the burning bush (Ex 3:2–4:17) appeared to Joshua as the commander of the Lord's army (Jos 5:14-15) with a message from the Lord (6:2). The city of Jericho will fall without a siege and ensuing battle. Israel's response to Jericho's preparedness for war (cf. 24:11) was strange, but the presence of the ark and the blowing of the trumpets symbolized that the Lord would fight for Israel, even as he had promised. However, Israel could not take any of the spoil. Because Yahweh fought for Israel, everything was to be devoted to him (6:17). The Lord honored the vow to Rahab, made by the spies, so that she and her family were kept alive (vv 17, 25), but they were temporarily placed outside the camp (v 23). The valuable metals were placed into the treasury (vv 19, 24), whereas everything else was burned by fire (v 24). Nothing was to be taken for personal gain; otherwise God's judgment would rest on Israel (v 18). In order to emphasize God's absolute ownership of Jericho, Joshua put a curse on anyone who would attempt to rebuild the city (6:26; cf. 1 Kgs 16:34). The rumors of Jericho's destruction spread, and the peoples of Canaan knew that the Lord was with Joshua (Jos 6:27; cf. 1:5, 9).

►TRAGEDY AND TRIUMPH AT AI, 7:1–8:29 Victory was short-lived because Achan defied God's "ban," took some of the objects, hid them in the ground under his tent (7:21), and brought God's wrath on all of Israel (v 1). Israel was stunned by their defeat at Ai (vv 2-5). Joshua and the elders responded to the disaster by fasting and lamenting (vv 6-9). What a contrast between the reports of victory spread through the land and the anguished cry of God's servant, fearful that the Canaanites would amass strength and wipe out Israel (v 9). Only after the people had consecrated themselves (v 13) and Achan was exposed and his memory removed (vv 25b-26) could they renew the attack on Ai with the encouraging promise of God's presence and victory (8:1-2). Ai, too, was taken (vv 3-19) and the population execrated (vv 20-26), but Israel enjoyed the spoils by direct permission from the Lord (v 27). The ruins of Ai, the pile of stones covering the body of Ai's king (vv 28-29), and the heap of rocks over Achan's body were sobering reminders to Israel that God's faithfulness requires absolute loyalty from his people.

►RENEWAL OF THE COVENANT, 8:30-35 Joshua led Israel in a ceremonial covenant renewal at Shechem, as Moses had instructed (Jos 8:31; cf. Dt 11:29; 27). Joshua took care in the proper preparation of the altar (cf. Ex 20:25) on which dedicatory and communal offerings were presented. He copied the law as a symbol of his royal leadership and his devotion to the Lord (Jos 8:32; cf. Dt 17:18). All Israel (officers and people, aliens and native-born Israelites) together presented themselves for the reading of the blessings and the curses (Jos 8:33-35). The whole book of Deuteronomy (i.e., "the Book of the Law," cf. Dt 31:26) was read in their presence. Half the tribes stood on Mt Gerizim and said "Amen" to the blessings, and the other six stood on Mt Ebal, saying "Amen" to the curses (cf. Dt 27:9-26).

➤ COVENANT WITH THE GIBEONITES, 9:1-27 The rumors of God's mighty acts had brought fear on the Canaanite kings (cf. Jos 2:8-11, 24; 5:1; 6:27). The first defeat at Ai had given them a ray of hope that Israel could be put down. Rather than submit themselves to Israel and suffer from humiliation as servants of Israel, they joined forces against Joshua and Israel (9:1-2).

The Hivites from Gibeon, Kephirah, Beeroth, and Kiriath-jearim (9:7, 17) did not join with their fellow Canaanites. Instead, they developed an intricate plan to deceive Israel and to sue for full treaty status. The purpose of the treaty was that of friendship (namely, "peace"), promising each other to be of mutual assistance in case of attack. The concern was with the preservation of life (vv 15, 24). Their deception included a ruse about the great distance they had traveled (vv 11-14) and a false report of Israel's victories in Transjordan with no mention of their crossing the Jordan (9:9-10; cf. 5:1). The law permitted the submissive city to subject its population to a type of suzerainty treaty, in which Israel defined the terms and expected the subjugated populace to serve as its forced laborers (Dt 20:11; cf. Jgs 1:28-35; 1 Kgs 9:15-21). However, the treaty permitted the Hivites to maintain their way of life with the advantage of Israel's military protection.

➤ THE SOUTHERN CAMPAIGN, 10:1-43 The king of Jerusalem, Adoni-zedek, led the cities of Hebron, Jarmuth, Lachish, and Eglon in an alliance against Gibeon as a military ploy to take a stand against Israel (Jos 10:1-5). The Gibeonites appealed to Israel for help based on their covenantal relationship (v 6). Joshua led Israel on a 25-mile (40-kilometer) hike through the wilderness from Gilgal up to Gibeon during one night (vv 7-9). The Israelite attack surprised the Canaanites, who were already frightened of the Israelites. The camp of the Canaanites was thrown into confusion, and the soldiers fled the hill country via the road of Beth-horon to Azekah and Makkedah (v 10). But while running, they were tormented with large hailstones (v 11). The victory was the Lord's. Miraculously, Israel could push the Canaanites farther from the hill country because of the long day (vv 12-14). The marvel of this day was long remembered in the Book of Jashar (cf. 2 Sm 1:18), because on it the Lord listened to a man, namely Joshua (Jos 10:14).

The five kings hidden in a cave at Makkedah were discovered, killed, hanged on trees, and buried in the cave (10:16-27). Their foolish attempt to make war on Israel came to a quick end. Since the coalition of large cities had been put down, Joshua led Israel in a rapid campaign of the other southern cities (vv 29-43). The region was taken in one campaign with the Lord's help (v 42).

➤ THE NORTHERN CAMPAIGN, 11:1-15 The Israelites were again forced into battle, this time by the leadership of Jabin, king of Hazor. Jabin rallied the kings of the northern cities who assembled their troops and horses by the waters of Merom for battle against Israel (11:1-5). The similarity to the southern campaign is a literary way to demonstrate that the kings of the south and north initiated the war and were consequently defeated. So it was with the northern kings, who were routed as far as the region of Sidon in Phoenicia (v 8). Their horses were hamstrung and their chariots burned (v 9), as the Lord had instructed (v 6). Israel was to depend on the Lord (cf. Ps 20:7). Hazor, the great and ancient city, the center

of Canaanite power in the north, was completely destroyed (Jos 11:10-13). The burning of Jericho, Ai, and Hazor were exceptions, because Israel had been promised Canaanite houses, wells, and cities (Dt 6:10-11; cf. Jos 24:13). The campaign narrative stresses again the absolute loyalty of Joshua to the Lord and to Moses, the servant of the Lord (Jos 11:9-15).

➤ SUMMARY OF THE CAMPAIGNS, 11:16-12:24 Joshua led Israel in victory and rest because of his careful adherence to the Lord's directions to Moses. Moses had described the land to be conquered in detail (Dt 1:7), and Joshua took the regions of which Moses had spoken. Though the cities could have sued for a peaceable arrangement under which they would have been forced laborers (Dt 20:11), none of the cities recognized Israel. In fear they plotted and schemed how to destroy Israel. They were the aggressors. God had hardened their hearts (Jos 11:20). The theological reason is a mystery, as it was in the case of Pharaoh. But the net result was that Canaan was conquered and the population exterminated, except for the Hivites at Gibeon and their surrounding cities (vv 19-20). Even the Anakites, who had brought fear on Israel some 40 years before (Nm 13:33; cf. Dt 2:10, 21), were execrated (Jos 11:21). Yet it is already apparent that not every square mile of land was taken (v 22), even though in a sense the entire land was Israel's, because major centers of Canaanite resistance had been broken. The tension between fulfillment and complete fulfillment is apparent in these verses.

The listing of defeated kings (ch 12) includes the victories over Sihon and Og under Moses' leadership. Their juxtaposition with the list of kings conquered under Joshua demonstrates the continuity of leadership and purpose—two leaders, many campaigns, but one battle. The Land of Promise is now a fulfillment. Through the campaigns the borders of the land of inheritance were now more apparent. In Transjordan the limits are from the Arnon to Mt Hermon (vv 2-5). In Canaan the boundary extends from the region south of Sidon to the Negev (vv 7-8).

The Division of the Land, 13:1-22:34

➤ THE COMMAND TO DIVIDE THE LAND, 13:1-7 Because of Joshua's advanced age, the "whole" land was not taken. Moses had forewarned Israel that the inheritance would result from conquest as well as from gradual extension of Israel's narrow boundaries. Slowly Israel was to inherit the whole land, lest it be overwhelmed by the size and be unable to use it properly (Ex 23:29-30; Dt 7:22). The areas still to be occupied were: the region to the north of Galilee, Mt Hermon (east of the Sea of Galilee), the area occupied by the Philistines, and remaining Canaanite enclaves (Jos 13:2-7; cf. Jgs 1). Israel was not to be concerned with the future rights of occupation, because the Lord promised to help them (Jos 13:6).

➤ DIVISION OF TRANSJORDAN, 13:8-33 Joshua did not alter the Mosaic arrangement concerning the allotments to the tribes of Manasseh, Reuben, and Gad (Jos 13:8, 32-33; cf. Nm 32; Dt 3:12-17). Their territory also excluded certain regions still occupied by Canaanites (Jos 13:13). The clans of Reuben had received the territory from the Arnon River north to Heshbon (vv 15-23). The clans of Gad had received the territory of Gilead, south of the Jabbok River to Heshbon (vv 24-28). Several clans of Manasseh received the region south of the Wadi Yarmuk to the Jabbok (vv 29-31). The Levitical towns are not listed here, but a reference is made to them as not receiving a patrimony, because they were to live off the offerings and sacrifices made to the Lord (Jos 13:14; cf. Nm 18:20-24; 35:1-8).

►THE TRIBAL DIVISIONS IN CANAAN, 14:1–19:51 Eleazar, the high priest, and Joshua together cast lots to determine the boundaries, size, and allocation for the remaining nine and a half tribes. Again the exclusion of the tribe of Levi is mentioned (Jos 14:4), because their cities will be dealt with in chapters 20–21. Another literary device is special mention of the inheritance of Caleb in the beginning (14:6-15) and of Joshua at the conclusion (19:49-50). These two were the only ones who had left Egypt as adults, had been faithful spies, and had entered into the Promised Land (Nm 14:24, 30; Dt 1:36-38).

Judah, 15:1-63 (cf. Jgs 1:10-15, 20) The boundaries of Judah extended from the Dead Sea westward to the Mediterranean (Jos 15:2-12). The cities of Judah are listed in its four regions: 29 in the Negev (vv 21-32), 42 cities in the Shephelah (or western foothills) and coastal plains (vv 33-47), 38 cities in the hill country (15:48-60), and 6 cities in the desert (vv 61-62). Judah was unable to take Jerusalem (v 63) until David made it his capital (cf. Jgs 1:21; 2 Sm 5:6-16).

Ephraim and Manasseh, 16:1–17:18 These two tribes, descended from Joseph, were richly blessed (cf. Gn 48; 49:22-26; Dt 33:13-17) and had obtained prominence among the tribes. They received one allotment as "the allotment for Joseph" (Jos 16:1). Part of Manasseh had already received a patrimony east of the Jordan (13:29-31). The limits for Ephraim and the west half of Manasseh were from Bethel to Mt Gilboa in the north and from the Jordan to the Mediterranean (16:1-3). Ephraim received the smaller portion in the south (vv 5-9) but was unable to drive the Canaanites out of Gezer. The clans of Manasseh are given, including Zelophehad (17:3-6; cf. Nm 27:1-11; 36:1-12), in order to clearly distinguish them from the clans of Manasseh in Transjordan. The region of west Manasseh extended from Shechem to Mt Gilboa (Jos 17:7-11); but Manasseh, also, was incapable of driving out the Canaanites completely (vv 12-13).

Though they had received the largest portion of the land (more than a third), the tribes of Joseph complained. They knew that the Lord had blessed them (17:14), and they expected to get more cultivable land. But Joshua urged them to use the available land by cutting down the forests (vv 15-18). When they expressed realistic concern about Canaanite military power, Joshua called on them to do their share in occupying the land.

Seven Tribes, 18:1–19:51 The Israelites assembled at Shiloh to set up the tabernacle (cf. 1 Sm 1). At that point seven tribes had not yet received their patrimony. Joshua called for each tribe to commission three men to survey the land. When they returned, Joshua cast lots at the tabernacle in Shiloh and divided the land (Jos 18:3-10). The territory of Benjamin was between Judah and Ephraim (vv 11-28). Simeon's allotment was in southern Judah (19:1-9), resulting in its absorption into Judah (cf. Gn 49:7). Zebulun (Jos 19:10-16), Issachar (vv 17-23), Asher (vv 24-31), and Naphtali (vv 32-39) received a portion north of Manasseh in the region of Galilee. Dan received the seventh lot and suffered subsequently, when it could not maintain the allotted territory because of the pressure of Judah on the east and the Philistines to the west (vv 40-48). They migrated northward and found the sources of the Jordan to be a fruitful region (Jos 19:47; cf. Jgs 18).

Conclusion, 19:49-51 The conclusion is symmetric with the beginning (Jos 14:1-14) in that Joshua also received a gift. Again, mention is made that all divisions were in the presence of the Lord, witnessed to and executed by the high priest Eleazar and Joshua (19:51; cf. 14:1).

►CITIES OF REFUGE AND THE LEVITICAL CITIES, 20:1–21:45 According to the instructions of Moses, six Levitical cities were set apart, three on each side of the Jordan, as cities of refuge (Nm 35:9-34; Dt 4:41-43; 19:1-10). The purpose was to provide "refuge" (asylum) for those who were guilty of manslaughter but had not intentionally killed someone. This practice was not to provide a way out for someone who was guilty, but to allow for the legal process to be completed (Jos 20).

The Levites received by clan a total of 48 cities, six of which also served as cities of refuge (21:1-42). The Levites could not cultivate the soil because they were dependent on the tithes of the people (Nm 18:21-24), but they were permitted to have land for grazing. The dimensions of the land are given in Numbers 35:4-5. A special allocation is made to the descendants of Aaron (Jos 21:9-19), because they served as priests and their 13 cities were in the Judah-Simeon region, in proximity to the Jerusalem temple of the Solomonic era.

With the allocation of the Levitical cities, the division of the land is concluded. The promise of the land is fulfilled (21:43-45). God is faithful! This section emphasizes the fulfillment, the power, and the grace of God, by which Israel entered into its rest. However, the book of Joshua also hints of the struggle that is still ahead of the Israelites and of the test that ultimately they will fail (cf. Ps 95:11; Heb 3:7-11).

►RETURN OF THE TRANSJORDAN TRIBES, 22:1-34 Joshua dismissed the two and a half tribes with a commendation for their loyalty to the other tribes and to the Lord (Jos 22:1-4), with a warning not to succumb to idolatry but to love the Lord in accordance with the Deuteronomic law, and with a blessing (vv 5-8). However, as they returned they set up a large altar by the Jordan on the western side. The other tribes heard about it and met at Shiloh (v 12). They wisely commissioned Phinehas, the son of the high priest, with ten representatives of the tribes, to investigate the matter. The commission charged the Transjordan tribes with treachery (Jos 22:15-20; cf. Nm 25; Jos 7).

The response of the Transjordan tribes demonstrated their concern for the unity of the tribes and for the worship of God. These tribes feared being excluded from the fellowship of God's people and had purposefully constructed an altar, identical to that prescribed in the law, in order to demonstrate their common heritage (Jos 22:21-30). The altar was not for sacrifice or worship but functioned as a symbol of the covenantal unity of the people of God.

Phinehas and the tribal representatives were pleased with the response and left with the assurance of God's presence (22:30-31). Their report to the tribes led to reconciliation of all the tribes on this matter. The narrative concludes with a mention of the name given to the altar: "A witness between us and them that the LORD is our God, too" (v 34, NLT).

Epilogue: The Land Is a Sacred Trust, 23:1–24:33 The last two chapters contain Joshua's farewell speeches to all the leaders and to all Israel.

►ADDRESS TO THE LEADERS, 23:1-16 Joshua reviews what the Lord has done for Israel in giving the land to the tribes. He has demonstrated his loyalty. And he will continue to be with his people so that no enemy can stand against them. He will fulfill every outstanding promise, even as he had already fulfilled promises.

However, they must persevere in their loyalty to the Lord. Loyalty to the Lord is not apart from loyalty to the law of Moses. Apostasy will be severely punished, first by leaving the nations to ensnare Israel, and then by consuming them in his wrath.

➤ADDRESS TO ISRAEL, 24:1-28 The address ends with a covenant renewal at Shechem (Jos 24:1, 25-28; cf. 8:30-35). In the ancient Near East it was common when making a treaty (covenant) to give a brief historical summary of the relationship of the parties involved. Joshua reviewed Israel's history from the patriarchs to their generation: patriarchs (24:2-4), exodus (vv 5-7), and conquest (vv 8-13).

The goodness, presence, and loyalty of Yahweh was evident to them. Yahweh also expected "faithfulness" from his people in the form of whole allegiance, without any form of idolatry (Jos 24:14-15). As the head of his family, Joshua vowed to be loyal (v 15). The people responded by giving reasons for being loyal to the Lord (vv 16-18). But Joshua pushed them to a deeper commitment by challenging their profession (vv 19-20), then recording their vow and setting up a stone of witness against them (vv 25-27).

➤END OF AN ERA, 24:29-33 The book began with a reference to the death of Moses (1:1-2) and concludes with the death and burial of Joshua (24:29-30) and of Eleazar the high priest (v 33). This marks the end of an era. The burial of Joseph's bones (Jos 24:32; cf. Gn 50:25; Ex 13:19) in a plot purchased by Jacob (Gn 33:19) brings together the hope characteristic of the epoch of Moses and Joshua.

See also Cities of Refuge; Conquest and Allotment of the Land; Israel, History of; Joshua (Person) #1; Levitical Cities.

JOSIAH

1. Sixteenth king of the southern kingdom of Judah (640–609 BC). A godly man, he stood in marked contrast to his grandfather Manasseh and his father, Amon. In fact, Scripture declares there was no king either before or after him who was as obedient to the law of Moses (2 Kgs 23:25). The Greek form of his name, Josias, appears in Matthew 1:10-11 (KJV).

The Times of Josiah When Josiah became king in 640 BC, the international scene was about to change drastically. After the great Assyrian king Ashurbanipal died in 633 BC, mediocre rulers followed him on the throne, and there was considerable unrest in the empire. Nabopolassar, father of Nebuchadnezzar, seized the kingship in Babylon and established the Neo-Babylonian Empire late in 626 BC. Soon Babylonians and Medes combined forces to topple the Assyrian Empire, and in 612 BC completely destroyed the city of Nineveh. As Babylonian power rose in the east, Assyrian control over the province that had once been the kingdom of Israel relaxed and Assyrian pressure on Judah virtually ceased. After the fall of Nineveh, the Assyrians established their capital at Haran. There they were defeated by Babylonians and Scythians in 610 BC. At that point Pharaoh Neco II of Egypt decided to support Assyria. In the late spring of 609 BC he advanced through Judah, defeated and killed Josiah, and spent the summer campaigning in Syria.

Before Josiah's reign, Judah had capitulated to gross idolatry during the reign of Manasseh (697–642 BC). Baalism, Molech worship, and other pagan religions had invaded the land, as had occultism and astrology. A false altar even stood in the temple in Jerusalem,

and human sacrifice to pagan deities was practiced near Jerusalem. The nation was thoroughly corrupt. Although some reform occurred in Manasseh's latter days, conditions reverted to their former baseness during the reign of his son Amon (642–640 BC). In 640 BC officials of Amon's household assassinated him, and the "people of the land" put Josiah on the throne (2 Kgs 21:26; 22:1; 2 Chr 33:25–34:1).

Josiah's Reform Activities Josiah was only eight years old when he became king. Evidently he had spiritually motivated advisers or regents; by the time he was 16, he began on his own accord "to seek the God of his ancestor David" (2 Chr 34:3). When he was 20, he became greatly exercised over the idolatry of the land and launched a major effort to eradicate the pagan high places, groves, and images from Judah and Jerusalem. So intense was Josiah's hatred of idolatry that he even opened the tombs of pagan priests and burned their bones on pagan altars before the altars were destroyed.

Josiah carried his reform movement beyond the borders of Judah, venting his fury especially on the cult center at Bethel, where Jeroboam had set up his false worship. In fulfillment of prophecy (1 Kgs 13:1-3), he destroyed the altar and high place and burned the bones of officiating priests to desecrate the site (2 Kgs 23:15-18). What he did at Bethel he did everywhere else in the kingdom of Samaria (vv 19-20).

When Josiah was 26, he launched a project to cleanse and repair the temple in Jerusalem (2 Kgs 22:3). Shaphan, the king's administrative assistant, commissioned the work; Hilkiah the priest supervised the renovation and construction. In the process of restoring the temple, Hilkiah found the Book of the Law, the nature and contents of which are otherwise unknown. Possibly in the dark days of Manasseh a deliberate attempt had been made to destroy the Word of God. At any rate, there was little knowledge of Scripture in Judah.

When Shaphan read the Book of the Law to Josiah, the king was devastated by the pronouncements of judgment against apostasy contained in it. He sent a delegation to Huldah the prophetess to find out what judgments awaited the land. The prophetess replied that the condemnation of God would indeed fall on Judah for its sin, but she sent word to Josiah that because his heart was right toward God, the punishment would not come during his lifetime.

The king called together a large representative group for a public reading of the law—evidently sections especially concerned with obligations to God. The king and the people made a covenant before God to keep his commandments.

Faced with the importance of maintaining a pure monotheistic faith, the king was spurred on to even more rigorous efforts to cleanse the temple and Jerusalem. He destroyed the vessels used in Baal worship, the monument of horses given by the kings of Judah for sun worship, the chariots dedicated to the sun, the homosexual community near the temple, and shrines built by Solomon and in use since his day. Moreover, he made stringent efforts to eliminate the pagan shrines and high places in all the towns of Judah (2 Kgs 23:4-14).

The Death of Josiah Precisely why Josiah opposed Pharaoh Neco's advance through Judean territory is unknown. He may have wanted to prevent aid from reaching the hated Assyrians or to maintain his own independence. Josiah was mortally wounded in the conflict and was greatly lamented by Jeremiah and all the people (2 Chr 35:25). Well they might weep, for their godly king was gone, and within a few years the judgment withheld during his lifetime would descend on the nation.

See also Chronology of the Bible (Old Testament); Israel, History of.

2. Son of Zephaniah, who returned to Jerusalem with other Jews after the captivity (Zec 6:10, 14; Hebrew "Hen").

JOSIAS* KJV spelling of Josiah, Jehoiachin's father, in Matthew 1:10-11. See Josiah #1.

JOSIBIAH* KJV spelling of Joshibiah, Jehu's father, in 1 Chronicles 4:35. See Joshibiah.

JOSIPHIAH Father of Shelomith, leader of a family of which 160 members accompanied Ezra back to Palestine (Ezr 8:10).

JOTBAH Hometown of Haruz, the father of Meshullemeth, who was the mother of King Amon of Judah (2 Kgs 21:19). Its location is uncertain; however, some identify it with the town later named Jotapata by the Romans, situated six miles (9.7 kilometers) north of Sepphoris (modern Khirbet Jefat).

JOTBATHAH Temporary camping place of the Israelites during their wilderness wanderings, located between Hor-haggidgad and Abronah (Nm 33:33-34). Later, following the death of Aaron, Israel journeyed from Gudgodah to this place, noted for its streams of water (Dt 10:7).

See also Wilderness Wanderings.

JOTHAM

1. Youngest of Gideon's 70 sons and the only survivor of Abimelech's slaughter of Jotham's brothers at Ophrah (Jgs 9:5). Upon learning of Abimelech's intrigue with the Shechemites, which led to the death of his brothers, Jotham traveled to Shechem and addressed its people from atop nearby Mt Gerizim. Using a parable, he portrayed Abimelech's rise as king and concluded his denunciation by issuing a curse on both his half brother (see 8:31) and the people of Shechem for their treachery (9:7). Jotham then fled to Beer for fear of a reprisal from Abimelech (v 21). Later, God fulfilled Jotham's curse; the people of Shechem were killed in a revolt and Abimelech was struck down at the hands of a woman (v 57).

2. Eleventh king of Judah (750–735 BC). He was the son of King Azariah (Uzziah) of Judah and Jerusa, daughter of Zadok (2 Kgs 15:7; 2 Chr 26:21; 27:1), and the father of Ahaz. Jotham, at 25 years of age, ascended Judah's throne in the second year of King Pekah of Israel (752–732 BC) and ruled for 16 years in Jerusalem. Initially he reigned as co-regent with Azariah, who was stricken with leprosy for tolerating pagan worship, until his father's death (2 Kgs 15:5).

Jotham was considered a righteous king in the eyes of the Lord. However, he also failed to cleanse the temple of its pagan influences, and subsequently the people of Judah continued in their evil ways (2 Chr 27:2-6). His building projects included the Upper Gate of the temple, work on the wall of Ophel, and the fortification of numerous towns in Judah's hill country (vv 3-4). Jotham also defeated the troublesome Ammonites in battle (v 5) and registered by genealogy the families of Gad living east of the Jordan (1 Chr 5:17). He was buried in Jerusalem after his

death (2 Chr 27:9). The prophets Isaiah and Micah ministered to Judah, and Hosea to Israel, during his tenure as king. Jotham is listed as an ancestor of Jesus Christ in Matthew's genealogy (Mt 1:9).

See also Chronology of the Bible (Old Testament); Genealogy of Jesus Christ; Israel, History of.

3. Second of Jahdai's five sons (1 Chr 2:47).

JOT OR TITTLE* An expression Jesus used in the Sermon on the Mount. In Matthew 5:18 *jot* is a transliteration of the Greek letter *iota*. In this context it originally referred to the Hebrew letter *yod*, the smallest letter in the Hebrew alphabet. *Tittle* is a Middle English word referring to the diacritical dot placed over abbreviated words. The KJV translators used it to render a Greek word meaning "little horn." The Jews used that word to refer to the small marking that distinguished certain Hebrew letters from one another. Jesus used the two terms to emphasize the importance of the law when he said not one jot or tittle would pass from the law until all was fulfilled.

JOY Positive human condition that can be either feeling or action. The Bible uses "joy" in both senses.

Joy as a Feeling Joy is a feeling called forth by well-being, success, or good fortune. A person automatically experiences it because of certain favorable circumstances. It cannot be commanded.

The shepherd experienced joy when he found his lost sheep (Mt 18:13). The multitude felt it when Jesus healed a Jewish woman whom Satan had bound for 18 years (Lk 13:17). The disciples returned to Jerusalem rejoicing after Jesus' ascension (24:52). Joy was also the feeling of the church at Antioch when its members heard the Jerusalem Council's decision that they did not have to be circumcised to keep God's law (Acts 15:31). Paul mentioned his joy in hearing about the obedience of the Roman Christians (Rom 16:19). He wrote to the Corinthians that love does not rejoice in wrong but rejoices in the right (1 Cor 13:6; see also 1 Sm 2:1; 11:9; 18:6; 2 Sm 6:12; 1 Kgs 1:40; Est 9:17-22).

Psalms 137:1-6 shows that the emotion cannot be commanded. The Jews' captors wanted them to sing in the land of their exile, something they were unable to do. Faraway Jerusalem was their chief joy.

Joy as an Action There is a joy that Scripture commands. That joy is action that can be engaged in regardless of how the person feels. Proverbs 5:18 tells the reader to rejoice in the wife of his youth, without reference to what she may be like. Christ instructed his disciples to rejoice when they were persecuted, reviled, and slandered (Mt 5:11-12). The apostle Paul commanded continuous rejoicing (Phil 4:4; 1 Thes 5:16). James said Christians are to reckon it all joy when they fall into various testings because such testings produce endurance (Jas 1:2). Joy in adverse circumstances is possible only as a fruit of the Holy Spirit, who is present in every Christian (Gal 5:22).

See also Fruit of the Spirit.

JOZABAD

1. Benjamite from Gederah and one of the military men who came to David's support at Ziklag (1 Chr 12:4).
2, 3. Leaders and mighty warriors from Manasseh's tribe who joined David at Ziklag to fight against Saul (1 Chr 12:20).
4. One of the Levites who assisted with the administration of the temple contributions in Jerusalem during King Hezekiah's reign (2 Chr 31:13).
5. One of the Levitical chiefs who generously gave

animals to the Levites for the celebration of the Pass-over feast during King Josiah's reign (2 Chr 35:9).

6. Levite, the son of Jeshua, and one who helped Meremoth, Eleazar, and Noadiah take inventory of the temple's gifts and precious metals during the days of Ezra (Ezr 8:33).

7. Priest and one of the six sons of Pashhur who was encouraged by Ezra to divorce his foreign wife during the postexilic era (Ezr 10:22).

8. One of the Levites who was encouraged by Ezra to divorce his foreign wife (Ezr 10:23).

9. One of the Levites who assisted Ezra with teaching the people the law during the postexilic period (Neh 8:7).

10. One of the Levites who relocated to Jerusalem and was put in charge of the work of the temple during the days of Nehemiah (Neh 11:16).

11. Alternate rendering for Shimeath's son in 2 Kings 12:21. *See* Jozacar, Jozachar.

JOZACAR*, JOZACHAR* Son of Shimeath the Ammonitess and one of the royal servants who conspired against the murdered King Joash of Judah (2 Kgs 12:21). He is alternately called Zabad in 2 Chronicles 24:26. *See* Zabad.

JOZADAK* Seraiah's son and one of the exiles transported by Nebuchadnezzar to Babylonia (1 Chr 6:14-15). He was the father of Jeshua (also called Joshua), the high priest in postexilic Jerusalem during the days of Zerubbabel (Ezr 3:2, 8; 5:2; 10:18; Neh 12:26; Hg 1:1-14; 2:2-4; Zec 6:11). Jozadak is alternately called Jehozadak.

JUBAL Son of Adah, wife of Lamech, a descendant of Cain. He is crredited with being the first musician, the inventor of the harp and flute (Gn 4:19-21).

JUBILEE YEAR* Year of emancipation and restoration to be kept every 50 years. For Israel, the seventh year expressed at length the values of the seventh day Sabbath (Lv 25:1-7). When a series of seven years reached the perfection of seven sevens, the 50th year was heralded by the trumpet of jubilee and a whole additional year was set aside as belonging to the Lord.

The word "jubilee" simply means a ram's horn; it came to mean a trumpet made from or in the shape of a ram's horn. Such horns were exclusively for religious use. The sacred trumpet gave its name to the year of the ram's horn, the jubilee year—a year to which the people of God were summoned in a striking and holy way. It was not simply a release from labor, not just a rest, but a year belonging to the Lord. In Leviticus 25 this exact expression occurs in connection with the seventh year rather than expressly with the jubilee year. Functionally such a year was a Sabbath rest for the land, and it brought enjoyment "to the LORD" (Lv 25:4). But nothing could more directly express the implications and orientations of the 50th year.

Lordship The first principle of the jubilee is God's lordship over the whole earth, acknowledged by his people in their obedience to his command to set the year aside in this way. Just as the Sabbath expressed his right to order life, giving it the shape of six days' work and one day's rest, and just as the seventh year, linked in Deuteronomy 31:9-13 with the reading of his law, expressed his right to command the obedience of his people, so the 50th year expressed his sovereign possession of all: land, people, means of production, and life itself. Take the

typical case of debtor and creditor. When God brought his people into possession of the land, he gave to each his inheritance. In a given circumstance a man might be compelled to sell his land in whole or part, but it must come back to him: "The land must never be sold on a permanent basis because it really belongs to me. You are only foreigners and tenants living with me" (Lv 25:23, NLT). In this verse "foreigners" carries the meaning "stateless persons," "refugees," "those who have sought political asylum"—in a word, those who have no rights except what mercy concedes. Such are the people of God and such they must acknowledge themselves to be when the jubilee year comes around. When a piece of real estate changed hands, the seller might congratulate himself on the astuteness with which he had solved his problem, and the buyer might rejoice in his skillful acquisitiveness, but in the Year of Jubilee seller and buyer alike are compelled to confess a different truth: neither is master, either of his own welfare or of the person and goods of another. Each has a Master in heaven.

Redemption According to the ordinance, the trumpet that heralded the year was sounded on the Day of Atonement (Lv 25:9). That was the day on which the Lord proclaimed his people clean before him from all their sins (16:30). Forgiveness of sins ushered in the jubilee year. The verb "to redeem" and the noun "redemption" had a strong commercial use in the recovery of property pledged against loans of money, and in the 50th year these words would have sounded and resounded as debtors confessed that they could not "redeem" and creditors forewent their "redemption" rights, each using the very vocabulary of the Lord's action at the exodus (Ex 6:6). This is what the Lord had done for his people, and the divine action must be the norm of the human. Brotherly generosity is urged (Lv 25:35-38), liberty is granted (vv 39-43), and slavery in perpetuity is forbidden (vv 47-55) simply because the divine redemptive act makes the redeemed into brothers, brings them into the Lord's servitude, and cancels the bondage that would otherwise be theirs forever.

Rest The correlative of redemption is rest. This rest is vividly illustrated and enforced as Moses legislates rest from all the toil connected with promoting next year's crop (Lv 25:4); rest from the toil of harvesting, for the people of God were to live hand to mouth, gathering only what and when need dictated (vv 5-7); rest from the anxious burden of debts incurred; and rest from slavery (vv 10). Like the Sabbath, this rest would have meant exactly what it said: freedom from toil; relaxation, refreshment, and recreation. Very likely tiredness was as endemic among the people of God then as now, and grace drew near to give them a holiday. But equally with the Sabbath, release from the preoccupations of staying alive created time to be preoccupied with the Lord, his worship, his Word, and the life that pleases him. We can understand Isaiah 58 as binding the ideals of Sabbath and jubilee together. The Lord frees his people not for unbroken idleness but for the redirection of life toward himself. The jubilee year was thus a deliberate opting out of the rat race; it called a halt to acquisitiveness; it abandoned concern over the pressure to stay alive. It reordered priorities, giving a chance to appraise the use of time and the selection of objectives. For a whole year the people of God stood back, rested, ceased from the good in order to attain the best.

Faith But this standing back from life was not in the style of a dropout. It was the action of responsible faith. No one on earth can escape questions such as "What shall we eat?" The Lord foresees and provides (Lv 25:20); grace provides so that God's people can enjoy the ordinances of grace (cf. Ex 16:29). When he commands a year off, he enables them to take it. The 50th year was a living testimony to his faithfulness. The last season of sowing and reaping would have been the 49th year; in the final 7th year in the series the people would live off the casual growth; and in the 50th year nothing but the sheer attentive faithfulness of their God could provide for them (Lv 25:21). Here indeed their faith would be put to the test, for God spoke a word of majestic promise and called on them to believe. At the heart of their jubilee they took God at his word and found him faithful.

Obedience Biblically, it is a central characteristic of the people of God that they do what he commands for no other reason than that he commands it. In the ordinance of the 50th year the people of God must show themselves as his obedient ones, and in fact their obedience is the guarantee of continuance in the land he has granted to them. Thus, for example, Leviticus 26:34-35 teaches that loss of tenure and loss of liberty is directly related to contravention of the principle of the Sabbath, found on the seventh day, seventh year, and jubilee year. Refusal to obey goes hand in hand with loss of possession, leaving behind an empty land, which then enjoys the Sabbath rest it never received from its disobedient inhabitants.

Hope In the 50th year the people lived in the light of the forgiveness of sins, walked by obedience in harmony with the God who redeemed them, and in freedom from toil, received from the ground its life-sustaining benefits without any sweat on their brows (Gn 2:16; 3:19). It was a sort of Eden restored, the curse momentarily held in abeyance—but also a prolonged foretaste of the coming day when the promises would all be fulfilled, the blood of the covenant efficacious without hindrance, the prisoners of hope (i.e., who had waited in hope for their release) freed, and the trumpet of liberation heard throughout the world (Is 27:13; Zec 9:11-14). The Year of Jubilee in a limited but real way foreshadowed what would yet be the eternal inheritance and bliss of the people of God.

See also Feasts and Festivals of Israel.

JUCAL* Alternate name for Jehucal, Shelemiah's son, in Jeremiah 38:1 (NLT mg). *See* Jehucal.

JUDA* (Person)

1. Alternate KJV spelling of Judas, Jesus' brother, in Mark 6:3. Judas is also called Jude in Jude 1. *See* Jude (Person).
2. Alternate KJV spelling of Joda, Joanan's son, in Luke 3:26. *See* Joda.
3. Alternate KJV spelling of Judah, Joseph's son, in Luke 3:30. *See* Judah (Person) #8.
4. Alternate KJV spelling of Judah, Jacob's son, in Luke 3:33. *See* Judah (Person) #1.
5. Alternate KJV spelling for Judah's tribe (Heb 7:14; Rv 5:5; 7:5). *See* Judah, Tribe of.

JUDA (Place) Alternate KJV spelling for Judah's territory (or "Judea") in Luke 1:39. *See* Judah, Tribe of; Judea, Judeans.

JUDAEA* *See* Judea, Judeans.

JUDAH (Person)

1. Fourth of Jacob's 12 sons (Gn 35:23; 1 Chr 2:1) and the fourth son born to Jacob by Leah, who, overjoyed

with the thought of bearing Jacob another son, named him Judah, meaning "praise" (Gn 29:35). Judah fathered five sons: Er, Onan, and Shelah by Bathshua the Canaanitess (Gn 38:3-5; 1 Chr 2:3); and the twins Perez and Zerah by Tamar, his daughter-in-law (Gn 38:29-30; 1 Chr 2:4). He eventually settled his family in Egypt with his father and brothers (Ex 1:2), although his first two sons, Er and Onan, were divinely killed in Canaan for their disobedience (Gn 46:12). Judah became the founder of one of Israel's 12 tribes (Nm 1:26-27).

Though reckless in his behavior with Tamar (Gn 38:6-30), Judah showed firm resolve in taking personal responsibility for Benjamin's safety in Egypt and acting as intercessor for his brothers before Joseph (44:14-18). At the time of Jacob's blessing, Judah was granted the birthright privileges of the firstborn; the leadership of Jacob's family would come through Judah's seed, as would the promised Messiah of Abraham's covenant (49:8-12). Later, Judah's family was praised at the time of Ruth's engagement to Boaz (Ru 4:12), and both the Davidic lines of kings (1 Chr 2:1-15; 3:1-24) and Jesus Christ's ancestors traced their descent from Judah (Mt 1:2-3; Lk 3:33).

See also Genealogy of Jesus Christ; Judah, Tribe of.

2. Forefather of a family of Levites who assisted Jeshua, the high priest, with rebuilding the temple during the postexilic era (Ezr 3:9, NLT mg). He is alternately called Hodaviah in Ezra 2:40 and Hodevah in Nehemiah 7:43. *See* Hodaviah #4.
3. One of the Levites who was encouraged by Ezra to divorce his foreign wife (Ezr 10:23).
4. Benjamite, son of Hassenuah, who was second in command over the city of Jerusalem during the days of Nehemiah (Neh 11:9).
5. One of the leaders of the Levites who returned with Zerubbabel and Jeshua to Judah after the exile (Neh 12:8).
6. One of the princes of Judah who participated in the dedication of the Jerusalem wall during the postexilic period (Neh 12:34).
7. One of the priests who played a musical instrument at the dedication of the Jerusalem wall during the days of Nehemiah (Neh 12:36). He is perhaps identical with #5 above.
8. Joseph's son, father of Simeon and an ancestor of Jesus Christ (Lk 3:30). *See* Genealogy of Jesus Christ.

JUDAH, Tribe of One of the 12 tribes of Israel.

Geographical Territory The frontiers of Judah are well defined in Joshua 15, which describes the inheritance of the tribe after the Conquest. Second Kings 23:8 describes Judah as extending from Geba to Beersheba: Geba is about 8 miles (13 kilometers) north of Jerusalem, and Beersheba about 40 miles (64 kilometers) south. Judah thus held a strip of mountain land on the central spine of southern Palestine, about 50 miles (80 kilometers) from north to south and 20 miles (32 kilometers) from east to west. Of this 1,000 square miles, half was desert (on the south and east); the rest was stony and not well watered. The central ridge, upon which are situated Jerusalem, Hebron, and Beersheba, rises to over 3,000 feet (914 meters) in places before tapering off into the desert in the south. Along this ridge, connecting these towns, runs the chief road. To the east, the ridge drops steeply to the Dead Sea, nearly 5,000 feet (1,524 meters) below. To the west it drops less sharply to the "lowlands," actually a plateau some 1,000 feet (305 meters) high, before descending to the Philistine plain, which stretches to the sea.

Judah proper (Jerusalem was a later addition) was remote and secure in its hills. Its true center and capital was Hebron, 3,500 feet (1,067 meters) up. Only on the north was it vulnerable to attackers marching south along the ridge road. However, three great valleys led up from the western lowlands into the hills: the valley of Ajalon, the valley of Sorek, and the valley of Elah. Battles would rage up and down these valleys from the days of Joshua to the time of David and long afterward. The few roads to the east (the one from Jerusalem to Jericho is the best known) were not so important, although it was by this "back door" that Joshua had invaded the hill country (Jos 10:9). Judah was thus geographically well out of the mainstream of Israelite life, since only the territory of Simeon lay to the south.

The area occupied by Judah falls easily into three natural regions: the central mountain ridge, fairly densely settled, especially on its western side, where rainfall and dew were greatest; the eastern slopes, almost uninhabited and mostly desert; and the southern pastoral region round Beersheba, where the mountains fall away into dry prairie, with sparse settlement throughout.

Economic Life To Israel, Palestine was a land flowing with milk and honey (Nm 13:27). Half of Judah might be desert, but the rest had reasonably good soil, and on the western slopes the rain was usually adequate. Wheat, barley, olives, figs, and especially vineyards, grew freely. The land might be stony, but stones could be collected and used for walls and buildings. Not as rich as the great northern valleys like Jezreel, Judah was still good mixed farming country, although it required hard work. Sheep and goats were plentiful, and that meant wool and milk. Cattle were probably rarer; Judah was not cattle country like Bashan (Nm 32:1). Wool meant cloth, and hide meant leather. In those days the hills were forested, which meant fuel and building materials. Clay for pottery was readily available for domestic utensils. Copper came from Edom in the south, and iron from Philistia in the west; these could be obtained by bartering agricultural produce. Whether they realized it or not, God had dealt graciously with the people of Judah in giving them adequate resources. Nonetheless, the climate was bracing: a cold, wet winter, with snow and hail at times, and a long, rainless summer, with low humidity and cool nights. This brought heavy dews on the eastern slopes (Jgs 6:38), and precious rainwater was conserved in rock-hewn cisterns (Jer 2:13). Permanent streams of any size did not exist in Judah, but springs or "wells" were abundant, from Jerusalem to Beersheba. It was not until Judah got caught up into the economic life of Solomon's trading empire that its simple pattern of life changed; even then, the change in the hills of Judah was far less than elsewhere. Judah had no seaport of its own and controlled no rich caravan routes. It had no coveted raw materials, like the copper of Edom or the cedars of Lebanon; no luxury goods for trade, like the purple dye of Phoenicia or the gold of Ophir; no lush land to tempt the greed of others. In God's mercy Judah's temptations were few. Its faith was also less liable to be corrupted: comparatively few Canaanites had ever settled in this area, while the Conquest had been more thorough in the south than in the north.

History and Significance The earliest blessings on Judah are recorded in Genesis 49:8-12 and Deuteronomy 33:7. After the exodus, the tribe of Judah took first place in the desert camping arrangement (Nm 2:3). Caleb, one of the two faithful spies, was a tribal chieftain of Judah

(13:6). In Joshua's invasion of Palestine, the highlands allotted to Judah were the first to be cleared of Canaanites, after the initial fighting around Jericho and Ai (Jos 6; 8). The book of Joshua is a summary account of the whole campaign.

After Joshua's death, Simeon and Judah continued the fight against the Canaanites and marched together against the hill country of the south, led by Caleb and Othniel. Although God's gift to Judah had been the whole land westward as far as the sea, Judah failed to take anything but the hills. The plain was controlled by iron-protected chariots and fortress cities. The king of Jerusalem was killed and Jerusalem was burned (v 8), but the Jebusites continued to occupy the area until David's day (v 21). The men of Judah, like other Israelites, might burn Canaanite towns, but they did not usually occupy the old sites themselves. Under the judges, the tribe of Judah was still isolated, though Othniel was of Judah (ch 3). In the great battle against Sisera, Judah is not even mentioned (ch 5). This tribal isolation was soon lost, first through Philistine invasions from the west, and then through David's capture of Jerusalem and the placing of the national and religious capital there. Although in Judges 15:11 the men of Judah are prepared even to hand over Samson to the Philistines, with Samuel as judge, everything changes. The ark returns (1 Sm 7:1); lost territory is regained (v 14). Indeed, Samuel's sons act as judges in Beersheba (8:2), although they are corrupt.

David finally breaks the power of the Philistines in a series of victories and rules as king first in Hebron, Judah's chief town (2 Sm 2:1-4). When he is crowned king of all Israel, however, he moves the capital to the newly conquered Jerusalem, on the northern frontier of the tribe of Judah (5:6-10). Here the ark was to be brought (ch 6), and here Solomon was to build the temple (7:13). All God's promises will henceforth cluster around Jerusalem, the temple, and David's line. Most important, the Messiah would come from Judah (Gn 49:10).

The division between the northern and southern tribes had begun in David's lifetime, after Absalom's revolt (2 Sm 20:1); after Solomon's death, the rift became complete (1 Kgs 12:16). Henceforth for 200 years, until the fall of the northern kingdom in 722 BC, there were two little kingdoms side by side: a larger one in the north and east, called Israel (the "ten tribes" of 1 Kgs 11:35), and a smaller one in the south, called Judah. With this, the history of Judah as a tribe virtually comes to an end, for although still called by the old tribal name, this little

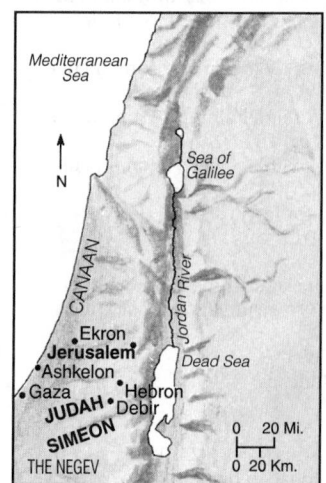

Judah Fights for Its Land The tribe of Judah wasted no time beginning their conquest of the territory allotted to them. With help from the tribe of Simeon, Jerusalem was conquered, as were the Canaanites in the Negev and along the coast. Hebron and Debir fell to Judah, and later so did Gaza, Ashkelon, and Ekron.

kingdom was really a "Greater Judah." It now contained not only the old tribe of Judah but also the newly conquered Jebusite territory of Jerusalem, some of the old Philistine country, and the tribes of Benjamin and Simeon, as well as many Levites (2 Chr 11:14) and other "loyalists" from the north. Indeed, from now on, "tribe" had far less meaning than before; it was more important where a person lived than of what tribe the person was, although, within the family, tribal origins continued to be remembered. For 250 more years the little kingdom of Judah persisted alone. Even after the exile it was the tiny province of Judah that emerged under Nehemiah (Neh 1:2-3), and Judea still remained as a district in NT days (Lk 3:1). In fact, the vast majority of later Jews were of the tribe of Judah, as the very name "Jew" shows. But the chief glory of the tribe of Judah, now as ever, was that the house of David sprang from it. When Jesus Christ was born, he was to be of David's line and Judah's tribe. So it is that in Revelation 7:5, when 12,000 are sealed from each tribe, Judah has pride of place in the list, as it had in Numbers (Nm 2:3) so long before.

See also Judah (Person) #1.

JUDAISM

JUDAISM Religion and culture of the Jewish people from the beginning of the postexilic period (538 BC) to modern times. The term "Judaism" is derived from "Judah," the name of the southern kingdom of ancient Israel, while "Jew" is a shortened form of "Judeans."

The Period of the Second Temple (515 BC–AD 70)

Historical Survey The united kingdom of Israel under Saul, David, and Solomon came to an end shortly after the death of Solomon. Rehoboam, his son, provoked a revolt about 930 BC on the part of the 10 northern tribes by levying unreasonably high taxes (1 Kgs 12). From that time on, the kingdoms of Israel (or Samaria, the northern kingdom) and Judah (the southern kingdom) maintained a separate existence. The northern kingdom fell to the Assyrians in 722 BC, and thousands of captives, primarily members of the upper class, were exiled forcibly and taken to Assyria, where they presumably intermarried with the native population and disappeared from history. The kingdom of Judah survived as an independent state until 597 BC, when it came under the control of the Babylonians under Nebuchadnezzar. The temple was finally destroyed in 586 BC and many captives were carried off to Babylonia, beginning a period of exile that was to last two generations. The Babylonians were defeated by Cyrus the Persian in 539 BC, and the following year the king issued a decree permitting all captive peoples to return to the lands of their origin (2 Chr 36:22-23; Ezr 1). At least four waves of Jewish expatriates returned from Mesopotamia to Judea during the century following the decree of Cyrus, under such leaders as Sheshbazzar, Zerubbabel, Ezra, and Nehemiah. Many Jews, however, chose to remain in their adopted Mesopotamian homeland. The dedication of the second temple in the spring of 515 BC provided a formal end to the exilic period of 70 years (Jer 29:10), and was a direct result of the prophetic exhortations of Haggai and Zechariah.

In Judea the Jewish people were ruled by governors who held office at the pleasure of the Persian king. One of the earlier governors was Zerubbabel (Hg 1:1; 2:1-2), a descendant of David (1 Chr 3:10-19). In some way he shared rule with the high priest Jeshua ben Jehozadak. Palestine was part of one of the 20 satrapies of the Persian Empire, which lasted from 539 to 331 BC, when it fell to the Greeks under Alexander the Great. Little is known about the historical developments in Palestine during most of the Persian period. When Alexander died in 323 BC, his empire was divided up among his generals; Egypt and Palestine fell to Ptolemy I. The Ptolemies were benevolent despots who allowed the Jews of Palestine a measure of freedom and autonomy. After the battle of Paneion in 198 BC, Palestine came under the rule of the Seleucid Empire, founded by Seleucus I, another of Alexander's generals.

The Seleucid Empire embraced a very large area with a diverse population, extending from Asia Minor and Palestine in the west to the borders of India on the east. Antiochus IV (Epiphanes) ascended the Seleucid throne in 175 BC and attempted to unify his vast empire by Hellenizing it (i.e., by forcing the adoption of Greek language and culture). Local cultures and religions were forcibly suppressed as a result of this policy, and the Jewish state in Palestine was perhaps the hardest hit of all. In 167 BC Antiochus IV dedicated the temple in Jerusalem to Olympian Zeus, sacrificed a sow on the altar, destroyed scrolls containing the Jewish Scriptures, and forbade the rite of circumcision. This repression triggered a revolt led by an aged priest named Mattathias and his sons. The Seleucids were repulsed, and finally in 164 BC the temple was retaken by Mattathias's son Judas the Maccabee (an epithet meaning "the hammer"). This Jewish victory has been commemorated annually by the festival of Hanukkah ("dedication"). Judas and his brothers, called Maccabees or Hasmoneans (Mattathias was of the house of Hasmon), and their descendants ruled Judea from 164 to 63 BC, when Palestine fell to the Roman general Pompey. Thereafter, Palestine remained a vassal of Rome.

Hyrcanus, a Hasmonean, was high priest after the conquest of Judea by the Romans, though Antipater (an Idumean) was the real power behind Hyrcanus. The sons of Antipater, Phasael and Herod, were governors of Jerusalem and Galilee, respectively. Upon the assassination of Antipater in 43 BC, and through his connections in Rome, Herod (later called Herod the Great) was named king of Judea by the Roman senate; he reigned from 37 to 4 BC. When he died, Palestine was divided up by the emperor Augustus (27 BC–AD 14) and placed under the governorship of three of Herod's sons: Herod Archelaus (ethnarch of Judea, Idumea, and Samaria from 4 BC to AD 6), Herod Antipas (tetrarch of Galilee and Perea from 4 BC to AD 39), and Herod Philip (tetrarch of Batanea, Trachonitis, and other small states from 4 BC to AD 34). These territories were generally placed under Roman procurators after the sons of Herod had died or been deposed. For a brief period (AD 41–44), Herod Agrippa I, the grandson of Herod the Great, ruled virtually the same territory as his grandfather. Upon his death (narrated in Acts 12:20-23), his territories were placed under Roman procurators. The greed and ineptitude of these procurators provoked the Jewish populace to rebel. The ill-fated Jewish revolt of AD 66–73 resulted in the destruction of the second temple by the tenth Roman legion under Titus in AD 70. The revolt was completely quelled in AD 73, when more than 900 Jews under siege in the desert fortress of Masada near the Dead Sea committed mass suicide rather than fall into Roman hands. These tragic events ended permanently the temple cult and the priestly system in Judaism.

Social and Religious Developments The Babylonian conquest of Judea and the destruction of the Solomonic temple in 586 BC produced dramatic social and religious changes in Jewish life. The cessation of the temple cult struck a serious blow at the heart of the Israelite religion, since the Jerusalem temple alone was the legitimate and divinely appointed place for discharging much of the ritual requirement of the Mosaic law, chiefly the sacrificial cult. Even the three annual pilgrimage festivals, Succoth (Tabernacles), Pesach (Passover), and Shavuoth (Weeks) could no longer be observed by pious Jews who had remained in Judea after 586 BC. When after 538 BC many exiles chose to return to Judea, many others elected to remain in their new homeland. For the latter, the temple cult, even when reinstituted in 516 BC, could no longer play a significant role in their religious lives.

During the exilic and early postexilic period, the peculiar Jewish institution of the synagogue (a Greek word meaning "gathering place") began to evolve. The synagogue became such a popular and useful institution for Jewish communities outside Palestine that in the centuries after the dedication of the second temple they sprang up throughout Palestine, many in Jerusalem itself. By the end of the second temple period, the synagogue had come to play three important functions in Jewish life: it served as a house of prayer, a house of study, and a place of assembly. First-century AD synagogue worship is illustrated in Luke 4:16-30 and Acts 13:13-42. The focus of the service was a reading of a selection from the Torah (Law of Moses), then one from the Haphtorah (Prophets). These readings were followed by a homily based on Scripture. Other elements in first-century AD synagogue worship included the recitation of the Shema ("Hear, O Israel"), a combination of biblical passages including Deuteronomy 6:4-9; 11:13-21 and Numbers 15:37-41, and the Shemoneh Esreh (Eighteen Benedictions) called the Amidah ("standing") because it was recited while standing upright. Jews also wore fringes on their garments in obedience to Numbers 15:38-39 (Mt 23:5), and phylacteries on their foreheads and left arms. Phylacteries are little boxes containing the portions of Scripture recited in Shema; they were used in literal fulfillment of the command in Deuteronomy 6:8. Archaeologists have discovered first-century phylacteries in the ruins of Masada.

Outside of Palestine, Mesopotamia became the second most important center of Judaism. The Babylonian Jewish community was known as the Golah ("captivity"), and its titular head was called the Resh Galuta or Exilarch (both terms mean "leader of the captivity"). By the end of the exilic period, the descendants of the ancient original captives had forgotten Hebrew and had adopted Aramaic, the international language of the ancient Near East and sister language to Hebrew, as their first language. Even in Palestine, Aramaic was the primary language spoken. Thus, when portions of Scripture were read in synagogue services in Hebrew, most of those present were unable to understand what was read. This problem was solved by providing a methurgeman (translator) who would translate orally short sections of Scripture. Eventually these targums ("translations") were reduced to writing, beginning in the second century AD.

By the first century AD, it had been estimated that there were from four to seven million Jews in the Greco-Roman world, perhaps three to four times the population of Palestine. Jews in lands outside of Palestine came to be known collectively as the Diaspora ("scattering"). After the Greeks dominated the Mediterranean world through Alexander and his successors, Greek became the common language throughout this region. Just as Mesopotamian Jews spoke Aramaic in place of Hebrew, so Jews in the Greco-Roman world came to speak Greek. By the middle of the third century BC, Hellenistic Jews began to translate the Hebrew Scriptures into Greek. This translation, called the Septuagint (a term meaning "seventy," based on a legend that it was translated simultaneously by seventy Jewish scholars), contained a more extensive canon of Scripture than that recognized by Palestinian Judaism. This reflects the more liberal attitudes of Hellenistic Jews.

During the second century BC, most of the major sects within Palestinian Judaism came into being. The Hasidim ("pious") were members of a religious association that aided the Hasmoneans in the revolt against the Seleucids (1 Macc 2:42; 7:13) but later opposed them when they claimed rights to the priesthood. Both the Pharisees and Essenes may have their origin in this religious sect. The Sadducees were perhaps connected with Zadok, a high priest appointed by David. Zadok's descendants were regarded as the only legitimate priestly line; they were devoted above the Levites in Ezekiel 40-48. The Sadducees were a wealthy, aristocratic class that monopolized the high priesthood. They did not believe in angels, spirits, life after death, or the resurrection (Acts 23:8), nor did they accept the validity of the oral law as developed by the Pharisees. They left no writings and disappeared with the destruction of the temple in AD 70.

The Pharisees ("separated ones") first appear in our sources toward the end of the second century BC and were involved primarily in political affairs. They represented the common people against the tyrannical Hasmonean ruler Alexander Janneus (103–76 BC), who had hundreds of Pharisees executed in reprisal. By the first century AD, the Pharisees seem wholly concerned with religious matters and were noted for the scrupulous observance of the Mosaic law as traditionally interpreted. On grounds of ritual purity, they separated themselves from other Jews who were not as scrupulous and who might contaminate them. Pharisees went about in groups called Haberim ("associates") in which they were insulated from those who were lax religiously. In their zeal to remain faithful to the Mosaic law, the Pharisees developed an oral law (later erroneously attributed to Moses) that served as a fence around the Torah. This oral law was an interpretation and expansion of the 613 commands in the Mosaic law; it was finally compiled and reduced to written form as the Mishnah ("teaching") in the late second century AD. Paul (Acts 22:3; 23:6; 26:5; Phil 3:5) and many other early Christians were converts from Pharisaism (Acts 15:5). Pharisaic Judaism survived the destruction of Jerusalem in AD 70 to form the rabbinic Judaism that dominated Jewish religious life from the second century AD to modern times.

The Essenes were another religious sect within Judaism that had its origins in the second century BC. Like the Pharisees, the Essenes were concerned principally with maintaining ritual purity in obedience to the law of Moses. The Essenes lived and worked in Jewish society; they tried to influence people by the simple, altruistic life they followed. Some Essenes also lived in their own communities, to which they returned each night after work. There were numerous religious factions within Judaism, and one such group, which may only have had vague connections with the Essenes, established a community on the western shore of the Dead Sea. This group regarded itself as the true Israel and in the wilderness prepared for the final visitation of God by keeping themselves pure from all defilement. Many documents written by members of this sect were discovered in caves near the Dead Sea where they had been hidden just before the Romans destroyed the settlement. These documents, the Dead Sea Scrolls, have provided detailed information about this religious sect and its beliefs.

The Zealots were another Jewish sect, who may be

related to the Sicarii ("dagger men"). This group of political activists flourished from AD 6 to 66. Regarding God alone as their sovereign, they attempted to overthrow the Romans and those who collaborated with them by violent means, including assassination. They helped to foment the Jewish revolt of AD 66–73 and perished with Jerusalem in AD 70.

Social class and status in first-century AD Palestine were determined in accordance with the rules of ritual purity. The upper class comprised members of the religious establishment, such as the Sadducees, scribes, Pharisees, and Jerusalem priests. The Sanhedrin was a deliberative body whose membership was drawn from these groups. For all practical purposes there was no middle class. The lower class consisted primarily of the Am Ha Arez ("people of the land")—Jews who were ignorant of the law through lack of education and who did not scrupulously observe those commandments with which they were familiar. The generally hostile attitude of the Pharisees toward the Am Ha Arez is expressed in John 7:49: "But this crowd, who do not know the law, are accursed" (RSV). There was yet another social class in first-century Palestine, which can be designated as "untouchables." This group was composed of Samaritans, tax collectors, prostitutes, shepherds, lepers, Gentiles, and perhaps worst of all, Jews who became as Gentiles (e.g., the prodigal son of Lk 15:11-32). The rules of ritual purity as generally observed prevented any form of social contact between the upper class and the untouchables, and made contacts with the Am Ha Arez highly undesirable. Against this background, the horror of the Pharisees over Jesus' association with tax collectors and sinners is throughly understandable (Mk 2:15-17).

A further consequence of this religious criterion for determining social class and status was an uneasy tension between Jerusalem and the rural areas of Palestine, particularly Galilee, during the last two centuries of the second temple period. Those in Jerusalem regarded Galilee as a place where ignorance of the Torah was the rule (Jn 1:46). Jerusalem was primarily a religious center, whose major industry was the temple cult. The total population of Jerusalem in the first century AD has been estimated at 25,000 to 40,000. Most of these were either artisans and craftsmen devoted to building and adorning the temple (still incomplete before it was destroyed; see Jn 2:20) or priests and Levites involved in the many ritual activities of the temple. Though Jews were expected to travel to Jerusalem for each of the three annual pilgrimage festivals, this requirement proved difficult for rural Palestinian farmers.

Further, the tithe demanded by Mosaic command was only on the produce of the land, not upon wages or bartered goods. The rural farmers, therefore, bore the brunt of this taxation and quite naturally resented the privileged position of urban artisans, merchants, and priests who were not obliged to tithe. The temptation not to tithe the produce of the land was very great, and many farmers succumbed to it. Their untithed produce was not kosher, and thus to be avoided by those, like the Pharisees, who were religiously scrupulous. In addition to the first and second tithes demanded of farmers (the second tithe had to be spent in the vicinity of Jerusalem), it has been estimated that Roman tax levies amounted to 10 to 15 percent of an individual's income. Religious taxes, together with Roman taxes, added up to a crushing tax burden of from 25 to 30 percent. The fact that the Jews finally revolted against their Roman oppressors in AD 66 is not difficult to comprehend. Throughout the first century AD, in fact, minor revolts in Palestine occurred with predictable frequency. Many of these occurred during the

three annual pilgrimage festivals in Jerusalem, when the normal population of 25,000 to 40,000 swelled to 500,000 or more. These festivals provided ideal opportunities for uprisings, and the Romans were particularly alert for such eventualities. Jesus was executed during one such Passover festival because he was suspected of being a political revolutionary (Mk 15:26).

The second temple period provided the setting for the rise and fall of apocalypticism within Judaism. Apocalypticism (from a Greek word meaning "revelation") was a kind of eschatology ("account of final events") that assumed that ideal conditions could not be restored on earth unless God first intervened climactically to destroy evil (particularly foreign oppressors) and vindicate the righteous (Israel). Apocalyptic visionaries composed many documents, called apocalypses, in which they attempted to read the signs of the times and predict the coming of the visitation of God. Since there was a widespread consciousness that the era of prophecy was over, these apocalyptists wrote not under their own names but under the names of ancient Israelite worthies, such as Moses, Abraham, Enoch, and Ezra. Among the more significant expectations of Jewish apocalypticism were (1) the coming of a Messiah; (2) the coming of a great period of tribulation, sometimes called the messianic woes; (3) the resurrection of the just; (4) the judgment of the wicked and the reward of the righteous. Apocalyptic beliefs probably provided the motivation for most—if not all—of the Jewish revolts against the Romans.

Jews Praying and Reading Scriptures before the Wailing Wall

Some portions of the Hebrew Scriptures were still in the process of composition at the beginning of the second temple period. The last three prophetic books—Haggai, Zechariah, and Malachi—were written from the end of the sixth century to the mid fifth century BC. Later rabbis expressed the opinion that the Spirit of God had been taken from Israel when these prophets ceased their labors. The Chronicler ends his work by referring to the decree of Cyrus (538 BC), and both Ezra-Nehemiah and Esther appear to have been written in the fifth century BC.

The second temple period witnessed not only the completion of those writings that were later regarded as inspired and authoritative in Judaism but also the full recognition of all 24 sacred books. Prior to the destruction of Jerusalem in 586 BC, the Mosaic law had not been observed with any consistency (according to 2 Kgs 22 it had been mislaid for an unknown period of time), nor had the classical prophets always received appropriate recognition. But after 586 BC the Torah occupied a position of unquestioned sanctity in the lives and thoughts of the Jewish people, replacing in many respects the temple cult even before its final dissolution in AD 70.

The Jewish Scriptures are divided into three sections, designated by Jews with the acrostic "Tanak": (1) Torah ("Law" or "Revelation"), (2) Nebi'im ("Prophets"), and (3) Kethubim ("Writings"). It is generally claimed that while the Law and Prophets enjoyed canonical status prior to the second century BC, the Writings were finally declared canonical at the rabbinic council of Jamnia (c. AD 90), though the historicity of this is disputed. The rabbis are thought to have discussed whether certain biblical books should continue to be part of Scripture. In reality, the Jewish canon of Scripture was fully defined from traditional usage by the first century BC. The Law consisted of five books: Genesis, Exodus, Leviticus, Numbers, and Deuteronomy. The Prophets consisted of two sections, the Former Prophets (Joshua, Judges, Samuel, and Kings) and the Latter Prophets (Isaiah, Jeremiah, Ezekiel, and the 12 Minor Prophets). The Writings included Chronicles, Ezra-Nehemiah, Esther, Job, Psalms, Proverbs, Ecclesiastes, Song of Songs, Lamentations, Ruth, and Daniel. The total number of books in this canon is 24, identical with the Protestant canon of 39 books, since Samuel, Kings, Chronicles, Ezra-Nehemiah, and the 12 are each counted as only one book. The Alexandrian canon of Hellenistic Judaism was more extensive, and the extra books (called Apocrypha by Protestants) are all found in the Roman Catholic OT canon of 46 books.

The Talmudic Period (AD 73–425)

Historical Survey According to Jewish legend, when the Romans were about to conquer Jerusalem in the revolt of AD 66–73, a prominent Pharisee, Rabbi Johanan ben Zakkai, feigned death and his disciples were permitted to carry him out of the besieged city in a coffin. The more likely scenario is that he received permission from the Romans to move his school from Jerusalem to Jamnia, on the coast of Palestine. The temple cult and the priestly system had disappeared, and rabbinic academies such as that of Rabbi Johanan set themselves to the enormous task of reconstructing Judaism. The older Sanhedrin was reinstituted as the Beth Din ("Court of Law"), and Gamaliel II, a grandson of Hillel, who had presided over the old Sanhedrin, became its leader with the title Nasi ("prince"), or Patriarch. The patriarchate continued until AD 425, when Emperor Theodosius II abolished the office upon the death of the last patriarch, Gamaliel VI. In Mesopotamia, Babylonian Judaism experienced a renaissance that lasted until the end of the fifth century AD. This period was called the Age of the Gaonim ("excellencies") after the heads of the two great rabbinic academies at Sura and Pumpeditha. It was there that the great Babylonian Talmud was compiled by the fifth century AD.

In AD 115 various Jewish communities throughout the eastern Mediterranean, including Egypt, Cyprus, and Cyrene, revolted against the Roman emperor Trajan. Without exception these revolts were all put down by Roman legions. Finally, when the emperor Hadrian was on the brink of founding the new city of Aelia Capitolina on the site of old Jerusalem, the Jews again revolted in AD 132, led by a self-proclaimed messiah, Simeon Bar Koziba, who was called Bar-Kochba ("Son of a Star") by his followers as an allusion to the messianic passage in Numbers 24:17. Bar-Kochba was aided by the famous rabbinic scholar Akiba. This revolt, though initially successful, was put down by the Romans under Julius

Severus in 135. Shortly thereafter, Hadrian issued a decree banning all Jews from the new Aelia Capitolina.

Social and Religious Developments During this period, the result of generations of rabbinical scholarship bore fruit with the compilation of the Babylonian and Jerusalem Talmuds. The rabbinic sages consciously saw themselves as the heirs of the ancient Israelite prophets, who in turn were the heirs of the Mosaic law. They distinguished consciously between their own legal interpretations of the Mosaic law (which they called Halakah, or "walking," i.e., a guide for life), and the commands in the Torah itself (called Mitvah, or "commandment"). The oral law, developed through generations of rabbinic discussion, was finally compiled and written down through the efforts of the patriarch Judah ha-Nasi (c. AD 135–220) during the last quarter of the second century AD and became known as the Mishnah ("teaching"). This is a topical arrangement of rabbinic discussions on such subjects as the Sabbath, firstfruits, sacrifices, and women. The Mishnah became the basis for further rabbinic discussion in both Palestine and Babylonia. The decisions of sages who flourished after the writing of the Mishnah were compiled about AD 450 in Palestine and about 500 in Babylonia. This second stage beyond the Mishnah was called the Gemara (meaning either "completion" or "repetition"). The Mishnah and the Babylonian Gemara make up the Babylonian Talmud, while the same Mishnah with the Jerusalem or Palestinian Gemara comprises the Jerusalem Talmud. Yet another type of rabbinic literature is the Midrashim ("interpretations"), which either follow the order of a particular biblical book or consist of homilies on particular biblical texts. The Targums, paraphrastic translations of Scripture into the Aramaic language, finally came to be written down beginning in the late second century AD.

After the destruction of the temple, rabbinic Judaism concentrated on the religious significance of the Torah and elevated scholarship to the central role that it still plays in Judaism. Rabbinic Judaism gradually exerted its influence upon diaspora Judaism under the initial leadership of Rabbi Johanan until a kind of rabbinic orthodoxy emerged during the second century. Christianity was one of the major ideological foes of rabbinic Judaism. In order to purge Jewish Christians from their midst, the rabbis introduced an additional benediction to the eighteen benedictions customarily recited at synagogue services. This 19th benediction was a curse upon the *minim* (Christians and other heretics), which Jewish Christians who attended synagogue services found impossible to recite. The line was firmly drawn between Judaism and Christianity by this device, which was employed late in the first century.

See also Dead Sea Scrolls; Essenes; Diaspora of the Jews; First Jewish Revolt; Israel, History of; Jew; Judah, Tribe of; Judaism; Pharisees; Philo, Judaeus; Postexilic Period; Sanhedrin; Talmud; Torah; Tradition; Tradition, Oral.

JUDAIZERS* Christian Jews who, during the apostolic and early postapostolic periods, attempted to impose the Jewish way of life on gentile Christians. The Greek verb, which literally means "to Judaize," is found only one time in the NT (Gal 2:14), where it actually means "to live according to Jewish customs and traditions." In that passage Paul quotes part of a brief conversation he had with Peter several years earlier: "If you, though a Jew, live like a Gentile and not like a Jew, how can you compel the Gentiles to live like Jews [i.e., to Judaize]?" (RSV). The issue that concerned Paul was not simply whether or not a person followed the Jewish way of life but whether one erroneously thought that salvation was attained thereby.

In the early days of Christianity, most—if not all—Christians were Jews prior to their conversion to Christianity. The few who were originally Gentiles, such as Nicolaus of Antioch (Acts 6:5), had converted to Judaism before turning to Christianity. At that time, conversion to Judaism was accomplished through three separate steps: (1) circumcision (for males); (2) a ritual bath in water; and (3) agreement to take upon oneself the "yoke of the law," that is, to obey the 613 commands of the Mosaic law as interpreted and expanded in Jewish Halakah (rabbinic legal decisions). Following Jewish customs and traditions and observing Jewish religious laws was a normal way of life for Jewish Christians, whether they were Jews by birth or through conversion. For them, belief in Jesus as the Messiah of Jewish expectation enhanced, but did not replace, their Judaism. Christianity was not regarded as a religion distinct from Judaism but rather as the truest form of Judaism. These Jewish Christians had all been circumcised as infants, or upon conversion to Judaism, and they also practiced the kosher dietary laws and rules of ritual purity prescribed in Mosaic legislation and rabbinic tradition. Further, they continued to worship at the temple in Jerusalem (Acts 3:1; 21:26) until its destruction by the Romans in AD 70, and certain Jewish Christians continued to meet in synagogues (see Jas 2:2, NLT mg).

While earliest Christianity began as a predominantly Jewish movement, it soon expanded into the Greco-Roman world. Jewish Christians were forced to leave Jerusalem as a result of persecutions (Acts 8:1; 11:19-24), and they proclaimed the gospel wherever they went. Philip was responsible for bringing the gospel to Samaria, where many Samaritans became Christians (8:4-25). On the Day of Pentecost, many Jews from places all over the Roman world became converts to the Christian faith (2:5-11). Presumably, when these newly converted Jewish Christians returned to their homes, they carried the gospel with them. Although the origin of the Christian community in Rome is shrouded in obscurity, this is probably how the gospel first came to Rome. One of the central concerns of Luke, the author of Acts, is to show how Christianity, which began as a small, persecuted sect of Judaism in Jerusalem, spread throughout the Roman world; in so doing, it was rejected by Jews and embraced by Gentiles. The major turning point in Acts is in chapter 10, where Peter is the means whereby the Roman centurion Cornelius, together with his entire household, accepted the gospel and began to manifest the gifts of the Holy Spirit. According to Acts 10:45, "The Jewish believers who came with Peter were amazed that the gift of the Holy Spirit had been poured out upon the Gentiles, too" (NLT).

The growing number of gentile converts to Christianity forced Jewish Christians to face a very difficult problem: Must a Gentile first become a Jew in order to be a Christian? Some Jewish Christians gave a positive answer to this question, and these became known as the circumcision party (Acts 11:2; Gal 2:12). Others, such as Peter and Barnabas, and especially Paul, vigorously disagreed. While these two radically different points of view could have split the early church into two major factions, that possibility did not occur. Luke tells the story of how, after a successful first missionary journey (Acts 13:1–14:28), Paul and Barnabas reported to the church at Antioch how God had opened a door of faith to the Gentiles (Acts 14:27). Opposition from the Judaizers in the circumcision party was soon felt, however, since some of them had come to Antioch from Judea for the express

purpose of advocating the idea that circumcision was absolutely necessary for salvation (15:1). Many Jewish Christians had, like Paul, once been Pharisees. These former Pharisees were particularly insistent that new converts who were Gentiles be circumcised and charged to keep the law of Moses (v 5). They were really demanding that Gentiles become converted to Judaism in order to be Christians.

Paul and Barnabas debated with members of the circumcision party before an assembly of apostles and elders in Jerusalem (Acts 15:4-12). The assembly, led by James the Just (the brother of Jesus), listened to both sides and decided to issue a compromise. A letter to the gentile churches was drafted in which it was recommended that gentile converts to Christianity adhere to only a few absolutely essential obligations: (1) abstention from meat sacrificed to idols, (2) abstention from eating blood or blood-saturated meat, and (3) abstention from unchastity (vv 23-29). These three obligations were probably singled out because they were thought to have been important features of those laws regarded as part of the covenant between God and Noah according to Jewish tradition. Since Noah was the ancestor of all mankind, Gentiles as well as Jews, such laws had universal validity. The Mosaic covenant, on the other hand, was incumbent only upon Jews, not upon Gentiles. For this reason the Jerusalem Council determined that abstention from meat sacrificed to idols, blood-saturated meat, and unchastity applied to all Christians, whereas the obligation of circumcision did not.

Judging from the remainder of the book of Acts, it might be supposed that the decision of the Jerusalem Council was satisfactory to the Judaizers of the circumcision party. However, from the details provided by Paul in many of his letters, we find that this was not the case. After Paul briefly summarizes the results of the Jerusalem Council for the Galatian Christians (Gal 2:1-10), he relates how, even after the Jerusalem Council, the Judaizers of the circumcision party were sufficiently powerful to cause even Peter and Barnabas to temporarily isolate themselves from gentile Christians. (According to rabbinic purity laws, one would become religiously impure if one ate with Gentiles.) The major reason Paul wrote the Letter to the Galatians was to combat Judaizers who had apparently invaded the Christian communities in Galatia after his departure. These Judaizers appear to have successfully persuaded some of the Galatian Christians that salvation was available only for those who were circumcised and who kept the Mosaic law (5:12; 6:13). At least some of the problems experienced by the Corinthian church appear to have been caused by Judaizers (2 Cor 11:12–15, 22), and they had infected the Christian community at Philippi (Phil 3:2-3). Judaizers also appear to have made some progress in the church at Colosse. Therefore, according to Colossians 2:16-17, "Let no one pass judgment on you in questions of food and drink or with regard to a festival or a new moon or a sabbath. These are only a shadow of what is to come; but the substance belongs to Christ" (RSV).

Of all the early apostles and elders, Paul was the one who most consistently opposed the Judaizers' view that Gentiles must first become Jews in order to be Christians. His dramatic conversion to Christianity, narrated three times in Acts (9:1-9; 22:6-16; 26:12-23) and occasionally referred to by Paul himself (1 Cor 9:1; 15:8; Gal 1:11-17), convinced him that salvation could be achieved only through faith in Christ. Since Jesus was the *only* way, all other means by which persons sought to obtain salvation were necessarily invalid and illegitimate. Paul was fully aware that it was not because of the fact that he was an observant Jew that he had become justified before God (Phil 3:2-11) but through his faith in Christ. Primarily because of the persistent activity of the Judaizers, Paul had to insist frequently on the invalidity of the law and the validity of faith as the means of being justified before God. This theme dominates his letters to the Romans and the Galatians.

Jewish Christianity gradually withered and disappeared, and with it went the insistence of the Judaizers that Gentiles live according to Jewish customs and traditions in order to receive salvation. The center of Jewish Christianity had traditionally been Jerusalem. Just before the destruction of Jerusalem and the temple at the end of the Jewish revolt of AD 66–70, many Jewish Christians fled to Pella in obedience to a divine revelation. The ill-fated revolt of Bar-Kochba (AD 132–135) further weakened the movement, when Jewish Christians experienced persecution at the hands of the Jewish insurgents. Thereafter Jewish Christianity grew weaker and eventually disappeared. With its disappearance the persistent notion that Gentiles must first become Jews in order to be Christians also died.

See also Acts of the Apostles, Book of the; First Jewish Revolt; Galatians, Letter to the; Jerusalem Council; Jew; Paul, The Apostle.

JUDAS

1. Simon's son, surnamed Iscariot; one of the 12 disciples of Jesus. The derivation of Iscariot is uncertain. In all probability it designated the place of his birth, the town of Kerioth. His childhood home was perhaps Kerioth of Moab, east of the Jordan (Jer 48:24; Am 2:2), or Kerioth-hezron of southern Judah, also known as Hazor (Jos 15:25). A less feasible suggestion identifies Iscariot with an Aramaic word meaning "assassin," a word eventually attached to Judas's name because of his betrayal of Jesus.

   Judas Iscariot's name appears last in the list of disciples (Mt 10:4; Mk 3:19; Lk 6:16), perhaps indicating his ignominy in the minds of later believers rather than his original importance among the Twelve. During Jesus' public ministry, he managed the treasury of the group (Jn 13:29), from which he was known to pilfer money (12:4). As a betrayer, Judas contracted to turn Jesus over to the chief priests for 30 pieces of silver. He accomplished this act of treachery by singling out Jesus with a kiss in the Garden of Gethsemane (Mt 26:14-47; Mk 14:10-46; Lk 22:3-48; Jn 18:2-5).

   Various suggestions have been offered to explain Judas's traitorous deed. (1) In keeping with his patriotic zeal, Judas turned Jesus over to the authorities after realizing that his Master did not intend to overthrow the Roman order and establish a Jewish state. (2) Judas believed Jesus to be the Messiah and planned his arrest in hope of urging Jesus to usher in his kingdom. (3) He was a scoundrel who had plotted wickedness since the start of Jesus' public ministry. (4) Prompted by a satanic impulse, Judas betrayed Jesus; however, after recognizing that he was deceived, out of remorse he took his own life. (5) With damaged pride and humiliated ego from Jesus' caustic rebukes, Judas, originally a loyal disciple, turned against him. (6) Judas, moved by his own greed, yielded to his selfish instincts, not realizing that Jesus would consequently be tried and killed; upon learning the outcome of his betrayal, he repented in despair and committed suicide.

   Judas, despondent over his act of betrayal, went out and hung himself in a field bought with his 30 pieces of silver (Mt 27:3-10). Acts 1:18 gruesomely adds that his body burst open, spilling out his intestines; for this reason the field was called the "Field of Blood" (Acts 1:19). Matthias later took Judas Iscariot's place among the Twelve (v 26).

2. Son of Joseph and Mary, and the brother of Jesus, James, Joseph, and Simon (Mt 13:55; Mk 6:3). Evidently Judas and his brothers rejected Jesus as Messiah (Jn 7:5) until after his resurrection (Acts 1:14). Later, it is thought, Judas (English "Jude") authored the epistle named Jude.

3. Son of James and one of the 12 disciples (Lk 6:16; Jn 14:22; Acts 1:13). He is identifiable with Thaddeus in Matthew 10:3 and Mark 3:18. *See* Thaddaeus, The Apostle.

4. Galilean who led a Jewish revolt against the Romans because of the census taken by Quirinius in AD 6. In Acts 5:37 the Pharisee Gamaliel mentioned Judas as an example of one who unsuccessfully tried to gain the support of the Jewish people. Josephus credited him with founding the Jewish Zealot party, an extreme revolutionary movement that attempted to throw off Roman rule and to reestablish Jewish autonomy (*War* 2.8.1).

5. Owner of a house along the street called Straight in Damascus. Here, following his conversion, Saul (Paul) found lodging and had his vision restored by Ananias (Acts 9:11).

6. Prophet and leader in the early Jerusalem church. Judas, surnamed Barsabbas, was selected with Silas to accompany Paul and Barnabas to Antioch, where they confirmed the Jerusalem Council's decision regarding the gentile church and subsequently encouraged its believers (Acts 15:22-32). *See* Joseph #12.

7. KJV spelling of Judah, Jacob's son (Mt 1:2-3). *See* Judah (Person) #1.

JUDAS BARSABBAS *See* Judas #6.

JUDAS ISCARIOT *See* Judas #1.

JUDAS MACCABEUS *See* Maccabeus, Judas.

JUDAS OF GALILEE *See* Judas #4.

JUDE (Person) Brother of James and author of the general epistle named Jude. Jude is the English form of the Greek name Judas (Hebrew Judah). Most scholars think Jude was the brother of Jesus called Judas. *See* Judas #2.

See also Brothers of Jesus; Jude, Letter of.

JUDE, Letter of Short, hard-hitting letter to a church being infiltrated by teachers who practiced all types of moral evil. Jude reveals the inner situation of a Jewish-Christian community and also presents some great difficulties for the Christian interpreter.

PREVIEW
• Author
• Date, Origin, and Destination
• Background
• Purpose and Theological Teaching
• Content

Author The Letter of Jude states that it was written by "Jude . . . [the] brother of James" (1:1). Many scholars understand this nomenclature to designate Jude (Greek "Judas"), Jesus' brother, whose brother James became the leader of the Jerusalem church. But other scholars think that perhaps another Jude wrote it, or some later author wrote it in the spirit of the leader whom he revered. The hypothesis that another Jude wrote it seems unlikely, for the apostle Jude (Lk 6:16; Acts 1:13) is the son of a certain James, not a brother of James; besides, Jude 1:17 appears to distinguish Jude from the apostles. And since there was only one James who was prominent in the early church, James the Lord's brother, it would be hard to believe that some other Jude would have a brother named James and would use such an identification in the title; it would have been too confusing. The title "brother of James" most likely means that Jude was James of Jerusalem's brother and therefore Jesus' brother; he did not use the title "brother of our Lord," perhaps, as Clement of Alexandria said, out of modesty.

The idea that a later author wrote using Jude's name presents a major problem: Why would he pick such an obscure name, instead of Paul or Peter or James, and why would he not use a more exalted and authoritative title? We must conclude that, despite the difficulties of date and background, Judas the Lord's brother wrote this letter.

Date, Origin, and Destination About date, origin, and destination, the letter says nothing directly. Since the content of the faith is clearly fixed (Jude 1:3) and the recipients have personally heard the apostles (who may have died already, v 17), the date is probably between AD 60 and 100.

Presumably, Jude traveled (with his wife and family) to promote the faith (1 Cor 9:5). Throughout his travels, he may have established some churches—or, at least, he probably taught at various local churches. It may be that he heard of false teachers infiltrating these churches and was prompted to write them this epistle.

Jude may have written from Galilee in his old age, or perhaps he had returned to Jerusalem. The best guess we can make about the recipients would be that they were members of Jewish-Christian churches in Syria. Still, these locations remain little more than guesses.

Background Three facts about the Letter of Jude make its background difficult to reconstruct. First, it is hard to be sure what type of heresy it was combating. Some scholars believe that this was early Gnosticism, and others that it was simply teaching infiltrated with ethical error. If the heretics were Gnostics, they believed in a hierarchy of angels or demigods. In this case they probably saw Jesus as a lower rung on the way to salvation. Perhaps they also considered God to be the lower creator (the demiurge) and spoke of wanting to serve the true God (Jude 1:4). This might explain the interest in angels

and demons (v 8) and the stress on the unity of God (v 25). But probably these were simply people who had found a way to rationalize immoral behavior and were unwisely mocking the evil powers. There is no clear evidence that they were Gnostic, while there is plenty of evidence that people turned the freedom of the gospel into an excuse for sin (e.g., Rom 6; 1 Cor 5–6). These teachers probably denied Christ by failing to follow his ethical teaching, and their blasphemy of angels (while they themselves were deep in sin) was another ethical sin. Such depravity is enough to explain the letter; however, knowing that doctrinal and ethical error often go hand in hand, we must not discount the possibility that some doctrinal error was also involved.

Second, Jude surprises us by quoting from two apocryphal books, the Assumption of Moses (Jude 1:4) and 1 Enoch (Jude 1:14-15 quotes 1 Enoch 1:9). This fact and other allusions in the book reveal that Jude and probably his readers were well read in Jewish apocryphal literature. Moreover, it also shows that Jude regarded books outside the canon of the OT as transmitting true traditions and authoritative prophecy. That Jude accepted these books is not surprising, since many apocryphal books were used by Jews of that period, alongside the OT, as a type of devotional literature. Early Christians often included apocryphal literature along with canonical books as part of their Bibles (sometimes they would also omit NT books that were not yet considered authentic). The canon of NT Scripture was not firmly established until the third century, long after Jude's epistle was written.

It is important to realize that while Jude probably believed in the historicity of these citations, the teaching of the letter does not depend on that historicity. Jude wrote about neither Moses nor Enoch but about how one should behave toward authorities (Jude 1:8) and what God will do to ungodly people (v 13). The citations illustrate Jude's teaching and probably carried weight with his first readers, but the fact that they are apocryphal should bother us no more than Paul's quotations from pagan writers or the writer of Hebrews' allusions to 2 Maccabees (Acts 17; Ti 1:12; Heb 11:35). The authority of Scripture rests in the point the author is making.

Third, Jude shows such a close relationship to 2 Peter 2 that either Jude is an expansion of 2 Peter 2 or else 2 Peter 2 is an abbreviation of Jude. Words, phrases, and illustrations are essentially identical in the two works. While it is hard to determine who borrowed from whom, probably the author of 2 Peter has adapted the strong denunciations of Jude to the more instructive tone

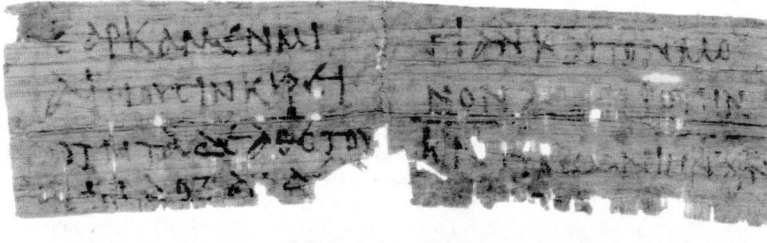

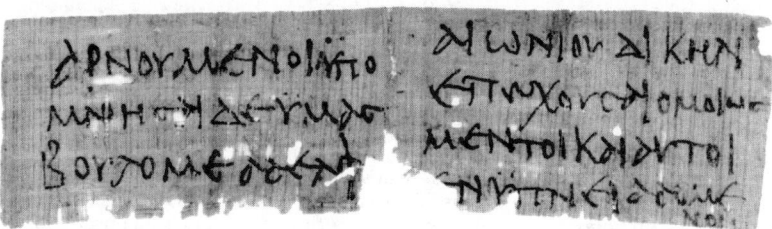

Ancient Papyrus Manuscript of Jude Jude in Papyrus Oxyrhynchus 2684 (c. 300)—P78

of his work. It would be hard to imagine anyone writing Jude if 2 Peter already existed. Christians should have no problem with this borrowing, for no writer of Scripture believed himself so original that he could not borrow from other Scriptures, from hymns, or from noncanonical literature. It is no more a problem for God to inspire a quotation or adaptation from another writing than for him to inspire a new composition. Indeed, some passages in Scripture are total repetitions of others (e.g., Ps 18 and 2 Sm 22).

Purpose and Theological Teaching Jude describes his work in terms of exhortation or encouragement (Jude 1:3). Obviously he wanted to strengthen the churches against false teachers who were perverting the gospel. Thus, he repeatedly urged the believers to hold fast or guard their purity and the gospel (vv 3, 20-21, 24). Yet he did not want the teachers simply kicked out, for he had hopes that the believers would be able to rescue some from this danger, although the rescue itself would be dangerous work (v 23).

In framing his exhortation the author did not produce any new doctrines; rather, he underlined some old ones: (1) He stressed the ethical nature of the gospel and the need to maintain purity in life and speech. (2) He showed a high regard for salvation through Christ and a strong belief in one God. (3) He demanded respect for authority, both temporal and spiritual (vv 8-11). (4) He had a clear apocalyptic belief, stressing the coming last judgment (vv 14-15) and affirming that the last days had already come (v 18). (5) He warned of the necessity to persevere in the faith both doctrinally and ethically (vv 19-21). (6) He demonstrated zeal to reclaim those who had erred, for they were outside the grace of God (v 23).

Content

Salutation (1:1-2) The author identifies himself humbly as a servant of Jesus Christ and addresses his letter to the faithful in the church—those who are loved, guarded, and called by God and Christ.

Called to Hold to the Faith (1:3-4) Jude had been planning to write these Christians about "the salvation we all share" (v 3). We will never know what instruction he had planned to give, for in the middle of his preparations he heard news that forced him to change his plans. Instead, he penned an epistle in defense of "the faith"— that is, the true apostolic teachings concerning Jesus Christ that all genuine believers embrace. Some people had joined the church, perhaps with ulterior motives, who were dangerous to the church. The Christians must fight hard to keep pure the body of doctrine (meaning ethics as well as theology) that they had received from Jude and the apostles. Jude makes two charges against these false believers: (1) they had perverted God's grace into licentiousness, perhaps openly flaunting sexual sins as a sign of freedom they had in Christ (cf. Rom 6; 1 Cor 5–6); and (2) they denied the Lord Jesus (by failing to follow his teachings).

Reminder of God's Judgment (1:5-7) Since the recipients were probably Jewish Christians, they had learned the OT and Jewish tradition well. The author chose three illustrations of the results of apostasy: (1) Judgment can come to those once considered as God's people (as it did to those "saved" from Egypt, Ex 32:28; Nm 11:33-34; 14:29-35). (2) The consequence of apostasy is eternal damnation (as in the case of the fallen angels of 1 Enoch 6–16—these ideas appear in other Jewish traditions as well). (3) Ethical corruption is in fact a type of apostasy and thus merits damnation (as in the case of Sodom— Gn 19; 2 Pt 2:4-6). The author stressed the homosexual-

ity of Sodom rather than its injustice, which Ezekiel 16:49 condemns, so perhaps sexual misbehavior was a problem with the false teachers. These three illustrations drive home the seriousness of the problems that the church was facing.

Denunciation of the False Teachers (1:8-16; cf. 2 Pt 2:10-17) The false teachers claimed to have received revelations in dreams as the basis of their evil behavior. Their sins were (1) sexual impurity (including, but not limited to, homosexuality); (2) rejection of Christ's authority (as embodied in his ethical teaching); and (3) evil speech about angels (whether good ones, which is probably the case, or evil). This latter practice is shown to be sin by an example from the Assumption of Moses: even an archangel rebuking the devil himself would not use the language these teachers used about angels. But since these people were unspiritual, they were totally ignorant of what they insulted (cf. 1 Cor 2:7-16), yet they were experts in bodily sin—like savage animals. Their sin was destroying them.

Therefore, the teachers were just like Cain (the embodiment of violence, lust, greed, and rebellion against God in Jewish tradition), Balaam (who tried to make money by leading people into sin—Nm 31:16; Dt 23:4), and Korah (who rebelled against God's authority in Moses—Nm 16). They were also dangerous to the believers, for they were turning the meal, which was part of the love feast and Lord's Table (Eucharist), into an orgy (cf. 1 Cor 11:20-22), and would thereby corrupt the practice of the rest of the church. They cared only for themselves and were devoid of real spiritual gifts from God (like waterless clouds or the dead trees of winter, cf. Lk 13:6-9), being ready for the second death (their fate was so sure that it is seen as having already happened). They produced only evil deeds; in this they are like the fallen angels (stars are considered angels in Jewish tradition—1 Enoch 18:13-16; 21:1-10).

The prophecy of Enoch in 1 Enoch 1:9 shows the certainty of their doom. Originally, the prophecy spoke of God coming in judgment, but Jude made it refer to Christ, who for Christians is the coming judge (Mt 25:31). Christ will come with the angelic hosts and execute justice on sinners for their sins (both evil deeds and evil words). That prophecy pertains to people who grumble or accuse God, as Israel did (Ex 16:7-12; 17:3); it also applies to people who do whatever they desire, are loud-mouthed, yet flatter when it is to their advantage.

Instructions for the Faithful (1:17-23) Faithful Christians must remember that the apostles (here meaning the Twelve, not the wider circle of apostles that included Paul, Barnabas, and others) had predicted just such a situation when they were alive: in the last days there would be scoffers, who would do any ungodly act they desired (2 Pt 3:3). These false teachers are such people. They divide the church, and although they claim to be spiritual and receive dreams, they are totally worldly, for they do not possess the Holy Spirit. The faithful must watch out that they remain in the love of God and do not drift into rebellion as these heretics have. This is done by (1) building themselves up (as opposed to causing divisions) on the basis of the faith, the apostolic teaching, and example; (2) praying in the Holy Spirit (Eph 6:18), which sets them off from those not having the Spirit; and (3) waiting expectantly for the mercy Jesus would show them in the soon-coming Last Judgment (1 Enoch 27:3-4).

Yet the Christians must still deal with those who had influenced by the false teaching. While the Greek text here is very uncertain (it is not clear whether Jude had two or three groups in mind), Jude probably intended that the church should act mercifully toward those who were wavering over whether to follow the false teaching, restore those it could from the followers of the false teaching as if snatching them from hell, and while keeping a merciful attitude (a readiness to accept them back quickly if they repented), strictly avoid any social contact with the unrepentant out of fear of God's judgment.

Benediction (1:24-25) Jude closes with a doxology very much like that found in Romans 16:25-27. In the midst of many who have fallen from the faith, God is praised as the one who is able to keep the believers from falling and to bring them safely into his very presence. It is to this one who is alone God our Savior through Jesus Christ (meaning God saves us by means of Jesus) that the four attributes—glory, majesty, dominion, and authority—belong, now and forever.

See also Apostasy; Brothers of Jesus.

JUDEA, JUDEANS "Land of the Jews," particularly after the Captivity. Since most of the Israelites who returned from the exile were from the tribe of Judah, they were called Judeans or Jews and their land, Judea. This part of the Holy Land has always been of great interest to the Bible student because of the location of such places as Jerusalem and Bethlehem within the area and because of the events of Christ's life and ministry that occurred here.

Definition First used in Ezra 5:8, the term there designates a province of the Persian Empire. It is also spoken of in the literature of the Maccabean period after Greece had taken control of the area from the Persians (1 Macc 5:45; 7:10). In Roman times Judea was annexed to the Roman province of Syria until the time of Herod the Great, who was declared king of Judea in about 37 BC. On occasion, the term Judea seems to mean all the territory occupied by the Jewish nation, that is, all of western Palestine (Lk 23:5; Acts 10:37; 26:20). Secular writers of NT times, including Strabo, Tacitus, and Philo, used the term in the wider sense. But in its ordinary and strict sense it denoted the southern district of Palestine. The other two districts or divisions were Galilee in the north and Samaria in the center.

Geography While the geographic boundaries of Judea were not always the same in different historical periods, the province did include the territories once belonging to the tribes of Judah, Dan, Benjamin, and Simeon. The northern boundary, separating Judea and Samaria, is less definite than the others since there is no natural geographic barrier—no valley, no body of water, no break in the terrain—to indicate a division. It is thought, however, that the northern boundary line ran from Joppa on the Mediterranean to a point on the Jordan River about 10 to 12 miles (16 to 19 kilometers) north of the Dead Sea.

The southern boundary extended from a point about seven miles (11 kilometers) southwest of Gaza near the coast through Beersheba to the Dead Sea. According to Judges 20:1, Beersheba was the southern boundary of the nation, and it is therefore properly considered the southern limit of Judea. The eastern boundary was the Dead Sea, and the western boundary the Mediterranean Sea. Judea therefore was in shape a square of territory approximately 45 miles (72 kilometers) wide on each side.

History The history of Judea begins in the Persian period (539–331 BC), when Cyrus allowed the Jews to return to rebuild their temple and their holy city of Jerusalem. In the Greek period (334–167 BC) the area came under the control of the Seleucids, descendants of one of Alexander's generals who ruled in Syria. Their attempts

to destroy the Jewish religion led to a Jewish revolt under the leadership of the Hasmonean family, and the Jews enjoyed nearly a hundred years of independence (167–63 BC). In 63 BC Pompey conquered Palestine for Rome, and eventually Herod the Great was made king (37–4 BC), being succeeded by his son Herod Archelaus (4 BC–AD 6). The Romans then appointed a series of imperial governors called procurators, and these ruled Judea, Samaria, and Idumea (south of Judea) until the Jewish revolt of 66–70, with the exception of the years 41 to 44, when the grandson of Herod the Great, Herod Agrippa I, ruled all of Palestine.

The fate of Judea has been the fate of all Palestine, and it has continued to know many cruel conquerors since the close of NT times. The country was under the heel of Rome until 330, when it came under Constantinople, or Byzantium, and saw the building of many Christian churches (330–634). The Persians again invaded (607–629), destroying Christian churches and killing many people. The Arab period (634–1099) saw the coming of Muslim control of Judea, which was interrupted by the Crusaders (1099–1263), who were determined to rescue the Holy Land from the Muslims. After the final defeat of the Crusaders, the Muslims regained control until the modern period (1917–present). After World War I, Judea was a part of the British mandate over Palestine. In 1948 it was partitioned between Israel and Jordan, and as a result of Israel's victories in the Six Day War of June 1967, Judea was reunited and came once again under the control of the Jews.

See also Diaspora of the Jews; Judaism; Palestine; Postexilic Period.

JUDGE An official authorized to decide matters brought before a court. The judge undertook a variety of tasks, mostly in legal and judicial areas, but at times in political areas. In the patriarchal period the elders of the tribes decided disputes. Moses appointed other judges to assist him, taking only the difficult cases himself (Ex 18:13-26; Dt 1:9-17). Samuel went on circuit judging cases (1 Sm 7:16-17); his sons became judges too (8:1). During the monarchy period, the office of judge was well established.

In the NT era two kinds of courts operated in Palestine, the Jewish and the Roman. Capital cases were tried before a Roman judge. Witnesses were produced at trials (Mt 18:16; 2 Cor 13:1; 1 Tm 5:19). Jesus himself was tried before Pontius Pilate, the Roman procurator (Mt 27:11-25; Mk 15:2-5; Lk 23:2-3; Jn 18:29-40), and Paul before Felix (Acts 24:1-26) and Festus (25:1-26).

See also Civil Law and Justice; Criminal Law and Punishment.

JUDGES, Book of Old Testament book named after the prominent leaders raised up by the Lord to deliver his people. The word "judge" in Hebrew also denotes the activity of governance, including warfare. Some scholars have argued that there were two kinds of judges: charismatic deliverers (or major judges) and local judicial sages (minor judges). It is uncertain why some judges receive cursory attention, whereas the exploits of other judges are given in great detail.

PREVIEW
•Author
•Date
•Literary Framework
•Purpose and Theological Teaching
•Content

Author The book reflects a final editing of the material in the period of the early monarchy. It may well be a polemic for the righteous rule of David over against the kingship of Saul, which was molded by a secular, Canaanite conception of kingship rather than by the law of God. The author was almost certainly not Samuel, as traditionally thought, but a later compiler who relied on ancient written materials.

Date Though the judges succeeded in giving the tribes some rest from the incursions of surrounding enemies, the Israelites were continually harassed over long periods of time. Scholarly opinion differs on the duration of the period of the judges. The dating of the exodus affects the dating of the beginning of the judges. Those who take an early date for the exodus put the beginning around 1370–1360 BC, whereas others propose a date close to the end of the 13th century BC. A related issue pertains to the chronology of the judges. Does Judges give a chronological, sequential account of the period, or is the book a representative account of judges from various parts of Canaan and Transjordan who "judged" a region, a tribe, or several tribes simultaneously?

Literary Framework There is no doubt that the stories in the book bear the marks of literary creativity. The stories are classics in their own right. The poetry of Deborah's song (Jgs 5) is very moving, and the fable of Jotham (9:8-15) is a fine example of figurative speech. The care given to the stories is also reflected in the construction of the book. There are two introductions: a political one (Jgs 1:1–2:5) and a socioreligious one (2:6–3:6). The political introduction connects Judges with the story of the Conquest, when the tribes attempted to occupy the land. It prepares the reader for the political and military problems of the era of the judges. The socioreligious introduction explains why Israel had so many adversities, why the institution of the judges arose, and why the Lord never gave Israel the promised lasting rest from its enemies. The main body of the book is the story of the judges (3:7–16:31). References to the minor judges (six in all) are set within the stories of the major judges in increasing frequency. As is evident from the schema, the number of minor judges increased in frequency in proportion to the decrease in number of major judges: two major, one minor; two major, two minor; one major, three minor; one major. There is a total of 12 judges, representative of the 12 tribes of Israel.

The purpose of the listing of 12 judges, representative of the various parts of Canaan and Transjordan, is to demonstrate that all tribes throughout the conquered territories experienced grave difficulties from a variety of enemies: Arameans, Moabites, Ammonites, Amalekites, Canaanites, and Philistines. Israel was hard pressed on nearly all its frontiers. The appendixes (chs 17–21), together with the two introductions, form the framework of the book. The political and socioreligious problems (1:1–3:6) are presented by way of several stories in the last chapters. The final editor who gave the book its canonical shape purposefully framed the stories of the judges so as to show lack of movement. The successes of the previous stages in redemptive history came to a standstill in the ebb and flow of the judges. Though the Lord delivered his people in many ways, they returned to the problems described in 1:1–3:6. The appendixes describe Israel's problems representative of the period of the judges, when "there was no king in Israel" (17:6; 18:1; 19:1; 21:25).

Purpose and Theological Teaching The cycle of apostasy, judgment, cry for deliverance, and God's raising up of a judge reflects a deuteronomic perspective with its warnings concerning disobedience and judgment. The repetitiveness of the cycle supports the contention of the anonymous narrator that Israel remained unchanged by the grace of God. However, in spite of the moral, religious, and political anarchy as well as the civil wars, the last chapter shows that the tribes are still concerned with each other's welfare. Though the unity of God's people has been gravely challenged, the situation is not hopeless. The book ends on a note of hope—hope for a king who may deliver Israel.

CYCLE OF OPPRESSION AND DELIVERANCE IN THE BOOK OF JUDGES

Judges/Oppression	Years	Dates (BC)
Mesopotamian oppression by Cushan-rishathaim (3:8)	8	1382–1374
Othniel (3:11)	40	1374–1334
Moabite oppression by Eglon (3:14)	18	1334–1316
Ehud (3:30), including Shamgar	80	1316–1236
Canaanite oppression by Jabin (4:3)	20	1236–1216
Deborah and Barak (5:31)	40	1216–1176
Midianite oppression (6:6)	7	1176–1169
Gideon, judge (8:28)	40	1169–1129
Abimelech's misrule (9:22 ff.)	3	1129–1126
Tola's deliverance (10:1-2)	23	1126–1103
Philistine oppression (10:7; 13:1), including Ammonites, etc., in the east	40	1103–1063
Samuel's judgeship (1 Sm 7:2), including his sons at the end (8:1)	20	1063–1043

Thus, there are several purposes of the book: (1) to demonstrate the meaninglessness of this stage in Israel's development; (2) to explain why the tribes did not occupy all the land promised to the patriarchs; (3) to justify the way of God, who was gracious and patient with Israel's repeated acts of disobedience; (4) to set forth the legitimacy of a "shepherd" king in contrast to a despotic form of kingship; and (5) to explain the urgent need for a new momentum, lest Israel succumb to the Philistines and intertribal warfare.

Content

The Political Introduction (1:1–2:5) In Joshua 1–12 the warfare under Joshua is portrayed as a mobilization of Canaanite forces against Israel. By the intervention of the Lord, the Canaanite resistance was put down and the land was occupied by the tribes (chs 13–21). Joshua 13–21, however, clearly shows that each tribe had problems ridding its territory of pockets of Canaanite resistance, which were usually centered around heavily guarded and well-fortified cities (cf. 13:2-6, 13; 15:63; 16:10; 17:12-18).

The book of Joshua emphasizes the successes and minimizes the problems, whereas the prologue to Judges sets the stage for the whole book by openly addressing Israel's problems and failures. As the book unfolds, it is precisely these problems and failures that in due time bring Israel to the brink of disaster.

The period of the judges began with the death of Joshua (Jgs 1:1; 2:8-9). The Israelites had inherited a legacy from Joshua: the law of the Lord (Jos 23:6; 24:26), the land, a challenge to obey the Lord (24:14-27), and a promise of God's presence and help in subduing the Canaanites (23:5, 10).

▶JUDAH AND SIMEON (JGS 1:2-20) The prominence of Judah and Caleb parallels the position of Judah in Joshua (Jos 14:6–15:63; cf. also the house of Joseph, Jgs 1:22-29; cf. Jos 16–17). Judah was victorious over the cruel Adoni-bezek, who ruled over Bezek, a town of uncertain location. Judah successfully occupied the hill country, the Negev, and the western foothills. They even took Jerusalem, or an outlying suburb identified with Jerusalem (Jos 1:8), but could not retain control there (v 21) until David's conquest of the city (2 Sm 5:6-9). Judah was victorious over the Canaanites in the region of Hebron, already conquered under Joshua (Jos 10:36). Hebron, also known as Kiriath-arba ("city of four" or "tetrapolis"), was a powerful ally of Jerusalem (v 3) and had been able to rally military support for a new assault on Israel, even after its first defeat. Caleb received Hebron, as Moses had promised (Jgs 1:20; cf. Jos 15:13). After the victory over Hebron, Judah extended its control over the southern hill country by an attack on Debir (Jgs 1:11-15; cf. Jos 15:14-19).

The Kenites (Jgs 1:16), descendants of Jethro and therefore related to Moses by marriage, settled in the Negev around Arad and the City of Palms, which here probably refers to Tamar rather than Jericho.

Judah secured the southern border by a victory over the Canaanites at Hormah (Jgs 1:17; cf. Nm 14:45; 21:3; Dt 1:44) and the coastal plain by victories at Gaza, Ashkelon, and Ekron. However, Judah's successes in the coastal plain were resisted by a well-armed Canaanite force (Jgs 1:18-19). It occupied the Judean hill country and the Negev, but could not retain control over the plains. The Philistines were soon to take control over Gaza, Ashkelon, and Ekron, and incorporate them into their pentapolis.

➤ BENJAMIN (1:21) Jerusalem was situated on the border between Judah and Benjamin. Judah took the city or a suburb (Jos 1:8) but was too far removed to retain control over it. Benjamin was too weak to subdue the Jebusites. Only David succeeded in this (2 Sm 5:6-9); he incorporated it into Judah (cf. Jos 15:63), even though it originally was allotted to Benjamin (Jos 18:28).

➤ JOSEPH: EPHRAIM AND MANASSEH (1:22-29) Ephraim took Bethel, known from the patriarchal stories as a significant cultic site (Gn 12:8; 13:3-4; 28:19; 31:13; 35:1-15). However, Manasseh was unsuccessful in taking the fortified cities in the valley of Jezreel (Esdraelon): Beth-shan, Taanach, Dor, Ibleam, and Megiddo. These cities controlled traffic along the east-west and north-south roads as well as the important passes through the Carmel range and the ford of the Jordan. Ephraim could not take full possession of the coastal plain, controlled by Gezer. The success of both Ephraim and Manasseh was limited.

➤ THE OTHER FOUR TRIBES (1:30-36) The other four tribes in Canaan receive brief mention. They, too, were only partially successful. Zebulun, Asher, Naphtali, and especially Dan did not fully succeed in driving out the Canaanites. At best they later subjected most of them to forced labor.

➤ THE FAILURE OF ISRAEL (2:1-5) The failure to subdue the land and to wipe out the Canaanites and their culture led to intermarriage and idolatry (cf. Ex 23:33; 34:12-16; Nm 33:55; Dt 7:2-5, 16; Jos 23:7, 12).

The identity of "the angel of the Lord" who appears at Bokim is far from certain. It may be a reference to the Lord himself, to an angelic messenger, or to a prophet (cf. Jgs 6:8). He rebuked the people in the prophetic spirit and pronounced God's judgment as taking the form of continual confrontation between Israel and the Canaanites (2:3). Their weeping and sacrificing were to no avail (2:4-5; cf. Mal 2:13). Israel stood condemned within a generation after Joshua's death.

The Theological Introduction (2:6–3:6) The theological introduction begins where Joshua left off (Jos

24:28-31). The generation of Joshua was characterized by loyalty, but their loyalty to the Lord did not last long after the excitement of the Conquest and the demonstration of God's presence (Jgs 2:10). Israel served Canaanite gods (Baal and Astarte) instead. Baal was the storm god, symbolic of rain and fertility, and Astarte was his cohort. The plural (Baals and Ashtaroth, 2:11-13) signifies the many local ways in which the Canaanite gods were worshiped. The religious unity was broken up into a great diversity. Thus Israel angered the Lord (vv 12-14), who sent them enemies and plunderers. Israel was unsuccessful in dealing with them, as Moses and Joshua had forewarned (Dt 28:25, 33; Jos 23:13, 16). The cycle of apostasy, judgment, cry for mercy, and deliverance is found throughout Judges. The people were rooted in the apostasy of their forefathers, even though the previous generation had been sensitive to God. Israel did not submit to the leadership of the judges, except to free itself from the oppressors. In fulfillment of the curses of the covenant, God swore not to give his people rest but to test them and to train them for warfare (Jgs 3:1-4), so that they might learn to respond to the challenges of a real world.

The Judges of Israel (3:7–16:31)

➤ OTHNIEL (3:7-11) Othniel is a transitional figure, linking the Conquest and the judges. He had involved himself in the conquest of Kiriath-sepher and was related to Caleb as his cousin and son-in-law (1:13). He repelled the Arameans led by Cushan-rishathaim, so that the land enjoyed peace for some 40 years.

➤ EHUD (3:12-30) The Moabites, allied with the Ammonites and Amalekites, came against Israel from the east and oppressed them for 18 years under the leadership of Eglon. Ehud led the mission to bring tribute to Eglon at his palace, located probably by Jericho (the City of Palms). Ehud was uniquely qualified for this mission; being left-handed, he was able to use his double-edged sword in an unsuspecting manner to stab the king. Ehud's success was the result of careful plotting and the element of surprise. He paid the tribute and left, only to return with a supposed oracle from the gods. The king fell for the deception and was murdered. The delay at the Moabite court gave the Israelites an opportunity to bring their forces together at the fords of the Jordan. Ehud's success was complete; no Moabite escaped, and Israel enjoyed peace for 80 years.

➤ SHAMGAR (3:31) Shamgar's exploits were against the Philistines in the coastal plains. He had a non-Israelite name but was probably an Israelite by birth. Like Samson he fought the Philistines with an unconventional weapon (an ox goad). His name is also mentioned in the song of Deborah (5:6).

➤ DEBORAH AND BARAK (4:1–5:31) The narrative now turns to the Canaanite aggressors in the north under the leadership of Jabin, king of Hazor, and Sisera, of Harosheth-haggoyim (4:1-3). The ruins of Hazor (Jos 11:13) had been rebuilt, and another Jabin (cf. v 1) ruled over the region. He had regained his military power, as he had as many as 900 chariots of iron. He oppressed Israel for 20 years (Jgs 4:3).

God had a prophetess in Israel who led his people during this dark time (4:4). She rendered judgments under a palm tree in southern Ephraim near Benjamin (v 5). She called on Barak to muster the armies of Naphtali and Zebulun, the tribes affected by the Canaanite raids, and to engage Sisera in a surprise attack by the Kishon River (vv 6-7). Barak's hesitancy led him to request Deborah's presence, which resulted in his forfeiture of the honor of killing Sisera, the commander of the Canaanite forces (vv 8-10). The Lord gave success to the surprise attack from Mt Tabor, so that the Canaanites were routed, unable to use their heavy chariots, which were mired down in the swamps of the Jezreel Valley (5:20-22). The Canaanites were routed, and Sisera was killed by Jael, the wife of Heber, a Kenite who had separated from the Kenites around Arad (4:17-18; cf. 1:16). She offered him hospitality, as her family had friendly relations with the Canaanites, but heroically put him to death with a tent peg (4:18-21; 5:26-27). In successive campaigns the Israelites gained freedom from Jabin, until they destroyed his power (4:24).

The song of Deborah (ch 5) celebrates, in poetic fashion, the victory over Jabin. It is one of the oldest poems in the Bible. It praises the God of Israel as the King who comes to protect his covenant people, and before whom the mountains move (5:2-3). He is the God of Mt Sinai (Jgs 5:4-5; cf. Dt 33:2; Ps 68:7-8; Hb 3:3-4). Though the oppressors had despoiled Israel and had made the roads unsafe for travel, and Israel was unable to defend itself (Jgs 5:6-8), the Lord raised up Deborah and Barak to lead the nobles to war (vv 9-13). They came from Ephraim, Benjamin, Zebulun, Issachar, and Naphtali (vv 14-15a, 18), but the Transjordan tribes and Asher did not want to get involved (vv 15b-17). The song then moves to the battle scene, where torrential rains bogged the chariots down (vv 19-23). Jael is celebrated as "most blessed of women," who used her simple way of life to bring an end to Sisera (vv 24-27). She stands in contrast to Sisera's mother, who is portrayed with all her culture waiting in vain for Sisera's return with all of his spoils (vv 28-30). The Lord has used the simple to confound the powerful. The conclusion is a prayer for God's judgment on all of Israel's enemies (Jgs 5:31a; cf. Ps 68:1-3).

➤GIDEON (6:1–8:35) Israel's rest for 40 years (Jgs 5:31b) was disturbed by the invasion of Midianites and Amalekites from the East (6:1-3). They destroyed the economy by invading the country at harvesttime (vv 4-6). In response to Israel's cry, God sent a prophet with a message similar to that of the angel of the Lord (2:1-5). Then an angel appeared to Gideon and called him to lead the people in battle (6:11-14). The Lord assured him of his presence (v 16) by a sign (vv 17-22). Gideon knew that he had been visited by the Lord and built an altar called "The LORD Is Peace" in Ophrah (v 24). He responded by destroying the cultic site dedicated to Baal and Asherah at Ophrah (vv 25-28) and by initiating worship at the new altar (v 28). Baal did not protect his own altar (vv 29-32), even when challenged by Gideon's father (v 31). Consequently, Gideon was known as Jerubbaal (meaning, "let Baal contend with him," v 32).

Next, Gideon mustered an army of 32,000 men from Asher, Zebulun, and Naphtali (6:35; cf. 7:3b). In order to assure himself of the Lord's presence, he asked for another sign: the sign of the fleece (6:36-40). It must be kept in mind that Gideon lived in an area in which the wonders of God had been scarce (v 13) and that he, like Moses, needed reassurance that God was with him. God responded to his growing faith. Gideon went forth with a greatly reduced army of 300 against the enemy. Of his original army, 22,000 had left because they were afraid (7:2-3; cf. Dt 20:8). Another 9,700 were sent home, though they were valiant men (7:4-8). After assuring Gideon by a dream of an enemy soldier, God used the 300 in a marvelous way to confound the Midianites (vv 9-15). God gave Israel victory over the Midianite leaders Oreb, Zeeb, Zebah, and Zalmunna (7:16–8:21). Gideon wisely avoided a possible military confrontation with

Ephraim (8:1-3), pursued the enemy deep into the Transjordan, and punished the leaders of Succoth and Penuel, who did not assist him (vv 4-9, 13-16).

This glorious victory created a new wave of interest in the idea of kingship. The men of Israel wished to establish the family of Gideon as their royal dynasty (8:22). Gideon refused, and instead wrongly set up an ephod, cast from the gold taken in battle (vv 23-27). The ephod was probably used for cultic practices, possibly divination (cf. 17:5).

Gideon's era also came to an end. He was God's instrument, giving Israel rest for 40 years. He fathered 70 sons and died in old age. God had richly blessed him, even though he had led Israel astray with his ephod. Thereafter, Israel returned to Baal worship (8:33-35).

In the wake of Gideon's era, his son Abimelech attempted to establish dynastic continuity by having himself installed as king at Shechem (9:1-6). With the support of his relatives at Shechem, Abimelech had all his brothers killed except Jotham (vv 4-5). After Abimelech's coronation, Jotham set forth his opposition to his brother in a proverbial manner (vv 7-20), and went into hiding. Three years later Abimelech's evil schemes entrapped him when the citizens of Shechem rebelled. He furiously attacked the city and destroyed it. A short time later, however, he was wounded at Thebez by a millstone dropped by a woman from the tower in which she had sought refuge from him. His servant put him out of his misery as per his request. This episode demonstrates how bad a despotic king may be. Again, God's justice prevailed.

➤TOLA (10:1-2) Tola was a minor judge from Issachar who judged Israel for 23 years.

➤JAIR (10:3-5) Jair was a minor judge from Gilead who judged Israel for 22 years.

➤JEPHTHAH (10:6–12:7) A recapitulation (10:6-16) of the cycle (idolatry, enemies, cry for help, momentary repentance) sets the introduction to the Jephthah narrative. Under attack from the Ammonites, the elders of Gilead requested help from Jephthah (10:17–11:8), who promised to help them on the condition that he remain their leader even after the war (vv 9-10). At a solemn ceremony he becomes their "head" at Mizpah (v 11). Jephthah opened up correspondence with the Ammonite king, in which he argued for Israel's rights on the basis of the Israelites' historic claim to the land as granted to them by the Lord (vv 12–27). Instead of going out immediately to war, he hoped that "the Lord, the Judge" would settle the dispute (v 27); but the Ammonite king was unimpressed. When the Spirit of God came over him, Jephthah led Israel into battle, but only after making a rash vow. He was victorious but found out that his vow to sacrifice whatever came first out of his house required him to sacrifice his daughter. Debate continues as to whether he offered her up as a human sacrifice or whether she sacrificed marriage (see discussion under Jephthah).

The Ephraimites seemed to have had an insatiable desire for war. Earlier they had complained to Gideon, who successfully defused their threats (8:1-3). Jephthah fought them, however, because the Israelites living in Transjordan had been reviled as "renegades" (12:1-4). Forty-two thousand Ephraimites were killed by the fords of the Jordan in this civil war. Thereafter, Jephthah ruled for only six years.

➤IBZAN (12:8-10) Ibzan was a minor judge from Bethlehem who ruled Israel for seven years.

➤**ELON (12:11)** A minor judge from Zebulun, Elon ruled Israel for ten years.

➤**ABDON (12:13-15)** Abdon was a minor judge from Pirathon, the location of which is uncertain. He ruled for eight years.

➤**SAMSON (13:1–16:31)** Samson's greatness in the history of redemption is due to his miraculous birth (13:1-24), his service as a Nazirite (13:7; cf. Nm 6:1-21), the repeated overpowering by the Spirit of the Lord (Jgs 13:25; 14:6, 19; 15:14), the single-handed exploits against the Philistines (Ashkelon, 14:19; the fields, 15:1-6; Ramath Etam, 15:7-17; Gaza, 16:1-3, 23-30), and his occasional dependence on the Lord (15:18-19; 16:28-30). However, his personal life was flawed because of his weakness for Philistine women (chs 14, 16). Having been seduced by Delilah, he was imprisoned at Gaza. He died in the collapse of Dagon's temple, praying that the Lord would permit him to get revenge (16:28-30). He was buried in his father's tomb in the territory of Dan (16:31).

Epilogue (17–21) The cyclical nature of Israel's existence was without movement. Rest from enemies was always temporary. Israel was not yet ready for dynastic kingship, and whatever one may say of the three years of Abimelech, it was a kingship of the worst sort. Israel vacillated between idolatry and belief in the true Lord. The period of the judges was unstable, marked by petty individualism and provincialism. Yet God remained sovereign in the affairs of his people. The epilogue contains two stories: the story of Micah and the Danite migration (chs 17–18) and the civil war (chs 19–21). The epilogue is bound together by the phrase "In those days Israel had no king; everyone did as he saw fit" (17:6; 18:1; 19:1; 21:25, NIV). The symmetric recurrence (two times in each narrative) emphasizes the anarchy and inability of the tribes to unite together to serve God as a covenant people.

➤**MICAH AND THE DANITES (17–18)** Micah was an Ephraimite who established a shrine and hired one of his own sons, and then a Levite from Bethlehem, to serve as its priests (ch 17). Unable to keep their patrimony, the Danites left to establish themselves at the foot of Mt Hermon. They took the idols and the Levite from Micah's shrine and set up a cultic city at the newly established city of Dan, built on the ruins of Laish (ch 18). Thus, they set up a cultic center that rivaled the tabernacle at Shiloh (18:31).

➤**THE CIVIL WAR (19–21)** The people of Gibeah, which belonged to Benjamin, sexually abused the concubine of a Levite so that she died. Like the Levite of chapters 17 and 18, he was from Bethlehem (19:1). Dramatically, the Levite sent pieces of her corpse to all the tribes, which assembled against the Benjamites because they protected the criminals of Gibeah (19:29–20:19). In the ensuing battle the population of Benjamin was decimated (20:20-48). The 11 tribes gave them 400 virgins taken in a civil war against Jabesh-gilead (21:6-15). These were not enough, however. Because of the threat of the extinction of Benjamin and the vow not to give their daughters in marriage to any Benjamite, the Israelites devised a plan by which the Benjamites could take Israelite virgins dancing in the festival at Shiloh. Benjamin thus was able to rebuild its towns and settlements.

See also Gideon; Jephthah; Samson.

JUDGES*, Period of *See* Judges, Book of.

JUDGMENT Concept in Scripture closely related to the concept of God's justice. In all his relationships God acts justly and morally. Human beings, created by God, have a moral dimension, so that they may positively respond to God's righteous demands in their lives. Divine judgment, involving God's approval or disapproval upon each human act, is a natural consequence of the Creator-creature relationship. Thus judgment, simply defined, is the divine response to human activity. God the Creator must also be God the Judge. Since God is just, he responds with either punishment or reward to what each person does. A human's moral accountability to God (a quality not shared by the rest of creation) is an essential ingredient of being created in God's image. Creation in the divine image means that God and man can communicate with each other in such a way that all people are able to understand God's moral requirements and willingly respond to them. Among the various positive commands given to people in his original creation— including marriage, the subduing of the earth, and enjoyment of the Garden of Eden—was the negative command prohibiting the eating of the fruit from one tree. Defiance of this prohibition carried the threat of death as punishment (Gn 2:16-17). Genesis 3 contains the account of God's first judgment, the one against Adam. He was punished by death since he had not lived within the moral regulations set by God (3:17-19). In a purely technical sense, judgment includes God's approval upon acts that please him; more frequently, judgment is understood negatively in the sense that God punishes those who violate his commands. Since the fall, all human activity stands under God's negative judgment (Rom 2:12).

Judgment in This Life The Christian idea of the atonement, that Christ died for sin in the place of man, depends on the premise that God holds humans accountable for their sins. But God sent his Son to deal with this problem. The Son willingly placed himself under God's judgment, and in people's place he received the divine punishment (Gal 3:13). Christ's death for sin may therefore be considered the extreme manifestation of divine judgment. God as judge visits upon the soul of Christ in his crucifixion the total divine judgment against sin.

Through faith, brought about by the Holy Spirit and fed by the Word, a believer becomes one with Christ and thus escapes divine judgment and is rescued from punishment (Rom 3:22). Those who, by faith, share in the benefits of Christ's death stand before the divine Judge and receive a verdict of "not guilty," and instead of punishment and divine retribution, receive a sentence of eternal life. Jesus says of those who believe in him that they have already passed through judgment, have escaped death, and are already sharing in eternal life (Jn 5:24).

Though sins have been atoned for by Christ, each person—believer and unbeliever alike—still suffers certain consequences of his or her sins here in this life. For every human action there is a divine reaction (Rom 2:6). Paul speaks about the conscience, which carries out a series of judgments even upon the actions of those who do not know the true God (v 15).

Governments are also manifestations of divine judgment upon man's public performances with respect to the law. Civil justice, though often corrupted, is a means through which God carries out temporal judgment upon any infringement of the law in this life (Rom 13:1-2). Public crimes against society are not the only sins subject to divine judgment.

In addition to the accusations of the conscience

against even the most private of sins, each human action carries with it potential reward or punishment. Living within the moral bounds established by God, especially as they are revealed in the Ten Commandments and further explicated in the rest of Scripture, results in certain physical benefits in this life. Living in disregard of the moral law results in penalties and hardships appropriate to the infraction (Gal 6:7-8). For example, refusal to work can result in poverty, and overindulgence can result in poor health. Some activities bring their own penalties. Christians should not conclude, however, that the presence of calamities in a person's life must indicate a specific judgment of God against a particular sin. God can use calamities in the life of a Christian to guide him providentially to the goal of eternal life (1 Pt 4:12-13).

On account of Adam's sin, the creation was subject to a judgment of corruption (Gn 3:17). All of human life participates in a deterioration that is a manifestation of divine judgment against the sin that originated with Adam. God remains sovereign even over the universal corruption and is able to direct and control it for his ultimate purposes (Rom 8:20). Thus he can use calamities for the benefit of the Christian's life (v 28), but he can also use them to manifest his anger on those who persist in deliberate sin and who reject his Son Jesus Christ as the Redeemer from sin. Pharaoh, who recognized Moses as God's prophet and still rejected him and his message, is a prime example of a person who received God's judgment (Ex 10:20). The Jews who saw the miracles of Jesus and rejected his claims to be the Messiah are also among those who received God's judgment while living (Mt 12:22-32).

Through wars and the creation and destruction of nations, God carries out judgment collectively against entire peoples. The OT records the rise and fall of nations and of kings. The refusal to acknowledge and worship the true God and to follow his laws eventually and most certainly results in national extinction. The destruction of Nineveh and Israel in the OT and Jerusalem in the NT are clear examples of God's judgment against entire peoples who reject his message of salvation. Public disregard of the moral law must result in national disintegration, which is then frequently compounded by invasion by a foreign nation. The destruction of Sodom and Gomorrah was the direct result of immoral license (Jude 1:7).

Last Judgment Judgment in its final and ultimate sense is best understood as the appearance of Jesus Christ on the last day. At that time believers will inherit eternal life and unbelievers will be damned. The Christian does not fear this moment, because he has already been acquitted in Christ Jesus. The unbeliever rightfully fears death. The cause of horrible and unchangeable judgment is the persistent rejection of God's offer of salvation. This is the sin against the Holy Spirit (Mt 12:32). Those who fall under its condemnation are those who have heard God's special message to them and are convinced of its truth but who nevertheless persist in rejecting this salvation. As the unbeliever has rejected God in this life, so God rejects him in his death forever.

In addition to this individual judgment, all nations will appear before Jesus (Mt 25:31-32). The fate of all those who appear before the Judge has already been sealed. The Scriptures teach that there is a judgment on that last day that will be made on the basis of works (vv 31-46). This should not be seen as a denial and contradiction of the principle that one is saved by faith alone. People enter into a saving relationship with Jesus Christ

through faith alone, without works. Faith is known only to God and of itself is not visible to others. The evidence for the presence of faith is works.

God's judgments upon people in this life can be of benefit because through these judgments he is calling them to repentance. The judgment of the last day will be final; no one will be permitted to repent or change his or her mind about God. On that day all will recognize the truthfulness of God's claims in Christ Jesus, but only those who have believed in him and carried out his will in their lives will receive the invitation to enter eternal life (v 34).

Practical Implications Christians live a positive and confident life knowing that Jesus has taken the divine judgment for them and thus they are free from any further divine retribution. At the same time they are aware of God's judgment against all sins, including those of Christians, and that apart from Christ they would suffer the worst possible divine punishment. They see the evil and calamities of this life as God's continued displeasure with sin. When they come, Christians use them as opportunities for searching their own souls and for repentance. Though they are not aware of the exact date of the last day, they prepare themselves each day for the final judgment.

Conclusion The concept of judgment covers the entire history of the human race—from the fall to the last day. God, as a just God who sees a decisive difference between good and evil, has no choice but to carry out judgment upon all people in their daily lives and especially at life's conclusion. God in his grace has sent his Son to suffer the judgment we deserved, and in his mercy delays the final Day of Judgment so that we can come to repentance by faith in Jesus Christ (2 Pt 3:9). The great concepts of creation, justice, law, salvation, and atonement reach their climax in the divine judgment of the last day.

See also Hell; Judgment Seat; Justification, Justified; Last Judgment; Second Coming of Christ; Wrath of God.

JUDGMENT*, Hall of KJV translation in Jn 18:28, 33; 19:9; Acts 23:35 of a NT word also translated "Praetorium" (Mk 15:16) and "common hall" (Mt 27:27). The word was first used to refer to the place where the Roman general's tent stood in an army camp and hence was a reference to the headquarters of the camp. It then came to mean the military council that met in the general's tent. Later, it was used in reference to the palace in which the Roman governor or procurator resided while ruling a province. It also designated the army headquarters and barracks that were housed in connection with the governor's residence. In Jerusalem it was the palace that Herod the Great had built for himself. When the Roman governor came from his normal residence in Caesarea to Jerusalem, he occupied Herod's palace and conducted his official business there. It was there that Pilate questioned Jesus (Jn 18:28; 19:9), but it was at another place called the "Pavement" that Pilate sat in judgment and gave Jesus to the Jews.

JUDGMENT SEAT Place before which people will one day stand to give an account of their lives to God.

In the Old Testament The NT concept of divine judgment has its roots in the OT. There God is seen as Judge of the whole world, and especially of his own people.

During his intercession for Sodom, Abraham spoke of God as the Judge of all the earth (Gn 18:25). Moses' position as judge over the Israelites was based on the belief that God gave judgments through Moses. A similar relationship existed between God and the judges who led Israel after the conquest of the Promised Land. That understanding of God became explicit in Jephthah's message to the king of Ammon: "Let the LORD, who is judge, decide today which of us is right—Israel or Ammon" (Jgs 11:27, NLT). When God called Samuel, he told Samuel that he (God) would judge Eli's house.

The concept of God as the Judge of his people is prevalent in the Psalms and Prophets. In Psalm 9:4 David said of God, "For you have judged in my favor; from your throne, you have judged with fairness" (NLT). He added, "But the LORD reigns forever, executing judgment from his throne. He will judge the world with justice and rule the nations with fairness" (9:7-8, NLT). Isaiah described a future day when God shall judge the nations (Is 2:4). Joel also spoke of God as the judge of the nations (Jl 3:12).

In the New Testament Statements like those above formed part of the background for the NT understanding of the judgment seat of God or Christ. The image of a judgment seat came from the fact that in the Roman world judgment took place on a platform (Gk, *bema*) or tribunal, from which a judge would hear and decide cases. Thus, most of the NT references to a judgment seat occur when Jesus, or the apostle Paul, was brought before a ruling authority. For example, Pilate sat on his judgment seat when he tried Jesus (Mt 27:19; cf. Jn 19:13; Acts 18:12, 16-17; 25:6, 10, 17).

The two passages in the NT that speak directly of the judgment seat of God or Christ are Romans 14:10 and 2 Corinthians 5:10. In Romans 14:10 Paul addressed the urgent problem of unity within the church—unity based on a loving acceptance of those with different understandings of the effects of faith in a Christian's daily life. Paul urged the Christians, both Jews and Gentiles, to accept one another in spite of differences concerning eating certain foods and observing certain days. All, he reminded them, must eventually stand before the judgment seat of God to give an account of the way they had lived. Further, since God is the ultimate Judge, Christians should not judge one another. Again, in 2 Corinthians 5 Paul told the Corinthian Christians why Christians strive to please the Lord: all must appear before the judgment seat of Christ to be recompensed for their deeds. The judgment seat of Christ or God, therefore, expresses the ultimate accountability of the Christian.

See also Bema; Judgment; Last Judgment; Second Coming of Christ.

JUDITH (Person)

1. Daughter of Beeri the Hittite and one of Esau's wives (Gn 26:34). In Genesis 36:2 she is alternately called Oholibamah. *See* Oholibamah.
2. Heroine in the book of Judith, a beautiful Judean widow from Bethulia who beheaded the Assyrian general Holofernes, thereby saving her people from destruction. *See* Judith, Book of.

JUDITH, Book of
A deuterocanonical book, named from its leading character. There is general agreement that the book was originally written in Hebrew, but it never was admitted into the Hebrew canon, although it was recognized as canonical by the third Council of Carthage (AD 397) and also by the Council of Trent (AD 1545).

The Maccabean era, and more specifically the persecutions by Antiochus Epiphanes (175–164 BC), are thought to have been the occasion most likely to have produced literature of this kind. The book is an attempt by a Palestinian Jew to encourage his fellow Jews in resisting their enemies and in continuing to observe the law of God faithfully. Judith, the heroine, is blest with the happy combination of a rigorous observance of the law and a cunning bravery amidst great danger.

The book recounts that when Nebuchadnezzar sought to enlist the forces of Persia, Cilicia, Damascus, Lebanon, Antilebanon, all those who lived along the seacoast, Palestine, and Egypt to assist him in war against the Medes, they refused to respond (Jdt 1:7-11). Consequently, he vowed to avenge himself on the whole territory (v 12). After defeating King Arphaxad of the Medes and overthrowing his army, he conquered Ecbatana, killed Arphaxad, and returned to Nineveh to celebrate his victory for four months (vv 12-16) and to recoup his military strength. Nebuchadnezzar commissioned Holofernes to lead a great army of 120,000 foot soldiers and 12,000 cavalry and contingents from other nations (ch 2) against the nations who disobeyed him. The seacoast cities surrendered unconditionally and the Assyrians destroyed local shrines, insisting that all the subjugated peoples should henceforth worship Nebuchadnezzar alone as god (ch 3). When the people of Israel in Judea heard of the devastation being wrought by Holofernes, they determined to thwart his advance against Jerusalem by mobilizing forces and setting up supply depots at strategic passes in the hills north of Jerusalem. At the same time, they sought divine favor (4:1-15). Holofernes, enraged because the people of Israel prepared to fight against him, inquired of the chiefs of Moab and Ammon who these people were (5:1-4) and was informed by Achior, the leader of the Ammonites, of their history and of their invincibility so long as they do not sin against their God (vv 5-21). In anger, Holofernes ordered Achior to be bound and abandoned near the Jewish camp so that he might be destroyed with the nation he had said was invincible (5:22–6:9). Achior was found by the men of the city of Bethulia; Uzziah, the chief ruler of the city, treated him kindly and the Jews continued to call on the God of Israel for help (6:10-21). The next day Holofernes moved his entire army into the valley near Bethulia, terrifying the inhabitants. He decided to cut off the water supply and wait until famine forced the Jews to surrender (7:1-18). Uzziah, after a siege of 34 days, was asked by the elders to surrender to the Assyrians, but he pled with them to hold out for five more days, agreeing that he would capitulate if help was not forthcoming within that time (vv 19-32).

Judith was a wealthy and beautiful widow who was also deeply pious. She reproached the leaders for limiting God and inspired them to believe that God would deliver them by her hand (8:2-36). Judith prepared herself by earnest prayer and dressing in elaborate finery. She packed some kosher food, and with her maid went into the valley toward the camp of the enemy. When she told the Assyrian patrol that she was a Jewess fleeing from the impending fall of the city and that she would show Holofernes how to take the hill country without losing a man (10:11-13), Holofernes assured Judith that she had nothing to fear and encouraged her to tell what her mission was (10:14–11:4). With persuasive words and expressions that had a double meaning, she indicated that her people were about to sin, disobeying the law because of the rigors of the siege. She promised to inform Holofernes when the people had committed their sins so that he might have an easy conquest of all Judea (11:11-19).

Holofernes ordered food and wine for her, but she explained that she must conform to the dietary laws of the

Jews. On the fourth night after her arrival a banquet was staged and Holofernes lay drunk after all the servants had been dismissed (12:5–13:2). With a prayer for strength, she drew his sword and with two powerful strokes severed his head from his body. Putting the head in her bag, she went out calmly, as on previous nights, into the darkness beyond the borders of the camp and came to the gates of Bethulia (13:3-11). Unbounded joy greeted Judith as the people learned what she had done. Uzziah and all the people gave thanks to God and praised Judith for her daring exploit (13:12-20). They arranged for the Jews to make an attack on the morrow (14:1-4). When Achior was summoned and shown the head of Holofernes, he converted to Judaism (vv 5-10). When the Assyrians realized that their general was murdered, they fled in terror and utter confusion, while the Jews pursued them beyond Damascus (14:11–15:7). The high priest Joakim and the members of the Sanhedrin came from Jerusalem to pay homage to Judith for her bravery, and all joined in praising her in song and dance (15:8-13). Judith responded in a hymn of praise to God for granting them deliverance (16:1-17), after which all the people went up to Jerusalem to worship the Lord with sacrifices and feasting for three months (vv 18-20). The book closes with the account of Judith's return to Bethulia, where at the age of 105 she died and was buried with her husband and was mourned for seven days (vv 21-25).

JULIA

1. Woman greeted by the apostle Paul (Rom 16:15). Her name follows that of Philologus, who may have been her brother or husband.
2. According to a variant reading, a woman noted by Paul as being one of his coworkers, as well as a distinguished apostle (Rom 16:7, NLT mg). She was probably Andronicus's wife. The couple, like Aquila and Priscilla, formed an apostolic team. In other manuscripts, the reading is Junia—which, in the Greek, can be understood as a masculine name or feminine, depending on the accent. However, the most ancient manuscripts do not have an accent mark on this name; therefore, the interpreter must decide if this apostle was male or female.

JULIUS Roman centurion of the Augustan cohort who escorted the apostle Paul and other prisoners from Palestine to Rome (Acts 27:1). Jewish leaders in Jerusalem accused Paul of teaching false doctrine and defiling the temple. Because indecision by two successive Roman governors kept Paul in prison for more than two years, he finally appealed to Caesar. Julius was a kind man. He allowed Paul to leave the ship in Sidon to be comforted by his friends (v 3). However, in his eagerness to get his prisoners to Rome, Julius ignored Paul's advice to spend the winter in Fair Havens. Instead, he ordered the ship to sail to Phoenix, another harbor in Crete, which was more suitable for harboring in winter (vv 9-12). During the trip, a storm wrecked the ship. The soldiers on board wanted to kill the prisoners for fear of their escaping, but Julius prevented that massacre, ordering all to jump ship and swim to shore. This decision spared Paul's life (vv 42-44). Some scholars have conjectured that Julius was the soldier who stayed with Paul in Rome (28:16).

JUNIA A Jew who, along with Andronicus, was greeted by Paul in his letter to the church in Rome—according to the reading of some manuscripts (Rom 16:7). Paul recognized Junia as an apostle who had been a prisoner with Paul for the sake of the gospel. This person could have been a male or female. See Julia #2.

JUNIPER* KJV mistranslation for "broom," a desert shrub (1 Kgs 19:4-5; Job 30:4; Ps 120:4). See Plants.

JUPITER* Supreme Roman deity, equivalent to Zeus in Greek mythology. He was Saturn's son and Juno's husband and brother. Jupiter (also called Jove) was the god of destiny. His weapon was the thunderbolt; the eagle and the oak and olive trees were considered sacred in his worship. A temple of Jupiter stood in Rome on the Capitoline Hill. During Hadrian's reign (AD 117–138), a temple of Jupiter Capitolinus was erected on the foundation of the Jewish temple ruins in Jerusalem.

As a result of Barnabas and Paul's ministry in Lystra during their first missionary journey, the people of Lystra thought they were Zeus and Hermes (Jupiter and Mercury) come down to visit them (Acts 14:12-13).

JUSHAB-HESED One of Zerubbabel's seven sons (1 Chr 3:20). Jushab-hesed means "lovingkindness is returned."

JUST See Righteousness.

JUSTIFICATION*, JUSTIFIED The act of God in bringing sinners into a new covenant relationship with himself through the forgiveness of sins. It is a declarative act of God by which he establishes persons as righteous—that is, in right and true relationship to himself.

Since the time of the Reformation, when Martin Luther reestablished the doctrine of justification by faith alone as the cornerstone for theological understanding, this term has had special significance in the history of theology. To Luther it represented a rediscovery of the writings of Paul and a fundamental counterthrust to medieval Catholicism with its theology of works and indulgences. The doctrine of justification by faith alone affirms the thoroughgoing sinfulness of all persons, their total inability to deal effectively with their own sin, and the gracious provision through the death of Jesus Christ of a complete atonement for sin, to which persons respond in simple trust without any special claims or merit of their own.

The noun "justification" and the verb "to justify" are not used often in Scripture. In the KJV, for example, the verb is found only in the OT, and there fewer than 25 times. In the NT both terms are used only 40 times. The more frequent and more important terms that translate the same Hebrew and Greek words are "righteousness" and "to declare (or make) righteous." Any understanding of justification, therefore, directly involves a biblical understanding of righteousness.

In common Greek, "justification" and "justify" are frequently forensic terms; that is, they relate to the law court and the act of acquitting or vindicating someone. It has to do with the innocence or virtue of a person. But more broadly it has to do with the norm of any relationship.

In the Old Testament In the OT righteousness has to do with relationship and the obligations of that relationship. At times one is referred to as righteous because he or she stands in right relationship to another. At other times one is righteous because he or she fulfills certain obligations in a relationship (Gn 38:26). But more important, these terms are used with reference to God, who is viewed as just. He governs with justice (18:25), and his judgments are true and righteous (Ps 19:9). Both the innocent and the guilty know well the justice of God; the former know they will be vindicated and the latter know his law prevails.

Justification and righteousness have technical significance because of their close association with the saving activity of God on behalf of his covenant people. The righteousness of God is bound up not so much with justice as with his intervention on behalf of his people under the covenant. The righteousness of God or the act of justification is, therefore, to be viewed not primarily in terms of law but in terms of covenant. The most important expression of this is the example of Abraham, who was reckoned righteous, that is, brought into personal relationship by virtue of his response of faith to the covenant offered by God (Gn 15:6). Abraham could not justify himself, but on the basis of the covenant, God established him as righteous. All persons share the helplessness of Abraham. In the sight of God no one shall stand justified (Ps 143:2). The hope of humanity is that God will remember his covenant. Righteousness is hence a product of the mercy or grace of God, who deals with his people according to his lovingkindness (Is 63:7). Justification is thus derived from the nature of God; it is primarily a religious term, and only secondly ethical.

In the New Testament Almost all discussion of justification in the NT is found in the letters of Paul, primarily in those to the Romans and Galatians. In these two letters it is one of the fundamental terms by which Paul seeks to set forth the consequences of the work of Christ for sinful humanity. Justification by faith is set primarily against the background of Jewish legalism and its attempts to make the law the basis of salvation. Paul regards this as an alien message requiring the strongest condemnation (Gal 1:6-9). The word and work of Christ, embedded in the message that Paul proclaimed, was a reminder that righteousness or justification is the gift of God through the blood (*covenant* blood, Heb 13:20) of Jesus Christ. All this is entirely apart from the law (Rom 3:21). The law, in fact, is not capable of leading one to righteousness, nor was it given to bring about righteousness.

Galatians 3:15-25 is especially instructive in understanding the function of the law, which came 430 years after the covenant by which Abraham was brought into a living, personal relationship with the holy God. Whatever purpose the law had, it was not given as a means of righteousness. "For if a law had been given which could make alive, then righteousness would indeed be by the law" (Gal 3:21, RSV). The atoning work of Christ for the justification of people is to be seen in terms of covenant rather than law. This is the essential argument of Paul in this section of Galatians, namely, that justification, from the time of Abraham, has been through faith in the God who keeps covenant and has never come by the law. "Righteousness" is therefore a relational term and is affirmed by one who by faith has been brought into right relationship with God. The law brings judgment; it confronts one with his incapacity to cope with sin (Acts 13:39; Rom 8:3). Justification, then, has its forensic (judicial) dimensions in that it copes with, and represents salvation to, the problem of sin and guilt. The believer is set free from condemnation (Rom 8:1). Yet the fundamental understanding of justification is to be gained in moving away from the law and judgment to the covenant and grace. The appeal to Abraham in both Romans and Galatians is to show that the covenant has always been the only hope of humanity. God keeps his covenant, even though his covenant people violate it daily.

In Paul's formulation of the gospel, God is both just and the one who justifies. Sin demands judgment and must be dealt with. God's pattern of bringing people into personal relationship now stands manifest apart from the law in the ministry and death of Christ, whom God put forth as the atoning agent (Rom 3:21-26). Sin is dealt with directly in the death of the sinless one who became sin for us so that we might in him become the righteousness of God (2 Cor 5:21). In his substitutionary death he bears the guilt of all humanity so that by responding in trust mankind might know God in true relationship.

For Paul, then, justification in view of human sinfulness is rooted in the nature of God who alone is able to take initiative in the healing and redeeming of humanity. Justification is by grace alone. Rooted in the nature of God, it is also made available through the work of Christ as God's gift. Thus, we have the often repeated confession that Christ died "for us" (Rom 5:8; 1 Thes 5:10), or "for our sins" (1 Cor 15:3). The means of appropriation is by faith and faith alone (Rom 3:22; 5:1). This faith is a simple trust in the sufficiency of the work of Christ, a trust by which one freely and wholeheartedly identifies with Christ, loves and embraces his Word, and gives himself to the value system expressed in the kingdom of God. The basic self-consciousness of the justified person is that his right relationship with the living God has nothing to do with merit or achievement. It is from beginning to end a gift of infinite love. His own

---

PAUL AND JAMES ON JUSTIFICATION
The Letter of James is often seen to be in conflict with Paul's teaching on justification by faith apart from works of the law. In fact, James quotes the same text (Gn 15:6) concerning Abraham and concludes, "You see that a man is justified by works and not by faith alone" (Jas 2:24, RSV). Martin Luther even repudiated this letter because it seemed at variance with Paul. But two factors should be observed:

(1) Paul and James are faced with two completely opposite crises. Paul is compelled to oppose a legalism that made the law the basis for righteousness and enabled one to stand justified before God. The legalists were trying to maintain the law of Moses (in particular the obligation of circumcision) for those who would be justified. For these, the law was front and center. James, on the other hand, seeks to cope with an antinomianism that shows no concern for the law of God and says that faith is enough. For these persons the law is of no consequence. Paul's opponents would put the law at the heart of justification, so Paul's response is expressed largely in negative terms: "No one will be justified by works of the law" (Rom 3:20). The opponents of James remove the law altogether and negate the significance or meaning of works in the name of faith. As a result James speaks positively of the law in relation to faith.

(2) When Paul and James speak of "works," they speak of different concepts. Paul is speaking of works of the law, that is, works as an expression of the law, or what might be called "law-works" (Rom 3:20). James, on the other hand, never speaks of works of the law but rather of works that give expression to faith, or what might be called "faith-works." James regards faith without works as dead—that is, as no faith at all (Jas 2:17). For him faith is expressed and perfected by works. Paul and James both affirm that one comes into, and continues in, living relationship to God through faith—apart from the law but not without the love and obedience that is born of faith.

powerlessness is resolved in the power of the gospel in which God's saving work is revealed (1:17).

In the Gospels justification appears in the parable of the Pharisee and the tax collector who went into the temple to pray. The former drew attention to his pious works and moral superiority. The latter, humbled by a deep sense of sin and unworthiness, could only cry for mercy. This man, according to Jesus, went down to his house justified (Lk 18:14). Though this is the only instance of the terminology of justification by faith, the entire ministry of Jesus was among people preoccupied with their own piety and the task of justifying themselves before God, people who set themselves over against sinners and undesirables, people who were so involved in their own works that they were offended by the language of grace and the full pardon of sinners (7:36-50). Jesus spoke to the same issue that later plagued Paul. Only the humble before God will be exalted (Mt 18:4; 23:12). Only the sinner hears the word of grace (Lk 5:32; 15:7, 10; 19:7). The unworthy find healing (Mt 8:8).

Justification (or righteousness) by faith is always to be reaffirmed, for within each person there is the almost inevitable and natural desire to establish personal righteousness, to be able to stand before God on the basis of personal character and piety. But the revival and well-being of the church (note that both Luther and Wesley turned from works to faith upon their study of Romans) is rooted in the understanding that the just live by faith (Rom 1:17; Heb 10:38; 11:7).

See also Adoption; Faith; Law, Biblical Concept of; Sanctification.

JUSTUS
1. Surname for Joseph Barsabbas (Acts 1:23). *See* Joseph #12.
2. Godly Corinthian man (presumably a convert of Paul), who opened his home to Paul and the Christians after the Jewish synagogue was closed to Paul's preaching (Acts 18:7). There is disagreement among the manuscripts as to the exact form of his name. Various readings are Justus or Titius Justus. He has also been identified as the Gaius of Romans 16:23.
3. Surname of a believer named Jesus, a Jewish Christian (Col 4:11). *See* Jesus #3.

JUTTAH One of the cities of refuge assigned to Aaron's descendants (Jos 21:16). It was in the hill country of Judah's territory and in the district of Maon (15:55). It has been identified with modern Yatta, about five and a half miles (8.8 kilometers) southwest of Hebron.

See also Cities of Refuge.

K

KAB* According to Josephus, a dry measure equaling about a quart. Other authorities think the kab was larger (see 2 Kgs 6:25, NASB mg). *See* Weights and Measures.

KABZEEL City located in the extreme south of Judah's territory adjacent to neighboring Edom (Jos 15:21; also called Jekabzeel in Neh 11:25). Benaiah, one of David's valiant warriors, came from there (2 Sm 23:20; 1 Chr 11:22). The reference in Nehemiah indicates that Judah's tribe returned to this area after the exile. Its exact site is not known, but Khirbet Hora has been suggested.

KADESH, KADESH-BARNEA Home of the wandering Israelites for nearly 38 years. In the vast area of the Sinai there are two main oases: in the south is Wadi Feiran, near the mountain of Moses (Mt Sinai or Horeb); in the north is Kadesh, or Kadesh-barnea. The former was the place where the law was given; the latter, the main campsite of the 12 tribes during their exodus from Egypt (Dt 1:46).

Kadesh-barnea (Gn 14:7, "En-mishpat") was raided by Chedorlaomer, king of Elam, during the time of Abraham. In this area Hagar was driven from the tent of Sarah, her mistress (16:14), and here Miriam died and was buried (Nm 20:1). The great contention over water took place here, giving rise to the name Meribah or Meribath-kadesh (Nm 20:2-24; Dt 32:51; Ez 47:19; 48:28). This was also the scene of Korah's rebellion against the leadership of Moses and Aaron (Nm 16–17). This area would long remain in the memory of the Israelite tribes as the place of their unbelief following the report of the 10 spies and a delay of 38 years before their occupancy of the Promised Land (Ps 95:8-11; cf. Heb 3:7-19).

Because of the water, pasture, and agricultural lands, plus its proximity to Canaan, the Israelites found this area the best spot in which to spend most of their time prior to entering the Promised Land.

See also Meribah #2; Wilderness Wanderings.

KADMIEL Head of a Levite family who returned from the exile with Zerubbabel (Ezr 2:40; Neh 7:43; 12:8). His name appears in the list of those who supervised the temple rebuilding project (Ezr 3:9), participated in sealing the covenant (Neh 10:9), and were prominent in the praise service (9:4-5; 12:24).

KADMONITES Semitic tribe whose land was promised to Abraham's descendants (Gn 15:19). The name of the tribe is the same as the Hebrew adjective "eastern" and suggests that references to peoples or lands of the east (Gn 25:6; Jgs 8:10; 1 Kgs 4:30; Jb 1:3) may be synonymous with the tribal name.

KAIN (Place) Town in the Judean hill country (Jos 15:57). Its place in the same district as the known cities of Maon, Carmel, Ziph, and Juttah (v 55) favors its identification with Khirbet Yuqim, southwest of Hebron.

KAIN* (Tribe) Clan name synonymous with the Kenites (Nm 24:22; Jgs 4:11). The name is Hebrew for "spear," suggesting a tribe of metalworkers. The nomadic tribe was friendly (1 Sm 15:6) and was eventually absorbed by Judah. *See* Kenites.

KAIWAN Mesopotamian astral deity, called "Chiun" in the KJV and "Kiyyun" in the NASB (Am 5:26). *See* Sakkuth.

KALLAI Priest and the head of Sallu's (Sallai's) priestly family during the days of Joiakim the high priest (Neh 12:20).

KAMON City in Gilead where Jair the judge was buried (Jgs 10:5). While the place has not been identified with certainty, modern Kameim, a small village southeast of the Sea of Galilee, probably reflects the original name, if not the exact location.

KANAH
1. Brook forming Ephraim's northern border and the southern border of Manasseh's tribe (Jos 16:8; 17:9). It flowed westward, joining the Yarkon River about five miles (8 kilometers) from the Mediterranean just north of the modern city of Tel Aviv (biblical Joppa). It is dry most of the year. Kanah is today called Wadi Qana.
2. City situated along Asher's border (Jos 19:28). It lay about six miles (9.7 kilometers) southeast of Tyre on one of the major northeast-southwest routes through northern Galilee. Qana (in modern Lebanon) still bears the name and marks the site.

KANATHA* One of the original 10 Greek cities rebuilt by Rome after Pompey's conquest of Palestine and Syria around 63 BC. The region of these cities became known as the Decapolis. Kanatha (also spelled Canatha), positioned about 60 miles (96.5 kilometers) east of the Sea of Galilee, formed the easternmost boundary of the Decapolis. Some suggest that the city is identifiable with Kenath of Numbers 32:42 and the subsequent modern town of Qanawat, a short distance northeast of es-Suweideh in the Hauran region.

See also Decapolis; Kenath.

KAREAH Father of Jonathan and Johanan (2 Kgs 25:23). After Jerusalem fell to Nebuchadnezzar's army, his sons joined Gedaliah at Mizpah (Jer 40:8–43:5).

KARKA Unidentified town marking a part of Judah's southern boundary (Jos 15:3). It was located in the southwest section of Palestine between Kadesh-barnea and Wadi el-Arish (Besor Brook).

KARKOR City in the Transjordan where Gideon attacked the armies of the two Midianite kings, Zebah and Zalmunna (Jgs 8:10). Indications of its location are sketchy. Judges 8:11 places it east of Nobah and Jogbehah, a town identified with Jubeiah, which is seven miles (11.3 kilometers) northwest of Amman in Jordan. A more feasible site is in the vicinity of ancient Succoth (Tell Dier 'Alla) and Penuel (Tell edh-Dhahab esh-Sherqiyeh), both assigned to Gad's tribe in Gilead.

KARNAIM Town situated along the King's Highway and along one of the northeastern tributaries of the Yarmuk River, 22 miles (35.4 kilometers) east of the Sea of Galilee on the Transjordan Plateau. The prophet Amos prophesied against Karnaim (also spelled Carnaim), foretelling its impending destruction on account of its wickedness (Am 6:13).

It was the leading town in the area after the decline of its sister city, Ashtaroth, and became the main center of an Assyrian province in the seventh century BC. In 163 BC it was captured by Judas Maccabeus (1 Macc 5:26, 43-44). Christian and Jewish traditions believe it to be the home of Job.

See also Ashteroth-karnaim.

KARTAH Levitical city in Zebulun's territory. The list of cities assigned to the Merarite clan of Levites in Joshua 21:34 mentions Kartah, but the parallel passage in 1 Chronicles 6:77 (in the Hebrew) does not.

KARTAN Levitical town assigned to the Gershonites from the tribe of Naphtali (Jos 21:32). It is called Kiriathaim in 1 Chronicles 6:76. *See* Kiriathaim #2; Levitical Cities.

KATTATH Town assigned to Zebulun (Jos 19:15), perhaps the same as the Kitron of Judges 1:30. *See* Kitron.

KEBAR Canal in Babylonia. The prophet Ezekiel, who was among the exiles from the southern kingdom of Judah, received visions from God while living in the area of the Kebar Canal (Ez 1:1, 3; 3:15, 23; 10:15, 20, 22; 43:3). Secular Babylonian texts refer to a *nar Kabaru* that is believed to be the same canal.

KEDAR
1. Second son of Ishmael, Abraham's son (Gn 25:13; 1 Chr 1:29).
2. Tribe or area appearing mainly in the prophetic writings from Solomon to the exile. In Isaiah's prophecy against Arabia, Kedar is mentioned twice (Is 21:13-17). Along with Arabia, Dedan, and Tema, the Kedarites are threatened with destruction. The pomp attributed to them in verse 16 indicates some degree of affluence (see also Ez 27:21), and the militaristic tone of verse 17 points to the fact that they were a warring people. In Jeremiah 49:28 Kedar is linked with Hazor as victims of Nebuchadnezzar's conquests. Although there is no extrabiblical record of Nebuchadnezzar's march on Kedar, Ashurbanipal, the king of Assyria, does mention the conquest of Kedar. That would have been about 650 BC, or a half a century earlier than the Babylonian conquest. Apart from Ashurbanipal's account, the only other ancient extrabiblical reference to Kedar is found on a silver bowl offered to the Arabian goddess Han-'ilat in the Egyptian Delta. The inscription on the bowl reads, "Cain, son of Geshem, king of Kedar," and the date is firmly fixed in the fifth century BC. This Geshem was very likely the enemy of Nehemiah (Neh 2:19; 6:1-6).

The picture the Bible gives of Kedar is that of a desert nomadic people descended from Ishmael. They were not initially believers in Yahweh but are included in Isaiah's prophecy of the future kingdom of God (cf. Is 42:11; 60:7). Their desert environment limited their work to sheep herding and trading. Because of unpre-

dictable water supplies in the desert, they were constantly moving—a way of life best handled by living in tents rather than permanent houses (cf. Ps 120:5; Sg 1:5). For this reason archaeologists have found no site named Kedar. All we can surmise is that the area of Kedar lay to the east and slightly to the south of Israel in what is today the southern part of Jordan. The people of Kedar presumably died out or were assimilated into the surrounding nations.

KEDEMAH Son of Ishmael (Gn 25:15) who gave his name to the tribe he fathered (1 Chr 1:31).

KEDEMOTH City east of the Jordan, probably located on the upper course of the Arnon River. From the wilderness of Kedemoth, Moses sent messengers to Sihon, king of Heshbon, asking permission to pass peaceably through his land (Dt 2:26). In the division of the land, Kedemoth was given to Reuben's tribe (Jos 13:18) and then set aside as one of the Levitical cities for the Merarites (Jos 21:37; 1 Chr 6:79).

See also Levitical Cities.

KEDESH
1. Town in the Judean Negev (Jos 15:23); its appearance alongside Adadah (Aroer) argues against its identification with Kadesh-barnea.
2. City of refuge in upper Galilee, in the territory of Naphtali (Jos 20:7), set apart for the Gershonite clan of Levi (Jos 21:32; 1 Chr 6:76), and the home of Barak (Jgs 4:6). It was conquered by Tiglath-pileser III in 732 BC (2 Kgs 15:29). Jonathan Maccabeus defeated the army of Demetrius there (1 Macc 11:63, 73). It is identified with Tell Qades, four and a half miles (7.2 kilometers) northwest of Lake Huleh.

See also Cities of Refuge.
3. Levitical city in Issachar (1 Chr 6:72); the parallel passage has Kishion (Jos 21:28).

See also Levitical Cities.

KEDORLAOMER King of Elam who participated with three other kings in a campaign against five cities near the southern end of the Dead Sea plain (Gn 14). Although Kedorlaomer is initially third in the list (v 1), he was evidently the leader of the four kings. Elsewhere in the chapter his name comes first or stands alone.

For 12 years the five cities of the plain were vassals of Kedorlaomer. In the 13th year the cities rebelled, and the next year Kedorlaomer enlisted allies to enforce his lordship. The victorious kings looted the cities and took prisoners. Because the patriarch Abram's nephew Lot was among the captives, Abram mustered his servants and allies and pursued Kedorlaomer as far as Damascus. Kedorlaomer was defeated, and the captured loot and prisoners were rescued.

The first half of the name Kedorlaomer is a common Elamite word meaning "servant." The second half is probably the name of an Elamite deity. Although both elements of the name are known outside the Bible, the combination is not. It fits, however, with an early second-millennium BC date for the encounter, coinciding with the biblical account.

KEHELATHAH One of the places where the Israelites encamped on their journey from Egypt to Mt Sinai, located somewhere between Rissah and Mt Shepher (Nm 33:22-23).

KEILAH (Person) Caleb's descendant from Judah's tribe, called the Garmite in 1 Chronicles 4:19. Some identify this reference with the city in Judah instead of a person.

KEILAH (Place) City assigned to Judah's tribe (Jos 15:44; 1 Chr 4:19), located in the southeast Shephelah near the Philistine border. It is identified with modern Khirbet Qila, eight and a half miles (13.7 kilometers) northwest of Hebron.

David led a daring expedition to Keilah to deliver it from marauding Philistine bands, who were stealing grain from its threshing floors. He made it his residence for a time and expected to gain the loyalty of its people. However, when it became evident that the men of Keilah were plotting to turn him and his men over to Saul, he retreated into the wilderness of Ziph (1 Sm 23:1-14).

Keilah was reinhabited by Jews after the Captivity and was divided into two districts, ruled by Hashabiah and Bavvai. Its rulers were included in the roster of those who participated in rebuilding the Jerusalem wall under Nehemiah (Neh 3:17-18).

KELAIAH A Levite who was guilty of marrying a pagan wife (Ezr 10:18). According to verse 23 Kelaiah is also called Kelita. A Levite named Kelita is also found in Nehemiah 8:7, 10:10, and 1 Esdras 9:48, where he is one who helped Ezra in expounding the law and who set his seal on Ezra's covenant. It cannot be determined with certainty whether Kelaiah and Kelita are the same individual.

KELAL See Chelal.

KELITA A Levite sometimes thought to be the same as Kelaiah. See Kelaiah.

KELUB See Chelub.

KELUBAI* See Chelubai.

KELUHI One of Bani's sons, who was encouraged by Ezra to divorce his foreign wife after the exile (Ezr 10:35).

KEMUEL
1. Third son of Nahor (Abraham's brother) and the father of Aram (Gn 22:21).
2. Shiphtan's son from Ephraim's tribe; one of 12 men appointed to divide the land among the Israelite tribes (Nm 34:24).
3. Hashabiah's father, a ruler of the Levites during David's reign (1 Chr 27:17).

KENAANAH
1. Father of Zedekiah, the false prophet who incorrectly prophesied victory for kings Ahab and Jehoshaphat over the Syrians (1 Kgs 22:11, 24; 2 Chr 18:10, 23).
2. Bilhan's son, who was chief of the subclan of Jediael in Benjamin's tribe in the time of King David (1 Chr 7:10-11).

KENAN Fourth-generation descendant of Adam (Gn 5:9-14; 1 Chr 1:2); alternately called Cainan in Luke's genealogy of Christ (Lk 3:37, RSV). See Genealogy of Jesus Christ.

KENANI Levite who participated in Ezra's public reading of the law after the exile (Neh 9:4).

KENANIAH
1. Levite chief who led processional singing when King David brought the ark of the covenant to the new tabernacle in Jerusalem (1 Chr 15:1-3, 22, 27).

2. Public administrator during David's reign. His sons also served as public officials (1 Chr 26:29).

KENATH Town in the Hauran taken by Nobah (Nm 32:42) but later lost to Geshur and Aram (1 Chr 2:23). It was a Canaanite city known from Egyptian execration texts of the 19th and 18th centuries BC and from the conquest by Thutmose III and the Amarna letters. In the Hellenistic period it became one of the cities of the Decapolis; Jewish returnees from Babylon had settled there, and the rabbis considered it a border town of the Promised Land. It was also called Kanatha.
See also Kanatha.

KENAZ Singular form of the name of the Kenizzite tribe, whose land was promised to Abraham's descendants (Gn 15:19). The appearance of three men by this name in the OT may be explained by the spread of the Kenizzite tribe over Edom and southern Judah before the Israelite conquest.

1. Grandson of Esau and chieftain of Edom (Gn 36:11, 15, 42; 1 Chr 1:36, 53).
2. Father of Othniel (Jos 15:17; Jgs 1:13; 3:9-11) and Seraiah (1 Chr 4:13).
3. Caleb's descendant (1 Chr 4:15). See Kenizzites.

KENEZITE* KJV spelling of Kenizzite in Numbers 32:12 and Joshua 14:6, 14. See Kenizzites.

KENITES One of 10 tribes living in Canaan during Abraham's time (Gn 15:19). The Kenites, however, are not included in the parallel statement from Moses' day (Ex 3:17). The apparent reason for this is a more favorable relationship with Israel by that time. That Israel continued to accord special treatment to the Kenites is clear from 1 Samuel 15:6. When Saul mobilized his army against the Amalekites, he gave a warning before the attack. This kindness seems to reflect the aid given by Hobab, son of Reuel, who was their guide in the wilderness (Nm 10:29-31).

By the time of Barak the judge and Deborah the prophetess, there was a branch of the Kenites in Galilee. Judges 4:11 says, "Now Heber the Kenite, a descendant of Moses' brother-in-law Hobab, had moved away from the other members of his tribe and pitched his tent by the Oak of Zaanannim, near Kedesh" (NLT). This Kedesh was in Galilee and was not the Kadesh-barnea of the Sinai wilderness.

Since the name Kenite is closely related to the word for (copper) smith in both Arabic and Aramaic, it may be that this tribe was something of a trade guild of wandering smiths who offered their skills where needed. Nomadic tribes of metalworkers were known to have moved about in the ancient Near East from the early second millennium BC. Such artisans are found among the party of Asiatics pictured on the Beni-Hasan tomb in Egypt, dating from the 19th century BC. In modern times at least one Arab tribe of gypsylike traveling smiths or tinkers has followed the trade routes in search of employment.

In light of the biblical information about the Kenites, the major question is the influence this seemingly ubiquitous tribe had on the life and culture of the Hebrews. The least likely suggestion is that Moses was dependent on his Kenite/Midianite father-in-law, Jethro, for making the bronze serpent (Nm 21:4-9). However, it is likely that the Kenites, if indeed expert in metallurgy, may have taught this technology to God's covenant people to help them achieve settled nationhood. More serious is the suggestion that Jethro (also called Reuel), "priest of Midian," was the source of Moses' theology—the monotheistic religion of Jehovah (or Yahweh). This suggestion can be countered from two angles—one biblical and the other historical.

The biblical reference specifically stating that Jehovah was the personal God known to godly men from the earliest generations is Genesis 4:26: "And to Seth, to him also there was born a son; and he called his name Enosh. Then began men to call upon the name of Jehovah" (ASV). Equally significant is the fact that Moses' mother (or ancestress, as some would conclude) bore the name Jochebed, "Jehovah is glory." Obviously, then, Moses did not first hear of Jehovah from his father-in-law during his exile in the wilderness of Midian. The historical evidence indicates that no cultic sites (worship centers) other than the mobile tabernacle were located in Sinai or anywhere south of Beersheba. It was south of that city that the God who earlier revealed himself to the patriarchs at various localities in the north announced to Moses that he was none other than the God of Abraham, of Isaac, and of Jacob (Ex 3:6). The Israelites never returned to Sinai for worship, even though God had first revealed himself to them there.

Jethro clearly learned of Jehovah through Moses, not vice versa. Those Kenites who became part of the family of God's people did so by adoption, by introduction through Israel's witness into the covenant relationship with the God of Jacob.

Interestingly, 1 Chronicles 2:55 includes the Kenite Hammath, father of the Recabites, within the genealogy of Judah's tribe, into which they had been assimilated. David also links the Kenites with other inhabitants of southern Judah (1 Sm 27:10). Jeremiah 35 states that the Recabites preserved the simple nomadic life of their ancestors down to the time of the Babylonian captivity. This, too, conforms to what is known about the nature of the Kenites.

KENIZZITES A people related to Kenaz, grandson of Esau (Gn 36:11, 15). The Kenizzites were of Edomite stock and resided to the southeast of Judah in the vicinity of the Kenites. They are thought to belong to the pre-Israelite population of Canaan (Gn 15:19). Their territory was to be given to the Israelites along with that of the Kenites, the Amorites, and the Canaanites (vv 19-21).

In Numbers and Joshua, Caleb, the faithful spy, is reckoned to belong to the Kenizzites (Nm 32:12; Jos 14:6, 14). According to 1 Chronicles 4:15, Caleb's genealogy is traced back to Judah (1 Chr 4:1). The relationship of Caleb to the Kenizzites is far from clear. Caleb established his patrimony at Kiriath-sepher (Jgs 1:11-13), which is in Judah but which is also situated close to the territory of the Kenizzites. Critical opinion views the Kenizzites as non-Israelites who occupied Hebron, Debir, and the southernmost hill country of the Negev and became politically incorporated into Judah.

KEPHAR-AMMONI City allotted to Benjamin's tribe for an inheritance after the initial conquest of Canaan by Joshua (Jos 18:24).

KEPHIRAH Hivite city included in a treaty with Joshua that the Gibeonites secured by deception (Jos 9:17). When the Israelites conquered the land of Canaan, Kephirah became the property of Benjamin's tribe (18:26). Many inhabitants of this city came back to Judea with the repatriates after the exile (Ezr 2:25; Neh 7:29). The site is now identified as Khirbet Kefireh, located southwest of ancient Gibeon.

KERAN Dishon's son, a member of the Horite tribe during Esau's time (Gn 36:26; 1 Chr 1:41).

KEREN-HAPPUCH Job's third daughter and the sister of Jemimah and Keziah. She was listed as a member of Job's family at the time of his restoration (Jb 42:14).

KERETHITES Members of a tribal group that lived in southern Judah near Hebron (1 Sm 30:14), mentioned along with the Pelethites (2 Sm 8:18). The Kerethites were associated with the Philistines, according to Ezekiel 25:15-17 (cf. Zep 2:5). They were judged with "the rest of the seacoast" for the Philistines' offense against Israel. Since the Philistines most likely originated in the islands of the Mediterranean, including Crete, the word Kerethite probably means Cretan. "Pelethite" is probably an alternate spelling of Philistine.

Because of the Kerethites' Philistine connections, what is known about the Philistines may shed light on them. Archaeological evidence from Cretan murals and Egyptian tomb paintings and temple reliefs shows Philistines wearing plumed headdresses. Similarities between Philistine, Cretan, and Greek pottery designs also suggest a strong link among these Mediterranean peoples.

Kerethites and Pelethites were hired by David as mercenaries, forming an elite corps of foreign soldiers faithful to him through all his troubles (2 Sm 15:18; 20:7, 23; 1 Kgs 1:38). Later kings may have continued to use them as soldiers, as suggested by the mention of "Carites" (Kerethites?) in 2 Kings 11:4, 19.

KERIOTH

1. Town in the Negev of Judah (Jos 15:25), called Kerioth-hezron. The Hebrew text understands Kerioth and Hezron to be separate towns, the latter being identical to Hazor (v 23).
2. Town in Moab (Jer 48:24, 41; Am 2:2). From the Moabite Stone, it can be located in the southwest tableland of Moab opposite Ataroth. It is not counted among the towns of Reuben and Gad (Nm 34: Jos 13); in other lists it is absent while Ar is mentioned (Is 15–16), which leads scholars to equate Ar with Kerioth.

KERIOTH-HEZRON Town mentioned in Joshua 15:25. *See* Kerioth #1.

KERITH, The Brook Also rendered the "Kerith Ravine" (NIV), it was the place where the Lord told the prophet Elijah to hide from King Ahab during a famine Elijah had predicted. There he had sufficient water to drink and was fed by ravens each morning and evening (1 Kgs 17:2-6). The brook, or gorge, has traditionally been identified as the Wadi Qelt, west of the Jordan River near Jericho. More likely Kerith, indicated in Scripture as "east of the Jordan River," was located in Gilead, Elijah's homeland (v 3).

KEROS One of the temple servants whose descendants returned to Jerusalem with Zerubbabel (Ezr 2:44; Neh 7:47).

KERUB One of five Babylonian cities from which Israelites who could not trace their ancestry returned after the exile (Ezr 2:59; Neh 7:61).

KERYGMA* Basic evangelistic message proclaimed by the earliest Christians. More fully, it is the proclamation of the death, resurrection, and exaltation of Jesus that leads to an evaluation of his person as both Lord and Christ, confronts one with the necessity of repentance, and promises the forgiveness of sins. The kerygma is drawn from two sources: (1) the fragments of pre-Pauline tradition that lie embedded in the writings of the apostle, and (2) the early evangelistic speeches of Peter in the book of Acts. When these two sources are compared, a single basic message emerges.

The kerygma is essentially the same as the gospel, although the term itself emphasizes the *manner* of delivery somewhat more than the *message* that is being proclaimed. In the ancient world the king made known his decrees by means of a *kerux* (a town crier or herald). This person, who often served as a close confidant of the king, would travel throughout the realm announcing to the people whatever the king wished to make known. It is this note of authoritative declaration that is so appropriately transferred to the evangelizing activities of the primitive church.

The simplest outline of the kerygma is made up of (1) a proclamation of the death, resurrection, and exaltation of Jesus, seen as the fulfillment of prophecy and involving human responsibility; (2) the resultant evaluation of Jesus as both Lord and Christ; and (3) a summons to repent and receive forgiveness of sins. However, on the basis of a careful study of the actual texts themselves, the kerygma did *not* contain (1) a declaration of the dawn of the messianic age; (2) any reference to the life and ministry of Jesus (in contrast to his death and resurrection); or (3) a major emphasis on the Second Coming as part of the evangelistic proclamation. While all of these issues are part of the larger theological presentation of the NT, they do not appear to have been included in the essential apostolic gospel. In any case, they are missing from the various texts that provide the source for the kerygma.

It is evident that the resurrection plays the central role in the drama of redemption. The kerygma always focuses on the resurrection. This supernatural act of God in history authenticates the words and works of Jesus and constitutes the basis for the Christian hope of immortality. Without the resurrection, the church would be no more than a group of well-intentioned religious people who had placed their faith in the superior philosophical and ethical teachings of an unusually fine man. The resurrection is proof positive that Jesus is who he said he was. Only if he is the Son of God can his death provide an appropriate and sufficient sacrifice for human sin. Essentially, the kerygma is a declaration that Christ is risen from the dead and that by that great act God has brought salvation.

The kerygma is not a dull recital of historical facts but a dynamic confrontation between the Holy Spirit and the sinful heart of man at the point of its basic need. Who can deny that the reality of the resurrection validates the claims of Christ? Who can resist the compelling logic of the resurrection as it leads irresistibly to the conclusion that Jesus of Nazareth is the living Lord? To repent and believe is to enter the kingdom of God. The kerygma has as its ultimate goal not a sophisticated theology but a transformed life. It is the declaration that in Christ the new order of eternal life has already entered into time and history.

See also Acts of the Apostles, Book of the; Gospel.

KESALON City in northern Judah near the border of Dan, situated on the northern slope of Mt Jearim; usually identified with modern Kesla, about nine miles (14.5 kilometers) west of Jerusalem. Kesalon is mentioned only in the period of Israel's initial settlement of Canaan under Joshua (Jos 15:10).

See also Jearim, Mount.

KESED Son of Milcah and Nahor, Abraham's brother (Gn 22:22).

KESIL City situated along the borders of Edom in the Negev, allotted to Judah's tribe for an inheritance (Jos 15:30). In parallel lists of towns Kesil is replaced by Bethul (Jos 19:4), Bethuel (1 Chr 4:30), and perhaps Bethel—not to be confused with the Bethel north of Jerusalem (1 Sm 30:27). Bethuel or Bethul is considered by many textual critics to be the original name, with Kesil as a later textual variant.

See also Bethuel, Bethul (Place).

KESITAH* Weight of unknown value (Gn 33:19; Jos 24:32; Jb 42:11). *See* Money.

KESULLOTH Town in Issachar (Jos 19:18); also called Kisloth-tabor in Joshua 19:12. It is probably to be identified with the modern Iksal, about three miles (4.8 kilometers) southeast of Nazareth.

KETURAH Second wife of Abraham. It is unclear whether he married her before or after Sarah's death (Gn 25:1). He had six sons with her: Zimran, Jokshan, Medan, Midian, Ishbak, and Shuah (v 2). Keturah's status was not identical to that of Sarah. She is called a concubine (Gn 25:6, cf. 1 Chr 1:32), and her sons were presented with gifts instead of receiving a share in the inheritance. Keturah's sons were the ancestors of tribes with which Israel came into contact after the Conquest, especially Midian and Jokshan's sons Sheba and Dedan (Gn 25:3). As far as can be determined, the tribes settled in the north and central regions of the northern Euphrates, as far as the central sections of the Arabian Desert. They were merchants (ch 37) and shepherds (Ex 2:16). They were involved in international trade (Is 60:6). For example, the queen of Sheba, a descendant of Jokshan (Gn 25:3), came to Solomon to initiate trade relations (1 Kgs 10:2).

See also Abraham.

KEYS OF THE KINGDOM Symbolic description of the authority given by Jesus to Peter in Matthew 16:19: "I will give you the keys of the kingdom of heaven, and whatever you bind on earth shall be bound in heaven, and whatever you loose on earth shall be loosed in heaven" (RSV).

Many ancient peoples believed that heaven and hell were closed by gates to which certain deities and angelic beings had keys. In Greek mythology, for example, Pluto kept the key to hades. In Jewish writings near the time of Jesus give God the key to the abode of the dead. In the book of Revelation, John sees Christ holding the keys of death and hades (Rv 1:18; see 3:7).

In Matthew's Gospel the keys symbolize the authority to open and shut the kingdom of heaven. In response to Peter's declaration that Jesus is the Christ, the Son of the living God (Mt 16:16), Jesus entrusts authority to "bind" and "loose" to Peter (v 19). This authority is later extended to the other disciples (18:18). The words "bind" and "loose" were used by rabbis near the time of Christ to declare someone under a ban ("binding") and relief of the ban ("loosing"). Sometimes this referred to expulsion or reinstatement at a synagogue. At other times binding and loosing indicated consignment to God's judgment or acquittal from it. The "power of the keys" (or binding and loosing) of which Jesus speaks is a spiritual authority like that he gave the disciples in John 20:23: "If you forgive the sins of any, they are forgiven; if you retain the sins of any, they are retained" (RSV).

The Pharisees and scribes assumed that as teachers of the law they had power to shut the kingdom of heaven against others (Mt 23:13). Yet as blind guides they failed to recognize what Peter had acknowledged—that Jesus was the one in whom God's kingdom had come. The keys of the kingdom authorized the pronouncement of judgment and the promise of forgiveness—not by human authority, but on the basis of Christ's word.

See also Kingdom of God, Kingdom of Heaven.

KEZIAH Job's second daughter, born after his restoration (Jb 42:14).

KEZIB Alternate name for Aczib, a city in Judah's territory, in Genesis 38:5. *See* Aczib #1.

KEZIZ*, Valley of KJV rendering of Emek-keziz, a city allotted to Benjamin's tribe for an inheritance, in Joshua 18:21. *See* Emek-keziz.

KIBROTH-HATTAAVAH Location in the wilderness where the Israelites who were killed by plague for craving meat from Egypt were buried (Nm 11:34-35; 33:16-17; Dt 9:22). It was situated between Mt Sinai and Hazeroth, but its exact site is unknown. The name, meaning "graves of craving," accords with the account of the quails.

See also Wilderness Wanderings.

KIBZAIM One of several cities in Ephraim given to the Levitical family of Kohath after the conquest of Canaan (Jos 21:22). It is probably the same as the Jokmeam of 1 Chronicles 6:68.

KID Young goat. *See* Animals (Goat).

KIDNEY One of the body parts of sacrificial animals used for offerings to God. The kidneys, along with their fat, were to be burned on the altar (Ex 29:13; Lv 3:4-15) and represented the blood that the Israelites were not permitted to eat.

In a more figurative sense the kidneys are thought of as the seat of human emotions (Ps 73:21) and the rational and moral faculties (Ps 16:7; Jer 12:2). They are closely associated with the "heart" and "soul," standing for one's innermost self-consciousness. The NLT translates the Hebrew word as "mind," "heart," and "soul" in several passages.

As in the OT Jehovah had knowledge of man's inmost thoughts (e.g., Pss 7:9; 26:2; Jer 20:12), so Christ was identified in the book of Revelation as the one who "searches the minds and hearts" (Rv 2:23), making an indirect but clear identification of Jesus with Jehovah. This is the only reference to the kidneys in the NT.

KIDON* Threshing floor where Uzzah was struck down by God as he attempted to steady the ark of the covenant (1 Chr 13:9, NLT mg). The parallel passage in 2 Samuel 6:6 refers to this place as "the threshing floor of Nacon." Following the death of Uzzah, the place was renamed Perez-uzzah, which means either "the breach of Uzzah" or "the outbreak against Uzzah" (2 Sm 6:8; 1 Chr 13:11).

KIDRON Valley and streambed running below the southeast wall of Jerusalem and separating the city from the Mt of Olives on the east. It then turns southeast from Jerusalem and follows a winding course to the Dead Sea. The Kidron can be described as a torrent bed that is nearly always dry, since the watercourse flows only in the rainy season, partly maintained by the two irregular springs Gihon and En-rogel.

The Gihon was the vital water source for the old City

of David, and in Hezekiah's day an underground tunnel was cut in the rock to guarantee a water supply in time of siege, thus supplying the pool of Siloam within the city walls.

The term "brook" found in John 18:1 (KJV) would be better translated "winter flow" or "winter course," since the original word intends to convey this seasonal character of the creek rather than to suggest a river.

The two most important functions of the Kidron Valley for the city of Jerusalem are military and funerary. The walls of the city have always towered over the valley, and its steepness made it extremely difficult for any attack to succeed from that side. Over the centuries rubble from nearby ruins has raised the floor of the valley. In places the present floor is some 40 feet (12.2 meters) above earlier historic levels; it is not certain how many ancient caves and tombs must lie below the present surface. The wide space just south of the city, where the Kidron meets and merges with the Tyropean and Hinnom Valleys, has always been a favorite spot for the royal gardens, irrigated from the two nearby springs.

Aerial View of the Kidron Valley

Since the fourth century AD, the Kidron has been called "the valley of Jehoshaphat" (Jl 3:12), scene of the judgment of nations at the last day, and this tradition is strong among both Muslims and Jews. Today the sides of the valley are crowded with tombs. Even before the exile it was a popular place for burial (2 Kgs 23:4-12 refers to the graves of the common people and to the dumping of idolatrous refuse there; see also 2 Chr 34:4-5).

The first reference to the Kidron Valley is in 2 Samuel 15:23, where the people and David crossed over toward the desert. This strategic move would give them a way of escape if rebellious Absalom's forces decided to attack the city. The people and the king wept bitterly during this move (2 Sa 15:30) because it had such a depressing significance; David was abandoning Zion without a fight. Later the offensive Shimei was forbidden to cross the Kidron by Solomon (1 Kgs 2:36-38) on pain of death. Josephus mentions that the wicked queen Athaliah was put to death in the Kidron Valley (*Antiquities* 9.7.3), but it is not clear from 2 Kings 11:16 whether the horses' entrance to the palace opened onto the Kidron.

The last reference to the Kidron is the occasion of Jesus' crossing it with his disciples on the eve of his betrayal (Jn 18:1). The parallels with the crossing of David are interesting, considering the place David holds in the establishment of the biblical symbolism of king

and kingdom. Eschatologically, Jeremiah foretells a time when the Kidron will be sacred to the Lord (Jer 31:38-40) as part of the restoration of Israel.
See also Jerusalem.

KILEAB David's second son, and the first born to him by Abigail (2 Sm 3:3); alternately called Daniel in 1 Chronicles 3:1.

KILION One of the two sons of Elimelech and Naomi (Ru 1:2). He married a Moabite girl named Orpah (v 4) and eventually died in Moab (v 5).

KILLING *See* Civil Law and Justice; Criminal Law and Punishment; Commandments, The Ten.

KILMAD Mesopotamian city listed with Haran, Canneh, Eden, and Asshur as traders with Tyre (Ez 27:23).

KILN Large furnace used in firing pottery. *See* Pottery.

KIMHAM Son of Barzillai (according to Josephus), a very wealthy man who supplied David and his men with food while they were in Mahanaim during their flight from Absalom (2 Sm 19:32). David offered to take Barzillai back to Jerusalem with him, but Barzillai declined and suggested that David show kindness to Kimham instead (vv 37-40). David accepted the proposal and ordered his son and successor, Solomon, to grant Kimham a pension at the palace (1 Kgs 2:7). His name is reflected centuries later in Geruth-kimham, a place near Bethlehem where the people Johanan had rescued from Ishmael stayed, intending to go to Egypt later (Jer 41:17).

KINAH Town in the Negev of Judah (Jos 15:22), perhaps named after the Kenites who lived in the area (Jgs 1:16). According to a letter discovered at Arad, troops were sent from Kinah to reinforce Ramoth-negev against an Edomite attack. The ancient name is preserved in Wadi el-Qeini, in the eastern Negev.

KINDNESS State of being that includes the attributes of loving affection, sympathy, friendliness, patience, pleasantness, gentleness, and goodness. Kindness is a quality shown in the way a person speaks and acts. It is more volitional than emotional.

The Bible is filled with illustrations of kindness. Joseph wanted Pharaoh's butler to show kindness by remembering him to Pharaoh (Gn 40:14). Rahab requested kind treatment from Israel for her protection of the two spies who had come into her home (Jos 2:12). Before he attacked Amalek, Saul asked the Kenites to leave the Amalekite territory, not wanting to kill them along with the Amalekites because of the kindness they had shown Israel when Israel came up from Egypt (1 Sm 15:6). David commended the men of Jabesh-gilead for the kindness they had shown Saul in giving his body a decent burial (2 Sm 2:5). Jonathan requested "unfailing kindness" of David so that he would not be killed (1 Sm 20:14-15). David extended this kindness to Jonathan's son by granting him the right to eat at the king's table (2 Sm 9:1-7).

It is the worst kind of ingratitude to return evil for kindness. Abimelech wanted Abraham to swear that he would return kindness for kindness to his offspring (Gn 21:23). Abner showed kindness to Ishbosheth by not delivering him over to David, while Ishbosheth, in return, charged Abner with guilt regarding Saul's concubine, Rizpah (2 Sm 3:8). Hanun received David's kind

act of sending condolences on his father's death by humiliating David's messengers, thereby bringing on war between the two nations (10:2-19). Absalom rebuked Hushai, David's friend, for supposedly leaving David's side when he needed him. Absalom asked Hushai if that was the way he was repaying David's friendship (2 Sm 16:17; see also 2 Chr 24:22).

God's actions provide the outstanding illustrations of kindness in the Bible. The Levites praised God because he had proved to be a God of forgiveness, graciousness, compassion, and abundant lovingkindness (Neh 9:17-31). To highlight God's virtue even more, they declared his kindness against the backdrop of Israel's unfaithfulness. God did not forsake his people, even though they forsook him for a golden calf. He gave them his Spirit to instruct them. He gave them manna to eat and water to drink for 40 years in the wilderness. He gave them Canaan, a land in which to dwell.

The high point of God's kindness was his provision of salvation for sinners, not on the basis of their works but on the basis of his mercy (Ti 3:4; see also Eph 2:7). Because of God's great kindness toward them, in giving both physical and spiritual blessings, Christians are exhorted, as God's elect, to put on hearts of compassion, kindness, humility, gentleness, and patience; that is, to show kindness to others in return for God's kindness (Col 3:12). The apostle Peter commanded Christians to add to their faith, along with other excellences, the excellence of brotherly kindness (2 Pt 1:7, KJV).

KINE* Cows. *See* Animals (Cattle).

KING The word *melek* (king) occurs more than 2,000 times in the Hebrew OT. It may refer to God (Ps 95:3) or to human rulers. Generally it designates one invested with ultimate authority and power over his subjects. In the OT, the word *melek* designates the ruler of a tribe ("the kings of Midian," Nm 31:8), a city (Jericho, Ai; cf. Jos 12:9-24, where 31 kings of city-states conquered by the Israelites are listed), a nation (Israel, Judah, Ammon, Moab, Aram), or an international power (such as Egypt, Assyria, Babylonia, or Persia). Other words may also refer to royalty. The Philistines introduced the title *seren* (lord) into Hebrew vocabulary. The five Philistine cities were ruled by five lords. Another word for an Israelite king is *nagid* (ruler). Both Saul and David were anointed as *nagid* over Israel (1 Sm 10:1; 16:13). In the NT and the Septuagint, the Greek version of the OT, the Greek word *basileus* has a meaning similar to the Hebrew *melek*. The NT *basileus* refers to secular rulers living in the first century, kings of Israel, rulers of the past, and the divine King, Jesus Christ.

The phrase "King of kings," attributed to Jesus (1 Tm 6:15), is a Hebrew expression meaning supreme or greatest king. For example, in Ezekiel's prediction of the fall of Tyre, Nebuchadnezzar is named the "king of kings" (Ez 26:7). The great rulers of Assyria and Babylon introduced this title. Before their time, rulers were called either "king" or "great king," as in 2 Kings 18:28: "Hear the word of the great king, the king of Assyria" (RSV). Later rulers had their titles adjusted to keep up with the expanse of their empires.

Kingship in Israel God chose Abraham as the father of nations; through him and his descendants the messianic rule would be established on earth. In his promises to Abraham, God repeatedly assured him that he would become the father of a mighty nation, to whom God would give the land of Canaan, and that kings would arise from his descendants (Gn 17:6). Abraham showed his acceptance of the rule of God over his family by obeying God's command to be circumcised, which set the clan of Abraham apart for the service of God (vv 10-14). The ultimate purpose of God's relation with Abraham and his descendants was that God would be King over Israel and that his people would show their acceptance of his rule by their faithful obedience to him (v 9).

At the heart of the covenant was God's expectation of loyalty to his rule. Abraham and his descendants were to exercise their God-given "rule" over the nations by living in fellowship with the great King. Thus the Lord reestablished his dominion over mankind. Through Abraham and his descendants, he would raise up a "royal nation" to whom the full privileges of rule over his creation would be restored.

The Lord also made a covenant with Israel. This covenant was a sovereign administration of grace and promise by which the Lord consecrated the people unto himself by the sanctions of divine law and by his very presence. The nation, witnessing God's care for them, had to learn that by their obedience to God's expectations the theocratic kingdom might become a reality on earth. In the Sinaitic covenant the theocracy (the rule of God) was established. Israel was entrusted with the commandments, so that they might show themselves to be a theocratic nation, as God revealed to Moses: "Now if you will obey me and keep my covenant, you will be my own special treasure from among all the nations of the earth; for all the earth belongs to me. And you will be to me a kingdom of priests, my holy nation" (Ex 19:5-6, NLT). They were God's elect for the sake of the nations; through Israel's priestly obedience and intercession, the whole earth might know the Creator-Redeemer.

The qualities of God's kingship were power, glory, fidelity, wisdom, concern, service, delegation of power to man, blessing and protection, just rule, judgment, vindication, and deliverance. Israel's kingship was to be no different from God's. Their varied and sometimes complex laws taught Israel to distinguish between what was holy and common, clean and unclean, the ways of God and the ways of the nations. The ways of God enhanced love, fidelity, justice, peace, harmony, service, concern for others, wise living, defense of the needy, and judgment of the guilty. The ways of the kingdoms of the world all too often promoted selfishness, anarchy, despotism, and disregard for justice.

The Lord also instituted an organizational structure designed to promote his theocratic purposes. In the wilderness Moses and the chosen leaders of Israel (Ex 18:19-26; Nm 11:24-25; cf. Dt 1:15-18) were God's instruments for upholding his kingship in Israel. Upon Moses' death, Joshua took over the theocratic rule. The Lord was with him as he had been with Moses, and all Israel recognized the continuity of God's rule in Joshua's leadership (Dt 34:9; Jos 3:7; 4:14). Like Moses had before his death, Joshua charged the leadership and Israel to persevere in the gracious covenant relationship (Jos 23-24). However, Israel perished because of its greed, immorality, strife, and idolatry. During the period of the judges, each one did what was right in his own eyes (Jgs 17:6; 18:1; 19:1; 21:25). There was no king in the land in those days. The judges were military leaders whom the Lord raised up to deliver his people from their foreign oppressors. But God remained King, regardless of the fact that Israel lived as if he were not. The period of the judges demonstrated that apostate Israel, disobedient to their King, was unsuccessful in dealing with the surrounding nations.

The theocratic leadership was restored to Israel by the ministry of Samuel. He was born into a Levitical family and served the Lord at the Shiloh tabernacle. He was called to be a prophet—an office which had not been filled since Moses' death (1 Sm 3:20-21). He was recognized as a judge in Israel (7:15). In Samuel the offices of priest, prophet, and king were combined. He is never called king, as his lifestyle was that of a prophet rather than that of a ruler. The carefully calculated request of the people for a king was a rejection of Samuel's ministry. The people were not satisfied with the spiritual, charismatic leadership of Samuel. In their search for a more dynamic leader they found in the kings of the surrounding nations attractive elements: power, manifestation of glory, and stability. Thus far the tribes had experienced several civil wars that endangered the unity of Israel. It was thought that a king would remedy all of the social and political problems. Though God had foreseen the days of the monarchy in the law (Dt 17:14-20), the people were motivated to introduce the kingship for secular rather than religious reasons: "Give us a king like all the other nations have" (1 Sm 8:5); "We want to be like the nations around us. Our king will govern us and lead us into battle" (v 20, NLT). Samuel never accepted the idea of kingship; it was foreign to the theocratic ideal.

The crucial difference between kingship in Israel and kingship in neighboring lands lay in the fact that God endowed the king of Israel with his Spirit to establish his rule on earth. God ruled for his people, and his people benefited from his rule; he was their provider, protector, and divine warrior.

Samuel was instrumental in anointing Saul (a sad example of kingship) and David (a good example of kingly rule under God). Saul's kingship revealed a despotic, uncaring attitude and self-aggrandizement. He was intent on establishing his dynasty, while not caring sufficiently for the people of God. Therefore, the Lord rejected his kingship (1 Sm 15:23).

David's kingship, in contrast to Saul's, was in line with God's because it reflected the glory of Yahweh's kingship. David's life and rule are taken up in the two books of Samuel as a commentary on the pros and cons of kingship. Positively, David was a man after God's heart, who sought the will of his sin, repented of his sin, and sought the glory of God. Negatively, David failed in his personal and family life to uphold the high standards of God's law. Yet God was pleased to choose David's dynasty as the lineage through which Jesus Christ would come. The prophet Nathan assured David that his dynasty would last: "Your dynasty and your kingdom will continue for all time before me, and your throne will be secure forever" (2 Sm 7:16, NLT). But God did not promise that it would be immune from prosecution or banishment.

The outstanding qualities of the kingship of David and his son Solomon reflect the true theocratic intention: concern for the Lord, for a heart of wisdom and integrity, and for the well-being of God's people. Concern for the Lord found expression in the preparation and actual building of the temple (cf. Ps 132). Concern for integrity and wisdom is clearly evident, especially in David's response to Nathan's rebuke (2 Sm 12) and in Solomon's request to have a heart of wisdom (1 Kgs 3). Concern for the people comes to expression in their securing the borders against enemies, achieving national unification, and bringing opportunity for economic growth. The era of David and Solomon represented a true reflection of God's kingship on earth.

The accounts in Kings and Chronicles unfold the subsequent history of kingship in Israel and Judah. The good kings followed the examples provided by David and Solomon in securing Jerusalem against foreign invaders, in supplying for the needs of the temple, in having God's people instructed in the word of God, and in modeling their rule after the law of Moses. A good Davidic king loved the Lord, the temple, the law, and God's people. He served them as a good shepherd. Evil kings were those who rejected this model of kingship in favor of the pagan models. So Omri and Ahab introduced the Phoenician culture with its Baalism, utterly disregarding the heritage of Israel.

The Davidic king was treated as a member of God's household, being a "son" of the great King (cf. 2 Sm 7:14-16; Ps 2:6-7). The Davidic king was to be loyal to the great King, Yahweh. He, like Moses and Joshua, received his orders directly from the Lord; but unlike with Moses, the word of the Lord was mediated through the prophets. He, like Moses and Joshua, was expected to serve his God and his people.

The Messiah-King The descendants of David failed to maintain and expand the theocracy. By the eighth and seventh centuries BC, it was apparent that even the greatest kings were dwarfed by the stature of David and Solomon. The prophets (Is 9:2-7; 11:1-9; Jer 33:14-16; Ez 34:22-31; Mi 5:2-5) spoke of another king, the Messiah, a descendant of David who would rule permanently and by whose rule the reign of God would extend to the ends of the earth. He would put down all opposition to God's rule, remove all enemies, and bring in an era of universal peace and righteousness. The Messiah-King would reveal the perfections of divine rule, as the Spirit of God would be upon him. His kingship would be marked by service to the people of God, so that they would be a well-cared-for flock; he would serve them as their shepherd.

In the coming of Jesus the messianic kingdom is more clearly revealed. He is the King of whom the angels said, "The Savior—yes, the Messiah, the Lord—has been born tonight in Bethlehem, the city of David!" (Lk 2:11, NLT). These magnificent words show continuity with the prophetic word. Jesus is the Savior, whose role includes deliverance from sin but also deliverance from all causes of adversity, evil, and the effects of the curse. His mission pertains to both forgiveness and to the establishment of peace on earth (1:77-79). In this light we must look at Jesus' ministry of healing, feeding, opposing the forces of evil, suffering, and teaching as the establishment of God's kingdom on earth. He is the King who serves, fights against the demonic powers, and overcomes. The resurrection marks his victory, and he is crowned with glory by being seated at the right hand of the Father (Acts 2:33-36; cf. 1 Cor 15:25). In being the Savior he is none other than Christ the Lord. The early apostolic preaching proclaimed that Jesus is the Messiah of God and the Lord. The lordship of Jesus is corollary to his being the Messiah. To those who call on him, he is the Savior-Messiah-Lord (Rom 10:9-15), but to those who reject him, he is the divine warrior, before whom all knees will bow and who will bring in the era of the Father's judgment (cf. Rv 1:12-16; 19:11-21).

Jesus taught his disciples that at his coming in glory he would be seated on his throne and all mankind would pay him obeisance. The enemies of God will be cast out from his presence, and the people of God will fully inherit the kingdom (Mt 25:31-46). In accordance with Jesus' teaching, the members of his body, the church, are expected to work out the theocratic ideal in their lives, that by their works and faith they may glorify the Father and show that they are his (Jn 17:20-26; cf. Mt 25:33-40). This is the biblical manner of witness that Israel failed to give and that the church is privileged to give; as Paul wrote to Timothy:

> I command you before God, who gives life to all, and before Christ Jesus, . . . that you obey his commands

with all purity. Then no one can find fault with you from now until our Lord Jesus Christ returns. For at the right time Christ will be revealed from heaven by the blessed and only almighty God, the King of kings and Lord of lords. He alone can never die, and he lives in light so brilliant that no human can approach him. No one has ever seen him, nor ever will. To him be honor and power forever. Amen. (1 Tm 6:13-16, NLT)

Then Paul gives several instructions as to how the people of God must demonstrate their allegiance to Jesus. Throughout the book of Revelation, Jesus is viewed as King over the church (Rv 4:2, 9-11; 5:1, 9-13). At his return his kingship will be established. At this time, the enemies of the cross will see the one whom they have rejected and will bow before the messianic King (1 Cor 15:25-28). "After that the end will come, when he [Jesus] will turn the Kingdom over to God the Father, having put down all enemies of every kind" (v 24, NLT).

See also Israel, History of; Kingdom of God, Kingdom of Heaven.

KINGDOM OF GOD, KINGDOM OF HEAVEN
The sovereign rule of God, initiated by Christ's earthly ministry and consummated when the kingdom of the world becomes the kingdom of our Lord and of his Christ (Rv 11:15).

PREVIEW
• Introduction
• Old Testament Background
• In the New Testament

Introduction According to the testimony of the first three Gospels, the proclamation of the kingdom of God was Jesus' central message. Matthew summarizes the Galilean ministry with the words "Jesus traveled throughout Galilee teaching in the synagogues, preaching everywhere the Good News about the Kingdom" (Mt 4:23, NLT). The Sermon on the Mount is concerned with the righteousness that qualifies people to enter the kingdom of God (5:20). The collection of parables in Matthew 13 and Mark 4 illustrate the "mystery" of the kingdom of God (Mt 13:11; Mk 4:11). The establishment of the Lord's Supper looks forward to the establishment of the kingdom of God (Mt 26:29; Mk 14:25).

The NT reports two different forms of the expression: "the kingdom of God" and "the kingdom of the heavens." The latter is found only in Matthew, but Matthew also has "the kingdom of God" four times (Mt 12:28; 19:24; 21:31, 43). "The kingdom of heaven" is a Semitic phrase that would have been meaningful to Jews but not to Greeks. The Jews, out of reverence for God, avoided uttering the divine name, and contemporary literature gives examples of substituting the word "heaven" for God (1 Macc 3:18, 50; 4:10; see Lk 15:18).

The key to an understanding of the kingdom of God is that the basic meaning of the Greek word *basileia*, as also of the Hebrew *malkut*, is rule, reign, dominion. We frequently find in the OT the expression "in the year of the kingdom of . . . ," meaning in the year of the reign of a given king (e.g., 1 Chr 26:31; 2 Chr 3:2; 15:10; Ezr 7:1; 8:1; Est 2:16; Jer 10:7; 52:31). When we read that Solomon's kingdom was firmly established (1 Kgs 2:12), we are to understand that his authority to reign was settled. To "turn the kingdom of Saul over to [David]" (1 Chr 12:23, KJV) indicates that the authority that had been Saul's was given to David. As a result of having received legal authority, David became king. This abstract idea of *malkut* is evident when it is found in parallelisms with such ideas as power, might, glory, and dominion (Dn 4:34; 7:14).

When *malkut* is used of God, it almost always refers to his authority or to his rule as the heavenly King. "They will talk together about the glory of your kingdom; they will celebrate examples of your power. . . . For your kingdom is an everlasting kingdom. You rule generation after generation" (Ps 145:11, 13, NLT).

Further, if a king rules, there must be a realm or sphere over which he reigns. This is also called *malkut*. "So the realm of Jehoshaphat was quiet, for his God gave him rest round about" (2 Chr 20:30, RSV; see Est 3:6; Jer 10:7; Dn 9:1; 11:9).

This same twofold use of *basileia* is found in the NT. In fact, *basileia* could be translated by the expression "kingly power" in Luke 23:42 (NIV mg) and by "kingship" in John 18:36. When a nobleman went into a far country to get a "kingdom" (Luke 19:12, NASB) he went to the governing authority to get an appointment as king. When Jesus said, "My kingship is not of this world" (Jn 18:36, RSV), he did not mean to say that his rule has nothing to do with the world but rather that his kingship—his dominion—does not come from man but from God. Therefore, he rejects the use of worldly fighting to gain his ends.

This central meaning of *basileia* makes it easy to understand many sayings in the Gospels. In the Lord's Prayer the petition "Thy kingdom come" (Mt 6:10) is a prayer for God to manifest his reign so that his will may be done on earth as it is in heaven. When we read that we are to "receive the kingdom of God like a child" (Mk 10:15, RSV), we must open our hearts and lives to the rule of God.

Also in the NT are sayings about being *in* the kingdom or of *entering* the kingdom (Mt 8:11; Mk 9:47; 10:23-25; Lk 13:28). There is no philological or theological objection to understanding "the kingdom of God" first as the divine reign or rule and second as the sphere of blessing in which that reign is experienced.

Old Testament Background The expression "the kingdom of God" is not found in the OT, but the idea appears throughout the prophets. God is frequently spoken of as the King, both of Israel (Ex 15:18; Nm 23:21; Dt 33:5; Is 43:15) and of all the earth (2 Kgs 19:15; Pss 29:10; 47:2; 93:1-2; 96:10; 97:1-9; 99:1-4; 145:11-13; Is 6:5; Jer 46:18). Although God is not the earthly King of Israel, other references speak of a day when God shall become King and shall rule over his people (Is 24:23; 33:22; 52:7; Ob 1:21; Zep 3:15; Zec 14:9-11).

This brief summary of God's kingship provides the outline for the entire OT concept. While God is King over all the earth, he is in a special way King over his people, Israel. God's rule is therefore something realized in Israel's history. However, it is only partially and imperfectly realized. Israel again and again rebelled against the divine sovereignty. Furthermore, Israel was constantly plagued by wars with its pagan neighbors in which it was not always victorious. Again, there are evils in nature and the physical world that often bring suffering to God's people. Therefore, the prophets look forward to a day when God's rule will be fully experienced, not by Israel alone, but by all the world. The main emphasis of the prophets is on hope, the establishing of God's perfect rule in the world.

The prophets describe the final establishment of God's kingdom in terms of a theophany—a divine visitation (Mi 1:3-4). Zechariah foresees a "Day of the Lord" when all nations will be gathered in battle against Jerusalem, when the Lord will go forth and fight against those nations (Zec 14:3, 5). Israel will be visited by the Lord (Is 29:6) and delivered from its enemies (35:4; 59:20). God's coming will also mean judgment (2:21; 26:21). This final coming of God will mean the salvation of the Gentiles as well as of Israel (Zec 2:10-11; cf. Is 66:18-24).

Behind this language is a distinct theology of "the God who comes." It is a fact widely recognized in contemporary OT theology that the God of the OT is not a nature god, like the gods of other peoples, but a God of history—a God who visits his people in history to bless or to judge them. God visited Israel in Egypt to deliver them from bondage and to constitute them as his people. The rescue from Egypt was not merely an act of deliverance; it was an act through which God made himself known and through which Israel was to know and serve him.

Because God has visited his people again and again in their history, he must finally come to them in the future to judge wickedness and to establish his kingdom. Israel's hope is thus rooted in history, or rather in the God who works in history. God will finally break into history in a glorious theophany to establish his rule in all the earth. The source of the kingdom is not history itself but God.

While the prophets visualize the kingdom as coming from God, the kingdom is always on earth. The divine irruption into the natural order is not designed to accomplish its destruction but to make way for a new, perfect order arising out of the old, imperfect one. The prophets do not present a single consistent picture of the new order. Sometimes the new order is described very much in this-worldly terms. "The terraced vineyards on the hills of Israel will drip with sweet wine" (Am 9:13, NLT). On the other hand, God will create new heavens and a new earth (Is 65:17; 66:22), where there will be untroubled joy, prosperity, peace, and righteousness. The final visitation of God will mean the redemption of the world, for a redeemed earth is the scene of the kingdom of God. The prophets look forward again and again to the deliverance of creation "from the bondage to decay." The description is often couched in simple physical terms. The wilderness will become fruitful (32:15); the desert will blossom (35:2); sorrow and sighing will flee away (v 10). The burning sands will be cooled and the dry places become springs of water (v 7); peace will return to the animal world so that all injury and destruction are done away with (11:6). All this results because the earth becomes full of the knowledge of God (v 9).

Such language is not mere poetry but reflects a profound theology of creation. Humans as creatures were made to dwell on the earth, and the earth shares in human destiny. The main point is that creation as such is good and not a hindrance to true spirituality, as was often true in Greek thought. Redemption always includes redemption of the earth, which then becomes the blessed environment God intended it to be. Salvation does not mean deliverance from creaturehood, for this is not an evil thing but an essential and permanent element of true, human existence. Salvation does not mean escape from bodily creaturely existence, as in some Greek thought. On the contrary, ultimate redemption will mean the redemption of the whole person. The emergence of the doctrine of bodily resurrection is a reflection of this theology of creaturehood. The corollary of this is that creation in its entirety must share in the blessing of redemption.

A distinctive element in prophetic eschatology is the tension between history and eschatology. That is, as the prophets looked into the future, they saw an immediate historical judgment as well as a more remote eschatological visitation. For Amos, the Day of the Lord is both the immediate judgment of Israel by the Assyrians and a final eschatological salvation. Joel sees an imminent historical visitation of drought and locusts, but beyond this he sees the eschatological Day of the Lord. Zephaniah sees an imminent Day of the Lord in some undesignated historical visitation (Zep 1:2-18), but beyond it he sees the salvation of the Gentiles (3:9). The same God who acts in history to bless and judge his people will act at the end of history in an eschatological act of judgment and salvation. The prophets do not sharply distinguish between these two days, for it is one and the same God who is concerned to judge and save his people.

The eschatological hope of the prophets is always an ethical hope. That is to say, the prophets are not interested in the future for its own sake but for the impact of the future on the present. The prophetic predictions were given that, in light of future judgment and salvation, Israel might be confronted in the present by the will of God. "Prepare to meet your God as he comes in judgment, you people of Israel" (Am 4:12, NLT) might well be taken as the keynote of all the prophets.

In the New Testament

The Synoptic Gospels Jesus' teachings about the kingdom of God embodied the same contrast between the present order and the future age as that of the prophets, and he expressed it in the idiom "this age and the age to come." This fact is obscured in the KJV, which translates the word for "age" by "world." These are, however, two different concepts. A rich man asked Jesus what he must do to inherit eternal life (Mk 10:17). The context makes it clear that he was asking about eschatological life—the life of the resurrection (Dn 12:2). Jesus speaks of the difficulty of entering the kingdom of God. (The parallel passage in Matthew 19:23-24 has both "kingdom of God" and "kingdom of heaven," proving that they are interchangeable terms.) In their reaction the disciples ask, "Then who can be saved?" Jesus' answer contrasts the lot of his disciples "in this time" with the "age to come" (Mk 10:29-30) when they would inherit eternal life. It is clear from this passage that in some sense the kingdom of God, the kingdom of heaven, salvation, and eternal life all belong to the age to come. So far as this saying is concerned, God's people will not experience eternal life until they do so in the new age.

Matthew alone records the expression "the close of the age." This age will be terminated by the coming of the Son of Man (Mt 24:3) and by the judgment of humanity (13:39-42). Then the righteous will be separated from the wicked (v 49). The same expression occurs in the promise of the risen Jesus assuring his disciples of his presence until the consummation of the age (28:20). It follows that if this age is to come to its consummation, it must be followed by another age—the age to come.

The eschatological kingdom will be inaugurated by an apocalyptic event—the glorious coming of the Son of Man. This is made clear by two of the parables about the kingdom of God. In the parable of the tares, "the Son of man will send his angels, and they will gather out of his kingdom all causes of sin and all evildoers, and throw them into the furnace of fire" (Mt 13:41-42, RSV). The parable of the sheep and goats reflects the same eschatology. When the Son of Man comes in his glory, he will sit on his glorious throne to judge the nations, separating the sheep from the goats. The righteous—the sheep—are to "inherit the kingdom prepared for you from the foundation of the world"; and entrance into the kingdom is synonymous with entrance into life (25:31-46, RSV).

The eschatological character of the kingdom of God is seen also in the other two parables of Matthew 25. "The kingdom of heaven shall be compared to ten maidens who took their lamps and went to meet the bridegroom" (v 1, RSV). However, five of them were foolish and did not provide an adequate supply of oil for their lamps. Thus they were late for the wedding and were excluded from the wedding feast—a symbol of the eschatological kingdom—while those properly prepared entered the kingdom. In the same way the two faithful servants who had been "faithful over a little" were granted to "enter into the joy of your master" (vv 21, 23), while the unfaithful servant was excluded from the kingdom and cast into outer darkness.

Jesus almost never showed any interest in descriptions of the eschatological kingdom, but it is clear that its coming was constantly in his thoughts. The pure in heart will see God (Mt 5:8). The harvest will take place and the grain will be gathered into the barn (13:30, 39; Mk 4:29). Jesus frequently used the metaphor of a feast or table fellowship to describe life in the eschatological kingdom. He will drink wine again with his disciples in the kingdom of God. They will eat and drink at Jesus' table in the kingdom (Lk 22:30). People will be gathered from all corners of the earth to sit at a table with the OT saints (Mt 8:11-12; Lk 13:29). The consummation is likened to a wedding feast (Mt 22:1-14) and a banquet (Lk 14:16-24). All of these metaphors picture the restoration of communion between God and people, a union that had been broken by sin.

In most of the sayings cited to illustrate the future character of the kingdom, "kingdom" refers to the eschatological order—the eschaton, the age to come. However, when Jesus taught his disciples to pray "Thy kingdom come" (Mt 6:10), he was not referring to the new eschatological order; he was referring to the kingdom as God's kingly rule, his reign. It is a prayer that God will effectively establish his sovereign rule in the world.

In his teaching about the kingdom of God as the apocalyptic consummation, Jesus does not differ essentially from the OT prophets. The most distinctive element in Jesus' teaching—indeed, the fact that characterizes his entire mission and message—is the fact that in some real sense of the word, the kingdom of God has come in history in an utterly unexpected way. This sets Jesus' teaching apart from all contemporary Jewish thought.

This is seen first of all in his repeated teaching that his mission is a fulfillment of the OT messianic prophets. Mark summarizes Jesus' message with the words "The Kingdom of God is near! Turn from your sins and believe this Good News!" (Mk 1:15, NLT). This saying can have one of two meanings. It may refer to the imminent coming of the apocalyptic kingdom. Matthew summarizes the message of John the Baptist with nearly the same words: "Turn from your sins and turn to God, because the Kingdom of Heaven is near" (Mt 3:2, NLT). The Baptist expounds what he means by the approach of the kingdom of God: "He is ready to separate the chaff from the grain with his winnowing fork. Then he will clean up the threshing area, storing the grain in his barn but burning the chaff with never-ending fire" (v 12, NLT). John proclaimed an apocalyptic act; "unquenchable fire" can mean no strictly historical event but only an apocalyptic judgment. John expected Jesus to be the one in whom the cosmic event expected by the prophets would be carried out.

It is possible that this was also Jesus' meaning. However, another interpretation is possible that is better supported by the actual course of his mission: "The time is fulfilled." The messianic promises of the prophets were not only about to be fulfilled; they were actually in process of fulfillment in his mission. In Jesus, God was visiting his people. The hope of the prophets in some real sense was being realized.

The meaning of this can be seen in Luke's introduction of Jesus' ministry. Luke selects an event that occurred in Nazareth later in Jesus' ministry (Lk 4:16-21) and places it at the beginning of his Gospel in order to sound this note of fulfillment. Jesus read from Isaiah a promise that looked forward to the messianic salvation: "The Spirit of the Lord is upon me, for he has appointed me to preach Good News to the poor. He has sent me to proclaim that captives will be released, that the blind will see, that the downtrodden will be freed from their oppressors, and that the time of the Lord's favor has come" (vv 18-19, NLT). Then Jesus astonished his audience by the assertion "This Scripture has come true today before your very eyes!" (v 21, NLT).

Here was an amazing claim. John the Baptist had announced an apocalyptic visitation of God that would mean the fulfillment of the eschatological hope and the consummation of the messianic age. Jesus proclaimed that the messianic promise was actually being fulfilled in his person. This is no apocalyptic kingdom but a present salvation. In these words Jesus did not proclaim the imminence of the apocalyptic kingdom. Rather, he boldly announced that the kingdom of God had come. The presence of the kingdom was a happening, an event, the gracious action of God. This was no new theology or new idea or new promise; it was a new event in history.

The note of fulfillment is again sounded in Jesus' answer to the question about fasting. "Do wedding guests fast while celebrating with the groom? Of course not. They can't fast while they are with the groom" (Mk 2:19, NLT). The marriage feast had become a metaphor in Judaism for the messianic consummation. In these words Jesus announced the presence of the messianic time of salvation. It would be a contradiction in terms for the disciples to fast when they were enjoying the blessings of the messianic age. The time of fulfillment had come.

A saying found in different contexts in Matthew and Luke touches this central note of the fulfillment in history of the OT hope: "Blessed are the eyes which see what you see! For I tell you that many prophets and kings desired to see what you see, and did not see it, and to hear what you hear, and did not hear it" (Lk 10:23-24, RSV; cf. Mt 13:16-17). Both Matthew and Luke associate this saying with the kingdom of God, and both agree that the hope of former generations has become an object of experience. Many prophets and kings looked forward to something, but they looked in vain, for it did not come to them. What they longed for has now come, and this can be nothing less than the promised messianic salvation.

Fulfillment in history is again asserted in Jesus' answer to John's question about the one who is to come (Mt 11:2-3). "The deeds of the Christ" (Messiah) were not the deeds John had announced. Wicked rulers like Herod were not being judged in fire. Instead, Jesus was helping people, not bringing an apocalyptic kingdom. Jesus replied in words that echo the promise of the messianic salvation in Isaiah 35:5-6: "Go and tell John what you hear and see: the blind receive their sight and the lame walk, lepers are cleansed and the deaf hear, and the dead are raised up, and the poor have the gospel preached to them" (Mt 11:4-5, RSV). In these words Jesus claimed that the blessings of the messianic salvation are present. There was indeed reason for John's perplexity, for the fulfillment was not taking place along expected lines. The apocalyptic consummation did not appear to be on the horizon. The point of Jesus' answer was that fulfillment was taking place without the eschatological consummation. Therefore, Jesus pronounced a special blessing upon those who were not offended by the character of the messianic fulfillment (v 6). The fulfillment was indeed taking place, but not the apocalyptic consummation.

The most unambiguous statement of the presence of the kingdom is found in the words about the binding of Satan. One of Jesus' most characteristic acts was the exorcism of demons—deliverance from satanic power. The Pharisees admitted his power but attributed it to Satan. Jesus replied, "If Satan casts out Satan, he is divided against himself; how then will his kingdom stand? . . . But if it is by the Spirit of God that I cast out demons, then the kingdom of God is come upon you" (Mt 12:26, 28, RSV). Here the verb has the clear meaning "to come, to arrive" (cf. Rom 9:30; 2 Cor 10:14; Phil 3:16). Here is a clear affirmation that the kingdom of God has come among men.

In explanation Jesus said, "Or how can one enter a strong man's house and plunder his goods, unless he first binds the strong man? Then indeed he may plunder his house" (Mt 12:29, RSV). The strong man is Satan; this "present evil age" (Gal 1:4) is his "house"; his "goods" are demon-possessed men and women. Jesus has invaded the strong man's house to snatch away from him men and women whom he has in his power, and this is the work of the kingdom of God. The kingly reign of God has come into history in the person of Jesus before the apocalyptic consummation when Satan will be destroyed, to render Satan a preliminary defeat. Jesus has already "bound" Satan (i.e., curbed his power). This has been accomplished by the presence of the kingdom of God in the mission of Jesus.

A similar saying is found in Luke 10:18. Jesus had sent a band of his disciples on a preaching mission. Like Jesus, they were to proclaim the nearness of the kingdom of God (Lk 10:9). They, too, were to exorcize demons. When they returned to Jesus to report their success, Jesus said, "I saw Satan fall like lightning from heaven" (v 18, RSV). This again is metaphorical language that asserts that in the mission of Jesus' disciples, as well as in Jesus himself, Satan has fallen from his place of power. Both "binding" and "falling" are metaphors that describe the same truth: the victory of the kingdom of God over Satan.

Here is the element that sets Jesus apart from the OT and from all of contemporary Judaism. The prophets conceived of the kingdom being established by a heavenly supernatural being (Dn 7) or ruled by a powerful Davidic messianic king (Is 9, 11). The fulfillment of the messianic hope is everywhere in the prophets an eschatological hope. The same is true of the Jewish writers who despaired of history and cast all hope into the future.

In contrast to all that had gone before him, Jesus proclaimed the kingdom of God as an event taking place in his own person and mission. God had again assumed the initiative; God was acting. No first-century Jew had any idea of the kingdom of God coming into history in the person of an ordinary man—a teacher who was meek and lowly.

The presence of the kingdom is further seen in the fact that the rule of God, present in Jesus, is a gift to be received. This is also true of the kingdom in its eschatological consummation, where the kingdom is freely inherited by the righteous (Mt 25:34). In answer to the young man's question about inheriting eternal life (Mk 10:17), Jesus spoke of entering the kingdom (vv 23-24) and receiving the gift of eternal life (v 30) as though they were synonymous. The kingdom is a gift that the Father is pleased to bestow upon the little flock of Jesus' disciples (Lk 12:32).

If God's eschatological rule brings to his people the blessings of that kingdom, and if God's kingdom is his rule invading history before the eschatological consummation, then we may expect God's rule in the present to bring a preliminary blessing to his people. This fact is reflected in numerous sayings. The kingdom is something to be sought here and now (Mt 6:33) and to be received as children receive a gift (Mk 10:15; Lk 18:16-17). Although it is present in an unexpected form, the kingdom of God in Jesus' person is like a hidden treasure or a pearl of great price whose possession outranks all other goods (Mt 13:44-46). The gift of the kingdom is also seen in that the deaf hear, the blind see, lepers are cleansed, and the poor have good news preached to them (11:5).

John's Gospel In the Gospel of John the concept of eternal life takes the place of the kingdom of God in Jesus' teaching. The kingdom of God is mentioned twice (Jn 3:3, 5), and it is placed in connection with eternal life. The kingdom of God is here the eschatological kingdom, and eternal life is the life of the kingdom. Thus, as the kingdom of God in the synoptic Gospels is both future and present, so eternal life is both the life of the age to come (12:25) and also a present blessing (3:16, etc.).

Acts In Acts it seems the earliest disciples generally failed to understand Jesus' message about the kingdom of God as a present spiritual blessing. They gathered together to await the coming of the eschatological kingdom to Israel (Acts 1:6). Acts relates that the disciples continued to preach the kingdom of God, but usually it is an eschatological blessing (8:12; 14:22; 19:8; 20:25; 28:23, 31). However, the last two references make the kingdom of God synonymous with the gospel about Jesus Christ.

One important theme in Acts is linked to that of the kingdom of God. On the Day of Pentecost, Peter announces that God has seated Jesus at his right hand in fulfillment of Psalm 110:1 (Acts 2:33-35). In the Psalms this is a prophecy of the enthronement of the Davidic king in Jerusalem. Peter asserts that this prophecy is now fulfilled in the heavenly reign of Jesus. Therefore, he has been made both Lord and Christ (Messiah). These are interchangeable terms, "Lord" meaning absolute sovereign, "Christ" meaning the messianic king.

Paul's Writings Paul carried further this theme of the heavenly rule of Christ, the anointed King. The kingdom is both an eschatological inheritance (1 Cor 6:9; 15:50; Gal 5:21; Eph 5:5; 1 Thes 2:12; 2 Thes 1:5; 2 Tm 4:1, 18) and a present blessing into which believers now enter (Rom 14:17; Col 1:13). The key to this is the interchangeable character of lordship and messianic kingship. Jesus is now exalted as Lord over all (Phil 2:11), and even as his lordship is invisible, it will become manifest to all at his second coming. In the same way, he has been enthroned as messianic King by virtue of his resurrection and heavenly session, and he must reign as King until he has put all his enemies under his feet (1 Cor 15:25; Eph 1:22). The last enemy to be destroyed is death.

Revelation The central message of the Revelation to John is the consummation of God's redemptive purpose, when the kingdom of this world becomes the kingdom of our Lord and of his Christ (Rv 11:15). Revelation pictures the plight of a persecuted church in a hostile world, but it assures the church that Christ has already won a victory over the powers of evil (5:5), by virtue of which he can finally destroy them (19:11–20:14). Again, the last enemy to be destroyed is death (20:13-14). Revelation closes with a highly symbolic picture of the kingdom of God (chs 21–22) when God comes to dwell among his people, and "they shall see his face" (22:4). Thus the NT ends: divine order is restored to a disordered world. This is the kingdom of God.

See also Jesus Christ, Teachings of; King; Parable.

THE MYSTERY OF THE KINGDOM

A "mystery" is a divine truth hidden in the heart of God but in due time revealed to people (see Rom 16:25-26). The mystery of the kingdom (Mt 13:11; Mk 4:11) is precisely this: that prior to its eschatological consummation, the kingdom has come in an unexpected form in the historical mission of Jesus. This mystery is illustrated in Jesus' parables (Mt 13; Mk 4). Modern scholarship recognizes two critical norms in interpreting the parables. First, a parable is not an allegory but a story taken from daily life, teaching essentially a single truth. Second, the parables must be interpreted in the life setting of Jesus' mission.

The parable in Mark 4:26-29 is not a parable of stages of growth but an illustration that "the earth produces of itself" (v 28, RSV). The kingdom is God's reign—a supernatural thing, not a human work.

The parable of the four soils (Mt 13:3-9, 18-23) does not intend to teach that there are precisely four kinds of hearers of the word of the kingdom. The central truth is that the word of the kingdom must be *received;* otherwise it does not bear fruit. In other words, the kingdom as Jesus proclaimed and embodied it requires a human response to be effective.

The parable of the wheat and weeds (Mt 13:24-30) teaches that the kingdom of God has actually come into history without effecting the eschatological judgment that will separate the good from the bad. Both are to grow together in the world (v 38) until the Day of Judgment, when the eschatological separation will take place.

The parables of the mustard seed and leaven (Mt 13:31-33) are parables of contrast between present insignificance and future magnificence. The emphasis is not upon how the kingdom progresses from small beginnings. Jesus never spoke of the growth of the reign of God. What is now like a tiny seed—a Galilean prophet and a handful of followers—will one day be like a great tree.

The parables of the treasure and pearl (Mt 13:44-46) teach that this apparently insignificant appearance of the kingdom in Jesus nevertheless merits every effort to attain it.

The parable of the net (Mt 13:47-50) teaches that the movement set up by the presence of the kingdom in Jesus brings together a mixed people. (Jesus' disciples even harbored a traitor.) There will nevertheless be an eschatological separation.

KINGS, Books of First and Second Books continuing the history of the covenant people as recorded in Joshua, Judges, and the books of Samuel. The record in Kings begins with the events at the end of David's reign (1 Kgs 1–2). It continues through the reign of Solomon (chs 3–11); the histories of the divided kingdoms (1 Kgs 12—2 Kgs 17); and the history of the surviving kingdom in the south, through its fall in 586 BC and the subsequent kindness shown Jehoiachin by Evil-merodach, king of Babylon, around 561 BC (2 Kgs 18–25).

PREVIEW
• Authorship and Date
• Sources
• Theology and Purpose
• Content

Authorship and Date Kings was originally regarded as one book in the Hebrew canon; the division into two books of approximately equal length appeared first in the Septuagint and finally entered the Hebrew Bible in the 15th century AD.

The book itself is anonymous, and information about its author can only be deduced by examining the concerns and perspectives of the work. The Babylonian Talmud (*Baba Bathra* 15a) attributes Kings to Jeremiah. Although this identification could have arisen from the tendency of later Jewish tradition to assign biblical books to prophetic authors, the theory of origin in prophetic circles fits the evidence quite well. Substantial portions are given to the lives of the prophets; 16 of 47 chapters are devoted to the lives of Elijah and Elisha (1 Kgs 17—2 Kgs 10), and there is considerable interest in other prophetic figures such as Ahijah (1 Kgs 11:29-39; 14:1-16), an unnamed man of God (13:1-10), and Micaiah (22:13-28). Possible dependence on Isaiah (2 Kgs 18–20; cf. Is 36–39) and Jeremiah (2 Kgs 24–25; cf. Jer 52) also suggest prophetic origin. The author-compiler also shows intense concern with the efficacy of the prophetic word, frequently calling attention to the fulfillment of words spoken earlier by the prophets.

One might initially think that such a history would be unlikely for a prophet, but the evidence is to the contrary. The prophets were the guardians of the covenant relationship and are known to have produced accounts used as sources by other biblical historians. The following are among such sources: the acts of Samuel the seer, the acts of Nathan the prophet, the acts of Gad the seer (1 Chr 29:29); the acts of Nathan the prophet, the prophecy of Ahijah the Shilonite, the visions of Iddo the seer (2 Chr 9:29); the chronicles of Shemaiah the prophet and of Iddo the seer (12:15); the annotations of the prophet Iddo (13:22); and the acts of Uzziah by Isaiah the prophet (26:22). Add to this the fact that Kings is positioned in the Hebrew canon in the Former Prophets (Joshua to 2 Kings), and a consistent picture of prophetic origin emerges.

The date of the final part of the book must be after the last events recorded. Evil-merodach's kindness toward Jehoiachin (c. 561 BC) is the terminus of the book and therefore fixes the earliest date. Since the work shows no knowledge of the restoration period, a date before 539 BC is probable. The author's selection of his data to answer the burning theological questions of the exilic community also suggests a date between 561 and 539 BC.

Sources The compiler of Kings specifically names three of the sources that he used in his work, and biblical scholars have suggested the presence of a number of other sources that may have been cited. Of course, the sources not mentioned specifically by the compiler are only the speculations of those who have studied his work and can have only varying degrees of probability. The sources both specified and alleged are as follows.

The Book of the Acts of Solomon As 1 Kings 11:41 says, "The rest of the events in Solomon's reign, including his wisdom, are recorded in *The Book of the Acts of Solomon*" (NLT). Presumably additional materials of a biographical nature were included, specifically accounts similar to the

judgment between the two mothers (3:16-28) or the visit of the queen of Sheba (10:1-10). There has been debate as to whether these materials were official court records or nonofficial documents. Some scholars have attempted to isolate further materials within this section by identifying descriptions of the buildings as from temple archives (chs 6–7) and lists of administrators as from administrative documents (chs 4–5), but this must remain speculative.

The Book of the History of the Kings of Israel This source is mentioned 17 times in Kings, usually in the closing formulas at the end of the account of the reign of a northern king. Some idea of the nature of these chronicles can be derived from looking at the type of information to which the compiler refers his readers (see 1 Kgs 14:19; 16:27; 22:39; 2 Kgs 13:12; 14:28). These passages suggest that this source was the official annals covering the reigns of the kings.

The Book of the History of the Kings of Judah This source is mentioned in 15 passages, and as with the kings of Israel, is found in the concluding formulas to the accounts of the reigns. This source was to be consulted for additional details on individuals' reigns (for example, see 1 Kgs 15:23; 22:45; 2 Kgs 20:20; 21:17). These sources for the histories of the two kingdoms were probably similar to the annals known from the surrounding cultures, particularly from the reigns of Assyrian kings. They were likely official court histories kept in Samaria and Jerusalem.

In addition to these explicitly mentioned sources, scholars have suggested the compiler drew on other sources that he does not name.

Davidic Court History Second Samuel 9–20 is often identified as a unit of material in the composition of the books of Samuel; it is variously called "the court history" or "the succession narrative." Because of similar vocabulary and outlook, 1 Kings 1–2 are often associated with this material from Samuel. The statement of 1 Kings 2:46, "so the kingdom was now firmly in Solomon's grip," is taken to be the end of this record.

Sources for the House of Ahab The reigns of individual kings are ordinarily given only brief notices; for example, the father of Ahab, Omri, is given eight verses, even though when judged by political and economic significance, he was among the greatest of the northern kings (1 Kgs 16:21-28). However, beginning with the reign of Ahab, the record becomes quite expansive, and extensive coverage is given the dynasty of Ahab through the coup by Jehu (1 Kgs 16—2 Kgs 12). The use of the stereotyped formulas for the reigns is suspended in this material, and the existence of other literature used by the compiler is probable. This material is commonly subdivided into further sources for the lives of Elijah and Elisha and the reign of Ahab.

The Elijah section covers material in the following chapters: 1 Kings 17–19, including the feeding by the ravens, the incidents with the widow of Zarephath, the drought, the fire on Carmel, and the revelation of God at Sinai; 1 Kings 21, the affair of Naboth's vineyard; and 2 Kings 1, the death of Ahaziah's messengers. The reign of Ahab, which gets so much attention in Kings, is primarily a backdrop for the accounts concerning Elijah.

The Elisha material found in 2 Kings 2–13 may have had an independent literary development from that of the Elijah accounts. It includes the following: chapter 2 (Elisha's succession to the prophetic office, the purification of a spring, the death of mocking children); chapter 3 (on the campaign against Moab); chapter 4 (the widow's oil, the Shunammite woman); chapter 5 (Naaman's leprosy); chapter 6 (the Aramean attempt to capture Elisha); chapter 7 (the famine in Samaria); chapter 8 (the Shunammite's property, the coup of Hazael); chapter 9 (the anointing of Jehu); and chapter 13 (the death of Elisha). No other portion of the OT takes the sheer delight in the miraculous that is seen in the Elisha narratives.

In 1 Kings 16 to 2 Kings 13 there are additional incidents not directly related to the biographies of Elijah and Elisha; accounts such as the military campaigns of 1 Kings 20:1-34 and further details of Jehu's coup (2 Kgs 9:11-10:36) are often attributed to a third source containing accounts of the dynasty of Ahab and his successors. In all three of these possible sources the orientation is toward affairs in the northern kingdom.

Isaiah Source The account of the reign of Hezekiah contains a section (2 Kgs 18:13-20:19) that is nearly a verbatim citation of material also found in Isaiah (Is 36:1-39:8). The section records the invasion of Sennacherib, the mission of the Rabshakeh, Hezekiah's prayer, Isaiah's prophecy, Hezekiah's illness, the regression of the sun, and the envoys from Merodach-baladan. The material must be regarded as based on the book of Isaiah or some other source used in both Isaiah and Kings.

A Prophetic Source Because Kings shows great interest in the prophets and their ministries, various scholars have suggested that yet another source was used by the compiler; this would be an independent literary unit containing accounts of the prophets. This source would have contained the records for the material on Ahijah (1 Kgs 11:29-39; 14:1-16), unnamed prophets (ch 12; 20:35-43), Micaiah (22:13-28), and other references.

Apart from the sources explicitly mentioned and inferences about their character, the remainder of the sources suggested have only varying degrees of probability. Considerable scholarly effort has gone into identifying and characterizing such sources, but it remains speculative. When considering the sources the compiler may have used, one important caution must be kept in mind. Even if such sources did exist, one cannot have confidence in a reconstruction of the compositional history. Which sources had already been integrated into a larger composition before they were used by the compiler of Kings? We cannot be certain that the life situation out of which these other sources grew has been correctly identified, nor can we know that even the compiler himself was aware of the past history of his sources. Biblical scholarship has expended considerable energy in trying to delineate the past history of the book of Kings, but it has often been at the neglect of the unity of perspective that is the product of the final compiler(s) in whose hands the book received its canonical form.

What is important to understanding the book is not the perspective of its various sources (of which the compiler himself may have been unaware), but the perspective of the book as a whole on the history of the kingdoms. It is the outline that the compiler has imposed on the sources that establishes the teaching of the book; his sources are used in accord with his own purposes, a fact that makes the purposes for which the sources had been prepared largely irrelevant to the teaching of the book in its present form. Exploring possible sources, worthwhile in itself, must not eclipse the message of the book as a whole. This is not to imply that the books of Kings are simply a compilation of unaltered sources. The writer(s) undoubtedly exercised a measure of selectivity and literary skill in composing the historical narrative.

One compositional technique of the compiler is quite prominent in the histories of the divided kingdoms: this is the use of formulaic introductions and conclusions to the various reigns. The formulas for both kingdoms are quite similar, differing only in minor details. For the kings of Judah, the full introductory formula is as follows: (1) year of accession synchronized with the regnal year of the northern king; (2) age of the king at his accession; (3) length of his reign; (4) name of his mother; (5) judgment on the character of the reign. The account of a Judean king's reign is concluded as follows: (1) a reference to the chronicles of the kings of Judah for further information; (2) a statement regarding the death of the king, including the place of burial; (3) successor: "And his son reigned in his stead" (RSV). The full formula for a Judean king can be seen, for example, in the reign of Rehoboam (1 Kgs 14:21-22, 29-31).

The formulas differ slightly for the kings of Israel; the introduction is as follows: (1) year of succession synchronized with the regnal year of the southern king; (2) length of his reign; (3) location of the royal residence; (4) condemnation for idolatry; (5) name of the king's father. The account of an Israelite king's reign ends as follows: (1) a reference to the chronicles of the kings of Israel for further information; (2) a statement regarding his death; (3) a statement of the succession of his son, unless a usurper follows. The full formula for an Israelite king can be seen, for example, in the reign of Baasha (1 Kgs 15:33-34; 16:5-6).

There is some variation in the use of these patterns, but on the whole, they are consistently followed and provide the basic framework for the history of the divided kingdom. The synchronisms of the reigns provide data for constructing the chronology of the period. The variations in the formulas may reflect the characteristics of the sources the compiler was using or may reflect his own interests. The name of the mother of a Judean king is recorded, but not of an Israelite king, perhaps reflecting concern with a more exact and fuller record of the Davidic succession. The royal residence is presumed to be Jerusalem for the southern kings (though it may be mentioned) but is recorded for the northern kings since it moved several times, from Shechem to Penuel to Tirzah to Samaria. The mention of the king's father for a northern ruler also reflects the frequent change in dynasties there, as opposed to the dynastic stability of Judah, which is reinforced by mentioning the burial of almost all its kings in the city of David.

Theology and Purpose The books of Kings record the history of the covenant people from the end of the reign of David (961 BC) through the fall of the southern kingdom (586 BC). Yet it is not history written in accord with modern expectations for history textbooks. Rather than concentrating on economic, political, and military themes as they shaped the history of the period, the compiler of Kings is motivated by theological concerns.

Evaluation of the theology and purpose of the books of Kings is made easier by the fact that there is a parallel history for much of Kings found in the books of Chronicles. By comparing the two accounts, especially where the later Chronicler adds or deletes material found in Kings, the interests of both histories are thrown into clearer relief.

The books of Kings were composed during the exile, likely between 560 and 539 BC. Jerusalem had been turned into rubble, and there was no longer a throne of David. Those two pillars of the popular theology—the inviolability of the temple and the throne of David (Jer 7:4; 13:13-14; 22:1-9; see 1 Kgs 8:16, 29)—had tumbled.

If Israel's faith was to survive, the burning questions that had to be answered were "How did it all happen? Can't God keep his promises to David and to Zion? Have the promises failed?" The writer of Kings aims to deal with the bewilderment of the chosen people in response to the disasters of 722 BC (fall of Samaria) and 586 BC (fall of Jerusalem). Kings, like the book of Job, is a theodicy, a justification of the ways of God to men.

In order to answer the question "How did it happen?" the compiler adopts the procedure of recounting the history of the covenant people in light of standards propounded in the Law. For this reason Kings could be called Pentateuchal history, or even more pointedly, Deuteronomic history, for standards propounded only in the book of Deuteronomy in the Pentateuch are used by the compiler to measure the kingdoms. Among the prominent themes selected from Deuteronomy and applied to the kingdoms are the centralization of worship, the institution of the monarchy, the efficacy of the prophetic word, and the outworking of the covenant curses on disobedience.

Centralization of Worship The primary concern of the writer is the purity of the worship of the Lord. His major criterion for measuring this purity is the attitude of the kings toward centralization of worship in the Jerusalem temple as opposed to the worship of the Lord elsewhere and the continuation of Canaanite cults mingled with Yahwism at the high places. Centralization of worship at the central shrine is called for in Deuteronomy 12. Perhaps "centralization of worship" is a misnomer, for worship was always centered around the tabernacle in the periods prior to the temple; the change that is envisaged in Deuteronomy is not the centralizing of worship but rather the fact that the shrine would no longer be mobile but stationary. For the kings of the northern kingdom, this criterion becomes virtually a stereotyped formula that "he did that which was evil in the sight of the Lord and walked in the way of Jeroboam son of Nebat, who sinned and made all Israel sin along with him" (see 1 Kgs 14:16; 15:30; 16:31; 2 Kgs 3:3; 10:31; 13:2, 11; 14:24; 15:9, 18, 24, 28; 17:22). The compiler of Kings sees the rival altars with the golden calves at Dan and Bethel as the great sin of which the northern kings never repented (1 Kgs 12:25–13:34). Rejecting the primacy of Jerusalem, these altars became the rod with which to measure the northern kings. All the kings of Israel are condemned by this standard (except for Shallum, who reigned but a month, and Hoshea, the last of the northern kings)—even Zimri, the murderer of Elah, who ruled only one week before committing suicide in the flames of his own palace (16:9-20). For the kings of Judah, a different standard is used: what their attitude was to the high places where heterodox worship was allowed to flourish in the environs of Jerusalem. Only Hezekiah and Josiah receive the compiler's unqualified endorsement for following the ways of David (2 Kgs 18:3; 22:2). Six others are commended for their zeal in suppressing idolatry, though they did not remove the high places (Asa, 1 Kgs 15:9-15; Jehoshaphat, 22:43; Jehoash, 2 Kgs 12:2-3; Amaziah, 14:3-4; Azariah, 15:3-4; Jotham, 15:34-35). The remainder of the Judean kings are condemned for their participation in the high places and their desecration of the temple itself. This one theme is the preeminent motif in the book.

History of the Monarchy A second prominent interest for the compiler was to trace the history of the monarchy. Deuteronomy 17:14-20 provides for the day when Israel would ask for a king and charges that king with the

basic religious responsibility for the people. This provision for a king, again a feature found only in Deuteronomy, becomes the basis for the compiler's intense interest in the history of the monarchy, and particularly the religious fidelity of the kings. David becomes the model of the ideal king, the one by whom the others are measured, the one whose sons "continue long in his kingdom in the midst of Israel" (17:20; see also 1 Kgs 15:11; 2 Kgs 18:3; 22:2 for following in the ways of David, and 1 Kgs 14:8; 15:3-5; 2 Kgs 14:3; 16:2 for the reverse). The compiler wanted to show that God had been faithful to David even though David's sons were not faithful. While both kingdoms had about the same number of kings, the northern kingdom is marked by repeated dynastic changes and regicide through its 200 years, while the dynasty of David is maintained as a lamp in the south through 350 years (1 Kgs 11:13, 32, 36; 15:4-5; 2 Kgs 8:19; 19:34; 20:6). It is the disaster that had befallen the house of David, and the consequent doubts about the promises of God, that prompted the compiler to write.

Efficacy of the Prophetic Word Another reason why Kings can be called Deuteronomic history is its concern with the efficacy of the prophetic word. There are three passages in the Pentateuch that deal with the institution of the prophetic order: Numbers 12:1-8; Deuteronomy 13:1-5; and Deuteronomy 18:14-22. It is only in Deuteronomy 18 that the test of a true prophet is given: that what he has spoken comes about, that his words are fulfilled. Notice the number of instances where the writer calls attention to the fulfillment of the words of the prophets: 2 Samuel 7:13 in 1 Kings 8:20; 1 Kings 11:29-36 in 12:15; 1 Kings 13:1-3 in 2 Kings 23:16-18; 1 Kings 14:6-12 in 14:17-18 and 15:29; 1 Kings 16:1-4 in 16:7, 11-12; Joshua 6:26 in 1 Kings 16:34; 1 Kings 22:17 in 22:35-38; 1 Kings 21:21-29 in 2 Kings 9:7-10, 30-37 and 10:10-11, 30; 2 Kings 1:6 in 1:17; 2 Kings 21:10-15 in 24:2; 2 Kings 22:15-20 in 23:30. The writer is concerned to show that the words of the prophets were efficacious, powerful words. His concern with the prophetic order is also seen in the material devoted to Elijah and Elisha and to other prophetic figures.

Fulfillment of the Curses Another aspect of the compiler's interest in Deuteronomy is seen in his concern to trace the fulfillment of the covenant curses on disobedience. God's covenant with Israel would issue in curses or blessings depending on the obedience of the people; the compiler of Kings sees the curses inflicted on the two kingdoms because of their failure to meet the demands of the covenant. He takes care to show that most of the curses of Deuteronomy 28:15-68 had some historical realization in the life of the people. Moses had warned that disobedience would "bring a nation against you from afar, from the end of the earth, as the eagle swoops down" (Dt 28:49, NASB), and the Assyrians came to Samaria and the Babylonians to Jerusalem (28:52). The siege of Samaria lasted from 724 to 722 BC, and the siege of Jerusalem from 588 to 586 BC. The dire conditions of the siege would drive the people to devouring their own children; women would feed on their afterbirths. It happened to Israel in the siege of Ben-hadad (2 Kgs 6:24-30). Just as the Lord had delighted to prosper and multiply his people, so he would not refrain from destroying them and scattering them among the peoples of the earth (Dt 28:63-67).

In these and other ways the writer of Kings set out to write the history of Israel and Judah to solve a theological dilemma. How was one to reconcile the exile with

God's promises to the nation and David? His answer is twofold: (1) the problem was not with God but with the people's disobedience—God remains just; (2) the end of the state does not equal the end of the people or the house of David. Here the ending of the book is instructive: Evil-merodach releases Jehoiachin from prison, elevates him above the other kings, and provides his rations (2 Kgs 25:27-30). Even during the exile, though cut down to almost nothing, the house of David still enjoys the favor and blessing of God. God has not abandoned his promises; the people should keep hope.

Other themes in Kings also show the theological motivations underlying the compiler's selection and arrangement of the data, particularly his use of Deuteronomy as a framework for examining the history of the people. Compare the laws governing the observance of Passover in Exodus 12:1-20 and Deuteronomy 16:1-8: whereas the Passover is centered in the family in Exodus, it is celebrated at the sanctuary in Deuteronomy. The writer of Kings is careful to show that the Passover during the reign of Josiah was celebrated in accordance with the requirements of Deuteronomy (2 Kgs 23:21-23). A passage in Deuteronomy is explicitly cited with reference to Amaziah's keeping the law (Dt 24:16 in 2 Kgs 14:6).

Contrast with Chronicles The interests of Kings are further highlighted when compared with the parallel accounts in Chronicles. While the writer of Kings worked in the aftermath of the destruction of Jerusalem and had to answer the "how?" and "why?" questions, the Chronicler is part of the restoration community. Here the burning theological questions were not "how?" and "why?" but rather "What continuity do we have with David? Is God still interested in us?" The need is not to account for the exile but rather to relate the postexilic and the preexilic. The building of the second temple and the ordering of worship there show up in increased detail in Chronicles in any matter pertaining to the former temple. Chronicles is a history of Judah and of the Davidic line, reflecting the fact that it alone survives after the exile. Interesting, too, are the things omitted from the account by the Chronicler. Since he is not building a case for an indictment, as was done in Samuel and Kings, he is free to omit references to David's sin with Bathsheba (2 Sm 11) or to Solomon's difficulties in gaining the throne (1 Kgs 1-2). Since in his day the northern kingdom had not survived, the Chronicler did not go into detail about the sins of Jeroboam (chs 13-14). Chronicles is interested more in the affairs of the temple and does not show the marked interest in prophetic matters found in Kings, so that the lives of Elijah and Elisha are omitted (1 Kgs 16—2 Kgs 10). Nor does the Chronicler recite the sins that led to the demise of the northern kingdom (2 Kgs 17:1-18:12). In all these examples one can see the interplay of the historical moment and theological concerns of the people and the compilers. Each compiler has selected and arranged the data in accordance with the concerns and needs of the community in which he was a member; comparing the two accounts throws the interests of each into sharp relief.

Content The books of Kings fall into three parts: (1) the reign of Solomon (1 Kgs 1–11); (2) the history of the divided kingdom (1 Kgs 12–2 Kgs 17); (3) the history of the surviving kingdom in Judah (2 Kgs 18–25).

The Reign of Solomon (1 Kgs 1–11) The record begins with an account of the court intrigue surrounding Solomon's accession to the throne, set against the backdrop of the abortive coup by Adonijah (ch 1). The dying David charges Solomon to obey the commandments of God (2:1-4) and also to take vengeance on his enemies (vv 5-9). After David's death Solomon orders the deaths of Adonijah, Joab, and Shimei, and the banishment of Abiathar, the priest who had supported Adonijah in his bid for the throne (vv 13-46). Enemies eliminated, the kingdom was firmly established by Solomon (v 46).

The remainder of Solomon's reign is divided into two parts: Solomon the good, who follows in the ways of his father, David (chs 3–10); and Solomon the bad, whose heart is led astray (ch 11). While sacrificing at Gibeon, Solomon asks God to give him the gift of wisdom to rule—wisdom promptly demonstrated in the quarrel of two prostitutes about a child (ch 3). An account is given of the administrative organization of the kingdom and the incomparable wisdom of Solomon (ch 4). The

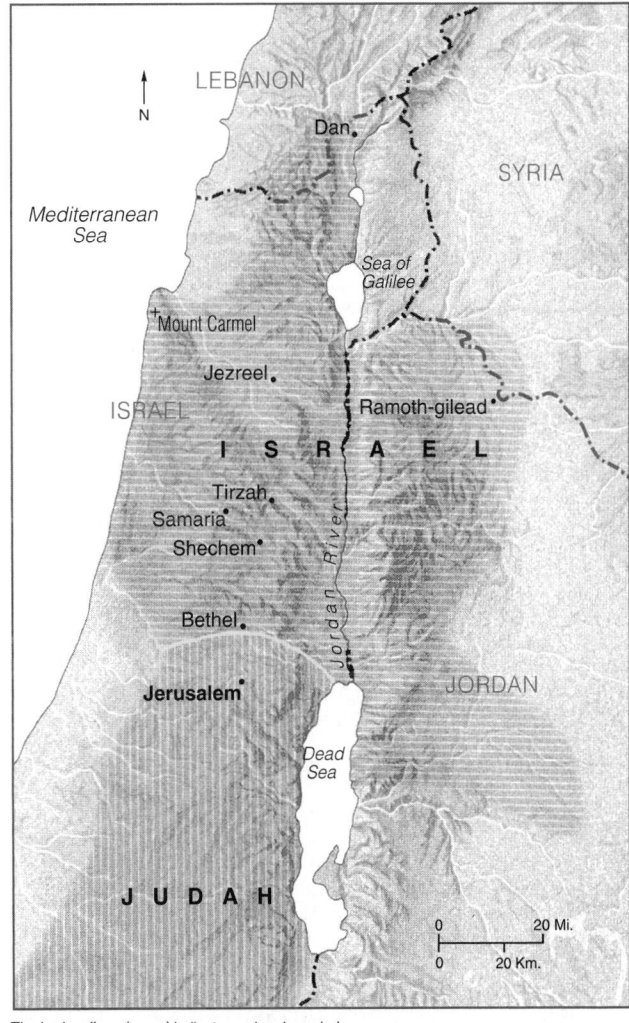

The broken lines (—·—·) indicate modern boundaries.

Key Places in 1 Kings

compiler of Kings gives extensive coverage to the preparations (ch 5), building (chs 6–7), and dedication (ch 8) of the temple. God appeared to Solomon a second time, reminding him to keep his commandments as David had done (9:1-9). Details are given of the king's building and commercial activities (vv 10-27). The account of the visit by the queen of Sheba is followed with elaboration of Solomon's splendor (ch 10). But Solomon did not keep God's commands; seduced to pagan worship by his foreign wives, he was not fully devoted to the Lord as David had been (11:4), and God determined to take away the northern tribes from the rule of his son (vv 11-13). As punishment from the hand of God, Solomon faced rebellion among conquered peoples (vv 14-25) and within Israel in the person of Jeroboam (vv 26-40).

History of the Divided Kingdom
(1 Kgs 12—2 Kgs 17) The united monarchy dissolved after the death of Solomon. The northern kingdom (Israel) would exist for about two centuries, would be ruled by 20 kings from nine different dynasties, and would show a history of internal weakness riddled with regicide and usurpation. In contrast, the southern kingdom would last for three and a half centuries and would be ruled by 19 kings of Davidic descent (apart from a short period under the dynastic interloper Athaliah).

There had been a long history of independent action and even warfare between the northern and southern tribes prior to David and Solomon, so it is no surprise that the division would take place along the lines that it did. The immediate cause, however, was the unwise severity with which Rehoboam replied to the representatives of the northern tribes while negotiating for the kingship. Jeroboam, the popular hero of the earlier insurrection against Solomon, became king in the north. He immediately erected the rival sanctuaries at Dan and Bethel (1 Kgs 12); these rival altars became the measure by which the kings of Israel were condemned for following in the sins of Jeroboam.

For two generations there would be warfare between Israel and Judah over the border areas in Benjamin claimed by both sides. Fifty years of sporadic fighting on their mutual frontier, interlaced with invasions from the Arameans in the north or the Egyptians in the south, would consume the reigns of Jeroboam, Nadab, Baasha, Elah, and Zimri in Israel and of Rehoboam, Abijam, and Asa in Judah (1 Kgs 13–16:20).

The accession of Omri in Israel introduced a ruling house that would last for a total of four generations and end the dynastic instability of the northern kingdom. Though Kings gives Omri a scant eight verses (1 Kgs 16:21-28), he was among the greatest of the northern kings, forging alliances with the Phoenicians and Judah; for over a century, the Assyrians would call Israel "the house of Omri."

The reigns of Omri's successors, Ahab, Ahaziah, and Jehoram, are treated at disproportionate length, taking almost a third of the total book, 16 of 47 chapters (1 Kgs 17—2 Kgs 10). This is due to the fact that the compiler of Kings incorporated extensive coverage of the lives of Elijah and Elisha, weaving a contrast between good and evil by paralleling the dynasty of Omri with these prophets. Ahab and Jezebel were used as foils for the account of Elijah, so that Ahab became a paradigm of the evil king (e.g., 2 Kgs 21:3).

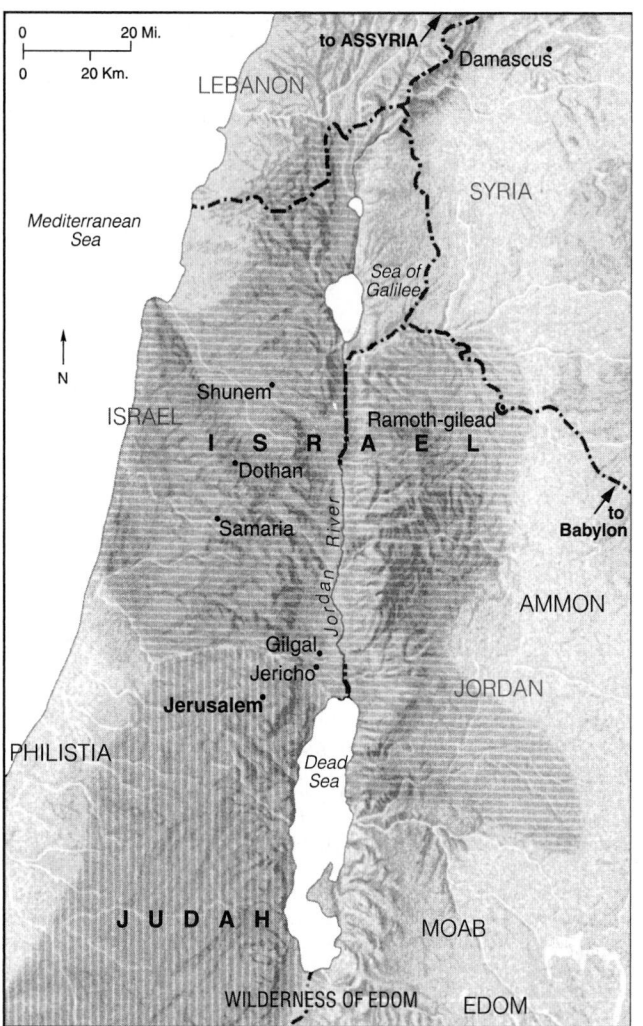

The broken lines (—·—·) indicate modern boundaries.

Key Places in 2 Kings

Because of this preoccupation with the dynasty of Omri and the lives of Elijah and Elisha, the equivalent period in Judah is not given as extensive coverage. During this period, the northern kingdom appears to have exercised some hegemony over Judah, as attested by the marriage of an Omride (Athaliah, 2 Kgs 8:18, 26) to Jehoram of Judah and the subservient role of Jehoshaphat to Ahab at the battle of Ramoth-gilead (1 Kgs 22). Judah's fortunes declined in this period when Edom revolted against Jehoram (2 Kgs 8:20-22), costing Judah control over the port at Ezion-geber and consequent economic losses.

In 842 BC Jehu, after being anointed king by a prophet (2 Kgs 9:1-13), led a coup ending the house of Omri and also killing Ahaziah of Judah (vv 14-29).

Jehu's purge also brought the death of Jezebel, Ahab's family, members of the family of Ahaziah, and the ministers of Baal (9:30–10:36). The consequences were severe politically: the murder of the Phoenician princess Jezebel and the king of Judah cost Israel its allies to the north and south.

Jehu's dynasty had the longest succession of any in Israel, including Jehoahaz, Jehoash, Jeroboam II, and Zechariah, a period spanning 90 years. Jehu's murder of Ahaziah of Judah set the stage for the one threat to the continuity of the Davidic dynasty. Queen Athaliah, herself an Omride, seized the throne and attempted a purge of Davidic pretenders. She ruled for six years, until the faithful priest Jehoiada staged a countercoup to place the child Joash on the throne of David (ch 11).

Israel endured a half century of weakness as a result of Jehu's coup, during which the Arameans had a free hand, reducing the forces of Jehu's son Jehoahaz to a small army and bodyguard (2 Kgs 13:1-7).

The reemergence of Assyria early in the ninth century BC gave relief to Israel and Judah. Assyrian armies conquered the Arameans; with that threat removed, Israel and Judah enjoyed a dramatic resurgence. Jehoash of Israel, grandson of Jehu, reconquered cities lost to the Arameans (2 Kgs 13:25); Elisha died during his reign (v 20). In the south Amaziah reconquered the Edomites (14:7). Amaziah and Jehoash renewed the warfare between the kingdoms, with the north again victorious (vv 8-14).

Under Jeroboam II, Israel enjoyed a period of prosperity when the borders of the kingdom reached the same extent as they had under Solomon (2 Kgs 14:23-28). Uzziah (Azariah), his contemporary in Judah, also fortified Jerusalem and undertook a program of offensive operations extending Judah's sway to the south (14:21-22; 15:1-7).

Yet this resurgence was but a brilliant sunset in the history of the two kingdoms. After the death of Jeroboam II, the history is one of successive disasters, culminating in the fall of Israel and the subjugation of Judah to the might of Assyria. The next 30 years in Israel would see four dynasties, three represented by only one king, and repeated regicides as the northern kingdom hastened to its demise. A period of civil war and anarchy would see five kings in just over ten years (2 Kgs 15). Heavy tribute was paid to Tiglath-pileser III in both the north and south (15:19-20; 16:7-10). Israel and the Arameans forged a coalition to throw back the Assyrians and sought to press Ahaz of Judah into the fight; Ahaz appealed to Tiglath-pileser III for help. The coalition was destroyed, and Israel and Judah became vassals. Hoshea defected as soon as he felt safe, looking to Egypt for help, but it was suicide for the northern kingdom. Shalmaneser V retaliated, and the political history of the state of Israel came to an end (17:1-23). The area was resettled with other displaced populations (vv 24-41).

Israel had faced the Arameans and survived, only to fall to Assyria. And now, similarly, Judah would outlast Assyria, only to fall to Babylon.

History of the Surviving Kingdom of Judah (2 Kgs 18–25)

Ahaz's appeal for Assyrian aid cost him his liberty, and Judah became a vassal of the Assyrian Empire. Illegitimate worship flourished under his rule (2 Kgs 16:1-19). Ahaz was succeeded by the first of the outstanding reform kings of Judah: Hezekiah. Much of the account of his reign is given to his rebellion against Sennacherib of Assyria: the rebellion, the Assyrian envoys and threats, Isaiah's assurances of deliverance, and the destruction of the Assyrian armies (18:9–19:37).

Hezekiah's illness was averted after a sign and oracle from Isaiah (20:1-11). As part of what appears to be negotiations toward an anti-Assyrian alliance, Hezekiah also entertained envoys from Babylon, a decision that the prophet announced would be costly (vv 12-21).

Hezekiah was followed by Manasseh, who ruled longer than any other king of Judah (a total of 55 years). His reign was marked by great apostasy—apostasy so severe that the compiler of Kings regarded his reign as sufficient reason for the exile that was unavoidable (2 Kgs 21:1-18; cf. 23:26; 24:3-4; Jer 15:1-4). Manasseh was followed by his son Amon, a carbon copy of his father, who ruled only two years before he was deposed by the people (2 Kings 21:19-26).

The second great reform king of Judah, Josiah, followed. In his reign the Book of the Law was found while the temple was being refurbished; he led the people in a renewal of the covenant and suppressed illegitimate worship (2 Kgs 22:1–23:14). The Assyrian Empire was in rapid decline, so Josiah extended his borders to the north, destroying the altar at Bethel and the high places throughout Samaria (23:15-20). A great Passover celebration was convened in Jerusalem, and further measures were taken to rectify worship (vv 21-25). Josiah tried to block Pharaoh Neco's foray to assist Assyria, and he lost his life at Megiddo (vv 26-30).

Josiah was the only king of Judah to have three of his sons succeed him. At his death the people put Jehoahaz on the throne, but Neco removed him three months later and took him to Egypt in chains (2 Kgs 23:31-33), replacing him with another son of Josiah, Eliakim, whose name was changed to Jehoiakim (vv 34-37). During his reign, Nebuchadnezzar conquered Judah, and Jehoiakim became his vassal. Late in his life Jehoiakim rebelled against Nebuchadnezzar. Jehoiakim died, leaving his son Jehoiachin to face retaliation from Babylon (24:1-10). Nebuchadnezzar besieged Jerusalem; when the city fell, Jehoiachin, the queen mother, the army, and the leaders of the land were carried away captive. Nebuchadnezzar put Mattaniah (uncle of Jehoiachin and third son of Josiah) on the throne, changing his name to Zedekiah (vv 11-17). Nine years later Zedekiah, too, would rebel against Babylon. Nebuchadnezzar besieged the city for two years and, when it fell, utterly destroyed it. Zedekiah's sons were killed before his eyes, and then his own eyes were put out, and he was taken to Babylon (24:18–25:21). Nebuchadnezzar appointed Gedaliah to rule as governor from nearby Mizpah; he was assassinated, and the conspirators fled to Egypt (25:22-26).

The book concludes by showing that God had not forgotten his promise to David, mentioning that in captivity Jehoiachin enjoyed favor from the hand of Evil-merodach, successor of Nebuchadnezzar (2 Kgs 25:27-30).

See also Chronicles, Books of First and Second.

KING'S DALE* KJV name for the King's Valley near Salem, the city of Melchizedek, in Genesis 14:17. *See* King's Valley.

KING'S GARDEN Probably an area of the royal estates, situated outside the walls of Jerusalem near the pool of Siloam (2 Kgs 25:4; Jer 39:4; 52:7) in the Kidron Valley, near where the Kidron meets the valley of Hinnom. Upon the return from the exile, Nehemiah set the families to work, each building a part of the wall. Fountain Gate is recorded as being near the pool of Siloam by the king's garden (Neh 3:15). It is not certain whether the site now called the king's garden outside the walls of modern Jerusalem is the original site.

KING'S HIGHWAY* The road running north-south across the Transjordanian plateau. It appears in the OT only twice in requests by the Israelites to use this road when passing through Edom (Nm 20:17) and the Amorite kingdom of Heshbon (21:22). The route may also be called simply "the highway" (20:19). The northern segment is called "the way of Bashan" (Nm 21:33; Dt 3:1).

This highway connected Damascus with the caravan route running through the Hijaz down to southern Arabia and the rich sources of spices, perfumes, and other exotic products (1 Kgs 10:2; Ez 27:22). Control over it was a key factor in the geopolitics of Israel and its rivals.

The local topography limits the possible lines of march to two parallel routes. A double watershed exists the full length of the Transjordanian plateau. One is created by the shorter streams that bisect the mountains from east to west; they leave a watershed about 13 to 16 miles (21 to 26 kilometers) east of the Jordan Valley. The larger streams, the Yarmuk, Jabbok, Arnon, and Zered, begin some 25 to 30 miles (40 to 48 kilometers) to the east, usually running north before curving westward. The route bypassing them on the east must follow the fringes of the north Arabian Desert. Though the latter has an easier course to follow, it passes fewer good water sources and settlements where supplies could be obtained. The former, on the western watershed, had ample water and was lined with major towns; however, the caravans had to negotiate the steep canyons of the four large wadis.

The earliest record of movement along this route is in Genesis 14. The four kings went from Ashtaroth, the capital of Bashan, to Ham in northern Gilead, then to Shaveh-kiriathaim on the Moabite plateau, and finally to Mt Seir as far as El-paran. The patriarchs probably always came this way when traveling to Canaan; Jacob came through Gilead (Gn 31:21) and established a base at Succoth before crossing the Jordan to Canaan (33:17).

KING'S POOL Reservoir in the king's garden in Jerusalem (Neh 2:14), also called the pool of Siloam (3:15).

KING'S VALLEY Valley near Salem, the city of Melchizedek, where Abraham encountered the king of Sodom and rejected his offer of a morally compromised truce (Gn 14:17); also called the valley of Shaveh. If Salem is the same site as Jerusalem, the "king's valley" is probably either the Kidron Valley or the valley of Hinnom. This would be the site where Absalom raised a pillar as a monument to himself (2 Sm 18:18).

KINNERETH

1. Fortified town in the territory allotted to Naphtali's tribe (Jos 19:35). It is also mentioned in an Egyptian list of towns conquered by Thutmose III in the 15th century BC. The site has been identified as Tell el-'Oreimeh on the northwest shore of the Sea of Galilee. Archaeological evidence suggests that the site was inhabited from about 2000 to about 900 BC.
2. A district in Naphtali's territory that included #1 above. It was conquered by Ben-hadad, king of Syria, in the reign of Baasha, king of the northern kingdom of Israel in the early ninth century BC (1 Kgs 15:20).
3. Early name for the Sea of Galilee (Nm 34:11; Dt 3:17; Jos 11:2; 12:3; 13:27). It is hard to say whether the city (see #1 above) was named after the sea or vice versa. The name, however, means "lyres," which could be an allusion to the Sea of Galilee's shape, which roughly resembles that of a lyre. In NT times the pro-

nunciation of the name was corrupted to Gennesaret (Lk 5:1). *See* Sea of Galilee.

KINSMAN A relative of the same family. In ancient Israel the tribe was the largest social and political unit. The smallest social unit within the tribe was the family. The relationship of one family to another was carefully regulated by the list of those to whom one should not be married (Lv 18). Those who were related, even though somewhat distantly, received by law privileges and obligations for all members of the family. It was the right of the "kinsman" to receive the inheritance of a family without heir (Nu 27:11). He was also obligated to reclaim property of a kinsman who had gone into debt (Lv 25:25-28), especially if it involved someone's enslavement to a non-Israelite (vv 47-49). In this function the kinsman *(karov)* becomes the kinsman-redeemer *(go'el)*. In the book of Ruth, Boaz is the kinsman-redeemer: "The man is our close relative; he is one of our kinsman-redeemers" (Ruth 2:20, NIV). On legal grounds Boaz had a right to reclaim the property of Naomi, but he was required by law to wait for his turn, as he was not the *nearest* relative (4:4). Only after this nearest relative refused (v 6) did Boaz proceed with his obligation as kinsman.

KIOS Rocky, mountainous island in the east-central area of the Aegean Sea. On his third missionary journey, Paul's ship anchored opposite Kios between stops at Mitylene and Samos en route to Jerusalem (Acts 20:15). Though not particularly fertile, Kios was nevertheless noted for its wine, figs, and gum mastic. It is separated from the mainland by a five-mile (8-kilometer) strait. In Paul's day its principal city, Kios (modern Scio), was a free city in the Roman province of Asia.

KIR

1. Mesopotamian city from which the Syrians migrated to Damascus and back to which they were later exiled by the Assyrians (Am 1:5; 9:7). Escape from Kir to Aram paralleled the exodus of the Israelites. It must have been a terribly bitter experience to have been deported (by Tiglath-pileser) back to Kir (2 Kgs 16:9). Whether the city actually existed or not is debatable. It could have become a metaphor for enslavement and exile.
2. Fortress usually identified with the ancient capital of Moab. Soldiers from Kir were associated with those from Elam (Is 22:6). Likewise, Kir was paralleled with Ar in Isaiah's lament over Moab (15:1). Kir of Moab, therefore, is probably the same as Kir-haraseth (2 Kgs 3:25; Is 16:7), located at Kerak, 11 miles (17.7 kilometers) east of the southern end of the Dead Sea.

KIR-HARESETH Fortified city often identified with the ancient capital of Moab. *See* Kir #2.

KIRIATHAIM

1. Town on the Moabite plateau, mentioned in the march of the four kings against the five (Gn 14:5) where the indigenous Emim were attacked. It was taken by the Israelites from Sihon (Nm 32:37) and included in Reuben's inheritance (Jos 13:19). The Moabite Stone records that Sihon fortified the place after gaining control of the plateau; in the seventh century BC it was still under Moabite control (Jer 48:1, 23; Ez 25:9). Eusebius placed it 10 Roman miles west of Medeba. Two identifications have been proposed—either Khirbet el-Qureiyeh or Qaryat el-Mukhaiyet, six miles (9.7 kilo-

meters) northwest and three miles (4.8 kilometers) northwest of Medeba respectively.

2. Levitical town in Naphtali's territory (1 Chr 6:76), called Kartan in Joshua 21:32; the latter is probably a dialectical variant. The suggested identification is with Khirbet el-Qurieyeh, northeast of 'Ain Ibl in southern Lebanon.

   See also Levitical Cities.

KIRIATH-ARBA Ancient name of Hebron, near which is the cave of Machpelah, the burial place of the patriarchs (Gn 23:2; Jos 14:15; Jgs 1:10). *See* Hebron (Place) #1.

KIRIATH-ARIM* Alternate name for Kiriath-jearim in Ezra 2:25 (NLT mg). *See* Kiriath-jearim.

KIRIATH-BAAL Alternate name for Kiriath-jearim in Joshua 15:60 and 18:14. *See* Kiriath-jearim.

KIRIATH-HUZOTH Town in Moab to which Balak and Balaam went before going to Bamoth-baal (Nm 22:39).

KIRIATH-JEARIM Village on the road from Jerusalem to Tel Aviv, about 10 miles (16 kilometers) northwest of Jerusalem. Excavations by the French revealed a settlement 7,000 years old in which the residents changed from grazing to farming. Its modern name is Abu Ghosh, so named after a family of Arab sheiks who robbed pilgrims en route to Jerusalem until Ibrahim Pasha of Egypt terminated the practice early in the 19th century. The Crusaders mistakenly identified this village as Emmaus, where Jesus revealed himself to two people after his resurrection (Lk 24:13). Because of this, they built a church there (in the 12th century). The massive walls of the church were built over the remains of a Roman fort where Titus had stationed his veterans of the Jewish Revolt. The large crypt under the church contains a spring, mentioned in memoirs of the First Crusade as the "Emmaus Spring."

In the time of the judges this village was one of the four cities of the Gibeonites who, under false pretenses, made a mutual defense pact with Joshua and the elders of Israel (Jos 9:3-27). Because it was on the border between Judah and Benjamin, it was integrated into the tribe of Judah (15:9; 18:14). During the time of Samuel, after the Philistines captured the ark (1 Sm 4:11) and found its possession to be dangerous, they were advised to return it to Israel. This they did; the ark arrived in Beth-shemesh, where 70 men who peered into it perished. Because of the danger its presence presented, it was sent on to Kiriath-jearim, where it remained in the house of Abinadab (1 Sm 7:1) for 20 years. One of King David's first official acts after arriving in Jerusalem was to bring the ark from Baalah (Kiriath-jearim) to Obed-edom's house, then on to Jerusalem (2 Sm 6).

Uriah the prophet, who condemned the reign of King Jehoiakim and was later executed (Jer 26:20-23), was a native of Kiriath-jearim. Among the returnees from the exile were citizens originally from Kiriath-jearim (Ezr 2:25; Neh 7:29).

KIRIATH-SANNAH Alternate name for Debir, a Judean city, in Joshua 15:49. *See* Debir (Place) #1.

KIRIATH-SEPHER Older name for the Judean city Debir in Joshua 15:15. *See* Debir (Place) #1.

KIRIOTH* KJV alternate spelling of Kerioth, the Moabite city, in Amos 2:2. *See* Kerioth #2.

KIRJATH* KJV spelling of Kiriath, an abbreviation of Kiriath-jearim, in Joshua 18:28. *See* Kiriath-jearim.

KIRJATHAIM* KJV spelling of Kiriathaim (Nm 32:37; Jos 13:19; 1 Chr 6:76). *See* Kiriathaim.

KIRJATH-ARBA* KJV form of Kiriath-arba, the ancient name of Hebron. *See* Hebron (Place) #1.

KIRJATH-ARIM* KJV form of Kiriatharim, an alternate name for Kiriath-jearim, in Ezra 2:25. *See* Kiriath-jearim.

KIRJATH-BAAL* KJV spelling of Kiriath-baal, an alternate name for Kiriath-jearim, in Joshua 15:60 and 18:14. *See* Kiriath-jearim.

KIRJATH-HUZOTH* KJV spelling of Kiriath-huzoth, a Moabite town, in Numbers 22:39. *See* Kiriath-huzoth.

KIRJATH-JEARIM* KJV spelling of Kiriath-jearim. *See* Kiriath-jearim.

KIRJATH-SANNAH* KJV spelling of Kiriath-sannah, in Joshua 15:49. *See* Debir (Place) #1.

KIRJATH-SEPHER* KJV spelling of Kiriath-sepher in Joshua 15:15-16 and Judges 1:11-12. *See* Debir (Place) #1.

KISH

1. Benjamite of Gibeah, father of King Saul and a man of some position in the community (1 Sm 9:1). His genealogy is traced for four generations, as is that of Elkanah, the father of Samuel, who would anoint Saul king (1:1).

   There is some obscurity in the genealogical information about Kish. His father's name is listed as Abiel in 1 Samuel 9:1. If the Kish mentioned in 1 Chronicles 8:30 is the same person, then we must conclude that Abiel was also known as Jeiel. But it may be that this second Kish was an uncle of Saul's father. A further obscurity results from 1 Chronicles 8:33 and 9:39, where Ner, not Abiel, is said to be the father of Kish. Yet in 1 Samuel 14:51 Abiel is said to be the father of two sons whose names were Ner and Kish. The solution probably lies in the assumption that Ner in the Chronicles references was an earlier ancestor, probably Abiel's father or grandfather. If that should be the case, then the father-son relationship between Ner and Kish should be taken in an extended sense, as elsewhere in the OT. No other details of Kish's life are available. His grave was in Zela of Benjamin (2 Sm 21:14). The KJV of Acts 13:21 spells his name Cis.

2. Levite, grandson of Merari, Mahli's son and the father of Jerahmeel (1 Chr 23:21-22; 24:29).

3. Abdi's son, another Levite of the family of Merari. He was one of the Levites who assisted Hezekiah in the cleansing of the temple (2 Chr 29:12).

4. Benjamite and the great-grandfather of Mordecai. Mordecai was carried into exile by Nebuchadnezzar in 597 BC (Est 2:5), together with King Jehoiachin and the prophet Ezekiel.

KISHI Levite of Merari's family whose son Ethan was a singer and musician in the sanctuary during David's reign (1 Chr 6:44). He is also known as Kushaiah in 15:17.

KISHION City allotted to Issachar's tribe (Jos 19:20) and given to the Gershonite Levites (Jos 21:28). *See* Levitical Cities.

KISHON

1. KJV variant of Kishion in Joshua 21:28. *See* Kishion.
2. River draining the valley of Jezreel. It is a mere 25 miles (40 kilometers) in length but gathers into itself numerous small streams that originate in the hill country to the south and the north along its course. It rises in the north of the Samaritan highlands where the watershed directs some waters north and others west down the plain of Dothan. Numerous small wadis empty into the main watercourse as it moves northwest down the slopes of the north Samaritan hills into the plain of Esdraelon. These upper reaches are dry in summer but in winter (the rainy season) can become torrential. From Jenin to the narrow gap at Tell el-Qassis (the "mound of the priest"), the fall is about 250 feet (76.2 meters). The course of the river follows the Mt Carmel ridge, and numerous streams join the main stream from the Carmel ranges to the south and the hills of Galilee to the north. Because this region has a much better rainfall than the area of the upper reaches of the river, the Kishon becomes a perennial stream for the last part of its course. It flows for the last six miles (9.7 kilometers) of its length beside Mt Carmel and empties into the Mediterranean Sea about two miles (3.2 kilometers) north of Haifa. Just before it reaches the sea, it attains a width of 65 feet (19.8 meters).

The heavy runoff from the hills, especially at the time of the spring rains, combined with the flat terrain of the plain of Esdraelon, produced swampy conditions along its course and provided a serious obstacle to transportation in early times. Its middle course has been largely drained in recent years.

Two important biblical events took place in the region of the Kishon River. The defeat of Sisera by Barak and Deborah took place here. Canaanite chariots were caught in the swamps of the Kishon and were overcome by the Israelite attack (Jgs 4–5). The river was praised in the Song of Deborah (5:21), and the event was recalled in Psalm 83:9 (where it is called Kison in the KJV). Later, the prophets of Baal, humiliated by Elijah on Mt Carmel, were killed along the banks of the Kishon (1 Kgs 18:40). The river is mentioned by the Roman historian Pliny, by Arab writers, and by the Crusaders. In recent years the last part of the river has been deepened and widened so that a channel 984 feet (300 meters) long, 164 feet (50 meters) wide, and 13 feet (4 meters) deep provides an auxiliary harbor for Haifa, especially for fishing vessels.

KISLEV* Month in the Hebrew calendar, about mid-November to mid-December; also spelled Chislev or Chisleu. *See* Calendars, Ancient and Modern.

KISLON Father of Elidad, leader of Benjamin's tribe during the Israelites' wilderness wanderings and one of those appointed by Moses to divide the land of Canaan among the tribes (Nm 34:21).

KISLOTH-TABOR City mentioned in Joshua 19:12. *See* Kesulloth.
See also Tabor (Place).

KISON* KJV spelling of the river Kishon in Psalm 83:9. *See* Kishon #2.

KISS, KISS OF PEACE* Common salutation symbolizing love and fellowship. In the Bible, kissing is referred to in a wide variety of contexts. In addition to its ordi-

nary expression among relatives (Gn 29:11; 33:4), its sensual aspect is noted (Prv 7:6-13; Sg 1:2). It is well attested as an act of homage (1 Sm 10:1; Jb 31:27), although such expressions may be heinous in God's sight (1 Kgs 19:18; Hos 13:2). Hypocrisy, even betrayal, may accompany a kiss (Mt 26:48-49).

Five NT texts refer to a "holy kiss," called later in church liturgy a "kiss of peace" (Rom 16:16; 1 Cor 16:20; 2 Cor 13:12; 1 Thes 5:26; 1 Pt 5:14). Peter speaks of a "kiss of love" and mentions peace in conjunction with it. Although the practice is neither described nor limited by Scripture, the kiss was evidently exchanged between Christians as a pledge of brotherly friendship and fidelity (1 Thes 5:25-27).

In the generations following the apostolic era, the kiss of peace came to occupy an established place in liturgical worship. In the latter part of the second century, Justin Martyr spoke of the exchange of kisses throughout the congregation following the conclusion of prayer. Eventually, the church placed the ceremony immediately prior to Holy Communion. Later on, the actual kiss was largely replaced by a simple bow. Other variant forms of the practice are still observed in various churches.

KITCHEN *See* Food and Food Preparation; Homes and Dwellings.

KITE Bird of prey declared unclean by the law (Lv 11:14; Dt 14:13). *See* Birds.

KITHLISH*, KITLISH City assigned to Judah's tribe for an inheritance (Jos 15:40).

KITRON City allotted to the tribe of Zebulun from which the Canaanite inhabitants could not be driven out (Jgs 1:30). It has been identified with Kattath (Jos 19:15), Tell el-Far, and Tell Qurdaneh. *See* Kattath.

KITTIM Ancient Hebrew name for the island of Cyprus (Gn 10:4; Dn 11:30). *See* Cyprus.

KNEELING Position often denoting worship, respect, or submission. A strong knee symbolically implied a man with strength of faith and purpose, and thus bowing the knee indicated submission to a superior. The knee was bowed before a king, a ruler, a governor, or God. Genesis 41:43 describes the people who were kneeling before Pharaoh and Joseph. Kneeling in reverence before the Lord was common (Is 45:23; Rom 14:11; Phil 2:10). In a time of famine, when the Israelites turned away from the Lord, those who remained faithful were described as "all the knees that have not bowed to Baal" (1 Kgs 19:18, RSV; see Rom 11:4).

As firm knees represented strength, so smiting those knees represented the destruction of power (Dt 28:35). Isaiah pleaded with the Lord for the strengthening of weak knees (Is 35:3). References to weak or feeble knees were generally used to show a lack of firmness of faith (Jb 4:4; Heb 12:12) but could sometimes refer to failing health (Ps 109:24). Ezekiel referred to those who had knees "as weak as water" (Ez 7:17; 21:7).

Kneeling before the Lord was a posture representing worship (Ps 95:6) and also prayer (Dn 6:10). Christ himself knelt to pray in the garden of Gethsemane (Lk 22:41), and Peter, Paul, and Stephen all did the same (Acts 7:60; 9:40; 20:36; 21:5). Solomon knelt in prayer and supplication before the Lord (1 Kgs 8:54), and even on one occasion had a scaffold built so that he could climb up and be seen by the whole congregation of Israel kneeling before the Lord (2 Chr 6:13).

Some knelt in penitence, as Ezra did at the evening sacrifice (Ezr 9:5) and as Peter did when begging the Lord's forgiveness for his lack of faith and trust (Lk 5:8). Those who were beseeching the prophet Elijah knelt before him as God's representative (2 Kgs 1:13), and many came kneeling and begging the Lord for healing (Mt 17:14; Mk 1:40). Daniel knelt in wonder and awe before an angel (Dn 10:10), and a sign of Belshazzar's fear was that his "knees knocked together" (Dn 5:6). In the NT a regal and patient Christ is subjected to the taunting and mockery of the soldiers who knelt before him and sarcastically cried, "Hail, King of the Jews" (Mt 27:29; Mk 15:19).

KNIFE Small, handheld, single- or double-edged cutting instrument, usually made of flint or metal.

KNOWLEDGE Observation and recognition of objects within the range of one's senses; acquaintance of a personal nature that includes a response of the knower.

The word "know" or "knowledge" occurs more than 1,600 times in the Bible. The specific connotation of the word group provides insight into the basic messages of both the OT and the NT.

The Hebrew view of man is one of differentiated totality—the heart, soul, and mind are so interrelated that they cannot be separated. "To know" thus involves the whole being and is not simply an action of the mind. The heart is sometimes identified as the organ of knowledge (cf. Ps 49:3; Is 6:10). The implication is that knowledge involves both will and emotions. It is in light of this connotation that the OT uses "to know" as an idiom for sexual intercourse between husband and wife.

The Jew's concept of knowledge is beautifully illustrated in Isaiah 1:3: "Even the animals—the donkey and the ox—know their owner and appreciate his care, but not my people Israel. No matter what I do for them, they still do not understand" (NLT). Israel's failure lay not in ritual behavior but in refusal to respond in loving obedience to the God who has chosen her. Only the fool refuses to respond to this revelation. Thus the person who does not respond in obedience obviously has an incomplete knowledge of the Lord. "To know God" involves relationship, fellowship, concern, and experience.

The NT continues this basic idea of knowledge and adds some variations of its own. In the Gospel of John the knowledge of God is mediated through Jesus as the Logos. Jesus has perfect knowledge of God's purpose and nature, and reveals it to his followers: "If you had known who I am, then you would have known who my Father is" (Jn 14:7, NLT). The identification of Jesus' own relationship with the Father as a model for the relationship of the disciples indicates that knowledge signifies a personal relationship that is intimate and mutual.

The definition of eternal life in John 17:3 adds further content to this concept: "And this is the way to have eternal life—to know you, the only true God, and Jesus Christ, the one you sent to earth" (NLT). This concept is vastly different from that of Hellenistic mysticism, in which contemplation and ecstasy are consummated in the gradual merging of the knower and God. In John, by contrast, the result of knowledge is having a personal relationship with God through his Son.

Paul also places the revelation of God in Christ as the source of knowledge. God has made known the "mystery of his will" to the one who is "in Christ." The spiritual person is taught by the Spirit of God (1 Cor 2:12-16) and responds to the truth as it is revealed in Jesus Christ. Again, there is emphasis on relationship and encounter as essential elements in the concept of knowledge.

Christian knowledge of God is not based simply on observation or speculation but is the result of experience in Christ. This knowledge is contrasted sharply with natural wisdom, which operates from an incorrect perspective. Paul is quick to point out that the mystery of God's redemptive plan has been made known and there is now no room for ignorance. Knowledge, then, is the whole person standing in relationship with God through Christ.
See also Revelation; Truth.

KOA People probably living northeast of Babylonia. They are named along with Babylon, Pekod, and Shoa as people who would come against Jerusalem as instruments of God's judgment on Israel (Ez 23:23). They are perhaps identifiable with the Kutu, mentioned frequently in Assyrian inscriptions.

KOHATH, KOHATHITES Son of Levi (Gn 46:11; Ex 6:16), father of Amram, Izhar, Hebron, and Uzziel (Ex 6:18; Nm 3:19, 27; 1 Chr 6:2), and progenitor of the Kohathite branch of Levitical families who were responsible for the tabernacle service (Nm 3:31-32). Moses, Aaron, and Miriam were descendants of Kohath (Ex 6:18-20; Nm 26:59; 1 Chr 6:3; 23:13-17).

The three main divisions of the tribe of Levi bore the names of Gershon, Kohath, and Merari, who were traditionally the original sons of Levi (Gn 46:11; Ex 6:16; Nm 3:17; 1 Chr 6:1, 16; 23:6). The Kohathites, therefore, were a prominent Levitical family. The order of their names in Numbers 4, Joshua 21, 1 Chronicles 6:16, and 2 Chronicles 29:12 indicates that they were assigned a more honorable office than either Gershon or Merari. Their position and responsibilities—whether referred to as "the Kohathites," or "the sons of Kohath"—are noted throughout the early writings of the Hebrews (Ex 6:18; Nm 3:19, 27-30; 4:2-4, 15, 18, 34, 37; 7:9; 10:21; 26:57; Jos 21:4-5, 10, 20, 26; 1 Chr 6:2, 18, 22, 33, 54, 61, 66, 70; 15:5; 23:12; 2 Chr 20:19; 29:12; 34:12).

During the wandering of the Israelites in the desert following their exodus from Egypt, the Kohathites were assigned a position on the southern side of the tabernacle (Nm 3:29). When the tabernacle was moved, they were to carry the ark and other sacred things on their shoulders (7:9). At the time of the building of the tabernacle, a census was taken to determine the number of male Kohathites who would be involved in the service of the Lord (3:27-28; 4:1-4, 34-37).

After the settlement of the tribes in the land of Canaan, the service of the Kohathites appeared to have ended. God, however, specifically stated that they should be cared for in the same manner as the other Levitical families. The Kohathites were given numerous cities (Jos 21:4-5, 20-26; 1 Chr 6:66-70).

When David became king, he organized the Levites into three divisions (1 Chr 23:6). Heman, who represented the Kohathites, was charged with the musical service in the house of the Lord (6:31), and another group of Kohathites was made responsible for the "bread of the presence" each Sabbath (9:32). When David brought the ark of the covenant to Jerusalem, Uriel, a Kohathite, was commissioned to supervise its transportation (15:3-5).

During the period of the divided kingdom, the combined forces of the Moabites and Ammonites attacked Judah. King Jehoshaphat admitted his inability to repulse the aggressors and sought the aid of the Lord. The Kohathites led the people in a song of praise and probably led the army when, the next morning, the king and the fighting men of Judah went out against the invaders (2 Chr 20:19-22).

Two important reform movements characterized the

declining years of the kingdom of Judah. The first took place during the reign of Hezekiah (715–686 BC; 2 Kgs 18; 2 Chr 29–30); the second in the reign of Josiah (640–609 BC; 2 Kgs 22–23; 2 Chr 34). The climax of Josiah's reform came in 621 BC with the discovery of the Book of the Law. In both these movements the Kohathites played an important role. In the reign of Hezekiah they were numbered among those who cleansed the house of the Lord (2 Chr 29:12-16), and in Josiah's time two notable Kohathites were among those appointed to supervise the work of the temple (34:12).

Following the exile, mention is again made of the Kohathites. The paucity of evidence precludes any judgment of the significance of their ministry. In all probability they were numbered among those who attempted to serve the Lord faithfully in the midst of general spiritual decline. The few whose names are forever enshrined in Scripture were appointed to humble offices. In the absence of evidence to the contrary, it may be assumed that they discharged their duties faithfully (1 Chr 9:19, 31-32; Ezr 2:42; Neh 12:25).

See also Levi, Tribe of; Priests and Levites; Tabernacle; Temple.

KOHELETH* *See* Qoheleth.

KOINE GREEK* Type of Greek that was "common" *(koine)* to the Near Eastern and Mediterranean lands in Roman times. It is the Greek in which the NT was written. *See* Bible.

KOLA Kola is mentioned in the book of Judith (Jdt 15:4) as a place-name. It may be identified with Holon (Jos 15:51).

KOLAIAH
1. Benjamite; forefather of a family who lived in Jerusalem after the exile (Neh 11:7).
2. Father of Ahab, the false prophet who, along with Zedekiah, prophesied falsely in the name of God during Jeremiah's day (Jer 29:21).

KONA Town referred to in the apocryphal book of Judith (Jdt 4:4).

KOR* Dry commodity measure equivalent to one homer (about 3.8 to 7.5 bushels). *See* Weights and Measures.

KORAH
1. Third son of Esau by Oholibamah, daughter of Anah (Gn 36:5,14,18; 1 Chr 1:35).
2. Esau's grandson; fifth son of Eliphaz (Gn 36:16).
3. Eldest son of Izhar, Kohath's son from Levi's tribe (Ex 6:21, 24), who led a rebellion against Moses and Aaron in the wilderness, accusing them of exalting themselves above the assembly of the Lord (Nm 16:1-3). Numbers 16:1 also records a revolt led by two brothers, Dathan and Abiram, and a man named On, all of the tribe of Reuben, who also challenged the authority of Moses. Dathan and Abiram accused Moses of making himself a prince over the people and then failing to lead them into the Promised Land (vv 12-14). The stories of the two rebellions are interwoven in such a way that it is difficult to separate them. It may be that the two revolts occurred simultaneously.

Moses challenged Korah and his followers to a trial by ordeal. Together with Aaron, they were to take censers filled with fire and incense to the tent of meeting the next day; the Lord would then select from among them whoever should be the holy priest before the Lord (Nm 16:4-10, 15-17). Moses accused Korah and his company of rebelling against God rather than against Aaron (v 11). When the men gathered as Moses had instructed, the glory of the Lord appeared to all the people. The Lord ordered Moses to tell the congregation to separate themselves from the tents of Korah, Dathan, and Abiram (vv 19-24). Moses proposed a test to show the source of his authority, but while he was still speaking, the earth opened and swallowed all the rebels, their families, and their possessions. Fire consumed the 250 men who were offering the incense. The rest of the Israelites were terrified and fled from the scene (vv 31-35). Numbers 26:11 adds, however, that "the sons of Korah did not die that day" with the others.

Then, through Moses, the Lord instructed Eleazar, the son of Aaron, to take the censers of the men who had died and have them made into hammered plates to be used as a covering for the altar; thus, they would serve as a reminder to the Israelites that no one who was not a priest and a descendant of Aaron should ever draw near to burn incense before the Lord, lest that person meet the same fate as Korah and his company (Nm 16:36-40).

Instead of being convinced that God had vindicated Moses and Aaron, the next day the congregation began complaining that they had killed the Lord's people. For this act of rebellion God threatened to destroy the congregation and sent a plague among them. Moses interceded and averted complete catastrophe, but not before 14,700 Israelites had died (Nm 16:41-50). The rebellious incident of the Korahites is last mentioned in Jude 1:11.

See also Korahite, Korathite.

4. Eldest son of Hebron, included in the genealogy of Caleb (1 Chr 2:43); the reference has been understood as a geographical name, possibly a town in Judah.
5. Aminadab's son and grandson of Kohath, second son of Levi (1 Chr 6:22).

KORAHITE, KORATHITE* Member of Levi's tribe, of the division of Kohath (Ex 6:18, 21). Their ancestor, Izhar, was a member of the priestly family and was related to Moses and Aaron. The rebellion led by Korah, Dathan, and Abiram against Moses and Aaron ended with the death of many members of the Korahite family (Nm 16:31-35). Only those who did not participate survived (v 11). They settled around Hebron in the Levitical cities (26:58).

The Korahites were known as temple singers, according to the superscriptions of Psalms 42, 44–49, 84–85, and 87–88. David put them in charge of the musical service in the house of the Lord after the ark was brought to Jerusalem (1 Chr 6:31-33). They also acted as gatekeepers (9:19; 26:19) and bakers of sacrificial cakes (9:31). They are mentioned as singers during the celebration of Jehoshaphat's victory over Ammon and Moab (2 Chr 20:19).

See also Korah #3.

KORAZIN Palestinian city on which Jesus pronounced woe (Mt 11:21-24; Lk 10:13-14). It was in Korazin, Bethsaida, and Capernaum that "most of his miracles" had been done, but the people were generally unresponsive and had not repented (Mt 11:20).

From the biblical references, Korazin was probably in the vicinity of Capernaum and Bethsaida. The church father Jerome (c. AD 400) located it two miles (3.2 kilometers) from Capernaum, which is on the northwest shore of the Sea of Galilee. Scholars generally agree that the ruins of Khirbet Kerazeh on the basalt hills north of Capernaum are those of Korazin. The ruins indicate that it was a fairly important city. Remains of a synagogue, probably from the fourth century AD, include a carved seat with an inscription, an example of a "Moses' seat" (Mt 23:2). According to the Jewish Talmud, Korazin was known for its wheat.

KORE

1. Kohathite Levite who, with his brothers, was responsible for the service at the entrance to the tent of meeting in David's time (1 Chr 9:19; 26:1).
2. KJV alternate name for Korahite in 1 Chronicles 26:19. *See* Korahite, Korathite.
3. Imnah's son, a Levite who was a keeper of the East Gate in Hezekiah's reign. He had charge of the freewill offerings of the people (2 Chr 31:14).

KORHITE* KJV alternate spelling of Korahite, a descendant of Korah, Hebron's son, in 1 Chronicles 12:6. *See* Korah #4.

KOZ

1. Descendant of Judah and possibly an ancestor of the priestly house of Hakkoz (1 Chr 4:8).
2. KJV rendering of the priestly family of Hakkoz (Ezr 2:61; Neh 3:4, 21; 7:63); perhaps identifiable with #1 above. *See* Hakkoz.

KUB* A place in Ezekiel 30:5 identified as Libya (NLT mg).

KUE* Name of Cilicia in OT times. From there Solomon imported horses (1 Kgs 10:28; 2 Chr 1:16, NLT mg). It included two geographical areas, the plain on the east (Cilicia Pedias) and the mountains on the west (Cilicia Tracheia). It was bounded on the south by the Mediterranean, on the west and northwest by the Taurus ranges, on the northeast by the anti-Taurus, and on the east by the Amanus.

The Akkadian rulers of the late third millennium, Sargon the Great and his grandson Naram-Sin, claimed to have reached the "cedar forest" and the "mountain of silver," evidently the Amanus and Taurus, respectively. The name of the plain in the middle Bronze Age was Adaniya; during the late Bronze Age a kingdom called Kizzuwatna, composed of Luwian and Hurrian elements, came into being there but was subjugated by the Hittite Empire.

The Iron Age (first millennium BC) saw the rise of the Neo-Hittite kingdom of Kue; it acted as a middleman, bringing horses down from the north (cf. Ez 27:14). In the ninth century BC Kue joined a coalition of states to resist the aggression of Shalmaneser III (858 BC), who finally conquered Kue in 839–833 BC. When the Assyrians withdrew, Kue was third in importance after Aram-Damascus and Arpad (according to the stela of Zakir, king of Hamath). By the end of the eighth century, Urikki, king of Kue, paid tribute to Tiglath-pileser III (738 BC), and somewhat later Kue was annexed by Assyria. With the death of Sargon (705 BC), all the Assyrian provinces in Cilicia and Anatolia rebelled; Sennacherib did not reconquer them until 695 BC. In spite of pressure from the neighboring Tabal and the tribes of the Khilakku (who later gave the name Cilicia to the plain), Esar-haddon and Ashurbanipal managed to keep their hold on Kue. The Chaldean Nebuchadnezzar conducted campaigns there in 593 and 591 BC. Later, Chaldean kings also controlled it and campaigned against neighboring Lydia. With the fall of Babylon to the Persians, the Khilakku took advantage of the situation to occupy the plain. This brought an end to Kue and the beginning of the classical Cilicia.

KUSHAIAH Alternate name for Kishi, a Merarite Levite, in 1 Chronicles 15:17. *See* Kishi.

L

LAADAH Shelah's son and the father of Mareshah from Judah's tribe (1 Chr 4:21).

LAADAN*
1. KJV spelling of Ladan, Joshua's ancestor, in 1 Chronicles 7:26. *See* Ladan #1.
2. KJV spelling of Ladan, an alternate name for Libni the Gershonite, in 1 Chronicles 23:7 and 26:21. *See* Libni #1.

LABAN (Person) Bethuel's son (Gn 24:24, 29), brother of Rebekah (vv 15, 29), father of Leah and Rachel (29:16), and the uncle and father-in-law of Jacob. Laban's forebears lived in Ur, but his father, Bethuel, was called the Aramean of Paddan-aram, and Laban also is referred to as the Aramean (KJV "Syrian," 25:20; cf. 28:5). Their hometown was Haran, which was in Syria and which, like Ur, was a center of the worship of the moon god, Sin or Nannar.

When Isaac came of age, Abraham sent his servant Eliezer back to Haran to find a wife for Isaac. Laban greeted Eliezer hospitably and made provision for him and his camels (Gn 24:29-33, 54). Laban acted as the head of the house; he made the decision concerning Rebekah's marriage to Isaac (vv 50-51), and it was to him and his mother that Eliezer made gifts of costly ornaments (v 53).

Laban figures largely in the narrative of his nephew Jacob in his quest for a wife. After the deception of Isaac by Rebekah and Jacob, Rebekah feared that Esau would kill Jacob, so she suggested that he flee to her brother, Laban (Gn 27:43); meanwhile, she persuaded Isaac that Jacob should go to Haran to find a wife from among their own people. When Jacob arrived in the area of Haran, he met Rachel, the younger daughter of Laban, and was warmly welcomed (29:13). Laban hired Jacob to tend his flocks, and it was agreed that after seven years of work Jacob would receive Rachel as his wages. At the end of that period Laban substituted Leah, his older daughter. Jacob protested, but the two men finally decided that Jacob should serve another seven years for Rachel.

Both Jacob and Laban were schemers and had serious disputes about wages. Jacob proposed that his wages should be a certain portion of the flocks. When this was accepted, the Lord blessed Jacob and his flocks, and Laban became angry. Jacob claimed that Laban had changed his wages ten times (Gn 31:7, 41).

Jacob fled from Haran. Laban pursued him because he was missing his household gods, whose possession made the holder heir to Laban's estate. Rachel had taken them but adroitly concealed them from her father's search.

Laban and Jacob parted after making a covenant of peace and erecting a pillar of stones to serve as a witness between them (Gn 31:46-50).

See also Jacob #1.

LABAN (Place) Israelite camping place in Sinai (Dt 1:1). Some equate it with the Libnah of Numbers 33:20-21. Proposals for its location have ranged from just south of Rabbath-ammon to the Arabian coast south of Elath. Its site is still unknown.

LACHISH Place first mentioned in the Bible in connection with Joshua and the Israelite conquest of Palestine. At that time, its king and army were among the coalition of southern Palestinian towns that faced Joshua at Gibeon. After Joshua's victory, he executed the king of Lachish and later took the town itself (Jos 10:26, 32). Though David probably brought the town to life again, it gained new significance when King Rehoboam of Judah (c. 920 BC) made it one of his fortified cities to protect the realm against Egyptian and Philistine attacks (2 Chr 11:9). About a century later, Amaziah, king of Judah, was killed at Lachish, where he had fled to escape from conspirators (2 Kgs 14:19).

Aerial View of Lachish

Lachish resisted valiantly when Sennacherib of Assyria invaded in 701 BC, but it ultimately fell under furious onslaughts (2 Kgs 18:13-17; Is 36). Reoccupied and rebuilt by the Judeans, it was one of the last outposts of Jerusalem to fall to the Babylonians when Nebuchadnezzar invaded in 588–586 BC and brought the southern kingdom to an end (Jer 34:7). In addition to biblical references, the Egyptian Amarna letters and Assyrian records allude to Lachish.

The location of Lachish was long debated. Originally, it was placed at Umm Lakis, then in 1891 at Tell el-Hesi, and finally in 1929 at Tell ed-Duweir, 30 miles (48.3 kilometers) southwest of Jerusalem and 15 miles (24.1 kilometers) west of Hebron. This last identification has now been confirmed by a variety of indicators.

See also Lachish Letters.

LACHISH LETTERS* Collection of letters, sometimes described as "a supplement to Jeremiah," which was J. L. Starkey's most important discovery at Lachish. In 1935 he found 18 ostraca in a guardroom between the outer and inner gates of the city, in a layer of ash deposited by the fire that Nebuchadnezzar kindled when he destroyed the city. Probably the Chaldeans breached the walls late in 589 BC after the olive harvest, since numerous burned olive pits appear in the nearby ruins. Having taken this and other outlying towns, Nebuchadnezzar then laid siege to Jerusalem in January of 588. In 1938 three other letters were found at Lachish. Of uncertain date, these were short and fragmentary. All 21 of these texts were written in black carbon ink with a wood or reed stylus on pieces of broken pottery. The scribes used the Phoenician script, in which classical Hebrew was written.

Nearly all of the 21 documents were letters, and most of them were written by some subordinate officer at an outpost to the commander at Lachish. Unfortunately, only seven of the texts are sufficiently legible to make connected sense; on the others, only isolated sentences and words can be read. Some of the signs are blotted out and unfamiliar abbreviations and symbols are used. Scholars differ in their interpretations.

One of the most interesting of the letters is no. 4, which says, "We are watching for the fire signals of Lachish, according to all the signs which my lord has given, for we cannot see [the signals of] Azekah." Jeremiah 34:7 mentions Lachish and Azekah (12 miles, or 19.3 kilometers, northeast of Lachish) as two of the last surviving cities of Judah. Now it would appear that Azekah too has fallen and the Chaldean noose is tightening on the Judean kingdom. However, the signals of Azekah temporarily may not have been visible for climatic or other reasons. It is important to note the external evidence here for the use of fire signals in ancient Israel. The Hebrew word for fire signal is the same as that used in Jeremiah 6:1.

Letter no. 6 alludes to the fact that the princes are weakening the hands of the people. Evidently this refers to some insubordination or defeatism. The text reads: "And behold the words of the princes are not good, but to weaken our hands and to slacken the hands of the men who are informed about them." This is almost identical to the charge that some of the princes lodged against Jeremiah: "For he is weakening the hands of the soldiers who are left in this city, and the hands of all the people, by speaking such words to them" (Jer 38:4, RSV).

Letter no. 3 refers to a journey of the Judean army commander to Egypt. Whether he went with an appeal for troops or supplies is not known. This allusion points to the intrigues of the pro-Egyptian party during the reign of Zedekiah. The reason for the present expedition must have been much different from that referred to in Jeremiah 26:20-23. Letter no. 3 also refers to a letter with a warning from a prophet. Efforts to identify this prophet as Uriah or Jeremiah have not been convincing.

Letters 2–6 refer to a defense that a certain Hoshaiah (a name that appears in Jer 42:1; 43:2), the writer of several of the Lachish texts, makes to his superior, Ya'osh. Though the charges are not always clear, they have something to do with reading confidential documents and presumably divulging some of the information contained therein. One scholar has suggested that this collection of letters in the Lachish guardhouse constituted a "file" used in the court-martial of Hoshaiah. The guardhouse was not only a military post but was also located by the gate where Palestinian trials were held in biblical times.

The Lachish letters have epigraphic, linguistic, and historical value for the Bible scholar. They indicate the kind of language and script the Hebrews were using in the age of Jeremiah, and they give information for textual criticism. They are firsthand documents of the disturbed political and military situation during the months before Nebuchadnezzar's destruction of Jerusalem, when Jeremiah was the leading prophet in Judah. They help to make possible a study of Hebrew proper names in the last days of the monarchy and provide numerous historical references (e.g., no. 20 refers to the ninth year of King Zedekiah).

See also Letter Writing, Ancient.

LADAN

1. Member of Ephraim's tribe who was Joshua's ancestor (1 Chr 7:26).
2. Gershonite Levite, named as the head of several families (1 Chr 23:7; 26:21). He is also called Libni. *See* Libni #1.

LAEL Levite of the family of Gershon and father of Eliasaph (Nm 3:24).

LAHAD Jahath's son from Judah's tribe (1 Chr 4:2).

LAHAI-ROI* KJV form of Beer-lahairoi, the name of a well mentioned in Genesis 24:62 and 25:11. *See* Beer-lahairoi.

LAHMAM Judahite town in the Shephelah district of Lachish (Jos 15:40), usually identified with modern Khirbet el-Lahm; alternately spelled Lahmas in some versions (NIV, NASB).

LAHMI Brother of Goliath the Gittite. According to 1 Chronicles 20:5, he was killed by Elhanan. However, 2 Samuel 21:19 says that Elhanan killed Goliath rather than his brother Lahmi. Most interpreters accept the 1 Chronicles passage as the correct reading, the 2 Samuel text being a textual corruption.

LAISH (Person) Father of Paltiel (Palti), to whom Saul gave his daughter Michal, who was formerly David's wife (1 Sm 25:44; 2 Sm 3:15-16).

LAISH (Place)

1. Early name for the city of Dan (Jgs 18:7, 14, 27-29). *See* Dan (Place) #1.
2. KJV spelling of Laishah, a Benjamite town, in Isaiah 10:30. *See* Laishah.

LAISHAH Town in Benjamin mentioned between Gallim and Anathoth (Is 10:30). Its site is possibly Khirbet el-'Isawiyeh.

LAKE OF FIRE Final abode of Satan, his servants, and unrepentant human beings.

This place is mentioned only in Revelation (Rv 19:20; 20:10, 14-15; 21:8), but its terrible nature is abundantly clear. It is described as a lake of fire or lake of burning sulphur into which are cast (1) the "beast" and his "false prophet" after the Lamb defeats them, (2) Satan after his last rebellion, (3) Death and Hades, and (4) all whose names are not found in the "Book of Life." It is called the second death, for it is the ultimate separation from God beyond the resurrection and final judgment.

The lake of fire is probably the same place that Jesus calls Gehenna (Mt 10:28; Mk 9:43; Lk 12:5), the "outer darkness" (Mt 8:12; 22:13; 25:30), and the eternal fire prepared for the devil and his angels (Mt 25:41; cf. Is 66:24). The imagery is drawn from the fires in the valley of Hinnom outside of Jerusalem and perhaps the stream of fire issuing from God's throne (Is 30:33; Dn 7:10; cf. Is 34:9-10). The picture was known to Jewish as well as Christian writers (Assumption of Moses 10:10; 2 Esd 7:36). Whatever the image or name, they all point to a place of eternal torment and separation from God where the unrepentant will suffer forever.

See also Gehenna; Last Judgment.

LAKKUM, LAKUM* Fortified border town within the territory of Naphtali (Jos 19:33). Its site is identifiable with Khirbet el-Mansurah, about three miles (4.8 kilometers) southwest of Khirbet Kerak, at the head of Wadi Fejjas.

LAMB *See* Animals (Sheep).

LAMB OF GOD General term used twice by John the Baptist (Jn 1:29, 36), adding on the first instance "who takes away the world's sin!" He does not explain what the term means. Christians use the term freely, but what do they mean by it? Why would anyone be called "God's Lamb"?

Some maintain that John saw Jesus fulfilling all that the Passover means and that this is a way of referring to the Passover lamb. It is true that the fourth Gospel places the death of Jesus at the time the Passover sacrifices were killed. But "Passover lamb" is a modern expression; not one example of its use is known to occur in antiquity. When people wanted to refer to the animal killed for this sacrifice, they simply called it "the Passover" (Ex 12:21, cf. 1 Cor 5:7, KJV). The Passover victim was not necessarily a lamb; it might be, and often was, a kid. There is no reason for seeing the Passover in this expression.

Some scholars think the image comes from Isaiah 53. They see the lamb led to the slaughter (v 7) as a way of referring to the Messiah.

Other scholars think there is an allusion to the triumphant lamb of the apocalypses. The writers of apocalyptic literature used vivid imagery to reveal their meaning to initiates and to conceal it from outsiders. They sometimes used the lamb as a symbol of a conqueror (cf. the use of "the Lamb" for "the Mighty One" in Revelation). These scholars think that John was pointing to Jesus as the Messiah, King of Israel. Many find this view attractive. The royalty it ascribes to Jesus is certainly congenial to John. But against it is the weighty consideration that John was speaking about a Lamb who takes away sin, while the apocalyptic lamb is normally a conqueror. The roles are different. Further, it is not easy to see how non-Jewish readers of the Gospel at the time it was written would have been able to discern the point of apocalyptic imagery.

There are other suggestions. The "gentle lamb" (Jer 11:19), the daily sacrifice in the temple, the scapegoat, and the guilt offering have all been put forward with some confidence. But no one has produced evidence that any of these was ever called "God's lamb."

In the OT passages referring to a lamb, nearly all of them speak of sacrifice (85 out of the total of 96). Combined with a reference to the taking away of sin, it is difficult to see how a reference to sacrificial atonement is to be rejected. Characteristically the lamb in Scripture puts away sin by being sacrificed. "God's Lamb" means that this provision is made by God himself. A reference to sacrifice seems undeniable, but a connection with any one sacrifice is hard to make. All that the OT sacrifices foreshadowed, Christ perfectly fulfilled. God's Lamb puts sin away finally.

See also Feasts and Festivals of Israel; John, The Apostle; John, Gospel of.

LAMECH

1. Methushael's son, a descendant of Cain, and the husband of Adah and Zillah. Lamech's sons by Adah were Jabal, "the father of those who dwell in tents and have livestock," and Jubal, "the father of all those who play the lyre and pipe." A son, Tubal-cain, "the forger of all instruments of bronze and iron," and a daughter, Naamah, were Lamech's children by Zillah (Gn 4:18-22). In the account of beginnings given in the early chapters of Genesis, the sons of Lamech are the first herdsmen, musicians, and metalworkers. His song of vengeance (vv 23-24) is an example of early Hebrew poetry. In the song Lamech declares that he has killed a man for wounding him and compares the act to his forebear Cain's slaying of Abel (cf. vv 8-12). He asserts that "if anyone who kills Cain is to be punished seven times, anyone who takes revenge against me will be punished seventy-seven times!" Lamech's song indicates that, as civilization became more complex, pride and the propensity for violence increased. Jesus' word about forgiving "seventy times seven" (Mt 18:22) stands in sharp contrast to Lamech's example.

2. Methuselah's son, and the father of Noah (Gn 5:25-31; 1 Chr 1:3). When Noah was born, Lamech expressed his hope that the child would bring relief to humanity from the curse placed upon Adam (Gn 5:29; cf. 3:17). His life span—777 years—is one of the longest in the listing of those who lived before the Flood. Fanciful conversations in old age between Lamech and his father, Methuselah, are recorded in the Dead Sea Scrolls. Lamech is listed as an ancestor of Jesus in the genealogy recorded in Luke 3:36.

See also Genealogy of Jesus Christ.

LAMENT, LAMENTATION* *See* Mourning.

LAMENTATIONS, Book of Book consisting of five poems that constitute a formal dirge lamenting the fall of Jerusalem.

PREVIEW
- Author
- Date
- Background
- Structure
- Purpose and Theological Teaching
- Content

Author The book of Lamentations has been traditionally ascribed to the prophet Jeremiah. This ascription is supported by the Latin Vulgate and the Septuagint.

The Jeremaic authorship of the book has been questioned by many scholars, however. The chief reasons for this are the different literary styles of the books of Jeremiah and Lamentations and the alleged conflicting viewpoints in the two books.

The literary styles of these books are strikingly different. The prophecies of the book of Jeremiah are flowing pronouncements that create an impression of spontaneity and are quite unlike the contrived literary structures of Lamentations. But it is somewhat arbitrary to assert that Jeremiah could not have written the book of Lamentations on the basis of style. The choice of the acrostic form would naturally limit the scope of the writer's freedom and profoundly affect his style. It is clear from 2 Chronicles 35:25 that Jeremiah composed the same type of material as that found in Lamentations. Since the sermons of the book of Jeremiah were intended for public proclamation, they would naturally have a spontaneity that the book of Lamentations would not possess. Certainly, the sensitive nature reflected in Jeremiah's prophecies characterized the author of Lamentations as well.

Typical of the alleged differences of viewpoint used to deny Jeremaic authorship is the role of the nations in the destruction of Jerusalem. In his prophecy Jeremiah saw the invading Babylonians as a tool of God's punishment, and appealed to the Jews to surrender to the invaders (Jer 28:3). The book of Lamentations seems to make God the direct author of the punishment and sees the enemy nations only as onlookers who will also experience God's wrath (Lam 1:21; 3:59-66). It must be noted, however, that the enemies referred to in Lamentations are not only the Babylonians but all of the hostile powers that threatened Judah and gloated over its destruction (1:21). The assurance that God will judge these enemies is not a denial of the message of the book of Jeremiah, for it would be artificial for Jeremiah to suppose that the Babylonians, even though they were an instrument of God's anger, were exempt from punishment. Such a concept is at variance with Jeremiah 12:14-17.

A number of phrases used in the book of Jeremiah are found in Lamentations as well. The expressions "terrors on every side" (Lam 2:22; cf. Jer 6:25; 20:10) and "wormwood" (Lam 3:15, 19; cf. Jer 9:15; 23:15) are examples of these. This fact lends support to the concept of Jeremaic authorship of the book.

Other reasons cited for the denial of Jeremaic authorship are the absence of the name of Jeremiah in Lamentations and the position of the book in the Writings, not the Prophets, in the Hebrew Bible. The absence of Jeremiah's name is not a cogent argument against his authorship; there are a significant number of OT books whose authors are not cited. Since the book of Lamentations is a formal dirge, and is thus unlike the book of Jeremiah with its numerous autobiographical references, one would not expect personal allusions by the author.

The position of Lamentations in the third division of the Hebrew Bible is sometimes appealed to by those who question Jeremaic authorship. Since Jeremiah is in the second division, it is argued that Lamentations was written too late for it to have been authored by Jeremiah. It should be noted, however, that there is a lack of unity in the early lists of the canonical books in the third division. It is difficult to assign a late date to a book of the third division only because of its inclusion in that division. The early church father Jerome indicated that Lamentations was once on the same scroll with Jeremiah.

Date If the book of Lamentations was written by Jeremiah, the time of writing would be shortly after the fall of Jerusalem (586 BC). It is extremely difficult to imagine an author living in later times writing such a poignant lament over Jerusalem's fall. The vivid descriptions of the suffering endured by the inhabitants of Jerusalem support the position that the book was written by an eyewitness to the events.

Background After many months of siege by the Babylonian armies, Jerusalem fell, and the final deportation of the people of Judah took place. Extrabiblical confirmation of the devastation caused by the Babylonian invasion may be found in the Lachish letters, which record the message from a soldier in the field who indicates that he is watching for the signals of Lachish but cannot see the signals of Azekah (cf. Jer 34:7).

The time preceding Jerusalem's fall was one of internal strife and political intrigue. Jeremiah counseled surrender, while the chauvinistic leaders of Jerusalem tried to encourage the Judahites to fight on against the Babylonian onslaught. The role of Jeremiah in those final events was a tenuous one. His life was threatened, and he suffered numerous imprisonments.

The fall of Jerusalem meant more than ignominious defeat and exile. While these would have been hard to bear, the theological emergency brought about by the event would have been the most difficult thing for

believing Jews to comprehend. The fall of the city in which God chose to reveal himself would have signaled the end of God's promises. The OT clearly set forth a glorious future for Jerusalem. It was to be the center of the messianic kingdom in the end time (Mi 4). The destruction of the city would cause many to question the veracity of God's Word. The laments in this book are not only for the suffering that accompanied the fall of the city but also for the deep spiritual questions posed by its demise.

Structure Each poem has a distinct symmetrical pattern. The first (Lam 1) is an elaborate acrostic composed of three-line segments. There are 22 segments, each beginning with a different letter of the Hebrew alphabet, proceeding in order from the first to the last. The second poem (ch 2) is similar except for a transposition of two Hebrew letters. The third poem (ch 3) is also composed of three-line segments, but each line begins with a different letter of the Hebrew alphabet, rather than only the first line of each segment as in the first two poems. The same Hebrew letters are transposed. The fourth poem (ch 4) is an acrostic composed of two-line segments. The first line of each segment begins with the appropriate Hebrew letter. The last poem (ch 5) is not an acrostic, but it contains the same number of letters as the Hebrew alphabet.

The reason for this complex structure is unknown. It has been suggested that it is a device to aid memorization. Another suggestion is that the Hebrews may have seen the alphabet as representing the concept of totality or completeness. This idea derives from the fact that the Hebrew alphabet represented numbers as well as letters. This concept of totality may be reflected in the reference to the first and last letters of the Greek alphabet in Revelation 1:8: "I am the Alpha and the Omega." It is quite possible that the expression of lamentation in the structure of the Hebrew alphabet could have represented the full range of sorrow felt by the author as he pondered the fall of the city of Jerusalem.

Purpose and Theological Teaching A major purpose of the book of Lamentations was to give expression to the deep grief that Jeremiah felt as a result of Jerusalem's catastrophe. By writing the book, he expressed the grief of all the Jews of his time and gave them a vehicle that would give vent to their sorrow.

The book does not contain only lamentation, however, for it expresses hope and comfort as well. Thus another of its purposes was to lift the hearts of the people and point them to God, the source of all comfort. One of the greatest expressions of hope in the book is found in 3:22-23: "The unfailing love of the LORD never ends! By his mercies we have been kept from complete destruction. Great is his faithfulness; his mercies begin afresh each day" (NLT).

Perhaps the most important purpose of the book was to explain the theological reason for the catastrophe. The book places the reason for Jerusalem's fall in clear focus and demonstrates what can be learned about God from this. The reason given for Jerusalem's demise is the sin of the people (1:8-9, 14; 4:13). The fall of the city is a vivid illustration of God's justice in not overlooking sin even in those who are his own (1:18). It demonstrates the fact that God may seem like an enemy to his people when they are disobedient (2:5-7). It shows that the catastrophe was not outside the purposes of God (v 17) and vividly describes the results that can come from willful disobedience. But God is envisioned as a God of mercy and faithfulness as well. Even though Jeremiah saw his beloved homeland crumbling about him, there remained one great element of stability: God's loyalty to his promises. Jeremiah knew that this was not the end, for he trusted in the steadfast love of the Lord and learned to wait quietly for God to act in his time (3:22-27).

Content The first chapter is a lamentation over the captivity of the citizens of Jerusalem and the resultant desolation of the city.

The author alludes to Deuteronomy 28:64-65 at the beginning of the first lamentation (Lam 1:3). In that passage Moses warned the people that their disobedience to God would result in their dispersion among the nations, with no resting place. Lamentations 1:3 says that this warning has been realized.

The cause of Israel's misfortune was their sin (1:8a). This is a remarkable example of the results of disobedience to God. The dire results of sin permeate this first lamentation in a series of pictures of deep pathos (vv 11-12, 16-17). In the midst of this suffering Israel confesses that God was in the right (v 18). The righteousness of God involves his acting in integrity. He punishes sin even in his own people.

The first lamentation ends with a prayer in which the people cry out for God's judgment on their enemies (1:21-22). Such imprecations are the OT believer's way of expressing his longing for an end to evil as it was personified in the godless nations.

The second lamentation also concerns the destruction of Jerusalem but places more emphasis on God's judgment. The tone is more strident than in the previous lamentation. Throughout the passage words expressing anger appear (2:1-3, 6-7). It is as though the terrible wrath of God evident in the destruction of the city is still vivid in the mind of the writer.

The author lays the blame for God's anger squarely on the false prophets (2:14); but he does not exempt the people from guilt, as is clear from other passages (e.g., 1:5, 8). It was the false prophets of the time who failed to warn the people of the results of their sin (2:14). Because of this, destruction came, and the writer can give no comfort to the people (v 13).

The second lamentation begins with a reference to God's footstool (2:1), probably referring to the ark of the covenant (1 Chr 28:2). The ark was the focal point of God's revelation of himself. This verse reflects the theological emergency of the time; the writer laments the fact that God has not remembered his "footstool." Even the holy ark, which marked God's presence with his people, has not prevented God from destroying Jerusalem.

The same thought is expressed in verses 6-7, where the traditional aspects of Israelite worship, as well as the sanctuary, are seen as having been destroyed by God. This important truth demonstrates the viewpoint of the whole book, which sees God as the direct cause of the misfortune.

The third lamentation is very personal. At its conclusion, sorrow and complaint pass into a prayer of assurance (3:61-66). In the first 18 verses of this chapter, the writer describes how the Lord has afflicted him. He refers to God in the third person, not addressing him as Lord until he speaks the words of verse 18. Only after he has poured out his grief in this fashion can he speak the name of the Lord. This poignant grief suddenly changes to an expression of joy. He can affirm the covenant faithfulness of the Lord, and in the midst of the deepening sorrow, he sees God's mercies as new every morning (vv 22-24). The chapter closes with a sudden burst of assurance (vv 58-66), in which the writer affirms his belief that God will vindicate him before his enemies. Only after he meditates on the nature of God's loving-kindness (vv 22-27) can he speak these words. The desperate isolation and separation from God expressed in verses 1-17 give way as he affirms

God's goodness. Assurance comes as he reflects on the nature and goodness of God.

The fourth lamentation emphasizes the fact that the judgment was well deserved. The author describes the various classes of the population (4:1-16) and indicates how each has been affected by Jerusalem's downfall. Verses 12-20 affirm that the judgment of God is a direct consequence of sin. This lamentation also becomes a joyous statement of hope (vv 21-22), as the writer affirms that God will punish Israel's enemies. Israel's sin will be forgiven, and the guilt of "the daughter of Edom" will be punished. The "daughter of Edom" undoubtedly stands for all the enemy nations. (Edom is used in Isaiah 63:1 in the same fashion.) This salvation of the nation of Judah will not take place until their guilt is atoned for. It occurs when God conquers the godless nations. This conquest of the nations is an event that takes place in the end time, according to numerous OT and NT passages. It represents the manifestation of God's total sovereignty over his creation.

The last chapter is a poignant prayer in which the author describes their sufferings and asks God to restore the fortunes of the people. It begins with a request to God, asking him to consider all that has befallen the people (5:1-18). Part of the ignominy of the captive Jews is that "slaves" rule over them (v 8). This is an apparent reference to the Babylonian captors, who themselves were subject to despotic rule for many decades. The author's perspective changes in verse 19, where he affirms that the Lord reigns forever. While Jerusalem, the earthly dwelling place of the Lord, has come to an end, the Lord's throne endures forever. Because his throne is everlasting, the author asks, "Why do you continue to forget us? Why have you forsaken us for so long? Restore us, O LORD, and bring us back to you again! Give us back the joys we once had! Or have you utterly rejected us? Are you angry with us still?" (5:20-22, NLT). The question is based on the belief that because God's reign is eternal, he cannot utterly forsake his people. He will restore his kingdom.

The book of Lamentations is neglected by many Christians. It deserves to be studied more. Its powerful statement concerning the blessings that may come from tragedy is a relevant message in any age, and it is one of the most powerful illustrations of the results of sin to be found in the OT. Its theology is clear and precise, painting a brilliant picture of God's faithfulness against the dark background of the collapse of the city of Zion.

See also Jeremiah (Person) #1; Jeremiah, Book of.

LAMP, LAMPSTAND Israelite lamps developed from those in general use among the Canaanites in the second millennium BC. Their shape was similar to a shell or saucer with a lip. Lamps of stone, metal, and shells were used, although the majority were made of pottery. A multitude of clay lamps, fashioned in a variety of designs, have been excavated in Palestine.

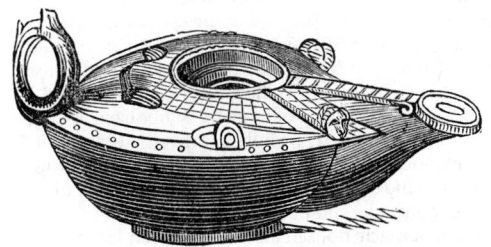

An Ancient Lamp

The clay bowl was fashioned first, and the rim was folded over to help contain the oil. A spout was pinched in place at one end, into which the wick would be placed. When the clay had dried, the lamp would be fired to a dull brown shade. Gradually a style with an increasingly sharply pinched lip was developed. The wick was generally made of flax (Is 42:3, KJV), although an old piece of linen cloth was sometimes used. Salt could be added to the wick for a brighter flame, and frequently extra wicks were used. This led to the development of multispouted lamps like those found at Tell Dotha from 1200 BC.

Olive oil provided the most common form of lamp fuel (Ex 27:20), and the average lamp could hold enough oil to burn through the night. Despite this, the housewife would have to get up several times to tend the wick and keep her precious lamp lit (Prv 31:18). Tongs were used for extinguishing the flame of a lamp in the tabernacle or temple (Ex 25:38; 37:23; Nm 4:9; 1 Kgs 7:49; Is 6:6). Since candles were not known in biblical times, the translation in the KJV is incorrect.

The saucer lamp, which would have spilled easily, was not suitable for night travel, so a torch was probably used for that purpose (Jgs 7:16-20). In addition, the wick of the open saucer lamp could easily have blown out at night.

Lamps were commonly found in burials along with food offerings. Because the lamp's flame was associated with life, lamps were frequently placed in tombs as a symbol of life being rekindled.

Although a more elaborate cup-and-saucer style of lamp was developed in which the flame came from the central area, the saucer lamp remained the most popular. The earliest Hellenistic lamp found in Palestine dates from 630 BC and already shows indications of the later covered model. During the sixth and fifth centuries BC, a flat-bottomed, saucer-style lamp was developed.

In the third century BC the more elaborate wheel-made, covered Greek style took precedence. These lamps were often simple in design, rounded, with a central hole for the oil and one in the small spout for the wick.

In the second century BC the wheel-made lamp was replaced by a molded ceramic lamp of finer design with a larger spout. Imported Egyptian lamps of this type have been found in southern Palestine. Multispouted lamps were probably used on festive occasions. From the same period comes the Hellenistic-influenced bronze lamp of a seated figure holding out a saucer lamp in his hands. At the end of the Hellenistic age the form of lamps deteriorated as the spouts became thick and squat.

Small, round wheel-made lamps of simple design were prevalent in the time of Christ; this would be the type of lamp used by the woman searching the house for her gold coin (Lk 15:8). With wicks trimmed, the lamps of the foolish virgins would probably have lasted approximately five hours, from dark until about midnight (Mt 25:1-12).

Jewish lamps were part of the religious symbolism of the home, probably dating back to the prohibition against lighting a fire on the Sabbath (Ex 35:3). References to light abound in Scripture. We read of the eye as a lamp (Mt 6:22-23; Lk 11:33-36) and of Christ as the Light of the World (Jn 8:12). We are warned to pay attention to teaching as to a light shining in the dark (Prv 6:23; 2 Pt 1:19). Both God and the spirit of man are symbolized as lamps (2 Sm 22:29; Prv 20:27), while in Proverbs 13:9 "lamp" is synonymous with the essence of life itself. Lamps, with or without stands, were also part of the Jewish ritual of death, mourning, and burial.

The tabernacle housed an ornate golden lampstand, or menorah. On either side three branches came out from the main central stem, and seven lamps could be lighted in the flower-shaped holders. The menorah from the Jerusalem temple is represented in relief on the Arch of Titus in Rome. This particular seven-branched lampstand resembles the ten that were part of the furnishings of Solomon's temple.

The seven-branched lampstand has been a particular symbol of the Jewish faith from the time of its earliest appearance on a coin in the reign of Antigonus (40–37 BC) up to the present day.

See also Menorah.

LANCE* Long, spearlike weapon. *See* Armor and Weapons (Javelin and Spear).

LAND The relationship of humans to the land is a prominent theme in the OT. In Genesis the earth with its dry land was created as a place for humans to dwell in fellowship with God. Humans were given the task of subduing the earth and ruling over the animal creation to satisfy their own needs and to bring glory to the Creator. Subsequent to humanity's fall into sin they suffered alienation not only from God and their fellow human beings but also from the land on which they lived. They were driven from the Garden of Eden, and the earth became cursed. They were forced to toil and sweat in order to subdue the earth and provide for their own subsistence because the harvest was choked by thorns and thistles.

After murdering his brother, Cain receives an individual intensification of the land curse as punishment. He is told that the earth will not yield its produce for him even with hard labor, forcing him to wander from one place to another. With no permanent homeland, Cain is denied the enjoyment of rest and prosperity. Because of sin, the important human aspiration for a sense of place is refused to Cain (Gn 4:12).

After the Flood, which was God's judgment on an exceedingly wicked human race, humans again provoked God's wrath; the construction of the Tower of Babel exalts human might apart from God. God intervenes to confuse the people's language and "scatter them abroad upon the face of the earth" (11:9). Genesis 1–11 is thus characterized by a sequence of narratives describing land loss with its attendant deprivations as a consequence of sin and rebellion against God.

Land and the Abrahamic Covenant In the time of Abraham, God intervened in human affairs to provide a special homeland for a select group of people who are set apart unto himself. It is here that the Promised Land theme is introduced in Scripture. God said to Abraham, "Leave your country, your relatives, and your father's house, and go to the land that I will show you. I will cause you to become the father of a great nation" (Gn 12:1-2, NLT). This promise to Abraham is enlarged upon in Genesis 12:7; 13:14-18; 15:7-21; 17:7-8. Abraham is told that the land of Canaan is to be the "everlasting possession" of his descendants (17:8).

The OT narrative then traces Abraham's line of descent through Isaac and Jacob, and tells of the migration of Jacob's family to Egypt, where during approximately four centuries they became a great and numerous people. During this period, the promise of possession of the land of Canaan is reiterated (Gn 28:15; 35:11-12; 46:3-4; 50:24) and held before Abraham's descendants as an integral feature of God's covenantal promises.

Land and the Mosaic Covenant When God called Moses to lead the Israelites out of Egypt, he associated Moses' task with the fulfillment of the promises to the patriarchs: "I have remembered my covenant with them. . . . I will make you my own special people, and I will be your God. . . . I will bring you into the land I swore to give to Abraham, Isaac, and Jacob. It will be your very own property" (Ex 6:5-8, NLT). Israel is to be delivered from Egypt for two reasons: first, in order to be established as God's covenant people at Mt Sinai, and second, in order to possess the land promised to their fathers. It is of utmost significance, however, that with the establishment of the Mosaic covenant the continued possession of the land is made dependent on obedience. Should Israel violate the covenantal obligations, it will bring upon itself the covenant curses, the most severe of which is banishment from the Promised Land (Lv 26:32-33). This does not mean that God will abandon his people and the land totally or forever, because God also promises that when the people repent, "then I will remember my covenant with Jacob . . . and I will remember the land" (Lv 26:42, NLT).

During the reign of King David, the promise of land received at least a provisional fulfillment. Although it is true that initial fulfillment occurred when Joshua entered the land, at that time the territory did not extend to the borders promised Abraham (Gn 15:18) and much of the land that was occupied still contained pockets of resistance by the former inhabitants (Jos 13:1-6; Jgs 1). It was not until the time of David that the land was fully possessed as originally promised (2 Sm 8; 1 Kgs 4:21, 24).

The responsibility of the king to observe the law, and the connection between covenantal obedience and possession of the land is again made clear when Solomon dedicates the temple (1 Kgs 9:4-9). Disobedience will bring not only expulsion from the land but also the destruction of the temple.

The subsequent history of the divided-kingdom era is for the most part a history of covenant abrogation, by the people as well as the kings. The Lord sent repeated warnings through the prophets that such disobedience could only lead to expulsion from the land. But their message fell on deaf ears (Is 6:11-12; Am 5:27; 7:17; Hos 9:17). The kings repeatedly proved themselves to be unworthy of the office.

As the people persisted in their evil way, Jeremiah announced that Nebuchadnezzar was to be the Lord's agent to drive them from the land (Jer 21:2; 22:25; 25:8-9; 27:6; 28:14; 29:21). However, Jeremiah and other prophets also looked beyond the exile to a future restoration and return to the land (Jer 32:6-25). Historically, this was accomplished under the rule of Cyrus the Great of Persia (538 BC) and is described in the books of Ezra and Nehemiah.

A difficulty of interpretation arises in finding an adequate fulfillment of certain prophecies of the return (cf. Ez 37; Am 9:14-15), which envision great prosperity and permanent possession of the land under the rule of a Davidic king. The intertestamental period does not seem to be a suitable fulfillment for these predictions.

Land and the New Covenant In the NT the land theme is much less prominent and seems mostly to be given a spiritual symbolism. The writer of Hebrews suggests that Abraham understood the land promise as something that pointed beyond a merely geographical fulfillment to a higher and far more satisfying heavenly home. Realizing the imperfection and transitory nature of all that this world offers, Abraham looked beyond the temporal fulfillment of the land promise for a city whose builder and maker is God (Heb 11:10), and he sought a "better country, that is, a heavenly one" (v 16). In the NT it appears that Israel's land promise and entrance into Canaan is to be understood as typifying something of

the future heavenly rest awaiting God's people (Heb 3–4). Perhaps this explains the OT stress on the connection between Israel's living in obedience to God's law and their possession of the land. When the Israelites do not typify a condition of holiness, they disqualify themselves from typifying a condition of blessedness, and thus are either denied access to or driven from the land. The NT indicates that it is God's purpose to prepare an eternal homeland for his people where the rule of the divine King is direct and just, where all things are subject to his will, where death and sin are abolished, and where the needs of his people are completely satisfied (Heb 11:13-16; Rv 21).

The OT land promises have been viewed by some as having only typical significance. In the light of Christ's incarnation any statement of Scripture concerning a future for the land is to be interpreted as fulfilled in a spiritual sense in the church. The church is now the new Israel and heir of the OT promises. Because God's kingdom is now a spiritual reality, it is considered a misunderstanding of the OT to expect yet future fulfillments of the OT prophecies of Israel's return to the land and an establishment of a period of peace and prosperity under the rule of Christ, the Son of David (cf. Is 2:1-5; 11:6-11; Ez 37; Am 9:14-15). To abide in Christ is considered an adequate fulfillment of the physical and geographical promises of the OT economy.

Others, while not denying typical significance for these OT realities, would suggest that the land promises are still operative in the physical and geographical categories in which they were given. It is pointed out that Paul argues in Romans 9–11 that there is yet a future for national Israel. In spite of Israel's history of disobedience, climaxing in the rejection of the Messiah, the election and calling of God is irrevocable, and Israel is yet to be reingrafted in the olive tree from which it had previously been cut off. Luke says that Jerusalem will be trodden down by the Gentiles until the times of the Gentiles are fulfilled (Lk 21:24), indicating that there is to be a future time when Jerusalem will again be possessed by the Jewish nation. This does not necessarily mean that one must view the present state of Israel as the direct fulfillment of the OT promises of return to the land. The OT indicates that the return will be occasioned by belief (Dt 30:1-16). The present return is in unbelief. At the same time, the remarkable preservation of the Jewish people over the centuries and the recent reestablishment of the nation are perhaps to be understood as anticipations or signs of a future and more complete realization of the OT land promises.

LANDMARK* Inscribed stone that denoted a boundary of fields, districts, or nations (Gn 31:51-52). In most Near Eastern countries the removal of a landmark was a serious crime; in Israel it was a violation of the law of Moses (Dt 19:14; 27:17). Removing landmarks (NLT "boundary markers") could be represented as changing ancient customs and laws (Prv 22:28; 23:10; cf. Jb 24:2).
See also Inscriptions.

LAODICEA, LAODICEANS* Largest of three cities and its residents in the broad valley area on the borders of Phrygia, Laodicea stood where the Lycus Valley joined the Meander. Significantly, the western entrance to the city was called the Ephesian Gate. The traveler left the city on the east by the Syrian Gate, for the great road ran to Antioch, where other roads branched to the Euphrates Valley, to Damascus, and to the northeast, where the desert trade routes ran toward the mountains, the Gobi, and the remote lands of the East.

Ancient Laodicean Water Pipe This water pipe brought cold water into Laodicea.

Laodicea was not a natural fortress. The low eminence, on which its Seleucid fortifications stood, might have presented a challenge to invaders, but Laodicea had a serious weakness. The water supply came principally via a vulnerable aqueduct from springs six miles (9.7 kilometers) to the north in the direction of Hierapolis. Fragments of the aqueduct can be seen today, the conduit badly narrowed by thick deposits of calcium carbonate. A place with its water so exposed could scarcely stand a determined siege. The double conduit was buried, but it was not a secret that could be kept.

With the Roman peace, Laodicea lost all of its frontier character. Under Rome, the city grew in commercial importance. Cicero traveled that way in 51 BC on his way to the provincial governorship of Cilicia, and the fact that he cashed drafts in Laodicea shows that the city had outgrown neighboring Colosse and was already a place of financial importance and wealth. One product was a glossy black wool, and the strain of long-haired black sheep bred for the trade were common until the 19th century. The wool was the basis of a textile industry centered in both Colosse and Laodicea. Various types of Laodicean garments are listed in Diocletian's price-fixing edict of AD 300, a copy of which recently came to light from neighboring Aphrodisias.

A Flock of Sheep with Some Goats in Laodicea

Laodicea had a medical school. The names of its physicians appear on coins as early as the principate of Augustus. It was probably the medical school of Laodicea that developed the Phrygian eye powder, famous in the ancient world. It is a fair guess that this was the dried mud of the Hierapolis thermal springs, which could be mixed with water to form a kaolin poultice, an effective remedy for inflammation.

It can be readily seen how these features of the city pro-

vided the pattern for the scornful imagery of Revelation 3:17-18: "You say, 'I am rich. I have everything I want. I don't need a thing!' And you don't realize that you are wretched and miserable and poor and blind and naked. I advise you to buy gold from me—gold that has been purified by fire. Then you will be rich. And also buy white garments so you will not be shamed by your nakedness. And buy ointment for your eyes so you will be able to see" (NLT). The black garments exported all over the Mediterranean world, the famous eye ointment, and the city's wealth form a basis for the writer's stinging reproaches.

See also Revelation, Book of.

LAPIS LAZULI* Semiprecious stone (silicate) known for its rich blue color. *See* Minerals and Metals; Stones, Precious.

LAPPIDOTH Husband of Deborah the prophetess (Jgs 4:4).

LAPWING* KJV translation for hoopoe, an unclean bird according to the Law, in Leviticus 11:19 and Deuteronomy 14:18. *See* Birds (Hoopoe).

LASCIVIOUSNESS* Extreme indulgence in sensual pleasures. Modern Bible translations commonly use the words "licentiousness," "debauchery," or "sensuality" instead. Lasciviousness occurs when the pursuit of pleasure is carried to the extreme of complete disregard for the integrity of others and for the environment.

Among biblical examples of lasciviousness are the people of Sodom and Gomorrah, who filled their lives with lawless deeds (2 Pt 2:7); the false teachers, who promised freedom but were themselves slaves of corruption (2 Pt 2:2, 18-19; compare Jude 4); and the Gentiles, who were greedy to practice every kind of uncleanness (Eph 4:19). The apostle Paul used "lasciviousness" to refer to sexual excesses (Rom 13:13; 2 Cor 12:21; Gal 5:19), which is likely the word's sense in Mark 7:22.

LASEA Seaport city on the island of Crete, about five miles (8 kilometers) east of Fair Havens. Paul's ship passed Lasea on its way to Italy (Acts 27:8). Little is known about Lasea; it is probably in ruins near Fair Havens. It may be the same as the Lasos that Pliny the Elder mentions in his *Natural History* (4.12.59). He says it was famous in the ancient world, for its region contained 100 cities and it was one of Crete's most important ports.

LASHA Place-name, otherwise unknown, used in an ancient description of the southern boundary of the territory occupied by the Canaanites (Gn 10:19). In this passage Lasha is associated with other cities usually located near the southern end of the Dead Sea.

LASHARON Town in Canaan conquered by Joshua (Jos 12:18). Another early manuscript reads "the king of Aphek in Sharon," perhaps indicating that Lasharon was not the name of a town but part of a phrase distinguishing this city from the other Apheks mentioned in the Bible.

LAST DAYS Expression used in Scripture to describe the final period of the world as we now know it. In the OT the last days are anticipated as the age of messianic fulfillment (see Is 2:2; Mi 4:1), and the NT writers regard themselves as living in the last days, the era of the gospel. Thus, for example, Peter explains that the events of the Day of Pentecost are the fulfillment of Joel 2:28: "In the last days,

God said, I will pour out my Spirit upon all people. Your sons and daughters will prophesy, your young men will see visions, and your old men will dream dreams. In those days I will pour out my Spirit upon all my servants, men and women alike, and they will prophesy" (Acts 2:17-18, NLT). The author of the letter to the Hebrews declares, "Long ago God spoke many times and in many ways to our ancestors through the prophets. But now in these final days, he has spoken to us through his Son" (Heb 1:1-2, NLT). The last days, then, are the days of evangelical blessing in which the benefits of the salvation procured by the perfect life, death, resurrection, and glorification of Jesus Christ are freely available throughout the world. They are the days of opportunity for unbelievers to repent and turn to God, and of responsibility for believers to proclaim the gospel message throughout the world.

The plural "last days" gives the impression of a period of some duration, and the correctness of this impression is confirmed by the fact that this final age has already lasted for many centuries. But in the perspective of eternity it is no more than a short time, and in every generation the end of this final age is always imminent, so much so that John speaks of it as "the last hour." To this the presence of antichrist even within the church of the apostolic period bears witness. "It is the last hour," John says, "and as you have heard that antichrist is coming, so now many antichrists have come; therefore we know that it is the last hour" (1 Jn 2:18, RSV). The end of these last days is always at hand, and one day it will certainly come; hence the need, insisted on by Christ, for constant vigilance, in view of the consideration that we know neither the day nor the hour of his return in majesty, the climactic event that will bring these last days to a close (Mt 24:44; 25:13).

This leads naturally to the further teaching that these last days will have their culmination in "the Day": the last days will be terminated by the last day. The use of the term "day" in the singular corresponds in the NT to the concept of the "Day of the Lord" familiar in the OT, where it is generally presented as an awful day of final judgment against the unrepentant, but with the implication that it is also the day of the salvation and vindication of God's people (see, e.g., Is 2:12-22; Ez 13:5; Jl 1:15; 2:1, 11; Am 5:18-24; Zep 1:7, 14). The climax of these last days, and therefore of all history, will be "the day of the Lord," which will overtake the world suddenly (1 Thes 5:2). This last of the last days will be the day of the last judgment for rejecters of the gospel, the purification of our present fallen world, the restoration of the created order, so that in the new heaven and the new earth all of God's purposes in creation are brought to fulfillment. Then, at the consummation of our redemption, at last fully conformed to our Redeemer's likeness, we will enter into the enjoyment of his eternal glory (Rom 8:19-25; 1 Jn 3:2; Rv 21:1-8).

Moreover, Christians are reminded by the apostle Paul that on this last day, which he calls simply "the Day," the quality of their building will be revealed—i.e., what they have done with their lives will be known. It is not that the security of their salvation in Christ is in any way at stake; rather, it is to measure whether they will meet him with confidence or with shame at his coming (cf. 1 Jn 2:28). "Each man's work will become manifest," Paul writes; "for the Day will disclose it. . . . If the work which any man has built on the foundation survives, he will receive a reward. If any man's work is burned up, he will suffer loss, though he himself will be saved" (1 Cor 3:13-15, RSV).

This last of the last days is followed by the everlasting day of Christ's kingdom when God will be all in all (1 Cor 15:28; Phil 3:20-21). The last day is also, accordingly, the day of triumph and resurrection, when Christ has promised to raise up everyone who believes in him (Jn 6:39-44,

54). The last days are like night compared with the glory that will be revealed at Christ's return, so that the end of these last days will also be the beginning of God's unending day (see Rom 13:11-12). The realization that we are in the last days and that the last day is approaching ought to have a dramatic effect on the quality and intensity of our living here and now (see 2 Pt 3:11-14).

The last days, then, are the days of the gospel of our Lord Jesus Christ. They are preliminary to and preparatory for the last day of final judgment of unbelievers and the dawn of eternal glory for believers. For Christ's faithful followers they are days of joy and blessing, but still days in which the fullness of redemption is awaited. They are days, too, of trial and affliction for the church of Christ. But God has given us the assurance of his Spirit in our hearts, the foretaste that guarantees the full banquet hereafter, the down payment that pledges the payment in full (Rom 8:23; 2 Cor 1:22; 5:5; Eph 1:14). Meanwhile, we should be assured with the apostle Paul that the sufferings of these last days are not worth comparing with the glory that is to be revealed to us (Rom 8:18). They are days, moreover, of responsibility and opportunity: responsibility because Christians are under orders to proclaim the gospel throughout the world (Mt 28:19-20; Acts 1:8) and all people everywhere are commanded by God to repent (Acts 17:30).

See also Day of the Lord; Second Coming of Christ.

LAST JUDGMENT* Time at the end of history when God will judge the deeds of all humankind. In their preaching concerning the Day of the Lord, various OT prophets anticipated the time when God would wage war against all wicked nations and establish his rule in the eternal city of Zion (Is 4:2; 11:10; Jer 50:3-32; Jl 2:1-3; 3:9-16; Am 5:18-20; 9:11; Zep 1:7-18). The NT writers continue this theme, restating it in the light of the words and work of Jesus. He has been appointed by God to be judge of the living and the dead (Acts 10:42; 17:31). Both believers and unbelievers must appear before the judgment seat of Christ, so that each one may receive good or evil, according to what they have done with their lives (2 Cor 5:10; cf. Rom 14:10).

The focus of God's judgment is human behavior. Those faithful to the covenant will prosper, but those who are disloyal will perish. The prophet Habakkuk identifies the righteous person as the one who is faithful (Hb 2:4). NT writers state that one will be judged according to whether or not his deeds are pleasing to God (2 Cor 5:10; Rv 20:12). However, the NT also states that no one has met the perfect standards of God. All have sinned and therefore deserve to be punished (Rom 3:9, 23). The issue to be determined at the time of judgment is not one's guilt but rather whether or not one has been acquitted. The NT speaks of this acquittal as justification and reconciliation (3:21-28; 5:1-21). The means of acquittal is the death and resurrection of Christ, for Jesus' act of righteousness leads to acquittal and life for all people (5:18). The one who trusts in Christ is not condemned (Jn 3:16-18) and can enter the Day of Judgment with confidence (1 Jn 4:17). His name is written in the Lamb's Book of Life (Rv 21:27). The unbeliever must face the Day of Judgment with no assistance. He will be judged by what is written in the books; that is, by what he has done (20:11-12).

See also Day of the Lord; Eschatology; Judgment; Judgment Seat; Last Days; Wrath of God.

LAST SUPPER* *See* Lord's Supper, The.

LAST TIMES *See* Last Days.

LATIN One of the primary languages of the Greco-Roman world. The supremacy of Rome, and the ramifications of its official relations with the people under its control, made the widespread use of Latin, Rome's vernacular, inevitable. This led to a considerable Latin contribution to *koine* (common) Greek. From the beginning

Old Latin Text of Genesis Genesis 5:4–6:2 from Oxyrhynchus, fifth century AD

of the Roman sway in Greece, Roman politics and commerce contributed a constantly increasing number of Latin words to Greek.

Traces of Latin in the NT are, therefore, not surprising. But Latin influence on NT Greek has left its mark mainly upon vocabulary, in the transliterated words and literally translated phrases. Latin was one of the three languages in which the inscription on the cross was written (Lk 23:38, KJV; Jn 19:20). Only in these two passages does the term "Latin" occur in the NT. Latin was the language of Roman law and court procedure. Greek might be allowed, but only by favor of the court. This explains why the superscription was written in Latin as well as Greek and Aramaic. Every educated Roman would understand Greek, but Latin was used as the official and military, as well as legal, language. This is reflected in the NT where Latin judicial and military terms occur, along with the names of coins, articles of apparel, utensils, and so on. For example, Latin words are used for farthing, denarius, centurion, colony, guard or watch, legion, towel, parchment, palace, assassin, napkin, and superscription. In addition, over 40 Latin names of persons, titles, and places occur in the NT. Among the better known are Agrippa, Claudius, Caesar, Felix, and Cornelius. Romans 16 reveals that Latin proper names were common among Christians.

In Mark's Gospel more Latin words, apart from proper names, occur than in other NT documents. This is to be expected if the Gospel were indeed written in Rome, but this is by no means established. The occurrence of numerous Latin words in this shortest of the four Gospels is not necessarily evidence of its Roman origin, because they are usually terms that the Roman government would make familiar in all parts of the empire. Also, Latinisms found in Mark's Gospel are found in the other three Gospels. For example, Matthew uses Latin words for mile, tribute, guard or watch, and to take counsel. Because of the close grammatical affinity between Latin and Greek, the influence of the former upon the grammar of the latter is more difficult to trace.

For over 100 years after the founding of the Christian church, Greek dominated over Latin in Christian circles. The providential spread of common Greek made it possible for the church to use one Bible: the Greek OT. To freedmen and slaves, Latin was a foreign, and largely unknown, language. This explains why the earliest traces of a Latin translation of any part of the Scriptures are relatively late.

See also Bible, Versions of the (Ancient).

LATTER DAYS *See* Last Days.

LATTER RAIN* Annual spring rainfall in Palestine from late March to early April, following the citrus harvest and preceding the wheat and barley harvests. The spring rains normally conclude the rainy season until the resumption of the fall (early) rains in October. In Scripture the occurrence or absence of the spring rains was often associated with God's favor or displeasure with Israel (Dt 11:13-17; Jb 29:23; Prv 16:15; Jer 3:3; Hos 6:3; Jl 2:23; Zec 10:1; Jas 5:7).

LAUGHTER Expression of a variey of emotions. Laughter can express overjoyed happiness when circumstances change for the better, as for the Jews in returning from exile (Ps 126:2). Such joy is sincerely but facilely offered to Job by one of his comforters (Jb 8:21). Laughter can be good-humored and friendly, to encourage others (29:24). There is "a time to cry and a time to laugh" (Eccl 3:4), but the Preacher had his doubts: life is no laughing matter, and sorrow can be a better teacher (2:2; 7:3). Yet it is good to be able not to take certain things seriously. The well-prepared housewife "laughs with no fear of the future" (Prv 31:25). Job is promised that war and famine would be nothing to worry about (Jb 5:22; cf. Hb 1:9).

Laughter can be a negative, derisive thing. We can laugh at people and laugh them to scorn. This element comes very much to the fore in the OT. Job and Jeremiah complain of being laughingstocks (Jb 12:4; Jer 20:7). The nation complains that their enemies laugh at their distress (Ps 80:6; cf. 2 Chr 30:10). Sometimes there is every justification. In Psalm 52:6 the righteous are promised the last laugh, at the expense of the wicked unbeliever who thinks that he can leave God out of his life. In Proverbs 1:26, personified Wisdom warns that she will laugh at the calamity of those who refuse to take her advice: it will serve them right. In this sense laughter is ascribed to God three times in the Psalter. He laughs at the nations plotting against his anointed King (Ps 2:4). He laughs at wicked people, knowing they are heading for disaster (37:13). He is invited to laugh at the psalmist's enemies (59:8). This divine laughter is a way of expressing that the truth will eventually prevail.

Laughter has a special place in the Abraham narratives. It is used in connection with the name of his son Isaac, which means "He laughs" or "May [God] smile [upon him]." Hebrew stories like to bring out the meaning of words, and so the human reaction to the birth of Isaac, the channel of God's patriarchal promises, is described in terms of laughter. It is theologically important because it tends to be contrasted with faith. In Genesis 17:17 laughter is Abraham's incredulous response to God's unrealistic promise of a son, in view of Sarah's elderliness. In Genesis 18:12 Sarah cannot smother her laughter as she eavesdrops—it seems so absurd that she will become pregnant in her 90s. But finally in Genesis 21:6, when the impossible becomes true, Sarah's laughter is a mark of God-given joy.

LAVER* Basin filled with water that the priests used to wash their hands and feet before entering the Holy Place and before returning to serve at the altar (Ex 30:17-21). In Solomon's temple a large laver called the "molten sea" was placed between the altar of burnt offerings in the courtyard and the entrance to the inner temple. This consisted of the large basin and the pedestal on which it sat (Ex 30:18); it was made of bronze or brass, melted and shaped from mirrors of highly polished metal given by Israelite women (38:8).

In Solomon's temple, in addition to the molten sea (1 Kgs 7:23), there were ten smaller lavers, five on the north and five on the south sides of the sanctuary (1 Kgs 7:38-39). Each held 40 baths (320–440 gallons, or 1,211.2–1,665.4 liters), one-fiftieth the capacity of the large laver. The lavishly decorated molten sea was used for the ablutions of the priests, while the ten lavers were no doubt used for the sacrifices (2 Chr 4:6). Later King Ahaz, possibly for religious or financial reasons, severed the lavers from their bases and the sea from its base, placing it on a stone pediment (2 Kgs 16:17). The prophet Jeremiah, during King Jehoiakim's reign, predicted that the molten sea and the bases would be carried into Babylon (Jer 27:19-22), which in fact happened, according to Jeremiah 52:17. No mention is made of the ten small lavers, which were perhaps already melted down and sold.

In Ezekiel's description of the temple to come (Ez 40–42), there is no mention of a laver or molten sea. The apostle John, however, in Revelation 4:6 and 15:2 mentions a "sea of glass," perhaps reminiscent of Solomon's molten sea.

See also Bronze Sea.

LAW, Biblical Concept of God's means of consecrating his people to himself. The nature and content of "law" may change, but the goal remains the same: maturity and conformity to the image of God.

PREVIEW
• Historical Context
• Law in the Old Testament
• Israelite Law and the Ancient Near East
• Old Testament Laws
• Purposes of the Law

Historical Context When man was created in God's image, he received glory, rule, and provision for his daily sustenance from the Creator-King (Gn 1:27-30). However, in his exalted status as ruler over God's creation on earth, man had to prove his loyalty to the Lord. For this purpose God set up a simple test: the tree of the knowledge of good and evil. Man was prohibited from eating the fruit of that tree (2:17). His disobedience marked him as unfit for fellowship with the great King. He was rebellious and by nature full of treachery, as the subsequent accounts of Cain (4:1-16), the generation of the Flood (6:1-13), Ham and Canaan (9:18-26; 10:6-20), and the Tower of Babel (11:1-9) demonstrate.

Yet in the midst of all this the Lord graciously called Abraham. He promised to bless him, his seed, and the families of the earth that would join in a common expression of faith (Gn 12:2-3; 17:4-7). Abraham responded to God in faith (15:6), willingly observed the ritual of circumcision as a sign of the covenant (17:10; cf. 21:4), and walked before God with integrity of heart (17:1). Abraham subsequently learned that God had sovereignly and graciously chosen him with the purpose that Abraham's family might distinguish itself from the nations "by doing righteousness and justice" (18:19). The Lord was pleased with his servant Abraham, who, though he had not received detailed laws, was a man of integrity. His heart was right with God, so that he willingly did what God commanded.

The father of faith was the father of the faithful; the Lord testified that Abraham "obeyed me and kept my requirements, my commands, my decrees and my laws" (Gn 26:5, NIV). His faith resulted in the fruits of righteousness (Jas 2:21-24).

However, Israel, blessed by the Lord in the increase of descendants, the exodus, the crossing of the Red Sea, and his presence, did not respond to him in faith. They murmured and complained at Mt Sinai, at Kadesh-barnea, and in the plains of Moab. They proved themselves to be a rebellious and stiff-necked people (Ex 32:9; 33:3, 5; 34:9; Dt 9:6, 13). Though they had shown their character, the Lord was faithful to Abraham by covenanting himself to them. Israel became his people, his royal priesthood, his holy nation (Ex 19:5-6; Dt 26:18-19). He gave Israel the Ten Commandments, the law, and the covenant, symbolized by the two tablets of the testimony (Ex 32:15-16). Even after Moses had broken them in anger because of the people's idolatrous worship of the golden calf, the Lord renewed his covenant by writing again the words of the covenant (34:28). On one hand, the context in which the law was given reflects God's grace and forbearance with Israel's sins (vv 6-7) and his determination to use Israel in the unfolding of his plan of redemption for the world. On the other hand, the context reflects Israel's immaturity and stubbornness.

Therefore, the law in the OT has positive and negative purposes.

Law in the Old Testament The OT has many words for God's law. The most general word is *Torah*, which signifies instruction of any kind: religious and secular, written and oral, divine and human. Law in Israel was God's law, mediated through Moses (Ex 20:19; Dt 5:23-27). Because Israel rejected the direct revelation of God's oracles, the law was mediated through Moses the servant of God (Jn 1:17).

Synonyms for law are, in various translations, word (cf. Ex 24:3; 34:27), judgment (cf. Ex 24:3), decree (cf. Nm 30:16; Dt 4:1), ordinance (cf. Nm 9:12, 14; Dt 6:2), command(ment) (cf. Dt 6:1, 25), statutes (Lv 3:17; 10:11), precepts (a Hebrew word used only in Psalms; cf. 119:4, 15, 27, 40, 45, 56, 63, 69, 78, 87, 93, 94, 100, 104, 110, 128, 134, 141, 159, 168, 173), stipulations, requirements, testimonies (cf. Dt 4:45; 6:20; 1 Kgs 2:3), precept (a Hebrew term not in the Pentateuch; cf. Ps 119:15), or simply the "way(s)" (cf. 1 Kgs 2:3; Pss 18:21; 25:9; 37:34).

These words form a semantic field, and it is far from easy to distinguish clearly among the various forms of laws. Generally "the words" pertain to the duties of man toward God, especially the Ten Commandments (Ex 20:1; 34:27). The "judgments" contain civil regulations and duties to one's fellows and to the social environment (21:1–23:9); these are often in the form of "if . . . then. . . ." In Leviticus and in cultic formulations the word "ordinances" has the technical sense of cultic regulations—the ceremonial laws. However, in other contexts, especially in a series of synonyms for law, it signifies any expectation or regulation. The "commandments" are those regulations given by a higher authority. Though the OT has many words for law, the connotation of one word is often indistinguishable from that of other words, especially in series such as "the decrees and laws" (Dt 4:1, 5; 5:1), "the commands, decrees and laws" (6:1), "walk in his ways, and keep his decrees and commands, his laws and requirements, as written in the Law of Moses" (1 Kgs 2:3, NIV).

The motivation for keeping the divine law lies in the acts and presence of the Lord. The prologue to the Decalogue reminds us of God's mighty acts: "I am the LORD your God, who brought you out of the land of Egypt, out of the house of bondage" (Ex 20:2, RSV). In the historic acts of Israel's redemption, revelation at Mt Sinai, and consecration of Israel to be his people, he involved himself with Israel as a "father." He adopted Israel to sonship and consecrated them; that is, he declared them holy (Ex 19:6; 31:13; Lv 20:8; 22:32; cf. Rom 9:4). Sometimes the two concepts of redemption and consecration are placed together, but whether they are or not, they are inseparable: "I am the LORD, who makes you holy" (Lv 22:32b, NIV). The ground of obedience can be stated simply by an appeal to God's name: "I am Yahweh" (cf. Lv 18:6, 21, 30; 19:10, 14, 16, 18, 28, 30-31, 34, 36-37). The requisite of practical holiness is also based on the experience of God's presence. The Lord commanded Israel to be holy because he is holy (Lv 11:44-45; 19:2). The "holy one of Israel" dwelt in the midst of his people (Ex 25:8; 29:45; Nm 5:3; 35:34).

How could rebellious Israel grasp what God required, if it were not by precise moral, social, civil, and cultic regulations? The Lord had observed that they did not have "the heart" to serve him as a covenant-loyal people (Dt 5:29). By Israel's very nature, it could not develop an adequate moral and cultic system to please God. Because of the people's hardness of heart, God had to reveal (i.e., "spell out") his will.

Israelite Law and the Ancient Near East Israel's law reflected the practices of its ancient Near Eastern context. Ancient Babylonian law codes (Eshnunna, Hammurabi) show similarities with the biblical codes. The similarities go beyond similarity of cases and include legal formulations (casuistic law). Israelite law is distinct in that it is divine law. Moses is the mediator and not the promulgator of the law, as was the practice of a king who, like Hammurabi, put into force a legal code. The Lord himself gave Israel its laws (cf. Dt 4:5-8). The laws in the ancient Near East dealt with the ordering of society. But Israel's laws were given to regulate every aspect of life: personal, familial, social, and cultic. The laws were to teach Israel to distinguish between holy and profane, between clean and unclean, and between just and unjust.

Old Testament Laws The legal corpus of the OT is not given in one book or in one section. Moreover, the laws reflect the development from the desert context (Exodus) to the context of the land (Deuteronomy). The OT legal material is complex, full of variations and duplications. It is found in Exodus (chs 20–24; 25–31), Leviticus, Numbers (chs 3–6; 8–10; 15; 18; 19; 28–30), and Deuteronomy (chs 5–26).

The Ten Commandments The commandments are simply designated as "the words" of God (Ex 20:1). They appear in Exodus 20:1-17 and in Deuteronomy 5:6-21, but minor variations and individual commandments occur in other contexts (e.g., Ex 34:14, 17, 21; Lv 19:1-8; Dt 27:15-16). As a part of the covenant, the commandments were first addressed to Israel; they now form the basis of morality in Christianity. The abiding relevance of the moral law is clear from the NT. Our Lord established his authority as interpreter of all the commandments (Mt 5:17-48; 12:1-14; 23:23-24). He summarized the law in terms of love for God and man (cf. Mt 22:37-40; Mk 12:28-34; Lk 10:27; cf. Rom 13:8-9; Gal 5:14). Since he is also the Lord of the Sabbath, the Sabbath cannot be divorced from the other commandments (Mt 12:8). The apostle Paul also upheld the law, as his "ethics of the Spirit" reflects an internalization of the law of God in the hearts of believers (cf. Rom 8:1-17; 12:1–15:13; 1 Cor 2:6-16; 5:1-8; 10:23–11:1; Gal 5:13-6:10; Eph 4:17–6:9; Phil 2:1-18; Col 3:1–4:6; 1 Thes 4:1-12; 5:12-24; 2 Thes 3:6-15; 1 Tm 6:3-10; Ti 3:1-11).

The commandments were written on both sides of the two tablets by the Lord (Ex 32:15-16). It is unclear whether the tablets were duplicate copies, how the commandments were divided, and how the commandments were numbered. They were kept in the ark of the covenant as a testimony to the covenant (40:20).

The Book of the Covenant (Ex 20:23–23:19) The purpose of the covenant code was to exemplify and to set into motion the legal machinery by which Israel as a nation could reflect God's concern for justice, love, peace, and the value of life. The laws in the Book of the Covenant are mainly of the casuistic type. They regulate life in an agricultural society with servants, donkeys, bulls, oxen, sheep, and fields of grain. The regulations pertain to relations with women (including widows), aliens, orphans; to legal concerns (liability, damages, ownership); as well as to religious obligations (altar, Sabbath). Often the law requires restitution, but restitution is not the rule when human life is involved (Ex 21:12-29; 22:2-3), especially when it involves one's family (21:15-17, 22-25). The penal code attached to the case laws makes clear the value of human life, which is protected by the *lex talionis* ("law of retaliation"). The *lex talionis* does not point to a lack of forgiveness under the OT but rather was intended to be a legal principle giving coherence and justice to a society. The Book of the Covenant explicates by means of principles and cases how Israel must live together as a nation embracing the law of God and applying it *justly* (without discrimination or twisting of rights), *lovingly* (with a concern for the parties involved), and *peaceably.*

The Priestly Law God's concern for holiness and purity comes to expression in the priestly laws (Ex 25–31; 35–40; Lv 1–27; Nm 4–10). The regulations pertain to the construction of the tabernacle, the consecration and ordination of priests, the offerings and sacrifices, rules of purity, the holy days, and vows.

The tabernacle was set in the middle of Israel's camp in the wilderness. It symbolized the presence of God with his people. The priests and Levites were encamped around the tabernacle to serve and protect God's holiness. All the tribes were situated around the tabernacle, and though the members of the tribes did not have access to all parts of the tabernacle, they had to be ritually clean to live in the camp. Anyone who was ritually defiled (Lv 13:46; Nm 5:1-3) or had sinned grievously was put outside the camp (Lv 24:10-23; Nm 15:32-36). This regulation even included objects that had become defiled (Lv 8:17; 9:11).

By means of prescribed offerings and sacrifices (Lv 1–7; 16; Nm 15:1-31; 28), God assured Israel, individually and corporately, of forgiveness when it had unwittingly sinned. The offerings and sacrifices concretely embodied the purpose of the offerer, whether forgiveness, dedication, or fellowship.

The priests and Levites taught the law of God (Dt 31:9-13), applied its regulations, and served in courts (17:8-13).

The Holiness Code (Lv 17–26) The holiness code forms a significant part of the book of Leviticus. Here Moses addressed all of Israel (cf. Lv 17:2; 18:2; 19:2; 20:2; 21:24; 23:2; 24:2; 25:2; 26:46; 27:2).

The laws are in the form of prohibitions and direct commands. They pertain to the place of sacrifice and the prohibition of eating meat with blood in it (ch 17); the prohibition of sexual relations with specified family members (ch 18); and regulations promoting godliness, holiness, justice, and love in society (ch 19). The penal code applies penalties to those who sin against the regulations (ch 20; 24:10-23). Chapters 21–24 apply the cultic regulations to the priests and to all Israelites. The institutions of the sabbatical year and the Year of Jubilee regulate the remission of debts, freedom of people, and restitution of land (ch 25).

The holiness code spells out the qualities required of a holy people: devotion to God (offerings, sacrifices, priests) and love for man (Lv 19:18b) demonstrated in concern for justice, peace, freedom, the value of human life, and a concern for the family. Many of the laws reflect the spirit of the Decalogue (ch 19).

Both promises and curses are attached to the holiness code (ch 26). The curses predict exile as a consequence of breaking the laws. But always underlying the laws and penalties is the grace of the Lord, who promises freely to forgive the people's sins and to renew the broken covenant (26:44-45).

Laws of Deuteronomy The Deuteronomic laws are explications and new applications of the Book of the Covenant in view of Israel's new historical situation. Israel was about to enter the Promised Land when Moses outlined to them the law of God (Dt 1:5). The impersonal element of the Book of the Covenant is here transformed by personal appeal. Moses strongly appeals to Israel to be loyal to the Lord, the covenant, and the covenantal stipulations. The Deuteronomic laws envision the people in the land of promise, with a central sanctuary (12:5, 11-18; 14:23; 15:20; 16:5-7, 16, 21; 17:8; 18:6; 26:2; 31:11) and with a king (17:14-20). The blessings and the curses motivate covenant loyalty (ch 28). However, Israel is also here assured that even if it breaks God's law, the Lord remains gracious and forgiving.

Purposes of the Law The law revealed at Mt Sinai was intended to lead Israel closer to God. Rebellious though they were, God used the law as his righteous instrument to teach, in a very specific way, what sin is (cf. Rom 5:20; 7:7-8) and how they should walk on a path that kept them undefiled by sin and holy to the Lord. The law was the teacher and the keeper of Israel (Gal 3:24). The detailed explications of the laws in all areas of life (work, society, family, cult, and nation) had an important place in God's dealings with Israel. Israel was a nation in a special land, with a theocratic government, and was in need of a legislative corpus. Moreover, Israel's condition at Mt Sinai was such that it could not receive direct revelation. The revelation had to be mediated through Moses. It had to be set forth in detail because Israel had no intuitive grasp of what the revelation of God's holiness, justice, righteousness, love, and forebearance required of them. They had adopted Egyptian ways and had to learn the divine will by revelation. However, Moses and the prophets emphasize that the purpose of the law is not strict adherence to the law for its own sake (legalism) or for a reward (Pharisaism). Keeping the law is an act of devotion to God, for the sake of God. Our Lord confirmed the purpose of the law: to establish a dynamic way of life in which one continually seeks God's kingdom and his righteousness (Mt 6:33).

The law of God is his means of sanctification. He consecrated Israel by an act of grace, and he required Israel to remain holy. Jesus confirmed those uses of the law whereby one may know his sinfulness and by which he may be driven to Christ. On the cross our Lord carried the penalties of the law, fulfilled in a greater way the tabernacle/temple presence of God, fulfilled the Father's expectations of atonement, and demonstrated the love of the Father. He, the Son and greater than Moses, gave the essence of the law in the summary of God's requirements: love of God and love of neighbor (Mt 23:23-24; Lk 11:42-44). Jesus taught that the purpose of obedience is not primarily to receive a reward but to serve as salt (Mt 5:13) and light (Mt 5:14-16; cf. Eph 4:17–5:20), and to bear fruit (Jn 15:1-17). The purpose of the law of God is the gradual transformation of the children of God to reflect the image of the Son (Rom 8:29; 2 Cor 3:18; Col 3:10), to be an imitation of the Father (Eph 5:1-2), and to be filled with the Spirit of God (Gal 5:18, 22-24). For this purpose Jesus gave us the Beatitudes and the Sermon on the Mount, which summarize the intent of the teaching of Moses and the prophets (Mt 5–7).

The purpose of the law is to transform regenerated believers into maturity. Spiritual maturity is not a privilege that was reserved for believers after Christ; OT saints also walked with God (Enoch, Gn 5:22-24; Noah, 6:9; Abraham, 17:1). These were mature men who lived with integrity in the presence of God (cf. Gn 17:1; Dt 18:13; Pss 15:1-2; 18:26; 101:2, 6; 119:80; Prv 11:5).

Maturity, or integrity, is that response to God whereby the believer no longer needs to live by individual stipulations or in fear of mistakes and sins of omission, but delights in doing the Lord's will (Pss 1:2; 112:1). Since the coming of Christ and Pentecost, the Holy Spirit has been poured out on every believer. He has come not only to internalize the law of God (Jer 31:33) but also to help us develop Christian maturity by giving the fruits of godliness in greater fullness (Gal 5:22-24). Whereas maturity and freedom were experienced by some OT saints, it is God's gift to all his children in Christ (Acts 2:39; 1 Cor 12:13). The purpose is still the same, "so that the man of God may be thoroughly equipped [mature] for every good work" (2 Tm 3:17, NIV), but the means to accomplish this and the status of the child of God is so much better since Pentecost.

See also Civil Law and Justice; Cleanness and Uncleanness, Regulations Concerning; Criminal Law and Punishment; Galatians, Letter to the; Hammurabi, Law Code of; Justification; Romans, Letter to the; Commandents, The Ten; Torah; Tradition.

LAWLESS ONE* Name Paul used for the Antichrist (2 Thes 2:8-9). *See* Antichrist.

LAWYER* Term used primarily by Luke in his Gospel in reference to those learned in the law of Moses. *See* Scribe.

LAYING ON OF HANDS *See* Hand.

LAZARUS
1. Lazarus the beggar. In one of Jesus' most familiar parables (Lk 16:19-31), he contrasted the earthly circumstances of a beggar named Lazarus with that of a nameless rich man. From the adjective for "rich" in the Latin Vulgate, the rich man came to be called in English "Dives." The rich man relished the luxury of his wealth, while he ignored an ulcerated blind beggar lying at his gate. Jesus said that Lazarus died and went to Abraham's bosom, while Dives suffered everlasting torment.

   The parable of Lazarus has been misinterpreted sometimes as a condemnation of wealth instead of a warning against enjoyment of wealth without regard for the poor. It teaches that decisions in the present life determine eternal destiny.

   In no other parable did Jesus identify a character by name. Some Bible students have therefore concluded that he was telling a true story. The name's symbolism, however, seems to account for its use, since Lazarus was cast in the role of one "whom God helped." In the Middle Ages the beggar Lazarus was venerated as the patron saint of lepers. Leper hospitals were called lazar-houses.
2. Lazarus of Bethany. Jesus performed the most spectacular of all his miracles (excluding his own resurrection) when he restored Lazarus of Bethany to life four days after death. Lazarus lived with his two sisters, Mary and Martha. They were among Jesus' most intimate friends (Jn 11:3-5, 36). On several occasions he visited in their home, which also served as his headquarters during his final week on earth (Mt 21:17; Lk 10:38-42; Jn 11:1–12:11). Lazarus was at the banquet in Jesus' honor when Mary anointed Jesus' feet with costly ointment (Jn 12:1-3).

   The raising of Lazarus, the climax of the signs in John's Gospel, receives the fullest treatment of Jesus' miracles. It produced three notable results: (1) many Jews in the vicinity of Jerusalem believed in Jesus (Jn 11:45) and some weeks later escorted him into the city (12:17-18); (2) the Jewish leaders, hardened in their rejection of Jesus, resolved that he must die (11:53); (3) those leaders also plotted Lazarus's death (12:10-11). The miracle not only showed Jesus' power over death but set the stage for his own resurrection.

LEAD Heavy, soft, blue-gray metal. *See* Minerals and Metals.

LEAH Laban's daughter, the wife of Jacob, and the older sister of Rachel.

After deceiving his father, Isaac, into giving him the blessing intended for Esau (Gn 27:5-40), Jacob left home and went to his uncle Laban (27:43; 28:2) in distant Mesopotamia, in order to find a wife (27:46–28:2) and escape the revenge of Esau, who had determined to kill him (27:41-42). Here he fell in love with his cousin Rachel and arranged with her father to marry her in exchange for seven years of work (29:17-18). When the time for the wedding feast came, Laban deceived Jacob in an apparent scheme to keep his services for seven more years; he gave Leah instead of Rachel to Jacob on the wedding night (vv 21-25). His lame excuse that custom required the giving of the older daughter in marriage before the younger (v 26) was hardly appropriate at that point and certainly should have been explained from the beginning. Leah is described as "weak-eyed," perhaps to be understood as "dull-eyed," in contrast with Rachel, who is described as "beautiful and lovely" (v 17).

Jacob's love for Rachel (Gn 29:20) induced him to agree to work for another seven years in order to receive her also as his wife. Because of the intense rivalry between the two sisters and Jacob's favoring of Rachel, the Lord blessed Leah with six sons and a daughter (Reuben, Simeon, Levi, Judah, Issachar, Zebulun, Dinah) before Rachel was given any children (29:31–30:22). This barrenness became a great burden for Rachel over the years. At one point she bargained with Leah for mandrakes, a plant believed to ensure conception, in exchange for conjugal rights. The result was to increase her sister's advantage, however, because Leah conceived and bore her fifth son, Issachar (30:14-17).

Leah was given the honor of being the mother of the two tribes that played the most significant roles in the history of the nation of Israel. The tribe of Levi became the tribe of the priesthood. The tribe of Judah became the tribe of royalty through which the promised seed (Gn 3:15; 12:2-3; 2 Sm 7:16; Mt 1:1) ultimately came in the person of Jesus Christ.

See also Jacob #1.

LEATHER Prepared animal hide, used extensively in Bible times for a wide variety of purposes. It was used as clothing in early times (Gn 3:21). At the beginning of the period of the prophets, their raiment, made from animal skins, became a means of identifying them (2 Kgs 1:8; Zec 13:4). Elijah's mantle (1 Kgs 19:13, 19; 2 Kgs 2:8, 13-14) is described in the Greek OT as sheepskin. Animal skins were also used to make shoes (Ez 16:10), girdles (Mt 3:4), and other articles of clothing (Lv 13:48).

Some household utensils were made of leather. The most common was the container for holding liquids, such as milk (Jgs 4:19), wine (Mk 2:22), and water (Gn 21:14). Oil, extracted from olives, then purified and refined, was also stored in skins, until required for cooking, toiletry, or medicinal purposes, or as fuel for lamps. In all probability leather was used for beds, chairs, and other household articles. There is no reference to leather being used to make tents, but animal skins were employed in the construction of the tabernacle (Ex 25:5; Nm 4:8). Clearly, the references are to tanned skins. Their use would ensure that the roof was waterproof.

The Bible is silent concerning the use of leather for making armor or weapons; however, it would be a natural choice for helmets and shields for defense, slings for offense, and quivers to hold arrows. Rubbing oil into the surface of shields, presumably to keep them from becoming brittle and therefore useless, is referred to in 2 Samuel 1:21 and Isaiah 21:5 and points to their being made of leather. A painting in the tomb of an Egyptian nobleman from about 1900 BC supplements the meager knowledge that the Bible provides concerning the use of leather in OT times. In the painting the men wear sandals and the women boots. A leather water bottle is strapped to one man's back. Another, an archer, carries a quiver on his back. The asses are carrying objects that have been identified as two pairs of goatskin bellows.

Leather was used extensively as writing material, but early on almost wholly in Egypt. There, parchment, also derived from animal hides, has a very ancient history. The difference between leather and parchment is that the former is tanned, whereas the latter is produced by treating the skins with solutions of lime, salt, or dyes, scraping off the hair on one side and the flesh on the other, stretching and drying them in a frame, then rubbing them with a pumice stone to produce smooth surfaces on both sides. The use of prepared skins for writing material was known before 2000 BC in Egypt, but according to Pliny, the term "parchment" did not come into use until about 160 BC in other areas.

No leather documents have been recovered from Assyria or Babylonia, probably because leather was used much less extensively there than elsewhere in the ancient East. Middle East literary allusions point to its having come into use there at a later period. The term "parchment" is not found before the Persian period, and the phrase "written on parchment" does not occur before the early years of the Seleucids (312–64 BC). Even then papyrus was the chief writing material.

Another leather product, vellum, is fine parchment made from calf, kid, lamb, or antelope skins. In Rome, from the first century BC through the second century AD, vellum was in restricted use. Not until the third and fourth centuries did vellum prevail. It was at this time that the celebrated Codex Vaticanus and the Codex Sinaiticus were produced. The whole Bible now could be gathered into a single codex, which was in the form of a modern book with folded sheets, whereas previously a set of from 30 to 40 rolls of papyrus would be required for the Bible. Vellum also allowed for the palimpsest, from which the original writing could be erased and written upon again.

In the OT leather or skins are not mentioned in connection with writing. Books in roll form are mentioned in Psalm 40:7, Jeremiah 36, and Ezekiel 2:9–3:3, but these were probably papyrus. Before the discovery of the Dead Sea Scrolls, the earliest reference to Jews using parchment or leather as writing material is found in Josephus, toward the end of the first century AD. However, we now know that around 100 BC parchment was used by Jews. The Talmud requires the Law to be written on skins of clean animals, a regulation that still stands for books to be used in the synagogue, but it is not certain that this points to an ancient tradition.

Some of the Dead Sea Scrolls were written on leather. For example, the great scroll of Isaiah, written about 100 BC, consists of 17 sheets sewn together into a length of almost 23 feet (7 meters). The autographs of the NT were probably written on papyrus. Certainly John wrote his second letter on papyrus (2 Jn 1:12) within the last quarter of the first century.

Tanning is not mentioned in the OT, but it is implied in Exodus 25:5 and Leviticus 13:48. The possible use of skins of unclean animals and the constant contact with dead bodies made tanning an unclean trade, and it was

forbidden in the city. However, the preparation of skins for parchment was considered an honorable calling.

See also Letter Writing, Ancient; Writing.

LEAVEN* Any substance that produces fermentation when added to dough. Leaven may signify the dough already infected by leaven, which was put into the flour so that the leaven could pass through the entire mass before baking, or it may refer to dough that had risen through the influence of the leaven. The early Hebrews apparently depended on a piece of leavened dough for transmission of the leaven; not until much later were the lees of wine used as yeast.

The ancient Israelites regularly ate leavened bread (Hos 7:4), but in the commemoration of the Passover they were forbidden to eat leavened bread or even to have it in their homes during the Passover season (Ex 13:7). This annual observance ensured that the people would not forget their hasty exodus from Egypt, when God's command gave no time for the preparation of leavened bread. The people were forced to carry with them their kneading troughs and the dough from which they baked unleavened cakes to sustain them as they journeyed (Ex 12:34-39; Dt 16:3).

Possibly because fermentation implied disintegration and corruption, leaven was excluded from all offerings placed on the altar to be sacrificed to God (Ex 23:18; 34:25). It was also not permitted in grain offerings (Lv 2:11; 6:17). Scripture does not tell us whether or not the showbread (or bread of the Presence) was unleavened, but the historian Josephus states that it was leavened (*Antiquities* 3.6.6).

Two exceptions to this rule should be noted. Leaven could be used in offerings that were to be eaten by the priests or others. Leavened bread could accompany the peace offering (Lv 7:13), and it was sacrificed at the Feast of Weeks (Pentecost) because it represented the ordinary daily food that God provided for his people (23:17).

The slow working of the leaven proved to be a problem during the agricultural stage of Hebrew development, especially during the first busy days of harvest. Unleavened dough, therefore, became increasingly common for ordinary baking. This practice was encouraged by the growth of the idea that leaven represented decay and corruption, as did other fermented things. This view excluded leaven as inconsistent with the concept of the perfect holiness of God. Plutarch was expressing a long-held belief current also among other peoples when he wrote, "Now leaven is itself the offspring of corruption and corrupts the mass of dough with which it has been mixed." The apostle Paul quotes a similar proverb in 1 Corinthians 5:6 and Galatians 5:9.

The significant thing about leaven is its power, which may symbolize either good or evil. Usually, though not always, leaven was a symbol of evil in rabbinic thought. Jesus referred to leaven in the adverse sense when he used the word to describe the corrupt doctrine of Pharisees and Sadducees (Mt 16:6, 11-12) and of Herod (Mk 8:15). The leaven of the Pharisees is elsewhere identified as hypocrisy (Lk 12:1; cf. Mt 23:28).

Paul applies the same concept to moral corruption, warning that "a little leaven leavens the whole lump" and admonishing his readers to clean out the old leaven, that is, the vestiges of their unregenerate lives, and to live the Christian life with the "unleavened bread of sincerity and truth" (1 Cor 5:6-8).

On the other hand, Christ uses the concept of leaven's effect upon dough in its good sense to provide his disciples with a brief but memorable parable (Mt 13:33;

Lk 13:20-21), wherein leaven illustrates the cumulative, pervasive influence of the kingdom of God on the world.

See also Bread; Feasts and Festivals of Israel; Food and Food Preparation; Unleavened Bread.

LEBANA*, LEBANAH Head of a family who returned to Jerusalem with Zerubbabel following the exile (Ezr 2:45; Neh 7:48).

LEBANON Region mentioned only in the OT, although its towns, including Tyre and Sidon, are named in the NT. The name Lebanon generally refers to the double range of mountains that commences near Tyre and runs northeast following the Mediterranean coast. The two Lebanon ranges are parallel to one another, Lebanon to the west and Anti-Lebanon to the east. The name Lebanon is derived from the Hebrew root l-b-n, meaning "white," which may reflect either the white limestone of the mountains or the snow that lay on the mountains for six months of the year (Jer 18:14).

Geography At the southern end the Lebanon ranges are a direct continuation of the hills of northern Galilee, with Mt Hermon (Sirion, Senir) very prominent in the Anti-Lebanon range, rising to 9,230 feet (2,813.3 meters). The two ranges are divided by a broad valley, the valley of Lebanon (Jos 11:17) or "the entrance of Hamath" (Nm 34:8), the modern Beqa'a.

In the south the Lebanon range is separated from the Galilee hills by a deep east-west gorge through which the Litani River flows, entering the Mediterranean just north of Tyre. In its upper courses it follows the Beqa'a Valley in a northeasterly direction almost to Baalbek. The Lebanon ridge, about 100 miles (160.9 kilometers) long, stretches north to the east-west valley of the Nahr el-Kebir and is marked by a series of peaks. In the south are Gebel Rihan, Tomat, and Gebel Niha (ranging from 5,350 feet to nearly 6,230 feet, or 1,636.7 to 1,898.9 meters, high) east of Sidon. In the center lie Gebel Baruk, Gebel Kuneiyiseh, and Gebel Sunnin (7,220 feet, 6,890 feet, and 8,530 feet high, or 2,200.7 meters, 2,100.1 meters, and 2,599.9 meters high, respectively) east of Beirut. Further north, to the east of Tripoli, lies Qurnet es-Sauda, which reaches 9,840 feet (2,999.2 meters), and Qurnet Aruba, about 7,320 feet (2,231.1 meters) high.

These high mountains trap the rain coming from the Mediterranean, providing both the mountain areas and the coastal strip below with good rainfall; beyond the mountains, the rainfall drops. It is along the coastal strip between the mountains and the sea that the Phoenicians flourished and towns like Tyre, Zarephath, Sidon, Berytus (Beirut), Byblos (Gebal), and Tripoli were established. The coastal area has a number of headlands that are extensions of the mountain range. The coastal road had to be cut around or through these spurs. A good example is the headland of Nahr el-Kelb, a little to the north of Beirut.

On the east side of the Lebanon range is the Beqa'a Valley. The Orontes River rises in the north of this valley and flows north to enter the Mediterranean north of ancient Ugarit. This whole valley region was known in classical literature as Coele-syria (Hollow Syria). It was the "breadbasket" of the Romans.

To the east of the Beqa'a Valley is the Anti-Lebanon range, in which the Barada River rises and flows east toward the fertile oasis of Damascus. Mt Hermon, in the southern part of the range, was known as Sirion by the Phoenicians and Senir by the Amorites (Dt 3:9).

Resources Lebanon was famous in antiquity for its rich forests of fir and cedar. The coastal areas, the Beqa'a Val-

ley, and the lower slopes of the mountains were suitable for olive trees, fruit trees, and vineyards, as well as some grain crops. One important product came from the sea: a mollusk of the gastropoda class from which a red or purple dye was obtained. The name "Phoenician" derived from the Greek *phoinos*, red-purple. Wool dyed purple was available in Ugarit about 1500 BC. The Phoenicians had a monopoly on this industry for centuries. The people of Israel, who used a great deal of purple dye in their tabernacle furnishings (Ex 26) and the garments of their priests (Ex 28:4-6; 39:1, 28-29), probably obtained the dye from the Phoenicians.

King Solomon had significant trading relations with Phoenicia. To build the temple in Jerusalem, cedar and fir were obtained from Hiram I of Tyre (1 Kgs 5:6, 9, 14; 7:2; 10:17, 21; 2 Chr 2:8, 16). Solomon paid for this timber in wheat and olive oil (1 Kgs 5:11). The trees were floated down by sea to a point in Solomon's domain and transported from there to Jerusalem. Cedar and fir trees from Lebanon and Anti-Lebanon provided ships for Tyre (Ez 27:5), sacred barges and furniture for Egypt, and timber for building the second temple in Jerusalem (Ezr 3:7).

From the ports of Lebanon, the Phoenicians traded with many lands. They mastered the art of shipbuilding, and their ships were used in peace and in war. A vivid picture of the trading activities of traders from Tyre, Sidon, Gebal, and Arvad is given in Ezekiel 27, where the extent and nature of their trade is given in considerable detail.

History The area became of interest to the Egyptians during the fourth dynasty (c. 2600 BC) when Pharaoh Snofru acquired 40 shiploads of cedar from Lebanon. Byblos fell under Egyptian influence during the 12th dynasty (c. 1980–1800 BC) and Egyptians gave golden ornaments in exchange for cedar. During the 18th dynasty (c. 1552–1306 BC), Egypt conquered Syria, and the records speak regularly of cedar being taken as tribute. Later an envoy of Ramses XI named Wenamon paid dearly for the cedar (c. 1100 BC).

When Egyptian power waned, the Assyrians controlled the area and took vast quantities of cedar as tribute from the days of Tiglath-pileser I (c. 1100 BC) onward. Nebuchadnezzar and the Babylonian nation likewise controlled Lebanon and took away large quantities of cedar to build temples and palaces. The spoiling of Lebanon's forests was spoken of by Isaiah (Is 14:8) and Habakkuk (Hb 2:17). In later centuries Lebanon passed successively under the domination of Persians, Greeks, and Romans.

In NT times the towns of Tyre and Sidon are generally coupled together (Mt 15:21; Mk 3:8; 7:24, 31; Lk 6:17; 10:13-14; Acts 12:20), though sometimes they are referred to alone (Acts 21:3, 7). A Greek woman who was a Syro-Phoenician is referred to in Mark 7:26. Jesus preached in these areas during his ministry. In biblical poetry the tall cedars of Lebanon were a symbol of majesty and strength (Jgs 9:15; 2 Kgs 14:9; Pss 92:12; 104:16; Is 35:2; 60:13). They were also a symbol of earthly pride that would be broken before the wrath of God one day (Ps 29:5; Is 2:13; 10:34; Jer 22:6; Ez 31:3).

LEBAOTH Town in the Negev of Judah (Jos 15:32) occupied by the tribe of Simeon under the name Beth-lebaoth (19:6). The parallel list of Simeonite towns has Beth-biri in this place (1 Chr 4:31). The element *beth*, "house of," is undoubtedly original, denoting a place of worship of the goddess of the lions *(lebaoth)*;

Beth-biri might be another place or just a textual variant typical of the list in 1 Chronicles.

LEBBAEUS* Alternate name given to Thaddaeus, one of the 12 disciples, in Matthew 10:3 (KJV only). Most versions omit the name, which comes from a textual variant followed by the KJV translators. *See* Thaddaeus, The Apostle.

LEBO-HAMATH Town on the Orontes River below Riblah; perhaps the correct reading for the phrase "entrance of Hamath" in numerous OT passages (Nm 34:8; 1 Kgs 8:65; 2 Kgs 14:25; Ez 47:15). *See* Hamath #1.

LEBONAH Town located between Shiloh and Shechem (Jgs 21:19). It is usually identified with modern Lubban, about three miles (4.8 kilometers) northwest of Shiloh.

LECAH Either a person, descendant of the Judahite Er, or an otherwise unknown place in Judah settled by Er, depending on one's understanding of "father" (1 Chr 4:21).

LEECH Blood-sucking, segmented worm, mentioned only in Proverbs 30:15. *See* Animals.

LEEK Garden herb (Nm 11:5). *See* Plants (Onion).

LEES* Thick substance, or dregs, that forms at the bottom of a wine container as fermentation takes place.

The term appears in three different situations in the OT, each apparently representing a particular phase of fermentation. Isaiah 25:6 refers to wine at its best ("well-aged," NLT) after a proper fermentation: strong, clear, and filtered. "Wines on the lees" in context refers to the blessings of peace and plenty that God's people will enjoy in the age to come. Jeremiah 48:11 and Zephaniah 1:12 refer to wine that is overfermented, having become syrupy in appearance and weak and bland in taste. Figuratively, the term applies to the Jews and Moabites about to receive impending judgment for having allowed themselves to be lulled into an ungodly indolent and indifferent life style. Psalm 75:8 uses "dregs" to refer to the bitter sediments and grounds left after the wine has been poured out, which the ungodly will be forced to consume.

LEGION A unit of the Roman army. In NT times the standard size of the legion was 6,000 men, to which some 120 cavalry were added.

Because it represented a large body of men, the word "legion" came to be used symbolically for an indefinitely large number; this use occurs four times in the NT. In the story about the demoniac in the country of the Gerasenes, Jesus asked the man, "What is your name?" and the reply was, "My name is Legion, for we are many" (Mk 5:9, 15; Lk 8:30; cf. Mt 12:45; Lk 8:2, which speak of a number of demons possessing a single individual).

Another use of the word is in Matthew 26:53, where at the time of Jesus' arrest one of those with him drew his sword to defend his Master. Jesus forbade such action, saying, "Don't you realize that I could ask my Father for thousands [legions] of angels to protect us, and he would send them instantly?" (NLT; see mg). Thus he spoke of the vast number of angels that could be summoned to his aid.

The word "legion" is never used in the NT in its military sense, but either of the spiritual powers of evil that oppose men (cf. Eph 6:12) or of the spiritual powers that can be summoned to their aid (cf. Heb 1:14).

See also Warfare.

LEHABIM*, LEHABITES One of several peoples associated with Egypt (Gn 10:13; 1 Chr 1:11). The Lehabim are either an unidentified people near Egypt or—as many scholars hold, probably correctly—identical with the Lubim (Libyans). The latter are often seen in the Bible as fighting in alliance with Egypt (Dn 11:43; Na 3:9), sometimes against Israel, as in the time of Rehoboam (2 Chr 12:3) and Asa (2 Chr 16:8).

LEHI Place in Judah where the Philistines assembled to capture Samson (Jgs 15:9). The place was evidently in the hills, and after Samson's victory (using a jawbone of an ass for a weapon), it was called "the height of the jawbone" ("Jawbone Hill," NLT), that is, Ramath-lehi (v 17). It was apparently near a spring in a crater or depression (v 19). An adjacent cliff was called Etam (v 11). Other than somewhere in the hills behind Beth-shemesh, there is no hint of where to locate (Ramath-) Lehi.

LEMUEL King credited with writing Proverbs 31:1-9. In these verses he sets forth teachings given him by his mother on good government, sexual relations, and wine. Although he has been identified with Solomon, most modern interpreters reject this identification.

LENTILS Pealike vegetable; specifically, the seeds of the lentil plant. *See* Food and Food Preparation; Plants.

LEOPARD *See* Animals.

LEPER, LEPROSY One afflicted with a chronic infectious disease caused by *Mycobacterium leprae*, a bacterium similar to the tuberculosis bacillus. The disease is manifested by changes in the skin, mucous membranes, and peripheral nerves. In the skin there are often patches of depigmentation but rarely a total loss of pigment, so a pure white patch of skin is definitely not characteristic of leprosy. Loss of sensation to touch and temperature is frequently associated with the depigmented patches. Thickening of the skin and nodule formation cause the lionlike facial appearance commonly associated with leprosy. Peripheral nerve involvement may cause paralysis of a hand, leg, or face, or it may cause loss of sensation so complete that serious injury or ulceration to an extremity may occur without the afflicted person knowing it. The eyes, ears, and nose are also frequently involved. An effective, though prolonged, treatment has been developed, and sometimes spontaneous arrest may occur. The disease is spread through prolonged contact with an individual having leprosy. Children are more susceptible than adults, but in any case the transmissibility is low.

The early history of leprosy is shrouded in uncertainty. Possible references to leprosy have been cited in ancient Egyptian, Babylonian, and Indian writings, but authorities disagree over whether the records refer to modern leprosy. The ambiguity in these early records is significant because it limits the help they might give toward our understanding of the meaning of "leprosy" in the OT.

In the Old Testament Leviticus 13 and 14 contain the most details about what is called "leprosy" in the Scriptures (in traditional versions such as the KJV and RSV). However, careful study of the descriptions of the disease given in these passages strongly suggests that what is now called leprosy is not the skin disease described in Leviticus. If a priest today used the criteria given in these verses, he would probably declare many leprosy patients unclean, but he would also pronounce unclean many individuals with a variety of other skin conditions. The disease we call leprosy (or Hansen's disease) does not fit the description given in Leviticus. The white hairs referred to so frequently in these verses are not typical of leprosy and may be found in many skin diseases. A white patch of skin is not characteristic of leprosy, nor is the scalp ordinarily affected. A 7- to 14-day period is usually inadequate to observe changes in the disease. If modern leprosy is being described in these verses, it seems strange that the more obvious characteristics of the disease are not mentioned. The bacillus of leprosy has defied attempts by bacteriologists to cultivate it, so leprosy of garments or houses is most unlikely to occur. Therefore, biblical leprosy is not synonymous with modern leprosy. Consequently, modern versions do not use the word "leprosy" in Leviticus 13 and 14; rather, it is rendered as "contagious skin disease" in the NLT and "infectious skin disease" in the NIV.

In the New Testament In the NT there is no description of the disease referred to as leprosy, so again we cannot be certain whether it is the modern disease or not. Modern leprosy was known to the people of that day, but it is doubtful whether they were always able to accurately distinguish it from other skin conditions. The Greek word translated "leprosy" in the NT basically means "scaly." The Greeks used it to designate psoriasis-like skin conditions, and they referred to leprosy by the word we translate as "elephantiasis," a word not found in the NT. Confusion concerning the use of the word "leprosy" extends even to the Middle Ages, leaving historians uncertain at times concerning the historical spread of the disease. When we read in the NT that Christ cleansed lepers, we know only that he healed chronic skin conditions considered to be defiling.

The attitude of Jesus toward those afflicted with leprosy was in marked contrast to that of the rabbis of his day. One rabbi would not eat an egg purchased in a street where there was someone with leprosy. Another rabbi threw stones at lepers in order to keep them away. But Jesus touched a man with leprosy, thereby demonstrating his power to overcome uncleanness as represented by leprosy (Mt 8:3; Mk 1:41-42; Lk 5:12-13).

See also Medicine and Medical Practice; Plague.

LESHEM* Alternate name for Laish, the early name for the city of Dan, in Joshua 19:47 (NLT mg). *See* Dan (Place) #1.

LETHECH* Dry measure equaling about two to three measures. *See* Weights and Measures.

LETTER OF JEREMIAH The Letter of Jeremiah is a book accepted as part of the Deuterocanonical works. It was originally written in Hebrew or Aramaic by an unknown Jewish author. The work is no longer extant in the original but has come down to us in the Greek Septuagint. The book cannot be clearly dated; most scholars agree that the Letter was composed between the third and first centuries BC.

The Letter aims at demonstrating the folly of idolatry. Its claim to have been written by Jeremiah to the captives in the Babylonian exile is spurious. Rather, it was written by a pious Jew for Jews who, living in the Diaspora, were challenged by the dangers of idolatry—"So take care not to become at all like the foreigners. . . . But say in your heart, 'It is thou, O Lord, whom we must worship' " (Letter of Jeremiah 6:5-6). Ridicule is heaped on the gods made by craftsmen out of raw materials. The idols tarnish and may easily be burned up in a fire. They collect dust, are blackened by the smoke of the temple, and are a resting place

for animals. They cannot speak and are impotent to protect themselves against offenders and pillagers. They cannot see the lamps lighted in the temples. The idols cannot receive the sacrifices brought by the devotees and are also not in a position to bless or help those who believe in them. Since the idols are frauds, fashioned by craftsmen, they are incapable of providing people's needs and of delegating divine authority to kings. The Letter concludes with several comparisons: the idol's protection is likened to a scarecrow in a plot of cucumbers and to a thornbush in a garden, or to a corpse cast out in the dark (vv 70-71).

The Letter was printed as chapter 6 of the book of Baruch in the Latin Vulgate. *See also* Baruch, Book of.

LETTER WRITING*, Ancient A communication, especially from a king or high official, usually containing commands, promulgations, or reports. There are letters extant from Arad-Nana, the royal physician, to his master Ashurbanipal on the matter of the monarch's spondylitis and a young prince's eye trouble. The famous Amarna letters are reports and appeals from petty subject princes in Palestine disturbed over the weakness of Pharaoh Akhnaton's foreign policy in the area. There is a tantalizing letter from Tutankhamen's widow to a Hittite king on the subject of a marriage arrangement.

Examples of OT letters are David's deadly letter to Joab about Uriah (2 Sm 11:14-15), Jezebel's equally evil letter over Ahab's forged signature to the elders of Jezreel (1 Kgs 21:8-9), and the Syrian king's letter to the king of Israel about Naaman's leprosy (2 Kgs 5:5-7). All these are reported in the OT record without the customary greetings and the polite forms of address. In Ezra (Ezr 4:11-23; 5:7-17; 7:11-26), Nehemiah (Neh 6:5-7), and Jeremiah, correspondence appears that purports to be the full text. Commonly there is paraphrase, abbreviation, or mere report of content (Neh 2:8; Est 9:20-31).

Official communications in letter form like those noted in the OT are found in the Egyptian papyri. For example, there is the letter of Claudius sent in AD 42 to the turbulent Alexandrians about the Jewish problem in that city. A circular letter of the early second century AD from the governor of Egypt about the approaching census, and highly relevant to the story of the Nativity, is known. The letters of Cicero provide invaluable information on the stormy period in which senatorial rule ended and the Roman Empire was established. The letters of Pliny show Roman society at its best at the turn of the first century of the Christian era, when the writer was governor of Bithynia, and they give much information about the first clash between the state and the church.

Ancient correspondence throws vivid light on common life and the mundane occupations of ordinary people in Greco-Roman times and the early Christian centuries in a manner only to be paralleled in the documents of the NT. It provides background, illustration, comment, and sometimes direct historical evidence—as, for example, the letter file of the leader of the second rebellion of the Jews (AD 132–35), Bar-Kochba. A cache of Bar-Kochba's letters and campaign documents was discovered in a cave by the Dead Sea. In one letter he orders, "Whatever Elisha says, do." Another orders the arrest of Tahnun ben Ishmael and the confiscation of his wheat. Another calls for punishment of some who had repaired their homes in defiance of some scorched-earth policy.

Paul observed, with some care, the forms of letter writing common in his day. There is an opening word of salutation, followed by thanksgiving and prayer for the person or company addressed. Then comes the special subject of communication, greetings to friends, and perhaps a closing word of prayer. Here is a second-century letter that shows strikingly the Pauline style in brief:

> Ammonous to her sweetest father, greeting. When I received your letter and recognized that by the will of the gods you were preserved, I rejoiced greatly. And as at the same time an opportunity here presented itself, I am writing you this letter being anxious to pay my respects. Attend as quickly as possible to the matters that are pressing. Whatever the little one asks shall be done. If the bearer of this letter hands over a small basket to you, it is I who sent it. All your friends greet you by name. Celer greets you and all who are with him. I pray for your health.

In subject matter Paul ranges from delicate irony over Corinthian pretensions to stern rebuke for heresy, and from news of friends to some precious books and the warm cloak he left at Troas.

The NT letters continue and adapt a mode of didactic correspondence that can be traced back to Plato and Aristotle, except that the NT writers address themselves to groups or communities (Romans, Corinthians, Galatians, Philippians, Ephesians, Colossians, Thessalonians, Hebrews), to the church at large (the letters of Peter, Jude, James, and John's first epistle), or to individuals or a specific Christian community. The apostolic letter recorded in Acts 15 may have inspired this practice. Revelation 2 and 3 are genuine letters to seven churches on John's Asian circuit.

See also Lachish Letters; Writing.

LETUSHIM*, LETUSHITES
Tribe founded by the second of Dedan's three sons, a descendant of Abraham and Keturah through Jokshan's line (Gn 25:3). Some suggest that the tribe eventually settled in northern Arabia.

LEUMMIM*, LEUMMITES
Tribe founded by the third of Dedan's three sons, a descendant of Abraham and Keturah through Jokshan's line (Gn 25:3). The tribe probably settled in northern Arabia.

LEVI (Person)
1. Jacob's third son by Leah (Gn 29:34). The etymology of the name is uncertain. Levi's name is associated with the tragedy at Shechem, where the male inhabitants of the city were ruthlessly murdered when Levi and Simeon sought to avenge the violation of their sister Dinah by Shechem the Hivite. Jacob condemned the act and before his death pronounced a judgment on Levi's behavior (49:5-7). According to these words, Levi's descendants were to be dispersed among the tribes.

    The tribe of Levi was composed of the descendants of Levi's three sons: Gershon (Gershom), Kohath, and Merari. Moses, Aaron, and Miriam traced their genealogy to Kohath (Ex 6:16). The Levites remained faithful to Yahweh at the occasion of the golden calf by Mt Horeb. They were rewarded with the right to special service in and around the tabernacle (ch 32) and later in the temple.

    See also Levi, Tribe of.
2. Tax collector in Capernaum (Mk 2:14); one of the 12 disciples who was also named Matthew (Mk 2:14; Lk 5:27; cf. Mt 9:9). *See* Matthew (Person).
3. Son of Melki and ancestor of Jesus (Lk 3:24). *See* Genealogy of Jesus Christ.
4. Son of Simeon and ancestor of Jesus (Lk 3:29). *See* Genealogy of Jesus Christ.

LEVI, Tribe of
Israelite tribe taking its name from the third son of Leah and Jacob (Gn 29:34). The meaning of the name ("attached") is a pun on Leah's position as an unloved wife: now that she has borne three sons to Jacob, surely he will be "attached" to her. Elsewhere, by a similar pun, the tribe of Levi is described as "attached" to Aaron (Nm 18:2).

Levi appears with Simeon at the treacherous slaughter of the inhabitants of Canaanite Shechem (Gn 34:25-29). This brings Jacob's rebuke at the time (v 30) and his deathbed curse (49:5-7), foretelling that the descendants of Levi and Simeon will be scattered throughout Israel. This does not seem a likely background for God's priestly tribe, but so it proved to be, for it was as a priestly tribe that Levi was scattered through Israel, while Simeon merely melted into the desert south of Judah.

At first Levi was apparently a "secular" tribe like any other. True, Moses and Aaron were of Levi (Ex 2:1), but no stress is laid on this. Levi's later position was God's reward for its costly faithfulness when Israel rebelled against God (32:25-29); this inaugurated the "covenant with Levi" (Nm 18:19). Henceforth the tribe of Levi would be accepted by God instead of Israel's firstborn sons, who belonged to him by the law of "firstfruits" (3:11-13). Levi, as a tribe, could therefore own no tribal territory: God himself was their inheritance (18:20). However, they were given 48 villages, with their pasturelands, in which to live (Jos 21:1-42). These included the six cities of refuge (ch 20).

Since Levi could not amass wealth, the tribe was to be supported by gifts and tithes (Nm 18:21); like the widow, orphan, and stranger, they were commended to the care of God's people (Dt 14:29). Since they were God's tribe, Joab was unwilling to include Levi in David's census (1 Chr 21:6; cf. Nm 1:49). Naturally, Levi did not serve in war except in a religious capacity (2 Chr 20:21). Their service pertained to the meeting tent (Nm 1:50-53) and later the temple (1 Chr 23:25-32). Within Levi the Bible makes a clear distinction between (1) the high priest (sometimes merely called "the priest," 1 Sm 1:9), who came from one branch of Aaron's family; (2) the rest of the priests, also of particular families; and (3) a mass of subordinate Levites, who had lesser tasks. In early days they packed and moved the portable tent of meeting (Nm 1:50-51), as well as did other duties; in later days they served as porters and choristers (1 Chr 16:42). The duties of Levi are summarized in Deuteronomy 33:8-11, where oracular guidance and theological instruction are just as important as their priestly duties. It is therefore no surprise that Jehoshaphat later used them as teachers of law (2 Chr 17:7-9). Nevertheless, the ordinary Israelite thought of them primarily as priestly (Jgs 17:13).

Later references to the lasting covenant with Levi are found in Jeremiah 33:20-26 and Malachi 3:3-4. Members of the tribe returned from the exile (Ezr 2:36-42), apparently more coming from the priestly than the wider Levitical section. Barnabas, in NT days, belonged to the tribe of Levi (Acts 4:36). Indeed, among modern Jews, wherever the surname Levy is found, a member of the tribe probably lives on.

See also Priests and Levites.

LEVIATHAN
Great sea monster or large aquatic reptile (Jb 3:8; Pss 74:14; 104:26; Is 27:1). *See* Animals.

LEVIRATE MARRIAGE*
Israelite custom in which a man, upon the death of his brother, marries his brother's widow and raises up children for his brother. *See* Marriage, Marriage Customs.

LEVITES
See Levi (Person) #1; Levi, Tribe of; Priests and Levites.

LEVITICAL CITIES
Special areas set aside for the tribe of Levi in place of a regular territorial inheritance

(Nm 18:20-24; 26:62; Dt 10:9; 18:1-2; Jos 18:7). The Levites were allotted 48 cities, including the six cities of refuge (Nm 35:6-7). Each town and a limited zone around it was for the Levites (vv 3-5); their property enjoyed a special status with regard to the laws of redemption (Lv 25:32-34).

Two lists of the Levitical cities are given (Jos 21; 1 Chr 6:54-81). Thirteen towns were for the priests (Jos 21:4), including the six cities of refuge. In spite of some variation between the two lists, it seems clear that they go back to one original. The distribution of the Levitical towns tells much about their purpose. They were distributed among the 12 tribes but not usually placed at the tribal centers. Those in Judah and Simeon were actually in the southern hill country, the area where the satellite clans of the Calebites and the Kenizzites had settled. Those in Benjamin were grouped along the southern half of that tribe's inheritance, the part later attached to Judah; the family of Saul was located there. Levitical towns were placed in border areas where garrisons were required—for example, on the eastern desert fringes in Reuben and facing Philistia in Dan. Other key territories were in the plains where Asher, Manasseh, and other Galilean tribes had originally failed to conquer the Canaanite cities (Jgs 1:27, 31). Thus, the Levites were assigned places where the special task of controlling strategic areas was necessary. Many of the towns were not taken during the initial conquest and only came under Israelite control in the reign of David.

Though the Levites were not the exclusive residents of any one city (they shared them with other Israelites), they were posted there for specific duties. They tended to the work of the Lord and the service of the king (1 Chr 26:30-32). Collecting tithes (Nm 18:21; Dt 14:28), handling legal and judicial matters (1 Chr 26:29; 2 Chr 17:8; 19:8-10), military garrison duties (1 Chr 26:1-19), and managing the storehouses (v 22) were all Levitical responsibilities. Though they served by rotation in the capital (27:1), they also had similar duties the year round in their home districts (26:29-32). Their loyalty to the house of David caused them to lose their status in the northern kingdom, so most of them joined Judah when the kingdom was split (2 Chr 11:13-14).

See also Cities of Refuge.

LEVITICUS, Book of
Third book of the OT, largely concerned with the duties of the Levitical priests.

PREVIEW
• Author
• Date
• Background
• Purpose and Theology
• Content

Author A traditional alternative title of Leviticus is the Third Book of Moses, which gives proper credit to the man who most deserves to be called its author. For though the book never says that Moses wrote down any of the material, it repeatedly states that God revealed the contents of Leviticus to Moses. It may be that Leviticus was not put into writing as soon as it was revealed, but there is little to commend the common critical view that it was composed nearly a thousand years after Moses. The spelling and grammar of Leviticus was, like other books of the OT, revised from time to time to make it understandable to later generations of Jewish readers, but that does not mean the essential content of the book was modified.

Date God revealed some of the laws in Leviticus by speaking to Moses from the tent of meeting, or tabernacle (Lv 1:1). Other laws were revealed on Mt Sinai (26:46). Such statements show that Moses learned the contents of Leviticus after the tabernacle had been built but before the Israelites left Mt Sinai. This fits in with Exodus 40:17, which says that the tabernacle was erected exactly a year after the Israelites left Egypt. They then spent another month at Sinai, during which time the laws in Leviticus were given to Moses. Then one month later (Nm 1:1) Moses was commanded to prepare the people to leave Sinai to conquer the Promised Land of Canaan.

It is difficult to give an exact date for the Israelite exodus from Egypt. Dates at the end of the 15th century BC or early in the 13th century are put forward by different scholars. Whichever view is adopted, the origin of Leviticus must be one year later than the exodus. But certainty about the absolute date of Leviticus is unimportant so long as the religious setting of the book is understood.

Background About 400 years before the exodus, God promised Abraham that his descendants would be very numerous and live in the land of Canaan. The family of Abraham multiplied, but as a result of famine they had to go and live in Egypt. Afraid of the Israelites, the rulers of Egypt turned them into slaves.

The book of Exodus tells how God, acting through Moses, brought the Israelites out of Egypt in a miraculous way. Moses led them to Mt Sinai, where God appeared in fire and smoke on the top of the mountain. Moses went up the mountain, and there God gave him the Ten Commandments and explained various laws. Through these acts God showed that he had chosen the nation of Israel to be his special holy people, different from all the other nations because they would show God's character through their behavior (cf. Ex 19:5-6).

God's revelation at Sinai was unique and unrepeatable. But he disclosed to Moses that he wanted to live among the people of Israel permanently. They were told

Ancient Hebrew Text of Leviticus Leviticus 27:11-19 in 11^{Q}paleoLev

to build a portable royal palace that would be suitable for the divine King of kings. The building of this portable palace, traditionally called the tabernacle, is described in Exodus 35–40. When it was completed, the fire and cloud that had been seen on Mt Sinai appeared over the tabernacle as a sign that God was now dwelling in it (Ex 40:34-38).

Exodus also tells how Moses was told to appoint his brother, Aaron, and Aaron's sons to serve in the tabernacle as priests (Ex 28–29). Unfortunately, before the Israelites even began to build the tabernacle, they made a golden calf under Aaron's leadership and started to worship it instead. The people were spared only as a result of Moses' prayers. The book of Exodus therefore leaves the reader in suspense. The tabernacle has been built, but no one knows how to worship God in it. Though Aaron and his family are alive, we are left wondering whether they will still be allowed to lead the worship of God after the idolatry of the golden calf. The book of Leviticus answers this question.

Purpose and Theology The Ten Commandments explain briefly and simply how God expects his people to behave. The first four commandments explain our duty toward our neighbor. The book of Leviticus follows a similar scheme. Chapters 1–17 show how God wanted Israel to worship him, while chapters 18–27 are mainly concerned with how people should behave toward each other. Whereas the Ten Commandments are general and can be applied quite easily to every society, the book of Leviticus is much more detailed and specifically geared to the special circumstances of ancient Israel. If modern readers are to profit from reading Leviticus, they must look behind the specific regulations to the underlying religious principles that do not change—in other words, to the theology of Leviticus.

Four themes are very important in the theology of Leviticus: (1) the presence of God, (2) holiness, (3) sacrifice, and (4) the Sinai covenant.

The Presence of God God is always present with Israel in a real way. Sometimes his presence becomes visible in fire and smoke. But even when there is no miraculous sign, God is present. He is especially near when people worship him and offer sacrifice. The many animal sacrifices mentioned in the book are all brought to the Lord. When the animals are burnt, God is pleased with the smell (1:9). The priests who offer the sacrifices must be especially careful since they come closer to God than other people do. If they are careless in their duties and break God's commands, they may die (10:1-2).

God is present not just in worship but in all the ordinary duties of life. The recurring refrain of the later chapters, "I, the LORD, am your God" (18:2; 19:3), reminds the Israelites that every aspect of their life—religion (chs 21–24), sex (chs 18, 20), and relations with neighbors (chs 19, 25)—matters to God. The behavior of every Israelite must mirror that of God himself (20:7). The fear of God should prompt persons to help the blind, the deaf, the elderly, and the poor. Though such people may have no redress against unfair treatment, God cares about what happens to them (19:14, 32; 25:17, 36, 43).

Holiness "You must be holy because I am holy" (11:44-45; 19:2; 20:26) could be termed the motto of Leviticus. "Holy," "clean," and "unclean" are common words in this book. God is the supremely holy person in the Bible, and holiness is the distinctive feature of his character. But earthly creatures can become holy too. To become holy, a person must be chosen by God and undergo the correct ceremony. Thus, at Sinai all Israel

became a holy nation (Ex 19:6). Leviticus 8–9 explains how Aaron and his sons were ordained priests. This made them more holy than ordinary Israelites and therefore able to approach God and offer sacrifice.

Before anyone could become holy, they had to be "clean." Cleanness in Leviticus means more than just being free of dirt, though this idea is included. It means being free of any abnormality. Whenever a person appears to fall short of perfection, he is described as "unclean." Thus, the worst uncleanness is death, the very opposite of perfect life. But bleeding and other discharges and patchy skin diseases can make someone unclean. Animals that move in peculiar ways or have strange habits are also called unclean (Lv 11–15).

Holiness and its opposite, uncleanness, can describe behavior as well as outward appearance. To be holy means to obey God and to act like God. Chapters 18–25 explain what holiness means in daily living. It means avoiding illicit sexual relations, caring for the poor, being honest, being fair, and loving your neighbor as yourself. This sort of behavior made Israel different from other peoples. Through their holiness the whole nation was supposed to demonstrate what God was like.

Sacrifice In practice, unfortunately, the nation and the individuals within it rarely lived up to these ideals of holiness. Even if one did not commit a grievous sin, he or she was always liable to become unclean through contact with someone else, touching a dead animal, or in some other way. To maintain contact with a holy God, Israel's sins and uncleanness had to be removed. This is what the sacrifices were for. They brought the forgiveness of sins and cleansing from uncleanness. Because sin affects relations between God and humans in various ways, Leviticus provides four different types of offerings to cover the different cases (Lv 1–6), and explains which sacrifices must be offered on which occasions (chs 7–17). All these rituals served to underline the seriousness of sin and helped preserve peace and fellowship between God and humanity.

The Sinai Covenant All the laws contained in Leviticus form part of the Sinai covenant. They fill out and apply the principles of the Ten Commandments to the specific circumstances of ancient Israel. But they are more than a set of detailed rules, because they were given as part of the covenant. Three things have to be remembered about this covenant. First, the covenant created a personal relationship. The Lord became Israel's king, and Israel became his special treasure set apart from the other nations of the world. Second, the covenant was based on God's grace. He had made a promise to Abraham and, in saving the people from Egyptian slavery, he demonstrated his faithfulness to his promise and his love for Israel. Israel, in turn, was to show its gratitude for salvation by keeping the law. In no way did keeping the law earn them salvation. The law was given to a redeemed people. Finally, there were promises and threats built into the covenant (Lv 26). When the nation keeps the law, God promises they will enjoy good harvests, victory over their enemies, and God walking among them as he did in Eden. But if they reject God's laws, terrible calamities will befall them: drought, famine, defeat, and even expulsion from the land God had promised to give them. These covenant curses form the background to the prophets' warnings in later times.

Content

Kinds of Sacrifices (1–7) These chapters explain how the different kinds of sacrifices were to be offered. Most of these sacrifices also formed part of the regular worship in the tabernacle and later in the temple. But these chapters are concerned with personal offerings made when someone had sinned or made a vow or recovered from an illness. They explain what the offerer must do and what the priest must do, which parts of the animal must be burned, which parts may be eaten by the priest, and what is to be done with the blood of the animal.

First, the offerer brought the animal into the outer court of the tabernacle. In the presence of the priest he put his hand on the head of the animal and explained why he was bringing the sacrifice. Then the worshiper killed the animal and chopped it up. The priest then took over. He caught the blood as it ran out of the dying animal and splashed it over the altar, and burned at least some of the animal on the great altar in the court of the tabernacle. These acts were performed with all the animal sacrifices.

The special feature of the burnt offering (Lv 1) was that the whole animal, which had to be unblemished, was burned on the altar. All that the priest received was the skin. This was the most common sacrifice and was offered on many different occasions. In giving the whole animal to God in the sacrifice, the worshiper dedicated himself or herself totally to God's service. "Lay your hand on its head so the Lord will accept it as your substitute, thus making atonement for you" (1:4, NLT).

Chapter 2 deals with the grain offering that always accompanied the burnt offering, but which could also be offered alone. Only part of this offering was burned; the rest was given to the priests to eat. The sacrifices formed an important part of their income.

The peace (fellowship) offering's special feature was that it was the only sacrifice where the offerer was allowed to eat part of the meat (Lv 3). Since in the earliest period Israelites were not permitted to kill animals except for sacrifice (ch 17), every meal that included meat had to be preceded by a peace offering. Leviticus 7:11-18 mentions three occasions that might prompt a peace-offering "thanksgiving": when someone had something to praise God for or some sin to acknowledge; a vow promising a sacrifice if God would help one out of a difficulty; and a voluntary offering, made just because the person felt like it.

Despite its name, the sin offering (Lv 4) was not the only offering dealing with sin. The other sacrifices also made the forgiveness of sin possible. The special significance of this sacrifice is emphasized by its unusual ritual. Instead of the blood being splashed over the altar, as in the other sacrifices, it was carefully smeared over the horns (corners) of the large altar in the courtyard (4:30) or over the small altar inside the holy place (v 18); once a year the blood was sprinkled over the ark in the Holy of Holies (16:14). Sin makes these different parts of the tabernacle unclean, unfit for the presence of God. And if God is not present in the tabernacle, worship has no point. The blood acts as a spiritual disinfectant, making the tabernacle clean and holy again. The sin offering was required whenever a person inadvertently broke one of the commandments or had suffered from a discharge or skin disease that made him or her unclean for a week or more (chs 12, 15).

The guilt offering (5:14–6:7) was for more serious offenses, such as stealing holy property or deliberately using God's name in a false oath. Such an offense was seen as robbing God. Therefore, a ram had to be offered as a sort of repayment. Whereas the poor person could offer just a bird for the other sacrifices, a ram was always required for a guilt offering.

Chapters 6:8–7:38 contain various other regulations about sacrifice, mainly specifying how much of each sac-

rifice the priests may eat and how much must be burned. One important rule for those who weren't priests was that they were not to eat any fat or blood or eat sacrificial meat when they were unclean. If they did, they could be cut off from Israel (7:21-27).

Beginnings of the Priesthood (8–10) Though Leviticus looks like a law book, because it contains so many regulations, it is really a history book describing the events that occurred about a year after the exodus. These chapters remind us of the true character of the book, for they tell how Moses ordained Aaron and his sons to be priests and how they offered their first sacrifices.

Awed by the complexity of the ordination rituals, the modern reader may miss the marvel that Aaron should have been appointed high priest. For it was Aaron who had presided over the making of the golden calf and encouraged its worship (Ex 32). Had not Moses interceded for Israel, the whole nation would have been destroyed in the wilderness. Here the gracious forgiveness of God is most clear. Aaron, the chief sinner, is appointed chief mediator between God and the people. In the NT the career of Peter parallels Aaron's in some respect.

The greatness of the high priesthood is symbolized by the richly decorated robes Aaron wore. He and his sons were anointed with oil, and then Moses offered the three most common sacrifices on their behalf. They were confined to the court of the tabernacle for a week, and it seems likely that some of the rituals were repeated each day. By this means they were set apart from the rest of the people and entirely consecrated to their holy office.

By the eighth day the process was complete. Now Aaron and his sons could offer sacrifice. This time, Moses only told them what to do; he did not offer sacrifices himself. Chapter 9 concludes by telling that, after they had offered the sacrifices for themselves and the people, fire came out of the tabernacle to burn up the offerings, thereby displaying God's approval of their actions.

After this, 10:1-2 presents an unexpected turn of events: "Aaron's sons Nadab and Abihu put coals of fire in their incense burners and sprinkled incense over it. In this way, they disobeyed the Lord by burning before him a different kind of fire than he had commanded. So fire blazed forth from the Lord's presence and burned them up, and they died there before the Lord" (NLT). We do not know exactly what is meant by unholy fire. What is important is that the priests did something that God had not commanded them. The priests were supposed to set an example of total obedience to God's word: this is the essence of holiness. Instead, they decided to follow their own plans and the consequences were dire.

"Aaron was silent" (10:3). He was warned not even to mourn his sons' deaths, lest he be suspected of condoning their sin (vv 6-7). Yet, despite his sons' actions, Aaron and his surviving sons were confirmed as priests. They were reminded that their job was "to distinguish between what is holy and what is ordinary, what is ceremonially unclean and what is clean. And you must teach the Israelites all the laws that the Lord has given through Moses" (vv 10-11, NLT). The chapter closes on another note of grace. Although the priests made a mistake in offering one of the sin offerings, God would overlook it on this occasion.

Cleanness and Uncleanness (11–16) Distinguishing between the unclean and the clean is the theme of chapters 11–15, which prepare for the great Day of Atonement ceremonies of chapter 16. These are designed to cleanse the tabernacle from the uncleannesses of the people of Israel, thereby ensuring that God would continue to dwell among them (16:16, 19).

Chapter 11 discusses unclean animals, that is, animals that may not be eaten. Land animals are dealt with first, then fish and birds, and finally various miscellaneous creatures such as locusts and reptiles. To be clean, a land animal must have cloven hooves and chew the cud; that covers sheep and cattle but excludes pigs and camels. Fish must have fins and scales to be edible; without them, they count as unclean. Birds are clean unless they are birds of prey or scavengers that eat carrion. Insects that resemble birds in having wings and two large legs to hop with—for example, locusts—are clean. Other flying insects are unclean. All squirming creatures that dart hither and thither, such as lizards, are unclean.

The reasons for declaring some animals clean and others unclean has long been a great puzzle. One suggestion is that the unclean animals were used in sacrifice by pagan worshipers or were thought to represent pagan deities. Certainly some unclean animals were used in pagan worship, but so were some clean ones, and that fact makes this explanation unsatisfactory. A second possibility is that the rules were hygienic: the clean animals were safe to eat whereas the unclean were not. There may be some truth in this explanation, but it is not completely adequate, for some clean animals can be harmful while some unclean ones are all right to eat.

Unclean animals could not be eaten, but there was no harm in touching them. Israelites could ride camels, for example. However, all dead animals, unless killed for sacrifice, were unclean. Anyone who touched the carcass of a dead creature became unclean himself and therefore could not enter the tabernacle that day (11:39-40).

The following chapters deal with other conditions that make people unclean. Chapter 12 states that childbirth, or more precisely the bloody discharge that follows childbirth, makes a woman unclean. In OT theology death is the ultimate uncleanness, and conditions that are abnormal or threaten to lead to death are also unclean. When the discharge has ceased, after a fixed period the mother must bring a burnt offering and a sin offering to atone for any sin she may have committed, and to purify the tabernacle that may have been polluted through her uncleanness.

Chapters 13–14 deal with the uncleanness caused by skin diseases. Detailed regulations are given to distinguish between different diseases so that the priests can decide whether people are unclean or not. If they are unclean, they must live outside the camp until their skin heals. Traditionally the unclean skin disease has been called leprosy. But this is unlikely to be correct, since leprosy was unknown in the Middle East in OT times. Rather, it was any disease that led to the skin peeling off in patches, such as psoriasis. This explains why the disease might spontaneously get better.

If the disease did retreat sufficiently, the sufferer could call the priest, and if the priest was satisfied with the cure, the sufferer could be readmitted to the community after following the rituals prescribed in chapter 14. This also explains what is to be done if patches of mold are found in pieces of cloth or house walls.

Chapter 15 explains how men can become unclean through discharges from their sexual organs, due to gonorrhea or sexual intercourse, while women become unclean through menstruation or a long-term discharge. Part of the purpose of these regulations is to prevent the sacred prostitution that was common in the ancient world. Since sexual intercourse made people unclean, they could not go to worship immediately afterward. Further, the uncleanness of menstruation should have discouraged men from being overfamiliar with unmarried girls.

The broad scope of these uncleanness regulations meant that nearly every Israelite would be unclean at some time in his or her life. This uncleanness could contaminate God's dwelling place, the tabernacle, making it impossible for God to continue to live there. To avert this catastrophe, a Day of Atonement was held once a year. This is the most solemn day in the Jewish calendar, and the ceremonies for it are described in detail in Leviticus 16.

There are three acts on the Day of Atonement that are described in this chapter. There was first the special sin offering offered by the high priest, in the course of which the outer altar of burnt offering, the incense altar inside the Holy Place, and finally the ark itself in the Holy of Holies were sprinkled with blood to purify each part of the tabernacle. This was the one occasion in the year when the high priest entered the presence of God in the Holy of Holies, and elaborate precautions were taken to screen the high priest from God's holiness (16:2-4, 11-17). There was another public act that pictured the sins of Israel being taken away. A goat was chosen by lot. Then the high priest placed his hands on its head and recited over it the nation's sin. This goat was then led away and driven into a solitary place; in later times it was pushed over a precipice. These actions pictured Israel's sins being carried away, so that they could not disturb the peace between God and his people. The third important feature of the Day of Atonement was public prayer and fasting. This showed that sin could not be eliminated without effort, but only through a complete change of heart by every person in Israel.

Rules for Daily Life (17–25) Whereas the opening chapters of Leviticus are entirely concerned with the Godward side of religion, the later chapters are more concerned with practical religious duties toward other persons. However, chapter 17 repeats some of the rules about sacrifice and makes one new one: that all sacrifice must be offered in the tabernacle courtyard. This was to prevent people from secretly worshiping heathen gods.

Chapters 18 and 20 spell out the rules governing sexual relations in ancient Israel. Chapter 19 gives further examples of what holiness means in everyday life. Positively, it means helping the poor by leaving some grain behind in the fields at harvesttime (19:9-10); paying people promptly (v 13); avoiding gossip (v 16); honoring the elderly, helping the immigrant, and being honest in business (vv 32-36). But holiness goes beyond deeds and words. It should transform thoughts: "Never seek revenge or bear a grudge against anyone, but love your neighbor as yourself" (v 18, NLT).

Chapters 21 and 22 discuss how the holy men of Israel, the priests, are to demonstrate their holiness in their lives. First, they must avoid approaching dead bodies unless the dead are very close relatives. Second, they must marry women of known moral uprightness. Third, deformed priests—for example, a blind or lame priest—may never offer sacrifices. Here the principle is plain that men who represent God must reflect the perfection of God in normal, healthy bodies. However, those who are temporarily unclean, through skin disease or a discharge, may resume their duties as soon as their uncleanness is cured.

Chapter 23 lists the main holy days and the sacrifices that had to be offered on each one. Chapter 24 deals with the lamp and special bread kept within the tabernacle. A case of blasphemy that occurred in the wilderness is mentioned. Because the man actually used the sacred name of God in a curse, he was sentenced to death.

Chapter 25 deals with the jubilee year. In every society people fall into debt. Today the effects of debt are somewhat cushioned by state welfare payments and bank overdrafts, but ancient societies did not have such aid available. People in debt had to sell off their family land, on which they depended for their living, or in more serious situations, they could sell themselves into slavery. Once impoverished in this way, it was exceedingly difficult ever to recover one's land or one's freedom. But this law in Leviticus provided an escape. Every 50 years was a jubilee. In this year every slave was released from bondage, and everyone who had sold his land was given it back free. Thus, everyone who fell into debt was given a chance to make a fresh start. Though this law was primarily designed to help the poor, it also served to prevent the accumulation of too much wealth in the hands of a few rich men.

Blessings, Curses, and Vows (26–27) Chapter 26 contains the blessings and curses that traditionally concluded a covenant. Israel is promised great material and spiritual prosperity if she keeps the law but is warned that tragedy will befall if she is disobedient.

Chapter 27 is an appendix dealing with vows and other gifts made to God. When a person promises to give something to God, it becomes holy and cannot be retracted unless a suitable payment is made instead. This chapter sets out the rules about such dedications.

See also Aaron; Moses; Offerings and Sacrifices; Priests and Levites; Tabernacle; Temple.

LEVITICUS AND THE CHRISTIAN
The laws in Leviticus were given many years before Christ and seem very remote from Christian living at the onset of the 21st century. However, though our circumstances are very different, the basic religious message of Leviticus still is vital and valid today. It is in terms of the sacrifices mentioned in Leviticus that the NT understands the death of Christ. Jesus was the true burnt offering, the Lamb of God, who takes away the sin of the world (Jn 1:29). Jesus was the perfect sin offering whose blood cleanses us from all sin (1 Jn 1:7). His death has, of course, made animal sacrifices obsolete, but these old Levitical sacrifices show us what Jesus achieved for us.

In other ways the theology of Leviticus still applies to the Christian. Christians are still called to be holy because God is holy (1 Pt 1:16). As those who ate sacrifices while they were unclean were warned in Leviticus that they would be cut off, so Paul warned the Corinthians that those who partook of the Lord's Supper unworthily would face judgment (1 Cor 11:27-32). Leviticus insists that the priests must be examples of perfect holiness in their behavior; so Christian ministers are expected to be models of Christian virtue (1 Tm 3:1-13).

The practical exhortations to care for the poor, the blind, and the deaf; to be fair and honest; and to be faithful in marriage are just as applicable now as they were 3,000 years ago. Our Lord summed up the whole Law and the Prophets with a quotation from Deuteronomy 6:5, "You must love the LORD your God with all your heart," and another from Leviticus 19:18, "Love your neighbor as yourself" (NLT; cf. Mt 22:37-40). By studying and meditating on Leviticus, the modern Christian can learn much about the character of God and his will for holy living.

LIBATION* Ritual of pouring a liquid such as oil or wine upon the ground as a sacrifice. *See* Offerings and Sacrifices.

LIBERTINES* Freedmen of Jewish extraction. The only reference to Libertines in the NT is Acts 6:9 (KJV). Most modern versions render this Latin term with the more Anglicized "freedmen" ("Freed Slaves," NLT) on the assumption that the designation is legal-political, not geographical. The appearance of Libertines with groups from various parts of the empire could be taken to mean that the Libertines were a group from the region of Liberatum in North Africa, at that time under Roman jurisdiction. A more probable understanding, however, is that the people who met in the synagogue of the Libertines were Jews who had formerly been slaves. Philo, a Hellenistic Jew of Alexandria, writes about Jews who had been captured during Pompey's conquests and taken to Rome in 63 BC, where they were sold as slaves but later released. When these Jews were set free, they settled in various parts of the empire: Cyrene, Alexandria, Cilicia, and Asia.

These Greek-speaking Jews, according to Acts 6:9, worshiped in a synagogue of their own in Jerusalem. They could not speak the Aramaic of their Palestinian counterparts. In 1913 R. Weill found an inscription in Jerusalem relating to a certain Theodotus, son of Vettenos. The inscription refers to a synagogue that fits the description of Acts 6:9. The early church found it necessary to debate its faith with the Libertines of this synagogue. Stephen, a man appointed earlier to deal with problems arising in the Greek-speaking element of the church (Acts 6:1-6), appears as the able exponent of faith in Christ Jesus against the synagogue of the Libertines.

See also Freedmen.

LIBERTY* Quality or state of being free. In the ancient world slavery was universal. The law of Moses provided that a Hebrew slave serve six years and go free in the seventh (Ex 21:2). This provision of the law lies behind Jeremiah 34, a passage that makes two things plain: (1) what the law required was recognized, but (2) many failed to comply with it. But whatever the practice, the law enshrined the principle of freedom. After each 49 years there was to be a jubilee year when all property would be returned to its original owners and slaves would be freed (Lv 25:8-24; cf. Ez 46:17).

Liberty might be given a slave for other reasons. If his owner destroyed the sight in an eye or knocked a tooth out, the slave must be freed for the loss of his eye or tooth (Ex 21:26-27). In a somewhat gloomy passage Job reflects that in Sheol "the slave is free from his master" (Jb 3:19). In another vein he appreciates the freedom of the wild ass (39:5).

When the Messiah comes, one of his tasks will be "to proclaim liberty to the captives" (Is 61:1). OT believers thought of this liberty in terms of freedom from foreign domination. But the Messiah is concerned basically with setting people's spirits free. Liberty is a way of life before God, as well as a state of being free from shackles.

In the NT freedom is sometimes seen as a literal release from captivity. For example, all four Gospels refer to the Jewish custom of having a prisoner set free at Passover (see Mk 15:6-15). There are references also to the release of prisoners (see Acts 3:13; 16:35). Paul encouraged Christian slaves to get their freedom if they could (1 Cor 7:21), and he personally advocated the freedom of Onesimus, a slave who had run away from his master, Philemon (see Phlm). But Paul did not advocate freedom from slavery as part of the Christian gospel. Rather, he emphasized freedom in Christ for all the believers—both those who are free and those who are slaves.

The freedom that matters is the freedom Christ gives. Jesus says plainly that people are really free when the Son sets them free (Jn 8:36). Paul exults in the freedom that Jesus Christ brings (Rom 7:24-25). The same idea can be expressed in terms of the truth making people free (Jn 8:32); of course, these words must be understood in light of the fact that Jesus is himself the truth (Jn 14:6). This is not the philosophical concept that error enslaves men while truth has a liberating effect. Truth here is that truth that is associated with Jesus, "the word of the truth, the gospel" (Col 1:5). Paul says, "Now the Lord is the Spirit, and where the Spirit of the Lord is, there is freedom" (2 Cor 3:17, RSV).

The NT is insistent that, left to themselves, people cannot defeat sin. And this is a fact of life of which the modern world affords ample proof. We may earnestly desire to do good, but evil is too powerful for us. We cannot do the good we wish to do (Rom 7:21-23). But because of Christ's atoning work, the power of sin is broken. "For the law of the Spirit of life in Christ Jesus has set me free from the law of sin and death" (Rom 8:2, RSV). This truth is insisted on again and again, and is expressed in a variety of ways.

But there is another freedom that belongs to the Christian—freedom from the law. There were many in the first century who saw the way of salvation as keeping the commandments of God. This was commonly urged among the Jews, and some of the first Christians seem to have taken up the idea from them. After all, it seems so obvious: if we lead good lives, we will be all right with God. The trouble with this position is that we do not lead good lives, for sin is too strong. But there is a further defect; namely, that the way of law is not the way for which Christ died. This is given special emphasis in Galatians, where Paul argues strongly that salvation is not by way of the law but by faith (Rom 4; Gal 3). He complains of people who slipped in to spy on the freedom they had in Christ Jesus (Gal 2:4). He points out that since Christ freed us, we ought not to get caught up in any form of bondage (5:1).

In one striking passage Paul looks for the whole creation to be liberated from the bondage of decay (Rom 8:21). It will in some way share in the liberty of the glory of God's children. This points to a wonderful destiny for creation. And we should not miss the "glory" that the liberty of God's children means.

There is an obvious temptation to presume on our freedom, since we do nothing to merit our salvation. But we are more than once warned not to misuse our liberty (Rom 6:1-4; Gal 5:13; 1 Pt 2:16). We must live as free people without making our liberty the means of bringing us into a new form of slavery of our own devising.

See also Slave, Slavery.

LIBNAH

1. One of the stations at which the Israelites encamped during the wilderness journey. It was situated between Rimmon-perez and Rissah (Nm 33:20-21). See Wilderness Wanderings.
2. Canaanite city-state in southern Palestine, conquered and destroyed by the Israelites under Joshua (Jos 10:29-31; 12:15). It was located within Judah's territory (15:42) and later given to the Levites for an inheritance (Jos 21:13; 1 Chr 6:57).

Three details in the city's subsequent history are noted in Scripture: (1) During the reign of King Jehoram of Judah, at the time of Edom's uprising, Libnah joined in the revolt but was subdued (2 Kgs 8:22; 2 Chr 21:10). (2) After King Sennacherib of Assyria took the city of Lachish, he proceeded to attack Libnah (2 Kgs 19:8; Is 37:8). Earlier Isaiah had affirmed to King Hezekiah that a rumor would cause the invading king to interrupt his military campaign

against Judah and return to his own land; it was while Sennacherib was besieging Libnah that Isaiah's affirmation was confirmed (2 Kgs 19:7-8). (3) The mother of Jehoahaz and Zedekiah, two of Judah's last kings, was a native of Libnah (2 Kgs 23:31; 24:18; Jer 52:1).

LIBNI

1. Gershon's son, the grandson of Levi, and Shimei's brother (Ex 6:17; Nm 3:18; 1 Chr 6:17, 20). He was the father of three sons and the founder of the Libnite family (Nm 3:21). Libni is alternately called Ladan in 1 Chronicles 23:7-9 and 26:21.
2. Mahli's son, the father of Shimei, and a descendant of Levi through Merari's line (1 Chr 6:29).

LIBNITE Descendant of Libni, Gershon's son, from Levi's tribe (Nm 3:21; 26:58). See Libni #1.

LIBYA, LIBYANS Country and its inhabitants to the west of Egypt. Three different Hebrew words are so rendered, but there is some confusion of meaning, partly because of textual uncertainties and partly because classical writers tended to use "Libya" to describe non-Egyptian Africa in general.

From the 12th century BC, Libyans served in the armies of Egypt and Ethiopia (2 Chr 12:3; 16:8; Na 3:9). The great invader Shishak himself was of Libyan origin. Ezekiel prophesied that Libya would share in the doom of the nations (Ez 30:5), and Libyans are counted among the peoples forced into submission in Daniel 11:43. There is passing reference to the Libyans (Hebrew, "Pul") in Isaiah 66:19.

Simon, "a man from Cyrene" in eastern Libya, was forced to carry the cross of Jesus (Mt 27:32; Mk 15:21; Lk 23:26). Libyans are listed among those who thronged Jerusalem on the Day of Pentecost (Acts 2:10).

LICE* KJV translation for some sort of small insects, probably gnats; the third plague in Egypt (Ex 8:16-18). See Animals (Gnat).

LICENTIOUSNESS* See Lasciviousness.

LIFE In biblical perspective, life flows from the living Father through the Son (his agent in creation and redemption) into a world thirsting for "real" life (see Jn 6:57).

The Living Father God the Father is above all else "the living God" (Jer 10:10; Jn 5:26). God, the source of all life (1 Tm 6:13), "inbreathed" humans at creation and sustains them continually (Jb 34:14-15). God alone gives life (Gn 17:16) and takes it away (Gn 3:22-24; 6:3; Ps 104:29; Lk 12:20).

The sign of life is movement; man is a "lively," animated body (Mt 27:50; Lk 8:55). Animals also have this animating "breath-soul" (Hebrew of Gn 1:24; 6:17). Thus, all nature is instilled with life deriving from God (Acts 17:24-28). Life is therefore sacred, but unfortunately it is as transient as grass, clouds, dew, shadow (1 Chr 29:15; Jb 7:6, 9; Jas 4:13-16; 1 Pt 1:24). Long life is desired (Gn 35:29); any life is preferable to death and of infinite value (Eccl 9:4-6; Mt 6:25; 16:26), for Sheol houses a ghostly "nonliving life," bereft of feeling, hope, or divine help (Ps 88:3-12). One's life can be enhanced by loving and serving God (Dt 30:15-20; 1 Pt 3:8-12), by experiencing God's deliverance (Is 38:16), and by receiving divine blessings (Mt 5:3-12).

Christ as Life The Greek word for "life" is zoe. In classical Greek this word was used for life in general. There are a few examples of this meaning in the New Testament (see Acts 17:25; Jas 4:14: Rv 16:3), but in all other instances the word was used to designate the divine, eternal life—the life of God (Eph 4:18). This life resided in Christ, and he made it available to all who believe in him. Human beings are born with the natural life—called *psuche* in Greek (translated "soul," "personality," or "life"); they do not possess the eternal life. This life can be received only by believing in the one who possesses the *zoe-life,* namely, Jesus Christ.

The overflowing, vibrant quality of life made available in Christ was evident in the authority of his speech and the power of his touch (Mt 9:18; Mk 1:27, 41-42; 5:27-29). He is "the author of life" (Acts 3:15), who provides the way into life (Mt 7:14; 25:46; Mk 8:35-37; 9:42-47). And he raised the dead with his life-giving power. His own resurrection made him "a life-giving spirit," with the power of "an indestructible life" (Rom 8:2; 1 Cor 15:45; Heb 7:16). Thus, Jesus Christ is "our life" (Col 3:4)—in union with whom we find "newness of life" (Rom 6:4) and are newly created, living henceforth not for ourselves but for him (2 Cor 5:15-17).

John, especially, dwells on the theme that Christ is the source of this new life (Jn 3:14-16; 5:21) for the children of God (1:12; 3:3, 5). This life is enjoyed already by those who know God and Christ (5:24; 17:3; 1 Jn 5:11-12), for they have already passed from death into eternal life (Jn 10:28; 11:26). Such life is abundant (10:10), enlightened (8:12), free and satisfied (10:9), victorious (Rom 6:6-14), full of peace and joy (Rom 5:1-11), inexhaustibly refreshed (Jn 4:13-14; 7:37-38) and immortal (Jn 5:24; 1 Cor 15:51-57).

All this is possible because from the beginning "all that came to be was alive with his life" (Jn 1:4, NEB). Thus, the life within the Father flows into the world through the Son, who also "has life in himself" and gives it to whom he will (5:26). He is "the resurrection and the life" (11:25; 14:6) and demonstrates it by restoring life to paralyzed limbs, raising the dead, and conquering death (5:5-9; 11:43; ch 20). People remain in death only because they will not "come" and "have life" (5:40; cf. 1 Jn 3:14).

See also Eternal Life.

LIFE, Book of *See* Book of Life.

LIFE EVERLASTING *See* Eternal Life.

LIGHT Illumination that makes sight possible.

In the Old Testament Light is a many-sided concept in the OT. The term is often used of ordinary, sensible light, but it also speaks of communicating spiritual truth. Light was the first thing God created after the heavens and earth (Gn 1:3). God also made individual lights such as the sun, moon, and stars (v 16). Sometimes light is personified, as when its inaccessibility is indicated by saying that it is impossible to reach the place where it lives (Jb 38:19; cf. v 24). There are also manufactured light sources, such as those used in the tabernacle (Ex 25:37).

Light is a natural symbol for what is pleasant, good, or uplifting, or what is associated with important people and more especially with God. "Light is pleasant," says the preacher (Eccl 11:7). During one of the plagues in Egypt, the Egyptians were in thick darkness while the Israelites had light (Ex 10:23). When the Israelites left Egypt, they were led in the wilderness by a pillar of cloud by day and of fire by night (13:21). The pillar gave them light when their enemies were in darkness (14:20). In later days Israel remembered that God did not abandon

his people even when they sinned; the pillar of fire was always there to show them the right way (Neh 9:19; cf. Neh 9:12; Pss 78:14; 105:39).

Light symbolizes the blessing of the Lord. Job said, "He floods the darkness with light; he brings light to the deepest gloom" (Jb 12:22, NLT). In his time of trouble Job recalled earlier, better days: "I long for the years gone by when God took care of me, when he lighted the way before me and I walked safely through the darkness" (Jb 29:2-3, NLT). Similarly Eliphaz pictured the happiness that would befall Job if he would take Eliphaz's advice: "Whatever you decide to do will be accomplished, and light will shine on the road ahead of you" (Jb 22:28, NLT). Eliphaz's use of that expression shows what is commonly conveyed in his day. The psalmist counted it a blessing when God himself lighted his lamp (Pss 18:28; 118:27; cf. 97:11; 112:4).

Light is closely linked with God; indeed, God can be said to be light: "No longer will you need the sun or moon to give you light, for the LORD your God will be your everlasting light, and he will be your glory. The sun will never set; the moon will not go down. For the LORD will be your everlasting light" (Is 60:19-20, NLT). The psalmist exulted, "The LORD is my light and my salvation" (Ps 27:1). God is said to be robed with light (104:2), and light dwells with him (Dn 2:22). Darkness is no problem to God; darkness and light are alike to him (Ps 139:12). Micah saw God as light and also as bringing his servants into the light (Mi 7:8-9). Both are ways of affirming that there is blessing and victory with God, so that a servant of God need never be dismayed.

God's blessing, described in terms of light, is also related to "the light of his presence." Something of that expression's meaning is seen from its use in Psalm 4:6: "Many people say, 'Who will show us better times?' Let the smile of your face shine on us, LORD" (NLT). The parallelism shows that "good" and the lifting up of the light of God's countenance are much the same. Similarly, it was the light of God's countenance that brought victory (Ps 44:3; here it is linked with God's right hand and arm and his delight in his people). Those who walk in the light of God's countenance are blessed (89:15). There is another side to that expression, for secret sins are exposed in his light (90:8). There is a close scrutiny from which no one and nothing can escape. But the predominant idea is that of the blessing that follows from God's looking upon his people. On one occasion the phrase is used of a person showing favor to others (Jb 29:24). An extension of the Lord's blessing is the light God gives to the world through his servants (Is 42:6; 49:6). God's servants can guide others to the revelation and blessing of God.

Light is associated with justice when the Lord says, "A law will go forth from me, and my justice for a light to the peoples" (Is 51:4, RSV). God's light in that act of justice is a consuming fire. Sometimes light is connected with good behavior: "The path of the righteous is like the light of dawn, which shines brighter and brighter until full day" (Prv 4:18, RSV).

The OT uses the absence of light as a synonym for disaster. There are those who grope in the dark without light (Jb 12:25). Bildad saw the light of the wicked put out in punishment and death (18:5-17). The wicked will be "thrust from light into darkness" (v 18). In the aftermath of the Babylonian destruction of Jerusalem there came the lament "He has brought me into deep darkness, shutting out all light" (Lam 3:2, NLT).

In the New Testament New Testament references to light are often figurative. Thus, on the Damascus road, Saul of Tarsus encountered "a light from heaven" (Acts

9:3; cf. 22:6-11; 26:13). Was that light as we know it or something else? Likewise, what quality of light shone in the apostle Peter's cell (12:7)? The light in the heavenly city is not the kind of illumination seen on earth, "for the Lord God will be their light" (Rv 22:5; cf. 21:11, 23-24).

The association of God with light is recurrent in the NT. The apostle John wrote that "God is light and there is no darkness in him at all" (1 Jn 1:5, NLT). The apostle James referred to God as "the Father of lights" (Jas 1:17). Or God may be thought of as living in light, light that no person can approach (1 Tm 6:16; cf. 1 Jn 1:7). Jesus said, "I am the light of the world" (Jn 8:12; see also 9:5), and "I have come as light into the world, that whoever believes in me may not remain in darkness" (Jn 12:46, RSV). Jesus told his followers to believe in the light while it was with them (v 35). Such passages emphasize that Christ brought a revelation from God, but he was more than a revealer. He was himself that revelation, according to the apostle John (Jn 1:1-10). John the Baptist came to bear witness to the light for the purpose of bringing people to believe (vv 7-8). Those who received Jesus, who believed in the light, received the right to become children of God (vv 9-12). Sometimes light is used to express the illumination that happens when people come to the knowledge of God and his salvation (Mt 4:16; Lk 2:32; Acts 13:47; 26:18).

Perhaps thinking of a then-popular concept of a war between light and darkness, John wrote that the light shines in the darkness and adds that the darkness has not overcome it (Jn 1:5; cf. 1 Jn 2:8). John tells us that "the light from heaven came into the world, but they loved the darkness more than the light, for their actions were evil" (Jn 3:19, NLT). To love darkness brings condemnation, now and at the final judgment. John pointed out that evildoers keep away from the light; they do not want their evil exposed. But those who "do the truth" come to the light (vv 20-21). In John's account of the raising of Lazarus, Jesus speaks of the possibility of walking without stumbling in the light of day, but then he goes on to the way a man stumbles in the night because he has no light (11:10). The lack of light "in" the man shows that it is a spiritual process with which Jesus is concerned and not with making physical progress by daylight. He who follows Jesus will have the light of life (8:12), which indicates what Jesus has in mind.

Those who respond to the light may be characterized as "sons of light" (Jn 12:36). Their allegiance is to the light and their conduct has been shaped by this fact. The concept is not confined to John's Gospel, for we also see it in Luke (Lk 16:8). We find it in Paul's affirmation that the Thessalonian Christians are children of light and of the day, not of the night or darkness (1 Thes 5:5). John speaks of walking in the light (1 Jn 1:7) and sees the conduct of the Christian as aptly symbolized by light.

This way of looking at the Christian's manner of life reaches its high point in the words of Jesus to his followers: "You are the light of the world" (Mt 5:14), thus applying to them words that are also applied to himself. Of course, we are not the world's light in the same sense as he is. When light refers to Christ, there is a reference to him as Savior and not merely as one who reveals great truths. When believers are called the light of the world, there is clearly no saving significance in the description: they do not accomplish the world's salvation. But they do point it out. It is their function to live as redeemed people. They are to show the quality of life proper to the people of God and in this way act as light to the people of the world. They are to let their light shine before the world in such a way that people will see their good deeds

and so come to praise God (not, be it noted, those who do the deeds, Mt 5:16). It is important for those in this position to make full use of the light they have. It is tragic when the light that is in them is darkness (Mt 6:23; Lk 11:35).

This metaphor is worked out in a way not congenial to modern men and women, but the basic lesson is clear. Christians have been illuminated by the light that is Christ, who dwells within his people. If they ignore the illumination he brings and live like those in the dark, then indeed they are in deep darkness. They are worse than others because they know what light is and what it can mean to them, and have turned away from it.

See also Darkness.

LIGHTNING The flashing of light. When the Bible speaks of lightning, it usually has to do with God making an appearance. It occurs, therefore, at very dramatic moments, as when God comes down upon Mt Sinai just before giving the Ten Commandments to Moses (Ex 19:16); or referring to the return of Jesus (Mt 24:27), where lightning is only one of many spectacular signs of the event (Ez 1:14; Dn 10:6). It is a common symbol also in Revelation (Rv 4:5; 8:5; 16:18), a book whose chief concern is to give a vision of God.

Sometimes the figure of lightning speaks of God in special ways. It can accompany judgment against God's enemies (2 Sm 22:15; Rv 16:18). More often, it points to God's power and kingship over all creation (Ps 135:7). Lightning is one of the things God mentions to Job (Jb 38:35) to show him how great is the creation and the Creator, and how small Job is by comparison (compare Ps 77:16-18).

LIGN ALOES* KJV translation for aloes in Numbers 24:6. *See* Plants (Aloe).

LIGURE* KJV translation for jacinth in Exodus 28:19 and 39:12. *See* Stones, Precious.

LIKHI Shemida's son from Manasseh's tribe (1 Chr 7:19).

LILITH* Hebrew for the night creature referred to in Isaiah 34:14. According to Hebrew mythology, Lilith was Adam's first wife, who was replaced by Eve; subsequently, Lilith became a female demon.

LILY *See* Plants.

LILY-WORK* Design of a lily or lotus used on ancient pillars, inspired by the large water lily found along the Nile. It appeared at the vestibule of Solomon's temple (1 Kgs 7:19-22), around the brim of the basin (v 26), and in numerous artistic creations of the Assyrians, Persians, and other Near Eastern peoples.

See also Bronze Sea; Laver.

LIME* White substance (calcium oxide) obtained by applying heat to materials containing calcium carbonate, such as limestone or shells. *See* Minerals and Metals.

LINEN Cloth made from flax. *See* Cloth and Cloth Manufacturing.

LINTEL* Horizontal beam placed above a doorway, supported by structures called "jambs" or simply "doorposts."

In Exodus 12, the Israelites are instructed to prepare

for the tenth plague, the plague of death, and for the first Passover. After killing a lamb, the people were to take the blood and "put it on the two doorposts and the lintel of the houses" (Ex 12:7).

First Kings 6:31 describes Solomon's building of the temple. The KJV says, "He made doors of olive tree: the lintel and side posts were a fifth part of the wall." The meaning in the Hebrew is a little difficult to determine. The NASB translates it as "the lintel and five-sided doorposts." The NEB replaces the word "lintel" with "pilasters." It may be that the top of the doorway was slanted, formed by beams leaning toward each other (archlike) instead of one horizontal beam.

In Amos 9:1 the KJV has "lintel," whereas the RSV has "capital." The Hebrew word here appears to mean the capital of a column. The same is true in Zephaniah 2:14, where the KJV has "lintels" and the NASB has "tops of her pillars." See Architecture.

LINUS Christian at Rome who joined Paul in sending salutations to Timothy (2 Tm 4:21). According to Irenaeus and Eusebius, the apostles Peter and Paul made a man named Linus bishop of Rome. Eusebius identified him with the Linus referred to by Paul at the end of 2 Timothy and said that he served for 12 years. The *Apostolic Constitutions*, along with other early church documents, also makes this identification.

LION See Animals.

LION OF THE TRIBE OF JUDAH A title of the Messiah that appears only in Revelation 5:5: "the Lion of the tribe of Judah, the heir to David's throne, has conquered" (NLT). This is an allusion to the messianic promise of Genesis 49:9-10, "Judah is a young lion. . . . The scepter will not depart from Judah" (NLT). The expression summarizes the OT hope that the Messiah would come as a conquering hero, delivering his people from every form of spiritual, political, and social evil (cf. 2 Esd 11:37; 12:31). The OT frequently employs the lion as a symbol of power and the complete ability to subdue one's enemies (Jb 10:16; Ps 10:9; Ez 1:10; Dn 7:1-4).

The author of Revelation expressed the belief of all Christians—that Christ is the deliverer who would defeat all the powers of evil. However, in contrast to the OT hope, the deliverer comes not as the conquering Lion of military power, but rather as the Lamb, who suffers and is sacrificed for the sins of his people (Rv 5:6).

LITTER* Large couch used for carrying dignitaries (Sg 3:7-10; Is 66:20); it is also translated as "carriage" or "palanquin." See Travel.

LIVER Large abdominal organ that performs many functions necessary for life. The writer of Proverbs understood the critical nature of the liver when he noted that an arrow injury to the liver (NLT "heart") was fatal (Prv 7:23). In most instances, in Scripture the liver is mentioned in connection with the description of animal sacrifices (Ex 29:13, 22; Lv 3:4, 10, 15).

In ancient Babylon, sheep liver was occasionally used in fortune-telling; the shape of each small detail of the liver was carefully examined for possible omens. Bronze and baked-clay anatomical models of sheep livers have been recovered from archaeology sites dating to the 16th century BC. Evidently this is the use of the liver made by the king of Babylon in Ezekiel 21:21. This use of the sheep liver was popular until the time of the Greeks and rivaled astrology for many centuries.

LIZARD Small reptile with scaly skin, four legs, and a long tail. See Animals.

LO-AMMI Symbolic name, meaning "Not My People" (Hos 1:9), given by the prophet Hosea to his son. See Ammi.

LOAN Money lent at interest. See Money; Banker, Banking.

LOCUSTS Various insects known especially for their swarming, mass migration, and tremendous destruction of vegetation. See Animals.

LOD City on the coastal plain of Palestine. The modern city, called Ludd, is located 10 miles (16.1 kilometers) southeast of Tel Aviv. The name of the city first occurs in a list of Canaanite towns that goes back to 1465 BC, to the reign of the Egyptian pharaoh Thutmose III, who supplied the list. The founder of the city is said to have been Shemed, a Benjamite (1 Chr 8:12). It is included in a list of places that were resettled by returning exiles from Babylon (Ezr 2:33; Neh 7:37), and is included in the list of Benjamite settlements (Neh 11:35). The history of the city can be traced continuously from Maccabean times, through the Roman period, including the first and second Jewish wars against the Romans, to the Byzantine and Crusader periods, through to modern times.

In the NT era Jewish sources emphasize the importance of the city, at that time named Lydda. It had a large market and was noted for the raising of cattle. Textile, dyeing, and pottery industries flourished there. And it was the seat of a Sanhedrin; famous Talmudic scholars taught there. This, then, was the kind of bustling, flourishing community that existed when Peter visited the city and ministered to its Christians (Acts 9:32-35).

LO-DEBAR Alternate name for Debir, the Gadite city, in 2 Samuel 9:4 and Amos 6:13. See Debir (Place) #2.

LOG* Liquid measure mentioned only in Leviticus 14. The log was equal to one-twelfth of a bath or one-half pint (236.6 milliliters). See Weights and Measures.

LOGIA* Term used for many of Jesus' sayings as collected and later employed by the Gospel writers. See Jesus Christ, Life and Teachings of.

LOGOS* English transliteration of a Greek term for "word." The term is significant because in John's writings it refers to Jesus. The prologue of John's Gospel (Jn 1:1, 14) and the beginning of 1 John (1 Jn 1:1) use *logos* to show how Jesus can be God and yet be an expression of God in the world. The divine Word took on human form and became a historical personage. Logos is also the title of Christ in the vision of his divine glory (Rv 19:13). Writers outside the NT, such as Philo of Alexandria, used the term but with a different meaning.

See also John, Gospel of; Word, Word of God.

LOINS Region of the body from the chest to the lower part of the hip; an expression in the KJV ("out of his loins") for that part of the body that involved procreation (Gn 35:11; 46:26; Ex 1:5; 1 Kgs 8:19). In most instances, the word describes physical features, although occasionally emotion, power, or strength is meant (see Na 2:1). As was the custom of the Hebrews and other Near Eastern peoples, a man would tie up his clothes around the loins before traveling a long distance on foot

(Ex 12:11; 1 Kgs 18:46; 2 Kgs 9:1). In the NT girded loins signified that a man was ready for service or heavy battle (Lk 12:35). Metaphorically, girding the loins is a symbolic way of saying that one is standing firm and/or exercising self-control (Eph 6:14; 1 Pt 1:13, KJV).

LOIS Maternal grandmother of Timothy (2 Tm 1:5), whose family, including Timothy's mother, Eunice, lived at Lystra (Acts 16:1). Lois was a deeply committed Jew who probably converted to Christianity during Paul's first missionary trip (ch 14). Paul comments that Timothy shared the faith of his grandmother and mother.

LONGSUFFERING* Word denoting long and patient endurance. This is a word used in the KJV four times in the OT (Ex 34:6; Nm 14:18; Ps 86:15; Jer 15:15) and 13 times in the NT. The NLT and other modern versions use "forbearance" and "patience" and other synonyms.

Longsuffering is usually applied to God (Rom 2:4). A holy God must punish sin. Yet his loving nature delays that punishment to give the sinner time to repent and turn away from his sin (1 Tm 1:16; 1 Pt 3:20). Longsuffering is also a Christian virtue, a fruit of the Spirit (Gal 5:22). Christians need to exercise this in their relationships with each other.

LOOM Frame or machine for weaving. *See* Cloth and Cloth Manufacturing.

LORD "Lord" in English is the rendering of the Hebrew *'adonai* or of the Greek *kurios*. The Hebrew YHWH is usually rendered "LORD"; *see* Yahweh (YHWH).

God's rule and authority as Lord rests ultimately upon his creation and ownership of all things and people (Ps 24:1-2). God's total supremacy over nature is emphasized by his being called the Lord over earthquakes, wind, fire (1 Kgs 19:10-14), stars (Is 40:26), beasts and sea monsters (Jb 40–41), and primeval chaos (Pss 74:12-14; 89:8-10).

The later prophets indicated that God is Lord or King of history because he directs the affairs of humans and nations (1 Kgs 19:15-18; Is 10:5-9; Am 9:7) and he is the Lord of universal morality (Ez 25–32; Am 1:3–2:16). But he is especially the Lord of Israel; his expressed will represents their civil and religious constitution and demands absolute obedience (Ex 20:2). The divine sovereignty was, however, Israel's comfort under oppression and hope for the future, when a triumphant Day of the Lord would right its wrongs, punish its oppressors, and restore its glory (Is 2:2-4, 11-12; 34:8; Ez 30:1-5; Jl 2:31–3:1).

In the Septuagint, the regular expression for "Lord/lord/master" is *kurios*, which in the Greek NT also is used of masters, husbands, and rulers (Mt 25:11; Lk 14:21; Acts 25:26; 1 Pt 3:6); of God (Mt 11:25; Heb 8:2); and of pagan gods (1 Cor 8:5). It is used of Jesus as a customary title of respect ("sir," Mt 8:2; 15:25); it also retains its Septuagint associations of faith, reverence, and worship (Mt 3:3; Lk 7:13; Acts 5:14; 9:10; 1 Cor 6:13-14; Heb 2:3; Jas 5:7); it appears in phrases like "the Lord Jesus," "the Lord's Day," "the Lord's Table," "the Spirit of the Lord" (who is also "Lord," 2 Cor 3:17), "in the Lord," "from the Lord," "light in the Lord," "boast in the Lord." Sometimes it is not clear whether God or Christ is intended (Acts 9:31; 2 Cor 8:21). The title is attributed to Jesus himself in John 13:13-14; in John 20:28 Jesus accepts the title "My Lord and my God!"

In the first Christian sermon Jesus' lordship is made central to salvation (Acts 2:21). It appears that the public confession of Jesus as Lord was the approved focus and expression of Christian faith, and the basis of membership in the apostolic church (Acts 16:31; Rom 10:9; 1 Cor 12:3; Phil 2:11). Thus, it could become more a formal statement than a sincere expression of belief—hence, the warnings in Matthew 7:21 and Luke 6:46.

From the first, such a confession was fraught with meaning. In common usage "lord" reflected the slave system and implied the absolute power exercised by the master over the purchased slave. So Paul unhesitatingly expounds the moral implications of Christian redemption (1 Cor 6:19-20; 7:22-23; *see* photo on p. 822). To Jewish minds, the title had messianic overtones of kingship and authority (Lk 20:41-44), offending both Jews and Romans. Politically, "Lord" was a title claimed by Caesar. Therefore, it is significant that Jesus is called "King of kings and Lord of lords" during the age of Domitian when Caesar worship was mandated (Rv 17:14; 19:16).

Among Greek-speaking Jews of the dispersion, familiar with the Septuagint, as among Gentiles, for whom "Lord" was the customary title for the many gods of polytheism, the application to Jesus of the epithet belonging to godhead was blasphemous, especially when associated with "Son of God," prayer, praise, total devotion, and hope (1 Cor 8:5-6; Phil 2:9-11; 1 Thes 4:14-17). On every level, therefore, the adoring tribute given to Jesus was loaded not only with spiritual meaning but with positive and imminent danger.

See also Christology; God, Being and Attributes of; God, Names of.

LORD OF HOSTS* Old Testament name for God found mostly in the prophets. The hosts are the heavenly powers and angels that act at the Lord's command. *See* God, Names of.

LORD'S DAY, The Expression occurring once in the NT (Rv 1:10), where John says, "On the Lord's Day I was in the Spirit" (NIV); synonym for "Sunday" in modern usage.

The earliest reference to Christian activity on Sunday comes in a brief allusion Paul makes to "the first day of the week" (1 Cor 16:2, NLT mg). He instructs individual members of the church in Corinth to remember their poverty-stricken fellow believers in Jerusalem by setting aside a sum of money each Sunday.

Why Sunday? Obviously the first day of the week had taken on a special significance among Christians in Corinth before Paul wrote this letter (AD 55–56), and he makes it clear that the observance was not merely local (1 Cor 16:1). Sunday was the day when special church meetings took place (Paul alludes several times to these in 1 Cor—see 5:4; 11:18-20). Collections were taken on these occasions to meet local needs (cf. 1 Cor 9:7-14). So Paul was saying, "When the collection bag comes around on Sundays, and you are reminded of your local needs, set aside something—privately—for the needs of your brethren in Jerusalem."

There is a more detailed account of a Christian Sunday meeting in Acts 20:6-12. The all-night service Luke describes there took place in Troas about three years after Paul wrote 1 Corinthians. Luke's main aim is to tell the story of sleepy Eutychus's miraculous recovery, so some of the details of the meeting that would interest us most are missing. Nevertheless, the account is full enough to indicate the kind of things the first Christians did when they met together on Sundays.

The fact that Luke mentions the day of the week at all is significant. Elsewhere he rarely identifies a day, unless it is a Sabbath or a special feast. His word for "gathered" (Acts 20:7) is important too. It is a semitechnical term the NT uses for Christians gathered together for worship (1 Cor 5:4). So this was not a special meeting convened to hear Paul (who had already been in town six days) but a regular weekly event. The church in Troas may have met daily, like the church in Jerusalem (Acts 2:42, 46), but the Sunday meeting was obviously treated as a special occasion.

"Lord Jesus Christ" Written as a Nomen Sacrum Closing page of 2 Corinthians, Chester Beatty Manuscript II, late second century—P46. The third to the last line shows K͞Y I͞H͞Y X͞P͞Y, *Κυριου Ισου Χηριστου* (Lord Jesus Christ).

Luke uses the same word to describe Paul's preaching (Acts 20:7) that he used earlier for the apostle's preaching ministry in the synagogues at Ephesus and Corinth (18:4; 19:8). This preserves an interesting link between the Jewish Sabbath and the Christian Sunday. When a local church separated from the synagogue, it probably modeled its worship on synagogue practice. Although the three main components of synagogue worship (Scripture reading, teaching, and prayer) are not found together in the few NT accounts of Christian worship, each is separately attested.

The main purpose behind the church's Sunday meeting at Troas, however, was distinctively Christian. It was "to break bread" (Acts 20:7), the NT's term for eating the Lord's Supper (and including, probably, the less formal table fellowship of the love feast—cf. 1 Cor 11:17-34). The Lord's Supper very quickly became a focal point of the early church's Sunday worship. As a memorial of the resurrection and the promise of Christ's presence in the worshiping fellowship, it was an obviously appropriate Christian way of celebrating the first day of the week.

The third clear reference to Sunday in the NT (and the only one that calls it the Lord's Day) takes us from the Turkish mainland to the Aegean island of Patmos, probably about 40 years after Paul's visit to Troas. In Revelation 1:10 John describes how he was worshiping on the Lord's Day when he received his great vision. It is just possible that the expression "Lord's Day" here means Easter, or even the great day of God's judgment that the OT prophets foretold, but in view of the way later Christian writers used this phrase, it is far more likely to mean simply "Sunday."

The immediate context of Revelation 1:10 makes it clear that John saw Sunday as the Lord's Day because on it Christians expressed together their total commitment to Jesus as Lord and Master (Rv 1:8). It was Jesus' resurrection on the first day of the week that demonstrated his lordship most clearly (see Rv 1:18 and Jn 20:25-28). One day the whole world will have to acknowledge that he is "King of kings and Lord of lords" (Rv 19:16; cf. Phil 2:11), but in the meantime it is in the church's worship that his lordship is recognized.

LORD'S PRAYER, The*

Pattern for prayer Jesus gave his followers to use. There are two versions of the Lord's Prayer (Mt 6:9-13; Lk 11:2-4). The former is included in the Sermon on the Mount; the latter is Jesus' response to a disciple's request that he teach them to pray. There are considerable differences between the two versions.

Some scholars devote a good deal of attention to the question of which is the earlier of the two. Generally speaking, they conclude that in most points Luke's is the earlier form. This is largely because it is shorter, and there is no reason why someone should leave out anything in a prayer as short as this, whereas it is easy to see why additions might be made. These scholars usually hold that in some of the wording Matthew is likely to have retained the earlier form.

This approach, however, does not take into account the fact that Jesus seems to have regarded the prayer as a pattern, not as a formula. In Matthew he introduces it with the words "Pray then like this." If the prayer was seriously meant as a model, it is unlikely that it would be recited only once. On the contrary, it is to be expected that Jesus would have used it on a number of occasions. And if he seriously meant people to pray "in this way" (and not invariably in these words), then variations in the wording are to be expected.

Some recent writers regard the whole prayer as eschatological—that is, concerned with the end of the world. They take the petition "Thy kingdom come" as central and

understand all the other petitions to refer in one way or another to the coming kingdom. The prayer about hallowing the name is then seen as a prayer for the destruction of God's enemies who do not revere his holiness; the line about the bread becomes a petition for the messianic banquet; and so on. But this is to take the words in an unnatural sense. Christians are, of course, always living in the "last days," and there is no reason why they should not see an application of Jesus' words to the eschatological situation. It seems much more probable, however, that we should understand the prayer with reference to the help we need in our daily lives.

> Our Father which art in heaven,
>   Hallowed be thy name.
> Thy kingdom come.
> Thy will be done in earth,
>   as it is in heaven.
> Give us this day our daily bread.
> And forgive us our debts,
>   as we forgive our debtors.
> And lead us not into temptation,
>   but deliver us from evil:
> For thine is the kingdom,
>   and the power,
>   and the glory, for ever.
> Amen.

The first person singular pronoun is not used anywhere in the prayer. We say, "Our Father, . . . give us. . . ." This prayer is meant for a community. It may profitably be used by an individual, but it is not meant as an aid to private devotion. It is a prayer to be said by God's people; it is the prayer of the Christian family.

In Matthew the opening words are "Our Father in heaven," whereas Luke has simply "Father." Those who pray like this are members of a family, and they look to God as the head of the family, one who is bound to them by ties of love. Matthew's "in heaven" brings out something of his dignity, and this is seen also in the petition "Hallowed [Honored] be thy name" (identical in the two). In antiquity "the name" meant far more than it does to us. In some way it summed up the whole person. Thus this petition is more than a prayer that people will use the name of God reverently rather than blasphemously (though that is important and is included). It looks for people to have a reverent attitude to all that God stands for. They should have a proper humility before God, being ready to honor him as he is in all his holiness.

"Thy kingdom come" is the petition that most of all looks for the eschatological activity of God. Christians have always longed for the day when God will overthrow the kingdoms of this earth and when all will become the kingdom of our Lord and of his Christ (Rv 11:15). This is included in the meaning of the petition. But there is another sense in which the kingdom is a present reality, a kingdom that is now in human hearts and lives. This aspect of the kingdom is brought out in the words added in Matthew's version, "Thy will be done on earth as it is in heaven" (Mt 6:10). The servant of God looks for the rule of God to become actual in more and more lives.

In the petition about bread Jesus is concerned with the material necessities of daily life. Jesus' followers are, it is true, not to be anxious about the things they need to eat and to wear (Mt 6:25). But Jesus also taught that they should constantly look to God for such needs to be supplied (vv 32-33). The view that the messianic banquet is in mind does not reckon with the fact that the banquet is regarded as a feast, while it is bread, not some festive food, that is mentioned here. The big problem in this petition is the meaning of the word usually translated "daily." It is an exceedingly rare word, and many scholars think that it was coined by Christians. Since it is impossible to establish meaning from the way it is used, discussions center on its derivation. It could mean any number of things: "daily," "for today," "for the coming day," "for tomorrow," or "necessary." The traditional understanding, "daily," seems most probable. But however we translate it, the prayer is for the simple and present necessities of life. Jesus was counseling his followers to pray for necessities, not luxuries, and for what is needed now, not a great store for many days to come. By confining the petition to present needs, Jesus taught a day-by-day dependence on God.

The petition about forgiveness differs slightly in the two accounts. In Matthew it is "Forgive us our debts," while Luke has "Forgive us our sins." Without question it is the forgiveness of sins that is in mind, but the Matthean form sees sin as an indebtedness. We owe it to God to live uprightly. He has provided all we need to do this. So when we sin, we become debtors. The sinner has failed to fulfill his obligations, what he "owes." Matthew goes on to say, "as we also have forgiven our debtors," and Luke, "for we ourselves forgive everyone indebted to us." The tense in Matthew indicates that the person praying is not only ready to forgive but has already forgiven those who have sinned against him; in Luke, that he habitually forgives. Further, he does so in the case of every debtor.

In neither form of the prayer is it implied that human forgiveness earns God's forgiveness. The NT makes it clear that God forgives on account of his mercy, shown in Christ's dying for us on the cross. Nothing we do can merit forgiveness. There is also the thought that those who seek forgiveness should show a forgiving spirit. How can we claim the forgiveness of our sins if we do not forgive others who sin against us?

There is dispute as to the precise meaning of the petition traditionally translated "lead us not into temptation." Some favor a rendering like that of the NEB, "do not bring us to the test." The word usually understood as "temptation" does sometimes mean a proving or a testing. But it is the kind of testing that the evil one engages in, testing with a view to failure. It is thus the normal word to be used when temptation is in mind. If the whole prayer is to be understood eschatologically, then "do not bring us to the test" is no doubt the way this petition should be taken. The great testing time that comes with the upsurge of evil in the last days is something from which every Christian naturally shrinks, and the prayer would give expression to this. But it is much more likely that the prayer refers to life here and now. Even so, it may mean "severe trial," and some scholars favor this. They think that Jesus was counseling his followers to pray for a quiet life in which they would not meet serious misfortune. But a prayer to be delivered from temptation is much more likely. Christians know their weakness and readiness to sin, so pray that they may be kept from the temptation to go astray. It is true that God does not tempt people (Jas 1:13). But it is also true that it is important for the believer to avoid evil. One should not see how close to sinning one can come without actually doing it, but one should keep as far away from it as possible (cf., e.g., 1 Cor 6:18; 10:14).

Matthew adds, "but deliver us from evil" (as do some manuscripts of Luke). This is a further development of the prayer just offered. There is uncertainty as to whether the last word means "evil" generally or "the evil one." Either meaning is possible. Christians pray that they may not be tempted, and this leads naturally to the thought either that they may not become the prey of evil or that

they may be free from the domination of the devil. It is the general thrust of Jesus' teaching that should decide the point, not the precise language used here.

This is where the prayer ends in Luke and in the oldest manuscripts of Matthew. Few would doubt that here is where the prayer ended in the teaching of our Lord. But many manuscripts, some of them fairly old, add the familiar words, "for thine is the kingdom and the power and the glory for ever." This is the kind of doxology that is often found in prayers in antiquity, both Jewish (cf. 1 Chr 29:11) and Christian. The early Christians used the Lord's Prayer in worship services and doubtless found this a splendid way to end it. In time, what was so acceptable in worship found its way into some of the manuscripts. We may well continue to end the prayer in this way. It is good to remind ourselves that all ultimate sovereignty, power, and glory belong to God forever. But we should not see this as part of the prayer Jesus taught his followers to use.

See also Prayer; Sermon on the Mount; Worship.

LORD'S SUPPER, The The supper Jesus shared with his disciples a few hours before he was arrested and taken to his trial and death (thus often called "The Last Supper"); the ceremony of partaking of the bread and wine that Christians have come to call the Lord's Supper (1 Cor 11:20), the breaking of bread (Acts 2:42, 46; 20:7), Holy Communion (from the expression of 1 Cor 10:16), the Eucharist (the Greek word for "thanksgiving," see Mk 14:23), or the Mass. The apostle Paul speaks of handing on what he had "received from the Lord" concerning the institution of this supper "on the night when he was betrayed." Like Luke, Paul gives the Lord's command to his disciples: "Do this in remembrance of me" (1 Cor 11:24-25). According to Acts 2, the early Christians from the beginning of the life of the church met regularly for "the breaking of bread."

PREVIEW
• The Accounts of the Institution
• The Time of the Institution
• Words and Actions of the Institution
• The Practice of the Early Church
• Paul's Teaching

The Accounts of the Institution The institution of the Lord's Supper is recorded in Matthew 26:26-30; Mark 14:22-26; and Luke 22:14-20. John's Gospel (ch 13) tells of the Last Supper Jesus shared with his disciples, of his washing the disciples' feet and the teaching associated with that, but does not mention his institution of Communion. Many see the Lord's Supper reflected in the teaching of John 6, following the miracle of the feeding of the 5,000 and Jesus' speaking of himself as "the bread of life," but this is open to question. First Corinthians 11:23-26 gives Paul's version of the institution, which he speaks of as "receiving" and "delivering" to the Corinthian Christians.

In Luke 22:17-18 Jesus is said to have passed the cup to the disciples with the words "Take this, and divide it among yourselves" before taking the bread and giving it to them. In most early manuscripts there is then a second cup after the giving of the bread. This difference of Luke from the other Gospels and from Paul has been variously explained, but whether there are two cups of wine at the supper or a different order in the giving of the bread and the wine, it makes no essential difference to the fact and the meaning of the institution.

The Time of the Institution All of the narratives—the three Gospels and 1 Corinthians—speak of the Last Supper when the Eucharist was instituted as taking place a few hours before Jesus' arrest. All four Gospels tell, in this context, of Jesus' words to his disciples, about Judas's betrayal, and about Jesus telling Peter that he would deny his Master. Matthew (Mt 26:17-20), Mark (Mk 14:12-17), and Luke (Lk 22:7-14) all say clearly that this Last Supper was prepared by the disciples and kept by Jesus with them as a Passover meal. John speaks of it as happening "before the feast of the Passover" and then says that at the time of the trial of Jesus before Pilate the Jewish leaders "did not enter the praetorium, so that they might not be defiled, but might eat the passover" (Jn 13:1; 18:28, RSV).

Various explanations of this difference between John and the other Gospels have been suggested, such as that different groups of the Jews kept the Passover at different times, that the meal in the upper room was not strictly a Passover but a fellowship meal at the Passover season, or that Jesus deliberately chose for his own special reasons to celebrate the Passover before the normal time. Luke 22:15 gives his words, "I have earnestly desired to eat this passover with you before I suffer" (RSV). However the differences between the Gospels may be explained, and whenever the gathering around the table took place, it is clear that the Last Supper had the significance of a Passover meal.

Thus, there is an inevitable similarity between the celebration of the Passover as a feast of the old covenant and the Lord's Supper as a feast of the new. The former looks back with thankful remembrance to the people's redemption and liberation from Egypt by the act of God, associated with the sacrifice of the Passover lamb. The latter looks back with thankful remembrance to redemption by the act of God through the sacrifice of Christ. The apostle Paul links the two: "Christ, our Passover lamb, has been sacrificed" (1 Cor 5:7, NIV).

Words and Actions of the Institution The association of the Last Supper with the Passover points to the importance of the OT background for our understanding of the meaning of the Lord's Supper. This OT background is equally important in understanding the words and actions of Jesus in the upper room.

"This is my body." The actions of Jesus in taking the bread are described similarly in Matthew (Mt 26:26), Mark (Mk 14:22), Luke (Lk 22:19), and 1 Corinthians (1 Cor 11:23-24). Jesus took the bread, gave thanks to God ("blessing" has the same meaning in the biblical context), and broke it. It is noteworthy that the same three actions are described in the records of the feeding of the 5,000 and of the 4,000 (Mk 6:41; 8:6). What he said, according to all four accounts of the Last Supper, was "This is my body." Christians in Catholic, Orthodox, and various Protestant traditions have differed in their understanding of the precise meaning of those words. What is clear is that in the taking of the bread there is the realization of Jesus' giving himself, his body to be broken on the cross, his life offered that we, in and through him, might have life. First Corinthians 11:24 gives the words as "This is my body which is for you," and some early manuscripts have "broken for you."

"Do this in remembrance of me." This specific instruction is found only in Luke 22:19 and 1 Corinthians 11:24. Some have argued that the absence of the words in the other Gospel records indicates that it was not the explicit intention of the Lord that what he did at the Last Supper was to be repeated as a Christian sacrament. Yet all the Gospels were written when the breaking of bread had been a regular practice in the life of the church for years. Matthew and Mark, therefore, may have thought it

unnecessary to express Jesus' intention with those words. They were taken for granted.

It must also be said that these words have been interpreted differently in various Christian traditions. Many Protestant Christians have understood them to mean that in the Holy Communion we are to recall with great thankfulness that Christ loved us and gave himself to die for us. In the Roman Catholic Church the word "remembrance" has been understood as a memorial before God, a representing of the sacrifice of Christ before the Father. "This do" has been interpreted as meaning "offer this," and even in the second century Christian writers spoke of the Eucharist as a "sacrifice." Protestant Christians generally have felt the danger of this way of speaking; it can detract from, or even deny, the biblical understanding of the sacrifice of Christ having been offered once and for all, sufficiently atoning for the sins of the world (cf. Heb 7:27; 9:12). It must be said, however, that many Roman Catholic statements today stress the sufficiency and completeness of Christ's sacrifice on the cross; and many Protestant scholars, while not wishing to introduce a sacrificial understanding of the Lord's Supper, stress that "remembrance" is more than simply calling to mind a past action. In biblical thinking "remembrance" often involves a realization and appropriation in the present of what has been done or what has proved true in the past (see Pss 98:3; 106:45; 112:6; Eccl 12:1; Is 57:11).

"This is my blood of the [new] covenant." Jesus took the cup of wine, gave thanks, and handed it to his disciples for them all to drink. In essence the four accounts of the institution agree. Matthew (Mt 26:28) and Mark (Mk 14:24) give the words of Jesus as "This is my blood of the [new] covenant." Luke 22:20 has "This cup which is poured out for you is the new covenant in my blood," and 1 Corinthians 11:25 is similar to this. This refers back to the ritual of making a covenant with the offering of sacrifice, as the covenant between God and Israel after the exodus (Ex 24:1-8). Implied also is that the prophetic hope of the new covenant (Jer 31:31-34) was fulfilled in Jesus, as Hebrews 8–9 describes.

"Poured out for many for the forgiveness of sins." The meaning of the death of Jesus as a sacrifice is linked with the understanding of the Passover and of the covenant. It is also linked with what Isaiah 53 says of the suffering Servant making himself "an offering for sin" (Is 53:10). Luke 22:37 includes among the words of Jesus in the upper room the statement, "This scripture must be fulfilled in me, 'And he was reckoned with transgressors.' " That verse, Isaiah 53:12, also says, "he poured out his soul to death" and "he bore the sin of many." Mark 14:24 appears to allude to these Scriptures when Jesus speaks of his blood "poured out for many," and Matthew 26:28 adds "for the forgiveness of sins."

Expectation for the Future All four accounts of the Last Supper associate, though in different ways, an expectation for the future with the institution of the Eucharist. In Mark 14:25 it comes in the words of Jesus, "Truly, I say to you, I shall not drink again of the fruit of the vine until that day when I drink it new in the kingdom of God" (RSV). In Matthew 26:29 that future drinking of the fruit of the vine is said to be "with you in my Father's kingdom." In Luke 22:18 there are similar words, and two verses earlier the statement about fulfilling the Passover "in the kingdom of God." All of these can be understood as the ultimate realization of another hope that both OT and later Jewish apocalyptic writings set forward: the messianic banquet, the feast on the mountain of the Lord of which Isaiah 25:6 speaks. In 1 Corinthians

11:26 that future hope is quite explicitly that of Christ's second coming; for, says the apostle, "As often as you eat this bread and drink the cup, you proclaim the Lord's death until he comes" (RSV).

The Practice of the Early Church In Acts 2:42, after the record of what happened at Pentecost, it says "they devoted themselves to the apostles' teaching and fellowship, to the breaking of bread and the prayers" (RSV). Further, "day by day, attending the temple together and breaking bread in their homes, they partook of food with glad and generous hearts" (Acts 2:46, RSV). Two questions are raised about these words and the practice that lay behind them. Do they simply mean that the Christians shared fellowship meals together? Acts 2:46 seems to speak of breaking bread and partaking of food as two separate actions. Moreover, Acts 20:7 in speaking of Christians at Troas "on the first day of the week . . . gathered together to break bread" seems clearly to allude to a Christian service and not just a meal. From 1 Corinthians 10 and perhaps from the reference to "love feasts" in Jude 12, we may reasonably deduce that a meal in Christian fellowship and the celebration of the Lord's Supper often took place together. A second question is whether the earliest "breaking of bread," as in the Jerusalem church, may have been a different rite from that with the bread and wine, the former recalling the fellowship of the disciples with the risen Lord, the latter especially recalling his sacrificial death. There is no direct evidence to support such a view. The Lord's Supper to which the Gospels bear witness involved the breaking of bread and the sharing of the cup in remembrance of the blood of Christ "poured out for many." We may assume, too, that the tradition that the apostle Paul received, followed, and passed on to others went back to his earliest years as a Christian and so involved the breaking of the bread and the sharing of the cup in remembrance of Christ, and thus proclaiming the Lord's death until his return.

Paul's Teaching In Paul's teaching, as in the Gospels, the Lord's Supper clearly involves the backward look in thankful remembrance for the sacrifice of Christ offered once for all for the sins of the world, the realization of the Lord being with his people in the present, and the look forward in hope. Other aspects of teaching relating to the Eucharist are brought out in 1 Corinthians 10–11. The teaching arises from practical aspects of the situation in the Corinthian church; the need to be aware of the danger of turning back in any way to the worship of idols; and the potential divisions in the Christian fellowship, including that between rich and poor.

Fellowship with Christ To partake of the bread and to drink of the cup is spoken of as having part with Christ, as sharing in sacrificial meals would mean partaking at "the table of demons" (1 Cor 10:21). "The cup of blessing which we bless, is it not a participation in the blood of Christ? The bread which we break, is it not a participation in the body of Christ?" (v 16, RSV). "Participation" is the translation of the Greek word *koinonia*, so often rendered "fellowship" in NT passages. When the Lord's Supper was celebrated, there must often have been a recalling not only of the Last Supper on the night before Jesus died, but also of his presence with his disciples on the first Easter and his making himself known to them in the breaking of the bread (Lk 24:30-35). They continued to experience that fellowship with him.

Feeding on Christ Of the two Christian sacraments, baptism has a once-for-all nature, while Holy Communion is repeated. The life of Christ has been offered for sins once for all on the cross, and we find life in turning to him—baptism signifies that. At the same time that life is also offered to us constantly for the nourishing of our spiritual lives day by day—of this regular feeding on Christ the Eucharist speaks. First Corinthians 10:3-4 speaks of "supernatural food" and "supernatural drink" and finds in the events at the sea and in the wilderness in the days of Moses foreshadowings of what Christians find in Christ. Christ said, "I am the bread of life," and "My flesh is food indeed, and my blood is drink indeed"; thus what we have in John's Gospel (Jn 6:35, 55, RSV) is close to what Paul implies about the Lord's Supper expressing the truth of Christians spiritually feeding on Christ.

LO-RUHAMAH Symbolic name, meaning "Not pitied" (Hos 1:6-8), given by the prophet Hosea to his daughter, indicating God's rejection of Israel. *See* Ruhamah.

LOT Abraham's nephew; progenitor of both the Moabites and the Ammonites. Like Abraham, he was born in Ur. When his father died, he was put in the care of his grandfather Terah, and accompanied him and his uncle Abram to Haran (Gn 11:27-32). After the death of Terah, he joined Abram in the journey to Canaan and subsequently to Egypt and back to Canaan.

By the time the pair returned to Canaan, their flocks and herds were too numerous for them to live together in a single area. Generously, Abram gave Lot his choice of where he would like to settle; Lot chose the fertile plain of the Jordan, which was like a "garden of the Lord" (Gn 13:10) before the divine judgment and catastrophe fell on the region. Thus, Lot became increasingly involved with and contaminated by the corruption of the cities of the plain and took up his residence in Sodom.

While Lot was living in Sodom, four Mesopotamian kings (probably of small city-states) defeated the kings of the five towns in the area in battle, and in the subsequent plundering they carried off Lot and his family and possessions. When word of the loss reached Abram, he launched a rearguard action against the invaders and recovered all the prisoners and the loot at Hobah, north of Damascus (Gn 14).

Subsequently, two angelic visitors called on Lot in Sodom to hasten his departure from the doomed city. The homosexual attack on them illustrated the depravity of the city, and Lot's willingness to sacrifice his daughters shows how the corruption of his environment was rubbing off on him. As further evidence of the evil influence, Lot was unwilling to leave Sodom; his future sons-in-law refused to accompany him; and his wife looked back and was turned to a pillar of salt (Gn 19).

The sequel to the story was as sordid as the scene at Lot's door. His daughters, despairing of husbands of their own, got him drunk enough to engage in sexual relations with them. The result was the birth of two sons, Moab and Ben-ammi, ancestors of the Moabites and Ammonites, inveterate enemies of Israel (Gn 19:30-38).

In spite of his waywardness the NT declares that Lot was a "righteous man" (2 Pt 2:7-9), apparently meaning that his faith in God was sufficient to guarantee his salvation. To critics who question the historicity of Lot and the destruction of Sodom, it must be noted that Jesus vouched for both in Luke 17:28-29.

See also Sodom and Gomorrah.

LOTAN Seir's eldest son (Gn 36:20) and a chief of the native Horite inhabitants of Edom (vv 22, 29). Lotan had two sons, Hori and Homam (1 Chr 1:38-39).

LOTS, Casting of Practice common in the OT, less common in the NT prior to Pentecost, and absent in the biblical narrative after Pentecost.

In the Bible the practice was used in a variety of circumstances, including (1) the selection of the scapegoat (Lv 16:8-10); (2) the allocation of the tribal inheritance in the Promised Land (Nm 26:55-56; Jos 14:2; Jgs 1:3); (3) the determination of the families who had to relocate to give a proper distribution of the populace or of those warriors who had to go to war where only a percentage was required (Jgs 20:9; Neh 11:1); (4) the order of the priests and their duties (1 Chr 24:5-19; Neh 10:34); (5) the determination of an offender (Jos 7:14-18; cf. Prv 18:18).

According to biblical usage, lots seem to have been used only when the decision was important and where wisdom or biblical injunctions did not give sufficient guidance. One of the advantages of the casting of lots was the impartiality of the choice. It was held that the Lord directed the lots (Prv 16:33). The method of casting lots is not specified or described and seems to have varied according to the need of the situation (cf. Lv 16:8; Nm 26:55-56; Jgs 20:9).

The practice of casting lots was never condemned by God and on several occasions was sanctioned by him (Lv 16:8; Prv 18:18; Is 34:17). The principle behind the procedure is set forth in Proverbs 16:33, which affirms that the disposition or result of the lot is determined by God; therefore, the theory was that the lot pronounced the will of God.

In the NT the soldiers cast lots over Jesus' garments (Mt 27:35), and the disciples cast lots when they selected Matthias to the apostleship in place of Judas (Acts 1:26). After the outpouring of the Holy Spirit upon the church, the practice of casting lots ceased. Some scholars think that there was no further need for the practice to continue, as the Holy Spirit guided the church in its decisions.

See also Urim and Thummim.

LOTUS Water plant common in the Near East, mentioned only in Job 40:21-22. *See* Plants (Lotus Bush).

LOVE Prominent virtue in Christian theology and ethics. It is therefore important to understand clearly this exceedingly important term.

In the Old Testament Sexual love *(ahabah* and *dod)* is spoken of in the stories of Adam and Eve and of Jacob and Rachel, as well as in the Song of Songs. A higher form of love, involving loyalty, steadfastness, and kindness, is expressed by the Hebrew word *hesed,* which is sometimes rendered "loyalty" (2 Sm 22:26, RSV), but more often "steadfast love" or "loving-kindness."

The connotation of this significant word is clear in Hosea 2:19-20: "I will make you my wife forever, showing you righteousness and justice, unfailing love and compassion. I will be faithful to you and make you mine, and you will finally know me as LORD" (NLT); in Job 6:14-15, where kindness is compared with treachery; and in 1 Samuel 20:8, which speaks of covenanted kindness. This unshakable, steadfast love of God is contrasted with the unpredictable, capricious moods of heathen deities. *Hesed* is not an emotional response to beauty, merit, or kindness but rather a moral attitude dedicated to another's good, whether or not that other is lovable, worthy, or responsive (see Dt 7:7-9).

This enduring loyalty, rooted in an unswerving purpose of good, could be stern, determined to discipline a wayward people, as several prophets warned. But God's love does not change. Through exile and failure it persisted with infinite patience, neither condoning evil nor abandoning the evildoers. It has within it kindness, tenderness, and compassion (Pss 86:15; 103:1-18; 136; Hos 11:1-4), but its chief characteristic is an accepted moral obligation for another's welfare.

Nevertheless, response was expected. The Law enjoined wholehearted love and gratitude for God's choosing and redeeming of Israel (Dt 6:20-25). This was to be shown in worship and especially in humane treatment of the poor, the defenseless, the resident alien, slaves, widows, and all suffering oppression and cruelty. Hosea similarly expected steadfast love among people to result from the steadfast love of God toward people (Hos 6:6; 7:1-7; 10:12-13).

Love for God and for "your neighbor as yourself" (Lv 19:18) are thus linked in Israel's law and prophecy. While much love of another kind lies within the OT, these are the major points: God's loving initiative, the moral quality of love, and the close relationship between love for God with loving others.

In the New Testament Of the Greek words available to describe love, *eros* (sexual love) does not occur in the NT. *Phileo,* connoting natural affection, occurs some 25 times, with *philadelphia* (brotherly love) five times, and *philia* (friendship) only in James 4:4. *Storge,* connoting natural affection between relatives, appears occasionally in compounds. By far the most frequent word is *agape,* generally assumed to mean moral goodwill that proceeds from esteem, principle, or duty rather than attraction of charm. *Agape* is very similar in meaning to *hesed* in that both denote dedication. *Agape* specifically means to love the undeserving, despite disappointment and rejection. The difference between *agapao* and *phileo* is difficult to sustain in all passages. *Agape* is especially appropriate for divine love. *Agape* was long believed to be a Christian coinage, but pagan occurrences have recently been claimed. The verb *agapao* was frequent in the Greek OT. Though *agape* has more to do with moral principle than with inclination or liking, it never means the cold religious kindness shown from duty alone, as scriptural examples abundantly prove.

In the Synoptic Gospels In a sinful and suffering world, Jesus' divine love showed itself supremely in compassion and healing for the distressed and in redemptive concern for the alienated and the self-despairing. Hence, the kingdom Christ proclaimed offered good news to the poor, captives, blind, and oppressed (Mt 11:2-5; Lk 4:18), while the attitude of Jesus toward those ostracized, despised, or grieving over sin in some far country of the soul assured them of forgiveness and a welcome return to the Father's house (Lk 15). Such forgiveness was free, its only precondition being readiness to receive it in repentance and faith.

Moreover, the good news of divine love does impose its own obligation: to love God and to love others as God does (Mt 5:44-48). The first and greatest commandment in God's law is "You shall love the Lord your God. . . . And a second is like it, You shall love your neighbor as yourself. On these two commandments depend all the law and the prophets" (Mt 22:35-40, RSV; cf. Lv 19:18; Dt 6:5).

The first commandment is not identical with, lost in, or only fulfilled through the second; it is separate and primary. What Jesus meant by loving God is indicated by his own habits of public worship, private prayer, and absolute obedience. Love for one's neighbor is nowhere defined but everywhere illustrated. In the parable of the good Samaritan, "neighbor" is shown to mean anyone near enough to help, and love involves whatever service the neighbor's situation demands. The parable of the sheep and goats shows love feeding the hungry, clothing the naked, visiting the sick and the imprisoned. In the untiring example of Jesus, love heals, teaches, adapts instruction to the hearers by parable and symbolic language, defends those criticized or despised, pronounces forgiveness, comforts the bereaved, befriends the lonely. We are to love others as he has loved us and as we love ourselves. Such imaginative transfer of self-love does good without expecting return, never returns ill treatment, ensures unfailing courtesy even to the lowliest, sustains thoughtful understanding that tempers judgment.

To Jesus, the outstanding sin was lovelessness, the willful omission of any possible good, passing by on the other side while others suffer, ignoring the destitute at one's gate, withholding forgiveness. Lovelessness was made worse by self-righteousness, censoriousness, the religious insensitivity that ignores another's distress to preserve some petty ritual regulation. In the end, obedience to or neglect of the law of love will determine everyone's eternal destiny (Mt 25:31-46).

In the Writings of Paul The apostolic church quickly grasped the revolutionary principle that love is enough. Paul's declaration that love fulfills the whole law is almost a quotation from Jesus. His exposition of various commandments against adultery, killing, stealing, and coveting is summarized in loving, because love can do no wrong to a neighbor (Rom 13:8-10). Ephesians 4:25–5:2 makes the same point another way: all bitterness, anger, lying, stealing, slander, and malice are to be replaced by tenderness, forgiveness, and kindness.

Love is, for Paul, "the law of Christ," supreme and sufficient (Gal 5:14; 6:2), and Paul neatly defines what alone "avails" in Christianity as "faith working through love" (5:6). He insists that the supreme manifestation of the Spirit that Christians should covet is "the more excellent way" of love (1 Cor 12:27–13:13; cf. Rom 5:5; Gal 5:22). Here, too, he contrasts love with five other expressions of religious zeal much prized at Corinth in order to show that each is profitless without love (1 Cor 13:1-3). He ends the chapter by comparing love with faith and hope, the other enduring elements of religious experience, and declares love to be the greatest.

Paul's description of love in action includes liberality, acts of mercy, and hospitality; avoidance of revenge; sympathy; rejoicing with others; sharing of weakness, shame, or need; restoring, supporting, and edifying others, giving them all honor, kindness, forgiveness, encouragement; restraining criticism, even of the divisive, overscrupulous "weaker brother"—the list is almost endless. More generally, love is revealed as a quality of activity, of thinking, and of suffering (1 Cor 13:4-8). In brief, love does no harm and omits no good; it is God's law.

According to Paul, God showed his love for us in that Christ died for us. Because of his great love, he made us alive in Christ; in that love we live, by it we conquer, and from it nothing shall separate us (Rom 5:8; 8:32-39; 2 Cor 13:14; Eph 2:4; 2 Thes 2:16; Ti 3:4-5). Our love reflects the love first "poured into our hearts" (Rom 5:5), and it is directed toward Christ (1 Cor 7; 16:22; Eph 6:24) and toward others, whom we love for his sake.

In the Writings of John What John later recalled, and reflected upon, forms the crown of biblical teaching about love. For John, love was the foundation of all that had happened—"God so loved the world" (Jn 3:16; 16:27; 17:23). This is how we know love at all: Christ

laid down his life for us (1 Jn 3:16). The mutual love of Father, Son, and disciples must be the fundamental fact in Christianity because God himself is love (4:8, 16).

We know this by the Incarnation and by the cross (1 Jn 4:9-10). Thus we know and believe the love God has for us, and that love itself is divine ("of God"). It follows that "he who loves is born of God." "He who does not love does not know God." Such a person "is in the darkness," "is not of God," and "remains in death." No one has ever seen God; nevertheless "if we love, . . . God abides in us" and we in God.

God's love is thus prior and original; if we love at all, it is "because he first loved." Our love is directed first toward God, and John is exceedingly searching in his tests of that Godward love. It demands that we "love not the world," that we "keep his word [and] his commandments," and that we love our Christian brothers and sisters. This commandment we received from Christ, "that he who loves God should love his brother also," for "if God so loved us, we also ought to love one another." Twelve times John stressed the duty of mutual loyalty and love. Indeed, if one closes his heart against his brother or sister, "how does God's love abide in him?"

This emphasis upon the mutual love of Christians has been held a serious limitation of the love Jesus required. "Your brother" appears to have supplanted "your neighbor." In this respect the commandment given in the upper room (Jn 13:34) is "new" compared with that in Matthew 22:39 (citing Lv 19:18), and the circumstances explain why. The night on which Jesus was betrayed was shadowed by the surrounding world's hostility, the imminent crucifixion, and the defection of Judas. All the future depended upon the mutual loyalty of the 11 disciples, standing together under social pressure. By the time of John's letter, new defections had rent the church. A perversion of the gospel called Gnosticism, essentially intellectualist, proud, "giving no heed to love" (Ignatius), had drawn away leaders and adherents (1 Jn 2:19, 26). Once again mutual loyalty was all-important, and John wrote expressly to consolidate and maintain the apostolic fellowship (1 Jn 1:3).

However, love for one's fellow Christians does not exclude, but instead leads on to, a wider love (cf. 2 Pt 1:7). John insists that God loved the whole world (Jn 3:16; 1 Jn 2:2; 4:14). Moreover, if love fails within the Christian fellowship, it certainly will not flourish beyond it but evaporate in mere words (1 Jn 3:18).

In countering the loveless conceit of Gnostic Christianity, John's concern was with the basic commandment of love to God and people as at once the criterion and the consummation of true Christian life. He does not, therefore, detail the many-sided expressions of love. For description of love in action, his mind recalls Christ's words about "keeping commandments" and "laying down life" in sacrifice (Jn 15:10, 13; 1 Jn 3:16), and he mentioned especially love's noticing a brother's need, and so sharing this world's goods (v 17). Terse as these expressions are, they contain the heart of Christian love. John's forthright realism in testing all religious claims ensures that for him love could be no vague sentimentalism.

The Christian ideal can only be socially fulfilled within a disciple band, a divine kingdom, the Father's family, the Christian fellowship. In Scripture, love is no abstract idea, conceived to provide a self-explanatory, self-motivating "norm" to resolve the problem in every moral situation. It is rooted in the divine nature, expressed in the coming and death of Christ, experienced in salvation, and so kindled within the saved. Thus it is central, essential, and indispensable to Christianity. For God is love.

See also God, Being and Attributes of; Grace; Mercy; Wrath of God.

LUBIM* KJV form of Libyan, an inhabitant of Libya, in 2 Chronicles 12:3, 16:8, and Nahum 3:9. *See* Libya, Libyans.

LUCAS* KJV spelling of Luke in Philemon 1:24. *See* Luke (Person).

LUCIFER* Appellation from a Latin word meaning "light bearer." The Latin term refers to the planet Venus appearing in the evening and the morning, which is the brightest object in the sky except for the sun and moon. Others have identified it with the crescent moon. It is also said by some to be the planet Jupiter. The Hebrew term, from which the Latin *lucifer* is derived, is found in Isaiah 14:12: "How you have fallen from heaven, O morning star, son of the dawn! You have been cast down to the earth, you who once laid low the nations!" (NIV). The Hebrew word means the "shining one." It has cognates in Akkadian, Ugaritic, and Arabic. The Septuagint, Targum, and the Vulgate translate it as "morning star," quite fitting in view of the appositional "son of the dawn."

The Hebrew expression was probably never meant to be a name, but it has come to be used thus because the verse in which it occurs is applied to Satan. This apparently was done first by two of the church fathers, Tertullian and Origen. However, the popularity of Lucifer as a name for Satan may be attributed to its use in John Milton's *Paradise Lost.*

The event recorded in Isaiah 14:12 may be an example of a story quite commonly known in the time of Isaiah. This old Canaanite story concerned the morning star, who had attempted to rise high above the clouds and establish himself on the mountain where the gods assembled, in the uttermost part of the north. He had desired to take the place of the highest god, becoming ruler of the world. His attempts were thwarted, and he was cast into the underworld. This story of the minor star deity aspiring to ascend above the throne of the most high god served, in the purposes of Isaiah, as an excellent analogy to the pride and aspirations of the king of Babylon, the person with whom chapters 13 and 14 are concerned. Isaiah states (14:3-4) that Yahweh, the God of Israel, would give the people relief from the tyranny of their oppressors, and they would take up a taunt song against the king. Although he had sought to be great, he would be brought low; he who sought to be a god would, with his descendants, cease to exist on the earth. Though the Hebrews had no myths, illustrations from familiar gentile mythology often were used to express spiritual truth.

There are many who believe the expression (and surrounding context) refers to Satan. They believe the similarities among Isaiah 14:12, Luke 10:18, and Revelation 12:7-10 warrant this conclusion. However, although the NT passages do speak of Satan's fall, the context of the Isaiah passage describes the defeated king of Babylon. The Babylonian king had desired to be above God and so fell from heaven. His doom is pictured as already accomplished. Though defeat is certain for Satan, he yet continues his evil acts against God's people. Not until the final judgment (Rv 12–20) will his fate be sealed and his activity stopped. Isaiah, then, is not speaking of Satan in 14:12 but of the proud, and soon to be humiliated, king of Babylon.

See also Satan.

LUCIUS

1. Man from Cyrene, listed among the prophets and teachers in Antioch (Acts 13:1). He may have been among the Jewish Christians from Cyprus and Cyrene who preached to the Gentiles in Antioch in the face of persecution (11:19-21). Various attempts have been made to identify him with Luke, the author of Acts, or with the Lucius of Romans 16:21, but these have been unsuccessful.

2. Jewish believer (cf. Rom 9:3) and one of the companions of Paul who sent greetings to those in Rome (16:21). This casts doubt on Origen's identification of this Lucius with the Luke of the Gospel and Acts, who was most likely a Gentile (Col 4:12-14).

LUD, LUDIM*, LUDITES Names occurring in the table of nations in Genesis 10. Ludim is listed as the first son of Mizraim, and Lud is listed as the fourth son of Shem. On the basis of this, it is probably better to consider them as having different ethnic origins. Some, however, have suggested that both names refer to a people of Asia Minor, the Lydians, who are mentioned on Ashurbanipal's inscriptions as *Luddu.* There is little question that Lud, at least, is to be associated with Lydia. Josephus makes this identification (*Antiquities* 1.6.4.). In Isaiah 66:19, it is listed among other nations of Asia Minor.

Lud is often mentioned in contexts that suggest the men were well known as good soldiers. According to Jeremiah 46:9, they fought with the Egyptians against the Babylonians at the battle of Carchemish in 605 BC. In the lament over Tyre in Ezekiel 27:10, they are listed among others who were mercenaries in the army of Tyre. Perhaps Ezekiel 30:5 is another case of Lydians serving as mercenaries—this time in the Egyptian army. Such military aid to Egypt goes back to the Assyrian period when Gyges sent military aid to Psammetichus of Egypt against the Assyrians.

See also Lydia (Place).

LUHITH Moabite city mentioned in connection with the flight of the Moabites to Zoar (Is 15:5). Since it was also listed with Horonaim, it was perhaps situated between these two cities in the southeastern area around the Dead Sea.

LUKE (Person) Companion of the apostle Paul; author of the third Gospel and Acts.

Accepting the author of Luke-Acts as Luke the companion of Paul, much can be learned about him from this two-volume work. The preface to the Gospel indicates that Luke was not an eyewitness or immediate disciple of the Lord. Luke states that he had carried out extensive research and had written an orderly account about Jesus.

Luke's writings have some features not found in the other Gospels. The extraordinary feature of Luke's work is the inclusion of the book of Acts as a sequel to the Gospel. The two books together—Luke and Acts—show the actual fulfilling of the prophecies of Isaiah in the proclamation of the gospel to the ends of the earth. This inclusion of the Gentiles is often referred to as Luke's universalism or concern for all humanity (Luke 2:14; 24:47). The Gospel of Luke displays a keen interest in individuals, social outcasts, women, children, and social relationships, especially situations involving poverty or wealth. This Gospel has a special stress on prayer and the Holy Spirit, which results in a striking note of joyfulness and praise. These features tell us something about Luke as a person and his understanding of Christianity.

If Luke is accepted as the companion of Paul, then the "we" passages of Acts disclose that Luke was in Philippi (possibly his hometown) when he first joined Paul (Acts 16:10-17). Then he later rejoined Paul when the latter returned to Philippi (20:5-15). Luke then journeyed with

Paul on his way to Jerusalem and stayed with Philip at Caesarea (21:1-18). Then, after Paul's two-year imprisonment in Caesarea, Luke sailed with him to Rome (27:1–28:16).

Further references to Luke in the epistles of Paul (Col 4:14; 2 Tm 4:11; Phlm 1:24) give some valuable information about Luke. Colossians 4:11 and 14 seem to indicate that Luke was a Gentile and a physician. The latter is supported, but not proved, by the interest shown by Luke in medical matters, as in Luke 4:38, 5:12, and 8:43. It is also interesting that early tradition adds that Luke was a physician of Antioch who wrote his Gospel in Achaia and died at the age of 84.

LUKE, Gospel of Third book of the NT; also the third of the synoptic Gospels (Matthew, Mark, Luke).

PREVIEW
• Author
• Date, Origin, and Destination
• Background
• Purpose and Theological Teaching
• Content

Author Tradition attributes the authorship of the Gospel to the esteemed companion of Paul, Luke the physician (Col 4:14). The Gospel does not identify its author by name, but he is apparently well known in the company of early believers. He had obviously been gathering information for his project for some time. In both Luke and Acts the recipient is identified as Theophilus.

The internal testimony of Acts for Lucan authorship must also be weighed, since there is a close relationship between the two books. In three extensive "we" passages the author reports his presence (Acts 16:10-17; 20:5–21:18; 27:1–28:16). These appear to be excerpts from a travel diary; the last of them places the author in Rome with the apostle Paul. We can, by the process of elimination, virtually establish Luke as the author.

Date, Origin, and Destination The dating of Luke is debatable. Some argue for a date after AD 70, but this robs Luke 21:20 of its predictive value. Others suggest a date prior to the death of Paul (AD 64). The latter would readily account for Acts concluding with his ministry in Rome while in prison.

The Gospel may have been written in Rome, but this is by no means certain. Asia Minor and Greece have also been suggested as possibilities. The *Monarchian Prologue to Luke* promotes the latter option, but its reliability is suspect. It was at Rome that Luke could have used the time profitably to put the finishing touches on the third Gospel.

Luke wrote to Theophilus. Theophilus ("beloved of God") is probably not, as some suggest, a generic term for all believers. He was a person apparently unfamiliar with the geography of Palestine, for Luke takes care to detail it from time to time. He has a much better grasp of the Greco-Roman world as a whole, for Luke predictably assumes his reader's familiarity with it. Luke also avoids terms that might prove puzzling to a gentile reader, such as "hosanna" in connection with Jesus' triumphant entry into Jerusalem.

In all probability the third Gospel was composed in Rome while Paul awaited trial, on or before AD 64. It was dedicated to the "most excellent Theophilus" (Lk 1:3), as an appropriate custom of the time. He was a prominent Gentile who had become a believer. Luke wanted to instruct him (and others) more carefully in the faith.

Background Jesus lived out his life within an area roughly 50 miles (80.5 kilometers) wide and 150 miles

(241.4 kilometers) long, from Dan in the north to Beersheba in the south. Apart from Jerusalem, the places he is reported to have visited are not important to the secular history of the region. He was raised in the humble village of Nazareth and lived there until about 30 years of age. Capernaum became the center for his Galilean ministry. He passed through Samaria on occasion, and he ministered in Perea. He was betrayed and crucified in Jerusalem. He was raised in triumph on the third day.

Luke writes in retrospect. His perspective had shifted during the interim—geographically from Palestine to the Roman Empire, politically from Israel to Rome, socially from Jewish society to pagan, and religiously from the temple to the horizon of Christian mission. It is as if one era were superimposed on the other, so that the significance of the life and ministry of Jesus can be seen for the early church.

Purpose and Theological Teaching Simeon beautifully expressed the redemptive theme of Luke's Gospel when he held Jesus in his arms and exclaimed: "I have seen the Savior you have given to all people. He is a light to reveal God to the nations, and he is the glory of your people Israel!" (Lk 2:30-32, NLT). He pointed to Jesus as the long-anticipated Savior, the hope of Gentiles and Jews alike.

Luke wove the work of the Holy Spirit into the life and ministry of Jesus. Jesus was conceived by the Holy Spirit (Lk 1:35); the Spirit descended on him at his baptism (3:22); he was led into the desert by the Spirit to be tempted (4:2); he was anointed by the Spirit for his ministry (v 18). The Spirit is, as it were, in the background with regard to Jesus' subsequent labors, but the relationship is understood even when it is not repeated.

Luke accented the experience of messianic joy. The angelic host announced Jesus' birth with the words, "Glory to God in the highest heaven, and peace on earth to all whom God favors" (2:14, NLT). Then, as he was approaching Jerusalem, the multitude that accompanied him began to praise God, saying, "Bless the King who comes in the name of the Lord! Peace in heaven and glory in highest heaven!" (19:38, NLT).

All this suggests that the redemptive theme in Luke is complex in character. It points to Jesus as the Christ. It invites the favorable response of Gentiles no less than Jews. It blends in the empowering of the Holy Spirit for Jesus' ministry and that of his disciples. It emphasizes the joy that accompanies the publication of the gospel. These are simply variations on the one redemptive design of Luke.

Other concerns surface incidentally. Luke's interest in historical accuracy is one of these. His apologetic burden is another. The critical place he gives to prayer is a third. The list could be extended.

Content

Prologue (1:1-4) The Gospel begins with a formal prologue. Luke sought to record in orderly fashion what others had handed down as a legacy of faith. He did so in order to establish the historical credentials of the faith and to assure his readers of their validity.

Nativity and Childhood of Jesus (1:5–2:52) None of the Gospels is a thoroughgoing biography of Jesus. But Luke took a special interest in historical incidents, first with regard to the nativity and childhood narratives. He recounted 10 episodes in all: the annunciation of John the Baptist's birth as the forerunner of Christ; the announcement of Jesus' birth to Mary; the visit of Mary to Elizabeth; the birth of John the Baptist; John the Baptist's time in the wilderness; the birth of Jesus; the visit of the shepherds; the circumcision of Jesus; Jesus' presentation in the temple; and the visit to the temple as a youth.

John the Baptist received considerable attention from the outset. Luke recorded that it was during the reign of Herod (Herod the Great, 37–4 BC) that Zechariah the priest was ministering in the temple. (Twenty-four platoons of priests served in this capacity for two separate weeks out of the year. The privilege of burning incense was determined by casting lots, and once the priest had done so, he was disqualified from repeating the act.) An angel of the Lord appeared to Zechariah as he was about to burn incense, announcing that he and his wife, Elizabeth, would have a son, whose name should be John. He was to live as a Nazirite (see Nm 6:1-4) and prepare the way for the Messiah. When Zechariah was reluctant to believe (he and Elizabeth were of advanced age), the angel struck him dumb until the time of the promised birth.

We next hear of John in connection with Mary's visit to Elizabeth. The baby leaped within Elizabeth's womb as she heard Mary's greeting (Lk 1:41). Luke immediately followed this account with the birth of John the Baptist. Zechariah named the child as he had been directed, received back his speech, and proceeded to prophesy concerning the coming Messiah and the preparatory role his son would play. The child grew and became "strong in spirit," abiding in the wilderness until his public ministry began.

Luke told the nativity

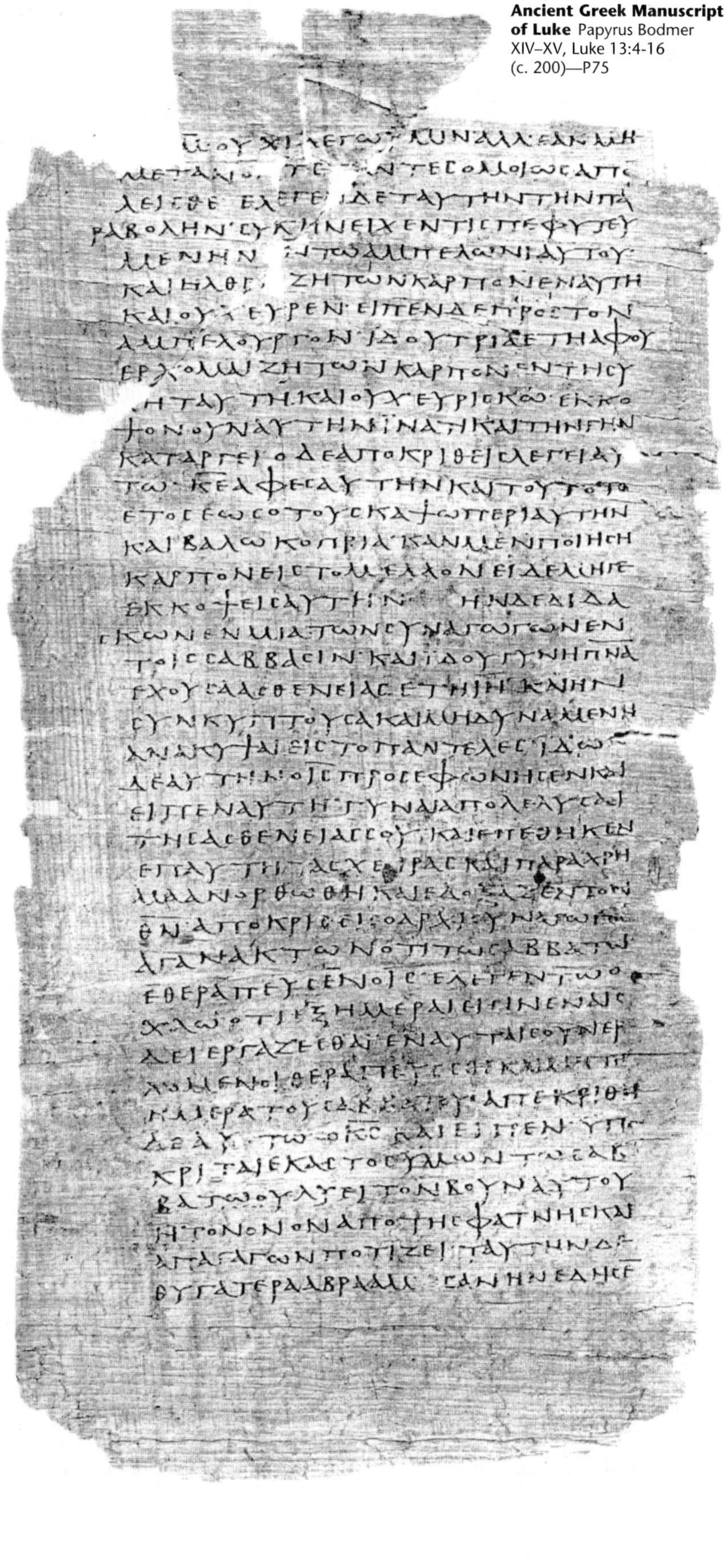

Ancient Greek Manuscript of Luke Papyrus Bodmer XIV–XV, Luke 13:4-16 (c. 200)—P75

story from the perspective of Mary. The angel Gabriel visited her and announced that she would give birth to the Messiah (1:26-38). She would conceive miraculously by the Holy Spirit. Mary is portrayed as being devoutly submissive to the purposes of God.

The birth is said to have taken place when Quirinius was governor of Syria, and persons had to travel to their ancestral towns to register for a census. Mary gave birth in a Bethlehem stable. Angels announced the birth to shepherds, who left their flocks to observe the child. Mary treasured these events and continued to ponder their significance.

After Mary had observed her 40 days of ritual purification, she went with Joseph to the temple to present Jesus to the Lord (2:21-40). There Simeon and Anna, two elderly and devout persons, recognized the infant as the promised Messiah. Simeon concluded that Jesus would cause many in Israel to fall and rise, and would bring deep sorrow to the heart of Mary.

The nativity and childhood narratives close with Jesus' visit to the temple at age 12 to celebrate the Feast of the Passover. Joseph and Mary left Jesus behind in the temple, supposing that he was among relatives or friends. They retraced their steps and found him in the temple conversing with the rabbis—listening to them and amazing them with his own understanding. Luke concluded by saying that "Jesus grew both in height and in wisdom, and he was loved by God and by all who knew him" (2:52, NLT).

Beginning of the Public Ministry (3:1-4:30)

Luke then recorded those events related to the inauguration of Jesus' ministry. These include the ministry of John the Baptist, the baptism of Jesus, his genealogy, his temptation, and the public announcement in Nazareth. Luke dated the beginning of John the Baptist's ministry in no fewer than six ways: with the terms of office of Tiberius Caesar, Pontius Pilate, Herod Antipas, Philip, Lysanias, and Annas and Caiaphas. John came preaching a baptism of repentance in preparation for the coming of the Messiah. Multitudes came out into the wilderness to hear him and to be baptized by him.

Jesus also came to be baptized. (Luke does not record John's protest that Jesus ought rather to baptize him, or Jesus' insistence that it had to be done—apparently to identify with the people and anticipate his vicarious death on their behalf.) The baptism marked Jesus' entry into public ministry. Luke inserted what may be the genealogical record through Mary, consistent with his earlier efforts to narrate the events from her perspective.

The temptation of Jesus was a probationary test of his messianic ministry. The introduction to two of the temptations, "If you are the Son of God," was calculated to make him doubt the words heard at his baptism, "You are my Son" (3:22; 4:3, 9). Satan hoped to persuade Jesus to seek to fulfill his calling and yet avoid the cross. Each time Jesus parried the temptation with a quotation from Scripture.

Jesus returned to Galilee and to the synagogue in Nazareth. Here he announced his public ministry in words borrowed from the jubilee observance and associated with the messianic age (4:18-19; cf. Is 61:1-2). They reflected both the religious focus and broad social implications of the ministry to come. The announcement especially held out hope to those who were downtrodden and ostracized by society. When those in attendance challenged his credentials, Jesus replied, "No prophet is accepted in his own hometown" (Lk 4:24). And when they would have cast him from the brow of a hill, he passed through their midst and went on his way.

The Galilean Ministry (4:31-9:50)

Jesus moved the center of his activity to Capernaum. Luke records a variety of episodes associated with the Galilean ministry that follows. Approximately 30 instances are mentioned. About a third involve some extraordinary occurrence, such as healing, exorcism, raising from the dead, or feeding a multitude. These were events associated with the messianic age.

However, it was Jesus' teaching that first seems to have caught the people's attention. He did not teach as the rabbis, by drawing upon traditional precedent, but he taught in the authority of his messianic office. Luke interlaced his narrative with a considerable amount of Jesus' teaching. There is a fairly extended section on the observance of the Sabbath (6:1-11). But it is less prominent than Jesus' sermon "on the plain," with its extended comments concerning blessings and woes, love for enemies, judging others, knowing one by his fruit, and wise and foolish builders (6:12-49). Jesus taught by way of parables, and Luke recorded those of the sower and lamp (8:1-18). In the former instance, the seed represents the word of God, and the soil the varying preparation to receive the Word. Thereby the disciples might better understand the mixed results of Jesus' ministry and their own. Others would be perplexed by the parables.

Luke described the calling of select disciples. He mentioned Peter, James, and John, and at a later point Levi (5:1-11, 27-32). The former were called from their fishing boats and the latter from his tax booth. All were summoned to follow Christ in his messianic ministry through the Galilean countryside. Later on, when there were 12 disciples, Jesus sent them out to preach the kingdom and heal the sick (9:1-11). No doubt many contributed to the extended ministry. Luke recorded certain women who traveled with them and "were contributing from their own resources to support Jesus and his disciples" (8:3, NLT).

One senses a rising tide of enthusiasm with regard to the Galilean enterprise. It begins with Jesus alone, working in obscurity; it terminates with a faithful band of followers, multitudes hanging on his words, and his name circulated throughout the region. The section peaks with Peter's confession of Jesus as the Christ and the transfiguration of Jesus (9:10-36). The presence of Moses and Elijah represents the Law and Prophets as subordinate to the Messiah.

The scene shifts abruptly to the foot of the mount, where the disciples have been ineffective in delivering a demon-possessed boy. Here Jesus pointed out the need for spiritual resources to accomplish kingdom needs, and thereafter (in response to the disciples' argument over who would be greatest) an appeal to humility.

The Journey toward Jerusalem (9:51-19:27)

Luke next reported Jesus' ministry on the way to Jerusalem. This has sometimes been called the Perean ministry, assuming that much of it took place across the Jordan in the district of Perea. It has also been graphically described as "the road to the cross." The number of incidents are roughly the same as those in the preceding section, although the text is about 25 percent longer.

Opposition is seen building at the outset. Jesus sent messengers ahead to prepare for his arrival at a Samaritan village. But the inhabitants would not welcome him, because he was on the way to Jerusalem. There was bad blood between the Jews and Samaritans. The latter had been settled in the land during the Assyrian occupation and brought with them foreign religious and social customs, resulting in a syncretism repugnant to the Jews. Certain disciples asked if Jesus would have them bring down fire from heaven on the village, but Jesus rebuked them. He evidenced a more conciliatory spirit.

Luke reintroduced the Samaritans in connection with a story Jesus tells (10:25-37). It seems that a man was attacked by thieves, who left him for dead. First a priest and then a Levite came along, each walking by on the opposite side of the road. Another passed that way and took pity on the injured stranger. He bound up his wounds and brought him to an inn where he could be cared for at the expense of his benefactor. Jesus added the detail that the man who stopped to help was a Samaritan. He alone understood that a neighbor is the one we befriend rather than the one who befriends us. (The Samaritans reappear once more in the account of 10 lepers who were healed, of whom only a Samaritan returned to give thanks—17:11-19.)

The story of the good Samaritan suggests the opposition Jesus was encountering from the religious establishment centered in Jerusalem. Even as the crowds increased, Jesus observed: "The queen of Sheba will rise up against this generation on judgment day and condemn it, because she came from a distant land to hear the wisdom of Solomon. And now someone greater than Solomon is here—and you refuse to listen to him" (11:31, NLT). So also will the men of Nineveh stand to condemn the present generation, because they repented at the preaching of Jonah, and now one greater than Jonah is here.

Jesus reserved the severest rebuke for those Pharisees who had come to contest his every move. Jesus and the Pharisees traveled in much the same circles. Some had been sympathetic to his message, but these seem to have been in the minority. Jesus pictured the Pharisees as meticulous legalists (11:37-44). Events were building to a climax. Jesus had prophesied his impending death and subsequent resurrection. His face was set toward Jerusalem. When some solicitous Pharisees warned him of Herod Antipas's plan to have him killed, he refused to be intimidated (13:32-33).

Parables abound in this section of the Gospel. They include those of the Good Samaritan, mustard seed, yeast, narrow door, invitation to a marriage feast, great banquet, tower builder, king who goes to war, lost sheep, lost coin, Prodigal Son, unjust steward, rich man and Lazarus, Pharisee and publican, and ten minas. These seem to fall into one of three categories, although perhaps not exclusively so. The one has to do with accepting sinners. (While Scripture reveals that we are all sinners, "sinners" in the synoptic Gospels refers to nonobservant Jews.) A classic instance is the story of the Prodigal Son (15:11-32).

The second category might be called kingdom parables. They suggest that while the kingdom begins in some relatively insignificant fashion, it will expand to incredible proportions. They also warn that not all that seems a part of the growth is a true extension of the kingdom. These emphases can be recognized by comparing the parables of the mustard seed, yeast, and narrow door (13:18-30).

The third category deals with stewardship. Jesus told one such parable as they neared Jerusalem (19:11-27). It involved a man of noble birth who went to a far country, leaving his servants with ten minas each (a mina was about a three-month wage for laborers). They were to invest the minas so that the man would have a good profit when he came back. Upon returning, the nobleman called his servants to get an accounting from them. Those who were found faithful in lesser things were given greater opportunity, but one who failed lost even that which he had been given.

There are some especially touching scenes in the Gospel narrative. One shows Jesus welcoming little children (18:15-17). Another describes a rich ruler who inquired of Jesus how he might obtain eternal life (vv 18-30). Still another episode concerns a tax collector called Zacchaeus (19:1-10). These help us to gain a better appreciation of Jesus' diversified ministry.

Slowly but surely Jesus had worked his way to Jerusalem. He had met increasing opposition. The cross was just over the horizon. He ministered while time allowed.

Jesus' Death and Resurrection (19:28-24:53) Luke concluded his account with the Passion week. First is the Triumphal Entry of Christ (19:28-44). As those with Jesus came over the crest of the Mt of Olives, they began to praise God for all the miracles they had seen: "Bless the King who comes in the name of the Lord! Peace in heaven and glory in highest heaven!" (19:38, NLT). The jubilation of the multitude stands in sharp contrast to Jesus' weeping over an unrepentant city and lamenting the destruction to be visited upon it.

Entering the temple area, Jesus began driving out those who were selling goods there. God's house should be a house of prayer, but—Jesus protests—they have made it a den of robbers. He continued to teach daily in the temple precincts, while the religious leaders plotted how to put him to death without inciting the anger of the people.

Luke recorded some of the interchange with the leaders and people (chs 20-21). This includes a challenge to Jesus' authority, the parable of the wicked tenants, the question about paying taxes to Caesar, another question concerning the resurrection, Jesus' question about how to understand the Messiah's Davidic ancestry and lordship, warning against the scribes, comments on the widow's offering, and discourse on the end of the age. This broad range of topics is related to the messianic disputation in progress.

The problem as Luke represents it seems less an intellectual than a moral one. The religious establishment was determined to retain its privileged position at all costs. This Galilean rabbi was a serious threat that had to be eliminated. It was only a matter of waiting for the right opportunity. It appeared when Judas Iscariot offered to betray Jesus (22:1-6).

The Last Supper and the prayer vigil in Gethsemane intervene between the plot of the leaders and the arrest of Jesus (22:7-46). From the upper room Jesus and the disciples made their way across the Kidron Valley to the Mt of Olives. Here Jesus prayed in preparation for the crucifixion to follow. The disciples slept, being weary from the heavy demands of those days. Soon Judas appeared to point Jesus out, and the soldiers rushed him away to stand before the high priest. Peter denied Christ, fearing for his own life. Jesus was condemned by the Sanhedrin. (Commentators debate whether this was a formal session of the council of Jewish elders.) He was sent to the Roman governor, Pontius Pilate, then to Herod Antipas, and back again to Pilate. Pilate saw no reason for putting Jesus to death, but the multitude was stirred up by the Jewish leaders to demand his crucifixion. Pilate yielded to their pressure when alternatives seemed to escape him.

Jesus was led away to be crucified. Luke alone mentioned those who mourned him (23:27). Jesus warned them rather to mourn for themselves and their children. Here and hereafter we see Jesus' concern for others in the midst of his own agony: those crucifying him, the repentant criminal, and his mother, Mary.

Luke records a mixed response to the crucifixion. The people stood watching, as if immobilized by the rush of events. They may have felt helpless to intervene even if disposed to do so. Some of the religious leaders went so far as to mock Jesus; "He saved others, . . . let him save himself if he is really God's Chosen One, the Messiah" (23:35, NLT). One hardened criminal joined in their derision; the other asked for clemency.

Darkness shrouded the scene. The curtain of the temple was torn, as if to suggest that access was being made available through the shed blood of Christ. Jesus commended his spirit to the Father. He breathed his last. His body was laid in the tomb of Joseph of Arimathea. Women went to prepare spices and perfumes for the interment, but they rested on the Sabbath in obedience to the commandment.

Early on the first day of the week the women approached the tomb, only to find the stone guarding its entrance rolled away and the body of Jesus missing. Suddenly two figures in gleaming array stood by them. They announced to the frightened women: "He isn't here! He has risen from the dead!" (24:6, NLT). The women returned to report to the apostles. Peter ran to confirm their findings. He discovered the strips of linen laid out as they had been, but with the body absent. He wondered what had happened.

The same day two disciples were going to a village called Emmaus. They were discussing what had happened in Jerusalem when Jesus joined them. They were kept from recognizing him until later on when he broke bread with them. They hurriedly returned to Jerusalem to reassure the fellowship that it was true that the Lord was risen.

While they were still talking, Jesus appeared in their midst. "Look at my hands. Look at my feet. You can see that it's really me. Touch me and make sure that I am not a ghost, because ghosts don't have bodies, as you see that I do!" (24:39, NLT). Then he helped them understand the implications of what had happened: "Yes, it was written long ago that the Messiah must suffer and die and rise again from the dead on the third day. With my authority, take this message of repentance to all the nations, beginning in Jerusalem: 'There is forgiveness of sins for all who turn to me.' You are witnesses of all these things. And now I will send the Holy Spirit, just as my Father promised. But stay here in the city until the Holy Spirit comes and fills you with power from heaven" (vv 46-49, NLT).

Luke concludes his Gospel with an account of the ascension (24:50-53). It was as Jesus blessed them that he was lifted up before their eyes. They worshiped him as the ascended Lord and returned to Jerusalem with great joy. There they remained in the temple precinct, praising God and anticipating the coming of the Holy Spirit to empower them for witnessing to all the world.

See also Acts of the Apostles, Book of the; Jesus Christ, Life and Teachings of; Luke (Person); Synoptic Gospels.

LUTE

LUTE Guitarlike musical instrument with strings stretched along a neck and over a sounding box, usually plucked or strummed. *See* Musical Instruments (Asor).

LUZ

1. Original Canaanite name of the city of Bethel (Gn 28:19; 35:6). It was here that Jacob had a vision of God. In recognition of God's presence he called the place "the house of God" (beth-El). Jacob may not have been in the city itself, which might account for the seeming discrepancy in Joshua 16:2. The phrase "from Bethel to Luz" in the description of the border of the land allotted to Joseph (Ephraim and Manasseh) seems to distinguish Bethel from Luz as though they were two different cities. Perhaps the

solution is to be found in that originally the name Luz continued to be used of the city, while at the same time the Israelites knew, through tradition, of the place where Jacob had named Bethel outside the city of Luz. According to Joshua 16:2, then, Bethel would be an area lying east of the city of Luz. At the time of Conquest (Jgs 1:22-25), or subsequently, the Israelites changed the name of Luz to Bethel.

See also Bethel (Place), Bethelite #1.

2. Hittite city named after Luz in Palestine by one of its inhabitants who migrated to the Hittite region after the Israelites captured this city (Jgs 1:26).

LYCAONIA Region in the southern interior of the Roman province of Asia (also called Asia Minor), north of the Taurus Mountains. Prior to Roman occupation, it was bordered on the north by Galatia, on the south by Cilicia, on the east by Cappadocia, and on the west by Phrygia and Pisidia. Like many of its neighboring states, Lycaonia was ruled by the Seleucids after the conquest of Alexander the Great. When the Romans defeated the Seleucids in western Asia Minor (190 BC), Lycaonia was given to the Attalids of Pergamum. It remained under their control until 130 BC, when their king died and their kingdom was dissolved. The area was subsequently administered by the Romans, who attached the northern section of the Lycaonian territory to Galatia, the eastern section to Cappadocia, and the southern section to Cilicia. In AD 37 eastern Lycaonia gained independence from Cappadocia and was known as Lycaonia Antiochiana. By the time of Christ, Lycaonia had essentially been reduced to an ethnic area in southern Galatia and should be considered as such in all NT references.

The territory was situated on a high, barren plateau. The soil was generally of poor quality, though fertile areas existed in the south around the principal cities of Lystra and Derbe. Consequently, the primary occupations were the herding of sheep and goats, with some agriculture in the south. Lycaonia was bisected by a major trade route between Syria, Ephesus, and Rome.

It is debatable whether Iconium was a city of Lycaonia. Some scholars believe it was the capital and principal city. Others consider it a Phrygian city. The latter position seems to be supported in Acts, where Paul is said to flee Iconium for Lystra and Derbe, "cities of Lycaonia" (Acts 14:6)—places where the Lycaonian language was spoken (v 11). It is likely that within the political territory of Galatia there were several ethnic areas and that Paul crossed an ethnic border in an attempt to find safety from the disgruntled Jews of Iconium.

The apostle Paul made three visits to Lycaonia. During his first missionary journey, the preaching of the gospel was very effective and many disciples were made (Acts 14:21-22). In fact, when Paul healed a crippled man in Lystra, the leaders of the pagan cult wished to worship him as a god (vv 11-18). He visited the area again on his second missionary journey. It was here that he met Timothy and asked him to join his company (16:1-5). A final visit (during his third journey, where his purpose was to strengthen the believers) is indicated by Acts 18:23.

Later Christian inscriptions indicate that by the end of the third century the region of Lycaonia possessed one of the most mature ecclesiastical systems in Asia Minor.

LYCIA Country located in the southwest part of the Roman province of Asia (commonly known as Asia Minor), bounded on the northwest by Caria, on the north by Phrygia and Pisidia, on the northeast by Pamphylia, and on the west, south, and east by the Mediterranean Sea. The geography of the region combines rugged mountainous terrain with fertile valleys formed by the descent of several small rivers to the sea. The mountainous regions produce olives, grapes, and timber, while the valleys are responsible for the production of the area's cultivated grains. At the mouths of the rivers are located the major seaports of the country. Two of these, Patara and Myra, are of interest to students of the NT.

Patara, located in southwest Lycia in the valley of the Xanthus River, was the seat of the oracle of Apollo. Acts 21:1 mentions it as the port where Paul, at the conclusion of his third missionary journey, boarded a ship sailing for Phoenicia (some manuscripts include here an additional stop at Myra). Myra, located in southeast Lycia, is mentioned in Acts 27:5-7 as the port where Paul and Julius, a Roman centurion, boarded an Alexandrian ship bound for Rome. When winds were from the west, it was the practice of Alexandrian grain ships headed for Italy to work north along the shore of Palestine and Syria and west along the southern coast of Asia Minor. This would make the ports of Lycia natural places for ships to harbor in preparation for the final leg of the trip to Italy.

The history of the region is tied closely to that of Asia Minor. Among all the peoples of western Asia Minor, Lycia was alone able to withstand the onslaught of the kings of Lydia. However, in 546 BC it was forced to submit to Persian domination. With the invasion of Alexander the Great in 333 BC, Lycia came under the control of the Ptolemies (308–197 BC) and the Seleucids (197–189 BC). When the Romans defeated Antiochus III at Magnesia (189 BC), Lycia was given to Rhodes, an island off its western coast. Twenty years later Rome granted Lycia the status of an independent state. This status held until AD 43, when Emperor Claudius declared Lycia a Roman province. Under the provincial reorganization of Vespasian in AD 74, it was joined with Pamphylia.

First Maccabees 15:23 gives evidence of a sizable Jewish community in Lycia around 139 BC. The NT provides no evidence of Christians in this area. However, a letter from Lycia written in AD 312 to Emperor Maxim in opposition to Christianity indicates the presence of Christians in this region in the early centuries of the church.

LYDDA New Testament name for Lod, a town located southwest of Jerusalem in the Shephelah (Acts 9:32-38). See Lod.

LYDIA (Person) Gentile woman who was converted under the preaching of Paul in Philippi (Acts 16:14, 40). Lydia was a dealer in purple cloth and came from the city of Thyatira in the region of Lydia in the western part of the Roman province of Asia (commonly known as Asia Minor). The description of her as "a worshiper of God" (or "God-fearer") indicates that she was a Gentile who had been attracted to Judaism. After her conversion to Christianity and her baptism, she hosted Paul and Silas during their stay in Philippi.

LYDIA (Place) Name designating a geographical area occurring in Jeremiah 46:9, Ezekiel 27:10, and 30:5 in the NLT. In other versions, it is listed as "Lud" (see NLT mg) or "Ludim." But the identification of Lydia with Lud or Ludim in the OT is not certain. Jeremiah mentions Lud in connection with the North African countries of Put (Libya) and Ethiopia (Jer 46:9). Ezekiel mentions Lud in connection with Put and Persia (Ez 27:10), as well as Arabia (30:5). Josephus considered the Lydians to have been founded by Lud (*Antiquities* 1.6.4).

In any event, it appears that Lydia refers to a province in the western part of the Roman province of Asia (modern Turkey) bounded on the north by Mysia, on the east by Phrygia, on the south by Caria, and on the west by the Greek cities in Ionia. It is listed among the provinces taken by the conquering Romans from the Syrian king Antiochus the Great and given to Eumenes II, the king of Pergamum, after the battle of Magnesia in 190 BC.

The capital of Lydia, Sardis, was considerably inland, and the province never showed any significant maritime development. Herodotus referred to Lydia as a fertile land and to its abundance of silver (*Persian Wars* 5.49), while Tacitus spoke of the rich countries around Sardis (*Annals* 4.55). According to Herodotus, the Lydians "were the first nation to introduce the use of gold and silver coin, and the first who sold goods by retail" (*Persian Wars* 1.94).

By NT times, Lydia had become a part of the Roman province of Asia, having been given to Rome in 133 BC by the Pergamene king Attalus III. Five of the churches to which the book of Revelation was addressed were in Lydia (Ephesus, Smyrna, Sardia, Philadelphia, and Laodicea).

See also Lud, Ludim, Ludites.

LYE Strong alkaline substance (probably potassium carbonate) used for cleaning purposes. *See* Minerals and Metals.

LYRE Stringed instrument consisting of a body, crossbar, and sometimes a sounding box. *See* Musical Instruments (Kathros, Kinnor).

LYSANIAS Tetrarch of Abilene (the area west of Damascus) in AD 27–28. The Gospel of Luke mentions Lysanias as among those who ruled at the beginning of John the Baptist's ministry (Lk 3:1). This is the only reference to him in the NT.

Josephus mentions a Lysanias who succeeded his father, Ptolemaeus, as the king of Chalcis. However, he was killed by Mark Antony in 36 BC. Since there is no other known reference to a Lysanias in the writings of antiquity, and since this second Lysanias could not have lived during John the Baptist's lifetime, some biblical scholars assume Luke is inaccurate in his chronology. In defense of Luke, other scholars indicate that Josephus mentions "Abila of Lysanius," an area given to Agrippa II by Claudius in AD 53; however, that reference may be to the Lysanias who ruled Chalcis 90 years earlier.

The most conclusive evidence in support of Luke is found in an inscription that records the dedication of a temple at Abila, "for the salvation of the Lord Imperial and their whole household by Nymphaeus, a freedman of Lysanias the tetrarch." The title "Lord Imperial" was bestowed jointly only on Emperor Tiberius and his mother, Livia, Augustus's widow. That would fix Lysanias's date between AD 14 (when Tiberius became emperor) and AD 29 (when Livia died). On that basis Luke's chronology may be assumed accurate.

LYSIAS
1. Roman commander who wrote a letter to Felix concerning the apostle Paul (Acts 23:26). See Claudius Lysias.
2. Appointed regent of Syria by Antiochus IV Epiphanes while the king was fighting the Parthians (1 Macc 3:31-37; 166–165 BC). Lysias (d. 162 BC) sent generals Ptolemy, Nicanor, and Gorgias to subdue Judas Maccabeus in Judea and then himself led an attack on Judas. Eventually, a peace treaty was signed and approved by Antiochus Epiphanes (2 Macc 11). This

removed the severe religious restrictions against the Jews, and Judas proceeded to cleanse the temple and reinstate the daily sacrifice.

When Antiochus Epiphanes died in 164, Lysias, accompanied by the boy-king Antiochus V Eupator, entered Judea again, defeated Judas at Bethzacharia, and laid siege to Jerusalem. But the political situation in Antioch forced Lysias to withdraw and return to Syria, where he and his young charge, Antiochus V, were overthrown by Demetrius I and executed (162 BC).

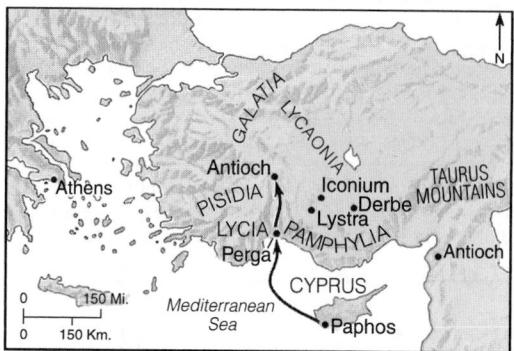

Paul and Barnabas's Ministry in Lystra Paul and Barnabas, thrown out of Antioch in Pisidia, descended the mountains, going east into Lycaonia. They went first to Iconium, a commercial center on the road between Asia and Syria. After preaching there, they had to flee to Lystra, 25 miles (40.2 kilometers) south. Paul was stoned in Lystra, but he and Barnabas traveled the 50 miles (80.5 kilometers) to Derbe, a frontier town. The pair then boldly retraced their steps.

LYSIMACHUS

1. According to the Additions to Esther, the son of Ptolemy of Jerusalem and translator of the book of Esther into Greek.
2. Menelaus appointed his brother Lysimachus to function as his deputy in the high priesthood. He himself had supplanted Jason as high priest. An evil man,

Menelaus consented to acts of sacrilege by Lysimachus against the temple, including the theft of many gold vessels. The people reacted against Lysimachus, who then attempted to subdue them with 3,000 men. He failed. In the process the people, using stones and blocks of wood, routed Lysimachus and his men, killing Lysimachus near the treasury.

LYSTRA City in the region of Lycaonia in the Roman province of Galatia. Events in the town in the NT are confined to the book of Acts (and referenced in 2 Tm 3:11). On Paul's first missionary journey, Paul and Barnabas encountered opposition at Iconium and fled to Lystra, Derbe, and the surrounding region (Acts 14:6). While at Lystra, Paul healed a crippled man (v 8). This miracle excited the local crowd to cry out that Barnabas must be Zeus, and that Paul was Hermes (later called by their Latin counterparts Jupiter and Mercury in some English versions) because of his role as chief speaker (vv 9-21).

The town of Lystra was largely inhabited by the remnants of a small Anatolian tribe who spoke their own dialect, attested today by a number of inscriptions found in the area and still spoken as late as the sixth century AD. Evidently the old Anatolian village system prevailed in this market town even when Roman rule was established there.

The Greek deities Zeus and Hermes were worshiped in that area, and archaeological evidence confirms Luke's picture in Acts. One inscription records the dedication to Zeus on a statue of Hermes. Another records a dedication to "Zeus before the town," throwing light on Acts 14:13 with its reference to the priest "of Zeus before the gate."

Geographically Derbe and Lystra both belonged to the same political region, while Iconium lay in another. Lystra was closer to Iconium than to Derbe geographically, commercially, and socially—in spite of the political boundary separating them. There was evidently a good deal of communication between the two towns. In Acts 16:1-2 Lystra and Iconium are linked together as places where Timothy was well known and respected.

M

MAACAH, MAACHAH* (Person) Common Hebrew name, often spelled Maachah in the KJV.

1. Last of the four children of Nahor, Abraham's brother, by Reumah his concubine (Gn 22:24).
2. Daughter of Talmai, king of Geshur, a wife of David, and Absalom's mother (2 Sm 3:3; 1 Chr 3:2).
3. Achish's father. Achish, king of Gath, housed two of Shimei's slaves during Solomon's reign (1 Kgs 2:39). He is identified with Maoch in 1 Samuel 27:2. *See* Maoch.
4. Daughter of Absalom (Abishalom) (1 Kgs 15:2, 10), the wife of Rehoboam, king of Judah (930–913 BC), and the mother of King Abijah (913–910 BC) and grandmother of King Asa (910–869 BC) of Judah (1 Kgs 15:10; 2 Chr 11:20-22). Later, Asa removed her as queen mother because she had an idol made for Asherah (1 Kgs 15:10-13; 2 Chr 15:16). Maacah is spelled Micaiah (Michaiah) in 2 Chronicles 13:2.
5. Caleb's concubine and the mother of four sons (1 Chr 2:48).
6. Sister of Huppim and Shuppim, the wife of Makir the Manassite and mother of Peresh and Sheresh (1 Chr 7:15-16).
7. Benjamite, the wife of Jeiel, and an ancestress of King Saul (1 Chr 8:29; 9:35).
8. Father of Haman, one of David's mighty warriors (1 Chr 11:43).
9. Father of Shephatiah, chief officer of Simeon's tribe during David's reign (1 Chr 27:16).

MAACAH, MAACHAH* (Place) Small kingdom in northern Transjordan alternately named Aram-Maacah in 1 Chronicles 19:6 (KJV "Syria-maachah"). According to Joshua 13:11, the states of Geshur and Maacah were between Gilead and Mt Hermon and they bordered the kingdom of Og, ruler of Bashan (Jos 12:4-5). Its people were reckoned as descendants of Nahor (Gn 22:24) and were the southernmost of the Nahorite tribes.
See also Aram (Person) #2; Aram (Place).

MAACATHITE, MAACHATHI*, MAACHATHITE* People of Maacah who held the territory neighboring the Geshurites and the boundary of land granted to the half-tribe of Manasseh (Dt 3:14; Jos 12:5; 13:11). It was taken over by Jair, who with his companions were unable to dislodge the Maacathites and Geshurites living among them (Jos 13:13).

From the Maacathites came Eliphelet, who joined David's army of "mighty men" (2 Sm 23:34). The parallel passage in 1 Chronicles 11:36 calls him a Mekerathite.

Their unfriendliness persisted throughout Israel's history. When Jerusalem fell to Nebuchadnezzar, Jaazaniah, the son of a Maacathite, sought to join Ishmael the Ammonite against Gedaliah, whom Nebuchadnezzar had left to govern the city (2 Kgs 25:23; Jer 40:8).
See also Maacah, Maachah (Place).

MAADAI Bani's son, who obeyed Ezra's exhortation to divorce his pagan wife after the exile (Ezr 10:34).

MAADIAH* Head of a priestly family who returned to Jerusalem after the exile (Neh 12:5, NLT mg) and whose house was headed by Piltai in the next generation during the days of Joiakim the high priest. He is called Moadiah in v 17. He is perhaps identifiable with the priest Maaziah, who set his seal on Ezra's covenant (10:8).

MAAI Priestly musician who participated in the dedication of the rebuilt Jerusalem wall (Neh 12:36).

MAALEH-ACRABBIM* KJV rendering of "ascent of Akrabbim," a site on Canaan's southern border, in Joshua 15:3. *See* Akrabbim.

MA'ANEH* Unit of measure equivalent to the length of a furrow (20–30 yards, or 18.3–27.4 meters). *See* Weights and Measures.

MAARATH One of Judah's cities of inheritance located in the hill country (Jos 15:59), perhaps modern Biet Ummar, seven miles (11.3 kilometers) north of Hebron. It may be the same as Maroth, mentioned in Micah 1:12.

MAASAI Priest who returned to Jerusalem with Zerubbabel after the exile (1 Chr 9:12).

MAASEIAH
1. One of the singers appointed by the Levites to accompany David when he brought the ark from Obed-edom's house to Jerusalem (1 Chr 15:18-20).
2. Commander who agreed to assist Jehoiada the priest in crowning Joash king (2 Chr 23:1).
3. Officer who served King Uzziah by assisting in the organization of the king's army (2 Chr 26:11).
4. Son of Judah's royal house who was slain when Pekah the king of Israel invaded Judah (2 Chr 28:7).
5. Ruler in Jerusalem whom Josiah appointed to assist in repairing the temple (2 Chr 34:8).
6–8. Three priests who obeyed Ezra's exhortation to divorce their foreign wives during the postexilic era (Ezr 10:18-22).
9. Pahath-moab's son (Ezr 10:30).
10. Father of Azariah, a repairman of the Jerusalem wall (Neh 3:23).
11. Ezra's attendant when he read the law to the people (Neh 8:4).
12. Levite who, with others, helped the people to understand the law Ezra read (Neh 8:7).
13. Leader who set his seal on Ezra's covenant under Nehemiah's leadership (Neh 10:25).
14. Judahite leader and the son of Baruch, who lived in Jerusalem with those chosen by lot to inherit the rebuilt city (Neh 11:5). He is sometimes identified with the Asaiah mentioned in 1 Chronicles 9:5.
15. Ithiel's son from Benjamin's tribe who was chosen to live in Jerusalem (Neh 11:7).
16. Priestly trumpeter at the dedication of the Jerusalem wall (Neh 12:41).

17. Priestly singer at the dedication of the Jerusalem wall (Neh 12:42).
18. Father of Zephaniah the priest. Zephaniah, with Pashhur, was sent to Jeremiah by King Zedekiah to inquire of the Lord concerning the future of Nebuchadnezzar's war against Jerusalem (Jer 21:1-2; 29:25) and to request that Jeremiah pray for Jerusalem (37:3).
19. Father of Zedekiah the false prophet, an opponent of Jeremiah's prophecy about Jerusalem's fall under Nebuchadnezzar's siege (Jer 29:21).
20. KJV form of Mahseiah, Baruch's forefather, in Jeremiah 32:12 and 51:59. See Mahseiah.
21. Keeper of the threshold during Jehoiakim's reign (Jer 35:4).

MAASIAI* KJV spelling of Maasai, a postexilic priest, in 1 Chronicles 9:12. See Maasai.

MAATH Ancestor of Jesus in Luke's genealogy (Lk 3:26). See Genealogy of Jesus Christ.

MAAZ Ram's son from Judah's tribe (1 Chr 2:27).

MAAZIAH
1. Levite who served in the temple during David's reign (1 Chr 24:18).
2. Levite who set his seal on Ezra's covenant (Neh 10:8); sometimes identified with Maadiah, a postexilic priest (Neh 12:5).
   See also Maadiah.

MACBANNAI See Machbanai, Machbannai.

MACBENAH See Machbenah.

MACCABAEUS, JUDAS See Maccabeus, Judas.

MACCABEAN PERIOD* Period of Israel's history when the Maccabeans fought for Israel's freedom and governed the country. This period lasted from 167 BC to approximately 40 BC, when the priest Mattathias and his descendants, particularly his son Judas, surnamed Maccabeus, were active opponents of all attempts to introduce Hellenistic practices into Jewish life and religion.

From the conquest of Alexander the Great in 332 BC, Judea became alternately a pawn and a battleground as the Egyptian descendants of Ptolemy, the Syrians, and later the Romans vied for political control. The Ptolemies, though directing activities from Egypt rather than from Athens, were themselves Greeks and, like the Syrian kings of the Seleucid dynasty, were descendants of Alexander's generals. Thus the Ptolemies were also Hellenists. They believed in the superiority of everything Greek. They encouraged the extension of learning and built the library of Alexandria to develop a center of Greek culture in competition with Athens itself.

The aim of the pro-Greeks or Hellenists was to introduce Greek culture to the Near East, to establish Greek-style cities and colonies, and to encourage intermarriage between Greeks and Asians. In this way nationalism would be engulfed in the overall Greek plan, national heritage would be lost, and national or regional religions would give way to the legends and symbolism of the colorful Greek gods.

Judah represented a small nation in this vast picture. The chances for the survival of the religion, heritage, or political freedom of this group would have appeared to be minimal. In their favor, however, was the faith and assurance that God was with his people and that, if they followed his dictates, they would survive. They realized that as a people they might face suffering and exile, but they knew that, if they held firm in their faith, the nucleus of a nation would be preserved. They were also upheld in their attitude by the belief that the coming of the Messiah was imminent.

Before 200 BC, neither Egypt nor Syria seemed able to gain long-term control over Judea, until an agreement was reached assigning the jurisdiction to Syria, and this was supported by Judea. In appreciation, Antiochus the Great of Syria canceled Judean taxes for three years and promised compensation for the cities destroyed in the preceding battles. Priests, scribes, and temple singers were exempted from certain taxes, and duties on imported timber were removed temporarily to facilitate reconstruction in Jerusalem. Money was made available for sacrifices, and many Jewish prisoners were freed.

By 175 BC, the picture had changed considerably. Antiochus IV Epiphanes had gained the throne of Syria by assassinating both his brother and the rightful heir to the kingdom. Prior to this, Antiochus IV had lived in Athens and had also been held hostage in Rome for 14 years. He understood and respected the political power of Rome, and to prevent a takeover of the Near East, he decided to expand his own position by conquering Egypt and bringing the entire area under Syrian control. Impressed by Greek philosophy and traditions, he aimed to use a program of Hellenization as a tool to unite the diverse peoples under his control. A dangerous madman, he would stop at nothing to achieve his political ends.

The most influential position in Jerusalem at the time was that of the high priest. It seemed to be as much a political as a religious office. Traditionally the high priest had been a descendant of Aaron, and during this period of unrest, it was essential for the position to be held by a strong and inspiring leader, firm in his own faith, who could be an example and help to rally those who opposed the encroachments of Hellenism. Thus the right to select the high priest became vested in the one who held military control over the area. When Syrian power was strong, the king attempted to install his own nominee as high priest. When Syria was involved in internal political squabbles or external military engagements, or was being defeated by the followers of Judas Maccabeus, the Jewish people were permitted temporarily to choose their own high priest and simultaneously to enjoy a certain amount of political independence and relief from taxes.

It is understandable, therefore, just how upset the Jews were when Antiochus first attempted to install his own nominee, Menelaus, as high priest. Since he was not of the line of Aaron, he had no claim to the position, having actually obtained it by making Antiochus a high monetary offer that swelled the coffers of the financially impoverished king. While Antiochus was busy invading Egypt, the people of Jerusalem took advantage of the opportunity to oust Menelaus and reinstate the former high priest. In revenge, Antiochus ordered that the city be sacked. Many of the inhabitants were killed, the temple was desecrated, and its treasure was removed. After this, the city was left in the hands of a Syrian military commander (1 Macc 1:20-29; 2 Macc 5:14-22; Josephus's Antiquities 12.5.3).

Still eager to obtain control of Egypt, Antiochus invaded it again, but retreated rapidly when he received orders to do so from the Senate in Rome. Fearful of the power and extent of Roman authority, he determined to secure the loyalty of the Jewish state by pressing his program of Hellenization. He thus hoped to use Judea as a partial buffer between himself and Rome.

The observance of the Sabbath, religious festivals, sacrifices, and the circumcision of male children were forbidden by law, and copies of the Torah were destroyed. Altars to Greek gods were set up, and the Jews were ordered to eat the flesh of pigs, which was prohibited to them (2 Macc 6:18; see Lv 11:7). The temple in Jerusalem became a shrine dedicated to Zeus, and a pig was offered in sacrifice on the altar (1 Macc 1:41-64; 2 Macc 6:1-11; see Dn 11:31-32).

In each Judean village an altar was set up and sacrifice offered under the watchful eye of a Syrian officer. In 166 BC, when the time came for Mattathias, an aged priest with five sons, to offer a sacrifice of unclean flesh to a pagan god, he refused on behalf of himself and his sons. In anger Mattathias killed both an apostate Jew, who had offered sacrifice, and the Syrian officer supervising the enactment of the new law. Prior to this, resistance had been steady but isolated, and although there were those who accepted the edict, many refused and faced death for their faith (1 Macc 1:60; 2:29-37; 2 Macc 6:18-31).

Mattathias called upon supporters of the Hebrew law to follow him (1 Macc 2:15-27), and he and his sons fled to the hills. Mattathias was joined by an ardent religious group called the Hasidim, and together with other supporters, they waged a most successful guerrilla war from bases in the Judean hills.

Attacks were made on isolated villages, heathen altars were torn down, and uncircumcised Jewish boys were circumcised. With the death of Mattathias in 166 BC, a more warlike phase of the struggle began under the direction of his son Judas Maccabeus, who became the symbol of Jewish resistance. He was a leader who waged a vigorous campaign in a righteous cause. He brought into focus the nationalistic sentiment of his people, and above all he was successful in the face of huge odds. His forays were more than a thorn in the flesh to Antiochus, for Judas's tactics and victories earned the respect of his friends and fear of his enemies.

The success of Judas gave him virtual control of the country. He immediately set about the restoration of the temple. The altar that had been used for sacrifice to Zeus was destroyed, and faithful priests rededicated the temple so that daily worship could be resumed (1 Macc 4:36-59; 2 Macc 10:1-8; Josephus's Antiquities 12.7.6-7). The practice of the Jewish faith was restored in symbolism and in fact for all to see, with the institution of the Feast of Dedication or Lights (Hanukkah). With the spiritual house in order, Judas set about rebuilding the city walls so that Jerusalem would be able to withstand the next Syrian onslaught.

Then Judas and his brothers broadened their sights, hoping to secure freedom not only for Judea but for the whole of Palestine. Therefore, attacks were made against the Idumeans in Transjordan (1 Macc 5:1-8) and against Philistia (vv 9-68; Josephus's Antiquities 12.8.1-6). Judas then set about achieving political freedom for Judea. He opposed the appointment of a high priest who, although of the line of Aaron, was a Hellenist (1 Macc 7:14; 2 Macc 14:3-7; Josephus's Antiquities 12.9.7). The Hasidim broke ranks with Judas and accepted the new high priest, but certain promises were not honored, and 60 of them were slain. The remainder realized their mistake and rededicated their allegiance to Judas (1 Macc 7:15-20; Josephus's Antiquities 12.10.2). A Syrian army that was dispatched to secure the high priest's position in Jerusalem was destroyed, and the Syrians, together with their priestly nominee, fled ignominiously.

Throughout the period, Rome was an overshadowing presence, and Judas hoped to use the might of Rome for his own political advantage in the perennial fight against Syria. A warning was sent to Demetrius stating that Judas was under the protection of Rome, but it arrived after a huge Syrian army had set out on a mission of revenge. Some of the Maccabean army deserted before the mighty hordes of Syria, and in the ensuing battle Judas was killed.

While the Maccabeans regrouped under Judas's younger brother, Jonathan, the Syrians and the Hellenists were in control of Jerusalem, rebuilding the walls and strengthening other cities against a possible Maccabean attack. Over the next few years, the Syrians suffered a defeat, and their support of the Hellenists in Judea was weakened. No new high priest was appointed by the Syrians, to the satisfaction of Jonathan, who did not want to see his own authority curtailed. When the Maccabees gained the ascendancy once more, they punished the Hellenists (1 Macc 9:23-73; Josephus's Antiquities 13.1.1-6), and for the following five years there was peace.

From 152 BC, Syria was embroiled in internal struggles, both major factions vying for Jonathan's support, while he in turn used the situation to strengthen his own position. Promises to Jonathan from these two factions ranged from the title of high priest to exemption from taxes and an increase in territory. Ultimately Jonathan was appointed high priest, being the first of the Maccabees to be offered this prestigious position. Judas would probably have liked the office as a crown to his military successes, but his family was not of the house of Aaron, and at that time the people would not have been prepared to accept him as high priest.

As the throne of Syria changed hands through death in battle and assassination, Jonathan sided first with one faction, then with the other. He also sent an embassy to Rome to reconfirm his support in that quarter. Jonathan was then held hostage and murdered by the Syrians and was succeeded by Mattathias's sole surviving son, Simon, in 143 BC.

Simon extracted a treaty from the young Syrian king Demetrius II whereby Judea became virtually independent and considerably larger in territory. Simon was even given the right to mint coinage (1 Macc 15:6), a sure sign of independence, but as soon as Antiochus came to power in 139 BC, the right was withdrawn. In the period of peace that followed Simon's treaty with Demetrius, many expected that the coming of the Messiah was near. They thought that perhaps he would be a descendant of Simon, despite the fact that the standards and tactics of some of the Maccabean leaders had been most questionable. Simon retained the title and office of high priest, and it became a hereditary position for his family.

There was by no means universal support for Simon as high priest, however, even among the anti-Hellenists and the Hasidim, who had previously supported the Maccabeans. Some Jews also maintained that the priesthood should remain in the hands of the Aaronic line. The peace and relative prosperity continued until Simon was murdered by his son-in-law about 135 BC.

Simon, the first of the Hasmonean line, was succeeded by his son John Hyrcanus. He was a strong ruler, despite the troubled period that opened his reign. Antiochus VII, who had gained the throne of Syria a few years previously, attacked Jerusalem, and although the city held out for a year, it finally succumbed. Judea once again became tributary to Syria, not regaining its freedom until the death of Antiochus, about 128 BC.

At this time John Hyrcanus gained the enmity of the Hasidim (from then on known as Pharisees), whose disciple he had once been. It would seem likely that a claim to kingship had angered the Pharisees, who considered that this right rested with the Davidic line, whether or not there was a claimant ready to accept the throne.

In his role as high priest, John Hyrcanus would have had close dealings with the Sadducees, a party as political as it was religious. It gained its support chiefly from the upper levels of society, whose descendants were the rulers of the Sanhedrin in NT times. The Pharisees, who observed the Torah in minute detail, must have constrained any ruler who tried to govern within their limitations.

During the earlier Judean struggles, the Hasidim had sometimes sided with the Maccabeans but at other times had been content to remain quietly under the Syrian yoke so long as their freedom of worship was guaranteed. Under John Hyrcanus, however, they began to enjoy the privilege of influencing the national policy, and thriving on that taste of power they were reluctant to relinquish it. Their dismay at seeing political control pass into the hands of the Sadducees can be imagined.

As dissension and dissatisfaction spread among the Pharisees, a leader emerged in Judea whom we know from the Qumran literature as the "Teacher of Righteousness." As well as advocating strict adherence to the law, he taught that the present generation was the last generation and that final preparations for the imminent coming of the Messiah should be made. During the subsequent reign of Alexander Janneus, those who adhered strictly to the law were persecuted actively, and the "Teacher of Righteousness," along with his immediate followers, left to set up their own establishment at Qumran in the Judean wilderness. They felt that since wickedness in the person of Alexander Janneus was prevailing, then God must have abandoned Israel and that he would, instead, be pleased to dwell with the surviving righteous remnant in Qumran.

The group dissociated themselves completely from the Jewish leaders in Jerusalem by not finding it necessary to offer sacrifices in the temple and by resorting to the ancient calendar that had been preserved in Samaria, so that the great festivals were even celebrated on different dates. The success of the group also helped to undermine the authority of the temple and of the remainder of the Pharisees.

After the death of John Hyrcanus, the throne passed to a younger son, Aristobulus, who reigned for one year only, and then to the eldest son, Alexander Janneus, in 103 BC. At this time Jewish hopes ran high. The Syrians were too involved in their own political turmoil to be a threat and the new king set out on a path of successful conquest. In the midst of fighting, torture, and death, he was in his element, and from what we know of his character, it would seem that there was ample reason why the throne had passed first to his younger brother.

He was extremely successful, however, in extending the boundaries of the Jewish nation from the Mediterranean coast to the frontiers of Egypt. His success was dearly won, as he frequently lost almost as many troops as his enemy. Most of his army consisted of mercenaries, whose pay came from a heavy tax burden for the Jewish people.

For six years he was engaged in a bitter civil war and remained feared and unpopular. He seemed to have little genuine interest in religion, and it was unacceptable to many that a man with such a lust for blood should hold the office of high priest. He had also married his brother's widow, Alexandra (Salome), which although permitted under the laws of levirate marriage (Dt 25:5-10), was strictly forbidden to the high priest (Lv 21:13-14; cf. Ez 44:22). The bitter feelings of the people toward Alexander Janneus were seen in the year 90 BC, when festival pilgrims pelted him with lemons as he was attempting to perform his priestly function at the Feast of Tabernacles. He reacted predictably by turning his guards on the crowd and killing 6,000 people (Josephus's *Antiquities* 13.13.5).

Since the king was supported by the Sadducees, the loyalty of the people veered toward the Pharisees. As opposition to Alexander Janneus built up, Syrian help was requested from Demetrius III. Fifty thousand Jews were estimated to have been killed in the subsequent fighting. Alexander Janneus suffered a severe defeat at Shechem, but Demetrius withdrew, leaving the shattered Pharisaic party to face the terrible wrath of their king. Many were executed, and approximately 8,000 went into exile (Josephus's *Antiquities* 14.14.2).

The Pharisees considered that Alexander Janneus had secularized the Jewish kingdom. His own Hellenistic upbringing in Galilee did not endear him to them. They were concerned, too, not only with his conquests but also with his attempts to impose the Jewish religion on other groups by force. On his deathbed Alexander Janneus handed the throne over to his wife, Alexandra Salome, instructing her to make peace with the Pharisees by giving them a share of power. She may have been the daughter of a prominent Pharisee, and she certainly heeded the advice, relinquishing almost complete power to the Pharisaic party (Josephus's *Antiquities* 13.16.2).

Revenge was sweet for the Pharisees, and many of the old traditions of the Sadducees were set aside. The situation was complicated further by the fact that the queen's elder son, Hyrcanus, supported the Pharisees, while the younger, Aristobulus, followed the Sadducees. Though high priest and heir apparent, Hyrcanus, the elder son, was quiet and lacking in ambition. Contrary to this, Aristobulus grew in the image of his father and was appointed commander of the army.

The Sadducees, claiming threats to national security, obtained permission from the queen to occupy several strongholds in the country. During Alexandra's nine-year reign, the law had been upheld and well administered by the Pharisees. But with the death of the queen in 67 BC, the stage was set for turmoil between her two sons.

As Aristobulus gathered an army and attacked his brother, many of the troops deserted Hyrcanus and he relinquished both crown and priesthood to Aristobulus. Instead of being able to retire quietly to his country estate as he had hoped, Hyrcanus was still looked on by the Pharisees as their leader.

An Idumean named Antipater, father of the future king Herod the Great, then schemed to restore Hyrcanus to his unwanted throne. Quite clearly, Antipater hoped to be the power behind the figurehead Hyrcanus. Antipater and Hyrcanus, with outside support, defeated Aristobulus and besieged him in Jerusalem. Many devout Jews, eager to abandon the squabbling and bitterness, left for a new life in Egypt. The siege of Jerusalem aroused the interest of the nearby Roman army, and both sides appealed for assistance, offering large bribes. The Roman commander decided to support Aristobulus, but two years later, in 63 BC, Pompey intervened personally.

Aristobulus, having aroused the suspicion of the Romans, attempted to defy the might of the approaching army. Followers of Hyrcanus opened the gates of the city to the Romans, and the temple was stormed on the Sabbath after three months of resistance by the supporters of Aristobulus. Pompey marched sword in hand into the Holy of Holies but did not remove the temple treasure. Although Aristobulus was spared, many of his principal supporters were executed. Judea lost any semblance of authority over many of the surrounding areas, and it became a tributary to Rome.

The amount paid to Rome in taxes, although substantial, must have seemed small compared with the taxes that had been necessary to underwrite the incessant fighting of the previous century. Judea then entered upon a period of relative calm. To the Romans, the area was unimportant in the sense that major trade routes now focused on Rome. The routes to the East were no longer either useful or accessible because of the political barriers to the east, and the north-south trade route to Egypt was declining in importance.

In 57 BC Aristobulus raised a minor revolt, the only result of which seems to have been the whittling away of what little authority remained to Hyrcanus. Aristobulus and his supporters continued their unsuccessful attempts for several years, but to no avail.

Antipater, meanwhile, continued firm in his support of Hyrcanus and of Rome. During the civil war that began in 49 BC, Antipater changed sides from Pompey to Caesar, acting in the name of Hyrcanus, and when Caesar was successful, the Jews were rewarded with a remission of Roman taxes.

They were confirmed in their religious freedom, and in Jewish matters they were allowed to be tried in their own courts. They were also exempt from Roman military service. Their territory was increased, and they were permitted to raise their own taxes. Antipater was personally rewarded by the Romans, and as his authority increased, so did the hatred and distrust of him by the Sadducees. Antipater appointed his son Herod as governor of Galilee.

Herod immediately undertook to rid the area bordering on Syria of a group of "brigands" or "Judean patriots" who were under the leadership of Hezekiah. They had considerable local support, but many of the group were subsequently captured, including their leader, and they were executed. Since under Jewish law no man could be executed without the sentence being sanctioned by the Sanhedrin, Herod himself was called to account by the Jewish elders of the Sanhedrin.

During the years of turmoil that followed, Antigonus was responsible for the death of Hyrcanus. Herod went to Rome and was confirmed as king of the Jews by the Senate, while Antigonus, the last of the Hasmoneans, was executed in Antioch. Thus the stage was set for the coming of a new and strong religious leader for the Jewish people, the long-awaited Messiah.

MACCABEES, 1 and 2 Two deuterocanonical books that cover the period of Israel's history from 167 BC to 100 BC. The books are named after Judas Maccabeus, who initiated the Jewish revolt in 166 BC against Rome. The chief value of these books is that they provide historical accounts of Israel's struggles during the time between Malachi (the last book of the Jewish canon) and the time of Christ (6/5 BC–AD 30).

1 Maccabees This work was written, much as Chronicles was, to record a "spiritual" history of the nation, except that it deals exclusively with the Maccabean period up to 100 BC. The author, who is unknown, drew upon some genuine literary sources, although the authenticity of parts of the work has been questioned.

2 Maccabees This book (written c. 100 BC) is even more theologically oriented than 1 Maccabees. Whereas 1 Maccabees endeavors to present a reasonably objective account of the Hasmoneans, 2 Maccabees comprises a rhetorical summary of a considerably larger work on the subject of the Maccabean era. *See* Maccabean Period.

MACCABEES*, 3 and 4 *See* Apocrypha (Introduction).

MACCABEUS, Judas Third son of Mattathias; leader of the Jewish insurrection against Rome in 166 BC. His surname, Maccabeus (perhaps from an Aramaic word

meaning "the Hammerer"), was later applied to all of the Hasmonean family.

Judas Maccabeus was one of the great generals in Jewish history. With but a few thousand followers, he faced the superior Syrian armies sent by Lysias under generals Ptolemy, Nicanor, and Gorgias with direct orders from Antiochus IV Epiphanes to "wipe out and destroy the strength of Israel and the remnant of Jerusalem; . . . to banish the memory of them from the place, settle aliens in all their territory, and distribute their land" (1 Macc 3:35-36, RSV). When confronted with over 40,000 infantry and 7,000 cavalry, the Jewish insurrectionists said, "It is better for us to die in battle than to see the misfortunes of our nation and of the sanctuary. But as his will in heaven may be, so he will do" (vv 59-60). First Maccabees 4:1-25 records their resounding victory over Gorgias, "Israel had a great deliverance that day" (v 25).

Judas won the peace from Lysias (165 BC), and in 164 BC his army occupied Jerusalem, where the temple was purified from the defilement of the worship of Zeus and the daily Jewish sacrifice was restored. This event is commemorated by the Jewish festival Hanukkah, or the Feast of Dedication (Jn 10:22). Judas continued the fight by opposing enemies in and around Judea, thus consolidating his authority, and extended the reach of his power north to Galilee and east to Gilead. In 163 BC Syria recognized the religious liberty of the Jews. As 1 Maccabees quotes Lysias: "Let us come to terms with these men, . . . and agree to let them live by their laws as they did before; for it was on account of their laws which we abolished that they became angry and did all these things" (1 Macc 6:58-59).

The rebellion against religious oppression that began with Judas's father, Mattathias, had become a war for political independence. To this end, Judas initiated a pact of friendship with Rome (1 Macc 8:1ff). But the ascension of Demetrius I to the Syrian throne had an effect on Judea. A traitorous Jew named Alcimus, who had designs on the position of high priest, brought accusations against Judas to the new king. Therefore, Demetrius sent Bacchides and Alcimus with an army to punish Judas Maccabeus (7:1ff). They tried to overcome him by deceit but only succeeded in slaughtering 60 innocent Hasidim.

So Nicanor, "who hated and detested Israel" (1 Macc 7:26), was sent with yet another Syrian army. He also met with defeat at the hands of Judas (161 BC), and "the land of Judah had rest for a few days" (1 Macc 7:50). Finally Bacchides and Alcimus returned and again joined in battle with Judas. The Jews were outnumbered 20 to 1 because of the desertion of the majority of their forces, and Judas was killed in the ensuing battle at Alasa (9:1ff). Israel mourned, "How is the mighty fallen, the savior of Israel!" (v 21), and the Maccabean leadership fell to Jonathan and his brother Simon.

MACEDONIA Roman province in NT times, beginning as a kingdom in the seventh century BC. Little is known about the first several centuries of its history, but with the coming to power of the Greek king Philip II (359–336 BC), and especially of his son Alexander III (the Great, 336–323 BC), Macedonia became a world power. After Alexander's death, the empire was divided among his successors into several regions, one of them the original Macedonian kingdom. Instability held sway for the next 150 years, and in 167 BC Macedonia came under Roman rule. Initially divided into four districts by the Romans (Acts 16:12 is a possible reference to this division), this territory was made into a Roman province in 14 BC with Thessalonica as its capital. Briefly, from

AD 15–44, Macedonia was combined with Achaia and Moesia (other parts of Greece) into one large province; however, in AD 44, the three were again separated. Macedonia's importance continued through the Roman era, and it remained a separate entity down to modern times, though at present no Macedonian state exists.

The Roman province of Macedonia included the northern region of Greece and southern sections of present-day Albania, Yugoslavia (former Yugoslav Republic of Macedonia), and Bulgaria. Noted for its gold, silver, timber, and farmlands, the region also served as a land route for trade between Asia and the West. Shortly after the Romans incorporated Macedonia as a province, they built the Via Egnatia, a paved road over 500 miles (804.5 kilometers) long, running from the Adriatic coast to the Aegean, no doubt traveled by the apostle Paul as he moved through the Macedonian cities of Neapolis, Philippi, Amphipolis, Apollonia, and Thessalonica (Acts 16:11-12; 17:1).

The gospel was introduced to Europe by way of Macedonia when Paul responded to a vision while on his second missionary journey (Acts 16:9-12). Details of that work, centering in Philippi and Thessalonica, are described in Acts 16:11–17:15. On his third journey, though delayed initially (19:21-22), Paul later returned to Macedonia, and again after a stay in Corinth (20:1-3; see 1 Cor 16:5; 2 Cor 1:16 and 2:13 for other references to Macedonia visits).

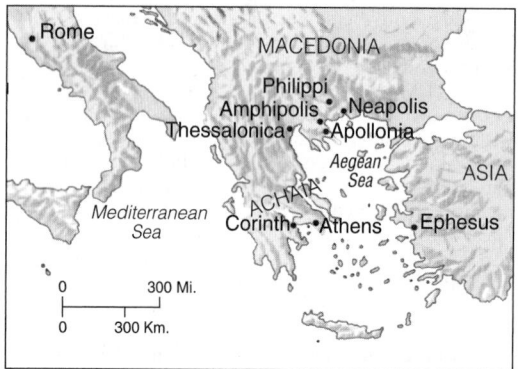

Paul Travels to Macedonia When Paul received the "Macedonian call," he went to Neapolis and on to Philippi in Macedonia.

Macedonian believers played an important part in the collection Paul gathered for the poor in Jerusalem (Rom 15:26; 2 Cor 9:2-4); Paul commended them for their liberality (2 Cor 8:1-2). He also praised them for their example of faith, even in times of adversity (2 Cor 7:5; 1 Thes 1:7), and for their love of others (1 Thes 4:10). Some of the Macedonians worked directly with Paul in carrying out the gospel commission (Acts 19:29; 20:4; 27:2), and he addressed letters to churches in two Macedonian cities, Philippi and Thessalonica.

See also Greece, Greek.

MACHAERUS* Fortified castle where John the Baptist was imprisoned and later beheaded by Herod Antipas (according to Josephus's *Antiquities* 18.5.2). The name does not occur in canonical Scripture nor in the Apocrypha, but it was one of the strongest fortresses in all Palestine, having been built by Alexander Janneus (Josephus's *War* 7.6.1-4). It was destroyed by Gabinius in the wars of Pompey (*War* 1.8.5) but restored and greatly enlarged by Herod the Great, who built a magnificent palace within the enclosure. It was situated east of the Dead Sea at the southern extremity of Perea on a promontory overlooking the Dead Sea. It is identified with the modern M'Khaur.

Matthew (Mt 14:1-12) and Mark (Mk 6:17-29) report that Herod, upon hearing of the fame of Jesus, attributed his miracle-working power to John the Baptist, whom he believed had been restored to life. The confinement of John the Baptist was apparently not so rigorous as to exclude the visit of friends (Mt 11:2-3; Lk 7:18-20). It was from this castle that the Arabian wife of Herod, who had been repudiated by him for the sake of Herodias, fled to her father, Aretas, the king of Arabia. This precipitated the war between Herod and Aretas (Josephus's *Antiquities* 18.5.1) and resulted in the defeat of Herod.

MACHBANAI*, MACHBANNAI* Warrior from Gad's tribe who joined David at Ziklag in his struggle against King Saul (1 Chr 12:13).

MACHBENAH* Evidently a place-name among the geographical names in the genealogy of Caleb and Judah (1 Chr 2:49). It is followed by Gibea, which is probably the same town mentioned in Joshua 15:57; thus, Machbenah was probably located in the eastern district of the hill country south of Hebron, an area where Calebites were to be expected.

MACHI* Father of Geuel from Gad's tribe. Geuel was one of the 12 spies sent to search out the land of Canaan (Nm 13:15).

MACHIR*

1. Joseph's grandson and the firstborn son of Manasseh through his Aramean concubine (Gn 50:23; 1 Chr 7:14). Machir was the father of Gilead and the founder of the Machirite family (Nm 26:29). His descendants dispossessed the Amorites living in the land of Gilead east of the Jordan during the days of Moses (Nm 32:39); later, they were assigned this land along with Bashan for an inheritance (Dt 3:15; Jos 17:1-3). In Judges 5:14, the whole tribe of Manasseh is called by this name.
2. Ammiel's son living at Lo-debar, a town east of the Jordan. Machir provided shelter for Mephibosheth (2 Sm 9:4-5) and later, with Shobi and Barzillai, took care of David's domestic needs during his flight from Absalom (2 Sm 17:27).

MACHIRITE* Descendant of Machir, Joseph's grandson from Manasseh's tribe (Nm 26:29). *See* Machir #1.

MACHNADEBAI* A son of Bani (Binnui), who obeyed Ezra's exhortation to divorce his foreign wife during the postexilic era (Ezr 10:40).

MACHPELAH Small field of trees and a cave with two chambers near Mamre in the district of Hebron, which was purchased by Abraham as a burial place for Sarah. The seller was Ephron, a Hittite, and the price was 400 shekels of silver (Gn 23:8-19). Later, Abraham (25:9), Isaac and Rebekah (49:30-31), and Jacob (50:13) were buried here.

The details of Abraham's purchase of Machpelah, if compared with Hittite laws, support the trustworthiness of the story in Genesis 23. Attention is drawn to the number of the trees, the weighing of silver at the current buyer and seller valuation, and the witnesses at the city gate where the transaction was officially made known. All these details are in accordance with Hittite laws, which would have been forgotten after the time of the patriarchs. Coin was not a circulating medium before 700 BC. The implication that the shekel was a weight and not a coin in the time of Abraham also indicates an early date for the story of the purchase.

MACNADEBAI *See* Machnadebai.

MADAI Third of Japheth's seven sons (Gn 10:2; 1 Chr 1:5).

MADIAN* KJV spelling of Midian, a geographical region in northwest Arabia, in Acts 7:29. *See* Midian, Midianite.

MADMANNAH (Person) Shaaph's son and a grandson of Caleb (1 Chr 2:49).

MADMANNAH (Place) Alternate name for Bethmarcaboth, a city in southern Judah, in Joshua 15:31. *See* Beth-marcaboth.

MADMEN Town in Moab, according to Jeremiah's oracle (Jer 48:2). It may be a form created by dittography from an original Dimon, as in the oracle against Moab by Isaiah (Is 15:9). If so, Khirbet Dimneh, seven and a half miles (12.1 kilometers) northwest of Kerak at the head of Wadi Beni Hammad, would be a possible site. In any case, there is a word play in the Jeremiah passage between the place-name and the Hebrew word "be silent."

MADMENAH Benjamite town positioned north of Jerusalem along the route taken by the Assyrian army during Sennacherib's military incursion into Judah (c. 701 BC) against King Hezekiah (715–686 BC) and the Holy City (Is 10:31).

MADON One of the many Canaanite cities allied against Joshua in a vain attempt to stop the progress of the Israelites into Palestine. A disastrous battle fought at Meron brought these cities under Israelite control (Jos 11:1; 12:19). Madon is probably the modern Qarn Hattin, about five miles (8 kilometers) from the Sea of Galilee.

MAGADAN Locality visited by Jesus after he crossed the Sea of Galilee (Mt 15:39). The correct spelling was most likely Magdala. The only NT reference to this town is in the name of one of the Marys, namely, *Magdalene*. Magadan was known by several names; many Greek sources have Taricheae, "factories for salting fish" (Strabo 16.2.45; Pliny 5.71). Rabbinic sources have Migdal Nunnayah or Migdal Sab'aiyah, "Tower of the Fishes/ Dyers." It was el-Mejdel about three miles (4.8 kilometers) northwest of Tiberias, on the southern end of the great plain of Gennesaret, famous for its fertile soil and year-round tropical climate.

See also Dalmanutha.

MAGBISH Town reoccupied after the exile by 156 descendants of its former residents (Ezr 2:30).

MAGDALA* KJV place-name used in Matthew 15:39. Recent versions and translations have the name Magadan. Sources dating from NT times locate the town of Magdala a short distance north of the city of Tiberias on the western shore of the Sea of Galilee.

See also Magadan.

MAGDALENE, Mary Name of one of several Marys who followed Jesus. This Mary was the first to see the risen Christ (Jn 20:11-18). *See* Mary #3.

MAGDIEL One of the chiefs of Edom (Gn 36:43; 1 Chr 1:54).

MAGGOT Fly larvae (Jb 25:6; Is 14:11). *See* Animals (Fly).

MAGI* "Wise men" (NLT, KJV) appearing in Matthew 2:1-12 who, following a star, came to Jerusalem and then to Bethlehem in order to pay homage to the newborn "king of the Jews." Matthew's account forms a significant introduction to his Gospel by drawing attention to the true identity of Jesus as King and by foreshadowing the homage paid by the Gentiles to Jesus throughout that Gospel.

The Magi in the Ancient World Extrabiblical evidence offers various clues that shed light on the place of origin and positions held by the magi of Matthew 2. The historian Herodotus mentioned magi as a priestly caste of Media, or Persia, and, as the religion in Persia at the time was Zoroastrinism, Herodotus's magi were probably Zoroastrian priests. Herodotus, together with Plutarch and Strabo, suggested that magi were partly responsible for ritual and cultic life (supervising sacrifices and prayers) and partly responsible as royal advisers to the courts of the East. Believing the affairs of history were reflected in the movements of the stars and other phenomena, Herodotus said, the rulers of the East commonly utilized the magi's knowledge of astrology and dream interpretation to determine affairs of state. The magi were, therefore, concerned with what the movement of the stars (as signs and portents) might signify for the future affairs of history. Such an interest could account not only for the magi's interest in the star in Matthew, but also their conclusion, shared with Herod, that the star's appearance signified the birth of a new ruler of great importance (2:2). Several centuries before Christ, a similar correlation was noted between a stellar phenomenon and the birth of Alexander the Great.

Identity in Matthew's Gospel Matthew's infancy narrative contains little information concerning the identity of the magi. Matthew states only that the magi were "from the East" (2:1-2), an ambiguous point of origin that left room for many subsequent hypotheses. Some church fathers proposed Arabia on the basis of where the gifts (gold, frankincense, and myrrh, 2:11) were likely to have originated. Others suggested Chaldea or Media/Persia because Persia had a caste of priests (magi), which would fit the description in Matthew.

Significance in Matthew's Gospel The visit of the magi plays a significant role in introducing Matthew's Gospel. From the beginning it reveals the true identity of the infant as the long-expected and prophesied royal Messiah of Israel. This is brought out first in the appearance of the "star," which carried clear messianic connotations: "a star shall come forth out of Jacob, a scepter shall arise out of Israel" (Nm 24:17; see also Is 60:3). Second, the interchange between the magi, Herod, and the chief priests and scribes (Mt 2:2-6) reveals that Jesus is the fulfillment of the messianic prophecy of Micah 5:2, the ruler of Israel coming from the small village of Bethlehem. Third, the offering of the gifts (Mt 2:11) may also echo the possible messianic promises of Psalms 68:29 and 72:10.

In addition to confirming that Jesus is the long-awaited Messiah, the account of the magi's visit, as part of the introduction to Matthew's Gospel, introduces several prominent themes that reappear in subsequent chapters. First, the account establishes that Jesus' messiahship has bearing not only on the Jews but even on the gentile world (symbolized in the "wise men from the East"). A second theme, which surfaces later, is the surprising Gentile's faith, a faith that is lacking among Jesus' own people. Even as the foreign magi honor the infant Messiah, Herod and possibly the chief priests and scribes of the people plot the baby's death (Mt 2:3-6, 16). So also elsewhere in the Gospel, Gentiles exhibit faith in Jesus, which often contrasts markedly with the faithlessness of the Jews (see 8:5-13; 15:21-28; 27:19, 54).

THE MYSTERIOUS MAGI

Matthew did not tell how many magi came to honor the infant Jesus. The Eastern church believed there were 12 travelers, although this may simply derive from the biblical penchant for that number (12 tribes of Israel, 12 disciples). The Western church settled on 3 magi or wise men, based presumably on the 3 gifts brought in homage. The exact number is not known.

A similar silence exists in Matthew regarding the names of the wise men. The names Gaspar, Melchior (Melkon), and Balthasar are legendary; they do not come from Matthew's text. Similarly, the later tradition that Gaspar was a king of India, Melchior a king of Persia, and Balthasar a king of Arabia has no basis in fact.

MAGIC Attempt to influence or control people or events through supernatural forces. These forces are called upon by means of ceremonies, the recitation of spells, charms, incantations, and other forms of ritual.

There are a number of terms used in the Bible that might fall into the broad category of magic. Several of the words are mentioned in Deuteronomy 18:9-14. The use of magical and occult practices by Israel is not permitted. The people of God are instructed to avoid magical practices because God provides them with his personal revelation through his prophets. Human magical practices lead to either false hope or false fear and therefore lead away from the truth of God. Yet while magical practices cannot measure up to the accuracy of God's prophet, the Bible does leave open the possibility that there may be supernatural reality behind some magical practices.

Magicians are prominent in the OT book of Exodus, where the magicians of Egypt contend with Moses. The text does not discount the success of the magicians as mere trickery, for they were at least partially successful at first (chs 7–8). But their failures begin to become clear in chapter 8 and continue through chapter 9. The Bible does not flatly deny that there may be certain evil supernatural power at work in the person of the magician. What the Bible does make clear is that this power is not in accord with, nor can it defeat, the will of God.

The NT addresses the issue of magic in the book of Acts. When Philip went to Samaria, he encountered Simon the magician. Simon had drawn a great deal of attention to himself by amazing the people with his magic (Acts 8:11). Philip's message was believed and people began to be drawn to him. Simon saw the wonders that Philip was able to perform and thought that these powers were received through the ritual of the laying on of hands. Philip made clear that the wonders of his work could not be purchased but came through the gracious gift of God to the penitent.

Another important passage is found in Acts 19:11-20. Certain Jewish exorcists thought they could magically use the name of Jesus in their work. The result was violent reaction: the man in whom resided the evil spirit

leaped on them, mastered all of them, and overpowered them, so that they fled out of that house naked and wounded. This passage shows that the power responsible for the apostolic miracles was based upon the personal relationship of the apostle with the Lord Jesus Christ. The result of the above incident is also important; it led the people of Ephesus to make a clear decision between the word of the Lord and their magical practices. Several who practiced magic arts brought their books together and burned them in the presence of everyone. This dramatic display of the power of God and the need for clear loyalty to him led to further expansion of the gospel.

The biblical stand against magic is stated strongly in the last book of the Bible, where sorcerers are condemned to the lake of fire (Rv 21:8). The biblical view is consistent in its opposition to magic. The Bible does not preclude the possibility that Satan can use magic for evil purposes, and magical practices are condemned because they may lead to false hope or false fear and away from loyalty to God's Word.

See also Amulet; Canaanite Deities and Religion; Frontlet; Omen; Soothsayer; Sorcery; Psychics.

MAGISTRATE Title of a public official who acted as judge and administrator of a given municipality. King Artaxerxes ordered Ezra to select magistrates along with judges to govern the people when they returned to Palestine (Ezr 7:25). This official was one of the officers of Nebuchadnezzar's court invited to the dedication feast (Dn 3:2-3). Luke 12:58 portrayed the magistrate as a ruling authority whose verdict was final.

During the Roman era, each Roman colony was assigned two magistrates (called *duumviri*) who were primarily responsible for judging criminal offenses against the state. Hence, Paul and Silas were brought before the magistrates at Philippi for allegedly advocating customs unacceptable to the Romans (Acts 16:20-38). Before this *duumvir*, they were ordered to be stripped, beaten, and thrown into prison. A chief magistrate was sometimes called a "praetor" (Greek *strategos*), a deferential title given to a leading *duumvir*.

MAGNIFICAT* The song of Mary found in Luke 1:46-55. This poem is in the style of the OT psalms and is strongly reminiscent of the prayer of Hannah in 1 Samuel 2:1-10. At an early date it found a place in Christian worship. It was chanted in the vesper service of the Roman Catholic Church and was carried over into Lutheran and Anglican usage. From the time of the Renaissance, countless musical settings have been written for this beautiful canticle, both in Latin and in various Western languages.

MAGOG Term found only five times in the Bible but significant because of its use in the well-known prophetic passages of Ezekiel 38–39 and Revelation 20. In the register of nations in Genesis 10:2 (see also 1 Chr 1:5), Magog was listed among the sons of Japheth, identifying both an individual and the nation that came forth from him. In Ezekiel and Revelation, Magog came to refer either to a land, a people, or both.

Magog is not mentioned in the contemporary literature of biblical times. Therefore, a definition must come primarily from the witness of Scripture, though writers from later times have given additional clues for the identification of the word. Magog was first identified biblically as a son of Japheth (Gn 10:2; 1 Chr 1:5), along with Tubal and Meshech (cf. Ez 38:2). Ezekiel 38:2 associates Magog with the person Gog, indicating that Magog was the land (along with Tubal and Meshech) over which

Gog ruled. Ezekiel 39:6 uses the term Magog to speak of the people from the land of Magog. Together, Ezekiel 38 and 39 present an invasion of Israel in the latter days (cf. Ez 38:8-16) by Gog and his people from the land of Magog, along with peoples from every corner of the known world (cf. vv 5-6).

Revelation 20:8 depicts Gog and Magog as invading the land of Israel with a great company of nations from every part of the world. It certainly appears that Ezekiel and Revelation had the same event of the latter days in mind. Revelation 20:8 can be understood to identify Gog as Satan and to see Magog as invading peoples who come with Satan. Some see "Gog and Magog" in Revelation 20:8 as a symbol of a future great battle at the end of the millennium that is similar to the invasion in Ezekiel 38–39, but the terms themselves are not identified specifically. Some see Magog in Revelation 20 as another person along with Gog.

Extrabiblical writings give additional clues. Josephus's *Antiquities* 1.6.1 equates Magog with the Scythians of the north who lived in the area of present-day Turkey and south-central Russia. Jubilees 7:19 and 9:8 refer to Magog as the "northern barbarians." In the OT, Magog is associated with Tubal and Meshech, geographical areas normally believed to lie in the mountainous region between, and south of, the Caspian and Black Seas.

The available data argue for the identification of Magog in Ezekiel and Revelation with the northern barbarian hordes (perhaps the area of the Scythians) from the modern geographical region of Turkey and south-central Russia who will invade Israel under the leadership of Gog in the latter days. However, there is no warrant in the Scripture or elsewhere to conjecture that these modern nations are *the* identification of these terms.

MAGOR-MISSABIB* Name given by Jeremiah to Pashhur, the chief officer in the house of the Lord. Jeremiah did this because Pashhur put him in stocks for prophesying judgment upon Judah (Jer 19:14–20:2). The name Pashhur means "prosperity round about" and was changed to "terror on every side" (20:3) because Pashhur was to see the horrors of the Babylonian invasion.

MAGPIASH Political leader who signed Ezra's covenant during the postexilic period (Neh 10:20).

MAGUS*, Simon Magician mentioned in Acts 8:9. *See* Simon #8.

MAHALAB* Reconstructed name of a town in Asher's tribe (Jos 19:29, NLT "Mehebel"); the Hebrew text has a transposition of the last two consonants, but the town is probably the same as Ahlab and Helbah of Judges 1:31. The correct name is preserved in the Assyrian annals of Sennacherib as Mahalliba; another text has Mahalab. The town is sometimes identified with Khirbet el-Mahalib, northeast of Tyre.
See also Ahlab.

MAHALAH* KJV rendering of Mahlah, Hammoleketh's son, in 1 Chronicles 7:18. *See* Mahlah #2.

MAHALALEEL*, MAHALALEL
1. Kenan's son and the father of Jared in Seth's line (Gn 5:12-17; 1 Chr 1:2), also mentioned in Luke's genealogy (Lk 3:37). *See* Genealogy of Jesus Christ.
2. Perez's son and a postexilic Judahite (Neh 11:4).

MAHALATH* (Music) Musical cue, perhaps meaning "sadness," listed in the title of Psalm 53 (see RSV),

which would designate the way in which and/or the melody to which the psalm should be sung. *See* Music.

MAHALATH (Person)
1. Daughter of Ishmael, Nebaioth's sister, Esau's third wife, and Reuel's mother (Gn 28:9); alternately called Basemath (KJV "Bashemath") in Genesis 36:3-17.
2. Jerimoth's daughter and King Rehoboam's first wife (2 Chr 11:18).

MAHALATH LEANNOTH* Hebrew phrase in the title of Psalm 88, translated "The Suffering of Affliction"; perhaps a familiar ancient melody to which the psalm was performed. *See* Music.

MAHALI* KJV form of Mahli, Merari's son, in Exodus 6:19. *See* Mahli #1.

MAHANAIM Settlement east of the Jordan in Gilead. Jacob met angels there and named the place "God's camp." He divided his household and possessions into two camps (Mahanaim means "two camps" in Hebrew) to keep from losing everything when he confronted Esau (Gn 32:1-11).

The city was located along the border between Manasseh and Gad's tribes (Jos 13:26, 30) and was given to the Levites for an inheritance (Jos 21:38; 1 Chr 6:80). After Saul's defeat at Mt Gilboa, Ishbosheth, his son, fled to Mahanaim to set up a capital in exile. He managed to control much of Israel from there (2 Sm 2:8, 12, 29) until he was assassinated by Recab and Baanah (4:5-7). David fled to this city when Absalom rebelled against him. Here he received supplies from Barzillai and some Gileadites (17:24-27). At this city gate he wept as he received the news of Absalom's death. Solomon chose the city for the capital of his seventh district and established Ahinadab as its governor (1 Kgs 4:14).

Biblical references point to a location somewhere along the Jabbok River in central Gilead. Outside of this, the city could have been located virtually anywhere. It was earlier identified with Khirbet al-Makhna, two miles (3.2 kilometers) north of Aijalon. Most recent attention, however, has moved to the twin hills of Tulul al-Dhahab on the Jabbok. Aharoni suggests that the western mound of Tulul al-Dhahab is Mahanaim and the eastern mound is Penuel.

MAHANEH-DAN Place west of Kiriath-jearim between Zorab and Eshtaol, where the Spirit of the Lord began to stir in Samson (Jgs 13:25) and where Dan's tribe encamped on the way to the hill country of Ephraim (18:12).

MAHARAI One of David's mighty men and a Zerahite from Netophah in the hill country of Judah. He was appointed commander of a division (24,000 soldiers) during the 10th month of the year (2 Sm 23:28; 1 Chr 11:30; 27:13).

MAHATH
1. Levite, son of Amasai, and ancestor of Heman the temple singer in David's time (1 Chr 6:35).
2. Levite who assisted in the cleansing of the temple during Hezekiah's time (2 Chr 29:12). He was appointed an overseer of the contributions, the tithes, and the things dedicated to God (31:13).

MAHAVAH, MAHAVITE* Term used in 1 Chronicles 11:46 to designate Eliel, one of David's mighty men. The word was probably added to indicate where he came from so as to distinguish him from the Eliel in verse 47.

MAHAZIOTH One of the 14 sons of Heman the Kohathite, and head of the 23d course of tabernacle musicians who ministered with cymbals, harps, and lyres (1 Chr 25:4, 30).

MAHER-SHALAL-HASH-BAZ Name of Isaiah's son, meaning "swift to plunder and quick to spoil" (NLT mg), which prophetically described the imminent destruction to befall Damascus and Samaria by the hand of the Assyrians (Is 8:1, 3).

MAHLAH
1. Manassite; one of Zelophehad's five daughters. She, with her sisters, appealed to Moses to work out an arrangement that would allow them to retain their inheritance in spite of having no brothers (Nm 26:33; 27:1; 36:11; Jos 17:3).
2. Hammoleketh's son from Manasseh's tribe (1 Chr 7:18).

MAHLI
1. Merari's son and Levi's grandson (Ex 6:19; Nm 3:20; 1 Chr 6:19, 29; 23:21; 24:26-28; Ezr 8:18), and the founder of the Mahlite family (Nm 3:33; 26:58). The Mahlites, along with the other families of Merari, were appointed to carry the frames of the tabernacle and the pillars of the court (Nm 4:29-33).
2. Mushi's son and the nephew of #1 above (1 Chr 6:47; 23:23; 24:30).

MAHLITE Descendant of Mahli, Merari's son from Levi's tribe (Nm 3:33; 26:58). *See* Mahli #1.

MAHLON Son of Elimelech and Naomi, and Chilion's brother. While with his family in Moab, he married Ruth, the Moabitess. He died in Moab, however, and Ruth later married Boaz (Ru 1:2, 5; 4:9-10).

MAHOL Father of three famous wise men (Heman, Calcol, and Darda) during the Solomonic era (970–930 BC; 1 Kgs 4:31).

MAHSEIAH Forefather of Baruch (Jer 32:12) and Seraiah (51:59), spelled Maaseiah in the KJV.

MAID, MAIDEN Young unmarried woman, often of the servant class. In the OT, five Hebrew words with varying shades of meaning are translated by the English word "maiden."

One of these words is *'amah*. Various English translations of this word include "bondmaid," "bondwoman," "handmaid(en)," "maid(en)," "maid servant," "female servant," "female slave," "slave girl," and "girl."

Another term is *shiphchah*. This Hebrew word is of similar meaning to *amah*. It is translated variously as "handmaid," "maid(en)," "female slave," and "slave girl." Although both *shiphchah* and *'amah* refer to female slaves, *shiphchah* seems to imply that a closer relationship existed between the slave and the family to whom she belonged. In the patriarchal story this term is often employed in reference both to female slaves in general and specifically to the concubines who were also slaves to the free wife of their husbands (Gn 16, 29–30).

Still another Hebrew term for "maiden" is *bethulah*. This term refers specifically to a virgin, or a young woman of marriageable age (Gn 24:16; Ex 22:16). The OT prophets sometimes used this term figuratively to refer to a city or country as a "virgin" (Jer 31:21; Am 5:2).

Another word, *na'arah*, is itself used in several ways in the OT. Often it refers to an unmarried girl (Est 2:4); at other times it is used in speaking of a servant (Est 4:4;

Ru 2:23). This same word is the base of the proper name of a woman (Naarah, the wife of Ashhur, in 1 Chr 4:5-6) and of a city in Ephraim near Jericho (Jos 16:7).

For many years controversy has surrounded the meaning of *'almah*, the word for maiden used in Isaiah 7:14. The dispute arises because of the varied definitions of the word throughout the OT ("girl," "young woman," "young woman of marriageable age, presumably a virgin"). Only context can accurately determine the meaning of *'almah* in any given instance. Looking at Isaiah 7:14 from a NT perspective, *'almah* is a reference to the virgin Mary, the mother of Jesus (see Mt 1:23).

Several Greek words are translated as "maiden" in the English NT. The meaning of *korasion* is simply "girl," "little girl," or "maiden" (Mt 9:24-25). Another word, *paidiske*, originally referred to a "young woman" but later came to mean "a female slave," "a servant-maid" or "a servant girl" (Mk 14:66; Lk 12:45). It is a diminutive of *pais* (a Greek word denoting "a young girl," "maiden," or "child") (Lk 8:51, 54). *Numphe* is the Greek word meaning "young wife," "bride," and "daughter-in-law" (Lk 12:53; Rv 21:2). *Parthenos* is the usual Greek term for "virgin" and occurs 14 times in the NT.

See also Slave, Slavery.

MAIL, Coat of Body armor consisting of small interlaced metal plates sewn onto a leather jacket. *See* Armor and Weapons.

MAKAZ One of the 12 cities that provided food one month out of the year for King Solomon and his household (1 Kgs 4:9). Situated in northwest Judah, it may be identified with Khirbet el-Mukheizin, south of Ekron.

MAKHELOTH One of the stopping places of the Israelites on their way to Canaan, situated between Haradah and Tahath (Nm 33:25-26). *See* Wilderness Wanderings.

MAKI *See* Machi.

MAKIR *See* Machir.

MAKIRITE *See* Machirite.

MAKKEDAH One of the Shephelah towns conquered during the southern campaign led by Joshua (Jos 10:10-29; 12:16). It belonged to the same district as Lachish (15:41). Eusebius placed it eight Roman miles east of Eleutheropolis (Beth-guvrin), which would lead to Beit-Maqdum, a Roman-Byzantine ruin beside the Roman road from Eleutheropolis to Hebron. The biblical site may have been at Khirbet el-Qom about one-half mile (.8 kilometer) to the southwest.

MAKTESH* Locality within the topography of Jerusalem (Zep 1:11). Since the word means "mortar," the expression here should refer to some basinlike depression. It is probably the Tyropeon Valley opposite the temple mount, though the Targum equates it with the Kidron.

MALACHI (Person) Author of the last book of the OT (Mal 1:1). The prophet Malachi lived about 500–460 BC. His name means "my angel" or "my messenger" and is so translated in Malachi 3:1 and elsewhere. Apart from the book that bears his name, nothing else is known about him from the Bible. In the apocryphal book of 2 Esdras 1:40 he is identified as "Malachi, who is also called a messenger of the Lord." Rabbinic tradition suggests that Malachi may be another name for Ezra the scribe, although there is no supporting evidence for this identification.

See also Malachi, Book of; Prophet, Prophetess.

MALACHI, Book of Last prophetic book of the Jewish canon; last book of the Old Testament.

PREVIEW
• Author
• Background
• Date
• Purpose and Theology
• Content

Author The name Malachi means "my messenger" or "messenger of the Lord." Since the word appears in 3:1, some scholars think that it is not a proper name at all and does not provide the name of the author of the book. According to one ancient tradition, the "messenger" was Ezra, the priest responsible for the books of Ezra and Nehemiah. Yet it would be most unusual for the Jews to preserve a prophetic book without explicitly attaching to it the name of the author. All of the other major and minor prophets—including Obadiah—are named after a particular prophet. Moreover, "messenger of the Lord" would be a most appropriate name for a prophet (cf. 2 Chr 36:15-16; Hg 1:13).

Background During the fifth century BC, the struggling Jewish community in Judah was greatly assisted by the return of Ezra and Nehemiah. In 458 BC Ezra was encouraged by King Artaxerxes of Persia to lead a group of exiles back to Jerusalem and to institute religious reform. About 13 years later, in 445 BC, a high-ranking government official named Nehemiah was allowed to go to Jerusalem to rebuild the city walls, a task he accomplished in 52 days (Neh 6:15). As governor, Nehemiah led the people in a financial reform that provided for the poor and encouraged tithing to support the priests and Levites (5:2-13; 10:35-39). Like Ezra, Nehemiah urged the people to keep the Sabbath and avoid intermarrying with pagan neighbors. After a 12-year term, Nehemiah returned to Persia and the spiritual condition of Judah deteriorated. Perhaps discouraged by their lack of political power, tithing became sporadic, the Sabbath was not kept, intermarriage was common, and even the priests could not be trusted. When Nehemiah came back to Jerusalem sometime later, he had to take firm action to straighten out the situation (13:6-31).

Date Since Malachi had to deal with the same sins mentioned in Nehemiah 13 (see Mal 1:6-14; 2:14-16; 3:8-11), it is likely that the prophet ministered either during Nehemiah's second term as governor or in the years just before his return. The reference to "the governor" in Malachi 1:8 implies that someone other than Nehemiah was in office, so it may be best to place Malachi just after 433 BC, the year Nehemiah had returned to Persia.

Purpose and Theology Malachi was written to shake the people of Judah from their spiritual lethargy and to warn them that judgment was coming unless they repented. The people doubted God's love (1:2) and justice (2:17) and did not take his commands seriously (1:6; 3:14-18). Yet God was "a great King" (1:14) with a great name that was to be feared even beyond the border of Israel (vv 5, 11). Malachi repeatedly urged both the priests and the people to revere God and give him the honor he deserved. God was Israel's Father and Creator (2:10), but the nation showed contempt for his name (1:6; 3:5). In response to this contempt, God would send

his messenger to announce the Day of the Lord (3:1). John the Baptist did call the nation to repentance, and Christ came to cleanse the temple (Jn 2:14-15) and to establish the covenant (Mal 3:1-2). Most of the work of refining and purifying will take place at the Second Coming, when Christ returns to purify his people (cf. vv 2-4) and judge the wicked (4:1).

Content

God's Great Love for Israel (1:1-5) To introduce the book, Malachi presents a contrast between God's love for Israel and his hatred for Edom. Yet the assertion of God's love is greeted with a strange question: "How have you loved us?" God loved Israel by entering into a covenant with the nation at Mt Sinai, just after he had freed them from the prison of Egypt. He had chosen them as his special people (cf. Gn 12:1-3; Ex 19:5-6), whereas the descendants of Esau were not chosen (cf. Rom 9:10-13). Both Israel and Edom endured invasion and destruction, but only Israel was restored and rebuilt after the exile. The people of Edom were driven from their homeland by the Nabateans between 550 and 400 BC, and they never regained their territory. Through the judgment of Edom, God demonstrated that he is the great Ruler over the nations (Mal 1:5) and that he will not forget Israel.

The Unacceptable Sacrifices of the Priests (1:6-14) Although God deserved the honor and reverence of the Israelites, both the people and the priests openly disdained his laws and regulations. Strangely, it was the priests who led the way into disobedience. Sacrifices and offerings were supposed to atone for sin, but the animals offered by the priests only served to pollute or defile the altar (1:7, 12). According to Leviticus, animals with defects were unacceptable as sacrifices, but Malachi mentions that the priests were offering to the Lord animals that were stolen and mutilated, crippled and sick (v 13; cf. v 8). To emphasize their contempt, the Lord challenged the priests to bring comparable presents to the governor. Would they dare to insult him in this fashion and face sure rejection? Rather than having the priests continue to bring unfit sacrifices to the altar, the Lord asked them to close the temple doors entirely (v 10). Going through the motions never pleased God, either in ancient times (cf. Is 1:12-13) or modern. By calling the altar and its sacrifices "contemptible" (Mal 1:7, 12), the priests were no better than the wicked sons of Eli, whose disregard of the rules for sacrifices sent them to a premature death (cf. 1 Sm 2:15-17).

In sharp contrast to the attitude of the priests stands the emphasis upon God's greatness in Malachi 1:11 and 14. God is more powerful than the gods of other nations, and even if Israel's priests and people dishonor the Lord, eventually pure offerings will be brought to God by believing Gentiles. Perhaps these offerings refer to prayer and praise (cf. Ps 19:14; Heb 13:15; Rv 5:8), but others interpret the reference more literally (cf. Is 56:7; 60:7). Peter may be alluding to this verse in connection with the conversion of Cornelius (Acts 10:35).

The Punishment of the Priests (2:1-9) One of the functions of the priests was to pronounce blessings upon the people in the name of God, but their disgraceful behavior turned the blessings into curses (Mal 2:2). Because of the priests' sinfulness and the poor condition of the animals, their sacrifices were also worthless, and the entrails of the animals will be spread on their faces as a sign that God holds them in contempt. The disgrace heaped upon the priests differs sharply from the honor enjoyed by Aaron and his descendants. Malachi refers to a covenant of life and peace (v 5) made with Levi and more particularly with Aaron's grandson Phinehas, who courageously took action against the Jews involved in idolatry and immorality (Nm 25:10-13). In those days the priests revered the Lord and turned many from sin (Mal 2:6).

Another responsibility of the priests was to teach the nation the law handed down by Moses (cf. Lv 10:11). Like prophets, they were messengers of the Lord (Mal 2:7) who were supposed to walk close to the Lord, but now the priests disregarded the law and were dishonest in handing down judicial decisions (Mal 2:9; cf. Lv 19:15).

The Unfaithfulness of the People (2:10-16) In light of the attitude of the priests, it is not surprising to discover that the people at large were unfaithful to the Lord. God had formed Israel to be his special people, but the people had broken faith with him. A major factor in their unfaithfulness was intermarriage with foreigners, a sin mentioned in Ezra 9:1-2 and Nehemiah 13:23-29. By marrying pagan women, the men of Israel invariably began to worship pagan gods and turn from the Lord. When such intermarriage occurred, it sometimes followed the divorce of an Israelite wife. In Malachi 2:14-15 God underscores the sacred commitment that he himself witnesses when two people marry. If that marriage covenant is shattered by divorce, God is deeply displeased. And it is even more tragic if divorce became an excuse to marry a more attractive or appealing foreigner.

The Coming of the Messenger of the Covenant (2:17–3:5) The sins of the priests and the people did not go unnoticed, even though the nation doubted that God would take action (2:17). But the third chapter opens with the announcement that the messenger of the covenant will indeed come to his temple. His way will be prepared by another messenger—a prophecy of John the Baptist, who prepared the way for the ministry of Christ (cf. Mt 11:10; Mk 1:2-3). When Christ came, he revealed his anger when he cleansed the temple (cf. Jn 2:13-17) and denounced the scribes and Pharisees (cf. 9:39), but most of his purifying and refining work awaits the Second Coming. Someday the priests and Levites will bring acceptable sacrifices, as they did in the days of Moses and Phinehas (cf. Mal 3:3-4 and 2:4-5). Verse 5 of chapter 3 broadens the scope of the judgment to include the whole nation, as sorcerers, adulterers, and those who oppress the poor are condemned.

The Benefits of Faithful Tithing (3:6-12) Another specific weakness of postexilic Judah was the failure of the people to bring their tithes to the Lord. Encouraged by Nehemiah, the nation promised to tithe faithfully (cf. Neh 10:37-39), but apparently their good intentions were short-lived (cf. 13:10-11). According to Malachi 3:8-9, the tithes of the nation were so dismal that the people were, in effect, robbing God and were therefore under a curse. In verses 10-12 Malachi challenges the nation to bring their tithes; then God would pour out his blessing upon them. Just as the opening of the "windows in heaven" meant the end of a famine in 2 Kings 7:2, 19, so God promises that their crops will be so abundant that they will run out of storage space. The hope of "blessing" in Malachi 3:10 and 12 provides welcome relief from the curses mentioned in 1:14, 2:2, 3:9, and 4:6.

The Day of the Lord (3:13–4:6) Faced with the challenge of Malachi 3:10-12, the people of Israel responded in two different ways. One group denied that serving God brought any benefit (3:13-15), while another segment of the nation bowed low before him with deep reverence (vv 16-18). The unbelievers argued that obeying the Lord was useless and that arrogant and evil people were the ones who prospered. In response to their

charge, Malachi noted that God would remember who the righteous were in the Day of Judgment. Although all of Israel was included in the promise made to Abraham, only those who genuinely believed would be God's treasured possession (3:17; cf. Ex 19:5), with their names written in the Book of Life (cf. Mal 3:16). As for the arrogant and evildoers, the Day of the Lord will consume them and they will have no survivors (4:1). Those who revere the Lord will enjoy spiritual and physical health under the blessing and protection of God, who is called the "sun of righteousness" (v 2). Like calves just released from confinement, the righteous will trample down the wicked and triumph over them (v 3).

In view of the judgment associated with the Day of the Lord, Malachi urged the people to repent. To do this they needed to heed the law of Moses and take seriously the decrees and commands given at Mt Sinai (4:4; cf. 3:7). Just as Elijah called on Israel to turn back to God, so a new "Elijah" will preach repentance to a rebellious nation. When John the Baptist prepared the way for Christ (cf. Mal 3:1), he ministered "in the spirit and power of Elijah" and begged the Jews to turn from their sin and humble themselves before God (Lk 1:17). If they refused to listen, the nation faced the prospect of total destruction, the curse placed upon the people of Canaan (cf. Jos 6:17-19) and upon the nation of Edom, whose collapse was described in Malachi 1:2-5.

See also Israel, History of; Postexilic Period; Prophecy; Prophet, Prophetess.

MALCAM
Shaharaim's son from Benjamin's tribe (1 Chr 8:9).

MALCHAM*
1. KJV form of Malcam in 1 Chronicles 8:9. *See* Malcam.
2. KJV form of Milcom, an Ammonite god, in Zephaniah 1:5. *See* Milcom.

MALCHIAH*
1. KJV spelling of Malchijah, Gershon's descendant, in 1 Chronicles 6:40. *See* Malchijah #1.
2. KJV spelling of Malchijah, Parosh's son, in Ezra 10:25. *See* Malchijah #4.
3. KJV spelling of Malchijah, Harim's son, in Ezra 10:31. *See* Malchijah #6.
4. KJV spelling of Malchijah, Recab's son, in Nehemiah 3:14. *See* Malchijah #7.
5. KJV spelling of Malchijah the goldsmith in Nehemiah 3:31. *See* Malchijah #8.
6. KJV spelling of Malchijah, Ezra's assistant, in Nehemiah 8:4. *See* Malchijah #9.
7. KJV spelling of Malchijah, Adaiah's forefather, in Nehemiah 11:12. *See* Malchijah #2.
8. KJV spelling of Malchijah, the royal prince in whose cistern Jeremiah was imprisoned (Jer 38:6). Malchiah is also spelled Melchiah (21:1). *See* Malchijah #12.

MALCHIEL*, MALCHIELITE*
Beriah's son, a grandson of Asher (Gn 46:17; 1 Chr 7:31), and the founder of the Malchielite family (Nm 26:45).

MALCHIJAH*
1. Gershon's descendant, appointed by David, along with the rest of his family, to serve as a temple musician (1 Chr 6:40, KJV "Malchiah").
2. Priest who served in the time of David (1 Chr 9:12). His descendants were among those who returned to Jerusalem with Zerubbabel (Neh 11:12).
3. Priest in David's reign (1 Chr 24:9); perhaps the same as #2 above.

4. Parosh's son, who obeyed Ezra's exhortation to divorce his pagan wife after the exile (Ezr 10:25, KJV "Malchiah").

5. KJV rendering of Hashabiah, another of Parosh's sons, in Ezra 10:25. See Hashabiah #9.

6. Harim's son, who obeyed Ezra's exhortation to divorce his pagan wife after the exile (Ezr 10:31, KJV "Malchiah"). He repaired part of the Jerusalem wall under Nehemiah (Neh 3:11).

7. Recab's son and the ruler of Beth-hakkerem. Under Nehemiah's direction, he repaired the Dung Gate of the Jerusalem wall (Neh 3:14).

8. Goldsmith who worked under Nehemiah's direction to help repair the Jerusalem wall (Neh 3:31).

9. One who stood to Ezra's left during the public reading of the law (Neh 8:4).

10. Priest who signed Ezra's covenant of faithfulness to God with Nehemiah and others after the exile (Neh 10:3).

11. Participant in the dedication of the rebuilt Jerusalem wall (Neh 12:42).

12. Royal prince who owned a cistern in which the prophet Jeremiah was imprisoned (Jer 38:6). Malchijah's son Pashhur (21:1; 38:1) was one of those who, after hearing the harsh prophecies of Jeremiah, appealed to King Zedekiah to put Jeremiah to death. The princes attempted to do so by throwing him into Malchijah's cistern.

MALCHIRAM* Son of Jeconiah (Jehoiachin), and a descendant of David (1 Chr 3:18).

MALCHI-SHUA* King Saul's third son (1 Sm 14:49; 1 Chr 8:33; 9:39). He was killed by the Philistines at the battle of Gilboa (1 Sm 31:2; 1 Chr 10:2).

MALCHUS Name of a slave of the high priest in John 18:10. At the time of Jesus' arrest, Peter struck Malchus with a sword, cutting off his right ear. In Matthew 26:51, Mark 14:47, and Luke 22:50-51, no name is given for this person. According to Luke, Jesus immediately healed the wound.

MALELEEL* KJV form of Mahalaleel, an ancestor of Jesus, in Luke's genealogy (Lk 3:37). See Mahalaleel, Mahalalel #1.

MALKIEL, MALKIELITE See Malchiel, Malchielite.

MALKIJAH See Malchijah.

MALKIRAM See Malchiram.

MALKISHUA See Malchi-shua.

MALLOTHI One of Heman's 17 children (1 Chr 25:4-5), who became leader of the 19th of 24 divisions of singers for service in the sanctuary during David's reign (v 26).

MALLOW* Shrubby plant (Jb 24:24; 30:4). See Plants.

MALLUCH
1. Merarite Levite and ancestor of Ethan the singer in Solomon's temple (1 Chr 6:44).
2. Bani's son, whom Ezra required to divorce his foreign wife (Ezr 10:29).
3. Harim's son, whom Ezra required to divorce his foreign wife (Ezr 10:32).
4. Priest who set his seal on Ezra's covenant (Neh 10:4).
5. Another priest who set his seal on Ezra's covenant (Neh 10:27).
6. Priest who returned from the exile with Zerubbabel (Neh 12:2).

MALLUCHI* Father of a house headed by Jonathan during the days of the high priest Joiakim in the postexilic period (Neh 12:14, NLT mg). Possibly the same person as Malluch #6.

MALTA Island in the Mediterranean Sea, south of Sicily. The name Malta occurs only once in the Bible (Acts 28:1, KJV "Melita"), in connection with the shipwreck that occurred on Paul's voyage to Rome (25:11-12). This voyage was undertaken during the winter, the season in which storms are most likely to be encountered on the

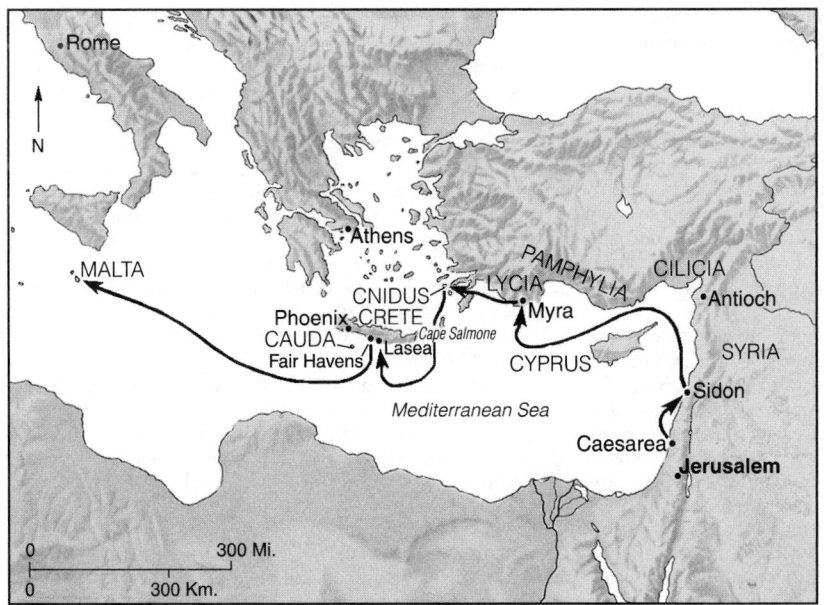

Shipwrecked at Malta
Paul began his 2,000-mile (3,218-kilometer) trip to Rome at Caesarea. To avoid the open seas, the ship followed the coastline. At Myra, Paul was put on a vessel bound for Italy. It arrived with difficulty at Cnidus, then went to Crete, landing at the port of Fair Havens. The next stop was Phoenix, but the ship was blown south around the island of Cauda, then drifted for two weeks until it was shipwrecked on the island of Malta.

Mediterranean. The ship proceeded cautiously, for contrary winds were blowing (27:4). With difficulty they reached the harbor of Fair Havens on Crete (vv 7-8). In spite of a warning by Paul, the decision was made to try to reach the Cretan port of Phoenix, which was more suitable for wintering (vv 9-12).

Caught by a severe storm and driven helplessly by the wind for 14 days, the ship finally neared land during the night. In the morning, the ship tried for the beach but ran aground and was pounded to pieces by the surf. Everyone managed to reach the shore safely. While putting wood on a fire, Paul was bitten by a viper. The natives of the island supposed that he was a criminal whose life was being taken by the bite of a snake. When he did not fall down dead, they radically changed their opinion of him and regarded him as a god (Acts 28:6).

The island of Malta is about 60 miles (96.5 kilometers) from Sicily and has an area of 95 square miles (246.1 square kilometers). St. Paul's Bay marks the traditional site of the shipwreck of Acts. The island is essentially agricultural, but production is poor because of the thin calcareous soil. Terracing is practiced in order to utilize the soil to the fullest extent. The island has no rivers and is dependent on rainfall and springs for its water. The climate in general is mild, but in the summer the island is subject to the hot, dust-laden sirocco from the deserts of Libya.

MAMMON* Aramaic word, meaning wealth or property, transliterated by the Gospel writers in Greek letters. Some English translations preserve the Greek form of the word in English (KJV, RSV, NASB); others translate it with the words "wealth" or "money" (NEB, TEV, NIV, NLT). In Matthew 6:24 and Luke 16:13, "mammon" is personified as a rival to God for the loyalty of the disciples: To which master will obedience be given? In Luke 16:9-11 the term designates material wealth or property. Mammon itself does not carry a negative value, as the parallel phrasing in Luke 16:11 makes clear: "If then you have not been faithful in the unrighteous mammon, who will entrust to you the true riches?" (RSV).

MAMRE (Person) Owner of a parcel of land called "the plain of Mamre." He was an Amorite and is recorded as having two brothers: Aner and Eshcol (Gn 14:13). These became confederates of Abraham when he fought to save his nephew Lot.

MAMRE (Place) Important oak grove near which Abraham lived, and named for an Amorite who helped him defeat Chedorlaomer and rescue Lot (Gn 14:13, 24). Abraham erected an altar under the oak of Mamre (13:18). Abraham was sitting by the sacred tree when he welcomed three mysterious guests (ch 18). Mamre is also a possible site for the scene of Abrahamic covenant ceremonies (ch 15). Isaac and Jacob also lived there (35:27).

MAN Human being, whether male or female.

The biblical teaching on man begins with a right notion concerning God. The biblical perspective of anthropology (i.e., the study of man) is centrally displayed in the context of an elevated theology (i.e., the study of God). A high and reverent view of God leads to a noble and dignified view of man, whereas a poorly developed concept of God often produces a distorted perspective on man. Hence, man may be viewed more importantly than he ought, or man may be seen less important than is biblical. Either view is subbiblical. The place to begin a study of man (which in this article is used as a generic term for both male and female human beings) is with a view of God, his Creator.

Man's Origin Against the naturalistic, materialistic theories of origins, the biblical view starts with the assertion that the eternal God has created man, the most significant of all his created works. It is not necessary for one to subscribe to a particular chronological scenario for God's work in the creation of man. Some Christians believe the Bible teaches a closed chronology in Genesis 1 made of six literal 24-hour days (cf. Gn 1:5, 8, 13, etc.), with the stunning, sudden appearance of man coming perhaps just some 6,000 years ago (cf. the chronologies associated with but not limited to Archbishop James Ussher, *Annales*, 1650–58). Some who hold this general viewpoint (sometimes called creation science) extend the creation of man to about 10,000 years ago, based on a view of some elasticity in the chronologies of Genesis 5 and 11.

Others believe the texts of Genesis 1 and 2 may be interpreted far more broadly to speak of a most remote antiquity for the creation of man (extending to millions of years). They argue that process (under God's control and direction) may have played a significant role in God's creative work. This viewpoint is best termed progressive creationism, and is to be contrasted with theistic evolution, in which God is usually viewed as initiating the process but having little involvement once the processes are in motion. In the former approach, the Hebrew term "day" *(yom)* in Genesis 1 may refer to an extended period of time (e.g., the "day-age" theory); thus, the phrasing "an evening and a morning, the *x*th day" may be a literary device to present successive scenes in the creative works of God through the processes of time.

Many Christians find themselves somewhere between a conservative and a broad chronology for man's origin. Yet in spite of individual preferences, one must give assent to God's creative work in producing man in order to think biblically about man. The essence of faith begins in the words "I believe in God the Father Almighty, Creator of heaven and earth."

Man is not only God's creation but also the pinnacle of his creative effort. Long before modern precision in such things, the ancients were aware of man's anatomical similarities with members of the animal kingdom. Yet despite these similarities, the biblical viewpoint never places man on the same level as animals—man is distinct, the high point of God's creative work, the apex of his handicraft. The progression of the created things in Genesis 1 is climactic; all of God's created work culminated in his fashioning of man.

The distinct behavioral characteristics of man include language, toolmaking, and culture. Distinct experiential characteristics include reflective awareness, ethical concern, aesthetic urges, historical awareness, and metaphysical concern. These factors individually and collectively separate man from other forms of animal life. Man is far more than the "naked ape" of some modern evolutionary theories. But sociology alone does not suffice to explain the full nature of man. That is the subject of divine revelation.

While man bears a continuity with God's creation (assumed in the words of Gn 2:7, being fashioned from the dust of the earth), man is also distinct from all that precedes him because God breathed into him the breath of life so that he became a living soul (2:7). Man was created by God as male and female (1:27), meaning that what is said generally of man must be said of both the male and the female, and that the truest picture of what it means to be human will be found in the context of man and woman together. The commands to multiply and exercise sovereignty over the earth were given to both sexes as shared responsibility. Similarly, it is man as male and female that rebelled against God and bears the consequences of that primeval sin in the postfall world, and it is man as male and female that Christ came to redeem (cf. Gal 3:28). At the same time, the words "male" and "female" denote true distinctions. Many perceived gender differences may be culturally conditioned, yet the prime sexual distinctions between male (Hebrew, *zakar*, "the piercer") and female (Hebrew, *neqeba*, "the pierced") are divinely intended. It takes both male and female to exhibit the full image of God (see Gn 1:27).

Indeed, the most stunning biblical assertion respecting man is that God made man *in his image*. Of no other creature, not even the angels, is such a statement found. The words "in God's image" in Genesis 1:26-28 are the basis for the psalmist's paraphrase in Psalm 8:5, "for you have made him to lack but little of God" (literal translation; "lower than the angels," Septuagint translation). The meaning of the phrase "the image of God" (Latin, *imago Dei*) has been the subject of much debate. Some have thought the phrase to refer to a physical representation of God, but this is doubtful in that God is spirit (cf. Jn 4:24). Others think the phrase refers to man's personhood, which corresponds to the personality of God (having intellect, sensibilities, and will). Such qualities of man may be found in God's image; however, these varied aspects of personality are also shared by other members of the animal kingdom and are not unique to the human species.

The basic meaning of the word "image" (Hebrew, *tselem*) is "shadow," "representation," or "likeness." The image of God in man reveals God's perspective of man's worth and dignity as a representation or a shadow of himself in the created world. Ancient kings of Assyria were known to have physical images of themselves placed in outlying districts as a reminder to those who might be prone to forget that these areas were a part of the empire. So God has placed in man a shadow of himself, a representation of his presence, in the world that he has made.

This view of God's image in man seems to be confirmed by the immediate context in Genesis 1. Man, created in God's image, is to have dominion over all of God's other works (Gn 1:26; see also Ps 8:5). Further, as a representative of the Creator, man is to respond to him. Jesus' assertion of the spirituality of God results in a response of worship in spirit and in truth (Jn 4:21-24).

Man's Nature One may tend to think of man in parts, but the biblical emphasis is on man as a whole. Debates continue on the tripartite (threefold) nature of man (cf. 1 Thes 5:23)—spirit, soul, and body—as against a bipartite (twofold) nature of man, material and immaterial. Though the Bible does seem to support both positions, the most important issue respecting the nature of man is his unity rather than the number of his parts. Hence, a biblical view of man begins in the assertion that one is a person made up of physical and nonphysical properties. In the words of Karl Barth, the human person is "bodily soul, as he is also besouled body." There is no person in body only, nor can one easily think of a bodiless spirit as a person, except in a temporary, transitional state. The Hebrew term *nephesh*, often translated "soul," is best rendered "person" in most contexts. The Hebrew word *ruach* ("breath," "wind," "spirit") and the Greek words *pneuma* ("spirit") and *psuche* ("soul") often speak of the immaterial part of man. This is no less real than the physical. A purely material, physical view of man is frightfully deficient. At the same time, an overemphasis on the spirit and a deemphasis on the physical is neither realistic nor balanced. One may say, "I am a person whose existence is presently very dependent upon my physical body. But I am more than body, more than flesh. When my body dies, I still live. When my flesh decays, I exist. But one day I shall live in a body again. For the notion of a disembodied spirit is not the full measure of my humanity. God's ideal for me is to live my life in my [new] body. So in hope of the eternal state, I believe in the resurrection of the body and life everlasting."

One cannot go far in thinking of the nature of man from the biblical vantage point without first facing the problem of the fall. Genesis 3 suggests that unfallen man was immortal, that his powers of sexual reproduction were not originally bound in the pain in childbearing, and that his work was not troubled by reversals in nature. After the fall, however, all was changed: within man himself, between the male and the female, in his interaction with nature, and in his relationship with the Creator.

As a result of the fall, man has become profoundly fallen, a fallenness extending to every part of his person. The phrase "total depravity" need not mean that one is as evil as he or she might be, but rather that the results of sin affect one's whole being. At the time, the image of God in man continues in some way after the fall, providing the divine rationale for salvation (cf. Rom 5). It is essentially because of God's estimation of the intrinsic worth of man that the divine justification of salvation may be maintained.

The old debate between the essential goodness and the evil disposition of man finds its quandary and resolution in the Genesis account: God made man to consciously reflect the dignity and nobility of the Creator, yet man, by his own deliberate rebellion, turned against his Creator and continues, except by God's grace, in the ensuing sin that marks his life. This resultant sin is both a quality of being in the fallen person, as well as numerous, continuing acts of pride and selfishness. Though the image of God in man was marred by the fall, it may be stimulated anew by the effective work of the Spirit of God as one comes to newness of life in Christ. This gracious work of God brings personal renewal, restoration of relationships with others, and fellowship with God.

Man, then, who was created good by God, has become evil by his own devices, yet in God's power he may recapture the good again. The rediscovery of what it means to be fully human is found in the life of Jesus, whose human life is the new beginning for man. Hence, Jesus is the new Adam; in his model there is a new beginning that replaces the former pattern.

Man's Destiny A biblical view of man must include a balanced statement respecting his divine origin, his rebellion against the grace of God, his judgment, and his prospect for redemption in the person of the Savior Jesus with the promise of eternal life. Man has a beginning and will live forever. This assertion is in stark contrast to naturalistic theories of origins and destinies. One of the most deceptive tendencies of modern thought is the concept "coming to terms with death." People with no thought of God and no hope for eternity are encouraging each other to accept the inevitable decline and demise of their bodies as the natural end to human life. The biblical notion is that death in man is not natural at all.

Death is an acquired trait, not the natural destiny of man. Death may be said of the body but not of the spirit. The biblical teaching is that while the body dies and decays, the person lives on in hope of a renewed body. Those who have come to know Christ go to be with him when their bodies die (Phil 1:23) and anticipate the resurrection of the body for eternal life to come

(1 Cor 15:35-49). Those who die apart from Christ do not cease to exist but rather are assigned an eternal existence of conscious knowledge that they are separated from God and have fallen short of their destiny to enjoy his presence forever. The biblical teaching on the destiny of the lost is quite unpalatable for modern man. Even Christians who have generally high views of biblical inspiration may find themselves blanching at the thought of eternal punishment of the wicked. Yet the biblical doctrine of the final judgment of the wicked is as well established as most teachings in the Bible.

One of the most dramatic truths in Scripture respecting the nature of man is to realize that it was for man that God initiated the salvation work that led to the incarnation of the eternal son of God. After his resurrection and ascension, the Lord Jesus Christ returned to his eternal position of glory and majesty in heaven, where he forever remains the God-man. As God, he shares all the attributes of the Father and the Holy Spirit, and as man, identifies with man. He reveals himself in a physical body, albeit the resurrection body, the firstfruits of the resurrection of all who are his. The incarnation, then, brought about an eternal change in deity. Only a very high view of the worth of man could have brought God to such a fundamental change in himself. As the writer to the Hebrews states, "Because God's children are human beings—made of flesh and blood—Jesus also became flesh and blood by being born in human form" (Heb 2:14, NLT).

The final measure of our humanity is that man was made to worship God and to enjoy him forever. Such thoughts are not attributed to any other created being. Even the angels, who have maintained their perfect state and who worship the Father in conscious bliss, do not have quite the same relationship with God as do redeemed men (Heb 2:16).

What is man? In Christ, man is all God means him to be, in majesty and dignity, and in joy before his throne forever.

See also Image of God; Man, Natural; Man, Old and New.

MAN*, NATURAL Expression occurring in 1 Corinthians 2:14 (RSV mg). The adjective translated there by "natural" is also found in 1 Corinthians 15:44 (twice), 46; James 3:15; and Jude 1:19. This adjective is related to the Greek noun usually translated "soul." Its meaning, however, is primarily determined by its various contexts, particularly in 1 Corinthians, where all four occurrences are contrasted pointedly with "spiritual," an adjective occurring frequently in the NT, mostly in Paul's writings. In almost every instance it refers to the work of the Holy Spirit. Applied to things, "spiritual" means derived from, or produced by, the Holy Spirit (the law—Rom 7:14; gifts—1 Cor 12:1; blessings—Eph 1:3; sacrifices—1 Pt 2:5). When it is applied to persons, it means indwelt, motivated, and directed by the Holy Spirit (1 Cor 2:15; 14:37; Gal 6:1). "Natural," then, when contrasted with "spiritual," generally describes what is devoid of or in opposition to the Holy Spirit and his work. In 1 Corinthians 2:14-15 "natural man" is set over against "spiritual man" (see RSV). Within this context the natural man is one who does not accept the things that come from the spirit of God (1 Cor 2:14). Rather, these things are "foolishness" to him. He cannot understand them because they are "spiritually discerned." This foolishness is the foolishness of unbelief (1:21), and the discernment lacking is insight produced only by the Holy Spirit. Plainly, Paul has in view someone utterly without and even opposed to the Holy Spirit and God's revealed truth.

In 1 Corinthians 15:44-46, the contrast between spiritual and natural occurs in a different context—that of the "body" in death as compared to the "body" in resurrection. The body of the believer laid in the grave ("sown") is a natural body (v 44a). The body of the believer raised from the dead will be a spiritual body, that is, a body renewed and transformed by the Holy Spirit (Rom 8:11). In 1 Corinthians 15:44b and 45a, however, the natural body is traced back by appeal to Genesis 2:7 to Adam before the fall, at Creation. This shows that biblically what is natural refers to the Creation. Originally, as created by God, the "natural" was "very good" (Gn 1:31) but subsequently it has been subjected to corruption and death by the sin of man. Therefore, the sinful rebellion of the natural man, measured by the original creation, is thoroughly unnatural and abnormal. The opposing work of the Holy Spirit now, in Christ, not only removes this abnormality but brings the original purposes of Creation to their consummation (Rom 8:19-22; 2 Cor 5:17).

See also Man; Man, Old and New.

MAN, Old and New Biblical terms used to describe the state of man in relation to Christ. Human beings are created in the image of God and are made to have fellowship with him (Gn 1:26-27). God made known to Adam and Eve his will in a specific situation (2:15-17), yet they used the freedom of their will to disobey God's command (3:1-7). So the human race is dead in sin (Rom 5:12-21; Eph 2:1-3). The sin of Adam and Eve has been passed on to all humanity (original sin). Born with the tendency toward sin (Ps 51:5), as soon as the age of moral responsibility is reached, individuals begin to commit their own sins. Paul uses the term "old man" to refer to this condition. The old man can keep certain parts of the law and do various good things. But no old man can ever do enough good things to earn his own salvation. The old man must be made into a new man or he will suffer the consequences of his sin. Only God can bring about that radical change. Human beings can only accept by faith God's gracious gift.

David, in Psalm 51, cries out for God to take away the guilt of his sins. In verse 10 he pleads, "Create in me a clean heart, O God, and put a new and right spirit within me" (RSV). God promises in Ezekiel 11:19, 18:31, and 36:26 to give repentant sinners a new heart and a new spirit. In Romans 6:5-11 Paul shows how the old nature has been crucified with Christ, so he can conclude, "So you also must consider yourselves dead to sin and alive to God in Christ Jesus" (6:11). In Ephesians 4:22-24 and Colossians 3:9-10 he shows the believer that he has put off the old man and put on the new man. Jesus speaks of this radical transformation as being born anew—not a second physical birth, as Nicodemus thought, but a spiritual birth (Jn 3:6). Only the grace of God can change the old man into the new man. The old man accepts God's gracious gift by faith, but even that faith is a gift of God (Eph 2:8). The new man becomes a child of God. He does not immediately become perfect. He must fight against sin throughout this life as he strives to come closer and closer to the ideal of perfect holiness. He will attain that perfection only in the resurrection to come (1 Cor 15:42-45), when all things are made new (Rv 21:5).

See also Adam (Person); Man; Man, Natural; Regeneration.

MAN, Son of *See* Son of Man.

MANAEN One of the prophets and teachers in the church at Antioch (Acts 13:1), identified as a close companion of Herod the tetrarch. The name is a Greek form of the Hebrew name Menahem.

MANAHATH (Person) One of Shobal's five sons (Gn 36:23; 1 Chr 1:40).

MANAHATH (Place), MANAHATHITE Evidently a place in the Judean hills near the Benjamite border (1 Chr 8:6). The Manahathites (1 Chr 2:54), the people of Manahath, had connections with the Judean and Calebite clans in northern Judea. Its site is apparently that of Malha, three miles (4.8 kilometers) southwest of Jerusalem on the northern slope of the valley of Rephaim.

MANASSEH (Person)

1. Firstborn son of Joseph and his Egyptian wife, Asenath (Gn 41:50-51). Manasseh, along with Ephraim his brother, visited their grandfather Jacob on his deathbed. Jacob announced that Manasseh and Ephraim were to be considered his own, not Joseph's sons (Gn 48:5-6), and that Manasseh, the firstborn, would have descendants not quite as great as those of Ephraim (vv 13-20). This explains why Ephraim and Manasseh (in that order) provided their names for two of the 12 tribes of Israel but Joseph did not, at least in most listings (cf. Rv 7:6). Manasseh also founded the Manassite family (Dt 4:43; 2 Kgs 10:33).

   See also Manasseh, Tribe of.

2. KJV translation for Moses in Judges 18:30. In Hebrew the two names differ by only one letter. Apparently an early scribe was offended that this verse connected Moses' grandson with idolatry, so he changed the name to Manasseh to preserve Moses' reputation. See Moses.

3. Thirteenth king of Judah (697–642 BC) and Jesus' ancestor (Mt 1:10); notorious for his long and wicked reign, described in 2 Kings 21:1-26 and 2 Chronicles 33:1-20. His father was the godly king Hezekiah, and his mother was Hephzibah (2 Kgs 21:1).

   At the age of 12 he became co-ruler with his father. In 686 BC his father died and he became sole monarch at only 23. His 55-year reign (2 Kgs 21:1) is dated from the beginning of his co-regency, so he ruled 11 years as co-regent and 44 years as sole king—longer than any other king in Judah or in Israel. Regrettably, he was the most wicked of all the Judean kings, even resorting to a series of murders, presumably to stay in power (21:16; 24:4). In addition to murder, among his sins listed in 2 Kings 21:2-9 are rebuilding the high places for pagan worship; encouraging Baal, sun, moon, and star worship; and burning his son as a child sacrifice (21:6; cf. 23:10; Jer 7:31).

   Second Chronicles 33:11-16 indicates that he was taken as a prisoner of war to Babylon, that he genuinely repented there, that God restored him as king, and that he tried to abolish his former pagan practices and to restore proper worship of God alone. Skepticism about this account is not warranted, even though unparalleled in 2 Kings. Surviving Assyrian records twice mention Manasseh, saying that he faithfully provided men to transport timber from Lebanon to Nineveh for the Assyrian king Esar-haddon (681–669 BC) and that he paid tribute to King Ashurbanipal (669–627 BC) after an Assyrian military campaign in Egypt in 667 BC. Though Pharaoh Neco's similar captivity and release is mentioned, Manasseh's is not.

   When Manasseh died in 642 BC, at the age of 67, he was buried in his own garden (2 Kgs 21:18), rather than with highly regarded kings like Jehoiada and Hezekiah (2 Chr 24:16; 32:33). His son Amon reverted to his father's wicked practices, and reigned only two years (642–640 BC) before being assassinated. It was his godly grandson Josiah (640–609 BC) who led the people back to the true worship of Yahweh (2 Kgs 23:4-14). But even his reforms could not avert the judgment promised on account of Manasseh's sins (vv 26-27).

   See also Prayer of Manasseh.

4. Pahath-moab's son, who obeyed Ezra's exhortation to divorce his pagan wife after the exile (Ezr 10:30).
5. Hashum's son, who obeyed Ezra's exhortation to divorce his pagan wife after the exile (Ezr 10:33).

MANASSEH, Tribe of Geographically, the largest of the 12 tribes of Israel, and unique in having two territories, a half-tribe in each. Isolated from each other by the Jordan River valley, they developed separately. The half-tribe west of the Jordan was more important, both in OT and NT times, because it was the main tribe of the northern kingdom of Israel (931–722 BC) and one of the main ancestral stocks of the Samaritans.

Early History

Its Roots Its families traced their origins back to Joseph's elder son Manasseh, to Manasseh's son Makir or grandson Gilead, or to later descendants such as Zelophehad and Jair. A fair harmony can be constructed from the biblical genealogical data in Gn 48:5-6; Nm 26:28-34; Jos 17:1-3; 1 Chr 2:21-23; and 7:14-19, a text corrupted by several copyists' errors. The mention of Asriel in 1 Chronicles 7:14 seems to be a copyist's mistake; otherwise, the accounts are capable of being reconciled, even if each list preserved different data and none is complete in itself.

Its Size One year after the exodus, Manasseh had the smallest army, according to Moses' first census (Nm 1:34-35). On the eve of the conquest of Canaan, after wandering 38 years in the Sinai wilderness and then conquering Transjordan, it had the sixth largest fighting force, according to a second census (Nm 26:28-34)—52,700 men.

Its First Settlements The soldiers of the eastern half-tribe of Manasseh settled their families in Gilead, which they captured under Moses' leadership from the Amorite king Og (Nm 21:32-35; 32:39-42; Dt 3:1-15). Then, under Joshua, they crossed the Jordan to help the other tribes conquer Canaan (Nm 32:1-32; Jos 1:12-18). Subsequently, the western half-tribe received its allotment and began to settle in the central hill country (Jos 16:1-9; ch 17). After the remaining tribes received their shares of land, the army from the eastern half-tribe returned home (22:1-9). En route to their families in Gilead, they helped to build an altar by the Jordan River. This act was intended to preserve national unity, but it nearly started a civil war (vv 10-34).

The Eastern Half-Tribe

Its Territory Moses allotted the eastern half-tribe nearly 3,000 square miles (7,770 square kilometers) of territory in three geographical regions (northern Gilead, Bashan, and Mt Hermon), but it succeeded in controlling only about 800 square miles (2,072 square kilometers)—the half of Gilead north of the Jabbok River (and south of the Yarmuk River)—despite successful initial conquests (Nm 32:39-42; Dt 3:12-15; Jos 13:8-13) and gradual northern expansion much later (1 Chr 5:23).

   The territory occupied was mostly a high plateau with a mountainous center. It was watered well by rains in winter and by a heavy dew in summer. Olive trees, grapevines, and wheat thrived, and goats and sheep could find adequate pasture on the eastern slopes, which merged gradually into the desert to the east.

People and Places Prominent citizens of the eastern half-tribe included the "judges" Jair and Jephthah

(Jgs 10:3-5; 11:6-12) and David's benefactor Barzillai (2 Sm 19:31-39). Principal cities were Jabeth-gilead and Ramoth-gilead, a city of refuge and a Levitical city, respectively (originally in Gad—Jos 20:8; 21:38).

The eastern territory was usually called simply "the half-tribe of Manasseh," until David (c. 1000–961 BC) made it an administrative district (1 Chr 27:21). Solomon (970–930 BC) divided and incorporated it into two new districts (1 Kgs 4:13-14). Under Jeroboam I (930–909 BC), it joined, on equal terms, with eight other tribes and with the western half-tribe, to form a confederacy of ten tribes—the northern kingdom of Israel—in 930 BC. Syria and Assyria both held eastern Manasseh temporarily, in the ninth and eighth centuries BC (cf. 2 Kgs 10:32-33; 13:7 with 14:25; and 2 Kgs 15:29 with 2 Chr 34:6-7). King Tiglath-pileser III (745–727 BC) of Assyria invaded the area, conquered it, deported its people, and scattered them throughout his empire (1 Chr 5:26; cf. 2 Kgs 15:29) about ten years before the rest of the northern kingdom fell to the Assyrians in 722 BC. Most of the western Manassites who were left behind intermarried with the foreigners, began to worship pagan gods, and became ancestors of the Samaritans (2 Kgs 17:24-41). Subsequently, the region was known as Gilead. By NT times the region was partly in the Decapolis and partly in Perea.

MANASSES*
1. KJV form of Manasseh, king of Judah, in Matthew 1:10. *See* Manasseh (Person) #3.
2. KJV form of Manasseh, one of Israel's 12 tribes, in Revelation 7:6. *See* Manasseh (Person) #1; Manasseh, Tribe of.

MANASSITE* Descendant of Manasseh, Joseph's first-born son (Dt 4:43; 2 Kgs 10:33). *See* Manasseh (Person) #1; Manasseh, Tribe of.

MANDRAKE Mediterranean herb believed to have had aphrodisiac properties (Gn 30) and noted for its fragrance (Sg 7:13). *See* Plants.

MANEH* KJV rendering of mina, a weight in Ezekiel 45:12. *See* Weights and Measures.

MANGER Feeding trough for domesticated animals. The Greek term for manger is found only four times in the NT. Three of these instances are in the Nativity narrative of Luke and are translated with the English word manger (Lk 2:7, 12, 16). The fourth occurrence, also in Luke's Gospel, is translated "manger" in the RSV and NEB, but "stall" in 13:15 in the KJV, NIV, NASB, NLT.

The most common OT equivalent is the Hebrew term translated "crib" or "stall" in Job 39:9, Proverbs 14:4, and Isaiah 1:3. The context of these passages favors the use of the Greek word for manger. In the Septuagint, however, three other Hebrew words are also translated by this same Greek term. They are the Hebrew terms for "a stall," that is, an enclosure for animals (2 Chr 32:28); "a mash" or "fodder" (Jb 6:5); and "pens" or "stalls" (Hb 3:17).

Through a study of modern Middle Eastern customs and biblical archaeology, two possible locations of the stable and manger area have been determined. In the home of a poor family, the stable was generally a room adjacent to and slightly lower than the living quarters. The stone manger was either located against one of the wooden walls of the stable or carved from a natural outcropping of rock. The other possible location of the stable was in a cave near the house or in the limestone foundation beneath the living quarters of the house. An example of the first of these was found at the ancient site of Megiddo. At Lachish a cave (c. 1200 BC), which seems to have been used as a stable, was discovered beneath the remains of a building.

Traditionally, the manger area in which Jesus was born was a cave stable; it is over such a cave that the present Church of the Nativity was erected. However, the evidence recorded in Luke's Gospel could as easily refer to an area adjacent to a house. *See* Jesus Christ, Life and Teachings of.

MANIUS, Titus Roman legate who wrote to the Jews concerning political concessions (2 Macc 11:34). *See* Titus (Person) #1.

MANNA Miraculous food the Lord provided for the Israelites in the desert. It originally appeared in the form of thin flakes, like frost on the ground, around the Israelite camp (Ex 16:14-15). It is compared elsewhere with coriander seed and bdellium, or resin (Nm 11:7). Its taste is said to have been like that of honey or of fresh oil (Ex 16:31; Nm 11:8). Since the experience of taste and color is somewhat subjective, these descriptions do not necessarily conflict. The word comes from the Hebrew *man*, which means, "what?" When the Israelites saw the manna, they asked, "What is it?" (Ex 16:15).

Attempts have been made to link manna with substances discovered by modern travelers in Sinai and Arabia. In early summer (June–July) the tamarisk tree in these regions exudes a sweet-tasting liquid, produced as the result of the activity of a tiny insect. This liquid falls to the ground, where it forms small grains that disappear when the sun gets hot. Reference also has been made to an edible lichen that in parts of southwest Asia is used instead of grain in years of famine. But the regularity, periodicity, and abundance of the manna cannot be explained on any but miraculous grounds. The Israelites were to gather it for one day at a time. Anything collected above that measure was subject to spoiling (16:20). Only the Sabbath day was an exception to that rule. Manna was no longer provided after Israel entered Canaan (Jos 5:12). When Israel craved other food besides manna, the people were punished with an excess of quail (Nm 11:4-6, 18-20). In poetic literature it was called "the grain of heaven" (Ps 78:24; cf. 105:40), and "the bread of angels" (78:25). Jesus pointed to himself as the true manna, the bread from heaven, which, when eaten, would nourish man unto life everlasting (cf. Jn 6:25-59).

See also Wilderness Wanderings.

MANOAH Danite from Zorah whose wife was barren. Through encounters with the Angel of the Lord, the couple learned that God was about to give them a son who would judge the Philistines and deliver Israel from its oppression. Manoah later fathered Samson, who fulfilled these promises (Jgs 13; 16:31).

MAN OF LAWLESSNESS, MAN OF SIN* Expression used by the apostle Paul of the Antichrist in 2 Thessalonians 2:3. *See* Antichrist; Mystery of Lawlessness.

MANUAL OF DISCIPLINE* Book of community rules of conduct belonging to the Essenes at Qumran. *See* Dead Sea Scrolls; Essenes.

MAOCH* Father of Achish, the Philistine king of Gath. David sought refuge with this king in order to escape Saul's plots to kill him (1 Sm 27:2). *See* Maacah, Maachah (Person) #3.

MAON (Person), MAONITE Son of Shammai, and Bethzur's father (1 Chr 2:45). He was either the founding father of the people of Bethzur and/or the founder of the city. His descendants are perhaps the Maonites of Judges 10:12.

MAON (Place) Chief town in the hill country of Judah (Jos 15:55), about nine miles (14.5 kilometers) south of Hebron. David and his men hid in this area while fleeing from Saul (1 Sm 23:24-25), and David's wife Abigail was from this town (25:2-3). It has been identified with modern Tell Ma'in, where pottery was found dating from the time of David.
See also Meunim, Meunites.

MARA A name, meaning "bitter," which Naomi gave to herself when she returned as a widow to Judah from Moab (Ru 1:20). *See* Naomi.

MARAH Spring of water in the wilderness of Etham, the first camping place of the Israelites after crossing the Red Sea (Ex 15:23; Nm 33:8-9). The accepted identification is with 'Ain Hawarah, a pool of bitter water on the eastern coastal plain of the Gulf of Suez, about 44 miles (70.8 kilometers) southeast of Suez, and about 5 miles (8 kilometers) northwest of 'Ain Gharandel, south of Wadi Amarah (which may preserve an echo of the ancient name).
See also Wilderness Wanderings.

MARALAH KJV and NLT rendering of Mareal, a site on Zebulun's western border, in Joshua 19:11. *See* Mareal.

MARANATHA* Aramaic expression used by Paul in 1 Corinthians 16:22, meaning either "Our Lord, come!" or "Our Lord has come."

Quite certainly the use of *maranatha* (cf. *amen* and *abba*) originated in the worship services of early Jewish Christians whose mother tongue was Aramaic. Since Paul wrote in the Greek language, he needed to transliterate (writing the Aramaic phrase with Greek letters), a process that sometimes creates ambiguities. In addition, words were not written separately in ancient documents. Therefore, since *maranatha* consists of two words, it can be analyzed in different ways.

Most scholars agree that the first word in the phrase is *maran* or *marana*, meaning "Lord," or more probably "our Lord," and that the second word represents the Aramaic verb "to come." This verb, however, may be taken either as a prayer (imperative *tha* or *etha*, "come!") or as a statement (perfect tense *atha* "has come"). Five different interpretations are then possible: (1) If the words are considered as a prayer, Paul is praying for either Jesus' spiritual presence, with possible reference to the Lord's Supper, or (2) Jesus' second coming. As a statement, the expression may refer to the Incarnation; it may be translated (3, 4) "Our Lord is present," either with reference to the Lord's Supper or to Jesus' more general promise in Matthew 18:20; or (5) it may be translated "Our Lord is coming" (the so-called "prophetic perfect," although some prominent Aramaic scholars argue that this is not really possible).

In support of rendering the expression as a statement ("our Lord has come") is the fact that the Syriac (a form of Aramaic) version translates the verb in the perfect tense; further, the early church fathers usually interpreted it the same way. A majority of scholars, however, believe that such an interpretation does not fit the context well. Further, if the phrase is understood as a prayer, it can be related to other passages (Phil 4:5b; 1 Pt 4:7; cf. Rv 22:20b, which may be a translation of *maranatha*).

The fact that *maranatha* occurs immediately after Paul's imprecatory curse (1 Cor 16:22) has led many to the view that the Aramaic expression is part of the curse itself. The KJV rendering ("let him be Anathema Maran-atha") leaves the impression that the two words are a unit, whereas *anathema* is a Greek word meaning "curse" and probably ends the sentence. It is nevertheless quite possible, some modern scholars believe, to relate *maranatha* very closely to the curse, since the prayer for Jesus to come in judgment reinforces the solemnity and reality of Paul's imprecation. Interestingly, a church council in the seventh century anathematizes dissidents with the words "anathema maranatha, let him be condemned at the Lord's coming."

MARBLE *See* Minerals and Metals; Stones, Precious.

MARCION*, Gospel of Heretical gospel of the early second century.

Marcion was a native of the Roman province of Pontus who went to Rome about AD 138 and became the founder of a sect called the Marcionites. He seems to have been a member of the Roman church for a time before he went off into heresy. The basic tenet of this later heretical position was that there existed a radical difference between the Old Testament and the New, between the law of the Old and the love and grace of the New, and between the creator God of the Old and the Christian God of the New. For him the God of the Old Testament was the author of evil, which he associated with matter and the world in general, while the God of the New was our Father and the giver of everything good.

This being his belief, Marcion set out to establish for himself a canon of Scripture to support it. This canon included his gospel, which was the Gospel according to Luke, purified of anything connected with the Old Testament, the Jews, the creation of this sinful material world, and anything that related to a true humanity for our Lord. As Irenaeus writes in *Against Heresies* (1.17.2), "Besides this, he [Marcion] mutilates the Gospel which is according to Luke, removing all that is written respecting the generation of the Lord, and setting aside a great deal of the teaching of the Lord, in which the Lord is recorded as most clearly confessing that the Maker of this universe is His Father." Irenaeus goes on to say, "In like manner, too, he dismembered the Epistles of Paul, removing all that is said by the apostle respecting that God who made the world, to the effect that He is the Father of our Lord Jesus Christ, and also those passages from the prophetical writings which the apostle quotes, in order to teach us that they announced beforehand the coming of the Lord." In summary, Marcion's canon consisted of his gospel, which was a mutilated copy of Luke, and 10 of the Pauline epistles (excluding the Pastoral Epistles).

MARCUS* KJV alternate spelling of Mark (Col 4:10; Phlm 1:24; 1 Pt 5:13). *See* Mark, John.

MARDUK Supreme Babylonian deity, worshiped as the god of creation and destiny. Marduk (also called Bel) was originally the local city god of Babylon. However, as Babylon increased in power, Marduk achieved preeminence over the whole Mesopotamian pantheon of deities. His rise to supremacy is told in the creation epic *Enuma Elish*, where Marduk is credited with defeating Tiamat, primeval chaos; he then created the heavens and the earth. Zarpanit (Sarpanit) was Marduk's consort, and the temple Esagila at Babylon was erected for them. Jeremiah foretold that Marduk would be put to shame for his inability to keep Babylon from destruction (Jer 50:2; Merodach—the Hebrew pronunciation of Marduk).

MAREAL* Town defining part of the western border

MAREAL* Town defining part of the western border of the land allotted to Zebulun's tribe for an inheritance. It was positioned between Sarid and Dabbesheth (Jos 19:11, NLT "Maralah").

MARESHAH (Person)

1. Caleb's firstborn son and the father of Hebron (1 Chr 2:42; RSV, based on the Greek text). He is alternately called Mesha in the Hebrew text (RSV mg). *See* Mesha (Person) #2.
2. Perhaps a Judahite son of Laadah (1 Chr 4:21).

MARESHAH (Place)

MARESHAH (Place) City (Greek *Marisa;* Josephus, "Marissa") on the road from the coastal plain of Judah toward Hebron and Jerusalem. Remains of Jewish pottery indicate occupation from at least 800 BC. The site is now called Tel Mareshah.

Aerial View of Tell Mareshah Mareshah overlooks the Elah Valley, the scene of the battle between David and Goliath.

At Israel's occupation of Canaan, Mareshah was allotted by Joshua to Judah (Jos 15:44). Later, at the division of the kingdom, Rehoboam fortified it as a protective outpost covering Jerusalem from the southwest, from which many invaders were to approach (2 Chr 11:8). Zerah the Ethiopian, with a million men and three hundred chariots, penetrated as far as Mareshah and was defeated there

by Asa (14:9). In the following reign, that of Jehoshaphat, the prophet Eliezer, born at Mareshah, foretold the destruction of the proud fleet the king had built (20:37).

The prophet Micah, who was born at Moresheth-gath (a few miles to the north), uttered a moving elegy upon the fate of the regions he knew from boyhood, as the Assyrians approached (whether under Sennacherib, 701 BC, or Sargon, 711 BC). Punning upon each familiar place-name, he warned Mareshah of a coming "possessor" (Mi 1:15).

MARI* Influential city-state, located in eastern Syria, which became important in the early second millennium BC. It seems to have been settled by Semitic nomads, who adopted the values of city dwellers and progressed so far as to adapt cuneiform to their own Akkadian language.

The importance of this cosmopolitan city, which was an outpost of Sumerian civilization, is highlighted by the fact that it became the capital of an empire extending over a great part of northern Mesopotamia, about 22 miles (35.4 kilometers) along the Euphrates River.

Archaeological excavations at Mari yielded a monumental discovery: archives containing over 20,000 documents. These records virtually rewrite the history of western Asia. In addition to the tablets, a well-preserved palace was also unearthed. Original mural paintings were still intact, as were some kitchen and bath installations. These artifacts and tablets shed a great deal of light on life during the period from 1810 to 1760 BC.

As one viewed Mari from a distance, a great defensive wall was seen that encircled the city, protecting it from invading forces. One prominent structure rose portentously above the town, probably to an approximate height of 150 feet (45.6 meters). This was the ziggurat, a temple tower built in a lofty pyramidal structure with successive stages. One ascended its heights by means of outside staircases, which led to the shrine at the top. There were smaller temples at its base.

Not far away, the royal palace commanded about six acres (2.4 hectares) of land. The palace was constructed of extremely thick walls made of brick covered with clay, rising to a height of 16 feet (4.9 meters). An elaborate drainage system was also discovered that effectively carried away rainwater through its bitumen-lined clay pipes, some 30 feet (9.1 meters) underground. The palace at Mari contained nearly 300 rooms. It was not only the royal residence but also the center of business, diplo-

Mari Tablet: Side, Front and Back

matic services, and military leadership. It even had room to store merchants' goods and military equipment, such as battering rams and siege towers. The royal court enjoyed such foods as fish, meat, four varieties of bread, cucumbers, peas, beans, garlic, dates, grapes, and figs. Beverages were beer and wine. The religious observances involved sacrifices and temple prostitution, which was common in the ancient Near East.

The clay tablets of the archives reveal a great deal about the everyday life of the people. Some of the records are bilingual, some literary, but most deal with a period between Jahdun-Lim of Hana, the founder of Mari, to the decline under Zimri-Liom, his son. The recovered information at Mari reveals that the king held court every day, listening to officials and ambassadors presenting affairs of state. He also was called upon to settle certain serious legal disputes. The state religion demanded the daily participation of the king, who visited the temples, officiated at rituals, sacrificed animals, reported to the gods, and attended religious feasts, and who was sometimes considered divine. The king also was responsible for regulating the calendar, which necessitated an extra month every three years.

The commercial and economic records indicate that there were metalworkers, weavers, fullers, gem cutters, jewelers, painters, perfume makers, boatmen, carpenters, leather workers, fishermen, potters, and masons. Payment for services rendered was largely made in goods, though sometimes in gold or silver. Such commodity payments were corn, wool, clothing, wine, or oil.

See also Inscriptions.

MARINER* *See* Sailors.

MARJORAM* Small mint growing as high as three feet (.9 meter) tall. It was perhaps the "hyssop" of the OT. *See* Plants (Hyssop).

MARK, Gospel of Second book of the NT, probably written by John Mark of Jerusalem sometime between AD 60 and 68.

PREVIEW
• Author, Date, Provenance
• Distinctives
• Structure
• Occasion, Purpose, Theology
• Content

Author, Date, Provenance Our most ancient testimony about who wrote the second Gospel comes from Papias (c. 60–130), author of several expositions of Jesus' teachings, in which he reports various traditions from "the Elder John" (possibly to be identified with the apostle John, although this is by no means certain). At one point Papias states, "The Elder used to say this also: Mark became Peter's interpreter and wrote down accurately, though not in order, all that [Peter] remembered concerning the things both said and done by the Lord." (This quotation was preserved by the fourth-century writer Eusebius of Caesarea in his *Ecclesiastical History* 3.39.15.) One need not doubt the basic reliability of this statement. Mark—almost surely to be identified with the John Mark of Acts 12:12 (see also 1 Pt 5:13)—was a disciple of Peter, and the second Gospel owes its existence, at least in part, to the apostle's reminiscences. It does not follow, however, that one has adequately characterized Mark's work if that is all one says. For instance, Papias's qualification, "though not in order," indicates that Mark did not intend to write a chronological biography. Fur-

thermore, Papias goes on to comment (according to one interpretation of his ambiguous words) that Mark (or Peter?) adapted the material to the teaching situation and that therefore Mark is absolved from any (implied) charges of inaccuracy. It appears that from the earliest times Christians appealed to the purposes and circumstances of Mark's writing in order to account for difficulties in harmonizing the material found in the various Gospels.

Other statements from Christian writers in the second, third, and fourth centuries seem dependent on Papias's testimony, but some additional data they provide may possess independent value. For example, a fairly early document (date uncertain) known as the Anti-Marcionite Prologue asserts that Mark wrote his Gospel somewhere in Italy after Peter's death (in the mid-60s), and this testimony is considered reliable by many scholars. Still, the possibility that Mark composed his work before Peter's martyrdom cannot be ruled out completely.

Papias says nothing specific about *when* the Gospel was written. A small minority of scholars date Mark shortly after AD 70. Another minority suggest a date in the 40s or 50s on the basis of a papyrus fragment discovered in Qumran called 7Q5. (According to José O'Callaghan, the fragment, which has been dated about AD 50–68, should be identified as Mark 6:52-53.) This fragment contains only 20 letters on one side, making the Markan reconstruction very uncertain. Few scholars are convinced that the text is Mark; some think it is part of 1 Enoch or Zechariah. An impressive majority of scholars date Mark in the 60s, with conservatives usually preferring the early years of the decade. Why this preference? If the theory of Markan priority is accepted, then clearly Mark was written before Luke; and since Luke is normally dated by conservatives about AD 62, Mark can be no later than AD 60 or 61. This line of argument, though strong, is not decisive. In the first place, Luke cannot be dated with complete certainty. Second, the view that Matthew and Luke used Mark (the working assumption of most scholars) is only a hypothesis, and one that is vigorously opposed by some writers. Third, a tradition going back to the second century (see above) asserts that Mark wrote his Gospel *after* Peter's death, no earlier than AD 64. Fourth, one persuasive view regarding the occasion of this Gospel assumes that the Neronian persecution (AD 64) had begun. (According to a different view of the occasion, Mark was written after the beginning of the Jewish revolt in AD 66.) Therefore, while a date in the early 60s remains possible, it does not require committal.

With regard to the authorship of the second Gospel, there seems to be no compelling reason to deny Papias's report that Mark (no doubt the John Mark of Acts 12:12) took down Peter's reminiscences and that these became the basis of his work. Some scholars argue that the Gospel contains geographical inaccuracies (e.g., we have no evidence of a region called Dalmanutha, Mk 8:10) and that a native of Jerusalem such as Mark would have been more reliable in his information. However, the topographical problems in Mark, though real, need not be interpreted as inaccuracies (present ignorance of a place named Dalmanutha is hardly conclusive proof that it did not exist). Furthermore, in other respects (e.g., 14:54, 66) the Gospel reveals an impressive knowledge of local details. Many writers also point out bits of information that support a Petrine background, such as the healing of Peter's mother-in-law (1:30-31). In short, the internal evidence, while falling short of proof, does not at all undermine the tradition preserved by Papias. A generation ago, the trustworthiness of Papias's testimony was almost universally accepted. This situation has changed somewhat, but even those scholars who adopt a skeptical attitude toward this tradition concede that it *may* be true.

As attention turns to the provenance of the Gospel, the task becomes more difficult. Tradition going back to the second century asserts what may be already implied by Papias—namely, that Mark wrote his Gospel in Rome. Although some scholars have suggested other possibilities, such as Galilee and Antioch, these have not proved satisfactory. Mark did spend some time in Rome, and some characteristics in the Gospel (such as Latinisms in the Greek and the explanation of Jewish customs, as in 7:3-4), while proving nothing, are certainly consonant with a Roman origin. Furthermore, one persuasive view of the occasion that gave rise to the Gospel assumes a background of persecution in Rome.

Distinctives A number of characteristics of Mark set it apart from the other Gospels. For example, a word usually translated "immediately" occurs more than 40 times in Mark and only a dozen times in the rest of the NT. While this feature could be interpreted as a simple "mannerism," consonant with Mark's unpretentious, colloquial style, it certainly adds to the rapid flow of his narrative, which, dwelling more on Jesus' activity than on his discourses (in contrast to Matthew and Luke), shifts from scene to scene with hardly a pause. Since the Gospel is also quite brief (Luke is nearly twice as long), one may wonder whether the author intended for it to be read at a sitting; even if read aloud, this would take only about one and a half hours. At any rate, there can be little doubt that the work conveys a sense of urgency.

Other characteristics, however, prove more significant. Someone unfamiliar with the story of Jesus who happened to read Mark for the first time would no doubt be taken aback by its rather abrupt beginning. After a brief clause that stands as a sort of title (1:1), Mark moves on to describe in brief the ministry of John the Baptist. Then he introduces Jesus as coming from Nazareth without telling us anything whatever of his earlier life. Furthermore, over one-third of the book (including the so-called Passion narrative) is devoted to Jesus' last week. These and other factors lend to the work a note of mystery, accentuated by the fact that at various points Mark calls attention to the fear or amazement gripping those who came in contact with Jesus (2:12; 4:41; 5:15, 33, 42; 6:51; 9:6; and several other passages, especially the strange words of 10:32). In addition, if one assumes that the Gospel originally ended with 16:8, Mark wished to leave his readers with the same sense of awe that the disciples experienced at Jesus' resurrection.

But how does one account for this fear and amazement? Mark's clear answer is that Jesus, though truly a man, is also divine. While Mark's Gospel exhibits the humanity of Jesus Christ (1:41; 3:5; 8:12; 10:14), his chief emphasis is on the Lord's deity. Indeed, Mark introduces his book by referring to Jesus as "the Son of God" (a phrase omitted in some manuscripts, however), a position that is recognized by the demons (3:11; 5:7) and by God himself (9:7). What may well be the true climax of the Gospel occurs at 15:39, where Mark writes that a Gentile, a Roman centurion, upon hearing Jesus' death cry, exclaimed, "Truly this man was the Son of God!"

Structure The author organized his Gospel according to a simple plan. The first eight chapters summarize the nature of Christ's public ministry by alternating stories that show his growing popularity with stories that stress the disapproval of the Jewish leaders. This first half of the book, while indicating some of the tensions created by Jesus' coming, gives the basic impression of success

and general optimism. A significant shift then strikes the reader toward the end of chapter 8, particularly beginning with verse 31. At Caesarea Philippi, Peter has just confessed that Jesus is the Messiah, and now for the first time Jesus reveals that as Messiah he must die. The disciples become perplexed and discouraged and their pessimism mounts as this thought is brought home to them repeatedly (9:9, 31; 10:32-34; 14:17-25). In the end they desert their master (14:50).

Interestingly, this pessimistic note is anticipated in the earlier part of the Gospel at three points: 3:6 (Jesus' enemies plot his death); 6:6 (faithlessness in Nazareth); and 8:21 (lack of understanding in the disciples). Some scholars suggest that Mark used these three verses to indicate the first three divisions of his book. In addition, other scholars note that two healings of blind men (8:22-26; 10:46-52) seem to provide the opening and the conclusion of a section that emphasizes the spiritual blindness of the disciples. One more structural clue is 14:1, which clearly marks out the final section of the Gospel.

Mark in Codex Vaticanus Mark 16:3-8, with the short ending, in a replica of Codex Vaticanus (fourth century)

Occasion, Purpose, Theology A few scholars think that Mark may have been combating a heretical sect that stressed the miracles of Jesus and viewed him purely as a divine wonder-worker. Although this view has not gained acceptance as originally formulated, a number of writers do see the Gospel as a theological corrective. Ralph Martin, who links Mark very closely with Paul, suggests that the evangelist is opposing some heretical groups who have distorted Paul's message by placing exclusive stress on Christ as a *heavenly* figure (cf. the views that Paul himself opposes in Colossians). Mark responds to these aberrations by emphasizing, in Martin's words, "the paradox of Jesus' earthly life in which suffering and vindication form a two-beat rhythm." Even if one decides that this reconstruction, too, is rather speculative, one may nevertheless retain certain elements in it as valid.

Other scholars, such as H. Kee, place emphasis on the apocalyptic background of Mark. Kee and others tie this element to the Jewish revolt of AD 66, but commitment to this particular historical connection is unnecessary to appreciate the great significance of Mark 13 (Jesus' apocalyptic discourse) for those original readers of the Gospel who may have been undergoing persecution.

Perhaps the most satisfactory reconstruction links this Gospel to the Neronian persecution in the mid-60s. Mark, for example, is the only Gospel that records that Jesus, after being driven to the wilderness, found himself in the company of wild animals (1:13). This detail, according to William Lane, "was filled with special significance for those called to enter the arena where they stood helpless in the presence of wild beasts." This interpretation, while not without difficulties, has the advantage of accounting for most of the available data. First, it is compatible with the strong tradition that assigns the origin of Mark's work to Rome. Second, Mark speaks distinctly to those suffering persecution by introducing them quickly to John's imprisonment and several other details. Third, related to this is Mark's emphasis on discipleship. Christians facing persecution must have been tempted to relax the standards (4:17-19). Fourth, given this general situation, one can hardly doubt the significance of our Lord's apocalyptic message in chapter 13, intended to encourage the disciples in the midst of their trials by reminding them of the glory to follow. Finally, Mark's clear concern for the Gentile mission fits in with the needs of pagan Rome. The suffering Christians cannot afford to forget the unbelieving society in which they live. In the light of this particular responsibility, Mark assures his readers of what even the Roman centurion began to recognize—surely Jesus *is* the Son of God (15:39).

Content The development of Mark's narrative can be presented in six major divisions within a twofold structure:

Introduction (1:1-13)
Part I: Popularity and Opposition (1:14-8:21)
  1. Jesus' authority and the Pharisees' enmity
    (1:14-3:6)
  2. The people's response (3:7-6:6a)
  3. The disciples' misunderstanding (6:6b-8:21)
Part II: Darkness and Death (8:22-15:47)
  4. The Messiah's mission and the disciples' blindness (8:22-10:52)
  5. Final ministry (11:1-13:37)
  6. The Passion narrative (14:1-15:47)
Conclusion (16:1-8)

Although one can hardly claim that this outline corresponds exactly to the author's original plan (Mark may

not have consciously worked out a detailed outline), the sixfold division provides a useful starting point for an interpretive summary of the contents.

Jesus' Authority and the Pharisees' Enmity (1:14-3:6)
Immediately after the introductory portion (1:1-13), which describes John the Baptist's ministry as well as Jesus' baptism and temptation, Mark opens the body of the work with a summary statement (vv 14-15). In these two verses he seems to suggest that Jesus' public ministry, characterized by the proclamation that God's kingdom is about to be inaugurated, was occasioned by John's imprisonment. This is followed by the call of the first disciples (vv 16-20) and then by a complex of stories (vv 21-38), all of which report incidents that took place in Capernaum, apparently within a 24-hour period: synagogue instruction followed by the healing of a demoniac; the healing of Peter's mother-in-law; numerous other healings in the evening; prayer in a lonely place. The statement that Jesus proceeded to expand his ministry throughout the province of Galilee (v 39) is followed by the story of a leper's cure (vv 40-45). Next are found a very important group of incidents (2:1-3:6), all of them focusing on Jesus' conflicts with Jewish leaders: the healing and forgiveness of a paralytic; the call of Levi, whose dinner (attended by Jesus as well as by the hated tax gatherers) occasioned some disputes, particularly on the issue of fasting; and two significant stories regarding proper behavior on the Sabbath.

The People's Response (3:7-6:6a) Mark opens this second section as he opened the first: a summary statement (Jesus' healings by the lake—3:7-12) followed by the official appointment of 12 apostles (vv 13-19). Then follows a section that focuses on the kinds of charges brought against Jesus by his own family and by the scribes (vv 20-22), leading to a response touching on Satan, on blasphemy against the Holy Spirit, and on what constitutes true membership in his family (vv 23-35). Most of chapter 4 is devoted to Jesus' parables of the kingdom—the sower, the seed growing secretly, the mustard seed—and includes statements on the nature and purpose of his teachings (4:10-12, 21-25, 33-34). In the evening Jesus and his disciples set out to cross the Sea of Galilee, leading to the stilling of the storm (vv 35-41), the healing of the Gerasene demoniac on the other side of the lake (5:1-20), and, on their return to Capernaum, the healing of a hemorrhaging woman and the raising of Jairus's daughter (vv 21-43). The section concludes with Jesus' visit to his hometown, Nazareth, and the rejection he suffered there (6:1-6a).

The Disciples' Misunderstanding (6:6b-8:21) The third section begins with two introductory passages: the sending out of the 12 (6:6b-13) and the story of John the Baptist's death (vv 14-29). When the disciples return, Jesus determines to seek some rest, but the crowds follow them; Jesus then teaches and feeds the 5,000 (vv 30-44) and, after crossing the lake (vv 45-52, which includes Jesus' walk over the water), he performs numerous cures in and around Gennesaret (vv 53-56). Then follows a controversy with the Pharisees regarding the hand-washing ritual (7:1-8), and this incident leads to Christ's assertion of the authority of God's word over human tradition (vv 9-13) and to some general instructions on true purity (vv 14-23). The next several stories describe Jesus' withdrawal from Galilee, first to Tyre, where a gentile woman's daughter is healed (vv 24-30), then to the Decapolis, where he cures a deaf-mute (vv 31-37) and feeds a crowd of four thousand (8:1-10). The demand of the Pharisees for a sign (vv 11-12) leads to Jesus' warning against the "leaven" of the Pharisees, a statement misunderstood by the disciples (vv 13-21).

The Messiah's Mission and the Disciples' Blindness (8:22–10:52) Still away from Galilee, but now in the nearby town of Bethsaida, Jesus heals a blind man (8:22-26). He then leads his disciples north toward Caesarea Philippi, which sets the stage for Peter's confession (vv 27-30). This recognition on the part of the disciples (of whom Peter is in effect a representative) leads Jesus to prophesy his death, but Peter's refusal to accept the prophecy calls forth a rebuke and instruction on discipleship (vv 31-38). The failure of the disciples to understand the necessity of Christ's death provides the background for the Transfiguration (9:1-8), which assures Peter, John, and James that God's kingdom will indeed come (note v 1); further, the Father himself enjoins them to believe Jesus' prophecy (v 7). After some words about the resurrection and about the coming of Elijah (vv 9-13), Mark relates the healing of a demoniac boy (vv 14-29). Back in Galilee, a second prophecy of Jesus' death (vv 30-32) is followed, sadly, by a trivial discussion among the disciples as to who is the greatest (vv 33-37). Appropriately, one finds some further instructions concerning discipleship (vv 38-50). Mark next writes that Jesus left Galilee for the last time and began his journey toward the south. During this journey, Jesus delivered teachings on divorce and on the spiritual privileges of children (10:1-16), then met the rich young ruler (vv 17-22), an incident that leads to further words on discipleship (vv 23-31). A third prophecy of Jesus' death (vv 32-34) is again followed by selfish behavior on the part of the disciples, in this case an ambitious request from James and John (vv 35-40). The incident produces indignation among the rest of the disciples, thus necessitating another rebuke from their master, who himself came to serve and to die (vv 41-45). The section ends as it began—by reporting the cure of a blind man, Bartimaeus of Jericho in this story (vv 46-52).

Final Ministry (11:1–13:37) This section seems naturally to divide into three balanced subsections. The first one (11:1-26) includes three events: the Triumphal Entry, the withering of the fig tree, and the cleansing of the temple. The second subsection (11:27–12:44) is particularly important, for here is found Jesus' final series of controversies with the Jewish leaders. The topics covered are the source of Jesus' authority (11:27-33), the parable of the wicked husbandmen (12:1-12), the legitimacy of Caesar's tax (vv 13-17), the Sadducees' denial of resurrection (vv 18-27), the chief commandment (vv 28-34), and the question regarding David's son (vv 35-37). This subsection ends with a warning against the scribes and with the story of the widow's mite (vv 38-44). The third subsection (ch 13) is devoted completely to the Olivet discourse, with its prophecies of destruction, calamities, persecutions, deceivers, and final vindication. The discourse ends with various admonitions to keep alert.

The Passion Narrative (14:1–15:47) This final section, which is introduced by a report of the priests' plot (14:1-2), may be divided into two subsections. The first one relates the events leading up to Jesus' trial (vv 3-52). They include the anointing of Jesus (vv 3-9), Judas's betrayal (vv 10-11), the incidents connected with the Last Supper (vv 12-31), the scene at Gethsemane (vv 32-42), and the arrest (vv 43-52). The second subsection relates Jesus' trial before the Jews (vv 53-65), Peter's denials (vv 66-72), the trial before Pilate (15:1-15), the crucifixion (vv 16-41), and the burial (vv 42-47).

The Gospel concludes somewhat mysteriously, but no less triumphantly, with the news that Jesus has risen from the dead (16:1-8). The earliest surviving Greek manuscripts, usually regarded as the most reliable, end at verse 8; the majority of manuscripts, however, include an additional 12 verses that report Jesus' appearances to his disciples.

See also Jesus Christ, Life and Teachings of; Mark, John; Matthew, Gospel of; Luke, Gospel of; Synoptic Gospels.

MARK, John Cousin of Barnabas; companion to both Paul and Peter; author of the second Gospel.

A member of a Jewish family in Jerusalem who were early believers in Jesus Christ, John Mark had both a Jewish and a Roman name. The Roman name Mark was perhaps a badge of Roman citizenship, as in Paul's case, or was adopted when he left Jerusalem to serve the gentile church in Antioch (Acts 12:25). When an angel of the Lord freed Peter from prison, the apostle went directly to "the house of Mary, the mother of John whose other name was Mark" (v 12, NRSV). This house, described as having an outer gate, being of adequate size to accommodate a gathering of many believers and served by a slave named Rhoda (vv 12-13), was obviously the dwelling of a wealthy family. By the time of this event (c. AD 44), Mark may have already been converted through the personal influence of Peter (1 Pt 5:13). The fact that he was chosen to accompany Barnabas and Saul (Paul) to Antioch indicates that Mark was held in high esteem by the church in Jerusalem (Acts 12:25).

John Mark accompanied Barnabas and Saul to assist them on their evangelistic expedition (Acts 13:5). He soon left the apostles, however, and returned to Jerusalem (v 13). Scripture does not reveal the cause of this desertion. Perhaps the rigors and hardships of the journey overwhelmed the young man. Another possible explanation was that at Paphos, shortly into the journey, Paul stepped to the front as leader and spokesman (v 13). Thereafter, Acts (with the natural exception of 15:12, 25) speaks of Paul and Barnabas rather than Barnabas and Paul. Perhaps it offended Mark to see his kinsman Barnabas, who had preceded Paul in the faith (4:36-37) and had ushered him into the apostles' fellowship (9:27), take second place in the work of the gospel. But there may have been a deeper and more significant cause for Mark's withdrawal. Like Paul, Mark was "a Hebrew born of Hebrews" (Phil 3:5, NRSV). Because of this, Mark may have objected to Paul's offer of salvation to the Gentiles based only on faith without the prerequisite of keeping the Jewish law. It is noteworthy that the Bible uses only the Hebrew name John when recording Mark's presence on the gospel journey (Acts 13:5) and his departure at Perga in Pamphylia (v 13). Also important is the fact that John Mark returned, not to the gentile church in Antioch, the site of his former service, but to the Jewish church in Jerusalem (v 13). Luke's history records that "the disagreement [between Paul and Barnabas over Mark] became so sharp that they parted company" (Acts 15:39, NRSV). Nothing stirred Paul's feelings more than the question of justification by faith, and Barnabas had demonstrated his weakness on this point (Gal 2:13). Therefore, it may have been the cause of their separation: Barnabas and Mark to Cyprus, and Paul and Silas into Asia Minor to strengthen the new churches (Acts 15:39-41).

About 11 years pass before Mark again appears in the biblical record. In Colossians 4:10 and Philemon 1:24, he is in Rome with "Paul the aged," who is there as "a prisoner of Jesus Christ" (Phlm 1:19). The fracture had been healed, such that Paul says that Mark and others are "the only ones of the circumcision [the Jews] among my co-workers for the kingdom of God" (Col 4:11, NRSV). Paul, in his last epistle, pays Mark his final tribute. He tells Timothy, "Do your best to come to me soon. . . . Only Luke is with me. Get Mark and bring him with you, for he is useful in my ministry" (2 Tm 4:9, 11, NRSV). Although all had deserted Paul in his trial before Caesar Nero (v 16), Mark, who in his youth had also deserted the apostle, traveled from Ephesus to Rome, endeavoring to come to the beloved Paul with Timothy.

According to 1 Peter 5:13, the apostle Peter sent Mark's greeting along with that of the church in Babylon (signifying Rome), indicating Mark's close relationship with the apostle to the circumcision (Gal 2:9). The most important and reliable extrascriptural tradition concerning Mark is that he was the close attendant of Peter. The early church fathers said this association produced the Gospel of Mark, inasmuch as Mark took account of Peter's teachings about Jesus and then used them to shape his Gospel, perhaps written in Rome between AD 60 and 68.

MARKET, MARKETPLACE Place for the buying and selling of goods in antiquity. Generally, the marketplaces of the ancient Near East would be much like the open air bazaars one can still see in any city throughout Israel, Greece, and Turkey.

The marketplace of NT times known as the *agora* was a place for buying and selling goods (Mk 7:4); a place for children to play (Mt 11:16; Lk 7:32); a place for idlers and for men seeking work (Mt 20:3); a place where public events, including healings, occurred (Mk 6:56); the center of public life and debate (Acts 17:17); and a place where trials were held (16:19).

MARK OF GOD*, MARK OF THE BEAST Ensignia placed on people either by God or by the Antichrist. Though the phrase is limited to the book of Revelation, a mark was used in Ezekiel 9:4-6. In his vision Ezekiel saw the inhabitants of Jerusalem slain for their wickedness, except those upon whose foreheads God had put a mark. The mark was one of identification for the purpose of protection.

The usage in the book of Revelation is quite similar. The idea begins in Revelation 7:3 (though the word does not occur here), where the 144,000 servants of God are sealed on their foreheads to protect them from the coming wrath of God. This sealing is referred to again in Revelation 9:4, where it is noted that the demonic locusts of the fifth trumpet are not to harm those with the seal of God.

In Revelation 13 the specific phrase "the mark of the beast" is used. The context is John's vision of the two beasts. The one from the sea (13:1-10) symbolizes the Antichrist with political power over the inhabitants of the earth. The beast from the earth (vv 11-18) symbolizes the Antichrist's assistant, which is the religious leadership dedicated to securing universal worship of the Antichrist. This false religious leader causes all to receive upon their right hand or their forehead the mark (of the Antichrist), or the name (cf. v 12), or the number of the name of the antichrist (vv 16-17). This mark of the beast is necessary for a person to engage in business or economic transactions involved in physical survival. Perhaps it also serves to identify such people for martyrdom (vv 7-10). It stands in sharp contrast to the seal of God marking out the servants of God in chapter 7:1-8 (cf. 14:1). Thus mankind as depicted in this vision is divided into two classes—those belonging to Christ and those belonging to the Antichrist.

Revelation 13:18 contains a challenge to the church to have wisdom and to recognize what that mark or number of the beast is. Two things are stated. First, it is of a man or refers to a man. Second, his number is 666 (or 616, according to some manuscripts).

The interpretation of this number has been discussed at length by biblical scholars without reaching a general consensus. Many think that it was a first-century cryptic (Hebrew) reference to Nero. In that context of preliminary fulfillment, it would have simply been an appeal for Christians to recognize the true nature of the godless Nero as having the character of Antichrist and to refuse to give him their allegiance. Perhaps this identity indicates that the number or mark of the beast is an expression of one's allegiance to the Antichrist as expressed in the cult of emperor worship. Thus it would be this activity of worship and not a literal number on one's body that is intended.

When the prophecy is completely fulfilled by the Antichrist, believers must be wise and refuse to give their loyalty to him through whatever form or test of allegiance this takes.

The importance of believers' steadfastness is shown in Revelation 14, where the faithful 144,000, with the name of Christ and God on their foreheads, are seen standing victoriously with the Lamb on Mt Zion. This steadfastness is spoken of as keeping the commandments of God and the faith of Jesus (14:12). A similar vision of those who overcome the beast is given in 15:2-4. Here they are pictured as standing before God singing the song of Moses and the song of the Lamb.

There are four further references in Revelation to the mark of the beast. The angel warns that those who receive the mark of the beast and worship him will drink the cup of God's wrath (14:9-11). When the first angel pours out the first bowl of wrath, this falls on those who have the mark of the beast and who worshiped his image (16:2). At the destruction of the beast and the false prophet, the latter is described as deceiving those who received the mark of the beast and worshiped his image (19:20). Finally, those who reign with Christ during the millennium are those who did not worship the beast or receive his mark (20:4).

In summary, the phrase "mark of the beast," or the number 666, is a way of referring to the identity of the followers of the Antichrist in the book of Revelation. Believers are warned not to become a part of those who are deceived but rather to remain steadfast and faithful to the Lamb and to own his name upon their foreheads.

See also Antichrist; Beast #4.

MAROTH City in Palestine, mentioned only by Micah (Mi 1:12). It may be the same as the Maarath in Joshua 15:59; if so, it would be an ancient Canaanite city, part of the inheritance of Judah's tribe.

MARRIAGE*, Levirate *See* Marriage, Marriage Customs.

MARRIAGE, MARRIAGE CUSTOMS The joining together of male and female in matrimony, as practiced by various cultures.

The idea of marriage was ordained by God in his instruction to Adam that a man should leave his father and mother, and that he and his wife should be as one flesh (Gn 2:24).

Several forms of marriage are referred to in the OT, the earliest of which seems to be based on a matrilineal principle. Although there appears to be some evidence for this in the middle Bronze Age and in the early monarchy, it is difficult to be certain about the matter, despite the importance in Egypt, and perhaps elsewhere, of the role of the mother in determining descent.

Generally, the bride left her parents when she married and went to live with her husband's clan, as Rebekah did (Gn 24:58-59). The phrase "to marry a wife" is from a root meaning to "become master" (Dt 21:13), and the wife frequently treated her husband as, and referred to him as, master.

Hebrew genealogical lists indicate that descent was reckoned through the male line (Gn 5:10; 36:9-43; Nm 1:1-15; Ru 4:18-22; 1 Chr 1:1-9). The important right of naming a child, indicating power and authority over that child, was exercised almost equally between father and mother in biblical references (cf. Gn 4:1, 25-26; 5:29; 35:18; 1 Sm 1:20; 4:21; Is 8:3; Hos 1:4-9). Sons were frequently named after their fathers and were identified with them.

The father was the authority figure in the home in a patriarchal society. His wife and children were regarded as his possessions in somewhat the same way as his fields and livestock (Ex 20:17; Dt 5:21). He had the right to sell his daughters (Ex 21:7; Neh 5:5), and even had the power of life and death over his children.

The ease with which a man could terminate a marriage by divorcing his wife also shows the measure of his authority in the family (Dt 24:1-4; cf. 22:13-21).

A levirate marriage was instituted to preserve a family name and inheritance. When a man died, the responsibility for maintaining his widow and any children that she might have fell upon her husband's closest male relative. The order of responsibility is set out in Deuteronomy 25:5-10. Normally, the brother of the deceased husband living with the clan was expected to enter into a levirate marriage with the widow. If she was childless, the firstborn of the new marriage was regarded as a child of the deceased. Levirate marriage was also known to the Canaanites, Assyrians, and Hittites.

The most familiar levirate situation in the OT, although not conforming strictly to the law of Deuteronomy 25, is described in the book of Ruth. It was essential for Ruth to find some close male relative to marry her so that the family name and property could be preserved. The closest male relative declined the responsibility, feeling that it was a double imposition, first, to have to purchase the land and support Ruth, and second, to know that the first son would be regarded as her dead husband's child, bearing his name and inheriting the land. Boaz agreed to undertake the responsibility (Ru 2:20–4:10).

Despite numerous examples of polygamy cited in the OT, there is no doubt that the vast majority of the Israelites were monogamous. There are no examples given of large polygamous marriages in the families of commoners.

The original instruction to Adam was that a "man . . . cleaves to his wife" (Gn 2:24). Hebrew laws generally imply that a marriage with one wife is the most acceptable form of marriage (Ex 20:17; 21:5; Lv 18:8, 16-20; 20:10; Nm 5:12; Dt 5:21). Although this seems to have become the norm by the time of the monarchy, a king such as Solomon did not follow Hebrew traditions in this matter. In the postexilic period marriages were predominantly monogamous, although they were being terminated increasingly by divorce. In the NT period monogamy seems to have been the rule, although persons such as Herod the Great were polygamous. Christ taught that marriage should last the lifetime of the partners, and if a man divorced his wife and married another woman during his previous spouse's lifetime, he committed adultery (Mt 5:31-32).

Marriage generally took place with those who were close to the immediate family circle, and it was imperative, therefore, that limits on acceptable consanguinity should be imposed. In patriarchal times a man could marry his half sister on his father's side (Gn 20:12), and this continued to be the case even under David (2 Sm 13:13), although it was specifically forbidden in Leviticus 20:17. As there is some contradiction between the marriage laws of Deuteronomy and those in the Law of Holiness (Dt 25:5; Lv 18:16), it is possible that there was some modification of the stricter Levitical regulations. Marriages between cousins, such as Isaac with Rebekah, and Jacob with Rachel and Leah, were common. When a close relative was interested in marriage, it was almost impossible to refuse (Tb 6:13; 7:11-12). Moses was the offspring of a marriage between nephew and aunt (Ex 6:20; Nm 26:59), which would have been forbidden in Leviticus 18:12-13 and 20:19, as would Jacob's marriage with two sisters at the same time (Gn 29:30).

When the Israelites settled in Canaan, many of them married Canaanite women, much to the consternation of those who desired to maintain the purity of the Hebrew religion (1 Kgs 11:4). Such intermarriage was prohibited under Mosaic law (Ex 34:15-16; Dt 7:3-4), although many Israelites ignored these regulations and continued to indulge in mixed marriages. If a woman was captured in war and was prepared to abandon her native country, an exception could be made (Dt 21:10-14). By contrast, Samson married a Philistine woman who remained with her own people, but who received conjugal visits from her husband periodically (Jgs 14:8–15:2).

The danger of intermarriage affecting the purity of Hebrew religion was considered so great that in the postexilic period wholesale divorce was ordered where Jews had married foreign wives (Ezr 9:2; 10:3, 16-17). The intent was that the national religion should remain pure, even though homes and families were destroyed. Even in NT times, Paul denounced marriage with non-Christians (2 Cor 6:14-15).

It is difficult to estimate at what age young people married. A boy was considered to be a man by his early teens, and late in Jewish tradition this transition was celebrated by the bar mitzvah, which generally occurred when the boy was 13.

Normally the young man's parents chose the bride. The resulting discussion about the marriage occurred between the groom's parents and the bride's parents, and often neither of the young people was consulted. It was not essential for the eldest in the family to be married first (Gn 29:26). When Abraham decided that Isaac should be married, a servant was sent to choose a bride from among Abraham's relatives in Mesopotamia. The servant made contact with the bride's brother and mother (24:33-53), and it was only afterward that Rebekah was asked to give her consent (vv 57-58). Her father was possibly incapacitated; otherwise, it would have been unlikely that her consent would have been asked at all.

One of the reasons why the average young man would not have been able to afford more than one wife was the practice of the bride-price, which had to be paid to the bride's father. It was possible to substitute service for the bride-price (Gn 29:15-30), or the completion of an appointed task (1 Sm 18:25-27). A specific sum is mentioned for the bride-price in the case of a virgin who had been raped and who had to be purchased by her seducer. The price was set at 50 shekels, but this was considered to be a punishment; it is probable that the normal amount was between 10 and 320 shekels (Lv 27:4-5).

At the time of the second temple, a virgin bride was

considered to be worth 50 shekels, and a widow or divorced woman about half that sum. During this period, a virgin bride was normally married in midweek so that, if her husband found her not to be a virgin, he could bring proof to the court the following day, which would still be in advance of the Sabbath. A widow or a divorced woman normally married on the equivalent of a Thursday, giving her a full day with her husband before the Sabbath.

Marriage was a covenant or alliance between two families. It thus united them, and by extending the kinship, the overall size of the group was increased. This was important in a society where responsibilities for relatives, however distant, were accepted unhesitatingly. The covenant concept also could have political overtones, as with the marriage between Solomon and the Egyptian princess (1 Kgs 11:1) or Ahab of Israel and Jezebel of Tyre (16:31).

The sealing of the covenant included the transfer of gifts, which would establish the wealth and status of the donor and of the bride (Gn 34:12). In the ancient Near East, the giving of a gift was thought to include a part of the donor, so that the giver was actually offering a portion of himself. The gift that sealed the covenant also established the donor's authority over the bride.

The next stage in the marriage procedure was the betrothal. First mentioned in Exodus 22:16, the term is used several times in Deuteronomy (Dt 20:7; 22:23-24). The betrothal had the legal status of a marriage (Dt 28:30; 2 Sm 3:14), and anyone violating a betrothed virgin would be stoned, according to the law of Deuteronomy, for violating his neighbor's "wife" (Dt 22:23-24). The meaning of a betrothal involved taking possession, in a manner similar to that of receiving tribute. Nevertheless, there remained a distinction between betrothing a woman and taking her as a wife (20:7). During the period of betrothal, the prospective groom was exempt from military service. It was assumed that the betrothal was a formal part of a permanent relationship (Mt 1:18; Lk 1:27; 2:5).

A man who was to marry another's daughter was already regarded as a son-in-law at the time of betrothal (Gn 19:14). Mary, as Joseph's betrothed, was actually considered his wife, although he did not have intercourse with her until after the birth of Jesus.

The first biblical record of a wedding being celebrated by a feast is in the story of Jacob (Gn 29:22). There was no actual marriage contract recorded until its mention in the book of Tobit (Tb 7:12). This contract was not considered valid until the couple had cohabited for a week (Gn 29:27; Jgs 14:12, 18). When Samson left his bride before the end of the seven-day period, the bride's parents considered the marriage void and gave her to another man (Jgs 14:20).

The wedding was an occasion of great family rejoicing. The special clothing of the bride and groom (Is 61:10; Ez 16:9-13) included for the bride a fine dress often adorned with jewels (Ps 45:14-15; Is 61:10) and other ornaments, while the bridegroom had fine clothing and wore a diadem (Sg 3:11; Is 61:10). The bride wore a veil (Gn 24:65; Sg 4:3), which was removed in the bridal chamber. This would account for Rebekah's need to veil herself in the presence of Isaac, her fiancé (Gn 24:65), and also for the ease with which Laban was able to replace Rachel with Leah on Jacob's wedding night (29:23-25).

Symbolic ceremonies may sometimes have been included as part of the betrothal or wedding ceremonies, such as Ruth's request that Boaz spread his skirt over her to indicate that he was taking her to wife (Ru 3:9). Another ritual may have been the ceremonial removal of the bride's girdle by the groom in the nuptial chamber, which was a room or tent specially prepared for the newly married couple. The marriage was normally consummated on the first night (Gn 29:23; Tb 8:1), and the stained linen would be retained as evidence of the bride's virginity.

In a contrast to the elaborate procession and feasting of the marriage, divorce was simple. A man could divorce his wife if he found fault with her in any particular matter, and this right was not abolished until the 11th century AD. Divorce was discouraged, however, and gradually the procedure became more complex, being hedged about with a number of deterrents.

As the laws regarding divorce became more complex, so the procedure became increasingly expensive. At a later time a lawyer, or sometimes a rabbi, would give advice, especially on such matters as the return of property rightly belonging to the bride or her family.

If a bride was found to have committed adultery, the husband was thought to be entitled to a divorce. This was also the case if he even suspected her of infidelity. He could also divorce his wife if he felt that she had violated normal morality, had become apostate, or had been less than efficient in the management of her household. If a woman refused her husband his conjugal rights for a period of at least one year, she could be divorced. Other grounds for divorcing a wife included insulting behavior to a husband or his relatives, contracting an incurable disease, or refusing to accompany her husband when he moved the domicile to a new area.

In general, the status of the wife was low. Despite the fact that she gave advice, managed the household, educated the young children, and worked alongside her husband when necessary, he was still her master, and her role was to obey. She was little more than a servant, although better than a slave, for she could not be sold even though she could be divorced.

In the frequent figurative uses of marriage in the OT, the Hebrew people and God are referred to in terms of bride and bridegroom (Is 62:4-5; Jer 2:2). The desolation that is about to overtake Judah is contrasted by Jeremiah with the celebration of a wedding feast (Jer 7:34; 16:9; 25:10). Figurative forms are used again in Hosea, where God rejects the relationship with his wife, Israel (Hos 2:2), but is prepared to accept her again if she resumes her faithful practices (vv 19-20).

In the NT, John the Baptist compares his sense of joy with that of a friend of the groom at a wedding (Jn 3:29), while Jesus himself made reference to the wedding preparations in the parable of the wise and foolish virgins (Mt 25:1-12). In the story of the marriage feast (22:1-14) Christ mentions quite incidentally the fact that wedding robes were provided for the guests at such ceremonies. The theme of the Christian church as the bride of Christ occurs in such books as 2 Corinthians, Ephesians, and Revelation.

Jesus' Teachings on Marriage and Adultery In the realm of civil law there are changes of emphasis in Jesus' teaching over against the OT. For example, the OT did not regard infidelity by a husband as adultery against his wife. When challenged by the Jews, Jesus said that originally God had made one wife for a man; therefore, there should be no divorce (Mk 10:2-9). Further, he stated if a man does divorce his wife and marry again, he "commits adultery against her" (v 11). Thus, Jesus made man and woman equal as regards adultery. An unfaithful husband is just as adulterous as an unfaithful wife. This revolutionary teaching struck the disciples as severe (see

Mt 19:10), but it illustrates what Jesus meant when he said their righteousness must be greater than that of the Jewish leaders (5:20).

There is a slight difference in Matthew's account of Jesus' teaching, which has led some scholars to argue that Jesus was not quite as strict as the above summary suggests. According to Matthew 19:9, a wife's "unchastity" (probably some sexual misconduct) allows an aggrieved husband to divorce her and marry again. If this remark concluded the passage, this interpretation would be the simplest. However, from the context it is more likely that Jesus allowed innocent spouses to separate from their wives but not to remarry. This explains why the disciples were so shocked and why Jesus went on to speak about some who refuse to marry for the sake of the kingdom of heaven (Mt 19:12). This was also the way the church interpreted the passage for the first five centuries. They allowed Christians to separate but not to remarry (cf. 1 Cor 7:11).

See also Adultery; Civil Law and Justice; Concubinage, Concubines; Divorce; Family Life and Relations; Sex, Sexuality; Virgin.

MARSENA One of the seven princes of Persia and Media who served Ahasuerus, ranking next to him in authority in the kingdom (Est 1:14).

MARSH HEN* Alternate name for water hen in Leviticus 11:18 and Deuteronomy 14:16. *See* Birds (Water Hen).

MARS' HILL* Alternate KJV translation for Areopagus, the name of a small hill northwest of the Acropolis in Athens and the site of Paul's address to the Athenians (Acts 17:16-34). *See* Areopagus.

MARTHA Sister of Mary and Lazarus, and friend of Jesus. Martha's family lived in Bethany, a small town on the eastern slope of the Mt of Olives.

Luke gives an account of an incident concerning Martha when she was busy preparing and serving food while her sister, Mary, was listening to Jesus. Martha complained to Jesus that Mary was not helping her; Jesus corrected Martha gently: "My dear Martha, you are so upset over all these details! There is really only one thing worth being concerned about. Mary has discovered it—and I won't take it away from her" (Lk 10:41-42, NLT). In saying this, Jesus challenged Martha's anxiousness by pointing out that fellowship with him was life's highest and most rewarding priority.

In John's account of the death and resurrection of Lazarus, it is Martha who, upon Jesus' arrival, goes out to meet him while Mary remains in the house (Jn 11:20). Once again, Martha complains to Jesus, this time saying that if he had come earlier Lazarus would not have died (v 21). When Jesus replied that her brother would rise again, Martha naturally assumed that Jesus was speaking of the future resurrection. Jesus reassured Martha that he was the resurrection and the life and that she must trust in him (vv 23-26). Martha then confessed her belief that Jesus was the Christ (v 27). When Jesus asked that the tomb be opened, Martha protested that the smell would be unpleasant. Jesus replied firmly to her doubts, "Did I not tell you that if you would believe you would see the glory of God?" (v 40, RSV). Jesus then proceeded to raise Lazarus from the dead.

In John 12:1-11 Martha is again serving a meal for Jesus and Lazarus; this time she does not protest Mary's elaborate show of affection for Jesus.

MARY Popular feminine name among first-century Jews, borne by six (or seven) women in the NT.

1. Mary, the mother of Jesus. According to the infancy narratives of Matthew and Luke, Mary was a young Jewish virgin, probably from the tribe of Judah, who during her engagement to Joseph (of Davidic descent from the tribe of Judah) was discovered to be pregnant. This was due to her submission to the Holy Spirit (Mt 1:18-25; Lk 1:26-38). The couple married and lived first in Nazareth of Galilee, then traveled to Bethlehem (Joseph's hometown) for a census, where Jesus was born (Mt 2:1; Lk 1:5; 2:4-5). Matthew informs us that shortly after the birth the family had to flee to Egypt to escape Herod (Mt 2:13-14). Later, the family resided again in Nazareth (Mt 2:23; Lk 2:39).

   We have little other information about Mary. She was certainly a concerned mother (as her scolding of Jesus in Lk 2:48 shows), and she later had a high estimate of Jesus' ability (as at the wedding in Cana, Jn 2:1-4). She had several other sons and daughters to care for. She appeared at the foot of the cross, where Jesus asked "the beloved disciple" to care for her in her grief (Jn 19:25-27). After the resurrection she and Jesus' brothers were among the disciples who experienced the outpouring of the Spirit on Pentecost (Acts 1:14). No further mention is made of her.

   Mary's song of praise, "The Magnificat" (Lk 1:46-55) displays her sterling humility and trust in God's will. She is truly "blessed among women" (v 42).

2. Mary, the mother of James and Joseph. This woman goes by several names, but in each account she appears among Jesus' faithful female disciples, standing by the cross and witnessing the empty tomb. Matthew calls her "Mary the mother of James and Joseph" or just "the other Mary" (27:56, 61; 28:1); Mark names her "Mary the mother of James the younger and of Joses," "Mary the mother of Joses," or "Mary the mother of James" (15:40, 47; 16:1); in John's Gospel, she is "Mary wife of Clopas" (19:25), though she may possibly be a separate Mary. Tradition has it that this Mary was Jesus' aunt, as Clopas was Joseph's brother (Eusebius's *Ecclesiastical History* 3.11).

3. Mary Magdalene. We know little about this woman other than that her name indicates that she was from Magdala in Galilee. Somewhere in Galilee she met Jesus, who cast seven demons out of her. She then joined the band of disciples and followed Jesus wherever he went (Lk 8:2), ending up in Jerusalem at the foot of the cross when all the male disciples had fled (Mk 15:40; Jn 19:25). She observed Jesus' burial (Mk 15:47) and witnessed the events surrounding the resurrection. Matthew 28:1, Mark 16:1, and Luke 24:10 group her with the other women who went to the tomb. John says that she was the first among these women to discover the empty tomb, the first to report to the disciples, and the first to see the risen Christ as she lingered by the tomb after all the others had left (Jn 20:1-2, 11-18). This faithful disciple, however, was not allowed to touch her Lord (v 17).

4. Mary of Bethany. This Judean Mary was the sister of Martha and Lazarus. We know three facts about her. First, she was such a devoted follower of Jesus that she neglected her household duties to listen to him (Lk 10:38-42; Jesus approved this). Second, she was apparently upset with Jesus when he did not come to heal her brother before he died (Jn 11:20, 28-33). Finally, before Jesus died, she anointed him with an expensive ointment while he feasted at her home in Bethany (Mt 26:6-13; Mk 14:3-9; Jn 12:1-8).

5. Mary, mother of John Mark. This woman appears only once in Scripture (Acts 12:12). Her house was the meeting place of the persecuted church. Since it was apparently large and she had servants, she was a wealthy woman, probably a widow (since no husband is mentioned). In her house the church prayed for Peter, and Peter came there after being released from prison. Her son John Mark accompanied Paul and probably Peter as well.

6. Mary of Rome. In Romans 16:6 Paul greets a woman in Rome named simply "Mary, who has worked hard among you." At some time she had been in Greece or Asia Minor, perhaps being expelled from Rome with Aquila and Priscilla (Acts 18:2; c. AD 49). While there she had met Paul, perhaps being converted by him, and had worked hard with him in his work of evangelism or caring for the church. By AD 56 (a probable date for the book of Romans), she had returned to Rome. She was distinguished by the praise Paul heaped upon her and his other coworkers living in Rome.

MARY MAGDALENE *See Mary #3.*

MASADA* Rock fortress on the western shore of the Dead Sea, opposite the Lisan, about 10 miles (16.1 kilometers) south of En-gedi where the Jewish Zealots made their last stand against the Romans in AD 73. Today it is called in Arabic Qasr es-Sebbe, and in Hebrew, Metsada.

The rock rises some 1,400 feet (426.7 meters) above the Dead Sea, about 2,000 feet (609.6 meters) from north to south, and about 980 feet (298.7 meters) from east to west, with sheer cliffs on all sides. The top, which slopes gently toward the south and west, is almost flat, about 20 acres (8.1 hectares) in area, or the equivalent of about two large city blocks. It is situated about two miles (3.2 kilometers) west of the shore of the Dead Sea.

Aerial View of Masada

According to Josephus (*Wars* 7.8-9), this almost impenetrable rock was first fortified by Jonathan the high priest, who gave it the name Masada ("mountain stronghold"). The "Jonathan" mentioned by Josephus, long the subject of scholarly debate, is probably to be identified as Alexander Janneus (103–40 BC) on the basis of scores of coins found at Masada. It was Herod the Great who expended a great amount of effort to build

and fortify the place, partly out of fear that the Jews might overthrow him and restore the former kings, and partly because he was afraid that Cleopatra would convince Antony to cut him off and give the kingdom of Judea to her.

Present knowledge of Herodian Masada comes not only from Josephus but also from the excavations of Yigael Yadin in 1963–65. The archaeological discoveries confirm many of the statements found in Josephus.

Herod installed his family at the stronghold during the period when he was in Rome to claim his kingdom (40–39 BC). Subsequently, he built palaces, a Roman bath, storerooms, an elaborate water supply system, and a wall. The wall entirely surrounded the top of the rock, a length of 4,250 feet (1,295.4 meters), with 30 towers and 8 gates, and was of casemate construction—that is, it consisted of an outer and an inner wall, between which were about 110 rooms. The space between the walls was 13½ feet (4.1 meters). The water supply consisted of drains from the wadis in the west, designed to collect water in the rainy season, and 12 cisterns in two rows on the northwest side of the fortress, having a capacity of 10.5 million gallons (39.7 million liters). A three-tiered palace villa was built in a spectacular location on the northern end of the rock. Other palaces, administrative buildings, and storerooms were located on the top of the rock, at the northern end, at the western side, and in the central region toward the southern end. It is possible that Josephus is correct in reporting that crops were raised, since there was a layer of soil toward the southern end of the rock. The royal buildings contained fine mosaic floors and frescoed walls, and the bath was a typical Roman bath with a caldarium (hot or steam room), tepidarium (warm room), and frigidarium (cold room). The entire bath complex was 33 feet by 36 feet (10.1 by 11.0 meters) with walls six feet (1.8 meters) thick.

When the first Jewish revolt began in AD 66, a number of Zealots led by Menahem took over Masada, which had been occupied by a small Roman garrison. The Zealots made a number of alterations, building a synagogue and two ritual baths and converting the palaces and administrative buildings into living quarters. Coins struck in the first, second, third, fourth, and fifth years of the Jewish revolt (i.e., AD 66–70) have been found, putting the date of occupation beyond question. Included in the discoveries were fragments of scrolls, including portions of Leviticus, Deuteronomy, Psalms, the Wisdom of Jesus ben Sirach (Ecclesiasticus), the book of Jubilees, and a portion containing the words "the song of the sixth sabbath sacrifice on the ninth of the second month." These words, and the calendar system used, connected the scroll with one found in cave 4 at Qumran. This led Yadin to conclude that some of the Qumran Essenes joined the Zealots in the revolt against Rome, bringing scrolls from Qumran with them to Masada.

After the destruction of Jerusalem (AD 70), the Romans removed all pockets of Jewish resistance until only the fortress of Masada remained. When Flavius Silva became the Roman procurator, he determined to bring to an end the last of the revolt. The Zealots at Masada, 960 in number, according to Josephus, were led by Eleazar. Silva surrounded the stronghold with eight camps and a wall six feet (1.8 meters) thick and 11,400 feet (3,474.7 meters) long, with 12 towers at intervals of 240 to 300 feet (73.2 to 91.4 meters). The camps could hold about 9,000 troops, but it is estimated that Silva had about 15,000 men, including a large number of Jewish prisoners, to mount the siege. It seems obvious that his intent was to prevent a single Zealot from escaping to stir up a new revolt.

There were two routes to Masada, the "snake path" up the eastern side and a path on the western side. The snake path is tortuous and narrow, requiring about 50 minutes of dangerous climbing. The Zealots had amassed a supply of large boulders near the top, apparently expecting an attack at this point. Silva selected the western approach, ordering his soldiers to build an earthen ramp, about 180 feet (54.9 meters) in height, about 645 feet (196.6 meters) in length, and about the same width at the base as the length. It did not quite reach to the top of the fortress, ending about 60 feet (18.3 meters) below the casemate wall.

By means of a battering ram and missile catapult, Silva breached the wall, but the Zealots repaired it overnight with timbers and earth. Silva then burned the timbered repair. When Eleazar ben-Ya'ir saw that the Romans were about to capture Masada, he delivered a stirring speech, given at length (and probably with considerable imagination) in Josephus. Some excerpts may be quoted: "It is still in our power to die bravely, and in a state of freedom. . . . Let our wives die before they are abused, and our children before they have tasted of slavery; and after we have slain them, let us bestow that glorious benefit upon one another mutually, and preserve ourselves in freedom, as an excellent funeral monument for us. But first let us destroy our money and the fortress by fire . . . and let us spare nothing but our provisions, for they will be a testimonial when we are dead that we were not subdued for want of necessaries; but that, according to our original resolution, we have preferred death before slavery."

There was reluctance to perform this mass suicide, and Eleazar had to follow the speech with a second, both shaming them and encouraging them. While he was still speaking, they cut him off and began the bloody work: "The husbands tenderly embraced their wives and took their children into their arms, and gave the longest parting kisses to them, with tears in their eyes." Then the men killed their wives and children, and laid all their possessions in a heap and set fire to them. After that, they chose ten men by lot to slay the rest, "every one of whom laid himself down by his wife and children on the ground, and threw his arms about them, and they offered their necks" to those chosen to slay them. Finally, the ten remaining cast lots "that he whose lot it was should first kill the other nine, and after all, should kill himself." Yadin tells of finding 11 ostraca (pottery sherds) each with a single name inscribed on it, which he suggests may have been the means used to select the one to put the others to death. One of the sherds bore the name "ben-Ya'ir," quite likely that of Eleazar ben-Ya'ir.

The plan was carried out almost to the last detail. Two women, however, hid themselves and five children in one of the caverns. The Romans entered the fortress the next day, expecting to meet some kind of resistance, but all they found was silence and the ashes of a great fire, plus vast stores of food in the storehouses. The women who had hidden in the caverns told the story to the Romans.

See also First Jewish Revolt; Herod, Herodian Family; Judaism; Zealot.

MASCHIL* KJV rendering of maskil, a musical cue in the titles of numerous psalms. *See* Maskil.

MASH Aram's fourth son (Gn 10:23), a descendant of Shem. He is called Meshech in 1 Chronicles 1:17. *See* Meshech #2.

MASHAL Alternate spelling of Mishal, a Levitical town in Asher, in 1 Chronicles 6:74. *See* Mishal.

MASKIL* Hebrew term in the superscriptions of 13 psalms; perhaps a musical cue denoting the manner in which the designated psalms were to be performed. *See* Music.

MASON, MASONRY Worker in and craft of brick and stonework. The mason prepared stone from the quarry for use in building. In Israel's early days masons were brought from Phoenicia (2 Sm 5:11; 1 Kgs 5:17-18; 1 Chr 14:1), but later Israelite masons did their own work (2 Kgs 12:12; 22:6; 2 Chr 24:12; Ezr 3:7).

MASORA*, MASORETES* Oral tradition concerning the pronunciation and accuracy of the Hebrew text of the OT, and the scholars who were responsible for putting those traditions into writing.

At the background of the work of the Masoretes lay the efforts of the Sopherim, or scribes, who, from about 400 BC to AD 200, tried to establish and maintain the true text of the OT. In connection with this effort they made a practice of counting the verses, words, and letters of each Bible book and appending this information in order to give future copyists some standard against which to check the accuracy of their copies. The traditional Hebrew text, called the Masoretic Text, achieved its standard form early in the second century AD. It was based on and substantially agreed with a much earlier textual tradition, as the Dead Sea Scrolls demonstrate. But the text of the scribes or custodians of the Bible was still only consonantal; it had no vowels or accent marks.

The work of the Masoretes picked up where that of the Sopherim left off. They are called Masoretes because they preserved in writing the oral traditions (Masora) concerning the biblical text. These Jewish scholars lived primarily in Tiberias on the western shore of the Sea of Galilee during the period AD 500 to 950. Most prominent among them were the learned Moses ben Asher and his son Aaron; the present text of the Hebrew Bible is based on a ben Asher text.

The Masoretes sought not only to determine the exact text handed down to them but to pass it on to future generations without change. To protect against copyists' errors and alterations, they filled the side margins with all sorts of data concerning how often and where various words and phrases appearing in a given line of the text could be found elsewhere.

The special contribution of the Masoretes was to provide the text with vowels and accent marks. They achieved this with a system of dots and strokes. Their task was not to invent pronunciations but to pass on received or accepted pronunciations and to decide between debatable ones. Of course, the issue was not merely correct pronunciation, because a slight change in vowel pointing or pronunciation would, for instance, turn a noun into a participle.

As the Masoretes sought to vocalize, determine, and protect the true text, they had to engage in a certain amount of textual criticism. But their reverence for the text would not permit making changes in it, so they worked out an ingenious system of editorial notes. Where it appeared to them that a copyist's error had occurred, they left the error written in the text (a *kethib* working—that which is written) but put vowel markings with it for a preferred wording (*qere*—that which is to be read) and inserted the consonants for that reading in the margin. They also indicated a limited number of words that probably should be omitted altogether.

One of the most interesting of the *qere* readings involved the pronunciation of God's name. As early as the fifth century BC, Jews began to grow uneasy about pronouncing God's covenant name, properly vocalized as Yahweh. So they substituted the vowel markings for Adonai (Lord), indicating that Adonai was to be uttered instead of Yahweh. This substitute vowel marking of the Masoretes has led to the modern pronunciation of Jehovah (using the vowels of Adonai).

The meticulous efforts of the Masoretes and the Sopherim before them resulted in a marvelously successful preservation of the OT text. What the Masoretes passed on to later centuries was meticulously copied by hand until the advent of the printing press. So it may be confidently asserted that, of ancient Near Eastern literature, the OT is unique in the degree of accuracy of preservation.

See also Bible, Manuscripts and Text of the (Old Testament).

MASORETIC TEXT *See* Masora, Masoretes.

MASREKAH Home of an Edomite king named Samlah (Gn 36:36; 1 Chr 1:47).

MASSA Ishmael's seventh son and Abraham's grandson (Gn 25:14; 1 Chr 1:30). His descendants inhabited northwestern Arabia. Tiglath-pileser III mentions these people, along with the inhabitants of Tema (cf. Gn 25:15) and others who were ruled by him and paid tribute to him. The people of Tema probably were descendants of Massa's brother Tema.

Massa forms part of the titles of Proverbs 30:1 and 31:1. The definite article precedes it in 30:1 and can be translated "the burden" or "the oracle." It is frequently used in prophetic passages in the ominous sense of God's impending judgment (Is 13:1; Na 1:1; Hb 1:1).

MASSAH AND MERIBAH Two Hebrew words meaning, respectively, "to put to the test" and "to find fault, quarrel." According to Exodus 17:7, after Moses got water from the rock at Rephidim, he called the place by these two names to memorialize the Israelites' "testing" of God's faithful provision.

Massah is mentioned four times as the site of the rebellious rejection of God by the Israelites (Dt 6:16; 9:22; 33:8; Ps 95:8). In contrast, Numbers 20:13, 24; 27:14; and Deuteronomy 32:51 place Meribah near Kadesh in the wilderness of Zin where Moses struck the rock twice to produce water. Psalm 81:7 and Deuteronomy 33:8 suggest that God was testing the Israelites in these instances.

See also Meribah.

MASTER Word used to translate five different Hebrew words and seven different Greek terms with root meanings of owner (Is 1:3), elder (Dn 1:3), sovereign (1 Pt 2:18), teacher (Lk 6:40), superintendent (Lk 5:5), lord (Gn 39:3), sir (Jgs 19:11), rabbi (Mk 9:5), and captain (Acts 27:11); often used to describe Jesus.

One of the Greek words, *kurios*, has multiple meanings with important implications for interpretation. It variously means sir or mister (Lk 14:21), master (Mt 6:24), lord (Acts 25:26), and the Lord God (Eph 6:9). Usually the context clearly indicates the specific meaning intended.

MASTIC* Small Mediterranean tree that exudes a gum used to make numerous products. *See* Plants (Balm).

MATHUSALA* KJV rendering of Methuselah, Enoch's son, in Luke 3:37. *See* Methuselah.

MATRED Mother of Mehetabel, the wife of King Hadad (Hadar) of Edom (Gn 36:39; 1 Chr 1:50).

MATRI*, MATRITES Family of Benjamin's tribe. Saul, the first king of Israel, came from this family (1 Sm 10:21).

MATTAN
1. Priest of Baal killed at the time when Jehoiada the priest had Queen Athaliah killed and Joash placed on the throne of Judah (2 Kgs 11:18; 2 Chr 23:17).
2. Father of Shephatiah, a prince under King Zedekiah and among those who persecuted Jeremiah (Jer 38:1-6).

MATTANAH Place of encampment for Israel following the exodus as the company moved east of the Dead Sea from the Arnon River northward into the territory of Sihon, king of the Amorites (Nm 21:18-19). Its exact location is unknown, but Khirbet el-Medeiyineh on the left bank of Wadi eth-Themed is considered its most likely setting.

MATTANIAH
1. Last king of Judah, whom King Nebuchadnezzar of Babylon enthroned in place of his nephew Jehoiachin; his name subsequently was changed to Zedekiah (2 Kgs 24:17), and as such he was known in the other references to him in 2 Kings, 2 Chronicles, and Jeremiah. *See* Zedekiah.
2. Asaph's descendant, named among the Levites living in postexilic Jerusalem (1 Chr 9:15; Neh 11:17, 22; 12:8, 35).
3. Heman's son, who helped lead music in the sanctuary during David's reign (1 Chr 25:4, 16).
4. Levite of the sons of Asaph, who was an ancestor of Jahaziel, a messenger of God in the days of King Jehoshaphat (2 Chr 20:14).
5. Another Levite of the sons of Asaph who helped cleanse the temple during King Hezekiah's reign (2 Chr 29:13).
6–9. Four men of Israel who were exhorted by Ezra to divorce their foreign wives during the postexilic era (Ezr 10:26-27, 30, 37).
10. One of the gatekeepers at the time of the dedication of the reconstructed wall of Jerusalem in Nehemiah's day (Neh 12:25).
11. Grandfather of Hanan, a treasurer of the temple storehouse in Nehemiah's day (Neh 13:13).

MATTATHA Ancestor of Jesus, according to Luke's genealogy (Lk 3:31). *See* Genealogy of Jesus Christ.

MATTATHAH* KJV spelling of Mattattah, Hashum's son, in Ezra 10:33. *See* Mattattah.

MATTATHIAS
1. Member of the priestly family of Joarib (his genealogy can be traced in 1 Macc 2:1 and in Josephus's *Antiquities* 12.6.3). He was a native of Jerusalem who settled in Modein and became the father of the nationalistic leaders, the Maccabeans, who led the Jewish revolt against the Syrians (167 BC). In his attempt to wipe out Judaism and establish Hellenism, Antiochus Epiphanes, king of Syria, outlawed Jewish sacrifices, built pagan altars (including one to Zeus in the temple), and executed anyone who possessed the law (1 Macc 2:1-49). Mattathias ignited the revolt against this oppression when Greek officers set up a pagan altar at Modein and ordered that

sacrifices be offered to heathen gods. Mattathias refused, killed the Jew who volunteered, killed the Greek officer, destroyed the altar, and fled to the hills with a band of followers. He led guerrilla warfare against the Syrians, continued to circumcise children, and made strenuous efforts to preserve the law. His motto was "Let everyone who is zealous for the law come after me."

He led the revolt for about a year and died, probably in 167 BC. His last bequest to his sons was "Obey the ordinance of the law." He was succeeded in military leadership by his son Judas, and the Hasmonean dynasty of priests were his descendants. He is remembered in special Hanukkah prayers because of his zeal in fighting for religious freedom.
2. Amos's son and an ancestor of Jesus, according to Luke's genealogy (Lk 3:25). *See* Genealogy of Jesus Christ.
3. Semein's son and an ancestor of Jesus, according to Luke's genealogy (Lk 3:26). *See* Genealogy of Jesus Christ.

MATTATTAH Hashum's son, who obeyed Ezra's exhortation to divorce his pagan wife after the exile (Ezr 10:33).

MATTENAI
1. Hashum's son, who obeyed Ezra's exhortation to divorce his pagan wife after the exile (Ezr 10:33).
2. Bani's son, who obeyed Ezra's exhortation to divorce his pagan wife after the exile (Ezr 10:37).
3. Head of Joiarib's priestly house during the days of Joiakim the high priest in postexilic Jerusalem (Neh 12:19).

MATTHAN Ancestor of Jesus (Mt 1:15); perhaps identifiable with Matthat in Luke 3:24. *See* Genealogy of Jesus Christ.

MATTHAT
1. Ancestor of Jesus (Lk 3:24), perhaps the same as Matthan (Mt 1:15).
2. Ancestor of Jesus (Lk 3:29).

See also Genealogy of Jesus Christ.

MATTHEW (Person) Son of Alphaeus; a tax collector by occupation; chosen by Jesus to be one of the 12 apostles; credited with the authorship of the Gospel of Matthew.

Matthew is listed in each of the four rosters of the 12 (Mt 10:3; Mk 3:18; Lk 6:15; Acts 1:13). Aside from these lists, Matthew is mentioned only in the account of his calling (Mt 9:9; Mk 2:13-14; Lk 5:27). Before his apostolic call, the Gospels refer to Matthew as Levi (Mk 2:14; Lk 5:27; compare Mt 9:9). The identity of Levi as Matthew is beyond all doubt. It is improbable that Matthew was the brother of James the Less whose father was also named Alphaeus (Mt 10:3), since this fact would have been mentioned in the record of Scripture, as it is in the cases of Peter and Andrew and the sons of Zebedee.

Matthew served King Herod Antipas in Capernaum of Galilee, collecting tariffs on goods passing on the road from Damascus to the Mediterranean Sea. To function in this capacity Matthew would have been an educated man, acquainted with the Greek language as well as the native Aramaic, thus qualifying him to write the Gospel of Matthew. As a tax collector, Matthew may have been a man of wealth, but this occupation also caused him to be despised by the Jews and to be considered among the lowest of people. The Pharisees consistently spoke of tax collectors in the same breath with sinners (Mt 11:19; Mk 2:16; Lk 7:34; 15:1).

Matthew was called while he was working at his tax booth. Jesus passed by on the road and said to him, "Follow me" (Mk 2:14). Matthew left everything and did so (Lk 5:28). Immediately he gave Jesus a great banquet at his house, and a large crowd of his fellow tax collectors and others were there to enjoy it. It was at this feast that the Pharisees and their scribes made the well-known complaint "Why do you eat and drink with tax collectors and sinners?" (Lk 5:30, NLT mg).

It is not certain when Matthew was called, but it is probable that the first six disciples were present on that day, since the Pharisees complained to Christ's disciples during Matthew's feast. Unlike the first men Jesus called, Matthew was not originally a follower of John the Baptist.

MATTHEW, Gospel of First Gospel and first book of the NT.

PREVIEW
• Author
• Date and Provenance
• Purpose
• Content

Author Nowhere does the text of Matthew itself clearly identify the author. Yet, as did the ancient church, we may ascribe authorship to Matthew the apostle. He was otherwise known as Levi (see Mk 2:14; Lk 5:27, 29). Before Jesus called him, he was a tax collector (Mt 9:9 ff.). It is interesting to note that Matthew called himself a tax collector, while none of the other Gospel writers did. Perhaps he did this to show how great an ascendancy he had been granted when the Lord called him, for tax collectors were despised and considered the lowest of people. The Gospel itself bears the impress of one knowledgeable of currency, for the Gospel writer speaks quite specifically about a two-drachma tax (Mt 17:24), a four-drachma coin (v 27), and the various talents (18:24; 25:15 ff.).

Date and Provenance Scholars are divided about the date when Matthew was written primarily because there is still debate about which Gospel was first written: Matthew or Mark. If Mark was written before Matthew, then Matthew was very indebted to Mark for a great deal of material, and vice versa. Those who argue for Matthew's priority do so on the basis that Matthew's Gospel was (1) recognized in the early church as the first Gospel, (2) written to those who first needed a written account—the Jews, and (3) placed first in the NT canon. Whether it preceded or followed Mark, most scholars are certain that it was written before the destruction of Jerusalem (AD 70) because the temple is spoken of as still standing (Mt 24:15). Irenaeus indicated that Matthew wrote this Gospel while Peter and Paul were in Rome. This would make the time of writing in the 60s.

Purpose

Apologetics Matthew wrote to a community of Greek-speaking Jewish Christians, located in a center such as Antioch in Syria. The community was surrounded and beset by Jews hostile to the claims of Jesus and the Christian community.

Matthew wrote as a Jew for Jews. In Jesus of Nazareth, Matthew contends, the OT reached its appointed goal. Jesus is the Messiah of Israel's expectation. In the opening chapter Matthew identifies him as "the son of David, the son of Abraham" (1:1), indeed as "God with us" (v 23). In later chapters Jesus is revealed as the Son of Man of Daniel 7 and the Suffering Servant of Isaiah 53. Throughout the book (Mt 1:22–27:10) the events of Jesus' life are represented as the "fulfillment" of OT prophecies. He comes to offer Israel salvation from sin (1:21). Nevertheless, the Jews have rejected him as their Messiah, and have thus placed themselves in the most perilous position (11:20-24; 21:33-46). One explanation for Israel's rejection of Jesus is the failure of the Jewish religious leadership to prepare the people for his coming. In the strongest language, Matthew denounces the teachers of the law and the Pharisees. They have forsaken the Word of God in favor of their own traditions (ch 15).

Teaching the Church Matthew also wrote as a Christian for Christians. He presents Jesus as a new Moses, indeed as Yahweh incarnate, expounding his own law for his people (ch 5), now newly constituted around his person under the leadership of the apostles (10:2-4; 16:18-19; 23:8-10). If the Christian church is to function properly, the teaching of the Messiah on a host of moral and spiritual issues must be taken with utmost seriousness (chs 5–7, 18). To aid this purpose, Matthew takes the form of a theological textbook or a handbook for the church, to instruct the people of God concerning the person and work of Jesus. That these teachings may be more readily and firmly grasped, Matthew presents them in a highly organized and memorable way. To facilitate the learning of the material, he arranges Jesus' teachings in five major discourses (interlocked with narrative portions) in which teachings of the same kind are clustered together (e.g., ch 10 consists of a charge to missionaries, and ch 13 consists of seven parables of the kingdom). Matthew's leading theological themes may be identified as the *Son* of God (Jesus is Yahweh incarnate, "God with us"), the *kingdom* of God (in Jesus, God is invading history to inaugurate his final rule), the *salvation* of God (as the servant-king, Jesus has come to "save his people from their sins," 1:21), and the *people* of God (Jesus has come to build his church, a redeemed community consisting of both Jews and Gentiles).

Content

The Coming of the Savior (1:1–2:23) His name reveals his mission: "Jesus" (1:1) means "Yahweh saves." He is "the son of Abraham," who comes to fulfill God's ancient promises to Jews and Gentiles (Gn 12:1-3). He is "Christ [or Messiah]," the son of David (Mt 1:1), who comes to inaugurate the kingdom of God (4:17). More than that, as evidenced both by prophecy (1:22-23) and by the nature of his conception (vv 18-20), he is "God with us"—now come to "save his people from their sins" (v 21). As the son of David, and in accord with prophecy, he is born in Bethlehem (2:1-6). Drawn by the star of Israel's Messiah (cf. Nm 24:17), Gentiles come to worship him (Mt 2:1-12). When Herod seeks to destroy him, Jesus finds sanctuary in a gentile land; God's calling his Son from Egypt marks the beginning of a mighty saving work—nothing less than a new exodus under Jesus, the new Moses (vv 13-20). Having been born in the humblest of circumstances, Jesus now comes to live in Nazareth (vv 21-23).

The Beginnings of Ministry (3:1–4:25) In face of the judgment that Jesus is about to execute (as evidence of the kingdom's arrival), John the Baptist calls Israel to repentance (3:1-12). Jesus' submission to John's baptism, and the voice from heaven, show him to be a King

who serves his subjects by taking their sins upon himself (vv 13-17). Like Israel at the exodus, Jesus is led into the wilderness for a period of testing (4:1). When the devil seeks to turn him away both from God and from his appointed mission, Jesus gains victory by depending upon God and his Word (vv 1-11). Returning to Galilee, Jesus deliberately settles in territory with both Jewish and Gentile inhabitants (vv 12-16) and begins a ministry of preaching (like John, he calls for repentance in face of the dawning kingdom), teaching (he calls his first disciples), and healing (vv 17-25).

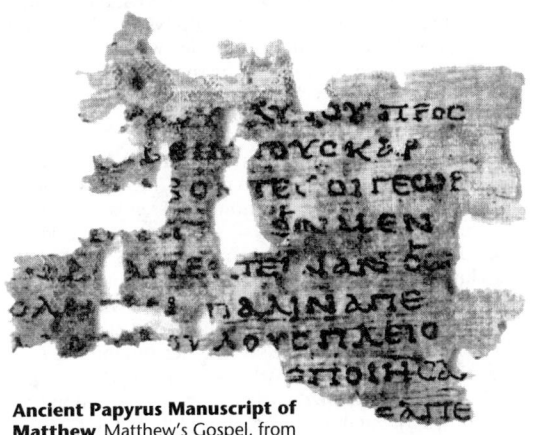

Ancient Papyrus Manuscript of Matthew Matthew's Gospel, from Oxyrhynchus Papyrus 4404 (second century)—P104

The Sermon on the Mount (5:1–7:29) Just as Moses ascended Sinai to receive God's law for Israel, so Jesus—as both the new Moses and as God incarnate—ascends the mountain to set forth his instruction for the citizens of the kingdom of God (5:1-2). He begins with *gospel* (not law), declaring that God shall surely save those who—beset by sin—trust in God's mercy, obey his commands, and long for him to establish his righteous rule in the earth (vv 3-12). Toward that end, disciples are a preservative (salt) and a witness (light) in a sinful society (vv 13-16). As the one who has come not to abolish the Law and the Prophets but to bring them to completion (i.e., to usher in the new age to which the OT pointed—v 17), Jesus calls his disciples to steadfast obedience to God's law as now expounded by the Lawgiver himself (vv 18-20). God's commands embrace inner desires as well as outward actions, must not be watered down or rationalized, and call for more radical obedience than ever before, now that the end has come (vv 21-48). In their giving, praying, and fasting, disciples are to combat hypocrisy by God-centeredness and self-forgetfulness (6:1-18). The Lord's Prayer (vv 9-13) calls upon God to honor his name by establishing his rule on earth, and to pardon, protect, and provide for his children. Given this prayer, and given the disciples' God-centered view of reality (vv 19-24), there is no cause for anxiety (vv 25-34). Disciples must be discerning without being judgmental (7:1-6), and depend on God for the power needed to love others (6:7-12). Having completed his exposition of the law (5:21–7:12), Jesus now calls would-be disciples to follow him (7:13-14), warns against false teachers (vv 15-20), and insists that true disciples do God's will (vv 21-23).

The Authority of Jesus (8:1–9:38) Having given his authority *verbal* expression in teaching (7:28-29), Jesus now gives it *visible* expression in a series of healing miracles, again revealing himself as the servant of Isaiah

(8:17). He heals a leper, a centurion's servant, and a bleeding woman by his word (8:1-13; 9:20-22). His touch dispels a fever and raises a dead person (8:14-15; 9:23-25). A combination of word and touch cures the blind (9:27-31). As "God with us," Jesus calls for unqualified allegiance (8:18-22). Though lacking even the natural protection enjoyed by animals (v 20), he demonstrates his sovereignty over the natural world—and thus his deity—by calming the storm (vv 23-27). In direct confrontations with demons, he shows his superiority over them (8:28-34; 9:32-33). Exercising God's own authority, he declares sins forgiven (9:1-8) and calls sinners to repentance and to discipleship (vv 9-13). Joy over the kingdom's inauguration is mingled with longing for its consummation (vv 14-17). The summary of 9:35-38 echoes 4:23-25, recalls chapters 5–7, and prepares for the next major discourse.

Jesus' Charge to the Missionaries (10:1-42) In response to the prayers that he has commanded, Christ now invests 12 disciples with apostolic authority and sends them out into his harvest field (9:37–10:4). The discourse speaks both of the apostles' immediate mission (10:5-15) and of the church's broader mission (vv 16-42). For now, the apostles are to concentrate on evangelizing Jews (v 6), in preparation for the mission to Gentiles (28:19). The "worthy" are those who welcome the apostles and their message; the "unworthy," those who reject them (10:11-15). In the broader mission, there is sure to be persecution (vv 16-19, 24-25), but this will actually aid the witness (vv 17-23). God will save his faithful missionaries (vv 19-23) but judge those who oppress them and who disown Christ (vv 26-39). A sure reward awaits both the herald and the recipient of the message (vv 37-42).

Christ the Lord (11:1–12:50) The judgment John predicted is already under way; one's stand in the last judgment would be determined by his response to the words and works of Jesus (11:2-6). Like his herald, Jesus meets with widespread hostility and indifference (vv 7-19). Given the finality of the grace attending his ministry, those who reject him will suffer the severest judgment (vv 20-24). Yet there are others—the lowly, the burdened, the teachable—who learn (by revelation from God the Father and God the Son) that the "Lord of heaven and earth" is also the "gentle and humble" God who comes to give rest to those who trust in him (vv 25-30). As the one who ushers in the new age (12:6), Jesus claims that he is the Lord of the Sabbath (vv 1-8). True rest (11:29) comes to those who come to Jesus.

Viewing Jesus as the destroyer of the Sabbath, the Pharisees ascribe his miraculous powers to Satan (12:22-24). On the contrary, says Jesus, the rule he is inaugurating is crushing Satan's empire (vv 25-29). To reject this truth in the full awareness of what one is doing is to commit the unforgivable sin against the Holy Spirit (vv 30-32); the words of Jesus' accusers expose them as persons destined for condemnation (vv 33-37). The requested sign from heaven will not be given. Jesus' resurrection is the only sign they need.

The Parables of the Kingdom (13:1-58) This, the third of Matthew's five great discourses, contains seven parables. In the parable of the sower, four kinds of soil— hard, shallow, cluttered, and fruitful—illustrate the various responses to Jesus' preaching (13:3-9, 18-23). As those who have received Jesus' proclamation of the kingdom (4:17), the disciples are given more light, but the crowds must accept that initial proclamation before further light is given (13:10-17, 34-35). In both the parable of the weeds (vv 24-30, 36-43) and the parable of the net

(vv 47-50), Jesus assures his disciples that the final judgment will separate true believers from false, and warns against hasty, premature judgments (cf. 7:1-5). The parables of the mustard and the yeast (13:31-33) contrast the smallness of the kingdom's inauguration with the fullness of its consummation. The parables of the hidden treasure and the pearl (vv 44-46) depict the kingdom as a value far surpassing all others (cf. 6:33). Thus illuminated by Jesus, disciples have new treasures to add to their old (13:51-52). The people of Nazareth, on the contrary, echo the crowds' lack of understanding and the Pharisees' hostility (vv 53-58).

Spiritual Conflict (14:1–16:12) In 14:1-12 the preaching of John exposes the weakness of Herod, and the beheading of John anticipates the crucifixion of Jesus (cf. 17:12). The true king is not Herod but Jesus. He is sovereign over nature itself (14:13-36)—God incarnate, "God with us," who feeds the hungry multitude in the wilderness (as God once provided manna) and walks upon and calms the sea (see Ps 89:9). Peter models Christians' faith, fear, and utter dependence on Jesus (Mt 14:28-31). The Pharisees and teachers of the law appear to worship God but in fact are devoted to their own traditions, which they offer not as supplements but as *rivals* to the Word of God (15:1-9). In verses 10-20 Jesus teaches both that ceremonial law apart from moral law becomes empty ritual, and that the old distinction between clean and unclean foods (Lv 11) is now as obsolete as the distinction between Jews and Gentiles. To underscore the point, Jesus enters pagan territory, heals a Canaanite (15:21-28) and feeds a Gentile multitude (vv 29-39). Pharisees and Sadducees, for all their differences, are united in their opposition to Jesus (16:1-12).

The Coming Salvation (16:13–17:27) Going beyond the crowds' respectful but inadequate estimates, Peter confesses Jesus to be "the Christ, the Son of the living God"— a recognition of Jesus' deity granted by divine revelation (16:13-17; cf. 11:25-26). As it is God the Son who possesses and builds the church, Satan and death are victims rather than victors. Jesus will build his church on Peter's confession that Jesus is the Christ, the Son of the living God. The apostles' prohibiting and granting entry into the church ("binding" and "loosing," respectively) depends upon the prior decision of heaven (i.e., God's revelation of apostolic teaching). In face of Peter's confession and the persistent false notions of messiahship (16:20, 23), Jesus now (for the first time) predicts his sufferings and coming glory (vv 21-28). In anticipation of that glory, Jesus is transfigured before certain disciples; Moses and Elijah join God the Father in bearing witness to the unique splendor of God the Son (17:1-8). Jesus then demonstrated his power by combating demonic powers (vv 14-18) and exhibited his authority by choosing to pay the temple tax using miraculous means (vv 24-27).

Greatness in the Kingdom (18:1-35) In this, the fourth of Matthew's five great discourses, Jesus concentrates on the character and attitudes of church members. He calls upon his followers both to *become* and to *welcome* the lowliest (18:1-5). Leaders especially are enjoined to deal harshly with themselves but gently with those under their care (vv 6-9). Remembering the Father's love for sinners, Christians are to make every effort (both by prayer and by personal initiative) to restore offending brothers, with excommunication being the last resort (vv 10-20). Church members who really understand the Father's amazing grace will never stop offering forgiveness and compassion to those who wrong them (vv 21-35).

Instructions on the Way to Jerusalem (19:1–20:34)

Given God's creation ordinances, says Jesus, divorce itself is never *commanded*; it is only *permitted* in the case of sin—that is, where the marital bond has already been severed through infidelity (19:1-9). As in 5:17-48, Jesus calls his followers to radical obedience (19:10-12). Besides instructing disciples to become like children (18:1-4), Jesus embraces children themselves with his love (19:13-15). He appeals likewise to the rich young man (vv 16-22); but the man, while faithful to the commands about love of neighbor, is too bound by his wealth to give himself unreservedly to loving God. Yet those who abandon all to follow Jesus will receive wealth untold in the coming kingdom (vv 27-30). The basis for such blessings lies not in human merit but in the astonishing generosity of the gracious God (20:1-16). None—not even the rich—are beyond the power of his grace. But God offers free salvation at great cost to himself (vv 17-19). Confronting competitiveness and ambition among his followers, Jesus teaches them that true greatness lies not in lording it over others but in serving them (vv 20-34), as shall be supremely demonstrated in his death as "a ransom for many" (v 28).

Confrontations in Jerusalem (21:1–22:46)

As the Servant-King (cf. 3:17), and as the Messiah destined for suffering (cf. 16:16-21; 20:28), Jesus enters Jerusalem not upon a war horse but upon a donkey's colt, for he purposes not to declare war on his enemies but to hand himself over to them—and thus achieve his triumph through defeat (21:1-11). As Lord of the temple, he demands that its commerce be halted and that it become (as God ordained) a place of worship for everyone, including the sick, the young, and the alien (21:12-17; cf. Mk 11:17). He outwits those who refuse to acknowledge the heavenly source of his and John's authority (Mt 21:23-27). In dramatic and devastating fashion, first visibly (by cursing the fig tree—vv 18-22) and then verbally (in the three parables of 21:28–22:14), Jesus pronounces judgment upon those Jews who have refused to acknowledge him as Messiah and Son of God. Henceforth, the true people of God are those who believe in Jesus, whether Jews or Gentiles. He calls upon his people to pledge their supreme allegiance to God. In the resurrection what will matter most is one's relationship to God (22:23-33). Indeed, he who loves God with his whole being and his neighbor as himself has kept the two foundational commandments of the OT (vv 34-40). Henceforth, submitting to God means rightly recognizing Jesus; he is indeed David's son (Mt 1:1), but he is supremely David's Lord—the exalted Son of God (22:41-46; cf. 16:16).

Woes upon the Scribes and Pharisees (23:1-39)

Five reasons are stated for Jesus' denunciation of the Jewish religious leaders. First is their hypocrisy: their practice contradicts their teaching (23:1-4), their external purity conceals inner rottenness (vv 25-28), and they appear to champion God's cause but are really enemies of God's servants (vv 29-36). Second is the pride that prompts their hypocrisy (24:5-12). Third is their exploitation of, and their baleful influence upon, those under their charge (vv 13-15). Fourth is their preoccupation with the minutia of the law to the neglect of its weightier matters (vv 16-24). Fifth is their responsibility for the dreadful judgment that the whole nation is about to experience (vv 33-39).

The Coming of the End (24:1–25:46)

The introduction to this, the fifth and last of Matthew's great discourses, makes it plain that there is the closest connection (for both Jesus and his disciples) between the coming destruction of Jerusalem and the end of the age (24:1-3). Jesus first characterizes the time between his first advent and his return: there will be natural catastrophes, international warfare, the rise of false messiahs, the persecution of God's people, and the universal proclamation of the gospel of the kingdom (vv 4-14). Then Jesus speaks of the catastrophe that is soon to befall the Jewish nation in particular (as already foretold in 22:7; 23:38), culminating in the destruction of Jerusalem and its temple in AD 70 (24:15-25). Sometime thereafter (but after an interval known only to God the Father—v 36), the Son of Man will return in great glory, amid apocalyptic signs, to gather his people (vv 26-31). The present generation will not pass away before judgment falls upon Israel (vv 15-25), so let listeners take heed (vv 32-35). The same warning applies to the more remote coming of the Son of Man (vv 36-51): both the certainty of the event and the uncertainty of its time call for vigilance and faithfulness in the interval, for that event will bring both salvation and judgment. To drive the lesson home, Jesus tells the parables of the wise and foolish virgins (25:1-13) and the talents (vv 14-30). The concluding parable of the sheep and the goats (vv 31-46) speaks of the urgent necessity of making the right response to the "brothers"—that is, the messengers—of Christ; those who feed, clothe, and otherwise care for the messengers of Christ thereby testify to their reception of the apostles' message and their Lord (cf. 10:40-42).

The Road to Golgotha (26:1–27:26)

As though in response to Jesus' own prediction, the chief priests and the elders hatch their murderous plot (26:1-5), soon to be aided by Judas (vv 14-16). The anointing at Bethany (vv 6-13) testifies to the extravagance of love and the imminence of death. At the Passover meal (vv 17-30), signaling at what sacrifice the new exodus comes about (cf. 2:15), Jesus interprets his forthcoming death as an atoning sacrifice for the forgiveness of sins (26:26-28; cf. 1:21) and anticipates the day of final victory over sin and death in the consummated kingdom (26:29). Jesus' agony in Gethsemane (vv 36-46) expresses his horror over taking his people's sins upon himself. By a stupendous act of filial obedience, he submits his will to the Father, that the Scriptures might be fulfilled (26:54; cf. Is 53). As the servant of God destined to suffer, Jesus resists attempts to thwart his arrest (26:47-56). The Jews' supreme court (the Sanhedrin) and their loftiest religious official (the high priest) condemn Jesus as a blasphemer because he dares to identify himself as "the Christ, the Son of God" (26:57-68; cf. 16:16). As though joining the court's repudiation, Peter—in fulfillment of Jesus' prophecy (26:31-35)—disclaims knowledge of Jesus (vv 69-75). Judas's disillusionment finds expression in suicide (27:3-10). The Jews hand Jesus over to Pilate the Roman governor (vv 1-2), he alone having the authority to pronounce the death sentence. Knowing that the charge of blasphemy will carry no weight with Pilate, the Jews now represent Jesus as a threat to Caesar. In the end, Pilate responds not to specific charges and evidence but to pressure from the crowd and the threat of riot (vv 11-25). He releases Barabbas and delivers Jesus to be crucified (v 26).

The Death of Jesus (27:27-66)

Following his humiliating treatment at the hands of the Roman soldiers, Jesus is led to the place of execution; weakened by the beatings, he requires assistance (27:27-32). He refuses the proffered narcotic so that he might keep his head clear (v 34). His being executed with malefactors (v 38) testifies to the purpose of his death (cf. 1:21). A steady stream of abuse is hurled at him, in blasphemous disregard of the truth of the superscription "This is Jesus the King of the Jews" (27:37-44). Finally, out of the darkness Jesus utters the cry of dereliction; now is revealed the ultimate horror (that from which his soul shrank in Gethsemane), the sin-bearer's supreme agony—the beloved Son's abandonment by the Father (vv 45-49). Having cried out with a loud voice (cf. Jn 19:30), Jesus dies (27:50). Immediately, the saving effects of his death become evident (vv 51-53): sinners, now forgiven, have access to the holy God (the veil of the temple is rent asunder), and there is hope of resurrection for those who have died. As at the beginning (2:1-12), Gentiles instead of Jews confess Jesus (27:54; contrast 26:63-65). Joseph's careful attentiveness to Jesus' burial contrasts with the ongoing attempts of the chief priests and Pharisees to resist Jesus' power (27:57-66).

The Triumph of the Savior (28:1-20) Amid great glory and power and joy, the Savior's victory over death is announced and attested (28:1-7). The risen Jesus appears first to the women who stayed with him during his crucifixion (28:8-10; cf. 27:61; 28:1). The Jews' response to the guards' report signals their growing desperation before irresistible reality (28:11-15). Meeting with the 11 disciples on the mountain in Galilee (vv 16-20), Jesus, the new Moses, continues his instructions. He now reveals the evangelistic purpose for which Matthew has been preparing readers from the very threshold of his Gospel. The apostles are to disciple all peoples by baptizing them into the name of the triune God and by teaching them to obey all that Jesus has commanded. The apostles go forth in the assurance that Jesus—as the Lord—stands over them, and that Jesus—as Immanuel—stands with them until the very end of the age.

See also Jesus Christ, Life and Teachings of; Luke, Gospel of; Mark, Gospel of; Matthew (Person); Synoptic Gospels.

MATTHIAS
Disciple of Jesus, mentioned by name only in Acts 1:23-26, chosen to take the place of Judas Iscariot.

Shortly after Jesus' ascension, Peter voiced the need for another apostle, the stipulations being that the candidate must have been a follower of Jesus from his baptism to his ascension and have been a witness to his resurrection. The assembly put forward two men who met these criteria: Joseph called Barsabbas, surnamed Justus, and Matthias. They then cast lots (some scholars believe they cast ballots). Whatever the method, Matthias was chosen. Later, the apostolate was widened to include others such as Paul, Andronicus, and Junias. Scripture never mentions Matthias again, though tradition says that he preached in Judea and was finally stoned to death by the Jews.

See also Apostle, Apostleship.

MATTITHIAH
1. Levite and Shallum's firstborn son, who was in charge of making the baked cakes that accompanied the offerings in the temple (1 Chr 9:31).
2. Musician appointed by the Levites to play the lyre, along with five others, when the ark was brought to Jerusalem in David's time (1 Chr 15:18, 21; 16:5).
3. One of Jeduthun's six sons, who was a musician in David's time (1 Chr 25:3, 21); perhaps identifiable with #2 above.
4. Nebo's son, who divorced his foreign wife as commanded by Ezra (Ezr 10:43).
5. One who stood to Ezra's right when Ezra read the law to the people after the exile (Neh 8:4).

MATTOCK* Agricultural tool used for grubbing or breaking up the soil (1 Sm 13:20-21, NLT "pick"). *See* Agriculture.

MAUL* KJV translation for "war club" (NLT "ax") in Proverbs 25:18. *See* Armor and Weapons; Warfare.

MAYOR *See* Town Clerk.

MAZZAROTH* Word appearing in Job 38:32 that may refer to a constellation. The Hebrew form is feminine in Job 38:32 and masculine in Job 9:9, where it has usually been thought to refer to the Hyades. Some hold that Mazzaroth refers to the constellation of the Bear, while others think it refers to the 12 signs of the zodiac, the Corona Borealis, or the Hyades.

See also Astronomy.

MEAH*, Tower of KJV translation for "Tower of the Hundred" in Nehemiah 3:1 and 12:39. *See* Hundred, Tower of the.

MEAL OFFERING* An offering of grain or fine flour. It has also been translated "grain offering" (NLT, NIV), "cereal offering" (RSV) and "meat offering" (KJV). *See* Offerings and Sacrifices.

MEALS, Significance of The meal played a significant role in family, social, and religious life. The evening meal was the time when all family members normally were gathered together, and was thus an important time of fellowship. Providing food for the traveler was both a social and a religious responsibility, while the ideal of a quiet social life was realized by having friends break bread with the family and discuss the problems of the day by the light of small oil lamps. The significance of the meal retains its central focus both in the Jewish religion with the Passover meal and in Christianity with the celebration of the Lord's Supper.

In the ancient Near East two meals were normally eaten during the day. The first was the noonday meal, usually consumed by laborers in the field and consisting of such items as small cakes or flat loaves, figs or olives, and possibly cheese or curds of goats' milk. This was considered a small meal, eaten for sustenance and refreshment at a time of relaxation and respite from the heat of the sun and the labor of the day (Ru 2:14). Breakfast was considered unnecessary, and biblical references to any such form of early morning meal are very few (Jgs 19:5; Jn 21:12).

Whereas in Egypt the main meal was served at noon, among the Hebrews the evening meal was the most important social occasion of the day. Then the exhausted field workers could return home to relax after their day's work and enjoy the feeling of communal warmth as the family gathered together for their principal meal. This occasion coincided with the arrival of darkness, a time when there was insufficient light for fieldwork to continue.

The laborer's meal consisted of bread or cakes made of hand-ground grain, goats' cheese or curds, vegetables (especially beans, lentils, leeks, and peas, which were popular for the sake of variety although not always plentiful), and figs, olives, raisins, and dates. Meat was usually available, but for the majority was a luxury item. Food was cooked in olive oil, and honey was used for sweetening.

The meal was eaten together by the entire family. There was no separate dining room in the average house, and during the patriarchal period, meals were consumed while the family was seated on the floor, a mat often serving as a table (Gn 37:25). Canaanite seating habits were adopted subsequently, and chairs and small tables were used (1 Kgs 13:20; Ps 23:5; Ez 23:41). Eating in the Egyptian fashion in a reclining position became popular and continued throughout the Roman period. Musical entertainment, dancing, and riddles were sometimes provided on festive occasions for family and guests, since the meal period was the normal time for entertainment in Near Eastern society.

By NT times, a separate upper room often served as a dining room. Guests reclined by leaning on the left elbow so that they were close enough together on their couches to facilitate easy conversation. There was a strict hierarchy to the seating arrangements (cf. Gn 43:33; 1 Sm 9:22; Mt 23:6; Mk 12:39; Lk 14:8) at all formal meals, the "highest" place being that to the right of the servants as they entered the room and the lowest to their left.

Guests washed their hands before and after meals, and normally partook of a form of meat and/or vegetable stew from a common bowl placed in the center of the table. Instead of cutlery, pieces of bread held in the fingers were made into the shape of a small scoop and dipped into the bowl. There would usually be only one main dish requiring preparation, so that the woman who had cooked the meal could partake of it with her guests, thus fulfilling the ideals of community at mealtimes.

On several occasions in the NT Jesus is mentioned as eating meals with disciples and friends. He and his followers were guests at the wedding feast held in Cana of Galilee (Jn 2:1-10), and also at a dinner given by Matthew (Mt 9:10), as well as at another given by Simon the Pharisee (Lk 7:36-50). Jesus also was entertained at dinner somewhat unexpectedly by Zacchaeus (19:6-7). On several occasions Jesus was a guest at a family gathering held at the home of Martha, Mary, and Lazarus in Bethany (Lk 10:38-42; Jn 12:2). Following the customs of smaller towns and villages, passersby may well have called into the house to greet Jesus and perhaps converse with other guests.

There are two important meals described in Scripture, one involving the old covenant and the other the new, in which meals had a redemptive meaning for the people of God. The first was the institution of the Passover at the time of Israel's departure from Egypt under Moses (Ex 12). The second was the institution of the Lord's Supper. Both are discussed in detail in separate articles.

See also Food and Food Preparation; Feasts and Festivals of Israel; Lord's Supper, The; Passover.

MEARAH Region of Palestine that the Israelites had not possessed (Jos 13:4, NIV "Arah"). Its location is uncertain. Suggestions include the district of caves (Mearah means "cave") near Sidon called Mughar Jezzin, and the towns Khirbet 'Arah and Mogheiriyeh.

MEASURE *See* Weights and Measures.

MEAT *See* Food and Food Preparation; Meals, Significance of.

MEAT OFFERING* KJV form of "meal" or "grain" offering. *See* Offerings and Sacrifices.

MEBUNNAI* Alternate name (probably a textual corruption) of Sibbecai, a warrior among David's "mighty men," in 2 Samuel 23:27 (NLT mg). *See* Sibbecai, Sibbechai.

MECHERATHITE* Designation for Hepher in 1 Chronicles 11:36. The parallel passage in 2 Samuel 23:34 calls him "the son of the Maachathite" (KJV) or

"from Maacah" (NLT). *See* Maacah, Maachah (Place); Maacathite, Maachathi, Maachathite.

MECONAH Settlement mentioned beside Ziklag (Neh 11:28) and presumably in the western Negev.

MEDAD Elder of Israel who, with Eldad, prophesied in the wilderness to Joshua's consternation. Moses, however, defended Medad's right to speak in God's name (Nm 11:26-27).

MEDAN Third son of Abraham by his second wife, Keturah (Gn 25:2; 1 Chr 1:32).

MEDEBA Moabite town in the fertile plain northeast of the Dead Sea, about 25 miles (40.2 kilometers) south of Philadelphia (modern Amman). It was situated 6 miles (9.7 kilometers) south of Heshbon on the Roman road to Kerak.

Here the Amorites defeated Moab (Nm 21:30). Later, Israel defeated Sihon, king of the Amorites, at Medeba and assigned it to Reuben's tribe (Jos 13:9, 16). At this place David routed an Aramean army hired by the Ammonites to attack his forces (1 Chr 19:7).

According to the Moabite Stone, the town was once controlled by Omri and Ahab of Israel; however, when Mesha reasserted Moabite dominance in the eighth century BC, he rebuilt Medeba and other Moabite cities. Medeba is named in Isaiah's prophecies against Moab (Is 15:2). In later times Joram and Jehoshaphat made unsuccessful attempts at capturing this city.

MEDES, MEDIA, MEDIAN* Indo-European-speaking people appearing in the highland area of the ancient Asian country called Media. They were closely related to the Persians, with whom they are often identified or confused by writers who referred to the people of the area by the almost generic term "Medes." In fact, the Medes inhabited a defined area in the Zagros Mountains positioned between 3,000 and 5,000 feet (914.4 and 1,524 meters) above sea level in a mountainous region divided by valleys. The capital, Ecbatana (now Hamadan), was on the major trade route from Mesopotamia. The elevation provided a temperate summer climate that encouraged the use of Ecbatana as a summer retreat for Persian kings.

As no texts are extant in the Median language recording the history and culture of the Medes, information must be obtained from references to them in contemporary writings of the Greeks, Neo-Babylonians, and Assyrians. As the Medes and Chaldeans were instrumental in bringing down the Assyrian Empire, it is understandable that they should figure prominently in the Neo-Babylonian texts. Valuable additional information is available from Herodotus, possibly from cuneiform sources.

The Assyrian king Shalmaneser III recorded the activity of the Medes in the area around Ecbatana in the ninth century BC, but historians are uncertain exactly how long before that date they had migrated into the region.

Shalmaneser organized a raid into the plains controlled by the Medes in order to steal herds of carefully bred horses, the reputation for whose excellence was already deservedly high. Over generations, Assyrian kings continued this type of raid, not only for the purpose of obtaining fresh supplies of horses but also to ensure the free passage of traders on this major route. During the eighth century BC, Assyrian kings such as Adad-nirari (810–781 BC), Tiglath-pileser III (743 BC), and Sargon II (716 BC), all claim to have conquered

Media. The OT records that the Israelites were transported there at the time of Sargon's incursions (2 Kgs 17:6; 18:11).

When Esar-haddon was king of Assyria (681–669 BC), he expected the Medians to acknowledge his overlordship and pay tribute according to their treaty, but taking advantage of the declining strength of Assyria, the Medians joined forces with the Scythians and Cimmerians in 631 BC. The ebbing strength of the Assyrians was further eroded under a series of attacks led by Phraortes culminating in the fall of Nineveh in 612 BC and of Haran in 610 BC. Under the leadership of Cyaxares of Media, who organized a strong, disciplined army, the Median forces and their allies, having gained control of the major cities, extended their sphere of influence to the northern part of Assyria, negotiating peace with Lydia in 585 BC.

The Elamites, also a people involved in the ebb and flow of the power struggle in the region over the centuries, came into the ascendency in 550 BC when Cyrus of Anshan overcame Astyages. Cyrus was of half-Persian, half-Median ancestry. Ecbatana, capital of Media, was captured, and the entire area was controlled by Elam. Cyrus took on the additional title "king of the Medes." The laws and the heritage of the Medes were incorporated with those of the Persians (Dn 6:8, 15). Medes were entrusted with high office in the administration. The Medes and the Persians were referred to in almost synonymous terms (Est 1:19; Dn 8:20). They were also involved in the capture of Babylon (Is 13:17; Jer 51:11, 28; Dn 5:28). Being of Median heritage (Dn 9:1), Darius, son of Ahasuerus, was referred to as "the Mede" (Dn 11:1) from the time he took over as ruler of Babylon. His administration was not altogether peaceful, however, and restlessness led to outright rebellion both in his reign and during that of Darius II (409 BC).

A description of the sumptuous feasting and luxurious appointments of the court apartments are described in the book of Esther (Est 1:3-7). The Medians subsequently were subjected to the control of the Syrians (Seleucids) and the Parthians. In the NT there is a single combined reference to Parthians, Medes, and Elamites (Acts 2:9), but thereafter Media seems to have become only a geographical term, the people no longer appearing in history as a group in their own right.

MEDIATE, MEDIATOR The act of an intermediary, go-between, or expert in divine things, not to negotiate agreement or compromise but to approach God on behalf of others, and so to convey desired knowledge and reassurance with divine authority.

In the Old Testament Job voices longing for such a mediator (translated here from the LXX): "God is not a mortal like me, so I cannot argue with him or take him to trial. If only there were a mediator who could bring us together, but there is none. The mediator could make God stop beating me, and I would no longer live in terror of his punishment. Then I could speak to him without fear, but I cannot do that in my own strength" (Jb 9:32-35).

More familiar is the mediation of instruction concerning the divine character and will. The Mosaic covenant was given through the mediation of angels and of Moses (Ex 20:18-21; Dt 33:2; Acts 7:53; Gal 3:19; contrast Heb 6:13-17, where God, acting alone, "mediated" an oath). The terms of the covenant law were expounded by prophets who "stood in God's council," and by priests who communicated God's mind by oracle, sacred lot,

and pronounced blessing (Dt 10:8; 33:8-10; 2 Chr 15:3; Jer 23:10-11, 18-22, 31-34; Mi 3:11; Mal 2:7).

Most familiar is the liturgical mediation of the priest, whether by Moses (Ex 24:4-8) or by an appointed person trained in the rituals of worship (28:1). Because of Israel's emphasis upon the holiness of God, sacrificial expiation, or "covering," of sin figured largely in priestly mediation. The priest represented before God the people's penitence, confession, and prayers for forgiveness, bearing the tribes' names on shoulders and breastplate, and represented God, in turn, assuring his favor, forgiveness, and protection (see Heb 5:1-4; 7:27–10:11).

In the New Testament It was natural that the mission of Jesus should be described in mediatorial terms, and first as that of a prophet speaking for God to humans, making God known (Mk 6:15; 8:28). Where applied to Jesus, the actual title "mediator" refers mainly to his institution of a new covenant, establishing God's new relationship with people (Heb 8:6; 9:15; 12:24). The one other instance is 1 Timothy 2:5, where the unity of God requires a sole, unrivaled mediator, namely, Christ.

This last reference mentions Christ's giving himself as "a ransom for all." This essentially priestly function is the theme of Hebrews. Christ as Son of God, divinely appointed, sinless, suffering, tempted, sympathizing, and obedient, is uniquely qualified to be High Priest of his people. As priest, he offers a perfect sacrifice and lives forever to intercede for those who draw near to God through him. This mediatorial ministry places Jesus at "the right hand of God." His intercession for people is mentioned also in Romans 8:34 and probably in 1 John 2:1, where ancient Greek commentators, NEB, and other authoritative sources so understand "paraclete," here applied to Jesus. His mediatorial sacrifice is mentioned in Matthew (Mt 26:28), John (Jn 1:29), Romans (Rom 3:25), and 1 John (1 Jn 1:7; 2:2; 4:10).

Still more significant is the insistence, everywhere in the NT, that man's knowledge of God, salvation, and hope come through Christ alone. Made poor for our sakes, he died and rose "for us"; our peace, access to God, reconciliation, expiation of sin, grace, truth, prayer, and "all spiritual blessings" are "through him," "in him," "through his blood," and "in his name." The purpose of God focuses in him; he mediated at Creation and at redemption (Col 1:15, 22); in him all the fullness of God dwells, and the face of Christ reveals God's glory. No one knows the Father except the Son and those to whom the Son reveals him; no one comes to the Father but by him; neither is there salvation in any other.

Christ's mediation is the fulfillment and end of all mediation between God and humankind. The book of Hebrews opens with the assertion that Christ surpasses all other mediators—angels, Moses, the Aaronic priesthood. His is a timeless priesthood, like Melchizedek's. His sacrifice is unrepeatable, "once for all time," and by it we have been consecrated to God "for all time." The covenant he established between God and people offers better promises, sacrifice, sanctuary, and hope (Heb 7:19; 8:6; 9:1, 11-15). Christ's mediation so far excels all others that it can never be superseded; he is priest without rival and forever (cf. 1 Tm 2:5).

Without using the priestly analogy, John emphasizes the same truth. The gulf between divine and human has been crossed, decisively and finally, by the Incarnation. Instead of standing between God and man, Christ unites both within himself by becoming man. Mediating in the beginning at Creation, Christ is himself the Word, which from God's side mediates God's mind, embodies God's message, and conveys God's power. No one has seen

God at any time, but as unique Son and divine, Jesus "expounds" God (Jn 1:18). From the human side, Jesus prays for the disciples (ch 17), offers perfect obedience, lays down his life for his flock, and offers the unblemished sacrifice that bears away the sin of the world.

See also Reconciliation.

ANY OTHER MEDIATORS?

Despite the sufficiency and finality of Christ's continuing mediation, the desire for additional mediators has lingered in the church, where people have prayed to martyrs, angels, departed saints, celibates, and the Virgin Mary. Biblical grounds for this kind of extended mediation were sought in the oneness of the church on earth and in heaven; in saints in either realm interceding for each other; in allusions to departed souls still praying for others (Lk 16:27-28; cf. Rv 6:9-11); and especially in the vision of Judas Maccabeus, in which Jeremiah and the high priest Onias, both deceased, invoked blessing on the Jews (2 Macc 15:12; cf. Jer 15:1).

At the same time, John 20:23 was held to show Jesus conferring mediatorial powers of absolution and excommunication upon the apostles and their successors. To these were soon added exclusive powers through the sacraments. This extended mediation was held to complement, not to supplant, that of Christ.

Most Protestants, however, deny the mediation of Mary, angels, departed saints, or the clergy, asserting instead the priesthood of all believers (1 Pt 2:5, 9; Rv 1:6; 5:10). This was understood to mean for all Christians the privilege of individual direct access to God (Rom 5:2; Eph 2:18; Heb 10:19-22) and the duty of intercession for others (Rom 15:30; Eph 6:18; Jas 5:16). John 20:23 is held to emphasize the responsibility of all Christians to bring Christ's forgiveness to others by witnessing to the gospel. Protestants insist upon the sufficient and final mediation of Christ, who came to show us the Father, died to bring us to God, and ever lives to make intercession for us.

MEDICINE AND MEDICAL PRACTICE The field of knowledge dealing with the diagnosis, treatment, and prevention of diseases, as well as the actual substances used to diagnose, treat, or prevent disease.

Medicine as a branch of knowledge received little attention from the Hebrew people of OT times, in contrast to the surrounding cultures found in Mesopotamia and Egypt, where medical knowledge had a prominent place. Extant in the library of Assyrian king Ashurbanipal are 800 tablets relating to medicine. From these writings it can be seen that medicine at that time was a mixture of religion, divination, and demonology. Their pharmacopeia was extensive and included agents such as dog dung and human urine. Surgical operations were performed by some physicians. An unusual method of diagnosis practiced in Babylon was to inspect the liver of a freshly killed animal and compare it with a clay model of a liver from a normal animal. Differences between the two were used to diagnose the condition of the patient. An interesting example of this, and divination, is found in Ezekiel 21:21.

The art of medicine was more advanced in Egypt than in Mesopotamia, depending more upon logic and observation. The Edwin-Smith papyrus is the oldest surgical treatise known. It discusses a variety of fractures, dislocations, wounds, tumors, and ulcers. Adhesive plaster, surgical stitching, and cauterization were used in treatment. The heart was recognized as the center of the circulatory system, and the pulse was observed. The Ebers papyrus deals with problems of internal medicine and their treatment. Enemas were a popular form of therapy, and their *materia medica* contained an assortment of remedies ranging from castor oil to animal fat to hot sand. Other papyri deal with gynecological problems and contain formularies and many magical incantations. Mummification was a highly developed art; Joseph had his father Jacob embalmed (Gn 50:2).

The outlook of the Hebrew people in OT times toward disease was entirely different from that of their heathen neighbors. They did not believe in the heathen superstitions or gods and, consequently, did not develop a medical knowledge similar to the Egyptians and Babylonians. Instead, the Hebrews regarded sickness as a judgment from God (Ex 15:26; Dt 28:22, 35, 60-61; Jn 9:2) and recovery also was attributed to God (Ex 15:26; Ps 103:3). In accordance with this philosophy, King Asa's reliance on physicians instead of on God is referred to in a reproachful way in 2 Chronicles 16:12. Therefore, while medical treatment was available in Israel, its use and development was less advanced than in neighboring lands.

The most significant contribution the Hebrews gave to medicine was in the hygienic measures outlined in the Law, particularly Leviticus 11–15. While these had primarily a religious significance, they undoubtedly improved the general level of health and physical well-being of the people. The Hebrew priest was not the counterpart of the physician-priest found in other cultures. Although the Hebrew priest was expected to determine what physical conditions rendered a person ceremonially unclean, there is no intimation in Scripture that he treated diseases.

The only surgical operation mentioned in Scripture is circumcision. This was performed by the Hebrews for religious rather than medical purposes, and it was not done by a physician but by the head of the house or someone else (Ex 4:25). In Ezekiel 30:21 reference is made to treating a fracture of the arm by immobilizing and splinting it with a roller bandage.

Obstetrical care was given by women who were experienced midwives (Gn 35:17). In Genesis 38:27-30 there is an account of the birth of twins complicated by a transverse presentation. This is a difficult problem for even the most skilled obstetrician, and the fact that the mother and both babies survived speaks highly for the skill of this midwife. In Exodus 1:15-21 the use of birth stools for delivery is mentioned. This was a device to hold the laboring woman in a position favorable for delivering the baby.

In NT times, Greek medicine had a dominant influence in the Mediterranean world. Although the practice of medicine was still in a primitive state, Hippocrates and other Greek physicians of his day laid the basis for modern medicine by rejecting magical explanations of diseases and through careful observation attempted to give a rational basis for medical treatment. From Mark 5:26 it is known that physicians were available in Israel. Indeed, the rabbis ordained that every town must have at least one physician, and some rabbis themselves practiced medicine.

Specific medical remedies are occasionally mentioned in the Bible. Mandrakes were used as an aphrodisiac (Gn 30:14; Sg 7:13). When Job was afflicted with generalized boils, he removed the devitalized skin with a piece of pottery and sat in ashes (Jb 2:7-8). The ashes would have a drying effect on the draining sores, giving this treatment a rational basis for its use. Jeremiah refers in a rhetorical way to the balm in Gilead, indicating its medicinal use (Jer 8:22; 46:11). The exact nature or use of this balm is not known. When Hezekiah was mortally ill, he was instructed by Isaiah to put a lump of figs on the boil (2 Kgs 20:7). This probably should not be considered a treatment, however, any more than the dipping seven times in the Jordan by Naaman or the application of mud to the eyes of the blind by the Lord. The therapeutic effect of merriment on the mind found in Proverbs 17:22 is in accord with modern mental health beliefs.

Medicinal use of wine is recorded several times in Scripture. Its mood-changing ability is alluded to in Proverbs 31:6, and apparently the sour wine offered to the Lord on the cross was intended to ameliorate his suffering through its analgesic property (Jn 19:29). Paul suggests to Timothy that he use a little wine for his stomach and other infirmities (1 Tm 5:23). It is significant that Paul said "a little" because pharmacologists today agree that wine in moderate amounts aids digestion and helps blood circulation; however, excessive amounts are deleterious to the health in numerous ways. The good Samaritan used oil and wine to treat the wounds of the injured man (Lk 10:34). Because of its alcoholic content, the wine would have an antiseptic action, but at the same time it would tend to coagulate the surface of the raw wound and permit bacteria to thrive under the coagulum. The oil, by its emollient effect, would tend to nullify this latter undesirable side effect of wine and would also be soothing due to its coating action. A dressing was then applied, and the patient was taken to a resting place.

In Revelation 3:18 the Laodicean church is admonished to use eye salve. Since Laodicea was famous for a powder used for weak and ailing eyes, this illustration is uniquely appropriate to use in warning this church concerning its lack of spiritual vision.

See also Disease; Physician; Plague.

MEDITERRANEAN SEA Body of water often called the Great Sea, bordering Palestine on the west (Nm 34:7; Jos 9:1; Ez 47:10, 15). The sea is approximately 2,196 miles (3,533.4 kilometers) long, from Gibraltar to Lebanon, varies in width from 600 miles to 1,000 miles (965.4 to 1,609 kilometers), and has a maximum depth of 2.7 miles (4.3 kilometers). Its various subdivisions consist of the Adriatic, Aegean, Ionian, Ligurian, and Tyrrhenian seas.

From the Bay of Iskenderun on the north to el-Arish on the south, a distance of about 450 miles (724.1 kilometers), the eastern coastline is rather straight, with a few deep bays or headlands. Along the Syrian coast as far south as Beirut, the coastline contains rocky formations rising sharply from the water. At Acco the coast recedes and the land slopes gently upward toward the plain of Esdraelon. South of this, the sharp ridge of Mt Carmel projects into the water. From the southern slope of Carmel, the vale of Sharon spreads southward to merge with the plains of Philistia. From there the coast is an almost unbroken curve to the Nile Delta.

Several good harbor areas indented the Syrophoenician coast in antiquity, and the sea played an important role in the development of that region. Byblos was a sea power prior to 1000 BC, and Tyre and Sidon were known for their maritime prowess after 1000 BC. Following their conquest of Palestine under Pompey (63 BC), the Romans made extensive use of the sea and referred to it as "Our Sea."

Although located on the Mediterranean Sea, and having neighbors who were seafaring people, the Israelites never developed any extensive commercial or military use of it. Various reasons have been given for this. First, Israel was a pastoral and agricultural people whose roots were in the soil rather than the sea and who, therefore, looked inland for their development. Second, the primary efforts of Israel in Palestine were directed toward conquest and retention of the lands taken, and this left little time to develop maritime interests. Third, the sea was controlled by Phoenicia, and to a lesser degree by Philistia. From the time of the exodus, the Phoenicians had established themselves at points along the coast and formed an essentially maritime confederation extending from the Orontes on the north to Joppa on the south. South of this point, the Philistines controlled the coastline during much of Israel's history. At one time Solomon had a fleet of ships at Ezion-geber on the Red Sea (1 Kgs 9:26-27), and Jehoshaphat also had a fleet in that vicinity (22:48). Finally, there were no natural harbors along the Israelite-occupied coastline. A few harbors existed, such as Ashkelon, Dor, Joppa, and Acco, but the only port to which Israel had access apparently was Joppa during the monarchy. When Solomon was building the temple, lumber from Lebanon was shipped to Joppa and transported to Jerusalem from there.

The NT records one visit by Jesus to the coastal area, when he went to "the district of Tyre and Sidon" (Mt 15:21) and healed the demon-possessed daughter of the Syrophoenician woman. The apostle Paul in his missionary journeys had many contacts with the Mediterranean Sea from Caesarea on the Palestinian coast to Puteoli on the coast of Italy. Under Roman rule, the Mediterranean was widely traveled by merchants, government officials, soldiers, and teachers. Paul and other early Christians took advantage of the Roman roads of land and sea to spread the gospel throughout the world surrounding the Mediterranean.

Aerial View of the Mediterranean Sea outside of Mount Carmel

MEDIUM Person who acts as a channel of communication between human beings and the spirit world. *See* Magic; Necromancer, Necromancy; Psychics.

MEGIDDO, MEGIDDON* City standing at the southwest edge of the plain of Esdraelon on the main route between Mesopotamia and Egypt. It overlooks the historic route where a pass through the Mt Carmel range led from the plain of Sharon into the plain of Jezreel. This strategic position made Megiddo one of the most important commercial and military centers of

Aerial View of Megiddo

Palestine in the second millennium and the early first millennium BC. From earliest times, the environs have been the scene of major battles. Great military men, such as Thutmose III of 15th-century BC Egypt, Napoleon in 1799, and General Allenby during World War I, have fought for mastery there.

At the time of the conquest, Joshua defeated the king of Megiddo but did not take the city (Jos 12:21). In the subsequent allotments to the tribes of Israel, Megiddo was assigned to Manasseh, but they could not conquer it from the Canaanites (Jos 17:11-12; Jgs 1:27). During the days of the judges, Deborah and Barak defeated the forces of Hazor under the command of Sisera near Megiddo (Jgs 4:15; 5:19) but did not take the city either. Perhaps David conquered it as part of his program for establishing the kingdom. At any rate, by the time of Solomon, Megiddo served as the headquarters of one of his 12 administrative regions (1 Kgs 4:12). Solomon rebuilt it to serve as one of his chariot and garrison cities (9:15-19).

King Ahaziah of Judah died there (841 BC) after being wounded by Jehu while on a visit to the northern kingdom (2 Kgs 9:27). King Josiah of Judah met and intercepted Pharaoh Neco of Egypt (609 BC) at Megiddo in a vain effort to prevent him from going north to aid the Assyrians; he was mortally wounded in the battle (23:29-30). The plain of Megiddo (KJV "valley of Megiddon") is referred to in Zechariah's prophecies of restoration for Israel and Jerusalem (Zec 12:11). Revelation predicts a great future war that will take place at Armageddon (Har Megiddon, the "mount of Megiddo," Rv 16:16).

MEGIDDO*, Waters of Scene of the battle between Sisera and Barak, mentioned in the victory song of Deborah (Jgs 5:19, NLT "Megiddo's springs"). It refers to a perennial stream near Megiddo, probably the Wadi el-Lejjun, which drained the basin behind Megiddo.
See also Megiddo, Megiddon; Armageddon.

MEGILLOTH* Plural form of the Hebrew word for scroll. The word occurs several times in Jeremiah 36, where King Jehoiakim, rejecting the word from God, burned the scroll that the prophet sent to him.

Megilloth is also used collectively of the OT books of Song of Songs, Ruth, Lamentations, Ecclesiastes, and Esther. These are the "five rolls," which are read by the Jews during the major festivals of the Jewish year: the Song of Songs at Passover, Ruth at Pentecost (Firstfruits), Lamentations on the anniversary of the destruction of

Jerusalem by the Babylonians, Ecclesiastes at the Feast of Tabernacles, and Esther at Purim.

MEHETABEL
1. Matred's daughter and the wife of Hadar (Gn 36:39; 1 Chr 1:50), king of Edom in pre-Israelite times.
2. Shemaiah's grandfather. Shemaiah was hired by Tobiah and Sanballat to discredit Nehemiah by frightening him into fleeing into the temple (Neh 6:10).

MEHIDA Head of a family of temple servants in Ezra's time (Ezr 2:52; Neh 7:54).

MEHIR Kelub's son from Judah's tribe (1 Chr 4:11).

MEHOLAH, MEHOLATHITE* Location used to describe Adriel the son of Barzillai, who was the husband of Merab, Saul's eldest daughter (1 Sm 18:19; 2 Sm 21:8). He was probably from Abel-meholah, an important city of Gilead. The marriage of Adriel and Merab was probably a political move by Saul, agreed to by David, who was to have married Merab himself (1 Sm 18:17-19).

MEHUJAEL Irad's son and the father of Methushael in Cain's line (Gn 4:18).

MEHUMAN One of the seven chamberlains King Ahasuerus sent to bring Queen Vashti to the royal banquet (Est 1:10).

MEHUNIM*, MEHUNIMS* KJV forms of Meunim and Meunites in Ezra 2:50 and 2 Chronicles 26:7, respectively. *See* Meunim, Meunites.

ME-JARKON Topographical designation in the description of Dan's inheritance (Jos 19:46). It is probably not a settlement; Jarkon seems to be the name of the river (el-'Awjah) flowing across the coastal plain from the springs at Aphek to the coast four miles (6.4 kilometers) north of Joppa. It was a formidable obstacle to north-south travel, but the numerous ancient sites along its banks testify to its importance as an entryway from the sea to the interior of the country.

MEKERAH, MEKERATHITE* *See* Mecherathite.

MEKONAH* KJV spelling of Meconah, a Judean city, in Nehemiah 11:28.

MELATIAH Descendant of Gideon who helped repair the Jerusalem wall next to the Old Gate during Nehemiah's time (Neh 3:7).

MELCHI*
1. Jannai's son, according to Luke's genealogy (Lk 3:24).
2. Addi's son, according to Luke's genealogy (Lk 3:28).

See also Genealogy of Jesus Christ.

MELCHIAH* KJV spelling of Malchiah, Pashhur's father, in Jeremiah 21:1. *See* Malchiah #8.

MELCHISEDEC* KJV rendering of Melchizedek, the priest and king of Salem who blessed Abraham, in Hebrews 5-7. *See* Melchizedek.

MELCHI-SHUA* KJV alternate form of Malchi-shua, King Saul's third son, in 1 Samuel 14:49 *See* Malchi-shua.

MELCHIZEDEK Mysterious biblical personality whose name means "king of righteousness." The historical record about this priest-king is contained in Genesis 14:18-20, and he is spoken of in Psalm 110:4 and Hebrews 5:10; 6:20; 7:1-17.

In Genesis 14:18-20 Kedorlaomer, king of Elam, with three other Mesopotamian kings, raided a vassal confederacy of five kings near the shores of the Dead Sea. In the ensuing massacre and rout by the Mesopotamian confederacy, Abraham's nephew Lot and his family and possessions were captured (Gn 14:1-12). Abraham led an attacking force in pursuit of Lot's captors, achieved victory, retrieved the plunder, and secured the release of Lot and his family (vv 13-16).

Upon his return, Abraham was greeted not only by the grateful kings of the Dead Sea confederacy but also by Melchizedek, king of Salem, who gave Abraham bread and wine along with his blessing as "priest of the most high God" *(El Elyon)* (Gn 14:18). Salem is Jerusalem (cf. Ps 76:2). El Elyon is not the pagan deity of Canaanite worship by the same name but rather the title of the true God who created heaven and earth—an idea foreign to Canaanite religion (cf. Gn 14:22; Pss 7:17; 47:2; 57:2; 78:56). Melchizedek correctly viewed Abraham as worshiping this same God (Gn 14:22) and praised God for giving victory to Abraham. Abraham identified himself with the worship of the one true God represented by Melchizedek in that he received his gifts and blessing and gave him a tenth of everything, thus recognizing Melchizedek's higher spiritual rank as a patriarchal priest. In contrast, Abraham disassociated himself from Canaanite polytheism by declining gifts from the king of Sodom.

It is interesting to speculate whether Melchizedek's knowledge of the true God was received by tradition from the past ages closer to the Flood, or whether he, like Abraham, had been uprooted from paganism to monotheism by direct divine revelation. It is at least clear from Hebrews 7:3 that his priesthood was isolated and not received through a priestly pedigree.

In Psalm 110:4 In this messianic psalm, David envisioned one greater than himself whom he called "Lord" (v 1; cf. Mk 12:35-37). Thus the perfect messianic king was not an idealization of the present ruler but someone to come. Also, he was to be not merely a man but more than this. The Messiah would be the Son of God as well as the son of David. The divine oracle of Psalm 110:4 is addressed to the Messiah: "You are a priest forever in the line of Melchizedek." The significance of this statement is left for the inspired author of the letter to the Hebrews to develop.

In Hebrews 5:6-11; 6:20–7:28 The argument of the writer of Hebrews is that the priesthood of Aaron has been superseded by the superior priesthood of Christ and that the superiority of Christ's priesthood is demonstrated by its Melchizedekian character. First, both Christ and Melchizedek are kings of righteousness and kings of peace (Heb 7:1-2). Second, both have a unique priesthood that does not depend on family pedigree (v 3). Third, both exist as priests continually (v 3).

Melchizedek was superior to Abraham, the father of Levi, because Melchizedek gave gifts to and blessed Abraham, and received tithes from him (7:4-10); David predicted the succession of the Melchizedekian priesthood over the Levitical priesthood, showing the imperfection of the latter (vv 11-19); the Melchizedekian priesthood of the Messiah was confirmed by a divine oath, which was not true of the Levitical priesthood (vv 20-22); and the Melchizedekian priesthood possessed an unchangeable and permanent character (vv 23-25).

Certain scholars have thought that Melchizedek was an appearance of the preincarnate Christ in the OT (technically called a Christophany). They argue this on the basis of Hebrews 7:3, which says that there is no record of his father or mother or any of his ancestors—no beginning or end to his life. However, this statement is simply to be understood in the sense that his priesthood was not connected to any priestly family line. Melchizedek had a priestly office by special divine appointment, and was thus a type of Jesus Christ in his priesthood. The writer of Hebrews says that Melchizedek was one "resembling the Son of God" (7:3); this clearly indicates that he was not himself the Son of God.

See also Hebrews, Letter to the; Priests and Levites.

MELEA Ancestor of Jesus, according to Luke's genealogy (Lk 3:31). *See* Genealogy of Jesus Christ.

MELECH Micah's son from Benjamin's tribe (1 Chr 8:35; 9:41).

MELICU* KJV form of Malluchi the priest in Nehemiah 12:14. *See* Malluchi.

MELITA* KJV form of Malta, an island south of Sicily, in Acts 28:1. *See* Malta.

MELKI *See* Melchi.

MELKON* Name that tradition has given to one of the wise men (also called Melchior) who brought gifts to Jesus (Mt 2:1-2). *See* Magi.

MELON Generic name for many-seeded fruit of the gourd family. *See* Food and Food Preparation; Plants.

MELZAR* Steward responsible for the food given to Daniel (Dn 1:11, 16). The KJV translates the word as a proper name, but the RSV translates the word as a title. Most likely Melzar is a Hebraization of a Babylonian title.

MEMORIAL Something that keeps remembrance vivid. The ideas represented by the words "remember," "remembrance," and "memorial" are closely connected in common parlance as well as in biblical usage. The Hebrew and Greek words translated as "memorial" in the OT and NT are nominal derivatives of the verbal roots meaning "to remember." It is for this reason that one cannot fully grasp the significance of the term "memorial" without first understanding something of the usage and meaning of the term "to remember."

Although "remember" is usually understood as simply recalling to the mind something from the past, and "memorial" as that which serves to preserve the memory of something from the past, there is often another dimension to these terms in biblical usage. In the Bible, the verb "to remember" often represents a broader idea than simply to recall something from the past because it implies and includes resultant action as well. It is not just recalling, but recalling in a way that affects one's present feeling, thought, or action. For example, when it is said in Genesis 8:1 that God "remembered Noah," this does not mean that God merely recalled that Noah was in the ark. It includes this idea to be sure, but more than this it means that God is acting on Noah's behalf. In a similar way, when Genesis 30:22 says that God "remembered Rachel," the meaning is that after a long period of barrenness God is going to answer Rachel's prayer for a child.

One of the most prominent uses of the idea to remember in the OT is the exhortation to the Israelites to remember the mighty acts of the Lord on their behalf in the past (Pss 77:11; 78:7; 105:5). This also means much more than simply recalling events from past history. It means to live in the present in the light of God's past actions. By drawing consequences for the present from the acts of God in the past, Israel's faith is to be strengthened for the challenges and difficulties encountered in the present. Israel's failure to remember in this way repeatedly led to apostasy and disobedience (78:11, 42; 106:7, 13, 21-22).

A brief survey of the usage of the term "memorial" demonstrates that it also often carries this added dimension of meaning. Here one notices in particular its use in connection with the Passover. Exodus 12:14 says that the Passover "shall be for you a memorial day" (RSV). It is to be an observance that causes the Israelites to live in the present in the light of God's past action in delivering them from sin and bondage in Egypt. This is much more than simply recalling the exodus as a historical occurrence.

In a similar way Joshua 4:7 describes setting up a monument of 12 stones in the midst of the Jordan River as a "memorial" to the miraculous provision for Israel's crossing and entering Canaan. This memorial is to be "for the people of Israel for ever." It is to remind them of God's past deliverance so that they may take courage in their present circumstances.

Another usage of the term is found in connection with the "stones of remembrance" attached to the front of the ephod worn by the high priest (Ex 28:12, 29; 39:7). The significance of these stones was that they were to bring the names of the sons of Israel before the Lord. This is not simply in order for the Lord to recall their names but to assure the Israelites of his present concern for their well-being.

The term "memorial" is used with a somewhat different connotation in connection with the grain offering in Leviticus 2:2, 16. The "memorial of the grain offering" is that portion that the priest offers upon the altar. The remainder is used for the sustenance of the priests themselves. The memorial is that which represents the whole: it does not serve just to remind God of the entire offering, but is viewed as an embodiment of it. A memorial in this sense may be viewed as embodying something of that which it represents.

In the NT the words "memorial" or "remembrance" occur rather infrequently, but in one instance with particular significance. When Jesus instituted the observance of the Lord's Supper, the NT counterpart to the OT Passover, he said, "This is my body which is given for you. Do this in remembrance [or memorial] of me" (Lk 22:19). The Lord's Supper is observed as a remembrance of the suffering and death of Christ. It is much more, however, than simply recalling a historical fact; it is remembering in a way that fills the believer with thanksgiving and determines how he lives and acts in the present.

MEMPHIS City located about 15 miles (24.1 kilometers) southwest of Cairo, once the sprawling capital of Egypt; now, for all practical purposes, it does not exist.

When the city was founded about 3000 BC, it was known as "White Wall" and was later called Men-nefru-Mine or Menfe in Egyptian. From the latter the Greeks got the name Memphis. Though one Hebrew reference follows the Greek (Hos 9:6), Memphis is commonly called Noph in the OT (Is 19:13; Jer 2:16; 44:1; 46:14, 19; Ez 30:13, 16); presumably this is a corruption of the middle part of the Egyptian name.

History of Memphis According to the fifth-century BC Greek historian Herodotus, King Menes founded the city of Memphis and built the temple of Ptah there shortly after unifying the country. Whether or not Menes was a historical person, it is commonly concluded today that shortly after the unification of Egypt (c. 3100 BC) a new capital was built on the border between Upper and Lower Egypt. Although the rulers of the first two dynasties after Egypt's unification had come from Thinis, north of Thebes, the fact that they were buried at Saqqara west of Memphis seems to indicate that they made Memphis their capital.

Memphis continued as the capital of Egypt during the Old Kingdom period (c. 2700-2200 BC). And Memphis, or the nearby city of It-Towy, continued as capital during much of the Middle Kingdom (c. 2050-1775).

During the New Kingdom or Empire period (c. 1580-1100), the capital was moved to Thebes. But Memphis was Egypt's second capital during most of that period, and some rulers lived there because of its central geographical location. Ramses II moved his residence to Tanis in the Delta during the 13th century BC, but he built a number of structures at Memphis and engaged in large-scale renovation and restoration there. As early as the 16th or 15th century BC, Memphis began to take on a cosmopolitan character. Syrians, Phoenicians, Greeks, and Jews eventually established separate residential quarters there.

Though some decline set in at Memphis during the invasions and uncertainties of the first millennium BC, the city remained virtually intact. Even after the founding of Alexandria in the fourth century BC, the city maintained its greatness; some of the Ptolemies were crowned there instead of at the primary capital of Alexandria.

Memphis lost its importance as a religious center after the Christian emperor Theodosius closed its temples and ordered them torn down in the fourth century AD.

Prophecy against Memphis As noted above, the only places Memphis is referred to in the OT are in the Prophets. Of course, Memphis shared in the general condemnation of Egypt, but it was signaled out for special attention. Ezekiel declared that God would destroy the idols of the city (Ez 30:13) and bring great distress upon it (v 16). Jeremiah went further, prophesying that Memphis would be utterly destroyed and without inhabitants (Jer 46:19).

Evidently, there are several reasons for this judgment. First, the punishment will come on all nations for their sinfulness and idolatry. Second, they will be punished for their animosity and cruelty to the Jews. In the generations before the exodus the Egyptians made their name hated by the Hebrews. After the death of Solomon and the division of the Hebrew kingdom, Shishak of Egypt invaded Palestine in the fifth year of King Rehoboam and wrought considerable destruction (926 BC; 1 Kgs 14:25). Then in 609-608 BC Pharaoh Neco held Israel under tribute.

Fulfillment of prophecies against Memphis occurred especially in connection with two major events. The Christian Roman emperor Theodosius (AD 379-395), in his campaign against paganism, ordered destruction of the temples of Memphis and desecration of its statues. Then in the seventh century Muslim monotheists conquered Egypt and likewise tried to obliterate evidences of ancient polytheism. After the Arabs began to build Cairo in 642, Memphis became a quarry for the new city. Gradually the ruins have been carted away until virtually nothing is left. A fallen 40-foot statue of Ramses II, one of his sphinxes, a few column bases, and other minor ruins lie among the palm trees and cornfields at the site. The largest remaining portion sits in a lake because the breaching of the ancient dikes has permitted the place to be inundated.

See also Egypt, Egyptian.

MEMUCAN One of the seven princes of Persia and Media under King Ahasuerus (Est 1:14-21). He brought charges against Vashti, the Persian queen, who had refused to make a royal appearance that the king had commanded (v 16). Memucan proposed that she be divested of her position and the queenship given to another; the king took his counsel and issued a decree to that effect (v 21). Hence Esther was chosen as queen over Media and Persia.

MENAHEM King of Israel who ruled from 752–742 BC. He was the son of Gadi, a name not attested in the OT except in 2 Kings 15:14-22.

Virtually everything that the OT records about the career of Menahem is contained in a few brief verses in 2 Kings 15. Three important points may be noted from these verses.

First, 2 Kings 15:14 records the assassination of Shallum, which enabled Menahem to seize the throne. Verse 16 then recounts the actions of Menahem against the town of Tappuah (Tiphsah). The entire verse is troublesome but may be translated as follows (NLT): "At that time Menahem destroyed the town of Tappuah and all the surrounding countryside as far as Tirzah, because its citizens refused to surrender the town. He killed the entire population and ripped open the pregnant women." Two things are unusual. First, the actions of Menahem are quite without precedent in Israelite history. Second, the location and identity of the town that Menahem attacked are uncertain. The Hebrew text reads "Tiphsah" (see NLT mg), using the spelling of a town normally identified as Thapsacus on the Euphrates. Menahem's reasons for attacking a town this far away from his own territory and interests would be difficult to determine. Accordingly, some scholars have followed the Lucianic version of the Greek Bible that reads the Hebrew letters as if they were "Tappuah," a town 14 miles (22.5 kilometers) southwest of Menahem's hometown of Tirzah. If this reading is correct, and the textual evidence for it is limited to the one version, the meaning of 2 Kings 15:16 is that Menahem began just outside the boundaries of his hometown (Tirzah) and put to the sword the entire population of a neighboring town (including its citizens who lived outside the city proper) that failed to support his bid to become king.

Second, 2 Kings 15:19-20 provides the biblical view of the way in which Menahem dealt with the Assyrian crisis posed by the campaign of Tiglath-pileser III into the Syro-Palestinian region (c. 744). Evidently hoping to persuade the Assyrians to support his claims to the throne in Israel, Menahem levied a stiff tax upon the wealthy citizens of his nation to be used to pay tribute to Tiglath-pileser (called by his Babylonian name "Pul" in v 19). Evidently Menahem hoped this payment would convince the Assyrian king "to gain his support in tightening his grip on royal power" (v 19). Politically at least, Menahem appears to have guessed correctly, because the Assyrians withdrew (v 20) and Menahem was left in power.

Finally, the reign of Menahem is introduced (2 Kgs 15:17) and concluded by the standard literary forms employed throughout the books of Kings. Despite the fact that Menahem was judged to be just as sinful as the original apostate (Jeroboam I) had been, 2 Kings 15:22 appears to attest an unusual fact about his death. Of the last six kings of Israel, only he died a peaceful death.

See also Chronology of the Bible (Old Testament); Israel, History of.

MENAN* KJV form of Menna, an ancestor of Jesus in Luke's genealogy (Lk 3:31).

MENE, MENE, TEKEL, PARSIN Mysterious prophetic words in Daniel 5:25 pointing to the judgment of God against Babylon and her king. A decade or so following the death of King Nebuchadnezzar of Babylon (562 BC), a man of lesser moral stature, Belshazzar, became monarch of the empire. The fifth chapter of Daniel tells of a great banquet that Belshazzar made to which 1,000 of his nobles and their wives had been invited. Under the influence of wine, Belshazzar ordered his servants to bring the gold and silver vessels taken from the temple in Jerusalem by Nebuchadnezzar a generation earlier. The sacred vessels, kept in storage until then, were distributed to the guests at the feast and sacrilegiously used to offer praise to the gods of Babylon (Dn 5:4).

In the midst of the revelry, the fingers of a man's hand appeared and wrote upon the plaster of the banquet room wall. The king's composure was altogether shattered by the event and he cried out for someone to interpret the writing. None of his wise men were able, however, to discern the meaning of the words. Finally, the queen proposed a solution to the dilemma: Daniel the prophet—a gifted man in matters such as these—could be summoned to interpret the writing.

Daniel was brought in before the king and immediately rebuked him for his foolish and godless arrogance. His sermon before Belshazzar (Dn 5:17-23) powerfully proclaimed the judgment of God against all sinful pride, a message decisively revealed in the enigmatic words that Daniel then proceeded to interpret.

The words, given in the Aramaic script, are transliterated into English as *"Mene, Mene, Tekel, Parsin"* (*"Upharsin,"* KJV). The mystery of the words lay not in the decipherment of the language but in the significance attached to each of the words. Superficially, they simply denoted a series of weights or monetary values. In truth they prophesied the immediate judgment of God against Babylon and its king.

Daniel's explanation of the inscription is recorded in Daniel 5:26-27. *Mene* means "numbered" and its double entry indicated that God had both numbered the days of Belshazzar's kingdom and had reckoned its termination. *Tekel* means "weighed." Applied to Belshazzar, it signified his moral and spiritual inadequacy. He was, as it were, too light to balance out on the scales of God's standard of righteousness. The final participle, *parsin* means "broken" or "divided." Daniel gives the singular form of the word in his interpretation *peres*, indicating that Belshazzar's kingdom was about to be divided between the Medes and the Persians. There is a bit of wordplay in that the noun for Persians (*paras*) is virtually the same as the root used here. Daniel 5:30-31 notes that the words of this prophecy were fulfilled later that evening.

See also Daniel, Book of.

MENELAUS It is thought that this conscienceless, conniving high priest was the leader of the Jewish supporters of the Seleucid kings during the reign of Antiochus IV Epiphanes. Second Maccabees 4:23-50 relates the story of how Menelaus outbid Jason for the priesthood by paying Antiochus 300 talents of silver above Jason's price.

See also Maccabees, 1 and 2.

MENI* Pagan god of destiny or luck worshiped by apostate Jews (Is 65:11). The name is rendered "destiny" in NASB, NIV, NLT; "fortune" in NEB; and "unto that number" in KJV, reflecting the meaning of the Hebrew word "to count, apportion," as it were, by fate. Meni has been identified with the Arabic god Maniyyat, Babylonian Manu, and Edomite Manat. The reference in Isaiah has to do with preparing meals for pagan deities.

MENNA Ancestor of Jesus, according to Luke's genealogy (Lk 3:31). *See* Genealogy of Jesus Christ.

MENORAH* Lamp or lampstand in the tabernacle. It refers to the seven-branched lamp (candelabrum) that was to lighten the tabernacle: these seven lamps gave light in front of the lampstand (Nm 8:2). In Solomon's temple there were ten such lampstands, five on each side before the inner sanctuary (1 Kgs 7:49). The design of the original lamp was conceived by Bezalel, the son of Uri and the grandson of Hur, of the tribe of Judah, a man filled with the Spirit of God who was an excellent craftsmen (Ex 31:1-4). Bezalel was also responsible for designing the other utensils for the tabernacle.

Exodus 25:31-40 and 37:17-24 provide us with details regarding the lamp and its decorations. Made of a single piece of pure gold and ornamented with almond flowers and knobs in the shape of apples, it consisted of a central shaft branching out into three arms on either side. Each branch was surmounted with a cup narrowed into a lip to hold the wick and the special olive oil.

The Golden Lampstand The seven-branched lampstand, called a menorah, has been a symbol of the Jewish faith for over 2,000 years.

Archaeologists have dug up clay bowls with seven spouts, which date back to the middle Bronze Period. According to Josephus, the central shaft was fixed to a base, and from it extended slender branches placed like prongs of a trident—with the end of each one forged into a lamp. Josephus's account of the temple lamp tallies well with that of Zechariah in his vision of the restored temple after the exile (Zec 4:2-3). Several facsimiles have come down to us from archaeological finds, as well as the famous sculpture of the menorah with some of the other temple vessels on the Arch of Titus in Rome. The menorah on the panel in Rome differs from Josephus's description, being a massive object with thick arms carried by five men on either side.

According to Exodus 37:24, the weight of the menorah

was one *kikar* in pure gold. This equals a Babylonian talent, which is computed to weigh 34 kilograms (or 75 pounds). But from Exodus 25:39 it would appear that this weight included accessories, such as snuffers, trays, etc. (cf. 2 Chr 4:22). There is also another discrepancy regarding the base of the lamp. On the panel of Titus's Arch the pedestal consists of two tiers and is rectangular, whereas archaeologists have uncovered ancient designs of the lamp that end in a tripod. Scholars are undecided which is the more original, and there are several theories to explain the difference. In Jewish mystical lore the menorah symbolizes the tree of life, the seven planets, and the seven days of creation.

In the NT the lampstand in the book of Revelation is a carryover of the temple tradition, with special reference to Zechariah 4:2, 11. By an association of ideas it refers to the witness of the seven churches, to Christ who is the Light of the World, and to God, who is the source of all light (Rv 1:12-13, 20; 2:1; 11:4).

MENUHOTH* People descended from Judah through Shobal, mentioned only in 1 Chronicles 2:52 (rendered Manahethites in NEB, KJV; Manahathites in NIV, NASB, NLT). The RSV transliterates the Hebrew word Menuhoth, which derives from the same root as "half of the Manahathites" in verse 54.

See also Manahath (Place), Manahathite.

MEONENIM*, Plain of KJV mistranslation for the diviners' oak, a place near Shechem, in Judges 9:37. *See* Diviners' Oak.

MEONOTHAI Othniel's son from Judah's tribe (1 Chr 4:13-14).

MEPHAATH One of the cities of Reuben's tribe on the plain near Heshbon, which was allotted to the Merari family of Levites (Jos 13:18; 21:37; 1 Chr 6:79). Later, it was numbered among Moabite towns during Jeremiah's ministry (Jer 48:21). It has been identified with modern Jawah, six miles (9.7 kilometers) south of Ammon. *See also* Levitical Cities.

MEPHIBOSHETH

1. Son of Jonathan, David's friend. The original form of the name was undoubtedly Merib-baal (1 Chr 8:34; 9:40), but when the word *baal* became predominantly associated with the chief male deity of the Canaanite fertility cult, it was replaced, in some instances, by the Hebrew word *bosheth* (meaning "shame"). As the grandson of Saul, Mephibosheth was born into a situation of privilege, which changed dramatically when the Philistines attacked. Saul, Jonathan, and two of his brothers were killed in the battle on Mt Gilboa (1 Sm 31:1-6). When news of the catastrophe reached the Israelite palace at Jezreel, the five-year-old Mephibosheth was snatched up by his nurse. In a panicked scramble for safety, she fell, dropping Mephibosheth, whose legs or ankles were broken. The lack of adequate medical attention meant that he became completely crippled (2 Sm 4:4). Eventually, he found refuge at Lo-debar in Transjordan, with Makir, who later on befriended David himself (9:4; 17:27). Mephibosheth's uncle, Ishbosheth (Saul's only surviving son), who had been made Israel's puppet king (2:8-10) was murdered (ch 4). Mephibosheth, although apparently next in succession, appears not to have been considered. When David was established on the throne of a now united kingdom and wished to show kindness to any surviving members of Jonathan's family, he was informed of

Mephibosheth's existence by Ziba, once an influential steward in Saul's palace (9:1-13). Summoned to Jerusalem, Mephibosheth was naturally apprehensive, probably fearing that David might want to eliminate all possible rivals (see 19:28). But David's generous nature showed itself in restoring to Mephibosheth all of Saul's original land, with Ziba and his family continuing to manage the estate, and in granting the cripple a permanent place at the royal table.

When Absalom's rebellion broke out, Ziba met the fleeing David and supplied him with welcome provisions, taking the opportunity to curry favor at the expense of his master. Mephibosheth, he suggested, even entertained hopes of gaining the kingdom for himself. David, in the stress of the crisis, was taken in by this unlikely story and promised Ziba all Mephibosheth's property (2 Sm 16:1-4). The civil war over, Mephibosheth himself came to David with clear evidence of his grief at the latter's exile and therefore of Ziba's duplicity. But David, not willing to alienate Ziba and probably grateful for his earlier gift, compromised, dividing the land between the two. Mephibosheth's genuine joy at the king's restoration was such that the loss of his land was of no account in comparison (19:24-30). Later, when seven descendants of Saul were slain to appease the Gibeonites, David's continuing remembrance of Jonathan resulted in Mephibosheth's being spared (21:7). Mephibosheth's son, Mica (9:12), became the head of a considerably large family (1 Chr 8:35; 9:41).

2. Son of Rizpah, Saul's concubine. Unlike his better-known namesake, he was one of Saul's seven descendants who had to be hung in order to appease the Gibeonites, whose ancient treaty with Israel had been violated by Saul, causing a three-year famine (2 Sm 21:8; see Jos 9:3-27). In the sequel (2 Sm 21:10-14), Rizpah's untiring vigil over the corpses prompted David to give them a decent burial, together with the remains of Saul and Jonathan, in the family sepulcher.

MERAB Eldest of Saul's two daughters (1 Sm 14:49), who was promised as a wife to David (18:17-18). Saul unexplainedly did not keep the agreement, instead giving him Michal.

MERAIAH Head of Seraiah's priestly family during the priesthood of Joiakim in postexilic Jerusalem (Neh 12:12).

MERAIOTH
1. Levite, six to seven generations removed from Aaron (1 Chr 6:6-7; Ezr 7:3).
2. Ahitub's son and the father of Zadok (1 Chr 9:11; Neh 11:11); perhaps identifiable with #1 above, despite differences in genealogy.
3. Priestly house whose head was Helkai during the days of Joiakim in postexilic Jerusalem (Neh 12:15). Its forebear is given as Meremoth (v 3). Some regard Nehemiah 12:15 as a scribal error and identify the names in verses 3 and 15 as the same person.

MERARI, MERARITE Transliteration of a Hebrew word meaning "bitter," "bitter drink," or "to be bitter." It means the same in Arabic and Akkadian, but in Ugaritic it means "to strengthen, to bless." Traditionally, the word has been understood to be derived from the Hebrew and thus to mean "gall" or "bitterness." But the Ugaritic root meaning "to strengthen, to bless" is not foreign to the Hebrew way of thinking. When used as a person's name, it probably should be understood to mean "strength" or "blessing." Such an understanding may be preferred in many biblical references. In the case of Merari, the third son of Levi, this understanding is preferable in noting his importance and that of his family. It is inconsistent for the youngest son to have a name meaning "gall" or "bitterness" and then to have the greatest responsibility and the greatest reward for his service.

The Bible makes numerous references to Merari the son of Levi. He was the youngest of Levi's three sons (Gn 46:11; Ex 6:16-19; Nm 3:17-20, 33; 1 Chr 6:1). He was the father of two sons, Mahli and Mushi (Ex 6:19; Nm 3:20), who had the responsibility of carrying the frames (KJV "boards"), bars, pillars, bases (KJV "sockets"), vessels, and accessories of the tabernacle (Nm 3:36-37; 4:31-33; 7:8; 10:17; Jos 21:7, 34, 40). His descendants are known as Merarites. Chronicles makes numerous references to Merari's family as an indication of its importance (1 Chr 6; 9; 15; 23; 26; 2 Chr 29; 34).

See also Priests and Levites; Levi, Tribe of.

MERATHAIM Name that Jeremiah uses in reference to God's judgment upon Babylon (Jer 50:21). Though it means "double rebellion" or "twofold rebel," it is a wordplay on the name for southern Babylonia, Marratu. Thus, God says, "Go up against the land, Two-fold rebel . . . and utterly destroy it!"

MERCHANT A person who buys and sells commodities for profit. The barter system of trade gave way in time to a system where professional merchants facilitated the exchange of goods. At first, it was for payment in silver pieces (Gn 23:16) and then in coinage or some other medium of exchange. Merchants operated locally and internationally with Arameans (1 Kgs 20:34; Ez 27:16-18), Canaanites and Phoenicians (Is 23:2, 8), Assyrians (Na 3:16), Babylonians, Persians, Greeks, and Romans. Some merchants traveled afar (Neh 13:16-20). Desert peoples with caravans traded their wares in many lands (Ez 27:15, 20-23; 38:13). They operated in bazaars and set up shops for trade (1 Kgs 20:34; Neh 3:31; 13:19-20). Commodities were held in storehouses (Gn 41:49; 1 Kgs 9:19). The sons of Jacob traded in Egypt (Gn 43:11). In Solomon's day, trade greatly expanded (1 Kgs 9:26-27; 10:28). During the exile, Jews became involved in merchant activity in Babylonia, and many never returned to Palestine. In Jerusalem the merchants helped Nehemiah to rebuild the wall (Neh 3:31-32).

MERCURIUS*, MERCURY* Roman god. *See* Hermes #1.

MERCY A divine quality by which God faithfully keeps his promises and maintains his covenant relationship with his chosen people despite their unworthiness and unfaithfulness (Dt 30:1-6; Is 14:1; Ez 39:25-29; Rom 9:15-16, 23; 11:32; Eph 2:4).

The biblical meaning of mercy is exceedingly rich and complex, as evidenced by the fact that several Hebrew and Greek words were used to express the concept. Consequently, there are many synonyms employed in translation to express the dimensions of meaning involved, such as "kindness," "lovingkindness," "goodness," "grace," "favor," "pity," "compassion," and "steadfast love." Prominent in the concept of mercy is the compassionate disposition to forgive offenders or adversaries and to help or spare them in their sorry plight.

Theological Significance At the heart of the concept of mercy is the love of God, which is freely manifested in his gracious saving acts on behalf of those to whom he has pledged himself in covenant relationship. In the OT it was his chosen people Israel whom he elected to be his own and to whom he showed mercy (Ex 33:19; Is 54:10; 63:9). God persistently puts up with his disobedient and wayward people and continuously seeks them out to draw them back to himself. The psalmist describes God as a father who pities his children who revere and trust him (Ps 103:13). Hosea pictures God as a loving father who looks down from heaven with a yearning heart of compassion upon his rebellious and wayward people (Hos 11; cf. Jer 31:20). He also regards Israel as an unfaithful and adulterous wife whom God loves as a faithful husband in spite of her apostate and sinful condition (Hos 1–3; cf. Is 54:4-8). Isaiah depicts God as a mother who has compassion on the son of her womb (Is 49:15). These pictures reveal God's mercy in rich and different ways. Other dimensions include forgiveness and restoration to favor (2 Kgs 13:23; Is 54:8; Jl 2:18-32; Mi 7:18-20), and deliverance from distress and perils (Neh 9:19-21; Pss 40:11-17; 69:16-36; 79:8-9; Is 49:10).

Because of what Israel as a covenant nation had learned about the steadfast love and faithfulness of God, devout Jews instinctively lifted their voices in petition for divine mercy and forgiveness in times of need, eloquently expressed in the penitential psalms (Pss 6; 32; 38; 51; 102; 130; 143), as well as other OT passages (Ex 34:6; Neh 9:17; Pss 57; 79; 86; 123; Is 33:1-6; Dn 9:3-19; Jl 2:13). It is the remembrance of God's mercy that gives the repentant person the hope and assurance of divine favor and of reconciliation with the offended Lord.

In the NT a very descriptive Greek word is used for Jesus' mercy toward the needy (Mt 9:36; 14:14; 20:34). It expresses his pity and compassion by means of an intense verb literally translated "to be moved in one's bowels." The Hebrews regarded the bowels as the center of the affections, especially that of the most tender kindness. Jesus was described as being deeply moved in his inner feeling of benevolence toward the needy and spontaneously acting to relieve their suffering—to heal (Mt 20:34; Mk 1:41), to raise the dead (Lk 7:13), and to feed the hungry (Mt 15:32).

The OT concept of God's mercy expressed in his faithfulness to the covenant people is found also in the NT (Lk 1:50, 54, 72, 78; Eph 2:4; 1 Tm 1:2; 1 Pt 1:3; 2:10). The most characteristic use of mercy in the NT is that of God's provision of salvation for mankind in Jesus Christ (Rom 11:30-32; Eph 2:4). God is "the Father of mercies" (2 Cor 1:3), which he bestows on those who believe in his Son. It is because he is "so rich in mercy" that he saved those who are spiritually dead and doomed by their sins (Eph 2:4-6). It is out of God's mercy that one is forgiven and granted eternal life (1 Tm 1:13-16).

People's Responsibility to Show Mercy to Others
Because God has freely extended his mercy irrespective of worthiness or faithfulness, people are to respond by showing mercy to others, even though they do not deserve it or seek it. Indeed, people are commanded to be merciful, especially to the poor, the needy, widows, and orphans (Prv 14:31; 19:17; Mi 6:8; Zec 7:9-10; Col 3:12). God regards mercy more than the ritual sacrifice (Mt 9:13). God's mercy in Christ actually puts people under obligation to act toward others as God himself has acted toward them. The Lord made mercy a foundation for his teaching (Mt 5:7; 9:13; 12:7; 23:23; Lk 6:36; 10:37; Jas 3:17). His coming was anticipated and announced in the context of the mercy that would characterize his mission (Lk 1:50, 54, 72, 78).

Members of the Christian church are to show compassion and practical concern for each other. They are to give aid and relief, love and comfort to one another, as Christ freely gave to them in their need. The apostle James teaches the essential nature of such good works as being of the very essence of genuine faith (Jas 2:14-26). It was the mercy that the good Samaritan had toward the man who was beaten and robbed that was singled out by the Lord for special commendation (Lk 10:36-37). To be full of mercy is a distinguishing virtue of the citizens of the kingdom of heaven (Mt 5:7).

See also God, Being and Attributes of; Grace; Love.

MERCY SEAT* Gold slab placed on top of the ark of the covenant with cherubim attached to it on either end, termed the "mercy seat" in many English versions of the Bible (cf. Ex 25:17-22). The Hebrew word for which "mercy seat" is the translation is technically best rendered as "propitiatory," a term denoting the removal of wrath by the offering of a gift. The significance of this designation is found in the ceremony performed on the Day of Atonement, held once a year, when blood was sprinkled on the mercy seat to make atonement for the sins of the people of Israel (Lv 16). Because of the importance of this covering on the ark and the ceremony associated with it, the Holy of Holies in which the ark was housed in the temple is termed the "room for the mercy seat" in 1 Chronicles 28:11 (RSV). The term "mercy seat" came into English use from Luther's German rendering of the Hebrew term, which is difficult to translate appropriately from the Hebrew (cf. NIV "atonement cover" and NLT "Ark's cover").

The Mercy Seat—a lid or cover on the Ark of the Covenant

The mercy seat measured two and a half cubits (45 inches, or 114.3 centimeters) by one and a half cubits (27 inches, 68.6 centimeters). The cherubim on each end were also made of gold and faced each other with their wings spread upward over the ark. It was in this space above the ark that the Lord's presence with his people was localized in a special sense, and from which the Lord made his commandments known to Moses (Ex 25:22; cf. also Lv 16:2). Because of the close association of the Lord's presence with the space above the ark, he is said to be enthroned between the cherubim (1 Sm 4:4; 2 Sm 6:2). The ark itself contained the tables of stone inscribed with the Ten Commandments that summarized the covenantal obligations of the Israelites to their divine King. When the children of Israel fell short of their covenant obligations by sinning against God and breaking his commands, the blood of the sacrifice sprinkled on the mercy seat made atonement for their sin and reconciled them with God.

The propitiatory or mercy seat points forward to Jesus, who is termed by Paul (Rom 3:25) the "means of propitiation" through faith in his blood for all who have sinned and fallen short of the glory of God. Here in Romans 3:25 the Greek term translated "propitiation" is the same Greek word consistently used in the Septuagint and in Hebrews 9:5 to translate the Hebrew word for mercy seat in the OT.

See also Ark of the Covenant; Propitiation; Tabernacle; Temple.

MERED Ezrah's son from Judah's tribe, who had two wives. One wife, Bithiah, was the daughter of Pharaoh, and one was a Jewess (1 Chr 4:17-18).

MEREMOTH
1. Priest, son of Uriah, grandson of Hakkoz (Ezr 8:33; Neh 3:4, 21). The family of Hakkoz was unable to prove its descent; therefore, they were excluded from the priesthood. Meremoth appears to be an exception. He weighed silver and gold (a priestly function [Ezr 8:24-30]), repaired part of the Jerusalem wall (Neh 3:4, 21), and sealed the covenant (10:5).
2. Priest and Bani's son, who severed ties with his foreign wife and children at Ezra's request (Ezr 10:36).
3. Priest who returned from Babylon with Zerubbabel (Neh 12:3) and established the house of priests called Meraioth in Nehemiah 12:15 (though some identify the two references as the same person).

MERES One of the seven princes of Persia and Media who acted as personal adviser to King Ahasuerus (Est 1:14).

MERIBAH
1. Noun meaning "strife," named for a place at Horeb, near Rephidim (Wadi Feiran), where Israel contended with Moses for water near the beginning of the wilderness wanderings (Ex 17:7). This is the place probably alluded to in Deuteronomy 33:8 and Psalm 95:8, and is alternately called Massah.
2. Another place, near Kadesh-barnea in the wilderness of Zin, where Israel also quarreled with Moses for water, and God again provided it from a rock (Nm 20:13, 24; 27:14); alternately called Meribath-kadesh in Deuteronomy 32:51. This episode took place toward the close of the desert wanderings. The waters of Meribah were waters of contention. Here God's anger was provoked against Moses and Aaron because they did not listen to him and sanctify him before Israel. Instead of speaking to the rock as God commanded, Moses—angered at Israel's hardness of heart—struck the rock twice with his rod. The psalmist records that here God tested Israel (Ps 81:7), and Israel's subsequent rebellion prodded Moses to sin (106:32). Meribah-kadesh is mentioned as a place on Israel's southern border (Ez 47:19; 48:28).

See also Massah and Meribah.

MERIBAH-KADESH, MERIBATH-KADESH*
Alternate names for Kadesh-barnea (Dt 32:51; Ez 47:19; 48:28), a place for lengthy encampment by the Israelites during the wilderness wanderings. *See* Kadesh, Kadesh-barnea.

MERIBBAAL Original name for Mephibosheth, the handicapped son of Jonathan (1 Chr 8:34; 9:40). The name means "Baal contends" and is displaced by the later name (Mephibosheth, meaning "idol breaker") in 2 Samuel 4:4 and 9:6. The substitution of *bosheth* ("shame") for *baal* ("lord") was not uncommon when the term acquired its idolatrous connotation (cf. 2 Sm 11:21). *See* Mephibosheth #1.

MERODACH* Hebrew pronunciation of Marduk, the chief Babylonian deity. *See* Marduk.

MERODACH-BALADAN Name meaning "Marduk has given a son!" Second Kings 20:12-19 and Isaiah 39 present a parallel account of Merodach-baladan, son of Baladan, king of Babylon, sending envoys to King Hezekiah of Judah.

Shalmaneser V, king of Assyria, captured Samaria in 722 BC and threatened King Hezekiah in Jerusalem but then died within a year's time. Sargon II succeeded him in 722 BC. At that time Merodach-baladan, living south of Babylon in the land called Bit-Yakin, formed an alliance with the Elamites and seized the throne of Babylon, referred to as the second jewel of the Assyrian crown. Sargon II immediately made efforts to regain Babylon as a province in the Assyrian Empire. He must not have been successful initially, for Merodach-baladan reigned over Babylon for 10 years. In 710 BC Sargon succeeded in defeating him and captured the Babylonian fortresses. Merodach-baladan escaped. After Sargon died in 705 BC, Merodach-baladan, in 703 BC, was able to recapture and hold the throne of Babylon for a short period. It is considered most plausible that during this short reign Merodach-baladan sent envoys to Hezekiah in Jerusalem, as he also is thought to have sent them to Edom, Moab, Ammon, and others, seeking to form an alliance against Assyria. The Arabian desert between Babylon and Palestine made such an alliance ineffective, and the new king of Assyria, Sennacherib, thoroughly destroyed Merodach-baladan and then turned to the nations on Palestinian soil.

Isaiah rebuked Hezekiah for receiving the envoys from Babylon, the province that had broken away from the Assyrian Empire and that in a very short time was again forced into the Assyrian Empire. In Isaiah's rebuke lies the prediction that Babylon would become the invading and despoiling nation in the future. Hezekiah, knowing Assyria's power and Babylon's inability to cope with it at that time, felt quite safe as far as Babylon was concerned (2 Kgs 20:19).

MEROM*, Waters of Site of Joshua's victory over Jabin, king of Hazor, and his allies, mentioned only twice in the Bible (Jos 11:5-7). Jabin's allies included Jobab, the king of Madon, and the kings of Shimron, Achshaph, and the northern hill country, as well as those of the lowland south of the Sea of Galilee. The site of the battle is not clear but a likely place for "the waters of Merom" is near the foot of Har Merom (on modern Israeli maps), or on older maps, Jabel Marun—the highest mountain in Israel (3,962 feet, or 1,207.1 meters). Near the base of the mountain is the town of Merom, where several roads leading into northern Galilee converge. It is on the road between Hazor and Acco on the coast; hence, it was a convenient place for Joshua's enemies to rendezvous. Merom is about eight miles (12.9 kilometers) southwest of Hazor. The "waters of Merom," therefore, would be the springs that emerge from the mountain to flow down Wadi Leimun into the Sea of Galilee. Merom is mentioned in Egyptian texts of the second millennium BC associated with the campaigns of Thutmose III. The Assyrian monarch Tiglath-pileser III also reported his expedition into this region in 733–732 BC, at the time when he conquered Damascus. The allied forces defeated by Joshua fled northwest, in the direction of Sidon, suggesting an attack by Joshua from the southeast, from the area west of the Sea of Galilee, the natural approach from the south.

MERONOTH The hometown of Jehdeiah (1 Chr 27:30) and Jadon (Neh 3:7).

MEROZ Town in northern Palestine whose inhabitants were cursed for not assisting Deborah and Barak in their war against Sisera and the Canaanites (Jgs 5:23).

MESECH* KJV spelling of Meshech, Noah's grandson, in Psalm 120:5. *See* Meshech #1.

MESHA (Person)
1. King of Moab in the ninth century BC whose name is derived from a root meaning "to save or deliver." According to 2 Kings 3:4-5, Mesha was a sheep breeder who paid heavy tribute to Israel during the time of Ahab but rebelled after Ahab's death (2 Kgs 1:1). Later, Jehoram the son of Ahab joined with Jehoshaphat of Judah and the king of Edom in an attempt to reestablish hegemony over Moab. When the battle went against the Moabites, Mesha took his eldest son and offered him as a human sacrifice upon the wall of the city to the Moabite god Chemosh (3:27).
2. Caleb's son and the father of Ziph (1 Chr 2:42). In the Greek text the latter part of this verse appears to say that Mesha was the father of Hebron, though the Hebrew text here substitutes the name Mareshah for Mesha. The RSV (following the Septuagint) reads Mareshah in both places. *See* Mareshah (Person) #1.
3. Benjamite and one of the sons of Shaharaim born by Hodesh in the land of Moab (1 Chr 8:9).

MESHA (Place) Place in southern Arabia defining the western boundary of the territory in which the descendants of Joktan settled (Gn 10:30). Its location is unknown. Some suggest that Mesha was a seaport town situated along the eastern shores of the Red Sea in the vicinity of what is modern Yemen; others place it along the Persian Gulf's northwestern banks near the region of Mesene.

MESHACH One of the three companions of the prophet Daniel who was thrown into the fiery furnace (Dn 1:7; 2:49; 3:12-30). *See* Shadrach, Meshach, and Abednego.

MESHECH
1. Son of Japheth and Noah's grandson (Gn 10:2). His descendants are usually mentioned in connection with Tubal, Gog, or Magog (Ps 120:5; Ez 27:13; 32:26; 38:2-3; 39:1). They are called Muski in Assyrian records and inhabited the mountains north of Assyria during the reigns of Tiglath-pileser I (1115–1102 BC), Shalmaneser III (859–824 BC), and Sargon (722–705 BC). The people of Meshech are characterized as aggressive and pagan, traders in bronze and slaves with Tyre.

2. Shem's son according to 1 Chronicles 1:17, but rendered Mash in the parallel passage in Genesis 10:23. The latter is generally accepted.

MESHELEMIAH Korahite Levite, Kore's son from the house of Asaph, and a gatekeeper of the sanctuary with his sons in the time of David (1 Chr 9:21; 26:1-2, 9); alternately called Shelemiah in 1 Chronicles 26:14.

MESHEZABEEL*, MESHEZABEL
1. Ancestor of Meshullam who helped repair the Jerusalem wall (Neh 3:4).
2. Political leader who signed Ezra's covenant of faithfulness to God during the postexilic period (Neh 10:21).
3. Father of Pethahiah, an adviser to King Artaxerxes regarding the people in Judah (Neh 11:24).

MESHILLEMITH Alternate spelling of Meshillemoth in 1 Chronicles 9:12. *See* Meshillemoth #2.

MESHILLEMOTH
1. Father of Berekiah, a chief of Ephraim (2 Chr 28:12).
2. Ancestor of the postexilic priest Amashsai (Neh 11:13); alternately spelled Meshillemith in 1 Chronicles 9:12.

MESHOBAB Prince of Simeon's tribe in the days of Hezekiah, who, with 12 other princes, moved to Gedor, dispossessed its pagan people (the Meunim), and settled his family there (1 Chr 4:34).

MESHULLAM
1. Forefather of Shaphan, the royal secretary to King Josiah of Judah (2 Kgs 22:3).
2. Zerubbabel's son and a descendant of David (1 Chr 3:19).
3. Gadite leader registered during the reigns of Jotham, king of Judah (950–932 BC), and Jeroboam II, king of Israel (993–953 BC; 1 Chr 5:13).
4. Benjamite and a descendant of Elpaal (1 Chr 8:17).
5. Benjamite and the father of Sallu, a resident in Jerusalem during the postexilic period (1 Chr 9:7; Neh 11:7).
6. Benjamite and the son of Shephatiah, who resided in Jerusalem during the postexilic period (1 Chr 9:8).
7. Priest, the son of Zadok and the father of Hilkiah, whose descendants served in Jerusalem's sanctuary during the postexilic era (1 Chr 9:11; Neh 11:11). He is probably identical with Shallum in 1 Chronicles 6:12-13.
8. Priest, the son of Meshillemith and a forefather of Adaiah. Adaiah served in Jerusalem's sanctuary during the postexilic era (1 Chr 9:12).
9. Kohathite Levite who was appointed to oversee the repair of the temple during King Josiah's reign (2 Chr 34:12).
10. One of the Jewish leaders whom Ezra sent to Iddo at Casiphia to gather Levites and temple servants for the caravan of Jews returning to Palestine from Babylonia (Ezr 8:16).
11. One who opposed Ezra's suggestion that the sons of Israel should divorce the foreign women they had married since returning to Palestine from exile (Ezr 10:15).
12. Bani's son, who was encouraged by Ezra to divorce his foreign wife during the postexilic era (Ezr 10:29).
13. Berekiah's son, who rebuilt a section of the Jerusalem wall during the days of Nehemiah (Neh 3:4, 30). His daughter married Jehohanan, the son of Tobiah the Ammonite (6:18).

14. Besodeiah's son, who with Joiada repaired the Old Gate in the Jerusalem wall (Neh 3:6).

15. One of the men who stood to Ezra's left when Ezra read the law to the people (Neh 8:4).

16. One of the priests who set his seal on the covenant of Ezra (Neh 10:7).

17. One of the leaders of Israel who set his seal on the covenant of Ezra (Neh 10:20).

18. Head of Ezra's priestly family during the days of Joiakim, the high priest, in postexilic Jerusalem (Neh 12:13).

19. Head of Ginnethon's priestly family during the days of Joiakim (Neh 12:16).

20. One of the gatekeepers during the days of the high priest Joiakim (Neh 12:25); perhaps identifiable with Shallum in 1 Chronicles 9:17.

21. One of the princes of Judah who participated in the dedication of the Jerusalem wall during the postexilic era (Neh 12:33).

MESHULLEMETH Mother of Amon, king of Judah (642–640 BC) and the daughter of Haruz of Jotbah (2 Kgs 21:19).

MESOBAITE* KJV spelling of Mezobaite, a title given to Jaasiel, in 1 Chronicles 11:47. *See* Mezobaite.

MESOPOTAMIA Name given by the Greeks to the land between the Tigris and Euphrates Rivers, an area today called al-Jazira, "the island," by the Arabs. Mesopotamia, which means literally "between the rivers," is applied to the land between and near those rivers down to the Persian Gulf. Much of it is included in Iraq, but some of it is in Syria, and a small part in Turkey.

Mesopotamia played a significant role in OT history. Much of the tightly compressed account of Genesis 1–11 was centered here. The Garden of Eden was situated in this area, for two of the rivers of Genesis 2:10-14 are identified as the Euphrates and the Tigris.

The prehistoric cultures of Mesopotamia are unknown. The historical periods are labeled by the names of various cities that dominated them, such as Ur and Isin-Larsa, or by the names of dynasties established in those places, for example, Ur III.

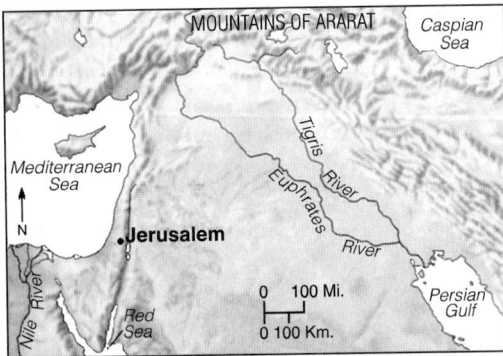

Mesopotamia: The Land between the Tigris and Euphrates

The southernmost part of Mesopotamia is known as Sumer and was populated by the Sumerians, who had a distinctive culture and a non-Semitic language, which was written in cuneiform script, as were most of the other languages of Mesopotamia. Farther north was the district called Akkad, which was also named Agade and had a Semitic population. Still farther north, along the

Tigris, was the land that became Assyria, while to the far west was Syria, or Aram, and in between was Mitanni (c. 1400 BC). As portions of Mesopotamia slipped from hand to hand, various sections became parts of different empires, such as Hittite, Assyrian, Babylonian, Persian, Greek or Hellenistic, and Roman.

In the Hebrew OT the name for Mesopotamia is Aram-naharaim, "Aram of the two rivers." Abraham sent his servant, Eliezer, to Aram-naharaim to find a wife for Isaac (Gn 24:10). In this context it has been suggested that the two rivers were the Euphrates and the Khabur. The account of the adventures of Jacob in this area does not use the term Aram-naharaim but employs instead the name Paddan-aram, "the field [or garden] of Aram" (28:2).

Balaam, the son of Beor, was from Pethor in Mesopotamia (Dt 23:4). During the period of the judges, Cushan-rishathaim, king of Mesopotamia, oppressed Israel for eight years, but the Lord brought deliverance through Othniel (Jgs 3:8-10).

When the Ammonites expected David to invade their territory because they had insulted his ambassadors, they hired chariotry from Mesopotamia and elsewhere to bolster their forces (1 Chr 19:6).

In the NT Mesopotamia is mentioned only twice. People from Mesopotamia were present on the day of Pentecost (Acts 2:9). Stephen, in his defense before the Sanhedrin, states that Abraham lived in Mesopotamia before he lived in Haran (Acts 7:2; see Gn 11:31).

MESSENGER One who carries a message, a herald. The word "messenger" is used in the Bible in four ways.

1. The word is used of messengers carrying messages from one person to another. Such messengers might bring news (2 Sm 11:22), requests or demands (1 Sm 11:3; 16:19), or act as envoys of one nation to another (Is 37:9). In the NT we read of messengers of the churches (2 Cor 8:23; Phil 2:25). The blessing of a good messenger is spoken of in Proverbs 25:13: "Faithful messengers are as refreshing as snow in the heat of summer. They revive the spirit of their employer" (NLT).

2. The word is used of messengers bringing messages from God. Israel was intended to be God's messenger but often showed herself blind and deaf (Is 42:19). Prophets (Hg 1:13) and priests (Mal 2:7) were God's messengers. God sent many such messengers to his people, even though they were often unheeded (2 Chr 36:15-16). In Malachi 3:1 we have the prophecy of a special messenger, "Look! I am sending my messenger, and he will prepare the way before me. Then the Lord you are seeking will suddenly come to his Temple. The messenger of the covenant, whom you look for so eagerly, is surely coming" (NLT). This verse is quoted in the NT in Matthew 11:10, Mark 1:2, and Luke 7:27 as fulfilled in John the Baptist.

3. In both the OT and NT the most common word for "messenger" is also that for "angel." God's angels are distinctively his messengers. *See* Angel.

4. The word is used in a metaphorical sense, as in Proverbs 16:14, "The wrath of a king is as messengers of death" (KJV), and in 2 Corinthians 12:7, where Paul's constant physical ailment is called "a messenger from Satan to torment" him.

MESSIAH Title derived from the Hebrew, *mashiach*, a verbal adjective meaning "anointed one." Along with its NT equivalent, *christos* (Christ), it refers to an act of consecration whereby an individual is set apart to serve God and then anointed with oil. The verbal root (mashach) conveys this idea as well.

Israel's practice of ceremonially anointing with oil is present in several contexts. Priests were regularly anointed prior to their divinely given service at the altar of sacrifice (Lv 4:3). While there is evidence for a literal anointing of prophets (1 Kgs 19:16), this does not appear to have been a standard practice. The anointing of Saul and David by Samuel established the act as a significant prerequisite for Hebrew kings before they assumed their positions of royal leadership. The king was especially considered to be the Lord's anointed and as such was viewed to hold a secure position before men (1 Sm 12:14; 2 Sm 19:21) and God (Pss 2:2; 20:6). Along with numerous messianic prophecies, these proceedings helped inform the Jews of the Anointed One, par excellence, who would eventually come to bring salvation to Israel.

Concluding the 13 articles of Hebraic faith attributed to Moses Maimonides (13th century AD) is the statement still found in many Hebrew prayer books: "I believe with a perfect heart that the Messiah will come; and although his coming be delayed, I will still wait patiently for his speedy appearance."

Messiah in the Old Testament Jewish hope for the advent of the Messiah developed dynamically from the period of David's reign, when it was prophesied that his kingdom would endure to the end of time (2 Sm 7:16). Israel was told that, through David's descendants, his throne would exert a never-ending dominion over all the earth (2 Sm 22:48-51; Jer 33). It is with this aspect of messianic salvation that Jewish minds have traditionally been preoccupied (cf. Acts 1:6).

Among Orthodox rabbis there has never been a lack of conjecture respecting the details of the Messiah's ministry. At one time the rabbis applied no less than 456 passages of Scripture to his person and salvation. Preoccupation with the Messiah is evident in the tractate Sanhedrin (Babylonian Talmud), where passages state that the world was created for him and that all the prophets prophesied of his days (Sanhedrin 98b, 99a). By and large, Orthodoxy still retains its time-worn belief in the Messiah's reign in Jerusalem, the rebuilding of the temple, and the reestablishment of both priesthood and sacrifice.

While later Judaism looked for the Messiah as an eschatological figure who will reign at the end of time, modern Jewish thought has largely jettisoned the traditional notion of a personal Messiah in favor of belief in a messianic age. Prevalent liberal Judaism envisions the world ultimately perfected through the influence of the twin Judaic ideals of justice and compassion. Such conviction, ignoring the plight of fallen humans and the teaching of Scripture, substitutes humanistic thinking for miraculous heavenly intervention.

While the Messiah's origin is linked firmly to the house of David (2 Sm 7:14; Hos 3:5), the promise for a Messiah was given long before David lived. In fact, the hope for the Messiah is implicit in the first promise of the establishment of the kingdom of God. Addressed to Satan, Genesis 3:15 declares that God will place hostility between the serpent and the woman until, in the fullness of time, the "seed" of the woman inflicts a fatal blow to the head of the serpent.

The nature of messianic prophecy is progressive; each prophecy casts more light on the subject. This occurs, for example, respecting the concept of the "seed": Messiah is to be born of a woman (Gn 3:15), through the line of Shem (9:26) and specifically through Abraham (22:18).

Yet even as late as Genesis 22:18, the "seed" is not clearly presented as a person, since zerah (seed) may indicate a singular or plural object. Still less apparent in these early stages of messianic prophecy is the nature of the "bruising" that is to occur. Yet the idea of the Messiah being crushed for sin is implicit in the Genesis pronouncement, as is the violence associated with that act. Chief among the messianic prophets, Isaiah gives full range to the axiom that the Anointed One must endure extensive suffering (Is 53:1). Under the figure "the Servant of the Lord," four "servant songs" delineate the mission of the future deliverer (Is 42:1-7; 49:1-9; 50:4-11; 52:13–53:12). While it is true that Isaiah does not explicitly link the title Messiah with the Servant of the Lord, identifying both figures as one and the same person is justifiable. Both figures are uniquely anointed (61:1); each brings light to the Gentiles (55:4; cf. 49:6); neither is pretentious in his first appearance (7:14-15; 11:1; cf. 42:3; 53:1); and the title of Davidic "branch" rests upon them both (11:1-4). Equally significant are the dual facts of their humiliation and exaltation (49:7; 52:13-15). Jewish scholars of the early Christian era in the Aramaic Targum on the prophets paraphrase Isaiah 42:1, "Behold my Servant Messiah" and begin Isaiah 53, "Behold my Servant Messiah will prosper." While Cyrus may be spoken of as "anointed," no final salvific work is attributed to him (45:1-5). Israel, although elect and loved by God (41:8), is ill-equipped as God's servant to bring his redeeming work to mankind (42:18). The collapse of David's dynasty points eloquently to Israel's need for an anointed monarch who will heal the apostasy and disobedience (Ex 33:5; Hos 4:1). More and more, OT history presents Israel's comprehensive moral failure. Her problem, which she shares with mankind, can only be solved by the making of a covenant whose surety and focal point is both a personal Savior and sovereign Lord (Jer 31:31-34). The advent of such a champion lives in the recorded promise of a shoot from the stump of Jesse's fallen tree, who will bring the light of life to God's benighted people (Is 9:2; 11:1).

It is difficult to get away from the idea that the concept of servanthood and lowliness belongs within the sphere of royalty (Zec 9:9). The concept of the Messiah filling the complementary offices of priest and king is incontrovertible (Ps 110:1-4); a suffering priest-king is far less obvious. Some among the Talmudic writers apparently recognized the likelihood that the Messiah would have to suffer. In the Babylonian Talmud, tractate Sanhedrin 98b, the Messiah is said to bear sicknesses and pain. Among the prayers for the Day of Atonement may be found the words of Eleazar ben Qalir (perhaps as late as AD 1000): "Our righteous Messiah has departed from us; we are horror-stricken, and there is none to justify us. Our iniquities and the yoke of our transgressions he carries, and is wounded for our transgressions. He bears on his shoulders our sins to find pardon for our iniquities. May we be healed by his stripes." In a similar vein Rabbi Eliyya de Vidas writes, "The meaning of 'He was wounded for our transgressions, bruised for our iniquities,' is that since the Messiah bears our iniquities, which produce the effect of His being bruised, it follows that whosoever will not admit that the Messiah thus suffers for our iniquities must endure and suffer for them himself." For all this, it is highly doubtful that anyone imagined the Messiah would accomplish his salvational work by means of his own death (cf. Is 53:12). When rabbinic speculation failed to satisfactorily harmonize the paradoxical facts of humiliation and exaltation, some hypothesized that God would send a Messiah to suffer as well as a Messiah to reign. Biblically, it is evident that the

Anointed One's terrible ordeal of suffering is but the necessary prelude to infinite glory. He is pictured not only as a great king (52:13; 53:12) but also as humble (53:2), humiliated (52:14), rejected (53:3), and bearing the consequences of mankind's rebellion (vv 5-6). Yet he is raised up to intercede for, and richly bless, his people (v 12). The Messiah, having accomplished that full obedience that Adam and Israel failed to achieve, will bring Israel and the nations back to God (42:18-19; 49:3, 6).

The writings of Daniel contain important messianic data. Daniel is unique in that he boldly speaks of "Messiah the Prince" (Dn 9:25), identifies him as the "Son of Man" (7:13), and says he suffers ("cut off," 9:26). This statement of the cutting off (i.e., death) of the Messiah makes possible his work of atonement (9:24). The doctrine of a vicarious substitutionary atonement is the only doctrine of atonement found in the Bible (cf. Lv 17:11). Israel understood that to bear sin meant enduring the consequences, or penalty, for sin (cf. Nm 14:33). The same penal substitution is evident in the working principle of the Messiah's atoning sacrifice. He is the victim's substitute to whom is transferred the suffering due the sinner. The penalty having been thus borne vicariously, the supplicant is fully pardoned.

Psalm 22:1 records the plaintive cry of the Messiah bearing man's penalty for sin (cf. Mt 27:46) as he becomes sin on behalf of his people (2 Cor 5:21). Yet his cry, "My God," indicates an intimate relationship that cannot be radically severed. Once again the motif of messianic humiliation prior to great exaltation is in view (Ps 22:27). In the so-called "royal psalms" (e.g., 2; 72; 110) it is the priestly intercessor who is also ordained to function as monarch and judge.

Jeremiah brings the portrait a step further. The one who will enable humans to enter into a salvational covenant with God conveys God's imputed righteousness: the Messiah, God's righteous branch, becomes "the Lord our Righteousness." Paradoxically, under the law no one could be crucified who was not guilty of sin (Dt 21:22). But it is Christ the righteous one who was crucified, thereby forever undermining any supposed legalistic confidence (Dt 21:23; Gal 3:13). More than forgiven, believers are deemed righteous in him (Jer 23:5-6).

While the birthplace of the Messiah was well established (Mi 5:2), his deity was a hotly contested matter. Although few in ancient Israel disputed the belief in a superhuman Messiah, it is doubtful that anyone imagined him to be "God with us" in the fullest sense of the expression (cf. Heb 1:3).

Messiah in the New Testament The NT writers present the picture that he who was the child of supernatural origins (Is 7:14; Mi 5:2) carried the full weight of divinity (Is 9:6; Phil 2:6; Col 1:19). He is the Son of God, worthy to receive the worship of all people (Ps 45:6-7; cf. Heb 1:8-9).

The Jews of first-century Palestine knew that the messianic promise would be fulfilled in the coming of one like Moses (Dt 18:18). Parallels between Jesus and Moses are abundant. As mediators, innovators, and propagators of new phases of spiritual life for the people, they are unexcelled. Specifically, both are miraculously spared in infancy (Ex 2; Mt 2:13-23); both renounce a royal court for the sake of serving the people of God (Phil 2:5-8; Heb 11:24-28); both exhibit intense compassion for others (Nm 27:17; Mt 9:36); both commune "face to face" with God (Ex 34:29-30; 2 Cor 3:7); and each mediates a covenant of redemption (Dt 29:1; Heb 8:6-7). But, as Luther observes, "Christ is no Moses." In the final analysis Moses

is but a household servant; the Messiah is the maker and master of all things (Heb 3:3-6; cf. Jn 1:1-2, 18).

Family genealogies are important in Scripture. Rabbis agreed upon the absolute necessity of the Messiah's Davidic lineage based on Hosea 3:5 and Jeremiah 30:9. The angelic announcement immediately establishes the correct lineage for Jesus (Lk 1:32-33; cf. 2:4), as does Matthew's (Mt 1:1-17). The Lukan list, like that of Matthew, sets forth the exclusive kingly descent verifying Jesus as Messiah (Lk 3:23-38). Although variations occur between the two genealogies, there is a firm solidarity emphasizing an ancestry within the unique messianic stock. Fully aware of the messianic focus of Scripture (Jn 5:46; 8:56), Jesus acknowledged himself to be the Christ on numerous occasions. He accepted the title from blind Bartimaeus (Mk 10:46-48); from the crowds when he entered Jerusalem (Mt 21:9); from the children at the temple (v 15); and in other contexts as well (Mt 16:16-18; Mk 14:61-62; Lk 4:21; Jn 4:25-26). Nonetheless, he warned his disciples not to broadcast his mighty acts as Messiah prior to his resurrection (Mt 17:9; cf. Lk 9:20-21). Owing to the commonly held (but false) notion that the Messiah's role was primarily that of a political liberator, Jesus actually avoided use of that term and preferred to identify himself as "the Son of Man." It was by no means assumed that both designations referred to the same person (cf. Mk 14:61-62). Borrowing essentially from Daniel's vision of a heavenly conqueror (Dn 7:13-14), Jesus consistently employed this less-known title and filled it with the true character and scope of messianic salvation. Jesus' teaching in this regard enabled his disciples to correct their erroneous views concerning his mission (Mt 16:21-23). In the fullness of time they would come to see him not only as Messiah but also as the theme of the entire OT (Mt 5:17; Lk 24:27, 44; Jn 5:39; cf. Heb 10:7). When Jesus expounded the Scriptures beginning with the Torah (Lk 24:27), he did so as the living exegesis of God, the Word made flesh (Jn 1:14, 18). Legitimate messianic exposition is found in a host of texts, such as Psalms 2; 16; 22; 40; 110; Isaiah 7:14; 9:6; 11:1; 40:10-11; 50:6; 52:13–53:12; 61:1; 63:1-6; Jeremiah 23:5-6; 33:14-16; Ezekiel 34:23; 37:25; Daniel 9:24-27; Hosea 11:1; Micah 5:2; Zechariah 9:9; 11:13; 12:10; 13:7; Malachi 3:1; 4:2.

The messiahship of Jesus is firmly proclaimed by all four evangelists (Mt 1:1; Mk 1:1; Lk 24:26; Jn 20:31). Peter on Pentecost, Philip before the Ethiopian eunuch, and Apollos in open debate all argue convincingly that Jesus is the Messiah (Acts 2:36; 8:35; 28:28). Peter says he was "made" both Lord and Christ (2:36), signifying that the resurrection rightfully confirms him as such. Similarly, the apostle Paul speaks of Jesus' resurrection as a patent declaration of his inalienable right to the title (Rom 1:4). For the ex-Pharisee and former persecutor of the church, "Jesus the Christ" is the very heart and soul of Paul's preaching. Nothing is worthy to be compared to the glory of the Messiah; everything pales by comparison (Phil 3:5-10). The apostle's all-consuming passion is for others to know the fullness of God in the person of his only Son (Eph 3:14-19).

The Holy Spirit in Scripture speaks of Jesus with wide-ranging appellatives—Holy One, Judge, Righteous One, King, Son of God, and Lord—but these are not exhaustive. In him all the lines of messianic prediction converge; he is the touchstone whereby their validity is firmly established. The Lord Jesus Christ is himself the heart and substance of that covenant through which sinful people may be reconciled to a holy God (Is 42:6; Jn 14:6). That Jesus is the Messiah of Israel, God incarnate, exhaustively fulfills prophecy, type, and symbol—all shadows of his coming. Therefore, all should trust in him, the source of all grace, the only abiding treasure (Mt 12:21; Jn 1:16-17; Col 2:3). Anointed as prophet, he leads us into all truth (Jn 6:14; 7:16); as priest he intercedes for us (Heb 7:21); and as king he reigns over us (Phil 2:9-10).

See also Atonement; Branch; Christology; Jesus Christ, Life and Teachings of; Redeemer, Redemption; Son of God; Son of Man.

METALLURGY* Science and technology of metals. See Coppersmith; Goldsmith; Ironsmith; Minerals and Metals; Silversmith.

METHEG-AMMAH* Place (whose name means "Bridle of the Mother City") conquered by David (2 Sm 8:1, NLT mg). Most likely it refers to the Philistine capital, Gath (1 Chr 18:1). The capital city was often referred to as the "mother" city, and surrounding cities as "daughters"; the "bridle" represented control or authority.

METHUSAEL* KJV spelling of Methushael, Mehujael's son, in Genesis 4:18. See Methushael.

METHUSELAH Son of Enoch, Lamech's father, and the grandfather of Noah through Seth's line (Gn 5:21-27; 1 Chr 1:3). Living 969 years, Methuselah is the oldest recorded person in the Bible. His lineage is included in Luke's genealogy of Christ (Lk 3:37).

See also Genealogy of Jesus Christ.

METHUSHAEL Mehujael's son and the father of Lamech in Cain's line (Gn 4:18).

MEUNIM, MEUNITES People living in Edom (Mt Seir, 1 Chr 4:41-42) who were dispossessed of their rich pasturelands by the Simeonites. Later, Meunites from Edom attacked Judah's King Jehoshaphat (2 Chr 20:1); later still, King Uzziah of Judah defeated them (26:7). Their original land possession, association with Arabs and Ammonites, and prolonged hostility recall Judges 10:11-12, where "Maonites" are named oppressors of Israel. This word, by Hebrew rules of vocalization, could well become "Meunites," suggesting Maon (Ma'in, Maan) in the Edomite area south of the Dead Sea as their home.

The Meunim are listed among the families of temple servants returning to Jerusalem following the exile (Ezr 2:50; Neh 7:52). However, because ancient enemies seem unlikely temple servants, some suggest that these Meunim were descendants of the Caleb clan within Judah to whom another town named Maon, west of the Dead Sea and south of Hebron, was allotted (Jos 15:20, 55). This Maon gave David refuge and another wife (1 Sm 23:24-28; 25).

This reconstruction involving two groups, two Maons, and temple servants with very foreign names, is tentative. An alternate view holds that hostile foreigners, formerly captured to become temple slaves (cf. Jos 9:7; Ez 44:6-8), attained freedom during the exile and temple-guild status on returning.

See also Maon (Place).

MEZAHAB Matred's father and the grandfather of Mehetabel, the wife of the Edomite king Hadar (or Hadad) (Gn 36:39; 1 Chr 1:50).

MEZOBAITE* Designation for Jaasiel, one of David's "mighty men" (1 Chr 11:47). The meaning is unknown, though some suggest "from Zobah" (NLT).

MEZUZAH* A Hebrew word, used about 20 times in the OT, that means the upright framework of a door or gate. The blood of the Passover lamb was smeared on the "mezuzah" of the house (Ex 12:7, 22-23).

In Deuteronomy 6:9 and 11:20, the Hebrews were instructed to write the commandments on the doors of the houses and on the city gates. This practice is still followed by the Jewish community. Every Jewish home has a small metal or wooden container mounted about shoulder-height on the doorpost of the house. This container, which itself became known as a mezuzah, has inside a small piece of parchment inscribed on one side with the words of Deuteronomy 6:4-9 and 11:13-21, and on the other side with the word *Shaddai*, the Hebrew name for God Almighty. On the outside the mezuzah has embossed the Hebrew letter *shin*, the first letter of the name *Shaddai*. Every time a pious Jew enters or leaves the house, he or she will touch the mezuzah and then kiss the fingers as he repeats to himself the words of Psalm 121:8: "The LORD keeps watch over you as you come and go, both now and forever" (NLT).

MIAMIN*
1. KJV rendering of Mijamin, Parosh's son, in Ezra 10:25. See Mijamin #2.
2. KJV rendering of Mijamin, a postexilic priest, in Nehemiah 12:5. See Mijamin #4.

MIBHAR Warrior among David's mighty men, who were known as "the thirty" (1 Chr 11:38).

MIBSAM
1. One of Ishmael's sons and the founder of a tribe named after him (Gn 25:13; 1 Chr 1:29).
2. Shallum's son and the father of Mishma (1 Chr 4:25).

MIBZAR Chief of Edom (Gn 36:42; 1 Chr 1:53). The name means "fortress." Eusebius connects Mibzar with Mibsara, a large town in Edom.

MICA Common name interchangeable with Micah and probably a contracted form of Micaiah.

1. Mephibosheth's son. He shared in the fortunes of David's generosity to his father, and in Ziba's treachery (2 Sm 9:12).
2. Levite and Zicri's son from Asaph's clan (1 Chr 9:15), who performed musical service in the temple. He appears to have been one of the exiled priests whose son Mattaniah was among the first group of returning exiles (also called "the son of Zabdi," Neh 11:17, 22, and Micaiah, the son of Zaccur, 12:35).
3. One who set his seal on Ezra's covenant during the postexilic era (Neh 10:11).

MICAH (Person)
1. Ephraimite judge who had idols made and then hired a Levite to become his priest (Jgs 17–18).
2. Shimei's descendant from Reuben's tribe (1 Chr 5:5).
3. Alternate spelling of Mica, Mephibosheth's son and the great-grandson of King Saul, in 1 Chronicles 8:34-35; 9:40-41. See Mica #1.
4. KJV spelling of Mica, Zicri's son, in 1 Chronicles 9:15. See Mica #2.
5. Levite and Uzziel's son from Kohath's clan, whose temple responsibilities included care of the furniture and equipment (1 Chr 23:20; 24:24-25).
6. Alternate spelling of Micaiah, Acbor's father, in 2 Chronicles 34:20. See Micaiah #2.

7. Prophet and author of the OT book that bears his name (Mi 1:1). A native of Moresheth, a town about 21 miles (33.8 kilometers) southwest of Jerusalem, Micah prophesied to both northern and southern kingdoms during the reigns of Jotham, Ahaz, and Hezekiah (750–686 BC). According to Micah 1:9, he was still prophesying in 701 BC when the Assyrian armies under Sennacherib (cf. Is 36–37) besieged Jerusalem. About 100 years later, Micah is used as an example of an early prophet who predicted the destruction of Jerusalem (cf. Jer 26:16-19).

See also Micah, Book of; Prophet, Prophetess.

MICAH, Book of
Sixth in the order of the books of the 12 minor prophets.

PREVIEW
•Author
•Date
•Audience
•Background
•Purpose and Message
•Content

Author Micah 1:1 says that the word of the Lord came to Micah of Moresheth. Micah was God's spokesman to the people of his day. Micah is not called a prophet in his book. There is no account of God's call for him to be a prophet, but he does claim to be God's witness (v 2). Five times in the book some form of the messenger formula, "thus says the LORD," is used (2:3; 3:5; 4:6; 6:1, 9), asserting that the message is from God. Micah, like a true prophet, claims, "As for me, I am filled with power and the Spirit of the LORD. I am filled with justice and might, fearlessly pointing out Israel's sin and rebellion" (3:8, NLT).

Micah's name was common in ancient Israel. At least seven different individuals in the OT are called Micah or Michaiah. The prophet is mentioned by name only in Micah 1:1 and Jeremiah 26:18 in the OT.

The superscription of Micah (Mi 1:1) gives his hometown as Moresheth, which may be identified with the modern village of Tell el Judeideh about 25 miles (40.2 kilometers) southwest of Jerusalem on the road from Azekah to Lachish. Moresheth, in Micah's time, was a frontier village near the Philistine border city of Gath. As a border town, Moresheth often took the brunt of enemy attacks on Judah from the south and west (1:15). Such an attack may be reflected in verses 10-16, where 12 towns in southwest Judah are named as being in the path of an invader. Moresheth-gath is ninth in that list. Because Micah lived in this border town, he seems to have developed an international concern with "the peoples" (1:2; 4:1-5, 11; 5:7-15; 7:16-17). As a citizen of a small town, Micah could identify with peasants and small land holders who were often victims of foreign aggressors and of the politicians and greedy land grabbers in Jerusalem (2:1-4). Although Micah may have left Moresheth to live and preach in Jerusalem, he had harsh words for cities (1:5-6; 3:12; 4:10; 5:11, 14; 6:9).

Date The date for Micah's ministry was sometime during the reigns of three kings of Judah: Jotham (c. 750–735 BC), Ahaz (c. 735–715 BC), and Hezekiah (c. 715–686 BC). The maximum period covered by the reigns of these three kings was over 60 years (750–686 BC), but it is not likely that Micah was active as a prophet during all of that time. Jeremiah dates Micah's ministry in the reign of Hezekiah (Jer 26:18). Some of Micah's oracles seem to predate the fall of Samaria (Mi 1:2-7;

6:16), an event that took place in 722 BC. The Assyrians appear to be Israel's primary enemy in Micah's time (5:5-6), a situation that prevailed during the reigns of the three kings listed above. Some striking parallel passages between Micah and Isaiah (Mi 4:1-4; Is 2:2-4) and between Micah and Amos (Mi 6:10-11; Am 8:5-6) make it probable that Micah's ministry was in the last part of the eighth century BC.

Audience Micah's message was universal. It was addressed first in a broad sense to "all the people of the world" (Mi 1:2), but the focus narrows quickly to the capital cities of Jerusalem and Samaria (1:1). Other cities in Judah are the object of one oracle (1:10-16). A group of wealthy land grabbers (2:1), false prophets (2:6-11; 3:5-7), judges, prophets, priests, and dishonest merchants (3:1, 11; 6:10-12) are the objects of other messages.

Background In order to understand the book of Micah properly, one needs a knowledge of the Assyrian crisis in the history of ancient Israel. During the early part of the eighth century BC, the northern and southern kingdoms of Israel and Judah experienced a period of peace and prosperity under the long and stable reigns of Jeroboam II (793–753 BC) and Uzziah (792–740 BC). Radical changes in the economic structure occurred within Israel and Judah during this long period. There was a rise of cities and a new wealthy class. Commerce grew enormously. The rich got richer and abused their power over the poor, the priests, and the judges. A class system appeared that struck at the heart of OT covenant religion.

During the reigns of Jeroboam II and Uzziah, Israel and Judah were relatively free from outside intervention. But in 745 BC Tiglath-pileser III became king of Assyria and set out to create an empire. He captured Damascus in 732 BC and made vassals of the small states of Israel, Judah, and Philistia. Tiglath-pileser III died in 727 BC and was succeeded by Shalmaneser V. In 724 BC Hoshea, the last king of Israel, withheld tribute from Assyria and incurred the wrath of the Assyrians. Shalmaneser V began his siege of Samaria in 724 BC, but the people were not subdued until 722 BC. By that time, Sargon II was the king of Assyria. Many of the wealthy and influential people of Samaria were carried into captivity to Assyria (2 Kgs 15:29-30; 17:1-41). Judah did not escape the crisis. Although a fragmentary government of Judean kings was left in Jerusalem by the Assyrians, practically all of their liberties were taken away (2 Kgs 16:10). Judah never fully recovered politically nor religiously from the Assyrian crisis.

Purpose and Message The book of Micah is made up of about 20 separate sections or oracles. There is a variety of material in the book about different subjects, coming perhaps from different periods. With such variety in the book, it is difficult to speak of *the* message of the book. However, certain themes are prominent in the book, the most prominent being judgment. It is coming on Samaria (Mi 1:2-6) and on Jerusalem (3:9-12). It is coming on guilty land grabbers (2:3-5), on false prophets, corrupt judges, and hireling priests (3:5-12). Judgment is coming on the cheater, the violent, the liar, and the deceiver (6:9-12). Judgment is coming on the nations (4:11-13; 5:5-9, 15; 7:16-17). Judgment is due to sin (1:5). Sin takes many forms in Micah, ranging from idolatry (1:7; 5:13), to practicing the occult (5:12), to theft (6:11), to lying (6:12), to contempt for parents (7:6), to murder (7:2).

What is Micah's remedy for sin? For the nations it is a knowledge of and obedience to the ways of God (4:2). For Israel it is "to do what is right, to love mercy, and to walk humbly with your God" (6:8). All of this is possible because God pardons iniquity and is not always angry. He is a God of compassion who treads iniquities underfoot, casts sins into the depth of the sea, and keeps his covenant with Abraham (7:18-20). Micah caught a glimpse of the future kingdom of God when he saw that a future ruler of Israel would be born in Bethlehem. He will stand and feed his flock in the strength of the Lord. He will provide security because he will be great to the ends of the earth (5:2-4).

Content Some scholars divide the book into two parts. The first part (chs 1–5) is addressed primarily to the nations, while the second (chs 6–7) is addressed primarily to Israel. The first part ends with a threat of judgment on the nations (5:15) and the second ends with a hymn to the compassion of God. That outline seems too simple, however, and does not cover the diverse materials in the two parts. Other scholars divide the book into three parts: chapters 1–3 (judgment); chapters 4–5 (hope); and chapters 6–7 (judgment and hope). Again, this outline is too simple because all three sections contain both judgment and hope. Perhaps it is better to divide the book into three parts beginning with chapters 1, 3, and 6. Each section begins with words of judgment (1:2–2:11; 3:1-12; 6:1–7:6) and ends on a note of hope (2:12-13; 4:1–5:15; 7:7-20). Such an outline can be valuable in attempting to see the book as a whole, but a closer look at each oracle or unit is needed to interpret the book properly. This discussion marks off each of the 20 units by chapter and verse, identifies its literary form, and determines its major motif or theme.

The first unit, "The Lord Is Coming," consists of 1:2-7. Its form is that of a lawsuit and a theophany. The peoples of the world are called to listen to what the Lord will witness against them. He is described as leaving his heavenly temple to come to earth to tread on top of the mountains that melt under him (1:2-4). God's coming is due to the sins of the people. Samaria, the capital of the northern kingdom of Israel, is to be destroyed primarily because of idolatry (vv 5-7).

The second passage is "The Prophet's Lament" (1:8-16). The prophet sees an enemy army coming from the southwest. Twelve cities are in its path. Desolation, refugees, and hostages are the result. There is a wordplay on the name of each of the cities except Gath, designed to express the fate of each city. Some of the cities are well known, such as Lachish, Jerusalem, Moresheth-gath, and Adullam. Others cannot be identified. This passage indicates that even though the first oracle was addressed to the nations and specifically announced the fall of Samaria, Judah was the real concern of Micah.

The third passage is "Woe to the Wealthy Wicked" (2:1-5). It is a woe oracle, meaning that it is a message of judgment. This time, judgment is on a certain group of wealthy men who wickedly devise schemes at night to seize houses and lands from unsuspecting farmers. Micah says their plans will boomerang. Their own lands will be snatched from them.

"Micah and the Wealthy Wicked" is the theme of the fourth section (2:6-11). This passage records a dispute between Micah and those who snatched houses and fields from unsuspecting victims. Micah's wicked listeners could not accept his message of judgment. They found it offensive and commanded him to stop preaching such things. They did not believe that evil would overtake them because they thought God would not do such things (vv 6-7). But Micah enumerates a number of crimes of these wicked men, such as taking the robes off travelers' backs and driving women and children from

their homes (vv 8-9). Such wicked men follow false prophets (v 11).

The fifth passage is "A Remnant to Be Restored" (2:12-13). The Lord will gather a remnant of his people like sheep in a fold (v 12), then the Lord as their king will lead them out through the gate ahead of them (v 13). This section is open to various interpretations. The passage does not indicate the place where the Lord will gather the remnant. Some assume the place is Babylon and take the passage as a reference to the exile. Others believe the place is Jerusalem and relate the incident to refugees fleeing to Jerusalem before Sennacherib's invasion in 701 BC.

The sixth passage is about "Guilty Rulers" (3:1-4). Micah charges that the heads and leaders of his people act like cannibals. They should know justice but they hate the good and love evil. They will cry to the Lord, but he will not hear them.

"Peace Prophets and Micah" is another disputation passage (3:5-8). Micah accuses the false prophets of preaching for money and asserts that they have no vision or message from God. By contrast, Micah claims to speak in the power and Spirit of God.

"Corrupt Leaders and Zion's Fall" is the subject of the eighth passage (3:9-12). This oracle seems to be a summary of all Micah has been saying to the various groups of leaders in Jerusalem. Because of their sins and crimes, Jerusalem and the temple will be destroyed.

"Zion's Future Exaltation," the ninth section, contains the surprising announcement of Zion's fall and the temple's destruction (4:1-5). This oracle of salvation was probably deliberately placed after the previous oracle of judgment to indicate that even though the temple might be destroyed, it would be restored in grander style to be the worship center for all nations. A parallel to this passage is found in Isaiah 2:1-4.

"Restoration of a Remnant and Zion" is the subject of the tenth section (4:6-8). The opening phrase, "in that coming day," indicates that this is an eschatological oracle in that the Lord is seen as reigning over his restored flock in Zion.

The next three passages (4:9-10; 4:11-13; 5:1-4) all begin with the word "now" (in the Hebrew) and end with an assertion that the present evil situation will be changed for the better. The first of the three is "From Distress to Deliverance" (4:9-10); the second is "From Siege to Victory" (vv 11-13); and the third is "From Helpless Judge to Ideal King" (5:1-4). The last passage in this series is one of the most familiar passages in Micah. It contains the promise of the birth of a new king in Bethlehem who will be great to the ends of the earth.

The fourteenth section, "Peace and the Overthrow of Assyria" (5:5-6), is followed closely by "The Remnant among the Peoples" (vv 7-9). The remnant is portrayed as dew on plants and as a lion among sheep. Dew on plants is usually taken to signify a blessing, but in 2 Samuel 17:12 it is a metaphor for judgment as a lion is among sheep.

The sixteenth passage is "Purge of the Military and False Religions" (5:10-15). The expressions "cut off," "throw down," "cause to perish," "root out," and "destroy" suggest radical surgery. It is an oracle on those things that might take the place of God in people's minds.

"God's Lawsuit" (6:1-8) is probably the most familiar passage in Micah. It is one of the great summaries of true religion.

The next passage presents "More Charges and the Sentence" (6:9-16). The further charges are dishonest business practices, lying, and acts of violence. The sentence is a life of futility, frustration, scorn, and destruction.

The nineteenth pericope in Micah is a "Lament over a Decadent Society" (7:1-6). The prophet begins with a woe because he seems to be the only godly or righteous man left (vv 1-2). He cannot trust anyone. Everyone may be setting a trap for another. People do evil with both hands. Even the members of families rise against each other. Jesus applied the words of 7:6 to his own times (Mt 10:21, 35-36).

The last section of Micah (Mi 7:7-20) is a prophetic liturgy. It is made up of a psalm of trust (vv 7-10); a prophetic promise of restoration (vv 11-13); a prayer for God to bless Israel and judge their enemies (vv 14-17); and a hymn or a doxology declaring God incomparable in "grace and truth," showing faithfulness to Jacob and steadfast love to Abraham (v 20).

See also Israel, History of; Prophecy; Prophet, Prophetess.

MICAIAH

1. Prophet and Imlah's son, called by Ahab to forecast the result of projected battles against the Syrians. At first Micaiah mocks him with glad news, then tells the cruel truth. Ahab casts the prophet into prison as a kind of ransom, but the wicked ruler dies in battle, just as Micaiah predicted (1 Kgs 22:8; 2 Chr 18:7-25).
2. Father of Acbor, one of the court officials whom King Josiah sent to the prophetess Huldah to get an opinion on the Book of the Law that Hilkiah the high priest had found in the temple (2 Kgs 22:12; 2 Chr 34:20, "Abdon, son of Micah").
3. Alternate rendering of Maacah, mother of Judah's King Abijah, in 2 Chronicles 13:2. *See* Maacah, Maachah (Person) #4.
4. Teacher commissioned by King Jehoshaphat to teach the law of the Lord throughout Judah (2 Chr 17:7).
5. Alternate spelling of Mica, Zicri's son, in Nehemiah 12:35. *See* Mica #2.
6. Priest who blew a trumpet at the dedication of the Jerusalem wall (Neh 12:41).
7. Gemariah's son, who reported the words of the Lord to Jewish princes during the reign of King Jehoiakim (Jer 36:11-13).

MICHA*

1. KJV spelling of Mica, Mephibosheth's son, in 2 Samuel 9:12. *See* Mica #1.
2. KJV spelling of Micah, Uzziel's son, in 1 Chronicles 23:20. *See* Micah (Person) #5.
3. KJV spelling of Mica, a Levite, in Nehemiah 10:11. *See* Mica #3.
4. KJV spelling of Mica, Mattaniah's father, in Nehemiah 11:17, 22. *See* Mica #2.

MICHAEL
Name meaning "Who is like God?" used of 10 men in Scripture and also of one who is described as an archangel.

1. Father of one of the spies sent by Moses into Canaan (Nm 13:13).
2-3. Gadites named in the lists of those who settled in the land of Bashan (1 Chr 5:13-14).
4. Forefather of Asaph, a temple singer in the days of David (1 Chr 6:40).
5. Chief man of Issachar in the temple lists (1 Chr 7:3).
6. Benjamite named in the temple lists (1 Chr 8:16).
7. Man of Manasseh who joined David in Ziklag when he was fleeing from Saul (1 Chr 12:20).
8. Father of Omri, a top political officer in the days of David (1 Chr 27:18).

9. Son of King Jehoshaphat of Judah (2 Chr 21:2).
10. Father of Zebadiah, a returnee with Ezra to Jerusalem (Ezr 8:8).
11. Angel in the OT, intertestamental literature, and the NT. In Daniel 10:13 it is said that "the spirit prince of the kingdom of Persia" sought to oppose the purpose of God, but Michael, "one of the archangels," contended against this evil spirit at the Lord's side (Dn 10:21). His conflict on behalf of Israel is referred to further in Daniel 12:1.

In the book of Enoch, Michael is one of four (Enoch 9:1; 40:9) or of seven (20:1-7) special angels or "archangels." In Enoch, in the War Scroll (of the Dead Sea Scrolls), and in other intertestamental literature, Michael regularly is presented either as the champion of the cause of the righteous or as the patron angel of Israel.

The book of Jude, apparently alluding to the Assumption of Moses, speaks of the archangel Michael as having contended with the devil in a dispute about the body of Moses (Jude 1:9; cf. 2 Pt 2:10-11; see also the reference to "the archangel" in 1 Thes 4:16). The only other reference to Michael in the NT is Revelation 12:7-8, where it is said, "Then there was war in heaven. Michael and the angels under his command fought the dragon and his angels. And the dragon lost the battle and was forced out of heaven" (NLT).

See also Angel.

MICHAH* KJV spelling of Micah, Uzziel's son, in 1 Chronicles 24:24-25. *See* Micah (Person) #5.

MICHAIAH*

1. KJV spelling of Micaiah, Acbor's father, in 2 Kings 22:12. *See* Micaiah #2.
2. KJV spelling of Micaiah, the mother of Judah's king Abijah, in 2 Chronicles 13:2. *See* Maacah, Maachah (Person) #4.
3. KJV spelling of Micaiah, one of King Jehoshaphat's officials, in 2 Chronicles 17:7. *See* Micaiah #4.
4. KJV spelling of Micaiah, an alternate name for Mica, Zicri's son, in Nehemiah 12:35. *See* Mica #2.
5. KJV spelling of Micaiah, a postexilic priest, in Nehemiah 12:41. *See* Micaiah #6.
6. KJV spelling of Micaiah, Gemariah's son, in Jeremiah 36:11-13. *See* Micaiah #7.

MICHAL Younger daughter of Saul (1 Sm 14:49). She fell in love with David after his defeat of Goliath (18:20). Saul, jealous of David, offered his first daughter, Merab, to David, but the recent victor graciously declined. When Michal's love became known to Saul, he renewed his offer of a wife, providing David produce evidence of having killed 100 Philistines—a condition Saul felt would surely lead to David's death.

David met Saul's condition in double measure and married Michal. Saul's jealousy was only fanned, and he plotted to have David murdered. Michal heard of the plot and assisted in her husband's escape (1 Sm 19:8-17). During David's exile, Saul gave Michal to Palti (25:44).

Following Saul's death, Abner negotiated with David, part of the agreement being the return of Michal to David's household. This was done despite Palti's remorse (2 Sm 3:12-16). But youthful ardor had apparently suffered strain. When David returned with the ark to Jerusalem, dancing before it, Michal voiced her harsh criticism. David's reply was equally severe. Michal would remain childless as punishment for her candidness. (The KJV, using inferior manuscripts, reports Michal as the mother of five sons in 2 Samuel 21:8. Adriel, however, was the husband of Merab—a correction reflected in modern versions.)

David's overwhelming popularity should not overshadow the courage and passion displayed by Michal. She let her love be known when women hardly took the initiative in courtship, saved David's life at the risk of her own, was emotionally victimized by her forced marriage and separation from Palti, and voiced her critical convictions against the tide of public opinion.

MICHMASH* Town in southern Mt Ephraim near the edge of the wilderness that descends eastward toward the Jordan Valley. Though it must have been an Israelite settlement in the territory of Benjamin, it is absent from the list of Benjamite towns (Jos 18:21-28). The ancient name is preserved in that of the Arab village of Mukhmas, situated on a narrow ridge to the east of Wadi Suweinit (valley of Zeboim) overlooking the deep canyon through which it runs. It is about two miles (3.2 kilometers) northeast of Geba (Jaba'), which stands on the western side of the same valley. A lateral road passed by Michmash to Jericho, and a longitudinal road also followed the watershed beside it. The latter route was of only secondary importance but still could serve as an alternate to the main route, the highway west of Bethel.

The town played its best-documented role in biblical history during the reign of Saul. When he mustered his troops, part were with him in Michmash while the rest were with Jonathan at Gibeah of Benjamin (1 Sm 13:2). After Jonathan had smitten the Philistine commissioner at Geba, the Philistines came out in force and encamped at Michmash (v 5) since Saul had withdrawn to Gilgal to assemble the rest of his forces. Then he went back to Geba, on the opposite side of the valley from the enemy. Using their base at Michmash (vv 11, 16), the Philistines sent out raiding parties north to Ophrah, west to Bethhoron, and southeast along the edge of the valley of Zeboim (vv 17-18); this passage serves to illustrate the value of Michmash as a strategic crossroads.

An outpost south of Michmash was manned by Philistines facing the Israelites on the opposite ridge (1 Sm 13:23). Jonathan went out to the canyon where the two cliffs Bozez (on the side of Michmash) and Seneh (beside Geba) face one another. He and his armor bearer made a surprise attack on an outpost of soldiers, who then fled to Michmash. The resultant confusion among the Philistines was taken advantage of by Saul and his troops (14:1-23). The Philistines withdrew under heavy Hebrew harassment by way of the lateral road via the Aijalon Valley (v 31).

MICHMETHATH* See Micmethath.

MICHRI* See Micri.

MICHTAM* KJV rendering of miktam, a musical cue, in the titles of Psalms 16, 56, 57, 58, 59, and 60. See Miktam.

MICMASH See Michmash.

MICMETHATH Geographical location describing part of the boundary dividing the territory assigned to Ephraim (Jos 16:6) and Manasseh's tribes (17:7), situated in the mountains west of the Jordan, midway between the Dead Sea and the Sea of Galilee.

MICRI Ancestor of a family who returned to Jerusalem with Zerubbabel after the Babylonian captivity (1 Chr 9:8). Also spelled Michri.

MIDDIN One of the six cities in the wilderness west of the Dead Sea allotted to Judah's tribe for an inheritance, located between Beth-arabah and Secacah (Jos 15:61).

MIDIAN, MIDIANITE Person, place, or people, the latter living on the eastern edge of Gilead, Moab, and Edom south into northwest Arabia. They had few, if any, permanent settlements.

Midian and his descendants figure prominently only in the early history of Israel, in connection with Abraham (Gn 25:1-6), Joseph (37:25-36), Moses (Ex 2:15–3:1), Balaam (Nm 22:1-6; 25; 31:1-20), and Gideon (Jgs 6:1–8:28).

Midian was Isaac's younger half brother, the fourth of six sons born to Keturah, whom Abraham married as an old man (Gn 25:1-2; cf. 23:1-2; 24:67; 1 Chr 1:32). By calling Midian and his full brothers "the sons of Keturah" (Gn 25:4; 1 Chr 1:32-33), the Bible carefully distinguishes them from Isaac, the son of Sarah, who was the one through whom God's promise to Abraham would be fulfilled (Gn 12:1-3; 17:15-21). In fact, Abraham and the Israelites regarded these other sons as having no more inheritance rights than a concubine's sons (Gn 25:5-6; 1 Chr 1:31).

Expelled from Abraham's family, for Isaac's sake, they became seminomadic peoples of the deserts east and south of Palestine (Gn 25:5-6).

The Land of Midian Of uncertain location, Midian was probably far south of Edom on the eastern side of what is today called the Gulf of Aqaba. The Alexandrian geographer Ptolemy (second century AD) mentions a city named Modiana on the coast and a Madiana 26 miles (41.8 kilometers) inland (modern el-Bed') in this region, an identification supported by the Jewish historian Josephus (first century AD) and the Christian church historian Eusebius (early fourth century).

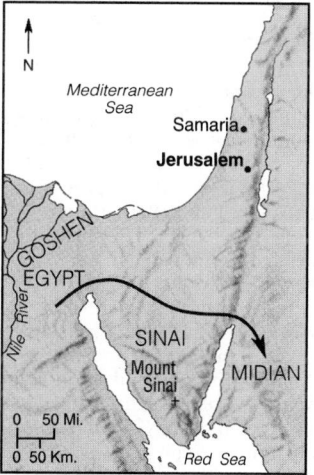

Moses Flees from Egypt to Midian
After murdering an Egyptian, Moses escaped into Midian. There he married Zipporah and became a shepherd.

In early OT times Midian seems to have been the land on the edge of the deserts bordering Gilead, Moab, and Edom south even into eastern Sinai.

In Joseph's day, some Midianite clans must have lived in the northern Transjordanian desert adjacent to Gilead or Bashan because they were part of an Ishmaelite caravan traveling the trade route from Damascus across Gilead past Dothan to Egypt (Gn 37:17, 25-28, 36).

When Moses fled from Pharaoh, he settled in Midian and eventually married Zipporah, the daughter of a Midianite priest (Ex 2:15-22). Moses asked his Midianite relative Hobab to act as a guide from Horeb to Kadesh-barnea (Dt 1:19); Hobab was familiar with the wilderness of Paran (Nm 10:11-12, 29-31), even though his own land and relatives were elsewhere (v 30).

In the Balaam episode and its bloody aftermath (Nm 22:31), a substantial group of Midianites appears to have been living on the eastern frontier of Moab. The Moabite king Balak, who was subject to the Amorite king named Sihon (21:26-30; Jer 48:45), discussed the Israelite threat with the elders of Midian, and a joint delegation was sent to Balaam (Nm 22:2-7). At Acacia in the plains of Moab (Nm 22:1; 25:1), an Israelite met and married a Midianite princess (Nm 25:6-18; 31:8). The Midianite kings were considered puppet kings of King Sihon (Jos 13:21). All the indications are that Midianite clans lived nearby, on the borders of Moab. Since Moab is north of Edom, the reference to an Edomite victory over Midian (Gn 36:35) might indicate a northern encroachment by the Midianites on Edomite territory.

The Midianite invasion that Gideon repulsed had all the appearances of an invasion from the east. It would therefore seem that while "the land of Midian" is a term that may refer to a territory south of Edom, Midianites were living over a much wider area—on marginal land—east of Moab and Edom and south of Edom into east Sinai and northwest Arabia.

MIDRASH* Transliteration into English of a Hebrew word that occurs twice in 2 Chronicles. Second Chronicles 13:22 refers to the literary source used for recording the reign of King Abijah of Judah (913–910 BC) as the "midrash" of the prophet Iddo. Second Chronicles 24:27 mentions, in connection with the reign of King Joash of Judah (835–796 BC), the "midrash" of the book of the kings.

Although these are the only times that midrash is mentioned in Chronicles, they do fall into a pattern of appeals to literary sources. For instance, Chronicles often cites *The Book of the Kings of Israel and Judah* or the like (e.g., 2 Chr 16:11; 20:34; 27:7; 33:18). It is probable that the title in 2 Chronicles 24:27 incorporating the term "midrash" is just a variant title of a main source. Again, Chronicles often alludes to various prophetic sources; the otherwise unknown prophet Iddo features also in a work called *The Visions of Iddo the Seer* in connection with the reign of Jeroboam I of Israel (930–909 BC; 2 Chr 9:29), and also *The Record of Shemaiah the Prophet*, with reference to King Rehoboam of Judah (930–913 BC; 2 Chr 12:15). Here, too, it is probable that a single prophetic work is labeled with different names.

But what did the term "midrash" mean, precisely, to the author of Chronicles? The ancient Greek version translated it simply as "book, writing," and it is likely that it meant nothing more than that. The underlying Hebrew verb means to inquire or study, and accordingly the noun could signify "a result of research, a study." Alternatively, it may mean "commentary" in the sense of a presentation of history from a certain perspective.

Apart from these instances in Chronicles, the other usage of importance for the OT is its meaning as a procedure or product of interpretation of the biblical text, which was eventually incorporated into the Jewish commentaries called Midrashim. In the literature of Qumran, midrash appears in the general sense of "interpretation of the law." But in later rabbinic literature it became a technical term for a collection of traditional teachings of the rabbis arranged in order of chapter and verse of biblical books. The overall aim of these studies was to apply the ancient text to contemporary circumstances in a variety of ways.

See also Talmud.

MIGDAL-EL One of the fortified cities belonging to Naphtali's tribe (Jos 19:38).

MIGDAL-GAD Village in Judah located in the Shephelah district of Lachish (Jos 15:37). It is perhaps identifiable with Khirbet el-Mejdeleh, southeast of Tell el-Nuweir.

MIGDOL Town in the eastern delta of Lower Egypt. In the narrative of the exodus it appears between the place called Pi-hahiroth and Baal-zephon (Ex 14:2; Nm 33:7). Some scholars who think the exodus route must have taken the Israelites south into the Sinai Mountains think these three sites were somewhere near Suez. Others who think the Serbonitic Lake is the Reed Sea accept the identification of this Migdol with that mentioned by Jeremiah as the dwelling place of exiled Jews in the sixth century BC (Jer 44:1; 46:14). That place must be identical with the Migdol that represents the north (eastern) extremity of Egypt in juxtaposition to Syene in the far south (Ez 29:10; 30:6). Not all scholars agree on whether Migdol is a single location or two separate locations. Nonbiblical sources refer to Migdol—for example, Papyrus Anastasi 5.19, where it appears in association with Succoth in a message about runaway slaves. It also appears on the wall relief of Seti I as a fortress between Sillo (Sele) and the other northern Sinai forts. The Antonine Itinerary places Magdolo between Pelusium and Sele, which would make the equation with Tell el-Heir, 12 miles (19.3 kilometers) north, most likely.

MIGRON Site where Saul rested under a pomegranate tree, near Gibeah (1 Sm 14:2); also mentioned as part of the line of march of the Assyrians (Is 10:28). The first reference is to a site south of Michmash, the second is probably north of Michmash. Some scholars, however, try to identify both with the site south of Michmash, though this is doubtful.

MIJAMIN

1. Priest who ministered during the time of David (1 Chr 24:9).
2. Parosh's son, who was encouraged by Ezra to divorce his foreign wife during the postexilic period (Ezr 10:25).
3. One of the priests who signed Ezra's covenant during the postexilic period (Neh 10:7).
4. Priest who returned to Jerusalem with Zerubbabel after the exile (Neh 12:5, NLT "Miniamin").

MIKLOTH

1. Resident of Gibeon, son of the Benjamite Jeiel, and father of Shimeah (1 Chr 8:32; 9:37-38).
2. Officer in David's army who served under Dodai (1 Chr 27:4), according to some manuscripts.

MIKNEIAH Levite of the second order who was a gatekeeper and musician during David's reign (1 Chr 15:18, 21).

MIKTAM* Title in Psalms 16 and 56–60 (see NIV), possibly also of Hezekiah's recovery psalm, Isaiah 38:9. The precise meaning of the term is uncertain. Its similarity to the Akkadian word "to cover, expiate" suggests the title may mean a psalm of expiation or sin covered. Other suggestions include a psalm of problems or mysteries.

See also Music.

MILALAI Participant in the dedication of the rebuilt Jerusalem wall (Neh 12:36).

MILCAH

1. Daughter of Haran and half sister of Nahor who became Nahor's wife (Gn 11:29). She bore Nahor eight sons (22:20-23). Through her son Bethuel she was the grandmother of Rebekah (24:15-47).
2. One of the five daughters of Zelophehad. Because Zelophehad had no sons, his daughters petitioned Moses to allow them to receive their father's inheritance in west Manasseh after their father's death (Nm 26:33; 27:1-11; 36:5-13; Jos 17:3-4).

MILCOM* National god of the Ammonites, better known as Molech or Moloch. Worship of this deity, which was accompanied by sacrificing children in the fire, was strictly prohibited to Israel (Lev 18:21; Jer 32:35). Solomon built Milcom a worship site (1 Kgs 11:5, 33), which Josiah later tore down (2 Kgs 23:13). Milcom is rendered as "king" in 2 Samuel 12:30 and 1 Chronicles 20:2 (see also Jer 49:1-3; Zep 1:5, KJV "Malcham").

See also Ammon, Ammonites.

MILDEW Superficial growth produced on organic matter or living plants by fungi. Mildew was caused by a common fungus in Palestine, *Puccinia graminis*, and was regarded as divine punishment for disobedience. The root meaning of the Hebrew word is "pale greenish yellow."

MILE Measurement of distance. A Roman mile was somewhat shorter than the English mile. *See* Weights and Measures.

MILETUM*, MILETUS Important Greek city located at the mouth of the Meander River. It was settled by Crete as early as 1339–1288 BC. Miletus had contact with the Hittite Empire. Her king, in fact, was claimed as a vassal by the Hittite ruler. Excavations indicate that Miletus, once destroyed by fire, was later surrounded by a defensive wall (13th century BC).

Miletus was attacked by the kingdom of Lydia around 650 BC and ruled by a military dynasty headed by King Gyges. Its citizens still managed, however, to colonize Abydos on the narrows of the Dardenelles. Over 70 such colonies were founded by the merchants of Miletus along the Black Sea, the most important being Sinope. Miletus became an important city, therefore, in the ancient world. Her traders carried the furniture and woolens for which she was known to many foreign ports.

Ancient Theater in Miletus

The city had its own poet, like many other Greek centers, famous in his own time but known today only in a few verses. Phocylides wrote: "A little city on a rock, with order, is better than madness in Nineveh." Again, "all virtue is summed up in justice."

Miletus was also the birthplace of philosophy and scientific speculation. The philosopher Thales predicted an eclipse in 585 BC, and his disciple, Anaximander, propounded evolution from sea creatures. Much of the city's strength, however, was wasted on bitter civil strife. Two parties, known as the rich and the workers, kept the city torn by inner feuding. In approximately 495 BC, the city was sacked by the Persians and never again regained world importance, though it was retaken by Alexander.

Miletus was, of course, well known in NT times, though it was not an important center to early Christianity. The apostle Paul stopped there on the last missionary journey recorded in the book of Acts (Acts 20:15-17). While there, he called for the Ephesian elders and exhorted them to care for the flock in their charge (vv 28-35). From Miletus he sailed for Tyre. Second Timothy 4:20 says that Paul left Trophimus in Miletus (KJV "Miletum") because he was sick.

MILK *See* Food and Food Preparation.

MILL Two circular stones (millstones) used in the grinding of grain. The grinding of grain as depicted in ancient art is attested in archaeological excavations in the Middle East from at least the Neolithic period (c. 8300–4500 BC) in the shape of various concave stones with flat grinding pieces accompanying them. These were essentially handmills. Over the centuries improvements in technique took place. But two elements were always necessary, the lower one on which the grain was spread and the upper one, which was moved over the surface of the lower one under pressure, to grind the grain into flour. The Hebrew term for "mill" is grammatically a dual—that is, it refers to two elements.

Millstone

The earliest mill, the saddle quern, consisted of a rough base stone, slightly concave, and a convex rubbing stone. The base stone varied from 18 to 30 inches (45.7 to 76.2 centimeters) across with one end a little thicker than the other. It was known in Hebrew as "the underneath portion" (Jb 41:24). The upper stone, called the "rider portion" (Jgs 9:53; 2 Sm 11:21), varied from 6 to 15 inches (15.2 to 38.1 centimeters) in length and was flat on one side and convex on the other. It could be held easily in the hand. Grinding was done by pushing the upper stone backward and forward over the grain, which lay on the lower stone. Only a small quantity of grain could be ground at one time using this method (Gn 18:6).

A second type of handmill consisted of two round stones. The lower one could be either convex or concave on top and the upper one was either concave or convex so as to fit nearly over the lower stone. Some examples of this type of mill have a funnel-shaped hole in the center of the top stone through which grain was poured. The upper mill was turned on the lower one by means of a wooden peg inserted on its outside edge. As the grain was crushed, it escaped along the edges of the upper stone. Commonly the stone used was black basalt because its rough and porous surface provided good cutting edges. The normal type of handmill could be operated by one person, but sometimes two persons were required (Mt 24:41).

So important was the handmill in the life of the people that it was prohibited by law to take a man's millstone as a pledge against the payment of a debt, for this would deprive his family of the means of making flour for bread (Dt 24:6). These stones were heavy enough to kill a man when thrown on his head, as in the case of Abimelech (Jgs 9:53; cf. 2 Sm 11:21).

Normally, the grinding of grain was the task of servants (Ex 11:5) or of women (Is 47:2). The noise of grinding could be heard each day in every village in Palestine. When that sound ceased, the village had come to an end (Jer 25:10).

There seems to have been larger community mills that required animal power. A heavy round stone, perhaps four to five feet (1.2 to 1.5 meters) in diameter, was rolled on its edge by means of a pole through its center. This pole rotated around a vertical post in much the same way as one finds in some Eastern lands even today. It may have been a large mill of this type that Samson was forced to use to grind grain for the Philistines (Jgs 16:21).

See also Food and Food Preparation; Bread; Agriculture.

MILLENNIUM* Biblical term (taken from the Latin word meaning "a thousand") referring to the thousand-year reign of Christ. The primary biblical context for the doctrine of the millennium is found in Revelation 20:1-6 (where the Greek word for thousand is used five times). The idea of a thousand-year reign may also be supported by passages such as Acts 3:19-21 and 1 Corinthians 15:23-26, which speak of a future restoration and reign of Christ. This doctrine, however, is explicitly taught only in the book of Revelation, and is characterized by differences of interpretation, as well as considerable uncertainty about its importance.

The *a*millennial (*no* millennium, at least of a visible, earthly nature) interpretation stresses the symbolism of Revelation and holds that now, during the present age, Satan is bound and the church is experiencing the millennium. Perhaps the most serious difficulty with the amillennial view is that it interprets the two resurrections of Revelation 20 differently. Though the same Greek word is used for both, the first (v 4) is interpreted as a spiritual resurrection, while the second (v 5) as a physical resurrection, while the passage itself does not indicate that the writer intended a difference of meaning. Hence, the amillennial position is often accused of improperly spiritualizing the meaning of the Bible. Another perspective on the *a*millennial position is that the thousand-year reign of Christ is a symbolic expression of Christ's unlimited rule—as opposed to an actual reign of 1,000 years.

The *post*millennial (Christ will return *after* the millennium) view sees the progress of the gospel as producing the millennium. The essential idea in this interpretation is progress. It may be held that this era of peace is yet future or that it began with the first advent of Christ and is continuing on until the gospel triumphs over the world, with the majority being won to Christianity. However, the variant forms of postmillennialism stress that Christ does not return until *after* the millennium. It is not the second coming of Christ and his visible presence that brings about the millennium.

Different from the above two views is the *pre*millennial (Christ returns *before* the millennium) interpretation, which maintains that Christ will return to earth and establish his peaceful reign in a visible and powerful manner.

The premillennialist emphasizes that the visions of the book of Revelation must be interpreted sequentially. First is the return of Christ in chapter 19, followed by the binding of Satan for a thousand years and the first resurrection of the saints to reign with Christ for the thousand years (20:1-6). This, in turn, is followed by a release of Satan and the battle of those deceived—"Gog and Magog"—against Christ and his people and the final destruction of the devil (vv 7-10). Next is the account of the final judgment and the last resurrection (vv 11-15), followed by the new heaven and new earth (ch 21).

The premillennialist strongly affirms that this sequence demands that the millennium, the reign of Christ, be understood as a real, future event following Christ's return. None of the variations of amillennialism or postmillennialism that see the millennium in the present church age before Christ returns or even in the future before Christ comes again, adequately accounts for the sequence of events in Revelation.

In addition to the literary argument, there is the theological point that the premillennial position places the real triumph of Christ within history. That is, the victory that the church believes was accomplished through Christ's death on the cross will be made visible to the world and the forces of evil at Christ's return and reign on earth. This is not faith in a merely spiritual or heavenly triumph, but faith that God will genuinely intervene in the course of the world to bring justice and peace.

However, implicit within this is the greatest weakness of the premillennial viewpoint. The Bible does not explain the details of how Christ and his resurrected saints will reign over an earth not yet made new and over nations still living in their natural state. This unresolved problem has led many interpreters to explain Revelation 20 by one of the other interpretations.

See also Eschatology; Judgment; Resurrection; Revelation, Book of; Second Coming of Christ.

MILLET Small-seeded grass grown for food and foliage (Ez 4:9). *See* Plants.

MILLO

1. Earthen embankment or fortification mentioned in Judges 9:6, 20. *See* Beth-millo.
2. Fortress or embankment mentioned in connection with the construction of the city of David (2 Sm 5:9; 1 Chr 11:8). Solomon apparently either rebuilt or expanded this fortification (1 Kgs 9:15; 11:27).

   Two kings of Judah are mentioned in connection with this structure: Joash was slain in "the house of Millo" (2 Kgs 12:20), and Hezekiah strengthened Millo due to the threat of invasion by Sennacherib (2 Chr 32:5).

MINA Small weight used in the measure of precious metals as well as other substances. *See* Weights and Measures.

MIND

One's intellectual processes in a narrow sense or, more broadly, the sum total of a person's mental and moral state of being. To the Hebrew way of thinking, there is no distinctive terminology for the concept of the mind. To the Greek world, the mind plays a very important role in the understanding of humans.

Since in the OT there was no separate word that could be used for the human mind, translators of the English versions have supplied other words ("soul," "spirit," or "heart"), as the context dictates. Thus, precise distinctions among these terms are hard to define. A person is a soul, having a spirit and a heart. Any of these terms may represent the mind. This means that the widely held distinction between the mind as the seat of thinking and the heart as the seat of feeling is alien to the meanings these terms carry in the OT.

While the "mind" denotes a person's thoughts, the prominent idea of "mind" in the OT is that it denotes the heart (1 Sm 2:35; Ez 11:5; 20:32). The heart is often intended to include the entire inner person and thus often relates especially to the mind. In these instances it relates primarily to the functions of will and memory (Is 46:8; 65:17; Jer 3:16).

The basic patterns of Hebrew reasoning continue in the Gospel accounts. The conception of mind appears quite rarely. When used, it is mostly in connection with the heart—for example, the imaginations of the heart (Lk 1:51). The only other occurrences of the word "mind" come in the statement of the great commandment: "You shall love the Lord your God with all your heart, and with all your soul, and with all your strength, and with all your mind" (cf. Mt 22:37; Mk 12:30; Lk 10:27). The Gospel writers are unanimous in their agreement that Jesus added "with all your mind" to Deuteronomy 6:5. In Mark, however, the questioner repeats the command of Jesus but with a word for "understanding" in place of the word for "mind" (Mk 12:33).

With the writings of Paul, one moves into the Greek world. Paul understood the mind as distinct from the spirit of man. It possesses the ability to understand and to reason (1 Cor 14:14-19); it is the seat of intelligence. In other places, "mind" is used in a broader sense that includes the entire mental and moral process or state of being of a human (Rom 12:2; Eph 4:23). A human's actions flow from the inclinations of his or her mind. Whether a person is good or evil depends on the state of the mind.

The state of a person depends upon what or who controls the mind. Romans 8:6-7 speaks of a person's mind being controlled either by the flesh or by the Spirit. The person whose mind is controlled by the flesh is evil. The mind controlled by the Spirit leads to good. Other passages refer to the inclination of a person's mind being controlled by the god of this world (2 Cor 4:4). People whose minds are controlled by the "god of this world" will have their minds darkened and will not be able to understand the world as it really is (3:14). It is as a veil over one's understanding. But the Lord can open people's minds. For example, Jesus opened the minds of the disciples who walked the Emmaus road with him so that they might understand the Scriptures (Lk 24:45).

For Paul, the action of conversion is considered to be a "renewing of the mind" (Rom 12:2; Eph 4:23). In both cases, the process is one whereby God takes control of the mind of a person through the Holy Spirit and leads the thoughts of that person into proper channels. Thus, the renewed person is given power to make proper value judgments. Such people have new minds with which to make spiritual discernments (1 Cor 2:15-16).

See also Man; Heart; Soul.

MINERALS* AND METALS

A "mineral" is a naturally occurring substance, normally an ore that must be mined and treated before the metal can be extracted. A "metal" is a chemical element such as iron or copper, which is free from contamination by other materials. Metals in a pure form generally do not occur in nature, though there are exceptions.

In Palestine, mining and smelting are ancient arts, practiced long before the Israelites arrived. The quarrying of suitable stones, such as flint, for toolmaking goes back to the Stone Age; the quarrying of stone for building is also an ancient craft. In particular, metals, native gold, copper, and meteoric iron were known and used in the Middle East before 4000 BC. From 4000 to 3000 BC, native silver became known as well as copper and lead ores. The art of smelting was discovered probably almost by accident, resulting in the production of alloys like bronze. Then the reduction of oxidized iron was discovered. From 3000 to 2000 BC, important advances were made. Copper sulfides and tin oxides were reduced to metal, and metallic tin and copper became important items of trade.

In the years 2000 to 1000 BC, bellows came into use for furnaces, and iron was reduced from its ores and forged. The art of making brass from copper and zinc was discovered about 1500 BC but did not become significant till somewhat later. Bronze, known for many centuries, was made sometimes with a high tin content to form speculum for mirrors. By this time the Israelites were settled in the land and the kingdom was established. From 1000 BC to the start of the Christian era, the production of metals, especially iron, greatly expanded. A form of steel was made and used for weapons and tools.

By the time of David and Solomon, the Israelites had learned many skills in the preparation and working of metals. Under David, Edom, with its rich copper and iron deposits, was conquered (2 Sm 8:13-14) and there was a lot of activity in the casting of metals in the Jordan Valley (1 Kgs 7:13-14, 45-46). In this activity Solomon had the assistance of Hiram, a Phoenician artisan. Israelite tradition associated the origins of metallurgy with Tubal-cain (Gn 4:22), who is said to have forged all kinds of tools out of bronze and iron. Deuteronomy 8:9 refers to the presence of iron and copper in the land to which Israel was going.

While the Israelites eventually undertook their own metalworking processes, it is evident from 1 Samuel 13:19-22 that on at least one occasion, in the days of Philistine domination, they were obliged to have their agricultural tools made by their enemies. Similarly, the manufacture of cult vessels for Solomon's temple was supervised by Phoenician artisans (1 Kgs 7:13-50).

Minerals, metals, and precious stones were also important items of trade. Israel was never a land rich in these commodities and was obliged to import a wide variety of them. The visit of the queen of Sheba was partly diplomatic and partly for trade (1 Kgs 10:2, 10-11).

Metals and precious stones featured also among the booty carried off by invaders, notably—but not only—by the Egyptians and Assyrians. These items were in constant demand as they were needed for agriculture and making weapons of war, and for the manufacture of jewelry and items of personal adornment.

Minerals A mineral is an inorganic substance with a definite chemical composition and structure, sometimes occurring alone or sometimes combined with others. "Ore" refers to any mineral or mineral aggregate containing chemical compounds of metals in sufficient quantity and grade to make the extraction of the metal commercially profitable. The essential element, the metal, occurs in nature as a chemical compound, such as a sulfide, an oxide, a carbonate, or some other compound, though the sulfides and oxides are the most common. Minerals exhibit a variety of properties, such as color, luster, crystal form, cleavage, fracture, hardness, and density, which help in their identification and exercise control on the commercial and industrial uses of the particular mineral.

Metals A metal in its pure form is a chemically pure element with its own fixed physical properties, such as density, tensile strength, crystalline structure, melting point, ductility, conductivity, and the like. Metals form alloys with other metals, but this process destroys their purity. In both the ancient world and the modern world the alloy is extremely important.

In order to obtain a pure metal, the ore in which the metal is contained must be smelted—a process known as metallurgy. In ancient Israel pure metals were widely used—among them were gold, silver, iron, and lead. Yet alloys such as bronze and brass were even more widely used.

Metallurgy and Metal Extraction The method of producing hard wrought iron was discovered by the Hittites of Asia Minor about 1300 BC, and was taken up by the Philistines (1 Sm 13:19-20). At first, the iron obtained from simple furnaces was drawn off and hammered to drive out slag (Dt 4:20; 1 Kgs 8:51; Jer 11:4). Later, the addition of carbon produced an early form of steel.

The lead sulfide ore is heated with lime in a flow of air. A slag with rock particles forms. The air is then cut off and the temperature is raised. Finally, the lead flows free.

The OT refers to the mining of silver (Jb 28:1), the refining of the metal (Zec 13:9; Mal 3:3), the melting of scrap metals or jeweler's remnants (Ez 22:20-22), and of multiple refinings in a crucible (Prv 17:3; 27:21) to produce refined silver (1 Chr 29:4; Ps 12:6; Prv 10:20).

Specific Metals Although several OT passages suggest that the science of metallurgy was known in biblical times, comparatively little archaeological evidence is available. The processing plants were small and were used for the treatment of copper and iron. The archaeological record is far from complete, but the general impression is that metallic ores were comparatively rare in Palestine; imports must have been considerable. However, numerous molds for casting agricultural and military tools have come to light in excavations. Evidently, some refined metal was available locally, but perhaps most of it was imported. The metal was then heated and poured into the appropriate earthenware or pottery mold.

There are many references to metals in the Bible, but especially to gold, silver, iron, and lead. While copper was widely used, it was normally in the form of its alloys, bronze and brass. There are comparatively few references to tin as such, though it was used in manufacturing bronze. Similarly zinc, though used in the manufacture of brass, is not mentioned in the Bible.

Gold is referred to hundreds of times in the OT and NT, more frequently than any other metal. It is often mentioned together with silver, and in the majority of cases silver is mentioned first, reflecting a time when gold was less valued.

Gold was used in the manufacture of ornaments for personal use (Gn 24:53; 41:42; Ex 3:22; 11:2; 12:35). Gold was important in worship both in Israel and among the non-Israelites. References to pagan gods occur in several passages (Ex 20:23; 32:2-4; Ps 115:4; Is 2:20; 30:22; 31:7; 40:19; 46:6; Hos 8:4). It seems that the gold was melted down and later engraved so that the replicas could be called both molten images (Ex 32:24) and graven images. The tabernacle and the temple used a great deal of gold. The wooden ark was covered inside and outside with gold (25:11). Other timber pieces were overlaid with gold (25:11; 1 Kgs 6:20-22, 30).

The vessels and utensils used in the tabernacle and temple were made of "pure gold": the cherubim (Ex 25:18; 37:7), the mercy seat (25:17; 37:6), the candlestick (Ex 25:31; Zec 4:2), various vessels (Ex 25:38; 2 Kgs 24:13), chains to carry the ephod (Ex 28:14), and the bells on the high priest's robe. The high priest's crown, ephod, and breastplate were also of gold (39:2-30). The offerings collected for the manufacture of such articles in the wilderness include golden dishes weighing 120 shekels (Nm 7:86). The more lavishly adorned temple apparently used more gold than the tabernacle (1 Kgs 6:20-28; 1 Chr 29:2-7; 2 Chr 3:4–4:22). The number of specific references to gold in the tabernacle and temple is far too great to mention all of them here. The large amount of gold used in the temple was attractive to invaders, who would strip the temple of its gold and carry it off as booty (1 Kgs 14:26; 2 Kgs 16:8; 18:14; 24:13; 25:15; 2 Chr 12:9).

Gold had commercial value. It was imported in Solomon's day, and up to 666 talents were brought to Israel annually (1 Kgs 10:14). Hiram of Tyre gave Solomon 120 talents of gold (9:14), possibly as a loan. Certainly Solomon used a lot of gold in the temple (10:16-17). Gold was useful, too, for buying off an enemy (2 Kgs 16:8) or simply as tribute (18:14). Evidence of this comes also from the Assyrian annals, where the tribute taken from various lands often included gold.

The possession of gold was not in itself an evil thing, but preoccupation with its accumulation was condemned (Jb 28:15-17; Prv 3:14; 8:10, 19; 16:16). The possession of wisdom and the knowledge of God was of greater value than the possession of much gold (Pss 19:10; 119:72, 127; Prv 20:15). Job rejected trust in gold (Jb 31:24). Gold would not save a man in the day of judgment (Zep 1:18).

In the NT gold was regarded as perishable (Jas 5:3; 1 Pt 1:18) and as an unnecessary burden to carry (Mt 10:9; Acts 3:6). The wearing of a gold ring was certainly no measure of a man's worth (Jas 2:2); indeed, both Paul and Peter forbade it (1 Tm 2:9; 1 Pt 3:3).

The use of gold in itself was no measure of piety. The elders of Revelation 4:4 wore golden crowns, but the great harlot was "bedecked with gold" (Rv 17:4), as was the harlot city Babylon (18:16). By contrast, there are some positive statements in the NT about the value of gold (3:18). The wise men brought gold to the infant Jesus as a symbol of his kingly character (Mt 2:11), and the Holy City, the new Jerusalem, was a city of gold, clear as glass (Rv 21:18).

In the OT, silver is mentioned in several connections. Being a precious metal, once considered more precious than gold, it was regularly used in commerce for the payments of debts. Small pieces of silver were weighed into a balance against a standard weight. Abraham bought the cave at Machpelah as a burial place for Sarah for 400 shekels of silver and weighed out the "money" according to the weight's current value with the merchant (Gn 23:15-16). Joseph's brothers received 20 pieces of silver in payment for Joseph (37:28), and Benjamin was given a money gift by Joseph in pieces of silver (45:22).

There are other examples of payment in silver for

commodities or services (Gn 20:16; Ex 21:32; Lv 27:16; Jos 24:32; Jgs 17:10; 2 Sm 24:24; Neh 7:72; Jb 28:15; Is 7:23; 46:6; Am 2:6; 8:6). Silver was a measure of a man's wealth (Gn 13:2; 24:35; Ex 25:3; Nm 22:18; Dt 7:25; Zep 1:18; Hg 2:8; Zec 6:11). An unusual comment in 1 Kings 10:21 notes that in Solomon's day "it was not considered as anything," apparently because it was so plentiful. It was regularly taken as booty (Jos 6:19; 7:21; 1 Kgs 15:18). Sometimes the drinking cup of an important man was made of silver (Gn 44:2). Sometimes, too, a royal crown was made of gold and silver (Zec 6:11). It was important in the manufacture of personal ornaments (Gn 24:53; Ex 3:22; 12:35), and one example is given of ornaments of gold studded with silver (Sg 1:11).

The process of refining silver was used as a metaphor for the trying of people's hearts (Ps 66:10; Is 48:10), and the tarnishing and deterioration of silver was a picture of the disintegration of one's character (Is 1:22; Jer 6:30). God's Word is pictured as "pure" silver refined and purified in a furnace. Despite silver's great value, wisdom excels it (Job 28:15; Prv 3:14; 8:19; 10:20; 16:16; 22:1; 25:11).

Native copper is mentioned in Deuteronomy 8:9, though the reference may be to one of its ores. More commonly, biblical references are to brass, the alloy of copper and zinc. However, the chemical analysis of copper-based tools and implements during the middle and late Bronze Ages (c. 2000–1200 BC) shows that the material was bronze. References to brass in the KJV are therefore to bronze.

By NT times, copper in the form of alloys (bronze and brass) was widely used. Bronze coinage was well known and this may be the sense of Matthew 10:9. The widow's mite was a tiny bronze coin, the lepton. Bronze utensils and vessels were well known (Rv 9:20; 18:12). The reference to "sounding brass" (KJV) in 1 Corinthians 13:1 may actually be to brass, which was a bright, shining alloy, and was used in musical instruments. In the vision of John in Revelation (Rv 1:15; 2:18), the Son of Man had feet of fine brass (NLT "bronze").

The Iron Age began in Palestine about 1200 BC, that is, in the days of the judges, though native iron had been known in Egypt in the predynastic period. Archaeological evidence suggests that the smelting of iron ore was discovered by the Hittites about 1400 BC. The Philistines seem to have introduced iron to Palestine about 1300 BC. In the days of Moses an encounter with the Midianites produced much tribute, among which iron is mentioned (Nm 31:22). When Israel captured Jericho, the spoils included iron (Jos 6:24). Manasseh's half-tribe also took booty including iron (22:8). In the days of the judges the Canaanites were equipped with chariots of iron (Jos 17:16-18; Jgs 1:19; 4:3).

These early references point to the arrival of iron at the start of the Iron Age. The Philistines enjoyed a local monopoly in its use (1 Sm 13:19-21), and their mighty warrior Goliath was armed with an iron spear (17:7). It was not long, however, before Israel learned the use of iron (2 Sm 12:31; 23:7). Evidently, by Solomon's time, iron was widely used, because builders of the temple were forbidden to use iron tools (1 Kgs 6:7). The false prophet Zedekiah in Ahab's day used the horns of iron to thrust toward Syria as he spoke of their defeat (22:11).

The prophet Isaiah in the eighth century BC referred to iron (Is 10:34), and Jeremiah later spoke of the metal in several places (Jer 1:18; 6:28; 11:4; 15:12; 17:1; 28:13-14). Ezekiel made use of an iron plate in one of his symbolic actions (Ez 4:3), referred to iron in his description of smelting (22:18, 20), and listed it as a commodity for

trade (27:12, 19). The prophet Amos spoke of threshing instruments of iron (Am 1:3). Micah used iron as a symbol for military might (Mi 4:13). The book of Daniel makes several references to it (Dn 2:33-35, 40-45; 4:15, 23; 7:7, 19).

By Roman times, iron weapons were the regular implements of war. Gates of iron were used to close prisons (Acts 12:10), and in a symbolic usage powerful rulers were said to rule with a rod of iron (Rv 2:27; 9:9; 12:5; 19:15). The term "iron" was used also in some metaphorical expressions. The smelting of iron was a symbol of testing and suffering (Dt 4:20; 1 Kgs 8:51; Jer 11:4; Ez 22:18), a pillar of iron was symbolic of strength (Jer 1:18), and an iron rod of harsh rule (Ps 2:9; Rv 2:27; 12:5; 19:15).

See also Coppersmith; Goldsmith; Ironsmith; Mason; Masonry; Silversmith; Stones, Precious.

MINIAMIN

1. Levite who assisted Kore, the son of Imnah, with the distribution of the "contribution reserved for the Lord" among the priests in the cities of Judah (2 Chr 31:14-15).
2. Head of a priestly house during the postexilic era (Neh 12:17). He was also called "Mijamin" (12:5).
3. Participant in the dedication of the Jerusalem wall (Neh 12:41).

MINISTER, MINISTRY *See* Bishop; Body of Christ; Church; Deacon, Deaconess; Elder; Ordain, Ordination; Presbyter; Priesthood; Spiritual Gifts.

MINNI People mentioned in Jeremiah 51:27, along with Ararat and Ashkenaz, as aggressors against Babylon. The Minni first appear in Assyrian inscriptions during the reign of Shalmaneser III (858–824 BC), who pillaged and subdued the people. They lived between Lake Urmia and Lake Van, north of Babylon, and are identified with the Mannean people, regularly associated with Urarteans (Ararat) in Assyrian manuscripts. The Minni were restless subjects. They revolted against Assyria in 716 and 715 BC. Further agitation occurred in the reign of Ashurbanipal (669–627 BC). After Nineveh's fall to the Babylonians in 612 BC, the Minni disappear from the extrabiblical record.

MINNITH One of the 10 cities conquered by Jephthah in his defeat of the Ammonites (Jgs 11:33). The city was a center for the wheat trade (Ez 27:17).

MINSTREL* Archaic term for musician (2 Kgs 3:15; Ps 68:25; Mt 9:23; Rv 18:22).

MINT* Sweet-smelling herb used in cooking and medicine (Mt 23:23; Lk 11:42). *See* Plants.

MIPHKAD*, Gate of KJV translation for Muster Gate ("Inspection Gate," NLT), a city gate in northeast Jerusalem, in Nehemiah 3:31. *See* Muster Gate.

MIRACLE A divine act by which God reveals himself to people. The classical definition of miracle assumes that it is contrary to natural law, but this is a misnomer for two reasons. First, many of the miracles of the Bible used nature rather than bypassed it (e.g., the wind that parted the Red Sea, Ex 14:21). Second, there no longer is a concept of "absolute natural laws"; rather, a phenomenon that is not readily explainable may reflect laws that scientists do not yet fully understand. In Scripture the element of faith is crucial; a natural approach cannot prove or disprove the presence of "miracle." The timing and content of the process can be miraculous, even though the event may seem natural. The revelatory significance is also important. In every case God performed the miracle not merely as a "wonder" to inspire awe but as a "sign" to draw people to himself.

The Vocabulary of Miracles In the OT the two main terms are "sign" and "wonder," which often occur together (e.g., nine times in Dt alone, 4:34; 13:1; etc.). More than one Hebrew term is used for "wonder"—one referring to it as an act of supernatural power and another as being beyond man's understanding. On the whole, they are used synonymously for God's providential acts within history. The "sign" refers to an act that occurs as a token or pledge of God's control over events and as a revelation of God's presence with his people.

The NT uses the same basic idiom, "signs and wonders," with the same general thrust (cf. Mt 24:24; Mk 13:22; Jn 4:48; Acts 2:43). A third term is that for "power" or miracle, and this becomes the predominant term in the synoptic Gospels. It signifies the mighty act itself by which God is revealed in Christ. A fourth term is "work," which along with "sign" is preferred in the Gospel of John. This term is used in John to show that in Jesus the work of the Father is revealed. While the terms are often synonymous (the first three occur together in Rom 15:19-20; 2 Thes 2:9; Heb 2:4), they designate three different aspects of miracles. "Signs" point to the theological meaning of miracle as a revelation of God; "power," to the force behind the act; "work," to the person behind it; and "wonder," to its awesome effect on the observer.

Miracles in the Old Testament To the Hebrew, a miracle was nothing more nor less than an act of God. Therefore, nature herself was a miracle (Jb 5:9-10; Pss 89:6; 106:2), and an act of kindness or victory over one's enemies is so described (Gn 24:12-27; 1 Sm 14:23). The natural order is totally under Yahweh's control, so a miracle was observable not because of its supernatural nature but because of its character as part of the divine revelation. This connection with salvation history is crucial, for Israel at all times tried to guard against a desire for the spectacular. Deuteronomy 13:1-4 warns against accepting a wonder as authenticating a prophet; rather, the authentication must come from the fact that he worships Yahweh.

Miracles in the OT are restricted to critical periods of redemptive history. Many have discussed the act of Creation as the first miracle, but in actuality it is not presented as such in the Genesis account. A miracle is signified by its revelatory significance and/or its connection with crucial points in the history of God's people—the exodus, the conquest of Jordan, the battle against the insidious Baal worship of the prophetic period. Creation is characterized by one major theme: a chronicle of the beginnings. The miracles of Genesis—striking blind the inhabitants of Sodom, the Flood, Babel—all signify the wrath of God upon those who have turned against him. This is the other side of redemptive history, the judgment of God upon those who are not his people.

The miracles of the exodus account have two foci: The plagues represent the absolute power of Yahweh over the gods of Egypt, and the miracles of the wilderness show God's absolute care and protection of his people. The plagues are particularly interesting because each one is directed at one of the gods of Egypt and reveals Yahweh as the only potentate. The basic theme is found in Exodus 7:5 and is repeated throughout the account (cf. 7:17; 8:6, 18; 9:14-16, 29; 12:12): "When I show the Egyptians

my power and force them to let the Israelites go, they will realize that I am the LORD" (NLT). In this regard they were directed not only at the Egyptians but also to the Israelites, who needed to know that their God would vindicate them against the Egyptians. This is borne out in the major miracle, the crossing of the Red Sea. The plagues themselves show a gradual increase in severity.

The wilderness miracles are intimately connected to the basic theme of the wandering narratives, the trial of Israel in times of desperate need and God's providential protection of his people when they turn to him. The basic organization of the stories concerns the need itself, which leads to Israel's complaint; this is followed by Moses' intercession and then by God's sovereign intervention. The miracles are interspersed with other stories that tell of God's punishment when the people's murmuring tries him too far. The miracle is God's self-revelation regarding his involvement in the needs of his own; Israel must then respond, and her response determines her blessing or punishment at the hands of Yahweh.

Miracles are conspicuously absent in the period of the united monarchy. This was a time of self-sufficiency, when God worked through the monarchy and did not intervene directly in the life of the nation. The reason is that Israel's eschatological hopes had been realized and made concrete in the presence of the Holy City and the temple.

It was different during the prophetic period. In the lives of Elijah and Elisha, miracles were predominant. This was a time of apostasy, and under the reign of Ahab and Jezebel the nation turned to paganism and the worship of Baal. The very existence of the Hebraic religion seemed to be threatened, and so the times called for extraordinary measures. Here the wondrous nature of the miracles is more evident than anywhere else in the OT. There are conscious allusions to the exodus miracles, perhaps looking to Elijah as a new Moses reinstituting the true worship of Yahweh. Parallels are seen in the challenge to the priests of Baal (1 Kgs 18; cf. Ex 7); the revelation of God on Mt Horeb with the wind, earthquake, and fire (1 Kgs 19; cf. Ex 19); and the parting of the Jordan (2 Kgs 2:10-14; cf. Ex 14). Many of the miracles were intended to demonstrate the impotence of Baal, such as the drought, the contest on Mt Carmel, and the miraculous sustenance supplied by God. Again, God's actions within history were part of his self-revelation, the vindication of his messengers, and the punishment of his enemies.

Miracles are infrequent in the writing prophets, perhaps due to the proclamation form of the writings (i.e., they dealt with message rather than deeds). The two major exceptions (apart from the recovery of Hezekiah chronicled in Is 38) are Jonah and Daniel. In Jonah, the miracle is addressed not to the Ninevites but to the Israelites, who are called back to their covenant obligations as the spokesmen for Yahweh. In Daniel the direction is reversed, and the situation is the same as that in Exodus or Kings. The miracles are directed to the Babylonians and Persians and have the same foci as the earlier events of the exodus and Elijah-Elisha chronicles, that is, the supremacy of Yahweh over the foreign gods and the vindication of his messengers. This is the third and final time of crisis and illustrates the major theological use of miracles in the OT.

Miracles in the New Testament The presence of the miraculous has a similar purpose in the NT; it occurred at a crisis point in salvation history to authenticate the presence of God in historical acts. It differs, however, in that it is transcended by the presence of the very Son of God, who himself is the greatest miracle of all. God now has not only acted in history; he has entered history and has turned it to himself. The parallels with the exodus events are obvious and show that the miracles of Jesus paved the way for the entrance of the new covenant in the same way that the exodus miracles prepared for the old.

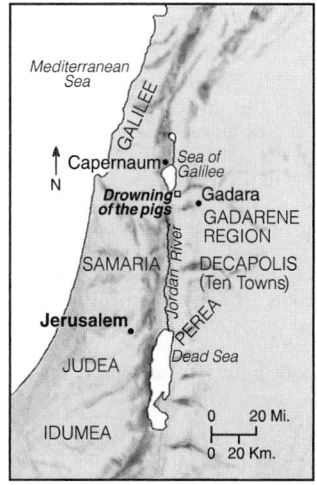

Jesus' Miraculous Powers Displayed Jesus calmed the storm on the Sea of Galilee, then cast out demons from two men in Gadara.

Jesus' Understanding Jesus stressed the connection between his miraculous ministry, especially the casting out of demons (exorcism), and the coming of the kingdom of God. As in the OT, the miracles signify the presence of God, but here it is more direct and also signals the inauguration of his kingdom (Mt 12:28). As such, then, the exorcism miracles mean the binding of Satan and the institution of the reign of God (Mk 3:23-27). At the same time all the miracles signify the dawning of the age of salvation, as expressed in Jesus' inaugural address at Nazareth (Lk 4:18-21, from Is 61:1-2).

Yet these miracles are not automatic signposts to the act of God; they must be interpreted by faith. Jesus was well aware of the presence of other miracles in his day (Mt 12:27) and so stressed the presence of faith in the healing miracles (Mk 5:32; 10:52). This faith must be directed to the presence of God in the event and in Jesus himself. The necessity of faith also helps to understand Jesus' refusal to provide his contemporaries with a "sign" (Mk 8:11-12); miracles could never "prove" the presence of God. For a better understanding of the connection between faith and miracles, it is best to note each Evangelist's individual portrait of the theological use of miracles.

Miracles in Mark Mark, the first of the four Gospels to be written, has often been called the "action Gospel" because of its emphasis on Jesus' deeds rather than his teaching. This is also true regarding Jesus' miracles, for Mark contains more proportionally than any of the others. There are five groups or five kinds of miracles in Mark. The first group centers on Jesus' authority over demons (Mk 1:21-39). The second concerns Jesus' authority over the law and conflict with his opponents (1:40-3:6). They result in fame but occasion his refusal to allow his true identity as Son of God to be known. The third group (3:7-30) contains exorcisms and the Beelzebub controversy, centering on his power over Satan. The fourth group (4:35-6:43) contains especially powerful miracles (stilling the storm, the Gaderene demoniac, the raising of Jairus's daughter) and probably

centers on the disciples, as Jesus thereby reveals to them the meaning of the kingdom and seeks to overcome their own spiritual dullness. The fifth and final group (6:30-8:26) continues the theme of the disciples' misunderstanding and prepares the way for the Passion, with the message regarding the bread, blindness, and the judgment of God.

The miracles in Mark center on conflict, first with Jesus' opponents and then with his own disciples. While the miracles are harbingers of God's kingdom, their purpose is to force an encounter with Jesus' true significance. They do not show Jesus as a Hellenistic wonder worker; in fact, they lead only to amazement and then disbelief in those who do not have faith. Jesus' personhood has been hidden and can only be understood in light of the cross. The miracles are not proofs but powers; God does not authenticate himself through them but shows himself to those with eyes to see.

Miracles in Matthew Matthew's is the teaching Gospel, where dialogue takes precedence over action. Matthew compresses Mark's narrative in order to make room for didactic material. Therefore, his stress is on the theological implications of faith rather than on the results they contain. Matthew's groups of miracles are isometric to teaching passages, in keeping with his general practice of combining narrative portions and organizing them around didactic sections. The first group (chs 8-9) combines miracles from Mark's first, second, and fourth groups and stresses Jesus' significance as the servant of Yahweh who exercises sovereign power and forgives sins. The secondary theme teaches discipleship and shows the awakening faith of the disciples and their involvement in Jesus' ministry. The second group (ch 12) centers on his authority over the law (the man with the withered hand) and over Satan (the Beelzebub controversy). The third group (chs 14-15) parallels Mark's fifth group but has a different purpose. Rather than arousing conflict, the disciples are seen in positive guise, actively involved in the Master's work. So the disciples become the means by which Jesus' ministry is continued. Therefore, the disciples are involved as "learners" (the meaning of "disciple") in his miraculous ministry.

Miracles in Luke Luke-Acts is remarkable and extremely important because it establishes beyond dispute the early church's belief that it was in absolute continuity with Jesus and was continuing the work of God in the world. Luke's major stress is on salvation history, and so one of his major stylistic methods for showing this direct connection is miraculous deeds. Especially enlightening here is Acts 9:32-42, where in two healing miracles Peter duplicated the Lord's miracles (the paralytic Aeneas, Lk 5:18-26; the raising of Dorcas, Lk 8:49-56).

From this respect also Luke returns to Mark's interest in the deed more than the teaching. However, Luke goes even further than Mark, for the miracles validate Jesus more directly. The first group follows the inaugural address (4:18-22), which itself presents the miraculous deeds as authenticating signposts to Jesus' personhood. They center on Jesus' power and authority (vv 31-41) and validate God's power in Jesus (5:17; 8:39) as well as faith in Jesus (seen in the "praise" motif, 5:25; 7:16; etc., but especially in Acts 9:35; 13:12; 19:17). The presence of "fear" at the miracles is a human response to having witnessed God's power (Lk 5:26; 7:16; 8:35-37; 24:5). The call to the disciples occurs in the presence of miracles (5:1-11, at the miraculous catch of fish; vv 27-28, after the healing of the bedridden paralytic).

Therefore, Luke views miracles as having redemptive

significance. However, this is not contrary to Mark's picture. Luke still avoids picturing Jesus as a mere wonder worker; Jesus still refuses to satisfy people's curiosity for an external sign (Lk 11:29-32; cf. also 9:9), and in the parable of the rich man and Lazarus (16:19-31) he teaches that the unbelieving heart can never be convinced by such events. Nevertheless, they can lead to repentance (10:13-16).

Miracles in John John is the most directly theological of the Evangelists, and miracles are characteristically given a distinctive Johannine coloring. In the Synoptics, miracles are "acts of power" signifying the entrance of God's reign into this world via Jesus; thereby, Jesus establishes Satan's defeat and God's sovereign control of history. John, however, contains no exorcisms, and the miracles are seen as "signs." At the same time miracles are part of the larger category of "works" (the other term for miracles used in John), by which Jesus shows the Father's presence in himself (Jn 10:32, 37-39; 14:10) and they give witness to Jesus as the sent one (5:36; 10:25, 38).

John selects only seven "sign miracles" from many others (20:30) and uses them as part of the thematic development in the respective section of each. For instance, changing the water into wine is a messianic act, signifying the outpouring of the kingdom blessing in the ministry of Jesus, the Messiah (ch 2); the multiplication of the loaves builds upon the "bread of life" and points to the messianic banquet as spiritually present in Jesus (ch 6).

The paradoxical nature of miracles in the Synoptics is even greater in John. He gives more stress to the wondrous nature of the events by providing such details as the stupendous amount of water changed into wine (2:6, approximately 120 gallons, or 454.2 liters); the distance over which Jesus' healing power works (4:46, almost 20 miles, or 32.2 kilometers); the length of time the man of Bethesda had been lame (5:5, 38 years; cf. 9:1, where the man had been born blind); the amount of bread needed to feed the 5,000 (6:7, where Philip said 200 denarii, or days' wages, would not have bought enough); and the proof of Lazarus's death (11:39; he had already begun to decay). John has a great interest in the miraculous. Yet at the same time there is even greater stress on the inadequacy of miracles for faith. The miracles as "signs" have saving value and point to the true significance of Jesus but are related to an awakening faith and in themselves are insufficient (2:11; 4:50). They have christological force, looking to Jesus' sonship and the Father's authentication of him but are based on the soteriological decision of the individual. As "signs," they contain the very presence of God in Jesus, the spiritual reality of the "sight" and "life" he brings (9:35-38; 11:24-26). Yet their purpose is to divide the audience and confront it with the necessity of decision. Two camps result—those seeking understanding and those considering only the outward aspects. Some refuse to consider the signs, and thus they reject them (3:18-21; 11:47-50), while others see them shallowly as mere wonders and fail to see in them the true significance of Jesus (2:23-25; 4:45). On the other hand, some view them with the eye of faith and go on to a realization of his personhood (2:11; 5:36-46; 11:42). In John the highest faith of all is that which does not need external stimulation (20:29).

Miracles in the Rest of the New Testament Apart from Acts, several passages in the NT speak of the value of miracles. Paul in 2 Corinthians 12:12 and Romans 15:18-19 considered them as "sign-gifts," which authenticated the divine authority of the "true apostle." He listed healing and miracles as specific "gifts of the Spirit" in 1 Corinthians 12:9-10. In Galatians 3:5 he considered them evidence for the presence of the Spirit. The author of the letter to the Hebrews in 2:4 said "God bore witness" to the true message of salvation via miracles. Therefore, in the apostolic age the miracles of God's servants were seen more directly as authenticating signs of God's action in his messengers.

See also Sign; Spiritual Gifts.

MIRIAM

1. Daughter of Amram and Jochebed and the sister of Aaron and Moses (Ex 15:20; Nm 26:59; 1 Chr 6:3). Miriam first appears in Scripture as a young girl commissioned with the task of watching her infant brother's cradle hidden in the reeds of the Nile River (Ex 2:4)—the result of a scheme conceived by her parents (Heb 11:23)—to escape the pharaoh's edict that all Hebrew males be drowned at birth (Ex 1:22). Miriam evidences not only courage and concern, but also displays a certain wisdom when her brother is discovered by the Egyptian princess (2:5-6). Taking the initiative, she offers to secure a nurse for the child, and when this plan is accepted, she gets her mother (vv 7-8).

Miriam first appears by name after the Israelites have crossed the Red Sea (Ex 15:20). She is given the title of "prophetess" and is, with her brothers, appointed a leader in the nation (Mi 6:4). Following the death of the Egyptian charioteers she leads the women of Israel in an anthem of praise accompanied with dancing and instrumental music (Ex 15:21).

Miriam appears in disgrace after her jealousy of and rebellion against Moses. With Aaron she murmurs against Moses because of his superior influence in the nation and because of his marriage to a Cushite woman (Nm 12:1-2). For this attack against God's chosen spokesman, she is struck with leprosy (v 10). Moses, however, intercedes on her behalf (Nm 12:9-13), and she was restored, but only after seven shameful days spent outside the camp while Israel waits to resume its march (Nm 12:14-15). This sad incident is the last recorded event in Miriam's public life. She died near the close of the wilderness wanderings at Kadesh and was buried there (20:1).

2. Child of Mered, descended from Ezra of Judah's tribe (1 Chr 4:17).

MIRMA*, MIRMAH
Son of Shaharaim and Hodesh from Benjamin's tribe (1 Chr 8:10).

MIRROR
Smooth surface for reflecting images. The word does not occur in the KJV, but the idea is there, translated from the Hebrew or Greek as "glass," "glasses" or "looking glass." Modern translations use the word "mirror."

In the biblical era, mirrors were made of copper, bronze, silver, gold, or electrum. They were highly polished so as to reflect the face as clearly as possible. Glass was in existence but was usually opaque (except Roman glass) and was not used for mirrors until after the biblical period.

The Bible first mentions mirrors in the time of Moses in relationship to the building of the tabernacle in the wilderness of Sinai just after the exodus from Egypt (Ex 38:8). When Alexander the Great spread Greek culture, the use of mirrors became even more widespread in the biblical world. Until that time, they were the possession of either court ladies or prostitutes.

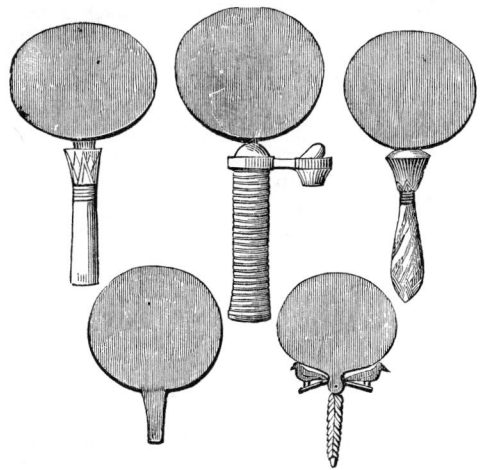

Ancient Bronze Mirrors

Archaeological excavations have unearthed bronze mirrors in Palestine along with various items of women's jewelry and clothes. Most of these date from the postexilic era up through Roman times. The mirrors are usually circular in shape with handles of wood or ivory, if they have handles at all.

MISCARRIAGE Spontaneous abortion of a nonviable fetus. It occurs in both human (Jb 3:16; Hos 9:14) and animal (Gn 31:38; Jb 21:10) pregnancies. The major problem is not in being unable to conceive or to become pregnant but in carrying the pregnancy to full term. The curse of a "miscarrying womb" results in not being able to have children (Hos 9:14), while the blessing of God results in successful pregnancies and long life (Ex 23:26).

The time factor is the key abnormality as indicated by premature delivery or "untimely birth" (Ps 58:8; Jb 3:16). While miscarriages occur for many reasons, Scripture mentions two: improper care (in animals) (Gn 31:38) and trauma to a pregnant woman (Ex 21:22).

Numbers 5 gives the test for an unfaithful wife. If she is guilty of adultery, then "her abdomen will swell and her thigh waste away" (v 27, NIV). These phrases may be euphemisms for miscarriage or for sterility (see NLT).

Paul underscores his inherent unworthiness to be an apostle by comparing his spiritual birth to an untimely physical birth (1 Cor 15:8).

See also Barrenness.

MISGAB* KJV translation for a place in Moab (Jer 48:1), rendered "the fortress" in the NLT.

MISHAEL
1. Uzziel's son (Ex 6:22), who, with his brother Elzaphan, was summoned by Moses to remove the bodies of Nadab and Abihu after they were killed for defiling the altar of the Lord (Lv 10:1-5).
2. One who stood beside Ezra when the law was read (Neh 8:4).
3. Hebrew name for one of Daniel's companions in Babylon (Dn 1:6), who, with Daniel and two others, remained faithful to God (vv 11, 19) and was delivered from the fiery furnace into which he had been cast for refusing to obey the king's edict (ch 3). His Babylonian name was Meshach (1:7).
See also Shadrach, Meshach, and Abednego.

MISHAL Levitical town in Asher's territory (Jos 19:26; 21:30; 1 Chr 6:74). *See* Levitical Cities.

MISHAM Elpaal's son from the tribe of Benjamin, who helped to build Ono and Lod with its towns (1 Chr 8:12).

MISHEAL* KJV spelling of the Levitical town Mishal in Joshua 19:26. *See* Mishal.

MISHMA
1. Son of Ishmael, Abraham's grandson, and the father of an Arabian tribe (Gn 25:14; 1 Chr 1:30).
2. Mibsam's son from Simeon's tribe (1 Chr 4:25-26). His omission in Genesis 25 and inclusion in the 1 Chronicles genealogy may indicate either that he was born after Jacob moved his family to Egypt or that he represented an Arabian tribe that affiliated with Simeon when Simeon's tribe expanded to the south (1 Chr 4:38-43).

MISHMANNAH Warrior from Gad's tribe who joined David at Ziklag in his struggle against King Saul (1 Chr 12:10).

MISHNAH* Series of interpretations of the meaning of the law; according to rabbinic tradition, they were given when Moses received the law from God on Mt Sinai, and they were to be passed down in oral form. This "oral tradition" was the "law" to which Jesus referred, for example, in Matthew 15:1-9. By about AD 200, under Rabbi Judah, the work begun by Rabbi Akiba around 120 was completed, and the oral tradition was finally written down. This written material is called the Mishnah. The word is derived from a verb that reflects the way the material had been repeated orally from teacher to disciple for many generations.

The Mishnah is divided into six "orders"; each order is divided into sections called "tractates," which in turn are divided into chapters. The orders deal with specific areas of legal concerns as follows:

1. *Seeds* is concerned with agricultural laws, and is introduced with a tractate dealing with daily prayers.
2. *Festivals* deals with feasts, fast days, and Sabbath regulations.
3. *Women* records marriage and family laws.
4. *Injuries* deals with civil/criminal law and ethical standards.
5. *Holy Things* concerns the ritual laws and the activities of the priesthood.
6. *Purifications* elaborates the laws of ritual purity.

The Mishnah, which is essentially a commentary on the OT law, forms the basis for the Gemara and the Talmud.

See also Gemara; Talmud.

MISHRAITE Descendant of Caleb and a member of Kiriath-jearim's family from Judah's tribe (1 Chr 2:53).

MISPAR, MISPERETH* One of the men who returned with Zerubbabel to Palestine following the Babylonian captivity (Ezr 2:2); alternately called Mispereth in Nehemiah 7:7.

MISREPHOTH-MAIM One of the northernmost places to which the Israelites pursued the fleeing Canaanite armies defeated at the waters of Merom (Jos 11:8). Misrephoth-maim, meaning "burning of water," defined part of the boundary of land remaining yet to be possessed by Israel during the days of Joshua (13:6). In all probability, Misrephoth-maim is identical with the cluster of springs at Khirbet el-Musheirifeh near the Mediterranean Sea, 20 miles (32.2 kilometers) south of Sidon and 6 miles (9.7 kilometers) north of Tyre, at the base of Ras en-Nakurah.

MITE* Small bronze or copper coin worth only a fraction of a cent (Mk 12:42, KJV). *See* Coins; Money.

MITHCAH, MITHKAH* One of the temporary camping places of the Israelites during their wilderness wanderings. It was mentioned between Terah and Hashmonah (Nm 33:28-29).

See also Wilderness Wanderings.

MITHNA Town of Joshaphat, one of David's mighty warriors (1 Chr 11:43, NLT). Other translations describe him as "the Mithnite."

MITHREDATH

1. Name of the treasurer of King Cyrus of Persia, who was given charge of the sacred vessels to give to the Judean prince Sheshbazzar as the exiles prepared to return to Jerusalem (Ezr 1:8).
2. Persian officer stationed in Samaria who, along with others, wrote a letter to King Artaxerxes of Persia, protesting the restoration of the city and walls of Jerusalem (Ezr 4:7).

MITRE* KJV translation for turban, a kind of headdress, worn by the high priest of Israel, in Exodus 28:4. *See* Priests and Levites.

MITYLENE Main city on the island of Lesbos in the Aegean Sea near the northwestern coast of Asia Minor. Mitylene was a seaport with two harbors. Originally it had been built on a small island separate from Lesbos. In NT times it was connected with the main island by a raised roadway across a narrow stretch of water. Acts 20:14 identifies Mitylene as one of the overnight stopping places where Paul and his traveling companions lodged as they journeyed by ship toward Jerusalem.

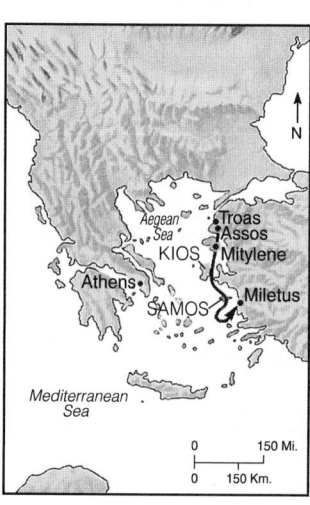

Mitylene On his third missionary journey Paul stopped at Mitylene before going on to Miletus. In Miletus he summoned the elders of the Ephesian church to say farewell to them, because he knew he would probably not see them again.

MIXED MARRIAGE* Marriages between Jews and Gentiles. Marriages to the original inhabitants of Canaan were forbidden lest Israel become idolatrous (Dt 7:1-5;

cf. 2 Cor 6:14). Nevertheless, this prohibition was often neglected in the period of the judges (Jgs 3:6) and thereafter (2 Sm 11:3; 1 Kgs 11:1-8). No explicit prohibition was given against marriages with other nationalities (Nm 12:1; Dt 23:7; Ru 1:4). After the exile, marriages to Gentiles were repudiated by Ezra and Nehemiah (Ezr 9:1-4; Neh 13:23-27).

See also Marriage, Marriage Customs.

MIZAR Small hill apparently situated in northern Palestine on the Transjordan plateau near Mt Hermon (Ps 42:6).

MIZPAH Name meaning "watchtower" in Hebrew (alternately spelled Mizpeh) used to designate a number of different locations mentioned in the OT and Apocrypha.

1. Place in Gilead where Jacob and Laban made a covenant (Gn 31:49) and set up a heap of stones to mark the borders between their territories.
2. Place referred to as "the land of Mizpah" (Jos 11:3) or the "valley of Mizpah" (Jos 11:8) near Mt Hermon and inhabited by the Hivites.
3. Town in Judah near Lachish referred to in Joshua 15:38.
4. Place in the tribal area of Benjamin (Jos 18:26). It was here that the Israelites gathered to war against the tribe of Benjamin (Jgs 20:1; 21:1) after the men of Gibeah had abused and killed the concubine of a visiting Levite. It was here that Samuel called all Israel together to pray for victory over the Philistines (1 Sm 7:5-8). Later, Samuel called for an assembly at Mizpah to publicly designate Saul as king and to instruct the people and king in the ways of the kingdom (10:17-25). In the time of Asa, Mizpah was a fortified town on the border between Israel and Judah (1 Kgs 15:22). After the fall of Jerusalem in 586 BC to the Babylonians, Mizpah became the residence of Gedaliah the governor (2 Kgs 25:23-24; Jer 40:10), who was murdered there by Ishmael of the "royal seed" (Jer 41:3). Two days later Ishmael murdered a company of pilgrims who were going to Jerusalem to bring their offerings at the ruined temple, and he cast their bodies into a cistern that had been constructed centuries earlier by Asa.

   In the intertestamental period Mizpah continued to be an important religious center. Judas Maccabeus called the people together at Mizpah "because Israel formerly had a place of prayer in Mizpah" (1 Macc 3:46).
5. Home of Jephthah, from which he led the Israelites in battle against the Ammonites, and to which he returned to carry out his vow (Jgs 10–11). This is possibly the same place as the Ramath-mizpeh of Joshua 13:26 and is thought by many to be identified with Khirbat Jal'ad just south of the Jabbok.
6. Town in Moab to which David fled from Saul (1 Sm 22:3).

MIZPAR* KJV spelling of Mispar in Ezra 2:2. *See* Mispar, Mispereth.

MIZPEH Alternate spelling for Mizpah (Jos 11:3, 8; 15:38; 18:26). *See* Mizpah.

MIZRAIM Hebrew word for the land of Egypt and/or its people, though some scholars suggest that Mizraim refers to a site either on the Edomite border or in northern Syria. In Genesis 10:6, Mizraim (Egypt) is identified as one of the sons of Ham who settled south of Canaan. Genesis 10:14 and Isaiah 11:11 distinguish Mizraim from Pathrushim, that is, Upper Egypt (the southern half of the United Kingdom of Egypt), but in the majority of the nearly 700 known references to Mizraim, there is no distinction between the two parts of the kingdom, and the term refers simply to the Egyptian territory.

See also Egypt, Egyptian.

MIZZAH Reuel's son and a chief of an Edomite clan (Gn 36:13, 17; 1 Chr 1:37).

MNASON Name of a Christian in Jerusalem (Acts 21:16). He is identified as a native of the island of Cyprus and a disciple of long standing. On their arrival at Jerusalem, Paul and his traveling party were entertained as guests by Mnason.

MOAB, MOABITES Name of a small kingdom in central Transjordan and also its inhabitants. The land of Moab was situated on the high plateau immediately east of the Dead Sea; the escarpment of the Jordan Rift formed an effective boundary between Moab and Judah. Moab's northern boundary shifted in accordance with the kingdom's military might, with the Heshbon vicinity forming the northern limit of Moab in periods of strength, and the Arnon River (modern Wadi el-Mojib) functioning as the northern border in times of weakness. The kingdom's eastern boundary was formed by the fringe of the Syrian desert, since the latter demarcated Moab's agricultural zone. On the south, Moab was separated from Edom by the Zered River (modern Wadi el-Hesa). Thus, even at its peak, ancient Moab encompassed a relatively small territory, measuring only about 60 miles (96.5 kilometers) north-south by about 20 miles (32.2 kilometers) east-west.

Most of Moab is gently rolling tableland that is divided by numerous ravines. Running through the heart of Moab is the King's Highway, a route that probably had military and commercial importance throughout this region's history (Nm 21:21-22; Jgs 11:17). The plateau has always been famous for its abundant pasturage (2 Kgs 3:4), and Moab's soil and climate are quite suitable for growing wheat and barley.

Moab: East of the Promised Land

Origin and History According to Genesis 19:37, the Moabites descended from Moab, the son of Lot and his oldest daughter. Deuteronomy 2:10-11, a passage whose context relates to the Moabites at the time of the Hebrew invasion, says that the pre-Moabite inhabitants of this region were the Emim, but the connection between Lot's descendants, the Emim, and the occupants of Moab at the time of the Hebrew invasion is not identified. There is thus far no specific information concerning the establishing of the Moabite kingdom proper, which existed from around

1300 BC to 600 BC. Knowledge of this period of Moabite history and culture is derived from archaeological and textual sources, including Egyptian, Assyrian, and OT texts.

Prior to the Israelites' passage through Transjordan, the Moabites had lost control of the land north of the Arnon and were dominated by Sihon, the Amorite king who ruled at Heshbon (Nm 21:13, 26). Having been refused permission to travel through Edom and Moab along the King's Highway, the Hebrews defeated Sihon in one of their most celebrated military campaigns. Fearing that Israel might conquer his land, King Balak of Moab waged war against the Hebrews (Nm 22:6; Jos 24:9) and hired the Mesopotamian diviner, Balaam, to pronounce a curse upon his enemies (Nm 22–24). The tribes of Reuben and Gad settled in Sihon's territory, and the Arnon formed the border between Israel and Moab (ch 32). From the time of the Israelites' apostasy at Shittim onward (ch 25), the Moabite tableland north of the Arnon was a source of contention between Moab and Israel.

Until his assassination by Ehud, the Moabite king Eglon oppressed the Hebrew tribes on both sides of the Jordan (Jgs 3:12-30). By Jephthah's day, northern Moab was once again under Israelite control (11:26). Obviously, as the book of Ruth indicates, there were also periods in which Moab and Israel lived in peace.

During the reigns of Saul and David, from the late-11th until the mid-10th centuries BC, Moab and Israel were at war, with the latter usually holding the upper hand (1 Sm 14:47; 2 Sm 8:2). Solomon's harem included Moabite women, and he also built a high place for Chemosh, the chief god of the Moabites (1 Kgs 11:1, 7). Following the division of the Israelite monarchy in 930 BC, Moab experienced a brief period of independence, but this ended when Omri and Ahab dominated the Moabites and their king, Mesha, during the ninth century BC. (The famous Moabite Stone, which describes Mesha's conflict with the Omride dynasty, and several shorter texts demonstrate that the language of Moab was closely related to OT Hebrew.) Conflict between Moab and her neighbors (e.g., Israel, Judah, Edom, and most importantly, Assyria) continued until the Babylonian king Nebuchadnezzar destroyed the Moabite kingdom early in the sixth century BC (Ez 25:8-11). This conflict is documented in the Assyrian literature, which indicates that Moab became an Assyrian vassal in the late eighth century BC, and in the OT (2 Kgs 3; 10:32-33; 13:20; 24:2). Indeed, the enmity between Moab, Israel, and Judah is especially evident in a series of prophetic oracles leveled against the Moabites (Is 15–16; Jer 9:25-26; 48; Am 2:1-3; Zep 2:8-11). These passages call attention to some of the major towns in ancient Moab (Nebo, Medeba, Heshbon, Dibon, Ar, Kir, and Horonaim).

Following the Babylonian conquest, the region of Moab fell under Persian control and was occupied by various Arab peoples, most notably the Nabateans. Although a Moabite state was never reestablished, people of Moabite ancestry were recognized in late OT times (Ezr 9:1; Neh 13:1, 23), since the postexilic Jewish community was concerned about observing the law recorded in Deuteronomy 23:3-6. In AD 106 the region of Moab became part of the Roman province of Arabia. Archaeological research has added much to the body of information that relates to Moabite history and culture from the prehistoric through Ottoman periods.

Religion During the third and second millennia BC, Moabite religion was probably similar to that practiced by the Canaanites, though the religion of Moab eventually developed into a relatively distinct system. Although other deities were worshiped by the Moabites, Chemosh was their national god. The OT refers to the Moabites as "people of Chemosh" (Nm 21:29; Jer 48:46), and the frequent appearance of "Chemosh" in Moabite personal names points to this god's elevated status. In general, the Moabite Stone's dozen references to Chemosh portray him as a god of war who leads his people against their enemies.

Divine guidance and favor were sought, and diviners and oracles were respected (Nm 22–24). A priesthood (Jer 48:7) and sacrificial system (Nm 22:40–23:30; 25:1-5; 2 Kgs 3:27; Jer 48:35) were important aspects of Moabite religion. No Moabite sanctuary has been discovered, but their existence is mentioned in the Moabite Stone and the OT (1 Kgs 11:7; 2 Kgs 23:13). Elaborately furnished tombs, like those found at Dibon, point to the Moabites' belief in the afterlife.

See also Canaanite Deities and Religion; Moabite Stone.

Drawing of Moabite Stone

MOABITE STONE* Longest literary source outside the OT dealing with the history of the region of Palestine and Transjordan during the period of 1300–600 BC. It is a particularly important source for the history of the Moabites, a people who lived in an area east of the Dead Sea. The stone was discovered in the 1860s and has a fairly complete narrative of the reign of Mesha, a Moabite king in the middle of the ninth century BC. When found, the stone was a hard slab with rounded top and 39 lines of Hebrewlike writing three feet, ten inches (1.2 meters) high by two feet (.6 meter) wide by two and a half inches (6.4 centimeters) thick.

On August 19, 1868, F. Klein, a German employed by the Church Missionary Society, saw the stele and reported its existence. When the German and French consuls showed an interest in the stone, the Arabs who had discovered it wanted to get the best price they could from the two governments. The Arabs then began to quarrel among themselves over how much to charge the foreigners, and the dispute became so bitter that one group heated the stone over a fire and then poured water on it, causing the stone to break into pieces. The Arabs then distributed the various pieces among the granaries of the countryside. There they were to act as a blessing or offering for a good harvest. Fortunately, a messenger from the French Consulate had obtained an impression of the writing on the stone. But the impression began to break apart as the messenger returned to the consulate on horseback. Impressions were also taken of the larger sections when they could be gathered at a later date. Finally, many of the other, smaller pieces were located, and the whole stone was put back together as closely as possible. Although parts were missing, the stone did contain a clear description of the history of the Moabites.

The text begins with a dedication to Chemosh, the god of the Moabites. Mesha, the king of the Moabites for 30 years, states that in gratitude for being delivered "from all the kings and letting" him see his "desire over all . . . enemies" he had erected a high place for the god. The place where the stele was found may also have been the location of the high place.

As the text continues, a short sketch of the history of the Moabites appears that can be related to the OT narrative. "Omri, king of Israel," had oppressed Moab for many days because Chemosh was angry with his land [Moab]. Omri's son "succeeded him and he too said, 'I will oppress Moab.' In my [Mesha's] time he said [this] but I triumphed over him and over his house, while Israel has perished for ever." The 40-year domination of Israel over Moab must involve the reigns of Omri (885–874 BC; 1 Kgs 16), his son Ahab (874–853 BC), Ahaziah (853–852), and the first half of Jehoram's reign (852–841). Thus the son mentioned in the text would be Omri's grandson. That would be more consistent with Scripture, which states that Jehoram (NLT, NIV "Joram") had tried to destroy Moabite rebels (2 Kgs 3:4-27). The rest of the text describes the victories over the Israelites, Mesha's public works, and the call of the god Chemosh for Mesha to fight the Hauranites.

See also Inscriptions; Moab, Moabites.

MOADIAH Head of a family of postexilic priests, whose house was headed by Piltai during the days of Joiakim the high priest (Neh 12:17); alternately called Maadiah in verse 5. See Maadiah.

MODIUS* Dry measure equivalent to about one peck.

MOLADAH One of the cities belonging to Judah's tribe (Jos 15:26), later assigned to Simeon (Jos 19:2; 1 Chr

4:28). The people of Judah resettled that area after the exile (Neh 11:26).

Some consider Moladah identical to Malatha, which became an Idumean fortress occupied by the Edomites (Josephus's *Antiquities* 18.6.2). Others place it by Jattir, at modern Khureibet el-Waten, as do Jerome and Eusebius. The evidence is, however, too obscure to make certain identification.

MOLE Small, burrowing rodent (Is 2:20). *See* Animals.

MOLECH Ammonite god worshiped with human sacrifice (Lv 18:21; Jer 32:35). *See* Milcom.

MOLID Son of Abishur and Abihail from Judah's tribe (1 Chr 2:29).

MOLOCH* Alternate spelling of Molech, an Ammonite god (Acts 7:43). *See* Milcom.

MOLTEN SEA* Alternate name for the laver in King Solomon's temple in 1 Kings 7:23. *See* Bronze Sea; Laver; Tabernacle; Temple.

MONEY Medium of exchange, measurement of value, means of payment.

Money was developed as a convenient medium of exchange to supplement and later to replace bartering, although the two systems operated concurrently for many centuries. From the patriarchal period to the present day, wealth has been measured in terms of goods and precious metals, particularly gold and silver, which remain universally acceptable mediums of exchange. Genesis 13:2 describes Abraham as "very rich in cattle, in silver, and in gold."

Wealth in a nomadic or seminomadic society was frequently measured by the number of cattle a person possessed, and because of this, cattle were a readily acceptable and easily valued, if rather large, medium of exchange. The degree to which cattle were commonly recognized as the standard for value, wealth, and exchange is reflected in the Latin form for money, *pecunia*, which is derived directly from *pecus*, meaning "cattle." For religious purposes, taxes or donations paid in cattle were most acceptable, and this not only increased the general recognition for this medium but also made the temple a repository for large herds of cattle, as well as smaller animals and produce, which, if they could not be used directly in the temple rituals, could be bartered for whatever commodities were required. Perishable foods were less popular for purposes of exchange than animals such as sheep and asses, although timber, wine, and honey were regularly used as a form of currency (1 Sm 8:15; 2 Kgs 3:4; Ez 45:13-16). Both public and private taxes, tribute, and debts of all kinds were settled by this means. Solomon paid Hiram, king of Tyre, in wheat and olive oil for his assistance in the construction of the temple (1 Kgs 5:11), and in the eighth century BC taxes were commonly paid in jars of wine or olive oil. Tribute in the form of sheep and wool is recorded in 2 Kings 3:4.

All the means of exchange mentioned represented goods that could be measured or counted, and attempts were made to establish a standard rate of exchange for them in relation to each other.

Silver was the precious metal most readily available in the ancient Near East and was therefore the one most frequently mentioned in connection with purchases by weight, and at a later period by coin. The first recorded instance in the Bible of silver being used as a medium of exchange occurs in Genesis 20:14-16, where Abraham received a payment of 1,000 shekels by weight of silver, as well as animals and slaves. Abraham also purchased the field and cave of Machpelah for 400 shekels of silver (Gn 23:15-16), which according to the custom of the day had to be weighed out in front of the vendor and checked by witnesses (cf. Jer 32:9-10).

As these events occurred about the beginning of the second millennium BC, the term "shekel" would not represent the coin familiar from later periods but rather a certain weight of silver. At a later time the brothers of Joseph sold him to traveling merchants for 20 shekels of silver (Gn 37:28). Genesis 33:19 mentions another unit of weight for metal, *the kesitah* (NLT mg), in connection with the purchase of a field by Jacob; the term occurs again in Joshua 24:32 and Job 42:11. This unit may have represented an amount equivalent to the currency value for a lamb.

In time large animals and material objects came to be considered extremely cumbersome as a means of exchange, and metal became increasingly popular. Transportation of large quantities of precious metal remained a problem, however, and a method had to be devised for easy recognition, accessibility, and storage of particular metals of value.

Over the years, fairly uniform shapes were designed for metals used in transactions. Silver could be piled or tied in bundles, as shown in Egyptian bas-reliefs, and the sons of Jacob took advantage of a similar method in transporting the purchase price of the grain they were buying from Egypt (Gn 42:35). About 1500 BC, pieces of metal shaped in the form of ingots, bars, tongues, or heads of animals were in use, as well as gold discs and rings of gold wire. Perhaps the most popular pieces acceptable as currency were those that had also been designed as jewelry. The valuables listed among the spoil of the Midianites included gold chains, bracelets, signet rings, and earrings (Nm 31:50). The bracelets and rings in particular probably represented a standardized weight, and could therefore be used easily as currency. Rebekah received gifts from her fiancé that were in the form of jewelry of specific weight: a gold ring weighing half a shekel and two bracelets weighing ten gold shekels (Gn 24:22). Job was given a fine ring of gold by a number of relatives, and it is unlikely that they would all have given him the same gift if it did not in fact represent a certain monetary value (Jb 42:11).

The requirement in Deuteronomy 14:25 to "bind up your money" would again imply either thin strips of silver that could be bundled together or rings that could be strung. In either event, transportation would be facilitated.

The value for weights of silver mentioned in Mosaic times can best be understood in terms of purchasing power. A ram could be bought for two shekels, while fifty shekels was the price of about four bushels of barley (Lv 27:16). In the time of Elisha, during a good year, one and one-half pecks of fine flour or three pecks of barley could be bought for one shekel (2 Kgs 7:16). Needless to say, monetary valuations of this kind would be affected by such economic considerations as supply and demand.

Estimation by eye was an inaccurate means of judging the value of currency, and there is no doubt that cheating was prevalent in the weighing and examination of metal. The weighing, an essential part of every major transaction, was also very time-consuming. In order to ensure the correct value of the weights, which were usually pieces of bronze, iron, or dressed stones, they carried some sort of stamp. Once this practice was generally established, it was a short step to the stamping of the individual pieces of metal, whether tongues, bars, or bracelets, being used as currency. The next logical development was stamping a piece of silver to authenticate its value for purposes of currency. This was the precursor of the coin, which was not known in the ancient Near East prior to the exilic period. Therefore, any reference to money before that time indicates bars, bracelets, rings, or other metal objects, stamped or unstamped.

The earliest minted coins came from the kingdom of Lydia in Asia Minor, being credited traditionally to Croesus (560–546 BC), the fabulously wealthy ruler of that land. The coins from Lydia were made of electrum, a natural alloy of silver and gold, and they depicted a lion and a bull. Like most of the early coins, the reverse simply contained a punch mark.

Originally a coin not only represented a value, but also its weight was worth the amount of silver or gold of its face value. Thus many of the early coins were slashed heavily by some ancient skeptics, who wished to be sure that the coin was of pure silver and not a less valuable metal coated with silver.

The purity of silver or gold was also a factor in the popularity and acceptance of particular coins. Thus in Greek and Roman times the tetradrachma from Tyre was one of the most widely accepted silver coins because of the purity of its metal content.

The use of coins did not eliminate the necessity for weighing, because the fraudulent clipping of the edges of coins was prevalent from their introduction in the sixth century BC. This particular problem plagued all subsequent issues of coinage, and it was only in the late 18th century in Britain that it was surmounted by a process involving the milling, or reeding, of the edges of the more valuable coins.

In the sixth century BC, when the Jews returned from exile in Babylonia, coins were donated for the rebuilding of the temple in Jerusalem, as well as silver and gold in other forms. The gold coin mentioned is a "daric." The term, apparently derived from the name of the great Persian king Darius I (521–486 BC), was in wide current use and even appears in biblical passages written at a later date but referring to a period before the reign of Darius (cf. 1 Chr 29:7).

Few craftsmen with the skills required for the manufacture of coins would have been available before the sixth century BC, so the earliest gold darics were probably minted at Sardis. The mint itself was taken over by the Persians when they occupied the territory, with production continuing as before.

Western sections of the Persian Empire probably used silver coins more frequently than gold. According to some traditions, coinage developed in Greece at Aegina about the time that the Lydians first adopted the concept. The earliest of these silver coins to be excavated so far dates from the sixth century BC and was minted in northern Greece.

Also in current use were the popular fifth-century BC tetradrachmas from Athens, which had dies on both sides of the coin. These depicted the head of the goddess Athena and the sacred owl.

Although the silver content of many coins in contemporary use was lowered, that of the Athenian tetradrachma remained consistently at its original high standard of purity. This circumstance naturally increased its acceptability, especially in areas caught up in political turmoil where the purity of the local currency was particularly questionable. Because of the stability of the silver content of the coin and the rapidity with which the Greek Empire was expanding, the Athenian tetradrachma was minted and used almost unchanged over a period of

200 years. Many of these coins have been found in hoards all over the eastern Mediterranean.

There is no doubt that by the fourth century BC there was a local mint in Judea, for silver coins imitating the Athenian tetradrachma, but also bearing the legend "Jehud," have been excavated there.

Because of the extent of trade in Greek and Roman times, the coins from the larger centers had a general acceptance in all the Mediterranean coastal areas. They were also favored in the inland areas, especially in those traversed by trading routes or those that were part of a larger empire.

Mints in Gaza, Joppa, and Tyre were established about the end of the fourth century BC to produce local currency. At this period Sidon continued to be an important supplier of silver coins, as it had been since the fifth century BC.

As the Seleucids gained control of Judea in 198 BC, a period of political turmoil commenced when the Syrians tried to Hellenize the Jewish people. Resentment toward Greek culture and resistance to all tampering with the traditional Jewish faith increased steadily until it found an outlet in the leadership of Mattathias, father of the Maccabees, who began a guerrilla uprising in 167 BC.

When the fortunes of war shifted temporarily to the Maccabeans, King Antiochus of Syria granted Simon Maccabeus the right to mint his own coins (1 Macc 15:6), but before he could take advantage of this prime symbol of independence, the balance of power changed once more. Judea returned to its status as a tributary, and the permission to mint coinage was hastily withdrawn.

Simon's son, John Hyrcanus, succeeded in overcoming the weakened Syrians and declared independence in 129 BC. The small bronze coins minted about 110 BC showed a wreath on the obverse bearing the inscription "Johanan the high priest and the community of the Jews." The reverse displayed a double cornucopia with a poppy head, both of which were Greek symbols of plenty. These were the first genuinely Jewish coins.

With the lack of skilled craftsmen and of a good mint it is hardly surprising that the resulting coins were simple and unpretentious. In consequence they were quite unlike the elaborate, and often delicate, designs of many contemporary coins.

Meanwhile, silver coins continued to be struck in the Phoenician cities of Tyre and Sidon on the orders of the Seleucids, and they remained the most popular silver coins in everyday use in Palestine until Roman times. Even then they continued to circulate side by side with the Roman coinage.

See also Banker, Banking; Coins; Money Changer.

MONEY CHANGER Ancient profession that undertook many of the services performed by the modern banker, particularly in the area of exchanging the currency of one country or province into that of another, or of exchanging small coins for coins of greater value or vice versa. Naturally, a fee was charged for such a service.

Standardized coinage as such does not go back beyond the seventh century BC. In earlier periods pieces of silver were weighed out in payment for commodities (Gn 20:16; 37:28; Jgs 17:2). Once the standardized coin was adopted in Asia Minor the idea was copied in other lands, but since coins differed from country to country, equivalents had to be worked out by the money changers.

The need for such procedures was particularly important in Palestine, where every adult male Jew had to pay a half-shekel offering (Ex 30:11-16). Jews from various countries who came to pay this sum might bring a variety of types of coinage. Temple authorities had to authorize a coin appropriate for the purpose. This was the silver Tyrian half-shekel or tetradrachma (cf. Mt 17:27, where Peter was told to pay the temple tax for Jesus and himself with the coin he found in the mouth of a fish). The Mishnah states (*Sheqalim* 1:3) that money changers operated in the provinces on the 15th of the month of Adar (the month before the Passover) to collect this tax. Ten days before the Passover the money changers moved to the temple courts to assist Jews from foreign countries.

Jesus encountered the money changers in the temple courtyard when he "cleansed the temple" (Mt 21:12-13; Mk 11:15-16; Lk 19:45-46; Jn 2:13-22). The reason for this action has been a matter of debate. Worshipers needed to procure the half-shekel to pay their tax. But they needed also to purchase birds, animals, or cake offerings in some cases. This wholesale activity in buying and money changing seemed inappropriate in the temple precincts, which constituted a sacred area (cf. Mk 11:16), although Jesus evidently approved the payment of the temple tax as such (Mt 8:4; 17:24-26; Mk 1:44; Lk 5:14). There is also the possibility that the charge made by money changers and by those who sold sacrificial birds and animals was exorbitant, whether for their own profit or for the profit of the temple authorities. Such operations could be carried on at a suitable distance from the sacred area so that the haggling and noise associated with such activities in an Eastern setting did not unnecessarily disturb the prayer and the offering of sacrifices carried on in the temple courts (cf. Jer 7:11).

See also Coins; Money.

MONOTHEISM* Belief that there is only one God. It is distinguished from polytheism, which posits the existence of more than one god; from henotheism, which worships one god without denying the existence of other gods; and from atheism, which denies the existence of any God. The three great monotheistic religions of the world are, in their historic order, Judaism, Christianity, and Islam.

If there is only one God, it follows that the deity is personal, sovereign, infinite, eternal, perfect, and almighty. This is, in fact, what Scripture declares of God in his essential being. It is only in the biblical revelation that we can know clearly and certainly who God is and what he is like. He must be distinct from the world (thus avoiding pantheism) in such a way that he is the only Creator and sustainer of the universe and the Lord of history. He is above and beyond his creation (divine transcendence), and yet he enters into time and human affairs (divine immanence). The biblical doctrine of monotheism is known both through historical events involving "the God who acts" for the salvation of the human race and through his verbal communication as "the God who speaks" to chosen servants for the instruction and edification of those who believe. It is in such dimensions that monotheism embraces the possibility and reality of direct encounter between the eternal and infinite God and the finite, sinful creature. The NT makes it clear that this is accomplished through Jesus Christ.

According to the Bible, man was originally a monotheist. No other conclusion is possible from the Genesis records (Gn 1–3). Polytheism developed later as a sinful corruption of the pristine belief in one true God, the God of Creation, revelation, and redemption. This corruption had set in at least by the time of Abraham, for God's call of Abraham to leave Ur of the Chaldees and journey toward Canaan, the land God had promised him and his posterity, undoubtedly involved a break with the polytheism of his ancestors in the area of Ur (11:31–12:9).

When Abraham reached Canaan, the Promised Land, he and his family found people worshiping a multitude of gods. Each ethnic grouping in Palestine had its own god or many gods (Gn 31:3-35; Jgs 11:24; 1 Sm 5:2-5; 1 Kgs 11:33). In their disobedience, the sons of Abraham were continually losing faith in God and lusting after the gods of the Canaanites or diluting the true worship of God with the heathen practices associated with the worship of the Canaanite gods (Gn 35:2-4; cf. Jos 24:2; 1 Kgs 16:30-33). One of the major roles of the prophets was to call the Jews back to true worship and faith in the one God, "the God of Abraham, the God of Isaac, and the God of Jacob" (Ex 3:6, 15-16; cf. 1 Kgs 18:17-18). This reminder of their monotheistic heritage was constantly needed because of the ever-present danger of losing it through contact with the polytheistic beliefs and practices of their idolatrous neighbors. Such reminders were necessary even for leaders like David (1 Sm 26:19), and certainly for Solomon (1 Kgs 11:1-7) and later kings (12:28-32; 2 Kgs 10:31; 22:17).

The early prophets did not clearly delineate a formal doctrine of monotheism; rather, they showed the importance and unreality of the pagan gods (1 Kgs 18:24). It was the eighth-century BC prophets who asserted a monotheistic faith in the face of a persistent polytheism. It was not until the time of the exile that the Jews were cured of their idolatrous polytheism, when their enemies took away their idols and demonstrated their impotence (Ps 115; Is 46). Then Israel learned that God alone was their refuge and help in the time of trouble, because he only is the true and living God who can save his people when they repent of their sins and obey the divine will.

See also God, Being and Attributes of.

MONSTER Term designating various creatures of the water. *See* Animals (Crocodile; Dragon).

MONTH *See* Calendars, Ancient and Modern.

MOON Lesser luminary of the heavens (Gn 1:16). Many Semitic languages use the same word for moon as the Hebrew. In three passages in the Hebrew OT (Sg 6:10; Is 24:23; 30:26), the moon is called "the white one," and paired with "the hot one," the sun. Another term, "crescent," is used in other languages such as Aramaic and Arabic, and "crescent ornaments" (Jgs 8:21, 26; Is 3:18) are mentioned.

In the creation account, it is said concerning the functions of the two luminaries: "They will be signs to mark off the seasons, the days, and the years" (Gn 1:14, NLT)— that is, "times" are determined by their movements. For this reason, when telling about the mighty deeds of the Lord in Creation, the poet says, "You made the moon to mark the seasons" (Ps 104:19, NLT). The ancient Hebrew calendar was lunar (Sir 43:6-7), the months beginning with the new moon, marked by special rituals (Nm 10:10; 28:11-14; 2 Chr 2:4). Two great festivals, Passover and Tabernacles, began in midmonth when the moon was full (Lv 23:5-6; Ps 81:3-5; and Lv 23:34, respectively). The seven-day week is a division of the 28-day lunar cycle into logical and convenient units, so the moon may be said to provide the basis for the significance of the number seven. As a corollary, the beginning of the seventh month, the Festival of Trumpets (Lv 23:24), marked the climax month of the sacred feasts; it also signified the New Year for regnal years and for agriculture (Josephus's *Antiquities* 1.1.3; Mishnah, *Rosh Hashanah* 1:1).

One verse in the creation story speaks of the sun's dominion over the day and the moon's over the night

(Gn 1:16; cf. Ps 136:9). The moon is also mentioned (alongside the sun) in the general order of creation when the spheres of the universe were established (Jer 31:35). From this the luminaries symbolize the continuity of the world order (Pss 72:5; 89:37-38). The darkening of the moon (and the sun) is a sign of the change of the order in creation in the latter days (Is 13:10; Ez 32:7; Jl 2:10; Hb 3:11; Mt 24:29; Mk 13:24; Rv 6:12; the converse is stated in Is 30:26). Since the moon resembles the sun, it also has the power to smite (Ps 121:6) and to influence the growth of crops in the field (Dt 33:14). In the book of Deuteronomy, the Israelites were warned against worshiping the moon and the rest of the host of heaven (Dt 4:19; 17:3), but this foreign worship made its inroads into the Judean kingdom (2 Kgs 21:3; 23:4-5; Jer 7:18; 8:2).

To keep an accurate control over the calendar and the feasts, the new moon was carefully observed seven times during the year in Jerusalem. This assured that the major feasts fell on the proper days. The Sanhedrin would gather early in the morning on the last day of the preceding month, and watchmen were posted to observe the moon's first appearance. When the evidence became clear, the sacred word was pronounced and the day became the first of the new month. Fire signals beginning from the Mt of Olives announced the new moon; later they were replaced by messengers because the Samaritans had set up false signals along the way.

See also Astronomy; Calendars, Ancient and Modern; Feasts and Festivals of Israel.

MOON, New *See* Calendars, Ancient and Modern; Feasts and Festivals of Israel; Moon.

MORASTHITE* KJV designation for the prophet Micah, taken from the name of the town Moresheth (Jer 26:18; Mi 1:1). *See* Micah (Person) #7.

MORDECAI

1. Jewish leader during the exile. Our knowledge of Mordecai comes exclusively from the book of Esther, which, according to some rabbinic sources, Mordecai himself wrote. Mordecai's activities are set against the period in which Xerxes (Ahasuerus) reigned over ancient Persia, a vast empire stretching over 127 provinces. Mordecai was a Benjamite descendant of Kish, the father of King Saul. His relatives were among those Jews who left Palestine during the captivity of Nebuchadnezzar. While his name reveals a Babylonian etymology, his heart burned with love for his countrymen who, notwithstanding the decree of Cyrus permitting their return to the Holy Land (538 BC), determined to colonize in dispersion rather than face the hardships of resettling in Palestine.

His remarkable life's drama is intertwined with Hadassah (Esther), his cousin, who became his ward following the death of her parents. Esther's sudden, unexpected exaltation to the position of queen following Vashti's deposition was an essential link to the deliverance of her people; Mordecai's forceful influence upon this beautiful Jewess was another. Behind them both, however, moved their sovereign God, whose love for Israel provided protection against the malevolent designs of Xerxes' prime minister, Haman.

Haman, the very incarnation of evil, had determined to exterminate the Jews of Persia because of Mordecai's unwillingness to pay him homage. Mordecai, learning of the plot, communicated the matter to Esther by way of Hathach, one of the king's officers. Her initial hesitancy to intervene on behalf of her people was met with her cousin's concise and stern answer: "Do not think that because you are in the king's house you alone of all the Jews will escape. For if you remain silent at this time, relief and deliverance for the Jews will arise from another place, but you and your father's family will perish. And who knows but that you have come to royal position for such a time as this?" (Est 4:13-14, NIV).

Several days elapsed during which Haman erected an enormous gallows upon which to hang Mordecai. On the evening of its completion, Xerxes, being unable to sleep, ordered the book containing the record of his reign to be read to him. Upon hearing of the actions of Mordecai in frustrating an earlier assassination attempt against him, he inquired as to what honors Mordecai had received in recognition of his service. Finding he had not been rewarded, Xerxes summoned Haman and asked him what fitting thing should be done for the man the king had purposed to honor. Haman, thinking that he was the object of the king's query, responded with three grand ideas (Est 6:7-9). Ironically, Haman was chosen to carry out his recommendations on behalf of Mordecai. A final touch of irony is seen in the execution of Haman on the very instrument he had prepared for Mordecai.

Following Haman's death, Mordecai and Esther had to act quickly to counteract the irrevocable edict directed against the Jews at Haman's instigation. Xerxes, now solicitous of the Jews' well-being, issued another edict allowing the Jews the freedom both to defend themselves and to retaliate against any aggressors. Apparently, the Persian officials to whom Mordecai forwarded this follow-up directive cooperated fully in protecting the Jews from their adversaries, thousands of whom were slain.

Consequently, Mordecai instructed all Jews to celebrate the time of their deliverance annually on the 14th and 15th days of Adar (roughly, March). The name of the festival, Purim, is derived from the word *pur* ("lot"), which was cast by Haman to determine the day for the Jews' annihilation.

See also Esther, Book of.

2. One of the 10 leaders who returned with Zerubbabel after the exile (Ezr 2:2; Neh 7:7).

MOREH, Hill of Hill close to the valley of Jezreel, near which the Midianites camped when they were attacked by Gideon (Jgs 7:1). It was probably called by this name because it was the location of a sanctuary where divination was practiced. Its name may imply instruction or divination. It is generally identified with Jebel Nabi Dahi, across the valley from Mt Gilboa.

MOREH, Oak of Abraham's first recorded stopping place upon entering Palestine after leaving Mesopotamia. Here he built an altar to God (Gn 12:6). Later, Moses mentioned this place as a geographical landmark to identify the whereabouts of Mt Gerizim and Mt Ebal (Dt 11:30). The KJV improperly reads "plain" of Moreh. The oak of Moreh was located near Shechem.

MORESHETH Micah's hometown (Jer 26:18; Mi 1:1). *See* Micah (Person) #7.

MORESHETH-GATH Town in the lowland country of Judah included in Micah's lament (Mi 1:14); perhaps the same as Moresheth, Micah's hometown. The "gath" in Moresheth-gath suggests that the town was in close proximity to the major Philistine city by that name. Its exact location is uncertain. Jerome (a fourth-century AD church father) suggested that Moresheth-gath was situated a short distance east of Eleutheropolis, identifiable with modern Khirbet el-Basel. Another possible site is Tell ej-Judeideh, six miles (9.7 kilometers) southeast of Gath.

MORIAH Name used twice in the OT. Abraham was sent to sacrifice his son Isaac in "the land of Moriah" (Gn 22:2). Because in the narrative it is said that the ram was "provided" in the place of Isaac when God "appeared" to Abraham, it has been suggested that the form of the name "Moriah" may be connected with this. (The Hebrew verb ra'ah can have the meanings "see," "provide," and "appear," and the ending -iah is the shortened form of the name of the Lord that is found in many Hebrew names.)

In 2 Chronicles 3:1, Mt Moriah is the place of Solomon's temple, specifically identified with the threshing floor of Ornan the Jebusite (cf. 2 Sm 24; 1 Chr 21), but not explicitly with the place of Abraham's sacrifice. Some, however, see in the description of the Lord's appearing to David a reminder of his appearing to Abraham there. The Jewish historian Josephus (Antiquities 1.13.2; 7.13.4) clearly connects the place of the temple with the place where Isaac was offered up, as does the second-century BC book of Jubilees (Jubilees 18:13). Samaritan tradition linked Moriah with Mt Gerizim. Muslim tradition connects the Dome of the Rock that stands today on the site of the Jerusalem temple with Abraham's sacrifice of Isaac on the great rock under the dome of the mosque.

MORNING SACRIFICE *See* Offerings and Sacrifices.

MORNING STAR Literally, Venus. The phrase is closely related to the idea of the "dayspring" (Jb 38:12; Lk 1:78) and the "daystar" (2 Pt 1:19). The identity of the star is settled when Christ says, "I am the morning star" (Rv 22:16). It is another way of saying, "I am the light of the world" (Jn 8:12; 9:5: 12:46). The central concept found in the symbol is that of Christ as light shining in darkness (Lk 2:32; Jn 1:4, 7-9; 3:19; 12:35; 2 Cor 4:6; Eph 5:14; 1 Pt 2:9; 1 Jn 2:8; Rv 21:23). With the birth of the Messiah, the morning star arose—the gospel light dawned (Is 9:1-2; Mt 4:15-16). The phrase points to Christ's glory, as the source of light, and to his grace in the sharing of life. Christ not only described himself as the morning star but also declared that he gives the morning star to those who overcome (Rv 2:28).

MORTAR*, The Name given by Zephaniah to a hollow place or depression resembling a mortar in Jerusalem. The "mortar" (Hebrew, *Maktesh*) was a place of business whose merchants were soon to grieve for their loss of trade (Zep 1:11). Its location is variously identified with the Phoenician quarter, the Kidron Valley, or the Tyropoeon Valley.
See also Jerusalem.

MOSERAH, MOSEROTH Temporary camping place of the Israelites during their wilderness wanderings. It was positioned between Hashmonah and Bene-jaakan (Nm 33:30-31). Later, Aaron died and was buried there (Dt 10:6). Moseroth is the plural form of Moserah.

MOSES Great leader of the Hebrew people who brought them out of bondage in Egypt to the Promised Land in Canaan; also the one who gave them the law at Mt Sinai that became the basis for their religious faith through the centuries. Focused in this one person are the figures of prophet, priest, lawgiver, judge, intercessor, shepherd, miracle worker, and founder of a nation.

The meaning of his name is uncertain. It has been explained as a Hebrew word meaning "to draw out" (Ex 2:10; cf. 2 Sm 22:17; Ps 18:16). If, however, it is an Egyptian name given him by the daughter of Pharaoh who found him, it is more likely from an Egyptian word for "son" (also found as part of many well-known Egyptian names such as Ahmose, Thutmose, and Ramses). No one else in the OT bears this name.

Without question, the greatest figure in the OT (mentioned by name 767 times), his influence also extends to the pages of the NT (where he is mentioned 79 times). The first 40 years of his life were spent in the household of Pharaoh (Acts 7:23), where he was instructed in all the wisdom of the Egyptians. The next 40 years he spent in Midian as a fugitive from the wrath of Pharaoh, after killing an Egyptian who was mistreating a Hebrew. His last 40 years were devoted to leading the Israelites out of bondage in Egypt to the land God had promised to Abraham and his descendants (Gn 12:1-3). He died at the age of 120 after leading the Israelites successfully through 40 years of wandering in the wilderness to the very edge of the Promised Land on the east side of the Jordan River (Dt 34:7). He is one of the great figures in all of history, a man who took a group of slaves and, under inconceivably difficult circumstances, molded them into a nation that has influenced and altered the entire course of history.

PREVIEW
• Background
• The First 40 Years—In Egypt
• The Second 40 Years—In Midian
• The Third 40 Years—From Egypt to Canaan
• Moses in the New Testament

Background The only source of information for the life of Moses is the Bible. Archaeology confirms the credibility of the events associated with Moses, but it has never provided any specific confirmation of his existence or work. His story begins with the arrival in Egypt of Jacob, his sons, and their families during a time of famine in Canaan. Invited by Joseph and welcomed by Pharaoh, the family settled down in northeast Egypt in an area known as Goshen, where they remained for 430 years (Ex 12:40). With the passing of time, their numbers grew rapidly, so that the land was filled with them (1:7). A new king arose over Egypt who did not know Joseph. The biblical account does not give the name of this pharaoh, and there has never been agreement as to his identity. He has most frequently been identified as Thutmose III (1504–1451 BC), Seti I (1304–1290 BC), or Ramses II (1290–1224 BC). Out of fear that their growing numbers might become a threat to the security of his nation, Pharaoh determined to take measures to reduce their number. He put them to work building the store cities of Pithom and Rameses, but the severity of the work did not diminish them. He next tried to enlist the cooperation of the midwives to destroy the male babies, but they would not carry out his orders. He then ordered his own people to drown the male infants in the Nile River. Against the background of this first-known Jewish persecution, the baby Moses was born.

The First 40 Years—In Egypt

Birth and Early Life A man of the family of Levi named Amram married his father's sister Jochebed (Ex 6:20; cf. 2:1). Their first son, Aaron, three years older than Moses, was born before the command to drown the Hebrew babies was given, as there is no indication that his life was in danger. However, the cruel order was in force when Moses was born, and after three months, when his mother could no longer hide him, she took a basket made of bulrushes and daubed it with bitumen and pitch. She put the baby into the basket and placed it among the reeds along the banks of the river. An older sister, Miriam, stayed near the river to see what would happen. Soon the daughter of Pharaoh (identified by Josephus as Thermuthis and by others as Hatshepsut, but whose actual identity cannot be determined) came to the river to bathe, as was her custom. She discovered the baby, recognized it as one of the Hebrew children, and determined that she would raise the child as her own. Miriam emerged from her hiding place and offered to secure a Hebrew woman to nurse the child, an arrange-ment that was agreeable to the princess. Miriam took the baby to his own mother, who kept him for perhaps two or three years (cf. 1 Sm 1:19-24). Nothing is recorded of those formative years. Whether his mother continued seeing him during his later childhood and young man-hood or revealed his true identity to him or taught him the Hebrew faith are matters of speculation. Moses was instructed in all the wisdom of the Egyptians, as would befit a member of the royal household, and he became mighty in his words and deeds (Acts 7:22).

Identification with His Own People Just when Moses became aware that he was a Hebrew rather than Egyptian cannot be known, but it is clear that he knew it by the time he was 40 years old. One day he went out to visit his people and to observe their treatment, for the cruel measures taken against them by Pharaoh at the time of Moses' birth had not been lifted. Seeing an Egyptian beating a Hebrew, Moses in great anger killed the Egyp-tian and buried him. He thought the deed had gone unnoticed until the next day when he encountered two Hebrews fighting with each other. When he tried to act as peacemaker, they both turned on him and accused him of murder: "Who made you a prince and a judge over us? Do you mean to kill me, as you killed the Egyp-tian?" (Ex 2:14, RSV). Acts 7:25 adds: "He supposed that his brethren understood that God was giving them deliv-erance by his hand" (RSV). Aware that being a member of Pharaoh's household would not exempt him from pun-ishment now that the deed was known, Moses fled for his life to the land of Midian.

The Second 40 Years—In Midian

Marriage into the Family of Jethro Soon after arriving in Midian, Moses sat down by a well, where he observed the seven daughters of the priest of Midian who had come to the well to draw water for their father's flock. Shepherds came and drove them away, but Moses intervened and helped them water their animals. When Jethro (Ex 3:1; also called Reuel, 2:18; Hobab, Nm 10:29) learned what had happened, he invited Moses to stay with his family and gave him Zipporah as his wife. (There is some dis-agreement among scholars regarding the identity of Hobab in Numbers 10:29; some think he was Moses' father-in-law, while others maintain that Hobab was Moses' brother-in-law. *See also* Hobab). Two children, Gershom (Ex 2:22) and Eliezer (18:4), were born to Moses and Zipporah during the years in Midian. Forty years passed, and Moses' thoughts about his former life in Egypt must have faded into the past. He could not have foreseen that God would soon thrust him back into the midst of the court in Egypt, where he would confront the son of the now-dead pharaoh with the demand to release the Hebrew people from the bondage they had endured for so many years. God had not forgotten his people and was now ready to deliver them.

Encounter with God at the Burning Bush One day, while Moses was taking care of the flocks of his father-in-law, he led them to Mt Horeb (known also as Sinai), where God appeared to him in a flame of fire out of the midst of a bush that burned but was not con-sumed. Moses approached to observe the strange sight more closely and heard God speak to him out of the bush, "Moses, Moses!" Moses replied, "Here am I." Before he could come any nearer to the bush, God said, "Do not come near; put off your shoes from your feet, for the place on which you are standing is holy ground" (Ex 3:4-5, RSV). He further identified himself as the God of Abraham, Isaac, and Jacob. He assured Moses that he was aware of the cruel afflictions of his people and had heard their cries. Then he told of his plan to send Moses to Egypt to deliver his people from their bondage.

Faced with a challenge that seemed beyond his capa-bilities, the aged Moses began making excuses for not accepting the task. God assured Moses that he would be with him (Ex 3:11-12). To his excuse that he would not be able to give an answer if the people asked him the name of the God he represented, God revealed his name in the cryptic statement, " 'I AM THE ONE WHO ALWAYS IS' . . . Just tell them, 'I AM has sent me to you' " (vv 13-14, NLT). Many interpretations have been proposed for the name. Whatever else it means, it undoubtedly suggests the self-existence and all-sufficiency of God. Moses then argued that the people would not believe him when he told them that God had sent him to deliver them from Egypt. In response God gave him three signs: When he cast his shepherd's rod to the ground, it became a ser-pent. When he put his hand to his bosom, it became lep-rous. He was also told that when he would pour water from the Nile on the ground, it would become blood (Ex 4:1-9). Even armed with these powerful evidences of the presence of God with him, Moses raised still another objection, "O Lord, I'm just not a good speaker. I never have been, and I'm not now, even after you have spoken to me. I'm clumsy with words" (v 10, NLT). God told him that he would teach him what to say, but despite such assurance, Moses asked God to send someone else. In anger mingled with compassion, God made Moses' brother, Aaron, the spokesman, but said his instructions would still be given directly to Moses.

Return to Egypt Moses took his wife and sons and set out for Egypt, telling his father-in-law only that he wanted to go back to Egypt to visit his kinsmen there (Ex 4:18). The biblical account says he put his wife and sons on the same donkey to journey back to Egypt (v 20). The fact that all three rode the same animal indicates that both children were quite young and had not been born in the early years of Moses' marriage. At a lodging place along the way a strange thing happened. The Lord met him and sought to kill him (v 24), apparently because Moses had failed to circumcise the baby before leaving Midian. When Zipporah realized that Moses' life was in danger, she performed the rite herself and said to her husband, "What a blood-smeared bridegroom you are to me!" (v 25, NLT). Whatever else may have been involved in this unusual encounter with God, it was a solemn reminder that the one who was to be the leader of the covenant people must not himself neglect any part of the covenant (Gn 17:10-14).

God told Aaron (who was still in Egypt) to go to the mountain where Moses had encountered God at the burning bush and meet his brother there. Moses told Aaron everything that had happened, and together they went to Egypt, gathered the elders together, and informed them of these matters. When Moses and Aaron performed the signs in the presence of the people, they believed these leaders had been sent by God to deliver them from their affliction (Ex 4:30-31).

The Third 40 Years—From Egypt to Canaan

The Encounter with Pharaoh Soon after his return to Egypt, Moses, accompanied by Aaron, went to Pharaoh and repeated the demands of the Lord, "Let my people go, for they must go out into the wilderness to hold a religious festival in my honor" (Ex 5:1, NLT). Pharaoh rejected the demand with the observation that he had never heard of this God of Moses. When one realizes that Egyptian kings considered themselves to be gods, the affront to Pharaoh becomes even more acute. Not only did he reject Moses' demands, but he intensified the burdens of the Hebrews. Their work had up until then required them to make brick using straw provided for them, but now Pharaoh said they would have to gather their own straw and still produce the same number of bricks. The Hebrews turned in anguish and anger to Moses and blamed him for making them offensive in the sight of Pharaoh. Even Moses could not understand the turn of events and complained bitterly to God. God reassured Moses that he would deliver the Hebrews from their bondage, and moreover, he would bring them into the land he had promised Abraham, Isaac, and Jacob. He then instructed Moses to return to Pharaoh and repeat the demand to release the Hebrews upon threat of severe reprisal if the demand were ignored.

Ushered again into Pharaoh's presence, Moses repeated his request for release of the Israelites. He attempted to impress Pharaoh by turning his rod into a serpent, but the Egyptian wise men, through their secret arts, were able to duplicate the miracle, so Pharaoh's heart remained hardened and he would not listen to Moses. In rapid succession Moses brought nine plagues upon the land of Egypt to show the omnipotence of God to force the compliance of Pharaoh. These included a plague in which the water of the Nile turned to blood, a plague of frogs, one of gnats, then of flies, a plague on the livestock, boils on the people, plagues of hail, locusts, and complete darkness. During the plagues of the frogs, flies, hail, locusts, and darkness, Pharaoh was distraught and would temporarily relent and agree to Moses' demands, but as soon as the plague was lifted, his heart hardened and he would retract his promise. The outcome of the first nine plagues was terrible devastation of the land of Egypt, but the Israelites were not released. There was yet one more plague in store, the most terrible of all.

The First Passover God told Moses that there remained one more plague in store for the Egyptians: "All the firstborn sons will die in every family in Egypt, from the oldest son of Pharaoh, who sits on the throne, to the oldest son of his lowliest slave. Even the firstborn of the animals will die" (Ex 11:5, NLT). Furthermore, he assured Moses that the plague would not touch a single household of the Hebrews, "Then you will know that the LORD makes a distinction between the Egyptians and the Israelites" (v 7, NLT).

God instructed the people through Moses and Aaron to make their preparations for leaving the land in haste. They were to go to the Egyptians and ask them for their jewels of silver and gold (Ex 11:2-3), a request to which the Egyptians agreed, perhaps out of fear of the Hebrews and in the belief that the gifts would bring about an end of the terrors that had struck the land. The Hebrews were also instructed to prepare a lamb for each family—small families could share—for the last meal to be eaten in the

land of Egypt (a rite that became the pattern for the Jewish observance of the Passover for many centuries). Blood of the lamb was to be put on the doorposts and lintels of the houses in which the Passover meal was being eaten that night. The Hebrews were promised that wherever the blood was on the door, no harm would come to that household. They were also instructed to prepare unleavened bread. At midnight the death angel of the Lord killed all the firstborn in the land of Egypt, from the firstborn of Pharaoh himself to the lowest captive in a dungeon; not a single house of the Egyptians escaped tragedy. When Pharaoh saw what had happened, he ordered Moses and the people to leave the land at once (12:31-32). The biblical record says that about 600,000 Hebrew men left Egypt. Together with women and children, the total would have been in excess of 2 million people.

The Exodus from Egypt The exodus is the central event of the OT and marks the birth of Israel as a nation. The Jewish people still look back to that event as the great redemptive act of God in history on behalf of his people, much as Christians look upon the cross as the great redemptive act of their faith.

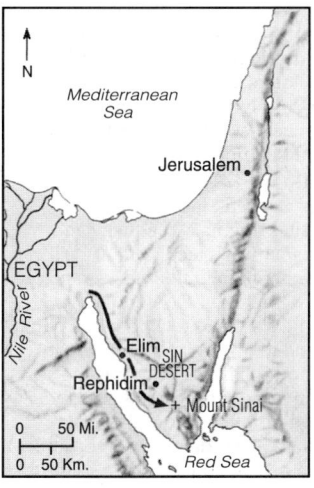

Moses Leads the Israelites to Mount Sinai

The exact route taken by the Hebrews out of Egypt cannot be determined today, though many possibilities have been proposed. They did not take the shortest, most direct route to Canaan (which would have been about a 10 days' journey along the Mediterranean coastline), but set out in the direction of Mt Sinai, where Moses had earlier met God at the burning bush. As a sign that Moses had been sent to deliver the people, God told Moses he would bring them to that same spot, where they would worship God (Ex 3:12). The Hebrews did not forget the request of Joseph to carry his bones with them when they returned to their own land (Gn 50:25; Ex 13:19).

As the people journeyed, they were preceded by a pillar of cloud during the day and a pillar of fire at night. The cloud represented the presence of God with his people and guided them along the route they should travel.

Back in Egypt, Pharaoh was having second thoughts about letting the Hebrews leave the land and decided to pursue them with his army and bring them back. When the Hebrews saw the approaching cloud of dust and realized that the Egyptian army was pursuing them, they were terrified. The sea lay ahead of them and the Egyptians were behind; there seemed to be no way of escape. The people turned on Moses, blaming him for bringing them out of Egypt. God again assured them that they did not need to be afraid or do anything to defend themselves. He promised to fight the battle for them and give them victory (Ex 14:14).

The Lord parted the water of the Sea of Reeds (traditionally but erroneously referred to as the Red Sea) by a strong east wind and allowed the Israelites to pass through the sea on dry ground to the other side. The Egyptians rushed after the Israelites, following them into the dry bed of the sea. But before they reached the other side, the waters rushed back together, destroying the Egyptian army in the midst of the sea and leaving the Israelites safe on the other side. The people celebrated their great deliverance in song (Ex 15) and then continued their journey. The narrative that follows describes the struggle of the Israelites to survive in the desert—problems of food and water, internal dissension, murmurings against Moses, and battles with enemies. Through all their experiences, Moses towers as the unifying force and great spiritual leader.

In spite of having seen God's great act of deliverance so recently, the faith of the Israelites was not strong. Three days later they came to a place where the water was not fit to drink, and they began complaining against Moses. The Lord showed Moses how to purify the water, and the people's needs were satisfied (Ex 15:22-25). When they reached the wilderness of Sin, they complained again, this time because of lack of food. God met their need by supplying manna, a breadlike substance that would serve as their food until they came to Canaan (16:1-21). Later, camped at Rephidim, the people complained again, this time for lack of water. Once again God met their needs by supplying water from the rock at Horeb (17:1-7). The Amalekites attacked them while they were still camped at Rephidim, but God gave a great victory to the Israelites (vv 8-13).

Moses and the people reached Sinai and camped there. Jethro came to visit, bringing Moses' wife and sons. Zipporah had apparently decided to return with her children to stay with her father rather than to go on to Egypt with Moses. It was a joyful reunion, and Jethro made a burnt offering and sacrifices to God (an act that has evoked the suggestion that Jethro was a true worshiper of God, though nothing is known of his links to the Hebrew faith). When Jethro observed Moses trying to settle all the disputes and problems of the Hebrews unaided, he proposed that Moses delegate responsibility for some of the lesser matters to able men chosen from among the people. Moses accepted the suggestion, and shortly afterward Jethro returned to his own land. He did not remain at Sinai to participate in the ratification of the covenant (Ex 18:13-27).

Giving of the Law at Sinai God had kept his promises to Moses. He had delivered the Hebrews from their Egyptian bondage and brought them to the very place where he had commissioned Moses to be their leader. He was now ready to enter into a covenant relationship with Israel. Amid a spectacular and terrifying scene of lightning, thunder, thick clouds, fire, smoke, and earthquake, God descended to the top of Sinai and called Moses to come up the mountain, where he remained 40 days to receive the law that would become the basis of the covenant.

At Sinai, God was revealed as the God who demands exclusive allegiance in all areas of life and, at the same time, as the God who desires personal fellowship with his people.

Apostasy of the People While Moses tarried on Mt Sinai, the people below became impatient and skeptical about his return, so they went to Aaron and asked him to make idols for them to worship. They contributed the gold earrings they were wearing. "Then Aaron took the gold,

melted it down, and molded and tooled it into the shape of a calf. The people exclaimed, 'O Israel, these are the gods who brought you out of Egypt!' " (Ex 32:4, NLT). The next day they joined in the worship of the idol with sacrifices and revelry. God told Moses what was taking place below and angrily declared that he was going to destroy the people but would make a great nation of Moses and his descendants. Moses immediately interceded on behalf of the people, and God's wrath abated. Moses descended the mountain, carrying the two tablets of stone on which the law had been written, but when he entered the camp and saw what was taking place, he could not restrain his anger. He threw the stone tablets to the ground, ground the golden calf to powder, mixed it with water, and forced the people to drink it. He turned angrily to Aaron and demanded an explanation for the great sin that had been committed. Aaron lamely tried to shift the blame by minimizing his own role: "I threw them [the gold] into the fire—and out came this calf!" (v 24, NLT). Moses called for volunteers to carry out God's judgment on the people for the great sin they had committed. Men of the tribe of Levi responded and executed about 3,000 men. Later they were commended and rewarded (Dt 33:9-10). Moses again interceded for the people, requesting that he be destroyed with the rest if God could not forgive them. God relented and promised Moses that the angel of the Lord would go with them still (Ex 32:34).

Then Moses made a special request that he might be allowed to see the glory of the Lord. God instructed Moses to hew out two more tablets of stone like the ones he had destroyed and to return to the top of the mountain the next day. There the Lord passed before him and proclaimed his name: "I am the LORD, I am the LORD, the merciful and gracious God. I am slow to anger and rich in unfailing love and faithfulness" (Ex 34:6, NLT). Moses remained on the mountain another 40 days, where he received renewed warnings against idolatry and further instructions from the Lord, together with another copy of the Ten Commandments on tablets of stone. When Moses came down from the mountain, he was not aware that the skin of his face shone as a result of talking with God. At first the people were afraid to come near him, but he called them together and repeated all the Lord had said to him on the mountain. Afterward, he covered his face with a veil, which he removed only when he went into the presence of the Lord. Paul said the purpose of the veil was to prevent the people from seeing the heavenly light gradually fade from Moses' face (2 Cor 3:13).

The Tabernacle and Establishment of the Priesthood When Moses went up to the mountain the first time to receive the law from God, he was instructed to collect materials to be used in the construction of the tabernacle or tent. Gold, silver, bronze, blue and purple and scarlet yarn, fine twined linen, goats' hair, tanned rams' skins, goatskins, and acacia wood would be needed, along with oil for the lamps, spices for the anointing oil and for the fragrant incense, onyx stones, and stones for setting (Ex 25:3-7). The pattern for construction was also given to him, together with the ritual to be used for the consecration of the priests. A man named Bezalel was put in charge of the construction of the tabernacle, assisted by Oholiab (31:1-6). The tabernacle was portable like a tent so that it could be taken down and moved from place to place as the Hebrews continued their journey toward Canaan.

In addition to giving Moses directions for the tabernacle, God also instructed him concerning the sacrifices that were to be brought: the burnt offering, grain offering, peace offering, sin offering, and guilt offering (Lv 1–7). The solemn ceremony for ordaining Aaron and his sons as priests and for inaugurating the worship practices were to be performed by Moses (chs 8–9).

Sometime after this solemn inauguration of the religious ritual actually took place, Nadab and Abihu, two of Aaron's four sons, offered unauthorized fire before the Lord. A fire came out from the Lord and destroyed them. Moses forbade Aaron and his sons Eleazar and Ithamar to express grief because of the sinfulness of the act (Lv 10:1-7). The nature of their sin is difficult to determine, but it surely involved a violation of God's holiness. Therefore, it is appropriate that a large part of the remainder of the book of Leviticus gives regulations that stress the holy living that God expected from his people.

From Sinai to Kadesh A year had elapsed from the time the Israelites left Egypt until the census was taken (Nm 9:1). God reminded the people that it was time to observe the Passover, which they did, and a month later they set out from Sinai and came to the wilderness of Paran. Along the way they complained about the unvarying diet of manna and they longed for the fish, cucumbers, melons, leeks, onions, and garlic they had eaten in Egypt (11:4-6). In anger God sent quail in abundance, but even while the people were devouring the meat, God sent a great plague that killed many Israelites. The complaining attitude of the people was shared even by Miriam and Aaron. They began to speak against the Cushite woman Moses had married (12:1-2). It is not certain whether the Cushite was an Ethiopian or whether this was another way of referring to Zipporah. If Moses did marry a second time, no mention is made of it elsewhere in the OT. Moses made no reply to the accusations of his brother and sister. It was not necessary, for God intervened in defense of his servant. He smote Miriam with leprosy for her part in speaking against Moses, and when Aaron saw what had happened to Miriam, he acknowledged that they both had sinned. Miriam's leprosy was removed in response to Moses' fervent intercession.

While the people were encamped at Kadesh (also called Kadesh-barnea—Nm 32:8) in the wilderness of Paran, Moses sent 12 men into Canaan, one from each tribe, to spy out the land in preparation for the Israelite entry. After 40 days the spies returned and, though they acknowledged that the land was fertile and inviting, 10 of them were afraid of the Canaanite inhabitants and advised against going into the land. Only Joshua and Caleb were willing to go ahead and occupy the territory. The entire congregation joined the protest against going in and determined to choose a new leader and return to Egypt rather than risk death by the sword in Canaan. They threatened to stone Moses and Aaron. At that moment God intervened and would have destroyed all

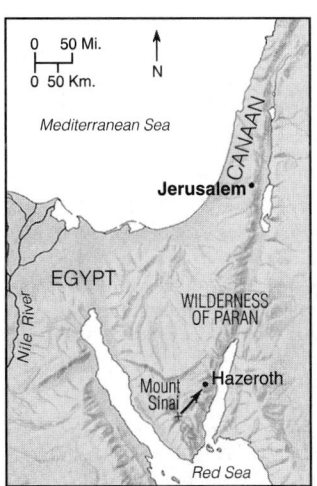

Moses Leads the Israelites toward the Promised Land

the people on the spot except for the intervention of Moses (13:1–14:19). He declared that, if God did not bring the people into Canaan, the nations round about would conclude that the God of the Israelites was unable to bring them into the land. Once again God acquiesced to Moses' request to pardon the people but said that none of them 20 years and older who had complained against him would be allowed to enter the land. All the people would wander in the wilderness for 40 years until that generation died, and then their children would be allowed to enter Canaan (14:29-33). When they heard the Lord's sentence upon them, the people quickly decided to lift the sentence of judgment by entering the land at once, but God was not with them, and they suffered a disastrous defeat at the hands of the Amalekites and Canaanites.

Forty Years in the Wilderness Very little is known about events during the 40 years of wilderness wanderings. In spite of the judgment that had already come upon them, the people did not seem to change their ways. A man named Korah led another rebellion against the authority of Moses and Aaron. God would not listen to the pleas of Moses and Aaron on behalf of these dissidents (Nm 16:22-24), but told the congregation to separate itself from the tents of Korah and his conspirators. While the people watched, the ground split open and swallowed up the rebellious factions together with their households and all their possessions. Though the rest of the Israelites witnessed the fate of the rebels, it did not deter them from again turning on Moses and Aaron. At this, God told Moses to remove himself from the murmuring congregation in order that he could take vengeance. Though Moses offered atonement for the people's sins, 14,700 died by plague before the punishment was ended. To demonstrate further to the people that Moses was his chosen leader, the Lord instructed Moses to take rods, one for each tribe, and to deposit them in the tent of meeting. God would cause the rod of the man chosen by him to sprout, and so silence the murmurings of the people. The rod belonging to Aaron sprouted and budded and bloomed, but the people only complained more.

As the people neared the end of their years of wilderness wanderings, Miriam died in Kadesh and was buried there (Nm 20:1). Soon after, the people began to complain once more for lack of water. God instructed Moses to speak to a rock that would bring forth water to satisfy the needs of the people. Instead of speaking to the rock, Moses struck it twice with his rod. The water came forth, but God rebuked Moses and Aaron: "Because you did not trust me enough to demonstrate my holiness to the people of Israel, you will not lead them into the land I am giving them!" (v 12, NLT). The nature of the sin is not clear, but Moses and Aaron were apparently taking to themselves honor that belonged to God alone. Because of the sin, they were denied the privilege of leading the Israelites into the Promised Land. The punishment may seem too severe for the sin, but it shows that the privileged role of leadership given to Moses and Aaron carried with it an unusual measure of responsibility.

The people then journeyed from Kadesh to Mt Hor on the border of the land of Edom, where Aaron died. Moses took his priestly garments from him and gave them to Eleazar, his son, thereby transferring the priestly office (Nm 20:28).

As the people came closer to their destination, resistance on the part of the native population increased. There was a skirmish with the king of Arad and his forces at Hormah, resulting in a victory for Israel (Nm 21:1-3). As they journeyed around Edom, some of the Israelites began speaking against God and Moses because there was no food or water and they were tired of eating manna. This time the Lord sent poisonous snakes among the people, and many of them died of the venomous bites. Those who had not yet been bitten came to Moses, acknowledged their sin, and asked that the serpents be removed from their midst. God instructed Moses to make a serpent of bronze and set it on a pole. If a person bitten by a serpent looked up at the bronze serpent, he or she would live.

As the Israelites approached the territory of Sihon, king of the Amorites, they sent messengers asking permission to pass peaceably through his land. Instead of granting the request, Sihon gathered his army together and fought against Israel. He was killed in the battle, and his land and cities were taken and occupied by the Hebrews (Nm 21:21-25).

Arrival at the Jordan River After their victory over Sihon, the Israelites set out again and encamped in the plains of Moab on the east side of the Jordan River facing Jericho, in full view of the Promised Land. The Moabites were terrified by the presence of these people because they had heard what happened to the Amorites. Their king, Balak, hired a magician named Balaam to curse the Israelites. Three times Balaam attempted to curse them, but each time God turned his words into a blessing (Nm 22–24). Though unable to curse the Israelites, Balaam was responsible for an even greater calamity. He advised the Moabites to entice the Israelites to sacrifice to their gods and bow down to them (Nm 25:1-3; 31:16; 2 Pt 2:15; Rv 2:14). While the people were worshiping the Moabite deity, Baal of Peor, God's anger was kindled against them, and he sent a plague that killed 24,000 of them (Nm 25:9). It was Israel's first encounter with the seductive allurement of licentious idolatry and an ominous foreview of what would happen after they settled down in Canaan. Their continued attraction to idolatry would be their final undoing.

After the plague, God instructed Moses and Eleazar to take another census of the people like the one almost 40 years earlier. A whole generation of Israelites had died in the wilderness, but they had been replaced by an almost equal number, so that now there were 601,730 men 20 years and older who were able to go to war (Nm 26:51). Not a man remained of those who had been counted in the first census, except Caleb and Joshua.

The Lord instructed Moses to lay hands on Joshua and commission him as the new leader in the sight of Eleazar the priest and all the congregation (Nm 27:12-23). In addition, the Lord gave Moses instructions concerning feasts and offerings and vows (chs 28–30). God ordered Moses, as his last act as leader, to avenge the Israelites on the Midianites. In that battle the armies of Israel gained a great victory over the Midianites, killing their kings, their men, and also Balaam.

The Lord gave instructions to Moses concerning the boundaries that would mark the Promised Land and named the men who would divide the land among the tribes (Nm 34). He also ordered that 48 cities be given to the Levites, the priestly tribe, as their portion. Six of these were designated as cities of refuge where murderers could flee so that they would not be killed by those seeking vengeance without having an opportunity to stand before the congregation for judgment (ch 35).

Moses' Death The book of Deuteronomy has often been called Moses' valedictory speech to the people, for in it Moses is not merely the chief speaker but the only speaker. With the congregation of his people gathered before him, he rehearsed all that God had done for them

since leaving Sinai, and he reminded them of their failure to enter the Promised Land 38 years earlier (Dt 2:14). He recalled his plea that God would let him cross the Jordan and see the land that was to be the home of the people, but God responded that Moses would only be allowed to view the land from the top of Pisgah. Moses then exhorted the people to obey the statutes and ordinances that had been given to them in order to experience God's blessings in the land.

The Death of Moses Not allowed to enter the Promised Land, Moses climbed Mt Nebo to look at it just before his death.

As the day of Moses' death approached, the Lord ordered Moses and Joshua to present themselves at the tent of meeting in order for Joshua to be commissioned as the new leader (Dt 31:14-23). Before his death, Moses pronounced a blessing upon all the Israelites (ch 33). Having completed these tasks, Moses went up from the plains of Moab to Mt Nebo, and to the top of Pisgah. From there God showed him the land promised long ago to Abraham, Isaac, and Jacob—the land that was soon to be the home of the wandering Israelite tribes. Again God told him that he would not be allowed to cross over the Jordan. Moses died there and God buried him somewhere in the valley in the land of Moab opposite Bethpeor (34:6). Moses was 120 years old when he died, and the Israelites mourned his death for 30 days. The finest tribute to Moses is found in the closing words of the book of Deuteronomy, "There has never been another prophet like Moses, whom the LORD knew face to face" (v 10).

Moses in the New Testament All Jews and Christians in apostolic times considered Moses the author of the Pentateuch. Such expressions as "the law of Moses" (Lk 2:22), "Moses commanded" (Mt 19:7), "Moses said" (Mk 7:10) "and Moses wrote" (12:19) shows that his name was synonymous with the OT books attributed to him. He is mentioned in the NT more than any other OT figure, a total of 79 times. His role as lawgiver is emphasized more than any other aspect of his life (Mt 8:4; Mk 7:10; Jn 1:17; Acts 15:1). He appears at the transfiguration of Jesus as the representative of OT law, along with Elijah as the representative of OT prophets (Mt 17:1-3).

Moses' role as prophet is also mentioned in the NT. As a prophet, he spoke of the coming Messiah and his sufferings (Lk 24:25-27; Acts 3:22). The NT also draws from the life and experiences of Moses to show patterns of life under the new covenant. The nativity story of Jesus parallels the Mosaic story of the infant deliverer being rescued from the evil designs of an earthly despot (Mt 2:13-18). Jesus' proclamation of a new law in his Sermon on the Mount parallels the giving of the law at Sinai (Mt 5–7) and presents Jesus as the authoritative interpreter of the will of God. Contrast between the old law and the new relationship with God is especially marked in the book of Galatians. The comparison of Moses with Christ is an important emphasis of the book of Hebrews (Heb 3:5-6; 9:11-22). John contrasted the law that was given through Moses with the grace and truth that came through Jesus Christ (Jn 1:17). He also contrasted the manna in the wilderness to Jesus as "the bread of life" (6:30-35).

Other references to Moses or to events associated with him include his birth (Acts 7:20; Heb 11:23), the burning bush (Lk 20:37), the magicians of Egypt (2 Tm 3:8), the Passover (Heb 11:28), the exodus (3:16), crossing of the sea (1 Cor 10:2), the covenant sacrifice at Sinai (Mt 26:28), the manna (1 Cor 10:3), the glory on Moses' face (2 Cor 3:7-18), water from the rock (1 Cor 10:4), the bronze serpent (Jn 3:14), and the song of Moses (Rv 15:3).

See also Egypt, Egyptian; Exodus, The; Israel, History of; Plagues upon Egypt; Priests and Levites; Tabernacle; Temple; Commandments, The Ten; Wilderness Wanderings.

MOSES, Books of
See Deuteronomy, Book of; Exodus, Book of; Genesis, Book of; Leviticus, Book of; Moses; Numbers, Book of; Pentateuch.

MOSES, Law of
See Covenant; Deuteronomy, Book of; Exodus, Book of; Leviticus, Book of; Moses.

MOSES, Song of
One of two archaic poems: the Blessing of Moses (Dt 33) and the Song of Moses (ch 32). The Song of the Sea (Ex 15) is set at a much earlier period of Moses' life, while these two poems are virtually his "last will and testament."

Moses had already written books of the Law as a witness against Israel, should they turn away from God. But the law itself required at least two witnesses to establish any charge (Dt 17:6). Moses was then commanded to write down the song as a further witness against Israel (31:19).

The song is therefore a witness to the greatness and goodness of God, and in particular, his goodness to Israel (Dt 32:10-14). This grace underlines all the more the sinfulness of Israel's response, which can only call forth the anger of God and consequent punishment. God will use "natural disasters," wild beasts, and wars to carry out his purposes. Yet even this is not the end. God, in his grace, will turn his hand against Israel's enemies instead, and rescue his own people (v 36).

This song carries the consistent message of every great prophet of the OT, a message that Psalm 78 expresses in terms of Israel's historical situations. The song outlines the very nature of God, so it is not strange that the song of heaven is "the song of Moses, the servant of God, and the song of the Lamb" (Rv 15:3).

See also Moses.

MOSES' SEAT*
Biblical expression occurring only in Matthew 23:2, where Jesus speaks of the scribes and the Pharisees as having sat down on the seat of Moses. In biblical times, the seat that one occupied usually indicated the degree of rank or respect one claimed for himself or was to receive from others (Mt 23:6). Sitting on "Moses' seat" referred to a place of dignity and the right to interpret the Mosaic law. The scribes were the succes-

sors and the heirs of Moses' authority and were rightfully looked to for pronouncements upon his teaching.

In the context of Matthew 23:2, Jesus does not seem to challenge this right, for he commands his hearers to practice and observe whatever the scribes and the Pharisees speak, that is, all they teach that is in accordance with the law. But Jesus warned the people against doing their works, because they did not practice what they spoke. On other occasions Jesus condemned their unbiblical traditions relative to the law of Moses (Mt 15:3-6; 23:4, 16-22).

MOST HIGH
Ancient name for God (Ps 21:7; Acts 7:48). See God, Names of.

MOST HOLY PLACE
Inner room of the tabernacle and temple in which the ark of the covenant was kept. See Tabernacle; Temple.

MOTE*
Term used in the KJV to describe a small particle lodged in the eye of a "brother" (Mt 7:3-5; Lk 6:41-42). More recent translations prefer the term "speck."

MOTH
Winged insect noted for its destruction of clothes while it is in the larval stage (Jb 13:28; Mt 6:19-20). See Animals.

MOUNT, MOUNTAIN
Elevated topographical feature. In Israel, as in surrounding countries, mountains were places where people expected to meet God. Many significant events in Israel's religion took place on Mt Sinai or Horeb (see Ex 3:1-4; 16; 19–23; 1 Kgs 19:8-18), and Mt Zion became almost as important when David was king (Ps 50:2; Is 2:2-4).

Whereas the Hebrews' neighbors sometimes thought mountains were magical places where their gods actually lived, the Israelites knew that their God lived in heaven and only descended upon the mountain at significant times (Ex 19; cf. 1 Kgs 8:27).

In the NT much of Jesus' activity takes place on mountains. He preached there (Mt 5:1); he retired there to pray (Lk 6:12); and he was transfigured on a mountain (9:28-36).

MOUNT EBAL
See Ebal, Mount.

MOUNT GAASH
See Gaash.

MOUNT GERIZIM
See Gerizim, Mount.

MOUNT HERMON
See Hermon, Mount.

MOUNT HOR
See Hor, Mount.

MOUNT HOREB*
See Sina, Sinai.

MOUNT NEBO
See Nebo, Mount.

MOUNT OF ASSEMBLY*
See Congregation, Mount of the.

MOUNT OF CORRUPTION
See Corruption, Mount of.

MOUNT OF OLIVES
See Olives, Mount of.

MOUNT OF THE AMALEKITES*
See Amalekites, Hill Country (Mount) of the.

MOUNT OF THE AMORITES* *See* Amorites, Hill Country (Mount) of the.

MOUNT OF THE BEATITUDES* Place where Jesus delivered the Sermon on the Mount. *See* Beatitudes, The.

MOUNT OF THE CONGREGATION* *See* Congregation, Mount of the.

MOUNT SINAI *See* Sina, Sinai.

MOUNT TABOR *See* Tabor, Mount.

MOURNING Established ritual for grieving, observed by a dead person's relatives and friends. It began with the closing of the eyes of the dead (Gn 46:4), the embracing of the body (50:1), and its preparation for burial. The hot climate necessitated that burial take place immediately (Acts 5:1-10). But detailed information about burial earlier than NT times (Mt 27:59; Jn 11:44; 19:39-40) is extremely meager. Excavations suggest that the dead were buried fully clothed but not in coffins. The Israelites practiced neither embalming nor cremation, but decent burial was essential.

At the news of a death, it was customary to tear one's garments (Gn 37:34; 2 Sm 1:11; Jb 1:20), put on sackcloth (2 Sm 3:31), and take off one's shoes (2 Sm 15:30; Mi 1:8) and headdress; a man might cover his beard or veil his face (Ez 24:17, 23). Mourners put earth on their heads (Jos 7:6; 1 Sm 4:12; Neh 9:1; Jb 2:12; Ez 27:30) or rolled themselves in the dust (Jb 16:15; Mi 1:10) or sat on a heap of ashes (Est 4:3; Is 58:5; Jer 6:26; Ez 27:30). Such mourning rites as shaving the hair and the beard and making cuts on the body (Jb 1:20; Is 22:12; Jer 16:6; 41:5; 47:5; 48:37; Ez 7:18; Am 8:10) were condemned (Lv 19:27-28; Dt 14:1) because of pagan associations. Mourners refrained from washing and discontinued the use of perfumes (2 Sm 12:20; 14:2).

Fasting was also a mourning rite (1 Sm 31:13; 2 Sm 1:12). Neighbors or friends brought mourning bread and the "cup of consolation" to the relatives of the deceased (Jer 16:7; Ez 24:17, 22). Food could not be prepared at the house of the dead because death rendered a place unclean. The dead were unclean to the extent that a priest could "profane" himself by taking part in mourning rites, except for his nearest blood relatives (mother, father, son, daughter, brother, and sister, provided she was still a virgin; Lv 21:1-4, 10-11). These mourning rites were not acts of worship directed toward the dead, nor did they constitute a cult for the dead, but rather they were expressions of grief and affection.

At the graveside, lamentation for the dead was made (1 Kgs 13:30; Jer 6:26; Am 5:16; 8:10; Zec 12:10) by men and women in separate groups (Zec 12:11-14). These exclamations of sorrow might develop into a rhythmic lament (2 Sm 1:17-27; Am 8:10). However, professional mourners, men and especially women (Jer 9:17-19; Am 5:16), were employed. The book of Lamentations is a fine example of laments and is a reminder that among Jews mourning was not always associated with death. It expressed brokenness of spirit for sin, individual and national. National calamity also evoked great lamentation.

These mourning rites were expressive of great grief. But some of them—tearing clothes, wearing sackcloth, disfiguring oneself with dust and ashes, self-mutilation—point to paroxysms of grief, the religious significance of which now escapes us. This was far removed from mourning as an inner feeling or a mood of the mind. It was not just an involuntary outburst of feeling but rather a deliberate,

established ritual. When death occurred, the Israelite wept because it was customary and seemly. The erection of monuments or memorials was not unknown (2 Sm 18:18), but the average Israelite was too poor for this to be a common practice.

Mourning practices in NT times differed little from those described in the OT. Mourning was associated with Christ's second advent (Mt 24:30), with repentance (Jas 4:8-10), with Christ's leaving the 12 (Mt 9:15), with deep spirituality (5:4), as well as with death (Mk 5:38-39; Lk 7:13; Jn 11:33).

True, the overthrow of death by Jesus Christ robbed death of its sting and the grave of its victory (1 Cor 15:54-57), but the Christian still mourns, though not as those who have no hope (1 Thes 4:13; Rv 21:4).

See also Burial, Burial Customs; Funeral Customs.

MOUSE Small rodent considered unclean by the law (Lv 11:29). *See* Animals.

MOZA
1. Caleb's son by his concubine Ephah (1 Chr 2:46).
2. Zimri's son, the father of Binea and a descendant of Saul and Jonathan (1 Chr 8:36-37; 9:42-43).

MOZAH Town in the territory assigned to Benjamin's tribe (Jos 18:26); tentatively identified with the village of Qalunyah. It has been suggested that the name is preserved in the modern Khirbet beit Mizza, a small village about four miles (6.4 kilometers) northwest of Jerusalem.

MULBERRY Tree with a darkish blue edible berry. *See* Plants.

MULE Offspring of a male ass and a female horse (2 Sm 13:29). *See* Animals.

MUPPIM One of Benjamin's 10 sons (Gn 46:21). He is elsewhere called Shephupham (Nm 26:39) and Shuppim (1 Chr 7:12) and is perhaps identifiable with Shephuphan (1 Chr 8:5). *See* Shephupham.

MURDER, MURDERER *See* Civil Law and Justice; Criminal Law and Punishment; Commandments, The Ten.

MUSHI, MUSHITE Son of Merari, the grandson of Levi, and Mahli's brother (Ex 6:19; Nm 3:20; 1 Chr 6:19, 47). He was the father of Mahli, Eder, and Jeremoth (1 Chr 23:21-23; 24:26, 30) and the founder of the family of Mushites (Nm 3:33; 26:58).

MUSIC A natural human expression that probably began with speech-singing and developed into songs, which were then accompanied by instruments. Music as we know it has become quite complex, a luxury and entertainment; music in antiquity, however, was a functional expression of daily life, work, and worship.

The phrase "sing to the Lord," common to the OT (Ex 15:21; 1 Chr 16:9; Pss 68:32; 96:1-2; Is 42:10; Jer 20:13), was not unique to the Jewish nation. All religions draw on the natural human impulse to sing. The injunction "sing to the Lord" was a signal for the people to pour out their praise in song.

The Bible, however, is limited in its treatment of music in ancient Israel. Since there was no written musical notation, the primary record of songs sung by the Hebrews is the collection of texts, particularly the psalms, and a few enigmatic musical instructions. The biblical writers were writing a history not of their culture but of their relationship with God; hence, their comments about music are not critical. Also, the biblical documents cover a long span of history and are grouped according to category rather than in chronological order, thus making it difficult to order the development of musical style with precision. Finally, there is the problem of understanding the biblical descriptions of music and its performance. Only in this century have scholars been able to interpret the information provided in the Bible in terms of Eastern music systems.

PREVIEW
•Music in the Old Testament
•Music in the Psalms
•Music in the New Testament

Music in the Old Testament The first musician mentioned in the Bible is "Jubal, the first musician—the inventor of the harp and flute" (Gn 4:21, NLT). The importance of this description of a musician so early in history lies in the equality Jubal is given with his brothers Jabal, the herdsman, and Tubal-cain, the smith. Music making is recognized among the earliest professions of nomadic peoples. The name Jubal is believed to be a derivative from the Hebrew word for "ram." The ram's horn *(shophar)* was an early instrument of the Jewish people and was significant in signaling important events.

For the most part, the music described in early biblical history was of a functional nature. Music gained special significance as it became an important part of temple worship. Many of the descriptions of music making in ancient Israel, before David's time, are quite utilitarian. There are accounts of music at times of farewell (Gn 31:27), at times of rejoicing and feasting (Ex 32:17-18; Is 5:12; 24:8-9), at military victories (2 Chr 20:27-28), and for work (Nm 21:17, the song of the well diggers; Is 16:10; Jer 48:33). Most of this music was probably rather crude and primitive in nature, especially the music associated with military advances, which was meant to terrify the enemy (Jgs 7:17-20). The music and dancing that greeted Moses as he descended from the mountain was described as if it sounded like "war in the camp" (Ex 32:17-18).

In the early history of the Jewish people, women played an important part in the performance of music. The image of women dancing and singing for joy accompanied by percussion instruments is repeated several times: Miriam led the women in a hymn of thanksgiving after the deliverance from the Red Sea (Ex 15); Jephthah's daughter welcomed her father in his victory (Jgs 11:34); Deborah joined with Barak in singing a song of victory (Jgs 5); and women hailed David after his defeat of the Philistines (1 Sm 18:6-7). There is little mention of women as musicians following the establishment of the temple in Jerusalem, but there are a few allusions to the fact that women did participate in singing and dancing. The account of the return from exile in Babylon includes both male and female singers (Neh 7:67), confirming that women still took part in musical performance.

As Jerusalem became the religious center of the Hebrew people (950–850 BC), the role of the professional musician became more important. The women's songs became insignificant compared to the pomp and ceremony associated with the temple and the royal court. While the Levitical singers took most of the musical responsibility at the temple, the development of antiphonal singing allowed the people to join in on responses in the singing of psalms.

Musical Style and Use The Jewish people seem to have been especially musical. Of course, they were influenced by other ancient cultures, but there is evidence that they were in demand as musicians by other peoples. According to an Assyrian document, King Hezekiah gave as tribute to King Sennacherib many male and female Jewish musicians. The Babylonians demanded that the captive Jews sing to them and entertain them (cf. Ps 137:3).

Since the OT's purpose was to narrate the relationship between the Jewish nation and God, most of the references to music deal with its function in worship. However, evidence reveals that there was also a large body of secular musical literature. There may have been guilds of poets and singers early in Jewish history. The kinds of songs recorded in the early part of the OT represent a folklike poetry. The song of thanksgiving to the Lord by Moses and the people of Israel after their escape at the Red Sea is a stirring national song. Many descriptions of the biblical writers reflect the spirit of bardic song. This would be logical, as these stories were meant to be passed on. Marching songs (2 Chr 20:27-28), and songs of triumph (Jgs 5) also indicate a secular body of music.

Music in Worship The singers and musicians for the temple worship were chosen from the tribe of Levi. King David assembled the Levites for a census, and out of the total of 38,000 men over the age of 30, 4,000 were chosen as musicians. These 4,000 were subsequently given specific jobs. "David and the chiefs of the service also set apart for the service certain of the sons of Asaph, and of Heman, and of Jeduthun, who should prophesy with lyres, with harps, and with cymbals. . . . The number of them along with their brethren, who were trained in singing to the LORD, all who were skilful, was two hundred and eighty-eight" (1 Chr 25:1, 7, RSV). The singers were further divided into 24 groups of 12 singers, who rotated in participating in the weekday, Sabbath, and high holy day services.

According to a later source, there were minimum and maximum numbers of singers and instrumentalists required at each service. The minimum number of singers was twelve, the maximum was unlimited. There had to be in attendance at least two harps but no more than six, at least two flutes but no more than twelve, a minimum of two trumpets with no maximum, and a minimum of nine lyres with no maximum. There was only one player with a pair of cymbals.

A singer was admitted to the Levitical choir at the age of thirty following a five-year apprenticeship (1 Chr 23:3). Five years is a relatively short time considering the amount of material these singers had to memorize (for there was no notation) and the liturgical ritual they had to master; it is speculated that they actually were in training from childhood. The Levites lived in villages outside the city wall and may have been actively involved in the musical education of their children (Neh 12:29). The Levites performed other duties connected with the sacred service, but the singers were excused from all other duties because they were on duty day and night (1 Chr 9:33). Their skills were an important part of the temple worship, and they were able to devote their entire life to the development of their musical ability. A singer served in the choir for 20 years, from age 30 to 50, and the music was of a high quality due to strict discipline and continuous practice and performance.

From the beginning of Jewish formal worship connected with the tabernacle, music and sound was

important. In Exodus 28:34-35 the descriptions of
Aaron's robe include bells attached to the lower hem
that sounded as he entered the Holy Place. The first
liturgical music mentioned in the OT is found in
2 Samuel 6 in the descriptions of the transfer of the ark:
David and the Israelites sang, played instruments, and
danced to the glory of the Lord. This music bore little
resemblance to the stately ceremony described later in
Solomon's temple. In 2 Chronicles 7:6, David is given
recognition for inventing the musical instruments used
in the temple. In the postexilic era Levitical singers are
mentioned as the descendants of Asaph, the "singing
master" appointed by David (Ezr 2:41; Neh 7:44;
11:22-23). From passages such as these, we have a definite indication that liturgical music and organization
stemmed from David's time.

The ceremonies in the Jewish temple were organized
around the sacrifice. Singing formed an integral part of
the sacrificial service and was necessary to validate the
sacrificial action. There were special musical settings for
each sacrifice; thus the daily burnt, expiatory, and lauda-
tory offerings and libations had individual liturgies. Particular psalms became associated with certain sacrifices
as well as with certain days of the week. The psalm of the
day was intoned as the high priest started to pour out the
drink offering. The psalm was divided into three sections, each signaled by the blowing of the trumpets, on
which signal the people would prostrate themselves. This
is the only time the trumpets were used together with the
other instruments in orchestral fashion on solemn occasions (2 Chr 5:12-13).

Music in the Psalms

Musical Psalm Titles The collection of 150 lyric poems
known as the book of Psalms contains the most information on music making in ancient Israel. The Psalter
contains not only religious songs but also songs that
have their roots in secular or popular songs, such as
work songs, love songs, and wedding songs. The majority are songs of praise, thanksgiving, prayer, and repentance. There are also historic odes that relate great
national events—for example, Psalm 30, "a song at the
dedication of the temple," and Psalm 137, which portrays the sufferings of the Jews in captivity.

The psalms were an important part of all the services
of the temple; the Psalter became the liturgical hymnal
of the Israelites. Worship included an appointed psalm
for each day of the week. On the first day of the week,
Psalm 24 was sung in remembrance of the first day of
creation, Psalm 48 was sung on the second day, Psalm
82 on the third, Psalm 94 on the fourth, Psalm 81 on the
fifth, Psalm 93 on the sixth, and Psalm 92 on the Sabbath. After the sacrificial offerings, Psalm 105:1-5 was
sung at the morning service and Psalm 96 at the evening
service. The Hallel psalms (Pss 113–118, 120–136,
146–148) were sung during the offering of the paschal
lamb at the Passover feast.

While most of the liturgical music was performed by
Levites, texts of the psalms suggest that there was also
congregational participation. The forms of music found
both in synagogal and ecclesiastical chant had their
source in the forms of the poetic text of the psalms. The
simplest is the plain psalmody sung by one person (e.g.,
Pss 3–5, 46). In responsorial psalmody the soloist is
answered by the choir (e.g., Ps 67:1-2; the soloist sang
verse 1 and the choir answered with verse 2). Antiphonal
psalmody involves two groups singing alternately (e.g.,
Ps 103:20-22). The congregation would chant a refrain
such as appears in Psalm 80: "Restore us, O God; let thy

face shine, that we may be saved!" recurs throughout the
psalm (RSV).

Even though the synagogue had no altar for sacrifice,
psalm singing retained an important place. After the
Romans destroyed the temple, the worship heritage of
the Jews could have been lost if the customs, including
musical customs, had not become an integral part of
synagogue worship.

The most enigmatic part of the psalms is the headings
that are not part of the poetic text. The first question is
whether these should even be considered as superscripts.
Greek, Latin, Hebrew, and other ancient languages were
written in such a way that the text ran together without
any break between chapters or paragraphs. This means
that the verses, and even the division of the psalms
themselves, were partially determined by copyists,
chiefly the Masoretes. There is some question as to which
psalms the extrapoetic texts actually belong with; they
may actually be subscripts instead of superscripts.
Sumerian and Babylonian poetry had information such
as the name of the author, the musical instrument used
for accompaniment, the tune, the purpose, and such
listed at the end of the poem. Hence, some of the headings may actually be endings.

The indications at the beginning of a psalm fall into
three categories. They are either musical terms giving
direction for the actual performance, musical cues designating the tune to which the psalm would be sung, or
comments indicating the function of the psalm. These
terms have been interpreted in various ways.

Originally, these headings may have been marginal
notes for the choir leaders. Realizing that these terms
were not related to the psalm text proper, early biblical
scribes may not have been overly careful with their placement in the text, which may explain some of the discrepancies among the early manuscripts—why certain words
are left out in some and why terms assigned to only a
few psalms may originally have been indicated on more
of them.

All but 50 of the psalms contain a proper name in the
heading. These names possibly indicate the author; other
commentators, interpreting the preposition appearing
before the names to mean "for," think the names are a
dedication. Thus the title would be "A Psalm for David,"
not "A Psalm of David." This may be the case with the
names of Asaph, Heman, Ethan, and especially the sons
of Korah, where it would make better sense for the psalm
to be written for rather than by the family. Seventy-three
psalms have David's name in the heading, hence the
common reference to the Psalter as the Psalms of David.
Twelve include the name of Asaph, eleven the children
of Korah, two Solomon, and one each contains Moses,
Heman, and Ethan.

Musical Terms in the Psalm Titles Numerous musical
terms are included in the superscriptions to cue the kind
of instrumental accompaniment, mood, and style of performance for the psalm.

Alamoth is one of the most controversial terms found
in the psalm headings. It appears at the beginning of
Psalm 46 and also in 1 Chronicles 15:20. One meaning
for the Hebrew word is "maiden," and musicologists
interpret this as an instruction that the psalm should be
sung in the range of the female singing voice. The reference in Chronicles is to harps in the range of women's
voices. This interpretation does not seem to fit Psalm 46,
but if we look at the preceding psalm and read the term
as a subscript, it becomes logical. Psalm 45 is a song of
love, actually a nuptial ode; it would be natural for
women to sing the second half (vv 10-17). While there is

little mention of women singing in the temple, there is speculation that young boys in training may have sung along with the Levitical singers. Also this may be a case where the term appears only once in the modern text but may have been used more often in the original. Another possible meaning for *Alamoth* is "flutes," perhaps describing the kind of musical accompaniment for the performance of the psalm.

Gittith is a term found in the superscriptions of Psalms 8, 81, and 84. It may be a musical cue, indicating a mood for the performance of these psalms, but a more common explanation is that it is a collective term for the stringed instruments that would have accompanied them.

Mahalath has been left in its original Hebrew form by early translators and is found in the headings of Psalms 53 and 88. It may have roots in the Hebrew *mahaleh* "sickness" or *mahot* "dance," though neither of these words can be related to the psalm texts. Another explanation is a musical one. *Mahalath* may come from the word *halal* meaning "to pierce," implying that the psalm was to be accompanied with pipes.

Maskil (KJV "Maschil") appears in the headings of 13 psalms (Pss 32, 42, 44–45, 52–55, 74, 78, 88–89, 142). The term is probably derived from the verb *sakal*, "to have insight or comprehension," but there is no agreement among commentators. By looking at the psalms themselves, their didactic nature and the structure of stanzas and refrains, musicologists conclude the term represents a song of praise, possibly sung by a soloist with participation by the choir.

Menazzeah appears in the heading of 55 psalms. It appears 52 times in the first three books of Psalms (Pss 1–89), not at all in book four (Pss 90–106), and 3 times in book five (Pss 107–150). The most common modern translations are "to the Choirmaster" (RSV), "to the choir director" (NASB, NLT), "to the director of music" (NIV), "to the chief Musician" (KJV, NKJV). The word is derived from the Hebrew verb *nazzah*, appearing in 1 Chronicles 23:4 and Ezra 3:8-9 in the sense of "administering." In 1 Chronicles 15:21 the word is found in relation to leading or directing song in the temple. *Menazzeah* relates to the choirmaster and represents the singer chosen to lead the music who probably was involved in rehearsing and instructing. It is now assumed that *menazzeah* indicates the psalm was to be sung partially or entirely by a soloist. This is evidenced by the change in some texts from "I" where the soloist sang, to "we" where the choir or congregation sang. Psalm 5 is an example of a text divided for solo and choral singing: verses 1-3 solo; verses 4-6 choral; verses 7-8 solo; verses 9-10 choral; and verses 11-12 end the psalm with the combined soloist and choir.

Miktam (KJV "Michtam") is another term that has no clear musical meaning, due mainly to the fact that its etymology is unknown. It occurs in Psalms 16 and 56–60, all of which have a character of lamentation or supplication. In a musical sense, it probably meant that a certain well-known tune was to be selected as the melody of the psalm.

Mizmor (Hebrew, meaning a song sung to instrumental accompaniment) is found nowhere else in the Bible; it is included in the superscriptions of 57 psalms. It probably indicated a song accompanied by melodic instruments as opposed to a dance song accompanied by rhythmic instruments.

Neginah appears in the superscriptions of Psalms 4, 6, 54–55, 61, 67, and 76. The term *neginah* and its plural *neginoth* are found in Psalm 77:7, Lamentations 5:14, Isaiah 38:20, and Habakkuk 3:19. *Neginah*, from the Hebrew root *naggen*, "to touch the strings," instructs that stringed instruments accompany the singing.

Nehiloth is found only in the introduction to Psalm 5 (KJV). The origin of the word is problematic. It could come from the verb *nahal*, "to possess or inherit," or more feasibly from *halal*, meaning "to pierce." The latter implies the idea of a pierced instrument (the flute or pipe) to be used for accompaniment.

Sheminith appears in Psalms 6 and 12 and also in 1 Chronicles 15:21. The Hebrew word means literally "over the eighth." Some scholars feel it had something to do with an octave, but the Hebrew musical language probably did not include a musical unit divided into eight parts. Other scholars interpret *sheminith* as meaning an eight-stringed instrument. A more logical interpretation comes from examining its use in 1 Chronicles. In 15:20 the instructions are for musicians to play the harps according to *alamoth* and in verse 21 to play the lyres according to *sheminith*. Here the terms *alamoth* and *sheminith* seem to be used in opposition. If *alamoth* implies a register of the female voice, then *sheminith* would imply a lower register. Thus, it may have been an instruction to use a lower pitched instrument for accompaniment.

Psalm Varieties in the Titles Some of the notes in the psalm headings are indications of the type or variety of psalm.

Hazkir is found in the headings of Psalms 38 and 70. According to the Targum, this is an indication that the psalm was sung at the sacrificial rite called *askara* and is translated "for a memorial offering."

Lammed appears in the superscription of Psalm 60 in the phrase *le-lammed*, translated "to teach." According to tradition, this was a psalm, though undoubtedly not the only one, taught to young people as part of their education. This is another example of a term that may have been omitted from other psalms in later versions of the Psalter.

Shiggaion is in the heading of Psalm 7 and also in Habakkuk 3:1. The word probably comes from the Hebrew verb *shagah*, "to wander," but may also be connected with the Assyrian liturgical term *shigu*, which represented a plaintive song in several stanzas. Biblical scholars have assumed *shiggaion*, plural *shigionoth*, was a lament or penitential song.

Shir is the simplest word for "song" and was probably used in the headings at an early stage of the Psalter; it is usually found with *mizmor* (13 times). Fifteen psalms have this heading. It was probably the term for a specific type of praise song, usually performed by the choir.

Shir Hamaalot and *Shir Lamaalot* occur in the headings of Psalms 120–134, which are often referred to as the Psalms of Ascent (KJV "Psalms of Degrees"). Most explanations offered relate to the fact that the temple was situated on high ground. Often these 15 psalms are associated with the 15 steps leading from the Court of the Women to the Court of the Israelites. But most contemporary scholars believe the idea of "going up" referred to the pilgrims' journey to Jerusalem to worship at the temple. These psalms are short, with popular appeal, making them appropriate for singing during the journey.

Shir Hanukkat Habayit is found only in the heading of Psalm 30. This phrase tells that the psalm was to be used for the dedication or rededication of the house of God.

Shir-yedidot appears only in Psalm 45. It refers to a love song that was probably sung at wedding ceremonies.

Tefillah is a common term for "prayer" and appears in the headings of Psalms 17, 86, 90, 102, and 142, and also in Habakkuk 3:1. The word probably refers to a specific form of poetic prayer.

Selah is one of the most frequently used, but most enigmatic, terms found in the book of Psalms. It occurs in 39 psalms, appearing a total of 71 times in the Psalter—67 times within the text and 4 times at the end of a psalm. It is most frequent in the first three books. In the first book *selah* appears in 9 psalms; in the second book, 17 psalms; in the third book, 11 psalms. In the fourth book it is not found at all and in the fifth book in only two psalms. Thirty-one of these psalms also include the term *menazzeah* in their superscriptions, which implies that they were sung by a soloist and choir. Most commonly, *selah* is interpreted as a signal for a break in the singing and possibly for an instrumental interlude. It never appears at the beginning of a psalm but only in the middle of the text or at the end. The regularity of its appearance within a psalm is not consistent, and in only a few instances do these divisions break the psalm into equal sections. Because of the random placement of the term, some scholars believe that, like the headings, *selah* was not always carefully copied into the text. It may have been a note appearing only in the texts of the musicians, which would explain this inconsistency. An explanation of *selah* is found in the Talmudic tradition: "Ben Azra clashed the cymbal and the Levites broke forth into singing. When they reached a break in the singing they blew upon the trumpets and the people prostrated themselves; at every break there was a blowing of the trumpet and at every blowing of the trumpet a prostration. This was the rite of the daily whole offering in the service of the House of our God." *Selah,* then, would be an instruction for the musicians that the singing was to cease and the instrumentalists were to play.

The term *higgaion selah* appears once, in Psalm 9:16. The word *higgaiaon* comes from the root *hagah,* "to murmur, to growl, to produce a low sound." This may have been an instruction for the interlude to be more subdued than a normal *selah.*

Ancient Melodies in the Titles Many psalms contain headings that are not direct musical references but are cue words to suggest well-known tunes. They probably refer either to names or the first words of popular secular songs *(makams)* whose melodic patterns were used in singing the psalm. Many biblical scholars have tried to find hidden meaning in these headings, but most musicologists believe these are simply references or introductions to melodies.

Aijeleth Shahar, in Psalm 22 (KJV), is translated "according to The Hind of the Dawn" (RSV), and "To the tune of 'The Doe of the Morning' " (NIV), "To the tune 'Doe of the Dawn' " (NLT).

Al-taschith, in Psalms 57–59 and 75 (KJV), is translated "To the tune 'Do Not Destroy!' " (NLT).

Jonath-elem-rechokim, in Psalm 56 (KJV), is translated "according to The Dove on Far-off Terebinths" (RSV), and "To the tune 'Dove on Distant Oaks' " (NLT).

Mahalath Leannoth, in Psalm 88, is translated "To the tune 'The Suffering of Affliction'" (NLT).

Muthlabben, in Psalm 9, is translated "To the tune 'Death of the Son' " (NLT).

Shoshannim, in Psalms 45 and 69 (KJV), is translated "To the tune 'Lilies' " (NLT).

Shoshannim-Eduth, in Psalm 80 (KJV), is translated "To the tune 'Lilies of the Covenant' " (NLT).

Shushan-eduth, in Psalm 60, is translated "To the tune 'Lily of the Testimony' " (NLT).

These melody types appear only in the first three books of the Psalter, and this may imply that these popular *makams* had fallen into disuse by the time the final books of the Psalter were written. Other *makam*-types had probably become popular, and the authors, realizing the rela-

tively short life of a popular tune, did not include them in the headings of the Psalms but left the choice up to the performer.

Music in the New Testament

First-Century Influences

➤ THE SYNAGOGUE By the time of Christ, the synagogue had become the chief place of worship for the Jewish people. It began as a place for study of the law but gradually became the center of worship for Jews unable to attend the temple. The liturgical service of the temple could not be duplicated in the synagogue as there was no sacrificial rite, and the music could not be exactly reproduced as there were no trained Levitical singers. Scholars do not agree about the amount of continuity between the music of the temple and the music of the synagogue, but there is evidence that certain musical practices did remain constant between the two places of worship.

Information on the customs and rituals of the synagogue come from Talmudic writings. The musical elements of worship in the synagogue were the chanting of Scripture, psalmody, and spiritual songs. The choral singing of the temple was replaced by a single cantor. The cantor was a layman who, according to tradition, had to have the following qualifications: "He had to be well educated, gifted with a sweet voice, of humble personality, recognized by the community, conversant with Scripture and all the prayers; he must not be a rich man, for his prayers should come from his heart." His most important job was the cantillation of the Law and the Prophets. A series of accents and punctuations, forerunners of actual musical notation, were indications for the cantor in the musical interpretation of the Scripture.

Psalm singing was gradually transplanted from the temple to the synagogue, which in turn influenced the early Christian church. Gregorian psalm tones have their roots in Hebrew psalmody.

➤ GREEK AND ROMAN CULTURES While both the temple and the synagogue were familiar to the early Christians (Acts 2:46-47; 3:1; 5:42; 9:20; 18:4; etc.), the Greek and Roman cultures also played a major part in shaping the young church. Hellenistic influences by the time of Christ had long been felt in the Middle East, and while it was strongly opposed by some Jewish leaders, the Greek arts had permeated Jewish culture. Greek philosophers considered music a cathartic force that could lead humans into metaphysical knowledge. This understanding led to the belief that music had a moral substance that could influence people to either good or evil. If this philosophy had totally encompassed Judeo-Christian thought, certainly Paul would have encouraged the use of music in the spread of the gospel. However, Paul's omission of this theory implies that the Judeo-Christian world at that time had rejected the Greek ideal, at least in part.

While the Jewish rabbis considered music an art form for the praise of God, and while the Greek philosophers thought of it as a powerful moral force in creation, the Romans considered music mainly as entertainment. The music of the Roman games was neither religious nor philosophic and, from the accounts of witnesses, it was not technically exceptional. In the Roman Empire musicians were given a lower status and looked on as mere entertainers. One reason the early church did not include instrumental music in their worship was in reaction to the debased secular use of instruments by the Romans.

In the New Testament Writings One of the few mentions of instruments in the NT is the use of flutes at a wake (Mt 9:23). As in the OT, music is associated with

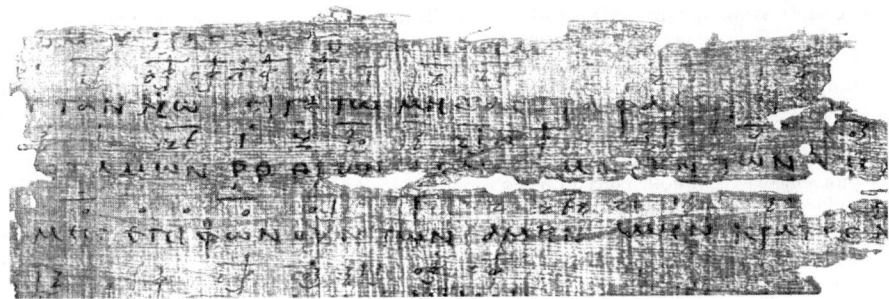

Ancient Christian Hymn Greek hymn to the Trinity with words and musical notations, from Papyrus Oxyrhynchus 1786 (third century)

feasting and merrymaking (e.g., the return of the prodigal son, Lk 15:25). Five passages mention music metaphorically (Mt 6:2; 11:17; Lk 7:32; 1 Cor 13:1; 14:7-8). The most well known of these is Paul's celebration of love in 1 Corinthians 13. The denunciation of the gong and cymbals must be understood in light of the attitude of the early Christians toward the music of the Pharisees. Here the signal instruments of the temple were used to represent pompous display of religious pietism.

Most references to music are found in the eschatological visions and prophetic passages scattered throughout the NT—most frequently in the book of Revelation (also Mt 24:31; 1 Cor 15:52; 1 Thes 4:16; Heb 12:19). Many of these descriptions have a direct association with musical references in the OT (e.g., the use of harps and trumpets and the singing of the Hallelujah). But the value of many of the passages in Revelation comes from their literary style. These doxological and psalmlike passages were probably spontaneous "spiritual songs" composed by the young church (e.g., Rv 5:9-10).

The passages that mention religious or liturgical music are often more conceptual than literal. Two parallel passages describing the Last Supper (Mt 26:30; Mk 14:26) mention that Christ and his disciples sang a hymn. This is the only direct account of Jesus singing, but it is probable that when he read in the synagogue he did so in the accepted vocal style (Lk 4:16-20). There is much controversy surrounding the actual events at the Last Supper, but we can assume that the hymn sung was a traditional Jewish hymn, probably associated with the Passover.

From the account in Acts 16:25 we know that Paul and Silas sang hymns while in jail. Paul gives instruction for music making in 1 Corinthians 14:15, 26 in terms of a balance between rationalism and emotion. And, as with all the gifts of the Spirit, Paul asks that singing be done for edification.

In two similar passages (Eph 5:19; Col 3:16) Paul groups together three musical terms—psalms, hymns, and spiritual songs. The singing of psalms was an obvious carryover from the synagogue, and we can assume that the early Christian psalm singing followed the Jewish style. The term for "hymns" probably refers to poetic texts, possibly modeled after the psalms, but in praise of Christ. "Spiritual songs" may refer to a spontaneous, ecstatic form of musical prayer, possibly wordless (perhaps related to glossolalia), in a style that was popular in mystical Judaism. These outbursts of song were probably melismatic (sung on one tone) and are perhaps the forerunners of the later Alleluia chant.

Hymnody in the New Testament It can be assumed that the early Christians composed hymns in praise of Christ. Logically, most of the hymns found in the NT are based on Hebrew poetic psalm forms, but there is Greek and Latin influence also. The hymns from the Gospel of Luke have become well-known canticles adopted by the church:

the Magnificat (Lk 1:46-55), the Benedictus (1:68-79), the Gloria (2:14) and the Nunc Dimittis (2:29-32). While patterned after the psalms of the OT, these hymns are full of confidence in the salvation of Christ and in his imminent return. Other Christological hymns found in the NT include the prologue to the Gospel of John, Ephesians 2:14-16, Philippians 2:6-11, Colossians 1:15-20, 1 Timothy 3:16, Hebrews 1:3, and 1 Peter 3:18-22.

MUSICAL INSTRUMENTS Stringed, wind, and percussion instruments used to make music.

In contrast to the detailed accounts of liturgical music in the OT, the descriptions of the musical instruments themselves are rather sparse. Because of the injunction of the second commandment, interpreted by the Hebrews as discouraging pictorial representations, there are few drawings of Hebrew instruments. In addition to the instruments used in the temple, the book of Daniel lists six instruments played in King Nebuchadnezzar's court.

The ancient Hebrews made certain distinctions among the instruments, not on musical but on ethical grounds. Some instruments were considered "unclean" and were not allowed in temple worship.

Stringed Instruments The stringed instruments were favored by the Jewish people. In many ancient civilizations the strings were considered the most masculine and noble (e.g., David playing the lyre); the Jews considered them the most suitable for accompaniment in the temple service. The term *minim* is used in Psalm 150:4 to designate the entire family of stringed instruments used in the praise of God.

Asor appears three times in the book of Psalms (Pss 33:2; 92:3; 144:9). Although the word derives from a Hebrew root meaning "ten," the actual description of the instrument remains unclear. The most common theory identifies it with the Phoenician zither having ten strings; it is perhaps the lute.

Kathros was a stringed instrument included in the list of those played at Nebuchadnezzar's court and was probably a kind of lyre (Dn 3:5, 7, 10, 15).

Kinnor is the most frequently mentioned instrument in the Bible, found in 42 places. It is often called David's harp and is the most beloved instrument of the Jewish people. We can say with reasonable certainty that it was a lyre and not a harp. The strings, the number of which is not clear, were made of sheep tripe and the sounding box was at the bottom of the instrument. It is not certain whether it was played with a plectrum or with bare hands, but the specific comment that David "played it with his hand" (1 Sm 16:23, RSV) may have implied that this was not the common practice. The biblical descriptions of the sound of the *kinnor* include "pleasant" and "sweet" (Ps 81:2). The *kinnor* was played mainly in worship but also in celebrations (Is 5:12), for state occasions (1 Sm 10:5; 2 Sm 6:5), and by shepherds (1 Sm 16:16).

Nebel was another stringed instrument (literally meaning "skin" or "skin bottle") mentioned 27 times in Scripture. Its shape was probably similar to a bottle, with the belly-shaped sounding box on the bottom. It definitely belongs to the family of harps (2 Sm 6:5; 1 Kgs 10:12; Neh 12:27; Ps 57:8; Am 5:23) and may have been influenced by similar Egyptian instruments. The *nebel* was probably played without a plectrum and was a larger and louder instrument than the *kinnor*. It is translated as "harp" in most modern English translations, compared to the KJV ("psaltery," or "viol").

Psantrin or *pesanterin* was a Greek instrument, mentioned in the description of King Nebuchadnezzar's orchestra. It may have resembled a dulcimer, having strings played with hammers (Dn 3:5-15).

Sabcha or *sabbeka*, identical with the Greek *sambyke* and the Roman *sambuca*, was a stringed instrument (RSV "trigon," KJV "sackbut") played in the Babylonian court. It was a triangle with four strings, having a high and harsh tone (Dn 3:5-15).

Wind Instruments The wind instruments can be divided into two groups: pipes and horns.

Halil is mentioned only six times in the Bible but was referred to frequently by postbiblical writers. This kind of piped instrument was similar to the Greek *aulos* (Mt 9:23; 1 Cor 14:7; Rv 18:22), a primitive oboe, rendered "flute" in many translations. The root word *halal* means "to pierce," thus the meaning "hollow tube." The early pipes were made from reedlike plants. The *halil* had a double-reed mouthpiece and probably produced a shrill and penetrating sound. It was connected with joyful events such as banquets (Is 5:12) and prophetic frenzies (1 Sm 10:5), but its tone was also associated with wailing and mourning (Jer 48:36).

Hatzotzrot was a sort of trumpet. Modern scholars have more information about this horn than many of its ancient Hebrew counterparts. The triumphal arch built by Titus in Rome includes depictions of the captured implements of the temple, among which are two trumpets. The form of these horns may have been influenced by the Israelites' knowledge of Egyptian trumpets. Similar instruments were also known in Assyria, in the Hittite

Empire, and in Greece. Moses was commanded to make two silver trumpets (Nm 10:2); playing these instruments became the exclusive privilege of the descendants of Aaron. These trumpets were made of silver or gold, about a yard (.9 meter) long, but narrow, with a pronounced bell. The descendants of the *hatzotzrot* are the herald trumpets. Numbers 10:10 says the trumpets were used "for a memorial before . . . God." Trumpets and horns were used to signal the gathering of the congregation to the tent of meeting, to sound alarm, to alert the camps to move forward, and to announce when war was at hand. The *hatzotzrot* became an important part of the temple service. There were at least two trumpets in the daily services, but at high holidays the number could be increased indefinitely (1 Chr 15:28; 2 Chr 15:14; Ps 98:6; Dn 3:5-15; Hos 5:8).

Mashroqita, considered by modern scholars to be a Pan's pipe similar to the Greek *syrinx*, is included in the list of orchestral instruments of King Nebuchadnezzar's court (Dn 3:5, 7, 10, 15).

Shophar is mentioned in the Bible 72 times, more than any other Hebrew instrument. It is the only instrument of ancient Israel that survives in its original form and is still used in Jewish liturgy. The early *shophar* was curved like a ram's horn, but the later form was straight with a bend near the bell of the horn. There is some question whether any of the hornlike instruments can actually be considered musical instruments. The *shophar* could produce two, maybe three tones, and was used for giving signals, not for playing music. It was used in such religious ceremonies as the transfer of the ark (2 Sm 6:15; 1 Chr 15:28), the renewal of the covenant by King Asa (2 Chr 15:14), thanksgiving to God (Ps 98:6; 150:3), and was blown at the new moon and the beginning of the jubilee year. Its secular use included such royal occasions as Absalom's accession to the throne (2 Sm 15:10), Solomon's anointing as king (1 Kgs 1:34), and Jehu's accession to the throne (2 Kgs 9:13).

Sumponia is an uncertain term included in Daniel 3. Many commentators have interpreted it as a bagpipe (RSV), but musicologists strongly argue that at the time of King Nebuchadnezzar there was no such instrument. It has been suggested that *sumponia* was not a musical

Musical Instruments from Ancient Times Musical instruments used in New Testament times included trumpets, lutes, cymbals, and stringed instruments. Also pictured is a musical procession of people playing various instruments.

instrument at all but signified the playing of the entire ensemble. This could come from the Greek root *symphonia*, meaning "sounding together." The word is also found in Luke 15:25, where it is translated as "music."

Ugab, a flutelike instrument, is mentioned in Scripture four times (Gn 4:21; Jb 21:12; 30:31; Ps 150:4; KJV mistranslates it as "organ"). It is only in Psalm 150 that the *ugab* is connected with a sacred occasion.

Percussion Instruments Most of the accounts of percussion instruments are found in the early history of the Hebrew people. They were gradually eliminated from the temple orchestra, perhaps because of their association with idolatrous practices.

Mena anim was a loud metal rattle, constructed with a frame carrying loose rings. It is included in a list of instruments in 2 Samuel 6:5 (RSV "castanet"; KJV mistranslates as "cornet"). It was likely a form of the *sistrum*, an Egyptian instrument.

Pamonim were the bells attached to the lower hem of the priest's garment, described in Exodus 28:33-34 and 39:25-26. They were not loud but indicated the position of the high priest as he entered the sanctuary.

Shalishim, often translated as *sistrum* or *timbrel*, is a kind of rattle. It is not clear whether this term actually refers to a musical instrument. It appears in 1 Samuel 18:6 as part of the reception of King Saul and David after the battle with the Philistines.

Toph or *tof* was an instrument used mainly by women, but there are some indications that men might have played it as well (1 Sm 10:5; KJV "tabret"; 2 Sm 6:5; 1 Chr 13:8). The mention of this kind of hand drum appears 15 times in the Bible. A wooden or metal hoop was covered with the skin of a ram or wild goat and was played with the hand. It is not clear whether the *toph* had skin on just one side or two. Some commentators have described it as a tambourine or timbrel but there is no indication that it included jangles. The *toph* was used in merrymaking and was rather loud (Ex 15:20; Ps 81:2).

Zelzelim or *meziltayim* were cymbals. Both of these words come from the Hebrew root *zala*, meaning "to resound" or "to tingle," and the noun forms represent the instrument known as the cymbal. Sometimes these terms are wrongly translated as "castanets." These were the only percussion instruments included in the temple music and were always referred to in a dual form, suggesting a pair of cymbals, but played by one man. Cymbals made of metal were known to most ancient cultures. They appear for the first time in the Bible when the ark was transferred to Jerusalem (2 Sm 6:5; 1 Chr 13:8). Later they were played in the temple by the leaders of the Levitical singers (1 Chr 15:19). The function of the cymbals was less musical than liturgical, being used as signals for the singing to begin and between the sections of the psalms. Two different kinds of cymbals are mentioned in Psalm 150, but their difference is not clear, probably involving either size or material.

MUSICIAN *See* Music; Musical Instruments.

MUSTARD Herb noted especially for its small seed (Mt 13:31). *See* Plants.

MUSTER GATE* RSV translation for the Jerusalem gate located opposite the house of the temple servants and the merchants during the days of Nehemiah (Neh 3:31; KJV "Miphkad Gate"; NIV "Inspection Gate"). Its exact location is uncertain. Some suggest that it was a temple gate or a gate in the wall of the old city of David. *See* Jerusalem.

MUTENESS The inability to speak. Muteness, or aphasia, can be a momentary phenomenon or a permanent handicap. It may result from mental retardation, brain lesion, or deafness.

The Bible records several examples of muteness. Zechariah was made mute by the angel Gabriel for not believing he would become the father of John the Baptist (Lk 1:18-22). That condition persisted at least nine months, until the baby was born and named (vv 62-64).

Inability to speak is usually associated with neurological diseases or severe structural deformities. When Jesus healed people who were thus afflicted, or hearing-impaired (Mt 9:32-33; 12:22-23; 15:30-31; Mk 7:32-37; 9:17-27; Lk 11:14), observers were understandably astonished.

Other scattered biblical passages refer to muteness in people (Prv 31:8; Is 35:6) and in animals (Is 56:10; 2 Pt 2:16). The fact that false gods and idols cannot speak (Hb 2:18-20; 1 Cor 12:2) was frequently pointed out by the prophets, who contrasted them with the living, speaking God of Israel.

See also Medicine and Medical Practice.

MYRA Port city on the southern coast of Asia Minor in the province of Lycia, identified with the modern Demre in Turkey. According to Acts 27:5-6, Paul and his military escort briefly stopped here to change ships on their journey to Rome, where Paul was to stand trial.

MYRRH Fragrant gum resin obtained from various shrubs. *See* Plants.

MYRTLE Evergreen shrub with small leaves and scented flowers (Neh 8:15; Is 41:19). *See* Plants.

MYSIA Region in northwest Asia Minor (modern Turkey). It had a long history, leading up to its annexation into the Roman Empire in 133 BC as part of the province of Asia. For about 150 years before that it had been part of the kingdom of Pergamum. The travel account in Acts 16:7-8 indicates that the apostle Paul passed through this region on his second missionary journey but did not preach there.

See also Pergamos, Pergamum.

MYSTERY Counsel, or secret plan, that God shares only with his people. In most biblical passages it relates to the wise counsel of God in his guidance of history to its destiny. The most specific and significant application of the concept of mystery is to the plan of God regarding the death of Christ. It does not refer to a secret that God is unwilling to tell or to something so obscure that it could not be understood even if told.

The passages in which its theological meaning is most clearly seen (among over 30 occurrences in Scripture) are Daniel 3:18-28; 4:6 (Septuagint); Matthew 13:11; Mark 4:11; Luke 8:10; Romans 11:25; 16:25; 1 Corinthians 2:7; 4:1; 15:51; Ephesians 1:9; 3:3-6, 9-12; Colossians 1:26-29; 2:2; 2 Thessalonians 2:7; 1 Timothy 3:9, 16; Revelation 1:20; 10:7; 17:5-18.

In the passages in Daniel, the emphasis is on the revelation that God gave Daniel concerning the content and meaning of King Nebuchadnezzar's dream about the future. It is important to note here that the dream was about what God was going to do. No wise man, enchanter, magician or diviner could explain it, but "there is a God in heaven who reveals mysteries" (Dn 2:28).

Scholarly studies in recent years have determined that similar themes are found in other Jewish writings, including the Dead Sea Scrolls. The stress is on the decisions God has made about the future, especially the end time. The world wrestles with such matters as the problem of evil (i.e., Why, if God is both good and powerful, do people still suffer?). The believer identifies with these problems but knows that God has his providential plans and that one day he will make all things clear. The way God will bring vindication for those who are wronged in this world and judgment to those who do wrong is part of the content of the "mystery" and was a major emphasis in the writings around the time of Christ. God controls the affairs of the universe. The nations will eventually fulfill his purposes.

Matthew 13:11, Mark 4:11, and Luke 8:10 are part of the parables of the kingdom. The kingdom itself is related to the final climactic work of God in history. This is seen in some of the imagery of the parables, such as the harvest, which symbolizes future judgment. Therefore, the word "mystery" is appropriate and significant here. In the immediate context Jesus is explaining why he uses parables. They both vividly illustrate truth and conceal truth from those who are not receptive to it. Therefore, the word "mystery" (plural in Mt and Lk) describes the inner meaning of Jesus' teaching about the kingdom. Those who accept the message will know its meaning; those who do not will lose not only the meaning but apparently also the opportunity to hear and respond to the message of salvation (Mt 13:12-15).

Another aspect of this passage lies in the unasked question as to why, if the Messiah has come, evil still persists in the world. The servants in one of the parables wanted to pull up the weeds, symbolizing evil or evil persons, but were told to allow them to grow until the time of harvest—that is, the judgment (Mt 13:24-30). The persistence of evil in the world and the way God will eventually deal with it is one of the "mysteries."

Romans 11:25 occurs in a large section (chs 9–11) that deals with the people of Israel and their future. Once again, the issue concerns a present problem and its future resolution. In this case the problem is the unbelief of Israel. The hardening of Israel during the present time is called a "mystery" (Rom 11:25). God's purposes will not be thwarted, however, "and so all Israel will be saved" (v 26). This emphasis on the purposes of God is closely intertwined with the concept of the "mystery" and is basic to this entire passage.

Romans 16:25 is broader in its scope, connecting the "revelation of the mystery hidden for long ages past" with Paul's "gospel and the proclamation of Jesus Christ." Here the focus is more closely on the meaning of the death of Christ.

God's "secret wisdom" is mentioned in 1 Corinthians 2:7. The context is the message of the cross that Paul preaches. This message is foolishness to those who consider themselves wise but are lost, and it is the "foolishness" of what is preached that brings salvation to believers (1:18-25). Paul does not attempt to proclaim worldly "wisdom," but he does declare a "message of wisdom" to those who are spiritually mature (2:6). To these he speaks the "secret wisdom," or literally, "wisdom in a secret" (v 7). This passage clearly connects the basic concept of "mystery" as the counsel of God with the death of Christ as the means of salvation. It also connects mystery with the process of history ("the rulers of this age") and with the sweep of God's purposes from OT times into the future. Verse 10 emphasizes the fact that God has indeed revealed these mysteries to us.

In 1 Corinthians 4:1 Paul again speaks from the context of a contrast between God's wisdom and that of the world (3:18-23). He speaks not only of secret things or mysteries but also introduces the concept of stewardship.

He has been entrusted with the revelation of God's mystery and must be faithful in his ministry of declaring it. This theme will reappear in Ephesians 3:2-6.

Paul returns to the relationship of mystery and the end time in 1 Corinthians 15:51. The earlier passage (2:9-16) showed that human knowledge cannot possibly anticipate what God has planned, but God has revealed this mystery to believers. A major aspect of this revealed mystery is the way in which the faithful will be brought into the presence of God: "Lo! I tell you a mystery. We shall not all sleep, but we shall all be changed, in a moment, in the twinkling of an eye, at the last trumpet" (15:51-52, RSV). The other references to mystery in 1 Corinthians occur in the broad context of chapters 12–14 dealing with spiritual gifts, which include receiving divine revelation, so the term "mysteries" in 13:2 and 14:2 is appropriate.

Ephesians opens with a series of statements about God's purpose in history, culminating in the universal headship of Christ (Eph 1:10). These statements include such terms as "chose," "destined," "will," "purpose," "plan," and "counsel." This is clearly the range of ideas associated with the word "mystery" in ancient Jewish writings, and these ideas shed light on Paul's use of the summary expression: "For he has made known to us . . . the mystery of his will" (v 9, RSV).

Part of God's purpose was to form a body of believers, reconciled to himself and to each other through the cross (Eph 2:14-18). In this body, Jewish and Gentile believers have been made members together of one body and sharers together in the promise in Christ Jesus, a new phase of God's revealed plan, which Paul here calls a "mystery" (3:6). As noted above, Paul himself has a responsibility to minister the truth of this "mystery" faithfully (3:2-5; cf. 1 Cor 4:1-5).

Colossians continues to show Paul's sense of responsibility regarding this "mystery," which is now identified with the "word of God" (Col 1:25-29). Once again there is the idea of the span of history linked with the mystery that is known only by revelation: "the mystery that has been kept hidden for ages and generations, but is now disclosed to the saints" (v 26). As in Ephesians, the church is the locus for the working out of God's mystery, "which is Christ in you, the hope of glory" (v 27). This Christ is proclaimed in wisdom, so that believers may reach mature completion in him (v 28). The Colossian believers are asked to pray for Paul as he preaches this "mystery" (4:3).

It is made clear in 1 Timothy 3:16 that the "mystery of godliness" includes the basic elements associated with the "mystery," such as its manifestation in the world and ultimate vindication. However, this grand plan of God does not unfold without opposition. In connection with the coming of the end time, Paul again mentions a mystery. This time it is a dark mystery, called the "secret power of lawlessness" (2 Thes 2:7). A similar evil force, "Babylon the Great, the Mother of Prostitutes," is introduced in the book of Revelation with the word "mystery" (Rv 17:5). Perhaps the idea is that there are forces counter to God whose workings are also impossible for humans to understand. God's truth and power will, however, prevail over these, as he brings his own mystery, his wise counsel, to fulfillment.

Revelation 10:6-7 declares this fulfillment. The ages of waiting in perplexity, of enduring evil, are over, as the angel announces, "There will be no more delay!" The time has finally come when "the mystery of God will be accomplished." Note the dynamic quality of the mystery in this context. It is not just static truth but something that can be "accomplished." This great climax to history is in accord with God's previous revelation "to his servants, the prophets." The mystery, then, is God's wise counsel, which both guides history and is revealed in its culmination. It expresses God's answer to the problem of evil and the vain opposition by evil powers. It declares the meaning of the central event in history, the death of Christ, and reveals the results of the resurrection in the ultimate transformation of all believers at the coming of Christ.

MYSTERY OF LAWLESSNESS*

Phrase used by the apostle Paul to describe a lawless power or force threatening the world. The expression is found only in 2 Thessalonians 2:7 and must be considered in the light of its context.

Evidently, some members of the church at Thessalonica were convinced that Christ had already returned (2 Thes 2:1-2). In order to counter this belief Paul describes some of the events that must occur before the return of Christ. These events center around the coming of "the man of lawlessness," an evil figure who takes his seat in the temple of Jerusalem and proclaims himself to be God (vv 3-4). Although the man of lawlessness is presently being restrained, the evil that he will perpetrate is already at work (v 6). Paul calls this evil "the mystery of lawlessness."

The identity of the man of lawlessness, the restrainer, and the content of the mystery of iniquity have been subject to much debate. Among the suggestions that have been made, the following three predominate:

1. The mystery of lawlessness is the tyranny of the Roman Empire, and the man of lawlessness is a future Roman emperor who is being kept from power by the present Roman ruler. In support of this position it can be said that the Jewish apocalypses of Paul's day considered Rome to be the quintessence of evil. In addition, approximately 10 years before the writing of 2 Thessalonians, Caligula, the Roman emperor, ordered his statue to be erected and worshiped in the Jerusalem temple (Josephus's *Antiquities* 18.8.2-6; *War* 2.10.1-5).

2. The mystery of lawlessness is the religion of Judaism, and the man of lawlessness is the high priest who is restrained by apostolic preaching. However, it is doubtful that Paul would have considered Judaism in this light (cf. Rom 9:1-5).

3. Dispensational theology identifies the mystery of lawlessness as the whole course of evil, consummated in the figure of the Antichrist (the lawless one) and presently restrained by the Holy Spirit. In such a context, it is difficult to establish a scriptural basis for the Holy Spirit being "taken out of the way" (2 Thes 2:7).

See also Antichrist; Eschatology; Second Coming of Christ; Thessalonians, First Letter to the; Thessalonians, Second Letter to the.

NAAM Caleb's descendant from Judah's tribe (1 Chr 4:15).

NAAMAH (Person)
1. Daughter of Zillah and Lamech in the list of Cain's descendants (Gn 4:22).
2. One of Solomon's many wives, an Ammonitess (1 Kgs 14:21, 31; 2 Chr 12:13). She was surely responsible in part for Solomon's idolatry. Her son Rehoboam ruled Judah after Solomon's death (1 Kgs 14:21-24).

NAAMAH (Place) One of the 16 cities located in the Shephelah assigned to Judah's tribe for an inheritance, mentioned between Beth-dagon and Makkedah (Jos 15:41).

NAAMAN
1. Grandson of Benjamin and son of Bela, who gave his name to the Naamite clan (Gn 46:21; Nm 26:38-40; 1 Chr 8:4, 7).
2. Commanding general of the Aramean army during the reign of Ben-hadad, king of Syria (2 Kgs 5). He was held in honor by the king, evidently for his character as well as for military achievements, "but he had leprosy." This did not exclude him from society, as it would have done in Israel (cf. Lv 13–14), but the possibility of a cure suggested by a captive Israelite girl sent Naaman, with Ben-hadad's approval and gifts, to the court of his highly suspicious neighboring monarch (unnamed, but probably Jehoram). Elisha the prophet intervened and prescribed an unlikely mode of healing. The reluctant Naaman followed through because of the good sense of his servants, who said, "If the prophet had told you to do some great thing, would you not have done it?" Naaman confessed that the one true God is in Israel, and he returned home with two mule-loads of earth, perhaps on the assumption that this was a God who could be worshiped only on his own ground (cf. Ex 20:24). In Luke 4:27 Jesus reminds his synagogue listeners of how Naaman, a non-Israelite, was the only one of his time to be cleansed of leprosy.

NAAMATHITE Resident of Naamah in northwest Arabia. Zophar, one of Job's friends, was a Naamathite (Jb 2:11; 11:1; 20:1; 42:9).

NAAMITE Descendant of Naaman, Bela's son from Benjamin's tribe (Nm 26:40). *See* Naaman #1.

NAARAH (Person) One of Ashhur's two wives, who bore him four sons (1 Chr 4:5-6).
See also Maid, Maiden.

NAARAH (Place) City on the eastern border of Ephraim's tribe, just north of Jericho (Jos 16:7); alternately called Naaran in 1 Chronicles 7:28. Josephus locates it near Jericho and associates it with abundant water supply in Archelaus's day (*Antiquities* 17.13.1). Some locate Naarah at modern Tell el-Gisr near 'Ain Duq at the foot of the mountains northwest of Jericho. A synagogue dating to the fourth or fifth century AD has been excavated here; it contains a mosaic floor with a zodiac, an ark of the law, and other figures.

NAARAI* One of David's mighty men (1 Chr 11:37, NLT mg); perhaps the same as Paari (2 Sm 23:35).

NAARAN Alternate name for Naarah, an Ephraimite border town, in 1 Chronicles 7:28. *See* Naarah (Place).

NAARATH* KJV spelling of Naarah, an Ephraimite border town, in Joshua 16:7. *See* Naarah (Place).

NAASHON* KJV spelling of Nahshon, Amminadab's son, in Exodus 6:23. *See* Nahshon.

NAASSON* KJV form of Nahshon, Amminadab's son, in Matthew 1:4 and Luke 3:32. *See* Nahshon.

NABAL Wealthy, successful farmer of Maon in the southern wilderness of Judah. Unlike his godly forefather, Caleb, Nabal was hard of heart and wicked in all his ways (1 Sm 25:3).

When he enters the story of David (1 Sm 25), it is sheep-shearing time, which seems to have been a time of festivity and hospitality. Fleeing from Saul, who wanted to kill him, David decided to ask Nabal for a gift, not only to mark the occasion, but also because David's presence in the area had served to protect Nabal's flocks. Nabal refused in a most insulting way, suggesting that David was no better than a runaway slave.

David decided on revenge. But Abigail, Nabal's quick-witted wife, saved Nabal by bringing David the presents he had asked for and by begging him not to stain his record by acting in anger. David agreed. But when Nabal heard what had happened, he was struck down by what appears to have been a stroke and died 10 days later.

Nabal, whose name means "fool," stands as a reminder of the deep folly of opposing God. God himself, not David, took revenge.

NABATAEANS*, NABATEANS Inhabitants of an independent kingdom bordering Judea, which existed from 169 BC to AD 106. The reader of the Bible and of standard histories often overlooks them for two reasons: their achievements are of recent discovery, and they flourished in a period when other major events, including the life of Christ and the beginning of the church, vastly overshadowed their existence.

The Judeans and Nabateans of the Hellenistic-Roman era shared borders and politics. The mother of Herod the Great, son of the Idumean ruler Antipater, was herself a Nabatean. Herod fled to Petra, the Nabatean capital, in 40 BC, when the Parthians attacked Jerusalem. Relations between the two kingdoms were strengthened by the marriage in the next generation of Herod Antipas to a daughter of the powerful Nabatean king Aretas IV (9 BC–AD 40); relations soured again due to his divorce to marry his niece and sister-in-law, Herodias.

The NT alludes to the extent of Nabatean influence in the region, when Paul tells of his narrow escape from incarceration following his return from the Arabian desert: "At Damascus, the governor under King Aretas guarded the city . . . in order to seize me, but I was let down in a basket . . . and escaped his hands" (2 Cor 11:32-33, RSV).

Nabatean origins are obscure. The best-known remains of Nabatean culture are the funerary monuments of Petra. Aramaic inscriptions abound, standardized on coins and dedicatory items, with papyri and ostraca (sherds) revealing a cursive variation that anticipates Arabic script. Adoption of Aramaic language and Syrian deities shows the pragmatism by which they also adapted to their hostile environment. Only their Byzantine heirs approached their ingenuity for capturing precious water to sustain life in an arid region. Caravan travel was enhanced and permanent control thereof made possible only by skillful engineering.

The earliest historical reference to the Nabateans associates them with Antigonus, Alexander's successor in Syria (312 BC). The succession of known kings begins with Aretas I, around 170 BC (2 Macc 5:8). Josephus writes that about 100 BC the citizens of Gaza looked to "Aretas [II], king of the Arabs," for aid against Alexander Janneus. Aretas III controlled Damascus (80–70 BC).

The golden age at Petra lasted from 50 BC to AD 70 and included the reigns of Malichus I and Obodas II (period of Herod the Great), Aretas IV, and Malichus II. The rule of Rabbel II marks the end of the Nabatean kingdom. His predecessor, Malichus III, had moved the capital to Bostra, 70 miles (112.6 kilometers) east of Galilee. This in turn became the capital of the Roman province of Arabia, following Trajan's conquests, in AD 106. The Nabateans were absorbed into the population, while their distinctive script continued into the fourth century.

See also Petra.

NABOTH Owner of a vineyard that Ahab, king of Israel, coveted (see the story in 1 Kgs 21). Ahab's request was perhaps not unreasonable, and Naboth's refusal may have been a little curt. While Ahab sulked, however, Jezebel had two scoundrels accuse Naboth of blasphemy, the greatest crime an Israelite could commit, which was punishable by death (Lv 24:10-23). Two witnesses secured a conviction, according to the law of Moses (Dt 17:6-7). The murder that was carried out had the appearance of being a legal and just execution. A fast was proclaimed and held according to royal instructions. The accusation and trial of Naboth was supervised by the elders of the city, and he was stoned to death in accordance with the law.

The prophet Elijah, however, knew the real wickedness that lay behind the deed. He faced Ahab with it and prophesied that he and Jezebel and all their family would be wiped out because of it.

The words came true. Ahab got a temporary reprieve when he repented but was later killed in battle (1 Kgs 22:34-40). The blood of Jezebel was indeed licked up by dogs (2 Kgs 9:36), and the body of Joram, their son, was flung into Naboth's vineyard (v 25).

NACHON* KJV spelling of Nacon in 2 Samuel 6:6. *See* Nacon.

NACHOR* KJV form of Nahor, Abraham's ancestor, in Joshua 24:2 and Luke 3:34. *See* Nahor (Person) #1.

NACON A place David passed when he brought the ark from Baale-judah (Kiriath-jearim) to Jerusalem. At the threshing floor of Nacon, Uzzah was struck dead for touching the ark (2 Sm 6:6). Hence, this place was called Perez-uzzah, meaning "the breaking forth upon Uzzah" (v 8). Nacon is alternately called Kidon in 1 Chronicles 13:9 (see NLT mg).

NADAB

1. Eldest son of Aaron and Elisheba, the daughter of Amminadab (Ex 6:23; Nm 3:2; 1 Chr 24:1), who became one of Israel's first priests together with his brothers and father. He participated in the ratification of the covenant with God on Mt Sinai (Ex 24:1, 9) and was ordained to the priesthood (28:1).

Nadab and his brother Abihu, Aaron's second son, died because they offered "strange fire" to the Lord (Lv 10:1-2; Nm 3:4; 1 Chr 24:2). Incense offered in the morning usually preceded the cutting up of the sacrifice. In this case "fire from the Lord devoured them." The offering of "strange fire" does not appear anywhere else in the Bible.

Rabbis have offered various explanations of the offense committed by Nadab and Abihu. Since an admonition against drinking wine in the tent of meeting follows this tragedy (Lv 10:9), an early tradition held that the brothers were drunk. Death was the penalty for any priest drinking in this sacred tent.

An interesting point arises in the instructions that Moses gave to the grieving father of Nadab and Abihu. Moses exhorted Aaron not to mourn or to interrupt his priestly functions. Since Aaron had been sanctified by the sacred anointing oil, he had to continue serving God. He was not allowed to go out of the door of the tent "lest he die." Instead, the rest of Israel mourned for Nadab and Abihu (Lv 10:3-7).

2. Son of Jeroboam, whom he succeeded to the throne of Israel (909–908 BC). Nadab ruled two years (1 Kgs 14:20; 15:25), coming to power in the second year of Asa's reign in Judah; he was succeeded in the third year of Asa's reign (15:28). His rule may have been arranged before the death of Jeroboam, for he surely recognized the dangers of the charismatic ideal that continued among the northern tribes. However, Nadab was not successful in stabilizing the kingdom. To gain the acclamation of the army, he went into battle against the Philistines at Gibbethon, about two and a half miles (4 kilometers) southwest of Gezer. Baasha from the tribe of Issachar, presumably a military officer, assassinated Nadab and all his sons and usurped the throne. So he fulfilled the prophecy predicted by Ahijah the Shilonite against the house of Jeroboam (v 29).

3. Jerahmeelite, the son of Shammai and grandson of Onam, and the great-grandson of Jerahmeel. Nadab in turn had two sons, Seled and Appaim (1 Chr 2:26-30).

4. Son of Jeiel and Maacah, a Gibeonite (1 Chr 8:30; 9:36).

NAGGAI, NAGGE* Ancestor of Jesus, according to Luke's genealogy (Lk 3:25, KJV "Nagge"). *See* Genealogy of Jesus Christ.

NAG HAMMADI MANUSCRIPTS* A collection of 12 Coptic codices containing 52 tractates, or Gnostic documents.

In 1947 the area of Jabal al-Tariff (near Chenoboskion and Nag Hammadi in Egypt) yielded a magnificent collection of 12 Coptic codices containing 52 tractates, or documents, 6 of which are duplicates. One volume was smuggled out of Egypt and was finally purchased in 1952 by the Jung Institute in Zurich. (Gnosticism is important to the study of the psychology of religious experience.) After publication, the owners agreed to return the pirated manuscript to Egypt, and together with the remainder of the Nag Hammadi documents, it is now housed in the small but very significant Coptic Museum in Cairo. The documents in the Nag Hammadi library can be divided into several categories.

Gnostic Texts with Christian Orientation In this category, those documents that have received considerable attention are The Gospel of Thomas, which is a series of sayings and is thought by some scholars to be a sayings-source for the canonical Gospels of Matthew and Luke; The Gospel of Truth, which some scholars have thought came from the pen of the well-known heretic Valentinus; The Gospel of Philip, which contains a unique series of logia related to Gnostic sacraments; and the Apocryphon of John, which has close affinities to the theories of the Ophites and Sethians as described by the heresiologs and provides a full-scale primary source for the Syrian Gnostic reinterpretation of the Garden of Eden story. Some of the other documents in this category that show indisputable signs of Christian influence on Gnosticism are The Treatise on the Resurrection, the several apocalypses of Peter and James, The Book of Thomas the Contender, and Melchizedek.

Gnostic Texts with Less Than Clear Christian Orientation Some scholars have considered that these texts suggest a pre-Christian Gnosticism, but such a conclusion does not seem to be fully substantiated. *Eugnostos* is the document usually cited in this matter and is frequently viewed as an undeveloped stage of the more Christianized form of the text known for some time as The Sophia of Jesus Christ. Even the so-called pre-Christian *Eugnostos*, however, seems to bear unmistakable signs of being related to the Alexandrian school of Christian writings and has been found to contain some allusions to the NT. The Paraphrase of Shem is another document frequently assigned to this category. Its references to baptism and the Redeemer, however, may be the result of a reinterpretation of Christian views and may reflect the conflict between the church and the Gnostics. Other documents in the library usually assigned to this category are The Apocalypse of Adam, The Three Stelaes of Seth, and The Thunder.

Non-Gnostic, Christian Documents There are also in the library several non-Gnostic, Christian documents, which include The Acts of Peter and the Twelve, The Sentences of Sextus, and The Teachings of Silvanus.

Miscellaneous Documents There are several documents that are neither Christian nor technically Gnostic but that were probably read with great interest by the Gnostic scribes. Of particular note are the hermetic treatises that are Egyptian in orientation but contain a less radical dualism than is evident in typical Gnostic literature. Hermetic literature has long been known by scholars through the publication of a hermetic library known as the *Corpus Hermeticum* (English translation, *Thrice-Greatest Hermes*). The first tractate, "Poimandres," is probably of the greatest interest to biblical students because of its rather positive view of creation and its interesting parallels with some of the theological ideas, such as "light" and "life," in the fourth Gospel.

See also Apocrypha.

NAHALAL City in Zebulun's territory (Jos 19:15), given to the Levites for an inheritance (21:35). Zebulun's tribe was unable to drive the Canaanites from the city, so they forced them into hard labor (Jgs 1:30, "Nahalol"). The exact location of the city is unknown. Some possible locations include Tell el-Beida, south of modern Nahalal, and Tell en-Nahl, north of the Kishon River and near the southern end of the plain of Acco, near modern Nahalal.

See also Levitical Cities.

NAHALIEL Temporary camping place for the Israelites during their wilderness wanderings, situated east of the Dead Sea in the vicinity of Moab between Mattanah and Bamoth (Nm 21:19).

See also Wilderness Wanderings.

NAHALLAL* KJV spelling of Nahalal, a city of Zebulun, in Joshua 19:15. *See* Nahalal.

NAHALOL A city of Zebulun, in Judges 1:30. *See* Nahalal.

NAHAM Judahite chief and the brother of Hodiah's wife (1 Chr 4:19).

NAHAMANI One of the leading officials who returned with Zerubbabel to Palestine following the exile (Neh 7:7). His name is omitted in the parallel list of returning officials in Ezra 2:2.

NAHARAI One of David's mighty warriors, who was also Joab's armor bearer. Naharai was from the city of Beeroth (2 Sm 23:37; 1 Chr 11:39).

NAHASH
1. King of the Ammonites who laid siege to Jabesh-gilead during the days of Saul. The men of the city, offering themselves in servitude, petitioned Nahash to make a treaty with them; he agreed to do so on the condition that he gouge out each one's right eye to shame all of Israel. Given a week's reprieve from his threat, the men of Jabesh organized a secret war plan with Saul and Israel, resulting in the destruction of Nahash's Ammonite army (1 Sm 11:1-2; 12:12). He later honored a reconciliation with David, which his son Hanun, on bad counsel, disregarded (2 Sm 10:2; 1 Chr 19:1-2).
2. Father of Abigail and Zeruiah (2 Sm 17:25). In 1 Chronicles 2:16, Abigail and Zeruiah are listed as the daughters of Jesse and the sisters of David and his brothers. Various theories have been offered to resolve this difference. The most feasible suggests that Nahash's wife bore him Abigail and Zeruiah; after his death, his widow married Jesse and subsequently bore David.
3. Father of Shobi from Rabbah, the chief Ammonite city east of the Jordan. Shobi, along with Makir and Barzillai, took care of David's domestic needs during his flight from Absalom (2 Sm 17:27). He is perhaps identifiable with #1 above.

NAHATH
1. Chief of a clan in Edom and Reuel's firstborn son (Gn 36:13, 17; 1 Chr 1:37).
2. Levite of the family of Kohath and Elkanah's grandson (1 Chr 6:26).
3. Levite who oversaw the temple during King Hezekiah's reign (2 Chr 31:13).

NAHBI Son of Vophsi; the head of Naphtali's tribe and one of the 12 spies sent to search out the land of Canaan (Nm 13:14).

NAHOR (Person)

1. Abraham's grandfather (Gn 11:22-25; 1 Chr 1:26); also an ancestor of Jesus according to Luke's genealogy (Lk 3:34, where some English translations follow the Greek spelling, Nachor). The Genesis and 1 Chronicles passages show that Nahor is from Shem's line. Hence, Abraham and his descendants are part of the Semitic family of nations.
2. Son of Terah and Abraham's brother (Gn 11:26-29; Jos 24:2). He married Milcah, Haran's daughter, and his family is named in Genesis 22:20-23. Abraham sent his servant to seek a wife for Isaac at Nahor's residence in Mesopotamia (see Gn 24:10, which possibly suggests that the city itself was called Nahor). There he found Rebekah, Nahor's granddaughter (Gn 24:1-51). Nahor is also named as the father (perhaps grandfather) of Laban, to whom Jacob went when he fled from his brother Esau (Gn 29:5). Both of these texts link Abraham's family with related Semitic people. In Genesis 31:53 God is spoken of as "the God of Abraham and Nahor."

    See also Nahor (Place).

NAHOR (Place)
Northwestern Mesopotamian city; home of Rebekah, Isaac's wife, and Nahor, Abraham's brother (Gn 24:10). Nahor is frequently mentioned in the Mari documents (18th century BC) as the town of Nakhur, located near Haran in the Balikh River Valley. This city was probably the home of some of the ancient Habiru people. Its site is unknown.

See also Nahor (Person) #2.

NAHSHON Amminadab's son; brother of Elisheba and Salmon's father (Ex 6:23; 1 Chr 2:10-11). Nahshon, the prince of Judah's tribe at the start of Israel's wilderness wanderings (Nm 1:7; 2:3; 10:14), represented his kinsmen at the altar's dedication (7:12). In Ruth 4:20 he is listed as David's forefather and a descendant of Judah through the line of Perez, and in Matthew and Luke's genealogies as an ancestor of Jesus Christ (Mt 1:4; Lk 3:32).

NAHUM (Person)

1. A prophet of Judah whose name means "consolation" or "consoler." This name fits his message, as he wrote to encourage the people of Judah while they were being oppressed by the Assyrians (Na 1:1). Other than being the prophet who wrote the book of Nahum, nothing is known of him except that he came from the village of Elkosh. Its exact location is unknown, but four suggestions have been made. First, it was the town of Alqush, near Mosul on the Tigris River just north of Nineveh. A tradition declares this to be the site of Nahum's tomb, but it is first mentioned by Masius in the 16th century. The tomb and its location have no archaeological confirmation, and its authenticity is highly suspect. Second, Jerome recounts a Jewish tradition identifying it with "a village in Galilee called 'Helcesaei'" (Helcesei or Elcesi), and writes, "A very small one, indeed, and containing in its ruins hardly any traces of ancient buildings, but one which is well known to the Jews and was also pointed out to me by my guide." This village is located about 15 miles (24.1 kilometers) northwest of the Sea of Galilee. Third, on the northern edge of the Sea of Galilee rest the ruins of Capernaum, meaning "village of Nahum." But there is no proof that this name goes back to the prophet. Finally, some believe it should be identified with Elcesi, near Bet-gabre, about

halfway between Gaza and Jerusalem in the territory of Judah. Internal evidence seems to support this position (Na 1:15).

It is entirely possible that Nahum may have been a member of the northern tribes but migrated to Judah after the conquest of 722 BC and ministered there.

See also Nahum, Book of; Prophet, Prophetess.

2. Ancestor of Jesus, according to Luke's genealogy (Lk 3:25). *See* Genealogy of Jesus Christ.

NAHUM, Book of
Seventh book in the canonical grouping of the 12 Minor Prophets. Its significance and importance lie in the strategic place it holds in delineating the plan and program of God in relationship to both Judah and the nations of the world.

PREVIEW
•Author
•Date
•Background
•Purpose and Theological Teaching
•Content

Author Nahum is identified as an Elkoshite in the superscription to the book (Na 1:1). The term is somewhat doubtful in meaning but probably refers to a city now unknown. If the term does refer to a geographical location, it may be the village of Elcesi in Judah.

Date The book of Nahum deals with the fall of two great cities, Nineveh and Thebes. The fall of Thebes is cited in 3:8-10, and the entire book deals with the destruction of Nineveh, the capital of Assyria, which was yet future. Thebes was destroyed by the Assyrians around 663 BC, and Nineveh fell in 612 BC. Within this range of history a number of dates for the composition of Nahum have been suggested. Some scholars prefer a date very close to the fall of Nineveh, perhaps during the time when Assyria was being invaded. However, Assyria's influence extended to Judah at the time of the writing of the book (1:13-15; 2:2), a fact that is hardly consonant with the impending downfall of that nation. Since the influence of Assyria in the western provinces began to decline in the latter half of the seventh century, it is best to place the writing of the book in the middle of the seventh century, subsequent to the destruction of Thebes but before the erosion of Assyrian power in Syro-Palestine.

Scholars who deny the validity of biblical prophecy generally date the book in the period subsequent to the fall of Nineveh.

Background The extent of Assyrian dominance in the mid-seventh century was unparalleled. Never before had Assyrian influence extended so far. The destruction of Thebes brought to an end any significant resistance to Assyria by Egypt, their most powerful foe.

The destruction of Thebes occurred during the reign of Manasseh of Judah (696–642 BC), who was, for all intents and purposes, a vassal of the Assyrians. Assyrian influence in Judah led to the intrusion of non-Yahwistic influences, such as the revival of fertility cults and the worship of Assyrian astral deities (2 Kgs 21:1-9).

Within the structure of Assyria's enormous expansion there were many weaknesses that would bring about the decline and eventual demise of that empire. For one thing, it had overextended itself. The task of keeping hostile captive countries in line, many of which were at vast distances from the capital, became increasingly difficult.

Assyria began to experience internal difficulties, particularly with the Chaldeans, a group of loosely knit tribes who had been absorbed into the Assyrian Empire. Egypt also began to withhold tribute. Numerous border raids by barbarians caused the empire to gradually weaken.

The situation worsened as the internal strife began to burgeon into a major crisis. Finally a coalition of Babylonians, Medes, and Scythians brought about the collapse of Assyria when, after a three-month siege, Nineveh fell in 612 BC.

The site of Nineveh was excavated in 1840 by Henry Layard. The excavation revealed that the city was heavily fortified. Evidence still remains of the moats and bulwarks constructed for its defense. The palace of Sennacherib, with its 71 rooms decorated with artistic works, was also uncovered by Layard. Even though the palace lay buried for millennia, it still revealed the splendor of the days of Nineveh's greatness.

The prophet Nahum predicted that the city would be burned (Na 2:13). In his description of the city, Layard indicated that a great fire had destroyed Nineveh. This became evident even when only two small portions of the tell had been explored. The massive gates of the city, which Nahum said would be open to its enemies (3:13), were also burned. The massive sculptures that originally stood by the gates were found buried in debris of earth, brick, and stones mixed with charcoal.

An important archaeological find is a Babylonian chronicle recording events in the reign of the Babylonian king Nabopolassar (625–605 BC). This chronicle fixes the date of the fall of Nineveh, placing it in the 14th year of Nabopolassar—that is, 612 BC.

Purpose and Theological Teaching The purpose of the book of Nahum is to predict the downfall of the Assyrian Empire as prefigured in its capital city, Nineveh. It sets forth the mighty power of God revealed in the arena of history.

At first glance the book may seem to be lacking substantial theological teaching. It is, after all, an extended ode celebrating the downfall of a pagan city. However, when one looks at history from the perspective of a prophet, history becomes the context for the revelation of many of God's attributes.

In chapter 1 the prophet weaves several significant theological themes into his account of the demise of the city. He sets forth the fact that God loves and cares for his own. In 1:7 he describes the Lord as knowing those who take refuge in him. In 1:13 God promises the end of Assyrian oppression of Judah.

God's sovereignty is set forth as well. God is sovereign over the nations that oppose him (1:2). He is sovereign over nature, for the clouds are but the dust of his feet (v 3). God cannot be defied (v 6). He is the sovereign of his people (v 13).

Basic to the theological structure of the book is its affirmation that God is the Lord of history. History is the arena of his activity. God is not merely an abstract concept to the prophet, nor is he a disinterested deity. He brings nations into being and he destroys them. History is not under the control of godless nations or fortuitous events; it is under the control of the Creator.

Nahum points out that God does not deal with people only in wrath. His wrath is revealed against those who oppose him. He deals in tenderness and love with those who find him to be their refuge.

Content

Superscription (1:1) Like other prophetic books, Nahum begins with a superscription. It attributes the authorship of the book to the prophet Nahum. The first part of the superscription reads, "An oracle concerning Nineveh," which indicates the book's content.

The Prophet Considers the Wrath and Might of God (1:2-6) The message of the prophet begins with a descriptive account of a number of attributes of God, specifically his anger and sovereign power. The statement that God is a jealous God (1:2) is not to be understood as attributing selfish motives to God. Rather, it expresses God's intense devotion and loyalty to those who are his own.

Basic to this section is the affirmation that God takes vengeance on his foes. This theological principle is the basis for Nahum's description of the fall of Nineveh. That Assyria was an enemy of God was made clear in history. The Assyrians were not only an instrument used by God to punish his people, but also they were a pagan people who opposed and harassed the Hebrews at every opportunity. Their conquest and exile of the kingdom of Israel was the ultimate manifestation of their opposition to Yahweh. Perhaps it was this dreadful period in Hebrew history that was uppermost in Nahum's mind.

An opening statement in this book says, "The LORD is slow to get angry, but his power is great, and he never lets the guilty go unpunished" (1:3, NLT). Even toward his enemies God acts in grace; he does not lash out in uncontrolled rage but deals with them to change their ways. The statement "he never lets the guilty go unpunished" is an allusion to the great affirmation of God in Exodus 34:6. It is best translated, "He will not completely clear the guilty," which affirms that God forgives but often allows the effects of sin to have their course. This is illustrated in the case of David, whose sin with Bathsheba was forgiven, but the child of the union died. The destruction of Nineveh was thus certain to occur, according to the theological principle established by Nahum: God punishes those who oppose him.

The sovereignty of God over the sphere of nature is established in Nahum 1:3b-6. It, too, is the arena in which his awesome power is revealed.

The Fall of Nineveh and the Deliverance of Israel (1:7-15) The prophet then turned to the city of Nineveh in direct address. In verse 11 he speaks of one who comes forth from Assyria plotting evil against the Lord—a reminder of the Rabshakeh, the Assyrian emissary cited in Isaiah 36:14-20 as counseling the people to give in to his demands for surrender. The words of doom for Nineveh become words of comfort for Judah, for Nahum says that Assyria will afflict them no longer (Na 1:12).

The ultimacy of the destruction of the city is set forth in verses 13-15. No longer would Assyria rise to afflict the Jews. This great truth is celebrated in verse 15, where the prophet encourages the people to return to their worship of God, for they will no longer have Assyria as an enemy.

The Fall of Nineveh (2:1-13) The literary style of Nahum in this section is superb. The fast-moving action, expressed by concise, almost clipped phrasing, lends an atmosphere of excitement and urgency to the description of the collapse of the city. One hears the orders of the defenders in these words: "Sound the alarm! Man the ramparts! Muster your defenses, and keep a sharp watch for the enemy attack to begin!" (2:1, NLT).

Nahum seems to describe the rush into the city just moments after the walls had been breached. One sees the flashes of red as shields are brandished (2:3) and hears the crushing sound of the madly dashing chariots (v 4), but the defenders are too late (v 5).

An important part of Nineveh's defensive structure were the moats that surrounded the city. These moats, fed by two rivers in the vicinity, are alluded to in 2:6, 8. But these moats can't keep back the invaders.

The language again becomes vivid, punctuated with brisk commands: "Stop, stop!" (2:8). And the invaders are heard to say, "Loot the silver! Plunder the gold!" Finally the siege is over, and there is only desolation and ruin (v 10).

This section closes with a reference to lions (2:11-13). Lions in the OT often stand for the wicked, particularly when the wicked devour the righteous. Assyria was very lionlike in its treatment of the Jews. But God declares that he is against the Assyrians (v 13) and will completely cut them off.

This section, vivid and colorful in its style, contains a deep theological message that should not be overlooked. It affirms God's activity in history and assures the believer that the enemies of God will never ultimately conquer the people of God. For God is almighty; he is an avenging God who jealously cares for his own.

A Lament for Nineveh (3:1-19) The prophet pronounces "woe" on the city in a lengthy ode celebrating Nineveh's fall. If he seems to get undue satisfaction from Nineveh's destruction, it is not necessarily because he has a cruel nature. The OT writers viewed the godless nations of the world as the personification of evil. When Nineveh fell, the sphere of history witnessed God's conquest of evil in that particular realm.

In 3:1-7 the prophet speaks of the shame that Nineveh will experience as a result of her fall. He describes one of the causes of Assyria's downfall as her sorceries and harlotries (3:4). This is an evident reference to the idolatrous religion of Assyria. The Assyrian priests were noted for their use of divination and omens. Particularly noteworthy were their attempts to predict the future by observing the motions of the heavenly bodies.

The prophet pointed to other countries that fell prey to their enemies (3:8-11) and affirmed that Assyria is no better than these. He closed by describing the grandeur and might of Nineveh, but he vividly showed how all of that would pass away. Whether it is fortifications (v 12) or extensive trade (v 16), or soldiers (v 17)—all will crumble.

See also Israel, History of; Nahum (Person) #1; Prophecy; Prophet, Prophetess.

HOW SHOULD CHRISTIANS READ THE BOOK OF NAHUM? The book of Nahum could be a problem for Christians. They could wonder how a prophet could rejoice in the carnage of battle, or how he could take delight in describing the death and destruction of the collapse of the Assyrian Empire. What the prophet was rejoicing over was the fact that God had proved himself active in history and victorious over his foes. Christians will also rejoice when the Great Babylon—the enemy of God—is destroyed (see Rv 18–19).

NAIN Village in southern Galilee near the border of Samaria. It is the location of the miracle in which Jesus brought a dead man back to life (Lk 7:11). The man was the son of a widow who lived in this village.

NAIOTH Place where David was given refuge from Saul (1 Sm 19:18–20:1). Here Samuel supervised a group of prophets. According to verses 19 and 23 of chapter 19, Naioth was located within Ramah, Samuel's hometown.

The derivation of the term is enigmatic. The word occurs nowhere else in Scripture, and the Hebrew text seems intentionally obscure. The word perhaps stems from a Hebrew root meaning "pastoral abode" or "dwelling place." In 2 Samuel 15:25 another derivative of the Hebrew root refers to the Lord's habitation, prompting some to suggest that Naioth is a proper noun referring to a sanctuary in Ramah (see 1 Sm 10:5, where prophets were also associated with a sanctuary). Others conclude that Naioth alludes to a school, cloister, or settlement of prophets, of which Samuel was head.

NAMES OF GOD *See* God, Names of.

NAMES, Significance of In biblical times names were given in order to express something about a person, or to express something through him, and not simply to hang a convenient label around his neck. At least seven motivations appear in the choice of names:

1. To record some aspect of a person's birth. Moses was so called by his adoptive mother because he was drawn from the water, the sound of the name recalling a Hebrew verb "to draw out" (Ex 2:10). The circumstances surrounding their births gave Jacob (Gn 25:26) and also Samuel (1 Sm 1:20) their names. In Samuel's case it is interesting to note that his name, meaning "heard by God," records not the offering of prayer but the hearing and answering of it. Something of the deeper and more far-reaching implications of naming is seen in the fact that while the names Jacob and Samuel arise from birth circumstances, they also reveal in advance the person the child will become: Jacob the sneaky opportunist (cf. Gn 27:36), Samuel the man of prayer (1 Sm 7:5-9; 8:6, 21; 12:19-23).

2. To express parental reactions to the birth. Isaac means "laughter" (cf. Gn 17:17; 18:12; 21:3-6). Nabal (1 Sm 25:25), which means "fool," must have been the essence of a mother's prayer—"Let him not be a fool"—though sadly he was! Abimelech (Jgs 8:31) means "My father is king" and may express a secret ambition of Gideon's, at variance with his public testimony (Jgs 8:22-23).

3. To secure the solidarity of the family. This may explain the proposal to call the baby Zechariah in Luke 1:59.

4. To reveal the nature of the person, his function, or some other significant thing about him. The preeminent example of this is Jesus (Mt 1:21), named for his saving vocation. Isaiah seems to have seen his own name as significant of his message "the Lord saves" (see Is 8:18 NLT mg).

5. To communicate God's message. Isaiah (see Is 7:3) called his first son Shear-jashub ("a remnant shall return") in order to embody the double-sided thrust of his message: as a result of faithlessness, the people will be reduced to a mere remnant ("only a remnant shall return"); as a result of God's faithfulness, his people will be preserved in life ("a remnant shall indeed return"). He called his second boy Maher-shalal-hash-baz (8:3), ("speed-prey-haste-spoil"), indicating the certainty of the imminent onset of a victorious foe.

6. To establish religious affiliation. All the names in the Bible with the endings -iah (alternatively -jah) or -el (e.g., Jeremiah, Nathanael) are in fact statements with "the Lord" (-yah) or "God" (-el) as subject. For example, Adonijah (2 Sm 3:4) means "the Lord is Sovereign"; Nathanael (Jn 1:47) means "God gave." Such names were often chosen in times of religious decline in order to affirm the true faith of the parents.

7. To affirm authority over another. In the ancient Near East, the naming of an object or person implied power

and authority over what was named (Gn 2:19-20). Thus, a person not knowing another's name could do neither harm nor good to that person (Ex 33:12, 17). In the ancient world a name described the person or his work in some way. When the individual or his situation changed, so did the name, as with Abram (Abraham) and Jacob (Israel). Pharaoh, as master of the patriarch Joseph, changed Joseph's name when his status altered, calling him Zaphenath-paneah (Gn 41:45). When Eliakim was made king of Judah, the pharaoh changed the Jewish king's name to Jehoiakim (2 Kgs 23:34). In captivity, Daniel, Hananiah, Mishael, and Azariah were forced to change their names to Belteshazzar, Shadrach, Meshach, and Abednego by order of the eunuch (Dn 1:6-7).

In the NT, John the Baptist was named by an angel who represented God, and similarly Jesus was given his name by an angel. The naming of those children symbolized God's authority over John the Baptist and his special relationship as Father to Jesus.

New Names The ability of the name to reveal the nature or status of the person who bears it is well illustrated in the biblical practice of giving new names, as when Sarai became Sarah (Gn 17:15). Three motivations are possible:

1. The new name replaces the old in order to signify the bestowal of powers not hitherto possessed. In this case the new name is equivalent to the experience of regeneration. The childless Abram becomes the "father of a multitude of nations," Abraham (Gn 17:5).
2. The new name may indicate a new character and status with God, as when Jacob the trickster became Israel the man of power with God (Gn 32:27; Hos 12:3-4); thus also, Simon became Peter (Jn 1:42).
3. The new name may cement a new loyalty in the place of an old. Daniel the captive was given the name Belteshazzar, incorporating the name Bel, one of the gods of Babylon—presumably to turn him from the God of his fathers to that of his captors (Dn 1:7).

See also God, Names of.

NANEA Persian goddess mentioned in 2 Maccabees 1:13. In a temple to her in Elymais, a certain Antiochus was assassinated.

NAOMI Wife of Elimelech and the mother of Mahlon and Chilion. A member of Judah's tribe, she lived in Bethlehem during the period of the judges. Her story is told in the book of Ruth. Because of a severe famine in Canaan, Naomi temporarily resettled with her family in the land of Moab, east of the Dead Sea (Ru 1:1-2). Following the death of her husband and two sons in Moab (vv 3-5), Naomi returned to Bethlehem with Ruth, her Moabitess daughter-in-law (vv 8-22). Upon meeting her friends, she told them not to call her Naomi, meaning "pleasant," but Mara, meaning "bitter," for she said, "I went away full, but the LORD has brought me home empty" (vv 20-21, NLT). Naomi's domestic problems were eventually resolved when Ruth married Boaz, Elimelech's near kin (chs 2–4).

NAPHATH-DOR* Region or town identified with Dor, a site on the Mediterranean coast, in Joshua 12:23 and 1 Kings 4:11. *See* Dor.

NAPHISH Eleventh of Ishmael's 12 sons (Gn 25:15; 1 Chr 1:31) and the founder of a tribe that later went to war against the tribes of Israel living east of the Jordan (1 Chr 5:19).

NAPHOTH-DOR Alternate form of Naphath-dor, a site on the Mediterranean coast, in Joshua 11:2. *See* Dor.

NAPHTALI (Person) One of Jacob's 12 sons (Gn 35:25; 1 Chr 2:2). He was the second of two sons borne to Jacob by Bilhah, Rachel's maid. Overjoyed with giving Jacob another son, Rachel named the boy Naphtali, meaning "my wrestling," for her conflict with Leah— "with mighty wrestlings I have wrestled with my sister, and have prevailed" (Gn 30:8, RSV). Naphtali eventually moved his family with Jacob to Egypt (Gn 46:24; Ex 1:4). He fathered four sons (Nm 26:50; 1 Chr 7:13) and founded one of the 12 tribes of Israel (Nm 1:43).

See also Naphtali, Tribe of.

NAPHTALI*, Mount of Hill country comprising the majority of Naphtali's territory, in which the town of Kedesh was set apart as a city of refuge (Jos 20:7).

See also Cities of Refuge; Naphtali, Tribe of.

NAPHTALI, Tribe of One of the 12 tribes of Israel that migrated from Egypt to Canaan, ultimately settling in northern Canaan in the high country of Galilee.

During the period of the Israelite exodus from Egypt, Naphtali's tribe is mentioned only incidentally. Acting as the leader of the tribe, Ahira, Enan's son (Nm 2:29; 7:28), helped conduct the census of Naphtali (1:15) as Israel prepared for the prospect of war. The first census records 53,400 men ready for war (vv 42-43), whereas a later census taken near the end of their desert sojourning records 45,400 men capable of battle (26:48). When Moses sent the 12 spies to search out the land of Canaan, Nahbi, Vophsi's son, represented Naphtali's tribe (13:14). Other significant activities involving Naphtali's tribe during the wilderness wanderings include the position of encampment around the tabernacle while in the desert (2:29); the distribution of the land, in which Pedahel, Ammihud's son, represented Naphtali in the ceremony of choosing lots (34:28); and the ratification of the covenant at Shechem (Dt 27:13). Finally, like the rest of the tribes, Naphtali was the recipient of a blessing from Moses (Dt 33:23).

The tribal inheritance of Naphtali was located on the eastern side of upper Galilee, bordered on the south by Zebulun and by Asher on the west (Jos 19:34). Within its borders were several Levitical cities (Jos 21:6; 1 Chr 6:62) and a city of refuge, Kedesh (Jos 20:7; 1 Chr 6:76). Though they successfully occupied the region, they did not initially drive out the Canaanites (Jgs 1:33). They did, however, subjugate the inhabitants of the Canaanite cities Beth-shemesh and Beth-anath to forced labor. As a result of their location, they were involved in some major conflicts with the indigenous population and foreign invaders. The most significant of these was the war with Jabin, king of Hazor. Barak, son of Abinoam, from Kedesh in Naphtali joined Deborah, the prophetess, and together they led the tribes of Zebulun and Naphtali against the Canaanites (chs 4–5). Along with the tribes of Asher, Zebulun, and Manasseh, the tribe of Naphtali was also called by Gideon into battle against the Midianites (6:35).

During the united monarchy, the tribe of Naphtali sent troops to Hebron, demonstrating their support of David's kingship over all of Israel (1 Chr 12:34). Naphtali's continued allegiance to the Davidic dynasty was evidenced in their support of Solomon's administrative system. Ahimaaz of Naphtali's tribe was one of 12 officers who administered the various regional districts for the king; this same Ahimaaz also married Basemath, the daughter of Solomon (1 Kgs 4:15).

The history of the tribe during the divided monarchy is sketchy, and references to Naphtali occur in the contexts of military conflicts. During the reign of Asa in Judah, Baasha, king of Israel, sought to build a fortress at Ramah on the central Benjamite plateau. Feeling threatened, Asa encouraged Ben-hadad of Syria to attack the northern kingdom. The Syrian monarch complied, and the brunt of his attack was felt by Naphtali's tribe (1 Kgs 15:16-24). Baasha withdrew his troops from the Benjamite plateau only to encounter the powerful onslaught of the Syrian army. The other major foreign power to exert its influence in the region of Naphtali was Assyria, particularly during the reign of Tiglath-pileser III. During the rule of Pekah in Israel and Rezon in Syria, this Assyrian monarch came and captured Gilead, Galilee, and Naphtali (2 Kgs 15:29) in 732 BC.

According to the prophet Isaiah (Is 9:1), though the Lord had made Naphtali's land contemptible, he would make it glorious once again. Matthew sees the fulfillment of this prophecy in the person of Christ, who brought the message of God's kingdom to the Jews living in the region of Naphtali's tribe (Mt 4:13-15). In the book of Revelation (Rv 7:6), 12,000 members of Naphtali's tribe are included among the sealed multitude of Israel.

NAPHTUHIM*, NAPHTUHITES Egyptian descendants of Noah through Ham's line (Gn 10:13; 1 Chr 1:11), listed between the Lehabim and Pathrusim tribes. Some scholars suggest that the Naphtuhim were the inhabitants of Middle Egypt, situated between the Libyans of Lower Egypt and the Pathrusim of Upper Egypt. However, the exact site of their ancient settlements is uncertain.

NARCISSUS (Person) Christian whose household knew the Lord and received greetings from Paul in his letter to Rome (Rom 16:11).

NARCISSUS* (Plant) Fragrant plant growing profusely on the plains of Sharon (Is 35:1). *See* Plants.

NARD Perennial herb with strong, fragrant roots. *See* Plants.

NATHAN

1. Son of David by Bathsheba, the third son to be born in Jerusalem (2 Sm 5:14; 1 Chr 3:5; 14:4). Nathan, Solomon's older brother, is featured in the apocalyptic oracle of Zechariah 12:12 and Christ's line of descent via Joseph (Lk 3:31).
   See also Genealogy of Jesus Christ.
2. One of the early prophets and adviser of David. When David's military campaigns were almost completed, he shared with Nathan his desire to erect a suitable dwelling place for God. Nathan's immediate reaction was favorable, but on receiving direct instructions from the Lord, he countermanded his initial approval. He foretold that one of David's sons would build God a house, and that God would establish a house (dynasty) for David through his son Solomon. The prophecy includes not only the Davidic line but also the messianic king. Nathan's oracle, therefore, was of vital importance, since it dealt with two great institutions, the temple and the Davidic monarchy (2 Sm 7:1-7; 1 Chr 17:1-15).

   During the Ammonite war, David, having fathered an illegitimate child, tried to cover his sin by involving the woman's husband, Uriah (2 Sm 11:1-13; 23:39). When this attempt failed, he had Joab, the general of the army, engineer Uriah's death, whereupon David

took Bathsheba openly as his wife (11:14-27). Nathan confronted the king, courageously exposing the enormity of David's crime by a parable that provoked the king's righteous anger and turned the finger of condemnation upon David himself (12:1-9). Nathan foretold the fearful consequences for David's family resulting from his sin and evil example (vv 10-12). This prophecy was fulfilled in rape, the deaths of three of David's sons, and civil war (2 Sm 13–18; 1 Kgs 1). Bathsheba's child also would not live (2 Sm 12:14).

When David was near death, one of his sons, Adonijah, seized power (1 Kgs 1:1, 10). Nathan prompted Bathsheba to remind David of an earlier promise concerning Solomon's succession, supporting her by his own timely intervention (vv 10-27). David immediately authorized Solomon's coronation (vv 28-53).

Nathan was an important chronicler (1 Chr 29:29; 2 Chr 9:29). With David he played a vital part in developing the musical aspects of temple worship (2 Chr 29:25).
3. Man of Zobah and the father of Igal, one of David's 30 heroes (2 Sm 23:36). He was possibly the Nathan noted as the brother of Joel (1 Chr 11:38).
4. Father of two important court officials (1 Kgs 4:5); probably either the prophet or David's son.
5. Descendant of Judah, in the clan of Jerahmeel, the son of Attai and the father of Zabad (1 Chr 2:36).
6. One of a deputation sent by Ezra to secure Levitical reinforcements for the Israelites returning to Jerusalem (Ezr 8:16). Possibly Nathan was among those who covenanted to divorce their foreign wives (10:39), but the name, meaning "gift," was a very common one.

NATHANAEL Jew from Cana of Galilee whom Jesus called to be a disciple (Jn 1:45-50; 21:2). Initially skeptical when Philip described Jesus as the fulfillment of the whole OT (1:45-46), Nathanael proclaimed Jesus to be the Son of God and the King of Israel (v 49) after an astonishing personal encounter.

The fact that the only NT references to Nathanael occur in the Gospel of John has led some scholars to identify him with several personalities appearing in the synoptic Gospels. Because his call appears with those of Andrew, Peter, and Philip, some have speculated that he was one of the 12, possibly Bartholomew. Three pieces of evidence are cited in support of this position: (1) the name Bartholomew is patronymic (literally "son of Tolmai") and would be accompanied by another name; (2) each of the Synoptic lists of the 12 apostles place Bartholomew after Philip (Mt 10:2-4; Mk 3:16-19; Lk 6:14-16), paralleling the call of Nathanael after Philip in John's account; and (3) Bartholomew's name does not appear in the fourth Gospel.

A second position identifies Nathanael as James, the son of Alphaeus. According to this view, Jesus' comment in John 1:47 should read "Behold, Israel [not "an Israelite"] indeed, in whom is no guile!" Israel is the name God gave to Jacob, and the NT form of Jacob is James. John addressed James, the son of Alphaeus, as Nathanael in order to distinguish him from others who had become prominent in the early church.

Two less plausible identifications equate Nathanael with either Matthew or Simon the Cananaean. The first is precariously founded on the similar etymologies of the names Matthew ("gift of Yahweh") and Nathanael ("Yahweh has given"). The second identifies the two on the basis of the common hometown of Cana.

In the final analysis, Nathanael was most likely a disciple who was not a member of the 12 and was known only to John. This suggestion conforms to early patristic evidence. In the fourth Gospel, Nathanael serves as a symbol for the true Jew who overcomes initial skepticism to believe in Christ. This is confirmed by three observations: (1) his initial reaction to Jesus parallels that of others who believed in the Law and the Prophets (Jn 7:15, 27, 41; 9:41); (2) Jesus' perception of Nathanael under a fig tree (1:48) identifies the latter's devotion to the Torah (in rabbinic literature the proper place to study the Torah is under a fig tree); and (3) Jesus identifies Nathanael with Jacob, the father of the Israelite nation. In Genesis 25–32, Jacob is certainly sly and cunning in his dealings with Esau and Laban. John 1:51 strengthens the ties between Nathanael and Jacob by presenting the imagery of angels ascending and descending, reminiscent of Jacob's dream, and by locating the event in Galilee close to Bethel and Jabbok, the sites of Jacob's experiences. Nathanael is thus a symbol of the pious Israelite for whom Christ came. His response typifies what the fourth Evangelist understands as the appropriate response of the true Israelite to Jesus—from initial skepticism to faith (cf. Rom 9:6).

See also Apostle, Apostleship.

NATHAN-MELECH Official during King Josiah's reign. Horses for sun worship were kept near his quarters but were removed by Josiah (2 Kgs 23:11).

NATIONS Groups formed on the basis of political or social interests or on kinship. Generally, the word "nations" implies peoples of the world other than the Hebrews, although it can also include the Jews.

Origins The book of Genesis attributes to the three sons of Noah the origin of the various "families" or ethnic groups (about 70 in all) who inhabited the eastern Mediterranean regions (Gn 10). The narrative presupposes that each group has its own individual geographical location and language (vv 5, 20, 31). The story of the tower (ziggurat) of Babel, whose peak was to reach to heaven (ch 11), explains that ethnic groups were separated by language barriers and scattered geographically so that they might not collaborate on presumptuous ventures.

Paul, in his sermon in Athens, assumes that the various nations had a common origin, just as the writer of Genesis did, and accepts as part of the design of God the fact that nations should be separated by geographical boundaries (Acts 17:26). The prophet Zephaniah looked forward to the day when God would reverse this state of affairs and cause all the nations to speak one language (Zep 3:9). The writer of Revelation, in his vision of the new heaven and the new earth, saw these natural boundaries abolished. The nations freely intermingle in the new Jerusalem (Rv 21:22-26).

The distinction between "Israel" and "the nations" is not clear-cut. "Israel" evolved from various ethnic groups, and several of "the nations" traced their origins to prominent figures in the Israelite community. Abraham, the father of the Jewish nation, lived in Ur of the Chaldees in the delta region of the Tigris-Euphrates valley. With his father he migrated north to Haran, and finally southwest to the land of Canaan (Gn 11:31–12:9). Deuteronomy 26:5 ("a wandering Aramean was my father") suggests Abraham's residence was in the district of Mesopotamia known as Aram-naharaim. When Abraham entered into covenant with God, God gave him the token of the covenant relationship: circumcision. Foreigners purchased as slaves were circumcised, thus including them in the covenant community. When Moses led the Israelites out of

Egypt into the wilderness, a mixed multitude also went up with them (Ex 12:38), which suggests again that people not biologically related nevertheless identified themselves with the people of Israel.

The nation of Israel did not include all of those physically descended from Abraham. The first son of Abraham, Ishmael, had an Egyptian mother and is the ancestor of the Ishmaelites, bedouins who roamed the southern wilderness region (Gn 16). Of the twin sons born to Isaac and Rebekah, Esau, the firstborn, is the father of the Edomites living in the southeast, traditional enemies of Israel (Gn 25:23; Nm 20:21).

God and the Nations Scripture presents negative and positive attitudes toward the nations. The nations inhabiting the territory between the Tigris-Euphrates valley and the Nile River were wicked nations. Therefore, God took away their land and gave it to the descendants of Abraham (Gn 15:16-20). Incestuous relationships, adultery, homosexuality, and sexual relationships between men and animals characterized the nations and incurred God's displeasure (Lv 18). The nations indulged in the practice of spiritism, augury, witchcraft, and necromancy, so the Hebrews were instructed to avoid such activities (19:26; 20:6). The nations worshiped many gods and included in their worship the practice of human sacrifice, often the sacrifice of children—a ritual that God abhors (Lv 20:1-5; 2 Kgs 17:29-34). The prophet Isaiah spoke scathingly of the craftsman who, taking a branch of a tree, used part of it to kindle a fire and fashioned from the remainder a graven image that he then worshiped (Is 44:12-20). The Baalim and Ashteroth, fertility gods of the Canaanites, were a constant source of temptation to the people of Israel. The message repeated throughout Scripture is that for these reasons God would drive out the nations and give their territory to Israel (Ex 34:24; Dt 12:29-31). The prophetic oracles against the nations reinforced this negative attitude (Jer 46–51; Am 1:3–2:3).

However, the Scripture also reflects a more positive attitude toward the nations. As revealed in the book of Psalms, God is not only concerned about Israel; his eyes keep watch over the nations, and all the earth praises and worships him (Ps 66:1-8). The psalmist prays that God's saving power may be known among all the nations. He affirms that God righteously judges the peoples and guides the nations. All the ends of the earth should fear him (67:7). The prophet Isaiah declares that the Jerusalem temple is to be a house of prayer for all peoples and that God welcomes the foreigner who comes with sacrifices and offering worship (Is 56:6-8). Isaiah's vision of hope for the latter days pictures people of all nations pouring into Jerusalem to worship the Lord and learn his ways. Instead of nation warring against nation, all will live in peace, ruled by God (2:2-4).

The Nations in the New Testament According to the Gospels, Jesus ministered not only to the Jews but also to the Gentile nations in accordance with ancient prophecy (Mt 4:15-16). Jesus taught in Galilee, a predominantly non-Jewish area, traveled to Tyre and Sidon (Mk 7:24) and through the Decapolis (v 31). He ministered to a Roman centurion (Lk 7:1-10), the widow of Nain (vv 11-17), and a Syrophoenician woman (Mk 7:26). People from Idumea came to observe his miracles (3:8).

The teaching of Jesus was also wide in scope. The narrative of the great judgment (Mt 25:31-46) depicts all nations gathered before the Son of Man, and Jesus commissions the apostles to "make disciples of all nations" (Mt 28:19).

Although the book of Acts does not overlook the

nations' role in the death of Jesus (Acts 4:27) and their role in opposing the ministry of Paul (26:17), it nevertheless clearly indicates that the church fulfilled its commission to present the gospel to non-Jewish peoples. Peter proclaims the message about Jesus to the household of Cornelius, a Roman soldier of the Italian Cohort (ch 10). Although the early church resisted the fact that non-Jewish peoples might freely receive the gift of the Spirit, they eventually welcomed this conclusion (11:1-8; 15:1-29). Paul traveled through Cyprus, Asia Minor, Greece, and Italy, founding or visiting churches that were predominantly Gentile. The book of Acts ends dramatically with Paul preaching the gospel in the city of Rome, the heart of the Roman Empire.

NATURAL MAN* *See* Man, Natural.

NAUM* KJV spelling of Nahum, an ancestor of Jesus (Lk 3:25). *See* Nahum (Person) #2.

NAZARENE Native or inhabitant of Nazareth, a NT town in lower Galilee.

Nazareth was Jesus' hometown during the first 30 years of his life. Since the name Jesus was a common name among the Jews, and since surnames were not used, perhaps the designation Nazarene differentiated Jesus of Nazareth from others with the same name (see Greek texts of Mt 27:16-17; Acts 7:45; Col 4:11; and Heb 4:8, where the name Jesus refers to other men).

In the original texts, the designation Jesus the Nazarene was used by demons (Mk 1:24; Lk 4:34), the crowd outside Jericho (Mk 10:47; Lk 18:37), a servant girl (Mk 14:67), soldiers (Jn 18:5-7), Pilate (Jn 19:19), the two disciples on the road to Emmaus (Lk 24:19), and the angel at the tomb (Mk 16:6).

The apostles in Acts used the designation to identify Jesus. Peter speaks of Jesus the Nazarene in his sermon on the day of Pentecost (Acts 2:22), and at the temple gate in a subsequent healing (3:6; 4:10). Paul identifies Jesus as such in Acts 26:9.

One hostile reference to the name is in Acts 6:14. The false witnesses against Stephen accused him before the Sanhedrin of saying, "This Nazarene, Jesus, will destroy this place [temple] and alter the customs that Moses handed down to us" (see Greek). Another antagonistic reference is in Acts 24:5, the only reference to Jesus' followers as Nazarenes. Tertullus accused Paul, saying, "For we have found him to be a troublemaker, a man who is constantly inciting the Jews throughout the world to riots and rebellions against the Roman government. He is a ringleader of the sect known as the Nazarenes" (NLT).

With regard to the name "Nazarene," Matthew 2:23 has always been problematic: "So they went and lived in a town called Nazareth. This fulfilled what was spoken by the prophets concerning the Messiah: 'He will be called a Nazarene' " (NLT). No OT prophecy directly states that the Messiah would be called a Nazarene. Some scholars relate Matthew's reference to Isaiah 11:1, which speaks of the Messiah as a Branch, a Hebrew term derived from the same root as "Nazareth." Others suggest that the OT prophecies concern the despising and reviling of the Messiah as having been thought by others to be a Nazarene, when it was well known that the Messiah was supposed to come from Bethlehem, the city of David. Of course, that is where Jesus was born, but he was raised in Nazareth and subsequently was known as a Nazarene and thereby ridiculed. Thus, the prophecy was fulfilled when some of his contemporaries called him a Nazarene, from the despised town of Nazareth (Jn 1:46; cf. Mt 13:54; Mk 6:2-3; Lk 4:22).

See also Nazareth.

NAZARENES Name given to those who followed Jesus of Nazareth. Since Jesus was known as Jesus of Nazareth or Jesus the Nazarene, it was easy to transfer that title to his followers. They were "followers of the Nazarene" or "Nazarenes." The earliest use of the term is in Acts 24:5, where Tertullus accused the apostle Paul of being "a ringleader of the sect of the Nazarenes." Certainly, he did not intend the title as a compliment. The early Christians probably did not use that name for themselves, whereas later Jewish-Christian and Gnostic groups did call themselves Nazarenes. One early writing was even called *The Gospel of the Nazarenes.*

NAZARETH Village in the Roman province of Galilee, the home of Joseph, Mary, and Jesus. Always small and isolated, Nazareth is not mentioned in the OT, the Apocrypha, intertestamental Jewish writings, or the histories of Josephus. The town lies just north of the plain of Esdraelon in the limestone hills of the southern Lebanon range. It is situated on three sides of a hill. This location forms a sheltered valley with a moderate climate favorable to fruits and wildflowers. Trade routes and roads passed near Nazareth, but the village itself was not on any main road. Nazareth is about 15 miles (24.1 kilometers) west of the Sea of Galilee and 20 miles (32.2 kilometers) east of the Mediterranean. Jerusalem lies about 70 miles (112.6 kilometers) south. Archaeological remains indicate that the ancient town was higher on the western hill than the present village (cf. Lk 4:29). In the time of Christ, Nazareth, along with the entire region of south Galilee, lay outside the mainstream of Jewish life, providing the background for Nathanael's wry remark to Philip, "Can anything good come out of Nazareth?" (Jn 1:46).

Aerial View of Nazareth

Nazareth is first mentioned in the NT as the home of Mary and Joseph (Lk 1:26-27). Sometime after Jesus was born at his parents' ancestral town of Bethlehem (about 80 miles, or 128.7 kilometers, to the south), Mary and Joseph returned to Nazareth (Mt 2:23; Lk 2:39). Jesus grew up there (Lk 2:39-40, 51), leaving the village to be baptized by John in the Jordan River (Mk 1:9). When John was arrested, Jesus moved to Capernaum (Mt 4:13). Though Jesus was often identified by his boyhood city as "Jesus of Nazareth" (see Mk 10:47; Jn 18:5, 7; Acts 2:22), the NT records only one subsequent visit by Jesus to Nazareth. On this occasion, Jesus preached in the syna-

---

THE NAZARETH DECREE

A fascinating document comprising some 20 lines of rather poor Greek inscribed on a simple slab of white marble was discovered in Nazareth in the latter part of the nineteenth century. This document reads:

"Ordinance of Caesar. It is my pleasure that graves and tombs remain undisturbed in perpetuity for those who have made them for the cult of their ancestors, or children, or members of their house. If, however, any man gives information that another has either demolished them, or has in any other way extracted the buried, or has maliciously transferred them to other places in order to wrong them, or has displaced the sealing or other stones, against such a one I order that a trial be instituted, as in respect of the gods, so in regard to the cult of mortals. For it shall be much more obligatory to honor the buried. Let it be absolutely forbidden for anyone to disturb them. In the case of contravention I desire that the offender be sentenced to capital punishment on charge of violation of sepulture."

In order to understand the full significance of this text we need to be able to make a very close approximation to the date by means of the style of writing. According to this text, the inscription is to be dated to about AD 50. The most likely emperor under whom such a decree was issued was Claudius (AD 41–54). He is known to have taken an interest in the regulation of Jewish affairs in other lands.

The secular historian Suetonius, in his biography of Claudius, made reference to riots that broke out within the Jewish community "at the instigation of Chrestus," that is Christ, as the name appears misspelled in the text (*Life of Claudius* 25.4). We may conjecture that Christian Jews in Rome who preached Jesus to their fellows provoked riots in that city. Claudius seems to have expelled all the Jews from Rome (Acts 18:2). Another copy of a letter of Claudius was found among papyri in Egypt in 1920, dating to AD 41. It forbade the Alexandrian Jews "to bring or invite other Jews to come by sea from Syria. If they do not abstain from this conduct, I shall proceed against them for fomenting a malady common to the world."

Against this background we may propose an explanation of the Nazareth Decree. The early Christians were proclaiming that Jesus Christ had risen from the dead. The rabbis of the time claimed that "his disciples came and stole away the body" (Mt 28:13). Whatever the truth of the matter from the viewpoint of Claudius, he did not wish to encourage theories about the disappearance of bodies from tombs. The Nazareth Decree thus becomes a strong pointer to the resurrection of Christ, which was at that time upsetting the Roman world. So Claudius took steps to curb the spread of these disturbing ideas.

---

gogue and was rejected by the townspeople (Lk 4:16-30; cf. Mt 13:54-58; Mk 6:1-6). Jesus' followers were also derisively called "Nazarenes" (Acts 24:5).

Nazareth remained a Jewish city until the time of the emperor Constantine (d. AD 327), when it became a sacred place for Christian pilgrims. A large basilica was built in Nazareth about AD 600. Arabs and Crusaders alternately controlled the village until 1517, when it fell to the Turks, who forced all Christians to leave. Christians returned in 1620, and the town became an important Christian center.

See also Nazarene.

NAZARITE*, NAZIRITE   Person who was either chosen or consecrated for life or for a set period of time to complete a vow to God. The Nazirite (Nazarite) devoted himself to self-imposed discipline in order to perform some special service (Nm 6:1-21).

Israelite tradition viewed the Nazirite as consecrated for life. Samson was the ancient hero of the Nazirites. He was "consecrated to God" through the vow of his mother (Jgs 13:5; 16:17) and remained under that vow to the "day of his death" (13:7). As long as Samson's hair was not cut, he was able to receive the Spirit of the Lord and thereby perform amazing physical feats.

Early Nazirite vows may have been associated with holy-war ceremonies. Combatants were consecrated to God and perhaps wore long hair (Jgs 13:5). The prophet Samuel did not cut his hair because of his mother's vow that no razor would touch his head (1 Sm 1:11); the Septuagint adds that he was not to drink wine. The Nazirite vow of uncut hair was associated with being consecrated to God's service and was especially common during the charismatic days of Israel's early leaders.

Naziritism developed into a ritual for those who sought to consecrate themselves temporarily to God. During the period of consecration, the devotee abstained from drinking wine, allowed his hair to grow, and avoided all contact with dead bodies.

Uncut hair symbolizes strength and life. Perhaps this is

the intended meaning of *nazir* when used to describe Joseph in the blessing of Jacob (Gn 49:26) and in the blessing of Moses (Dt 33:16). Vineyards that were not pruned in sabbatical or jubilee years were said to be *nazir*.

In later times, touching or coming in close proximity to a dead body was the most serious offense against the vow. Should anyone die in his presence, a Nazirite became impure. Such a contaminated Nazirite was expected to shave his "defiled head" on the day of cleansing. Next, he would bring two young pigeons to the priest, who would offer one as a sin offering. And finally, he must bring a male lamb for a guilt offering (Nm 6:9-12). Because of this defilement, the Nazirite had to begin his days of separation again.

At the end of his period of separation he "desecrated" himself through a ceremony: he offered a sacrifice for sin and a communion sacrifice, then he shaved his head and burnt the hair. Thereafter, the Nazirite returned to his normal life and could drink wine (Nm 6:13-21).

Paul completed a similar vow at Cenchrea in NT times (Acts 18:18) and, then again, along with four other Nazirites in Jerusalem (Acts 21:23-24). In the Talmud the period of time for the consecration was usually 30 days. It was customary for the wealthy to aid poor Nazirites in the purchase of their offerings. During the Maccabean period, the Nazirites were unable to complete their rites because the temple was profaned (1 Macc 3:49-51).

NEAH   Border town in Zebulun's territory (Jos 19:13).

NEAPOLIS   Port city of Philippi, identified with modern Kavalla. Neapolis, whose name comes from a Greek word meaning "new city," existed as early as the fifth century BC, and in Roman times was clearly dependent upon the city of Philippi.

After Paul's dream of the man from Macedonia, he left Troas and the continent of Asia for the continent of Europe. The party passed by the island of Samothrace and then came to Neapolis. Thus, Neapolis was the first city of Europe visited by Paul (Acts 16:11).

Roman Double Aqueduct in Neapolis

NEARIAH
1. One of Shemaiah's six sons and a descendant of David (1 Chr 3:22-23).
2. Captain of 500 men of Simeon's tribe who went to Mt Seir, where they destroyed the remnant of the Amalekites and settled their own people in Hezekiah's time (1 Chr 4:42).

NEBAI Political leader who signed Ezra's covenant of faithfulness to God with Nehemiah and others after the exile (Neh 10:19).

NEBAIOTH Firstborn of Ishmael's 12 sons (Gn 25:13; 1 Chr 1:29) whose sister, Mahalath (also called Basemath, cf. Gn 36:3) later married Esau (Gn 28:9). The identification of Nebaioth's descendants is uncertain, though possibly they are the ancestors of the Nabatean Arabian tribe who possessed the land of Edom and parts of the Transjordan as far north as Palmyra (ancient Tadmor). The descendants of both Nebaioth and Kedar are noted for their superb flocks of sheep (Is 60:7) and are mentioned in the inscriptions of the Assyrian king Ashurbanipal (seventh century BC).

NEBALLAT Town situated in the hills overlooking the southeastern region of the plain of Sharon, settled by Benjamites after the exile (Neh 11:34). It is identified with modern Beit Nebala, four miles (6.4 kilometers) east of Lod and two miles (3.2 kilometers) north of Hadid.

NEBAT Ephraimite of Zeredah in the Jordan Valley, a servant to Solomon, and the father of King Jeroboam (1 Kgs 11:26).

NEBO (Deity) Marduk's son and a chief god among the Babylonian pantheon. Nebo (Hebrew spelling; pronounced Nabu in Akkadian) was the patron deity of wis-

dom, education, and literature. Originally the local city god of Borsippa, Nebo grew in prominence with the rise of the Babylonian Empire. Numerous inscriptions affirm his popularity among the Babylonian and Assyrian kings. At Kalkhi (modern Nimrud), an ancient capital of Assyria, a temple was built and maintained for Nebo and his consort Tashmit. Isaiah ridiculed Nebo for his inability to save even himself from being carried into captivity (Is 46:1). *See* Babylon, Babylonia.

NEBO (Person) Forefather of 52 descendants who returned with Zerubbabel to Judah following the exile (Ezr 2:29; Neh 7:33), 7 of whom were encouraged by Ezra to divorce their foreign wives (Ezr 10:43). Some suggest that Nebo refers to a town in Benjamin's tribe from which some inhabitants went into exile to Babylon.

NEBO (Place)
1. City located on the pastoral tablelands of the Transjordan and desired by the sons of Gad and Reuben (Nm 32:3). Reuben was apportioned this town (Nm 32:38; 1 Chr 5:8) but eventually lost it to King Mesha of Moab around 850 BC. Later, Isaiah (Is 15:2) and Jeremiah (Jer 48:1, 22) predicted Nebo's destruction as part of God's judgment against Moab.
2. Summit in the Pisgah portion of the Abarim mountain range, situated eight miles (12.9 kilometers) east of the Jordan River at the northeastern corner of the Dead Sea, atop of which Moses viewed the Promised Land of Canaan before he died (Dt 32:49; 34:1). Its site has been variously identified with Jebel en Neba or with Khirbet el-Mekhaiyet.
   See also Nebo, Mount.

NEBO, Mount Name of a high mountain on the east side of the Jordan River opposite the city of Jericho. The Israelites encamped near it on the last stage of their journey to the Promised Land (Dt 32:49). The mountain with which Nebo is now identified has two peaks; in the OT the peak of Nebo is called Pisgah (34:1). From this high vantage point Moses beheld the Promised Land (vv 1-5).

NEBUCHADNEZZAR, NEBUCHADREZZAR* Babylonian king (605–562 BC) who captured and destroyed Jerusalem in 586 BC. He was the son of Nabopolassar and the foremost ruler of the Neo-Babylonian Empire (612–539 BC); his name is alternately spelled Nebuchadrezzar in Jeremiah and Ezekiel (see NLT mg).

Nebuchadnezzar states that he conquered all of "Hatti-country," which is a term used for all of Palestine and Syria, including Judah. Jehoiakim had been made king of Judah by Pharaoh Neco (2 Kgs 23:34) and initially submitted to Nebuchadnezzar (24:2; cf. Dn 1:1-2), but three years later rebelled. Jehoiakim died and his son Jehoiachin succeeded to the throne (2 Kgs 24:6); however, he reigned for only three months. Nebuchadnezzar came to Jerusalem in 598 BC and took Jehoiachin captive to Babylon (vv 10-17). He replaced Jehoiachin with his Uncle Mattaniah, whom he renamed Zedekiah (2 Kgs 24:17; 2 Chr 36:10).

Zedekiah rebelled against the king of Babylon (2 Kgs 24:20). Nebuchadnezzar's armies besieged the city of Jerusalem and captured Zedekiah. He was brought to Nebuchadnezzar at Riblah, where Zedekiah's sons were slain before his eyes. He was then blinded, bound, and taken captive to Babylon (25:6-7). The temple was looted and burned, the city walls were dismantled, and the city was plundered and razed (vv 9-17). The leading people of the nation were either killed or taken into captivity.

The remnant of the people in Judah were put under the charge of Gedaliah, the appointed governor. After his treacherous murder, the Jews fled to Egypt. Both Jeremiah (Jer 43:8-13; 46:13-24) and Ezekiel (Ez 29–32) prophesied that Nebuchadnezzar would invade Egypt. Josephus gives the date as the 23d year of Nebuchadnezzar (582/581 BC), but a fragmentary historical inscription dating to the 37th year of Nebuchadnezzar (568/567 BC) indicates that the defeat of Egypt occurred during the reign of Amasis.

Nebuchadnezzar's military successes were in many respects overshadowed by his building activities in Babylon. The king voiced his pride when he declared, "Is not this great Babylon, which I have built by my mighty power as a royal residence and for the glory of my majesty?" (Dn 4:30, RSV). The hanging gardens were acclaimed as one of the seven wonders of the ancient world. They were built on terraces in an effort to cure his Median queen of her homesickness for the mountains of her homeland.

The events of the book of Daniel center on Babylon and Nebuchadnezzar. Daniel was among the captives taken to Babylon in 605 BC. Nebuchadnezzar became aware of Daniel when the king had a dream that none of his occult experts could interpret (ch 2). The Lord gave to Daniel the interpretation of the dream; the human image that the king saw in his dream represented the various governments from the New Babylonian Empire to the reign of the Messiah.

Nebuchadnezzar set up a large human statue that was 90 feet (27.4 meters) high and 9 feet (2.7 meters) wide. Failure to worship the image would incur death by fire. The three compatriots of Daniel refused and were thrown into a furnace from which the Lord delivered them unhurt (ch 3).

The king had another dream about a great tree that was cut down but later sprouted from the stump (4:4-27). Again the "wise men of Babylon" could not give the interpretation, but Daniel informed the king that the dream prophesied a humbling experience lasting seven years as a consequence of the king's pride (vv 28-33).

See also Babylon, Babylonia; Daniel, Book of.

NEBUSHASBAN*, NEBUSHAZBAN Babylonian officer among those ordered to provide safety for Jeremiah after the Babylonians conquered Jerusalem (Jer 39:13).

NEBUZARADAN Chief Babylonian official and captain of the bodyguard during Nebuchadnezzar's reign (605–562 BC). Nebuzaradan was one of the officials whom Nebuchadnezzar authorized to oversee Jerusalem and Judah and the deportations of Jewish exiles to Babylon (2 Kgs 25:8-20; Jer 39:9-10; 52:12-30). On the king's orders, he appointed Gedaliah governor of Judah and Jeremiah's guardian (Jer 39:11-13; 41:10; 43:6).

NECKLACE *See* Jewelry, Jewels.

NECHO*, NECHOH*, NECO, NECOH* Pharaoh of the 26th dynasty of the Saite kings, who succeeded his father, Psammetichus, in 610 BC. Psammetichus had ruled 54 years over Egypt and was instrumental in the renewal of archaic art forms and in the revival of religious fervor. In addition to this, Psammetichus had fortified the borders with garrisons and driven the Assyrians beyond the northeast border into Canaan. The alliance

of the Babylonians and Medes made Psammetichus realize the potential threat to Egypt's independence, and he allied himself with Assyria, his former enemy.

Neco fell heir to the accomplishments of his father and to an international political scene out of which he could not easily withdraw. He was allied with a losing power, as Nineveh, Assyria's capital, fell in 612 BC. Neco was called upon to assist the king of Assyria, who had retreated to Harran from the Babylonian forces under Nebuchadnezzar. Neco moved his troops through Judah on his way to Carchemish to engage in battle with the Babylonians. As the troops moved through the Megiddo pass, they were ambushed by Judean troops under King Josiah. Neco had requested safe passage, but Josiah foolhardily refused. Josiah was killed in the field (2 Kgs 23:29-30; cf. 2 Chr 35:20-25). Neco continued onward to Carchemish. The battle (605 BC) turned out to be a great victory for the young Nebuchadnezzar. Nebuchadnezzar recorded it in glowing terms: "As for the rest of the Egyptian army which had escaped from the defeat . . . the Babylonian troops overtook and defeated them; so that not a single man escaped to that country." The OT briefly observes: "The king of Egypt never returned after that" (2 Kgs 24:7, NLT).

Neco strengthened Egypt by a policy of isolation. He made Judah a buffer zone and fortified the borders successfully in order to keep the Babylonians from penetrating into Egypt. He had deposed Jehoahaz, the newly enthroned king of three months, brought him to Riblah in Syria, and later to Egypt (2 Kgs 23:33-34). Jehoiakim succeeded to the Davidic throne in Jerusalem, and Judah was forced to pay a tribute of 100 talents of silver and a talent of gold (vv 33-36). When Judah fell to Babylon, the Judeans considered the Egyptian interest in their survival as vital to Egypt's independence and requested help against Babylonia. The prophet Jeremiah strongly spoke against this dependence on Egypt (Jer 46:17-24). Whether Neco risked his forces to penetrate into Judah, a Babylonian province, is not certain. Nebuchadnezzar quickly moved his forces to Judah, exiled Jehoiakim to Babylon, and enthroned Zedekiah (597 BC). Shortly thereafter, Neco died (595 BC). His son, Psammetichus II, succeeded him.

See also Egypt, Egyptian; Israel, History of; Josiah #1.

NECROMANCER*, NECROMANCY* Practice of communicating with the dead; a practice strictly forbidden by the law (Dt 18:11). *See* Magic; Medium; Psychics.

NEDABIAH Son of Jeconiah (NLT "Jehoiachin"), king of Judah (1 Chr 3:18).

NEEDLE Object used in Jesus' lesson about the rich man and entrance into God's kingdom. Following his discussion with the rich young ruler, Jesus told his disciples that "it is easier for a camel to go through the eye of a needle than for a rich person to enter the Kingdom of God!" (Mt 19:24, NLT; Mk 10:25; Lk 18:25). Jesus was not condemning riches or wealth but rather the change of will and false security that they may engender, as was the case with the rich young ruler (cf. Mt 19:21-22; Mk 10:21-22; Lk 18:22-23). Entrance into God's kingdom is an act of God, not of man. Using the largest land animal in Palestine, Jesus paralleled the absurdity of a camel's passing through the eye of a needle with a rich man's attempt to use his position and possessions to gain entrance into heaven. A similar expression is found in rabbinic literature, where the elephant is pictured as passing through the eye of a needle.

NEGEB*, NEGEV Southernmost region of Palestine. The name comes from the root "to be dry, parched," although its basic meaning is "south country, south." It is an area with no precise geographical boundaries. From north to south, the Negev covers the area between Beersheba and Kadesh-barnea. From west to east it extends from near the Mediterranean to the Arabah, a distance of some 70 miles (112.6 kilometers).

Avedat Canyon in the Negev

This is an arid section of the country, with infrequent and limited rainfall. With limited water resources, there was restricted opportunity for agriculture, although in the northern area some grain farming was done on a small scale, with possibly one crop failure every three years. A pastoral economy existed based primarily on the raising of sheep, goats, and camels. Simeon received this territory, including the cities, such as Arad and Rehoboth, in the tribal division of the Promised Land. Later, Judah absorbed this tribe. During the monarchy, the Israelites pushed into the Negev. During the reigns of Solomon and Jehoshaphat, there was commercial traffic to and from the port of Ezion-geber on the Gulf of Aqaba. In Greco-Roman times the Nabateans inhabited the Negev. Through careful preservation of rainwater, they developed limited agriculture and sustained a number of towns. During NT times the Idumeans controlled the Negev.

The KJV does not use the term Negev but ordinarily translates it as "the south." On the other hand, the NIV, NASB, and NLT regularly use the name for the territory. Abraham was often associated with the Negev (Gn 12:9; 13:1-2; 20:1). David told Achish, king of Gath, that he had raided "the Negev of Judah," "the Negev of Jerahmeelites," and "the Negev of the Kenites" (1 Sm 27:10), while the Egyptian captured by David stated that the Amalekites had made incursions against "the Negev of the Cherethites," "the Negev of Judah," and "the Negev of Caleb" (1 Sm 30:14).

NEGINAH*, NEGINOTH* Hebrew terms in the superscriptions of Psalms 4, 6, 54–55, 61, 67 and 76 (KJV); musical cues, meaning "stringed instruments," describing the kind of musical accompaniment for the performance of the designated psalms. *See* Music.

NEHELAMITE Ancestral name or the geographical designation for Shemaiah the false prophet (Jer 29:24, 31-32). Its derivation is unknown. Etymologically similar to the Hebrew word for "dream," Nehelamite is perhaps an epithet coined by Jeremiah to deride Shemaiah, the false prophet, as a dreamer.

NEHEMIAH (Person) Name of three men mentioned in the OT after the period of the exile. The name means "the Lord comforts" and was appropriate for this time of hope and fulfillment.

1. Leader mentioned in a list of Jewish exiles who returned from Babylon with Zerubbabel sometime after 538 BC (Ezr 2:2; Neh 7:7).
2. Ruler of half the district of Beth-zur who helped rebuild the Jerusalem wall in 444 BC (Neh 3:16).
3. Governor of Judah during the restoration. Originally cupbearer to the Persian king Artaxerxes I (464–424 BC), Nehemiah pleaded to be sent to Judah to aid his fellow Jews in their difficulties and in particular to rebuild Jerusalem (Neh 1:1–2:8). He was appointed governor of Judah for 12 years.

After inspecting the walls upon his arrival, he realized that their repair was to be his prime task. This repair would guarantee the security of the city and could provide a focal point for the Jewish community scattered throughout Judah. That he was able to marshal support for this project and to complete it attests to his skills in management and administration. He also had a strong personal faith, as his prayers (Neh 1:4-11; 2:4) and conviction of divine guidance and help (2:8, 18, 20) attest. He had to overcome hostility and intimidation from powerful neighboring authorities in Samaria, Ammon, and Arabia (4:1-9; 6:1-14). He also required economic justice (ch 5). A few rich Jews were exploiting a food shortage by exacting high interest from their poorer brothers.

Included in Nehemiah's concern for Jerusalem was a strong interest in the maintenance of temple worship. He was involved in the production of a document in which the Jewish community pledged themselves to support the temple personnel and to provide offerings (Neh 10:1, 32-39). Clearly, he realized that Judah needed at its heart a religious emphasis as well as political stability. These particular religious reforms are linked with those of his second period as governor (ch 13). Other reforms of that period concerned the observance of the Sabbath (13:15-22) and the problem of marriages to non-Jews (13:23-27). Nehemiah was a forceful leader (v 25) who used his imperial powers to restore to the settlers a national and religious identity in a period of political and economic weakness.

See also Nehemiah, Book of; Ezra (Person) #1; Ezra, Book of; Postexilic Period.

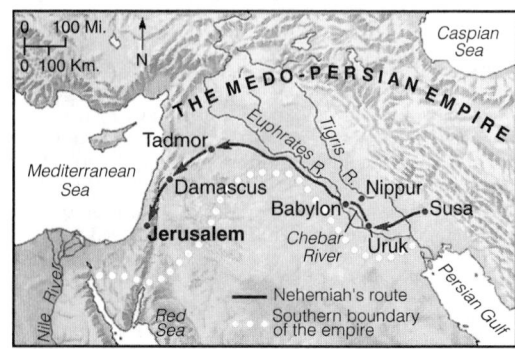

Nehemiah's Journey to Jerusalem When Nehemiah heard that the rebuilding projects in Jerusalem were progressing slowly, he asked the king of the Medo-Persian Empire, for whom he worked, for permission to go there to help his people complete the task of rebuilding their city's walls. The king agreed to let him go; so he left as soon as possible, traveling along much the same route Ezra had taken seven years earlier.

NEHEMIAH, Book of One of the last of the Jewish historical books.

PREVIEW
•Background
•Author
•Historical Authenticity
•Chronology
•Significance
•Content

Background In 597 BC Nebuchadrezzar of Babylon took away the first exiles from Jerusalem. In 586 BC the Babylonians returned, pillaged and burned the city and its temple, and took an estimated 60,000 to 80,000 Judeans into exile. The expatriates settled in various districts where they enjoyed a measure of freedom. They engaged in agriculture and commerce and in some instances acquired considerable wealth. The elders continued to function, prophets like Ezekiel ministered among the exiles, and resistance to religious apostasy was kept alive in the popular mind.

With the appearance of the Persian king Cyrus the Great (559–530 BC), the Jewish exiles' prospects altered dramatically. Cyrus was a civilized and enlightened statesman, and within a short time after his conquest of Babylon, he issued an edict (Ezr 1:2-4) that granted the expatriates permission to return to their homeland. Two separate groups of exiles returned to Judah and built a new sanctuary in Jerusalem on the site of Solomon's temple in 516 BC. Then, under King Artaxerxes I (464–424 BC), two separate groups returned from Babylon under Ezra (458 BC) and Nehemiah (445 BC), respectively. From this seedbed there sprang the theocratic people of Judah, the Jews, dedicated to the law of God, isolated from foreign influence, and centered in Jerusalem.

Author Nehemiah's personal memoirs form a considerable portion of the book that bears his name. These memoirs reveal a man of nobility and piety, who was compassionate, prudent, and patriotic. He was a man of generosity and fidelity, political acumen, and religious zeal, of total dedication to God, outstanding organizational ability, and dynamic leadership. At the same time Nehemiah possessed a capacity for ruthlessness when confronting the sin and waywardness of his compatriots (Neh 5:1-13) and the intrigues of powerful non-Jewish enemies (13:8, 28). Not surprisingly, then, a dispirited and dejected people awoke from their lethargic and apathetic state and responded to Nehemiah's stringent approach to their situation (2:4; 13:14, 22, 31).

Historical Authenticity According to Josephus and other early writers, the books of Ezra and Nehemiah formed one book in the early Hebrew Bible entitled the book of Ezra. The earliest Hebrew manuscript in which the two books are divided is dated 1448, and modern Hebrew Bibles refer to them as the books of Ezra and Nehemiah. In manuscripts of the Greek OT (LXX) they also formed one book. Origen, in the beginning of the third century, is the first to attest to a division. There is general acknowledgment of the genuineness of the personal memoirs of Nehemiah, which constitute a major part of the book.

The historical framework of the book is confirmed by papyri that were discovered between 1898 and 1908 in Elephantine, an island in the upper Nile. Here Psammetichus II (593–588 BC) established a Jewish colony. The Elephantine papyri are well preserved, written in Aramaic, and are the fifth-century BC literary remains of this Jewish colony of the Persian period.

The most important item among the papyri is a copy of a letter sent to the Persian governor of Judah in 407 BC. Three years earlier the Jewish temple in Elephantine had been destroyed. This disaster was the occasion of a letter to Jehohanan, the high priest in Jerusalem (see Neh 12:12-13). Now, in their letter to the governor in Judah, they asked permission to rebuild their temple and said that they had sent a similar request to Delaiah and Shelamiah, the sons of Sanballat (Nehemiah's enemy, 2:10, 19; 4:1). The Elephantine papyri reveal that Sanballat was governor of the province of Samaria and that Tobiah was governor of the province of Ammon in Transjordan (2:10, 19). Here, then, is evidence that there was in Judah a twofold authority, civil and religious, and that the high priest of 408–407 BC was Jehohanan (12:13).

Chronology The question about whether Ezra or Nehemiah came to Jerusalem first has been hotly debated. There is no doubt that Nehemiah arrived in the city in 445 BC. The objections to the view that Ezra came to Jerusalem 13 years earlier, in 458 BC, raise questions concerning historical and textual data that are of such complexity as to preclude discussion of them here. However, achieving an understanding of the spiritual values of the book does not depend on a correct interpretation of the details of chronology. Arguments against the traditional chronology are neither altogether decisive, nor do they dispel the inherent complexities.

Significance When the exiles returned to Jerusalem, Judah had neither nationhood nor political status. Only one thing remained to them: their religion. They were the "remnant" of Yahweh's chosen people, from whom would rise the new and glorious Israel. It was this vision that explains Nehemiah's insistence that the Jewish people maintain the purity and exclusiveness of their religious faith and practice in order to rejuvenate their national life and rebuild the city walls (6:15), because this symbolized the racial and the religious purity of the people. He also insisted on separation from paganism, prohibition of marriage with non-Jews (13:23-28), and careful observance of the laws of the Sabbath (vv 15-22).

It is, therefore, difficult to exaggerate the significance of the book of Nehemiah. Along with the book of Ezra, it furnishes the only consecutive Hebrew account of that period in Jewish history when the foundations of Judaism—with its inflexible segregation of the Jews and its passionate veneration of the Mosaic law—were laid. Of course, Haggai, Zechariah, and Malachi also contribute to knowledge of the period, but Nehemiah (with Ezra) provides a progressive narrative of this epoch. The return of the expatriates from Babylon to Jerusalem constitutes a resumption of the saving purposes of God for his ancient people, leading to the advent of Jesus Christ.

The account of the return from Babylon under Nehemiah emphasizes the religious aspect of the community of repatriates in Jerusalem. But other, secondary factors should be noted: Nehemiah's preoccupation with Judah's political security and constitutional status to ensure its independence of Samaria; the rebuilding of the city walls; Nehemiah's resettlements of population (7:4; 11:1-2); and his appointment to the governorship of the new province. However, there is no reference in the book of Nehemiah (or for that matter in Ezra) to a restoration to nationhood under a scion of the house of David— no mention of a Messiah, no allusion to the universal kingdom of God. Nehemiah manifests absolute loyalty to the Persian overlord who, while showing remarkable openness to Nehemiah's request (2:4-9), still continues to levy taxes (5:4, 15).

The repatriates retreated behind their city's new walls and congregated around the second temple, completed in 516 BC. "The book of the law of Moses" (8:1), recognized by the Persian overlord as the law of the land of Judah, became central to Jewish devotion and worship. Judaism was the product of the restoration, which became both a protective barrier against, and a wall of separation from, the Gentiles. Religious institutions initiated during the Babylonian exile and transplanted to Jerusalem took deep and firm root: the synagogue where the Law and the Prophets were read and the prayers were offered; the scribes who worked with single-minded devotion; and the Sanhedrin that continued to serve the new theocracy.

The Jewish remnant of the fifth century BC parallels the modern Christian church in that both share the challenge of spiritual reconstruction and renewal essential to God's purposes.

Content In the winter of 445 BC, the Persian court was in Susa, the ancient capital of Elam (1:1). There Nehemiah occupied a position of honor and influence (2:1). From Jerusalem, a company of Judeans arrived, among them Nehemiah's brother, whose description of conditions in Jerusalem horrified and grieved Nehemiah (1:2-4). Four months later, and after much prayer, he reached Jerusalem with an armed escort (1:5–2:11). After a three-day inspection of the situation, Nehemiah realized that rebuilding the walls would be his primary task (2:12–3:32).

An outburst of new national spirit caused latent opposition to surface. Sanballat, Tobiah, and Geshem were powerful, resourceful, astute antagonists. Through ridicule and rumors, they insinuated that work on the walls was a form of rebellion against the king (2:19; 4:1-3, 7-14; 6:1-9). But Nehemiah countered every subterfuge and stratagem with prayer and with an adamant refusal to deviate from his goal. There was also hostility from traitors within the camp (6:10-19). Despite all opposition, Jerusalem's walls were reconstructed (v 15) and rededicated amid enthusiastic celebration (12:27-43).

The community's response to the reading by Ezra, priest and scribe, of the law of Moses and to its interpretation by the Levites (8:1-8), was a complex response of sorrow for sin and rejoicing in God (vv 9-18); of fasting and prayer (9:1-37); of renewing the covenant (9:38–10:29); and of self-commitment to obey God's commandments, ordinances, and statutes (10:30-39). Chapters 11 and 12 refer to various offices and duties, civil and religious, and the names of the people appointed to them. Then follows the decision to exclude all people of foreign descent from Judaism (13:1-3).

At this juncture Nehemiah traveled to Susa to give an account of his stewardship; a further leave of absence being granted, he returned to Jerusalem to find that serious irregularities were again present. His enemy Tobiah and the priest Eliashib were embroiled (13:4-9); the people failed to provide the Levites with adequate maintenance (vv 10-14); the laws of the Sabbath were being violated (vv 15-22); and Jews were marrying non-Jews (vv 23-32). Due to the increase of intermarriage with foreigners, the offspring could not speak Hebrew (vv 23-25). The danger of assimilation was halted by enforcing a policy of exclusivism.

The book of Nehemiah ends rather abruptly with a description of his vigorous and ruthless handling of these deviations from the newly established principles and precepts of Judaism.

See also Chronology of the Bible (Old Testament); Ezra, Book of; Ezra (Person) #1; Israel, History of; Judaism; Nehemiah (Person) #3; Postexilic Period.

NEHILOTH* Hebrew term in the superscription of Psalm 5 (KJV); musical cue, meaning "flutes," describing the kind of musical accompaniment for the performance of the psalm. *See* Music.

NEHUM* One of the men listed in Nehemiah 7:7 who returned with Zerubbabel to Palestine following the Babylonian captivity. His name is alternately spelled Rehum in Ezra 2:2. *See* Rehum #1.

NEHUSHTA Mother of Jehoiachin, king of Judah, who was deported with her son to Babylon (2 Kgs 24:8-15).

NEHUSHTAN Name given to the bronze serpent that Moses made during the wilderness wanderings. At the time of King Hezekiah's reforms, it was destroyed (2 Kgs 18:4). *See* Bronze Serpent, Bronze Snake.

NEIEL Border town in Asher's territory (Jos 19:27). Its site is perhaps identifiable with modern Khirbet Ya'nin, on the east end of the plain of Acco.

NEIGHBOR Concept apparently limited in the OT period and late Judaism to one's fellow Israelite, or member of the covenant, and extended by Jesus to include anyone encountered in life.

In the Old Testament Although it is never explicitly limited as such, the prominent connotation of "neighbor" in the OT is that of a fellow member of the covenant community; that is, another Israelite (see Lv 6:1-7; 19; Dt 15:2-3). In Leviticus 19:18, a passage often quoted in the NT, the Israelite is commanded to "love your neighbor as yourself." In 19:34, it is explicitly stated that such love should also be shown to the foreigner (or "sojourner") passing through the land. If "neighbor" (v 18) implied a more encompassing notion, such as "mankind" or "fellow man," there presumably would have been no need to include the further stipulation in verse 34. "Neighbor" was therefore probably taken to mean one's immediate neighbor, the fellow Israelite.

Within the covenant community, love of neighbor involved certain responsibilities explicitly set forth in the law. The neighbor was to be treated fairly (Ex 22:5-15; Lv 6:2-7; 19:9-18) and respected (Ex 20:16), as were his belongings (Ex 20:17). To foster such just and merciful relationships within the covenant community, the neighbor was to be thought of as a "brother" (Lv 25:25; Dt 22:1-4). What one did to one's neighbor was to be returned in kind (Lv 24:19-23; Dt 19:11-19).

The grave importance attached to treatment of the neighbor is understandable when seen as part of one's wider relationship with God and was considered something that could affect significantly the divine-human relationship (Lv 6:1-7; 19; 25:17; Dt 24:10-13; Ps 12). Israelites were to treat their neighbors in the same loving way they had themselves been treated by God (Ex 22:21; Lv 25:35-38).

The importance of the neighbor relationship within the covenant community is also demonstrated by the fact that when such responsibilities were ignored, a societal breakdown or national turmoil followed (Dt 28:15-68; Hos 4:1-3; Am 2:6-7). That the Israelites often did neglect love for neighbor, particularly the neighbor in need, is a contributing cause for the divine punishment of the exile (Jer 5:7-9; 7:1-15; 9:2-9; Hos 4:1-3; Am 2:6-7; 5:10-13; 8:4-6). The mere fact that proper love of neighbor was also part of Israel's hope for the messianic age to come (Jer 31:34; Zec 3:10) also points to its common neglect within the OT covenant community.

In Late Judaism From the exilic experience, Israel recognized that divine blessing was conditional somewhat on justice and love exercised toward one another (Zec 8:14-17). The identity of the "neighbor" was debatable, however. Several factors suggest that "neighbor" was limited in this period to the fellow Israelite and the proselyte (gentile convert to Judaism). Evidence from rabbinic material excludes Samaritans and the Gentiles living in the land from being considered "neighbors" and thus worthy of love. Within the Jewish Essene community at Qumran, the "neighbor" to be respected and treated fairly was restricted to one's fellow community members. Finally, when Jesus recalls, "You have heard that it was said, 'You shall love your neighbor and hate your enemy'" (Mt 5:43), he is quoting only partially from the OT (Lv 19:18—"You shall love your neighbor"). The last phrase ("and hate your enemy") reflects the contemporary Jewish feeling toward outsiders; that is, God did not require love toward those considered "enemies" but only toward fellow countrymen.

In the New Testament Jesus differed dramatically from his Jewish contemporaries by eradicating the limitations on the neighbor to be loved. In contrast to those who would limit love to one's fellow countrymen, Jesus advocated extending the obligation reserved for the neighbor to the enemy as well (Mt 5:43-48), and in so doing, he destroyed the distinction between neighbor and enemy altogether.

On another occasion, a scribe asked Jesus what was the greatest commandment given by God (Mk 12:28-31). In response, Jesus cited Deuteronomy 6:5 concerning the nature of God and man's obligation to love God with his entire being: heart, soul, and mind. Of significance is that Jesus did not stop there but linked with this a second commandment to "love your neighbor as yourself" (Lv 19:18). Some scholars suggest that this dramatic and close association of love of God and love of neighbor originated with Jesus. If Jesus was the first to tie these commands together (see Mt 22:37; Mk 12:29-31), it reveals our Lord's own understanding of the relation of these two obligations; proper love for neighbor derives from love for God, and conversely, love for God is inseparable from meeting the needs of a neighbor in love.

The debate in Jesus' time was not over how to properly treat a neighbor but who, in fact, was the neighbor. Jesus is asked this very question by an expert of the law (Lk 10:29). Jesus had complimented the lawyer for his clear understanding of what was required to inherit eternal life, namely, love of God and love of neighbor. Luke suggests that the lawyer asked the further qualifying question in order to "justify himself," that is, justify his actual behavior of limited love toward his fellow man. Jesus chose not to respond directly but through the use of a parable, in this case, the familiar parable of the Good Samaritan (vv 30-35).

In order to open the lawyer's eyes to the tragic shortsightedness of his question, Jesus related an everyday story of a man traveling the treacherous road from Jerusalem down to Jericho, a road particularly plagued by robbers. The traveler is robbed, stripped, beaten, and left half dead. To this point, the lawyer might have assumed Jesus was offering an example of who constitutes a "neighbor"—a fellow Jew in need. Jesus proceeds, how-

ever, to introduce two figures, a priest and a Levite who, in an academic discussion, could have argued quite ably on who is the neighbor God calls one to love. The lawyer would no doubt have anticipated such experts in the law to act rightly toward the victim. In contrast, the priest and Levite, upon seeing the man in need, respond by "passing by on the other side." Unable to determine whether the victim was dead or barely alive, and possibly not wanting to risk uncleanness, the experts of the law pass by, thus violating the greatest of the commandments just identified by the lawyer (10:25-28).

Enter a Samaritan—a figure especially despised by the Jews. Viewed as heretics by the Jewish religious authorities, the Samaritans were disqualified in rabbinic circles from being considered a "neighbor" and thus worthy of love. In fact, previous centuries had witnessed the slaughter of many Samaritans by Jewish rulers, and animosity clearly existed between the two peoples (see Jn 4:9). While the lawyer listening to the parable would have expected the priest and Levite to act justly toward the victim, he must have been surprised that a hated Samaritan would show compassion and thus fulfill the greatest commandment. Jesus intentionally spelled out the extent of the Samaritan's compassion (immediate care in dressing wounds, transport to the inn, care for the victim there and extended care in paying for care by others while he is away, Lk 10:34-35) to such a degree that the lawyer would have no doubt as to the genuineness of the Samaritan's love. The irony of the story is that one not considered worthy to be called "neighbor" by Jews was precisely the one who showed himself to be "neighbor" to the victim (vv 36-37).

The parable, like the statement in Matthew 5:43-48, reveals Jesus' own understanding of "neighbor" and what "love of neighbor" demands. Jesus sets no limitation on who qualifies as the neighbor commanded by God to be loved.

The forcefulness and power of Jesus' teachings on the love of neighbor and its relationship to one's love for God are demonstrated by a similar emphasis within the early church. Paul on two occasions called the love of neighbor the fulfillment of the entire law (Rom 13:8-10; Gal 5:14), while James referred to the same commandment as "the royal law" (Jas 2:8).

NEKEB* KJV rendering of a town defining the boundary of the territory allotted to Naphtali's tribe for an inheritance, positioned between Za-anannim and Jabneel (Jos 19:33). *See* Adami, Adami-nekeb.

NEKODA
1. Father of a family of temple servants who returned to Jerusalem following the exile (Ezr 2:48; Neh 7:50).
2. Father of a family of returned exiles who could not prove their Israelite descent (Ezr 2:60; Neh 7:62).

NEMUEL
1. Reubenite and the son of Eliab (Nm 26:9).
2. One of Simeon's sons (Nm 26:12; 1 Chr 4:24), also called Jemuel (Gn 46:10). *See* Jemuel.

NEMUELITE Member of Nemuel's family from Simeon's tribe (Nm 26:12; alternately called Jemuel in Gn 46:10). *See* Jemuel.

NEPHEG
1. Levite of the family of Kohath and the second of Izhar's three sons (Ex 6:21).
2. David's son born to him during his reign in Jerusalem (2 Sm 5:15; 1 Chr 3:7; 14:6).

NEPHILIM* Early group of the human race, mentioned only twice in the OT (Gn 6:4; Nm 13:33; NLT mg). The Greek translation of the Hebrew Scriptures (the Septuagint) rendered the name "Nephilim" as "giants," and other versions followed this rendering, including the KJV. Modern translations, however, usually designate them as Nephilim, thus identifying them with the Anakim (Nm 13:33; Dt 2:21) and the Rephaim (Dt 2:20). The latter two were reputed to be large physically, hence the rendering "giants."

The Nephilim are of unknown origin. Some writers have taken the Hebrew verb *naphal*, "to fall," to imply that the Nephilim were "fallen ones"—that is, fallen angels who subsequently mated with human women. But Christ taught that angels do not have carnal relationships (Lk 20:34-35), and therefore this view can only be maintained by assuming that Genesis 6:1-4 reflects Greek mythology, in which such unions occurred. The Genesis passage, however, deals with anthropology, not mythology.

The Nephilim were evidently not the "sons of God" and seem to be different also from the "daughters of men." The best classification is with the Anakim and Rephaim as ancient peoples of unknown origin.

See also Giants.

NEPHISH* KJV spelling of Naphish, Ishmael's son (1 Chr 5:19). *See* Naphish.

NEPHISHESIM*, NEPHISIM* A group of people who returned to Jerusalem with Zerubbabel after the exile, counted among the temple servants (Ezr 2:50; Neh 7:52).

NEPHTHALIM* KJV rendering of Naphtali's tribe in Matthew 4:13, 15. *See* Naphtali, Tribe of.

NEPHTOAH, Waters of Geographical landmark situated between Mt Ephron to the west and the valley of Hinnom to the east, defining part of the boundary separating the tribes of Judah and Benjamin (Jos 15:9; 18:15). Its site is generally identified with Ain Lifta, three miles (4.8 kilometers) northwest of Jerusalem.

NEPHUSHESIM*, NEPHUSIM, NEPHUSSIM* Alternate spellings of Nephisim in Ezra 2:50, Nehemiah 7:52. *See* Nephishesim, Nephisim.

NEPTHALIM* KJV rendering of Naphtali's tribe in Revelation 7:6. *See* Naphtali, Tribe of.

NER Benjamite, father of Abner and brother of Kish; he was probably the uncle of Saul (1 Sm 14:51; 26:5; 2 Sm 2:8; 1 Kgs 2:32; 1 Chr 26:28). Although Ner's father's name was given as Abiel (1 Sm 14:51), disputed readings put Ner among the sons of Jeiel (1 Chr 8:29-30; 9:35-36). Elsewhere he is listed as the father of Kish, the father of Saul (8:33; 9:39). Ner was, then, the grandfather or the uncle of Saul, probably the latter. One suggestion is that there were two men called Kish, one of whom was Ner's brother, the other his son. Another is that there were two men called Ner. These speculations demonstrate that genealogical tables were sometimes incomplete or ambiguous.

NEREUS Roman Christian to whom Paul sent greetings in the salutation of his letter to Rome (Rom 16:15).

NERGAL Heathen deity worshiped by the men of Cuth after the fall of Israel in 722 BC (2 Kgs 17:30). Nergal,

lord of the netherworld and associated with the sun god, was the city god of the northern Babylonian city of Cuthah (cf. v 24). *See* Assyria, Assyrians.

NERGAL-SHAREZER Babylonian prince who held the title "Rabmag." Nergal-sharezer participated with Nebuchadnezzar and the Chaldean army in conquering Jerusalem after a three-year siege from 588 to 586 BC (Jer 39:3) and later entrusted Jeremiah to Gedaliah's care (v 13).

NERI Ancestor of Jesus in Luke's genealogy (Lk 3:27). *See* Genealogy of Jesus Christ.

NERIAH Father of Baruch the scribe (Jer 32:12, 16; 36:4, 8) and Seraiah the quartermaster (51:59), both of whom served Jeremiah the prophet.

NERO* Roman emperor from AD 54 to 68. *See* Caesars, The.

NET *See* Fishermen.

NETAIM Habitation of the potters who were employed in the king's service (1 Chr 4:23).

NETHANEEL*, NETHANEL Common OT name spelled Nethaneel in the KJV.

1. Zuar's son and the prince of Issachar's tribe at the start of Israel's wilderness wanderings (Nm 1:8; 2:5; 10:15), who represented his kinsmen at the altar's dedication (7:18, 23).
2. Judahite, the fourth son of Jesse and David's brother (1 Chr 2:14).
3. One of the priests assigned to blow a trumpet before the ark in the procession led by David when the ark was moved to Jerusalem (1 Chr 15:24).
4. Levite and the father of Shemaiah, the scribe who recorded the 24 divisions of priests founded during David's reign (1 Chr 24:6).
5. Korahite Levite and Obed-edom's fifth son in David's reign (1 Chr 26:4).
6. One of the princes sent by King Jehoshaphat to teach the law in the cities of Judah (2 Chr 17:7).
7. One of the Levitical chiefs who generously gave animals to the Levites for the celebration of the Passover feast during King Josiah's reign (2 Chr 35:9).
8. Priest and one of Pashhur's six sons who was encouraged by Ezra to divorce his foreign wife during the postexilic era (Ezr 10:22).
9. Head of Jedaiah's priestly family during the days of Joiakim, the high priest, in postexilic Jerusalem (Neh 12:21).
10. One of the priestly musicians who performed at the dedication of the Jerusalem wall during Nehemiah's day (Neh 12:36).

NETHANIAH
1. Elishama's son, father of Ishmael and a member of the royal family of Judah (2 Kgs 25:23-25; Jer 40:8-15; 41:1-18).
2. One of Asaph's four sons and the leader of the fifth of 24 divisions of musicians trained for service in the sanctuary during David's reign (1 Chr 25:2, 12).
3. One of the Levites sent by King Jehoshaphat of Judah to teach the law in the cities of Judah (2 Chr 17:8).
4. Shelemiah's son and the father of Jehudi. Jehudi served in the court of King Jehoiakim of Judah (Jer 36:14).

NETHINIM* Term appearing only in the books written after Israel's return from exile (1 Chronicles, Ezra, Nehemiah). *Nethinim* derives from the verb *nathan*, "to give, set apart, dedicate," and means "those given" or "those set apart or dedicated." The Septuagint translates the word *dedomenoi*. Some recent translators have followed Josephus (*Antiquities* 11.5.1) by referring to them as "temple slaves." The NLT reads "Temple assistants."

Before the exile, the Nethinim were active in temple service. First Chronicles 9:2 lists them with the priests and Levites who took possession of their allotted cities. Their listed order—priests, Levites, and Nethinim—suggests their subordinate role to the Levites (see also Neh 7:73; 11:3, 20-21). They returned from exile as temple personnel (Ezr 2:43, 58; 7:7, 24; 8:17, 20; Neh 7:46, 60). They had their dwelling in Jerusalem (Ezr 7:7; Neh 3:31; 11:21) and joined in the repair of the walls (Neh 3:26).

The identification of the Nethinim is not absolutely certain. Numbers 31:47 records that the Levites received captives who were assigned laborious and menial tasks. When the Gibeonites were accepted within Israel as servants, they too were appointed as water carriers and wood choppers for the entire community and the altar of the Lord (Jos 9:9-27). David augmented the number of tabernacle servants by assigning captives taken in war to these duties (Ezr 8:20). At the completion of the temple, the temple services called for more workers, and Solomon added to their number. This new group became known as "Solomon's men." Ezra records that from the Nethinim, 392 returned from exile to Jerusalem (2:58) and performed the work in the rebuilt temple that had been done by their ancestors before the exile. Considered full members of the restored covenant community, the Nethinim devoted themselves to God (Neh 10:28).

NETOPHAH, NETOPHATHITE Home and designation for two of David's thirty mighty men (2 Sm 23:28-29; 1 Chr 11:30; 27:13-15). Seraiah, one of the captains who came to Gedaliah, the governor in Jerusalem after its fall to Babylon in 586 BC, was a Netophathite (2 Kgs 25:23; Jer 40:8). Fifty-six men of Netophah are mentioned as among the exiles who returned from Babylon with Zerubbabel and Joshua (Ezr 2:22).

First Chronicles 9:16 speaks of Levites who lived in the villages of Netophathites, while Nehemiah 12:28 says that temple singers were gathered from the villages surrounding Jerusalem and from the villages of the Netophathites. Both of these references suggest that Netophah was the name of a district and not just of a town.

The linking of Netophah with Bethlehem (see 1 Chr 2:54; Neh 7:26) indicates that it was in that vicinity. The actual site of Netophah is not known; however, the most probable location is the modern Khirbet Bedd Faluh, three miles (4.8 kilometers) southeast of Bethlehem.

NETTLE *See* Plants.

NEW That which has just been made or come into existence—often replacing that which already existed, thereby turning the old into new.

That the second part of the Bible is called the *New* Testament indicates how fundamental the idea of "new" is to biblical revelation. Many key theological expressions incorporate the idea: new creation (2 Cor 5:17), new birth (Jn 3:3), new man (Eph 2:15; Col 3:10), new commandment (Jn 13:34), new covenant (Jer 31:31), new life (Rom 6:4), and various others.

The Expectation of the New The totality of the expectation of the *new* is best expressed in Jeremiah and Ezekiel and in the reference in the Psalter to the "new song" to be given to the people to sing (e.g., Pss 33:3; 40:3; 149:1; cf., also Is 42:10). Jeremiah speaks of the day when God will make a new covenant with the house of Israel (Jer 31:31-34; cf. Ez 34:25-31; 37:26-28). In contrast with the old, this new covenant will be written upon the heart—that is, it will be internalized. Similarly Ezekiel (Ez 36:22-32) tells of the day when God, as an expression of his own holiness, will cleanse his people and will give a heart of flesh in place of the heart of stone. This will usher in the age of the Spirit and will bring about a new existence, characterized by security and freedom, in which the laws of God are carried out. The supreme feature of this new time is the new spirit within them (Ez 11:19). Joel speaks also of that day when the Spirit of God will be poured out on all flesh (Jl 2:28). Isaiah 65:17 states the promise of "new heavens and a new earth," words that often reflect national circumstances and hopes (for example, after the exile). However, they came to take on new eschatological significance beyond the hope of the nation Israel.

The Coming of the New The central proclamation of the presence of the kingdom in the world through Jesus is a declaration that the promised new age has broken into time in powerful ways. Jesus' ministry is one of fulfillment; what has been promised by prophets has begun to take place. John the Baptist had prepared the way for the one who would bestow the promised Spirit. The giving of this Spirit is the giving of new life. Through faith in Christ, one is born anew (Jn 3:3-7). But Jesus had to die in order for this new life to be given. At the Last Supper the cup of wine Jesus shared with his disciples symbolized the blood of the new covenant (Mk 14:24).

The early church expressed this significance in varying metaphors. This "newness of life" is expressed sacramentally through baptism (Rom 6:4). The eucharistic cup is the new covenant through blood (1 Cor 11:25). An extended discourse on the old and new covenants shows that by the shedding of his blood Christ has become mediator of a new covenant (Heb 9:15); by his blood he has opened up a new and living way into the Holy Place (10:19-20). Paul restates the promise of Ezekiel for a heart of flesh (2 Cor 3:3), after which he gives an account of the ministry of the new covenant in contrast to the old. The church represents the appearance of the new age in the domain of the old.

The one who comes to Christ by faith is declared a new person, a new creation, for whom the old has passed away (2 Cor 5:17; Gal 6:15). Jewish-Gentile hostility disappears in the resulting "new humanity" (Eph 2:15). All other social distinctions (such as male-female, slave-free) pass away in the new humanity created afresh in Christ Jesus (Col 3:10-11).

The newness of a person in Christ is the foundation for NT ethics (Eph 4:24; Col 3:12). The new commandment (Jn 13:34; 1 Jn 2:8) is not really new (1 Jn 2:7), but now has new possibility and dimension by virtue of the power and pattern of Jesus. Though this new life is a gift of God, the *process* of being made new continues. Transformation by the renewing of the mind (Rom 12:2) brings realization of the will of God. Paul declares the inner man being renewed day by day (2 Cor 4:16).

The Realization of the New As real as the new life of the believer may be, Scripture recognizes a tension between the new age that has come in history but is not yet fully realized. There is a projection to that time when all things are made new (Rv 21:5). With the end of the old, there is a new heaven and new earth. The new Jerusalem (v 2) "descends" as the dwelling place of God. The people of God receive a new name (3:12) as the former things pass away. To the redeemed of the Lord, a new song is given, the song of the Lamb slain from the very foundation of creation: "Worthy is the Lamb who was slain, to receive power and wealth and wisdom and might and honor and glory and blessing!" The antiphonal song returns, "To him who sits upon the throne and to the Lamb be blessing and honor and glory and might for ever and ever!" (5:12-13, RSV).

See also Commandment, The New; Covenant, The New; Jerusalem, New; Man, Old and New; New Creation, New Creature; New Heavens and New Earth; Regeneration.

NEW BIRTH* See Regeneration.

NEW COMMANDMENT Expression used by Jesus (Jn 13:34) to designate his teaching concerning the love of Christians for each other. See Commandment, The New.

NEW COVENANT Expression used by Jesus (Lk 22:20; cf. Jer 31:31) to designate the meaning of his death. See Covenant, The New.

NEW CREATION*, NEW CREATURE* Concept of redemption developed throughout the OT and NT to its final consummation in the second coming of Jesus Christ.

The most fundamental truth of the Bible is that God is the Creator of heaven and earth, who sustains and controls everything (e.g., Gn 1; Pss 33:6-11; 104; Mt 6:25-32). The most basic consideration about men and women is that they are creatures made in God's image (Gn 1–2). Accordingly, the Bible's message of salvation is unintelligible apart from what it teaches about God as Creator. The true nature and perversity of humanity's sin stem from the fact that they "worshiped and served created things rather than the Creator" (Rom 1:25, NIV). God is Redeemer because he is Creator. By the same token, the objects of God's saving activity are his rebellious creatures who, along with the entire created order, are cursed with futility and decay (Gn 3:17-18; Rom 8:20-21).

In the Old Testament The tie between creation and salvation is especially prominent in the latter part of Isaiah (Is 40–66). The prophet surveys the grandeur of the final redemption God will accomplish for Israel. Repeatedly the perspective on this promised eschatological deliverance is that God is the Creator of heaven and earth and of Israel in particular (see also the full statement of 40:12-31; e.g., 44:24; 45:18; 48:13; 51:16; 64:8).

In this context, expectation centers on "the new heavens and the new earth" (65:17; 66:22). This reference to the new creation gives the broadest conceivable scope to the eschatological salvation prophesied by Isaiah. God's work of renewal and restoration at the end parallels his work of creation in the beginning (48:12). What God will do in bringing all things to their consummation is of the same order of magnitude as what he did in calling them into existence out of nothing. At the same time, the new creation concept reveals that the end-time salvation promised to Israel has universal and cosmic proportions. The underlying hope is the ultimate entrance of the faithful from among the nations, as well as in Israel, into the bliss of the eternal, new creation order. These themes

from Isaiah are taken up and developed by the NT writers, and are integral to their message.

The New Creation and Christ The NT ties together creation and redemption. Several writers either parallel or in other ways relate the saving work of Christ to his activity at creation (Jn 1:3; Col 1:15-18; Heb 1:2-3; Rv 3:14). What he has done at the end, in "the fullness of time" (Gal 4:4; Eph 1:10), "in these last days" (Heb 1:2), roots in what he did in the beginning. The redemption accomplished by Christ is a work of new creation.

This association of the new creation with Christ's work is unmistakable when Paul designates Christ as the "last Adam" and "second man" (1 Cor 15:45-47; cf. v 22; Rom 5:14). This description has close affinities with "Son of Man," a self-designation of Jesus. Paul's use of the last Adam designation is obviously intended to heighten the contrast between Adam and Christ (Rom 1; 1 Cor 15). In antithesis to Adam, who through his disobedience brought into the world sin and the consequent condemnation of death, Christ by his obedience has established righteousness, resulting in justification and life.

Paul discloses something of the full range and implications of the Adam-Christ contrast in 1 Corinthians 15:42-49. He contrasts the believer's present bodily existence, in its weakness and mortality, with the body to be received at the resurrection. He sums up this contrast: the one body is "natural," the other is "spiritual." Adam and Christ exemplify these two bodies, the natural and the spiritual. At the same time, however, Adam and Christ are brought into view as whole persons. They are the representatives of others and heads over contrasting orders of life. Adam, the first man, is representative head of the natural earthly order of existence, made subject to corruption and death by his sin (Rom 5:12-19). Christ, the second and last Adam, is the representative head over the spiritual, heavenly order, characterized by life, power, and glory. Ultimately, the contrast in this passage is between two successive world orders, creation and its consummation (new creation), each beginning with an Adam.

Two other points also bear on the new creation gospel of Paul and the other NT writers. First, the believer's resurrection is fully dependent on the resurrection of Christ, who, as the last Adam, became life-giving Spirit in resurrection (v 45). The controlling emphasis is on the unity between the resurrection of Christ and that of believers (cf. 1 Cor 15:12-20; Col 1:18). In the NT proclamation, the resurrection of Christ is the great redemptive counterpart to creation (Rom 4:17). According to the NT, the new creation is a present reality, dating from the resurrection of Christ. Second, in stating that the last Adam became life-giving Spirit, 1 Corinthians 15:45 points to the unity that exists between the exalted Christ and the Holy Spirit in their life-giving activity. The Holy Spirit is the power of the new creation (cf. Heb 6:5). Where the Spirit is at work as the gift of the glorified Christ, the new creation is present.

The new creation is the eschatological fulfillment promised and anticipated in the OT. As such it has already been inaugurated and realized by the work of Christ (the last Adam), particularly by his death and resurrection, and will be consummated at his return. The interval in between receives its fundamental character from the coexistence of the two creations; the new has begun, while concurrently the old continues to pass away (1 Cor 7:31). The concept of new creation closely parallels that of the kingdom of God. According to the synoptic Gospels, it is the central theme of Jesus' proclamation. Tied to his own person and work in its coming, the kingdom is announced by him as both present (Mt 12:28; 13:11, 16-17) and future (Mt 8:11; 25:34). In terms of the two-age distinction, coined by contemporary Judaism to express its eschatological expectations and taken over by Jesus and the early church (e.g., Mt 12:32; Eph 1:21), the new creation is the longed-for "age to come." "New creation" serves to indicate the comprehensive nature of this eschatological reality; redemption involves nothing less than the renewal of all things (Rv 21:5).

The New Creation and the Church Salvation, according to the NT, is from beginning to end a matter of union with Christ and sharing in all the benefits resulting from his once-for-all redemptive work. Accordingly, because Christ died and was raised, anyone in Christ is already a participant in the new ceation order (2 Cor 5:15). The reference is not only personal but cosmic, as seen from the context with its correlative emphasis on the reconciliation and its scope (vv 17-19).

In the only other NT occurrence of the expression "new creation" (Gal 6:15), the perspective is cosmic as well as individual. The new creation, in which neither circumcision nor uncircumcision matters, stands in opposition to the world, to which the believer has been crucified with Christ (Gal 6:14; cf. Col 2:20). "When anyone is united to Christ, there is a new world; the old order is gone, and a new order has already begun" (2 Cor 5:17, NEB).

Resurrection is not only a future hope for believers but a present reality; they have already been raised with Christ (Eph 2:5-6; cf. Col 2:12-13; 3:1). Consequently, believers are "created in Christ Jesus for good works" (Eph 2:10). Further, the church is the new covenant reality of "the new man," made up of Israel and the nations (v 15). As such, its members are already being renewed inwardly (2 Cor 4:16) by the Lord-Spirit according to the glorified image of the last Adam (2 Cor 3:18; 4:4-6; cf. Rom 8:29; Eph 4:24; Col 3:10). And they will bear this same image bodily at his return (1 Cor 15:49). The deepest motive for holy living is not gratitude for the forgiveness of sin but the determination of the believer's existence as a new creature. The ethics of the NT are new creation ethics (Rom 12:2; Col 2:20).

The new creation is not only a present reality but a future hope. For the new creation, too, the church lives "by faith, not by sight" (2 Cor 5:7). Reminiscent of Isaiah's expectation, believers are looking to Christ's return for "new heavens and a new earth in which righteousness dwells" and where sin and its effects are nothing more than memories (2 Pt 3:13; Rv 21:1-4).

This hope raises the question of the relationship between this final, eternal order and the original creation. The picture of destruction by burning (2 Pt 3:10-12) and some of the images in Revelation 21 and 22 (e.g., no sun, moon, night; cf. 6:12-14) seem to suggest an absolute disjunction. Other passages, however, interpret this as imagery. With all the radical differences before and after the resurrection, the natural and spiritual bodies (1 Cor 15:44) are not distinct from each other as bodies. This body, sown in corruption, dishonor, and weakness, will be raised up incorruptible, glorious, and powerful. And what holds true for the believer's body also holds for creation. The anxious longing and groaning of the entire (nonpersonal) creation is not for annihilation but that it may be set free from bondage to futility and decay and may share in the glorious freedom of the children of God, which will be revealed in the redemption (resurrection) of the body

(Rom 8:19-23). The new creation is not merely a return to conditions in the beginning but a renewed creation, the consummation of God's purposes set from before the beginning and realized, despite man's sin and its destructive effects, by the redemption in Christ, the last Adam. *See* Adam (Person); Creation; Eternal Life; Man, Old and New; New; New Heavens and New Earth.

NEW GATE One of the gates of the temple during Jeremiah's ministry (Jer 26:10; 36:10).

NEW HEAVENS AND NEW EARTH Concept of a new or renewed universe first found in the book of Isaiah. God declares, "For behold, I create new heavens and a new earth; and the former things shall not be remembered or come into mind. . . . For as the new heavens and the new earth which I will make shall remain before me . . . so shall your descendants and your name remain" (Is 65:17; 66:22, RSV).

Some scholars think that long before Isaiah's time there existed among many ancient peoples the belief that the end of human history would correspond to its beginning and therefore some sort of universal restoration would take place. The world renewal taught in Scripture regards the event as supernatural and as taking place in a different and higher sphere.

That God is Creator of the heavens and earth is basic to all biblical theology. "In ages past you laid the foundation of the earth, and the heavens are the work of your hands" (Ps 102:25, NLT). If God created the heavens and earth, then it is entirely appropriate that, once they have served their purpose, God may do with them what he wishes. "Even they will perish, but you remain forever; they will wear out like old clothing. You will change them like a garment, and they will fade away" (v 26, NLT). The same metaphor is found in Isaiah 51:6, which speaks of the earth wearing out like a garment.

Scripture (quoted below from the NLT) gives considerable attention to the passing away of the old order, speaking of a future time when heaven and earth will disappear (Is 34:4; 51:6; Mt 24:35; Rv 21:1). A number of related phrases portray the same idea: "And this world is fading away" (1 Jn 2:17); "They [the heavens and earth] will wear out like old clothing" (Heb 1:11; cf. Ps 102:26; Is 51:6); "But the day of the Lord will come as unexpectedly as a thief. Then the heavens will pass away with a terrible noise, and everything in them will disappear in fire, and the earth and everything on it will be exposed to judgment" (2 Pt 3:10). This consummation by fire will take place at the time of final judgment. It will be "the day when God will set the heavens on fire and the elements will melt away in the flames" (v 12).

This judgment, which brings to a close the old order, clears the way for new heavens and a new earth. Peter continues, "But we are looking forward to the new heavens and new earth he has promised, a world where everyone is right with God" (2 Pt 3:13). It will be so wonderful that no one will even remember the old (Is 65:17). Peter, preaching in Solomon's Colonnade, says that Jesus will remain in heaven until the time comes for establishing all that God spoke by his holy prophets (Acts 3:21). This recovery or renewal is eagerly awaited by the created order. Paul writes, "For all creation is waiting eagerly for that future day when God will reveal who his children really are" (Rom 8:19) because "all creation anticipates the day when it will join God's children in glorious freedom from death and decay" (v 21).

The heaven that will be renewed is not the heaven of God's presence, but the heaven of human existence, the starry expanse that constitutes the universe. In the book of Revelation we learn that the new Jerusalem comes down from heaven to earth (Rv 21:2, 10) and forms the eternal dwelling place of God and his people. The new earth will be a place of perfect righteousness (Is 51:6), divine kindness (54:10), eternal relationship to God (66:22), and total freedom from sin (Rom 8:21).

See also Eschatology; Heaven; Kingdom of God, Kingdom of Heaven; New; New Creation, New Creature.

NEW JERUSALEM *See* Jerusalem, New.

NEW MAN*, NEW PERSON Expression used by the apostle Paul to refer to Jesus Christ and his body, the church (Eph 2:15). *See* Man, Old and New.

NEW MOON Monthly celebration involving grain offerings, burnt sacrifices, and trumpet blasts. *See* Feasts and Festivals of Israel; Moon.

NEW TESTAMENT *See* Bible.

NEW TESTAMENT CANON* *See* Bible, Canon of the.

NEW TESTAMENT CHRONOLOGY* *See* Chronology of the Bible (New Testament).

NEZIAH Forefather of a family of temple servants who returned to Jerusalem with Zerubbabel following the Babylonian captivity (Ezr 2:54; Neh 7:56).

NEZIB One of the cities in the lowland allotted to Judah for an inheritance (Jos 15:43). Its site is identified with modern Khirbet Beit Nesib, east of Lachish.

NIBHAZ The name of a god worshiped by displaced Avvites after they were forcibly resettled in Samaria by the Assyrians in 722 BC. They brought the worship of this idol, as well as that of Tartak, with them at that time (2 Kgs 17:31). Although purported to be of Mesopotamian origin, this is not likely because the worshipers were Syrian. The word Nibhaz may be a Hebrew corruption of "altar" and hence a reference to a deified altar that was the object of worship.

NIBSHAN One of the six cities in the wilderness allotted to Judah for an inheritance (Jos 15:62).

NICANOR
1. The son of Patroclus, "one of the king's chief friends" (2 Macc 8:9) and a Syrian general under Antiochus IV Epiphanes and Demetrius Soter. This general may have been the supreme commander over Ptolemy and Gorgias in Lysias's first campaign against Judas Maccabeus (1 Macc 3:38 ff.) during the reign of Antiochus IV Epiphanes. He was slain in the battle at Adasa and Beth-horon (161 BC). According to 2 Maccabees, Judas hung Nicanor's head from the citadel as a clear proof of the Lord's victory (15:35).
2. One of the seven chosen by the early church to supervise the daily distribution to the poor saints in Jerusalem (Acts 6:5).

NICODEMUS Pharisee and member of the Sanhedrin mentioned only in John's Gospel (Jn 3:1-15; 7:50-52; 19:39-41). According to John 3, Nicodemus came to Jesus at night and acknowledged him as a teacher sent by God. He was convinced that Jesus could not perform such things if God were not with him. Following an exchange concerning the need to be born again, Jesus asked how Nicodemus, a member of the Jewish religious court, could fail to understand such things. At that time he evidently made no profession of faith, but later he did defend Jesus before the Sanhedrin (7:50-52). After Jesus' death, Nicodemus openly assisted Joseph of Arimathea with the burial of his body (19:39-42).

Some scholars suggest that Nicodemus was one of the Jewish leaders who believed in Jesus but did not confess him openly for fear of excommunication (12:42). Tradition subsequently held that he belonged to the household of faith, as one persuaded to believe through the message and deeds of Jesus, but remained intimidated by the religious establishment.

See also John, Gospel of.

NICOLAITANS Heretical sect in the early church that is mentioned by name twice in the book of Revelation. The church at Ephesus was commended for hating the works of the Nicolaitans (Rv 2:6), and the church at Pergamum was criticized for having some members who held their doctrine (v 15).

Since the specific sins condemned at Pergamum—the eating of food sacrificed to idols and the practice of immorality—were also present at Thyatira (Rv 2:20), it is commonly thought that the woman Jezebel was a leader of the Nicolaitans in that church. In the letter to Pergamum, their sins are equated with the teaching of Balaam (Rv 2:14; cf. Nm 25:1-2; 31:16; 2 Pt 2:15; Jude 1:11), who advised Balak, the king of the Moabites, to bring about Israel's downfall by inviting them to worship the Moabite gods and engage in intermarriage and the sexual immoralities connected with Moabite religious practices. Thus, the Jews would have been separated from God and his protection. In Jewish thought, Balaam was the symbol of all that led men to obscene conduct and the forsaking of God. The ungodly practices at Thyatira are called the "deep things of Satan" (Rv 2:24).

The early church was also threatened by the combination of idolatry and immorality so prevalent in the world. The necessity for frequent warning in the NT reveals the gravity of the problem. The Jerusalem Council (Acts 15:20) called upon the Gentiles to abstain from eating food that had been offered to idols and sexual immorality. Paul called for a voluntary avoidance of this kind of fare for the sake of those who were weak or immature in the faith (1 Cor 8). He strongly condemned actual participation in idol feasts (1 Cor 10:14-22) as well as fornication in general and temple prostitution in particular (6:12-20).

Who the Nicolaitans were is more difficult to determine. The tendency among the church fathers was to identify them as followers of Nicolaus of Antioch, a Gentile convert to the Jewish faith, who had become a Christian and was chosen to be one of the original seven deacons (Acts 6:5). Both Irenaeus and Hippolytus believed that he had fallen from the faith. Clement claimed that the heretical and immoral Nicolaitans were not actual followers of Nicolaus but falsely claimed him as their teacher. In any event, there is no direct evidence available.

Since the 19th century it has been common to view the name as a translation into Greek of the Hebrew name Balaam. This is in accord with the allegorical, symbolical nature of Revelation and the apparent linking of the two names in the letter to Pergamum (Rv 2:14-15).

NICOLAS, NICOLAUS* One of the seven men named in Acts 6:5, who was enlisted for service in the Jerusalem church in its early days. His duty as specified in Acts 6:1-4 was to direct the fair and equal distribution of food. Due to the use of terms in Acts 6:1 ("daily distribution" or "service") and 6:2 ("to distribute at tables" or "to serve"), these seven men traditionally have been called "deacons" (or "servers").

Nicolas, the last-named in the list, is identified as a proselyte. Thus, he was a Gentile convert to Judaism before he became a Christian. His name is Greek, and the city of Antioch is mentioned as his home. The NT writings provide no further information about him.

See also Deacon, Deaconess.

NICOPOLIS
Name meaning "Victory City," a popular choice in the Roman Empire when a newly founded city required a name, especially when a newly built town was created to commemorate some military victory in days of warfare.

In his letter to Titus, Paul directs him to leave Crete, where he had been ministering (Ti 1:5), and make his way to Nicopolis, where the apostle was working and intended to spend the winter (3:12). Of the nine Nicopolises throughout the empire, Paul almost certainly meant the city situated northwest of the Gulf of Corinth and southeast of the promontory of Epirus.

Octavian founded this city in 31 BC to celebrate his victory over Mark Antony in the great battle of Actium fought nearby. Nicopolis was Greek both in name and constitution. The center of a number of nearby towns, the new Nicopolis was a metropolis, enjoying an independence similar to that of neighboring Athens. Temples, theaters, a stadium, and an aqueduct were built, and games were instituted for the four yearly festivals. Nicopolis's most famous citizen, Epictetus, the Stoic philosopher, lived there around AD 90. Paul made this splendid metropolis and its satellite communities a field for evangelism.

NIGER*
Surname of Simeon, one of the leaders in the church at Antioch (Acts 13:1). *See* Simeon (Person) #4.

NIGHT
Word in Scripture denoting that time of darkness from dusk until dawn when no light of the sun is visible. For example, Joseph took Mary and Jesus to Egypt by night (Mt 2:14). The shepherds were keeping watch over their flocks at night (Lk 2:8). Nicodemus came to see Jesus at night (Jn 3:2). An angel from the Lord came and opened the prison doors at night in order to let the disciples out (Acts 5:19).

According to Genesis 1, the day-night cycle was instituted by God and "night" was the name given to the period of darkness (Gn 1:5). Later, God put the lights in the expanse of the heavens, appointing the sun to rule or dominate the day, and the moon, the lesser light, to dominate the night (vv 16-18). The covenant of the Lord is the basis of the regularity of the rotation of day and night.

The night in OT times was apparently divided into three periods or "watches." The latter name originated with the changing of the guard at these times. Gideon's 300 men blew their trumpets and broke their pitchers at the beginning of the middle watch (Jgs 7:19). Although no references in the OT give the limits of these three periods, night was considered to begin at sunset, and consequently the periods may have been 6:00 to 10:00 PM, 10:00 PM to 2:00 AM, and 2:00 to 6:00 AM.

Later, according to the Roman calculation of time, night was divided into four watches. Some historians think they began at 9:30 PM, at midnight, at 2:30 AM, and at 5:00 AM. Others think that the nighttime period between 6:00 PM and 6:00 AM was divided equally into four periods, the first beginning at 6:00 PM, the second at 9:00 PM, the third at midnight, and the fourth at 3:00 AM. Mark 13:35 contains the popular designations for these four watches, namely late in the day (early evening), midnight, the cock-crowing, and early in the morning.

Apparently, Matthew 14:25 and Mark 6:48 follow the Roman calculation when they locate Jesus' walking on the water at about the fourth watch of the night.

A specialized use of the word "night" along with the word "day" emphasizes the continuance of activity. For example, the man with an unclean spirit is said to have been in the mountains and in the tombs "night and day" (Mk 5:5). Paul refers to his having labored, working night and day, so as not to be a burden to the church (1 Thes 2:9). Later in the same book he refers to his continuous praying night and day (3:10).

Along with this literal usage of the word "night," there is also a figurative or metaphorical usage. In some references it refers to divine judgment (Am 5:8-9; Mi 3:6). Jesus uses "night" to refer to death (Jn 9:4). Once the night (death) comes, time for working is over.

Paul compares this present age (soon to be over with) to the night that is almost gone (Rom 13:12). Again, Paul speaks of himself and his readers as children of the light and of the day, not the night and darkness (1 Thes 5:5). In this context he links night with separation from God, sin, intemperance, careless living, as well as spiritual blindness and ignorance, especially regarding the Lord's return.

See also Day.

NIGHT HAG*
Designation for a bird of the wasteland (Is 34:14). *See* Birds (Owl, Scops).

NIGHT HAWK
See Birds (Goatsucker).

NIGHT MONSTER*
Designation for a bird of the wasteland (Is 34:14). *See* Birds (Owl, Scops).

NILE RIVER
Life-giving river of Egypt in northeast Africa. Perhaps no other river has been so vital to the history of the nation through which it flows. With an attributed length of some 4,160 miles (6,693.4 kilometers), the Nile is the longest river in the world, although its drainage system is ranked third (other sources say sixth) in area (nearly 1.3 million square miles, or 3.4 million square kilometers).

The origin and meaning of the name "Nile" are unknown. To the ancient Egyptians the Nile was simply "the river." The Egyptians found it hard to conceive of any river different from the Nile, so when they reached the Euphrates, they assumed it was running backward, since it flowed south, whereas the Nile flows north.

Unusual Features Among the characteristics that distinguish the Nile are its six cataracts, areas where the river has failed to erode a clear channel through hard rock formations. These are numbered from north to south, in order of their discovery by modern explorers. The first cataract is at Aswan in Egypt, near the famous islands of Elephantine and Philae. The other five cataracts lie in the Sudan, with the second just above the city of Wadi Halfa.

Another distinguishing feature of the Nile is that it flows from south to north. This was of importance to Egyptian river transport, for sailing vessels could take advantage of the prevailing north wind for going upstream, while the current propelled travelers downstream.

The Nile River determined the three seasons of about four months each: (1) inundation (mid-July to mid-November); (2) winter (mid-November to mid-March); (3) summer (mid-March to mid-July).

The inundation culminated in late October, softening the soil of the agricultural land for planting.

Course and Tributaries The Nile has two main streams named for their respective colors, the White Nile and the Blue Nile. These streams owe their existence to the annual rains in equatorial Africa.

The White Nile has its origin in the lake country. Lake Victoria is usually said to be its source, but some geographers pinpoint the source as a little stream that flows into the lake. The only outlet at Lake Victoria is the Victoria Nile, northeast of the lake at Ripon Falls.

The most important junction of the river is at Khartoum, where the Blue Nile and White Nile are united. At this point one can often clearly see the color difference in the waters of the two rivers.

The Blue Nile, only about 850 miles (1,367.7 kilometers) long, originates at Lake Tana in the highlands of Ethiopia. A much more precipitous stream than the White Nile, it is also dependent upon the rainy season in the high country. The White Nile begins its flooding first, but when the onrush of the Blue Nile sets in, it holds in check the water of the White Nile. During flood season, the Blue Nile has twice the volume of the White Nile and provides the greater part of the alluvium that built up the soil of Egypt.

To the north of Khartoum is the sixth cataract, the first of the natural barriers. The Atbara, the last tributary of the Nile, enters from the east. At the fourth cataract, near Napata, is a group of cemeteries and ruins associated with the Ethiopian or Kushite (25th) dynasty of Egypt. Farther downstream is the important archaeological site of Kerma, where the Egyptians maintained a trading post during the Middle Kingdom.

Downstream from the second cataract is the celebrated temple of Abu Simbel, the work of Ramses II, with the smaller temple honoring Nefertari, his wife. These temples were moved to the cliff above their original position before Lake Nasser engulfed the site.

Just above Aswan and the first cataract is the new High Dam and the older Aswan Dam. Between the two dams is the island of Philae, with its well-known temples. A short distance above the Delta lies Cairo and the Giza pyramids, and farther south are the ruins of Memphis, the first capital of Egypt.

The Delta measures some 125 by 115 miles (201.1 by 185.0 kilometers). Seven ancient streams of the Nile found their way into the sea, but there are only two modern ones: the Rosetta on the west, which gave the name to the Rosetta Stone, and the Damietta to the East.

Importance to Egypt Without the water of the river, life would be impossible in northeast Africa, and the civilizations of Egypt could not have come into being. The Greek writers, first Hecataeus and later Herodotus, commented that Egypt is the gift of the Nile. The fertile soil of Egypt, which has produced such abundant crops over so long a span of time, is the alluvium laid down by the river over the course of centuries. Not only was the river the source of the soil itself, but with the annual inundation the Nile fertilized the land by bringing down new alluvium and by depositing organic materials. At the same time, the inundation thoroughly soaked the soil, so that it was possible to produce good crops with a minimum of effort expended on irrigation.

The Nile also satisfied many personal needs of the people, providing drinking water and a washing place for both the people and their clothing. In ancient times,

even members of the royal family came to the river to bathe (see Ex 2:5; 8:20).

The Nile teemed with fish and waterfowl, and sport fishing (mostly spearfishing) and waterfowling were traditional diversions of the upper classes. Fish and fowl were also regular food, especially for the wealthy. A more hazardous sport, in which nobles traditionally engaged, was the hunting of hippopotami in reed watercraft with harpoons.

The Nile River

The Nile was the primary means of communication, with boats plying up and down its channels. Riverboats of large size moved goods from one end to the other. The building of temples, palaces, and tombs throughout the land demanded the moving of granite for hundreds of miles along the river.

The river was also a feature of the religious life of the Egyptians. The river was deified in the form of the god Hapi, a man who is shown in the various forms of art as having pendulous breasts and a somewhat corpulent body, probably to represent luxuriant overabundance, along with the fish and vegetation from the river.

The Nile and the Bible The biblical references to the Nile River are naturally found in those parts of the Bible that have to do directly with Egypt, which means that many occur in the Joseph narrative in the latter part of Genesis and in the account of the Israelite bondage in Egypt and subsequent exodus in the early chapters of Exodus.

The first reference to the Nile appears in the mysterious dream of Pharaoh (Gn 41). In his dream the king stood on the riverbank and saw seven well-fed cows, followed by seven lean cows, which came out of the river and devoured the fat cattle (cf. 41:1-4, 17-21). This agrees with grazing practices of ancient Egypt and coincides with the depiction of cattle on the funerary monuments.

During the sojourn in Egypt, when the Israelites multiplied and became a possible threat to Egyptian security, Pharaoh decreed that every Israelite male child should be thrown into the river upon birth (Ex 1:22). This led to the events that marked the early life of Moses.

Moses declared the judgments of the Lord at the river (7:15; 8:20). The first plague, the turning of water to blood (7:15-24; 17:5; Ps 78:44), was directed against the river and against the Nile god, Hapi. The second plague (frogs) was also associated with the river (8:3, 5, 9, 11), for the swarms of frogs came up out of the river and enveloped the land (cf. Ps 78:45), discrediting the frog-headed goddess Heket.

There are numerous references to the Nile in the books of prophecy. Isaiah often mentions the Nile, but not always in the same context. In 7:18 Isaiah writes that Israel would be invaded and humiliated by armies from the Nile. In the "oracle concerning Egypt" (Is 19), the prophet foresees both evil and good for the land of the Nile. The natural vegetation and sown crops along the river will be destroyed, while the fishermen will lament. These dire prospects are offset by the prediction of final blessing for Egypt.

In the burden of Tyre (Is 23) the revenue of the Sidonian merchants was "the harvest of the Nile" (v 3), indicating the importance of agricultural produce in the Nile valley. In verse 10, Tyre casts off all restraint and is told to overflow the land like the Nile, for the Lord is bringing the pride of Tyre to an end. Jeremiah also predicted a severe defeat for Egypt and speaks of Egypt rising like the Nile, like rivers whose waters surge (Jer 46:7-8).

The prophecy of Ezekiel concerning Egypt (Ez 29) singles out Pharaoh, king of Egypt, and describes him in figures of speech drawn from the Nile. He is described as the great dragon that lies in the midst of his streams—a reference to the mighty crocodile. Pharaoh boasts, "My Nile is my own," but the Lord said that he would put hooks into the king's jaws and draw him out of the water of his streams with all of the fish sticking to his scales. The king and the fish of the streams will perish in the wilderness. Because of the proud boasts of the king, the Lord declares that he is against him and his streams and that Egypt will become a desolation and a waste.

Amos described the northern kingdom of Israel as being tossed about, and sinking again, like the Nile of Egypt (Am 8:8; 9:5). Finally, Zechariah spoke of an ingathering of Israel by the Lord and comments that in this process the Nile would be dried up (Zec 10:11).

Although the prophetic references to the Nile primarily deal with severe judgments, the prophets looked forward to a time beyond judgment to eventual blessing for this land of the Nile.

See also Egypt, Egyptian.

NIMRAH Alternate rendering of Beth-nimrah, a city in Moab, in Numbers 32:3. *See* Beth-nimrah.

NIMRIM, Waters of One of the places in the southern extremity of Moab denounced by Isaiah (Is 15:6) and Jeremiah (Jer 48:34) in their oracles of judgment against the nation. The waters of Nimrim were spring-fed streams originating in the Transjordanian hills, following a northwesterly track down into the Arabah Valley, and eventually emptying into the southeast corner of the Dead Sea. The region surrounding the streams was evidently well known for its lush vegetation (see Is 15:6). This watercourse is probably identifiable with the modern Wadi en-Numeirah positioned about eight miles (12.9 kilometers) north of the Brook Zered.

NIMROD Cush's son and grandson of Ham the son of Noah (Gn 10:8; 1 Chr 1:10). He is described as "the first man of might on earth" and "a mighty hunter" (Gn 10:8-9). Nimrod was the first to establish a great empire and was a well-known hunter. Tradition makes him ruler over Babylon and Akkad in southern Mesopo-

tamia, and over Nineveh in Assyria. The phrase "land of Nimrod" seems to be synonymous with Assyria (Mi 5:6).

The OT references to Nimrod indicate that in ancient tradition he was a man of indomitable personality, possessing extraordinary talents and powers. Some scholars identify him with a Mesopotamian king who united Assyria and Babylon in the 13th century BC. This conflicts with the statement connecting him with Cush the son of Ham and pointing to an association with the south of Egypt where Cush was located (Gn 10:8).

The name and fame of Nimrod have a secure place in Talmudic Judaism and in Islamic tradition. In the former he personifies both rebellion against God and military might in the earth. In rabbinic tradition, the Tower of Babel (Gn 11:1-9) is "the house of Nimrod" where idolatry was practiced and divine homage offered to Nimrod. In Islam, Nimrod persecutes Abraham and has him thrown into a fiery furnace.

NIMSHI Father of Jehoshaphat and grandfather of Jehu, who was king of Israel (1 Kgs 19:16; 2 Kgs 9:2-20; 2 Chr 22:7).

NINEVEH, NINEVITE* One of the capitals of the Assyrian Empire and, at the height of that empire, one of the great cities of the world. Nineveh was situated in what is now northern Iraq and is represented today by the mounds of Kouyunjik and Nebi Yunus to the east of the Tigris River and opposite the main part of the city of Mosul.

The larger mound, Kouyunjik, to the northwest (approximately a mile by 650 yards [1.6 kilometers by 594.4 meters] in area and some 90 feet [27.4 meters] in height above the plain), is separated from Nebi Yunus by the Khosr River. A village, a cemetery, and a mosque said to contain the tomb of Jonah occupy Nebi Yunus, preventing extensive archaeological work.

Nineveh's surrounding brick wall, about 8 miles (12.9 kilometers) long with 15 gates (of which 5 have been excavated) was guarded by the colossal stone bulls that typify Assyrian city architecture of this period.

History The occupation of the site dates to prehistoric times (c. 4500 BC), in agreement with the record of the founding of the city in Genesis 10. Materials from the various early cultures (Hassuna, Samarra, Halaf, Ubaid) have been found at Nineveh.

Sargon of Akkad (mid-24th century BC) was acquainted with Nineveh, which flourished during his time. A record from the reign of a later king, Shamsi-Adad I (c. 1800 BC), relates that a son of Sargon, Manishtusu, restored the temple of Ishtar at Nineveh.

Ishtar (Inanna), the goddess of love and war, was a fitting deity for the rapacious and warlike Assyrians. Many other deities were worshiped at Nineveh, and gates of the city were named after them. The Assyrians worshiped at the temple of Nabu, the god of writing and of arts and sciences, who reflects the Assyrian interest in records, literature, and sculpture in relief and in the round.

Shamsi-Adad I and Hammurabi also restored the temple of Ishtar at Nineveh, Shalmaneser I and Tukulti-Ninurta I enlarged and strengthened the city, and other rulers built their palaces here—Tiglath-pileser I, Ashurnasirpal II (883–859 BC), and Sargon II (722–705 BC). But Sennacherib (705–681 BC) made Nineveh the capital and went to great lengths to beautify the city. In addition to his famous palace, he undertook many projects, rebuilding the city walls, creating parks, making botanical and zoological collections, and constructing aqueducts to bring water for the city from 30 miles (48.3 kilometers) away. To Nineveh came the tribute

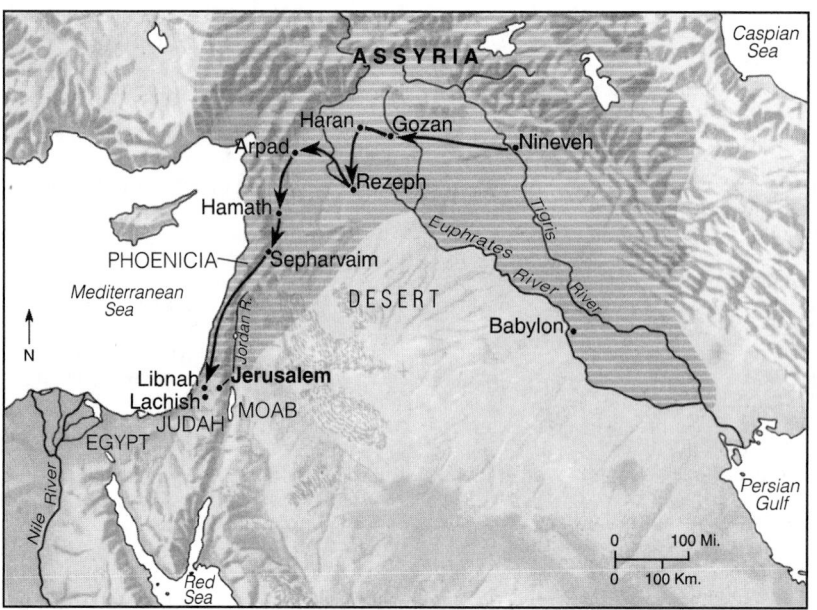

Sennacherib Leads His Troops from Nineveh toward Israel

in 612 BC; the city fell and King Sinshariskum (Sardanapalus) perished in its flames.

Although a Ninevite remnant under Ashuruballit held out at Haran until 609 BC, Nineveh had been destroyed: the divine predictions of the Hebrew prophets had their complete fulfillment.

Nineveh and the Bible Six books of the OT refer to the city of Nineveh. In Genesis the only mention of Nineveh appears in the table of nations (Gn

that the conquering Assyrians exacted from the nations, including Israel and Judah, which fell victim to their awesome armies.

After the assassination of Sennacherib, his son and successor, Esar-haddon (681–669 BC), captured Nineveh from the hands of rebels. He built a palace at Nineveh and had another at Calah, where he spent most of his time.

Esar-haddon's son Ashurbanipal (669–633 BC) made his residence at Nineveh, where he had been educated and trained in sports and military skills. He was something of an antiquarian and mastered the reading of Akkadian and Sumerian. In his palace was housed the famous library for the study of Assyriology. The temple of Nabu contained a library dating at least to the time of Sargon II, but the royal library of Ashurbanipal far surpassed it in size and importance. Sargon and his successors had collected many tablets, but Ashurbanipal sent scribes all over Assyria and Babylonia to gather and to copy tablets, so that tens of thousands of tablets accumulated. Like the library of Nippur, the Nineveh collection covers a great range of materials: business accounts, letters, royal records, historical documents, lexicographical lists and bilingual texts, legends, myths, and various other kinds of religious inscriptions, such as hymns, prayers, and lists of deities and temples. Among the tablets were 7 that preserved a Babylonian creation story and 12 that bore the epic of Gilgamesh, with a version of the Flood. Other writings that sometimes are cited as parallels to Bible accounts include the story of Adapa, with the lost opportunity to achieve immortality, and the legend of Etana, a shepherd who ascended to heaven.

Ashurbanipal was also well known for his wars and for his cruelty. The palace relief showing a peaceful banquet scene also displays the severed head of an Elamite leader hanging in a tree.

In the later years of the aging king, and after his demise, the vassal kingdoms rebelled. Babylon became independent and joined with the Medes to take Ashur and Calah in 614 BC. Cyaxares the Mede, Nabopolassar of Babylon, and a Scythian force laid siege to Nineveh

10), which states that Nimrod went out from the land of Shinar to Assyria and built Nineveh, Rehoboth, Calah, and Resen between Nineveh and Calah (vv 11-12; the KJV attributes this building to Asshur).

The tribute paid by Menahem (2 Kgs 15:19-20) and the spoil taken at the fall of Samaria (Is 8:4) were brought to Nineveh. To this city also came the tribute that Sennacherib received from Hezekiah (2 Kgs 14–16).

Among the scenes commemorated in the reliefs found in Sennacherib's palace at Nineveh is the depiction of the siege and capture of Lachish (cf. 2 Kgs 19:8). Sennacherib is shown on a throne, with suppliant captives before him. The siege itself is shown in progress, with archers and battering rams on the attack, while defenders on the walls use bows and arrows and firebrands to repulse the onslaught. From one gate people are emerging with bundles on their backs as if in surrender or flight. At the lower right three naked men have been impaled on poles.

On the prism at the Oriental Institute of the University of Chicago and on the Taylor Prism at the British Museum there is Sennacherib's account of this invasion of Judah. Since the Assyrians did not take Jerusalem, Sennacherib had to be content with boasting: "As to Hezekiah the Jew, he did not submit to my yoke. I laid siege to 46 of his strong cities, walled forts and to the countless small villages in their vicinity, and conquered them. . . . Himself I made a prisoner in Jerusalem, his royal residence, like a bird in a cage."

The Assyrian kings associated with Nineveh played an important part in the history of Israel, but the name Nineveh occurs only once in the historical books of the Bible. Second Kings 19:36 states that after the loss of 185,000 soldiers at the hand of the angel of the Lord, Sennacherib went home and stayed in Nineveh. There, in 681 BC, he was murdered by his sons (cf. 2 Kgs 19:37; 2 Chr 32:21; Is 37:38).

There are many references to Nineveh in the book of Jonah, for the prophet was expressly sent to that city to warn it of impending judgment. Nineveh is called "that great city" (Jon 1:2; 3:2) and it is described as "a city so large, that it took three days to see it" (3:3). Nineveh must have included more than the area represented by the mounds of Kouyunjik and Nebi Yunus. Some commentators believe that Nineveh encompassed other cities associated with it, including the "Assyrian triangle," the angle of land between the Tigris and the Great Zab rivers, reaching from Khorsabad in the north to Nimrud in the south.

The Lord speaks of "that great city, in which there are more than a hundred and twenty thousand persons who do not know their right hand from their left" (Jon 4:11, RSV). Some writers interpret this statement as indicating the number of innocent children in the city and therefore arrive at a total population of some 600,000 for greater Nineveh. However, it is more reasonable to conclude that the entire population is meant and that the descriptive clause relates to the utter spiritual darkness of the Ninevites—as is translated in the NLT.

Jonah preached a message of judgment and destruction, but the repentance of the city brought about its deliverance (3:6-10). Nahum declared the final downfall of the city in language that is vivid and stirring. Zephaniah also foretold the doom of Nineveh and prophesied that it would be a desolation, a place for flocks to lie down, as even the casual visitor to the site would note (Zep 2:13-15).

Nineveh was destroyed by a coalition of Babylonians, Medes, and Scythians. The devastation of the city was overwhelming and complete; within several centuries the very location of the city was forgotten. Xenophon and the Greek armies retreated past the site in 401 BC without realizing it. In the second century AD the Greek satirist Lucian commented: "Nineveh is so completely destroyed that it is no longer possible to say where it stood. Not a single trace of it remains."

The only NT references to Nineveh in the Gospels also have to do with judgment. Jesus asserted, in response to a demand from the scribes and Pharisees, that an evil generation looks for a sign; as Jonah had been a sign to the Ninevites, so Jesus would be a sign to his generation (Mt 12:38-40; Lk 11:29-31). He went on to declare that the people of Nineveh would rise at the judgment with his generation and condemn it, for the Ninevites repented at the preaching of Jonah. Now one greater than Jonah had come (Mt 12:41; Lk 11:32).

See also Assyria, Assyrians; Hammurabi, Law Code of.

NISAN* Babylonian name for a Hebrew month (Neh 2:1; Est 3:7). *See* Calendars, Ancient and Modern.

NISROCH The god of King Sennacherib, in whose temple at Nineveh the king was assassinated by Adrammelech and Sharezer, his sons (2 Kgs 19:37; Is 37:38). Nisroch was the city god of Nineveh, the chief capital of the Assyrian Empire; he was perhaps identical with the Assyrian god Nusku.

See also Assyria, Assyrians.

NO* KJV form of Thebes in Nahum 3:8. *See* Thebes.

NOADIAH

1. Binnui's son and one of the two Levites present when the temple treasure that was brought back to Jerusalem by Ezra was weighed and recorded (Ezr 8:33).
2. Prophetess who, along with Tobiah, Sanballat, and some false prophets, attempted to intimidate Nehemiah when he was engaged in rebuilding Jerusalem's walls after the exile (Neh 6:14).

NOAH

1. Son of Lamech and the grandson of Methuselah, a descendant of Seth, third son of Adam (Gn 5:3-20). Lamech named his son Noah, a name that sounds like

a Hebrew term that can mean "relief" or "comfort." When Lamech gave him this name, he said, "He will bring us relief from the painful labor of farming this ground that the LORD has cursed" (v 29, NLT).

Determined to destroy creation because of rampant wickedness (cf. Mt 24:37-39; Lk 17:26-27), God made an exception with Noah, a man righteous in God's sight and blameless before people (Gn 6:3-9). Following God's precise instructions, Noah constructed an ark into which went only eight people—Noah and his wife and his three sons and their wives—and all kinds of creatures in pairs. They were thus protected from the ensuing deluge in which all other living things perished (6:14–8:19). When they emerged from the ark, Noah built an altar and sacrificed burnt offerings that pleased God, who promised that the Flood would never be repeated or the sequence of the seasons disrupted, despite man's sin (8:20–9:17).

Noah had withstood mighty temptations, but, whether through carelessness or old age, he became drunk. Family members reacted differently and were judged accordingly. Shem and Japheth received blessing. Ham received no blessing, but his son Canaan was cursed (9:20-27). Noah was 950 years old when he died, 350 years after the Flood.

Noah, Daniel, and Job are specifically cited for "their righteousness" in Ezekiel 14:12-14, 19-20. The Letter to the Hebrews commends Noah, who by faith, holy fear, and rejection of the world became the heir of righteousness (11:7), and 2 Peter 2:5 calls him "a preacher of righteousness."

See also Flood, The; Gilgamesh Epic.

2. Daughter of Zelophehad of Manasseh's tribe (Nm 26:33). When their father died without a son, she and her four sisters successfully petitioned for a change in the law that would protect their inheritance rights (Nm 27:1-11; cf. Jos 17:3-6). They were, however, restricted to marrying within their own tribe (Nm 36:1-12).

NO-AMON* Alternate reading for No, the Hebrew name for Thebes, capital of upper Egypt (Na 3:8, NLT mg). *See* Thebes.

NOB City located on the eastern slopes of Mt Scopus opposite the Mt of Olives and northeast of Jerusalem. An important religious center; 86 priests resided there, as did the ephod (1 Sm 22:13-20). Nob was the central sanctuary in which the priests served who had fled from Shiloh when the Philistines destroyed the sanctuary there.

The episode of David and the priests of Nob (1 Sm 21:2-7) attests to the antiquity of the details of the table and the bread of the presence (Ex 37:10-16). Jesus cites David's hunger as a just reason for breaking the ritual laws governing Sabbath observance (Mk 2:23-28). David, fleeing from Saul and needing food, went into the sanctuary at Nob and took the loaves laid out each Sabbath as an offering to the Lord.

Ahimelech, a descendant of Eli and leader of the priests of Nob, gave the showbread to David, along with the sword with which Goliath had been slain. This incensed Saul, who ordered the murder of Ahimelech and the massacre of all the priests and citizens of Nob (1 Sm 22:6-23), an act that sealed the fate of the king. Abiathar, a priest who evaded the massacre, played a prominent role in the reign of David until Solomon eventually removed him from his position (1 Kgs 2:26-27). The phrase "where God was worshiped" may refer to the sanctuary at Nob (2 Sm 15:32).

NOBAH (Person) Manassite who conquered and settled the town of Kenath, east of the Jordan, and subsequently renamed it after himself (Nm 32:42).

NOBAH (Place)
1. Town east of the Jordan, previously named Kenath, allotted to Nobah the Manassite for an inheritance, at which time he called it Nobah after his own name (Nm 32:42). Nobah is perhaps also identifiable with Kanatha, the easternmost city of the Decapolis during the Roman era.
    See also Decapolis; Kanatha.
2. Place near the Gadite town of Jogbehah east of the Jordan, near which Gideon ambushed the Midianites (Jgs 8:11).

NOD Land east of Eden to which Cain went after he murdered his brother Abel (Gn 4:16).

NODAB*, NODABITES Forefather of an Arabian tribe that joined forces with the Hagarites to fight against the tribes of Israel who were living east of the Jordan (1 Chr 5:19). Though not included in the list of Ishmael's sons (cf. Gn 25:13-15), he was perhaps a distant relation.

NOE* KJV rendering of Noah in Matthew 24:37-38 and Luke 3:36; 17:26-27. *See* Noah #1.

NOGAH One of 13 sons of David born in Jerusalem after David established his kingdom (1 Chr 3:7; 14:6).

NOHAH (Person) Fourth son of Benjamin (1 Chr 8:2).

NOHAH* (Place) Place west of Gibeah in Benjamin's territory (Jgs 20:43, RSV). Other translations consider Nohah (meaning "quiet") an adverb and translate it accordingly, "with ease" (KJV), because no town by that name is known.

NON* KJV form of Nun, Joshua's father, in 1 Chronicles 7:27. *See* Nun.

NOPH* KJV translation of the Hebrew word for Memphis (Egypt). *See* Memphis.

NOPHAH Place delineating the boundaries between Israel and the Moabites and Amorites (Nm 21:30). Some scholars equate Nophah with the Nobah of Judges 8:11.

NORTH, NORTH COUNTRY Cardinal point on a compass opposite the south, often having the connotation of "dark," perhaps because the north side is often in shadow. In biblical literature, notably in the books of Joshua and Ezekiel, the term "north" is used frequently to designate direction, whether of tribal boundaries or of a temple.

An enemy from the north is mentioned at least 40 times in the prophecies of Jeremiah, Ezekiel, Daniel, and Zechariah. During the time of the exile (Jeremiah and Ezekiel), it referred to invaders who came from the East, pushed westward north of the Syrian desert, and then turned south to invade Judah from the north. Hence, they were viewed as invading from the "north country"; this latter phrase occurs at least 10 times in Jeremiah and Zechariah.

Jerusalem is vulnerable only from the north. The topography of the country is such that seldom in history has any invader conquered the Holy City from any direction except from the northern approach. The city was protected by deep valleys on each of the other three sides. In biblical times only the Egyptians and the Philistines threatened Jerusalem from the west; even the Philistines, during the time of Saul, were successful only in the areas north of Jerusalem. In Daniel the "king of the north" doubtless refers to Syrian forces in mortal combat with the "king of the south" (Egypt).

NORTHEASTER Name given to the stormy wind of Acts 27:14, encountered by Paul on his journey to Rome. Against his advice, the ship weighed anchor from a harbor near Lasea. Their course was "close in" along the Cretan coast, as a gentle breeze encouraged them along. Probably no further than nine miles (14.5 kilometers) out, a sudden squall threatened their tiny craft. Luke calls it a typhoon (KJV "tempestuous wind"), its name being Euroclydon, meaning "the southwest wind, that stirs up waves."

NOT LOVED, NOT PITIED* Symbolic name given by the prophet Hosea to his daughter (Hos 1:6-8) as a warning of the coming judgment of God upon Israel. *See* Ruhamah.

NOT MY PEOPLE Symbolic name given by the prophet Hosea to his third son (Hos 1:9) as a warning of the coming judgment of God upon Israel. *See* Ammi.

NUMBERS AND NUMEROLOGY* Individual numbers have a symbolic as well as a literal sense in the Bible. In Daniel, and to a lesser extent in Revelation, there is a developed system of numerology where interrelated systems of numbers are used in a definite pattern.

Traditionally, conservative Christians have been suspicious of numerology because of its unwise use by groups of Christians who see theological symbolism in every number in the OT, even the most factual. This view was inherited from mystical, pre-Christian Jewish groups, and later carried to extremes by the Kabbalists.

PREVIEW
• Expression of Numbers
• Ways of Writing Numerals
• Problems of Large Numbers
• Counting by Generations
• Approximate Use of Numbers
• Symbolic Use of Numbers
• Exact Statistics
• Numerology

Expression of Numbers Hebrew, and indeed any other Semitic language, has a simple but adequate system of numeration. The number one is an adjective. After that, the numerals are nouns, in parallel masculine and feminine forms, although the masculine is used with the feminine noun and vice versa. Ordinal numbers (first, second, third, etc.) exist alongside cardinal numbers (one, two, three), but as in most languages, the second set can be used instead of the first ("day two" instead of "second day"). From ten to nineteen, there is one composite form built like English "thirteen" ("three-ten"), but "twenty" is literally "tens" (the plural of "ten"). Thirty, forty, and so on are literally "threes," "fours" (the plural of the words "three" and "four," respectively) and so on, up to a hundred, which is a new word. There are also separate words for "thousand" and for "ten thousand," as in Greek, Chinese, and many other languages. Larger numbers must be expressed by multiples of these ("ten thousand times ten thousand" and "thousands of thousands"), suggesting that large figures, rarely needed for small populations and tiny kingdoms, were expressed approximately. Hebrew has not only a singular and plural but also a dual form to express two of anything (two hundred, two thousand). Fractions (a half, a third, a tenth, etc.) could be expressed, and multiplication, division, addition, and subtraction were used. Indeed, instances of all four operations can be found in the Bible. The Hebrew mathematical system was basically part of the larger western Asian mathematical system, of which we know a great deal from Mesopotamia and Egypt. These countries, however, used a more highly developed mathematical system than Israel.

Ways of Writing Numerals In the Bible, numbers are always written out in words, as on the famous Moabite Stone and the Siloam Inscription. But every nation in the ancient world could also express numbers by using figures or ciphers of various kinds (like our 1, 2, 3, . . .). Because of this danger of error, in later days numbers were normally written out in full, in words, where confusion, although still possible, was not nearly so likely. An additional way of writing numbers, known both to the Hebrews and the Greeks, was the use of consecutive letters of the alphabet instead of consecutive numerals (as if we used A for 1, B for 2, etc.). This system, in wide use by NT times, is the usual system in modern Hebrew and has the advantage that numerical combinations can be pronounced by inserting arbitrary vowels, thus making artificial words. For example, if the number of the beast (Rv 13:18), 666, is expressed in alphabetical letters, it can spell out the consonants of "Nero Caesar," although other names are possible, especially if the variant reading 616 is used.

Problems of Large Numbers Even allowing for all these possibilities, there remain certain problems connected with large numbers, particularly in the OT. The most obvious is that of the ten long-lived patriarchs, whose ages are recorded in Genesis 5. Different figures (varying by whole centuries) are recorded for their ages in the Hebrew text, the Samaritan text, and the earliest Greek translation (known as the Septuagint), but all figures are very large. Some interpret these figures literally and point out that there is a steady reduction from the ages attained by these patriarchs to the more modest 120 years allotted to man in Noah's time (Gn 6:3) and the 70 years accepted later as the human life span (Ps 90:10). This would correspond to the progressive spiritual deterioration of mankind after the fall, from the perfect state of Adam to the present condition. Whatever the explanation of the figures, there is no doubt that this is the theological intent of the Bible.

The large number of Israelites who left Egypt is also problematic. If there were actually 600,000 fighting men (Nm 1:46), this would correspond to a whole nation of some 2 million or more. Possibly the word translated "thousand" means "clan units"; it would clearly be a much smaller total body, whatever its exact size. Of course, God could have maintained any number of people in the desert. The evidence of archaeology as to the population of Canaan both before and after the Israelite onslaught seems to support a lower number. The same principle might explain the large numbers given for the fighting men of the various Israelite tribes, and the huge totals for Israel and Judah's military strength given at later times in the historical books of the OT.

To the ordinary Bible reader, perhaps one of the biggest problems is the different numbers recorded in Chronicles and Kings, when the same incidents are being described. Manuscript errors, or confusion of numbers written by signs or single letters of the alphabet, may account for numerous individual inconsistencies, but not for wholesale differences, particularly as the figures in Chronicles are consistently much larger. These very large round numbers may have symbolic significance and may not be intended to be taken in their literal sense at all. Indeed, since the Jews had before them the book of Kings and the book of Chronicles at the same time, they can hardly have taken both sets of numbers literally themselves.

Counting by Generations One of the problems of the OT is that of the dating of events. Even with an exact number system, there is no absolute fixed point from which to reckon. Later Jews and Christians counted from the presumed date of the Creation. Not until after the time of David and Solomon are both internal reference between the comparative dates of kings of Judah and Israel and external reference to monarchs outside Israel used. This open-endedness accounts for the vague period of "forty years" used so often in the OT (e.g., the book of Judges) for any long but indeterminate period of time, almost certainly corresponding to a generation (Hebrew, *dor*). Counting by generations is specific in some places in the Bible and may be implicit in others. For instance, Abraham's descendants are to return to Canaan "in the fourth generation" (Gn 15:16), and the genealogy of Christ is neatly constructed on a pattern of three groups of fourteen generations (Mt 1:17), rather than on periods of years. Wherever people use and recite genealogies, such counting by generations is natural. But Abraham's descendants are said to have returned to Canaan approximately four centuries later (Gal 3:17), and therefore the word "generation" sometimes stands for 100 years. The Hebrew word for "generation" may mean 120 years (Gn 6:3). Usually, the ancient Hebrews used vague phrases like "in those days" or "after those days" or "the days are coming," which expressed past, present, and future without any specific mention of number. In other words, the Bible writers were more concerned with theology than with mathematics.

Approximate Use of Numbers In the OT, Israel's 40 years in the desert is a good example of the approximate use of numbers (Nm 14:33). In the NT, Jesus was in the wilderness 40 days during the temptation (Mt 4:2), and there were 40 days between his resurrection and ascension (Acts 1:3). Moses was 40 years old at his call (Acts 7:23), apparently lived 40 years in Midian (Ex 7:7), and spent 40 years leading Israel out of Egypt and through the desert (Dt 34:7), for he is said to be 120 years old at his death. However, two generations of 40 years is the normal maximum for a healthy man (Ps 90:10), and even this is often shortened to 70 years by the rigors of life. Seventy is also used at times in this approximate sense.

Symbolic Use of Numbers In Scripture, seven symbolizes completeness or perfection. On the seventh day God rested from his labors and creation is finished (Gn 2:2). Pharaoh in his dream saw seven cattle coming from the Nile (41:2). Samson's sacred Nazirite locks were braided in seven plaits (Jgs 16:13). Seven devils left Mary of Magdala, signifying the totality of her previous possession by Satan (Lk 8:2); "seven other devils" will enter the purified but vacant life of a person (Mt 12:45). However, on the positive side, there were the seven spirits of God (Rv 3:1). In the seventh year the Hebrew slave was to be freed (Ex 21:2), having completed his time of captivity and service. Every seventh year was a sabbatical year (Lv 25:4). Seven times seven reiterates the sense of completeness. In the Year of Jubilee (at the completion of 7 x 7 years = the 50th year), all land is freed and returns to the original owners (Lv 25:10). Pentecost, the Feast of

Weeks, is seven times seven days after Passover. "Seventy," which is literally "sevens" in Hebrew, strengthens the concept of perfection. There are 70 elders (Ex 24:1) in Israel. Israel was exiled to Babylon for 70 years (Jer 25:12) to complete its punishment. "Seventy times seven" (Mt

18:22) reiterates this still further. The Lord was not giving Peter a mathematical number of times that he should forgive another person, but rather was insisting on limitless forgiveness for a brother's sin.

"Three" may well share in this meaning of completion

The Number 666 in an Ancient Greek Manuscript The number 666 (written as χξϲ) in the ninth line of Chester Beatty Papyrus III, Revelation 13:18 (c. 300)—P47

or perfection, although not so forcibly (2 Kgs 13:18). Many things happen "on the third day" (Hos 6:2). Jonah spent three days in the stomach of the fish (Mt 12:40), and the Lord rose again on the third day (1 Cor 15:4). David was offered a choice of divine punishments— three years, three months, three days (2 Sm 24:13). For the Christian, "three" takes on a far deeper significance as the number of Persons of the Trinity. The three Persons are clearly expressed, for instance, in the Great Commission (Mt 28:19) and in the Pauline benediction (2 Cor 13:13). Many echoes of this threefold expression are in the NT, and many anticipations of it in the OT, of which the thrice-repeated "Holy" in Isaiah 6:3 is the most famous.

Some scholars see four as another symbol of completeness (four winds of heaven, Dn 7:2; four horsemen, Rv 6:1-7; four living creatures around the throne of God, Rv 4:6). Five is certainly used in an indefinite sense as a small number (Is 19:18; 30:17). Nor do eight or nine seem to have any special significance, although, like other numbers, they may be used in a factual sense to describe any of God's activities (nine plagues on Egypt, Ex 7–10). "Ten" does have significance because of the Ten Commandments (Ex 20:1-17), but not any special symbolism earlier in the Bible. If anything, "ten" is elsewhere used in a vague way. Laban changes Jacob's wages ten times (Gn 31:7); Daniel and his friends are ten times better than all other students (Dn 1:20); ten times over, the Jewish settlers will be warned of impending enemy attacks (Neh 4:12).

Eleven appears to have no special biblical significance, but 12 certainly has. The clearest proof of this is the existence of the 12 tribes in Israel. In Revelation 7:4-8, where it is mathematically important that the number of tribes be limited to 12, the tribe of Dan is altogether omitted— probably on account of Dan's sin of idolatry (Jgs 18:14-20). Ishmael's descendants were also divided into 12 clans (Gn 17:20), so that the number 12 was apparently significant outside Israel as well. In the NT Christ chose 12 apostles (Mt 10:1-4). The link with the number of tribes is made specific when Christ tells the apostles that they will sit on 12 thrones, judging the 12 tribes (Mt 19:28). However, it is interesting that, after the election and appointment of Matthias (Acts 1:26), the Christian church apparently made no subsequent efforts to maintain the number of apostles. Like "seven times seven," "twelve times twelve" increases the force of the number. When this is further multiplied by a thousand, the figure becomes the 144,000 redeemed (Rv 7:4), who were sealed "out of all the tribes of Israel."

Exact Statistics As distinct from the metaphorical use of numbers to denote completion, immensity, and the like, numbers in Hebrew were often used to give exact tallies or measurements. Such usage is known to us only from clay tablets and ostraca (broken pieces of potsherd engraved in ink, used as rough notebooks). However, ascertaining exactly what the text was in its earliest form and what that text means is difficult.

An example is the number of the sons of Jeconiah among the inhabitants of Beth-shemesh. They were struck down by the Lord because of their failure to rejoice with the others when God's ark returned to Israel from the Philistine country (1 Sm 6:19). The Greek text (LXX) reads "seventy"; the later Hebrew manuscripts add "fifty thousand." But, as Beth-shemesh itself was only a small frontier town, and the "sons of Jeconiah" was presumably only one clan among several, the smaller number is obviously the original, and the large addition due to some later manuscript confusion.

A good rule in trying to decide whether a number is statistical or impressionistic is to determine whether it is a small number, or an unusual number for which there is no obvious theological explanation. When the men of Ai killed some 36 Israelites at the first assault on the city (Jos 7:5), the smallness of the number is evidence that this is a vividly remembered factual detail. Similarly, in the case of the number of Abraham's 318 men (Gn 14:14) or the catch of 153 fish after the resurrection (Jn 21:11), the numbers, though large, are not round numbers but unusual combinations, and are obviously meant in a literal or statistical sense. Irrelevant details like this have a habit of remaining in the memory, and are the best guarantee of the trustworthiness of the narrative.

Numerology Numerology may be said to be an extended application of the metaphorical significance of numbers (7, 40, etc.) already discussed. In the Bible, this systematization of numbers always goes with a strong sense of the sovereignty of God, his control over human history, and a belief in his ongoing purpose and its triumphant conclusion.

Perhaps the first clear instance of numerology in the Bible is 1 Kings 6:1, where Solomon began to build the temple 480 years after the exodus, a period 5 times 10 times 12, or 4 times 120, the ideal life span of man in early days (Gn 6:3). First Chronicles 6:3-8 gives 12 generations of men (presumably 40 years each) to cover the same period, so "twelve generations" is probably the real basis for the computation, rather than any exact year-by-year tally. A tally would have been impossible in the days of the judges and unlikely before the monarchy. David was the first to establish an official scribe or recorder to keep daily annals in Israel (2 Sm 8:16-17), as was common in the great kingdoms from far earlier times. Such Israelite annals are later mentioned as sources of the books of the kings (2 Kgs 14:18). The number 480 is probably a rough approximation rather than exact and denotes the end of one of God's epochs.

When Jeremiah prophesies an exile of 70 years for Judah (Jer 25:11; 29:10), it is not only a historical prediction that was literally fulfilled but also a symbol of completeness; Judah's punishment is complete (cf. Is 40:2). Isaiah (Is 23:15) had made a similar prophecy of a 70-year punishment for Tyre, and Ezekiel (Ez 29:11-13) prophesied a 40-year "exile" for Egypt. When these 70 years are regarded as sabbatical years, where the land must lie untilled to compensate for the 7 times 70 years of sin before, then true numerology begins (2 Chr 36:21). Here numerology is used only as an explanation of past and present, but it can also be used to explain the future, especially in the book of Daniel.

Daniel (Dn 9:2) refers to the literal 70 years of the exile as foretold by Jeremiah. In Daniel 9:24, this has been extended to 70 weeks of years (490 years) applied to the distant future. Daniel 9:25 sees 69 of these (483 years) as elapsing before Messiah appears. Presumably, the last week of the 70 is therefore thought of as the time of his activity. However this may be interpreted in terms of actual dates, it must be harmonized with 9:26, where the Messiah is "cut off" after 62 weeks of years (434 years). The difficulty lies in establishing the starting point for this long period. This is an example of an elaborate numerology, embracing centuries of history, all ultimately based on the 70 years of Jeremiah. According to biblical principles, this can have both an "immediate" fulfillment in the return from exile, and a "prophetic" fulfillment in the far distant future in connection with the coming of Christ.

The other major example of extended numerology in Daniel is in connection with the "time, times, and half a time" (7:25). This must stand for three and a half "times," that is, half of seven "times." Thus, it refers either to three and a half years (half a "week" of years) or three and a half "weeks" of years (cf. "seven times" in 4:16, where "seven years" is clearly meant). Whatever may be its ultimate prophetic fulfillment in Christ, the "initial" or "partial" fulfillment is the roughly three and a half years of bitter persecution of God's people by Antiochus Epiphanes (167–164 BC). This figure of three and a half years reappears in Revelation 11:2 ("forty-two months"), and 12:14 ("a time, and times, and half a time"), to describe the period of Rome's persecution of the Christian church. The figure had possibly become a symbol of any bitter but limited persecution. The "two thousand three hundred evenings and mornings" of Daniel 8:14 may mean 1,150 days, which is approximately the same length of time.

The three and a half years of Daniel 7:25 reappear in Revelation 11 in the form of "forty-two months," the time when the heathen will trample down Jerusalem (Rv 11:2). The 1,290 days of Daniel 12:11 reappear here (in the slightly different form of 1,260 days) as the time that God's two witnesses will prophesy (Rv 11:3). The 42 months reappear in Revelation 13:5 as the period that the wild beast will be allowed to blaspheme. While the "thousand years" of 20:6 is not derived from Daniel at all, the metaphorical use of "thousand" is familiar to the OT. The closest direct parallel is in Deuteronomy 7:9, where God's covenant will be kept with a "thousand generations" to come.

NUMBERS, Book of
Fourth book of the English Bible. Its title is the English translation of the Latin Vulgate title, *Numeri*. The book takes this name from the fact that several rosters of various kinds are recorded in the book, specifically, the two army musters in chapters 1 and 26, the tribal camp and march arrangements in chapter 2, and the Levitical censuses in chapters 3 and 4.

PREVIEW
•Author
•Background
•Purpose
•Content
•Theological Teaching

Author The question of the authorship of Numbers is part of the larger question of the authorship of the Pentateuch. Until the appearance of the higher-critical documentary theories of the 19th century, the Mosaic authorship of the Pentateuch was almost universally held by both Jews and Christians alike. This time-honored tradition is supported by the Pentateuch itself (e.g., Ex 17:14; 24:4; 34:27; Nm 33:2; Dt 31:9, 24), the rest of the OT (e.g., Jos 23:6; Jgs 3:4; Mal 4:4), as well as Jesus' teaching (e.g., Jn 5:46-47), and the rest of the NT (e.g., Acts 28:23; Rom 10:19; 1 Cor 9:9). Although discrepancies in the Pentateuch were widely and openly acknowledged, nevertheless Moses, the 15th-century BC lawgiver, was affirmed as the primary author of the Pentateuchal literature.

Background

Sinai Peninsula The historical background of Numbers begins primarily in the geographical region of the Sinai Peninsula of the mid-second millennium BC.

The Sinai Peninsula is in the shape of an inverted tri-

angle with the base on the north. It is approximately 240 miles (386.2 kilometers) long from north to south and 175 miles (281.6 kilometers) wide at the northern base, with an area of approximately 22,000 square miles (56,980 square kilometers). It is bounded on the north by the Mediterranean Sea and the southern border of Canaan, on the west by the Bitter Lakes and the Gulf of Suez, and on the east by the Arabah and the Gulf of Aqaba. Beginning in the north at the Mediterranean coast and moving south, for about 15 miles (24.1 kilometers) the soil is sandy. South of this coastal plain is a high plateau (Et-Tih) of gravel and limestone (about 2,500 feet, or 762 meters, above sea level), stretching south into the peninsula for approximately 150 miles (241.4 kilometers). Rising above the plateau at this point is a granite mountain formation with peaks up to 8,000 feet (2,438.4 meters) above sea level. In this mountainous region at the apex of the peninsular triangle, Jebel Musa (7,363 feet, or 2,244.2 meters, high), the traditional site where Israel camped before Mt Sinai and Moses received the law, rises above the plain.

The peninsula itself is comprised of five wilderness areas. In the north and immediately east of the land of Goshen is the approximately 40-mile- or 64.4-kilometer-wide wilderness of Shur, which runs past the River of Egypt (Wadi el-Arish) to the region of Kadesh-barnea and northeast to Beersheba. East of this region is the wilderness of Zin, extending east from the wilderness of Shur to the southern tip of the Dead Sea. Kadesh-barnea is located on its southern border (Nm 20:1; 33:36). South of the wilderness of Shur is the wilderness of Etham, and east of this wilderness in the east-central region of Sinai is the great wilderness of Paran (Dt 1:19). Kadesh-barnea is on the northern border of this territory (Nm 13:26). In this area the Israelites spent 38 of their 40 years of wandering. Southwest of the wilderness of Paran, on the western slopes of the peninsula, not far from the granite mountains standing in the southern apex of the triangle, is the wilderness of Sin.

While the region is generally desolate and barren, it is not impassable or incapable of sustaining travelers. Wells and springs dot both the western and eastern borders at reasonable distances from each other. The water table is fairly close to ground level, making the digging of wells possible (Nm 20:17; 21:16-18). The limestone rocks are also capable of holding great amounts of water (20:11). Vegetation is sparse except around the more permanent streams where vegetation and date palms flourish. The rainy season in winter is approximately 20 days. Quail (11:31-32) are known to migrate across the peninsula to Europe in the spring.

The Peoples Israel Confronted

➤AMALEKITES AND CANAANITES (14:25, 43-45; 24:20) The Amalekites were descendants of Amalek, son of Eliphaz and grandson of Esau (Gn 36:12, 16). They were generally a nomadic people. In the Sinai Peninsula they were the first to war against Israel at Rephidim (cf. Nm 24:20), perhaps the Wadi Refayid in southwest Sinai (Ex 17:8-16), before Israel reached Horeb. A year later, the Amalekites settled in the hills and valleys north of Kadesh-barnea. In league with the Canaanites, the inhabitants of Palestine, they blocked the effort of Israel to invade the land of promise from the south (Nm 14:45). Israel's will to wage war appears to have been completely broken for years to come.

➤EDOMITES (20:14-21; 21:4, 10-11) Edom, or Seir (24:18), is the territory south of the Dead Sea occupied by Esau's descendants. Stretching from its northern border at the

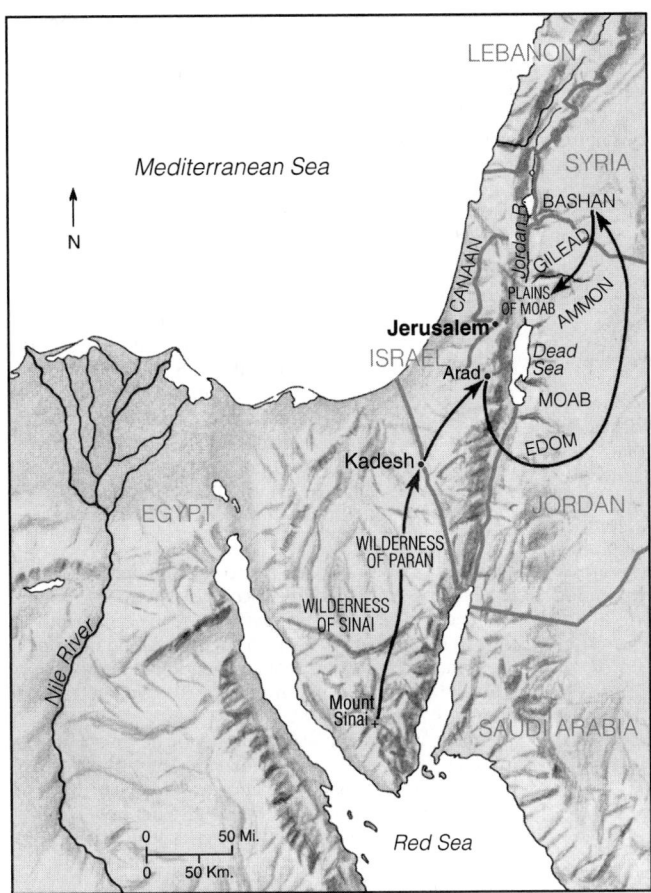

Modern names and boundaries are shown in gray.

Key Places in Numbers The book of Numbers begins at Mt Sinai and ends at the plains of Moab. From there, the Israelites entered the Promised Land.

Wadi Zered (21:12), which flowed into the Dead Sea at its southern tip, 100 miles (160.9 kilometers) south to the Gulf of Aqaba, it occupied both sides of the Arabah, with Kadesh-barnea again standing on the edge of its western border (20:16), giving it a land area of approximately 4,000 square miles (10,360 square kilometers). It is a rugged mountain region with peaks rising to 3,500 feet (1,066.8 meters). The "king's highway," an ancient trade route from Damascus through the Transjordan to the Gulf of Aqaba, passed through its territory and major cities, Bozrah and Leman. While Edom was not fertile, it did have cultivable areas (20:17-19).

During Israel's march to the Transjordan region, Edom refused to let Israel journey directly east from Kadesh through its territory but forced Israel to move southeast into and up the Arabah (21:4, 11). In spite of this hostility to God's people, Israel was forbidden to attack (Dt 2:2-8) or to hate the Edomites (23:7), and so Edom was spared from destruction during the conquest of the land. The area was later conquered by David (2 Sm 8:13-14) according to Balaam's prophecy (Nm 24:18).

➤ARAD (21:1-3) Arad was a south Canaanite settlement in the Negev. Its king, after fighting against Israel and taking some captives, was later defeated at Hormah.

➤MOABITES (21:11-15; 22:1–24:25) Moab, occupied by the descendants of Lot (Gn 19:37), is the territory east of

the Dead Sea lying primarily between the Wadi Arnon (Nm 21:13) and the Wadi Zered with a land area of approximately 1,400 square miles (3,626 square kilometers).

In the late middle Bronze Age, the Moabites had overflowed their main plateau and had extended well to the north of the Arnon all the way to the northern end of the Dead Sea (21:20). At the time of the events recorded in Numbers, however, the Amorites occupied the area from Arnon all the way north to the Wadi Jabbok (vv 13, 21-24), having earlier taken this land from Moab (vv 26-30). The Moabite kingdom was highly organized, with agriculture and livestock, splendid buildings, distinctive pottery, and strong fortifications around her borders. Its god was Chemosh (v 29).

Balak, king of Moab during the period of the conquest, in league with Midian, hired Balaam to curse Israel (chs 22–24). When this failed, the two heathen powers sought to neutralize Israel by luring the people of God into the worship of Chemosh and into idolatry (25:1-2). In the war that ensued, Israel defeated Midian (31:1-18), but by God's express command (Dt 2:9-13) spared Moab. But as Balaam had prophesied earlier (Nm 24:17), David in the 11th century warred against and defeated Moab (2 Sm 8:2, 13-14).

➤AMORITES (21:21-35) The Amorites, the people who had occupied northern Moabite territory (Nm 21:25-30), were descendants of Canaan (Gn 10:16) who had scattered throughout the hill country on both sides of the Jordan River. Heshbon was their capital city. Both Sihon of Heshbon and Og of Bashan were Amorite kings (Dt 3:8).

As for Bashan (Nm 21:33-35; cf. Dt 1:4; 3:1-12), it is the fertile grazing region (Nm 32:1-5) east of the Sea of Kinnereth (Galilee), whose northern border extended to Mt Hermon and whose southern border, while normally the river Yarmuk, in the Mosaic age was the Wadi Jabbok (Jos 12:4-5). Its land area covered approximately 5,000 square miles (12,950 square kilometers). Its major cities were Ashtaroth, Edrei, and Golan. After the conquest of the land, this territory fell to the half-tribe of Manasseh, with Gad occupying southern Gilead, and Reuben the region south to the Wadi Arnon.

➤MIDIANITES (25:16-18; 31:1-54) The Midianites, descendants of Abraham through the concubine Keturah (Gn 25:2), were desert dwellers in Transjordan from Moab to the region south of Edom. The elders of Moab and Midian cooperated in hiring Balaam to curse Israel (Nm 22:4-7). Later, when that effort proved fruitless, the Midianites, again with Moab, led Israel into idolatry and immorality (25:1-6, 14-15). Cozbi, the Midianite woman who was executed for her wickedness (25:8), was the daughter of Zur, one of the five Midianite kings confederate with the Amorite king Sihon (Jos 13:21) who were later killed in Israel's holy war against Midian (Nm 31:8). This war with Midian apparently broke the back of any remaining Amorite resistance, for Joshua 13:15-23 clearly intimates that as a result the tribe of Reuben occupied this territory.

Purpose Numbers serves a twofold purpose. First, as a historical book, it contains the account of Israel's fortunes from Mt Sinai to the plains of Moab on the eve of the conquest of Canaan—that almost-40-year period spent in the wilderness of Sinai and in Transjordan (1447–1407 BC). While recounting Israel's many failures and God's many faithful acts, it depicts Moses, Israel's leader, in all of his greatness and in all of his weakness. The two army rolls (chs 2 and 26) introduce the "acts" of the main drama of its history: the first in preparation for entering the land, which failed due to Israel's unbelief; the second, after the death of the entire generation that left Egypt, in preparation for the successful invasion of Canaan under Joshua's leadership.

Second, in line with Paul's general belief that "whatever was written in former days was written for our instruction, that by steadfastness and by the encouragement of the scriptures we might have hope" (Rom 15:4, RSV), and in keeping with his specific teaching that "these things [that befell Israel in the wilderness] happened to them as a warning, but they were written down for our instruction, upon whom the end of the ages has come" (1 Cor 10:11, RSV), Numbers serves a doctrinal, typical, and hortatory purpose (cf. v 12). Historical events are divinely invested with spiritual truths, thereby becoming object lessons for the Christian.

Content

Chapter 1 The Lord commanded Moses to register (Nm 1:18) the men able to go to war (vv 2-3). The total number of soldiers in Israel was 603,550 (v 46). The Levites were not numbered in this roll (vv 47-54), since they were to be set apart for special service pertaining to the tabernacle.

Chapter 2 The Lord instructed Moses concerning the arrangement of the tribes while encamped and on the march. With the tabernacle in the center of the camp, Judah, Issachar, and Zebulun, totaling 186,400 (v 9), were to camp on the east; Reuben, Simeon, and Gad, totaling 151,450 (v 16), were to camp on the south; Ephraim, Manasseh, and Benjamin, totaling 108,100 (v 24), were to camp on the west; and Dan, Asher, and Naphtali, totaling 157,600 (v 31), were to camp on the north.

On the march, Judah's east group (v 9) was to set out first, followed by Reuben's south group (v 16). The Levites with the tabernacle were to follow (v 17). Then Ephraim's west group (v 24) was to follow the Levites, with Dan's north group (v 31) bringing up the rear. This means that the Levites were flanked by two groups, before and behind.

Chapter 3 Aaron, the great-grandson of Levi through Kohath (Ex 6:16-20), and his descendants were designated to serve as priests at the tabernacle (Nm 3:2-3). The remaining descendants of Levi, from the families of Gershon, Kohath, and Merari, were to serve the Aaronic line at the tabernacle (vv 5-10). The Gershonites were responsible for the tabernacle coverings, hangings, and screens (vv 25-26); the Kohathites were responsible for the "furniture" in the tabernacle (v 31); and the Merarites were responsible for the frames, bars, and foundations for the tabernacle (vv 36-37).

God instructed Moses to number the three Levitical families. Gershon's descendants, totaling 7,500 (v 22), were to camp on the west, between the western group of tribes and the tabernacle. Kohath's descendants, totaling 8,600 (v 28), were to camp on the south, between the southern group of tribes and the tabernacle. Merari's descendants, totaling 6,200 (v 34), were to camp on the

north, between the northern group of tribes and the tabernacle. Moses and the Aaronic family were to camp on the east, between the eastern group of tribes and the tabernacle (v 38). Both in camp and on the march, then, the tabernacle was in the midst of Israel.

The census of Israel's firstborn males disclosed 273 more male babies than Levites (vv 40-46), and since the Levites were a ransom for Israelite males on a one-to-one basis, the 273 additional male children had to be ransomed by atonement money (vv 46-51).

Chapter 4 God instructed Moses that only Levites between the ages of 30 and 50 were to serve at the tabernacle. A census disclosed that there were 2,750 Kohathites (v 36), 2,630 Gershonites (v 40), and 3,200 Merarites (v 44), making a total of 8,580 (v 48) who were eligible to serve the Aaronic priests.

God further ordered the Aaronic priests, when the tabernacle was being dismantled for the march, to cover all the tabernacle "furniture" before the Kohathites even looked at them (v 20) lest the Kohathites, either looking at or touching them (v 15), should die (vv 15, 20).

Chapter 5 For ceremonial purposes, God demanded that lepers, those with a bodily discharge, and those who had touched the dead, must be put outside the camp until they were purified (vv 1-4). Furthermore, God instructed those making restitution for a wrongdoing, if the wronged person was no longer alive, to give the restitution price to a priest (vv 5-10).

Finally, if a woman was suspected by her husband of infidelity but there was no evidence of such, the woman was to undergo a trial by water ordeal to relieve the man of his suspicions. The priest was to give her holy water with dust from the floor of the tabernacle in it to drink. If she was guilty, the water by divine direction would cause her pain, make her abdomen swell, and her thigh waste away (vv 11-31).

Chapter 6 Laws pertaining to the Nazirite were given next. A Nazirite was a person who determined to take a vow to separate himself wholly to the Lord. To dramatize this separation, the Nazirite was to drink no intoxicating beverage, let the hair grow long, and touch no dead body (vv 3-6). Should he defile himself, he was to follow prescribed rules for ceremonial cleansing (vv 9-12). When his vow had run its course, he was to follow prescribed rules for terminating his vow (vv 13-21). Finally, God instructed the Aaronic priesthood concerning the blessing they were to pronounce upon the Israelite worshiper (vv 22-27).

Chapter 7 The leaders in Israel brought six wagons and twelve oxen for use in the transfer of the tabernacle (7:3). Moses gave two wagons and four oxen to the Gershonites (v 7), and four wagons and eight oxen to the Merarites (v 8). (The Kohathites were to carry the "furniture" of the tabernacle on their shoulders, v 9.) For twelve consecutive days, to consecrate the altar after it was anointed (vv 10, 88), the tribal leaders, in the order of march (cf. ch 2), brought similar offerings. God demonstrated his pleasure with this gesture by speaking to Moses from the mercy seat (v 89).

Chapter 8 God granted the prerogative to light the seven-branched lampstand to the Aaronic priests (vv 1-4). Following divine instructions, Moses and Aaron consecrated the Levites to the service of the tabernacle by means of a purification ceremony (vv 5-22).

Chapters 9:1–10:10 For the benefit of the worshiper who was ceremonially unclean or away on a journey at the time of the Passover, God granted permission to observe the Passover a month later (6-12; see also ch 27).

God gave final instructions to the people before their departure from Sinai. They were to prepare for marching when they saw the cloud ascending from the tabernacle, and they were to stop at the place where the cloud settled down (9:15-23). The people were to assemble at the tabernacle if two silver trumpets were blown; only the leaders were to come if one was blown; and at the blast of a military alarm, the several groups of tribes were to prepare for an immediate march (10:1-10).

Chapters 10:11-14:45 The next section recounts the march from Sinai to Kadesh-barnea, a period of time approximately one and a half to two months in length (cf. 10:11; 13:20). Almost immediately the people began to complain as they passed through the terrible wilderness of Paran (Dt 1:19), angering the Lord at Taberah (Nm 11:1-3) and at Kibroth-hattaavah (Nm 11:4-35; Pss 78:26-31; 106:13-15). Miriam and Aaron challenged Moses' sole right to speak for God to the people, which resulted in temporary leprosy as punishment for Miriam (doubtless the leader in the provocation). Through Moses' intercession, the two were forgiven (Nm 12). Out of this event, however, came the remarkable description of Moses' relationship to God as a unique means of revelation (vv 6-8).

From Paran (Kadesh-barnea) Moses dispatched the spies to survey the land (ch 13). Deuteronomy 1:22 suggests that the plan to spy out the land originated with the people, with Moses (at God's behest) acquiescing. At the end of 40 days, they returned. Only Caleb and Joshua urged the people to advance to the conquest; the other 10 spies spoke of foes too formidable for them to defeat. The people, greatly discouraged, attempted to stone Caleb and Joshua (Nm 14:10), and were prevented from doing so only by the sudden appearance of the glory cloud at the tabernacle. God swore in his wrath (Nm 14:21; cf. Heb 3:7-4:10) that, with the exception of Caleb and Joshua, none of that generation would enter the land of promise (Nm 14:21-35). He then struck down the 10 unbelieving spies (v 37). Presumptuously, and in spite of God's express command to the contrary (Dt 1:42), Israel attempted to advance on the land, leaving Moses and the ark of the covenant in the camp. They were challenged by the Amalekites and Canaanites.

Israel remained in this general area with tribal families fanning out over the wilderness and settling around springs and oases (Dt 1:46). Numbers 15:1-21:20 relates the account of the 38 years of wilderness wandering. Much of this time was probably spent around Kadesh-barnea (Dt 1:46).

Chapter 15 Further priestly legislation was given (Nm 15:1-21). Also, the procedure to be followed when an Israelite committed a sin deliberately and defiantly was spelled out in terms of excommunication: there was no atonement for such an attitude (vv 22-31). A Sabbath violator was executed (vv 32-36), perhaps as an illustration of the foregoing legislation. Finally, to assist them in obeying God's laws, the Israelites were instructed to tie blue tassels to their outer garments as reminders (vv 37-41).

Chapter 16 Korah challenged Aaron's high priesthood, and Dathan, Abiram, and On challenged Moses' leadership (vv 1-14). God, at Moses' word, opened up the earth and swallowed the offenders (Nm 16:32; cf. Dt 9:6; Ps 106:16-18). Korah is regarded in the NT (Jude 1:11) as a classic example of a rebellious malcontent.

Numbers 26:11 states that Korah's young children did not perish with him. Perhaps they became the ancestors of the "sons of Korah," the sacred musicians of the temple who composed 12 Korahite psalms (Pss 42-49, 84-85, 87-88).

Chapter 17 God then instructed the leaders of each tribe to bring rods, 12 in all, to write the names of the tribes upon them (with Aaron's name on Levi's rod), and to deposit them in the tabernacle. The following day, Aaron's rod had sprouted with blossoms and ripe almonds, thus vindicating Aaron's special high-priestly status.

Chapters 18-19 Further priestly legislation was given. In 18:1-7, the full responsibility for the priestly service was given to the Aaronic priests—a very natural consequence of the preceding chapter. The Levites were to assist the Aaronic order (v 6). Since the tribe of Levi received no land inheritance, they were to be supported from the offerings of the people (vv 8-20).

In 19:1-22 instructions concerning ceremonial impurity were given. When an Israelite became ceremonially unclean through contact with death (vv 11-16), God required that he be purified from his sin (vv 9, 17) by the sprinkling of specially prepared water upon him.

Chapter 20 With Israel once again at Kadesh on the southern border of the wilderness of Zin in the first month of the 40th year of wandering, Miriam died and was buried (v 1). According to the encampment list in chapter 33, 18 encampments may have occurred for Israel since the nation had last been at this site (cf. 33:18-36).

At this time the nation complained once again because there was little water (20:2). Moses, at God's instruction, brought forth water from a rock (vv 8-11), but because of a gross infraction by Moses and Aaron on this occasion, God announced that they would not be permitted to lead Israel in the conquest of the land (vv 12, 23-24).

The chapter closes with Edom refusing Israel passage across its territory (vv 14-21) and Aaron dying on Mt Hor on the border of Edom (vv 22-29) in the fifth month of the 40th year (33:38). Eleazar, Aaron's son, assumed the office of high priest.

Chapter 21 After a quick victory over Arad (vv 1-3), Israel started south to encircle Edom. Becoming impatient with God and with Moses, the people expressed their disgust with God's provision of manna. The Lord sent poisonous snakes to the camp, causing many to die. But at God's command Moses fashioned a snake out of bronze and placed it atop a standard. All who looked to the bronze snake survived (vv 4-10). The bronze snake was preserved and later was destroyed by Hezekiah, the symbol having become by his time an idol (2 Kgs 18:4). Later still, Jesus drew an analogy between these wicked sinners looking to the bronze snake and being delivered and men looking to him by faith and being saved (Jn 3:14-15).

Leaving that fateful place, Israel journeyed into and up the Arabah, crossed the Wadi Zered in an eastern swing around Moab, finally crossing the Arnon into Amorite territory. Journeying north, they camped at Pisgah (Nm 21:10-20).

At this point the conquest of the Transjordan begins. In quick succession Israel defeated Sihon of Heshbon (vv 21-31) and Og of Bashan (vv 33-35) and settled in the plains of Moab (22:1). This encampment was the scene for the remainder of the activities of Numbers, Deuteronomy, and Joshua 1-3. In a real sense, one can say the wilderness wanderings were now over.

Here is the place, then, to summarize the spiritual condition of Israel on the eve of the conquest of Canaan. Numbers makes it quite evident that the entire generation that left Egypt, with the exception of Joshua and Caleb, was to die in the wilderness because of its apostasy (cf. Am 5:25), unbelief, and general failure to keep covenant with God. None of the generation of male children born in the wilderness had been circumcised (Jos 5:2-9). Psalm 90 underscores Israel as the recipient of God's wrath in the wilderness. It is in this pitiable spiritual condition that Israel arrived on the plains of Moab.

Chapters 22–24 Balak, king of Moab, frightened by Israel's presence, joined with Midian to hire Balaam, the false prophet, to curse Israel. For gain, Balaam agreed (2 Pt 2:15; Jude 1:11), but God prevented him, causing him rather to bless Israel in his four oracular utterances (Nm 23:7-10, 18-24; 24:3-9, 15-19) and to predict the destruction of Moab, Edom, Amalek (24:20), the Kenites (24:21), and Asshur (24:24). With that, Balak and Balaam separated. Balaam, in collusion with Midian, agreed to counsel Israel to commit idolatry and immorality (31:16). And so, where Balak failed to turn the Lord against Israel, Balaam succeeded (ch 25).

Chapter 25 Israel sinned against God by idolatrous and immoral acts with the people of Moab (vv 1-3). In carrying out the command of God to destroy the reprobate Israelites, Phinehas killed Zimri and Cozbi, the latter being a daughter of one of the five kings of Midian (vv 4-14). This event provided the occasion for God to declare a holy war against Midian (vv 16-18; cf. ch 31).

Chapter 26 The Lord commanded Moses to take a roll of the men of the second generation who were capable of warring against Israel's enemies. The total number came to 601,730 (v 51), a reduction of 1,820 men from the first count. With a smaller force than the first generation, Israel conquered Canaan, clearly indicating that Israel could have spared itself the years of wandering if only the nation had obeyed God 38 years before Kadesh. The Levites totaled 23,000 males a month old and upward (vv 57-62).

Chapter 27 At the request of the daughters of Zelophehad (cf. 26:33) that they be granted the right to inherit their father's possessions since he had no sons, the Lord agreed that they could, using the occasion to give further laws of inheritance (vv 1-11).

Reminded that he would soon die in Abarim, Moses requested that God appoint his successor. God selected Joshua, and Moses commissioned him (vv 12-23).

Chapters 28–30 Further priestly legislation regarding offerings for various occasions was given. God also instructed Moses to inform the people concerning vows. When a man made a vow, it was inviolable (30:2), but if a woman made a vow, the man (father, husband) responsible for her could nullify it if he felt that it was rash (vv 1-16).

Chapter 31 The account of the holy war declared against Midian in 25:16-18 is given. With Phinehas accompanying 12,000 warriors, Israel defeated Midian, killing Balaam along with the five kings and many male adults of Midian (31:1-8). The Midianite women and children were taken captive, but Moses commanded that all the male children and the nonvirgin women be killed (vv 9-18). One must not conclude that this war meant the end of Midian as such, for Midian later proved a formidable foe of Israel in the time of the judges (Jgs 6).

After the battle, the warriors were instructed to purify themselves, their clothing, and the booty from the war before coming into the camp (Nm 31:19-24). Furthermore, they were instructed to divide the booty in half and to contribute one-fifth of one percent of their half to the high priest ("the Lord's tribute"). The other half was divided among the people who had remained in camp, after the Levites received a two percent contribution (vv 25-31).

Verses 32-47 give the tally of the booty after its division into two parts and the amount that was given from each part to Eleazar and the Levites. The tally is said by some to be too high to be authentic, but there is no evidence that disputes the recorded figures.

In thanksgiving to God because no Israelite had been killed in the war (v 49) and to make atonement for themselves (v 50), the army officers brought a special offering of gold trinkets to Moses and Eleazar, which was placed in the tabernacle as a memorial (vv 48-54).

Chapter 32 At their request and on the condition that they aid the other tribes in the conquest of Canaan, Reuben, Gad, and the half-tribe of Manasseh were allotted the Transjordan region. Moses earnestly besought the Lord to change his mind about not permitting him to enter the land of promise (Dt 3:23-27). But God would not let him.

Chapters 33–34 At God's command, Moses kept a written record of Israel's itinerary from Egypt to the plains of Moab. Here is biblical evidence of the Mosaic authorship of Numbers.

The boundaries of the Promised Land were now given. The southern boundary would run from the southern tip of the Dead Sea, south of Kadesh-barnea up to the River of Egypt (Wadi el-Arish), and on to the Mediterranean Sea (34:3-5). The western boundary would be the coastline of the Mediterranean Sea itself (v 6). The northern boundary, not realized until the times of David and Solomon (2 Sm 8:3-12; 1 Kgs 8:65), was to extend from the Mediterranean Sea east to Hamath, at the head of the Orontes River (Nm 34:7-9). The eastern boundary was to be practically on a vertical line, with the Jordan Valley running north to the northern boundary (vv 10-12). The nine and a half tribes were to divide this area among themselves (vv 13-15).

The Lord then selected the men who were to bear the responsibility of dividing the land of Canaan among the western tribes after the conquest (vv 16-29).

Chapter 35 God instructed Israel to give 48 cities throughout the land on both sides of the Jordan to the Levites for a permanent possession (vv 1-8), since that tribe was not included in the land allotments to the other tribes. The number of cities each tribe was to give was to be determined by its size (v 8). Six of the Levitical cities, three on each side of the Jordan, were to be designated "cities of refuge" for the manslayer (v 6; cf. Jos 20).

Legislation concerning the manslayer follows (vv 9-34). If the slayer committed murder, the kinsman avenger had the right to fulfill his role as executioner (vv 16-21). If, however, the killing was unintentional, the manslayer was to flee to the nearest city of refuge for a trial. If found innocent of murder, he was assigned to remain within the city of refuge until the death of the high priest. If he left the city before then, the kinsman avenger was permitted to execute him (vv 22-34).

Chapter 36 Basing their question on the earlier law established in chapter 27, the leaders from Manasseh asked whether an heiress should be allowed to marry outside her tribe, with the accompanying transfer of property from one tribe to another that would ensue. God directed that an heiress would have to marry within her tribe (vv 1-12).

The last verse of the book refers to all the laws given in the plains of Moab (26:1–36:12; cf. Lv 27:34).

Theological Teaching In the book of Numbers God is revealed as the unchangingly faithful God of the covenant (Nm 23:19). This faithfulness to his covenant required that he both guide and care for his people and punish their sins against him. But no impediment was so great that God's design to bring his people to the land of promise was thwarted (11:23).

Both by his wrathful reaction to Israel's sin and by the numerous priestly laws, God highlights his awesome holiness. The legislation expressly teaches that the person who approaches God must be clean. Even to look with unholy eyes upon the holiness of God meant death (4:20).

His sovereignty over all of life is evident from the attention he displays over even the minutest aspects of life. The phrase "And the Lord said unto Moses" occurs over 50 times, and the words that follow in each case deal with all kinds of matters.

As the God of the covenant, God's "christological" character is also apparent. God's blessing and faithfulness reflect the christological motif. Finally, Moses' prophetic leadership (Acts 7:37-38) and intercessory ministry (e.g., Nm 11:2; 12:13; 14:19), in the Aaronic priesthood (e.g., ch 16), in the animal sacrifices (cf. 19:9; Heb 9:13), and in the symbols (the manna, the water, the bronze snake) foreshadow the future Christ.

In Israel's responses to God, the people depict all of human sinfulness and faithlessness. Israel's wanderings illustrate the results of unbelief. The punishments of Israel prove the maxim of Numbers 32:23: "But if you fail to keep your word, then you will have sinned against the LORD, and you may be sure that your sin will find you out" (NLT). Numbers forcefully teaches that safety and blessing are to be found only in trust in the Lord. Only he is capable of bringing men and women to the place of rest (Heb 4:9).

See also Deuteronomy, Book of; Exodus, Book of; Genesis, Book of; Leviticus, Book of; Moses; Wilderness Wanderings.

NUMENIUS Son of Antiochus, a Jewish diplomat sent first by Jonathan, and later by Simon the Hasmonean to Rome and Sparta to strengthen alliances. Numenius and Antipater, son of Jason, were warmly received in Sparta, and according to Josephus, a friendly alliance with the Jews was decreed (*Antiquities* 13:169-170). The writer of Maccabees said, "What they said we have recorded in our public decrees, as follows, 'Numenius the son of Antiochus and Antipater the son of Jason, envoys of the Jews, have come to us to renew their friendship with us. It has pleased our people to receive these men with honor and to put a copy of their words in the public archives, so that the people of the Spartans may have a record of them. And they have sent a copy of this to Simon the high priest' " (1 Macc 14:22-23, RSV). Since Jonathan probably died during the mission, the correspondence from Sparta was went to Simon, his successor (1 Macc 14:20 ff.). Simon sent Numenius to Rome in 141 BC with a special gift, a gold shield weighing 1,000 pounds (453.6 kilograms) in honor of the new pact. When Numenius returned two years later, he brought with him copies of Lucius's letters to the surrounding states, in which the Roman council declared friendship for the Jews and forbade the surrounding nations to hurt the Jewish people: "We

therefore have decided to write to the kings and countries that they should not seek their harm or make war against them and their cities and their country, or make alliance with those who war against them" (1 Macc 15:19, RSV). Moreover, the rulers of the surrounding nations were requested to hand over any traitors who had left Judah to seek asylum in another country. The traitors were to be punished in accordance with the Jewish laws. According to Josephus, Numenius made another journey to Rome to strengthen the diplomatic ties during the priesthood of Hyrcanus II.

NUN Ephraimite, Elishama's son, and the father of Joshua, the great leader of Israel (Ex 33:11; Nm 11:28; Dt 1:38; Jos 1:1; Jgs 2:8).

NURSE A woman who took care of an infant that did not belong to her, or a man who took care of young children. The work was limited to the nursing and caring of an infant. Women usually took care of their own children, such as Sarah (Gn 21:7) and Hannah (1 Sm 1:23). A wet nurse often became a part of the family circle and had a special place. Rebekah had a nurse, and when she passed away, the woman was even mentioned in the biblical text: "Now Deborah, Rebekah's nurse, died and was buried under the oak below Bethel. So it was named Allon Bacuth" (Gn 35:8, NIV). Moses' mother became his nurse, as she was being paid by Pharaoh's daughter (Ex 2:7). Royal sons were cared for by nurses, as in the case of Joash, who was hidden with his nurse by Jehosheba his aunt (2 Kgs 11:2). Since Joash was hidden for six years and was seven when he acceded to the throne, Joash was about a year old when he was hidden—and his nurse must have been a wet nurse.

Royal sons received special care and were under the supervision of a nurse after they had been suckled. Children were nursed up to the age of three, and when they were weaned, there was a feast (Gn 21:8; 1 Sm 1:23-24). Thereafter, a nurse-teacher took charge of the youngster. Mephibosheth was five years old when his nurse fell with him, causing him to be lame (2 Sm 4:4). Naomi took care of her grandson as a nurse (Ru 4:16). It is probable that male nurses were used as teachers for the young aristocrats, such as we find in 2 Kings 10:1, when it is said that Ahab's children had tutors (cf. also v 5). In this sense we must understand Moses' reference to himself, too, as a "nurse": "Did I conceive all these people? Did I give them birth? Why do you tell me to carry them in my arms, as a nurse carries an infant, to the land you promised on oath to their forefathers?" (Nm 11:12, NIV). Paul saw himself, too, as a "nurse" to the church (1 Thes 2:7).

NURTURE* KJV rendition of a Greek word (*paideia*, Eph 6:4) better translated as "discipline." *See* Discipline.

NUT *See* Food and Food Preparation; Plants (Almond; Pistachio).

NUZI*, NUZI TABLETS* Town in northeastern Mesopotamia, about nine miles (14.5 kilometers) southwest of present-day Kirkuk. In ancient times the site was called Gasur, but the modern name is Yorgan Tepe. Excavations at Yorgan Tepe were carried out from 1925 to 1931 by an expedition of a number of cooperating archaeologists who made many interesting finds. But Yorgan Tepe is best known for its clay tablets, which primarily deal with business transactions.

In the third millennium BC the population of Gasur was largely Semitic, but by the middle of the second millennium, the inhabitants were Hurrians, and the name of the city had been changed from Gasur to Nuzi. The Hurrians are identified as the Horites of the Bible (cf. Gn 14:6; 36:20-21; Dt 2:12, 22).

Many clay tablets of the third millennium BC were unearthed, including one tablet inscribed with a map regarded as the oldest map in the world. The records also show that installment buying was practiced even then.

In the 15th to 14th centuries BC, Hurrian scribes wrote on thousands of clay tablets, mostly in the Babylonian language. These records provide much information about Near Eastern customs and legal practices, and shed light on the patriarchal period of the Bible.

The following examples may serve as illustrations of possible relationships between Nuzi and the Bible. In Nuzi a childless wife could give her handmaid to her husband so that the maid could bear children in the name of the wife. This practice was followed by Sarai, who gave her maid, Hagar, to her husband, Abram (Gn 16:1-4); by Rachel, who gave Bilhah to Jacob (30:1-8); and by Leah, who gave Zilpah to Jacob (vv 9-13). In such a case, the father had a responsibility to rear the child as the offspring of his legal wife, and the wife could not drive away the child. According to this rule, Sarai had no right to drive out Hagar's son, Ishmael (cf. 16:4-6).

In Nuzi there was a law against the sale of property outside one's own family. Several schemes were employed to circumvent this prohibition, including adoption and the exchange of property. In return for a guarantee of lifelong care and burial costs, a wealthy landowner would have himself "adopted" by land-holding peasants so that he received their property. The records indicate that the very same man could be adopted by 300 or 400 peasants. A couple without children could legally adopt someone to provide for them in their old age and for their burial. The adopted person would be the heir to the property of his adopting parents; this may have been the relationship between Abram and his servant Eliezer (Gn 15:2). One could also exchange property of little value for valuable property. In some instances, the difference in value could be made up in money. At Nuzi a man named Tehip-tilla sold his inheritance rights in a grove to his brother, Kurpazah, in exchange for three sheep, paralleling Esau's sale of his birthright to Jacob for a serving of stew (25:27-34).

In Nuzi an oral will or blessing given on one's death-bed was legally binding and irrevocable. A man named Huya was lying on his sickbed at the point of death. He took the hand of his son, Tarmiya, and gave to him a woman, Sululi-Ishtar, to be his wife. Tarmiya's two brothers challenged his claim in court, but the court recognized the validity of Tarmiya's case. Although Jacob obtained the blessing of his blind and aged father by deception, Isaac had to stand by what he had done (Gn 27:33).

The Nuzi tablets also indicate that the person who had possession of the teraphim, or household gods, was the heir to the property of the owner of the idols. For this reason, Rachel took the teraphim of her father Laban (Gn 31:19), who was very disturbed over their disappearance (vv 30-35).

Another case of adoption parallels the relationship between Jacob and Laban. Nashwi adopted Wullu and gave his daughter, Nuhuya, to him in marriage. If Wullu married another wife, he would have to forfeit the property he had received from Nashwi. Laban also made a covenant with Jacob that he would not take a wife other than Laban's two daughters, Leah and Rachel (Gn 31:50).

See also Inscriptions.

NYMPHA Christian woman living in Laodicea (or perhaps Colossae), in whose house believers gathered for worship. Paul sent greetings to her and the church (Col 4:15, KJV uses the masculine form "Nymphas").

OAK *See* Plants.

OAK, Diviners' Tree near Shechem (Jgs 9:37). *See* Diviners' Oak.

OAK OF MEONENIM* Tree near Shechem (Jgs 9:37, ASV). *See* Diviners' Oak.

OAK OF THE PILLAR Sacred meeting place in Shechem where the citizens of that city and the inhabitants of Beth-millo made Abimelech king (Jgs 9:6, ASV, NAS). It is perhaps identifiable with the Oak of Moreh. *See* Moreh, Oak of; Plain of the Pillar.

OAK OF WEEPING Tree near Bethel under which Deborah, Rebekah's nurse, was buried (Gn 35:8), hence called *Allon-bacuth,* meaning "Oak of Weeping."

OAK OF ZAANANNIM Site regarded as a border point in the territory of Naphtali (Jos 19:33; Jgs 4:11). *See* Zaanannim.

OAKS OF MAMRE* Site associated with Abraham and Isaac (Gn 13:18). *See* Mamre (Place).

OATH Solemn vow or promise to fulfill a pledge. There are two terms in Hebrew that mean "oath": *'ala* and *sebu'a.* The latter, more general term in ancient times meant to enter into a solemn (even magical) relationship with the number seven, although ancient connections are lost. Even so, when Abraham and Abimelech entered into an oath at Beersheba (the well of seven, or the well of the oath), Abraham set aside seven ewe lambs as a witness to the fact that he had dug a well (Gn 21:22-31). The former term *'ala,* often translated "oath," properly means "curse." At times the two terms are used together (Nm 5:21; Neh 10:29; Dn 9:11). Any breach of one's undertaking affirmed by an oath would be attended by a curse. The Lord affirmed that he had established a covenant and a curse with Israel—that is, a breach of covenant would be followed by a curse (Dt 29:14ff.).

An oath was taken to confirm an agreement or, in a political situation, to confirm a treaty. Both in Israel and among its neighbors, God (or the gods) would act as the guarantor(s) of the agreement and his name (or their names) was invoked for this purpose. When Jacob and Laban made an agreement, they erected a heap of stones as a witness (Gn 31:53). If either party transgressed the terms, it was a heinous sin. For this reason one of the Ten Commandments dealt with empty affirmations: "Do not misuse the name of the LORD your God. The LORD will not let you go unpunished if you misuse his name" (Ex 20:7, NLT). The people of Israel were forbidden to swear their oaths by false gods (Jer 12:16; Am 8:14). To breach an international treaty, where the oath was taken in the Lord's name, merited death (Ez 17:16-17). It was one of the complaints of Hosea that the people of his day swore falsely when they made a covenant (Hos 10:4). Judgment would attend such wanton disregard of the solemnity of an oath. Certain civil situations in Israel called for an oath (Ex 22:10-11; Lv 5:1; 6:3; Nm 5:11-28). This practice provided a pattern for the Israelite covenantal oath of allegiance between God and his people.

Christ taught that oaths were binding (Mt 5:33). In the kingdom of God oaths would become unnecessary (vv 34-37). At his trial before Caiaphas, Jesus heard an imprecatory oath from the high priest (26:63-65), and Paul swore by an oath on occasion (2 Cor 1:23; Gal 1:20). God himself was bound by his own oath (Heb 6:13-18) to keep his promise to the patriarchs (Gn 50:24; Pss 89:19-37, 49; 110:1-4).

See also Covenant; Vows.

OBADIAH (Person)

1. Governor of Ahab's house (1 Kgs 18:3-16). Elijah met him after the years of drought, and requested Obadiah to bring Ahab to him, while both Ahab and Obadiah were looking for water and grass (v 5). Obadiah was an important officer in charge of Ahab's house. Unlike his master, Obadiah was faithful to the Lord, as he hid 100 prophets in caves and provided them with food and drink.
2. Descendant of David (1 Chr 3:21).
3. Descendant of Izrahiah from Issachar's tribe (1 Chr 7:3).
4. Azel's son and a descendant of King Saul from Benjamin's tribe (1 Chr 8:38; 9:44).
5. Son of Shemaiah, who was among the first Levites returning from exile to Jerusalem. He lived in one of the villages of the Netophathites (1 Chr 9:16). He is called Abda in Nehemiah 11:17. *See* Abda #2.
6. Gadite who joined David at his stronghold in the wilderness. He was a mighty warrior, able to handle shield and spear, and was extremely fast (1 Chr 12:8-9).
7. Father of Ishmaiah, commander over the forces of Zebulun (1 Chr 27:19).
8. Prince of Judah in Jehoshaphat's time (2 Chr 17:7). He joined four other officers and the Levites in teaching the law throughout the cities of Judah.
9. Levite overseer in Josiah's time (2 Chr 34:12), in charge of the repair of the temple.
10. Son of Jehiel (Ezr 8:9), who joined Ezra in his journey from Babylon to Jerusalem, leading 218 men with him.
11. Priest who signed Ezra's covenant (Neh 10:5).
12. Gatekeeper and Levite charged with the oversight of the storehouses by the gates in the days of Joiakim, son of Jeshua (Neh 12:25-26).
13. Prophet who prophesied against Edom, which had rejoiced at the Babylonian victories in Jerusalem in 597 BC. Obadiah described the behavior of the Edomites (Ob 1:11-14) in his prophecy, the shortest book in the OT, and predicted God's judgment on Edom (vv 2-10, 15).

See also Obadiah, Book of; Prophet, Prophetess.

OBADIAH, Book of Fourth book of the Minor Prophets; shortest book in the OT.

PREVIEW
• Author
• Background
• Content
• Theological Significance

Author Practically nothing is known about Obadiah the prophet. Not even the name of his father or his home region is given in the superscription (Ob 1:1).

Background It would seem likely that Obadiah came from Judah, because he expresses deep concern over the inroads made into his land by the Edomites in the day of Judah's destruction (v 12). He probably had his vision concerning Edom (v 1) shortly before the fall of Jerusalem and the devastation of Judah by Nebuchadnezzar in 586 BC. Nebuchadnezzar may have invaded Edom in 582 BC, although no certain reference to such an invasion exists. The Babylonian king Nabonidus stayed at Teima for several years, and the town of Tell el Kheleifeh near the Gulf of Aqaba flourished early in the century. However, Edom entered a period of decline in the sixth century BC, due to interference from its trading partners from Arabia and the south, such as Teima and Dedan.

Content Edom's fall is announced by the prophet (vv 1-4). Evidently, a coalition of neighboring Arab tribes was conspiring to attack Edom, which added weight to his message (v 1). Little did these tribes know that their planned assault on Edom was part of the divine plan.

Edom's destruction is declared (vv 2-9) and its actual downfall is described (vv 2-4). Edom, apparently strong and safe in the rocky bastion in the high mountains (v 3), would be brought low (v 4). Edom's overthrow would be complete (vv 5-6). As thieves and marauders ravage a place by night, so Edom would be stripped, its houses and vineyards plundered. Edom would know no merciful alleviation as sometimes happens when robbers raid a house. Even allies would prove treacherous (v 7), confederates would deceive, and guests would set snares. Taken by surprise, Edom would fall an easy prey. When the day of Edom's doom came, the wise would be destroyed (v 8) and soldiers demoralized and slaughtered (v 9).

Edom's wrongdoing is spelled out (vv 10-15). Edom showed ill will toward Judah on the day when the Babylonians attacked. Rather than helping Judah, Edom stood aloof and behaved like one of Judah's foes. To make matters worse, Edom gloated over Judah's misfortune, jeered at the people, and laid hands on their property. Edom collaborated with Babylon, cutting off Judah's refugees from escape and handing them over to Judah's enemies. Such deeds would return to Edom.

On the Day of the Lord (vv 15-21), guilty Edom would be caught up in the wider scale of God's judgment on all nations. Beyond the day of disaster endured by Jerusalem in 586 BC stood another day, a day of vindication and judgment in Israel's favor.

Positively, the remnant of Judah (vv 17, 21) would be preserved; the sacred site, Mt Zion, would be rehabilitated; and the Edomites would come under the control of the remnant of Israel. Like a fire, Israel would consume the stubble of Edom (v 18) and regain lost territories (vv 19-20).

Theological Significance Theologically, the prophecy stresses divine sovereignty in the midst of the cruel invasion of Judah's restricted sovereignty. The Lord of history works out his purposes in the midst of past and present events. In the future, he would execute judgment on Israel's foes. Zion would be reestablished as the proud capital of a glorious nation, freed from pagan defilement forever.

See also Israel, History of; Prophecy; Prophet, Prophetess.

OBAL Alternate spelling of Ebal, Joktan's descendant, in Genesis 10:28. *See* Ebal #2.

OBED
1. Ruth and Boaz's first child, listed among the ancestors of Jesus (Ru 4:17, 21-22; 1 Chr 2:12; Mt 1:5; Lk 3:32). *See* Genealogy of Jesus Christ.
2. Jerahmeelite and Ephlal's son (1 Chr 2:37-38).
3. One of David's mighty men (1 Chr 11:47).
4. Shemaiah's son and an able leader who ruled his father's house (1 Chr 26:6-7).
5. Father of Azariah, a captain of Jehoiada (2 Chr 23:1).

OBED-EDOM
1. Man under whose care David placed the ark of the covenant when he was transferring it from Gibeah to Jerusalem (2 Sm 6:10-12; 1 Chr 13:5-14). He is called a Gittite, which indicates that his birthplace was Gath. This was not the Philistine city of Gath but the Levitical town in the territory of Dan known as Gath-rimmon (Jos 19:45). It is likely that Obed-edom was a Levite and therefore qualified to care for the ark of the covenant. Uzzah's rash action in steadying the ark when the oxen stumbled brought upon him immediate death. David's consternation and fear at this turn of events led him to reconsider his intention of bringing the ark to Jerusalem. Apparently Obed-edom's home was nearby and it was convenient to leave the ark in his care. When David was informed after three months that the Lord had greatly blessed Obed-edom, he realized that the judgment that fell on Uzzah was incurred because the ark was carried contrary to the method prescribed in the Law (Nm 4:15; 7:9) and not because the Lord was angry with Uzzah. He ordered that the ark be taken from Obed-edom's home and carried to Jerusalem in the proper manner (1 Chr 15:25-28). Apparently Obed-edom was rewarded for his faithful service by being appointed a gatekeeper for the ark in Jerusalem (15:24; 26:4, 8, 15). But some scholars believe that Obed-edom the gatekeeper was a man other than the one referred to above.
2. Levitical musician who ministered before the ark (1 Chr 15:21; 16:5, 38). He was the son of Jeduthun, one of David's chief singers. Some scholars think that the musician and singer were different men.
3. Levitical guardian of the sacred vessels of the temple taken hostage by Joash (2 Chr 25:24).

OBEDIENCE Act or instance of submitting to the restraint or command of an authority; compliance with the demands or requests of someone over us. The general words for obedience in both Hebrew and Greek refer to hearing or hearkening to a superior authority. Another major Greek word includes the idea of submission to authority in the sense of arranging or ordering oneself under someone in a place of command. A third Greek word suggests obedience that is a result more of persuasion than of submission.

Obedience to God and human authorities is an obligation stressed in both the OT and NT. Abraham was additionally blessed on one occasion because he obeyed God in offering Isaac on the altar (Gn 22:18; cf. 26:5). God's continued blessing upon Israel by virtue of the Sinai covenant was contingent upon their obeying his voice and keeping his covenant (Ex 19:5). On the verge of entering Canaan, Moses placed before Israel a blessing and a curse—the former if they listened to and obeyed the commandments of the Lord, and the latter if they did not (Dt 11:22-28).

Deuteronomy warns that the penalty for stubborn and rebellious children is, first of all, chastisement, and then death by stoning if they persistently refuse to listen (Dt 21:18-21).

One evidence that a person is a child of God is continued obedience to the commandments of God (1 Jn 2:3-5). Jesus said that those who love him would keep his commandments (Jn 14:15). And Peter, speaking of Christians, calls them "obedient children" (1 Pt 1:14; see also Heb 5:9; 11:8).

Christians are to render obedience to a variety of people: believers to the Lord (Jn 14:21-24; 15:10), wives to their husbands (Eph 5:22-24; Col 3:18; Ti 2:5; 1 Pt 3:1, 5), children to their parents (Eph 6:1; Col 3:20), citizens to their governmental officials (Rom 13:1-7; Ti 3:1; 1 Pt 2:13-14), and servants to their masters (Eph 6:5; Col 3:22; Ti 2:9; 1 Pt 2:18).

However, in spite of the strong stress on obedience in the Bible, such obedience is never made the grounds for justification before God. Paul declares that salvation is a gift of God that will produce good works (Eph 2:8-10). So, too, James speaks of works of obedience as flowing from faith (Jas 2:14-26).

Jesus himself, on the night of his betrayal, emphasized by repetition that love for him is measured by obedience to his commandments (Jn 14:15, 21, 23-24; 15:10). He underscored this by asserting that his own love for the Father was evidenced by his obeying the Father's commands (14:31). The Bible mentions many people whose obedience to God comes from their faith and love for him (Heb 11). For example, Abel believed God and offered a more excellent sacrifice (v 4); Noah put his faith in God's word and prepared an ark (v 7); by faith Abraham left Ur at God's direction, not knowing his destination (v 8); Moses put his faith in God and refused the privileges of being called Pharaoh's son, choosing rather to identify with Israel, God's people (vv 24-25). The greatest example of obedience based on trust in God is Jesus Christ himself. He emptied himself, taking the form of a bond servant; he humbled himself and became obedient to death, even death on a cross (Phil 2:7-8).

OBIL Ishmaelite steward of King David's camels (1 Chr 27:30).

OBLATION* *See* Offerings and Sacrifices.

OBOTH Temporary camping place of the Israelites during their wilderness wanderings, mentioned between Punon and Iye-abarim (Nm 21:10-11; 33:43-44). Although its exact location is uncertain, some have attempted to identify it with 'Ain el-Weiba, 33 miles (53.1 kilometers) south of the Dead Sea in the Arabah Valley. *See* Wilderness Wanderings.

OCHRAN* *See* Ocran.

OCINA A town on the coast south of Tyre (Jdt 2:28). Its location is uncertain, and it has been identified with both Sandaliam and Acco.

OCRAN Father of Pagiel, the leader of Asher's tribe during the wilderness journeys (Nm 1:13; 2:27; 7:72, 77; 10:26).

OFFEND, OFFENSE Words used two ways in the Bible: doing what is wrong oneself, or causing someone else to do wrong or to stumble.

Doing Wrong In both the Hebrew of the OT and the Greek of the NT there are several words for sin or wrongdoing having a variety of different translations. With the word "offend" or "offense," the emphasis is on the sin being against a person or against the law, an offense against either God or man.

Sin is fundamentally an offense against God. For example, the people of Edom had grievously offended in taking vengeance on Judah, and so the hand of the Lord was against them in judgment (Ez 25:12-13). Israel commited an offense in their worship of Baal (Hos 13:1). The breaking of God's law is spoken of as an "offense committed" (Dt 19:15; cf. 22:26; 25:2). In the NT, James (Jas 2:10; 3:2) speaks of offenses against God and against his law.

There are many passages in the Bible addressing one man's offense against another: for example, Abraham's against Abimelech (Gn 20:9), or Pharaoh's chief butler and chief baker against their master (40:1). Sometimes it is an alleged offense and no actual wrong has been done (e.g., Gn 31:36; 2 Kgs 18:14; Jer 37:18). Paul, in his defense before the Roman governor Festus, said, "Neither against the law of the Jews, nor against the temple, nor against Caesar have I offended at all" (Acts 25:8, RSV).

Finally, the Bible speaks about dealing with real offenses against God and people. Offenses should be acknowledged and confessed (Hos 5:15). One's proper resolution before God is "I will not offend any more" (Jb 34:31, RSV). One needs to make amends for offenses (Eccl 10:4) and to forgive the offenses of others (Prv 17:9; 19:11). Jesus Christ died for our offenses (Rom 4:25; 5:15-21), so that in turning to him there is forgiveness for all sins.

Causing Another to Sin The noun "offense" and the verb "offend" are also used in reference to a person being caused to stumble or to do what is wrong. There are three ways in which this may happen:

1. There may be something in the individual that causes him or her to stumble. Jesus expressed the seriousness of this, and though speaking metaphorically, he indicated the strenuous steps of prevention (Mt 5:29-30; 18:8-9).

2. There may be something in a person that causes offense to others. Jesus said, "Woe unto the world because of offences! for it must needs be that offences come; but woe to that man by whom the offence cometh!" (Mt 18:7, KJV). There are, in fact, many NT passages that insist that one should live so as not to cause others to stumble (Rom 14:13). The apostle Paul says, "Don't tear apart the work of God over what you eat. Remember, there is nothing wrong with these things in themselves. But it is wrong to eat anything if it makes another person stumble. Don't eat meat or drink wine or do anything else if it might cause another Christian to stumble" (Rom 14:20-21, NLT; cf. 1 Cor 10:32; 2 Cor 6:3).

3. However, people may be offended at the truth through no fault of the person who presents it. Isaiah speaks of God as "a stone that causes people to stumble and a rock that makes them fall" (Is 8:14) in that people would not always accept his demands and the way of faith in him. The NT takes these same words and applies them to the offense of the gospel of Christ (Rom 9:32-33; 1 Pt 2:8). In the time of his ministry there were those who were offended at Jesus—at his

lowly birth (Mt 13:57), at what he said and did (15:12), or because of the cost of following him (13:21). Even disciples were capable of being offended and turning aside (Jn 6:61). In the end all were offended and fled from him (Mt 26:31, 56). Finally, the apostle Paul spoke of the offense in the preaching of the cross of Christ. He could have chosen to preach a popular message and avoided persecution, a "message that doesn't offend anyone" (Gal 5:11). He chose rather to preach the cross even though it was a stumbling block to Jews and folly to Gentiles (1 Cor 1:23).

See also Sin.

OFFERINGS AND SACRIFICES
Major ritual expressions of religious life with accompanying rites, such as libations, effusions, and sacred meals. The ideology expressed in Israel's ritual complex made its religion unique in the ancient Near East. The concepts of OT ritual also underlie NT theology with regard to sin and reconciliation to God through the atoning death of Jesus Christ.

Performance and Order of Sacrifices The main source for a description of the correct performance of sacrificial ritual is the opening section of Leviticus (Lv 1–7). It consists of two separate parts. The first (1:1–6:7) is didactic, dealing with two categories of sacrifice: those of a "pleasing odor," namely, the burnt (1:1-17), the grain (2:1-16), and the peace offerings (3:1-17); and the expiatory sacrifices, namely, the sin (4:1–5:13) and the guilt or trespass offerings (5:14–6:7). Attention is paid to the minute details of each ritual, and they are grouped according to their logical or conceptual associations.

The grain (or cereal) offering follows the burnt offering because it always accompanied it in actual practice (Nm 15:1-21; chs 28–29); it also went with the peace offering (Lv 7:12-14; Nm 15:3-4). Special emphasis is placed on burning the inward parts of a sacrifice on the altar to make a "pleasing odor to the Lord" (Lv 1:9, 17; 2:2, 9, 12; 3:5, 11, 16). When the Lord smelled the pleasing odor (Gn 8:21), it was a sign of divine favor; refusal indicated God's displeasure (Lv 26:31). The officiating priest evidently knew how to read the signs and would tell the offerer whether his sacrifice had been accepted (1 Sm 26:19; cf. Am 5:21-23).

The sin and guilt offerings were expiatory (Lv 4:1–6:7, 20). The situations requiring such offerings are listed, and special emphasis is laid on the handling of the blood in the ritual.

The second major section in this passage (Lv 6:8–7:38) stresses the administrative details for the various offerings. This section consists of a series of "instructions" for each type of offering pertaining to the distribution of the sacrificial materials. Some went to the priest(s), some went to the offerer, and others were burned on the altar or disposed of outside the camp. Those sacrifices designated as "most holy" were to be eaten only by qualified members of the priesthood (Lv 2:3, 10; 10:12-17; 14:13; Nm 18:9).

The burnt offering is discussed first because it was entirely consumed on the altar (and thus not eaten by anyone). After it, there follow the sacrifices distributed to the officiants (Lv 6:17, 26, 29; 7:1, 6), and at the end come the peace offerings, a significant portion of which was returned to the offender.

The order in which the sacrifices are treated in this passage also corresponds to their relative frequency in the rituals of the sacred calendar (Nm 28:19; 2 Chr 31:3; Ez 45:17). This would be particularly important for the priests and Levites on duty at the temple because they were responsible for the logistics of the daily sacrificial ritual, especially on the high holidays; management of the temple storehouse was a formidable task (1 Chr 23:28-32; 26:15, 20-22; 2 Chr 13:10-11; 30:3-19; 34:9-11).

Each section concerning a particular offering concludes with the logistic or administrative details peculiar to it. There then follows a summary of the matters treated thus far (Lv 7:7-10), and the section concludes with a treatment of the peace offerings (vv 11-36). The latter did not play a role in the sacred calendar except during the Feast of Weeks (23:19-20); on all other occasions, with the two exceptions of the Nazirite vow and the installation of the priesthood, peace offerings were purely voluntary sacrifices and thus not subject to any fixed bookkeeping.

In other biblical contexts, the sacrifices are listed according to the same "bookkeeping" or "administrative" order: burnt, grain, and drink; sin (or guilt); and sometimes peace offerings. An example is the roster of donations made by the tribal leaders for dedication of the altar (Nm 7). The information is organized like an everyday ledger from the temple storehouse; the summary classifies the animals as burnt, grain, sin, and peace offerings (vv 87-88) in accordance with the respective entries from each donor (vv 15-17). The Levitical scribe had two purposes for such a record: to credit the offerers and to record the treasures and food supplies coming in. Much of the foodstuffs being given as offerings was actually apportioned to the officiating priests (Nm 18:8-11; 2 Chr 31:4-19).

When prescriptions were made as to the type and number of offerings to be brought (e.g., Nm 15:24), the "bookkeeping" order is generally followed. This was true of the calendarial sacrifices; burnt and grain offerings and libations were listed, followed by a sin offering for each of the following: New Moon (Nm 28:11-15), each day of Passover (vv 19-22), the Festival of Weeks (Lv 23:18-19; 28:27-30), Trumpets (29:2-5), Day of Atonement (vv 8-11), and each day of the Feast of Tabernacles (vv 12-16).

For sacrifices required in specific cases, the instructions as to what offerings to bring follow this sequence (e.g., the purification of a woman after giving birth, Lv 12:6-8). Note also the offerings given at the successful termination of a Nazirite vow; the Nazirite brought burnt, sin, and peace offerings (with some special grain offerings, Nm 6:14-15). However, the priest conducted the actual ritual according to a different order; the sin offering was made first, followed by the burnt offering and finally the peace offering (vv 16-17). In the case of an incomplete vow, the first step was to offer a sin offering and then a burnt offering to renew the vow (v 11). The reconsecration of the Nazirite required a separate guilt offering—a distinct ritual act (v 12).

The description of the offerings made by the prince of Israel in the latter days presents the same contrast between the two orders of sacrifices. On festival holidays the prince brought burnt, grain, and drink offerings, but he offered them as sin, grain, burnt, and peace offerings (Ez 45:17). This second order of sacrifices in which the sin offering precedes the burnt offering was also followed in the rededication of the altar (43:18-27).

The same "procedural" sequence of sacrifices appears in other instances: the purification of the leper—guilt and sin offerings (Lv 14:19), followed by a burnt offering (vv 12-20); the man with a discharge—sin and burnt offerings (15:15); likewise the woman with a discharge (v 30). The same order is followed for the sacrifices on the Day of Atonement (16:3-6, 11, 15, 24).

The book of Leviticus furnishes two examples of the proper order in which sacrifices were offered. One is the ordination of Aaron and his sons. The sin offering came first and then the burnt offering (Ex 29:10-18; Lv 8:14-21). The focal point in this ritual was the sacrifice of ordination, or literally "installation," a special form of peace offering (Ex 29:19-34; Lv 8:22-29). The second passage is the formal inauguration of the sacrificial system at the tabernacle (Lv 9). The sacrifices for Aaron were sin and burnt offerings, followed by those for the people: sin, burnt, grain, and peace offerings (9:7-22).

The same sequence is followed at the cleansing and restoration of the temple in Jerusalem conducted by King Hezekiah (2 Chr 29:20-36). A great sin offering was first, followed by the burnt offerings accompanied by music and song. Then the king proclaimed that the people had committed themselves to the Lord; in this new state of purity they could now share in the sacrifices of devotion (burnt offerings) and thanksgiving (peace offerings).

The procedural order of the sacrifices embodies the OT ideology of how God may be approached. First, atonement for sin had to be made and then total consecration of self; these are symbolized by the sin and/or guilt offerings and the burnt and grain offerings, respectively. When these conditions were met, the offerer could express his continued devotion by more burnt offerings and also take part in the fellowship sacrifices (peace offerings) in which he himself got a large portion of the slaughtered animal (to share with his friends and the poor in his community; Dt 12:17-19).

Description of Sacrifices The ensuing description of the different types of sacrifice will treat them in accordance with the "procedural" order, that is, as symbolic stages in one's approach to God.

Expiation These two offerings were required for making atonement for sins and trespasses:

1. Sin offering (Lv 4:1–5:13; 6:24-30). Different animals were specified in accordance with the rank of the offerer. A high priest had to bring a young bull (4:3), as did the congregation as a whole (v 14), except when the matter was a ritual infraction (Nm 15:24). A ruler would bring a male goat (Lv 4:23), but a commoner could provide a female goat (v 28; Nm 15:27) or a lamb (Lv 4:32). If he was indigent, he could offer two turtledoves or two young pigeons (one of which would be a burnt offering; 5:7), or if he was extremely poor, he might even substitute a tenth of an ephah of fine flour (Lv 5:11-13; cf. Heb 9:22).

Sacrificial Offering According to OT law, a lamb or other animal was sacrificed in order that God's people could be forgiven of their sins.

The offerer brought the animal to the entrance of the temple court and laid his hand on it (Lv 4:4). He did not confess his sin in this act because the animal was not being sent away (cf. the goat for Azazel,

16:21); rather, he was identifying himself with the sacrifice. The offerer had to kill the animal on the north side of the altar (4:24, 29). The animals were never slaughtered on the altar proper. The officiating priest collected the blood; when it was a bull for himself or for the congregation, he sprinkled some of the blood before the veil inside the tent of meeting and put some on the horns of the incense altar (vv 5-7, 16-18). On the Day of Atonement he brought the sacrificial blood for himself and for the people into the Holy of Holies (16:14-15). From all other animals, the blood was applied to the horns of the altar of burnt offering (4:25, 30, 34); the blood of fowl was sprinkled on the side of the altar (5:9). Finally, the remaining blood from any offering was poured or drained out at the base of the altar (4:7).

The choicest of the internal organs, namely, the fatty tissue over and on the entrails, the two kidneys and their fat, and the appendage to the liver, were all offered to the Lord on the altar (Lv 4:8-10). The carcass and the other entrails were burned outside the camp when it was a bull for the priest or for the people. This was also true of the bull for the ordination of the priests (Ex 29:10-14; Lv 8:14-17). Otherwise, the priest who conducted the rites received the edible flesh as his portion. He had to eat it within the temple area, and its preparation was governed by strict rules of ritual purity (Lv 6:25-30; cf. 10:16-20). A sin offering of one male goat was presented at each of the sacred holidays: the New Moon (Nm 28:15), each day of Passover (vv 22-24), the Festival of Weeks (v 30), the Festival of Trumpets (29:5), the Day of Atonement (v 11), and each day of the Feast of Tabernacles (vv 16, 19). The high priest also offered a bull for himself and then sacrificed one of the two goats on the Day of Atonement. Certain purification rites required lesser sin offerings, namely, lambs or birds: childbirth (Lv 12:6-8), cleansing from leprosy (14:12-14, 19-22), and abscesses and hemorrhages (15:14-15, 29-30) or after defilement while under a vow (Nm 6:10-11).

2. Guilt offering (Lv 5:14–6:7; 7:1-7). The guilt or trespass offering was a special kind of sin offering (cf. 5:7) required whenever someone had been denied his rightful due. Reparation of the valued amount that had been defrauded had to be made, plus a fine of one-fifth (5:16; 6:5). The animal was usually a ram (5:15, 18; 6:6). The cleansed leper and the defiled Nazirite had to bring a male lamb (Lv 14:12, 21; Nm 6:12). The offerer apparently handled the sacrifice as he would a sin offering, but the priest had to sprinkle the blood around the altar (Lv 7:2). Viscera were burned on the altar as usual (vv 3-5). Some of the blood was then applied to the tip of the cleansed leper's right ear and to his right thumb and big toe (14:14). Again the priest received most of the animal's flesh for food (7:6-7; 14:13). A guilt offering was required whenever another party had suffered some loss. Ritual infractions, such as eating the "holy things" without proper authorization (5:14-19; 22:14), called for payment of the sum that should have gone to the Lord plus the fine of one-fifth that went to the priest (Lv 5:16; 2 Kgs 12:16). The leper belongs in this category, since during the time of his infection he was unable to render service to God (Lv 14:12-18). The same applies to the Nazirite who had suffered defilement while he was set apart to God by the vow; thus a guilt offering was required (Nm 6:12). Violation of another person's property rights could be expiated only by the guilt offering and its additional one-fifth. Such matters included cheating on deposits

or security, robbery or oppression, failing to report the find of some lost property, or false swearing or failing to testify (Lv 6:1-5). Intercourse with a betrothed slave girl was also a violation of property rights (19:20-22). If the offended party was no longer living and had no surviving kinsmen, the payment went to the priest (Nm 5:5-10).

Consecration Offerings These rituals usually come to mind when one hears the word "offering." They represent acts of personal commitment that must accompany the repentance expressed in the sin and guilt offerings. They were also a prerequisite for the fellowship or communal sacrifices that might follow.

1. Burnt offering (Lv 1:3-17; 6:8-13). The burnt offering could be a bull, a sheep, or a bird. The offerer presented the animal, laid his hand on it, and killed it on the north side of the altar. The bird was simply given to the priest. The latter collected the blood, presented it before God, and then sprinkled it around the altar. When the offering was a bird, he wrung off its head and drained the blood at the side of the altar. Though the slaughtering and sprinkling of the blood relates the burnt offering to the expiatory sacrifices of the previous section, the main emphasis here is on killing the animal, washing its unclean parts, and then carefully arranging all of the pieces on the altar. All of this was then consumed on the altar as a pleasing odor to the Lord. Since burnt offerings were offered morning and evening, a good supply of wood by the altar was necessary. The officiating priest, dressed in proper garments, had to keep the fire burning continuously (6:8-13).

Burnt offerings played a prominent role in the sacrifices of the ritual calendar. The continual burnt offering was made twice a day, a male lamb morning and evening (Ex 29:38-42; Nm 28:1-8). Two additional lambs were sacrificed each Sabbath (Nm 28:9-10).

Except for these daily offerings, a sin offering of one goat was usually made along with the burnt offerings on the following holidays: For the New Moon at the beginning of each month, two young bulls, one ram, and seven male lambs were offered (Nm 28:11-14). The same were required for each day of the Passover festival (vv 19-24) and again on the Feast of Weeks (vv 6-29). On the Festival of Trumpets and the Day of Atonement, the requirement was one bull, one ram, and seven lambs (29:2-4).

The great Feast of Tabernacles was characterized by a series of elaborate burnt offerings, plus one goat per day as a sin offering. On the first day, 13 young bulls, 2 rams, and 14 male lambs were offered (Nm 29:12-16). Each successive day, the number of bulls was decreased by one until on the seventh day there were only seven (the rams and lambs remained the same; 29:17-25). On the eighth day the animals required for Trumpets and Atonement were offered, namely, one bull, one ram, and seven lambs.

Certain rituals of purification also required burnt offerings in addition to sin offerings: after childbirth (Lv 12:6-8), abscesses (15:14-15), and discharges (vv 29-30); or after defilement while under a Nazirite vow (Nm 6:10-11). Though it is not stated that grain offerings were required in these cases, they certainly were for the cleansing from leprosy (Lv 14:10, 19-22, 31) and the completion of the Nazirite vow (Nm 6:14-16).

2. Grain (Cereal) offering (Lv 2; 6:14-23). The Hebrew term referring to this particular offering means "gift,"

or "offering," including animals (Gn 4:3-5; Jgs 6:18; 1 Sm 2:17). But in the specific sacrificial context it signifies a combination of fine flour, olive oil, and frankincense that could be made up in the form of baked loaves, wafers, or morsels. The offering of firstfruits was to be crushed heads of new grain (Lv 2:14). No leaven or honey was permitted on the cakes, although those same commodities could be accepted as a firstfruit offering. They would not go to the altar but were given to the priest. The offerer had to bring the prepared loaves or wafers to the temple. The priest would burn one handful on the altar as its "memorial portion" (v 2), keeping the remainder for his own food (6:16; 7:9). But when the priest was making a grain offering on his own behalf, he burnt it all on the altar (6:22-23).

A grain offering was usually given with every burnt offering, especially those pertaining to the sacred calendar (Nm 28–29). The amounts of flour and oil were set according to the animal being sacrificed: three-tenths of an ephah of flour and one-half a hin of oil for a bull, two-tenths ephah and one-third hin for a ram, and one-tenth ephah plus one-fourth hin for a lamb (15:2-10). Other happy occasions for a grain offering included the cleansing of a leper (Lv 14:10, 20-21, 31; unspecified quantity of grain with a bird) and the successful consummation of a Nazirite vow (Nm 6:13-15).

Peace offerings were invariably followed by grain offerings (Lv 7:12-14; Nm 15:4). The priest received one of each pair of cakes or wafers. The remainder was returned to the offerer to be eaten with the flesh of the sacrificial animal at a place of his choice.

A special case where such offering was used was the one-tenth of an ephah of barley meal required in the jealousy ritual. It was to have no oil or frankincense (Nm 5:15, 18, 25-26). A very poor individual was permitted to bring one-tenth of an ephah of fine flour without oil or frankincense as a sin offering (Lv 5:11-13).

3. Drink offering (Nm 15:1-10). The standard libation was one-fourth of a hin of wine for a lamb, one-third for a ram, and one-half for a bull. The wine (Ex 29:40), also called "strong drink" (Nm 28:7), is probably an intentional substitute for the blood used by other nations (Ps 16:4). The libation was classed as a "pleasing odor" offering (Nm 15:7). As with the burnt offering, the entire drink offering was expended; nothing was given to the priest (28:7).

Drink offerings accompanied the daily offering (Ex 29:40-41; Nm 28:7) and the Sabbath offering (Nm 28:9), as well as the New Moon festival. Reference is also made to them in connection with the second and following days of the Feast of Tabernacles (29:18, 21); for the first day their absence is probably unintentional. The same might hold true for the Passover, Firstfruits, and Feast of Trumpets (Nm 28:16–29:11; cf. Ez 45:11). A libation was required for the rites concluding a Nazirite vow (Nm 6:17) but not for cleansing a leper (Lv 14:10-20).

Fellowship Offerings These sacrifices were voluntary on the part of the offerer and generally not imposed by regulations except for the Nazirite (Nm 6:17) and the Feast of Weeks (Lv 23:19-20). An offerer who had already fulfilled the ritual requirements for atonement and personal consecration was permitted to make a fellowship offering. Burnt offerings often accompanied the fellowship sacrifices as a further expression of devotion.

1. Peace offering (Lv 3; 7:11-36; Am 5:22). This is the basic class of all fellowship or communal offerings; the others are simply subclasses of the peace offering. In terms of holiness, or restrictedness, they were not so rigidly confined as the other offerings. Animals from the herd or flock, male or female (Lv 3:1, 6, 12), were permitted. The usual stipulation of freedom from blemish was in force, except in the case of the freewill offering, in which the animal could have one limb longer than the other (22:23). Unleavened cakes were also required, at least for the thank (7:12-13) and Nazirite (Nm 6:15-19) offerings. Each of these three types of peace offerings will be discussed below, with their special features.

The first parts of the ritual—the presentation and laying on of the hand—were identical to those of the other sacrifices. However, the animal was slaughtered at the door of the sanctuary courtyard and not on the north side of the altar (Lv 3:1-2, 7-8, 12-13; 7:29-30). The priest collected the blood and tossed it against the altar as he did with the burnt offering (3:2, 8, 13). The choice viscera were offered up as a "pleasing odor" (3:3-5, 6-11, 14-16).

The priest also received a certain portion of the offering. He was allowed to eat it in any ritually clean place and to share it with his family (Lv 7:14, 30-36; Nm 6:20), in contrast to his portion of other sacrifices, which he had to eat somewhere in the temple compound (Nm 18:10-11). He received one of the cakes and the breast as a wave offering and the right thigh as a contribution for the offerer. This latter is the so-called "heave offering"; the technical term developed from a root signifying "to be high" and meaning "that which is lifted up." The heave offering did not really represent a special kind of ritual ceremony.

The ritual act of the peace offering culminated with a fellowship meal. Except for those parts on the altar or given to the priest, the body of the animal was returned to the man who offered it. He had to prepare it as a communal meal for himself, for his family, and for the Levite in his community (Dt 12:12, 18-19). This would have to be at the official sanctuary (Dt 12:6-7, 11-12, 15-19; cf. 1 Sm 1:3-4) and the participants had to observe strict rules of purity (Lv 7:19-21; 19:5-8). It may be contrasted with the ritual slaughtering of animals for a banquet that was permitted at any local altar (Dt 12:16, 20-22). The flesh of the thank offering had to be eaten on the same day of the sacrifice (Lv 7:15), while that of the votive or freewill offerings could be finished off on the following day (vv 16-18). Whatever remained then had to be burned before the time limit expired.

Only three times is there a specific demand for a peace offering: in the Feast of Weeks (Lv 23:19-20), upon completion of a Nazirite vow (Nm 6:17-20), and at the installation of the priesthood (Ex 29:19-22, 28). Other public ritual occasions included the inauguration of the temple (1 Kgs 8:63; 2 Chr 7:5). Events on a national level that evoked the peace offering were the successful conclusion of a military campaign (1 Sm 11:15), the end of a famine or pestilence (2 Sm 24:25), confirmation of a candidate to the throne (1 Kgs 1:9, 19), or a time of religious revival (2 Chr 29:31-36). On the local level, they were offered at the annual family reunion (1 Sm 20:6) or other festive occasions, such as the harvest of the firstfruits (Ex 22:29-31; 1 Sm 9:11-14, 22-24; 16:4-5).

2. Wave offering. The first portion of the peace offering was "waved" before the Lord to signify that the priest was eating it as a representative of God (the actual motion evidently resembled the wielding of a saw or a staff, Is 10:15). The same technical term, "wave offering," was also used for other kinds of offering: precious metals donated for making the cultic artifacts (Ex 35:22; 38:29) and the guilt offering of the cleansed leper (Lv 14:12).

3. Freewill offering. These gifts, brought to the holy convocations that took place three times per year (Ex 23:16; 34:20; Dt 16:10, 16-17; 2 Chr 35:8; Ezr 3:5), were voluntary (Lv 7:16; 22:18, 21-23; 23:28; Nm 15:3; 29:39; Dt 12:6, 17). Like the voluntary offering, the freewill offering could be a burnt rather than a peace offering (Lv 22:17-24; Ez 46:12). If it was the latter, the flesh could be eaten on the second day but must be burned before the third (Lv 7:16-17). Unlike some other peace offerings, the animal being sacrificed could have one limb longer than the other (22:23).

4. Installation offering. This Hebrew term refers to the settings of precious stones (Ex 25:7; 35:9, 27; 1 Chr 29:2), so "installation" seems an appropriate translation. It had to do with "filling the hand," a ritual act that consecrated someone to divine service (Ex 28:41; cf. 32:29) and required ritual purity and spiritual devotion (2 Chr 29:31). The details of the original ceremony at the installation of the first priest is described in two passages (Ex 29:19-34; Lv 8:22-32).

See also Atonement; Cleanness and Uncleanness, Regulations Concerning; Feasts and Festivals of Israel; Tabernacle; Temple.

OFFICERS IN THE CHURCH *See* Bishop; Deacon, Deaconess; Elder; Pastor; Presbyter; Spiritual Gifts.

OG King whose fame partly came from his being a giant. "King Og of Bashan was the last of the giant Rephaites. His iron bed was more than thirteen feet [4.1 meters] long and six feet [1.8 meters] wide" (Dt 3:11, NLT).

Og, king of Bashan, fell before Moses' assault immediately after the defeat of King Sihon the Amorite (Nm 21:33-35). Bashan lay along the northern part of the Transjordan. Og's land stretched northeastward from the lower course of the Jarmuk (Yarmuk) River, and lofty mountain ranges protected him on the east from scorching desert winds.

Og and his people had several settlements, primarily Ashtaroth and Edrei (Jos 13:12). Og had fortified his land with 60 walled cities and was probably overconfident before Moses' army. Moses completely destroyed the populace of those cities; he spared only the livestock and the spoils of war (Dt 3:5-6).

Three tribes of Israel found the Transjordan particularly suitable for grazing their herds. So at the defeat of Sihon and Og, Moses assigned the newly won lands to the tribes of Gad, Reuben, and half of Manasseh (Nm 32:33; Jos 12:4-6).

OHAD Simeon's son (Gn 46:10; Ex 6:15), whose name does not appear in the list of Numbers 26:12-14.

OHEL Descendant of Jehoiakim and King David (1 Chr 3:20).

OHOLAH AND OHOLIBAH Names given to the northern kingdom (KJV "Aholah"), with its capital at Samaria, and to the southern kingdom (KJV "Aholibah"), with its capital at Jerusalem, respectively, by Ezekiel in his allegory depicting the unfaithfulness of God's people (Ez 23). The names characterized the basic attitude of each of the twin kingdoms toward God and his worship. Samaria (Oholah) had "her own tent" (the literal meaning of the name) and had invented her own centers of worship; Jerusalem (Oholibah, literally "my tent is in her") prided herself in being the custodian of the temple.

Rather than being true to the Lord, Samaria had committed spiritual adultery. Not being content with her spiritual infidelity in wooing the gods of Egypt, she had lusted after the idols of Assyria and the worldly attractions that the Neo-Assyrian culture held out before her. Both courses of action are adequately documented by archaeological discoveries from the ancient Near East, such as Jehu's act of homage as portrayed on the Black Obelisk of King Shalmaneser III of Assyria (859–824 BC). Samaria's conduct had been judged by God; her new-found desire had proved to be her destruction, God giving her over into the hands of the Assyrian conqueror.

Far from learning from Israel's example, Judah had not only courted Assyria and its idolatry (e.g., 2 Kgs 16:10-18) but also had added to her affections the Neo-Babylonian Empire (e.g., 20:14-18) and then had turned once again to Egypt (e.g., Jer 37; 46), her earlier lover (Ez 23:11-21). Therefore, God would sorely punish her at the hands of the Babylonians, and she would know the just judgment of God.

Ezekiel closes his allegory with a rehearsal of God's charges against the two kingdoms. God's people were doubly guilty. Not being content with their apostasy, they had gone so far as to profane the sanctuary of God and his Sabbath by entering the temple with hands bloodied in the sacrifice of their own children in pagan rites.

OHOLIAB Man assigned by Moses to assist Bezalel, the master craftsman, in the construction and ornamentation of the tabernacle. Son of Ahisamach and member of Dan's tribe, Oholiab was specifically noted as a designer and embroiderer. Along with Bezalel, he taught the skills necessary for the construction of the tabernacle (Ex 31:6; 35:34; 36:1-2; 38:23; KJV "Aholiab").

OHOLIBAMAH

1. Esau's wife, the daughter of Anah the Hivite (Gn 36:2, 5, 14, 18, 25, KJV "Aholibamah"), who bore to him Jeush, Jalam, and Korah before Esau left Canaan for Seir.

   The absence of her name from the other lists of Esau's wives (see Gn 26:34; 28:9) has occasioned a great deal of discussion. The considerable variation in these lists may indicate either a confusion in the scribal transmission or may point to the use of alternate names, gained either at marriage or as a result of some memorable event in the women's lives. Whether or not she is identified with Judith, as some have suggested, the scriptural observation that she was "a source of grief to Isaac and Rebekah" is true (26:35).

2. Edomite clan chieftain descended from Esau (Gn 36:41; 1 Chr 1:52, KJV "Aholibamah").

OIL Substance most commonly produced from the olive berry, although the word could also apply to oil of myrrh (Est 2:12). Oil was used primarily in cooking, but additionally as a cosmetic for anointing the body, for medicinal purposes, as a source of light, for anointing kings and priests, and in religious offerings.

The growth of olive trees was widespread, and the Israelites took advantage of this major crop to establish a thriving trade in oil with Tyre and Egypt. Like precious metals and animals, oil became an established medium of exchange. Solomon used it as part of the payment to Hiram for construction expenses connected with the temple (1 Kgs 5:11; Ez 27:17).

Because oil was essential for everyday life, it was an effective and acceptable medium of barter. Oil was used in the preparation of most food (1 Kgs 17:12-16). The common cake or patty of grain, which formed the basis of the noon meal, would be cooked on a griddle with a little oil.

As a cosmetic, oil was used for anointing the body after a bath (Ru 3:3; 2 Sm 12:20). It was frequently used on festive occasions, and at Egyptian banquets the heads of both the guests and the female entertainers were anointed. In the NT, the anointing of the sick is mentioned (Jas 5:14). Olive oil could also be taken internally as a medicine for the relief of gastric disorders. It had a soothing effect and was also used as a mild laxative. It was applied externally as an ointment for bruises, burns, cuts, and abrasions (Is 1:6; Mk 6:13; Lk 10:34).

As soon as the sun set, the only source of light was the oil lamp. Often the small portable one could be placed easily on a shelf, but in large homes, palaces, synagogues, or temples, the lamp could rest on a tall metal base like a standard lamp. The wick of flax (Is 42:3) or hemp was placed in the oil that gave out a flame until it was extinguished or the supply of fuel ran out. Torches were used in the streets both to light the way and for additional security. They added immeasurably to the festive atmosphere of evening processions. Torches were an essential part of the wedding procession, and normally those carrying the torches brought a quantity of oil in a container in case there was a delay and their supply was exhausted. This scene is vividly portrayed in Jesus' parable of the wise and foolish virgins (Mt 25:1-13).

In other ceremonial events, oil had a special meaning when used for the anointing of kings (1 Sm 10:1; 1 Kgs 1:39) and priests (Ex 29:7). It was symbolic of the office and of the recognition of God's blessing on the office-holder.

Quantities of oil were used in the temple. It was donated as part of the firstfruit offering (Ex 22:29) and was also subject to tithing (Dt 12:17). Oil was frequently used for the ceremonial aspect of temple life or as part of the offering. The grain offering was mixed with oil (Lv 8:26; Nm 7:19), and the oil in the lamp that burned in the sanctuary constantly needed replenishing (Lv 24:2). The daily sacrifice required the use of oil (Ex 29:40), although the sin offering (Lv 5:11) and the jealousy offering (Nm 5:15) specifically did not use oil.

A pestle and mortar, or a stone press, pressed oil from the olives (Ex 27:20). Where the latter was used, the pulp initially produced by the press was often trodden out or subjected to further extensive pressing. Stone presses were set up to process the quantities of berries available at the Mt of Olives. The word for "oil press" was *gatt-semen*, hence the name Gethsemane.

Oil was symbolically associated with joy, festivity, ceremony, honor, light, and health (both spiritual and physical), while its absence spelled sorrow (Jl 1:10) and the withdrawal of all that is good in life.

See also Anoint; Food and Food Preparation; Medicine and Medical Practice; Ointment; Plants (Olive, Olive Tree).

OIL, Anointing *See* Anoint.

OIL TREE* Small tree bearing an olivelike fruit that yields a medicinal oil. *See* Plants.

OINTMENT Various preparations, generally of a spicy nature with an oil base. In Palestine, olive oil was the chief base of ointments and was itself considered an ointment. The OT does not distinguish between "oil" and "ointment." In Egypt and Mesopotamia, numerous vegetable oils and animal fats formed the basis of ointments. Among the vegetable oils, some of the more important include castor oil, sesame oil, linseed oil, radish oil, colocynth oil, and oil from various nuts.

Ointments played an important and visible role in antiquity. In the hot and dry climate of the Near East, ointments gave a measure of protection. Widespread medicinal uses, soothing qualities, and effectiveness in masking odors made the use of ointments a virtual necessity among all classes. The OT mentions apothecaries or perfumers (1 Sm 8:13; 2 Chr 16:14), artisans who were organized into guilds (Neh 3:8).

In general, ointments were made by boiling aromatic substances in oil (cf. Jb 41:31). Perfumed ointments were combinations of certain raw materials with specially prepared oil. In the OT, qualifying terms such as "fragrant" (Sg 1:3) or "precious" (Eccl 7:1) signify perfumed oils. Ointments could be stored in a variety of vessels, but flasks made of alabaster were preferred. An alabaster jar held the expensive ointment with which Mary anointed Jesus in Bethany (Mk 14:3).

Ointments had a variety of uses. Among the Semites in particular, ointments acquired important associations. Aaron, his sons, the tabernacle, and its furnishings were all consecrated by holy anointing oil. This compound consisted of myrrh, cinnamon, calamus, and cassia mixed with olive oil (Ex 30:23-25). Kings and prophets were anointed, but not with the holy anointing oil mixture.

As a cosmetic, perfumed ointments controlled unpleasant odors. Applications were made to the body (2 Sm 12:20), clothing (Ps 45:8), or personal objects (Prv 7:17). Women utilized ointments for cleansing the skin and enhancing the attractiveness of their skin (Est 2:12). The fragrance of certain ointments attracted the attention of the opposite sex (Sg 4:10). Not surprisingly, the Song of Songs has several references to fragrant ointments.

The use of ointments to refresh and soothe guests was a mark of hospitality in the ancient Near East. Cones of ointment placed on the heads of guests and allowed to drip down over the body were used by the Egyptians (cf. Ps 133:2). As a sign of respect and honor, the head of a guest was anointed with oil. Jesus chided a Pharisee who neglected this traditional mark of hospitality (Lk 7:37-40). Mary anointed Jesus with a costly flask of nard, a fragrant ointment obtained from the roots of an aromatic herb from India (Mk 14:3).

Aerial View of the Mount of Olives

Ointments were used in the burial process. In the NT a corpse would be washed (Acts 9:37) and anointed with ointments (Mk 16:1). The body was wrapped in linen garments with spices and ointments (Lk 23:56; Jn 19:40). Both the Jews and the Romans utilized nard for burials. A mixture of myrrh and aloes was used in the burial of Jesus.

Medicinal uses of ointment were frequent. Oil was applied to wounds (Lk 10:34). Balm (probably an aromatic gum) had well-known medicinal uses and is associated with Gilead (Jer 8:22). Balm was an item of export from Palestine (Gn 37:25; Ez 27:17). Biblical reference is made to a famous eye ointment produced and exported by the city of Laodicea (Rv 3:18). Ointments formed an important commodity for merchants in the Roman period (18:13).

Anointing with oil came to be associated with gladness and joy (Ps 45:7; Is 61:3). Thus, one was to refrain from anointing during times of mourning (2 Sm 14:2). The lack of oil for anointing was viewed as judgment (Mi 6:15). Shields were anointed with oil to make them supple and possibly to help deflect projectiles (2 Sm 1:21).

See also Medicine and Medical Practice; Oil; Plants (Olive, Olive Tree).

OLD GATE Jerusalem gate repaired by Joiada and Meshullam under Nehemiah's supervision (Neh 3:6), and subsequently mentioned in the northerly route traveled by one of the companies of celebrants during the Jerusalem wall's dedication (12:39). The Old Gate was located in the city's northern wall between the Fish Gate and the Gate of Ephraim (12:38-39).

See also Jerusalem.

OLD MAN *See* Man, Old and New.

OLD TESTAMENT *See* Bible.

OLD TESTAMENT CANON* *See* Bible, Canon of the.

OLD TESTAMENT CHRONOLOGY* *See* Chronology of the Bible (Old Testament).

OLD TESTAMENT QUOTATIONS IN THE NEW TESTAMENT* *See* Bible, Quotations of the Old Testament in the New Testament.

OLIVE, OLIVE TREE *See* Agriculture; Food and Food Preparation; Plants.

OLIVES, Mount of Prominent ridge running north-south in the Judean mountains, lying due east of Jerusalem and the Kidron Valley. Three summits with two intervening valleys distinguish the mountain. The northern summit is Mt Scopus. To its south is a small saddle through which the ancient Roman road to Jericho passed. The central hill is the traditional Mt of Olives (2,684 feet, or 818.1 meters) standing across from the temple platform (the *Haram esh-Sherif*). Here Constantine built the great Church of the Ascension dedicated to his mother, Helena. Another saddle to the south contains the modern road to Bethany. The southern hill, overlooking Jebusite Jerusalem and the city of David, is called the "Mt of Offense" since here Solomon built temples for his foreign wives. Beneath it is the Arab village of Silwan and the confluence of the Kidron and Hinnom valleys.

The Mt of Olives gained its name from its extensive olive groves, which were renowned in antiquity (Zec 14:4; Mk 11:1). Its western face collects rainfall from the Mediterranean, which, together with decomposed limestone, makes for fertile orchards. The eastern side marks the boundary of the arid Judean wilderness. Bethany and Bethphage are two NT villages hugging these eastern slopes.

In the OT the Mt of Olives is first mentioned when David fled from Absalom's conspiracy. He departed from Jerusalem, went up the Mt of Olives in the east, and continued on toward the Rift Valley (2 Sm 15:30). Solomon chose this mountain for the construction of "high places" for the foreign deities of Sidon, Moab (1 Kgs 11:7), and Ammon—each of which was later destroyed by Josiah (2 Kgs 23:13). Ezekiel (Ez 11:23) records the vision of the glory of God departing from the temple and resting on the Mt of Olives. The most famous description appears in Zechariah's apocalyptic vision (Zec 14:1-5): "On that day [the LORD's] feet will stand on the Mount of Olives, which faces Jerusalem on the east. And the Mount of Olives will split apart, making a wide valley running from east to west, for half the mountain will move toward the north and half toward the south" (v 4, NLT).

In the NT Jesus appears at the Mt of Olives during Passion week. The only exceptions are the Bethany stories when Jesus visits Mary and Martha (Lk 10:38-42) and raises Lazarus from the dead (Jn 11:17-44). On his triumphant entry to Jerusalem, Jesus came from Jericho, crossed the mountain from the east, and then descended into the Kidron Valley (Mk 11:1-10). On his descent he paused and wept over the city (Lk 19:41-44).

During his final week, Jesus taught on the Mt of Olives (Mk 13) and spent his evenings there (Lk 21:37, although this may refer to Bethany). Following the Last Supper, Jesus came to this mountain for prayer (Mk 14:26). In a garden near an olive oil press ("Gethsemane"), he was arrested (v 32). The final event of Christ on earth, his ascension, was viewed from the mount by his followers (Acts 1:12).

A REVERED SITE: THE MOUNT OF OLIVES
The Mt of Olives quickly became a center of Christian devotion. In the Byzantine era the mountain had 24 churches with vast numbers of monks and nuns. Constantine's church dominated the summit, celebrating Christ's ascension. In the fourth century it had even become the customary burial site for Jerusalem's bishops.

Jews and Muslims likewise revere the site because it will be the place of judgment. According to the Talmud, the righteous will be resurrected between Jerusalem and the Mt of Olives. This explains the vast Muslim and Jewish cemeteries, especially on the western slope of the Mt of Olives. Christian, Jew, and Muslim alike view the Mt of Olives as the focal point for the final Day of the Lord.

OLIVET* See Olives, Mount of.

OLYMPAS Member of the church in Rome to whom Paul sent personal greetings (Rom 16:15).

OLYMPIAN ZEUS, Temple of Name given to the temple of Jerusalem by Antiochus Epiphanes in 168 BC when he turned the holy place into a shrine for the chief of the pagan gods of Greece (2 Macc 6:2). Jews were forced to abandon ancestral customs and could no longer observe God's law. The desecration included temple prostitution, forced cannibalism, and humiliation for the Jews.

OMAR Second son of Eliphaz, grandson of Esau and the great-grandson of Abraham (Gn 36:11, 15; 1 Chr 1:36); an Edomite clan chief.

OMEGA English spelling of the name of the last letter of the Greek alphabet. See Alpha and Omega.

OMEN Natural sign or occurrence prefiguring the outcome of a future event. Augury was listed among the abominable pagan practices forbidden to Israel (Dt 18:10). Balaam, upon seeing that the Lord was pleased with his blessings on Israel, did not seek omens as he normally did (Nm 24:1). The men of Syria looked for an omen to see if King Ahab of Israel (874–853 BC) would be favorably disposed to release the Syrian king Benhadad from captivity (1 Kgs 20:33). Isaiah reveals the Lord as one "who frustrates the omens of liars, and makes fools of diviners" (Is 44:25, RSV).

See also Magic; Sorcery.

OMER Measuring unit used in gathering manna (Ex 16:16, 18, 22, 36). See Weights and Measures.

OMNIPOTENCE* God's unlimited authority to bring into existence or cause to happen whatsoever he wills. See God, Being and Attributes of.

OMNIPRESENCE* Aspect of God's infinity in which he transcends the limitations of space and is present in all places at all times. See God, Being and Attributes of.

OMNISCIENCE* God's infinite knowledge and understanding of things past, present, and future. See God, Being and Attributes of.

OMRI
1. King of Israel who first appears in Scripture as general of the army during the reign of Elah, king of Israel. In 885 BC Elah sent Omri to besiege the Philistine fortress of Gibbethon. During the siege, Zimri, another military leader, launched a coup against Elah, killed him, and immediately wiped out all of Elah's male relatives. When Omri heard of the assassination, he had the army declare him king and marched to the capital at Tirzah to deal with Zimri. When Zimri saw that the siege of Tirzah was going to be successful, he set fire to the king's palace and died in the flames after only seven days on the throne.

But Omri's rule over Israel was not yet established. Tibni seized control of part of the state and held it for about four years. Finally, Omri was able to crush Tibni and extend his power over all Israel. He established Israel's fourth ruling dynasty, which was destined to continue through three more generations after his own. His reign lasted a total of 12 years (885–874 BC), including the years of sovereignty disputed with Tibni.

International Developments To the northeast of Israel, the Arameans of Syria were building a strong state with its capital at Damascus. A few years before Omri took the throne, Asa of Judah had sought the help of Syria against Baasha of Israel. Soon Syria would become a threat to both Hebrew kingdoms.

Farther east, Assyria was growing in strength under the leadership of Ashurnasirpal II (883–859 BC), the founder of the empire. He marched into Phoenicia, but Israel was spared Assyrian attack until the days of Omri's son Ahab.

Omri's Reign Since the purpose of Scripture is not to provide a political, military, or even social history of Israel or the countries surrounding it, administrations of the kings of Israel and Judah are often very briefly treated. For a fuller picture, it is necessary to turn to nonbiblical sources. From Assyrian records, it is evident that Omri must have been an impressive ruler. Generations later, Assyrians still spoke of Israel as the "land of Omri."

Perceptive leader that he was, Omri recognized that the nations needed a capital that was centrally located and militarily defensible. He settled on the site of Samaria, the third and most significant capital of the realm (Shechem and Tirzah had previously served as capitals). Located seven miles (11.3 kilometers) northwest of Shechem on the main road leading to Galilee and Phoenicia, it perched on a free-standing hill that rose some 300 to 400 feet (91.4–121.9 meters) above the surrounding plain. Thus it could be quite easily defended; it had a prosperous hinterland to supply it with food and taxes; and it was conveniently located on a main road. Omri bought the hill from Shemer and named the city after its owner. Then he leveled the top of the hill and built the palace compound. He also built a 33-foot- (10.1-meter-) thick wall around the summit of the hill.

Omri's expansionist activities are not mentioned in 1 Kings, but Scripture is supplemented by discovery of the Moabite Stone in 1868 at Dibon, east of the Jordan River. On this stela, Mesha, king of Moab, tells that Omri conquered Moab. Israel had continued to subjugate the land in the days of Ahab, but during his days, Mesha successfully rebelled against Israel (2 Kgs 3:4). That Omri could mount a successful war against Moab soon after becoming king shows that he was a capable ruler, because previously the kingdom of Israel had been greatly weakened by insurrection and political instability.

Omri also reestablished the friendly relations with Phoenicia that had been initiated in the days of David and Solomon. Presumably, he made a full alliance with King Ethbaal of Tyre and then sealed it with the marriage of his son Ahab to the Phoenician princess Jezebel. Such an alliance would have been mutually beneficial, for it would have brought cedar, beautifully crafted goods, and Phoenician architectural and technical expertise to Israel, and it would have provided Israelite grain and olive oil to Phoenicia. Moreover, it would have linked their forces against the threat of the rising power of Assyria.

This pact was destined to corrupt Israel, however, for it brought Baal worship into the land. Probably this is what the writer of Kings had in mind when he said that Omri "did worse" than the other kings of Israel before him (1 Kgs 16:25) because he practiced the idolatrous ways of Jeroboam. Baal worship was regarded as more degrading than the calf worship Jeroboam had introduced. Omri, and his son Ahab after him, subscribed to both.

Omri was one of the most powerful kings of Israel, building its new capital, winning for the state a reputation for prowess, and setting a course for future kings to follow. But unfortunately that course was morally corrupt; the introduction of Baal worship was one of the terrible results of Omri's alliance with Tyre.

2. One of Beker's sons from Benjamin's tribe (1 Chr 7:8).
3. Descendant of Perez, son of Judah (1 Chr 9:4).
4. Son of Michael, prince of the tribe of Issachar during David's reign (1 Chr 27:18).

ON (Person)
Reubenite, Peleth's son who joined Korah's rebellion against Moses and Aaron in the wilderness (Nm 16:1).

ON* (Place)
Hebrew name for Heliopolis, an Egyptian city (Gn 41:45, 50; 46:20). *See* Heliopolis.

ONAM
1. Grandson of Seir and Shobal's fifth son (Gn 36:23; 1 Chr 1:40).
2. Son of Jerahmeel and Atarah, the father of a clan in Judah (1 Chr 2:26-28).

ONAN
Second son of Judah and a Canaanitess named Shua (Gn 38:4-10; 46:12; Nm 26:19; 1 Chr 2:3). Judah forced him to enter into a levirate marriage with Tamar, the wife of his deceased brother, Er. Er and Tamar had no children. Onan refused to have children by Tamar, knowing that they would be heirs to his brother's estate. As a result of Onan's refusal to raise up descendants for his brother, the Lord punished him with death (Gn 38:8-10).

ONESIMUS
Slave on whose behalf Paul wrote the Letter to Philemon. A slave of Philemon, he had robbed his master and run away from him. He is also mentioned with Tychicus as a bearer of the Letter to the Colossians (Col 4:9), indicating that he came from that region. Paul became acquainted with him, converted him, and developed a close friendship with him (Phlm 1:10). Paul wanted to keep Onesimus with him during his imprisonment because he had been helpful to him (in Greek, Onesimus means "useful"). However, Paul returned the slave to his master, confident that the runaway slave would be received by his former owner as a Christian brother and that Philemon would charge any wrong that Onesimus had done to Paul's account.

See also Philemon, Letter to.

ONESIPHORUS
Christian who took care of Paul during his confinement in Ephesus. After Paul's transfer to Rome, Onesiphorus eagerly sought him out and ministered to him there (2 Tm 1:16). In the salutation of his Second Letter to Timothy, Paul sent greetings to Onesiphorus and his household (4:19).

ONIAS
Onias is the family name of four high priests in the intertestamental period. They were descendants of Zadok, the high priest in Solomon's reign. Their lives spanned a period from the end of the fourth century BC down to the second. In their times the high priesthood was not only a religious office but included great political power.

Little is known of Onias I, except that he was son and successor to Jaddua, who was high priest at the time of Alexander the Great (336–323 BC). Onias II was his grandson. He eventually succeeded his father, Simon I, after two relatives had held office until he was old enough to take over. According to Josephus, Onias II was an old man by the reign of Ptolemy III of Egypt (246–221 BC). It was probably to Onias II that King Arius of Sparta sent the famous letter preserved in 1 Maccabees 12:20–23, claiming that the Jews and Spartans were both descended from Abraham. Josephus claims that Onias III was the recipient, but there is no knowledge of a Spartan king Arius in his period. During this time, Judea was under the control of Egypt. Onias II attempted to secede by refusing to pay taxes. During the period of office of his successor, Simon II, Palestine changed hands and became subject to the Seleucid kings of Syria.

The powerful family of the Tobiads became political rivals to the Oniads, especially to Simon's son and heir, Onias III, who succeeded him about 180 BC. Their rivalry included religious tensions, since Onias stood for ortho-dox Judaism, while the Tobiads represented liberal con-cessions to Hellenism. In the power struggle Onias III was denounced as being pro-Egyptian, after a Syrian attempt to plunder the temple failed (2 Macc 3:4-40). In 175 BC, when the Seleucid king Antiochus IV came to the throne, he was removed from office and exiled to Antioch. His brother Jason was appointed high priest in his place. Eventually Jason, in turn, was succeeded by Menelaus, who had bribed the Syrians to displace Jason. Fearing opposition from the exiled Onias, Menelaus arranged to have him assassinated (4:33-38). Eventually, the Syrians deposed Menelaus.

The legitimate successor, Onias IV, son of Onias III, was prevented from taking over and fled to Egypt. In Egypt he built a temple at Leontopolis, probably as a sanctuary for the local Jewish military colony rather than as a religious center for Egyptian Jews generally, who continued to support the Jerusalem temple. According to the Jewish Mishnah, the religious authorities in Jerusa-lem apparently regarded its sacrifices as legitimate but refused to allow its (authentically Zadokite) priesthood to officiate in the temple at Jerusalem. It remained in use until the Roman emperor Vespasian had it closed down in AD 73.

ONION *See* Food and Food Preparation; Plants.

ONLY BEGOTTEN* Phrase deeply entrenched in Christian language as descriptive of Jesus. The word tra-ditionally translated "only begotten" does not carry the idea of birth at all. Literally, it means "only one of its kind," "unique." This can be readily seen in the way it is used in the NT and in the Septuagint (the Greek transla-tion of the OT).

The Greek word for this phrase appears nine times in the NT, but only five of these occurrences, all from the Johannine writings, make reference to Jesus (Jn 1:14, 18; 3:16, 18; 1 Jn 4:9). Three of the other occurrences are of an only son or daughter (Lk 7:12; 8:42; 9:38; cf. Jgs 11:34 in the LXX). Because of its frequent use for an only child, the word often conveys the idea of some-thing especially favored or precious. The remaining non-Johannine reference, in Hebrews 11:17, is to Isaac as Abraham's "favored" or "unique" son. Isaac was not Abraham's "only begotten," since he had other chil-dren, but Isaac was his favored and unique son fulfill-ing God's promise. In the Septuagint for Psalm 22:20 and 35:17, the psalmist, in his plea for deliverance, even uses this word of his own soul as that which is of great value. The Hebrew word that stands behind each of these OT texts also means "only" and does not carry any idea of birth.

Where the word is used of Jesus, its meaning is like-wise not "only begotten" but "only" or "unique." The word is used with "son" and should be understood as God's *only* Son, indicating both God's favor toward him and his uniqueness (Jn 3:16, 18; 1 Jn 4:9). The statement at the baptism and transfiguration of Jesus in the Synoptics ("This is my beloved son") expresses virtually the same idea. In fact, the word "beloved" is used in the Septuagint as an equivalent to the word "only" to translate the same Hebrew word. In John 1:14 the word "only" is used by itself to stress that the incarnate Word comes as a unique one from the Father. The final reference (Jn 1:18) is especially inter-esting because of the fact that some texts read "the only son" while others read "the only God." Because scribes could easily have written "only son" due to their famil-iarity with the other texts in John and because of the

superiority of the texts that read "only God," this latter reading is preferred. The attitude expressed toward the incarnate Word is the highest possible. No one has ever seen God, but the unique (or only) God who is in the bosom of the Father has revealed him.

See also Christology.

SHOULD TRANSLATORS USE THE EXPRESSION "ONLY BEGOTTEN"?
The phrase "only begotten" is not an accurate translation and should not be used in any of the nine passages noted above. This phrase is derived from the Latin Vulgate (a translation of the Bible from about the fifth century that has been quite influential on other translations) and reflects cer-tain theological debates about the person of Christ. While the language of the Word being born of God is present in the second century, the most notable occurrence of this language is the creed from the Council of Nicaea in AD 325. This creed speaks of the Son of God as begotten of the Father, unique—that is, from the substance of the Father—God from God, light from light, true God from true God, begotten and not made, of one substance with the Father. This creed was the result of the rejection of the heresy that the Son of God was the first created being. Ultimately, the phrase "begotten, not made" leads to what theo-logians call the doctrine of the eternal generation of the Son. It is an attempt to say that the Son is derived from the Father but that he is eternal with the Father. However, this discussion is an attempt to explain the mystery of the Trinity and goes far beyond the biblical text.

Whether there is any biblical passage that speaks of the Son being born from the Father is doubtful at best. The use of Psalm 2:7 in Acts 13:33, Hebrews 1:5, and 5:5 ("You are my son, today I have begotten you") refers to the resurrec-tion and exaltation of Christ. The use of "first-born" (Rom 8:29; Col 1:15, 18; Heb 1:6) stresses sovereignty rather than birth. The only text that possibly points to the idea of the Son's being born from the Father is 1 John 5:18, but the meaning of the words "the one having been born from God" is debated both because of a textual variant and because of the grammar. The words may refer to Christians instead of the Son.

In the end it must be said that "only begotten" is an incorrect translation. The idea being stressed is the uniqueness of Jesus' relation to the Father, not any kind of birth per se.

ONO Benjaminite town built by Shemed (1 Chr 8:12). Some of its inhabitants returned to Palestine with Zerubbabel following the exile (Ezr 2:33; Neh 7:37). Its location was variously known as the plain of Ono (Neh 6:2) or as the valley of craftsmen (11:35). Ono is identi-fied with Kefr 'Ana, seven miles (11.3 kilometers) south-east of Joppa.

ONYCHA* One of the sweet spices used in the sacred incense of the tabernacle (Ex 30:34). Its identification is uncertain. Some suggest that onycha was derived from the shell of a certain mussel found in India that exuded a musklike fragrance when burned.

ONYX Semiprecious stone used on the breastplate of the high priest (Ex 28:9). *See* Stones, Precious #18.

OPHEL

1. Hill or mound in Samaria where Elisha's house stood (2 Kgs 5:24).
2. Fortification in the southeast portion of ancient Jerusalem high above the slopes of the Brook Kidron, strengthened by Jotham (2 Chr 27:3) and Manasseh (33:14). Isaiah described the destruction of such a fortress when prophesying the judgment of God upon Jerusalem (Is 32:14). After the exile, the temple servants lived there and repaired its walls (Neh 3:26-27; 11:21). Josephus states that it was near the temple. Archaeological excavations at the traditional site in Jerusalem reveal fortifications dating from pre-Israelite times to the Maccabean period.

OPHIR (Person)
Joktan's son and a descendant of Shem through Arphaxad's line (Gn 10:29; 1 Chr 1:23).

OPHIR (Place)
Place to which Solomon sent a fleet of merchant ships to bring back gold and all sorts of precious and exotic products. The location of Ophir is not certain; most scholars place it in southwest Arabia. There may be a relationship between the place and the man named Ophir who appears in the table of nations as a son of Joktan (Gn 10:29; cf. 1 Chr 1:23), a descendant of Shem. The names of Joktan and his sons are connected with the southern and western parts of Arabia.

First Kings 9:26-28 reports that Solomon built a fleet of merchant ships at Ezion-geber, which was near Elath on the Gulf of Aqaba. Hiram, king of Tyre, provided seamen to accompany those of Solomon. This expedition returned with 420 talents of gold for Solomon. First Kings 10:11 adds that the fleet of Hiram brought from Ophir a great amount of almug wood and precious stones.

Later, Jehoshaphat built "ships of Tarshish" to go to Ophir for gold, but the ships were wrecked at Ezion-geber. Then Ahaziah, the son of Ahab of Israel, offered to send his men with the seamen of Judah, but Jehoshaphat refused (see 1 Kgs 22:48-49).

The premier product of Ophir was fine gold. Eliphaz the Temanite comments that the Almighty should be one's gold rather than the gold of Ophir (Jb 22:24). Job himself declares that wisdom is far more valuable than all the gold of Ophir (28:16). In his description of the glories of the king, the psalmist describes his queen at his right hand as wearing jewelry of finest gold from Ophir (Ps 45:9).

Some suggest that the ships of Tarshish mentioned (1 Kgs 10:22) were those ships that went to Ophir and returned every three years with gold, silver, ivory, apes, and peacocks. Traders brought the products, some from as far away as India, to the ports of Ophir, where Solomon's representatives bought them.

OPHNI
Village allotted to Benjamin after Israel had taken possession of Palestine (Jos 18:24). Its precise location is unknown, but some early writers suggest the town of Gophna (modern Jifna) on the highway from Samaria to Jerusalem, a day's march north of Gibeah. This identification assumes that the boundary of Benjamin turned north near Bethel on the northern boundary. The modern Jifna is located three miles (4.8 kilometers) northwest of Bethel.

OPHRAH (Person)
Meonothai's son from Judah's tribe (1 Chr 4:14).

OPHRAH (Place)

1. City in Benjamin, probably identical with Ephraim (2 Sm 13:23; 2 Chr 13:19, "Ephron"; Jn 11:54).

Ophrah is usually identified with the modern et-Taiyibeh, five miles (8 kilometers) north of Michmash and four miles (6.5 kilometers) northeast of Bethel.
2. City in Manasseh owned by Gideon's father, Joash the Abiezrite, and Gideon's home (Jgs 6:11). There the angel appeared to Gideon, commissioning him as God's agent of relief from the Midianites (vv 12-24). Following his spectacular victory, Gideon was nominated for kingship, but he refused. Strangely, he constructed an ephod from the spoils of battle (8:22-28), which Israel worshiped. The idol at Ophrah became a snare to Gideon and his family. Gideon died at Ophrah, an old man (vv 29-32). His son Abimelech, ambitious for power, slaughtered his sibling rivals at Ophrah; only one of the 70, Jotham, escaped (9:1-6).

ORACLE
Divine revelation communicated through God's spokesperson (prophet, priest, or king), usually pronouncing blessing, instruction, or judgment. Contrary to Balak's request for Balaam to curse Israel, Balaam spoke an oracle of blessing (Nm 24:3-16). God instructed Moses through "living oracles" (Acts 7:38), and entrusted them with the Jewish people (Rom 3:2). The book of Proverbs records two oracles of wisdom: one given by Agur, Jakeh's son (Prv 30:1), and the other by King Lemuel (31:1). Oracles of judgment were uttered against kings Joram of Israel (2 Kgs 9:25) and Joash of Judah (2 Chr 24:27). The prophets often delivered them against evil nations: Isaiah delivered oracles against Babylon (Is 13:1; 21:1), Damascus (17:1), Egypt (19:1), Jerusalem (22:1), Moab (15:1), Philistia (14:28), and Tyre (23:1). Nahum delivered one against Nineveh (Na 1:1); Habakkuk, one against Judah (Hb 1:1); and Malachi, one against Israel (Mal 1:1). Sometimes false and misleading oracles were given by false prophets (Lam 2:14).

See also Prophecy.

ORDAIN, ORDINATION
The act of officially investing someone with religious authority. Several synonyms are "appoint," "institute," "make," and "establish." In current usage, the words "ordain" and "ordination" are applied to persons, signifying selection and appointment to God's service.

In the Old Testament Throughout the OT, emphasis falls upon God's choosing and appointing whom he wills. Priestly functions passed very early from the head of each household to the divinely chosen tribe of Levi (Dt 33:8-11; Jgs 17:13). Through all subsequent clan rivalries—"Zadokite," "Aaronic," "Hasmonean"—this claim to inherited privilege persisted. Divine appointment through Levi was traced back to Moses (Ex 4:14; 28:41; 29:9), claimed for the Ephraimite Samuel (1 Chr 6:28), and still celebrated by Sirach (Ecclus 45:6-22, c. 180 BC). As the book of Hebrews states (Heb 5:1, 4), no one takes the honor upon himself; he is "called by God, as Aaron was," by birth into an inherited status.

The first Levites were presented at the tabernacle in the presence of the people, and acknowledged by "the laying on of hands" (Nm 8:10, 14-18). Similarly, Moses received instructions for the week-long consecration of Aaron and his sons, with elaborate sacrifices, vestments, anointing, and ritual (Ex 29; Lv 8). In both cases, the careful preservation of these detailed instructions suggests that the ceremonies were retained, to some degree, in later years, though no repetition is recorded.

Alongside the priests there existed establishments of recognized prophets, or prophetic communities, sometimes with royal patronage (1 Sm 10:5; 1 Kgs 1:9-10; 18:17-19; 20:35; 22:5-28; 2 Kgs 2:3-7; 23:2). The line of prophecy was also traced back to earliest days (see Gn 20:7; Dt 34:10; Jgs 4:4; Jer 7:25). The phrase "sons of the prophets," and an obscure hint in Jeremiah 35:4, may imply that prophecy, like priesthood, was sometimes hereditary, but the manner of appointment and installation is unknown. The outstanding prophets were frequently opposed to the prophetic "schools" (Elijah, 1 Kgs 17; Micaiah, 1 Kgs 22:5-28; Jeremiah, Jer 27:14-16; 28). Such men were appointed by direct, divine call (1 Kgs 17:1; 21:17; Is 6; Jer 1; Am 7:15), though by God's instruction Elisha was called and anointed by Elijah (1 Kgs 19:16; cf. Is 61:1). Authentication of the prophet's message lay not in appropriate installation ceremonies but in its self-evident truth; in the case of predictions, in their fulfillment (1 Kgs 22:13-14, 26-28; Jer 28:5-9).

In the New Testament Christian ordination is also a matter of divine choice. Neither Jesus, nor any disciple, came from the professional religious classes. In ordaining the 12 apostles, Jesus called to him those whom he desired, later insisting, "You did not choose me, but I chose you and appointed you" (Jn 15:16, RSV). The selection of Matthias rested upon prayer and the divine lot (Acts 1:24-26). Paul contended that he had been set apart by God before he was born and did not receive his apostleship from or through men (Gal 1:1, 15). Paul and Barnabas were commissioned by direction of the Spirit during worship, probably through a Christian prophet. Similarly, Timothy was first chosen as assistant to Paul by prophetic utterances that pointed to him (1 Tm 1:18; 4:14).

At Corinth, various ministries of speaking, teaching, healing, and administration were directly conferred as gifts of the Spirit, who apportions as he sees fit (1 Cor 12:8-11, 28; cf. Eph 4:11). Elders of the church at Ephesus were made guardians of the flock by the Holy Spirit (Acts 20:28). The divine prerogative is everywhere clear: any attempt to obtain the privilege of ministry by personal initiative and unworthy means meets with sharpest condemnation (8:18-24).

On the other hand, the assembled church "nominated" Barsabbas and Matthias before submitting the final choice to God (Acts 1:15, 23). The believers chose the seven servers, then presented them to the apostles (6:2-6). An assembled church, at the Spirit's command, commissioned and sent off Paul and Barnabas (13:3). Paul and Barnabas themselves appointed elders (14:23), as Titus is instructed to do (Ti 1:5), and probably Timothy also (1 Tm 5:22). Elders at Lystra and Iconium, with Paul, obeying a Christian prophet, appointed Timothy to leadership (1 Tm 4:14; 2 Tm 1:6). By the time letters were written to Timothy and Titus, elaborate lists of qualifications were required for church leaders (1 Tm 3:1-13; 2 Tm 2:2).

The congregation of believers also participated in selecting leaders. This could have involved prayer, fasting, and casting lots (Acts 1:26; 6:6; 13:2-3; 14:23); sometimes "selection by hands" (Greek, *cheirotonein*, originally meaning "election by raising hands," later "selection by pointing to"; cf. Acts 14:23; 2 Cor 8:19); and sometimes selection by group choice (Acts 1:15, 23; 6:2-5; 13:3; 16:2; 1 Tm 4:14).

See also Foreordination.

OREB One of two Midianite chieftains (the other being Zeeb) put to death by men from Ephraim's tribe (Jgs 7:25). The occasion for this execution was Gideon's sur-

prise attack on the Midianite encampment at the hill of Moreh in the valley of Jezreel. The Midianites' line of retreat eastward required them to recross the Jordan River. Gideon sent word to the Ephraimites to seize the fording places on the river to prevent the Midianites from escaping. The Ephraimites, following the orders, intercepted a contingent of fleeing Midianites, including the prominent leaders Oreb and Zeeb. They beheaded these two leaders and sent their heads as a war prize to Gideon, who was then pursuing the Midianites on the east side of the Jordan (8:3).

During Israel's later history, the deaths of Oreb and Zeeb were recognized as a great triumph of God over the enemies of his people. The psalmist implores God to overthrow the nobles among Israel's current enemies just as he did the Midianite chieftains (Ps 83:11). The Lord, speaking through his prophet Isaiah, pledged that the Assyrians would be overthrown like the slaughter of Midian at the rock of Oreb (Is 9:4; 10:26), implying that the earlier victory amounted to more than the capture of two leaders; it was an important and strategic defeat of the Midianite invasion force.

OREB, Rock of Place where the Ephraimites killed the Midianite chieftain Oreb (Jgs 7:25; Is 10:26). *See* Oreb.

OREN Descendant of Judah and the third son of Jerahmeel (1 Chr 2:25).

ORGAN* KJV mistranslation for pipe in Genesis 4:21, Job 21:12, 30:31, and Psalm 150:4. *See* Musical Instruments (Ugab).

ORION Septuagint name for a constellation widely believed to resemble a giant hunter, belted or fettered. Various legends grew about this hunter—in Greece, that he had been banished to the sky for foolish boasting; in Semitic lands, for foolishly asserting his strength against God (the Hebrew means both "sturdy" and "fool"). Job 9:9 mentions the "making" of Orion among the great, unsearchable things God does in nature (cf. Am 5:8). God challenged Job to attempt what only God could do—loose Orion's fetters (Jb 38:31-32). The real significance of the question lies in the fact that the appearance of the Pleiades ushers in the spring and Orion ushers in the winter, both under the direction of God.

See also Pleiades.

ORNAN* Alternate rendering of Araunah, the Jebusite, in 1 Chronicles 21:15 (NLT mg). *See* Araunah.

ORONTES* River of the Great Rift Valley, flowing northward from the watershed and reaching the Mediterranean at Seleucia Pieria, the harbor city for Antioch. The Orontes never provided Syria with an economy as did the Nile for Egypt or the Tigris-Euphrates for Mesopotamia.

The countries that form the Fertile Crescent include Syria, which powerfully affected Israel's history, principally through the cities that stood on the Orontes; for example, the city of "Hamath the great" (Am 6:2) on the Orontes against which Solomon fought (2 Chr 8:3-4) and which Jeroboam II much later recovered for Israel (2 Kgs 14:28). When Samaria fell to Assyria, Sargon deported its inhabitants and replaced them with people from Hamath (17:24, 30). The inscriptions of Shalmaneser III say that Ahab of Samaria fought in the battle of Qarqar on the Orontes in 854 BC. Jehoahaz of Judah was summoned by Pharaoh Neco to Riblah on the Orontes (23:33), an event that Jeremiah mourned in a dirge (Jer 22:10). At Riblah, Nebuchadnezzar had Zedekiah blinded and led in chains to Babylon (2 Kgs 25:20).

ORPAH Woman of Moab who married Chilion (Ru 1:1-14), son of Elimelech and Naomi. After her husband and sons died, Naomi decided to return to Judah. Both Orpah and Ruth resolved to go with Naomi, but at Naomi's urging Orpah remained in her homeland.

See also Ruth, Book of.

ORPHAN Word coming from a Hebrew root meaning "to be alone" or "bereaved," often rendered as "fatherless." The idea describes any person who is without legal standing in the covenant community of Israel, who is unprotected or needy, and who is especially exposed to oppression. It also speaks of one who is bereft of one or both earthly parents (cf. Lam 5:3).

Since God has a special concern for the fatherless (Ex 22:22-24; Dt 10:18; Pss 10:14, 18; 27:10; 68:5; 146:9; Is 1:17; Hos 14:3), OT legislation made special provision for them by protecting their rights of inheritance (Nm 27:7-11; Dt 24:17; Prv 23:10), ensuring their freedom to glean the fields and vineyards (Dt 24:19-21), allowing their participation in the great annual feasts (16:11, 14), and allotting them a portion of the tithe crops collected every three years (14:29; 26:12). Strong condemnation awaits those who oppress them (Dt 24:17; 27:19; Mal 3:5).

While the orphans of Israel were sometimes aided by friends and relatives (Jb 29:12; 31:17), there was general failure to meet the requirements of the law, as is witnessed by the accusations of the inspired writers (Jb 6:27; 22:9; 24:3, 9; Ps 94:6; Is 1:23; 10:2; Jer 5:28; Ez 22:7). Consequently, the prophets never tire of pleading the orphan's cause (Jer 7:6; 22:3; Zec 7:10).

The word is used only twice in the NT—once in a general sense to describe those who are "desolate" or "comfortless" (Jn 14:18), and once in the specific sense to describe the "fatherless" (Jas 1:27). In the spirit of an OT prophet, James declares that true religion involves the care of orphans.

ORTHOSIA A city north of Tripolis in Phoenicia to which the Syrian usurper Trypho fled after being defeated by Antiochus VII Sidetes during the time of Simon Maccabeus (1 Macc 15:37).

OSHEA* KJV form of Hoshea, the alternate name for Joshua, in Numbers 13:8, 16. See Joshua (Person) #1.

OSIRIS* See Egypt, Egyptian.

OSNAPPER* Aramaic name for the Assyrian king Ashurbanipal (Ezr 4:10, NLT mg). See Ashurbanipal; Assyria, Assyrians.

OSPRAY*, OSPREY Large predatory bird, also known as the black vulture, considered unclean (Lv 11:13; Dt 14:12, NLT). See Birds (Vulture, Black).

OSSIFRAGE* Largest of the vulture family, also known as the bearded vulture, considered ceremonially unclean (Lv 11:13; Dt 14:12, KJV). See Birds (Lammergeier).

OSSUARY* A small stone coffin (Latin, ossuarium), vase, or casket for the reception of the calcined remains of the dead, or a sepulchral house, where the bones of the dead were deposited. Sarcophagus was the name given by the Greeks and Romans to a big stone coffin. Some religious ideas were involved in calling a coffin a "body

eater" (Greek, sarx, "flesh," and phagein, "to eat"). In many cases, the burial was not completed until the bones were taken up from the earth or from the sarcophagus. The bones were cleaned and put into their final deposit, that is, into an ossuary, usually a small coffin of stone. The tendency to postpone the final burial, where it involves exhumation or the collection of bones, is accentuated by making a common ossuary for a number of the departed. This exhuming and collecting the bones is connected with the idea of final reunion with one's fathers.

THE OSSUARY OF THE ST. CATHERINE MONASTERY
The famous ossuary of the St Catherine Monastery in Sinai is situated in the corner of a garden. For the bone remains of the monks, there is a house, where the bones are piled up in regular order, arranged according to their kind, as skulls, legs, and arms. In an uncovered porch before the bone house, there are vaults and pits in which the corpses of the monks are usually interred without coffins until the flesh is changed into dust, and then the bones are collected into the common ossuary.

OSTRACA* Inscribed pieces of pottery. See Inscriptions; Potsherd; Pottery; Writing (Potsherds).

OSTRICH See Birds.

OTHNI Levite; Shemaiah's son and a gatekeeper in Solomon's temple (1 Chr 26:7).

OTHNIEL Judge of Israel, mentioned as the son of Kenaz and Caleb's nephew (or perhaps brother), who delivered Israel from the tyranny of Cushan-rishathaim, and who earlier distinguished himself by capturing Debir (Jos 15:15-17; Jgs 1:11-13; 3:8-11).

At Caleb's prompting (promising his daughter Achsah to anyone who could conquer Debir), Othniel took Kiriath-sepher (Debir) and received Achsah for his wife. When Caleb gave her and her land as a present, Achsah asked for a water source and was given the upper springs and the lower springs (Jos 15:19; Jgs 1:15).

Later, Othniel delivered the Israelites from the oppressive Cushan-rishathaim, king of Mesopotamia (Aram-naharaim), whom the Israelites had served for eight years on account of their sin (Jgs 3:7). When the people cried for relief, the Lord raised up Othniel. Delivering them, he was described as someone that the "Spirit of the Lord came upon" (v 10). The effects of his work as judge lasted for a generation (vv 9-11).

See also Judges, Book of.

OUTCAST English translation of two related Hebrew terms whose primary meanings are to push away, banish, or cast out. In five of seven passages the term refers to exiles from Israel who are to be regathered by the Lord (Ps 147:2; Is 11:12; 27:13; 56:8; Jer 30:17). In two other passages it refers to fugitives from Moab (Is 16:3-4) and from Elam (Jer 49:36).

OUTWARD MAN* Part of a person outwardly observed. Used in contrast to "inner man," the term is not to be confused with other terms, both biblical and extrabiblical, such as "old man and new man," "natural man and spiritual man," "body and soul." Near Eastern, and particularly Semitic, thinking dealt in wholes instead of dichotomies, so the inner and outward man were viewed as parts of a whole rather than as irreconcilable opposites.

Although the phrase appears only in 2 Corinthians 4:16, similar terms, such as "outward appearance," are found elsewhere in Scripture (1 Sm 16:7; Mt 23:27-28; 2 Cor 10:7). From the biblical perspective, appearance should correspond to that which is inside a person. The Talmud says, "A scribe whose inner man does not correspond to the outer is no scribe."

See also Inner Man; Man.

OVEN *See* Food and Food Preparation.

OVENS, Tower of the Structure in the Jerusalem wall restored by Nehemiah and his workmen after the exile (Neh 3:11; 12:38). Malkijah, son of Harim, and Hasshub, son of Pahath-moab, are named as its builders. The tower was likely a defensive work on the northwest section of the wall, named for its proximity to nearby baking ovens.

OVERSEER Word appearing 12 times in the OT (KJV) and once in the NT. The NIV uses it at least six times in the NT to translate the word *episkopos*, which is derived from "peer" or "watch over." In the OT "overseer" is used to translate three words, which literally mean (1) one with authority who visits, (2) the preeminent one, or (3) the head writer.

Joseph was given authority to watch over and administer all aspects of Potiphar's house (Gn 39:4-5), advising Pharaoh to appoint 50 men to regulate and watch over the abundant harvest for seven years (41:34). Solomon appointed 3,600 overseers ("supervisors," NASB) to make the people work (2 Chr 2:18). In Josiah's time of temple renovation, there were overseers over all the workmen in every job (34:13, 17). Nehemiah appointed men to oversee the rebuilding of the wall (Neh 11:9, 14), to oversee the Levites (v 22), and to be in charge of the Levitical singers (12:42).

The word "overseer" speaks of the highest person of authority who exercised oversight over others. Included in this authoritative oversight was the idea of watching, directing, and protecting the master's interests. The NT carries these ideas also in regard to men appointed to serve the church on behalf of Jesus Christ (Acts 20:28; Phil 1:1; 1 Tm 3:1-2; Ti 1:7). Jesus Christ himself is the great Overseer (1 Pt 2:25, NIV).

See also Bishop; Elder.

OWL *See* Birds.

OX *See* Animals (Cattle).

OX (Person) Descendant of Israel, grandfather of Judith, the heroine of Maccabean times (Jdt 8:1).

OZEM
1. Sixth son of Jesse and a descendant of Hezron (1 Chr 2:15).
2. Fourth son of Jerahmeel by his first wife (1 Chr 2:25).

OZIAS* KJV rendering of Uzziah, king of Judah in Matthew 1:8-9. *See* Uzziah #1.

OZIEL Ancestor of Judith, the heroine of Maccabean times (Jdt 8:1).

OZNI, OZNITE Alternate names for Ezbon and his descendants (Nm 26:16). *See* Ezbon #1.

P

PAARAI One of David's mighty men, said to be from Arba, in Judah (2 Sm 23:35); perhaps the same as Naarai the son of Ezbai (1 Chr 11:37).

PACE (Measure) Linear measure equivalent to the average distance of a man's stride, or about one yard (.9 meter). *See* Weights and Measures.

PADDAN, PADDAN-ARAM Northwestern Mesopotamian district whose name means "Field of Aram," distinguishing this flatland from the mountainous regions to the north and east. Paddan-aram is alternately called Paddan in Genesis 48:7, the "land of Aram" in Hosea 12:12, and Aram-naharaim in Genesis 24:10 meaning "Aram of the two rivers" (see NLT mg). The two rivers probably referred to the Euphrates and Balih rivers, between which this tract of land was situated.

See also Aram-naharaim.

PADON Forefather of a family of temple servants who returned with Zerubbabel to Palestine following the Babylonian captivity (Ezr 2:44; Neh 7:47).

PAGANS *See* Gentiles.

PAGIEL Ocran's son from Asher's tribe, who was appointed by Moses to help number the people in the wilderness. He also served as leader of his tribe during that time (Nm 1:13; 2:27; 7:72, 77; 10:26).

PAHATH-MOAB Head of a family of Israelites who returned with Zerubbabel to Palestine after the Babylonian captivity (Ezr 2:6; Neh 7:11). Other members of his family, about 200 men, came with Ezra (Ezr 8:4). After the return, certain of his sons were included among the Israelites who vowed to sever their relationships with foreign wives (10:30). Hasshub, Pahath-moab's son, helped rebuild the Jerusalem wall and the tower of furnaces in Nehemiah's day (Neh 3:11). Pahath-moab, called a chief of the people, set his seal on Ezra's covenant (10:14).

PAI* Alternate form of Pau, an Edomite city, in 1 Chronicles 1:50 (see NLT mg). *See* Pau.

PALACE Residence for royalty. Excavations suggest that any city that enjoyed royal patronage would boast of a building that could be described as a palace. Royal cities had a second surrounding wall that shut off the royal palace and its outbuildings, forming the acropolis of the city. Jerusalem had the equivalent in the City of David, which formerly was the Citadel of Zion (2 Sm 5:7-9).

The OT's references to palaces in Palestine are vague—for example, David's palace (2 Sm 11:2, 9), the palace of Tirzah (1 Kgs 16:18) and Ahab's palace in Jezreel (21:1). Even the references to Solomon's palace in Jerusalem are quite imprecise. In 1 Kings 7:1-12 the construction of public and private buildings close to the temple went on for 13 years. Only the choicest of materials were used. But from the details supplied, it is quite impossible to reproduce plans of the House of the Forest of Lebanon, the Porch of Pillars, the Porch of the Throne, the palace for Solomon's Egyptian wife, or the royal palace. What the situation of these buildings was in relation to one another is matter only for conjecture. Round about the whole complex was a great court of hewn stones and cedar beams.

Forced labor was universal in the ancient Near East. Samuel's warning that a king would introduce the system into Israel (1 Sm 8:12-17) was fulfilled, and it came to full development under Solomon when he undertook his massive building program, including his palace. Solomon raised his workforce from all over Israel. The system incited Jeroboam to revolt (1 Kgs 12:4, 16). King Asa used it (15:22), and it continued on into Jeremiah's time (Jer 22:13). Nehemiah's builders were volunteers (see Neh 3:5).

Prominent among Solomon's royal buildings was the temple. Apparently, it stood in the middle of a courtyard called the inner court (1 Kgs 6:36), by contrast with the great court (7:12), which included both the temple and the palace. The palace itself had an inner court too (v 8), the northern wall of which was common to the inner court of the temple. Hence it was but a step from the king's domain to the Lord's domain.

The king's enthronement took place in the palace, in the Porch of the Throne (1 Kgs 1:46; 2 Kgs 11:19). When he took his seat on the throne, it marked his assumption of power (1 Kgs 16:11; 2 Kgs 13:13). Solomon's throne in his palace became the symbol of royal power, although his throne was still called the throne of David (1 Kgs 2:24, 45; Is 9:7). Solomon's palace throne is described as one of the wonders of the world (1 Kgs 10:18-20). It was around this throne that the high officials came to do him homage (1:47).

The king's daughters lived in the palace until their marriage under the care of women (2 Sm 13:7). They wore a distinctive dress (vv 18-19). The king's sons were reared in the palace by nurses (2 Kgs 11:2) and tutored under leading men of the city (10:1, 6-7), until they were able to perform certain duties at the court (2 Sm 8:18; 1 Chr 18:17). Then they led an independent life and were provided for by the king (2 Chr 21:3). Amnon evidently lived outside the palace (2 Sm 13:5), and Absalom had his own house (13:20; 14:24), lands, and livestock (13:23; 14:30). Palace or court officials surrounded the royal family (1 Kgs 10:4-5). Whatever their office, they were called the king's "servants." There were those "who saw the king's face," meaning they were admitted to the king's presence (2 Sm 14:24, 28, 32), or stood before the king (1 Sm 16:21-22; Jer 52:12). It was a signal mark of favor to be admitted to the royal table (2 Sm 9:7, 13).

PALACE OF THE FOREST OF LEBANON Name for Solomon's palace in Jerusalem, adjacent to the temple, given this designation because of the amount of Lebanese cedar used in its construction. The structure was about 150 feet (45.7 meters) long, 75 feet (22.9 meters) wide, and 45 feet (13.7 meters) high (1 Kgs 7:2-5). Three hundred gold shields were made to decorate it, and all the vessels of the house were made of gold. A large ivory throne overlaid with gold was constructed and placed within the palace (2 Chr 9:16-20). Besides providing housing and a formal palace for Solomon, it was also used to store arms (Is 22:8).

PALAESTRA* Greek word designating a place for athletic exercise (2 Macc 4:14).

PALAL Uzai's son, who helped rebuild the Jerusalem wall in Nehemiah's day (Neh 3:25).

PALESTINA* KJV rendering of Philistia, a country along the southwest coast of Canaan, in Exodus 15:14 and Isaiah 14:29-31. *See* Philistia, Philistines.

PALESTINE* Country on the eastern shore of the Mediterranean Sea, also known as Canaan and Israel. Palestine was situated at the west end of the Fertile Crescent—that arching stretch of highly productive land that ran from the Persian Gulf through Mesopotamia and Syria to Egypt. Palestine lay in a unique position, for it constituted a land bridge between Mesopotamia and Egypt, the two primary cultural centers of the ancient Near East. It also served as a connection between the continents of Asia and Africa and as a continental link between Africa and Europe. Trade moved by well-defined routes as goods were brought into the Fertile Crescent from as far as northern Europe, India, and south of Egypt. The same roads were followed by prospective conquerors as they moved their armies from area to area in quest of power and wealth.

It was the land promised by God to Abraham and his descendants, the homeland of God's chosen people, and the geographical scene for much of biblical history. It has become a land sacred to three great world religions: Judaism, Christianity, and Islam. Physically, Palestine is a kind of microcosm. In a stretch of 150 miles (241.4 kilometers) one can find almost every kind of climate and terrain known on the earth. It has fertile plains, sandy deserts, rocky wastes, forests, mountains, lakes, and rivers. With such a variety in so small an area, the land provides sharp contrasts. In the north, Mt Hermon stands perpetually snowcapped at an altitude of about 9,100 feet (2,773.7 meters), while a scant 100 miles (160.9 kilometers) distant in the subtropical depression of the Jordan Valley is the Dead Sea, representing the deepest spot on the earth.

PREVIEW
• Name
• Territory
• Climate
• Geography

Name This land has been known by many names over its long history. The country seems to have been named after the maritime region, perhaps because this was the area that most foreigners contacted. So the land was called Canaan and later named after Philistia. In the table of nations, Canaan is said to have extended from Sidon in the north toward Gerar as far as Gaza and east toward the Cities of the Plain (Gn 10:19). The name Canaan appears in the Bible; the first occurrence of the name as that of a country or region is in Genesis 11:31.

After the Israelite conquest of Canaan, the country was known as the land of Israel (1 Sm 13:19; 1 Chr 22:2). With the division of the kingdom in the reign of

Rehoboam (930 BC), the name Israel went with the northern kingdom, and the southern kingdom was known as Judah (later, Judea).

Territory The earliest reference to the extent of Palestine appears in the promise of the land to Abraham and to his descendants (Gn 15:18-21). Here the borders are given as the River of Egypt (Wadi el-Arish) in the southwest to the Euphrates River in the northeast. It is further defined in terms of the peoples who occupied it at that time, 10 in all, including the Kenites, the Kenizzites, the Kadmonites, the Hittites, the Perizzites, the Rephaim, the Amorites, the Canaanites, the Girgashites, and the Jebusites. In Genesis 17:8 the land is called simply "all the land of Canaan."

The Lord gave more detailed directions to Moses concerning the borders of the land that Israel was to occupy (Nm 34:1-12). The southern boundary was to be from the River of Egypt to the south of Kadesh-barnea and along the wilderness of Zin to the southern extremity of the Dead Sea. The western boundary was the Mediterranean, the northern border was set at the entrance to Hamath, and the eastern limit was the Jordan River and the Dead Sea.

The greatest extent of the Promised Land is seen in the Lord's declaration to Moses that he would set the bounds of Israel from the Red Sea to the Sea of the Philistines (Mediterranean) and from the wilderness to the Euphrates River (Ex 23:31). Historically, during the period of the judges and the reign of Saul, Israel did not conquer the land that had been given to the tribes in the division under Joshua. The military strength of David and the diplomacy of Solomon enabled them to achieve a marked expansion of Israelite rule. David defeated Hadadezer, king of Zobah, and thus pushed his northern frontier to the Euphrates River; he defeated Syria, Ammon, Moab, Edom, and Amalek, enlarging the kingdom also to the east and south (2 Sm 8:1-14; 1 Chr 18:1-13). Solomon had a fleet of merchant ships stationed at Ezion-geber on the Gulf of Aqaba. He also engaged in copper mining in that area.

Climate It has been said that the climate of Palestine is more varied than that of any other area of comparable size in the world. Generally, the climate may be described as temperate; at Jerusalem, for example, the temperature extremes range from 26° F (-3.3° C) to 107° F (41.6° C), and the average annual rainfall is about 20 inches (50.8 centimeters). The coastal plain is warmer and has been compared to the east coast of Florida. The average annual temperature at Jaffa (Joppa) is 67° F (19.4° C). The Jordan Valley in the area of the Dead Sea is subtropical; in summer its temperatures may reach 120° F (48.8° C).

Rainfall is seasonal, with rain coming in the cooler months of the year as the prevailing west wind brings moisture over the comparatively colder land area, much like the "lake effect" snows of the Great Lakes region of the United States. The rainy season extends from October to April. Within this time the Israelites singled out two periods (Jer 5:24; Jl 2:23), the former rain and the latter rain, with the former rain occurring in the months of October and November and the latter rain falling in March and April. The coastal area receives about 28 inches (71.1 centimeters) of rain annually, while the average for the country in general is 22 to 24 inches (55.9–70 centimeters).

Geography For purposes of description, the land of Palestine may be conveniently divided into five longitudinal sections:

1. The Maritime or Coastal Plain
2. The Shephelah

3. The Western Plateau or Hill Country
4. The Arabah or Jordan Valley
5. The Eastern Plateau or Transjordan

These divisions are based essentially on differences in elevation, but other geographic elements also serve to mark their limits or otherwise distinguish them.

with an elevation of about 500 to 1,000 feet (152.4–304.8 meters) and a width of only a few miles. It extends from the valley of Aijalon to Beersheba.

The valleys of the Shephelah produced grain crops, while the hills were well suited for grapes and olives. The region was very important strategically, because it afforded approaches to Jerusalem.

Aerial View of Jerusalem in Judea

The Maritime or Coastal Plain The Maritime or Coastal Plain may be divided into three separate plains from south to north: the plain of Philistia, the plain of Sharon, and the plain of Acre.

1. The plain of Philistia begins with the Wadi el-Arish, or River of Egypt, and extends north to the Nahr el-Auja, about five miles (8 kilometers) north of Joppa. This plain is about 70 miles (112.6 kilometers) long and reaches its greatest width in the latitude of Gaza, where it measures about 30 miles (48.3 kilometers). Along the Mediterranean there were dunes of sand, but for the most part, this area was very fertile and admirably suited for the production of grain.
2. The plain of Sharon is not sharply demarcated from the Philistine plain and was probably under Philistine control, but the OT recognizes it as a separate entity (cf. Sg 2:1; Is 65:10). The plain extends north to Mt Carmel. On the coast are the town of Dor, which is mentioned in "The Tale of Wenamon," and the city of Caesarea, where Herod the Great did much building.
3. Beyond the promontory of Carmel lies a bay on which was situated the city named Ptolemais (Acts 21:7), also known as Acre or Acco (Jgs 1:31). Here a narrow plain stretches some 20 miles (32.2 kilometers) to the Ladder of Tyre (Ras en-Nakurah). The Kishon River (Jgs 4:7, 13; 1 Kgs 18:40) flows through this plain to the sea.

The Shephelah The Shephelah constitutes a kind of "midlands," intermediate between the lowlands of the coastal plain and the highlands of the Western Plateau,

The Western Plateau or Hill Country The Western Plateau or Hill Country ranges from 1,000 to 4,000 feet (304.8–609.6 meters) in elevation and covers some 150 miles (241.4 kilometers) from Lebanon to Beersheba. It may also be divided into three areas: Galilee, Samaria, and Judea.

1. Galilee may be regarded as two parts, Upper Galilee (2,000–4,000 feet, or 609.6–1,219.2 meters) and Lower Galilee (below 2,000 feet, or 609.6 meters). The area was agricultural and pastoral, like much of Palestine, and was open to invasion. The highways that traversed Galilee made it a cosmopolitan district, so that Isaiah 9:1 calls it "Galilee of the nations."
2. Samaria was also suitable for crops and pasture. The brothers of Joseph were grazing their flocks in the plain of Dothan when Joseph visited them and became the victim of their conspiracy (Gn 37:17).
3. Judea has an elevation of about 2,000 to 3,500 feet (609.6–1,066.8 meters) and reaches some 60 miles (96.5 kilometers) from Bethel to Beersheba. The city of Jerusalem stands at an elevation of 2,654 feet (808.9 meters), surrounded by mountains and valleys that served as part of its defense system (Ps 125:2). This was the heart of the nation, for from the time of David onward, the capital was here, and more important, the ark of the covenant had been brought here during David's reign. As the Lord had long foretold, Jerusalem had become the center of his worship; here Solomon built the temple, one of the greatest structures ever made.

The Arabah or Jordan Valley The Arabah or Jordan Valley presents the extremes of height and depth. Mt Hermon rises to 9,166 feet (2,793.8 meters), while the surface of the Dead Sea lies 1,275 feet (395 meters) below sea level, and at its deepest part the sea plunges another 1,300 feet (396.2 meters).

1. The North Arabah or Upper Jordan Valley. The Jordan River has four sources, all near Mt Hermon. The Jordan flows through what was Lake Huleh, now partly drained and designated as a wildlife refuge. Two miles (3.2 kilometers) below the Huleh basin is the Bridge of Jacob's Daughters, by which the old road to Damascus crossed the river. The Jordan then flows into a gorge some 1,200 feet (365.8 meters) deep.

2. The Sea of Galilee, about 10 miles (16.1 kilometers) from Huleh, has an elevation of -685 feet (-208.8 meters). It measures 15 by 8 miles (24.1 by 12.9 kilometers), with a maximum depth of 750 feet (228.6 meters). The shape of the lake gave it the OT name, Chinnereth, meaning "harp" (Nm 34:11; Jos 13:27). In the NT it was also called the Lake of Gennesaret (Lk 5:1) and the Sea of Tiberias (Jn 6:1; 21:1).

3. The Middle Arabah, or Ghor. The name Jordan means "descender"; in the 60 miles or 96.5 kilometers (in a straight line) from the outlet of the Sea of Galilee to the northern end of the Dead Sea there is a fall of more than 600 feet (182.9 meters), or 10 feet per mile. The river flows in a series of S-curves or zigzags, so that its actual course between Galilee and the Dead Sea covers some 200 miles (321.8 kilometers).

   This stretch of the Jordan Valley is known as the Ghor, or Rift. Six miles (9.7 kilometers) below the Sea of Galilee the Yarmuk River enters from the east. Some smaller streams empty into the Jordan, but the next river of consequence is the Jabbok (Gn 32:22). Just south of the Sea of Galilee the Ghor is about four miles (6.4 kilometers) wide; near Beth-shan it reaches seven miles (11.3 kilometers) wide; beyond that for some 15 miles (24.1 kilometers) the mountains close in on the river on both sides, narrowing the valley to two to three miles (3.2 to 4.8 kilometers); near Jericho it broadens to about 12 miles (19.3 kilometers).

4. The Dead Sea is unique. Its surface is the deepest point on the face of the earth and its waters are of tremendous wealth. In the OT it is known as the Salt Sea (Gn 14:3; Nm 34:12; Jos 12:3) and the Sea of Arabah (Jos 12:3). Josephus calls it Lake Asphaltitis.

   This body of water is 46 miles (74 kilometers) long, 10 miles (16.1 kilometers) wide, and 1,300 feet (396.2 meters) deep and consists of about 25 percent mineral matter, making it a chemical deposit of great value. In addition to the flow of the Jordan, the Dead Sea receives the water of other streams, such as the Arnon River on the east. Much of the runoff of the seasonal rains also finds its way into the Salt Sea. Temperatures in the valley may reach 120° F (48.8° C) in summer; with the extreme humidity the climate is very debilitating and almost unbearable. It is estimated that the daily evaporation from the sea is 6 to 8 million tons (5.4–7.3 million metric tons).

5. The Southern Arabah, mostly a barren wilderness, extends from the Dead Sea to the Gulf of Aqaba, a distance of 150 miles (241.4 kilometers). There is a gradual ascent from the Dead Sea to a watershed just west of Petra. Near the tip of the Gulf of Aqaba were the ports of Elath (modern Eilat) and Ezion-geber.

The Eastern Plateau or Transjordan The Eastern Plateau, or Transjordan, was not named as part of the land of promise, but it was taken by the tribes of Reuben, Gad, and half of Manasseh. The region is better supplied with water than the Western Plateau and has perennial streams, such as the Yarmuk, Jabbok, and Arnon. A principal north-south road was the King's Highway, followed by the Israelites during the exodus (Nm 21:22) and probably also the route taken by the invading kings of Genesis 14.

The northern section of Transjordan was known as Bashan, noted for its cattle (Ps 22:12; Ez 39:18) and for its oak trees (Is 2:13; Zec 11:2).

Gilead, famed for its balm (Gn 37:25; Jer 8:22), was often mentioned in the OT (e.g., Dt 3:10-16; Jgs 11). It extended from the Yarmuk River to the city of Heshbon. This area was heavily forested in David's time (cf. 2 Sm 18:8).

In Palestine proper there were two important divisions: the plain of Esdraelon and the Negev. The plain of Esdraelon, often associated prophetically with Armageddon, lies between Galilee and Samaria. This is one of the most fertile areas of Palestine and also was the scene of numerous battles. The plain was guarded by fortress cities on its southern side (Megiddo, Ibleam, and Taanach). In the OT the valley of Jezreel was not regarded as a part of Esdraelon but as the valley between the hill of Moreh and Mt Gilboa. At the eastern end was the stronghold of Beth-shan.

In the extreme south of the land is the wilderness area called the Negev, or South Country. This begins in the region of Beersheba and extends roughly to Kadesh-barnea. A district of infrequent and irregular rainfall, its agriculture is restricted, although a nomadic pastoral life has been widely practiced there. *See* Arabah; Conquest and Allotment of the Land; Dead Sea; Decapolis; Sea of Galilee; Jordan River; Negev; Shephelah; Transjordan.

PALLU, PALLUITE Reuben's son, father of Eliab (Gn 46:9; Ex 6:14; Nm 26:8; 1 Chr 5:3) and the founder of the Palluite family (Nm 26:5).

PALM *See* Plants.

PALMERWORM* KJV designation for the cutting locust in Joel 1:4, 2:25, and Amos 4:9. *See* Animals (Locust).

PALMS, City of Designation for Jericho in Deuteronomy 34:3 and 2 Chronicles 28:15. *See* Jericho.

PALSY* *See* Paralysis, Paralytic.

PALTI

1. One of the 12 spies Moses sent to explore the land of Canaan before the Israelite conquest. Palti represented Benjamin's tribe (Nm 13:9).
2. Laish's son, to whom King Saul gave Michal, his daughter and David's wife, after the break between Saul and David (1 Sm 25:44). Michal was recovered from him and returned to David (2 Sm 3:15); in that reference he is called Paltiel.

PALTIEL

1. Son of Azzan and a leader of Issachar's tribe (Nm 34:26). He was appointed by Eleazar and Joshua to assist in the distribution of the land west of the Jordan River among the ten tribes to whom it was given.

2. Alternate rendering of Palti, Laish's son, in 2 Samuel 3:15. *See* Palti #2.

PALTITE*, The Designation for Helez, one of David's mighty men and possibly a descendant of Palti (2 Sm 23:26, NLT mg). He may have lived in Beth-pelet. In 1 Chronicles 11:27 he is called a "Pelonite." *See* Beth-Pelet.

PAMPHYLIA Coastal region on the southern shore of Asia Minor (Turkey) stretching 80 miles (128.7 kilometers) from Lycia on the west to Cilicia on the east, and about 20 miles (32.2 kilometers) wide from the seacoast to the Taurus Mountains. Being little more than a narrow coastal plain with an unpleasantly hot and humid climate, this province produced few important cities. This, combined with its general inaccessibility—lying as it did deep at the north end of the bay of Adalia and separated from the rest of inland Asia by a rugged mountain range—made it a haven for pirates. In 102 BC the Roman senate established patrol stations on the coasts of Pamphylia and western Cilicia to police the area, but no effective control was established until 67 BC, when Pompey was given unlimited resources to clean up the Mediterranean.

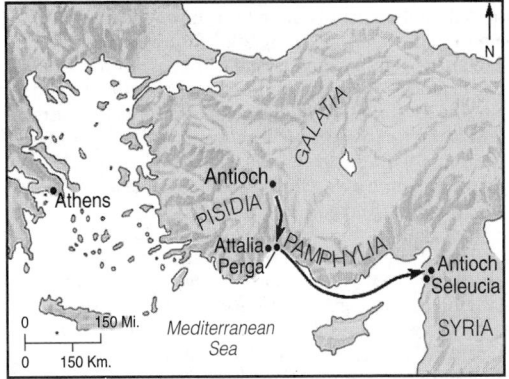

Paul and Barnabas Travel through Pamphylia at the End of the First Missionary Journey

There was evidently a Jewish population in the province because Luke names Pamphylia among 15 countries from which Jews came to Jerusalem to the feast of Pentecost (Acts 2:10). Some have argued that Pamphylia could not have possessed any significant numbers of Christians because it and Lycia are not mentioned in 1 Peter 1:1, which seems to sum up the whole of Asia Minor. That argument is not convincing, however, because the date of the writing of 1 Peter is not known, and if it was written during the period from AD 43 to 74, when Pamphylia was considered a part of Galatia, Pamphylia could have been included in that designation. Peter may also have considered Lycia in the broad designation of Galatia because his introduction mentions only the larger political divisions of Asia Minor. Nevertheless, it must be noted that Paul apparently had little success in the Pamphylian city of Perga, because there is no statement of opposition to him there or of any converts being made. He did not revisit the province on his second journey, even though his plan was to return and visit the Christians in every city where they had preached (Acts 15:36). Perhaps Paul's separation from Barnabas was the reason for this, and it may be that Barnabas and John Mark visited Pamphylia after Cyprus (vv 37-41).
See also Attalia; Perga.

PAMPHYLIA AND THE CRITICS
Some critics have doubted the accuracy of Luke's designation of Pamphylia as a separate province from Lycia (Acts 27:5) because of an apparent contradiction by the early Roman historian Dio Cassius who stated that Claudius combined Pamphylia and Lycia into one imperial province in AD 43. However, an inscription from Pamphylia establishes that it remained an independent province for a while longer, was eventually connected with Galatia to the north, and finally was united to Lycia about AD 74 by the Roman emperor Vespasian. Therefore, when Paul traveled through the region on his first missionary journey (Acts 13:13; 14:24; 15:38), it is correctly referred to by Luke as Pamphylia.

PANNAG* KJV rendering of millet (Ez 27:17), an annual grass whose seeds are used in making bread. *See* Plants (Millet).

PANTHER *See* Animals (Leopard).

PAPER Word in English translations of the Bible better understood as papyrus. *See* Writing.

PAPHOS Originally a Phoenician settlement in southwest Cyprus. "Old Paphos" was supplemented by a Greek settlement, "New Paphos," some 10 miles (16.1 kilometers) distant; the new one became the administrative center when Cyprus became a senatorial province of Rome in 22 BC. The combined city was famous for its temple, dedicated originally to the Syrian goddess Astarte, worshiped (according to Tacitus) with ancient Phoenician rites involving anointing of a conical stone (meteorite?). The Greeks identified her with Aphrodite, claiming she sprang from the sea.

At Paphos, Paul first met vigorous opposition to the gospel from Elymas. Here Paul performed his first recorded miracle. Mercifully, Elymas's blindness was only "for a time" (Acts 13:11).

PAPIAS* Early church leader of Hierapolis; chronicler of early Christianity. The information we have about Papias (AD 60–130) and his work was given by Eusebius of Caesarea and Irenaeus of Lyons. Irenaeus stated that Papias had heard the apostle John preach and also knew Polycarp. Eusebius mentioned his *Explanation of the Sayings of the Lord*. In the preface to this work Papias maintains that his primary purpose was to bring forth a truthful record of a collection of the words and deeds of the apostles that were told to him by a presbyter. Irenaeus understood him to be alluding to the apostle John, but Eusebius contended that he referred to two Johns, one who was the apostle and the other who was the companion of Aristion.

Papias claimed that Mark, the Evangelist, who had never heard Christ, was the interpreter of Peter, and that he carefully gave an account of everything he remembered from the preaching of Peter. The statement that Matthew wrote down sayings of Jesus in Hebrew was affirmed by Papias. Irenaeus understood this as a reference to Hebraisms in Matthew's Gospel, whereas Origen took this to mean that Matthew originally wrote his Gospel in Hebrew.

The statements of Papias have raised many questions concerning (1) the formation of the Gospels, (2) a possible Hebrew (Aramaic) version of Matthew, and (3) the possibility and identity of two Johns. According to tradition, Papias died a martyr.

PAPYRUS Ancient Egyptian writing material derived from the papyrus plant. *See* Plants; Writing.

PARABLE A particular form of Jesus' teaching in the Gospels.

PREVIEW
• Introduction
• History of Interpretation
• The Meaning of "Parable"
• The Purpose of Parables
• The Reason Jesus Taught in Parables

Introduction An understanding of parables is essential if one is to understand the teaching of Jesus, since the parables make up approximately 35 percent of his recorded sayings. At no point are the vitality, relevance, and appropriateness of his teaching so clear as they are in his parables. While the parable form is not unique to Jesus, he was certainly a master at using parables as a way of teaching. The parables are not merely illustrations for Jesus' preaching; they *are* the preaching, at least to a great extent. Nor are they simple stories; they have been truly described as both "works of art" and "weapons of warfare." How one interprets the parables is not as easy a task as one might think. The way one understands the nature of a parable and the essence of Jesus' message obviously will determine the method and content of interpretation.

History of Interpretation A great deal of insight can be obtained by following the course of treatment the parables have received over the centuries. Not surprisingly, they have been subjected to radically different approaches. But the questions that underlie all interpretations are these: (1) How much of the parable is really significant—all the details or only one point? (2) What is the meaning of the parable in the teaching of Jesus? (3) Of what relevance is the parable to the interpreter?

The Allegorizing Approach From the second century even to the present, many people have allegorized the parables. In effect, they have said that every detail in the account is significant and that the meaning and relevance of a parable are to be found in the way it portrays Christian theology. This method, often identified as the Alexandrian school of interpretation, is best illustrated by a classic example that comes from Augustine (AD 354–430), the scholar who, despite his allegorizing, was a great theologian. His interpretation of the parable of the good Samaritan views Christ as the good Samaritan, the oil as the comfort of good hope, the animal as the flesh of the Incarnation, the inn as the church, and the innkeeper as the apostle Paul (to say nothing of the other details). Obviously, this interpretation has nothing in common with Jesus' intention but rather reads into the story preconceived ideas of the interpreter. Such an approach can sound good theologically, but it prohibits the hearing of the Word of God. Medieval interpreters went even further than the allegorizing approach by finding multiple meanings in the text. Usually four were listed: (1) the literal meaning; (2) an allegorical meaning relating to Christian theology; (3) a moral meaning giving direction for daily life; (4) a heavenly meaning indicating something about future life.

Not all of the church was dominated by such allegorizing interpretations. The school of Antioch was known for its commonsense approach to hearing the text. However, its influence was limited when compared to the Alexandrian school and, apart from notable excep-

tions, most of the church's efforts at understanding the parables over the centuries have involved allegorizing.

The Approach of Adolph Julicher (1867–1938) Julicher was a German scholar who published two volumes on the parables toward the end of the 19th century. His major contribution was the wholesale rejection of allegorizing as a means of interpreting the parables. In his reaction against allegorizing, Julicher went to the opposite extreme to say that a parable of Jesus has only one point of contact between the story and the fact being portrayed. He believed that this one point alone is important in interpretation and that it will usually be a general religious statement. Julicher went so far as to say that not only was allegorizing wrong but that Jesus did not use allegories, since they tend to hide rather than reveal. He said that any allegory appearing in the NT comes from the writers of the Gospels rather than Jesus. Julicher was correct to reject allegorizing (i.e., making an allegory of what was not intended to be allegory), but the rejection of allegory itself as a legitimate means of communication for Jesus is unfounded.

The Historical Approach Twentieth-century study of the parables, particularly the work of C. H. Dodd (1884–1973) and Joachim Jeremias, has rightly emphasized the historical context in which the parables were originally told. Focus is placed on cultural factors that help in understanding the details of the parables and on the context of Jesus' original preaching about the kingdom of God. Usually this approach has assumed that the first-century church changed the original thrust of some of the parables to meet her own needs, and consequently various procedures have been proposed to recover the original intent. It is true that the parables have been shaped, edited, and collected in units by the Gospel writers (note, e.g., Matthew's collection of eight parables in Mt 13:1-52). Also, the aim of an interpreter should be to hear the parables as they were originally intended by Jesus and as his original audience heard them. The attempt to go behind the Gospel accounts, however, is a delicate task, and some of the procedures proposed for doing so need to be questioned. Notice must be taken of the way each of the Gospel writers has used his material, but the extent to which one can go behind the Gospels is limited.

Modern Trends in Parable Research In the past few decades a number of attempts to interpret the parables have suggested new avenues of approach. Basically these new approaches have been somewhat dissatisfied with (although appreciative of) both Julicher and the historical approach in that both limit the impact of the parables on today's reader. Julicher reduced Jesus' teaching to pious moralisms, and the historical approach tended to focus on 2,000 years ago while ignoring both the artistic and psychological features of the parables. Consequently, numerous attempts have been made to convey the same impact the parables had for the original hearers to today's hearers. Increasingly, less focus is placed on the historical meaning of the parables and more emphasis is placed on their artistic, existential, and poetic effect. Jesus' parables are regarded as works of art that can be regarded as open-ended as far as meaning is concerned. A parable, then, would have an original meaning and the potential for a series of further possible meanings. While the original meaning would provide some control for reinterpretation, these approaches are not bound by the author's intention.

A great deal can be learned from modern approaches, especially from their concern to make sure that the parables speak to our day with their original vitality. However, there is also the danger of abusing the parables in a way similar to earlier mistreatments. Those allegorizing the parables in the history of the church were not bound by the meaning of Jesus and found their own meaning. Modern interpreters, too, can find their own meaning, and even though the explanations may sound convincing (as no doubt Augustine's did to his hearers), they will not be a communication of the Word of God. If God and his ways are revealed by Jesus, then we err if we do not hear his parables as they were intended in their original context. There is indeed a dynamic interaction between the text and the interpreter, but the interpreter is brought to a moment of truth most effectively when the Spirit confronts him or her with the parable as Jesus intended it for his hearers.

The Meaning of "Parable" The usual definition of a parable as "an earthly story with a heavenly meaning" will not suffice for understanding Jesus' parables. Nor are parables merely comparisons or illustrations of what Jesus wanted to say. The situation is much more complex with regard to the biblical meaning of the word "parable." In fact, one must distinguish between three uses of the word "parable" in biblical studies.

First, one should be aware that the Greek word for parable and its Hebrew counterpart are both broad terms and can be used for anything from a proverb to a full-blown allegory, including a riddle, a dark saying, an illustration, a contrast, or a story. For example, the Greek word for parable is used in Luke 4:23 with reference to the saying "physician, heal yourself" and most translations render it as "proverb." In Mark 3:23 "parables" is used with reference to the riddles Jesus asks the scribes, such as "How can Satan cast out Satan?" Similarly, Mark 13:28 uses "parable" of a simple illustration. In Luke 18:2-5 the unjust judge is *contrasted* with God, who brings justice quickly. If one compares the Hebrew OT and the Septuagint (an ancient Greek translation of the OT), the word for parable is used most frequently with reference to a proverb or dark saying. The broad meaning of "parable," then, can refer to any of these methods used to stimulate thought.

Second, "parable" can be used of any story with two levels of meaning (literal and figurative) that functions as religious and ethical speech.

Third, "parable" can be used technically in modern studies to distinguish it from other types of stories, such as similitudes, exemplary stories, and allegories. In this case a parable is a fictitious story that narrates a particular event and is usually told in the past tense (e.g., the parable of the lost son). A similitude, however, is a comparison that relates a typical or recurring event in real life and is usually told in the present tense (e.g., Mt 13:31-32). An exemplary story is not a comparison at all; rather, it presents character traits as either positive or negative examples to be imitated or avoided. Usually four exemplary stories are identified: the good Samaritan (Lk 10:30-35), the rich fool (12:16-20), the rich man and Lazarus (16:19-31), and the Pharisee and the tax collector (18:10-13).

Allegory is the most difficult to define and has caused considerable debate. Usually allegory is defined as "a series of related metaphors." A metaphor is an implied comparison that does not use "like" or "as." This definition is used broadly, but it is not entirely satisfactory for two reasons: (1) It does not indicate whether obscurity is an essential element in allegory. Some view allegory as needing to be decoded and as being understandable only to a select few. If, however, the allegory uses customary metaphors that all could understand, it would not be obscure. (2) It does not specify how much of the story is important as related metaphors. If there were only two or three related metaphors, would the story be an allegory? At the other extreme, do minor details in the story (such as the three levels of harvest in the parable of the sower) have significance? An example of an allegory would be the parable of the sower.

This raises the problem of the difference between a parable and an allegory—a frequently debated issue. On definitions one and two above, allegory is included in parable. But on definition three, a distinction is made between them because a parable is not a series of related metaphors. The details of the story of the lost son (the swine, the far country, etc.) do not stand for something else as they would if they were in an allegory but rather convey in dramatic terms the depths to which the son had sunk. However, a parable is *not* thereby limited to one point of comparison between the story and the fact being portrayed. There may be several items that need to be mentioned from a particular parable. The parable of the lost son emphasizes the rejoicing that takes place at repentance (note the repetition of this theme in Lk 15:24, 32), but the receptivity of the father obviously parallels the grace of God and the younger and elder sons reflect sinners and religious authorities, respectively. The distinction between parable and allegory is vague at best and will vary, depending on what definitions are assigned the terms. One should note that what can be said about parable usually can also be said about allegory.

The Purpose of Parables The purpose of parables and a description of their characteristics will assist understanding. The parables focus on God and his kingdom and in doing so reveal what kind of God he is, by what principles he works, and what he expects of humanity. Because of the focus on the kingdom, some of the parables reveal many aspects of Jesus' mission as well (note the parable of the wicked tenants in Mt 21:33-41).

The following characteristics of parables should be observed: (1) Parables are usually concise and symmetrical. Items are presented in twos or threes with an economy of words. Unnecessary people, motives, and details are usually omitted. (2) The features in the story are taken from everyday life, and the metaphors used are frequently common enough that they set up a context for understanding. For example, the discussion of an owner and his vineyard would naturally make hearers think of God and his people because of the OT use of those images. (3) Even though the parables speak in terms of everyday life, often they contain elements of surprise or hyperbole (an exaggeration used as a figure of speech). The parable of the good Samaritan (Lk 10:30-35) introduces a Samaritan in the story where one would probably expect a layperson. The parable of the unforgiving servant (Mt 18:23-34) puts the debt of the first servant at $10 million, an unbelievable sum in that day. (4) Parables require their hearers to pass judgment on the events of the story and, having done so, to realize that they must make a similar judgment in their own lives. The classic example is the parable of Nathan to David (2 Sm 12:1-7), where David judges the man in the story as worthy of death and then is told that he is the man. Because they force one to decide, to come to a moment of truth, the parables force their hearers to live in the present without resting on the laurels of the past or waiting for the future. The parables are the result of a mind that sees truth in concrete pictures rather than abstractions, and they teach that truth in such a compelling manner that the hearer cannot escape it.

GUIDELINES FOR INTERPRETING PARABLES

Interpreting the parables is not easy, but certain guidelines can be presented that will avoid past errors and make sane interpretation possible.

1. Analyze the parable thoroughly. Note the characters and movement of the story, its climax, and the repetition of key words or ideas. If it appears in more than one Gospel, do a comparative analysis of the various accounts to note both similarities and differences.
2. Listen to the parable without any preconceptions as to its form or its meaning. Attempt to hear the parable as if sitting at the feet of Jesus without knowing the parable, its meaning, and Christian theology. While it is impossible for a modern reader to become a first-century Jewish hearer, it is imperative that a parable be interpreted in its original context and in the ways its author originally intended it to be understood.
3. Look for help in the surrounding context, but realize that the original context for many of the parables has not been preserved. Often the parables appear where they do in the Gospels because of the arrangement of the Gospel writers.
4. Notice features in the parable that reflect the life and thinking of the first-century world. An understanding of cultural and religious factors, and an awareness of the OT ideas reflected in a parable, will greatly assist in its interpretation.
5. Note how the parable fits into the purpose and plan of the entire book. If the parable is present in the other Gospels, note its location and how it has been shaped to fit into the purpose of each Gospel writer.
6. Determine as explicitly as possible the message of the parable in the teaching of Jesus. There may be several points that need to be made in a given parable, as was indicated above for the parable of the lost son. There may be legitimate secondary features in the parable, but be careful not to push the story too far. One should exercise caution since it is easy to violate a parable's intention. No one would want to suggest that God has tormentors on the basis of the parable of the unforgiving servant (see Mt 18:34); rather, this verse points out the seriousness of the sin and its judgment. However, some people wrongly overemphasize minor features of other parables. If one will interpret the parable as a whole—in keeping with its original intention—such errors will be minimized.
7. Note where the teaching of the parable conforms to the teaching of Jesus elsewhere. Jesus' nonparabolic teaching may provide the key for, or strengthen, the interpretation of a parable.
8. Give due emphasis to the "rule of end stress." Usually the climax and the most important part of a parable comes at its conclusion. Consequently, the focus of the interpretation should be there as well. Often, the end of the parable will include the theme of reversal. As elsewhere in the teaching of Jesus, his statement on a given topic is often the exact reverse of what others say or expect. Note Matthew 10:39: "If you cling to your life, you will lose it; but if you give it up for me, you will find it" (NLT). The parable of the workers in the vineyard tells of those who receive less than they expected and closes with a classic reversal statement: "the last shall be first and the first last" (Mt 20:16; cf. 19:30). Note the reversal in Matthew 21:31 at the end of the parable of the two sons (21:28-30). After the religious authorities had made a judgment on the basis of the parable, the reversal is accomplished as they are told that the tax collectors and prostitutes were going into the kingdom of God before them (vv 31-32).
9. Determine what principles are present in the parable that reveal the nature of God, his kingdom, the way he deals with humanity, or what he expects of humanity.

The Reason Jesus Taught in Parables There is little doubt that Jesus taught in parables because they are both interesting and compelling and therefore are one of the most effective means of communicating. When one reads Mark 4:10-12, however, it seems that Jesus taught in parables in order to *keep* people from understanding so that they would not turn and be forgiven. It seems as well that there is a mystery that is given to the *in* group and that the *out* group is prohibited from learning. Herein is the meaning of the term "mystery." Rather than being that which is not known or understood, as the word is used today, the biblical use of this word is usually for that which has been revealed by God and would not have been known had God not revealed it. The content of the mystery is not explained here, but from Jesus' teaching on the kingdom elsewhere, it probably refers to the fact that the kingdom is present in Jesus' own words and actions.

The other factor crucial for understanding this passage is that the word "parable" in biblical usage has a broad meaning referring to any striking speech or dark saying intended to stimulate thought. Jesus did not spoon-feed his hearers; rather, he taught in such a way as to bring about a response, and where there was a response, he gave additional teaching. Consequently, it is not merely that parables are interesting, poetic, and arresting (as important as those characteristics are). In addition, para-

bles stimulate thought and bring about response—if hardness of heart does not prevent it. It is as if Jesus were saying, "If you cannot hear what I am saying, I will reveal my thought in parables." Where there is response to this initial teaching, additional information is given.

PARACLETE* Transliteration of a Greek word meaning "one who is called to someone's aid" or "one who advocates for another." Thus, the term may be used technically for a lawyer. More generally, the word denotes one who acts in another's behalf as a mediator, an intercessor, or an encourager. In 1 John 2:1 Christ is called a paraclete because he represents people to God. This function is akin to his ministry as High Priest (cf. Heb 7:25-28).

The most numerous uses of "paraclete" come in John's Gospel, all referring to the work of the Holy Spirit (Jn 14:16, 26; 15:26; 16:13). In these passages Jesus declares that the Holy Spirit will come from the Father when he departs. The Paraclete, also called "the Spirit of truth," will lead them into all truth and aid them in their ability to recall correctly Jesus' message. He is to become their special replacement for the departed Lord.

See also Spirit of God.

PARADISE Term borrowed from Persian that means "garden of god." The Hebrews originally used a word that they applied not only to ordinary gardens but also to God's garden in Eden (Gn 2–3; Is 51:3; Ez 28:13). Comparatively late in their history, they adapted from the Persian language the word that afterward became "paradise"; it appears three times in the OT referring to a park or orchard (Neh 2:8; Eccl 2:5; Sg 4:13). Later still, when the OT was translated into Greek, there was a Greek form of the same word, and the translators used it extensively for "garden"; for Greek-speaking Jews, the garden of Genesis 2 became *paradeisos*.

The idea of the original Persian word was that of an enclosure or walled garden. It referred particularly to the royal parks of the Persian kings, and this was how the Greeks came to know it. Both ideas fit well with the Hebrews' picture of a garden where the Lord God walked (Gn 3:8) and from which his subjects could be excluded (v 24). Further important features of the Genesis paradise were its fruit trees and its rivers.

By NT times, this picture of God's garden had developed in various ways, which are paralleled, not unexpectedly, in the folk beliefs of many nations. Like the Golden Age in Greek and Roman mythology, paradise was first of all something belonging to the remote past. But the Jews came to believe that it still existed in some undiscoverable place; like the Elysian fields, it was inhabited by the deserving dead. Then, with ever more elaborate descriptions of its glories, they wrote of its eventual reappearance at the end of this age.

Thus, in the idea of paradise converge all myths of another world, past, present, and future, where death and evil have no place. The NT witnesses to the truth that is at the core of all such beliefs. Paradise is the place into which, as an actual but otherworldly reality, Paul was once mysteriously "caught up" during his lifetime (2 Cor 12:4). It is also the place where the repentant thief on the cross was promised he would be, with Christ, immediately after his death (Lk 23:43). The third and last NT reference, a similar promise (Rv 2:7), tells us in addition that paradise is where the tree of life grows, and so identifies it both with the original world of Genesis 2 and with the future world of Revelation 22, complete with the life-giving tree and river, the encircling wall, and the presence of the king.

See also Heaven; New Heavens and New Earth.

PARADOX* Form of expression that seems to be either self-contradictory or absurd but at another level expresses fundamental truth. It is often employed to get hearers to think at a deeper and more critical level. It may often be closely related to hyperbole, an exaggerated statement, except that for the paradox there is an apparent element of contradiction, which arrests attention and demands consideration.

In the ministry of Jesus one finds it in such expressions as grown persons being born again. "Can a man enter a second time into his mother's womb," Nicodemus asks, "and be born?" (Jn 3:4). Or again, in response to the attempts of rich men to enter the kingdom, Jesus says that it is easier for a camel to go through the eye of a needle (an impossibility) than for a rich man to enter the kingdom (Mk 10:25). The point is not to focus on the literal statement or take it word for word but to understand its essential purpose. In this instance, it is a form of "shock treatment" to force the wealthy to see how their attitudes toward wealth have excluded them from the kingdom.

Much of the use of paradox in Jesus' ministry has to do with his attempts to show that the perspective, or value system, of the kingdom represents a complete reversal of the values by which people live. Whosoever will lose his life will find it (Mt 10:39). The last shall be

first, and the first last (Lk 13:30). Whoever would be greatest of all must be servant of all (Mk 10:43; Lk 22:26). Indeed, the servant ministry of Jesus himself underscores this great reversal of the kingdom. After washing the feet of the disciples, Jesus says, "You call me Teacher and Lord; and you are right, for so I am. If I then, your Lord and Teacher, have washed your feet, you also ought to wash one another's feet" (Jn 13:13-14, RSV).

Paradox also enters Christian expression when one attempts to speak of God in the language of men. Thus God is "before all time." Even "God in flesh" is paradoxical yet profoundly true. People inevitably and of necessity speak of God in terms of their own experience, yet God cannot be limited by such experience or language, for he is infinitely greater. Hence, language is a limited instrument for speaking of him who is not limited.

PARAH City belonging to Benjamin's inheritance (Jos 18:23). It is undoubtedly Khirbet el-Farah, approximately five and a half miles (8.8 kilometers) northeast of Jerusalem.

PARALYSIS*, PARALYTIC*, PARALYZED Symptom of an organic disease of the central nervous system affecting the temporary or permanent loss of sensation and/or voluntary muscle control. This degenerative condition was usually incurable. A few cases of paralysis (palsy) are mentioned in the NT, all of which occur in connection with Christ's healing ministry.

Paralytics were included in the group of ailing people seeking Jesus' healing in Galilee (Mt 4:24), numbered among the sick at Bethesda in Jerusalem (Jn 5:3), and represented among those cured by Philip in Samaria (Acts 8:7). The paralyzed servant of the centurion was described by Luke as very sick and at the point of death (Lk 7:2). This man was probably victimized by an often fatal form of paralysis that begins in the legs and spreads rapidly upward through the rest of the body. The paralytic at Capernaum was most likely ailing from paraplegia, a paralysis of the lower half of the body (Mt 9:2, 6; Mk 2:3-10; Lk 5:18, 24). This disease may have been brought on by an injury at birth or by damage to the spinal cord. Perhaps Aeneas, whom Peter healed at Lydda, also suffered from paraplegia (Acts 9:33).

See also Disease; Medicine and Medical Practice.

PARAN Desert region in the northeast Sinai Peninsula west of the Arabah (Rift Valley). The settlement of Kadesh-barnea is its northernmost limit. Some scholars identify the great Et-Tih plateau of the central Sinai as a part of this wilderness.

The wilderness of Paran is a wild, arid expanse of tableland, mountains, gorges, and wadis. The lack of water and vegetation made it a most inhospitable place and a stark contrast to the land flowing with milk and honey that was promised to Israel.

This wilderness became the home of Ishmael (Gn 21:20-21). The nation of Israel camped there on the way from Egypt to Canaan (Nm 10:12; 12:16). From Kadesh-barnea, at the northern edge of the wilderness, Moses sent spies to reconnoiter the Promised Land (13:3, 26). David is said to have led his band of men to this region after the death of Samuel so as to distance himself from King Saul (1 Sm 25:1).

See also Palestine; Sina, Sinai; Wilderness Wanderings.

PARAPET* Protective barrier around the circumference of house roofs. The parapet was required by the Law (Dt 22:8) since flat roofs were widely used (Jos 2:6; Jgs 16:27; 1 Sm 9:25; Is 22:1). Construction of a parapet would relieve the dweller from liability should a person fall from the roof.

See also Architecture; Homes and Dwellings.

PARCHMENT* *See* Writing; Pergamos, Pergamum.

PARDON *See* Forgiveness.

PARENT *See* Family Life and Relations.

PARMASHTA One of the 10 sons of Haman killed by the Jews (Est 9:9).

PARMENAS One of the seven men full of the Spirit and of wisdom chosen by the Jerusalem church to minister to the widows (Acts 6:5).

PARNACH Elizaphan's father from Zebulun's tribe (Nm 34:25).

PAROSH Head of a family who returned to Jerusalem with Zerubbabel after the Babylonian exile (Ezr 2:3; Neh 7:8). One of his descendants, Pedaiah, participated in rebuilding the Jerusalem wall (Neh 3:25); other descendants are mentioned as having taken foreign wives (Ezr 10:25).

PAROUSIA* Transliteration of a Greek word meaning "presence," "arrival," "appearance," or "coming." While it is used often with reference to people (1 Cor 16:17; 2 Cor 7:6; 10:10; Phil 1:26; 2:12) and once with reference to the Antichrist (2 Thes 2:9), the word is employed most frequently with reference to Christ (Mt 24:3, 27, 37-39; 1 Cor 15:23; 1 Thes 2:19; 3:13; 4:15; 5:23; 2 Thes 2:1, 8). Consequently, the Parousia has come to denote the second coming of Christ at the end of the ages.

Paul was probably responsible for the technical emphasis on Christ's return. While rejecting all attempts to calculate the time (1 Thes 5:1-2; 2 Thes 2:2-3; cf. Mt 24:4-36), he nonetheless paints a vivid picture of the Parousia (1 Thes 4:13-18; 2 Thes 1:7–2:8; see also 1 Cor 15:20-28, 50-55). According to his teaching, it will be a personal, visible, sudden, and glorious coming (1 Cor 15:23; 1 Thes 2:19; 3:13; 4:15-17). Though apparently he felt he and his readers would experience Christ's return (1 Thes 4:15; cf. Rom 8:23; 13:11), his approaching martyrdom caused him to moderate his thinking (Phil 1:23). James, also sensing the delay in Christ's return, called for patience (Jas 5:7-8). Peter, too, cautioned against allowing the delay to create doubt (2 Pt 3:8-10). The message is not myth (2 Pt 1:16), and scoffers will be silenced (3:3-4). John encouraged consistent faith lest the believer be put to shame at his coming (1 Jn 2:28).

See also Eschatology; Second Coming of Christ.

PARSHANDATHA One of the 10 sons of Haman slain by the Jews (Est 9:7).

PARSIN Aramaic word interpreted as "divided" (Dn 5:25, 28). *See* Mene, Mene, Tekel, Parsin.

PARTHIA*, PARTHIANS Land (roughly corresponding to modern Iran) lying beyond the eastern boundaries of the Roman Empire, and so almost outside the world of the NT.

It is included, however, in maps of the OT world, which generally encompass Eastern territory. Many Jews deported from Palestine after the Assyrian and Babylonian invasions were living in this area when in the sixth century BC it became part of the vast Persian Empire of Cyrus, and thousands stayed on in spite of Cyrus's offer of repatriation. Two centuries afterward, that empire was conquered by Alexander the Great. But 100 years later several parts of it, including Parthia, threw off the yoke of his successors and became independent.

Parthia eventually became a great empire, stretching from the Euphrates to the Indus. In the NT period, even mighty Rome regarded it as a potential threat. The first confrontation between the two powers actually resulted in a defeat for the Romans (at Carrhae, the biblical Haran, in 53 BC). Only in the second century AD did the balance shift, and even then, though twice annexed, Parthia twice recovered its independence. It fell eventually in AD 226, not to the Romans, but to a neo-Persian coup within its own borders.

Wealthy because of their position astride Asian trade routes, and militarily strong because of their famous mounted bowmen, who won many a battle by apparently retreating and then shooting at the pursuing enemy (hence the phrase "parting [or 'Parthian'] shot"), the Parthians seem also to have been a tolerant people. A large Jewish community continued to live among them, and at the time of Pentecost (Acts 2) their province of Babylonia had, curiously enough, a Jewish governor. More important, Jews from Parthia, and possibly also Parthian converts to Judaism ("proselytes"), were in Jerusalem on that epoch-making day (v 9). By them the gospel may have been taken, within weeks of the resurrection, well on its way to India.

PARTRIDGE *See* Birds.

PARUAH Father of Jehoshaphat from Issachar's tribe. Jehoshaphat was appointed to provide food for King Solomon and his household one month out of the year (1 Kgs 4:7, 17).

PARVAIM Geographical area from which Solomon obtained gold for use in the temple (2 Chr 3:6). According to rabbinic sources, the gold had a reddish hue and was used to make the vessel with which the high priest removed the ashes from the altar of burnt offering on the Day of Atonement. Parvaim was probably located in Arabia.

PASACH Japhlet's son from Asher's tribe (1 Chr 7:33).

PAS-DAMMIM Alternate form of Ephes-dammim, a place in Judah's tribe, in 1 Chronicles 11:13. *See* Ephes-dammim.

PASEAH

1. Eshton's son, the brother of Beth-rapha and a descendant of Kelub from Judah's tribe. Paseah was mentioned as one of the men of Recah (1 Chr 4:12).
2. Ancestor of a family of temple servants who returned to Palestine with Zerubbabel after the Babylonian captivity (Ezr 2:49; Neh 7:51).
3. Joiada's father. Joiada, along with Meshullam, repaired the Old Gate of Jerusalem under Nehemiah's direction during the postexilic period (Neh 3:6).

PASHHUR, PASHUR*

1. Forefather of a family of priests who returned to Jerusalem with Zerubbabel after the exile (Ezr 2:38; Neh 7:41). He was perhaps also the son of Malkijah and the grandfather of Adaiah the priest. Adaiah served in the sanctuary during the postexilic period (1 Chr 9:12). Six of Pashhur's sons were encouraged by Ezra to divorce their foreign wives (Ezr 10:22).

2. One of the priests who with Nehemiah set his seal on the covenant of Ezra (Neh 10:3).
3. Immer's son and the priest and chief officer of the sanctuary during the reign of King Zedekiah of Judah (597–586 BC). Frustrated with Jeremiah's predictions of doom for Jerusalem, Pashhur beat him and had him put in stocks at the temple's Benjamin Gate. Upon his release, Jeremiah exposed Pashhur's false prophecies and foretold his exile and death in Babylon (Jer 20:1-6).
4. Son of Malkijah and perhaps the grandson of King Zedekiah of Judah (597–586 BC; Jer 21:1; 38:1; cf. 38:6). The king sent Pashhur, with Zephaniah the priest, to Jeremiah, requesting that he ask the Lord to deal favorably with Judah. It was in his father's cistern that Jeremiah was imprisoned (Jer 38:6).
5. Father of Gedaliah. Gedaliah—with Shephatiah, Jucal, and Pashhur—opposed Jeremiah and attempted to kill him by imprisoning him in Malkijah's cistern (Jer 38:1).

PASSION* A derivative from Latin meaning "suffering." It is used in some translations (KJV and RSV) in Acts 1:3 to refer to the sufferings of Jesus. Throughout the centuries Christians have referred to Jesus' sufferings as his Passion.

The Nature of the Passion Each of the four Gospels has what is called a Passion narrative, which is the section recording the sufferings of Jesus on the night of his arrest and the following day leading up to his death. Matthew includes it in chapters 26–27, Mark in chapters 14–15, Luke in chapters 22–23, and John in chapters 18–19.

On the physical side of his Passion, Luke describes most graphically the agony Jesus experienced while at prayer in the Garden of Gethsemane (Lk 22:41-44). John (Jn 18:12) tells us that Jesus was then bound and led to the high priest's house, where he was first interrogated by Annas, the father-in-law of Caiaphas, current holder of that office. This interrogation is recorded in John 18:19-24.

Annas sent Jesus on to Caiaphas for further examination (Jn 18:24). At this stage the soldiers guarding Jesus indulged in some foul play—beating him and asking him (when blindfolded) to prophesy who had hit him (Lk 22:63-65). At daybreak the Sanhedrin, or Jewish Council, assembled and attempted to convict him but could not obtain consistent evidence against him.

Finally, the high priest asked him a question that led him to incriminate himself (in their eyes)—a procedure that was quite contrary to Jewish law (Mk 14:55-64). By putting a direct question concerning Jesus' messiahship, they compelled him to commit what they regarded as blasphemy, for they had closed their minds to the possibility that this could in fact be true.

Matthew 26:67-68 and Mark 14:65 suggest that it was at this point that Jesus was ill-treated by his guards and possibly some members of the council. He was then taken under arrest to Pilate's residence in Jerusalem, the Praetorium or garrison headquarters. Pilate appears to have conducted a preliminary examination of Jesus, and when he found that his hometown was in Galilee, sent Jesus to Herod as being under the latter's jurisdiction. Jesus refused to answer any of Herod's questions, and so the Jewish tetrarch sent Jesus back to the governor—after mocking Jesus (Lk 23:1-12). Pilate then appears to have wanted to enlist the crowd's sympathy for Jesus and so had him scourged, after which he was dressed in a purple robe (possibly the one given him by Herod; Lk 23:11) and

a crown of thorns. The scourging could have been the regular prelude to crucifixion, or it may have been an attempt to suggest that he had punished Jesus enough (v 16). It was inflicted by the flagellum (Mk 15:15)—a leather whip whose thongs were weighted with jagged pieces of bone and lead—while the victim's hands were tied to a pillar. Even after this, Jesus faced more buffeting by the soldiers (Mt 27:27-31; Mk 15:16-20; Jn 19:3) and then had to stand by while Pilate tried weakly to negotiate with the mob, who by now had been stirred up by his opponents to clamor for Jesus' death (Jn 19:1-16; cf. Mt 27:11-26; Mk 15:1-15; Lk 23:18-25). All was in vain, and Pilate handed him over to the execution squad. It is not surprising that after all this ill-treatment, Jesus appears to have been unable to carry the cross (either the cross piece only or the whole of this instrument of execution) to Calvary, and so Simon of Cyrene was pressed into carrying it for him (see Mk 15:21 and parallels). Once this grim destination was reached, the soldiers lost little time in nailing him to the cross. Traditionally, this was done by driving a nail through each hand and a longer nail through both feet together. The cross was then set upright into a socket in the ground (or the cross piece hauled up on the piece already standing upright), and Jesus was left to hang there until he expired from loss of blood after the scourging (which in itself sometimes proved fatal) or from a ruptured heart caused by the strain on the muscles of the diaphragm.

Apart from the physical side of the Passion, we must not forget that Jesus also experienced the mental agony of being betrayed by his friends and forsaken by his followers. There was the further suffering of knowing that all he went through was totally undeserved, him being completely innocent of all the charges trumped up against him. The Jews prided themselves on the quality of their religion, and the Romans on the standards of their law, and yet it was paradoxically the misunderstanding of Jewish religion and the misuse of Roman law that enabled his enemies to hound him to the cross.

Most of all, there was the spiritual suffering of knowing that he was going to be "made sin, who knew no sin" (2 Cor 5:21) and consequently separated from God. This was why Jesus, at a moment when many martyrs have known the presence and reality of God in a marked degree, uttered his stark cry of dereliction—"My God, my God, why have you deserted me?" (Mk 15:34 and parallels).

The Uniqueness of the Passion It is evident from the pages of the NT that the "good news" with which the first Christians turned the ancient world upside down was that "Christ died for our sins just as the Scriptures said he would, and that he was buried, and that three days afterwards he arose from the grave just as the prophets foretold" (1 Cor 15:3, TLB). This was the basic message of Peter (Acts 2:22-36; 3:12-21; 10:36-43; 1 Pt 2:24; 3:18) and Paul (Acts 13:26-39) and is also central to the thinking of John (1 Jn 1:7; 2:2; 4:10 and Rv 1:5; 5:9) and the writer of the Letter to the Hebrews (Heb 2:9, 17; 9:28; 10:12). The fact that Jesus was sinless qualified him to bear the sins of the whole world and thus achieve what no human being has ever been able, or will ever be able, to do: bear the consequences of, and punishment for, human sin.

PASSOVER Important Jewish festival celebrating Israel's redemption from Egypt. *See* Feasts and Festivals of Israel; Meals, Significance of.

PASTOR Word literally meaning "shepherd," used in both the OT and NT in a figurative sense for rulers and leaders. Of the 12 times the word is used in the NT as a metaphor for "leader," it is translated as "pastor" only in Ephesians 4:11 (KJV, ASV, RSV, NIV, TEV, NLT).

Pastors and teachers together formed a group who complemented the work of apostles, prophets, and evangelists. The titles "bishop" and "elder" refer to the same office in the NT (cf. Acts 20:17, 28; Ti 1:5-7), and "pastor" seems to be practically synonymous with them, as shown by Jesus being referred to as "the Shepherd and Bishop of your souls" (1 Pt 2:25, KJV). The verb "to shepherd" is used to describe the work of local church leaders (Jn 21:16; Acts 20:28; 1 Pt 5:2), and often the congregation is called a flock. It is the pastor's responsibility to build up the body of Christ by watching over the congregation (Acts 20:28; Heb 13:7) and countering false teaching (Acts 20:29-30). More detailed information regarding the duties and responsibilities of pastors is found in Paul's letters to Timothy and Titus, which have come to be called the Pastoral Letters.

See also Bishop; Deacon, Deaconess; Elder; Presbyter; Shepherd; Spiritual Gifts.

PATH A worn track or road. "Path(s)" and "pathway(s)" are used to translate a variety of words used in the Bible: (1) a well-trodden and much-used roadway (Gn 49:17; Pss 16:11; 139:3; Prv 2:8, 19); (2) a thoroughfare or highway (Is 59:7; Jl 2:8); (3) a beaten track as across fields, over hills, and through valleys (Jb 30:13; Ps 119:35; Prv 3:17); (4) a track or passage in which the idea of flowing along is included (Ps 77:19; Jer 18:15); (5) a circular path, as in a trench or in a parapet (Ps 65:11; Prv 2:9); and (6) a narrow passage, as through a hole (Nm 22:24). "Path" is used to translate the Greek words meaning a worn track (Mt 3:3; Mk 1:3; Lk 3:4) and a wheel rut (Heb 12:13).

A careful review of the use of the terms "path(s)" and "pathway(s)" reveals that the Bible uses them literally to speak of a stretch of ground over which traffic passes. This could be in the form of a crooked mountain path, an unpaved and much-traveled way, or a well-prepared pavement. Biblical writers also used the words metaphorically to speak of or to describe the way human life

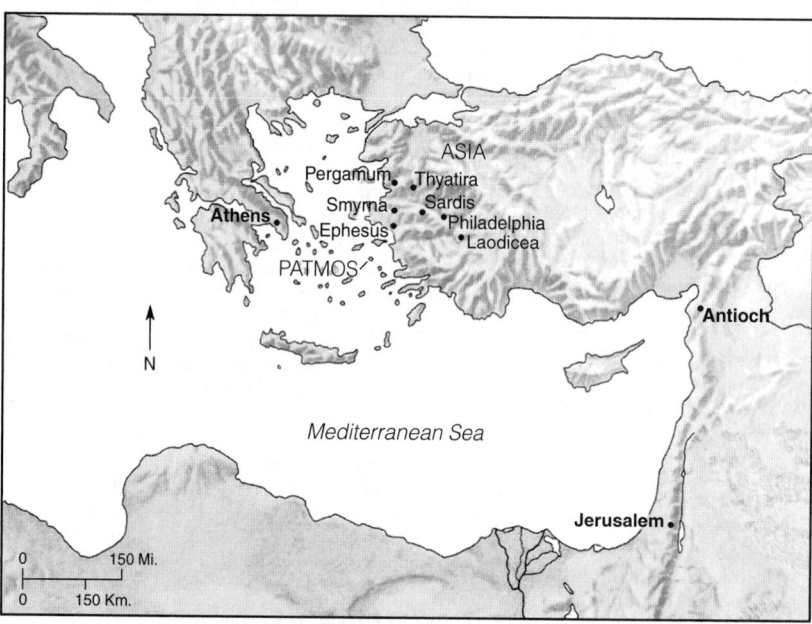

Patmos and the Seven Local Churches in Revelation
John wrote to seven churches in the Roman province of Asia while he was in exile on the island of Patmos.

PASTORAL LETTERS* Descriptive phrase used in modern biblical study to designate the letters known as 1 and 2 Timothy and Titus. In Christian tradition these three writings have been grouped together since the second century. They are addressed to individuals rather than to churches. The benediction at the end of each letter assumes a group of readers, however. In general, the letters offer advice to their recipients about church order, false doctrine, leadership standards, and pastoral oversight of church life.

See also Paul, The Apostle; Timothy, First Letter to; Timothy, Second Letter to; Titus, Letter to.

PATARA Seaport of the ancient region of Lycia, now located in modern Turkey. The ancient city, one of the largest and most prosperous of the region, was a center of trade and commerce. A temple to Apollo stood in Patara. Remains of a theater and baths can still be seen there. Prevailing winds made Patara a convenient place for ships to begin their voyages to the eastern Mediterranean. The apostle Paul changed ships at Patara on his final journey to Jerusalem (Acts 21:1-2).

is lived in relation to God, and how God directs, and can and does either enrich or impoverish human life. Writers used the terms figuratively to refer to human conduct and experiences in the midst of the various dimensions of human life. Especially colorful in the last two uses are such expressions as the path of life (Ps 16:11), the plain (level) path (27:11), the good path (Prv 2:9), the path of the wicked (4:14), the path of the just (v 18), the path of judgment (Is 40:14), the right paths (Prv 4:11), and paths of peace (3:17).

PATHROS The region of Upper Egypt, mentioned five times in the Hebrew OT (Is 11:11; Jer 44:1, 15; Ez 29:14; 30:14). Each time it occurs in conjunction with a city in Lower Egypt (Noph = Memphis, or Zoan = Tanis). The Hebrew is *Pathros,* and the Egyptian is *pa to resy* ("the Southern Land"). Egyptologists believe that the Hebrew form is a corruption of *Pethoris* or *Pethores.* Isaiah 11:11 suggests that *Mitsrayim* is to be equated with Lower and Middle Egypt, and *Pathros* is the region south of it up to the border of Cush (i.e., Upper Egypt). According to Ezekiel 29:14, Pathros is the original home of the Egyptians. The prophets spoke about God's judgment on Pathros: "I will lay waste Upper Egypt ["Pathros," mg], set fire to Zoan and inflict punishment on Thebes" (Ez 30:14, NIV). After the exile, Jews migrated to Egypt and some settled in Pathros. Jeremiah warned that God's judgment on Egypt was to come and that they would not escape it: "This word came to Jeremiah concerning all the Jews living in Lower Egypt—in Migdol, Tahpanhes and Memphis—and in Upper Egypt [Pathros]: 'This is what the LORD Almighty, the God of Israel, says: You saw the great disaster I brought on Jerusalem and on all the towns of Judah. Today they lie deserted and in ruins' " (Jer 44:1-2, NIV).

PATHRUSITES Inhabitants of Pathros, a region of southern Egypt (Gn 10:14; 1 Chr 1:12). *See* Pathros.

PATIENCE Ability to take a great deal of punishment from evil people or circumstances without losing one's temper, without becoming irritated and angry, or without taking vengeance. It includes the capacity to bear pain or trials without complaint, the ability to forbear under severe provocation, and the self-control that keeps one from acting rashly even though suffering opposition or adversity.

The usual Hebrew expression for patience is related to the verb "to be long" and involves the idea of being long to get riled or slow to become angry. Two different Greek words were translated by the KJV translators with the word "patience." One of the words has the idea of "remaining firm under" tests and trials and is better translated "endurance" or "steadfastness." The other Greek word is related to the above Hebrew meaning and refers to patience as "long-spiritedness" or "calmness of spirit" even though under severe provocation to lose one's temper.

The Island of Patmos

The great biblical illustration of patience in operation is God himself. Several passages speak of him, in conjunction with other gracious attributes, as "slow to anger." In a context that stresses Israel's rebellion and provocation of God, he is contrasted as a God who is forgiving, gracious, compassionate, slow to anger, and abounding in lovingkindness (Neh 9:17). The psalmist declares, "Thou, O Lord, art a God merciful and gracious, slow to anger and abounding in steadfast love and faithfulness" (Ps 86:15, RSV; see also Ex 34:6; Nm 14:18; Ps 103:8; Jl 2:13; Jon 4:2). In addition, the virtue of a patient spirit on the part of mankind is extolled in the OT, especially in Proverbs (Prv 14:29; 15:18; 16:32; 25:15; see also Eccl 7:8).

The NT also stresses the patience of the Lord. It is God's kindness, forbearance, and patience that lead people to repentance (Rom 2:4). God was patient in holding off the Flood for the sinners of Noah's day while the ark was being built, thereby giving more time for repentance (1 Pt 3:20). Probably the greatest of the NT references to God's patience is in 2 Peter 3:9. The delay in Christ's return is not an indication of slowness on God's part, says Peter, but of his long-suffering, not being willing that anyone should perish. A specific reference to Jesus Christ's patience is made by Paul, who claimed that, in his case, Jesus was able to demonstrate perfect patience (1 Tm 1:16).

Patience, which is an attribute of our God and of our Lord Jesus Christ, is also to characterize each Christian. Paul's prayer for the Colossians is that they might demonstrate this quality (Col 1:11). It is one of the fruits of the Spirit (Gal 5:22), an attribute of love (1 Cor 13:4), and a virtue (Col 3:12; see also 2 Tm 3:10). In addition, Christians are exhorted to be patient (1 Thes 5:14). If we are not, we will be treated as the slave in a parable that Jesus told. This slave pleaded with his lord, to whom he owed a great sum, for patience, promising to pay all. The lord was patient and forgave all the debt, until he found out that the slave had refused to show the same patience to a fellow servant who owed him a pittance in comparison (Mt 18:26-29).

In some contexts, the word "patience" takes on the more general meaning of waiting long and expectantly for something. The farmer waits patiently for the crop to come (Jas 5:7b). Abraham waited patiently for God's promise to give him the land of Canaan to be fulfilled and died without seeing what was promised, although still believing (Heb 6:15; 11:39). Finally, all Christians are commanded to be long-suffering until the coming of the Lord (Jas 5:7a).

PATMOS Small island in the Aegean Sea, located about 35 miles (56.3 kilometers) west of the city of Miletus off the coast of Asia Minor. Patmos is about ten miles (16.1 kilometers) long and six miles (9.7 kilometers) wide at its northern end, consisting of rocky volcanic hills.

In Revelation 1:9 John says that he was on the island of Patmos "for preaching the word of God and speaking about Jesus" (NLT). He also indicates that he is a fellow participant in their "suffering." The Roman historian Tacitus informs us that the Romans used some of the Aegean islands as places of banishment and exile during the first century (*Annals* 3.68; 4.30; 15.71). Thus the language of the author and the evidence of Tacitus, joined to Christian traditions from the second and third centuries about John's banishment, support the likelihood that Patmos was a place of exile or political confinement.

In a time when the Asian churches were undergoing persecution, John wrote to them from this island. He addressed each of seven churches by means of a letter of encouragement and warning. The series of letters is followed by the author's account of the divinely sent vision of impending judgment, which "must soon take place" (Rv 22:6). Patmos, then, was the location from which this NT writing originated.

See also Revelation, Book of.

PATRIARCHS, Period of the Period of time during which the biblical fathers of Israel lived. The Bible tells of long-lived patriarchs before the Flood (Gn 1–5), of Noah (chs 6–9), and of a line of patriarchs after the Flood (chs 10–11). However, the word in the narrower sense usually refers to Abraham, Isaac, and Jacob (chs 12–36), with the addition of Joseph (chs 37–50).

Date Exact dating of the patriarchs is difficult because, apart from the kings mentioned in Genesis 14:1-2, we do not have any fixed external point of reference from which to calculate. While this chapter does refer to historical persons and places, we cannot identify with certainty any one of the kings. The Italian excavators of Tell Mardikh (ancient Ebla) have reported finding the names of the "Cities of the Plain" of Genesis 14:2 (whose destruction is reported in Gn 19) and even the name of one of their kings on the clay tablets excavated. These clay tablets seem to date from well before 2000 BC, which is too early for Abraham; all that they would prove is that the cities were in existence long before his time. What we can say is that the patriarchs must have belonged to the middle Bronze Age, probably early in the second millennium BC, and that this was the general period of the Amorite "drift" into Palestine from the north and the west. The most usual modern view is that the Amorite migration was in two "waves," the earlier one being seminomadic (like Abraham's friends Aner, Eshcol, and Mamre, Gn 14:13), and the second and later wave, probably from Syria in the north, being urbanizers and settlers (the group usually described as "the Amorites" in the catalog of the various races in Canaan, e.g., Ex 3:8). The society of the time of the patriarchs has been described as "dimorphic," or twofold. On the one hand, there were the city communities, while on the other there were open village settlements and semi-nomadic tribes that at times were loosely grouped around the towns and at times drifted away from them. It is against this sort of background that we must imagine the patriarchs. Joseph, of course, lived in the fully settled world of Egypt, but Scripture does not give us the name of the pharaoh of his day.

Geographical Range For such an early period, and seeing that it is really only the chronicle of one family, the patriarchal history has a remarkable geographic and climatic range, covering many hundreds of miles of varied country. It begins at Ur, an old Sumerian city on the Persian Gulf at one extreme end of the Fertile Crescent. Then the center of interest moves far to the northwest, to Haran on the Balikh River, between the Tigris and the Euphrates Rivers in their upper courses. Then the action sweeps far southwest to Palestine. But twice the interest moves back to Haran, and twice it goes into the Egyptian Delta. This is truly history on a wide canvas. Even when in Palestine, there is no fixed, quiet center of life. The patriarchs are endlessly on the move, backward and forward, mostly along the north-south mountain spine, but sometimes also in the coastal plain and even in Transjordan. Nor is there steady development; some groups slip away from the seminomadic life to join the city cultures (like Lot in Gn 13:12), while others melt back into the desert or semidesert (like Ishmael in 25:18, or Esau in 36:6-8). Yet always at the center the life of the patriarchs goes on.

Importance It is impossible to exaggerate the importance of the place of the patriarchs in God's gradually unfolding plan of redemption. The process that is to culminate in the coming of Christ begins with Abraham (Jn 8:56). This is not, of course, to deny that in a more general sense God's plan of salvation begins to unfold in the opening chapters of Genesis. But in a more special way, God's particular revelation begins with the call of Abraham (Gn 12:1-3) and continues, with ever-increasing clarity, through the lives of the other patriarchs. It is no accident that the Bible speaks of God as the God of Abraham, Isaac, and Jacob even at the moment when a further revelation is about to be made to Moses (Ex 3:6).

This is because the revelation made to the earlier patriarchs is the foundation of all that follows; indeed, we in the New Covenant look back to Abraham as our "father" too (Rom 4:16).

See also Abraham; Chronology of the Bible (Old Testament); Isaac; Israel, History of; Jacob #1; Joseph #1.

PATRIMONY* Inheritance from a father or ancestor (Dt 18:8). *See* Heir; Inheritance.

PATROBAS One of the Christians in Rome to whom Paul sent greetings (Rom 16:14).

PATROCLUS Father of Nicanor (2 Macc 8:9), the Syrian general whose 20,000 soldiers were routed by a numerically inferior band led by Judas Maccabeus. Patroclus is mentioned only in connection with his embarrassed and dishonored son.

PAU City located in Edom, in which King Hadar reigned (Gn 36:39); alternately called Pai in 1 Chronicles 1:50.

PAUL, The Apostle Prominent leader of the first-century church; apostle to the Gentiles; author of 13 NT epistles.

PREVIEW
• Family and Cultural Background
• Education
• Saul the Persecutor
• Conversion and Calling
• Preparation for Ministry
• Sent Out from Antioch
• Traveling with Barnabas
• The Council of Jerusalem
• Further Travel
• Labor in the Gospel
• The Arrest in Jerusalem
• Voyage and Stay in Rome
• Final Years and Martyrdom

Family and Cultural Background Paul was born around AD 10, a Jew in a family of Pharisees (Acts 23:6) of the tribe of Benjamin (Phil 3:5) in Tarsus of Cilicia (Acts 9:11; 21:39; 22:3), a center of commerce and learning that embraced the Hellenistic spirit and Roman politics. It was a city of which he could be proud (21:39). His parents named him Saul, perhaps after the first king of Israel, who was also a Benjaminite (1 Sm 11:15; Acts 13:21), but Acts 13:9 notes that he "was also called Paul." He uses the Roman name Paul throughout his letters.

From religious parents Paul received knowledge of the Law and Prophets and the Hebrew and Aramaic languages (Acts 21:40; 22:2-3; 23:6; Gal 1:14; Phil 3:5-6). Tarsus, however, was not a Jewish city. Rather, it had a Greek character, being a place where the Greek language was spoken and Greek literature was cultivated. This accounts for Paul's familiarity with Greek (Acts 21:37), the language of the streets and shops of Tarsus.

Jews were brought to Tarsus, the capital of the Roman province of Cilicia, in 171 BC to promote business in the region. At that time Paul's ancestors were probably given Roman citizenship. Paul inherited from his father both Tarsisian and Roman citizenship, which would prove to be of great value to Paul in his later life as he traveled with the gospel throughout the Roman Empire (Acts 16:37; 22:25-29; 23:27). Paul may have had several brothers and sisters, but Acts 23:16 mentions only one sister, whose son performed a lifesaving act for his uncle.

Paul was a tent maker (Acts 18:3). He may have learned this trade from his father, or he may have selected it as a means of self-support, as was the custom of those in rabbinical training. Tarsus was well known for the goat's-hair cloth called cilicium. It was the weaving of this cloth and the fashioning of it into tents, sails, awnings, and cloaks that gave Paul his economic independence during his apostolic ministry (Acts 18:3; 20:34; 28:30; 2 Cor 11:9; 1 Thes 2:9; 2 Thes 3:8).

Education Although born in Tarsus, Paul testified to the Jews in Jerusalem that he had been brought up in this city and studied under Gamaliel (Acts 22:3). It is not clear when Paul was first brought to Jerusalem, but it is likely that sometime between the ages of 13 and 20 he began his formal rabbinical studies. His teacher, Gamaliel, was the grandson of Hillel, founder of a Pharisaic school whose teachings run through the Talmudic writings to this day. This is the same Gamaliel whose wisdom persuaded the Sanhedrin to spare the lives of Peter and the apostles (5:33-40). No doubt, it was while studying under Gamaliel in Hillel's school that Paul began to advance in Judaism beyond many Jews of his own age and became extremely zealous for the traditions of his fathers (Gal 1:14). Perhaps then also Paul began to experience the struggles with the law he would later describe in Romans 7.

While Paul was studying the Jewish law in Jerusalem, Jesus was working as a carpenter in Nazareth. Then Jesus gathered the disciples who would one day be Paul's coworkers in the gospel, fulfilled his ministry, and accomplished redemption on the cross of Calvary (AD 30). Christ's resurrection gave birth to the church, which was baptized in the Holy Spirit at the Feast of Pentecost in Jerusalem.

Saul the Persecutor Shortly after these world-changing events, the members of certain synagogues in Jerusalem, including the Cilician synagogue, that of Paul's native land (Acts 6:9), could not withstand the wisdom and spirit (v 10) of a member of the church in Jerusalem named Stephen (vv 5, 8). They accused him of blasphemy before the Sanhedrin (vv 11-15) and after his eloquent defense (7:1-53) dragged him out of the city, where he was stoned to death. He became the first Christian martyr. The record does not fully reveal the role Paul played in these proceedings, but we know that he was present and prominent because the witnesses against Stephen, who were required to throw the first stones in the execution, "laid their clothes at the feet of a young man called Saul [Paul]" (v 58, NIV).

At Stephen's trial, Paul heard Stephen's historical method of defense, and he later used it himself at Antioch of Pisidia (Acts 13:16-41). He witnessed the man with the face of an angel (6:15), full of the Holy Spirit, looking above and proclaiming "the heavens opened, and the Son of man standing at the right hand of God" (7:56). Stephen's death initiated the events that would culminate in Paul's conversion and commission as the apostle to the Gentiles. But at that time Paul was a leader of the oppressors of the church. He breathed threats and murder against the disciples of the Lord (9:1); he persecuted the church of God and tried to destroy it (Gal 1:13) by imprisoning Christians, both male and female (Acts 22:4), in many cities.

Conversion and Calling Paul had obtained letters from the high priest in Jerusalem to the synagogues in Damascus authorizing him to arrest the believers there and bring them to Jerusalem for trial (Acts 9:1-2). Paul traveled to Damascus for this purpose. Then, on the out-

skirts of the city, came the event that was to transform this law-keeping persecutor of Jesus Christ and blasphemous destroyer of the infant church into the chief propagator of the gospel of grace and master builder of the church (1 Cor 3:10; 1 Tm 1:13). This was the occasion of Paul's conversion (c. AD 31-33). It was of such revolutionary and lasting importance that three detailed accounts of it are given in the book of Acts (Acts 9:1-19; 22:1-21; 26:1-23), and many references are given to it in Paul's own writings (1 Cor 9:1; 15:8; Gal 1:15-16; Eph 3:3; Phil 3:12).

At that time a light from heaven, brighter than the midday sun, shone around Paul and his traveling companions, and they fell to the ground (Acts 26:13-14). Only Paul, however, heard the voice of Jesus instruct him in his commission as a minister and witness to the Gentiles (vv 14-18). Temporarily blinded, Paul was led into Damascus (9:8). There, the disciple Ananias and the Christian community forgave Paul, baptized him, and helped him through the bewildering event of his conversion (vv 10-22). After a short time with the church there, Paul was threatened with death by the Jews to whom he preached Jesus (vv 20-22), but he was protected by the believers and ingeniously delivered from his persecutors (vv 23-25).

Preparation for Ministry Then began a period of preparation, which lasted about 13 years. During this time, Paul first was in the desert of Arabia for three years. Here was his opportunity to pray and reflect on Stephen's defense to the Sanhedrin, the momentous significance of his conversion, the vision he received of Jesus Christ, and the meaning of all this in the light of Jewish theology. Following this, Paul returned to Damascus and then visited Peter for 15 days (Gal 1:17-18).

At first, the disciples in Jerusalem were afraid of him because they did not believe he was a disciple of Jesus (Acts 9:26), but he was championed by Barnabas and thus accepted by the believers in Jerusalem (vv 27-28). While there, Paul may have heard the oral gospel, a summary of the words and deeds of Jesus, handed down to all converts. This would have included the institution of the Lord's Supper (1 Cor 11:23-25), specific words of the Lord (Acts 20:35; 1 Cor 7:10; 9:14), the appearances of the resurrected Christ (1 Cor 15:3-8), and the spirit and character of Jesus (2 Cor 10:1; Phil 2:5-8). Paul also preached in Jerusalem, perhaps in the same synagogues in which he had heard Stephen. However, when his life was again threatened by the Jews, the believers sent him away to Tarsus (Acts 9:29-30; Gal 1:21).

The end of Paul's preparation came when Barnabas went to Tarsus to look for him and bring him to Antioch. By this time Paul had lived for 10 years in Cilicia. Since his conversion, before being sent to Tarsus, he had proclaimed Jesus (Acts 9:20), speaking boldly in the name of the Lord (v 27). There is no reason to think he did otherwise while living among the Gentiles in Cilicia. In fact, his work may have been so effective that he began to attract attention in Antioch. During these years, Paul probably underwent many of the sufferings mentioned in 2 Corinthians 11:24-26. Several scholars think that the ecstatic experience mentioned in 2 Corinthians 12:1-9, with its accompanying thorn in the flesh, also took place before he came to Antioch.

Sent Out from Antioch The church in Antioch had its origins in the persecution fomented by Paul after the death of Stephen. Until they arrived in Antioch, the scattered believers had only spoken the word to Jews (Acts 11:19). It was here that the Gentiles first heard the Good News (v 20), and many became believers (v 21). It is

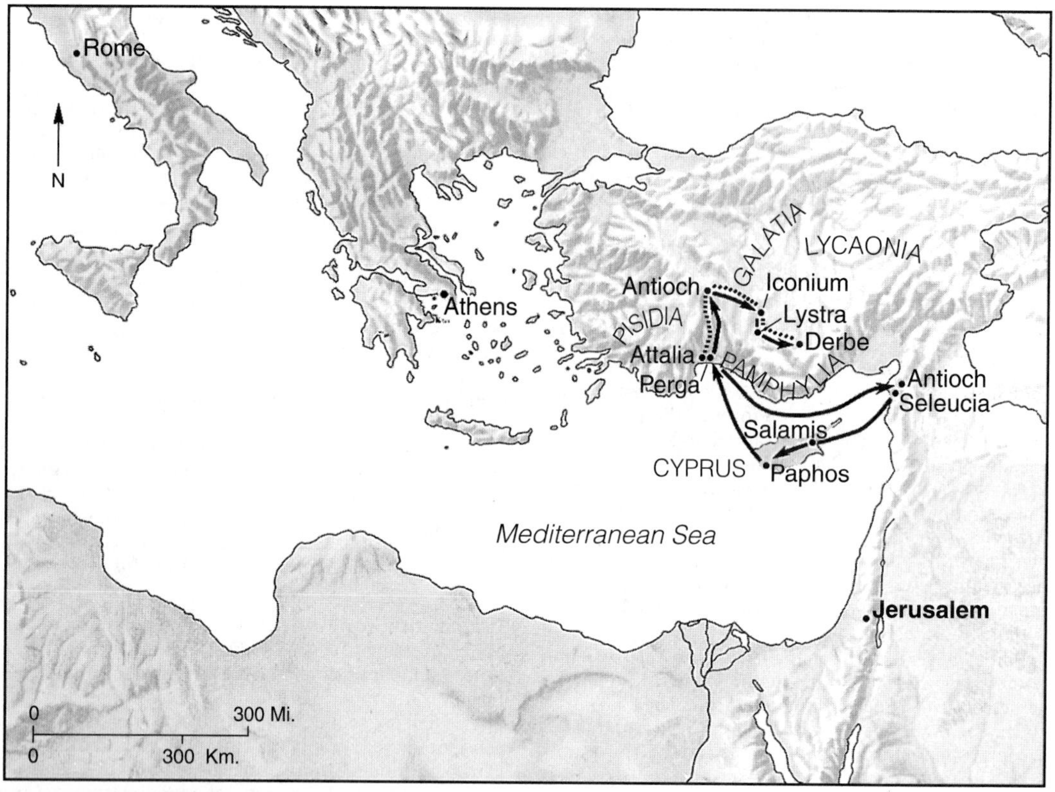

PAUL'S FIRST MISSIONARY JOURNEY (ACTS 13:1—14:28)

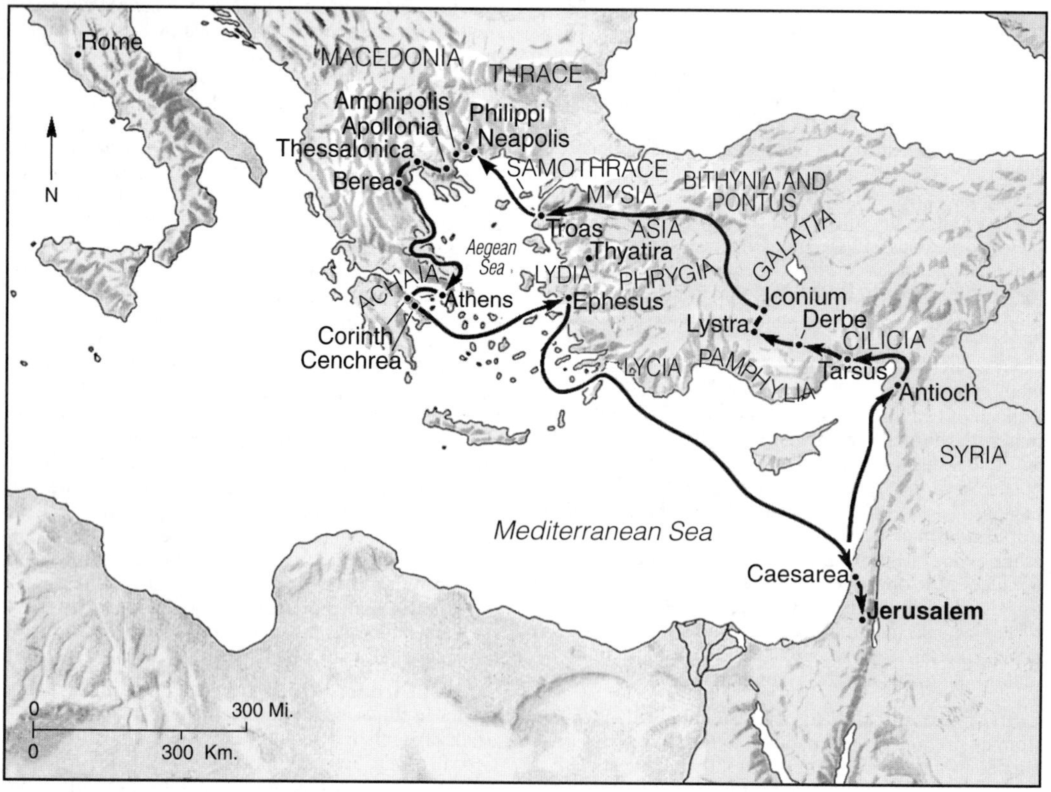

PAUL'S SECOND MISSIONARY JOURNEY (ACTS 15:36—18:22)

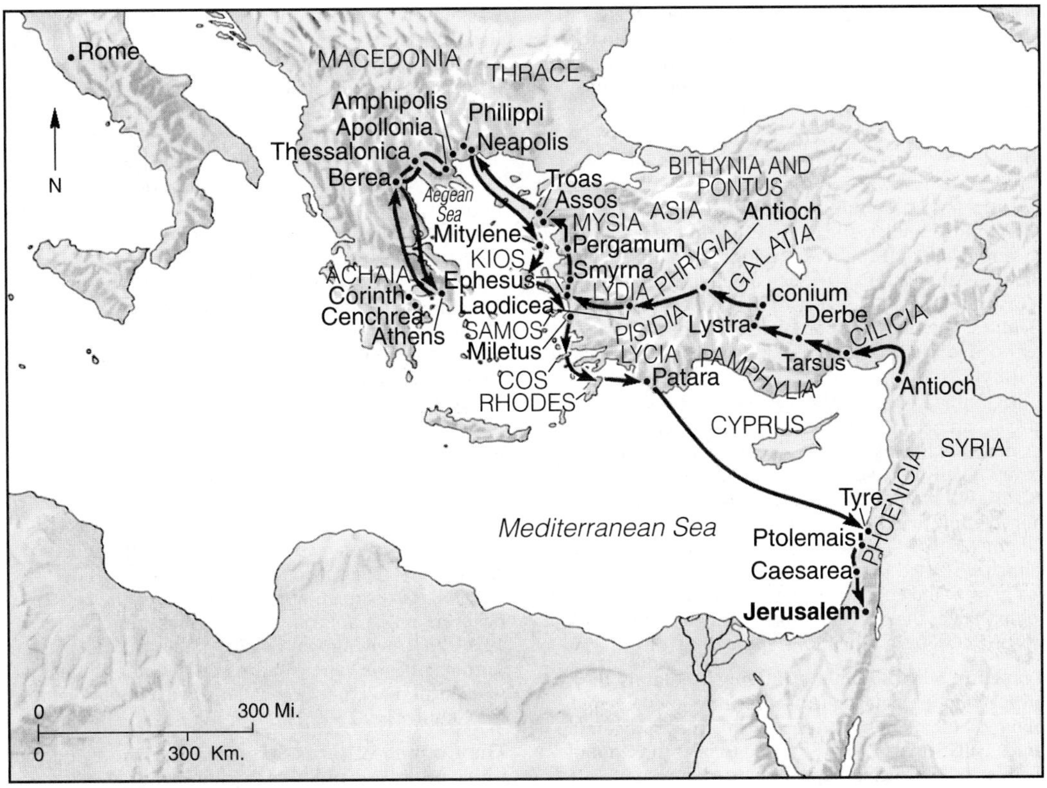

PAUL'S THIRD MISSIONARY JOURNEY (ACTS 18:12—21:16)

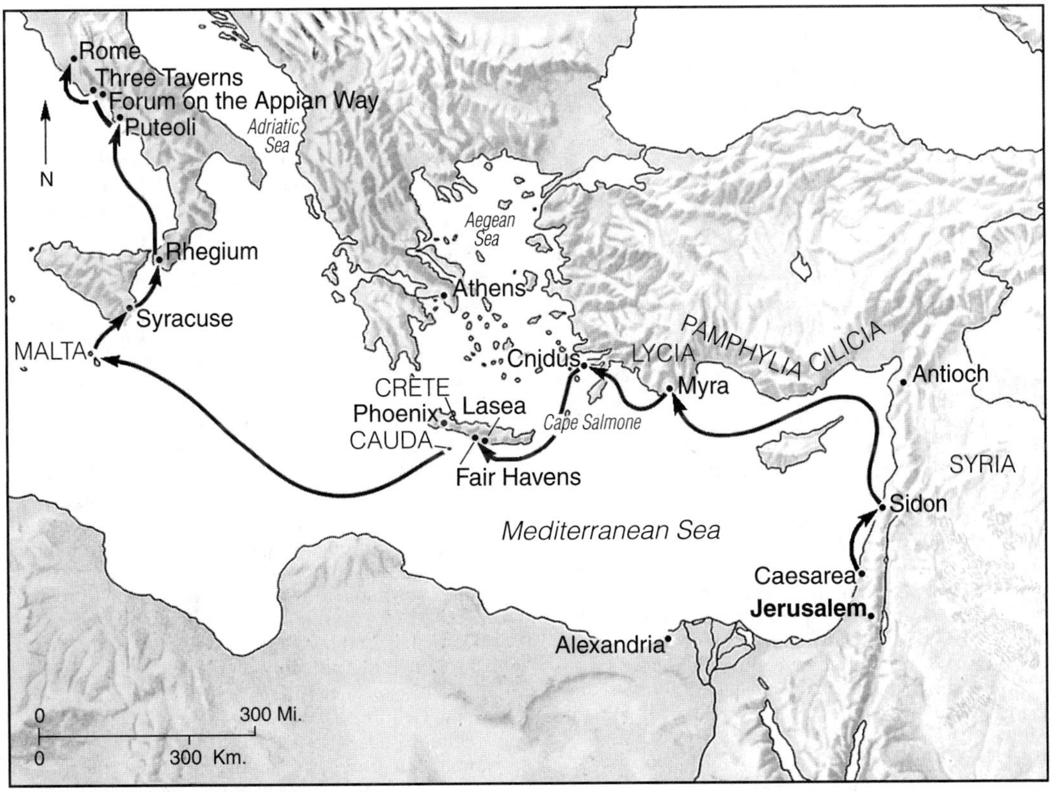

PAUL'S JOURNEY TO ROME (ACTS 21:17—28:31)

fitting that Paul, the apostle to the Gentiles (Acts 22:21; Rom 11:13), who was as yet unknown by sight to the churches of Judea (Gal 1:22), should appear in Antioch to formally begin the ministry to which he was called (Acts 26:17-18).

Barnabas and Paul stayed with the church in Antioch for a year. Their work there was so blessed that a new name, Christian, was coined to distinguish the believers in Antioch from Gentiles and Jews (Acts 11:26). Hearing of a famine in Judea, the disciples in Antioch determined to send relief to the believers in Judea and did so by Barnabas and Paul (v 30). Such a gift displayed to the Jewish churches the potency of the gospel among the Gentiles. Their mission complete, Barnabas and Paul returned to Antioch with John Mark (12:25), Barnabas's cousin (Col 4:10).

Beginning from the Day of Pentecost, the work in the gospel had been casual and incidental. Contacts were made in the homes, the marketplace, the streets, synagogues, highways, etc. (Acts 3:1; 5:12, 42; 8:26-29; 10:22). But in Antioch the Holy Spirit initiated a determined effort to evangelize a section of the Roman Empire (13:1-3). By the Holy Spirit's instructions, the church separated Barnabas and Paul for this work. With the prayers and encouragement of this church, and with John Mark as their assistant, Barnabas and Paul, sent out by the Holy Spirit, sailed for Cyprus (v 4).

Traveling with Barnabas Arriving in Salamis, they preached in the synagogues as they traveled the length of the island to Paphos (Acts 13:5-6). There the Roman proconsul, Sergius Paulus, wanted to hear the word of God (v 7). A magician named Elymas Bar-Jesus tried to prevent the proconsul from believing in Jesus but was stricken with temporary blindness by Paul's command (vv 8-11). This was the first manifestation in Paul of the signs of an apostle (2 Cor 12:12). From then on, the name Paul, not Saul, is used in Luke's record of the Acts of the Apostles (Acts 13:9), and Paul replaced Barnabas as the leader of the party. So "Paul and his company" set sail from Paphos and arrived in Perga of Pamphylia (v 13). John Mark deserted them at Perga and returned to his home in Jerusalem (v 13). This caused discord (15:39), but Paul and Mark were later reconciled (Col 4:10; 2 Tm 4:11).

Paul's travels with the gospel now continued through the Roman province of Asia, specifically in the southern portion of Galatia, the areas of Pamphylia, Pisidia, and Lycaonia. The coastal area where the party landed is a hot, malarial region. It is thought that Paul contracted malaria there and so traveled inland through the mountains to the 4,000-foot- (1,219.2-meter-) high tablelands. Such a journey would have been full of dangerous rivers and bandits (2 Cor 11:26), but Paul was well cared for by the Galatian highlanders when he arrived (Gal 4:13-15) and was rewarded with a warm reception to his message (Acts 13:48-49).

Paul and Barnabas were asked to speak at the synagogue of Antioch in Pisidia (Acts 13:15), and Paul delivered a discourse full of the characteristics of the gospel he would later record in his letters to the churches (vv 16-41). He was invited to speak the next week (v 42); nearly the whole city gathered together to hear the word of God (v 44). This stirred up jealousy in the Jews who opposed Paul's words (v 45), causing the apostles' dramatic turn to the Gentiles (vv 46-47). Many Gentiles in Antioch believed and spread the word throughout the region, but Paul and Barnabas were forced out and went to Iconium in Lycaonia (vv 48-51).

The success in Antioch was duplicated in Iconium as was the Jews' opposition (Acts 14:1), and the apostles fled from the threat of a stoning to Lystra and Derbe in Lycaonia (vv 5-6). In Lystra the signs of an apostle were again seen when Paul healed a man who had been crippled since birth (vv 8-10). The idolatrous citizens of the town, however, primed by the popular belief that Jupiter, accompanied by Mercury, had once visited their region, worshiped Paul and Barnabas as these deities (vv 11-13). Even the convincing words of Paul, whom they mistook for Mercury, hardly restrained the crowds from offering a sacrifice (vv 14-18).

It was in Lystra that Paul was first given a taste of the same medicine he had once administered to Christians. The Jews stoned him, dragged him out of the city, and left him for dead (Acts 14:19). Timothy (16:1-3) may have been among the new disciples surrounding Paul as he lay outside the gate (14:20). Timothy was Paul's son in the faith (1 Cor 4:17; 1 Tm 1:2), eyewitness to his suffering (2 Tm 3:10-11), faithful companion, and fellow worker (Acts 19:22; 20:4; Rom 16:21; 1 Thes 3:2). The next day Barnabas and Paul went on to Derbe (Acts 14:20).

After making many disciples in Derbe, the apostles retraced their steps through Lystra, Iconium, and Antioch of Pisidia, strengthening and encouraging the new believers and appointing elders in each church (Acts 14:21-23). Arriving again in Perga, they sailed back to Antioch of Syria, where they reported to the church the wonderful news that God had opened a door of faith for the Gentiles (vv 25-27).

The Council of Jerusalem The Jews, who had dogged the steps of Paul and Barnabas throughout Galatia, followed on their heels to bewitch the Gentiles there, convincing them to desert the grace of Christ and submit to the Jewish law (Gal 1:6; 3:1). Shortly after the apostles' return to Antioch, Judaizers came from Judea to Antioch, teaching salvation by the law (Acts 15:1). This began the war against the gospel of grace, which Paul preached.

The church in Antioch sent Paul, Barnabas, and others to Jerusalem to settle the controversy of the law versus grace with the apostles and elders there (AD 49, Acts 15:2). Along the way to Jerusalem they spread the news of the conversion of the Gentiles. This brought great joy to the believers (v 3). Such joy was not shared by some in Jerusalem, who in the first meeting of the council said that the Gentiles should be ordered to keep the law of Moses (v 5).

After this meeting, Paul and Barnabas met privately with Peter, John, and James (Gal 2:1-10) and explained the gospel they had been preaching to the Gentiles. These three leaders of the church in Jerusalem saw the grace that had been given to Paul to bring the gospel to the Gentiles and extended to him the "right hand of fellowship." This private meeting seems to have decided the question of compliance to the Jewish law because in the next general meeting Peter said, "We believe that we shall be saved through the grace of the Lord Jesus" (Acts 15:11, RSV), and James reached the decision that "we should not trouble those of the Gentiles who turn to God" (Acts 15:19, RSV). This was a great victory for Paul and Barnabas, and the news was received with rejoicing by the church in Antioch (vv 30-35).

Later, Peter visited Antioch and freely associated with the Gentile believers as he had timidly done in Cornelius's house (Acts 10:28). This continued until "certain men came from James." Their presence brought fear to Peter, clouding the light of the gospel of grace, and causing him to separate himself from the Gentiles.

Peter's action influenced others, including Barnabas, to do the same (Gal 2:12-13). Paul rose to the challenge of this serious crisis, confronted Peter publicly, and charged him with Judaizing and hypocrisy (v 14). Paul won the battle and rescued Peter and Barnabas with eloquent words on justification by faith (vv 15-21), but the Judaizers had resumed their war. From this time on, they did not rest; rather, they tormented and persecuted Paul all over the world. But the apostle did not submit to them for a moment. He was engaged in the fight of his life, so that the truth of the gospel might remain with the Gentile believers (v 5).

Further Travel Paul wanted to visit the new believers and see how they were doing. So he proposed to Barnabas that they return to the cities where they had previously preached about Jesus (Acts 15:36). Barnabas wanted to take John Mark with them, but Paul would not take him since he had deserted them during their earlier journey (13:13). This sharp disagreement ended Barnabas's association with Paul (15:37-39). Silas, a leader among the brothers in Jerusalem (v 22), accompanied Paul as he set out by land through Syria and Cilicia, strengthening the churches (vv 40-41).

Beginning from Derbe in Galatia, Paul and Silas revisited the churches Paul had established with Barnabas. While in Lystra, they were joined by Timothy (Acts 16:1-3). The apostles delivered to these young churches the letter drafted by the elders and apostles in Jerusalem concerning the observance of the law (15:23-29), thus strengthening and increasing them (16:4-5).

It is likely that Ephesus, a major city in the Roman province of Asia, was the party's main objective for the advancement of the gospel, but they were "forbidden by the Holy Spirit to speak the word in Asia" (Acts 16:6). Then they attempted to turn north and enter the region of Bithynia, "but the Spirit of Jesus did not allow them" (v 7). In this way they were forced by God to continue straight westward to Troas on the Aegean Sea, where Luke joined them ("we" in v 10), and Paul had a vision in which he was called out of Asia into Macedonia (vv 8-9). Paul and his party immediately crossed by boat into Europe (v 11) where they carried the gospel to Philippi, Thessalonica, Berea, Athens, and Corinth.

Philippi was a Roman colony and military outpost where there were few Jews, so Paul went to a place by the river where the local Jews prayed. He spoke to some women there, notably Lydia, who believed and with her household was baptized (Acts 16:12-15), beginning the first church in Europe. Paul cast a spirit of divination out of a girl in Philippi, and as a result he and Silas were jailed (vv 16-24). The events of their night in jail made the jailer a believer in God (vv 25-34), and he and his family were added to the church in Philippi, which met in Lydia's home (v 40). When Paul disclosed his Roman citizenship, he was released and was asked to leave the city (vv 35-39).

At Thessalonica the Jews, aroused to jealousy by the success of Paul's gospel message, raised a mob to search for the apostles. They complained to the city authorities that the people "who have turned the world upside down have come here also" and accused the apostles of "saying that there is another king [besides Caesar], Jesus" (Acts 17:5-7).

Paul and Silas quickly left Thessalonica by night and arrived in Berea, a city thereafter distinguished by its citizens who eagerly and thoughtfully received the gospel (Acts 17:10-12). The Thessalonian Jews did not rest but trailed Paul to Berea to incite the crowds. The believers

then sent Paul away to Athens, while Silas and Timothy stayed behind (vv 13-15).

The Athenians called Paul a babbler but let him air his views before the Areopagus. Paul's speech there was alive with his broad knowledge. He alluded to Greco-Roman philosophy (Acts 17:27), poetry (v 28), sculpture (vv 25, 29), architecture (v 24), and religion while proclaiming the existence of an "unknown god" (v 23). But he was rudely cut short by scoffing and indifference when he mentioned the resurrection (v 32). Paul's words delighted the minds of many but influenced the wills of few, so when he arrived in Corinth, he determined not to proclaim the mystery of God in lofty words of wisdom so that the believers' faith would not rest on human wisdom but on the power of God (1 Cor 2:1-5).

In Corinth Paul met Aquila and Priscilla (Acts 18:2-3), Roman Jews with whom he lived and worked as a tent maker and who would become prominent among the churches (Acts 18:26; Rom 16:3; 1 Cor 16:19; 2 Tm 4:19). He stayed in Corinth 18 months from AD 50 to 51, raising up a church (Acts 18:11) on the strength of a vision from God (vv 9-10) and in spite of the attacks of the Jews (vv 12-17). Paul wrote the first and second letters to the Thessalonians from Corinth to establish the believers in a holy, industrious life (1 Thes 3:13; 5:23; 2 Thes 3:7-12) in hope of the second coming of Jesus Christ (1 Thes 4:15-18; 2 Thes 2:1 ff.).

Accompanied by Priscilla and Aquila, Paul sailed from Corinth for Syria. He left his fellow workers in Ephesus, sailed to Caesarea, briefly visited Jerusalem, and returned to Antioch (Acts 18:18-22). Paul stayed in Antioch for awhile but did not remain absent from the field of his labors for long. Alone, he departed from Antioch, went from place to place in Galatia and Phrygia strengthening all the disciples, and eventually arrived in Ephesus (18:23; 19:1).

Labor in the Gospel A Jew named Apollos had ministered in Ephesus prior to Paul's arrival and had recently gone over to Corinth (Acts 18:24-28). There Apollos innocently became the cause of such discord (1 Cor 3:3-9) that he left and refused to return even at Paul's request (16:12). Paul's earlier visit to Ephesus (Acts 18:19-20), Apollos's ministry, and the presence of Priscilla and Aquila had prepared Ephesus for the apostle's preaching of the gospel of Christ.

Paul began his work in Ephesus by setting straight some ill-informed disciples of John the Baptist (Acts 19:1-7). He then spent three months preaching at the local synagogue until members of the congregation "spoke evil of the Way" (v 9). Paul then took the disciples and continued his arguments on the neutral ground of Tyrannus's school (vv 8-9), where Jews and Greeks were free to come. He continued there for two years and "all the residents of Asia, both Jews and Greeks, heard the word of the Lord" (v 10).

The work in Ephesus was a great success (Acts 19:10, 20, 26). Paul enjoyed an open door for effective work (1 Cor 16:9), bolstered by extraordinary miracles (Acts 19:11-17), a public burning of valuable books of sorcery (vv 18-19), and the assistance of friendly officials from the province of Asia (v 31). There were also many adversaries (1 Cor 15:32; 16:9), especially among the artisans associated with the temple of Diana. Paul's ministry had hurt their trade to the extent that they were incited to riot (Acts 19:23-41). Paul had intended to stay in Ephesus until Pentecost (1 Cor 16:8), but this tumult seems to have hastened his departure (Acts 20:1).

During his stay in Ephesus, the household of Chloe sent word to Paul from Corinth that there were divisions in the church there (1 Cor 1:10-13). This report generated a flurry of letters and travels. Paul wrote a letter, which is now lost, to this church (5:9). The church in Corinth wrote a letter (7:1) and sent messengers to Paul (16:17), and Paul sent Timothy to them (4:17; 16:10). Paul then wrote 1 Corinthians (AD 53) and sent it by Titus, who was to meet him in Troas to report the results (2 Cor 2:12-13).

After his hasty exit from Ephesus, Paul found an open door for the gospel in Troas, but he so longed to hear from Corinth that he pushed on into Macedonia (2 Cor 2:12-13). There he was finally comforted by Titus (7:5-7) and rejoiced at the news of the Corinthians' repentance, earnestness, longing, and zeal (vv 8-16). From Macedonia Paul wrote 2 Corinthians (AD 54), toured northwest to proclaim the good news of Christ in Illyricum (Rom 15:19), and then turned south for Achaia and his third visit to Corinth (Acts 19:21; 20:1-3; 2 Cor 13:1).

The time and place from which Paul wrote his letter to the Galatians is a topic of controversy. Some date it before the council at Jerusalem, about AD 45. Others say he wrote it from Corinth at this stage in his history. The latter opinion is the choice of this narrative.

A three-month winter stay in Corinth (AD 55–56) produced the Letter to the Romans, which firmly set the benchmark of the gospel for all the ages. Paul had many personal friends in Rome (Rom 16) and had long intended to visit there (1:10-15). His plans were to deliver a collection from the Gentile churches to Jerusalem (Acts 20:35; Rom 15:25-26; 1 Cor 16:1) and then visit Rome (Acts 19:21) on his way to Spain (Rom 15:23-24).

The Arrest in Jerusalem Paul's trip from Corinth to Jerusalem was marked by abundant warnings of the danger awaiting him in Jerusalem. The Judaizers' acrimony toward Paul was common talk everywhere, but all alarms went unheeded (Acts 20:22-24, 38; 21:4, 10-15). However, the request for prayer in Romans 15:30-32 shows that Paul knew he might soon need a divine rescue from the unbelievers in Judea.

The travelers, carrying the collection for Jerusalem, journeyed swiftly in order to reach Jerusalem by Pentecost (Acts 20:16). They proceeded by land from Achaia, through Macedonia, to Philippi in time for the Passover (spring AD 56, v 6). Crossing by sea to Troas, they visited the believers there (vv 7-12) and then sailed through the archipelago of the eastern Aegean Sea to Miletus (vv 13-16). From Miletus, Paul sent for the elders of Ephesus, to whom he delivered an impassioned speech containing his own dire warnings for them (vv 17-38).

Parting from them, Paul and his companions set sail to Cos, to Rhodes, and then to Patara, where they changed ships for Phoenicia (Acts 21:1-2). A straight course to Tyre brought them within sight of Cyprus, with its memories of Barnabas and Sergius Paulus (v 3). "Through the Spirit" the disciples in Tyre "told Paul not to go on to Jerusalem" (v 4), but he pressed on to Caesarea, where he and his company stayed with Philip, who had formerly served with the martyred Stephen (21:8; cf. 6:5). In Caesarea, Paul would not be persuaded by an especially dramatic prophecy of his coming arrest (21:10-14).

In Jerusalem the apostolic band stayed with Mnason, an early disciple, and were warmly welcomed by the brothers there (Acts 21:15-17). James and the elders of the church praised God when they heard of the things he had done through Paul among the Gentiles (vv 18-20), and when they received the collection from the churches (24:17). They told Paul of his bad reputation among the

thousands of Jewish believers in Jerusalem and urged him to set right the Judaizers' misrepresentation that he encouraged Jewish Christians to forsake the Mosaic customs (21:21-24). Acts 21:25 shows the Jerusalem elders understood that the Gentiles were under no obligation to Moses; their concern was for Paul to demonstrate that Jewish believers were free to continue their traditional observances.

Paul had kept the Jewish feasts (Acts 20:6), as had Jesus and the early disciples in Jerusalem. He had also cut his hair in a vow at Cenchreae (18:18), so it was a small matter for him, a Jew, to ceremonially purify himself after becoming a Christian, especially if it would undermine the arguments of the Judaizers. To have refused the elders' request would have lent credence to the Judaizers' charge. The success of this plan is seen in that it was the Jews from Asia, visiting Jerusalem for the Pentecost feast of AD 57, who stirred up trouble for Paul (21:27-29)—not the Judaizers from Jerusalem.

The whole city was aroused by Paul's persistent persecutors. A violent crowd dragged him out of the temple just as Stephen had once been hauled to his martyrdom. They tried to kill him, but he was rescued by Roman soldiers as the mob cried, "Away with him!"—just as they had done to Jesus (Acts 21:30-36). At this juncture the educational and cultural diversity of Paul's life came to his rescue. As he was carried for safety to the Roman barracks, he spoke in Greek to the tribune, who had mistaken him for an Egyptian assassin (vv 37-38). Given permission to speak to the crowd, he did so in the Aramaic language then common in Israel (vv 39-40). The hushed crowd eagerly heard Paul's defense until he uttered the word "Gentiles." At this, the crowd resumed its threatening and violence, and Paul was brought into the barracks (22:1-24). There the Romans prepared to flog him, until Paul revealed that he was not only a Jew from Tarsus but also a freeborn Roman citizen. The tribune was afraid, since he had bound a Roman citizen. Wanting to know the charges against Paul, he brought him to the Sanhedrin (vv 25-30).

This meeting of the Jewish judiciary was shortly reduced to dissension and violence. Paul resorted to tactics justifiable in such a war and hopelessly divided the Sanhedrin on the subject of the resurrection (Acts 23:1-9). Paul again was rescued, this time from the contending factions of the Jewish leadership, and taken to the barracks, where the Lord encouraged him, promising that he would go to Rome (AD 56, vv 10-11).

In the meantime 40 Jews entered into a murderous plot against Paul. They vowed not to eat or drink until they had killed the apostle (Acts 23:12-15). They almost succeeded, but with the help of the son of Paul's sister (v 16), the conspiracy was exposed. For safety, Paul was taken from Jerusalem to Caesarea under guard of 470 soldiers and handed over to the custody of Felix the governor (vv 16-35). Inconclusive hearings before Felix (Acts 24), his successor, Festus (25:1-12), and King Agrippa (25:23–26:32) occupied Paul in his two years of imprisonment in Caesarea. Festus, wanting to please the Jews, suggested that Paul be returned to Jerusalem for trial, but Paul knew the murderous intent of his accusers and again utilized his Roman citizenship by making a dramatic appeal to Caesar (25:9-12).

Voyage and Stay in Rome To plead his case at Caesar's court, Paul and his companions, Aristarchus and Luke, were taken on a perilous voyage (AD 58, Acts 27:1–28:16). Their passage by ship from Caesarea to Rome is one of the most remarkable on record. Luke's detailed account is a treasure of information on ancient ships, navigation, and seamanship. It is also a beautiful portrait of a heroic and dignified apostle Paul, the gospel's ambassador in chains (Eph 6:20), who with the guidance and assurance of his God (Acts 27:23-26), led the 276 people on board to safety (v 37).

Luke traces the voyage stage by stage through every crisis, with a change of ship at Myra, delay at Fair Havens on Crete, and the shipwreck on Malta. Finally, in the spring of AD 59, they arrived at Puteoli, Italy, and made their way to Rome, welcomed by the believers along the Appian Way (Acts 28:13-16).

Luke provided a peaceful denouement to the Acts, notwithstanding the fact that the apostle was an imperial prisoner of Caesar Nero. Paul lived by himself in his own house, chained to a Roman guard (Acts 28:16, 30). There he received the local Jewish leaders—to calm any misgivings they may have had about him and, at the same time, to convince them about Jesus. His efforts had mixed success (vv 17-28). During Paul's two or more years in Rome, the Judaizers seem to have withdrawn, only to be replaced by the peril of Eastern Gnosticism. This is seen in Paul's letters to the Philippians, Colossians, and Ephesians, and to Philemon, all written at this time. It is unlikely that Paul's accusers appeared in Rome to bring formal charges before Caesar, so Paul was probably released in AD 61.

Final Years and Martyrdom It is here assumed that the Pastoral Letters (1 Timothy, 2 Timothy, and Titus) are truly Paul's work. Only through them can the probable course of events in Paul's final years be traced. Romans 15:28 shows that Paul intended to deliver the collection to Jerusalem and then to "set out by way of you [Rome] to Spain." The arrest and imprisonment in Jerusalem not only destroyed these plans but also extracted five precious years from the prime of a most productive life. Although Clement of Rome implied that Paul did fulfill his desire to go to Spain (*Clement to the Corinthians* 5), it is certain that the daily pressure of Paul's anxious care for all the churches (2 Cor 11:28) did not abate.

If Paul went to Spain, he may have been there when Rome was burned on July 19, AD 64. Tradition says that Paul traveled as far as Britain, but there is no evidence to confirm this. Returning east, he left Titus in Crete (Ti 1:5) and traveled through Miletus, south of Ephesus, where he left Trophimus sick (2 Tm 4:20). Traveling toward Macedonia, Paul visited Timothy in Ephesus (1 Tm 1:3). On the way, Paul left his cloak and books with Carpus in Troas (2 Tm 4:13). This indicates that he intended to return there for his possessions. From Macedonia Paul wrote his loving yet apprehensive first letter to Timothy (AD 62–64). He had decided to spend the winter in Nicopolis (Ti 3:12), northwest of Corinth on the Adriatic Sea, but was still in Macedonia when he wrote his letter to Titus. This letter is similar to 1 Timothy, yet with a somewhat harsher tone. In it is a final glimpse of the eloquent and zealous Apollos (Ti 3:13), who is still in association with Paul 10 or more years after his first appearance in Ephesus (Acts 18:24).

From here Paul's path is obscure. He may have wintered in Nicopolis, but he did not return to Troas for his winter cloak (2 Tm 4:13). At some point he was arrested by the Romans, because he spent a winter in Rome's Mamertine Prison, suffering from the cold in that rock cell before he wrote his second letter to Timothy (AD 66–67). He may have been anticipating the coming winter when he requested that Timothy bring his cloak (vv 13, 21). It is possible that the charges against Paul were related to the burning of Rome; this is unknown. It was,

however, now "illegal" to be a Christian since the "new religion" was no longer protected by Roman law as being part of Judaism (which was a legalized, recognized religion by Roman law).

It was dangerous to be associated with Paul at this time. Many deserted him (2 Tm 4:16), including all his coworkers in Asia (1:15) and Demas, who loved the world (4:10). Only Luke, the physician and author of Luke and Acts, was with him when he wrote his second letter to Timothy (v 11). Faithful believers still in hiding in Rome were also in contact with the apostle (1:16; 4:19, 21). He told Timothy to come to him in Rome and bring Mark also (4:11). Apparently Timothy did come and was imprisoned (Heb 13:23). Paul's request for the books and parchments (2 Tm 4:13) discloses that he was reading and studying the Scripture to the end.

The apostle Paul had two hearings before Caesar Nero. At his first defense only the Lord stood by him (2 Tm 4:16). There he not only pleaded his own cause but also that of the gospel, still longing that all the Gentiles would hear its message. Perhaps no decision was made, and thus he was "rescued from the lion's mouth" (v 17). Though he knew he would soon die, he was not afraid, but was assured that the Lord would give him a crown of righteousness on the last day (v 8). Finally, the apostle himself recorded his seminal encouragement to all believers: "The Lord be with your spirit. Grace be with you" (v 22, RSV). After this, the Scripture is silent regarding Paul.

Nothing is known of Paul's second hearing but that it resulted in the sentence of capital punishment. History does not record Paul's end. Nero died in the summer of AD 68, so Paul was executed before that date. As a Roman citizen, he must have been spared the lingering torture that had recently been suffered by his fellow martyrs. Tradition says that he was decapitated by the sword of an imperial headsman on the Ostian Road just outside of Rome, and buried nearby. This fulfilled Paul's desire "to depart and be with Christ, for that is far better" (Phil 1:23, RSV).

PAUL WRITES HIS OWN EPITAPH
Paul wrote his own epitaph in 2 Timothy 4:6-8:

> As for me, my life has already been poured out as an offering to God. The time of my death is near. I have fought a good fight, I have finished the race, and I have remained faithful. And now the prize awaits me—the crown of righteousness that the Lord, the righteous Judge, will give me on that great day of his return. And the prize is not just for me but for all who eagerly look forward to his glorious return. (NLT)

This is a model for all true believers to emulate.

PAULUS, Sergius *See* Sergius Paulus.

PAVEMENT Term occurring ten times in the Bible, usually alluding to the stone floor of the temple(s). Particular interest focuses on the reference in John 19:13 to the pavement on which Jesus stood trial before Pilate. It was at the decisive moment of the Roman phase of the trial of Jesus when "Pilate had Jesus brought out, and seated himself on the chair of judgement at a place called the Pavement, in Hebrew Gabbatha" (Jn 19:13, NJB). This verse has played an important role in determining the location of Jesus' trial. Until recently scholars located this pavement where Pilate's judgment seat was placed under the present street level in Jerusalem at the site of Herod's fortress Antonia. This enormous stone pavement consists of large blocks of limestone, excavated in the 1930s by Père Vincent. Today, scholars disagree about whether this is the most historically plausible site for the pavement where Jesus was condemned.

PAVILION* A translation of the Hebrew word *sukkah* and *sokoh* in the KJV. The word *sukkah* is also translated as "booth" (Gn 33:17), "tabernacle" (Lv 23:34), and "tent" (2 Sm 11:11). Other translations of *sokoh* are "den" (Ps 10:9), "tabernacle" (76:2), and "covert" (Jer 25:38). The words *sukkah* and *sokoh* signify a shelter or covering, which may be in the form of a tent (booth or tabernacle), hut, or den.

The word "pavilion" is used to refer to the tents of Ben-hadad's royal entourage and allies as they were in a drunken stupor when Ahab attacked them (1 Kgs 20:16). Other versions read "booths" (RSV), "temporary shelters" (NASB); "quarters" (NEB), and "tents" (NIV, NLT).

The metaphorical use is found in the book of Psalms. In Psalms 27:5 and 31:20 the psalmist speaks of the Lord's special protection as a place where one may find refuge from the evildoers. The word may also refer to the clouds that, in the pictorial language of the psalmist, cover the presence of the Lord, "He made darkness his covering, his canopy around him—the dark rain clouds of the sky" (Ps 18:11, NIV).

PEACE Total well-being, prosperity, and security associated with God's presence among his people. Linked in the OT with the covenant, the presence of peace was conditional, based on Israel's obedience. In the prophetic writings, true peace is part of the end-time hope of God's salvation. In the NT, this longed-for peace is understood as having come in Christ and can be experienced by the believers.

In the Old Testament *Shalom*, the most prominent OT term for "peace," held a wide range of connotations (wholeness, health, security, well-being, and salvation) and could apply to an equally wide range of contexts: the state of the individual (Ps 37:37; Prv 3:2; Is 32:17), the relationship of person to person (Gn 34:21; Jos 9:15) or nation to nation (e.g., absence of conflict—Dt 2:26; Jos 10:21; 1 Kgs 5:12; Ps 122:6-7), and the relationship of God and people (Ps 85:8; Jer 16:5).

The presence of *shalom* in any of these contexts was not considered ultimately as the outcome of human endeavor but as a gift or blessing of God (Lv 26:6; 1 Kgs 2:33; Jb 25:2; Pss 29:11; 85:8; Is 45:7). It is not surprising, therefore, to find "peace" tied closely to the OT notion of covenant. *Shalom* was the desired state of harmony and communion between the two covenant partners—God and his people (Nm 6:26; cf. Is 54:10). Its presence signified God's blessing in the covenant relationship (Mal 2:5; cf. Nm 25:12), and its absence signified the breakdown of that relationship due to Israel's disobedience and unrighteousness (Jer 16:5, 10-13; cf. Ps 85:9-11; Is 32:17).

Shalom becomes a pivotal term in the prophetic writings. It was the "false" prophets who, forgetting the conditions for national well-being within the covenant relationship, assumed God's loyalty to Israel (Ps 89) would guarantee political peace forever (Jer 6:14; 8:15; Ez 13:10, 16; Mi 3:5). Against such popular but false security, the preexilic prophets proclaimed the coming judgment precisely as a loss of this *shalom* due to Israel's persistent disobedience and unrighteousness (Is 48:18; Jer 14:13-16; 16:5, 10-13; 28; Mi 3:4, 9-12).

The prophets did, however, point beyond the crises of exile and subsequent setbacks to a time when *shalom*, characterized by prosperity and well-being (Is 45:7; Ez 34:25-26), absence of conflict (Is 2:2-4; 32:15-20; Ez 34:28-31), right relations (Is 11:1-5; Mi 4:1-4; Zec 8:9-13), restoration of harmony in nature (Is 11:6-9; Ez 47:1-12), and salvation (Is 52:7; 60:17; Ez 34:30-31; 37:26-28) would again return. Often this eschatological (or end-time) expectation of peace in the OT was associated with a messianic figure, as in Isaiah 9:6, where the future Messiah is termed the "Prince of Peace." Moreover, his reign would be one of "peace" not only for Israel but throughout the whole earth (Zec 9:9-10). The OT ends with this hope of peace still unrealized in its full sense.

In the New Testament The Greek term for "peace" used predominantly in the NT is *eirene*, a word expanded from its classical Greek connotation of "rest" to include the various connotations of *shalom* discussed above. As with *shalom*, *eirene* could be used as a greeting or farewell (as in "peace be with you"—Lk 10:5; Gal 6:16; Jas 2:16; cf. Jn 20:19), or could signify the cessation of conflict (national—Lk 14:32; Acts 12:20; or interpersonal—Rom 14:19; Eph 4:3), or the presence of domestic tranquillity (cf. 1 Cor 7:15).

The chief issue concerns how Jesus incorporated the OT hope for the eschatological peace of God into his ministry. In the "benedictus" of Zechariah (Lk 1:67-79), the coming of Jesus as the Messiah is expected to "guide our feet into the way of peace" (v 79). So also the angelic testimony to the shepherds proclaims Jesus as the bringer of God's peace to people (2:14). That is, Jesus as the Messiah would usher in God's reign of peace. Jesus' self-understanding as expressed in the fourth Gospel corresponds to this association. This long-expected peace of God is Jesus' farewell gift to the disciples (Jn 14:27); it is given to them when he breathed his Spirit into them (20:19-22).

The nature of this gift of peace brought by Jesus may be easier to explain by stating what it is not. It is not an end to tension or the absence of warfare. It is not domestic tranquillity nor anything like the worldly estimation of peace (Lk 12:51-53; Jn 14:27; 16:32-33). Its presence may, on the contrary, actually disturb existing relations, being a dividing "sword" in familial relations (Mt 10:34-37). Jesus' gift of peace is, in reality, the character and mood of the new covenant of his blood that reconciles God to people (Rom 5:1; Col 1:20) and forms the basis of subsequent reconciliation between divergent people (Eph 2:14-22).

The early church understood "peace" to be the final, end-time salvation of God given already through Jesus Christ (cf. Phil 4:7-9). This understanding of "peace" altered the content of the common greeting "go in peace" as it was taken up in the Christian community. In Paul's common "grace and peace" greeting (1 Cor 1:3; 2 Cor 1:2; Gal 1:3; Eph 1:2, etc.; cf. also 1 Pt 1:2; 2 Jn 1:3; Jude 1:2; Rv 1:4), it is no longer a mere wish for peace that Paul extends to his readers but is a reminder of the messianic gifts available in the present time through Christ to the man of faith. In accord with this, Jesus is described as "peace" itself (Eph 2:14), while God, too, because of his act of reconciliation through Christ, is known as a "God of peace" (Phil 4:9; Col 3:15).

This gift of peace or reconciliation with God, made available through Christ, places an ethical demand on the Christian; it calls for the exercises of "peace" (as reconciliation between persons) within the church. Peace, as a fruit of the Spirit (Gal 5:22), is to be the goal of the Christian's dealings with others (Rom 12:18; 14:19; Heb 12:14).

PEACE OFFERING *See* Offerings and Sacrifices.

PEACOCK *See* Birds.

PEARL
Gem formed within the shell of certain mollusks. The word appears only once in the OT (Jb 28:18). However, some think that the reference to a reddish stone in Lamentations 4:7 may be to the pink pearl found in the Red Sea. By the NT period, the pearl was a prized piece of feminine jewelry (1 Tm 2:9), an item of trade (Mt 13:45-46; Rv 18:12-16), and an object of high price. Being familiar objects, pearls were frequently used by Jesus in his illustrations. A fine pearl was an object of such great value that a man might sell all his accumulated wealth to purchase it (Mt 13:45-46). A pearl (used figuratively for the word of the Lord) would not be given to those who, like pigs, had no appreciation for its value (7:6).

See also Stones, Precious.

PEDAHEL
Ammihud's son from Naphtali's tribe, appointed to work with Joshua and Eleazar in distributing Canaanite territory west of the Jordan River among the Israelites (Nm 34:28).

PEDAHZUR
Gamaliel's father from Manasseh's tribe (Nm 1:10; 2:20; 7:54, 59; 10:23).

PEDAIAH
1. Maternal grandfather of Judah's King Jehoiakim. Pedaiah was from Rumah (2 Kgs 23:36).
2. Jeconiah's third son (1 Chr 3:18-19).
3. Joel's father from the half-tribe of Manasseh (1 Chr 27:20).
4. Parosh's son, who worked with the temple servants in repairing the Jerusalem wall opposite the Water Gate (Neh 3:25).
5. One who stood beside Ezra during the public reading of the Law (Neh 8:4).
6. Kolaiah's son and Joed's father (Neh 11:7). He was a member of Benjamin's tribe and lived in Jerusalem after the return from exile.
7. Levite appointed by Nehemiah as treasurer of the storehouse to distribute grain, wine, and oil to the priests who served in the temple (Neh 13:13).

PEKAH
Son of Remaliah and 18th king of Israel. His name means "he has opened [the eyes]." It is an abbreviated form of the name of his predecessor, Pekahiah, "Yahweh has opened [the eyes]." The name has been found on a fragment of an eighth-century-BC wine jar from Hazor stratum V, the level destroyed by Tiglath-pileser in 734 BC. It is thought that this is a reference to Pekah and to a kind of wine. It is likely that the usurper Pekah was so eager to ensure his position as king that he deliberately assumed the name of his predecessor. Moreover, Isaiah refers to him as the "son of Remaliah," almost scornfully, to indicate his nonroyal descent. But when Isaiah refers to his heathen ally, he uses the specific name "Rezin, the king of Syria" (Is 7:4-9; 8:6).

Accession to the Throne Pekah, an officer of Pekahiah, was the third man in a chariot, apart from the driver and the warrior. He was the shield and armor bearer of the warrior. In time the term came to signify a royal aide-de-camp.

The account of Pekah's murder of Pekahiah has been somewhat obscured because of the difficulty in understanding the terms Argob and Arieh (2 Kgs 15:25). Some translators and commentators have thought these referred to persons, whereas others have held these are place-names. Some scholars radically alter the text here and eliminate the troublesome words by claiming they were a scribal mistake or emendation. A key seems to have been found by comparing them with the Ugaritic. The terms mean "eagle" and "lion," respectively. Thus, Pekah was murdered "near the eagle and the lion." It is suggested that this means he was put to death near the guardian sphinxes of his palace. Such sphinxes were a common motif in ancient eastern palaces and were duplicated on ivory plaques erected in the gateway. This interpretation seems very plausible, since it avoids critical emendation and solves the major problems in the text.

Political Significance The brilliant Tiglath-pileser III, leading the kingdom of Assyria to prominence, appeared on Israel's border. Menahem deemed it wise to become tributary to him. Apparently Pekahiah, Menahem's successor, could not appease the Assyrians during his short reign. The conciliatory efforts of Menahem and Pekahiah may well have prompted the Syrians to conspire with Pekah, the army officer, to gain control of the throne of Samaria in order to present a united military front against Assyrian encroachment. Once Samaria was under control, the Syrians led by Rezin, Israel ruled by Pekah, and several Transjordanian kingdoms formed a powerful alliance.

In time Pekah and Rezin began to pressure the kingdom of Judah in order to induce it to join their alliance against the impending Assyrian attack. Jotham resisted their invitations and fortified the Judean hill country. Jotham's son, Ahaz, continued his father's policy of noncooperation with the Samaria-Damascus coalition. Pekah and Rezin invaded Judah with the intent of taking Jerusalem and placing "the son of Tabeel" on the throne of Judah in Ahaz's place (Is 7:1-6). He presumably was a son of Uzziah or Jotham by a princess of Tabeel. Although the actual siege of Jerusalem was unsuccessful, Pekah and Rezin inflicted severe casualties upon Ahaz's army. In one day of battle they killed 120,000 men of Judah and carried away 200,000 captives, including women and children. However, the prophet Oded prophesied in Samaria before the army. He urged the leaders of Samaria to return the captives. The leaders heeded the prophetic word and sent the captives back to Jericho (2 Chr 28:8-15).

Rezin's revolt against Assyria brought a quick response from Tiglath-pileser, who laid siege to Damascus in 734 BC. The city fell in 732 BC. Another detachment of the Assyrian army descended on the upper districts of Syria and Samaria. Second Kings 15:29 lists the districts and cities that were overrun. They included Gilead (regions beyond Jordan), Naphtali (regions lying to the west of the lakes of Galilee and Merom), and all Galilee as far south as the plain of Esdraelon and the valley of Jezreel. Isaiah refers to this lost tribal territory (Is 9:1-7). From this Assyrian-controlled region the messianic ruler would arise and give light to those who lived in a land of darkness (v 2). Thus Pekah's kingdom was reduced to a third of its original size by the Assyrian campaign of 734–732 BC. In 732 a palace conspiracy led by Hoshea plotted the assassination of Pekah. He was put to death in the coup d'état and the throne was usurped by Hoshea.

The author of Kings evaluates the reign of Pekah as follows: "But Pekah did what was evil in the LORD's sight. He refused to turn from the sins of idolatry that

Jeroboam son of Nebat had led Israel to commit" (2 Kgs 15:28, NLT). It is likely that he continued the calf worship at the shrines at Dan and Bethel. The continuation of the apostasy during successive regencies was the cause for the judgment that befell the northern kingdom. Pekah is the last king of Israel given such an evaluation.

PEKAHIAH Son of Menahem, king of Israel. Pekahiah (whose name means "Yahweh has opened [his eyes]") was among the 20 kings who ruled Israel from Samaria following its decline consequent to the fracture of the Solomonic monarchy in the tenth century BC. The brief account in the Bible concerning him (2 Kgs 15:22-26) points to the godlessness of his life (v 24). His sin, like that of his father (Menahem), was linked to the false worship of Jeroboam, who built shrines at Dan and Bethel to rival worship in the temple at Jerusalem. Such religious activity threatened the true worship of God by attempting to fuse biblical concepts with the fertility cult of Baal, a movement sharply denounced by the Word of God (1 Kgs 13:1-5). Like many of Israel's kings, Pekahiah ruled briefly, being assassinated in the second year of his reign. The chief instigator of the plot against him, a captain named Pekah, took 50 men of Gilead and killed the king, along with two aides, in the citadel of the royal palace at Samaria. His successor, Pekah, was regrettably as evil as Pekahiah and received the condemnation of Scripture typical of virtually all the Israelite kings: he "did what was evil in the LORD's sight" (2 Kgs 15:28, NLT).

See also Pekah.

PEKOD Place mentioned as the location of an Aramean tribe living in southern Babylonia between Babylon and Elam and more exactly on the eastern bank of the Lower Tigris by modern Kut-el-Amara and the confluence of the Kerkha (Jer 50:21; Ez 23:23). Tiglath-pileser III (745–727), Sargon II (722–705), and Sennacherib (705–681) subjugated the population and exacted tribute of horses, cattle, and sheep from Pekod.

PELAIAH
1. Elioenai's son and a remote descendant of David (1 Chr 3:24).
2. Levite who helped Ezra explain (or translate) the Law to the people after it was read to them (Neh 8:7; 10:10).

PELALIAH Forefather of Adaiah, a priest living in Jerusalem during Ezra's day (Neh 11:12).

PELATIAH
1. Hananiah's son, in a list of King Solomon's descendants (1 Chr 3:21).
2. Military leader among the Simeonites who helped destroy an Amalekite remnant at Mt Seir during Hezekiah's reign (1 Chr 4:42).
3. Political leader who signed Ezra's covenant of faithfulness to God with Nehemiah and others after the exile (Neh 10:22).
4. Benaiah's son and one of the two princes seen by Ezekiel in a vision of judgment, identified by the Spirit of the Lord as one who devises wickedness and gives wicked counsel in the city (Ez 11:1-2, 13).

PELEG Son of Eber and father of Reu (Gn 10:25; 11:16-19; 1 Chr 1:19, 25; Lk 3:35). During his lifetime, the earth was divided (Peleg means "division" or "watercourse"). Precisely what the division refers to is still debated. Suggestions include (1) the geographical and linguistic dispersion following the Tower of Babel fiasco (Gn 11:1-9); (2) dispersion of Noah's descendants;

(3) separation of the people of Arphaxad from Joktanide Arabs (Gn 10:24-29); and (4) the division of land by irrigation canals (the term is so used in Jb 29:6; 38:25; Is 30:25; 32:2). The origin of the name is usually traced to the city of Phalga, north of the junction of the Euphrates and Khabur rivers.

See also Genealogy of Jesus Christ.

PELET
1. Jahdai's son from Judah's tribe (1 Chr 2:47).
2. Warrior from Benjamin's tribe who joined David at Ziklag in his struggle against King Saul. Pelet was one of David's ambidextrous archers and slingers (1 Chr 12:2-3).

PELETH
1. On's father from Reuben's tribe (Nm 16:1).
2. Jonathan's son and a Jerahmeelite from Judah's tribe (1 Chr 2:33).

PELETHITES* Bodyguards of David, and loyal mercenaries during the king's political setbacks. They are always associated with the Cherethites, and both are believed to be of Philistine stock with Crete as their place of origin (Caphtor, home of the Philistines, generally taken to be Crete—Am 9:7). The Pelethites accompanied David when he fled Jerusalem under threat from Absalom's forces (2 Sm 15:18) and fought for David in the rebellion of Sheba (20:7). Their leader, Benaiah, supported Solomon's claim to David's throne against the ambitions of Adonijah, and the presence of the Pelethites at Solomon's anointing surely contributed to Adonijah's demise (1 Kgs 1:38, 44). Mercenaries from the Aegean were common.

PELICAN *See* Birds.

PELLA* City located east of the Jordan River in the Decapolis region. There is no reference to this city in the Bible, but records show that it was an important Canaanite city, influenced by Egypt and later by Greece and Rome. During the Jewish revolt against Rome (AD 66–70), Pella became a refuge for many Christians and a center for the early church.

PELONITE* Designation given to two of David's mighty men, Helez and Ahijah (1 Chr 11:27, 36; 27:10, NLT "from Pelon"). No sources for the designation are known, which has led some scholars to consider it a textual corruption. In 2 Samuel 23:26, Helez is called a Paltite, and Ahijah is probably identical to Eliam the Gilonite in 2 Samuel 23:34. The latter are preferred over "Pelonite" in both cases. Others suggest that Pelonite is derived from the town Beth-pelet (see Jos 15:27; Neh 11:26).

PELUSIUM City known for its flax and wine, but also a strategic fortified town on Egypt's Mediterranean coast, situated on the trade route between Egypt and Mesopotamia (Ez 30:15-16). Today the site is called Tell Farama and is located about 20 miles (32.2 kilometers) southeast of Port Said. The Hebrew OT uses the old Egyptian name for the town, *Sin*, meaning "fortress." Some English translations of the OT (KJV) use this English name. When the Greeks controlled Egypt, they renamed the town Pelusium, "the muddy city," apparently confusing the Egyptian name with a similar Egyptian word *sin*, meaning "mud" or "clay." In Ezekiel it is called "the stronghold of Egypt" because it provided a defense against the ever-present danger of attack from the north.

PEN Writing implement used with ink. *See* Writing.

PENCE* KJV form of denarius in Matthew 18:28, Mark 14:5, Luke 7:41, 10:35, and John 12:5. *See* Coins; Money.

PENCIL* A carpenter's outlining tool named in RSV in connection with the manufacture of idols (Is 44:13). Other translations are "line" (KJV), "red chalk" (NASB), "a scriber" (NEB), "a marker" (NIV).

PENIEL Alternate form of Penuel, the Palestinian city where Jacob wrestled with the "angel" of God, in Genesis 32:30. *See* Penuel (Place).

PENINNAH One of Elkanah's two wives, the other and more favored being Hannah (1 Sm 1:2-6). Peninnah's fortune in bearing children was the source of much domestic friction for the childless Hannah, especially at the time of the annual sacrifice at Shiloh. Rabbinic tradition explains Peninnah's taunts as attempts to provoke Hannah into pregnancy, but the biblical record portrays the women as rivals.

PENKNIFE* Iron tool used to sharpen reed pens, cut papyrus, and carve letters in stone. It is mentioned by name only in Jeremiah 36:23 (RSV), but it is referred to elsewhere as a pen or tool of iron (Jb 19:24; Jer 17:1).

PENNY
1. KJV translation of denarius (Mt 20:2, 9-10, 13; 22:19; Mk 12:15; Lk 20:24; Rv 6:6).
2. The RSV and NLT translation of the Roman assarion, equivalent to one-sixteenth of the denarius (Mt 10:29; Lk 12:6).
3. The RSV and NLT translation of the Roman quadrans, equivalent to one-fourth of the assarion or one sixty-fourth of the denarius (Mt 5:26; Mk 12:42).

See also Coins; Money.

PENTATEUCH* Word formed by two Greek words, *pente* ("five") and *teuchos* ("case") and commonly used to refer to the first five books of the OT (Genesis, Exodus, Leviticus, Numbers, Deuteronomy), which were encased together, as in one book. This portion of God's Word was written by Moses (Ex 17:14; 24:4; 34:27; Nm 33:1-2; Dt 31:9, 22) and constitutes the foundation upon which all other Scripture rests. The Pentateuch begins with the creation of the universe and records God's dealings with mankind in the Garden of Eden, his preparation of a seed-bearing line (the patriarchal stories), and the formation of the nation Israel. A substantial portion of the Pentateuch consists of laws governing the religious and civil life of the theocratic nation.

See also Deuteronomy, Book of; Exodus, Book of; Genesis, Book of; Leviticus, Book of; Numbers, Book of; Torah.

PENTECOST Word derived from the Greek word *pentekoste* ("fiftieth"), which stood for the festival celebrated on the 50th day after Passover. In the OT this festival, called *Shavu'oth* (Weeks) in Judaism, is referred to as the Feast of Weeks (Ex 34:22; Dt 16:10) because it occurs seven weeks after Passover. Other names include the Feast of Harvest (Ex 23:16), because of its relationship with harvest season, and the Day of Firstfruits (Nm 28:26), because two loaves of newly ground grain were presented before the Lord. (This latter name should be distinguished from the offering of firstfruits at the beginning of the harvest season, as mentioned in Lv 23:9-14.)

The Feast of Weeks was one of three OT pilgrimage fes-

tivals when individuals were to appear before the Lord with gifts and offerings (Ex 23:14-17). The festival was primarily a harvest festival and celebrated the end of the barley harvest and the beginning of the wheat harvest. Traditionally, grain harvest extended from Passover, when the first grain was cut (Dt 16:9) around mid-April, to Pentecost, which marked its conclusion in mid-June. Josephus's statement that Pentecost was called "closing" illustrates this understanding (*Antiquities* 3.10.6).

Each year the priest waved a sheaf of newly harvested grain before the Lord on the day after the Sabbath during the Festival of Unleavened Bread (the period of seven days following Passover). The people then counted 50 days from the offering of that first sheaf of grain until the day after the seventh Sabbath to observe the Feast of Weeks (Lv 23:11). On this day two loaves, made of two-tenths of an ephah of flour and baked with yeast, were waved before the Lord (v 17) and freewill offerings were encouraged (Dt 16:10). This harvest festival was a time of great rejoicing and a holy assembly when no work was to be done (Lv 23:21; Dt 16:11). Observance of the Feast of Weeks during Solomon's time (2 Chr 8:13) is the only OT reference outside of the Pentateuch, for Ezekiel makes no mention of it in his calendar for future festivals (Ez 45–46).

Pentecost is first mentioned in the NT as the occasion for the outpouring of the Holy Spirit upon the disciples of Christ, an event that many theologians understand as marking the beginning of the church (Acts 2:1). Since this was a required festival, Jews gathered from great distances to observe Pentecost in Jerusalem, making it an appropriate time for God's work. On two occasions Paul takes into consideration the Festival of Pentecost when anticipating his travels. In the first instance he writes to the Corinthians about delaying his visit to them until after Pentecost (1 Cor 16:8), while later he was desirous of traveling to Jerusalem to get there in time for Pentecost (Acts 20:16).

See also Feasts and Festivals of Israel.

PENTECOST CELEBRATIONS FOR JEWS AND CHRISTIANS
Jews today celebrate the giving of the law at Sinai on Shavu'oth, in addition to observing aspects of the Harvest Festival. After the destruction of the temple in AD 70, this association became stronger and is now a central part of the festival. In addition to readings from the Pentateuch, the book of Ruth is read because of its harvest background. Much later in Judaism, this festival came to commemorate the anniversary of David's death, so the Psalms are also read.

Christians annually celebrate Pentecost on a designated Sunday on the assumption that 50 days from Passover to the Feast of Weeks were counted until the day after the seventh Sabbath (our Sunday) as prescribed by Leviticus 23:15-16. While the early church celebrated God's gift of the Holy Spirit on Pentecost, in time it became a popular occasion for baptisms. The white dress of the candidates gave rise to the name Whitsunday (White Sunday) in Christian tradition.

PENUEL (Person)
1. Descendant (possibly son) of Hur and father (in the sense of progenitor) of Gedor from Judah's tribe (1 Chr 4:4).
2. Shashak's son from Benjamin's tribe (1 Chr 8:25).

PENUEL* (Place) Name given to the place near the Jabbok River where Jacob strove all night with God (Gn 32:31); alternately called Peniel in verse 30. During the period of the judges, Gideon destroyed the tower of Penuel and killed the men of the city for refusing to join him in war against the Midianites (Jgs 8:8-9, 17). Later, King Jeroboam rebuilt the town (1 Kgs 12:25). It was positioned near Succoth east of the Jordan River, though its exact location remains uncertain.

PEOPLE OF GOD
Designation for the collective group that believes in God. It is a common strand of Israel's faith that it became the people of God because he chose it to be his own possession (Ex 6:6-7; 19:5; Dt 7:6; 14:2; 26:18). The idea of the covenant is linked to this (Lv 26:9-12). In the preaching of the prophets, where the judgment of God is often seen as leading to complete destruction, there is also the vision of the reestablishment and re-creation of the people of God (Jer 32:37; Hos 2:1, 23; Ez 11:20; 36:28). In the development of Judaism after the exile, the idea emerges that it is only the Israel of the future, the final messianic community, that will be "people of God" in the full sense of that term.

It is evident from a number of passages in the NT that the church knew itself to be this future people of God. The clearest passage is 1 Peter 2:9 (RSV): "You are a chosen race, a royal priesthood, a holy nation, God's own people." The expressions "royal priesthood" and "holy nation" are taken from Exodus 19:6, which so powerfully expresses both the participation in God's reign and the priestly service of the people of God in the world. Just as the original people of God were called to proclaim God's mighty acts of deliverance (Is 43:20-21, LXX), so the new people of God are called to "declare the wonderful deeds of him who called you out of darkness into his marvelous light" (1 Pt 2:9).

See also Body of Christ.

PEOPLE OF THE EAST*
Tribes located east and northeast of Canaan, many of them overtly hostile to the Jews. Genesis 29:1 provides the first reference to these peoples. Jacob, en route to Haran, crossed through territory designated as "the land of the people of the east."

The comprehensiveness of the term is evident in the way it is used to refer to nomads (Ez 25:10) or Mesopotamians (1 Kgs 4:30). The term also occurs in association with specific tribes, such as the Amalekites (Jgs 6:3), Ammonites (Ez 25:4), Edomites (Is 11:14), Kedarites (Jer 49:28), Midianites (Jgs 6:33), and Moabites (Ez 25:10).

The most distinguished OT personality linked to the term is the patriarch Job, who is called the greatest man among all the people of the east (Jb 1:3). Job's homeland, the land of Uz, was probably in the vicinity of Edom to the southeast of the Dead Sea.

PEOPLE OF THE LAND*
OT phrase also known by its Hebrew transliteration, 'Am-Ha'arets. In a generic sense, 'Am-Ha'arets referred to a political or ethnic group of people, such as the Hittite sons of Heth (Gn 23:7), the Egyptians (42:6), the Israelites (Ex 5:5), the nations of Canaan (Nm 13:28; Neh 9:24), and the Ammonites (Nm 21:34). With the expansion of Israel as a nation, this expression was used to define the general class of people who were not part of the upper religious and political levels of society (2 Kgs 11:14-20; 25:3; 2 Chr 33:25; Jer 52:25). During the postexilic period, the mixed race of Jews who had intermarried with heathen peoples were called the people of the land and mostly shunned by Ezra and his followers (Ezr 4:4; 10:2, 11; Neh 10:28-31). Later, rabbinic Judaism labeled the Jewish people who were unwilling or unable to observe the whole law as 'Am-Ha'arets.

PEOPLES
See Nations.

PEOR (Deity)
Contraction for the Canaanite god of Baal-peor, or for the place itself (Nm 23:28; 25:3, 5). *See* Baal-peor; Canaanite Deities and Religion.

PEOR (Place)
1. Mountain east of the Jordan and north of the Dead Sea where Balak led Balaam in a final effort to evoke a curse on Israel (Nm 23:28). The camp of Israel at Shittim was visible from the site (24:2). There Israel initiated a sexual orgy with the Moabite women, and worshiped Baal (25:1-13). The exact location of the mountain is not certain, though Eusebius and Jerome place it opposite Jericho on the way to Heshbon. It is thus believed to be near Mt Nebo in the Abarim range.
2. Place cited in the Septuagint in Joshua 15:59, but not in Hebrew manuscripts. It is identified as the modern Khirbet Faghur, southwest of Bethlehem.

PERAEA*
See Perea.

PERAZIM, Mount
Mountain mentioned in Isaiah 28:21, apparently near Baal-perazim, the "Baal of Breaches," where David defeated the Philistines. From the context of 2 Samuel 5:20, this battleground was evidently located in the valley of Rephaim, southwest of Jerusalem.

PERDITION*
Term used eight times in the KJV NT to express the eternal aspect of the destruction of life and self. In Philippians 1:28, "perdition" is the opposite of "salvation." Hebrews 10:39 contrasts it with "preserving one's soul." Second Peter 3:7 links perdition with the day of judgment, while 1 Timothy 6:9 has both present and future in view. "Son of perdition" is a label affirming the destiny of the betrayer Judas (Jn 17:12) and of the antichrist (2 Thes 2:3). In Revelation 17:8, 11 perdition designates the final abode of the beast. Revelation 19:20 and 20:10 identify this abode as the "lake of fire," a place of everlasting torment.

"Perdition" occurs four times in the RSV NT (Jn 17:12; 2 Thes 2:3; Rv 17:8, 11) and twice in the OT (2 Sm 22:5; Ps 18:4). In the latter, the parallel lines of Hebrew poetry show that perdition is the equivalent of death.

See also Antichrist; Death; Judgment; Lake of Fire.

PEREA*
Term not occurring in the NT except in the fourth-century manuscript Codex Sinaiticus and the fifth-century manuscript Codex Washingtonianus, where it appears in Luke 6:17 and is treated as a variant reading by most editors of the Greek NT. It was used in the first century AD by Josephus to refer to the region "beyond the Jordan" (he derived the word Perea from the Greek for "beyond"). The geographical location of the area is therefore best understood from Josephus's *War of the Jews* (3.3.3): "Now the length of Perea is from Machaerus to Pella, and its breadth from Philadelphia to Jordan; its northern parts are bounded by Pella, as we have already said, as well as its western with Jordan; the land of Moab is its southern border, and its eastern limits reach to Arabia, and Silbonitis, and besides to Philadelphene and Gerasa." Gadara is called "the metropolis of Perea" by Josephus because it was a "place of strength" and because "many of the citizens of Gadara were rich men" (*War* 4.7.3). This Gadara is not to be confused with the Gadara of the Decapolis, modern Um Qeis, but is to be identified with Tell Gadura,

about 15 miles (24.1 kilometers) northwest of modern Amman, Jordan.

The Decapolis is separated from Perea in Matthew 4:25, where it is listed among the various sections of Palestine from which people came to hear Jesus. Perea is here called the region "beyond the Jordan," and is so designated also in Mark 3:8. In one place Matthew referred to Perea as "the region of Judea beyond the Jordan" (Mt 19:1). This is perplexing because politically Perea was never a part of Judea, belonging to the jurisdiction not of Archelaus but of Herod Antipas, who also controlled Galilee. The parallel passage in Mark 10:1 reads, "the region of Judea and beyond the Jordan." Perhaps Matthew was using the phrase to refer to that part of Perea that, though politically not a part of Judea, was Jewish in population. In his *Natural History* (AD 77) Pliny spoke of Perea as a place "separated from the *other parts* of Judea by the River Jordan" (5.70), and the *"rest"* of Judea by the River Jordan" (5.70), and the *"rest"* of Judea" as being divided into 10 local government areas, as though he considered Perea to be a part of Judea. However, this may be a mistaken assumption, since Pliny's knowledge of the immediate area is somewhat questionable—in the same context he erroneously asserts that the Dead Sea is "more than 100 miles long and fully as wide at its widest part" (*Natural History* 5.72), whereas in reality it is less than 50 miles (80.5 kilometers) long and only 11 miles (17.7 kilometers) wide.

The area was well known and often mentioned in the OT by the phrase "beyond the Jordan" (Nm 22:1; Dt 1:1, 5), and was occupied in its southern portion by the two Israelite tribes Gad and Reuben (Jos 1:12-14). Stretching from the brook Kerith in the north almost to the Arnon River in the south, Perea was virtually synonymous with OT Gilead (Jos 22:9; Jgs 5:17).

It seems to have been an important district in the decades before the birth of Christ (Hellenistic period) when Jewish (Maccabean) leaders controlled it after 124 BC. Under Roman rule, it was given to Herod the Great until his death in 4 BC, when it passed (according to his will) into the hands of his son Herod Antipas, along with Galilee. Because the area was beautiful and productive and had trees noted for their medicinal balm (Jer 8:22; 46:11), it was always well populated and supported numerous well-known cities, such as Pella, Jabesh-gilead, Succoth, Penuel, and Gerasa (modern Jerash). Herod Antipas even had a fort named Machaerus in the southern extremities of Perea, where he imprisoned John the Baptist and had him put to death (see Josephus's *Antiquities* 18.5.2).

It was customary for Jews traveling back and forth from Galilee to Judea to cross the Jordan into Perea in order to avoid contact with the Samaritans. Before his death, John the Baptist had been baptizing in Bethany beyond the Jordan when he announced Jesus as the Lamb of God (Jn 1:28-29), and Jesus returned here during his ministry once when he was being severely persecuted (10:40).

PERES* Singular form of Parsin, meaning "divided" (Dn 5:28). *See* Mene, Mene, Tekel, Parsin.

PERESH Son of Maachah and Makir from Manasseh's tribe, and the grandson of Manasseh (1 Chr 7:16).

PEREZ, PEREZITE Son of Judah whose name is derived from a Hebrew word meaning "he who bursts forth"; his name refers to the manner in which he unexpectedly came first from Tamar's womb before his twin brother, Zerah (Gn 38:29). He fathered two sons, Hezron and Hamul, and became the ancestral head of the Perezite family (Gn 46:12; Nm 26:20-21; 1 Chr 2:4-5; 4:1). The KJV and the Apocrypha translate the name variously as Pharez, Phares, and Pharzite.

Through the descent of his son Hezron, he became the ancestor of David and Jesus Christ (Ru 4:18-22; Mt 1:3; Lk 3:33). The esteem this clan enjoyed in the tribe of Judah is evidenced by the blessing pronounced upon it by the men of Bethlehem (Ru 4:12). A descendant named Jashobeam commanded David's captains for the first month of each year (1 Chr 27:2-3). Upon the return from captivity in Babylon, 468 Perezites were chosen to live in Jerusalem (1 Chr 9:4; Neh 11:4-6).

PEREZ-UZZAH Alternate name given to the site associated with the threshing floor of Nacon in 1 Chronicles 13:11 and 2 Samuel 6:8, respectively. *See* Nacon.

PERFUME Term covering a wide range of materials prepared from ground-up minerals, vegetable oils, and roots, which were used from the earliest times to enhance one's personal presentation or to produce pleasing fragrances both for secular and religious purposes. The Bible mentions a wide variety of perfumes, such as aloes, balm, balsam, bdellium, cassia, cinnamon, frankincense, gum, myrrh, nard, sweet cane, spice, ointment, and so on. There must have been a vigorous perfume trade with such lands as Arabia (frankincense, myrrh), India (aloes, nard), Ceylon (cinnamon), Persia (the spice galbanum), and Somaliland (frankincense). In the Bible there are several references to those who traded in these items; for example, the Arabian (Ishmaelite) merchants who took Joseph to Egypt (Gn 37:25), the caravans of the queen of Sheba (1 Kgs 10:10), and the traders of Sheba and Raamah who brought spices to Tyre (Ez 27:22).

There are several biblical references to those who prepared perfumes. For example, Bezalel prepared holy anointing oil and sacred incense for the tabernacle (Ex 37:29). The holy anointing oil was a mixture of four constituents (30:22-25): myrrh, cinnamon, aromatic cane, and cassia mixed in olive oil. In postexilic times, some priests were given the responsibility of mixing perfumes for incense (1 Chr 9:30), and a perfumer is mentioned among those who built Nehemiah's wall (Neh 3:8).

Modern excavation has produced tangible evidence of a variety of cosmetic vessels and appliances, although, strangely enough, little is said in the Bible about these (Is 3:20; Mt 26:7; Mk 14:3; Lk 7:37). The reference to alabaster containers gains support from their use in Egypt and from archaeology. Some ancient sites in Palestine have yielded numerous small decorated cosmetic bowls, often made of alabaster; small bottles for scents and oils; and palettes for mixing cosmetics. Some of these items are imports from lands like Egypt.

There was a wide range of uses for the various perfumes, whether powders or oils. Perfumed oils were regularly used to anoint the body in order to soothe sun-dried skin (2 Sm 12:20; Ru 3:3). On one occasion, King Ahaz clothed, fed, and anointed men who returned home from captivity (2 Chr 28:15). The rich in the land could afford the "finest oils" (Am 6:6), although such extravagance could be costly (Prv 21:17). This biblical picture is corroborated by evidence from Egypt and Mesopotamia. In particular, there was a lavish use of oils and ointments in the royal palaces of the East.

An Alabaster Vase Small alabaster containers like this one were used in ancient Egypt and Palestine to store perfumes, oils, and other cosmetic materials.

Ointments and oils of various kinds that gave off a pleasing fragrance were regularly used. The Song of Songs has many references to such ointments (Sg 1:3), some of which are specifically named: spikenard (1:12; 4:13-14), myrrh (1:13; 3:6; 4:6; 5:1, 5, 13), frankincense (3:6; 4:6), spices (5:13; 6:2; 8:14), henna (1:14; 4:13), fragrant powders (3:6), saffron (4:14), calamus, and cinnamon (4:14). And there are references in other parts of the Bible to perfumes and ointments of various kinds (1 Kgs 10:2, 10; 2 Kgs 20:13; Prv 27:9; Is 3:24).

Perfumes were put on clothes (Ps 45:8; Sg 4:11) and sprinkled on couches (Prv 7:17). Perfumes and spices also played an important role in the burial of the dead. They were used in embalming (Gn 50:2-3, 26) and were sprinkled on the bier or burned in the fire at some funerals (2 Chr 16:14). Nicodemus brought a mixture of myrrh and aloes to be used in wrapping the body of Jesus (Jn 19:39-40). In the funeral of Herod the Great, 500 slaves carried the spices (Josephus's *Antiquities* 17.8.3).

Besides the personal use of such materials, there was a wide range of oils, perfumes, and incense used in worship. A holy anointing oil was used to anoint the tabernacle and its furnishings and the Aaronic priests at their induction (Ex 30:22-25; Ps 133). An interesting prescription for the sacred incense to be prepared by the perfumer is given in Exodus 30:34-35. The items listed are well known both in Israel and in other parts of the ancient East.

The NT contains a number of figurative references. Christ gave himself as a fragrant offering to God (Eph 5:2). The gifts of the Philippians to Paul were described as a fragrant offering (Phil 4:18) and the prayers of the saints are described as bowls of incense (Rv 5:8).

See also Cosmetics; Oil; Ointment; Perfumer.

PERFUMER* Also known as an "apothecary" (Ex 30:25, KJV) or a "confectionary" (1 Sm 8:13, KJV). This person prepared oils, powders, and mixtures for medicinal use, for perfumes and cosmetics, and for religious use in incense. A wide variety of plants, when crushed, provided oils or powders giving off distinctive odors. *See* Perfume.

PERGA City probably of very early Greek origin and the religious capital of ancient Pamphylia. In the second century BC, the Romans overthrew a Syrian garrison there, and thereafter the city apparently had a substantial degree of independence from external control.

On their first missionary journey, Paul and his colleagues passed through the city on their way to Pisidian Antioch. The Acts of the Apostles reports no preaching activity on that occasion but notes only that it was at Perga that John Mark left his companions and returned to Jerusalem (Acts 13:13-14).

If we assume that Luke would have recorded the fact that Paul had preached during this visit, we can only

speculate why he did not do so. The presence nearby of a renowned temple of Artemis, an Anatolian nature goddess, would surely have challenged rather than deterred him. The apostle may have been ill (some commentators suggest a possible connection with the reference in Gal 4:13), but in that case we might have expected Barnabas to have taken his place. It has been suggested that at this point the group had disagreed about outreach to and acceptance of Gentiles, and that it was his differences with Paul (and perhaps his resentment at the latter's leadership) that precipitated John Mark's departure.

On the homeward journey, however, Paul and Barnabas "preached the word in Perga" before going on down to Attalia, where they took a ship to Antioch of Syria (Acts 14:25-26). The results from that preaching are not known, but it is evident that Christianity did not flourish in Perga, as it did in other cities of Asia Minor.

PERGAMOS*, PERGAMUM City just north of the Caicus River, in the southern part of Mysia (eastern Turkey), and one of the greatest cultural centers of the Hellenistic era. The early geographer Strabo (63 BC–AD 24?) called the area around Pergamum the richest land in Mysia. It is mentioned only twice in the Bible (Rv 1:11; 2:12; KJV "Pergamos"), both times referring to one of the seven churches of Asia to which the last book of the NT was written.

The province of Mysia was combined with Lydia and Caria to form the Roman district of Asia, comprising the western portion of modern Turkey. Pergamum lies less than 20 miles (32.3 kilometers) inland from the sea and about three miles (4.8 kilometers) north of the Caicus River on a large conical hill, 1,000 feet (304.8 meters) high, which is sandwiched between two smaller streams that flow into the Caicus, the Selinus on the west and the Cetius on the east. This natural position of strength, combined with its religious significance as a temple site, made it a desirable place to store wealth. Lysimachus, one of Alexander the Great's generals, deposited an enormous sum of money here (9,000 talents), which was later used by Pergamene kings to create the glory of Pergamum. Although coins were minted in Pergamum before 400 BC, it was not a great city until long after the death of Alexander.

The splendor of Pergamum began with Attalus I (241–197 BC), who took the title of king and founded the Attalic dynasty. His wealth, success in battle (defeating the Gauls who moved into Galatia in 278 BC), and his judicial alliance with the rising power of Rome contributed to his ability to embellish his kingdom with Hellenistic culture. He adorned it with temples, theaters, a library, and other public buildings.

He was succeeded by his son Eumenes II, who, because of his help in Rome's conquest of the Seleucid kingdom of Syria, was given in 189 BC all Seleucid territory northwest of the Taurus mountains, thus extending the Pergamene kingdom from the Taurus to the Dardanelles. Under Eumenes (197–159 BC), Pergamum attained the height of its power and glory. He expanded the library to 200,000 volumes, almost rivaling the great one at Alexandria, and he constructed the altar of Zeus, which stood on a hill 800 feet (243.8 meters) above the city and could be seen for miles. It is tempting to imagine this altar as the place "where Satan's throne is" (Rv 2:13), especially since Pergamum was the chief center of worship for four of the greatest pagan deities—Zeus, Athena, Dionysus, and Asclepius. However, it may be that Revelation is referring to the fact that Pergamum was the center of emperor worship in Asia at that time.

The last king of the Attalic dynasty, Attalus III, died

without leaving an heir in 133 BC. In his will he gave all of his kingdom to Rome, with the exception of Pergamum and other Greek cities, which were given freedom as independent administrative units and were exempt from tribute. In order to reduce its obligation to police, the Roman consul bequeathed the easternmost territory of Phrygia to Pontus and Cappadocia. Thus, the newly created Roman province of Asia was smaller than the Pergamene Empire had been. Even though after 120 BC Phrygia was reclaimed by the Roman senate (upon the death of Mithridates, king of Pontus), it was not actually incorporated into Asia until 85 BC. At that time, the Roman provincial unit was again roughly comparable in size to the old Pergamene kingdom.

Remains of Ancient Library at Pergamum

Pergamum was built across the centuries in three separate areas. The upper city on top of the mountain was the northernmost area and was largely the domain of the royal family, the nobility, and the military commanders. It had an air of officialdom. The middle city, further south and lower down the mountain, contained the part of the city visited by the common people and included sports fields for the youth and temples frequented by those of less education. These facilities were not controlled directly by the city and the priesthood, and the general citizenship of Pergamum had unrestricted access to them. The third area, across the Selinus River to the southwest, contained the famous Asclepian of Pergamum, a center for the healing arts. This center had a medical school that produced the celebrated physician Galen. Here the god Asclepius was worshiped in a cylindrical temple, which was a small replica of the famed Pantheon built in Rome some 20 years before (AD 130). There was also a lovely fountain, theater, pool, medical building, library, and various temples, the striking remains of which may still be seen.

The references in Revelation 2:12-15 to the Nicolaitans and those who held the doctrine of Balaam probably refers to the extensive influence of the immoral and idolatrous worship of Dionysus and Aphrodite, which was especially offensive to the known Jewish population (Josephus's *Antiquities* 14.10.22), as well as to true Christians. Pliny (*Natural History* 5.30) considered Pergamum to be the most distinguished city of Asia and as such it would have been the natural place for emperor worship. The reference to the martyrdom of Antipas, "my faithful witness" (Rv 2:13), can easily be understood in the light of the Jewish and Christian refusal to worship the emperor in this city.

Because of the extensive manufacture of writing mate-

rial from sheepskin in Pergamum, the name parchment (Latin, *pergamena*) was given to the product.

PERIDA* Alternate rendering of Peruda, the ancestor of a family of servants who returned to Jerusalem after the exile (Neh 7:57, NLT mg). *See* Peruda.

PERIZZITE One of several population segments occupying the land of Palestine prior to and subsequent to the Israelite conquest (Gn 15:20; Ex 3:8, 17; 23:23; 33:2; 34:11; Dt 7:1; 20:17; Jos 3:10; 9:1; 11:3; 12:8; 24:11; 1 Kgs 9:20; 2 Chr 8:7; Ezr 9:1; Neh 9:8). The enumeration of these peoples throughout the OT serves a variety of purposes, none of which is strictly historical or geographical. It serves to inform the reader that, no matter how numerous, the doom of these people is sure when God's time has come (Gn 15:20; Ex 3:8). At other times, they are mentioned to illustrate the hostility of the enemies of God against Israel's onward march into the land promised to them by the Lord (Jos 9:1; 11:3; 24:11). But they are also portrayed as conquered and reduced to servile labor (Jos 12:8; 1 Kgs 9:20). In the postexilic period, they continue to be a threat to the purity of life of the covenant community recently settled in the land of their fathers (Ezr 9:1).

There are a few instances where the word "Perizzites" occurs in conjunction with "Canaanites" (Gn 13:7; 34:30; Jgs 1:4-5), and in one instance it is combined with "Rephaites" (Jos 17:15). The name "Pirizzi" also occurs once in the tablets of El Amarna.

The exact identity of the Perizzites has thus far remained obscure. In a few instances in which the name occurs in conjunction with "Canaanites," it seems to refer to one of the major components of Canaan's population. Some have even suggested that the Perizzites were the pre-Canaanite population of Palestine, in view of the omission of them in the list of Genesis 10. But this cannot be proven. Others have attempted to read this name as an appellative meaning "inhabitants of unwalled villages." This view finds some support in another Hebrew word, *perazoth*, "unwalled villages" (Est 9:19; Ez 38:11; Zec 2:4; cf. also *perazi*, "open country," Dt 3:5; 1 Sm 6:18). But the fact that the name occurs so frequently among other peoples whose identity is known should caution against such an approach.

Several commentators, instead of regarding the Perizzites as one of the major components of Canaan's population, have sought to localize them, either in the vicinity of Bethel (cf. Gn 13:7) or of Shechem (34:30), or in the territory of Judah (Jgs 1:4-5). But these locales are by no means contiguous. The reference to the Rephaim (NLT, NIV "Rephaites") in Joshua 17:15 has prompted the suggestion that the Perizzites belonged to the Transjordan region, but this does not follow either from the immediate context or from the use of the word "Rephaim" elsewhere.

See also Canaan, Canaanite.

PERSECUTION Infliction of suffering, injury, or death on others because of their identity or beliefs. The Bible begins with an account of the persecution of the righteous by the unrighteous (Gn 4:3-7, "regard for Abel"; Mt 23:35; Heb 11:4). The Wisdom of Solomon (Wisd of Sol 2:12-20) dramatically illustrates the envy and guilt that prompt such persecution. Lot's experience, likewise, illustrates the suffering involved in refusing to conform to popular behavior (Gn 19:9; 2 Pt 2:7-8). The ill-treatment of Israel in Egypt, like her later oppression by the Philistines, Midianites, and others, had economic and political grounds. For those refusing to accept the royal policy of syncretism, official tolerance of injustice, and pagan immoralities, persecution becomes frequent—from Elijah's period onward (1 Kgs 19:10). Later prophets, as spokesmen of uncompromising truth and the claims of divine law in the face of social evils, suffered severely at the hands of the ruling classes, so that persecution became, in Jewish eyes, the hallmark of the true prophet (2 Chr 36:15-16; Mt 5:12; 23:29-37; Acts 7:52; Heb 11:32-38).

Daniel's stories illustrate persecution during the exile. On the return under foreign rule, strict Jews sought to preserve the nation's identity and religion amid alien pressures and the compromises of lax Jews anxious for accommodation and prosperity (1 Macc 1:11-15; 2:42-48). The result was the social oppression and harassment that made the repeated pleas for vindication and divine intervention, in such psalms as 10, 69, 140, and 149, painfully relevant in postexilic worship. This persecution reached a horrifying climax of cruelty during the Maccabean age, provoking armed resistance in response (2 Macc 6–7; Heb 11:35-38).

Thus, despite her confidence in God's sovereignty and "protection," Israel learned that right does not always prosper in this world, that faithfulness to truth does not ensure immunity from suffering, sacrifice, or martyrdom.

This acceptance of the high cost of righteousness was inherited by Christianity. Jesus repeatedly warned of persecution, even within households, and urged "armed" preparation for it, promising the Spirit's assistance at judicial examinations (Mt 5:11-12; 10:16-23, 34-36; 23:34; Lk 6:26; 22:35-36). Jesus was deeply angered by the murder of John the Baptist by Herod (Lk 23:9), and he foresaw his own fate. Because he criticized the legalism and nationalism of the Pharisees, and the compromises of the Sadducees to protect their own privileges (Jn 11:47-50), and because he disappointed the militaristic hopes set upon the Messiah by the common people, Jesus knew he would be rejected. His call to discipleship came to include warnings of danger, reviling, slander, accusation, flogging, arraignment before courts, hatred, and death. He frankly invited followers to prepare for his crucifixion, as the only way to life and the kingdom (Mt 16:21-26; 20:17-22; Mk 10:29-30; Jn 15:18-25; 16:1-4). Jesus was killed on the charges of subverting the nation, forbidding payment of taxes to the Romans, and claiming to be king (Lk 23:2).

The first persecution of the church by Jewish authorities was provoked mainly by Peter's accusations concerning the murder of the Messiah. As apostolic influence increased, official action came to include imprisonment and beating (Acts 5:17, 40). The powerful advocacy of the Hellenist Stephen provoked a Jewish mob to stone him (Act 6–7)—the signal for "a great persecution," scattering most Christians from Jerusalem. The conversion of the archpersecutor Saul of Tarsus marked a resounding victory over opposition, and Herod's sudden death just after attacking the church "to please the Jews" was another (Acts 12:1-3, 20-24).

As Christianity moved into the Gentile world, a new cause of Jewish persecution arose as disturbances began to occur in the synagogues (Acts 13:44-45, 50; 14:1-6, 19; 17:1, 5, 13; 18:4-6, 12). In addition, the healing of the slave girl at Philippi led to the disciples' imprisonment (16:19-24); at Ephesus, the effect of Christian preaching on the trade of idol makers occasioned a dangerous threat, which the authorities averted (19:23-41). Paul averted the plot of more than 40 men who vowed to ambush him and kill him (21:4-36; 23:12-15). And the book of Acts closes with Paul awaiting trial before Caesar (28:30-31).

Throughout this period, persecution of Christians was sporadic, local, and mainly Jewish, provoked by envy of the church's missionary success. Officially, Christianity, as a Jewish sect (Acts 24:5, 14), shared the state's legal recognition won by the Jews. Thus, Paul received Roman protection at Paphos, Philippi, Corinth, Ephesus, and Jerusalem from governors Felix and Festus and their adviser Herod Agrippa, as well as from the centurion conveying him to Rome. This explains Paul's confident appeal to Caesar; an imperial acquittal would ensure Christianity freedom from harassment throughout the empire.

Paul's attitude to persecution included regretful remembrance of his own persecuting days (Acts 22:4; 26:9-11; Gal 1:22-24), deliberate acceptance of risks in obedience to Christ (Acts 20:22-24; 21:13), continual warning that tribulation is inseparable from discipleship (Acts 14:22; Rom 5:3; 12:12; 1 Thes 3:4), and assurance that in every form of tribulation Christians are more than conquerors (Rom 8:35-37).

Almost certainly, Paul was beheaded during fierce persecution at Rome following the fire for which the Christians were blamed. Christians were often accused of "atheism" (rejecting polytheism), of appealing only to slave classes, of "scandalous" love feasts, and unsociable, austere behavior (cf. Jn 15:19), making them a popular target for blame.

About this time, Peter warned Christians in the East of the danger confronting the church. For a little while, "various trials" only prove the genuineness of faith (1 Pt 1:6). Slander should be answered by blameless living. Honor should be paid to the authorities. Suffering for righteousness should be accepted without fear. Let Christians prepare respectful defenses, with consciences clear of blame. If they suffer for doing right, remember that Christ did too—for them. Thus they must "arm" themselves for suffering (4:1), and not be surprised at persecution as "something strange" (v 12). They are sharing Christ's sufferings. His final word is "Stand fast!"

Mark, too, is thought to have written at this time for the benefit of the suffering Roman church. His Gospel dwells upon Christ's conflict, its causes and forms, and vividly portrays Christ's own heroic death. Like Peter, Mark meets persecution by pointing back to the suffering Lord.

Somewhat later, Christianity was exposed as an "illegal religion," no longer a protected sect of Judaism, by the introduction into synagogue services of a prayer against "Nazarenes," which Christians could not offer. Thereafter, the church was liable to official suppression. Rome readily incorporated old, national religions into state rituals for the sake of imperial unity, but she resisted new, nonconformist movements, especially those with secret meetings (i.e., the Eucharist), as politically dangerous (cf. Acts 17:6-7).

Toward the end of the century, faced with a growing church and political unrest, the state required public "worship" of "the genius of Rome" alongside any other religious rites. In Domitian's reign (AD 81–96) this became worship of the living emperor, with elaborate temples and an official priesthood. When Christians refused, acknowledging Jesus alone as divine Lord, official, and increasingly barbaric, persecution began. It is probable that Revelation reflects this situation (Rv 1:9; 2:13; 6:9; 13; 19:2). So the Bible ends as it began, with the theme of the persecution of the people of God.

See also Suffering; Tribulation.

PERSEUS Last king of Macedonia (1 Macc 8:5). Perseus was the illegitimate son of Philip III of Macedonia. He succeeded his father to the throne in 179 BC. In 168 BC Rome defeated Macedonia in the battle of Pydna. Macedonia became a Roman province, and Perseus died in captivity.

PERSEVERANCE Action or condition of steadfastness. OT Israel waited generations for fulfillment of promises that many believers never lived to see (Heb 11:1, 13, 21-22, 39). The promise to Abraham sustained hope for centuries before Canaan was possessed. The lesson of the wilderness journey, when the waning of initial zeal prevented the people from entering the Promised Land, was never forgotten (3:16-19). Prophets looked constantly beyond failure and tragedy to distant horizons, and they nourished a patient faith (Jer 31:1-15; Hos 3:4-5; Jl 2:28-29; Hb 2:1-3; Dn 12:11-13).

The NT everywhere urges similar perseverance. Among several Greek expressions, the usual word, *proskartereo*, has the root meaning "to attend continually, adhere steadfastly" (Mk 3:9; Acts 8:13; 10:7; Rom 13:6), and is variously translated "devoted," "continued," "constant," "[be] steadfast."

This persistent patience is called for in prayer (Lk 18:1-8; Col 4:2); in well doing (Rom 2:7; Gal 6:9); in Christian teaching (Acts 2:42; 2 Tm 3:14); in affliction (2 Thes 1:4); in grace (Acts 13:43; 2 Cor 6:1); in faith (Acts 14:22; Col 1:23); in divine love (Jn 15:9; Jude 1:21); in standing firm (1 Cor 16:13; 2 Thes 2:15); in abiding in Christ (Jn 15:4-10; 1 Jn 2:28); in running with patience (Heb 6:12; 12:1); in not falling away (Heb 3:12; 4:1-10); and in being zealous to confirm our call and election (2 Pt 1:10).

The failure in perseverance of Judas (Jn 6:71), Demas (2 Tm 4:10), and Hymenaeus (2 Tm 2:17) must be kept in mind, as well as the dread possibility of neglecting so great a salvation (Heb 2:3), being disqualified (1 Cor 9:27), falling while we think we stand (1 Cor 10:12), and committing apostasy (Heb 6:1-8). For, as Jesus said, "He who endures to the end will be saved" (Mt 10:22; 24:13). Such extraordinary emphasis cannot be accidental. The pressures of pagan society, the danger of persecution, emotional reaction after a wonderful initial experience, and the apparent implication of "instant salvation," made it imperative for Christians to understand that by their endurance they would inherit eternal salvation (Lk 21:19; Rom 5:3; Col 1:11).

Yet Scripture never implies that perseverance depends entirely upon human effort. In the OT, the redeeming purpose of God is unswerving; God's covenant stands, though it needs to be renewed (Jer 31:31-34). Divine love (Hebrew, *hesed*) connotes changeless loyalty; God "will never fail nor forsake" for "his own name's sake." The NT assurance is that Christ will raise his own at the last day—none shall pluck them from his hand or the Father's. Christ will keep us from falling. God is faithful; he works in us to will and work for his good pleasure, and will not allow us to be tempted beyond our strength. Nothing, in heaven or earth, present or future, shall separate us from divine love. We are already sealed by the Holy Spirit as a guarantee of eternal salvation, and we are kept by the power of God unto a salvation yet to be revealed.

The scriptural tension between exhortation to perseverance and assurance of salvation has given rise to much debate. The intellectual paradox is resolved only in spiritual experience.

See also Assurance; Backsliding.

PERSIA, PERSIANS Country lying just to the east of Mesopotamia (modern Iraq) and covering virtually the same territory as present-day Iran. It was known in ancient times by various forms of Fars or Pars, which came down to us as Persia. It continued to be known as Persia until 1935, when its name was changed to Iran. The official modern language of the country is Persian, an Indo-European language written in Arabic characters.

Geography and Climate Persia served as a geographical link between inner Asia and the plateau of Asia Minor. It has been described as a triangle set between two depressions, the Persian Gulf on the south and the Caspian Sea to the north. The sides of the triangle are made up of mountain ranges that enclose an area of desert. On the west the Zagros Mountains run northwest-southeast, with many fertile valleys that are suitable for agriculture. Severe summer heat requires that animals be taken to cooler elevations during that season.

On the north is the Elburz range, with Mt Demavend reaching a height of more than 19,000 feet (5,791.2 meters). The most heavily populated area of Persia is Azerbaijan, which, because of routes leading from various northern points, was one of the most accessible parts of the country and therefore had to be protected by strong fortifications.

Farther east, the Elburz becomes the mountains of Khorasan, which also afford easy passage into the country. This district, which has been called the "granary of Iran," has been susceptible to foreign invasion over the centuries. On the south, the third side of the triangle, is another mountain range, the Makran. Within these ranges is a saline depression, the southern part of which has been regarded as more arid than the Gobi Desert.

One of the important sections of the country was actually an extension of the Mesopotamian plain; this was known in ancient times as Susiana and now is called Khuzistan. Here the capital, Susa, was situated. Adjoining it to the north is a mountain spur that was the location of Luristan, famous for its bronzes. Another plain, near the Caspian Sea, is tropical in climate; because of heavy rainfall, it produces an abundance and variety of food.

Lacking a river like the Nile or the Tigris-Euphrates system, and having no regular seasonal rains as in Palestine, the agriculture of Persia is dependent on irrigation. Rainfall varies dramatically from one region to another and the climate differs markedly with the topography.

In antiquity the lower mountains were heavily forested with many kinds of trees sought for building by the Sumerian kings of Mesopotamia. Alabaster, marble, lapis lazuli, carnelian, and turquoise were used from early times. Iron, copper, tin, and lead were found here. In modern times the oil resources of Iran have been widely exploited.

History The Medes (a term often used synonymously with Persians, since the two are so closely related) are a people about whom relatively little is known. They were pictured in Assyrian reliefs. It was the Median Cyaxares who teamed up with the Babylonian Nabopolassar to bring about the destruction of Nineveh in 612 BC.

In the seventh century BC, a small kingdom of Persians was established at Parsumash under Achaemenes, after whom the great Persian dynasty was named. Teispes (675–640 BC), the son and successor of Achaemenes, was under the domination of the Medes, who were gathering forces to overthrow Assyria. Trouble for the Medes freed Teispes from their control, and the weakness of Elam enabled him to gain the province of Parsa (modern Fars). The Assyrians under Ashurbanipal destroyed the nation of Elam and came into contact with the Persians under Cyrus I, son of Teispes.

Cambyses, son of Cyrus, married the daughter of the Median king Astyages; their son, Cyrus II the Great (559–530 BC), built a great palace complex for himself at

Pasargadae. The Babylonian king, Nabonidus, allied himself with Cyrus against the Medes. Cyrus fought and defeated his grandfather, Astyages, and made the Median capital, Ecbatana, "place of assembly" (Hamadan), his own capital and set up his archives there (cf. Ezr 6:2).

Cyrus, and later Darius, exhibited an attitude of benevolence and generosity toward defeated enemies, a policy that sometimes worked to the disadvantage of the Persians. A capable military leader, Cyrus invaded Asia Minor and defeated Croesus, king of Lydia, and brought the Greek cities of the area into subjection. He then solidified his eastern frontier. In 539 BC he captured Babylon with virtually no resistance and decreed that the exiled Jews could return to Jerusalem to rebuild the temple (Ezr 1:1-4).

trilingual inscription that lauds his person and reign. Later kings were buried in tombs cut in the same cliff.

Darius was succeeded by his son Khshayarsha, better known as Xerxes (485–465 BC). An inscription at Persepolis lists the nations subject to him at the time of his accession and confirms his devotion to Ahura Mazda. During his rule, the Persian fleet was defeated at Salamis (480 BC).

Artaxerxes I Longimanus (Artakhshathra, 464–424 BC) was followed by Darius II (423–405), Artaxerxes II Mnemon (404–359), Artaxerxes III Ochus (358–338), Arses (337–336), and finally Darius III (335–331).

The loss of the empire has been attributed to the cowardice of Darius III, whose armies were defeated by Alexander the Great at Issus in 333 BC and ultimately at

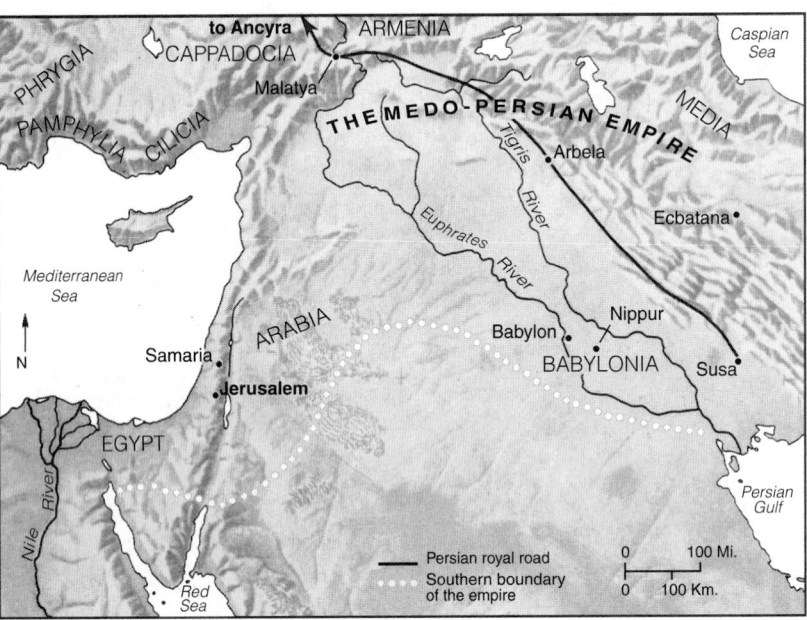

The Medo-Persian Empire
The Medo-Persian Empire included the lands of Media and Persia, much of the area shown on this map and more. The Jewish exiles were concentrated in the area around Nippur in the Babylonian province. The decree by King Cyrus that allowed the Israelites to return to their homeland and rebuild the temple was discovered in the palace at Ecbatana.

The son of Cyrus, Cambyses II (529–522 BC), conquered Egypt. Upon his suicide, the empire nearly disintegrated. Cambyses was succeeded by Darius I the Great (521–486 BC), the son of Hystaspis, satrap of Parthia. Darius put down the internal revolts and consolidated the empire. For efficient administration of his vast empire, he created 20 provinces or satrapies, each under a satrap or "protector of the kingdom." Other offices were instituted to check on the activities of the satraps. Darius changed the principal capital from Pasargadae to Persepolis, where his building activities were continued by later Achaemenid kings to make a tremendous palace complex. He was a follower of Zoroaster and a worshiper of Ahura Mazda, as were Xerxes and Artaxerxes.

The early victory of Darius over the rebels is commemorated on the famous rock of Bisitun (Behistun). This memorial took the form of reliefs and a long cuneiform inscription in three languages: Persian, Elamite, and Akkadian. A copy of these records was made by Henry C. Rawlinson in 1855 at considerable risk, for the monument was difficult to approach, situated some 500 feet (152.4 meters) above the plain. This accomplishment played a large part in the deciphering of languages in the cuneiform script. During the later part of Darius's reign, he suffered defeat at the hands of the Greeks at Marathon (491 BC). Upon his death, Darius was buried in a rock-cut tomb at Naqsh-i-Rustam, a short distance northeast of Persepolis. This was a memorial consisting of reliefs and a

Gaugamela, near modern Erbil (Arbela) in 331 BC. Upon the death of Alexander in 323 BC, Persia became the lot of Seleucus, one of his generals. Persian sources say little of the period between Darius III and the beginnings of Sassanian rule in the early third century AD.

Persia and the Bible The biblical references to Persia occur in the later period of OT history and in the writings of the prophets who ministered during that time. The earliest mention is the reference to Cyrus in Isaiah 44:28–45:1, a passage that has confounded scholars who have felt that the prophecy could not be so precise. This predictive prophecy was given to Isaiah by God more than 150 years before Cyrus captured Babylon and decreed the return of the captive Jews to Jerusalem.

The chronological notations in Daniel, Ezra, Nehemiah, Zechariah, Haggai, and Esther enable us to set chronological markers with some degree of certainty. The first year of Cyrus's reign over Babylon (Ezr 1:1) may be fixed at 538 BC. The rebuilding of the temple met with opposition from enemies of the Jews in the time of Cyrus and Darius (Ezr 4).

It was at this time that the prophets Haggai and Zechariah encouraged the Jews and urged the completion of the temple. Haggai 1:1 places the message of that prophet on the first day of the sixth month of the second year of Darius I. That translates into August 29, 520 BC. Similarly, Zechariah 1:1 is dated to the eighth month of the year, that is, October/November 520 BC. The letter that was sent to Darius concerning the decree for rebuilding the temple (Ezr 5:6-17) brought about a search of the royal archives that Cyrus had set up at Ecbatana (cf. 6:1-2). The finding of the decree of Cyrus enabled the Jews to complete the temple project, which was finished on March 12, 515 BC (the third day of the month Adar in the sixth year of Darius, Ezr 6:15).

The work of Nehemiah occurred in the reign of Artaxerxes I Longimanus. Nehemiah's request that he be allowed to return to Jerusalem to rebuild the wall was made in the month of Nisan in the 20th year of Artaxerxes (Neh 2:1, April/May 445 BC). This building project also met with strong opposition. The date is generally confirmed by a letter from the 17th year of Darius II (408 BC) and found among the Elephantine papyri in Egypt. Two personal names found in Nehemiah also occur in this letter: the sons of Sanballat, Nehemiah's most virulent enemy (cf. Neh 2:19; 4:1-8), and Johanan the grandson of Eliashib, who was high priest at Jerusalem when Nehemiah arrived there (3:1). Another letter among these papyri grants Persian authority to the Jews at Elephantine to celebrate the Passover according to their custom.

The book of Esther is set in the time of King Ahasuerus, who is Xerxes, referred to in Ezra 4:6 between Darius and Artaxerxes. The Hebrew Ahasuerus represents Khshayarsha, whom the Greeks called Xerxes. On the one hand, the Septuagint has Artaxerxes, and Josephus names Artaxerxes as the king mentioned in the book of Esther. Esther provides a number of details of the life and customs of Persian royalty.

Persia also figures in the prophecies of Ezekiel, where Persia is named among the armies of Tyre (Ez 27:10). It is also listed as an ally of Gog in the invasion of Israel (38:5). The recorded history in Daniel refers to Persia (Dn 10:1), as do the prophecies of that book (8:20; 11:2).

See also Postexilic Period; Medes, Media, Median.

PERSIS Christian woman in Rome to whom Paul sent greetings (Rom 16:12).

PERUDA Head of a family of Solomon's servants (Ezr 2:55); alternately called Perida in Nehemiah 7:57. His descendants formed part of the remnant of Israel that returned to Jerusalem after the exile (1 Esd 5:33).

PESTILENCE Derivative of a Hebrew word referring to a contagious epidemic disease of devastating proportions. Pestilence is never portrayed in the Bible as an aimless, naturally occurring phenomenon. It is always regarded as a judgment or punishment sent by God.

Pestilence was one form of chastisement brought upon Israel for neglect of her covenant obligations (Lv 26:25; Dt 28:21). This is the reason for the frequent use of the word by both Jeremiah and Ezekiel. These prophets were prosecuting God's covenant lawsuit against his people. The sentence had been determined, and they announced that its infliction was impending. For this reason, pestilence almost always occurs as part of a list of scourges, such as the formula "sword, famine and pestilence" used throughout Jeremiah's prophecy (Jer 14:12, etc.). Because pestilence is a punishment for sin, it is not applied indiscriminately upon all. The one who remains faithful will be protected from its effects (Ps 91:1-3). The enemies of Israel could also be objects of this form of judgment (Ps 78:50; Ez 28:23; 38:22).

Pestilence is not identical with plague in the OT. Plague often denotes such diseases as bubonic plague, measles, and smallpox, whereas pestilence might refer to cholera, typhus, typhoid, and dysentery—diseases often

afflicting a city under siege. There is some overlap in the terms, however. The death of 70,000 Israelites after David's census is an example of the severity and virulence of this form of divine chastisement (2 Sm 24:13-15).

The Greek word *loimos* occurs three times in the NT. In Acts 24:5 (KJV) Tertullus used this term as a derogatory description of Paul—"a pestilent fellow." Jesus predicted that the destruction of the temple would be preceded by several judgments, including pestilence or plague (Lk 21:11).

See also Disease; Plague.

PETER, First Letter of
First of two general epistles authored by Peter.

Author The author says he is the apostle Peter (1 Pt 1:1), a witness of Christ's sufferings (5:1)—thus one of the original apostles chosen by Jesus (Mk 3:14-19) as an authoritative spokesman. Also known as Simon and Cephas, Peter probably saw and felt Jesus' last hours of suffering more keenly than any of the other apostles (14:54) because he had denied Jesus three times (vv 66-72). In 1 Peter the sufferings of Jesus are mentioned at least four times (1 Pt 1:11; 2:23; 4:1; 5:1).

Peter was known as the apostle to the Jews, just as Paul was the apostle to the Gentiles (Gal 2:7). Since Peter was a traveling missionary (1 Cor 1:12; 9:5), he could have actually visited the Asia Minor churches to whom this letter was sent.

That Peter had been with Jesus during his earthly ministry may help account for the strong influence of Jesus' teaching in 1 Peter. Except for James, 1 Peter probably echoes more of Jesus' words than any other NT letter. The chart below presents similarities between Peter's words and Jesus' words in the Gospels:

SIMILARITIES BETWEEN PETER'S WORDS IN 1 PETER AND JESUS' WORDS IN THE GOSPELS

1 Peter Reference	Gospel Reference
1:3, 23	Jn 3:3, 7
1:4	Lk 12:33
1:8	Jn 20:29
1:10-12	Lk 24:25-27
1:13	Lk 12:35
1:22; 4:8	Jn 13:34; 15:12
2:4, 7	Mk 12:10; Mt 21:42
2:12	Mt 5:16
2:19-20	Lk 6:32-35
2:25	Jn 10:11, 14
3:9	Lk 6:27-28
4:13	Mt 5:12
5:3	Lk 22:24-27
5:5-6	Lk 14:11; 18:14

Some scholars think the Greek of this letter is too good to have been written by a former fisherman whose native language was Aramaic; that the doctrine is too much like Paul's to have been written by an apostle whose position was different from Paul's; and that someone wrote the letter after Peter's death and used his name to give apostolic weight to it.

Other scholars answer that if the author wanted to

give authority to a letter whose teaching resembles Paul's, he would have used Paul's name, not Peter's; that most Galileans probably learned Greek as well as Aramaic early in life; and that there is no evidence that the teaching of Peter and Paul fundamentally differed. When Paul rebuked Peter (Gal 2:11-14), it was due to a temporary lapse in conduct, not a basic disagreement in teaching. Besides, some key doctrines of Paul are missing from 1 Peter (e.g., justification), and those similar to Paul's were the common possession of all the early churches. We may reasonably conclude that the apostle Peter authored this letter. However, it seems quite clear that Silas (otherwise know as Silvanus) helped Peter write this epistle (1 Pt 5:12), which means (1) he functioned as an amanuensis (secretary) for Peter, (2) he translated Peter's letter (from Aramaic to Greek) as Peter dictated it, or (3) he composed a letter based on Peter's thoughts.

Destination, Origin, Date The people to whom 1 Peter is addressed lived in Pontus, Galatia, Cappadocia, Asia, and Bithynia. These Roman provinces covered all but the southernmost part of Asia Minor, the bulk of modern Turkey.

Christianity may have been brought back by pilgrim Jews converted in Jerusalem on the day of Pentecost (cf. Acts 2:9). More likely, these churches included some founded by Paul on his first and second missionary journeys, and others by unknown missionaries. Peter does not explicitly include himself among "those who preached to you" (1 Pt 1:12).

Whether the readers were Christian Jews or converted pagan Gentiles is not known. First Peter 1:1 reads: "to God's chosen people who are living as foreigners in the lands of Pontus, Galatia, Cappadocia, the province of Asia, and Bithynia" (NLT). That the readers are in some sense exiles is confirmed by 1:17 and 2:11. These verses could refer to a literal exile of Jews outside of Palestine or to a spiritual exile of all believers on earth because their true home is in heaven. No one denies that there was (and is) a literal Jewish dispersion (Diaspora). Peter, viewing the church as the true Israel (cf. Rom 2:29; Gal 6:16; Phil 3:3), may simply have transferred the language of exile from the nation Israel onto the church. The phrase used by Peter in 1 Peter 2:11 is almost identical to the one in Hebrews 11:13 (cf. Gn 23:4; Ps 39:12).

Against the view that construes the dispersion of 1 Peter 1:1 as Christians (Jew and Gentile), rather than Jews only, one may argue that Peter was specifically the apostle to the Jews (Gal 2:7) and that the use of so much OT in 1 Peter demands a Jewish readership. But there is evidence that Peter did not restrict his ministry to Jews (1 Cor 1:12; Gal 2:12), and the use of the OT is not surprising even if the readers were not Jews, because so many Gentile God-fearers (like Cornelius, Acts 10:2) were familiar with the OT.

Whether the readers were Jews or mainly Gentiles is decided by several texts that reflect the pagan background of the readers. Peter says in 1 Peter 2:10 that his readers were once "not a people," a reference to Hosea 2:23 (cf. Rom 9:25). Then in 1 Peter 4:3 Peter describes their past "immorality and lust, their feasting and drunkenness and wild parties, and their terrible worship of idols" (NLT). This does not describe unbelieving Jews, whose problem was not gross immorality but hypocrisy and legalism. Thus the recipients of this letter must have included many Gentile Christians in Asia Minor, characterized as aliens and strangers in the world.

Most scholars think 1 Peter was written from Rome. The clue is found in 5:13: "She who is in Babylon, cho-

sen together with you, sends you her greetings" (NIV). Babylon (which had come to symbolize a big, powerful, evil city) was substituted as a kind of code name for Rome in much early Christian literature (e.g., Rv 14:8; 16:19; 17:5; 18:2, 10, 21; cf. Sibyllene 5:143, 159).

The date of 1 Peter is probably AD 64 or 65 (see next section).

Background While other NT writings refer now and then to Christian suffering, 1 Peter is preoccupied with it. How Christians should conduct themselves when abused is often discussed (1 Pt 1:3-7; 2:12, 20-23; 3:13-17; 4:12-19; 5:9-10). Official state persecution cannot be clearly affirmed; abuses seem to be the common lot of all Christians everywhere (5:9). Cruel masters may sometimes abuse their Christian servants (2:18-20); Christian wives may have to endure harsh, unbelieving husbands (3:1-6); and in general, people are on the lookout to revile Christians as wrongdoers (2:12; 3:9, 16; 4:15-16).

Even though no official state persecution is in view, the letter apparently indicates that there is something worse on the horizon (4:12-19). Peter seems to sense that the present tension between believers and their society could flare into something much worse.

Early church tradition says that Peter was crucified in Rome during Nero's persecution, and there is no good reason to doubt it. Moreover, since 1 Peter was written from Rome, and since 4:12 and 17 imply an impending crisis like the one that struck the Christians in Rome in AD 65, we may suppose that this letter was written not long before Nero began to oppress the Christians in Rome. According to the historian Tacitus, Nero blamed the Christians for burning Rome, in order to squelch the rumor that he himself had done it (so that he could build a greater city). His relentless persecution of Christians had not yet broken out when 1 Peter was written (cf. 2:14; 3:13), but Peter may have seen it coming and may have wanted to prepare the churches outside Rome, should the holocaust reach them, too. Nero's persecution apparently did not affect the Christians in the provinces outside Rome, but that does not diminish the value of Peter's letter, because mostly it deals with how Christians should relate to their society and how they should respond when abuse and suffering come.

If this is a correct picture of the background of 1 Peter, its date would be the early to mid 60s, since the fire of Rome broke out on July 19, AD 64, and the persecution occurred later that year or in the spring of 65.

Purpose and Theological Teaching The main purpose of 1 Peter is to exhort Christians to conduct themselves properly among the community of believers (3:8; 5:1-7), but especially in non-Christian society (2:12), testifying clearly to their hope in Christ (3:1, 15) for God's glory. The letter aims to help Christians understand and endure the abuses that often come from relationships with non-Christians (1:6-7; 2:12, 18-25; 3:9, 14-17; 4:1-5, 12-19; 5:8-10).

Peter's exhortation is based on the good news of God's salvation through the death, resurrection, and second coming of Christ. God is merciful (1:3; 2:10), "the God of all grace" (4:10; 5:12), and there is hope in grace's ultimate display at Christ's coming (1:13). God foreknew and determined a plan of redemption by which to create a holy people for his own possession (2:9-10). Accordingly, Christ was sent into the world to accomplish this redemption for the sake of God's elect (1:20). Although he was "chosen and precious" to God, he was "rejected by men" (2:4) who did not believe him (v 7). But his sufferings (1:11; 4:1, 13; 5:1) were not a meaningless tragedy; they were for the sake of his people

(2:21, 24; 3:18), to redeem them with his precious blood from their empty way of life (1:18-19).

Put to death in the flesh, he was "made alive by the Spirit" (3:18), raised from the dead and glorified (1:21; 2:7), and holds the place of authority at God's right hand (3:22). Further still, we must try to explain the link between the good news of God's saving activity and our good conduct. The good news must be proclaimed if it is to change anybody's life. This proclamation happens in the power of God's Holy Spirit (1:12). It is not merely a "newscast" but is "the living and abiding word of God" (1:23; cf. 4:11), by which God calls his people into being and summons them "out of darkness and into his wonderful light" (2:9; cf. 1:15), "to his eternal glory in Christ" (5:10). This change is described in 1 Peter as a "new birth" (1:3, 23); what distinguishes a newborn person is the "living hope" that he has in Christ (1:3, 13).

This hope, grounded in Christ's resurrection and his sure return, transforms behavior (1:13-15). No longer will we have to seek satisfaction and fulfillment in harmful, unloving ways, but rather by entrusting our souls to a faithful Creator (4:19; 5:7), we can endure unjust suffering patiently (2:20), not return evil for evil (3:9), and seek to extend the mercy of God to others in doing good (2:12, 15; 3:11, 16; 4:19).

Lively Christian hope does not lead us *out* of non-Christian society but rather changes our behavior *in* it. Christians are addressed as citizens of the state (2:13-17), as slaves of cruel masters (vv 18-25), and as wives of unbelieving husbands (3:1-6). By living as new and hopeful persons *in* the institutions of society, others see our good deeds and give glory to our Father in heaven (2:12; cf. Mt 5:16).

Content

1:1–2 This section describes God's election of his people, which is often translated using three prepositional phrases.

First, it is "according to the foreknowledge of God" (NIV). This means more than God's knowing ahead of time whom he would elect. As in 1:20, foreknowledge probably also includes God's purpose (cf. Am 3:2; Acts 2:23; Rom 8:28-30; 11:2; 1 Cor 8:3; Gal 4:9).

Second, the election is "by the sanctifying work of the Spirit" (NASB). Election involves the Spirit's effectual work in making a person obedient to the gospel (see Rom 1:5). In Ephesians 1:4 election is described as "before the foundation of the world" (KJV).

Third, our election is "for obedience to Jesus Christ and for sprinkling with his blood" (RSV). The latter probably refers to the moral effect of Christ's death in purifying our conscience and our behavior as we trust in him (see Heb 9:13-14).

Thus, the elect people of God have their origin in the eternal, purposed foreknowledge of God; owe their call and conversion to the work of the Holy Spirit; and have as their goal in life obedience to God (cf. 1 Pt 1:14).

1:3-12 This section describes how tremendously valuable salvation is—a vast inheritance, absolutely perfect, never diminishing in beauty or worth (v 4), the goal of our faith (v 9), the basis of inexpressible joy (vv 6-8). Searched into and desired by the holy prophets of old, it is so amazing that even angels desire to peer into it (vv 10-12).

It originates in the great mercy of God and was made available to people through the resurrection of Jesus from the dead (v 3). Even though a *future* inheritance is ready to be revealed in the last time (v 5), it offers many *present* spiritual benefits for those who trust in Christ. One of them is the promise of God's present power to cause the believer to persevere in faith (v 5). This does not mean Christians escape hardship; it may be necessary that they suffer (v 6). If so, they should not grumble but see suffering as a refining fire for their good, because it burns away false dependencies and leaves only the pure gold of genuine faith (v 7). So suffering may be an important preparation for the full experience of salvation, since it is faith alone that will be blessed in the end.

Faith is not the same as sight, for believers have never seen Jesus, yet they trust him and love him (v 8). There are good grounds for hope (3:15), founded mainly on the resurrection of Jesus (1:3)—a real historical event.

1:13-25 Peter now gives a command: hope fully in the grace coming to you at the revelation of Christ (v 13), and lead a new life of obedience to God (vv 14-15). Hope is

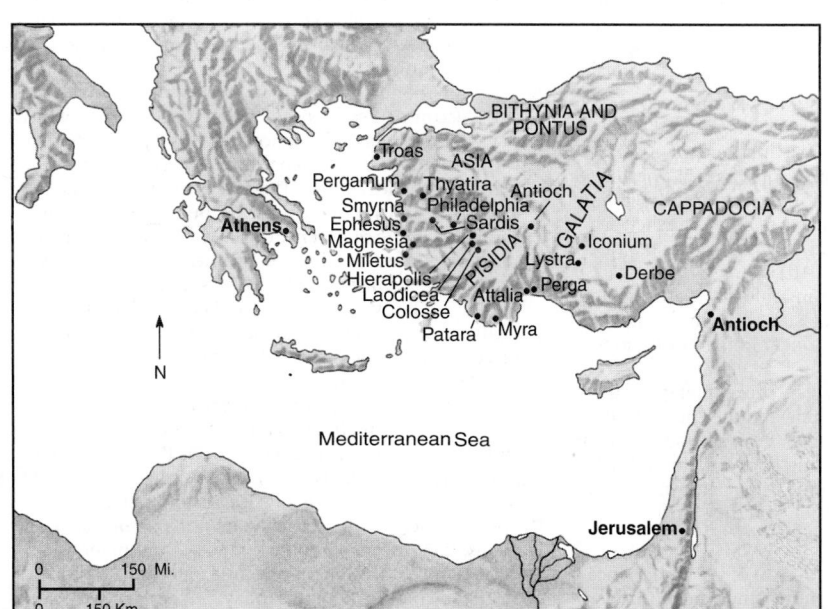

The Churches of Peter's First Letter
Peter addressed his letter to the churches located throughtout Bithynia, Pontus, Asia, Galatia, and Cappadocia. Paul had evangelized many of these areas; other areas had churches that were begun by the Jews who were in Jerusalem on the day of Pentecost and heard Peter's powerful sermon (see Acts 2:9-11).

an intense desire for something and a confidence that it will come. So Peter was commanding the churches to *desire* Christ strongly and be assured of his glory and his coming. Thus, believers must use their minds and keep clearheaded (sober) about what is truly valuable in life (v 13). Full hope in Christ always results in holiness of life. If we delight in being God's children (v 14), we will surely imitate our Father (vv 15-16; cf. Lv 19:2).

But there is another motivation for good conduct: fear of God, who judges each person according to his or her works (1 Pt 1:17). While Peter motivates with fear, he also assures us that we have been redeemed from our futile conduct with the precious blood of Christ (vv 18-19). We are saved by faith, not by good works. Probably Peter means us to fear God's displeasure with unbelief. When the letter says he will judge our works, it probably means that he will look for evidences of obedient, loving conduct, which is the sure sign of hope and faith. If we are lacking in this, fear of his judgment should drive us back to God's mercy, where we can have peace and joy, which in turn lead to love.

This love is commanded toward believers in verse 22. Hope is not mentioned in verses 22-25, but it is implied when Peter says we are born anew through the *abiding* Word of God. Since "the word of the Lord abides forever" (v 25 = Is 40:6-8), those whose life depends on it will abide forever.

2:1-10 This passage is filled with OT quotations and imagery, as shown in the following chart:

OLD TESTAMENT QUOTATIONS AND IMAGERY FROM 1 PETER 2:1-10

1 Peter Reference	Old Testament Reference
2:3	Ps 34:8
2:4, 7	Ps 118:22
2:6	Is 28:16
2:8	Is 8:14
2:9	Ex 19:5-6; Is 9:2; 43:20-21
2:10	Hos 2:23

Verses 9 and 10 indicate that Peter considered the Christian church a new Israel. He probably saw the experience of the church in the world as that of an *exile* like the Jews in Babylonian exile (1:1, 17; 2:11), and considered conversion as a kind of *exodus* out of the darkness of an old futile life into God's light, like the Jewish exodus out of Egypt.

Verses 6-8 show that Jesus is a precious jewel for some but a stumbling stone for unbelievers. Behind that stands God's inscrutable predestination (v 8). Those who trust him are chosen (v 9; cf. 1:1) as a royal priesthood (see below on 2:5), as a nation having God's own holy character (cf. 1:14-15), and as a people cherished as God's special possession. All of this is not due to our merit but to God's mercy (v 10).

Verses 1-3 are again a command—to desire the kindness of Christ that we have tasted through the milk of the Word and so to grow stronger in faith or to hope fully in the grace of Christ.

Verses 4-5 portray a complex, mixed metaphor that pictures Christ as a living stone and the church both as a spiritual house of stones and as a priesthood. The church is, on the one hand, a dwelling place for God (cf. 1 Cor 3:16; Eph 2:21-22), and on the other, a group of ministers in that dwelling who offer God the sacrifices of obedience (cf. Rom 12:1-2).

2:11-12 This is the central concern of the letter. Since Christians are exiles in this world, they must not share the same desires as unbelievers. Such fleshly desires are ephemeral and destroy the soul that follows them. Instead, God's new people should devote themselves to good deeds, even though people may slander them, for this will ultimately cause people to glorify God. The sequence, again, is changed desires, changed behavior, God glorified (cf. Mt 5:16).

2:13-17 Christians should show proper respect to everyone (vv 13-14). That Christ died for sinners is a very humbling truth that forbids Christians to be arrogant or to think that they do not owe others love (cf. Rom 13:8-10). Rather, they are adjured to count others better than themselves (Mk 10:44; Phil 2:3).

Peter declares, then, that believers should be subject to the king and to the civil authorities under him. They should positively devote themselves to doing good so that those who say Christianity makes no difference in life will be silenced.

However, subjection to the state is not absolute, for Christians are first and foremost slaves of God. It is out of freedom that they acknowledge the propriety of a God-ordained state to preserve orderly life. Because Christians serve God first, and the king is merely God's creature, subjection to him is a subjection for the Lord's sake, not the king's sake.

2:18-25 Christian slaves have consciences oriented toward and shaped by God (v 19). They also have experienced his grace and are here told to rely on it by enduring unjust suffering patiently. They are not to strike back: they were called to live this way because Jesus suffered *for them* and because he suffered *as an example*. Verses 21-23 describe the example. Verses 24-25 describe Christ's redemption and its effects. That is, Jesus not only modeled the life of nonretaliation but also enabled his followers to live this way by dying *for* them that they might live for righteousness (v 24). Only when Christians are secure and content in the hope Christ achieved *for them* can they have the freedom and inclination to follow his costly example. When believers are tempted to take vengeance into their own hands, they should recall that even Jesus entrusted himself to God, who judges justly (v 23; cf. Rom 12:19-20).

3:1-7 Here are six verses for wives and one for husbands. How shall a believing wife win her unbelieving husband (v 1)? Peter warns against preoccupation with making the body more attractive (v 3). Instead, he stresses the adornment of the heart with a meek and tranquil spirit (v 4), accompanied by pure, loving conduct (v 2), which may win the husband "without talk" (v 1). This is not a call to mindless subservience but to poise, to free and confident service in love. The wife is not to be afraid even of an abusive husband (v 6). But how? By following Sarah's example of *hoping* in God (v 5). So it is again said that hope transforms life and enables believers to be subject to others. The wife is bound first to the Lord and only secondarily to her husband. Like the slave, the Christian wife will use her God-oriented conscience (2:16) to decide when, for Christ's sake, she cannot follow the lead of her husband.

Husbands are admonished in verse 7 to bring their relationships to their wives into conformity with natural and revealed truth. The *natural* truth is that women are physically weaker. This does not mean that they are inferior mentally or emotionally. It is a simple statement of observed fact: women's bodies are not as strong as men's. In a culture without all kinds of automatic devices, physical strength was much more crucial for survival and comfort than it is today. So the man is urged to use his superior strength for the sake of his wife. The *revealed* truth is that the wife is an "equal partner in God's gift of new life," to be honored and respected.

3:8-12 This concludes the section 2:13–3:12 and admonishes the whole church first to love the brotherhood (3:8) and then to love the hostile outsider (vv 9-12). Verse 9 recalls Jesus' behavior and his commands (Lk 6:27-36). Not only are Christians to endure abuse patiently (1 Pt 2:19-20), they are also to react positively and "bless" those who revile them (3:9). To bless means to wish them well and turn the wish into a prayer. Believers' real desire for their enemies is that they be converted and come to share in the blessing that the Christian will inherit (vv 1, 9). Psalm 34:12-16 is brought in to support the logic of verse 9. If Christians want to inherit the blessing of salvation (1:4-5; 3:9), they must bless those who revile them. This does not mean they *earn* their salvation but that salvation is the goal of faith (1:9), and true faith always makes a person loving.

3:13-17 Generally speaking, when Christians do good, they will not be harmed for it (v 13). Nevertheless, it may be God's will that Christians suffer for doing good (v 17) and that is far better than suffering for doing evil. It is better not only because they ought never do evil but also because they are "blessed" when they suffer for righteousness' sake (v 14; cf. 4:14; Mt 5:10-12). So instead of being afraid of people, believers should fear displeasing Christ and be at peace in his faithfulness (cf. 1 Pt 3:14-15 with Is 8:12-13). Thus, their consciences will be clear and believers will be freed so that when they explain the reason for their hope, even their demeanor will bear witness to its truth (cf. 1 Pt 3:15 with 1:3). The Christians' abusers may be put to shame (v 16) and be won over (3:1) and give glory to God (2:12).

3:18-22 Similar to 2:21-25 and 1:18-21, this unit affirms Peter's call for patient suffering. Since Christ died once for all for mankind's sins and thus freed everyone from guilt and opened a way into the fellowship of the merciful God, believers should be able to bear unjust suffering meekly. Refusing to bear undeserved suffering would be a mark of unbelief in the all-faithful Creator (4:19) who cares for his children and wants to bear their anxieties for them (5:7).

Just as in the days of Noah, only a few were saved (cf. 3:1, 20; 4:17), so now only a few were being saved in Peter's hostile generation, through baptism (3:18-21). Peter defined very carefully in what sense he meant that baptism saves—not by the cleansing function of the water, but rather by the resurrection of Jesus Christ and the pledge of a good conscience toward God (v 21).

4:1-6 Christians should live according to the will of God (cf. 1:14; 2:1-2, 11-12, 15). This will mean a break with the behavior of their unbelieving friends and will probably result in being slandered (4:4). But this should not cause believers to avenge themselves, for God will take care of judgment (v 5).

Believers have this command (v 1): "So then, since Christ suffered physical pain, you must arm yourselves with the same attitude he had, and be ready to suffer, too. For if you are willing to suffer for Christ, you have decided to stop sinning" (NLT). Some have taken this to mean that through a process of suffering we are increasingly sanctified; however, if suffering here refers to dying (as the parallel with 3:18 and the "therefore" of 4:1 suggest), then probably verse 1 is to be understood along the lines of Romans 6:6, 10-11.

First Peter 4:6 is difficult. Some think it refers to the same preaching referred to in 3:19. Another, perhaps preferable, interpretation is that there is no preaching to the dead here but rather a preaching of the gospel to those who subsequently died. That is, those who heard the gospel, believed, and then died did not hear the gospel in vain. For the purpose of the preaching was that, while from a merely human standpoint these believers have been judged in the flesh (i.e., have died), from the divine standpoint they live in the Spirit. The purpose of verse 6 is thus a great encouragement to live by God's will, even when former friends scorn the Christian hope by pointing out that even Christians die.

4:7-11 Activity among believers in the church is again the theme here. Peter saw contemporary events as the beginning of the end (vv 7, 17). This gave an earnestness to his exhortation that believers keep their minds clear and sober for prayer.

By steadily drawing upon God in prayer, Christians find the help they need to love each other and to overlook many offensive things (cf. Eph 4:1-3). This love should manifest itself in joyful hospitality, especially important in times of persecution (1 Pt 4:9), and should move believers to use all their varied gifts and talents to build each other up in faith (v 10). Two examples are given: speaking and ministering (the work of the preacher and the work of the deacon). Most important in speaking and ministering is to recognize what the goal of these gifts is and how to reach that goal. The goal is "that in all things God may be praised" (v 11). This may be done by recognizing that he gives the strength for service and the words for edifying speech.

4:12-19 Here the situation of suffering and bearing reproach for being Christians is again in view. The prospect of a "painful trial" (v 12) is impending (cf. 1:6-7). Peter saw these sufferings (probably from hostile associates rather than official state persecution) as God's judgment on the world, beginning with the church (vv 17-18; cf. Prv 11:31). But God's judgment on the church is not punitive but purgative (1 Pt 4:14; cf. 1:6-7).

Peter gives a reminder that suffering is a normal Christian experience (v 19; cf. 3:14; Acts 14:22; 1 Thes 3:3) and that Christ himself was so mistreated (1 Pt 2:21-25; Mt 10:25). Christians are encouraged to entrust their souls to a faithful Creator (1 Pt 4:19), to rejoice (v 13), and to persevere in doing good (v 19), thereby glorifying God (v 16). When believers respond to suffering in this way, they are blessed (v 14), for God manifests himself to them in an intimate and reassuring way.

5:1-7 Again (as in 3:8; 4:7-11) Peter treats relations within the church. He tells the elders how to be good shepherds of the flock (5:1-4), the younger people how to treat their elders (v 5), and everyone how to be humble toward each other.

Peter reminds believers that God opposes the proud but gives grace to the lowly (v 5; cf. Mt 23:12; Jas 4:6), whom he will exalt in the age to come (1 Pt 5:6; cf. Lk 14:11; 18:14; Jas 4:10). Most important, God invites his people to throw all their anxieties on him because he cares for them (1 Pt 5:7; cf. Ps 55:22; Mt 6:25-30).

The young people who are thus made humble will be subject to their elders and respect them (1 Pt 5:5). The elders who are thus made humble will not lord it over the flock (v 3) or be greedy or begrudging in their service (v 2), but will lead the flock by a humble example.

5:8-11 Peter returns to his concern with suffering. Suffering is the universal lot of believers (v 9; cf. 4:12).

Although in one sense willed by God (1:6; 3:17; 4:19), it is used by Satan to try to destroy their faith. So Peter appeals to the church to be wakeful and sober (5:8; cf. 1:13; 4:7) so that they can resist the lion by faith.

5:12-14 In conclusion, Peter describes his "brief" writing as an exhortation and a testimony concerning the true grace of God. So the letter is not a call for hard labor for God; rather, it is a call to recognize, enjoy, and live by the hard labor that God graciously has exerted and will exert for his children. As was noted above, the letter was written by Silas (Greek *Silvanus*, probably the same person as in Acts 16:25; 1 Thes 1:1; 2 Thes 1:1). It was written from Rome, and greetings were sent from Mark (probably the Gospel writer and former missionary companion of Paul—Acts 13:13; 15:37; 2 Tm 4:11) and the whole church. Peter's last word is to invoke peace upon the churches and to urge them to keep the affection warm among themselves.

See also Suffering; Peter, the Apostle; Spirits in Prison.

PETER, Second Letter of The second, general epistle authored by Peter.

PREVIEW
• Author
• Date, Origin, Destination
• Background
• Purpose and Theological Teaching
• Content

Author The author is clearly identified in 1:1 as Simon Peter, one of the 12 apostles chosen by Jesus. However, two things should be noted. First, its style differs markedly from that of 1 Peter. Second, because 2 Peter is obviously a later work (see Date below) and incorporates Jude in abstract, it is possible that a trusted coworker (e.g., John Mark) put together Peter's final concerns, incorporating an abstract of Jude's epistle after Peter's death. Thus, 2 Peter is the final words of Peter, a type of posthumous testament directing the church in the postapostolic age. It is also possible that Peter was the author behind this work, but not the writer, as was suggested in the section on "Author" for the First Epistle. As such, the epistle could have been prepared by someone other than Silas (as was done for Peter's first epistle) and therefore would explain the difference in style between the two epistles. Furthermore, the actual written document may have been published posthumously.

Date, Origin, Destination Tradition tells us that Peter was martyred about AD 64 in Rome. If that is so, this work was probably written in Rome before AD 70 (before his last teaching was forgotten) and after AD 60 (the earliest date when Peter might have known Paul's letters). Furthermore, it was written after Jude, for 2 Peter 2 incorporates a shortened form of Jude. The Roman place of origin also accounts for 1 Clement's apparent knowledge of 2 Peter in AD 96, the earliest use of the letter. If 3:1 refers to the same churches mentioned in 1 Peter, then the letter is destined for northeastern Asia Minor. The group of churches includes some to which Paul wrote letters (3:15). But the churches could just as well be all the churches, to whom Peter was sending a general message.

Background In a context of many attractive libertine cults, the church was constantly in danger from teachers promoting immorality. Corinth certainly had similar problems, and Romans 6 may show that Paul was aware of a like misuse of his teaching that had reached Rome. Paul's declaration that Christians are free from the law (see Gal 3–5) always carried the danger that instead of yielding to the Spirit, people would yield to their fallen desires, ignoring Paul's warning that those who did such things would not inherit the kingdom of God. This tendency in the early church seems to lie behind 2 Peter.

Purpose and Theological Teaching As 1:12-15 makes clear, the letter is a testament, a final reminder of truth written in the face of the divisions caused by false teachers. It is one final attempt to stabilize the church.

Three main theological themes stand out: (1) a call to Christian virtue and faithfulness and to the apostolic tradition on which the church had been founded; (2) a basing of this call on the exalted status of Jesus Christ and his return in judgment, making all other goals of life irrelevant; and (3) an apocalyptic denunciation of those who had compromised with the world and were therefore living with a sub-Christian ethic.

Content

Greeting (1:1-2) The greeting stresses the authority both of Peter and of his teaching by using the title "apostle," and solidarity with his readers by including the word "servant" and mentioning "a faith of equal standing" with respect to the readers.

Call to Virtue (1:3-21) God has already acted to call Christians to himself. He has, by sovereign grace, given them all that is needed to truly live in a godly manner. And he has set fantastic promises before them. They must not allow themselves to be caught again in the moral morass of the world, for it was God's purpose in saving them to enable them to escape from this trap. Instead, they should become like Christ ("participate in the divine nature") and must therefore grow in Christian virtue. If they fail in this growth, they miss God's promises, but zealousness to move forward will confirm their election and their future in heaven (1:3-11).

Since Peter was about to die, as Jesus predicted (cf. Jn 21:18-19), he wanted to give his readers a final word of encouragement. Peter's encouragement was important for two reasons. First, he was truly an eyewitness of Christ's glory (i.e., the Transfiguration, an event that must have deeply impressed Peter, but is cited here because it revealed the glory, power, and authority of Jesus and bound the OT and NT together). Unlike the false teachers, his tradition is based on what God really did, not on mere speculation. Second, his experience confirms OT prophecy. Like Peter and his followers in the apostolic tradition, the OT prophets were inspired by the Holy Spirit. Thus, the Spirit alone gives the true interpretation, and the idiosyncratic interpretations of the false teachers are therefore wrong (2 Pt 1:12-21).

Denunciation of False Teachers (2:1-22) Christians need to be encouraged to stand firm in virtue because there have always been false teachers in the church who twist the OT Scriptures to support their own behavior. One cannot be sure exactly who these teachers were, but some of their actions are clear. First, they were libertine in their morals, probably twisting Paul's teaching on freedom from the law to support their actions (cf. 3:15; 1 Cor 6:12-20 shows a similar problem in Corinth). Second, they were forming groups loyal to themselves, exploiting these people and leading them into sin (cf. 1 Cor 1–3 for another example of building splinter groups). Third, they were teaching about angelic and demonic powers, some of which they were cursing, which revealed a general disrespect for authority (2 Pt 2:10; cf. Col 2:8). Fourth, while ultimately sectarian, they were still celebrating the Lord's Supper (which at that time was still a common meal, as it would be for another century) with the church and thus defiling the whole celebration (2 Pt 2:13).

Peter's great concern is that these people are sectarian. ("Destructive heresies" refers to groups split from the church, not to doctrinal differences, which is the meaning "heresy" took centuries later.) These teachers formed groups marked by their immoral behavior. They denied the authority of Christ, even though he once bought them out of sin. They denied Christ by rejecting his clear teaching against greed and immorality, and led others in their wake, making the whole Christian faith disreputable before the world. Their motivation was greed, and their predicted destiny was judgment, although it might not be apparent to those unfamiliar with the Scriptures.

This judgment is sure, as OT examples of the judgment of immoral persons (along with the salvation of the righteous) show: for example, of angels (Gn 6:1-4), of the people of Noah's day (vv 5-22), and of Sodom (chs 18–19). In each case God delivered the few righteous individuals, even though he severely judged the evil majority; this encouraged the readers to be righteous like Noah and Lot. Furthermore, the readers might identify with Lot in their own distress at the immorality going on in their church (2 Pt 2:4-10; cf. Jude 1:6-7).

Like those judged in the OT, these false teachers were both proud and ignorant, cursing spiritual powers they did not really understand (probably demonic powers, for Peter was following Jude, who drew on a tradition from the Assumption of Moses). Even angels, who know far more than these teachers do and are more powerful, are not so disrespectful. Even Satan is to be spoken of with respect, according to Scripture. The teachers were not only proud but were also immoral and greedy, even at the Lord's Table ("reveling in their pleasures while they feast with you," 2 Pt 2:13). They claimed to teach freedom but were themselves ensnared in desire, so their words were empty. Their teaching seemed impressive, but it was all sound and wind. Because they had returned to evil after experiencing freedom from sin in Christ, they became worse off than if they had never heard the gospel. They were like dogs (cf. Prv 26:11) or like pigs (2:11-22; cf. Jude 1:8-13).

Warning of Coming Judgment (3:1-16) Both the OT and Jesus himself speak of coming judgment. The false teachers may scoff at the idea, but the story of Noah shows that God does eventually judge. God judged the world in Genesis by water (the very water from which he once separated land in Gn 1); he will judge again, but this time by fire (2 Pt 3:1-7).

Judgment has not yet fallen, because God is wonderfully patient; time does not have the same meaning for him as for humans. The scoffing of the false teachers simply reveals their ignorance of God. And they also do not know God's motives for his seeming delay—that is, that God wants to forgive people, not condemn them. He takes no pleasure in sending people to hell but wills that everyone be saved; not everyone, however, will accept God's offer, and eventually his judgment will come and the universe will be burned. All that is now visible is transitory (3:8-10).

Therefore, Christians ought to live holy lives, preparing for the new and permanent world God has promised them, instead of indulging in the desires of this temporary, perishing world as the false teachers do (3:11-16; cf. Jude 1:20-21).

Closing (3:17-18) In closing, Peter exhorts Christians to be on guard against false teaching. Instead of copying the life of the false teachers, they are to imitate the life of Jesus. A doxology to Christ ends the letter.

See also Peter, The Apostle.

PETER, The Apostle One of the 12 disciples; rose to prominence both among the disciples during Jesus' ministry and among the apostles afterwards.

There are actually four forms of Peter's name in the New Testament: the Hebrew translated into Greek, "Simeon" to "Simon," and the Aramaic translated into Greek, "Cephas" to "Petros" (meaning "rock"). His given name was Simeon bar-Jonah (Mt 16:17; cf. Jn 1:42), "Simon the son of John," which was common Semitic nomenclature. It is most likely that "Simon" was not merely the Greek equivalent of "Simeon" but that, having his home in bilingual Galilee, "Simon" was the alternate form he used in dealings with Gentiles. In fact, it was quite common for a cosmopolitan Jew to employ three forms of his name depending on the occasion: Aramaic, Latin, and Greek. The double name "Simon Peter" (or "Simon called Peter") demonstrates that the second name was a later addition, similar to "Jesus, the Christ." The number of times that the Aramaic equivalent "Cephas" is used (once in John, four times each in Galatians and 1 Corinthians), as well as its translation into the Greek (not common with proper names), indicates the importance of the secondary name. Both Aramaic and Greek forms mean "the rock," an obvious indication of Peter's stature in the early church (see below on Mt 16:18). It is obvious that he was called "Simon" throughout Jesus' ministry but came to be known as "Peter" more and more in the apostolic age.

PREVIEW
•Peter's Background
•Peter's Conversion and Call
•Peter's Place among the Twelve
•Peter the Rock
•Peter the Apostle
•Peter's Future Ministry

Peter's Background Peter was raised in bilingual Galilee. John 1:44 says that the home of Andrew (his brother) and Peter was Bethsaida, the whereabouts of which is difficult to place archaeologically. The only site about which we know is east of the Jordan in the district called Gaulanitis. Yet John 12:21 places Bethsaida in Galilee; however, it is possible that John is reflecting the popular use of the term "Galilee" rather than the legally correct one. Peter and Andrew had a fishing business centered in Capernaum (Mk 1:21, 29) and perhaps were partners with James and John (Lk 5:10). It is also likely that they intermittently continued in their business while disciples, as indicated in the fishing scene in John 21:1-8.

One difficulty with this is the series of statements saying, "We have left all and followed You" (Mt 19:27; Mk 10:28; Lk 18:28, NKJV). The majority of interpreters have given this an absolute sense of "sold" or "left" their business. However, Luke 18:28 occurs in the context of leaving their homes but obviously is not meant in an absolute sense. It seems most likely that the disciples did leave the practice of their fishing businesses to follow Christ, but kept the tools of their trade and returned to their trades when necessary.

They certainly did not abandon their families, as evidenced by Peter, who returned to his home at the end of each tour. The New Testament tells us that Peter was married. In Mark 1:29-31 Jesus heals his mother-in-law, who perhaps was living with Peter. In fact, it is possible that his home became Jesus' headquarters in Galilee. (Matthew 8:14 may indicate that Jesus dwelt there.) First Corinthians 9:5 says that Peter, along with the other married apostles, often took his wife with him on his missionary journeys. Later tradition speaks of his children (Clement of Alexandria's *Stromateis* 2.6.52) and says that Peter was present at the martyrdom of his wife (Eusebius's *Ecclesiastical History* 3.30.2).

Peter's Conversion and Call Peter's brother, Andrew, was a disciple of John the Baptist, according to John 1:35-40. This follows the witness of John in 1:29-34 and is the second stage of John's discipleship drama in chapter one—i.e., after bearing witness he now sends his own followers to Jesus. Andrew and the unnamed disciple (perhaps Philip as in Jn 1:43 or the "beloved disciple," whom many identify with John himself) then "follow" Jesus (a term used often in John for discipleship). The next day Andrew follows the Baptist's example and finds his brother Simon, saying, "We have found the Messiah" (Jn 1:41, NKJV). Peter's conversion is presupposed in John 1:42, where Simon is brought to Jesus by Andrew and there given a new name.

There are three separate episodes in the Gospels in which Simon is called, and these overlap with three episodes in which he is given the name "Cephas" ("Peter," which means "rock") by Jesus. John locates the event in Judea where John the Baptist was baptizing. The synoptic Gospels have two different scenes. The first call takes place at the Sea of Galilee (Mk 1:16-20; Mt 4:18-22). Jesus is walking along the shore and sees Peter and Andrew along with James and John casting their nets into the sea. At this time he calls them to become "fishers of men." Luke then expands this into a fishing scene (Lk 5:1-11), in which the disciples have fished all night and caught nothing but at the command of Jesus lower their nets and catch an amount of fish so great that the boat starts to sink. The episode concludes exactly like the Markan abbreviated form: Jesus says that from now on they will "catch men," and as a result they leave everything and follow him.

The second synoptic episode involving Peter's call (and his new name) is the official choice of the Twelve upon the mountain (Mk 3:13-19 and parallels); in the list of the names we have "Simon he surnamed Peter." The final occurrence dealing with Peter's new name is found in Matthew 16:17-19, in connection with Peter's confession at Caesarea Philippi.

It is somewhat difficult to harmonize these episodes properly. Were there three different episodes in which Simon was called (Jn 1:42; Mk 1:20; 3:16) and three separate incidents in which he was given the name Cephas/Peter (Jn 1:42; Mk 3:16; Mt 16:18)? It is attractive to a broad spectrum of academia to assume that one single event, which happened at some indeterminate time toward the beginning of Jesus' ministry, was later expanded into these diverse traditions. However, a closer examination of the Gospel data does not necessitate such a conclusion. John 1:35-42 is not an institutional scene that connotes an official call. Rather, it describes the first encounter with Jesus and realization regarding his significance. The "renaming" is in the future tense and looks to a later event. Moreover, John deliberately omits most of the crisis events in Jesus' life (the baptism, the choice of the Twelve, the Transfiguration, the words of institution at the Last Supper, Gethsemane) and replaces them with highly theological scenes that teach the spiritual significance of the events. This is what he has done here.

The same is true of the first synoptic call, i.e., the fishing scene. Again, there is no hint of official ordination to

office here but rather a proleptic or prophetic hint of future ministry. This is especially true of the highly theological scene in Luke, which promises abundant results. Again in all three accounts the future tense is employed: "I will make you fishers of men" (Matthew and Mark), "You will catch men" (Luke, NKJV). The call in Mark 1:20 and Matthew 4:21 and their reaction (leaving all behind and following Jesus) is the opening gambit that is finalized in the actual institutional scene in Mark 3:13-19 and parallels. The wording does not indicate that these two episodes are doublets, for the actual appointment of the disciples occurs in the second passage. We must differentiate between the original call to one segment (who became the so-called "inner circle" of the Twelve) and the final choice of all the disciples.

Peter's Place among the Twelve The prominence of Simon Peter in the Gospels and Acts cannot be disputed. While some have attempted to attribute this to his leadership role in the later church, there is no basis for that in the text of the NT. From the very beginning Simon attained preeminence above the others. In the lists of the Twelve just mentioned, Simon's name always appears first, and in Matthew 10:2 it introduces his name as "the first." Moreover, the Twelve are often designated "Peter and those with him" (Mk 1:36; Lk 9:32; 8:45, NKJV).

Throughout the accounts Peter acted and spoke on behalf of the other disciples. At the Transfiguration it is Peter who wanted to erect tents (Mk 9:5), and he alone had sufficient faith to attempt walking on the water (Mt 14:28-31). It is Peter who asks the Lord to explain his teaching on forgiveness (Mt 18:21) and parables (Mt 15:15; Lk 12:41) and who speaks the disciples' minds in Matthew 19:27, "Behold, we have left everything and followed you; what's in it for us?" (paraphrased). The collectors of the temple tax come to Peter as leader of the group (Mt 17:24). As a member of the inner circle (with James and John, possibly Andrew in Mk 13:3) he was often alone with Jesus (at the raising of Jairus's daughter, Mk 5:37 and parallels; at the Transfiguration, Mk 9:2 and parallels; at Gethsemane, Mk 14:33 and Mt 26:37). Jesus asks Peter and John to prepare the Passover meal in Luke 22:8, and in Mark 14:37 (and Mt 26:40) he directs his rebuke to Peter as representing the others ("Could ye not watch with me one hour?"). Finally, the message of the angel at the tomb as recorded in Mark 16:7 said, "Go your way, tell his disciples and Peter." Certainly Peter held a very special place among the Twelve.

This was especially evident in the Caesarea Philippi episode (Mk 8:27-33 and parallels). It was Peter whose confession became the high point of the Gospel accounts, "Thou art the Christ" (Luke adds "of God"; Matthew, "the Son of the living God"). After Jesus then spoke of the suffering of the Son of Man, Peter rebuked him, and in Mark's description Jesus then turned, gazed at all the disciples, and said to Peter, "Get thee behind me, Satan: for thou savourest not the things that be of God, but the things that be of men" (v 33, KJV). This was obviously directed at them all through Peter.

The portrait of Peter that comes through all four accounts pictures him as impulsive, often rash; he is the first to act and speak his mind and was typified by his enthusiasm for everything in which he had a part. At the sight of Jesus walking on the water, Peter asked that the Lord command him to do the same and then immediately leaped out of the boat and began doing just that. At the Transfiguration, while the others were awed into silence by the appearance of Moses and Elijah, Peter the man of action said, "If thou wilt, let us make here three tabernacles" (Mt 17:4, KJV). Mark and Luke both add here that Peter did not know what he was saying. Peter's unguarded and unthinking tendency to protest Jesus' statements is seen not only at Caesarea Philippi but also at the foot-washing scene in John 13:4-11 when he said first, "You shall never ever wash my feet"; and then after Jesus' strong retort, "If I do not wash you, you have no part with Me," he reversed himself completely, stating, "Lord, not my feet only, but also my hands and head" (13:8-9, NKJV). Finally, in the account of the race to the tomb (Jn 20:2-10), the beloved disciple, reaching the tomb first, paused while Peter immediately and impulsively entered it. Peter was certainly one who "rushed in where angels fear to tread." However, this very trait aligns him with all of us and may be one of the major reasons why he becomes the representative disciple throughout the Gospels.

Peter the Rock The key to the significance of Simon Peter is obviously the controversial addendum to the Caesarea Philippi episode, found only in Matthew 16:17-19, Jesus' testimonial to Peter. There are several crucial aspects of this saying. The most important for this study is verse 18, "And I say also unto thee, That thou art Peter, and upon this rock I will build my church" (KJV). There have been many interpretations of this down through history: (1) It refers to Peter as the "rock" or first bishop of the church. This was the Roman Catholic interpretation from the third century on and was employed as a prooftext for apostolic succession, but it is not hinted at anywhere in the context or even in the epistles: it was not a first-century concept. (2) The majority of Protestants since the Reformation have taken this to be a reference to Peter's statement of faith rather than to Peter himself; but this neglects the wordplay, which is even more pronounced in Aramaic, which has only one form for "Cephas" (rock). (3) An alternative has been to take "this rock" as a reference to Jesus himself, but that is fanciful and is hardly in the context. In conclusion, "this rock" is almost certainly a reference to Peter, but it must be understood in two ways. First, Peter was to become the foundation upon which Christ would build his church, a position clearly attested to in Acts. This does not mean that Peter had an authority above the other apostles. Paul's rebuke of Peter in Galatians 2:11-14 demonstrates that he was not above them, and at the Jerusalem council in Acts 15 it is James who has the position of leadership. Second, Peter is seen here not merely as an individual but as the representative of the disciples. This view is coming to increasing prominence today. It recognized the Jewish concept of "corporate identity" in which the leader was identified with the corporate body (e.g., the king or high priest representing the nation before God). This concept is also in keeping with Matthew 18:18-20, which passes on the same authority to the church as is here given to Peter. In this view Peter as the rock becomes the first of the building blocks upon which Christ, the chief cornerstone (to continue the metaphor), will build his church (see Eph 2:19-20).

Two other aspects are worthy of note here. First, verse 18 says, "the gates of hell shall not prevail against it." The "gates of hell" is a common Jewish euphemism for death's inevitable and irrevocable power. Jesus is saying that Satan will not be triumphant over the church, and his sphere of operations, death, will be defeated (cf. 1 Cor 15:26, 54-55). The church would undergo persecution and martyrdom, but the church would be triumphant.

Second, verse 19 promises, "I will give unto thee [singular] the keys of the kingdom," another statement used of apostolic succession by the medieval church. Again, this must be understood in light of corporate identity; Peter, as the preeminent figure in the early church, here embodies the community in his leadership. The "keys of the kingdom" are in direct contrast to the "gates of hell" (cf. Rev 1:18, "the keys of hell and death" and Rev 3:7, the "key of David"), and this follows the imagery of the building seen in the rock upon which Christ will build his church. Here Peter is given the keys that will unlock the power of the kingdom in building God's community, the church. The future tense ("will give") undoubtedly points to the postresurrection period, when that power was unleashed and the church erected.

Peter the Apostle Two events led to the new Peter who fills the pages of Acts: his reinstatement described in John 21:15-17 and the resurrection appearance of the Lord, which is never described but alluded to in Luke 24:34 and 1 Corinthians 15:5. His denial was certainly proof that he was not yet able to assume his predicted position as the rock of the church. Both Luke and Paul seem to state that the risen Lord appeared to Simon Peter before the others, which would be fitting in light of his preeminence in the early church. During the Palestinian era, the fifteen-year period prior to the Gentile mission, Peter was the leading figure. The others mentioned in Acts 1–12 are all secondary to Peter, the dominant director of church policy. These include John, who is with Peter in the temple (3:1), the prison (4:13), and Samaria (8:14); Stephen, who was one of the Seven and whose revolutionary preaching led to his martyrdom (chs 6–7); Philip, another of the Seven who proclaimed the gospel in Samaria and to the Ethiopian eunuch (ch 8); Barnabas, who set an example of communal sharing (4:36-37) and was an official delegate to Antioch (11:20-30); Paul, a miraculous convert and witness (9:1-30; 11:25-30; 12:25); and James, who became the first apostolic martyr (12:2). It is Peter who proposes the choice of the 12th disciple (1:15-17), who proclaims the gospel at Pentecost (2:14-40), who utters the healing word (3:6), and who defends the gospel before the Sanhedrin (4:8-12, 19-20; 5:29-32). The episode regarding Ananias and Sapphira is particularly poignant, for here Peter functions as the avenging messenger of God; nowhere is his authority more evident. We would also note his authority in the scene at Samaria concerning the attempt of Simon the Sorcerer to buy the charismatic power (8:18-24). Again, it is Peter whose influence commands the situation. In these two incidents we certainly see the "binding and loosing" jurisdiction (cf. Mt 16:19) exhibited in Peter.

Yet Peter and the church still came under the strictures of their Jewish heritage. The evidence points to a Jewish proselyte self-consciousness on the part of the early church. They viewed themselves as the righteous remnant, living in the age of Messianic fulfillment, but still interpreted themselves in a Jewish sense and conducted their evangelism in the proselyte form of Jewish particularism (i.e., Gentiles could only be converted through Judaism). Two events altered this. First, the Hellenistic Jewish branch of the church rebelled against the Hebrew Christians, which resulted in the appointment of the seven deacons and a change in the orthodox policy of the Palestinian church. Second, this then led to a new preaching ministry, first by Stephen, whose insights ended in his martyrdom and the dispersal of the Hellenistic branch in chapter 8; then by Philip and others, who extended the gospel even further, to the Samaritans and God-fearers. As a further result, Peter and John came to Samaria (8:14), the next significant step toward the

Gentile mission. Thus ended the centrality of Jerusalem in the unfolding story.

The two miracles of Peter, at Lydda (the paralytic) and Joppa (raising the dead woman) in Acts 9:32-42, are probably intended to parallel similar miracles of Jesus in Luke's first work (Lk 5:18-26; 8:49-56). This is part of a major theme in Acts whereby Jesus' life and ministry are paralleled and continued in the work of the Spirit through the church. Again Peter is seen in a representative role.

The new relationships are extended in two further scenes. First, Peter stays with "Simon, a tanner," in Joppa, an unclean trade; no pious Jew would knowingly have social contact with such a one. Even more important, God teaches Peter through a dream (10:10-16) that the old dichotomy between clean and unclean has been broken. This then leads Peter to the home of an uncircumcised Gentile, the most serious social taboo for the Jew, and subsequent events force Peter to admit Gentiles into the church without the necessity of Jewish proselyte requirements. The serious consequences of this are seen in the debate that ensued in Jerusalem (Acts 11:2-3) and later at the council (Acts 15:1-21). The centrality of this event is demonstrated in the extent to which Luke reproduces Peter's speech, which seems to be a repetition of chapter 10 but is meant to highlight this crucial episode. Often forgotten in the significance of this for the early church is the fact that for Luke the Gentile mission begins with Peter, not Paul. He is the one upon whom the salvific act of God descends; and as the leader of the church, he was the first important witness to it.

The persecution of Herod Agrippa (Acts 12:1-4) was likely due to the furor caused by this free intercourse with Gentiles; and it ended the period of Peter's leadership in Jerusalem. The Jewish people were greatly offended by the new Christian push; and according to Luke in Acts, the idyllic period of popularity, in which the common people supported the church, effectively ceased at this time. Peter's miraculous release and the dramatic scene at Mary's house typified the special place of Peter, but the momentum shifts. Peter is forced to flee Jerusalem, and in the interim James arises to leadership (Acts 12:17); at the Jerusalem council it is the latter who has the chair and presents the council's decision (Acts 15:6-29).

The exact relationship between Peter and the other disciples, especially with the so-called pillars—James and John—and the apostle Paul, cannot be ascertained. The evidence is too vague. Many have thought that indeed there were no truly universal leaders, for the early church was too diverse. However, that is unlikely, and Luke's portrayal in Acts parallels Paul's statement in Galatians 2:8 that Peter was the apostle par excellence to the "circumcised" and Paul to the "Gentiles." They were the universal leaders, while James became the local leader of the Jerusalem eldership. However, neither Peter nor Paul had dominical status similar to that of later popes (i.e., neither was the absolute spokesman of the church and above criticism). So-called emissaries from James could have such an influence on Peter that he would hypocritically change his behavior before Gentiles (Gal 2:12), and Paul could rebuke Peter publicly for doing so (Gal 2:11-14). Paul never claimed authority over the other disciples and even sought their approval and "the right hands of fellowship" for his ministry to the Gentiles (Gal 2:1-10).

Peter's Future Ministry We have very little hard evidence for Peter's other movements. It seems as though Peter gradually turned from leadership to missionary work. However, this is an oversimplification. It is most likely that, following the similar pattern of Paul, he combined the two. The presence of a "Cephas party" at Corinth (1 Cor 1:12; 3:22) may indicate that Peter had spent some time there. This is made even more likely when Paul uses Peter as the main example for taking one's wife on missionary expeditions (1 Cor 9:5). The "Cephas party" probably consisted of those who were converted under his ministry; it is probable that they were Jewish Christians and opposed the "Paul party" on Jewish-Gentile debates reflected elsewhere in 1 Corinthians.

The First Epistle of Peter was sent to churches in northern Asia Minor—the provinces of Pontus, Galatia, Cappadocia, Asia, and Bithynia. The problem here is that there is no hint that Peter had been there and no personal notations in the epistle to demonstrate his acquaintance with these churches. However, it does show that he was very interested in them. In fact, some believe that the reason why Paul was not allowed into this district according to Acts 16:7-8 was that Peter was already ministering there. In short, the question of Peter's involvement in Asia Minor must remain an open one.

There is no final NT evidence that Peter went to Rome. First Peter 5:13 says that the epistle was sent from "Babylon," and it is doubtful that this was the literal Babylon, because there is no tradition that Peter ever went there, and Babylon was sparsely populated back then. It is probably a cryptic symbol for Rome, the "Babylon of the West." It is most likely that the "Babylon" of Revelation 14:8 and 16:19 is also a symbol of Rome. This would fit the strong tradition in the early church that indeed Peter did minister there.

There are four early external witnesses concerning Peter's death. John 21:18 mentions only the martyrdom of Peter but does not give any hint as to the place. First Clement was written at the end of the first century and reports the martyrdom of Peter and Paul among others. While 1 Clement 5:4 testifies only to the fact and not the place of Peter's martyrdom, a study of two aspects favors Rome—the reference to a "great multitude" of martyrdoms, which best fits the Neronian persecution, and the phrase "glorious example among us," which shows that the people of Clement's own church (Rome) were involved. Ignatius's letter to the Romans (4:3) also testifies generally to the martyrdom of Peter and Paul, and again the context favors Rome as the place. He says, "I did not command you as did Peter and Paul," which shows that they had ministries in Rome. The Ascension of Isaiah 4:2-3, a Jewish Christian work of the same period, speaks of Beliar (probably Nero) who martyrs "one of the Twelve," almost certainly Peter. Therefore the earliest evidence does not explicitly point to Rome as the place of Peter's death, but that is the most likely hypothesis.

Definite statements to that effect appear toward the end of the second century. Dionysius, bishop of Corinth, in a letter dated c. 170 (preserved in Eusebius's *Ecclesiastical History* 2.25.8) says that Peter and Paul taught together in Italy. At the end of that century Irenaeus says (in *Against Heresies* 2.1-3) that Peter and Paul preached in Rome, and Tertullian in the same general period adds that Peter was martyred "like . . . the Lord" (*Scorpiace* 15). Clement of Alexandria and Origen both allude to Peter's presence in Rome, and the latter adds the belief that he was "crucified head-downwards" (Eusebius's *Ecclesiastical History* 2.15.2; 3.1.2). The tradition that Peter was crucified may be supported in John 21:18: "when thou shalt be old, thou shalt stretch forth thy hands, and another shall . . . carry thee wither thou wouldest not" (KJV).

The fact that Paul's Epistle to the Romans (c. 55–57) does not mention Peter tells us that he could not have gone there earlier than that. If 1 Peter was written during the Neronian persecution, as those who hold to Petrine authorship believe, he must have gone there sometime in the late 50s or early 60s. Of course, the extent of his ministry in Rome also cannot be known. Some indeed have posited that he had little or no extensive stay in Rome. The facts, as they can be recovered, point to certain tentative conclusions. Peter did have some type of ministry in Rome, though the extent of it cannot be known. However, it is doubtful, in light of the early testimony to his preaching ministry there, that he was merely passing through Rome when caught in Nero's pogrom. Therefore he most likely spent the last years of his ministry in Rome and there suffered martyrdom under Nero, perhaps by crucifixion.

Petra

Simon Peter, along with Paul, was the leading figure in the early church. His impact has been tragically dimmed by the acrimonious debates of Roman Catholic–Protestant circles, but the biblical evidence is clear. He was the leading disciple of Jesus and indeed the "rock" who provided the foundation for the church. As the representative disciple, his enthusiasm and even his weaknesses have made him the supreme example of the developing disciple, one who, through the power of the risen Lord, rose above his faults to become a towering figure on the church scene.

PETHAHIAH

1. Levite and ancestor of one of the postexilic priestly families (1 Chr 24:16).
2. Levite who obeyed Ezra's exhortation to divorce his pagan wife after the exile (Ezr 10:23).
3. Levite who assisted Ezra at the Feast of Tabernacles (Neh 9:5).
4. Meshezabel's son from Judah's tribe, who served as an adviser to the Persian king (Neh 11:24).

PETHOR Hometown of Balaam (Nm 22:5). Pethor is located in Upper Mesopotamia at the confluence of the Sajur River and the Euphrates. Balaam the son of Beor is said to have come from Pethor of Mesopotamia (Dt 23:4). Pethor is identified with Pi-it/ti-ru of the inscriptions of Shalmaneser III (859–824 BC) as a site on the Sajur River. The city was known according to the inscrip-

tions as Pethor by the Hittites (i.e., Syrians or Arameans). It went from Assyrian control to Aramean dominion, was taken again by Shalmaneser, and resettled with Assyrians.

PETHUEL Father of the prophet Joel (Jl 1:1).

PETRA* Capital of the Nabateans, who first appeared in history in 312 BC. The Nabateans were of Arabic origin, though their ancestry is uncertain. They occupied the old land of Edom and made Petra their capital. Petra lay in an impressive valley about 1,000 yards (914.4 meters) wide among the mountains of western Edom, some 60 miles (96.5 kilometers) north of Aqaba. The only access to the valley is through a narrow gorge called the Siq. On all sides, massive cliffs of reddish sandstone arise. Today, ruins of many temples, houses, tombs, and other structures hewn out of the reddish sandstone remain. A Roman basilica and theater are still to be seen. The place continued through Roman times and later had a Christian church and a bishop. It fell into ruins during the days of the Muslim conquest in the seventh century AD.

See also Nabataeans, Nabateans.

PEULLETHAI, PEULTHAI* Obed-edom's son, who was a Levite gatekeeper in the sanctuary during David's reign (1 Chr 26:5).

PHALEC* KJV rendering of Peleg, a descendant of Shem and an ancestor of Jesus, in Luke 3:35. *See* Peleg.

PHALLU* KJV spelling of Pallu, Reuben's second son, in Genesis 46:9. *See* Pallu, Palluite.

PHALTI* KJV spelling of Palti, Laish's son, in 1 Samuel 25:44. *See* Palti #2.

PHALTIEL* KJV spelling of Paltiel, an alternate name for Palti, Laish's son, in 2 Samuel 3:15. *See* Palti #2.

PHANUEL Father of Anna the prophetess. Anna prophesied in connection with the presentation of the infant Jesus at the temple (Lk 2:36).

PHARAOH Ruler over Egypt also known as "the King of Upper and Lower Egypt." He lived in a palace known as the "great house," which was the symbol of his authority. The Egyptian word for the palace was applied to the kings themselves during the New Kingdom (c. 1550–1070 BC). As king, the pharaoh personified the rule of the gods over Egypt. The 18th and 19th dynasties frequently employed the term "pharaoh" without giving the actual name of the pharaoh.

The title was not used officially. Rather, it was a popular designation for the king. In the OT the title was used to refer to men who lived in different historical periods. They were representatives of various dynasties. The use of the royal designation without the name was sufficient for the period in which the pharaoh ruled or for people who were acquainted with the pharaoh. For us today it is often difficult to ascertain who the pharaoh was at any given period and what dynastic period he ruled in.

In the OT the title pharaoh appears by itself (Gn 12:15), as well as with the additional description "king of Egypt" (Dt 7:8), and the name of the pharaoh, such as Neco (2 Kgs 23:29). The pharaoh was considered to be a representative of the gods Ra and Amon on earth. They upheld the divine order in Egypt and were supportive of the temples. The position of the pharaoh as civil and religious head of state gave him unique authority. Unlike his counterparts in the surrounding nations, the authority of the Egyptian king was not easily upset by insurrection.

It remains difficult to identify the pharaohs during the period of the patriarchs. Abraham and Joseph had dealings with the pharaohs of the Middle Kingdom and the second intermediate period. Also, the identity of the pharaoh of the oppression of the Israelites and of the exodus is not satisfactorily resolved. Those who hold to the early date of the exodus see Thutmose III as the pharaoh who began the oppression of the Israelites in Egypt (Ex 1:8). In this view Amenhotep II (c. 1440 BC), who succeeded Thutmose upon his death (2:23), is the pharaoh of the exodus. Another view is that the oppression began under the 18th dynasty and continued until the 19th dynasty. In this view Ramses II is the pharaoh of the exodus (c. 1290 BC).

During the united monarchy, Israel's position as an international power grew. David subdued the nations on Israel's border zones. When Joab took Edom, an Edomite prince, Hadad, fled to Egypt to find protection at pharaoh's court. The 21st dynasty ruled in Egypt during David's time, and it may be that Pharaoh Siamun welcomed Hadad as a political weapon to be used against the growing strength of Israel (1 Kgs 11:14-22). Pharaoh Siamun is possibly also to be identified with the pharaoh who made an incursion into the Philistine coastland, conquering Gezer to be given as dowry to Solomon at the marriage of his daughter to Solomon (3:1-2). At the collapse of Israel's unity, Pharaoh Shishak (Shishong I) of the 22d dynasty made a campaign against Judah and Israel and took much booty with him (14:25-26).

Pharaoh Neco defeated the Judean forces at Megiddo, killing King Josiah in action (2 Kgs 23:29). The last king of Judah (Zedekiah) hoped in vain for help from Egypt, where Pharaoh Hophra of the 26th dynasty ruled. The prophet Ezekiel spoke harshly against the king of Egypt: "Thus says the Lord GOD: 'Behold, I am against you, Pharaoh king of Egypt. . . . It [Egypt] shall be the most lowly of the kingdoms, and never again exalt itself above the nations; and I will make them so small that they will never again rule over the nations' " (Ez 29:3, 15, RSV). Under the Persian regime, the power of the pharaohs dwindled, in fulfillment of the prophetic word.

See also Egypt, Egyptian.

PHARAOH HOPHRA Fourth king of the 26th dynasty (Egypt), he ruled 589–570 BC (Jer 44:30). *See* Hophra.

PHARAOH NECHO*, PHARAOH NECHOH*, PHARAOH NECO, PHARAOH NECOH* Alternate names for Neco, pharaoh of the 26th dynasty (Egypt), who ruled 609–594 BC (2 Kgs 23:29). *See* Necho, Nechoh, Neco, Necoh.

PHARAOH'S DAUGHTER
1. Egyptian princess who rescued the infant Moses and adopted him as her own son (Ex 2:5-10; Acts 7:21; Heb 11:24). If one accepts an early date for the exodus, this foster mother of Moses could have been Hatshepsut. Some scholars who accept a later date for the exodus believe the pharaoh of the oppression was Ramses II; if so, this princess may have been the daughter of Seti I or the daughter of a pharaoh of the later 18th dynasty. It is likely that she was born to a concubine from a royal harem near the region of Goshen.
2. An Egyptian princess, one of the two wives of Mered (a descendant of Caleb) who gave birth to three children (1 Chr 4:17). Her name, Bithiah (meaning

"daughter of the LORD"), implies that she was converted to the worship of Israel's God. It is not known which pharaoh was her father.
3. Princess whom Solomon married in order to seal an alliance with Egypt. Her father was probably Siamun (978–959 BC). He gave to Solomon the town of Gezer as a marriage dowry (1 Kgs 3:1; 9:16; 11:1). Solomon built her a palace in Jerusalem because he would not have her live in David's house (1 Kgs 7:8; 9:24; 2 Chr 8:11).

PHARES*, PHAREZ* KJV forms of Perez, Judah's elder son by Tamar. *See* Perez, Perezite.

PHARISEES Religious sect active in Palestine during the NT period. The Pharisees are consistently depicted in the Gospels as Jesus' antagonists. It is commonly held that the Pharisees represented mainstream Judaism early in the first century and that they were characterized by a variety of morally objectionable features. Accordingly, most Bible dictionaries and similar works of reference depict the Pharisees as greedy, hypocritical, lacking a sense of justice, overly concerned with fulfilling the literal details of the law, and insensitive to the spiritual significance of the OT. These and other characteristics are furthermore viewed as giving shape to Judaism more generally.

There are several problems with this common perception of Pharisaic Judaism. In the first place, the Gospels themselves give some important information that appears inconsistent with this view. Second, the primary documents of rabbinic Judaism (such as the Mishnah, the Talmud, and the Midrashim) are positive and praiseworthy. Third, it has become increasingly clear, especially since the discovery of the Dead Sea Scrolls, that prior to AD 70 the Pharisees constituted only a small movement in a highly diversified society; whatever their popularity and influence, they can hardly be taken as representative of Judaism in general.

Origin The origins of the Pharisees are obscure. According to Jewish tradition, Pharisaic (= rabbinic) Judaism can be traced back to Ezra and the beginnings of the scribal movement in the fifth century BC. At the opposite extreme, a few scholars argue that, since there are no explicit references to the Pharisees in historical documents prior to the second century BC, Pharisaism appeared suddenly after the Maccabean revolt (167 BC). Many specialists take the position that perhaps as early as the third century BC one can find evidence of an incipient form of Pharisaism (as in The Wisdom of Joshua [Jesus] ben Sirach, also known as Ecclesiasticus). It may well be, moreover, that the intellectual pursuits associated with the work of the scribes did have something to do with the development of the Pharisees. It is also probable that prior to the Maccabean revolt some distinctive Pharisaic concerns appeared in connection with the development of the Hasidim ("the faithful ones"—traditionalists who opposed Greek influence in Jewish society).

According to a popular and reasonable interpretation, the Hasidim became disillusioned with the Maccabean rulers, whose conduct violated Jewish sensibilities in several respects. Some of the Hasidim separated themselves from the nation and developed into nonconformist sects, such as that of the Essenes. Those who remained tried to exert their influence on Jewish life and developed into the sect of the Pharisees.

The Pharisees no doubt played a significant role in Jewish affairs during the next century, even though at times they had little political clout. By NT times, they were widely recognized as religious leaders. Josephus, who tells us that he belonged to this sect, wrote toward the end of the first century AD that the Pharisees were "extremely influential among the townsfolk; and all prayers and sacred rites of divine worship are performed according to their exposition. This is the great tribute that the inhabitants of the cities, by practicing the highest ideal both in their way of living and in their discourse, have paid to the excellence of the Pharisees" (*Antiquities* 18.15). We cannot determine whether this description applies to the period before AD 70, but the evidence of the Gospels themselves confirms it to some extent. For example, the parable of the publican and the Pharisee (Lk 18:9-14), while it condemns the Pharisee, makes sense only if we appreciate the role reversal it announces: the wicked publican, not the one generally regarded as righteous, goes home justified.

Basic Characteristics It is not possible to give an accurate characterization of the Pharisees, since scholars disagree sharply concerning their fundamental distinctiveness. Some stress the notion of "separateness," partly on the basis of the supposed etymology of the name (from Hebrew *parush*, "separated one," though other suggestions have been made). A more carefully nuanced viewpoint calls attention to the Pharisees' concern with ritual purity (cf. Mk 7:1-4). Some of the evidence indicates that the Pharisees wished to apply the priestly rituals to the people generally (this factor may help to explain the relative ease with which the Pharisees adapted to the absence of the temple and its sacrifices after AD 70). Still another position sees the Pharisees as the scholar class. The close connection between them and the scribes (experts in the law) gives credence to this view, as does the fact that much of the later rabbinic literature reflects an intellectual pursuit, particularly in its detailed logical argumentations regarding the meaning and application of the Torah.

These various approaches are not mutually exclusive. Moreover, there appears to be widespread agreement about one theological conviction that was foundational to Pharisaism, namely, their commitment to the notion of a twofold law: the written Torah (the OT, principally the Pentateuch) and the oral Torah (the traditions handed down through many generations of rabbis). This is certainly one feature that distinguished them from the Sadducees (cf. Josephus's *Antiquities* 13.297-98). The latter accepted only the authority of the books of Moses and argued strongly that the importance that the Pharisees attached to oral traditions represented an unjustifiable innovation. These traditions, which sought to regulate the lives of the people before God, became more and more detailed over the course of time and were eventually brought together and written down as a single document, the Mishnah (dated c. AD 210). Somewhere in its development the view arose that the oral law itself had been given by God to Moses and thus shared divine authority with the Scriptures.

A careful look at the NT helps in understanding that this feature more than anything else explains the nature of the conflict between the Pharisaic viewpoint and the message of the gospel. The apostle Paul, for example, stresses the distinctiveness of his apostolic preaching by contrasting it to "the traditions of the fathers," which he zealously pursued in his youth (Gal 1:14). Especially instructive is the key passage in Mark 7, where it is written that the Pharisees complained to Jesus, "Why don't your disciples live according to the tradition of the elders instead of eating their food with 'unclean' hands?" (v 5, NIV). Christ's reply counters their criticism with a serious indictment: "You have let go of the commands of God

and are holding on to the traditions of men. . . . Thus you nullify the word of God by your tradition that you have handed down" (vv 8, 13 ; cf. Mt 15:1-6).

The importance the Pharisees attributed to their interpretations of the law compromised the authority of God's own revelation. To make matters worse, the genius of those interpretations was to distort the doctrine of grace by relaxing the divine standards. The very example used by Jesus in Mark 7:10-12 indicates that a rabbinic regulation—the Corban—made it possible for people to ignore the fifth commandment and feel justified in so doing.

The Pharisaic regulations were numerous and aggravating, but at least they could be fulfilled. Those who followed scrupulously the rabbinic traditions were in danger of concluding that their conduct satisfied God's demands (cf. Paul's description of his own preconversion attitude, Phil 3:6). And a muted sense of one's sin goes hand in hand with a false sense of spiritual security; the need to depend on God's mercy no longer appears crucial. This is, of course, the point of the parable of the publican and the Pharisee (Lk 18:9-14). In contrast, Jesus calls for a much higher righteousness than that of the Pharisees: "Be perfect, as your Father in heaven is perfect" (Mt 5:48; cf. v 20).

See also Essenes; Jew; Judaism; Sadducees; Talmud; Torah; Tradition; Tradition, Oral.

PHAROSH* KJV spelling of Parosh, the ancestor of a postexilic family, in Ezra 8:3. *See* Parosh.

PHARPAR One of two rivers named by Naaman as in or near Damascus (2 Kgs 5:12). Its exact identity is uncertain. One tradition identifies it with the Taura, one of seven waterways branching off the Barada River, which flows through Damascus. Another identifies it with the Awaj, a river originating in the eastern foothills of Mt Hermon and flowing south of Damascus. In its early going, its course is steep and swift. The Awaj swells during the spring because of the melting of the snows on Mt Hermon, and subsides as the heat of the summer sets in. The river accounts for the good productivity of the southern Damascan plain and flows much more rapidly than the sluggish Jordan.

PHARZITE* KJV form of Perezite, a member of Perez's family, in Numbers 26:20. *See* Perez, Perezite.

PHASEAH* KJV spelling of Paseah, the head of a family of temple servants, in Nehemiah 7:51. *See* Paseah #2.

PHASIRON Victims of a raid by Jonathan (1 Macc 9:66). The tribe, situated near Bethbasi, is otherwise unknown.

PHEBE* KJV spelling of Phoebe, a Christian woman, in Romans 16:1. *See* Phoebe.

PHENICE*
1. KJV form of Phoenicia, the country on the east Mediterranean coast and north of Palestine, in Acts 11:19 and 15:3. *See* Phoenicia, Phoenicians.
2. KJV form of Phoenix, a harbor along Crete's southern coastline, in Acts 27:12. *See* Phoenix.

PHENICIA* KJV spelling of Phoenicia in Acts 21:2. *See* Phoenicia, Phoenicians.

PHICHOL*, **PHICOL** Commander of Abimelech's army, mentioned in connection with his ruler's treaty negotiations with Abraham and Isaac (Gn 21:22, 32; 26:26). The presence of an army commander should have indicated Abraham's vulnerability, but the adversaries acknowledged the superior power of Abraham's God and thus sought peaceful coexistence with him.

PHILADELPHIA

1. City of the Decapolis, not specifically mentioned in any NT writing. It was located on the plateau about 25 miles (40.2 kilometers) east of the Jordan River. In 63 BC Palestine came under Roman domination. Pompey, the Roman general who conquered the region, reorganized the territory. He established a league of 10 self-governing cities or city-states. Most of these were located on the eastern side of the Jordan River. Philadelphia was the southernmost, and Damascus the northernmost, of the 10. In the Gospels this territory is referred to as the Decapolis.

    See also Decapolis.

2. City in western Asia Minor. It was one of the seven Asian cities to which the author of the book of Revelation addressed letters, mentioned in 1:11 and 3:7-13.

    This city was founded about 140 BC by Attalus II of the city of Pergamum. Attalus II was also known as "Philadelphus"; the name of the city was derived from this royal nickname. He intended that it would serve as a center for the spread of Greek culture throughout the region, especially to the people of Phrygia. Situated on a fertile plain, it was rich with vineyards and wine production. Asian Philadelphia was heavily damaged by an earthquake in the year AD 17. For the purpose of rebuilding, it was granted disaster aid by the Roman emperor Tiberius.

    When John wrote from Patmos near the end of the first century, the churches of western Asia were undergoing persecution. The church in Philadelphia was one of them. This church was enduring the persecution faithfully, and the letter to it (Rv 3:7-13) contains no words of reproach or warning. Instead, Jesus gave them encouragement and precious promises.

    Some years later, the Christian bishop and martyr Ignatius of Antioch also wrote a letter to the church in Philadelphia. He expressed appreciation for his recent visit with them, and encouraged them in Christian unity.

PHILEMON (Person)

Christian known only from the letter addressed to him by the apostle Paul. He is mentioned nowhere else in the NT. From Colossians 4:17 it is clear that Archippus, mentioned along with Philemon in Philemon 1:2 (and perhaps his son), was a man of Colosse. Although Paul had never visited that city (Col 2:1), he obviously knew Philemon well. He addressed him as "our beloved co-worker" (Phlm 1:1); perhaps Philemon had been a colleague during Paul's three-year mission in Ephesus (Acts 19:8-10; 20:31), and Paul knew that he could appeal to him on behalf of his runaway slave, Onesimus.

See also Philemon, Letter to.

PHILEMON, Letter to

The shortest of Paul's Prison Epistles.

PREVIEW

• Author
• Origin
• Recipient
• Background
• Purpose
• Teaching

Author In keeping with his custom and with the contemporary canons of the epistolary genre, the apostle Paul identifies himself as the author of this letter. He says that he was a prisoner at the time of writing (Phlm 1:9-10, 13, 23) because of his witness to Jesus Christ.

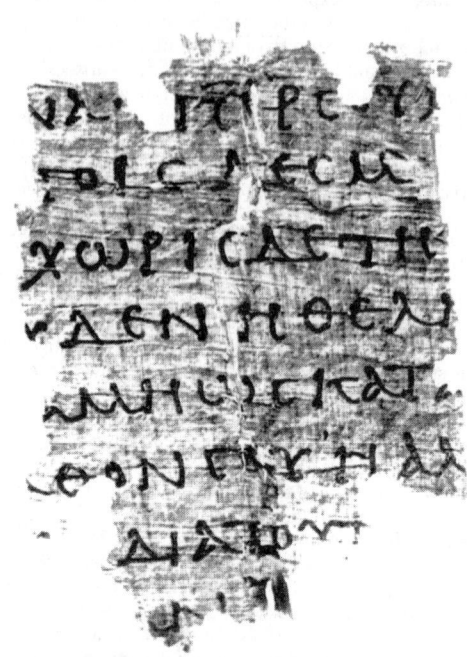

Ancient Greek Manuscript of Philemon Philemon 1:13-15, from Köh Papyrus 12 (c. 200)—P87.

Origin It is difficult to ascertain the location of Paul's imprisonment at the time of writing. Of Caesarea, Ephesus, or Rome, either of the latter locations seems to correspond to the data available in this epistle and in Colossians, with which it is closely related (Col 4:7-14; cf. Phlm 1:23-24). The mention of Mark and Luke as Paul's companions favor Rome as the point of origin of the letter (Phlm 1:24). However, the relative proximity of Ephesus to Colosse, where Philemon resided (about 100 miles, or 160.9 kilometers, away), and the announcement of Paul's forthcoming visit to Colosse (v 22) suggest Ephesus as the place of confinement. Although an Ephesian imprisonment is not explicitly mentioned in the book of Acts, the account of Paul's missionary endeavors in that city make it clear that he met with considerable opposition (Acts 20:19), which Paul describes in terms that could imply a time spent in prison (1 Cor 15:32; 2 Cor 1:8-10).

Recipient This document is often improperly viewed as a personal note from Paul to Philemon, his convert and friend, church leader in Colosse, and slave owner. In reality, the epistle is addressed to Philemon, to Apphia (presumably Philemon's wife), to Archippus, and to the congregation of believers that met in Philemon's house (Phlm 1:1-2). Greetings are sent by the medium of the epistle on behalf of Epaphras, Mark, Aristarchus, Demas, and Luke, who represent together an impressive contingent of church leaders (vv 23-24). Paul's purpose in mentioning them is to make Philemon realize that his response to Paul's plea will not be a private decision but one for which he will be accountable to the community of believers of which he is a part. In the body of Christ, matters that pertain to relationships of believers among themselves are of concern to the whole community. Such matters may not be treated as private issues, since they necessarily affect the well-being of the entire church (Mt 18:15-20).

The epistle makes it clear that a warm bond of brotherly love existed between Paul and Philemon. The apostle calls Philemon his "beloved co-worker" (Phlm 1:1); he commends him in effusive terms for Philemon's involvement in the missionary enterprise (vv 5-7); he appeals to him on the basis of love (v 9); he evokes their sharing of a common partnership (v 17); he gently reminds Philemon that he owes his salvation to Paul (v 19), and he says he trusts him to do what is requested of him and even more (v 21).

Background The object of Paul's letter pertains to a third party—Onesimus, the runaway slave of Philemon. After having committed some indiscretion not revealed in the letter (v 18), the slave had escaped, and having traveled to the big city, he had sought anonymity among the heterogeneous groups of people that form the underclass of any metropolis. Through providential circumstances that remain shrouded in mystery, the fugitive slave had come under Paul's influence; he had been converted by him (v 10), had endeared himself to Paul's heart (v 12), and had become involved with him in the work of the gospel to the extent that Paul would have been glad to keep him in his service as his faithful and dear brother (v 13; Col 4:9).

Paul knew that, had he kept Onesimus at his side as a coworker, Philemon would have been compelled to assent to his decision (Phlm 1:13-14). However, Paul decided to use the ambiguous situation that had developed as the occasion to make Philemon think through the implications of his faith on slavery, and to cause him to free Onesimus and elevate him to the status of brother, not only in a spiritual sense ("in the Lord") but also in regard to his civil status ("in the flesh," v 16). That Philemon acceded to Paul's request and granted freedom to Onesimus is attested to by the preservation of this document. Had Philemon rejected Paul's request, he would likely have destroyed the letter in order to erase from human memory what would have become incriminating evidence of his recalcitrance.

An intriguing postscript has been added to this story by the discovery of the repeated references to an elderly bishop named Onesimus who led the church at Ephesus in the early part of the second century, according to Ignatius's letter to the Ephesians. The identification of the bishop with Philemon's slave is suggested by the use in Ignatius's letter of Paul's play on words with the name of Onesimus in verses 11 and 20 (Onesimus means "useful" or "beneficial"). Should this be the case, it is conceivable that the former slave was the individual who collected the Pauline letters that were eventually integrated into the NT canon, including the letter to Philemon.

Purpose The purpose of Paul's letter to Philemon was to dramatize the incongruity of the institution of slavery with Christianity and thus obtain the release of Onesimus. There is no evidence in the epistle that Paul was worried about Philemon's inflicting upon Onesimus the harsh punishments that were prescribed by Roman law for runaway slaves. However, Paul was concerned that Onesimus not be reinstated as a slave but that he be received as a full-fledged member of Philemon's family, and that he be treated with at least the same deference and dignity that might have been extended to Paul himself (vv 17, 21).

Teaching Among the many teachings contained in this small epistle, three deserve special mention.

First, the letter bears witness to the revolutionary challenge brought by the gospel to the sin-laden institutions of society. As such, it constitutes a condemnation of the practice of slavery. Jesus had denied his followers the right to own or control other human beings. Within the Christian community, mastery or leadership was to be exercised in servanthood from the bottom of the social ladder rather than hierarchically along lines of authority (Mk 10:42-45). As a result, class differences had become irrelevant among Christians. In Christ, there was neither slave nor free but all were one in him (Gal 3:28). Enslaved Christians who could obtain their freedom were to avail themselves of the opportunity (1 Cor 7:21), and those who were free were to avoid becoming slaves of men (1 Cor 7:23; Gal 5:1). Conversely, Christian slave owners were to act as servants to their slaves (Eph 6:9), and all Christians were to be servants to one another (Gal 5:13). Consequently, Philemon was to receive Onesimus "no longer as a slave" (Phlm 1:16).

Second, if adherence to the gospel prohibits a conservative maintenance of the status quo, it also rules out its violent overthrow. The revolutionary temper of the gospel is expressed in a posture of servanthood rather than in militant hostility. Onesimus was advised by Paul to demonstrate this theology of liberation by returning in submission to Philemon so as to allow the Holy Spirit to effect radical change in their relationship. The employment of Satan's methods to achieve kingdom results rules out divine intervention and results in increased oppression.

Finally, the epistle provides a masterful model of inspired churchmanship. The situation that had developed between Philemon and Onesimus required the mediation of an advocate who could command the respect of the former in order to speak successfully on behalf of the latter. To win his case, Paul used the psychology of commendation (vv 4-7); he emphasized his own self-sacrificial suffering for the sake of the gospel (v 9); he played on Philemon's goodwill (v 14); he appealed to personal bonds of friendship (vv 17, 20); he offered to assume responsibility for losses incurred (v 18); he reminded Philemon of his own indebtedness to Paul (v 19); and he announced a forthcoming encounter that might have caused embarrassment had Philemon demurred at his request (v 22). Paul's approach is personal and pastoral, friendly but fervent. It exhibits a perfect balance of firmness and finesse. It demonstrates how genuine Christian leadership is to be exercised through persuasion and entreatment rather than by heavy-handed authoritarian impositions.

Although it is one of the shortest documents in the Bible, the Letter to Philemon stands as a timeless monument to the dignity and equality conferred by Christ on all humans regardless of rank, gender, class, or status. It also offers Christians a mandate and a methodology to pursue effective social reform.

See also Paul, The Apostle; Philemon (Person).

PHILETUS False teacher who, along with his companion Hymenaeus, held an erroneous view of the resurrection of believers—that the resurrection had already happened (2 Tm 2:17; cf. v 11).

PHILIP

1. Apostle whose name is placed fifth in each of the lists of the twelve after the two pairs of brothers, Simon Peter and Andrew, and James and John (Mt 10:3; Mk 3:18; Lk 6:14). John says that when John the Baptist bore witness to Jesus with the words, "Behold, the Lamb of God!" two of his disciples began to follow Jesus, and that one of these two was Andrew, who

then declared to his brother Simon Peter, "We have found the Messiah," and brought him to Jesus. (The other unnamed disciple was quite probably John himself, the writer of this account.) On the next day Jesus went to Galilee and there found Philip and addressed the call to him: "Follow me." John adds that Philip was from Bethsaida. Philip in turn found Nathanael and told him, "We have found him of whom Moses in the law and also the prophets wrote," and invited Nathanael, who was skeptical that any good could come out of Nazareth, to come and see for himself (Jn 1:35-51, RSV). From this is concluded that Philip was one of the first to follow Jesus and that he lost no time in persuading others to do the same.

Like the other apostles, however, he still had much to learn about the person and the power of Christ. Hence, the testing question of Jesus to him on the occasion of the feeding of the 5,000, "How are we to buy bread, so that these people may eat?" and Philip's puzzled response that even if they had 200 denarii (i.e., a large sum, roughly a person's wages for half a year), it would not buy enough bread for each one to be given just a little to eat (Jn 6:5-7). The miracle that followed taught him that the feeding of this multitude presented no problem to the one who is the Lord of all creation. Philip's next appearance is in Jerusalem after Christ's triumphal entry into the city, when "some Greeks" (i.e., Greek-speaking non-Jews) approached him with the request "Sir, we wish to see Jesus." Philip informs Andrew, and together they bring them to Jesus (12:20-22). This perhaps indicates that Philip was a person whom others found readily approachable, and also that he spoke Greek. In the upper room, prior to his arrest and trial, Jesus took the opportunity to impart further instruction to Philip, who had said, "Lord, show us the Father, and we shall be satisfied." Philip hoped perhaps, in all devoutness, for the privilege of some special revelation (reminiscent of the request of Moses, Ex 33:18). But Jesus taught him that he himself, the incarnate Son, is the all-sufficient revelation of the Father to humanity (Jn 14:8-10).

There is a tendency to confuse the apostle with the evangelist (see below) of the same name. It seems probable, however, that after preaching in various parts, the apostle settled in Hierapolis, a city of the Roman province of Asia, and died there. Whether his was a natural or a martyr's death is uncertain.

See also Apostle, Apostleship.

2. Hellenistic Jew and one of the seven men appointed by the church in Jerusalem to supervise the daily ministry of assistance to the impoverished widows of the Christian community. They all, including Philip, had Greek names, and one of them, Nicolaus, was a proselyte (i.e., not a Jew by birth). Whether or not they were regarded as deacons in the technical sense is not absolutely clear from the account; this occasion has, however, been generally accepted as the origin of the order of the diaconate (Acts 6:1-7). Of the seven, Stephen and Philip are the only ones of whom we have any further record in the NT. They are described as men of good repute, full of the Spirit and of wisdom (v 3).

That Philip became known as "the evangelist" is apparent from Acts 21:8. The designation was well deserved, for when the Jerusalem Christians were scattered by the persecution led by Saul of Tarsus, Philip went to a city of Samaria and proclaimed the gospel with such power there that a great number of people joyfully turned to Christ (Acts 8:1-8). In the midst of this spectacular work, Philip was divinely instructed to

leave Samaria and go down to the desert area in the southern part of the country. Humanly speaking, for him to turn away from the multitudes, who were so eagerly responding to his preaching and to go to the uninhabited territory in the south, must have seemed foolish. Yet Philip showed himself not only sensitive but also obedient to the will of God and followed this guidance without question. In the desert he found not a crowd but a single person, an important Ethiopian court official who had visited Jerusalem and was now returning to Africa. The wisdom of God in directing Philip to this place was fully vindicated, for the Ethiopian was reading Isaiah 53, the great gospel chapter of the OT. Philip gave him the good news that this prophecy pointed to Jesus Christ. The Ethiopian subsequently believed and was baptized and went on his way rejoicing (vv 25-40). The conversion of this one person meant not only that Philip was the first to proclaim the gospel to a Gentile but also that the gospel was taken by this Ethiopian courtier to the continent of Africa.

The prevailing nationalistic pride of the Jews was such that they despised the Samaritans and regarded the Gentiles as ceremonially unclean. But Philip, by his eager preaching of Christ first to the Samaritans and then to the Ethiopian, reflected the way in which the gospel penetrated social barriers and dissolved racial prejudices and demonstrated that the grace of God in Christ Jesus is freely available to all. Subsequently, Philip made his home in the coastal town of Caesarea. There he hospitably entertained Paul and Luke when they were en route to Jerusalem at the conclusion of the apostle's third missionary journey. Luke tells us that Philip had four unmarried daughters who were prophetesses (Acts 21:8-9). Not long after this, when Paul was in custody in Caesarea for two years, the kindness and friendship of Philip must have meant much to him (23:31-35; 24:23, 27).

3. Son of Herod the Great and Cleopatra and half brother of Antipas, whose mother was Malthace. He is called Herod in Luke 3:1. The latter was tetrarch of Perea and Galilee from 4 BC to AD 39; Philip was tetrarch of Iturea and Trachonitis (plus certain other territories) to the northeast of Galilee for 37 years (4 BC to AD 33). His wife was his niece Salome, who danced for Herod in exchange for the head of John the Baptist (Mt 14:3-12; Mk 6:17-29).

See also Herod, Herodian Family.

4. Son of Herod the Great and Mariamne and husband of Salome's mother, Herodias, who left him to become the mistress of his half brother Herod Antipas. It was for this immoral relationship that John the Baptist rebuked Herod and was later imprisoned and beheaded (Mt 14:3-12; Mk 6:17-29; Lk 3:19-20).

PHILIPPI Minor village of Thrace (known in antiquity as "The Springs") until about 357 BC, when the father of Alexander the Great, Philip II of Macedon, conquered the site and rebuilt it. He gave the village his name ("Philip's City"), fortified it as a military stronghold in subduing the area, and exploited the nearby gold mines. Two hundred years later, in the Roman era, it became a chief city of one of the four Roman districts into which Macedonia was divided. But because it was about 10 miles (16.1 kilometers) inland from the port of Neapolis, its growth was limited. Nearby Amphipolis (southwest) was the center of Roman government.

Philippi gained worldwide fame in 42 BC, as the site where the imperial armies of Antony and Octavian defeated the republican generals Brutus and Cassius (the assassins of Julius Caesar). The victory opened the way for the emergence of the Roman Empire under the rule of Octavian (Augustus).

Veterans from the war of 42 BC and other battles commonly settled in Philippi. When Paul came to the city, it still reflected its Latin military heritage. Situated on the Ignatian Way, it was one stop on that great military highway connecting the Adriatic with the Aegean. It possessed distinct civic pride inasmuch as it was a Roman colony (enjoying numerous privileges, such as tax exemptions), promoted Latin as its official language, and hosted numerous Roman citizens. Its government was modeled on the municipal constitution of Rome (its leader bearing Roman titles throughout), and the people lived as if they were indeed located in Italy. As Luke records in Acts 16:21, the citizens viewed themselves as Romans.

Ancient Amphitheater at Philippi

Paul visited the city on his second missionary tour and years later wrote one letter to the church. The account of Acts gives detailed attention to Paul's visit. The narrative frequently refers to the city's Roman heritage: not only does Paul successfully employ his Roman citizenship in his defense (Acts 16:37), but the city magistrates bear the dignified Latin title *praetor* (given in its Greek translation, *strategos*—vv 20-22, 38—and which English Bibles translate "magistrate"). There appears to have been a small Jewish community here. The church began with believing Jewish women who met outside the city because there was no synagogue. Later, they convened in the home of an important woman convert named Lydia (vv 14-15, 40).

Some have suggested that Luke may have had a special interest in Philippi. This is surmised not only by his careful attention to the city but also by the "we" sections of the book of Acts. The first "we" section (when Luke joins Paul) begins and ends at Philippi (Acts 16:10, 40). This suggests that Luke stayed behind in the city after Paul's departure. Then on the third tour Luke joins Paul again when the apostle passes through Philippi (20:6).

PHILIPPIANS, Letter to the One of Paul's Prison Epistles.

PREVIEW
• Author
• Date and Origin
• Background
• Theological Themes
• Content

Author Philippians is like 2 Corinthians, Colossians, 1 and 2 Thessalonians, and Philemon in that Paul shared its authorship with Timothy. The appearance of Timothy's name at the start of these letters, however, probably does not mean that he had any greater part in their composition than perhaps to act as Paul's secretary.

Date and Origin While it is clear that Paul was writing from prison (Phil 1:12-13), it is not clear where he was imprisoned. The most likely possibility is Rome, in which case the date would be around AD 62. But some have thought that all the journeys implied in 4:14 and 2:25-26 make such a distant place unlikely (the Philippians hear that Paul is in prison and send a gift by Epaphroditus; Epaphroditus hears in Rome that the Philippians have heard that he has been ill). So the alternatives of Ephesus (c. AD 55) and Caesarea (c. AD 58) have been proposed. We know that Paul was imprisoned in Caesarea (Acts 23:33-35), but the greeting "from those of Caesar's household" is difficult to explain if it was written there, in spite of the coincidence of name. Ephesus is certainly near enough to Philippi for plenty of interchange, but no imprisonment is recorded in the account of Paul's ministry there in Acts. So we would have to assume that Luke's account in Acts 19 is not complete and that Paul had been placed in protective custody at the time of the riot (see esp. 19:30-31). But such an imprisonment could hardly have led Paul to wonder whether his time "to depart and be with Christ" had now come (Phil 1:23). At the time of writing, he was clearly facing a capital charge.

The traditional location (Rome) seems the most satisfactory, especially when one reflects that Paul was imprisoned there for at least two years (Acts 28:30), and that it took about three weeks to travel from Rome to Philippi.

Background Philippi had the distinction of being a Roman colony (Acts 16:12), a privilege accorded to only a few cities outside Italy. Some 90 years before the gospel arrived there (c. AD 50), the city had been greatly expanded by large numbers of Roman soldiers, who were settled there by their commanding officers. As a consequence, the town acquired its coveted status as a colony, which meant that for all intents and purposes its citizens were treated as if they lived in Italy, and the town had a fully Roman administration. Paul alludes to this status in Philippians 3:20, where he teaches that Christians likewise are citizens of another city, the heavenly one, while yet residents elsewhere. It was a rich and busy place, one of the main centers of life in Macedonia, and consequently was "home" to the adherents of many different religions, from both east and west. There was a strong Jewish community there, as well as pagans of many sorts.

Theological Themes In a sense Paul's imprisonment is not just background material but lies at the heart of the letter's message. In his imprisonment he was experiencing the abasement that he mentions in 4:12, using there the same word found in 2:8 to describe the self-humbling of Christ unto death. The pattern of the ministry of Jesus described in the great "hymn" of 2:6-11—humiliation followed by glorification—becomes the pattern of Paul's own life and of the vision he holds out before the Philippians. So alongside abasement and suffering, joy is the other great theme of the letter. Within suffering and self-sacrifice, true joy is born. In fact, Philippians could justly be titled "The Epistle of Joy." Other prominent themes include the gospel, the Day of the Lord, and in addition to the famous "hymn" in chapter 2, a comparison of Paul's Jewish past with his present Christian experience (3:4-16).

ΡΟΛ

ΤΩΝ ΑΥΤΟΝ ΑΓΩΝΑ ΕΧΟΝΤΕϹ ΟΙΟΝ ΕΙΔΕΤΕ
ΚΑΙ ΕΝΕΜΟΙ ΚΑΙ ΝΥΝ ΑΚΟΥΕΤΕ ΕΙΤΙϹ ΟΥΝ
ΠΑΡΑΚΛΗϹΙϹ ΕΝ ΧΩ Ε
ΙΤΙ ΠΑΡΑΜΥΘΙΟΝ
ΑΓΑΠΗϹ ΕΙΤΙ ϹΚΟΙΝΩΝΙΑ ΠΝϹ ΕΙΤΙϹ ϹΠΛΑ
ΓΧΝΑ ΚΑΙ ΟΙΚΤΕΙΡΜΟΙ ΠΛΗΡΩϹΑΤΕ ΜΟΥ
ΤΗΝ ΧΑΡΑΝ ΙΝΑ ΤΟ ΑΥΤΟ ΦΡΟΝΗΤΕ ΤΗΝ ΑΥΤΗ
ΑΓΑΠΗΝ ΕΧΟΝΤΕϹ ϹΥΝΨΥΧΟΙ ΤΟ ΕΝ ΦΡΟΝΟΥ
ΤΕϹ ΜΗΔΕΝ ΚΑΤΑ ΕΡΙΘΕΙΑΝ ΜΗΔΕ ΚΕΝΟΔΟ
ΞΙΑΝ ΑΛΛΑ ΤΗ ΤΑΠΕΙΝΟΦΡΟϹΥΝΗ ΑΛΛΗΛΟΥϹ
ΤΙ ΡΟΗΓΟΥΜΕΝΟΙ ΤΟΥϹ ΥΠΕΡΕΧΟΝΤΑϹ ΕΑΥΤΩΝ
ΜΗ ΤΑ ΕΑΥΤΩΝ ΕΚΑϹΤΟϹ ϹΚΟΠΟΥΝΤΕϹ ΑΛΛΑ
ΚΑΙ ΤΑ ΕΤΕΡΩΝ ΕΚΑϹΤΟΙ ΤΟΥΤΟ ΓΑΡ ΦΡΟΝΕΙΤΕ
ΕΝ ΗΜΕΙΝ Ο ΚΑΙ ΕΝ ΧΩ ΙΗΥ ΟϹ ΕΝ ΜΟΡΦΗ ΘΥ
ΥΠΑΡΧΩΝ ΟΥΧ ΑΡΠΑΓΜΟΝ ΗΓΗϹΑΤΟ ΕΙΝΑΙ
ΙϹΑ ΘΩ ΑΛΛΑ ΕΑΥΤΟΝ ΕΚΕΝΩϹΕΝ ΜΟΡΦΗΝ
ΔΟΥΛΟΥ ΛΑΒΩΝ ΕΝ ΟΜΟΙΩΜΑΤΙ ΑΝΘΡΩΠΟΥ
ΓΕΝΟΜΕΝΟϹ ΚΑΙ ϹΧΗΜΑΤΙ ΕΥΡΕΘΕΙϹ ΩϹ ΑΝ
ΘΡΩΠΟϹ ΕΤΑΠΕΙΝΩϹΕΝ ΕΑΥΤΟΝ ΓΕΝΟΜΕΝΟϹ
ΥΠΗΚΟΟϹ ΜΕΧΡΙ ΘΑΝΑΤΟΥ ΘΑΝΑΤΟΥ ΔΕ ϹΤΡΥ
ΙΟΚΑΙ Ο ΘϹ ΑΥΤΟΝ ΥΠΕΡΥΨΩϹΕΝ ΚΑΙ ΕΧΑΡΙϹΑ
ΤΟ ΑΥΤΩ ΤΟ ΟΝΟΜΑ ΤΟ ΥΠΕΡ ΠΑΝ ΟΝΟΜΑ ΙΝΑ
ΕΝ ΤΩ ΟΝΟΜΑΤΙ ΙΗΥ ΠΑΝ ΓΟΝΥ ΚΑΜΨΗ ΕΠΟΥ
ΡΑΝΙΩΝ ΚΑΙ ΕΠΙΓΕΙΩΝ ΚΑΙ ΚΑΤΑΧΘΟΝΙΩΝ
ΚΑΙ ΠΑϹΑ ΓΛΩϹϹΑ ΕΞΟΜΟΛΟΓΗϹΗΤΑΙ ΟΤΙ
ΚϹ ΙΗϹ ΧϹ ΕΙϹ ΔΟΞΑΝ ΘΥ ΠΡϹ ΩϹΤΕ ΑΓΑΠΗ
ΤΟΙ ΜΟΥ ΚΑΘΩϹ ΠΑΝΤΟΤΕ ΥΠΗΚΟΥϹΑΤΕ ΜΗ ΩϹ
ΕΝ ΤΗ ΠΑΡΟΥϹΙΑ ΜΟΝΟΝ ΑΛΛΑ ΝΥΝ ΠΟΛΛΩ
ΜΑΛ ΛΟΝ ΕΝ ΤΗ ΑΠΟΥ ΚΑΙ

Ancient Greek Manuscript of Philippians
Philippians 1:30–2:12, from Chester Beatty Manuscript II
(late second century)—P46.

Content

Greeting and Opening Prayer (1:1-11) In the opening paragraph of his letter, Paul presents the themes that will be uppermost in his mind throughout. His personal warmth toward the Philippians is immediately striking: "I have you in my heart. . . . I long for all of you" (1:7-8), and this thought of outgoing and suffering love undergirds the whole letter. It is notable, too, that the letter begins and ends with the themes of "grace" and of "the saints" (1:1-2; 4:21-23). The grace of Christ, which reaches out to sinful people and transforms them, separating them from the world, occupies Paul throughout. "The saints" are the ones who, touched by that grace, are transformed in heart and mind, so that their love abounds more and more in knowledge and depth of insight (1:9).

Two more great themes appear here. The Greek word *phroneo,* "to think," is used more in Philippians than in any other letter of Paul, no fewer than nine times (as against seven in Romans). Unfortunately, it is not uniformly translated in the English versions, and so it is hard for the English reader to notice its repeated appearance and the emphasis on the right use of the mind that goes with it. But for Paul this is vital: the way we think is at the heart of the Christian life, and in these opening verses he makes it clear that the love he feels for the Philippians is actually the Christian way of thinking about them (v 7: literally, "It is right for me to think this way about you"). This leads naturally to another emphasis—growth. For the "Christian mind" does not appear overnight. So Paul prays that this mind may grow, giving the Philippians powers of discernment that will transform their character and prepare them for "the day of Christ" (vv 10-11; cf. v 6).

Finally, we note in this opening prayer the twin emphases on the gospel and on fellowship—linked in Paul's prayer of thanksgiving for the Philippians' partnership in the gospel (v 5; cf. v 7)—and also the introduction of the great theme of joy (v 4). All three are vital to the whole letter.

Paul and His Imprisonment: Christ Exalted (1:12-26) Paul writes about his own situation to present the heart of his message. For when he writes, "For me to live is Christ" (v 21), he means more than that his every waking moment is taken up by fellowship with his Lord and service for him. He means also that, in his own person and experience, he displays Christ and "lives" him. Later he will say, "Keep putting into practice all you learned from me and heard from me and saw me doing" (4:9, NLT). Few Christian ministers would dare make such a claim today! Yet Paul believed that, as an apostle of Christ, it was his privilege not just to speak on Christ's behalf but also to live out Christ's life in his own person, even if that meant suffering and humiliation.

There are two historical difficulties here. First, it is hard to reconstruct the situation to which Paul refers in 1:12-18. The church in Rome (if that is where he is) was clearly divided about his imprisonment—some believers actually being glad that he was behind bars. It seems as though they were prompted by his imprisonment to get on with preaching their own version of the gospel. Far from being upset by this, Paul is delighted! "What does it matter?" he asks (v 18). Whether by friend or foe, Christ is being proclaimed in a new way as a result of his imprisonment (v 14). He was normally quick to defend the purity of the Word proclaimed, so these rivals of Paul could not have been heretics.

The other historical difficulty surrounds verses 19-26. At one moment Paul seems not to know what the outcome of imprisonment will be (vv 19-21). Yet he then suggests that

he can choose whether to live or die (v 22), and finally tells the Philippians that he is sure he will remain alive (v 25). The best explanation is that Paul believed he had received a personal assurance from the Holy Spirit that his imprisonment would not end with his execution.

At any rate, his attitude about his own death is most moving. He expected deliverance, whether by life or by death (vv 19-20), and had an unshakeable confidence that to die is "better by far" (v 23), because it means being "with Christ." This section ends with a note of joy.

The Life Worthy of the Gospel (1:27-2:18) This section ends with "joy," just as the last did, and its whole message is summed up in the opening exhortation of verse 27. Paul wanted the Philippians to be people in whom there is no gap between profession and practice, in whom the gospel believed is the gospel lived. The section falls into four portions, which might be entitled as follows: (1) 1:27-30—the worthy life in a hostile world; (2) 2:1-4—the worthy life in Christian fellowship; (3) 2:5-11—the gospel that inspires us; (4) 2:12-18—priorities for lives worthy of the gospel.

Paul refused to let the Philippians feel that he was worse off than they. He wrote, "We are in this fight together. You have seen me suffer for him in the past, and you know that I am still in the midst of this great struggle" (1:30, NLT). For suffering at the hands of a hostile world is part and parcel of Christian discipleship. If we profess to believe a gospel about one who, though equal with God, left aside the glory of heaven and submitted not just to incarnation but also to a horrible death (2:6-8), then we must think of suffering not as an unfortunate necessity but as a privilege! "For you have been given not only the privilege of trusting in Christ but also the privilege of suffering for him" (1:29, NLT).

The essential quality the believers need, in order to face successfully the hostility of the world, is unity. They must be "standing side by side, fighting together for the Good News" (1:27), and believing one gospel will produce a united front against the world—and not a purely defensive front, either. The theme of unity continues into chapter 2, where Paul turns to life within the fellowship (2:1-4), as if to say that external unity before the world will not be possible unless their hearts and minds are truly united in one love, spirit, and purpose (v 2), whatever their outward situation. Such a unity will come only if there is tenderness and compassion among them (v 1). The lovely progression in verse 1 reaches a climax with this phrase, and that in turn leads into the famous "hymn" in 2:6-11. Such tenderness will not find its home in their hearts unless they believe the gospel about which the hymn sings.

Whether 2:6-11 was in fact a real hymn, sung in the context of early Christian worship, is now impossible to know for sure. Certainly Paul's language here takes on a hymnic quality, though it is not in poetic form. Many scholars have thought that Paul did not write these verses himself but was quoting a well-known piece of liturgy. All one can say for certain is that his language changes in style, and he expressed here ideas that are unique in his writings.

The hymn blends in with its context beautifully, and in fact forms the core of the whole letter. For we see here how the experience of imprisonment and deliverance, and of suffering and joy, is an entering into the experience of Jesus himself, who died and rose, was humbled and glorified.

Two Worthy Examples and Friends (2:19-30) Paul again writes about his own situation and plans, but as before, this section is not just concerned with practical arrangements. On the face of it, he was simply explaining why he was sending the letter by the hand of

Epaphroditus instead of Timothy. But actually he was holding them up as practical examples of the life lived by the gospel, about which he had just written. Timothy "genuinely cares about your welfare" (2:20), because, unlike everyone else, he did not seek his own interests but those of Jesus Christ (v 21). He lived the gospel! He was committed to the work of the gospel (v 22). And Epaphroditus was the same, though in a different way. His union with Jesus was expressed not so much in his self-giving service for the gospel and his fellow saints, as in the illness that he suffered and the pains of separation that he endured. Like Jesus, he put his life on the line (v 30), and like Jesus, he was restored to life again (v 27). Now he was to be restored to his beloved Philippians, and the joy that they would experience together would be a further outworking of the gospel.

Pressing Forward and Standing Firm (3:1–4:1) This section also begins and ends on the note of joy (3:1; 4:1)—not accidentally. The way of the cross that Paul describes is also the way of joy (cf. Heb 12:2). It begins and ends also with the address "dear brothers and sisters," and this, too, is not accidental, for once again in this passage Paul writes about himself, and once again the underlying thought is that his experience is typical and that his readers should expect and seek to see the same pattern in their lives. He wrote, "Dear brothers and sisters, pattern your lives after mine, and learn from those who follow our example" (3:17, NLT). Having put forward Timothy and Epaphroditus as examples in 2:19-30, Paul now does the same with himself.

The tone seems to change dramatically in 3:2, as Paul turns to warn the Philippians against "those dogs," who are probably the same as those to whom he refers in 1:28 as "your enemies." There, he was much concerned about the inner foundation of the Philippians' stand against them, so he did not specify who they were. But now he examines them more closely, in order to show the Philippians that the Christian life entails a complete reversal of the values held by their opponents.

It seems that they were Jews, the sort in Acts 17:5 who opposed Paul's ministry in nearby Thessalonica. They believed that they were God's chosen race, but Paul thought that was nothing more than placing confidence in the flesh (Phil 3:4). They thought they knew the way of righteousness—it is the way of rigorous and disciplined obedience to God's law in every detail of life. But Paul thought that was to seek a righteousness of one's own (v 9), having nothing to do with the righteousness that God wants to give. The true way to be God's people, he movingly insists, is the way of self-renunciation, so that all he previously held dear as a Jew came to be seen as rubbish (v 8), considered as loss for the sake of Christ (v 7). The only way to attain righteousness is through faith in Christ (v 9), for Christians must become like him in his death if they are to know the power of his resurrection (v 10). For Paul, dying with Christ meant not just suffering imprisonment and many other indignities for Christ's sake but also renouncing all the prized possessions that his Judaism had given him.

Thinking, Rejoicing, Sharing (4:2-23) Again, the tone changes suddenly (both at 4:2 and at 4:10)—so much so that some scholars have suggested that Philippians was compiled by an editor using several different letters. But when Paul turns (in v 2) to address Euodia and Syntyche, he was not really changing the subject. The link with the last section is the same as that between 1:27-30 and the first paragraph in chapter 2: how can Christians expect to be able to hold their own in the face

of some enemies of the cross of Christ (3:18) if they are disunited and at odds with each other? For if there is just one gospel, disharmony between Christians means that the gospel is not having its full effect. So Euodia and Syntyche are urged (literally) to "think the same thing in the Lord" (4:2), and are then reminded of how they once found a wonderful unity in striving side by side in the cause of the gospel (v 3).

The agreement that Paul urges them to come to does not mean complete identity of opinions on all subjects. It means a oneness of heart in a common love for Christ and the gospel. In the rest of the letter Paul spells out what this oneness means in practice—both what it should mean and what it has meant for the Philippians. The use of the mind is vital, and in verses 4-9 Paul paints a picture of the Christian life in which careful and intelligent prayer (vv 6-7) and the deliberate directing of the mind toward "whatever is true and honorable" (v 8) will produce a life marked by the two qualities of peace and joy, whatever the circumstances.

That leads to the final paragraph, in which Paul gives thanks that, in spite of the disharmony evident in one part of the Philippian church, the church as a whole has already displayed this true Christian "mind." For they have shown their oneness with Paul in the cause of the gospel by sending him a gift by Epaphroditus. "You have done well to share with me in my present difficulty," Paul writes (4:14), and our thoughts go back again to the hymn in 2:6-11. From the gospel about the one who came from heaven to bear our burdens comes this mutual sharing—and so does Paul's wonderful attitude to his circumstances: "I know how to be humbled [the same word as in 2:8], and I know how to abound" (4:12). Joined to Christ, we do not anxiously seek provision for our needs (v 17; cf. v 6), but share with him and with others whatever humiliation and exaltation he sends, confident that God will meet all our needs "from his glorious riches, which have been given to us in Christ Jesus" (4:19, NLT).

See also Paul, The Apostle; Philippi.

PHILISTIA, PHILISTINES Small country situated in southwestern Palestine, along the Mediterranean coast (also called "Palestina" in KJV, Ex 15:14; Is 14:29-31); Aegean people who settled on the maritime plain of Canaan.

PREVIEW
•Territory
•The People
•Government
•Religion and Ritual Objects
•The Philistines and Israel

Territory Strictly speaking, Philistia is that part of the maritime plain that is called the plain of Philistia, extending from the Wadi el-Arish (River of Egypt) in the south some 70 miles (112.6 kilometers) north to the Nahr el-Aujah, five miles (8 kilometers) north of Joppa. Near Gaza the plain reaches its greatest width, about 30 miles (48.3 kilometers). There are sand dunes near the shore, but most of the area is very fertile and produces an abundance of grain (cf. Jgs 15:1-5) and fruit.

The main highway between the East and Egypt lay along the coast. This was of commercial advantage for the Philistines, but it left them open to foreign invasion. God did not lead Israel from Egypt to Canaan by this shortest route through the land of the Philistines, because he did not want them to encounter fierce fighting from the Philistines (or perhaps from an Egyptian garrison stationed there) so soon (Ex 13:17). Apparently, the Philistines had little to fear from the Egyptians, for some scholars think that the Egyptians had a hand in locating the Philistines in Palestine.

From this constricted area the Philistines soon felt a necessity to expand. The passes through the Shephelah provided natural access to the hill country of Israel. They established outposts in Israelite territory, and at the time of the battle in which Saul and his sons were killed, the Philistines exercised control over the city of Beth-shan (1 Sm 31:10).

The People The Bible states that the Philistines came from Caphtor (Dt 2:23; Jer 47:4; Am 9:7), which is generally regarded as Crete, although some scholars place it in Asia Minor. The attire of the Philistines, as shown at Medinet Habu, is like that of Cretans, especially the headdress. The name of the Cherethites has been equated with Cretans, for the names have the same consonantal base: *c, r,* and *t.* The Cherethites were apparently a Philistine subgroup who lived in the Negev not far from Ziklag, David's home among the Philistines (cf. 1 Sm 30:14). The Cherethites and the Pelethites were among David's bodyguards, along with 600 Gittites (men from Gath) (cf. 2 Sm 15:19; 20:7, 23; 1 Chr 18:17).

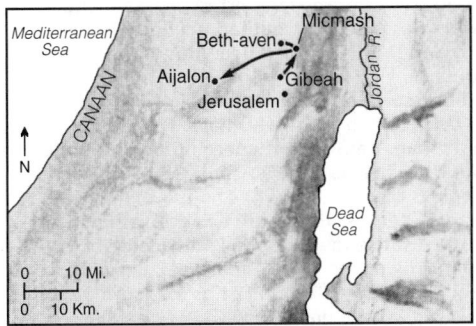

Jonathan Defeated the Garrison at Gibeah Jonathan, Saul's son, left the camp at Gibeah and crept to the Philistine camp at Micmash. With God's help, Jonathan and his armor bearer surprised the Philistines, who panicked and began killing each other! Saul's army heard the commotion and chased the Philistines as far as Beth-aven and Aijalon.

The name Philistines is recognizable in several languages. In Hebrew they are known as the *Pelishtim,* which has been translated into English as Philistines. In the Egyptian sources they are listed among the Sea Peoples and are called the *Peleset* or *Peleste.* They are best known for their part in the invasion of Egypt by the Sea Peoples, who were vanquished by Ramses III in a land and sea battle in the Delta. Detailed scenes of this fighting are shown in deep-sunk relief on the north exterior wall of the temple of Ramses III at Medinet Habu, opposite Luxor. These depictions give some idea of the attire and armament of the Philistines, who are easily identified by their headdress, which was made of feathers (or reeds?).

These people settled along the coast of Palestine after their defeat by Ramses, but it is possible that some stayed in Canaan on their way to Egypt. Possibly an earlier migration to Palestine occurred, perhaps before the time of the patriarchs.

Government Philistia had no single ruler over their entire land; the cities were independent, so they operated as city-states. The heads of these cities were not called kings but were spoken of in the Bible as "lords" or "rulers" (e.g., 1 Sm 5:11; 6:12; 29:2), and there were five of them, corresponding to the five major cities that comprised the Philistine Pentapolis: Gaza, Ashkelon, Ashdod, Gath, and Ekron (1 Sm 6:17; cf. Jer 25:20). The people had a voice in matters that related to them—for example, the return of the ark of the covenant (1 Sm 5:6-12)—but the great decisions were made by majority vote of the five lords. While David and his men were living at Ziklag, for example, the Philistines planned a big military campaign against Israel. David was subject to Achish, king of Gath, who asked David to join forces with the Philistines against Israel. David agreed to this, but when the Philistine lords found that David was present, they complained and voted him out (ch 29).

Religion and Ritual Objects Whatever gods the Philistines brought with them seem to have been abandoned relatively early in favor of Canaanite deities. A primary Philistine god mentioned in the Bible is Dagon, a grain god. Temples to Dagon have been found at Ras Shamra (Ugarit) and Mari. The Bible refers to a temple of Dagon at Gaza (Jgs 16:23-30) and another at Ashdod (1 Sm 5:1-5).

The Philistines and Israel The various forms of "Philistine" and "Philistia" appear almost 300 times in the OT, mostly in the books of Judges and Samuel. The earliest occurrence is in Genesis 10:14, where it is said that the Philistines came from the Casluhim, an unidentified people related to the Caphtorim (cf. 1 Chr 1:12).

Both Abraham and Isaac had contacts with the Philistines at Gerar, in parallel incidents involving their wives (Gn 20; 26). Here, however, the Philistines are not on the coast but at Gerar and as far east as Beersheba (26:33). In both references the king of Gerar is called Abimelech—a good Semitic name. It has been suggested that the Philistines of that time had earlier migrated from Crete, but this has not been demonstrated.

After the Israelite conquest of Canaan, the Philistines began to exercise superiority over the Israelites. An aggressive and militant people, the Philistines had the advantage of superior weapons, for they used iron and exercised a monopoly on iron making in the area. Their control over Israel allowed them to prohibit blacksmithing in Israel, forcing the Israelites to go to the Philistines even for sharpening tools (1 Sm 13:19-22). The Israelites were so poorly armed that only Saul and Jonathan had a sword or a spear (v 22). Facilities for smelting iron have been found at Ashdod, Tell Qasile, Tell Jemmeh, and Tel Mor.

The Medinet Habu reliefs show the Philistines armed with spears and long, straight swords, with large, round shields for protection. They had three-man chariots with six spoked wheels, and they transported people by means of solid two-wheel carts pulled by four oxen. Their ships were rigged with a square sail, like those of the Egyptians, and had a duck-shaped prow, which possibly was used for ramming enemy vessels.

Apostasy came early in Israel, and the Lord used the Philistines to chasten his people. Shamgar delivered Israel by killing 600 Philistines with an ox goad (Jgs 3:31). The account of Samson has many touches of Philistine life (13:1–16:31). This record demonstrates that there was intermarriage between Israelites and Philistines, contrary to the OT law.

Warfare between Israel and the Philistines is reported in 1 Samuel 4:1, when the Israelites were camped at Ebenezer and the Philistines at Aphek. The Philistines won that round and captured the ark of the covenant (1 Sm 4:17), which they returned after seven months because the Lord sent plagues upon them (5:1–6:21). Later, when Samuel had become leader, the Philistines attacked Israel at Mizpah, but God gave the victory to Israel. On this occasion Samuel set up a memorial stone and named it Ebenezer ("Stone of Help," 7:12). The Philistines did not invade Israel again during the lifetime of Samuel, and Israel recovered cities that had been taken by the Philistines (v 14).

The greatest activity of the Philistines in Israelite territory came during the reign of Saul, Israel's first king. More than 80 references to the Philistines are related to that period. The Philistines established outposts or garrisons in various parts of Israel (cf. 1 Sm 10:5; 13:3). Jonathan defeated the garrison at Geba (13:3); his exploit related in 1 Samuel 14:1-15 led to a rout of the Philistines.

A confrontation of the Philistine and Israelite armies took place in the valley of Elah, where the Philistines challenged Israel to provide an opponent to meet their champion, Goliath, in single combat (1 Sm 17:1-11). The young shepherd David killed Goliath; David became a hero, but Saul's jealousy made David a hunted man. In the course of dodging Saul's army, David's men rescued the town of Keilah from the Philistines (23:1-5). Eventually David sought political asylum with Achish, king of Gath, who gave him the town of Ziklag, from which David made raids in the Negev (ch 27).

When the Philistines were preparing for war against Israel, Achish asked David to join the Philistine forces, and David agreed. The lords of the Philistines voted down this participation, for they feared that David would turn against them (1 Sm 28:1-2; 29). In the ensuing battle Saul and his sons were killed on Mt Gilboa by the Philistines (31:1-7). The Philistines cut off Saul's head, placed his armor in the temple of Ashtaroth in Beth-shan, and hung his body on the wall of that city (vv 8-11).

When the Philistines learned that David had become king, they made an effort to destroy him, but he defeated them "from Geba to Gezer" (2 Sm 5:17-25). David broke the Philistine power, and although they again attempted war against Israel, they met with no success (21:15-21).

Uzziah warred against the Philistines; he broke down the walls of Gath, Jabneh, and Ashdod and built cities in Philistia (2 Chr 26:6-7). In the reign of Ahaz, the Philistines invaded the Shephelah and the Negev and captured a number of cities (28:18). Hezekiah fought against the Philistines as far as Gaza (2 Kgs 18:8).

References to the Philistines in the Prophets are relatively few, although Jeremiah devotes a short chapter to the Philistines (Jer 47). The Philistines were gradually assimilated into Canaanite culture and they disappeared from the pages of the Bible and from secular history, leaving the name Palestine as a monument to their presence.

PHILO*, Judaeus Hellenistic Jewish philosopher (c. 25 BC–AD 40) whose thought presents the first major confrontation of biblical faith with Greek thought.

Son of a prominent Alexandrian family, Philo was educated both in the Jewish faith and in Greek philosophy and culture. Of the events of his life we know little, except that in AD 40 he headed a delegation from the Jewish community in Alexandria to the emperor Caligula in Rome. Ethnic tension in Alexandria had grown as the Jewish populace increased and prospered. The tension erupted in AD 42 into riots by the Greeks and the expulsion of Jews from the Gentile sections into which they had spread. Jewish commercial success, particularly in the wheat trade, led to intensified anti-Semitism. Out of the riots came two apologetic treatises by Philo Judaeus, *Against Flaccus* (Flaccus was governing in Alexandria) and *Embassy to Caligula* (Caligula was emperor in Rome). The Jewish community in Alexandria was thoroughly

HOW DO WE KNOW ABOUT THE PHILISTINES?
Most of the knowledge of the Philistines comes from the Bible, the monuments and records of Egypt, and the archaeological excavations of Philistine cities. The biblical information centers in the historical books, but there are references to the Philistines in the Prophets and Psalms as well.

The historical records of Egyptian kings tell of their contacts with the Philistines. Other Egyptian written sources include the Amarna letters, "The Story of the Capture of Joppa," "The Tale of a Mohar," the Harris Papyrus I, and "The Adventures of Wenamon." Paintings and reliefs of Philistines are found in the Theban necropolis and particularly in the temple of Ramses III at Medinet Habu.

Most of the information concerning the material culture of the Philistines comes from excavated pottery, which was distinctive and homogeneous. The earliest Philistine pottery at Ashdod had fish designs and other decorative motifs that resemble Cypriot ware. Decorations included several bands of designs, with carvings of geometric pattern. Paintings of birds were common, particularly the preening bird, with one wing raised and the head turned back. Interesting pottery forms included kraters (large, wide-mouthed bowls with two handles) and single-handled beer jugs with strainer spouts.

The excavation of the University Museum of the University of Pennsylvania at Tell el-Husn (Beth-shan, Beth-shean) unearthed two temples from the 11th century. Possibly the southern temple is that of Dagon (1 Chr 10:10) and the northern temple the House of Ashtaroth (1 Sm 31:10). Ashtaroth was not a Philistine deity but one borrowed from the Canaanites. Ekron had a god named Baal-zebub (2 Kgs 1:2-3; Mt 12:24; Mk 3:22), who is equated with Beelzebul.

At Tell Qasile there was a Philistine temple with two pillars in the holy place, suggestive of the Gaza temple. This temple contained many objects associated with the cult, including a bird-shaped vessel and an incense altar. In houses and small shrines in Ashdod there were numerous clay figurines, both male and female, regarded as a pair of deities. There was also a strange ritual object of clay called an "Ashdoda," best described as a four-legged chair, whose back becomes the stylized upper part of a nude goddess. Another pottery form of religious use was the kernos, which is a hollow ring vase with attached miniature vessels and figurines of heads of animals and birds.

Hellenized. Even the Scriptures were read in the Greek translation called the Septuagint. In spite of the fact that these Jews were living and participating in Greek culture, they remained orthodox. Philo was no exception. On the one hand, he carefully observed the Mosaic law and held that it is the infallibly revealed will of God, both for God's chosen people—the Jews—and for the Gentiles. On the other hand, Philo was very Greek. He probably knew Hebrew only imperfectly and received a liberal education under Greek tutors. His Bible was the OT, especially the Pentateuch, which he held to be most authoritative, but he read it in Greek translation. Because he held that the Septuagint was divinely inspired, Philo had no need to refer to the original Hebrew text.

To understand Philo's work, one must recognize that the need to come to terms with Greek culture stemmed not merely from practical necessity but also from the fact that Judaism is a missionary religion. Jews could not simply turn their backs on the Greek world, for the prophets had called Israel to be a light to the Gentiles. From his studies Philo was also convinced that there is much that is true in Greek philosophy. Consequently, he was anxious to find some way of correlating and harmonizing biblically revealed truth with the teachings of the philosophers. As a Jewish believer considering the claims of Greek philosophy, Philo was confronted with problems very similar to those posed for a Christian by scientific theories of evolution in our day.

The method that Philo used to harmonize Scripture with the teachings of the philosophers was allegorical interpretation. This method of interpretation had been practiced by many before Philo, and many others followed his example. Through the use of this method, Genesis could be read as a contemporary myth about the human condition and man's search for salvation, rather than as an ancient and somewhat crude legend (as the Greeks would see it). The proper reading of the text gives not ancient history and geography but philosophical and moral truth. According to Philo, Moses—both because he was divinely instructed and because he had attained the summit of philosophy—did not resort to mythical fictions, as poets and sophists do; he was able to make ideas visible. By using allegorical interpretation, Philo found in the historical narrative and ceremonial law an inward, spiritual meaning that incorporates the truth he found in Greek thought.

In dealing with the conception of God, Philo approached Greek views critically and rejected what was opposed to Scripture. However, in dealing with the structure and composition of the world, Scripture is quite vague, and so Philo felt free to adopt whatever seemed most reasonable in the writings of the philosophers. He believed that God is the source of both the Mosaic law and the truths of Greek philosophy. The human mind is made in the image of the divine Logos, and so it has some capacity to receive and discover truths about realities beyond the sensible.

Among the philosophers, Philo found Plato's view closest to the truth. God existed from eternity without a world, and after he made the world, he continued to exist above and beyond it. God is the active cause, and this world is passive, incapable of life and motion by itself, but a most perfect masterpiece when set in motion, shaped, and quickened by God. Moreover, God does not neglect his creation but cares for it and preserves it. This care is called providence. While the Greeks had spoken of a universal providence that preserves natural processes, for Philo providence acquired a new meaning. It is God's care for individual beings, so that it includes the power to suspend the laws of nature.

God is one but is the source of all multiplicity. He is immutable and self-sufficient and hence does not need the world. Creation has its source in his goodness. Although Moses said that the world was created in six days, God must be thought of as doing all things simultaneously. The account of six days serves to show that there is order in things. The visible world was created out of nonbeing, from nothing. All the available matter was used in creation, so the world is unique. The world was created by God's will, and it may be imperishable. Philo thought that Plato followed Moses in thinking that the world was created by God.

Concerning the doctrine of the Logos, Philo is both dependent upon and yet critical of the Greek philosophers. Plato had affirmed that there are eternal ideas to which the Craftsman or Maker looked when forming the world. Philo could not accept this position, because God alone is eternal. He harmonized the two views by affirming that from eternity the ideas existed as thoughts of God, but they became a fully formed intelligible world only when God willed to create the visible world. The universe of the ideas, which has no location other than the divine reason, is the pattern according to which the sensible world was made.

To Philo, the Logos is much more than just the instrument by which the visible world was made. It is also described as "the idea of ideas," the first-begotten Son of the uncreated Father and "second God," the archetype of human reason. The Logos is the vital power that holds together the entire hierarchy of created beings. As God's viceroy, he mediates revelation to the created order. He stands on the frontier between Creator and creature. He is the high priest who intercedes with God on behalf of mortals. He appeared in the burning bush and dwelt in Moses. Some think that the Logos is God, but he is really God's image. While one can be quite certain that the Logos was not a person for Philo, the exact status of this power in relation to God is by no means clear.

Various aspects of this teaching have been taken up by Christian writers, most notably John, who taught that the Logos (the Word) is the instrument by means of which God created the world (see Jn 1:1-4). About the origins of this view much less is known. It appears that the notion of the Logos was current in Hellenistic Judaism. Its function in Philo's thought seems to indicate that it was philosophical considerations, rather than biblical ones, that were most significant in his teaching.

Philo had other views about the creation. He believed that while the heavenly bodies are living creatures endowed with mind and not susceptible to evil, man is of a mixed nature, liable to failure. He can be both wise and foolish, just and unjust. God made all good things by himself, but man, because he is liable to both good and evil, must have been made by lesser deities. This is why we are told by Moses that God said, "Let *us* make man" (Gn 1:26, emphasis added). In the case of man, then, being created involved a Fall. Here also there are two steps in Creation. First, there is man created after the divine image, and this is an idea or type, an object of thought only, incorporeal, neither male nor female, and by nature incorruptible (Gn 1:26). Later it says that "God formed man of the dust of the ground, and breathed into his nostrils the breath of life" (Gn 2:7). This man became an object of sense perception, consisting of body and soul, man or woman, by nature mortal. Woman became for man the beginning of blameworthy life. When man and woman saw each other, desire was aroused, and this desire produced bodily pleasure. This pleasure is the beginning of wrongs and violation of law. The Garden of Eden is also meant to be taken symbolically rather than literally. There never have been trees of life or of understanding, nor is it likely that any will ever appear on earth. The tree of life signifies reverence toward God; the tree of knowledge of good and evil signifies moral prudence.

One sees in Philo, then, a tendency to dualism in which spirit is good and matter evil, a tendency derived from Platonism and read into the OT. This led Philo to agree with the Stoics that the only good is the good of the soul. God gives us the world to use, not to possess. To rise to the eternal world of the mind, a man must suppress all responses to the sensible world. In general, Philo tended toward a world-denying asceticism.

The only temple worthy of God is a pure soul. True religion consists in inner devotion rather than externals. In this life the soul is a pilgrim, like Abraham or like the

Israelites wandering in the desert. Through spiritual self-discipline, the soul comes to realize that the body is a major obstacle to perfection. The goal of this spirituality is to draw near to God, who has drawn the mind to himself. God is knowable by the mind, but he is unknowable in himself. We can know only that he is, not what he is. For Philo, the soul in its search for perfection ultimately comes to discover that it must cease to rely on itself and must acknowledge that virtue is a gift of God. The man who has discovered his own limitations comes to know God and his own dependence upon God.

Although Josephus borrowed some from Philo, Philo's greatest influence was on Christian writers. Hellenistic Judaism became less significant as the Judaism of the rabbis became the norm during the next two centuries. By contrast, second- and third-century Christians had much in common with Philo. Parts of his work were translated into Latin and Armenian. Clement and Origen, among the Greek fathers, and Ambrose, among the Latin fathers, were especially indebted to him.

PHILOLOGUS Early Christian acquaintance or friend of the apostle Paul to whom he sent greetings (Rom 16:15). In the series of greetings, he seems to be paired with a woman named Julia.

PHILOMETOR Name of Ptolemy VI, ruler in Egypt (2 Macc 4:21). *See* Ptolemaic Empire.

PHILOSOPHY Logically disciplined, self-critical inquiry into the basic questions of life. "Philosophy" itself means "love of wisdom." This "love" treasures pursuing, discovering, analyzing, and justifying wisdom. Although the word "philosophy" appears only once in the Bible, both Judaism and Christianity were considered philosophies in the Hellenistic world. In fact, from their very earliest encounters with Jewish scholars in Alexandria in the third century BC, Greek philosophers referred to the Jews as a philosophical race. Biblical religion is philosophical because, unlike Greek religion, it makes holistic claims about the nature of reality and it sets out concrete values that can guide community life and individual decisions.

In the only explicit use of the word "philosophy" in the Bible (Col 2:8-10), a point of contrast is made between pagan and Christian philosophy. Paul wanted the Colossians to develop philosophy according to Christ, not according to empty deceit, human tradition, or "the elemental spirits of the universe." In contrast to empty philosophy based on pagan deceit and human tradition, Christ is himself the fullness of deity dwelling bodily—a sound foundation for wisdom and philosophy. In contrast to the mere "elemental spirits," Christ himself is the "head of all rule and authority," the greatest source of truth and justice. The discipline of philosophy is not condemned, for the alternative to deceit and human tradition is "philosophy . . . according to Christ."

As a discipline, philosophy developed in Greece only after the OT was complete, so it could not have been mentioned in the OT. Nevertheless, the biblical Wisdom Literature serves a function quite similar to some philosophical writings. It provides either proverbial instruction for wholesome living (especially Proverbs) or inquiry into the puzzles of human existence (especially Job and Ecclesiastes).

Some characteristics of biblical revelation are shared with the pagan philosophy of its time. For example, the idea of "conversion" was an assumed pattern in the Hellenistic world of the NT, because to change one's philosophy meant to adopt a new form of life. Moreover, the literary form of an epistle was developed by philosophers prior to the NT. Plato and Isocrates started the practice of using letters to defend doctrines or ways of life.

Also, a concern for practical life was central to philosophy at the time of the NT; to learn a philosophy came to mean to acquire the art of living well. Furthermore, to be a philosopher meant to be someone who is interested in the question of God, however one understood that question. The NT world was ripe for guidance in right living and in knowing God.

Two specific philosophies are mentioned in the NT: Epicureanism and Stoicism (Acts 17:18). Epicureans followed the teachings of Epicurus (342?–270 BC), an Athenian philosopher who had taught practical ways of achieving a pleasant life through moderate behavior and stable human relationships. He believed that human beings are merely material objects produced by chance combinations of atoms—small, indestructible material pieces.

Stoics also emphasized moderate living, but they believed that there is an ultimate purpose in the world. This purposefulness is established by an all-pervading substance called Logos, or reason. However, like Epicureans, Stoics were materialists, believing all things to be made of matter, including humans, the divine, and the Logos (which they sometimes treated as God).

In Athens, Paul may have also encountered the "academic skeptics." These philosophers emphasized the fallibility and finitude of human understanding to the point of withholding judgment whenever possible. However, they knew they had to make daily personal decisions, and they remained very curious about other people's ideas. In fact, all the Athenians and the foreigners who lived there at the time of Paul's visit seemed to sustain a high level of curiosity about new ideas (Acts 17:21), providing a mentally lively atmosphere.

It was only appropriate for Paul to present the gospel to these curious minds, and he was convincing enough to win some converts. He established a common ground by agreeing with ideas from two Greek philosophers: Epimenides (sixth century BC), "In him we live and move and have our being"; and Cleanthes the Stoic (third century BC), "We are his offspring." Nevertheless, Paul inevitably offended most of his philosophic listeners by defending the uniqueness of a particular man, Jesus Christ, and by claiming that he had been resurrected from the dead—a claim that contradicted these philosophers' materialist resignation to the finality of death. Clearly, Christianity entailed a dramatically different "philosophy."

See also Epicureans; Stoicism, Stoics.

PHINEHAS

1. Eleazer's son, grandson of Aaron (Ex 6:25), and Abishua's father (1 Chr 6:4, 50). During the high priesthood of Eleazer, Phinehas had charge over the gatekeepers of the tabernacle (9:20), as did Eleazer his father, when Aaron served as chief priest (cf. Nm 3:32). Phinehas, grieved by Israel's sin with Baal of Peor at Shittim, killed an Israelite man and a Midianite woman for their licentious behavior (25:7). Following this act, the Lord turned away his anger toward Israel and made a covenant of peace with Phinehas, which was a covenant of a perpetual priesthood for him and his descendants (vv 11-13); his deed was reckoned to him as righteousness from generation to generation forever (Ps 106:30). Except for the brief interval when Eli acted as high priest

(cf. 1 Sm 1–3; 14:3), Phinehas and his posterity officiated at the high priestly position until the destruction of the Jerusalem temple by the Romans in AD 70.

Following the Baal of Peor incident, Phinehas joined Israel in defeating the Midianites in war (Nm 31:6). After Israel took possession of the land of Canaan, Phinehas was given the town of Gibeah in the hill country of Ephraim for an inheritance (Jos 24:33). He was sent with a small delegation of Israelite leaders to question the building of an altar on the west bank of the Jordan River by the tribes of Israel living east of the Jordan (Jos 22:13, 30-32). Later, at Bethel, Phinehas promised Israel victory over Benjamin's tribe in battle (Jgs 20:28). His descendants Ezra the scribe (Ezr 7:5) and Gershom (8:2) returned with their families to Jerusalem following the exile.

2. One of Eli's two sons, who served as a priest at Shiloh (1 Sm 1:3). According to 1 Samuel, Phinehas was a despicable priest, who, along with Hophni his brother, profaned the offered sacrifices (2:12-17) and the sanctuary (v 22), and scorned Eli (v 25). His death was foretold to his father by a man of God (v 34). In a subsequent war with the Philistines, Phinehas was killed on the same day his wife bore him a son, named Ichabod (4:11, 17-19; 14:3).

3. Eleazer's father. Eleazer helped Meremoth and the Levites, Jozabad and Noadiah, take inventory of the temple's precious metals and vessels during the postexilic era (Ezr 8:33).

PHLEGON Christian in Rome to whom Paul sent greetings (Rom 16:14).

PHOEBE Christian woman of the church at Cenchrea, the eastern port for the city of Corinth. In Romans 16:1-2, Paul commended Phoebe to the recipients of the letter on the basis of her valuable service to other Christians. He asked that they give her whatever assistance she needed.

The term "deacon" is applied to Phoebe. It probably designates an official position in the church, as in Philippians 1:1, although it may mean "minister" in the same sense that Paul uses it elsewhere of himself and others (1 Cor 3:5; 2 Cor 3:6; 6:4).

PHOENICIA, PHOENICIANS Group of city-states (and their residents) that occupied a strip of the Syrian coastal plain at the foot of the Lebanon Mountains. "Phoenicia" was also spelled "Phenice" or "Phenicia." At one time these states extended from Carmel in the south to Arvad in the north, a distance of less than 200 miles (321.8 kilometers). Nowhere is the Phoenician plain more than four miles (6.4 kilometers) wide. In these fertile plains rose independent city-states, so Phoenicia was neither a political nor a geographical unity.

Bereft of good natural ports, the Phoenicians were forced to build their own. Fortunately, they had abundant supplies of magnificent cedar on the western slopes of the Lebanon Mountains, which they dominated. Thus they had good ship timber and an important source of revenue in a wood-starved region of the world. Offshore grew some of the finest dye-producing creatures (sea snails) of the Mediterranean, making possible quality textiles and dyestuffs. These two sources of income were supplemented by superior industrial production in metal and glassware and the transport of the goods of other peoples in Phoenician ships. With the passage of time, Phoenician colonies grew up along their trade routes. Prominent among them was Carthage.

PREVIEW
- History
- Cultural and Historical Significance
- Religion
- Phoenicia and the Bible

History Though peoples of Mediterranean stock occupied Lebanon by about 4000 BC, there was no significant political or cultural development in the area until after 3000 BC, when the Canaanites arrived. Canaanite (Hamitic) culture and ethnic stock were diluted by an Amorite (Semitic) invasion of Phoenicia, Syria, and Palestine about 2000 BC. Subsequently, Semites became dominant in the area.

Long before the Semites arrived, Egyptians established commercial contacts with Phoenicia. During the Old Kingdom (c. 2700–2200 BC), Egyptians seem virtually to have controlled Byblos, about 25 miles (40.2 kilometers) north of Beirut. It was the main port through which Phoenician timber moved to Egypt and Egyptian papyrus and influences entered Phoenicia.

Though Egyptian influence slipped during Egypt's first intermediate period (2200–2050 BC), it was fully restored during the Middle Kingdom. In fact, some scholars like to speak of much of Phoenicia falling within an Egyptian Middle Empire at this time (2050–1800 BC), but others think that Egypt's control was only economic. Subsequently, the Hyksos dominated the whole eastern end of the Mediterranean.

During the Egyptian empire period (c. 1580–1100 BC), the Egyptians at first effectively controlled the cities of Phoenicia, even stationing garrisons in them. But during the latter part of the period, Egyptians and Hittites fought for the mastery of Phoenicia. By 1100 BC, both the Egyptian and the Hittite empires had come to an end and Phoenicia entered a period of independence.

During the next two centuries, Tyre built up her power and established a hegemony over the other Phoenician cities. Of special significance in this rise to power were the efforts of Hiram I. At the same time, the Hebrew united monarchy was building, and the two powers reached out to each other in ventures of mutual advantage.

Conditions changed in the ninth century. In 868 BC Ashurnasirpal of Assyria forced the Phoenician states to pay tribute, and their freedom was lost again. But under the Assyrians, the Phoenicians prospered and planted numerous colonies in the west. By the end of the eighth century, Isaiah could wax eloquent about the prosperity of Tyre (Is 23:3-8).

But as time wore on, the Phoenicians grew restless under increasing Assyrian restriction of liberties. About 678 BC Sidon led a revolt against Esar-haddon of Assyria, which turned out to be a total failure. The furious Assyrians killed or captured most of the inhabitants and leveled the city of Sidon, thus intimidating all the Phoenicians. But Assyrian power subsequently diminished, and Tyre became independent about 625 BC. Her greatness largely remained, and Ezekiel penned a remarkable description of her attainments (Ez 27).

After Nebuchadnezzar of Babylon destroyed Jerusalem in 586 BC, he turned his attention to Phoenicia, easily conquering the rebuilt Sidon but requiring 13 years to subjugate Tyre. At that time he took only the mainland city of Tyre, however. The island city was safe because Nebuchadnezzar had no fleet. The greatness of Tyre was gone; the mainland city was never rebuilt.

When Cyrus the Great conquered the Babylonian Empire in 539 BC, the Phoenicians were absorbed peacefully. But about two centuries later, they participated in a rebellion against the Persians. When the Persian army stood before Sidon in 352 BC and the inhabitants faced the destruction of their homes and the prospect of being sold into slavery, they set fire to their homes and perished with them. It is said that 40,000 died in the flames. The other Phoenician cities had no heart to continue the rebellion.

When Alexander the Great came through Phoenicia in 332 BC, most of the cities welcomed release from Persian rule and opened their gates to him. Tyre did not, however, and was totally destroyed after a seven-month siege. When the city was rebuilt, it was populated with immigrants from Asia Minor and had little ethnic connection with the earlier period. Phoenician maritime supremacy was forever broken.

Subsequently, Phoenicia came under the control of the Ptolemies (286 BC), the Seleucids (198 BC), and the Romans (64 BC). During the Roman period, Phoenicia was part of the province of Syria and enjoyed new prosperity during the Pax Romana (the Roman peace) of the first two centuries of the Christian era. By that time, it was largely Hellenized and its former Semitic character was gone.

Cultural and Historical Significance As the finest mariners of the ancient world, the Phoenicians dominated the Mediterranean during the first half of the first millennium BC, as well as the Aegean Sea for much of that time. As intrepid seafarers, they not only shipped products but also transmitted ideas and processes and engaged in much cultural cross-fertilization.

Though there is no evidence that the Phoenicians invented the alphabet, they disseminated it so widely that it became known as the Phoenician alphabet. Especially important was their transmission of it to the Greeks (at least by 750 BC), who then added vowels and passed it on to the Western world.

The Phoenicians also planted colonies in numerous places in the western Mediterranean, notably during the eighth century BC. Most powerful of these colonies was Carthage, which at its height controlled the western part of north Africa, much of Spain, and numerous Mediterranean islands, and which almost brought Rome to her knees during the third century BC.

Furthermore, the Phoenicians developed advanced techniques in metalworking; some scholars think the Egyptians and possibly even Aegean peoples derived some of their processes from the Phoenicians. Though they may not have invented glass-making, as many ancient authors claim, they certainly contributed much to its development and the spread of its knowledge in the ancient world. The Phoenicians exported quantities of purple dye or dyed cloth and their famous cedars. Cedars of Lebanon found their way not only to Palestine but also to Egypt, Mesopotamia, and faraway Iran.

Of all Phoenician exports, the one most severely censured in Scripture was Baal worship, which found its way into the kingdom of Israel through the marriage of Jezebel to Ahab, and into the kingdom of Judah through the marriage of their daughter Athaliah to Jehoram.

Religion Less is known about Phoenician religion than that of most other peoples of antiquity. This is primarily because the Phoenicians' own literature has not been preserved. One cannot be sure that information from ancient Ugarit in nearby Syria correctly reflects religious practices and beliefs of the Phoenician cities. Nor should it be assumed that the religion of Phoenicia's colonies was transported without modification from the mother country. Unfortunately, what the OT says about Canaanite religion does not differentiate the beliefs or practices of individual Phoenician cities. The following information has been gleaned almost exclusively from Phoenician sources.

Several general names appeared in Phoenician religion. El was both the Semitic word for god and the name of a specific god who was head of the pantheon. Baal simply means "lord," but it also applies to the son of El. Baalat means "lady," but it often designated a specific deity as the Baalat of Gebal or Byblos. The Hebrew word *melek* meant a "king" or "ruler," but it might form part of a name of a deity such as Melqart ("ruler of the city"), chief god of Tyre.

As in the Greek city-states, Phoenician cities had patron deities that were not necessarily the head of the pantheon. On the female side, there was really only one deity worshiped in all the cities, the mother and fertility goddess Ashtart or Astarte (Hebrew, *Ashtoreth*), the Babylonian Ishtar. She was regarded as the genetrix of the gods and man as well as of plants. Promiscuity characterized her conduct, and religious prostitution was carried on in her name.

Baalat Gebal, who symbolized fertility and thus corresponded to Astarte, was the preeminent deity of Byblos, but Adonis was also very important. As the young god who died and was resurrected, he was linked to the annual death and rebirth of vegetation.

Astarte was also predominant in the pantheon of Sidon, as is demonstrated by numerous inscriptions, temples built in her honor, and the fact that kings and queens called themselves her priests. The male deity most involved in Sidonian life was Eshmun, thought to correspond to Adonis in function. By the Greeks, he was identified as Asklepios, god of healing.

The chief god of Tyre was Melqart, the baal or lord of Tyre. Since an annual feast of resurrection was celebrated in his honor, he was equated with Eshmun of Sidon and Adonis of Byblos. The Greeks identified Melqart with Heracles or Hercules. When Tyre came to dominate the other Phoenician cities, Melqart rose to a place of prominence in their pantheons. Melqart would have been the Baal introduced to Israel in the days of Ahab, who married Jezebel of Tyre. The main female deity of Tyre was Astarte. Hiram built temples to both Melqart and Astarte at Tyre, and Solomon brought the worship of Astarte (Ashtoreth) to Jerusalem in his day (1 Kgs 11:5). Her shrine remained to plague the Jews until the reform of Josiah late in the seventh century BC (2 Kgs 23:13).

The places for worship of Baal were either high places in the hills (consisting of an altar and a stone pillar representing the Baal, and a tree or pole representing Astarte) or stone enclosures with an altar, a stone pillar, and a tree. Sometimes they were covered temple buildings. Sacrifices consisted of animals and vegetables, and in times of great disaster, of human beings. Great religious festivals were held in observance of the god's connection with the rhythm of the seasons. When he and nature died, there were mourning, funeral rites, and perhaps self-torture. The spring festival, which celebrated his resurrection and new life in nature and which sought the fertility of nature, commonly was accompanied by sacramental prostitution. The idolatry, human sacrifice, and sexual promiscuity connected with Baal worship brought upon it God's special condemnation.

Phoenicia and the Bible Phoenicia first became involved in biblical history shortly after 1000 BC, when David obtained from Hiram I of Tyre some of the much-coveted cedars of Lebanon for construction of his palace. Solomon also bought cedar from Hiram for his palace and the temple. He hired Phoenician craftsmen for building the temple, for constructing fortifications at strategic centers, and for creating a major port facility at Ezion-geber on the Gulf of Aqaba, an arm of the Red Sea. Phoenician architectural design was employed in various Hebrew building projects in Solomon's day, and Phoenician shipbuilding expertise made possible Solomon's merchant marine. Phoenician sailors manned the ships after they were launched (see 1 Kgs 9:10-28).

During the first half of the ninth century BC, Phoenician impact on Israel was largely religious. It was then that Jezebel, a princess from Tyre, married Ahab and introduced Baal worship to the northern kingdom. More than a century later, Phoenicia was the subject of prophetic condemnation. Isaiah (before 700 BC, see Is 23) and Ezekiel (about 600 BC, see Ez 26:2-19; 28:1-23) hurled predictions of suffering and destruction at both Tyre and Sidon.

In NT times the apostle Paul spent a week at Tyre with a group of Christians on his return to Jerusalem at the end of his third missionary journey (Acts 21:2-7).

See also Canaanite Deities and Religion.

PHOENIX Harbor town on the southern coast of Crete, where Paul and his shipmates hoped to spend the winter during their voyage to Rome (Acts 27:12, KJV "Phenice"). Phoenix was situated west of Fair Havens near the island of Cauda. Against Paul's better judgment, the ship was ordered to leave the bay of Fair Havens and sail westward to Phoenix. While en route to this harbor town, the ship was struck by a powerful gale from the northeast. This wind drove the ship southwest past the island of Cauda and threatened to push it across the Mediterranean Sea into the treacherous north African shoals of Syrtis Major (vv 9-17).

cisely. The Phrygians were originally Europeans, called Phryges by the Greeks, who crossed the Hellespont from Macedonia and Thrace and settled here. This migration followed the general pattern of invasions from Europe into this section of Asia Minor. The Phrygians formed a powerful confederacy that flourished between the downfall of the Hittite Empire and the rise of the Lydian Empire, that is, between the 7th and the 13th centuries before Christ.

Their religious capital was at "Midas City," modern Yazilikaya, about 150 miles (241.4 kilometers) southwest of Ankara. This "city of Midas" consisted of an acropolis, defended by a wall with towers, and a lower city. Within a large cave was a spring, approached by steps cut in the rock, which supplied water for the upper and lower cities. The famous tomb or monument of King Midas has a Phrygian inscription that mentions the goddess "Mida," identified with Cybele the mother goddess, considered to be the mythical mother of the king. French archaeologists in 1948–49 discovered remains that indicate the city was destroyed in the sixth century BC, rebuilt about a century later, and finally destroyed in the third century BC.

Their chief goddess was Cybele. She later became the fertility goddess of all Anatolia. Orgiastic rites were performed in her honor, leading to sensuality intended to facilitate reproduction among humans, animals, and crops. When the Ionians and the Greeks settled in Miletus and Ephesus, Cybele was transformed into Artemis the Greek goddess of fertility, whose temple in Ephesus was one of the seven wonders of the world. Her image originally was a black meteorite stone (cf. Acts 19:35). She became the consort of Adonis, a vegetation

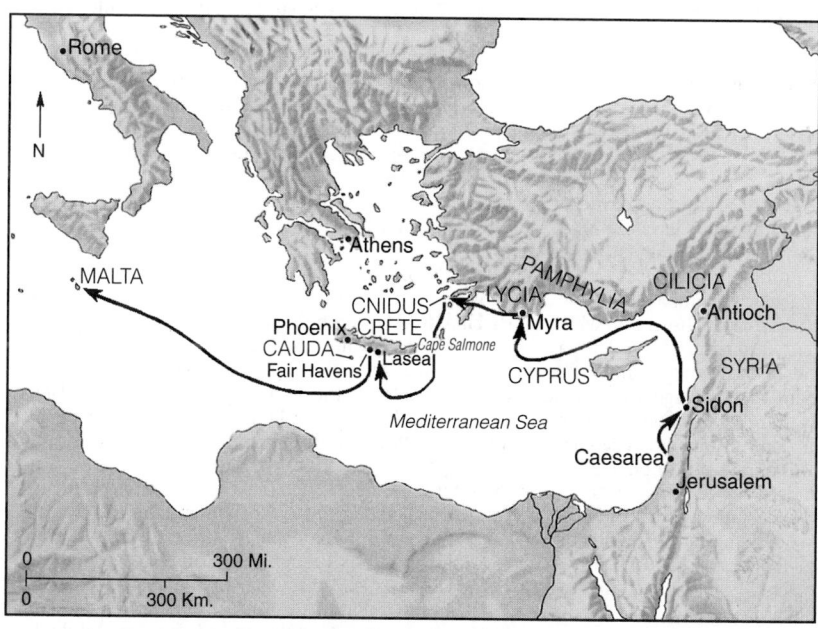

Phoenix, Harbor Town in Crete On Paul's journey to Rome, a storm forced the ship to bypass Phoenix on its way to Italy.

Luke's description of Phoenix as facing northwest and southwest (Acts 27:12) suggests that this place was the same as the modern Phoinika, a town on the western edge of Cape Mouros. In antiquity, this deep harbor was apparently accessible to ships and afforded protection from the winter winds. The name Phoenix is retained in Phoinika.

PHRYGIA Area in western Turkey on the Anatolian plateau, the boundaries of which cannot be defined pre-

god, and their fertility rites were common throughout the Middle East. This goddess was imported into Rome; a temple in her honor was built on the Capitoline Hill soon after the organization of the empire.

Gallic tribes invaded the region some three centuries prior to Paul. This changed the demographic situation, with the result that the political, geographical, and ethnic divisions did not always coincide. What was formerly Phrygia became known as Galatia because of the new inhabitants. Yet the old names persisted.

Jews were encouraged to settle in this area by the Syrian kings. They were an important part of society, and their synagogues were to be found in every major city. Paul passed through this area on his way from Lycaonia to Troas (Acts 16:6) after having been forbidden by the Holy Spirit to speak the word of God in Asia. The gospel probably came to this area from the pilgrims who went to Jerusalem and heard Peter preach. There, in astonishment, they heard the early believers proclaiming the works of God in their own native language (2:8-11). Some were converted and went home to spread the Good News.

That Christianity made early inroads and received a wide following here is indicated by the fact that in the middle of the second century Montanus, a zealous leader of the church, arose and called the church back to the primitive dynamism that characterized Pentecost. Thus arose the sect of Montanism, in which the leader was sometimes viewed as the incarnation of the Holy Spirit or the oracle of God. In better light, the movement is seen as a return to primitive Christianity and a protest against the increasing formalism among the churches. By the third century, the entire region was almost entirely Christian, according to Eusebius.

PHURAH* KJV spelling of Purah, Gideon's servant, in Judges 7:10-11. *See* Purah.

PHUT*
1. KJV spelling of Put, Ham's third son, in Genesis 10:6. *See* Put (Person).
2. KJV spelling of Put, a region close to Egypt along the Mediterranean Sea, in Ezekiel 27:10. *See* Put (Place).

PHUVAH* KJV spelling of Puvah, Issachar's son, in Genesis 46:13. *See* Puvah.

PHYGELLUS*, PHYGELUS Asian Christian who, along with others, abandoned Paul (2 Tm 1:15). Phygelus is mentioned with Hermogenes, also otherwise unknown.

PHYLACTERY* Small prayer case containing Scripture passages worn at times of prayer by pious Jews. Orthodox Jewish males wear two small, black leather cubes or boxes, with Scripture inside, at the time of prayer.

In its original form the phylactery was probably not a box containing Scripture but a strip of parchment on which four passages from the OT were written in Hebrew. The passages were Exodus 13:1-10 and 11-16, Deuteronomy 6:4-9, and 11:13-21. The Deuteronomy 6:4-9 passage contains the "Shema"—the confession of God being one Lord. All four passages contain the idea that God commands his people to bind his ordinances and commandments upon their hands and have them as "frontlets" between their eyes. Some Jews took this figuratively or spiritually and did not actually wear them. Other Jews took the command literally and began wearing portions of their Scriptures on their foreheads and on their hands. Exactly when they began to do this is not agreed upon by scholars. There is an explicit mention of the practice as early as 100 BC in a Jewish nonbiblical document. It is thought by some to have begun as early as the fourth century BC, if not earlier.

In Matthew 23:5 Jesus condemned the scribes and Pharisees for, among other things, making "broad their phylacteries." The context of the passage is Jesus' condemnation of ostentation in religion. Apparently, the broad phylactery would impress others with how religious the wearer was. It was evidence of pride, pretense, and hypocrisy in religion.

See also Amulet; Frontlet.

PHYSICIAN One trained in medicine. The physician tended to and repaired wounds and administered medicines to the sick. In early Israel the diagnosis and treatment of sick people was officially the concern of the priests, although many nonprofessional people practiced the healing art in the small towns and villages. King Asa sought their help for his feet (2 Chr 16:12). Jeremiah inquired about physicians in Gilead (Jer 8:22). Job complained that his friends were useless physicians (Jb 13:4). Scientific medicine and the careful training of physicians awaited the rise of Greek medicine, which by NT times saw medical schools established in various countries in the Greco-Roman world. Remarkable collections of surgical instruments have come from places like Pompeii. The NT refers to a number of sicknesses, and the word "physician" occurs several times in the Gospels (Mt 9:12; Mk 2:17; 5:26; Lk 4:23; 5:31; 8:43). Luke is given special mention as a beloved physician (Col 4:14). Physicians were not always able to effect a cure (Mk 5:26; Lk 8:43), but Jesus the healer succeeded where others failed.

See also Medicine and Medical Practice.

PI-BESETH* City mentioned together with Thebes, Memphis, and On in Ezekiel's oracle about Egypt's fall (Ez 30:17, NLT mg). In Egyptian the name is translated "house of the goddess Bastet." Bastet was first represented as a woman with the head of a lioness, and in later periods by the head of a cat. In Greek she was known as Boubastis or Bubastis. The city of Boubastis was extensively described by Herodotus. It was located on the right shore of the Old Tanite branch of the Nile, also known as the Branch of Boubastis. Boubastis is the present Tell Basta. Archaeological excavations in 1866-67 unearthed evidence that it is a very old city, dating from the Old Kingdom. It was not until Shishak I, the founder of the 22d (Libyan) dynasty, that Pi-beseth became the capital. Hence, the dynasty is also known as the dynasty of Boubastis. The 23d dynasty kept Boubastis as the capital. It served about two centuries as the capital (c. 950-750 BC). The city was destroyed around 350 BC by Persian forces.

PIG *See* Animals.

PIGEON *See* Birds.

PI-HAHIROTH Stopping place of the Israelites on their journey from Egypt to the Promised Land (Ex 14:2). It was here that the pursuing Egyptians overtook them (v 9), which led to the deliverance at the Red Sea. Israel never forgot how the Lord had saved them. The precise location of Pi-hahiroth is uncertain, as with Baal-zephon and Migdol, also mentioned as being in the same vicinity. After the Israelites had departed from Egypt, they camped first at Succoth in Goshen and then at Etham (Nm 33:6). After Pi-hahiroth, they journeyed three days to Marah and Elim, thought to be on the east shore of the Gulf of Suez, en route to Sinai. It seems that Pi-hahiroth was on the northeast border of Egypt, possibly on the west shore of the Bitter Lakes. Israel did not travel by the expected route of the Way of the Philistines, but southeast by the desert route (cf. 13:17-18), eventually linking up with the old Egyptian road to the copper and turquoise mines of Sinai.

See also Wilderness Wanderings.

PILATE, Pontius Appointed by Tiberius as the fifth prefect of Judea, Pilate served in that capacity from AD 26-36. He appears prominently in the trial narratives of the Gospels as the Roman governor who authorized

Jesus' crucifixion. In addition, he appears in a variety of extrabiblical sources as a dispassionate administrator who relentlessly pursued Roman authority in Judea.

Tacitus (*Annals* 15.44) mentions Pilate in connection with the crucifixion of Jesus but adds little to the Gospel account. Josephus, on the other hand, provides three narratives. First, he describes Pilate's arrival as the new prefect (*War* 2.9.2; *Antiquities* 18.3.1; cf. Eusebius's *Histories* 2.6). Offending Jewish law, Pilate brought ensigns into Jerusalem that bore the image of Caesar. A large gathering of Jews then came to Caesarea in protest, fasting there for five days. Pilate called in troops to dismiss them, but he learned his first lesson about Jewish intransigence. The Jews were ready to die rather than tolerate the ensigns. Soon thereafter Pilate relented.

A second incident occurred when Pilate appropriated temple funds in order to construct a 35-mile (56.3-kilometer) aqueduct for Jerusalem (*War* 2.9.4; *Antiquities* 18.3.2). Again, there was a major protest. Pilate ordered his soldiers to dress in tunics and infiltrate the crowds in disguise. At his command, the troops used clubs to beat the offenders. Many Jews were killed. Josephus records the horror with which Jerusalem perceived the affair.

Finally, Josephus records the story of Pilate's dismissal (*Antiquities* 18.4.1-2). In AD 36 a Samaritan false prophet (pretending to be the *Taheb*, or Samaritan messiah) promised to show his followers sacred vessels hidden by Moses on Mt Gerizim. Pilate sent a heavily armed contingent of footmen and cavalry who intercepted the pilgrims and slaughtered most of them. The Samaritans complained to Vitellius, the prefect of Syria, whereupon Pilate was ordered to report to the emperor Tiberius. Another prefect, Marcellus, was then sent by Rome as Pilate's replacement.

Philo records yet another event (*Leg. to Caius* 299-305). While extolling the liberal policies of Tiberius toward Judaism, he cites a negative example in Pontius Pilate. The prefect had erected gilded shields in Herod's former palace in Jerusalem that bore the name of the emperor. Refusing to hear Jewish complaints, the sons of Herod appealed to Tiberius, who ordered Pilate to transfer the shields to the temple of Augustus in Caesarea. The similarities with the parallel story in Josephus have led many scholars to believe that Philo is merely recounting another version of the same event.

Luke mentions a minor incident that contributes to this same portrait. In Luke 13:1 some Jews tell Jesus about the Galileans whose blood Pilate had mixed with their sacrifices. While this story is not corroborated by any other witness, it conforms to the impressions of Pilate's character given by Philo and Josephus. In fact, Luke adds another detail of interest in his trial narrative. In Luke 23:12 he says that prior to the crucifixion of Jesus, Herod Antipas (in Galilee) and Pilate had been at enmity with each other. This may have stemmed not simply from Pilate's usual antagonism but particularly from the Galilean incident.

Pilate's role in the death of Jesus is recorded in each Gospel (Mt 27:2; Mk 15:1; Lk 23:1; Jn 18:29) and was remembered as a historical datum in the preaching of the apostles (Acts 3:13; 4:27; 13:28; 1 Tm 6:13). In order to secure the conviction and death of Jesus, Caiaphas and the Sanhedrin brought their charges to Pilate. While the accusations took on a political flavor to evoke the governor's interest, he still could find no grounds for condemnation. In the end, Pilate unexpectedly accommodates the Jewish leaders and has Jesus crucified.

All of the Gospels and particularly John show Pilate's repeated verdict of Jesus' innocence. According to Matthew 27:19, Pilate's wife had an ominous dream about

Jesus' conviction, and she warned her husband. Pilate tried to have Jesus released, but the crowd cried for Barabbas. Matthew even records that Pilate washed his hands (27:24-25), declaring his own innocence in this. And finally, John says that Pilate refused to alter the title over the cross (Jn 19:19-22). These accounts, therefore, take the full blame for Jesus' death from Pilate and place it on the Jewish leaders of the Sanhedrin. They are ultimately responsible.

But why would Pilate act in behalf of the Sanhedrin? Two answers are possible. First, there may have been collusion between Caiaphas and Pilate that stemmed from a long-standing relationship and coterminous reign. Ten of Caiaphas's eighteen years in power were under Pilate, and when the prefect was dismissed in AD 36, Caiaphas was simultaneously removed. Second, if Jesus' trial occurred in AD 33, Pilate may have been concerned about his impeachment. He had originally been appointed by Sejanus (prefect of the praetorians in Rome who had appointed men to colonial office under Tiberius), but in the autumn of AD 31 Sejanus died. This explains why a Jewish delegation could report directly to Tiberius during the votive shield incident. Hence, the charge recorded in John 19:12 ("If you release this man, you are not Caesar's friend") would have had genuine power over Pilate. Pilate perceived his jeopardy and was anxious to pacify the Jews and please the emperor.

The history of Pilate after his dismissal in AD 36 is unknown. Eusebius reports that Pilate ultimately committed suicide during the reign of the emperor Caligula, AD 37–41 (*History* 2.7).

PILDASH Sixth son of Nahor and Milcah; nephew of Abraham (Gn 22:22).

PILEHA*, PILHA Political leader who set his seal on Ezra's covenant during the postexilic era (Neh 10:24).

PILLAR OF FIRE AND CLOUD One of the most frequent modes of God's appearing to humans in the OT; a visual manifestation of the presence of God common in the narratives of the exodus, Sinai covenant, the wilderness wanderings, and the dedication of the temple. The Bible refers to this phenomenon in a variety of ways: the pillar of cloud and of fire (Ex 14:24); pillar of cloud (Ex 33:9-10; Nm 14:14); pillar of fire (Ex 13:21; Nm 14:14); cloud (Ex 40:34-35; Dt 1:33); fire (Dt 1:33; 4:12). Though the Bible itself does not use this designation, the cloud and associated theophanies (God-appearances) are often called the "Shekinah glory" or simply "the Shekinah"—terms that have entered Christian theology from rabbinic literature.

The cloud theophany is associated with a variety of functions; common to all of them is that it is a visible expression of the presence of God. The cloud filled the tabernacle and was there day and night as a witness to the presence of God (Ex 40:34-38). God appeared in the cloud on the Day of Atonement (Lv 16:2). God's acceptance of the temple built as his dwelling is shown when the cloud comes at the dedication (1 Kgs 8:10-11; 2 Chr 5:13-14).

The cloud was also a protection for Israel. At its first appearance in the events of the exodus, the cloud positioned itself between the armies of Egypt and Israel, engulfing the Egyptians in darkness on the one side while lighting the way with its fire for Israel on the other (Ex 14:19-20). The psalmist recalled how God "spread out a cloud as a covering, and a fire to give light at night" (Ps 105:39, NIV).

The pillar also served as Israel's guide during the

exodus and wandering in the wilderness. "The LORD guided them by a pillar of cloud during the day and a pillar of fire at night. That way they could travel whether it was day or night. And the LORD did not remove the pillar of cloud or pillar of fire from their sight" (Ex 13:21-22, NLT). Whenever the cloud lifted from above the tent, the Israelites set out; wherever the cloud settled, the Israelites encamped (Nm 9:17). In spite of the sins of the people, the Lord God went ahead of them on their journey, in fire by night and in a cloud by day (Dt 1:33). Subsequent generations would recount how God was their guide by day and night (Neh 9:12, 19; Ps 78:14).

The cloud also had an oracular function (Ps 99:7). Not only did God speak from the cloud at Sinai (Ex 19:9, 16; 34:1-25; Dt 4:11-12; 5:22), he also spoke from there when Israel rebelled (Ex 16:10; Nm 14:10; 16:42-43), when Aaron and Miriam had a quarrel with Moses (Nm 12:1-15), and when the 70 elders were appointed. Only Moses had this ready access to the very words of God. When Moses went into the tabernacle, "the pillar of cloud would come down and hover at the entrance while the LORD spoke with Moses" (Ex 33:9, NLT). At the death of Moses the Lord appears in the pillar at the tent and speaks of the coming apostasy of the nation (Dt 31:14-29).

Other theophanies having the features of cloud, fire, and light—or some combination—should probably be associated with the pillar of fire and cloud. Ezekiel saw an immense cloud with flashing lightning and surrounded by a brilliant light (Ez 1:4); when he looked inside the cloud, he saw a fire, creatures in the service of God, the throne of God, and the awesome presence of the one who sat upon it and spoke (vv 5-28). Ezekiel also had a vision of the glory of God leaving the temple, and later a vision of its return (chs 10; 43). In Daniel's vision of the Ancient of Days, he sees one "like a son of man, coming with the clouds of heaven" to receive authority, glory, and power (Dn 7:13, NIV). The phrase "son of man" becomes Jesus' favorite self-designation in the Gospels. At the Transfiguration, when he reveals his own glory, the clouds envelop him (Mt 17:5; Mk 9:7; Lk 9:34). At his ascension he is received into the clouds, and angels remind the apostles of his promise to return in the same way (Acts 1:9-11; see Mt 24:30; Mk 13:26; Lk 21:27; Rv 1:7).

See also Glory; Shekinah; Theophany.

PILTAI Priest and head of Modiah's house during the days of Joiakim the high priest in the postexilic period (Neh 12:17).

PIM* Weight measurement equivalent to about two-thirds of a shekel. *See* Weights and Measures.

PINE TREE *See* Plants.

PINON One of the "chiefs" (NLT "leaders") descended from Esau (Gn 36:41; 1 Chr 1:52).

PIPE English word that translates a number of Hebrew and Greek words designating various tubular wind instruments. *See* Musical Instruments.

PIRAM King of Jarmuth, a Canaanite city located southwest of Jerusalem. After joining an alliance with four Amorite kings against Joshua, Piram—along with other kings—was defeated and killed (Jos 10:3).

PIRATHON Home of Abdon, one of the minor judges (Jgs 12:13-15). It is described as being in the land of Ephraim and in the hill country of the Amalekites. This may indicate that it originally belonged to the Amalekites or that it was seized by them during one of their invasions. Benaiah, one of David's mighty men, is also called a Pirathonite (2 Sm 23:30; 1 Chr 11:31; 27:14). It is generally identified with Ferata, situated on a high rock six miles (9.7 kilometers) southwest of Samaria.

PISGAH, Mount Mountain located at the northeast end of the Dead Sea near the ancient city of Jericho. Balak took Balaam to the top of Pisgah (Nm 23:14), and Moses was told to go to its summit to view the Promised Land (Dt 3:27). Later, Moses returned to the top of Pisgah to die (34:1). Pisgah's slopes border the Dead Sea, or Sea of the Arabah (Dt 3:17; 4:49; Jos 12:3; 13:20). The KJV sometimes refers to these slopes as "Ashdoth-pisgah." Many scholars identify Mt Pisgah with modern Ras es-Siyaghah, just north of Mt Nebo.

See also Nebo, Mount.

PISHON First of four divisions of the river that flowed out of the Garden of Eden (Gn 2:11). Suggestions for its identity include the Rion, the Indus, the Ganges, a canal connecting the Tigris and Euphrates, and a symbol of the Milky Way. No consensus exists on Pishon's identity.

PISIDIA Region included in the Roman province of Galatia at the time of the visit of Paul and Barnabas about AD 48.

It is north of the Taurus mountain range that parallels the coastline of Cilicia and Pamphylia. Separated from these coastal provinces by the mountain range, it lies in the central plateau of Anatolia about 3,600 feet (1,097.3 meters) above sea level. The territory includes the foothills of the Taurus range and measures about 400 miles (643.6 kilometers) long and 165 miles (265.5 kilometers) wide. It was joined by the large province of Asia on the west, by Galatia on the north, and by Lycaonia on the east. The inhabitants of the mountainous terrain were predatory tribesmen who were subjugated with great difficulty over a period of years by the Seleucids and later by the Romans. To assist in controlling these tribes, the city of Antioch was founded by Seleucus I Nicator (312–280 BC). Concern with security led Amyntas of Galatia to strengthen the city (c. 26 BC). At his death in 25 BC, Pisidia was absorbed into the province of Galatia. Augustus undertook the final phase of pacification of the populace by founding five cities in addition to Antioch: Crimma, Comana, Olbase, Parlais, and Lystra, all linked to Antioch by military roads. An inscription, discovered in 1912, indicates that Quirinius (cf. Lk 2:2) was administrator of the district and responsible to Augustus. Its capital, Antioch, was on the main road between Ephesus to the west and Derbe and Tarsus to the east. It was primarily a Roman colony and included a sizeable Jewish community, introduced by the Seleucids for the purpose of trade.

Paul and Barnabas passed through the country at least twice (Acts 13:14; 14:24) in the journey between Perga and Derbe. It was in Antioch of Pisidia that one of the most important decisions in the history of Christian missionary strategy was made and announced. After being rebuffed by a majority of his Jewish audience, accompanied by a more cordial response from the Gentiles, Paul and Barnabas announced, "Since you thrust it [the word of God] from you, and judge yourselves unworthy of eternal life, behold, we turn to the Gentiles" (13:46, RSV). Henceforth, the strategy of Paul and his associates was oriented more specifically to the non-Jewish peoples, thus making Christianity a world religion rather than another Jewish sect.

PISON* KJV translation for the Pishon River in Genesis 2:11. *See* Pishon.

PISPA*, PISPAH Jether's son from Asher's tribe (1 Chr 7:38).

PISTACHIO *See* Food and Food Preparation; Plants.

PIT Word used frequently in the OT to denote the grave, the abode of the dead, or Sheol—that is, a shadowy existence that the living feared because it cut them off from light, joy, and vitality. Godly people abhorred it because it seemed to them that it would negate their fellowship with God: Hezekiah (Is 38:17-18), Job (Jb 17:13-16; 33:22), and the psalmists (Pss 28:1; 30:3; 55:23; 88:4-6).

See also Bottomless Pit; Dead, Place of the; Death; Sheol.

PITCH *See* Asphalt; Bitumen.

PITCHER *See* Pottery.

PITHOM One of the store cities (along with Rameses) built by the Israelites during their Egyptian captivity (Ex 1:11). There has been considerable debate among Egyptologists for over a century as to the identification of these sites. The identification of Rameses is fairly well established as being associated with Pirameses, the capital of Pharaoh Ramses II (1290–1224 BC). A number of ancient sites have been suggested for Rameses, but Tanis in the northeastern Delta for many years was the assumed location. However, Qantir, in the same general region, is the more likely spot.

Pithom is derived from the Egyptian phrase meaning "House of [the god] Atum." This would have been a temple dedicated to the worship of the solar deity Atum. The Israelites would have been involved in building the storage facilities of the temple. Storage facilities from the mortuary temple of Ramses II in Thebes are well-preserved, long rectangular structures with arched roofs. They were built side by side and covered a significant portion of the mortuary complex. This gives us a fairly accurate picture of the sort of structures for which the Israelites were forced to provide bricks.

While the etymology of Pithom is known, its location continues to be a subject of scholarly discussion. The two sites most frequently associated with Pithom are Tell er-Retabah and Tell el-Maskhutah, both located in the Wadi Tumilat, which extends eastward from the Nile Delta to Lake Timsah. Excavations have taken place at both sites in recent years, and both tells have yielded evidence for the presence of Asiatics from Palestine and Syria. Since there might be a link between the Arabic name Maskhutah and Hebrew Succoth (mentioned in Ex 12:37 as a stopping-off point on the route of the exodus), Tell er-Retabah is now thought to be the best possible location for Pithom, and Maskhutah would be Succoth.

See also Egypt, Egyptian; Rameses (Place).

PITHON Benjaminite, Micah's son and a descendant of Jonathan (1 Chr 8:35; 9:41).

PITY *See* Mercy.

PLAGUE Word used to refer to a disease, disaster, or pestilence. Although there is a specific disease known as plague, the term "plague" as used in Scripture is not restricted to a single disease (1 Kgs 8:37; Lk 7:21). Plague can indicate an epidemic disease or refer to widespread calamity like the 10 plagues of Egypt (Ex 7–12).

There is no question that in the Hebrew mind plagues were part of the judgment God sent to individuals, families, and nations. God himself threatened to send plagues to the Israelites in proportion to their sins (Lv 26:21) and took full responsibility for the Egyptian plagues (Jos 24:5). The OT plagues demonstrated God's control over the processes of nature, just as Christ's miracles do in the NT.

At one point in the history of Israel, the Philistines won a battle and captured the ark of God (1 Sm 4:10-11). When the ark was kept at Ashdod, however, God showed his power by allowing a fatal disease characterized by swellings or tumors to be prevalent (5:6). The Philistines sent the ark on to Gath, but people of all ages began to have tumors in the region of the groin (v 9). A similar occurrence at the next city, Ekron, resulted in many deaths (v 12).

Finally, after seven months, the Philistines decided to return the ark of God to Israel along with a guilt offering of five golden rats and five golden tumors (1 Sm 6:1-4). The selection of this unusual offering was made because the Philistine diviners associated the swarms of rodents that marred the land with the plague that was upon them (v 5). The first Israelite village to receive the ark of God from the Philistines was punished with the same disease for looking into it (v 19). The epidemic in Beth-shemesh left 50,070 people dead (cf. NLT mg).

See also Disease; Exodus, Book of; Pestilence; Plagues upon Egypt.

PLAGUES UPON EGYPT Unprecedented series of disasters striking Egypt, probably culminating in spring or early summer (c. 1400 BC). They struck particularly the Nile Delta, although apparently not affecting the area called Goshen. These disasters were of such magnitude that the Egyptians from their earliest history could recall nothing like them (Ex 9:24).

PREVIEW
• The Plagues
• Pharaoh and the Plagues
• The Nature of the Plagues

The Plagues The plagues are described in Exodus 7–11. At first sight one might imagine that the plagues took place in succession within a few weeks, but casual notes of time (see 7:25; 9:31-32), as well as the nature of some of the plagues, would suggest that several months may well have been involved. The first plague was the turning of water into blood (7:20), so that the fish died and the water stank. Next came a plague of frogs (8:6); even after their death, the land was strewn with piles of their bodies (v 14). Next came a plague of lice (v 17), or possibly gnats, sandflies, or mosquitoes. The exact sense of the word is not clear, but it obviously means some small irritating creature. After that came "swarms of flies" (v 24). Again, the meaning is not quite clear. Later Jewish tradition made it swarms of wild beasts, but flies is a much more likely sense. Then some sort of cattle plague struck (9:3), affecting the domestic animals. After that came boils on humans (v 9), boils that erupted into painful blisters and vesicles, apparently irritating rather than fatal. Hail followed (v 18), so severe that nothing like it had been seen before—hail associated with thunder and lightning (v 24). This was so heavy that it could be fatal (v 19), and naturally did great harm to the crops of Egypt (v 31). After that came locusts in vast numbers (10:13)—again on an unparalleled scale. Then came three days of complete darkness (v 22) that brought Egyptian life to a standstill. Finally, all the firstborn of the Egyptians died (12:29)—from Pharaoh's household down to the lowliest homes in the land.

All the plagues are seen in the Bible as successive judgments of God. Normally, each is preceded by a warning from Moses, which is disregarded by Pharaoh, and then each is lifted as a result of temporary repentance on the part of Pharaoh. But it is also clear that the plagues gradually increase in severity and intensity, until the climax comes in the death of the firstborn—with that, even Pharaoh is broken. The first plagues represent discomfort rather than danger for the Egyptians; then their animals and crops are struck down; finally death takes the firstborn, the flower of the nation.

There are certain common features that run through the account of the plagues. At first, Pharaoh's magicians try to belittle the plagues, and the signs that precede them, by producing similar effects themselves (7:11-12; 8:7). This is an interesting warning that miracles may be produced from various sources and that this sort of sign is therefore not important in itself. But the time comes when the magicians are beaten and can no longer compete (8:18); even they admit that this is God's hand (v 19). When the plague of boils comes, the magicians cannot even present themselves before Pharaoh, so bad is their condition. After that, the magicians disappear from the story.

Another motif that becomes increasingly clear as the account of the plagues continues, is the increasing emphasis on the way in which God's people, living in Goshen, were delivered from the plagues that affected the Egyptians. It could be assumed anyway that, as Goshen was not on the Nile, the water that turned to blood and the plague of frogs and mosquitoes might affect them less. But in the case of the later swarms of flies (8:22), the cattle plague (9:4), the hail (v 26), and the darkness (10:23), we are specifically told that Israel was spared; in the case of the death of the firstborn, the Lord "passed over" Israelite homes.

At first, it seems as if the hearts of all the Egyptians are just as hard as that of the pharaoh (7:13). Yet as the story goes on, his own people keep urging him to yield to God. The magicians admit God's role in the plague of lice (8:19). Pharaoh's servants who heeded God's warning through Moses brought their servants and cattle indoors before the great hailstorms, and thus escaped loss and death (9:20). Only the unbelieving suffered. Finally, Pharaoh's own servants exhorted him to let Israel go, bluntly telling him that the land was being ruined by his stubbornness (10:7).

Pharaoh and the Plagues Pharaoh's reaction to God's word is remarkable. Scripture describes the hardness of Pharoah's heart in three ways. Exodus 7:3 speaks of God hardening Pharaoh's heart; 7:14 has the neutral statement that Pharaoh's heart was hardened; and 8:15 has Pharaoh hardening his own heart. Obviously, these all refer to the same process, which must be taken into account in any explanation. Furthermore, Paul must be allowed to have the last word on the matter (Rom 9:18).

But, within this theological framework, there is quite a movement, not merely a succession of shallow repentances designed to secure the removal of the plague, and then a renewed stubbornness, calling down a fresh judgment. There is also a typically Asian bargaining session between Pharaoh and Moses. After Pharaoh's broken promises to let the people go (8:8), he tries to bargain: the people should sacrifice to God in Egypt, without going at all (v 25); only the men should go (10:11); they should all go, but leave their flocks and herds as hostage

(v 24). But there can be no bargaining of this sort in response to the call of God, as Pharaoh was to learn. After the death of the firstborn, he was glad to see the Israelites leave (12:31-33).

In this sense, the whole story of the plagues is a struggle. It has sometimes been seen as the struggle of the prototype prophet, Moses (Dt 18:15), against the prototype king, Pharaoh; while it may be that, it is far more. It is the struggle of Moses, the servant of God, against the magicians. It is the struggle of Moses against mighty Pharaoh, or rather, the confrontation of Pharaoh by God, in the form of the word brought by his servant. At the deepest level, it is a victory won by God over the false gods of Egypt. This gives to many of the stories their peculiar relish. For the Nile is the god Hapi; Hept the frog is a god of fertility and childbirth; Ra the sun (outraged by the darkness) is a god; Hat-hot had the form of a heifer, and Apis that of a bull; the flying hornet symbolized Egypt; and Pharaoh himself was a god. Yet all were helpless before the God of Israel.

The Nature of the Plagues It is not known how God brought about the plagues, and some may think it vain even to ask, since God is free to use whatever means he pleases. Yet the statement that God turned back the waters of the "Reed Sea" by a strong east wind (Ex 14:21) indicates that God could use natural means to bring about his will. The Hebrew concept of "miracle" was not the same as the modern one, which usually regards miracles as "supernatural" and sees all else as "natural" and thus as nonmiraculous. The Hebrews, however, regarded everything in nature as the work of God; it was only that in certain instances he had acted more "wonderfully" (perhaps one would say more "obviously") than others. Therefore, there is nothing in any way rationalistic in saying that on this occasion God may have sent a series of "natural" disasters (the sort of disasters to which Egypt was geographically prone) but so heightened them—and sent them in such rapid succession—that they constituted miracles.

Most of the explanations of this sort assume a year of unusual climatic conditions, and in particular, a variation in the annual rise of the Nile. For instance, either an exceptionally low rise of the Nile (leading to red and muddy water) or an exceptionally high rise of the Nile (bringing down red earth from the Ethiopian highlands) have been suggested as explanations of the first plague. If one feels that the description "turned into blood" would be satisfied by thick blood-colored water, then either would be satisfactory. Another attractive suggestion is the multiplication of red plankton in the water. This phenomenon is fairly common across the world, especially in tropical and subtropical areas. This would make the likeness to blood much closer. In either of these cases, death of fish in foul water, and migration of frogs from the river would be understandable. If the Nile was flooding more widely than usual, the plague of frogs would be even more understandable. Some have seen the sudden death of the frogs as due to some type of internal anthrax; and, with piles of stinking frogs' bodies in the fields, the way was laid wide open both for the carriers of the plagues (flies, etc.) and the plagues that followed.

The next plague, for instance, was one of mosquitoes, sandflies, gnats, or possibly lice. At least the first and the last are potent carriers of disease, and all would cause irritant sores by their bites. The flooding of the stagnant waters of the Nile would give perfect breeding conditions for mosquitoes in particular.

If we are right in assuming that the swarms that followed were swarms of flies, then everything would fit into a divine pattern. Piles of dead frogs, piles of rubbish strewn over the land by the flood (including, no doubt, raw sewage), foul and muddied Nile waters—this would be a prime breeding place for flies. Further, Jewish interpreters suggest that the flies in question were biting or stinging flies (like our gadflies or horseflies). Perhaps these were the agents of the disease of the cattle. Modern interpreters have suggested a particular type of fly, still known in the area, which multiplies very rapidly amid rotting vegetation. The flies and the dust (9:9) between them could have produced that dreaded tropical scourge "prickly heat," easily becoming infected.

Again, in the providence of God, if the Israelites were not in the Delta area, nor actually living along the Nile itself, but concentrated in the Wadi Tumilat to the east, they would be spared these plagues—a fact that did not escape Pharaoh's notice (9:7). The miracle thus lay in God's overruling providence, using his world and its geographic and climatic conditions to do his work of judgment on the stubborn-hearted.

Hail, accompanied by violent thunderstorms (9:24), would be easily explicable (although rare in Egypt), especially in the "funnel" conditions of the Nile Valley, surrounded by hot, dry desert on either side. As to the severity of the hail (more common in Palestine), there are biblical parallels (Jos 10:11). With this plague there is a valuable note of time, given incidentally (Ex 9:31-32) in connection with the crops destroyed by the hail.

In the case of the plague of locusts, God's use of the elements of nature is made plain in the text, where an "east wind" brings them and a "sea wind" takes them away (10:13, 19). The "plague" here is both the enormous number of locusts (see Jl 1:1-12 for another illustration of this scourge) and the timing of their arrival. There are many other places in the OT where the precision of God's timing is shown and where indeed the miraculous element lies in the timing of the event.

The locusts may have darkened the land with their numbers (Ex 10:15), but that was nothing compared with the three days of darkness that followed. Most commentators are agreed that this is the dreaded *khamsin,* the hot desert wind bringing dust storms or sandstorms that fill the sky and may last for days without respite. If the red earth from the Ethiopian highlands had been brought down by the floodwaters of the Nile and deposited widely over the land, some commentators have suggested that it was whipped into the air by this wind, thus giving an even darker pall over the land.

In the case of the last plague, the death of the firstborn, we have no indication of what, if any, particular disease was used by God. Scripture gives us no clue. What can be said is that the Egyptians suffered but the Israelites did not. After this plague, they were free. Henceforth, it was their glad knowledge that none of "the plagues of Egypt" would strike them as God's people (15:26). It was their unshakable belief that these plagues were God's judgment, a punishment on stubborn Pharaoh, but the means of their salvation. Therefore, the plagues are not only a warning to us but also an encouragement. *See* Egypt, Egyptian; Exodus, Book of; Moses; Plague.

PLAIN OF THE PILLAR* KJV for "oak of the pillar," a sacred tree at Shechem, in Judges 9:6. *See* Oak of the Pillar.

PLANE TREE Large spreading tree having a wide trunk and scaly bark, indigenous to Palestine (Gn 30:37; Ez 31:8). *See* Plants.

PLANTS
Identifying biblical plants has always been a difficult task, partly because people continue to identify the biblical elm, sycamore, lily, rose, and vine with modern plants, and also because they assume that all the plants now growing in the Holy Land were there in ancient biblical days, or that the plants referred to in the Bible are still to be found there today. Unfortunately, many plants now quite common in the Holy Land were not there in biblical days. Many plants that once grew in abundance in the Holy Land are now extinct. Some have been driven out by foreign invaders; others have been exterminated or nearly exterminated by overcultivation of the land, the destruction of forests, and the resulting changes in climatic and other environmental conditions. At one time the Holy Land was a land of palm trees, with the date palm as abundant and characteristic there as it was in Egypt, but today the date palm is much less common. Similarly, in antiquity, the towering cedars clothed the slopes of Lebanon and other mountain ranges. Now the few remaining specimens must be carefully fenced in to protect them against trampling and the ravages of goats.

PREVIEW

•Acacia	•Cypress	•Nutmeg
•Acanthus	•Dandelion	Flower
•Algum	•Darnel Grass	•Oak
•Almond	•Dill	•Oil Tree,
•Almug	•Ebony	Oleaster
•Aloe	•Endive	•Oleander
•Apple	•Fig, Fig Tree	•Olive, Olive
•Apricot	•Fir Tree	Tree
•Ash	•Flax	•Onion
•Aspen	•Frankincense	•Palm
•Balm	•Galbanum	•Papyrus
•Barley	•Garlic	•Pine Tree
•Bdellium	•Gourd, Wild	•Pistachio
•Bean	•Hedge	•Plane Tree
•Bitter Herbs	•Henna	•Pomegranate
•Boxthorn,	•Hyacinth	•Poplar
European	•Hyssop	•Quince
•Box Tree	•Juniper	•Reed
•Bramble	•Laurel or Sweet	•Rue
•Broom	Bay	•Rush
•Buckthorn	•Leek	•Saffron
•Bush	•Lentil	•Sage
•Buttercup	•Lettuce	•Spelt
•Calamus	•Lily	•Storax Tree
•Cane	•Lotus Bush	•Sycamore
•Caper Plant	•Mallow	•Tamarisk
•Carob Tree	•Mankdrake	•Terebinth
•Cassia	•Melon	•Thistle, Thorn
•Castor Oil Plant	•Millet	•Tulip
•Cedar	•Mint	•Tumbleweed
•Chicory	•Mulberry	•Vegetable
•Cinnamon	•Mustard	•Vine
•Citron Tree	•Myrrh	•Walnut
•Coriander	•Myrtle	•Water Lily
•Cotton	•Narcissus	•Wheat
•Cucumber	•Nard	•Wormwood
•Cummin	•Nettle	

Acacia *(Acacia tortilis* and *A. seyal)* Any tree or shrub of the mimosa family of plants growing in warm regions. The plant referred to in the KJV as "shittah" (singular) or "shittim" (plural) is undoubtedly the acacia tree, the only timber tree of any considerable size in the Arabian desert. *Acacia tortilis* is by far the largest and most common tree in the desert in which the Israelites wandered for 40 years. It is especially conspicuous on Mt Sinai and was probably the species used for the tabernacle furnishings. *A. seyal* is less common, at least today. It can grow as high as 25 feet (7.6 meters), and bears yellow flowers on twisted branches. The wood is close grained, heavy and hard, orange-brown in color, and much valued in cabinetwork. The ancient Egyptians clamped shut mummy coffins with acacia wood.

Acanthus *(Acanthus syriacus)* The acanthus, perhaps referred to in Job 30:7 and Zephaniah 2:9, is a perennial thistlelike herb or small shrub about three feet (.9 meter) tall, and is a common weed in all Eastern countries. It has been used since time immemorial as a model for the leaf or scroll decorations in art.

Algum *(Juniperus excelsa Bieb)* The timber from Lebanon referred to in 2 Chronicles 2:8 is probably the juniper. Some translators hold, however, that algum and almug are Hebrew variants for the same tree (see NLT mg, 2 Chr 2:8).

See also Almug (below).

Almond *(Amygdalus communis)* The almond is a peachlike tree with saw-toothed pointed leaves and gray bark. It grows to a height of from 10 to 25 feet (3 to 7.6 meters). It blooms very early in the year; its Hebrew name has its roots in "watch for." To the Jews it was a welcome harbinger of spring (Jer 1:11).

Almond Trees

Almug *(Pterocarpus santalinus)* The precious wood imported by King Solomon and used in making the pillars for the temple and for making harps and psalteries (1 Kgs 10:11-12). This timber was brought by sea from Ophir to Ezion-geber, near Elath. Modern authorities suggest that Ophir was either in Arabia, India, or East Africa near Mozambique. The reference to "algum" in 2 Chronicles 2:8 is possibly to this tree. *See* Algum (above).

Aloe *(Aloe succotrina, Aquilaria agallocha)* Chiefly African, lilylike plant of the genus *Aloes*, certain species of which yield a drug and a fiber. Aloe is an aromatic substance mentioned in the Bible, together with myrrh, balm, and other fragrant plants (Ps 45:8; Prv 7:17; Sg 4:14; Jn 19:39). Most scholars think these passages refer to two different plants. The OT plant is likely to have been *Aquilaria agallocha*, the eaglewood, a large tree growing up to 120 feet (36.6 meters) tall with a trunk 12 feet (3.7 meters) in circumference. It is native to northern India, Malaya, and Indochina. The decaying wood is highly fragrant, and as such is highly valued as perfume and incense and for fumigation.

The aloe of John 19:39 is thought to be the true aloe *(Aloe succotrina)*, the juice of which was used by the Egyptians in embalming. Its smell, however, is not very agreeable, and it has a bitter taste. It is sometimes used by veterinarians as a horse medicine.

Apple *(Malus sylvestris)* The identity of the fruit identified by the Hebrew word *tappuach* (Prv 25:11; Sg 2:3, 5; 7:8; 8:5) continues to be debated. In most English translations it has been rendered "apple" because of its close linguistic tie to the Arabic word *tuffah*. Many scholars identify this tree as the apricot, questioning whether apples fit the biblical description "apples of gold" and whether the apple tree was cultivated in ancient Palestine. Recent excavations at Kadesh-barnea, however, have uncovered carbonized apples, probably a crab apple *(Malus sylvestris)*, dating to the ninth century BC. This would certainly allow for this ornamental apple's cultivation in Solomon's gardens.

See also Apricot (below).

Apricot *(Prunus armeniaca)* The identification of the Hebrew word *tappuach* with the apricot continues to be debated. The apricot tree produces yellow-orange peachlike edible fruit and is native to western Asia and Africa. It is abundant in the Holy Land and probably has been so since early biblical times. The tree is a round-headed reddish-barked tree growing 30 feet (9.1 meters) tall. Most translations render this Hebrew word "apple," though many scholars identify it with the apricot because of its descriptions in the biblical text (see Prv 25:11; Sg 2:3, 5; 7:8; 8:5; Jl 1:12).

See also Apple (above).

Ash *(Alhagi maurorum, Fraxinus ornus, Tamarix mannifera)* There are several ash trees found in the Near East. One of these, the prickly alhagi *(Alhagi maurorum)*, is a member of the pea family. It is a low, many-stemmed, much-branched shrub growing about three feet (.9 meter) tall with somewhat hairy twigs and pealike flowers. During the heat of the day, leaves exude a sweet, gummy substance that hardens in the air and is collected by shaking the bushes over a spread-out cloth.

The manna tamarisk *(Tamarix mannifera)* is a multi-branched shrub or a small tree 9 to 15 feet (2.7 to 4.6 meters) tall with rigid branches that have tiny pink flowers. It is found on deserts from the Holy Land to Arabia and the Sinai.

The flowering or manna ash *(Fraxinus ornus)* is a tree that grows from 15 to 50 feet (4.6 to 15.2 meters) tall. The fruits are very similar to those produced by our species of ash. The ash of Isaiah 44:14 (KJV) is believed to be the Aleppo pine.

Aspen *(Populus euphratica or P. tremula)* Any of several trees of the genus *Populus* with leaves attached by flattened leafstalks so that they tremble or "quake" in the wind.

Balm *(Balanites aegyptiaca, Pistacia lentiscus, Commiphora opobalsamum)* An oily aromatic resin exuded by chiefly tropical trees and shrubs and used medicinally; trees and shrubs producing this substance. References in Genesis 37:25, Jeremiah 8:22, 46:11, and 51:8 are thought to be either the Jericho balsam *(Balanites aegyptiaca)* or the lentisk or mastic tree *(Pistacia lentiscus)*. The Jericho balsam is very common in Egypt, North Africa, the plains of Jericho, and the hot plains bordering on the Dead Sea. It is a small desert-loving plant, 9 to 15 feet (2.7 to 4.6 meters) tall, with slender, thorny branches and small clusters of green flowers.

The lentisk or mastic tree is native to the Holy Land, and the reference in Genesis 43:11 is probably to this plant, since the implication is that this is a native product of the Holy Land unknown in Egypt at the time. This tree is a shrubby or bushy tree 3 to 10 feet (.9 to 3 meters) tall with evergreen leaves. The "balm" is a fragrant gummy exudation of the sap secured by making incisions in the stems and branches, usually in August. The best grades are in the form of yellow-white translucent tears or drops; they are employed in medicine as an astringent. The poorer grades are used extensively as a varnish. Children in the East use it as chewing gum.

References to spices in 1 Kings 10:10, 2 Kings 20:13, Song of Songs 3:6, Isaiah 39:2, and Ezekiel 27:17 are thought to be the balm of Gilead (*Commiphora opobalsamum*), which in spite of its name is not a native of Gilead or even of the Holy Land but is indigenous to Arabia, especially the mountainous regions of Yemen. The trees were still in existence on the plain of Jericho at the time of the Roman conquest. The Roman conquerors carried branches to Rome as trophies of their victory over the Jews.

This tree is a small, stiff-branched evergreen tree seldom more than 15 feet (4.6 meters) high with straggling branches. The "balm" is obtained by making incisions in the stem and branches of the tree. The sap soon hardens into small irregular nodules that are collected. Gum is also procured from green and ripe fruit.

See also Myrrh (below).

Barley (*Hordeum distichon*) A cereal grass bearing bearded flower spikes and edible seeds. The common barley (*Hordeum distichon*), the winter barley (*H. hexastichon*), and the spring barley (*H. vulgare*) have been cultivated in temperate regions of the world since time immemorial and today still constitute one of the principal grain foods. Barley and wheat were the two staple cereal crops of Egypt and the Holy Land. Being less expensive, barley was mostly used for feeding cattle, although it was also used by itself or mixed with wheat and other seed as food for man (Ez 4:9-12). Barley is mentioned in the Bible over 30 times, either as a plant growing in the fields or in reference to products made from it, such as barley meal, barley bread, barley cakes, and barley loaves. As the common food of the poor, barley was also regarded as a symbol of poverty and cheapness or worthlessness (Hos 3:2).

Bdellium (*Commiphora africana*) Aromatic gum resin similar to myrrh, produced by various trees of the genus *Commiphora* of Africa and western Asia. The reference in Genesis 2:12 and Numbers 11:7 to bdellium is thought by most scholars today to refer to a gum resin, obtained from a shrub, *Commiphora africana*, that grows in south Arabia and northeastern Africa. The resin is yellowish, transparent, and fragrant, and looks like a pearl.

Bean (*Faba vulgaris*) The references in 2 Samuel 17:27-28 and Ezekiel 4:9 are generally regarded as referring to the broad bean. This species, an annual plant, is thought originally to have grown in northern Persia, but it was extensively cultivated in western Asia in very early times as a food plant. Beans have been found in the mummy coffins of Egyptian tombs, and they were also cultivated by the Greeks and Romans.

Bitter Herbs (*Cichorium endivia, Taraxacum officinale, Lactuca sativa*) The "bitter herbs" of Exodus 12:8 and Numbers 9:11 seem to have been plants like endive (*Cichorium endivia*), the common chicory (*Cichorium intybus*), lettuce (*Lactuca sativa*), or the common dandelion (*Taraxacum officinale*). These are all weedy plants common in modern Egypt and western Asia and are still eaten by people living there. The leaves of the ordinary garden lettuce are intensely bitter when bleached. This is also true of the common dandelion. Others suggest that the bitter herbs were derived from thorns and thistles.

Boxthorn, European (*Lycium europaeum*) Various thorny shrubs, some species of which bear purplish flowers and brightly colored berries. The reference in Judges 9:14-15 is thought to be to the European boxthorn or desert-thorn. It is a thorny shrub 6 to 12 feet (1.8 to 3.7 meters) tall with clustered leaves and small violet flowers eventually producing small globular red berries. It is native to and common throughout the Holy Land, especially in the region from Lebanon to the Dead Sea.

Box Tree (*Buxus longifolia*) The long-leaved box tree is a hardy evergreen tree found in the mountainous regions of the northern part of the Holy Land, the Galilean hills, and Lebanon. It grows to a height of about 20 feet (6.1 meters) with a slender trunk seldom more than six to eight inches (15.2 to 20.3 centimeters) in diameter. Its wood is very hard and takes a fine polish. It was cultivated by the Romans for its hard wood, which they inlaid with ivory for cabinets and jewel caskets. Scriptural references include Isaiah 41:19 and 60:13.

Bramble (*Rubus sanctus, R. ulmifolius*) The Palestinian bramble (*Rubus sanctus*) and the closely related elm-leaf bramble (*R. ulmifolius*) are prickly evergreen shrubs that spread by means of suckers. The stems and young shoots are covered with a characteristic bloom or whitish powder and short hairs. The prickles are strong, erect, and hairy. The flowers are white, pink, rose, or purple in color, and the fruit is round and black.

See also Thistle, Thorn (below).

Broom (*Retama raetam*) A shrub native to Eurasia. The word translated "juniper" in the KJV has nothing to do with the true junipers but refers rather to a species of broom, known as the white broom (*Retama raetam*). Its branches are longer and flexible, forming an erect, dense bush 3 to 12 feet (.9 to 3.7 meters) tall. The leaves are small and sparse, yet it forms an agreeable shade in a desert region. The white pealike flowers are sweet and very fragrant and are borne in clusters along the twigs. It is a beautiful shrub that grows in the desert regions of Palestine, Syria, and Persia. In many desert areas it is the only bush that affords any shade (1 Kgs 19:4-5).

The "juniper roots" of Job 30:4 are not the roots of either the juniper or white broom. The roots of the latter are very nauseating and could not be eaten in the manner described by Job. Job's "juniper roots" were probably an edible parasitic plant (*Cynomorium coccineum*). This plant grows in salt marshes and maritime sands. It is frequently eaten in times of food scarcity and at one time was highly prized for its supposed medicinal value in the treatment of dysentery.

Buckthorn (*Rhamnus palaestina*) The Palestinian buckthorn is a shrub or small tree attaining a height of three to six feet (.9 to 1.8 meters) with velvety, thorny branches, evergreen leaves, and clusters of small flowers blooming in March or April. It grows in thickets and on hillsides from Syria and Lebanon through the Holy Land to Arabia and the Sinai.

Bush (*Acacia nilotica, Loranthus acaciae*) Low, branching, woody plant, usually smaller than a tree. There are differences of opinion in regard to the bush out of which the Lord appeared to Moses (Ex 3:2-4). From the biblical account, it seems most likely that the event was a miraculous one. However, some seek a natural explanation and believe that the burning bush may have been the crimson-flowered mistletoe or acacia strap flower (*Loranthus acaciae*), which grows in great profusion as a partial parasite on the various acacia shrubs, such as the thorny acacia (*Acacia nilotica*), in the Holy

Land and Sinai. When in full bloom, the mistletoe imparts to the shrub or tree the appearance of being on fire because its brilliant flame-colored blossoms stand out against the green foliage and yellow flowers of the host plants.

Buttercup (Ranunculus asiaticus) The Persian buttercup is one of the flowers or grasses of the field (Mt 6:28-30). It is a showy plant blooming in all brilliant colors except blue, with double flowers sometimes measuring two inches (5.1 centimeters) across.

Calamus (Acorus calamus, Andropogon aromaticus) A plant, or its aromatic root; any of a variety of tropical Asiatic palms. One of the plants that grew in Solomon's garden (Sg 4:14). The sweet flag (Acorus calamus) and the beardgrass (Andropogon aromaticus) have been suggested as the plants from which calamus came. The sweet flag is highly aromatic and grows in Europe and Asia, but it is not known in the Holy Land. Indigenous to India, beardgrass is highly odoriferous when bruised and is thought to have furnished the calamus of the Bible. It yields an oil known as ginger-grass oil.

Cane (Saccharum officinarum) It is thought that there were two species of sugarcane indigenous to and growing wild in the Holy Land. One of these, Saccharum sara, is known to be only from Lebanon. The other native species is S. biflorum, which grows on the banks of ditches and streams from Syria and Lebanon through the Holy Land south to Stony Arabia and the Sinai. This may be the wild cane familiar to the Jews. Most authorities, however, think that the "sweet cane" of Isaiah 43:24 was the true sugarcane (S. officinarum). This plant is thought to have originated in the tropics of the eastern hemisphere. It has been cultivated by people since time immemorial and is not now known in the wild state anywhere. It is a tall, stout perennial grass, maizelike in aspect with many jointed stems and a large plumelike terminal cluster of flowers.

Caper Plant (Capparis sincula) Spiny, trailing shrub of Mediterranean region; the flower bud of this shrub. The word "desire" in Ecclesiastes 12:5 may actually refer to the caper berry. The common caper or caper berry grows profusely in Syria, Lebanon, the Holy Land, and in the mountain valleys of Sinai. The plant may sometimes grow upright but more generally spreads itself weakly over the ground like a vine, covering rocks, ruins, and old walls like ivy. The young flower buds, pickled in vinegar, were used by the ancients as a condiment for meat. The berries were also used in cooking.

Carob Tree (Ceratonia siliqua) Evergreen of the Mediterranean region having edible pods. Scholars generally agree that the pods of the carob or locust tree were the "husks" of Jesus' parable of the prodigal son (Lk 15:16). The carob is an attractive evergreen leguminous tree that is very common throughout the Holy Land, Syria, and Egypt. The pods are most abundant in April and May and contain numerous pealike seeds embedded in an agreeably flavored mucilaginous sweetish pulp. The pods are also used abundantly now as they were in antiquity for feeding cattle, horses, and pigs. In time of scarcity, they are used as human food and perhaps even regularly by the very poor. The carob is frequently mentioned in the Talmud as a source of good food for domestic animals. The seeds of the carob were formerly employed as a standard of weight and are the source of the term "carat." Some commentators suggest that the "locusts" eaten by John the Baptist (Mt 3:4) were not insects but the fruit of the carob tree.

Cassia (Cinnamomum cassia, Saussurea lappa) Tree of tropical Asia with bark similar but inferior to cinnamon. The "cassia" of Exodus 30:24 and Ezekiel 27:19 is the cassia bark tree, Cinnamomum cassia. In Psalm 45:8 the reference seems to be to the Indian orris, Saussurea lappa.

Castor Oil Plant (Ricinus communis) Large plant, native to tropical Africa and Asia, cultivated for ornamental reasons and for extraction of oil from its seeds. The gourd of Jonah 4:6-7 was probably the ordinary castor bean. The castor bean is a tender shrub, growing 3 to 12 or more feet (.9 to 3.7 meters) tall with huge leaves that resemble the outstretched human hand. The castor bean plant is found in waste places, especially near water, in both Lebanon and the Holy Land and often is cultivated. In hot climates it becomes treelike and affords a dense shade by the abundance of its huge, umbrella-like leaves. It is known in the Orient for the rapidity of its growth. The oil extracted from the seeds of the castor bean was used by the Jews in ceremonial rites and is mentioned among the five kinds of oil that rabbinical tradition sanctioned for such use. The seeds themselves are poisonous when eaten.

Cedar (Cedrus libani) Any of several coniferous evergreen trees of the genus native to the Old World. With few exceptions, the references to "cedar" are to the well-known cedar of Lebanon. This is a noble tree, the tallest and most massive with which the Israelites were acquainted. It grows quite rapidly, attaining a height of up to 120 feet (36.6 meters) with a trunk diameter of as much as 8 feet (2.4 meters). In Solomon's day these trees were obviously abundant on the mountains of Lebanon, but now, because of excessive lumbering, they are very rare. The cedar of Lebanon was held in high esteem not only for its vigor, beauty, and age but also for the fragrance and remarkable lasting qualities of the wood. It symbolizes grandeur, might, majesty, dignity, lofty stature, and wide expansion. References in Ezekiel 17:3, 22-24, and 31:3-18 beautifully illustrate how these lofty kings of the forest symbolize and typify worldly strength, power, and glory.

Chicory (Cichorium intybus) See Bitter Herbs (above).

Cinnamon (Cinnamomum zeylanicum) Two varieties of trees of this genus, native to tropical Asia, with aromatic bark that, when ground, is used as a spice. The cinnamon of Exodus 30:23, Proverbs 7:17, Song of Songs 4:14, and Revelation 18:13 is undoubtedly Cinnamomum zeylanicum. The tree is a rather low-growing one, never getting more than 30 feet (9.1 meters) high, with a smooth, ash-colored bark and widespread branches and white flowers. Its shiny, beautifully veined evergreen leaves grow about nine inches (22.9 centimeters) long and two inches (5.1 centimeters) wide.

The Jews always regarded cinnamon as a deliciously fragrant substance and valued it highly as a spice and a perfume. It was one of the principal ingredients used in the manufacture of the precious ointments, or "holy oil," that Moses was commanded to use in the tabernacle for anointing the sacred vessels and officiating priests. It was undoubtedly very costly and precious.

Citron Tree (Tetraclinis articulata) Tree native to Asia bearing lemonlike fruit with a thick, fragrant rind. It seldom exceeds a height of 30 feet (9.1 meters) and has hard, dark-colored, durable, fragrant wood that takes a fine polish. The wood was one of the most highly prized woods of the ancients, who employed it extensively for cabinetwork. It was commonly referred to as being worth its weight in gold. The wood, owing to its resinous properties, is slow to decay and remains practically uninjured by insects.

Coriander (*Coriandrum sativum*) The references in Exodus 16:31 and Numbers 11:7 are clearly to the common coriander plant. The coriander was found quite commonly growing along with grain in cultivated fields throughout the Holy Land. It grows wild in Egypt and was used by the ancients both as condiment and as a medicine. The leaves are quite aromatic and are used in soups and for flavoring puddings, curries, and wines. The coriander is still used today as a spice by the Arabs. In Scripture it is mentioned only in connection with manna, which was said to resemble coriander seeds in size, shape, and color.

Cotton (*Gossypium herbaceum*) Any of various plants or shrubs of this genus grown in warm climates for the soft white fiber attached to their seeds and the oil from these seeds. The "green" of the KJV in Esther 1:6 is undoubtedly a reference to the Levant cotton (*Gossypium herbaceum*) that was cultivated since time immemorial in the Far East. Alexander the Great brought it back from India. It is probable that the Jews became acquainted with cotton during the period of their Persian captivity under King Ahasuerus.

Cucumber (*Cucumis chate, C. sativus*) The cucumber is an annual climbing or trailing vine, the origin of which is unknown. It has been cultivated in all the warm countries of the Old World since prehistoric times. Cucumbers are usually eaten raw; a cucumber and a barley cake or some other kind of bread often constitute a meal. The reference to "a lodge in a garden of cucumbers" (Is 1:8) refers to the crudely built small house or lodge often set up in Palestinian cucumber fields and vineyards.

Cummin (*Cuminum cyminum*) The references in Isaiah 28:25-27 and Matthew 23:23 are clearly to the cummin—a common, annual plant of the carrot family said to be native to Egypt and the region of the eastern Mediterranean. It has long been cultivated for its powerfully aromatic and pungent seeds, which are similar to caraway seeds but larger. They do not have as agreeable a taste as caraway seeds but nevertheless were used extensively as a flavor or spice and sometimes were even mixed with flour in making bread. Cummin was also used medicinally and as a condiment with fish and meats.

Cypress (*Cupressus sempervirens horizontalis*) The cypress is a massive, tall-growing evergreen with scalelike leaves and is widely distributed in the mountainous regions of the Holy Land. On Mt Lebanon and Mt Hermon it grows together with the cedar and oak. Its usual height is 50 to 60 feet (15.2 to 18.3 meters), but it may grow as tall as 80 feet (24.2 meters). It is said to have been used extensively in shipbuilding by the Phoenicians, Cretans, and Greeks. There is general agreement that the "gopher wood" of Genesis 6:14 is cypress because the wood is very durable.

Dandelion (*Taraxacum officinale*) *See* Bitter Herbs (above).

Darnel Grass (*Lolium temulentum*) It is generally agreed that the "tares" of the KJV (Mt 13:24-30) are the annual or bearded darnel grass. It is a strong grass closely resembling wheat or rye in appearance. The seeds are much smaller than those of wheat or rye, but it is extremely difficult to distinguish it from wheat or rye in its early stages. If it is not eradicated early but is left until the time of harvest, it is cut down with the wheat and the

two are subsequently very difficult to separate. The seeds are poisonous, either due to some chemicals naturally present or because of a fungus that grows within the seeds.

Dill (*Anethum graveolens*) Dill is a weedy annual plant resembling parsley and fennel, 12 to 20 inches (30.5 to 50.8 centimeters) tall with yellow flowers. The reference in Matthew 23:23 (KJV) to anise is probably a reference to dill. This plant is widely cultivated for seeds that are aromatic and carminative.

Ebony (*Diospyros ebenaster, D. ebenum, D. melanoxylon*) Chiefly tropical tree of southern Asia with hard, dark-colored heartwood. Ebony comes from the date plum or date tree (*Diospyros ebenaster* and *D. melanoxylon*) of India and is quite different from the date palm. It was sent by Phoenician ships across the Arabian Sea and up the Red Sea to the market in Tyre, from which it was carried overland by camel caravans. The outer wood of these trees is white and soft, but when old, the interior wood becomes hard, black, heavy, and durable and still constitutes most of the costly ebony of commerce. Ebony takes on a fine polish and is highly valued for cabinetwork, for turnery, for the manufacture of fancy ornamental articles and instruments, and as a veneer for other woods.

Ezekiel mentions ivory and ebony together (Ez 27:15). Ebony was and still is frequently inlaid with ivory, with which it contrasts so strikingly in color.

Endive (*Cichorium endivia*) *See* Bitter Herbs (above).

Fig, Fig Tree (*Ficus carica*) Any of several trees or shrubs of this genus, native to the Mediterranean region; its edible fruit. The common fig, mentioned some 60 times in the Bible, is one of the most important Bible plants. Its leaves are spoken of first in Genesis 3:7. The fig is generally regarded as native to southwestern Asia and Syria, but already in early times it was also cultivated extensively in Egypt and the Holy Land, where it was one of the principal foods. First Samuel 25:18 states that a part of the gift sent by Abigail to David consisted of 200 cakes of figs.

The fig tree has a very peculiar type of fruit called a syconium, which is actually a very much enlarged and fleshy receptacle. It is pollinated by a wasp, without which it cannot get its fruit; this was discovered when it was first transplanted to California.

The fig puts out its earliest fruit buds before its leaves, the former in February and the latter in April or May. When the leaves are out, the fruit ought to be ripe (Mt 21:19).

Whenever the prophets of old berated the people for their wickedness, they often threatened that the vine and the fig crops would be destroyed. And when they held out the promise of great rewards, they said that the vine and fig crop would be restored (Jer 8:13; Hos 2:12; Jl 1:7, 12; Mi 4:4; Zec 3:10).

Fir Tree (*Abies cilicica*) This a generic term for various evergreen trees having flat needles and erect cones. In all probability, most of the references in Scripture to the fir are references to the pine, cypress, or juniper. The only true fir in the Holy Land grows in the higher parts of Lebanon and the mountains northward. It attains a height of 30 to 75 feet (9.1 to 22.9 meters) and is widely cultivated.

Flax (*Linum usitatissimum*) Any of several plants of this genus, one particularly being widely cultivated for the linseed oil from its seeds and the fine textile fibers from its stems. Flax is the oldest known of the textile fibers. Cotton is identified only once in the Bible (Est 1:6). There is no mention of any other fiber plant being cultivated in Egypt or the Holy Land in biblical days, and for that reason it is thought that linen was the material out of which clothes other than woolen ones were made. Linen was also used for domestic purposes such as towels (Jn 13:4-5), napkins (11:44), girdles and undergarments (Is 3:23; Mk 14:51), nets (Is 19:8-9), and measuring lines (Ez 40:3). The priests serving in the temple were to wear nothing but linen clothes; a mixed cloth of wool and flax together was strictly forbidden to the Jews (Lv 19:19; Dt 22:11).

At least three kinds of linen were used in biblical times, and apparently there were particular uses for each kind. Ordinary linen of coarsest texture is mentioned in Leviticus 6:10, Ezekiel 9:2, Daniel 10:5, and Revelation 15:6. The second type of linen of superior quality is mentioned in Exodus 26:1 and 39:27. A third type of linen of finest texture and high cost is mentioned in 1 Chronicles 15:27, Esther 8:15, and Revelation 19:8.

The common flax plant grows from one to four feet (.3 to 1.2 meters) tall with a simple, slender, wirelike stem and numerous small, pale, lancelike green leaves. The failure of the flax crop is listed as one of God's punishments (Hos 2:9). The manufacture of linen from flax fibers was a domestic industry of Jewish women (Prv 31:13, 19), ranging from ordinary clothing to the robes and aprons worn by the priest and temple attendants. Linen was also used for wicks in lamps (Is 42:3).

Frankincense (Boswellia) Aromatic genus resin used chiefly as incense. Frankincense is obtained from three species of a single genus of plants that grow in southern Arabia, Ethiopia, Somaliland, India, and the East Indies. The trees are large in size, related to the turpentine or terebinth tree and to those that produce balsam and myrrh. The gum has a bitter taste and gives off a strong odor in the form of a volatile oil when warmed or burned. It is obtained by successive incisions in the bark of the trunk and in the branches of living trees. It is thought that the Hebrews imported all their frankincense from Arabia, especially from the region about Sheba.

Frankincense is mentioned 21 times in the Bible (e.g., Ex 30:34; 1 Chr 9:29; Neh 13:9; Sg 3:6; 4:6, 14; Mt 2:11; Rv 18:13) and was probably employed almost exclusively in the sacrificial services of the tabernacle and temple until the time of Solomon. It has always been the most important incense resin in the world.

Galbanum (Ferula galbaniflua) Galbanum is a malodorous yellowish or brownish gum resin containing the chemical substance umbelliferone, obtained from several species of plants related to the fennel, native to Syria and Persia. The gum is a natural exudation of the stem or is obtained by making a transverse incision in the young stem a few inches above the ground. The milky juice soon hardens and forms one of the kinds of commercial galbanum. Its odor is strongly balsamic, pungent, and disagreeable when burned. Galbanum was one of the ingredients used to form the "holy incense" (Ex 30:34).

Garlic (Allium sativum) *See* Onion (below).

Gourd, Wild (Citrullus colocynthis) There has been considerable difference of opinion regarding the meaning of the words translated "wild gourds" (2 Kgs 4:39) or "gall" (Dt 29:18; 32:32; Ps 69:21; Jer 8:14; 9:15; 23:15; Lam 3:5, 19; Am 6:12; Mt 27:34; Acts 8:23). Most scholars today believe the plant referred to was the colocynth, a cucumber-like vine that trails on the ground or climbs over shrubs and fences. The fruit contains a soft spongy pulp, which is intensely bitter, strongly cathartic, and sometimes poisonous.

Hedge (Rhamnus palaestina, Balanites aegyptiaca, Lycium europaeum) Row of closely planted shrubs or low-growing trees forming a fence or boundary. A number of plants were used to provide hedges in Bible times. One of these was the Palestine buckthorn, *Rhamnus palaestina*. This plant is a shrub or a small tree growing from three to six feet (.9 to 1.8 meters) tall with velvety, thorny branches, evergreen leaves, and clusters of small flowers blooming in March and April. It grows in thickets and on hillsides from Syria through the Holy Land to Arabia and the Sinai. The Jericho balsam *(Balanites aegyptiaca)* and the European boxthorn *(Lycium europaeum)* are also prickly shrubs widely used as hedges in the Holy Land and may be the plants referred to in Proverbs 15:19 and Hosea 2:6.

Henna (Lawsonia inermis) Tree or shrub of Asia and northern Africa with fragrant reddish or white flowers and leaves from which a reddish dye is made. The plant referred to in Song of Songs 1:14 and 4:13 and translated as "camphire" (KJV) is thought by scholars today to refer to the henna plant. It is a native of northern India and grows wild in the Sudan, Egypt, Arabia, Syria, Lebanon, and the Holy Land. It grows from 4 to 12 feet (1.2 to 3.7 meters) tall, and its scent is similar to that of roses.

Henna leaves are dried, crushed into a powder, mixed with water, and made into a paste that has been used since time immemorial as a cosmetic. A number of mummies have been found decorated with henna. Henna was used to provide a bright yellow, orange, or red color to the fingernails, toenails, the tips of the fingers, the palms of the hand, and the soles of the feet of young girls. Men also used it for coloring their beards and the manes and tails of horses. The dye had to be renewed once every two or three weeks. This use of henna as a cosmetic was common in Egypt at the time the children of Israel were there as slaves; they were undoubtedly familiar with it.

Hyacinth (Hyacinthus orientalis) The lily referred to in Song of Songs 2:1-2, 16; 4:5; and 6:2-4 may well be the garden hyacinth. It is native to, and very common in, the fields and rocky places in the Holy Land, Lebanon, and northward. Its flowers in the wild form are always deep blue and very fragrant.

See also Lily (below).

Hyssop (Origanum maru) Woody plant native to Asia with spikes of small blue flowers and aromatic leaves used as a condiment and in perfumery. There is little agreement among botanists as to the exact identity of the biblical "hyssop." Some have suggested *Hyssopus officinalis,* the well-known garden herb now called hyssop. However, this plant is not native either to the Holy Land or Egypt, being found only in southern Europe. Moreover, it does not fit the requirements of the biblical plant.

The "hyssop" of the OT is likely the Syrian or Egyptian marjoram *(Origanum maru).* It is referred to in Exodus 12:22; Leviticus 14:4-6, 52; Numbers 19:6, 18; 1 Kings 4:33; Psalm 51:7;

Hyssop

and Hebrews 9:19. The marjorams are mints growing (under favorable conditions) about two or three feet (.6 to .9 meter) tall, but more often are dwarfed when growing in rock crevices and walls (cf. 1 Kgs 4:33). An aromatic substance is obtained from the crushed and dried leaves. If gathered together in a bunch with leaves and flowers, the hairy stems of the marjoram would hold liquid very well and would make an excellent sprinkler.

The hyssop of the crucifixion passage in the NT (Jn 19:29) is probably the sorghum, a tall cereal plant grown primarily for food but also used for brushes and mops.

Juniper (Juniperus) Variety of evergreen tree or shrub. The plant referred to in Jeremiah 17:6 and 48:6 and translated in the KJV "heath" is probably the savin or Phoenician juniper. The Phoenician juniper, *Juniperus phoenicia*, is found in the hills and rocky places of Arabia. The savin juniper, *J. sabina*, is common throughout the deserts, plains, and rocky places of Syria and Palestine. These references are to the brown-berried cedar, or sharp cedar.

Laurel or Sweet Bay (Laurus nobilis) Shrub or tree native to the Mediterranean region. While the reference in Psalm 37:35 may be to the cedar of Lebanon, most scholars refer the "green bay tree" (KJV) of the psalmist to the sweet bay, a native of the Holy Land, inhabiting thickets and woods from the coast to the middle montane zone. It is an evergreen tree attaining a height from 40 to 60 feet (12.2 to 18.3 meters).

Even though the tree is abundant on Mt Carmel and around Hebron, it is generally not common in the Holy Land. Its leaves are still used as a condiment, and its fruit, leaves, and bark have long been used in medicine.

Leek (Allium porrum) See Onion (below).

Lentil (Lens esculenta) The lentil plant to which Genesis 25:29-34, 2 Samuel 17:27-29, 23:11, and Ezekiel 4:9 refer is a small, erect, annual, vetchlike plant with slender stems and tendril-bearing leaves. It produces small, white, violet-striped flowers with flat, pealike pods in which the lentils are borne.

Lettuce (Lactuca sativa) See Bitter Herbs (above).

Lily (Lilium) Any of various plants of the genus *Lilium* having large, variously colored, trumpet-shaped flowers; and related plants. The lily is one of the most famous of all the plants in the Bible, but it is also one about which there has been considerable difference of opinion. It seems probable that several kinds of plants, perhaps five or six, are called lilies in the KJV. Most authorities regard the Palestine anemone or wind flower, *Anemone coronaria*, as the "lily of the field" (Mt 6:28, KJV) that surpassed Solomon in all his glory. These flowers are found in every part of the Holy Land in profusion; the most common forms are scarlet or yellow, but the Palestine anemone may also be blue, purple, rose, or white in color. The flower attains a diameter of two and three-quarter inches (7 centimeters).

An alternative suggestion is the Palestinian chamomile, *Anthemis palaestina*, a common, white, daisylike plant. The chamomile is gathered like dry grass and thrown into the furnace when it dries up.

Another proposed plant is *Lilium chalcedonicum*, the scarlet or Martagon lily. The statement in Song of Songs 5:13—"his lips like lilies"—would better fit this plant than the Palestine anemone. The reference is apparently to a rare plant of exceptional beauty. The scarlet lily is rare in the Holy Land; indeed, some botanists doubt that it lives there.

The references in 1 Kings 7:19, 22, 26 and 2 Chronicles 4:5 are probably to the water lily, *Nymphaea alba*, which served as the pattern. The water lily is quite common in Europe and also in the Holy Land and northern Africa.

Lotus Bush (Zizyphus lotus) The "shady trees" of Job 40:21-22 (KJV; cf. NLT "lotus plants") may refer to the lotus bush of the Middle East, *Zizyphus lotus*, a shrub or low tree that grows to a height of about five feet (1.5 meters) with smooth, zigzag, whitish branches.

Other commentators believe that the shady trees of Job are large-leafed trees such as the plane tree, *Platanus orientalis*, or the oleander, *Nerium oleander*. This suggestion is based on the assumption that the animal described in Job 40 is the hippopotamus, and it seems unlikely that the hippopotamus would live under a lotus bush or even be found in places where this shrub grows. These individuals regard the plane tree or the oleander as more likely.

Mallow (Atriplex) The Hebrew word used in Job 30:4 implies saltiness, and for this reason botanists believe that it refers to one of the species of the saltwort or orach. Twenty-one species of saltwort occur in the Holy Land, almost all of which are common and could well meet the requirements of the text. *Atriplex halimus* is the species usually suggested, a strong-growing bushy shrub related to the spinach.

Mandrake (Mandragora officinarum) The mandrake or love apple is a stemless herbaceous perennial related to the nightshade, potato, and tomato. It has a large, beetlike, often forked taproot from the top of which arise many dark leaves about a foot (30.5 centimeters) long and four inches (10.2 centimeters) wide. The plant is slightly poisonous, and the thick taproots have some resemblance in shape to the lower parts of the human body. For this reason certain aphrodisiac properties were ascribed to it (cf. Gn 30:14-16).

The love apple was a common plant in deserted fields throughout the Holy Land. It is native to the entire Mediterranean region, southern Europe, and Asia Minor. The mandrake is mentioned in Song of Songs 7:13, though some scholars believe the writer may actually have been referring to the citron or to the common edible field mushroom, *Agaricus campestris*.

Melon (Cucumis melo, Citrullus vulgaris) Any of several varieties of these two related vines having a hard rind and juicy flesh. The melons of Numbers 11:5 may be either the muskmelon (*Cucumis melo*) or the watermelon (*Citrullus vulgaris*). It may be that both fruits are referred to.

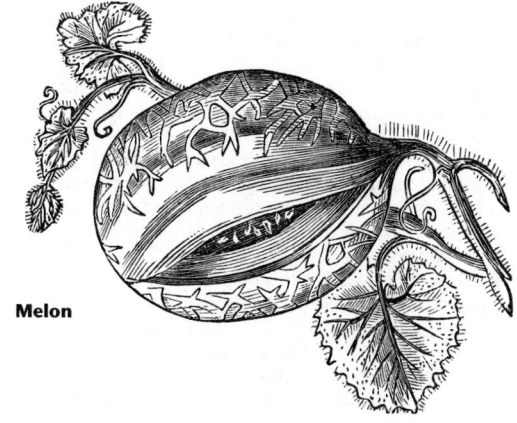

Melon

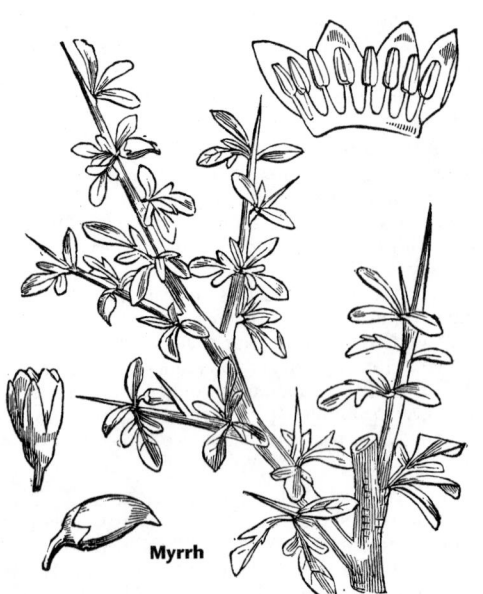

Myrrh

Millet (Panicum miliaceum) A grass grown in Eurasia for its edible seed. Millet seeds are the smallest of all the grass seeds cultivated as food but are produced profusely. Millet is an annual grass seldom more that two feet (.6 meter) tall. The small seeds of the millet are used on cakes and eaten uncooked by the poor of the land.

Mint (Mentha) Any of various plants of this family with aromatic foliage that is processed for flavoring. Quite a few mints are common in the Holy Land, but the horse mint (Mentha longifolia) is probably the one referred to in Matthew 23:23 and Luke 11:42. Mints were employed by the ancient Hebrews, Greeks, and Romans for flavoring, as a carminative in medicine, and as a condiment in cooking.

Mulberry (Morus nigra) Any tree of this family, some bearing dark-purple fruit and one bearing white fruit, having leaves used as food for silkworms. The sycamine tree of Luke 17:6 (KJV) is evidently the black mulberry, *Morus nigra*. It is a low-growing, thick-crowned, stiff-branched tree standing from 24 to 35 feet (7.3 to 10.7 meters) tall, though rarely more than 30 feet (9.1 meters) tall. Originally native to northern Persia, it is now cultivated throughout the Middle East for its fruit. The Chinese or Indian species, *M. alba*, was until recently widely cultivated in Syria and the Holy Land but is not indigenous.

Mustard (Brassica nigra, B. arvensis) Various plants of this genus are native to Eurasia, some of which are cultivated for their edible seeds. While there is disagreement about the identity of the "mustard" of Matthew 13:31-32, 17:20, Mark 4:31, Luke 13:19, and 17:6, it is generally thought to be the ordinary black mustard, *Brassica nigra*.

The mustard Jesus referred to may be the charlock or wild mustard, *B. arvensis*, which normally grows from one to three feet (.3 to .9 meter) tall. Some have suggested that it was actually *Salvadora persica*, found in thickets around the Dead Sea. The plant has a pleasant aromatic taste resembling that of mustard, and if taken in considerable quantity, it will produce an irritation of the nose and eyes similar to that of mustard. However, this plant does not grow as far north as Galilee, and the fruits are rather large and stony, thus hardly fitting the description of the parable.

While the seeds of the mustard are not the smallest known, they were probably the smallest familiar to the common people who comprised Jesus' audience in Galilee.

Myrrh (Commiphora myrrha, C. kataf) Shrub or tree exuding an aromatic gum resin used in perfume and incense. Most of the references in Scripture to myrrh are to *Commiphora myrrha*, although *C. kataf* may also be involved since it grows in the same region and is similar. The two trees are native to Arabia, Ethiopia, and the Somali coast of east Africa. They yield a gummy exudation that constitutes most of the myrrh of commerce. Both species are low, scrubby, thick- and stiff-branched thorny shrubs or small trees that grow in rocky places, especially on limestone hills. In the East it is highly regarded as an aromatic substance, perfume, and medicine. The ancient Egyptians burned it in their temples and embalmed their dead with it; the Jews also used it for embalming (Jn 19:39). The Hebrews held it in high regard as a perfume (Ps 45:8).

Myrtle (Myrtus communis) The myrtle tree is common in the Holy Land, especially around Bethlehem, Lebanon, Hebron, and the slopes of Mt Carmel and Mt Tabor. It is native to western Asia and in good environments grows into a small evergreen tree 20 to 30 feet (6.2 to 9.1 meters) tall. More often, however, it is a straggling bush 1½ to 4 feet (.5 to 1.2 meters) tall.

In the Bible, myrtle is referred to chiefly as a symbol of God's generosity. Branches of myrtle trees were included among those that Nehemiah ordered to be gathered for the Feast of Tabernacles (Neh 8:15). The myrtle was symbolic not only of peace but also of justice.

Myrtle

Narcissus (Narcissus tazetta) Widely cultivated plant of this family with narrow leaves and usually white or yellow flowers with a cup-crown or trumpet-shaped crown. The polyanthus narcissus (*Narcissus tazetta*) appears to be the plant referred to in Isaiah 35:1. This narcissus grows abundantly on the plains of Sharon and elsewhere in Palestine. Being sweet-smelling, it is a great favorite.

Nard (Nardostachys jatamansi) The nard is a perennial herb with strong, pleasantly scented roots. It is native to high altitudes in the Himalayas, and its range extends from there into western Asia. The roots and spikelike wooly young stems are dried before the leaves unfold and are used for making perfume. It is still used in India as a perfume for the hair, and there is every reason to believe that the spikenard of Scripture (Sg 1:12; 4:13-14; Mk 14:3; Jn 12:3) came originally from India.

Nettle (*Urtica*) Plant of this genus having toothed leaves covered with hairs that exude a stinging flush. Four species of nettle are found in the Holy Land: the common or great nettle, *Urtica dioica*; the Roman nettle, *U. pilulifera*; the small nettle, *U. urens*; and *U. caudata*, which is similar to the small nettle. Some nettles attain a height of five to six feet (1.5 to 1.8 meters). They are common pests of waste places and fields. They are often seen occupying ground that was once cultivated but has since been neglected (Is 34:13; Hos 9:6).

Nutmeg Flower (*Nigella sativa*) The "fitches" of Isaiah 28:25-27 (KJV) are probably the nutmeg flower, an annual plant of the buttercup family. The plant grows wild in southern Europe, Syria, Egypt, north Africa, and other Mediterranean lands, where it is extensively cultivated for its strongly pungent, pepperlike aromatic seeds. These are sprinkled over some kinds of bread and cakes in the East and are used for flavoring curries and other dishes in the Holy Land and Egypt. Cummin and nutmeg flowers are still gathered in the Holy Land in the same way described by Isaiah.

Oak (*Quercus*) At least five species of oaks are found in Palestine. One of these is the kermes oak (*Quercus coccifera*), the host of the insect *Coccus ilicis*, which produces the scarlet dye used in coloring linen and wool (Gn 38:28-30; Ex 25:4; 26:1; 28:33; 35:23; 39:24; Lv 14:4-6, 51-52; Nm 19:6; 2 Chr 2:7, 14; 3:14; Is 1:18; Heb 9:19; Rv 18:12). The kermes oak grows from 6 to 35 feet (1.8 to 10.7 meters) tall and is found in the mountainous regions of Syria, Lebanon, and the Holy Land. When it grows alone, the kermes oak often becomes a large tree. It was regularly planted by tombs in the East. The oak was always respected and even venerated in biblical times for its large size and strength, and great men were usually buried in its shade. Abraham's oak in Hebron is an example.

A second oak is the valonia oak (*Q. aegilops*), perhaps the oak of Isaiah 2:13 and 44:14. It is common in the middle montane zones and probably was abundant in the area around Bashan. The oak of Genesis 35:4, 8 is thought to have been the holm oak (*Q. ilex*), an evergreen oak that grows to a height of 60 feet (18.3 meters). Still another oak is *Q. lusitanica*, the cypress oak, a small deciduous tree seldom more than 20 feet (6.1 meters) tall. The very large acorns of this tree were sometimes eaten.

The word translated "plain" (KJV) in Genesis 12:6, 13:18, 14:13, and 18:1 should probably be translated "oak."

The many references to "groves" in the OT, usually in connection with the worship of Baal or other heathen gods (Ex 34:13; Dt 16:21; Jgs 3:7; 1 Kgs 14:23; 18:19; 2 Kgs 17:16—all KJV), were probably groves of sacred oak trees.

Oil Tree, Oleaster (*Elaeagnus angustifolia*) Small Eurasian tree with oblong silvery leaves, greenish flowers, and olivelike fruit. There is question as to which tree is referred to when 1 Kings 6:23, 31-33 and 1 Chronicles 27:28 refer to "olive trees." The same word occurs in Isaiah 41:19 and Micah 6:7. The plant referred to is probably the narrow-leaved oleaster (*Elaeagnus angustifolia*), a small stiff-branched tree or graceful shrub growing from 15 to 20 feet (4.6 to 6.1 meters) tall, common in all parts of the Holy Land except in the Jordan Valley. At one time it was particularly common on Mt Tabor and at Hebron and Samaria. The wood is hard and fine-grained and therefore well suited for carving of images and figures. The oil that it yields is a rather inferior type used in medication but not for food; this may be the oil of Micah 6:7.

Oleander (*Nerium oleander*) Any poisonous evergreen shrub of this genus growing in warm climates. One of the suggestions for the plants identified as "roses" in various translations (Ecclus 24:14, KJV) is the oleander. This plant, originally native to the East Indies, has been cultivated throughout the warm regions of the world for centuries. It flourishes in the Holy Land today and forms dense thickets in some parts of the Jordan Valley. It is usually a shrub from 3 to 12 feet (.9 to 3.7 meters) tall. Every part of the plant is dangerously poisonous.

Olive, Olive Tree (*Olea europaea*) Old world semitropical evergreen tree bearing edible fruit. The olive, *Olea europaea*, was unquestionably one of the most valuable trees known to the Jews. There are innumerable references to it in Scripture, as well as to olive oil, which was used for anointing. The tree is quite common in the Holy Land, and in many places it is the only tree of any substantial size. The branches of the wild olive are rather stiff and spinescent, and the typical cultivated tree is a multi-branched evergreen, 20 or more feet (6.1 meters) tall, with a gnarled trunk and smooth, ash-colored bark. The leaves are leathery and the flowers are small, yellow or white. The fruits are large, black or violet, ripening in September, and it is the outer fleshy parts of the fruit that yield the valuable olive oil of commerce. Thirty-one percent of the ripe fruit is oil. The ripe fruit is eaten raw, as is the green, unripe fruit. The wood of the trunk and limbs is hard, rich yellow or amber in color, and fine-grained, often handsomely variegated. It is still used today for the finest cabinetwork and turnery. The tree grows very slowly, but it attains a great age. It is difficult to kill the olive tree by cutting it down, because new sprouts are sent up from the root and all around the margins of the old stump, often forming a grove of two to five trunks, all from a single root that originally supported only one tree.

Onion (*Allium*) The onions referred to in Numbers 11:5 are undoubtedly *Allium cepa*, the Egyptian onion, which is made up of a compact coated bulb formed of layers consisting of broad fleshy bases of closely overlapping leaves. The leaves are slender and hollow. The entire plant has a characteristic pungent taste and odor.

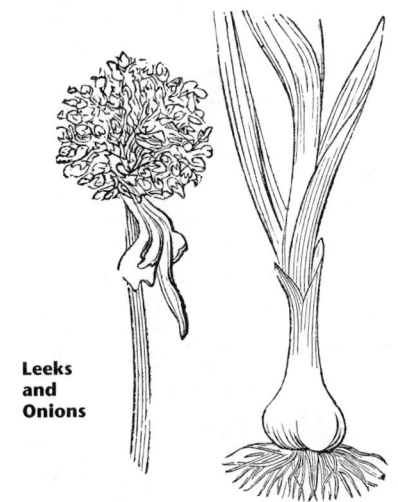

Leeks and Onions

Closely related to the onion is the garlic, *A. sativum*. The common garlic is a hardy, bulbous perennial plant that is cultivated in Europe, western Asia, and Egypt. The leaves are narrow, flat, and ribbonlike. It is extremely popular with people of the Mediterranean region.

Still another one of the onions is the leek, *A. porrum*. The bulb of the leek differs from that of the onion and garlic in that it is slender, cylindrical, and more than six inches (15.2 centimeters) in length. The flavor resembles that of the onion but is more pungent. The leaves are eaten as a relish or are cooked in soups. The bulbs are cut into small pieces and employed as seasoning for meat.

Palm *(Phoenix dactylifera)* The palm tree of the Bible is undoubtedly the date palm. At one time it was as characteristic of the Holy Land as it is still today of Egypt. It is characterized by a branchless, tapering stem of up to 80 feet (24.2 meters) or more in height and a large terminal cluster of feathery leaves, each six to nine feet (1.8 to 2.7 meters) or more long. Because of its height and unusual structure, it was natural that it should be used as a form of ornamentation in Eastern architecture. The stem and leaves were favorite subjects of architectural embellishment. The immense, branchlike leaves that are referred to as branches in the Bible were symbols of triumph and were used on occasions of great rejoicing (Jn 12:13; Rv 7:9). The large leaves are still used to cover the roofs and sides of houses and to give solidity to reed fences. Mats, baskets, and even dishes are made of them. Small leaves are used as dusters, and the wood of the trunk is used for timber. Rope is made from the weblike integument in the crown. The fruit, borne in an immense drooping cluster, which may weigh from 30 to 50 pounds (13.6 to 22.7 kilograms), is the chief food of many natives of Arabia and north Africa. A single tree may yield up to 200 pounds (90.7 kilograms) of dates a year. They may be dried for future use.

Papyrus *(Cyperus papyrus)* The Egyptian bulrush or papyrus (Ex 2:3-5; Jb 8:11; Is 18:2; 19:6-7; 35:7; 58:5) has smooth three-sided stems ordinarily attaining a

Papyrus

height of 8 to 10 feet (2.4 to 3 meters), but sometimes even 16 feet (4.9 meters), and a thickness of two to three inches (5.1 to 7.6 centimeters) at the base with a large tuft of florets at the end. The papyrus formerly grew in great abundance along the banks of the Nile, forming what was almost a dense jungle. Today it is practically extinct in lower Egypt, although it is still found along the White Nile and in the Sudan. The papyrus still grows in parts of the Holy Land, especially around the north end of the plain of Galilee and the Huleh swamps.

In addition to being used for making small vessels to float in water (Ex 2:3), for mats, and for various other domestic purposes, it is best known as the source of ancient paper. In manufacturing paper from papyrus, the stems of the plant were first peeled and the pitch then cut longitudinally into thin slices that were laid side by side. These were then sprinkled with water and pressed to unite the whole into one piece. The sheet was then dried and cut into pieces of the required size. In the better grades of papyrus paper, several layers of stem slices were laid crosswise on each other.

The pale, fawn-colored, tassel-like inflorescences at the summit of the stems were used to adorn Egyptian temples and to crown the statues of gods. They were also worn as crowns by famous men and national heroes.

Pine Tree *(Pinus brutia, P. halepensis)* Various evergreen trees of this family with needle-shaped leaves in clusters and seed-bearing cones. While there is considerable confusion concerning the conifers of the Bible, it seems apparent that pines are referred to in such passages as Leviticus 23:40; Nehemiah 8:15; Isaiah 41:19; and 60:13. One of the Holy Land's pines is the Brutian pine *(Pinus brutia)*, a mountain-inhabiting species of the northern regions of Palestine. It attains a height of 10 to 35 feet (3 to 10.7 meters) with a rather diffuse growth and branches in whorls.

Another of the pines is the Aleppo pine, *Pinus halepensis*. Most of the instances of the occurrence of "fir" or "fir tree" in the KJV probably refer to the Aleppo pine (2 Sm 6:5; 1 Kgs 5:8, 10; 6:34; 2 Kgs 19:23; 2 Chr 2:8; Ps 104:17; Sg 1:17; Is 14:8; 37:24; 55:13; 60:13; Ez 27:5; 31:8; Hos 14:8; Na 2:3; Zec 11:2). It grows from 9 to 60 feet (2.7 to 18.3 meters) tall with diffuse ascending branches and yellowish or brownish branchlets.

Pistachio *(Pistacia terebinthus, P. vera)* The Palestine terebinth or turpentine tree is a large deciduous tree with straggling boughs. In the winter, without its leaves, it looks much like the oak. It grows from 12 to 25 feet (3.7 to 7.6 meters) tall. Every part of the tree contains a fragrant, resinous juice. It is common on the lower slopes of the hills throughout Syria, Lebanon, Palestine, and Arabia, generally growing as a solitary tree and found mostly in localities too warm or too dry for the oak that it generally replaces. Since it is native to Gilead, it is quite probable that its resinous juice formed part of the spicery that the Israelites carried to Egypt from Gilead (Gn 37:25).

The nuts of Genesis 43:11 are apparently pistachio nuts from the pistachio tree, *Pistacia vera*, closely related to the terebinth. It attains a height of 10 to 30 feet (3 to 9.1 meters) with a spreading top. It is found wild in many rocky parts of Lebanon and the Holy Land. The nut has a light-colored shell and the kernel has a sweet delicate flavor much relished wherever it grows.

Plane Tree *(Platanus orientalis)* Any of several trees of this family with bell-shaped fruit clusters and usually an outer bark that flakes off in patches or strips. The references in Genesis 30:37 and Ezekiel 31:8 are apparently not to the chestnut tree, which is not indigenous to Palestine, but to the oriental plane tree, *Platanus orientalis.*

The plane tree is a massive tree 60 feet (18.3 meters) or more tall with a trunk often of vast circumference, sometimes as much as 40 feet (12.2 meters). The outer bark peels off in sheets or scales, thus exposing a smooth whitish or yellowish inner bark. The tree is common throughout Lebanon, Syria, and the Holy Land, growing even in subalpine regions. However, it is primarily a tree of the plains and lowlands, growing on the edges of streams and lakes and in marshy places.

Pomegranate *(Punica granatum)* The pomegranate is usually a small, bushlike tree but may occasionally become a large, branching shrub or small tree reaching a height of 20 to 30 feet (6.1 to 9.1 meters). The branches are often thorny. The showy bell-like flowers are usually scarlet, though sometimes yellow or white. The globular fruit is as large as an orange or medium-size apple. It has a hard rind of a bright red or yellowish color when ripe and is surmounted by the dry sepals that resemble a crown. The fruit itself is a crimson juicy pulp in which many red seeds are imbedded. The flowers of the pomegranate undoubtedly served as a pattern for the golden bells referred to in Exodus 28:33-34 and 39:24-26, and the open flowers of 1 Kings 6:32. The erect calyx lobes on the fruit served as a model for crowns of kings.

The pomegranate is native to Asia, but it has been cultivated since prehistoric times and is now quite common in the Holy Land, in Egypt, and along the shores of the Mediterranean. It is listed as one of the pleasant fruits of Egypt (Nm 20:5) and one of the promised blessings of the Holy Land (Dt 8:8).

Poplar *(Populus euphratica, P. alba)* Fast-growing deciduous tree of the same genus as the aspen and cottonwood. The KJV references in 2 Samuel 5:23-24 and 1 Chronicles 14:14-15 to mulberry trees are more probably to the Euphrates poplar or aspen, *Populus euphratica.* This tree grows to a height of 30 to 45 feet (9.1 to 13.7 meters) with spreading branches. The Euphrates aspen is found only on rivers and stream banks throughout the area from Syria through the Holy Land to Stony Arabia. It is especially common in the Jordan Valley.

The white poplar *(Populus alba)* is common in wet places in Syria, Lebanon, the Holy Land, and Sinai. It attains a height of 30 to 60 feet (9.1 to 18.3 meters) with spreading branches. Some suggest that the altars of various pagan religions were usually erected on the top of a hill and in the shade of a poplar grove.

Quince *(Cydonia oblonga)* Tree native to western Asia, having white flowers and applelike fruit that is edible when cooked. Some believe that the "apples" of the OT were quinces, *Cydonia oblonga.* The quince tree is quite common in the Holy Land, though chiefly as a cultivated tree. It may occur wild in the northern parts of Syria. It is native to northern Persia and Asia Minor. The fruit is yellowish and highly fragrant, and it is the fragrance that caused it to be held in high regard by the ancients.

Reed *(Juncus, Scirpus, Typha angustata, Arundo donax)* Numerous species of the rush and bulrush grow in the Holy Land. There are at least 21 varieties of rushes. The common soft rush or bog rush *(Juncus effusus)* is found in wet places, even in the Sinai and other deserts. The sea or hard rush *(J. maritimus)* is found in damp places throughout the Holy Land and even in Sinai.

At least 15 kinds of bulrushes *(Scirpus)* are known in the Holy Land. The cluster-headed club rush *(Scirpus holoschoenus)* is common in damp places throughout the Holy Land to the Sinai. The lake club rush or tall bulrush *(S. lacustris)* is found in swamps and ditches throughout northern Africa to the Dead Sea. The sea club rush or salt marsh club rush *(S. maritimus)* is found in ditches and swamps in many places of the Holy Land. Any of these species may be the one referred to in Job 8:11; Isaiah 9:14; 19:6, 15.

The reference in Genesis 41:2 to the feeding of cattle in the meadow seems to be to the tall reed *(Arundo donax),* which grows 18 feet (5.5 meters) or more in height. This plant is also known as the Persian reed and is common throughout the Holy Land, Syria, and the Sinai peninsula. It is a gigantic grass that may have a stem diameter of two or three inches (5.1 to 7.6 centimeters) at the base and is terminated by a plume of white flowers similar to those of the sugarcane or pampas grass. The plant was used for many purposes by the ancients: for walking sticks, fishing rods, measuring rods, and musical pipes. It is, therefore, quite possible that the "reed" of Matthew 2 7:48 and Mark 15:36 was a carpenter's reed or measuring rod.

See also Papyrus.

Rue *(Ruta chalepensis, R. graveolens)* Aromatic Eurasian plant with evergreen leaves that yield an acrid, volatile oil once used in medicine. There is little question as to the correctness of the translation of "rue" in Luke 11:42, but there is some doubt as to the exact species. Most writers think that it was the common rue *(Rue graveolens),* a perennial shrubby plant with erect stems two to three feet (.6 to .9 meter) tall and deeply cut leaves. A very strong odor emanates from the foliage. This species is native to the Mediterranean region and grows wild in the Holy Land, especially on Mt Tabor.

Rue was highly thought of by the ancients as a medicinal, supposed to prevent dizziness, dumbness, epilepsy, eye inflammations, insanity, and the "evil eye." Rue was also used for seasoning dishes.

Rush *(Butomus umbellatus)* Generic term for any of various grasslike marsh plants having pliant, hollow, or pithy stems. There is considerable uncertainty about the identification of the plant referred to in Genesis 41:2 translated in the KJV as "meadow," and in Job 8:11 as "flag." Since it is mentioned along with the papyrus in the Job passage, it seems that it refers to a specific kind of plant rather than to an aggregate of plants in a meadow. From the description in Genesis as being a plant on which Pharaoh's cattle might feed along the banks of the Nile and yet not the papyrus, it may refer to the flowering rush or water gladiola *(Butomus umbellatus),* which flourishes both in Egypt and in the Holy Land, along with the papyrus.

See also Reed.

Saffron *(Crocus sativus)* Saffron, referred to in Song of Songs 4:14, is the product of several species of *Crocus,* especially of the blue-flowered saffron crocus *(C. sativus),* which is native to Greece and Asia Minor. The commercial product consists of the stigma and upper portions of the style, the top parts of the flower ovary, which are collected shortly after the flower opens. It requires at least 4,000 stigmas to make an ounce of saffron. After being gathered, the stigmas are dried in the sun, pounded, and made into small cakes. Saffron is used principally as a yellow dye and also as a fruit coloring for curries and stews.

Another, entirely different kind of dye-producing plant *(Carthamus tinctorius)* called carthamine, bastard saffron, or safflower is a member of the thistle family. Its red florets yield a dye used extensively for coloring silk, in cooking, and for adulterating genuine saffron. It is an annual spiny plant three to four and a half feet (1.4 meters) tall, native to Syria and Egypt. In Egypt the grave clothes of mummies were dyed with this material, and it is quite possible that this plant may also have been the saffron of the Bible.

Sage (Salvia judaica) The Judean sage grows to three feet (.9 meter) tall in the mountains and hills of Palestine. Its stems are four-angled, stiff, and rough. The plant grows from Syria south through Nazareth, Hebron, Tiberius, Samaria, and Judea.

This plant is the origin of the design of the seven-branched lampstand of Exodus 37:17-18, which is known as the menorah, the traditional Jewish symbol. The inflorescence of the plant, when pressed flat, has almost exactly the same shape and form as the seven-branched candlestick, with its central spike and three pairs of side branches each bending upward and inward in a symmetrical fashion. On each branch of the plant's inflorescence are whorls or buds that perhaps give the idea for the "knops" (KJV) or "knobs" on the biblical golden candlesticks.

Spelt (Triticum aestivum) Hardy member of the wheat family. The rye of Exodus 9:32 and Isaiah 28:25, as well as the fitches of Ezekiel 4:9 (all KJV) are thought to be spelt. It is a hard-grained species of wheat with loose ears and grains triangular in cross-section, and was the most common form of wheat in early times. It has a stouter stem than wheat and strong spikes of grain. Bread made of its flour is much inferior to that made from wheat, but spelt will thrive in almost any kind of soil and will yield a crop on land that is unfit for wheat. The ancients preferred it to barley for bread.

Storax Tree (Styrax officinalis) Various trees of this genus yielding an aromatic resin. Today it is thought that the stacte of Exodus 30:34 was derived from the storax tree. It is an irregularly stiff-branched shrub or small tree 9 to 20 feet (2.7 to 6.1 meters) tall. This tree is abundant on low hills and rocky places from Lebanon through the Holy Land. Its gum is obtained by making incisions in the stems and branches. It is highly perfumed and is still prized today as a perfume.

Sycamore-fig (Ficus sycomorus) Tree of northeastern Africa and adjacent Asia, related to the fig. The word translated "sycamore" in 1 Kings 10:27; 1 Chronicles 27:28; 2 Chronicles 1:15; 9:27; Psalm 78:47; Isaiah 9:10; Amos 7:14; and Luke 19:4 undoubtedly refers to the well-known sycamore-fig, which is also known as the mulberry-fig or fig-mulberry. It should not be confused with the common sycamore of the North American continent, which is actually a plane tree. The sycamore-fig of the Bible is a strong-growing, robust, wide-spreading tree growing 30 to 40 feet (9.1 to 12.2 meters) tall and sometimes attaining a trunk circumference of 20 feet (6.1 meters) or more with a crown 120 feet (36.6 meters) in diameter. It is a tree that is easily climbed and is frequently planted along roadsides, which accounts for the reference in Luke 19:4. It produces an abundant amount of fruit in clusters on all parts of the tree, on both young and old branches and even on the trunk itself. It is very similar to the common fig, only smaller and much inferior in quality. In David's day it was so valuable that he appointed a special overseer for the sycamore trees (1 Chr 27:28). It is thought that Amos was not a gatherer of sycamore fruit but rather a dresser of sycamore trees.

Tamarisk (Tamarix) The references in Genesis 21:33 and 1 Samuel 22:6 and 31:13 seem to be to the tamarisk. These trees or shrubs are small and fast-growing with a durable wood. They are abundant in deserts, dunes, and salt marshes. *Tamarix aphylla* is leafless and has small white flowers. These trees or shrubs often provide a soothing touch of green foliage and a promise of cooling shade to the traveler. Tamarisks are able to survive because they either have small, scalelike leaves, which lose little moisture by transpiration, or no leaves at all. The larger of the tamarisks are valued for their wood in a region where wood is scarce. The wood was used for building and also as a source of an excellent type of charcoal.

Terebinth (Pistacia terebinthus) See Pistachio (above).

Thistle, Thorn (Lycium europaeum, Solanum incanum, Centaurea, Silybum marianum, Ruscus aculeatus, Agrostemma githago, Paliurus spina-christi, Zizyphus spina-christi) There are 22 different Hebrew and Greek words used in Scripture to refer to spiny or prickly shrubs or weeds, and these are translated as "bramble," "brier," "cockle," "thorn," and "thistle." At present, there are about 125 species of thorns and thistles that grow in the Holy Land.

The bramble in the allegory of Judges 9:14-15 is believed to refer to the European boxthorn or desert-thorn, *Lycium europaeum*.

The general consensus is that the "briers" of Isaiah 10:17, 55:13, Micah 7:4, and Hebrews 6:8 are the Palestine nightshade (*Solanum incanum*), or "Jericho potato."

The thistles of Genesis 3:17-18, 2 Kings 14:9, 2 Chronicles 25:18, Hosea 10:8, and Matthew 7:16, as well as the thorns of Matthew 13:7 and Hebrews 6:8, are thought to be one of the species of the thistle, *Centaurea*. Among the more common thistles in the Holy Land are the true star-thistle (*Centaurea calcitrapa*), the dwarf centaury (*C. verutum*), the Iberian centaury (*C. iberica*), and the lady's thistle (*Silybum marianum*). Some thistles attain a height of five to six feet (.9 to 1.8 meters). Thistles are characteristic of an area that is uncultivated and neglected. Many have beautiful flowers, but all are covered with sharp spines.

The references in Ezekiel 2:6 to "briers" and Ezekiel 28:24 to a "pricking brier" may be to the prickly butchers-broom or knee-holly, *Ruscus aculeatus*. The plant is common in rocky woods in the northern regions of the Holy Land, especially around Mt Tabor and Mt Carmel.

The cockle of Job 31:40 (NLT "weeds") perhaps refers to the corn cockle, *Agrostemma githago*. This plant is common in grainfields throughout the Holy Land. It is a strong-growing and troublesome weed in grainfields, growing from one to three feet (.3 to .9 meter) tall.

Many commentators think that the "thorns" out of which the crown of thorns (Mt 27:29; Jn 19:2) was made were from the Christ-thorn (*Paliurus spina-christi*). This belief has led to its specific name; the Christ-thorn is a spiny plant that ordinarily grows as a straggling shrub three to nine feet (.9 to 2.7 meters) tall. The flexible branches are armed at the base of each leaf with a pair of unequal, stiff, sharp spines. The unusual pliable texture of the young branches renders it particularly easy to plait into a crownlike wreath.

The thorns of Judges 8:7, Isaiah 7:19, 9:18, 55:13, and Matthew 7:16 may refer to the Syrian Christ-thorn (*Zizyphus spina-christi*), a shrub or small tree 9 to 15 feet (2.7 to 4.6 meters) tall, sometimes growing into a 40-foot (12.2-meter) tree with smooth white branches bearing a pair of stout, unequal, recurved spines at the back of each leaf.

See also Bramble; Buckthorn (above).

Tulip (Tulipa montana, T. sharonensis) Any of several bulbous plants of this family native to Asia. The rose of Sharon in Song of Songs 2:1 may be the mountain tulip, *Tulipa montana,* or the closely related Sharon tulip, *T. sharonensis.* The former is an attractive plant that grows from a bulb and has leaves that are often wavy-margined. The species is common in the mountainous regions of Syria, Lebanon, and the Anti-Lebanon. It is primarily a mountainous species. The Sharon tulip (*T. sharonensis*) is found in sandy places on the Sharon coastal plains.

Tumbleweed (Gundelia tournefortii, Anastatica hierochuntica) The references in Psalm 83:13 to "whirling dust" and in Isaiah 17:13 to "wheel" or "rolling thing" (NIV "tumbleweed") seem to be to the Palestinian tumbleweed (*Gundelia tournefortii*), a member of the thistle family. It is a prickly herb with milky juice. It rolls over the land and gathers in tremendous heaps in hollows.

Vegetable Scriptural references to vegetables are probably, in most cases, to the dried leguminous seeds of beans and lentils.

Vine (Vitis vinifera) Any plant with a flexible stem that climbs, twines, or creeps along a surface or support. The common grapevine (*Vitis vinifera*) is mentioned throughout the Bible. The fruitful vine (Ez 17:5-10) and the vine brought out of Egypt (Ps 80:8) were symbolic of the Jewish people. Jesus compares himself to the true vine, of which his disciples were the branches (Jn 15:1-6).

The grapevine of the Old World sometimes assumes the characteristics of a tree, with stems up to a foot and a half (45.7 centimeters) in diameter, the branches then being trained on a trellis and bearing bunches of grapes 10 to 12 pounds (4.5 to 5.4 kilograms) in weight, with the individual grapes the size of small plums. Bunches have been produced weighing as much as 26 pounds (11.8 kilograms). The vines of the Holy Land were always renowned both for the luxuriance of their growth and for the immense clusters of grapes they produced. Thus it does not seem improbable that the spies sent to the Promised Land should have employed a pole to transport some of the clusters home (Nm 13:23-24).

The wild grape (*Vitis orientalis*) is referred to in Isaiah 5:2-4, Jeremiah 2:21, and Ezekiel 15:2-6. It is known as the native wild fox grape and has small, black, acidic berries about the size of currants with little juice.

Walnut (Juglans regia) Any of several trees of this genus having round, sticky fruit enclosing an edible nut. The reference in Song of Songs 6:11 to "nuts" is thought to refer to the Persian or common walnut, *Juglans regia.* The tree is believed to have been indigenous to northern Persia, but it is actually found wild in many parts of northern India, eastward as far as China, and westward through Persia. At the time of Solomon, it was widely cultivated for its fruit throughout the East. Perhaps Solomon's garden of nuts was a part of his extensive gardens at Etham, six miles (9.7 kilometers) from Jerusalem.

Water Lily (Nymphaea) Any of numerous aquatic plants of this genus with floating leaves and showy flowers. The carved lily ornamentation of 1 Kings 7:19-26 and 2 Chronicles 4:5 was probably patterned after the flowers of the water lily. Few flowers can equal the Egyptian lotus or water lily (*Nymphaea lotus*) in beauty. It looks very much like a large white rose and at one time floated in profusion on the waters of the Nile.

The common European white water lily (*N. alba*) was also familiar to the children of Israel. It grows not only in Europe but also in the Holy Land and North Africa. It is, however, not as common in Egypt as is the white lotus.

Another water lily with which the Israelites were probably familiar is the blue lotus, *N. caerulea.* Its leaves are 12 to 16 inches (30.5 to 40.6 centimeters) across and it has light-blue flowers that are three to six inches (7.6 to 15.2 centimeters) in diameter.

Wheat (Triticum aestivum, T. compositum) Various cereal grasses of this family widely cultivated for its edible grain. Five kinds of wheat are native to—and still wild in—the Holy Land, and at least eight others are cultivated there today; probably most, if not all, were known in Bible times. The wild varieties were probably more abundant then than they are today. Among these are the einkorn (*T. monococcum*), the thaoudar (*T. thaoudar*), and the wild emmer (*T. dicoccoides*). The composite wheat (*T. compositum*), with its branched spikes, often bearing as many as seven heads per stalk, is definitely referred to in Genesis 41:5-57. It is depicted on numerous Egyptian monuments and on inscriptions and is still commonly seen in the Nile Delta, where it is known as "mummy wheat." It is also cultivated in the Holy Land.

The most frequently mentioned wheat of the Bible is undoubtedly the commonly cultivated summer and winter wheat, *Triticum aestivum.* It is an abundant annual grass cultivated in Egypt and other Eastern lands since earliest times. The exact place of its origin is unknown. Grains of wheat have been found in the most ancient Egyptian tombs and in the remains of prehistoric lake dwellings in Switzerland. It was certainly the chief grain of Mesopotamia in Jacob's time (Gn 30:14).

Corn in biblical days often included a mixture of peas, beans, lentils, cummin, barley, millet, and spelt, but wheat was always its main constituent. Egypt was a great grain-producing country, and Abram (Gn 12:10) and Joseph's brothers (ch 42) naturally turned to Egypt for wheat when famine visited Canaan.

The mills, millstones, granaries, and threshing floors mentioned in the Bible all refer to equipment employed in processing grain to produce flour. The fine flour of which the showbread loaves were made (Lv 24:5) was unquestionably wheat flour. Wheat intended for home consumption was often stored in the central part of the house; this explains the story told in 2 Samuel 4:6. It was also sometimes stored in dry wells (2 Sm 17:19).

Wormwood (Artemisia judaica, A. herba-alba) Wormwood is a general name given to a group of woody plants with a strong aromatic odor. Wormwood plants have a strong, bitter taste, and their young shoots and branch tips furnish the "wormwood" of commerce. Its bitter taste accounts for its being spoken of with gall—as being symbolic of bitter calamity and sorrow (Prv 5:4; Jer 9:15; 23:15; Lam 3:15, 19). *Artemisia herba-alba* is the common species of wormwood in the Holy Land today. It is strongly aromatic, smelling like camphor, and bitter. *A. judaica* occurs only in the Sinai.

Absinthe is made from species of this group. It first leads to greater activity and pleasant sensations and fills the mind with grandiose ideas (Lam 3:15). The habitual use of it, however, brings on a stupor and gradual diminution of intellectual faculties, ending in delirium and even death. Perhaps the hemlock of Amos 6:12 was wormwood.

PLEDGE *See* Banker, Banking.

PLEIADES Name of a constellation in the eastern sky composed of six bright and many other less visible stars. Telescopic photography has captured the appearance of these stars as being strung together by currents of matter. Job is asked a question that reflects this phenomenon: "Can you hold back the movements of the stars? Are you able to restrain the Pleiades or Orion?" (Jb 38:31, NLT).

See also Orion.

PLOW, PLOWMAN, PLOWSHARE *See* Agriculture.

PLUMB LINE, PLUMMET* Cord with a weight attached, used to ensure the straightness of a wall.

POCHERETH-HAZZEBAIM*, POCHERETH OF ZEBAIM* Head of a family of Solomon's servants who returned from the exile with Zerubbabel (Ezr 2:57; Neh 7:59). The KJV renders the name Pochereth of Zebaim, making the latter part a place-name.

POETRY, Biblical Poetic language in Scripture.

In the Old Testament The OT contains all that we know of the poetry of Israel, and what we have occupies an important place in that literature. It was presumably well known throughout the ancient Near East, for its fame had spread even to Babylon (Ps 137:3). Much of the OT is poetic in spirit and structure—a feature of the prophetic writings as well as the poetic literature. In the former are found passages of elevated poetry, studded with brilliant gems of imagery. The movement is rhythmical, with meter, parallelism, and strophic arrangement, as in the poetry books.

The English Revised Version of the Bible (1881) first rendered a great service to English readers by printing OT poetry in parallel lines. Where this is not done in the prophetic literature, the poetic quality of these books is obscured. Note that besides the OT books recognized as poetry—the Psalms, Job, Lamentations, Song of Songs, and Proverbs—Ecclesiastes and the Prophets consist of prose and poetry. The historical books also contain fine examples of poetry.

The Hebrew language was an ideal instrument for expressing poetic speech. Its simplicity of form combined intensity of feeling and pictorial power and allowed great play of imagination. Figures, metaphors, and hyperboles are extremely common. In its powerful imagery the genius of Hebrew poetry comes to its finest expression.

The normal unit of Hebrew verse is the couplet of two parallel lines. But this is not the only grouping of lines in Hebrew poetry. Units of three (Pss 1:1; 5:11; 45:1-2), four (Pss 1:3; 55:21; Prv 27:15-16), five (Ps 6:6-7; Prv 24:23-25), six (Ps 99:1-3; Prv 30:21-23), and even larger combinations of parallel lines occur.

As far as can be determined, meter is absent from biblical poetry. Certainly there is little concern for the careful meter that marks classic Greek and Latin, as well as much of English, poetry. The only exception is found in wailing songs or laments (Jer 9:18-20; Lam 1–4). This is called the lamentation meter, where the verse is in two parts. Rhyme also is so rare as to be almost nonexistent.

On the other hand, Hebrew poetry is rhythmical—one of its distinguishing features. Its rhythm recurs with stressed and unstressed syllables in relatively regular succession. There are usually three or four accents or beats to a line, but the rhythmic unit is not uniform. Rhythm in Hebrew poetry, however, is not confined to the balance of accents or beats in a line. The meaning of the words and their position in the line are also significant—a feature

called parallelism. This distinguishing characteristic was first clearly recognized by Dr. Robert Lowth, who in 1753 developed the principle of parallelism.

He distinguished three types. The first is *synonymous parallelism,* where the thought expressed in the first part of the verse is repeated in the second part, in different but equivalent terms (Pss 2:4; 19:1; 36:1-2; 103:11-12; Prv 3:13-18). The second is *antithetic parallelism,* where the thought in the first part of the verse is contrasted with its opposite in the second (Ps 1:6; Prv 10:1-4, 16-18; 13:9). The third is *synthetic parallelism,* where the idea expressed in the first line of a verse is developed and completed in the following lines (Pss 1:1; 3:5-6; 18:8-10; Prv 26:3). There are more complicated forms of parallelism, but these three are the most common.

Another characteristic of biblical poetry is the use of the letters of the Hebrew alphabet. Psalms in which verses are linked together by this means are called acrostic. Today, an acrostic is formed by taking a name and beginning the successive lines of the short poem with the letters that make up the name. The Hebrews took only the alphabet and arranged the lines of the poem according to the succession of the letters.

Each line of a psalm may begin with a different letter, as in Psalm 25. Or each of the stanzas may begin with the same letter until all 22 letters of the alphabet are exhausted, as in Psalm 119. However, this psalm, which is the most conspicuous example of a Hebrew acrostic poem, is quite complicated in its arrangement. Not only does each stanza begin with a letter, but each of the eight lines of every stanza begins with the same letter, so that eight alphabetic arrangements move through the psalm in parallel lines. Other elaborate acrostics are Psalms 9, 10, 34, 37, 111, 112, and 145.

The first four chapters of Lamentations also follow an acrostic arrangement. This example of acrostic arrangement is less noticeable to the English reader because the names of the Hebrew letters do not mark the beginning of the stanzas. In Lamentations 3 each letter of the alphabet begins three successive lines numbered as verses. Another acrostic occurs in Proverbs 31:10-31. It is an alphabetic description of the virtuous woman.

Another poetic device giving unity to a poem and marking its divisions is the refrain. Psalm 136 is an outstanding example of this arrangement. The refrain is "His faithful love endures forever" and is used to conclude every verse.

The meter of Hebraic poetry is dependent on accentuation; the unit is the couplet, in which the members may be of equal or varying length. Couplets are often arranged into strophes. The fundamental category of Hebrew poetry is the song or lyric. The song was accompanied by music (Gn 31:27; Ex 15:20; 1 Chr 25:6; Is 23:16; 30:29; Am 6:5) and could be associated with dance (Ex 15:20-21).

Some complete poems in the OT are embedded in the narrative books and represent various types of Hebrew poems. The first recorded poem in the Bible is a battle song (Gn 4:23-24). Other famous examples of this type are the Song of Moses (Ex 15:1-18) and the Song of Deborah (Jgs 5:1-31). Then there is the Taunt Song (Nm 21:27-30), the Song of the Well (vv 17-18), and songs of blessing. Of this latter type, well-known examples are the Blessing of Jacob (Gn 49:1-27), the Blessing of Moses (Dt 33:2-29), and the four Blessings of Balaam (Nm 23:7-10; 23:18-24; 24:3-9; 24:15-24). There are also laments for the dead (2 Sm 1:19-27) and didactic poems that warn against improvidence (Prv 6:6-11) and drunkenness (23:29-35). Common throughout all of these various types of poems is religious emotion and fervor. The songs of Moses and Deborah praise God as the giver of victory.

Most poems of distinctively religious fervor characterize the worship of the sanctuary. The psalms are religious poems sung with musical accompaniment. Many are private prayers, while others were composed for public worship, especially hymns of thanksgiving sung at the tabernacle or temple. It is in the Psalter that the soaring spirit of Hebrew poetry rises to a level never achieved by Israel's pagan neighbors; the Hebrews worshiped God in spirit and in truth, and as they did so, they were giving expression to a personal experience of the living God in their soul.

The internal qualities of Hebrew poetry are in part influenced by the age, social conditions, and environment in which the writers lived. Although the OT is of divine authorship, it also comes within the scope of literature and should be appreciated as such. Though the Holy Spirit inspired the message of the Hebrew writers, their individual writing styles remain clearly evident. Using simple and vivid diction, figures of speech, and literary devices, each poet expressed a wealth of religious thought, experience, and emotion; simile, metaphor, allegory, hyperbole, personification, irony, and wordplay all variously enhanced each writer's pattern of thinking. Hebrew poetry is the expression of the poet's human spirit, and it is the literature of revelation—the Word of God to humankind.

In the New Testament The NT has a limited number of poetical passages. Probably the NT contains less poetry than the OT (relatively speaking) because the early Christians found the OT Psalter (in the Hebrew and LXX) adequate for their devotional purposes. All the writers of the NT were Jews, except Luke. He has given us some memorable poems: the Magnificat (Lk 1:46-55), the Benedictus (vv 68-79), and the Nunc Dimittis (2:29-32). Interestingly, these poems are strongly Hebraic in form, character, and content. Matthew has given us the poetic Beatitudes (Mt 5:3-12). These Beatitudes have the parallelism that is common in OT poetry—specifically, synthetic parallelism (where the second line of each verse completes the meaning of the first line). There is also a definite rhythmic quality in Matthew 11:28-30. John's Prologue to his Gospel of John (1:1-18) is a fine example of Hellenistic poetry.

The NT Epistles contain a number of poetic passages, especially in the doxologies (see, for example, Rom 16:25-27; Jude 1:24-25). Other sections are distinctly poetry and/or early Christian hymns. These include Philippians 2:6-11 ("The Humility of Christ" hymn/poem); Colossians 1:15-20 ("The Preeminence of Christ" hymn/poem); and 1 Timothy 3:16 ("The Incarnation" hymn/poem). The writer to Hebrews also produced a noteworthy poetic prologue (1:1-3). Other sections of Paul's writings display poetic language, where rhythm and exalted diction are prominent (see, for example, 1 Cor 13; 15:54-57).

The book of Revelation also contains a number of poems of praise as well as hymns (see Rv 5:9-10, 12-13; 7:12; 11:17-18; 15:3-4).

See also Ecclesiastes, Book of; Job, Book of; Lamentations, Book of; Music; Proverbs, Book of; Psalms, Book of; Song of Solomon; Wisdom; Wisdom Literature.

POKERETH-HAZZEBAIM *See* Pochereth-Hazzebaim.

POLLUX* Son of Zeus and Castor's twin brother in Greek mythology. The twin brothers (Acts 28:11) are also called the Dioscuri. *See* Dioscuri.

POLYCARP* Early Christian leader and martyr in the postapostolic era.

Born to a Christian family, Polycarp identified himself as a disciple of "John," presumably the apostle. Polycarp was appointed bishop of Smyrna in Asia Minor. Ignatius of Antioch, on his way to Roman martyrdom (c. 116), wrote letters to Polycarp and to the church at Smyrna. Near the end of his life, Polycarp visited Rome. He was serving as representative of the Asia Minor churches in a discussion over the observance of Easter. Polycarp was later arrested by civil authorities, who attempted to convince him to renounce his faith. When he refused, he was burned at the stake. The story of Polycarp's death (recounted in a letter from the church of Smyrna to the church of Philomelium) is the earliest record of Christian martyrdom outside the New Testament.

As bishop of Smyrna, Polycarp wrote many letters to various churches. Only one of Polycarp's letters has survived, however. This letter, addressed to the Philippians, was written in response to a letter they had sent him. Apparently, while Ignatius was on his way to martyrdom in Rome, his guards chose to make a stop in Philippi. While there, Ignatius encouraged the local church to write to the church in Antioch. So they sent a letter by way of Polycarp. They also requested copies of Ignatius's letters to the Asian churches.

Polycarp's reply to Philippi is the document now called his *Epistle to the Philippians,* written around AD 120. It is the only example of the writing of this early church father. In his letter Polycarp assumes that Ignatius had already suffered death, but it seems that he was not certain of this. He asks the Philippians to send him what news they may have of Ignatius.

In his epistle Polycarp mentions the fame of the Philippians among the churches from the early days to that time. He refers to the apostle Paul's instructions for the church there, making reference to more than one letter from the apostle. Polycarp warns against the love of money, which caused the downfall of one of the leaders of the church (Judas Iscariot). He also warns against those who deny the resurrection of Christ, the Docetist heretics. Polycarp instructs the Philippians on the duties of church leaders and other Christians.

While many critics have labeled Polycarp's letter "unoriginal," containing no new theological insights, the letter does provide insight into the available NT writings for the churches. There are no citations from the OT in this epistle, but there are quotations and allusions to Matthew, Acts, Romans, 1 Corinthians, Galatians, Ephesians, 2 Thessalonians, 1 Timothy, and 1 Peter. He also makes use of Clement's epistle and the Ignatian letters. It is interesting to note that Polycarp makes no reference to the Gospel of John, though tradition insists that he was a disciple of the apostle John.

The letter ends with Polycarp's promise to forward the Philippians' letter to Antioch. He also promises to send them Ignatius's letters.

POLYGAMY* *See* Marriage, Marriage Customs.

POMEGRANATE *See* Plants.

POMMEL* KJV for "bowl," part of the capitals of the temple pillars (2 Chr 4:12). *See* Architecture (Palestinian); Tabernacle; Temple.

PONTIUS PILATE *See* Pilate, Pontius.

PONTUS Roman province in northeastern Asia Minor, located along the southern coast of the Black Sea.

Galatia, Cappadocia, and Armenia bordered Pontus. About 1000 BC the first Greeks started to colonize the southeastern coast of the Black Sea, founding Sinope and Trebizond. Here Xenophon and his men reached the sea after their great eastern adventure. The famous geographer Strabo, to whom is owed knowledge of the ancient history of Pontus, was born in the inland city of Amasia. Mithridates Eupator, king of Amasia, was, according to the Romans, the most formidable enemy the republic ever encountered. He waged three wars against the Romans until his final defeat by Pompey around 60 BC.

Aquila, the tentmaker who, with his wife, Priscilla, was a helpful coworker of the apostle Paul, was born in Pontus. Unlike Paul, however, he was not a Roman citizen; hence, he was subject to the edict of Claudius and expelled from Rome because he was a Jew (Acts 18:2; 22:25-28).

The Christians who were resident there in Peter's day (1 Pt 1:1) were probably converts of those who returned from Jerusalem after the first Pentecost when Peter spoke (Acts 2:9).

POOLS OF SOLOMON* *See* Solomon, Pools of.

POOR, The Those lacking material wealth.

Poverty as a Bad Thing At times the Bible gives a very simple explanation of why people are rich or poor. If a person delights in the law of the Lord, he or she will get wealth and riches. Such people will prosper in everything they do (Pss 1:3; 112:3). With regard to Israel in OT days, these ideas are not quite so naive as they might seem. There was indeed a connection between sin and poverty. Israelite society was built on rules laid down by God, so if there was poverty, that must mean that somewhere the rules were being broken.

Whether a person's poverty was due to his or her own sin or to someone else's, the OT saw it as an evil to be combated, and the law made many provisions for the relief of it (e.g., Ex 22:21-27; Lv 19:9-10; Dt 15:1-15; 24:10-22). God cared for the needy and expected his people to do the same.

During the period between the testaments, that care continued to be exercised within Jewish communities scattered around the Mediterranean, and it was in due course taken up as a practical responsibility by the Christian church (Acts 11:29; 24:17; Rom 15:26; 1 Cor 16:1; Gal 2:10; Jas 2:15-16; 1 Jn 3:17); for Christians also, the giving of alms was a duty plainly expected by their Lord (Mt 6:2-4; Lk 12:33). It was not really a primitive communism that the early church practiced, for had they renounced personal possessions, they could not have done what they in fact did—namely, to *give* in cash or in kind "as any had need" (Acts 2:45; 4:35).

Poverty, then, although it provides the wealthy with a chance to show the virtue of generosity, is in itself (in the NT as in the OT) a bad thing.

Poverty as a Good Thing As we can see, there is a certain sense in which righteousness will make people prosperous and sin will make them poor. But ordinary life is more complicated than that. Psalms 1 and 112, referred to above, show only one side of the matter. What about the prosperity of the wicked (Ps 73:3) and its corollary, the person who is righteous yet poor? The answer of Scripture (e.g., Jb 21; Pss 37, 49, 73) is that the wealth of bad people is a fleeting thing and that the righteous, though poor in worldly goods, have spiritual riches.

This thought—that far from being prosperous, the good person may often be poor—is sometimes curiously inverted. The righteous may be poor, but Scripture sometimes appears to reckon that to be poor is to be righteous. Of course, it is not automatically so (Prv 30:8-9), but such references are frequent enough, especially in the Psalms (e.g., Pss 9:18; 10:14; 12:5; 34:6; 35:10; 74:19), to deserve careful consideration. And on reflection, they are not so strange. As God is specially concerned about the poor, so the poor may be specially concerned about God, for two good reasons. First, if there was poverty in Israel, it was because those with power were misusing it; therefore, the poor would claim God's help first because it is his rule that was being flouted, and he must vindicate himself. And second, poverty turns people to God because in those circumstances there is no one else to turn to. In this way "poor" becomes almost a technical term. "The poor" are the humble, and the humble are the godly (Pss 10:17; 14:5-6; 37:11; Zep 3:12-13). Just as being rich can foster self-indulgence, self-confidence, pride, and the despising and oppression of one's fellow human beings, so being poor should encourage the opposite virtues.

Instead of being an evil to be shunned, poverty thus becomes an ideal to be sought. Following the OT use of "the poor" and "the pious" as almost interchangeable terms, personal property was renounced by many Jews during the period between the testaments. Among them were the sect of the Essenes and the related community that was set up at Qumran near the Dead Sea. The latter actually called themselves "The Poor." This tradition continued into NT times. Possibly "the poor" at Jerusalem means a definite group within the church there (or even the Jerusalem church as a whole; Rom 15:26; Gal 2:10). Certainly there emerged later a Jewish-Christian sect called the "Ebionites" (from a Hebrew word for "poor").

The NT teaches clearly, of course, that what really matters is the attitude of the heart. It is quite possible to be poor yet grasping, or rich yet generous. Even so, with the OT background outlined above, the general sense of these words in the Gospels is that rich = bad, poor = good. On the one hand, the Sadducees are rich in worldly wealth and the Pharisees in spiritual pride, and men of property are selfish, foolish, and in grave spiritual peril (Mk 10:23; Lk 12:13-21; 16:19-31). On the other hand, it is devout and simple folk, like Jesus's own family and friends, who generally represent the poor.

In truth, therefore, the two versions of the first beatitude (Matthew's and Luke's) amount to the same thing. Matthew's has the depth: "Blessed are the poor in spirit" (Mt 5:3). But Luke's has the breadth. When he says simply "Blessed are you poor" (Lk 6:20), he means those who in their need—in *any* kind of need—turn to the Lord. It was to bring the gospel to such people that Christ came into the world (Mt 11:5; Lk 4:18). Jesus Christ himself embodies the same ideal. As Paul put it, "Though he was very rich, yet for your sakes he became poor, so that by his poverty he could make you rich" (2 Cor 8:9, NLT). Our helpless poverty is an evil from which he comes to rescue us; his deliberately chosen poverty is the glorious means by which he does so.

See also Alms; Riches; Righteousness; Wages; Wealth.

POPLAR *See* Plants.

PORATHA One of the ten sons of Haman killed by the Jews (Est 9:8).

PORCH Court associated with the temple or palace. In the KJV, it is the translation of several Hebrew words. In 1 Kings 7 and Ezekiel 40, the KJV has many mentions of porch as a part of the temple. The porch separated the Holy Place from the rest of the world. By means of several steps, one would enter into the porch, which was elevated above the surrounding area. Both the steps and the elevation emphasized the separation of the temple. On both sides of the entrance to the porch stood the supporting pillars, the Jachin and the Boaz. In the NT the KJV has "porch" for *proaulion* and *stoa* ("portico"). The *stoa* was a roofed portico supported by pillars. Solomon's portico was the famous collonaded porch around the temple area facing the temple (cf. Jn 10:23; Acts 3:11; 5:12).

See also Architecture; Tabernacle; Temple.

PORCIUS FESTUS *See* Festus, Porcius.

PORCUPINE *See* Animals.

PORTER* KJV rendering of "gatekeeper."

PORTICO*, Solomon's *See* Porch; Tabernacle; Temple.

POSIDONIUS Ambassador for Nicanor. Posidonius was sent with Theodotus and Mattathias by Nicanor to arrange a truce with Judas the Maccabee after having engaged in battle with Judas and realizing that it was better to negotiate a settlement (2 Macc 14:19).

POSSESSION, Demon *See* Demon; Demon-possession.

POSTEXILIC PERIOD* A period in the Jews' history after their exile to Babylon. This period extends from 539–c. 331 BC.

PREVIEW
• The Biblical Perspective
• The Collapse of the Babylonian Empire
• The Policy of Persia
• The Return from Exile
• The Return of Ezra
• Nehemiah's Return and Ministry
• The Remainder of the Persian Period
• Religious Features of the Postexilic Period

The Biblical Perspective The books that specifically cover the history of the postexilic or Persian period are Ezra, Nehemiah, Haggai, and Zechariah. These cover a period of over a century, only a portion of which is dealt with in detail, as the following table shows:

BOOKS OF POSTEXILIC TIMES

Reference	Dates
Ezr 1:1–4:6, 24	538–536 BC
Ezr 5:1–6:22; Hg; Zec	520–515 BC
Ezr 7–10	458 BC
Ezr 4:7-23	c. 447 BC
Neh 1:1–13:3	445–433 BC
Neh 13:4-31	c. 431 BC

The Collapse of the Babylonian Empire This occurred with dramatic suddenness, largely because of internal resistance to the policies of the last Babylonian king, Nabonidus (555–539 BC). His neglect of the traditional Babylonian deity, Marduk, in favor of the moon god, Sin, was particularly resented. Nabonidus lived in Taima during the last decade of his reign, refusing to enter Babylon, where his son Belshazzar ruled as virtual king, as noted in Daniel 5. Babylon fell to the Persians in October 538 BC and the entire empire passed into their control.

The Policy of Persia This is well documented through contemporary inscriptions, notably the record of Cyrus, the first king of the Persian Empire (559–530 BC), in the "Cyrus Cylinder." A new phase in the relationship of conqueror to conquered peoples opened up, which contrasted with the policy of the Assyrian and Babylonian empires of crushing any opposition by massive force. Cyrus and his successors followed a conciliatory line, allowing exiled groups to return home, encouraging local faiths, posing as the champions of the territorial deities, and allowing local autonomy except where Persian interests were affected adversely. The cost of this operation, although considerable, must have been infinitesimal compared with that of keeping rebellious subjects under constant subjection.

The new enlightened policy is reflected in the decree of Cyrus, dated 538 BC (Ezr 1:1) and preserved in two versions. The first (vv 1-4) is clearly the official proclamation, while the second (6:3-5) is a more prosaic memorandum dealing with building specifications, a record of Cyrus's commitment stored in the official archives (vv 1-2). The critical tendency to question the narrative in Ezra 1, especially on the score of the favorable references to the God of Israel and the vast financial support promised, has been nullified by the archaeological evidence, which shows an identical policy elsewhere. The Cyrus Cylinder, for example, notes, "The gods who live within them [i.e., the cities] I returned to their places. . . . All of their inhabitants I collected and restored to their dwelling places."

In Judah itself there is no evidence for any warfare in this period, which suggests that the Persian takeover of the area was nonviolent. Judah was incorporated into the fifth Persian province, which included the entire area west of the Euphrates River (Ezr 7:21). It was no more than a minor subdistrict, governed through Samaria.

The Return from Exile The continuance of a large Jewish community in Babylonia shows that not all the Jews responded to the invitation to return to their homeland, probably because of the prosperity acquired in exile. But 42,360 dedicated Jews (Ezr 2:64) braved the challenge of a four-month 900-mile (1,448-kilometer) journey under Sheshbazzar (1:8), the officially appointed leader, and Zerubbabel his nephew (3:2), who was probably the one to whom the Jews looked as leader. With great enthusiasm the Jews rebuilt the altar of sacrifice and resumed the observance of the traditional feasts (vv 1-6), revealing both a sense of stewardship (2:68-69) and careful attention to the requirements of the Law (3:2-4). Soon after, work on the second temple commenced—the materials and master craftsmen being imported from Tyre and Sidon (Ezr 3:7-9; cf. 1 Kgs 5). When the foundations were laid, the worshipers were doubtless aware that they were fulfilling God's promise through Jeremiah (Ezr 3:10-11; cf. Jer 33:10-11). But their high hopes were thwarted when there was opposition from neighboring areas (Ezr 4:4-5), selfishness in giving their own accommodations a higher priority than the Lord's house (Hg 1:2-4, 9), and a series of crop failures that further reduced morale (1:6, 10-11; 2:17).

Work on the temple was not resumed until Haggai and Zechariah appeared in 520 BC. They encouraged Zerubbabel and Joshua (Jeshua) the high priest, rebuked the people for their apathy and selfishness, and promised God's presence and blessing upon the temple project (Hg 1:12–2:9). Zechariah's preaching went beyond the building of the temple, including the rebuilding of Jerusalem itself (Zec 2:1-5) and its world reputation (2:1-5, 11-12; 8:22). The two leaders were addressed in ways that anticipated the Messiah (Hg 2:21-23; Zec 6:10-14). But the Persian king Darius (521–486 BC) was not alarmed when the rebuilding operation was reported to him (Ezr 5:1–6:13) and allowed the work to continue. In February 515 BC it was dedicated (6:14-16). The Jewish community again had a focal point for its religion, but the political situation remained difficult, with no real security in a still-shattered city.

The Return of Ezra The traditional date of Ezra's return is 458 BC (preceding that of Nehemiah in 445 BC). This is based on the premise that the King Artaxerxes noted in Ezra 7:7 was Artaxerxes I Longimanus (464–424 BC) and not Artaxerxes II Mnemon (404–359 BC). However, some scholars, allowing that the king was Artaxerxes I, but believing that Nehemiah preceded Ezra, suggest that a tens unit has dropped out of "seventh" in Ezra 7:7, and that the date of Ezra's return should be the 27th (438 BC) or 37th year (428 BC) of Artaxerxes I, making Ezra's return a few years after Nehemiah's. While this is plausible, there remains strong support for the traditional view. It accords with the order of the two books in the OT and requires no textual emendation. It also accounts for the section in Ezra 4:7-23, where, in the reign of Artaxerxes, an abortive effort was made by a recently returned group to rebuild the wall of Jerusalem. Nehemiah 1:1-4 suggests that this was regarded as important and its abrupt termination, by a decree of the king, caused Nehemiah great distress. The probability is that Ezra, recently returned, realized that little could be done in the way of major religious reformation until Jerusalem was secure, but in attempting to rebuild the wall he exceeded his mandate and was not able to function adequately until Nehemiah arrived, when the new security of Jerusalem allowed the great Law-reading ceremony of Nehemiah 8:1-12 to take place.

Ezra's ministry concerned the teaching of the Law of Moses, the Pentateuch, which had long been extant in its final form by this time. Ezra 7 shows that Artaxerxes was following the traditional Persian policy of encouraging good relationships with his subject peoples. Ezra's appointment (Ezr 7:12) was to a state office; it has frequently been paraphrased as "Secretary of State for Jewish Religious Affairs."

Nehemiah's Return and Ministry Hanani and others (Neh 1:1-3) informed Nehemiah of the complete failure of a recent attempt to rebuild the wall, probably that recorded in Ezra 4:7-23, and sought his mediation before the very king who had authorized the decree that compelled work on the wall to cease. A friend in high places was vital, and Nehemiah, a trusted and influential member of the court (Neh 1:11), was approached for this delicate and dangerous task. Nehemiah 1:4–2:8 shows how well he prepared for and seized his opportunity. His appointment as the governor of Judah (5:14) involved

the removal of this area from the control of the governor of Samaria, which accounts for the unrelenting hostility of Sanballat (2:19; 4:1). The evidence of Nehemiah 3 suggests that the extent of Judah at this time was limited, probably not reaching as far north as Bethel or as far south as Hebron. Nehemiah was faced with opposition that included ridicule (2:19; 4:1-3), armed force (4:8, 11), discouragement (v 10), internal economic problems (5:1-18), intrigue (6:1-2), intimidation, and blackmail (vv 5-14). In spite of these obstacles, the wall was completed in the incredibly brief period of 52 days (v 15).

In addition to this monumental achievement, Nehemiah completely reorganized the social and economic life of Jerusalem, dealing with alienated mortgages, excessive interest rates (Neh 5:1-13), mixed marriages (10:30; 13:23-30), Sabbath observance (10:31; 13:15-21), and temple supplies (10:32-40; 13:10-13). Almost certainly, it was this political and economic security that allowed Ezra, who probably arrived 13 years earlier, to proceed with his great religious reformation based on the Law. Nehemiah's book, usually called the "Nehemiah Memoirs," was probably presented by him in the temple as a "votive offering" (as indicated by the form of 5:19; 13:14, 22, 31).

The Remainder of the Persian Period Persian control, which probably centered on Lachish, was traditionally mild, except when her interests were directly threatened. There is no evidence of any major discontent in Judah, which enjoyed a considerable degree of autonomy. The Phoenician revolt of 351 BC, which took Artaxerxes III (359–338 BC) three years to subdue, was the only serious disturbance in the area. While Artaxerxes deported some Jews to Hyrcania, southeast of the Caspian Sea, that was probably a precautionary measure, and Judah does not appear to have been greatly involved

THE THREE RETURNS FROM EXILE

	First Return	Second Return	Third Return
Scripture	Ezra 1–6	Ezra 7–10	Nehemiah 1–2
Date	538 BC	458 BC	445 BC
King of Persia	Cyrus	Artaxerxes	Artaxerxes
Leader of Return	Zerubbabel	Ezra	Nehemiah
Leader's Tribe and Ancestry	Judah (through David and Jehoiakin)	Levi (through Aaron, Phinehas, Zadok)	
Leader's Role	governor	priest	governor
Number	49,897	1,774	armed escort
Other Leaders at the Time	Jeshua the priest, Haggai, Zechariah	Nehemiah, Malachi	Ezra, Malachi
Result	Temple built	Law taught; people separated	Jerusalem's walls rebuilt

in the revolt. The Jerusalem priests were allowed to mint their own coinage and levy a temple tax. Under the wider influence of the Persian Empire, Hebrew gradually fell out of popular usage as a spoken language, being replaced by Aramaic. As the international stature of Greece increased, so the influence of Hellenism began to be felt, even in Judah.

Religious Features of the Postexilic Period

The Decline of Prophecy There were three main reasons for this:

1. The prophetic movement as a whole became discredited after Jerusalem fell in 586 BC. The large number of popular cult prophets who had foretold a sudden end to the Babylonian oppression (e.g., Jer 28:1-4) were proved decisively wrong. The suspicion that henceforth became attached to prophecy was increased further in the Persian period, when large numbers of itinerant "prophets" of various religions

traveled widely. Zechariah 13:2-6 shows the stern measures advocated against such false prophets and fortune-tellers.

2. There was a markedly different historical situation. The chastened remnant that survived had turned away from the blatant apostasy that characterized the preexilic period, so that the prophetic condemnation was not required with the same urgency. The temple and the Law had acquired a new prominence, and postexilic prophecy generally was concerned either with the rebuilding of the temple (e.g., Haggai and Zechariah) or the purification of its cult (e.g., Malachi). Once this goal had been realized, the role of the prophet was diminished. Another historical factor was the relatively large number of priests who returned from captivity, doubtless encouraged by the prospect of serving in the rebuilt temple. The main need at this time was for the priest, who revealed God's will on the basis of the Law.

3. There was an increasing stress on the transcendence of God, caused partly by an emphasis upon priestly mediation and partly by a fear of God that resulted from the recent judgment. The apocalyptic movement, with its emphasis on angelic intermediaries between humans and a transcendent God, encouraged this tendency. Correspondingly, the prophetic appeal for a personal, moral walk with God weakened.

The Rise of the Synagogue Some type of local worship, independent of the temple and its sacrifices, must have developed in the Captivity, with the Law increasingly occupying a dominant position. Later on, the prophetic books were read and expounded, but the primary stress was always on the Law. This mode of worship later took root in the homeland, and the synagogue gradually developed into the focal point of the community for social relationships, education, and worship. It facilitated the worldwide continuance and expansion of the Jewish faith, independent of Jerusalem.

See also Chronology of the Bible (Old Testament); Diaspora of the Jews; Ezra, Book of; Haggai, Book of; Israel, History of; Nehemiah, Book of; Zechariah, Book of.

POT *See* Pottery.

POTENTATE* A term used in 1 Timothy in the KJV and the ASV to translate the royal title ascribed to God in this passage. Most recent versions use the terms "Sovereign" or "Ruler."

POTIPHAR Officer who purchased Joseph when he arrived in Egypt after being sold by his brothers to the Ishmaelites or Midianites (Gn 37:36; 39:1). The word translated "officer" is derived from an Akkadian word for a court official. By the first millennium, the meaning "eunuch" was attached to the term; hence, the NEB, following the Septuagint tradition, has "eunuch" in Genesis 37:36. But most English versions are correct in rendering it "officer" or "official." Little, if anything, is known of eunuchs in Egypt, and certainly they played no role in Pharaoh's court in the second millennium BC.

A second title held by Potiphar was "captain of the guard," which seems to be a Semitic expression for an Egyptian title rather than a transliteration of an Egyptian phrase. This same title is applied to Nebuzaradan, Nebuchadnezzar's general (see 2 Kgs 25:8, 11, 20; Jer 39:9-11). The Egyptian counterpart to this title suggests that this officer was an instructor for retainers who were attached to the king. The titles indicate that Potiphar was a man of some importance and status. His purchase of a

Semitic slave to serve in domestic affairs is in keeping with the practice of Egyptians from 1800 BC onward.

The name Potiphar seems to be a transliteration of the Egyptian name, meaning "he whom Re [the sun god] has given." This name formula is known in Egypt beginning around the 13th century BC.

When falsely accused of trying to seduce Potiphar's wife, Joseph was placed in prison (Gn 39:20). Some think that Potiphar as "captain of the guard" would have been the warden. But Genesis 39:21 tells us that the "keeper of the prison" was impressed with Joseph's abilities (something Potiphar had already learned—cf. vv 2-6), and so gave him special responsibilities. The warden's discovery of Joseph's talents while in prison suggests that he was a different man.

See also Egypt, Egyptian; Joseph #1.

POTIPHERA Priest of On whose daughter, Asenath, was given to Joseph as his wife by Pharaoh (Gn 41:45, 50; 46:20). On (or Heliopolis) was the center of the sun-god cult, and Potiphera was likely a high-ranking priest in the cult. His name, which means "he whom Re [the son god] has given," does not appear in Egyptian records until the tenth century BC, a fact employed by those who prefer a late date for the book of Genesis. Yet the name is known from the 15th century (the time of Moses), and its full form may be a modernization of a name common in Joseph's era (20th century BC).

See also Egypt, Egyptian; Joseph #1.

POTSHERD* Piece of broken pottery used in OT times to carry hot coals or to dip water. Potsherds were also used as lids for storage containers or cooking kettles, as a medium for written communication, or to add grit to waterproofing compounds. The symbolic importance of sherds is clear in Psalm 22:15, Isaiah 30:14, 45:9, and Ezekiel 23:34.

See also Pottery; Writing (Potsherds).

POTSHERD GATE Gate in the south section of the preexilic Jerusalem wall. It led to the valley of Hinnom and to the Potter's Field. Potters could dispose of sherds there, hence its name. The KJV (relating the term to the Hebrew word for sun) renders it "east gate" (Jer 19:2).

See also Jerusalem.

POTTAGE* Red-colored vegetable stew commonly served in the OT (Hg 2:12). Pottage was made of lentils, herbs, onions, and sometimes meat. Its aroma proved strong enough to shift a birthright from Esau to Jacob (Gn 25:29-34). Elisha's disciples relished its nourishment (2 Kgs 4:38-41).

POTTER *See* Pottery.

POTTER'S FIELD Name of a burial ground outside Jerusalem (Mt 27:7, 10). *See* Blood, Field of.

POTTERY The manufacture of clayware and earthenware.

History and Development The first pottery was made by hand, molded into the desired shape and dried in the sun. There are no records describing the work of the ancient potter and his or her place in society, although the walls of tombs and palaces in Egypt abound with pictures of potters at work and a great deal can be learned by observing the activities portrayed. The first potters are thought to have been women who, out of necessity, produced vessels for food preparation, while the men were out trying to bring in the food. This still seems to be the pattern in places like Africa, Anatolia, Kurdistan, and the southwestern United States. Eventually, the making of pottery became a profession, apparently practiced by certain people in a large village and often by itinerant craftsmen moving from village to village making pottery to meet the demand and then moving on.

Ancient Egyptian Bowls and Vases

The discovery that moved pottery making from an occasional activity of a housewife to that of a profession was the invention of the potter's wheel. The speed with which vessels could then be made industrialized the craft, and it eventually became primarily a male occupation, although there is evidence that people (one would assume women) continued to make some vessels at home. Until the discovery of the potter's wheel, the techniques of making pots by laying coils of clay, one on top of the other, was the predominant method used, especially for large vessels. The first potter's wheel found in excavations in the lands of the Bible come from Ur in Sumer around 3500 to 3000 BC. It may have been developed in emerging urban settlements due to a greater market for pottery. Jeremiah speaks of a potter's workshop in the sixth century BC: "So I did as he told me and found the potter working at his wheel. But the jar he was making did not turn out as he had hoped, so the potter squashed the jar into a lump of clay and started again" (Jer 18:3-4, NLT). There is evidence in Greece of large workshops in the classical period employing more than 50 workers.

Clay must be spun at least 100 revolutions a minute to create the centrifugal force necessary to "throw" the vessel. The oldest wheels were made of two stones, a lower one with a hole in the center and an upper one with a protrusion that fits into the lower hole, allowing the upper stone to be turned. The upper stone, with a larger board attached to it on which the vessel rested, was undoubtedly turned by an apprentice. By the Hellenistic period, after 300 BC, the foot wheel was invented.

Another technique used in ancient pottery making was the mold. Molds were carved out of soft stone or made from clay for use in mass production of the same kind of vessel. Lamp molds are rather common in museums of the Middle East from the Hellenistic and Roman periods. Small oil lamps were made in two parts in the molds, an upper half and lower half, and then fused together before firing. Herodian lamps also had spatulated spouts that were formed independently of the other two parts.

The amount of diversity in both the size and shape of ancient pottery is remarkable. An average ancient home would have within it large vessels (amphorae and pithoi) to hold liquids such as wine or water. These were pointed on the bottom and designed originally to lie against the slope of a ship's hull while being transported. In homes of the common people they were partially set into the ground and leaned against the wall. In taverns in Pompeii and Herculaneum they were stored in wooden racks. Large, open-mouthed jars would be partially buried in the ground to keep the liquid contained in them cool. Also, grains of various kinds could be kept in these, some of

which were four feet (1.2 meters) in height and three feet (.9 meter) wide. Smaller water decanters holding a quart (.9 liter) or more were commonly used. Globular jugs were used to serve wine, having spouts that prevented spilling the precious liquid. Round canteens, with handles on either shoulder, were used to carry water on a journey. Bowls and dishes were common in various sizes and depths in ancient homes. Large-mouth dishes known as kraters were used for drinking. Cooking was done in medium-sized (about one gallon, or 3.8 liters) pots with rounded bottoms that would sit easily in the fire or in a dug-out place in the floor after being taken from the fire. They also had two looped handles, which allowed them to be hung over the fire.

Vessels were painted in classical Greece with vivid descriptions of religion, sex, warfare, and community life. Earlier vessels of Minoan and Mycenaean cultures contain beautiful artwork in the form of plants, animals, and marine life as well as geometric designs. From earliest times in the Middle East, variations in design were created by the use of dark and light shades of slip painted or poured randomly on vessels.

Pottery in Scripture There are many references to the potter and his work in the Bible. Typical are the following: "Israel, can I not do to you as this potter has done to his clay? As the clay is in the potter's hand, so are you in my hand" (Jer 18:6, NLT); "LORD, you are our Father. We are the clay, and you are the potter. We are all formed by your hand" (Is 64:8, NLT). In the Creation story God is portrayed as a potter making man from the ground (Gn 2:7). His absolute sovereignty in the election of Israel is argued by Paul (Rom 9:20-21) from an illustration used by Isaiah (Is 45:9) concerning a pot arguing with its potter: "Does a clay pot ever argue with its maker? Does the clay dispute with the one who shapes it, saying, 'Stop, you are doing it wrong!' Does the pot exclaim, 'How clumsy can you be!' " (NLT).

Jeremiah graphically prophesied the destruction of Jerusalem by breaking a potter's earthen flask into so many pieces that it could not be restored (Jer 19:11). The Jews, at the time of the destruction, though precious in God's sight, were "treated like pots of clay" (Lam 4:2)—an expression of their human frailty; they could be easily broken and destroyed.

A broken pottery vessel in the ancient world was considered so worthless that the pieces were swept aside or thrown out the window and a new one made. The potter's art was widely known and vessels were readily available at a cheap price. People normally did not transport their vessels when they moved. It was easier to make or buy new ones than to try to carry them, especially the larger ones. Broken pieces, however, were not without some use. Job scraped the secretion from his sores with a potsherd, which is a broken piece of pottery (Jb 2:8). At a much later time, potsherds were used to write notes on and were called ostraca. The psalmist spoke of his strength as having dried up like a potsherd (Ps 22:15)—a reference to the lack of moisture in a dried and fired pottery vessel. The eventual defeat of polytheistic and idolatrous pagan nations is described as vessels of pottery being dashed to the ground and broken to pieces by the righteous (Ps 2:9; Rv 2:27).

See also Archaeology and the Bible; Brick, Brick Kiln; Inscriptions.

POUND

1. KJV for "mina," a weight equivalent of about one pound or half a kilogram (1 Kgs 10:17; Ezr 2:69; Neh 7:71-72). *See* Weights and Measures.

2. Greek coin *(mina)* equivalent to about three month's wages (Lk 19:13).

3. Roman measure (Greek *litra*) equivalent to about three-quarters of a pound (12 ounces, or .3 kilogram); mentioned only in John 12:3 and 19:39. *See* Weights and Measures.

POWER

POWER Ability to do things, by virtue of strength, skill, resources, or authorization. In the Hebrew of the OT and the Greek of the NT, there are several different words used for power. What the Bible says about power may be subsumed under four headings: (1) the unlimited power of God; (2) the limited power God gives to his creatures; (3) the power of God seen in Jesus Christ; and (4) the power of God (by the Holy Spirit) in the lives of his people.

The Unlimited Power of God God is almighty and all other power is derived from him and subject to him. Much that the Bible says is summed up in the words of 1 Chronicles 29:11-12 addressed to God in praise: "Thine, O LORD, is the greatness, and the power, and the glory, and the victory, and the majesty; for all that is in the heavens and in the earth is thine; thine is the kingdom, O LORD. . . . thou rulest over all. In thy hand are power and might; and in thy hand it is to make great and to give strength to all" (RSV). Using human terms, the OT often speaks of God's "mighty hand" and his "outstretched arm," both being used for the power of God in action (Ex 6:6; 7:4; Ps 44:2-3). His power is seen in creation (Ps 65:6; Is 40:26; Jer 10:12; 27:5), in his rule over the world (2 Chr 20:6), in his acts of salvation and judgment (Ex 15:6; Dt 26:8), and in all that he does for his people (Ps 111:6). The NT, as well as the OT, speaks of the mighty power of God. Ephesians 1:19 speaks of the immeasurable greatness of his power, and the words of Jesus in Matthew 26:64 show that the word could be substituted for the very name of God when he said that the Son of Man would be seen "seated at the right hand of Power."

The Limited Power God Gives to His Creatures Animals have power, as is particularly evident in the wild ox, the horse, and the lion (Jb 39:11, 19; Prv 30:30). There is power in wind and storm, thunder and lightning. Power is given to humans: physical strength (Jgs 16:5-6), power to fight (6:12), and the power to do good and the power to do harm (Gn 31:29; Prv 3:27; Mi 2:1). Rulers have God-given power and authority (Rom 13:1). The Bible also speaks of the power of angels (2 Pt 2:11) and of spiritual beings known as "principalities and powers." Certain powers are given to Satan (see Jb 1:6-12; 2:1-6). Sin, evil, and death are allowed to have some power over men (Hos 13:14; Lk 22:53; Rom 3:9). All of these, however, have only limited power, and God is able to give his people strength to conquer all these powers. He can save them from the power of animals (Dn 6:27; Lk 10:19) and from the power of other people over them. To Pilate Jesus said, "You would have no power over me at all unless it were given to you from above" (Jn 19:11, NLT). He is able to deliver people from the power of sin and death, from Satan, and from all the spiritual forces of evil (2 Cor 10:4; Eph 6:10-18). The "ruler of this world" could ultimately have no power over Christ (Jn 14:30) and so cannot have power over those who rely on him.

The Power of God Seen in Jesus Christ The Gospels and the book of Acts bear frequent witness to the power of Christ. Power was shown in his miracles (Mt 11:20; Acts 2:22), in his works of healing and exorcism (Lk 4:36; 5:17; 6:19; Acts 10:38). Power is shown supremely in his resurrection. Jesus speaks of his power

to give up his life and power to take it again (Jn 10:18), but the NT speaks most frequently of the power of God the Father shown in the raising of his Son from the dead (Rom 1:4; Eph 1:19-20). In the end he will be seen coming on the clouds of heaven with power and great glory (Mt 24:30). With regard to his human life on earth, however, it may be noted in the light of what follows that he lived and did his mighty works in the power of the Holy Spirit (Lk 4:14; Acts 10:38).

The Power of God in the Lives of His People In the OT it is often said that the weak are made strong by the power of God. He empowers those who are weak (Is 40:29) so that they may increase from strength to strength (Ps 84:7; see also Pss 68:35; 138:3). We read in particular of his power being given to prophets (Mi 3:8) and kings (1 Sm 2:10; Ps 21:1), and it is said that in an outstanding way power will be given to the Messiah (Is 9:6; 11:2; Mi 5:4). But to all God's people power is offered that they may live for him and serve him (Is 49:5). When we turn to the NT, we read of the gospel itself as being the power of God for salvation—to everyone who has faith (Rom 1:16). "To all who received him [Jesus Christ], who believed in his name, he gave power to become children of God" (Jn 1:12, RSV). In that life as children of God, power is received from the Holy Spirit (Acts 6:8), inner strength to live in his service (Eph 3:16), power to be his witnesses (Lk 24:49; Acts 1:8), power to endure suffering (2 Tm 1:8), power for ministry (Eph 3:7), power in the face of weakness (2 Cor 12:9), power through prayer (Jas 5:16), and power to be kept from evil (1 Pt 1:5). Those who do great things in the service of Christ do not do them in their own strength (Acts 3:12); he sent out his disciples confident only in the assurance that all things are under his authority and that they would have the power of his unfailing presence with them (Mt 28:18-20).

See also God, Being and Attributes of; Principalities and Powers.

POWERS *See* Principalities and Powers.

PRAETORIUM*, PRAETORIAN GUARD* Term appearing in the Greek NT in Mark 15:16; Matthew 27:27; John 18:28, 33; 19:9; Acts 23:35; and Philippians 1:13. It is a Latin word borrowed from the Romans, who dominated the Mediterranean world in NT times. It was used primarily in military and governmental affairs. Originally it designated the tent of the general *(praetor)* in a military encampment. The meaning was extended to include the residence of a governor or other Roman official, as, for example, that of Pontius Pilate, the procurator of Judea. In looser usage the term may also have referred to a part of the residence—for instance, the barracks of the soldiers.

In English translations of the NT, the variety of terms used by translators indicates the uncertainty about the specific reference. The general reference to the headquarters of the Roman representative and military force is clear, however. According to the Gospels of Matthew and Mark, the praetorium was the location of the Roman soldiers' mocking of Jesus after his appearance before Pilate. Mark also calls this place a "palace" (RSV) or "courtyard" (NEB, TEV). According to the Gospel of John, the "praetorium" was the place within which Pilate examined Jesus about the charges brought against him. He went outside the praetorium to meet with the accusers who brought the charges.

Within Jerusalem, two locations are possible for Pilate's headquarters. One is the fortress known as the

Tower of Antonia at the northwest corner of the temple area. The other is the old palace of Herod the Great, in the western part of the city. Either one could have served as the praetorium, but the Gospel sources identify neither by name or description.

In Acts 23:35, on the other hand, the praetorium in which Paul is held in Caesarea (pending the arrival of his accusers) is called "Herod's praetorium." This probably means that the procurator Felix (and his predecessors) had taken over the old official residence of King Herod as their coastal headquarters.

The location of Paul's imprisonment at the time he wrote to the Philippians is not clear. His mention of the "praetorium" in Philippians 1:13 suggests some center of Roman government. The phrase "the whole praetorium," however, indicates that in this context he was referring to the personnel rather than to a building or a place. Recent translations reflect this meaning: "the whole praetorian guard" (RSV); "all at headquarters" (NEB); "all the soldiers in the palace guard" (NLT).

PRAISE Honor, commendation, and worship.

To Whom Praise Is Offered The one Lord who is God over all is alone worthy of praise. Frequently, the OT stresses that the praise due him is not to be offered to other gods or to idols of any kind (e.g., Is 42:8). There is a place for the commendation of men and women for their qualities of life and their right actions (Prv 31:28-31; 1 Pt 2:14). Ultimately, however, they should seek the praise and commendation of God (Rom 2:29), not the praise of their fellows (Mt 6:1-6; Jn 12:43), that others may be led to glorify God for whatever good is found in them (Mt 5:16). Frequently the Bible speaks of praising "the name" of God (e.g., Ps 149:3), meaning that he is to be praised for all that he is and has revealed himself to be. The often repeated word "Hallelujah" is simply the Hebrew equivalent of "Praise the Lord."

By Whom Praise Is Offered God is praised perfectly by his angels in heaven (Pss 103:20; 148:2). They caroled their praise when Jesus was born (Lk 2:13-14), and the book of Revelation (e.g., Rv 7:11-12) speaks about their continual praise in heaven. All creation praises God in the sense that it shows his greatness as Creator (Ps 19:1-6). Psalm 148 lists sun, moon and stars, fire and hail, snow, rain, wind and weather, mountains and hills, fruit trees and cedars, wild animals, cattle, snakes and birds—all these—as praising God together. Heaven and earth are spoken of as involved in the praise of God (Pss 89:5; 96:11; 98:4). The Psalter closes with the words "Let everything that lives sing praises to the LORD!" (150:6). In the OT we read of the special role of priests and Levites (Ps 135:19-20) and of the temple singers (2 Chr 20:21) and of those who, like Miriam (Ex 15:20) and David (2 Sm 6:14), led others in God's praise. But it was the duty of all God's people to praise him; their praise was intended, moreover, to lead the nations to know and to praise him (Ps 67:2-3). The NT has this same emphasis (Rom 15:7-12), and it stresses that God's gifts are given to his people to be used to his praise and glory (Eph 1:6, 12, 14). It is by a life of righteousness as well as by word of mouth that people are to praise him (Phil 1:11). The redeemed people of God are appointed to show forth the praises of him who has called them out of darkness into his marvelous light (1 Pt 2:9). The last book of the NT presents the praise of God in heaven, where the four living creatures (representing all creation) and the 24 elders (representing the people of God under the old and new covenants) unite in worship, adoring the mighty God who created them and the Lamb of God who redeemed them (Rv 4–5).

When God Is to Be Praised In the OT there were times of special praise, Sabbaths, new moons, and festivals. In Psalm 119:164 the psalmist says he praised the Lord seven times a day. "Everywhere—from east to west—praise the name of the LORD" is the exhortation of Psalm 113:3 (NLT). Psalm 145:1 says, "I will praise you, my God and King, and bless your name forever and ever" (NLT). A dedication to a life of praise is expressed in Psalm 146:2: "I will praise the LORD as long as I live. I will sing praises to my God even with my dying breath" (NLT). In the NT, likewise, there are special times of praise, but the whole of the Christian's life is intended to be devoted, in word and action, to the praise of God.

Where Praise Is to Be Offered In the OT the temple (and thus "Zion" or "Jerusalem," where the temple was located) had a special place in the purpose of God: his people should praise him there. Psalm 102:21 pictures people declaring "in Zion the name of the Lord, and in Jerusalem his praise." People are to praise God publicly before the congregation and before the leaders of the nation (Ps 107:32), but they may also do so alone. For the whole of life is to be praise. Thus praise can come from unexpected places. Godly men and women can sing for joy as they lie on their beds (149:5). Paul and Silas can sing praises to God in a Philippian prison (Acts 16:25).

How God Is to Be Praised As there is no limit to time or place, so there is no limit to the ways in which God may be praised. He may be praised with singing (Ps 47:7), with dancing (149:3), or with instruments of music (144:9; 150:3-5). The Psalter provides us with many songs of praise, and others are scattered throughout the OT. The NT speaks of "psalms and hymns and spiritual songs" (Col 3:16; see also Eph 5:19), and examples of Christian songs of praise are probably to be seen in Ephesians 5:14, Philippians 2:6-11, 1 Timothy 1:17, and 2 Timothy 2:11-13.

Why God Is to Be Praised Creation provides impetus for the praise of God (Ps 8:3), as does his preserving love and care (21:4) and the fact that he is a prayer-answering God (116:1). His redeeming work leads his people to worship him (Ex 15:1-2). Some of the psalms (e.g., Ps 107) list many reasons why he should be praised. With the coming of the Lord Jesus Christ, there is a fresh outburst of praise because the Messiah, the Savior, has come to his people (Lk 2:11). All that he did by his life, death, and resurrection calls for praise. But ultimately praise will be made perfect when God reigns victorious over all. Thus John speaks in the book of Revelation (19:6): "Then I heard again what sounded like the shout of a huge crowd, or the roar of mighty ocean waves, or the crash of loud thunder: 'Hallelujah! For the Lord our God, the Almighty, reigns' " (NLT).

See also Prayer; Tabernacle; Temple; Worship.

PRAYER The addressing and petitioning of God. Prayer to a god or gods is a feature of many, if not all, religions, but here attention will be restricted to the biblical teaching and some of its implications. A classic definition of Christian prayer is "an offering up of our desires unto God, for things agreeable to his will, in the name of Christ, with confession of our sins, and thankful acknowledgment of his mercies" (Westminster Shorter Catechism). Christian prayer is the end product of a long process of change and development in God's relation to people, as a survey of the biblical data shows.

Prayer in the Old Testament Newly created humans, made for fellowship with God, lived in close communion with him. Sin broke this intimate, direct relationship. Nevertheless, when the Lord formed his covenant with Abraham (Gn 15), the relationship between the covenant partners was open again. Abraham's prayer for Sodom and Gomorrah (ch 18) is a striking combination of boldness and persistence and is a recognition of his own smallness and inferiority compared to God. The same could be said about Jacob's wrestling with the angel at Peniel (ch 32). But boldness and directness are not to be confused with familiarity. Biblical prayer is characterized by the reality that there is a distance between the Creator and the creature due to human sin, bridged only by God's grace. The basis of a person's approach to God in prayer is never simply "man's search for God" but God's gracious initiative, the establishing of the covenant, and the promise of help and deliverance on the basis of that covenant. It is this covenant relationship that gives the *warrant* for prayer. Thus, in patriarchal times prayer was conjoined with sacrifice and obedience.

The reestablishing of the national consciousness of Israel at the time of their deliverance from Egypt marks another phase in the biblical development. Moses was not only the political leader of Israel but also their divinely appointed mediator and intercessor with the Lord. Repeatedly he "pleads the name of the Lord" in the face of the human uncertainties of the wilderness journey and his own people's unbelief and disobedience. Pleading the name of the Lord is not to be thought of as an incantation but as a reminder to God of who he has revealed himself to be. (God's revelation of himself to Moses at the burning bush is fundamental to an understanding of this.) In this revelation of himself, God made promises to his people, and in prayer Moses held God to these promises. Moses was by no means the only intercessor. Aaron, Samuel, Solomon, and Hezekiah were among those who interceded for the people.

With the formation of the priesthood and the establishment of the ritual worship of the tabernacle and later the temple, the worship of God seems to be characterized by distance. There is little indication that the people personally prayed to God, and—with the exception of Deuteronomy 26:1-15—there is nothing about prayer in all the instructions for worship given to the people. However, there is indication in the psalms that sacrifice and prayer would be coupled together (Pss 50:7-15; 55:14). Many of the psalms are remarkable for the way in which personal perplexities are acknowledged, leading to "arguments with God" and an ultimate resolution of the conflict (e.g., Ps 73).

The prophets were men who prayed, and it seems that God's Word came to them in prayer (Is 6:5-13; 37:1-4; Jer 11:20-23). Jeremiah's ministry was characterized by times of conflict in prayer (Jer 18:19-23; 20:7-18) as well as more settled times of fellowship with God (10:23-25; 12:1-4; 14:7-9; 15:15-18). At the exile, with the establishment of the synagogue, corporate prayer became an element in Jewish worship. After the exile there was an emphasis on spontaneity in prayer and on the need for devotion to be more than mechanical and routine (Neh 2:4; 4:4, 9).

Prayer in the New Testament The NT's teaching on prayer is dominated by Christ's own example and teaching. His dependence on his Father in his mediatorial work expresses itself in repeated prayer, culminating in his High Priestly prayer (Jn 17) and the agony of Gethsemane with the prayer from the cross. His teaching on prayer, particularly in the Sermon on the Mount, is to be understood as contrasting with the Jewish practices at that time, not with OT ideals. Prayer is an expression of sincere desire. It is not to inform God of matters that he would otherwise be ignorant of, and the validity of prayer is not affected by length or repetitiveness. Private prayer is to be discreet and secret (Mt 6:5-15).

The parables are another important source of Christ's teaching, emphasizing persistence in prayer (Lk 18:1-8), simplicity and humility (vv 10-14), and tenacity (11:5-8). A third source of teaching is the Lord's Prayer. Once again there is the blend of directness ("Our Father") and distance ("who art in heaven. Hallowed be thy name"). The requests given in the Lord's Prayer are concerned first with God, his kingdom and his glory, and then with the disciples' needs for forgiveness and for daily support and deliverance. Occasionally, it seems from our Lord's teaching that anything that is prayed for will, without restriction, be granted. But such teaching ought to be understood in the light of Christ's overall teaching about prayer ("Thy kingdom come. Thy will be done in earth, as it is in heaven").

Christ stated that when the Holy Spirit, the Comforter, came, the disciples would pray to the Father in the name of Christ (Jn 16:23-25). Accordingly, we find that after the coming of the Spirit on the day of Pentecost, the early church is characterized by prayer (Acts 2:42) under the leadership of the apostles (6:4). The church praises God for the gift of his Son and his Spirit, and petitions God in times of difficulty (4:24; 12:5, 12).

It is in Paul's writings that the theology of prayer is most fully developed. The NT believer is a son, not only a servant. The Spirit who, as a result of Christ's triumph, has come to the church is the Spirit of adoption, enabling the Christian to come to God as his Father, with all his needs. Prominent among these needs, in the mind of the apostle, are a deepening of faith in Christ, love for God, and a growing appreciation of God's love in turn (Eph 3:14-19). Prayer is a part of the Christian's armor against satanic attack (6:18), the effective ministry of the Word of God depends on the prayers of God's people (vv 18-19), and the Christian is encouraged to pray for all sorts of things, with thanksgiving (Phil 4:6), and so to be free from anxiety. Paul's own example in prayer is as instructive as the teaching he gives.

The Christian's prayer is rooted, objectively, in Christ's intercession; subjectively, in the enabling of the Holy Spirit. The church is a kingdom of priests, offering spiritual sacrifices of praise and thanksgiving (Heb 13:15; 1 Pt 2:5), but Christ is the "great High Priest." This thought is developed fully in Hebrews. Because of Christ's human sympathy, the power of his intercessory work (i.e., the triumph of his atonement), and his superiority over the old Aaronic priesthood, the church is encouraged to come to God boldly, to find grace when it is needed (Heb 4:14-16; 9:24; 10:19-23). Nowhere in either the OT or NT is there any encouragement to pray to individuals other than God. Nowhere in Scripture is it suggested that there is any other mediator between God and men except Christ (1 Tm 2:5).

The Elements of Prayer Although prayer is, typically, an unself-conscious activity in which the person praying devotes himself to God, it is possible to distinguish various elements in prayer, as will be apparent from the discussion of the biblical data. *Praise* involves the recognition of who God is and what he does. It is "giving God the glory," not in the sense of adding to his glory, which would be impossible, but of willingly (and where appropriate, publicly) recognizing God as God. Typical expressions of such praise are to be found in the

DIFFICULTIES IN PRAYER

Why does God answer some prayers and not others?

In attempting to answer this question it is necessary to bear in mind that prayer is not to be thought of in mechanical terms. Prayer involves a personal relationship with God. So the reason why God answers one prayer and not another has nothing to do with the volume or length of the prayers themselves. Because prayer involves a personal relationship with God, sincerity and unaffectedness in that relationship are of paramount importance. There must be no hypocrisy or mere formalism in prayer. Length of prayer may be an indication of strength of desire, or it may not. Scripture contains examples of both long and short prayers.

Assuming sincerity, the most fundamental factor is the relationship between the one who prays and the express will of God. The only warrant for praying at all is that God commands it and desires it, and the only warrant for praying for some particular thing rather than for some other thing is that God wills it or may will it. A knowledge of the will of God as it is revealed in Scripture is basic to a proper understanding of petitionary prayer and to proper conduct in prayer.

It is necessary to distinguish between those matters that God has declared he will unfailingly grant upon true prayer being made and those matters that he may grant upon true prayer being made. The guide for prayer is not the petitioner's own needs, either real or imaginary, nor his feelings or state of mind when he prays, nor his or others' speculations about the future. The guide is Scripture alone. And the Scriptures distinguish between (1) those things a person may pray for that are desirable or good in themselves, and yet that are not for every believer's highest good, and (2) those things that concern redemption. For instance, health or wealth, or a particular career, though each is desirable and lawful, may nevertheless not be best, in the wisdom of God, for a particular individual at a particular time. Paul's "thorn in the flesh" (2 Cor 12:7-9) and the death of the child of David and Bathsheba (2 Sm 12:15-23) are examples of unanswered prayer. So although health or wealth may be sincerely and warrantably prayed for, God in his wisdom and sovereignty may decline to grant these things—because these things may not be included in that particular array of things that are working together for the good of the believer concerned (Rom 8:28).

By contrast, the blessings of redemption—such as forgiveness of sins, sanctification, and strength and wisdom for the fulfilling of duties—are always given to those who truly pray for them (Ps 84:11; Lk 11:13; Jn 6:37; 1 Thes 4:3; Jas 1:5). Even such unqualified or unconditional blessings may come after apparent delay, or from an unexpected source, and allowance for factors such as these must be made when judging whether or not prayer has been answered. An important part of petitioning God is the discipline of conforming one's desires to the revealed will and the ongoing providence of God. In this sense prayer is educative for the believer. "Not my will but thine be done" is the concern of the sincere petitioner. The exercise of faith in prayer to God is seen in submission to the express will of God. Otherwise, faith becomes presumption, and humility becomes arrogance.

psalms (Pss 148; 150). When the recognition of God's goodness is in respect to what he has done for the one who prays, or for others, then the prayer is one of *thanksgiving,* for life itself, for the use and beauty of the physical universe, for Christ and his benefits (see 2 Cor 9:15), and for specific answers to prayer. *Confession* of sin recognizes the holiness of God and his supreme moral authority, together with the personal responsibility of the one making the confession. Confession thus involves the vindicating or justifying of God and an explicit and unreserved recognition of sin, both as it takes its rise in sinful motives and dispositions and as it finds outward expression. Psalm 51, David's confession of sin regarding Bathsheba, is the classic biblical instance of a prayer of confession. *Petition* can be thought of as it concerns the one praying, and also as it concerns others, when it is *intercession.* Scripture never regards prayer for oneself as sinful or ethically improper, as can be seen from the pattern of prayer given in the Lord's Prayer. Prayer for others is an obvious expression of love for one's neighbor, which is fundamental to biblical ethics.

See also Lord's Prayer, The; Praise; Worship.

PRAYER*, Lord's *See* Lord's Prayer, The.

PRAYER OF AZARIAH *See* Daniel, Additions to.

PRAYER OF MANASSEH* This short prayer, ascribed to King Manasseh of Judah, is often regarded as the finest composition in the entire English Apocrypha. During the Reformation, Protestants highly valued its piety. However, neither Protestants, Roman Catholics, nor the Eastern Orthodox regard it as Scripture.

The older title, The Prayer of Manasses King of Judah When He was Holden [Held] Captive in Babylon (KJV, ERV), is more helpful than the one commonly used today (RSV, NEB) or the Latin one, *Oration Manassae.* The older title alerts the reader to the supposed connection between this prayer and King Manasseh (696–642 BC), who was taken captive to Babylon, where "at last he came to his senses and cried out humbly to God for help. And the Lord listened, and answered his plea by returning him to Jerusalem and to his kingdom!" (2 Chr 33:12-13, TLB; on the historicity of this account, see Manasseh #3). The writer of 2 Chronicles indicates that this prayer was available to him from national archives and from another work (2 Chr 33:18-19). The prayer was composed by an anonymous author, though the date is uncertain. On internal evidence it has been dated between 250 BC and AD 50. The oldest surviving Greek biblical manuscript containing it is Codex Alexandrinus (fifth century AD), but the earliest evidence for its existence is its inclusion in a Syriac manual of church procedures known as *Didascalia* (third century AD), which, in a revised and expanded form, also appeared as a part of the *Apostolic Constitutions* (AD 380).

Most scholars believe that the prayer was originally composed in Greek, but for such a short book—about 400 words in English—the problem of determining the original language is difficult. Because the Prayer of Manasseh survives both in Greek and in Syriac, Latin (two forms), Ethiopic, Armenian, and Old Slavonic translation, it was clearly popular in the first three Christian centuries, among both Jews and Christians.

The Prayer of Manasseh is the prayer of a self-confessed sinner to a merciful God. The RSV (which is quoted below unless otherwise noted) and NEB divide the Prayer of Manasseh into 15 verses. KJV and ERV do not indicate verses, and a rarer system divides the prayer into 19 verses. The prayer uses several descriptions of God drawn from the OT. It begins by identifying God as "Lord Almighty" (Prayer of Manasseh 1:1; cf. 2 Cor 6:18) and "God of our fathers" (Prayer of Manasseh 1:1, cf. 2 Chr 20:6; 33:12) and of their righteous descendants. God is the Creator—glorious and powerful, wrathful yet merciful (Prayer of Manasseh 1:2-7a). He "made heaven and earth" (v 2; cf. Ex 20:11; Neh 9:6; Ps 146:6) "in their manifold array" (Prayer of Manasseh 1:2, NEB). He "shackled the sea" and "confined the deep" (v 3; cf. Jb 38:8-11). No one can endure his glorious majesty (Prayer of Manasseh 1:5a; contrast 2 Pt 1:16-17). His power makes every creature "shudder, and tremble" (Prayer of Manasseh 1:4), but his goodness is demonstrated in mercy and salvation (vv 7, 14; cf. Is 63:7 and Rom 2:4), for he is compassionate, patiently long-suffering (forbearing), and very merciful (Prayer of Manasseh 1:7; cf. Ps 86:5, 15). God is "the Lord Most High" (Prayer of Manasseh 1:7; cf. Ps 7:17; 47:2).

Even so, Manasseh confesses that "none can endure thy menacing wrath against sinners" (Prayer of Manasseh 1:5b, NEB). He recognizes that his idolatry has been evil in God's eyes all along, even though he has just become aware that he has been "piling sin upon sin" (v 10, NEB). He also knows now that he finds himself in irons and rejected by God because his idolatry has provoked God's wrath (v 10; cf. 2 Chr 33:6 and Ps 107:10). God's mercy is his only hope. It is unmeasurable and unfathomable (Prayer of Manasseh 1:6), boundless (v 7, NEB), and great (v 14). God's mercy is also available, because the Lord himself has "appointed repentance for sinners, that they may be saved" (v 7; cf. Acts 5:31), and for him in particular (v 8).

The heart of the prayer (vv 9-13a), in which he confesses his sin and appeals for forgiveness, contains three memorable lines: "My transgressions abound, O Lord, my transgressions abound. . . . Forgive me, O Lord, forgive me!" The turning point in the prayer comes in verse 11, after his confession of sin. The RSV preserves the figure of speech: "And now I bend the knee of my heart, beseeching thee for thy kindness." Despite his unworthiness (vv 9, 14), he pleads with God not to destroy him, nor be eternally angry with him, nor condemn him to the grave, because the Lord is "the God of those who repent" (v 13). Manasseh becomes confident that God, in his goodness and mercy, will save him (v 14), and he shows the appropriate response of a forgiven sinner when he says, "I will praise thee continually all the days of my life" (v 15). A brief doxology about God's praise and eternal glory concludes the prayer.

Despite its admirable parts, this prayer differs from Christian teaching in one significant way. The author erroneously assumes that there are two categories of people—those who are basically good (the righteous) and those who are basically bad (sinners). The prayer presents Abraham, Isaac, and Jacob as righteous men who did not sin and did not need to repent. This is not true, but it shows Jewish thinking prior to Christian preaching (cf. Mt 9:13). Paul made it quite plain that no person is righteous on his own merit, because every person has sinned (Rom 3:10-12, 21-26). Abraham's righteousness was not inherent; it came by faith (Rom 4:3; cf. Phil 3:8-9).

See also Apocrypha.

PRECIOUS STONES *See* Stones, Precious.

PREDESTINATION* *See* Elect, Election; Foreordination.

PREPARATION, Day of Term used in Scripture for the day before the Sabbath. Each of the Gospels refers to a day

that it calls "the Preparation" (Mt 27:62; Mk 15:42; Lk 23:54; Jn 19:14, 31, 42), Mark calling it "the day before the Sabbath." The Jews did not have specific names for the days (preferring to speak of "the first [second, etc.] day of the week." But the Sabbath was distinctive, and the previous day was used to prepare for this weekly day of rest and worship. Thus, what we call "Friday" the Jews called "Preparation." What was "prepared" is not said. But as no work could be done on the Sabbath, preparations had to be made for food and other necessities.

"The Preparation of the Passover" (Jn 19:14) is often understood to mean "Passover eve," the day before Passover, just as "the Preparation" means the day before the Sabbath. There appears, however, to be no specific extrabiblical examples of the day before Passover being called "the Preparation" or "the Preparation of the Passover."

PRESBYTER* NT term referring to an elder in the church. Following the OT pattern of synagogues governed by a council of elders, the church of the NT had officers (*presbuteroi*, "older persons") whose task was to tend the flock of God that was under their care (1 Pt 5:2). Thus, they were called to labor in preaching and teaching (1 Tm 5:17); visit, pray over, and anoint the sick (Jas 5:14); administer famine relief (Acts 11:29-30); and generally oversee the affairs of the church (15:4; 16:4). There is evidence to suggest that all elders were of equal status and that the terms "presbyter" and "bishop" were at first used interchangeably (Acts 20:17, 28; Phil 1:1; Ti 1:5-7). In the second century, however, the presiding presbyter gradually emerged as a distinctive figure with a position of preeminence and as the source of authority. As the years passed, the designation "presbyter" was contracted to that of "priest," and in churches of the episcopal order it remains so today. It is significant, nevertheless, that the NT nowhere links priestly functions with the office of presbyter. With the spread and development of Christianity, the priest became a powerful figure. With eucharistic theology, there grew up unbiblical accretions. These were exposed and rejected when the Reformers triumphed in the 16th century and stressed the priesthood of all believers. In Protestantism priests became ministers, pastors, or (in more modern times) clergymen. In non-Roman Episcopal churches, "priest" is found again today. Even where it is interpreted differently from Roman usage, most evangelical Anglicans refuse to use it. In Presbyterian and similar churches, the elders (whether teaching or ruling) are still officially called presbyters, and all are of equal status.

See also Bishop; Deacon, Deaconess; Elder; Pastor; Spiritual Gifts.

PRESENCE, Bread of the *See* Bread of the Presence.

PRESENCE OF GOD, The God's manifestation of his spiritual being. Since God is spirit, believers experience him by sensing his invisible presence. God also makes himself known in other ways. He appears in nature, particularly in catastrophic forces—fire, lightning, and earthquake (1 Kgs 19:11-13). He also appears in human form (Gn 18; 32:22-32). So God, who cannot be seen, has chosen ways to reveal himself.

In the Old Testament

The Angel of the Lord The angel of the Lord was God's emissary and Israel's special helper, although it is not said that the same angel is meant in every instance (Ex 14:19; 23:20; 33:2). After the angel vanishes, Hagar insists that she had seen God himself (Gn 16:13). In

Jacob's experience the angel identifies himself with God (31:11-13); while in Genesis 21:18, 22:11, Numbers 22:35, the "I" of deity signified God's presence in the angel. There is also oscillation between God and the angel in Exodus 12:23 and Genesis 48:15-16. Here God was temporarily incarnating himself within the form of the angel, assuring his own that he was immediately present with them.

The Glory of God Glory is what God possesses in his own right, a visible extension of his nature, a "concrete" form of his divine presence. The heavens are a visible form of God's presence (Pss 8; 19:1-6; 136:5), for they are his glory. The glory that appeared to Israel as devouring fire on Sinai (Ex 29:43) filled the tabernacle (40:34-38). By it God consecrated the tabernacle as the place of his presence. In Isaiah 6 the glory appears as the normal expression of the divine presence. In Ezekiel the glory is identical with God (Ez 9:3-4). Throughout the OT the glory of God is the transcendent God making his presence and nearness visible to his own.

The Face of God In the OT "presence" is used to represent the Hebrew word for "face"; when "face" is conjoined with a preposition, it means "in the presence of." In Genesis 32:30 Jacob saw God "face to face." A man's personality and character are made visible on his face. In this sense a man's face is the man. So, "the angel of his presence [face]" (Is 63:9) may mean "the angel who is his face," since the prophet may have intended the identification. The face of God is the revelation of the grace of God. So, when he hides his face, he is withholding his grace. But when he makes his face shine (Ps 31:16), there is blessing (44:3). The face of God, then, is the presence of God (Ex 33:14). To pray to God in a holy place was to "seek God's face" (Ps 24:6), his personal presence. Indeed, this sums up temple worship and private prayer in Israel (63:1-3; 100:2). The blessing of God consisted in his face shining upon them (Nm 6:25; Ps 80:3, 7, 19).

The Name of God Among Semites, the equation of the name and the person was a common idea. So also, the name of God was an interchangeable term for God himself, a symbol of his activity in revelation. The linking of man's worship of God with the divine name of God was the medium of his operation (Pss 44:5; 89:24; Is 30:27), a designation for the power of God that radiates help and energy universally. God could act by his name. The angel of the Lord's authority and power functioned because God's name was in him (Ex 23:20-21). As bearer of the divine name, he made real the hidden presence of God. The temple was the dwelling place of the name (1 Kgs 11:36), not only because God's name was invoked there but also because God's presence—God himself—dwelt there.

The Spirit of God In the Holy Spirit the transcendent God draws near to his people. The Spirit is the medium through whom God's presence becomes real among his people (Is 63:11-14; Zec 7:12) and by whom God's gifts and powers operate among them (2 Chr 15:1; 20:14; 24:20; Zec 4:6; 6:1-8). The Spirit was the presence and power of God with his people—God himself acting in accordance with his essential nature. The sinner cannot be in the presence of God without the aid of God's Holy Spirit; to be deprived of the Holy Spirit is to be deprived of God's presence (Ps 51:11). Without the Spirit, communion between God and humans is not possible.

In the New Testament In the NT a new mode of God's presence is revealed. It is in Jesus Christ the incarnate Word that God is present among his own (Jn

1:14-18; 17:6, 26). Jesus' mission was to reveal God to humanity. This he did through his whole life's work as well as through his words. His revelation of the name of God was expressed in his own name—Jesus ("The Lord Is Salvation"). And in the person of Jesus the function of the name of God found fulfillment. Christ was the new temple (Jn 1:14; 2:21; Col 2:9). He was the locus of the tabernacling presence of God. But that was only a first installment of the unveiling of God's presence.

The church now constitutes the temple of God in the NT. Christianity is essentially the religion of the presence of God and of communion with God. The body of Christ, "the spiritual temple" (Eph 2:22), made of "living stones" (1 Pt 2:5), is the residence of the presence of the glorious God.

And now, the individual Christian is also a temple of God (1 Cor 3:16-17; 6:19; 2 Cor 6:16). God is especially present in the Christian's spirit; there God reigns, for there is his kingdom; there he is worshiped, for there his glory and his presence have consecrated the inner being into a temple (see Jn 14:23).

See also God, Being and Attributes of.

PRIDE A reasonable or justifiable self-respect; or improper and excessive self-esteem known as conceit or arrogance. The apostle Paul expressed a positive kind of pride when speaking of confidence in Christians (2 Cor 7:4) or of strength in the Lord (12:5, 9). However, it is the latter, sinful meaning of "pride" that most frequently appears in the Bible, both in the OT and the NT.

The ten Hebrew and two Greek words generally used for pride refer to being high or exalted in attitude, the opposite of the virtue of humility, which is so often praised and rewarded by God. One other Greek word refers to a person's being puffed up or inflated with pride or egotism. The idea is that one gives the impression of substance but is really filled only with air (see, e.g., 1 Cor 5:2; 8:1; 13:4; Col 2:18).

Pride is basically a sin of attitude and of the heart and spirit. Hence one reads, "Haughty eyes and a proud heart, the lamp of the wicked, are sin" (Prv 21:4, RSV). Ecclesiastes 7:8 speaks of being proud in spirit and the psalmist declares, "O LORD, my heart is not proud, nor my eyes haughty" (Ps 131:1, NASB). Pride is cited in the two lists of the most glaring sins in the Bible. Along with the sins for which God is going to judge the Gentiles, one finds insolence, arrogance, and boasting (Rom 1:30). Included with the sins that will be prevalent in the last days, Paul includes boasting, arrogance, and conceit (2 Tm 3:2-4).

As so many of the sins of attitude, pride cannot remain internalized. It can infect one's speech; boasting is one way by which this sin can appear in one's speaking (see the passages referred to above and also Mal 3:13). Pride can also appear in the way one looks at another person. Hence, the Scriptures speak of "haughty eyes" in Proverbs 6:17, or, as it could also be rendered, "a proud look." The psalmist speaks of a person with haughty looks and arrogant heart (Ps 101:5; see also Prv 30:13). Pride may also take the ugly form of contemptible treatment of others (Prv 21:24). One of the illustrations of this in the Bible is the way in which the Pharisees and other Jewish leaders treated and spoke of those beneath their social level (e.g., Mt 23:5-12; Jn 9:34). They especially despised tax collectors and sinners.

Outstanding examples of proud people can be found in both Testaments. Pride was the downfall of King Uzziah, who, because of this sin, dared to offer incense on the altar of incense and was smitten with leprosy as his punishment from God (2 Chr 26:16). Hezekiah, after his healing by the Lord, became proud of heart and brought God's anger upon himself, Judah, and Jerusalem (32:25-26). The Pharisee praying in the temple, comparing himself with the humble tax collector, is another example (Lk 18:9-14). Herod's refusal to give God the glory for his greatness brought judgment from God; Herod was eaten by worms and died for his sin of pride (Acts 12:21-23). In fact, Ezekiel 28, which describes the pride of the leader of Tyre, is taken by many biblical scholars to refer, in a deeper sense, to the fall of Satan back in the beginning.

Pride can bring about the downfall not only of individuals but also of nations. This was the sin that is specifically mentioned as leading to other sins and that ultimately brought about the removal of both Israel and Judah from the land of Canaan (Is 3:16; 5:15; Ez 16:50; Hos 13:6; Zep 3:11). It is also the specific sin that brought about the downfall of the king of Assyria (Is 10:12, 33) and of the king of Moab (Jer 48:29). Because of its deadliness, Israel is specifically warned against pride and the tendency to forget God that so often stems from it (Dt 8:14).

In the light of the preceding discussion, it is no surprise to read in the Bible that pride is one of the seven things that the Lord hates (Prv 6:17). It is also said by two different writers that God opposes the proud but gives grace to the humble (see Jas 4:6 and 1 Pt 5:5; see also Prv 3:34 and 18:12, to which James and Peter may be referring). The words of Mary, the mother of Jesus, in her hymn of praise to God may summarize the attitude of God and the Bible toward pride: "His mighty arm does tremendous things! How he scatters the proud and haughty ones! He has taken princes from their thrones and exalted the lowly" (Lk 1:51-52, NLT).

PRIEST, High See Priests and Levites.

PRIESTHOOD
Office or function of a priest. The modern word "priest" (in French *prêtre* and in German *priester*) is used of a clergyman in episcopalian churches (Roman, Orthodox, and Anglican). It is also used in the description of the whole church as "a royal priesthood" (1 Pt 2:9). To ascertain how this usage arose and to see what priesthood means, it is necessary to look briefly at both biblical and theological developments.

In the Old Testament In the covenant made between God and Israel, the whole people was seen as a "kingdom of priests" and thus a holy people (Ex 19:6). Within this context, specific priestly activities belonged to three orders—high priest, priest, and Levite. "Priests" were male descendants of Aaron, who was a Levite (Nm 3:10), and "Levites" were other male members of the tribe of Levi. The chief functions of the priesthood took place in the temple. Priests looked after the ceremonial vessels and performed the sacrifices. In doing their duties they dressed in special, symbolic vestments. They were also teachers, passing on the sacred traditions of the nation as well as such matters as medical information (Lv 13–15). The high priest was the spiritual head of Israel and he had special functions, such as entering the Holy of Holies on the Day of Atonement (ch 16). The Levites assisted the priests and served the congregation in the temple. They sang the psalms, kept the temple courts clean, helped to prepare certain sacrifices and offerings, and also had a teaching function. Through this threefold order, the priesthood of the nation was exercised. By it the people offered worship to God, made intercessions and petitions, and learned of God's will. Thus what occurred in every pious home, as the head of the house

guided his family in worship, occurred in a larger and more ceremonial way in the temple.

In the New Testament It is remarkable that the term "priest" is never used in the NT of a minister or order in the church. Certainly the usage with reference to Judaism and paganism continues (Acts 4:1, 6; 14:13), but it is never introduced into the church. The Letter to the Hebrews presents the OT priesthood as fulfilled in Jesus Christ. First of all, he has been appointed high priest by God himself (Heb 5:4-6). Yet his is a superior priesthood to that of Aaron (ch 7). Second, being totally sympathetic to the needs of sinful people and tempted at all points like them, he is without sin (4:15; 7:26). Third, instead of offering animal sacrifices to take away sin, he offers himself, as the sinless Lamb, to take away sin. This is a perfect atonement (7:27; 9:24-28; 10:10-19).

Not only was the OT sacrificial system fulfilled; it was also finished by the unique, unrepeatable, and unlimited sacrifice of Christ. Having risen from the dead, he is a priest forever (Heb 7:17) and he remains the same yesterday and today and forever (13:8). Part of his high priest- hood is to offer intercession for his people (7:25). He is the mediator of a new and better covenant (7:22; 8:6; 9:15). Only through him are sinful human beings able to enter the holy presence of God and be accepted as children of God (Jn 14:6; 2 Cor 5:18-20; 1 Tm 2:5). Therefore, whatever priesthood Christians have, they have it only in and through Christ, their high priest and Mediator.

The NT (quoted from the RSV) describes believers as "a holy priesthood, to offer spiritual sacrifices acceptable to God through Jesus Christ" (1 Pt 2:5); "priests to his God and Father" (Rv 1:6); "a kingdom and priests to our God" (5:10); "priests of God and of Christ, and they shall reign with him a thousand years" (20:6).

What, then, does the priesthood of all believers mean in the NT? The high priesthood of Christ may be defined as his complete dedication and obedience to God, his Father, and unlimited compassion for his fellow human beings. At the center is his sacrificial death on the cross. On this basis and in union with him, the priesthood of Christians is their sacrificial obedience to God; this involves spiritual worship and love of God and compassionate activity and prayer for their fellow human beings. Paul wrote, "Present your bodies as a living sacrifice, holy and acceptable to God, which is your spiritual worship" (Rom 12:1, RSV). Each Christian offers his whole body to Christ and each local church offers itself wholly to Christ, and Christ offers his whole body (the church) to God the Father. Thus, in and by Christ, the priesthood of believers is exercised and made effectual. In the hearts of believers is the indwelling Spirit, and it is in his power that acceptable service and worship is offered. Christ is the pattern of priesthood as well as being high priest.

See also Offerings and Sacrifices; Priests and Levites; Tabernacle; Temple; Worship.

PRIESTS AND LEVITES
Servants of God in the OT. There were three basic classes of religious personnel in ancient Israel: prophets, wise men, and priests and Levites. The classical prophets fulfilled a vocation but were not professionals; they were not paid for their task and functioned only in response to the particular call of God. The wise men were involved in government and education; some of their duties were secular, though they were also involved in moral education. The priests and Levites fulfilled a variety of essentially religious duties and were equivalent approximately to the clergy in

modern times. They were professional men and were supported for their full-time religious work.

The role of the priesthood may be seen most clearly in the context of Israelite religion as a whole. At the heart of religion was a relationship with God; to be an Israelite or a Jew was to know and maintain a continuous relationship with the living God. This relationship found its outward expression in a variety of contexts: the covenant, the temple, worship, and every facet of daily life. Thus religion, understood as a relationship, had two perspectives: the relationship with God and that with fellow human beings. It had both a personal and a communal dimension to it. The priests were the guardians and servants of this life of relationship, which was at the heart of OT religion; all their functions can best be understood within the context of a relationship between God and Israel. The prophets, too, were servants of the covenant relationship. While the priests functioned as the normal servants of religion, the prophets' role was more that of calling a delinquent people back to the relationship with God in times of crisis.

In the OT, there are frequent references to both priests and Levites; in a number of biblical texts, however, the distinction is not clear (see, e.g., Dt 18:1-8). From the scholarly point of view, the precise relationship between priests and Levites is a continuing problem that has not yet been fully resolved. In general terms, only the sons of Aaron were to assume the role of priests; all other Levites would have religious functions, though technically they would not be priests. While this distinction is clear in most biblical texts, in others there is lack of certainty and clarity. It is clear, however, that *priests* (Levites descended from Aaron) and *Levites* (other than the descendants of Aaron) all had professional religious duties to perform. The precise nature of those duties varied from time to time in the course of Israel's history.

PREVIEW
• The Origins of the Priesthood
• The High Priest
• The Priests
• The Levites
• The History of the Institution
• The Priesthood in New Testament Times

The Origins of the Priesthood The priesthood in Israel began during the time of Moses and Aaron. The exodus from Egypt was not only the liberation of a group of Hebrew slaves but also the birth of the nation of Israel. The nation that was born in the exodus was given its constitution in the covenant of Sinai. The law of this covenant established the foundations and origins of Israelite priesthood. It provides insight into the three basic categories to be considered: the high priest, the priests, and the Levites.

The High Priest Any large and complex organization requires a head or leader, and this was true also of the Hebrew priesthood (though in its early days it was a small organization). The covenant was established through Moses, the prophet, through whom God gave the offer and substance of the covenant relationship; religious life within the covenant was to be the primary responsibility of Aaron, who was the first and chief priest.

In the earliest days of Israel's priesthood, it is probable that the high priest's office was relatively informal; he was chief or leader among his fellow priests. The office was significant, nevertheless, and involved a special ritual of investiture, special clothing, and certain special

responsibilities. While the high priest's duties were similar in principle to those of other priests, he had certain exclusive responsibilities. To some extent, his duties were administrative, pertaining to all the priests of whom he had charge. But his position was more weighty than that of an administrator; just as all priests were the servants and guardians of the covenant relationship, so the high priest was chief servant and chief guardian. In his hands rested spiritual responsibility for the entire people of God, and therein lay the true honor and gravity of his position.

**Chestpiece Worn by the
High Priest**

This spiritual seniority of the high priest is seen most clearly in certain tasks he undertook within Israel's life of worship. The clearest example may be seen in the annual observation of the Day of Atonement (Yom Kippur). On that day alone, the high priest entered the Holy of Holies and, standing before the "mercy seat," he sought God's forgiveness and mercy for the whole nation of Israel (Lv 16:1-19). It is in that ceremony that Israel's covenant faith is seen most clearly. Israel's religion was one of relationship with a holy God, and human evil disrupted that relationship. While all worship and sacrifices throughout the year were concerned with the continuation of the relationship, the Day of Atonement was the most solemn day of the year, in which the attention of all the people focused upon the meaning of their existence. Life held meaning only if the relationship with God could be maintained; the high priest had the great honor and heavy burden of seeking God's mercy for all Israel.

The special clothing worn by the high priest was symbolic of the nature and importance of his office; although all the symbolism cannot be determined, some of it is made clear in the biblical text. There are three particular themes in the symbolism. The first is beauty. The sense of beauty emerges from the quality and design of all the items of clothing, together with the use of color and precious stones. But beauty is dominant in the breastplate; the Hebrew word translated approximately as "breastplate" has as its basic sense "beauty" or "excellence." The clothing symbolizes beauty, while beauty describes the office; the two other themes associated with the symbolism bring out the excellence of the office.

The second theme is the role of the priest as representative of Israel before God. This essential dimension of the office of the high priest is explicitly identified in the names of the tribes of Israel in the two onyx stones in the ephod, and in the 12 precious stones attached to the breastplate. The high priest entered God's presence to seek deliverance from God's judgment (the breastplate is identified with judgment; Ex 28:15) for his people and in order to keep the people constantly in God's remembrance (v 12), as symbolized by the two onyx stones. The third theme is the role of high priest as the representative of God to Israel. This dimension of the office is seen in the Urim and Thummim, kept in the breastpiece, by means of which God made known his will to Israel. The high priest, Aaron, fully robed, was a splendid figure, and the splendor of his garments indicated the magnificence of the office with which he had been entrusted.

The high priesthood was to be passed on within the family (for the high priest was expected to be a married man), although in later history the practice was not always adhered to. On Aaron's death, the office passed to Eleazar, one of his four sons.

The Priests Priests took office not as the result of a particular vocation but by virtue of priestly descent. Thus the first priests were the four sons of Aaron: Nadab, Abihu, Eleazar, and Ithamar. These four were ordained at the same time that Aaron was ordained high priest (Ex 28:1). Like him, they had special clothing, which was basically similar, though it lacked the distinctive garments of the high priest (the special ephod, the breastpiece, and the crown). The priesthood would be passed down through their sons.

The sanctity of the priestly office was such that it was preserved from degeneration through specific laws. A man must be a descendant of Aaron to be a priest, but he was also required to meet a variety of other qualifications. He would not marry a divorcée or a former prostitute (Lv 21:7). If he was afflicted by certain kinds of disease or congenital defects, he was barred from priestly office (e.g., blindness, lameness, mutilation, being a hunchback or dwarf; vv 16-23). The principle involved was similar to that applying to animals used in sacrifice—only those free from defect or blemish were suitable for divine service.

In the earliest days of the priesthood there is some information provided in the biblical text concerning the specific duties of the priests. Eleazar had overall responsibility for the tabernacle and its offerings (Nm 4:16); assisted Moses in a number of duties, such as numbering the people and dividing the land (26:1-2; 32:2); and later served as an adviser to Joshua. Ithamar was responsible for the construction of the tabernacle (Ex 38:21) and supervised the families of the Gershonites and Merarites (Nm 4:28-33). Nadab and Abihu, however, died soon after their ordination as a result of a sinful act in their priestly duties (Lv 10:1-7), which may have been related in part to drunkenness (vv 8-9).

Priestly duties, in general, fell into three areas (Dt 33:8-10). First, priests were responsible, in conjunction with the high priest, for declaring God's will to the people. Second, they had responsibilities in religious education; they were to teach to Israel God's ordinances and law (v 10). Third, they were to be the servants of the tabernacle, participating in Israel's sacrifices and worship. There were a number of other duties that may have fallen to them, which they would have shared with the Levites in general.

The priests, along with all other Levites, did not own any land, as did the other Israelite tribes. Their task was to be entirely in the direct service to God. The absence of land, however, meant that they could not support and feed themselves as could other men and women. Consequently, the law specified that they could be supported for their services by the people as a whole. They were to receive, from worshipers, portions of animals that were brought to the tabernacle, as well as corn, wine, oil, and wool.

The Levites This term includes the priests, in a broad sense, for the sons of Aaron belonged to the tribe of Levi. For practical purposes, however, the Levites were those of the tribe other than the priests. The Levites also functioned in the service of the tabernacle, though they had a subordinate position. They, too, were professional men and were paid in money and in kind for their services. Though they did not inherit tribal territory of their own, there were a number of cities set aside for their use (Nm 35:1-8), and pasturelands were designated outside those cities for their livestock.

The Levites were divided into three principal families, the descendants of Kohath, Gershon, and Merari (Nm 4). Each of these families had particular responsibilities with respect to the care and transport of the tabernacle. The sons of Kohath carried the tabernacle furniture (after it had been covered by the priests), the sons of Gershon cared for the coverings and screens, and the sons of Merari carried and erected the tabernacle's frame. The priests, by contrast, were responsible for the transportation of the ark of the covenant. The role of each Levite, as servant of the tabernacle, was restricted; he undertook his professional duties between the ages of 25 and 50 (8:24-26).

Although many of the duties of the Levites were of a mundane nature, they also had a very significant religious role. The law required that all the firstborn, including firstborn sons, be given to God, recalling the slaying of the firstborn at the exodus from Egypt. The Levites' role in religion was that of being accepted by God in the place of the firstborn sons of Israel (Nm 3:11-13); their cattle, too, were accepted in place of the Israelites' firstborn cattle. In the census taken in the time of Moses, the firstborn Israelites exceeded the number of the Levites, and a five-shekel redemption fee had to be paid into the priestly coffers for each person in excess (vv 40-51). The representative and substitutionary nature of the Levites can be seen in Israelite religion. Like the priests, they played a part in the larger activity of mediation between God and Israel.

The law of Deuteronomy specifies a number of duties that may have fallen upon both priests and Levites (though the texts are ambiguous). These duties included participation in the activity of the law courts as judges, perhaps with special reference to religious crimes (Dt 17:8-9), taking care of the Book of the Law (v 18), controlling the lives and health of lepers (24:8), and participating directly in the conduct of covenant renewal ceremonies (27:9).

The History of the Institution In theory, the covenant law of Moses determined the nature and course of the offices of priests and Levites for the future history of Israel. In practice, however, changing historical circumstances and changes in the shape of Israel's religion and culture altered the shape of the priesthood and the role of the Levites from time to time. And even more significantly, the persons who held the offices shaped them and their effectiveness through their faithfulness or unfaithfulness.

The Priesthood before the Monarchy In the time of Joshua, the priests continued to undertake their important task of carrying the ark of the covenant. The Levites assisted in the division and allocation of the newly acquired land among the Israelite tribes. In Joshua 21, there is a detailed list of the allocation of cities to both priests and Levites, in fulfillment of the earlier legislation. In the days of the settlement, beyond the Conquest, there is some evidence that the Levites took over the priestly duty of transporting the ark (1 Sm 6:15; 2 Sm 15:24).

The writer of the book of Judges has recorded two stories that illuminate the lives of particular Levites. The first, the story of Micah (Jgs 17–18), describes the establishment of a local shrine in which Micah's son was appointed as a priest (though he was not of Levite or Aaronic descent). Later, Micah hired an itinerant Levite to function as a priest in his shrine, though subsequently that Levite was persuaded to serve the tribe of Dan as a priest. It is difficult to fit the details of this story into the theoretical model of priests and Levites, though the story may illustrate the confused state of Israel's religion at the time. What is particularly significant is that the role of the Levite-priest was primarily oracular (18:5-6). The second story in Judges is the rather horrifying account of a Levite and his concubine (ch 19). The story illustrates the moral decline and lack of law and order in Israel at the time, but it sheds little light on the role of the Levites.

More information is provided about the priesthood during the 11th century BC, immediately before the establishment of the monarchy. The tabernacle (by now probably a semipermanent structure) and the ark of the covenant were located in Shiloh. The priest in charge of the sanctuary in Shiloh was Eli, who may have been a descendant of Aaron's son Ithamar. His two sons, Hophni and Phinehas, also served as priests, indicating that the principle of family descent was still operative with respect to the priesthood. But although Eli was a faithful priest, his two sons abused the office.

The precise role of Samuel in this period is unclear. He was primarily a judge and a prophet, but it is difficult to determine whether he was also a priest. In the historical narrative, he is not called a priest, though Psalm 99:6 might be interpreted to indicate his priestly office. There are a number of passages, however, that indicate he acted like a priest. For example, he offered sacrifices (1 Sm 7:9-10); as a young man he served in the sanctuary of Shiloh and wore an ephod (ch 2). Furthermore, one of the biblical genealogies implies priestly descent (1 Chr 6:23-30). Nevertheless, he is not normally identified as a priest and the introduction to his story refers to him as an Ephraimite, by descent from his father (1 Sm 1:1), not a Levite. If the priest is perceived as a permanent servant of the sanctuary, as was Eli, then it is clear that Samuel was not a priest. But the priestly role of Samuel may perhaps be related to the fact that his mother "lent" him to God (v 28) while he was still a boy.

The Priesthood during the Time of David and Solomon Several radical changes took place during the reign of David and Solomon. These were a result, primarily, of the establishment of a permanent temple in Jerusalem and the installation of the ark of the covenant there. During the time of Saul, the first king of Israel, the social structure was essentially the same as it had been in the time of the judges. Saul, as king, was a military leader, but his relationship to religion and the priesthood was not clearly determined.

David changed the situation in many important respects. After his capture of the city of Jerusalem, he made that place the political and religious capital of his nation. The religious centrality of Jerusalem was assured by moving the ark of the covenant there, together with the tabernacle. Jerusalem now became the permanent location of the ark, and therefore the permanent center of religion; at the same time, the various regional shrines, which had developed in the premonarchical period, were gradually eliminated.

These changes had numerous implications for the priesthood and the Levites. During David's reign, there were two principal priests, Abiathar and Zadok. Abiathar, a former priest of Nob, had joined David before his rise to power; he appears to have been a descendant of Eli, and through him of Ithamar, one of Aaron's sons. Zadok's background is less clear, though his lineage appears to go back to Aaron's other son, Eleazar. These two priests are always named together in the texts describing David's reign, and Zadok is always mentioned before Abiathar. Although neither is explicitly identified as high priest in the ancient texts, there is some evidence to suggest that Abiathar functioned as high priest (1 Kgs 2:35); in NT times, he is identified as such (Mk 2:26). Zadok, during David's reign, may have been particularly responsible for the care of the ark of the covenant (2 Sm 15:24-25). These two priests had a significant position in David's royal establishment; they may also have shared overall responsibility for the priests, whose lives were now centered on the Jerusalem temple.

Much of David's time was focused upon the preparations for building a permanent temple for God. In the preparation for the temple, and in its completion during the reign of King Solomon, the new activities of the Levites may be seen. (The construction of a permanent temple automatically removed their former responsibilities related to the care and transportation of the tabernacle.) Large numbers of Levites were employed as laborers in the actual building of the temple. Others found new tasks in the worship of God in the tabernacle during David's reign and in the temple upon its completion. To the Levites, and especially to Heman, Asaph, and Ethan, was given primary responsibility for the music of worship; this involved not only singing but also the playing of a variety of instruments in the temple's orchestra or band. The Levites had also a variety of other tasks; they worked as gatekeepers at the sanctuary, assisted the priests in the preparation of sacrifices, kept the sanctuary clean, and functioned as general administrative and legal officers (1 Chr 23:1-32). Other Levites functioned as bankers, with primary responsibility for the temple treasuries (26:20-28).

Following David's death, there was a dispute over the royal succession, from which Solomon emerged as the new king. During his reign, the temple was brought to its completion and the regular worship of the nation was conducted there. In the matter of succession, however, Abiathar had supported a losing candidate, and when Solomon was made king, he lost his important office in the royal court. During Solomon's reign, the control of the priesthood passed into the hands of Zadok.

The Priesthood during the Divided Monarchy The great empire, which had been built by David and maintained by Solomon, collapsed after Solomon's death. From the ruins, two new and relatively insignificant states emerged. The southern kingdom, Judah, retained Jerusalem as its capital and the temple as its center of worship. The northern kingdom, Israel, located its first capital at Shechem, from where it was later moved to Tirzah.

In the southern state of Judah, the priests and Levites

continued to function normally within the Jerusalem temple. The office of high priest continued to be passed on by descent within the family of Zadok, who had held office in Solomon's reign. The continuity of office in this family was to be retained down into the time of the second temple, when the Zadokite succession was interrupted about 171 BC. Nevertheless, for all the continuity of religion in Jerusalem, all was not well with religion in Judah, neither during the reign of its first king, Rehoboam, nor during the reigns of his successors. During Rehoboam's reign, there was a decline in religion and also in the priesthood, when popular forms of religion were introduced as a result of foreign influence (1 Kgs 14:22-24). The history of the southern kingdom was marked by periods of religious decline followed by reform, often as a result of the activities of the prophets. The role of the priesthood was all too rarely one of spiritual leadership, and the priests themselves were often the subject of criticism by the prophets (e.g., Jer 2:8, 26).

The northern kingdom, whose first king was Jeroboam I, inevitably had to introduce some radical changes in religion. Jeroboam could not recognize the temple of Jerusalem, partly because it lay outside his state and partly because it was intimately associated with the royal line of David. Jeroboam established two principal shrines in his kingdom, both of which were to retain importance during the relatively short life of the northern kingdom (200 years). The first was at Bethel, in the southern part of his kingdom near the border of Judah (it was only about 12 miles, or 19.3 kilometers, north of Jerusalem). The second shrine, or sanctuary, was at Dan, in the far northern part of his kingdom.

Both these sanctuaries had ancient associations with the Hebrew traditions. Bethel is referred to as early as the time of Abram (Gn 12:8), and the sanctuary at Dan is known from the history of the judges (Jgs 18). There may indeed have been priests and Levites still residing in these two places, descendants of the former servants of the sanctuaries. But Jeroboam established a non-Levitical priesthood to serve in these sanctuaries and in various smaller shrines or "high places," thereby cutting off the religious tradition of the northern state even more radically from that of Judah. The royal sanctuary at Bethel, so close to the Jerusalem temple, may have been set up in deliberate competition with the Judean sanctuary.

The history of the priesthood in the northern kingdom is no more impressive than that of Judah. Many of the prophets, including Amos, Hosea, and Jeremiah, condemned the northern sanctuaries and their priests. Hosea was forceful in his condemnation: "As marauders lie in ambush for a man, so do bands of priests; they murder on the road to Shechem, committing shameful crimes" (Hos 6:9, NIV). Those to whom the spiritual lives of the chosen people had been entrusted only rarely lived up to their responsibilities.

Priests and Levites during and after the Exile The
northern kingdom came to its end in 722 BC, defeated by the armies of Assyria, but religious life continued in Judah for a while longer. Eventually, the end of the southern state came about 586 BC; the defeat of the state by the Babylonians was accompanied by the destruction of Jerusalem and its temple (Lam 2:20). The Babylonian commander took Seraiah, the high priest, and Zephaniah, his assistant, to Riblah, where, along with other officials, they were executed (2 Kgs 25:18-21). Then a policy of exile was established by the Babylonians; the most important and influential people of Judah were deported to Babylon, while the less significant were allowed to remain, for they were unlikely to cause trouble. Of those exiled from

Judah, many may have been priests (Jer 29:1), for they were men of influence. By way of contrast, it seems likely that a much smaller number of Levites was exiled, reflecting perhaps their inferior social position.

In the city of Jerusalem there was little normal religious life during the years of the exile; the altar had been destroyed and was not restored until after the exile. No doubt some kind of activity continued, but it was an impoverished form of religion. Most of the priests were in exile in Babylon, but they could not function, for there was no temple or sanctuary. Ezekiel implies that God himself was the only "sanctuary" for the exiles (Ez 11:16). Not until the return from exile and the restoration of Jerusalem and its temple could the normal functions of priests and Levites resume.

When the Babylonian Empire was defeated, the new Persian conquerors instituted a policy whereby the Hebrew exiles could return to their homeland. Of those returning, 4,289 are designated as priests and members of priestly families, while only 341 were Levites (Ezr 2:36-42); the imbalance probably reflects the imbalance in the number of those exiled initially. Under Joshua (Jeshua), the priest, and Zerubbabel, work began on the restoration. The priests played a significant role in the first year of the return, in the restoration of the altar in Jerusalem, so that sacrifice and worship to God could resume. Once the altar had been restored, the work began on the temple itself in the second year of the return. In this work, both the priests and the Levites were involved, and the laying of new foundations for the temple began. When the foundation had been laid, both priests, in their vestments, and Levites, in their role as singers and musicians, participated in the ceremony of dedication (3:8-13). Again, when the temple had been rebuilt, both priests and Levites participated in the ceremony of dedication (6:16-18). The restoration, however, was concerned with more than buildings; it also involved a moral and religious component. Though priests and Levites helped in this task, they were also affected by it. Many, for example, had married foreign wives (9:1), and thus had to conform to Ezra's reform laws.

To some extent, the priests and Levites resumed their normal duties in the worship of the postexilic period. The priests were engaged in the conduct of the temple worship. The Levites assisted, as temple servants (Neh 11:3), as treasurers and collectors of tithes (10:37-39), and as instructors or teachers of the law of God (8:7-9). Nevertheless, the history of the priesthood after the exile is not free of blemish. Condemnation of the abuses of the priestly office was delivered by the prophet Malachi (Mal 1:6-2:9). Malachi catalogues a list of priestly evils reminiscent of the evil priests who lived during the time of the monarchy.

The office of high priest continued after the exile among the descendants of Zadok, being held first by Joshua (Hg 1:1). The different political circumstances, however, changed the nature of the high priestly office. Whereas in the days of the monarchy the high priest was subservient to the king, there was no king, in the proper sense, after the exile. From a political perspective, the Jews were members of a province or colony; for practical purposes, they were a community based upon a common religion. The high priest was no longer subject to the secular authority of a Jewish king, but his religious authority was considerable, and in some ways his functions were similar to those of a king in preexilic times.

The Priesthood in the Maccabean Period During the
second century BC, some changes took place in the priesthood, particularly with respect to the office of high

priest, which marked the end of the OT era and set the background for the NT period. Judea, in the second century, was ruled by the Seleucid kings, who had inherited a portion of the massive Greek Empire established by Alexander the Great. The Judean province was controlled internally under the high priesthood, whose authority was received from the Seleucid kings.

For the first three decades of the second century BC, the high priesthood remained with the Zadokite line of descent. The high priests were members of the (Zadokite) Oniad family: first, Onias III (198–174 BC); then Jason, brother of Onias III (174–171 BC). It was in the period of Jason that there began a series of events that would terminate the Zadokite tradition.

Onias III had opposed the Hellenization policy of Antiochus IV (Epiphanes), which threatened to undermine the Jewish faith. Antiochus replaced Onias by Jason, who in effect purchased the high priesthood from the Seleucid king. In purchasing the priestly office, Jason had set a dangerous precedent; although he was of Zadokite descent, his act implied that the office could be bought and that descent was not vital. The opponents of Jason, the Tobiads, were able to remove him from office and have their own candidate, Menelaus (who was not a Zadokite), appointed in his place. This act resulted in a civil war between those supporting Jason and those supporting Menelaus, and the war in turn culminated in ruthless repressive measures by Antiochus Epiphanes; there were massacres in Jerusalem, and the temple was desecrated (167 BC). The desecration of the temple led to the Maccabean revolt, as a result of which the Jews regained their independence for a short time. Menelaus retained the office of high priest until 161 BC and was succeeded by Alcimus (161–159 BC).

There then followed a period during which there was no high priest for seven years. The political climate, however, was such that it became unlikely that the Zadokite line would ever regain the high priesthood, which had been established in the time of King Solomon. The Maccabean Jonathan gained control of Jerusalem, and in 152 BC, with the approval of the Seleucid king, he was formally invested with the high priest's robes of office. He was succeeded as high priest and ruler by his brother Simon in 143 BC, who also held the office with the approval of the Seleucids (Demetrius II). But in the third year of his reign (140 BC), the high priesthood of Simon received public approval in a great religious assembly, and the family of Simon became "high priest forever" (1 Macc 14:41-47). That event marked the real termination of the Zadokite tradition and the foundation of the Hasmonean line.

The establishment of the high priestly office outside the Zadokite line did not go without challenge. It is probable that a sect within Judaism, now known as the Essenes, was born in reaction to the high priesthood of Simon. The Essenes (better known for the Dead Sea Scrolls) appear to have been founded by a Zadokite priest who rejected the authenticity and authority of Simon. Thus, in a limited sense, the Zadokite priests continued to survive.

The Priesthood in New Testament Times In the early NT period, both priests and Levites continued to function within the Jewish religion. Zechariah, father of John the Baptist, was a priest belonging to the division of Abijah (Lk 1:5), and his wife was also of priestly descent. When Zechariah was visited by an angel, he was engaged at the time in priestly duties in the Jerusalem temple—various divisions of priests took responsibility for the temple services for a period of time and then returned to their homes (v 23), as another division took over. The distinction between priests and Levites is also maintained in the NT (Jn 1:19) and appears in Jesus' parable concerning the Good Samaritan (Lk 10:31-32). Both priests and Levites were among the earliest converts to Christianity; Barnabas was a Levite from Cyprus (Acts 4:36), and several priests responded to the proclamation of the gospel (6:7).

The office of high priest is frequently referred to in the NT. Several high priests are named, the plurality of current and former holders of the office reflecting the nature of the position as an essentially political appointment (as distinct from its oldest definition, that of an office passing from father to son on the death of the father). The two most significant high priests in the NT are those who held office during the lifetime of Jesus. Annas was high priest about AD 6 to 15, but even after he ceased to hold the office formally, he continued to exert considerable influence through his son-in-law, the high priest Caiaphas (c. AD 18–36). Both were significant figures in the trial of Jesus. At a later date, Ananias, son of Nedebaeus, was high priest (c. AD 47–58) and president of the Sanhedrin during the time in which Paul was brought to trial.

The priesthood held considerable authority in NT times. Most internal and religious matters in the Roman province of Judea were within the authority of the Sanhedrin, which functioned as a kind of provincial government, though its powers were limited in certain matters by Rome. Its membership included the ruling and former high priests and a large number of Sadducees, many of whom belonged to influential priestly families. This priestly influence in the Sanhedrin was indicative of the important role of the temple in Jewish life during the first century AD.

In AD 70, following the destruction of the temple in Jerusalem, a radical change came about in the significance of the priesthood in Judaism. The end of the temple removed in effect the purpose for the existence of the priesthood. Although the priesthood continued after a fashion until the Bar-Kochba rebellion in AD 135, its days were numbered after AD 70. Since the end of the first century AD, Judaism has developed without priests, and its course down to the present century has been charted by the rabbis, the spiritual descendants of the Pharisees.

See also Priesthood.

PRIMOGENITURE* Word not found in the Bible; derived from the Greek translation of the Hebrew word for "firstborn." Primogeniture refers specifically to the exclusive right of inheritance that belonged to the firstborn male. If the firstborn died, the next oldest living male did not receive that exclusive right; neither did a female if she were the firstborn; nor the firstborn if he was born of a concubine or of a slave woman (e.g., Gn 21:10). That the Scriptures attached much importance to the rights of the firstborn (primogeniture) can be seen in the distinction drawn between the firstborn and other sons (Gn 10:15; 25:13; 36:15), the double portion to be given to the firstborn (Dt 21:17), as well as the paternal blessing given to them (Gn 21:1-14; 27:1-29; 48:18).

See also Birthright; Firstborn.

PRINCIPALITIES AND POWERS* Phrase familiarized by the KJV, occurring several times in Paul's writings, and expressed by means of three Greek synonyms. The concept of principalities is signified by *exousia* and *archai*, while powers is represented by *dunamis*. In the NT, *exousia* describes the power inherent in authority as something confirmed by or derived from a position of prominence. There is nothing evil about this kind of authority; on the contrary, it is essentially right both morally and spiritually (Mt 21:23). It thus applies most appropriately to the authority of the Messiah (Mt 9:6; Mk 2:10), of the apostles (2 Cor 10:8; 13:10), and of human government (cf. Mt 8:9; Lk 20:20). *Archai* has several meanings but occurs 12 times in the sense of "command," "rule," or "sovereignty," 9 of which (Rom 8:38; 1 Cor 15:24; Eph 1:21; 3:10; 6:12; Col 1:16; 2:10, 15; Ti 3:1) appear in Paul's letters. Finally *dunamis,* a common word for power, denotes the ability or strength to achieve an impressive goal (Mt 25:15; Acts 3:12).

By using the expression "principalities and powers," Paul was referring to the hierarchy of supernatural agencies, such as angelic beings, who worship and serve the Creator of the universe. Some commentators have divided this hierarchy into five categories, namely thrones, principalities, powers, authorities, and dominions. This categorization, however, can be arrived at only by general inference, since there is nothing in Scripture that points directly to such distinct groups. In using the phrase, Paul was probably expressing the cosmic lordship of Jesus in as colorful and dramatic a manner as possible.

In giving Jesus a name above every other name, Paul was demonstrating the supreme lordship of Christ over all created beings, whether good or bad (Rom 14:11; Phil 2:10). As their Creator, the heavenly hosts were his subjects, acknowledging him as Lord of the universe. This affirmation was important for the Colossians, whose theology had apparently been tainted by unbiblical speculation (Col 2:8). The truth is that in Jesus there resided all the fullness of God, and this is transmitted to believers through the Lord's Spirit.

PRISCA* KJV rendering of the name of Priscilla, Aquila's wife, in 2 Timothy 4:19. *See* Priscilla and Aquila.

PRISCILLA AND AQUILA Christian couple who were friends and possibly converts of the apostle Paul during his ministry at Corinth (Acts 18:1-3). They are always mentioned together in the NT. Priscilla's personal character or her leadership role in the church may account for her name coming before her husband's in four out of six references (Acts 18:18, 26; Rom 16:3; 2 Tm 4:19).

Aquila was a Jew and a native of Pontus in Asia Minor. He had been expelled from Rome by the AD 49 edict of Claudius (Acts 18:2). Suetonius records that the emperor "banished from Rome all the Jews, who were continually making disturbances at the instigation of one Chrestus." From Rome, Aquila and Priscilla went to Corinth, where Paul (on his second missionary journey) met them. There they lived together and worked at the same trade of making tents. After such close association with Paul, they were able to instruct even the learned Apollos, a Jewish teacher who then became a Christian (vv 24-28).

Both Priscilla and Aquila were Paul's loyal friends and trusted coworkers (Rom 16:3-4). When he left Corinth, they accompanied him and remained at Ephesus after he returned to Syria (Acts 18:18-19). When Paul wrote the First Letter to Corinth, they were still at Ephesus, where their home was used as a place for Christians to gather (1 Cor 16:19). Since the decree of Claudius was temporary, Priscilla and Aquila were again in Rome when Paul wrote to the Roman Christians (Rom 16:3). When the Second Letter to Timothy was written, they were again in Ephesus (2 Tm 4:19).

PRISON *See* Criminal Law and Punishment; Punishment.

PRISON*, Court of the KJV rendering of "Court of the Guard," an open court where the prophet Jeremiah was kept prisoner, in Jeremiah 32:2. *See* Guard, Courtyard of the.

PRISON, Spirits in *See* Spirits in Prison.

PRISON GATE* KJV rendering of "Gate of the Guard," a gate in Jerusalem, possibly in the palace complex, in Nehemiah 12:39. *See* Guard, Gate of the.

PRIZE Reward given the winner of a contest. In the ancient Greek games (the Olympian and Isthmian), the prize usually consisted of a simple wreath woven with olive branches. The apostle Paul transposed this technical term from the athletic arena into the language of the early church for illustrative purposes. He alone uses the word, and in only two related passages: 1 Corinthians 9:24, where he employs it literally, and Philippians 3:14, where he applies it metaphorically.

Comparing the living of the Christian life to the running of a footrace, Paul exhorts his readers to live so that they may win the prize. The prize itself, whether defined as "eternal life" or "heavenly perfection" or "resurrection glory," is a gift of grace; therefore, Paul's figure of the race and the reward cannot be pressed to imply that man's effort is the causative agent in the securing of the prize (Rom 9:16), but only that strenuous effort must be exercised if the prize is to be enjoyed. The purpose of the illustration is to summon believers to live the Christian faith with the same self-denial, supreme exertion, and single-minded concentration as that manifested by the winner of the prize in the Grecian games.

PROCHORUS*, PROCORUS One of the seven men appointed by the apostles in Jerusalem for service in the early days of the church (Acts 6:5). They were to oversee the fair distribution of food in the Christian community.

See also Deacon, Deaconess.

PROCONSUL* Governor (NLT; KJV "deputy") appointed by the senate of Rome to govern a province. From the time of Augustus, the Roman senate appointed governors to administer certain of the Roman senatorial provinces, provinces considered secure enough that no army was kept in them. Proconsuls were appointed for the period of one year between a time when they were *praetor* and the time when they became consul of Rome. They are to be distinguished from procurators, who were appointed by the emperor to rule imperial provinces for an indefinite period. We meet two proconsuls in the book of Acts: Sergius Paulus of Cyprus (Acts 13:7-12) and Gallio of Achaia (18:12-17).

See also Gallio; Gallio Inscription; Sergius Paulus.

PROCURATOR* Financial officer of Rome (NLT "governor"), usually from the equestrian rank, whose responsibilities included the supervision and collection of imperial revenues in an assigned province. In Judea and other lesser provinces of the Roman Empire, the procurator acted at times as the governor of that region. He not only managed financial affairs but also exercised judicial and military authority, and he was primarily responsible for keeping peace in his jurisdiction. The NT mentions three Roman procurators: Pontius Pilate (AD 26–36; Mt 27; Jn 18–19), Antonius Felix (AD 52–59; Acts 23:24–25:14), and Porcius Festus (AD 59–62;

Acts 24:27–26:32). These administrators were held accountable and subordinate to the governor of Syria.

See also Felix, Antonius; Festus, Porcius; Pilate, Pontius.

PROMISE Declaration by one person to another that something will or will not be done, giving the person to whom it is made the right to expect the performance of whatever has been specified.

Types of Promise In biblical usage there are scattered examples of promises that people give either to one another (e.g., Nm 22:17; Est 4:7) or to God (e.g., Neh 5:12), but the promises that God gives to man are far more significant. These divine promises are absolutely trustworthy because the one who gives them is totally able to perform that which he has promised (Rom 4:21).

Divine promises in Scripture assure their recipients of many spiritual and temporal benefits, including sonship (2 Cor 6:16–7:1), forgiveness of sin (1 Jn 1:9), answer to prayer (Lk 11:9), deliverance from temptations (1 Cor 10:13), sustaining grace for difficult times (2 Cor 12:9), provision for all needs (Phil 4:19), reward for obedience (Jas 1:12), and eternal life (Lk 18:29-30; Jn 3:16; Rom 6:22-23). God's promises are certain and sure, but participation in their blessing often requires that certain conditions on which they are predicated be met. Divine promises also are not always guarantees of blessing. Indeed, there are promises announcing the certainty of judgment on those who refuse to obey the gospel of the Lord Jesus (2 Thes 1:8-9).

In addition to the promises of God, which have subjective and individual application to many different people in widely different times and places, there are a great many promises that pertain to the programmatic unfolding of God's plan of redemption in a grand procession of historical events. These promises have neither repeated applications nor conditional natures. In such cases, promise becomes nearly synonymous with prophecy, and promises of this type, along with their subsequent fulfillment, are intricately intertwined in the entire fabric of redemptive history.

Promises in the Old Testament The highlights of the promise theme in the OT can be seen in the promise of what is often termed the protevangelium (i.e., the first announcement of the gospel) given to Adam and Eve in the Garden of Eden immediately after the fall into sin (Gn 3:15). Subsequent promises are the covenants God made with Abraham (chs 12; 15; 17) and with David (2 Sm 7), followed by the promise of a new covenant (Jer 31).

The Protevangelium Genesis 3:15b says: "Your [Satan's] offspring and her [Eve's] offspring will be enemies. He will crush your head, and you will strike his heel" (NLT). This statement is a promise that at some future time the offspring of the woman will crush Satan. The offspring of the woman is individualized in the "he" of the last phrase. "He" shall strike you (i.e., Satan) on the head, although Satan will inflict a wound on the offspring of the woman. Here, then, is the promise that gives Adam and Eve, as well as their descendants, the basis to expect the eventual destruction of their adversary Satan through their offspring.

The Promise to Abraham In Genesis 12:1-7 Abraham is told to leave his people and country and to go to a land that the Lord would show to him. God, in turn, promises him that (1) his offspring would become a great nation; (2) he would be blessed and his name made great; (3) through him other nations would be blessed; and (4) the land of Canaan would be given to his descendants. Of particular significance among these promises given to Abraham is that through his offspring he will bless many nations. This promise is repeated five times in the book of Genesis (Gn 12:3; 18:18; 22:18; 26:4; 28:14) and points back to the promise of Genesis 3:15 as well as forward to Christ.

The Promise to David In 2 Samuel 7, God gave a promise to King David that his dynasty would endure forever (2 Sm 7:16; Ps 89:34-37). It is with this Davidic covenant that the promised line, which had previously run from Adam through Seth, Shem, Abraham, Isaac, Jacob, and Judah, is now narrowed to the royal line of the house of David. David is to be the ancestor of the Messiah-King to come (Ps 89:3, 27-37). David thus became a central figure in the history of God's plan to redeem the world. Jesus Christ is referred to as the son of David, the son of Abraham (Mt 1:1).

The Promise of a New Covenant In Jeremiah 31:31-37, it is promised that in future days the Lord would make a new covenant with the house of Israel and the house of Judah. The content of this new covenant reemphasizes and extends the basic promises of the former covenant: "I will be their God, and they will be my people. . . . I will forgive their wickedness and will never again remember their sins" (vv 33-34, NLT). It would appear that the "new covenant" of Jeremiah is to be viewed as a restatement of the same basic promises included in the Abrahamic and Davidic covenants.

The new covenant was inaugurated with the first advent of Christ, and believers in Christ are now recipients by the Holy Spirit of the blessings of that new covenant (Heb 8:6-13). The complete and final realization of these blessings in all their fullness awaits the return of Christ, the complete establishment of his kingdom in its outward and final form, and the blessedness of life in the new heavens and new earth. In the intervening time, God's people live in a day in which some of the benefits of the age to come are a present reality but the fullness of the new age is yet future.

The Promise Theme in the New Testament New Testament writers refer to the OT promises in a way that indicates that they did not view these promises as separate and isolated assertions but rather as portions of a unitary promise that is ultimately fulfilled in Christ (see Lk 1:54-55, 69-73; Acts 13:23, 32-33; 26:6-7; 2 Cor 1:20). Jesus is the fulfillment of the promises made to the patriarchs and David, and these promises are accordingly to be viewed as having a single focal point in him.

In the books of Galatians and Ephesians, Paul develops this idea in more detail, saying to the Gentile Christians that they are made "heirs together with Israel, members together of one body, and sharers together in the promise in Christ Jesus" (Eph 3:6, NIV). In fact, Paul says that Gentiles who trust in Christ are incorporated into the seed of Abraham and are thus heirs according to the promise (Gal 3:29), and he even goes so far as to equate the gospel with the promise given to Abraham when he states, "The Scripture foresaw that God would justify the Gentiles by faith, and announced the gospel in advance to Abraham: 'All nations will be blessed through you'" (Gal 3:8, NIV). These and other NT texts establish the close connection between the coming of Christ and the fulfillment of the promise. The promises of God find their point of convergence in Christ and all that he accomplished, and will yet accomplish, for his people.

One further aspect of the promise particularly emphasized in the NT concerns the coming of the Holy Spirit. Paul refers to believers as sealed with the promised Holy

Spirit (Eph 1:13), and as receiving the promise of the Spirit (Gal 3:14). The gift of the Holy Spirit is not only the fulfillment of an OT promise (Is 32:15; Ez 36:27; Jl 2:28), and that of Christ himself (Lk 24:49; Jn 14:16, 20; Acts 1:4), but it is also itself a promise of something yet future. Paul speaks of the Holy Spirit's presence within the believer as a guarantee of our inheritance (2 Cor 1:22; 5:5; Eph 1:14). The Holy Spirit is the "firstfruit" of future glory (Rom 8:23).

One final aspect of the promise theme in the NT concerns the assurance of Christ's second advent and the establishment of the new heavens and the new earth (cf. Jn 14:1-3; 2 Pt 3:4, 9, 13).

See also Covenant; God, Being and Attributes of; Hope; Prophecy; Prophet, Prophetess.

PROPHECY
Term, along with its English cognates ("prophet," "to prophesy," "prophetism," and "prophetic"), derived from a group of Greek words that, in secular Greek, mean "speak forth," "proclaim," "announce." In biblical Greek, however, these terms always carry the connotation of speaking, proclaiming, or announcing something under the influence of spiritual inspiration.

PREVIEW
- Prophecy in the Old Testament
- Types of Old Testament Prophets
- The Message of the Prophets
- Prophecy in the New Testament
- The Role of the Christian Prophet

Prophecy in the Old Testament One of the clearest and most significant statements on the nature of prophetic inspiration in the OT is found in Numbers 12:6-8: "The LORD said to them, 'Now listen to me! Even with prophets, I the LORD communicate by visions and dreams. But that is not how I communicate with my servant Moses. He is entrusted with my entire house. I speak to him face to face, directly and not in riddles! He sees the LORD as he is' " (NLT). Several important insights into the nature of prophetic inspiration are found in this passage: (1) The prophetic gift of Moses was unique in that he alone received revelations directly from God. (2) Ordinarily, prophetic revelation was received through the medium of a dream or a vision. (3) The meaning of prophetic revelation is not always completely clear; prophecy is sometimes ambiguous.

Further insight into the nature of prophetic revelation is found in Deuteronomy 18:18: "I [God] will raise up for them a prophet like you [Moses] from among their brethren; and I will put my words in his mouth, and he shall speak to them all that I command him" (RSV). While this passage is of interest because Jesus was identified as "the prophet like Moses" who came in fulfillment of this prediction (Acts 3:22; 7:37), the more immediate historical reference is to the succession of prophets that guided Israel from Joshua to Malachi. The phrase "I will put my words in his mouth" refers to the process of divine inspiration and is reminiscent of the common OT prophetic formula "the word of the Lord came to [such and such a prophet]" (for examples, see 1 Sm 15:10; 2 Sm 24:11; 1 Kgs 19:9; Jon 1:1; Hg 1:1; 2:1, 20; Zec 7:1, 8; 8:1). A true prophet is one who speaks (or repeats) all that God has told him.

Modes of Prophetic Inspiration Dreams were a commonly recognized mode of inspiration throughout the ancient world, though they were more highly regarded in Greece than in ancient Israel. Revelatory dreams in the Bible fall into two major categories: (1) dreams whose

meaning is self-evident, and (2) symbolic dreams that usually require the expertise of an interpreter of dreams. Both types normally involve both visual and auditory elements. In those dreams whose meaning is self-evident, normally a supernatural being (God or an angel) appears to the dreamer and speaks to him or her in a straightforward manner.

More frequently, revelatory dreams have symbolic elements that require interpretation. The two great dream interpreters of the OT are Joseph and Daniel; the latter is clearly a prophet. The two symbolic dreams that Joseph himself dreamed (Gn 37:5-11) had sufficiently self-evident meaning so that his brothers and father were able to interpret them immediately. More complex were the dreams of the butler and baker (40:1-19) and of Pharaoh (41:1-36), which Joseph was able to interpret with the help of God. Similarly, Daniel was enabled to interpret the dreams of Nebuchadnezzar (Dn 2:25-45; 4:4-27). The skill in interpreting such dreams was attributed by both Joseph and Daniel to God (Gn 40:8; 41:16, 25; Dn 2:27-30; cf. 4:9). While dreams are used almost interchangeably with visions in referring to modes of prophetic inspiration (Jl 2:28), dreams do not occupy a significant part in the prophetic revelations of any of the OT prophets, with the exception of Daniel.

One of the most characteristic modes of prophetic inspiration was the vision (Nm 12:6; 24:4, 16; Hos 12:10). The revelatory visions experienced by the prophets were not limited to visual phenomena alone but also included the auditory dimension as well. In Isaiah 1:1, the author describes his entire prophetic book as a "vision": "These visions concerning Judah and Jerusalem came to Isaiah son of Amoz during the reigns of Uzziah, Jotham, Ahaz, and Hezekiah—all kings of Judah" (NLT). Yet in the very next verse, Isaiah says, "Hear, O heavens! Listen, O earth! This is what the LORD says." Again, in Amos 1:1, "The *words* of Amos, who was among the shepherds of Tekoa, which he *saw* concerning Israel" (RSV, emphasis added).

Manifestations of Prophetic Inspiration All prophecy, whether biblical or not, presupposes that the prophet either possessed or was possessed by a personal supernatural power. The external behavioral manifestations of this possession can exhibit great variety.

The prophetic phenomenon generally designated "ecstatic" prophecy appears to have existed in Canaan prior to the arrival of the Hebrew tribes in the 13th century BC. The first reference to ecstatic prophecy in Israel occurs in 1 Samuel 10:5-13 (11th century BC), and it persisted at least till the sixth century BC (Jer 29:26).

The ecstatic prophet achieves a trancelike state by self-induced means. The most common devices used to achieve a state of ecstasy were musical instruments, such as the harp, tambourine, flute, and lyre (1 Sm 10:5). Among the prophets of Baal, self-flagellation was another means of inducing ecstasy (1 Kgs 18:28-29).

This kind of prophetic ecstasy was usually practiced by groups of prophets (1 Sm 10:5), and such ecstasy was contagious. When Saul met a band of such prophets, the Spirit of God came upon him and he, too, began to prophesy (vv 10-13), a phenomenon that occurred repeatedly to various messengers sent by Saul on a later occasion (19:20-22). At that time Saul again prophesied, and his ecstatic behavior is described in 1 Samuel 19:24. When Elisha was asked to prophesy for King Jehoram of Israel, he first requested a minstrel. When the minstrel played, the power of the Lord came upon him (2 Kgs 3:15).

Types of Old Testament Prophets There are two basic types of prophetic commission in the OT. One type is that of a narrative call by God to a particular individual whose objections to the call are gradually overcome in a dialogue between himself and God. The classic example of this type of prophetic commission is found in Jeremiah 1:4-8:

> The LORD gave me a message. He said, "I knew you before I formed you in your mother's womb. Before you were born I set you apart and appointed you as my spokesman to the world."
>
> "O Sovereign LORD," I said, "I can't speak for you! I'm too young!"
>
> "Don't say that," the LORD replied, "for you must go wherever I send you and say whatever I tell you. And don't be afraid of the people, for I will be with you and take care of you. I, the LORD, have spoken!" (NLT)

Similar prophetic commissions including such dialogues are associated with the calls of Moses (Ex 3:1–4:17) and Gideon (Jgs 6:11-17).

The second major form of prophetic commission is the "throne vision." An outstanding example is Isaiah 6:1-8:

> In the year King Uzziah died, I saw the Lord. He was sitting on a lofty throne, and the train of his robe filled the Temple. . . .
>
> Then I said, "My destruction is sealed, for I am a sinful man and a member of a sinful race. Yet I have seen the King, the LORD Almighty!"
>
> Then one of the seraphim flew over to the altar, and he picked up a burning coal with a pair of tongs. He touched my lips with it and said, "See, this coal has touched your lips. Now your guilt is removed, and your sins are forgiven."
>
> Then I heard the Lord asking, "Whom should I send as a messenger to my people? Who will go for us?"
>
> And I said, "Lord, I'll go! Send me." (NLT)

Here we have an account of the visionary presence of a prophet in the heavenly council; in this case, however, the prophet participates in the deliberations and thereby receives a prophetic commission. Though few prophets have left accounts of their divine commissions, most of them appear to have been conscious of having been "sent" by God (Is 48:16; Hos 8:1; Am 7:14-15). According to Jeremiah, false prophets did not receive such divine commissions (Jer 23:21, 32; 28:15).

The Message of the Prophets

The Form of the Message The most common introductory formula for prophetic oracles in the OT is the phrase "Thus says the Lord," which occurs hundreds of times in prophetic contexts. This formula clearly implies that the pronouncement so introduced is not the word of the prophet who utters the oracle but of the God of Israel who delivered his word to his prophet. The use of this formula also reiterates the prophet's sense of divine commission. In oracles introduced in this manner, God speaks in the first person. In fact, virtually all Israelite prophetic utterance is formulated as the direct speech of the God of Israel.

The prophets used many literary forms in which to express their oracles. Two of the more widely used forms of prophetic speech are the judgment speech and the oracle of salvation. The judgment speech is composed of at least two central elements: the speech of rebuke

or invective, and the pronouncement of judgment (see 2 Kgs 1:3-4). The second common prophetic speech form is the oracle of salvation (see Is 41:8-13). Other fixed forms of prophetic speech include the prophecy of salvation (43:14-21), the proclamation of salvation (41:17-20; 42:14-17; 43:16-21; 49:7-12), and the woe oracle (Is 5:8-10; 10:1-4; Am 5:18-24; 6:1-7; Mi 2:1-5).

The Content of the Message The common adage that OT prophets were not "foretellers" but "forthtellers" is not strictly correct. All of the prophets predict the future. Such prediction, however, is based not on human curiosity of what the future will hold but rather is rooted in the future consequences of past or present violations of the covenant, or on a future act of deliverance that will provide hope for a discouraged people. Most of the prophetic speeches that have been preserved in the OT were originally delivered as public proclamations or sermons. Most of these prophetic proclamations were evoked by the iniquity and apostasy of Israel. Hosea and Jeremiah condemned Israel because she had broken the covenant (Jer 11:2-3; Hos 8:1).

The prophets are frequently associated with social justice and social reform, and these elements were unquestionably an important dimension of their message. Amos denounced the rich who afflicted the poor (Am 2:6-8; 4:1; 5:11; 8:4-6). He railed against sexual immorality (2:6-8) and against those who take bribes (5:12). Hosea provided a list of prevalent vices, including lying, killing, stealing, adultery, and idolatry (Hos 4:2). Idolatry was a particular target for his denunciations (8:5; 11:2). The background for such heated denunciations of Israel's behavior is God's unquenchable love for Israel (Is 43:4; Jer 31:3; Hos 3:1; 11:1-4; 14:4; Mal 1:2), which is inseparable from his election of Israel (Is 43:1; Jer 33:24; Ez 20:5; Hos 3).

The prophets were concerned not only with the transgressions of Israel and the historical judgment that would inevitably follow but also with the achievement of a final future time of bliss. The message of many of the prophets is thoroughly eschatological (i.e., pertaining to the end times). One such eschatological concept is that of the Day of the Lord. The concept of the Day of the Lord first appears in Amos, where the emphasis lies on the disaster that will befall Israel on that day. Amos's emphasis on disaster notwithstanding, the Day of the Lord is a conception that had both salvific as well as judgmental overtones for Israel. While the disaster that will occur in the Day of the Lord can be viewed in terms of a literal historical fulfillment in the tragic events of 722 BC (the fall of Samaria) and 586 BC (the fall of Judah), there are nevertheless features of these predictions that transcend historical fulfillment and reach toward eschatological fulfillment.

Since the Israelite conception of "salvation" was largely temporal in its dimensions, it included such blessings as length of life, fruitfulness of the womb and field, peace and victory over one's enemies, the abundance of water, and so on. In harmony with this conception of salvation, the future age is conceived in precisely those terms, as in Amos 9:13-15.

The prophets pictured a time when David himself, or someone very much like him, would return and inaugurate a golden era reminiscent of the great Davidic and Solomonic period. The covenant of God with David was not a conditional covenant but rather one that was absolutely inviolable (2 Sm 7:4-17; Ps 89; Jer 33:19-22), and it was with this knowledge that the prophets could look forward confidently to a restoration of David's throne (Jer 17:24-26; 23:5-6; 33:14-15).

Prophecy in the New Testament

In contrast to the few self-proclaimed prophets of the intertestamental period, early Christianity began with a flurry of prophetic activity that lasted well into the second century AD. Jesus, his disciples and followers, and the early Christians were convinced that the times in which they lived were times in which OT prophecy was being fulfilled (Mk 1:14-15; Acts 2:16-21; Rom 16:25-27; 1 Cor 10:11). Yet this era was not only one of fulfillment but also one of the renewal of the prophetic gift.

John the Baptist John the Baptist is remembered in the NT primarily as the forerunner of Jesus whose coming was predicted by Malachi (Mal 4:5-6). Yet, in his own right, John proclaimed the imminent judgment of God with a flair of denunciation and rebuke reminiscent of the OT prophets. John's costume, consisting of a hairy cloak and a leather girdle (Mk 1:6), was reminiscent of the typical garb of OT prophets (1 Kgs 19:19; 2 Kgs 1:8; 2:13-14; Zec 13:4). John was regarded as a prophet by people everywhere (Mt 14:5; 17:10-13; Mk 9:11-13; 11:32; Lk 1:76; 7:26). Luke reports, in a style similar to the OT prophetic narratives, that "the word of God came to John" (Lk 3:2). Two short prophetic speeches have been preserved in Matthew 3:7-10 (cf. Lk 3:7-9) and Mark 1:7-8 (cf. Mt 3:11-12; Lk 3:15-18). In the first speech, John denounced those of his generation who had transgressed the covenant law and exhorted them to change their manner of life. In the second speech, John predicted the coming of the Mighty One, Jesus (Mt 3:11; Mk 1:7; Lk 3:16; Jn 1:15, 27, 30; Acts 13:25). John's style, however, was not precisely that of the OT prophets. His pronouncements were made on his own authority; never did he use formulas such as "thus says the Lord," or present his prophetic utterances as if they were speeches made by God. Yet, in spite of these differences, John is appropriately regarded as the last representative of the OT prophetic tradition (Mt 11:13; Lk 16:16).

Jesus of Nazareth Jesus was popularly regarded as a prophet (Mt 16:14; 21:10-11; Mk 6:14-15; 8:28; Lk 7:16, 39; 9:8, 19; Jn 6:14; 7:40, 52). This assessment was based as much on the mighty deeds Jesus performed as on his prophetic speeches and predictions. Though Jesus nowhere claimed prophetic status directly, that claim is implicit in Mark 6:4: "A prophet is honored everywhere except in his own hometown" (cf. Mt 13:57; Lk 4:24). It is implicit as well in Luke 13:33: "Yes, today, tomorrow, and the next day I must proceed on my way. For it wouldn't do for a prophet of God to be killed except in Jerusalem!" (NLT). In Acts, Jesus is regarded as "the prophet like Moses" predicted in Deuteronomy 18:18 (Acts 3:22; 7:37). Matthew presents Jesus as the New Moses, but he does not particularly emphasize his prophetic role. John, however, like Luke, emphasizes Jesus' role as the prophet (Jn 4:19; 6:14-15; 7:40).

While the Gospels and Acts reflect the notion that Jesus was a prophet, they also emphasize the fact that he was much more than a prophet. Nevertheless, the notion of prophetism was sufficiently important in early Judaism that Jesus' recognition as a prophet is very significant. There are 12 solid reasons for regarding Jesus as a prophet in the OT tradition: (1) The sovereign authority of Jesus' teaching (Mk 1:27), a feature underlined by his use of the introductory formula "(Amen) I say to you," which is reminiscent of the formula "thus says the Lord" used by the OT prophets. (2) The poetic character of many of Jesus' sayings is unlike contemporary rabbinic teaching but is similar to the poetic rhetoric of the OT prophets. (3) Jesus experienced visions (Lk 10:18) like the ancient prophets. (4) Jesus, like the prophets, made many predictions (Mt 23:38; Mk 13:2; 14:58; Lk 13:35; etc.). (5) Like the OT prophets, Jesus performed symbolic acts (such as the cleansing of the temple, the entry into Jerusalem, and the Last Supper). (6) Jesus, like the prophets, when necessary, rejected the formal observance of religious ritual and emphasized the moral and spiritual dimensions of obedience to God. (7) Jesus announced the imminent arrival of the kingdom of God—an eschatological proclamation similar to those made by the prophets. (8) Like the OT prophets, Jesus functioned as a preacher of repentance. (9) Jesus, like many of the prophets, was conscious of a special calling of God (Mt 15:24; Mk 8:31; 9:37; 14:36; Lk 4:18-26). (10) Jesus, like the prophets, received divine revelation through intimate communion with God (Mt 11:27; Lk 10:22). (11) Like the prophets, Jesus represented God; to obey him was to obey God, to reject him was to reject God (Mk 9:37; cf. Ez 33:30-33). (12) Like the prophets, Jesus was conscious of a mission to all Israel (Mt 15:24; 19:28; Lk 22:30).

Among the many prophetic predictions of Jesus are the following:

1. Predictions of the imminent arrival of the kingdom of God (Mt 10:7-8, 23; 23:39; Mk 1:15; 9:1; 13:28-29)
2. Predictions of the destruction of Jerusalem and the temple (Mt 23:37-39; 24:2; 26:61; 27:40; Mk 13:2; 14:58; 15:29; Lk 13:34-35; 21:6; Jn 2:19-21)
3. Predictions of the coming of the Son of Man (Mt 10:23, 32-33; 12:40; 13:40-41; 16:27; 24:27, 37-39; Mk 3:38; 13:26-27; 14:62; Lk 9:26; 11:30; 12:8-9; 17:24, 26)
4. Predictions of the end of the age. The longest prophetic section in the Gospels is the eschatological discourse of Jesus in Mark 13:1-32 (cf. Mt 24:1-36; Lk 21:5-33), in which a number of predictions concerning the destruction of Jerusalem and the end of the age are woven into a lengthy discourse to the disciples.

Prophecy as a Gift for the Believers The beginning of prophetic activity in early Christianity, according to Acts, coincided with the outpouring of the Holy Spirit upon the earliest Christians on the Day of Pentecost (Acts 2:1-21). Peter's sermon on the Day of Pentecost indicates that the outpouring of the Spirit fulfilled Joel's prophecy (Acts 2:4, 17-21; cf. Jl 2:28-32). Further, since the Spirit had been poured out upon all early Christians (that Spirit being a Spirit of prophecy), all are actual or potential prophets.

According to 1 Corinthians 12:28 (see also Rom 12:6; Eph 4:11), God has appointed in the church first apostles, second prophets, and third teachers. The names of several early Christian prophets have been preserved. These include Agabus (Acts 11:27-28; 21:10-11); Judas and Silas (15:32); Barnabas, Simeon Niger, Lucius of Cyrene, Manaen, and Paul (13:1); and the four virgin daughters of Philip the evangelist (21:8-9). John, the author of Revelation, was certainly a prophet (Rv 1:3; 22:9, 18), though he never directly assumed that title.

The Role of the Christian Prophet

Christian prophets were leaders in early Christian communities (1 Cor 12:28; Eph 4:11), who exercised their gift in church gatherings (Acts 13:1-3; 11:27-28; 1 Cor 12–14; Rv 1:10). Since the Spirit of God was particularly active in Christian worship, prophecy was a major means whereby God communicated with his people. Prophets, like apostles and teachers, did not hold offices in local communities like bishops, elders, and deacons. Rather, they were chosen, not by individual congregations, but by divine commission and so were honored and accepted in all local communities.

Early Christian prophets were both itinerant and settled, though itinerant prophets seem to have been more prevalent in Syria-Palestine and Asia Minor than in the European churches.

MESSIANIC PROPHECIES AND FULFILLMENTS

For the Gospel writers, one of the main reasons for believing in Jesus was the way his life fulfilled the Old Testament prophecies about the Messiah. Following is a list of some of the main prophecies.

	Old Testament Prophecies	New Testament Fulfillment
1. Messiah was to be born in Bethlehem	Micah 5:2	Matthew 2:1-6 Luke 2:1-20
2. Messiah was to be born of a virgin	Isaiah 7:14	Matthew 1:18-25 Luke 1:26-38
3. Messiah was to be a prophet like Moses	Deuteronomy 18:15, 18-19	John 7:40
4. Messiah was to enter Jerusalem in triumph	Zechariah 9:9	Matthew 21:1-9 John 12:12-16
5. Messiah was to be rejected by his own people	Isaiah 53:1, 3 Psalm 118:22	Matthew 26:3-4 John 12:37-43 Acts 4:1-12
6. Messiah was to be betrayed by one of his followers	Psalm 41:9	Matthew 26:14-16, 47-50 Luke 22:19-23
7. Messiah was to be tried and condemned	Isaiah 53:8	Luke 23:1-25 Matthew 27:1-2
8. Messiah was to be silent before his accusers	Isaiah 53:7	Matthew 27:12-14 Mark 15:3-4 Luke 23:8-10
9. Messiah was to be struck and spat on by his enemies	Isaiah 50:6	Matthew 26:67; 27:30 Mark 14:65
10. Messiah was to be mocked and insulted	Psalm 22:7-8	Matthew 27:39-44 Luke 23:11, 35
11. Messiah was to die by crucifixion	Psalm 22:14, 16-17	Matthew 27:31 Mark 15:20, 25
12. Messiah was to suffer with criminals and pray for his enemies	Isaiah 53:12	Matthew 27:38 Mark 15:27, 28 Luke 23:32-34
13. Messiah was to be given vinegar	Psalm 69:21	Matthew 27:34 John 19:28-30
14. Others were to cast lots for Messiah's garments	Psalm 22:18	Matthew 27:35 John 19:23-24
15. Messiah's bones were not to be broken	Exodus 12:46	John 19:31-36
16. Messiah was to die as a sacrifice for sin	Isaiah 53:5-6, 8, 10-12	John 1:29; 11:49-52 Acts 10:43; 13:38, 39
17. Messiah was to be raised from the dead	Psalm 16:10	Matthew 28:1-10 Acts 2:22-32
18. Messiah is now at God's right hand	Psalm 110:1	Mark 16:19 Luke 24:50-51

The Function of Prophecy According to Paul, the central purpose of prophecy (as of all other spiritual gifts) is that of building up or edifying the church. According to 1 Corinthians 14:3, "one who prophesies is helping others grow in the Lord, encouraging and comforting them" (NLT). Again, in 1 Corinthians 14:4, Paul states that the "one who speaks a word of prophecy strengthens the entire church." Paul discussed the subject of spiritual gifts, particularly tongues speaking and prophecy, because the Corinthians had placed an excessive emphasis on speaking in tongues. Paul did not object to speaking in tongues (1 Cor 14:18, 39), but he did point out that, since it was generally incomprehensible, the church could not be edified by it. Prophecy, which consisted of comprehensible speech inspired by the Spirit, contributed to the mutual edification, encouragement, and consolation of all present (1 Cor 14:20-25, 39).

The Content of Christian Prophecy We know only a little about the content of prophecies uttered in the first-century church. Prophetic utterance occasionally provided divine guidance in making important decisions in early Christianity. Through a prophetic utterance, Paul and Barnabas were selected for a particular mission (Acts 13:1-3; cf. 1 Tm 1:18; 4:14). Probably through prophetic utterance, Paul and Timothy were forbidden to preach the gospel in Asia (Acts 16:6), and they were similarly forbidden by the Spirit of Jesus to go into Bithynia (v 7). Perhaps the most frequent use of prophecy is the prediction of the future. Agabus predicted a universal famine (11:28) and the imminent arrest of Paul (21:11). Other prophets had also predicted his impending imprisonment (20:23). The prophecies contained in the Revelation of John are all oriented toward the future events that will gradually unfold in the last days. Yet the purpose of John's elaborate prophecy is not to satisfy the curiosity of his audience but rather to comfort and encourage them in the midst of persecution.

The Form of Christian Prophecy Unlike the prophets of the OT, Christian prophets did not always present their message in the form of a direct speech from God or

Jesus. There are few, if any, formal indicators of the presence of prophetic speech in early Christian literature. The book of Revelation is one notable exception.

See also Dreams; Oracle; Promise; Prophet, Prophetess; Prophets, False; Visions.

PROPHET, PROPHETESS
A man or woman chosen by God to speak for him and to foretell events in the divine plan.

PREVIEW
• Introduction
• The Titles and History of the Prophets
• Inspiration
• True and False Prophets
• The Function of the Prophet
• Methods of Communication

Introduction When Jesus raised the widow's son from the dead, the onlookers responded by saying, "A great prophet has arisen among us!" (Lk 7:16; cf. Mk 6:15; 8:28). In Jewish religious thought, the most vivid and formative religious happenings found their focus in the call and ministry of a prophet, through whom God communicated his word to his people. In their appraisal of Jesus, the people were in fact more correct than they knew, for in him God had in reality visited them and he, though so much more than a prophet, was in fact the crown and climax of the prophetic order predicted by Moses (Dt 18:15-19).

The Titles and History of the Prophets The main words used to describe such individuals in the OT are "prophet" (see Jgs 6:8), "man of God" (see 2 Kgs 4:9) and "seer" (see 1 Sm 9:9; 2 Sm 24:11).

The word translated "prophet" seems to have the idea "called" as its first emphasis: God takes the initiative, selects, summons, and sends the prophet (e.g., Jer 1:4-5; 7:25; Am 7:14). "Man of God" speaks of the relationship into which the prophet is brought by his call: he is now "God's man" and is recognized as belonging to him (2 Kgs 4:9). "Seer" indicates the new and remarkable powers of perception granted to the prophet. In Hebrew, as in English, the ordinary verb "to see" is used also of understanding ("I see what you mean") and of the power of perception into the nature and meaning of things ("He sees things very clearly"). In the case of the prophets, their powers of "perception" were raised far above normal because the Lord inspired them to become vehicles of his message.

The line of great prophets upon whose shoulders the story of the OT moves forward began with Moses, who is recognized as the prophet par excellence (Dt 34:10). This was a correct perception, for all the distinctive marks of a prophet belonged to Moses: the call (Ex 3:1–4:17; cf. Is 6; Jer 1:4-19; Ez 1–3; Hos 1:2; Am 7:14-15), the awareness of the importance of historical events as the acts of God in which he confirmed his word (Ex 3:12; 4:21-23), ethical and social concern (2:11-13), and championship of the helpless (v 17).

But the comment in Deuteronomy 34:10 not only looks back to the greatness of Moses but also looks forward to the coming of a prophet like Moses. This accords with his own prediction (Dt 18:15-19), which undoubtedly anticipates a single, great individual prophet. Moses makes a striking comparison with himself—the coming prophet will fill just such a role as Moses filled at Mt Sinai (Dt 18:16). On that occasion, Moses acted as the prophetic mediator of the voice of God in a unique sense, for at Sinai God fashioned the old covenant into

its completed form. In expecting a prophet cast in this mold, Moses was therefore looking forward to another covenant-mediator, Jesus Christ himself.

The expectation for this great prophet was kept alive as God kept sending prophets to his people. In each case, such a prophet was known to be true by his likeness to Moses; in each case he would be viewed with excitement by genuine believers to see whether he was the great one come at last. In this light we can understand the excitement of the people who saw Jesus raise the dead (Lk 7:16).

The OT mentions the existence of prophetic groups, sometimes called "schools." Elisha clearly had such a group under his instruction (2 Kgs 6:1), and "sons of the prophets" (e.g., 2 Kgs 2:3, 5; Am 7:14) probably refers to "prophet in training" under the care of a master prophet. "Guilds" would be a better description of the groups in 1 Samuel 10:5-11. Such groups enjoyed an enthusiastic, ecstatic worship of the Lord, touched with a marked activity of the Spirit of God. But at the heart of their devotion was "prophecy"—that is, a declaration of the truth about God himself. After this early period, the prophetic groups seem to have diminished in significance (judging by the disappearance of plain references similar to those in 1 Samuel), and the gradual change of things from ecstasy to a more direct ministry of the word could well lie behind the comment in 1 Samuel 9:9.

Inspiration The Spirit of the Lord whose inspiration lay behind the activities of the ecstatic groups (1 Sm 10:6, 10; 19:20, 23) was active in all the prophets, and the claim to divine inspiration is plainly registered from time to time (e.g., 1 Kgs 22:24; Neh 9:30; Hos 9:7; Jl 2:28-29; Mi 3:8; cf. 1 Chr 12:18; 2 Chr 15:1; 20:14; 24:20). The Spirit inspired men and women to speak the very words of God (cf. 2 Pt 1:21).

Jeremiah claims that the hand of God was laid on his mouth, putting the words of God into his lips (Jer 1:9); Ezekiel records how he was made to eat a scroll, by which means he received the words the Lord had written and was thus enabled to speak what the Lord called "my words" (Ez 2:7–4:4). The miracle is stated in a nutshell at the beginning of Amos (1:1, 3): "The words of Amos . . . Thus saith the LORD." Though the words were truly Amos's words, the words were also the Lord's.

True and False Prophets False prophets were to be separated from true prophets by means of three tests. The first test was doctrinal. In Deuteronomy 13 the motive of the false prophet was to draw the people away from the God who had revealed himself in the exodus (Dt 13:2, 5-7, 10). Notwithstanding that the word of the false prophet might be supported by apparent signs and wonders (vv 1-2), it was to be refused—not simply because it introduced novelty (vv 2, 6) but because that novelty contradicted the revelation of the Lord at the exodus (vv 5, 10). The first test was thus doctrinal and required that the people of God have knowledge of the truth whereby they could, by comparison, recognize error.

The second test was practical and required patience. It is stated in Deuteronomy 18:21-22: the word of the Lord always comes to pass. This requires patience because, as Deuteronomy 13:1-2 indicates, a false word may be supported by an apparent spiritual proof. The call of Deuteronomy 18:21-22 is a call for patience. Should there be any real doubt about whether a prophetic word is true or false, wait for the confirmatory turn of events.

The third test is moral and calls for watchful discernment. Jeremiah, of all the prophets, was most afflicted in his spirit by the presence of false prophets and gave the longest and most sustained consideration to the problem (Jer 23:9-40). His answer is striking and challenging: the false prophet will be found out as a man of unholy life (vv 11-14) whose message has no note of moral rebuke but rather encourages men in their sin (vv 16-22).

The Function of the Prophet It is sometimes said that prophets are not "foretellers" but "forthtellers." As far as the OT is concerned, however, the prophets are forthtellers (declaring the truth about God) by being foretellers (predicting what God will do). Prediction is neither an occasional nor a marginal activity in the OT; it is the way the prophet went about his work. Deuteronomy 18:9-15 explains the function of the prophet in Israel: the surrounding nations are revealed as probing into the future by means of a variety of fortune-telling techniques (vv 10-11); these things are forbidden to Israel on the ground of being abominable to the Lord (v 12). Israel's distinctiveness is maintained in that the nations probe the future by diviners, whereas the Lord gives Israel a prophet (vv 13-15). Elisha (2 Kgs 4:27) is surprised when foreknowledge is denied him; Amos teaches that foreknowledge is the privilege of the prophets in their fellowship with God (Am 3:7). But prediction in Israel was totally unlike prognostication among the nations, for in no way was it motivated by a mere curiosity about the future.

First, biblical prediction arose out of the needs of the present. In Isaiah 39 it is the faithless commitment of Hezekiah to rely for security on a military understanding with Babylon that prompts Isaiah to announce the future Babylonian captivity. Isaiah does not snatch the name Babylon out of thin air; it is given to him within the situation in which he was called to minister.

Second, prediction aimed at giving knowledge of the future was to result in moral reformation in the present. The moral exhortations of the prophets find their explanation in what the Lord is about to do (e.g., Is 31:6-7; Am 5:6).

Third, the predicted course of events was aimed at stabilizing the faith of the true believer in dark times. For example, various passages in Isaiah (Is 9:1-7; 11:1-16; 40:1-3) have the effect of lifting the eyes out of the immediately preceding grim tragedy to the coming glory.

Methods of Communication In foretelling, the prophets were forthtelling—they were proclaiming the wonderful works of God (cf. the definition of prophecy in Acts 2:11, 17). For the most part, this proclamation was by direct word of mouth. The prophets were men of the word. Their words were like messengers sent by God (Is 55:11), endowed with all the divine efficacy of the creative word of Genesis 1:3 (cf. Ps 33:6). Sometimes the efficacy of the word was enhanced by being accompanied by a sign or symbolic action (e.g., Jer 13:1-11; 19; Ez 4:1-17; 24:15-24), or identified intimately with a person (Is 7:3; cf. 8:1-4). Such things were like visual aids, whereby the word would be made clearer to those present. But it would seem that the intention of the symbolic action (sometimes called an "acted oracle") was not so much to make understanding easier but to give more power and effect to the word as it was sent like a messenger into that situation. This is the conclusion to be drawn from 2 Kings 13:14-19, where the extent to which the king "embodied" the word in action determined the extent to which the word would prove effective in bringing events to pass.

The final embodiment of the words of the prophets is in the books that have been preserved. Jeremiah 36 may be taken as an object lesson in the fact that the prophets took the time and trouble to record their spoken messages in writing: there was stress on careful word-by-word dictation (Jer 36:6, 17-18). But the actual literary

form of the messages themselves tells the same tale. What we find in the books of the prophets cannot be the preached form of their words but rather the studied wording in which they preserved (and filed away) their sermons. It stands to reason that men who were conscious of communicating the very words of God would see to it that those words were not lost. We may take it for granted that every prophet preserved a written record of his ministry. Whether each of the named prophets was himself directly responsible for the final form of his book, we are not told and have no way of knowing. The careful way in which the books of Isaiah or Amos, for example, are arranged is best suited by assuming that the author was also his own editor.

See also Prophecy; Prophets, False.

PROPHETS, False Spokesmen, heralds, or messengers falsely speaking for, or on behalf of, someone else. The false prophet was often motivated not by loyalty to God but by a desire for popularity. This was the main difference between Jeremiah and his contemporaries. While Jeremiah was foretelling doom (Jer 4:19), the false prophets were assuring the people of peace (6:14; 8:11). The people preferred it that way; they said, "Don't tell us the truth. Tell us nice things. Tell us lies" (Is 30:10, NLT).

The false prophet's message frequently appealed to national pride: Israel was God's people; God's temple was in their midst; therefore, all would be well (Jer 7:10). Jeremiah, however, warned them not to be fooled into thinking that just because they had the temple they would never suffer (vv 12-15). Such confrontation between the prophet of God and the national cult is exemplified in Amos's encounter with Amaziah the priest of Bethel, who accused Amos of conspiring against Israel (Am 7:10-13). Yet Amos was proved right when the northern kingdom fell to the Assyrians in 722 BC and the Jews were taken into exile.

The message of the false prophet was usually spurred by self-interest and given to please the people. It was not necessarily his intention to speak falsely, yet when spoken with wrong motivation, his message was often in error. This sometimes means that even a true prophet could become false and occasionally a false prophet could be used of God for the right purpose. For example, Balaam, a non-Israelite with whom God entrusted a vision, found himself in the difficult position of having to please Balak, who had hired him, and the God of Israel, who spoke to him (Nm 22–23). A fascinating story is told in 1 Kings 13 of two nameless prophets—one true and the other false—who abruptly change roles when the lying prophet speaks truth and the true prophet is proven false by disobedience. In the case of Jeremiah in confrontation with Hananiah the son of Azzur, the two prophets meet in the temple to pitch prophecy against prophecy. Hananiah was proved false, though he appeared as a legitimate prophet from Gibeon (Jer 28:1). He prophesied the very thing the people in Jerusalem wanted to hear, namely, the imminent fall of Babylon. Subsequent events, however, proved this thinking wishful. We may therefore say that false prophecy is self-centered, wrongly motivated, and detached from reality.

The concept of the false prophet is carried over into the NT. Our Lord warns against those who disguise themselves as harmless sheep but are in fact wolves ready for the kill. Jesus also warned his disciples that false christs would arise who would try to deceive God's elect (Mt 24:24). The early church must have been plagued by such pseudoprophets, for the apostolic letters further warn against such men (cf. 2 Pt 2:1; 1 Jn 4:1). In the context of these letters "prophets" and "teachers" are interchangeable, though the original text speaks of them as "false prophets." While pretending to be Christians, they are deceptive teachers because their instruction is perverse. These people even perform miracles, but with the help of evil spirits, not the Spirit of Christ (cf. Rv 13:11-15).

False prophets, fraudulent spirits, and wrong teachings are recurring problems in the church. Believers should constantly stand guard against those who cleverly lie about the truth (cf. Eph 4:14-16); they should discern the spirits of prophets to determine whether they are from the evil one or from God (1 Cor 12:10-11). We are told not to believe everyone who claims that his or her message is from God, but to "test" the spirits to see whether their message is from the Holy Spirit and whether it agrees with the truth that Jesus is the Son of God in human form (cf. 1 Jn 4:1-3).

See also Antichrist; False Christs, False Messiahs; Prophecy; Prophet, Prophetess.

PROPITIATION* The act of appeasing another person's anger by the offering of a gift. The word was often used by the pagans in antiquity, for they thought of their gods as unpredictable beings, liable to become angry with their worshipers for any trifle. When disaster struck, it was often thought that a god was angry and was therefore punishing his worshipers. The remedy was to offer a sacrifice without delay. A well-chosen offering would appease the god and put him in a good mood again. This process was called propitiation.

Understandably, some modern theologians have reacted against using the term in reference to the God of the Bible. They do not see him as one who can be bribed to become favorable, so they reject the whole idea. When they come to the term in the Greek NT, they translate it by "expiation" or some equivalent term that lacks any reference to anger. This is an unjustified avoidance because, in the first place, the Greek term for propitiation occurs in some important biblical passages (Rom 3:25; Heb 2:17; 1 Jn 2:2; 4:10). In the second place, the idea of the wrath of God is found throughout the Bible; it must be taken into account in the way sin is forgiven.

The idea that God cannot be angry is not based on the OT or the NT. God does have anger for the sins of the human race. Whenever his children sin, they provoke the anger of God. Of course, his anger is not an irrational lack of self-control, as it so often is with humans. His anger is the settled opposition of his holy nature to everything that is evil. Such opposition to sin cannot be dismissed with a wave of the hand. It requires something much more substantial. And the Bible states that it was only the cross that did this. Jesus is "the propitiation for our sins: and not for ours only, but also for the sins of the whole world" (1 Jn 2:2, KJV). This is not the only way of looking at the cross, but it is an important way. If God's anger is real, then it must be taken into account in the way that sin, which caused that wrath, is dealt with. When the NT speaks of "propitiation," it means that Jesus' death on the cross for the sins of mankind put away God's wrath against his people once and for all.

See also Atonement; Expiation; Wrath of God.

PROSELYTE* Gentile who converted to Judaism by being circumcised, baptized, and offering a sacrifice in the temple.

Foreigners who resided on some fairly permanent basis in Palestine in OT times were encouraged to become integrated into the full religious life of Israel through circumcision (Ex 12:48). But "proselytizing,"

or bringing willing Gentiles into the covenant community, occurred more frequently in the Jewish communities outside Palestine. Jews, living in most areas of the known world due to exile or commercial or military reasons, naturally carried their religious faith and practice with them. This Jewish way of life, particularly its monotheistic faith and high ethical standards, was attractive to many of the surrounding Gentiles accustomed to polytheism. The result was that many Gentiles attached themselves in varying degrees to the Jewish faith through the life of the synagogue (see Is 56:1-8; Mal 1:11). Extrabiblical Jewish sources (Philo, Josephus) and Roman sources (e.g., Horace, Seneca, Tacitus) reveal that Jews carried on an aggressive mission to Gentiles in the centuries immediately preceding the life of Christ and then on into the early NT era (see Mt 23:15).

The more zealous of those attracted to Judaism at this time became full members of the Jewish community through a rite involving three elements: circumcision (if male), a baptism representing a break with pagan background, and an offering in the temple at Jerusalem. Termed "proselytes," these converts were considered true Jews in the sense of being obligated to follow the entire OT law.

There were other Gentiles who admired the monotheism and moral superiority of Judaism and were attracted to synagogue life but did not desire to take such a final step as circumcision. These were termed "God-fearers" (see Acts 10:22; 13:16, 26) or "devout" ones (10:2; 17:4, 17) and were regarded favorably by some Jews. But they were disregarded by others as no better than Gentiles.

See also Diaspora of the Jews; God-fearer; Jew.

PROSPERITY *See* Bless, Blessing; Money.

PROSTITUTE, PROSTITUTION Person guilty of illicit sexual relationships; figuratively, one who worships an idol. The term "prostitute" translates four different words found in the Bible. One type of prostitute was the man or woman, married or unmarried, who committed immoral acts (Gn 34:31; Jgs 19:2; Prv 23:27). A different kind of prostitute was the temple prostitute of heathen religions in which fornication was part of the worship (Gn 38:21-22; Dt 23:17; Hos 4:14). Such prostitution was forbidden by the law of Moses (Lv 19:29; 21:9). The "strange woman" was another kind of prostitute (1 Kgs 11:1; Prv 5:20; 6:24; 7:5; 23:27). There are different opinions for why that name was given to prostitutes. One explanation is that it referred to a man leaving his own wife for another, who ought to be a stranger to him (Prv 5:17-20). It may also have referred to a foreign woman (Nm 25:1; Jos 23:13). "Prostitute" also refers to any woman, married or single, who practices unlawful sexual indulgence, whether for lust or monetary gain (Mt 21:31-32; Lk 15:30; 1 Cor 6:15-16; Heb 11:31; Jas 2:25).

Prostitution appeared early in Israel's life and continued throughout biblical history. Most biblical passages strongly condemn the practice of prostitution in any form. The priestly law of Leviticus 21:9 provided that a priest's daughter who practiced prostitution was to be burned to death. A priest could not marry a prostitute (Lv 19:29), and the wages of prostitution could not be used to pay vows in the temple (Dt 23:18). These prohibitions served to keep the worship of the Lord free from the practice of cult prostitution.

The sons of Jacob killed Hamor and his son Shechem, justifying their act by saying: "Should he treat our sister like a prostitute?" (Gn 34:31, NLT). Amaziah's wife was to become a prostitute (Am 7:17) as punishment for his treatment of the prophet Amos.

In the first century, prostitutes and tax collectors were equally detested by the Jews (Mt 21:32). According to Paul, the body of a Christian belongs to Christ and should not be joined to a prostitute's body (1 Cor 6:15-16). Proverbs is replete with warnings to those who would go in to prostitutes.

A few biblical passages do, however, seem to accept the prostitute as a member of the community. Tamar temporarily served as a prostitute to remind her father-in-law of his promise to her (Gn 38:14-15). Rahab the prostitute had a special place in Hebrew history because she had befriended the Hebrew spies (Jos 2:4-16; Heb 11:31).

The words "prostitute" and "prostitution" were used figuratively for idolatry, especially in the prophetic books (Jer 2:20; Rv 17:1, 5, 15-16; 19:2). This figurative use was based on the marriagelike relationship of the Lord and his people (Jer 3:20). When the people gave their allegiance to idols rather than to God, he charged that they were prostitutes for other gods (Jgs 8:33). The same idea is found in the NT (Rv 17).

PROTEVANGELIUM* The word means first *(protos)* gospel *(evangelion)*. Theologians have used the word in reference to the message of redemption God spoke after the fall of man. Speaking to Satan (embodied in a serpent), God said, "From now on, you and the woman will be enemies, and your offspring and her offspring will be enemies. He will crush your head, and you will strike his heel" (Gn 3:15, NLT). In the protevangelium we have the protorevelation of the humanity (her offspring) and the divinity (crushing the head of serpent) of the great Deliverer. In this proclamation, God promises a Deliverer who will destroy Satan in an ordeal in which he himself will suffer. This refers to Jesus' death on the cross. In suffering that death, Jesus defeated him who had the power of death, the devil (Heb 2:14).

PROVERBS, Book of Third poetical book in the OT. A collection of striking, epigrammatic expressions concerning practical wisdom by example, warning, or precept.

PREVIEW
•Authors
•Date
•Background
•Purpose and Theology
•Content

Authors While there is an underlying unity of thought in the book of Proverbs, there is no presumption of unity of authorship, since the writers of the seven or more sections into which the book is divided are, in most cases, clearly noted.

1:1–9:18 There is a division of opinion as to whether the opening verse refers to the Solomonic authorship of this section or whether it simply underscores the name of the main contributor to the entire book. It is objected that the man who wrote so carefully about the danger of promiscuous relationships with immoral women—one of the main themes of this section—is not likely to be Solomon, who failed significantly in the matter of mixed marriages (1 Kgs 11:1-8). There are flaws in such an argument. One may be capable of giving excellent advice without necessarily having the strength of character to follow it oneself, and there is a distinction between the seductive prostitutes or adulteresses of Proverbs 5:1-21,

6:20-35, 7:1-27 and Solomon's polygamous but respectable relationships. However, the question of authorship is probably best left open. Those who question the Solomonic origin of this section regard 1:2-7 as setting out the purpose of the whole book. Proverbs 1:8–9:18 is a series of 13 practical discourses on wisdom, lovingly and honestly given as by a father to a son. This provides an indispensable foundation for the more popular proverbial teaching in the remainder of the book.

10:1–22:16 Solomon is specifically noted as the author or compiler of this main section of Proverbs. The probability that he played a major part in the production of the book of Proverbs finds strong support in the historical books. Soon after his coronation he was endowed with the spirit of wisdom—in response to his request (1 Kgs 3:5-14). The incident concerning the two prostitutes (vv 16-28) provided public proof of this. His universal reputation, especially in connection with proverbial wisdom, is attested to in 1 Kings 4:29-34 and in the visit of the queen of Sheba (10:1-13).

22:17–24:34 The title "the words of the wise" (Prv 22:17, NEB) is incorporated into the opening verse of this section. An evident difference of style, replacing the simple, one-verse proverb by a more discursive approach that deals with a subject over several verses, and the title of the next subsection "These also are sayings of the wise" (24:23), strongly suggest the independence of this collection. Of major interest is the remarkably close parallel between 22:17–23:11 and the Egyptian book of Amenemope, which has been dated variously between the 13th and 7th centuries BC. Scholars have detected as many as 30 connections between the two. Most think that this section in Proverbs is an adaptation of an Egyptian original (such selection and modification being entirely congruous with the doctrine of inspiration). However, a minority of scholars, including several prominent Egyptologists, argue persuasively on the basis of grammatical structure that Amenemope is derived from a Hebrew original.

25:1–29:27 Some material of Solomon's has here been edited and incorporated by "the men of Hezekiah king of Judah" (25:1). In this section there is a tendency to group together proverbs dealing with specific subjects—for example, the relationship between a king and his subjects (vv 2-7), the lazy man (26:13-16), and the mischief maker (vv 17-27). Solomon and Hezekiah were frequently linked together in Jewish thought (e.g., 2 Chr 30:26), and rabbinic tradition credited Hezekiah with the production of both Proverbs and Ecclesiastes. The national prestige during the reigns of both kings would have been conducive to literary pursuits.

30:1-33 Nothing is known of Agur, of his father, Jakeh of Massa, or of the two other characters mentioned, Ithiel and Ucal. According to Genesis 25:14, Massa was one of the 12 sons of Ishmael, and it is likely that Agur came from north Arabia, an area traditionally renowned for its wisdom.

31:1-9 Lemuel, the author of this section, also came from Massa, but apart from this is unknown. The inclusion of wisdom sayings from sources outside Israel illustrates the international connections of the wisdom movement during the period of the monarchy.

31:10-31 It is possible that Lemuel's authorship includes this superb acrostic poem on the ideal wife; its inspiration may have come from his mother, like the earlier section. But the pattern of life would fit more easily into the context of a prosperous, agricultural community in Palestine rather than in an Arabian nomadic or seminomadic community. For this reason, most scholars regard the poem as anonymous.

Date The larger part of the book may, with confidence, be ascribed to Solomon (ruled c. 970–930 BC). But the considerable contribution of Hezekiah and his men rules out a date for the completion of the book before 700 BC. The inclusion of sections by non-Israelites, like Agur and Lemuel, is more likely in the preexilic period, with its wider international interests, than in the more particularistic atmosphere of postexilic Judaism. Probably the final, sophisticated acrostic poem was the last section to be included, but there is nothing in the book that demands a date later than the early seventh century BC. In rabbinic tradition Proverbs was invariably grouped with Psalms and Job in the third section of the Jewish canon, the Writings or Holy Books. While the content of the Writings was not authoritatively finalized until the end of the first century AD, it is likely that Proverbs was accepted as inspired long before this, as witnessed by its inclusion in the Septuagint, the principal Greek translation. The order in our English versions may have been influenced by the rabbinic tradition that linked the books of Job, Psalms, and Proverbs with Moses, David, and Hezekiah, respectively.

Background The book of Proverbs is included in the OT corpus of books known as the Wisdom Literature. This corpus is further represented in Scripture by the books of Job and Ecclesiastes and some of the Psalms (e.g., Pss 1, 37, 73, 119). Proverbs represents one major class of this literature. Individual proverbs contain sharp, practical applications of wisdom covering many facets of life. Job and Ecclesiastes focus on one major problem, or a group of interrelated problems, in monologue or dialogue form.

In the ancient Near East, wisdom was originally connected with all skills, manual as well as intellectual, and was considered to be the gift of the gods. Gradually it acquired a dominantly intellectual significance, particularly in a cultic setting, in such magical or semimagical arts as exorcism. A wide range of wisdom literature from Egypt, Canaan, and Mesopotamia, of the two basic types noted in the preceding paragraph, has survived, making it possible to see its Hebrew counterpart against this background. There is no duplication, however, and the spirit of the Hebrew Wisdom Literature is markedly superior to anything comparable in the ancient world. This is due principally to the strong religious foundation in Israel, where wisdom's first step was to trust and revere the Lord (Prv 1:7).

When Israel emerged as a nation in the Mosaic period, it was in a world where individuals or groups of "the wise" already existed. Israel shared this inheritance, with both men and women being involved, as witnessed by the wise women of Tekoa and Abel in Beth-maacah (2 Sm 14:2; 20:16) and the professional military or civic court counselors Ahithophel and Hushai (2 Sm 15:1-2, 31; 16:15-19). Proverbs shows this group of "the wise" at its best; the life of uprightness, diligence, honesty, and self-control that it advocates sets a standard of morality that accords with the law on which it was based. But it is probable that many proverbs predate the emergence of a class of the wise. Most communities develop their own collections of short, witty sayings that express practical wisdom and form a store of primitive philosophy. Solomon's part in giving definitive shape to Israel's proverbs (1 Kgs 4:32) has already been noted. The antithetic form of Hebrew poetry, where the parallelism of the second line allows either a sharp contrast (as generally in Proverbs 10–15) or further support (i.e., synonymous parallelism, as in chs 16–22) is an ideal medium for the proverb. When the class of "the wise" developed, this popular wisdom became part of their provenance.

Purpose and Theology

The Close Relationship between Religion and Everyday Life While the general tone of Proverbs is dominantly rational, the importance of fearing (showing reverence to) the Lord is stressed throughout the book (1:7; 2:5; 3:7; 8:13; etc.). This "fear of the Lord" is one of the main definitions of religion in the OT, the other being "the knowledge of God" stressed especially by Hosea and Jeremiah (Jer 9:24; Hos 4:1). Both are found in parallel in Proverbs 2:5 and 9:10. Far from there being an unbridgeable gap between religion and the secular world, Proverbs shows the results, in noble character and harmonious, happy homes, when the whole of life is brought under God's control. A danger exists when the moral elements are taken in isolation from the religious foundation that is assumed throughout. Then the pursuit for happiness or success can become selfish, inward-looking, and ultimately self-defeating.

Proverbs and the Prophetic Movement There are many similarities between Proverbs and the Prophets, including a down-to-earth realism; a championing of the poor and underprivileged groups (e.g., 14:31); a realization of the inefficacy of sacrifice apart from morality (15:8; 21:27); and an emphasis on the individual, which was sometimes overlooked because of the strong sense of corporate identity within the covenant community. Jeremiah and Ezekiel, especially, restated strongly the theme of individual responsibility (Jer 31:29-30; Ez 18). But there is a vital difference that Proverbs shares with the remainder of biblical Wisdom Literature, namely, the absence of any clear, historical reference to Israel's election and covenant relationship with God. This was the consistent point of appeal of the great preexilic prophets. Similarly, Jerusalem and its temple theology are not mentioned, although the wisdom movement, especially as reflected in Proverbs, flourished under the patronage of the Davidic monarchy. Even the name Israel does not occur. This has lent strength to the view that Proverbs is the clearest and most comprehensive manual of universal, practical ethics existing in the ancient world. An educated contemporary Egyptian would have found Proverbs readily comprehensible and uplifting, and although this was not its primary purpose, the book still has a strong appeal to the moral non-Christian.

Proverbs and Deuteronomy Proverbs shares many features with the book of Deuteronomy, especially its emphasis on retribution and reward (Prv 2:22; 3:9-10; 10:27-30; cf. Dt 28). This doctrine could be perverted into an invariable equation: the righteous are always rewarded and the wicked are always punished. That is a view against which Job (Jb 21:7-34) and Jeremiah (Jer 12:1-4) protested strongly. It could also result in a hypocritical, self-seeking approach; I want the blessings promised (e.g., Prv 3:9-10), therefore I will "honor" God in the matter of tithes. This substitution of an outward show for the inward dynamic of love, gratitude, and faith was often the curse of Israel's formalized religion. However, the principle itself—that those who honor God and live in cooperation with him and his laws are generally those who are God-blessed (not necessarily in material terms)—is a scriptural one, and the authors of Proverbs must not be blamed for the perversions that arose subsequently.

Content

Introduction: 1:1-7 Proverbs 1:1-7 sets out the purpose of the wisdom movement in Israel. The subtitle of the whole book is found in verse 2: "The purpose of these proverbs is to teach people wisdom and discipline, and to help them understand wise sayings" (NLT). The question of the authorship of this section has already been discussed, but there is certainly nothing incongruous about Solomon's authorship. In the earlier part of his reign, Solomon showed a deep longing for the wisdom that was required to govern his people rightly (1 Kgs 3:7-9), and there is the earnest desire here that his subjects might have a similar understanding. Verses 1-6 form one sentence in Hebrew and include no fewer than 11 different aspects of wisdom. The first of them, "wisdom," occurs 37 times in Proverbs and indicates an informed, skillful use of knowledge. It is only by taking the first step of trusting in the Lord that a person can enter into wisdom. Morality is not situational, nor an absolute in itself; it requires an unchanging point of reference that can only be found in God.

Lessons on Wisdom: 1:8–9:18 This section is composed of 13 distinct lessons on wisdom, most of which are introduced by "My son" or something similar. The final lesson (8:1–9:18) is given by Wisdom herself. This method indicates the warm, personal relationship between the teacher and his pupils, who, in the ancient Near East, would be exclusively male. A similar style is found in both Egyptian and Mesopotamian wisdom literature and could well have been adopted by Solomon, who, in the humility and God-fearing concern for the national well-being of his earlier years, would have been a teacher par excellence.

▶LESSON 1: AVOIDING EVIL COMPANIONS (1:8-33) Three voices are raised: (1) the specious voice of those who promise quick gains by violence (vv 10-14); (2) the wise man himself (vv 15-19), who reinforces the advice of parents patiently given over the years (vv 8-9) and who advocates a clean break with violent men doomed to a violent end; and (3) Wisdom (vv 20-33), whose appeal is not furtive but open and who seeks to give others her own spirit of wisdom (v 23). Those who spurn the voice of wisdom will experience judgment (vv 29-33).

▶LESSON 2: THE REWARDS OF WISDOM (2:1-22) While wisdom is ultimately God-given (v 6), people must seek it with an intensity of desire that characterized the psalmist (Prv 2:2-4; cf. Ps 63:1). There is no contradiction here, but a paradox that underlines the fact that God's gifts are not given lightly but are given to those who, by their attitude of heart and will, merit them. The benefits of wisdom outlined (Prv 2:7-22) have both negative and positive and both material and spiritual elements. The peril of associating with immoral women, which is referred to so frequently in Proverbs, is mentioned for the first time (vv 16-19).

▶LESSON 3: THE REWARDS OF COMPLETE TRUST IN GOD (3:1-10) For the Jew there was always the temptation to try to ensure blessing by an outward show of religion, and verses 9-10 could be misinterpreted. But the context stresses the requirement of heart loyalty and obedience (vv 1-8). "God first" (v 6) is the fundamental need; without this an individual or a nation is impoverished (cf. Hg 1:1-11).

▶LESSON 4: THE NEED FOR DISCIPLINE (3:11-20) One of the major themes in Proverbs is discipline, especially that of a father chastising his son (Prv 3:11-12; cf. Heb 12:5-11). The other theme here is the praise of wisdom and the benefits it bestows.

▶LESSON 5: WISDOM AND COMMON SENSE (3:21-35) Wisdom and common sense will result in safety (vv 23-26) and guard against unwise acts (vv 27-32). But the underlying security is found in verse 26: "The LORD is your security."

▶LESSON 6: DETERMINATION (4:1-9) Here the teacher gives his own testimony and shows that he is drawing on the accumulated wisdom of an earlier generation (vv 1-6). There is an emphasis upon determination, with the will resolutely set to gain wisdom, as the verbs in verses 5-9 show.

▶LESSON 7: THE STRAIGHT PATH (4:10-19) An equal determination is necessary to keep clear of evil men and their pursuits (vv 14-17). Note the graphic description, both beautiful and frightening, of the two paths (vv 18-19).

▶LESSON 8: PURSUING RIGHTEOUSNESS AND AVOIDING EVIL (4:20-27) The single-minded pursuit of righteousness and its corollary, the avoidance of every kind of evil (cf. 1 Thes 5:22), involves our hearing (Prv 4:20), memories (v 21), hearts (vv 21, 23), sight (v 25), and wills (vv 26-27). It means total commitment to God.

▶LESSON 9: SEXUAL PURITY (5:1-23) In blunt language that cannot possibly be misunderstood, the perils of sexual prostitution and the wisdom of faithfulness within marriage are underscored. In sexual relationships there can be no purely private morality; others are necessarily involved, and God is more than a concerned spectator (v 21).

▶LESSON 10: THE THINGS GOD HATES (6:1-19) First (vv 1-5), there is straightforward advice about the need to avoid rash pledges. If one is foolish enough to be already involved, the sensible thing is to swallow one's pride and extricate oneself as soon as possible. The second lesson—to emulate the ants in their diligent preparation for future need (vv 6-11)—anticipates the contrasting attention later given to the sluggard (22:13; 26:13-16). The third lesson describes in detail the slick, deceitful "con man" (6:12-19). He is to be avoided.

▶LESSON 11: ILLICIT SEXUAL RELATIONSHIPS (6:20-35) This section continues with the subject of illicit sexual relationships, showing God's attitude to this particular form of sin. The wounded husband will prove a formidable adversary, should he discover infidelity (vv 33-35), and the effect upon the adulterer himself will be utterly disastrous (vv 26-32).

▶LESSON 12: THE WILES OF THE PROSTITUTE (7:1-27) This chapter gives a graphic illustration of the wiles of a prostitute. Speciously, the pleasures she offers appear alluring, enhanced by the element of risk, but in fact the night's adventure invariably proves to be the road to hell (v 27).

▶LESSON 13: WISDOM'S DIRECT APPEAL (8:1–9:18) In contrast to the smooth-tongued, deadly seductress of chapter 7 and the brazen, loud-mouthed prostitute of 9:13-18, there are two complementary pictures of Wisdom. The first, in 8:1-36, is one of the most remarkable examples of personification in the OT. Wisdom seeks not the ruin of one but the welfare of all (vv 1-5). Wisdom and integrity, righteous conduct and frankness are pictured as inseparable entities (vv 6-13). But there remains an emphasis on the blessings that result from the quest for wisdom (vv 14-21). Kings, judges, and rulers are dependent on her, and success of the most desirable kind is her gift to her followers. Verses 22-31 are virtually a theological explanation for the preeminence of Wisdom, showing her close association with God's creative activity.

Understandably, many Christians have seen in these verses an anticipation of Christ himself. The NT sees Christ as the answer to two of the most vital religious issues: how does God approach mankind, and how did he create the world? Here is the answer—by Wisdom. The connection may be carried into the next section (vv 33-36), where Wisdom, like Christ in the NT, is seen as the one absolutely essential and desirable thing.

In the second picture of Wisdom (9:1-6), she is seen as a gracious, generous hostess, offering a banquet that issues in life (cf. Jesus' parable in Lk 14:15-24). A further contrast with the immoral woman in Proverbs 9:13-18 notes, pointedly, that the latter's guests end up in hell. A series of proverbs on the contrast between the wise and foolish (vv 7-12) come between the two pictures. They show how teachable the wise man is, in contrast to the fool. Once more the true foundation of life is clearly defined (v 10).

The Collected Proverbs of Solomon: 10:1–22:16 The 375 proverbs in this section were probably selected from the 3,000 for which Solomon is credited (1 Kgs 4:32). Each verse is a unit, with a contrast or a comparison between its two lines. There are understandable repetitions (e.g., Prv 14:12; 16:25), almost inevitable in a large collection of this kind. The common sense of the proverbial sayings, each of which has been proved in experience, is evident, but one must allow for varying levels; some appear rather mundane and close to worldly wisdom. But taken as a whole, they provide a practical guide, sanctioned by God, for everyday life. Again, it must be stressed that the religious life, based on the law and the covenant relationship, is assumed. God is vitally concerned with the minute details of life, and religious issues are not entirely bypassed (e.g., 10:27-29; 14:27; 15:16, 33; 18:10). This section in Proverbs cannot be read quickly; each verse demands a pause to allow its point to penetrate the mind. Since there is no systematic arrangement of the proverbs, the most helpful way of approach into this section may be by a consideration of the principal themes. It would be a valuable study to collate the references to each subject:

1. The rewards of the righteous and the end of the ungodly (10:2, 7, 16, 27-30; 11:3-9).
2. The fool. The three Hebrew words translated "fool" can all have the sense of stubborn rebelliousness as well as dullness of intellect, so "rebel" is often an apt rendering. The fool gives his parents grief and is a menace to society. His mind is completely closed to reason and his unbridled words cause untold damage. In his case, correction is pointless; he is beyond hope.
3. The simple. The reference here is to the large, uncommitted group, neither fools nor wise, but those who are open to the gentle persuasion of concerned wisdom teachers. The main appeal of this section is to this group rather than to the wise and prudent, who have already "graduated."
4. The lazy. This person is often contrasted with the industrious (e.g., 10:4-5) and is mercilessly satirized for his apathy and weak excuses.
5. The power of words. They can wound or heal (12:18). The stress on honest speech, in contrast to deceitful, thoughtless words, is well illustrated in the same chapter (e.g., 12:6, 13-14, 17-19, 22).
6. Wisdom. Chapter 13 shows how it may be derived from parents (v 1), the Scriptures (v 13), the class of the wise (v 14), and good company (v 20).
7. Justice. The stress on this echoes the great prophets. In particular, bribery is condemned (17:8, 23;

18:16), as are false witnesses (19:5, 9, 28), while open-mindedness is commended (18:17).
8. Neighborliness. Fair-weather "friends" are often referred to (e.g., 19:4-7) and contrasted with the true friend (17:17; 18:24).
9. Riches and poverty. These conditions are approached in a variety of ways, but always with an emphasis on moral and spiritual rather than merely material prosperity (e.g., 21:6; 22:1, 4). Care for the poor is frequently demanded (21:13)—to be accompanied with the highest motives (22:2).
10. Family life. There is an attractive picture of an ideal family, with its industrious husband, an understanding wife who is a blessing to him (12:4; 14:1; 18:22; 19:14), and obedient children, disciplined when necessary by punishment (13:24; 19:18; 23:13-14).

The Final Section—More Wise Advice: 22:17–31:31 While the subjects considered and the general outlook are unchanged, the proverbs in this section are generally longer and there is an evident attempt to group together proverbs dealing with particular subjects—for example, the perils of strong drink (23:29-35). The religious motive of the editor of this section is evident; he writes that people should trust in the Lord (22:19).

➤ADDITIONAL PROVERBS: 22:17–24:34 This may be viewed as a supplement to the previous section dealing further with the subjects of justice, wise business policy, slander, and laziness. The humorous but pointed proverb of the lazy man's field is the longest in the book.

➤ADDITIONAL SOLOMONIC PROVERBS: 25:1–29:27 From the many Solomonic proverbs not included in the main collection (10:1–22:16), the aides of Hezekiah selected and edited a further group of Solomon's proverbs. Again, there is evidence of an effort to group related proverbs—for example, the place of kings (25:2-7); unwise litigation (vv 8-10); the fool (26:1-12); laziness (vv 13-16); and the troublemaker (vv 17-27).

➤THE WISDOM OF AGUR: 30:1-33 The humility of the wise man in the presence of an all-wise God emerges clearly in Agur's introduction (vv 1-4), a passage paralleled in Job 38–39. His teaching method was apparently to confront his students with a number of examples of a point under discussion, the "two . . . three . . . four" method, indicating that the catalogue was not complete and encouraging them to add further illustrations from their own experience. Agur was evidently in close and perceptive touch with life at every level.

➤THE WISDOM OF LEMUEL: 31:1-9 This section, inspired by his mother, deals yet again with sexual relationships, the perils of intoxication, and the need to champion the poor and oppressed. Lemuel's name, meaning "belonging to God," probably tells us still more about his mother.

➤THE IDEAL WIFE: 31:10-31 Every verse of this poem, which was possibly anonymous, begins with a successive letter of the Hebrew alphabet, a device that often signified completeness. Coming at the end of Proverbs (a book that is forthright when dealing with the subject of the immoral woman), it gives, in antithesis, a refreshing picture of a cultured, well-to-do housewife and mother. At the same time, it provides an enlightening insight into several facets of contemporary life. As elsewhere in the book, her underlying relationship to God (v 30) results in desirable virtues that include trustworthiness (v 11), immense application (vv 13-19, 24, 27), charity (vv 19-20), foresight (vv 21, 25), wisdom, and kindness (v 26).

See also Poetry, Biblical; Solomon (Person); Wisdom; Wisdom Literature.

PROVIDENCE*

PROVIDENCE* God's activity throughout history in providing for the needs of human beings, especially those who believe in him.

Significance of Providence All through the centuries of human existence there have been those who took great comfort in God's providential care. God has not left this planet alone in the vast universe or forgotten for a moment the human situation. God visits, touches, communicates, controls, and intervenes, coming before and between people and their needs. Providence is ground for thankfulness.

Counterfeit Concepts of Providence The fact that the nonbelieving world has so many erroneous ideas about providence proves that this is an immensely realistic issue. At the heart of every nonbiblical proposal about providence is the denial of the personhood of God. In its place stands some cold principle or force dominating man and clashing with his life. It may be all-pervasive or local. It may be rational or irrational, consistent or arbitrary. False providences include:

Fate Countless numbers of people have believed themselves to be trapped by a sometimes fickle and always foreboding fate. "As fate would have it," they say.

Luck Life is indeed fortuitous at times. Optimists speak of "fortune," or less solemnly of "luck." But then, since this is all so impersonal, fortune-tellers arose, and someone dreamed up "lady luck."

Serendipity This is the term used by the one who takes credit for unintentional discoveries of good things along the way in life. But he refuses to acknowledge that God was there before him and so he does not give thanks.

History Some Marxist propagandists have championed their cause by saying, "History is on our side." They were appealing to a supposed inevitability of future events that would lead to a Communistic world. "History" in such a statement appears to have taken on a divine dimension. Likewise, when American leaders have affirmed a "manifest destiny" for the United States to be the superior power in the Western hemisphere or in the world at large, the same kind of reasoning is employed.

Progress The development of science and technology, education and social evolution, and territorial conquests have made some people believers in progress as something more than what is seen. Until the two world wars, there was the illusion of a relentless momentum pushing upward and onward forever. In some respects, progress is but providence by another name, but not to the degree that people assume for themselves the glory that belongs to God.

Nature Men like Ralph Waldo Emerson and Henry David Thoreau of 19th-century New England attributed to nature the gifts of providence. But nature is impersonal and abstract.

Natural Selection and the Survival of the Fittest
Charles Darwin's classic on biological evolution, *The Origin of the Species*, appeared in 1859. It popularized two relatively new theories. For millions of people, the mysterious decisions behind "natural selection" intrigued the thoughtful more than the notion of God's providence. And the idea that "the fit survive" necessarily makes providence altogether unnecessary.

These counterfeit views compete with the idea of God's providence. Of course, they cannot all be true. Nor can they satisfy the inquirer whose personhood calls insistently for a personal providence that reflects a knowledge of his individual needs and uniqueness. Only the Christian doctrine of providence provides that.

Biblical Meaning of Providence Providence is basically God's provision for the needs of people on time. The classic statement is found in Abraham's confession of faith in his life's most difficult test. He was under the duress of God's command to provide something he could not afford—his son in sacrifice. He struggled with the dilemma of losing his son or losing God's friendship. In answer to Isaac's question about a sacrifice for God, Abraham exclaimed, "God himself will provide the lamb for the burnt offering, my son" (Gn 22:8, NIV). The word "providence" means literally "to see before," and therefore by implication to do something about the situation. In this case, there was already upon Mt Moriah a suitable sacrifice, "a ram, caught in a thicket by his horns" (v 13). The unbelieving analysis of that situation would understand only that through an ordinary process an animal had become entangled in dense underbrush, and coincidentally Abraham and Isaac happened to arrive on the scene. But to believing Abraham, who was led for three days toward that one point in time and space in desperate need of a divine provision, it was altogether clear to him that God, by whatever process, had stationed the ram at the place of sacrifice for his use. "Provision" and "providence" are coordinately related to their verbal root, "provide," and are essentially and etymologically the same. However, they are theologically distinguished in usage by providence's having come to mean divine provision on the basis of foresight.

The great text on providence in the NT is also set in a context of sacrifice pleasing to God. Paul had reason to commend the Philippians' sacrificial support of his missionary work. To them he stated his unbounded confidence in the providential care of God: "This same God who takes care of me will supply all your needs from his glorious riches, which have been given to us in Christ Jesus" (Phil 4:19, NLT). The sacrifice of Christ Jesus for us confirms the doctrine of providence with a most reasonable certitude. What God initially required of Abraham but did not ultimately require (the sacrifice of his son), he required of himself and did fulfill two millennia later. It is God's nature to supply, to foresee man's need and to provide for him.

Providence and the Nature of God Immediately following his reassuring words to the Philippians about the treasury of providence ("his riches in glory"—Phil 4:19), the apostle Paul wrote a doxology to God "our Father" (v 20). Providence is appropriately pictured in the fatherhood of God. His fatherhood is the attribute, and providence is the act that expresses it. Fathers provide and guide. Fathers construct conditions of opportunity for children without crowding their freedom. They exercise governance in a context of caring. Providence, therefore, as an activity of God, flows naturally from God's fatherly nature.

See also Foreordination; God, Being and Attributes of.

PSALM 151*

PSALM 151* A noncanonical psalm that, prior to the Qumran discoveries, was known only through ancient translations (LXX, Latin, and Syriac). At Qumran the psalm was included in the Hebrew Psalm Scroll (11Q). The Hebrew text indicates two separate poems. The first poem (designated as 151A) is a commentary on 1 Samuel 16:1-13. It relates how David was set over his father's flocks but was made king over God's people after God had looked upon his heart. The second poem (151B) is a commentary on 1 Samuel 17 and deals with David and

Goliath. It is thought by some to show the bravery of David in contrast to his humility, as is shown in 151A.

PSALMS, Book of

Poems sung to musical accompaniment, originally the harp. The alternative title, the Psalter, refers to a collection of songs sung to harp accompaniment. The English title, therefore, broadly defines the form employed, whereas the Hebrew title of the book, "Praises," or "Book of Praises," suggests the content.

PREVIEW
• Authors
• Date
• Background
• Structure
• Canonicity
• Purpose and Theology
• Content

Authors

The Evidence of the Titles The Hebrew Bible credits David with 73 psalms, compared with 84 in the Septuagint and 85 in the Latin Vulgate. Korah and Asaph, the leaders of the Levitical singing groups, are connected with 11 and 12 psalms, respectively (although Ps 43 is almost certainly to be attributed to Korah also). Two psalms are ascribed to Solomon (Pss 72; 127), one to Moses (Ps 90), and one to Ethan (Ps 89), while Heman shares the credit for one psalm with the sons of Korah (Ps 88). The remainder are sometimes called "orphan psalms" because of their anonymity.

The preposition "of" found in the titles (for example, "A Psalm of David") usually indicates authorship. But in the case of groups, such as the sons of Asaph or Korah, it may simply indicate that the psalms were included in their repertoire. Less plausible is the idea that it may also be rendered "for the use of." For example, some of the "Psalms of David" might be "for the use of" the Davidic king on some occasion.

Historical Allusions in the Titles Many of the titles refer to specific events in the life of David (e.g., Pss 3; 7; 18; 30; 34; 51). There is evidence that the titles were added at an early date. When the psalms were translated into Greek, there appears to have been some difficulty in translating the titles, possibly because of their antiquity. If the historical references were added at a late date, there is no reason why plausible backgrounds could not have been supplied for all the Davidic psalms, instead of only a few. Moreover, the apparent disparity between the title and the actual content of some psalms (e.g., Ps 30) indicates that the titles were supplied by those who knew about a connection unknown to a later editor. Admittedly, there are minor discrepancies between the titles and the references in the historical books. For example, in Psalm 34 David acts the madman before Abimelech, whereas in 1 Samuel it is before Achish. But probably Abimelech was the general name (like Pharaoh for the kings of Egypt) for all the Philistine kings (e.g., Gn 21:32; 26:26).

Evidence of authorship and historical background in the titles, therefore, may be taken as a reasonably reliable guide. But the internal difficulties, together with the freedom exercised by successive translators into Greek, Syriac, and Latin, indicates that they were not regarded as inspired.

The Case for Davidic Authorship Five points can be offered to support David's authorship of several psalms:

1. The authenticity of David's lament over Saul and Jonathan (2 Sm 1:19-27) is generally accepted. This indicates a deeply poetic spirit and a generous temperament that prepares us to accept those psalms ascribed to David that evidence similar characteristics. "The last words of David" is another Davidic poem in the historical books (2 Sm 23:1-7).

2. David had a reputation as a skillful musician at Saul's court (1 Sm 16:16-18). Amos comments on his inventiveness as a musician (Am 6:5), while the Chronicler repeatedly stresses his contribution to the musical aspect of temple worship (e.g., 1 Chr 6:31; 16:7; Ezr 3:10). The Jewish historian Josephus said that David composed songs and hymns to God in varied meters. The probability is that David, as well as amassing materials and preparing the plans for Solomon's temple, also gave attention to the temple worship. This is his place in Jewish tradition.

3. The early monarchy, with a freshly secured independence, national prestige, and a new prosperity, would most likely be a time of artistic creativity. David was at the heart of this movement.

4. There is a close correspondence between David's life as described in the historical books and certain psalms, for example, his sin concerning Bathsheba and Uriah (2 Sm 11:2–12:25) and Psalm 51, as witnessed in the title. David's lapses and genuine repentance, as well as the varied aspects of his career—shepherd, fugitive, warrior, and so on—find expression in many of the psalms attributed to him. The correspondence between the David of the psalms and the David of the historical books is close, especially in the display of strong faith in God.

5. Although some scholars believe that when "David" is mentioned in the NT, it is simply a reference to the book of Psalms and not an ascription of authorship, a straightforward interpretation of the NT text strengthens the case for Davidic authorship. David is specifically named as the author of various psalms in Matthew 22:41-45; Acts 1:16; 2:25, 34; Romans 4:6; 11:9.

In conclusion, there is strong support for the view that the substantial nucleus of the Psalter is Davidic. Moreover, it is probable that some of the anonymous psalms were the work of the "sweet psalmist of Israel" (2 Sm 23:1). Hebrews 4:7 refers one of these, Psalm 95, to David (see also Acts 4:25 and Ps 2).

Date Once David's authorship of several psalms is established, then it must follow that these psalms are dated during David's life. Thus, most of the psalms formed the hymnbook of Israel in the period of the monarchy. Other psalms were written later. For example, Psalm 137 is clearly exilic, and Psalms 107:2-3 and 126:1 allude to the return from captivity. Psalms 44 and 79 are probably, but not conclusively, postexilic.

The book of Psalms was probably the product of a considerable period of growth. The incidence of Davidic psalms in the first section indicates that it was completed early, possibly toward the end of David's reign. The remainder of the process of compilation is difficult to reconstruct, but the fact that the titles, with their allusions to authors, events, and musical directions, become less frequent in the two final collections (Pss 90–150) lends support to the probability that the collections were combined chronologically in the sequence in which they are found today. Ezra is traditionally credited with the final grouping and editing of the psalms, a hypothesis that appears reasonable in light of his vital contribution to the systematic reshaping of the national religious life. In any case, the process was completed before the translation of the Psalter into Greek (the Septuagint) at the end of the third century BC, since the traditional order is found there. General, but not complete, support comes also from the evidence of the Dead Sea Scrolls. At some point minor dislocations occurred. Psalms 9 and 10 may have originally formed one psalm (as in the Septuagint), and there is a strong case for combining Psalms 42 and 43.

Background As the book of Psalms lies before us, its connection with temple worship is apparent. Fifty-five psalms are addressed to the choirmaster, and as we have noted, 23 or 24 are linked with the two main guilds of Levitical singers, Asaph and Korah. The musical instruments, such as stringed instruments (Ps 55 title) and flutes (Ps 5 title) are noted. Probably other terms concern musical directions: *Selah*, which occurs 71 times, may indicate a pause or crescendo; *Higgaion* (Ps 9:16) may recommend a meditative attitude. Seemingly obscure references like "The Hind of the Dawn" (Ps 22 title), "Lilies" (Pss 45 title; 80 title) and "The Dove on Far-off Terebinths" (Ps 56 title) may indicate the tunes to which the psalms were to be sung. The precise meaning of other terms, such as *Shiggaion* (Ps 7 title) or *Alamoth* (conjecturally a choir of ladies, Ps 46 title), may also be in the realm of musical directions.

Structure The Psalter, possibly in conscious imitation of the five books of Moses in the Law, is divided into five sections (Pss 1–41; 42–72; 73–89; 90–106; 107–150), separated by four doxologies (41:13; 72:18-19; 89:52; 106:48). While the editorial comment in Psalm 72:20 notes that the psalms of David were ended, Davidic psalms are found later in the book (Pss 86; 101; 103), suggesting that at least some of these sections circulated independently until their inclusion in the final collection. Such independence is further indicated by the duplications in the various sections (e.g., Pss 14 and 53; 40:13-17 and 70) and by the use of different names for God, who is usually referred to as "Lord" in the first collection and as "God" in the second.

Canonicity In the various recensions of the third section of the Hebrew canon, the Writings or Holy Books, the book of Psalms is almost invariably placed first. It was clearly regarded as the most important book in this section, and in Luke 24:44, "Psalms" is synonymous with "Writings" as its title. While the canonicity of all the contents of the Writings was not finalized until the end of the first century AD, it is likely that the book of Psalms was accepted as inspired long before this, probably by 300 BC.

It must not be inferred that all the psalms had their origin in the cultic life of the community, but the sanctuary was the focal point of Israel's worship for the greater part of the OT period. Prayer was possible elsewhere, but whenever practicable, it was customary for the worshiper to present his petitions at the main sanctuary. And thanksgiving in ancient Israel was almost invariably connected with a thank offering, vow offering, or freewill offering. The psalms could have been composed by individuals, like David, who had the requisite technical ability. And it must be appreciated that poetry, an unfamiliar medium to most Western civilizations, was the natural way for the ancient Easterner to express his emotions. Or the individual could have engaged a member of the Levitical guilds of musicians to frame either his supplication or his thanksgiving. Gradually, a comprehensive collection of psalms would be available for the use of individuals, the congregation, and even the entire nation in any conceivable situation. Once finalized, this collection served not only the subsequent needs of Israel but the devotional requirements of successive generations of Christians as well. Whatever the origin of an individual psalm, each has finally been incorporated in a cultic setting, and it may be assumed that the best of Israel's psalmody has thus been preserved.

Purpose and Theology

The Doctrine of God In both adversity and prosperity, the psalmists indicate a strong faith in God and a clear conception of his attributes. Understandably, anthropomorphisms (ascribing human characteristics to nonhuman things) abound, with references to God's voice, words, ears, eyes, face, or hands and fingers. No exception needs to be taken to this. Anthropomorphisms of this kind are, in fact, widely used by present-day Christians. Their great value is that they make God real to the worshiper. How else could humans describe God, except in terms of their own understanding?

The monotheism of the psalms emerges clearly in Psalms 115:3-8; 135:15-18; 139. God is viewed as the Creator (Pss 8:3; 89:11; 95:3-5), with references to the creation mythology of surrounding nations (e.g., Ps 89:10) serving merely as illustrations of his almighty creative power. He is proclaimed as the Lord of history (Pss 44, 78, 80, 81, 105, 106) and as the sovereign controller of nature (Pss 18:7; 19:1-6; 65:8-13; 105:26-42; 135:5-7). The psalmists never tired of celebrating God's absolute greatness.

The Human Perspective The Psalter is a God-centered book, but humanity has a worthy place, in spite of the vast gulf between them and their Creator (Pss 8:3-4; 145:3-4) and the limitations of their earthly life (Ps 90:9-10). By the will of God, humans occupy a responsible, mediating position between God and all other created beings (Ps 8:5-8). The relationship with a righteous God is endangered by sin (Ps 106), but God is gracious and long-suffering (Ps 103), faithful and forgiving (Ps 130). While references to the sacrificial system are not lacking (Pss 20:3; 50:8-9), the emphasis is upon a personal piety that demands obedience and a surrendered heart (Ps 40:6-8). Psalm 51 indicates a depth of sin with which the sacrificial system was totally inadequate to cope; the psalmist could only cast himself, in total penitence, upon God's mercy. Man's moral obligations (Pss 15; 24:3-5) and loyalty to the law (Pss 19:7-11; 119) are fully accepted. Throughout, there is the revelation of a strong personal relationship that encourages prayer and praise and invites trust.

The Afterlife The Psalms maintain the traditional Hebrew view of Sheol as the abode of the departed, without distinction between the good and evil, where all but mere existence has perished. The chief complaint of the devout man was that, in Sheol, all meaningful relationship with God ceased (Pss 6:5; 88:10-12). However, it was recognized that, since God was almighty, even Sheol was not exempt from his reach (Ps 139:8). Added to this was the preciousness and strength of fellowship with God, which could not be terminated even by death. Psalms 16:9-11, 49:15, and 73:23-26 well illustrate this insight. The Psalter, therefore, witnesses to an important transitional phase in Israel's belief.

Universal Recognition of God Passages like Psalms 9:11; 47:1-2, 7-9; 66:8; 67; and 117:1 call upon all nations to acknowledge and praise God and show an awareness of his sovereignty over all nations. But this universalism does not appear to involve any desire to convert the heathen nations and, indeed, it is balanced by strong particularistic elements. God's covenant relationship with his people and his mighty deeds on their behalf are the chief items for which the praise of all nations is summoned (Pss 47:3-4; 66:8-9; 126:2). As elsewhere in the OT, the role of Israel is passive; her continued existence witnesses to God's faithfulness and brings glory to him.

Lasting Value Whatever the emotion of the psalmists, be it bitter complaint, anguished lament, or joyous exultation, all the psalms reflect one or other of the many aspects of communion with God. The reader may look "into the heart of all the saints" (so said Luther) as they faced life's experiences in the awareness of a God who was all-seeing, all-knowing, and all-powerful. The strength of that personal relationship with God that typified OT worship at its best is exemplified here, and the many echoes of the psalms elsewhere in Israel's literature show the powerful influence of these testimonies on the faithful. The fact that, almost invariably, little specific detail is given of the psalmists' actual conditions has made it easier for the Psalter to become the universal hymnbook and devotional treasury of God's people, in both public and private worship, until and including the present day. Modern life, materially, is vastly different from that of ancient Israel, but God remains unchanged and so do the basic needs of the human heart. The Holy Spirit, therefore, can still use this spiritual treasury as a means of revelation and communication between God and man. Few books in the Bible have exercised so profound an influence or been so widely used.

Content

Introduction It is more helpful to describe the psalms in categories than to explain them one by one in canonical order. The psalms can be categorized as follows:

Psalms of praise
Royal, messianic psalms
Passion psalms
Psalms about Zion
Laments
Imprecatory psalms
Penitential psalms
Wisdom psalms and historical psalms
Psalms of trust

Psalms of Praise The Hebrew title, "Praises," defines accurately a large part of the contents of the book. Each of the first four sections concludes with a doxology, while the fifth section concludes with five psalms, each of which begins and ends with one or two "Hallelujahs." The last of these, Psalm 150, sounds the call to total praise. God is to be praised for his being, for his great acts in creation, nature, and history on both the individual and the communal level.

1. Individual praise. In comparison with the number of individual laments, there are relatively few psalms in this category. Those normally included are Psalms 9, 18, 32, 34, 116, and 138. This may, in part, be due to the universal tendency to complain rather than to express thanks. But a number of the laments do, in fact, include the note of thanksgiving for the anticipated deliverance, and the normal round of congregational thanksgiving would allow the individual to express his personal praise. However, it was customary in temple worship to give a verbal act of thanksgiving before the whole assembly whenever a vow offering or a thank offering was made. Such public testimony, and the communal meal associated with this type of sacrifice, is indicated in Psalms 22:22-26; 66:13-20;

116:17-19. The inclusion of such opportunities for personal praise and testimony must have added warmth and significance to worship. Each act of deliverance and every experience of God's mercy became part of salvation history, which was a cumulative, ongoing concept, not simply a recital of God's deeds in earlier centuries.

2. General communal praise. This is sometimes entitled "hymns" or "descriptive praise," its main feature being linked to a particular act of deliverance. God is usually referred to in the third person, not directly. Psalm 103 may be taken as representative of this group. It begins and ends with individual references (vv 1-5, 22b), but the central section (esp. vv 6-14) shows that the psalmist was part of a worshiping community. There is first of all the imperative call to praise God for the full range of his mercy to each individual, including physical and spiritual deliverance and his sustaining and satisfying grace. Then the focus changes to his great works in history (vv 6-7). This forms a natural basis for the recital of those gracious qualities revealed so consistently during the course of the national history, especially his tender, fatherly care (vv 8-14). The frailty of humanity contrasts with God's constancy (vv 15-18), and his rule, being universal and absolute (v 19), merits the praise of all things, living and inanimate, in heaven and on earth (vv 19-22). There is, however, a great number of possible variations in the way in which God is celebrated, as Psalms 113 and 136, which come within this class, illustrate.

3. Specific communal praise. Occasionally termed "declarative praise," this type of psalm connects with a particular outstanding evidence of God's mercy and would most naturally follow soon after the event itself. Deliverance from an enemy provides the occasion for most of the psalms in this category (e.g., Pss 124, 129). Psalm 66:8-12, now the nucleus of an expanded recital of God's goodness, was possibly once complete in itself. Psalms 46–48 may form a trilogy connected with the remarkable deliverance of Jerusalem from Sennacherib's Assyrians in 701 BC (2 Kgs 18:17–19:37). Psalm 67 was probably composed in gratitude for a particular harvest. It is easy to see how psalms of this type could, in the process of time, acquire a more general usage.

4. Praise for the God of nature. The first part of Psalm 19 pictures the praise of God sounding from the heavens; Psalm 29 celebrates him as the God of the thunderstorm, which, sweeping in from the Mediterranean near Lebanon, pursues its awe-inspiring path southward into the wilderness of Kadesh, with the result that "in his temple" (the created world?) all are praising, "Glory, glory to the Lord" (v 9). His sovereignty and self-sufficiency in this world are celebrated in Psalm 50:10-12; he is the God of growth and harvest (Ps 65:9-13); in Psalm 104, often called the "Hymn of Creation," he sustains and supplies everything on the earth and in the seas and is the absolute Lord of all life (vv 29-30). There is no confusion between God and his creation; even the seemingly permanent heaven and earth will perish, but "you go on forever" (Ps 102:25-27). Nature's role is to proclaim the glory of God (Ps 19:1) and to praise him (Ps 148). People see themselves as insignificant when set against those forces of nature, which are themselves dwarfed by God—hence, the awareness of the immeasurable gulf between God and people that God has bridged by his grace (Ps 8).

5. Praise for God's kingship. A relatively small group of psalms (Pss 47, 93, 96–99) celebrate the kingship of

God in a way that goes beyond the ascription of praise noted in the foregoing groups. They are marked by acclamation, by both shouting and clapping when God "ascends." Presumably, the reference is to his throne (Ps 47:1-5; cf. 99:1-2). "The LORD reigns" (Pss 93:1; 97:1; 99:1) is the frequent cry, and the nature of his reign is extolled (Ps 99:4-5).

Royal, Messianic Psalms Psalms 2, 18, 20, 21, 45, 61, 72, 89, 101, 110, 132, and 144 are usually included as the royal psalms. They do not form a literary category, since psalms of various types are included, but they all have some reference to the king, the nature of his rule, and his relationship to God. Since the Davidic monarchy was terminated in 586 BC, these psalms, almost certainly, were composed before that date. The language in these psalms often shows the king as being God's vice-regent. For example, Psalm 45, a royal marriage psalm, contains the assertion "Your throne, O God, endures for ever and ever" (45:6). But this is best understood in terms of the throne being regarded as the Lord's, occupied by the king as his representative. Similarly, the wording in Psalm 110:1, "Sit at my right hand," indicates the privileges and prerogatives that the king enjoys as God's vice-regent. The balance of the OT evidence concerning the king shows that the monarchy in Israel was qualified by the nature of God's covenantal relationship with his people; the king did not enjoy the absolutism claimed by most of the rulers of surrounding kingdoms.

Most of the royal psalms can also be called messianic psalms. They were interpreted as such in the early Christian church, as witnessed in Jesus Christ's general statement that the psalmists wrote of him (Lk 24:44) and by particular NT quotations. The main psalms concerned, and the NT references, are the following:

1. Psalm 2 (Acts 13:33; Heb 1:5; 5:5), while linked with the Davidic king, nevertheless speaks of a universal vindication and rule, which far transcended even David's rule. Further, the picture of the Davidic king, anointed to rule on the earth as the representative of God, who is enthroned in heaven, strongly suggests Christ's mediating, incarnate ministry.
2. Psalm 45 (Heb 1:8-9), a marriage psalm for one of the Davidic kings, possibly Solomon, speaks not only of love and marriage but also a permanence and quality of rule. In the most obvious translation of verse 6, the writer addresses God, "Your divine throne endures for ever and ever." The writer to the Hebrews clearly accepted this interpretation (Heb 1:8-9) and used it in contrast to the exalted status of even the angels, reinforcing it with two other quotations from the psalms that originally applied to God (Ps 97:7; 102:25-27; cf. Heb 1:6, 10-12).
3. Psalm 110 is the most frequently quoted messianic psalm (Mt 22:43-45; Acts 2:34-35; Heb 1:13; 5:5-10; 6:20; 7:21). The language, speaking of the privileges, universal victory and continuing priesthood of David and his successors, would be considered hyperbolic and possibly misleading except for its fulfillment in "great David's greater Son." In contrast to the angels, who are privileged to stand in God's presence (Lk 1:19), Christ the Son sits in the place of power and authority (Heb 1:13).

Other psalms that could also be designated messianic but are not specifically included among the royal psalms are Psalm 8 (1 Cor 15:27); Psalm 40 (Heb 10:5-10); Psalm 72, with its idealized picture of the nature, consequences, and extent of the rule of God's representative; Psalm 118:22-23; and Psalm 132 (Acts 2:30).

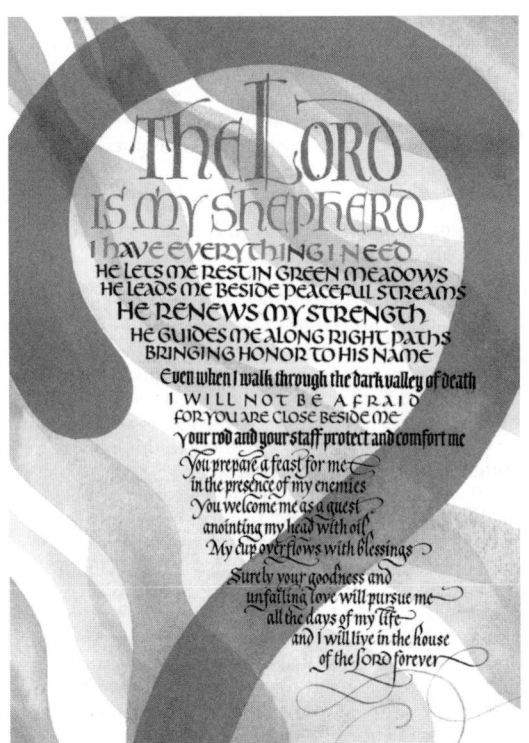

Psalm 23, NLT, rendition by Timothy R. Botts

Passion Psalms The four psalms in this group (Pss 16; 22; 40; 69; some scholars would also include Pss 102; 109) may also be regarded as messianic. They connect with that line of OT prophecy that interprets the Messiah's ministry in terms of the Suffering Servant who features prominently in Isaiah (e.g., Is 42:1-9; 52:13–53:12). Of these four, Psalm 22 is the most remarkable. Jesus recited part of it when he was on the cross (Ps 22:1; cf. Mt 27:46), and other connections with the crucifixion scene are noteworthy (e.g., Ps 22:6-8, 14-18). Some further considerations are even more significant: there is no suggestion of any awareness of sin; the suffering of the psalmist appears completely unjustified; there is no imprecatory element, even in the face of bitter persecution. This connects with the sinless Christ (2 Cor 5:21), who could even pray for his executioners (Lk 23:34). Psalm 16:10 anticipates the triumph of the incorruptible Christ over the grave (cf. Acts 2:24-31). Psalm 40:6-8 foreshadows the Incarnation and self-giving redemptive work of Christ (Heb 10:5-10). Psalm 69 refers to the isolation resulting from a commitment to God's cause (Ps 69:8-9) and anticipates the part played by Judas in what was fundamentally God's work in Christ (Ps 69:25-26; cf. Ps 109:8; Is 53:10; Acts 1:20).

Psalms about Zion This group could have been classified as a subsection of communal praise, but due to the close historical connection between God's choice of the house of David and Jerusalem (Pss 78:68-72; 132:11-13), and their subsequent interrelated fortunes, we consider them at this point. There was a biting satire in the request of the Babylonians to the refugees of a shattered city to "Sing us one of the songs of Zion!" (Ps 137:3, NIV), but it witnesses to the existence of such a collection. Praise of Zion was, in fact, almost synonymous with the praise of the Lord who dwelt there. Jerusalem's continued survival, in spite of its difficulties, was ample demonstration of God's enduring greatness (Ps

48:11-14) and peculiar affection for the city that housed his temple (Ps 87:1-3). Psalms 48, 76, 84, 87 and 122 are the main psalms in this category, but the theme itself appears widely throughout the psalms (e.g., 102:16; 125:1; 126:1-3; 133:3; 147:2). The basis of the NT concept of a heavenly Jerusalem, the spiritual home of the regenerate of all nations, finds its origin in this concept, especially in Psalm 87.

Laments These are associated with specific occasions of distress and are of two types:

1. National. The prophetic and historical books give several examples of the kind of occasion, such as drought, locust infestation, or enemy attack, that could prompt national laments, and also the inward and outward attitudes that accompanied them (e.g., Jgs 20:23, 26; Jer 14:1-12; 36:9; Jl 1:13-14; 2:12-17; Jon 3:5). There is a regular structure in the psalms of this class: the distressing situation is first described; God is petitioned to come to the aid of his people, often with the reminder of his past mercies for Israel; finally, there is often an expression of confidence that God would heed their cry. Israel's adversaries are clearly in mind in Psalms 14, 44, 60, 74, 80, and 83, while Psalms 58, 106, and 125 reflect situations less critical.

2. Individual. There are so many of this type (approximately 50) that it is frequently described as the backbone of the Psalter. Their most obvious features are the sharpness of complaint and the bitterness of attack upon those responsible. As in the national laments, there is often complaint against God, especially for his lack of attention or his tardiness in intervening. The basic components of this type are almost identical to the national laments, except that they often conclude with the avowal to praise God in anticipation of deliverance (e.g., Ps 13:5-6). Frequently, the lament is accompanied by thanksgiving for the deliverance sought and experienced, as illustrated in the two sections of Psalms 22:1-21 and 28:1-9.

Imprecatory Psalms Approximately 20 psalms contain passionate pleas for the overthrow of the wicked, in language that is often shocking. Any instant condemnation of this attitude must, however, be tempered by certain relevant considerations:

The cry for vengeance was not purely personal; it was firmly believed that God's honor was at stake (e.g., Ps 109:21). In an age where there was a less developed view of an afterlife, it was axiomatic that rewards and punishments resulting from obedience or disobedience to God, must be observable within this lifetime. Whenever this was not apparent, it would seem that no righteous God existed, and the name of God was dishonored (e.g., Ps 74:10). This burning desire for the eradication of evil and evil men sprang from a consciousness of a moral God and virtually demanded the triumph of truth.

The poetic language is also prone to hyperbole—a feature not confined to the psalms (e.g., Neh 4:4-5; Jer 20:14-18; Am 7:17). Such language is startling; indeed, part of its function was probably to startle—to express and promote a sense of outrage.

In the pre-Christian period, therefore, such outbursts were not completely unjustifiable. But in the light of the fuller revelation in the NT, such an attitude cannot be condoned. The Christian is to love as Christ loved (Jn 13:34), to pray for his enemies and to forgive them (Mt 5:38-48; Col 3:13). The theme of judgment continues into the NT and is indeed heightened there, since Christ's coming has left people without excuse to live in sin (Jn 16:8-11), but there can be no place for purely private vengeance.

Penitential Psalms Psalms 32, 38, 51, and 130 are the clearest examples of penitential psalms, although traditionally the church has also included Psalms 6, 102, 143, where there is no explicit confession of sin. In an age when adversity in its various forms was seen as God's judgment for wrongdoing, the admission of distress was tantamount to a confession of guilt. In the four main examples there is an intensity of feeling and a deep sense of the enormity of sin in God's sight, although, as elsewhere, there is no indication of specific sin, even in Psalm 51, which is surely to be connected with David's sin against Bathsheba (2 Sm 11–12). Significantly, David bypasses the sacrificial system, which was totally inefficacious in his case, casting himself entirely on the mercy of God (Ps 51:1, 16). The burden of unconfessed sin is clearly revealed in Psalm 32, and sin's searing and corrupting effect in Psalm 38.

Wisdom Psalms and Historical Psalms While it is accepted that prophets, priests, and wise men all functioned at the major sanctuaries, some overlap in their modes of expression is to be expected. Proverbial forms are not infrequently found in the psalms (Pss 37:5, 8, 16, 21-22; 111:10; 127:1-5). Psalm 1, probably an introduction to the whole Psalter, contrasts the diverging paths of the righteous and ungodly (cf. Ps 112), while Psalms 127 and 128 concentrate on the blessings given to the godly. Psalm 133 is written in praise of unity. The problem of explaining the sufferings of a righteous person and the apparent prosperity of evil people, dealt with in the Wisdom Literature in the book of Job and in the prophets also (e.g., Jer 12:1-4), is taken up in Psalms 37, 49, and 73.

The historical psalms should be included in this category, since they underscore the lessons arising from the favored nation's often bitter experience. It is apparent that Israel delighted in the recital of salvation history. The main psalms, and the periods covered are Psalm 78, from the exodus to the establishment of the Davidic monarchy (note the declared intention to teach in vv 1-4); Psalm 105, from Abraham to the conquest of Canaan; Psalm 106, from Egypt to the judges; and Psalm 136, from the Creation to the Promised Land.

Psalms of Trust While some of these may also be classified as laments, the dominant feature of this group is the serene trust in God revealed, which makes them particularly suitable for devotional use. Many of these psalms begin with an affirmation of gratitude to and affection for God. Psalms 23 and 27 are the outstanding examples of this type, which could also include Psalms 11, 16, 62, 116, 131, and 138.

Conclusion The difficulties in any precise categorization of psalms are obvious; many do not neatly fall into one group—hence, the occasional overlap. What is clearly evident is a pulsating, vital devotional life that has found its clearest expression in the book of Psalms. To say that it expresses the worship and devotion of the ordinary person is a simplification; kings and priests, wise men and prophets all contributed to this remarkable collection. Yet there remains the truth that, in God's sight, all people, regardless of human achievement or privilege, are "ordinary," for all are sinners in need of God's grace and goodness. So the worshiping community of ancient Israel, and the saints of every succeeding generation, in the vastness of their diversity, have found the expression of their own hearts' condition, desires, and devotion in this unique treasury—the Psalms.

See also David; Messiah; Music; Poetry, Biblical; Singers in the Temple; Tabernacle; Temple; Wisdom; Wisdom Literature.

PSALM TITLES* Superscriptions to numerous psalms. *See* Music; Psalms, Book of.

PSALTERY* KJV rendering of harp. *See* Musical Instruments (Nebel).

PSYCHICS People who have contact with supernatural forces and who claim to be able to interpret their intentions. In the OT, such people are grouped with "mediums"—that is, people who claim to mediate between supernatural forces and human beings. The Scriptures everywhere prohibit God's people to use the services of psychics or mediums (Lv 19:31; 20:6, 27).

See also Magic.

PTOLEMAIC EMPIRE* Empire named from Ptolemy I Soter, a Macedonian general of Alexander the Great who got himself appointed satrap, or governor, of Egypt shortly after Alexander died in 323 BC. At its height during the third century BC, the empire included Egypt, Cyrenaica (Cyrene), south Syria, Palestine, Cyprus, the south coast of Asia Minor, and some Aegean islands. Throughout the history of the empire, the Ptolemaic dynasty (all taking the name Ptolemy) occupied the imperial chair.

Ptolemy Soter was forced to engage in numerous struggles with governors of other parts of Alexander's empire. Generally successful, he felt secure enough to assume the title of king in 305 BC. The following year he fought on the side of Rhodes against Macedonia. For saving Rhodes's independence, he won the title of Soter (savior). The ancients did not number kings of the same name, as it is now customary to do, but distinguished them by titles instead.

Ptolemy Soter managed to win control of Palestine on his fourth invasion of the area (301 BC), and his successors were destined to hold it for over a century. On his abdication (285 BC), he left a well-ordered kingdom in which the Greek population was loyal to the administration and the native population had been wooed by efforts of conciliation. Alexandria had become his great capital. There he founded a famous library and museum and patronized the arts.

Ptolemy II Philadelphus (285–246 BC) maintained a splendid court in Alexandria, which is often compared to that of Versailles under Louis XIV for its pageantry and its vices. He patronized the arts and scientific research and added to the library in the capital. Ptolemy II was also a formidable power in the ancient world, and he came to exercise naval control over the Mediterranean and the Aegean. His commercial efforts were extensive and included the shores of the Red Sea after he dug a canal linking the Nile and the Red Sea.

Ptolemy III Euergetes (246–221 BC) continued to maintain the empire's naval power but allowed the army to decline after successful ventures against the Seleucids in Mesopotamia early in his reign. In fact, under Ptolemy III the empire may be regarded as having reached its height. He was also a liberal patron of the arts and built numerous public buildings and temples.

Ptolemy IV Philopator (221–203? BC) was a wretched and debauched person under whom the Ptolemaic Empire began its decline. During his rule, conflict with the Seleucids continued, but the Egyptians won a great victory over Antiochus III of Syria in 217 BC. This Egyptian triumph was accomplished in part because the Greek administration armed native Egyptians. This fact gave rise to a series of native rebellions during the next 30 years.

Ptolemy V Epiphanes (203?–181 BC) was only about five when he came to the throne. Antiochus III of Syria and Philip V of Macedon decided to take advantage of the weakness of Egypt at that time and divide the Ptolemaic Empire between them. In the process Syria took control of Palestine after a century of Ptolemaic rule. In this difficult period Egypt became quite closely linked with Rome, which intervened on Ptolemy's behalf.

Ptolemy VI Philometor (181–145 BC) likewise came to the throne as a minor and the country was further weakened under another regency. His regents launched a war against Syria to regain Palestine but were unsuccessful. When Syria invaded in 170 BC and captured him, Rome intervened and restored him to his throne. Rome again intervened and restored Ptolemy VI to his throne when Ptolemy VII sought to unseat him in 163 BC. As a kindly and reasonable man, Ptolemy Philometor is sometimes considered to be the best of the Ptolemies.

His successor, Ptolemy VII Physcon (145–116 BC), is represented as just the opposite—as a cruel man untouched by natural affections and afflicted with a loathsome corpulence. After his death, the royal household was plunged into domestic strife for several years, and the dynasty was never again destined to be very stable. During the first century BC, Rome increasingly intervened in Egyptian affairs on behalf of one or the other of the Ptolemies. After several weak reigns, Rome more effectively entered Egyptian affairs during the days of Ptolemy XII and Cleopatra VII, annexing Egypt after the suicide of Cleopatra in 30 BC.

PTOLEMAIS Alternate name for Acco, a city in northern Palestine, in Acts 21:7. *See* Accho, Acco.

PUA* KJV form of Puvah, Issachar's son, in Numbers 26:23. *See* Puvah.

PUAH
1. One of two Hebrew midwives ordered by Pharaoh to kill Hebrew males at birth. However, she feared God and did not carry out the order (Ex 1:15).
2. Father of Tola, a judge of Israel (Jgs 10:1).
3. Alternate form of Puvah, Issachar's son, in 1 Chronicles 7:1. *See* Puvah.

PUBLICAN* KJV translation for "tax collector."

PUBLIUS Name of a resident of the island of Malta, mentioned in Acts 28:7-8. He hosted Paul and others briefly after a shipwreck had stranded them on the island as they journeyed to Rome. Publius bore a title that indicated he was an important official on Malta at the time. His ailing father was healed by Paul during the visit.

PUDENS Companion of Paul mentioned in 2 Timothy 4:21. At the close of the letter his personal greetings are communicated to the recipient. Three other companions, who also send greetings, are named: Eubulus, Linus, and Claudia.

PUHITE* KJV spelling of Puthite, a member of a family of Judah's tribe, in 1 Chronicles 2:53. *See* Puthite.

PUITE *See* Punite.

PUL
1. Name given to Tiglath-pileser, the Assyrian ruler (745–727 BC), when he became king of Babylon (729–727 BC; 2 Kgs 15:19; 1 Chr 5:26). The meaning of the name is unknown, and Assyrian manuscripts do not mention it, suggesting to some scholars that Pul was Tiglath-pileser's original name. *See* Tiglath-pileser.

2. African people mentioned only in Isaiah 66:19 (KJV). Their connection with Tarshish and Lud has strongly suggested that Pul is a copyist's error for Put (as in various Greek manuscripts), a people related to the Egyptians and possibly a subculture of Libyans. *See* Put (Place).

PULSE* KJV translation of a Hebrew word perhaps better rendered as "vegetable" (Dn 1:12, 16). Not wishing to defile themselves with the king's food, Daniel and his friends requested permission to live on a diet of vegetables and water. The Hebrew word translated as "vegetable" literally refers to "things sown" and probably includes any kind of edible seed. *See* Plants.

PUNISHMENT The intentional infliction of pain or loss (e.g., loss of liberty or money) by an authorized individual on another because of an offense committed. There can be no punishment without authority, and none without a guilty party.

Some argue that punishment is justifiable if it will deter the offender (and other potential offenders) from committing offenses in the future, or if it will act as an instrument of reform. This means that punishment will influence the offender so that he will not want to commit other offenses. If punishment does not either reform or deter him, they contend, there is no justification for it.

There are others who argue that the guilty—simply because they are guilty and for no other reason—ought to be punished. Appeal is made either to the moral law of God or to some abstract principle of justice. This view, called the retributive view, is not to be confused with mere bloodthirstiness or the desire for revenge, which can often be selfish and unwarranted.

Both general views, the deterrent/reformative and the retributive, have the problem of what degree of punishment is to be inflicted in particular cases. Clearly, people could be deterred from committing fairly trivial offenses by severe punishments or the threat of them. In the case of retribution, only in comparatively rare cases could the punishment exactly match the offense.

According to the Bible, the death of Christ cannot be understood except in retributive terms. His atonement was a vicarious, penal offering to his Father to satisfy divine justice as the representative of those for whom he died. Christ's death removes the sinner's guilt by satisfying divine justice (Rom 5:8; Gal 3:13).

Given the retributive character of Christ's death, a Christian cannot consistently maintain that retribution should play no part in punishment. But the question can still be raised concerning the extent to which a system of punishment should today be retributive. In favor of the view that it should be retributive, the following arguments have been offered: (1) There are explicit scriptural injunctions regarding capital punishment (Gn 9:5-6), and such a divine command is not among those moral and ceremonial commands that are done away with in Christ. Coupled with this is the approving NT description of the powers that be as the bearer of the sword, God's minister of vengeance (Rom 13:1-5). (2) Besides such explicitly scriptural arguments, further support can be found from an appeal to principles of justice, and in particular to the important consideration that retribution can be a barrier against arbitrary and tyrannical government in that it sets clear and definite bounds to the power of the state in the punishment of offenders. For example, it cannot hold an individual indefinitely for "treatment" or order ferocious reprisals. Such a view of punishment emphasizes individual responsibility and the presumption of individual freedom until an offense has been committed, and hence it emphasizes predictability in human relations. The argument that capital punishment is only compounding the original offense would apply to all punishments.

Against these arguments for retribution are those that appeal to utilitarian considerations according to which it is argued that punishment ought only to be inflicted if a greater good is likely to be achieved by punishing than by not punishing. Further, there is the argument that since humanity is a brotherhood, no one person or group can have the right to punish another. The first of these arguments would appear to allow punishment without limit (provided that a greater good would probably result), while the second seems to be incompatible with government of any kind for fallible and sinful people.

One final matter concerns the kind of punishment to be permitted in a penal system. In earlier centuries many offenders were hung, drawn and quartered, broken on the wheel, or had limbs or ears or tongues cut off as a punishment for often trivial offenses. Most today would regard such punishments as barbaric and inherently degrading to the individual. There is clearly an element of relativity here. It is perhaps arguable, for instance, that corporal punishment of certain kinds is less degrading than the modern alternative of confinement with other criminals in filthy conditions.

Ultimately, Scripture teaches that the general judgment of all people, which follows death, will be final and retributive, guided by God's unerring wisdom, justice, and mercy.

See also Criminal Law and Punishment.

PUNISHMENT, Eternal *See* Hell.

PUNITE* Member of family in Issachar's tribe headed by Puvah (Nm 26:23). *See* Puvah.

PUNON Town identified with the modern Feinan, lying on the eastern side of the Arabah in the hill country of Edom. Punon lay conveniently on the road from Edom through the Negev to Egypt. It enjoyed an abundant supply of water and the presence of copper. Punon became an ancient smelting center of copper (c. 2000 BC), which was mined in the vicinity or was imported to Punon. When the Israelites passed by Punon on their way into Transjordan (Nm 33:42-43), Punon was at a low point in her industrial history. Remains of slag heaps abound in the vicinity. Archaeological evidence indicates that Punon was an extensive settlement at the time of the patriarchs (middle Bronze Age) and that after a period of 500 years of no settled occupation it was resettled around 1300 BC. The mining and smelting operations lasted until 700 BC and were then renewed in the age of the Nabateans. Eusebius reports that Christians worked in the mines along with criminals at Punon. In the Byzantine period the Christians built a basilica and monastery here. An inscription bearing the name of Bishop Theodore (c. 587 BC) was found in the monastery.

PUR* Hebrew word, meaning "lot," from which the name of the Jewish festival Purim, celebrating their deliverance from Haman, was derived (Est 3:7; 9:24-26). *See* Feasts and Festivals of Israel.

PURAH Gideon's servant, who accompanied his master on a secret night visit to the Midianite camp, where they were encouraged by the Lord (Jgs 7:10-11).

PURGATORY* According to the Roman Catholic Church, the place of temporal punishment and cleansing before entry into heaven. *See* Intermediate State.

PURIFICATION *See* Cleanness and Uncleanness, Regulations Concerning.

PURIM Hebrew name, meaning "lots," for the Jewish festival celebrating their deliverance from Haman (Est 9:26-32). *See* Feasts and Festivals of Israel.

PURPLE Highly prized dye extracted from sea snails. Purple was used for dyeing fabrics in the tabernacle and making the clothes of wealthy people (Ex 25:4; Jgs 8:26).
See also Animals (Snail); Color.

PURSE A small bag or receptacle in which money and often other small objects would be carried. There are basically three Hebrew words and three Greek words referring to such a purse or pouch. The first refers to a purse or bag in which money or stone weights used with the balance scales were carried (Dt 25:13; Prv 1:14; Is 46:6; Mi 6:11). It could be made of leather or stout cotton. Another Hebrew word referring to much the same kind of pouch is found in 2 Kings 5:23. This same word also appears in a list of ladies' finery in Isaiah 3:22 and may therefore have been a more ornamentally woven pouch than the first described above. The third Hebrew word appears in Genesis 42:35 and refers to a little bag with an open mouth. This was the small bag or purse in which Joseph's brothers' money had been placed before it was put into their sacks of grain.

The corresponding Greek word for the Hebrew words discussed above means a money bag or purse. When Jesus sent out his disciples two by two, he prohibited them from taking, among other things, a purse (Lk 10:4; 22:35-36). In Luke 12:33 this same word for purse is used figuratively for treasure in heaven that cannot be exhausted, stolen, or destroyed.

Another Greek word indicates another normal place for the carrying of money, the girdle or the belt, which was an essential part of dress for both men and women in the ancient East. When made of leather, they were made hollow or with slots for the purpose of carrying coins. When made of cloth, they were folded in such a manner that money could be carried in the folds, which served as pockets (Mt 10:9; Mk 6:8).

The Greek word for the "money bag" that Judas is said to have kept for the disciples refers to a case or container for the mouthpiece of a wind instrument. By NT times it had become the Greek word for a money box or possibly a money bag (Jn 12:6; 13:29), and hence another NT word for purse.

PUT (Person) Third of Ham's four sons, who most likely settled in northern Africa and is perhaps the forefather of the peoples of Egypt and Libya (Gn 10:6; 1 Chr 1:8).
See also Put (Place).

PUT (Place) Ancient nation, descended from a man of the same name. It is commonly identified as Libya, although it has been argued that it was the Punt of Egyptian records, somewhere along the northeast coast of Africa, perhaps Somalia. Its association with Egypt, Cush, and Canaan, and the usage of the name in the OT, make the Libyan location probable. In the OT the Libyan people are called Lubim, a name that always appears in the plural.

Ancient Libya was situated to the west of Egypt, the site of modern Libya, on the Mediterranean coast of North Africa. The Egyptians distinguished among several groups of Libyans. The Tjehenu, who inhabited the coastal region, were primarily herdsmen. They were represented in Egyptian art as having long hair and wearing only a belt and a penis sheath. They were listed among the Nine Bows—the nine traditional enemies of Egypt. The Tjemehu were nomads and were physically different from other African ethnic groups in that they had blond hair and blue eyes. Their relationships with Egypt date back to the Old Kingdom, and from time to time they tried to make their way into Egypt. The Libu (after whom the country was named) and the Meshwesh (western Libyans) are described as fair-skinned, tattooed, and with long leather garments.

The Egyptians had commercial and military contacts with Libya throughout its history. The Libyans periodically attempted to penetrate Egypt from the northwest. From the Middle Kingdom there is the story of Sinuhe (c. 2000 BC), which begins with the death of Amenemhet I while his son, Senusert (Sesostris), was fighting the Libyans in the western Delta. Later, Libyans did infiltrate the Delta, but Seti I and Ramses II kept them under control. The Stele of Merneptah (c. 1224–c. 1214 BC), which mentions Israel, is largely devoted to Egypt's victory over the Libyans. Ramses III drove them out of the western Delta in connection with his victorious land and sea struggles with the Sea Peoples.

Eventually, Libyans gained control of Egypt and made up the 22d (Bubastite) dynasty (c. 946–c. 720 BC) and the 23d (Tanitic) dynasty (c. 792–c. 720 BC). Their kings bore foreign names like Sheshonk (the Shishak of the OT, 1 Kgs 11:40; 14:25; 2 Chr 12:2-9), Osorkon, and Takelot.

The first occurrence of Put in the Bible is in the table of nations (Gn 10), where Put is listed as a son of Ham, along with Cush (Nubia, Ethiopia), Egypt, and Canaan (Gn 10:6; cf. 1 Chr 1:8).

Jeremiah 46 speaks of the battle of Carchemish and refers to the warriors of Ethiopia (Cush) and Put, "who handle the shield," among the hosts of Egypt (Jer 46:9). Ezekiel names Persia, Lud, and Put as being in the army of Tyre (Ez 27:10). Nahum mentioned "Put and the Libyans" among the allies of Thebes who were unable to stop the onslaught of the Assyrians against Egypt (Na 3:9). Daniel predicts that the Antichrist will have the Libyans, Egypt, Cush, and others in submission (Dn 11:43).

In Isaiah 66:19 the Hebrew text reads "Pul," while the Greek version gives "Put," which most of the English translations follow. (NLT reads "Libyans," with footnote to Hebrew and Greek readings.) Here, Put is listed between Tarshish and Lud in a list of nations that will be told of the glory of God. In Ezekiel 30:5 the Hebrew word *Put* is thought to be a country equivalent to Libya. However, other scholars consider *Cub* also to be Libya in this same verse (see NLT). In the records of King Xerxes of Persia (485–465 BC), Libya is listed among the nations subject to Xerxes.

PUTEOLI Italian seaport town on the Bay of Naples. It was a normal stopping place for seafaring travelers and cargo going to Rome. Paul, following his landing at Rhegium, resided with Christians in Puteoli for seven days before he was taken to Rome (Acts 28:13). The modern city is called Pozzuoli.

PUTHITE Family of Judah's tribe from Kiriath-jearim mentioned only in 1 Chronicles 2:53.

PUTIEL Father of Eleazer's wife and the grandfather of Phinehas (Ex 6:25).

PUVAH* Issachar's son, who went with Jacob and his household to Egypt, where they sought refuge from the severe famine in Palestine (Gn 46:13; NLT "Puah"). Puvah founded the Punite family (Nm 26:23) and is alternately called Puah in 1 Chronicles 7:1.

PYGARG* KJV translation for antelope in Deuteronomy 14:5. *See* Animals (Antelope).

PYRAMIDS* *See* Egypt, Egyptian.

PYRRHUS Father of Sopater of Berea, who, with others, accompanied Paul on his return trip through Macedonia (Acts 20:4).

Q

QERE* An anglicized Aramaic word meaning "what is to be read." Until the time of the Masoretes, the Hebrew Bible was written only with consonants. The Masoretes, however, thought that the vowels would clarify the Scriptures and therefore began to copy them with the vowels. When they came across a word they thought was unclear by its normal vowels, they would put the word in the margin with other vowels, changing the meaning or intent. The word that was written in the text was called the "Ketib," and what was to be read, "Qere." This is the variant marginal reading.

QESITAH* Weight of unknown value (Gn 33:19; Jos 24:32; Jb 42:11, RSV mg). *See* Money.

QOHELETH* Hebrew title for the book of Ecclesiastes, translated "the Preacher" or "the Teacher"; also spelled "Koheleth." Derived from a word meaning "to call an assembly," it came to mean "to address an assembly." The author of the book calls himself Qoheleth in numerous passages. *See* Ecclesiastes, Book of.

QUADRATUS*, Apology of An early Christian apology was written by Quadratus (c. AD 125) to the emperor Hadrian as a defense of Christianity. The only surviving fragment is found in the writings of Eusebius, where these words are credited to Quadratus:

> But the works of our Savior were always present (for they were genuine): namely, those who healed, those who rose from the dead; who were not only seen in the act of being healed or raised, but were also always present; and not merely when the Savior was on earth, but after his departure as well, they lived for a considerable time; insomuch that some of them survived even to our own day.

According to Eusebius, the apology was written in order to defend the church because "certain evil men tried to trouble those who belonged to us." Moreover, Quadratus hoped to persuade Hadrian of the truthfulness of Christianity so that he, being assured of the pure intents of the Christians, would call a halt to the persecutions. The apology of Quadratus is sometimes mistakenly identified with the "Letter to Diognetus."

QUAIL *See* Birds.

QUART *See* Weights and Measures (Choinix).

QUARTUS Christian who joined the apostle Paul in sending greetings to the church in Rome (Rom 16:23).

QUATERNION* KJV translation for "squad" in Acts 12:4. *See* Warfare.

QUEEN Word used to describe a reigning monarch, a queen consort, or a queen mother. The queen of Sheba became the epitome of wealth at the time of her visit to the luxurious court of King Solomon (1 Kgs 10:1; Mt 12:42; Lk 11:31), when she arrived with a large retinue and camels bearing gold, jewels, and spices. Candace, queen of Ethiopia, is mentioned when a eunuch, a senior minister in her court, is converted by Philip while on a visit to Jerusalem (Acts 8:27).

In Jewish history, Athaliah, thinking that she had murdered all rival claimants to the throne within the royal family, reigned for six years (2 Kgs 11:3). Also, Salome Alexandra succeeded her husband, Alexander Janneus, as ruler from 76 to 67 BC. A queen consort normally played a minor role, although Bathsheba (1 Kgs 1:15-31), who was determined to ensure the succession of her son, and Jezebel (ch 21), who plotted the false accusation leading to the death of Naboth, are notable exceptions. The powerful role was that of queen mother. She not only ruled over the royal household but also was held in respect both by the court and by the monarch (cf. Ex 20:12). Her requests were unlikely to be denied (1 Kgs 2:20). As the mother of the king, she was unique, whereas his wives might share their position with several others. Maacah, queen mother of Abijam, even retained her authority during much of her grandson's reign (1 Kgs 15:2, 10, 13; 2 Chr 15:16). The queen mother was crowned (Jer 13:18), and Bathsheba, powerful enough as queen, was seated at the right hand of King Solomon when she became queen mother (1 Kgs 2:19).

QUEEN OF HEAVEN Goddess mentioned by Jeremiah in his denunciations of Judah's idolatry (Jer 7:18; 44:17-19, 25). The women of Judah were especially involved in worshiping the Queen of Heaven. After the destruction and depopulation of Jerusalem in 586 BC, a group of exiles fled to Egypt, carrying Jeremiah with them. There he again condemned the idolatry that had brought this disaster. This provoked a sharp reaction from the men and their wives. In the recent catastrophe, they had seemingly vowed to return to the worship of the Queen of Heaven. They claimed that since they had given up this worship, nothing but trouble had befallen the nation—the complete reversal of Jeremiah's affirmation. To this, the prophet's response was that if this was their attitude, nothing remained to be said. He delivered them over to their reprobate mind, asserting that in Egypt, among the Jews who settled there, true worship would become extinct, so that even the name of the Lord would not be heard (44:25-28).

The goddess is generally identified with Ishtar, a Babylonian deity associated with the planet Venus, whose worship was probably imported into Judah during Manasseh's reign. Through the preaching of the prophets and the reforms of Josiah, worship of this god largely died out, but it must still have been cherished secretly, possibly among the women of the royal court.

See also Canaanite Deities and Religion.

QUIRINIUS Roman governor of Syria at the time of Jesus' birth (Lk 2:2). According to the Roman historian Tacitus (*Annals* 3.48), Publius Sulpicius Quirinius was elected consul of Syria in 12 BC. He was appointed around 7 BC, along with Varus, legatus (or governor) of Syria. His duties concentrated on military and foreign affairs, while Varus concerned himself with civil matters. Quirinius's first administration as governor lasted several years, during which time he led a successful expedition against the Homonadenses, an unruly group of rebel mountaineers who lived in the Cilician province of Asia Minor, and superintended in his region the empire-wide census decreed by Caesar Augustus. Luke records that Jesus' birth took place at the time of this first enrollment "when Quirinius was governor of Syria" (Lk 2:2), and according to Matthew, during the days of King Herod the Great (Mt 2:1)—presumably in 4 BC.

Quirinius became rector to Gaius Caesar in 1 BC and married Aemilia Ledipa in AD 2, whom he subsequently divorced. In AD 6, he was reappointed legatus of Syria, perhaps serving in this position for a couple of years. In this second administration Quirinius again supervised a census of Judea. However, the second census was not administered according to Jewish custom, as was the first. The second census taxed the Jews as a subservient people to the Roman state, thus causing Jewish opposition and rebellion toward Rome. This is probably the census referred to by the Jewish historian Josephus (*Antiquities* 17.13.5) and Gamaliel (Acts 5:37). The remainder of Quirinius's career was probably spent in Rome, where he died at an advanced age (c. AD 21).

See also Census; Chronology of the Bible (New Testament).

QUMRAN* Ancient Jewish religious community near the site where the Dead Sea Scrolls were found in 1947.

On the north side of the Wadi Qumran, about one mile (1.6 kilometers) south of Cave I, lie the ruins of a Jewish monastery known as Khirbet Qumran. The ruins had been noted by travelers for years.

Excavations at Khirbet Qumran Preliminary investigations of Khirbet Qumran were made in 1949 by Harding and de Vaux. Systematic excavations were carried out, beginning in 1951, under the auspices of the Jordanian Archaeological Museum and the École Biblique. They uncovered the main building in the complex, concluding that it was the center of a well-organized community. An estimated 200 to 400 people lived at Qumran at one time, most of them in tents outside the buildings or in nearby caves. A large cemetery, with smaller secondary graveyards, was located to the east toward the Dead Sea. De Vaux concluded that Khirbet Qumran was the headquarters of a Jewish sect called the Essenes.

Investigations at the site have shown that it was occupied at various times in antiquity. The earliest level of occupation dates back to the eighth and seventh centuries BC. Some have suggested that the buildings and cisterns may have been built during the reign of King Uzziah (cf. 2 Chr 26:10). Evidence of occupation of the site in the Greco-Roman period is abundant. A major settlement began shortly before 100 BC, probably in the time of Hyrcanus I (the first ruling priest of the Hasmonean dynasty, 134–104 BC), and ended with an earthquake in 31 BC. The site was probably reoccupied about the time of the death of Herod the Great (4 BC). That occupation ended when the area was captured by the Romans in AD 68. A Roman garrison remained there until about AD 90. Finally, Jewish rebels used the site in the second revolt against the Romans under Bar-Kochba in AD 132–135.

The largest building was the main assembly hall, with adjoining rooms. Pottery was found in abundance, not only for kitchen use but also (probably) for housing the scrolls, which were copied in the writing room, or scriptorium. Although no manuscripts were found in the ruins of Khirbet Qumran, the pottery was similar to that in which the scrolls were found in Cave I, thus establishing a link between the ruins and the manuscripts. Low plaster tables or benches, together with inkwells dating from Roman times, were found in the scriptorium.

An interesting feature of the area was an elaborate water system, with many round and rectangular cisterns that collected water from the mountains to the west. The cisterns were probably used for ritual purifications and baptismal ceremonies of the Qumran sect. Hundreds of coins from the Greco-Roman period have also helped in dating the various layers of occupation. An oasis and spring known as 'Ain Feshka, about two miles (3.2 kilometers) to the south, appears to have been an agricultural outpost of Khirbet Qumran.

Identity of the Qumran Sect The Qumran community was a sectarian group of Judaism. It originated in the second century BC, probably as a result of the imposition of Greek culture on the Jews by rulers of the Seleucid dynasty. The community repudiated the temple at Jerusalem and withdrew into the desert. "Damascus" was probably the designation of their community at Qumran. As the "community of God," the members believed they were obedient to God's will and were keeping his covenant.

The sect has been identified with various groups, including the Hasidim, Pharisees, Sadducees, Zealots, Ebionites, and others. The best identification seems to be with the Essenes, a sect mentioned by such first-century AD writers as Josephus, Philo, and Pliny the Elder. They described the Essenes as an ascetic group who lived along the western shores of the Dead Sea. In addition to the geographical and chronological arguments in favor of that identification, a more important argument is based on similarities in beliefs and practices between the Qumran community and the Essenes. Both had a probationary period of about two years for entrance into the group, ranked the members in their community, held their property and wealth in common, ate communal meals, practiced immersion and ritual cleansings, and were subject to the discipline and examination of overseers.

Aerial View of Qumran Compound

The Qumran sect was composed of priests and laity. The council of the community consisted of 15 men: 3 priests and 12 laymen. A superintendent or examiner was over the whole group. There are some discrepancies and alleged differences between the Qumran sect and the Essenes. Unlike the Essenes, the Qumran members were allowed to marry, and women were permitted entrance into the sect. Although the Essenes were pacifists, the people of Qumran were not.

Beliefs of the Qumran Sect Like both orthodox Jews and Christians, the Qumran sect held the Scriptures in high esteem. Considering themselves God's covenant people, they separated themselves from the mainstream of Jewish life to study the law of God and prepare the way of the Lord. As Jews, they believed in the God of the OT: the Lord of creation, sovereign over all things, predestining human beings to either salvation or condemnation. Angels played an important role in their theology as spirit creatures who would fight beside the "elect" in a final war against evil and darkness. The sect strongly emphasized knowledge and, within their basic framework of monotheism, viewed the world as evil and good—with God as the author of both.

Qumran teachings pictured humans as frail creatures of dust who were utterly sinful and who could be saved only by God's grace. Cleansing came only as one obeyed God's ordinances and the community's teachings as given by the Teacher of Righteousness. The anonymous Teacher of Righteousness described in the "Habakkuk Commentary" and other scrolls was not the founder of the sect but had been raised up by God to teach the community the way of life. He had been given special insight into God's purposes, which would be accomplished in the end times. He was a priest who had received understanding from God to interpret the words of the prophets, but he was not the Messiah. The Teacher was opposed and persecuted by a "Wicked Priest." Attempts to identify the Teacher of Righteousness and the Wicked Priest with specific historical figures, as some scholars have tried to do, are purely conjectural.

The Qumran sect had a strong messianic hope. They

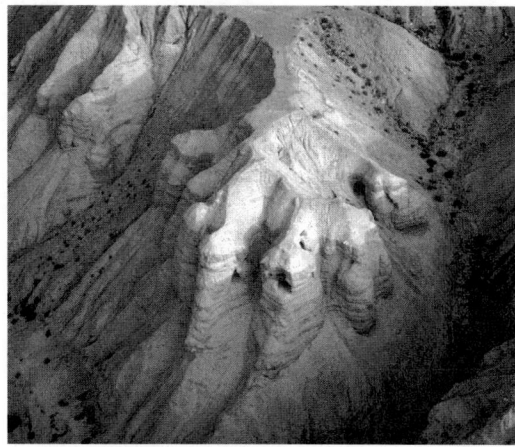

Aerial View of Qumran Caves In 1947, the first of the Dead Sea Scrolls were found in caves like these.

believed that they were living in the last days before the coming of the Messiah (or Messiahs) and the final battle with wickedness. The "Damascus Document" used the expression "the anointed ones [messiahs] of Aaron and Israel." Many scholars see in the expression a reference to two messiahs: a superior priestly messiah (descended from Aaron) and a lesser kingly messiah (descended from Israel). Some scholars even see three messianic figures: one descended from David, a messianic king; one from Aaron, a messianic priest; and one from Moses, a messianic prophet (cf. Dt 18:18). The Teacher of Righteousness may even have had the role of the anticipated prophet. Members of the community believed in the resurrection of the dead and the immortality of the righteous. The wicked, they taught, would be punished and annihilated by fire.

QUOTATIONS OF THE OLD TESTAMENT IN THE NEW TESTAMENT* *See* Bible, Quotations of the Old Testament in the New Testament.

R

RAAMA*, RAAMAH One of Cush's five sons and a descendant of Ham's line. He was the father of Sheba and Dedan (Gn 10:7; 1 Chr 1:9). Ezekiel 27:22 mentions the people of Sheba and Raamah trading spices and precious stones with the merchants of Tyre. Raamah's name was later given to a town perhaps identifiable with Ma'in in southwest Arabia.

RAAMIAH* One who returned with Zerubbabel to Palestine following the Babylonian captivity (Neh 7:7, NLT mg). Raamiah is alternately spelled Reelaiah in Ezra 2:2. The correct form of the word is uncertain. *See* Reelaiah.

RAAMSES* Alternate spelling of Ramses and Rameses. *See* Ramses (Person); Rameses (Place).

RABBAH One of the towns in the hill country assigned to Judah's tribe for an inheritance (Jos 15:60). Its location is uncertain. Some identify it with Rubute, mentioned in the Amarna tablets, or Khirbet Bir al-Hilu.

RABBAH OF THE AMMONITES Capital of the ancient Ammonite kingdom. Located near the sources of the Jabbok River, it stood about 25 miles (40.2 kilometers) east of the Jordan and lay astride the main caravan route leading from Damascus south along the length of the Transjordanian plateau. This road was also known as the King's Highway (Nm 20:17; 21:22). Modern Amman, the capital of Jordan, covers the ancient city. During the third century BC, Ptolemy II Philadelphus of Egypt rebuilt the city and renamed it Philadelphia. After the Romans took Palestine in 63 BC, the city became part of the Decapolis, and after AD 106 was part of the Roman province of Arabia.

Rabbah first appears in Scripture as the place where the great iron bedstead of Og, king of Bashan, was kept (Dt 3:11; KJV "Rabbath of the children of Ammon"). When Transjordan was divided among the tribes of Gad, Reuben, and the half-tribe of Manasseh, the territory of Gad extended to the vicinity of Rabbah but did not include it (Jos 13:25).

Rabbah figured most significantly in Scripture during David's reign. At that time Joab laid siege to the city, and during the battle, Uriah the Hittite lost his life by the specific command of the king (2 Sm 11:1; 12:26-29). The city was built in two parts—the upper city and the lower city, called the "city of waters" (12:27). Joab took the lower city and perhaps gained control of the water supply, and then waited for David to come and complete the conquest (vv 27-28). After a thorough sack of Rabbah, David did not station troops in the city but left it under the control of the Ammonites, who became vassals of Israel.

About 250 years later, Amos pronounced judgment on the then-prosperous city (Am 1:13-14). When Nebuchadnezzar stopped at Rabbah during his invasion of Transjordan, it was a significant place (Ez 21:20). It was at Rabbah that Baalis, king of the Ammonites, later plotted the attack that resulted in the death of Gedaliah (Jer 40:14ff.), the Babylonian governor of Judea, and the

exile of Jeremiah into Egypt. Jeremiah's prophecy against Rabbah is recorded in Jeremiah 49:2-3.

Since modern Amman covers ancient Rabbah, no excavation of the ancient city is possible. The Roman theater stands in the center of the city, with seating for 6,000 people. Dilapidated remains of an odeum, or music hall, and a fountain, also of the Roman period, stand nearby. Everything visible on the ancient citadel is Roman, Byzantine, or Arab, except at the northeast corner, where part of the Iron Age town wall is still exposed. The Roman temple at the southwest corner of the citadel was dedicated to Hercules.

See also Decapolis; Philadelphia #1.

RABBI Title of respect, meaning "my great one" or "my superior one," used in Jesus' day for Jewish religious teachers.

According to Matthew 23:7, "rabbi" was evidently used as a common title of address for the Jewish scribes and Pharisees. However, in the NT it is most commonly used as a title of respectful address when others were speaking to Jesus. It was used by Nathanael (Jn 1:49), by Peter and Andrew (v 38), by Nicodemus (3:2), by the disciples as a group (9:2; 11:8), and by a crowd generally (6:25). Mary Magdalene (Mk 10:51) and blind Bartimaeus (Jn 20:16) both use the longer form, "rabboni," to address Jesus directly, thus indicating even more profound respect than the use of the shorter title "rabbi." By the time of the writing of John's Gospel, the title "rabbi" meant "teacher"; John explicitly states this in 1:38 and implicitly says this in 3:2.

Jesus condemns the scribes and the Pharisees for their evident pride displayed in their love of being greeted in the marketplaces and their insistence on having people call them "rabbi" (Mt 23:7-8). Jesus prohibited the use of the title for his own disciples, saying, "You are not to be called rabbi." However, Jesus' prohibition was more against seeking to be called this and insisting on it than the legitimate possession of the title itself. In fact, when people did use the title of Jesus in a reverent way, they were not in any way rebuked.

RABBITH Town defining the border of Issachar (Jos 19:20) and perhaps identifiable with the Levitical town called Daberath (Jos 19:12; 21:28; 1 Chr 6:72). If so, its site is near Mt Tabor at modern Deburiyeh. *See* Daberath.

RABBONI* Variant of rabbi in Mark 10:51 and John 20:16. *See* Rabbi.

RABMAG* Title given to a certain Babylonian officer, Nergal-sharezer, who was in charge of Jeremiah's safety during the fall of Jerusalem (Jer 39:3, 13). The meaning of the title in uncertain.

RABSARIS* Title of a high-ranking Assyrian and Babylonian court official, usually a eunuch and sometimes supervisor of the royal harem. A rabsaris was part of the Assyrian delegation (2 Kgs 18:17), a judge at the gate

(Jer 39:3), the official who released Jeremiah from prison (v 13), and one of Nebuchadnezzar's officials (Dn 1:3, 7).

RABSHAKEH* High Assyrian official, originally a cup-bearer or chamberlain, but later a powerful palace official. The rabshakeh was the emissary of Sennacherib, who insultingly demanded that Hezekiah and Jerusalem abandon their reliance on both Egypt and God and surrender to Assyria. Hezekiah refused; the rabshakeh returned to find his king at war against Libnah (2 Kgs 18:17-37; 19:4, 8; Is 36:2-22; 37:4, 8).

RACA* Derogatory expression used by Jews of the first century AD to show open contempt for another. *Raca* is derived from an Aramaic and Hebrew term meaning "empty" or "worthless." Literally meaning "empty-headed," *raca* probably insinuates an intellectual stupidity or inferiority rather than a moral deficiency. In the OT it is comparable to the worthless lot that Abimelech hired to follow him (Jgs 9:4), the idle men who gathered around Jephthah (11:3), and the scoundrels who joined up with Jeroboam (2 Chr 13:7). Michal accused David of acting like one of the vulgar fellows [*raca*] who shamelessly uncovered himself (2 Sm 6:20). Rabbinic literature used this term to describe an immoral, untrained person.

Jesus warned against calling a brother *"Raca!"* (Mt 5:22, NLT mg). According to Jesus, the perpetrator of the insult was to be judged by the highest court of the land and punished by its severest penalty. The commandment against murder (Ex 20:13) not only prohibited the deed itself but also the thoughts of unrighteous anger and expressions of unwarranted contempt.

RACAL One of the towns in southern Judah in which David distributed the spoils taken from the defeated Amalekites (1 Sm 30:29). The city is named Carmel in the Septuagint.

RACHAB* KJV form of Rahab in Matthew 1:5. *See* Rahab (Person).

RACHAL* KJV form of Racal, a Judean town, in 1 Samuel 30:29. *See* Racal.

RACHEL Beautiful younger daughter of Laban; she was the favorite wife of Jacob. He first met her as she arrived at Haran in Paddan-aram. There he assisted her by attending to the needs of Rachel's father's sheep, removing a stone from the mouth of a well in order to water them (Gn 29:10). Jacob loved Rachel exceedingly and agreed to work seven years for Laban in return for her hand in marriage. His seven years' service seemed like only a few days because of his great love for her. Laban deceptively reneged on his bargain and required Jacob to marry Leah, his older, less attractive daughter, before finally giving him Rachel for his wife. Unlike Leah, Rachel was barren in the early years of her marriage to Jacob (30:1). Consequently, she gave her servant, Bilhah, to Jacob in order to have children. Thus, through this commonly accepted ancient custom, Dan and Naphtali were born. In time, Rachel herself conceived and bore Joseph (vv 22-25). After this, Jacob took his wives, children, and possessions away from Haran.

Somewhere between Bethel and Bethlehem, Rachel died while giving birth to Benjamin (Gn 35:16, 19). Jacob set up a pillar over her tomb there, a landmark known even in the days of Saul (1 Sm 10:2). Rachel and Leah are highly regarded as those who built up the house of Israel (Ru 4:11). In Jeremiah 31:15, Rachel is pictured as crying for her children being carried off into captivity.

Later, Matthew recalls Jeremiah's words in Herod's slaughter of the male infants (Mt 2:18).

See also Jacob #1.

RACHEL'S TOMB Landmark set up by Jacob at the site of Rachel's grave (Gn 35:19-20) that was still in existence at the time of Samuel (1 Sm 10:2). Two persisting traditions make its original location still questionable. The older tradition locates the tomb near Bethlehem, south of Jerusalem (Gn 35:19; 48:7; Mt 2:18). This option has won the impressive historical support of Josephus, Eusebius, Jerome, Origen, and the Talmudists. A second site is Ephrath (Gn 35:19), which was on the northern border of Benjamin, 10 miles (16.1 kilometers) north of Jerusalem (1 Sm 10:2; Jer 31:15), near ancient Bethel.

Rachel's tomb is the first recorded instance in the Bible of a sepulchral monument. A picture of the tomb is a common decorative piece in Jewish homes throughout the world.

RADDAI Fifth of Jesse's seven sons and the brother of David from Judah's tribe (1 Chr 2:14).

RAGAU* KJV rendering of Reu, Peleg's son, in Luke 3:35. *See* Reu.

RAGUEL
1. KJV spelling of Reuel, an alternate name for Jethro, Moses' father-in-law, in Numbers 10:29. *See* Jethro.
2. A member of the tribe of Naphtali living in Ecbatana who, according to Tobit 3:7, was the father of Sarah, soon to become the wife of Tobias, thanks to the intervention of the angel Raphael.

RAHAB* (Monster) Mythological sea monster that poetically represented Egypt (Ps 87:4). "For Egypt's help is worthless and empty, therefore I have called her 'Rahab who sits still' " (Is 30:7, RSV). The biblical writers, with Israel's crossing of the Red Sea and the Egyptian army's subsequent drowning (cf. Is 51:10), portray God as waging war against this monster and cruelly defeating it (Job 26:12; Ps 89:10; Is 51:9).

See also Egypt, Egyptian.

RAHAB (Person) Heroine of the battle of Jericho (Jos 2–6). Soon after Moses' death, God told Joshua that he and the people were to cross the Jordan and occupy the land of promise. Before the crossing, however, Joshua sent two spies into the land to reconnoiter the opposition, in particular the fortified city of Jericho. Upon entering the city, the spies found their way quickly to Rahab's house, which was perhaps an inn and/or a brothel. She apparently was a prostitute.

News of the arrival of spies was not long in reaching the king of Jericho, who quite naturally demanded that Rahab divulge their whereabouts. She cleverly admitted seeing them but insisted that they had left the city at nightfall. Actually, the spies were hiding under the stalks of flax on the roof of her house. When the king's search party left Jericho to hunt the spies, Rahab confessed to the spies the reason for her complicity with the Israelites' cause. She feared the God of the Jews, believing that he would surely give them victory (Jos 2:11).

For her help, the spies agreed to save Rahab and her family. The sign was to be a cord of scarlet thread hanging from her window, the same avenue the spies used to escape the city. Rahab and her family were indeed the only survivors of the subsequent battle. They were led to safety, on Joshua's command, by the very men Rahab had saved.

Rahab became the wife of Salmon and mother of Boaz, and thus an ancestor of Jesus (Mt 1:5). Rahab is listed, along with Moses, David, Samson, and Samuel, as an example of faith (Heb 11:31). Her deed is an example of good works and justification (Jas 2:25).

See also Conquest and Allotment of the Land; Joshua, Book of.

RAHAM Son of Shema, and father of Jorkeam (1 Chr 2:44). He was a descendant of Judah.

RAHEL* KJV spelling of Rachel, Jacob's wife, in Jeremiah 31:15. *See* Rachel.

RAIN *See* Palestine (Climate).

RAINBOW Sign of God's covenant with Noah following the flood (Gn 9:8-17). The normal Hebrew word for "war bow" is used. Jewish tradition interpreted this as a symbol that God's anger had ceased since the rainbow pointed downward, just as an antagonist lowers his bow to declare peace. In the NT, the rainbow forms part of the heavenly vision (Rv 4:3; 10:1).

See also Flood, The.

RABBIS' VIEW OF A RAINBOW
To the biblical account, the rabbis added the notion that the rainbow was created at evening on the sixth day of Creation, and that it did not appear during the lifetime of a saint whose good life was sufficient to preserve the world from destruction. To gaze directly at a rainbow risked injury, since the bow was a reflection of the glory of the Lord. A prescribed blessing was to be recited on seeing a rainbow: "Blessed are Thou O Lord our God, King of the universe, who remembers the covenant, is faithful to the covenant, and keeps His promise."

RAISIN Staple food in biblical lands made by drying grapes on housetops. Raisins were used as gifts (1 Sm 25:18; 2 Sm 16:1-3), sometimes offered to false gods (Hos 3:1), and considered a source of nourishment (1 Sm 30:12; 1 Chr 12:40).

See also Food and Food Preparation.

RAISIN CAKE Culinary delicacy of ancient peoples (Is 16:7). The cakes resisted deterioration and thus were useful for soldiers and travelers (2 Sm 6:19). They were used as cultic offerings (Hos 3:1) and sometimes served as aphrodisiacs (Sg 2:5).

RAKEM Manasseh's grandson (1 Chr 7:16).

RAKKATH One of 19 cities allotted to Naphtali's tribe for an inheritance (Jos 19:35). The city served as a buffer against military attack on the western shore of the Sea of Galilee. Jewish tradition identifies Rakkath with Tiberias, but modern scholars prefer its location at either Khirbet el-Quneitireh or Tell Eklatiyah.

RAKKON One of the cities assigned to Dan's tribe (Jos 19:46). It is identified today with Tell er-Ragguat, one and a half miles (2.4 kilometers) north of the mouth of the Yorkon River.

RAM *See* Animals (Sheep).

RAM (Person)
1. Ancestor of King David (Ru 4:19; 1 Chr 2:9-10), listed in Matthew's genealogy of Christ (Mt 1:3-4; called Arni in Lk 3:33). *See* Genealogy of Jesus Christ.
2. Jerahmeel's eldest son (1 Chr 2:25-27), and perhaps the nephew of #1 above.
3. Head of the family of Elihu, one of Job's friends (Jb 32:2).

RAMA* KJV spelling of Ramah, a Benjaminite city, in Matthew 2:18. *See* Ramah #1.

RAMAH
1. One of the cities located in the territory allotted to Benjamin's tribe for an inheritance, listed between Gibeon and Beeroth (Jos 18:25). In the proximity of this town, Rachel, Jacob's wife, was buried (Mt 2:18; cf. Gn 35:16-21; Jer 31:15). Ramah, positioned near Bethel, was the place where Deborah judged Israel (Jgs 4:5). This city was a temporary resting place for a Levite and his concubine traveling north from Bethlehem (19:13).

   During the period of the divided kingdom (930–722 BC), King Baasha of Israel (908–886 BC) fortified Ramah. From Ramah, Baasha was able to prevent an invasion of King Asa's (910–869 BC) Judean army. Baasha later abandoned the city and hurried his army north to repulse a Syrian offensive led by King Ben-hadad I (c. 885 BC). Asa dismantled Ramah's military fortifications, using the material to build the towns of Geba and Mizpah (1 Kgs 15:17-22; 2 Chr 16:1-6).

   The cities of Geba, Ramah, and Gibeah formed the route taken by the Assyrian army during Sennacherib's military incursion into Judah (c. 701 BC) against King Hezekiah and Jerusalem (Is 10:29). Later King Nebuchadnezzar used Ramah as a place of detainment for the Jews being deported to Babylon. Here Nebuzaradan, the captain of the guard, released Jeremiah from among the captives (Jer 40:1).

   Following the Babylonian captivity, inhabitants of Ramah returned with Zerubbabel to Palestine and rebuilt this city (Ezr 2:26; Neh 7:30). Some suggest that the postexilic town of Ramah was another Benjaminite town located farther west near the coastal plain (Neh 11:33). The site of Ramah is identified with the modern village of er-Ram, five miles (8 kilometers) north of Jerusalem.
2. City in the Negev marking the southern extremity of the territory allotted to the tribe of Simeon within Judah's inheritance (Jos 19:8); also called Ramoth of the Negev (1 Sm 30:27) and Baalath-beer (Jos 19:8; cf. 1 Chr 4:33). *See* Baalath-beer.
3. Town defining the boundary of the territory assigned to Asher's tribe for an inheritance, mentioned between Sidon and Tyre (Jos 19:29).
4. One of 19 fortified cities given to Naphtali's tribe for a possession, mentioned between Adamah and Hazor (Jos 19:36). Its location is identifiable with the modern town of er-Rameh, about 11 miles (17.7 kilometers) northwest of the Sea of Galilee.
5. Home of Samuel's parents, Elkanah and Hannah; the birthplace of Samuel (1 Sm 1:19; 2:11); and later his home (7:17; 16:13). Samuel judged Israel from Ramah, Bethel, Gilgal, and Mizpah (7:17). Saul first met Samuel at this city (9:6-10). Here the elders of Israel petitioned Samuel to appoint a king for them (8:4), and later this city provided David a place of refuge from King Saul (19:18–20:1). Samuel was buried at Ramah (25:1; 28:3). Ramah is alternately called Ramathaim-zophim in 1 Samuel 1:1.

6. Abbreviated name for Ramoth-gilead (2 Kgs 8:29; 2 Chr 22:6). *See* Ramoth-gilead.

RAMAH OF THE NEGEV, RAMAH OF THE SOUTH*
Alternate names for Baalath-beer, a town in Simeon's territory, in Joshua 19:8. *See* Baalath-beer.

RAMATHAIM
Alternate translation of Greek "Rathamin" (1 Macc 11:34, NLT mg). *See* Rathamin.

RAMATHAIM-ZOPHIM*
Alternate name for Ramah, Samuel's hometown, in 1 Samuel 1:1. *See* Ramah #5.

RAMATHITE*
Inhabitant of Ramah (1 Chr 27:27), though which Ramah is uncertain.

RAMATH-LEHI*
Place where Samson routed the Philistines with an ass's jawbone (Jgs 15:17, NLT mg). *See* Lehi.

RAMATH-MIZPEH
Alternate name for Mizpah, a town in Gad's territory, in Joshua 13:26. *See* Mizpah #4.

RAMATH OF THE SOUTH*
KJV rendering of Ramah of the Negev, an alternate name of Baalath-beer, in Joshua 19:8. *See* Baalath-beer.

RAMESES (Person)
Alternate form of the Egyptian Ramses of the 19th and 20th dynasties. *See* Ramses (Person).

RAMESES (Place)
Place (also called Ra'amses or Ramses) mentioned with Pithom in Exodus 1:11 (KJV "Raamses") as one of the locations where the Hebrews were engaged in a building program for the pharaoh. Here they were afflicted with heavy burdens by the pharaoh's officers. In due course they escaped their oppression and set out for the Promised Land (Ex 12:37; Nm 33:3). The identification of this place and the period is important for establishing the date of the exodus from Egypt.

The great Ramses II (c. 1290–1224 BC) built extensively in the east Delta region. The ambitious pharaoh determined to add a center of his creation, using as a nucleus the old family seat of Avaris, where his father had built a summer palace. On the north side of Avaris, he built a majestic palace that he named Piramesse. The location of its site is much debated, having been variously located at Pelusim (on the Mediterranean Sea) and at Tanis (or Zoan). This latter suggestion is now rejected since the stonework was reused material taken from elsewhere and not original. However, 19 miles (30.6 kilometers) south of Tanis, near the town of Qantir, considerable remains of a palace commenced by Seti I, with an adjacent glazing factory, dwellings of princes and high officials, and traces of a temple and public audience halls, are now recognized as the site of Ra'amses (Pirameses). The old Hyksos center was destroyed when these foreigners were expelled early in the 18th dynasty (c. 1552–1306 BC). The place was then abandoned but later rebuilt under the 19th dynasty. Ramses II lavishly adorned his father's palace and established nearby a marshaling place for his chariots, a mustering place for his infantry, and a mooring place for his ships.

See also Egypt, Egyptian; Pithom.

RAMIAH
Parosh's son, who obeyed Ezra's exhortation to divorce his foreign wife after the exile (Ezr 10:25).

RAMOTH* (Person)
KJV form of Jeremoth, Bani's son, in Ezra 10:29. *See* Jeremoth #8.

RAMOTH (Place)
1. Abbreviated form of Ramoth-gilead. *See* Ramoth-gilead.
2. Alternate name for Baalath-beer, a city in the Negev, in 1 Samuel 30:27. *See* Baalath-beer.
3. Alternate name (or textual alteration) of Jarmuth, a Levitical city, in 1 Chronicles 6:73. *See* Jarmuth #2.

RAMOTH-GILEAD
City lying in the Transjordan area of Gilead and probably identifiable with Tell Ramith, although the site of Tell el-Husn has also been suggested. Initially, biblical references pertain to Ramoth in Gilead (Dt 4:43; Jos 20:8; 21:38), while later it is called Ramoth-gilead. Combined names were used to avoid confusion with cities of the same name in other locations.

Ramoth-gilead, a possession of the tribe of Gad, first appears in the biblical narrative as one of three Transjordan cities of refuge (Dt 4:43) later included in the six cities of refuge for all Israel (Jos 20:8). It was allotted to the Merarites as one of 48 Levitical cities (21:38) and was most likely located along the King's Highway, which transversed that area.

During the time of Solomon, Ramoth-gilead enjoyed a place of prominence as the central city in his sixth administrative district and the residence of Ben-geber, chief officer of that district (1 Kgs 4:13). After the division of the kingdom, this border town was taken by the Arameans and became a site of contention between Israel and Aram. King Ahab's final battle began with his desire to retake Ramoth-gilead. In seeking to convince his ally Jehoshaphat, king of Judah, to support him in this maneuver, he produced many prophets who spoke favorable and victorious words to the king (1 Kgs 22; 2 Chr 18). Unconvinced, Jehoshaphat inquired of the word of the Lord through Micaiah, a prophet of the Lord, who warned of impending disaster. The message was ignored and Ahab was killed at Ramoth-gilead. Ahab's son Joram also fought with Aram here and was wounded in battle (2 Kgs 8:29; 2 Chr 22:6; also called Ramah). Shortly thereafter, Elisha sent one of the sons of the prophets to Ramoth-gilead, where he anointed Jehu to be king over Israel (2 Kgs 9:1-14).

See also Cities of Refuge; Levitical Cities.

RAMOTH OF THE NEGEV, RAMOTH OF THE SOUTH*
Alternate names for Baalath-beer, an unknown site in Simeon's territory, in 1 Samuel 30:27. *See* Baalath-beer.

RAMSES* (Person)
Name of 11 kings of the 19th and 20th Egyptian dynasties (also spelled Rameses). Ramses II reigned for some 67 years (c. 1290–1224 BC). He was known as Ramses the Great, mostly because of his extensive building activities, such as his mortuary temple at Thebes (the Ramasseum), the rock-cut temple of Abu Simbel in Nubia, and his additions to the temples of Karnak and Luxor. Pictured on his temple walls as a great military leader, he fought with the Hittites at Kadesh on the Orontes, where, because of a serious tactical blunder on his part, he nearly lost his life. The battle was at best a draw, but he depicted it as an Egyptian victory in the Ramasseum and Abu Simbel. His treaty with the Hittites is the earliest known international nonaggression pact. He has often been suggested as the pharaoh of the oppression (Ex 1:8-11), but this is improbable.

Ramses III (c. 1195–1124 BC), of the 20th dynasty, saved Egypt from an invasion by the Sea Peoples in a land and sea battle in the Nile Delta. He built a large mortuary temple complex and royal residence in the Theban area, at Medinet Habu. On the northern exterior wall of the temple area are the first known representations of a naval battle. Among the captives are the Peleset, who are believed to be Philistines. The exterior walls also bear excellent reliefs of lion and wild-bull hunts. From late in the reign of Ramses III comes the famous Harris Papyrus, which lists the benefactions of the king to Amon. Because of withheld wages in kind, workers in the royal necropolis went on strike. Similar strikes occurred in the times of Ramses IX and X. From the end of the reign of Ramses III come records of the court trial of a harem conspiracy in which Ramses III apparently was killed.

The other Ramessides were minor rulers who played no great part in history. The instability of the country is further illustrated by widespread looting of the royal tombs. A complicated and dubious investigation of these robberies was conducted in the reign of Ramses IX.

See also Egypt, Egyptian.

RAMSES* (Place) Alternate form of the Egyptian place-name Rameses. See Rameses (Place).

RAM'S HORN Primitive musical instrument made from an animal horn (Jos 6:4-6, 13). See Musical Instruments (Shophar).

RANSOM Price for redeeming or liberating slaves, captives, property, or life. Jesus described his entire ministry as one of service in giving his life as a ransom for many (Mt 20:28; Mk 10:45). Hence, "ransom" is closely linked to such terms as "redemption" and "salvation," to the satisfaction Christ made in atonement for sin.

TO WHOM WAS THE RANSOM PAID?
This question has perplexed scholars for hundreds of years. Origen (c. 185–254), a theologian of Alexandria, maintained that the ransom was paid to the devil. Origen's form of the theory was that Christ cheated the devil by escaping through his resurrection.

Although Jesus Christ defeated Satan and liberates believers from Satan's bondage, Scripture does not indicate that the ransom was paid to him. God was wronged by human sin, yet he showed his great love in providing redemption (Jn 3:16). God declared humans guilty for their sin and imposed the death penalty for human transgression. Thus Scripture indicated that the ransom was really directed by Christ to the Father. The biblical references to Jesus' life as a ransom are echoed in the satisfaction views of the atonement.

Anselm of Canterbury in 1098 developed the satisfaction view of the atonement, emphasizing that the honor of God required satisfaction for sin. Later views emphasized the justice of God in requiring payment (ransom) for the just demands of the law and for the removal of the curse of the law, which is death (see Eph 1:7, 14; Col 1:14). Paul emphasized the justice of God, which was met so that he would be just in justifying sinners who believe (Rom 3:23-26).

Reformed theology emphasizes the ransom as being paid by Christ's death to meet the satisfaction of God's justice in Christ's atonement. Without using the term "ransom," the same implications are carried in such condensed expressions as "Christ died for our sins" (1 Cor 15:3).

In the Old Testament In the OT God provided various regulations for his covenant people whereby life and property could be "redeemed," "bought back," or "set free" by payment of ransom (cf. Lv 25–27). Ransom involved a price paid as a substitute for that which was redeemed or set free.

The OT uses three different Hebrew words for ransom or redemption. Only when there is a clear indication of the payment of a price are these terms translated by "ransom." But even when another term, such as "redemption," is used in English translation, a ransom price is usually implied.

One of the Hebrew terms (*kopher*) means a "cover" or a "covering." It was a replacement payment made in exchange for punishment. A ransom could be paid to redeem the life of the owner of an ox that had gored a person to death (Ex 21:30). A half-shekel ransom price was required by God for each Israelite at census taking to prevent a plague (30:12), and this "atonement money" was an offering to the Lord for use in the tabernacle service. A murderer could not be ransomed, and anyone who found safety in a city of refuge could not be taken back by ransom (Nm 35:31-32). It was impossible to avoid death by paying a ransom (Ps 49:7-9). But in a few instances the term takes on the meaning of a "bribe" or "hush money" (1 Sm 12:3; Prv 6:35; Am 5:12).

A second Hebrew word-family for "ransom" and "redemption" is related to go'el. Go'el, meaning a "reclaimant" or "redeemer," derives from the root meaning of the Hebrew term "to restore, repair, deliver, rescue." The term refers to God's family-law regulations that place various obligations on a relative or kinsman (Lv 25:25-55). The kinsman had the right and duty of redeeming by ransom any family property that a person was compelled to sell (Lv 25:25-34; Ru 4:4-6); of ransoming a relative who was compelled by poverty to sell himself as a slave to a stranger or sojourner (Lv 25:47-55); and of acting as avenger of the blood of a dead relative, thus enforcing the claim for satisfaction for shedding his blood (Nm 35:19-27; Jos 20:3-5). The kinsman was also obligated to marry the wife of a dead brother who had died without leaving children so that the kinsman might raise up seed and the brother's name not be forgotten in Israel (Ru 3:9-13; 4:1-12). In a general sense the go'el was a "vindicator" or "redeemer"; a familiar example is Job's cry for God to vindicate him (Jb 19:25). In the highest sense, God is the kinsman and go'el of Israel, redeeming them from the bondage of Egypt (Ex 6:5-7), from captivity in Babylon, and from distress in general (go'el occurs 13 times in Is 40–46). Thus Israel is called "the ransomed of the Lord" (Is 35:10), having been "redeemed without money" (52:3). In such contexts, however, the cost is indicated in terms of God's might and power.

The OT uses a third Hebrew word (*pidyon*) from the area of commercial law for ransom or payment. Since God spared the firstborn in Israel at the time of Passover, the first offspring of every womb belonged to God, and the oldest male was redeemed by ransom (Ex 13:12-15; 34:20; Lv 27:27; Nm 18:15-17). Later the entire tribe of Levi was set aside as priestly substitutes for the firstborn. Since there were 273 more firstborn than Levites, a payment of five shekels was paid in ransom for each (Nm 3:40-46). This term was also used for the price paid to ransom a slave from slavery (Dt 15:15; 24:18); a slave concubine could also be ransomed (Ex 21:8-11; Lv 19:20). God motivates these provisions by his own ransoming of Israel as slaves in Egypt (Dt 15:15; 24:18). This Hebrew term is also applied to God's deliverance of Israel from Egypt (Dt 7:8; 9:26; 13:5; 2 Sm 7:23;

1 Chr 17:21; Ps 78:42) and from Babylonian captivity (Is 35:10; 51:11). Sometimes God ransoms without reference to a specific occasion (Hos 7:13; cf. Dt 21:8; Neh 1:10; Is 1:27; Jer 31:11). God also ransoms from the grave (Hos 13:14), from iniquities (Ps 130:8), and from troubles (25:22). This deliverance always implies some sort of payment or cost, such as "the mighty power" or "strong hand" of God needed for the redemption.

In the New Testament In the NT there is just one family of words used for ransom. The term basically means "to loose" or "to set free." It denotes releasing, redeeming, or liberating on payment of the ransom price. The translation "ransom" is restricted to approximately eight instances where there is a clear reference to the payment of some sort of price. The translators of the Septuagint restricted their use of this Greek word to those instances where the three Hebrew terms clearly meant ransom payment.

The most important occurrence in the NT is Jesus' description of his death "as a ransom for many" (Mt 20:28; Mk 10:45). Three features stand out in Jesus' words: his service is one of ransom; his self-sacrifice is the ransom price; and his ransom is substitutionary in character. "He gave his life to purchase freedom for everyone" (1 Tm 2:6). Jesus Christ "gave his life to free us from every kind of sin" (Ti 2:14). The ransom price was "the precious blood of Christ," who was an unblemished lamb (1 Pt 1:18-19), thus linking Christ's self-sacrifice to the sacrifices of the OT that pointed to him. The blood of goats and calves was not able to save, but an eternal redemption was obtained by Christ's blood (Heb 9:12). In heaven the redeemed sing the new song to the Lamb whose blood ransomed them (Rv 5:9; cf. 14:3-4).

See also Atonement; Redeemer, Redemption.

RAPE The act of a man forcing a woman to have sexual intercourse against her will. Two instances are recorded in the OT: Shechem the son of Hamor, a Hivite, raped Dinah (see Gn 34:2-7), and Amnon raped his sister Tamar (2 Sam 13:14). In both instances, their brothers got vengeance for the rape of their sister.

See also Dinah; Tamar (Person) #2.

RAPHA
1. Benjamin's fifth son (1 Chr 8:2). His name is omitted in the earlier list of Genesis 46:21.
2. KJV spelling of Raphah, an alternate name for Rephaiah, Binea's son, in 1 Chronicles 8:37. *See* Rephaiah #4.

RAPHAEL Major character in the deuterocanonical book of Tobit. When God heard the prayers of Tobit and Sarah, the angel Raphael was sent to their aid (Tob 3:17). This angel, posing as a dependable relative named Azarias (NLT "Azariah"), accompanied Tobit's son Tobias on his journey to retrieve a sum of money from Gabael (5:1ff.). Traveling with Tobias's dog, Toby, the two made camp by a river (6:1ff.). A fish leapt from the water and tried to swallow Tobias's foot. At the suggestion of Raphael, Tobias eviscerated the fish and set aside its gall, heart, and liver for future use as remedies. When queried by Tobias, the angel revealed that "the gall is for anointing a person's eyes when white patches have spread over them" (v 8). This happened to be the very malady that was plaguing Tobias's father, Tobit (2:9-10).

The journey continued, and Raphael became matchmaker to Tobias and Sarah (6:9ff.). At Sarah's home the two were married. In the bride's chamber, the fish's heart

and liver came in handy for exorcising the demon that had prevented the success of Sarah's previous seven marriages (8:2).

Meanwhile, Raphael continued on the errand to recover Tobit's money from Gabael (9:1ff.). He succeeded at this task. Finally, Tobias and his new wife, Sarah, accompanied by the angel Raphael, with the dog Toby faithfully following at their heels, returned at long last to the home of Tobit (11:1ff.). There Tobias applied the angel's fish-gall remedy to his father's eyes. Tobit's eyesight was immediately restored. At the urging of Tobit, Tobias offered to reward the disguised Raphael half of the money retrieved from Gabael. At this point the angel made his true identity known to them saying, "I am Raphael, one of the seven angels who stand in attendance on the Lord," and adding, "Take note that I ate no food; what you saw was an apparition" (12:15, 19). Raphael then ascended out of sight.

RAPHAH* Alternate form of Rephaiah, Binea's son, in 1 Chronicles 8:37. *See* Rephaiah #4.

RAPHANAH* One of the original 10 Greek cities rebuilt by Rome after Pompey's conquest of Palestine and Syria around 63 BC. Raphanah (also spelled Raphana) was situated in the Decapolis region. *See* Decapolis.

RAPHON A town where Judas Maccabeus and his troops defeated the Syrian commander Timothy (1 Macc 5:37-43). It was near Carnaim, and since Carnaim is the same as Ashteroth-karnaim (the modern Sheikh Sa'ad), Raphon is probably er-Rafeh on the Nahr el-Ehreir.

RAPHU Benjaminite and the father of Palti, one of the 12 spies sent to search out the land of Canaan (Nm 13:9).

RAPTURE* Christian term used to denote the ascension (or lifting up) of Christians at the time of Christ's second coming. This is the noun corresponding to the verb used in 1 Thessalonians 4:17, where those believers who are still alive at the coming of Christ are described as being "caught up" together with their resurrected fellow Christians to meet him "in the air." (It may be relevant to note that the verb of 1 Thes 4:17 is used in 2 Cor 12:2-3 to denote Paul's mysterious experience of being "caught up" into the third heaven, or paradise.) Differences of interpretation about the chronology of the rapture at the time of Christ's second coming in relation to other end-time events has led to the emergence of distinct schools of eschatological thought.

See also Eschatology; Second Coming of Christ.

RASSIS*, RASSISITES A place and its people, probably in Cilicia, which was devastated by the army of Holofernes (Jdt 2:23).

RATHAMIN* A territory transferred from the dominion of Samaria to Judah by Demetrius of Syria. A letter from Demetrius to his adjutant Lasthenes authorizing the transfer is mentioned in 1 Maccabees 11:34. The word is sometimes translated Ramathaim (NLT), the birthplace of Samuel and home of Elkanah and Hannah (1 Sm 1:1, 19; 2:19). In that case, it figures prominently in OT history, for there Saul first made acquaintance with Samuel (9:6, 10), there Samuel retreated after his last break with Saul, and there Samuel's grave is located (25:1). Textual variants Armathaim (TEV "Arimathea") and Ramatha are partly explained by the transposition of *m* and *th* in the Septuagint version. Two modern sites are recommended for the ancient district: Beit Rime, 13 miles (20.9 kilometers) east and north of Lydda, and Ramallah, 8 miles (12.9 kilometers) north of Jerusalem.

RAVEN *See* Birds.

RAVENOUS BIRDS* KJV translation for "birds of prey" in Isaiah 46:11 and Ezekiel 39:4. *See* Birds (Kite or Glede; Vulture, Griffon).

RAZIS A fiercely patriotic Jewish elder sought by the Syrian general Nicanor for opposition to Hellenism (2 Macc 14:37-46). He committed suicide, throwing his own innards at spectators, rather than face arrest by Syrian soldiers.

RAZOR A sharp tool used for shaving off the beard or hair (Nm 8:7; Ez 5:1). Use of the razor was proscribed for those under the Nazirite vow (Nm 6:5; 1 Sm 1:11). The instrument played a central role in Samson's life (Jgs 13:5; 16:17).

The razor is a simile for a slanderous tongue (Ps 52:2) and a metaphor for judgment (Is 7:20).

REAIA* KJV spelling of Reaiah, Micah's son, in 1 Chronicles 5:5. *See* Reaiah #2.

REAIAH
1. Shobal's son and the father of Jahath from the tribe of Judah (1 Chr 4:2), perhaps identifiable with Haroeh (2:52).
2. Reubenite, Micah's son and the father of Baal (1 Chr 5:5).
3. Head or founder of a family of temple servants who returned with Zerubbabel from captivity in Babylon (Ezr 2:47; Neh 7:50).

REAPER, REAPING *See* Agriculture.

REBA One of the five Midianite kings killed by Moses at the Lord's command for seducing the Israelite settlers to idol worship (Nm 31:8; Jos 13:21).

REBECCA*, REBEKAH Daughter of Bethuel and the wife of the patriarch Isaac. Her name, which means "well fed" or "choice," appears 31 times in Genesis (primarily in chs 24–27) and once in Romans 9:10.

Rebekah's father was Bethuel, who in turn was the son of Milcah and Nahor, Abraham's brother (Gn 22:20-23). Abraham was her great-uncle and eventually, of course, her father-in-law. Laban, the father of Leah and Rachel, was her brother. Thus her son Jacob married his two cousins, who were sisters.

Genesis 24 is the account of the successful search by Abraham's servant for a wife for Isaac. He went to Aram-naharaim (northwest Mesopotamia) in obedience to Abraham, who did not want his son to marry a local Canaanite. In answer to the servant's prayer, Rebekah not only gave a drink to the man but also watered his camels. After a certain amount of hospitality was extended and payment was made, Rebekah willingly went to meet her new husband.

Rebekah bore twins, Esau and Jacob (25:20-27). She preferred Jacob, the younger, over Esau and was a party to the deception of her husband in securing the right of the firstborn for Jacob. Disguising Jacob to feel, look, and smell like Esau the outdoorsman was her idea. She also prepared Isaac's favorite dish in order to facilitate the event (27:5-17).

Scripture records little more of her life but does report

that she was buried next to her husband in the cave of Machpelah near Mamre (49:31).

See also Isaac.

REBIRTH *See* Regeneration.

RECAB
1. Rimmon's son who, with his brother Baanah, commanded bands of raiders under Saul's son Ishbosheth. Hoping to please David, they killed Ishbosheth. David, however, angered with this killing, had the two put to death (2 Sm 4:1-3, 5-12).
2. Father of Jehonadab (or Jonadab), the violent supporter of Jehu who killed Ahab's supporters in Samaria (2 Kgs 10:15-27). Jeremiah refers to the followers and descendants of Recab as Recabites. These were nomadic people who lived by Jonadab's command that his descendants not drink wine, live in houses, sow seed, or plant vineyards. Jeremiah applauded the Recabites' loyalty to their forebear, contrasting them with Judah and Jerusalem's unfaithfulness to God. Jeremiah predicted doom for Judah and Jerusalem but promised that Recabites would be preserved (Jer 35:1-19).

RECABITE Descendants of Recab, Jonadab's father (Jer 35:2-18). *See* Recab #2.

RECAH Town in Judah occupied by Eshton, Beth-rapha, Paseah, Tehinnah, Ir-nahash, and their families (1 Chr 4:12).

RECHAB*, RECHABITE* Alternate spelling for Recab, Recabite. *See* Recab; Recabite.

RECHAH* KJV spelling of Recah, a Judean town, in 1 Chronicles 4:12. *See* Recah.

RECONCILIATION Restoration of friendly relationships and of peace where there had previously been hostility and alienation. Ordinarily, it also includes the removal of the offense that caused the disruption of peace and harmony. This was especially so in the relation of God with humanity, when Christ removed the enmity existing between God and mankind by his vicarious sacrifice. The Scripture speaks first of Christ's substitutionary death in effecting reconciliation of God with sinners; of sinners appropriating this free gift by faith; the promised forgiveness and salvation that become the sinners' possession by grace; and finally reconciliation with God (Rom 5:10; 2 Cor 5:19; Eph 2:16).

The term *katalassein* (Rom 5:10; 2 Cor 5:19) signifies first of all the reconciliation of God with the world, expressing God's initial change of heart toward sinners. The problem is not rightly addressed by questioning whether the unchanging God ever changes his mind; the situation rather is one where an altered relationship now exists between God and sinners by Christ's interposing sacrifice on behalf of fallen humanity. The point of the reconciliation is that God, for Christ's sake, now feels toward sinners as though they had never offended him. The reconciliation is complete and perfect, covering mankind both extensively and intensively—that is, all sinners and all sin. The cause of rupture between God and sinners has now been healed, a truth wholly independent of humanity's mood or attitude. While sinners were still the objects of God's just wrath, Christ, in full harmony with the gracious will of his heavenly Father, interposed himself for their sakes, for the restoration of harmony.

So basic is this truth that without objective reconciliation there is no thought of salvation, of regeneration, of faith, of Christian life. The initiative in reconciliation, moreover, is all on God's side; through his Word, the gospel, God reveals to sinners that he is fully reconciled with them because of Christ.

The vicarious atonement or redemption of Christ underlies God's reconciling activity. Reconciliation took place not by God's exercise of divine fiat or decree of power but through Christ interposing himself as the people's substitute for the law's condemnation. Thus the vicarious atonement is the key to understanding reconciliation as scripturally conceived and taught. Christ "became sin for us"; he assumed the full obligations of the law, perfectly fulfilling it and fully bearing the guilt and punishment. Sins and guilt were laid on him; his righteousness attained under the law was imputed to mankind.

The human predicament, simply and precisely, was the human inability to change or rectify in any way the broken, hostile relationship existing between humanity and God. Christ was the bridge. To carry out his substitutionary mission was the purpose of his incarnation. His sacrificial suffering and death, sealed by his triumphant resurrection, achieved mankind's redemption (Rom 4:25). Christ suffered death not as the common lot of all people but as the wages of sin.

His vicarious satisfaction for all sins is the central teaching of the Scripture. Everything literally depends upon the fact that the turning point for humanity came from God, who was working out reconciliation with the world through Christ. This is not simply an imagined or piously conceived idea, something presented as true by deeply concerned and thoughtful people, but a reality that happened (Is 53:6; 2 Cor 5:21; Heb 9:12-14; 1 Pt 1:19). It was God's solution for the grievous, hostile state that existed between a righteous, angry God and sinful, offending people.

The Scripture never loses sight of the sweeping extent of Christ's work, the atonement for the sins of all people (Jn 3:16; 1 Jn 2:2). Christ is the sinners' shield from and before the just wrath of God. Nor was it merely by God's accepting it as sufficient that Christ's atonement availed; it was in fact and in truth the adequate and full payment (Mt 20:28; Rom 3:25; Heb 7:26-28; 1 Tm 2:6; 1 Jn 2:2).

The gospel, therefore, is the message that informs the sinner of God's reconciliation with sinners through Christ and powerfully persuades the sinner to accept this truth in faith, or as the apostle Paul puts it: "For God was in Christ, reconciling the world to himself, no longer counting people's sins against them. This is the wonderful message he has given us to tell others. We are Christ's ambassadors, and God is using us to speak to you. We urge you, as though Christ himself were here pleading with you, 'Be reconciled to God!' " (2 Cor 5:19-20, NLT).

RECORDER The title of a high public official from David's reign until the end of the Israelite monarchy. Though precise duties are never specified in the OT, the recorder probably kept the official log or ledger and advised the king from the information available to him. A recorder is mentioned with other leading officers in 2 Samuel 8:16, 20:24, and 1 Kings 4:3. The recorder spoke for Hezekiah in his dealings with Rabshekah (2 Kgs 18:18), and during Josiah's reign, supervised temple repairs (2 Chr 34:8).

RED *See* Color.

REDEEMER, REDEMPTION English words derived from a Latin root meaning "to buy back," thus meaning

the liberation of any possession, object, or person, usually by payment of a ransom. In Greek the root word means "to loose" and so to free. The term is used of freeing from chains, slavery, or prison.

Old Testament and New Testament Words For a full understanding of the concept of redemption, it is necessary to look at the OT. There are three different words used in Hebrew, depending on the particular situation, that convey the idea of redemption. The meaning of these redemptive terms rests on legal, social, and religious customs that are foreign to modern culture. An understanding of the culture is needed for an understanding of the terminology and its use.

The first term used for redemption has a legal context. The verb *padah* is used when an animal substitutes for (or redeems) a person or another animal. The noun derived from the root means the ransom or the the price paid. When a living being, person or animal, requires redemption, the substitution must be made, or price paid; otherwise, the creature involved is killed (Ex 13:13; 34:20). However, there is evidence that this rule was not always strictly followed (Ex 21:8; Jb 6:23).

The concept of redemption had special significance for the firstborn. The firstborn male, both man and beast, belonged to God. In theory the firstborn was sacrificed to him. This was done in the case of many animals, but the human firstborn and some animals were redeemed (Ex 13:13; 34:20; Nm 18:15-16). In the redemption of the firstborn son, an animal was substituted, although later a sum of money was paid (Nm 18:16).

The second term involved is the Hebrew root *ga'al*, which is used primarily in relation to family rules and obligations, the laws governing family property rights and duties. For example, should a piece of property be lost by a family member, the next of kin had both the right and the obligation to redeem this property. This right of redemption protected the family inheritance. The noun derived from this root is equivalent to the English root "redemption," and the person who buys back the property is the *go'el* or redeemer.

An Israelite who was forced to sell himself into slavery to pay his debts could be redeemed by a near relative or even by himself (Lv 25:47-49). Land might also be redeemed in the same fashion (25:25-28; Jer 32:6-9).

The right of redemption extended also to persons in special circumstances. The obligation of a man to marry his brother's widow is well known. In the book of Ruth, the right of redemption is extended to a distant relative. In this story, Boaz redeemed not only the property but Ruth as well, and she became his wife (Ru 3:13; 4:1-6).

The third term used in Hebrew is the root verb *kaphar*, which means "to cover." From this root come the terms meaning to cover sin, atone, or expiate. The noun derived, *kopher*, means the price paid to cover sin, when the term is used in the religious sense.

The term is used to mean the payment made for any life that should be forfeited. A good illustration is the price paid by the owner of an ox that had gored a person to death. Under the law, the owner's life was forfeited, but he could redeem himself by paying the required ransom (Ex 21:28-32).

All three terms are translated by the same Greek verb, *luo*, meaning "to loose." The noun *lutron* (ransom), is used for all three terms on occasion. This indicates that while the Hebrew used different words for different situations, the same essential meaning of redemption was involved in all situations. The concept of redeeming or freeing was of primary concern.

God as Redeemer In the OT the object of God's redemption is generally the people as a whole, or the nation, rather than individuals. The beginning of this concept of national redemption is seen in God's freeing the people from slavery in Egypt. Though they were in bondage, their God ransomed them (Ex 6:6; Dt 15:15).

As indicated by the terms used for redeeming or ransoming, the payment of a set price or the substitution of another life was involved. When the redemptive concept is applied to God as the subject, he delivers—without the payment of a price—by his might or power: "I am the LORD, and I will free you from your slavery in Egypt. I will redeem you with mighty power and great acts of judgment" (Ex 6:6, NLT; cf. Dt 15:15). The same thought is carried forward in other times of need and deliverance, such as the time of exile. God is the national deliverer (e.g., Is 29:22; 35:10; 43:1; 44:22; Jer 31:11).

Again there is no suggestion that God paid a price to free his people. God redeems by his own power. "For this is what the LORD says: 'When I sold you into exile, I received no payment. Now I can redeem you without paying for you' " (Is 52:3, NLT). When Cyrus let the people free, it was again without payment of a price (45:13).

In the Christian community, especially in the early centuries of the church, there arose the idea that a ransom price was needed to pay for sins. In fact, it was often taught that the sinner was, in effect, held captive by Satan. Christ's death was the ransom price paid by God to Satan to free sinful people. This teaching is not supported by Scripture. The death of Christ is an atonement or expiation made for sin, but this does not mean that his death was a price paid to Satan. God is not pictured anywhere in Scripture as getting into such a commercial transaction with Satan. The redeeming work of the cross must always lie within the realm of divine mystery.

The Red Sea

Redemption and the Messiah In the OT redemption is closely linked with the messianic hope. From the time of the exodus on, God is revealed as deliverer. The hope of redemption is very strong during the Captivity. The prophets constantly speak of God as redeemer or deliverer. This hope was to be fulfilled ultimately through God's anointed one, or Messiah, who would be of the line of David (Is 9:1-6; 11:1-9; Jer 23:5-6).

The messianic hope grew stronger during the periods of exile and persecution. In fact, during the long centuries of persecution, this hope of a messianic deliverer was stronger than ever. This period, generally called the intertestamental period, lasted about four centuries and

extended from the last of the prophets until the time of John the Baptist and Jesus.

Christians believe that in Jesus the Christ (or Jesus the Messiah) we see the fulfillment of the OT redemptive concept. The redemptive image is very evident in the Gospels. John the Baptist depicted Jesus of Nazareth as the fulfillment of God's redemptive kingdom (Mt 3:12) and hence, the Messiah of Israel. Jesus, the Son of Man, came to give himself as a ransom for many (Mt 20:28; Mk 10:45). The work of the Messiah was vicarious and substitutionary.

The same thought occurs especially in the writings of Paul. Christ is the sin offering to the Father (Rom 3:25). Redemption is by the giving of his life (Acts 20:28) for a purchased people (1 Pt 2:9; see also 1 Cor 7:22-24; 2 Cor 5:14-17). These are all words or expressions used to present the central idea of redemption or atonement. Jesus Christ is the one who in himself fulfilled the redemption concept of Scripture and by his sacrifice provided for the redemption of sinners.

The concept of redemption has deep meaning for God's people. In the OT it illustrates the truth that God is the Savior of his covenant people. Although Israel fell into sin by denying God's law, God did not destroy them but restored them to favor upon repentance.

In the prophets, especially, God's redemptive work was to be completed through the Messiah and his redemptive sacrifice. The followers of Jesus believed that he was the Messiah who would provide redemption for the whole world. Coupled with the idea of redemption is the motivating force of divine love as the basis for restoration (Jn 3:16). The one who believes will be freed from the bondage of sin and find favor again with his redeeming God.

See also Atonement; Ransom; Salvation.

RED HEIFER *See* Animals (Cattle).

RED SEA Arm of the Indian Ocean, extending to the northwest and lying between the continents of Africa and Asia. It is a long, narrow body of water, some 1,350 miles (2,172.2 kilometers) long and averaging 180 miles (289.6 kilometers) in width. It is flanked on the east by the Arabian Peninsula, while its African shore includes Egypt, the Sudan, Eritrea, and Ethiopia. At the northwest, the peninsula of Sinai juts into the sea, with the Gulf of Suez on the west and the Gulf of Aqaba on the east. At the northwestern end of the Gulf of Suez is the city of Suez and the water connection with the Mediterranean Sea via the Suez Canal. At the tip of the Gulf of Aqaba is the Israeli port of Eilat and the sole Jordanian port, Aqaba. The waters of this sea are extremely rich in aquatic life; the fish and other animal life from the Red Sea could provide much of the food needs for this part of the world. There are few cities, few good roads, and little arable land adjoining the Red Sea.

In the Hebrew OT the Red Sea is called the "Sea of Reeds" or "Sea of Rushes," but English translations ordinarily give "Red Sea," following the Septuagint. This body of water could be different from what is known today as the Red Sea. In the NT the only references to the Red Sea by that name are in the defense of Stephen before the council (Acts 7:36) and in the "heroes of faith" chapter (Heb 11:29).

The crossing of the Red Sea by the Israelites at the time of the exodus is one of the most celebrated events of Hebrew history and has been memorialized by the Jewish people to the present time. The place of this crossing is much debated, but wherever it occurred, it is evident that the water was too deep to wade across and the distance too far to swim. And it was deep enough to cover all the Egyptian army and wide enough to drown all of their number. Confronted by the sea and closely pursued by the crack troops and skilled chariotry of the best army in the world at that time, the Israelites were delivered by the direct intervention of the Lord, who used an east wind to make a channel for their passage upon the bed of the sea (see Ex 14:10-31).

When the Lord overwhelmed the Egyptian forces in the sea, the deliverance of the Israelites from the Egyptian threat was complete. This victory was celebrated by songs (Ex 15:1-21) and was often recalled in accounts of the Lord's works in behalf of Israel (see Jos 4:23; 24:6-7; Pss 106:7-9; 136:13-15). Even the people of Jericho heard what God did at the Red Sea and fear fell upon them (Jos 2:9-10).

The route taken by Israel paralleled the eastern shore of the Gulf of Suez for some distance. After they left Elim, they camped beside the sea (Nm 33:9-11). Then they turned inland to head for Mt Sinai.

From Sinai they headed northeast, paralleling the Gulf of Aqaba as closely as possible and certainly touching the Red Sea at Ezion-geber (Nm 33:35). Following their failure to enter Canaan from Kadesh-barnea and their defeat at Hormah, they turned south to the point at which Mt Seir approaches the Gulf of Aqaba (cf. Dt 2:8).

The southernmost border of the Promised Land is indicated as the Red Sea (Ex 23:31). Solomon's kingdom extended to the Gulf of Aqaba, for at Ezion-geber near Eloth he built a fleet of ships that went to Ophir, from which gold and other precious and exotic commodities were brought (1 Kgs 9:26-28; cf. 2 Chr 8:17-18). Later, Jehoshaphat attempted to do the same, but his ships were wrecked at Ezion-geber (1 Kgs 22:48; 2 Chr 20:36-37).

See also Exodus, The; Exodus, Book of.

REED Tall grass that grows in damp places and beside bodies of water. *See* Plants.

REEDS*, Sea of Hebrew designation for the body of water crossed by the Israelites during the exodus from Egypt. *See* Red Sea.

REELAIAH Head of a family who returned to Jerusalem with Zerubbabel after the exile (Ezr 2:2); alternately called Raamiah (Neh 7:7). *See* Raamiah.

REFUGE, Cities of *See* Cities of Refuge.

REGEM Jahdai's son and a descendant of Caleb (1 Chr 2:47).

REGEMMELECH One of the delegation sent to inquire whether fasting to commemorate the temple destruction should continue (Zec 7:2). The name may refer to a person or could be a title meaning "friend of the king."

REGENERATION* Spiritual rebirth producing a new beginning. It describes the new life of the believer in Christ (Ti 3:5) and the new order that will begin at Christ's return (Mt 19:28). It occurs in the KJV of the Bible in only these two places. This does not mean, however, that the concept is unimportant. A variety of other words and figures are used frequently by the biblical writers to describe the same inner renewal of the heart.

Secular writers also speak of regeneration. For the Stoic philosophers, it meant a return to a former state of existence. They referred to the yearly cycle of the seasons as a regeneration. For the biblical writers, however, regenera-

tion means a renewal on a higher level. It is a radically new beginning rather than a mere restoration of previous conditions. This renewal involves a mighty change in the person. It is a work of the Holy Spirit, breaking the dominion of sin and implanting proper attitudes and desires. The regenerated person freely and joyously does the will of God. The ultimate goal of regeneration is the creation of a new heaven and earth that will be totally righteous and without sin (2 Pt 3:13). The present working of the Holy Spirit in the believer is a foretaste of this future cosmic regeneration (Eph 1:13-14). The new heavens and earth are still future. But God's renewal of his people, foreseen by the OT prophets, is already a reality (Is 65:17; 66:22; 2 Pt 3:13; Rv 21:1).

The believer now possesses a new life from God through the process of spiritual birth. Christians are born of God (Jn 1:12-13). And it is only through this spiritual birth that one may participate in the kingdom of God and receive his Spirit. Those born into God's family reflect his righteous character (1 Jn 2:29). They are freed from habitual sin (3:9; 5:18). In James 1:18 this process of birth is attributed to the power of the Word of God.

Extending this metaphor for regeneration, Jesus taught Nicodemus about the absolute necessity of being born again, or born from above, as a prerequisite to entering the kingdom of God. Those who are thus reborn possess a living hope (1 Pt 1:3). Again, this new birth is brought about through the power of the Word of God (v 23).

The initial experience of regeneration is followed by a continuing renewal in the life of the Christian. The newborn are to desire the pure milk of the Word of God in order to grow (1 Pt 2:2). Paul commands an ongoing transformation by the renewing of the mind (Rom 12:2; Eph 4:23). The new person remains in a process of constant renewal (Col 3:10), and the inner self is renewed daily (2 Cor 4:16).

The present result of the new birth is a new person or new creation for whom old things are replaced by new (2 Cor 5:17). It is this new creation, rather than superficial participation in religious practices, that is the goal of the Christian life (Gal 6:15). It involves laying aside the old nature (Eph 4:22) and putting on the new nature (v 24). In the final analysis, however, this is never the result of human effort alone. We are God's workmanship (2:10).

See also Atonement; Conversion; Redeemer, Redemption; Repentance; Salvation.

YOU MUST BE BORN AGAIN
The Bible insists that regeneration is absolutely necessary. Apart from it, all persons are dead in trespasses and sin (Eph 2:1). A shocking description of this condition is given in Ephesians 2:2-3. An unregenerated person is unable to understand the things of God, and no amount of good works can change it (1 Cor 2:14; Ti 3:5). This is why Jesus insisted, in his dialogue with Nicodemus, "You must be born again" (Jn 3:7).

REHABIAH Levite, son of Eliezer the priest and Moses' grandson (1 Chr 23:17; 24:21; 26:25).

REHOB (Person)
1. King of Zobah whose son, Hadadezer, was defeated by David at the Euphrates River (2 Sm 8:3, 12).
2. One of the Levites who set his seal on Ezra's covenant (Neh 10:11).

REHOB (Place)

1. Northernmost territory explored by the Israelite spies prior to occupation of Canaan (Nm 13:21). It agrees with the location of Beth-rehob (Jgs 18:28) and is mentioned with Zobah and Maacah as an opponent of David in the Ammonite war (2 Sm 10:6-8).
2. Two cities belonging to Asher's tribe (Jos 19:28-30). One was given to the Levitical family of Gershon (Jos 21:31) and became a city of refuge (1 Chr 6:75). The other remained in Canaanite hands (Jgs 1:31). Some scholars identify the references as one city.

   See also Cities of Refuge; Levitical Cities.

REHOBOAM

King (930–913 BC) especially remembered for his part in perpetuating the split of the Hebrew kingdom and for being the first king of the separate kingdom of Judah.

Split of the Kingdom When Solomon died (930 BC), his son Rehoboam ascended to the throne. Perhaps as a concession to the Ephraimites, who often seemed to have been piqued at their inferior status, Rehoboam agreed to hold his coronation in their town of Shechem instead of in Jerusalem, a traditional place of meeting on which "all Israel" could agree (1 Kgs 12:1).

At the conclave, leaders of the northern tribes, accompanied by Jeroboam, approached the new king for concessions. Jeroboam—an official under Solomon's administration who had fled to Egypt when Solomon suspected him of treason—had returned to Israel to assume a position of leadership. Jeroboam was destined to be the ruler of Israel because of Solomon's apostasy (1 Kgs 11). Solomon's numerous building projects and his ostentation seem to have bankrupted the kingdom, resulting in an intolerable tax burden. Especially objectionable was forced labor on various projects (see 1 Kgs 12:4; 2 Chr 10:4). The populace sought relief from high taxes.

The new king asked for a three-day grace period in which to study the request. Advisers from Solomon's administration counseled concessions; the younger men urged no moderation but an even greater tax burden. Following the advice of his peers, Rehoboam arrogantly threatened even higher taxes. The restless northern tribes broke away to establish a separate kingdom under the leadership of Jeroboam. Judah and Benjamin were the only tribes loyal to Rehoboam.

The separate existence of the northern kingdom was not a new development. After Saul's death, the north had gone its own way while David ruled in Hebron. Some 30 years later, it had briefly supported Sheba in a revolt against David. Now under the leadership of Jeroboam, the rupture was to become permanent.

Not accepting the apparent success of the secession, Rehoboam sent his tribute master or treasurer, Adoram (Adoniram), to try to heal the division. North Israelite partisans stoned him to death, and Rehoboam and his party fled to Jerusalem. Rehoboam immediately tried to subjugate the rebellious tribes. Raising a force of 180,000 men from Judah and Benjamin, he prepared to march north, but the prophet Shemaiah brought word from God to abandon the project since the breakup of the kingdom was part of the judgment of God on Israel for the sinfulness of the nation during Solomon's reign. Rehoboam promptly abandoned his military efforts, but intermittent military skirmishes plagued the relations of Rehoboam and Jeroboam throughout their reigns.

Reign of Rehoboam In the face of constant threat of attack, Rehoboam set about to fortify his kingdom. He built extensive fortifications with adequate supplies of weapons and food at Bethlehem, Etam, Tekoa, Beth-zur, Soco, Adullam, Gath, Maresha, Ziph, Adoraim, Lachish, Azekah, Zorah, Aijalon, and Hebron.

Military preparedness was supplemented by spiritual underpinning. As a result of the establishment of a new apostate religion in the northern kingdom, priests and Levites streamed to the south, where they greatly strengthened the spiritual fiber of the realm. Apparently, they helped to maintain the stability of Judah for three years.

However, the people built high places and pagan sanctuaries throughout the land. They began to engage in the corrupt religious practices of the heathen nations around them, including homosexuality (1 Kgs 14:22-24).

Soon Rehoboam forsook the law of the Lord, and all Israel followed him (2 Chr 12:1). Rehoboam was the son of Solomon, a preoccupied father who himself grew increasingly lax about spiritual things. Rehoboam's mother was Naamah, a pagan Ammonite princess who presumably lacked any spiritual perception (1 Kgs 14:21). His father's example of keeping a harem and having numerous children likewise had an impact on him. Rehoboam had 18 wives, 60 concubines, 28 sons, and 60 daughters. He spent a considerable amount of time providing living arrangements for them in the fortified cities of Judah (2 Chr 11:21-23).

At length, the apostasy of Judah became so great that God brought judgment on the nation in the form of a foreign invasion. In the fifth year of Rehoboam (c. 926 BC), Shishak I (Sheshonk I) of Egypt invaded Palestine with 1,200 chariots and 60,000 men (1 Kgs 14:25; 2 Chr 12:2-3).

After Shishak's initial successes, the prophet Shemaiah made it clear to the king and the nobility that the invasion was direct punishment for their sinful ways. When they repented of their waywardness, God promised to moderate their punishment. They were subjected to either heavy tribute or a plundering of their cities. The national treasury and the temple treasury were emptied to satisfy the demands of the Egyptians.

Shishak's invasion continued into the northern kingdom, for his inscription in the temple of Karnak at Luxor tells of his conquest of 156 towns in the two kingdoms. Only a fraction of the names listed can be identified.

Rehoboam's repentance was only temporary. Scripture indicates that his latter years were characterized by evil (2 Chr 12:14), and that his son and successor, Abijam, "walked in all the sins which his father did before him" (1 Kgs 15:3). Probably the sins of his father would not have been condemned if Rehoboam's last 12 years had been a good example to his maturing son.

Rehoboam was 41 when he ascended the throne, and he reigned for 17 years.

See also Chronology of the Bible (Old Testament); Genealogy of Jesus Christ; Israel, History of.

REHOBOTH

1. KJV name for Rehoboth-Ir, a city built by Nimrod, in Genesis 10:11. *See* Rehoboth-Ir.
2. Site of the third well dug by Isaac (Gn 26:22). This time Abimelech and the herdsmen of Gerar did not lay claim to it, and Isaac named the well "broad places" or "room." The well was located about 20 miles (32.2 kilometers) southwest of Beersheba.
3. Home of Shaul, an Edomite ruler (Gn 36:37; 1 Chr 1:48). The place is identified as "on the river," a frequent biblical reference to the Euphrates. Hence, versions such as the NASB, RSV, and NLT insert "Euphrates" into the text.

REHOBOTH-IR Name meaning "broad places of the city." It was the second city built by Nimrod the hunter (KJV "Asshur") in Assyria (Gn 10:11; KJV "Rehoboth"). Opinion differs as to whether it was a distinct municipality (a suburb of Nineveh) or, since the name of the town is not mentioned in Assyrian literature, open squares or broad streets within Nineveh itself.

REHUM

1. One of the 12 Jewish leaders who returned from captivity with Zerubbabel (Ezr 2:2; Neh 7:7, where "Nehum" is apparently a copyist's error). *See* Nehum.
2. Persian commander who, with Shimshai the scribe, wrote to Artaxerxes I, complaining of the Jews' temple-rebuilding project and promising dire consequences should the project be completed. The king's response halted construction until the second year of Darius's reign (Ezr 4:8-23).
3. Levite identified as Bani's son, who helped repair the Jerusalem wall under Nehemiah's direction (Neh 3:17).
4. Leader who set his seal on Ezra's covenant (Neh 10:25).
5. Priest who accompanied Zerubbabel (Neh 12:3); elsewhere he was called Harim (see NLT mg). *See* Harim #5.

REI Officer who supported Solomon when Adonijah attempted to become king near the end of David's reign (1 Kgs 1:8).

REKEM (Person)

1. Prince or king of Midian killed with his four accomplices in a battle waged by Moses at the Lord's command (Nm 31:8, Jos 13:21). Israelites living in the vicinity of Rekem's dominion had been seduced to the worship of Baal-peor.
2. Son of Hebron, a descendant of Caleb, and Shammai's father (1 Chr 2:43-44).

REKEM (Place) One of 26 cities assigned to Benjamin's tribe for an inheritance (Jos 18:27).

RELIGION The service and worship of God; an institutionalized system of religious beliefs and practices. The Israelites' service and worship of God had become institutionalized by the time Jesus lived. Jesus himself criticized several of its practices for having a show of piety but lacking true heart-felt adoration of God. The institutionalization of the Christian faith occurred in many churches long after the time of the apostles. Hence, it is not discussed in the NT.
See also Judaism.

REMALIAH Father of King Pekah of Israel (737–732 BC). Pekah, through treachery, claimed Israel's throne (2 Kgs 15:25-37) and later terrorized Jerusalem (Is 7:1-9).

REMETH Border town in Issachar's territory (Jos 19:21), and probably the same as Ramoth (1 Chr 6:73), also called Jarmuth. *See* Jarmuth #2.

REMISSION OF SINS* KJV phrase synonymous with "forgiveness of sins." The NT uses a variety of terms to describe a single truth. With the concept of forgiveness of sins, there are a number of expressions employed ("passing over," Rom 3:25; "covered," Rom 4:7; "not imputed," Rom 4:8; "remembered no more," Heb 10:17). One of the most significant is the word rendered

"remission" (Mt 26:28; Mk 1:4; Lk 1:77; 3:3; 24:47; Acts 2:38; 10:43; Heb 9:22; 10:18).

The word has an interesting tradition in the Greek language. In the legal sense, it was used to denote dismissal from office, release from obligation, remittance of debt or punishment. In time it also referred to amnesty or exemption from taxation. In NT usage the verb means "to let go," "to leave behind," or "to send away." Hence, the noun can be (and frequently is) translated "forgiveness" as well as "remission" (Acts 5:31; 13:38; 26:18; Eph 1:7; Col 1:14). While forgiveness can be exercised at both the human and divine levels, the forgiveness indicated by the word "remission" is almost always that of God (Mt 26:28; Acts 10:43).
See also Forgiveness.

REMMON* KJV form of En-rimmon, a town in Simeon's territory, in Joshua 19:7. *See* En-rimmon.

REMMON-METHOAR* KJV translation for "Rimmon it ends toward Neah," in Joshua 19:13. *See* Rimmon (Place) #2.

REMNANT Group of people who survive a catastrophe brought about by God, ordinarily in judgment for sin. This group becomes the nucleus for the continuation of mankind or the people of God; the future existence of the larger group depends on this purified, holy remnant that has undergone and survived the judgment of God. The remnant concept is found in all periods of redemptive history where catastrophe—be it natural disaster, disease, warfare, or other instruments—threatens the continuity of God's purposes. From the Creation account to the end of the OT, the concept is progressively sharpened.

The Problem The theological problem that the remnant concept addresses is the tension between the grace and promises of God over against his holiness and just judgment of sin. This tension between God's grace and his judgment presents a distinction between the true and false people of God and between the present and future people of God. The holy, pure, and true people of God will survive his judgment on sin as a faithful remnant and will become the nucleus of a renewed, chosen people. The purposes of God are not frustrated but are effected among that true and renewed people.

The concept is one that cuts in two directions. On the one hand, depending on the imminent expectation of the biblical author, it may emphasize judgment, that God is on the verge of destroying his people because of their sin; the remnant itself may even be threatened because the contemplated judgment is so severe. On the other hand, the fact that a remnant survives emphasizes both the grace of God (his favor shown to those he has kept safe) and the dawning of a new age and a new community, which inherits the promises of God as it springs from that remnant.

In the Old Testament

Prior to the Patriarchal Period The first passage exhibiting the remnant concept is the account of the fall of man. Though there is no immediate loss of life or numerical reduction, the judgment of God threatens the continued existence of mankind (Gn 3:15-19). Judgment is averted by God's grace, and Adam and Eve become the nucleus of humanity; the hopes of the future are focused in their offspring (3:16, 20; 4:1). God's purposes for mankind will be realized through the seed of the woman.

The Flood narrative is more specific. Because of the wickedness of mankind, God determined to blot out all life. However, a righteous man who was blameless before God, together with his family, received God's favor (Gn 6:8-9; Heb 11:7). Only Noah and those with him in the ark survived the judgment of God (Gn 7:23). The continued existence of mankind focuses in the fruitfulness and increase of his sons (9:1), introducing a new age and a new covenant (vv 8-17). God's purposes for mankind will be realized in the seed of Noah.

From the Patriarchal Period to the Monarchy Not all passages contributing to the development of the remnant motif involve the threat of universal judgment. The sins of the twin cities of Sodom and Gomorrah were so grievous that God determined to destroy them. For the sake of his servant Abraham (Gn 18:16-19; 19:29) and because of Lot's righteousness (2 Pt 2:8), God spared Lot and his two daughters. Abraham's negotiations with God to spare the entire city if 50, and finally even 10, righteous persons could be found there (Gn 18:22-33) emphasize again that the righteous escape judgment. God will not sweep away the righteous with the wicked; even when they hesitated, he was merciful and led them out of the city (19:16, 29).

The story of Joseph is the literary bridge from the children of Jacob, a family in Canaan (Gn 46:26-27), to the thousands of children of Israel at the time of the exodus. The dominant theological motif in the story is the preservation of the patriarch's family in the face of mortal threat from famine. God sent Joseph into Egypt to save lives and to preserve for his family a remnant (45:6-7). Joseph's brothers intended harm, but God turned it to good—to the saving of many lives (50:19-20). Once again the purposes of God are not thwarted but will be realized in these survivors from the threat of extinction.

Obedience to the commands of God and trust in his promises are at issue when the spies return from reconnoitering Canaan (Nm 13–14). Representatives from all the tribes had explored the land. In spite of their agreement about its excellence, all but two of the spies reported that the land could not be taken. Because of their grumbling, God announced his intention to destroy them all and to recreate a greater nation from his faithful servant Moses. After Moses interceded on behalf of the people, the Lord relented. Instead of destruction for all, only Joshua and Caleb would enter the promised inheritance because of their faithful report. The people would remain in the wilderness 40 years until all died except these two. The transgressors would die, but the faithful remnant would receive the promise.

The law, too, stipulates that faithfulness is required to retain possession of the land. Disobedience would bring disease, defeat in war, drought, crop failure, attack by wild animals, death by sword and famine, cannibalism, destruction of cities, and exile into enemy lands (Lv 26:1-39). But for those who were left, those who confessed their sins and repented—the remnant—God would keep his covenant with them, restore them to their land, and realize his purpose through them.

From the Monarchy to the Exile Even in the apostate northern kingdom the Lord kept his faithful remnant. At the end of a three-year drought in punishment for sins in the northern kingdom (1 Kgs 17:1; 18:1) and after the victory over the priests of Baal at Mt Carmel, Elijah went to Mt Sinai, fleeing for his life from Jezebel (ch 19). There he lamented that Israel had given itself totally to false worship and that he alone was left of the faithful. God replied by instructing him to anoint Jehu as king and Elisha as his prophetic successor. Jehu and Elisha would destroy the apostate, while God preserved for himself the 7,000 who had not bowed the knee to Baal. The faithful remnant would be spared destruction.

The preexilic prophets emphasized the smallness of the remnant that would survive the destruction under Assyria and Babylon. Amos warned of great judgment that would threaten even the remnant itself. God would destroy the sinful kingdom, though not totally. Isaiah, too, speaks of the smallness of the remnant. Israel is left like a shelter in a vineyard, a hut in a melon field only narrowly avoiding the fate of Sodom and Gomorrah (Is 1:8-9). It is left like a pole on a hilltop (30:17), like the stump of a felled tree (6:13). When the reaper gathers his harvest, Israel is the gleanings that are left, the few olives that remain in the top of the tree (17:4-6). But from the stump of that felled tree will spring new life (6:11-13). Those who survive in Jerusalem will be holy, and the Lord will bring a new shoot from the stump of Jesse, a righteous servant (the Branch) who will bring the remnant of the people of God from many nations (4:2-3; 11:1-16). After God has purged away the iniquity of the people, Jerusalem would be known as the city of righteousness (1:21-26).

During the Exile From his vantage point among the exiles by the Kebar River (Ez 1:1), Ezekiel was concerned about the future remnant and the promises of restoration. In a vision (ch 9), he saw a scribe pass through the city of Jerusalem placing a mark on the foreheads of all who grieved for the sins committed in the city. Behind the scribe came a group of warriors slaying all who did not have the mark on their foreheads. Fearing the destruction of all the people, Ezekiel called out, "O Lord, will you destroy the entire remnant of Israel?" Immediately thereafter, he saw the glory cloud—the visible presence of God in the midst of his people—rise and depart from the temple (ch 10). Ezekiel prophesied judgment on the leaders of Israel, and Pelatiah (whose name means "escape") died, prompting Ezekiel to ask again, "O Lord, will you destroy the entire remnant of Israel?" (11:13). The Lord will gather his people and restore them to their land as a pure people free of idolatry. Though their sins were great, there would yet be mercy and restoration for a purified nation. The glory cloud that Ezekiel saw departing from the temple will return to a new temple (ch 43). The people will no longer stray from God (14:11) but will enjoy a new and everlasting covenant (16:60-62). Ezekiel recalled the remnant motif as it applied to the wilderness community after the exodus: many will leave the land of bondage, and the rebellious will die along the way, not entering Israel (20:35-38). God will gather his flock, and they will have "one shepherd, my servant David" (34:20-24). God will remove their hearts of stone, give them hearts of flesh, and put his Spirit in them (36:24-27). Though Israel appears dead and incapable of living again, yet God will speak to these dry bones and bring them to life (37:1-14).

REMPHAN* KJV form of Rephan, a pagan deity, in Acts 7:43. *See* Rephan.

REPENTANCE Literally a change of mind, not about individual plans, intentions, or beliefs, but rather a change in one's attitude about God. Such repentance accompanies saving faith in Christ (Acts 20:21). It is inconsistent and unintelligible to suppose that anyone could believe in Christ yet not repent. Repentance is such an important aspect of conversion that it is often stressed rather than saving faith, as when Christ said that there is joy in heaven among the angels over one sinner who repents (Lk 15:7). The apostles described the conversion of the Gentiles to Christ as God granting them "repentance unto life" (Acts 11:18). Evangelical repentance and faith in Christ are in fact inseparable, though a convert may be aware of one aspect more than another.

Such penitence is not an isolated act but a disposition of the mind, providing a spur for behavior that accords with God's declared will. Recognition of daily sins and shortcomings provides the occasion for renewed acts of penitence and for fresh exercises of faith in Christ. One of the deepest and most noteworthy expressions of such penitence is David's account of his adultery with Bathsheba (Ps 51). Whole churches are, on occasion, called to repent (Rv 2:5). Second Corinthians 7 contains an interesting and full description of such corporate repentance involving the elements of sorrow for sin and a determined resolve to forsake old sinful ways and to behave properly. While repentance is often accompanied by deep feelings, it is not equivalent to such feelings but is rooted in convictions about the sinner's own need before a holy God.

Both John the Baptist (Mt 3:2; Mk 1:4) and Christ (Mk 1:15) were preachers of repentance, calling not the righteous but sinners to repent. And in accordance with the Great Commission (Lk 24:44-49), the apostles continued the same kind of preaching—beginning with Peter's preaching on the Day of Pentecost (Acts 2), with noteworthy results. *See* Confession; Conversion; Forgiveness; Regeneration; Salvation.

CAN GOD REPENT?
Occasionally, in some translations of the OT, God is said to "repent." A classic example is found in his treatment of Nineveh during Jonah's prophetic ministry there (Jon 3:10). God told Jonah to proclaim judgment to Nineveh, yet once the Ninevites repented, God relented (KJV "repented")—no judgment came. Such an attitude is not to be understood as denoting either personal sorrow on God's part or a change in his eternal purpose, but rather a change in, or an updating of, his announced purpose and in his relations with people as they themselves change. Such a way of describing God's relation to his creatures is one of many in which, as Calvin and others have stressed, God "accommodates himself" to humans.

REPHAEL Shemaiah's son and a temple gatekeeper in David's time (1 Chr 26:7-8).

REPHAH Resheph's father from Ephraim's tribe (1 Chr 7:25).

REPHAIAH
1. Jeshaiah's son and a descendant of Solomon (1 Chr 3:21).
2. Ishi's son and a captain from Simeon's tribe who led 500 Israelites to destroy the Amalekites at Mt Seir (1 Chr 4:42-43).
3. Tola's son and a warrior from Issachar's tribe in the days of David (1 Chr 7:1-2).
4. Son of Binea and father of Eleasah, a descendant of Saul (1 Chr 9:43); also called Raphah in 1 Chronicles 8:37 (KJV "Rapha").
5. Hur's son, who worked on the Jerusalem wall during the days of Nehemiah (Neh 3:9).

REPHAIM*
1. A Hebrew word referring to shades or departed spirits whose dwelling place was the habitation of Sheol (Prv 2:18; 9:18; 21:16). The *rephaim* of the underworld suffered anguish (Jb 26:5) and were separated from God

(Ps 88:10-12) and all living people (Is 26:14). Their immaterial being bore a weakened shadowlike resemblance to their former corporeality (Is 14:9).
2. A mighty people tall in stature living in Palestine during the days of Abraham. The Rephaim, along with the Zuzim, Emim, and Horite peoples, were defeated by Kedorlaomer and his allied armies (Gn 14:5). They were one of nine nations living in Palestine at the time when the Lord promised to give the land to Abraham's descendants (15:20). The ancient Rephaim were called the Emim by the Moabites and the Zamzummin by the Ammonites; they were comparable in size and number to the giant Anakim (Dt 2:11, 20). Og, king of Bashan, represented the last of the Rephaim. He was later killed and his kingdom dispossessed by the Israelites under Moses (Dt 3:11; Jos 12:4; 13:12). Perhaps the giants among the Philistines were descendants of the Rephaim (2 Sm 21; 1 Chr 20).
   See also Giants.

REPHAIM, Valley of Geographical landmark forming part of the common boundary of the tribes of Judah and Benjamin (KJV "the valley of the giants" in Jos 15:8; 18:16); a broad valley in the southwestern outskirts of Jerusalem thought to be frequented by giants like the Anakim and the Nephilim. During David's reign, after hearing that he had been anointed king, the Philistine armies came up from the coast to search for him in the Valley of Rephaim (2 Sm 5:18-22; 1 Chr 14:9). This valley joined the Wadi Serar, which led down to the Philistine coast and was a fertile area where grain was grown (Is 17:5).

REPHAITES Alternate translation for Rephaim. *See* Rephaim #2.

REPHAN Pagan deity mentioned by Stephen in Acts 7:43 (KJV "Remphan"; NASB "Rompha") when he cited the text of Amos 5:26 (NLT "Kaiwan," see mg) to portray the paganism of the wandering Israelites. Stephen was quoting from the Septuagint, whose translators had taken *kaiwan* to refer to the Assyrian god of Saturn, or perhaps to the Egyptian Saturn god Repa. Some scholars argue that Amos 5:26 is a general reference to the Israelites' wilderness paganism and names no ancient deities at all.

REPHIDIM Camping place of Israel in the wilderness of Paran, following their exodus from Egypt. Exodus 17:1 lists Rephidim as Israel's stopping place after the wilderness of Sin. Numbers 33:12-15, however, specifies that after the wilderness of Sin, they camped at Dophkah and Alush, then Rephidim, before they journeyed on to the Sinai wilderness.

Several incidents occurred at Rephidim during the wilderness travels of Israel. Upon arriving at Rephidim, the Israelites learned that there was no water to drink. The thirsty, disgruntled people complained to Moses. In reply, Moses struck a rock in Horeb with his staff (according to the Lord's instruction) and water flowed out to satisfy the nation. Moses, however, named Rephidim Massah (meaning testing) and Meribah (meaning quarreling) because of Israel's doubt of the Lord's presence and provision (Ex 17:1-7).

Rephidim was the site near which the Israelites, led by Joshua, engaged the Amalekites in battle. The Lord promised to grant Israel victory as long as Moses kept his hands in the air. With the assistance of Hur and Aaron, Moses held up his hands for the duration of the day, and the Israelites prevailed over the Amalekites.

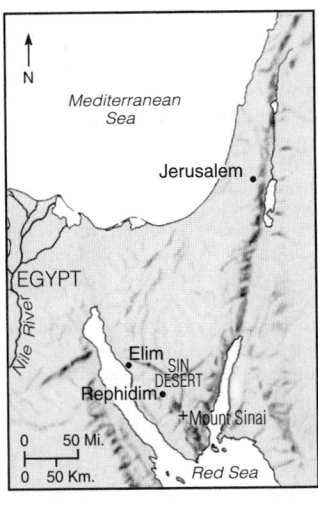

Rephidim The map shows the possible location of Rephidim. Here God supplied water from a rock for the Israelites.

The location of Rephidim is uncertain. Some suggest Wadi Refayid in southwest Sinai. Others variously place it near modern Jebel Musa at Wadi Feiran or at Wadi es-Sheykh.

See also Wilderness Wanderings.

REPTILE *See* Animals (Adder; Asp; Gecko; Lizard; Snake).

RESEN City built by Nimrod between Nineveh and Calah (Gn 10:12). It was part of the complex known as "the great city" and could have been a suburb of Nineveh. Some interpreters suggest it was a waterwork between Nineveh and Calah.

RESHEPH Rephah's son, a descendant of Ephraim and an ancestor of Joshua, son of Nun (1 Chr 7:25).

REST Freedom from work or activity. The source of the Christian doctrine of rest is the rest of God himself, who, after completing the work of Creation in six days, "rested on the seventh day from all his work which he had done" (Gn 2:2). This provides the basis for the Hebrew Sabbath as the weekly seventh day of rest (*sabbath* is the Hebrew term for rest), which is presented as an ordinance of Creation. The fourth commandment demands the consecration of the Sabbath day to God and the limitation of labor to six days precisely because God made all things in six days and rested the seventh day (Ex 20:8-11).

The biblical concept of rest, however, is not just past (Creation) and present (weekly) but also future. This future aspect received symbolic expression in the Israelites' pilgrimage under the leadership of Moses through the wilderness from the bondage of Egypt to the "rest" of the Promised Land. That rest was attained under Joshua, who led them into the land and settled them there (see Jos 23–24).

The 40 years of restless wandering in the wilderness meant that the whole adult generation that set out with Moses perished without entering the Promised Land. This was a judgment they brought upon themselves by their ingratitude and rebelliousness (Nm 14:26-35). Centuries later God warned their descendants against the danger of following this example of hard-heartedness and reaping a similar consequence of not entering his rest: "Today, when you hear his voice, do not harden your hearts" (Ps 95:7-11). The author of Hebrews cites this passage (Heb 3:7-8; 4:7) as evidence that God's rest

is not a matter of past history but that "the promise of entering his rest remains." The word "today" indicates that the day of grace is not closed: "For if Joshua had given them rest, God would not speak later of another day. So then, there remains a sabbath rest for the people of God" (4:8-9, RSV).

It is *God's* rest into which all persons are encouraged to enter. The weekly day of rest is a reminder and a reflection of that rest. The rest of the Israelites in the Promised Land after their wilderness wanderings is a symbol of God's eternal rest that his people will share. The rest that Christ gives to those who come to him (Mt 11:28) is a foretaste and a guarantee of the divine rest that awaits them. The rest after death of believers who have fallen asleep in Christ is a blissful intensification of the reality of this experience: "Blessed are the dead who die in the Lord. . . . They may rest from their labors" (Rv 14:13, RSV). But the completion of this rest in its inexpressible fullness will take place at the return of Christ, when at last all who are his will be fully conformed to his likeness (1 Jn 3:2). Salvation will be consummated as they are clothed with imperishable, glorified bodies (2 Cor 5), and the renewed order of creation in which righteousness dwells will be established (2 Pt 3:13).

This will be the climactic point of all history and the moment of the entry of God's people into the full and unending enjoyment of his rest. The completion of the redemption purchased by Christ at the cross will mean rest and freedom from all sin, and this in turn will mean rest and freedom from all sorrow, pain, suffering, persecution, frustration, injustice, and death (Rv 7:9-17; 21:1-7). The rest of mankind, moreover, will involve the rest of God's whole creation as it is brought to the perfection of that glorious destiny for which it was intended from the very beginning (cf. Rom 8:19-25).

Rest is not synonymous with inactivity. What God rested from was the work of Creation. He continues constantly to be active, however, in providentially sustaining all that he has created and in the work both of righteous judgment and gracious salvation. Jesus Christ, indeed, in his incarnation, life, death, rising, and glorification, is precisely God in action (2 Cor 5:19). Hence the assertion of Jesus: "My Father is working still, and I am working" (Jn 5:17, RSV). What the Christian will rest from is the struggle against the forces of evil and the afflictions by which this present life is marred. The rest into which the Christian will enter will not be a state of uneventful boredom. God himself is dynamic, not static, and so also is his rest.

Consequently, all that a Christian rests from simply sets him free to be active ceaselessly and joyfully in the service of God, the Creator and Redeemer. In perfect harmony with all God's works, and in complete fulfillment, Christians exultantly praise and serve the triune God. Joy will be full, without possibility of improvement or deficiency (cf. Rv 4:8-11; 5:8-14; 7:9-12). Such will be the rest without end of that eternal Sabbath that has a morning but no evening: "Let us therefore strive to enter that rest" (Heb 4:11, RSV).

See also Heaven; Lord's Day, The; Sabbath.

RESURRECTION Act of being raised from the dead, used in the Bible in three different contexts: (1) It refers to miraculous raising of the dead back to earthly life, such as when Elijah raised a boy (1 Kgs 17:8-24), Elisha raised the Shunammite's son (2 Kgs 4:18-37), Jesus raised both Jairus's daughter (Mk 5:35-43) and Lazarus (Jn 11:17-44), Peter raised Dorcas (Acts 9:36-42), and Paul raised Eutychus (20:9-12). There is no hint that these resuscitations would prevent future death.

(2) It refers most frequently to the resurrection of Jesus Christ. (3) It also refers to the eschatological resurrection of mankind at the end of time for punishment or reward (Jn 5:29; cf. Rv 20:5-6).

PREVIEW
- Resurrection in the Old Testament and Judaism
- The Resurrection of Jesus Christ
- The Resurrection Accounts
- The Significance of Christ's Resurrection
- Resurrection in General
- Resurrection and Gnosticism

Resurrection in the Old Testament and Judaism

The concept of resurrection to eternal life developed slowly in Israel. Life and death were limited to physical existence in this world. Death meant leaving this world and entering a shadowy existence known as Sheol, the place of the *rephaim,* or shades (Is 14:9), a place of hopelessness (2 Sm 12:23; Jb 7:9-10). The tragedy of Sheol was that a person was cut off from fellowship with God. At that stage of Israel's thought, there seemed little hope for resurrection (Pss 6:4-5; 88:10-12).

But in the midst of hopelessness concerning a personal future, Israel developed a sense of faithfulness to God. In spite of the fact that the future was not clear, Job cried helplessly, "If a man dies, will he live again?" (Jb 14:14). As Job sought for the seemingly impossible, the difficult passage in Job 19:25-26 suggests the reality of resurrection by a living redeemer (*go'el*).

While some would argue that Hosea 6:1-3 suggests a resurrection, it is more likely that Israel considered it to be a promise of God's continuing care, even when it experienced defeat at the hands of its enemies. Whether Paul saw in the third-day statement of Hosea a reference to Jesus is difficult to assess. This passage, along with texts like the dry bones of Ezekiel (ch 37), focus primarily on giving Israel hope in spite of defeat. But they may have become part of a developing sense in Israel that after death there should be something more.

In Daniel 12:2, however, there is a sure reference to the resurrection of the dead. Indeed, the text announced a twofold resurrection of Jews: some to eternal life and some to eternal contempt. But there was no general resurrection of all people suggested by this text.

In the intertestamental period, views began to solidify. The theologically conservative Sadducees would have nothing to do with the new ideas of resurrection and the afterlife. They continued to argue that there was no mention of resurrection in the writings of Moses, that life pertained to this earthly realm, and that the future hope was experienced through one's children (Ecclus 46:12). Sheol, the place of the dead, was devoid of relationship with God and was a place of hapless existence. The Sadducean opinion of the resurrection is generally well known to Christians because of the encounter between Jesus and the Sadducees when they sought to ensnare him concerning the wife of seven brothers. Jesus rejected their views of the resurrection, of God, and of the Scriptures (Mk 12:18-27).

The Pharisees, along with the Essenes and those at Qumran, believed in resurrection. A twofold pattern of resurrection was suggested by the famous eschatological passages of 2 Esdras 7 and the Apocalypse of Baruch 50–51. Both texts may be as late as the first century AD. In the Similitudes of 1 Enoch, the righteous Jews could generally expect resurrection, but not the wicked (1 Enoch 1:46, 51, 62). But elsewhere in Enoch there is a hint that some wicked may be raised for judgment (vv 22, 67, 90). The resurrection of the righteous in these texts would

generally be linked to a spiritual type of body, yet in 2 Maccabees 7:14ff., the view seems less developed and more physical. The ascetics at Qumran expected a resurrection in the great Day of the Lord.

While in Judaism there was a growing sense of an eschatological day of resurrection and reckoning, there was no hint anywhere of a resurrection of the Messiah. Such an idea had to await the historical reality of Jesus.

The Resurrection of Jesus Christ The resurrection of Christ is the central point of Christianity. So important was the resurrection for Paul that he hinged both preaching and faith upon its validity. He considered that a Christianity without the resurrection would be empty and meaningless (1 Cor 15:12-19). Indeed, the resurrection for him was the unveiling of God's power in Jesus (Rom 1:4).

The resurrection of Christ is the presupposition behind other texts of the NT as well. Rebirth to a living hope is based upon the resurrection (1 Pt 1:3). It is the foundation for witness and fellowship with God, because the living Lord has been seen and touched (1 Jn 1:1-4). It is the bedrock thesis for ministry and apostleship (Acts 1:21-25). The Gospels likewise would hardly have been good news if they did not conclude with Christ's resurrection. Christ's resurrection is the prototype for all the believers, who will experience resurrection when Christ returns.

The Resurrection Accounts While the resurrection of Jesus Christ is the very essence of Christianity, it has been the subject of considerable debate. Scholars have frequently noted the variations that are present in the accounts. How many and who were the women at the tomb? Was there one (Mt; Mk) or were there two (Lk; Jn) angels at the tomb? Did the women come to anoint the body (Mk; Lk) or to see the tomb (Mt)? Did the women say nothing to anyone because of fear (Mk), or did they report to the disciples (Mt)? What was the order of the appearances, and did they take place in Jerusalem (Lk; Jn 20) or in Galilee (Mt; Jn 21) or in both places? Can the appearances be harmonized? What kind of body did Jesus possess? These and many other questions have been the watershed for a great deal of contemporary scholarly debate.

Many of these questions were not first discovered by recent scholars. Tatian in the second century sought to remove the questions by composing his *Diatessaron* (harmony) in hopes that Christians would accept his work as a variant-free substitute for the Gospels. Although Christians liked the harmony, they continued to faithfully transmit the Gospels, because they believed that in them, by divine inspiration, God had provided a powerful witness concerning his Son. Many today still try the way of harmonization in an effort to deal with the minutia of historical questions, but they usually miss the uniqueness of each testimony. Others emphasize the differences and speculate on the Gospel constructs, but the fact of the resurrection usually becomes lost in the details of these human constructs. Both are attempts at protecting the essence of faith and reason in different ways.

The Empty Tomb Many explanations have been given concerning the empty tomb. Some said the body was stolen by the disciples (already suggested by Mt 28:13), but then one needs to explain the church on the basis of fraud. Others have said that the Jews could have stolen the body, or the disciples could have mistaken the tomb, but then the body would soon have been produced by the enemies. Others have said that Jesus could have lapsed into a swoon, reviving later in the cold tomb, but then the result would hardly have inspired the power of the Christian church. These explanations are all rationalistic attempts based upon a preconception that an actual resurrection of Jesus could not have happened.

In spite of the material differences, and while the Gospel writers have used a great deal of common material in their tomb stories, they themselves refrain from employing the tomb as a basis for resurrection faith. With the exception of John 20:8, the empty tomb engendered surprise and fear. Indeed, it seemed to be an idle tale (Lk 24:11). It is not the tomb stories but the appearances of Jesus after his resurrection that gave rise to faith.

The Appearances Unlike the tomb stories, there is little commonality of material in the appearances. Yet the appearances are the basis for faith that the unbelievable happened. An enemy like Paul was converted into a zealous apostle (Acts 9:1-22; 1 Cor 15:8). A fearful fisherman like Peter abandoned his nets (Jn 21). A doubter like Thomas uttered early Christianity's greatest confession, calling Jesus "my Lord and my God" (20:24-28). And two weary travelers to Emmaus found new zeal to return quickly to Jerusalem and share the news about their encounter with the risen Jesus (Lk 24:13-35).

Scholars have debated the nature of these appearances. Starting from Paul's list of appearances (1 Cor 15:5-8), some have argued that all appearances are of the same nature, and since the Damascus-road appearance to Paul recorded in Acts seems to have been of a spiritual nature (Acts 9:1-9; cf. 22:6-11; 26:12-19), then all the appearances must have been similar. Statements that the risen Jesus was touchable (Lk 24:41-43) are rejected as later accretions to an earlier vision-type tradition. This type of argument is based on presuppositions of the impossibility of a bodily resurrection.

Another theory was based on the division between the Jesus of history and the Christ of faith. According to this view, the resurrection was not to be regarded as a fact of history but as an experience of the faith of the disciples. The issue, however, is that the eyewitnesses of Jesus' resurrection proclaimed the event as a historical, palpable reality.

The Significance of Christ's Resurrection Several people were raised from the dead, as recorded in the Bible. A widow's son was raised by Elijah, another widow's son was raised by Jesus, and Lazarus was raised by Jesus. However, their revitalization (or resuscitation) is not the same as Christ's resurrection. They arose only to die again; he arose to live forevermore. They arose still doomed by corruptibility; he arose incorruptible. They arose with no change to their constitution; he arose in a significantly different form.

When the Lord arose, three significant things happened to him. He was glorified, he was transfigured, and he became spirit. All three happened simultaneously. When he was resurrected, he was glorified (see Lk 24:26). At the same time, his body was transfigured into a glorious one (Phil 3:21). Equally so—and quite mysteriously—he became life-giving spirit (1 Cor 15:45).

Prior to the Lord's crucifixion and resurrection, he declared, "The hour has come for the Son of Man to be glorified. Truly, truly, I say unto you, unless a grain of wheat falls into the ground and dies, it abides alone; but if it dies, it brings forth many grains" (Jn 12:23-24; literal). This declaration provides the best picture of resurrection. Paul also used this illustration. He likened the resurrection glory to a grain being sown in death and then coming forth in life. Actually, Paul used this illustration when answering two questions the Corinthians

posed about resurrection: (1) How are the dead raised? and (2) With what sort of body do they come? (1 Cor 15:35).

To the first question Paul responded, "Foolish man, what you sow is not made alive unless it dies" (1 Cor 15:36). This follows perfectly the Lord's saying in John 12:24, and the two explain each other. The grain must die before it can be quickened. Paul devotes more explanation to the second question; and the Spirit inspired his sublime utterance to unfold this mystery. Using the same natural example of the grain of wheat, Paul revealed that the body that comes forth in resurrection is altogether different in form from that which had been sown. Through an organic process, the single bare grain is transformed into a stalk of wheat. In essence, the grain and the stalk are one and the same—the latter simply being the living growth and expressed expansion of the former. In short, the stalk is the glory of the grain, or the glorified grain. This illustration shows that Jesus' resurrected body was altogether different from the one that was buried. In death, he had been sown in corruption, dishonor, and weakness; in resurrection, he came forth in incorruption, glory, and power. The natural body that Jesus possessed as a man became a spiritual body, and at the same time Christ became "life-giving spirit."

With this new spiritual existence, Christ, as spirit and through the Holy Spirit, could indwell millions of believers simultaneously. Before the resurrection, Jesus was limited by his mortal body; after his resurrection, Jesus could be experienced illimitably by all his believers. Before his resurrection, Christ could dwell only among his believers; after his resurrection, he could dwell in his believers. Because Christ became spirit through resurrection, he can be experienced by those he indwells. The Spirit of Christ now makes Christ very real and experiential to us.

The Lord Jesus entered into a new kind of existence when he was raised from the dead because he was glorified and simultaneously became spirit—or, to coin a term, he was "pneumafied" (from the Greek word for "spirit," *pneuma*). It appears that when he arose the indwelling Spirit penetrated and saturated his body so as to constitute his entire being with spirit. Recent studies in the area of pneumatology (the study of the Spirit) point out that the risen Christ and the Spirit were united via Christ's resurrection.

William Milligan, the author of the best English classic on the subject of the resurrection, said that the risen Christ is spirit. In that classic, called *The Resurrection of Our Lord*, he wrote the following:

> The condition of our Lord after His Resurrection was viewed by the sacred writers as essentially a state of *pneuma* (spirit). Not indeed that our Lord had then no body, for it is the constant lesson of Scripture that a body was possessed by him; but that the deepest, the fundamental characteristic of His state, interpenetrating even the body, and moulding it into a complete adaptation to and harmony with His spirit, was *pneuma*. In other words, it is proposed to inquire whether the word *pneuma* in the New Testament is not used as a short description of what our Lord was after His Resurrection, in contrast with what He was during the days of His humiliation upon earth.

Milligan went on from there to show that several Scriptures affirm that the resurrected Christ is spirit. He cited 1 Corinthians 6:17 to show that the believer who is joined with the risen Lord must be joined to him as spirit, because he who is joined to the Lord is said to be "one spirit" with him. He used 2 Corinthians 3:17-18 to demonstrate that the Lord who is the Spirit is none other than the risen Christ. He also employed 1 Timothy 3:16, Romans 1:3-4, and Hebrews 9:14 to prove that the risen Lord is spirit.

When we read the last chapters of the Gospels, we realize that a great change had transpired in our Lord after the resurrection. By entering into glory, he had entered into a new sphere of existence. At one moment he was visible; in another he became invisible (Lk 24:31). He was defying the limitations of space and perhaps even time. In the early morning of the day of resurrection, he appeared to Mary Magdalene in the garden (Jn 20:11-17), then to some of the other women (Mt 28:9). After this, he ascended to his Father (Jn 20:17). Then he returned to appear to Peter, who had gone home (Jn 20:10; Lk 24:34). On the same day, in the late afternoon, he took a seven-mile (11.3-kilometer) walk with two disciples on their way to Emmaus (Lk 24:13-33), following which he appeared to the disciples as they were assembled in a closed room somewhere in Jerusalem (Lk 24:33-48; Jn 20:19-23). It is nearly impossible to follow a sequential, chronological order of all these happenings. What Jesus did was humanly impossible. How could he make all of these appearances on the same day? All we can say is that resurrection greatly changed his sphere of existence. As spirit, and yet with a body—a glorified one—he was no longer limited by time and space.

Through resurrection, Jesus had acquired a different form (see Mk 16:12). As to his person, he was still the same; the Jesus who walked in Galilee and was crucified at Calvary is the same Jesus who arose. His person had not changed, nor will it ever; it is immutable. But his form did change; he is now life-giving spirit. As such, Christ is able to indwell all of his believers.

Resurrection and regeneration are closely linked in the Scriptures—in the same way that crucifixion and redemption form an inseparable unity. As redemption was not possible without Christ's crucifixion, so regeneration is not possible without Christ's resurrection. The Scripture plainly says that we have been born again through the resurrection of Christ (1 Pt 1:23).

After Christ was raised from the dead, he called the disciples his brothers (Mt 28:10; Jn 20:19), and he declared that his God was now their God, and his Father their Father. Through resurrection, the disciples had become the brothers of Jesus, possessing the same divine life and the same Father. As the firstborn from among the dead (Col 1:18; Rv 1:18), Jesus Christ became the firstborn among many brothers (Rom 8:29).

Resurrection in General Paul looked for the Day of the Lord when the dead in Christ would be raised and those who were still alive would join the dead in final victory (1 Thes 4:15-18). There was no doubt in his mind that this resurrection was a glorious expectation, that it involved some type of a personalized body, and that this body would not be physical but spiritual (1 Cor 15:35-44). Paul did not speak of two resurrections, as do the Johannine texts (e.g., Jn 5:29), but merely of the resurrection to life. Perhaps the Revelation of John provides the best clue in understanding NT thought on this issue because it refers to the blessing of being part of the first resurrection (Rv 20:5-6). Although in Revelation the term "resurrection" is not used in connection with judgment, the appearance at the judgment seat and the verdict of the second death in the lake of fire indicate that a resurrection to judgment will hardly be of the same essence as resurrection to life.

THE GREEKS' VIEW OF RESURRECTION
Greek dualism, the separation of body from soul, was not conducive to the acceptance of resurrection, with the exception of some miracle-story resuscitations.

Instead of a doctrine of resurrection, the Greeks developed a doctrine of the immortality of the soul. The body was thought to be a disposable physical outer garment, whereas the soul was related to the immortal forms and sustained from age to age. The Greek cyclical view of time lent itself to the development of a sophisticated view of the transmigration of the soul from body to body.

Whether the Athenians misunderstood Paul or not, their reaction to Paul's preaching of Jesus and the resurrection (Acts 17:16-32) is quite compatible with Greek thought. The idea of a genuine resurrection from the dead to an immortal state, whether for persons in general or for a specific person like Jesus, was foreign to Greek philosophy.

Resurrection and Gnosticism Gnostic eschatology is indebted to the Greek view of immortality and involves the shedding of the bodily husk in the spiritual ascent of the devotee to the Pleroma, or Gnostic heaven. Because of the way Gnostics used words, the Gospel of Philip is a helpful window for understanding the Gnostic twisting of ideas. There it is argued that "those who say that the Lord died first and [then] arose are in error; because he first arose and [then] died. If anyone does not attain the resurrection first, will he not die?" (Philip 56:15-19). The concept of resurrection is de-eschatologized and defined not in terms of a truly future expectation of resurrection but in terms of a realized spiritual awakening in this world. The Gospel of Philip is also useful in perceiving why in 2 Timothy 2:17-19 the criticism was so severe against Hymenaeus and Philetus for holding that the resurrection was past. Clearly, realized eschatology was rejected in the Pauline community and by the church when it appeared in Gnosticism. And it should continue to be rejected by the church in the present day.

See also Dead, Place of the; Eschatology; Second Coming of Christ; Spirit.

REU Peleg's son, the father of Serug, and a descendant of Shem (Gn 11:18-21; 1 Chr 1:25), listed in Luke's genealogy of Christ (Lk 3:35). *See* Genealogy of Jesus Christ.

REUBEN (Person) Eldest son of Jacob and Leah (Gn 29:32; 46:8) and forefather of one of the 12 tribes of Israel. Reuben was involved in the mandrake incident (30:14) and had sexual relations with Bilhah, his father's concubine (35:22). But he emerges into full adulthood as one of the more honorable of Jacob's sons. Reuben objected to the plot to kill Joseph and planned to rescue him from the pit (37:22-35). He moralized about the brothers' imprisonment in Egypt (42:22) and guaranteed the safety of Benjamin at immense risk to his own family. Yet at Jacob's pronouncement of blessing, Reuben is declared unstable and his birthright forfeited (49:3-4). He fathered four sons (1 Chr 5:3).

See also Reuben (Place); Reuben, Tribe of.

REUBEN (Place) Territory east of the Jordan given to Reuben's tribe on the condition that they assist in taking Canaan west of the Jordan (Nm 32). Moses agreed to the Reubenites' request for lands suitable for cattle grazing. The area was bordered on the south by the Arnon River, on the north and east by the wadi of Heshbon and the Ammonite kingdom, and on the west by the Jordan and Dead Sea. Reubenites dwelt there until taken into captivity by Tiglath-pileser III of Assyria around 732 BC.

See also Reuben (Person); Reuben, Tribe of.

REUBEN, Tribe of Tribe descended from Reuben, the eldest of Jacob's sons (Gn 29:32). The tribe of Reuben usually receives the place of honor in lists of the tribes, being named first (Nm 13:4). Similarly, in lists of the two and a half tribes residing east of the Jordan, Reuben is always mentioned first (Jos 1:12), though Gad seems to have held a larger portion.

Because of Reuben's sin (Gn 35:22), his father prophesied that his preeminence among his brothers would disappear (49:4). In spite of the prayer of Deuteronomy 33:6, this disaster did overtake the tribe in later years. In desert days, Reuben's tribal chief appears with all the others (Nm 1:5), and a spy goes forth from Reuben as with the other tribes (13:4). Reuben has his special place in camping and marching (2:10). Only the spies of Ephraim (Joshua) and Judah (Caleb) are faithful (14:6), but Reuben appears no worse than his brother tribes: all were equal in unbelief.

The revolt of Dathan and Abiram, men of Reuben, against the authority of Moses (Nm 16:1) and possibly against the special position of Levi may be significant. Reuben may be claiming his old primacy, forfeited by sin (Gn 49:3-4). The attempt failed, and God's judgment was a signal lesson (Nm 16:33).

Reuben was rich in herds of cattle (Nm 32:1) and presumably a powerful tribe. Reuben, Gad, and the half-tribe of Manasseh asked to remain in the richly timbered and well-watered lands to the east of Jordan, recently conquered from Sihon, the Amorite king, and Og, the ruler of Bashan. This selfish request (for it would involve no sharing in the hard fighting across the Jordan) was rightly denounced by Moses. However, on the promise of the two and a half tribes to bear the brunt of the fighting for their brothers in the west, their request was granted (vv 20-22). They were evidently good soldiers, and Joshua sent them home at the end of the campaign (Jos 22:1-6). Although living east of the Jordan, and separated from their brothers by what was sometimes an insuperable natural obstacle, they had no desire to form an independent state. They showed this by building a great memorial altar at the spot where they crossed the Jordan on their way home (v 10).

Reuben does not appear again until the time of Deborah the prophetess. When the clans of Israel rallied to God's call under Barak to fight Sisera the Canaanite, Reuben did not respond. The wording suggests that Reuben once again was influenced by material possessions, as the tribe had been in the days of the Conquest, when, because of their cattle, they chose the lush lands of Transjordan rather than the rugged hills of Canaan (Nm 32:5). The easy shepherd's life appealed more to them than warfare on the slopes of Mt Tabor (Jgs 5:16). Also the wording suggests long inconclusive discussions—or even, perhaps, great protestations of bravery and fidelity to God's cause—that finally led to nothing (v 15). Reuben has not changed; the tribe, like its ancestor, was still "unstable as water" (Gn 49:4).

Reuben's tribal lands, to the southeast of Gad, were probably overrun and occupied by the Moabites at a later date. Certainly the whole area to the east of the Jordan was an area of contention between Israel and Aram later (1 Kgs 22:3). Finally, Transjordan, with the north of Israel, was one of the first areas overrun and devastated by the Assyrians (2 Kgs 15:29). Although Ezekiel, in his vision, speaks of a strip of territory north of Judah for Reuben (Ez 48:6), it could only have been a small remnant, if any, that returned from the exile of the northern kingdom. Indeed, although Reuben finds his place in the list of the redeemed in Revelation (Rv 7:5), no man of Reuben plays a part in the NT.

REUBENITE Descendant of Reuben, Jacob's son (Nm 26:7; Jos 1:12). *See* Reuben, Tribe of.

REUEL
1. Son of Esau by his wife Basemath, and the father of four sons: Nahath, Zerah, Shammah, and Mizzah (Gn 36:4, 10-17).
2. Priest of Midian who gave his daughter to Moses for a wife. He is perhaps the same person as #1 above, and identical to Jethro (Ex 2:18; cf. 3:1). He is also called Raguel in Numbers 10:29 (KJV). *See* Jethro.
3. Alternate spelling of Deuel, Eliasaph's father, in Numbers 2:14. *See* Deuel.
4. Ancestor of Meshullam in Benjamin's tribe (1 Chr 9:8).

REUMAH Nahor's concubine (Gn 22:24). Her four sons became the ancestors of the Aramean tribes living north of Damascus.

REVELATION Term from the Latin *revelatio*, referring to either (1) the act of revealing for the purpose of making something known or (2) the thing that is revealed. In theology it designates God's own self-disclosure or manifesting of himself, or things concerning himself and the world; it may also mean the word itself, oral or written, that conveys such revelation. The equivalent NT terms are *apokalupsis* (apocalypse), which means unveiling, uncovering, or making someone or something known. The Greek word *phanerosis* is virtually synonymous, though usually with the nuance of clear, readily discernible presentation.

Rationalistic philosophy (as promoted by René Descartes, Immanuel Kant, J. G. Fichte, F. W. J. von Schelling, G. W. F. Hegel) finds in human reason the sole source for whatever shape revelation takes or is, acknowledging only natural religion and denying the reality of all supernatural divine revelation. Rationalists may at times admit the possibility of supernatural religion, but they cannot conceive of divine intervention.

Christian theology, on the other hand, is committed to the idea that the principle of knowledge is the Word of God, specifically the Scripture, despite the severe critique of higher criticism against any claim that the Scripture affords a secure, reliable, and independent base for theological truth. Modern critical theology has declared its support for what it calls "scientific theology," for the "sure" judgments of natural science and the supposed improbability of all supernatural happenings. This has forced the Scripture, as the inspired Word of God, out of its authoritative, normative position. What the Scripture contains is not the account of what actually happened, or what God actually said or did, but merely the early church's confession of faith as to what first-century followers of Christ supposed or contrived to have happened. The Bible, therefore, is not unique in its divine origin; it is only the unique product of early religious searchings and strivings.

Christian theology, on the other hand, asserts (on the basis of the scriptural text and the confirming mighty acts of God) that divine revelation is the first, last, and only source for theology. People have knowledge of God because of God's initiative and activity. God is always the initiator and author of revelation; people are the recipients. God discloses what otherwise would be unknown; he uncovers what otherwise would be hidden (Dt 29:29; Gal 1:12; Eph 3:3).

General Revelation God draws back the veil in a two-fold manner. There is first of all what has come to be called "general revelation." God reveals himself in nature, in history, and in all people as made in his image. The association of God's revelation with nature, by which people have an intuitive knowledge of God's existence, is of long standing and is a truth supported throughout Scripture—both in the OT (Pss 10:11; 14:1, 19:1) and in the NT (Acts 14:17; 17:22-29; Rom 1:19-21). That there is a God, that God is the Creator with almighty power, that God deals justly as the supreme Judge, or rules as the "wholly other" over his creatures—these things are known and recognized by many people. Thus, the fact that God *is,* is undeniable. So, when people deny God's existence, as do atheists, it is a forced effort against an inner conviction worked by nature itself. Paul could expect concurrence from the Athenians when he asserted that it is in God, the one and only true God, that all people live and move and have their being (Acts 17:28). Knowing God through nature, however, is not the end of revelation. Full and complete revelation comes when people encounter the personhood of God.

his prophets and apostles to speak his Word, but in specific instances also inspired them to record in writing the thoughts, words, and promises that he wanted revealed and retained for all time. The sacred collection of writings forms a remarkably harmonious and unified whole by which God reveals his thoughts and purposes toward humanity. For this writing, the prophets and apostles were prompted to recount not only certain historical events and happenings but also what God revealed for special communication. The ultimate purpose of Scripture is to reveal Christ. To him all Scripture gives witness (Jn 5:39; 10:35; Acts 10:43; 18:28; 1 Cor 15:3).

See also Bible, Inspiration of the.

REVELATION, Book of Last book of the Bible, containing revelations concerning the events of the last days.

PREVIEW
• Author
• Date, Origin, Destination
• Background
• Methods of Interpreting Revelation
• Purpose and Teaching
• Content

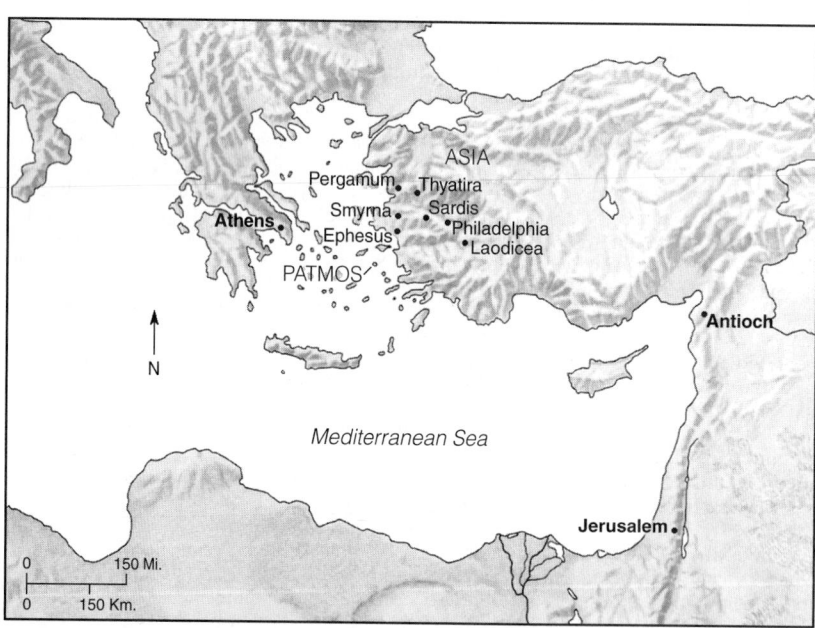

The Seven Churches of Revelation The seven churches were located on a major Roman road. A letter carrier would leave the island of Patmos (where John was exiled), arriving first at Ephesus. He would travel north to Smyrna and Pergamum, turn southeast to Thyatira, and continue on to Sardis, Philadelphia, and Laodicea—in the exact order in which the letters were dictated.

Special Revelation To know God from his revelation in nature still leaves him and his gracious purposes completely unknown. The gracious, loving heart of God intends the salvation of all people. By special revelation God purposes to share this with mankind in various ways. Mankind would know nothing at all of God's messianic purposes in Christ, if God had not revealed his heart and purposes throughout Scripture. By inner, immediate illumination of their hearts and minds by God, the prophets and apostles spoke his Word as he gave them utterance (Jer 1:4-19; 1 Cor 2:13; 1 Thes 2:13; 2 Pt 1:16-21). The zenith of God's revelation was the coming in flesh of his beloved Son, Jesus Christ (Jn 1:14-18; Gal 4:4-5; Heb 1:1-2). Jesus' revelation of the Father and the Father's gracious will toward all people was direct, accurate, and preeminent (Jn 14).

God did not merely illuminate the hearts and minds of

Author The earliest witnesses ascribe the authorship of Revelation to John the apostle, the son of Zebedee. Dionysius, the distinguished bishop of Alexandria and student of Origen (early third century), was the first within the church to question its apostolic authorship because it seemed to him that the writing style differed greatly from that found in the fourth Gospel, attributed to John. From the time of Dionysius, the apostolic origin of the book was disputed in the East until Athanasius of Alexandria (c. 350) turned the tide toward its acceptance. In the West, the book was widely accepted and was included in all the principal lists of canonical books from at least the middle of the second century on.

From the internal evidence, the following things can be said about the author with some confidence. He calls himself John (Rv 1:4, 9; 22:8). This is most likely not a pseudonym but rather the name of a person well known among the Asian churches. This John identifies himself as a prophet (1:3; 22:6-10, 18-19) who was in exile because of his prophetic witness (1:9). As such, he speaks to the churches with great authority. His use of the OT and Targums makes it virtually certain that he was a Palestinian Jew, steeped in the ritual of the temple and synagogue. John the apostle fits this profile. The difference between the style of the fourth Gospel and that of Revelation can be explained by the radically different genres of the two books. The Gospel is a composed historical narrative, whereas the book of Revelation is a record of visionary experiences and direct divine revelation. The writer of the Gospel could take his time in crafting a narrative word by word and sentence by sentence. The writer of Revelation was compelled by God to write down immediately whatever he was told or was shown. Thus, the apostle John could easily have been the writer of both. In any event, no convincing argument has been advanced against his authorship.

Date, Origin, Destination Only two dates for Revelation have received serious support. An early date, shortly after the reign of Nero (AD 54–68), is allegedly supported by references in the book to the persecution of Christians, to the *Nero redivivus* myth (a revived Nero would be the reincarnation of the evil genius of the whole Roman Empire), to the imperial cult (ch 13), and to the temple (ch 11), which was destroyed in AD 70. The alternate date rests primarily on the early witness of Irenaeus, who stated that the apostle John "saw the revelation . . . at the close of Domitian's reign" (AD 81–96).

The origin of the book is clearly identified with Patmos, one of the Sporades Islands, located about 37 miles (59.5 kilometers) southwest of Miletus, in the Icarian Sea (1:9). John was apparently exiled on the island due to religious and/or government persecutions arising from his witness to Jesus (1:9).

Likewise, the recipients are clearly the seven historic churches in the Roman province of Asia (modern western Turkey): Ephesus, Smyrna, Pergamum, Thyatira, Sardis, Philadelphia, and Laodicea (1:4, 11; 2:1, 8, 12, 18; 3:1, 7, 14).

Background The book of Revelation differs from the other NT writings, not in doctrine but in literary genre and subject matter. It is a book of prophecy (1:3; 22:7, 18-19) that contains both warning and consolation—announcements of future judgment and blessing—communicated by means of symbols and visions.

The language and imagery were not as strange to first-century readers as they are today. Therefore, familiarity with the prophetic books of the OT, especially Daniel and Ezekiel, will help the reader grasp the message of the Apocalypse.

While the symbolic and visionary mode of presentation creates ambiguity and frustration for many, it actually lends to the description of unseen realities a poignancy and clarity unattainable by any other method. Such language can trigger a variety of ideas, associations, existential involvement, and mystical responses that the straight prose found in most of the NT cannot achieve.

The letters to the churches indicate that five of the seven were in serious trouble. The major problem seemed to be disloyalty to Christ; this may indicate that the major thrust of Revelation is not sociopolitical but theological. John was more concerned with countering the heresy that was creeping into the churches toward the close of the first century than with addressing the political situation. This heresy seems to have been a type of Gnostic teaching.

Revelation is also commonly viewed as belonging to the group of writings known as apocalyptic literature. The name for this type of literature is derived from the Greek word for "revelation": *apokalupsis*. The extrabiblical apocalyptic books were written in the period from 200 BC to AD 200. Although numerous similarities exist, there are also some clear differences.

Much more important than the Jewish apocalyptic sources is the debt John owes to the eschatological teaching of Jesus, such as the Olivet discourse (Mt 24–25; Mk 13; Lk 21). Revelation is unique in its use of the OT. Of the 404 verses of the Apocalypse, 278 contain references to the Jewish Scriptures. John refers frequently to Isaiah, Jeremiah, Ezekiel, and Daniel, and also repeatedly to Exodus, Deuteronomy, and the Psalms. However, he rarely quotes the OT directly.

Methods of Interpreting Revelation Four traditional ways of understanding Revelation 4–22 have emerged in the history of the church:

Futurist This view holds that, with the exception of chapters 1–3, all the visions in Revelation relate to a period immediately preceding and following the second advent of Christ at the end of the age. The beasts (chs 13, 17) are identified with the future Antichrist, who will appear at the last moment in world history and will be defeated by Christ in his second coming to judge the world and to establish his earthly millennial kingdom.

Variations of this view were held by the earliest expositors, such as Justin Martyr (d. 164), Irenaeus (d. c. 195), Hippolytus (d. 236), and Victorinus (d. c. 303). This futurist approach has enjoyed a revival since the 19th century and is widely held among evangelicals today.

Historicist As the word implies, this view sees in Revelation a prophetic survey of history. It originated with Joachim of Floris (d. 1202), a monastic who claimed to have received a special vision that revealed to him God's plan for the ages. He assigned a day-year value to the 1,260 days of Revelation. In his scheme, the book is a prophecy of the events of Western history from the time of the apostles until Joachim's own time. In the various schemes that developed as this method was applied to history, one element became common: the Antichrist and Babylon were connected with Rome and the papacy. Later, Luther, Calvin, and other Reformers came to adopt this view.

Preterist According to this view, Revelation deals with the time of its author; the main contents of chapters are thus viewed as describing events wholly limited to John's own day. The beasts (ch 13) are identified as imperial Rome and the imperial priesthood. This is the view held by many contemporary scholars.

Idealist This method of interpreting Revelation sees it as being basically poetic, symbolic, and spiritual in nature. Thus Revelation does not predict any specific historical events at all; on the contrary, it sets forth timeless truths concerning the battle between good and evil that continues throughout the church age. As a system of interpretation, it is more recent than the other three schools.

Purpose and Teaching NT scholar H. B. Swete wrote of Revelation: "In form it is an epistle, containing an apocalyptic prophecy; in spirit and inner purpose, it is a pastoral." As a prophet, John was called to separate true from false belief—to expose the failures of the congregations in Asia. He desired to encourage authentic Christian discipleship by explaining Christian suffering and martyrdom in light of the victory over evil won by Jesus' death and resurrection. John was concerned to show that the martyrs (e.g., Antipas, 2:13) will be vindicated. He disclosed the end both of evil and of those who follow the Beast (19:20-21; 20:10, 15), and he described the ultimate victory of the Lamb and of those who follow him.

stant reminder to all churches throughout every age (cf. 2:7, 11, 17, 29; 3:6, 13, 22; esp. 2:23). Their order (1:11; 2:1–3:22) reflects the natural ancient travel circuit beginning at Ephesus and arriving finally at Laodicea.

Ancient Greek Manuscript of Revelation Revelation 5:5-8 in Oxyrhynchus Papyrus 1230 (c. 300)—P24.

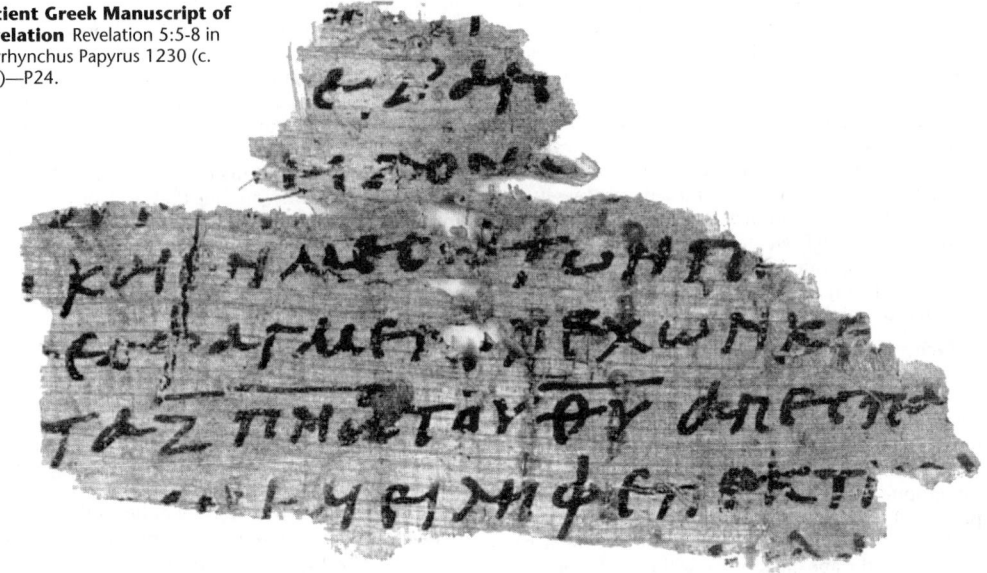

Content The main contents of Revelation are arranged in series of seven items, some explicit, some implied: seven churches (chs 2–3), seven seals (chs 6–7), seven trumpets (chs 8–11), seven bowls (chs 16–18), seven last things (chs 19–22). It is also possible to divide the contents around four key visions: (1) the vision of the Son of Man among the seven churches (chs 1–3); (2) the vision of the seven-sealed scroll, the seven trumpets, and the seven bowls (4:1–19:10); (3) the vision of the return of Christ and the consummation of this age (19:11–20:15); and (4) the vision of the new heaven and new earth (chs 21–22).

John's Introduction (1:1-8) The first three chapters of Revelation form a unit and are comparatively easy to understand. They are the most familiar and contain an introduction to the whole book (1:1-8); the first vision, of the Son of Man among the seven lampstands (1:9-20); and the letters or messages to the seven churches in Asia (2:1–3:22).

The first eight verses introduce the whole book. They are freighted with theological content and detail. After a brief preface (1:1-3), John addresses the book to the seven churches of Asia in an expanded ancient letter form (vv 4-8).

The Son of Man among the Lampstands (1:9-20) After a brief indication of the historical situation that occasioned it (1:9-11), John describes his vision of "someone, like a son of man," walking among seven golden lampstands (vv 12-16). The person identifies himself as the exalted Lord, Jesus Christ (vv 17-18), and then explains the meaning of the symbolic vision (vv 19-20). Finally, the Lord addresses a rather detailed and specific message to each of the seven churches in Asia (2:1–3:22).

The Letters to the Seven Churches (2:1–3:22) These seven churches contained typical or representative qualities of both obedience and disobedience that are a con-

Each message generally follows a common literary plan consisting of seven parts:

1. The addressee is given first, following a common pattern in all seven letters: "To the angel of the church in Ephesus, write. . . ."

2. Then the speaker is mentioned. In each case, some part of the great vision of Christ and of his self-identification (1:12-20) is repeated as the speaker identifies himself; for example, "This is the message from the one who holds the seven stars in his right hand, the one who walks among the seven gold lampstands" (2:1; cf. 1:13, 16).

3. Next, the knowledge of the speaker is given. He intimately knows the works of the churches and the reality of their loyalty to him, despite outward appearances. In two cases (Sardis and Laodicea) the assessment proves totally negative. The enemy of Christ's churches is the deceiver, Satan, who seeks to undermine the churches' loyalty to Christ (2:10, 24).

4. Following his assessment of the churches' accomplishments, the speaker pronounces his verdict on their condition in such words as "You do not love me as you did at first" (2:4) or "You are dead" (3:1). Two letters contain no unfavorable verdict (Smyrna, Philadelphia) and two no word of commendation (Sardis, Laodicea). In the letters, all derelictions are viewed as forms of inner betrayals of a prior relation to Christ.

5. To correct or alert each congregation, Jesus issues a penetrating command. These commands further expose the exact nature of the self-deception involved.

6. Each letter contains the general exhortation: "Anyone who is willing to hear should listen to the Spirit and understand what the Spirit is saying to the churches." The words of the Spirit are the words of Christ (cf. 19:10).

7. Finally, each letter contains a promise of reward to the victor. Each is eschatological and correlates with the last two chapters of the book. Furthermore, the prom-

ises are echoes of Genesis 2–3: what was lost by Adam in Eden is more than regained by Christ. We are probably to understand the seven promises as different facets that combine to make up one great promise to believers: wherever Christ is, there the "overcomers" will be.

The Seven-Sealed Scroll (4:1–8:1) In view of the elaborate use of imagery and visions from 4:1 through the end of Revelation, and in view of the question of how this material relates to chapters 1–3, it is not surprising that commentators differ widely in their treatment of these chapters.

➤THE THRONE, THE SCROLL, AND THE LAMB (4:1–5:14) Chapters 4–5 form one vision consisting of two parts: the throne (ch 4) and the Lamb and the scroll (ch 5). Actually, the throne vision (chs 4–5) and the breaking of all seven seals (chs 6–8) form a single, continuous vision and should not be separated; indeed, the throne vision should be viewed as dominating the entire vision of the seven-sealed scroll, and, for that matter, the rest of the book (cf. 22:3).

A new view of God's majesty and power is disclosed to John so that he can understand the events on earth that relate to the seven-sealed vision (4:1-11; cf. 1 Kgs 22:19). For the first time in Revelation, the reader is introduced to the frequent interchange between heaven and earth found in the remainder of the book. What happens on earth has its inseparable heavenly counterpart.

Chapter 5 is part of the vision that begins with chapter 4 and continues through the opening of the seven seals (Rv 6:1–8:1; cf. introduction to ch 4). The movement of the whole scene focuses on the slain Lamb as he takes the scroll from the hand of the one on the throne. The culminating emphasis is on the worthiness of the Lamb to receive worship because of his death.

➤OPENING OF THE FIRST SIX SEALS (6:1-17) The opening of the seals continues the vision begun in chapters 4 and 5. Now the scene shifts to events on earth. The scroll itself involves the rest of Revelation and has to do with the consummation of the mystery of all things, the goal or end of history for both the overcomers and the worshipers of the beast. The writer tentatively suggests that the seals represent events preparatory to the final consummation. Whether these events come immediately before the end or whether they represent general conditions that will prevail throughout the period preceding the end is a more difficult question.

The seals closely parallel the signs of the approaching end times spoken of by Jesus in his Olivet discourse (Mt 24:1-35; Mk 13:1-37; Lk 21:5-33). This parallel to major parts of Revelation is too striking to be ignored. Thus the seals would correspond to the "beginning of birth pains" in the Olivet discourse. The events are similar to those occurring under the trumpets (Rv 8:2–11:19) and bowls (15:1–16:21) but should not be confused with those late and more severe judgments.

➤FIRST INTERLUDE: THE 144,000 ISRAELITES AND THE WHITE-ROBED MULTITUDE (7:1-17) The change in tone from the subject matter in the sixth seal, as well as the delay until 8:1 in opening the seventh seal, indicate that chapter 7 is a true interlude. John first sees the angels, who will unleash destruction on the earth, restrained until the 144,000 servants of God from every tribe of Israel are sealed (vv 1-8). Then he sees an innumerable multitude clothed in white standing before the throne of God; these are identified as those who have come out of the great tribulation (vv 9-17).

Some scholars separate the two groups into Jews and Gentiles at large, while others see the two groups as one group viewed from different perspectives.

➤THE OPENING OF THE SEVENTH SEAL (8:1) After the interlude (ch 7), the final seal is opened and silence for half an hour occurs in heaven to prepare for judgment on earth or to hear the cries of the martyrs on earth (cf. 6:10).

The First Six Trumpets (8:2–11:14) After a preparatory scene in heaven (8:2-5), the six trumpets are blown in succession (8:6–9:19), followed again by an interlude (10:1–11:14).

➤THE FIRST SIX TRUMPETS (8:6–9:21) Opinion differs, but it may be best to see the first five seals as preceding the events of the trumpets and bowls. But the sixth seal enters into the period of the outpouring of God's wrath that is enacted in the trumpet and bowl judgments (6:12-17). The trumpet judgments thus occur during the seventh seal, and the bowl judgments (16:1-21), during the seventh trumpet's sounding. Therefore, there is some overlapping, but also sequence and advancement, between the seals, trumpets, and bowls.

As in the seals, there is a discernible literary pattern in the unfolding of the trumpets. The first four trumpets are separated from the last three, which are called "woes" (8:13; 9:12; 11:14) and are generally reminiscent of the plagues in the book of Exodus.

The last three trumpets are emphasized and are also called "woes" (8:13) because they are so severe. The first of these involves an unusual plague of locusts (9:1-11) and the second a plague of scorpionlike creatures (vv 13-19). Both of these plagues can best be seen as demonic hordes (cf. vv 1, 11).

➤THE SECOND INTERLUDE: THE LITTLE BOOK AND THE TWO WITNESSES (10:1–11:14) The major point of chapter 10 seems to be a confirmation of John's prophetic call, as verse 11 indicates: "You must prophesy again about many peoples, nations, languages and kings" (NIV). More specifically, the contents of the little scroll (book) may include chapters 11, 12, and 13.

Chapter 11 is notoriously difficult. It includes a reference to measuring the temple, the altar, and the worshipers, and to the trampling down of the Holy City for 42 months (11:1-2), as well as the description of the two prophet-witnesses who are killed and raised to life (vv 3-13). Opinions vary considerably here; some see this vision as depicting the restored Jewish nation, with the actual prophets Moses and Elijah being revived. Others see the temple as the true church being protected by God during the tribulation and the two witnesses representing the whole faithful church under persecution.

The Seventh Trumpet (11:15–14:20) The seventh trumpet sounds, and in heaven loud voices proclaim the final triumph of God and Christ over the world. The theme is the kingdom of God and Christ—a dual kingdom, eternal in its duration. The image suggests the transference of the world empire once dominated by a usurping power, now taken by the hand of its true Owner and King. The announcement of the reign of the King is made here, but the final breaking of the enemies' hold over the world does not occur until the return of Christ (19:11-21).

➤THE WOMAN AND THE DRAGON (12:1-17) In this chapter there are three main figures: the woman, the child, and the dragon. There are also three scenes: the birth of the child (vv 1-6), the expulsion of the dragon (vv 7-12), and the dragon's attack on the woman and her children (vv 13-17).

Since the context indicates that the woman under attack represents a continuous entity from the birth of Christ until at least John's day or later, her identity in the author's mind must be the Christian community.

The woman is in the throes of childbirth (v 2). The emphasis is on her pain and suffering, both physical and spiritual. The meaning of her anguish is that the faithful Christian community has been suffering as a prelude to the coming of the Messiah himself and of the new age (Is 26:17; 66:7-8; Mi 4:10; 5:3).

►THE TWO BEASTS (13:1-18) Turning from the inner dynamics of the struggle (ch 12), chapter 13 shifts to the actual earthly instruments of this assault against God's people—namely, the two dragon-energized beasts. The activities of the two beasts constitute the way the dragon carries out his final attempts to wage war on the offspring of the woman (12:17).

The dragon and the first beast enter into a conspiracy to seduce the whole world into worshiping the beast. The conspirators summon a third figure to their aid—the beast from the earth, who must be sufficiently similar to the Lamb to entice even the followers of Jesus. As the battle progresses, the dragon's deception becomes more and more subtle. Thus, the readers are called on to discern the criteria that will enable them to separate the lamblike beast from the Lamb himself (cf. 13:11 with 14:1).

►THE HARVEST OF THE EARTH (14:1-20) The two previous chapters have prepared Christians for the reality that, as the end draws near, they will be harassed and sacrificed like sheep. This section shows that their sacrifice is not meaningless. In chapter 7 the 144,000 were merely sealed; here, however, they are seen as already delivered. When the floods have passed, Mt Zion appears high above the waters; the Lamb is on the throne of glory, surrounded by the triumphant songs of his own; the gracious presence of God fills the universe.

Chapter 14 briefly answers two pressing questions: What becomes of those who refuse to receive the mark of the beast and are killed (vv 1-5)? What happens to the beast and his servants (vv 6-20)?

The Seven Bowls (15:1–19:10) The series of bowl judgments constitutes the "third woe," announced in 11:14 as "coming soon" (see comments on 11:14). These last plagues take place "immediately after the distress of those days" referred to by Jesus in the Olivet discourse and may well be the fulfillment of his apocalyptic words: "The sun will be darkened, and the moon will not give its light; the stars will fall from the sky, and the heavenly bodies will be shaken" (Mt 24:29, NIV).

►PREPARATION: THE SEVEN ANGELS WITH THE SEVEN LAST PLAGUES (15:1-8) Chapter 15 is related to the OT account of the exodus and is strongly suggestive of the liturgical tradition of the ancient synagogue. The chapter has two main visions: the first portrays the victors who have emerged triumphant from the great ordeal (vv 2-4); the second relates the emergence from the heavenly temple of the seven angels clothed in white and gold who hold the seven bowls of the last plagues (vv 5-8).

►THE POURING OUT OF THE BOWL JUDGMENTS (16:1-21) These occur in rapid succession with only a brief pause for a dialogue between the third angel and the altar, accentuating the justice of God's punishments (vv 5-7). This rapid succession is probably due to John's desire to give a telescopic view of the first six bowls and to hasten then on to the seventh, where the far more interesting judgment on Babylon occurs, concerning which the author will give a detailed account. The final three

plagues are social and spiritual in their effect and shift from nature to humanity.

►THE PROSTITUTE AND THE BEAST (17:1-18) To a majority of modern interpreters, Babylon represents the city of Rome. The beast stands for the Roman Empire as a whole, including its provinces and peoples. However, it is not sufficient simply to identify Babylon with Rome. For that matter, Babylon cannot be confined to any one historical manifestation, past or future; it has multiple equivalents (cf. 11:8). Babylon is found wherever there is satanic deception. Babylon is better understood here as the archetypal head of all entrenched worldly resistance to God. Babylon is a transhistorical reality that includes idolatrous kingdoms as diverse as Sodom, Egypt, Babylon, Tyre, Nineveh, and Rome. Babylon is an eschatological symbol of satanic deception and power; it is a divine mystery that can never be wholly reducible to empirical earthly institutions. Babylon represents the total culture of the world apart from God, while the divine system is depicted by the New Jerusalem. Rome is simply one manifestation of the total system.

►THE FALL OF BABYLON THE GREAT (18:1-24) Chapter 18 contains the description of the previously announced judgment on the prostitute (17:1). Under the imagery of the destruction of a great commercial city, John describes the final overthrow of the great prostitute, Babylon.

►THANKSGIVING FOR THE DESTRUCTION OF BABYLON (19:1-5) In stark contrast to the laments of Babylon's consorts, the heavenly choirs burst forth in a great liturgy of celebration to God.

►THE MARRIAGE OF THE LAMB (19:6-10) Finally, the cycle of praise is completed with the reverberating sounds of another great multitude (v 6): the redeemed throng (cf. 7:9). They utter the final Hallel in words reminiscent of the great royal psalms (Pss 93:1; 97:1; 99:1).

The Vision of the Return of Christ and the Consummation of the Age (19:11–20:15)

►THE FIRST AND SECOND LAST THINGS: THE RIDER ON THE WHITE HORSE AND THE DESTRUCTION OF THE BEAST (19:11-21) This vision, which depicts the return of Christ and the final overthrow of the beast, may be viewed as the climax of the previous section (vv 1-10) or as the first of a final series of seven last things—namely, the return of Christ; the defeat of the beast; the binding of Satan; the Millennium; the release and final end of Satan; the last judgment; and the new heaven, the new earth, and the new Jerusalem.

Although Satan has been dealt a death blow at the cross (cf. Jn 12:31; 16:11), he nevertheless continues to promulgate evil and deception during this present age (cf. Eph 2:2; 1 Thes 3:5; 1 Pt 5:8-9; Rv 2:10). Yet he is a deposed ruler who is now under the sovereign authority of Christ. Satan is allowed to continue his evil for a short time until God's purposes are finished. In this scene of the overthrow of the beast, his kings, and their armies, John shows us the ultimate and swift destruction of these evil powers by the King of kings and Lord of lords. They have met their Master in this final and utterly real confrontation (Rv 19:17-21).

►THE THIRD AND FOURTH LAST THINGS: THE BINDING OF SATAN AND THE MILLENNIUM (20:1-6) The Millennium has been called one of the most controversial and intriguing questions of eschatology. The main problem is whether the reference to a Millennium (thousand years) indicates an earthly historical reign of peace that will manifest itself at the close of this present age, or whether the whole passage is symbolic of some present experience of Christians or some future nonhistorical reality. The former view is called premillennial (i.e., Christ's second coming precedes the Millennium), the latter is amillennial (i.e., there is no literal Millenium).

The binding of Satan removes his deceptive activities from the earth (vv 1-3) during the time the martyred saints are resurrected and rule with Christ (vv 4-6).

▶THE FIFTH LAST THING: THE RELEASE AND FINAL END OF SATAN (20:7-10) In Ezekiel 38–39, "Gog" refers to the prince of a host of pagan invaders from the North, especially the Scythian hordes from the distant land of Magog. In Revelation, however, the names are symbolic of the final enemies of Christ duped by Satan into attacking the community of the saints.

▶THE SIXTH LAST THING: THE GREAT WHITE THRONE JUDGMENT (20:11-15) The language of poetic imagery captures the fading character of everything that is of the world (1 Jn 2:15-17). Now the only reality is God seated on the throne of judgment, before whom all must appear (Heb 9:27). His verdict is holy and righteous (expressed symbolically by the white throne). This vision declares that even though it may have seemed that the course of earth's history ran contrary to his holy will, no single day or hour in the world's drama has ever detracted from the absolute sovereignty of God.

▶THE SEVENTH LAST THING: THE NEW HEAVEN AND THE NEW EARTH AND THE NEW JERUSALEM (21:1–22:5) John here discloses a theology in stone, gold as pure as glass, and color. Archetypal images abound. The church is called the bride (21:2). God gives the thirsty "the springs of the water of life without charge!" (v 6). Completeness is implied in the number 12 and its multiples (vv 12-14, 16-17, 21), and fullness in the cubical shape of the city (v 16). Colorful jewels abound, as do references to light and the glory of God (21:11, 18-21, 23-25; 22:5). There is the "river of the water of life" (22:1) and the "tree of life" (v 2). The "sea" is gone (21:1).

Allusions to the OT abound. Most of John's imagery in this chapter reflects Isaiah 60 and 65 and Ezekiel 40–48. John weaves Isaiah's vision of the new Jerusalem together with Ezekiel's vision of the new temple. The multiple OT promises converging in John's mind seem to indicate that he viewed the new Jerusalem as the fulfillment of all these strands of prophecy. There are also allusions to Genesis 1–3: the absence of death and suffering, the dwelling of God with his people as in Eden, the tree of life, the removal of the curse. Creation is restored to its pristine character.

The connection of this vision with the promises to the overcomers in the letters to the seven churches (Rv 2–3) is significant. For example, to the overcomers at Ephesus was granted the right to the tree of life (2:7; cf. 22:2); at Thyatira, the right to rule the nations (2:26; cf. 22:5); at Philadelphia, the name of the city of God, the new Jerusalem (3:12; cf. 21:2, 9-27). In a sense, a strand from every major section of the Apocalypse appears in chapters 21–22.

John's Conclusion (22:6-21) With consummate artistry, the words of the introduction (1:1-8) are sounded again in the conclusion: the book ends with the voices of the angel, Jesus, the Spirit, the bride, and finally John: "Amen. Come, Lord Jesus" (22:20).

See also Apocalyptic; Daniel, Book of; Eschatology; John, the Apostle.

REVENGE, REVENGER See Avenger of Blood.

REWARD Recompense for good or evil; most often it suggests a benefit for favorable compensation. Both

good and evil are rewarded or punished, and man's responsibility and accountability are involved in an ethical sense. Related terms such as "wages," "hire," "recompense," or "requital" are a part of the broader concept. In this fullest sense, the operation of reward ranges from the consequences resulting from dealings between people to God's compensation for obedience or disobedience, from the consequences of actions felt in this life to divine recompense in the life to come.

To Greek and Hebrew minds, the concept of reward suggested the ideal of the wholeness of an action, the completion of a deed. Just as work was completed for a man in the payment of wages, so it was assumed that an action naturally carried certain results, either reward or punishment. The overtones of commercial transactions were not absent, as when the reward is referred to as "wages." Thus Paul says, "The wages of sin is death" (Rom 6:23). The idea involves an equal return commensurate with the action performed.

The biblical conception of reward was both ethical and religious. The covenant of God made with Israel was evidence of God's loving favor; it promised good things to Israel on the condition of their obedience to God's commands. Disobedience was a violation of the covenant and would bring disaster and death. Deuteronomy 28 spells out the blessings that obedience would bring and also the national disasters that would come upon Israel if they did not observe what was right and good in the sight of the Lord (see also Lv 26). In the period of the wilderness wanderings, failure to obey on the part of the people and their leaders brought suffering and death. The history of the judges and the kings was written in terms of reward for faithfulness and punishment for sin and idolatry. Earthly victory and the national welfare depended on obedience and faithfulness to the Lord (Jos 1:7-9; cf. Jgs 2).

The pattern of reward and punishment was not always carried out. The Jews believed that God would be a merciful, forgiving God. Forgiveness involved the removal of the punishment for sin. "He does not deal with us according to our sins, nor requite us according to our iniquities" (Ps 103:10, RSV).

The writer of Ecclesiastes found that life did not work out so neatly and that the doctrine of retribution did not always apply in the span of an individual life. There is a somewhat cynical note when the righteous suffer and the wicked prosper. Job's friends take the position that his sickness is the result of some hidden sin. Job maintains his integrity, and for him the answer lies outside the pattern of strict reward for righteousness and punishment for evil. In the outcome Job is rewarded for his good life.

In Jesus' day Judaism had changed significantly. The legal system of the judges had been replaced by Roman law. But Judaism had no hesitation about recognizing the merit of good works and exhorting people to accumulate a store of merit on a basis of which God would bless them (Tob 4:7-10; Ecclus 51:30). The Pharisees believed that accurate and conscientious observance of the law would oblige God to recompense them for their performances. The individual who did much was to expect reward from God, while every transgression entailed its corresponding recompense for evil. What was not repaid in this life would be a part of a future reward.

Reward was a significant part of Jesus' teaching, especially in the Sermon on the Mount (Mt 5–7). The Beatitudes proclaimed that the blessing of God would come upon all people who exhibited certain moral characteristics (Mt 5:1-12). The individual who acts to receive the praise of others shall receive that and nothing more, but the one whose motives call him to please God shall be rewarded by God (6:1, 4, 6, 18). However, Jesus sharply curbed this idea when he taught the parable of the laborers (20:1-16). Here each was paid the same amount no matter how long he had worked. Jesus calls us to work for motives higher than reward. In the discourse on the good shepherd, the hireling who only works for wages is contrasted with the shepherd who is willing to lay down his life for the sheep (Jn 10:11-14). The servant who had only done his duty deserves no reward (Lk 17:9-10).

Beginning with Paul, the idea of reward, especially as it relates to salvation, is seen in a drastically different light. No longer is salvation considered to be the result of an individual having done more good than evil in life. Salvation is an act of divine favor that no one can earn (Rom 4:4-5). Salvation is not earned but given by a loving, beneficent God. The idea of reward does not disappear. Reward results from good done after salvation is attained. First Corinthians 3:8-14 teaches that the quality of a person's works will be examined and rewarded but that salvation does not hinge upon good works. However, works do have an important place in one's eternal destiny (Col 3:24; Rv 14:13).

See also Crown; Judgment.

REZEPH City destroyed by the Assyrians. It was mentioned in a derisive letter sent from Sennacherib, king of Assyria, to Hezekiah of Judah. Rezeph was listed along with the conquered cities of Gozan and Haran and the sons of Eden in Telassar. The Assyrian king was reminding Hezekiah that just as the local deities of these cities were not able to protect them from Assyrian conquest, so neither could Hezekiah's God preserve Jerusalem (2 Kgs 19:12; Is 37:12). Rezeph was a notable Assyrian city, known for its commerce and governing seat. It was brought into the Assyrian Empire well over a century before Hezekiah's confrontation with Sennacherib. It is perhaps identifiable with the modern Syrian city of Resafa.

REZIA* KJV spelling of Rizia, Ulla's son, in 1 Chronicles 7:39. *See* Rizia.

REZIN

1. Syrian monarch who ruled in Damascus during the earlier part of Isaiah's prophetic ministry and during the last years that the northern 10 tribes existed as a nation. Rezin was used by God to humble both Israel and Judah because they had forsaken him and rejected his covenant (2 Chr 28:5-6).

Rezin was born in the town of Bit-hadara near Damascus in the land of Syria (also called Aram). Upon his accession to the throne, the Syrian people (also called Arameans) reasserted their independence from Israel's domination. During this period, Assyria was strengthening itself and expanding its empire throughout the Near East. Along with King Menahem of Israel, Rezin was forced to pay tribute to the Assyrian monarch Tiglath-pileser III in 738 BC. The heavy burden of vassalage to the Assyrians generated anti-Assyrian sentiment among the Syrian and neighboring people. During this time, Rezin seems to have helped Pekah in his successful coup to seize the throne of Israel. Immediately upon his accession to the throne, Pekah formed an anti-Assyrian coalition with Rezin. They soon realized that successful resistance against Assyria required a larger alliance. They invited King Ahaz of Judah to join their coalition, but Ahaz adamantly refused. With the intention of placing an Aramean of Davidic lineage upon the throne of Judah in order to effect a broader Syrian-Israelite alliance,

Rezin and Pekah joined in an attack on Judah. In spite of winning most battles, Rezin and Pekah were unsuccessful in their attempt to take Jerusalem and replace Ahaz (2 Chr 28:5-15; Is 7:1-9). During these dark days for Judah, Isaiah brought an encouraging word to the people. He prophesied the imminent destruction of Israel (Ephraim) and Damascus by Assyria (Is 7:1-9; 8:1-8). So certain was the destruction of these kingdoms that he referred to their two kings as "stubs of smoldering firebrands" about to be extinguished (7:4). Disregarding Isaiah's prophecy, Ahaz sent a large sum of money to Tiglath-pileser III, hoping to induce him to come to Judah's aid.

Rezin and Pekah moved their forces to the north to prepare for the impending Assyrian invasion. Tiglath-pileser attacked in 733 BC and captured much of the area of Galilee. He then turned his attention to Damascus, to which Rezin had fled. Assyrian records refer to Rezin as a "caged bird" in besieged Damascus. When Damascus fell in 732 BC, Rezin was executed and many citizens of Damascus were exiled. Samaria, the capital city of Israel, fell to the Assyrians in 722 BC. Damascus and the nation of Syria became an Assyrian province. Rezin thus was the last Syrian king to reign in Damascus.

2. Father of some of the temple servants who served in postexilic times (Ezr 2:48; Neh 7:50).

REZON Son of Eliada, who set himself up as ruler of Damascus and Syria following David's killing of Hadadezer, king of Zobah. Rezon was a God-appointed adversary who despised Israel and was a constant problem to Solomon during his reign (1 Kgs 11:23-25).

RHEGIUM Important Italian harbor visited by Paul in his journey to Rome (Acts 28:13). From Malta, Paul's ship traveled north to the Sicilian capital of Syracuse. Then, in the absence of a south wind, they may have tacked into the Strait of Messina, finding good harbor at Rhegium. Another south wind carried them from Rhegium to Puteoli in the Bay of Naples—the ship's destination, since Puteoli was southern Italy's chief port, receiving the great Alexandrian grain vessels.

The Strait of Messina was well known to every Roman navigator. Passage here was necessary in order to gain access to Italy's west coast, but its obstacles were numerous. Obstructions, shallows, and the narrow width forced ships to stay at Rhegium until an adequate south wind arose.

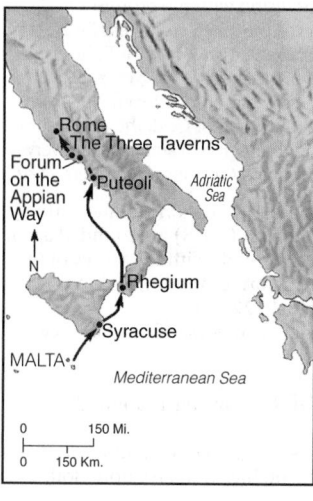

Rhegium Paul stopped by the Italian harbor of Rhegium on his way to Rome.

The name Rhegium (modern Reggio or Reggio di Calabria) may have come from a Greek verb meaning "to tear" or "rend." Sicily, it seemed, had been "torn from the mainland" and Rhegium was the nearest Italian port.

RHESA Descendant of Zerubbabel and an ancestor of Jesus Christ (Lk 3:27). *See* Genealogy of Jesus Christ.

RHODA Maid in the home of Mary the mother of John Mark in Jerusalem. Rhoda reported to those in the house that Peter was standing outside the door. Since they were unaware of his release from prison, the others at first did not believe her report (Acts 12:13-15).

RHODES Port of call on Paul's return trip to Jerusalem from his third missionary journey (Acts 21:1). The mention of Rhodes in Genesis 10:4, Ezekiel 27:15, and 1 Chronicles 1:7 is not based on the Hebrew text of the OT but on its Greek translation. The island of Rhodes, an area of more than 500 square miles (1,295 square kilometers), is situated near the southeast coast of modern Turkey.

In Paul's time the island had long been an important establishment of Dorian Greek culture, with several cities. Rhodes, the capital, lay on the busiest ancient sea route between the ports of Italy and the province of Asia to the west, and those of Syria and Egypt to the east. It was distinguished for its natural harbor and public works. Rhodes was a prominent center for business and supplied most of the precedents for Roman law of the sea. The second century BC marked the height of its political power, which included control of most of Caria and Lycia on the mainland of Asia Minor. Roman power first deprived Rhodes of its commercial domination, and during the Roman civil wars of the first century BC, it was reduced politically to little more than a provincial town in the Roman Empire.

To celebrate a military victory in 280 BC, the city of Rhodes erected an immense bronze statue of the Greek sun god, 121 feet (36.9 meters) tall—about the height of the Statue of Liberty. It was 12 years in the making, and soon after its completion, an earthquake broke it off at the knees (224 BC). But the fragmented ruins remained as a curiosity until Arab occupation of the island in the seventh century. This Colossus of Rhodes was included in some ancient lists of wonders of the world.

RHODOCUS A Jewish traitor who gave military information to the Syrians regarding the fortification of Beth-zur by Judas Maccabeus. When discovered, he was found guilty and imprisoned (2 Macc 13:21).

RIBAI Benjaminite of Gibeah and the father of Ittai, one of David's mighty men (2 Sm 23:29; 1 Chr 11:31).

RIBLAH
1. Town along the Orontes River located some 35 miles (56.3 kilometers) northeast of Baalbek, identifiable with modern Ribleh in Syria. Riblah was well situated topographically for military operations, especially when the great powers of Egypt and Mesopotamia were crossing the northern part of the Fertile Crescent. The Egyptians are mentioned in Scripture as the first people that troubled this town. After the death of King Josiah in his battle with the Egyptian pharaoh Neco, Jehoahaz was made king. Neco did not approve of the election. So the pharaoh imprisoned Jehoahaz at Riblah and made Eliakim (Jehoiakim), Jehoahaz's brother, king of Judah (2 Kgs 23:33).

After the defeat of Neco at Carchemish in 605 BC, Nebuchadnezzar of Babylon took control of the area, making Riblah his headquarters for his South-Syria and Palestine dominions. When Zedekiah, king of Judah, opposed Nebuchadnezzar, the Babylonians captured him and imprisoned him at Riblah (2 Kgs 25:6; Jer 39:5-6; 52:9-10). Consequently, many of Zedekiah's sons were killed at Riblah, and Zedekiah was bound and taken to Babylon (2 Kgs 25:20-21; Jer 52:26-27).

Riblah is also called Diblah (ASV) and Diblath (KJV) in Ezekiel 6:14.

2. Town defining part of the eastern boundary of Israel, located east of Ain (Nm 34:11). Its exact location is unknown, though it is probably not identifiable with #1 above.

RICHES Wealth measured by money or the amount of property owned, whether land and buildings (Is 5:8-10), livestock (1 Sm 25:2-3), or slaves (8:11-18). Great riches brought great influence and power, as the Hebrew word for wealth implies.

The Bible seems to speak with two voices on the subject of riches, sometimes describing material wealth as a sign of God's blessing and approval (e.g., Gn 24:35), at other times virtually identifying the rich with the wicked (e.g., Ps 37:7, 16).

God made all things for people to enjoy (1 Tm 6:17). That is why being rich is a matter for thanksgiving, not embarrassment. Every possession that a person can possibly own comes from the Creator (Ps 24:1), so all wealth can rightly be counted as a blessing from God. It was in this spirit that David could pray to God, "Riches and honour come of thee" (1 Chr 29:12, KJV). Even when wealth is earned by hard work, the Bible reminds its readers that both their talents and their resources are God-given. Jesus illustrates this important lesson in the parables of the 10 talents (Mt 25:14-30) and the 10 minas (Lk 19:11-26).

Nowhere, then, does the Bible say that having possessions and becoming wealthy are wrong in themselves. There would be no point in the Ten Commandments' ban on stealing and envy if it was wrong for God's people to own anything at all. Jesus himself never taught that it was sinful to be rich.

However, Jesus warned that riches could keep a person out of the kingdom: "How hard it is for rich people to get into the Kingdom of God!" (Mk 10:23, NLT). Affluence, he taught, can destroy peace (6:24-34), blind people to the needs of others (Lk 16:19-31), stand between individuals and the gateway to eternal life (Mk 10:17-27), and even bring God's judgment (Lk 12:16-21). He told his disciples not to accumulate personal wealth (Mt 6:19), and he praised those who gave up their possessions (19:29).

Jesus' warnings against wealth are not, in fact, directed against riches in themselves. What he condemns is the wrong attitudes many people have toward acquiring wealth, and the wrong ways in which they use it. Longing for riches, not having them, chokes the spiritual life like weeds in a field of grain (Mt 13:22). The greedy desire to have more wealth doomed the unforgiving servant (18:23-35). And the rich man's selfishness, not his wealth, sealed his fate (Lk 16:19-26). Paul captured the main theme in these parables when he said, "The *love* of money is at the root of all kinds of evil" (1 Tm 6:10, NLT, emphasis added).

The greatest danger of all arises when riches gain the mastery in a person's life. The whole Bible warns against this idolatrous attitude to material things (e.g., Dt 8:17-18; Lk 14:15-24). Satan tempted Jesus to put material wealth and power in God's place (Mt 4:8-9), and Jesus delivers the clearest warning against making money one's master (6:24). In this light Jesus instructs the rich young ruler to sell everything (Mk 10:17-22). Here was a wealthy man who had allowed his possessions to possess him. Jesus' aim was to make him recognize his bondage so he could escape from his self-made prison. The fact that he turned away from Jesus demonstrates the powerful pull of riches.

These blunt warnings are the most striking aspect of Jesus' teaching on wealth. But alongside his exposure of wrong attitudes he was careful to sketch in the outline of right attitudes. Those who recognize that they are God's trustees (not owners) of their possessions, he taught, will find many valuable outlets for their riches in the Lord's service (Lk 12:42-44). Instead of making them tight-fisted, their riches should allow them to express love in many practical ways (2 Cor 8:2). And instead of having their inward peace ruined by anxious greed, they would find the secret of serenity in an increasing sense of dependence on their heavenly Giver (Lk 12:29-31; 1 Tm 6:17).

According to the Bible, then, the morality of riches depends entirely on personal attitudes. And nowhere does this come out more than in the frequent comparisons Scripture draws between material and spiritual wealth. Those who make material riches their goal in life have wrong values. However wealthy they may appear, they are poverty-stricken in God's sight (Mt 16:26; Rv 3:17). In his view, the truly rich are those whose main aim in life is to serve him as King (Mt 13:44-46). Their wealth lies in the currency of faith and good works (1 Tm 6:18; Jas 2:5)—a heavenly bank balance that no one can steal and nothing can erode: "Wherever your treasure is, there your heart and thoughts will also be" (Mt 6:21, NLT).

See also Money; Poor, The; Wages; Wealth.

RIDDLE Word puzzle widely used and esteemed in the ancient world, both as an everyday amusement and as a test of wisdom at a more serious level. The point of a riddle was the discovery of a concealed meaning. Riddles, therefore, may be broadly distinguished from fables, which, like Jotham's celebrated plant fable (Jgs 9:7-15), contained an easily discerned significance. Obviously, there is an intermediate area where there is no sharp differentiation. For instance, Ezekiel's riddle (Ez 17) has sometimes been classified as a plant fable.

Samson's riddle at his wedding feast is the best-known biblical riddle (Jgs 14). Probably it was a form of diversion used on such occasions (vv 12-13). The riddle took the form of a couplet: "From the one who eats came something to eat; out of the strong came something sweet" (v 14). Samson's 30 young men threatened his betrothed, who wheedled the secret from him: "What is sweeter than honey? What is stronger than a lion?" (v 18).

Solomon's wisdom was demonstrated in his ability to answer the "hard questions" (lit., "riddles") of the queen of Sheba (1 Kgs 10:1-4). His reputation for this kind of wisdom is further demonstrated by Ben Sirach: "Your soul covered the earth, and you filled it with parables and riddles" (Ecclus 47:15).

Josephus notes a contest of wits between Solomon and Hiram, with riddles being exchanged. Solomon won the earlier exchanges, but Hiram finally outwitted him by enlisting outside help (*Antiquities* 8.5.5). Such wisdom to solve riddles was, understandably, claimed by Israel's wise men (e.g., Ps 49:4; Prv 1:6). In Daniel 8:23-24 there is the apocalyptic vision of "a master of intrigue [who]

will rise to power" (lit. "one who understands riddles"). Daniel himself possessed the same ability to "interpret dreams, explain riddles, and solve difficult problems" (Dn 5:12).

In the NT riddles figure infrequently. The various "hard sayings" of Jesus (e.g., Jn 6:60) are difficult to accept and are equally as hard to understand. Possibly the only true riddle is the number of the beast, 666 (Rv 13:18). Various attempts have been made to identify a person, after the pattern of numerical references in contemporary literature. Of these, the emperor Nero is the most plausible candidate.

RIE* KJV rendering of spelt, a common form of wheat in Bible times, in Exodus 9:32. *See* Food and Food Preparation; Plants (Spelt).

RIGHTEOUSNESS The establishment of a right relationship—primarily between God and people, secondarily between people themselves. Righteousness is the fulfillment of just expectations in any relationship, whether with God or other people. It is applicable at all levels of society and is relevant in every area of life. Therefore, righteousness denotes the fulfilled expectations in relationships between man and wife, parents and children, fellow citizens, employer and employee, merchant and customers, ruler and citizens, and God and people. Depending on the fulfillment of one's expectations, an individual could be called righteous and his or her acts and speech could be designated as righteous. The opposite of righteous is "evil," "wicked," or "wrong" (cf. Ps 1:6; Zep 3:5).

In Israel the concept of righteousness transformed all of life, both religious and secular. Israel had been called into existence as a separate nation through which Yahweh was to witness to the nations concerning his universal rule, his nature, and his expectations of life on earth. This meant that Israel required a revelation from God so that they might learn his will and be instructed in maintaining a relationship with him. The quality of a person's relationship with God is directly linked to his relationship with his fellow human.

God is righteous (2 Chr 12:6; Pss 7:9; 103:17; Zep 3:5; Zec 8:8). His righteousness is dynamic, since it describes his acts on behalf of his people and also the nature of his relationship with them. All of God's acts are righteous (cf. Dt 32:4; Jgs 5:11; Ps 103:6), and God's people rejoiced in the righteous acts of God (Ps 89:16). Because God is righteous, he expects righteousness of others, who are to reflect the nature of their Creator. The expected response to God's rule is in the form of righteousness, that is, conformity to his rule and will. In this basic sense, Noah is called "righteous" because he walked with God and showed integrity in comparison to his contemporaries (Gn 6:9). After humanity's fall and acts of rebellion, culminating in the Flood and the dispersion at Babel, God renewed his relationship with humanity in Abraham and his descendants. Abraham was righteous because he ordered his life by the revealed will of God (15:6; cf. 17:1; 18:19; 26:5).

The Lord revealed to Israel even more clearly how they were to relate to him and to each other. The law in Israel was for the purpose of helping the people of God to live in conformity to the will of God and thereby be righteous. The person who was devoted to the service of God in worship and life was called righteous (cf. Mal 3:18). Thus, righteousness is a state of integrity in relation to God and one's neighbor, expressing itself in one's acts and speech.

The hope for an era characterized by righteousness was

rooted in the prophetic revelation of the messianic rule and the establishment of God's kingdom on earth (Is 11:1-9), whose rule will extend to the nations (vv 10-16) and last forever (9:7). Isaiah developed the revelation of the glorious, victorious entrance of the kingdom of God in a most exquisite way, when his enemies will be subdued and his people will be gathered together and will live in a state of peace in his presence. The acts of restoration, extending from Israel's return from exile until the final coming of the external kingdom are, in his prophetic purview, the demonstration of God's righteous acts. He forgives, restores, remains faithful, loves, elects, and sends his Spirit to renew his people and to bestow on them all the benefits of the renewed covenant relationship. Both Jews and Gentiles will be the recipients of his righteous acts (Is 45:8, 23; 46:13, 48:18; 51:5, 8, 16; 56:1; 59:17; 60:17; 61:10-11).

Out of concern for the salvation of his people and the establishment of his everlasting kingdom, God revealed his righteousness in the sending of his beloved Son. The coming of Christ marks an era of renewal of his relationship with people, the renewal of the covenant and renewal of his kingdom on earth. The older covenant was mediated by Moses; the covenant was renewed by the Son of God, who came "to fulfill all righteousness" (Mt 3:15). The message of Jesus is consistent with the OT in the close identification of God's kingdom with his righteousness (6:33; 13:43). Jesus also taught that God expects all people to live in harmony with his will (7:21). Jesus is God's final revelation of what God requires of individuals so as to enter the kingdom and to live righteously.

But individuals cannot attain this righteousness by their own merits; it is a gift from God (Rom 3:21–5:21). There is no righteousness apart from Jesus Christ. In the proclamation of the gospel of Jesus we discover that "it is through faith that a righteous person has life" (Rom 1:17; cf. Hb 2:4). Therefore, the Father requires acceptance of his Son as his appointed means of justification (Rom 3:25-26; 5:9). God declares people to be righteous when they put their trust in his Son (Rom 8:33-34; 2 Cor 3:18; 11:15). God pardons sins, is reconciled with sinners, and grants his peace to them (Rom 5:1, 9-11; Eph 2:14-17). Those who have been declared righteous enjoy a new relationship. They are "sons of God" by adoption. The Father relates to his children righteously and expects them to relate righteously to him.

The fullness of righteousness will be manifest at the coming of the Lord Jesus, when all those who have been justified will also be glorified (Rom 8:30). The goal of salvation history moves toward the final glorious manifestation of God's kingdom, when all creation will be renewed in "righteousness"—that is, all creation will be right with God (2 Pt 3:13).

See also God, Being and Attributes of; Justification, Justified; Law, Biblical Concept of.

RIGHT HAND The word "right" in the Bible is often used in the sense of "being straight"; it is used to describe that which is just or righteous (cf. Gn 18:25). Figuratively speaking, God's right hand is the means whereby victories are obtained for the people of God (Pss 17:7, 98:1); it is also an instrument of punishment for the ungodly (Hb 2:16). While the right hand of man is impotent to save (Jb 40:14), God's right hand sustains his children in the hour of need (Ps 139:10). Furthermore, God promises to strengthen the right hand of the person he purposes to help (Is 41:13).

To be at the right hand of God is to occupy a place of the choicest blessings (Ps 16:11); it is the place where the Lord Jesus Christ now reigns in glory and intercedes for those he has redeemed (Rom 8:34).

To offer the right hand of fellowship is to extend the warmest and most accepting type of camaraderie (Gal 2:9). Giving the right hand as the sign of a pledge also has a biblical antecedent (2 Kgs 10:15).

Although the left hand is often linked to blessings (Prv 3:16), it may also be associated with treachery or other undesirable activity (Eccl 10:2).

See also Hand.

RIMMON (Person)
1. Benjaminite of Beeroth, whose two sons, Baanah and Recab, assassinated Ishbosheth (2 Sm 4:2, 5, 9).
2. Deity revered by the Syrians of Damascus, whose temple was frequented by Naaman, captain of the Syrian army, and his master (2 Kgs 5:18). *See* Syria, Syrians.

RIMMON (Place)
1. Alternate name for En-rimmon, a town in southern Judah, in Joshua 15:32 and 1 Chronicles 4:32. *See* En-rimmon.
2. Town in the territory allotted to Zebulun's tribe for an inheritance (Jos 19:13); alternately called Dimnah in Joshua 21:35.
3. Large cave about 12 miles (19.3 kilometers) north of Jerusalem and 2 miles (3.2 kilometers) south of biblical Ephraim (modern Taiyiba), also called the Rock of Rimmon. Six hundred refugees from the city of Gibeah found shelter in the cave for four months (Jgs 20:45-47; 21:13).

RIMMON, Rock of Large cave north of Jerusalem (Jgs 20:45-47; 21:13). *See* Rimmon (Place) #3.

RIMMONO A town in the territory of Zebulun (1 Chr 6:77).

RIMMON-PEREZ Temporary camping place of the Israelites during their wilderness wanderings, mentioned between Rithmah and Libnah (Nm 33:19-20). *See* Wilderness Wanderings.

RINNAH Shimon's son from Judah's tribe (1 Chr 4:20).

RIPHATH Gomer's son and the brother of Ashkenaz and Togarmah, non-Semitic descendants of Noah through Japheth's line (Gn 10:3). First Chronicles 1:6, a parallel passage, reads Diphath instead of Riphath, undoubtedly a latter copyist's misspelling that was never corrected.

RISSAH Stopping place for Israel in the wilderness between Libnah and Kehelathah (Nm 33:21-22). *See* Wilderness Wanderings.

RITHMAH Stopping place for Israel in the wilderness between Hazeroth and Rimmon-perez (Nm 33:18-19). *See* Wilderness Wanderings.

RIVER OF EGYPT*
1. Alternate name for the border of Egypt (possibly the Nile River) in Genesis 15:18.
2. Alternate name for the brook of Egypt. *See* Brook of Egypt.

RIVER OF THE WILDERNESS*
KJV reading for an unidentifiable brook in the Arabah in Amos 6:14; called brook of the Arabah in the RSV (NLT "valley of the Arabah"). *See* Brook of the Arabah.

RIZIA Capable leader and mighty warrior, Ulla's son from Asher's tribe (1 Chr 7:39).

RIZPAH Daughter of Aiah and a concubine of Saul. She bore two sons, Armoni and Mephibosheth, to Saul. In a dispute between Ishbosheth and Abner, Ishbosheth accused Abner of having relations with Rizpah, suggesting an attempt to become a royal claimant to Saul's throne. Infuriated at this apparent false accusation, Abner vowed to assist David in defeating Saul and to make David king of Israel (2 Sm 3:7-10). During the reign of David, Rizpah's two sons, along with five other sons of Saul, were killed by the Gibeonites as reparation for Saul's unwarranted slaughter of the sons of Gibeon. Rizpah courageously protected her son's exposed bodies from natural predators until they were buried by David (2 Sm 21:8-11).

ROBBER, ROBBERY *See* Criminal Law and Punishment.

ROBOAM* KJV rendering of Rehoboam, Solomon's son, in Matthew 1:7. *See* Rehoboam.

ROCK BADGER *See* Animals (Badger).

RODANIM Fourth son of Javan and a descendant of Noah through Japheth's line (1 Chr 1:7). An alternate spelling in Genesis 10:4 reads Dodanim, possibly a copyist's error. Both words probably refer to the Greek peoples of Rhodes and its neighboring islands in the Aegean Sea.

ROE*, ROEBUCK *See* Animals (Deer; Gazelle).

ROGELIM Home of Barzillai the Gileadite, who served David at Mahanaim, where David sought refuge from Absalom (2 Sm 17:27; 19:31). Rogelim was situated in the highlands east of the Jordan River.

ROHGAH Shemer's son from Asher's tribe (1 Chr 7:34).

ROLL* Leather or papyrus scroll. *See* Writing.

ROMAMTI-EZER Heman's son and a musician appointed by King David to serve in the sanctuary (1 Chr 25:4, 31).

ROMANS, Letter to the

PREVIEW
•Author
•Date, Origin, and Destination
•Background
•Audience
•Purpose and Theological Teaching
•Content

Author Written in the first person (Rom 1:5, 10, etc.), this epistle was authored by the apostle Paul. (The first words of the first verse are "Paul, a slave of Christ Jesus, called an apostle.") The actual transcription of the letter, however, was done by Tertius (16:22), who acted as Paul's amanuensis (secretary). The letter's authenticity has never been disputed by reputable scholarship, liberal or conservative, and Romans stands at the head of virtually every ancient list or collection of Pauline letters.

Date, Origin, and Destination The destination of the letter is stated to be Rome (1:7). That Paul was in Corinth at the time of the writing seems clear from his reference to Erastus in 16:23 as the treasurer of the city. An inscription in the stone pavement beside the large theater in Corinth states that it was laid by Erastus, the city treasurer, in appreciation for his election. This could hardly be coincidental. Erastus evidently remained in Corinth, because it is mentioned as his home (2 Tm 4:20). Furthermore, Paul refers to Gaius as his host at the time he wrote Romans (Rom 16:23), probably the same Gaius who lived in Corinth (1 Cor 1:14). Finally, Phoebe, likely the carrier of this epistle, was a deaconess of the church at Cenchrea, the eastern port of Corinth (Rom 16:1).

From the epistle itself we can determine when Paul wrote it. Romans 15:23-28 indicates that Paul was just about ready to make his visit to Jerusalem with a contribution for its Christian poor from the churches of Macedonia and Achaia, after which his purpose was to visit Rome on his way to Spain (15:23-28). He carried this contribution with him from Corinth, at the close of his third visit to that city, which lasted three months (Acts 20:2, 23; 24:17). On this occasion certain persons accompanied him from Corinth, whose names are given by the historian of Acts (20:4), and four of these are expressly mentioned in this epistle as being with the apostle when he wrote it—Timothy, Sosipater, Gaius, and Erastus (Rom 16:21, 23). Paul's visit to Jerusalem is usually dated around AD 57–58. As such, the Epistle to the Romans was written around the same time.

Background In a previous visit to Corinth, during his second missionary journey, Paul established the church there and remained in the city for 18 months (Acts 18:1, 11). His arrival coincided with the arrival of Priscilla and Aquila, who had recently come from Rome. At the end of his 18-month stay, Paul was brought before the newly appointed proconsul, Gallio (Acts 18:12), whose arrival can be dated from the Gallio inscription found at Delphi to the spring of AD 51. Thus, Paul arrived in Corinth in the winter of AD 49.

Leaving the city, he returned to Antioch, gave a report on his work, and set out on his last journey to collect the contribution for Jerusalem from the Gentile churches (Rom 15:25-29), for which he had previously prepared (1 Cor 16:1; 2 Cor 9:5). Continued problems in Corinth (1 Cor 1:11; 7:1) necessitated his return to the city (Acts 20:3), at which time he wrote Romans. It is clear from the last two chapters of the letter that he planned to take the contribution to Jerusalem almost immediately and from there go on to Rome (Rom 15:23-24). The occasion for the letter, therefore, is to alert the Romans to his coming so that they can assist him in his journey to Spain (15:24, 28). Rome was the only church, other than Colosse, which Paul did not establish. His letter, consequently, does not reflect awareness of specific problems in the membership there.

Audience The Roman church at this time was composed of both Jewish and Gentile believers. The church was probably started by Jewish believers who were at Jerusalem on the Day of Pentecost (Acts 2:10) and were among the 3,000 converts. Evidently, some of these took the gospel back with them to Rome. Probably some of the believers addressed in the salutations of the epistle were Christians already of long standing, if not among the earliest converts to the Christian faith. Thus, it is not improbable that up to the time of the apostle's arrival, the Christian community at Rome had been dependent upon its own members for the increase of its numbers, aided perhaps by occasional visits from preachers.

Evidently, the gospel had gone out to Gentiles,

Ancient Greek Manuscript of Romans Romans 15:11-19 in Chester Beatty Manuscript II (late second century)—P46.

because there were Gentiles in the church, as is evidenced by Paul's remarks throughout the letter. In fact, it is clear that the apostle wrote to them expressly as to a Gentile church (Rom 1:13, 15; 15:15-16). Perhaps the major constituency of the Gentiles were "God-fearers" (see Acts 10:2).

Purpose and Theological Teaching Of all the epistles of Paul, this is the most elaborate and, at the same time, the most glowing. It has just as much in common with a theological treatise as with a personal, heartfelt epistle. The major theme running throughout the book is that both Jew and Gentile have fallen short of God's glory and stand in need of salvation (Rom 3:21-31). God's righteousness has not been revealed only to the Jew—because God is not God only to the Jews but to the Gentiles as well, since there is only one God (3:29). He will justify the Jews on the basis of the saving work of Christ at Calvary, and the Gentiles on the basis of that same act of faithfulness to Abraham's promise (v 30). Their common faith gives them access to this grace (5:2). The gospel is thus to the Jew first and also to the Greek (1:16).

Once a person believes, that person is justified before God (chs 1–3). This new relationship with God provides the believer with a new life in Christ and makes him or her a part of God's people (chs 4–8). This is the deepest and most difficult part of the whole epistle; it carries us directly to the eternal springs of grace, sovereign love, and the inscrutable purposes of God. After this, we are told about the calling of the Gentiles, the preservation of a faithful Jewish remnant amidst the general unbelief and the fall of the nation, and the ultimate recovery of all Israel to constitute, with the Gentiles in the latter day, one universal church of God upon earth (chs 9–11). The remainder of the epistle is devoted to the practical application (in church life) of the truths previously revealed (chs 12–15). And then the epistle concludes with Paul's heartfelt salutations to several different believers in Rome (ch 16).

Content

Overview The thematic statement of the first eight chapters of the letter is set forth in 1:17: "It is through faith that a righteous person has life" (NLT). This quotation from Habakkuk 2:4 sets Paul's teaching on faith over against that of the OT on works. Thus, he affirms the fact that his teaching on faith is not new but is squarely rooted in the OT prophets. What was new was that the Gentiles would be fellow citizens with the Jews on the basis of faith in Christ (Eph 3:5-6). They would not have to become proselytes to Judaism in order to be acceptable to God, as some Jewish Christians demanded (Acts 15:1). This was the mystery of which Paul spoke in Ephesians (Eph 3:6).

The first part of the epistle dwells on the theme that righteousness is attained by faith. The first three chapters demonstrate that Jew and Gentile are under sin and that the redemption of Christ is applicable to both (Rom 3:21-22). The fourth chapter demonstrates that Abraham is the father of Gentiles as well as Jews, because he is the spiritual father of believing Israel just as he is of believing Gentiles. Then, in chapters 5–8, Paul deals with the latter part of the theme of how a justifed person *lives* by faith. Whether Jew or Gentile, the person who accepts the righteous acts of God on Calvary through Christ will live free from the wrath of God (ch 5), the power of sin (ch 6), the enslaving power of the law (ch 7), and the power of death (ch 8).

In chapters 9–11, Paul discusses the nation of Israel

"according to the flesh" (physical Jews) in relation to the future purpose of God, concluding that God has not cast off his people who were Israelites descended from Abraham (11:1-2). He can regraft them back into the tree from which they have been cut off, if they will accept Jesus as their Messiah (v 23).

Then in his closing section, he discusses the implications of the first 11 chapters for everyday Christian living (chs 12–16), closing the book with a reminder of the importance of the "offering of the Gentiles" through his own ministry (ch 15).

In Detail In the first chapter Paul argues that the pagan Gentile world was in a state of rebellion against God, and the wrath of God had been revealed against their ungodliness (1:18). Even though God had given sufficient revelation of his existence to them in the world of nature, they had nevertheless become polytheistic and idolatrous, with all the accompanying moral degradations (vv 20-23). Thus, three times Paul emphasizes that God gave them up to their lusts (v 24), to dishonorable passions (v 26), and to a base mind and improper conduct (v 28). The meaning is that he passed over their sins (3:25), overlooked their spiritual ignorance of his true existence (Acts 17:30), and did not put a stop to such idolatry (7:42).

The Jews fared little better because, even though they had received the law of Moses containing a revelation of the will of God for their nation, they had not kept the law (2:17-29). Even the Gentiles had those among them who did by nature the things contained in the law and were acceptable because their consciences were pure (vv 14-15). For a Jew, keeping the law was insufficient unless he did so as a spiritual conviction, not as a mere legal requirement (v 29). God-fearing Gentiles who kept the essence of the law were a model for condemning the Jews who did not (vv 14, 27). However, the faithlessness of the chosen nation did not nullify the faithfulness of God to the fulfillment of the promise to Abraham (3:3). Although the Jew had every advantage over the Gentile, he was no better off because both had given themselves over to the power of sin (vv 1, 9). The situation now was that "all have sinned [both Jew and Gentile] and fall short of the glory of God" (v 23, RSV).

God had therefore made Christ the Redeemer for the sins of the world (3:21-31). The righteousness of God had been manifested apart from the law, through the "faith of Christ" (v 22; i.e., the faithfulness of Christ to the promise) and was available to the Gentile as well as Jew on the basis of personal faith. If this righteousness were available only through keeping the commandments of the law, as good and holy as it was (7:12), then God was a God of Jews only and not of Gentiles, because the law was given to the Jews (3:29). But God is also the God of the Gentiles and justifies the Jew on the basis of Christ's faithfulness, and the Gentile on the basis of that same faithful act. Christ died for all who believe in him (v 22). Thus God's righteousness was manifested through Christ's faithfulness (vv 3, 22) and provides the basis of salvation for everyone who believes (5:9).

Several times in the fourth chapter Paul insists that Abraham was the father of the Jews and of the Gentiles (vv 11-12, 16-18). Christ's faithfulness to the promise to Abraham that all nations (Gentiles) would be blessed through his seed (the descendants of Isaac) enabled Abraham to become the father of all nations, that is, of all who believe (v 11).

Having laid this broad theological base, Paul then argues that the impact of this justification or righteousness is that all believers experience salvation from the wrath of God and thereby experience peace (5:1, 9). Sin entered the world through the first transgression and passed to all people (v 12). Justification, however, was brought by the second Adam, Christ, who gives salvation to those who believe and receive the abundance of his grace (vv 16-18).

The function of the law was not to save the Jew. It was added because of transgressions (Gal 3:19); it served to intensify the awareness of sin, present in all people, to the point of transgression of the law (Rom 5:20). Sin used the law to deceive and destroy those who tried to keep it (7:11). Paul had known what it was to covet before he knew the law, but when he became subject to the dictates and penalties of the law at age 12 or 13, the commandment against covetousness became even more demanding and destroyed him (7:11). After the law was known, the penalty for its disobedience was fully applicable. Sin had been intensified because it became a transgression of the law. This very fact caused the need for greater grace, because where sin abounded, grace abounded all the more (5:20). But it would be a gross perversion of what it means to live free from wrath, law, sin, and death to argue that one should therefore continue in sin that grace may abound (6:1). Paul argues that those who have been justified and saved by Christ have died to the power of sin, which no longer has enslaving power (vv 2, 6). The key thought here is that sin (i.e., Satan—sin personified) cannot exercise dominion over the believer (vv 9, 14); it cannot reign over him (v 12) and make him its slave (vv 17, 20).

In addition to being liberated from God's anger, the law, and sin, those who have been justified by faith have been freed from death, and God will give life to their mortal bodies through his Spirit (8:2, 11). If they live according to the flesh, they will die; but if they live by the Spirit, they will enjoy a liberating life (vv 6-13). Not even death will be able to separate them from the love of Christ (v 38). The Spirit leads them and helps in their human infirmity, praying and interceding for them just as Christ does (vv 14, 26, 34).

Paul does not discuss the pragmatic application of these theological principles until chapter 12. In between, he deals with the issue of how and why the Jews could have rejected the Messiah. How is it that they, of all people on earth, with the history of God's personal involvement with them, could have rejected the Promised One? Chapters 9-11 focus on this important question.

Paul's answer is fourfold. First, it was God's purpose by election. He chose Israel, knowing what would happen in the future. These were physical Jews, Israelites, who enjoyed all the special relationships to God that an elect people could experience: sonship, glory, covenants, the law, worship, the promises, the patriarchs, and Christ (9:1-5). God had elected them just as he had chosen Jacob over Esau before either was born, just as he had hardened the heart of Pharaoh, just as the potter molds the clay into the vessel he desires (9:6-26). It had nothing to do with their character or inherent worth; it was strictly a matter of God's purpose for them. There is no injustice on God's part in making this choice, because it was necessary in order for God to show his power through them so that his name might be proclaimed in all the earth. He had chosen Israel to serve his purposes just as he had chosen Pharaoh and Jacob and Moses; their salvation was a matter of faith (Heb 11). After all, only a remnant of Israel ever really believed (Rom 9:27-29).

Second, Paul argues that Israel, in rejecting the Messiah and his gospel, is following a precedent that appears repeatedly throughout history (9:30-10:21). The Jews did not seek righteousness by faith, and thus never found it. They based their righteousness on the law and thus stumbled over their own Messiah (9:30-33).

Third, he argues that since a "remnant" of Israel has already believed the gospel, it is a clear indication that Israel as a whole will yet do so (11:1-16, 26). So, even though he says that God has rejected Israel, he argues that God has not rejected them finally and irrevocably. He has broken them off the cultivated branch of the Abrahamic promise, but he has not rejected his people. The elect (remnant) obtained what it sought, but the rest were hardened for a period of time until they could be provoked to jealousy by the Gentiles' inclusion into the kingdom. So Israel's alienation is not necessarily final.

Fourth, Paul argues that since Israel's rejection has been such a blessing for the inclusion of the Gentiles, the scenario of their conversion in large numbers would be like a resurrection from the dead. This argument runs throughout the rest of the chapter (11:17-36). The Gentiles should not be haughty, because Israel stumbled so as to make their inclusion possible (vv 17-19). Israel did not stumble just so they could fall (v 11); their fall was a blessing to Gentiles and was a part of the purpose of God. And God, who broke them off for their unbelief, will be able to regraft them back into the tree from which they were cut off, if they do not persist in their unbelief.

Chapters 12-16 deal with the pragmatic implications of Paul's impressive arguments. Thus the chapter begins with "I appeal to you therefore . . ." (12:1). What follows is a lengthy list of Christian virtues and responsibilities. Paul frequently includes advice in his letters so as to assist the young converts in their transition from paganism into the Judeo-Christian ethical and moral value system. He often even modifies some behavior patterns among Jewish converts. Chapter 13 discusses the important relationship that should exist between Christians in the capital city of the Roman Empire and their government officials. They should recognize that civil government is, as such, ordained by God and has a right to exist even if those who hold the offices are corrupt. They are God's servants to execute judgment on the disobedient (13:4). Chapter 14 encourages Christians enjoying freedom in Christ to live without influencing others to violate their own consciences in various matters, such as eating meat. Nor should those with weaker consciences try to restrict others who have found this precious freedom. Mutual love and respect is the mark of a true disciple of Christ. Chapter 15 contains Paul's travel plans and his understanding of his role as a priestly minister to Gentiles, offering their conversion to God symbolically on the altar at Jerusalem in the form of a large collection of money taken up among the Gentile churches. Chapter 16 closes typically with greetings and commendations from various individuals. Twenty-seven people are greeted by name.

See also Paul, The Apostle.

ROME, City of City in Italy founded, according to tradition, in 753 BC on seven hills about 15 miles (24.1 kilometers) from the mouth of the Tiber River. It was of no biblical interest until NT times. There are nine explicit references to the city in the NT (Acts 2:10; 18:2; 19:21; 23:11; 28:14, 16; Rom 1:7, 15: 2 Tm 1:17), but Paul's sojourn there and his letter to the Roman Christians, written probably from Corinth around AD 57 and 58, make the imperial city of considerable interest to Bible readers.

History In the second millennium BC, Indo-European migrants moved into Europe and settled in the Italian peninsula. One group settled around the mouth of the Tiber River. A vigorous and more cultured group, the Etruscans from Asia Minor, occupied central Italy. At the time of Rome's emergence in the eighth century BC, the population of the Italian peninsula was mixed. The Latin-speaking enclave, which settled toward the mouth of the Tiber, were agriculturalists. The scattered groups formed leagues and communities to defend themselves against raiders. They built stockades on the hills to protect families and flocks while fighting off the raiders. From such beginnings Rome emerged as a dominant center with its focal point in the area of the seven hills (the Palatine, the Capitoline, the Aventine, the Caelian, the Esquiline, the Viminal, and the Quirinal). Traditionally these hills were considered to be seven in number; in fact, there are more than seven, although some are simply flat-topped spurs. The Tiber River winds in a large S-curve between the hills. At one point it divided to form an island where it was shallow enough to ford. The town that grew up there was linked by roads, north to the Etruscans, south to the Greek trading cities, west to the coast, and inland to the tribal areas on the highlands. Knowledge of early Rome is based largely on archaeological evidence from the remains of the simple forts and numerous burial sites in the area.

Rome developed politically in a remarkable fashion over the next 1,000 years. The loose association of the original chieftains, who comprised the earliest "senate," gave place to domination by Etruscan kings who seem to have trained the people in discipline and obedience. They constructed numerous works, draining the forum area and making it a social, commercial, industrial, and political center. They built a temple for Jupiter, Juno, and Minerva on the Capitoline Hill as a common shrine for all the people. When the kings became autocratic, the Latin population rebelled and expelled the kings.

The republic was established in 510 BC. This establishment marked the beginning of Rome's remarkable expansion to the dimensions of a world empire. The population, which was now spread out over the hills and valleys, despite their tribal differences, united and solved political problems without bloodshed. Strictly speaking, the term "republican" should not be understood in any modern sense as indicating a kind of democracy. Rather, the ancient families (patricians) dominated the senate and constituted an oligarchy. This arrangement was useful for Rome at that time. The small city-state soon broke out of its confined area, overcame the Etruscans, and dominated the Greek cities to the south. The Romans then looked farther afield. In 273 BC they made a treaty with the Ptolemies of Egypt. Before long, they expanded into North Africa, overcame the Carthaginians, pressed on into Spain, and developed ambitions to occupy the Middle East as well. Rome's many conquests brought enormous wealth.

With geographical expansion came social changes in Italy. During the second century BC, rich landowners bought out the small independent farmers, who subsequently drifted into Rome, landless and unemployed. Huge, overcrowded tenement houses appeared, which constituted creeping slums. Alongside this squalor there was evidence of vast wealth from Rome's conquests in distant lands. In the capital, many fine buildings appeared. Pompey, who subdued and organized the East, did much to adorn the great capital.

The next stage in Rome's political development came when the senate, the governing body of the republic, proved unable to control its more radical and violent members. As their political ambitions increased, aspiring leaders sought to gain popular support by granting privileges to the people without the concurrence of the sen-

The Roman Colosseum

ate. Civil strife broke out and plagued the last century of the republic. Military victories beyond Rome gave power to the generals. In the civil wars that followed, constitutional questions were decided by the power of the sword. Marius, Sulla, Pompey, Crassus, Julius Caesar, Antony, and Octavian were the real political forces in the land.

By 27 BC, Octavian emerged supreme and was given the title Augustus. Theoretically, a dual government existed between the senate and Augustus (the emperor), but a weak senate allowed the emperor to become the virtual ruler. As a result, Roman peace (*pax Romana*) reigned at home and abroad until well into the second century AD. The emperors of the first century AD cover the period of the life of Jesus and of the emerging church, and several are mentioned in the NT: Augustus (Lk 2:1), Tiberius (Lk 3:1), Claudius (Acts 11:28; 18:2), and Nero, who is referred to without being explicitly named (Acts 25:10-12; 27:24; 2 Tm 4:16-17).

The city of Rome was the capital of the empire and the home of the emperor, senators, administrators, military personnel, and priests. Augustus, the first of the emperors whose leadership and diplomatic endeavors gave peace to Rome after two civil wars and a century of strife, gave attention to the restoration and adornment of the city. He boasted that he found Rome built of brick and left it built of marble. His efforts at restoring Rome's ancient religions led to the building of many temples. On the Palatine hill, Augustus united several houses already there into a palace for his own residence. A new and sumptuous temple of Apollo, surrounded by colonnades in which the emperor housed a large library, was erected near the palace. The palace itself overlooked an imposing group of new marble buildings in the valley below: a basilica business hall, a senate house, a temple of "the divine Julius," a marble speaker's platform, two impressive new forums, the forum of Caesar, and the forum of Augustus. Later emperors added to this splendor. Beyond the central forum area, the palaces of Tiberius and Caligula, various baths, arches, and theaters, the Circus Maximus, and the Circus Nero were built. The whole was enclosed by a wall built outside the old rampart of Servius. Several aqueducts brought water into the city, and significant roads from north, south, east, and west converged on the central city area.

Rome's Military Presence in Palestine With the military intervention of Pompey in the internal affairs of Judea in 63 BC, Rome established its presence in Palestine. The census ordered by Augustus Caesar, affecting the eastern provinces as well as the rest of the Roman world (Lk 2:1-2), was a vivid reminder. Roman military presence is amply reflected on the pages of the Gospels and Acts (e.g., Mk 15:16; Lk 3:14; 7:1-8; Acts 5:37).

In the NT period, service in the legions was open to all Roman citizens. A professional volunteer army had replaced a conscripted militia. The permanent standing army was made up of legions recruited from the ranks of citizens. The legions were commanded by experienced officers of the rank of consul. Auxiliary forces were raised outside Italy, the inducement for enlistment being Roman citizenship for a soldier and his descendants after 25 years of service.

In the provinces supreme military command lay with the provincial governor or prefect. In Judea at the time of Jesus' public ministry, Pontius Pilate was designated "prefect of Judea" in a Latin inscription found in Caesarea in 1961. At the official center for administration of Judea, Caesarea Maritima, one or more legions at the disposal of the governor would be garrisoned. On special occasions, particularly at the great Jewish festi-

vals, when riots and disorders could be anticipated, the provincial governor would take up residence in Jerusalem some 60 miles (96.5 kilometers) to the south, accompanied by a substantial contingent of troops (cf. Lk 13:1).

Augustus established a standing army large enough to defend and pacify the empire. In 15 BC there were 28 legions, each composed of some 5,000 foot soldiers plus a mounted bodyguard of 128 men. After three legions were destroyed in uprisings by fierce Germanic tribes in AD 9, the number remained at 25 for some time. That suggests a standing army of about 125,000 legionaries in the first century.

Augustus was also responsible for establishing a permanent auxiliary army, almost the same size as the legionary army. The auxiliary forces, recruited from provincials who had not yet received Roman citizenship, included both cavalry and infantry. The cavalry was organized in squadrons, the infantry in cohorts of 1,000 under command of a military tribune (Act 21:31-33). When the apostle Paul was in Jerusalem, the tribune was Claudius Lysias, a man of Greek birth whose purchased Roman citizenship made possible his elevation to commander of an auxiliary cohort (22:28; 23:26). To send Paul from Jerusalem to Caesarea, Claudius could delegate a military escort of 200 soldiers commanded by two centurions, plus 70 mounted guards (23:23), without dangerously weakening the strength of the fortress garrison.

A cohort was made up of either ten or five "centuries," units consisting of 100 men under the command of a centurion whose duties resembled those of a modern army captain. Cornelius (Acts 10:1) was a Roman centurion assigned to one of the auxiliary cohorts in Judea. There is inscriptional evidence for the presence of his unit, "the Second Italian Cohort of Roman Citizens," in Syria about AD 69. Paul was sent to Rome in the custody of another centurion, Julius, who belonged to the Augustan or imperial cohort (27:1). The term Augustan was a title of honor sometimes bestowed on auxiliary troops. Julius was evidently a legionary centurion assigned to the corps of officer-couriers who maintained a communication service between the emperor and his provincial armies. He had a detachment of soldiers under his command on the voyage to Rome (v 3) and on arrival handed his prisoners over to the commander of the courier corps (28:16). Probably all of the Roman centurions mentioned in the Gospels or Acts (Mt 8:5; Mk 15:39; Lk 7:2) were officers assigned to an auxiliary cohort.

Christians in Rome It was to this magnificent city that Paul came under escort in March AD 59. He found that the Christian church had already been established there. Indeed, he had already communicated with the Christians in his letter to the Romans early in 57. There was a considerable Jewish colony in Rome in the first century AD, descended from the large number of Jewish slaves brought to the city by Pompey after the capture of Jerusalem in 63 BC. The emperor Claudius expelled Jews from Rome in AD 49, possibly when Jesus was proclaimed as Messiah in the synagogue. Who the preachers were is not known, but they were probably Christian travelers and traders. Paul's Letter to the Romans was his exposition to the Gentile churches that had come into existence independently of him. His first known contact with the people of Rome was when he met Aquila and Priscilla at Corinth (Acts 18:2). This couple was expelled from Rome in the time of Claudius. Later, Paul hoped to visit Rome (Acts 19:21) on his way to Spain (Rom 15:24). In his salutation he mentioned a considerable circle of

Christians in Rome (ch 16). The references to households in several places (vv 5, 10, 11, 14, 15) suggest
that these were house churches of the Roman Christian
church. During his captivity, Paul was a prisoner of
Roman authorities, but he was able to meet the local
leaders of the Jews, explain his experiences to them, and
expound the gospel to them in person (Acts 28:16-31).

In the book of Revelation, Rome is given a sinister significance. By the end of the first century AD, Rome had
already drunk the "blood of the martyrs of Jesus" (Rv
17:6), a reference to early martyrs.

See also Caesars, The; Romans, Letter to the.

ROOT OF JESSE* *See* Jesse, Root of.

ROSE *See* Plants (Oleander; Tulip).

ROSETTA STONE* The fame of this stone rests upon
the part it played in providing the clue for deciphering
ancient Egyptian inscriptions. Rosetta is the European
name for the town Rashid in the vicinity of which the
stone was discovered. It is a place near the mouth of the
arm of the Nile flowing through the western delta
toward the sea. A slab of black basalt—measuring about
three feet, nine inches (1.1 meters) in length; two feet,
four and a half inches (.7 meter) in width; and eleven
inches (27.9 centimeters) thick—makes up the famous
stone. Unfortunately, when discovered, it was in a damaged state, with the two top corners missing. It has been
computed that the original stone size was at least 12
inches (30.5 centimeters) longer than it is now.

The discovery of the stone goes back to Napoleon's
invasion of Egypt in 1799. There are two versions of the
legend: according to one account it was found lying on
the ground; according to the other, it was part of a wall
that was ordered to be demolished for material to construct a fortification, later known as Fort Julian. The
French officer, an engineer named Bouchard, who found
the stone, recognized that the writing on it in three different scripts might be of great archaeological value. The
bottom of the stone was in Greek lettering. Bouchard
and his colleagues therefore assumed it to be the translation of the mysterious script at the top. The stone was
later shown to Napoleon, who ordered copies to be sent
to Europe for scholarly investigation. Two Frenchmen,
Jean-Joseph Marcel and Remi Raige, soon recognized
that the middle script, wedged between the hieroglyphic
and Greek texts, was a cursive form of Egyptian writing.
Scholars call it demotic writing, i.e., a popular, conventional form allowing for abbreviation, as distinct from
the elaborate hieratic, i.e., priestly, writing. The stone in
its present mutilated state consists of 14 lines of hieroglyphic text; 32 lines of demotic text; and 54 lines in
Greek, of which the last 26 lines are marred at the ends.
Fortunately, scholars were able to supplement a large
portion of the missing hieroglyphic lines from inscriptions of two related texts. The Rev. Stephen Weston was
the first to translate the Greek text into English. The
French translation was accomplished by a man called
"citizen Du Theil." The demotic script was studied by
Sylvester de Sacy and a Swedish diplomat by the name of
Akerblad. It was the latter who first identified the
demotic of all the proper names as they occur in the
Greek text, plus the words "temples," "Greeks," and the
third person of the masculine pronoun. An important
clue to the puzzle was the discovery by Thomas Young,
otherwise known for his theory of light, that ancient
Egyptian writing was made up of phonetic signs. The first
clue appeared with the identification of the name Cleopatra rendered in hieroglyphics. This gradually led to the

identification of the name Ptolemy, except for the last
few signs in the cartouche. It was assumed that the royal
titles in the Greek text corresponded to these last
hieroglyphs. By a combination of letters, scholars were
able to translate the title "ever-living, beloved of Ptah."
Thomas Young's discovery of the phonetical structure of
the hieroglyphic script, together with the work of
Jean-François Champollion, laid the foundations for
unravelling the mystery of the ancient Egyptian inscriptions. By 1822 Thomas Young produced a list of hieroglyphic characters that were expanded and corrected by
Champollion. The latter even worked out the grammar
upon which the language was based. They thus laid the
foundation for the work of later Egyptologists.

We now know that the stone has engraved upon it a
decree passed by the priests of Egypt assembled at Memphis, in celebration of the coronation anniversary of

Rosetta Stone

Ptolemy V, Epiphanes, king of all Egypt. The date is probably spring, 196 BC. Scholars think the original text was in
Greek; the demotic and the hieroglyphic were renderings
from this text. The opening lines were adulatory, listing
the king's titles and praising his piety and love of his people and country. This is followed by a list of benefactions
conferred by the king for the good of the temples, the
priesthood, and the general public, specifying amnesties
to criminals, reduction of taxes, etc. In gratitude for the
king's bounty, the priestly council decided to "increase the
ceremonial observances of honor which are paid to Ptolemy, the ever-living, in the temples." To this end it was
decided: (1) to make statues of Ptolemy, as savior of
Egypt; (2) to place figures of Ptolemy in shrines next to
the gods; (3) to place 10 double crowns of gold on his
shrine; (4) to make the king's birthday and coronation
day public holidays; (5) to make the first five days of the
month Thoth festive days when all people wore garlands;
(6) to add to the priests the title "Priests of the beneficent
god Ptolemy Epiphanus, who appears on earth"; (7) that
citizens be allowed to borrow temple figures of Ptolemy
for their house and for processions; and (8) that copies

of the decree be cut upon slabs of basalt to be set up in temples "side by side with the statue of Ptolemy, the ever-living god." The stone was brought to England as a result of the Capitulation Treaty of 1801 and is on view in the British Museum, London.

ROSH Seventh of Benjamin's ten sons (Gn 46:21).

RUBY *See* Stones, Precious.

RUE* Perennial shrub whose leaves were used for medicinal purposes (Lk 11:42). *See* Plants.

RUFUS
1. One of the sons of Simon of Cyrene (Mk 15:21).
2. Christian to whom Paul sent greetings, adding a special endearing comment about his mother (Rom 16:13). He is perhaps the same as #1 above.

RUHAMAH One of two symbolic names showing God's altered perspective toward Israel from one of hostility to one of mercy. God's attitude of displeasure was symbolized by the name Lo-ruhamah (meaning "Not pitied"), which Hosea named his daughter. God had withdrawn his compassion from Israel because of their great sin (Hos 1:6, 8). His new attitude of mercy was portrayed by the name Ruhamah (meaning "She has obtained pity"), revealing God's revived spirit of compassion that was to be poured out on Israel (2:1, 23).

RULER The term represents a number of different functions and translates 13 Hebrew and 3 Greek words. In a political sense, a ruler was one who exercised political control over a state (2 Chr 7:18; Ps 105:20; Prv 23:1; 28:15; Eccl 10:4; Is 14:5; 16:1; 49:7; Jer 33:26; 51:46; Mi 5:2), or a state that exercised control over a subject people (Jgs 15:11). The usual term for ruler was "king," but because of its unsavory associations, many in Israel preferred the Hebrew term translated "leader," meaning "one placed in front." For example, Samuel rejected the former term but used the latter (1 Sm 9:16; 10:1; 13:14; 25:30; 2 Sm 5:2; 6:21; 7:8). Other Hebrew words are translated "ruler" in the KJV. However, most modern translations prefer alternatives to this more generic term.

In the NT the Greek word regularly translated "ruler" refers to administrative or religious leaders (in various modern versions, see Mt 9:18, 23; Lk 8:41; 18:18; 23:35; 24:20; Jn 3:1; 7:26, 48; 12:31; Acts 3:17; 4:5, 26; 7:27, 35; 13:27; 14:5; 16:19; 23:5; Rom 13:3). Ephesians 6:12 mentions the rulers of the darkness of this world.

See also King.

RULER OF THE SYNAGOGUE* Senior official in a synagogue of NT times. It is generally understood that there was only one such official in any one synagogue.

His functions were to take care of the physical arrangements for the services of worship, to manage the maintenance of the building, and to determine who would be called to read from the Law and the Prophets or to conduct the prayers. The office was sometimes held for a specified period, sometimes for life.

The NT refers to this official on four different occasions. Jairus apparently was the ruler of a synagogue at Capernaum. When his daughter was ill, he went to Jesus for help, and Jesus raised her from the dead (Mt 9:18-26; Mk 5:21-43; Lk 8:41-56). Luke 13:14 records the hostility of another ruler of a synagogue who objected to Jesus' healing on the Sabbath after teaching in that synagogue.

On his missionary journeys Paul generally began his ministry in each place he visited by going to the synagogue. At Pisidian Antioch (Acts 13:15), the rulers of the synagogue welcomed and encouraged him to preach the gospel and to return again the following week. Crispus, the ruler of the synagogue at Corinth, was converted (18:8), and later Sosthenes (Crispus's successor) was beaten by the mob after the Jews had made a charge against Paul before Gallio, the governor of Achaia.

See also Synagogue.

RUMAH Home of Pedaiah, the father of Zebidah, Jehoiakim's mother (2 Kgs 23:36). Some identify it with Arumah, near Shechem (cf. Jgs 9:41) or with Khirbet el-Rumah in Galilee.

RUSH* KJV form of reed in Job 8:11 and Isaiah 9:14. *See* Plants.

RUTH (Person) Moabitess and the widow of Mahlon, the son of Naomi and Elimelech, who were Ephrathites from Bethlehem living in Moab because of a severe famine in Judah. After the death of Elimelech and Naomi's two sons, Naomi returned to Bethlehem with her daughter-in-law Ruth during the time of the barley harvest (Ru 1:4-22). While gleaning in the barley fields of Boaz, Ruth found favor in his eyes (2:2-22). She later married Boaz, when he, serving as nearest kin to the childless Naomi, purchased Naomi's estate to keep it within the family (4:5-13). Ruth is mentioned in Matthew's genealogy of Christ as the mother of Obed and the great-grandmother of David (Mt 1:5).

See also Genealogy of Jesus Christ; Ruth, Book of.

RUTH, Book of

PREVIEW
• Author and Date
• Purpose
• Content
• Message

Author and Date The author of the book is unknown. The question of authorship has particular connection with the date of writing, and a few clues provide at least an educated guess. The book must have been written sometime after the beginning of David's reign. The information in Ruth 4:18-22, which pertains to the historical significance of Ruth as David's great-grandmother, bears this out. Since foreign marriages were not approved in the book of Ruth, it scarcely could have been written during the period in which Solomon began his policy of foreign marriages. Also, David's close friendship with Moab might have prompted someone in his kingdom to write the book, thus presenting objective rationale for David's actions (see 1 Sm 22:3-5). Consequently, the author may have been someone close to David, possibly Samuel, Nathan, or Abiathar.

The time of the narrative is indicated by the opening statement: "In the days when the judges ruled. . . ." The dates of the judges probably comprise a period of about 300 years, beginning with the judgeship of Othniel and concluding with that of Samson, though Samuel also served as a judge. If the genealogical information is complete in Ruth 4:18-22, the events took place during the life of David's great-grandfather and mark the birth of his grandfather. Allowing a 35-year generation span, the events would have taken place somewhere about the turn of the 11th century BC, or about 100 years before David's birth.

Purpose The book's purpose is closely related to its date of composition. Assuming an early date, that is, one close to David's lifetime, its principal thrust must be the authentication of the Davidic line. The book may be considered as a justification for including the godly Moabitess in the nation of Israel.

Content

Introduction (1:1-5) Driven by famine, Elimelech, with his wife, Naomi, and his two sons, Mahlon and Chilion, cross the Jordan to stay for a period of time in Moab, where there is sufficient provision. The two sons, after marrying Moabite women, die, and their father dies as well. Naomi is left a widow, with two foreign daughters-in-law.

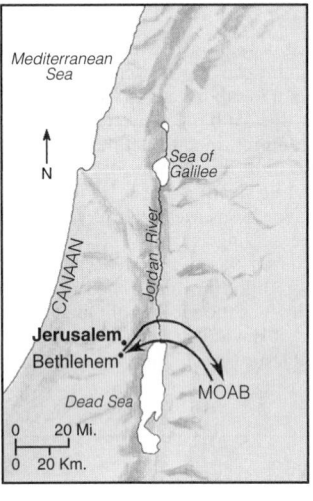

The Story of Ruth Elimelech, Naomi, and their two sons went to the land of Moab. Naomi returned to Bethlehem after her husband and sons died.

Return to Bethlehem (1:6-22) Hearing reports from Bethlehem that the famine has ended, Naomi makes preparations to return. Both of her daughters-in-law, Orpah and Ruth, accompany her for at least a portion of the journey. Probably thinking of the problems they might encounter as foreigners in Judah, Naomi strongly urges the girls to stay in their own land. Both of the young widows refuse, but Naomi presents the facts. First, she is not pregnant, so the chance of a younger brother fulfilling the levirate responsibility is not imminent. Second, she has no prospects of remarriage and consequently no prospect of further children. Then she also notes that even if the first two conditions were met immediately, the possibility of their waiting was impossible. Orpah is persuaded and kisses her mother-in-law good-bye.

But Ruth "clung to her" (1:18). The verb, having the connotation of being glued to something, is the same verb used of marriage (Gn 2:24). Ruth demonstrated her serious intentions by making five commitments (Ru 1:16-17). In essence, Ruth renounced her former life in order to gain a life that she considered of greater value. She decided to follow the God of Israel and his laws. Ruth's appeal to the God of Israel was more than equal to Naomi's pleas, and the two of them returned together.

Their arrival in Bethlehem was traumatic for Naomi. Having left Bethlehem with a husband and two sons, she returned empty. She told her friends to call her "Mara" (bitter). But she had returned at a propitious time, the beginning of the harvest season.

Reaping in the Fields of Boaz (2:1-23) The first verse of the chapter provides the setting for the narrative that fol-

lows by introducing Boaz, a wealthy relative of Elimelech.

In the second verse, Ruth volunteered to glean the fields by following the reapers and picking up the small amounts left behind. Gleaners were also permitted to harvest the grain in the corners of the fields—a provision for the poor contained in the law (Lv 19:9-10).

Ruth happened to come to the field of Boaz. When he visited this field, he noticed Ruth, inquired about her, and learned her identity. His overseer reported that she had industriously worked the fields from early morning until that time. Boaz, attracted to her because of her loyalty and concern for Naomi, graciously made additional provisions for her. She was given a favored position in reaping, directly behind the main body of reapers. Further, she was to receive water that had been drawn for her by the young men—an unorthodox arrangement.

Ruth, falling before Boaz in a gesture of great humility and respect, asked why she—as a foreigner—should receive such favor. Boaz gave two reasons: her kindness to her mother-in-law, and her spiritual insight, which led her to seek after Israel's God, "under whose wings you have come to take refuge" (Ru 2:12, NLT).

She was also given a place at the reapers' table and, upon Boaz's orders, returned to the fields, this time to reap from the unharvested grain. At the end of the day she returned home to Naomi and told her of the day's events. Naomi informed Ruth that Boaz had the right of redemption (see discussion below). Ruth returned to his fields until the end of the harvest season.

Relying upon the Kinsman (3:1-18) Naomi advised Ruth to approach Boaz as a *go'el*, or kinsman-redeemer. The plan suggested by Naomi seems peculiar, yet some thoughts may give a certain coloring to it. (1) Naomi seems to have believed that Boaz was the nearest kinsman, being ignorant of the yet nearer one (3:12). Consequently, according to Israelite law (Dt 25:5ff.), it would be the duty of Boaz to marry Ruth to produce offspring, since her husband died. (2) The general presentation of Naomi's character in this book is that of a God-fearing woman. It is certain that, however curious in its external form, there can be nothing counseled here that is repugnant to God's law or shocking to a virtuous man such as Boaz. Otherwise, Naomi would have been frustrating her own purpose.

Boaz's response to Ruth's actions demonstrated his gentlemanly concerns for her. He explained to her that he was not the nearest kinsman but promised that he would take care of the necessary procedures the next day. Protecting her reputation, Boaz sent her home before daylight. Naomi predicted that Boaz would settle the matter that very day.

Redeeming the Inheritance (4:1-22) Boaz went to the place of business, the city gate. The city gate area comprised the forum where the public affairs of the city were discussed. Boaz indicated that he wished to discuss a matter of business with the nearer kinsman. Ten of the city elders acted as witnesses. The first matter at hand was to deal with the issue of property. Boaz asked this nearer kinsman if he was willing to acquire property for Naomi. This is stated in the traditional stipulation: "Your purchase of the land from Naomi also requires that you marry Ruth, the Moabite widow" (4:5, NLT). The nearer kinsman was unwilling to marry Ruth because this would inevitably cost him some financial loss, since he would have to divide his own property with any son of his born to Ruth. Thus he relinquished his rights by the custom of taking off his shoe. (The shoe was symbolic of the land rights that belonged to the inheritance.) So

Boaz took the part of being the kinsman-redeemer. The marriage of Boaz and Ruth produced a son who, under Israel's laws, was reckoned as Naomi's child and heir.

Message First, the book of Ruth traces the lineage of Ruth to David. The completion of that line is in Matthew 1 and finds its fulfillment in Jesus.

A second teaching is the beauty of God's grace. A foreigner, even a Moabitess, can be linked with Israel's blessing.

Theologically, the concept of kinsman-redeemer as a type of Messiah is clearly evident. He must be a blood relative, have the ability to purchase, be willing to buy the inheritance, and be willing to marry the widow of the deceased kinsman.

And finally, the love that Ruth showed to Naomi provides a pattern of devotion. The women of Bethlehem told Naomi, "Your daughter-in-law . . . loves you so much and [is] better to you than seven sons!" (4:15, NLT).

S

SABACHTHANI One of the final words Jesus spoke during his crucifixion; it is Aramaic (Mt 27:46; Mk 15:34). *See* Eli, Eli, Lema Sabachthani.

SABAOTH Hebrew word meaning "hosts" or "army," as in the expression "Lord of hosts." *See* God, Names of.

SABBATH Derivation of a Hebrew word that means "cease" or "desist." The Sabbath was a day (from Friday evening until Saturday evening in Jesus' time) when all ordinary work stopped. The Scriptures relate that God gave his people the Sabbath as an opportunity to serve him and as a reminder of two great truths in the Bible—Creation and redemption.

In the Old Testament The relationship between Creation and the Sabbath is first expressed in Genesis 2:2-3. God "ceased" his work in Creation after six days and then "blessed" the seventh day and "declared it holy." In the fourth commandment (Ex 20:8-11), God's "blessing" and "setting aside" of the seventh day after Creation (the words used are the same as those in Genisis) form the basis of his demand that people should observe the seventh day as a day of Sabbath rest.

The idea of God resting from his work is a startling one. It comes across even more vividly in Exodus 31:17, where the Lord tells Moses how he was refreshed by his day of rest. This picture of the Creator as a manual laborer is one the Bible often paints. No doubt it is presented in vividly human terms in Exodus to reinforce the fundamental Sabbath lesson that people must follow the pattern their Creator has set for them. One day's rest in seven is a necessity for individuals, families, households, and even animals (Ex 20:10).

The Sabbath's setting in the biblical account of Creation implies that it is one of those OT standards that are meant for all people and not just for Israel. The inclusion of the Sabbath law in the Ten Commandments underlines this important truth. The Decalogue occupied a special place in OT law. Alone of all God's instructions, it was spoken by his audible voice (Ex 20:1), written by his finger (31:18), and placed in the tabernacle ark at the heart of Israel's worship (25:16). The NT, too, confirms the strong impression that the Decalogue as a whole embodies principles that are permanently valid for all people in all places at all times. Whether or not Sunday is recognized as the Christian Sabbath, one is obliged to accept the central principle of this biblical teaching as far as the Sabbath is concerned. God's instructions require people to observe a regular weekly break from work.

Significantly, the second main strand of the Bible's Sabbath teaching—that of redemption—also features in a list of the Ten Commandments. The Sabbath law (already noted in Ex 20:8-11) reappears in Deuteronomy 5:12-15, but here a different reason is attached to its observance: "Remember that you were once slaves in Egypt and that the Lord your God brought you out with amazing power and mighty deeds. That is why the Lord your God has commanded you to observe the Sabbath day" (v 15, NLT).

The differences between these two accounts of the fourth commandment are important. The first (Ex 20) is addressed, *through* Israel, to all people as created beings. The second (Dt 5) is directed *to* Israel as God's redeemed people. So the Sabbath is God's signpost, pointing not only to his goodness toward all people as their Creator but also to his mercy toward his chosen people as their Redeemer.

There is one other significant point in Deuteronomy's version of the Sabbath commandment that must not be missed. The prohibition of all work on the Sabbath day is followed by an explanatory note—"On that day no one in your household may do any kind of work. This includes you, your sons and daughters, your male and female servants, your oxen and donkeys and other livestock, and any foreigners living among you. All your male and female servants must rest as you do" (Dt 5:14, NLT). Practical concern for others is a feature of all the OT's covenant teaching. So God's loving concern for Israel in her Egyptian slavery must be matched by the Israelite family's loving concern for those who served them. The Sabbath offered an ideal outlet for the practical expression of that concern. Jesus was especially keen to rescue this humanitarian side of Sabbath observance from the mass of callous regulations that threatened to suffocate it in his day (see, e.g., Mk 3:1-5).

The OT's provision for a "sabbatical year" develops this humanitarian theme further (see Ex 23:10-12; Lv 25:1-7; Dt 15:1-11; also the regulations for the "year of jubilee" in Lv 25:8-55). Every seventh year the land was to lie fallow and be uncultivated (Lv 25:4). It needed a regular rest just as much as the people it sustained. The primary purpose of this law was benevolent: "But you, your male and female slaves, your hired servants, and any foreigners who live with you may eat the produce that grows naturally during the Sabbath year. And your livestock and the wild animals will also be allowed to eat of the land's bounty" (vv 6-7, NLT). Deuteronomy 15:1-11 extends the same humanitarian principle into the world of commerce. The sabbatical year must see the canceling of all debts within God's redeemed community. For the tight-fisted who might be tempted to refuse a loan if the sabbatical year was imminent, the law added a warning and a promise: "Do not be mean-spirited and refuse someone a loan because the year of release is close at hand. If you refuse to make the loan and the needy person cries out to the Lord, you will be considered guilty of sin. Give freely without begrudging it, and the Lord your God will bless you in everything you do" (Dt 15:9-10, NLT).

Observing the sabbatical year was obviously a great test of the people's obedience to God and of their willingness to depend on him for their livelihood. Sometimes the temptation to turn a blind eye was too strong. But history testifies to Israel's courage in observing the letter of this law on many occasions, despite threats of invasion and famine. Both Alexander the Great and the Romans excused Jews from paying taxes every seventh year in recognition of the depth of their religious convictions.

Returning from the seventh year to the seventh day, the OT law codes go to considerable lengths to buttress the Sabbath ban on work by defining what may and may not be done by God's people on the Sabbath day. The prohibitions were not meant to rule out activity of any kind. Their aim was to stop regular, everyday work, because if God had set aside the Sabbath (Ex 20:11), the most obvious way of profaning it was to treat it just like any other day. Rules were spelled out in specific terms that the farmer (34:21), the salesman (Jer 17:27), and even the housewife (Ex 35:2-3) would understand.

The details may seem trivial, but obedience to the Sabbath law was seen as the main test of the people's allegiance to the Lord. It was made quite clear that willful disobedience was a capital offense (Ex 35:2), and the fate of the person found gathering wood in defiance of Sabbath regulations showed that this was no idle threat (Nm 15:32-36).

Hemmed in by so many rules and regulations (and with the death penalty overhanging all), the Sabbath easily could have become a day of fear—a day when the people were more afraid of committing an offense than worshiping the Lord and enjoying a weekly rest. But the Sabbath was intended to be a blessing, not a burden. Above everything else, it was a weekly sign that the Lord loved his people and wanted to draw them into an ever-closer relationship with himself. Those who valued that relationship enjoyed the Sabbath, calling it a delight (Is 58:13-14). Nowhere does the OT express its sheer joy in Sabbath worship more exuberantly than in Psalm 92, which has the title "A Song for the Sabbath."

The later prophets, were, however, far from blind to the darker side of human nature. They knew that a great deal of Sabbath observance was a sham. Many people treated the Sabbath day more as holiday than holy day, an opportunity for self-indulgence rather than delighting in the Lord (Is 58:13). Some greedy tradesmen found its restrictions an annoying irritant (Am 8:5).

As God's spokesman, the prophets did not shrink from exposing such neglect and abuse (Ez 22:26). Those who go through the motions of Sabbath worship with unrepentant hearts nauseate the Lord, Isaiah said (Is 1:10-15). As a symptom of rebellion against God, Jerusalem's Sabbath breaking will bring destruction on the city, thunders Jeremiah (Jer 17:27). The Lord has been very forbearing with his people, warned Ezekiel, but prolonged neglect of his Sabbath makes judgment a certainty (Ez 20:12-24).

When the ax of judgment fell (in the exile to Babylon, 586 BC), the surviving remnant of the nation took the lesson to heart. Sabbath keeping was one of the few distinctive marks faithful Jews could retain in a foreign land, so it assumed extra significance. At the prompting of prophets like Ezekiel, who set out rules for Sabbath worship in the rebuilt temple at Jerusalem (Ez 44:24; 45:17; 46:3), and under the leadership of men like Nehemiah, the returning exiles were more careful than their predecessors in observing the Sabbath day (Neh 10:31; 13:15-22).

In the New Testament Prior to the first century, some Jews in Palestine developed several rules for promoting the observance of the Sabbath. Two tractates of the Mishnah are devoted exclusively to these Sabbath rules and regulations. Their main purpose is to define work (one tractate does so under 39 headings) in an attempt to show every Israelite what is and is not permitted on the Sabbath. Unfortunately, this led to such hairsplitting

complexities and evasions that ecclesiastical lawyers often differed among themselves in their interpretations, with the inevitable result that the main purpose of the Sabbath became lost beneath a mass of legalistic detail. The rabbis themselves were aware of how much they were adding to the straightforward teaching of the OT. As one of them put it, "The rules about the sabbath . . . are as mountains hanging by a hair, for Scripture is scanty and the rules many."

Jesus had many confrontations with the Jewish religious leaders over Sabbath observances. From their perspective, Jesus was a Sabbath breaker and therefore a lawbreaker. Jesus, however, never saw himself as a Sabbath breaker. He went to synagogue regularly on the Sabbath day (Lk 4:16). He read the lesson, preached, and taught (Mk 1:21; Lk 13:10). He clearly accepted the principle that the Sabbath was an appropriate day for worship.

His point of collision with the Pharisees was the point at which their tradition departed from biblical teaching. He made this clear when he defended his disciples by appealing to Scripture, after they had been accused of breaking Sabbath tradition by walking through grainfields and breaking off heads of wheat (which fell into the category of "harvesting," according to the Pharisees; Mk 2:23-26). He followed this up with a remark that took his hearers straight back to God's Creation purpose for the Sabbath: "The Sabbath was made to benefit people, and not people to benefit the Sabbath" (Mk 2:27, NLT).

Rabbinic tradition had exalted the institution above the people it was meant to serve. By making it an end in itself, the Pharisees had effectively robbed the Sabbath of one of its main purposes. Jesus' words must have sounded uncomfortably familiar in his opponents' ears. A famous rabbi had once said, "The Sabbath is given over to you, but you are not given over to the Sabbath."

More than anything else, Jesus' Sabbath healings put him on a collision course with rabbinic restrictions. The OT does not forbid cures on the Sabbath day, but the rabbis labeled all healing as work, which must always be avoided on the Sabbath unless life was at risk. Jesus fearlessly exposed the callousness and absurd inconsistencies to which this attitude led. How, he asked, could it be right to circumcise a baby or lead an animal to water on the Sabbath day (which tradition allowed) but wrong to heal a chronically handicapped woman and a crippled man, even if their lives were not in immediate danger (Lk 13:10-17; Jn 7:21-24)? The Sabbath, he taught, was a particularly appropriate day for acts of mercy (Mk 3:4-5).

Jesus, the man from heaven, claimed that he was Lord of the Sabbath (Mk 2:28; cf. Mt 12:5-8). Just as God kept working, despite his Creation rest, to sustain the world in his mercy, so Jesus would continue to teach and to heal on the Sabbath day (Jn 5:2-17). But one day his redemptive work would be complete, and then the Sabbath's purpose as a sign of redemption would be accomplished.

Living on the other side of Jesus' death and resurrection, Paul was quick to grasp the significance of both for Sabbath observance. He did not go so far as to ban all observance of the Jewish Sabbath. Indeed, he attended many Sabbath synagogue services himself in his evangelistic travels (see, e.g., Acts 13:14-16). Jewish Christians who insisted on keeping up their Sabbath practices were free to do so, provided they respected the opinions of those who differed (Rom 14:5-6, 13). But any suggestion that observing the Jewish calendar was necessary for salvation must be resisted (Gal 4:8-11). For Paul considered the Sabbath to be a shadow, while Christ himself is the reality of that shadow (Col 2:17).

Finally, it is the writer of the Letter to the Hebrews who explains how the twin biblical "sabbath themes" of creation and redemption find their joint fulfillment in Christ. He did so by linking together the ideas of God's rest after Creation and his redemptive act in bringing Israel to her "rest" in Canaan, and by showing how both relate to the present and future rest that Christians can and do enjoy in Jesus (Heb 4:1-11).

God intends all his people to share his rest—that is, his promise (Heb 4:1). He showed this intention clearly when he brought Israel to the Promised Land, but that did not mark the complete fulfillment of his promise. The full, complete rest still waiting for the people of God is in heaven. Christ has already entered there. He is resting from his work, just as God did after the Creation. And because of his redeeming work, he invites all those who believe in him to share that same "sabbath rest" now (v 9).

See also Lord's Day, The; Sabbath Day's Journey; Commandments, The Ten.

SABBATH*, Covert for the
Covered place in the court of the temple reserved for the king who stood there with his attendants on a Sabbath or feast day (2 Kgs 16:18, KJV; NLT "canopy").

SABBATH DAY'S JOURNEY*
Regulation derived from Jewish literature limiting travel on the Sabbath. The prohibition against work on the Sabbath was interpreted to exclude extensive travel (Ex 16:27-30). A person was permitted to travel 2,000 cubits (about a half mile, or 900 meters; see Jos 3:4, NLT mg) but no further. This was determined by the distance between the ark and the people following it (Jos 3:4) or from the pasturelands to the Levitical cities (Nm 35:4-5). Thus, in the former instance, one would not go further to worship or in the latter to pasture an animal. The only biblical reference describes the distance from the Mt of Olives to Jerusalem (which, according to Josephus, was 1,000 to 1,200 yards, or 914.4 to 1,097.3 meters) as "a Sabbath day's walk" (Acts 1:12).

The rabbis invented ways to at least double the distance. One could establish his home 2,000 cubits away by carrying food sufficient for two meals: one to be eaten and the other to be buried—thereby to mark a temporary domicile. He might alternatively fix his gaze upon a location 2,000 cubits away as his legal home for the Sabbath. He could, separately or in conjunction with a preceding modification, view the entire town as his home and so figure the Sabbath day's journey from the village limits.

See also Sabbath.

SABBATH YEAR, SABBATICAL YEAR*
Last year of the seven-year cycle established for keeping time in the Mosaic law. See Calendars, Ancient and Modern.

SABEANS
Inhabitants of Sheba (Saba), a country in southwest Arabia. The Sabeans were noted as men of stature (Is 45:14) and for their murder and theft of Job's servants and property (Jb 1:15).

See also Sheba (Place) #2.

SABTA*, SABTAH
One of Cush's five sons and a descendant of Noah through Ham's line (Gn 10:7; 1 Chr 1:9). Sabtah presumably settled along the southern coast of Arabia, where several cities bear his name.

SABTECA
One of Cush's five sons and a descendant of Noah through Ham's line (Gn 10:7; 1 Chr 1:9). Sabteca settled in Arabia.

SACAR, SACHAR*
1. Hararite and Ahiam's father. Sacar was one of David's

mighty men (1 Chr 11:35). In a parallel account he is alternately called Sharar the Hararite (2 Sm 23:33).

2. Korahite and one of Obed-edom's eight sons. Sacar and his brothers were listed among the families of gatekeepers (1 Chr 26:4).

SACHIA*, SACHIAH*
NASB and NKJV, respectively, for Sakia (NLT, NIV). See Sakia.

SACKBUT*
KJV rendering of trigon, a triangular-shaped harp, in Daniel 3:5-15. See Musical Instruments (Sabcha).

SACKCLOTH
Poor quality material or a garment of goat hair usually worn as a symbol of mourning, but also worn by some prophets and captives.

Sackcloth was coarse and probably dark in color (Is 50:3; Rv 6:12). The shape of the garment is disputed. Two views are prominent. One view is that the garment was rectangular, sewn on both sides and one end with spaces left for the head and arms. This shape resembles the grain sacks used by Joseph's brothers in Egypt (Gn 42:25-27, 35) and the sacks used by the Gibeonites (Jos 9:4; cf. Lv 11:32). A second view is that sackcloth was a small garment resembling a loincloth. Asiatic captives are pictured in such garb. The Hebrew practices of girding the loins with sackcloth (2 Sm 3:31; Is 15:3; 22:12; Jer 4:8) and the placing of sackcloth on the loins (Gn 37:34; 1 Kgs 20:31; Jer 48:37) support this view, though more than one type of garment could have been made from sackcloth. Sackcloth was associated primarily with mourning (Gn 37:34; 1 Kgs 21:27; Lam 2:10). National (2 Kgs 6:30; Neh 9:1; Is 37:1; Jon 3:8) as well as personal crises constituted times for the wearing of sackcloth. Kings (1 Kgs 21:27; 2 Kgs 6:30), priests (Jl 1:13), elders (Lam 2:10), prophets (Is 20:2; Zec 13:4), and cattle (Jon 3:8) all wore sackcloth. Sackcloth was found on the penitent (Neh 9:1; Jer 6:26; cf. Mt 11:21) though such usage was not restricted to Israel (Is 15:3; Jer 49:3; Ez 27:31; Jon 3:5). It has been suggested that the coarse fabric produced physical discomfort and was used to inflict self-punishment on the wearer. There is no evidence, however, to support this position.

See also Burial, Burial Customs; Mourning.

SACRIFICE
See Atonement; Offerings and Sacrifices.

SADDUCEES
Jewish sect cited 14 times in the NT, not referred to in the OT.

Their History A number of suggestions have been made as to the origin of the name. First, it has been connected with the Hebrew word for "righteous" (saddik). This is difficult from an etymological point of view, as there would have been a change from i to u in the word. Nor is there reason to think that they made such a claim to be the "righteous ones." Second, the name has been connected with Zadok (sometimes written Saddouk in Greek), a priest in the days of David (2 Sm 8:17; 15:24-29) who anointed Solomon (1 Kgs 1:32-39) and in his reign became chief priest (2:35). He is said to have descended from Eleazar, the son of Aaron (1 Chr 6:3-8), and Zadokite priests seem to have been responsible for priestly duties in the temple until the exile. In the blueprints for the restoration of the worship of the temple (Ez 40–48), it is the Zadokite priesthood that is again given charge to minister as "Levitical priests" (44:15-16; 48:11-12). After the exile, we read of Joshua (Jeshua) the son of Jehozadak as high priest (Hg 1:1), and his lineage was traced back to Zadok (1 Chr 6:8-15). The significance of the Zadokite priesthood continues to be stressed in writings of the early second century BC, but it is by no means clear that the Sadducees made a stand for the Zadokite priesthood. It may be added that the double *d* in the word is not readily explained by this view of Sadducean origins.

Third, a late rabbinic tradition is that the Sadducees took their name from another Zadok who lived in the second century BC. There is little to commend this view.

Finally, the British NT scholar T. W. Manson suggested that their name is to be connected with the Greek word *sundikoi,* meaning "members of the council," thus designating the Sadducees as councillors under the Hasmonean rulers.

The first historical knowledge of the Sadducees is in the time of Jonathan Maccabeus, who led the Jewish struggle against the Seleucids from 160 to 143 BC. Josephus (*Antiquities* 13.5.9) said that they were a party at this time, and that when John Hyrcanus was head of the Jewish state (135–104 BC) there was strife between the Pharisees and the Sadducees (*Antiquities* 13.10.6). It is possible that the Sadducees stood in some sense for the Zadokite priesthood or for the claim that the Jerusalem priesthood of their day was Zadokite in origin, but this is far from clear. Josephus says that the Sadducees had the rich on their side, while the Pharisees had a following among the common people. In the days of Salome Alexandra (76–67 BC), the Pharisees were in the ascendancy, but when Judea became a Roman province and Roman governors began to put one high priest down and raise another up, it appears that most of the high priests were from high-born Sadducean families. While they could temporize with the Romans, these Sadducean families had power and influence in the land. As hostilities developed between the Jews and their Roman overlords, the influence of the Sadducees declined. After the fall of Jerusalem to the Romans in AD 70, the Sadducees fade from history.

In the New Testament In the Gospel narrative they first appeared, together with Pharisees, at John's baptism. He addressed them as "sons of snakes" and challenged them to show repentance in their lives (Mt 3:7-10). Later, the Sadducees came along with some Pharisees to "test" Jesus, asking him to show them a sign from heaven (16:1). Jesus told his disciples to beware of the Sadducees (vv 6, 11-12).

A great difference begins to emerge between Pharisees and Sadducees in Matthew 22:23-33 (cf. Mk 12:18-27; Lk 20:27-38). The Sadducees, who, like others, wanted to embarrass Jesus with their questions, came with a trick question that showed their doubts concerning the resurrection of the dead. The Sadducees were described in this context as those who say there is no resurrection after death. They cited the case of a woman who had seven brothers as her husbands in succession. "Whose wife will she be in the resurrection?" they asked, implying that because of such a problem, the resurrection could not be a reality. Jesus answered by speaking of the error of their view caused by their ignorance of the Scriptures and of God's power.

In the early days of the church in Jerusalem, the priests and the captain of the temple police and the Sadducees became annoyed because the disciples were proclaiming the resurrection from the dead (Acts 4:1-2). The Sadducees seem to have led the opposition to the apostles and their preaching. Later the high priest and Sadducees determined to arrest the apostles and put them in the prison (5:17). The only other reference to them in the NT is in Acts 23:6-8, in the record of Paul's trial before the Jewish Sanhedrin. On that occasion, Paul deliberately spoke about his belief in the resurrection so as to cause a division between the Pharisees and the Sadducees, who did not believe in resurrection.

Thus from these NT passages one realizes something of the basic tenets of the Sadducees, of their prominence among the high priestly families, and of the differences between Pharisees and Sadducees.

Josephus, the Jewish historian who wrote in the closing years of the first century AD, adds to the information in the NT about this party. He said that the Sadducees, in contrast to the Pharisees and Essenes, gave no place to the overruling providence of God but emphasized that all that happens to us is the result of the good or evil that we do (*Antiquities* 13.5.9; *War* 2.8.14). Josephus, in a way comparable to the NT, spoke of the Sadducees' rejection of "the immortal duration of the soul, and the punishments and rewards in Hades" (*War* 2.8.14). "Souls die with the bodies" was what they said (*Antiquities* 18.1.4). Early Christian writers—Hippolytus, Origen, and Jerome—said that the Sadducees accepted only the Pentateuch and not the other OT books. It would seem, however, that they were not opposed to other OT books as a whole (though it is doubtful whether they accepted books such as Daniel, with its clear statement of the resurrection of the dead), but rather that they opposed the legal regulations introduced by the Pharisees and were saying that only the OT law should be considered mandatory. In this, as in their stand against belief in angels and in life after death, they appear to have regarded the Pharisees as innovators and themselves as conservatives.

The other main source of knowledge about the Sadducees is the Mishnah, the collection of the teaching of the rabbis, put down in writing in the second century AD. The Sadducees opposed many of the detailed regulations that the Pharisees sought to impose on the people (*Parah* 3.3,7). It also indicates that they had a greater tendency to compromise with the ways of the Gentiles than other Jewish parties (*Niddah* 4.2).

See Essenes; Judaism; Pharisees.

SADOC* KJV form of Zadok, an ancestor of Christ, in Matthew 1:14. *See* Zadok #9.

SAFFRON *See* Plants.

SAGE* Plant growing three feet (.9 meter) tall and indigenous to Palestine. When pressed flat, the inflorescence of this plant provides the pattern for the seven-branched lampstand used by the Jews (Ex 37:17-18). *See* Plants.

SAILORS Men trained in sailing ships at sea. The people of Israel were not generally seafaring and confined their activities on the water to the Sea of Galilee and the Jordan River. Occasionally, they may have had contact with large ships (Gn 49:13; Jgs 5:17). Solomon had a fleet of ships at Ezion-geber on the Gulf of Aqaba (1 Kgs 9:26-28; 2 Chr 8:17-18; 9:21). Jehoshaphat, too, had a fleet at Ezion-geber (1 Kgs 22:48; 2 Chr 20:35-37).

The NT frequently mentions ships and sailors—the numerous fishing boats on Galilee (Mt 14:22; Mk 1:19; 3:9; Lk 5:2; Jn 6:19, 22-24; 21:8) and the large ships such as the one in which Paul traveled to Rome (Acts 27:6-44). Shipmen or sailors are mentioned in Acts 27:27, 30. The term "mariner" (KJV) refers to a sailor (Ez 27:9, 27-29; Jon 1:5).

See also Travel.

SAINTS Name for believers meaning "holy ones" (which is the rendering in some modern versions—see NLT). The OT believers were called to be "holy," or consecrated to God (Ex 22:31; Lv 11:44). In the NT, "saints" became the apostle Paul's favorite name for Christians (Rom 1:7; 8:27; 12:13; 15:25-26, 31; 16:2, 15; plus 31 other places in Paul's letters). The name is also used 14 times in the book of Revelation. Other NT writers used it occasionally (Heb 6:10; 13:24; Jude 1:3). The name indicates that Christians are expected to be holy (Heb 12:10; Rv 22:11) because they have been consecrated to God as a holy priesthood and have rejected the ways of the world (1 Pt 1:15-16; 2:5, 9). More than that, they are the people of the coming age, who will reign with God over the earth and over angels.

SAKIA Son of Shaharaim and Hodesh from Benjamin's tribe (1 Chr 8:10).

SAKKUTH Name of the Babylonian Saturn, an astral deity in Mesopotamian religion (Am 5:26). Some suggest that Sakkuth reflects a corruption of *sukkah,* meaning "shrine" (NIV) or "tabernacle" (KJV), within which an image would be placed. *See* Kaiwan.

SALA*
1. Alternate name for Salmon, Boaz's father, in Luke 3:32 (see NLT mg). *See* Salmon (Person).
2. KJV rendering of Shelah, Eber's father, in Luke 3:35. *See* Shelah #1.

SALAH* KJV form of Shelah, Eber's father, in Genesis 10:24 and 11:12-15. *See* Shelah #1.

SALAMIS Seaport on the eastern shore of Cyprus where Barnabas and Saul landed near the beginning of their first missionary journey. They proclaimed the word of God in the synagogues of the Jews in this town (Acts 13:5). Tradition states that the city was 1,000 years old when the missionaries arrived, having been founded by Teucer after his return from the Trojan war.

For centuries, it was a major seaport, shipping copper, timber, ceramics, and agricultural products to Europe, Africa, and Asia. The Ptolemies encouraged Jews to settle there, which is why Barnabas and Saul found Jewish synagogues there. Barnabas's tomb is at nearby Ali Barnaba monastery (discovered in AD 477).

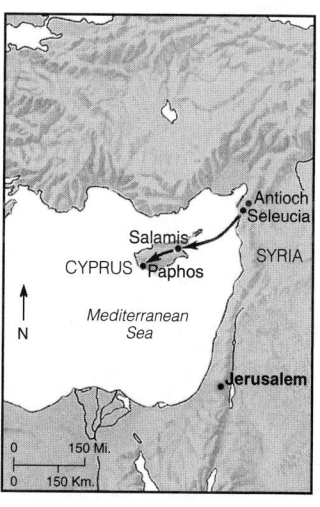

Salamis This city on the Mediterranean island of Cyprus was the first stop for Paul, Barnabas, and John Mark on the first missionary journey.

After the partial destruction of the city by Hadrian in AD 116 and further damage by earthquakes in AD 332 and 342, it was rebuilt by the Byzantine emperor Constantius II (AD 336–361). Prior to AD 332, Salamis had the largest

Jewish community on the island. Afterward, it apparently contained the largest Christian community, as it became the metropolitan see of the island.

After the destruction of the city by the Saracens in AD 647, the harbor silted up and the site was abandoned. During the centuries of Ottoman dominance, the harbor was replaced by the port of Famagusta.

> **ARCHAEOLOGICAL FINDS AT SALAMIS**
> Excavation of the site of Salamis reveals Roman baths, a Roman villa, a granite forum, the basilica, the agora, and the temple of Zeus. Portions of the city wall and ancient harbor have also been identified. The most impressive remains are at the north end and are called the Marble Forum. This vast complex includes remains of the gymnasium of the Greco-Roman period, the great hall, and baths from the early Byzantine period. The main forum, or market, measured 750 by 180 feet (228.6 by 54.9 meters), surrounded by large Corinthian columns. The basilica, or church building, is the largest known on the island. It was apparently built after Constantius II had renamed the city Constantia. The large Christian community that once flourished here bears witness to the pioneering work of Barnabas and Saul.

SALATHIEL* KJV alternate spelling of Shealtiel, King Jehoiachin's son, in 1 Chronicles 3:17, Matthew 1:12, and Luke 3:27. *See* Shealtiel.

SALCAH*, SALCHAH*, SALECAH City or district that formed the northeastern extremity of the Amorite kingdom of Og in Bashan, east of the Jordan River. Salecah (variously spelled Salcah and Salchah in the KJV) was located near the city of Edrei (Jos 12:5). The Israelites gained possession of this city when they defeated Og (Dt 3:10). Later, Salecah was included in the land received by Gad's tribe for an inheritance (Jos 13:11; 1 Chr 5:11). The city is identifiable with the modern town of Salkhad.

SALEM City from which the priest-king Melchizedek came (Gn 14:18; Ps 76:2; Heb 7:1-2). Salem is believed to be an ancient name of Jerusalem. *See* Jerusalem.

SALIM Location near Aenon on the west side of the Jordan River. Aenon was known for its many springs and was used by John as a place for baptism (Jn 3:23). Its location is not certain. Some scholars agree with Eusebius (an early church father) that its location was about seven miles (11.3 kilometers) south of Scythopolis (Beth-shan) in the Decapolis region. Others suggest it was the Salim east of Nablus near Shechem in Samaria, or perhaps the Wadi Saleim, six miles (9.7 kilometers) northeast of Jerusalem.

SALLAI
1. One of 928 Benjaminites who lived in the city of Jerusalem during the postexilic period (Neh 11:8).
2. Levitical household in the postexilic period during the days of Joiakim, the high priest (Neh 12:20; NLT "Sallu"); perhaps the same as Sallu in Nehemiah 12:7. *See* Sallu #2.

SALLU
1. Son of Meshullam and a Benjaminite, who resided in the city of Jerusalem during the postexilic period (1 Chr 9:7; Neh 11:7).
2. Levitical priest who returned to Jerusalem with Zerubbabel following the Babylonian captivity (Neh 12:7).

The Sallai mentioned in some translations of Nehemiah 12:20 is thought to be a variant spelling of Sallu.

SALMA

1. Hur's son of Caleb's family. He is considered the founding father of Bethlehem (1 Chr 2:51, 54).
2. An alternate spelling for "Salmon" in 1 Chronicles 2:11. See Salmon (Person).

SALMON (Person) Nahshon's son and an ancestor of David from Judah's tribe (1 Chr 2:11). Salmon fathered Boaz by Rahab (Ru 4:20-21) and is listed in Matthew's genealogy as a forefather of Jesus Christ (Mt 1:4-5); in the Greek his name is spelled Sala in Luke's genealogy (Lk 3:32).

   See also Genealogy of Jesus Christ.

SALMON* (Place) KJV spelling of Zalmon, a mountain in Bashan, in Psalm 68:14. See Zalmon (Place).

SALMONE Promonotory on the east side of Crete (Acts 27:7).

SALOME Name deriving from the Hebrew greeting shalom (peace), with the additional letter being a Greek suffix.

1. Woman who followed Jesus and was perhaps Mary's sister and the mother of James and John. In Mark 15:40, the evangelist describes the women who stood at the foot of the cross, and names three of them: Mary Magdalene, Mary the mother of James the lesser and of Joses, and Salome. Similarly, when describing the women who arrived at the tomb at dawn, Mark recounts that Mary Magdalene, Mary the mother of James, and Salome had brought spices to anoint the body (Mk 16:1). Matthew speaks of two women named Mary, and the mother of the sons of Zebedee, who could have been Salome (Mt 27:56). John speaks of four women: (1) Mary the mother of Jesus; (2) Mary the wife of Clopas; (3) Mary Magdalene; and (4) Mary's sister—unnamed (Jn 19:25). If Mary's sister was Salome, and she and the mother of the sons of Zebedee were one and the same, then James and John, the sons of Zebedee, were cousins of Jesus.
2. Daughter of Herodias, from her first marriage to Herod Philip. Although not specifically named in Matthew 14:6 or Mark 6:22, she is traditionally believed to be the girl whose dancing so pleased Herod that he promised her on oath anything she asked for up to half his kingdom. Prompted by her mother, she demanded the head of John the Baptist.

SALT, City of See City of Salt.

SALT*, Covenant of See Covenant of Salt.

SALT, Valley of Valley in the southern vicinity of the Dead Sea. The Valley of Salt was the scene of two major military campaigns recorded in the OT. Initially, it was where David made a name for himself by routing the Edomite army (2 Sm 8:13). Abishai, one of David's mighty men, was credited with killing 18,000 Edomites there (1 Chr 18:12). Later, King Amaziah of Judah defeated the Edomite army in this valley and captured Sela, an Edomite stronghold in the nearby hill country (2 Kgs 14:7; 2 Chr 25:11).

   The location of the Valley of Salt is not altogether certain. Some identify it with Wadi el-Milh (meaning "salt") east of Beersheba in Judah. A more probable suggestion

is with es-Sebkha, a lifeless saline plain south of the Dead Sea positioned in the Arabah, leading to the hill country of Edom.

SALT SEA* See Dead Sea.

SALTWORT* Family of bushy shrubs, of which numerous species can be found along the coasts of the Mediterranean Sea. See Plants (Mallow).

SALU Zimri's father from Simeon's tribe. Zimri, head of his father's household, was killed by Phinehas (Nm 25:14).

SALVATION God's way of providing people deliverance from sin and death. Scripture reveals God but it also reveals his plan to save the human race. In that sense, salvation is a major theme in both the OT and NT.

In the Old Testament The concept of salvation is represented by various terms and situations in both Testaments. Among several Hebrew words that mean "deliver" or "save," the Hebrew verb yasha' and derivatives are most frequently translated by English versions as "save" or "salvation." Frequency in the English Bible depends upon the version considered. For example, in the OT "salvation" is found 74 times in the NLT, 80 times in the NIV, 90 times in the RSV, 111 times in the NASB, and 119 times in the KJV. Salvation is not used as a technical term in the OT and is ascribed to both individuals and God. Leaders like Samson (Jgs 13:5) or David (2 Sm 8:6) are used of the Lord to bring deliverance to God's people.

   Israel's concept of salvation was rooted in the historical experience of the exodus. This momentous occasion was an opportunity to witness the salvation of the Lord (Ex 14:13) firsthand. Poets (Ps 106:8) and prophets (Is 43:3; Hos 13:4) later reiterated God's salvation when recalling the exodus experience. Israel's understanding of salvation was worked out in historical instances like Sennacherib's attack on Jerusalem in 701 BC, when the Lord declared that he would save the city for his name's sake (2 Kgs 19:34; cf. 18:30, 35). Israel's opportunity to see God's salvation through various leaders and situations corroborated this understanding of God as the God of salvation.

   Israel's response to God's deliverance was primarily praise, as evidenced so often in the psalms (Pss 3:8; 9:14; 21:1) and earlier poetic passages (Ex 15:2; 1 Sm 2:1). In addition, they directed petitions and pleas for help to the Lord for his salvation—whether from enemies (Pss 35:3; 38:22), sickness (69:29), or battle (140:7; 144:10-11)—and in faith expected his deliverance (35:9; 65:5).

   The prophets emphasized the eschatological (endtime) aspect of salvation. God's ability to save was revealed by his great works in the past, which thus promoted the anticipation of his work of deliverance in the future. This future hope was for the nation of Israel (Is 45:17) but anticipated universal deliverance (49:6). The prophets looked forward to deliverance and return from exile in Babylon (Is 49:25-26; Jer 46:27), yet they also spoke of an abiding future salvation (Is 45:17; 51:6-8). The messianic hope is indicated in passages that speak of an individual who will bring God's salvation. Isaiah speaks of the Servant who brings salvation to the ends of the earth (49:6), while Jeremiah writes of deliverance by God's righteous Branch (Jer 23:5-6). The mention of the king who brings salvation in Zechariah 9:9 reflects this messianic theme and is applied to Jesus Christ in Matthew 21:4-5.

In the New Testament In classical Greek the verb *sozo* ("to save") and noun *soteria* ("salvation") are used for the concept of "rescue," "deliverance" or "salvation," and even "well-being" or "health." The Septuagint most frequently uses *sozo* to render the Hebrew *yasha'* ("to save"), and the NT primarily employs *sozo* and its derivatives for the idea of salvation.

These Greek terms are generally used theologically in the NT, but examples of nontheological usage occur. In Acts 27, these words refer to the threat and deliverance of the soldiers, sailors, and prisoners from shipwreck (vv 20, 31), as well as their well-being (v 34).

In the Gospels "salvation" is clearly connected with the OT concept of salvation; it is applied to the coming of Christ in Zechariah's prophecy (Lk 1:69, 71; cf. Pss 106:10; 132:17) and in Simeon's hymn of praise (Lk 2:30). While *soteria* does not occur frequently in the Gospels, the concept of salvation is implied in Jesus' statement about entrance into the kingdom of God (Mt 19:24-26) and his miracles of healing (Lk 17:19; 18:42).

The NT teaches that salvation has its source in Jesus Christ (2 Tm 2:10; Heb 5:9), who is the "author" and mediator of salvation (Heb 2:10; 7:25). Salvation is God's work (1 Thes 5:9) and is offered by his grace (Eph 2:8-9). The message of salvation is contained in the Scriptures (2 Tm 3:15) and is carried by those who proclaim the word of truth (Eph 1:13). The appropriate response is repentance (2 Cor 7:10) and faith (2 Tm 3:15; 1 Pt 1:9). This was the preaching of the early church as it proclaimed the Savior Jesus (Acts 4:12; 13:23-26; 16:30-31). Paul especially proclaimed the universality of God's offer of salvation (Rom 1:16; Ti 2:11). His desire was for Jews to be saved (Rom 10:1), though he primarily preached the message of salvation to the Gentiles (11:11-13).

Within the Scriptures there are many other terms associated with the concept of salvation. The new birth speaks of being made alive in Christ ("born again," Jn 3:3). Justification envisions one's legal standing before God, while redemption speaks more of the means of salvation—the payment of a price to bring one back to God. Reconciliation speaks of a change in relationship and propitiation, which evokes the OT sacrificial system and points to the turning away of God's wrath. These terms and others share some common ground with the biblical concept of salvation, but all point to the person and work of Jesus Christ the Savior.

See also Justification, Justified; Reconciliation; Redeemer, Redemption; Savior.

SAMARIA Capital of the northern kingdom of Israel, identified with the hill on which the village of Sebastieh is located.

The hill was purchased by King Omri from Shemer, the clan who had occupied it. He built his new capital there (1 Kgs 16:24). A village was evidently there, dating at least from the 10th or perhaps the 11th century BC. It became the center of the revived kingdom and enjoyed the new prestige of the Omride dynasty. But it was also subject to siege. Ben-hadad of Syria (Aram-Damascus) came up against it with an alliance of 32 kings (1 Kgs 20), but the Israelites succeeded in driving them off. During the reign of Ahab's son Joram, Ben-hadad came again (2 Kgs 6:24–7:20) and almost conquered the city with a lengthy siege.

After a series of wars and the coup d'état by Jehu, which resulted in the slaughter of the priests of Baal in Samaria (2 Kgs 10:18-28), the city returned to the worship of Yahweh under Jehu's descendants. Nevertheless, the Asherah cult remained in Samaria under Jehoahaz (13:6). Syria continued to have the upper hand militarily (v 7).

During the eighth century, the balance changed in Israel's favor (2 Kgs 13:14-25), and under Jeroboam II, Samaria enjoyed great prosperity (2 Kgs 14:23-28; Am 3:10, 15; 4:1; 6:1, 4-6). In the late eighth century, the internal strife in Israel left the kingdom open to subjection by the Assyrians (2 Kgs 15). Finally, after Galilee, Transjordan, and perhaps the coastal plain were already detached, Samaria fell to Sargon II (18:9-12). During the ensuing decades, foreign exiles were transported there.

In the Persian period (sixth through fourth centuries BC), Samaria was the center of an administrative district governed by a dynasty of rulers whose names included several Sanballats (see Neh 2:10ff.), usually every other generation. The resultant Samaritan people considered themselves part of Israel but were rejected by the Judeans (Ezr 4:1-3). They were consulted, however, by the Jews of Elephantine when help was needed to rebuild the temple in Egypt.

Aerial View of Samaria

When Alexander the Great came to the Levant in 331 BC, the Samaritans at first curried his favor (Josephus, *Antiquities* 11.8.4), but later they murdered his governor. Their leaders evidently took refuge in the Wadi Dalieh cave, where they were trapped with their personal documents (papyri) and suffocated.

Samaria was taken in 108–107 BC (*Antiquities* 13.10.2; *War* 1.2.7) by John Hyrcanus, who destroyed the city. It was rebuilt by Pompey and further restored by Gabinius. King Herod changed the name of the city to Sebaste in honor of Caesar Augustus (Sebastos) and built a large temple to him there. At Sebaste, Herod entertained Agrippa, killed his wife Mariamne, and strangled his sons. During the first Jewish war, the Sebastenes went over to the Romans.

See also Samaritans.

SAMARITANS Schismatic group from the Jews. The group resided north of Judea and south of Galilee in hostile tension with its Jewish neighbors. Jesus' attitude toward this despised group radically contrasted with contemporary sentiment.

PREVIEW
• Origins of the Sect
• Relations between the Samaritans and the Jews
• Samaritan Beliefs
• Jesus and the Samaritans
• Samaria in the Mission of the Early Church

Origins of the Sect It is difficult to determine precisely when the Samaritan sect arose and when the final break with Judaism occurred. The OT conception of the origin of the Samaritan sect is that they stemmed from repopulated foreign peoples whose worship of God was only a veneer for underlying idolatry. According to 2 Kings 17, the Samaritan sect arose from the exchange of peoples following Israel's defeat by Assyria in 722 BC. Removing the Israelites from the land, the king of Assyria repopulated the area with conquered peoples from Babylon, Cuthah, and various other nations.

The Samaritans offer a vastly different interpretation of their origin. They claim descent from the Jewish tribes of Ephraim and Manasseh (see Jn 4:12) and hold that the exile of Israelites in 722 BC by Assyria was neither full-scale nor permanent. To account for the mutual hostility that developed between their group and the Jews, the Samaritan version holds that the Jews were guilty of apostasy, setting up heretical sanctuaries during the time of Eli, rather than staying with the only holy place on Mt Gerizim. The Samaritans therefore considered themselves true Israelites in descent and worship.

From Assyrian records of this period, an exchange of population is in fact affirmed for the northern kingdom, but apparently a total deportation was not carried out (see 2 Chr 34:9). This would suggest that there were two elements in the land: first, the native Israelite remnant not exiled; and second, the foreign exiles who were gradually won over to the faith of the native residents, although syncretism no doubt existed during the early period of assimilation.

Relations between the Samaritans and the Jews
The history of relations between the Samaritans—situated on the north around Mt Gerizim (their holy mountain), Shechem, and Samaria—and Jewish populations in Judea and then later in Galilee is one of fluctuating tensions. The ancient tension between the northern and southern kingdoms was revived with the return of exiles to Jerusalem under the Persian ruler Cyrus's edict (c. 538 BC). The entire southern area was at the time being governed from Samaria in the north by Sanballat, a native ruler of Palestine under Persian authority. The return of exiles to Jerusalem, particularly with their intentions of rebuilding the Jerusalem temple, posed an obvious political threat to his leadership in the north (Ezr 4:7-24; Neh 4:1-9).

Opposition was at first politically motivated but became religious when sometime later, possibly in the fifth century BC, a rival temple was erected on Mt Gerizim. An example of Jewish hostility toward the Samaritans about this time comes from Ecclesiasticus 50:25-26 (written approximately 200 BC), where the Samaritans are placed below the Edomites and Philistines in esteem and are termed a "foolish people" (cf. Test. Levi 7:2).

Jewish disregard for the Samaritans was increased by the Samaritans' lack of resistance to Antiochus Epiphanes' campaign (c. 167 BC) to promote Hellenistic worship in the area. While part of the Jewish community resisted the transforming of the Jerusalem temple to a temple for Zeus (1 Macc 1:62-64) and eventually followed the Maccabees in revolt (1 Macc 2:42-43), sources suggest that the Samaritans did not (see 1 Macc 6:2).

Poor relations came to a climax during the brief period of Jewish independence under the Hasmoneans, when the Jewish ruler, John Hyrcanus, marched against Shechem, conquering and destroying the Samaritan temple on Mt Gerizim (c. 128 BC).

Under Herod the Great, Samaria's fortunes improved, although animosity still continued between the Samaritans and Jews in Judea and Galilee. Holding the Jerusalem temple to be a false cultic center, and excluded from the inner courts by the Jerusalem authorities, a group of Samaritans desecrated the Jerusalem temple in approximately AD 6 by spreading human bones within the temple porches and sanctuary during Passover. Hostility toward Galilean Jews traveling through Samaria on the way to Jerusalem for various feasts was also not uncommon (Lk 9:51-53).

This animosity continued in Jesus' day. Both groups excluded the other from their respective cultic centers, the Jerusalem temple and the Samaritan temple on Mt Gerizim. The Samaritans, for example, were forbidden access to the inner courts of the temple, and any offering they might give was considered as if it were from a Gentile. Thus, although probably more accurately defined as "schismatics," it appears Samaritans were in practice treated as Gentiles. All marriage between the groups was therefore forbidden, and social relations were greatly restricted (Jn 4:9). With such proscribed separation, it is not surprising that any interaction between the two groups was strained. The mere term Samaritan was one of contempt on the lips of Jews (8:48), and among some scribes it possibly would not even be uttered (see the apparent circumlocution in Lk 10:37). The disciples' reaction to the Samaritan refusal of lodging (9:51-55) is a good example of the animosity felt by Jews for Samaritans at the time.

Although there is less evidence for similar attitudes from the Samaritan side, we can assume they existed. It is probable to speculate, therefore, that the Samaritan shunning of hospitality in Luke 9:51-55 was not uncommon toward other Jews whose "face was set toward Jerusalem."

Samaritan Beliefs The main beliefs of the Samaritans demonstrate both the close affinities with and obvious divergences from mainstream Judaism. They held in common with Judaism a strong monotheistic faith in the God of Abraham, Isaac, and Jacob. In contrast, however, there was an elevating of Mt Gerizim in the north as the only holy place for sacrifice, based on several divergent passages in Deuteronomy and Exodus in the Samaritan text. Mt Gerizim came to be identified with the site of Abel's first altar (Gn 4:4), the site of Noah's sacrifice after the Flood (8:20), the meeting place of Abraham and Melchizedek (14:18), the site of Isaac's intended sacrifice (ch 22), and many other associations.

The Samaritans held only the first five biblical books (Pentateuch) to be inspired and based their dogma and practice exclusively on these books. Such a narrow canon not only determined the direction of Samaritan theology but further separated them from contemporary Jewish thought. Moses, for example, was more highly exalted by the Samaritans than by the Jews. He was considered not only the chief prophet but also, in later thought, was described as the choicest of men, preexisting from Creation, interceding with God for Israel, and being to man "the light of the world." The messianic hope of Samaritan theology also reflects this narrow canon. A Messiah from the house of David could not be anticipated, as no evidence for such could be found in the Pentateuch. Rather, the Samaritans awaited a "prophet like Moses" based on Deuteronomy 18:15-18. This anticipated prophet was also designated the "Taheb," the Restorer, for he would in the last days restore proper cultic worship on Mt Gerizim and bring the worship of the heathen to that site.

It is clear, therefore, that it was primarily the claim of supremacy for Mt Gerizim that separated this group theologically and culturally from their Jewish neighbors.

Jesus and the Samaritans The common Jewish perspective on Samaritans as being nearly Gentile was evidently held to some extent by Jesus as well. Jesus refers to the Samaritan leper as "this foreigner" (Lk 17:18) and prohibits his disciples, during their commissioning, from taking the message of the kingdom to either the Samaritans or the Gentiles (Mt 10:5).

Yet the overwhelming evidence in the Gospels is that Jesus' attitude toward the Samaritans differed radically from that of his Jewish contemporaries. When his disciples display the usual Jewish animosity in asking to have the "fire of judgment" rain down upon the inhospitable Samaritans, Jesus "rebuked them" (Lk 9:55). Moreover, he did not refuse to heal the Samaritan leper but honored him as the only one of the ten who remembered to give glory to God (17:11-19). So also in the parable of the Good Samaritan (10:30-37) Jesus clearly breaks through the traditional prejudices in portraying the despised Samaritan, not the respected Jewish priest or Levite, as the true neighbor to the man in need. Here as elsewhere, Jesus, in confronting his audience with God's demand, breaks through traditional definitions of "righteous" and "outcast."

John 4:4-43 records not only the fascinating exchange between Jesus and the Samaritan woman but also Jesus' subsequent two-day stay in the town of Sychar, a Samaritan city. Here we see Jesus not only risking ritual uncleanness by contact with the Samaritan woman at the well (vv 7-9) but also offering the gift of salvation to her (v 10) and the entire Samaritan town (vv 39-41). Through Jesus' knowledge of her marital life (vv 16-18), the woman concludes he must be a "prophet." Remembering that the Samaritans were expecting a "prophet like Moses" in the last days, it is possible that the woman was wondering if Jesus was their long-awaited prophetic Messiah (vv 19, 25-26). Jesus not only breaks through the rigid animosity of Jews toward Samaritans by doing the unthinkable in staying with this despised people, but he also accepts their faith in him as "Messiah" (v 26) and "Savior of the world" (v 42). Here, as with his association with the outcasts of Jewish society, Jesus redefines righteousness not according to descent or religious practice but according to faith in himself. In so doing, he shatters the racial and cultural distinctions of his day and lays the foundation for the gospel's subsequent spread to the entire gentile world.

Samaria in the Mission of the Early Church In the great commission given prior to his ascension, Jesus told his disciples to take the gospel to Samaria (Acts 1:8). The missionary activity of the early church did indeed include this region. When, following the martyrdom of Stephen, many Christians were forced to leave Jerusalem (8:1), one such Christian, Philip, spread the gospel in the city of Samaria (v 5). The response was so great to the miracles performed that Peter and John (representing the apostles in Jerusalem) were sent to investigate and to confirm the presence of the Holy Spirit among them. Evidence from the second century AD suggests, however, that Christianity did not gain a strong foothold among the Samaritans. For the most part, the Samaritans retained their own religion. A small remnant of the Samaritan sect continues to exist to this day, living near Mt Gerizim (Shechem) and in various cities in Israel.

See also Bible, Manuscripts and Text of the (Old Testament); Samaria.

SAMGAR-NEBO* Babylonian prince who took part with Nebuchadnezzar and the Chaldean army in conquering Jerusalem after a three-year siege from 588–586 BC (Jer 39:3).

SAMLAH King of the Edomites from the town of Masrekah. Samlah came to power before any king ruled in Israel (Gn 36:36-37; 1 Chr 1:47-48).

SAMOS Small Greek island located off the coast of Asia Minor in the Aegean Sea near the promontory of Trogyllium. This Ionian island was positioned southwest of Ephesus and northwest of Miletus. In Paul's day, it was a prosperous commercial center and considered autonomous by Rome. In his wish to bypass Ephesus, Paul anchored near Samos on his journey to Jerusalem at the close of his third missionary journey. Paul's stay at Samos was mentioned between stops at Kios and Miletus (Acts 20:15).

Aerial View of Samos

SAMOTHRACE Island in the northeastern part of the Aegean Sea off the coast of the Roman province of Thrace. It was named Samothrace, or "Samos of Thrace," to distinguish it from the other Samos (cf. Acts 20:15), which was also in the Aegean Sea but a little southwest of Ephesus. Samothrace was about halfway between Troas and Neapolis, the seaport of Philippi.

This island was the stopping place for the apostle Paul on his way from Troas to Neapolis on his second missionary journey (Acts 16:11). It is not clear whether Paul landed on the island or whether his boat only anchored off its coast before sailing for Neapolis the next day. The usual anchorage was on the north side of the island, since boats were thereby protected from the southeast wind. Apparently, Paul's voyage from Troas to Neapolis via Samothrace was made with a fair wind behind the boat because it took two days. Returning, it took five days (see 20:6).

Samothrace

Samothrace is a mountainous island, with its central peak the highest point in the northern part of the Aegean, second in height only to Mt Athos on the mainland. The island has always been, in clear weather, an ancient landmark for sailors sailing between Troas and Neapolis. It is about 20 miles (32.2 kilometers) in circumference.

SAMSON Manoah's son, from Dan's tribe. His mother, whose name is not given in the Bible, had been barren.

The angel of the Lord announced to her that she would have a son, who was to be a Nazirite all of his life (i.e., he was not to drink wine or strong drink, not to eat anything ceremonially unclean, and not to allow a razor to touch his head, Nm 6:1-6). She was also told that he would begin to deliver Israel from the Philistines, who had subjugated them for 40 years (Jgs 13:1-5). She reported this to her husband, Manoah, and Manoah prayed concerning this angelic visit (v 8). The angel of the Lord appeared again and gave instructions about the child who was to be born. Manoah made a burnt offering, and the angel of the Lord ascended to heaven in the smoke. Manoah feared that they would die, for he now realized that they had seen God (v 22). The child was born and the Lord blessed him as he grew. The Spirit of the Lord moved upon him in Mahaneh-dan (v 25).

Samson went to Timnah and saw a Philistine woman whom he wished to marry. The Lord was seeking an opportunity against the Philistines, and in Samson's case these occasions came through Philistine women. When he and his parents went to Timnah to arrange the marriage, a lion came out of the vineyards, and Samson, upon whom the Spirit of the Lord came mightily, tore the lion in half. Later he found that a swarm of bees had made honey in the carcass of the lion (Jgs 14:2-9).

Samson made a feast at Timnah, as was the custom, and told the Philistine men a riddle that involved the lion and the honey. A wager was made on the riddle and the Philistines prevailed upon his wife to learn the answer and disclose it to them. When they came up with the answer, Samson knew what had happened, so he went out and killed 30 Philistine men to pay for his bet (Jgs 14:19). Samson went home, and his father-in-law gave Samson's wife to Samson's best man.

When Samson returned to see his wife, he was not allowed to visit her, so he took 300 foxes, tied them in pairs tail to tail, fixed a torch to each pair, and turned them loose in the grainfields of the Philistines, so that the shocks and standing grain were burned. Consequently, the Philistines came and burned his wife and her father. In revenge, Samson went out and slaughtered many of them (Jgs 15:1-8).

During these days, the Philistines came against Judah, and the people of Judah bound Samson with new ropes to turn him over to the Philistines. When they came to Lehi, where the Philistines were camped, the Spirit of the Lord came on him mightily. He snapped the ropes, seized the jawbone of a donkey, and killed 1,000 Philistines. Being very thirsty, he cried to the Lord, so God opened a spring of water at Lehi (Jgs 15:9-20).

Samson's weakness for Philistine women continued to create trouble for both him and the Philistines. He went down to Gaza, where he became involved with a prostitute (Jgs 16:1). The men of the city learned that he was there and plotted to kill him at dawn, but he arose at midnight and walked off with the doors, posts, and bar of the city gate and put them on top of the hill before Hebron.

Then he found Delilah, from the valley of Sorek. The Philistines enlisted her by bribery to find out the source of his strength (Jgs 16:4-5). She kept pestering him, so he told her that if they bound him with seven fresh bowstrings he would be as weak as other men. So she bound him and cried, "The Philistines are upon you." He easily broke the bowstrings. In response to her continued questions, he kept lying to her about the secret of his strength. In succession, she bound him with new ropes and seven locks of his hair woven together and attached to a loom. Finally, she wore him down and he told her the truth. If someone shaved his head and broke his

Nazirite vow, his strength would be gone. While Samson slept with his head on her knees, she called a barber, who shaved off his hair. This time when she cried, "The Philistines are upon you," the Philistines seized him, gouged out his eyes, and took him to Gaza (v 21).

At Gaza, Samson was bound with bronze fetters and forced to grind at a mill, during which time his hair began to grow again. At a time when the Philistines were having a great festival at the temple of their god, Dagon, they celebrated their victory over Samson and asked that he be brought so they could mock him. Some 3,000 people watched while Samson entertained them. At his request, Samson was placed between the two pillars supporting the temple. He asked the Lord for strength and pushed against the pillars, so that the entire building collapsed. Samson died with the Philistines as he had requested, but he killed more Philistines in this final act than he had previously (Jgs 16:1-30).

Samson's family came to retrieve his body, and they buried him between Zorah and Eshtaol in the tomb of his father, Manoah. He had served as "judge," or leader, of Israel for 20 years (Jgs 16:31).

See also Israel, History of; Judges, Book of.

SAMUEL (Person) Last of the judges, his name means "name of God" or "his name is El" (El is the name of the God of strength and power). The play on words in 1 Samuel 1:20 (cf. Ex 2:10) is not intended to be an explanation of the meaning of Samuel's name; Hannah's words recall only her prayer and the circumstances surrounding her son's birth.

Personal History Samuel's parents were a devout couple who went annually to the sanctuary at Shiloh (1 Sm 1:3). His father, Elkanah, was a Levite (1 Chr 6:26) and a resident of Ramah, territory of Ephraim. His mother, Hannah, was unable to bear children early in their marriage. Elkanah had a second wife, Peninnah.

On a visit to Shiloh, Hannah prayed in the sanctuary (1 Sm 1:6-11), vowing that, if the Lord would give her a son, she would dedicate him as a Nazirite (Nm 6:1-21) to God's service for life. The Lord heard Hannah's prayer and granted her request. She had no other children until after Samuel's dedication.

When Samuel was presented to Eli and began his service in the sanctuary, he bowed before the Lord and "worshiped the LORD there" (1 Sm 1:28). Three ingredients—a feeling of worth, a knowledge of his parents' love (cf. 2:19), and a sense of purpose—laid the foundation of his personality and his future accomplishments.

Further proof of Samuel's valuable early training is evidenced in 1 Samuel 2. Eli's sons had followed the licentious practices of the pagan religions around them. Eli was old, indulgent, and powerless to restrain them. Samuel neither developed irreverence for Eli nor followed his sons in the path of evil. God determined to judge Eli and his house for their sins. When God announced his purpose to Samuel, Samuel responded with reverence and respect. His personal and spiritual growth indicated that he had been marked out as a future prophet of the Lord.

When everyone did what was right in his or her own eyes (cf. Jgs 17:6; 21:25), God allowed an adjacent nation to serve as his instrument to chasten his people, until a judge arose to deliver them. When the Philistines again invaded the land (1 Sm 4-6), the Israelites mustered their army at Ebenezer, only to be defeated. Believing that the ark of the covenant would guarantee success, they sent to Shiloh for it. The next day the Israelites were again defeated and the ark captured. When this news reached Eli, he fell from his stool and died.

Twenty years elapsed before Samuel's name is mentioned again (1 Sm 7:2-3). Evidently, following the destruction of Shiloh (cf. Jer 7:12-14; 26:6, 9; Ps 78:60), he lived in Ramah and went on annual preaching missions that included Bethel, Gilgal, and Mizpah, "judging" the people in these places (cf. Dt 16:18-22; 17:8-13). Samuel probably also founded "schools of the prophets" during this period. Schools were established at Bethel (1 Sm 10:5; 2 Kgs 2:3), Gilgal (2 Kgs 4:38), Ramah (1 Sm 19:20), and elsewhere (2 Kgs 2:5), perhaps as a natural outgrowth of Samuel's ministry.

After a 20-year ministry, Samuel thought it timely to move toward spiritual and national unification. He convened a meeting at Mizpah (1 Sm 7). There, with a symbolic rite expressive of deep humiliation and in keeping with the libations of a treaty, the Israelites poured out water on the ground, fasted, and prayed.

The Philistines mistook the nature of the convocation and decided to attack the defenseless worshipers, who entreated Samuel to pray for them. He offered a sacrifice and the Lord sent a violent thunderstorm, causing the invaders to flee in panic. The pursuing Israelites won a significant victory at Ebenezer (1 Sm 7:12).

In Samuel's declining years, the elders rejected his leadership in favor of a king (1 Sm 8). Following earnest prayer, he received new direction from the Lord, acceded to their request, and later anointed Saul prince over God's people. Samuel then summoned the Israelites to Mizpah, where God's choice was made official, and Saul was hailed as king. Following Saul's victory over Nahash (ch 11), Samuel at Gilgal confirmed Saul's kingship. Thereafter, Samuel retired to Ramah to train men to carry on his ministry.

Samuel twice had to reprove Saul, first for impatience and disobedience (1 Sm 13:5-14), and then for disobeying the express command of the Lord (15:20-23), who rejected him as king. Samuel was then sent to the home of Jesse in Bethlehem, where he anointed David as the chosen one of the Lord (16:1-13).

In 1 Samuel 25:1 is a brief account of Samuel's passing, when all Israel gathered together and mourned for him. He was buried in Ramah. The only subsequent mention of Samuel is in 1 Samuel 28. Summoned by the witch of Endor at Saul's request, Samuel announced that on the following day Saul and his sons would die in battle (vv 4-19).

Character Samuel overcame many problems through piety, perseverance, and dedication to the service of the Lord. His overriding concern was for the good of his people. Wise and courageous, he boldly rebuked king, elders, and people when necessary, always from the sure ground of the revealed will of God.

While Samuel served as judge and priest, he was pre-eminently a prophet. Through his ministry the spiritual life of the Israelites improved. In inaugurating the monarchy, he led the people from tribal disunity to national solidarity. He appointed gatekeepers to the tent of meeting (1 Chr 9:17-26), organized observance of the Passover so memorably that it was still spoken about in Josiah's day (2 Chr 35:18), put into writing how a king and his kingdom should be (1 Sm 10:25), and penned "The Chronicles of Samuel the Seer" (1 Chr 29:29).

Samuel well deserves a place among the great men of faith (Heb 11:32). He was the last of the judges (1 Sm 7:6, 15-17) and the first of the prophets (1 Sm 3:20; Acts 3:24; 13:20).

See also Samuel, Books of First and Second.

SAMUEL, Books of First and Second

PREVIEW
- Name
- Author and Date
- Purpose and Theological Teaching
- Content

Name First and Second Samuel derive their names from the individual whom God used to establish kingship in Israel. Samuel is the most prominent figure in the early narratives of 1 Samuel. His key role in leading the nation of Israel through the transition from the period of the judges to that of the monarchy warrants the use of his name as the title for the book.

These books, however, have not always been so designated, nor was the material originally divided into two books. As far as is known, the Septuagint (the Greek translation of the OT dating from the third century BC) translators were the first to separate the material of Samuel into two books (they made a similar division in the material of Kings). The Hebrew original of these books was written, as is characteristic of Hebrew, with symbols only for consonants and none for vowels. When translated into Greek, it was necessary to use symbols for both vowels and consonants, thus greatly lengthening the manuscript. Presumably the practical consideration of the length of the scroll was the cause for dividing the material of both Samuel and Kings into two books (scrolls) instead of retaining just one. The Septuagint translators, recognizing the continuity of content and emphasis in Samuel and Kings, designated what is now known as 1 and 2 Samuel as "The First and Second Books of Kingdoms" and then designated what now is known as 1 and 2 Kings as "The Third and Fourth Books of Kingdoms." The Latin Vulgate (the Latin translation of the Bible prepared by Jerome in the late fourth century AD) slightly modified the Septuagint titles to "First, Second, Third, and Fourth Kings." These titles were utilized all through the Middle Ages and were modified into our present titles by the Protestant Reformers in the 16th century AD in agreement with Jewish rabbinic tradition. The Reformers, however, retained the division into two books, and this has been followed in modern English versions.

Author and Date Even though Samuel is prominent in the early part of the book, and the book bears his name in our English versions, it is clear that he is not the author of the entirety of 1 and 2 Samuel. Samuel's death is recorded in 1 Samuel 25:1, prior to the time of the accession of David to the throne in place of Saul. Who wrote the material of 1 and 2 Samuel if it was not Samuel? On the basis of the statement in 1 Chronicles 29:29, it has been suggested by some that Samuel composed the early narratives of the book and that his work was later supplemented by the writings of the prophets Nathan and Gad. Others have suggested one of David's contemporaries, such as Ahimaaz (2 Sm 15:27, 36; 17:17), Hushai (2 Sm 15:32; 16:16), or Zabud (1 Kgs 4:5). Presumably, these men would have had access to the writings of Samuel, Nathan, and Gad, as well as to other sources (see 2 Sm 1:18) pertaining to the life and reigns of Saul and David. Who the real author was, however, cannot be determined from available evidence. Whoever it was, it is clear that he lived after the death of Solomon and the division of the kingdom in 930 BC (see references to "Israel in Judah" in 1 Sm 11:8; 17:52; 18:16; 2 Sm 5:5; 24:1-9; and "kings of Judah" in 1 Sm 27:6).

Dead Sea Scrolls of 1 Samuel
Fragments containing 1 Samuel
1:22–2:24, from 4QSamᵃ

Thus, 1 and 2 Samuel was published in its final form sometime after 930 BC.

Purpose and Theological Teaching The theme binding together the narratives of 1 and 2 Samuel pertains to the relationship between kingship and the covenant. Kingship as requested by the people was a denial of the covenant; kingship as instituted by Samuel was compatible with the covenant; kingship as practiced by Saul failed to correspond to the covenantal idea; and kingship as practiced by David was an imperfect but true representation of the ideal of the covenantal king.

It has often been pointed out that there is ambivalence in the description of the establishment of kingship in Israel (1 Sm 8–12), because in some places it seems to be suggested that kingship is improper for Israel, while in other places it seems to be suggested that kingship was God's will for his people. Resolution to this tension is provided in 1 Samuel 12, when Samuel inaugurates Saul as Israel's first king in the context of a covenant renewal ceremony by which Israel renews its allegiance to the Lord.

Here it becomes clear that kingship in itself was not wrong for Israel; God desired Israel to have a king. But kingship of the type Israel desired ("like the other nations") and for the reasons she wanted a king (to give a sense of national security and lead her to victory in battle) involved a denial of the Lord as her ultimate sovereign. Samuel defined the role of the king in Israel and presented Saul to the people in a ceremony in which they renewed their allegiance to the Lord. The monarchy in Israel was first established in a form that was compatible with the covenant. The king in Israel, as every other citizen of the nation, was to be subject to the law of the Lord and to the word of the prophet. From this perspective, the author depicts the reign of Saul as failing to correspond to the covenantal requirements, while the reign of David, although imperfect, reflected the covenantal ideal.

There are at least two other important themes recorded in 1 and 2 Samuel. The first of these is that David conquers and acquires the land promised to Abraham. It is in the time of David that Israel's borders are extended from Egypt to the Euphrates, as had been promised. A second event of major significance for the remainder of the Bible is David's selection of Jerusalem to be the political and religious center of Israel.

Content

Samuel (1 Sm 1–7)

➤SAMUEL'S YOUTH (1 SM 1–3) God granted the request of Hannah for a son after a long period of barrenness. She named her son Samuel (a wordplay on the Hebrew expression "heard of God") and dedicated him to the service of the Lord—with Eli the priest at the tabernacle in Shiloh. Hannah's beautiful song of praise to God, who hears and answers prayer (2:1-10), exalts the sovereignty of God and prophetically anticipates not only the establishment of kingship in Israel but ultimately the highest fulfillment of the royal office in Christ himself (v 10). The evil practices of the sons of the priest Eli are described in verses 11-26. These men not only used their office for personal gain (vv 12-17) but also committed immoral acts with the women serving at the entrance to the tabernacle (v 22). Although Eli rebuked

his sons (vv 22-25), his warnings were too little too late. It was in this lax environment that Samuel grew up (vv 18-21, 26).

In 1 Sameul 2:27-36, an unnamed prophet pronounced judgment on Eli and his priestly line. The prediction of the imminent death of Hophni and Phinehas, Eli's sons, was fulfilled when the Philistines took the ark and destroyed the tabernacle at Shiloh (Is 4:11; Jer 7:14). In 1 Samuel 3:1–4:1, Samuel is called to be a prophet, and he too is given a message of judgment for the house of Eli (3:11-14). As the reliability of Samuel's words are attested, it is recognized by the people that he was a true prophet of the Lord (3:19–4:1).

➤THE LOSS AND RETURN OF THE ARK (1 SM 4–6) In a battle with the Philistines, the prophecy of 2:27-36 and 3:11-14 was partially fulfilled. The Israelites were defeated, the ark was taken, and Hophni and Phinehas were killed. Upon hearing the report of these calamities, Eli also died (4:17-18). The Philistines placed the ark of the Lord in the temple of their god Dagon in Ashdod (5:1-2). However, when the idol of Dagon broke in pieces and fell before the ark and a plague broke out in Ashdod, the ark was moved to Gath. When the plague broke out in Gath, it was moved to Ekron. When the plague erupted in Ekron, the Philistines were compelled to return the ark to Israel—as a test, it was placed on a cart pulled by two nursing cows. These cows, going against their motherly instincts, left their penned-up calves and headed for the Israelite border and the town of Beth-shemesh (6:1-21). By this the Lord demonstrated that the victory over the Israelites and the capture of the ark could not be attributed to the Philistines' god Dagon.

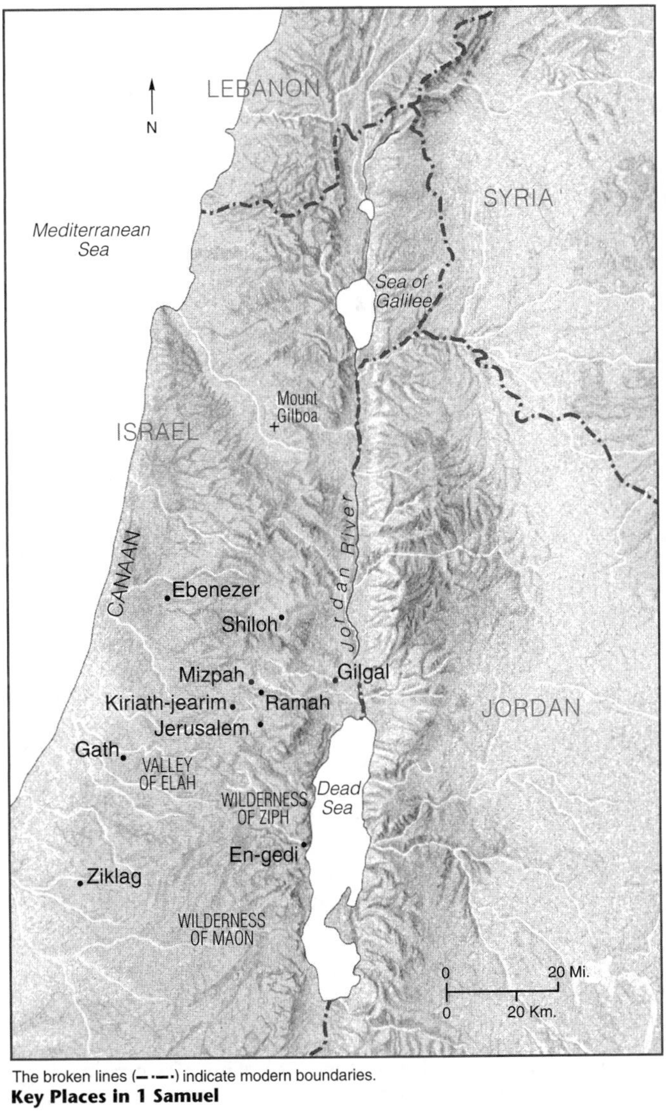

➤THE DEFEAT OF THE PHILISTINES (1 SM 7) Twenty years went by. Samuel assured the people of deliverance from Philistine oppression if they would confess their sin and turn from the worship of Baals and Ashtaroths. He called for a national assembly at Mizpah to renew allegiance to the Lord. While the Israelites were assembled, the Philistines attacked and the Lord gave the Israelites a miraculous victory, thereby demonstrating that obedience to covenant obligations would ensure national security (see Ex 23:22; Dt 20:1-4).

Kingship Established in Israel (1 Sm 8–12)

➤THE PEOPLE REQUEST A KING (1 SM 8:1-22) When Samuel was an old man, the elders of the nation approached him and requested that he give them a king. Samuel immediately perceived that their request was tantamount to a rejection of the Lord, who was their King, for the people desired a king "like the other nations"—as a symbol of national unity and military security. Nevertheless, the Lord told Samuel to give the people a king. At the same time, however, he told Samuel to warn the people concerning what having a king "like the nations" would mean. The warning, descriptive of

Mediterranean Sea

LEBANON

N

SYRIA

Sea of Galilee

Mount Gilboa

ISRAEL

Jordan River

CANAAN

Ebenezer
Shiloh
Mizpah
Kiriath-jearim Ramah
Jerusalem
Gath
VALLEY OF ELAH
WILDERNESS OF ZIPH
En-gedi
Ziklag
WILDERNESS OF MAON

Gilgal

JORDAN

Dead Sea

0   20 Mi.
0   20 Km.

The broken lines (— ·— ·) indicate modern boundaries.
Key Places in 1 Samuel

the practices of contemporary Canaanite kings, fell on deaf ears; the people persisted in their desire for a king.

➤ SAMUEL PRIVATELY ANOINTS SAUL (1 SM 9:1–10:16) The narrative of Saul's search for the lost donkeys of his father and his encounter with Samuel in the process of his search is given to explain how Samuel and Saul first met, and how the Lord indicated to Samuel who the person was that he was to anoint as Israel's first king (9:16-17). After Samuel privately anointed Saul (10:1), he was given three signs to confirm that his new calling came from the Lord.

➤ SAUL PUBLICLY CHOSEN BY LOT AT MIZPAH (1 SM 10:17-27) After the private designation and anointing of Saul to be king (9:1–10:16), Samuel convened a national assembly at Mizpah to make the Lord's choice known to the people (10:20-24) and to define the king's task (v 25). Again, at this assembly, Samuel emphasized that the people had rejected the Lord in requesting a king because they sought a king for the wrong reasons and failed to recognize the Lord's past faithfulness in delivering them from their enemies. But again it was clear that the time for kingship in Israel had come and it was the Lord's desire to give the people a king. Samuel's explanation of the "regulations of the kingship" was an important step in resolving the tension between, on the one hand, Israel's sin in desiring a king, and on the other, the Lord's intent to give them a king. This document, which was preserved at the tabernacle, probably contained an enlarged version of the "law of the king" in Deuteronomy 17:14-20 and spelled out regulations governing the role of the king in Israel for the benefit of both the king and the people. This document undoubtedly distinguished Israelite kingship from that of the kings of the surrounding nations.

➤ SAUL LEADS ISRAEL TO VICTORY OVER THE AMMONITES (1 SM 11:1-13) When Nahash, king of the Ammonites, attacked Jabesh-gilead, a town east of the Jordan in the territory of Manasseh, Saul left his farmwork to lead a volunteer army in support of the inhabitants of Jabesh-gilead. The victory over the Ammonites under Saul's leadership placed another seal of divine approval on his selection to be king. Saul attributed the victory to the Lord rather than to his own military strategies.

➤ SAUL INAUGURATED AS KING (1 SM 11:14–12:25) The victory at Jabesh-gilead prompted Samuel to call for a national assembly at Gilgal to renew the kingdom and make Saul king (11:14-15). At the Gilgal assembly, Samuel led the people in confessing the sin of their initial request for a king and in renewing their allegiance to the Lord. In the context of this covenant renewal ceremony, Saul was formally inaugurated in his office as king. By inaugurating Saul in this manner, Samuel effectively provided for covenantal continuity in the transition from the period of the judges to that of the monarchy.

Saul Rejected as King (1 Sm 13–15)

➤ SAUL'S DISOBEDIENCE (1 SM 13:1-22) When Saul was threatened with an imminent attack from the Philistines, he gathered troops at Gilgal and awaited Samuel, as he had been instructed (10:8; 13:8). When it appeared that Samuel would not come within the prearranged time, Saul became impatient and offered a sacrifice himself (13:9). Just as the sacrifice was completed, Samuel appeared and rebuked Saul for not keeping the commandment of the Lord. In disobeying Samuel's previous instructions, Saul had violated a fundamental requirement of his office. He was seriously mistaken in thinking he could strengthen Israel's hand against the Philistines

by sacrifice to the Lord when this was done in violation of the Lord's specific command. Samuel told Saul that because of his disobedience his dynasty would not endure (v 14).

➤ JONATHAN'S VICTORY (1 SM 13:23–14:52) Saul's son Jonathan and Jonathan's armor bearer skillfully and courageously attacked a Philistine outpost, killing about 20 men (14:8-14). The Lord used this defeat, along with an earthquake, to bring panic to the entire Philistine force. In the meantime, Saul sought divine guidance on whether to join the fray with his own forces. When the Lord's answer did not come immediately, Saul concluded that waiting for the Lord's word might jeopardize his military advantage. Here again he demonstrated that he trusted more in his own insight than in waiting upon the Lord. Saul further damaged his own stature in the eyes of his troops by pronouncing a foolish curse on any who would eat food before the battle was won. This nearly cost Jonathan his life; he was spared only because of the intervention of the troops in his defense.

➤ SAUL REJECTED AS KING (1 SM 15:1-35) Saul was commanded by the Lord through Samuel to attack the Amalekites and totally destroy them, sparing neither human nor animal life. The Amalekites had previously attempted to destroy Israel shortly after their exodus from Egypt while journeying to Sinai (Ex 17:8-16). Saul disobeyed the Lord in sparing the best of the animals for sacrifice and in sparing Agag, the Amalekite king. The Lord sent Samuel again to rebuke Saul for his disobedience. Samuel charged Saul with rebellion against the Lord and told him that, because he had rejected the word of the Lord, the Lord had rejected him as king.

Saul and David (1 Sm 16:1—2 Sm 1:27)

➤ SAMUEL ANOINTS DAVID (1 SM 16:1-13) The Lord instructed Samuel to go to the house of Jesse in Bethlehem to anoint one of his sons to be king in place of Saul. By divine leading, Jesse's youngest son, David, was shown to be the one whom the Lord had chosen. When Samuel anointed him as king, the Spirit of the Lord came upon him with power.

➤ DAVID IN THE SERVICE OF SAUL (1 SM 16:14–17:58) When Saul became plagued by an evil spirit, his attendants sought a harpist whose music would soothe him. David was the one chosen for this purpose. The position at the court, however, was not permanent, and David divided his time between the court and his home duties. In due time, the Philistines, led by the giant Goliath, encamped against the Israelites. Goliath challenged any Israelite who dared to meet him in individual combat. No Israelite ventured to accept his challenge until David, who was visiting the camp of the Israelite forces to bring food to his brothers, heard the challenge and responded in the strength and power of the Lord. The Lord gave David a great victory because he acknowledged that "the battle is the LORD's" (17:47, RSV).

➤ SAUL'S HATRED TOWARD DAVID (1 SM 18:1–19:24) In the aftermath of David's victory over Goliath, Saul's son Jonathan pledged loyalty to David in a covenant of friendship. As David achieved further successes in leading Israel's armies, and as his public acclaim grew, Saul began to fear that David was a threat to his throne (18:14-16, 28-30). Saul, hating David, made several attempts to kill him (18:17, 25; 19:1, 10). David was finally forced to flee and sought refuge with Samuel at Ramah. When Saul and three of his messengers went to Ramah to arrest David, they were so overcome by the

Spirit of God that they were incapable of fulfilling their mission.

➤DAVID AND JONATHAN (1 SM 20:1-42) David's absence from the royal table at the new moon festival provoked Saul to again threaten David's life. Jonathan met with David at a prearranged place to inform him of the danger and say good-bye. Jonathan and David again pledged themselves to mutual loyalty and kindness. In the encounter it is clear that both men knew that David, not Jonathan, would be the successor to Saul on the throne of Israel.

➤DAVID AT NOB (1 SM 21:1-9) David went to the priest Ahimelech at Nob and, indicating he was on a secret mission for Saul, asked for bread and for the sword of Goliath, both of which were given to him. One of Saul's servants, Doeg the Edomite, who was at Nob, observed the transaction.

➤DAVID AT GATH (1 SM 21:10-15) David then went into Philistine territory to King Achish at Gath. When his identity was discovered, he feigned insanity in order to escape.

➤DAVID AT ADULLAM (1 SM 22:1-5) From Gath David went to the cave of Adullam where he was joined by about 400 supporters. He took his parents to Moab for their own protection and then returned to the Forest of Hereth in Judah.

➤SAUL KILLS THE PRIESTS AT NOB (1 SM 22:6-23) Doeg the Edomite reported to Saul that Ahimelech the priest had given assistance to David. At Saul's command Doeg massacred all the priests at Nob except Abiathar, who escaped with the ephod and joined David.

➤DAVID AT KEILAH (1 SM 23:1-13) David and his men delivered the citizens of Keilah from Philistine raiders but were forced to leave the city when it was apparent that its unthankful inhabitants were prepared to hand David over to Saul.

➤DAVID IN THE DESERT OF ZIPH (1 SM 23:14-29) While David was in the desert of Ziph, he was encouraged by a visit from Jonathan, who again pledged to him his loyalty. Although the Ziphites promised to aid Saul in capturing David, a Philistine attack forced Saul to abandon his attempt to apprehend him.

➤DAVID SPARES SAUL'S LIFE (1 SM 24:1-22) While hiding deep in a cave at En-gedi, David was unexpectedly provided the opportunity to take Saul's life when Saul relieved himself at the entrance to the cave. Nevertheless, because Saul was "the anointed of the Lord," David spared his life and shamed him into confessing his own wickedness. David did this by showing Saul a piece of his robe that he had cut off while Saul was in the entrance to the cave.

➤DAVID, NABAL, AND ABIGAIL (1 SM 25:1-44) David was badly mistreated by a sheepherder named Nabal. David was deterred, however, from foolishly taking the man's life by the discerning words of Nabal's wife, Abigail. Shortly after this incident, Nabal died and David took Abigail as his wife.

➤DAVID SPARES SAUL'S LIFE A SECOND TIME (1 SM 26:1-25) For a second time, the Ziphites joined Saul in attempting to capture David. While Saul and his men were sleeping, David and Abishai crept into their camp and took Saul's spear and water jug. On the next day, David was again able to demonstrate to Saul that he did not seek to steal the kingship from his hands.

➤DAVID AMONG THE PHILISTINES (1 SM 27:1-12) David

eventually became weary of hiding from Saul in Israelite territory; in a time of discouragement, he went again to Philistia to seek refuge beyond Saul's reach. Ingratiating himself with Achish, a Philistine ruler, he was given the town of Ziklag as a place for himself and his men to reside. From Ziklag, David raided various tribes inhabiting the area south of Philistia, but deceived Achish into thinking he was raiding the territory of Judah.

➤SAUL AND THE MEDIUM OF ENDOR (1 SM 28:1-25) The Philistines again gathered an army to fight Israel, and Saul, terrified and seemingly anticipating an imminent defeat, vainly sought for some word from the Lord concerning the outcome of the battle. When this was denied, he went in disguise to a medium at Endor and requested her to bring up to him the spirit of Samuel. Saul was told by this spirit that Israel would be defeated and that he and his sons would die in the upcoming battle.

➤THE PHILISTINES MISTRUST DAVID (1 SM 29:1-11) Although Achish desired David to join the Philistine army in its battle with Israel, the other Philistine commanders mistrusted him and forced Achish to send David and his men back to Ziklag. This turn of events rescued David from a serious dilemma created by his apparent friendship with Achish.

➤DAVID DEFEATS THE AMALEKITES (1 SM 30:1-31) Upon returning to Ziklag, David discovered that in his absence the city had been raided and burned by the Amalekites and that their wives, children, and cattle had been taken captive. After inquiring of the Lord through Abiathar the priest, David and his men went in pursuit of the Amalekites and recovered all they had taken and more. He divided the plunder among his troops and sent gifts from it to various towns in Judah.

➤THE DEATH OF SAUL AND HIS SONS (1 SM 31:1—2 SM 1:27) As had been predicted, the battle with the Philistines ended in a disastrous defeat for Israel, in which Saul took his own life after being seriously wounded. Jonathan and two other sons of Saul were killed. David mourned for Saul and Jonathan and exalted their memory in his tribute to them recorded in 2 Samuel 1:19-27.

David (2 Sm 2–24)

➤DAVID ANOINTED KING OVER JUDAH (2 SM 2:1-7) Subsequent to Saul's death, the Lord instructed David to go to Hebron, where the tribe of Judah anointed him as their king.

➤DAVID, ISHBOSHETH, AND ABNER (2 SM 2:8-4:12) Although David became king over Judah, the remaining tribes—under the influence of Abner, commander of Saul's army—recognized Ishbosheth as Saul's successor (2:8-10). Ishbosheth was a son of Saul who had survived the battle with the Philistines. Conflict quickly broke out between the men of David, led by Joab, and the men of Ishbosheth, led by Abner. In this conflict Asahel, Joab's brother, was slain by Abner. As David grew stronger and Ishbosheth weaker, Abner shifted his allegiance from Ishbosheth to David (3:1-21). Joab, however, avenged the blood of his brother Asahel by murdering Abner under the pretense of negotiating with him. Although David detested this act, mourned for Abner, and cursed Joab, the crime was not punished until early in the reign of Solomon (see 1 Kgs 2:5-6, 29-34). Shortly afterward, Ishbosheth was killed by two soldiers, who brought his head to David at Hebron, expecting to be rewarded (2 Sm 4:1-8). David, however, had them both put to death. The only male survivor of Saul's line was the crippled son of Jonathan named Mephibosheth.

➤DAVID KING OVER ALL ISRAEL (2 SM 5) After Ishbosheth's death, David was made king over all the tribes at Hebron. One of David's first acts as king was to capture the fortress of Zion from the Jebusites. David established Zion as his capital and built a palace there for his residence.

➤THE ARK BROUGHT TO JERUSALEM (2 SM 6) Recognizing the importance of the ark as a symbol of God's presence with his people, David determined that it should be brought to Jerusalem from the obscurity of the house of Abinadab in Kiriath-jearim, where it had remained throughout the entirety of Saul's reign. Violation of prescriptions for handling the ark led to the death of Uzzah, one of Abinadab's sons, and delayed the ark's conveyance to Jerusalem for three months. In a second attempt David led a joyful procession into the city of Jerusalem, where the ark was placed in a tent that had been prepared for it.

➤DAVID, NATHAN, AND THE TEMPLE (2 SM 7) It soon became David's desire to build a temple to house the ark and provide a center for Israel's worship of the Lord. The Lord told David through Nathan the prophet that he was not to build the Lord a house (temple) but that the Lord would build him a house (a dynasty) that would endure forever. Here the line of the promised seed is narrowed to the house of David within the tribe of Judah. This promise finds its fulfillment in the birth of Jesus, who was the "son of David, the son of Abraham" (see Mt 1:1). It would be the task of Solomon, David's son, to construct the temple (2 Sm 7:13).

➤DAVID'S VICTORIES (2 SM 8) David was able to defeat numerous surrounding peoples, to extend Israel's borders, and to establish a time of prosperity and rest for the nation.

➤DAVID AND MEPHIBOSHETH (2 SM 9) Remembering his covenant with Jonathan (see 1 Sm 18:1-3; 20:13-16, 42), David inquired concerning survivors of the house of Saul to whom he could show kindness. When Mephibosheth was sought out, David brought him to the court to enjoy the honor of eating at the king's table.

➤DAVID AND BATHSHEBA (2 SM 10–12) During a war with the Ammonites, David committed adultery with the wife of one of his soldiers, Uriah the Hittite. When Bathsheba became pregnant, David attempted to get Uriah to sleep with her. When this failed, David arranged for Uriah's certain death in battle. These sinful acts provoked God's wrath (2 Sm 12:10-12) and David experienced the bitter fruits of his misconduct during the remainder of his life.

➤AMNON, ABSALOM, AND TAMAR (2 SM 13) David's oldest son, Amnon, feigned sickness in order to arrange for his half sister, Tamar, to care for him. When Tamar refused Amnon's sexual advances to her, he raped her. This incident enraged Tamar's full brother Absalom, who determined to avenge his sister by killing Amnon. Absalom waited two years and then arranged for the murder of Amnon during the festivities of the time of sheepshearing. He then fled to Geshur, a small city-state in Syria, where his maternal grandfather was king.

➤DAVID AND ABSALOM (2 SM 14–19) Absalom remained in exile for three years until Joab arranged for his return by securing a renunciation of blood revenge from David (14:1-27). Upon Absalom's return, however, David refused to see him for two years, until they were finally reconciled. In this whole episode David sidestepped the issues of repentance and justice and took no effective disciplinary action. In the meantime Absalom conspired to take the throne from David his father by attempting to discredit his administration of justice, and by seeking to win the favor of the people and members of David's court. After four years, Absalom proclaimed himself king in Hebron and gathered sufficient military strength to force his father to flee from Jerusalem (ch 15). Failure to immediately pursue

LEBANON
Abel-beth-maacah
ARAM
SYRIA
N
Mediterranean Sea
Sea of Galilee
Helam
ISRAEL
CANAAN
Jordan River
Forest of Ephraim
Mahanaim
Rabbah
AMMON
JORDAN
PHILISTIA
Jerusalem
Gath
Dead Sea
Hebron
Ziklag
MOAB
0   20 Mi.
0   20 Km.
EDOM

The broken lines (— · —) indicate modern boundaries.
Key Places in 2 Samuel

David led to the defeat of Absalom's forces and to Absalom's own death at the hand of Joab, David's commander. David mourned for his son Absalom (19:1-8), but he was able to return to Jerusalem and to reestablish his government. David disciplined Joab for killing Absalom by replacing him as commander of his troops with Amasa.

►REBELLION OF SHEBA (2 SM 20) In the unsettled conditions immediately after David's return to Jerusalem, another abortive revolt was attempted by Sheba of the tribe of Benjamin. Joab, in defiance of David's disciplinary action, killed Amasa, pursued Sheba, and crushed his revolt.

►DAVID AND THE GIBEONITES (2 SM 21:1-14) At some unspecified time during David's reign, the land suffered a three-year famine. It was revealed to David by the Lord that the famine was due to Saul's violation of an Israelite treaty with the Gibeonites (see Jos 9:15, 18-27). This offense was atoned for by giving seven descendants of Saul to the Gibeonites for execution.

►DAVID AND THE PHILISTINES (2 SM 21:15-22) In this pericope four episodes of heroic accomplishments by David's mighty men against the Philistines are recounted.

►DAVID'S SONG OF PRAISE (2 SM 22) In a beautiful song of praise, David described his deliverance from his enemies and the help with which the Lord sustained him. The same song occurs with minor variations in Psalm 18.

►DAVID'S LAST WORDS (2 SM 23:1-7) In a brief statement, David acknowledges the work of God's Spirit in enabling him to speak God's word, and proclaims his confidence in the realization of the Lord's promise to him and his dynasty.

►DAVID'S MIGHTY MEN (2 SM 23:8-39) This pericope contains a list of 37 of David's warriors and a description of some of their accomplishments.

►THE CENSUS AND DAVID'S PUNISHMENT (2 SM 24:1-25) David's decision to take a census of his fighting men reflected an improper trust in military-political organization and power. The Lord judged him by sending a plague on the land that killed many people. At the word of the Lord through Gad the prophet, David built an altar on the threshing floor of Araunah, which was later to become the site of the temple (see 2 Chr 3:1). The Lord responded to David's sacrifices and prayers on behalf of the people; the plague was stopped.

See also David; Samuel (Person); Saul #2.

SANBALLAT Leading political official of Samaria residing at Beth-horon in Ephraim. In a letter from Elephantine of Egypt, Sanballat was named as the governor of Samaria in 407 BC. Sanballat, along with Tobiah the Ammonite and Geshem the Arab, were adversaries of Nehemiah. They tried to prevent him from rebuilding the walls of Jerusalem during the postexilic period (Neh 2:10, 19; 4:1, 7; 6:1-14; 13:28). The Judean province probably had been included under Samaritan rule since its defeat by Babylon under Nebuchadnezzar in 586 BC. Nehemiah's determination to rebuild the walls of Jerusalem was in essence an assertion of Judean independence from Sanballat and Samaritan control.

SANCTIFICATION Term meaning "being made holy, or purified." It is used broadly of the whole Christian experience, though most theologians prefer to use it in a restricted sense to distinguish it from related terms, such as "regeneration," "justification," and "glorification."

Definition A comprehensive definition of sanctification by the New Hampshire Baptist Confession (1833) states,

> We believe that Sanctification is the process by which, according to the will of God, we are made partakers of his holiness; that it is a progressive work; that it is begun in regeneration; and that it is carried on in the hearts of believers by the presence and power of the Holy Spirit, the Sealer and Comforter, in the continual use of the appointed means—especially the Word of God, self-examination, self-denial, watchfulness, and prayer. (Article X)

This definition helps us to distinguish sanctification from regeneration in that the latter speaks of the inception of the Christian life. Sanctification is also distinguished from glorification, which focuses on the consummation of God's work in the believer. Put quite simply, then, regeneration refers to the beginning, sanctification to the middle, and glorification to the end of salvation.

The distinction between sanctification and justification, on the other hand, calls for more detailed attention, both because it is subtle and because it is fundamental. In the first place, "justification," like "regeneration," refers (though not exclusively) to the beginning of the Christian experience, whereas the above definition emphasizes the progressive character of sanctification. Second, justification refers to a judicial act of God whereby believers are at once absolved of all their guilt and accounted legally righteous, whereas sanctification, like regeneration and glorification, calls attention to the transforming power of the Holy Spirit upon the character of God's children.

This distinction played an important role at the time of the Reformation. The Roman Catholic Church, in the opinion of the Reformers, confused these two doctrines by insisting that justification "is not remission of sins merely, but also the sanctification and renewal of the inward man" (Decrees of the Council of Trent, Sixth Session, 1547, ch. VII). In contrast, the Reformers emphasized that the two doctrines, although inseparable, must be distinguished. Calvin argued that, to be sure, these two elements of God's saving act cannot be torn into parts any more than Christ can be torn: "Whomever, therefore, God receives into grace, on them he at the same time bestows the spirit of adoption, by whose power he remakes them to his own image. But if the brightness of the sun cannot be separated from its heat, shall we therefore say that the earth is warmed by its light, or lighted by its heat?" (*Institutes of the Christian Religion*, 3:11.6). In short, then, justification is a once-for-all, declarative act of God as Judge, whereas sanctification is a progressive change in the character of the person justified.

One more element in the New Hampshire Baptist Confession definition requires comment, namely, the statement that "we are made partakers of his holiness." A complete survey of what the Bible has to say about sanctification is not possible here, since practically the whole of Scripture addresses this issue in one way or another. One central theme in that teaching, however, must be emphasized: "You shall be holy as I am holy" (Lv 11:45; 1 Pt 1:16; cf. Mt 5:48). According to the Westminster Shorter Catechism (1647), by sanctification "we are renewed in the whole man after the image of God" (Question 34; see Col 3:10). Nothing can be more crucial to our view of sanctification than this truth. The standard of holiness is complete conformity to Christ's image (Rom 8:29); anything less than that is a lowering of the scriptural standard and thus a dilution of the doctrine. The definition above, however, implies that Christ is more than our pattern: he himself provides his holiness for those united with him—he *is* our sanctification (1 Cor 1:30).

Initial Sanctification The progressive nature of our sanctification is explicit in many passages, particularly Paul's statement that Christians are transformed "from glory to glory" into the Lord's image (2 Cor 3:18; see also Rom 12:1-2; Phil 3:14; Heb 6:1; 2 Pt 3:18). Moreover, the numerous commands found in Scripture imply that the Christian experiences growth.

At the same time, however, a number of expressions in Scripture reveal that sanctification is given to the believer concurrent with regeneration. For example, Paul frequently refers to Christians as "saints," that is, "holy ones" (Rom 1:7; Eph 1:1; etc.); this language suggests that sanctification is already the possession of believers. In fact, Paul specifically says that the Corinthian Christians "have been sanctified" (1 Cor 1:2), and he even coordinates sanctification with washing (= regeneration?) and justification as though all three elements had taken place at the same time (6:11). Perhaps more impressive is the apostle's declaration that Christians have died to sin (Rom 6:2). One can hardly think of a more powerful figure than death, suggesting as it does a permanent, irrevocable dissolution of the believer's relationship with sin.

It goes without saying, of course, that these passages do not teach absolute perfection for every Christian upon conversion. Such an interpretation would bring us into conflict with the clear teaching of Scripture as a whole. Furthermore, one should note that the Corinthian "saints" were marked by woeful immaturity (1 Cor 3:1-3; 6:8; 11:17-22).

How, then, should these passages be interpreted? Some writers have suggested that Paul is speaking of "potential" sanctification—that is, although our relationship with sin has not been actually severed, God has given us what we need for that to take place. There is an element of truth in this formulation, but it hardly does justice, by itself, to the force of Paul's language. Coming somewhat closer to an adequate explanation is to speak of "positional" sanctification. According to this view, Paul is speaking in judicial terms regarding our status before God. One should certainly recognize a judicial element in Paul's discussion (Rom 6:7 uses the word "justified"), but if that is all that is said, then it suggests that Romans 6 simply restates the doctrine of justification—a doubtful conclusion. Much more satisfactory is the view that Paul's teaching contains both a judicial element and an actual, experiential reference.

Progressive Sanctification

Historical Survey Although all Christian groups recognize the need to become transformed by the renewing of the mind (Rom 12:2), considerable differences are found among them regarding specific issues. The Reformers, generally speaking, held to what some call a "pessimistic" view of personal sanctification. This perspective is clearly reflected in the Westminster Confession of Faith (1647), which states that sanctification "is imperfect in this life; there abideth still some remnants of corruption in every part, whence ariseth a continual and irreconcilable war" within the believer (XIII.ii). Although the confession goes on to emphasize the overcoming power of

the Spirit, some Christians believe that its basic thrust obscures the need and possibility of spiritual victory.

To some extent, the teachings of John Wesley (1703–91) may be viewed as a reaction to the usual Calvinistic and Lutheran formulations. Strongly influenced by the Pietistic movement of his day, Wesley paid much attention to the experiential side of Christianity and eventually formulated, though not with great consistency, the doctrine that "entire sanctification" is possible in this life. During the 19th century, interest in the possibility of perfection (not understood in an absolute sense, however) spread to many Christian circles. According to some, perfection resulted from the eradication of sin; according to others, spiritual victory was gained by counteracting the sin that remains even in the Christian's heart. The latter approach became characteristic of the so-called Victorious Life Movement. These various "perfectionist" groups were subjected to a searching criticism by the Princeton theologian Benjamin B. Warfield (1851–1921). The debate has continued, though not as vigorously, ever since then.

The Agency in Sanctification Much of the controversy focuses on the human role in sanctification. While all Christians agree that holiness would be impossible without God's help, it is difficult to define precisely how that truth affects one's own activity. In the Roman Catholic tradition so much stress has been placed on the cleansing power of baptism and on the meritorious character of good works that one may rightly question whether the significance of divine grace is not thereby ignored. At the other extreme stand some exponents of the Victorious Life Movement, whose stress on "let go and let God" (a slogan that has some value if properly used) sometimes suggests that believers remain completely passive in sanctification.

No passage of Scripture is more relevant to this issue than Philippians 2:12-13, where Paul juxtaposes the command for one to work out one's own salvation with the declaration that it is God who provides the spiritual strength necessary for the task. It may be tempting to emphasize the first part of the statement so as to ignore the fundamental significance of the second, or else to become so arrested by Paul's stress (here and elsewhere) on divine grace that the weight of personal responsibility is overlooked. The apostle, however, appears to have deliberately and carefully preserved a fine balance between these two truths.

Sanctification requires discipline, concentration, and effort, as is clear by the many exhortations of Scripture, especially those where the Christian life is described with such figures as running and fighting (1 Cor 9:24-27; Eph 6:10-17). But Christians must always resist the temptation to assume that they in effect sanctify themselves, that spiritual power comes from within them, and that they may therefore rely on their own strength. This is a difficult tension, though no more puzzling than the paradox of prayer ("Why pray when God, who knows our needs and who is all-wise and sovereign, will always do what is best anyway?"). Yet perhaps the real "secret" of holiness consists precisely in learning to keep that balance: relying thoroughly on God as the true agent in sanctification, while faithfully discharging one's personal responsibility.

See also Holiness; Justification, Justified.

SANCTUARY Translation of two Hebrew words, *kodesh* and *midkosh*, both of which are derived from the verb "to be clean" and/or "to be holy." It appears approximately 60 times in Exodus, Leviticus, and Numbers where the building, moving, and initial use of the tabernacle is reported. Places of revelation, sacrifice, and worship are referred to in Deuteronomy but not by the term "sanctuary." The term appears over 60 times in Ezekiel, Daniel, and postexilic writings because of the importance the sanctuary had in the life of Israel during and after the exile.

"Sanctuary" refers to the place where God appeared and/or dwelt, as indicated by the presence of the ark. God's Word was kept there and issued forth from it. There God's people gathered for sacrifice, for hearing the covenant word, for worship and prayer, and for the celebration of the major feasts.

The patriarchs had places of worship (Gn 26:24-25; 28:16-22) but no actual sanctuary. The first reference to sanctuary (Ex 15:17) speaks of it as a symbol of God's dwelling among his people and ruling over them from within it. The tabernacle, moved from place to place, was the central sanctuary until the time when Solomon built the temple in Jerusalem. It must be emphatically stressed that God's people were to have one central sanctuary (Dt 12:4-7; 16:5-8).

The NT refers to the OT sanctuary as a type of a foreshadowing of God's eternal dwelling with and among his people (Heb 8:5-6; 9:1-14).

See also Tabernacle; Temple.

SANDALWOOD* *See* Plants (Almug).

SAND LIZARD *See* Animals (Lizard).

SANHEDRIN* Supreme judicial council (NLT "high council") of Judaism with 71 members, located in Jerusalem. It figures prominently in the Passion narratives of the Gospels as the body that tried Jesus, and it appears again in Acts as the judicial court that investigated and persecuted the growing Christian church.

History The history of the Sanhedrin is difficult to reconstruct. Jewish tradition recorded in the Mishnah views it as originating with Moses and his council of 70, but this is doubtful (Mishnah tractate *Sanhedrin* 1:6; cf. Nm 11:16). These were probably informal gatherings of tribal elders (1 Kgs 8:1; 2 Kgs 23:1). The likely origin of the Sanhedrin is to be found in the postexilic period, when those who reorganized Israel without a king made the ancient ruling families the basis of authority. The legislative assembly that emerged was a union of the nobility of the land and the priestly aristocracy (see Ezr 5:5; Neh 2:16). The influence of this council increased due to the relative freedom enjoyed under the Persians.

The advent of Hellenism in Israel in the fourth century BC affirmed this government. Hellenistic cities commonly possessed democratic assemblies and a council. Jerusalem hosted an aristocratic council that was given its appropriate Greek title, *Gerousia*. This council is first noted by Josephus, who records the decree of Antiochus III after his seizure of Jerusalem (*Antiquities* 12.3.3). Yet even though the political climate shifted drastically, the council still remained in force. Judas Maccabeus expelled the old line of elders and installed another hereditary rulership stemming from the Hasmonean families. Thus the Gerousia continued as a council of the nobility. But in the first century BC, as the tensions between Sadducees and Pharisees were pulling apart the fabric of Judaism, the council underwent a transformation. From the time of Alexandra (76–67 BC), scribes of Pharisee persuasion entered the council. Thereafter, the Gerousia was a mixture: aristocratic nobility on the one hand (both lay and priestly) and the popular Pharisees on the other.

The Romans left the council intact but more carefully defined the limits of its jurisdiction. As Judaism lost its self-government, the council lost much legislative and political power. Rome appointed the true powers of the land. For instance, Herod the Great began his rule in severe conflict with the old aristocracy, and in the end executed most of the Sanhedrin members (*Antiquities* 14.9.4). The prefects appointed the high priests and, as a symbol of control, from AD 6 to 36 they kept the priests' vestments in the Antonia fortress.

The name Sanhedrin (Greek, *sunedrion*, from *sun*, "together," and *hedra*, "seat") occurs for the first time in the reign of Herod the Great (*Antiquities* 14.9.3-5). This is the term used throughout the NT (22 times), along with "the elders" (Lk 22:66; Acts 22:5) and "gerousia" (Acts 5:21). The Mishnah provides still more titles: The Great Tribunal (*Sanhedrin* 11:2), the Great Sanhedrin (*Sanhedrin* 1:6), and the Sanhedrin of the 71 (*Shebuoth* 2:2).

After the great war of AD 70, when the final vestiges of Jewish autonomy were destroyed by Rome, the Sanhedrin reconvened in Jamnia. Its power, however, was only theoretical (addressing religious issues primarily), and the Romans gave it little consideration.

Character Little is known about the procedure for admission into the Sanhedrin, but because the council had aristocratic roots (and was not truly democratic), appointments were probably made from among the priests, leading scribes, and lay nobility. The Mishnah stipulates that the sole test of membership was rabbinic learning along with true Israelite descent (*Sanhedrin* 4:4). The council had 71 members (*Sanhedrin* 1:6) divided into the following three categories: the high priests, the elders, and the scribes.

The High Priests Usually from Sadducean backgrounds, these were the most powerful men of the Sanhedrin. Some scholars believe that they comprised an executive council of ten wealthy and distinguished citizens, on the pattern of several Greek and Roman cities. Tiberias in Galilee, for instance, was ruled by such a board, and Josephus refers to them as a body of "the ten foremost men" (*Antiquities* 20.8.11; cf. Acts 4:6). One was the captain of the temple, who supervised temple proceedings and was commander of the temple guard (Acts 5:24-26). Others served as treasurers who controlled the wages of priests and workers and monitored the vast amount of money coming through the temple. Income came from sacrifices and market taxes; the payroll included as many as 18,000 men during Herod's reconstruction of the temple. There was a president of the Sanhedrin who also headed this council and was called "the high priest" (*Antiquities* 20.10.5). In the NT he is a leading figure: Caiaphas ruled in Jesus' day (Mt 26:3), and Ananias in Paul's day (Acts 23:2). In Luke 3:2 and Acts 4:6, Annas is termed a high priest, but his title is emeritus, since his reign ended in AD 15.

The Elders This was a major category and represented the priestly and financial aristocracy in Judea. Distinguished laymen, such as Joseph of Arimathea (Mk 15:43), shared the conservative views of the Sadducees and gave the assembly the diversity of a modern parliament.

The Scribes These were the most recent members of the Sanhedrin. Mostly Pharisees, they were professional lawyers trained in theology, jurisprudence, and philosophy.

They were organized in guilds and often followed celebrated teachers. One famous Sanhedrin scribe, Gamaliel,
appears in the NT (Acts 5:34) and was the rabbinic
scholar who instructed Paul (22:3).

In Jesus' Day The domain of the Sanhedrin was formally
restricted to Judea, but there was a de facto influence
that affected Galilee and even Damascus (cf. Acts 9:2;
22:5). The council was chiefly concerned to arbitrate
matters of Jewish law when disagreements arose (*Sanhedrin* 11:2). In all cases, its decision was final. It prosecuted charges of blasphemy, as in the cases of Jesus (Mt
26:65) and Stephen (Acts 6:12-14), and participated in
criminal justice as well.

It is still not known if the Sanhedrin had the power of
capital punishment. Philo seems to indicate that violations to the temple could be prosecuted in the Roman
period (*Legatio to Gaius*, 39). This may explain the deaths
of Stephen (Acts 7:58-60) and James (*Antiquities* 20.9.1).
At any rate, Gentiles caught trespassing in the temple
precincts were warned about an automatic death penalty.
But the NT and the Talmud disagree with this. In the trial
of Jesus, the authorities are compelled to involve Pilate
who alone can put Jesus to death (Jn 18:31). According
to the Talmud, the Sanhedrin lost this privilege "forty
years before the destruction of the temple" (*Sanhedrin* I
18a, 34; VII 24b).

Judicial Procedure Despite the serious irregularities
of Jesus' trial, the formal procedures of Sanhedrin law
describe a court that was fair and exceedingly concerned
about the miscarriage of justice. Unfortunately, the procedural notes in the Mishnah only address guidelines for
lesser courts (Sanhedrins with 23 members), but it can
be reasonably conjectured that similar rules applied to
the Great Sanhedrin of 71. In sections four and five of
the Mishnah tractate *Sanhedrin*, these guidelines are carefully set forth.

The Sanhedrin sat in semicircular rows so that members could view one another. Two clerks sat at either end,
taking notes and recording votes. Facing the assembly sat
three rows of students, who were usually disciples of
leading scribes. The accused stood in the middle facing
the elders. He was required to show abject humility: he
was dressed in a black robe as if in mourning and wore
his hair disheveled (*Antiquities* 14.9.4). After questioning, he was dismissed and deliberations were private.

The procedures for capital cases illustrate the concern
for fairness. The defense would be heard first and then
the accusations. An elder who had spoken for the
defense could not then speak against the accused. Students could speak only for but never against the accused
(but in noncapital cases they could do either). Members
stood to vote, beginning with the youngest. Acquittal
required a simple majority, but condemnation
demanded a majority of two.

In noncapital cases, the trial was heard during the daytime and the verdict could be given at night. In capital
cases, both trial and verdict were during the day and thus
open to more public scrutiny. In noncapital cases, any
verdict could be reached the same day. In capital cases,
the verdict of guilt (which was immediately followed by
execution) had to be postponed one day because its consequences were irreversible. Hence, these trials were not
to be held on the eve of the Sabbath or a festival day
(*Sanhedrin* 4:1).

The trial of Jesus as recorded in the Gospels shows
many departures from the usual pattern of Sanhedrin
justice. It seems clear that a miscarriage of justice was evidenced in Jesus' arrest, interrogation, and death.

See also Courts and Trials; Jerusalem Council.

SANSANNAH One of 29 cities at the southern extremity of the land inherited by the sons of Judah (Jos 15:31).
It is possibly the same city as Hazar-susah mentioned in
a parallel description of the territory allotted to Simeon
within Judah's inheritance (19:5).

SAPH Descendant of the giants, killed by Sibbecai the
Hushathite (one of David's warriors) at Gad in a battle
between Israel and Philistia (2 Sm 21:18); alternately
called Sippai (1 Chr 20:4).

SAPHIR* KJV spelling of Shaphir, a place mentioned in
Micah 1:11. *See* Shaphir.

SAPPHIRA Member of the Jerusalem church and wife
of Ananias (Acts 5:1). *See* Ananias #1.

SAPPHIRE *See* Stones, Precious #21.

SARA* KJV rendering of Sarah, Abraham's wife, in
Hebrews 11:11 and 1 Peter 3:6. *See* Sarah #1.

SARAH
1. Wife of Abraham whose name was originally Sarai
(Gn 11:29). Her name was changed to Sarah ("princess") when she was promised that she would bear a
son and become the mother of nations and kings
(17:15-16). Sarah was both the wife and the half sister
of Abraham (20:12).

Sarah accompanied Abraham in his journey from
Ur of the Chaldees to Haran and eventually into the
land of Canaan (Gn 11:31; 12:5). She remained barren for much of her marriage. When God promised
Abraham that he would make of him a great nation
(12:2) and that the land of Canaan would be given to
his seed (v 7), Sarah was still barren.

After 10 years had passed (cf. Gn 12:4; 16:16) and
Sarah continued without children, she gave her Egyptian slave, Hagar, to Abraham as a concubine. Hagar
conceived and bore a son, Ishmael (16:3-4). God
promised that a nation would come from Ishmael
(17:20) but indicated that he was not to be the child
of the promise. Sarah herself was to be the mother of
this child, even though she laughed when the birth
was predicted. The fulfillment of this prediction took
place with the birth of Isaac (21:2-3), when Sarah was
90 years old, 25 years after the original promise of a
seed to Abraham (17:17; 21:5).

When famine forced Abraham and Sarah to journey
down into Egypt shortly after their entrance into
Canaan, Sarah was represented to the Egyptians as
Abraham's sister. This resulted in Sarah's being taken
into the harem of Pharaoh because of her great beauty
(Gn 12:11-15), and Abraham's being well treated and
rewarded by the Egyptians instead of being killed.
God intervened to protect the marriage of Abraham
and Sarah by plaguing the house of Pharaoh to force
Sarah's release. A similar tactic was followed by Abraham and Sarah on another occasion in Gerar (ch 20),
where she was taken into the household of Abimelech
the king of Gerar. Again God protected Sarah, preserved her as the mother of the promised seed, and
prevented any suspicion or doubt concerning who was
the father of Isaac. Significantly, Isaac was born not
long after this incident (21:1-5), his birth having been
promised about a year earlier (17:21; 18:10-14). Sarah
died at the age of 127 and was buried in the cave at
Machpelah, which Abraham had purchased from
Ephron the Hittite (ch 23).

Apart from the book of Genesis, Sarah is referred to

in the OT only in Isaiah 51:2. Reference is made to her in the NT in Romans 4:19, 9:9, Hebrews 11:11, 1 Peter 3:6, and Galatians 4:21-31, although in the Galatians text she is not mentioned by name.

   See also Abraham; Barrenness.

2. KJV spelling of Serah, Asher's daughter, in Numbers 26:46. *See* Serah.

3. The heroine of the book of Tobit. Her prayer of anguish was heard by God, who sent the angel Raphael as a matchmaker to arrange her marriage to Tobias (Tb 6:9ff.). She had been tormented by a demon, who had caused the death of her previous seven husbands but was exorcised by Tobias using a recipe of fish heart and liver that was given to him by the angel Raphael (8:2). After the death of Tobit and his wife, Anna, in Nineveh, Tobias and Sarah, and their children returned to Sarah's family in Ecbatana (14:12ff.).

SARAI Original name for Sarah, Abraham's wife (Gn 11:29). *See* Sarah #1.

SARAPH Shelah's son from Judah's tribe. Saraph ruled in Moab and later returned to Lehem. "Lehem" may refer either to his own countrymen or to a geographical location. The reading of the Hebrew text is unclear (1 Chr 4:22).

SARDINE STONE* KJV form of carnelian in Revelation 4:3. *See* Stones, Precious #22.

SARDIS Important city in the Roman province of Asia, once the capital of the ancient kingdom of Lydia. It lay astride great highways linking it to the coastal regions to the west and to eastern Asia Minor. It was a cultural, religious, and commercial center. Under King Croesus (c. 560–547 BC), its wealth became legendary. In his day gold and silver coinage came into use. The geography and topography of Sardis were advantageous. The Pactolus River lay on its eastern side and flowed eventually into the Hermus River. The broad ridge of Mt Tmolus, springing from the central plateau, dominates the Hermus Valley to its north, and a series of steep spurs jut out into the plain, offering strongholds. Sardis lay on one of these. The site of Sardis proper lay 1,500 feet (457.2 meters) above the plain and assumed a position of great importance from the earliest days of the Lydian kingdom (13th century BC), although it was occupied in earlier times; the lower city spread to the valley floor. The king lived in the great acropolis, which became a place of refuge in time of war.

Ancient Amphitheater at Sardis

   In 334 BC the city surrendered to Alexander the Great, who left a garrison on the acropolis. Following Alexander's death, Sardis changed hands several times. It was controlled first by Antigonus, then by the Seleucid rulers,

and then by Pergamum, which had broken away from the Seleucids. When Antiochus III (231–187 BC) sought to restore the city to his rule, the lower city was burned (216 BC) and the citadel entered (214 BC). After the defeat of Antiochus III by Pergamum and the Romans, Sardis was placed under Pergamum's jurisdiction until 133 BC. Later it became a Roman administrative center and, although enjoying considerable prosperity during the first three centuries AD, it never again held the prominence of earlier centuries. It was overlooked in AD 26 when the cities of Asia Minor vied with one another for the honor of building a second temple for the Caesar cult. A great earthquake destroyed the city in AD 17, and Emperor Tiberius assisted in its rebuilding on the valley floor.

   Christianity took root here before the end of the first century and later included a bishopric. The NT letter to "the angel of the church in Sardis" (Rv 1:11; 3:1-6) gives insight into the condition of the church at that time. After the Arab invasion of AD 716, the city declined. Today the small village of Sart preserves its name.

   Extensive excavations in recent years have identified many Roman public buildings: a theater, a temple of Artemis, a gymnasium, and an impressive late-Jewish synagogue, suggesting that it became an important center for the Jewish Diaspora.

SARDITE* KJV form of Seredite, a member of Sered's family, in Numbers 26:26. *See* Sered, Seredite.

SARDIUS* KJV form of carnelian in Ezekiel 28:13. *See* Stones, Precious #22.

SARDONYX* KJV form of onyx in Revelation 21:20. *See* Stones, Precious #23.

SAREPTA* KJV form of Zarephath, a Phoenician town, in Luke 4:26. *See* Zarephath.

SARGON Assyrian monarch from 722–705 BC, whose military campaigns are historically well documented. Excavations have revealed his palace at what was probably Nineveh as well as an incomplete palace at Khorsabad. Sargon II bore the name of an illustrious conqueror who lived and fought some 1,500 years earlier (Sargon I of Agade). His true identity has not been easily discerned. Previous generations, thinking that his name was an "alias," incorrectly identified him as Shalmaneser V (727–722 BC), Sennacherib (705–681 BC), or Esarhaddon (699–681 BC).

   The only place in the Bible where Sargon is specifically mentioned is Isaiah 20:1. Despite warnings of the prophet Isaiah against placing any trust in Egypt (Is 10:9), Judah was moving contrary to her best interests by considering just such an alliance. But in 713 BC the Philistine city of Ashdod rebelled against Assyria, thereby instigating a campaign by the forces of Sargon against this strategically important metropolis. A man named Yamani sought to secure support from Egypt, Ethiopia, and even Judah in mounting an effective coalition against the might of Sargon. However, in 711 BC Ashdod was subjugated by Sargon's army under his delegated official, "the Tartan" (Is 20:1, KJV).

   Sargon finished the task of conquering Samaria, begun by his predecessor, Shalmaneser V. Apparently, Shalmaneser V had besieged the northern kingdom of Israel for three years (2 Kgs 17:5-6) and had virtually completed that campaign when he died. While other military victories earmark the public life of Sargon, many of his battles were indecisive. A large part of his reign was spent suppressing rebellions and handling major domestic problems. He was finally killed on the battlefield in a remote area known as Tabal. Sargon's son, Sennacherib, succeeded him in 705 BC.

See also Assyria, Assyrians.

SARID Town located in the region of Zebulun near its southern border, situated between Maralah to the west and Kisloth-tabor to the east (Jos 19:10, 12). Some suggest that this town is the same as Tell Shadud, a town near the valley of Jezreel.

SARON* KJV spelling of Sharon, the large coastal plain in northern Palestine, in Acts 9:35. *See* Sharon #1.

SARSECHIM*, SARSEKIM* Personal name or title of an official who participated with Nebuchadnezzar and the Chaldean army in conquering Jerusalem (see Jer 39:3, NLT mg). Some modern translations read "Nebo-sarsekim."

SARUCH* KJV rendering of Serug, an ancestor of Jesus, in Luke 3:35. *See* Serug.

SATAN Spirit being who opposes God and seeks to frustrate his plans and lead his people into rebellion.

Satan is seldom mentioned in the OT. He is pictured as an angel who acts as the heavenly prosecutor (Jb 1:6-12; 2:1-7; Zec 3:1-2). As such, he is called "the satan" or "the accuser," and there is nothing in the context to indicate that the angel is evil. It is not until the late OT period that Satan appears as a tempter: in 1 Chronicles 21:1, the story of 2 Samuel 24:1 is retold with Satan (used for the first time as a proper name) substituted for God and pictured as an evil figure. The OT, then, has no developed doctrine of Satan but contains the raw material from which the later doctrine came. (Some people see Lucifer of Is 14:12 as a reference to Satan, but the context is clearly referring to the king of Babylon; it is therefore unlikely that any reference to Satan was intended.)

The Jews further developed the idea of Satan during the intertestamental period, also calling him Belial, Mastema, and Sammael. Three differing conceptions appear. First, the Satan of the OT reappears in the roles of tempting people, of accusing them in heaven before God, and of hindering God's saving plan (Jubilees 11:5; 17:16; Assumption of Moses 17; 1 Enoch 40:7). Second, the Dead Sea Scrolls present Satan (Belial) as the leader of the evil forces and attacker of the righteous. This development was probably influenced by the evil god of Zoroastrian religion. But unlike the Zoroastrian idea, the scrolls never present two gods but rather one God who has created both Belial and the Prince of Light (who is sure to win in the end, for God is with him). Third, in this literature Satan is often identified with OT stories from which his name was originally absent: he lusted after Eve and therefore caused the fall (Wisd of Sol 2:24), he controls the angels who fell in Genesis 6:1-4 (Jubilees 10:5-8; 19:28), or he is a fallen angel himself (2 Enoch 29:4).

The NT has a developed portrayal of Satan, and he comes with a whole list of names: Satan (Hebrew for "accuser"), devil (the Greek translation of Satan), Belial, Beelzebul, the Adversary, the Dragon, the Enemy, the Serpent, the Tester, and the Wicked One. Satan is pictured as the ruler of a host of angels (Mt 25:41) and the controller of the world (Lk 4:6; Acts 26:18; 2 Cor 4:4), who especially governs all who are not Christians (Mk 4:15; Jn 8:44; Acts 13:10; Col 1:13). He is opposed to God and seeks to alienate all people from God; therefore, he is an especially dangerous foe of Christians (Lk

8:33; 1 Cor 7:5; 1 Pt 5:8), who must steadfastly resist him and see through his cunning (2 Cor 2:11; Eph 6:11; Jas 4:7). Satan works his evil will by tempting persons (Jn 13:2; Acts 5:3), by hindering God's workers (1 Thes 2:18), by accusing Christians before God (Rv 12:10), and by controlling the evil persons who resist the gospel (2 Thes 2:9; Rv 2:9, 13; 13:2).

Most importantly, however, the NT teaches us that this being, who has been evil from the beginning (1 Jn 3:8), has now been bound and cast out of heaven through the ministry of Jesus (Lk 10:18; Rv 12). While Satan is still a dangerous enemy, Jesus himself prays for us and has given us the powerful weapons of prayer, faith, and the efficacy of his blood. Satan can still cause physical illness when allowed by God (2 Cor 12:7), and persons can be delivered over to him for punishment (1 Cor 5:5; 1 Tm 1:20). Satan will always be under God's control, who will eventually destroy him (Rom 16:20; Rv 20:10).

See also Angel; Demon; Demon-possession; Lucifer.

SATON* Greek word in Matthew 13:33 for a dry commodity measure equivalent to the OT seah, equaling about one peck (8.8 liters). The plural is *sata* (NASB mg). *See* Weights and Measures.

SATRAP* Governor who held jurisdiction over a number of provinces within the king's domain. This official represented the authority of the king in both civil and military matters, and supplied the means for maintaining the king's sovereignty over the whole empire. Satraps were listed among the high-ranking officers of the Babylonian and Persian empires (Ezr 8:36; Est 3:12; 9:3; Dn 6:1-7).

SATYR* Creature of uncertain identification, possibly referring to a demon, a goat, or a deity that resembles a goat. *See* Animals (Goat).

SAUL Name meaning "asked," with the implication being "asked *of God.*" A name with a usage extending far back into prebiblical times, it is attested in third-millennium texts from Tell Mardikh in Syria (ancient Ebla) and appears also to have been used in the second millennium in the city of Ugarit on the coast of Syria.

In addition to the conventional spelling, it is sometimes spelled Shaul in older English versions. Apart from King Saul, the most famous bearer of the name, one other person called Saul (Shaul) is referred to in the OT, though little is known about him (*see* Shaul).

1. Saul, king of Edom, is mentioned in an ancient list of kings who ruled Edom (in Transjordan) in pre-Israelite times (Gn 36:37-38; 1 Chr 1:48-49). He is described as coming from "Rehoboth on the river," the "river" perhaps referring to a small river in the vicinity of Edom.

2. Saul, the first king of Israel, is the best known and documented person with his name in the OT. He was a member of the tribe of Benjamin, one of the smallest of the Israelite tribes, whose territory was located just north of the Canaanite city of Jerusalem. His father was Kish, son of Abiel. Saul was born in Gibeah, a small town just a few miles north of Jerusalem in the hill country, and apart from his travels and military expeditions, Gibeah was Saul's hometown for his entire life. He was a married man with one wife, Ahinoam, and five children—three sons and two daughters (1 Sm 14:49-50). His best-known son, Jonathan, later served him in a senior military capacity; three of Saul's sons died with him in battle (31:2). Of

his two daughters, the best-known is Michal, the younger daughter, who married David.

Saul the Soldier Saul lived during a critical period in the history of the Israelite tribes. Though the dates cannot be determined with any certainty, he lived during the latter half of the 11th century BC and probably ruled as king from about 1020 to 1000 BC. Before he became king, the Israelite tribes were on the verge of military collapse. The Philistines, a powerful military people, had settled along the Mediterranean coast; they were well established on the coast and planned to move eastward and take control of Palestine as a whole. In order to do this, they first had to eliminate the Israelites, who were settled in the hill country on the west of the Jordan and also in Transjordan. The absence of any strong and permanent military authority among the Israelites meant that the Philistines were a grave military threat to the continued existence of Israel.

The immediate crisis, which was to contribute to Saul's rise to power, was a crushing defeat of the Israelite army by the Philistines at Ebenezer, in the vicinity of Aphek (1 Sm 4:1ff). The victory gave the Philistines more or less complete control of Israelite territories lying to the west of the Jordan; they attempted to maintain that control by establishing military garrisons throughout the country they had captured. Israel, weakened by the Philistine defeat, became vulnerable to enemies on other borders. The nation of Ammon, situated to the east of the Israelites' land in Transjordan, attacked and laid siege to the town of Jabesh (11:1). Saul, summoning an army of volunteers, delivered the inhabitants of Jabesh and defeated the Ammonites (v 11). It was after this event that Saul became king. He had already been anointed a prince or leader among the people by Samuel; after his military success at Jabesh, he assumed the office formally at the sanctuary in Gilgal (v 15).

The defeat of the Ammonites provided a significant boost to Israelite morale, but it did not change the military crisis and threat posed by the Philistines. Indeed, the location of Saul's appointment to kingship is significant. Gilgal, in the Jordan Valley near Jericho, was chosen partly because the earlier shrine of Shiloh was held by the Philistines. Gilgal was in one of the few areas remaining outside Philistine control. Hence, if Saul's kingship was to mean anything, he had to address the Philistine problem immediately; if he did not, there would be no Israel to rule.

Saul acted promptly. Although the precise historical details are difficult to reconstruct, a general view of Saul's anti-Philistine campaign is provided in the biblical text. He attacked garrisons at Gibeah and, later, at Micmash, about four miles (6.4 kilometers) northeast of Gibeah (1 Sm 13:16ff). He had great success at Micmash, thanks in part to the military aid of his son Jonathan. The Philistines were routed and retreated from that portion of the hill country (14:15-23). Saul established his military base in his hometown, Gibeah, and built a citadel there.

In the years that followed this initial campaign against the Philistines, Saul was constantly engaged in other military activities. He continued to fight with enemies on his eastern borders, particularly Ammon and Moab, to the east of the Dead Sea (1 Sm 14:47). He engaged in a major campaign on the southern border with the old enemies of the Israelites, the Amalekites (15:7); in this, too, he was successful. And throughout all this, he had to keep constant watch on Philistine activity on his western border.

Saul was faced with an extraordinarily difficult task

as military commander. His home ground had the advantage of being reasonably easy to protect, for most of it was mountainous countryside. But he was surrounded on all four sides by enemies who wanted his land, he had inadequate weapons (Philistines controlled the supply of iron), he had no large standing army, he had inadequate communication systems, and he did not have the wholehearted support of all the Israelites. For several years he was relatively successful against almost impossible odds, but eventually his military genius failed.

The Philistines assembled a large army in the vicinity of Aphek (1 Sm 29:1), but instead of attacking Saul's mountain territory directly, the army moved northward and then began to penetrate Israelite territory at a weak point in the vicinity of Jezreel (v 11). Saul attempted to gather an adequate military force to meet the Philistine threat, but he was unable to do so. With inadequate preparation and insufficient forces, he prepared for battle at Mt Gilboa (31:1); he should never have entered that battle, for it could not have been won. His sons were killed on the battlefield, and Saul, rather than fall into the hands of the Philistines, committed suicide (vv 2-6).

From a military perspective, Saul had become king at a time of crisis; he had averted disaster and gained some respite for his country. But the battle in which he died was a disaster for Israel; the country he left behind after his death was in worse straits than it had been on his assumption of power.

Saul the King If Saul had a difficult task as Israel's military commander, he had an even more difficult task as Israel's king. Before Saul's time, there had been no king in Israel. The absence of any form of monarchy in Israel was largely a religious matter. God was the one and only true King of Israel; he was the one who reigned (Ex 15:18). Consequently, although there had been single, powerful rulers in Israel's earlier history (Moses, Joshua, and certain judges), nobody had assumed the title or office of king, for it was thought that that would undermine the central position of God as King. However, provision had been made for the rise of kingship in the law (Dt 19:14-20); for more on kingship in Israel, *see* King, Kingship.

It was sheer necessity that brought a monarchy to Israel, a necessity created by the constant military threat of the Philistines. A brief external threat could have been met by a temporary ruler, a judge. But a permanent and serious threat to Israel's existence could not be thwarted by such temporary measures. If Israel was to survive as a nation (and it very nearly did not), it needed a central military government with recognized authority over the various tribes that constituted the nation of Israel. Thus the kingdom was established and Saul became the first king, facing incredible difficulties.

Since there had never been a kingdom before in Israel, there were no precedents. What were his responsibilities? Primarily, they were military, for that was why the monarchy had been established. In this area, Saul was successful in the early years of his reign. But apart from his military responsibilities, King Saul faced an enormously difficult task. Given the nature of Hebrew theology, it was inevitable that many Israelites were opposed to the idea of kingship from the beginning. Indeed, Samuel, who was instrumental in the initial anointing of Saul and then in the formal coronation, appears to have been ambiguous in his attitudes toward the kingship (1 Sm 8:6), and later toward Saul himself (15:23). Furthermore, nobody had specified precisely what it was that the leader could do. He was a soldier—that much was clear. But did he also have religious responsibilities? Though the judgment of history upon Saul is often harsh, it is wise to recall the difficulty of the task he undertook. The military problems alone would have been more than sufficient for most great men; Saul also had to fashion the new role as king. In practical matters, Saul's leadership was modest and praiseworthy. He sought none of the pomp and splendor of many Eastern kings. He had a small court, located in his military stronghold of Gibeah; there is little evidence that it was characterized by great wealth. For practical purposes, he had no standing army; he had only a few men close to him, in particular his son Jonathan and his general Abner. He also sought out young men of promise, like David. Saul's court was rustic and feudal in comparison to the later splendor of David and Solomon. But Saul, as national leader, ran into difficulties with Samuel, who had appointed him and had influenced Israel prior to his kingship. While the responsibility for the trouble may lie primarily with Saul, Samuel himself does not appear to have been particularly supportive and helpful. On one occasion, Saul was roundly criticized and condemned by Samuel for assuming the priestly role of offering sacrifices in the absence of Samuel at Gilgal (1 Sm 13:8-15). The judgment was no doubt deserved, though one can perceive Saul's dilemma. Did the king have a priestly role or not? This issue had not been made clear. Furthermore, Saul was at the time in a state of crisis; he had waited seven days for Samuel to turn up, and as each day passed, his army was reduced by deserters. So Saul acted. Perhaps he may not be excused, but his actions may easily be understood, and the incident itself is indicative of the difficulty of being a nation's first king. Again, after the Amalekite war, Saul was subject to divine condemnation through Samuel.

Saul was Israel's first king but not its greatest. Yet no criticism of Saul's leadership should be so harsh as to ignore his strengths. He faced extraordinary difficulties and for a while was successful. Few other men could have done what he did. Ultimately, he died in failure, yet his achievements might have been better remembered if he had been succeeded by any other leader than David. David's gifts and competence were so magnificent and unusual that Saul's modest achievements paled and only his failures are remembered.

Saul the Man The writers of the OT have presented the story of Saul in a fascinating manner. While some OT characters remain shadowy figures, Saul stands out, with all his strengths and weaknesses, as a fully human figure. He was, in many ways, a great man, but there were also flaws in his personality that emerged more and more in the later years of his life. Born of a wealthy father, Saul is described as being tall and handsome (1 Sm 9:1-2). He was a man of immense courage, and part of his military success was rooted in his fearlessness. In his early years as king, Saul is portrayed as a man whose basic instincts were generous; he was kind and loyal to his friends and did not easily carry a grudge or hatred toward those who opposed him (11:12-13). But the real strength of Saul, in his early days, was in his relationship to God. For all his natural gifts and abilities, Saul became king as a result of divine appointment (10:1) and because the "Spirit of the Lord" came upon him (v 6).

In his later life, a change came over Saul that transformed him into a tragic, pitiable person. The many incidents in Saul's relationship to the young David provide insight into the transformation. Once a friend, then perceived as an enemy, David became the object of Saul's unfounded suspicions and irrational jealousy. Saul's periods of sanity became punctuated by periods of depression and paranoia. The paranoia affected his rational thought. Instead of warring against the invading Philistines, his energy was diverted toward the pursuit of David. The biblical writers describe this change as "the departure of the Spirit of God from Saul" and "an evil spirit from the Lord tormenting him" (1 Sm 16:14). Many modern writers have interpreted this as the onset of a form of mental illness, perhaps manic-depression, the alternation between active and lucid periods, followed by intense depression and paranoia. But there is a certain danger in psychoanalyzing the figures of ancient history, principally because the literary sources are rarely adequate to the task. The biblical writers indicated a theological basis for the change in Saul: the Spirit of God had departed from him. From a simple human perspective, the man was not equal to the enormity of the task before him. Overcome by its complexity, and lagging in the faith of the one who appointed him to such awesome responsibility, Saul ended his days in tragedy.

See also David.

3. Saul, mentioned in the NT, whose name was changed to Paul (Acts 13:9). *See* Paul, The Apostle.

SAVIOR One who delivers or rescues. The term "savior" is most frequently applied to God and Jesus Christ in the Bible. The understanding of Jesus as Savior is a key truth in appropriating the biblical message. Versions of the English Bible use "savior" in the OT to translate various forms of the Hebrew *yasha'*, which means "to save," "to deliver," or "to rescue." Most frequently it is used to translate the participle of the verb, *moshia'*, meaning "the one who saves." Used in this way, "savior" is found 13 or 14 times in the OT, depending upon the version.

The basic understanding of the term "savior" as one who delivers or rescues is illustrated in Deuteronomy 22:27, where the law anticipated a situation when no deliverer was near in time of need. *Moshia'* is also used for individuals, as both Othniel and Ehud are called "deliverers" (Jgs 3:9, 15) and Nehemiah 9:27 speaks of the judges collectively as deliverers sent by God. Second Kings 13:5 reports that the Lord gave Israel a savior in reference to their deliverance from the Arameans. Some have identified this deliverer with King Jeroboam II of Judah; others with a foreign king, quite often Zakir of Hamath. But the text does not clearly indicate who this savior might have been. The point of the text is that God sent this deliverer for his people. The majority of references in the OT refer to God himself as Israel's savior, and even when other individuals are so termed, it is clearly stated that God sent them or raised them up. Israel understood that God was their savior and declared this in songs of praise (Pss 17:7; 106:1-12) and cries for help (Jer 14:8). David said this of God: "He is my stronghold, my refuge and my savior" (2 Sm 22:3, NIV). Quite often the psalmists refer to the Lord as their "help" or "salvation" (Pss 27:9; 38:22; 42:5, 11; 65:5; 68:19; 79:9; 85:4; 89:26; all rendered "Savior" by the NIV). The exodus was undoubtedly the greatest example of deliverance for Israel and undergirded their knowledge of God as the savior. The psalmist, in remembrance of Israel's sin of making a golden calf, proclaims, "They forgot God, their savior, who had done such great things in Egypt" (Ps 106:21, NLT; cf. Is 63:11; Hos 13:4-6). In Isaiah, where "savior" is a frequent title for God, the term is used to emphasize his uniqueness. God alone is seen as savior, in contrast to foreign gods and idols: "I, even I, am the LORD, and apart from me there is no savior. I have revealed and saved and proclaimed—I, and not some foreign god among you" (Is 43:11-12, NIV). Isaiah further states that God would show himself as savior by the future blessing and restoration of Israel (49:26; 60:16). The designation "savior" is not directly applied to the Messiah in the OT, but a passage like Zechariah 9:9 indicates that God's Anointed One would be a deliverer. Several apocryphal books use the term "savior" for God, some in lofty titles like "everlasting Savior" (Bar 4:22) or "the eternal Savior of Israel" (3 Macc 7:16). This later usage also illustrates the idea of God as the one who is able to save Israel.

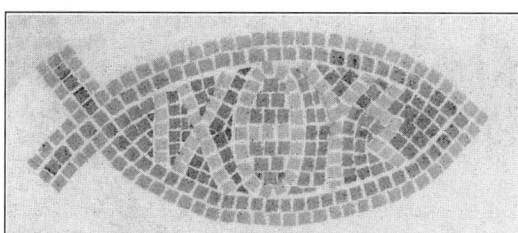

Sign of the Fish: A Special Insignia of Jesus' Names
The symbol came into use because the Greek word for "fish" (ΙΧΟΨΕ, or *ichthus*) is composed of the first letter of each word in the Greek phrase "Jesus Christ, God's Son, Savior."

ΙΗΣΟΥΣ (*iesous*) = Jesus
ΧΡΙΣΤΟΣ (*christos*) = Christ
ΘΕΟΨ (*theou*) = God's
ΨΙΟΣ (*huios*) = Son
ΣΟΤΗΡ (*soter*) = Savior

The Greek literature uses *soter* ("savior," "deliverer" from the verb *sozo* "to save," "to rescue") for both gods and humans. For example, at one point Herodotus refers to the Athenians as the "saviors" of Greece (*Persian Wars* 7.139.5). In the Septuagint *soter* ("savior") is used to render various forms of the Hebrew *yasha'* ("to save"). *Soter* occurs 24 times in the NT and is exclusively applied to God and Jesus Christ (to God 8 times and to Christ 16 times). Out of the 24 NT occurrences of *soter*, ten are in the Letters and five in 2 Peter. Dependence upon the OT can be seen in Luke 1:47, where Mary praises God as Savior in her hymn of praise. Jesus' name (Greek for Joshua) means "the Lord is salvation" and was given in anticipation of his function as the Savior (Mt 1:21). As the Savior, Jesus completes God's plan for a promised deliverer (Acts 13:23; Ti 3:4), provides redemption for humanity (Ti 2:13-14), and is the hope of the believer (Phil 3:20-21). Inherent in the term "savior" is the concept of one who saves or delivers from danger to a position of safety. Jesus has delivered the believer from sin and death into immortality and life (2 Tm 1:10). While Jesus never refers to himself as Savior (*soter*), he is announced as such by the angels at his birth (Lk 2:11), confessed as such by those who heard his words (Jn 4:42), and proclaimed as Savior by the early church (Acts 5:31; 13:23). Salvation is central to the mission of Jesus (Lk 19:10). Paul teaches that Christ is the Savior of the church in the present (Eph 5:23) and future (Phil 3:20).

Savior, as a title, is applied to God in the Pastoral Epistles and clearly represents God as Savior of all persons (1 Tm 2:3; 4:10). The Pastorals also clearly designate

Jesus as Savior (2 Tm 1:10; Ti 3:6), in some instances also declaring that he is God the Savior (Ti 2:13; 3:4-6). Savior is used as a title for Jesus Christ throughout 2 Peter (e.g., 2 Pt 2:20). John, in his first letter, uses it to describe Jesus as the Savior sent by the Father to save the world (1 Jn 4:14).

See also Salvation.

SCAB *See* Sore.

SCALL* KJV rendering for an eruption, a skin rash, in Leviticus 13:30-37 and 14:54. *See* Sore.

SCAPEGOAT Goat that, on the Day of Atonement, is sent into the wilderness, symbolically bearing away the sins of the people (Lv 16). *See* Atonement, Day of.

SCARLET *See* Color.

SCEPTER Long staff with an ornamental head and other decorations used to represent royal authority; a shorter staff was used as a battle mace to symbolize royal military power. It is of more than passing interest that those two ideas are also conveyed by the Bible when the word "scepter" appears in a passage. The scepter of royal authority is referred to in Genesis 49:10, indicating that Judah's descendants would exercise royal authority (so also in Ps 45:6, two times, and quoted in Heb 1:8). Amos (Am 1:5, 8) refers to the royal authority of the kings of Syria and Philistia, and Zechariah (Zec 10:11) refers to that of Egypt. King Ahasuerus held out this type of scepter to Esther (Est 4:11; 5:2; 8:4). The scepter of royal military power is referred to in Numbers 24:17 in reference to the coming messianic King. In Isaiah 14:5 it refers to the means by which Babylon exercised its oppressive military power, which was to be destroyed by God. Ezekiel 19:11, 14 uses "scepter" to refer to the authority, power, and dominion that Israel lost and was not able to regain.

SCEVA Father of seven sons and a Jewish chief priest in Ephesus at the time of Paul's visit on his third missionary journey. Sceva's sons attempted to imitate Paul's exorcism of evil spirits in the name of Jesus. The exorcisms failed, and their authority was not recognized. Consequently, they were attacked and harmed by the evil spirits they tried to rebuke (Acts 19:14).

SCHOOL* *See* Education.

SCHOOLMASTER* KJV rendering of "tutor" (NASB) in Galatians 3:24-25. *See* Custodian.

SCORPION *See* Animals.

SCOURGE *See* Criminal Law and Punishment.

SCREECH OWL *See* Birds (Owl, Barn; Owl, Scops).

SCRIBE Reference in early OT times to those employed for their ability to transcribe information. After the exile, scribes were a class of scholars who taught, copied, and interpreted the Jewish law for the people. They appear in the Gospels primarily as opponents of Jesus.

Scribes in Preexilic Times The ability to read and write was not widespread in ancient Israel, and professional secretaries were needed in the various aspects of public life. This appears to be the earliest biblical notion of the term "scribe" and has no particular religious connotation. Scribes were employed to keep accounts or transcribe legal information (Jer 32:12), military data (2 Chr 26:11), other public documents (Jgs 8:14; Is 50:1), or personal correspondence (Jer 36:18). These secretaries were essential to royal administrations, and there is frequent mention of a chief scribe who functioned as a court recorder (1 Kgs 4:3; 2 Chr 24:11), adviser (2 Sm 8:16-17; 2 Kgs 18:18; 22:12; 1 Chr 27:32; Is 36:3), and financial overseer (2 Kgs 22:3-4). Secretaries or scribes were associated with the priesthood as well, serving as recorders for temple affairs (1 Chr 24:6; 2 Chr 34:13-15).

Scribes in Postexilic Times With the restoration of Judaism under Ezra and Nehemiah, the term "scribe" begins to be associated more narrowly with those who gathered together, studied, and interpreted the Torah (Jewish law). They became, in essence, a separate profession of teachers (although unpaid), able to preserve accurately the law of Moses and interpret it to meet conditions in postexilic times. In this initial period, Ezra himself appears as the ideal "scribe who studied and taught the commands and laws of the LORD to Israel" (Ezr 7:11, NLT). In Ecclesiasticus, the scribe is portrayed as one who, because of his diligent study of the Law, the Prophets, and Writings (Ecclus 38:24ff; 39:1), is able to penetrate the hidden meanings of texts (39:2-3) and thus is able to serve as judge and counsel for the affairs of the people and state (38:33; 39:4-8). Because of his invaluable place in a society governed by the Torah, the scribe is worthy of praise and veneration throughout succeeding generations (39:9). By the second century BC, the scribes were a fairly distinct class in Jewish society. They appear as such during the Maccabean wars, acting as a negotiating body with the rival Syrians (1 Macc 7:12). It is also significant that, from this time forward, the history of the scribe in Jewish life is closely linked with the rise of the Pharisees. Although there were apparently some scribes affiliated with the rival Sadducean party, the party of the Pharisees, with its absolute devotion to the law (including the oral law), became the primary religiopolitical affiliation for the scribes (see the close connection in the NT: Mt 5:20; 12:38; 15:1; Mk 7:5; Lk 6:7).

Training and Status The training of scribes initially occurred within priestly family-based guilds that guaranteed the regulation and perpetuation of this position (1 Chr 2:55). Later, scribal training in the law became open to members of all classes, with the eventual result, by Jesus' time, of scribes from nonpriestly families being far more numerous and influential. Training in the law began at an early age under the personal supervision of a teacher (rabbi), who gave instructions in all matters pertaining to the law and its interpretation for present needs. Because the written law of Moses could not possibly speak directly to conditions in postexilic times, the oral interpretation and application of the written law to meet such current needs was a significant contribution by the scribes. Such oral law promulgated by them was regarded as equal to the written law and equally binding for those desiring to please God (see Mk 7:6-13). This important function, lying at the heart of Jewish life, accounts for the participation of the scribes in the Sanhedrin. The Sanhedrin, in order to make legal decisions in keeping with the law, obviously needed the presence of those most knowledgeable about the minutest details of the Torah and the principles governing its application to new circumstances. The scribes, consequently, were the only members outside the aristocratic high priests and elders to be represented in this Jewish supreme court (Mt 26:57; Mk 14:43, 53; Lk 22:66; Acts 23:9). Being the authoritative instructors of the law both within the tem-

ple (Lk 2:46) and within the various synagogues of Judea and Galilee (5:17), as well as prominent members of the Sanhedrin, the scribes were greatly respected within the Jewish community. They wore special robes (Mk 12:38) with memorial fringes at the bottom and phylacteries, or "prayer boxes," hanging from the arms (Mt 23:5). Such attire made their presence obvious and occasioned the rising or bowing of the common people when they passed (Mk 12:38). They were addressed with respect as "rabbi" or "master" (Mt 23:7) and were given the place of honor at worship as well as at social affairs (Mt 23:2; Mk 12:39; Lk 20:46). Indeed, the high regard the Jews held for their scribes is testified by the fact that such teachers of the law were buried alongside the tombs of the patriarchs and prophets.

The Scribes in Jesus' Day The scribes appear predominantly in the ministry of Jesus as those concerned with the circumspectness of legal observance. Luke refers to the scribes as "lawyers," thereby describing their chief function as interpreters of the Jewish law in a way that communicated to his gentile audience. It is often found, therefore, that the scribes were critical members of Jesus' audience, accusing him of violating the law on numerous occasions: in forgiving sins (Mt 9:1-3; Lk 5:17-26), in breaking their notion of Sabbath observance through work (Lk 6:1-2) and healing (vv 6-11), in not following their accepted ceremonial washings (Mk 7:2-5), and in ignoring their practice of fasting (Lk 5:33-39). Not surprisingly, they especially disapproved of Jesus' practice of mingling with the unclean and outcasts of Jewish society (Mk 2:16-17; Lk 15:1-2). In a similar light, they are not unfrequently found presenting questions concerning the law for the purpose of tricking Jesus (Mk 7:5; 12:28, 35; Lk 11:53; Jn 8:3-4). In a similar fashion, they demanded that Jesus make his identity clear (Mt 12:38) and reveal the source of his authority to perform miracles (Mk 3:22; Lk 20:1-4). Although there is evidence that a minority of the scribes accepted Jesus (Mt 8:19; 13:52; Mk 12:32; Jn 3:1-2), their primary attitude toward Jesus was one of hostility. As previously suggested, this was partly due to Jesus' differing expression of fidelity to the Mosaic law and his openness toward the outcasts. It was also partly due to the rising popularity of Jesus among the people, which posed a threat to their own authority (Mt 7:29) and to the safety of the city (Mt 21:15; Mk 11:18). Certainly, another major contributing factor of their opposition to Jesus was his exposure of their hypocrisy and corruption. In his rebukes of the scribes and the Pharisees, Jesus openly accused them of catering to public approval (Mt 23:5-7; Mk 12:38-39; Lk 11:43). While appearing to be outwardly correct and holy, they were inwardly corrupt (Mt 23:25-28; Lk 11:39-41). Jesus also attacked the principle of oral law taught by the scribes, which they demanded that the people follow. Jesus charged that the oral law was a "heavy burden" that the scribes themselves did not even bother to follow (Mt 23:2-4, 13-22; Lk 11:46). While emphasizing the minor points of the law, the scribes were also guilty of ignoring the weightier concerns of justice, mercy, and faith (Mt 23:23-24; Mk 12:40; Lk 11:42). Contrary to being the descendants of the prophets, as the scribes held themselves to be, the scribes (Jesus claimed) would have killed the prophets if they had lived in their day (Mt 23:29-36; Lk 20:9-19).

It is not surprising to find, therefore, the scribes anxious to get rid of Jesus (Mk 14:1; Lk 11:53). His more flexible interpretation of the law posed a clear threat to their position and authority within the community. The scribes joined forces with their normal opponents (the high priesthood) to engineer Jesus' arrest (Mk 14:43). When Jesus appeared before them and the rest of the Sanhedrin, they worked with the other leaders to construct a case against him worthy of death (Mt 26:57-66). When taking Jesus before Herod, they stood by and shouted their accusations with the others (Lk 23:10). Finally, they participated with other members of the Sanhedrin in mocking Jesus on the cross, demanding that Jesus save himself by coming down from the cross (Mt 27:41-43). Prior to the destruction of Jerusalem in AD 70, the scribes continued with the other elements of the Sanhedrin to oppose the early Christian church, and they brought about Stephen's martyrdom (Acts 6:12-14).

See also Judaism; Pharisees; Writer.

SCRIPTURE, SCRIPTURES The holy writings of Judaism and Christianity. Jews recognize 39 books as comprising their Scriptures. Christians recognize these same Jewish writings—categorized as Torah (Law), Prophets, and Writings—as Scripture, along with the four Gospels, 21 Epistles, the book of Acts, and Revelation. Some Christians also recognize the Apocrypha and/or Deutero-canonical books as Scripture. See Bible, Canon of the; Bible, Manuscripts and Text of the (New Testament); Bible, Manuscripts and Text of the (Old Testament).

SCROLL Roll of papyrus, leather, or parchment used as a writing document. See Writing.

SCROLLS*, Dead Sea See Bible, Manuscripts and Text of the (Old Testament).

SCURVY Term used three times in the Bible (Lv 21:20 and 22:22, KJV; Dt 28:27, NLT). In none of the instances does it refer to the modern disease by the same name, which results from severe vitamin C deficiency. In the Leviticus passages, "scurvy" is found in the sequence "scurvy or scabbed." This phrase is translated "oozing sores or scabs on his skin" in the NLT. See Disease; Medicine and Medical Practice.

SCYTHOPOLIS The Greek name for Beth-shan in 2 Maccabees 12:29. See Beth-shan, Beth-shean; Decapolis.

SEA A great body of salty water covering much of the earth.

The seas are mentioned in the very beginning of the Bible. In Genesis 1:1-2 we read that in the beginning all was shapeless, empty, and dark, "and the Spirit of God was moving over the face of the waters." Then God spoke and out of the chaos came order. Thus the voice of the Lord is powerful over all the waters of chaos. Psalm 29 celebrates this. From the account of the Creation in Genesis 1, two things stand out: (1) that the sea, like everything else in earth and heaven, was created by God; and (2) that by the word of God division was made between sea and land. These two facts are amplified in the Bible in a number of ways. Psalm 33:7 speaks of how "He made the oceans, pouring them into his vast reservoirs." Eloquently, God's ordaining of the limits of sea and land is expressed in the words of the Lord to Job: "Who shut in the sea with doors, when it burst from the womb; . . . and prescribed bounds for it, and set bars and doors, and said, 'Thus far shall you come, and no farther, and here shall your proud waves be stayed'?" (Jb 38:8-11, RSV).

God's control over the waters of the sea is described when the Bible says that God "trampled the waves of the sea" (Job 9:8). So in his life on earth, Jesus, the God-man, walked on the sea (Mk 6:48). He also stilled the storm, so that the disciples in awe and wonder asked, "Who then is this, that even wind and sea obey him?" (Mk 4:41).

The Hebrew people had a healthy respect for the sea and its power. Perhaps because of the lack of good natural harbors, and because they did not control the coastline for much of their history, they were not a seafaring people like the Phoenicians. It is only in the time of Solomon that we read of their having a fleet of their own (1 Kgs 9:26). The restless sea was to them a picture of the wicked (Is 57:20). "Breakers rolling upon a beach" (Is 17:13) or "the roaring of the sea" (5:30) made them think of forces able to do incalculable harm to men. In Daniel 7:3 and Revelation 13:1, powers hostile to God are pictured as beasts coming up out of the sea.

Yet, as we have seen, God controls the seas. He is able to rescue those who trust in him "out of many waters" (Ps 18:16). He is able to protect those who go out into the seas (107:23-31). It was always remembered that God had made a way in the sea for his people to pass when they came out of Egypt (Ex 15:19). Psalmists (Pss 74:13; 77:16; 78:13; 106:9) and prophets alike (e.g., Is 43:16-17) recalled this. See Dead Sea; Mediterranean Sea; Red Sea; Sea of Galilee.

SEA, Dead See Dead Sea.

SEA*, Molten Alternate name for the laver in King Solomon's temple (1 Kgs 7:23). See Bronze Sea; Laver; Tabernacle; Temple.

SEA, Red See Red Sea.

SEA, The Great See Mediterranean Sea.

SEA MONSTER* KJV rendering of "jackal" in Lamentations 4:3. See Animals (Dragon, Jackal).

SEA OF CHINNERETH*, SEA OF CHINNEROTH* Early names for the Sea of Galilee. See Sea of Galilee.

SEA OF GALILEE A large body of water in Palestine. It has had many names in its history. In the OT the Sea of Galilee was known as the Sea of Chinnereth or Kinnereth (Nm 34:11), named for the town (Jos 19:35), or as Chinneroth (12:3). Later, the name was changed to Lake of Gennesaret because the city of Gennesaret was located on the site of Chinnereth or Tell Ureime (Lk 5:1; 1 Macc 11:67). The most familiar name—the Sea of Galilee— was due to its connection with the province of Galilee to the west (Mt 4:18). It derived the name Sea of Tiberias (Jn 6:1, 23; 21:1) from the town of Tiberias on its southwestern shore. About AD 26 Herod Antipas, son of Herod the Great, built the town near the warm springs of Hamath by the sea and named it for the emperor. In the Gospels "the sea" usually identifies the Sea of Galilee. Its modern Hebrew name is *Yam Kinneret*.

Location The sea lies in the lower section of the Jordan Valley about 60 miles (96.5 kilometers) north of Jerusalem, located in a range of mountains. The mountains of Upper Galilee are northwest of the lake and rise to a height of 4,000 feet (1,219.2 meters) above sea level, while the mountains on the east and west ascend about 2,000 feet (609.6 meters). On the west, south, and east is the Decapolis.

At the northwest corner of the lake the mountain wall flattens into the rich plain of Gennesaret, and on the east at 2,000 feet (609.6 meters) above sea level it gives way to the fertile El Batila in the northeast, where the Jordan enters the sea. At the time of the NT the Sea of Galilee was surrounded by the towns of Capernaum, Bethsaida, Korazin, Magdala, Tiberias, and others.

The sea is an integral part of the Jordan River, which feeds it with water from the snowcapped Mt Hermon (towering over 9,000 feet, or 2,743.2 meters, above sea level) and the Lebanon mountains. In its 65-mile (104.6-kilometer) course from the Sea of Galilee to the Dead Sea, the Jordan River drops 590 feet (179.8 meters), an average of about nine feet per mile.

Description The lake is approximately 13 miles or 20.9 kilometers long and 6 miles or 9.7 kilometers wide (7½ miles or 12.1 kilometers at its broadest point opposite Magdala). It lies almost 700 feet (213.4 meters) below the Mediterranean Sea, and its greatest depth is 200 feet (60.9 meters). Its shape resembles a harp, and some scholars think the name Chinnereth comes from a Hebrew word meaning "harp." The climate is semitropical. Because of this climate, combined with the sulphur springs at Tiberias, it became a resort to which sick people traveled. The lake abounds in fish, so fishing became an important industry (Mt 4:18-22; Mk 1:16-20; Lk 5:9-11). Sudden and violent storms (Mt 8:23-27; Mk 4:35-41; Lk 8:22-25), caused by the collision of warm and cold air, occur regularly.

Importance Most of the events of Jesus' life took place in Galilee, especially around Gennesaret, the most densely populated area of Palestine. He is said to have lived at Capernaum (Mt 4:13), and he did many miracles there (11:23). Because the area on the west of the lake was a health resort, Jesus found many infirm people there and healed them (Mk 1:32-34; 6:53-56). Other important occurrences in relation to the sea were the Sermon on the Mount, traditionally near Capernaum (Mt 5:1 ff.; cf. 8:1, 5); the drowning of the swine in the region of the Gadarenes (8:28-34); the curse on Korazin (11:21); the calming of the sea (8:23-27; Mk 4:35-41; Lk 8:22-24); and Jesus' walking on the water (Mt 14:22-23; Mk 6:45-51; Jn 6:16-21).

See also Galilee; Palestine.

SEA OF GLASS A body of water in the vision of heaven described by John in the book of Revelation (Rv 4:6). It appears again later, in a different vision (15:2), and is perhaps connected with other "sea" references in the same book (13:1; 21:1). It probably depicts the vast expanse before God's throne. The crystal clearness of this sea may symbolize that everything is translucent and revealed in the presence of God.

SEA OF KINNERETH* Early name for the Sea of Galilee. *See* Sea of Galilee.

SEA OF REEDS* Hebrew designation for the body of water crossed by the Israelites during the exodus from Egypt. *See* Exodus, The; Red Sea.

SEA OF THE ARABAH* Alternate name for the Dead Sea (Dt 3:17; 2 Kgs 14:25). *See* Dead Sea.

SEA OF TIBERIAS Alternate name for the Sea of Galilee (Jn 6:1; 21:1). *See* Sea of Galilee.

SEAGULL *See* Birds.

SEAH* Unit of dry measure mentioned twice in the Bible (Gn 18:6; 1 Kgs 18:32). *See* Weights and Measures.

SEAL Small engraved object widely used in the ancient Near East to produce an image in soft clay.

Origin The exact origin of seals cannot be determined. The first seal probably developed from the amulet, whose purpose was to give protection to its wearer or to ward off evil. At one time a seal was believed to have some kind of magical protective power that would bring a curse or harm to the unauthorized person who dared to break it to obtain the contents it protected. Primitive seals were little more than tiny clay spools scratched with twigs to produce simple designs or figures. Glyptic art (the technical name for engraving or carving of seals on gems) flourished in the ancient Near East from the fourth millennium BC to the end of the Persian period in the fourth century BC.

Types of Seals

Stamp Seals Seals were produced in many shapes and sizes, the earliest being the stamp seal, a flat engraved gem or bead that produced a copy of itself when pressed against soft clay. It was superseded about 3000 BC in Mesopotamia by the cylinder seal and began to be used again only at the end of the eighth century BC; by Hellenistic times it had replaced the cylinder seal altogether.

Cylinder Seals The cylinder seal first appeared in Mesopotamia before 3000 BC and became the most widely used kind of seal until the middle of the first millennium BC. Its use in Egypt is evidence of early Mesopotamian cultural influence upon Egypt; however, it was soon replaced there by the scarab (beetle-shaped) seal, which was better adapted for sealing papyrus documents. Symbols or designs were carved on the outside of the cylinder, which left their imprint when the seal was rolled over the wet clay. Some of the earliest symbols used were geometric designs or representations of some magical symbol. Later seals depicted everything from mythology (deities seated conversing with each other, receiving worshipers in audience, riding in a boat or chariot, or fighting an enemy) to scenes from everyday life (hunting, marrying, banqueting, feeding animals, fighting wild beasts, offering sacrifices to the deity, warring, leading prisoners away) and representations of animals, flowers, and birds. Writing (e.g., the owner's name or a declaration of loyalty to a god or king) began to appear on seals in the third millennium BC. Because of the great number and variety of seals that have been found, they are invaluable for what they reveal about ancient peoples—how they dressed, their hairstyles, furniture, utensils, and religious beliefs.

Seals were so widely used and have been unearthed in such quantity in the ancient Near East that they can be dated within a century or two of their origin, though sometimes it is difficult to determine the exact period or country of origin. Herodotus observed that every Babylonian gentleman "carries a seal and a walking stick" (Book I, 195). The seal was suspended by a cord about the neck or the wrist or attached to some part of the owner's clothing (cf. Gn 38:18; 41:42; Sg 8:6; Jer 22:24). Graves have been found with cylinders tied to the wrists of the skeletons.

Another type of seal was the jar handle seal. Cloth was placed over the neck of a bottle, soft clay was smeared on top of the binding cord, and then the seal was pressed into the wet clay. The unbroken seal showed that the merchandise had not been opened before delivery. In Judea the seal was impressed on jar handles as evidence of ownership. Some jar handle stamps were probably trademarks of pottery factories; some bear private names (perhaps the owner of the factory). The so-called royal jar handle stamps contain either a four-winged or two-winged symbol and a short inscription consisting of two lines. The line above reads "belonging to the king," and the lower line contains the name of a city, probably where the jar was made.

Uses

Functional Uses Since their first creation as amulets, seals continued to serve as signals of protection. An unbroken seal proved that the contents had not been tampered with, whether on a document, a granary door, or a wine jar. The lions' den into which Daniel was cast was sealed with the king's signet and those of his nobles (Dn 6:17). Jesus' tomb was secured by sealing the stone (Mt 27:66). The seal also served as a mark of ownership or as a trademark (e.g., placed on pottery before firing). It was also used to validate documents (letters, bills of sale, government documents, etc.). Jezebel wrote letters in her husband's name and sealed them with his seal, thus bringing about the death of Naboth (1 Kgs 21:8-13). Jeremiah sealed a deed of purchase when he bought a kinsman's land (Jer 32:10-14). An edict with the Persian king's seal could not be revoked (Est 8:8).

Symbolic Use Symbolic use of the seal is found both in nonbiblical and biblical literature. A Babylonian prayer says, "Like a seal may my sins be torn away." The OT says, "Seal the teaching among my disciples" (Is 8:16, RSV). Zerubbabel was told he would become God's signet ring (Hg 2:23). The earth took shape like clay pressed by a signet ring (Jb 38:14).

The word is used symbolically in the NT to designate God's personal ownership. For example, the Scriptures say that God's seal is on Jesus, his Son (Jn 3:33; 6:27). This means that Jesus bears God's personal name; Jesus is God's personal expression. The Scriptures also say that the Holy Spirit seals the believers (2 Cor 1:22; Eph 1:13; 4:30). This means that the Spirit is God's mark of ownership on the believers, and it means that the Spirit protects and preserves the believers throughout their lives.

See also Archaeology and the Bible; Inscriptions.

SEASONS *See* Calendars, Ancient and Modern.

SEAT*, Moses' *See* Moses' Seat.

SEBA
Semitic people descended from Cush (Gn 10:7; 1 Chr 1:9; Is 43:3) and possibly to be identified with the people of Sheba. *See* Sheba (Person) #2.

SEBAM
City located on the pastoral tablelands of the Transjordan and desired by the sons of Gad and Reuben (Nm 32:3). Reuben was apportioned this area (Jos 13:19) but eventually lost it to the marauding Moabites. This city was known for its vineyards (Is 16:8-9; Jer 48:32). Sebam is alternately called Sibmah in the Hebrew text (cf. Nm 32:38; Jos 13:19; Is 16:8-9; Jer 48:32).

SEBAT*
KJV spelling of Shebat, the Hebrew month extending from about mid-January to about mid-February, in Zechariah 1:7. *See* Calendars, Ancient and Modern.

SECACAH
One of six cities situated in the wilderness region immediately west of the Dead Sea in the valley of Achor and included in the territory allotted to Judah, mentioned between Middin and Nibshan (Jos 15:61). Its location is perhaps three miles (4.8 kilometers) southwest of Khirbet Qumran at the modern town of Khirbet es-Samrah.

SECHU*
KJV spelling of Secu in 1 Samuel 19:22. *See* Secu.

SECOND ADAM* *See* Adam, The Second.

SECOND COMING OF CHRIST*
The return of Jesus Christ to earth to complete the work of salvation.

Terms Used The doctrine is expressed by verbs such as "come," "descend," "appear," and "is revealed" with Christ as the subject (e.g., "I will come again," Jn 14:3; "the Lord himself will descend," 1 Thes 4:16; "when he appears," 1 Jn 2:28; 3:2; "the day when the Son of man is revealed," Lk 17:30; "when the Lord Jesus is revealed from heaven," 2 Thes 1:7). It is expressed also by a variety of nouns, principally by "coming" (which is the regular translation of the Greek word *parousia,* meaning "presence," "visit," "arrival," "advent," especially of a royal or distinguished person) but also by "appearing" (as in 2 Tm 4:8; Ti 2:13), "revealing," or "revelation" (1 Cor 1:7). These different verbs and nouns point to the same event but highlight different aspects of it, especially the manifestation of God's glory in Christ when he comes. The time of this event is repeatedly referred to as "the Day," sometimes absolutely (as in Rom 13:12; 1 Cor 3:13; Heb 10:25), more often with a qualification, such as "the day of Christ" (Phil 1:10; 2:16), "the day of the Lord" (1 Thes 5:2; 2 Thes 2:2), "the day of the Lord Jesus" (1 Cor 5:5; 2 Cor 1:14), "the day of Jesus Christ" (Phil 1:6), and "the day of our Lord Jesus Christ" (1 Cor 1:8). When such expressions are used, there is often some reference to the judgment to be passed at the coming of Christ: his day is "the day of judgment" (1 Jn 4:17) or "the day of wrath" (Rom 2:5). For the people of God, however, it is "the day of redemption" (Eph 4:30).

The Proclamation of the New Testament That the second coming of Christ was an essential element in the gospel as preached in the apostolic age is clear from many NT writings (quoted below from the RSV).

The origin of the Second Coming is found in the teachings of Jesus before his death. Speaking of himself as the Son of Man, Jesus said, "The day when the Son of man is revealed" (Lk 17:30) he will come "in clouds with great power and glory" (Mk 13:26). This language is derived from the OT, especially from Daniel's vision in which "one like a son of man" is brought "with the clouds of heaven" to receive everlasting dominion from the Ancient of Days (Dn 7:13-14). A cloud or clouds regularly enveloped the divine glory in the OT (as in Ex 40:34; 1 Kgs 8:10-11); their mention in connection with the coming of the Son of Man indicates that, when he comes, the glory of God will be manifested in him. Jesus' last reference to his second coming came at his trial before the Jewish authorities when, asked by the high priest to say whether or not he was "the Christ, the Son of the Blessed," he replied, "I am; and you will see the Son of man seated at the right hand of Power, and coming with the clouds of heaven" (Mk 14:61-62).

After the Gospels, the rest of the NT affirms the eventuality of Christ's second coming. The record of Acts begins with the angels' assurance at the ascension of Christ that "this Jesus, who was taken up from you into heaven, will come in the same way as you saw him go into heaven" (Acts 1:11). The summaries of apostolic addresses that the book contains make repeated references to Jesus as "the one ordained by God to be judge of the living and the dead" (10:42; cf. 17:31).

Writing to his converts in Thessalonica (c. AD 51) a few weeks after they first heard and believed the gospel, Paul reminds them how they had "turned to God from idols, to serve a living and true God, and to wait for his Son from heaven, whom he raised from the dead, Jesus who delivers us from the wrath to come" (1 Thes 1:9-10).

Here Jesus' expected deliverance of his people from end-time judgment is put on the same plane as his historical resurrection; the Christian way of life embraces both serving God and waiting for Christ. This note of waiting for Christ is repeated and amplified several times in this short letter. A few years later Paul uses similar language when writing to his converts in Corinth (cf. Acts 18:1-18): "You are not lacking in any spiritual gift, as you wait for the revealing of our Lord Jesus Christ" (1 Cor 1:7). And in what may have been his last letter he speaks of "the crown of righteousness" that the Lord will award him "on that Day, and not only to me," he adds, "but also to all who have loved his appearing" (2 Tm 4:8). To love his appearing and to wait for him are two different ways of expressing the same attitude.

The writer to the Hebrews encourages his readers with the assurance that in a little while "the coming one shall come and shall not tarry" (Heb 10:37). James says that "the coming of the Lord is at hand" (Jas 5:8). Peter speaks of the time "when the chief Shepherd is manifested" (1 Pt 5:4). The Revelation to John ends with the risen Lord's promise, "Surely I am coming soon," and the church's response, "Amen. Come, Lord Jesus!" (Rv 22:20).

The Second Coming and the Resurrection In 1 Thessalonians, written not more than 20 years after the death and resurrection of Christ, his coming again is presented by way of comfort and encouragement to those whose Christian friends had died. Paul had been compelled to leave Thessalonica before he had time to give his converts there as much teaching as they required, and when some of their number died shortly after his departure, their friends wondered if they would suffer some serious disadvantage at the Second Coming, in contrast to those who would still be alive to greet the returning Lord. No, says Paul, "those who have fallen asleep" will suffer no disadvantage. On the contrary, the first thing to happen when "the Lord himself will descend from heaven" is that "the dead in Christ will rise." Only after that will those who survive until then be caught away to join them and be forever "with the Lord" (1 Thes 4:15-17). Fuller information on the same subject is given in 1 Corinthians, written about five years later. There the resurrection of believers is the full harvest that was inaugurated by the resurrection of Christ: "Christ the first fruits, then at his coming those who belong to Christ" (1 Cor 15:23). An additional revelation is imparted: not only will each believer who has died be raised in a "spiritual body" (v 44) but also those who are still alive will be "changed" so as to have bodies suitable for life in resurrection. For dead and living believers alike, Paul proclaimed that "as we have borne the image of the man of dust [i.e., Adam; cf. Gn 2:7], we shall also bear the image of the man of heaven [i.e., the risen Christ]" (1 Cor 15:49). To the same effect, Paul writes (a few years later still) in Philippians 3:20-21 that from heaven "we await a Savior, the Lord Jesus Christ, who will change our lowly body to be like his glorious body." A deeper unveiling of what this will involve is made in Romans 8:18-23, where the resurrection of the people of Christ is the catalyst for the liberation and glorious renewal of all creation.

The Second Coming and Judgment The association of judgment with the Second Coming arises in Jesus' teaching in the Gospels. The association is equally plain in the epistles of the NT. Paul, in particular, put the subject on a personal level. He forbade premature judgment of fellow Christians: "Do not pronounce judgment before the time, before the Lord comes" (1 Cor 4:5). The Lord will conduct an investigation that will bring to light the hid-

den motives of the heart. Paul knew that his own apostolic work would be assessed on "the day of Christ" (Phil 2:16; 1 Thes 2:19). Elsewhere, Paul urges his converts to bear in mind that they, with himself, must appear before the divine tribunal, variously called "the judgment seat of God" (where "each of us shall give account of himself," Rom 14:10-12) or "the judgment seat of Christ" (where each will "receive good or evil, according to what he has done in the body," 2 Cor 5:10). It seems clear that this judgment is to take place at the second coming of Christ, who will then "judge the living and the dead" (2 Tm 4:1). Because Paul was writing to Christians, he tended to concentrate on the judgment or assessment that the believers would experience at the Lord's return. But he also made it plain that the same coming would bring judgment to those who opposed the Christian faith (2 Thes 1:6-10). This is made explicit in Acts 17:31, where Paul told the Athenians that God "has fixed a day on which he will judge the world in righteousness by a man whom he has appointed."

See also Day of the Lord; Eschatology; Judgment; Judgment Seat; Last Days; Rapture; Resurrection; Revelation, Book of; Tribulation.

SECOND DEATH, The See Death, The Second.

SECOND JEWISH REVOLT* This Bar-Kochba Revolt, so-called after its leader, lasted from AD 131 to 135. The cause was twofold: (1) the emperor Hadrian made circumcision a crime punishable by death; and (2) he decided to rebuild Jerusalem and erect a shrine to Zeus on the derelict temple site. This incensed Jewish fury.

Bar-Kochba—whose name means "son of a star" and was therefore believed to be the "star out of Jacob" (Nm 24:17)—was hailed by many Jews as the Messiah. His guerrilla warfare tactics involved Jews and Romans in colossal losses, but Julius Severus finally eradicated Jewish resistance.

Hadrian rebuilt Jerusalem, renamed it Aelia Capitolina, resettled it with Gentiles, and forbade Jews even to enter it, on pain of death.

See also Bar-Kochba, Bar-Kokba.

SECOND TEMPLE*, Period of the Time interval from the dedication of the rebuilt Jerusalem temple in 516 BC to its destruction by the Romans in AD 70. See Judaism.

SECU Town or topographical landmark where Saul stopped to ask the whereabouts of Samuel and David, located between Gibeah and Ramah. It was especially noted for its large well—a natural place to go for information (1 Sm 19:22).

SECUNDUS A Thessalonian believer; traveling companion of Aristarchus. Secundus accompanied Paul on his third missionary journey through Macedonia and Greece and awaited him at Troas in Asia Minor (Acts 20:4). It is not known whether Secundus remained at Troas or went with Paul on his final trip to Jerusalem.

SEER See Prophecy; Prophet, Prophetess.

SEGUB
1. Youngest son of Hiel the Bethelite. Hiel rebuilt Jericho during the reign of King Ahab of Israel. His violation of Joshua's curse against anyone rebuilding the city (Jos 6:26) cost him his oldest and youngest sons. Segub was killed as a result of the rebuilding of the city gates (1 Kgs 16:34).

2. Son borne to Hezron by the daughter of Makir, the father of Gilead. Segub was the father of Jair (1 Chr 2:21-22).

SEIR (Person) Father of seven sons and a descendant of Abraham through Esau's line. Originally a Horite tribe dwelling in the land of Edom, the nation descended from Seir was first dispossessed by, but later intermarried with, Esau's descendants. Perhaps for this reason Seir and his offspring were included in the genealogies of Abraham (Gn 36:20-21; 1 Chr 1:38).

SEIR (Place)
1. Mountain range of Edom extending from the Dead Sea southward to the Gulf of Aqaba. Mt Seir was bordered by the great valley of Arabah on the west and by desert on the east. Seir is the modern Jebel esh-Shera.
   Seir was formerly inhabited by the Horites, whose defeat to King Kedorlaomer is recorded in Genesis 14:4-6. The Horites were later dispossessed from this region by Esau (Dt 2:12); however, a remnant of Horite chiefs was listed among the descendants of Esau living in Seir (Gn 36:20-30). As this area was given by the Lord as an inheritance to Esau (Jos 24:4), the Israelites were warned not to provoke the sons of Esau to war as they passed through Seir on their wilderness travels (Dt 2:1-8). During Israel's occupation of Palestine, they were drawn into a number of battles against the people of Seir. A band of Simeonites destroyed the Amalekites dwelling in Seir and resettled it with their own people (1 Chr 4:42). Jehoshaphat, king of Judah (872–848 BC), gained an incredible victory over the allied armies of Ammon, Moab, and Seir (2 Chr 20:10-23). King Amaziah of Judah (796–767 BC) routed an army from Seir in the valley of Salt (25:11-14). And finally, the prophet Ezekiel pronounced a curse of destruction on the inhabitants of Seir for their antagonism against Israel (Ez 35:1-15).
   See also Edom, Edomites.
2. Place defining part of the northern boundary of the land assigned to Judah's tribe (Jos 15:10). It was positioned west of Kiriath-jearim and northeast of Beth-shemesh. Mt Seir is perhaps the ridge on which the modern town of Saris is built.

SEIRAH Place where Ehud sought refuge after murdering Eglon, the king of Moab, and from where he summoned Israel to war against the Moabites (Jgs 3:26).

SELA
1. Unidentified site on the border of the Amorites (Jgs 1:36).
2. Edomite stronghold (2 Kgs 14:7). On this site the Nabatean city of Petra was built. *See* Petra.
3. Unidentified place mentioned in Isaiah's prophecy against Moab (Is 16:1).

SELAH* Musical notation, perhaps designating a pause in performance, occurring over 70 times in psalm texts and in Habakkuk 3:3, 9, 13. *See* Music; Psalms, Book of.

SELA-HAMMAHLEKOTH* Cliff in the wilderness of Maon, meaning "the Rock of Escape." Saul, in his desire to kill David, attempted to catch him in the steep-ravined mountains of Judah, where David had fled. Saul's attentions were diverted by a Philistine raid, thus enabling David to escape (1 Sm 23:28, NLT mg). The wadi el-Malaqi, about eight miles (12.9 kilometers) northeast of Maon, is a suggested location for this cliff.

SELED Nadab's son from Judah's tribe (1 Chr 2:30).

SELEUCIA Name of several ancient Near Eastern cities, all founded by Seleucus I Nicator (312–281 BC). The most important is Seleucia in Syria on the northeast corner of the Mediterranean, five miles (8 kilometers) north of the mouth of the Orontes River and 15 miles (24.1 kilometers) from Antioch, for which it was the port. Built by Seleucus I in 301 BC and strongly fortified to guard his capital from the west, it changed hands several times in the disputes between the Seleucid rulers in Syria and the Ptolemies of Egypt (Dn 11:7-9; 1 Macc 11:8-19). In 109 BC the Seleucid ruler, having shaken free of the Ptolemies, granted freedom to the city, along with the privilege of coining money. When the Romans appeared in the east, Pompey conferred the status of "free city" on Seleucia. However, he broke the power of the Seleucids and formed the Roman province of Syria with the free city of Seleucia as a port of entry to the east. Its fine natural harbor and artificial defenses were improved.
   In NT times Seleucia remained a free city and harbored Rome's Syrian fleet. Barnabas, Saul, and John Mark sailed from here on their first missionary journey (Acts 13:4-5) and returned to Antioch via Seleucia (14:26). Later, on Paul's second missionary journey, Paul and company again set out from Seleucia (15:39-41). The city was undoubtedly an attractive place with many public buildings, a temple, and an amphitheater cut out of a cliff.

SEM* KJV form of Shem, Noah's son, in Luke 3:36. *See* Shem.

SEMACHIAH*, SEMAKIAH Korahite Levite, Shemaiah's son and a gatekeeper in the temple (1 Chr 26:7).

SEMEI*, SEMEIN Descendant of Josech and an ancestor of Jesus Christ (Lk 3:26). *See* Genealogy of Jesus Christ.

SENAAH Father of a family of Israelites who returned with Zerubbabel to Palestine following the exile (Ezr 2:35; Neh 7:38). They helped Nehemiah rebuild part of the Jerusalem wall (Neh 3:3; Hassenaah is an alternate spelling for Senaah). Hassenuah is a possible variant for Senaah (1 Chr 9:7; Neh 11:9, where KJV reads "Senuah"). *See also* Hassenuah.

SENEH Name of one of the two rocky crags at a pass across the Wadi es-Suweinit over which Jonathan and his armor bearer crossed in their skirmish against the Philistines. The crag opposite Seneh was called Bozez and faced the town of Micmash to the north. Seneh was visible to the town of Geba to the south (1 Sm 14:4-5).

SENIR Amorite name for Mt Hermon in Deuteronomy 3:9 and Song of Songs 4:8. *See* Hermon, Mount.

SENNACHERIB King of the Assyrian Empire from 705 to 681 BC. His name, meaning "son has replaced brothers," may refer to a specific family situation by means of which he, a younger son of Sargon II, came to succeed his father. Before the death of his father, Sennacherib acted as military governor of the northern provinces of the Assyrian Empire. He was successful in quelling unrest in those areas. When Sargon II was assassinated in 705 BC, Sennacherib lost no time in claiming the throne.
   As king of Assyria, he was a bold administrator. He was soon known to be a just and tolerant man, for thus the biblical account speaks of him. Extrabiblical sources indicate that, while he was conducting military campaigns, he also developed a strong rule at home and,

employing slave labor acquired through his military victories, he did much building in Nineveh, his capital city. Many of the decorations of his palace, as well as inscriptions he prepared, are housed in museums today.

Shortly after Sennacherib became king, he was confronted by rebellion in the eastern and western provinces. It is at this point that the biblical record refers to Sennacherib. Judah was a vassal state of Assyria. It is likely that Merodach-baladan in Babylon and Hezekiah, king of Judah, joined in this insurrection (2 Kgs 18:7-8).

Sennacherib was ready for the challenge from Babylon and Palestine. In 703 BC he first led his forces to Kish near Babylon, where he defeated Merodach-baladan's army and then captured the city of Babylon itself. Turning west in 701 BC, Sennacherib led his armies against the Palestinian alliance headed by Hezekiah. He captured the cities of Tyre and Sidon and then continued his campaign southward. Several of the Philistine cities submitted before the Assyrian onslaught, but Ashkelon, Beth-dagon, and Joppa resisted and were captured and plundered. The leaders of the city of Ekron were put to death by being skinned alive because they had delivered up their pro-Assyrian king to Hezekiah. Sennacherib then turned to Judah. He besieged the Judean city of Lachish and captured 46 other towns, taking 200,150 Jewish captives. Hezekiah began to realize his desperate situation as Sennacherib's military victories came one after the other, so he sent tribute to Sennacherib at Lachish. The tribute amounted to 300 talents of silver and 30 talents of gold (2 Kgs 18:13-16). From his camp at Lachish, Sennacherib sent envoys to Jerusalem to demoralize the city inhabitants. In their effort to convince Jerusalem that it should surrender, the Assyrians referred to Hezekiah's removal of altars and places of worship. This act was considered an affront to the God the Judeans worshiped and on whom they relied for victory; he would not aid a people led by an idol-breaking king such as Hezekiah.

While Sennacherib was threatening Jerusalem, Tirhakah, the Ethiopian king of Egypt, led his army to Libnah. Sennacherib was able to defeat this Egyptian force. He then turned his full attention to Jerusalem again (2 Kgs 19:15-19). Isaiah was sent by God to inform Hezekiah that the mocking Sennacherib would be humbled and Jerusalem would be spared for David's sake. The Lord's word was fulfilled. Sennacherib's plans to take Jerusalem by siege had to be abandoned when 185,000 of his troops died of a miraculous plague.

Sennacherib returned to Nineveh, the capital city of Assyria. He was murdered in the temple of Nisroch by Adrammelech and Sharezer, two of his sons. A third son, Esarhaddon, succeeded him upon the throne of Assyria.
See also Assyria, Assyrians.

SENUAH* KJV form of Hassenuah in Nehemiah 11:9. See Hassenuah.

SEORIM Levite and head of the fourth of 24 divisions of priests formed during David's reign (1 Chr 24:8).

SEPARATION*, Water of KJV translation of "the water for the purification ceremony," a water denoting cleansing from sin or impurity, in Numbers 19:9, 13, 20-21; 31:23. See Cleanness and Uncleanness, Regulations Concerning.

SEPHAR Geographical landmark defining one of the boundaries of the territory settled by the sons of Joktan (Gn 10:30). Undoubtedly located in southern Arabia, Sephar is most often identified with one of two towns

bearing the Arabic name Zafar: the seaport town in central Yemen's Hadhramaut province, or the site in southern Yemen, once the capital of the Himyarites.

Sennacherib on the Throne

SEPHARAD* Place of exile for the Jews of Jerusalem (Ob 1:20, NLT mg). Its location is not certain; however, good evidence is available to support Sardis, the capital of Lydia, in Asia Minor as the place of captivity. Other less feasible suggestions are Saparda in eastern Assyria, where Sargon transported Jews, and Spain, as mentioned in the Targum of Jonathan.

SEPHARVAIM, SEPHARVITES* One of five cities and its inhabitants who were transported to Samaria after the fall of Israel to Sargon II, king of Assyria, in 722 BC (2 Kgs 17:24). The Sepharvites were remembered for their abominable practice of offering their children as burnt sacrifices to their gods Adrammelech and Anammelech. In a taunting message to King Hezekiah of Judah (715–686 BC), King Sennacherib of Assyria (705–681 BC) warned that as the gods and kings of Sepharvaim were not able to prevent her fall to the Assyrians, so too it would be with Jerusalem and Hezekiah's God (2 Kgs 18:34; Is 36:19; 37:13). The location of Sepharvaim is uncertain. It is probably identifiable with the Syrian city of Sibraim near Damascus (Ez 47:16).

SEPTUAGINT* See Bible, Versions of the (Ancient); Bible, Canon of the.

SEPULCHER* See Burial, Burial Customs.

SERAH Asher's daughter (Gn 46:17; Nm 26:46; 1 Chr 7:30).

SERAIAH
1. Royal secretary of King David (2 Sm 8:17); alternately called Sheva in 2 Samuel 20:25, Shisha in 1 Kings 4:3, and Shavsha in 1 Chronicles 18:16.
2. Chief priest in Jerusalem at the time of its destruction by the Babylonians in 586 BC. He was taken by Nebuzaradan, the captain of the guard, to Nebuchadnezzar at Riblah, where he was put to death (2 Kgs 25:18; Jer 52:24). First Chronicles 6:14 records

Seraiah as the son of Azariah, the father of Jehozadak and a descendant of Levi through Aaron's line.

3. Son of Tanhumeth the Netophathite and one of the captains of the Judean forces who sought clemency from Nebuchadnezzar under Gedaliah (2 Kgs 25:23; Jer 40:8).

4. Judahite, the son of Kenaz, the brother of Othniel and Joab's father (1 Chr 4:13-14).

5. Simeonite, the son of Asiel and Joshibiah's father (1 Chr 4:35).

6. One of the men who returned with Zerubbabel to Judah following the exile (Ezr 2:2); called Azariah in Nehemiah 7:7. See Azariah #23.

7. Father of Ezra the scribe. Ezra returned to Jerusalem during the reign of King Artaxerxes I of Persia (464–424 BC; Ezr 7:1). He is perhaps identical with #2 above, in which case Jehozadak would be Ezra's brother.

8. One of the priests who set his seal on the covenant of Ezra (Neh 10:2).

9. Son of Hilkiah and a priest living in Jerusalem during the postexilic era (Neh 11:11); called Azariah in 1 Chronicles 9:11. See Azariah #10.

10. One of the leaders of the priests who returned with Zerubbabel and Jeshua to Judah after the exile (Neh 12:1). His house in the next generation was headed by Meraiah. He is perhaps identical with #6 above.

11. Son of Azriel who, with Jerahmeel and Shelemiah, was ordered by King Jehoiakim of Judah (609–598 BC) to capture Baruch and Jeremiah (Jer 36:26).

12. Son of Neriah and the official who accompanied King Zedekiah of Judah (597–586 BC) to Babylon. Seraiah was to relay Jeremiah's message against Babylon (Jer 51:59-61).

SERAPH*, SERAPHIM Angelic beings mentioned only twice in the Bible, both occurring in the same chapter of Isaiah (Is 6:2, 6). The word *seraphim* is plural in number, but it is impossible to say from Isaiah's vision just how many he saw. The prophet spoke of them as though they were quite familiar spiritual beings, which seems a little curious since they are not mentioned elsewhere.

Isaiah described each seraph as having six wings: two shielded the face, two covered the feet, and the remaining pair enabled the seraph to fly. The most that can be said from the available evidence is that they were exalted spiritual entities who were occupied constantly in the praise and worship of God. Most probably the seraphim were an order of celestial beings comparable in nature to the cherubim and engaged in a somewhat similar form of service around the divine throne.

See also Angel; Cherub, Cherubim.

SERED, SEREDITE One of Zebulun's sons (Gn 46:14) and the father of the Seredite family (Nm 26:26).

SERGIUS PAULUS Proconsul of Cyprus, described as a "man of intelligence" (Acts 13:7). Paul and Barnabas, on their first missionary journey, evangelized the Cyprian city of Paphos, Sergius Paulus's residence. Here they met the Jewish false prophet and sorcerer named Bar-Jesus (or Elymas), who strongly opposed their gospel message before the proconsul. Paul, however, rebuked Elymas and cursed him with blindness. When Sergius Paulus witnessed what had happened, he believed. Thus, he became the first recorded convert on Paul's first missionary journey.

It is here that we find the transition from the name Saul to that of Paul. Origen and many since his time

have believed that Paul made the change at this point in honor of his famous convert.

SERMON ON THE MOUNT* *See* Beatitudes, The; Jesus Christ, Teachings of.

SERPENT A snake or sea monster. Various words are used in the Bible for serpents or snakes. In general, the serpent belongs to a class of reptiles often characterized by their ability to wound by striking or biting and then poisoning with venom. There are particular kinds of snakes mentioned in the Bible, such as the adder (Is 11:8) and the viper (Acts 28:3). "Serpent" also denotes the monstrous sea serpent mentioned in Job 26:13, Isaiah 27:1, and Amos 9:3.

In Genesis 3:1 the temptation that came to Adam and Eve is described as coming through the serpent, that "shrewdest of all the creatures the LORD God had made" (NLT). And in consequence of this, he was told, "You will grovel in the dust as long as you live, crawling along on your belly" (Gn 3:14, NLT). Reference is made in 2 Corinthians 11:3 to the fact that the serpent deceived Eve by his cunning, and Revelation 12:9 speaks of the "ancient serpent, who is called the Devil and Satan, the deceiver of the whole world" (RSV; see also Rv 12:14-15 and 20:2).

Most of the biblical references to serpents or snakes allude (in figurative application) to the ability of the snake to bite and to poison with venom (e.g., Gn 49:17; Eccl 10:8, 11; Is 14:29; Am 5:19; Rv 9:19). In Psalm 58:4-5 the wicked are likened to snakes. In Psalm 140:3, people's tongues are also spoken of as being as sharp as a serpent's, and their lips as poisonous as vipers. In Proverbs 23:32 it is said that strong drink "bites like a poisonous serpent; it stings like a viper" (NLT). Then in Jeremiah 8:17 the enemies of Israel are spoken of as coming, in God's judgment against his people, as "poisonous snakes you cannot charm. No matter what you do, they will bite you, and you will die" (NLT).

Positively, the serpent is seen to have great wisdom as the "craftiest" of creatures. And so we have the words of Jesus to his disciples, "Be wise as serpents and innocent as doves" (Mt 10:16). But the primary image is negative. The serpent is a symbol of deceit. Thus, Jesus addressed the scribes and Pharisees as "Snakes! Sons of vipers!" (23:33). John the Baptist also addressed the Pharisees and Sadducees with the words "You sons of snakes!" (3:7). See Animals.

SERPENT, Bronze *See* Bronze Serpent, Bronze Snake.

SERPENT'S STONE* Place where Adonijah, the son of David, sacrificed sheep and oxen and attempted to secretly set himself up as king (1 Kgs 1:9, NLT mg). The serpent's stone was located near En-rogel, a spring in the Kidron Valley located just south of Jerusalem. Some suggest that this stone was named for the large stone conduits nearby that emptied into the pool of Siloam, for a steep rock formation, or perhaps for a cultic shrine with the serpent used as its emblem. The Stone of Zoheleth is the English equivalent for the Hebrew term.

SERUG Reu's son from Shem's line (Gn 11:20-23), Abraham's forefather and an ancestor of Jesus Christ (Lk 3:35; KJV "Saruch"). See Genealogy of Jesus Christ.

SERVANT A person under obligation to serve a master, who in turn would provide a measure of protection. Some servants were slaves under legal bondage; others were servants voluntarily. It is not always possible to distinguish among "servant," "slave," "bondman," and "bondwoman." Several words in both Hebrew and Greek have been translated "servant," although newer translations sometimes prefer other words.

The Hebrew word for "lad," "youth," or "boy" often means servant (Ex 33:11; Nm 22:22; 2 Kgs 4:12). A word meaning "free-born servant" referred to the servants of the Lord, like the Levites (Ezr 8:17; Is 61:6; Ez 44:11) or priests (Ex 28:35; Jl 1:9; 2:17). Sometimes ministers of the king are called servants (1 Chr 27:1; Prv 29:12), as are angels who minister before the Lord (Pss 103:21; 104:4). The hired servant or hireling was also considered a free person (Ex 12:45; Jb 7:1; Mal 3:5).

The most common Hebrew term, occurring nearly 800 times in the OT, denotes a slave held in bondage (Gn 9:25; 12:16; Ex 20:17; Dt 5:15; 15:17). Yet the same word is used for people of noble rank, such as ministers and advisers to the king (2 Kgs 22:12; 2 Chr 34:20; Neh 2:10) or a servant of God (Gn 24:14; Nm 12:7; Jos 1:7; 2 Kgs 21:8), in such expressions as "Moses [or also David, Isaiah, Israel, Job, etc.] my servant." One of the noblest expressions is "the servant of Yahweh [the LORD]" (Dt 34:5; Jos 1:13; 8:31-33; Is 49:1-6; 50:4-9; 52:13–53:12). The proper name Obadiah means "servant of Yahweh."

The NT variously defines servant as a hired servant or hireling (Mk 1:20; Lk 15:17-19; Jn 10:12-14), more widely as a slave (Mt 8:9; 10:24-25; 13:27-28; Mk 10:44; 12:2-4; Lk 7:2-3, 8-10; Jn 4:51; 8:34; 13:16; Eph 6:5; Col 1:7), and also as a domestic servant (Lk 16:13).

See also Slave, Slavery.

SERVANT OF THE LORD

Title applied to a variety of persons in the Bible. The basic term, "servant," covers a range of meanings. Used some 800 times in the OT alone, "servant" refers to a slave, to an officer close to the king, or to the chosen leader of God's people.

Isaiah 41:8-9 defines this highest servanthood as something granted by God's grace: "But you, Israel, my servant, Jacob whom I have chosen . . . ; you whom I took from the ends of the earth, and called from its farthest corners, saying to you, 'You are my servant. . . .' " (RSV). This title is thus applicable to heroes of faith and action—to the patriarchs (Gn 26:24; Ez 28:25; 37:25), to Moses (Ex 14:31; 1 Kgs 8:53, 56), to David (2 Sm 7:26-29; Jer 33:21-26; Ez 37:24) and his descendants (as Hezekiah, Eliakim, Zerubbabel—Hg 2:23), to the prophets (2 Kgs 10:10; 14:25), and to other faithful Israelites, such as Joshua and Caleb (Nm 14:24; Jos 24:29; Jgs 2:8).

Prophets other than Isaiah employ this term, but only Zechariah joins him in giving an apparently messianic prediction to this name. Zechariah 3:8 says, "Hear now, O Joshua the high priest, you and your friends who sit before you, for they are men of good omen: behold, I will bring my servant the Branch" (RSV). Some would see Zerubbabel as the individual in view here (cf. Zec 6:12); however, the use of "Branch" is decidedly messianic in Isaiah (Is 11:1) and Jeremiah (Jer 33:15).

"*The* servant of the Lord," in specialized biblical usage, points to the Messiah while also alluding to Isaiah's central message. Though Isaiah, with others, employs "servant" with a range of significations, he composed some passages known as the Servant Songs. These distinctive sections of his book are distinguishable in content, but they cannot be extracted from the surrounding context without disrupting the flow of prophecy. Isaiah's focus is on the future Messiah-servant. None can question the NT's unanimous messianic interpretation of Isaiah's servant, nor its application of this understanding to Jesus Christ.

A "servant Christology" pervades Acts (Acts 3:13, 26; 4:27, 30), and 1 Peter, with numerous allusions in the Gospels. Jesus himself quotes Isaiah 53 explicitly only in Luke 22:37, but he seems to allude to it in Mark 10:45, 14:24, and possibly 9:12. Peter not only emphasizes vicarious, redemptive suffering (1 Pt 2:21-25; 3:18) but seems to highlight the theme of Isaiah 53 in summing up OT prophecy (1:11) as predicting "the sufferings of Christ and the glories that would follow." Paul includes these elements (1 Cor 15:3; Phil 2:6-11; cf. Rom 4:25; 5:19; 2 Cor 5:21), and John's "Lamb of God" title derives from Isaiah 53:7 no less than from the entire sacrificial system.

See also Christology; Isaiah, Book of.

SERVITOR*

KJV rendering of "servant" in 2 Kings 4:43.

SETH

Third son of Adam and Eve, replacing Abel, whom Cain murdered (Gn 4:25). He appears as the first-born son of Adam in the genealogies of Genesis 5:3-8, 1 Chronicles 1:1 (KJV "Sheth"), and Luke 3:38. It was through Seth's line that Jesus was born. Seth was the father of Enosh and lived 912 years.

See also Genealogy of Jesus Christ.

SETHUR

Asherite, Michael's son and one of the 12 spies sent by Moses to search out the land of Canaan (Nm 13:13).

SEVEN

See Numbers and Numerology.

SEVEN LAST SAYINGS OF JESUS*

Recorded words of Jesus between the time he was crucified and the time he died. These seven sentences (quoted below from the KJV) are not found in any one Gospel. Instead, the first two and the seventh occur only in Luke; the third, fifth, and sixth, only in John; and the fourth, in both Matthew and Mark. The order is traditional; because no Gospel records them all, it is uncertain in which order they really came. Also unknown is whether Jesus said other things from the cross or whether the seven sayings are summaries of longer statements. But considering the trauma of crucifixion, it would not be surprising if this were all he said.

1. "Father, forgive them; for they know not what they do" (Lk 23:34).

This is the only one of the seven last words whose genuineness is questioned, for several of the best Greek manuscripts do not contain it. Even if an element of doubt exists (the evidence is fairly evenly balanced), it certainly fits what is known of Jesus and his love, whether or not Luke originally recorded it. Just a few verses before, Jesus showed more concern for others than for himself (Lk 19:41; 22:50-51; 23:28). Jesus lived his own teaching and prayed for those who were torturing him (Lk 6:27-28)—no greater impulse for mankind to go and do likewise could be given. Certainly the soldiers and Jewish leaders were not totally unaware of what they were doing (cf. Acts 3:17), but in that they did not know the real import of their action, they were ignorant. For Christians, the request "Father, forgive" is more important than the reason, as Stephen recognized when he paraphrased it at his own martyrdom (Acts 7:60). In the end, forgiveness demands no reason; it is grace.

2. "Verily I say unto thee, To day shalt thou be with me in paradise" (Lk 23:43).

Luke does not record this statement to teach about the abode of the dead but to express the response of the Lord to faith. One criminal quite understandably joins with the jeering crowd and gets only silence (Lk 23:40), but the other quite remarkably recognizes not only the innocence of Jesus but also that the cross was only a prelude to the kingdom (vv 40-42). Jesus promised the man that he would be with him in paradise. Here again is grace, asked for and received.

3. "Woman, behold thy son! . . . Behold thy mother!" (Jn 19:26-27).

John pictures Jesus as fully in control of the situation. At this point that control is apparent, as he calmly cares for his mother instead of focusing on his own suffering. Mary was also suffering as the "sword" pierced her heart (Lk 2:35). Jesus, now much more her Lord than her son, remembers his natural as well as his spiritual relationships. It is not known why Jesus' brothers were not around to care for Mary, or why they missed the Passover festival. It also is unknown why the beloved disciple was chosen, but perhaps the choice fell on him because he was there at Calvary and he was trustworthy.

4. "My God, my God, why hast thou forsaken me?" (Mt 27:46; Mk 15:34).

It is now hours later than the first three words, deep in the darkness that covered Calvary for the last three hours. Suddenly Jesus cried out the first words of Psalm 22. Mark recorded them in Jesus' native language, Aramaic, while Matthew changed them to Hebrew. The meaning of the cry (called the cry of derelection) has been variously explained as an expression of human feeling, a statement of disappointment that God did not deliver him, an expression of separation from God because he was bearing sin, or a citation of the whole psalm with its triumphal ending being intended. Although the full depth of this cry is a mystery known only to Jesus and his Father, it is probable that, because the psalm is a cry to God for vindication, Jesus is here asking for that. He cries to God to show that he is truly God's chosen one. The petititon is answered in that God raised his Son from the dead three days later.

5. "I thirst" (Jn 19:28).

At the beginning of the crucifixion, Jesus was offered a drugged wine as a soporific to deaden the pain of crucifixion. He refused it (Mt 27:34; Mk 15:23). Now, severely dehydrated, Jesus accepts the soldiers' sour wine (Jn 19:29), which would sharpen his senses for his final cry. He needed it, for he had been hanging there six hours. Perhaps at no place in the life of Jesus do we see his full humanity quite so clearly as here. John saw this action as a fulfillment of Psalm 22:15 (and perhaps Ps 69:21).

6. "It is finished" (Jn 19:30).

John completes the crucifixion account with this simple statement (a single word in Greek). The sentence naturally reveals relief and satisfaction that the pain and agony are over, that death will soon release him, but John's context gives the word a deeper meaning. According to John, Jesus was in control of the whole crucifixion. He said that no one could take his life from him—he would lay it down of his own accord (Jn 10:18; 19:10-11). So here, knowing that he had totally completed the will of the Father, he voluntarily laid his life down. What is finished, then, is not simply his dying, nor his life per se, nor the work of redemption, but the total reason for his being in the world. The last act of obedience has been accomplished; the last scripture has been fulfilled. Jesus proclaims his life "finished" and exits from the stage until the resurrection begins a new act.

7. "Father, into thy hands I commend my spirit" (Lk 23:46).

Luke has a different picture of the end than John and the other Evangelists. Matthew and Mark report only "a great cry" after the cry of derelection, ending on a dark note. John ends with the completed work. Luke, who reports no feeling of forsakenness, ends by telling us the

great cry was a quotation of Psalm 31:5 (cf. Stephen in Acts 7:59). The quotation is prefaced by "Father," the familiar *Abba*, a form of address to God characteristic of Jesus. His relationship to God is unbroken to the end. Jesus is not leaping into the dark or fighting against the unknown but placing himself in death into the hands of the same Father he had served in life.

See also Crucifixion; Eli, Eli, Lema Sabachthani.

SEX, SEXUALITY* Unlike some religious and philosophical systems, the Bible takes a positive view of

---

THE SEVEN LAST SAYINGS IN THE CHURCH
The seven last words have a deep pastoral content that has captured the imagination of the church. Many forms for Christian meditation focus on these words. They have been celebrated in liturgy (especially Good Friday liturgies). They have been put to music (e.g., Heinrich Schutz in the 1700s). They have been an example of Christian behavior and a basis for Passion theology (particularly the fourth). Thus, they form an invaluable part of church tradition.

---

human sexuality. According to the OT's account of Creation, it was God himself who made people sexual beings. Being male or female is part of what it means to be created in the image of God (Gn 1:26-28). Above everything else, therefore, sexuality is a precious aspect of what a person *is*, not merely a description of what he or she *does*.

In line with this positive approach, the OT sees nothing embarrassing in the bodily differences between the sexes (Gn 2:25) and nothing shameful in physical expressions of lovemaking (Prv 5:18-19; Eccl 9:9). The Song of Songs, in particular, is a most beautiful love poem. Its powerful language should not be so spiritualized that the physical passion it describes is stripped of its delight and candor.

Paul strikes the same positive note in his letters to Corinth and to Timothy at Ephesus. Sexual vice was rampant in both these cities. Partly as a reaction to this, a negative, ascetic attitude was threatening to take control in the life of Christians. Marriage was being forbidden (1 Tm 4:3) and married couples were abstaining from sexual intercourse in the belief that this would help them to become more spiritually mature (cf. 1 Cor 7:5).

Paul had no hesitation in branding such attitudes as heretical. Recalling his readers to the message of Genesis, he encouraged them to receive God's gifts thankfully (1 Tm 4:3-5). Husbands and wives, he writes, are mutually obliged to satisfy each other's sexual needs (1 Cor 7:3-4).

Most obviously, God made sex for procreation (Gn 1:28). But sex is for relationship as well as procreation. Genesis 2 describes how God made woman to fill man's relationship vacuum (2:18-24). The relational purpose of human sexuality embraces far more than physical intercourse. In this broad sense, being male or being female is a God-given aid to making all sorts of relationships, including some not normally thought of as sexual at all.

The Bible does not, of course, ignore the darker side of human nature. Having described the goodness of sex in the Creator's perfect plan, Genesis goes on to explain how man's disobedience to God spoiled sex, just as it spoiled every other aspect of human life.

Nudity became a matter of embarrassment and fear, as men and women eyed each other as sex objects instead of as people with physical differences (Gn 3:7-10). On the relational side, trust and tenderness gave way to betrayal and harshness. Here lies the root cause of all the discrimination and abuse that fuel modern feminist protests. And procreation was spoiled, too, as the marvelous experience of childbirth was marred by unnecessary pain and distress.

This is the context in which the Bible's ban on extra-marital intercourse should be read; it prohibits adultery (Ex 20:14) and any kind of extramarital or premarital sex (1 Cor 6:18; 1 Thes 4:3). The Bible does not usually pause to back up its prohibitions with arguments, but on the rare occasions when it does expand its veto on extra-marital intercourse, the reasons given are highly instructive. There is no appeal to consequences (these things are wrong because they result in disease and unwanted babies) or even to motives (these things are wrong if they are done in an unloving spirit). All extramarital sex is wrong *in itself*, simply because the body is not meant for sexual immorality and those who commit sexual sins sin against their own bodies (1 Cor 6:13, 18). Sexual intercourse is a unique kind of body language that the Creator has designed to express and seal that special, exclusive, life-long relationship between a man and a woman which the Bible labels "marriage."

The Bible also prohibits homosexuality (Lv 18:22; Rom 1:26-27; 1 Cor 6:9-10; 1 Tm 1:9-10). The only verses that provide an explanation for this prohibition are Romans 1:24-27. Essentially, these verses indicate that God gave up on those who gave up on him when they turned from worshiping the Creator to worshiping things God made—that is, when they became idolaters. As such, God abandoned them, as they abandoned themselves to their own sinful and sexual desires, especially practicing homosexuality. Thus, homosexuality is seen as a violation of the natural created order and thereby an offense to God the Creator who created men and women, male and female, for procreation.

The Bible's advice to anyone caught up in sexual temptation is practical: flee from temptation. When Joseph was invited by another man's wife to go to bed with her, he left his cloak in her hand and ran out of the house (Gn 39:12). And Paul tells his Christian readers to follow Joseph's good example (1 Cor 6:18; 2 Tm 2:22). This is an acknowledgment of the power of the normal person's sex drive, not a counsel of despair. The power of the Holy Spirit, Paul taught, gives any believer the strength to win the war against sexual temptation. He knew Christians who had found the Spirit's power to gain self-control and conquer the most deeply ingrained habits (1 Cor 6:9-11; Gal 5:22-23; 2 Tm 1:7).

Finally, there is a strong hint in the NT that God is going to end human sexuality just as he began it. There will be no marriage, Jesus taught, in heaven (Mt 22:30). That is an unlikely but fitting climax to the Bible's teaching on sex and sexuality. When there is no more death, the need to procreate will be over. And when relationships are perfectly loving, there will no longer be any need for a sexual prop to support them. So both of God's main purposes for human sexuality will be perfectly fulfilled in eternity.

See also Divorce; Family Life and Relations; Man; Marriage, Marriage Customs; Virgin; Woman.

SHAALABBIN, SHAALBIM, SHAALBON Amorite

city known by three names, assigned to Dan's tribe for an inheritance, mentioned between Ir-shemesh and Aijalon (Jos 19:42). The Danites, however, were unable to defeat the Amorites and take possession of the city. When the house of Joseph grew strong, the Ephraimites conquered Shaalbim and reduced the Amorites to forced labor (Jgs 1:35). Later, Shaalbim, along with the cities of

Makaz, Beth-shemesh, and Elon-bethhanan made up Solomon's second administrative district (1 Kgs 4:9). Eliahba the Shaalbonite was one of David's 30 mighty men (2 Sm 23:32; 1 Chr 11:33).

SHAALIM Region within the land of Ephraim or Benjamin where Saul searched for his father's donkeys (1 Sm 9:4).

SHAAPH

1. Jahdai's sixth son, included in the genealogy of Caleb, Jerahmeel's brother (1 Chr 2:47).
2. Son of Caleb by his concubine; the brother of Jerahmeel; the father of Madmannah (1 Chr 2:49).

SHAARAIM

1. One of 14 cities in the lowland region of the territory allotted to Judah's tribe for an inheritance, listed between Azekah and Adithaim (Jos 15:36). Shaaraim was in the direction in which the Philistines tried to escape from the pursuing Israelites following David's slaying of Goliath (1 Sm 17:52).
2. One of 14 cities where the sons of Shimei, a descendant of Simeon, lived until David's reign (1 Chr 4:31). It is possibly the same city as Sharuhen (Jos 19:6), mentioned in a parallel passage, and Shilhim, located in the southern portion of Judah near Edom's border (15:32).

SHAASHGAZ Eunuch of King Ahasuerus, in charge of the concubines (Est 2:14).

SHABBETHAI

1. Levite who opposed Ezra's suggestion that the sons of Israel should divorce the foreign women they had married upon returning to Palestine from exile (Ezr 10:15). He explained the law to the people at Ezra's reading (Neh 8:7).
2. One of the chiefs of the Levites who oversaw the outside work of the sanctuary during the postexilic period (Neh 11:16). He is perhaps identical with #1 above.

SHACHIA* KJV for Sakia. *See* Sakia.

SHADDAI* Part of the Hebrew name *El Shaddai* for God, meaning "God Almighty" (Ps 68:14). *See* God, Names of.

SHADRACH, MESHACH, AND ABEDNEGO

Babylonian names of three Hebrew youths, Hananiah, Mishael, and Azariah, who along with Daniel and others were taken to Babylon as hostages by Nebuchadnezzar in 605 BC (2 Kgs 24:1; Dn 1:1-4). They may have been of royal descent (2 Kgs 20:18; Is 39:7), and thus their presence in Babylon would be thought to guarantee the good behavior of the Judean king Jehoiakim. Nebuchadnezzar, desiring to grace his court with intelligent and handsome men and provide able administrators for his kingdom, directed that certain of the Judean hostages be selected for special training. Among those chosen were Daniel and his three friends. Their Hebrew names, each of which exalted Yahweh, were changed to Babylonian names whose meanings are not clear but may have been intended to honor a Babylonian god. Thus, Hananiah ("The Lord is gracious") was changed to Shadrach ("Command of Aku"—the Sumerian moon god), Mishael ("Who is what God is") was changed to Meshach ("Who is what Aku is"), and Azariah ("The Lord has helped") was changed to Abednego ("Servant of Nabu"—the Babylonian god of wisdom). Also Daniel ("My judge is God") was changed to Belteshazzar ("Bel protects"—the chief Babylonian god). These young men underwent a three-year course of instruction in the languages and literature of the Chaldeans, the learned men of Babylon. This instruction no doubt included the Aramaic, Akkadian, and Sumerian languages; cuneiform writing; and perhaps also astronomy, mathematics, history, and agriculture.

Nebuchadnezzar provided food for this academy. The four Hebrew youths refused to defile themselves with it because it likely had been sacrificed to one or more of the pagan gods. It had not been properly prepared, therefore, and was unfit for Jewish consumption (cf. Ex 34:15; Lv 17:10-14). Fearing the king's displeasure should the young scholars appear undernourished, the chief eunuch expressed his concern to Daniel. Daniel proposed a substitute diet of vegetables to be tested for ten days. At the end of that period, the four Hebrew youths appeared healthier than their colleagues and were allowed to continue their diet. When the course of their instruction was completed, the four stood out from the rest because of their academic excellence and superior competence in every area of knowledge. Their intellectual superiority had been bestowed upon them by God.

Apparently, these four young men joined the ranks of the "wise men of Babylon" (Dn 2:12-49). When the others (the enchanters, sorcerers, and wise men) were unable to tell Nebuchadnezzar the nature and interpretation of a dream, he lashed out at them in a fitful rage and ordered them all put to death. Daniel appealed to the king, and their lives were spared when the dream and its interpretation were made known to him in a vision. Later, Shadrach, Meshach, and Abednego refused to comply with the king's command to prostrate themselves before an enormous golden image that Nebuchadnezzar had erected (ch 3). Confronted by Nebuchadnezzar and threatened with terrible punishment for their intransigence, they replied that their trust was fully in the Lord. A blazing furnace was stoked for the immediate execution of the faithful Hebrews. The Lord was with his faithful servants and preserved their lives by sending his angel to protect them in the furnace. In the end it was Nebuchadnezzar who had to acknowledge that his own kingdom and power could not compare to that of the true God.

See also Daniel, Book of; Daniel, Additions to (Prayer of Azariah and the Song of the Three Young Men).

SHAGEE Hararite and Jonathan's father (2 Sm 23:33; 1 Chr 11:34). Jonathan was one of David's mighty men.

SHAHARAIM Benjaminite living in Moab, father of nine sons, who divorced two of his three wives (1 Chr 8:8).

SHAHAZUMAH Town situated between Tabor and Beth-shemesh on the border of the land allotted to Issachar's tribe for an inheritance (Jos 19:22).

SHALIM* KJV for Shaalim. See Shaalim.

SHALISHA*, SHALISHAH One of the regions (mentioned between the hill country of Ephraim and the district of Shaalim) through which Saul traveled in search of his father's lost donkeys (1 Sm 9:4).

SHALLECHETH*, SHALLEKETH*, Gate of Gate located on the western side of the temple, which was guarded by Shuppim and Hosah (1 Chr 26:16, NLT mg).

SHALLUM
1. Son of Jabesh and Israel's 16th king (752 BC). In a conspiracy against King Zechariah, Shallum murdered

the monarch at Ibleam and declared himself ruler of Israel during the 39th year of King Uzziah's (Azariah's) reign in Judah (792–740 BC). However, in like manner, he was killed at the hands of Gadi after ruling for only one month (2 Kgs 15:10-15). See Chronology of the Bible (Old Testament); Israel, History of.
2. Son of Tikvah (alternately spelled Tokhath, see 2 Chr 34:22), who was keeper of the wardrobe and the husband of Huldah the prophetess, living in Jerusalem during the days of King Josiah (640–609 BC; 2 Kgs 22:14).
3. Sismai's son and the father of Jekamiah from Judah's tribe (1 Chr 2:40-41).
4. Alternate name for Jehoahaz, the youngest of King Josiah's four sons and later Judah's 17th king, in 1 Chronicles 3:15 and Jeremiah 22:11. See Jehoahaz #2.
5. Shaul's son, Simeon's grandson, and the father of Mibsam (1 Chr 4:25).
6. Alternate name for Meshullam, Zadok's son and Ezra's forefather, in 1 Chronicles 6:12-13 and Ezra 7:2. See Meshullam #7.
7. Alternate name for Shillem, the youngest of Naphtali's four sons, in 1 Chronicles 7:13. See Shillem, Shillemite.
8. Alternate name for Meshullam, Kore's son and chief of the gatekeepers (1 Chr 9:17-19, 31; Ezr 2:42; Neh 7:45). See Meshullam #20.
9. Ephraimite and the father of Jehizkiah (2 Chr 28:12).
10. One of the Levitical gatekeepers who was encouraged by Ezra to divorce his foreign wife during the postexilic era (Ezr 10:24).
11. One of the descendants of Binnui who was encouraged by Ezra to divorce his foreign wife (Ezr 10:42).
12. Hallohesh's son and a ruler of Jerusalem who, along with his daughters, repaired the section of city wall next to the Tower of the Ovens (Neh 3:12).
13. Col-hozeh's son and ruler of the Mizpah district, who rebuilt the Fountain Gate and the wall of the pool of Shelah of the king's garden (Neh 3:15).
14. Uncle of Hanamel and Jeremiah, who sold to the latter his field at Anathoth during King Zedekiah's reign (597–586 BC; Jer 32:7). He is perhaps identifiable with #2 above.
15. Maaseiah's father. Maaseiah, keeper of the threshold, owned a chamber in the sanctuary during Jehoiakim's reign (609–598 BC; Jer 35:4, KJV; cf. 52:24).

SHALLUN* KJV and NIV spelling of Shallum, Col-hozeh's son, in Nehemiah 3:15. See Shallum #13.

SHALMAI Alternate rendering of Shamlai in Ezra 2:46 and Nehemiah 7:48. See Shamlai.

SHALMAN Unknown conqueror whose brutal destruction of Beth-arbel was descriptive of Israel's approaching judgment (Hos 10:14). Several suggestions as to the identification of Shalman are the following: Salamanu, the king of Moab who paid tribute to Tiglath-pileser of Assyria; one of the Shalmaneser kings of Assyria; and Shalmah, a north Arabian tribe that invaded the Negev.

SHALMANESER Name of several Assyrian rulers, two of whom had direct contact with the people of Israel. However, only Shalmaneser V is known by name in the Bible.

1. Shalmaneser I (1274–1245 BC), the first king of this name, was active in the days when Israel was emerging as a significant group in Palestine. He had no direct contact with Israel.

2. Shalmaneser II (1030–1019 BC) was roughly contemporary with King Saul, but he had no contact with Israel.
3. Shalmaneser III (859–824 BC) had the first significant contact with Israel. This ruler made frequent raids into the lands west of Assyria during his reign. In his annals he left accounts of his exploits and gave lists of small kingdoms he overwhelmed. Another significant entry in the annals of Shalmaneser III is his reference to a campaign against Syria in 841 BC in which he claimed to have defeated Hazael of Damascus (1 Kgs 19:15-18). He did not capture Damascus but moved farther west to the region of Lebanon, where he received tribute from "Jehu, son of Omri." The black obelisk on which he recorded these events portrays Jehu, the king of Israel (842–814 BC), on his knees submitting to Shalmaneser while Israelites carry booty to the king. This event is not mentioned in the Bible.
4. Shalmaneser IV (782–772 BC) had no contact with Israel. He ruled Assyria during a period of decline. His successor Tiglath-pileser III (745–727 BC) was an exceedingly vigorous and able ruler who conducted campaigns in Syria and farther west from 743 BC onward and made several contacts with Israel (2 Kgs 15:17-29).
5. Shalmaneser V (727–722 BC) was able to bring Hoshea, the last king of Israel (732–723 BC), under his control (2 Kgs 17:3). Hoshea failed to pay his annual tribute in his seventh regnal year and was visited by Shalmaneser V, who placed Samaria, the capital of Israel, under siege. The king of Egypt was implicated in this treachery in some way, for he gave encouragement to Hoshea in his rebellious intentions. The siege of Samaria lasted for three years, and in Hoshea's ninth year the city fell. The biblical record seems to attribute the fall of the city to Shalmaneser. Unfortunately, there are no extant records for the reign of Shalmaneser V, and the capture of Samaria was claimed by Shalmaneser's son Sargon II (721–705 BC) in his own annals as an important event in his accession year.

See also Assyria, Assyrians; Black Obelisk.

SHAMA One of the mighty men of David's army, son of Hotham the Aroerite and the brother of Jeiel (1 Chr 11:44).

SHAMARIAH* KJV spelling of Shemariah, King Rehoboam's son, in 2 Chronicles 11:19. *See* Shemariah #2.

SHAMED* KJV spelling of Shemed, one of El-paal's sons, in 1 Chronicles 8:12. *See* Shemed.

SHAMER*
1. KJV spelling of Shemer, Bani's son, in 1 Chronicles 6:46. *See* Shemer #2.
2. KJV spelling of Shemer, Heber's son, in 1 Chronicles 7:34. *See* Shemer #3.

SHAMGAR Son of Anath from Beth-anath; a judge of Israel. Two brief references in the OT (Jgs 3:31; 5:6) tell us little of the man except for his one major exploit: the killing of 600 Philistines with an oxgoad. How such a feat was performed is not recorded. The oxgoad could have had a sharpened metal tip and may have been used as a spear. The timing of the reference indicates that his deeds took place early in the period of Philistine settlement in Canaan. Judges 5:6 would place him prior to the battle of Kishon (c. 1125 BC).

See also Judges, Book of.

SHAMHUTH* Alternate form of Shammah the Izrahite in 1 Chronicles 27:8. *See* Shammah #4.

SHAMIR (Person) Micah's son from Levi's tribe (1 Chr 24:24).

SHAMIR (Place)
1. One of the 11 towns in the hill country allotted to Judah. First in the list of towns, Shamir is followed by Jattir (Jos 15:48). Its location is perhaps at el-Bireh, about 12 miles (19.3 kilometers) southwest of Hebron.
2. Town where Tola the judge lived and was later buried. Shamir was in the land of Ephraim (Jgs 10:1-2).

SHAMLAI* Father of a family of temple servants returning to the land of Canaan with Zerubbabel after the Babylonian captivity; alternately spelled Shalmai in Ezra 2:46 and Nehemiah 7:48.

SHAMMA Zophah's son from Asher's tribe (1 Chr 7:37).

SHAMMAH
1. One of Reuel's four sons, the grandson of Esau and a chief in the land of Edom (Gn 36:13, 17; 1 Chr 1:37).
2. Third of Jesse's eight sons, the brother of David (1 Sm 16:9; 17:13) and the father of Jonathan (2 Sm 21:20-21) and Jonadab (2 Sm 13:3 ff.). Shammah is alternately called Shimea in 1 Chronicles 2:13 and 20:7, Shimeah in 2 Samuel 13:3, and Shimei in 21:21.
3. Son of Agee the Hararite and one of the elite among David's mighty men. He was renowned for his valiant stand against the Philistines at Lehi (2 Sm 23:11-12).
4. Harodite and one of David's 30 valiant warriors. He was listed between Elhanan and Elika (2 Sm 23:24-25). The parallel passage of 1 Chronicles 11:27 reads Shammoth, the plural form of Shammah. In 27:8 Shamhuth the Irahite, the commander of a division of David's soldiers, is no doubt the same man.
5. Hararite and one of David's mighty men, listed between Jonathan and Ahiam (2 Sm 23:33).

SHAMMAI
1. Onam's son, brother of Jada and the father of Nadab and Abishur from Judah's tribe (1 Chr 2:28, 32).
2. Rekem's son and the father of Maon from Caleb's house (1 Chr 2:44-45).
3. Mered's son by Bithiah, Pharaoh's daughter, and a descendant of Caleb (1 Chr 4:17-18).
4. Prominent rabbi whose life spanned the period 50 BC to AD 30. His name is most frequently coupled with that of his equally famous contemporary, Hillel, who was president of the Sanhedrin while Shammai was vice-president. Shammai had the reputation for being strict and rigid in his application of the law and severely literal in his interpretation of the Scriptures, while Hillel was more liberal and humane in applying the law and more imaginative in the use of the Scriptures. Shammai was renowned for his hatred of Roman domination and tried to forbid Jewish people from buying food or drink from Gentiles.

Two schools of interpretation followed these two contemporaries—"the house of Shammai" and "the house of Hillel"—continuing to the time of the compilation of the Mishnah, though the house of Hillel seems to have gradually gained ascendancy over the house of Shammai. The debates and conversations between the two rabbis or the two schools are recorded in the Mishnah and the Talmud, pertaining to such matters as offerings, priestly dues, tithes, Levitical cleanness and uncleanness, the observance of the Sabbath, marriage and divorce.

See also Hillel; Judaism; Pharisees; Talmud.

DID JESUS SIDE WITH HILLEL OR SHAMMAI?
According to Matthew 19:3, it is said that some Pharisees approached Jesus and tested him by asking, "Is it lawful to divorce one's wife for any and every reason?" They wanted to see whether he would side with the school of Shammai or the school of Hillel. The Shammai school would allow divorce only for immorality, while the school of Hillel allowed a husband to divorce his wife for a variety of lesser reasons. Jesus' response indicated that he did not affirm any kind of divorce, unless one partner had commited adultery (Mt 19:4-9).

SHAMMOTH* The plural form of Shammah the Harodite in 2 Samuel 23:25; 1 Chronicles 11:27 (NLT mg). See Shammah #4.

SHAMMUA
1. Reubenite, Zaccur's son and one of the 12 spies sent by Moses to search out the land of Canaan (Nm 13:4).
2. Alternate name for Shimea, David's son, in 2 Samuel 5:14 and 1 Chronicles 14:4. See Shimea #2.
3. Alternate name for Shemaiah, Galal's son, in Nehemiah 11:17. See Shemaiah #6.
4. Head of a family who returned to Jerusalem with Zerubbabel after the Babylonian exile (Neh 12:18).

SHAMSHERAI Jeroham's son and a chief in Benjamin's tribe (1 Chr 8:26).

SHAPHAM Leader in Gad's tribe (1 Chr 5:12). He is believed to have lived in Bashan and served during the days of Jotham, king of Judah (v 17).

SHAPHAN
1. Son of Azaliah and the father of Ahikam, Elasah, and Gemariah. He and his household favored Josiah's reforms, supported the prophet Jeremiah, and complied with Babylonian hegemony.
 Shaphan served as the royal secretary to Josiah, king of Judah (640–609 BC). He read the Book of the Law to the king after it was found by the high priest Hilkiah in the sanctuary of Jerusalem. Later, Josiah sent him with a small delegation to hear the words of the prophetess Huldah (2 Kgs 22:3-14; 2 Chr 34:8-28).
 Shaphan's sons were mentioned among the political leaders of Judah during the days of its desolation by Nebuchadnezzar of Babylon (605–586 BC). Ahikam assisted with the repair of the sanctuary and protected Jeremiah from the men who sought his death during the reign of King Jehoiakim (609–598 BC; 2 Kgs 22:12; Jer 26:24). Elasah delivered a message from King Zedekiah of Judah (597–586 BC) to Nebuchadnezzar in Babylon (Jer 29:3). Gemariah was the prince of Judah from whose chamber Baruch read the scroll of Jeremiah to the people (36:10-12).
 Shaphan was the grandfather of Micaiah (Jer 36:11-13) and Gedaliah. Gedaliah was appointed governor of Judah by Nebuchadnezzar (2 Kgs 25:22; Jer 40:5-11) and ordered to protect Jeremiah (Jer 39:14).

Gedaliah was later murdered by a mob led by Ishmael (41:2).
2. Father of Jaazaniah and, in Ezekiel's vision, a leader of idolatrous practices in Israel (Ez 8:11).

SHAPHAT
1. Simeonite, Hori's son and one of the 12 spies sent by Moses to search out the land of Canaan (Nm 13:5).
2. Father of the prophet Elisha from the town of Abelmeholah (1 Kgs 19:16, 19; 2 Kgs 3:11; 6:31).
3. Youngest of Shemaiah's six sons from Judah's tribe and a descendant of David (1 Chr 3:22).
4. Gadite chief in Bashan, a region west of the Jordan River (1 Chr 5:12).
5. Adlai's son and a member of King David's staff. Shaphat had charge of David's cattle in the valleys (1 Chr 27:29).

SHAPHER* KJV form of Shepher, the name of an unidentified mountain, in Numbers 33:23-24. See Shepher, Mount.

SHAPHIR One of the towns spoken against by Micah the prophet (Mi 1:11). Its exact location is not certain. Eusebius (a fourth-century church historian) suggested that it was a village positioned between the cities of Eleutheropolis and Ashkelon, placing Shaphir in Philistine territory. If this is correct, perhaps Shaphir is identifiable with one of three villages known as es-Suwafir near the city of Ashdod. Another possible site is Khirbet el-Kom, situated west of Hebron in the hill country of Judah.

SHARAI One of Binnui's sons who was encouraged by Ezra to divorce his foreign wife during the postexilic era (Ezr 10:40).

SHARAIM* KJV spelling of Shaaraim, a city in Judah's territory, in Joshua 15:36. See Shaaraim #1.

SHARAR Alternate name for Sachar, Ahiram's father, in 2 Samuel 23:33. See Sacar, Sachar #1.

SHAREZER
1. One of the sons of Sennacherib, the king of Assyria. In 681 BC he, along with his brother Adrammelech, killed Sennacherib while he was praying in the house of Nisroch (2 Kgs 19:37; Is 37:38).
2. One who was sent from Bethel to inquire of the priests and prophets as to whether or not the mourning and feasting in commemoration of the destruction of the temple should be confined to the fifth month of that year. Since the temple was nearing its restoration, there was some question about the commemoration on the part of the populace at Bethel (Zec 7:2-3).

SHARON
1. Section of the plain on the Mediterranean coast of Israel. It extends from Joppa in the south to the Crocodile River, which serves as the northern border and separates it from the plain of Dor. The largest of the northern coastal plains, it is 50 miles (80 kilometers) from north to south and 10 miles (16.1 kilometers) wide. Its shore is straight and consists of beach and cliffs. There are no natural harbors along the coast, so the plain had no large trading ports. The Via Maris, a major north-south trading route, skirted the eastern edge of the plain.
 Five streams or wadis cross the Sharon Plain: Nahal Tanninim (Crocodile River), Nahal Hadera, Nahal Alexander, Nahal Poleg, and Nahal Yarqon. These

streams drain water from the Samaritan hills and empty into the Mediterranean. Until recent times, the streams formed extensive swamps that were infested with malaria-carrying mosquitoes. Sharon also has sand-dune hills that rise to an elevation of 180 feet (54.9 meters) above sea level in the central part of the plain. In biblical times the elevated areas of Sharon were covered with oak trees. The combination of swamps, sand dunes, and forests made the area almost impenetrable. The plain was granted to Manasseh's tribe by Joshua (Jos 17), but it was not effectively controlled by Israel until the time of David (1 Chr 27:29), and even then it was only used for pasturage.

In the book of Isaiah, Sharon is ranked with the regions of Carmel and Lebanon for its fertility and luxuriance (Is 33:9; 35:2). When Isaiah speaks of the final restoration, he refers to the Sharon pastures as the place for flocks (65:10). The "rose of Sharon" (Sg 2:1) may have been one of several varieties of red flowering plants that grow in the plain. The beauty of the rose is contrasted with the dense bramblelike underbrush characteristic of the plain.

2. Place perhaps identical with the town of Lasharon in Joshua 12:18. *See* Lasharon.
3. Area east of the Jordan called "the pasture lands of Sharon" in 1 Chronicles 5:16.

SHARONITE* Designation for Shitrai, a royal steward in charge of David's flocks in the plain of Sharon (1 Chr 27:29).

SHARUHEN Alternate name for Shaaraim, a city in Simeon's territory, in Joshua 19:6. *See* Shaaraim #2.

SHASHAI Binnui's son, who was encouraged by Ezra to divorce his foreign wife during the postexilic era (Ezr 10:40).

SHASHAK Benjaminite, Elpaal's son and the father of 11 sons (1 Chr 8:14, 25).

SHAUL

1. Alternate name for Saul, an Edomite king, in Genesis 36:37-38 and 1 Chronicles 1:48-49. *See* Saul #1.
2. Son of Simeon by a Canaanite woman (Gn 46:10; Ex 6:15; 1 Chr 4:24) and head of the Shaulite family (Nm 26:13).
3. Levite and Uzziah's son from the house of Kohath (1 Chr 6:24).

SHAULITE Descendant of Shaul from Simeon's tribe (Nm 26:13). *See* Shaul #2.

SHAVEH, Valley of Alternate name for the King's Valley near Jerusalem in Genesis 14:17. *See* King's Valley.

SHAVEH KIRIATHAIM* Plain east of the Dead Sea near the city of Kiriathaim and occupied by the people of Emim. The Emimites in Shaveh Kiriathaim are listed with a number of other tribes and nations that King Kedorlaomer and his allies defeated (Gn 14:5; NLT, "Kiriathaim"). This plain was later inherited by the sons of Reuben.

SHAVSHA* Alternate name for Seraiah, the secretary to King David, in 1 Chronicles 18:16 (see NLT mg). *See* Seraiah #1.

SHEAL One of Bani's sons who was told by Ezra to divorce his foreign wife (Ezr 10:29).

SHEALTIEL Son of King Jeconiah (Jehoiachin) of Judah (598–597 BC) and the father of Zerubbabel. Zerubbabel led the Jews back to Palestine and there ruled as governor of Judah during the postexilic period (Ezr 3:2; 5:2; Neh 12:1; Hg 1:1, 12-14). In the genealogies of Jesus Christ, Shealtiel is variously mentioned as the son of Jeconiah (Mt 1:12) and as the son of Neri (Lk 3:27). In 1 Chronicles 3:17-19, Shealtiel appears to be the grandfather or perhaps the uncle of Zerubbabel. One probable solution is that Shealtiel was the son of Neri and the heir apparent to the throne of Jeconiah and that, at Shealtiel's death, Zerubbabel was next in succession.

Aerial View of Sharon Plain

SHEARIAH One of Azel's six sons, a descendant of Jonathan, son of King Saul, from Benjamin's tribe (1 Chr 8:38; 9:44).

SHEARING HOUSE* KJV translation for Beth-eked, a place on the road between Jezreel and Samaria, in 2 Kings 10:12-14. *See* Beth-eked.

SHEAR-JASHUB Isaiah's son whose name, meaning "a remnant shall return," symbolized the prophecy that, although Israel and Judah would be destroyed, a remnant would be saved and later return (Is 7:3).

SHEBA (Person)

1. Son of Raamah, the brother of Dedan and a descendant of Noah through Ham's line (Gn 10:7; 1 Chr 1:9).
2. One of the 13 sons of Joktan and a descendant of Noah through Shem's line (Gn 10:28; 1 Chr 1:22).
3. Son of Jokshan, the brother of Dedan and the grandson of Abraham and Keturah (Gn 25:3; 1 Chr 1:32).
4. Benjaminite and the son of Bicri. After the death of Absalom, Sheba incited Israel to rebel against David. Under the command of Joab, the revolt was subdued and Sheba was beheaded at Abel-beth-maacah (2 Sm 20:1-22).
5. One of the Gadite leaders ruling in Bashan, registered during the reigns of Jotham king of Judah (750–732 BC) and Jeroboam II king of Israel (793–753 BC); see 1 Chr 5:13, 16-17.

SHEBA (Place)

1. One of 14 cities listed in Joshua 19:2 that were assigned to Simeon's tribe within the southern portion of Judah's inheritance. Since the verse says there were 13 cities, not 14, it is possible that "Shebe" was repeated in the list as a shortened form of "Beersheba," as many translations indicate. The LXX, however, names this town Shema (cf. Jos 15:26).

2. Territory located in southwestern Arabia known also as the kingdom of Saba (Hebrew *Seba'*). The Sabeans were of Semitic descent and were governed by a priest-king in the royal city of Ma'rib.

They were a merchant people holding trade relations with Israel and other countries as far east as India. Rich in spices, precious stones, and agricultural commodities, the people of Sheba (Saba) established a network of overland and sea routes to trade their wares (Ps 72:10, 15; Is 60:6; Jer 6:20; Ez 27:22-23). Numerous inscriptions have been found, attesting to the Sabean civilization in southern Arabia and their travels.

During the Solomonic era (970–930 BC), the queen of Sheba traveled to Jerusalem to see Solomon's riches and to test his wisdom with riddles. Solomon exceeded her expectations on both counts (1 Kgs 10:1-13; 2 Chr 9:1-12).

SHEBA, Queen of *See* Sheba (Place) #2.

SHEBAH* KJV rendering of Shibah, a well near Beersheba, in Genesis 26:33. *See* Shibah.

SHEBAM* KJV spelling of Sebam, a city in Reuben's territory, in Numbers 32:3. *See* Sebam.

SHEBANIAH
1. One of the seven priests assigned to blow a trumpet before the ark of God in the procession led by David, when the ark was moved to Jerusalem (1 Chr 15:24).
2. One of the Levites who led the people in worship when Ezra read the law (Neh 9:4-5).
3. Head of a priestly family who set his seal on the covenant of Ezra (Neh 10:4; 12:14) and perhaps the same person as Shecaniah in Nehemiah 12:3. *See* Shecaniah, Shechaniah #9.
4. Another Levite who set his seal on the covenant of Ezra (Neh 10:12).

SHEBARIM* Location between Ai and Jericho to which the men of Ai pursued the fleeing Israelites. This region was evidently situated near the place of descent from the hill country to the lowlands (Jos 7:5, see NLT mg). Shebarim means "breaches" or "ruins" and might possibly refer to the rough, rocky conditions that would characterize the region at the top of a steep mountain slope. Its location is unknown.

SHEBAT* Name of the Hebrew month extending from about mid-January to about mid-February in Zechariah 1:7. *See* Calendars, Ancient and Modern.

SHEBER Caleb's son by his concubine Maacah (1 Chr 2:48).

SHEBNA Eighth-century official of the kingdom of Judah. The name Shebna is Aramaic in form and has been interpreted to mean "return, please [O Lord]," relating it to either a fuller spelling (Shebaniah) or to a Semitic root meaning "youthful." Because of the Aramaic spelling, some have argued that Shebna was of foreign birth. The appearance of the name, however, on several contemporary Palestinian inscriptions (e.g., from Lachish) may make such a view unnecessary.

Two major passages mention Shebna by name: Isaiah 22:15-25 and 2 Kings 18:17–19:7. The unlikelihood of two men with the same name, both holding high-ranking positions in the Judahite government in the same general time period, has caused most scholars to argue that the two passages in Isaiah and 2 Kings refer to a single individual.

Because of his arrogance in building an ostentatious tomb for himself, and because of excessive pride in his position and importance, Shebna was denounced by the prophet Isaiah. In fact, the prophet even predicted that Shebna would go into exile and die in a foreign country (Is 22:18). The events described in 2 Kings 18:17–19:7 (cf. the parallel account in Is 37) are clearly traceable to the year 701 BC and the invasion of Sennacherib. If the Shebna described in this story is the same person denounced by Isaiah in the passage just discussed, as seems likely, the date of the prophetic denouncement must be placed sometime earlier than 701.

In 701 the Assyrian ruler Sennacherib captured virtually all of the cities of Judah and clearly had his heart set on the capture of Jerusalem. King Hezekiah of Judah sent three official representatives to negotiate with the invading Assyrians. At this time, Eliakim was titled "the one who is in charge of the [king's] household" (2 Kgs 18:18) and Shebna held the rank of *sopher*, an important position, probably equal to that of a secretary of state.

SHEBUEL
1. Gershon's son and Moses' grandson from Levi's tribe (1 Chr 23:15-16); father of Jehdeiah (24:20, "Shubael"). He was the chief officer in charge of the treasuries (26:24).
2. Levite, Heman's son and a musician in the tabernacle (1 Chr 25:4, 20, "Shubael").

SHECANIAH, SHECHANIAH*
1. Descendant of David through the line of Zerubbabel living in postexilic Palestine (1 Chr 3:21-22).
2. Levite and the head of the 10th of 24 divisions of priests formed during the reign of David (1 Chr 24:11).
3. One of six priests serving under Kore during the reign of King Hezekiah of Judah (715–686 BC). Shecaniah assisted with the distribution of the temple offerings among his fellow priests living in the priestly cities (2 Chr 31:15).
4. Father of Hattush, who returned with Ezra to Judah following the Babylonian captivity during the reign of King Artaxerxes I of Persia (464–424 BC; Ezr 8:3).
5. Son of Jahaziel who returned with Ezra to Judah during the reign of King Artaxerxes I of Persia (Ezr 8:5).
6. Son of Jehiel in the house of Elam, who urged Ezra to command the sons of Israel to divorce the foreign women they had married (Ezr 10:2).
7. Father of Shemaiah. Shemaiah, the keeper of the East Gate, helped Nehemiah rebuild a section of the Jerusalem wall (Neh 3:29).
8. Father-in-law of Tobiah the Ammonite and the son of Arah (Neh 6:18).
9. Head of a priestly family who returned to Judah with Zerubbabel following the exile (Neh 12:3). Shecaniah is perhaps identical with Shebaniah in verse 14. *See* Shebaniah #3.

SHECHEM (Person)
1. Son of Hamor the Hivite. He raped Dinah, the daughter of Jacob, and was later killed along with his father and all the males of his town by Simeon and Levi (Gn 34; Jos 24:32).
2. One of Gilead's six sons, a descendant of Joseph through Manasseh's line, and the founder of the Shechemite family (Nm 26:31; Jos 17:2).
3. One of Shemida's four sons from Manasseh's tribe (1 Chr 7:19).

SHECHEM (Place) Town in the center of western Palestine, near the watershed that separates the waters that

flow to the Jordan from those that descend to the Mediterranean. The site is 40 miles (64.4 kilometers) north of
Jerusalem at the eastern entrance to the pass between Mt
Ebal and Mt Gerizim. The ancient town stood on the
lower southeastern slope or shoulder of Mt Ebal, hence
the meaning of the name (Shechem = shoulder).
Samaria, later capital of Israel, was about eight miles
(12.9 kilometers) northwest. Although strategically
located—the town controlled all roads through the central hill country of Palestine—it was without natural
defenses and required extensive fortifications.

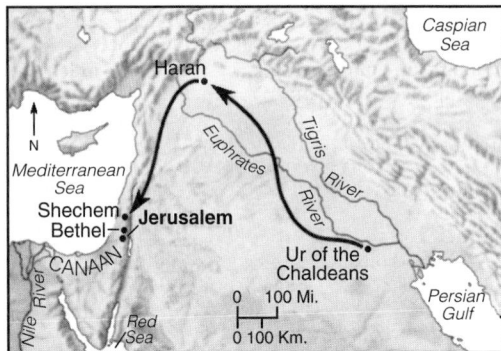

Shechem Abram's journey from Ur to Shechem

Biblical References Shechem first appears in the Bible
as the initial campsite of Abram after he entered Canaan
from Mesopotamia. There God promised him the land of
Canaan, and there Abram built his first altar in the land
(Gn 12:6-7). After Jacob's 20-year sojourn in northern Mesopotamia at Paddan-aram, he returned to Shechem and
bought a piece of land. By this time, the place was already a
walled city with a gate (34:20, 24). After the defilement of
their sister Dinah, Simeon and Levi massacred Shechem's
male population in revenge. Years later, when the patriarchal family was living in the Hebron area, Joseph went to
Shechem to look for his brothers (37:12-14).

After the Conquest, the ceremony of antiphonal blessing and cursing on Mt Gerizim and Mt Ebal, respectively,
was fulfilled in the vicinity of Shechem (Jos 8:30-35).
In the division and settlement of the land, Shechem
became one of the cities of refuge (20:7; 21:21) and one
of the 48 Levitical cities (21:21). There Joshua delivered
his farewell address (24:1, 25), and the bones of Joseph
were buried on the land Jacob had bought there (v 32).

During the unsettled days of the judges, Gideon's son
Abimelech set himself up as king of Israel there, at first
with the support of the inhabitants. But a later revolt
against him resulted in destruction of the city (Jgs 9:1-7,
23-57). Rehoboam was crowned there just before the
split of the kingdom (1 Kgs 12:1), and Jeroboam, first
king of the northern kingdom, rebuilt the city and made
it the first capital of the kingdom.

History Excavations reveal that the earliest settlement at
the site dates back to the fourth millennium BC, but the
first significant settlement occurred during the first half
of the second millennium and was the work of Amorites
or Hyksos. The Hyksos surrounded the city with an
immense sloping embankment about 80 feet (24.4
meters) wide and 20 feet (6.1 meters) high, upon which
they built a brick wall. There was a two-entry gate on the
east side and a three-entry gate on the northwest side.
On the acropolis they built what has been interpreted as
a fortress temple, which was rebuilt several times and
finally destroyed by the Egyptians in about 1550 BC.

About a century later, the Canaanites rebuilt Shechem

on a smaller scale. A new fortress temple was built on the
ruins of the old one and measured 53 feet (16.2 meters)
wide and 41 feet (12.5 meters) deep, with an entrance on
the long side. It had three sacred standing stones next to
an altar in the open court. This temple is believed to be
the house of Baal-berith destroyed by Abimelech about
1150 BC (Jgs 9:3-4, 46), and its sacred area was never
rebuilt. Before that, however, there is no archaeological
evidence of destruction for some 300 years, confirming
the biblical indication that the Hebrews did not take the
city at the time of the Conquest and that the inhabitants
lived peaceably among the Hebrews.

Evidently, Solomon rebuilt Shechem as a provincial
capital, but it suffered great destruction late in the 10th
century, probably at the hands of Shishak of Egypt when
he invaded Palestine in 926 BC (1 Kgs 14:25). Shortly
thereafter, Jeroboam I refortified the city and made it the
capital of the kingdom of Israel. Either he or a successor
built a government warehouse on the ruins of the temple. Israelite Shechem met its end at the hands of the
Assyrian king Shalmaneser V in 724 BC, just before the
destruction of Samaria, and the town was virtually uninhabited for about 400 years.

In the fourth century, Alexander the Great established
a camp on the site for his soldiers, and subsequently the
Samaritans moved from Samaria and settled there. They
built their temple on Mt Gerizim. John Hyrcanus probably
destroyed Shechem for the last time in 128 BC. His violent
opposition to the Samaritans involved destruction of their
temple on Mt Gerizim and of Samaria at the same time.

SHECHEM, Tower of Fortress erected on the acropolis of Shechem, housing the temple of Baal-berith and
situated inside the city walls. The city of Shechem was
located in the hill country of the tribe of Ephraim near
Mt Gerizim.

The tower of Shechem served as the citadel to which
the leaders of Shechem fled from the onslaught of
Abimelech. They sought refuge in the inner chamber of
the temple of Baal-berith. Abimelech, however, set the
upper parts of the inner chamber on fire, killing all the
men and women housed within (Jgs 9:46-49).

The remnants of the tower of Shechem have been
found within the ancient town of Shechem at Tell
Bala'ta, a short distance northeast of modern Nablus in
central Palestine. Modern excavations show that the
tower of Shechem was used as a temple and a fortress.

SHECHEMITE Descendant of Shechem, Gilead's son
from Manasseh's tribe (Nm 26:31). *See* Shechem (Person) #2.

SHEDEUR Elizur's father. Elizur represented Reuben's
tribe in Moses' census of the men capable of bearing
arms (Nm 1:5; 2:10; 10:18), and in the dedication of the
altar (7:30-35).

SHEEP *See* Animals.

SHEEP GATE Jerusalem gate repaired by Eliashib and
the priests under Nehemiah's supervision during the
postexilic era (Neh 3:1, 32; 12:39). It was positioned east
of the Fish Gate by the Tower of the Hundred, near the
pool of Bethesda (Bethsaida) and a short distance from
the modern St Stephen's Gate. In John 5:2 the KJV translates it "Sheep Market" and the NEB, "Sheep-Pool."

SHEERAH Daughter or granddaughter of Ephraim. Her
offspring built lower and upper Beth-horon and Uzzen-
sheerah, named after her (1 Chr 7:24).

SHEHARIAH Jehoram's son and a chief of Benjamin's tribe in Jerusalem after the exile (1 Chr 8:26).

SHEKEL Weight, and later also a coin. *See* Coins; Weights and Measures.

SHEKINAH* Transliteration of a Hebrew word meaning "the one who dwells" or "that which dwells." The term enters Christian theology from its use in the Targums and rabbinic literature to describe the immanent presence in the world of the transcendent Deity. Although the word is not itself used in either Testament, it clearly originates in OT passages that describe God as dwelling among a people or in a particular place (Gn 9:27; Ex 25:8; 29:45-46; Nm 5:3; 1 Kgs 6:13; Pss 68:16-18; 74:2; Is 8:18; Ez 43:7-9; Jl 3:17, 21; Zec 2:10-11); God, whose dwelling is in heaven, also dwells on earth. The term is also applied to the "shekinah glory," the visible pillar of fire and smoke that dwelled in the midst of Israel at Sinai (Ex 19:16-18), in the wilderness (40:34-38), and in the temple (1 Kgs 6:13; 8:10-13; 2 Chr 6:1-2).

The NT frequently alludes to the concept of the shekinah, even though the term itself is not used. God's presence in the NT is frequently associated with light and glory (Lk 2:9; 9:29; Acts 9:3-6; 22:6-11; 26:12-16; 2 Pt 1:16-18). John's Gospel emphasizes both the concept of glory and the concept of dwelling. When the Word became flesh, he dwelt among men who beheld his glory (Jn 1:14). The Spirit of God remained on him (v 32) and would be with his followers forever (14:16). He would abide in those who abide in Jesus (15:4-10). The same themes of dwelling in Christ and of his dwelling in his people occur repeatedly also in John's letters (1 Jn 2:6, 14, 24, 27-28; 3:6, 14-15, 24; 2 Jn 1:9).

Paul also identifies Christ as the shekinah of God. All the fullness of the Godhead dwells in him bodily (Col 1:19; 2:9). The dwelling of Christ in the church constitutes the saints as the people of God (1:15-23). Paul's message was the "gospel of the glory of Christ," for God had caused light to shine to give "knowledge of the glory of God in the face of Christ" (2 Cor 4:4-6, NIV). Finally, the writer of Hebrews sees Christ as "the radiance of God's glory and the exact representation of his being" (Heb 1:3, NIV). *See* Glory; Pillar of Fire and Cloud; Theophany.

SHELAH

1. Arphaxad's son and the father of Eber (Gn 10:24; 11:12-15; 1 Chr 1:18). Shelah is listed in Luke's genealogy of Christ as the son of Cainan the son of Arphaxad (Lk 3:35). *See* Genealogy of Jesus Christ.
2. Judah's third son by Bathshua the Canaanitess. He was born at Kezib, a small town in Judah (Gn 38:5; 1 Chr 2:3). Shelah founded the Shelanite family (Nm 26:20), which should possibly be read instead of "Shilonite" in Nehemiah 11:5; 1 Chronicles 9:5.

SHELAH*, Pool of Reservoir in the King's Garden in Jerusalem (Neh 3:15). *See* Siloam, Pool of.

SHELANITE Descendant of Shelah, Judah's son (Nm 26:20). *See* Shelah #2.

SHELEMIAH

1. Korahite from the tribe of Levi and a gatekeeper who was chosen by lot to guard the east gate of the sanctuary during David's reign (1 Chr 26:14); also named Meshelemiah (vv 1-2). *See* Meshelemiah.
2-3. Two of Binnui's sons, who were encouraged to divorce their foreign wives during Ezra's postexilic reforms in Israel (Ezr 10:39-41).
4. Father of Hananiah. Hananiah repaired a section of the Jerusalem wall under Nehemiah (Neh 3:30).
5. Priest and one of the three men appointed by Nehemiah as the treasurers of the temple in Jerusalem. Their task was to oversee the distribution of the tithes among their fellow priests (Neh 13:13).
6. Son of Cushi, the father of Nethaniah, and a forefather of Jehudi (Jer 36:14).
7. Son of Abdeel who, with Jerahmeel and Seraiah, was commanded by King Jehoiakim of Judah (609–598 BC) to seize Baruch and Jeremiah (Jer 36:26).
8. Father of Jehucal (Jer 37:3), alternately spelled Jucal in 38:1 (NLT mg).
9. Son of Hananiah and the father of Irijah. Irijah arrested Jeremiah for apparently deserting to the Babylonians (Jer 37:13).

SHELEPH Joktan's son and the founder of an Arabian tribe living in Yemen (Gn 10:26; 1 Chr 1:20).

SHELESH Helem's son and a chief of Asher's tribe (1 Chr 7:35).

SHELOMI Ahihud's father. Ahihud represented Asher's tribe in the division of the land of Canaan among Israel's ten tribes west of the Jordan (Nm 34:27).

SHELOMITH

1. Dibri's daughter and the mother of a man from Dan's tribe who blasphemed the Lord's name, for which he was subsequently stoned to death (Lv 24:11-16).
2. Sister of Meshullam and Hananiah, all of whom were descendants of David (1 Chr 3:19).
3. KJV spelling of Shelomoth, Shimei's son, in 1 Chronicles 23:9. *See* Shelomoth #1.
4. Alternate spelling of Shelomoth, Izhar's son, in 1 Chronicles 23:18. *See* Shelomoth #2.
5. KJV spelling of Shelomoth, Zicri's son, in 1 Chronicles 26:25-28. *See* Shelomoth #3.
6. Son of Rehoboam and Maachah (2 Chr 11:20).
7. One of Ezra's companions (Ezr 8:10).

SHELOMOTH

1. Gershonite Levite and one of Shimei's sons serving in the sanctuary during David's reign (1 Chr 23:9).
2. Levite and priest from the family of Izhar during David's reign (1 Chr 23:18, "Shelomith"; 24:22).
3. Zicri's son, who was in charge of the royal treasuries during David's reign (1 Chr 26:25-28).

SHELTERS, Festival of Alternate name for the Festival of Tabernacles. *See* Feasts and Festivals of Israel.

SHELUMIEL Simeonite, Zurishaddai's son and one of the leaders who assisted Moses in taking a census of Israel in the wilderness (Nm 1:6; 2:12; 7:36, 41; 10:19). He is the forefather of the apocryphal Judith (Jdt 8:1, where his name is Salamiel and his father's Sarasadai).

SHEM Eldest son of Noah (Gn 5:32; 6:10; 7:13; 9:18, 23, 26-27; 11:10; 1 Chr 1:4, 17-27; Lk 3:36) and the ancestor of the Semitic peoples (Gn 10:1, 21-31). Shem lived 600 years (11:10-11). In Hebrew, Shem means "name," perhaps implying that Noah expected this son's name to become great.

After their deliverance from the great Flood, Shem and Japheth acted with respect and dignity toward their drunken father Noah on an occasion when their brother

Ham dishonored him (Gn 9:20-29). Because of this act, Noah later pronounced a curse on Canaan, the son of Ham, and a blessing on both Shem and Japheth.

In Genesis 11:10-27, the line of descent for the promised seed, which was to crush Satan (Gn 3:15; 5:1-32), is traced through Shem to Abraham, and ultimately through Judah and David to Christ (cf. Lk 3:36). The blessing of Noah on Shem is thus to be taken as an indication that the line of Shem will be the line through which the seed of Genesis 3:15 will come. This is the first time in the Bible that God is called the God of some particular individual or group of people. The statement that Canaan would be a servant to Shem was fulfilled centuries later when the Israelites, who descended from Shem, entered the land of Canaan and subdued the inhabitants of the land (cf. 1 Kgs 9:20-21).

Noah also said that Japheth would be enlarged and dwell in the tents of Shem (Gn 9:27), the latter of which would seem to imply sustenance and protection. After Japheth would be greatly increased in numbers, the Japhethites would be brought into contact with Shem and would share in the blessings and promises of the Semitic faith. Many scholars see fulfillment of this prophecy in the opening of the gospel to the Gentiles during the NT era of the establishment of the church.

In the "table of nations" recorded in Genesis 10, five descendants of Shem are mentioned (Elam, Asshur, Arphaxad, Lud, and Aram). Receiving particular emphasis among these descendants is Eber from the line of Arphaxad, whose line is traced to Abraham in Genesis 11:16-27.

See also Abraham; Genealogy of Jesus Christ; Nations; Noah #1.

SHEMA (Person)

1. Judahite, Hebron's son and a descendant of Caleb (1 Chr 2:43-44).
2. Reubenite and Joel's son (1 Chr 5:8). He is perhaps identifiable with Shemaiah or Shimei in 1 Chronicles 5:4.
3. Benjaminite and head of a family in Aijalon, who helped defeat the inhabitants of Gath (1 Chr 8:13).
4. Levite who explained to the people passages from the law read by Ezra (Neh 8:4).

SHEMA (Place) One of the 29 cities located near the border of Edom in the southern extremity of the land inherited by Judah, mentioned between the cities of Amam and Moladah (Jos 15:26). In the parallel list at Joshua 19:2, Sheba (the LXX has "Shema") was one of 13 cities assigned to Simeon's tribe within the southern portion of Judah's inheritance. *See* Sheba #1.

SHEMA*, The The declaration "Hear, O Israel, Yahweh our God is one Yahweh" (Dt 6:4). *Shema* comes from the first Hebrew word of the verse, *shema*, "hear." Verses 4-9 make up the whole of this foundational biblical truth. While several translations of verse 4 are grammatically correct, Jesus' words in Mark 12:29 correspond most closely to the one given above. Religious Jews recite the Shema three times daily as part of their devotional life; no Sabbath worship is conducted in the synagogue without its proclamation.

Within the Shema is found both a fundamental doctrinal truth and a resultant obligation. There is an urgency connected to the teaching: the word *shema* demands that the hearer respond with his total being to the fact and demands of this essential revelation.

With regard to the teaching pertaining to the nature of God, the word "one" (*echad*) designates a compound unity rather than an absolute singular. While the eminent medieval Jewish theologian Maimonides insisted that God was *yachid* (an absolute singular), the OT does not use this word to define God's nature. The compound singular word for "one" first occurs in Genesis 2:24 where a man and woman, though separate entities, are seen to be one (*echad*) in marriage. Understandably, Jesus could freely quote Deuteronomy 6:4 without infringing upon the truth of his own deity.

See also Deuteronomy, Book of.

SHEMAAH Father of Ahiezer and Joash, two bowmen who joined David at Ziklag (1 Chr 12:3).

SHEMAIAH

1. Prophet during the reign of Rehoboam, king of Judah (930–913 BC). He warned the king not to go to war against Jeroboam and the ten northern tribes of Israel (1 Kgs 12:22-24; 2 Chr 11:2-4). Five years later he spoke words of comfort to a repentant Rehoboam and people of Judah (2 Chr 12:5-7). Shemaiah chronicled the life of Rehoboam in a book that has since been lost.
2. Son of Shecaniah, the father of six sons and a descendant of David through Rehoboam's line (1 Chr 3:22).
3. Simeonite, father of Shimri and an ancestor of Jehu (1 Chr 4:37).
4. Reubenite and a son of Joel (1 Chr 5:4).
5. Levite and the son of Hasshub, who returned to Jerusalem after the exile (1 Chr 9:14). He was made a leader in the work of the temple during the days of Nehemiah (Neh 11:15).
6. Son of Galal and the father of Obadiah, a Levite who returned to Jerusalem following the Babylonian captivity (1 Chr 9:16); called Shammua in Nehemiah 11:17.
7. Levite and the leader of his father's house. Shemaiah was summoned by David to help carry the ark from Obed-edom's house to Jerusalem (1 Chr 15:8-11).
8. Son of Nethanel and the Levitical scribe who recorded the 24 divisions of the priests during David's reign in Israel (1000–961 BC; 1 Chr 24:6).
9. Oldest of Obed-edom's eight sons and the father of sons who served as the gatekeepers of the south gate and storehouse of the sanctuary during David's reign (1 Chr 26:4-7).
10. One of the Levites sent by King Jehoshaphat of Judah (872–848 BC) to teach the law in the cities of Judah (2 Chr 17:8-9).
11. Son of Jeduthun and Uzziel's brother, who was among the Levites chosen by King Hezekiah of Judah (715–686 BC) to cleanse the house of the Lord (2 Chr 29:14-15).
12. One of the Levites assisting Kore with the distribution of the offerings among his fellow priests living in the priestly cities of Judah during the days of King Hezekiah (2 Chr 31:15).
13. One of the Levitical leaders who generously gave animals to the Levites for the celebration of the Passover feast during King Josiah's reign (640–609 BC; 2 Chr 35:9).
14. Son of Adonikam, who returned with Ezra to Judah after the exile during the reign of King Artaxerxes I of Persia (464–424 BC; Ezr 8:13).
15. One of the Jewish leaders whom Ezra sent to Iddo at Casiphia to gather Levites and temple servants for the caravan of Jews returning to Palestine from Babylon (Ezr 8:16-17).
16. Priest and one of Harim's five sons who was encouraged by Ezra to divorce his foreign wife during the postexilic era (Ezr 10:21).
17. Son of another Harim who was encouraged by Ezra to divorce his foreign wife (Ezr 10:31).
18. Son of Shecaniah and the keeper of the East Gate

who repaired a section of the Jerusalem wall under Nehemiah's direction (Neh 3:29).

19. Son of Delaiah and a false prophet hired by Tobiah and Sanballat to frighten Nehemiah and hinder him from rebuilding the Jerusalem wall (Neh 6:10-13).

20. One of the priests who set his seal on the covenant of Ezra (Neh 10:8).

21. One of the leaders of the priests who returned with Zerubbabel and Jeshua to Judah after the exile (Neh 12:6).

22. One of the princes of Judah who participated in the dedication of the Jerusalem wall during the postexilic period (Neh 12:34).

23. Son of Mattaniah, grandfather of Zechariah, and a descendant of Asaph. Zechariah was one of the priests who played a trumpet at the dedication of the Jerusalem wall (Neh 12:35).

24–25. Two priestly musicians who performed at the dedication of the Jerusalem wall (Neh 12:36, 42).

26. Father of Uriah the prophet from Kiriath-jearim. Like Jeremiah, his contemporary, Uriah spoke words of doom against Jerusalem and Judah during the reign of King Jehoiakim of Judah (609–598 BC), who deplored Uriah's message and eventually had him killed (Jer 26:20-21).

27. Nehelamite and a Jew deported to Babylon by Nebuchadnezzar, from where he opposed Jeremiah. He sent letters to the priests in Jerusalem that criticized Jeremiah for predicting a long captivity for Judah. Jeremiah exposed Shemaiah as a false prophet and foretold that he and his descendants would not live to see the return to Palestine (Jer 29:24-32).

28. Father of Delaiah, a prince of Judah during the reign of King Jehoiakim (Jer 36:12).

29. A kinsman of Tobit (Tb 5:14); also spelled Shemeliah.

SHEMARIAH

1. Warrior from the tribe of Benjamin who joined David at Ziklag in his struggle against King Saul. Shemariah was one of David's ambidextrous archers and slingers (1 Chr 12:5).

2. One of Rehoboam's sons (2 Chr 11:19; KJV "Shamariah").

3. Harim's son, who obeyed Ezra's exhortation to divorce his foreign wife after the exile (Ezr 10:32).

4. Binnui's son, who obeyed Ezra's exhortation to divorce his foreign wife (Ezr 10:41).

SHEMEBER
King of Zeboiim, who joined a confederacy with four other kings in rebellion against Kedorlaomer and his allies. Abraham rescued Lot from captivity after Shemeber, along with Sodom and Gomorrah, was defeated (Gn 14:2).

SHEMED
Elpaal's son and a descendant of Benjamin through Shaharaim's line. Shemed rebuilt the towns of Ono and Lod after the Babylonian exile (1 Chr 8:12).

SHEMER

1. Owner of the hill of Samaria, which Omri, king of Israel, bought as the site of his new capital city and named after Shemer (1 Kgs 16:24).

2. Merarite Levite, Mahli's son and the father of Bani; he was a temple singer during David's reign (1 Chr 6:46).

3. Asherite, Heber's son and a leader among his people (1 Chr 7:34).

SHEMIDA, SHEMIDAH*, SHEMIDAITE
Father of the family of Shemidaites (Nm 26:32) in Manasseh's tribe (Jos 17:2; 1 Chr 7:19).

SHEMINITH*
Obscure Hebrew term, meaning "the eighth," in 1 Chronicles 15:21 and the superscriptions of Psalms 6 and 12 (see RSV and NLT mg), whose function as a musical cue or instrument is uncertain. *See* Music.

SHEMIRAMOTH

1. One of the Levites whom David commanded to play the harp when the ark of God was brought from the house of Obed-edom to Jerusalem (1 Chr 15:18-22), and who retained a permanent position under Asaph as one of the ministers of the ark (16:4-5).

2. Levite commissioned by Jehoshaphat to teach the law "through all the cities of Judah" (2 Chr 17:8).

SHEMUEL

1. Ammihud's son and the representative of Simeon's tribe in the division of the land of Canaan among Israel's 10 tribes west of the Jordan (Nm 34:20).

2. KJV rendering of Samuel, Elkanah's son, in 1 Chronicles 6:33-34. *See* Samuel (Person).

3. Tola's son and chief in Issachar's tribe (1 Chr 7:2).

SHEN*
Alternate form of Jeshanah, a town near which the prophet Samuel set up the Ebenezer stone, in 1 Samuel 7:12. *See* Jeshanah.

SHENAZAR*, SHENAZZAR
Fourth son of Jeconiah (Jehoiachin), captive king of Judah (1 Chr 3:18).

SHENIR*
KJV alternate spelling of Senir, the Amorite name for Mt Hermon, in Deuteronomy 3:9 and Song of Songs 4:8. *See* Hermon, Mount.

SHEOL*
Hebrew term for the place of the dead. In ordinary usage it means "ravine," "chasm," "underworld," or "world of the dead." In the OT it is the place where the dead have their abode, a hollow space underneath the earth where the dead are gathered in. Synonyms for Sheol are "pit," "death," and "destruction" (Abaddon). Sheol is a place of shadows and utter silence. Here all existence is in suspense, yet it is not a nonplace, but rather a place where life is no more. It is described as the Land of Forgetfulness. Those who dwell there cannot praise God (Ps 88:10-12). In Revelation it is called the "bottomless pit" presided over by Abaddon, the prince of the pit (Rv 9:11).

It is not, however, a place where God is entirely absent; there can be no escape from God even in Sheol (Ps 139:8). This omnipresence of God is graphically described in Job: "Sheol is naked before God, and Abaddon has no covering" (Jb 26:6, RSV). A similar thought is expressed in Proverbs: "Sheol and Abaddon lie open before the LORD, how much more the hearts of men!" (Prv 15:11, RSV). In both texts Sheol and Abaddon are used interchangeably. Abaddon means literally "destruction," but in Revelation it is used as a personal name.

In the Bible, death is not a natural occurrence. It violates the principle of life, which is a gift from God. Sheol is therefore not only a place of rest but also of punishment. Korah and his associates who instigated rebellion against Moses were swallowed up by the open pit and perished in Sheol (Nm 16:30-33). Fear of death is natural to man; Sheol therefore serves as a symbol of the journey without return (Ps 39:12-13). King Hezekiah of Judah laments on his sickbed: "In the noontide of my days I must depart; I am consigned to the gates of Sheol for the rest of my years" (Is 38:10, RSV).

Sheol, as conceived in the OT, differs from the later doctrine of hell or Hades in that it is the place where all the dead are gathered indiscriminately, both the good and the bad, the saints and the sinners. To die means to be joined to those who have gone before. When a Jew dies, he is "gathered unto his people" (cf. Gn 25:8, 17; 35:29; 49:29). Beyond Sheol there seemed to be no hope (cf. Eccl 9:10). The utter despondency of death is expressed pathetically in the book of Job: "I go whence I shall not return, to the land of gloom and deep darkness, the land of gloom and chaos, where light is as darkness" (Jb 10:21-22, RSV). Yet this is not Job's last word. He also knows of the power of God, which reaches beyond the grave: "For I know that my Redeemer lives . . . ; and after my skin has been thus destroyed, then from my flesh I shall see God" (19:25-26, RSV).

The idea that the dead abide in the underworld persists in the OT. The incident in the case of Saul with the medium of Endor (1 Sm 28:11) is a good illustration. Samuel is brought "up out of the earth" to be consulted by the king at a time of crisis. Such necromancy was strictly prohibited both by the law of Moses (Dt 18:9-11) and by the king himself (cf. 1 Sm 28:3, 9). Apparently, those in the underworld, though separated from the living, were thought to be familiar with the affairs of men.

Sheol is roughly equivalent to the Greek word often found in the NT, *hades*, as that which also describes the place of the dead.

See also Dead, Place of the; Death; Hades; Hell; Intermediate State.

SHEPHAM
One of the places used by Moses to establish the eastern border of the Promised Land, mentioned between Hazar-enan, which marked the northeastern corner of the land, and Riblah (Nm 34:10-11).

SHEPHATHIAH*
Alternate KJV spelling of Shephatiah, Meshullam's father, in 1 Chronicles 9:8. *See* Shephatiah #2.

SHEPHATIAH
1. One of six sons born to David during his seven-year reign at Hebron. Shephatiah's mother was Abital, one of David's wives (2 Sm 3:4; 1 Chr 3:3).
2. Benjaminite and the father of Meshullam, a returnee to Jerusalem after the Babylonian captivity (1 Chr 9:8).
3. Haruphite from Benjamin's tribe and one of the men of military prowess who came to David's support at Ziklag (1 Chr 12:5).
4. Son of Maacah and chief official of the Simeonites during David's reign (1 Chr 27:16).
5. One of the seven sons of King Jehoshaphat of Judah (872–848 BC) and the brother of Jehoram who became sole regent (853–841 BC) after his father's death (2 Chr 21:1-2).
6. Forefather of 372 descendants who returned with Zerubbabel to Judah following the exile (Ezr 2:4; Neh 7:9). Later, 81 members of Shephatiah's house accompanied Ezra back to Palestine during the reign of King Artaxerxes I of Persia (464–424 BC; Ezr 8:8).
7. Founder of a household of Solomon's servants that returned with Zerubbabel to Judah after the Babylonian captivity (Ezr 2:57; Neh 7:59).
8. Descendant of Perez and an ancestor of a Judahite family living in Jerusalem during the postexilic period (Neh 11:4).
9. Son of Mattan and a prince of Judah during the reign of King Zedekiah (597–586 BC). Annoyed with Jeremiah's prophecies of doom for Jerusalem, Shephatiah (with Gedaliah, Jucal, and Pashhur) tried to put him to death. With Zedekiah's permission, they hoped to achieve their ends by imprisoning Jeremiah in a cistern (Jer 38:1).

SHEPHELAH*
Lowlands or foothills of Judah (see NLT mg, Jos 15:33; 1 Chr 27:28).

SHEPHER, Mount
Temporary camping place for the Israelites during their wilderness wanderings. Mt Shepher was located between Kehelathah and Haradah (Nm 33:23-24).

See also Wilderness Wanderings.

SHEPHERD
One who took complete care of a flock of sheep. His task was to find grass and water for the sheep, to protect them from wild animals (Am 3:12), to look for and restore those that strayed (Ez 34:8; Mt 18:12), to lead the flock out of the fold each day, and to return the flock to the fold at the close of the day (Jn 10:2-4).

The figure of the shepherd and his sheep is important in the NT. Jesus is the Good Shepherd who gives his life for the sheep (Mt 18:10-14; Mk 6:34; Jn 10; Heb 13:20). The analogy of the shepherd and the flock finds rich expression in Psalm 23, Ezekiel 34, and John 10. God was the Shepherd of Israel (Gn 49:24; Pss 23:1; 80:1; Is 40:11). When unfaithful shepherds failed Israel, God intervened and appointed his servant David as a faithful shepherd over them (Ez 34:11-16, 23-24).

The NT imagery comes from an OT and Palestinian background. In the Jewish economy, the shepherd who tended a flock of sheep or goats held a responsible position. Great flocks had to be moved from place to place, and it was necessary that they be guarded from wild animals and robbers. Because of the fundamental role of shepherding in the ancient world, the word "shepherd" became a common term for a ruler. The kings of Assyria, Babylon, and Egypt were often referred to as shepherds who protected their people. This imagery formed the background for the OT, where the same usage is found. God is pictured as the shepherd of Israel, concerned for every aspect of his people's welfare. Rulers and leaders of the people are often referred to as shepherds (Nm 27:17; 1 Kgs 22:17; Jer 10:21; 12:10; 22:22; 23:1-2).

By the time of Jeremiah, "shepherd" began to be used as a title for the coming Messiah. God himself would provide for his flock (Jer 23:3; 31:10; Ez 34:11-22) and promised to provide faithful shepherds who showed concern for his people (Jer 3:15; 23:4). He explicitly promised that he would be their God and would set the messianic Son of David as shepherd over them (Ez 34:23-24). In the NT Jesus referred to himself as the promised messianic Shepherd (Mt 10:16; 25:32; Mk 14:27; Jn 10:1-30; cf. Heb 13:20; 1 Pt 2:25). Ephesians 4:11 speaks of leaders of the church as shepherds or pastors, and this usage continued in the early church and down until the present day. Paul said they are special people given to the church by God to care for God's people as a shepherd does his sheep, leading and teaching them in the ways of God. Peter also spoke of the leaders as shepherds; he encouraged them to remain faithful shepherds until the time that the Chief Shepherd, Jesus Christ, appeared (1 Pt 5:1-4).

SHEPHERD OF HERMAS*
Volume composed by Hermas. Not much is known of Hermas other than the details he includes of himself in his work The Shepherd. In this story, Hermas states that he was originally a slave. He eventually gained his freedom, married, started a business, lost nearly everything, watched his children stray, and finally reunited his family. Hermas indicates that he knew Clement, the first-century bishop of Rome. From internal evidences, it is impossible to tell whether this biography is fictional or not. As to external facts, references to Hermas are contradictory. In the third century, Origen thought Hermas was the individual Paul mentioned in Romans 16:14. Other authorities, including the second-century Muratorian Canon, identified Hermas as a brother of Pius, bishop of Rome around 150. Most scholars today favor

this second position. Irenaeus, bishop of Lyons, provided the first recorded reference to The Shepherd in 185.

In The Shepherd Hermas describes a series of visions about Christian life and morality. Throughout the story, Hermas is both the hero and the narrator. The story is set in Rome and is divided into three parts: 5 visions, 12 mandates, and 10 similitudes, or parables.

Five visions in the book allegorize Christian ethical truths with such symbolism as a tower under construction and an older woman who becomes youthful. The visions begin with Hermas as he is smitten by the beautiful Rhoda, to whom he is sold as a slave. In the second vision Rhoda reappears as an old woman, representing the church. This old woman becomes more youthful each time she appears. The visions portray the church growing and spreading, purified by suffering and, in the fourth vision, by the terrors of judgment.

It is in the fifth vision, while Hermas is in his own house, that he no longer sees the church, but a bright, glowing man appears dressed like a shepherd. The man has been sent to live with Hermas to teach him until his death. The man is "the Shepherd, the angel of repentance" who gives Hermas 12 mandates and 10 similitudes, which form the remaining sections of the work.

In brief, the 12 mandates depict Christian virtues—humility, chastity, truthfulness, long-suffering, simplicity, respectfulness, and good cheer. The mandates also exhort believers to purity and repentance. Prominent here is the "Two Ways" pattern of moral instruction (the way of life and the way of death). This mirrors the Didache and other early Christian ethical writings.

Finally, the 10 similitudes describe principles by which the Christian virtues may be attained. The similitudes consider such topics as Christians as strangers, the rich and the poor, the sinners and the righteous, blossoming and withered trees, the purpose of the commandments, fasting, and punishment. They also include long parables about branches, a tower, maidens, and mountains. The 10th similitude is not a parable but a concluding chapter to sum up the work of the Shepherd. Here Hermas sums up the focus of the book: "I, too, sir, declare to every person the mighty works of the Lord; for I hope that all who have sinned in the past, if they hear these things, will gladly repent and recover life."

Throughout the early church, leaders gave Hermas's book high respect. Eusebius of Caesarea noted that The Shepherd was read widely in the early church. Some important leaders, such as Irenaeus and Clement of Alexandria, even considered it canonical Scripture. For Athanasius, the work was not Scripture, but it did offer, like the Didache, help for Christian learners. Because of its simplicity and candor, some have compared Hermas's work with Bunyan's *The Pilgrim's Progress*. The Shepherd serves as a valuable index to Christian ethics and moral instruction in Christianity's earliest decades.

Hermas's work exists in some Greek manuscripts and in many medieval Latin translations. Printed editions of the book began to appear in the early 1500s.

See also Hermas #2.

SHEPHI*, SHEPHO One of Shobal's five sons and a descendant of Seir the Horite. Shepho is listed in the genealogy of Abraham through Esau's contact with the nation (Gn 36:23); his name is alternately spelled Shephi (1 Chr 1:40; see NLT mg).

SHEPHUPHAM* Benjamin's fourth son (called "Muppim" in Gen 46:21) and the father of the Shuphamite family (Nm 26:39; see NLT mg). In the corresponding genealogy of Benjamin (1 Chr 7:12) he

is called Shuppim, appearing as Benjamin's great-grandson. *See* Shuppim #1.

See also Shephuphan.

SHEPHUPHAN Bela's son from Benjamin's tribe. Bela was the firstborn of Benjamin's sons (1 Chr 8:5). The exact position of Shephuphan in Benjamin's genealogy is unclear, and he is perhaps identifiable with Shephupham (1 Chr 7:12).

SHERAH* *See* Sheerah.

SHEREBIAH
1. Levite, a descendant of Mahli. Sherebiah, described as a man of understanding, was sent as a priest for the temple at Jerusalem following the exile (Ezr 8:18; Neh 12:8). During the return journey, he was one of 12 chief priests appointed to guard the silver, gold, and vessels presented for temple use (Ezr 8:24).
2. One who helped the people understand the law read by Ezra (Neh 8:7), and among the Levites who stood on the stairs leading the praise service (9:4-5).
3. One of the leaders of the Levites who led the songs of praise and thanksgiving (Neh 12:24).

It is possible that the above references refer to the same person.

SHERESH Makir's son and the brother of Peresh from Manasseh's tribe (1 Chr 7:16).

SHESHACH* Term that is probably a cryptic name for "Babel" (Babylon) found in Jeremiah 25:26 and 51:41 (NLT mg).

SHESHAI Descendant of Anak who was at Hebron when the 12 spies searched out the land of Canaan (Nm 13:22); he was defeated and displaced by Israel (Jos 15:14; Jgs 1:10).

SHESHAN Descendant of Judah through Jerahmeel, whose family line is traced in 1 Chronicles 2:25-41 to Elishama, evidently a contemporary of the writer. In verse 31 Sheshan's son Ahlai is named, but verse 34 says that Sheshan had no sons. Perhaps two men of the same name are denoted here, or Ahlai may be identical with Attai, Sheshan's grandson.

SHESHBAZZAR Jewish leader who found favor with Cyrus the Great, king of Persia. In the first year of his reign, Cyrus issued a decree that the temple in Jerusalem should be rebuilt (Ezr 1:1-4; cf. 6:1-5). He appointed Sheshbazzar governor of Judah (Ezr 5:14) and handed over to him the gold and silver vessels that Nebuchadnezzar had carried off when he took Jerusalem (1:7-9). Sheshbazzar fulfilled this commission by taking the vessels to Jerusalem with the returning exiles (v 9) and beginning the restoration of the temple (5:16).

Sheshbazzar is mentioned in the Bible only four times, all in the book of Ezra (1:8-9; 5:14-16). For many years it was commonly held that Sheshbazzar was another name for Zerubbabel. Both were of the royal line; Sheshbazzar is called "the prince of Judah," which may mean that he was heir apparent to the throne. Since his genealogy is not given, he may be represented in that listing by some other name, either Zerubbabel or Shenazzar (1 Chr 3:18-19). In the record of people who returned to Jerusalem, Sheshbazzar's name does not appear. The name of Zerubbabel is at the head of this list, where one would expect Sheshbazzar's to be; both were governors of the province of Judah. Zerubbabel is associated with the laying of the foundation of the temple (Ezr 3:8-11), but that work is attributed to Sheshbazzar in 5:16, in accordance with chapter 1. It is evident that the name Sheshbazzar is found only in connection with the Persians, for chapter 1 relates his dealings with Cyrus, and in chapter 5 the two occurrences of his name are in a letter written by the Persian official, Tattenai. One may conclude that the Persians knew him as Sheshbazzar, but the Jews called him Zerubbabel. Both names are Akkadian, so there is no parallel here to the renaming of Jewish captives in Babylon (Dn 1:7).

SHETH

1. Reference to the sons of Moab, who were the cause of tumult and war to Israel (Nm 24:17).
2. KJV spelling of Seth, Adam's son, in 1 Chronicles 1:1. See Seth.

SHETHAR One of Ahasuerus's seven counselors who, when Queen Vashti defied the king's command, advised him to deprive her of her title and to seek a new queen, as an example of domestic discipline (Est 1:14).

SHETHAR-BOZENAI, SHETHAR-BOZNAI* Persian official in a province west of the Euphrates River, who joined with Tattenai and his colleagues in writing a letter to Darius Hystaspeis, king of Persia, protesting the rebuilding of the temple and walls of Jerusalem under Zerubbabel (Ezr 5:3, 6). Darius warned them not to interfere with Zerubbabel's work, and they obeyed him (Ezr 6:6, 13).

SHEVA

1. Scribe or personal secretary of David (2 Sm 20:25). He is called by various names elsewhere. See Seraiah #1.
2. Caleb's son in the family of Hezron from Judah's tribe and the father of Macbena and Gibea (1 Chr 2:49).

SHEWBREAD* KJV rendering of showbread. See Bread of the Presence.

SHIBAH* Name of the fourth well dug by Isaac's servants, so named for the covenant made between Isaac and Abimelech, king of Gerar. The city at the location of the well was called Beersheba (Gn 26:33, NLT mg).

SHIBBOLETH Term used by Jephthah to detect the Ephraimites at the banks of the Jordan River (Jgs 12:6). After the battle, many Ephraimites tried to escape by crossing the Jordan and returning to their own land. When each of them came to the river, he was asked by one of Jephthah's soldiers to say "shibboleth." An Ephraimite could not pronounce the word with the same accent as Jephthah's men and was thus discovered and immediately killed.

The exact problem in pronunciation is not known. Two possibilities exist. First, the Ephraimites had no sound comparable to "sh." Thus, they pronounced "sh" as "s" ("shibboleth" becoming "sibboleth"). Second, the Gileadites pronounced "sh" as "th," a sound which was unknown to the Ephraimites, who pronounced it as "s." Thus, "shibboleth" was pronounced "thibboleth" by the Gileadites and "sibboleth" by the Ephraimites.

SHIBMAH* KJV form of Sibmah, an alternate name for Sebam, a city in Reuben's territory, in Numbers 32:38. See Sebam.

SHICRON* KJV form of Shikkeron, a city in Judah's tribe, in Joshua 15:11. See Shikkeron.

SHIELD, SHIELD BEARER Protective armor and the soldier or servant who carried the shield and weapons of a warrior. See Armor and Weapons.

SHIGGAION*, SHIGIONOTH* Hebrew words in the titles of Psalm 7 and Habakkuk 3, respectively, perhaps denoting a hymn, a psalm of distress, or a psalm accompanied with instruments. See Music.

SHIHOR Body of water in Egypt. The name is Egyptian and is given as a boundary of the land to be possessed by the Hebrews (Jos 13:3). First Chronicles 13:5 refers to Shihor as the southwestern limit of Israelite settlement in the time of David. Isaiah speaks of grain from the region of Shihor as a source of income for the city of Sidon (Is 23:3). Jeremiah describes Shihor as "the waters of the Nile" (Jer 2:18). Some believe that the Shihor was the easternmost branch of the Nile Delta. Others identify the Shihor with the Wadi el-Arish, 90 miles (144.8 kilometers) east of the Suez Canal. Still others identify it with the Brook (or River) of Egypt, a body of water whose precise location cannot be determined with certainty.

See also Brook of Egypt; Nile River.

SHIHOR-LIBNATH Place defining the southern boundary of Asher's tribe (Jos 19:26). Some have identified it with the Nahal Tanninim (Crocodile River), which flows into the Mediterranean Sea.

SHIKKERON Town near the Mediterranean Sea on the northern border of the land allotted to Judah's tribe for an inheritance, mentioned between Ekron and Mt Baalah (Jos 15:11). Its locality is uncertain, though perhaps identifiable with Tell el-Ful.

SHILHI Grandfather of King Jehoshaphat of Judah (1 Kgs 22:42; 2 Chr 20:31).

SHILHIM Alternate name for Shaaraim, a town in southern Judah, in Joshua 15:32. See Shaaraim #2.

SHILLEM, SHILLEMITE Fourth son of Naphtali (Gn 46:24), and father of the Shillemites (Nm 26:49); alternately called Shallum in 1 Chronicles 7:13.

SHILOAH* Name of an aqueduct in Jerusalem (Is 8:6; see NLT mg). See Siloam, Pool of.

SHILOH Town identified with Tell Seilun, located 10 miles (16.1 kilometers) northeast of Bethel, 12 miles (19.3 kilometers) southeast of Shechem, and 3 miles (4.8 kilometers) east of the road between Shechem and Jerusalem, precisely fitting the description of its location in Judges 21:19. In addition to the continuity of the name of the site and its fitting the biblical requirements for location, excavation results agree with the history of Shiloh as far as it is known from the Bible and confirm the identification.

The town is not mentioned in any prebiblical sources. Excavations show that Shiloh flourished as a fortified town in the early second millennium.

The site was abandoned and resettled in the early Israelite period. The Bible provides no information as to how the site passed into Israelite hands. Joshua established the tabernacle there (Jos 18:1), and Shiloh became the center of religious life during the period of the judges. There Joshua cast lots to apportion the inheritance of land to seven of the tribes (18:1-19:51) and to designate the Levitical cities (21:1-42). A dispute regarding an altar erected by the two and a half tribes that settled in Transjordan was settled at Shiloh (22:9-34). Some

Benjaminites abducted women from there during a religious festival (Jgs 21). Elkanah and Hannah often traveled to the tabernacle at Shiloh, where Hannah vowed to give her child to the service of the Lord (1 Sm 1:3, 9, 24). The sons of Eli who ministered there had dishonored their office and were rejected, so the Lord appeared to Samuel (1 Sm 2:14; 3:21). When the ark was taken from Shiloh to a battle with the Philistines, news of its loss to the Philistines reached Eli and brought about his death (1 Sm 4:1-18). The ark was never returned to Shiloh; the psalmist records that God had "abandoned the tabernacle of Shiloh, the tent he had set up among men" (Ps 78:60, NIV).

The town of Shiloh would presumably have suffered some destruction at the time of the fall of the northern kingdom in 722 BC. The sudden scarcity of ceramic remains in the Iron III period suggests that the site was

---

IS SHILOH A MESSIANIC NAME?

The transliteration of a Hebrew word in Genesis 49:10 was taken as a messianic name by the translators of the KJV: "The sceptre shall not depart from Judah, nor a lawgiver from between his feet, until Shiloh come; and unto him shall the gathering of the people be."

A nonmessianic interpretation of the verse understands the term "Shiloh" to be nothing more than a reference to the city of that name, a city that was prominent during the period of the judges. Given this view, the last clause of the verse is translated "until he comes to Shiloh." The basic objection to this approach is historical: Judah does not come into prominence until the time of the monarchy, at which time Shiloh was no longer an important center.

Many Christians since the time of Reformation have understood the word as a messianic proper name, as reflected in the translation of the clause in the KJV. Luther and Calvin viewed the word as derived from a Hebrew word they translated as "son." This interpretation is forced: the word in question is not the same as the word *shiloh*, and its more precise meaning is "embryo." Others associate the word with a Hebrew term meaning "be at ease, at rest" and translate the word as "rest-bringer." The basic objection here is also the fact that this title is not further developed in the messianic expectation of the Bible.

Some commentators and translations divide the word in two, and translate it "as long as tribute comes to him" or "until tribute comes to him." This approach is followed in the TEV, the NEB, and the NASB. Others identify the word *shiloh* as a Hebrew equivalent to a term in cognate languages meaning "ruler, prince." The translation would read "until his ruler comes."

The ancient translations (Septuagint, Peshitta, and Targums) understood the word *shiloh* as meaning "he to whom they belong." This translation also has the support of Ezekiel 21:27; Ezekiel appears to be alluding to Genesis 49:10 and paraphrases the last clause "until he comes to whom it rightfully belongs." Commentators and translations following this interpretation usually also understand the word translated "lawgiver" as "lawgiver's staff," so that the entire verse would read as follows: "The scepter will not depart from Judah, nor the ruler's staff from his descendants, until the coming of the one to whom it belongs" (NLT).

There are difficulties with these and other approaches taken to the word *shiloh* in Genesis 49:10. While a degree of uncertainty remains about the precise force of the term, the immediate context is brought into association with the Messiah in the NT (Rv 5:5).

---

largely abandoned around 600 BC. After the destruction of the temple in 586 BC, people came from Shiloh to offer sacrifices in Jerusalem (Jer 41:5). Shilonites were possibly also among the first returnees from the Babylonian captivity (1 Chr 9:5). The site was resettled around 300 BC and flourished through the Roman period. It is mentioned by Eusebius and Jerome and in Talmudic sources. It lost much of its importance after the Islamic conquests.

SHILONI* *See* Shilonite #2.

SHILONITE
1. Inhabitant of Shiloh, the hometown of Ahijah the prophet (1 Kgs 11:29; 12:15; 15:29; 2 Chr 9:29; 10:15). *See* Shiloh.
2. Hometown of the forefather of a family of exiles who returned to Jerusalem following the Babylonian captivity (1 Chr 9:5; Neh 11:5). This place is probably the same as #1 above. However, "Shilonite" should possibly be "Shelanite"; the NIV and NLT read "Shelah" in Nehemiah 11:5 (KJV "Shiloni"). *See* Shelah #2.

SHILSHAH Zophah's son and a chief of Asher's tribe (1 Chr 7:37).

SHIMEA
1. Alternate name for Shammah, Jesse's third son, in 1 Chronicles 2:13 and 20:7. *See* Shammah #2.
2. David's son borne to him by Bathsheba during his reign in Jerusalem (1 Chr 3:5). He is called Shammua in 2 Samuel 5:14 and 1 Chronicles 14:4.
3. Uzzah's son, the father of Haggiah and a descendant of Levi through Merari's line (1 Chr 6:30).
4. Gershonite Levite, Michael's son, the father of Berekiah, and the grandfather of Asaph. Asaph, with Heman and Ethan, was appointed by David to lead the musicians before the sanctuary (1 Chr 6:39).

SHIMEAH*
1. Alternate name for Shammah, David's brother, in 2 Samuel 13:3, 32. *See* Shammah #2.
2. Mikloth's son and the grandson of Jeiel from Benjamin's tribe (1 Chr 8:32); called Shimeam in 1 Chronicles 9:38.

SHIMEAM Alternate spelling of Shimeah, Mikloth's son, in 1 Chronicles 9:38. *See* Shimeah #2.

SHIMEATH Ammonitess mother (2 Chr 24:26) or perhaps father (2 Kgs 12:21) of one of the royal servants who conspired against and murdered King Jehoash of Judah (835–796 BC).

SHIMEATHITE One of three families of scribes living at Jabez in Judah. They were perhaps Kenites and descendants of Hammath (1 Chr 2:55). Their history is not certain. The Shimeathites may be identified with one of the nomadic Kenite tribes that settled with the Amalekites in southern Palestine during Saul's reign in Israel (1020–1000 BC).

SHIMEI
1. Son of Gershon, the grandson of Levi, and the brother of Libni (Ex 6:17; Nm 3:18; 1 Chr 6:17). He was the father of four sons and the founder of the Shimeite family (Nm 3:21; 1 Chr 23:7, 10; Zech 12:13).
2. Benjaminite, and the son of Gera from the house of Saul. He met King David at the village of Bahurim during the king's journey from Jerusalem to Mahanaim. Here Shimei bitterly opposed David, cursing him for the ruin of Saul's house (2 Sm 16:5-13). Later, Shimei

repented of his shameful behavior, entreated David's forgiveness, and received the king's pardon (19:16-23). After David's death, King Solomon ordered Shimei to settle in Jerusalem and never to leave the city for any reason. Shimei disobeyed the decree and was killed (1 Kgs 2:8, 36-44).

3. Brother of David and the father of Jonathan (2 Sm 21:21); alternately called Shammah in 1 Samuel 16:9. *See* Shammah #2.
4. One of David's court officials who did not support Adonijah's attempt to set himself up as king (1 Kgs 1:8).
5. Benjaminite, the son of Ela and one of King Solomon's officials who oversaw the royal household (1 Kgs 4:18); perhaps identical with #4 above.
6. Judahite, the son of Pedaiah, the brother of Zerubbabel, and a descendant of David through Solomon's line (1 Chr 3:19).
7. Simeonite, the son of Zaccur and the father of 16 sons and 6 daughters (1 Chr 4:26-27).
8. Reubenite, the son of Gog and the father of Micah (1 Chr 5:4).
9. Son of Libni, the father of Uzzah, and a descendant of Levi through Merari's line (1 Chr 6:29).
10. Gershonite Levite, the son of Jahath, the father of Zimmah, and an ancestor of Asaph who served as a leader of the musicians in the sanctuary during David's reign (1 Chr 6:42).
11. Benjaminite, the father of nine sons and a head of his father's house (1 Chr 8:21); alternately called Shema in verse 13. *See* Shema (Person) #3.
12. Gershonite Levite, and the father of three sons in the house of Conaniah appointed by Ladan (1 Chr 23:9).
13. Son of Jeduthun and the leader of the 10th of 24 divisions of musicians trained for service in the sanctuary during David's reign (1 Chr 25:3, 17).
14. Ramathite, and a member of King David's staff who had charge of David's vineyards (1 Chr 27:27).
15. Son of Heman, the brother of Jehuel, and one of the Levites selected to cleanse the house of the Lord during King Hezekiah's reign (715–686 BC; 2 Chr 29:14).
16. Levite, and the brother of Conaniah appointed by King Hezekiah of Judah to oversee the administration of the temple contributions in Jerusalem (2 Chr 31:12-13).
17–19. Three men, a Levite, Hashum's son, and Binnui's son, who were encouraged by Ezra to divorce their foreign wives during the postexilic era (Ezr 10:23, 33, 38)
20. Son of Kish and grandfather of Mordecai (Est 2:5).

SHIMEITE* Family of Levites founded by Shimei, Gershon's descendant (Nm 3:21; Zec. 12:13). *See* Shimei #1.

SHIMEON Harim's fifth son, who was encouraged by Ezra to divorce his foreign wife whom he had married during the postexilic era (Ezr 10:31).

SHIMHI* KJV form of Shimei, an alternate name for Shema, in 1 Chronicles 8:21. *See* Shema (Person) #3.

SHIMI* KJV spelling of Shimei, Gershon's son, in Exodus 6:17. *See* Shimei #1.

SHIMITE* KJV spelling of Shimeite. *See* Shimeite.

SHIMMA* KJV spelling of Shimea, an alternate name for Shammah, Jesse's son, in 1 Chronicles 2:13. *See* Shammah #2.

SHIMON Head of a Judahite family (1 Chr 4:20).

SHIMRATH Shimei's son from Benjamin's tribe (1 Chr 8:21).

SHIMRI
1. Simeonite, Shemaiah's son and the father of Jedaiah (1 Chr 4:37).
2. Father of Jediael (and perhaps Joha), two of David's mighty men (1 Chr 11:45).
3. Merarite Levite, Hosah's son and a temple gatekeeper during David's reign (1 Chr 26:10).
4. Levite, of the family of Elizaphan, who assisted in Hezekiah's temple reforms (2 Chr 29:13).

SHIMRITH* Moabitess mother of Jehozabad, a royal servant, who along with Zabad conspired against and murdered King Joash of Judah (2 Chr 24:26, NLT mg). She is alternately called Shomer in 2 Kings 12:21; Shimrith is the feminine form of Shomer. *See* Shomer #1.

SHIMRON (Person) Issachar's fourth son (Gn 46:13; 1 Chr 7:1) and the founder of the Shimronite family (Nm 26:24).

SHIMRON (Place) Canaanite town whose king joined the confederacy of King Jabin of Hazor in unsuccessful resistance to the Israelites under Joshua (Jos 11:1). Its site is uncertain, though it was in Zebulun's territory (19:15-16).

SHIMRONITE Family founded by Shimron, Issachar's son (Nm 26:24). *See* Shimron (Person).

SHIMRON-MERON Canaanite city destroyed by Joshua on his northern military campaign in Palestine. The king of Shimron-meron was one of 31 kings defeated by Joshua (Jos 12:20). This king was perhaps one of the northern kings summoned by Jabin, king of Hazor, to combine forces in an attempt to defeat Joshua (11:1). In all probability, Shimron-meron was one of the 12 cities included in the territory allotted to Zebulun for an inheritance (19:15).

SHIMSHAI Persian government official whose territory included Palestine. With another official (Rehum), he wrote a letter to Artaxerxes opposing the rebuilding of the temple by the Jews returned from exile (Ezr 4:8-9). He succeeded in halting the rebuilding project.

SHINAB King of Admah, who joined an alliance with four neighboring rulers against King Kedorlaomer. Kedorlaomer defeated this confederation of kings in the valley of Siddim—the southern region of the Dead Sea (Gn 14:2).

SHINAR* Name for a district of Babylonia mentioned exclusively in the Bible. The plain of Shinar comprised the region approximately from modern Baghdad to the Persian Gulf. In the ancient world this was the region of Sumer (south) and Akkad (north), which later became generally known as Babylonia (Dn 1:2, NLT mg). The renowned cities of Erech, Akkad, and Babel (Babylon) all were in Shinar as a part of the kingdom of Nimrod, son of Cush (Gn 10:10). Genesis 11:2 also mentions Shinar in connection with the Tower of Babel. In Genesis 14:1 and 9, we read about Amraphel, "king of Shinar," who was part of an eastern league in war with Abraham and the residents of Transjordan. Shinar's identification with a district of Babylon becomes clear in Israel's exile. Shinar is the destination of Nebuchadnezzar's new subjects (Dn 1:2) and the place of Israel's later rescue (Is 11:11; cf. Zec 5:11).
See also Babylon, Babylonia.

SHION One of 16 cities in the territory allotted to Issachar's tribe for an inheritance, mentioned between Hapharaim and Anaharath (Jos 19:19).

SHIPHI Ziza's father and a prince in Simeon's tribe (1 Chr 4:37).

SHIPHMITE* Designation for Zabdi (1 Chr 27:27). *See* Zabdi #3.

SHIPHRAH One of two Hebrew midwives who refused to kill Hebrew male infants at Pharaoh's command (Ex 1:15).

SHIPHTAN Father of Kemuel, a prince of Ephraim appointed by Moses to help divide the land among Israel's 10 tribes west of the Jordan (Nm 34:24).

SHIPS AND SHIPPING *See* Travel.

SHISHA Alternate name for Seraiah, King David's scribe, in 1 Kings 4:3. *See* Seraiah #1.

SHISHAK Egyptian pharaoh, descendant of a powerful family of Libyan chieftains, and founder of Egypt's 22d dynasty. His Egyptian name was Sheshonk. He was a contemporary of Solomon, Jeroboam, and Rehoboam. His years as ruler are variously given as 940–915 BC or 935–914 BC.

During Solomon's reign, he afforded asylum to Jeroboam, Solomon's servant and subsequent adversary, who escaped to Egypt to avoid being killed by his lord, against whom he had rebelled (1 Kgs 11:40). Since Jeroboam was to set up the northern kingdom after Solomon's death—an event used by God to punish his people for Solomon's sin—Shishak's readiness to harbor the fugitive rebel played a part in God's design to bring about his purposes.

God used Shishak a second time to further his plans. When Judah under Rehoboam became sinful and engaged in idolatrous practices, allowing male shrine prostitutes to operate in the land (a practice not to be equated with the phenomenon of homosexuality as presently known), God used Shishak's invasion of Palestine to punish his people. This invasion took place in the fifth year of Rehoboam's reign (1 Kgs 14:25; cf. 2 Chr 12:2-9). A great number of Judean towns were taken, but God spared Jerusalem from being captured, when the princes and the king showed repentance and humbled themselves (2 Chr 12:7). However, Shishak showed his mastery by plundering both the temple and royal palace in Jerusalem and by carrying off the gold shields that Solomon had made. Although the biblical account focuses on Shishak's invasion of the Judean area only, extrabiblical data indicate that he also

invaded the territory of Jeroboam, to whom he had previously given refuge.

See also Egypt, Egyptian; Israel, History of; Jeroboam; Rehoboam; Solomon (Person).

SHITRAI David's chief shepherd in charge of his flocks in Sharon (1 Chr 27:29).

SHITTAH TREE* KJV rendering of acacia, a common desert tree, in Isaiah 41:19. *See* Plants (Acacia).

SHITTIM* (Place) Site on the plains of Moab where the Israelites made their final Transjordan encampment after defeating Sihon and Og (Nm 21:21-35) and prior to their crossing of the Jordan (25:1). According to Numbers 33:49, this camp was near the Jordan, spreading from Beth-jeshimoth as far as Abel-shittim. Here Abel-shittim appears to be the full name of the place, while Shittim is the more common abbreviated toponym.

At Shittim, Balak of Moab attempted to thwart the Israelite penetration of Canaan by hiring Balaam to curse the people of God (Nm 22–24), and later, apparently incited by Balaam's counsel, Israel "played the harlot" with women from Midian and Moab (25:1-5; cf. 31:15-16). Israel's apostasy, participating in idolatrous rites and engaging in ritual prostitution, was punished by Yahweh with the plague at Peor (Nm 25:1-18; cf. 1 Cor 10:6-8). Moses and Eleazar organized a census of the tribes while encamped at Shittim, and here Joshua was publicly proclaimed as Moses' successor (Nm 27:18-22). Joshua dispatched two spies from Shittim to reconnoiter Jericho (Jos 2:1); later the Israelites prepared for the river crossing by breaking camp at Shittim and traveling to the Jordan (3:1).

Outside the Hexateuch the place-name Shittim occurs only in Joel 3:18 and Micah 6:5. The reference in Joel to the "valley of Shittim" or "wadi of the acacias" seems to be a symbol of barren aridity transformed into well-watered land when Yahweh restores his people in the eschaton, not a literal geographical location. Micah charges the people to remember "what happened from Shittim to Gilgal," no doubt a reference to the crossing of the Jordan and the covenant promise of a land ultimately realized, as he recites the "saving acts" of Yahweh on Israel's behalf.

SHITTIM WOOD* KJV rendering of acacia wood. *See* Plants (Acacia).

SHIZA Reubenite and the father of Adina, one of David's select warriors (1 Chr 11:42).

SHOA Assyrian people listed with the Babylonians, Chaldeans, and other Assyrian tribes, who were used by the Lord to punish Judah (Ez 23:23).

SHOBAB
1. Second of David's four sons by Bathsheba (2 Sm 5:14; 1 Chr 3:5; 14:4).
2. Caleb's son by his wife Azubah (1 Chr 2:18).

SHOBACH Commander of the army of Hadadezer, king of Zobah, who led the Ammonite-Syrian campaign against Israel. David's army killed Shobach and so completely destroyed his forces that the Ammonite-Syrian alliance was broken, and the kingdoms that were tributary to Hadadezer became subject to David (2 Sm 10:16-18). He is also called Shophach in 1 Chronicles 19:16-18.

SHOBAI Ancestor of a group of people who returned to Jerusalem with Zerubbabel after the Babylonian exile (Ezr 2:42; Neh 7:45).

SHOBAL

1. One of the seven sons of Seir the Horite in Edom (Gn 36:20; 1 Chr 1:38). Shobal became the father of five sons (Gn 36:23; 1 Chr 1:40) and a chief among the Horites (Gn 36:29).
2. Hur's son, the father of Haroeh, and the founder of the families of Kiriath-jearim (1 Chr 2:50-52).
3. One of Judah's five sons and the father of Reiah (1 Chr 4:1-2); perhaps the same as #2 above.

SHOBEK Leader who signed Ezra's covenant of faithfulness to God during the postexilic era (Neh 10:24).

SHOBI Ammonite prince, son of King Nahash, who, along with Makir of Lo-debar and Barzillai of Rogelim, generously supplied David with food and equipment at Mahanaim during Absalom's rebellion (2 Sm 17:27).

SHOCHO*, SHOCHOH*, SHOCO* KJV variant spellings of the city listed in Jos 15:35; 1 Sm 17:1; 2 Chr 11:7; 28:18. *See* Soco (Place), Socoh #1.

SHOHAM Merarite Levite, and Jaaziah's son in David's reign (1 Chr 24:27).

SHOMER

1. Father (2 Kgs 12:21), or perhaps the Moabite mother (2 Chr 24:26), of Jehozabad, a royal servant, who, with Jozacar, conspired against and murdered Joash, king of Judah. Shimrith is the feminine form of Shomer. *See* Shimrith.
2. Alternate name for Shemer, Heber's son, in 1 Chronicles 7:34. *See* Shemer #3.

SHOPHACH* Alternate form of Shobach in 1 Chronicles 19:16-18 (NLT mg). *See* Shobach.

SHOPHAR* Primitive musical instrument made from an animal's horn. *See* Musical Instruments.

SHOSHANNIM*, SHOSHANNIM-EDUTH*

Hebrew word and phrase in the superscriptions of Psalms 45, 69 and 80 (KJV), translated "according to Lilies" (RSV; see also NLT); perhaps a familiar ancient melody to which the psalms were performed. *See* Music (page 922).

SHOWBREAD* Bread that was kept in the Holy Place of the temple (2 Chr 2:4). *See* Bread of the Presence.

SHRUB *See* Plants.

SHUA

1. Canaanite whose daughter Judah married. She bore Judah three sons: Er, Onan, and Shelah (Gn 38:2-5, 12). *See* Bathshua #1.
2. Asherite, Heber's daughter and the sister of Japhlet, Shomer, and Hotham (1 Chr 7:32).

SHUAH

1. One of six sons borne to Abraham by Keturah (Gn 25:2; 1 Chr 1:32). He was perhaps the forefather of the Shuhite Arab tribe that dwelt near the land of Uz (Jb 2:11).
2. KJV spelling of Shua, Judah's father-in-law, in Genesis 38:2, 12. *See* Shua #1.
3. KJV spelling of Shuhah, Kelub's brother, in 1 Chronicles 4:11. *See* Shuhah.

SHUAL (Person) Zophah's son and a leader in Asher's tribe (1 Chr 7:36).

SHUAL (Place) Region that included the town of Ophrah and was perhaps situated in the territory of Benjamin and Ephraim (1 Sm 13:17). Shual was located to the north of Micmash.

SHUBAEL

1. Alternate form of Shebuel, Gershon's son, in 1 Chronicles 24:20. *See* Shebuel #1.
2. Alternate form of Shebuel, Heman's son, in 1 Chronicles 25:20. *See* Shebuel #2.

SHUHAH Kelub's brother from Judah's tribe (1 Chr 4:11).

SHUHAM, SHUHAMITE Alternate name for Hushim, Dan's son, and his descendants in Numbers 26:42-43. *See* Hushim #1.

SHUHITE Arab tribe, apparently descended from Shuah, the son of Abraham by Keturah. They were located near the land of Uz. Bildad, one of the three friends of Job, is identified as a Shuhite (Jb 2:11; 8:1; 18:1; 25:1; 42:9).

SHULAMMITE* Name or title of Solomon's lover in his Song (Sg 6:13). Her identity is not certain. Some suggest that Shulammite refers to a woman from the city of Shunem. Her designation as Shunammite was perhaps changed to Shulammite for its similarity in sound to Solomon's Hebrew name. Shunem was situated in the land of Issachar near Mt Gilboa (1 Sm 28:4). It was from this city that Abishag the beautiful Shunammite woman was called to nurse King David in his later years (1 Kgs 1:1-4, 15; 2:17-22). It is possible that Abishag became the beloved Shulammite maiden of Solomon's song.
  See also Shunem.

SHUMATHITE Family of Judah, descended from Shobal of Kiriath-jearim. Shobal was the son of Hur from Caleb's line (1 Chr 2:53).

SHUNAMMITE* Inhabitant of Shunem; hometown of Abishag (1 Kgs 1:3, 15). *See* Shunem.

SHUNEM Village of Issachar's tribe (Jos 19:18) strategically located in the Jezreel Valley. Shunem (modern Sulem) is about three and a half miles (5.6 kilometers) north of Jezreel, situated on the outer hills of Mt Moreh. Both Shunem and Jezreel guard the eastern approach to the Jezreel Valley from Beth-shan through the valley of Harod. This strategic location explains the appearance of Shunem on city lists of various foreign invaders: the lists of Thutmose III (15th century BC); the Amarna Letters (15th century BC), which mention it in conjunction with Megiddo; and the tenth-century BC record at Karnak of the Egyptian Shishak, who listed Shunem's importance.

The Philistines used Shunem to launch their siege of the Israelite forces at Jezreel (1 Sm 28–31). Because Shunem was on a well-used route, Elijah frequented the town and even resided there (2 Kgs 4:8). Later, Elijah raised a woman's son from death (vv 32-37). During the latter years of the reign of David, a beautiful woman from Shunem named Abishag was summoned to care for the ailing king (1 Kgs 1:3, 15). After David's death, Abishag appears in the story of the rivalry between Adonijah (David's eldest son) and Solomon. Adonijah requests Abishag for his own, once Solomon gains the throne, but the king views his brother's interest as presumption—and a possible attempt at his throne (2:13-25).
  See also Abishag; Shulammite.

SHUNI, SHUNITE Third of Gad's seven sons (Gn 46:16) and the family he founded (Nm 26:15).

SHUPHAM, SHUPHAMITE Benjamin's son and descendants. Shupham is the KJV spelling of Shephupham in Numbers 26:39. *See* Shephupham.

SHUPPIM
1. Son of Ir and a great-grandson of Benjamin (1 Chr 7:12). Shuppim is perhaps a shortened form of Shephupham (Shupham), mentioned in Numbers 26:39 as the son of Benjamin. It could also be an alternate spelling for Muppim (Gen 46:21). *See* Shephupham.
2. Levite gatekeeper, who, with Hosah, watched the gate of Shallecheth on the western side of Jerusalem (1 Chr 26:16).

SHUR Wilderness region located in the Sinai Peninsula east of Egypt's Nile Delta and west of the Negev. In antiquity, a caravan route passed through this region from Egypt to Palestine. Abraham lived for a time between Shur and Kadesh (Gn 20:1), and it was part of the territory occupied by the Ishmaelites (25:18). After crossing the Red Sea, Moses led Israel on a three-day trek through this arid wasteland (Ex 15:22). King Saul of Israel (1020–1000 BC) conquered the Amalekites in the vicinity of Shur (1 Sm 15:7), and later David (1000–961 BC) defeated the Geshurites, Girzites, and Amalekites here (27:8). The wilderness of Etham in Numbers 33:8 is identical with the wilderness of Shur.

See also Sina, Sinai; Wilderness Wanderings.

SHUSHAN* KJV form of Susa, the Persian capital. *See* Susa.

SHUSHAN EDUTH* Hebrew phrase in the superscription of Psalm 60, translated "To [the tune] of 'The Lily of the Covenant' " (NIV), perhaps a familiar ancient melody to which the psalm was performed. *See* Music (page 922).

SHUTHELAH
1. Ephraim's son, the brother of Beker and Tahan, and the father of Eran and Bered. He founded the Shuthelahite family and was an ancestor of Joshua the son of Nun (Nm 26:35; 1 Chr 7:20, 27).
2. Zabad's son from Ephraim's tribe (1 Chr 7:21).

SHUTHELAHITE Descendant of Shuthelah, Ephraim's son (Nm 26:35). *See* Shuthelah #1.

SIA*, SIAHA Ancestor of a group of temple assistants who returned to Jerusalem with Zerubbabel following the exile (Neh 7:47, NLT mg); spelled Siaha in Ezra 2:44.

SIBBECAI, SIBBECHAI* Zerahite from the town of Hushah and one of David's "mighty men" (1 Chr 11:29; 20:4; 27:11). He is credited with killing the giant Saph when Israel fought Philistia at Gob (2 Sm 21:18). In 2 Samuel 23:27 he is called Mebunnai, probably a later erroneous reading of the original.

SIBBOLETH Spelling of the Gileadite password as mispronounced by the Ephraimites (Jgs 12:6). *See* Shibboleth.

SIBMAH Alternate rendering of Sebam, a city in Reuben's territory, in Numbers 32:38 and Joshua 13:19. *See* Sebam.

SIBRAIM Geographical landmark between Damascus and Hamath, marking the northern boundary of Israel (Ez 47:16).

SICHEM* KJV form of Shechem in Genesis 12:6. *See* Shechem (Place).

SICKLE *See* Agriculture (Harvesting).

SICKNESS *See* Disease; Medicine and Medical Practice; Plague.

SIDDIM VALLEY Location of the battle between four kings from Mesopotamia and five allied kings living near the Dead Sea (Gn 14:3, 8-10). The precise location of the battle in the vicinity of the Dead Sea has proved impossible to determine; one is left with conjectures. The valley is described as being full of tar pits (Gn 14:10). This description suits the areas adjacent to the Salt or Dead Sea.

The account in Genesis describes an important military campaign believed to have occurred in the middle Bronze Age (c. 1900 BC), which would place it at the time of Abraham. The kings mentioned in the coalition from the East are unknown, since the alleged link of Amraphel with Hammurabi is now considered untenable. These four allies came south from Damascus and conquered a series of cities, including Karnaim, Ham, and the Horites in Mt Seir, as far south as the Gulf of Elat. They then turned northwest to Kadesh-barnea and from there northeast toward the Dead Sea. This seems to be the locality where they met resistance from the coalition of the kings of Sodom, Gomorrah, Admah, Zeboiim, and Zoar (Gn 14:2-9) south of the Dead Sea.

SIDON (Person) Canaan's firstborn son; Canaan was the son of Ham and grandson of Noah (Gn 10:15, 19; 1 Chr 1:13). Sidon founded a city (bearing his name) that set the northern boundary of the land of Canaan and later played a dominant role in Palestinian history.

See also Sidon (Place), Sidonian.

SIDON (Place), SIDONIAN City on the Phoenician coast, between Beirut and Tyre; frequently called Zidon in the KJV. The present town, Saida, is not regarded as a direct continuation of the ancient city but rather a development of post-Crusader times. The names Sidon and Sidonian appear 38 times in the OT, and Sidon occurs 12 times in the NT.

The relative antiquity of Byblos (Gebal, Jebeil), Tyre, and Sidon may be determined by the "table of nations" (Gn 10), which names Sidon as the firstborn son of Canaan, who was a son of Ham. The territory of the Canaanites extended from Sidon to Gaza and east to the Cities of the Plain.

Sidon is situated 22 miles (35.4 kilometers) north of Tyre, with which it is often associated (e.g., Is 23:1-2; Jer 47:4; Mt 11:21-22); both were much concerned with commerce and industry. Sidon was built on a headland that jutted into the sea toward the southwest. It had two harbors, the northern one having inner and outer ports. Sidon was also a center for the manufacture of the purple dye made from the Murex shellfish.

The Bible mentions Sidon several times in connection with the conquest of Palestine. Joshua defeated the northern confederation under Jabin, king of Hazor, and pursued the enemy as far as "Great Sidon" (Jos 11:8). Joshua also stated that the land of Israel included all of Lebanon, "even all the Sidonians" (13:4-6). The tribal allotment of Asher extended as far north as "Sidon the Great" (19:28), but Asher did not drive out the inhabitants of Sidon (Jgs 1:31).

The gods of Sidon are listed among the foreign deities that Israel served (Jgs 10:6); David's census included Sidon and Tyre (2 Sm 24:6-7); and during a famine in the time of Ahab, the prophet Elijah was sent to live at the home of a widow in Zarephath (Sarepta) in Sidon (1 Kgs 17:9; Lk 4:25-26). Sidon is referred to often by the Hebrew prophets (Is 23:2, 4, 12; Jer 25:22; 27:3; 47:4; Ez 27:8; Jl 3:4; Zec 9:2).

In the NT, Jesus healed the daughter of a woman of that area (Mt 15:21-28). People came from as far away as Tyre and Sidon to hear Jesus and to be healed by him (Lk 6:17). On Paul's voyage to Rome to appear before Caesar, the ship made its first stop at Sidon, where the centurion, Julius, allowed Paul to go ashore to visit friends (Acts 27:3).

SIEGE *See* Warfare.

SIGN Word connoting a visible event intended to convey meaning beyond that which is normally perceived in the outward appearance of the event.

In the Old Testament In a few instances in the OT, "sign" refers to the observances of heavenly bodies in an astrological sense (Gn 1:14; Jer 10:2), or to the "signs and wonders" as marks of the miraculous actions of God within the history of the world (Dt 4:34; 6:22; Neh 9:10; Ps 105:27; Jer 32:20). On other occasions, it is used as an insignia of the Mosaic covenant. Thus, the wearing of the law on the wrist and forehead and the keeping of the Sabbath are considered signs of the relationship between Israel and God (Dt 6:8; 11:18; Ez 20:12, 20).

The most numerous and significant usages of "sign" appear in relation to the OT prophetic ministry. Beginning with Moses, signs are used to confirm that God has spoken to the prophet. Thus, when Moses received the message of deliverance that he was to bring to the children of Israel in Egypt and the pharaoh, he was given two signs: his staff was changed into a serpent and his hand was afflicted with leprosy (Ex 4:1-8).

Signs and wonders were also used by false prophets. After a sign had been given and had come to pass, the leaders of Israel were to examine the message of the prophet to see if it led the people away from the true worship of God. If it did, the prophet who had given the sign was to be put to death (Dt 13:1-5).

The character of the sign varies and often is miraculous. Some of the great miracles of the OT are prophetic signs—for example, the moving of the shadow back up the steps of Hezekiah's palace to confirm Isaiah's prediction that the king would recover from what was a mortal illness (2 Kgs 20:8-9; Is 38:21-22). Often the sign is predictive only, and the people can know whether the prophet has spoken the truth by whether or not the event comes to pass—for example, the prophet's foretelling the death of both of Eli's sons on the same day (1 Sm 2:34; see also 14:10; 2 Kgs 19:29; Is 37:30). Sometimes the sign was carefully timed, and the recipient was told that the appearance of the sign would show when to act to fulfill the prophetic message (1 Sm 10:7-9). At other times, the events predicted were acted out in the life of the prophet. These symbolic actions demonstrated the truth of the prophet's message—for example, Isaiah's nakedness for three years to demonstrate the fate of those who preached trust in Egypt's power (Is 20:3; see also Ez 4:3).

In the New Testament The NT occurrences are much like those in the OT. There are references to heavenly signs that will occur as indications of the end of time, and those with special knowledge will understand that the end is drawing near (Mt 24:3, 30; Mk 13:4, 22; Lk 21:11, 25-26). These apocalyptic signs have no astrological connotations as in the OT. There is also mention of the sign as the seal of the covenant between God and Israel in reference to circumcision in Romans 4:11.

As in the OT, the NT uses of signs are confirmations of the message given by God, and this message comes through the apostolic community to the church. Thus, there is great emphasis on the way God confirms the message of the apostles through their ability to perform signs and wonders (Acts 2:43; 4:30; 5:12; 8:13; 14:3; Rom 15:19; Heb 2:4).

In Matthew, Mark, and Luke, Jesus' miracles are not called signs. Only in Acts 2:22 does Peter proclaim that Jesus' message was attested by signs he performed. Rather, Jesus' miracles are seen as acts of divine power and mercy. When the Jews ask for a sign, they are consistently refused, with the promise that the only sign they will receive is the sign of Jonah (Mt 12:38-39; 16:1; Mk 8:11-12; Lk 11:19, 30), a sign that refers to the death and resurrection of the Christ. As Jonah was in the belly of the whale for three days and three nights, so will the Son of Man be in the heart of the earth for three days (Mt 12:40).

In the Gospel of John, however, the miracles of Jesus are seen in a strikingly different light and are considered signs. Beginning with the changing of water into wine (Jn 2:1-11), the miracles are called signs and are intended to lead those who see them to faith (v 23). Jesus even laments that the people will not believe unless they see signs (4:48). John's purpose in writing his Gospel is to present the signs of Jesus so that those who come to faith may do so through seeing these signs (20:30). The signs in the Gospel are expressly chosen because they lend themselves to the development of true faith.

In the Gospel of John, the miracles of Jesus confirm the teaching of Jesus. In the synoptic Gospels, the miracles are seen as acts of mercy and divine power. In John they are carefully selected to demonstrate what Jesus has to tell the world about himself. In this respect, they are a bit like the symbolic actions of Isaiah and Ezekiel in that the action of the speaker dramatizes the message. After Jesus feeds the 5,000 with the five loaves of bread and the two fishes, he announces in the synagogue at Capernaum, "I am the bread of life which came down from heaven" (Jn 6:51). He tells them not to labor for the bread of this world that perishes. In much the same way, the healing of the man born blind is bound up with Jesus' teaching that he is the light of the world (9:5). The resurrection of Lazarus prepares the way for Jesus to proclaim that he is the resurrection and the life (11:25). In John's Gospel the signs are not only a demonstration of divine power but also a revelation of Jesus' divine character. In addition to confirming his divine message, they also proclaim his personhood and mission.

See also Miracle.

SIGNET *See* Seal.

SIHON King of the Amorites who ruled in Heshbon, about 14 miles (22.5 kilometers) east of the north end of the Dead Sea. His defeat by Israel under Moses, together with that of Og, king of Bashan, is frequently mentioned in OT prose and poetry, in narrative and song (Dt 1:4; 2:26-37; 4:46; 29:7; 31:4; Jos 2:10; 9:10; 12:2-6; 13:10-12). In the eyes of the sacred writers, this dual defeat is so significant that it can be ranked with the exodus as one of the singular manifestations of God's saving intervention on behalf of his people (Pss 135:11; 136:19-20), and as evidence of his everlasting love for them. In the postexilic period this event is recalled in prayer as a pleading ground for God's continuing mercy to the returned exiles (Neh 9:22).

Before Israel's arrival in Transjordan, Sihon had conquered Moab's territory as far south as the Arnon River (Nm 21:26). This conquest gives rise to a piece of ancient poetry that is incorporated into sacred Scripture (vv 27-30). Sihon's realm extends from the Arnon on the south to the Jabbok on the north, with the Jordan as its western boundary. It also includes the Jordan Valley as far as the Sea of Kinnereth (Jos 12:2-3), comprising part of the region known as Gilead. On the east it extends toward the desert and touches on Ammonite land.

Sihon's refusal to grant Israel passage through his domain is similar to that of Edom (cf. Nm 21:23 with 20:20). However, Sihon exhibits overt hostility toward Israel. Sihon was defeated and killed at Jahaz; his country was occupied by Israel. Subsequently, it was distributed to the tribes of Gad and Reuben (cf. Nm 32:33-38; Jos 13:10).

SIHOR* KJV form of Shihor, a body of water in northeast Egypt, in Joshua 13:3, Isaiah 23:3, and Jeremiah 2:18 (NLT mg). *See* Shihor.

SIKKUTH* *See* Sakkuth.

SILAS Respected leader in the Jerusalem church, also called Silvanus (2 Cor 1:19; 1 Thes 1:1; 2 Thes 1:1; 1 Pt 5:12). "Silas" is most likely the Aramaic form of the Hebrew name "Saul," which when given a Latin form became *Silouanos* (Silvanus). Silas thus carried two names—a Latin and a shorter, Semitic name. The name was known in the Hellenistic era and appears in various inscriptions. Luke used the name Silas when he narrated the history of the Jerusalem church in Acts. Paul and Peter used the Roman name in their epistles.

Silas is introduced in Acts 15:22 as a distinguished delegate who conveyed to Antioch the decree of the Jerusalem Council. Several manuscripts (of lesser quality than the best-attested ones) include 15:34; this added verse indicates that Silas remained in Antioch because shortly thereafter he joined Paul on his second missionary tour (Acts 15:40). His service as a prophet may be evident in Acts 16:6, when the Spirit redirected the company through Asia. Silas's name appears eight times within the second tour (Acts 16:19, 25, 29; 17:4, 10, 14-15; 18:5), as he accompanied Paul through the hardships suffered at Philippi, Thessalonica, and Berea. When Paul was safely ushered out of Macedonia by the Berean Christians (17:14), Silas remained behind with Timothy to oversee the work already begun in the region. Later in Corinth (18:5), Silas and Timothy rejoined Paul. Their report prompted Paul to correspond with the church at Thessalonica. This explains Silas's name in the prescript of both 1 and 2 Thessalonians.

It seems clear that Silas was well known to the Corinthians. Not only does he stay in the city with Paul for a year and a half (Acts 18:11), but it may be conjectured that he stayed behind in Corinth after the dispute before Gallio. Paul, on his final tour, wrote to Corinth from Ephesus and mentioned Silas again (2 Cor 1:19), reminding the Corinthians of the earlier ministry among them.

The subsequent history of Silas is obscure. Some believe Silas was a respected Christian scribe. Silas's involvement in 1 and 2 Thessalonians is often mentioned, pointing to Paul's sustained use of the first person plural. Some scholars find resemblances among 1 and 2 Thessalonians, the decree of Acts 15, and 1 Peter, where Silas is mentioned as a scribe (1 Pt 5:12). This latter association with Peter is intriguing and has led to the speculation that Silas ultimately joined Peter and ministered in north Asia.

SILK Fine, delicate thread extracted from the cocoon of the silkworm. Originating in China, silk may have been introduced into Palestine as early as Solomon's reign (970–930 BC), or perhaps not until the conquests of Alexander the Great (336–323 BC). A fine silken fabric was apparently included in the fashionable attire of Jerusalem (Ez 16:10-13). Revelation 18:12 lists silk as a valuable trade commodity of Babylon (Rome).

See also Cloth and Cloth Manufacturing.

SILLA Geographical landmark defining the whereabouts of "the house of Millo," the place of King Joash's murder (2 Kgs 12:20). Its exact location is unknown, though it was probably in the vicinity of Jerusalem.

SILOAH* KJV rendering of Shelah, an alternate name for the pool of Siloam, in Nehemiah 3:15. *See* Siloam, Pool of.

SILOAM, Pool of Pool mentioned in John 9. Jesus, after anointing with clay the eyes of a blind man, directed him to go and wash in the pool. The man obeyed. He washed and came back with his sight fully restored.

The pool of Siloam of NT days marked the emergence of Hezekiah's tunnel, dug during the threat of the Assyrian invasion about 700 BC. This tunnel is S-shaped and is described both in 2 Kings 20:20 and 2 Chronicles 32:2-4. Archaeologists found an inscription in the tunnel consisting of Hebrew letters chiseled into the side of the tunnel indicating the progress and the meeting place of the two groups of workmen (each of which had started on one side and worked their way to the middle). This inscription has since been removed and is now in the museum in Istanbul. The ancient Hebrew reads:

> When the tunnel was driven through . . . each man toward his fellow, and while there were still three cubits to be cut through—the voice of a man calling to his fellow. . . . And when the tunnel was driven through, the quarrymen hewed, each toward his fellow, axe against axe; and the water flowed from the spring toward the reservoir for 1200 cubits, and the height of the rock above the heads of the quarrymen was 100 cubits.

The purpose of the pool originally was to bring water inside the city walls and deny it to invaders of Jerusalem. It flowed through the temple mount to the inner part of the city, where it was accessible to the residents. Water from Gihon Spring flows through the tunnel, emerges at the pool (also called the King's Pool in Neh 2:14 and the pool of Shelah in 3:15), continues down the valley through the ancient area of the king's gardens, reenters the Kidron Valley, and makes its way toward the Dead Sea south of the Essene site at Qumran. The Gihon Spring, the only natural source of water in Jerusalem, is a copious perennial stream. This, together with a rugged terrain, explains the strength of Jerusalem and the reason why it had been chosen for a place of habitation since the early Bronze Age.

Siloam now lies outside the old city of Jerusalem. The pool today measures 50 feet (15.2 meters) long and 5 feet (1.5 meters) wide and lies 16 steps below street level. A Byzantine church stood over the pool until it was destroyed by the Persians in AD 614.

See also Aqueduct.

SILOAM, Tower of Edifice that collapsed, killing 18 people. Jesus compared those killed by the fallen tower to the rest of the people living in Jerusalem (Lk 13:4-5). Though nothing is known of this tower, it seems reasonable to conclude that it was situated in Jerusalem.

Perhaps it can be identified with the great tower built by Nehemiah on the wall of Ophel (2 Chr 27:3; Neh 3:26-27) or with one of the towers built on the wall of Jerusalem near the pool of Siloam.

See also Jerusalem.

SILOAM INSCRIPTION* Hebrew inscription in the Siloam tunnel, also known as Hezekiah's tunnel, which marked the progress of the tunnel as it was being built. *See* Siloam, Pool of.

SILOAM TUNNEL* Conduit, also known as Hezekiah's tunnel, built by Hezekiah at the time of the Assyrian invasion to bring water into Jerusalem (2 Kgs 20:20; 2 Chr 32:2-4). *See* Siloam, Pool of.

SILVANUS* Latin name for Silas, a companion of Paul and Peter (2 Cor 1:19; 1 Thes 1:1; 2 Thes 1:1; 1 Pt 5:12). *See* Silas.

SILVER *See* Coins; Minerals and Metals; Stones, Precious; Money; Banker, Banking.

SILVERSMITH One who refined silver-bearing ore and then cast it or beat it into the desired shape. Silversmiths produced musical instruments like trumpets (Nm 10:2), bases on which the frame of the tabernacle rested (Ex 26:19-25), and objects for use in the tabernacle and temple (Nm 7:13-85), as well as ornaments for private use. Silversmiths also made religious statues for false worship (Ex 20:23; Jgs 17:4). The silversmith Demetrius (Acts 19:24) made silver shrines for Artemis at Ephesus. The profession was well known in NT times (2 Tm 2:20; Rv 9:20).

SIMEON (Person)

1. Second of the 12 sons of Jacob (Gn 35:23; 1 Chr 2:1) and the second son borne to him by Leah (Gn 29:33). Simeon fathered six sons (Ex 6:15) and settled his family in Egypt with Jacob and his brothers (1:2). He was the founder of the Simeonites (Nm 26:12-14) and one of the 12 tribes of Israel (1:23). He is remembered most for his vengeance on the men of Shechem because of Dinah's rape (Gn 34:25).

   See also Simeon, Tribe of.
2. Pious Jew living in Jerusalem who was assured that he would not die before he saw the promised Messiah. Led by the Holy Spirit to the temple, Simeon met Mary and Joseph there, held Jesus in his arms, and prophesied about the Messiah's coming mission (Lk 2:25-35).
3. Ancestor of Jesus in Luke's genealogy (Lk 3:30). *See* Genealogy of Jesus Christ.
4. One of five prophets and teachers mentioned in Acts 13:1 who was serving in the church of Antioch. Simeon was surnamed Niger and was perhaps from Africa. Symeon is a better reading of the Greek in this text.
5. Reference to Simon Peter in Acts 15:14. *See* Peter, The Apostle.

SIMEON, Tribe of One of the 12 tribes of Israel descended from Jacob's second son. Because of Simeon's evil deed at Shechem, Jacob foretold that Simeon's descendants would be dispersed among the other tribes of Israel (Gn 49:7).

According to the book of Joshua, Simeon's inheritance was included in Judah's territory (Jos 19:1, 9). Judges 1:3 points to a close bond between the tribes of Simeon and Judah—they march and fight together as brothers to establish themselves in Canaan. In addition, the list of Levitical towns included Simeon's with Judah's (Jos

21:9-16). Inevitably, then, the Simeonites were linked to the kingdom of Judah throughout the period of the monarchy, and its tribal destiny was tied to that of the southern division of the divided monarchy. However, in spite of their minor inheritance within Judah's tribe, the Simeonites were able to preserve to some extent their own tribal identity, unity, and traditions, as indicated by the keeping of genealogical records, even to the days of Hezekiah, king of Judah (1 Chr 4:24-42).

During Hezekiah's reign, Simeonites took possession of and settled the Arab areas of Seir (1 Chr 4:24-43) and perhaps the hill country of Ephraim (2 Chr 15:9). Although Simeon was Jacob's second-oldest son, his progeny never achieved a position of prominence in Israel, either before or after the conquest and occupation of Canaan. For example, the tribe apparently provided no judges, and the Song of Deborah contains no references to this group (see Jgs 5). According to 1 Chronicles 4:28-33, Simeon's tribe settled in the southern extremes of Canaan (called the Negev in Hebrew)—an extensive region, consisting largely of dry, parched land, but with an annual rainfall and perennial springs that ensured fertility in the early summer. This explains why Simeon's territory is also called "the Negev of Judah," a phrase that serves to differentiate them from other racial groups occupying parts of southern Canaan (1 Sm 27:10; 30:14; 2 Sm 24:7).

The genealogies of the Simeonites reveal a certain amount of intermarriage with other Israelite tribes and, indeed, with non-Israelites as well. Shaul, Simeon's son, was the son of a Canaanite woman (Gn 46:10; Ex 6:15). Two of Simeon's sons (1 Chr 4:25) bear names of Ishmael's sons (Gn 25:13-14; 1 Chr 1:29-30), and Jamin (Gn 46:10; Ex 6:15) was a descendant of Ram (1 Chr 2:27).

In the NT, Simeon's tribe appears seventh in the list of the tribes who are sealed by God (Rv 7:7).

SIMEONITE* Member of Simeon's tribe (Nm 26:14; Jos 21:4). *See* Simeon (Person) #1; Simeon, Tribe of.

SIMON Greek form of a Hebrew/Aramaic name meaning "God has heard." Nine men in the NT had this name:

1. Son of Jona (Mt 16:17) or John (Jn 1:42), Andrew's brother (v 40), and surnamed Cephas and Peter (respectively Aramaic and Greek, for "rock," v 42) by Jesus. A fisherman of Bethsaida (Mk 1:16; Jn 1:44), he became an apostle of Jesus and author of two NT letters bearing his name. *See* Peter, The Apostle.
2. Brother of Jesus, named with other brothers, James, Joses or Joseph, and Judas (Mt 13:55; Mk 6:3).
3. Leper, perhaps cured by Jesus, in whose house at Bethany Jesus and his disciples were eating when a woman poured an alabaster flask of costly ointment on the Lord's head. Over the disciples' objections against the waste of what could have been sold to support the poor, Jesus commended the act as a wonderful thing (Mt 26:6-13; Mk 14:3-9). From John 12:1-8 it appears that Simon's house was also the house of Mary, Martha, and Lazarus, but their relationship to Simon is uncertain.
4. Man of Cyrene, a district of North Africa, whom the Romans forced to carry Jesus' cross (Mt 27:32; Mk 15:21; Lk 23:26). He was the father of Alexander and Rufus (Mk 15:21; cf. Rom 16:13).
5. Apostle of Jesus called a Zealot (Lk 6:15), presumably because of prior association either with the party of political extremists by that name, who adopted terrorism to oppose the Roman occupation of Palestine, or with one of a number of Jewish groups noted for their zeal for the law. In Matthew 10:4 and Mark 3:18 he is

designated the "Cananaean" (RSV)—from the Aramaic word for "zealot." He is mentioned again in Acts 1:13 as one of the 11 apostles in Jerusalem after Jesus' ascension. Otherwise, the NT is silent about him.

6. Pharisee whose treatment of Jesus evoked the parable of the two debtors (Lk 7:36-50). He invited Jesus to eat at his house but withheld courtesies customary for guests and disapproved of Jesus' acceptance of a "sinner" woman who wet the Lord's feet with her tears, dried them with her hair, and anointed them with ointment from an alabaster flask. Jesus' parable contrasted the woman's act of loving and repentant faith with Simon's unloving and self-righteous skepticism.

7. Father of Judas Iscariot, the disciple who betrayed Jesus in Gethsemane (Jn 6:71; 13:2, 26).

8. Magician (often called Simon Magus) of great repute in Samaria. Impressed by the signs and miracles performed by Philip the deacon-become-evangelist, he joined the crowd of baptized believers. He offered Peter and John money in exchange for the gift of the Holy Spirit, provoking Peter's emphatic rebuke (Acts 8:9-24). From the association of this incident with his name, the English word "simony" is derived; it denotes the sale or purchase of church positions, or any profiteering from sacred things.

9. Tanner of Joppa. Peter lodged at his house for many days (Acts 9:43; 10:6, 17, 32). On Simon's housetop, Peter experienced the vision of a great sheet let down from heaven, containing animals and birds prohibited as food in Jewish law (10:15). Peter later recognized this vision as his preparation for consenting to preach the gospel to the Gentiles (vv 28-29).

SIMON MACCABEUS The second son of Mattathias was successor to his brother Jonathan. In 142 BC Simon (d. 135 BC) negotiated a treaty with Syria by supporting Demetrius II against the plunderer Trypho. Under this treaty, Judea was recognized as politically independent. The Syrians were finally driven from the citadel at Jerusalem and "the yoke of the Gentiles was removed from Israel" (1 Macc 13:41). In 141 BC "the Jews and their priests decided that Simon should be their leader and high priest forever until a trustworthy prophet should arise" (14:41). These two offices were made hereditary in the Hasmonean family. Simon Maccabeus is considered perhaps the best leader of Israel in the postexilic period. Antiochus VII invaded Israel in 133 BC and was defeated by Simon's sons, Judas and John, at Modin. This was the single interruption in six years of prosperous rule. Simon and his sons were assassinated by his son-in-law and chief rival for power, Ptolemy son of Abub. John Hyrcanus (d. 104 BC), Simon's youngest son, escaped and succeeded to his father's position before Ptolemy could reach Jerusalem. John ruled from 134 to 104 BC.

SIMON MAGUS* Sorcerer of Samaria apparently converted by Philip (Acts 8:9-24). *See* Simon #8.

SIMON OF CYRENE* Man who was ordered to carry Jesus' cross on the road to Golgotha (Mt 27:32). *See* Simon #4.

SIMON PETER *See* Peter, The Apostle.

SIMON THE CANAANITE* KJV rendering for Simon the Zealot in Matthew 10:4; Mark 3:18. *See* Simon #5.

SIMON THE CANANAEAN* RSV rendering for Simon the Zealot in Matthew 10:4; Mark 3:18. *See* Simon #5.

SIMON THE ZEALOT One of Jesus' disciples (Mt 10:4; Mk 3:18; Lk 6:15; Acts 1:13). *See* Simon #5.

SIMON ZELOTES* KJV rendering for Simon the Zealot in Luke 6:15; Acts 1:13. *See* Simon #5.

SIMRI* KJV spelling of Shimri, Hosah's son, in 1 Chronicles 26:10. *See* Shimri #3.

SIN Evildoing that is not only against humanity, society, others, or oneself, but against God. The concept of God, therefore, gives to the idea of sin its many-sided meaning. Other gods, conceived of as capricious and characterless, exercised unlimited power in unbridled behavior; they engendered no such sense of sin as did Israel's one God, holy, righteous, and utterly good. This religious conception of wrongdoing with the terminology it created persists into the NT.

Terminology Israel's God sets the ideal, the standard for human behavior. The most frequent biblical words for sin speak of violating that standard in some fashion. The Hebrew word *hata'* and Greek *hamartia* meant originally "to miss the mark, fail in duty" (Rom 3:23). As Lawgiver, God sets limits to man's freedom; another frequent term (Hebrew, *'abar*; Greek, *parabasis*) describes sin as "transgression," "overstepping set limits." Similar terms are *pesha'* (Hebrew), meaning "rebellion," "transgression"; *'asham* (Hebrew) denotes "trespassing God's kingly prerogative," "incurring guilt"; *paraptoma* (Greek) denotes "a false step out of the appointed way," "trespass on forbidden ground." "Iniquity" often translates *'aon* (Hebrew, meaning "perverseness," "wrongness"), for which the nearest NT equivalent is *anomia* (Greek, "lawlessness") or *paranomia* (Greek, "lawbreaking").

In the Old Testament Genesis traces sin to deliberate misuse of God-given freedom in disobedience of a single limiting prohibition. Ezekiel insists eloquently upon individual responsibility against traditional theories of corporate guilt (Ez 18). Following Jeremiah, he urges the need for a cleansed, renewed inner life if outward behavior is to be reformed; the divine law must become a motivating force within a person if sin is to be overcome (Jer 31:29-34; Ez 36:24-29).

Psalm 51 offers a keen analysis of the inner meaning of sin. By affirming "in sin did my mother conceive me," the psalmist confessed that his life had been sinful from the first. His whole personality needed "purging"; he was defiled. Ritual sacrifices offer no solution. Only a broken, contrite heart can prepare a sinner for God's cleansing. The only hope, the sole ground of appeal, lies in God's steadfast love and abundant mercy. In spite of its rigorous view of sin, the OT also contains gracious assurance of forgiveness (Ps 103:8-14 Is 1:18; 55:6-7).

In Jesus' Teachings Jesus' teachings on the subject of sin took up the gracious offer of divine forgiveness and renewal, not only proclaiming with authority, "Your sins are forgiven," but showing many acts of compassion and social recognition that he came to be the friend of sinners, calling them to repentance, restoring their hope and dignity (Mt 9:1-13; 11:19; Lk 15; 19:1-10).

Jesus said little about the origin of sin, except to trace it to the human heart and will (Mt 6:22-23; 7:17-19; 18:7; Mk 7:20-23), but he significantly redefined sin's scope. Where the law could assess only people's actions, Jesus showed that anger, contempt, lust, hardness of heart, and deceitfulness are also sinful. He also spoke of sins of neglect, good left undone, the barren tree, the unused talent, the priest ignoring the injured, and the love never shown (Mt 25:41-46).

He especially condemns sins against love—unbrotherliness, implacable hostility, selfishness, insensitivity

(Lk 12:16-21; 16:19-31). And he condemned self-righteousness and spiritual blindness (Mt 23:16-26; Mk 3:22-30). Jesus spoke of sin as sickness (Mk 2:17) and sometimes as folly (Lk 12:20). Nevertheless, Jesus declared that fallen humans can be cured with God's help (7:36-50).

In John's Writings John's Gospel assumes sinful humanity's need, the sacrifice of Christ the Lamb to bear away the sin of the world, and the offer of light and life in Christ. The new note is an emphasis on sin that refuses to accept the salvation provided in Christ, by the love of God for the world—the refusal to believe. It is for loving darkness, rejecting light, and refusing to accept Christ the Savior that humans are judged already (Jn 3:16-21).

Against Gnosticism's claim that for advanced Christians sin does not matter, 1 John affirms 15 reasons why sin cannot be tolerated in the Christian life and emphasizes again that sin is both ignorance of the truth and lack of love (1 Jn 3:3-10). Yet God forgives those who confess their sins, while Christ atones for their sins and intercedes for them (1:7-2:2).

In Paul's Writings Paul argued strongly, from observation and from Scripture, that all have sinned (Rom 1-3). To him, sin is a force, a power, a "law" ruling within people (Rom 5:21; 7:23; 8:2; 1 Cor 15:56), producing all kinds of evil behavior—the hardening of the conscience (Rom 7:21-24), alienation from God, and subjection to death (Rom 5:10; 6:23; Eph 2:1-5, 12; Col 1:21). Humans are helpless to reform themselves (Rom 7:24). Paul's explanation of this desperate, universal condition is variously interpreted. Some readers think that Romans 5:12-21 says that Adam's sin is the source of all sin; others, that it is the "similitude" (KJV) of all sin. In any event, Paul essentially said that "every man is his own Adam," which means that each person is fully responsible for his or her sinful condition, even if the sinful nature was inherited from Adam.

The solution to sin, for Paul, lies in the believer's death with Christ—death to sin, self, the world. Concurrently, the new life of the invasive, effusive Spirit transforms one's life from within, making each person a new creation by sanctifying the personality into the likeness of Christ (Rom 3:21-26; 5:6-9; 6; 8:1-4, 28-29; 2 Cor 5:14-21).

See also Flesh; Justification, Justified; Sanctification; Sin unto Death; Unpardonable Sin, The.

SIN* (Place) Hebrew name for an Egyptian city named Pelusium (Ez 30:15-16, KJV). *See* Pelusium.

SIN DESERT* *See* Sin, Wilderness of.

SIN*, Man of KJV rendering of an inferior textual variant in the Textus Receptus in 2 Thessalonians 2:3. The correct reading is "man of lawlessness," an expression used by Paul of the Antichrist. *See* Antichrist.

SIN*, Wilderness of Arid, sandy region in the southwestern part of the Sinai peninsula, described in the Bible as being "between Elim and Sinai" (Ex 16:1). It is mentioned only four times in the Bible (Ex 16:1; 17:1; Nm 33:11-12) in itineraries of the exodus from Egypt. The wilderness of Sin lies to the southeast of Elim, which generally is regarded as the Wadi Gharandel.

See also Sina, Sinai; Wilderness Wanderings.

SINA*, SINAI Name of the mountain where God met Moses and gave him the Ten Commandments and the rest of the law. The name applies not only to the mountain itself but to the desert around it (Lv 7:38), as well as the entire peninsula embraced by the two arms of the Red Sea

known as the Gulf of Suez and the Gulf of Aqaba (or Elath).

The name is probably related to Sin (wilderness of) and may even be an alternate spelling (cf. Ex 16:1; 17:1; Nm 33:11-12). Sin is one name of the ancient moon god that desert dwellers worshiped. The mountain is also called Horeb, mostly in Deuteronomy (see also 1 Kgs 8:9; 19:8; 2 Chr 5:10; Ps 106:19; Mal 4:4).

Saint Catherine's Monastery at the base of Mount Sinai

The traditional location of Mt Sinai is among the mountains at the southern end of the Sinai Peninsula. Since at least the fourth century, Christians have venerated Jebel Musa (Mt Moses in Arabic) as the site where God molded the families of Jacob into the nation of Israel. A Greek Orthodox monastery of St Catherine at the base of the 7,500-foot (2,286-meters) peak has been there for over 1,500 years. Other candidates for the holy mountain have been the nearby Jebel Katerina (8,670 feet, or 2,642.6 meters) and Jebel Serbal (6,800 feet, or 2,072.6 meters). Some scholars prefer a northern location near Kadesh-barnea, while others argue for a volcanic mountain across the gulf to the east in ancient Midian or Arabia (Ex 3:1; Gal 4:25).

Most references to Sinai are in Exodus (13 times), Leviticus (5 times), and Numbers (12 times) because these are the books that report the giving of the law and the two-year encampment of the Israelites on the plains adjacent to the mountain. Exodus 19 and 34 especially are replete with references because these are the chapters that describe the encounters between Moses and Yahweh on the two occasions when the law was actually given.

In both the OT and NT, Sinai came to represent the place where God came down to his people. In the blessing of Moses (Dt 33:2), the song of Deborah (Jgs 5:5), Psalm 68 (vv 8, 17), the confession of the Levites in the time of Nehemiah (Neh 9:13), and the speech of Stephen (Acts 7:30, 38), Sinai was remembered as the scene of that momentous encounter. Paul, in Galatians 4:21-26, spells out an allegory in which Mt Sinai represents the old covenant, slavery, and the present city of Jerusalem. *See* Paran; Shur; Sin, Wilderness of; Commandments, The Ten; Wilderness Wanderings; Zin, Wilderness of.

SINGER The professional singer was important in temple worship. David first organized singers for worship in the tabernacle (1 Chr 9:33; 15:16, 19, 27). Later, they ministered in Solomon's temple (2 Chr 5:12-13) and for other kings (20:21; 23:13; 35:15). After the exile, the singers were again active (Ezr 2:41, 70; Neh 7:1, 44, 73;

10:28, 39). They sang psalms for temple worship (Pss 68:25; 87:7). Some were appointed "chief singers" (Hb 3:19). The sons of Asaph were prominent among them.
See also Music.

SINITE Canaanite tribe, possibly located in northern Lebanon, whose ancestry is traced to Canaan, Ham's son (Gn 10:17; 1 Chr 1:15).

SINLESSNESS OF CHRIST* The Scripture (quoted here from the RSV) leaves no question that Christ is regarded as sinless. He is declared to be the perfect Son of God in every respect. His human nature is holy, without any sin. This is repeatedly and explicitly affirmed in unmistakable terms. Paul states that Christ "knew no sin" (2 Cor 5:21). Peter says "he committed no sin; no guile was found on his lips" (1 Pt 2:22); he calls him "righteous" (3:18). The writer to the Hebrews says that Christ is "holy, blameless, unstained, separated from sinners" (Heb 7:26). James speaks of him as "the righteous man" (Jas 5:6), and John affirms that "in him there is no sin" (1 Jn 3:5). In the Gospels and in the apostolic preaching, Jesus is repeatedly witnessed to as the Holy Son of God, the Holy One of God, the Holy and Righteous One (Lk 1:35; Jn 6:69; Acts 3:14).

Jesus was able to ask his enemies with penetrating conviction, "Which of you convicts me of sin?" (Jn 8:46). He gives ample evidence of a holy self-consciousness throughout his entire lifetime. Numerous references and inferences are made to his exemption from the unrighteousness of sin and disobedience. He kept the entire law in every detail and in each respect (Rom 10:4; Heb 4:15). Pilate's wife regarded Jesus as a righteous man, and Pilate himself spoke of him as an innocent man (Mt 27:19, 24). Even Judas realized that he himself had sinned by "betraying innocent blood" (Mt 27:4).

The issue of Christ's sinlessness is not confined merely to the fact that he did not commit any sin. There is a deeper theological significance to the question, which has to do with the issue of whether Christ was at all able to sin. Was it even possible for him to sin? This concern has been spoken of in theology as his impeccability (Christ was unable to sin), or on the contrary position, his peccability (Christ was able to sin, even though he did not exercise his will in this direction). The problems on both of these views appear immediately: If Christ was unable to sin, how could he really have been tempted (and we have ample data in Scripture concerning Jesus' temptations)? If Christ could have sinned, even though he did not do so, does this mean that God can sin (for Christ was in every respect fully the Son of God, the second person of the Trinity)? It is useless to say that Jesus could have sinned with respect to his human nature but not so with respect to his divine nature, because this ignores the indissoluble unity of the person of the God-man. We may not separate the human nature from the divine nature, as though in his humanity he could have acted independently of his divinity. This was, in part, the error of the ancient Nestorian heretics. Whatever the Son of God does, he does with and in his entire divine-human nature.

Essentially, there is no contradiction between being tempted and being unable to sin. Of course, it is difficult for us to imagine how this can be possible. This is because we are sinners and stand within the experiential knowledge of evil. Christ's person is absolutely unique; we can little imagine how real were his temptations by the devil in the wilderness and throughout his life (Lk 22:28, 39-46), even though it was impossible for him to actually sin.

Perhaps an illustration may be helpful. Let us imagine there is an absolutely impregnable fortress that cannot be taken by the enemy as long as the defenses are maintained. (If we may, for the purpose of illustration, let us rule out the terrible destructive forces of modern warfare.) Because the fortress is incapable of being taken by assault and is in reality unconquerable, as long as the defenses are kept up, it does not mean that it cannot be besieged and furiously attacked. So it may be with respect to the reality of Christ's temptations and his inability to sin as the Holy Son of God.

His temptations were real. Therefore, "we have not a high priest who is unable to sympathize with our weaknesses, but one who in every respect has been tempted as we are, yet without sin. Let us then with confidence draw near to the throne of grace, that we may receive mercy and find grace to help in time of need" (Heb 4:15-16, RSV).

SIN OFFERING *See* Offerings and Sacrifices.

SIN UNTO DEATH* Sin mentioned in 1 John 5:16; in this verse John discourages prayer for those who sin in this way. Most likely, John was speaking of those who decisively turn their backs upon the truth, as well as those false teachers who deceive the church (Heb 6:4-6; 2 Jn 1:7-9).
See also Blasphemy; Sin.

SION*
1. KJV designation for Mt Hermon in Deuteronomy 4:48. *See* Hermon, Mount.
2. KJV form of Zion in Psalm 65:1 and in the NT. *See* Zion.

SIPHMOTH Town in southern Judah to which David gave part of the spoils of his victory over the Amalekites because its residents had aided him in his flight from Saul (1 Sm 30:28).

SIPPAI* Alternate form of Saph, a descendant of the giants, in 1 Chronicles 20:4 (NLT mg). *See* Saph.

SIRAH Well or cistern where Joab's messengers intercepted Abner as he returned from pledging allegiance to David in Hebron (2 Sm 3:26). Its site is probably the same as the present 'Ain Sarah, located about one and a half miles (2.4 kilometers) northwest of Hebron.

SIRION Sidonian name for Mt Hermon (Dt 3:9; 4:48; Ps 29:6; Jer 18:14). *See* Hermon, Mount.

SISAMAI* KJV form of Sismai. *See* Sismai.

SISERA
1. Commander of the army of Jabin, king of Canaan. Sisera resided in Harosheth-haggoyim, from where he attacked northern Israel for 20 years. His army, strengthened by 900 iron chariots, was routed at the swollen river of Kishon near Megiddo under the leadership of Barak and Deborah. Having fled the battlefield, Sisera was killed by the hand of Jael, the wife of Heber the Kenite, in the hill country overlooking the Jordan Valley (Jgs 4; 1 Sm 12:9). The events of this battle were remembered in the Song of Deborah (Jgs 5:19-30) and Psalm 83:9.
See also Judges, Book of.
2. Forefather of a family of temple servants who returned with Zerubbabel to Palestine following the Babylonian captivity (Ezr 2:53; Neh 7:55).

SISMAI Eleasah's son and the father of Shallum; a Judahite from the house of Hezron and Jerahmeel's line (1 Chr 2:40).

SISTER *See* Family Life and Relations.

SISTRUM* Ancient percussion instrument consisting of a thin metal frame with numerous metal rods or loops that jingled when shaken, translated as "castanets" (NLT) in 2 Samuel 6:5. *See* Musical Instruments (Mena anim; Shalishim).

SITHRI Kohathite Levite and Uzziel's third son. Sithri was the cousin of Aaron and Moses (Ex 6:22).

SITNAH* Well dug by Isaac's servants in the region of Gerar, receiving its name (meaning "enmity") from a dispute between Isaac's servants and the herdsmen of the region. Its location was possibly near Rehoboth (Gn 26:21-22; see NLT mg).

SIVAN* Name of a Hebrew month, perhaps of Babylonian origin (Est 8:9, NLT mg). *See* Calendars, Ancient and Modern.

SIX HUNDRED SIXTY-SIX Number of the beast of the earth envisioned in the book of Revelation (Rv 13:18). *See* Antichrist; Mark of God, Mark of the Beast.

SKULL HILL *See* Skull, Place of the.

SKULL, Place of the Place in Jerusalem where Jesus was crucified (Mt 27:33; Mk 15:22; Jn 19:17). Golgotha is the Greek transliteration of the Aramaic word for "skull." *See* Golgotha.

SLANDER The utterance of false charges or accusations that defame another person's reputation; when directed toward God, such accusations are considered blasphemy. *See* Blasphemy.

SLAVE, SLAVERY Person owned as property by another, and the relationship that bound the owner and the slave. Slavery was widespread in the ancient Near East, although the economy was not dependent upon it. By Roman times, slavery was so extensive that in the early Christian period one out of every two people was a slave. From at least 3000 BC, captives in war were the primary source of slaves (Gn 14:21; Nm 31:9; Dt 20:14; Jgs 5:30; 1 Sm 4:9; 2 Kgs 5:2; 2 Chr 28:8).

Slaves could be purchased locally from other owners or from foreign traveling merchants who sold slaves along with cloth, bronzeware, and other goods (Jl 3:4-8). Joseph was sold by Midianites and Ishmaelites to an Egyptian (Gn 37:36; 39:1) in this manner. Debt was the basic cause for many families being reduced to slavery; an entire family could be subject to slavery (2 Kgs 4:1; Neh 5:5-8). The law code of Hammurabi stipulated a maximum of three years of slavery for the family (Section 117), as opposed to a maximum of six years under Hebrew law (Dt 15:18). Voluntary slavery was widespread as a means of escape from abject poverty and starvation (Lv 25:47-48). Selling a kidnapped person into slavery, the crime of Joseph's brothers (Gn 37:27-28), was a capital offense under the law code of Hammurabi (Section 14) and the Mosaic law (Ex 21:11; Dt 24:7).

In Sumerian society, slaves had legal rights, could borrow money, and could engage in business. As the normal price for a slave was probably less than that for a strong donkey, the slave always had the hope that he could save sufficient money to purchase his freedom. Slaves performed tedious labor on farms and in households, though some gifted individuals occupied executive positions in households. Despite provisions in ancient law, the release of slaves was not always honored on schedule. A Hebrew who voluntarily entered slavery was normally released the next jubilee year, and theoretically no Hebrew could be enslaved for life (Ex 21:2; Lv 25:10-13; Dt 15:12-14).

The Israelites made a deliberate attempt to safeguard the slave from brutality by a master or overseer. By law, a maimed slave had to be released (Ex 21:26-27). The few Hebrew slaves in a household frequently toiled alongside their masters in the fields, and they and household slaves often had a reasonable and secure existence, compared with the threat of starvation and destitution of the poorest free men.

In Greek and especially in Roman times, when the number of slaves increased dramatically, household slaves remained the best treated. Many became servants and confidants; some even established good businesses to their own and their masters' benefit.

Information from Ur, Nuzi, and the book of Genesis shows that where a wife was childless, the female slave could bear the master's child (Gn 16:2-4). Legally a Hebrew master could agree to marry a young female slave, have his own son marry her, or establish her as a concubine. If subsequently she was discarded, or if the agreement was not fulfilled, she would be released from her slavery (Ex 21:7-11). Conquered people were required to perform forced labor for the state (2 Sm 12:31; 1 Kgs 9:15, 21-23), including the Israelites themselves in Lebanon (1 Kgs 5:13-18). Captured in war, the Midianites (Nm 31:28-30, 47) and Gibeonites (Jos 9:23-25) were made slaves to serve the temple. The practice continued through the reigns of David and Solomon (Ezr 2:58; 8:20). Nehemiah records that foreign slaves helped make repairs on the walls of Jerusalem (Neh 3:26, 31).

The NT attitude toward slavery indicates that the status of a slave was more like that of a servant and that the institution of slavery generally was declining. There was no strong opposition to slavery from Jesus or the apostles, but an admonition that slaves and servants should serve their masters faithfully and that masters should treat their slaves humanely and fairly (Eph 6:9; Col 4:1; 1 Tm 6:2; Phlm 1:16). Paul never

SLAVE: A NAME ADOPTED BY CHRISTIAN SERVANTS
Five NT authors called themselves "a slave [or servant] of Jesus Christ": Paul (Rom 1:1; Gal 1:10; Phil 1:1; Col 4:12; 2 Tm 2:24; Ti 1:1), James (Jas 1:1), Peter (2 Pt 1:1), Jude (Jude 1:1), and John (Rv 1:1). In many cases, the term is a synonym for "Christian." Why would such a term become a name for Christians? In the OT, God was viewed as a great king; the subjects of kings were their slaves. The people of Israel saw themselves in the same relationship to God: they were his slaves.

Often the title "slave of the king" meant that the person was an officer in the king's service; it was a title of honor. In Jewish literature Moses and others were called slaves of God (Nm 12:7-8; Rv 15:3). The term "slave" was thus a title both of honor and of subjugation; in the NT it is hard to know which sense is intended. Certainly subjection was often meant (1 Cor 7:22; Phil 2:7), but when applied to the apostolic writers, the term probably suggested their honored position in God's household. At the same time, it indicated their obedience to Christ; he commanded and they obeyed. Since obedience was characteristic of all Christians, "slave of Christ" became a title for members of the young church.

preached against slavery, but he personally tried to attain freedom for the slave Onesimus from his Christian master, Philemon (see the discussion on this in Philemon, Letter to).

See also Bond, Bondage; Liberty.

SLEEP Sleep is spoken of in three ways in the Bible: (a) to speak of natural sleep, (b) to refer to moral or spiritual inactivity, and (c) to refer to death.

Natural Sleep The sleep that the human body needs is seen as a precious gift of God (Pss 4:8; 127:2). Sleep may be withheld, as God chooses and to serve his purposes (Est 6:1; Dn 6:18). God may also, to fulfill his purposes, give people deep sleep (Gn 2:21; 15:12; 1 Sm 26:12), and during a person's sleep, God may make his will known by a dream or vision (e.g., Gn 28:11-16; Jb 4:13-17; Mt 1:20-24).

Several statements in the book of Proverbs rebuke the lack of discipline of life shown in the undue love of sleep. For example, one proverb says, "If you love sleep, you will end in poverty. Keep your eyes open, and there will be plenty to eat!" (Prv 20:13, NLT; see also 6:9-11; 10:5; 24:32-34).

Moral or Spiritual Inactivity In a figurative way, sleep is used as a symbol of laziness, carelessness, or inactivity. Isaiah 56:10 speaks of those who failed in their responsibility as leaders of God's people: "They love to lie there, love to sleep, to dream" (TLB). In the NT those who are the Lord's servants are called to watch and to be sure that when their Master comes he will not find them sleeping (Mk 13:35-37; see also Mt 25:1-13; 26:40-46). Likewise, the challenge to maintain spiritual alertness and to refrain from sleep comes in a number of places in the epistles: "Awake, O sleeper, and arise from the dead, and Christ shall give you light" (Eph 5:14, RSV); "So be on your guard, not asleep like the others. Watch for his return and stay sober" (1 Thes 5:6, TLB).

Death Very frequently, the Bible speaks of death as sleep. Commonly in the OT, when a person dies, he is said to go to sleep with his fathers (e.g., Dt 31:16; 2 Sm 7:12). Jesus spoke of death as sleep (Mt 9:24; Jn 11:11). So did the apostle Paul (1 Cor 11:30; 15:20, 51; 1 Thes 4:13-14). In some of these references, it would seem that it is the temporary nature of death that is the reason why it is spoken of as sleep. Even in Daniel 12:2 it is said that death is a sleep, until the dead "rise up, some to everlasting life and some to shame and everlasting contempt" (TLB). This is made more specific in many passages in the NT. When, however, we consider the full teaching of the Bible on the meaning of death for the Christian, we need to give full weight to such passages as Luke 23:43, 2 Corinthians 5:8, and Philippians 1:23, and especially 1 Thessalonians 5:13-14. In the first of these Jesus says to the dying thief on the cross, "Today you will be with me in paradise," and in the second Paul speaks of death for him as going to "be with Christ."

SLIME* KJV rendering of "asphalt" or "bitumen" in Genesis 11:3 and Exodus 2:3. *See* Asphalt; Bitumen.

SLIMEPITS* KJV rendering of asphalt pits or bitumen pits found in the valley of Siddim (Gn 14:10). *See* Siddim Valley.

SLING, SLINGER Weapon of war used to fire stones or lead pellets, and the thrower. *See* Armor and Weapons.

SMITH Worker in metals; a blacksmith. The earliest metalworker mentioned in the Bible is Tubal-cain (Gn 4:22). The term covers metalworkers of all kinds: copper, bronze, iron, silver, and gold. Silversmiths are mentioned in Judges 17:4 and Acts 19:24. Ironsmiths were rare or even nonexistent in Israel up to the time of Samuel, and the Israelites had to go to the Philistine smiths to have their iron tools sharpened (1 Sm 13:19). In the days of the kings, Israelite smiths were active and were subsequently taken into captivity by Nebuchadnezzar (2 Kgs 24:14-16; Jer 24:1; 29:2). Details of the work of the smith are given in several accounts (Prv 25:4; Is 44:12; 54:16). The smiths mentioned in Zechariah 1:20 are probably ironsmiths or blacksmiths.

See also Minerals and Metals; Stones, Precious.

SMYRNA Location of one of the seven churches mentioned in the book of Revelation (Rv 1:11; 2:8-11). It is the modern Izmir, located in Turkey.

Smyrna was inhabited at least 3,000 years before Christ. The Aeolian Greeks were replaced by the Ionians. The city, along with Miletus and Ephesus to the south, flourished under Ionian dominance. The city was conquered by the Lydians, whose capital was Sardis. The site was left in ruins for nearly three centuries until its refounding by Alexander the Great in 334 BC at a site farther south along the gulf. Although built by the energy of the Seleucids, the city recognized the coming dominance of Pergamum and entered into an alliance with its king. Later, with remarkable foresight, she transferred her allegiance to Rome, and in 195 BC built a temple in which Rome was worshiped as a deity. As a reward for Smyrna's early commitment to the rising Roman influence, the city prospered under Roman rule, partly as a rival to Pergamum and partly as a rival to the prosperous island of Rhodes. Because they had been an ally of the Romans, the people of Smyrna thought it would be to their credit to build (in AD 26) a temple in which the Roman emperor would be honored. This city became the seat of the Caesar cult that afflicted the church so seriously during the latter half of the first century.

Revelation 2:8 speaks of the city as being "dead and then alive," a possible allusion to the period of 300 years when it lay devastated until revived by Alexander and the Macedonians. Ancient writers, including Appollonius and Aristides, spoke of Smyrna as having the "crown of life." This was a way of describing the hilltop behind the city as if it crowned Smyrna on top, with its feet at the seashore. The promise of "the crown of life" to the Smyrnean believers probably plays off this image. This promise was given to those believers in Smyrna who would remain faithful through persecution. The reference to the "synagogue of Satan" (Rv 2:9) and to the devil putting them in prison (v 10) reflects the tribulation probably experienced under the Roman emperor Domitian (c. AD 95). It became a crime punishable by death to refuse to worship the image of the Roman emperor as "lord." Many Christians were compelled to choose between "Caesar as Lord" or "Jesus as Lord." To choose Jesus was to choose martyrdom.

See also Revelation, Book of.

SNAIL *See* Animals.

SNAKE *See* Animals (Adder; Asp; Serpent).

SNARE Literally, a trap used for entangling birds or others mammals; figuratively, anything that entangles or impedes another person. The word is often used in the Scriptures in the figurative sense to describe anything that ensnares people in sin (see Dt 7:25; Eccl 7:26).

SO A king of Egypt, mentioned once in Scripture (2 Kgs 17:4), with whom Hoshea, king of Israel, sought an alliance. This rebellious move, in part, prompted

Shalmaneser V of Assyria to imprison Hoshea (2 Kgs 17:3-5). It is difficult to identify So with any of the rulers of Egypt who are named in extrabiblical sources.

SOAP Cleansing agent extracted from a number of alkali-bearing plants. The alkali was gathered from the ashes of the burned plants and formed into a detergent. Saltwort, soapwort, and glasswort were alkali-bearing plants indigenous to western Asia and known to the ancient Hebrews. Soap was used primarily for cleansing purposes. In Jeremiah 2:22 soap is used to clean the body, and in Malachi 3:2, to wash clothes.

SOCHO* KJV form of Soco, Heber's descendant, in 1 Chronicles 4:18. See Soco (Person).

SOCHOH* KJV form of Socoh, a town in Sharon, in 1 Kings 4:10. See Soco (Place), Socoh #3.

SOCO (Person) Son of Heber, listed in the genealogy of Caleb (1 Chr 4:18). Since the Calebites were located in the southern hill country of Judah, Soco may be identified with the city in Joshua 15:48. See Soco (Place), Socoh #2.

SOCO (Place), SOCOH

1. One of 14 cities located in the Shephelah, in the territory allotted to Judah's tribe; it is listed between Adullam and Azekah (Jos 15:35). Jerome, in his Latin translation of Eusebius's *Onomasticon* (157:18–20), states that there were two settlements, one on the mountain and another on the plain. The description fits exactly the situation at Khirbet esh-Shuweikeh, a Roman-Byzantine site on the southern edge of the vale of Elah; just beside it to the east is a lofty mound with heavy fortifications from the Israelite period, called Khirbet 'Abbad. Socoh guarded the junction between two wadis that join to form the vale of Elah, a passageway to the central hill country, to Bethlehem or Hebron, respectively. This situation provides the background for 1 Samuel 17:1, when David killed Goliath during Saul's reign over Israel; the Philistines lined up their troops beside Socoh and extended toward Azekah. The Israelites were on the opposite ridge with the creekbed of the vale of Elah in between.

   Rehoboam included Socoh in his network of fortifications designed to place forces on the main lines of communication throughout his kingdom (2 Chr 11:7). The town apparently remained in Judah's hands from the tenth to the eighth century BC, at which time the Philistines, moving against King Ahaz, took it and several other key towns on the approach routes (2 Chr 28:18).
2. Town in the southernmost district of the Judean hill region (Jos 15:48). The reference to Soco in 1 Chronicles 4:18 in the genealogy of the sons of Caleb may refer to this same place. It is identifiable with another Khirbet Shuweikeh located about 10 miles (16 kilometers) southwest of Hebron.
3. Town in the Sharon Plain listed only once in the Bible (1 Kgs 4:10) but well known from nonbiblical sources. It appears three times in Egyptian records. First, in the topographical list of Thutmose III (no. 67), it comes after Aphek and before Yaham. The former is at Ras el 'Ain (Rosh Ha'Ayin) by the springs of the Yarkon River; the latter must be located at Khirbet Yamma on the eastern edge of the Sharon Plain. Next, Socoh is mentioned in similar geographical context in the Annals of Amenhotep II. Thus, it was a key town on the highway passing along the western edge of the

mountains of Samaria in the 15th century BC. Third, it comes in an identical position in the topographical list of Pharaoh Shishak (no. 38) from the late 10th century BC.

The town conquered by Shishak was that mentioned in 1 Kings 4:10 as being in Solomon's third administrative district, which was governed by Ben-hesed and comprised "the land of Hepher" and other subdistricts in the Sharon Plain.

All of these texts point to this Socoh as the ancient name of present-day Khirbet Shuweikeh er-Ras, just to the north of Tul-Karem. Between Aphek and Socoh there were no good water sources along the road, so these two towns mark the principal way stations in the southern Sharon Plain.

SODI Father of Gaddiel, one of the 12 spies sent by Moses to search out the land of Canaan (Nm 13:10).

SODOM*, Sea of Alternate name for the Dead Sea. See Dead Sea.

SODOM*, Vine of See Plants (Gourd, Wild).

SODOM AND GOMORRAH Two of the "cities of the plain [valley]" referred to in Genesis 13:12. There were five cities—Sodom, Gomorrah, Admah, Zeboiim, and Bela or Zoar (Gn 14:2)—all situated in the valley of Siddim (i.e., the Salt Sea). Of these, Sodom is mentioned most frequently in Genesis—36 times in all, of which 16 references are to Sodom alone. Sodom became known in biblical literature as the supreme example of a wicked city, and its destruction (19:24) was used as a warning of God's judgment in other biblical writings (Dt 29:23; Is 1:9-10; Jer 23:14; 49:18; Lam 4:6; Am 4:11; Zep 2:9). The story of Sodom's destruction found its place also in the NT (Mt 10:15; Lk 10:12; 17:29; Rom 9:29; 2 Pt 2:6; Jude 1:7; Rv 11:8).

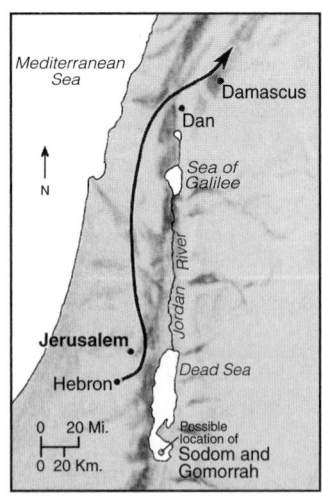

Possible Location of Sodom and Gomorrah This map shows one possible location for Sodom and Gomorrah. It also shows the route Abram took when chasing Kedorlaomer, who had conquered Sodom and taken many captives, among them Abram's nephew Lot (Gn 14:14-16).

The primary story of Sodom and Gomorrah occurs in Genesis 18 and 19, although the biblical interest in the city begins in chapter 13 with the decision of Lot, Abraham's nephew, to settle in the Jordan Valley, in the vicinity of Sodom, among people who were notorious sinners. It becomes clear that one of Sodom's most grievous sins was sexual perversion, especially homosexuality. Lot's offer of his virgin daughters to the men of Sodom to turn their attention away from his heavenly visitors is an indication of the demoralizing influence of the city.

Four rulers from the East descended on the region of Sodom and Gomorrah sometime after Lot settled there and subdued the area. They returned 14 years later to quell a rebellion (Gn 14:1-5). Among their captives was Lot, who was (subsequently) rescued by Abraham. The evil of Sodom and Gomorrah was so great that the Lord determined to destroy them. Abraham pleaded for mercy for them if ten righteous men could be found (18:20-33). The two heavenly visitors who went from Abraham to Sodom found Lot sitting in the gate of Sodom (19:1), revealed God's intentions to him, and persuaded Lot and his wife and two daughters to flee the city. Then the Lord rained brimstone and fire on Sodom and Gomorrah. The next morning Abraham saw the smoke from the destroyed cities rising like the smoke of a furnace.

See also Cities of the Plain.

SOJOURNER* *See* Foreigner.

SOLDIER The individual member in every army, whether part of the infantry, cavalry, or group engaged in siege warfare. *See* Warfare.

SOLOMON (Person) Third king over Israel, the second son of David and Bathsheba, who reigned 40 years (970–930 BC). His alternative name was Jedidiah, "beloved of the Lord."

Appointed to the Throne Once Amnon and Absalom were no longer in competition for the throne, the two most likely remaining candidates were Solomon and Adonijah, although the kingship had been assured to the former (1 Chr 22:9-10). Near the end of David's life, Adonijah contested the choice of Solomon and took steps to become king. With the help of Joab, general of the army, and Abiathar the priest, he was proclaimed the monarch. Solomon was not invited and neither were Nathan the prophet or Benaiah. Nathan brought word of this plot to Bathsheba, who in turn quizzed David as to his intentions. David then ordered Solomon to be proclaimed king over Israel; he was anointed by Zadok amidst the blowing of the trumpets and the shout of the people: "Long live King Solomon" (1 Kgs 1:34). Adonijah realized his claim had collapsed and asked for mercy, promising to be faithful to the new king.

Solomon moved swiftly to establish his hold on the government (1 Kgs 1–2). When Adonijah asked to marry Abishag, David's companion in his old age (1:1-4), Solomon refused and ordered his death because of possible claims to the throne (2:22-25). In addition, because Abiathar had joined with Adonijah, he was removed from his service as priest and sent back to Anathoth. Joab fled to the altar and there took hold of its horns and refused to let go. The king ordered his death at the hand of Benaiah, who then became commander-in-chief of the armies. Another contender, Shimei, of the house of Saul, was also executed.

One of Solomon's earliest recorded acts as king was to go to the high place at Gibeon and sacrifice 1,000 burnt offerings. On the following night, the Lord appeared to the king in a dream, asking as to his fondest wish. Solomon asked for wisdom to judge Israel, and God was pleased with the request (1 Kgs 3). Israel's king was given his wish, along with the gifts of long life, riches, and fame.

Solomon's Accomplishments

His Government David's efforts had brought about a union of the 12 tribes, but Solomon established an organized state with many officials to help him (1 Kgs 4). The entire country was divided into 12 major districts; each district was to ensure the provisions of the king's court for one month each year. The system was equitable and designed to distribute the tax burden over the entire country.

His Buildings One of Solomon's earliest building attempts was to construct the temple. David had wanted to build the temple, but this task was left to Solomon, the man of peace. Hiram, king of Tyre, provided cedar trees from Mt Lebanon for the temple (1 Kgs 5:1-12), and in return he was given an appropriate amount of food. In order to provide the necessary labor for these building projects, the Canaanites became slaves (9:20-21). Israelites likewise were compelled to work in groups of 10,000, every third month (5:13-18; 2 Chr 2:17-18). The workers for the temple alone comprised 80,000 stonecutters, 70,000 common laborers, and 3,600 foremen.

It took seven years to finish the temple, which by modern standards was a rather small building: 90 feet (27.4 meters) long, 30 feet (9.1 meters) wide, and 45 feet (13.7 meters) high. Nevertheless, the gold covering for both walls and furniture made it quite expensive.

In the 11th year of Solomon's reign, the dedication of the temple was celebrated in a great convocation (1 Kgs 6:38; 8:1-5). The presence of the Lord filled the temple, and Solomon then offered his great dedicatory prayer (8:23-53), marking it as one of the great peaks of his devotion to the Lord. Afterward, he offered up 22,000 oxen and 120,000 sheep as well as other offerings. The people were full of joy because David had so great a successor.

Solomon built other buildings: the House of the Forest of Lebanon, the Hall of Pillars, a hall for his throne, and a house for the daughter of Pharaoh (1 Kgs 7:2-8). Thirteen years were involved in the building of his own house, large enough to take care of his wives and concubines as well as the servants. A great fortress was also built, Millo, which was used to protect the temple (9:24), as well as other store and fortified cities.

His Trade with Other Nations The king had an agreement with Hiram, king of Tyre, to pay yearly for cedar trees, stonecutters, and other buildings; for 125,000 bushels (4.4 million liters) of wheat; and for 115,000 gallons (435,275 liters) of olive oil (1 Kgs 5:11). In addition, Hiram received 20 cities in Galilee to cover all indebtedness. Contrary to the instruction not to trade in horses (Dt 17:16), Solomon bought horses and chariots from the Egyptians, and some of these in turn were sold to the Hittites and Arameans at a profit (1 Kgs 10:28-29).

Furthermore, Solomon engaged in sea trade. Ships built at shipyards at Ezion-geber sailed to ports on the Red Sea and Indian Ocean. The mariners collected gold, ivory, and peacocks. From Ophir, the traders brought back 420 talents of gold, a considerable fortune.

His Wisdom Solomon wrote 3,000 proverbs and 1,005 songs (1 Kgs 4:32). Most of the book of Proverbs is attributed to him (Prv 25:1), as well as Ecclesiastes, Song of Solomon, and Psalms 72 and 127. His obituary notice mentions his literary accomplishments in the book of the acts of Solomon (1 Kgs 11:41).

The queen of Sheba came to see and hear if the reports of Solomon's fame and wisdom were correct. After viewing all he had in Jerusalem and hearing his wisdom, her final response was to bless the Lord God of Israel, who raised up such a wise person to sit upon such a magnificent throne (1 Kgs 10).

His Fall Solomon made many misjudgments during his reign, and one of them was his excessive taxation of the people. His worst blunder was adding more and more wives to his harem, accommodating their religious preferences with pagan shrines (1 Kgs 11:1-8). The Lord plagued Solomon, permitting Israel to be attacked on all sides. Although the kingdom was not damaged during Solomon's day, his son experienced its division. There is no record that Solomon repented, but it is quite possible that the book of Ecclesiastes does reveal his realization of his wrong decisions.

See also Chronology of the Bible (Old Testament); Ecclesiastes, Book of; Israel, History of; King, Kingship; Proverbs, Book of; Song of Solomon; Wisdom; Wisdom Literature.

SOLOMON*, Pools of Water-storage pools, whose construction has been attributed to Solomon. Solomon made pools for watering his vineyards, gardens, parks, and orchards (Eccl 2:4-6), but their location is uncertain.

The so-called pools of Solomon are situated in the valley of Etham, about ten miles (16.1 kilometers) south of Jerusalem and a little south of Bethlehem. The three reservoirs, which are somewhat rectangular in shape, are placed at different levels. They vary in size, with the highest the smallest and the lowest the largest. The lower pool is 582 feet (177.4 meters) long, 148 to 207 feet (45.1 to 63.1 meters) wide, and 50 feet (15.2 meters) deep. The small pool is also the most shallow, having a depth of only 15 feet (4.6 meters).

The pools are partly rock-cut and in part built of masonry; they are connected by conduits, and the lower end of the biggest pool serves as a dam. The water is supplied by springs and run-off rainwater. The estimated capacity of all three pools is about 40 million gallons (151.4 million liters).

See also Aqueduct.

SOLOMON*, Song of *See* Song of Solomon.

SOLOMON'S PORCH* Part of the outer court of Herod's temple (Jn 10:23; Acts 3:11; 5:12).
See also Temple.

SON *See* Family Life and Relations; Genealogy; Son of God.

SONG *See* Music; Musical Instruments.

SONG OF ASCENTS, SONG OF DEGREES* Title given to each of the Psalms from 120 to 134. Perhaps these psalms were sung by pilgrims journeying up to Jerusalem for the major feasts. *See* Music; Musical Instruments; Psalms, Book of.

SONG OF SOLOMON* Short OT book (eight chapters) containing only poetry. Its beautiful poetic passages describe the many dimensions of human love; there is little in this book that is explicitly religious. In addition to the popular title, the book is sometimes referred to as the "Song of Songs." This is the most literal translation of the short title of the book in the original language and means "the best of all possible songs." Some writers also entitle the book "Canticles"; this title is based on the name of the Latin version of the book, *Canticum Canticorum.*

PREVIEW
• Author
• Date
• Various Interpretations
• Purpose and Theological Teaching
• Content

Author There was an old tradition among the Jews that King Solomon (c. 970–930 BC) wrote the Song of Songs. This view is based on one of several possible translations of the first verse of the Song: "Solomon's song of songs" (1:1, NLT). This view could be correct, though there cannot be absolute certainty, for the last words of the verse in the original language could be translated in various ways. An English translation that preserves the ambiguity of the original would be "The song of songs, which is Solomon's" (KJV); the last words could mean that Solomon was author, but equally they could indicate that the song was "dedicated to Solomon" or "written for Solomon." As is often the case with the OT writings, authorship cannot be known with absolute certainty.

Date It follows that if the authorship is uncertain, there must also be uncertainty concerning the date at which the song was written. If Solomon was the author, it was written during the latter half of the tenth century BC. If he was not the author, then the song was probably written at a later date. But the contents indicate that the song must have been written and completed at some point during the Hebrew monarchy (before 586 BC). For those who do not accept Solomon as author, the precise date will depend to some extent upon the theory that is adopted concerning the interpretation of the song. If the song is an anthology of Israelite love poetry, then the many poems making up the song would have been written at different dates and gathered together into a single volume toward the end of the Hebrew monarchy.

Various Interpretations There are two major difficulties in interpreting this book. First, the song appears to be secular in its present form and God's name does not appear; the only exception to this statement is in 8:6, where some English versions translate the text to show God's name, though the original text uses the name in an unusual (adjectival) sense. The second problem is that, taken at face value, the song contains only secular poetry of human love. What is the theological significance of love poetry? These and other difficulties have led to a multitude of different interpretations of the song. A brief survey of some of the most significant interpretations will clarify not only the problem of understanding the book but also its content and meaning.

The Song as an Allegory One of the oldest interpretations of the song sees it as an allegory. This view was held by both Jewish and Christian scholars from an early date. The description of human love in the song is seen as an allegory of the love between Christ and the church. Augustine of Hippo (AD 354–430) believed that the marriage referred to in the song was an allegory of the marriage between Christ and the church.

This theory was valued for a long time. It influenced the translators of the KJV. They added chapter headings to their translations as an aid to readers in understanding the Bible. For example, at the beginning of the first chapter of the Song of Solomon, they wrote, "1. The Church's love unto Christ, 5. She confesseth her deformity, 7. and prayeth to be directed to his flock." It is important to stress, however, that the Hebrew text does not mention Christ or the church. The headings represent the understanding of the translators, not the content of the original Hebrew.

The Song as a Drama The view that the song is a drama is also an old one. Those who hold this theory begin by noting that there are several speakers or actors. Perhaps, then, the song is the script of an ancient dramatic play.

This theory has some strong points. In the manuscript of an ancient Greek translation of the OT, headings have been added to the Song of Solomon that identify the speakers. The cast includes bride, bridegroom, and companions. However, the headings were probably not a part of the original Hebrew text. They reflect the interpretation of the early Greek translators.

There is one major difficulty with this theory: there is no clear evidence that drama was a form of art used by the Hebrews. Although drama was common among the Greeks, it does not appear to have been employed in the Near East. It is possible, however, to suggest a slight variation to the drama theory. Perhaps the Song of Solomon is not a drama but simply dramatic poetry, similar to the book of Job. This possibility is more plausible, but it too has difficulties. A story or plot would be expected for either drama or dramatic poetry, but it is not clear that there is a story.

According to one interpretation, the story might go as follows. The song tells the story of true love. A maiden was in love with a shepherd lad. King Solomon, however, fell in love with the maiden and took her to his palace. There he tried to win her love with beautiful words but failed. She remained faithful to the shepherd lad whom she loved. Failing to win her, Solomon released her and allowed her to return to her true lover. The story is beautiful and simple, but it is not easy to see in the text without added headings and explanations. Other interpreters have discerned a quite different story in the Song of Solomon. In conclusion, it is not absolutely clear that there is a single story being told.

The Song as Reflecting a Fertility Cult Some modern scholars claim that the origin of the Song of Solomon is to be found in the fertility cults of the ancient Near East. In ancient fertility cults there was great emphasis on the fertility of the land, which would be seen in bountiful harvests. The cults were designed to ensure that the land remained fertile. They were accompanied by a mythology describing the gods responsible for fertility. This mythology included love poetry about the gods, and the poetry has some similarity to the Song of Solomon.

The theory might go like this: Originally the Hebrews also had a fertility cult. The Song of Solomon contains the love poetry associated with that cult. Later, the mythological references were omitted, so that the present song looks like secular love poetry.

The main difficulty with this theory is the lack of any firm evidence. There is no reference to God or any other gods in the Song of Solomon. There is no reference to a fertility cult or any other kind of cult. If the theory has some validity to it, the evidence no longer exists.

The Song as a Collection of Poems This last, most probable theory of interpretation involves two basic principles. First, the song is to be interpreted literally; it is what it seems to be—poetry celebrating human love. Second, the Song of Solomon is a collection, not a single piece of poetry. Just as the book of Psalms contains songs, hymns, and prayers from many different periods of Israel's history, so too the Song of Solomon contains poetry from different periods and different authors. The common theme joining all the passages together is human love. Opinions differ concerning where one song ends and the next begins. There may be as many as 29 songs in the book, some consisting of only one verse and others much longer.

Purpose and Theological Teaching If the Song of Solomon is primarily an anthology of the poetry of human love, what is its significance as a biblical book? What are its theological implications? First, the presence of the song in the Bible provides a valuable insight

THE SONG OF SONGS, CHAPTER 4 (NIV)

Lover
How beautiful you are, my darling!
  Oh, how beautiful!
  Your eyes behind your veil are doves.
Your hair is like a flock of goats
  descending from Mount Gilead.
[2]Your teeth are like a flock of sheep just shorn,
  coming up from the washing.
Each has its twin;
  not one of them is alone.
[3]Your lips are like a scarlet ribbon;
  your mouth is lovely.
Your temples behind your veil
  are like the halves of a pomegranate.
[4]Your neck is like the tower of David,
  built with elegance;
on it hang a thousand shields,
  all of them shields of warriors.
[5]Your two breasts are like two fawns,
  like twin fawns of a gazelle
  that browse among the lilies.
[6]Until the day breaks
  and the shadows flee,
I will go to the mountain of myrrh
  and to the hill of incense.
[7]All beautiful you are, my darling;
  there is no flaw in you.

[8]Come with me from Lebanon, my bride,
  come with me from Lebanon.
Descend from the crest of Amana,
  from the top of Senir, the summit of Hermon,
from the lions' dens
  and the mountain haunts of the leopards.
[9]You have stolen my heart, my sister, my bride;
  you have stolen my heart
with one glance of your eyes,
  with one jewel of your necklace.
[10]How delightful is your love, my sister, my bride!
  How much more pleasing is your love than wine,
  and the fragrance of your perfume than any spice!
[11]Your lips drop sweetness as the honeycomb, my bride;
  milk and honey are under your tongue.
  The fragrance of your garments is like that of Lebanon.
[12]You are a garden locked up, my sister, my bride;
  you are a spring enclosed, a sealed fountain.
[13]Your plants are an orchard of pomegranates
  with choice fruits,
  with henna and nard,
  [14]nard and saffron,
  calamus and cinnamon,
  with every kind of incense tree,
  with myrrh and aloes
  and all the finest spices.
[15]You are a garden fountain,
  a well of flowing water
  streaming down from Lebanon.

Beloved
[16]Awake, north wind,
  and come, south wind!
Blow on my garden,
  that its fragrance may spread abroad.
Let my lover come into his garden
  and taste its choice fruits.

concerning human love. The love between a man and a woman is a noble and beautiful thing; it is a gift of God. It is characterized by a certain mystery and cannot be bought. But because human love is a beautiful and noble thing, it can easily be debased. In the modern world, the Song of Solomon provides a proper perspective and a balanced view of human love. Further, a high value of human love is essential. Since human love and marriage are employed in the Bible as an analogy of God's love for humanity, love in itself must be good and pure.

Content

The Woman Sings Her Love Song (1:2-7) In each of the songs, the reader is like an eavesdropper listening to the words of love spoken, sometimes privately and sometimes to the beloved one. The opening song is a song of praise, rejoicing in love and delighting in a particular loved one: "Let him kiss me with the kisses of his mouth—for your love is more delightful than wine" (v 2, NIV). This song, as many others, is characterized by a country setting, here highlighted by a contrast with the city. The young woman is from the country and tanned from working in the open air; it makes her self-conscious among the city women of Jerusalem. But love overpowers self-consciousness, and it is in the country that she will meet her lover.

The King Converses with the Woman (1:8–2:7) In this passage, both the man and the woman are talking, though it is not a conversation in the normal sense. They are talking about each other, rather than to each other, and the beauty of both the man and the woman emerges, not in an abstract sense, but through the eyes of the beholder. Though beauty may perhaps be defined in an abstract sense, the beauty perceived by lovers is of a different kind; it is rooted in the lover's perception of the loved one and in the relationship of love that acts like a lens to focus that perception.

A Song of Springtime (2:8-13) This beautiful song describes the young maiden watching her beloved come to her. He calls her to join him in the countryside, where the winter has passed and the new life of spring can be seen in the land. The beauty of young love is here likened to the blossoming forth of fresh life and fragrance that characterizes Palestine in spring.

The Woman Searches for Her Loved One (2:14–3:5) Now the woman sings and a new dimension of her love emerges from the words of her song. Love is full when the partners are together, but separation creates sorrow and loneliness. The words of the maiden evoke the desperation of separated lovers, a desperation that could only be dissipated when she held her lover again and would not let him go (3:4).

The King's Wedding Procession (3:6-11) The song begins with a description of the approach of the royal wedding procession, a palanquin surrounded by men of war. The king approaches the city for his wedding, and the young girls of the city go out to greet him. The song can be compared with Psalm 45, another wedding song.

The Woman's Beauty, Like a Garden (4:1–5:1) In sumptuous language, the man describes his maiden's beauty. To the modern reader, the language is sometimes strange: "your neck is like the tower of David" (4:4, RSV). But the strangeness lies principally in our unfamiliarity with the ancient metaphors. Nonetheless, much of the language here draws upon the imagery of nature and wildlife, which can be appreciated by all. Again, beauty is not described merely as something aesthetic, for it is intimately tied to the relationship of love: "How delight-

ful is your love, my sister, my bride! How much more pleasing is your love than wine" (v 10, NIV). And again, the maiden's beauty is not simply to be admired; it is to be given to the beloved. So when the man stops his words of adoration, the woman offers herself to him (v 16) and he accepts (5:1).

The Woman Speaks of Her Beloved (5:2–6:3) In this song, the woman is talking with other women, and the man is not present. As she speaks about her lover, there is a change from words expressing a sense of loneliness and separation (5:4-8) to a resurgence of delight as she contemplates her loved one. The sorrow of separation from her beloved is dispelled as she recounts to them the handsomeness of her man (vv 10-16).

The Man Speaks of His Loved One's Beauty (6:4–7:9) This long passage may contain more than a single song; there are words from the man, the maiden, and the female companions. The principal theme is further description by the man of his beloved's beauty (6:4-10; 7:1-9), a theme already known from an earlier passage (4:1–5:1). Each part of the maiden's body is exquisitely beautiful in the eyes of the one who loves her.

The Woman and the Man Reflect upon Love (7:10–8:14) Both partners speak in this complex passage, which may contain a number of short love songs. While some parts are difficult to interpret (especially 8:8-14), other verses reveal in the most profound language the meaning of love. Love, that most powerful of all human relationships, creates a sense of mutual belonging and mutual possession: "I belong to my lover, and his desire is for me" (7:10, NIV). And later, the girl speaks of love with words that convey one of the most powerful understandings of love in the entire Bible: "For love is as strong as death. . . . Many waters cannot quench love; rivers cannot wash it away. If one were to give all the wealth of his house for love, it would be utterly scorned" (8:6-7, NIV).

See also Solomon (Person).

SONG OF SONGS *See* Song of Solomon.

SONG OF THE THREE YOUNG MEN *See* Daniel, Additions to.

SON OF GOD Term used to express the deity of Jesus of Nazareth as the unique divine Son.

Jesus' unique sonship is antithetical to concepts of sonship popular in the ancient world. In Hellenism, people believed a man could be a "son of the gods" in many ways: in mythology, by cohabitation of a god with a woman whose offspring was imagined to be superhuman; in politics, by giving generals and emperors high honors in the cult of Roman emperor worship; in medicine, by calling a doctor "son of Asclepius"; and eventually by ascribing to anyone with mysterious powers or qualities the title or reputation of "divine man."

The Term in the Old Testament In the OT, certain men who lived before the time of Noah (Gn 6:1-4), "the angels" (including Satan, Jb 1:6; 2:1), and other heavenly beings (Pss 29:1; 82:6; 89:6, RSV mg) are called "sons of God." Israel as a people was the chosen son of God. This corporate sonship became the basis of Israel's redemption from Egypt: "Israel is my first-born son" (Ex 4:22; cf. Jer 31:9). Corporate sonship was the context for focus on personal sonship in the divine sanction of David as king: "I will be his father, and he will be my son" (2 Sm 7:14). David's "adoptive" sonship was by divine decree: "I will proclaim the decree: . . . 'You are my son; today I have become your Father' " (Ps 2:7); and it was the prophetic prototype of the "essential" sonship of Jesus, David's royal son (Mt 3:17; Mk 1:11; Lk 3:22; Acts 13:33; Heb 1:5; 5:5). Other messianic prophecies ascribe divine names to the Davidic Messiah: "Immanuel" (Is 7:13-14) and "Mighty God, Everlasting Father" (Is 9:6-7). These are fulfilled in Jesus (Mt 1:23; 21:4-10; 22:41-45).

In the Gospels Jesus' identity as the Son of God is revealed in the Gospels in three distinct ways.

The first is his *eternal, personal sonship.* Jesus' personal sonship is revealed in Peter's confession, "You are the Christ, the Son of the living God" (Mt 16:16) and in Jesus' identification of himself at his trial: " 'Are you the Christ, the Son of the Blessed One?' . . . 'I am,' said Jesus" (Mk 14:61-62). In both instances, the issue is his personal being or essence, his eternal identity.

Long before Creation, even from eternity, the Father and the Son enjoyed fellowship with each other. We know this because the Bible tells us so—but not in any great detail. For the most part, the Scriptures are silent about the premundane scene. And yet there are a few verses that lift the veil slightly and give us a glimpse into that sublime, divine relationship that always existed between the Father and the Son.

Of all the books in the Bible, the Gospel of John has the most to say about the relationship between the Father and the Son. It is from John's inspired pen that we read from the outset, "In the beginning was the Word, and the Word was with God, and the Word was God." This is a rather flat rendering. The Greek conveys something more picturesque: "In the beginning was the Word, and the Word was face to face with God, and the Word was himself God." Imagine, the Word, who was the preincarnate Son of God, was face to face with God. The expression "face to face" translates the Greek preposition *pros* (short for *prosopon pros prosopon*, "face to face," a common expression in koine Greek.) The expression signifies intimate fellowship. The Father and Son enjoyed such an intimate fellowship from eternity. How they must have delighted in each other!

After the Son of God became a man and began his ministry on earth, he referred to the relationship he enjoyed with the Father before the foundation of the world. Jesus spoke of what he had seen and heard together with the Father before coming to earth (see John 3:13 and 8:38). Jesus longed to return to that glorious sphere. In his prayer before going to the cross (in ch 17), he asked the Father to glorify him with the glory he had with the Father before the world was (v 5). Jesus wanted to recapture his primordial equality with the Father—something he had willingly relinquished for the sake of his Father's plan (see Phil 2:6-7). As he prayed to the Father, a wonderful utterance escaped from his lips: "Father, . . . you loved me before the foundation of the world" (Jn 17:24). God's Son, the unique Son, was the single object of the Father's love.

The second aspect of Jesus' sonship is his *nativity sonship.* The nativity of Jesus is traced to the direct, spiritual paternity of God. Jesus is the Son of God because his incarnation and birth into the human race was created by the Holy Spirit. In Matthew, Jesus' conception "is of the Holy Spirit" (Mt 1:20). He is to be named "Jesus" (meaning Yahweh is salvation) "because he will save his people from their sins" (v 21), and "Immanuel" (God with us) because he is himself the Son of God in human flesh (v 23). In Luke, Jesus' conception was by the Holy Spirit and the power of the Most High (Lk 1:31, 35), so Jesus was called "the Son of God" (v 35). If the father of Jesus had been the man Joseph, he would have been

called "Jesus, the son of Joseph." Luke's teaching clearly means that since the Spirit of God was the father of Jesus, this son of the virgin Mary is properly called "Jesus, the Son of God."

The third aspect is his *messianic sonship.* Jesus is the Father's Son and representative, whose earthly mission is to establish the kingdom of God. At his baptism, he began his mission with the Father's coronation: "This is my beloved Son, with whom I am well pleased" (Mt 3:17; cf. Ps 2:7). Jesus received a similar pronouncement from heaven at his Transfiguration (Lk 9:35). As the messianic Son, Jesus perfectly completed the redeeming work given him to do by his Father.

In the New Testament Epistles Paul spoke of the essential, ontological sonship of Jesus—not as an isolated fact, but in the context of his redemptive work. It was as God's Son that Jesus took human nature (Rom 1:3) and as "the Son of God" that he was resurrected and enthroned in power (Mt 28:18; Rom 1:4; 1 Cor 15:28). The Incarnation is spoken of as "God sending his own Son" (Rom 8:3; Gal 4:4) for humanity's redemption, a redemption that was accomplished "through the death of his Son" (Rom 5:10; 8:29, 32). As a consequence, believers can have "fellowship with his Son, Jesus Christ our Lord" (1 Cor 1:9), and they can live by faith in "the Son of God" (Gal 2:20). Paul's first preaching was "that Jesus is the Son of God" (Acts 9:20); this was later expounded by Paul in the light of Psalm 2:7 (see Acts 13:33).

In Hebrews, Jesus is "the Son," who is God's "firstborn" and personal "heir," who is creator and sustainer of the universe, and who is the "radiance of God's glory" (Heb 1:2-12; 3:6; 5:5). As the Son, he is the final and eternal High Priest who ascended to heaven and whose mediatorial work remains perfect forever (4:14; 6:6; 7:3, 28). In 1 John 4 and 5, belief in Jesus as the incarnate Son of God is essential for salvation; disbelief comes from the spirit of the Antichrist.

See also Christology; Jesus Christ, Teachings of; Messiah; Son of Man.

SON OF MAN Messianic title used by Jesus to express his heavenly origin, earthly mission, and glorious future coming. It does not refer merely to his human nature or humanity, as some church fathers or contemporary scholars believe. Rather, it reflects on the heavenly origin and divine dignity of Jesus, on the mystery of his manifestation in human form, and on his earthly mission that took him to the cross and then into glory.

The background of the term "Son of Man" is to be found in the OT. The book of Ezekiel is the general source, since this prophet was referred to as "son of man" 90 times. For example, God addressed him, "Son of man, stand upon your feet, and I will speak with you" (Ez 2:1, RSV). Jesus' use of the term "Son of Man" and numerous themes from Ezekiel suggest his desire to identify himself as the eschatological prophet who, like Ezekiel (chs 4, 7, 10, 22, 40–48), had the last word about the destruction of Jerusalem and the restoration of the kingdom of God to Israel (Mt 23–24; Acts 1:6-8).

The specific source of the term is Daniel 7:13-14, with its vision of one "like a son of man" who "comes with the clouds" into the presence of "the Ancient of Days," who gives him the universal and eternal kingdom of God. Jesus repeatedly quoted parts of this text in teaching about his second coming (Mt 16:27; 19:28; 24:30; 25:31; 26:64). Clearly, Jesus understood this passage as a prophetic portrayal of his own person: his incarnation, ascension, and inheritance of the kingdom of God.

In the Gospels, the term "Son of Man" is used by Jesus about 80 times as a mysterious, indirect way of speaking about himself (Mt, 32 times; Mk, 14 times; Lk, 26 times; Jn, 10 times). In all these texts, Jesus was always the speaker, and no one ever addressed him as "Son of Man." In some texts the reference is cryptic enough for some interpreters to insist that Jesus was speaking about another person. Such uncertainty is recorded in only one text in John, where the crowd asks Jesus, "Who is this 'Son of Man'?" (Jn 12:34). In most texts, the identification is clear. In some it is explicit: "Who do men say that the Son of Man is?"—followed by, "Who do you say that I am?" (Mt 16:13, 15). The conclusion generally drawn is that Jesus used the term as a messianic title for himself, so that he could speak modestly about his person and mission yet convey the exalted content he wished to reveal about himself. He could do this with considerable originality because the term was not fraught with popular misconceptions concerning the Messiah.

The term occurs only four other times in the NT. In Acts 7:56, Stephen says, "Look, I see the heavens opened and the Son of Man standing in the place of honor at God's right hand!" (NLT). Hebrews 2:6 quotes Psalm 8:4 as applying to Jesus. Finally, Revelation 1:13 and 14:14 record visions of someone "like a son of man," who is undoubtedly the glorified Jesus.

In the synoptic Gospels, the first theme in Jesus' self-revelation connected with his use of the title "Son of Man" concerns his coming to earth to accomplish his messianic mission. A general comparison of Jesus' present earthly condition with that of his previous heavenly glory is expressed in the saying "Foxes have holes, and birds of the air have nests; but the Son of Man has nowhere to lay his head" (Mt 8:20; see Lk 9:58). This saying indicates that the Son of Man gave up his heavenly home to suffer all the humiliations of his earthly ministry (Phil 2:5-11).

Jesus used the title to claim divine prerogatives, saying, "The Son of Man is Lord of the sabbath" (Mt 12:8; Mk 2:28; Lk 6:5). The Sabbath, a divine institution, may not be revised by ordinary men. But since Jesus is the Son of Man from heaven, he is free to rule as Lord even of the Sabbath, because he is the same Lord who instituted the Sabbath (Gn 2:2; Ex 20:8-11). After healing the paralytic at Capernaum, Jesus claimed that "the Son of Man has authority on earth to forgive sins" (Mt 9:6; Mk 2:10; Lk 5:24). Previously, forgiveness of sins came from heaven and from God, but now forgiveness comes from Capernaum and is given by Jesus.

The second aspect of Jesus' use of the "Son of Man" title concerns his suffering, death, and glorious resurrection as the mysterious method he would use to fulfill his earthly mission as the Son of Man. Jesus began expounding this passion theme after Peter confessed him to be Messiah and Son of God (Mt 16:16). Jesus' prediction of his passion as the Son of Man begins in Mark 8:31-32 and is repeated in several other texts. The Gospels expand the theme to include his suffering of mockery and scourging (Mt 17:12; 20:18; Mk 8:31; Lk 9:22), betrayal by Judas (Mt 17:22; 26:24-25; Mk 14:21, 41), rejection by the Jewish leaders (Mt 20:18), death by crucifixion (Mt 20:19; Mk 9:12, 31; 10:33), burial for three days (Mt 12:40; Lk 11:30), and resurrection (Mt 17:22-23; Mk 8:31).

In the famous text "The Son of Man did not come to be served, but to serve, and to give his life as a ransom for many" (Mt 20:28; Mk 10:45), Jesus teaches that his death was a vicarious sacrifice for the salvation of his people. This idea of substitutionary atonement is a new element in the Son of Man material and derives from

Jesus' understanding of himself as the suffering Servant of the Lord (Is 53).

Jesus also used the "Son of Man" title to teach about his second coming. As the Son of Man, Jesus will return to earth from heaven in the glory of his Father with the angels (Mt 16:27; Mk 8:38; Lk 9:26). First, he will be seated at the right hand of God, and then he will come again (Mt 26:64; Mk 14:62; Lk 22:69) with the clouds (Mt 24:30; Mk 13:26; Lk 21:27). This coming will be unexpected (Mt 24:27; Lk 12:40), like a flash of lightning or the flood of Noah (Mt 24:37; Lk 17:24). His coming will be for the gathering of the elect, the judgment of all the nations of the earth (Mt 19:28; 25:32), and the restoration of final righteousness in the world (19:28; 25:46).

In these passages, Jesus' focus shifts from the provisional victory in his passion and resurrection to the final victory of the Son of Man at his second coming. Here again, the dramatic emphasis is on the heavenly origin and divine prerogatives of the Son of Man. This man Jesus, the Son of Man, will be the final judge (cf. Acts 17:31).

The Gospel of John has its own distinctive material concerning the Son of Man. The angels are said to ascend and descend on the Son of Man (Jn 1:51), thereby signifying that he is a preexistent person who has come from heaven to earth (3:13; 6:62). His being lifted up (by crucifixion) will bring about eternal life for all who believe in him (3:14). The Son of Man (3:14) is also the Son of God (3:16), God's one and only Son (1:18; 3:18). Quite simply, in John's Gospel, the "Son of Man" title is equivalent to the title "Son of God." It reveals his divinity, preexistence, heavenly origin, and divine prerogatives. It affirms his present earthly condition for revelation and passion, and his future eschatological glory. The Father has given the Son of Man authority to raise the dead and to judge the world (5:25-27).

See also Christology; Jesus Christ, Teachings of; Messiah; Son of God.

SONS AND DAUGHTERS OF GOD*

Expression designating human beings who have been born of God and have become part of his family. When the Bible speaks of God's sons, it does not intend to exclude females. The term "sons" is inclusive of all believers. But the Scriptures nearly always have the word "sons"—with one exception in the NT, 2 Corinthians 6:18, in which God's people are called "sons and daughters."

From the beginning, God the Father desired to have many sons and daughters sharing the image and likeness of his beloved Son. It could be said that his one Son brought him so much satisfaction that he yearned to have many more. This may have been the impetus for the creation of the universe and, most specifically, of human beings (see Gn 1:26-27). Proverbs 8 indicates that God was delighted with the sons of men. This is again expressed in the NT, especially in the book of Ephesians. The opening verses in Ephesians resound with this note: the heart's desire of God was to obtain many sons in and through his Son. The many sons, in union with the unique Son, would bring great glory and satisfaction to the Father.

Paul used a Greek word in Ephesians 1:5, 9, and 11 that conveys the idea of desire, even heart's desire. The word is usually translated as "will"—"the will of God." But the English word "will" conceals the primary meaning. The Greek word (*thelema*) is primarily an emotional word and secondarily volitional. God's will is not so much God's intention as it is God's heart's desire. God does have an intention, a purpose, a plan. It is called *prothesis* in Greek (see Eph 1:11), and it literally means "a laying out beforehand" (like a blueprint). This plan was created by God's counsel (called *boule* in Greek, Eph 1:11). But behind the plan and the counsel was not just a mastermind but a heart of love and of good pleasure. Therefore, Paul talks about "the good pleasure of God's heart's desire" (v 5). Paul also says, "He made known to us the mystery of his heart's desire, according to his good pleasure which he purposed in him" (v 9).

The impetus of God's eternal purpose came from a heart's desire, and that heart's desire was to have many sons made like his only Son (see Rom 8:26-28). In love, he predestined many people to participate in this "sonship"—not by their own merits but by virtue of their being united to the Son (Eph 1:4-5). Notice how often in Ephesians 1 Paul speaks of the believers' position "in him." Outside of him (the Son), no one could be a son of God and no one could be pleasing to the Father. The many sons and daughters owe all their divine privileges to the Beloved, as ones given grace through him (v 6). If it were not for God's satisfaction in his beloved Son, there would not have been the inspiration for the creation of man in the first place. Humans exist because God wanted to obtain many sons and daughters, each bearing the image of God's unique Son. People are well pleasing to God and bring him satisfaction by being united to the one who has always satisfied him. Apart from the Son, no one has access to the Father. But because of the Son's redemption, all believers have the right to become children of God (Jn 1:12) and now have access to the Father through the Son (14:6).

SONS OF THE PROPHETS* "Band of prophets" whom Saul met (1 Sm 10:5-6, 10-13) and forerunners of the "schools," "guilds," or "sons of the prophets," which flourished under Israel's early kings. Jezebel persecuted those defending the worship of Yahweh and established rival "schools" to propagate worship of Baal and Asherah (1 Kgs 18:19-29; 22:6). Ahab's steward, Obadiah, sheltered two companies of 50 prophets of Yahweh in caves and gave them provisions (18:4).

First Kings 22:5-28 illustrates the political danger of such royal guilds, and chronicles the emergence of individual spokesmen claiming spontaneous inspiration. First Kings 20:35-43 shows another individual, acting strangely yet recognizable as a true prophet. From 2 Kings 2–6, we learn that groups persisted at Bethel (about 50) and Gilgal (about 100).

See also Prophecy; Prophet, Prophetess.

SONS OF THUNDER Translation of the word "Boanerges," the surname given by Jesus to James and John (Mk 3:17). *See* Boanerges.

SOOTHSAYER* One who foretells events; a pagan practice, soothsaying was forbidden in Israel (Dt 18:10, 14). In Scripture, soothsaying was practiced by Balaam, Beor's son (Jos 13:22) and King Manasseh of Judah (2 Kgs 21:6; 2 Chr 33:6); Jacob's descendants were likened to the soothsayers of Philistia (Is 2:6); they were listed among the false prophets of Judah (Jer 27:9). During NT times, soothsaying was the source of a lucrative trade in Philippi (Acts 16:16).

See also Magic; Sorcery.

SOP* KJV term for a thin piece of bread, dipped into a common dish and used as a spoon (Jn 13:26). *See* Lord's Supper, The.

SOPATER Man from the church at Berea who, with others, accompanied Paul to Jerusalem to deliver the offering collected by the gentile churches for the Jewish Christians who were suffering from the effects of a famine (Acts 20:4). Sopater is perhaps identical to Sosipater, the kinsman of Paul who sent greetings to the church at Rome (Rom 16:21).

SOPHERETH Alternate form of Hassophereth, the name of a postexilic Levitical family, in Nehemiah 7:57. *See* Hassophereth.

SORCERY Practice whose adherents claim to have supernatural powers and knowledge; the ability to foretell the future and to summon evil spirits through charms and magical spells. Sorcerers were present in the high courts of Egypt (Ex 7:11), Assyria (Na 3:4), and Babylonia (Dn 2:2). Sorcery was forbidden in Israel (Dt 18:10) and was punishable by death (Ex 22:18). Nonetheless, Israel sought out sorcerers (2 Kgs 17:17; 2 Chr 33:6; Mi 5:12), provoking God's anger against her (Is 57:3; Mal 3:5). Paul included it in a list of sinful works (Gal 5:20), and the book of Revelation condemned its practitioners to the lake of fire (Rv 21:8) and to eternal separation from the righteous (22:15).

See also Magic.

SORE Any localized abnormality of the skin. It was a well-demarcated skin abnormality with a definite border between the inflamed or abnormal skin and the normal skin. Even the person "covered with sores" from head to toe has some normal skin between each of the sores. As such, "sore" is a broad term encompassing all the following types of skin abnormalities: scall, scab, rising, emerod, plague, and scar.

The KJV uses the word "sore" in translating 32 different Hebrew or Greek words to mean "extremely," a nonmedical use, such as "and Hezekiah wept sore" (2 Kgs 20:3) or "sore afraid" (Ez 27:35).

See also Disease; Medicine and Medical Practice.

SOREK, Valley of Valley in which Delilah lived (Jgs 16:4). It began in the hill country of Judah, about 13 miles (20.9 kilometers) southwest of Jerusalem, and took a northwesterly course to the Mediterranean Sea. It is identifiable with the Wadi es-Sarar. The Danites attempted to settle this area but were driven out by the Philistines in the region by the Mediterranean. The town of Zorah, Samson's birthplace, was near the head of the valley of Zorek, which provided the setting for his intrigues and the concentration of his activities as judge.

SORGHUM* Medium to stout annual grass growing over six feet (1.8 meters) tall; perhaps the "hyssop" to which the sponge of vinegar was attached during Jesus' crucifixion (Mt 27:48; Mk 15:36; Jn 19:29). *See* Plants (Hyssop).

SOSIPATER Jewish Christian who joined Paul, Timothy, Lucius, and Jason in sending greetings to the church at Rome (Rom 16:21).

SOSTHENES
1. Leader of the synagogue in Corinth who brought legal action against Paul before Gallio, proconsul of Achaia. Upon hearing Gallio's dismissal of the Jewish accusations against Paul, a mob, possibly of Greeks, seized Sosthenes and beat him (Acts 18:17).
2. Christian brother and companion of Paul, known to the Christians at Corinth and mentioned by Paul in 1 Corinthians 1:1.

SOSTRATUS Governor of the citadel of Jerusalem under Antiochus IV (2 Macc 4:28). He attempted to secure from Menelaus, the high priest, the sum of money Menelaus had promised to pay the king for his appointment to the priestly office. When the payment was not made, both men were called to account by Antiochus.

SOTAI Head of a family of temple servants who returned to Jerusalem with Zerubbabel following the exile (Ezr 2:55; Neh 7:57).

SOUL Term translating the Greek word *psuche* and the Hebrew *nephesh*.

The Greek philosopher Plato (fourth century BC) perceived the soul as the eternal element in humans; whereas the body perishes at death, the soul is indestructible. At death the soul enters another body; if it has been wicked in this life, it may be sent into an inferior human being or even an animal or bird. By means of transmigration from one body to another, the soul is eventually purged of evil. In the early centuries of the Christian era, Gnosticism also taught that the body was the prison house of the soul. Redemption comes to those initiated into the Gnostic secrets, leading to the release of the soul from the body.

Biblical thought about the soul is different. In the OT the soul signifies that which is vital to humans in the broadest sense. The Hebrew and Greek words for soul often can be translated as "life"; occasionally, they can be used for the life of creatures (Gn 1:20; Lv 11:10). "Soul for soul" means "life for life" (Ex 21:23). In legal writings, a soul refers to a person in relation to a particular law (e.g., "If a soul shall sin . . . ," Lv 4:2, KJV). When people were counted, they were counted as souls, that is, persons (Ex 1:5; Dt 10:22).

In a narrower sense, the soul denotes human emotions and inner powers. People are called to love God with all their heart and soul (Dt 13:3). Knowledge and understanding (Ps 139:14), thought (1 Sm 20:3), love (1 Sm 18:1), and memory (Lam 3:20) all originate in the soul. Here the soul comes close to what today would be called the self, one's person, personality, or ego.

There is no suggestion in the OT of the transmigration of the soul as an immaterial, immortal entity. Man is a unity of body and soul—terms that describe not so much two separate entities in a person as much as one person from different standpoints. Hence, in the description of man's creation in Genesis 2:7, the phrase "a living soul" (KJV) is better translated as "a living being." The thought is not that men and women became *souls*, for clearly they had bodies. The use of the word in the original draws attention to the vital aspect of humans as "living beings." The Hebrew view of the unity of the person may help to explain why people in the OT had only a shadowy view of life after death, for it would be difficult to conceive how people could exist without a body (Pss 16:10; 49:15; 88:3-12). Where hope of an afterlife exists, it is not because of the intrinsic character of the soul itself (as in Plato). It is grounded in confidence in the God who has power over death and the belief that communion with him cannot be broken even by death (Ex 3:6; 1 Sm 2:6; Jb 19:25-26; Pss 16:10-11; 73:24-25; Is 25:8; 26:19; Dn 12:2; Hos 6:1-3; 13:14).

In the NT the word for soul (*psuche*) has a range of meanings similar to that in the OT. Often it is synonymous with life itself. Followers of Jesus are said to have risked their lives (souls) for his sake (Acts 15:26; cf. Jn 13:37; Rom 16:4; Phil 2:30). As the Son of Man, Jesus came not to be served but to serve and to give his life (soul) as a ransom for many (Mt 20:28; Mk 10:45). As the Good Shepherd, he lays down his life (soul) for the sheep (Jn 10:14, 17-18). In Luke 14:26 the condition of discipleship is to hate one's soul, that is, to be willing to deny oneself to the point of losing one's life for Christ's sake (cf. Lk 9:23; Rv 12:11).

Frequently "soul" can mean "person" (Acts 2:43; 3:23; 7:14; Rom 2:9; 13:1; 1 Pt 3:20). The expression "every living soul" (Rv 16:3, KJV) reflects the vital aspect of living beings. As in the OT, the soul can denote not only the vital aspect of the person on the physical level, but it can also connote one's emotional energies. It denotes the person himself, the seat of his or her emotions, one's inmost being. For example, when Jesus was agonizing about his death, he spoke of his soul being crushed (Mt 26:38; Mk 14:34; cf. Ps 42:6). In an entirely different setting, Jesus promised rest to the souls of those who come to him (Mt 11:29). Here, as elsewhere, "soul" denotes the essential person (cf. Lk 2:35; 2 Cor 1:23; 2 Thes 2:8; 3 Jn 1:2).

Several passages place the soul alongside the spirit. Luke 1:46 is probably a case of Hebrew poetic parallelism, which expresses the same idea in two different ways. Both terms denote Mary as a person in the depths of her being. Similarly, in Hebrews 4:12, dividing the soul and the spirit is a graphic way of saying how the Word of God probes the inmost recesses of our being. The prayer in 1 Thessalonians 5:23—that the readers may be kept blameless in spirit, soul, and body—is a way of speaking of the whole being. Here soul probably suggests physical existence, as in Genesis 2:7 and 1 Corinthians 2:14, whereas spirit may imply the higher or "spiritual" side of life.

In other passages, the emotions, the will, and even the mind come to the fore, though in each case there is the accompanying idea of a person's inmost being. People are to love God with all the soul (Mt 22:37; Mk 12:30; cf. Dt 6:5). The expression "from the soul" (Eph 6:6; Col 3:23) means "from the heart," with all one's being. In Philippians 1:27 believers are called to be of one mind (cf. Acts 4:32; 14:2). Passages that speak of the soul in relation to salvation include Matthew 10:28; Luke 12:5; Hebrews 6:19; 10:39; 12:3; 13:7; James 1:21; 5:20; 1 Peter 1:9, 22-23; 2:25; 4:19; and Revelation 6:9; 20:4. Such passages speak of the soul either to stress the essential human being, as distinct from the physical body, or to express man's continued existence with God prior to the resurrection.

See also Man; Spirit of Man.

SOWING *See* Agriculture.

SPAIN Name of the most westerly peninsula in southwestern Europe. Biblical references to the peninsula note the role of the Phoenicians, whose far-flung Carthaginian Empire reached into Spain. The Romans expelled the Carthaginians from Spain as early as 206 BC, but they did not conquer the local tribes until 25 BC. Only by then had the Romans gained control of the whole region (1 Macc 8:3).

The Phoenician traders of Tyre extended their commercial empire to Spain or historic Iberia as early as 1100 BC. From Carthage on the North African coast, which was a center of the Phoenician Empire, a series of colonial thrusts followed the trading contacts. The Carthaginians established many settlements on the Spanish coast during the flourishing of their republic. These included Carthago Nova (now Cartagena) and Malacca (now Malaga). Later, they took Tartessus and absorbed much of the peninsula into their empire. From this base in Spain, the Carthaginians sought to expand their empire into Europe. The Romans met the Carthaginian challenge. After beating

Hannibal back in his attack on Italy in the Second Punic War (218–201 BC), the Romans extended their territory by overcoming the Carthaginians on the Spanish peninsula. Finally, under Augustus, the Romans made Spain part of the empire. At that time the Romans built a magnificent road system circling and crossing the whole Spanish peninsula.

Roman civilization had a deep and lasting influence on Spain. Three emperors—Trajan, Hadrian, and the first Theodosius—were born in Spain. Several scholars and writers of note in Roman culture came from Spain. These included the two Senecas, Martial, Prudentius, Lucan, Quintialian, Pomponius, and Mela.

In the apostle Paul's scheme for reaching the uttermost regions of the civilized world with the good news

The Divine Spirit and Human Spirit in Special Written Form In John 3:6 (last line), the scribe of Bodmer Papyrus II (P66) wrote the word TINC to signal the divine Spirit, and then wrote out the word PNEYMA to signal the human spirit.

of Jesus Christ, he probably realized the potential of converts in Spain. The chief evidence that Paul included Spain in his strategic planning is in Romans 15:24, 28. In that letter Paul clearly sets forth his message to Romans and Gentiles throughout the empire. To follow up on this letter, he planned to visit Rome and then make his way to Spain. Testimony of Paul actually visiting Spain comes only from a vague reference after his death. Clement of Rome, an early Christian writer at the end of the first century AD, stated that Paul went to "the limits of the West" (1 Clement 1:5). Although most Romans considered Spain as the western limit of

their empire, this vague phrase does not give sufficient evidence for a Pauline visit. Yet clearly Paul saw Spain as a strategic place for mission work; thus, it stands to reason that he himself, or others whom he designated, planted the Christian church in Spain during the first century AD.

SPAN Hand measurement equaling one-half cubit (Ex 28:16; 39:9). *See* Weights and Measures.

SPARROW *See* Birds.

SPEAR, SPEARMAN *See* Armor and Weapons.

SPELT Hard-grained species of wheat that flourishes in various kinds of soils; hence, it was popular grain among the ancients (Ex 9:32; Ez 4:9). *See* Plants.

SPICE, SPICERY* *See* Incense; Perfume.

SPIDER* *See* Animals.

SPIKENARD* Perennial herb with strong, pleasant-smelling roots. *See* Plants (Nard).

SPINNER, SPINNING Fibers were spun into yarn by women in all periods of Israel's history, but a class of professional spinners arose alongside them. Women spinners are mentioned in Exodus 35:25-26. Among her other virtues, the good wife of Proverbs 31 engaged in spinning (Prv 31:19). Jesus spoke of the lilies of the field that did not need to spin (Mt 6:28; Lk 12:27).

SPIRIT Designation of that aspect of existence that is noncorporeal and immaterial. Its Latin derivation (as with the Hebrew and Greek words in the Bible—*ruach* and *pneuma*) denotes blowing or breathing (Jb 41:16; Is 25:4). So the noun *spiritus* signifies breath and life. God, the source of all life, is himself Spirit (Jn 4:24). He put a spirit within all human beings so that they could commune with him in his realm and in his nature. A Christian's experience of Jesus Christ is made real when that person experiences the Spirit of Jesus Christ in his or her spirit.

Three articles follow that describe three major aspects of spirit: (1) Spirit of God; (2) Spirit of Jesus Christ; (3) spirit of man.

SPIRIT OF GOD Description of God in action, God in motion. The word "spirit" (Hebrew, *ruach*; Greek, *pneuma*) is the word used from ancient times to describe and explain the experience of divine power working in, upon, and around people.

In the Old Testament There are three basic meanings evident in the use of "spirit" from the earliest Hebrew writings: It was a wind from God, it was the breath of life, and it was a spirit of ecstasy.

First, it was a wind from God (the same Hebrew word translated "Spirit" in Gn 1:2) that caused the waters of the Flood to subside (8:1). A wind from God blew locusts over Egypt (Ex 10:13) and quail over the camp of Israel. The blast of his nostrils separated the waters of the Red Sea at the exodus (14:21).

Second, it was the breath of God that made man a living being (Gn 2:7). It is one of the earliest perceptions of Hebrew faith that humans live only because of the stirring of the divine breath or spirit within them (Gn 6:3; Jb 33:4; 34:14-15; Ps 104:29-30). Later, a clearer distinction was drawn between divine Spirit and human spirit, and between spirit and soul, but at the earliest stage these were all more or less perceived to be synonymous manifestations of the same divine power, the source of all life—animal as well as human (Gn 7:15, 22; see Eccl 3:19-21).

Third, there were occasions when this divine power seemed to overtake and possess an individual fully, so that his or her words or actions far transcended those of normal behavior. Such a person was clearly marked as an agent of God's purpose and given respect. This was apparently how leaders were recognized in the premonarchy period—Othniel (Jgs 3:10), Gideon (6:34), Jephthah (11:29), and the first king, Saul (1 Sm 11:6), as well. So, too, the earliest prophets were those whose inspiration came in ecstasy (1 Sm 19:20-24).

In the earlier stages of Hebrew thought, ecstatic experience was seen as the direct effect of divine power. This was true even when the ecstasy was recognized as evil in character, as in the case of Saul's seizure by the Spirit (1 Sm 16:14-16). A spirit from God could be for evil as well as for good (see Jgs 9:23; 1 Kgs 22:19-23).

In the Writings of the Prophets For Isaiah, the spirit was that which characterized God and distinguished him and his actions from human affairs (Is 31:3). Later, the adjective "holy" appeared as that which distinguished the Spirit of God from any other spirit, human or divine (Ps 51:11; Is 63:10-11).

The problem of false prophecy emphasized the danger of assuming that every message delivered in ecstasy was the word of the Lord. Thus, tests of prophecy evaluated the content of the message delivered or the character of the prophet's life, not the degree or quality of inspiration (see Dt 13:1-5; 18:22; Jer 23:14; Mi 3:5). This sense of a need to discriminate between true and false inspiration and to distinguish the word of God from the merely ecstatic oracle may help to explain the otherwise puzzling reluctance of the major eighth- and seventh- century BC prophets to attribute their inspiration to the Spirit.

In the Exilic and Postexilic Writings In exilic and postexilic literature, the role of the Spirit is narrowed to two major functions: that of the prophetic Spirit and that of the Spirit of the age to come.

The later prophets again spoke of the Spirit in explicit terms as the inspirer of prophecy (see Ez 3:1-4, 22-24; Hg 2:5; Zec 4:6). As they looked back to the preexilic period, these prophets freely attributed the inspiration of "the former prophets" to the Spirit as well (Zec 7:12).

This tendency to exalt the Spirit's role as the inspirer of prophecy became steadily stronger in the period between the OT and NT, until in rabbinic Judaism the Spirit was almost exclusively the inspirer of the prophetic writings now regarded as Scripture.

The other understanding of the Spirit's role during exilic and postexilic times was that the Spirit would be the manifestation of the power of God in the age to come. That eschatological hope of divine power effecting a final cleansing and a renewed creation is rooted principally in Isaiah's prophecies (Is 4:4; 32:15; 44:3-4). Isaiah speaks of one anointed by the Spirit to accomplish complete and final salvation (11:2; 42:1; 61:1). Elsewhere, the same longing is expressed in terms of the Spirit being freely dispensed to all Israel (Ez 39:29; Jl 2:28-29; Zec 12:10) in the new covenant (Jer 31:31-34; Ez 36:26-27).

In the period prior to Jesus, the understanding of the Spirit as the Spirit of prophecy and as the Spirit of the age to come had developed into the widespread dogma that the Spirit was no longer to be experienced in the present. The Spirit had been known in the past as the inspirer of prophetic writings, but after Haggai, Zechariah, and Malachi, the Spirit had withdrawn (1 Macc 4:44-46; 9:27; 2 Bar 85:1-3; see also Ps 74:9; Zec 13:2-6). The Spirit would be known again in the age of the Messiah, but in the interim the Spirit was absent from Israel. Even the great Hillel (learned Jewish leader and teacher, 60? BC–AD 20?), a near contemporary of Jesus, had not received the Spirit—though if anyone was worthy of the Spirit, it was he. There is a tradition that at a meeting of Hillel and other wise men, a voice from heaven said, "Among those here present is one who would have deserved the Holy Spirit to rest upon him, if his time had been worthy of it." The wise men all looked at Hillel.

The consequence of this accepted dearth of the Spirit was that the Spirit in effect became subordinated to the law. The Spirit was the inspirer of the law, but since the Spirit could no longer be experienced directly, the law became the sole voice of the Spirit. It was this increasing dominance of the law and its authoritative interpreters that provided the background for the mission of Jesus and the initial spread of Christianity.

In the New Testament If we are to understand the NT's teaching on the Spirit, we must recognize both its continuity and discontinuity with the OT. At many points NT usage cannot be fully understood except against the background of OT concepts or passages. For example, the ambiguity of John 3:8 ("wind," "Spirit"), 2 Thessalonians 2:8 ("breath"), and Revelation 11:11 ("breath of life") takes us back to the basic Hebrew meanings of "spirit." Acts 8:39 and Revelation 17:3 and 21:10 reflect the same conception of the Spirit that we find in 1 Kings 18:12, 2 Kings 2:16, and Ezekiel 3:14. The NT writers generally share the rabbinic view that Scripture has the authority of the Spirit behind it (see Mk 12:36; Acts 28:25; Heb 3:7; 2 Pt 1:21). The principal continuity is that the NT brings the fulfillment of what the OT writers looked forward to. At the same time, Christianity is not simply fulfilled Judaism. Jesus' coming and his giving of his Spirit to live within his believers marks off the new faith as something new and distinct.

The Spirit of the New Age The most striking feature of Jesus' ministry and of the message of the earliest Christians was their conviction and proclamation that the blessings of the new age were already present, that the eschatological Spirit had already been poured out. With the exception of the Essenes at Qumran, no other group or individual within the Jewish religion of that time had dared to make such a bold claim. The prophets and the rabbis looked for a messianic age yet to come, and the apocalyptic writers warned of its imminent arrival, but none thought of it as already present. Even John the Baptist spoke only of one about to come and of the Spirit's operation in the imminent future (Mk 1:8). But for Jesus and first-century Christians, the longed for hope was a living reality, and the claim carried with it the exciting sense of being in "the last days." Without some recognition of that eschatological dimension of the Christians' faith and life, we cannot understand this teaching on, and experience of, the Spirit.

Jesus clearly thought of his teachings and healings as fulfillment of the prophetic hope (Mt 12:41-42; 13:16-17; Lk 17:20-21). In particular, he saw himself as the one anointed by the Spirit to provide salvation (Mt 5:3-6; 11:5; Lk 4:17-19). So, too, Jesus understood his exorcisms as the effect of the power of God and as manifestations of the end-time rule of God (Mt 12:27-28; Mk 3:22-26). The Gospel writers, especially Luke, emphasize the eschatological character of Jesus' life and ministry by stressing the role of the Spirit in his birth (Mt 1:18; Lk 1:35, 41, 67; 2:25-27), his baptism (Mk 1:9-10; Acts 10:38), and his ministry (Mt 4:1; 12:18; Mk 1:12; Lk 4:1, 14; 10:21; Jn 3:34).

The Christian church began with the in-breathing of the Holy Spirit on the day of Christ's resurrection (Jn 20:22), followed by the outpouring of the Spirit at Pentecost "in the last days." The overwhelming experience of vision and inspired utterance was taken as proof positive that the new age prophesied by Joel had now arrived (Acts 2:2-5, 17-18). Similarly, in Hebrews the gift of the Spirit is spoken of as "the powers of the age to come" (Heb 6:4-5). More striking still is Paul's understanding of the Spirit as the guarantee of God's complete salvation (2 Cor 1:22; 5:5; Eph 1:13-14), and as the first installment of the believer's inheritance of God's kingdom (Rom 8:15-17; 1 Cor 6:9-11; 15:42-50; Gal 4:6-7; 5:16-18, 21-23; Eph 1:13-14). The Spirit is here again thought of as the power of the age to come, as that power (which will characterize God's rule at the end of time) already shaping and transforming the lives of believers.

For Paul, this means also that the gift of the Spirit is but the beginning of a lifelong process that will not end until the believer's whole person is brought under the Spirit's power (Rom 8:11, 23; 1 Cor 15:44-49; 2 Cor 3:18; 5:1-5). It also means that the present experience of faith is one of lifelong tension between what God has already begun to bring about in the believer's life and what has not yet been brought under God's grace (Phil 1:6). It is this tension between life "in the Spirit" and life "in the flesh" (see Gal 2:20) that comes to poignant expression in Romans 7:24 and 2 Corinthians 5:2-4.

The Spirit of New Life Since the Spirit is the mark of the new age, it is not surprising that the NT writers understood the gift of the Spirit to be that which brings an individual into the new age. John the Baptist described the way the coming one would baptize with the Holy Spirit and with fire (Mt 3:11). According to Acts 1:5 and 11:16, this imagery was taken up by Jesus, and the promise is seen as fulfilled at Pentecost—the outpouring of the Spirit here being understood as the risen Christ's action in drawing his disciples into the new age (Acts 2:17, 33).

It seems to be one of Luke's aims in the book of Acts to highlight the central importance of the gift of the Spirit in conversion-initiation—it is that decisive "gift of the Holy Spirit" that makes one a Christian (Acts 2:38-39). People could have been followers of Jesus on earth, but it was only when they received the gift of the Spirit that they could be said to have "believed in the

Lord Jesus Christ" (11:16-17). When the Spirit's presence was manifested in and upon a person's life, that was recognized by Peter as proof enough that God had accepted that person, even though he or she had not yet made any formal profession of faith or been baptized (10:44-48; 11:15-18; 15:7-9). So too Apollos, already aglow with the Spirit (18:25), even though his knowledge of "the way of God" was slightly defective (vv 24-26), apparently was not required to supplement his "baptism of John" with Christian baptism. However, the 12 so-called disciples at Ephesus proved by their very ignorance of the Spirit that they were not yet disciples of the Lord Jesus (19:1-6). Paul asked these 12 men, "Did you receive the Holy Spirit when you believed?" (19:2).

This accords with Paul's emphasis in his letters. Belief and reception of the Spirit go together: to receive the Spirit is to begin the Christian life (Gal 3:2-3); to be baptized in the Spirit is to become a member of the body of Christ (1 Cor 12:13); to "have the Spirit of Christ" is to belong to Christ (Rom 8:9-11); to receive the Spirit is tantamount to becoming a child of God (Rom 8:14-17; Gal 4:6-7). The Spirit so characterizes the new age and the life of the new age that only the gift of the Spirit can bring a person into the new age to experience the life of the new age. For the Spirit is distinctively and peculiarly the life-giver; the Spirit indeed *is* the life of the new age (Rom 8:2, 6, 10; 1 Cor 15:45; 2 Cor 3:6; Gal 5:25).

In just the same way in John's writings, the Spirit is characteristically the life-giving Spirit (Jn 6:63), the power from above, the seed of divine life that brings about the new birth (Jn 3:3-8; 1 Jn 3:9), and a river of living water that brings life when one believes in Christ (Jn 7:37-39; so also 4:10, 14). Or again, reception of the Spirit in John 20:22 is depicted as a new creation analogous to Genesis 2:7. Consequently, in 1 John 3:24 and 4:13, possession and experience of the Spirit count as one of the "tests of life" listed in that letter.

Manifestations of the Spirit It will be clear from what has already been said that when the first Christians, like the ancient Hebrews, spoke of the Spirit, they were thinking of experiences of divine power. In the NT, as in the OT, "Spirit" is the word used to explain the experience of new life and vitality (see above), of liberation from legalism (e.g., Rom 8:2; 2 Cor 3:17), of spiritual refreshing and renewal (cf. e.g., Is 32:15; Ez 39:29 with Jn 7:37-39; Rom 5:5; 1 Cor 12:13; 1 Tm 3:5-6). It is important to realize how wide a range of experiences were attributed to the Spirit: ecstatic experiences (Acts 2:24; 10:43-47; 19:6; cf. 10:10; 22:17—"in ecstasy"; 2 Cor 12:1-4; Rv 1:10), emotional experiences (e.g., love—Rom 5:5; joy—Acts 13:52; 1 Thes 1:6; see also Gal 5:22; Phil 2:1-2), experiences of illumination (2 Cor 3:14-17; Eph 1:17-18; Heb 6:4-5; 1 Jn 2:20-21), and experiences issuing in moral transformation (1 Cor 6:9-11). Likewise, when Paul speaks of spiritual gifts, called *charismata* (acts or words that bring divine grace to concrete expression), he evidently has a wide range of actual events in mind: inspired speech (1 Cor 12:8-10; 1 Thes 1:5), miracles and healings (1 Cor 12:9; Gal 3:5; cf. Heb 2:4), and various acts of service and help, of counsel and administration, and of aid and mercy (Rom 12:7-8; 1 Cor 12:28).

In talking thus of the Spirit in terms of experience, we should not overemphasize particular experiences or manifestations, as though earliest Christianity consisted of a sequence of mountaintop experiences or spiritual highs. There clearly were such experiences, indeed a wide range of experiences, but no one experience is singled out to be sought by all (except prophecy). There is no distinctively second (or third) experience of the Spirit in the NT, and Paul warned against overvaluing particular manifestations of the Spirit (1 Cor 14:6-19; 2 Cor 12:1-10; cf. Mk 8:11-13). Where particular experiences are valued, it is as manifestations of a more sustained experience, particular expressions of an underlying relationship (cf. Acts 6:3-5; 11:24—"full of the Spirit"; Eph 5:18). What we are in touch with here is the vigor of the experiential dimension of earliest Christianity. If the Spirit is the breath of the new life in Christ (cf. Ez 37:9-10, 14; Jn 20:22; 1 Cor 15:45), then presumably the analogy extends further, and the experience of the Spirit is like the experience of breathing: one is not conscious of it all the time, but if one is not conscious of it, at least sometimes, something is wrong.

The Fellowship of the Spirit It was out of this shared experience of the Spirit that the earliest Christian community grew and developed, for this is what "the fellowship [*koinonia*] of the Spirit" properly means: common participation in the same Spirit (Phil 2:1; cf. Acts 2:42; 1 Cor 1:4-9). It was the gift of the Spirit that brought those in Samaria, Caesarea, and elsewhere effectively into the community of the Spirit (Act 8, 10). So also, it was the experience of the one Spirit that provided the unifying bond in the churches of Paul's mission (1 Cor 12:13; Eph 4:3-4; Phil 2:1-2). Here we see the real importance of the divine manifestations of the Spirit for Paul: it is out of the diversity of these particular manifestations that the body of Christ grows in unity (Rom 12:4-8; 1 Cor 12:12-17; Eph 4:4-16).

SPIRIT OF JESUS CHRIST The Spirit as identified with Jesus Christ.

The most important development and element in earliest Christian understanding of the Spirit is that the Spirit is now the Spirit of Jesus Christ (Acts 16:7; Rom 8:9; Gal 4:6; Phil 1:19; 1 Pt 1:11; see also Jn 7:38; 15:26; 16:7; 19:30; Rv 3:1; 5:6). The Spirit is to be identified as the Spirit that bears witness to Jesus (Jn 15:26; 16:13-15; Acts 5:32; 1 Cor 12:3; 1 Jn 4:2; 5:7-8; Rv 19:10), but also, and more profoundly, as the Spirit that inspired and empowered Jesus himself. This Spirit became available to the believers after Christ's resurrection.

The apostles John and Paul were quite clear in their writings about Christ becoming spirit through resurrection. The keynote verses penned by John are John 6:63; 7:37-39; 14:16-18; 20:22; and 1 John 3:24; 4:13. The critical passages written by Paul are Romans 8:9-10; 1 Corinthians 15:45; 2 Corinthians 3:17-18; and 1 Corinthians 6:17.

Revelation concerning the Spirit of Jesus is progressive in the Gospel of John. John does not tell us from the beginning that people could not actually receive eternal life until the hour of Christ's glorification. Throughout the Gospel, Jesus declares to various people that he can give them eternal life if they would believe in him. He promises them the water of life, the bread of life, and the light of life. But no one could really partake of these until after the Lord had risen. As a foretaste, as a sample, they could receive life via the Lord's words because his words were themselves spirit and life (Jn 6:63); however, it was not until the Spirit would become available that believers could actually become the recipients of the divine, eternal life. After the Lord's discourse in John 6, Jesus said, "It is the Spirit that gives life, the flesh profits nothing" (v 63). In the flesh Jesus could not give them the bread of life, but when the Spirit became available, they could have life. Again, Jesus offered the water of life—even life flowing like rivers of living water—to the Jews assembled at the Feast of Tabernacles. He told them to come and drink of him. But no one could, then and

COMMUNITY OF THE SPIRIT
The two-volume work of Luke the Evangelist, Luke–Acts, presents the church as that community of people in which, and through which, the Spirit of God is working. Insofar as the church is that, it is an extension of a reality already begun by Jesus of Nazareth. In Luke's Gospel, John the Baptist announces the coming of one who would baptize with the Holy Spirit (Lk 3:16). In Acts, this promise is seen fulfilled in the outpouring of the Spirit (Acts 1:5). As Jesus was empowered for his mission by the Spirit (Lk 3:21-22), so the early Christian community was empowered for its witness in the world (Acts 1:8). As Jesus, the man of the Spirit, was confronted at the outset of his ministry with great obstacles (the temptation, Lk 4:1-13), so the church, as the community of the Spirit, faced the temptation to yield to pressures that would compromise its mission (Acts 2:12-13; 4:1-22; 5:27-42). As Jesus, empowered by the Spirit, proclaimed the Good News and touched the lives of people with reconciliation, release, and restoration (Lk 4:18-19), so the church was empowered by the Spirit to become a caring and sharing community (Acts 2:43-47; 4:33-37). As Jesus, the man of the Spirit, reached out to the weak, poor, and rejects of the Palestinian society (this is a special emphasis throughout Luke's Gospel), so the community of the Spirit was concerned with taking care of people's needs (Acts 4:34; 5:1-6). These parallels illustrate Luke's understanding of the oneness of Jesus' ministry with that of the church—all because the Spirit of Jesus was, and is, in his church.

there, come and drink of him. So John added a note: "But this he spoke concerning the Spirit, for the Spirit was not yet because Jesus was not yet glorified" (7:39). Once Jesus would be glorified through resurrection, the Spirit of the glorified Jesus would be available for people to drink. In John 6, Jesus offered himself as the bread of life to be eaten by people; and in John 7, he offered himself as the water of life to refresh men. But no one could eat him or drink him until he became spirit, as was intimated in John 6:63 and then stated plainly in John 7:39.

In John 14:16-18, Jesus went one step further in identifying himself with the Spirit. He told the disciples that he would give them another Comforter. Then he told them that they should know who this Comforter was because he was, then and there, abiding with them and would, in the near future, be in them. Who else but Jesus was abiding with them at that time? Then after telling the disciples that the Comforter would come to them, he said, "I am coming to you." First he said that the Comforter would come to them and abide in them, and then in the same breath he said that he would come to them and abide in them (see 14:20). In short, the coming of the Comforter to the disciples was one and the same as the coming of Jesus to the disciples. The Comforter who was dwelling with the disciples that night was the Spirit in Christ; the Comforter who would be in the disciples (after the resurrection) would be Christ in the Spirit.

On the evening of the resurrection, the Lord Jesus appeared to the disciples and then breathed into them the Holy Spirit. This inbreathing, reminiscent of God's breathing into Adam the breath of life (Gn 2:7), became the fulfillment of all that had been promised and anticipated earlier in John's Gospel. Through this impartation, the disciples became regenerated and indwelt by the Spirit of Jesus Christ. This historical event marked the genesis of the new creation. Jesus could now be realized as the bread of life, the water of life, and the light of life. The believers now possessed his divine, eternal, risen life. From that time forward, Christ as spirit indwelt his believers. Thus, in his first epistle John could say, "And hereby we know that he abides in us, by the Spirit whom he gave to us" (1 Jn 3:24), and again, "Hereby we know that we abide in him and he in us, because he has given us of his Spirit" (4:13).

The apostles had quite an adjustment to make after Christ's resurrection. They had become so accustomed to his physical presence that it was difficult for them to learn how to live by his spiritual, indwelling presence. All through the 40 days after his resurrection, from the time the apostles received the inbreathing of the Spirit, Christ was teaching the disciples to make the transfer. He would physically appear and then disappear intermittently. His appearances were very frequent in the beginning and then they steadily diminished. His aim was to guide the apostles into knowing him in his invisible presence. However, this was so new to them that he had to keep appearing to them in order to strengthen and reassure them. But his real desire was to help them live by faith and not by sight. When he appeared to the disciples as they were all together the second time, with Thomas present, he chided Thomas for his unbelief. Then he pronounced this blessing, "Blessed are those who do not see me and yet believe" (Jn 20:29).

The apostle Paul was such a "blessed" one. He did not know Christ in the flesh. He knew only the risen Christ (2 Cor 5:15-16). In this regard, he had an advantage over the early apostles. They had a great adjustment to make, but from the very beginning, Paul knew the risen Christ as Spirit. Paul became the forerunner of all those Christians who have never seen Jesus in the flesh and who have come to experience him in the Spirit. Yes, Paul had seen the risen Lord; he was the last one to do so (1 Cor 15:8). And from that time onward he realized that Jesus was a glorified man, exalted far above all. Paul wrote much concerning this, but his writings did not leave the far-above-all Jesus far away because this was not what Paul experienced. Any experienced Christian should be able to testify that the Christ in the heavens is also the Christ in the heart.

In his writings, Paul often speaks of the Spirit and Christ synonymously. This is evident in Romans 8:9-10. The terms "Spirit of God," "Spirit of Christ," and "Christ" are all used interchangeably. The Spirit of God is the Spirit of Christ, and the Spirit of Christ is Christ. In these verses, it is evident that Paul identified the Spirit with Christ because in Christian experience they are absolutely identical. There is no such thing as an experience of Christ apart from the Spirit. The separation and/or distinction does exist in Trinitarian theology— and for very good reasons—but the separation is nearly nonexistent in actual experience. Several of Paul's statements are written from the vantage point of experience.

In 1 Corinthians 15:45, Paul says that the risen Jesus became life-giving spirit. Notice the verse does not say Jesus became the Spirit, as if the second person of the Trinity became the third, but that Jesus became spirit in the sense that his mortal existence and form were metamorphosed into a spiritual existence and form. Jesus' person was not changed through the resurrection, only his form. With this changed spiritual form, Jesus regained the essential state of being he had emptied himself of in becoming a man. Before he became a man, he subsisted in the form of God (Phil 2:6), which form is Spirit and thereby was united to the Spirit (the third of the Trinity), while still remaining distinct. Thus, when the scripture says that the Lord "became life-giving spirit," it does not mean that the Son became the Holy Spirit. But it does indicate that Christ, via resurrection, appropriated a new, spiritual form (while still retaining a body—a glorified one) that enabled him to commence a new spiritual existence (see 1 Pt 3:18).

In 2 Corinthians 3, Paul explains that the NT ministry is a ministry carried out by the Spirit of the living God (v 3), who is the Spirit that gives life (v 6). In fact, the whole NT economy is characterized as "the ministry of the Spirit" (v 8). At the same time, Paul emphasizes that the function of the NT ministry is to bring God's people to see and experience the glorious Christ (3:3, 14, 16-18; 4:4-6). It is in this context that Paul boldly declares, "The Lord is the Spirit" (3:17). He who turns his heart to the Lord is, in effect, turning his heart to the Spirit. If the Lord were not the Spirit abiding in the believers, how could they turn their hearts to him? And how could they be transformed into the same image? Second Corinthians 3:18 says, "But we all, with unveiled face mirroring the glory of the Lord, are being transformed into the same image from glory to glory, just as from the Lord-Spirit." According to the Greek, the last phrase of this verse could be rendered "the Lord, the Spirit" (see ASV) or "the Lord, who is the Spirit" (see RSV, NIV) because the expression "the Spirit" is in direct apposition to "the Lord" (i.e., it is a further description of the Lord). Thus, the Lord is the Spirit.

In conclusion, when the Scriptures identify the Spirit with Christ and vice versa, the identification is not equivocation. Christ is not the Holy Spirit. Christ and the Spirit are distinct persons of the Trinity, as is affirmed by the overall teaching of the Word. But the Scriptures do identify Christ and the Spirit in the context of Christian experience. It would be accurate to say that Christians experience Christ through his Spirit, the Spirit of Christ. One cannot know Jesus apart from the Spirit or other than through the Spirit.

See also Resurrection.

SPIRIT OF MAN* The innermost being of the human person, corresponding with the nature of God, which is Spirit. Some scholars think the spirit is the same as the soul; others see a distinction. As such, some believe in the tripartite (threefold) nature of a human (cf. 1 Thes 5:23), spirit, soul, and body, as against a bipartite (twofold) nature, material and immaterial.

First Thessalonians 5:23 clearly speaks of a tripartite design for mankind. Other Scriptures see soul and spirit as the same. A clear case of the parallel (synonymous) use of soul and spirit (as in Jb 7:11; Is 26:9, etc.) is in Mary's "Magnificat." She says, "My soul magnifies the Lord, and my spirit has rejoiced in God my Savior" (Lk 1:47, NKJV). Rather than divide the two as "parts," some have suggested that a human *has* a spirit and *is* a soul. Usually spirit indicates the vitalizing, energizing, empowering agent; it is that essence of the human being that corresponds with God's nature and can commune with God, who is Spirit.

Those who are united to Christ experience spiritual union with him—his Spirit with their spirit. This is what Paul meant when he said, "He who joins himself to the Lord is one spirit" (1 Cor 6:17). Note that Paul does not say, "he who joins himself to the Spirit is one spirit"; he uses the word "Lord" as synonymous with "the Spirit." Union with the Lord is a union of the human spirit with his Spirit. Since the day of regeneration, a believer's human spirit is united to Christ's Spirit. Look at John 3:6 ("that which is born of the Spirit is spirit") and Romans 8:16 ("his Spirit bears witness with our spirit that we are the children of God"). These scriptures show that one's union with Christ is based upon the regeneration of one's spirit by the divine Spirit.

SPIRITS Synonym for angels and demons. *See* Angel; Demon.

SPIRITS*, Discerning of *See* Spiritual Gifts.

SPIRITS, Unclean *See* Demon; Demon-possession.

SPIRITS IN PRISON Term used in 1 Peter 3:18-20a. There is little agreement among scholars as to what "spirits in prison" really refers to or why Jesus would have gone to preach to them. Martin Luther confessed that verse 19 "is an amazing text and as dark as any in the New Testament and I am not sure I know what St. Peter means." Because there is so much disagreement and uncertainty, several possible interpretations are presented here.

First, many commentators take "spirits in prison" to refer to the disembodied spirits of the people who disobeyed the preaching of Noah and are now in Sheol or hades—the place of the departed unbelievers. Some think Christ preached the gospel to them so that they could believe and be saved (though there is little, if any, support in the NT that a person who dies as an unbeliever can get a second chance). Others think that Christ simply proclaimed his victory over Satan and made known the blessings that these spirits once for all rejected.

Second, other commentators argue that the "spirits in prison" are not human spirits but rather are the same supernatural beings referred to in 1 Peter 3:22—the evil angels, authorities, and powers. They are related to the "sons of God" in Genesis 6:1-4. In support of this, they argue that the proclamation to these spirits is not before but after Jesus' resurrection, and so is probably not a *descent* to the dead but an *ascent* to the "heavenly places," where the rebellious spiritual powers live (see Eph 6:12). Furthermore, in the pre-Christian Jewish book of 1 Enoch, Enoch is pictured as proclaiming doom to the apostate angels. So Christ is seen as the new Enoch declaring to the "spirits in prison" his victory on the cross and their final defeat.

Finally, still others have suggested that the preaching of Christ was neither to supernatural spiritual beings nor to the departed spirits in Hades. Rather, the preaching took place in the days of Noah and was addressed to Noah's contemporaries, who, because they disobeyed, are now in prison. In other words, the Spirit of Christ, referred to in 1 Peter 1:11, and which existed before the Incarnation, inspired Noah to preach to the people. In this interpretation there is no "descent into hell" and no declaration to the fallen angels. The text simply says that Christ in his spiritual dimension preached in the days of Noah.

See also Peter, First Letter of.

SPIRITUAL GIFTS Phrase regularly used to translate two Greek words, *charismata* and *pneumatika* (the plural forms of *charisma* and *pneumatikon*). Both words are almost exclusively Pauline within the biblical writings; elsewhere in the NT, they appear only in 1 Peter 2:5 and 4:10. Other writers, of course, mention phenomena that fall within Paul's definition of "spiritual gifts," but for specific teaching on the subject, one must depend on Paul first and foremost.

Both words are derived from more familiar words, *charis* (grace) and *pneuma* (spirit). Both have similar

senses—*charisma* meaning "expression of grace," *pneumatikon* meaning "expression of Spirit." Their range of application, however, is somewhat different.

Charisma denotes God's saving action in Christ (Rom 5:15-16) and the gift of eternal life (6:23). More generally, in Romans 11:29 it probably refers to the series of gracious acts on behalf of Israel whereby God made Israel's calling and election sure. In 2 Corinthians 1:11 it probably refers to a particular action of God that brought Paul deliverance from deadly peril. Otherwise, the reference seems to be to divine grace as mediated through individuals, with Paul presumably thinking of the sort of utterances and deeds that he illustrates in Romans 12:6-8 and 1 Corinthians 12:8-10 (so in Rom 1:11; 1 Cor 1:7; 7:7; 12:4-11, 28-30; similarly 1 Pt 4:10).

Pneumatikon has a wider range of usage. It is more properly an adjective and so describes various things (and people) as "spiritual," as manifesting the Spirit, or as serving as the instrument of the Spirit. These include some particular word or act (Rom 1:11), the law (7:14), the manna, water from the rock, and the rock itself in the wilderness wanderings of Israel (1 Cor 10:3-4), the resurrection body (15:44-46), unspecified blessings "in the heavenly places" (Eph 1:3), particular insights into the divine will (Col 1:9), and songs in worship (Eph 5:19; Col 3:16). As a plural noun, it can be used of individuals ("the spiritual ones," 1 Cor 2:13, 15; 14:37; Gal 6:1) or of things ("the spirituals," "spiritual gifts," Rom 15:27; 1 Cor 2:13; 9:11; 12:1; 14:1), even "spiritual powers in heaven" (Eph 6:12).

From this brief survey, a more precise definition of "spiritual gifts" can be made. Whatever thing or individual serves as an instrument of the Spirit or manifests the Spirit or embodies the Spirit is a spiritual gift (*pneumatikon*). Whatever event, word, or action is a concrete expression of grace or serves as a means of grace is a spiritual gift (*charisma*). *Pneumatikon* is the more general word; *charisma* is more specific. Moreover, *charisma* is probably Paul's own word (Rom 1:11; 12:6; 1 Cor 7:7; 12:4) in preference to the more ambiguous *pneumatikon*, which seems to have been popular with those causing difficulty for Paul in Corinth (1 Cor 2:13–3:4; 14:37; 15:44-46). Consequently, attention will focus in what follows on *charisma*. Not forgetting those passages where Paul uses this word in broader terms for the direct act of God (Rom 5:15,16; 6:23; 11:29; 1 Cor 1:11), concentration will be on the passages where Paul speaks in more precise terms of particular manifestations of grace mediated through one individual to others—"spiritual gifts" in this the narrower sense of *charisma*.

The lists of *charismata* (Rom 12; 1 Cor 12; Eph 4; 1 Pt 4) are the obvious starting point because they provide the clearest indications of what Paul would include within the range of spiritual gifts. For Paul (the one who gave Christianity the concept of *charisma*), a spiritual gift is essentially an act of God's Spirit, a concrete manifestation in word or deed of God's grace through an individual for the benefit of others.

In its basic sense, a spiritual gift is a specific act of God, and this remains true even when it is mediated through any individual. This means that no one can hope to manifest such a gift except in conscious openness to and dependence on God. By extension Paul can speak of individuals "having" or "possessing" certain spiritual gifts (Rom 12:6; 1 Cor 7:7; 12:3), but this is presumably just shorthand for their being so open to God's grace that that grace regularly or constantly manifests itself through them in particular ways. Such language no more means that the *charisma* is an ability at the individual's command than does the similar talk of "having the Spirit" (Rom 8:9, 23). It is true, however, that in 1 Timothy 4:14 and 2 Timothy 1:6 this basic sense is beginning to be left behind.

A spiritual gift is any event, word, or action that embodies and expresses God's grace. In this sense sacraments can be "means of grace" (though they are never called this in the NT), as are many other utterances and actions as well. In recognizing this, one can recognize too that the lists of gifts (e.g., Rom 12:6-8; 1 Cor 12:8-10) are neither definitive nor exhaustive, simply typical manifestations of the Spirit (or those with which they needed some advice). The degree of overlap between these various lists shows that Paul was not concerned to specify a precisely defined catalog; he simply selected a number of activities and utterances through which he saw the grace of God manifesting itself in his churches.

THE CHURCH'S VIEW OF SPIRITUAL GIFTS
The spiritual gifts of prophecy, glossolalia, and healing seem to have disappeared from the mainstream of the church's life by the middle of the third century. The longer ending to Mark (Mk 16:17), Justin Martyr, Irenaeus, and Tertullian all testify to the continuing experience of such gifts before then, but in the fourth century Chrysostom and Augustine of Hippo thought of them as belonging to the past. This was in large part due to the increasing institutionalization of the church, in the course of which *chrismation* (anointing with oil) progressively replaced *charismata* as the sign of the Spirit. The body of Christ came to be conceived of as a hierarchical structure, and the phrase "gifts of the Spirit" was referred more frequently to Isaiah 11:2. Over the centuries there were successive claims that one or more of the more striking gifts had been restored—most notably by the early Montanists (second century), Joachim of Fiore (1132?–1202), many of the Anabaptists, and the early Quakers—but such claimants were usually either pushed to the fringes of Christianity or persecuted outright.

More recently, events have taken a different turn. Renewed interests in spiritual gifts, particularly healing and glossolalia, at the end of the 19th century heralded the emergence of Pentecostalism in the 20th century. With the acceptance of Pentecostalism as a third or fourth main stream of Christianity (beside Orthodoxy, Catholicism, and Protestantism), and charismatic renewal within the older denominations, the charismatic dimension of Christian life and worship has steadily gained recognition, not least among the Catholics.

It is important to grasp that Paul saw all Christians as charismatics. Whoever "has" the Spirit—that is, is open to and being led by the Spirit (Rom 8:9-14)—will inevitably manifest the grace of God in some way and should also be open to the Spirit's power coming to expression in particular words and deeds within the community of the Spirit. For Paul, the church is the body of Christ. The functions of that body's members are exemplified by the spiritual gifts (Rom 12:4-6; 1 Cor 12:14-30). Unless the individual is functioning charismatically, he is not functioning as a member of the body. The Spirit's gifts are the living movements of Christ's body. As the body is many different members functioning as one body, so the unity of the church grows out of the diverse functions (gifts) of its mem-

bers. It follows that a spiritual gift is given primarily with the community in view. It is given "for the common good" (1 Cor 12:7). That is why a selfish, loveless clutching after *charismata* is wrong and futile (13:1-3). A spiritual gift is never one's to use as one wants for one's own benefit (except perhaps glossolalia, but that is why Paul gives it lower value). It is given to one only in the sense that God chooses to act through one for others. More precisely, it is given only through one to the community, and one benefits only as the community benefits. The spiritual health and edification of the individual is inextricably bound up with the health and well-being of the whole body (12:14-26; Eph 4:16). *See* Apostle, Apostleship; Miracle; Prophecy; Teacher; Tongues, Speaking in.

SPIRITUALITY *See* Sanctification.

SPONGE *See* Animals.

SPRINKLING OF BLOOD *See* Offerings and Sacrifices.

STACHYS Christian in Rome to whom Paul sent greetings, calling him "my beloved" (Rom 16:9).

STACTE* One of the fragrant spices used by Moses to make the incense offering (Ex 30:34). *See* Plants (Balm; Storax Tree).

STADIUM* Greek unit of linear measure equivalent to about 200 yards or 182.9 meters (Mt 14:24). *See* Weights and Measures.

STAG *See* Animals (Deer).

STALLION *See* Animals (Horse).

STAR *See* Astronomy.

STAR IN THE EAST* Star that guided the magi to the infant Jesus (Mt 2:2, 7-10). The magi were residents of some Eastern land (possibly Parthia, Babylon, or Arabia) who came to Herod. They explained that they had seen the star of the King of the Jews in their homeland. Herod and the Jewish scribes directed the men to Bethlehem, but the star guided them to the place of Jesus' birth.

Numerous theories have been advanced to explain this phenomenon. In the 17th century Johannes Kepler suggested that the explosion of a distant star (supernova) would emit extraordinary light. While many such explosions are recorded each year (few visible to the naked eye), none are known from the time of Christ. The ancients were fascinated with comets. Halley's comet was first sighted and recorded in 240 BC and, if calculated at 77-year intervals, would have appeared in Judea in 12–11 BC. This, however, significantly antedates Jesus' birth; moreover, comets were usually associated with catastrophes in the ancient world. That the ancients practiced astrology, plotting the constellations and the course of the planets, is well known. Rare planetary conjunctions were studied and interpreted. For instance, in 7 BC Jupiter and Saturn came together in the zodiac constellation of Pisces (this occurs every 257 years). According to this view, Jupiter was associated with the world ruler, Saturn with the region of Syria-Palestine, and Pisces with the last days.

First-century readers—Jewish or Greek—would not have been surprised to read about a new star presaging the birth of Jesus. In Matthew 2:2 "in the east" might mean "at its rising." In other words, the wise men had witnessed a new star and interpreted it as hallmarking some new event. In Greco-Roman society, the heavens often foretold or explained historical events (e.g., the founding of Rome, the birth of Augustus, etc.). Judaism likewise emphasized stars: Josephus recorded astral phenomena during the fall of Jerusalem in AD 70. Moreover, rabbis were enthralled with the imagery of the Balaam story in Numbers 24:17 (see esp. Nm 24:17, LXX) and symbolized their messianic expectations in a star. This was also common at Qumran (CD 7:19 f.; 1QM 11:6; cf. T. Levi 18:3; Rv 22:16). Similarly, coins struck after the onset of the revolt of Simon Bar-Kochba ("son of a star") bore a star.

See also Astronomy.

STATER* Common coin in Jesus' day (Mt 17:27). *See* Coins.

STEALING *See* Criminal Law and Punishment; Commandments, The Ten.

STEER* *See* Animals (Cattle).

STEPHANAS Christian believer at Corinth. He and his household were evidently Paul's first converts in Achaia. The members of Stephanas's family were some of the few Corinthian believers personally baptized by Paul. Stephanas and his kin were praised for their devotion and service to the Corinthian church. Stephanas, with Fortunatus and Achaicus, visited Paul at Ephesus in Asia Minor. Their mission probably included bringing aid for Paul's personal needs and seeking his advice for resolving the problems in the Corinthian church. Undoubtedly, Paul wrote and sent his first letter to the Corinthian church with this small delegation when they returned to Corinth (1 Cor 1:16; 16:15-17).

STEPHEN One of the first deacons and the first martyr of the apostolic church. For Luke, Stephen represents the growing Hellenistic interest of certain members in the early Jerusalem church. In addition, Stephen's major speech (Acts 7:1-53) serves as a critique of traditional Judaism and suggests evangelization beyond Judea.

In Acts 6, Luke tells us of the first division in the early church. The community consisted of two Jewish groups described as "Hebrews" and "Hellenists." These terms no doubt indicate cultural and linguistic divisions: Jews who had emerged from either Aramaic- or Greek-speaking synagogues. Stephen was one of seven deacons nominated to serve the needs of the Hellenists. Yet even in his introduction it is evident that his importance stands out; he alone is described as "full of faith and of the Holy Spirit" (v 5). After their commission Stephen is mentioned again as "full of grace and power," and as doing "great wonders and signs among the people" (v 8).

Stephen's preaching put him in contention with the Hellenistic synagogues of Jerusalem (Acts 6:9). As his subsequent speech before the Sanhedrin indicates, Stephen propounded a radical abrogation of the ancestral customs of Judaism and the temple cult. Luke's account of his arrest and interrogation (6:10–7:60) is intended to evoke memories of Jesus' trial. While capital punishment was reserved for the Roman governor once Judea had become a province, offenses against the temple still could be prosecuted by the Sanhedrin. In the end, Stephen's execution by stoning is pursued with a vengeance (7:54-60). As the first martyr of the church, Stephen models Jesus even in death. He commits his spirit to Jesus (as Christ had done to the Father, Lk 23:46) and dies asking forgiveness for his prosecutors (Acts 7:59-60).

The speech in Acts 7 not only provides us with Stephen's defense but in addition serves Luke's broader interests in the spread of the gospel abroad (Acts 1:8). It is the longest speech in Acts and appears at a pivotal place in apostolic history. Stephen provides a critical recital of biblical history and argues that the major pillars upon which Judaism rested were in jeopardy. The temple, in which the Jews took pride, was not a divine invention—Solomon's temple was contrary to the earlier tabernacle in the wilderness. The Torah, in which religious security was sought, was used by Stephen to chronicle Israel's consistent disobedience. These same scriptures announced the coming of "the righteous one," whom Israel crucified.

The implications of the speech are vital. God is free to move beyond the national/religious boundaries of Judaism. The exclusivistic outlook of Judaism is artificial. God's work is dynamic. And if Stephen's conclusions are correct, the Jewish church ought to be free to take the gospel beyond Judea. Stephen's martyrdom introduced a major persecution in Jerusalem (Acts 8:1-3), which was followed by the proclamation of the gospel to the Samaritans and then the Greeks.

STOCKS Common form of punishment and confinement in Bible times (2 Chr 16:10; Acts 16:24). *See* Criminal Law and Punishment.

STOICISM*, STOICS A widespread Greek philosophy, well represented in the audience at Athens listening to Paul (Acts 17:16-34). The apostle was probably familiar with it, for it had begun in Athens around 300 BC, with Zeno's teaching in the "stoa" (porches) of public buildings, and had spread throughout the Greco-Roman world. It was known, for example, at Tarsus and on the island of Cyprus, so that Paul would no doubt have encountered Stoics earlier in his journeys and possibly even in his hometown. The scope and power of its influence are indicated by the fact that the Roman emperor Marcus Aurelius (d. AD 180) was himself a Stoic, some of whose philosophical writings have survived.

The earliest Stoics were primarily concerned with cosmology, that is, the study of nature's origin and its laws. They were materialists, who held that all things come from the one basic element of fire and will eventually return to that one element in a vast cosmic conflagration. They, therefore, had a cyclical view of cosmic history, in which one universe after another arises and is destroyed. Both the orderliness of things as we know them, and this cyclical pattern of history, were ascribed to the organizing and sustaining power of a pervasive force known as the *Logos* that is sometimes regarded as divine. Its laws were the laws of nature to which all creatures must conform. It gives to all things their essential nature and so gives life and reason to men. In fact, the Logos is in man, taking the form of the human soul. Hence, to live according to reason is to live according to the natural order of things, and this is good. Conscious obedience to natural law liberates a man from fear and concern about external circumstances over which he has no control but which are still ruled by nature's laws. The good life, then, is one in which reason, not passion, rules, and peace of mind and harmony with nature consequently prevail.

Stoic ideas proved attractive to some Christians because of the apparent similarities between the Stoic logos and the Logos of John 1:1-18, and between the idea of natural law and the law of God.

See also Epicureans; Philosophy.

STONECUTTER A stonemason who removed stone from the quarry and squared it up for use in large buildings like palaces, administrative buildings, the temple, and large houses (1 Kgs 5:18, 2 Kgs 12:12; 1 Chr 22:2, 15). At first, the Israelites used Phoenician artisans, but they soon learned the art themselves and produced many fine buildings, such as those in Samaria. Herod's masons left behind beautiful masonry in Jerusalem, Hebron, Samaria, and elsewhere. Some of these artisans produced fine work for the interior of buildings to be used in windows, doors, lintels, and capitals for pillars. One special class of stonecutters, the engravers (Ex 28:11), worked with precious stones to produce seals, ornamental pieces, and jewelry.

STONES, Precious A lengthy list of the precious stones used in OT times occurs in Exodus 28:17-20 and 39:10-13, where four rows of three stones, each engraved with the name of one of the 12 tribes of Israel, were set in the high priest's breastplate. Other lists occur in Ezekiel 28:13 and Revelation 21:19-21. It is difficult to properly identify all of these stones, since an accurate translation is not always possible. Some of the differences of translation are indicated in the following list, as translated in the RSV:

1. Agate, an oxide of silicon, a type of translucent quartz with layers of different colors (Ex 28:19; 39:12; Is 54:12; Rv 21:19).
2. Alabaster, a finely granular banded variety of calcium carbonate (gypsum), often white and translucent and widely used in Bible times for ornamental vases, bowls, kohl pots, statues, perfume jars, and so on (Sg 5:15; Mt 26:7; Mk 14:3; Lk 7:37).
3. Amethyst, an oxide of silicon, a purple or violet variety of transparent crystalline quartz (Ex 28:19; 39:12; Rv 21:20).
4. Beryl, a silicate of aluminum (Ex 28:20; 39:13; Sg 5:14; Dn 10:6). It is usually green in color (Rv 21:20) but can be blue, white, or golden and may be either opaque or transparent—the latter variety including the gems emerald and aquamarine.
5. Carbuncle. See Emerald below.
6. Carnelian, a silicon oxide reddish in color. In translations it is sometimes equated with sardius (Ex 28:17; 39:10; Ez 28:13), a type of deep brown or red quartz (Rv 4:3; 21:20).
7. Chalcedony. See Agate above.
8. Chrysolite, an aluminum fluosilicate, yellowish in color (Rv 21:20), probably equivalent to topaz (Ex 28:17) or beryl (Ez 1:16; 10:9; 28:13).
9. Chrysoprase, a nickel-stained apple-green chalcedony widely used in jewelry (Rv 21:20).
10. Coral, the hard calcareous skeleton of a variety of marine animals occurring in various colors—red, white, and black. It is not strictly a stone (Jb 28:18; Ez 27:16).
11. Crystal, a clear, translucent crystalline quartz (Jb 28:18). In Revelation 4:6, 21:11, and 22:1 the Greek word *krystallon* may be rock crystal or even ice.
12. Diamond, a stone of uncertain identification (Ex 28:18; 39:11; Ez 28:13). It may not be the equivalent of the modern diamond. In Jeremiah 17:1, adamant was probably a form of corundum, a very hard substance.
13. Emerald, probably a green stone like the modern

emerald (Ex 28:18; 39:11; Ez 27:16; 28:13). The Septuagint suggests a purple stone like a garnet. In the NT *smaragdinos* in Revelation 4:3 and *smaragdos* in Revelation 21:19 suggest an emerald.
14. Jacinth, perhaps a reddish-orange zircon or a blue stone such as turquoise, amethyst, or sapphire (Ex 28:19; 39:12). In Revelation 21:20 *huakinthos* is a blue stone. The exact identification is uncertain.
15. Jasper, a compact, opaque, often highly colored crystalline quartz substance (Ex 28:20; 39:13). In the NT the Greek term *iaspis* (Rv 4:3; 21:11, 18-19) is a green quartz.
16. Lapis lazuli, a deep blue stone; a compound of sodium, aluminum, calcium, sulphur, and silver containing a mixture of several minerals. It generally has golden flecks of iron pyrites and was widely used for ornamental purposes in the ancient world. It is akin to sapphire.
17. Marble, a limestone crystallized by metamorphism, taking a high polish, durable and suitable for building purposes (1 Chr 29:2; Est 1:6; Rv 18:12).
18. Onyx, a quartz consisting of straight layers or bands which differ in color (Gn 2:12; Ex 25:7; 28:9, 20; 39:6, 13; 1 Chr 29:2; Jb 28:16; Ez 28:13). See Sardonyx below.
19. Pearl, a hard smooth substance, white or variously colored, which grows in the shell of various bivalve mollusks. In the NT "pearls" are known as ornaments for women (1 Tm 2:9; Rv 17:4) or as items for trade (Rv 18:12, 16). The kingdom of heaven is likened to a fine pearl, which people seek at great cost (Mt 13:45-46).
20. Ruby, an uncertain translation of the Hebrew word *peninim* in six places (Jb 28:18; Prv 3:15; 8:11; 20:15; 31:10; Lam 4:7). This deep red or carmine stone was probably known in the ancient world, but there are difficulties in the translation of terms that may refer to it.
21. Sapphire, a deep blue stone (Ex 24:10; 28:18; 39:11; Jb 28:6, 16; Sg 5:14; Is 54:11; Lam 4:7; Ez 1:26; 10:1; 28:13), which may have referred at times to lapis lazuli as in Job 28:6 and Revelation 21:19.
22. Sardius, a red or deep brown form of quartz (Ex 28:17; 39:10; Ez 28:13 KJV). It is referred to also in Revelation 4:3 (KJV "sardine stone"), though in modern versions it is often rendered as "carnelian." See Carnelian above.
23. Sardonyx, a form of agate with layers of brown and white (Rv 21:20, KJV, NASB; "onyx" in NLT).
24. Topaz, a yellow stone, a fluosilicate of aluminum occurring in crystalline form (Ex 28:17; 39:10; Jb 28:19; Ez 28:13; Rv 21:20).

See also Minerals and Metals.

STONING *See* Criminal Law and Punishment.

STONY ARABIA* A division of Arabia, also called Rocky Arabia. See Arabia, Arabs.

STORAX TREE* Small, stiff-branched tree from which stacte was extracted for making incense (Ex 30:34). *See* Plants.

STORK *See* Birds.

STRAIGHT STREET Street in Damascus where Paul lodged after his encounter with the risen Jesus and where, in the house of Judas, he was baptized by Ananias and recovered his eyesight (Acts 9:11). The street is called "Straight" because, unlike many others, this one was straight. It still is straight, though it is on an elevation about 15 feet (4.6 meters) higher than the original thoroughfare; it is called by this same name (Rue Droite). It runs east and west on the south boundary of the Christian quarter. The "house of Judas" is no longer there, but in a lane off the eastern end of Straight Street is the "house of Ananias."

See also Damascus.

STRANGER *See* Foreigner.

STRANGLING One of four practices from which the early gentile Christians were asked to abstain out of respect for their Jewish Christian brothers and sisters. Jewish law prohibited the eating of any meat from which the animal's blood was not fully drained at the time of slaughtering. The Jerusalem Council requested the early church to observe this practice in order to keep peace between Jewish and gentile Christians (Acts 15:20, 29; 21:25).

Strangulation was also one of four forms of capital punishment administered by the Jewish law courts. Though it was not mentioned as a method of punishment in the Bible, strangulation was later adopted by rabbinic Judaism as the mode of execution.

See also Criminal Law and Punishment.

STRINGED INSTRUMENT *See* Musical Instruments.

STRONG DRINK Any intoxicating liquor. It was forbidden to Levites who were entering the tent of meeting (Lv 10:9); to those taking the Nazirite vow (Nm 6:3; Jgs 13:4-14); to kings and rulers (Prv 31:4); and to John the Baptist (Lk 1:15). The writer of Proverbs 20:1 suggests that the wise man does not become intoxicated by it. Isaiah pronounces woe on those addicted to it (Is 5:11, 22). Strong drink was used as a libation in the Levitical sacrifice (Nm 28:7) and was permitted in the menu of the feast at the time of tithing (Dt 14:26).

See also Wine.

STUMBLING BLOCK* Term used both literally and figuratively to refer to anything that might cause one to stumble.

The phrase is used literally in Leviticus 19:14, where the people of Israel are admonished not to "put a stumbling block before the blind," but to "fear the Lord your God." An isolated figurative use occurs in Jeremiah 6:21, where God promises to put a stumbling block before the people of Israel if they do not heed his warnings.

The most common OT usage, however, is found in Ezekiel, where the phrase is used to refer to idols and idolatry: "Son of man, these men have taken their idols into their hearts, and set the stumbling block of their iniquity before their faces; should I let myself be inquired of at all by them?" (Ez 14:3, RSV; also 7:19; 44:12).

In the NT the term essentially retains its Hebraic meaning. Even so, the phrase is employed figuratively to speak of the difficulties encountered by many Jews in believing Jesus to be the Son of God: "But we preach Christ crucified, a stumbling block to Jews and folly to Gentiles" (1 Cor 1:23, RSV; see also Rom 9:31-32). In Romans 11:11-12, Paul says that this resistance is actually part of God's plan to spread his riches to the world. Finally, 1 Corinthians 8:9 uses "stumbling block" to speak of some practices that might in themselves be appropriate but might also have the unintended effect of offending a weaker brother (see also Rom 14:13).

STYLUS* Instrument used for writing characters on clay tablets (Jb 19:24; Jer 17:1). *See* Writing.

SUAH Zophah's son, who was a leader in his father's household and a mighty warrior in Asher's tribe (1 Chr 7:36).

SUCATHITE Family of scribes living at Jabez of Judah and descendants of the Kenites (1 Chr 2:55).

SUCCOTH

1. Town in the Jordan Valley listed along with other towns as belonging to the tribe of Gad (Jos 13:27). It is located in the fertile valley called Ghaur Abu 'Udeidah, known in the Bible as the valley of Succoth (Pss 60:6; 108:7); it comprises the central portion of the Jordan Valley on the eastern side, between the Wadi Rejeb and the Jabbok River.

The place is mentioned for the first time in the account of Jacob's meeting with Esau, which occurred just south of Penuel. Jacob went from the meeting to Succoth and built some shelters for his cattle, which is given as the explanation for the name of the settlement (Gn 33:17)—Succoth means "shelters."

Later, the men of Succoth refused to give food to Gideon and his men when they were pursuing the Midianites (Jgs 8:5-9). Upon his return, Gideon made a point of punishing the elders of Succoth (vv 13-17). The form of social organization reflected in this passage has suggested that the population was not Israelite at the time of Gideon's visitation.

Finally, Succoth is mentioned with regard to Solomon's building projects. The metal casting for the important fixtures and implements of the temple was performed in the area between Succoth and Zarethan (1 Kgs 7:46; 2 Chr 4:17). It is possible that Succoth of the monarchical period was destroyed by Shishak of Egypt.

It has been proposed that the place-name occurs in two other passages: as the staging area for David's forces in the battle with Ammon, when the ark and the army were "living in shelters (*sukkoth*)" (2 Sm 11:11), and as the staging area for Ben-hadad's troops in his war against Samaria (1 Kgs 20:12, 16).

2. Town in Egypt mentioned as the first station of the Israelites in their exodus from Egypt (Ex 12:37; 13:20; Nm 33:5-6); it appears between Rameses and Etham.

Egyptian sources, texts of the Anastasi collection, refer to a place that is most likely the same as biblical Succoth. An Edomite tribe is recorded as bringing their herds in from the desert to pasture them in the Delta, passing by the strong point at *Tkw* [Old Egyptian for Succoth] (Papyrus Anastasi VI, 54). The military garrison there was commanded by a "commander" of (archer) troops, and the fort was named after Pharaoh Mernephta (Papyrus Anastasi, VI, 55).

Scholarly opinion usually places Succoth at Tell el-Maskhuta, a site near the mouth of the Wadi Tumeilat. *See* map, page 459.

SUCCOTH-BENOTH Deity and shrine worshiped by Babylonians settled in Samaria by Assyria after the fall of Israel in 722 BC (2 Kgs 17:30). Various opinions exist as to the specific understanding of Succoth-benoth. Some suggest that it refers to a place of prostitution honoring a Babylonian deity or to a small structure housing female idols. Others suggest it refers to Sarpanitu, the consort of Marduk (a Babylonian deity), or to Marduk himself.

SUCHATHITE* KJV spelling of Sucathite, a family of scribes, in 1 Chronicles 2:55. *See* Sucathite.

SUFFERING Anything causing pain or distress; calamity. From the biblical viewpoint, affliction began with the entrance of sin into the world. Both mankind and all creation were afflicted with "thorns and thistles," sin, death, and decay (cf. Gn 3:16-19; Rom 8:18-21). Because of sin, misery is a common human experience, and our short life is full of trouble (Jb 14:1-6). It is impossible for human beings to avoid natural calamity, physical injury, and interpersonal conflict (2 Chr 20:9), yet God uses affliction to instruct and discipline his people. This aspect of affliction is graphically portrayed by the oppression during the Israelites' sojourn in Egypt (Ex 4:31), by their troubles during the period of the judges (Neh 9:26-27), and by their exile in Babylon (Is 26:16). In Israel's distress they cried out to God, who delivered them and led them into obedience (Jer 10:18; Hos 5:15–6:3).

The Bible acknowledges that it is difficult to understand the many afflictions of the righteous (Pss 34:19; 37:39; 138:7). Even the prophet and "Servant of the Lord" (Messiah) were not spared (Is 53:2-12; Jer 15:15). Jesus Christ bore the griefs and sorrows of humanity as the culmination of the affliction begun by Adam's sin (Is 53:4-5; 1 Pt 2:24).

Jesus indicated that there would be many trials and sorrows for his followers (Jn 16:33). Paul taught that entrance to the kingdom of God comes with many tribulations (Acts 14:22), which must not shake a Christian's faith (1 Thes 3:3). They are to be understood rather as a finishing up of the remainder of Christ's suffering for his body, the church (2 Cor 4:10-11; Col 1:24). The biblical picture indicates that affliction will grow more intense as "the end" approaches (Mt 24:9-14; 2 Tm 3:13). The forces of Satan will attack in an effort to deceive and destroy the "elect" (Mt 24:24; 2 Thes 2:9-12; Rv 20:7-9). But when Jesus Christ is revealed from heaven in flaming fire, God will afflict those who have afflicted believers and will bring vengeance upon those who have not obeyed the gospel of Jesus Christ (Rom 2:9; 2 Thes 1:5-10; 2:7-8).

See also Persecution; Tribulation.

SUFFERING SERVANT* *See* Servant of the Lord.

SUICIDE The act of taking one's own life voluntarily and intentionally. Though the word "suicide" does not appear in most Bible translations (see, however, Jn 8:22, NLT), the OT records suicides by Saul and his armor bearer (1 Sm 31:3-6), Ahithophel (2 Sm 17:23), and Zimri (1 Kgs 16:15-19). Judas Iscariot is the only suicide victim mentioned in the NT (Mt 27:3-5).

The Bible does not directly condemn suicide but rather treats it as an indication of moral failure, often intensified by guilt or great personal loss. Saul had lost his sanity, his stability, and then his three sons on the battlefield. So he ended his life. Ahithophel, once a trusted counselor, was ruined by his ambition. When his plot against David was refused by Absalom, he felt disgraced. So he went home, set his affairs in order, and hanged himself. Judas Iscariot also hung himself, but his suicide was far more tragic. He, one of the twelve disciples, betrayed Jesus for thirty pieces of silver. Then he deeply regretted what he had done, and brought back the money to the Jewish leaders, saying "I have sinned in that I betrayed an innocent man" (Mt 27:3-4). As an expression of desperate remorse, Judas hanged himself.

SUKKIIM*, SUKKIIMS*, SUKKITES A tribe who joined forces with King Shishak of Egypt and entered Palestine to wage war against King Rehoboam of Judah (930–913 BC). The Sukkites are mentioned with the Libyans and the Ethiopians (2 Chr 12:3). They were probably a Libyan people.

SULFUR *See* Brimstone; Minerals and Metals; Stones, Precious.

SUMER*, SUMERIANS* Sumer was a region settled before 3500 BC in the lower part of Mesopotamia, now called Iraq. The Sumerians had a highly civilized society, developing cuneiform (a type of writing), medicine, mathematics, and astronomy. Thousands of clay tablets discovered in this region reveal their cultural, religious, and political endeavors. The Sumerian culture was absorbed by Semitic invaders who moved into Mesopotamia and slowly took over. By 2000 BC they had lost their political powers. Nevertheless, their culture formed the basis for the great Babylonian and Assyrian civilizations that developed there later.

See also Mesopotamia.

SUN A luminary created by God to be one of the great lights in the heavens, "to rule over the day" (Gn 1:14-15). The new day begins with its setting, and the daily sacrifices were offered in accordance with its position: the first burnt offering with its rising (Ex 29:39; Nm 28:4). The hours of the day in rabbinic Judaism vary with the length of the solar day throughout the year.

The months in the Israelite year were determined by the moon, but the fact that the major festivals fell in the fall (Trumpets, Atonement, Tabernacles) and the spring (Passover) show that account was taken of the solar year. The Gezer calendar has 12 months according to the agricultural activities of the solar year. The Jewish calendar is based on a 19-year cycle in which extra months are added to seven of the years, thus harmonizing the lunar and solar cycles. Silence in the Bible about this system has led scholars to assume the intercalation of a 13th month was a late innovation. However, Aramaic documents from the Jewish colony at Elephantine show that in the fifth century BC the Jews there were using the 19-year cycle in their reckonings. It is probable that the monarchies of Judah and Israel were using a system of intercalation, even though documentary evidence is lacking.

Rabbinic Judaism recognizes four seasons, while the OT usually mentions only two, "seedtime and harvest, cold and heat, summer and winter" (Gn 8:22). The four seasons are marked by phases of the sun. The fall (called *setav*, a word originally meaning rainy season, rain; Sg 2:11) begins with the fall equinox (September 21); the winter (*horeph*) begins with the winter solstice (c. December 22); the spring (*aviv*) begins with the spring equinox (March 21); and the summer (*qayits*) begins with the summer solstice (June 22). Recently, a temple was discovered at Beersheba, dating to the Hasmonean period (125 BC), that was oriented toward the sunrise of the summer solstice. A temple at Lachish with a similar ground plan and date seems to be oriented toward the winter solstice. The Arad temple from monarchical times faced almost due east, probably toward the equinox sunrise; such was probably the case with the Jerusalem temple.

The sun also plays a role in Hebrew poetic imagery. It was said to have a habitation (Hb 3:11), a tent set up by the Lord out of which he comes like a bridegroom (Ps 19:4-5). The sun is a symbol of constancy (72:5, 17), of the law (19:7), of the presence of God (84:11), and of beauty (Sg 6:10). Life in this temporal world is that which is "under the sun," according to Qoheleth (Eccl 1:3, 9, 14; 2:11).

A time of chaos and wrath upon the earth will be marked by the darkening of the sun (Is 13:10; Ez 32:7; Jl 2:10, 31; 3:15; Zep 1:15; Mt 24:29; Rv 8:12). This is obviously an allusion to an eclipse, something viewed with terror by the ancients. The sun's turning pale may also be derived from the effect of the sirocco, when sandstorms and hazy clouds often darken the sky. On the other hand, the day of the Lord's victory will be characterized by the sun's shining sevenfold brighter than at present (Is 30:26).

See also Astronomy; Calendars, Ancient and Modern; Day; Moon.

SUN, City of the Phrase in Isaiah 19:18; generally taken as a reference to Heliopolis. *See* Heliopolis.

SUNDAY *See* Lord's Day, The.

SUNDIAL Instrument used for telling time installed by King Ahaz of Judah (735–715 BC) in the royal palace of Jerusalem. Some suggest that this time indicator was not a sundial but a stairway. The time of day was determined by the position of the shadow of some object cast on the stairs. At Isaiah's command, the Lord miraculously caused the shadow to recede ten steps, divinely confirming to King Hezekiah of Judah (715–686 BC) that he would recover from his illness, live 15 more years, and be delivered from the Assyrian threat (2 Kgs 20:7-11; Is 38:7-8).

SUPH Region mentioned in Deuteronomy 1:1, which was "beyond the Jordan in the wilderness, in the Arabah over against Suph" (RSV; KJV "the Red Sea"). The exact location of Suph is uncertain. It may refer to the region of Suphah (cf. Nm 21:14), east of the Jordan River, or perhaps to the Gulf of Aqaba, the northeastern branch of the Red Sea.

SUPHAH Place east of the Jordan in the land of Moab (Nm 21:14); translated as "Red Sea" by the KJV. *See* Waheb.

SUPPER, Lord's *See* Lord's Supper, The.

SUPPLICATION* *See* Prayer.

SUR GATE Gate in Jerusalem linking the king's palace to the temple. It is mentioned in 2 Kings 11:6 in connection with the enthronement of Jehoash over Judah and the murder of Athaliah. Its parallel passage in 2 Chronicles 23:5 reads the "Gate of the Foundation," revealing perhaps a corruption within the Hebrew text.

SURGERY* *See* Medicine and Medical Practice.

SUSA Capital of the non-Semitic people and district of Elam. Susa (modern Shush) is located in southwest Iran, about 150 miles (241.4 kilometers) north of the Persian Gulf and due east of the well-known city of Babylon. French archaeologists began excavating the site in 1884, discovering that it was occupied as long ago as about 4000 BC. Its importance in the OT derives mainly from the fact that it was incorporated into the Persian Empire, founded by Cyrus in 550 BC. It became a royal city along with Ecbatana (the other main city in Elam), Babylon, and Persepolis. This was the great period of importance for Susa, although it had known an earlier golden age in the 12th century BC. (The first copy of the law code of

Hammurabi ever found was discovered at Susa, dated in the 12th century BC.)

The center of Persian Susa was an acropolis or citadel that rose above the city as a rectangular platform surrounded by a massive wall. This was the royal quarter within which the palace stood. The palace was the winter residence of the Persian kings.

Nehemiah was a cupbearer at the palace of Susa in the reign of Artaxerxes I (Neh 1:1, 11; 2:1). In Esther 1:2 and 2:8 the young Jewess Esther was introduced to the court of King Ahasuerus, who was evidently the Persian king Xerxes (485–465 BC). Most of the action of the book takes place in Susa (cf. Est 3:15; 8:14-15; 9:6-18).

According to Daniel 8:2, the place of Daniel's vision is Susa. Probably Daniel is not to be regarded as having been there literally, but rather he was spiritually transported there in the vision. Chronologically, Daniel's vision is set at the end of the Babylonian period, just before the Persian conquest (Dn 8:1; cf. 7:1). At this time Susa controlled the Medians and was not subject to Babylon.

See also Persia, Persians.

SUSANCHITE* KJV translation for "men of Susa" or "Shushanchites" in Ezra 4:9. *See* Susa.

SUSANNA
1. One of the women who ministered to Jesus out of her own resources (Lk 8:3).
2. The heroine of the apocryphal book Susanna and the Elders; a woman falsely charged with adultery but saved by the young prophet Daniel. This story, compacted into 64 verses, is considered a great piece of literature and the first true detective story. The book is economical in its characters, casting the prophet Daniel as the clever private investigator, Susanna as the beautiful and virtuous crime victim, and two community elders as unscrupulous, lustful villains. Characteristic of this story, like its counterparts in the modern genre, is the belief that right will prevail.

SUSANNA AND THE ELDERS *See* Daniel, Additions to.

SUSI Gaddi's father from Manasseh's tribe. Gaddi was one of the 12 spies sent to search out the land of Canaan (Nm 13:11).

SWADDLING CLOTHES* KJV translation of the kind of clothes that were wrapped around the baby Jesus. The NLT translation describes this in modern terms: "She [Mary] wrapped him snugly in strips of cloth" (Lk 2:7).

SWALLOW *See* Birds.

SWAN* *See* Birds.

SWEARING *See* Oath.

SWEET CANE *See* Plants (Cane).

SWEET STORAX* Small stiff-branched tree from which stacte was extracted for making incense (Ex 30:34). *See* Plants (Storax Tree).

SWINE *See* Animals (Pig).

SWORD *See* Armor and Weapons.

SYCAMINE* Black mulberry tree, valued for its fruit (Lk 17:6). See Plants (Mulberry).

SYCAMORE Large, spreading tree bearing a figlike fruit (1 Kgs 10:27; Lk 19:4). See Plants.

SYCHAR Town in Samaria, mentioned in the Bible only in John 4:5. The name has been taken as a variant form of the Greek transliteration of the Hebrew name Shechem. Many scholars favor an identification with the present-day village of Askar, which is located at the southeast foot of Mt Ebal, about one-half mile (.8 kilometer) north of Jacob's well. Excavations appear to favor the Shechem identification, which was proposed by Jerome. The Babylonian Talmud refers to a place called Sichar or Suchar, but its location is not known.

Sychar is said to be near the field that Jacob gave to his son Joseph (Jn 4:5). The record of the giving of this parcel of land is recorded in Genesis 48:22. When Jacob had concluded the blessing of Joseph's two sons, Manasseh and Ephraim, he told Joseph that he had given to him rather than to his brothers "one mountain slope which I took from the hand of the Amorites with my sword and with my bow" (Gn 48:22, RSV). The Hebrew word translated "slope" is the word for shoulder and the name of the city of Shechem. It was on this piece of property that Joseph was buried (Jos 24:32). This passage also states that Jacob bought the ground from the sons of Hamor, the father of Shechem, for a hundred pieces of silver (cf. Gn 33:19; Acts 7:16).

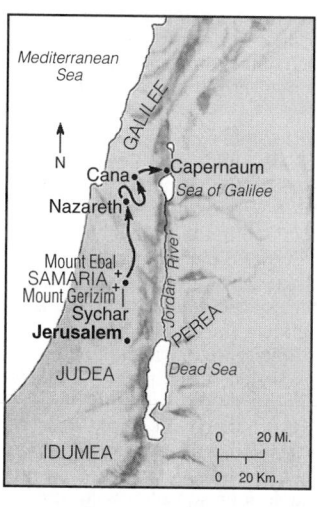

Sychar in Samaria
Jesus passed through Sychar on his way to various towns in Galilee.

The account of Jesus' visit to Sychar in John 4 is important. Jesus came to Sychar because of a spiritual, not geographical, imperative (Jn 4:4). One of the objectives of this mission was to break down barriers: the hostility between the racially pure Jew and the mixed-race Samaritan (v 9); the social restrictions between men and women (v 27); the societal separation between the ritually clean and the morally impure (this woman was ostracized; she came to the well alone and at an unusual time, v 6). The conversation between Jesus and the woman is instructive as to personal witness. The spiritual discernment and compassion of Jesus are evident. When the woman received the testimony of his identity as the Messiah, she too became an effective witness (vv 28-30). The new believers among the Samaritans asked Jesus to stay with them, so he remained for two days and many more believed in him (vv 39-41).

SYCHEM* KJV form of Shechem in Acts 7:16. See Shechem (Place).

SYENE* Southern Egyptian village (modern Aswan) demarcating Egypt's border with Ethiopia. The Hebrew form possibly derives from a word for "market" or "trading center," reflecting the importance of the outpost as a place of commerce. The remote location of Syene made it a useful geographical reference for designating the full span of Egypt's borders. "From Migdol to Syene" (Ez 29:10; 30:6) describes Egypt from northern delta to southern border (cf. Israel's description, "from Dan to Beersheba," 1 Sm 3:20; 1 Kgs 4:25). Syene was located on the east bank of the Nile just north of the first cataract. While valued by the Egyptians as a source of granite, Syene's fate was closely tied to Elephantine Island nearby. Elephantine was South Egypt's administrative center and was well fortified against attack. It was at Elephantine that Jews fleeing Judea in 587 BC found refuge and formed a colony.

SYMEON* Alternate spelling of Simeon, the name of a member of the church in Antioch (Acts 13:1). See Simeon (Person) #4.

SYNAGOGUE Transliteration of the Greek word *sunagoge*, meaning "a gathering together." It is used more than 50 times in the NT, mostly for the religious gathering places of Jewish communities in Palestine and throughout the Dispersion. The word *sunagoge* is usually the Greek rendering of Hebrew words in the OT that speak of the assembling or assembly of the people.

Origins and Early History It is unknown just how or when the synagogue as an institution first began. One can imagine the situation in Jerusalem after the destruction of the temple by the Babylonians in 586 BC. The people who remained in and around the city who wanted to keep true to their faith would have felt the need to meet for worship, where they would continue to teach the law and the message of the prophets. Some think, therefore, that synagogues may have had their origin in such a situation. Jewish people in the various places of the Dispersion would have been aware of a similar need. Jewish elders met together with Ezekiel in exile in Babylon (Ez 8:1; 14:1; 20:1). Yet there is no positive evidence of actual synagogues at this early stage. In Nehemiah 8:1-8 the postexilic community gathered in Jerusalem, and Ezra the scribe brought the law, read it from a wooden pulpit, and gave an interpretation so that the people understood the reading. When Ezra blessed the Lord, the people bowed their heads and worshiped. These were the basic elements of what came to be synagogue worship. The first undisputed evidence of a synagogue comes from Egypt in the third century BC. From the first century BC onward, the evidence of synagogues is abundant.

Synagogues in NT Times The Gospels give the impression of many synagogues existing throughout Palestine. Jesus frequently taught in synagogues (e.g., Mt 4:23; 9:35), especially during his Galilean ministry, but probably in Judea as well. In John 18:20 are the words of Jesus in his trial before the high priest: "I have spoken openly to the world; I have always taught in synagogues and in the temple, where all Jews come together" (RSV).

The Acts of the Apostles refers to synagogues in Jerusalem (Acts 6:9), Damascus (9:2), Cyprus (13:5), the Roman province of Galatia (13:14; 14:1), Macedonia and Greece (17:1, 10, 17; 18:4), and Ephesus in the

Roman province of Asia (19:8). Paul made it his practice to go directly to the synagogue and to preach there as long as he was given freedom to do so.

Synagogue Worship The Gospels and the Acts of the Apostles give abundant evidence for the meeting of Jewish people on the Sabbath to worship in the synagogue. People also met for worship on the second and fifth days of the week. Luke provides us with the earliest description of a synagogue service. The Mishnah describes the pattern of the synagogue service: the confession of faith, the Shema (which included reciting Deuteronomy 6:4-9; 11:13-21; and Numbers 15:37-41); prayer (such as the 18 Benedictions); Scripture reading (the reading of the Law was basic, see Acts 15:21, and was read according to a three-year cycle; the Prophets were also read, but more at random); interpretation (as the knowledge of biblical Hebrew diminished in Palestine, an Aramaic translation of the Scriptures was presented after the reading in Hebrew, and in the Dispersion, a Greek translation); address (following the reading, anyone suitably qualified might address the people, as Jesus and the apostle Paul often did); and blessing.

Ruins of an Ancient Synagogue in Capernaum

Judicial Functions Administration of justice was also part of the work of the synagogue. Offenders against the law and those whose actions were held to be contrary to Jewish religion were brought before the elders of the synagogue. They might, under extreme circumstances, excommunicate an offender (see Jn 9:22, 34-35; 12:42) or have him scourged. Jesus warned his disciples to be prepared to face either possibility (Mt 10:17; Jn 16:2). Saul, as persecutor of the Christians, had letters addressed to the synagogues at Damascus, giving authority to arrest Christians and bring them bound to Jerusalem (Acts 9:2). In Acts 22:19 he speaks of causing them to be both beaten and imprisoned. Paul himself received the 39 lashes that were administered in the synagogues (2 Cor 11:24).

Teaching of the Law The reading of the Law was of central significance in synagogue worship. The teaching of the Law to people generally, and especially to children, was intimately associated with the synagogue. Either the synagogue building or a school was used.

Organization The NT refers in particular (e.g., Mk 5:22; Lk 13:14; Acts 18:8,17) to two appointments in the synagogue: the "ruler of the synagogue," who was responsible for order and for selection of the Scripture reader; and an attendant (Lk 4:20), who brought out and put away the Scripture scrolls and also administered corporal punishment to unruly students. Later on, there was a person appointed as leader of the prayers.

Architecture In structure the synagogue was modeled after the temple. It was built, when possible, on high ground and often constructed so that the people could sit facing the direction of Jerusalem. There was a portable chest for the scrolls of the Law and the Prophets, and a platform for the reading of the Scriptures and for preaching. Men and women sat apart. The scribes loved the "chief seats" facing the people (Mk 12:39). Many synagogues had ornamentations of vine leaves, seven-branched candlesticks, the paschal lamb, and the pot of manna. Early synagogues also had a genizah, which was a cellar or attic where worn scrolls were put, because, as they bore the name of God, they were too sacred to be destroyed.

See also Judaism; Ruler of the Synagogue.

SYNOPTIC GOSPELS* Term (literally meaning "same view") applied to Matthew, Mark, and Luke because they see the ministry of Jesus from generally the same point of view, which is quite different from John's Gospel.

The similarities among these three Gospels include their use of a common outline: introduction; ministry of John the Baptist and the baptism and temptation of Jesus; Jesus' greater Galilean ministry; his journey and ministry through Samaria, Perea, and rural Judea; and the Passion week, death, and resurrection of Jesus in Jerusalem. The books also record the same emphasis in the teaching of Jesus—the presence, nature, and implementation of the kingdom of God. Furthermore, these three Gospels relate much of the same material, usually in the same order, and often with similar or identical words.

In addition to similarities, there are also striking differences among Matthew, Mark, and Luke. These fall into the same general categories as do the similarities—outline, material, organization, and wording. Matthew and Luke also have considerable common material not found in Mark, which, except for the healing of the centurion's slave, is composed exclusively of the words and teachings of Jesus. Each Gospel also contains accounts and teachings that are unique. The result is a rich diversity within the synoptic unity, each of which provides portrayals of Jesus from a variety of viewpoints. Matthew emphasizes Jesus' Jewishness and the continuity of his person and work with the message of the OT. Mark's fast-moving account presents Jesus as a man of action, the Son of Man who was a servant among men. Luke, in exquisite Greek literary style, seems to address cultured Gentiles and shows Jesus as a friend of disadvantaged groups.

Attempts to account for both the similarities and differences within these Gospels constitute the "synoptic problem." Solutions have been sought in many ways. As early as the second century, Tatian combined the four accounts into one; additional "harmonies" of the Gospel accounts have been continually produced. Since the 17th century, scholars have attempted to account for the similarities and differences by examining the stages through which the Gospel material is assumed to have passed before coming into its present form. Form criticism attempts to identify the influences from the period of oral transmission; source or literary criticism considers the alleged written documents from which the Evangelists drew information; redaction (or editorial) criticism seeks to determine the nature or purposes and personalities of the final editor-authors upon the accounts of the activities and teachings of Jesus. Other suggestions have called attention to the adaptation of material for a specific audience, the similarities between the synoptic accounts of Jesus' teachings and the parallel accounts of the Jewish rabbis in the Talmud, and more. No completely satisfactory solution to the synoptic problem is at hand. The fact remains that the Scriptures present Jesus in various perspectives; the conscientious reader must seek the divine purpose of both the similarities and the differences of these proclamations of "the good news of Jesus Christ, the Son of God" (Mk 1:1). *See* Gospel; Luke, Gospel of; Mark, Gospel of; Matthew, Gospel of.

SYNOPTIC PROBLEM* *See* Synoptic Gospels.

SYNTYCHE Woman encouraged by Paul to reconcile her differences with Euodia. Syntyche worked with Paul in proclaiming the gospel and evidently held a position of leadership in the Philippian church (Phil 4:2).

SYRACUSE Town on the east coast of Sicily and the island's most important city. Here Paul's ship, on which he traveled to Rome as a prisoner, made a three-day stop following his shipwreck and three-month stay in Malta (Acts 28:12). Syracuse had a fine harbor and was a natural port of call for a ship sailing from Malta through the straits of Messina between Sicily and Italy en route to Rome.

Syracuse Paul traveled from Malta to Syracuse on his way to Rome.

In the eighth century BC, Syracuse became a Greek colony, funded by Archias of Corinth. During the fifth century, it grew to great power and influence and was second only to Carthage as the most prominent city of the western Mediterranean. It played a significant role in the struggle between Rome and Carthage in the third century and was captured by Rome in 212 BC. Caesar Augustus settled Syracuse in 21 BC, making it a Roman colony (cf. Philippi). It is not stated in Acts 28 that Paul found Christians there, but later evidence from its catacombs indicates the existence of a church.

SYRIA, SYRIANS Terms used in the Septuagint and in some English translations to render the names Aram, Arameans.

History of the Arameans According to the "table of nations" in Genesis 10:22-23, the Arameans were a Semitic group, descendants of Shem. Another genealogy in Genesis 22:20-21 makes Aram a descendant of Nahor. According to Amos 9:7, the Arameans (Syrians) came from Kir, which is linked with Elam in Isaiah 22:6. The

exile of the Arameans to Kir (2 Kgs 16:9; Am 1:5) may suggest they were to go back to their original home. The precise origins of this group of people are, however, lost in antiquity. When they emerged clearly into history, they were settled around the central Euphrates from which they were spread out east, west, and north.

The Arameans were traditionally thought to have been established in upper Mesopotamia in the first part of the second millennium BC. Bethuel and Laban were known as Arameans (Gn 25:20; 28:1-7); the home of Bethuel was in Paddan-aram (25:20). The prophet Hosea recalls the tradition by noting that Jacob fled to "the field of Aram" (Hos 12:12) or "Aram-naharaim" (Aram of the two rivers), which was the northern part of Mesopotamia between the Euphrates and Tigris Rivers. In the creedal confession in Deuteronomy 26:5, the Israelite who brought his firstfruits confessed, "My father [probably Jacob] was a wandering Aramean."

Probably the best early evidence of an Aramean presence in this area comes from Tiglath-pileser I. In his annals of his fourth year (1112 BC), he speaks of a campaign among the "Akhlama, Arameans" in the Middle Euphrates area and the sacking of six Aramean villages in the Mt Bishri area.

The Arameans of upper Mesopotamia became important in biblical history. They set up a number of separate Aramean states, two of which were especially important for the people of Israel—Aram-zobah in the days of David, and Aram-damascus from the days of Solomon onward.

By about 1100 BC, the Aramean tribes had spread throughout Syria and had expanded into northern Transjordan, where they came into conflict with the Israelites. At his peak Hadadezer, king of Aram-zobah, embraced several vassals, such as Damascus, Maacah, and Tob. He was eventually defeated by King David (2 Sm 8:3-4; 10:17-19).

Events in Israel and Judah had some bearing on Damascus. After the death of Solomon, when the formerly united kingdom became divided into Judah and Israel, tension arose between the two small states. War broke out between Baasha of Israel and Asa of Judah in the years 890–880 BC. Asa sought aid from Ben-hadad I of Damascus (1 Kgs 15:18). Lands in Transjordan changed hands several times. The successors of Omri of Israel—namely Ahab, Ahaziah, Jehoram, Jehu, Jehoahaz, and Jehoash—had many conflicts with Damascus. Ahab fought Ben-hadad and his 32 allies who besieged Samaria (20:1), but Israel defeated him. A second time Ben-hadad entered Israelite territory and reached Aphek (20:26), but he was again defeated and captured. As a consequence of his defeat and for the price of his release, he was obliged to make bazaars available in Damascus for Israelite trade. After three years of peace between Israel and Damascus, hostilities broke out again and resulted in a battle in the region of Ramoth-gilead in which Ahab was killed (22:29-37). Aram-damascus was eventually defeated by King Jehoash of Israel (2 Kgs 13:25).

Syria after the Collapse of the Aramean Kingdoms After the collapse of Aram-damascus in 733–732 BC, the political character of the whole region changed. Over the centuries that followed and on into Christian times, the region passed under the control of several great powers and no independent Aramean state survived. When Assyria collapsed in 612–609 BC, the region came under Babylonian control, but only for a comparatively short period. With the rise of Cyrus the Persian, the Syrian region was quickly overrun by Persian armies. Palestine, Asia Minor, and Egypt were absorbed into the Persian Empire at the same time.

The next significant political change that affected the region came with the appearance of Philip of Macedon in 360 BC. His son Alexander the Great (336–323 BC) consolidated Greek power throughout western Asia and as far as the borders of India. On his death in 323 BC, at the age of 33, the control of western Asia passed to Alexander's generals. General Seleucus I (312–280 BC) controlled the southern half of Asia Minor, the region of Syria, Mesopotamia, and eastward to the borders of India. Syria thus fell under the influence of Hellenist rulers, the Seleucids, who founded a new capital at Antioch.

Ancient Site of Dura-Europos in Syria

Further west, Rome was rising to power and cast her eyes eastward. It was General Pompey who overcame Mithridates, the young king of Pontus, and moved to crush the remnants of the kingdom of the Seleucids. The western parts of Syria were formed into a Roman province in 64 BC. Pompey finally moved into Palestine, which came under Roman control in 63 BC.

The Roman province of Syria included Cilicia, a strip of territory in the southeastern corner of Asia Minor. The northern boundary reached to the Euphrates River. The boundary then swung south well to the east of Damascus and then turned west about halfway down the Dead Sea and continued west to the Mediterranean Sea. Syria was bound to the west by the Mediterranean up to the Gulf of Alexandretta, where it turned west. The province of Syria and Cilicia (Acts 15:23, 41; Gal 1:21) was governed by an imperial legate (*legatis*) who commanded a strong force of legionary troops. One such governor, Quirinius, governed Syria at the time of the census of Caesar Augustus; this census brought Joseph and Mary to Bethlehem for the birth of Jesus (Lk 2:2).

In the following centuries the population of Damascus was Christianized, and Christianity spread throughout the Roman province of Syria, giving rise to the Old Syrian Church, which remains to this day. It has left a remarkable legacy of Christian literature written in Syriac (Aramaic). The old Aramaic language remained, though a modified alphabet was used to write it.

It was the rise of Islam in the seventh century AD that brought about a considerable weakening of the Syrian church, although it has never been completely destroyed. Scattered communities of Aramaic-speaking people still survive in parts of Syria, and numerous remains of Christian churches have been brought to light as a result of modern archaeological work.

Language and Culture Aramaic was the language of the Arameans, of which numerous inscriptions have been discovered. The Aramaic script was adapted for use by the Israelites, and the language became the international language for diplomacy and administration all over the Near East. It was the *lingua franca* of the Persian period from Egypt to India and was widely spoken in

Palestine in Jesus' day. The words "*talitha cumi*" (Mk 5:41) and "*marana tha*" (1 Cor 16:22) are Aramaic.

Excavations in many sites have provided a good idea of the Aramean architecture, sculpture, pottery, and other arts. The religion of the Arameans was polytheistic. The people adopted many foreign deities as well. The principal Aramean deity was the ancient west Semitic storm god Hadad. In the days of Ahaz of Judah, the Damascus cult was forced on the people of Jerusalem when an altar based on a Damascus model was placed in the temple (2 Kgs 16:10-13). Arameans exiled to Samaria by the Assyrian ruler Sargon brought foreign Aramean cults with them (17:24-34).

Through the centuries that followed the disappearance of the Aramean states, the Aramaic language has survived. The Christian form of Aramaic, Syriac, has left behind a vast legacy of literature, histories, theologies, commentaries, treatises, and translations, which have been carefully preserved in ancient monastic libraries, particularly in northern Syria, northern Iraq, and southern Turkey.

See also Aramaic.

A Bedouin in Syria

SYROPHOENICIA* Homeland of the Greek woman who approached Jesus in the region of Tyre and Sidon and pleaded with him to cast a demon out of her daughter (Mk 7:26). The region of Phoenicia was located in the Roman province of Syria. Perhaps the designation of Syrophoenicia was used so as not to confuse this woman's country with the Phoenicia of North Africa called Libyphoenicia. In a parallel passage, this woman is identified as a Canaanite, a name by which Phoenicians called themselves (Mt 15:22).

SYRTIS Two bodies of water off the northern coast of Africa dreaded by ancient mariners. The larger was known as Syrtis Major and the smaller as Syrtis Minor. The former was the water to which Paul and his shipmates were dangerously drifting after leaving the island of Crete on their voyage to Rome. A furious northeasterly wind had crossed their course, threatening to push their ship southwestward across the Mediterranean into Syrtis Major (Acts 27:17).

Syrtis Major, now called the Gulf of Sidra, indents the coast of Libya and stretches 275 miles (442.5 kilometers) from the town of Misratah to the city of Banghazi. Syrtis Minor, now known as the Gulf of Gabes, is an indenture into the eastern coast of Tunisia. These bodies of water were feared for their quick shifting sandbars that produced unpredictable shoals and hazardous tides and currents.

T

TAANACH One of the Canaanite fortress cities bordering the plain of Esdraelon and the valley of Jezreel, including Jokneam, Megiddo, Ibleam, and Beth-shan. The modern site, about five miles (8 kilometers) southeast of Megiddo, retains the ancient name, Tell Taanak. Excavations reveal a 14th-century BC wall made of huge, irregularly shaped rocks, with smaller stones set in the chinks, along with ruins of a local king's palace. Some 40 cuneiform tablets of the 15th and 14th centuries BC were unearthed, and from a later period, brick houses possibly of Israelite construction. A terra-cotta incense altar was found in a house of Israelite date.

Taanach is first mentioned in the Bible in a list of kings conquered by the Israelites on the west side of the Jordan (Jos 12:21). In the tribal division of Palestine, Manasseh received Taanach (21:25), which was also named as a Levitical city. Manasseh, however, was not able to capture Taanach or any of the other strong cities in its inheritance (Jgs 1:27).

After the defeat of Sisera, Deborah and Barak sang a song in which it was said that the fighting took place at Taanach near the waters of Megiddo (Jgs 5:19). In the time of Solomon, Taanach was one of the towns mentioned in the enumeration of the administrative districts responsible for supplying monthly provisions for the king's household (1 Kgs 4:12). The last mention of Taanach in the Bible is in a genealogical list (1 Chr 7:29), where the city is said to have belonged to Ephraim, along the borders of the Manassites.

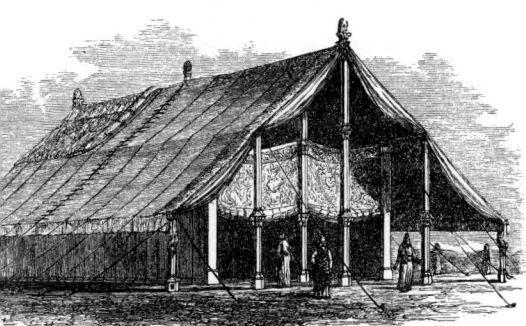

The Tabernacle

TAANATH-SHILOH City on the northeast border of the territory allotted to Ephraim's tribe for an inheritance, positioned between Micmethath and Janoah (Jos 16:6).

TABALIAH* *See* Tebaliah.

TABBAOTH Ancestor of a family of temple servants who returned to Jerusalem with Zerubbabel after the exile (Ezr 2:43; Neh 7:46).

TABBATH Town on the outskirts of Abel-meholah on the east side of the Jordan River in the hill country of Gilead, to which Gideon and his small army chased the fleeing Midianites (Jgs 7:22).

TABEAL*, TABEEL
1. Ruler in Samaria who, with his associates, wrote a letter to King Artaxerxes I of Persia (464–424 BC) protesting Zerubbabel's rebuilding of the Jerusalem wall (Ezr 4:7).
2. Father of the man whom King Pekah of Israel and King Rezin of Syria wanted to put on the throne of Jerusalem after they conquered it and subdued Ahaz, king of Judah (735–715 BC; Is 7:6).

TABERAH Temporary stopping place for Israel in the wilderness of Paran, listed with Massah and Kibroth-hattaavah as places where Israel complained against the Lord. Taberah was named for the fire that God used to judge the grumbling Israelites (Nm 11:3; Dt 9:22).

TABERNACLE Place of worship during the earliest years of the history of Israel.

PREVIEW
• Introduction
• Names for the Tabernacle
• Background
• The Tabernacle and Its Furniture
• The Tabernacle Proper
• The Outer Court and Its Furnishings
• The Construction and Consecration of the Tabernacle

Introduction The tabernacle was the precursor of the temple during most of the period between the formation of Israel at Sinai and its final establishment in the Promised Land in the early period of the monarchy. A portable sanctuary in keeping with the demand for easy mobility, it was the symbol of God's presence with his people and, therefore, of his availability, as well as a place where his will was communicated. At an early period it was anticipated that, when peace and security had been secured, a permanent national shrine would be established (Dt 12:10-11). This was not realized until the time of Solomon, when the temple was erected (2 Sm 7:10-13; 1 Kgs 5:1-5). Historical events, as well as the similarities in construction and underlying theology, illustrate the close connection between the tabernacle and temple.

Names for the Tabernacle Several words and descriptive phrases are used:

1. "Sacred residence," "sanctuary," or "holy place" (Ex 25:8; Lv 10:17-18) derive from the verb "to be holy."
2. "The tent" occurs 19 times and is also found in expressions such as "the tent of the testimony" (Nm 9:15), "the tent of the Lord" (1 Kgs 2:28-30), "the house of the tent" (1 Chr 9:23), and "the tent of meeting" (e.g., Ex 33:7). The last name appears approximately 130 times. The word involves the concept of meeting by appointment and designates the tabernacle as the

place where God met with Moses and his people to make known his will.

3. "Dwelling place" is the literal meaning of "tabernacle." In Exodus 25:9 the word indicates the whole tabernacle (including the outer court), but in Exodus 26:1 it refers to the tabernacle proper (that included the Holy Place and the Holy of Holies). A variant of this is "the tabernacle of the testimony" (Ex 38:21; NLT "Tabernacle of the Covenant"), which, with other expressions like "the tent of the testimony," stresses the presence of the two tablets of the law.

4. "The house of the LORD" (Ex 23:19).

Background The three-part construction of the tabernacle, composed of a general area and two restricted areas, was not unique. In other developed religions that included an organized priesthood there were three main levels of approach: one for all members of the community; one for the priests generally; and one for the chief religious leaders, which was an inner sanctuary, conceived as the dwelling place of the deity. Excavations of heathen sanctuaries in Palestine and Syria in the pre-Israelite period have revealed this type of divided sanctuary.

There is also widespread evidence of the use of portable, often complex, prefabricated structures during the second millennium BC, usually as either staterooms for kings and other high dignitaries, or as sanctuaries. Rulers of settled communities used these structures when traveling to other areas within their kingdoms (e.g., Egypt and, to a lesser extent, Canaan). Also, nomadic or seminomadic peoples, such as the Midianites, used portable sanctuaries. In pre-Mosaic Egypt, craftsmen used techniques similar to those used in the construction of the tabernacle.

The Tabernacle and Its Furniture The book of Exodus (Ex 25–40) describes the tabernacle and its furnishings in detail. The materials used included items ranging from precious to common materials. Three metals are mentioned in descending order of importance: gold, copper, and silver. Gold alone was employed in the principal sanctuary furnishings. The total amount of metals used was approximately one ton (.9 metric ton) of gold, three of copper, and four of silver (38:24-31). The relatively large amount of silver came from an offering (30:11-16), which augmented the silver and gold already given by the Egyptians (12:35).

Significantly, in God's building specifications, the starting point was the furniture of the inner sanctuary (the Holy Place and the Holy of Holies). In the actual construction, this furniture was made after the tabernacle itself, presumably so that it could be immediately and adequately housed (Ex 25:9–27:19; cf. 36:8–37:28).

The first item listed was the ark, the only furniture in the Holy of Holies. It was a wooden box sheathed in gold, approximately three and three-quarters feet (1.1 meters) long, with a width and height of two and a quarter feet (.7 meter). The supreme symbol of the covenant relationship between God and Israel, it was often called "the ark of the covenant of the LORD" (Dt 10:8). Unlike contemporary arks in some neighboring countries, it contained no representation of the deity, only the Ten Commandments (Ex 25:16), a jar of manna (16:33), and Aaron's rod (Nm 17:10)—all symbolic of various aspects of God's provision (see Heb 9:4).

The ark was transported by two poles that passed through rings attached to each lower corner (Ex 25:13-15). These poles, left in place, projected underneath the veil into the Holy Place, serving as a reminder of the presence of the unseen ark.

Resting upon the ark was the mercy seat (NLT "atonement cover"), a rectangular slab of solid gold, to which

were attached two cherubim. The inward-looking cherubim and the mercy seat formed a throne for the invisible God (Ex 25:22), who is frequently described as enthroned above or upon the cherubim (Pss 80:1; 99:1). The noun "mercy seat" comes from a verb meaning "to make atonement." The mercy seat was sprinkled with blood at the climax of the annual Day of Atonement (Lv 16:14). The fact that the ark was placed *under* the mercy seat (Ex 25:21) signifies that the law was under God's protection and explains the references to the ark as his footstool (e.g., Ps 132:7). Like the cherubim in the Garden of Eden (Gn 3:24), those in the Holy of Holies probably had a similar protective function. In the ancient world, symbolic winged creatures like the cherubim were frequently placed as guardians of thrones and important buildings.

Like the ark, the portable table of the bread of the Presence (Ex 25:30) was made of acacia wood overlaid with gold. It was marginally smaller, with a length of three feet (.9 meter), a width of one and a half feet (.5 meter) and a height of two and a quarter feet (.7 meter). The various auxiliary vessels and implements are detailed (v 29); presumably the dishes would be used for carrying the bread. On each Sabbath day, 12 loaves, symbolizing God's provision for the 12 tribes of Israel, were placed in two rows on the table (Lv 24:5-9). The table was located in the Holy Place, on the north side.

On the south side was the seven-branched golden lampstand (Ex 25:31-39; 37:17-24; 40:24). It was the most impressive item of furniture in the Holy Place; like the cherubim and the mercy seat, it was made of pure gold. Six golden branches, three on either side, extended from a central shaft, and the whole lampstand was ornamented with almond flowers. From the biblical evidence, it is not clear whether the lampstand gave continuous illumination (Ex 27:20; Lv 24:2) or night light only (1 Sm 3:3 in most versions). Leviticus 24:4 strongly supports the former, and the reference in 1 Samuel probably reflects the laxity that had crept in during the period of the judges. In Scripture, the golden lampstand symbolizes the continuing witness of the covenant community (Zec 4:1-7; Rv 2:1). The precise attention to the smallest detail is well illustrated in the listing of the supplementary items, all made of pure gold, required for the servicing of the lamps. Without this precise attention, the light would soon grow dim, and the sanctuary itself be defiled by carbon deposits (Ex 25:38). Moreover, only the best-quality olive oil was used, thus ensuring the brightest possible light (27:20).

The altar of incense (Ex 30:1-10) may have been deliberately played down to give greater prominence to the sacrificial altar in the outer court, which is frequently referred to as "*the* altar." In order to distinguish the altar of incense from the bronze altar of sacrifice, the former was called "the golden altar" (40:5). The altar of incense was located in the Holy Place, immediately opposite the ark in the Holy of Holies but just outside the veil, between the table of the bread of the Presence and the lampstand. Made of acacia wood overlaid with gold, it was 18 inches (45.7 centimeters) square and 3 feet (.9 meter) high, with horns and a golden molding around the four sides. Like the ark, it was made readily portable by the provision of rings and carrying poles. The altar was used for the offering of incense every morning and evening and for anointing the horns for the yearly atonement (30:7-10). The incense from a special recipe was forbidden for secular use. Originally, incense indicated something that ascended from a sacrifice, a pleasing aroma to God. Incense acknowledged God in worship (Mal 1:11) and at an early date signified the prayers of the godly (Ps 141:2). It also concealed God from human eyes (Lv 16:13).

The Tabernacle Proper The tabernacle was fundamentally a tent structure supported on a rigid framework. As with most of the other items, a triplication of detail underlines the importance of the tabernacle proper. The specifications are given in Exodus 26, the construction in Exodus 36:8-38, and the final erection in Exodus 40:16-19. The overall dimensions were approximately 45 feet (13.7 meters) long, 15 feet (4.6 meters) wide, and 15 feet high.

The basic framework was a series of upright supports, each 15 feet (4.6 meters) high and 2¼ feet (.7 meters) wide, and each standing on two silver bases (Ex 26:15-25). Scholars used to think these supports or frames were solid planks of acacia wood, but most modern scholars accept that each comprised two upright sides connected by horizontal pieces like a ladder. Such sections would be considerably stronger, would keep their shape better, and would allow a view of the beautiful inner layer of curtains from within the sanctuary. On the south and north sides were 20 such frames, with 6 more at the western end. In addition, on the western side were two corner pieces to which all the walls were attached by clasps (vv 23-25). A series of bars, which passed through gold rings attached to each upright frame, provided further security and alignment (vv 26-29). There were five such bars on each of the three sides. The central one on both the south and north sides extended the entire length; the other four probably extended halfway, so that each frame was effectively secured by three bars. All the wooden sections were sheathed in gold.

Over this framework several layers of coverings formed the top, sides, and back of the tabernacle. The first layer of ten linen curtains was dyed blue, purple, and scarlet, and embroidered with cherubim (Ex 26:1-6; 36:8-13). Each measured 42 feet by 6 feet (12.8 meters by 1.8 meters). Pairs joined along their length formed five sets of curtains. The two large curtains were themselves attached with 50 golden clasps that passed through a similar number of loops in each. Probably the curtains were stretched over the structure like a tablecloth.

Eleven curtains or tarpaulins of goat hair, each 45 feet by 6 feet (13.7 meters by 1.8 meters), formed the next layer. These were divided into two sets by joining together five and six curtains respectively, and were linked using a similar method as the under curtain, except that bronze clasps instead of gold were used. The extra length of the goat-hair tarpaulins provided an overlap to protect the under curtain, and the larger tarpaulin overlapped at both the front and the rear of the tabernacle (Ex 26:7-9, 12-13). Two further layers ensured complete weatherproofing, one of ram's skins dyed red and one of goatskins.

A veil made of the same material as the under curtaining divided the sanctuary and hung under the golden clasps that joined the two curtains, supported by four pillars of acacia wood plated with gold and resting in silver bases. The cherubim on both the veil and the curtains were symbolic guardians of the sanctuary. The positioning of the veil made the Holy of Holies a perfect cube of 15 feet (4.6 meters). The layers of overlapping material and the attention given to the joints emphasizes the darkness of the innermost shrine. God was surrounded by darkness, carefully isolated from any unauthorized sight (Ps 97:2). The Holy Place occupied an area 30 feet by 15 feet (9.1 meters by 4.6 meters), exactly twice the area of the Holy of Holies. A screen made from the same fabric as the main curtain stood between the Holy Place and the outer court and hung from golden hooks on five posts of acacia wood, overlaid with gold and resting on bronze sockets.

There is no mention of embroidered seraphim on this section, which formed the tabernacle's eastern wall.

The tabernacle, while probably having a somewhat squat appearance suggestive of strength, could be easily dismantled, transported, and reassembled. By the standards of that age, it was a fit dwelling place for God, constructed by the best human skills and the highest quality materials.

The Outer Court and Its Furnishings The court of the tabernacle was a rectangle 150 feet (45.7 meters) long on the north and south sides and 75 feet (22.9 meters) wide on the east and west (Ex 27:9-18; 38:9-19). The tabernacle itself was at the western end. Curtains of fine-twined linen 7½ feet (2.3 meters) high screened the entire tabernacle area. In the eastern section, there was a central entrance, 30 feet (9.1 meters) wide. An embroidered curtain of the same height screened this doorway, which was probably recessed to facilitate entrance on either side. Silver rods supported all the curtains. These rods passed through silver hooks attached to the silver-plated posts that rested on bronze bases (38:17).

The altar of burnt offering (Ex 27:1-8; 38:1-7), at the eastern end of the court adjacent to the entrance (40:29), was a reminder that there could be no approach to God except by the place of sacrifice. Seven feet (2.1 meters) square and four and a half feet (1.4 meters) high, it was small in comparison to the gigantic altar in Solomon's temple (2 Chr 4:1). Basically, it was a hollow wooden framework overlaid with bronze, light enough to be carried on bronze-plated poles that passed through bronze rings at each corner. The grating (Ex 27:4-5) was probably inside the altar at the middle, although some scholars believe that it extended around the lower, outer sides of the altar, to provide draft and to allow the sacrificial blood to flow to the base of the altar. The horns, possibly symbolizing the sacrificial victims, could be used to tether the animals about to be sacrificed. In Israel, a person could claim sanctuary by clinging to the horns of the altar (e.g., 1 Kgs 1:50), with the possible symbolism that he was offering himself as a sacrifice to God and so claiming his protection. The lower part of the altar may have been partly filled with earth to absorb the blood (Ex 20:24). All the accessories were bronze: ash buckets, shovels for removing the ashes and filling the base with earth, basins for the blood, carcass hooks, and fire pans (27:3).

No specifications concerning the size of the laver (NLT "washbasin") have survived (Ex 30:17-20; 38:8). It was made from the mirrors of the women who served at the entrance to the court. The laver stood between the altar of sacrifice and the tabernacle. Failure to wash at the laver prior to ministering was punishable by death—a solemn reminder of the need for cleanliness and obedience before undertaking any task for God. The bronze pedestal may have been merely a support for the laver, but possibly it incorporated a lower basin in which the priests could wash their feet.

The Construction and Consecration of the Tabernacle The God-given specifications required skills beyond the capabilities of Moses and Aaron. Prominent in the construction were Bezalel and Oholiab (Ex 30:1-11), with a large supporting group of experts, who must have learned their craftsmanship in Egypt. In a remarkable community effort, the Israelites gave so generously that the flow of gifts had to be stopped (35:20-24; 36:4-7). In addition, many gave of their special skills (35:25-29).

When all the items had been completed and placed in position (Ex 40:1-33), every piece except the mercy seat and the cherubim was anointed with special oil (30:22-33;

40:9-11) and symbolically consecrated for its particular function. The climax came when the glory of the Lord filled the tabernacle (40:34). He came to be present among his people, and thereafter the cloud by day and fire by night provided reassurance concerning his presence and guidance. Yet there could be no laxity in approaching him, and even Moses was excluded from the Holy of Holies. The tabernacle was erected exactly one year after the deliverance from Egypt and a mere nine months after the Sinai revelation.

Thereafter, when Israel camped, the Levites surrounded the tabernacle on three sides (Nm 1:53), with the families of Moses and Aaron occupying the remaining eastern side (Nm 3:14-38). This prevented any unauthorized intrusion into the sacred area. When the tabernacle was moved, the dismantlement was carefully regulated (4:5-15). The Kohathites were responsible for transporting the more sacred items, using the carrying poles; the Gershonites dealt with all the soft furnishings, the altar of sacrifice, and its accessories; and the Merarites carried the hard furnishings, such as the frames, bars, and bases. Even on the march, the tabernacle remained central, with six tribes preceding and the remaining six following (Nm 2).

See also Temple.

TABERNACLES*, Feast of Also known as the Feast of Booths, Shelters, or Ingathering. It was one of the three great festivals of Israel, celebrating the completion of the agricultural year. The Jews built booths or tabernacles (temporary shelters) to commemorate their deliverance from Egypt by the hand of God (Lv 23:33-43). *See* Feasts and Festivals of Israel.

TABITHA Aramaic name meaning "gazelle"; the name in Greek is Dorcas (Acts 9:36, 40). *See* Dorcas.

TABLE *See* Furniture.

TABLE OF SHOWBREAD* Piece of furniture in the tabernacle and temple upon which the bread of the Presence was placed (Ex 25:23-30). *See* Bread of the Presence.

TABLET *See* Writing.

TABOR (Place) City mentioned in 1 Chronicles 6:77 in a list of the towns of Zebulun. In a similar list in Joshua 19:12 the city is named Kisloth-Tabor; if the same city is meant, the Chronicler may have abbreviated the name here.

TABOR, Mount Important hill in lower Galilee located in the northeast area of the Jezreel Valley. About six miles (9.7 kilometers) east of Nazareth, Tabor rises abruptly from the valley floor. Appearing more prominent than its height would indicate (1,929 feet, or 587.9 meters), it became an important geographical reference point in antiquity. It defined the western boundary of Issachar's tribe (Jos 19:22) and was a useful navigation tool on the international coastal highway (the Via Maris) that passed through Megiddo in Galilee en route to Hazor. Its prominence invited comparison with Mt Hermon far to the north (Ps 89:12; cf. Jer 46:18).

In the OT, Mt Tabor is mentioned in the book of Judges when Deborah and Barak fight Sisera, the commander of a Canaanite army from Hazor (Jgs 4:1-24). Barak's troops from the nearby tribes of Naphtali and Zebulun met on Mt Tabor and at Deborah's command launched a successful campaign against Sisera. Later in the same book, Mt Tabor was named as the place where Gideon finally confronted the Midianite kings, Zebah and Zalmunna, who had killed his brothers (8:18).

Strategically located, Tabor's moderately sized top, less than a half mile square (1.3 square kilometers), was easily fortified. During the OT kingdom period, shrines may been located there (see Hos 5:1), but by the Hellenistic era, fortifications were built. The Ptolemies strengthened it, and by the time of Antiochus III (218 BC), Tabor may have become the administrative center of the Jezreel Valley. The Roman era witnessed various conflicts on Mt Tabor. In the major Jewish war of AD 66, Josephus fortified the hill with a large wall, which is still visible. Since the fourth century, Mt Tabor has been identified as the site of Jesus' transfiguration (Mk 9:2-13). This is uncertain, however, since the NT fails to mention Mt Tabor by name. Helena, the mother of Constantine, was convinced that the Transfiguration did take place there, and in AD 326 she built a church on the site. Other shrines, monasteries, and churches graced the hill until the 12th century, when everything was destroyed by the Arab conqueror Saladin. Today a Greek Orthodox monastery and a Latin basilica dating from the 19th century can be seen on the mountain.

TABOR, Oak of Place near Bethel and perhaps in Benjamin's tribal territory where Saul was to meet three men (1 Sm 10:3). This encounter was the second of four signs given to Saul to confirm his appointment as king.

TABRET* KJV rendering of tambourine in Genesis 31:27 and 1 Samuel 10:5, and timbrel in 1 Samuel 18:6, Job 17:6, Isaiah 5:12, 24:8, 30:32, and Jeremiah 31:4. *See* Musical Instruments (Toph).

TABRIMMON, TABRIMON* Hezion's son and the father of Ben-hadad I, king of Syria (1 Kgs 15:18).

TACHMONITE* KJV form of Tahkemonite, designation for one of David's mighty men, in 2 Samuel 23:8. *See* Tahkemonite.

TACITUS*, Cornelius Roman historian (c. AD 55–120).

Little is known of Tacitus personally, but his writings present an invaluable picture of Roman life during the first century AD. These works are *Dialogus de Oratoribus* (c. 77); *The Life of Agricola*, his father-in-law (c. 98); *Germania* (c. 98); *Histories* (c. 116); and *Annals* (c. 116). In this last-named work, Tacitus referred to the persecution of the Christians in Rome in AD 64, when the emperor Nero made them the scapegoats for the fire that he had ordered set. Though Tacitus believed the Christians to be innocent of the arson of which they were accused, he referred to their faith as "a detestable superstition," named Christ as the founder of this sect, and stated that he was crucified "in the reign of Emperor Tiberius by the Procurator Pontius Pilate." He further said that Nero accused the Roman Christians not only of arson but also of "hatred of the human race," and that Nero had some of them thrown to dogs, others crucified, still others burned in the imperial garden. Thus Tacitus provides independent secular confirmation for some basic events recorded in the NT, including Jesus' crucifixion.

TADMOR Ancient city whose name appears in a list of Solomon's building achievements in 2 Chronicles 8:4. The parallel verse in 1 Kings 9:18 reads "Tamar" in some Hebrew manuscripts and it is uncertain if the same city was intended.

Solomon built or rebuilt a number of cities, including store cities and cities for his horses and chariots. Among the cities mentioned is "Tadmor in the desert." Tadmor, situated some 140 miles (225.3 kilometers) northeast of

Damascus, is mentioned in the records of the Assyrian king Tiglath-pileser I (c. 1114–c. 1076 BC).

In Greek and Roman times, the city was known as Palmyra, whose ruins may be seen today. The oasis city was an important stopping place on the caravan route, and therefore could have been valuable to Solomon in his extensive trading ventures. It gained its greatest prominence during the reign of Queen Zenobia. The Roman Aurelian destroyed it in AD 273. Though rebuilt, it never regained its former position.

TAHAN
1. Ephraim's son and the father of the Tahanite family (Nm 26:35).
2. Telah's son and a descendant of Ephraim (1 Chr 7:25).

TAHANITE Descendant of Tahan from Ephraim's tribe (Nm 26:35). *See* Tahan #1.

TAHAPANES* KJV alternate spelling of Tahpanhes, an Egyptian city, in Jeremiah 2:16. *See* Tahpanhes.

TAHASH Son of Nahor and Reumah his concubine; Abraham's brother (Gn 22:24).

TAHATH (Person)
1. Son of Assir and a descendant of Levi through Kohath's line. He was an ancestor of Heman, one of David's musicians, and the father of Uriel and Zephaniah (1 Chr 6:24, 37).
2. Ephraimite, the son of Bered and the father of Eleadah (1 Chr 7:20).
3. Ephraimite, the son of Eleadah and the father of Zabad (1 Chr 7:20).

TAHATH (Place) Temporary camping place for the Israelites during their wilderness wanderings, mentioned between Makheloth and Terah (Nm 33:26-27).

TAHKEMONITE* Variant reading for Hacmonite in 1 Chronicles 11:11. There was probably an error in copying where the Hebrew letter "h" was confused for a "t." *See* Hacmonite.

TAHPANHES Important Egyptian center in the eastern Delta. Listed with Memphis among Israel's enemies (Jer 2:16), it is the place to which Jews fled after the murder of Gedaliah in 586 BC when Jeremiah was taken to Egypt (43:7-9; 44:1; 46:14). Ezekiel prophesied doom against this city (alternately spelled Tehaphnehes in Ez 30:18, RSV).

Today the site is identified with Tell Dephneh (Defenneh), 26 miles (41.8 kilometers) southwest of Port Said. There is little evidence of occupation here before the time of Psammetichus I (664–610 BC), who established a fortress at the site and left a garrison of Greek mercenaries. Pharaoh's palace in Tahpanhes, where Jeremiah buried stones as a promise of Nebuchadnezzar's invasion (Jer 43:9), has been identified with the fortress of Psammetichus. A fragmentary Neo-Babylonian text of the 37th year of Nebuchadnezzar refers to operations against Pharaoh Amasis and a Greek garrison.

TAHPENES Egyptian queen who lived during the reigns of David (1000–961 BC) and Solomon (970–930 BC). Pharaoh gave her sister to Hadad the Edomite in marriage. Tahpenes's sister bore to Hadad a son named Genubath (1 Kgs 11:19-20).

TAHREA A descendant of King Saul, in 1 Chronicles 8:35 and 9:41. An alternate spelling is Tarea.

TAHTIM-HODSHI One of the towns polled in David's census of Israel. Tahtim-hodshi is listed between Gilead and Dan-jaan (2 Sm 24:6).

TALENT* Unit of measure used in weighing gold or silver (Mt 25:14-30). *See* Coins; Weights and Measures.

TALITHA CUMI* Aramaic words spoken by Jesus and retained by Mark in his Gospel (Mk 5:41). Jairus, a synagogue official in the Galilean region, called on Jesus to heal his sick daughter; however, she died before Jesus arrived. Coming to the girl, Jesus took her hand and said, *"Talitha cumi,"* meaning "Little girl, arise." *"Talitha"* is a term of affection meaning "lamb" or "youth." *"Cumi"* is a command to rise up, translated by Mark as "I say to you, arise!"

In his Gospel, Mark includes other Aramaic phrases attributed to Jesus (Mk 3:17; 5:41; 7:11, 34; 11:9-10; 14:36; 15:22, 34). Matthew retains only two Aramaic phrases (Mt 27:33, 46), and Luke keeps none.

TALMAI
1. Son of Anak and brother of Ahiman and Sheshai. Talmai and his people were observed by the 12 Israelite spies when they searched out the land (Nm 13:22). Later, Caleb successfully defeated Talmai and his brothers, who were living in Hebron (Jos 15:14; Jgs 1:10).
2. Son of Ammihud and father of Maacah. Maacah gave birth to Absalom, David's third son (2 Sm 3:3; 1 Chr 3:2). Absalom eventually sought refuge in Talmai's small kingdom of Geshur after murdering Amnon (2 Sm 13:37).

TALMON Head of a Levite family who served as temple gatekeepers (1 Chr 9:17). His descendants returned from the exile with Zerubbabel and served as gatekeepers in the rebuilt temple (Ezr 2:42; Neh 7:45; 11:19; 12:25).

TALMUD* Word meaning "to study," "to learn." It is a body of literature in Hebrew and Aramaic, covering interpretations of legal portions of the OT, as well as wise sayings from many rabbinical sources; it spans a time period from shortly after Ezra, about 400 BC, until approximately the AD 500s.

Origin and Development of the Oral Law Traditional Jews believe that a second law was given to Moses in addition to the first or written word; this second one was given orally, and handed down from generation to generation in oral form. The Talmud itself makes this claim for an early origin, and *Pirke Aboth* 1:1 states that it is attributed to Moses. Other scholars do not agree on this origin of the oral law and insist that it had its beginning and development after Ezra. For example, there is no mention by the preexilic prophets concerning a lapse from the oral law, but the messages of the prophets abound in warnings about abandoning the written revelation given to Moses, thereby indicating the absence of a body of oral tradition prior to the Babylonian exile.

In the period succeeding Ezra ("a scribe skilled in the law of Moses," Ezr 7:6), teacher succeeded teacher in synagogues and schools, and their understanding of the OT was treasured and memorized. Across the centuries, many memorizing devices were employed to learn and remember the growing mass of opinions and interpretation. But eventually not even the best memory could retain all the available materials. It was finally necessary to compile a summary of all the essential teachings of preceding generations, and also to facilitate access for future generations to the immense treasure of thought, religious feeling, and wisdom for guidance and inspiration. The compilation is known as the Talmud, the basic repository of the oral law. Jewish people regard it as second to the Scriptures. A literature recognized as the genius of a national and religious creation, it has a profound influence upon the development of the Jewish world view.

Rationale for an Oral Law With the cessation of the postexilic prophets, and with the continual development of the complexity of life in Israel and its relationships to the outer world, there arose a need for further elaboration of the laws of the Pentateuch. The oral law, at first, was intended to be helpful so that people could obey the written Word of God.

The oral law contained in the Talmud has a twofold function. First, it provided an interpretation of the written Law. According to the rabbis, this is necessary since the oral law makes it possible to observe the written Law. Without the former, it would be impossible to observe the latter. A good example is the concept of not working, as indicated by the biblical Sabbath law. Everyone knew that work was not done on the Sabbath. The rabbis contend, however, that it took the oral law to define what was meant by work.

The second aspect of the oral law is that it modifies and seeks to adapt the written Law to fit new conditions and circumstances. The oral law is supposed to make the written Law a viable document from generation to generation. Without this oral law, the written Law would become obsolete. Therefore, the oral law is necessary for observance of prohibitions as well as for stressing what is good Jewish devotion and loyalty.

It is true that every generation must face new social, political, and economic conditions, which make necessary a different application of the Word of God. But the Word of God cannot be changed in order to accommodate personal desires or interpret new problems in different ages. Something of this is apparent in the first century AD, when Jesus challenged the Jewish leaders for having preempted the Word of God by their oral traditions (Mk 7:9-13).

Basic Antecedents to the Talmud One of the earliest means for teaching oral law was a running commentary, or Midrash ("to expound"), of the biblical text. If the teaching handled the legal portions of the OT, then it was referred to as Midrash Halakah (the latter emphasized a way by which one walks or lives). When treating nonlegal, ethical, or devotional portions of the OT, then the opinions and understanding was called Midrash Haggadah ("narration"). Ezra and his trained associates were using the method of Midrash, upon the occasion of the completion of the Jerusalem wall in 444 BC, when they "explained the law to the people while the people remained in their place. They read from the book, from the law of God, translating to give the sense so that they understood the reading" (Neh 8:7-8, NASB). This kind of oral Midrash is the method followed by generations of teachers after Ezra, when the religious leaders were known as Soferim ("bookmen" or "scribes"), until about 200 BC. Sometimes referred to as the "Great Synagogue," these scholars provided teaching to "hedge" the revealed moral and ceremonial word so that Israel would never stray into idolatry or ignorance again. The Soferim were succeeded by the Hasidim ("pious ones"), who tried to maintain a high level of religious devotion. In turn, the Hasidim were succeeded by the Pharisees ("separated ones") at about 128 BC. Each of these groups contributed to the Midrash method. This material continued to increase and

was transmitted orally. Succeeding generations learned these materials through continuous repetition. Therefore, the new method was called Mishnah ("repetition"), and the teachers of the Mishnah were known as Tannaim ("those who handed down orally"). Both Midrash and Mishnah existed side by side in ensuing generations. There came a time, however, when it was necessary to codify the oral law covered by Mishnah, since this became cumbersome to learn as a body of material. Eventually, this material was put into writing; it came to be known as Gemara ("completion"). The combination of Gemara and Mishnah constitute the Talmud.

See also Gemara; Haggadah; Halakah; Law, Biblical Concept of; Midrash; Mishnah; Pharisees; Torah; Tradition; Tradition, Oral.

TAMAH* KJV spelling of Temah in Nehemiah 7:55. See Temah.

TAMAR (Person)
1. Wife of Er, the firstborn son of Judah by a Canaanitess. Later, as a widow, Tamar bore two sons to Judah named Perez and Zerah (Gn 38:6-24; 1 Chr 2:4). Tamar preserved the line of Judah through Perez (Ru 4:12), and her name is recorded in the genealogy of Christ (Mt 1:3).
   See also Genealogy of Jesus Christ.
2. Sister of Absalom and the daughter of David by his wife Maacah, the Geshurite. Through deceit, Tamar was seduced by Amnon, her half brother. In vengeance, Absalom, her full brother, had Amnon murdered at Baal-hazor (2 Sm 13; 1 Chr 3:9).
3. Daughter of Absalom who was noted for her beauty (2 Sm 14:27). She perhaps married Uriel of Gibeah and became the mother of Maacah. See Maacah, Maachah (Person) #4.

TAMAR (Place) City located southwest of the Dead Sea in Judah's tribe (Ez 47:19; 48:28). Tamar is listed in some Hebrew manuscripts of 1 Kings 9:18 as one of the places built up by Solomon in his campaign to increase the might and grandeur of the Jewish empire. It may have been carefully fortified to safeguard the important trade route between the Elath seaport and southern Arabia.
   See also Tadmor.

TAMARISK Small, desert tree with small flowers (Gn 21:33). See Plants.

TAMBOURINE Percussion instrument consisting of a shallow one-headed drum with small metal discs attached on the side, which jingle when the instrument is tapped or shaken (1 Sm 10:5). See Musical Instruments (Toph).

TAMMUZ Chief Sumerian deity whose name derived from the Sumerian *dumuzi*. He is the god of fertility, of vegetation and agriculture, and of death and resurrection, and he is the patron deity of shepherds. The son and consort of Ashtar (Inanna), Tammuz represented the annual vegetation cycle of death during the heat of summer and the rebirth of life with the coming of the fall and spring rains, as mythically recounted in the Akkadian poem "Inanna's Descent into the Netherworld." This rejuvenation of life and defeat of death was annually celebrated during the Babylonian New Year Festival. In the OT, the prophet Ezekiel sees in a vision women weeping for Tammuz at the north gate of the temple; this is a prophetic description of coming desecrations of the Lord's house (Ez 8:14).

In subsequent cultures following the Sumerian civilization (third millennium BC), the Tammuz cult was carried on. It undoubtedly embodied the worship of Marduk of Babylon, Ashur of Assyria, Baal of Canaan, Attis of Phrygia, and Adonis of Syria (Aram) and Greece. Numerous liturgies and dirges have been found detailing Tammuz worship in ancient Mesopotamian culture. During the postexilic era, the fourth month of the Hebrew calendar was named Tammuz.

See also Calendars, Ancient and Modern.

TANACH* KJV spelling of Taanach, a Levitical town, in Joshua 21:25. *See* Taanach.

TANHUMETH Seraiah's father from the town of Netophah in Judah. Seraiah was the captain of an army of Netophathite men, who served under Gedaliah during the Babylonian suzerainty (2 Kgs 25:23; Jer 40:8).

TANNAIM* Teachers of the oral law mentioned in the Mishnah during the period beginning with the students of Shammai and Hillel in AD 10 and ending with the pupils of Judah HaNasi I in AD 220. *See* Talmud.

TANNED, TANNER*, TANNING* Worker and process of changing hide into leather (Acts 9:43). The tanner converted hides and skins into leather by soaking them in lime and the leaves and juices of certain plants. Tanners lived outside the towns because of the foul smells produced from their vats. The tabernacle coverings were made from the tanned skins of rams and goats (or perhaps sea cows). The leather was red in color either because of dye or as a result of the tanning process (Ex 25:5; 26:14; 35:7, 23; 36:19; 39:34). The only biblical reference to a tanner is to Simon in Acts (Acts 9:43; 10:6, 32).

See also Leather.

TAPHATH Solomon's daughter and the wife of Ben-abinadab, Solomon's officer in Naphoth-dor (1 Kgs 4:11).

TAPPUAH (Person) Hebron's son and a descendant of Caleb from Judah's tribe (1 Chr 2:43).

TAPPUAH (Place)
1. One of 14 cities located in the Shephelah assigned to Judah's tribe for an inheritance, mentioned between En-gannim and Enam (Jos 15:34). This locality is not to be mistaken for the land of Tappuah in Manasseh (17:8) or the town of Beth-tappuah at Hebron (15:53). *See* Beth-tappuah.
2. City situated in the hill country of Palestine defining part of the northern boundary of the territory allotted to Ephraim's tribe for an inheritance. From Tappuah the northern border ran westward to Kanah Brook, then followed its course to the Mediterranean Sea (Jos 16:8). The land of Tappuah was a district within the territory given to the tribe of Manasseh; however, the city of Tappuah, located on the border of Manasseh, belonged to the Ephraimites (17:8).

TARAH* KJV spelling of Terah, one of the stopping places during the wilderness journey, in Numbers 33:27-28. *See* Terah (Place).

TARALAH One of 26 cities in the land assigned to Benjamin's tribe for an inheritance, listed between Irpeel and Zelah (Jos 18:27). Taralah was possibly situated to the northwest of Jerusalem.

TAREA* *See* Tahrea.

TARES* KJV rendering of "weeds" (darnels) in Matthew 13:25-30. *See* Plants (Darnel Grass).

TARGUM* An Aramaic translation of the OT. While technically this Hebrew word may be used to refer to any translation, *targum* commonly designates an Aramaic paraphrase or interpretive translation of a portion of the OT. Targums were of inestimable importance in the development of ancient Judaism. Jewish tradition holds that oral targums were extant in the time of Ezra; Nehemiah 8:8 is cited as supportive evidence.

At the time of the Babylonian exile (seven centuries before Christ), the language of the Jews was Hebrew. During the Captivity, Aramaic (the native tongue of the Babylonians) gradually replaced Hebrew as the language for the average Israelite. It thus became a practical necessity for Jewish scholars to translate the Scriptures into Aramaic. In the synagogue, a reading of an excerpt from the Law would be immediately followed by an oral translation of it. Eventually these translations or paraphrases were committed to writings, many of which still survive. The earliest known manuscript of a Targum is of the book of Job. Found in a cave of the Qumran community, it antedates the time of Christ by more than a century. The most important Targums are Targum Onkelos and Targum Jonathon, in circulation by the fifth century AD. The former is a literal rendering of the Pentateuch; the latter is a freer interpretive version of the Prophets.

TARPEL, TARPELITES* KJV rendering of "officials" in Ezra 4:9. Its precise meaning is uncertain but possibly is a Persian title or an ethnic name.

TARSHISH (Person)
1. One of Javan's four sons and a descendant of Noah through Japheth's line (1 Chr 1:7).
2. Sixth of Bilhan's seven sons. He was a capable leader in Benjamin's tribe and numbered among those able to go to war (1 Chr 7:10).
3. One of the seven princes of Persia and Media. These men had personal access to King Ahasuerus's presence and positions of honor second only to the king himself (Est 1:14).

TARSHISH (Place) Place regarded as being very distant from Israel. Many countries have been proposed as the site for Tarshish, from Sardinia to Great Britain. The most commonly accepted identification is Spain, where the name Tartessus hints at Tarshish.

The Phoenicians, who were great sea voyagers, are often associated with Tarshish. Solomon used the sailors of Hiram, king of Tyre, for his fleet (cf. 2 Chr 9:21). They used sailing vessels that were called Tarshish ships (1 Kgs 10:22; 48:22); apparently they were a distinctive type used to journey to that place or were typical of Tarshish (Ps 48:7; Is 2:16; 23:1-14).

The most famous reference to Tarshish in the Bible is in the account of Jonah, who attempted to flee to Tarshish to escape doing the will of God (Jon 1:3; 4:2).

TARSUS Birthplace and hometown of Saul (Paul) and the capital and chief city of the Roman province of Cilicia in Asia Minor. The city is mentioned only five times in the Bible, all in the book of Acts. After Saul's conversion, the Lord directed Ananias to visit Saul; Ananias was told to ask for "a man of Tarsus named Saul" (Acts 9:11). Then, when Saul returned to Jerusalem and a plot against his life was discovered, the Christians sent him to Tarsus (v 30). When Barnabas was serving in Syrian Antioch and needed help, he went to Tarsus to get

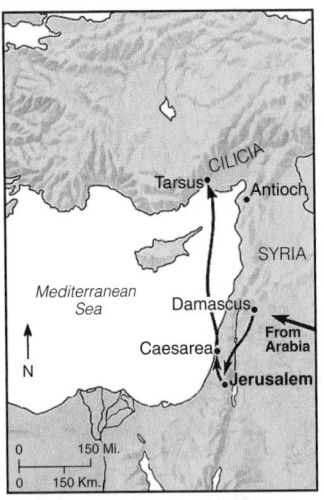

Paul's Return to Tarsus After time in Arabia, Paul returned to Damascus, then Jerusalem. After troubles in Jerusalem, he fled to Caesarea, then on to Tarsus.

Saul to work with him (11:25). On the occasion of Paul's rescue from the Jewish mob in the temple, the Roman tribune was concerned with Paul's identity. Paul identified himself: "I am a Jew, from Tarsus in Cilicia" (21:39). In the defense he made before that angry multitude, speaking in Hebrew, he declared, "I am a Jew, born at Tarsus in Cilicia" (22:3).

Tarsus was situated on the Cydnus River, 12 miles (19.3 kilometers) upstream from the Mediterranean Sea. The plain on which the city was built was very fertile, composed of alluvium carried down from the Taurus Mountains by the Cydnus and several other streams.

Although the river was navigable by small boats as far as Tarsus, the overland trade routes were the most important. Asia Minor was interlaced with roads long before the Romans came into the area. From the east there were two main routes, one of which began in northern Mesopotamia and went on to Carchemish or Aleppo, across the Amanus Pass. The other ran from Nineveh through Malatya and Antioch to the Syrian Gates. These two routes converged near Caesarea, 50 miles (80.5 kilometers) east of Tarsus. During the Roman Empire, "the Old Way to the East" ended at Babylon; coming westward it reached Aleppo, Syrian Antioch, Adana, Tarsus, the Cilician Gates, Derbe, Lystra, Iconium, Pisidian Antioch, Hierapolis, Colosse, Laodicea, Ephesus, Smyrna, and Troas, most of which are well known from the writings of Paul and from the book of Revelation.

Tarsus was an educational center; the university of Tarsus was famous for its scholarship, and Strabo indicated that Tarsus surpassed Athens, Alexandria, and other cities as a seat of learning. The university offered instruction in a wide range of studies; one of its specializations was the philosophy known as Stoicism, with which Paul was familiar. Although Paul does not say that he attended this institution, it has often been suggested that he studied there.

Tarsus was also a center for tent making, a vocation in which Paul had been trained (cf. Acts 18:3). The goats of the cold, snow-swept Taurus Mountains produced long hair that was made into a fabric particularly well suited for tents.

Tarsus has been described as "the heart of the Greco-Roman world" and "a meeting place of East and West." From such an environment, a man like Saul of Tarsus, at home with Greek and Roman culture and educated at the feet of Gamaliel, was singularly well equipped to bring the gospel to the Jew first and also to the Greek.

See also Paul, The Apostle.

TARTAK Deity worshiped by the Avvites in Samaria (2 Kgs 17:31). This deity may be a union of the deities Athtar and Anath, and thus a fertility god.

TARTAN* Title of the highest-ranking Assyrian official, second in command only to the king. The tartan was the commander in chief of the Assyrian army. The position is mentioned in two OT passages: (1) Sargon II, king of Assyria (722–705 BC), ordered his commander to subdue and capture the Philistine city of Ashdod (Is 20:1). (2) In 2 Kings 8:17 the tartan was one of three officials whom King Sennacherib of Assyria (705–681 BC) posted over the Assyrian army sent from Lachish to Jerusalem to confront King Hezekiah of Judah (715–687 BC).

TASKMASTER* An overseer of public workers who enforced their performance. Taskmasters are depicted on Egyptian bas-reliefs with whips in their hands to enforce discipline (Ex 1:11; 3:7; 5:6-14; Jb 3:18). The Hebrew verb means "to oppress." David and Solomon had such officers. Adoram was in charge of forced labor (2 Sm 20:24; 1 Kgs 4:6; 12:18; 2 Chr 10:18). The excesses of these men were a factor in the revolt of the northern tribes after the death of Solomon (1 Kgs 12:3-14).

TATIAN* Apologist and heretic; creator of the Diatessaron. See Bible, Versions of the (Ancient), page 202.

TATTENAI Persian governor of a province west of the Euphrates River who opposed the rebuilding of the Jerusalem temple and walls under Zerubbabel during the postexilic period (Ezr 5:3, 6; 6:6, 13).

TAX, TAXATION Amount of money or goods that was extracted by the powerful nations from those whom they subjected. It commonly consisted of gold, silver, animals, produce, or forced labor. Taxes were also levied on the people both by their ruler and by the priesthood to pay for the maintenance of the temple. The term "tribute" is first used in the KJV in Genesis 49:15 (NLT "forced labor"). In Numbers 31:28 the spoils of battle were divided up to include a tribute or levy for the priesthood. For the Hebrews the temple tribute was originally a voluntary offering to the Lord (Dt 16:10) but later became a prescribed tax (Mt 17:24).

Even in 2500 BC in the city of Lagash, taxes were imposed on most facets of life, from the means of earning a livelihood, to marriage, divorce, and death. Like many ancient peoples, the Sumerians believed that the land belonged to the god and his representative the king, and that therefore a rent or levy was payable to the owner.

In Egypt, Joseph exacted a burdensome 20-percent tax in grain during the seven years of plenty, which alleviated the food shortages during the subsequent seven years of famine (Gn 41:25–42:5). The tax on the crops was facilitated because in Egypt the ownership of the land was vested in the ruler.

Warrior kings, such as David, were able to maintain a healthy treasury without taxing their own people. The Canaanites and neighboring conquered peoples contributed great wealth to the treasury (2 Sm 8:6-14; 1 Chr 27:25-31), one list of which included silver, gold, bronze, 1,700 horsemen, and 20,000 foot soldiers. Forced labor was often required by David and his successors of aliens who remained within the boundaries of the Israelite kingdom (Jos 16:10; 17:13; Jgs 1:28).

Israel was probably first taxed during Solomon's reign. In this more stable period, income came from tribute but not from booty. To maintain the grandeur of the court and the extensive building program, Solomon divided

Israel into 12 areas, each under an officer, each of whom provided food and support for the king and his household for one month per year (1 Kgs 4:7). Solomon also derived considerable income from levying custom duties on trading caravans that passed regularly through his kingdom. In addition to all of this, both foreigners and native Israelites were subject to forced labor for major building projects, especially for the temple (1 Kgs 5:13; 9:20-21; 2 Chr 8:7-8). Handles from ten-gallon (37.9-liter) jars have been excavated, bearing a Hebrew stamp "to the king," indicating that they formed part of a levy (2 Chr 2:10).

Jehoshaphat was equally successful in taxing the people at home (2 Chr 17:5) and maintaining the tribute from abroad, including silver and gold from the Philistines and 7,700 rams and 7,700 he-goats from the Arabs (2 Chr 17:11-12). As the power of the surrounding empires increased, Judah found itself forced to pay tribute. Sennacherib, king of Assyria, required 300 talents of silver and 30 talents of gold, which necessitated the removal of the gold from the temple doors (2 Kgs 18:14-16). Approximately a century later, Pharaoh Neco required 100 talents of silver and a talent of gold from Judah (23:33), and shortly thereafter Nebuchadnezzar removed all the treasure from the temple and the royal palace, together with 10,000 captives, all the craftsmen, and 1,000 smiths, leaving few in Jerusalem except the poor (24:13-16).

A definite, regular, organized tax system was instituted by the Persians, whose satraps, ruling each province, were required to make payment of fixed sums into the royal treasury (Est 10:1). Tax exemption was introduced by Artaxerxes I, who stated that levies should not be collected from priests, Levites, or any others occupied in any way with the service of the temple (Ezr 7:24). An additional tax was required for the maintenance of the governor's household; it consisted of food, wine, and 40 shekels of silver (Neh 5:14-15). As governor, Nehemiah did not claim this allowance of food because he considered the taxes already burdensome, causing the mortgaging of fields, vineyards, and houses "for the king's tax." Simultaneously, a levy was imposed upon the Jews for the rebuilding of the walls of Jerusalem (4:6). Darius was politically astute enough to encourage the rebuilding of the temple and to allow the Jews to use some of the royal tax money for this purpose (Ezr 6:7-10).

Under the Seleucids, the Ptolemies, and subsequently the Romans, there was a change in the collection of taxes, whereby the office of tax collector was sold to the highest bidder, who in turn extracted the maximum payment from the people and built up his own wealth from the surplus generated. At times, the Jews were paying tithes for the maintenance of the temple, in addition to taxes of as much as one-third of the grain and half of the fruit grown. Excise, sales, and poll taxes were also collected.

After the extortionate level of tax imposed by Pompey, Julius Caesar reduced the amount paid by the Jews and exempted them from all payment in the sabbatical year. The provinces were considered booty by the Romans and were plundered physically by the army and financially by the tax collectors. In imperial times there was greater regulation of the tax system. An income tax was imposed on produce from the field and from artisans and tradesmen, as well as a poll tax, port duties, sales taxes, an auction tax, and an estate duty.

In addition to the taxes paid to foreign powers, all Jews worldwide who were 20 years of age and older (Ex 30:11-16) were assessed a half-shekel per person annually as a tax to support the temple in Jerusalem (Mt 17:24), a tax that continued to be levied even after the destruction of the temple in AD 70. Jesus was questioned on the validity of this tax (v 25) as well as the lawfulness of payment of taxes to Rome (Mt 22:17; Mk 12:14-15; Lk 20:22). Despite Jesus' famous reply—"render to Caesar that which is Caesar's and to God that which is God's" (Mt 22:21; Mk 12:17; Lk 20:25)—he was still accused before Pilate of forbidding the Jews to give taxes to Caesar (Lk 23:2). The early church also reinforced the legality of taxation as a legitimate responsibility required of all people (Rom 13:5-7).

See also Money; Banker, Banking; Tax Collector.

TAX COLLECTOR One who collected taxes for the government. In NT times the Romans collected a variety of taxes. Their own officers undertook some of this work but also delegated it to private individuals, Jews and others, who were required to return to the authorities an agreed-upon sum. Dishonest individuals collected far more than they were required to pay and became a hated group, especially the Jews who cheated fellow Jews. Zacchaeus, a Jew, was a "chief tax collector" who amassed considerable wealth in the Jericho area (Lk 19:2-10). Such men were regarded as sinners and were often linked in the phrase "tax collectors and sinners" (Mt 9:10-11; 11:19; Mk 2:15-16; Lk 5:30; 19:2-10).

TEACHER Teachers conserved the values and academia of a nation and passed them on to each new generation. In OT times the first teachers were often parents (Dt 6:7, 20-25; 11:19-21). Leaders like Moses and Aaron were charged with teaching the people (Lv 10:11), and later the priests and Levites had a teaching function (Dt 24:8; 33:8-10; 2 Chr 17:7-9; Ez 44:23; Mi 3:11). God himself was thought of as a teacher (Pss 25:8, 12; 27:11; 32:8; 86:11; Is 2:3).

In the NT the Greek noun for "teacher" and the verb "to teach" are widely used. John the Baptist was called a teacher (Lk 3:12). The term is used more than 30 times of Jesus (Mt 4:23; 5:2; 7:29; 9:35; 11:1; Mk 1:21; 2:13; 4:1-2; 6:2, 6, 34; Lk 4:15, 31; 5:3; 6:6; Jn 6:59; 7:14, 28; etc.). People recognized his teaching as authoritative (Mt 7:29; Mk 1:22; Lk 4:32). Even as a boy of 12 he conversed in a profound way with the teachers of the law in the temple (Lk 2:46). These men were often associated with the Pharisees (5:17). Gamaliel was a Pharisee and a teacher of the law (Acts 5:34). The term "rabbi" was often used to denote teacher. The rabbi was held in great honor. In the early church the teacher was widely recognized (Acts 13:1; 1 Cor 12:28-29; Eph 4:11; 2 Tm 1:11; Jas 3:1).

TEACHER OF RIGHTEOUSNESS* A designation of the founder of the Essene community at Qumran. The commentaries on biblical books found at Qumran provide us with some insight into the importance of the Teacher. He was a priest and as such was expected to officiate in the temple of Jerusalem. He separated himself with his followers from the established religion in Jerusalem when he began to teach an interpretation of the Law and the Prophets that differed from the established religious practices in Jerusalem. It is claimed that he received a special revelation from God: "to whom [the Teacher of Righteousness] God made known all the mysteries of the words of his servants the Prophets" (1QpHab 2:7-9). Based on the revelation he received, the Teacher taught another way of life and worship. Those who joined with him were discipled so that they might be saved from the day of judgment (1Qpap Micah 1:5).

The claims of the Teacher of Righteousness were exclusive. Only those who followed him by living in separation from corrupt Judaism in the desert were the elect. He felt himself called by God to establish a faithful remnant who would inherit the Abrahamic covenant. As the Teacher knew by revelation the mysteries of the future, he would assume that salvation was possible by faith in him: "This concerns all those who observe the Law in the House of Judah, whom he will deliver from the House of Judgment, because of their suffering and because of their faith in the Teacher of Righteousness" (1QpHab 8:1-3).

The priesthood of Jerusalem was upset with his teachings and exclusive claims. The Teacher was persecuted by one such person, known as the Wicked Priest. On the Day of Atonement, observed at Qumran according to a different calendar from that followed by the establishment, the Wicked Priest appeared at Qumran to force the devotees to defend themselves on their solemn day of rest (1QpHab 11:4-8). It is uncertain what happened to the Teacher of Righteousness. After his death, the Essene community continued to observe his teachings and to draw people dissatisfied with the established religion to its wilderness monastery at Qumran.

TEACHINGS OF JESUS *See* Jesus Christ, Life and Teachings of.

TEBAH (Person) Son of Abraham's brother Nahor (Gn 22:24). His mother was Reumah, Nahor's concubine.

TEBAH (Place) City of King Hadadezer from which David received a large quantity of bronze as booty (2 Sm 8:8; 1 Chr 18:8). Hadadezer was the king of Zobah, which is located in the region of Hamath in Syria, so the location of Tebah was likely in that region.

TEBALIAH Son of Hosah, a Merarite Levite and a temple gatekeeper who served during the postexilic period (1 Chr 26:11).

TEBETH* Month in the Hebrew calendar corresponding to about mid-December to mid-January (Est 2:16; see NLT mg). *See* Calendars, Ancient and Modern.

TEHAPHNEHES* Alternate spelling of Tahpanhes, an Egyptian city, in Ezekiel 30:18. *See* Tahpanhes.

TEHINNAH Forefather of the people of Ir-nahash in Judah's tribe (1 Chr 4:12).

TEIL* KJV rendering of terebinth in Isaiah 6:13. *See* Plants (Terebinth).

TEKEL Aramaic word interpreted as "weighed" in Daniel 5:25-27. *See* Mene, Mene, Tekel, Parsin.

TEKOA, TEKOITES* City about six miles (9.7 kilometers) southeast of Bethlehem on the edge of the Judean desert, and its residents. Tekoa may also be the name of a person, the son of Ashur of Judah's tribe; "father" could mean founder or leader of Tekoa (1 Chr 2:24; 4:5). Tekoa does not appear on the list of cities given to Judah (Jos 15). In an oracle predicting the siege of Judah, Jeremiah (Jer 6:1) makes a pun with the phrase "Sound the trumpet in Tekoa." The Hebrew word for "sound" is spelled with the same consonants (but not vowels) as Tekoa.

Tekoa is located on the high ground between two watersheds, both of which flow eastward to the Dead Sea. The southern slopes climb off to the upper reaches of the Nahal Arugot, which eventually comes out at En-gedi. The northern slopes are drained by the Nahal Darga. The ridge between them is the Ascent (or Pass) of Ziz (2 Chr 20:16). Because Tekoa lies between the desert and the town on the marginal land just east of the main north-south water-

shed, the area around it came to be known as the desert of Tekoa (2 Chr 20:20), a part of the larger desert of Judea. Tekoa marks the border where farming gives way to herding, explaining why Amos, a native of Tekoa, had two dimensions to his preprophetic career: a herdsman and a dresser of sycamore trees (Am 1:1; 7:14).

TEL-ABIB Village on the river Kebar where Ezekiel visited the Babylonian exiles (Ez 3:15). Although the exact location of the site is unknown, it was probably in the delta region of southern Babylonia. The Kebar was likely an irrigation canal that enhanced the fertility of the surrounding soil; hence, the name Tel-abib ("hill of corn").

TELAH Resheph's son, father of Tahan, and an ancestor of Joshua the son of Nun from Ephraim's tribe (1 Chr 7:25).

TELAIM Place where Saul organized Israel's army in preparation for war with the Amalekites (1 Sm 15:4). Telaim is perhaps identifiable with Telem, a city situated near Edom's border in the southern extremity of the territory allotted to Judah's tribe for an inheritance (Jos 15:24).

TEL-ASSAR Principal city of the people of Eden who were conquered by Sennacherib of Assyria (2 Kgs 19:11-12; Is 37:11-12). The conquest is mentioned in Rabshekah's taunt that the Lord would similarly be unable to protect Jerusalem.

TELEM (Person) One of the gatekeepers who was encouraged by Ezra to divorce his foreign wife (Ezr 10:24).

TELEM (Place) Alternate name of the city Telaim in 1 Samuel 15:4. *See* Telaim.

TEL-HARSHA One of the Babylonian villages from which some returning exiles could not establish their genealogy (Ezr 2:59; Neh 7:61). Its precise location is uncertain, though it is likely near the Persian Gulf in the lowland region of Babylonia.

TELL* Arabic word (Hebrew, *tel*) meaning an artificial mound composed of many layers of occupational debris, representing the ruins of successive cities, roughly like layers of a cake. The discerning of the strata, or building levels, is one of the biggest challenges of the field archaeologist. The levels are dated primarily by the pottery found in them.

Usually tells bear Arabic names, which sometimes have interesting or amusing meanings. Tell el Ful (Gibeah), the hometown of King Saul, means "the mound of the beans." Tell Beit Mirsim translates into "the mound of the house of the fast camel driver." Other modern names preserve the identity of ancient sites; for example, Tell Taanak is biblical Taanach; Tell Jezer is biblical Gezer.

There are numerous references to tells in the Bible, although in English tell may appear as "mound," "heap," or "heap of ruins." The Lord commanded Israel that a city which practiced abominable idolatry should be burned and "be a heap forever" (Dt 13:16). Joshua 11:13 states that Israel burned none of the cities that stood on mounds, except Hazor. Joshua burned Ai and made it "a heap of ruins for ever" (Jos 8:28). In a prophecy against the Ammonites, Jeremiah said that Rabbah "shall become a desolate mound" (Jer 49:2).

See also Archaeology and the Bible; Pottery.

TEL-MELAH One of the Babylonian towns situated in the vicinity of the Kebar River near the city of Nippur from which exiles, who were unable to establish their Israelite descent, returned to Palestine with Zerubbabel following the Babylonian captivity (Ezr 2:59; Neh 7:61).

TEMA (Person) Ninth son of Ishmael who became chief of a powerful nomadic tribe in the north Arabian wilderness (Gn 25:15; 1 Chr 1:30; Jer 25:23). The descendants of Tema were primarily caravan traders who controlled access to important routes across the desert (Jb 6:19). Tema was also associated with the territory and a town. *See* Tema (Place).

TEMA (Place) Town generally identified with Teima', an oasis located 200 miles (321.8 kilometers) north of Medina and 40 miles (64.4 kilometers) south of Dumah. Teima' was located on an ancient caravan route that connected the Persian Gulf with the Gulf of Aqaba. In prophetic literature Tema is mentioned with Dedan and Buz as Arabian oases that would not escape God's judgment (Is 21:14; Jer 25:23). The Jeremiah passage contains an obscure indication that the residents of Dedan, Tema, and Buz were among those who "cut the corners of their hair." The practice of cutting the corners of the hair would distinguish them from the Jews, who left the corners of their hair uncut (Lv 19:27). Like uncircumcision, the practice would identify the men of Tema as pagans.

TEMAH Forefather of a family of temple servants who returned with Zerubbabel to Jerusalem following the exile (Ezr 2:53; Neh 7:55).

TEMAN (Person) One of the chiefs of the Edomites and Eliphaz's firstborn son (Gn 36:11, 15, 42; 1 Chr 1:36, 53). He was likely either the founder or a chief of the Edomite city of Teman.

TEMAN (Place) In the prophetic writings, Teman seems to have been considered the principal city of Edom and is often used as a poetic parallel for the entire land of Edom (Jer 49:7, 20; Am 1:12; Ob 1:9). Since Teman means "south," it is likely that Teman was located in the far south of Edom; however, its precise location remains unknown. The residents of Teman were evidently well known for their wisdom (Jer 49:7; Ob 1:9). This reputation may well derive from Eliphaz the Temanite, who was one of Job's counselors (Jb 2:11, 4:1; 15:1; 22:1; 42:7-9).

TEMENI Ashhur's son by his wife Naarah, and a descendant of Judah (1 Chr 4:6).

TEMPLE

PREVIEW
- Background
- Solomon's Temple
- Zerubbabel's Temple
- Herod's Temple
- Significance of the Temple in the Old Testament
- Significance of the Temple in the New Testament

Background David's capture of Jerusalem (2 Sm 5:6-9) and his designation of it as the nation's capital is one of the great masterstrokes of history. Occupied by the Jebusites, it was a pocket of neutral territory between the northern and southern sections of David's united kingdom and was politically acceptable to both. Jerusalem was then established as the national religious center by the return of the ark, which had been largely neglected since its capture by the Philistines (2 Sm 6:1-17). Henceforth, God's choices of both David and Jerusalem ("Mount Zion") were indissolubly linked (Ps 78:67-72).

David's great impulse was to build an adequate dwelling place for Israel's God. The idea was initially approved by Nathan the prophet (2 Sm 7:1-3), but God revealed otherwise to him, and he conveyed the divine purpose to David (vv 4-17). In a significant wordplay, David was informed that, while he was not to build a house (temple) for God, God would build a house (dynasty) for him. David was not the one to build a temple because of the numerous wars during his reign; the temple would instead be built by his son (1 Kgs 5:3; 1 Chr 22:7-8; 28:3). Nevertheless, David enthusiastically amassed most of the necessary finances and materials and drew up the blueprints for the temple (1 Chr 22:3-5, 14; 28:2, 11-19). He also purchased the temple site (21:25).

Solomon's Temple

Date Construction commenced in Solomon's fourth year, about 966 BC, and took seven years to complete (1 Kgs 6:1, 38). Everything necessary for the temple, including the workers, had been prepared by David (1 Chr 28:21). The temple evidently had first priority among Solomon's building schemes, as he built his own palace later (1 Kgs 7:1).

Superintendents and Workforce The principal architect for the bronze furnishings was Huram (Hebrew "Hiram"), whose father was a metal craftsman from Tyre and whose mother was an Israelite (1 Kgs 7:13-14). Cedar for the temple came from Lebanon and was felled and transported by the skilled woodsmen of another Hiram—the king of Tyre, Solomon's ally (5:5-9). Thirty thousand Israelites, divided into three groups, were drafted to assist at Lebanon. Each group was on duty for one month in three. For the stonework, Solomon conscripted 153,600 foreigners resident in Israel to provide a self-contained group of carriers, stone cutters, and supervisors (vv 15-17; 2 Chr 2:17-18). Possibly the "men of Gebal," with their specialized skills, formed yet another group (1 Kgs 5:18). Building the temple was obviously a national project of immense size and effort. In order to preserve the sanctity

Solomon's Temple

of the site and to eliminate noise, the masonry and carpentry were not done at the temple site (6:7).

Description The details given in the Bible are sufficiently clear for us to make a reasonably accurate description of the temple. The accounts in Kings and Chronicles are supplemented by Ezekiel's depiction of the temple (see below), which was broadly based on his knowledge of the Jerusalem temple (Ez 40-48).

The side rooms probably rested on a foundation or platform that was separate from the temple itself (1 Kgs 6:5, 10; cf. Ez 41:8-9) and were arranged in three stories, each seven and a half feet (2.3 meters) high, extending around the whole building except for the porch side. Each successive story was one and a half feet (.5 meter) wider than the one below, these dimensions coinciding with the thickness of the side wall of the Holy Place. The ground floor rooms were seven and a half feet (2.3 meters) wide; the first story was nine feet (2.7 meters), and the second was ten and a half feet (3.2 meters). Access to the upper stories was possibly by winding staircases (1 Kgs 6:8). There is some uncertainty concerning the location of the entrances; there may have been one on either side, but only one is mentioned (v 8). As in Ezekiel's temple (Ez 40:17, 28), there were two adjacent courts, an inner and an outer (1 Kgs 6:36; 7:12), but no dimensions are given for these. The inner court, or "court of the priests," being next to the temple itself, was also called "the upper court" (2 Chr 4:9; Jer 36:10). The wall of the inner court was made of three layers of hewn stone held together by a layer of cedar beams (1 Kgs 6:36), and the doors of both courts were sheathed in bronze (2 Chr 4:9). The palace buildings were within the outer court area, probably with a private passageway between the palace and the temple that was later closed during the reign of Ahaz (2 Chr 4:9, 12; 2 Kgs 16:18).

The temple itself was 90 feet (27.4 meters) long, 30 feet (9.1 meters) wide, and 45 feet (13.7 meters) high (1 Kgs 6:2), with a porch or vestibule 15 feet (4.6 meters) deep stretching across the width. Probably the vestibule was on the east end of the temple, thus corresponding with the orientation of Ezekiel's temple (Ez 43:1; 44:1). The larger part of the main sanctuary, next to the porch, formed the Holy Place, which was 60 feet (18.3 meters) long (1 Kgs 6:17). Beyond this was the innermost sanctuary, the Holy of Holies (or the "Most Holy Place"), which was a perfect cube of 30 feet (9.1 meters). All the interior walls were paneled with cedar decorated with flower patterns, cherubim, and palm trees, so that no masonry was visible. The walls of both inner and outer sanctuaries were "overlaid" (v 22) with pure gold. Actually the gold decoration may have been inlaid, on the basis that a solid sheath of gold would spoil the natural beauty of the wood carving. The floor was made of cypress planks (v 15). Narrow windows set high in the walls above the level of the three-storied outer chambers provided light in the Holy Place (v 4). The ceiling was paneled with beams and planks of cedar. No detail is given about the exterior roofing, but probably the contemporary technique was employed, using a wooden, latticelike framework into which a waterproof, limestone plaster was packed and rolled.

The outer porch was apparently an open space, since no doors are mentioned. Access into the Holy Place was by double doors, both hinged to fold back on themselves, made of cypress and decorated in exactly the same way as the interior walls (vv 34-35). The doorposts were made of olive wood. Within the Holy Place was the altar of incense made of cedar overlaid with gold; it was placed centrally before the Holy of Holies. Also in the Holy Place were a table for the bread of the Presence of God, ten lampstands arranged in two groups of five on either side, and various

utensils required for maintaining the priestly duties (1 Kgs 7:48-50). All these were made or overlaid with gold. The ten tables, arranged five on each side, were presumably for the utensils and accessories (2 Chr 4:8).

Between the Holy Place and the Holy of Holies was a double door made of olive wood, carved with cherubim, palm trees, and flower patterns, and overlaid with gold. Inside these doors, veiling still further the Holy of Holies, was a blue, purple, and crimson curtain, made of the finest fabrics and ornamented with cherubim (2 Chr 3:14).

In the Holy of Holies were two cherubim, each 15 feet (4.6 meters) high and made of olive wood covered with gold (1 Kgs 6:23-28). Each wing measured seven and a half feet (2.3 meters). A wing of each touched the side walls; the other wings met at the center of the room. The divine throne had been considerably less impressive in the tabernacle, where a wing of each cherubim fused into the mercy seat above the ark (Ex 25:17-22). In Solomon's temple, the ark of the covenant was placed below the forward-facing cherubim, the symbolic protectors. The ark, the only major item surviving from the Mosaic tabernacle, still contained the tablets of the law, but the pot of manna and Aaron's rod were missing (1 Kgs 8:9).

Immediately outside the temple and on either side of the vestibule were two hollow bronze pillars (1 Kgs 7:15-20; 2 Chr 3:15-17). According to the book of Kings, these pillars were 27 feet (8.2 meters) high, with a circumference of 18 feet (5.5 meters). The metal itself was about four inches (10.2 centimeters) thick. The pillars were surmounted by bronze, lily-shaped capitals seven and a half feet (2.3 meters) high and six feet (1.8 meters) wide, intricately adorned with a chain latticework that supported two rows of pomegranates. The total weight must have been enormous, and their size is attested to by Jeremiah, who notes that the Babylonians had to break them in pieces before transporting them to Babylon (Jer 52:17, 21-23).

The bronze altar of sacrifice in front of the vestibule is not listed in the specifications of 1 Kings 7. However, it is mentioned in the temple dedication and subsequently (1 Kgs 8:22, 54, 64; 9:25) and clearly stood in the inner court. Its dimensions were 30 feet (9.1 meters) square and 15 feet (4.6 meters) high (2 Chr 4:1). In view of its weight, it was probably cast in sections at Solomon's foundry in the Jordan Rift valley (vv 17-18) and then transported to the temple site for assembly.

Probably the most striking article in the inner court was the "molten (bronze) sea," a huge, round tank made of bronze 3 inches (8 centimeters) thick, 7½ feet (2.3 meters) high, and 15 feet (4.6 meters) in diameter (1 Kgs 7:23-26). Its rim flared out like a lily (2 Chr 4:2-5). The tank was supported on 12 bronze oxen, four on each side, and had two rows of decoration, possibly gourds or pomegranates, under the brim. Its capacity was between 10,000 and 12,000 gallons (37,850-45,420 liters). The bronze sea was used for priestly ablutions (v 6). Presumably this involved a platform of sorts, for the brim of this vast basin would have been about 15 feet (4.6 meters) above ground level.

Hiram also constructed ten large lavers, mounted on moveable stands and placed in two groups of five, on the north and south sides of the inner court (1 Kgs 7:27-39). Basically the stands were bronze boxes, six feet (1.8 meters) square and four and a half feet (1.4 meters) high with a nine-inch (22.9-centimeter) rim around the top edge. Each corner was attached to braced posts to which the axles were fixed. The four-spoked wheels were 27 inches (68.6 centimeters) high. Into each stand there fitted a laver containing approximately 220 gallons (832.7 liters) of water, used for washing sacrificial animals (2 Chr 4:6). Probably each was adjacent to one of the ten tables that would be used to flay and otherwise prepare the sacrifices (v 8). Supplementary items, such as pots, shovels, and basins, all made of bronze, were also manufactured (1 Kgs 7:40, 45).

The Dedication Eleven months elapsed between the completion of the temple and its dedication (1 Kgs 6:38; 8:2), during which time the major items of furniture were set in place. The dedication itself took place in the seventh month, presumably in connection with the Feast of Tabernacles and the Day of Atonement (Lv 23:23-36). The ark of the covenant was brought into its final resting place (1 Kgs 8:3-4), but the inner court proved inadequate for the vast numbers of beasts sacrificed (1 Kgs 8:62-64; 2 Chr 7:7).

The temple employed the most sophisticated building techniques of the age, and no expense had been spared in construction, ornamentation, or equipment. Yet Solomon readily confessed its utter inadequacy to house the eternal God (1 Kgs 8:27). His prayer also underlined Israel's propensity to forsake the Lord, contrasting the nation with God, who, though a just judge, was also merciful and faithful. The climax of the proceedings came when fire from heaven consumed the sacrifices and the shekinah glory filled the temple (2 Chr 7:1-3).

Later History Like most ancient shrines, the temple became a treasury for national wealth and as such was often the target for attack. Shishak of Egypt plundered it within five years of Solomon's death (1 Kgs 14:25-38). Shortly afterward, King Asa (910–869 BC) depleted its gold and silver treasures to buy Syrian help against his oppressor, Baasha (908–886 BC), king of Israel (15:16-19). Joash, the king of Judah (835–796 BC) who was concealed in the temple from the vicious Athaliah during his youth (2 Kgs 11), made provision for its repair after protesting the priests' embezzlement of gifts (12:4-16). But after the death of Jehoiada, the high priest, Joash himself was adversely influenced by his nobles (2 Chr 24:15-19). As punishment for his apostasy, the Lord allowed the Syrians to attack, and Joash used the temple treasures to buy them off (2 Kgs 12:17-18). Hardly had provision for replacements been made, when Jehoash of Israel (798–782 BC), having shattered the arrogant pride of Amaziah of Judah (796–767 BC), again stripped the temple (14:8-14). Later, King Ahaz (735-715 BC) used the remaining resources of the temple to enlist support from the Assyrians (16:7-9), though he eventually became completely subservient to them.

Then Hezekiah (715–686 BC), one of the great reforming kings, thoroughly renovated the temple and restored worship after it had fallen into disuse during theclosing years of Ahaz (2 Chr 29:1-19; 31:9-21). Manasseh (696–642 BC), however, completely reversed his father's policy, bringing the practices of Canaanite and Mesopotamian worship into the temple (2 Kgs 21:3-7). His conversion experience, which probably occurred late in his reign and resulted in certain reform measures in the temple (2 Chr 33:12-19), was not far-reaching enough to escape the final judgment that his reign was the dark spot of Judah's history (2 Kgs 21:10-16).

Manasseh's grandson Josiah (640–609 BC), was the second great reforming king. He organized the repair of the temple in 622 BC, during which the lost Book of the Law (almost certainly the book of Deuteronomy) was discovered (2 Kgs 22:3-13). As a result, Josiah's reformation gained a new dimension and sense of urgency (22:14–23:3). The reformation included a thorough purge of all idolatrous elements from the temple (23:4-12) and the restoration of the traditional festivals. Sadly, however, Josiah's reformation died with him, and Judah's downward slide continued under the apostate Jehoiakim (609–598 BC). It was probably during this time that Jere-

miah preached his famous temple sermon foretelling its destruction (Jer 7:1–8:3; 26:1-19), which alienated him from the religious leaders. In Nebuchadnezzar's reprisal raid following Jehoiakim's rebellion in 601 BC (2 Kgs 24:1-4), Jerusalem was captured (596 BC) and many of the temple treasures were transported to Babylon (2 Chr 36:7). The temple itself appears to have escaped damage, but when Judah again rebelled under Zedekiah (597–586 BC), the temple was demolished (2 Kgs 25:8-10). The remaining temple treasures were taken away.

Zerubbabel's Temple

Construction Although the temple was devastated, the site still remained as a place of pilgrimage during the exile (Jer 41:4-5). In 538 BC the Persian king, Cyrus, in pursuance of a liberal policy diametrically opposed to that of the earlier empires, permitted the Jews to return from exile. And he authorized the rebuilding of the temple, financing it from the Persian treasury.

In the book of Ezra, the decree of authorization has been preserved in two forms: the general proclamation (Ezr 1:2-4) and a more prosaic memorandum in the national archives indicating the main temple specifications and the amount of promised Persian help (6:1-5). Probably only a minority of the Jews opted to leave the relative comforts of Mesopotamia for the dangers of a long journey to their desolated homeland. According to the book of Ezra, 42,360 dedicated individuals and their servants (2:64-65) responded under the leadership of Sheshbazzar (1:8-11; 5:14-16) and Zerubbabel (2:2; 3:2, 8; 4:2). With great enthusiasm, the altar was rebuilt on the temple site and the traditional pattern of worship reestablished (3:1-6). Utilizing the grant from Persia as well as their own freewill gifts (2:68-69; 3:7), the Jews began to plan the second temple and lay its foundations (3:7-13). The initial impetus quickly died as a result of local opposition (4:1-4, 24), selfish preoccupation, and crop failures (Hg 1:2-11). In 520 BC (Ezr 4:24; Hg 1:1; Zec 1:1), inspired by the prophets Haggai and Zechariah, the Jews under Zerubbabel and Joshua the high priest commenced rebuilding. Work continued in spite of official suspicion, if not direct opposition, and the temple was completed and dedicated in 515 BC (Ezr 5:1–6:22).

Little is known of the physical features of Zerubbabel's temple. The inference that it was vastly inferior to Solomon's temple (Hg 2:3) probably relates to an early stage in the building operation. In fact, the second temple stood for over 500 years. The dimensions noted in Ezra 6:3 are incomplete; the new temple was no doubt about the same size as its predecessor and was probably built on the same foundation. The construction technique appears to have followed the method of the original, with layers of timber providing a framework for sections of masonry (v 4). Clearly, there was auxiliary accommodation, probably like the side rooms of Solomon's temple (Ezr 8:29; Neh 12:44; 13:4-5). If Persian aid was forthcoming as promised (Ezr 6:8-12), the second temple was a more splendid, substantial structure than is generally supposed.

Later History Several references in the Apocrypha, pseudepigrapha, rabbinic writings, and the historian Josephus help to illumine the history of the temple and give more detail on its structure and furnishings. Josephus, quoting from Hecateus of Abdera (fourth century BC), states that the temple was a large building in an enclosure about 500 feet by 150 feet (152.4 meters by 45.7 meters), surrounded by a stone wall, with an altar of unhewn stones the same size as Solomon's bronze altar (cf. 2 Chr 4:1). Within the sanctuary was a golden altar of incense and a lampstand, the flame of which burned continually.

Josephus also notes that Antiochus III (223–187 BC) financially supported the temple when the Seleucids displaced the Ptolemies as masters of Jerusalem.

Ben Sirach, early in the second century BC, commended Simon, the son of Onias the high priest, for his work in fortifying and repairing the temple area. First Maccabees provides valuable evidence of the fate of the temple during the oppression under Antiochus IV Epiphanes (175–164 BC). The books of the Maccabees recount the defilement of the altar of burnt offering (1 Macc 1:54) and the plundering of the golden lampstand, altar of incense, table of offering, veil, and other treasures (2 Macc 5:15-16; 6:2-4). When the temple was recaptured and restored, the victorious Maccabees replaced the items taken by the Seleucids, except for the altar of sacrifice, which was considered so polluted that it was dismantled and replaced by a new one constructed of unhewn stone (1 Macc 4:36-61; 2 Macc 10:1-9). Clearly the temple area was used as a fortress, both in opposition to the Seleucid garrison that was maintained in Jerusalem in the Maccabean period and in the conflicts of the later Hasmonean period. When Pompey captured Jerusalem about 63 BC, he entered the temple to assert his authority but took no plunder, thus showing respect for it.

The history of Zerubbabel's temple closed when Herod, having carefully preserved it from any major damage when he gained control of Jerusalem with Roman aid in 37 BC, began to dismantle it about 21 BC in preparation for the construction of his own grand temple.

Herod's Temple Apart from over 100 references in the NT, our main sources of information about Herod's temple come from the Jewish historian Josephus and from the Middoth (a section of the Jewish rabbinic writings). There are considerable differences in detail between the two, which rules out any dogmatic interpretation in attempted reconstructions. Since Josephus was contemporary with the temple (he was born about AD 37 and died early in the second century), he is probably more reliable than the Middoth, which, dating from about AD 150, appears to exaggerate occasionally. Archaeological research has been helpful in determining the positions of the outer walls and gates.

Herod's motive in building his temple was political rather than religious. As an Idumean, he wished to placate his Jewish subjects by constructing a sanctuary as magnificent as Solomon's. Possible fears that the site might be profaned, or that the existing temple might be demolished and never rebuilt, were allayed by the training of 1,000 priests as masons and the amassing of materials before the work commenced. Herod's temple followed the tripartite plan of its predecessors, although its porch was much larger. It was built in the contemporary Greco-Roman architectural style and must therefore be regarded as distinct from Zerubbabel's temple. Work began in 20 BC, and while the main sanctuary was quickly erected (it was in full operation within ten years), the total project was not completed until AD 64, only six years before it was destroyed by the Romans.

Herod first prepared the site by clearing and leveling an area approximately 500 yards (457.2 meters) from north to south and about 325 yards (297.2 meters) from east to west. This involved cutting away sections of rock in some areas and building up with rubble in others. Considerable sections of the enclosing wall, constructed on stone blocks averaging about 15 feet (4.6 meters) long by 4 feet (1.2 meters) high, still survive. Some of the stones in the corners of the south wall weigh up to 70 tons (63.5 metric tons).

The sanctuary itself seems to have been based on the same dimensions as Solomon's temple. It was divided into the Holy Place, which was 60 feet (18.3 meters) long, 30 feet (9.1 meters) wide, and 60 feet high, and the Holy of Holies, which was 30 feet square. There was no furniture within the Holy of Holies, which was separated by a veil from the Holy Place. The Holy Place contained the seven-branch lampstand, the table for the bread of the Presence, and the incense altar. The main divergence from Solomon's temple was the imposing porch, 150 feet (45.7 meters) in width and height. Outside was a doorway approximately 30 feet (9.1 meters) wide by 40 feet (12.2 meters) high, with an inner doorway about half that size leading into the sanctuary. By allowing empty rooms over the Holy of Holies and the Holy Place, there was a uniform roof height of 150 feet (45.7 meters). Golden spikes on the roof discouraged birds from alighting and defiling the structure. Like its predecessors, the temple was oriented toward the east and was surrounded on the other sides by three stories of rooms rising to a height of 60 feet (18.3 meters). The stone used was the local white stone, cut in huge blocks and highly polished.

Access to the porch was by a flight of 12 steps from the Court of the Priests. Centrally placed before the porch and 33 feet (10.1 meters) away was the altar of sacrifice. Made of unhewn stone, it was a multilevel construction 15 feet (4.6 meters) high and about 48 feet (14.6 meters) square at its base. Male Israelites were allowed into this area once a year, during the Feast of the Tabernacles, to walk around the altar of sacrifice. Otherwise, they were restricted to the Court of Israel. To the east of the Court of Israel, and separated from it by a flight of 15 steps and by the ornate Great Gate, made of Corinthian bronze, was the Court of the Women. Here the offertory chests for temple expenses were located (Mk 12:41-44). The next court was the large, lower, outer Court of the Gentiles, which surrounded the inner courts and was separated from them by a balustrade and a series of warning notices. Two of these have been excavated, written in Latin and Greek and forbidding trespass by Gentiles into the inner areas, on pain of death. This outer court was widely used. Immediately inside its walls was a portico, supported by four rows of columns almost 40 feet (12.2 meters) high on the south side (the Royal Porch), and two rows on the other sides, the eastern portico known as "Solomon's Porch" or "Solomon's Colonnade." Here is the area where the stalls of the money changers and merchants were set up, where the Sanhedrin met, and where Christ and the scribes taught and debated (Mk 11:27; Lk 2:46; 19:47; Jn 10:23). Here, too, the infant church met before it was rejected by a hostile Judaism (Acts 3:11; 5:12). Just to the northwest of the temple enclosure was the Fortress of Antonia, where the Roman governor resided while in Jerusalem, and where a Roman garrison was on hand to deal with disturbances (Acts 21:31-40). Overlooking the temple area, it was separated from it by a wide moat. The high priest's vestments were stored in the fortress as a symbol of Roman authority. Access to the Court of the Gentiles was by four gates in the west wall; two in the south wall, where the ground fell away steeply into the valley, a site often identified as the pinnacle of the temple (Mt 4:5; Lk 4:9); and one gate in each of the east and north walls.

Significance of the Temple in the Old Testament

The temple in Jerusalem functioned as the focal point of the tribal confederation. In spite of the attempt of Jeroboam I, the first king of the northern kingdom, to divert attention from Jerusalem by establishing shrines at Bethel and Dan (1 Kgs 12:26-30), Jerusalem never lost its preeminence. Naturally, both Hezekiah and Josiah sought to extend their reformation into the area of the northern tribes (2 Chr 30:1-12; 34:6-7), and Jerusalem was a pilgrimage center for those areas even after its destruction (Jer 41:5). The prophets foretold its destiny as the focal point of universal worship (Is 2:1-4).

The temple was God's dwelling place among his people. God's presence, symbolized in the shekinah glory and the pillar of cloud, was associated with the tent of meeting (Ex 33:9-11), with the tabernacle (40:34-38), and finally with the temple (1 Kgs 8:10-11). The paradox is that while God is completely unrestricted, the temple was considered a place for God to live forever (vv 13, 27). God had chosen Zion, as he had chosen David (Pss 68:15-18; 76:2; 78:67-72), so the temple was regarded as God's house (27:4; 42:4; 84:1-4).

Ezekiel's Temple Ezekiel's detailed description of the ideal temple (Ez 40–48) was not used as the blueprint for Zerubbabel's temple. In fact, since Ezekiel must have been familiar with Solomon's temple before his deportation in 597 BC, his description is of greater help in determining uncertain details of the first temple. Ezekiel's concern was to show the nature of pure worship, safeguarded from all contamination. This worship would allow the glory of God, which had departed from corrupted Solomon's temple (9:3; 10:4, 18-19: 11:22-23), to return so that Jerusalem could again be named "the Lord is there" (43:1-5; 48:35). This thought, linked with Ezekiel's vital concept of God's Spirit indwelling his faithful worshipers (36:24-28), anticipated the NT teaching of the believers becoming God's temple.

Significance of the Temple in the New Testament

Christ and the Temple Christ showed considerable respect for the temple. When he was 12 years old, he entered into the rabbinic discussions in its porticoes and described it as his Father's house (Lk 2:41-50). To him "the house of God" was indwelt by God (Mt 12:4; 23:21). Although he twice cleansed it in righteous anger (Mt 21:12-13; Jn 2:13-16), he wept over the impending destruction of the city and temple (Lk 19:41-44). He often taught there, but he was "greater than the temple" (Mt 12:6). When his presentation to Jerusalem as the predicted Messiah was rejected, in spite of attendant miracles, he foretold its inevitable destruction (Mt 21:9-15; 24:1-2). For a brief period after Pentecost, the early church used the temple as its meeting place, until mounting opposition drove believers from Jerusalem (Acts 5:12, 21, 42; 8:1).

The Church as the Temple The NT writers used two different Greek words to describe the temple: *naos* and *hieron*. *Naos* refers to the actual sanctuary of the temple, the place of God's dwelling. *Hieron* refers to the temple precincts as well as to the sanctuary. Generally speaking, *naos* was used to designate the inner section of the temple known as the Holy Place and the Holy of Holies, whereas *hieron* included the outer court and the temple proper.

In Paul's epistles the word *naos* appears six times (1 Cor 3:16-17; 6:19; 2 Cor 6:16; Eph 2:21; 2 Thes 2:4) and *hieron* once (1 Cor 9:13). In these verses Paul maintains the distinction of definition noted above. When speaking of the actual physical temple, he used the word *hieron* to indicate the place where the priests offered up animal sacrifices on the altar (1 Cor 9:13), which was situated in the outer court (see Ex 27–29, 40). And when Paul referred to the abominable act of the lawless one in usurping God's place in the temple, he used the word *naos*—the word that designates the place of deity's presence (2 Thes 2:4).

In all the other Pauline passages, *naos* is used meta-phorically—to depict a human habitation for the divine Spirit. In one instance the sanctuary image is used to describe the individual believer's body (1 Cor 6:19); in every other instance the sanctuary depicts Christ's body, the church (1 Cor 3:16-17; 2 Cor 6:16; Eph 2:21). Mistakenly, many readers think 1 Corinthians 3:16-17 speaks of the individual, but according to the Greek text, it is unquestionably clear that Paul was speaking about the collective church (specifically, the church in Corinth).

When Paul told the church in Corinth that it was God's sanctuary, they would have understood the image from their knowledge of pagan temples. But Paul probably had in mind the one temple in Jerusalem. The Gentiles had many gods with many temples in one city; the Jews had one God with only one temple in all of Israel. This helped to preserve unity among the Israelites. The Corinthians needed spiritual unity; they were fragmented due to their individual preferences (see 1 Cor 1:10-13).

In Ephesians, Paul's masterpiece on the church, he speaks of the local churches as living, organic entities that are all (compositely speaking) growing into a holy sanctuary in the Lord (Eph 2:21). Paul pictured each local church as providing God with a spiritual habitation in that locality (v 22) and as growing together with all the other churches into one holy, universal sanctuary for the Lord's indwelling.

The Temple in John's Revelation In John's revelation there is no material temple, even though he continues to use the imagery of Jerusalem and Mt Zion (Rv 3:12; 14:1; 21:2, 10, 22). Three interrelated ideas dominate. First is the concept of the church made up of martyrs, whose faithful members are God's temple (3:12; 14:1). This temple grows gradually as the number of martyrs increases (6:11). Another aspect is the temple as the place of judgment (11:19; 14:15; 15:5–16:1). Finally, any temple in the new age is unnecessary, "for its temple is the Lord God Almighty and the Lamb" (21:22). The ultimate state will be God's dwelling with his people—the eternal, spiritual temple.

See also Altar; Ark of the Covenant; Bread of the Presence; David; Feasts and Festivals of Israel; First Jewish Revolt; Judaism; Mercy Seat; Offerings and Sacrifices; Priests and Levites; Sanctuary; Singers in the Temple; Solomon (Person).

TEMPLE ASSISTANTS*, TEMPLE SERVANTS *See* Nethinim.

TEMPT, TEMPTATION *See* Test.

TEMPTER *See* Satan.

TEN COMMANDMENTS, The *See* Commandments, The Ten.

TENTMAKER Artisans who made tents from the cloth of woven goats' hair. The Greek term for tentmaker may have served to denote a range of activities in cloth and leather. The single biblical reference (Acts 18:3) is to Aquila and Priscilla of Corinth, who worked in this trade. Paul joined them because he was trained in the same craft. He regularly earned his living at this trade during his missionary journeys (2 Cor 11:7-10; 1 Thes 2:9; 2 Thes 3:8).

TENT OF MEETING Designation for the tabernacle. *See* Tabernacle.

TERAH (Person) Father of Abram (Abraham), Nahor, and Haran (Gn 11:26, 1 Chr 1:26; Lk 3:34). Though Abram is listed first among his sons, it is likely that Abram was not the oldest. After Terah lived 70 years, he fathered Abram, Nahor, and Haran (Gn 11:26). Stephen reports in the NT, however, that Abram left Haran after the death of his father, at which time Abram was 75 years old (Gn 12:4; Act 7:4). Terah died at the age of 205 (v 32), which suggests that Terah was at least 130 when Abram was born. Terah initiated the trip to Canaan, though he failed to go beyond Haran (Gn 11:31-32). Abram was commanded there to leave his family and proceed to Canaan (12:1).

See also Abraham.

TERAH (Place) One of the stopping places of the Israelites during their wilderness wanderings, listed between Tahath and Mithcah (Nm 33:27-28).

TERAPHIM* Idols associated with pagan magical rites. In the OT, the term is often translated "household gods," indicative of talismans, which were kept in family shrines (Gn 31:19, 34). These were the idols that Rachel stole from her father and that occasioned Laban's angry pursuit. Many have postulated that Laban's anger reflects a Nuzian tradition where ownership of the household gods conferred inheritance rights to the owner. It is more likely that Rachel stole the teraphim simply to ensure good luck and safety.

Teraphim are also mentioned in connection with Micah's attempt to establish a private priesthood (Jgs 17:5). When the Danites moved to Laish, they stole Micah's teraphim and ephod for oracular use (18:14-20, 31). Teraphim were typically small idols but on occasion could be life-size as well. David escaped from Saul when Michal placed a teraphim in his bed as a dummy (1 Sm 19:13-16). During Israel's kingdom period, teraphim continued to be used in heretical cultic practices. Josiah attempted to rid the country of teraphim, wizards, and mediums, but his reforms appear to have been temporary (2 Kgs 23:24). The prophets regularly condemned the use of teraphim, identifying them with heathen abominations (Ez 21:21; Hos 3:4; Zec 10:2).

See also Idols, Idolatry.

TEREBINTH* Large deciduous tree, also called the turpentine tree (Is 6:13; Hos 4:13). *See* Plants.

TERESH One of two chamberlains who guarded the chambers of King Ahasuerus (Xerxes). When the two planned to kill the king, Mordecai discovered their plot and informed Esther, who in turn told the king. The guards were hanged (Est 2:21-23; 6:2).

TERTIUS Paul's amanuensis (secretary) for the book of Romans (Rom 16:22). Since his name is a common Roman name, he was probably Roman and known by the recipients of the letter. The supposition that Tertius is the same person as Silas because their names had similar meanings in Latin and Hebrew lacks any biblical or traditional evidence.

TERTULLUS Prosecuting attorney chosen by the Sanhedrin to lead in the trial of Paul before Felix, Roman procurator of Judea (Acts 24:1-2). It is not clear whether Tertullus was a Roman, Greek, or Jew. The chief arguments that he was a Jew come from references to "our law" and to the mention that Lysias had taken Paul from "our hands." However, these words are part of two verses (vv 6b-7) that are not included in the most ancient manuscripts.

From the speed with which the Jews were able to bring him forward, he was probably a professional attorney who practiced law regularly in the Roman court. His speech (Acts 24:2-8) begins with a word of flattery for Felix. Then he proceeds to charge Paul with being a public nuisance, a disturber of the peace, and a leader of the sect of the Nazarenes. All of these were serious charges in Roman law.

TEST The process of proving one's worth. When ascribed to God in his dealings with people, it means that God tests his peoples' faith and moral character. When the word is used in a negative way, it means "to tempt"—that is, to entice, solicit, or provoke to sin. Both senses of the word could be applied to Jesus' forty days of trial in the wilderness. He was tested by God and found faithful, while he was tempted by Satan and found sinless. The Spirit of God led Jesus into the wilderness to have his faith tried; but the agent in this trial was the wicked one, whose whole object was to seduce Jesus from his allegiance to God. It was temptation in the bad sense of the term. Yet Jesus did not give in to temptation; he passed the test (see 2 Cor 5:21; Heb 7:26).

TESTAMENT* English word translated from the Greek signifying the covenantal administrations of God. Prior to Christ, this covenant is known as the Old Testament; under Christ's administration, it is called the New Testament.

The Greek word, generally meaning "last will and testament," contains certain legal characteristics that have important theological implications. First, a testament was not an agreement between parties (especially equals) but rather was exercised solely by the testator. Second, the testament became effective upon the death of the testator. Third, the testament was irrevocable.

When the OT was translated into Greek, the translators had the option of two words to translate the Hebrew word for "covenant." One term carries the idea of a mutual agreement, and this often between equals. Since this would blur the divine initiative in God's covenantal dealings with the patriarchs and with Israel, the other word was used. It connoted the self-determined action of the sovereign in making the covenant. The NT writers saw additional significance in the word "testament." As a testament only becomes valid at the death of the testator, so the benefits of the new covenant are given to believers as a consequence of Christ's death (Heb 9:15-22; cf. 1 Cor 11:25; Lk 22:20).

See also Covenant; Covenant, The New.

TESTIMONY *See* Witness.

TETRAGRAMMATON* Term referring to the four consonants of one of the primary Hebrew names, for God (from Greek *tetra*, "four," and *gramma*, "a letter of the alphabet"). These letters are the Hebrew equivalents of English Y (or J), H, W, and H. The most widely accepted meaning of the name is "the one who is, that is, the absolute and unchangeable one." This is the name the Lord revealed to Moses (Ex 3:15; cf. vv 13-14; Jn 8:56-58). According to the Ten Commandments, the Jews were not to take this name in vain (Ex 20:2, 7). The Jews, therefore, regarded the name as so holy that they would not pronounce it but said instead *Adonai*, "Lord." Originally the text was written only with consonants, but when the scholars called Masoretes added the vowel points, they inserted the vowels for Adonai as a reminder not to read the sacred name. Non-Hebraists combined the vowels of Adonai with the consonants of JHWH, producing a new form, "Jehovah," which does not exist in the Hebrew language. The correct pronunciation of the name must have been Yahweh, but most translations render it LORD, using capital letters to distinguish it from other uses of the English word "Lord."

See also God, Names of.

TETRARCH* Title of a class of Roman provincial officials. Tetrarchs were tributary princes who were not deemed important enough to be designated kings. The title was used in the Roman provinces of Thessaly, Galatia, and Syria. The origin of the title appears to have come from governors who ruled over a fourth part of a region or country, as was the case in Syria after the death of Herod the Great. By NT times, the etymological significance had diminished, so that the title merely designated secondary princes. Three tetrarchs are mentioned in the Bible. Luke reports that Herod (Antipas) was the tetrarch of Galilee, Philip was the tetrarch of Iturea and Traconitis, and Lysanius was the tetrarch of Abilene (Lk 3:1). Of these, only Herod is mentioned elsewhere in the Bible (Mt 14:1; Lk 3:19; 9:7; Act 13:1). Herod's greater significance is indicated by the fact that he is also referred to as "king" by his Jewish subjects (Mt 14:9; Mk 6:14).

TEXTUS RECEPTUS* *See* Bible, Manuscripts and Text of the (New Testament).

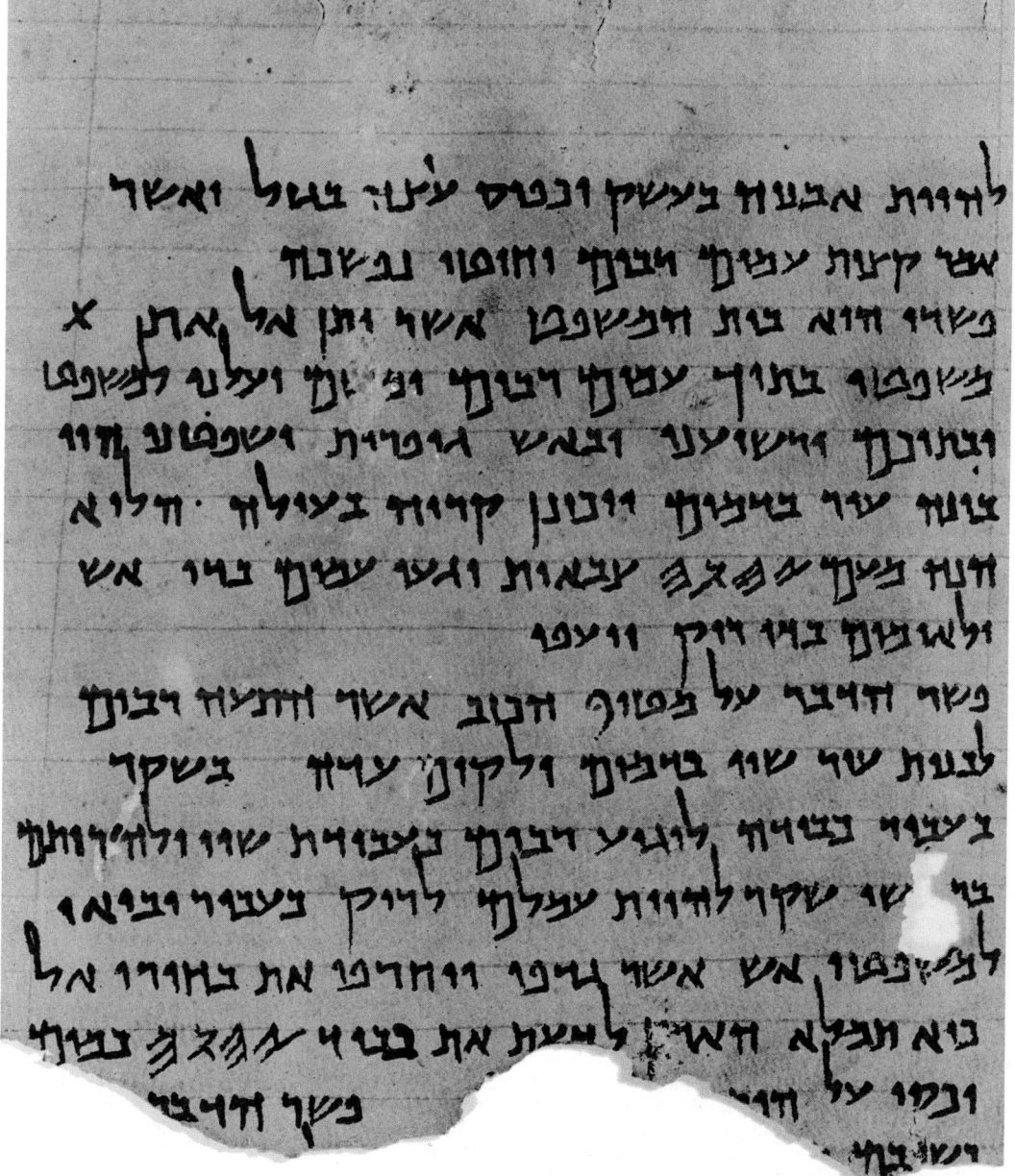

The Tetragrammaton YHWH in Ancient Hebrew Script Manuscript 1QpHab (Habakkuk), showing the Tetragrammaton יהוה in lines 7 and 14.

THADDAEUS, The Apostle One of the 12 original apostles according to the lists in Mark 3:18 and Matthew 10:3 (KJV "Lebbaeus, whose surname was Thaddaeus"). It is quite likely that this is the same person as Judas son of James (not Iscariot) in Luke 6:16 and Acts 1:13. *See* Apostle, Apostleship.

THAHASH* KJV spelling of Tahash, Reumah's son, in Genesis 22:24. *See* Tahash.

THAMAH* KJV spelling of Temah in Ezra 2:53. *See* Temah.

THAMAR* KJV spelling of Tamar, wife of Judah's first-born son, in Matthew 1:3. *See* Tamar (Person) #1.

THANK OFFERING* *See* Offerings and Sacrifices.

THANKSGIVING *See* Gratitude.

THARA* KJV form of Terah, Abraham's father, in Luke 3:34. *See* Terah (Person).

THARSHISH*
1. KJV alternate spelling of Tarshish, a port city, in 1 Kings 10:22 and 22:48. *See* Tarshish (Place).
2. KJV spelling of Tarshish, Bilhan's son, in 1 Chronicles 7:10. *See* Tarshish (Person) #2.

THEATER* A flat, semicircular orchestra surrounded by an open-air auditorium, a Greek creation in the sixth century BC. A chorus and actors performed in the orchestra, and the audience sat on the raised hillside before them. The earliest drama was tragedy, which celebrated the deeds of the god Dionysus and began with a sacrifice on the altar in the orchestra. Later, comedy developed.

The Golden Age of Athens (c. 450 BC) was also the golden age of Greek drama; Sophocles, Euripides, and Aeschylus wrote their dramas then. At that time audiences sat on the ground or on the wooden seats of the Theater of Dionysus in Athens, located on the south slope of the Acropolis. During the fourth century BC, theaters in Greece were equipped with stone seats arranged in concentric tiers against a concave hillside, and the orchestra was paved.

By the second and first centuries BC, great stone theaters were being built all over the Hellenistic East, and by that time a raised stage was constructed against the straight side of the semicircle of the orchestra. Action was now transferred to the stage. The auditorium of the typical theater consisted of three great bands of seats, which were divided into great wedges by the stairways that gave access to the seating. The elaborate stage was built in stone and had dressing and storage rooms. The orchestra was always paved.

Although initially the theater was intended for dramatic events, it came to be used for a variety of public meetings because it was one of the largest structures. For example, the great theater in Ephesus held about 25,000; the theater of Dionysus in Athens, about 17,000; and the south theater in Jerash of the Decapolis, about 5,000.

The theater should be distinguished from the odeum, which was shaped like a theater but was roofed. The odeum held only 1,000 or 2,000 people and was used primarily for musical events. It should also be distinguished from the amphitheater, which was a free-standing structure in stone, like the Colosseum of Rome and the arena of Verona, with an oval arena surrounded by concentric tiers of seats and used for gladiatorial combats, wild-beast hunts, and other such events. Only occa-

sionally, as at Salamis in Cyprus and Caesarea in Palestine, were theaters free-standing stone structures; almost always they were built into the side of a hill.

By NT times, theaters were built in Greco-Roman towns all over the Mediterranean world. They even made their appearance in Palestine, as a result of the Hellenizing activities of Herod the Great, who constructed Greek-style theaters in Samaria, Caesarea, and Jerusalem.

Only one theater, that of Ephesus, figures specifically in the NT (Acts 19:29-41).

See also Architecture.

THEBES City appearing in the OT as No or No-Amon. *No* means "city" and is equivalent to the Egyptian *Waset* or Greek *Thebes*. *No-Amon* means "city of Amon." Thebes appears only in the prophetic Scriptures of the OT and only in a context of judgment (Jer 46:25; Ez 30:14-16; Na 3:8). Thebes would suffer judgment and loss of population but would not be utterly destroyed. These prophecies were fulfilled in ancient times when Cambyses of Persia marched through Thebes in 525 BC and when the Roman Cornelius Gallus punished the city for a revolt in 30 BC.

Thebes was the capital of Egypt during most of the empire period (c. 1570–1100 BC), when the Hebrews were in bondage in the land and when the exodus took place. By that time, Amon had become the chief god, and the Pharaohs lavished their wealth on the great temples of Amon at Thebes, hoping for the god's help in overcoming their enemies.

The city of ancient Thebes was located on both the east bank of the Nile ("the side of the rising sun") and the west bank ("the side of the setting sun"). The city had an estimated population of nearly one million at its height.

Ancient Theater in Athens

THEBEZ City where Abimelech was killed when "a certain woman" dropped a millstone on him (Jgs 9:50). Abimelech had attacked Thebez after burning down the Tower of Shechem but had failed to capture the fortress within the city. After being critically injured by the millstone, Abimelech ordered his armor bearer to kill him lest it be said that he had been killed by a woman. Thebez was located about 11 miles (17.7 kilometers) northeast of Shechem, traditionally identified with modern Tubas.

THELASAR* KJV alternate form of Tel-assar in 2 Kings 19:12. *See* Tel-assar.

THEOCRACY* Form of government that acknowledges God alone as the highest political authority, whether or not he is represented by a human ruler such as a king. Thus, Deuteronomy 17:14-20 argues that a human king rules only as one designated for kingship by the Lord.

In ancient Israel, the concept of theocratic government developed through several historical stages. A fundamental theological conception of the sons of Israel in Egypt involved the belief that Yahweh, their special God, cared enough about their plight to become personally involved in redeeming them from slavery and establishing them in freedom from all earthly rulers (specifically the pharaoh). They would then be able to serve him alone (see Ex 3:7-10; 8:1; 9:1). It is necessary to remember that the conditions of oppression described in Exodus were everyday features in the lives of Egyptian peasants. Living under the rulership of the pharaoh as a peasant implied oppression, unreasonable work assignments, loss of freedom and self-respect, and many other things. By contrast, life under the rulership of Yahweh came to signify freedom, justice, and equality.

Upon arriving in Canaan, the young tribes encountered a system of kingship widely different from the Egyptian model but equally opprobrious. Ancient Canaanite rulers normally owned the city-state they governed, and rented out at least some of the land to their subjects. But the Israelites who occupied Canaan under Joshua were meant to be free inhabitants of the territory allotted to them and subservient to God alone.

In the period of the judges, the idea of theocracy continued to be expressed consistently and explicitly. The various groups comprising the "sons of Israel" were not welded together into a unified body by any external political structure. Rather, acceptance of the rulership of Yahweh alone continued to function as the foundational unifying element. Thus Gideon, when asked by some to accept kingship, could say in words acceptable to virtually all Israelites, "The LORD shall rule over you" (Jgs 8:23).

In this period, human leadership became necessary from time to time as threats arose to one or more of the tribes. These judges were regularly described as "raised up" for the specific task of averting immediate danger, but more specifically to lead the people back to the Lord (Jgs 2:16). But no judge was believed to have brought victory to Israel by means of his personal abilities. Yahweh alone was credited with having won the battle; hence, he deserved and received the loyalty of Israel.

Samuel bridges the time of the judges and a new era of monarchy in Israel. Philistine social and military pressure was confronting the Israelite theocratic government with a challenge of enormous proportions. For roughly 200 years preceding Samuel, the Israelites and the Philistines had coexisted, if not peaceably, at least short of open warfare. During the career of Samuel, however, the Philistines inaugurated a policy of open aggression toward Israel aimed at conquest and expansion. The tribal confederacy, which for years had successfully defended one or more tribal groups, now appeared incapable of resisting the Philistines. A new governmental structure had clearly become necessary. In the minds of many influential Israelites, only a kingdom headed by a king could enable Israel to survive (see 1 Sm 8:5, 19-20).

At this point the concept of theocracy received a severe test. Politically and militarily, a king appeared to be a wise and necessary choice. But the tradition of theocratic rule was deeply ingrained. Samuel viewed the desire for a king as rejection of the rulership of Yahweh (1 Sm 8:10-18; 10:19). On the other hand, he also appears to have received a prophetic word concerning Saul and the willingness of God to have him anointed as king (9:27-10:1).

In addition to his prophetic anointing, Saul also received a designation from "the spirit of God" (1 Sm 11:6), which closely paralleled the experiences of earlier judges. A third ingredient to Saul's claim to kingship was added when the people acclaimed him following a military victory over the Ammonites. Apart from the clarity of the biblical tradition that two opinions of kingship were represented among Israelites, clearly God chose the king and revealed his choice through his messenger-prophet.

One day God's people would no longer need a human king to rule them. This is portrayed in the book of Ezekiel (Ez 40–48), in which God would rule his people through the Zadokite priesthood. This began to be implemented through the work of Haggai and Zechariah in 520 BC. This was a particularly important feature of postexilic life and imparted a distinctive character to the Judean community. The work of Ezra made the theocracy normative for Judaism, and thereafter the priesthood exercised an important role in national life. Although the people were subjected to human rule under the Seleucids, they looked for the true king, a descendant of David. This man, the Messiah, would be the peaceful prince who would redeem Israel and bring the ancient covenantal values of justice, righteousness, and equity to fruition.

See also King.

THEOPHANY* An appearance or manifestation of God; a compound word derived from the Greek noun for "God" (*theos*) and the Greek verb "to appear" (*phano*). A theophany is a manifestation of God in temporary forms perceptible to the external senses. A theophany is regarded as one of the means by which God's special revelation comes to people; it is a divine revelation in which God's presence is made visible and recognizable to people.

God made himself known to people through a special messenger called the Angel of the Lord, through the pillar and cloud that accompanied the Israelites in their wilderness wanderings, and through the shekinah glory indwelling the tabernacle. *See* Angel (Angel of the Lord); Pillar of Fire and Cloud; Shekinah.

THEOPHILUS

1. Person to whom the books of Luke and Acts are addressed (Lk 1:3; Acts 1:1). Since Theophilus can be translated "lover of God" or "loved of God," many have suggested that Theophilus is a title rather than a proper name and that it designates the general audience of the books. However, the use of such generic titles is contrary to ordinary NT practice. Furthermore, the adjective "most excellent" generally designates an individual, particularly one of high rank. Paul addressed Festus as "most excellent," and Claudius Lysias and Tertullus addressed Felix in the same manner (Acts 23:26; 24:2-3; 26:25). Though Theophilus may well have had some noble standing, it is difficult to speculate what his position might have been.
2. Jewish high priest who was the son of Annas, the brother-in-law of Caiaphas, and the brother of Jonathan. The Roman prefect Vittelius installed him as high priest succeeding Jonathan in AD 37. He served until he was deposed by Herod Agrippa in AD 41, and was likely the high priest who gave Paul the authority to persecute the Christians. He is not mentioned by name in the NT.

THESSALONIANS, First Letter to the Paul's first epistle to the church at Thessalonica.

PREVIEW
•Author(s)
•Date, Origin, and Destination
•Purpose
•Content

Ancient Papyrus Manuscript of 1 Thessalonians First Thessalonians 5:8-10, 26-28 in Papyrus Oxyrhynchus 1598 (third century)—P30.

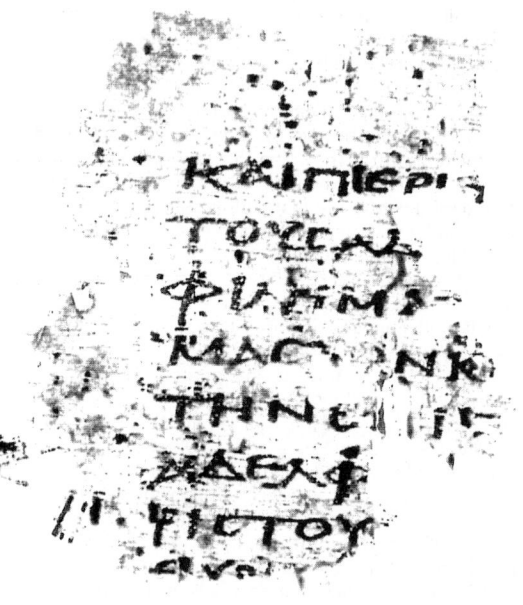

tudes among them imply a longer time, and Philippians 4:16 speaks of the Philippian Christians twice sending help to Paul in Thessalonica.

With Silas, and presumably Timothy, Paul went on to Berea, and his coworkers stayed there when Paul proceeded to Athens (Acts 17:10-15). When Timothy joined Paul at Athens, Paul sent Timothy to the Thessalonian Christians because he was concerned about how they were faring against their opposition. Timothy returned

Author(s) The names of Paul, Silas (Greek "Silvanus"), and Timothy stand at the head of this letter, and as with other letters of Paul, his coworkers may have had some share in the writing of the letter. Often the plural pronouns "we" and "us" are retained, but "I, Paul" (1 Thes 2:18) and the singular pronoun in other places (see 3:5; 5:27) show that the letter was essentially Paul's. From the 19th century, a few scholars have questioned the Pauline authorship of the epistle, but without convincing reasons. The issues dealt with in this letter are manifestly issues faced by a church in the earliest stages of its existence. In the light of differences of expression between this and other Pauline letters, some have suggested that Silvanus or Timothy may have had a significant part in writing it, but that is uncertain. The early church had no doubts about the authorship of the letter.

Date, Origin, and Destination The letter is addressed specifically to "the church of the Thessalonians" (1:1). According to Acts 17:1-9, Paul, with Silas (Silvanus) and Timothy, in the course of their missionary work in the Roman province of Macedonia, came from Philippi to Thessalonica. He went first, as was his custom, to the synagogue, and for three Sabbaths explained and proved from the Scriptures that the Christ should suffer and rise from the dead, declaring that Jesus was the Christ. Some Jews believed in Jesus as their Messiah, as did many God-fearing Greeks and several prominent women. But then the Jews stirred up opposition, so that Paul and his coworkers had to leave Thessalonica.

The actual time spent in Thessalonica was probably more than three weeks. In this letter Paul speaks of working for his support so as not to burden the Thessalonians (1 Thes 2:9). References concerning his actions and atti-

from Thessalonica with good news. Subsequently, Paul wrote this letter.

Acts 18:5 speaks of Timothy and Silas coming back from Macedonia to the apostle in Corinth. It was probably from Corinth, in the early part of his 18-month stay, that Paul wrote this letter. Since his work in Corinth can be approximately dated, this epistle was probably written early in the year 50, in all likelihood about a year after the first preaching of the gospel in Thessalonica.

Purpose Timothy's report of the situation in Thessalonica motivated Paul to write this letter. Possibly Timothy brought a letter from the Thessalonians. This is suggested by the way Paul introduced certain subjects ("concerning brotherly love," 4:9; "concerning those who are asleep," 4:13; "as to the times and the seasons," 5:1) and then said that he didn't need to write to them about these things. There were several reasons why Paul wrote to the Thessalonians:

1. He wanted to commend the Thessalonian Christians for their faith and devotion, which had become widely known as an example to others (1:7-10).
2. He realized that the persecution he had faced in Thessalonica had continued for those he left behind, and he wanted to encourage them to stand fast (2:13-16). He had feared for them but was delighted by the news of their steadfastness (3:1-10).
3. There were those who had been misrepresenting the apostle in Thessalonica, perhaps the Jews who had initiated opposition to him when he was there (Acts 17:5). They probably said that he was only a religious charlatan who had turned them away from their religion to his new faith, and they would never see him again. So the apostle reminded them of his methods

and attitudes among them (1 Thes 2:1-12) and told of his desires and plans to see them again (vv 17-18).

4. It was necessary also to urge the Thessalonian Christians to live true to Christian standards, especially in the matter of sexual morality (4:1-8). Other matters concerning their way of life and their relationships within the Christian fellowship also needed attention (4:9-12; 5:12-22).

5. Another major concern was to deal with the misconceptions of the Thessalonian Christians regarding those who had died and the second coming of the Lord (4:13-18). In relation to the future hope, there was also the question of "the times and the seasons," and Paul repeated the teaching he had given when among them (5:1-11).

6. There may also have been a danger of disunity that led the apostle to emphasize the fellowship of all believers (5:27), to urge them not to disparage any spiritual gifts (vv 19-21), and not to fail in respecting their leaders (v 12).

Content

Thanksgiving for the Thessalonians' Response to the Gospel (1:2-10) Paul prayed with gratitude that in their lives the fruits of faith, love, and hope were evident. The gospel had come to them in the power of the Holy Spirit, backed by the lives of its messengers. Even though receiving the gospel had involved suffering, their faith was an example to the Christians of the Roman provinces of Macedonia and Achaia. The Thessalonians had turned to the living God from idols, indicating that most of the believers were Gentiles rather than Jews.

Paul's Defense of His Ministry in Thessalonica (2:1-12) Because of false accusations made about him, Paul found it necessary to defend his ministry. He had come from an experience of persecution in Philippi and had to face "great opposition" in Thessalonica. There was no guile in his trying to persuade them of the gospel's truth. That gospel was entrusted to him by God, and his one desire was to communicate it to them in all integrity.

Their Acceptance of the Gospel (2:13-16) The Thessalonians had accepted the gospel as "the word of God" and had suffered at the hands of their own people. Such persecutors must face the righteous judgment of God.

Paul's Continuing Concern for Them (2:17-20) If Paul's accusers were saying that the Thessalonians would never see him again, he could give the assurance that he had often wanted to return but had been prevented. In saying "Satan hindered us," Paul may have been referring to the incident in which Jason was compelled to promise the authorities that Paul would leave the city and not return (Acts 17:9). In any case, the Thessalonian Christians are his "glory and joy." His delight will be for them to stand "before our Lord Jesus Christ at his coming."

Timothy's Mission (3:1-5) Fearful for the Thessalonian Christians facing persecution, Paul was willing to be left alone in the work of the gospel in Athens (see Acts 17:16-34) and sent Timothy to encourage and support them in all their "afflictions." Paul reiterated that Christians must always be prepared to face suffering.

The Good News That Timothy Brought (3:6-10) Paul himself had continued to have "distress and affliction" in the gospel's cause, but the news of their faith and love had revived his spirit and given him great cause for thanksgiving to God. He was praying that he might see them again and strengthen them further in faith.

Paul's Prayer (3:11-13) Paul's prayer was that God might return him to his friends in Thessalonica, and that they might overflow with love and be established in holiness of life, so as to appear "blameless, and holy when [they] stand before God our Father on that day when our Lord Jesus comes with all those who belong to him" (3:13, NLT).

Exhortation to Purity of Life (4:1-8) Holiness, not immorality, and sanctification, not uncleanness, are the Christian's calling. Paul stressed this by saying that living in a contrary way demonstrated disregard for the Holy Spirit. Christian standards must be utterly different from the prevailing standards among the heathen who don't know God. For example, sexual relationships must not be determined by lust but expressed in holiness and honor within the bonds of marriage.

Practical Exhortation (4:9-12) The Christian duty of mutual love had been demonstrated in Thessalonica, but Paul asked that it be shown in increasing measure. He exhorted them to live quietly and work for their living, and to not be dependent on others for support.

What Happened to Those Who Had Died Since Becoming Believers (4:13-18) The Thessalonians may have written Paul about this issue. Paul told them they didn't need to grieve, as those without hope, for their loved ones who had died. Those who are alive and those who have died will share together in the joy and triumph of the Lord's return. Those who have died "will rise first"; those who are alive on earth will be caught up to meet their Master; then together, living and departed, "shall always be with the Lord." With that assurance they can "comfort one another."

Living in Readiness for the Lord's Coming (5:1-11) Perhaps further questions had been asked about "the times and the seasons" in relation to the Second Coming. Neither they nor anyone else knows the time. The Lord will come unexpectedly like "a thief in the night." What matters, therefore, is that Christians should never be complacent but ready at all times, living as "children of the day," so that, waking or sleeping, "we might live with him."

Other Christian Duties (5:12-22) In the last main section of the letter, Paul urged the Thessalonian Christians to respect their leaders and to acknowledge their oversight; to live at peace, in unity; to do and encourage all that is good. The will of God for the Christian life is constant joy, prayer, and praise. The Holy Spirit is not to be quenched, the gift of prophecy is not to be despised, but all things claiming to be of God must be tested, so that the good can be embraced and the evil rejected.

Conclusion (5:23-28) The final prayer of the letter is for their holiness of life, so that they may stand "blameless at the coming of our Lord Jesus Christ." "Pray for us" is the apostle's plea. Greetings are to be passed on and the letter read to all the believers.

See also Eschatology; Paul, The Apostle; Second Coming of Christ; Thessalonians, Second Letter to the; Thessalonica.

THESSALONIANS, Second Letter to the Paul's second epistle to the church at Thessalonica.

PREVIEW
- Author(s)
- Date, Origin, and Destination
- Purpose
- Content

Author(s) This letter, like 1 Thessalonians, begins with the names of Paul, Silvanus, and Timothy, and like that letter often retains the plural pronouns "we" and "us" but also has the singular "I" (e.g., 2 Thes 2:5). The end of the letter reads: "Now here is my greeting, which I write with my own hand—PAUL. I do this at the end of all my letters to prove that they really are from me" (3:17, NLT).

Some scholars have questioned Paul's authorship, mostly because of the difference between the teaching about the future in this letter and that in 1 Thessalonians. In the light of the words of 2 Thessalonians 3:17, the first letter would have to be seen as a blatant forgery. And this is not the case. The early church did not question Paul's authorship of both.

Date, Origin, and Destination In the first verse, exactly as in 1 Thessalonians, the letter is addressed "to the church of the Thessalonians." Unlike 1 Thessalonians, this letter provides us with no other personal details of the movements of Paul and his coworkers. Thus, there is no direct evidence of the date and place of the letter.

Just as the difference between the teaching of this epistle from that of 1 Thessalonians has led some to question its Pauline authorship, so it has led others to a variety of explanations for its date and destination. These include:

1. It was written much later than 1 Thessalonians. This is improbable because both Silas and Timothy were still with Paul.
2. It was written earlier than 1 Thessalonians. In 2:15, however, there is a reference to a letter written previously to Thessalonica, and the early church from the second century certainly called this 2 Thessalonians.
3. It was written to Jewish Christians in Thessalonica, while 1 Thessalonians was written to gentile Christians. This, however, is most unlikely, as the apostle who had such concern for the unity of all Christians in one place (e.g., 1 Cor 1–3) and especially for the unity of Jewish and gentile Christians (see Eph 2:11-22) could hardly have done such a thing.
4. It was written to Christians in a different place (Berea or Philippi), and then came to be in the hands of the Thessalonian Christians. There is no evidence to support the idea that the letter was sent anywhere but to Thessalonica.

When this epistle was written, Paul had the same coworkers with him as when he wrote 1 Thessalonians (2 Thes 1:1). This indicates that probably a short time after writing 1 Thessalonians, Paul heard of further problems being faced by the Christians in Thessalonica, and in his concern for them, he wrote this second letter.

Purpose There were three main concerns in the mind of the apostle Paul as he wrote this letter.

As in all his letters, he wanted to encourage his readers to stand firm in their faith (2:15). He could thank God for his work in their lives (1:3; 2:13), made evident by their faith, love, and steadfastness in the face of persecutions (1:4). Paul assured them of the righting of wrongs in the ultimate judgment of God. Their task was to glorify the name of Jesus by their lives; then at his coming he would be glorified in his faithful people (vv 5-12).

There was false teaching, even purportedly from Paul, that the Day of the Lord had already come (2:2). The apostle rejected this teaching by saying that certain things must take place prior to the Second Coming. There must be a still greater manifestation of evil in the person of one called "the man of lawlessness" or "the son of perdition." This one will reject all true worship, show signs and wonders, and proclaim himself to be God. At present there is a restraining influence. The time will come, however, when the lawless one will be revealed. Then the Lord himself will come and "the lawless one" will be conquered and destroyed. This teaching (vv 1-12) is similar to that in the Gospels about the Antichrist or antichrists, claiming to be Christ, deceiving people by signs and wonders (Mt 24:5, 23-26; Mk 13:5-6, 20-23). In 1 Thessalonians, Paul emphasized that the time of the Lord's coming is unknown, and believers must be ready for him at any time. Here, in opposition to the idea that the Lord had already come, Paul spoke of those things that must take place before the Lord's coming. Both of these aspects were also presented by Jesus when he taught about the future (Mt 24; Mk 13; Lk 21).

Finally, the problem of laziness in the Christian community (referred to in 1 Thes 4:11; 5:14) remained, and probably had increased. Paul had to refer again to the example that he and his coworkers had given to them—they had worked with their own hands to earn a living instead of depending on those to whom they brought the gospel. Paul had a simple dictum that he applied: "If any one will not work, let him not eat" (2 Thess 3:10, RSV).

Content

Thanksgiving for Their Christian Lives (1:3-4) Paul praised God for the Thessalonians' growing faith, increasing love, and endurance of persecution.

A Reversal of Persecutors and Persecuted (1:5-10) At that time the Thessalonian Christians were having to suffer, but their persecutors would have to face the just judgment of God at the coming of the Lord Jesus "with his mighty angels." Those who reject the knowledge of God and the salvation offered in the gospel must "suffer the punishment of eternal destruction." His people will experience that glory of his coming and will realize that they have not believed or suffered in vain.

Prayer That the Lord Jesus Will Be Glorified (1:11-12) This is Paul's prayer for the Thessalonian Christians—a life worthy of their calling, the fulfilling of their resolves, and by the grace of God, that the name of Christ would be glorified in them.

Events That Must Precede Christ's Second Coming (2:1-12) In this section, Paul deals with the false teaching that the Day of the Lord had already come. Before this event, there must be the revealing of "the man of lawlessness," otherwise called the Antichrist (though it may be noted that the NT also speaks of "antichrists" and "the spirit of antichrist"—1 Jn 2:18; 4:3). Paul said, "That day will not come until there is a great rebellion against God and the man of lawlessness is revealed" (2 Thes 2:3, NLT).

At the present time, the mystery of lawlessness is restrained (vv 6-7). But in the future—just prior to the Lord's coming—the restraint will be taken away. In other words, all hell will break loose. Christians must be prepared for a supreme manifestation of evil "with pretended signs and wonders" (v 9, RSV) by which many will be deceived. The coming of Christ will mean the overthrow of evil and the judgment of those who oppose the truth and take pleasure in unrighteousness.

Renewed Thanksgiving, Encouragement, and Prayer (2:13–3:5) Subsequent to the discussion of the power of evil in people's lives, Paul gives thanks for the work of the Spirit of God in the lives of the Thessalonian Christians. He encourages them to continue in all that the apostle has taught them, when present with them or by letter. Paul's prayer is that God, as the great Giver of comfort and hope, will establish them in every good work and word. He also expresses his need of their prayers, that God may continue to prosper the word he preaches and deliver him from evil men. His Christian readers, for their part, can be assured of God's faithfulness. Paul's prayer for them is that, as they continue in the things in which they have been taught, they will be directed to the love of God and the endurance that comes from Christ.

Warning against Disorderliness and Idleness (3:6-15) Another of Paul's special purposes in writing was to stress that there is no place for idleness in the lives of Christians. He had taught this and exemplified this in his own life. Christian people are "to do their work in quietness," "earn their own living," and "not be weary in well-doing" (vv 12-13, RSV). There should be no associating with those who reject this teaching, but they should be admonished as brothers, not treated as enemies.

Conclusion (3:16-18) With a prayer for grace and peace and with his own personal signature, Paul concludes the letter. When he speaks of writing with his own hand in verse 17, it probably means that up to that point Paul had dictated his letter to someone else (cf. 1 Cor 16:21; Col 4:18).

See also Eschatology; Paul, The Apostle; Second Coming of Christ; Thessalonians, First Letter to the; Thessalonica.

THESSALONICA Chief city of Macedonia and the seat of Roman administration in the century before Christ. In addition to having a magnificent harbor, Thessalonica had the good fortune of being located on the overland route from Italy to the East. This famous highway, called the Egnatian Way, ran directly through the city. Two Roman arches, the Vardar Gate and the Arch of Galerius, marked the western and eastern boundaries.

According to Strabo, a famous Greek geographer, Thessalonica was founded in 315 BC by the Macedonian general Cassander, who named it after his wife, the daughter of Philip and stepsister of Alexander the Great. It was settled by refugees from a large number of towns in the same region, which had been destroyed in war. When Macedonia was divided into four districts (167 BC), Thessalonica was made the capital of the second division. Its influence continued to expand when the area became a Roman province. In the second civil war between Caesar and Pompey (42 BC), Thessalonica remained loyal to Antony and Octavian and was rewarded by receiving the status of a free city. This gift of autonomy allowed the city to appoint its own magistrates, who were given the unusual title of politarchs. The historical accuracy of Luke is seen in the fact that while the term "politarch" does not appear in earlier Greek literature, it is used in Acts 17:6-8 and has been found on an inscription on the Vardar Gate and in other inscriptions from the area. At the beginning of the first century, Thessalonica had a council of five politarchs. Cicero, a Roman statesman who lived shortly before the time of Christ, spent seven months in exile at Thessalonica.

The church at Thessalonica was founded by Paul on his second missionary journey (Acts 17:1-4). At Troas the apostle had been directed in a vision to cross over the Aegean Sea to Macedonia. After ministering at Philippi, where he was beaten and jailed, Paul's Roman citizenship secured his release and he traveled on to Thessalonica. On the Sabbath, Paul went into the synagogue and reasoned with the Jews that Jesus was the Christ. Some were persuaded, along with a number of God-fearing Greeks and quite a few prominent women (v 4).

Paul's success stirred the jealousy of the Jews, who gathered some rabble from the marketplace and started a riot. They rushed the house of Jason, where Paul was staying, but when they were unable to find the apostle, they dragged his host and some other believers before the city officials. They claimed that Paul was guilty of defying Caesar's decrees because he taught another king called Jesus. That very night Paul slipped out of town and made his way to Berea (Acts 17:5-10). The hostility of the Thessalonian Jews toward Paul is seen in the fact that when they learned that he was preaching at Berea they followed him there and stirred up the crowds against him (v 13).

Our basic knowledge of the church at Thessalonica comes from two letters by Paul from Corinth at a slightly later date. These early letters of the apostle supply an important insight into the life of a first-century Macedonian congregation that was primarily Gentile. In the centuries that followed, the city remained as one of the major strongholds of Christianity.

See also Paul, The Apostle; Thessalonians, First Letter to the; Thessalonians, Second Letter to the.

THEUDAS Rebel referred to by Gamaliel in his speech before the Sanhedrin as an example of the fact that false messiahs would fall without anyone's intervention (Acts 5:36). Theudas evidently led an unsuccessful rebellion against Rome in which he and 400 others were killed. A chronological difficulty is created by the fact that Josephus reports a rebellion led by Theudas during the reign of Claudius as occurring around AD 44, which is seven to ten years *after* Gamaliel's speech. While critics have offered this apparent anachronism as evidence that Luke (or some later editor) was in error, several other solutions are possible. Possibly the error is in Josephus's report rather than Luke's, or two different individuals named Theudas are intended. During the final years of Herod the Great, several rebellions occurred, one of which may have been instigated by Theudas. It has been suggested (without any direct evidence) that Herod's slave Simon may have adopted the name Theudas when he gained freedom and subsequently rebelled against Herod. While the identity of Theudas remains unknown, this fact does not necessarily discredit the historical accuracy of Luke's narrative.

THISTLE See Plants.

THOMAS, The Apostle One of the 12 apostles whose name appears in all four Gospels. The name is a transliteration of an Aramaic word meaning "twin" and appears in the NT as Thomas. Among Greek Christians, there was a tendency to use his Hellenistic name, Didymus (*didumos*, "twin"); this name appears three times in John (Jn 11:16; 20:24; 21:2). There is ample evidence from koine papyri that the name Didymus was well known in the NT era.

Thomas appears in each synoptic list of apostles (Mt 10:3; Mk 3:18, Lk 6:15; cf. Acts 1:13) but plays no further role. His celebrated appearance in the fourth Gospel is interesting. Here Thomas expresses the despair of the final approach to Jerusalem (Jn 11:16) and presses Jesus to explain his words of departure in the upper room (14:5). In the Gospel's closing scenes is the familiar episode in which Thomas doubts the Lord's resurrection (20:24) and then is given compelling proof (vv 26-28), after which Thomas called Jesus "my Lord and my God." Thomas is also named in John's epilogue (21:2).

Two apocryphal, pseudepigraphical works bear Thomas's name: the Gospel of Thomas (from Nag Hammadi), which records 114 "secret sayings which the living Jesus spoke" and which Thomas is said to have preserved; and the Acts of Thomas (extant in both Greek and Syriac), which says that Jesus and Thomas were twins (sharing similar appearances and destinies) and that the apostle obtained secret teachings. This apocryphal account even explains Thomas's fate. Against his wishes, Thomas traveled to India under the command of the Lord. There he was martyred with spears by the hand of an Indian king. He was raised up and his empty tomb took on magical properties. Today in St. Thomas, India, Christians assert that they are the spiritual descendants of the apostle.

See also Apocrypha: Thomas, Acts of, Thomas, Gospel of; Apostle, Apostleship.

THORN *See* Plants (Thistle, Thorn).

THREE TAVERNS Place where the believers came to meet Paul when he arrived in Rome (Acts 28:15). It was on the Appian Way located at milepost 33 (30.5 English miles or 49.1 kilometers). The Forum of Appius is ten miles (16.1 kilometers) further south along the same road. Three Taverns was near modern Cisterna at an important junction between the Appian Way and the road from Antium to Norba and was thus a common meeting place for travelers.

THRESHER*, THRESHING, THRESHING FLOOR
See Agriculture.

THRONE Elevated, ceremonial chair, symbolizing the importance and the authority of the person seated on it. With the widespread use of the word "throne," the term came to symbolize kingship and became equivalent in meaning to the kingdom itself. When Pharaoh elevated Joseph to the status and office of viceroy, he emphasized "only as regards the throne will I be greater than you" (Gn 41:40). The establishment of David as king of Israel was equivalent to the establishment of the throne of David (2 Sm 3:10). To occupy the throne indicated succession to the kingship (1 Kgs 1:46).

Only one throne is described in detail in the OT, the throne of Solomon (1 Kgs 10:18-20; 2 Chr 9:17-19). The description, combined with the representation of thrones on ancient monuments, gives an idea of the appearance of the throne of Israel. An elevated seat with six steps leading up to it, the throne was partly made of ivory and overlaid with gold. The throne had a backrest and arms; alongside it were statues of lions and six similar statues on either side of the steps. Although not mentioned in the OT's description, a footstool was an indispensable part of the throne (Is 66:1).

The Hebrew term *kisseh* is used of a seat of honor for any distinguished person; for example, a priest (1 Sm 4:13, 18), a ruler (Ps 94:20), a military officer (Jer 1:15), and a favored guest (2 Kgs 4:10), although it is principally used for a king's chair from which he discharged his royal duties. The OT refers to thrones of foreign kings (Ex 11:5; Jer 43:10; Jon 3:6), but particular emphasis is on the throne of Israel, especially on the throne of David.

The God of Israel is described metaphorically as sitting upon a throne (Is 66:1). The vision of God seated on a throne as seen in prophetic visions is described by Micaiah (1 Kgs 22:19), Isaiah (6:1-3), Ezekiel (1:4-28; 10:1), and Daniel (7:9-10). Later, Ezekiel's vision of the throne of God was of major significance in Jewish "throne mysticism." In Revelation 4 the throne of God is flanked by the 24 thrones of the elders, surrounded by an emerald rainbow and seven torches, with a crystal sea in front, and four living creatures on each side.

Usually, God's throne is spoken of as being in heaven (Ps 11:4; Mt 5:34), but Jerusalem (Jer 3:17), the temple (Ez 43:6-7), or the nation of Israel (Jer 14:21) may be called the throne of God. The concept of Christ's throne is rare in the OT (Is 9:7; Jer 17:25) but common in the NT (Lk 1:32; Acts 2:30). This throne symbolizes Christ's kingship and authority.

THUMMIM *See* Urim and Thummim.

THUNDER, Sons of Translation of the word "Boanerges," the surname given by Jesus to James and John (Mk 3:17). *See* Boanerges.

THUTMOSE* *See* Egypt, Egyptian.

THYATIRA Location of one of the seven local churches in the book of Revelation. The city was founded by the Lydian kingdom and later captured by Seleucus, Alexander's general. It then served as a border settlement to preserve his kingdom from Lysimachus, his rival to the west.

After the kingdom of Pergamum was founded (282 BC), Thyatira became the borderline between Pergamum and the Syrians. The city was without natural defenses. It was not built on a hill and therefore was subject to repeated invasions. The strength of the city lay largely in its strategic location and also upon the fertility of the area surrounding it. Its inhabitants were descendants of Macedonian solders and retained much of their ancestors' militancy. They were formidable defenders of the city.

When Rome defeated Antiochus in 189 BC, Thyatira was incorporated into the kingdom of Pergamum, Rome's ally. Peace and prosperity followed. Under the Roman emperor Claudius (AD 41–54), Thyatira rose to new prominence and was permitted to issue its own coins. The emperor Hadrian included this city in his Middle East itinerary (AD 134), a hint of the importance of Thyatira in the second century AD.

Prosperity attracted many Jews to this area. Among the commercial activities of the city were textiles and bronze armor. The armorers were in a guild, like the silversmiths in Ephesus. The first known Christian convert in Europe was a businesswoman from Thyatira named Lydia (Acts 16:14-15, 40). She specialized in the costly purple garments that were exported from Thyatira to Macedonia. Here the purple dye, from the madder root, offered a much cheaper cloth to compete with costlier garments dyed with the expensive murex dye from Phoenicia.

In the message to the church in Thyatira, the members are commended for their love, faith, service, and endurance (Rv 2:19). But the influence of paganism is still reflected in the sharp rebuke of those who tolerate the heresy of which "Jezebel" was the leader. Their temptation was similar to that of the Corinthian believers who were uncertain about eating food that had been dedicated to idols (1 Cor 8:1-13). The trade guilds held periodic festivals in which food offered to idols was consumed. This was sometimes accompanied by licentious rites in which religion and sex were mingled. This church was condemned for its accommodation to these pagan practices. Immorality was so rife among the pagans that the early church, with its uncompromising attitude toward unchastity, stood in constant tension with the mores of the community. Superstition and devil worship were apparently a great temptation as well. The "deep things of Satan" (Rv 2:24) is probably an allusion to one of the Gnostic sects that stressed "depth" and carried on secret rites in which only initiates participated. So serious was the temptation that the best hope was for survival of the remnant—hence, the exhortation "hold fast what you have, until I come" (v 25).

See also Revelation, Book of.

THYINE* KJV translation for "scented wood" in Revelation 18:12. Thyine was a dark-colored, fragrant, and valuable wood used for making furniture. *See* Plants (Citron Tree).

TIBERIAS City midway along the western shores of Lake Galilee, built about AD 20 by Herod Antipas, Herod the Great's son and the tetrarch of Galilee and Perea (4 BC–AD 39), who named the town in honor of the emperor Tiberius. The name is preserved in the modern town Tabariyeh. The site became his new capital after abandoning Sepphoris, which he built in 4 BC. The location of Tiberias had several advantages: it lay just below a rocky projection above the lake, a natural acropolis that offered good protection; it was a center where roads from north, south, and west met, allowing Herod to move readily to various parts of his domain; and a little to the south lay famous warm springs, which were known to the Roman writer Pliny the Elder, who spoke of their health-giving qualities. Herod built a lakeside palace, feeling secure in the knowledge that a naturally fortified acropolis lay behind him. From there he would have enjoyed a superb panorama, which took in the whole of Galilee at a glance.

During the building of the town, a necropolis was discovered, which led to the Jewish abandonment of the site. The town was subsequently settled by a heterogeneous company of Gentiles, some of whom were brought forcibly to the place by Herod. By offering good houses and land to all, Herod assembled a sizable population (Josephus's *Antiquities* 18.2.3). According to the Gospels, Jesus never went there, probably in deference to Jewish scruples about the pollution caused by corpses. The town is mentioned only once in the NT (Jn 6:23), where boats came from Tiberias following the episode of the feeding of the 5,000. The Sea of Tiberias, that is, Lake Galilee, is referred to in John 6:1 and 21:1.

TIBERIAS, Sea of Alternate name for the Sea of Galilee in John 6:1 and 21:1. *See* Sea of Galilee.

TIBERIUS Roman emperor (AD 14–37) during Jesus' earthly ministry. *See* Caesars, The.

TIBHATH* City of King Hadadezer (1 Chr 18:8, NLT "Tebah") called *Betah* in the Hebrew of 2 Samuel 8:8. *See* Tebah (Place).

TIBNI Ginath's son, who competed with Omri to be king of Israel after Zimri's suicide (1 Kgs 16:21-22). Tibni ruled over half of Israel from 884–880 BC before Omri defeated him in a civil war.

TIDAL King of Goiim who fought with Kedorlaomer's confederation against Sodom (Gn 14:1-9).

TIGLATH-PILESER Name of three Assyrian kings, the most important of whom was Tiglath-pileser III (745–727 BC). The name means "my trust is in the son of the temple Esharra," and appears in various forms (cf. 2 Kgs 15:29; also called Tilgath-pilneser in 1 Chr 5:6; 2 Chr 28:20).

Tiglath-pileser I (1115–1077 BC) was the son of Ashur-resh-ishi. Having gained independence from Babylonian overlordship, Tiglath-pileser consolidated his hold over the territory newly acquired in his father's reign, maintaining control and guarding against counterattacks from the former occupiers. Security brought increased trade and prosperity, and a large temple-building program was undertaken.

Tiglath-pileser II (c. 967–935 BC) was a weak king who ruled Assyria during a period of decline. Although he was able to maintain some degree of internal control, he was powerless to prevent outside peoples from encroaching upon Assyrian territory. In particular, the Arameans took advantage of Assyrian weakness to occupy large areas of land, and an Aramean ruler named Kapara built a palace at Guzana (the Gozan of 2 Kgs 17:6). Some of the Arameans who occupied the area have been identified from inscriptions found at the site. This period was of particular importance for the emergence of the Aramean Empire.

Tiglath-pileser III (745–727 BC) ascended to the throne at a time when he could stem and reverse another decline in Assyrian fortunes. Although not directly in line for the throne, he was probably of royal descent. On occasion, he used the name Pul (2 Kgs 15:19; 1 Chr 5:26), which may have been his real name as opposed to his throne name.

Tiglath-pileser III was a strong, able, resourceful king whose reign is remarkable for the rapid extension of Assyrian boundaries and for the peaceful administration of the newly acquired territories. He assisted Babylon by defeating the Arameans, and by his diplomacy retained Babylonian support while he concentrated his military efforts elsewhere. On the death of the vassal king Nabu-nasir of Babylon in 734 BC, Tiglath-pileser gained the support of some of the tribes and finally forced the submission of Marduk-apla-iddina (the Merodach-baladan of Is 39:1). According to the Babylonian Chronicle, he used the name Pul when acceding to the throne of Babylon himself in 729 BC. He was the first Assyrian king on the throne of Babylon in 500 years.

His reign, which was marked by a vast increase in territory coupled with a firm and able administration, also had long-term effects far beyond Assyria's immediate borders. The expansion into Syria and Palestine was bound to lead eventually to conflict with Egypt when that country wished once again to mount a more aggressive foreign policy. Tiglath-pileser was the father of Shalmaneser V (727–722 BC).

See also Assyria, Assyrians.

TIGRIS RIVER One of the two major rivers that drains the Mesopotamian plain. Unlike the Euphrates, it is seldom mentioned in the Bible. In the description of the Garden of Eden, it is listed as the third of the four rivers that flowed out of the river that watered the Garden (Gn 2:14). Unfortunately, this reference provides little help concerning the location of Eden. The river is not mentioned again until Daniel 10:4, where Daniel referred to it as the "great river" (KJV). Nahum was likely referring to the Tigris when he described the opening of the river gates of Nineveh during the Babylonian siege (Na 2:6).

When its two principal tributaries are included, the length of the Tigris is 1,146 miles (1,843.9 kilometers). Its primary source, a mountain lake called Golenjik, is only two or three miles (3.2–4.8 kilometers) from the channel of the Euphrates. As is the case with most of the rivers of the region, the flow of the Tigris varies considerably during the year. Flood season begins in early March, with its peak in early- to mid-May. Though the river is generally navigable, historical records suggest that the river never had great commercial significance. However, it did gain political significance during the period of Assyrian dominance. Nineveh, Asshur, and Calah were all located on the banks of the Tigris. Unfortunately for the Assyrians, the Tigris never proved to be a formidable natural barrier and thus failed to protect the empire from its enemies.

TIKVAH

1. Harhas's son, father of Shallum, and the father-in-law of Huldah the prophetess (2 Kgs 22:14); alternately called Tokhath (KJV "Tikvath") in 2 Chronicles 34:22.
2. Father of Jahzeiah, who was one of the four individuals on record who opposed Ezra's command to divorce foreign wives (Ezr 10:15).

TIKVATH* KJV spelling of Tokhath, an alternate name for Tikvah, Harhas's son, in 2 Chronicles 34:22. *See* Tikvah #1.

TILGATH-PILNESER* Alternate spelling of the Assyrian king Tiglath-pileser III's name in 1 Chronicles 5:6, 26 and 2 Chronicles 28:20. *See* Tiglath-pileser.

TILON Shimon's son from Judah's tribe (1 Chr 4:20).

TIMAEUS Father of Bartimaeus, the blind beggar whose sight Jesus restored near the gateway leading from Jericho (Mk 10:46).

TIMBREL* Small hand drum. *See* Musical Instruments (Shalishim; Toph).

TIME *See* Calendars, Ancient and Modern.

TIMEUS* *See* Timaeus.

TIMNA (Person)

1. Daughter of Seir, sister of Lotan, and a native Horite inhabitant of Edom (Gn 36:22; 1 Chr 1:39). She was a concubine to Eliphaz, Esau's son, and the mother of Amalek (Gn 36:12).
2. Edomite chief (Gn 36:40; 1 Chr 1:36, 51). This name may refer either to the name of the ancestor of the Edomite clan or to the geographical area occupied by the clan.

Solomon's Pillars This interesting formation at Timnah is also known as Chimney Rocks.

TIMNAH (Place)

1. One of the cities on the northern boundary of Judah's inheritance, located between Beth-shemesh and Ekron (Jos 15:10). This is the likely site of Judah's affair with Tamar, which resulted in the birth of Perez and Zerah (Gn 38:12-14). A frontier town between Judah and Philistia, Timnah was the place where Samson had his

first marital difficulties with one of the daughters of the Philistines (Jgs 14:1-5; 15:6). The town evidently changed hands frequently between the Israelites and the Philistines. Apparently, Israel did achieve control of Timnah during the conquest (cf. Jos. 19:43), but it was under Philistine control by the time of Samson (Jgs 14:1). Ahaz recaptured Timnah (c. 730 BC) from the Philistines (2 Chr 28:18).
2. One of the cities of the southern hill country that was part of the inheritance of Judah (Jos 15:57). It is possible that this is the site of Judah's encounter with Tamar (Gn 38:12-14; and perhaps the same as #1 above).

TIMNATH* KJV spelling of Timnah, a town in northern Judah, in Genesis 38:12-14 and Judges 14:1-5. *See* Timnah (Place) #1.

TIMNATH-HERES*, TIMNATH-SERAH The city that Joshua the son of Nun asked for and that was given to him as his inheritance when the land was divided among the tribes of Israel (Jos 19:49-50). Joshua rebuilt the city and settled there. When Joshua died, he was buried on the property located in the hill country of Ephraim, north of the mountain of Gaash (Jos 24:30). Judges 2:9 gives the same location, but the name is Timnath-heres (see NLT mg), which means "territory [or portion] of the sun." This seems to indicate that the city used to be a place for sun worship.

TIMNITE* Inhabitant from the town of Timnah in northern Judah (Jgs 15:6). *See* Timnah (Place) #1.

TIMON One of the seven men of the Jerusalem church of good repute, full of the Spirit and of wisdom, appointed to minister to the widows (Acts 6:5).

TIMOTHEUS* KJV spelling of Timothy. *See* Timothy (Person).

TIMOTHY (Person) Paul's convert and companion, whose name means "one who honors God."

Timothy first appears in Acts 16:1-3 as Paul's disciple whose mother "was a believer; but his father was a Greek" (v 1). He was a third-generation Christian after his mother, Eunice, and grandmother, Lois (2 Tm 1:5). The apostle Paul, undoubtedly Timothy's spiritual father, refers to him as "my true child in the faith" (1 Tm 1:2); he perhaps converted Timothy on his first or second missionary journey. The son of a Greek (or Gentile) father, Timothy was yet uncircumcised; however, when Paul decided to take Timothy with him on the second journey, he had him circumcised so as not to hinder their missionary endeavors among the Jews.

Timothy, who was well spoken of by the believers at Lystra and Iconium (Acts 16:2), became Paul's companion and assistant on his second missionary journey at Lystra. He traveled with Paul into Europe following the Macedonian vision. When Paul decided to go to Athens, he left Silas and Timothy at Berea to establish the church there (17:14). Timothy and Silas eventually joined Paul in Corinth (18:5). He next appears with Paul in Ephesus on his third journey (19:22), from where Paul sends him into Macedonia ahead of himself. In the last mention of Timothy in Acts 20:4, he was included in the list of goodwill ambassadors who were to accompany Paul to Jerusalem with the offering for the Christian Jews.

Timothy is often mentioned in the Pauline letters. His name is included in the introductory salutations of 2 Corinthians, Philippians, Colossians, 1 and 2 Thessalonians, and Philemon. Timothy's presence with Paul when he wrote these letters confirms the accuracy of the references to him in Acts. He was in Corinth on the second journey when Paul wrote 1 and 2 Thessalonians, at Ephesus on the third journey when Paul wrote 2 Corinthians, and in Rome during Paul's first Roman imprisonment, when he wrote Philippians, Colossians, and Philemon. He is mentioned in the introductions of 1 and 2 Timothy as the recipient of those two letters.

In the closing salutations of Romans 16:21, Timothy is listed along with others who send their good wishes to the believers in Rome. In 1 Corinthians 4:17 and 16:10, Paul speaks words of praise for Timothy as he sends him with a message to Corinth (see also Phil 2:19-23; 1 Thes 3:2-6). In 2 Corinthians 1:19 Timothy is named, along with Paul and Silas, as men who were proclaiming the good news about Jesus Christ. Paul put Timothy in charge of the church at Ephesus and wrote him two pastoral letters to help him perform that responsible task.

In Hebrews 13:23 the author (probably not Paul) tells his readers that Timothy had been released from prison, and that he hoped to come with Timothy to visit the readers of that letter. By this note, we know that Timothy experienced imprisonment.

See also Timothy, First Letter to; Timothy, Second Letter to.

TIMOTHY, First Letter to The first of Paul's epistles to his young coworker Timothy.

The authorship, date, and background of 1 Timothy must be considered together with those of the other two Pastoral Epistles, 2 Timothy and Titus, which were written to two young coworkers to help them deal with pastoral problems in the churches of Ephesus and Crete.

PREVIEW
• Author
• Date
• Background
• Theology
• Content

Author In 1 Timothy, as in 2 Timothy and Titus, Paul is named as the author in the first verse. And Paul's name is the only one assigned as author in the tradition of the early church since the time of Irenaeus (c. AD 185). Throughout all three letters are many personal references to the life of Paul, which constitute strong evidence that he was truly the author.

However, some scholars object to Pauline authorship on the following grounds:

1. The Greek vocabulary contains a large number of words that are not found in the other Pauline letters.

   But the subject matter in these letters is also different. In the Pastoral Epistles the author is dealing with the more technical matters of church organization and discipline—a church leader writing to other leaders. Paul was a highly educated man, with a large vocabulary at his disposal. None of the words peculiar to the Pastoral Letters would have been beyond Paul's own vocabulary. And if these weren't his words, they may have come from the scribes that Paul regularly used to compose his epistles.

2. There are notes about Paul's journeys that do not fit into the journeys described in the book of Acts.

   To believe that Paul wrote the Pastorals and did the things described in them, he must have been released from Roman imprisonment and then traveled to Crete, Ephesus, and Macedonia. These later journeys may not have been mentioned in Acts because the

writer of Acts concluded this book with Paul's imprisonment in Rome. There is some legal evidence that Paul would automatically have been released after two years, if he had not been convicted by that time.

3. The advanced development of the church described in the pastorals proves a date later than the life of Paul. Elders, bishops, and deacons are mentioned.

   However, elders existed in OT times and bishops, as officers within local churches, are almost certainly the same as elders. In addition, Paul refers to deacons elsewhere in his letters, such as Philippians 1:1.

Most conservative scholars, and many others as well, believe very strongly that Paul did write all three of the Pastoral Letters.

Date Assuming that Paul wrote the Pastorals, 1 Timothy would have been written after his release from the first Roman imprisonment, about AD 61 or 62, and before his second Roman imprisonment, somewhere between 64 and 67, the date of the death of Nero. As to the place, Paul left Timothy in Ephesus and then went on to Macedonia (1 Tm 1:3), where he may have written 1 Timothy. The letter was, of course, written to Timothy at Ephesus.

Background Paul left Timothy in charge of the church at Ephesus (1:2-3). Paul wanted to go to the Roman province of Asia, of which Ephesus was the chief city, on his second missionary journey, but the Spirit did not allow him to do so. He went on to Macedonia and Greece (Acts 16:6). He briefly visited Ephesus as he was completing his second journey (18:19-20). Then on his third journey he made Ephesus the center of his activity and spent three years there (19:1–20:1). During his first Roman imprisonment, he wrote an encyclical letter to Ephesus and the nearby churches. Only a few years later, he wrote 1 Timothy to Timothy at Ephesus.

ΚΑΙΟΜΟΛΟΓΟΥΜε
ΝΩϹΜΕΓΑΕϹΤΙΝ
ΤΟΤΗϹΕΥϹΕΒΕΙΑϹ
ΜΥϹΤΗΡΙΟΝΟϹΕ
ΦΑΝΕΡΩΘΗΕΝϹΑΡ
ΚΙ· ΕΔΙΚΑΙΩΘΗΕΝ
ΠΝΙΩΦΘΗΑΓΓΕΛΟΙϲ
ΕΚΗΡΥΧΘΗΕΝΕ
ΘΝΕϹΙΝΕΠΙϹΤΕΥ
ΘΗΕΝΚΟϹΜΩ·
ΑΝΕΛΗΜΦΘΗΕΝ
ΔΟΞΗ

1 Timothy 3:16 in Codex Sinaiticus Replication showing 1 Timothy 3:16, which in this manuscript reads, "And confessedly great is the mystery of godliness: who was manifested in flesh, justified in spirit, seen by angels, proclaimed among nations, believed on the world, taken up in glory."

Theology In general, the theology of 1 Timothy is consistent with that of the other Pauline letters and of the NT as a whole. The sovereignty and love of God are clearly presented time and again throughout the letter. Jesus is always presented as being truly God as well as man. Salvation is by faith in God through Christ. The law will not save a person, because all people have broken it. Yet the law is good and is God's guide for the saved person in living a life pleasing to God.

The church occupies a large place in the letter. All Christians should be a part of the church. They gain much from the church for the development of Christian character, and they can serve God far more effectively in the church than apart from it. The church needs organization to do its work effectively. And the church must strive always to avoid heresy and to teach the truths of the gospel.

Content

Salutation (1:1-2) The author names himself, Paul, and describes himself as an apostle, chosen by God and authorized by God the Father and his Son, Christ Jesus. Paul had the right to speak words of authority to the young pastor and to the church.

The letter is written to Timothy, Paul's beloved spiritual child, to whom Paul gave his triple blessing—grace, mercy, and peace from God.

Dealing with Heresy (1:3-20) One of the reasons Paul left Timothy in Ephesus was that he wanted him to "stop those who are teaching wrong doctrine" (1:3). Paul believed that what a person believed was as important as what he did. The heresy here is described as an early form of the Gnostic heresy, a dangerous heresy plaguing the church for centuries.

These early Gnostics claimed to have a deeper insight into truth than the average Christian. They separated God as Spirit from man as matter. For Gnostics, the bridge between the two was made up of innumerable angels of various ranks, emanations, aeons, and such, rather than the one mediator, Jesus Christ. They argued about myths and fables. They sought salvation by finding favor with an endless chain of angels rather than by accepting God's salvation by faith. But only the grace of God can save sinners, as Paul himself knew well.

Correct Worship in the Church (2:1-15) "I urge that supplications, prayers, intercessions, and thanksgivings be made for all men" (2:1, RSV). Prayer is an exceedingly important part of the worship of the Christian church. Paul emphasized the importance of special prayer for persons in high places of authority in the state (even though the state was the Roman Empire with Nero as its emperor). Paul had taught this clearly in Romans 13, and Jesus had told his disciples to give to Caesar the things that belonged to him (Mt 22:17).

Christian men and women should pray to God, lifting up holy hands to him, hands free from sin and anger and resentment. Paul specifically urged the sisters as follows: "And I want women to be modest in their appearance. They should wear decent and appropriate clothing and not draw attention to themselves by the way they fix their hair or by wearing gold or pearls or expensive clothes. For women who claim to be devoted to God should make themselves attractive by the good things they do" (1 Tm 2:9-10, NLT). Then Paul said, "I do not let women teach men or have authority over them" (v 12). This did not mean, however, that they could not function orally in the church meetings. According to Acts and 1 Corinthians, it is quite clear that women prayed, prophesied, and testified in church meetings. But teach-

ing was reserved for the men because it was the duty of the elders (who were male) to be the teachers. Thus, teaching and exercising authority went hand in hand.

Proper Organization in the Church (3:1-5:25) The first issue to resolve about the organization of the early church had to do with who the bishops were. The first verse of this section reads, "If any one aspires to the office of bishop, he desires a noble task" (3:1, RSV). In all the Pastoral Epistles, the bishop is clearly an officer within a local church rather than an official over a group of churches, such as the office of the episcopal bishop, which developed in the early second century. And in the light of Titus 1:4-6, where Paul passed directly from elders to bishops, most scholars believe that Paul used the two terms interchangeably. Timothy himself would be the closest thing to a modern pastor in the church, and there were elders (bishops) and deacons assisting him in governing the church.

To be an elder in the church is a worthy aspiration. But a person must have high qualifications to be elected to such a responsible position. He should be respected by other members of the church and by those outside the church. Most of the qualifications are quite clear but several of them deserve some attention.

"Now a bishop must be above reproach, the husband of one wife" (3:2, RSV). The Greek says literally, "a man of one woman." That would clearly prohibit polygamy and eliminate a man who was unfaithful to his wife. It would probably eliminate neither a man who had been divorced and remarried nor a bachelor who had never had a wife. The church should insist that its official leaders conform to a high view of sexual morality.

The elder should be able to discipline his own family life if he is to exert discipline in the church. The man also should not be a drunkard. Paul did not demand total abstinence, but he clearly demanded that an elder not be a person under the domination of strong drink. And a person occupying the high office of elder should not be a new Christian (lit. a neophyte), lest this go to his head and keep him from being a good elder. All in all, only a person of excellent character should be elected to the high office of elder, or bishop, in the church.

Then Paul went on to speak about the office of the deacon: "In the same way, deacons must be people who are respected and have integrity" (3:8, NLT). The qualifications for the deacons are virtually the same as those for elders. Before being elected as deacons, they should have experience in church work. First Timothy 3:11 applies the same qualifications to women aspiring to be deacons and/or to wives of deacons (NLT mg). Verse 12 continues with the qualifications of deacons in general.

In chapter 4 Paul urges Timothy to exercise his leadership in the church, especially in his relation to the heretics. Some of the Gnostic heretics taught a false kind of asceticism, forbidding marriage and the eating of various foods. But God has given these things to be used and appreciated for God's glory. Timothy's pastoral duty was to teach his people God's truths and not to allow himself to be caught up in arguing about the heretics' godless and silly myths (4:7). Paul urged Timothy to keep his spirit fit by constant spiritual exercise, which was even more important than exercise of the body.

Paul recognized that Timothy was a young man, and that some of the older Christians might be tempted to look down upon his youth. Timothy should strive even harder to deserve their admiration—"in speech and conduct, in love, in faith, in purity" (4:12). Because God had called Timothy and the church had ordained him by the laying on of hands, Timothy should strive to live up to these high responsibilities.

Paul gave Timothy practical advice as to how a young preacher should deal with the different age and sex groups in the church. He should treat the older men as his own father, the older women as his mother, the younger men as his brothers, and the younger women as his sisters—adding significantly, "in all purity" (5:2).

Paul also told Timothy how to deal with the problem of widows. At that time, when few women could work and before the days of insurance and Social Security, women who had lost their husbands were in a hopeless situation. The early church developed a roll for widows that would enable it to minister to their needs. Younger widows were to be encouraged to marry again and get new husbands to support them. Able families should recognize their responsibility to take care of their own needy ones. The church, then, would have the responsibility of taking care of the older widows who had no families to take care of them. The church, with its charitable obligations, must use its limited means responsibly, wisely, and fairly so that the greatest possible good can result.

Even in the early church, church leaders were paid for their work. Paul said that they should "be considered worthy of double honor" (5:17). Church leaders should not be chosen or ordained too quickly. Their sins should not be overlooked. Even Timothy himself was warned to keep himself free from sin. The section ends with another treatment of the sins of church leaders (vv 24-25). When the sins are clear, the sinner must be disciplined by the church. At times, a person's sins are not evident to other people, but God knows them and will deal with them. Conversely, the same is true about the many good deeds of the leaders.

Some Practical Teaching about the Christian Life (6:1-21) Slavery was a recognized institution in those days. Christian slaves should be good slaves, and Christian masters should be good masters. After many centuries, Christian principles would bring slavery to an end, but it would have been impossible for Paul or anyone else at that time to lead a crusade for the abolition of slavery.

Timothy was urged to avoid the teaching of the heretics but to be faithful in teaching the positive truths of the gospel.

Two sections (6:6-10, 17-19) deal with the Christian's attitude toward wealth. Here Paul closely followed the teachings of Jesus. Money can be made into a false god and bring all kinds of evil to the church member. But it can also be used in the service of God and be changed into treasure stored in heaven.

Finally, in two sections (6:11-16, 20-21), Paul encouraged Timothy to strive to do his very best to be truly God's man. He should fight a good fight as a soldier of God. This life will often be hard, but Timothy should keep his eyes fixed on the second coming of the glorious Christ.

See also Timothy, Second Letter to; Titus, Letter to.

TIMOTHY, Second Letter to

PREVIEW
•Author
•Place and Date of Writing
•Background
•Content

Author Many of those who deny the Pauline authorship of the Pastoral Epistles recognize that 2 Timothy

contains some true Pauline fragments in the numerous personal references in the letter. But the evidence in favor of the Pauline authorship is much stronger than the evidence against it. (See the discussion on authorship of the Pastoral Letters under "Timothy, First Letter to.")

Place and Date of Writing Paul was in prison when he wrote this letter to Timothy; 2 Timothy 1:15-18 tells specifically of his being in Rome and how Onesiphorus was faithful to him when others from the province of Asia had deserted him. Second Timothy 2:9 again refers to his being in jail for preaching the gospel. Toward the end of the letter, starting at 4:6, Paul relates his experience in prison—and that he has no hope for release. Second Timothy is a type of last will and testament of the apostle. Early, trustworthy tradition reports that Paul was martyred in Rome under Nero. Rome, then, was the place from which 2 Timothy was written.

The letter was written to Timothy in Ephesus, as is made plain throughout the letter.

As to the year in which it was written, two dates are possible. The year 64 AD was the date of the great fire in Rome. Nero tried to shift responsibility for the fire to the Christians. Possibly Paul was martyred at that time. Nero himself died in AD 67, so that would be the latest date that could be assigned. The letter was written between AD 64 and 67, with some preference being given to the earlier date.

Background Since the time of the writing of 1 Timothy, Paul made further travels and then came to Rome for his second imprisonment. See this section under "Timothy, First Letter to."

Content

Salutation (1:1-2) As was customary in ancient letters, the writer puts his name first. Then he gives a fuller identification of himself as an apostle, one belonging to Jesus Christ, and one commissioned to tell the whole world about the eternal life that God has made available through faith in Jesus Christ. Paul hereby indicates his authority and also gives a brief summary of the essence of the true Christian faith.

The person to whom the letter is written is "Timothy, my beloved child." Then follows a triple blessing, "Grace, mercy, and peace" from God the Father and his Son, Jesus Christ. As in all his letters, Paul changes the rather colorless Greek salutation, "greetings," to one of the greatest theological concepts, "grace," and adds the Greek translation of the regular Hebrew salutation, "peace." Then he adds here the great word, "mercy," as he did in 1 Timothy.

Exhortations to Timothy to Be a Good Minister (1:3–2:13) Paul begins this section by telling Timothy how often he offered prayers of thanksgiving to God on his behalf, to the God of his fathers, to the God whom it was his chief purpose in life to please. Paul greatly desired to see Timothy, especially as he remembered their tearful parting.

Paul reminded Timothy of his great trust in the Lord, a trust that was passed on to him by two godly women: his mother, Eunice, and his grandmother, Lois. Acts 16:1-3 states that Timothy's mother was a believing Jewess, and his father was a Greek, or Gentile. He had not allowed his son to be circumcised in infancy. But the believing mother had passed on her faith to her son. When Paul decided to take him along as an assistant on his second missionary journey, he had him circumcised so that he could work more effectively with the Jews. Thus, Timothy had a great heritage from Lois, Eunice, and Paul himself.

"Hence I remind you to rekindle the gift of God that is within you through the laying on of my hands" (2 Tm 1:6, RSV). First Timothy 4:14 adds this: "when the council of elders laid their hands upon you." This seems very much like there had been a formal service of ordination, when Timothy was set apart as a minister of the gospel by the laying on of hands accompanied by prayer. Timothy should have never forgotten that solemn moment, and the memory should have kept his life filled with strength and boldness. He was truly a man of God, a man filled with the Spirit of God, and a man not afraid to do his Christian work. Timothy might suffer for his faith, but he could be encouraged as he remembered the sufferings and imprisonment of his spiritual father, Paul. God would give Timothy strength to endure suffering, as he had done for Paul.

Then Paul reminded Timothy of how God had saved him and Paul, and how he had chosen them from all eternity to tell others of God's saving love through Jesus Christ, who came in time to work out that salvation, by breaking the power of death and showing the way to eternal life. Paul knew, of course, what he believed, but more importantly he knew whom he believed, or trusted—Jesus Christ. And in spite of the many uncertainties that must have been in Paul's mind, he could be absolutely sure of Christ. Paul was also sure that Christ would be able to guard what had been entrusted to him—guard it until the day Paul and Jesus saw each other. Paul was confident of that, and he wanted Timothy to have a similar assurance.

So Paul urged Timothy to hold fast to the pattern of truth Paul had taught him—that body of Christian doctrine, especially as it pertained to Jesus Christ and the faith and love in Christ. He should guard this gift carefully, with the help of the Holy Spirit.

Paul then shared with Timothy his great sorrow that all the Christians of the Roman province of Asia, of which Ephesus was the chief city, had deserted him. Paul mentions two of the deserters by name, Phygelus and Hermogenes. Evidently Timothy knew who they were. In striking contrast, Paul mentioned the good man Onesiphorus (also at 4:19), who had been such a wonderful and faithful helper of Paul, both in Ephesus and in Rome.

Paul again urged Timothy to be strong in the strength that Christ has given him (2:1). Timothy should pass on the Christian truths to others and train them to pass them on to still others. Paul was probably thinking especially of the elders and deacons (cf. 1 Timothy). Paul used three effective illustrations to encourage Timothy to give his best in his Christian service. He was to fight and suffer as a good soldier, play the game well as a good athlete, and work hard as a good farmer. The rewards will come to all three if they perform their tasks well. All three illustrations had been used by Jesus, and they were used by other NT writers.

In the midst of his exhortations, Paul provided a fine summary of true Christology in 2:8-10. Jesus was truly man and truly God. It is heretical to deny either the full humanity or the full deity of Christ, even though no human mind can full understand the mystery of the Incarnation. And this divine-human being died and then rose again from the dead.

Warnings against Heresy (2:14–4:5) This section begins with the affirmation "Remind everyone of these things, and command them in God's name to stop fighting over words. Such arguments are useless, and they can ruin those who hear them" (NLT). There are heretical beliefs that should be definitely condemned, but Chris-

tians are warned against arguing among themselves about insignificant matters. Christians can become angry with other Christians and spend time fighting one another rather than fighting Satan.

Timothy was to strive to make himself a good servant, meriting the approval of his Master, knowing well the truths of his word. In that way, he could combat the false teachings of the heretics. Two of the heretics are mentioned by name, Hymenaeus and Philetus. Philetus is named only here in the NT. Hymenaeus, though, was mentioned also in 1 Timothy 1:20, along with another heretic, Alexander; these two had been given over to Satan, or excommunicated, by Paul at that time. Their heresy was that they taught that the resurrection of believers had already happened (2 Tm 2:18). This heresy undermines the Christian hope of the final resurrection, which brings all believers into eternity. The heretics were denying the reality of that and redefining it as something that had already happened.

In various ways Paul urged Timothy to prove himself a true servant of God, one who is known by God and one who lives by the truths of God's word. He should avoid the evil thoughts that so often come to young men, and also the temptation to quarrel. Rather, he should be gentle, patient, and humble, seeking to help his people avoid the traps of Satan.

Second Timothy 3:1-9 gives Paul's strongest condemnation of the heretics in the church. They attend church but they do not believe the Christian truths. They do not live Christian lives themselves, and they strive to get others to follow their beliefs and practices; Paul likened the heretics of his day to the Egyptian magicians in Exodus 7 (who were given the names Jannes and Jambres by Jewish tradition). The heretics in Timothy's day would fail in their attacks against the truth, just as Jannes and Jambres had failed in their attacks against God and his spokesman Moses.

Paul contrasted his own life and beliefs with those of the heretics. He had been persecuted by heretics himself even on his first missionary journey, but he had continued to preach the truth and had brought many to accept Christ. Timothy should follow Paul's example.

The supreme way to overcome heresy is the diligent study of the Word of God. "All Scripture is inspired by God and is useful to teach us what is true and to make us realize what is wrong in our lives. It straightens us out and teaches us to do what is right. It is God's way of preparing us in every way, fully equipped for every good thing God wants us to do" (3:16-17, NLT).

Paul gave Timothy a solemn charge to preach that Word faithfully and diligently. Many would not be willing to listen to the truths of the Bible, but Timothy should try to correct and rebuke them, even though it may bring persecution upon himself.

Paul's Faith and Hope (4:6-18) Paul had been writing these important injunctions to Timothy because he knew that he had very little time left here on earth: "As for me, my life has already been poured out as an offering to God. The time of my death is near" (4:6, NLT). He can look back with satisfaction upon a life of true faith and service. So he can look forward in all confidence to his crown of victory in eternity. This kind of faith enabled Paul to face his death bravely, and it will do the same for all believing Christians for whom the Second Coming is a blessed hope.

Paul urged Timothy to come and be with him in Rome. Luke was the only one of his friends still with him. Paul told Timothy about other friends who had been with him but who had left. One, Demas, had proved to be a failure. Crescens, Titus, and Tychicus had left for other places. Paul asked Timothy to bring his coat, which he had left at Troas with Carpus, and also his books, especially those written on parchment (probably some copies of Scripture, both Old Testament and New). Paul warned Timothy against the evil man, Alexander the coppersmith (see 1 Tm 1:20).

At Paul's first trial, all of his friends had left him. But God had been with him and saved him. Paul had even had an opportunity of proclaiming the gospel for all the world to hear.

Concluding Greetings (4:19-22) Paul sent his greetings to a number of his friends in Ephesus. And he sent greetings to Timothy from some of the Roman Christians whom he evidently knew. He urged Timothy to try to come to him before winter, when traveling would be difficult or impossible. He then concluded with a short benediction: "The Lord be with your spirit."

See also Paul, The Apostle; Timothy, First Letter to; Titus, Letter to.

TIN *See* Minerals and Metals.

TIPHSAH

1. City on the northeastern boundary of Solomon's empire (1 Kgs 4:24). It is most likely identified with Thapsacus, a town mentioned frequently in Greek and Roman texts. Though its precise location is unknown, it was an important trading center on the Euphrates River that dominated an east-west caravan route and also served as a northern terminal for river traffic.
2. KJV rendering of Tappuah, one of the towns conquered by Menahem after he deposited Shallum in Samaria (2 Kgs 15:16). *See* Tappuah (Place) #2.

TIRAS Japheth's seventh son listed in the "table of nations" (Gn 10:2; 1 Chr 1:5). His descendants have been alternately linked to the Thracians, the Agathyrsi, the tribes of the Taurus mountain region, and the maritime Tyrrheni, but all of these identifications are purely speculative.

TIRATHITES First of three families listed as scribes living at Jabez; perhaps belonging to the Kenite family (1 Chr 2:55).

TIRHAKAH Ethiopian king who marched north to fight against the Assyrian army, thus diverting Sennacherib's siege of Jerusalem (2 Kgs 19:9; Is 37:9). The report of Tirhakah's intended invasion prompted the Rabshakeh's second threat against Jerusalem, Hezekiah's prayer for deliverance, and the subsequent divine destruction of the Assyrian army (2 Kgs 19:8-37). Tirhakah is almost certainly the Egyptian king Taharqa, who ruled from 689–664 BC during the 25th (Ethiopian) dynasty. Tirhakah probably served as commander of the army while he was crown prince, so that the reference to him as "king" refers to his then-future position.

TIRHANAH Hezronite and the second of Caleb's four sons by Maacah, his concubine (1 Chr 2:48).

TIRIA Jahallelel's son and a descendant of Judah through Caleb (1 Chr 4:16).

TIRSHATHA* KJV translation of a Hebrew word designating a title of authority with the connotation of "governor." It is appended to Zerubbabel's name (Ezr 2:63) and Nehemiah's name (Neh 8:9; 10:1), both of whom held the office in Jerusalem during the postexilic period.

TIRZAH (Person) One of the daughters of Zelophehad of Manasseh's tribe (Nm 26:33). Since her father had no sons, she and her sisters asked for and received their father's inheritance (Nm 27:1; Jos 17:3). This prompted the making of a new law concerning inheritance rights with the stipulation that daughters who obtained their families' inheritance must marry within the tribe (Nm 36:11).

TIRZAH (Place) Early capital city of the divided kingdom of Israel (1 Kgs 14:17; 15:21, 33; 16:6-23). It was one of the cities captured by Joshua (Jos 12:24), but it did not gain prominence until Jeroboam established it as his royal residence (1 Kgs 14:17). Although Baasha intended to move his capital to Ramah, he returned to Tirzah as a result of his war against Asa (1 Kgs 15:21). Tirzah also served as the capital for Elah, Zimri, and Omri during the first six years of Omri's reign. Omri built and established Samaria as his capital midway during his reign, resulting in the decline of Tirzah's significance. Perhaps as a result of the rivalry between Tirzah and Samaria, Menahem used Tirzah as his base to mount his revolt against Shallum in 753 BC (2 Kgs 15:14). Although it was known as a beautiful city located on a high hill (Sg 6:4), Tirzah's location has not been identified with precision.

Aerial View of Tirzah

TISHBE Native city of Elijah the prophet and its inhabitants (1 Kgs 17:1; 21:17, 28; 2 Kgs 1:3, 8; 9:36). The Hebrew form of Tishbe in 1 Kings 17:1 prompted the KJV to translate the word as "of the inhabitants [of Gilead]." Most translations follow the Septuagint, however, in considering Tishbe a proper noun. This reading is also supported by the fact that Elijah is elsewhere called a Tishbite. If Tishbe is considered a proper name, it is likely identified with Thisbe, a town in Naphtali that is mentioned in Tobit 1:2.

TISHRI* Hebrew month corresponding to about mid-September to mid-October. *See* Calendars, Ancient and Modern.

TITHE, TITHING Words deriving from Old English for "tenth" and representing a charge upon produce or labor levied for the maintenance of religious activities. The custom is very ancient (Abraham paid a tithe of the spoils of war to Melchizedek; see Gn 14:20) and widely practiced, being known in Athens, Arabia, Rome, Carthage, Egypt, Syria, Babylon, and China.

According to Deuteronomy (Dt 12:2-7, 17-19; 14:22-29), the centralization of worship meant that the tithe was taken annually at the sanctuary and shared by priests and Levites. Corn, wine, oil, and flocks were tithed.

Every third year, the Levites, foreigners, orphans, and widows were given the whole tithe in charity (Dt 26:12). According to Numbers 18:21-32, every tithe in Israel was given to the Levites in return for their priestly service.

The prophet Malachi (Mal 3:8-10), who scathingly declared the withholding of tithes to be "robbing God," promised full barns and vats, opened windows of heaven, outpoured blessing and deliverance from locusts, in return for faithful tithing. In the early tithe feasts, thanksgiving for God's gifts would seem appropriate (cf. Gn 28:22), though not emphasized. Maintenance of the service of God remained the chief purpose of tithing, along with a wide charity.

Apart from recalling Melchizedek's tithe (Heb 7), tithing is mentioned in the NT critically. According to Matthew 23:23 and Luke 11:42, Jesus spoke of those who meticulously paid tithes on three small garden herbs while neglecting three "weightier matters of the law," namely, justice, mercy, and faith. For him, this was an example of the lack of moral proportion, the lack of a right sense of priorities, that marked Pharisaism. The explicit rule, precisely observed, is so much easier and self-satisfying than the moral sensitivity that should govern all relations with others and with God. According to Luke 18:12, the Pharisee, congratulating himself in prayer for his superior virtues, mentions his tithing of all income among his claims to divine favor. Christ sternly devalued the pride-filled performance, compared with that of the humble penitent.

See also Offerings and Sacrifices.

TITIUS JUSTUS Believer in Corinth with whom Paul stayed (Acts 18:7). *See* Justus #2.

TITTLE* Tiny ornamental "horn" on certain Hebrew letters. *See* Jot or Tittle.

TITUS (Person)

1. One of Paul's converts—"my true child in a common faith" (Ti 1:4, NASB)—who became an intimate and trusted associate of the apostle in his mission of planting Christianity throughout the Mediterranean world (2 Cor 8:23; 2 Tm 4:10; Ti 1:4-5). Mentioned frequently in

Paul's letters (eight times in 2 Corinthians, twice in Galatians, once each in 2 Timothy and Titus), his name occurs nowhere in Acts. This is a puzzling silence that some scholars have sought to explain with the fascinating, but uncertain, suggestion that he was a brother of Luke, the author of Acts.

Unlike Timothy, who was half Jewish, Titus was born of gentile parents. Nothing is recorded of the circumstances surrounding his conversion and initial encounter with Paul. He is first introduced as a companion of Paul and Barnabas on a visit to Jerusalem (Gal 2:3). The occasion appears to have been the Jerusalem Council, about AD 50, which Paul and Barnabas attended as official delegates from the church at Antioch not long after the apostle's first missionary journey (Acts 15).

With the hotly contested issue of compulsory circumcision of gentile converts to Christianity before the council, Paul decided to make a test case of Titus. The council decided in Paul's favor against the Judaizing party, and Titus was accepted by the other apostles and leaders of the Jerusalem church without submitting to the rite of circumcision. Thus, Titus became a key figure in the liberation of the infant church from the Judaizing party.

Titus probably accompanied Paul from that time on, but he does not appear again until Paul's crisis with the church at Corinth during his third missionary journey. According to 2 Corinthians, while Paul was conducting an extended ministry in Ephesus, he received word that the Corinthian church had turned hostile toward him and renounced his apostolic authority. Other attempts at reconciliation having failed, he sent Titus to Corinth to try to repair the breach. When Titus rejoined Paul somewhere in Macedonia, where the apostle had traveled from Ephesus to meet him, Titus brought the good news that the attitude of the Corinthians had changed and their former love and friendship were now restored (2 Cor 7:6-7). In view of this development Paul sent Titus back to Corinth, carrying 2 Corinthians, which included instructions to complete the collection of the relief offering for the Jewish Christians of Judea (8:6, 16). In this venture also Titus was apparently successful (Rom 15:25-26).

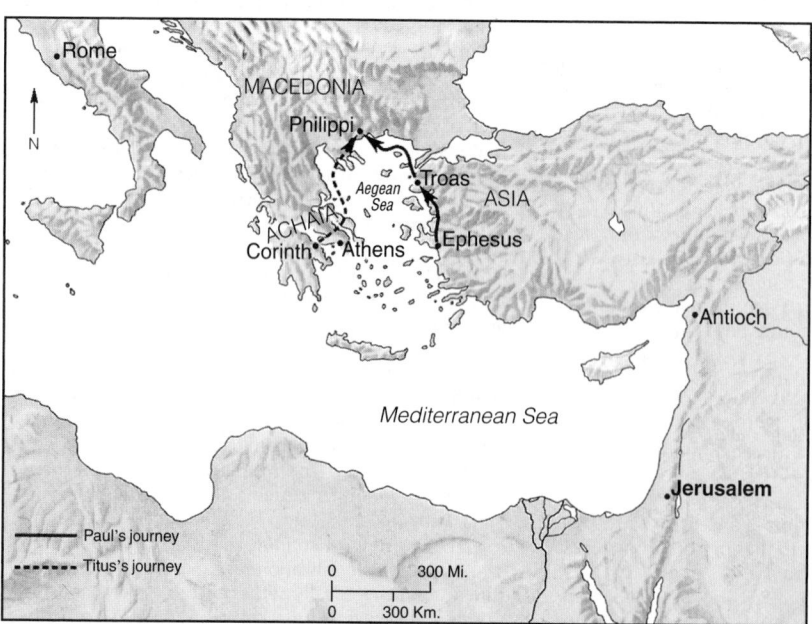

Paul Searches for Titus
Paul hoped to find Titus in Troas and receive news about the Corinthian church. Not finding him there, he went to Macedonia (most likely to Philippi), where he found Titus.

Rome

MACEDONIA

Philippi

N

Troas

Aegean
Sea

ASIA

ACHAIA

Corinth   Athens

Ephesus

Antioch

Mediterranean Sea

Jerusalem

———— Paul's journey

- - - - Titus's journey

0   300 Mi.

0   300 Km.

Assuming that Paul was released after his first Roman imprisonment, it appears that Titus accompanied him on a mission to the island of Crete. On departing from Crete, Paul left Titus behind to consolidate the new Christian movement there (Ti 1:5). The assignment was difficult, for the Cretans were unruly and the struggling church was already invaded by false teachers (vv 10-16). His handling of the Corinthian problem some years before, however, demonstrated that Titus possessed the spiritual earnestness, skillful diplomacy, and loving concern required to meet the present challenge, and Paul was confident that this new commission was therefore safe in his hands.

Paul's letter to Titus, one of his three Pastoral Letters, was written somewhat later to encourage Titus in his Cretan ministry. The letter closes with the apostle's request that Titus join him at Nicopolis, a town on the west coast of Greece, where he planned to spend the winter (Ti 3:12). Most likely it was from Nicopolis, or else later from Rome (where the apostle was imprisoned again and eventually martyred), that Paul sent Titus on the mission to Dalmatia, a Roman province in what is now Yugoslavia (see 2 Tm 4:10). If later tradition is correct, Titus returned to Crete, where he served as bishop until he was an old man.

See also Titus, Letter to.

2. Variant spelling of a gentile proselyte in Corinth, to whose house Paul went after the Jewish community in general rejected his message (Acts 18:7). Better manuscript evidence names him as Titius Justus. See Justus #2.

3. Vespasian's son; the emperor of Rome from AD 79–81. See Caesars, The.

TITUS, Letter to Paul's epistle to his coworker, Titus.

PREVIEW
•Author
•Recipient
•Date
•Purpose and Teaching
•Content

Author Though this letter begins with the name and greeting of Paul (Ti 1:1-3), Paul's authorship has been questioned by modern scholars on the grounds of its language and style, the church situation it presents, and the way that it sets forth Christian teaching. But Pauline authorship has been stoutly defended by eminent scholars and careful students who have argued that there is no reason for supposing that this epistle was written by someone else using Paul's name, after the apostle himself had died. The differences in this epistle and Paul's other letters are explained previously in the section on "Author" in the article "Timothy, First Letter to."

Recipient Titus appears to have been one of Paul's most trusted and valuable coworkers. Paul speaks of him (2 Cor 8:23) as "my partner and coworker." According to Titus 1:4, he owed his conversion to Paul. It is clear from Galatians 2:1-4 that he was a Gentile, as his was a test case whether gentile Christians should be compelled to be circumcised. At that time Titus was with Paul and Barnabas in Jerusalem. Much later, at the time of Paul's third missionary journey, he had two delicate missions to carry out for Paul in Corinth: the first pertained to the strained relationship between the apostle and the Corinthian Christians; the second related to the gentile collection for the Jerusalem church (2 Cor 2:12-13; 7:5-16; 8:1-24). If 2 Timothy 4:9-18 was written at the end of Paul's life, then Titus went to Dalmatia after the time of this letter.

Date To date this letter with precision is difficult. Titus was left by the apostle in Crete to continue his work (Ti 1:5). Paul was in Crete briefly on his voyage to Rome (Acts 27:7-13), but that could not have been the occasion referred to. In 3:12 Titus is called to come to Nicopolis (probably the Nicopolis in Epirus in Greece), as Paul had decided to winter there. Many have favored the view that after Paul's first imprisonment in Rome (Acts 28:16-31) he was released, carried out further ministry in various places (including Spain, Crete, and Greece), and then was arrested, imprisoned a second time, and finally put to death. Those who do not accept Pauline authorship of Titus, date this letter, like 1 and 2 Timothy, in the generation that followed Paul's death.

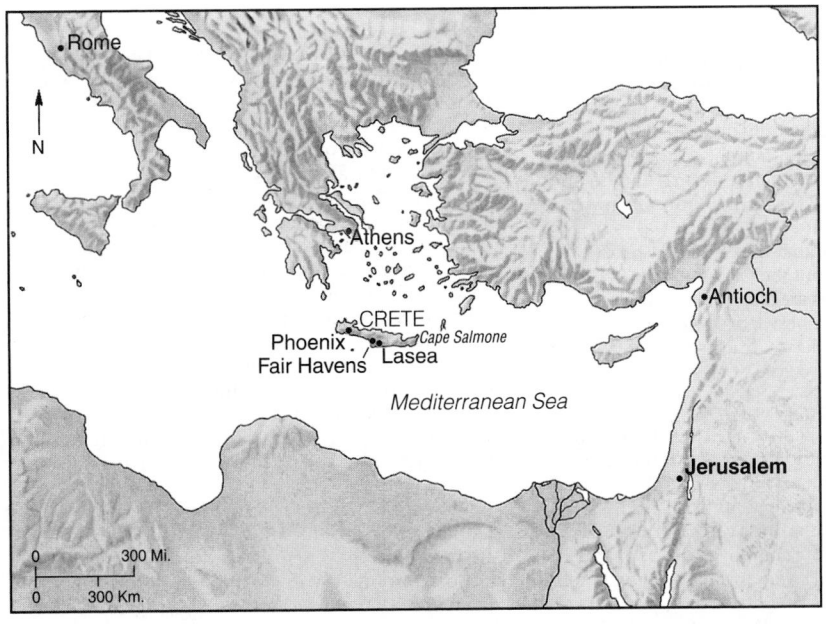

Titus Serves the Churches in Crete Tradition says that after Paul was released from prison in Rome (before his second and final Roman imprisonment), he and Titus traveled together for a while. They stopped in Crete, and when it was time for Paul to go, he left Titus behind to help the churches there.

Purpose and Teaching Although this letter is addressed to an individual colleague of the apostle, it has a minimum of personal references and exhortations. The growing and developing churches in Crete were Paul's main concern. They were being bothered by false teachings that appear to have had Jewish elements, ascetic emphases, and a great deal of speculative discussion (Ti 1:10, 14-15: 3:9). In short, it seems that they were dealing with an early Jewish form of Gnosticism. Its advocates promoted this teaching "for base gain" (1:11, RSV). Titus and those whom he would appoint as elders were called upon to refute the wrong teaching and to provide the believers with healthy teaching (v 9). Though this healthy teaching is not specified, it must have pertained to the saving grace of God in Christ, the renewing work of the Holy Spirit, and the future coming of the Lord Jesus (2:11-13; 3:4-7). In this letter there is constant emphasis on the lifestyle that bears out the truth of the gospel—with application to different groups in the Christian community: older men and women, young women, young men, and slaves.

Content

Salutation (1:1-4) Greetings come from Paul—whose apostleship is described as a stewardship of the gospel that promotes faith and strengthens the knowledge of the truth, hope of eternal life, and godliness of living—to Titus, spoken of as "my true son in our common faith."

Titus's Work in Crete (1:5-9) Titus was left behind in Crete to continue Paul's work and to appoint elders in every church (cf. Acts 14:23). These elders are also called bishops (cf. 20:17, 28)—that is, those with oversight of the church. The necessary qualities of life for these positions are described (cf. 1 Tm 3:2-7).

Dealing with False Teachings (1:10-16) The closing words of the previous section speak about the responsibility of elders "to encourage others with right teaching and show those who oppose it where they are wrong" (NLT). The opposers were upsetting people, indeed "whole families," by teaching what was not true. These false teachers were described by Paul in terms disparaging of Cretans, and as people whose lives do not demonstrate the knowledge of God that they professed to have.

Promoting Right Teaching (2:1-10) Titus had a particular responsibility to "promote the kind of living that reflects right teaching." He was charged to exhort the older men to exercise self-control (2:2), and he was supposed to teach the older women to live godly lives (v 3). In turn, these women were supposed to train the younger women to live pure and loving lives in their homes so that no one will malign the word of God (vv 4-5). Younger men were to show self-control (v 6), and Titus himself was to be an example in word and life so that the opponents would have nothing bad to say about the Christians (vv 7-8). Finally, in this section slaves are taught to submit to their masters, to give good and honest service with the motivation that "then they will make the teaching about God our Savior attractive in every way" (v 10, NLT).

God's Grace (2:11-15) What has been said leads now to a great statement of the purpose of the revelation of the grace of God in Jesus Christ: to bring salvation to all people, who will make a complete break with godless and sensual living so that they may live upright lives with the constant expectancy of the coming again of "our great God and Savior Jesus Christ." Their lives will show them to be a people who are God's very own, always eager to do what is right.

Doing What Is Good (3:1-8) In this section, Paul encourages Titus to tell the Christians at Crete that it is their duty to submit to rulers (cf. Rom 13:1-7; 1 Pt 2:13-17) and to be available in the community for honest work. Again, the quality of lifestyle is emphasized—in particular, courtesy and the desire for peace in relationships with others. This lifestyle comes from spiritual transformation. The means of that transformation is the saving work of Christ—not merited, but entirely of his mercy. He has brought cleansing from sin, "rebirth and renewal by the Holy Spirit."

Paul's Final Remarks and Greetings (3:9-15) In this final section, Paul encourages Titus to avoid those who like to debate about religion for the sake of debating. And he tells Titus how to deal with those who cause divisions.

Following this, Paul tells Titus that he will send him Artemas (not mentioned otherwise in the NT) or Tychicus. Then he encourages Titus to take care of Apollos and Zenas if they pass by Crete. Titus himself is supposed to come to Paul in Nicopolis before winter.

The epistle closes with a final exhortation to "good deeds" and to a spiritually fruitful life.

See also Paul, The Apostle; Timothy, First Letter to; Timothy, Second Letter to; Titus (Person) #1.

TIZ Village in which Joha lived (1 Chr 11:45).

TOAH Kohathite Levite and Samuel's ancestor (1 Chr 6:34).

TOB Place where Jephthah fled after his half brothers threw him out for being illegitimate (Jgs 11:3-5). During the reign of David, the Ammonites hired 12,000 men from Tob as mercenaries to fight against David (2 Sm 10:6-8). It is probably the same as the Aramite kingdom named Tob, which was located in the desert east or northeast of Gilead. During the Maccabean period, a Jewish colony was located in Tob.

TOB-ADONIJAH One of the Levites under Jehoshaphat who went out into the cities of Judah to teach the law (2 Chr 17:8).

TOBIAH

1. Forefather of a family of people who returned with Zerubbabel to Jerusalem following the exile. This family was not able to prove their Jewish descent (Ezr 2:60; Neh 7:62).
2. Ammonite who opposed Nehemiah when he arrived in Jerusalem about 445 BC. Tobiah was known as "the Ammonite official" (Neh 2:10, 19), a designation associated with a person of high office, such as a governor. He, together with Sanballat and Geshem, the other leading opponents of the reconstruction of the walls, were high-ranking officers in the Persian Empire. He was connected by marriage with the Jews in two ways. He married the daughter of Shecaniah, the son of Arah, and his son Jehohanan married the daughter of Meshullam son of Berekiah (6:18). These marriage relations to a prominent Jerusalem family gave him strong ties with the Jerusalem aristocracy (v 17).

Nehemiah had to face the threat posed by Tobiah and his influential allies. Nehemiah was charged with the intent of leading the Jerusalem population in a revolt against King Artaxerxes (Neh 2:19). As the work of rebuilding the wall progressed, Tobiah joined in the conspiracy of besieging Jerusalem (4:8). Nehemiah ordered the Jews to defend themselves. They continued their labors of repairing the wall with the protection of armed guards, and when the enemy forces came closer, every worker held a weapon in addition to his trowel (vv 17-19). They were encouraged by the belief that "our God will fight for us" (v 20). Tobiah also joined in the plot to assassinate Nehemiah after the walls were rebuilt (6:2-4). Nehemiah was further tested by libelous reports of insurrection and by a Jerusalemite hired by the allies to tempt Nehemiah into entering the temple proper and thereby discredit his standing among the faithful (vv 5-13).

After Nehemiah left Jerusalem in order to report to Artaxerxes, Tobiah succeeded in reestablishing himself with those who had remained faithful to him. The priest Eliashib was also related to Tobiah and gave in to Tobiah by preparing a large room previously used for offerings in the temple (Neh 13:4-5). Tobiah used these quarters when visiting Jerusalem. One of Nehemiah's first actions, upon his return, was to evict Tobiah from the temple (vv 8-9) and then restore the room for its proper use.

TOBIAS* The hero of the book of Tobit, who with divine aid marries his kinswoman Sarah, in spite of a jealous evil spirit, and restores his father Tobit's sight. *See* Tobit, Book of.

TOBIJAH

1. Levite sent by King Jehoshaphat to teach the law in the cities of Judah (2 Chr 17:8).
2. One of four men who returned from Babylon to Jerusalem with gold and silver used to make a crown for the high priest Joshua (NLT "Jeshua," Zec 6:10, 14).

TOBIT (Person) Primary character of the deuterocanonical book of Tobit. *See* Tobit, Book of.

TOBIT, Book of One of several deuterocanonical books of the Bible. It was received as canonical by the Council of Trent (1546) and is found in the Roman Catholic Bible, but it was never included in the Hebrew Old Testament and is placed with the Apocrypha by Protestants.

PREVIEW
•Author, Date
•Purpose
•Content
•Message

Author, Date The book, which may be described as a tale of pious fiction, was written by a devout Jew who was possibly a native of Palestine. A full-orbed monotheism is evident in the writer's conception of the transcendent deity who is referred to as "the God of our fathers" (Tb 8:5), as "our Lord and God, he is our Father for ever" (13:4), and as "the King of heaven" (vv 7, 11, 15).

The work has come down to us in three recensions of the Greek text, in two Latin versions, two Syriac versions, four Hebrew versions, and in Ethiopic. Hebrew and Aramaic fragments have been discovered at Qumran; from this some have argued for a Semitic original. There is no notice in the work of Maccabean history, which makes a date after that time most unlikely. A number of historical as well as geographical errors

militate against a date as early as the book purports to be from, and most scholars are inclined to date it around 200 BC or a little later.

Purpose Since the historical character of the work cannot be sustained, it is appropriate to ask what the writer's motivation and purpose might have been. He is apparently concerned to set forth the necessity of righteous conduct in view of the righteous character of God. Even when Tobit's fortunes took a turn for the worse, he continued to perform acts of charity to his fellow Jews and was especially concerned to bury those who had been the victims of the king's cruelty.

Content Tobit was a pious Israelite of the tribe of Naphtali living in Nineveh. Despite his good works and uprightness, he became blind when birds defecated in his eyes. Greatly afflicted, he asked God to let him die (Tb 1:1–3:6). On the very same day Sarah, Tobit's young relative who lived in Ecbatana, also prayed for death. She had been married seven times, and every one of her husbands was killed on their wedding night by Asmodeus, a jealous demon (3:7-15). And so the archangel Raphael was sent to help (vv 16-17). Tobit decided to send his son Tobias to the Median city of Rages (now Rai, near Teheran, Iran) to recover money left there with a friend. Raphael assumed a disguise and introduced himself as Tobit's kinsman Azariah (5:13). In this guise the angel went along as Tobias's guide. They were accompanied by Tobias's dog, Toby. Important things happened en route: Tobias caught a large fish; on the advice of Raphael, he kept its heart, liver, and gall for use as healing remedies (6:1-8); at Ecbatana, the angel arranged the marriage of Tobias and Sarah; in the wedding chamber Tobias used the fish's heart and liver to defeat Asmodeus (6:9–8:21). Raphael succeeded in recovering Tobit's money. Tobias, Sarah, Raphael, and the dog returned to Nineveh. There Tobias used the fish's gall to heal his father's eyes. Then, his mission accomplished, Raphael revealed his identity and disappeared. But Tobit was inspired by the archangel's final exhortation and so recited his own praises to God (ch 13). According to chapter 14, Tobit lived happily to the age of 112. Before his death, he predicted the destruction of Nineveh. Upon his father's advice, Tobias and Sarah returned to Ecbatana before this occurred.

Message Tobit gives us a good indication of the piety that characterized the Jews even prior to the period of the Maccabees. It is a beautiful portrayal of Jewish family life in postexilic times. The work was highly regarded by many of the church fathers. Luther spoke of it as "a truly beautiful, wholesome, and profitable fiction, the work of a gifted poet . . . a book useful and good for Christians to read."

In Tobit, the mercy of God is emphasized. His mercy is exalted, for "all his ways are mercy and truth" (3:2). He is a Father to his people (13:4). Although he afflicts them for their iniquities, he will show mercy (v 5). And though he scatters them among the nations, he will not hide his face from them (13:6; 14:5). Even the Gentiles will one day come to acknowledge him, for "many nations will come from afar to the name of the Lord God, bearing gifts in their hands, gifts for the king of heaven" (13:11). In its ethical teaching Tobit sets a high moral tone: honor and respect of parents (4:3-4); regard for God's commandments (v 5); the necessity of a disciplined life (v 14); and the exhortation "what you hate, do not do to anyone" (v 15). As a religious romance, it occupied a unique place in Jewish households, and its influence in the history of Christianity has also been evident.

TOGARMAH Third son of Gomer, a descendant of Japheth (Gn 10:3; 1 Chr 1:6). Beth-togarmah ("house of Togarmah") appears in Ezekiel's prophecy against the nations that opposed Israel (Ez 27:14; 38:6). Beth-togarmah was one of the principal trading partners of Tyre, providing war horses and mules. Since Togarmah is consistently linked with Javan, Tubal, Meshech, Dedan, and Tarshish, Ezekiel probably had the ethnographic lists of Genesis 10 in mind. As an ethnographic term, most have identified Togarmah with Armenia. The Armenians identify Togarmah (Thorgon) as the founder of their race.

TOHU Kohathite Levite and Samuel's ancestor (1 Sm 1:1).

TOI King of Hamath at the time David defeated the armies of Hadadezer (2 Sm 8:9-10; alternately called Tou in 1 Chr 18:9-10). He sent his son Joram to congratulate and give gifts to David.

TOKEN One of the villages settled by Simeon's tribe (1 Chr 4:32, KJV "Tochen"). The name does not appear in the parallel passage in Joshua 19, but in that list it does appear as Thokka in the Septuagint.

TOKHATH* Alternate form of Tikvah, the father-in-law of Huldah the prophetess, in 2 Chronicles 34:22 (see NLT mg). *See* Tikvah #1.

TOLA
1. One of the four sons of Issachar named among the 66 descendants of Jacob who accompanied him in the migration to Egypt to join Joseph (Gn 46:13); and the ancestor of the first of four families of the tribe of Issachar, as identified in the census of Israel undertaken by Moses and Eleazar (Nm 26:23). Tola's sons were Uzzi, Rephaiah, Jeriel, Jahmai, Ibsam, and Shemuel (1 Chr 7:2). The Israelite clan of the Tolaites took its name from him (Nm 26:23), and during the time of David the warriors of his family numbered 22,600 men (1 Chr 7:1-2).
2. One of the judges of Israel, the son of Puah and the grandson of Dodo (Jgs 10:1), of Issachar's tribe. Shamir, his home and burial place, was in the hill country of Ephraim. There he judged Israel for 23 years.
   Although he "delivered" Israel after the debacle of Abimelech's abortive attempt to establish a monarchy at Shechem, his accomplishment is covered in just two verses (Jgs 10:1-2). Like other "minor judges," mentioned only briefly (e.g., 12:8-15), he actually functioned in the judicial role—some more prominent "judges" (e.g., Gideon and Jephthah) were first, and perhaps solely, military heroes.
   See also Judges, Book of.

TOLAD Alternate form of Eltolad, a city in Simeon's territory, in 1 Chronicles 4:29. *See* Eltolad.

TOLAITE Descendant of Tola from Issachar's tribe (Nm 26:23). *See* Tola #1.

TOMB *See* Burial, Burial Customs.

TONGUES, Speaking in Supernatural manifestation of speech in a language not known to the speaker; the Greek term is *glossolalia*.
   Tongues-speaking was first manifested in the early church on the Day of Pentecost, when the Holy Spirit filled 120 Christians meeting together. They burst out in praise to God in a multitude of different languages. According to Acts 2:8-11, the audience of Jerusalem could understand them, since they were communicating the gospel in the hearers' own languages. (Verses 9-11 list about 16 nations whose representatives in Jerusalem hear the disciples speaking in their own language.) In subsequent occurrences, when a group of people were baptized in the Holy Spirit, the book of Acts indicates that they spoke in tongues (10:46; 19:6). But not all spoke in tongues when they received the Spirit (see 8:15-17), so it wasn't *the* unique sign for having received the Holy Spirit. The Scripture teaches that all believers are baptized by the Spirit as they become integrated into the body of Christ, the church (1 Cor 12:13). The genuine evidence of the work of the Holy Spirit is the "fruit of the Spirit" as defined in Galatians 5:22-23.

In the days of the early church, some Christians spoke in tongues and some didn't. According to Paul, speaking in tongues, when practiced in the church meetings, required interpretation. If no one could give an interpretation, it was to be practiced as a private devotional exercise, for one's own edification. As a means of private worship, the practice of glossolalia is tantamount to speaking to oneself and to God (1 Cor 14:28). However, under certain conditions formulated by Paul, glossolalia may become one of the spiritual gifts to be used in ministry to the church for the common good. In this case, the main concern is that the public use of glossolalia not be reduced to praying in tongues or speaking in tongues without interpretation.

In order to establish firmly the public practice of glossolalia as a ministry to the church and to prevent its abuse as a quest for personal fulfillment, Paul put forth a set of rules designed to control its corporate exercise (1 Cor 14:27-33):

1. A limit of one, two, or three persons is set for participation in tongues per worship session.
2. The one, two, or three tongues-speakers are to make their contribution in sequence, "one at a time" or "in turn," never simultaneously.
3. Before a worshiper decides to speak in tongues, he or she is to secure an interpreter. Should no such person be available, he or she is to refrain from speaking in tongues.
4. The person speaking in tongues should not be the one to provide the interpretation (1 Cor 12:10).
5. If there are too many believers speaking in tongues and not enough interpreters, the former should pray, instead, for the power to interpret (1 Cor 14:13).
6. When the contribution in tongues has been interpreted in intelligible language, it becomes a prophecy that needs to be evaluated by the recipients.
7. The genuineness of the experience is to be tested by those who have the ability to distinguish between spirits (1 Cor 12:10) so that they can test everything, hold fast to what is good, and abstain from every form of evil.

Persons participating in worship should be in control of their conduct at all times. They may not appeal to ecstatic states to excuse disorderly conduct or infractions to the rules of worship. Disorder and confusion are not inspired by God, since he is a God of peace and unity.

The gift of tongues is not to be desired or sought after. Only the "higher gifts" involving communication through directly intelligible speech are to be earnestly desired (1 Cor 12:31; 14:1, 5). However, should the gift of tongues be present, it should not be stifled, provided it can be used according to the rules and for the common good.

See Baptism of the Spirit; Spiritual Gifts.

TONGUES OF FIRE

Phrase occurring only in Acts 2:3, describing the visible manifestation of the Spirit. The tongues of fire seem to be the fulfillment of John the Baptist's proclamation that the Coming One would baptize with the Holy Spirit and fire (Mt 3:11; Lk 3:16). The disciples are described as filled with the Holy Spirit, thus fulfilling the OT promise reiterated by John the Baptist and Jesus of the baptism of the Spirit.

See also Pentecost.

TOPAZ *See* Stones, Precious.

TOPHEL

Place where Israel camped opposite the Jordan, "in the Arabah over against Suph, between Paran and Tophel" (Dt 1:1). Tophel has been identified with et-Tafileh, east of the Dead Sea. *See* Wilderness Wanderings.

TOPHETH

Location within the valley of Hinnom outside Jerusalem where Israel profaned the Lord by offering human sacrifices to Molech. As part of his religious reform, Josiah defiled Topheth and tore down its altars (2 Kgs 23:10). Josiah's reforms appear to have had only temporary impact, for the practice recurred under Manasseh (2 Chr 33:6) and was later condemned by Jeremiah (Jer 7:31-32). Jeremiah prophesied that the valley would be renamed the "Valley of Slaughter" because it would be the site where the Babylonians would rout Judah during their siege of Jerusalem. Jeremiah repeated the prophecy during his parable of the potter's flask, emphasizing the fact that Jerusalem would be destroyed so thoroughly that it would resemble Topheth (19:12). By this time, Topheth had evidently become a sort of city dump where broken pottery was thrown away and where burials that could not be accommodated in any of the city cemeteries would take place (v 11).

While Topheth is not mentioned in the NT, it is linked to Gehenna (Aramaic form of "valley of Hinnom"). Gehenna refers to the place of destruction and is typically translated "hell" in the NT (Mt 5:22, 29-30; 10:28; 18:9; Mk 9:43-47; Lk 12:5).

TORAH*

Word translated "law" in the OT, derived from the Hebrew verbal root *yarah*, which means "to throw" or "to shoot." The idea behind the word is to inform, instruct, direct, or guide. In Jewish tradition it is most frequently used to designate the text of the first five books of the Bible, also called the Pentateuch. Quite properly, however, the word has a wider meaning, acknowledged by OT usage, which embraces all directives that come from God. This is true in the NT as well where *torah*—represented by the Greek *nomos*—may refer to either the Mosaic legislation (Rom 7:14) or a broad behavioral principle (9:31).

For the Jew, the law includes what has been called the "oral Torah," that is, the sayings of the rabbis and venerated fathers of Judaism throughout the centuries. Such verbal tradition, while not part of the canonical books of the OT, seeks to interpret the texts of the Law to enable people to comply with the will of God. This method has often resulted in lessening the demands in the Law through reinterpreting them. Without temple worship, priesthood, or sacrifice—all prescribed by the Torah—such compromise with the Torah's demands became inevitable. These oral traditions were firmly entrenched at the time of Christ's advent and were held by many Jews to have been implicit in the Torah given to Moses (cf. Mk 7:3).

The Pharisees believed that the failure of the Jews to obey the Torah resulted in the great Babylonian captivity in the seventh century BC. Furthermore, it is commonly taught that until the Torah is rigorously subscribed to by all Jews, the Messiah will not appear upon the earth.

For the Sadducees, the Torah represented the only part of the OT that they accepted as authoritative. Their tendency, however, was to deemphasize the supernatural elements in the Pentateuch. Contrary to their viewpoint on resurrection, Jesus Christ quoted from the Torah to affirm eternal life (cf. Mt 22:31-32).

From the most ancient days, the reading of the Torah in the synagogue has been accompanied by great ceremony. To be called upon to read from these sacred scrolls is a high honor. It is written in Hebrew by a highly skilled craftsman known as a *sofer*, or scribe. The Torah is found in the form of a roll, the scroll for which is of parchment taken from the skin of ceremonially clean animals. The rods around which the Torah is rolled are usually of wood, silver, or ivory. Ornately designed ends of the rods are magnificent aesthetic creations frequently wrought in precious metals and stones. A person reading from the scroll uses a delicate pointer, called a *yad*, to follow the words. Use of the pointer safeguards the scroll, which would soon be damaged by the constant running of fingers over the fine manuscript. Moreover, the *yad* minimizes the possibility for error in oral recitation by preventing the reader from losing his place and possibly skipping some words of God's sacred revelation.

Among Jewish orthodoxy it is maintained that inasmuch as the Torah was the gift of God to Israel, the gentile nations are not required to submit to its regulations. However, Maimonides, the medieval Jewish scholar, taught that Gentiles would have a share in the world to come by obeying the covenant God made with Noah. Seven commands are commonly linked to that agreement, namely, the abstaining from idolatry, incest, shedding of blood, profaning the name of God, injustice, robbery, and eating the flesh of live animals.

The new covenant maintains that the Torah, while a necessary stage in the outworking of redemption, was never given to enable individuals to receive salvation on the basis of obeying the law. Although Leviticus 18:5 appears to hold out the possibility of working for righteousness, flawless obedience to God's will is beyond the reach of fallen humanity. The OT clearly bore witness to the role of grace in redemption by revealing the great patriarch Abraham to be justified by faith (Gn 15). Since that covenant preceded the Torah by four centuries, it presents an unalterable witness to the way in which God receives sinful people. A primary function of the law is to reveal people's fallen spiritual condition and thereby serve as a tutor leading them to Christ (Gal 3:24). As a sinner is exposed to the demands of the law, he or she is convicted of great sinfulness (Rom 7:7) and consequently seeks the grace of God in Christ. It is clear that Jesus Christ held the Torah in high regard, the purpose of his ministry being the fulfillment of its contents. That great work of satisfying the demands of the law is reckoned in the lives of all who entrust themselves to Christ; he is the end of the law so that everyone who has faith in him may be justified (Rom 10:4).

See also Judaism; Law, Biblical Concept of; Talmud.

TORTOISE* *See* Animals (Lizard).

TOU*

Alternate form of Toi, the king of Hamath, in 1 Chronicles 18:9-10 (see NLT mg). *See* Toi.

TOWER *See* Fort, Fortification; Watchtower.

TOWER OF BABEL *See* Babel.

TOWER OF SHECHEM *See* Shechem, Tower of.

TOWER OF SILOAM *See* Siloam, Tower of.

TOWER OF THE FURNACES* KJV translation for "Tower of the Ovens," a tower in Jerusalem, in Nehemiah 3:11. *See* Ovens, Tower of the.

TOWER OF THE HUNDRED *See* Hundred, Tower of the.

TOWN CLERK* An official in municipal administration whose duties included those of scribe or secretary. He published the decrees of the civic authority but also acted as a liaison officer between the administration of a city and the Roman provincial government. In Ephesus he was held responsible for the riotous assembly in Paul's day (Acts 19:35) and had the power to impose a severe penalty. Fortunately, he was able to calm the assembly.

TRACHONITIS*, TRACONITIS One of the five Roman provinces east of the Jordan River, along with Batanea, Gaulanitis, Auranitis, and Iturea. The region of Traconitis (apparently including Gaulanitis, Batanea, and Auranitis) was part of the tetrarchy of Philip, the brother of Herod (Lk 3:1). Traconitis was an extremely desolate region northeast of the Sea of Galilee. Its name in Aramaic was Argob, which signified that the region was a "heap of stones." Other than the reference in Luke, Traconitis is seldom mentioned in historical references. Josephus suggests that it was colonized by Uz, the son of Aram (cf. Gn 10:23). The Romans gained control of the region when Augustus deposed Zenodorus, a local robber-chieftain. Herod the Great was deeded the land on the condition that he control the local bandits. Philip received the land at the death of his father but apparently retained only nominal control over the region. The region is currently named el-Lejah and is located in southern Syria and northern Jordan.

TRADE ROUTES *See* Travel.

TRADITION Respect for tradition was particularly strong among Jews during the period at the beginning of the Christian era. Among these traditions, the most important collection was *Pirke Aboth* (Traditions of the Fathers). This consisted of comments by famous rabbis in explanation of the written Law. This and a growing collection of other rabbinic traditions interpreting the Law became an authoritative commentary on the written code. This collection was esteemed to be equal to the written Law.

The Pharisees used the expression "tradition of the elders" when speaking to Jesus about hand washing (Mt 15:2; Mk 7:5). In his response, Jesus referred to the "traditions of men," thus drawing attention to their human origin. In fact, in Mark 7:8, he definitely set the commandment of God over these traditions, which had become a burden to the people. Jesus strongly criticized the scribes and Pharisees for the way these traditions were enforced (Mt 23). He noted that adherence to the tradition had become more important than the moral and personal effect of the teaching.

See Judaism; Law, Biblical Concept of; Pharisees; Talmud; Tradition, Oral.

TRADITION*, Oral Oral tradition is both sharply distinguished from written tradition and yet closely con-

nected with it. Many literary traditions are based on oral traditions, making it necessary to investigate how transitions were made from one to the other.

In the ancient Near East, all significant events were committed to writing by the scribes. At the same time, an oral version of the occurrences would enable the information to be disseminated in contemporary society, and perhaps also to subsequent generations. It is important to realize the coexistence of written and oral forms of the same material, so that the way in which material was transmitted will be understood properly.

Oral transmission was very important in Judaism, and one of the strongest characteristics of rabbinic theology is the importance attached to the oral law in addition to the written Law. This oral law consisted of traditional interpretations that had been handed down from teacher to pupil. In the course of the passing on of the tradition, further explanations of basic principles were added. Rabbinic literature supplies many indications of the careful methods that were used in the schools for the study of the Law. The teacher's main aim was to ensure that the disciples accurately memorized the content of the teaching. There is no doubt that in rabbinic Judaism the passing on of the oral tradition had developed into a highly organized technique.

Such care is not surprising in view of the fact that the oral law carried equal weight with the written Law. It was essential that the transmission of this tradition should not be left to chance. Authorized oral tradition was an essential feature of Jewish life. There is little doubt that in the earliest period the words and works of Jesus were passed on by word of mouth. Whether Jesus himself followed the rabbinic teaching method is doubtful, but as much care went into preserving his teachings as the rabbis used in preserving their oral law.

See also Judaism; Pharisees; Talmud; Tradition.

TRANSFIGURATION* Event in Jesus' earthly ministry described in four passages in the NT (Mt 17:1-8; Mk 9:2-8; Lk 9:28-36; 2 Pt 1:16-18), wherein Jesus was glorified in the presence of three disciples: James, Peter, and John.

The Location of the Event The exact site where the Transfiguration took place is not given in the NT. Matthew 17:1 and Mark 9:2 simply state that it took place on a "high mountain." Various suggestions have been made as to which mountain, with the traditional site being Mt Tabor, a round hill located in the plain of Esdraelon approximately 10 miles (16.1 kilometers) southwest of the Sea of Galilee. There are, however, two major problems with this suggested location. For one, it is difficult to see how Mt Tabor can justifiably be called a "high mountain," for it is less than 2,000 feet (609.6 meters) above sea level. Second, in the time of Jesus a Roman garrison was stationed on Mt Tabor, and thus it would be unlikely that Jesus would have walked with his disciples up this mountain. A second suggestion for the site is Mt Carmel, which is located on the coast, but this seems off the main route of Jesus' travel after the events of Caesarea Philippi. A third suggestion is Mt Hermon, which is over 9,000 feet (2,743.2 meters) high and lies about 12 miles (19.3 kilometers) to the northeast of Caesarea Philippi. Mt Hermon is indeed a high mountain and has the additional advantage of being located near Caesarea Philippi.

The Event Six days after the events of Caesarea Philippi, Jesus took Peter, James, and John to be alone with him on a high mountain. As on several other instances, these three disciples alone accompanied Jesus (cf. also Mk

5:35-43; 14:32-42). According to the Gospel accounts, three things took place at the Transfiguration:

1. "He was transfigured." The various accounts all witness to an unusual transformation of Jesus. Jesus is transfigured: "his face shone like the sun, and his garments became white as light" (Mt 17:2). This transformation is described in Matthew and Mark by the Greek verb *metamorpheo*, the root for the word "metamorphosis." This indicates that a tremendous change occurred.

2. Moses and Elijah appeared and spoke to Jesus. These men, who undoubtedly represent the Law and the Prophets, are said to have spoken to Jesus of his "exodus," or departure (Lk 9:31). The term used in Luke 9:31 to describe Jesus' "exodus" (or death) is rather unusual and clearly portrays the death of Jesus not as a tragedy or defeat but as a victorious journey.

3. After Peter's remark that it was good for the three disciples to be present and witness this, and after his suggestion that they build three booths, a voice came from heaven saying, "This is my beloved Son; listen to him" (Mk 9:7). These words were clearly a rebuke for Peter having placed Jesus on the same level as Moses and Elijah. To make three booths (one for Moses, one for Elijah, and one for Jesus) loses sight of who Jesus is, and the voice from heaven pointed out Peter's error. The rebuke also must be understood in light of what Peter had said a few days earlier at Caesarea Philippi. Had Peter forgotten that he had just said to Jesus, "You are the Christ, the Son of the living God"?

The Meaning of the Event In order to understand the significance of the Transfiguration, it is important to contrast the heavenly voice at Jesus' transfiguration with the heavenly voice at Jesus' baptism. At the baptism both Mark 1:11 and Luke 3:22 indicate that the voice was addressed to Jesus: "You are my beloved Son." At the Transfiguration, however, the voice is not addressed to Jesus but to Peter, James, and John: "This is my beloved Son" (Mk 9:7). Clearly the events of the Transfiguration are primarily directed toward the disciples rather than Jesus. "He was transfigured before them" (v 2); "there appeared to them Elijah with Moses" (v 4); "a cloud overshadowed them . . . 'listen to him' " (v 7); "they no longer saw any one with them but Jesus only" (v 8). Evidently from these references, the incident is not meant so much for Jesus' sake as for the disciples'. Following closely after the events of Caesarea Philippi, God appeared to affirm at the Transfiguration what Peter had previously confessed at Caesarea Philippi: Jesus is indeed the Christ, the Son of God.

In 2 Peter 1:16-18 the writer recounts that he was an eyewitness of the Transfiguration. John seems to have done the same thing when he wrote the prologue to his Gospel and said, "We have beheld his glory" (Jn 1:14). At the Transfiguration the true form (Greek *morphe*) of the Son of God temporarily broke through the veil of his humanity and the disciples saw his preexistent glory. In this transformation of Jesus, the three disciples witnessed something of Jesus' preincarnate glory, as well as his future glory, which he received at his resurrection and which all will see when he returns to judge the world.

When Christ returns in his glory, all the believers will be transfigured and thereby receive a glorious, resurrected body. Thus, Christ's transfiguration is the preview of every believer's transfiguration (see 1 Cor 15:42-45; Phil 3:20-21; Col 3:4).

See also Jesus Christ, Life and Teachings of.

TRANSFORMATION An inward renewal and reshaping of the mind through which a Christian's inner person is changed into the likeness of Christ. Paul told the Roman believers, "Be transformed by the renewing of your minds" (Rom 12:2). As one's Christian life progresses, the person should gradually notice that his or her thought life is being changed from Christlessness to Christlikeness. Transformation does not happen overnight—regeneration is instantaneous, but transformation is not. Christians are transformed to Christ's image gradually as they spend time beholding him in intimate fellowship. Eventually, they will begin to mirror the one they behold. Paul said, "We all with unveiled face, mirroring the glory of the Lord, are being transformed into the same image, from one degree of glory to another, even as from the Lord who is the Spirit" (2 Cor 3:18—from the Greek). This does not come from conscious imitation but from spiritual communion with the Lord. The result will be beyond our expectations. The apostle John said it well: "We can't even imagine what we will be like when Christ returns. But we do know that when he comes we will be like him, for we will see him as he really is" (1 Jn 3:2, NLT).

TRANSGRESSION* *See* Sin.

TRANSJORDAN* Territory on the east side of the Jordan River. Although this name does not appear in the Bible, numerous events took place there in biblical history. Today the area is roughly equivalent to the kingdom of Jordan. In biblical times the area would have comprised Bashan, Gilead, Ammon, Moab, Edom, and the desert regions farther east. In the OT the expression "beyond the Jordan" is often used for the area (Gn 50:10-11; Dt 3:20; 4:47; Jos 9:10; 13:8; 18:7; Jgs 5:17), although the same expression is used occasionally for the area west of Jordan (Dt 3:25). In NT times, this area was known as Perea. *See* Perea.

TRAVEL In biblical times travelers found roads bad and often impassable. Sea voyages were made in comparatively small ships, usually by military and commercial personnel, and hardly ever for simple tourist traffic. With little reason to travel, ordinary citizens tended to remain in fairly limited areas. From time to time, there were group migrations, and sometimes people traveled for religious festivals or fled from war or famine.

The Appian Way

Travel in Old Testament Times Several accounts depict the people of Israel moving over restricted areas to graze their flocks. Joseph's brothers took their flocks from the south of the land up to Shechem and then to Dothan (Gn 37:12-17), but this was a mere 60 miles (96.5 kilometers). David traveled around Palestine and even went to Moab (1 Sm 22:3). The Danites moved from their home southwest of Jerusalem to the north, just south of the Lebanon Mountains (Jgs 18).

Examples of travel for pasturage, migration, and protection could be multiplied. Such travelers would normally walk, though the ass was used both for riding and as a pack animal. The ox was employed for transporting heavy loads and sometimes for people (Gn 46:5). Later the camel came into general use (1 Kgs 10:2; 2 Kgs 8:9). Little is known of resting places for travelers in OT times. There are only a few references to a "lodging place" (*malon*) in OT narratives (Gn 42:27; 43:21; Ex 4:24).

Travel in New Testament Times The Roman world knew a great deal of travel: to fulfill religious obligations at festival time, for trade, for government administration, for military purposes. Not the least among first-century travelers were the early Christian missionaries.

The advent of Roman peace and authority and the construction of well-made stone roads made travel relatively safe and quick. The modes of travel improved over that known in OT times. Long distances were traveled within the Roman Empire over good roads and in comparative safety. There were some hazards, however, notably in sea travel, from wind, storms, and pirates (Acts 15:39; 18:18-22; Rom 15:24-25; 2 Cor 11:25-26). Paul's sea journey to Rome, for example, was perilous (Acts 27:1–28:14).

The NT mentions a number of journeys on foot. Mary journeyed from Galilee to Judea to visit Elizabeth (Lk 1:39-40, 56). The baby Jesus was born in Bethlehem during the census (2:1-7); Jesus was brought to Jerusalem to comply with the Jewish purification law (v 22). Thus three trips were made from Nazareth to Jerusalem, a distance of about 70 miles (112.6 kilometers), from the time of Jesus' conception to Mary's purification. The annual Passover visit was made by Joseph and Mary (vv 41-51). Other journeys are mentioned (Jn 2:13; 5:1; 7:1-10; 12:1). Jesus himself walked to Jericho from Galilee (Mk 1:1-11) and also to the region of Tyre and Sidon (7:24). He was in Samaria more than once (Lk 17:11; Jn 4:4). His last journey to Jerusalem was via Jericho and up through the hills to Jerusalem (Mk 10:1, 46; 11:1). His last journey after the resurrection was to Emmaus (Lk 24:13-35).

Paul traveled by sea on each of his missionary journeys (Acts 13:1-14; 15:41–18:22; 18:23–21:17), generally accompanied by friends. He also made many journeys on foot in Palestine, Asia Minor, and the Greek peninsula. But not all travel was on foot in NT times. The ass, used for carrying loads, often carried people. Jesus once rode from Bethphage to Jerusalem, a short but highly symbolic journey (Mt 21:2-7; Mk 11:1-11; Jn 12:12-15). When Joseph traveled with his pregnant wife, Mary, to Bethlehem for the census at the time of Jesus' birth, Mary probably rode on an ass. The Ethiopian eunuch was riding in a chariot after worshiping at Jerusalem and was joined by Philip traveling on foot (Acts 8:26-38). Roman soldiers both marched and made wide use of horses. When Paul was brought to Caesarea from Jerusalem, mounts were prepared for him (23:23-24).

Roads and Sea Lanes The roads of biblical times figured prominently in the geography, topography, and history of Palestine—a land that served as a bridge between Egypt and centers of civilization and trade in the Middle East. Many of the roads were strategically important, both commercially and militarily. Some roads gained significance as pilgrim routes to facilitate travel to religious centers like Jerusalem. Roads in biblical times were of three main types: long-distance international roads, medium-distance intraregional roads, and a variety of roads inside each region or state.

Great International Roads These linked the Mediterranean coast to the northern Tigris Valley and southern Mesopotamia. Some linked Mesopotamia to Asia Minor, while others led south to Egypt, either along the coast or east of the Jordan River and the Dead Sea and across the Sinai Peninsula. There were trade routes between Anatolia and Assyria early in the second millennium BC. Apparently the military campaign referred to in Genesis 14 aimed to secure the great trade route, the King's Highway, from northern Mesopotamia to Egypt. Military invaders and travelers from Babylonia, Assyria, and Persia would head across the hinterlands of Syria toward the coast before turning south into Palestine and Egypt. The advent of European powers, Greece and Rome, into the Middle East opened up another vast network of international roads for the peoples of the East. Until Roman times, these roads were not surfaced with stone but were cleared pathways. They were very rough, ungraded, and in wet weather, impassable in many places. But they were evidently well defined by "waymarks" and "guideposts" (Jer 31:21). With the coming of the Romans, important roads were built with deep foundations and with large blocks of flat stone at the surface. The remains of these roads are still seen in many places in the Middle East and in Europe. Distance markers or milestones were regularly placed along the roads.

International North-South Roads in Palestine The roads that linked countries to the north with Egypt passed through Palestine, a natural land bridge. There were three major roads. The coastal road began in Damascus and passed via Hazor across the plain of Esdraelon, through the Megiddo Pass, down the coast past Gaza and into Egypt. This was probably "the way of the sea" (Is 9:1). The Sinai road led from Egypt into the southern Negev and then to Kadesh-barnea, Beersheba, Hebron, Jerusalem, Shechem, Acco, Tyre, and Sidon. The Red Sea road entered the Palestine area from the Gulf of Aqaba, where the ancient port of Elath and Solomon's port of Ezion-geber stood (Nm 33:35; 2 Chr 8:17). From there it led through the mountainous areas of Transjordan, crossing the deep wadis and then north through the Hauran region to Damascus. This was the road taken by caravans from southern Arabia to Damascus, the ancient King's Highway (Nm 20:17; 21:22).

There were other north-south roads of lesser importance. One coastal road led from Joppa via Caesarea and Dor to Acco, where it linked with the Sinai road. Evidently it was not very significant until Roman times, when the port of Caesarea was built. The marshes in the plain of Sharon posed many problems. The plain of Esdraelon was also marshy and interrupted the roads north in bad seasons. A raised road across the swampy sections was eventually constructed. Another road led north from Hazor, branching off the main trunk road to Damascus. The Jordan Valley road skirted the southwestern part of Galilee and led down the Jordan Valley to Jericho.

East-West Roads Several important roads ran east-west, intersecting the larger roads leading north. One such road led from Gaza to Beersheba and then down the Arabah, with an offshoot to Petra. Another led from Ashkelon, via Gath, to Hebron and on to En-gedi on the Dead Sea. Another road led from Joppa east up the valley of Aijalon (Jos 10:6-14) to Bethel and on to Jericho. One well-used road led from Joppa to Shechem, across the Jordan at Adam (3:16) and into Gilead in Transjordan. Other roads led from Acco eastward to Galilee and also up the coast to Tyre and Sidon. There were, indeed, numerous east-west roads that provided contact between various parts of Palestine. In Roman times, when the speedy movement of armies was essential, some of the old roads were greatly improved and new ones built.

Sea Lanes The people of Israel, unlike the Phoenicians, seldom used the sea lanes. When Solomon planned to send ships down the Red Sea to Ophir (1 Kgs 9:26-28), he used Phoenician seamen. Jehoshaphat planned a similar expedition, but his ships were wrecked (22:48-49). Coastal traffic in OT times was in the hands of Philistines and Phoenicians. There were several ports along the Mediterranean Sea coast, such as Gaza, Joppa, Dor, and Acco, but none was very good. There were also sea lanes linking the Mediterranean coast with Egypt and distant Tarshish (probably Spain). The other coastal water was the Gulf of Aqaba with its two ports— Ezion-geber for Transjordan, and Elath for west of the Jordan. Solomon's fleet used Ezion-geber as its home port.

Ancient Ship of the Largest Size

In NT times things changed considerably. The Middle East produced commodities used by peoples farther west, especially the Romans. Alexandria in Egypt and Antioch in Syria handled both cargo and travelers. Smaller ports like those in Palestine and many others around the coast of Asia Minor provided a haven for ships. One ingenious scheme to avoid a 200-mile (321.8-kilometer) journey around the Greek peninsula was to drag small boats across the five-mile- (8-kilometer) wide isthmus at Corinth. Even the largest ship in NT times was in danger from wind and storm at sea (Acts 27), so sea travel was undertaken preferably when the risk of storms was minimal, roughly from November to March. There was a lot of sea traffic in the Mediterranean Sea at appropriate seasons, largely for trade. Grain ships crossed regularly from Rome to Egypt and to the east.

Ships were driven by sail power supplemented as necessary by oars operated by slaves. Some indication of the size of ships comes from the discovery of ancient wrecks and from Latin and Greek literature. An old dry dock 130 feet (39.6 meters) long found near Athens was once used for Greek war vessels, which were smaller than the cargo vessels. The Roman writer Lucian refers to an Alexandrian grain ship 180 feet (54.9 meters) long, suggesting a capacity of about 1,200 tons (1,088.6 metric tons). Paul's ship carried 276 persons (Acts 27:37). Modern underwater archaeology is providing valuable information about these ancient ships.

Reasons for Travel The most important reason for travel in NT times was for trade and commerce, which involved far more than merely transporting goods. There were agents, supervisors, insurers of cargo, bankers, and a whole range of people involved in the acquisition and safe delivery of the cargo.

Military travel was considerable. A wide variety of tasks had to be undertaken in the way of reconnaissance, procuring of supplies, forward arrangements for the bivouacking of troops, and the transport of both troops and equipment.

Some travelers were tradespeople changing their place of employment, like Aquila and Priscilla (Acts 18:2-3). Aquila had traveled from Pontus on the Black Sea to Rome and then, in a time of persecution, he had fled to Corinth with his wife. Many others traveled for similar reasons.

People on religious pilgrimage traveled by land or sea. Jews from many lands journeyed to Jerusalem for the annual Passover festivities (cf. Acts 2:5-11). Non-Jews went to religious centers at Ephesus, Athens, and Eleusis, where there were important temples. Many minor temples also attracted pilgrims. The construction of new temples and a variety of government administration buildings brought craftsmen from afar. Often the materials used in construction had to be transported to the site. Some people made trips for health reasons to temples famed for healing miracles or to enjoy the benefits of hot springs like those at Capernaum or Tiberias. Athletes traveled to centers for important contests like the Olympic games, and crowds of people flocked to witness the spectacle. Some travelers were students or teachers going to great centers of learning—the universities of those times. Yet others traveled as official emissaries bearing important government and commercial documents. Despite all this activity, vast numbers of ordinary citizens hardly ever traveled more than a few miles from their homes.

TREASURER An officer in charge of financial matters. In OT times he had charge of the royal or sacred treasures, which consisted of goods, documents, money, and jewels. He was steward of the king's possessions and overseer of the treasury. David appointed Azmaveth over the king's treasuries, Jonathan over the treasuries in cities and villages (1 Chr 27:25), and Ahijah over the temple treasuries (26:20). Solomon's temple treasury was in the care of Jehiel (29:7-8). In Isaiah's day there was a treasurer for the household named Shebna (Is 22:15). An inscription found near Jerusalem may record his name.

Treasurers held positions in other lands too. King Cyrus of Persia entrusted his temple treasures to Mithredath (Ezr 1:8). Artaxerxes ordered the treasurers of the province "beyond the river" to supply funds to Ezra the priest (7:21-22). Nehemiah appointed treasurers over storehouses to distribute goods (Neh 12:44; 13:13).

In the NT, two treasurers are known. The Ethiopian eunuch was in charge of the treasury of Candace, queen of Ethiopia (Acts 8:27), and Erastus was the city treasurer of Corinth (Rom 16:23). An inscription left at Corinth by Erastus, a Roman treasurer, may be his.

See also Money; Banker, Banking.

TREE *See* Plants.

TREE OF KNOWLEDGE OF GOOD AND EVIL
Forbidden tree in Eden, whose fruit imparted knowledge and subsequent death, i.e., separation from God and ultimate expiration (Gn 2:9, 15-17; 3:1-24). The tempting serpent promised Eve equality with God if she ate the fruit. The result of Eve and Adam eating from this tree was that they indeed attained the "knowledge of good and evil." According to the usage of the phrasing "knowing good and evil" in the rest of the Bible (Dt 1:39; Is 7:15-16; Heb 5:14), the idea is that it describes a stage in a child's life when he or she passes from innocence to moral awareness.

Accompanying this knowledge is sexual self-awareness. Thus, when Adam and Eve partook of the fruit, they became aware of their own sexuality. At the same time, they were able to see as God saw and thereby thought that God would shame them for their nakedness. The story came to symbolize the loss of innocence and divine companionship through deliberate disobedience in an attempt to attain godhood.

The sad result of eating the fruit of the tree of the knowledge of good and evil was that Adam and Eve lost their innocence and were subsequently separated from God. Banishment from Eden followed to prevent the eating of fruit from a second tree, "the tree of life," which would have made them immortal. But they would have been immortal in their fallen, sinful state. Thus, it was a blessing to banish them.

See also Adam (Person); Eve; Garden of Eden; Fall of Man; Tree of Life.

TREE OF LIFE Tree placed by God in the midst of the Garden of Eden (Gn 2:8-9), a tree whose fruit could give eternal life. God told Adam that he could eat from every tree of the Garden except the tree of the knowledge of good and evil (vv 16-17). When Adam and Eve disobeyed God by eating from the tree of the knowledge of good and evil, they were expelled from the garden lest they "take also of the tree of life, and eat, and live for ever" (3:22).

The Genesis narrative suggests that God intended the tree of life to provide Adam and Eve with a symbol of life in fellowship with and dependence on him. Human life, as distinguished from that of the animals, is much more than merely biological; it is also spiritual—it finds its deepest fulfillment in fellowship with God. Life in the fullness of its physical and spiritual dimensions, however, could remain a person's possession only so long as he or she remained obedient to God's command (Gn 2:17). Apart from Genesis, the only other OT occurrences of the phrase the "tree of life" are found in Proverbs (quoted here from RSV), where it symbolizes the enrichment of life in various ways. In Proverbs 3:18 wisdom is referred to as "a tree of life to those who lay hold of her"; in 11:30 "the fruit of the righteous is a tree of life"; in 13:12 a fulfilled desire is as "a tree of life"; and in 15:4 "a gentle tongue is a tree of life."

The book of Revelation contains the only references to the tree of life in the NT (Rv 2:7; 22:2, 14, 19). The Bible begins and ends with a Paradise in the midst of which is a tree of life. The way to the tree of life, which was closed in Genesis 3, is open again for God's believing people. This was made possible by the second Adam, Jesus Christ. Those who have washed their robes in the blood of Christ (cf. Rv 7:14) and have sought forgiveness of their sin through the redemptive work of Christ, receive the right to the tree of life (22:14), but the disobedient will have no access to it.

See also Adam (Person); Eve; Fall of Man; Garden of Eden; Tree of Knowledge of Good and Evil.

TRESPASS* *See* Sin.

TRESPASS OFFERING* *See* Offerings and Sacrifices.

TRIBES, Territories of the *See* Conquest and Allotment of the Land.

TRIBULATION An experience of suffering, distress, affliction, trouble, or persecution. The Greek word appears in the NT about 45 times. There is a Hebrew equivalent that appears in four or five OT passages, never in the prophetic books. Therefore, it is appropriate to focus mainly on the NT for a definition of tribulation.

The NT contains a few references where the word "tribulation" is used to denote the hardships that occur in the lives of common people. The labor pains of a woman in childbirth (Jn 16:21), the worldly concerns that arise in marriage (1 Cor 7:28), and the affliction of widows (Jas 1:27) are all called tribulation. In a more general way, a scourge like the famine that afflicted Egypt and Canaan during the patriarchal age is characterized as "great tribulation" (Acts 7:11).

In a more narrow sense, the word "tribulation" refers to a specific Christian experience. The teachings of Christ provide basic definitions for this meaning of "tribulation." He said that whenever the gospel is present in the world, tribulation becomes its unavoidable corollary. As the word of the gospel is sown, tribulation and persecution appear spontaneously (Mt 13:21).

This concept of the ineluctable presence of tribulation during the church age is carefully developed in Jesus' teaching on future events in the Olivet discourse (Mt 24–25; Mk 13; Lk 21). This discourse provides the only explicit description of, and clear chronological reference available in the Bible to, the tribulation of his followers. In it, Jesus predicted the time of the beginning, the extent, and the end of tribulation. This teaching on the tribulation was handed down to the 12 disciples privately, as a matter directly relevant to their lives (Mt 24:3). Jesus told the Twelve that they would be delivered up to tribulation and that this tribulation would take the form of persecution to the death for his name's sake (v 9). The context of this teaching indicates that the tribulation taught by Jesus would affect Christians in many places throughout history. But the fact that Jesus predicted to the 12 disciples that they would fall victim to the tribulation, at the very beginning of the sufferings (v 8), provides a clear reference to the starting point of the tribulation during the disciples' lifetimes.

Likewise, the same group of disciples were to be witnesses of the "great tribulation" that would befall Jerusalem as predicted by the prophet Daniel (Mt 24:15-21). It is clear that, in the Olivet discourse, Jesus was referring to the destruction of Jerusalem in AD 70. The fall of Jerusalem at the hands of the Roman legions was to be viewed as an archetypal representation of the perennial tribulation. This is attested to by Matthew's parenthetical editorial comment in 24:15 ("let the reader understand"), intended to alert his original readers to the fulfillment of Jesus' prediction within their lifetimes. Moreover, the parallel section in Luke 21:20-24 makes it clear that the desolation of Jewish Jerusalem would be followed by a long period of gentile domination, which is precisely what happened after AD 70.

The NT forewarns believers of the inevitability of tribulation; it also prescribes the appropriate response of Christians. They should rejoice because tribulation produces perseverance and strength of character (Rom 5:3-4). They should bear it patiently (12:12), knowing that God comforts the faithful in all tribulations (2 Cor 1:4) and that the present tribulation prepares believers for incomparable glory in eternity (2 Cor 4:17).

Except for rare and exceptional circumstances that enable Christians to enjoy affluence and freedom, most believers throughout history have suffered tribulation. The normal vocation of the church has been to endure as a beleaguered and persecuted minority in a hostile world. For Christians providentially protected from tribulation, it is easy to relegate tribulation to a future period in history. For Christians suffering in the throes of opposition, however, the tribulation is an ever-present reality. The virulence and the severity of the tribulation may vary from time to time and from place to place, yet

Christ's promise remains true, "In the world you have tribulation; but be of good cheer, I have overcome the world" (Jn 16:33, RSV). *See* Suffering; Eschatology; Persecution.

TRIBUNE* Roman military official who served as the commander of a cohort (1,000 men). In NT usage it designated the commander of the Roman garrison in Jerusalem (e.g., Acts 21:31; 22:24; 23:10; 24:22). Paul was placed under the tribune's protection after his arrest in Jerusalem (21:33).

TRIBUTARY*, TRIBUTE *See* Tax, Taxation.

TRICHOTOMY* The threefold division of human nature into body, soul, and spirit (1 Thes 5:23). *See* Man.

TRIGON* Triangular-shaped harp mentioned in Daniel 3:5-15. *See* Musical Instruments (Sabcha).

TRINITY* Term designating the three members of the triune God: the Father, Son, and Holy Spirit.

The word "Trinity" does not appear in the Bible; it was created by scholars to describe the three members of the Godhead. Throughout the Bible, God is presented as being Father, Son, and Spirit—not three "gods" but three personas of the one and only God (see, e.g., Mt 28:19; 1 Cor 16:23-24; 2 Cor 13:13). The Scriptures present the Father as the source of creation, the giver of life, and God of all the universe (see Jn 5:26; 1 Cor 8:6; Eph 3:14-15). The Son is depicted as the image of the invisible God, the exact representation of his being and nature, and the Messiah-Redeemer (see Phil 2:5-6; Col 1:14-16; Heb 1:1-3). The Spirit is God in action, God reaching people—influencing them, regenerating them, infilling them, and guiding them (see Jn 14:26; 15:26; Gal 4:6; Eph 2:18). All three are a tri-unity, inhabiting one another and working together to accomplish the divine design in the universe (see Jn 16:13-15).

See also God, Names of (Father); Son of God; Spirit.

TRIUMPHAL ENTRY* A term that denotes Jesus Christ's entry into Jerusalem, where the multitudes welcomed him and hailed him as Son of David, King of the Jews. Ironically, this event occurred just a few days prior to his betrayal, arrest, trial, and crucifixion.

See also Jesus Christ (The Final Days in Jerusalem).

TROAS City in Turkey on the Aegean shore, 10 miles (16.1 kilometers) south of the ancient site of Troy, scene of the Trojan War immortalized by the poet Homer. Both the ancient city of Troy and the Roman city of Troas are on the Troad Plain, an area about 10 miles (16.1 kilometers) in length bordering the sea. Paul sailed from Troas into Macedonia in response to the call "Come over to Macedonia and help us" (Acts 16:9).

The Seleucid king Antigonus founded the city about 300 BC and named it after himself. Later, the name was changed to Alexandria Troas in honor of Alexander the Great, who had passed through it in pursuit of the Persians. The city became a Roman colony when Roman influence replaced that of the Greeks. According to some scholars, Julius Caesar envisioned Troas as his eastern capital, and Constantine considered making it his capital before deciding on Byzantium instead. It was an important seaport during the time of Paul because it was the easiest and shortest route from Asia to Europe.

On the second missionary journey, Paul and Silas came to Troas after being forbidden to preach the Word of God in Asia (Acts 16:6). Although this trip to Europe is not stressed in Acts, many scholars think this short voyage was as important historically as Caesar's invasion of Britain. After this vision, Paul and Silas embarked, passed the island of Samothrace, and landed at Neapolis (modern Kavalla), their first stop in Europe (v 11).

We know that a church must have been established in Troas because of events that are described later. After his mission in Ephesus was finished, Paul stayed and preached the gospel in Troas (2 Cor 2:12). On his way to Jerusalem for the last time, Paul stopped in Troas, where he preached until after midnight, causing one of the young men to fall asleep and fall from a window to his death. But Paul called him back to life and continued on with the meeting until morning (Acts 20:6-12). Paul visited Troas again and left behind a cloak and parchments, presumably when he was arrested there. In a letter to Timothy, Paul asks him to bring these to him at his prison in Rome (2 Tm 4:13).

TROGYLLIUM* Rocky straits between Samos and Miletus. In Acts 20:15, some manuscripts indicate that Paul's ship stopped at this place on his trip to Jerusalem near the end of his third missionary journey. Since Trogyllium is a promontory jutting out into the sea between Samos and Miletus, it is not unlikely for the sailing vessel to have landed there for the evening. However, most textual critics consider the phrase "after remaining at Trogyllium" (see Textus Receptus and KJV) to be a later insertion into the text.

TROPHIMUS One of the Asians who accompanied Paul on his final trip to Jerusalem (Acts 20:4). Because the Jews had seen Trophimus the Ephesian with Paul in Jerusalem, they incorrectly assumed that he had accompanied Paul into the temple (21:29). Since Trophimus was not a Jew, his alleged act of profaning the temple served as the pretense for Paul's arrest and subsequent imprisonment. Trophimus was traveling with Paul as one of the representatives of the Asian church who had been selected to superintend the collection for the Jerusalem church. Trophimus was probably one of the two brothers who accompanied Titus in the delivery of 2 Corinthians to Corinth (2 Cor 8:16-24). According to 2 Timothy 4:20, Trophimus had been accompanying Paul (prior to his final imprisonment) but then stayed behind in Miletus due to illness. Legend suggests that Trophimus was ultimately beheaded by the order of Nero.

TRUMPET *See* Musical Instruments (Hatzotzrot).

TRUMPETS, Festival of Day of solemn rest and remembrance of God's provision for his people through the Sinai covenant (Lv 23:23-25). *See* Feasts and Festivals of Israel.

Remains of Ancient Troas

TRUTH That which is real and verifiable by experience.

In Scripture, truth is a very important concept because God is the God of all truth (Pss 31:5; 108:4; 146:6), who speaks and judges truly (57:3; 96:13). He is the real source and cause of the whole universe. Scripture also focuses on the revealed truth in the gospel of God's redeeming grace through Christ. This is the truth Christ and the apostles proclaimed (Jn 8:44-46; 18:37; Rom 9:1; 2 Cor 4:2), which was foreshadowed in the OT (1 Pt 1:10-12), and witnessed to by the Holy Spirit (Jn 16:13). The OT teaching was never false, but it was shadowy and incomplete in comparison with the revealed truth of the NT. So Christ brought spiritual reality (Jn 1:17), and the Holy Spirit leads believers into the experience of all that is real in Christ (16:13).

Christ is the truth because, being God, his words carry divine authority. They are truth and life (Jn 6:63). In addition, the life of Christ epitomized truthfulness and utter reliability. When people live in obedience to the truth, they themselves are true and reliable. Scripture calls upon people to "do the truth" (Jn 3:21, KJV). Those who have experienced God's reality in Christ know, by experience, that Christ is the way, the truth, and the life (Jn 14:6).

TRYPHAENA*, TRYPHENA Christian woman of Rome. Along with Tryphosa, Paul called her one of the "Lord's workers" (Rom 16:12). They may have been sisters or codeaconesses.

TRYPHOSA Christian woman of Rome. Along with Tryphena, Paul called her one of the "Lord's workers" (Rom 16:12). They may have been sisters or codeaconesses.

TUBAL Fifth of the listed sons of Japheth in the table of nations (Gn 10:2; 1 Chr 1:5). Tubal later gained significance in the prophetic writings of Isaiah and Ezekiel as one of the nations that would be judged for threatening God's people (Is 66:19; Ez 27:13; 32:26; 38:2-3; 39:1). Tubal is typically mentioned with Javan and Meshech as either nations of the north or nations of the coastlands (Is 66:19; Ez 38:2). The fact that Tubal traded with Tyre (Ez 27:13) supports the premise that Tubal was located in a coastland region. Beyond this sketchy evidence, it is difficult to determine Tubal's precise ethnic identification or location. It has been identified with the Scythians, the Iberians, the region between the Black and the Caspian Seas, Thessaly, and various Hittite tribes.

TUBAL-CAIN Son of Lamech by his wife Zillah (Gn 4:22). He was "a forger of all instruments of bronze and iron." Though the text does not claim that he was the first or the "father" of all ironworkers, many scholars think that the text originally paralleled verses 20 and 21 to imply that he was the first.

TULIP* *See* Plants.

TUMBLEWEED* KJV rendering of "whirling dust" in Psalm 83:13 and Isaiah 17:13. *See* Plants.

TUMOR Abnormal swelling or growth in any part of the body. The only significant occurrence of this term is in 1 Samuel 5-6. After the Philistines captured the ark of God from Israel, a painful lethal disease afflicted the population of the Philistine city that kept the ark. Since the disease was associated with the presence of rats (1 Sm 6:4-5), the entire episode is consistent with the disease known as bubonic plague. In bubonic plague, the fleas of the rat are able to transmit to humans the pathologic bacteria *Yersinia pestis*. The bacteria invade the human body, causing fever and buboes, which are large soft swellings in the armpit and groin. Without treatment, the mortality rate is 60 to 90 percent. The Philistines sent the ark of God back to Israel with handcrafted golden images of rodents and tumors (vv 11, 17-18).

See also Medicine and Medical Practice.

TUNIC *See* Clothing.

TURTLEDOVE *See* Birds (Pigeon).

TWELVE, The Designation for the 12 apostles in 1 Corinthians 15:5 and other verses. *See* Apostle, Apostleship.

TWIN BROTHERS* Twin sons of Zeus. Paul sailed to Rome on a ship whose figurehead was the Twin Brothers (Acts 28:11). *See* Dioscuri.

TYCHICUS One of the believers who accompanied Paul in his trip to collect and deliver the offering for the Jerusalem church (Acts 20:4). Since he is often mentioned with Trophimus of Ephesus, Tychicus was likely also a native of that city. He served as the courier for Paul's letter to Ephesus (Eph 6:21) as well as Paul's letters to Philemon and the Colossians (Col 4:7). Most believe that he was also one of the two Christians (with Trophimus) who accompanied Titus in the delivery of 2 Corinthians (2 Cor 8:16-24). Paul mentioned Tychicus twice in his later letters, first sending him to Crete to be with Titus (Ti 3:12), and later mentioning to Timothy that he had sent Tychicus to Ephesus (2 Tm 4:12). Evidently, Tychicus and Paul were close friends as well as coworkers, since Paul frequently referred to Tychicus as a "beloved brother."

TYPE The English word "type" is derived from the Greek *tupos*, which has the basic meaning of "a visible impression or mark made by a blow or by pressure." In the Greek NT, the word occurs 16 times, with various meanings. A type is formed as a copy, print, or a form cast in a mold. In Acts 7:43 it is applied to "figures" of idols or false gods. A type can be a pattern according to which something is made (e.g., the tabernacle, Acts 7:44; Heb 8:5). It is an example or model, whether of evil to be avoided (1 Cor 10:6-11) or of good to be emulated (Phil 3:17; 2 Thes 3:9; 1 Tm 4:12; Ti 2:7; 1 Pt 5:3). It is like a form for pouring concrete, which determines both the shape and content of what is made.

A type is also an entity found in the OT that prefigures one found in the NT. The initial one is called the "type" and the fulfillment is designated the "antetype." Either type or antetype may be a person, thing, or event, but often the type is messianic and frequently refers to salvation.

A type can be distinguished from a symbol in that a symbol is a timeless sign. It can refer to past, present, or future, while a type always foreshadows that which is to come.

Some examples help to identify some biblical types and antetypes. The serpent lifted up on a pole in the wilderness to give healing to the Israelites was a type of Jesus being lifted up on a cross to give salvation to the world (Jn 3:14; cf. Nm 21:9). The Passover lamb (Ex 12:1-13) is a type of Christ (1 Cor 5:7). The rock from which Israel drank in the wilderness (Ex 17:6) prefigures

Christ (1 Cor 10:3-4). In Romans 5:14 Adam is called "a type of the one who was to come," that is, of Christ.

The book of Hebrews is full of examples of types that represent the Messiah. All of the sacrifices ordained by the ritual law that God gave at Sinai typify some aspect of the person and work of Jesus. The blood that was sprinkled on the altar spoke of the blood of the one who was slain once for all (Heb 9:12-22).

TYRANNUS, Hall of Place in Ephesus where Paul taught daily for two years (Acts 19:9). Paul's ministry in Ephesus had begun at the synagogue, where he had preached for three months. Finding increasing opposition there, Paul rented the Hall of Tyrannus (NASB "school of Tyrannus"), where he began a ministry to both Jews and Greeks (v 10).

In Greek, the term "hall" literally means "leisure" or "rest." It eventually became associated with the kind of activity carried on during times of leisure, that is, lectures, debates, and discussion. Finally, the term came to mean the place where these leisure activities occurred.

Virtually nothing is known about Tyrannus himself. Some scholars have suggested that he was a Greek rhetorician, sympathetic to Paul's preaching. This suggestion is made plausible by an addition in the Western text that states that Paul taught in the hall "from the fifth hour until the tenth," that is, from 11 AM until 4 PM (NRSV mg). This would mean that Paul used the hall only during afternoon rest periods, for in all Ionian cities, work ceased at 11 AM and did not resume until late afternoon because of the intense heat. Possibly these rest periods made the hall available for Paul's use, and Tyrannus himself lectured there before and after these hours.

TYRE Ancient Phoenician city-state located on the Mediterranean coast 20 miles (32.2 kilometers) south of Sidon and 23 miles (37 kilometers) north of Acre. Tyre consisted of two major parts: an older port city on the mainland and an island city a half mile (.8 kilometer) from the coast where the majority of the population lived. According to Herodotus, Tyre was founded around 2700 BC. Its earliest historical attestations, however, are references in a 15th-century Ugaritic document and an Egyptian citation from the same period. Tyre first appears in the Bible in the list of cities that comprised Asher's inheritance (Jos 19:29). At that time, it was described as a "strong city" and was evidently never conquered by the Israelites (2 Sm 24:7). Tyre was most significant as a mercantile center, with maritime contacts throughout the Mediterranean region and overland traffic with Mesopotamia and Arabia.

During David's and Solomon's monarchies, Tyre was a strong commercial ally of Israel. Both David and Solomon contracted with Hiram of Tyre for timber, building materials, and skilled laborers, for which they provided Tyre with agriculture produce (2 Sm 5:11; 1 Kgs 5:1-11; 1 Chr 14:1; 2 Chr 2:3-16). After the division of the kingdom, Tyre evidently maintained friendly relations with Israel for some time. Ahab's wife, Jezebel, was the daughter of "Ethbaal, king of the Sidonians," a king who is known elsewhere as Ithobal of Tyre (1 Kgs 16:31; cf. Menander). At some point, however, the pressure of Assyrian and Babylonian aggression dissolved the alliance, so that by the time of Samaria's fall, Tyre and Israel were no longer aligned and shortly thereafter became enemies.

During the later kingdom period, Tyre was the focus for some of the strongest prophetic denunciations recorded in Scripture (Is 23:1-18; Jer 25:22; 27:1-11; Ez 26:1-19; Jl 3:4-8; Am 1:9-10). Tyre's condemnation was justified for several reasons. Because of its commercial significance, Tyre was the focal point of Assyrian and Egyptian rivalries. Tyre managed, however, to play these rivals against each other while building its wealth and exploiting its neighbors. Additionally, the city of Tyre was not only a city of unscrupulous merchants but also a center of religious idolatry and sexual immorality. Foremost among Tyre's sins was pride induced by its great wealth and strategic location. Ezekiel's prophecy against Tyre offers a detailed picture of the city, its commercial empire, its sin, and its eventual demise (Ez 26:1-28; 29:18-20). The final destruction of Tyre did not come for almost 1,900 years (AD 1291), though it was besieged by Nebuchadnezzar for 13 years (587–574 BC), and conquered by Alexander the Great in 332 BC after a seven-month siege, during which he built a causeway out to the island. Ezekiel's description of Tyre's arrogance can be compared to that of Satan's, with Tyre's words "I am a God, I sit in the seat of God" (KJV) being the expression that led to the fall of both Satan and Tyre (Ez 28:2).

Despite Alexander's destruction of the city, Tyre had regained prominence by the NT period, being equal to or greater than Jerusalem in terms of population and commercial power. Jesus visited the region surrounding Tyre during his early ministry, healing the Syrophoenician woman's daughter (Mt 15:21-28; Mk 7:24-31). Jesus also compared the Galilean towns that had rejected him to Tyre and Sidon, suggesting that the Galileans would bear greater responsibility for their rejection because of the number of miracles he had performed among them (Lk 10:13-14).

U

UCAL* Disciple of Agur, the wise man whose sayings are recorded in the book of Proverbs (Prv 30:1; see NLT mg). The meaning of the passage is obscure. Many have suggested that the names Ithiel and Ucal are not proper nouns but should be translated, "I am weary and worn out, O God."

UEL Bani's descendant and a priest who was encouraged by Ezra to divorce his foreign wife during the postexilic era (Ezr 10:34).

UGARIT* City in northwest Syria during the second millennium BC. Though the city is not mentioned in the Bible, it is a significant archaeological site that illuminates OT language and history. Ugarit was located just east of the Mediterranean coast, approximately 175 miles (281.6 kilometers) north of Tyre.

Being known previously only from the Amarna letters, the ruins of Ugarit were discovered accidentally by a peasant farmer in 1928. The resulting discoveries were among the most important in the 20th century. Since Ugarit was a political and cultural center, its scribes created and transcribed documents in a wide variety of Near Eastern languages, including a language closely related to Hebrew that was written in an alphabetic cuneiform script. The discovery and subsequent deciphering of "Ugaritic" has influenced biblical studies both linguistically and culturally. Ugaritic has illuminated some otherwise obscure Hebrew passages and given greater attestation to others. For instance, the terms used to describe each of the various sacrificial offerings are very similar in Hebrew and Ugaritic, though the sacrificial systems themselves vary quite dramatically. Hebrew and Ugaritic poetry are quite similar stylistically, thus assisting in the understanding of Hebrew verse and also increasing the appreciation of its ancient heritage. Books like Job that often have been dated late by biblical critics exhibit significant Ugaritic parallels in style, vocabulary, and occasionally in literary allusion as well.

Perhaps the most significant contribution derived from the study of Ugaritic texts and cultural artifacts is the improved understanding of Canaanite culture and religion. The Ugaritic texts provide justification for the strongly negative assessment of Canaanite culture given in the Bible. Three principal religious epics have been discovered in the Ugaritic corpus, written in honor of Keret, Aqhat, and Baal, respectively. The Baal epic describes the way in which Baal becomes lord of the earth after battling Yam, the god of the sea. The epics further reveal a great deal about Canaanite religious ritual, reinforcing biblical contentions concerning the sexual permissiveness and degradation of the society. The strong biblical injunctions against the worship of Baal and the Asherahs and the command to utterly destroy the Canaanites are more easily understood in the context of the Ugaritic religious epics.

Finally, the Ugaritic texts potentially illuminate some historical questions relating to the OT. For instance, when Hezekiah was sick with a boil, he was instructed by Isaiah to treat it with a poultice of figs (2 Kgs 20:7; Is 38:21). This procedure is attested to in a Ugaritic text that prescribes it as a treatment for boils that infected horses.

See also Inscriptions.

ULAI River near the Persian capital city of Susa where Daniel received a vision concerning the end times (Dn 8:2-16). It is likely the same as the Eulaeus, which is described by both Greek and Roman geographers as a stream that flowed to the west of the citadel of Susa.

ULAM

1. Clan in Manasseh's tribe (1 Chr 7:16-17).
2. Eshek's firstborn son and a mighty warrior in Benjamin's tribe (1 Chr 8:39-40).

ULCER* *See* Sore.

ULLA Family in Asher's tribe (1 Chr 7:39).

UMMAH One of the villages inherited by Asher's tribe after the conquest of Canaan (Jos 19:30). Neither the location of Ummah nor the accompanying villages (Aphek and Rehob) are known.

UNCIRCUMCISION* Natural condition of the male, that is, with the foreskin covering his penis. Since the Jews, among many other peoples, surgically removed this as a sign of their covenant with God (Gn 17:9-14; Ex 12:48; Lv 12:3), the term came to designate "non-Jew" or "Gentile" (Philistines, Greeks, and Romans did not circumcise, but Egyptians and many Semitic peoples did). By extension, it connoted "those outside the covenant."

The term "uncircumcision" occurs 20 times in the NT, most of the time meaning simply "Gentile," as opposed to Jew. Paul argues strongly against making such distinctions. For Paul, the attitude of one's heart toward God is much more important than ritual law, which has nothing to do with his salvation (Rom 2:25-27). Abraham became a believer and was justified by God while he was uncircumcised, so circumcision has nothing to do with his salvation (3:30; 4:9-12). Formerly, Gentiles were excluded from the people of God (Eph 2:11-12), but now Jewish and gentile believers have become one in Christ (Gal 2:7; 5:6; 6:15; Col 3:11). Paul refuses to give way to those demanding circumcision for full church membership.

In one passage (Col 2:8-15), Paul speaks of uncircumcision metaphorically, meaning a person's unregenerate state. Here uncircumcision is equivalent to "the flesh" (meaning one's evil impulse or natural state). As literal flesh is cut away in the rite of circumcision, so this "flesh" is cut away by Christ at the time of conversion, as symbolized in baptism. The baptized person is one purified from "uncleanness" as a circumcised Gentile is purified from previous uncircumcised uncleanness.

See also Circumcision.

UNCLEAN, UNCLEANNESS *See* Cleanness and Uncleanness, Regulations Concerning.

UNFORGIVABLE SIN* *See* Unpardonable Sin, The.

UNICORN* KJV rendering for an animal called a "wild ox" in the NLT and most modern translations (Nm 24:8; Dt 33:17). Unicorn is an unfortunate translation (following the Septuagint) because the animal had two horns, not one. *See* Animals (Wild Ox).

UNLEAVENED BREAD Bread made without leaven (yeast). In ancient times, bread makers used a piece of dough remaining from a former baking process, a piece that had fermented and developed a certain acid content—the yeast that caused bread to rise.

Bread used at the Jewish Passover and most other religious observances was, by the command of God, unleavened (Ex 12:15-20; 23:15). Only under certain conditions were the people permitted to use leavened bread for spiritual purposes (Lv 7:13; 23:17). This was largely owing to the fact that leaven generally symbolized evil; fermentation implied decay and corruption.

With the exception of Jesus' teaching on the kingdom of God (Mt 13:33), the NT also speaks of leaven with a negative connotation. Jesus warned of the leaven of the Pharisees and Sadducees (16:6); Paul exhorted believers to guard against that tiny bit of yeast—unhealthy values—that can work through a whole batch of dough (1 Cor 5:6-8).

See also Bread; Food and Food Preparation; Leaven.

UNLEAVENED BREAD, Festival of *See* Feasts and Festivals of Israel.

UNNI
1. One of the musicians appointed by the chief of the Levites to sing and play the harp as part of the temple service during David's reign (1 Chr 15:18-20).
2. KJV spelling of Unno in Nehemiah 12:9. *See* Unno.

UNNO* One of the Levites who participated in the temple service during the postexilic era (Neh 12:9).

UNPARDONABLE SIN*, The Attributing to Satan what is actually the work of the Holy Spirit as demonstrated through Jesus Christ. This sin is blasphemy against the Holy Spirit.

The unpardonable sin must be defined by its context, which is found in Matthew 12:31-32 and Mark 3:28-30. In these passages, Jesus had just cast a demon from a man who was blind and mute. Incontrovertible evidence of the power of God had just occurred. But the Pharisees, with stubborn unbelief, credited this display of God's power to Beelzebul, the devil (Mt 12:24). Several Scriptures reveal that many Jews had expressed the same kind of fallacious opinion, namely, that Jesus was performing miracles by the power of the devil (Mt 9:34; 11:18; Lk 7:33; 11:14-20; Jn 7:20; 8:48, 52; 10:20). A group of Jews, mostly Pharisees, were guilty of attributing to the devil what was the work of the Spirit demonstrated through the Lord Jesus. They committed *the* unpardonable sin when they said that Jesus' actions, performed by the power of the Holy Spirit, originated from Beelzebul, the devil. Put simply, they sinned grievously by boldly characterizing Jesus' work as coming from the devil. Interestingly, many Jews perpetuated this false characterization about Jesus long after his death. They did not deny that he did miracles; they said he did miracles by the power of the devil.

What Isn't the Unpardonable Sin The unpardonable sin is not Israel's rebellion against God, even though this rebellion resulted in the eternal judgment of thousands and a temporary elimination of God's blessing. The "sin unto death" mentioned by John (1 Jn 5:16-17) is not the unpardonable sin. It would be impossible for a person who has redemption and the forgiveness of sin (Eph 1:7), cleansing for present and future sin (1 Jn 1:7), and eternal life (Jn 3:16) to commit an unpardonable sin. But those who commit the "sin unto death" are all Christians. First John 5:16 says the person who commits the "sin unto death" is a "brother" in Christ.

The unpardonable sin is not rejection of the Lord Jesus, until the rejecter dies in his unbelief. Such a sin will not be forgiven throughout eternity, but it is not the same sin as that which Jesus condemned with these words: "Anyone who blasphemes against me, the Son of Man, can be forgiven, but blasphemy against the Holy Spirit will never be forgiven, either in this world or in the world to come" (Mt 12:32, NLT). Numerous passages repeat the warning that unbelief in the Savior results in eternal death (Jn 3:18, 36; 1 Jn 5:12; Rv 20:15; 21:8), but these Scriptures do not directly speak of the unpardonable sin. Jesus asserted that a person could be an unbeliever in him, even to the degree of speaking against him, yet not be guilty of the unpardonable sin.

See also Justification, Justified; Sin unto Death.

UPHARSIN* Aramaic word interpreted as "divided" in Daniel 5:25 (KJV). *See* Mene, Mene, Tekel, Parsin.

UPHAZ Region well known for its gold (Jer 10:9; Dn 10:5). Some contend that Uphaz is a scribal error for Ophir (only one consonant is different), another region famous for its fine gold.

See also Ophir (Place).

UPPER GATE One of the gates leading to the temple mount in Jerusalem. It was built by Jotham (2 Kgs 15:35; 2 Chr 27:3) and served as the principal access between the royal palace and the temple area (2 Chr 23:20; Ez 9:2).

UPPER ROOM Second-story room of a Hebrew or a Greek house; often like a tower, built on the flat roof of a Hebrew home for privacy, for comfort during the hot season, or for the entertainment of guests. In some instances it could accommodate large gatherings of people. In at least one instance, the room was on the third story (Acts 20:8). Eutychus, sitting in the window, went to sleep and fell three stories to the street below (vv 9-10). It may have been a similar type of accident that caused Ahaziah's fatal injury when he fell through the latticework of his upper room (2 Kgs 1:2).

Elijah took the dead son of the widow of Zarephath to an upper room where he had been staying and raised him from the dead (1 Kgs 17:19-23). David went to an upper room for privacy to mourn the death of Absalom (2 Sm 18:33). The kings of Judah built strange altars near the upper room of Ahaz, which Josiah pulled down as part of his reform program (2 Kgs 23:12).

Jesus ate the Passover supper in an upper room with his disciples (Mk 14:15; Lk 22:12). The size of some of these rooms is evident from the fact that, after Jesus had left and ascended to heaven, the disciples went to the upper room where they all had been staying before. The congregation attending the meeting in Troas was not a small one either (Acts 20:8). Dorcas was laid in an upper room after she had died; later, Peter was taken up to the same room to pray for her restoration to life (Acts 9:36-41).

See also Architecture; Homes and Dwellings.

UR (Person) Father of Eliphal, one of David's mighty men (1 Chr 11:35); probably the same as Ahasbai in the parallel passage (2 Sm 23:34).

UR (Place) Hometown of Terah, the father of Abraham, and the birthplace of Abraham and Sarah. It is mentioned by name only four times in the Bible (Gn 11:28, 31; 15:7; Neh 9:7), always with the full name "Ur of the Chaldeans."

The modern site is known as Tell el Muqayyar, "The Mound of Bitumen." The results of archaeological investigations demonstrate that Abraham came from a great city, cultured, sophisticated, and powerful. The landscape was dominated by the ziggurat, or temple tower, and the life of the city was controlled by a religion with a multiplicity of gods. The chief deity was Nannar, or Sin, the moon god, who was also worshiped at Haran. Near his ziggurat was a temple dedicated to his consort, the moon goddess, Ningal.

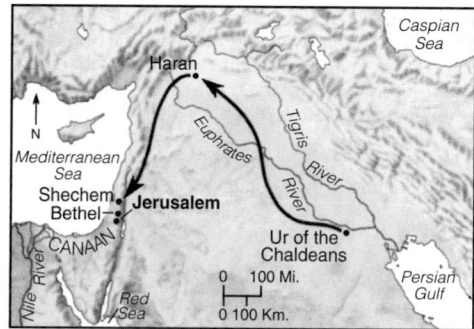

Ur of the Chaldeans

Many clay tablets found at Ur tell of the business life of the city, which focused on the temples and their income. There were factories here, such as the weaving establishment for the manufacture of woolen cloth. Some tablets dealt with religion, history, law, and education. Students were instructed in reading and writing in cuneiform script. They were taught multiplication and division, and some were even able to extract square roots and cube roots.

Domestic architecture was highly developed. Houses had two stories and many rooms (10 to 20), sometimes with a private chapel. Small clay religious figures (teraphim or household idols) were discovered. Many art objects made of precious metals and other costly materials have been excavated, especially in the royal tombs. These tombs also contained the remains of a number of retainers who must have been put to death at the time of the royal burials in order to accompany their masters in the afterlife.

URBANUS Believer greeted as one of Paul's coworkers in Christ (Rom 16:9).

URI
1. Father of Bezalel from Judah's tribe, and a builder of the tabernacle (Ex 31:2; 35:30; 38:22; 1 Chr 2:20; 2 Chr 1:5).
2. Father of Geber, one of Solomon's officers in Gilead (1 Kgs 4:19).
3. One of the temple gatekeepers who put away his foreign wife at Ezra's request (Ezr 10:24).

URIAH
1. Hittite who joined the people of Israel, became a leader in David's army, and was listed among the king's mighty men (2 Sm 23:39; 1 Chr 11:41). Uriah's wife was Bathsheba, with whom David committed adultery while Uriah was fighting the Ammonites. Upon learning that she was pregnant, David summoned Uriah to Jerusalem, hoping that Uriah would sleep with his wife and consider himself the child's father. However, Uriah slept in the servants' quarters because he was unwilling to enjoy the comforts of home while his companions were at war. The second night David again tried to entice him to sleep with his wife. Even after falling into a drunken stupor, Uriah still could not be persuaded to go home; instead, he spent the night at the palace. To deepen the intrigue, David sent Uriah back to the battle, ordering him positioned at a vulnerable place, where he was killed (2 Sm 11; Mt 1:6).

See also David; Genealogy of Jesus Christ.
2. Priest who built an altar at Jerusalem in imitation of an Assyrian model at King Ahaz of Judah's request (2 Kgs 16:10-16).
3. Priest who was the father of Meremoth. Meremoth weighed the silver, gold, and vessels for the temple (Ezr 8:33) and built portions of the Jerusalem wall during the days of Nehemiah (Neh 3:4, 21).
4. One of the men who stood to Ezra's right when Ezra read the law to the people (Neh 8:4). He is perhaps the same man as #3 above.
5. Priest whom Isaiah took as a witness (Is 8:2). He is perhaps the same man as #2 above.
6. Prophet and Shemaiah's son from Kiriath-jearim. Uriah enraged King Jehoiakim by prophesying against Judah and Jerusalem. Fearing for his life, Uriah fled to Egypt but was eventually abducted and brought back to King Jehoiakim, who subsequently put him to death (Jer 26:20-23).

URIAS* KJV spelling (in Matthew 1:6) of Uriah, Bathsheba's husband, whom David had killed. See Uriah #1.

URIEL
1. Levite of the Kohathite branch who is listed as the son of Tahath and the father of Uzziah (1 Chr 6:24).
2. Levite who officiated over the moving of the ark from the house of Obed-edom to Jerusalem (1 Chr 15:5-11). He was a Kohathite clan chief in charge of 120 men who participated in the ceremony, and he was personally sanctified for the purpose of carrying the ark.
3. Grandfather of King Abijah of Judah, and the father of the queen mother, Maacah (Hebrew *Micaiah*), the favored wife of Rehoboam (2 Chr 13:2). There is potential difficulty in that Absalom is also called the father of Micaiah (Maacah) in 2 Chronicles 11:20. Josephus explained this discrepancy by suggesting that Maacah's mother may have been Absalom's daughter Tamar, so that Uriel would be the father of Maacah and Absalom the maternal grandfather. While many adopt this suggestion, others have posited that Absalom was known by two different names, particularly after he had been disgraced.

URIJAH* KJV spelling of Uriah. See Uriah #2-4, 6.

URIM AND THUMMIM Two untranslated Hebrew words that might mean "lights and perfections." They refer to some kind of stones or tokens that the ancient high priests of Israel used for discovering the will of God (Nm 27:21). They were probably like dice or coins that had to land upright or upside down. According to Exodus 28:30, they were kept on or in the breastpiece of the high priest. They are not mentioned from the time of Saul

(1 Sm 28:6) until the time of Ezra and Nehemiah (Ezr 2:63; Neh 7:65), when they were used for reaccrediting returned priests. In 1 Samuel 14:41 (RSV, NIV mg, NLT mg), the Greek translation preserves what may have been lost from the Hebrew original, a mention of them in connection with Saul's effort to determine guilt in his army. That they could give answers to true-false or yes-no questions is evident from this verse. Hence, the system was probably akin to casting lots.

None of the major spiritual leaders (e.g., Abraham, Moses, David, or the prophets) ever used them for determining the will of God, and there is no mention of them in the NT. The Urim and Thummim belonged to the nation Israel in its developing years, not when there were prophets and surely not once the Holy Spirit was available to believers.

See also Lots, Casting of.

UTHAI

1. One who returned to Israel following the exile. He is listed as the son of Ammihud from the Perez branch of Judah's tribe (1 Chr 9:4).
2. One of Bigvai's sons who returned to Jerusalem with Ezra (Ezr 8:14).

UZ (Person)

1. Aram's firstborn son and a descendant of Shem (Gn 10:23). In the parallel passage in 1 Chronicles 1:17, Uz is linked directly to Shem without mention of Aram. He is perhaps the forefather of the Aramean nation situated in the Syrian desert regions.
2. Firstborn son of Abraham's brother Nahor by his concubine, Milcah (Gn 22:21).
3. Son of Dishan and the grandson of Seir the Horite (Gn 36:28; 1 Chr 1:42).

UZ (Place) Homeland of Job (Jb 1:1). The name appears in parallels with Edom and is associated with the Uz in the family tree of the original Horites in Seir (Lam 4:21). The book of Job does not locate the land of Uz, but it does say that the sons of the East (Kedem) lived there (Jb 1:3). Uz is also said to be close to the desert (v 15) and to the Chasdim (v 17). This indicates that it was located to the east of the land of Israel.

The associations with Edom strongly suggest that the land of Uz was populated by descendants of the Horites of Seir. Further support for this view is a verse in the Greek version at the end of the book of Job: "since he had lived in the land of Uz on the borders of Edom and Arabia." Certain ancient traditions place the home of Job in Bashan. Josephus also says that Job lived in Traconitis and Damascus (*Antiquities* 1.6.4), with reference to the Uz of the Aramean genealogy (Gn 10:23).

UZAI Father of Palal, a repairer of the Jerusalem wall during Nehemiah's day (Neh 3:25).

UZAL (Person) Son of Joktan, a descendant of Eber through Shem's line (Gn 10:27; 1 Chr 1:21).

UZAL (Place) Place mentioned with Dan and Javan in an obscure passage (Ez 27:19); it is identifiable with modern Sana (ancient Awzal), the capital of Yemen.

UZZA

1. Owner or initial planter of a garden that served as the burial place for kings Manasseh and Amon of Judah (2 Kgs 21:18, 26). The "garden of Uzza" was apparently adjacent to Manasseh's royal residence.

2. KJV spelling for Uzzah, Shimei's son, in 1 Chronicles 6:29. *See* Uzzah #2.
3. Son or descendant of Ehud from Benjamin's tribe (1 Chr 8:7), listed as an ancestor of Mordecai in extrabiblical texts.
4. KJV spelling for Uzzah, Abinadab's son, in 1 Chronicles 13:7-11. *See* Uzzah #1.
5. Forefather of a family of temple servants who returned to Jerusalem with Zerubbabel following the exile (Ezr 2:49; Neh 7:51).

UZZAH

1. Son of Abinadab who was killed while accompanying the cart that carried the ark of the covenant when it was returned from the Philistines (2 Sm 6:1-8; 1 Chr 13:7-11). He was struck dead by the Lord because he took hold of the ark while trying to steady it, thereby violating the instructions of Numbers 4:15. Uzzah's brother, Ahio, was apparently leading the oxen while Uzzah walked alongside. As a result of the incident, David renamed the site Perez-uzzah ("the breaking forth against Uzzah") and left the ark at the home of Obed-edom.
2. Levite from the clan of Merari who is listed as the son of Shimei and the father of Shimea (1 Chr 6:29).

UZZEN-SHEERAH Town built by Sheerah, who was either the daughter or granddaughter of Ephraim (1 Chr 7:24).

UZZI

1. Descendant of Eliezer who was in the direct ancestral line of high priests, though he apparently never served in that capacity (1 Chr 6:5-6, 51). He is listed as the son of Bukki and the father of Zerahiah; he was a lineal ancestor of Zadok and later Ezra (Ezr 7:4).
2. Clan chief and mighty warrior of the tribe of Issachar. He was one of the six sons of Tola and the father of Izrahiah, his successor as clan chief (1 Chr 7:2-3).
3. Clan chief and mighty warrior of Benjamin's tribe, listed as one of the sons of Bela (1 Chr 7:7).
4. Head of one of the Benjaminite clans that returned from Babylon, listed as the son of Micri and the father of Elah (1 Chr 9:8).
5. One of the overseers of the Levites in Jerusalem, listed as the son of Bani from the clan of Asaph (Neh 11:22).
6. Head of the priestly house of Jedaiah during the days of Joiakim the high priest (Neh 12:19).
7. One of the priests (or Levites) who participated in the dedication of the rebuilt temple (Neh 12:42). He may be the same as #5 or #6 above.

UZZIA One of David's mighty men (1 Chr 11:44). He was described as an Ashterathite, which probably means that he was from Ashtaroth, a town on the east side of the Jordan.

UZZIAH

1. Judah's king from around 792 to 740 BC (cf. 2 Kgs 14:21-22; 15:1-7; 2 Chr 26:1-23), the son of King Amaziah and Jecoliah of Jerusalem. Uzziah is the name he is called in Chronicles, but in Kings he is known as Azariah. Azariah means "the Lord has helped"; the meaning of Uzziah is "my strength is the Lord." Azariah may have been his given name and Uzziah a throne name taken upon his accession. He came to the throne at the age of 16, after the death of his father, who was assassinated in Lachish as a result of a conspiracy arising from his apostasy.

Uzziah was a capable, energetic, and well-organized

person, with many diverse interests. The Lord blessed him in all of his undertakings, so that he prospered. He is characterized as one who "did what was right in the eyes of the Lord" (2 Kgs 15:3; 2 Chr 26:4). He determined to seek God and went to Zechariah (not the postexilic prophet) for spiritual instruction. Consequently, "as long as he sought the Lord, God made him prosper" (2 Chr 26:5).

The prophets of the Lord were active during his reign. Isaiah, Hosea, and Amos began their prophetic work in the time of Uzziah (Is 1:1; Hos 1:1; Am 1:1). Uzziah was also active with military campaigns. His primary success was against Israel's strong historical enemy, the Philistines. He broke down the walls of Gath, Jabneh, and Ashdod and built his own cities in Philistia. He also built many fortifications, such as fortified towers in Jerusalem and in the wilderness. He defeated some Arabs and also the Meunites, and he brought the Ammonites under tribute (2 Chr 27:5-8). Uzziah had an army "fit for war," which was drafted according to census and organized into divisions. There were 2,600 officers and 307,500 fighting men who could wage war with mighty power. The army was well outfitted, with weapons, such as spears, bows, and sling stones, and with defensive equipment, including shields, helmets, and coats of armor (2 Chr 26:14). Second Chronicles 26:15 describes a kind of catapult, which was to be stationed on the towers and at the corners of walls for defensive purposes. This type of weapon could hurl arrows or large stones. Through his achievements and especially his military power, he became famous.

But Uzziah had a sad downfall. As Proverbs 16:18 says, pride goes before a fall. His pride became clearly evident when he presumed the function of a priest. When he entered the temple to offer incense on the altar of incense, he was confronted for his presumptuous behavior by Azariah the priest and 80 other priests. When Uzziah became angry, the Lord struck him with leprosy, so that he was forced to live in isolation and could not enter the temple. His son,

Jotham, became acting head of state and then succeeded to the kingship at the time of Uzziah's death.

2. Kohathite Levite and forefather of Samuel (1 Chr 6:24).

3. Father of Jonathan, David's treasurer (1 Chr 27:25).

4. One of Harim's five sons who was encouraged by Ezra to divorce his foreign wife during the postexilic period (Ezr 10:21; 1 Esd 9:21).

5. Descendant of Perez from Judah's tribe (Neh 11:4).

UZZIEL

1. Youngest of the sons of Kohath of Levi's tribe, who became the head of the Uzzielite division of the Kohathites (Ex 6:18; Nm 3:19, 27, 30; 1 Chr 26:23). He was Aaron's uncle, and his sons, Mishael and Elzaphan, carried Nadab and Abihu out of the camp when they rebelled against Aaron's authority (Ex 6:22; Lv 10:4). Several of his descendants were significant during Israel's history, including Amminadab, who officiated over David's transfer of the ark to Jerusalem, and Micah and Isshiah, who were chiefs among the Levites during the reign of Solomon (1 Chr 15:10; 23:20).

2. Son of Ishi who was one of the leaders of the Simeonite warriors who defeated the Ammonites at Seir during the reign of Hezekiah (1 Chr 4:42). As a result of defeating the Amalekites, who had not been defeated earlier by Saul or David, the Simeonites inherited the land.

3. Benjaminite clan chief who is listed as the son of Bela, the son of Benjamin (1 Chr 7:7).

4. Son of Heman of the Levite clan of Asaph (1 Chr 25:4). A variant name is Azarel (v 18, NLT mg).

5. Levite who participated in the reconsecration of the temple under Hezekiah (2 Chr 29:14), listed as the son of Jeduthun.

6. Goldsmith who worked on rebuilding the gates of Jerusalem (Neh 3:8). His name indicates that he was likely a priest who had the responsibility of making and repairing the temple instruments and vessels (cf. 1 Chr 9:29).

V

VAIZATHA, VAJEZATHA* One of Haman's ten sons, who was killed during the Jews' retaliation when Haman plotted to kill them (Est 9:9).

VALLEY GATE Gate from which Nehemiah went out to inspect the walls of Jerusalem and by which he re-entered (Neh 2:13-14). It was on the west side of the city facing the Tyropeon Valley. King Uzziah is said to have built and fortified a tower at this gate (2 Chr 26:9).

VALLEY OF CRAFTSMEN Translation and alternate name for Ge-harashim in Nehemiah 11:35. *See* Ge-harashim.

VALLEY OF DECISION* Valley near Jerusalem alternately called the valley of Jehoshaphat in Joel 3:2, 12. *See* Jehoshaphat, Valley of.

VALLEY OF HINNOM Valley on the south side of Jerusalem, called Gehenna in the Greek NT. *See* Gehenna.

VALLEY OF JEHOSHAPHAT *See* Jehoshaphat, Valley of.

VALLEY OF JEZREEL* *See* Jezreel Valley.

VALLEY OF REPHAIM *See* Rephaim, Valley of.

VALLEY OF SHAVEH Valley near Salem, also called the King's Valley in Genesis 14:17. *See* King's Valley.

VALLEY OF SIDDIM* *See* Siddim Valley.

VANIAH Bani's son and one of the priests who divorced his foreign wife at Ezra's command (Ezr 10:36).

VASHNI* KJV alternate name for Joel, Samuel's son, in 1 Chronicles 6:28. *See* Joel (Person) #2.

VASHTI Queen during the reign of Ahasuerus (Xerxes I) who was deposed for refusing to show herself to the guests at a royal banquet (Est 1:9-19). Since neither she nor Esther is otherwise known in secular history, many have suggested that they were inferior wives or concubines who were simply dignified with the title "queen." According to Plutarch, Persian custom dictated that the kings would ordinarily eat with their legitimate wives, but when they wanted to "riot and drink," they would send their wives away and call in their concubines. While this citation is often used to support the judgment that Vashti was called because she was only a concubine, the opposite conclusion better explains Vashti's refusal to come. Vashti's position as queen is indicated by the fact that she was supposed to appear with her "royal crown," that she was always called "queen" until the time of her dismissal, and that her behavior should serve as an example for all the women in the kingdom.

VEGETABLE *See* Food and Food Preparation; Plants.

VEIL OF THE TEMPLE* Curtain in the sanctuary separating the Holy Place from the Most Holy Place (Ex 26:31-33). *See* Tabernacle.

VESPASIAN* Roman general who entered Palestine in AD 66 to quell the rebellious Jews, and later became emperor of Rome (AD 69–79). *See* Caesars, The.

VESTMENTS* *See* Priests and Levites.

VINEDRESSER* *See* Vines, Vineyard.

VINEGAR *See* Food and Food Preparation.

VINE OF SODOM Designation for a plant that produces an enticing but inedible fruit (Dt 32:32). *See* Plants (Gourd, Wild).

VINES, VINEYARD Plants cultivated for the production of grapes, raisins, and wine. The grapevine is mentioned frequently in Scripture both in a literal and a figurative sense. Probably originating in the Ararat region (Gn 9:20), the vine was also cultivated in ancient Egypt, where tomb murals depict the wine-making process. The Canaanites provided wine for Abraham (14:18), and Moses described the vineyards in the Promised Land (Dt 6:11). Excellent grapes from the valleys and plains (Nm

The Grapevine

13:20, 24; Jgs 14:5; 15:5) provided fruit and wine to enhance the bland diet of the Hebrews. Wine was traded extensively in the late monarchy (cf. Ez 27:18), as well as in the Greek and Roman periods. For the Hebrews, an ideal picture of life was a sedentary one in which a man could remain peacefully in one place, cultivating his plot of land, and sitting under his vine (1 Kgs 4:25).

The typical vineyard was surrounded by a protective hedge or fence, and at harvesttime a watchtower was manned to guard the crop from thieves (Jb 24:18; Is 1:8; Mk 12:1). The vines were planted in rows within the enclosed area, and as the plants grew, the tendrils were trained along supports to raise the fruit-bearing branches off the ground (Ez 17:6). The vines were pruned and tended by vinedressers (Lv 25:3; Is 61:5; Jl 3:10; Jn 15:2). At harvesttime the mature fruit was picked and taken to the winepresses (Hos 9:2). A festive atmosphere accompanied the treading of the grapes (Is 16:10; Jer 25:30), and the fermenting juice was collected in new goatskin bags (Mt 9:17) or large pottery jars.

People working in the grape harvest were exempted from military service, which attests to its importance. Taxes and debts were often discharged by payments of wine, and the law provided for the poor to glean in the vineyards as in the wheat fields (Lv 19:9-10). Nonproductive vines were used for producing charcoal (Ez 15:4; Jn 15:6).

Christ frequently used the vineyard as a background for his parables (Mt 20:1-16; 21:28-43; Mk 12:1-11; Lk 13:6-9; 20:9-18). Wine-making methods were commonly known and understood, so that an allegory of placing new wine in old wineskins (Mt 9:17) was immediately familiar and significant. In a symbolic sense, Christ described himself as the true vine (Jn 15:1-11), and his blood became the sacramental wine of communion.

See also Agriculture; Plants (Vine).

VIOL* KJV rendering of harp in Isaiah 5:12; 14:11; Amos 5:23; and 6:5. *See* Musical Instruments (Nebel).

VIPER *See* Animals (Adder).

VIRGIN Word used only of women and (metaphorically) of places, nations, and the church. Literally, it describes a woman who has reached physical maturity but has not experienced sexual intercourse. Mary, mother of Jesus, is an obvious example (Mt 1:18-25).

The OT puts a high value on premarital virginity. One of Rebekah's qualities that made her a suitable bride for Isaac was her virginity (Gn 24:16). The law prescribed that priests, as men whose lives should conform most closely to God's standards, must marry only virgins (Lv 21:7, 13-14).

Undoubtedly this reflects the whole Bible's teaching on marriage, with its ideal of exclusive faithfulness. The NT expresses that ideal by its ban on premarital intercourse (1 Cor 6:13, 18), and by its use of "virgin" language to describe Christians who remain faithful to their Lord (Rv 14:4; cf. 2 Cor 11:2).

Negatively, the OT highlights the same principle in the penalties it lays down for the loss of a woman's virginity. If the man is morally responsible, he must either marry her or compensate her father (Ex 22:16-17). If the woman herself is to blame, the punishment is death (Dt 22:20-21). The OT says little, however, to commend lifelong virginity. Jeremiah was told not to marry, only to reinforce God's warning of coming judgment (Jer 16:2). From the woman's point of view, it was a tragedy to remain an unmarried virgin and therefore childless for life (cf. Jgs 11:37).

The NT echoes the value of marriage but brings out more clearly the advantages of a commitment to virginity for Christian men as well as women. Celibacy for

some is God's gift, declared Paul, because it has positive gains for Christian service (1 Cor 7:7, 25-38). Jesus commended those who "make themselves eunuchs" for the kingdom of heaven's sake (Mt 19:12).

See also Family Life and Relations; Marriage, Marriage Customs; Sex, Sexuality; Virgin Birth of Jesus; Woman.

VIRGIN BIRTH OF JESUS* Doctrine, drawn from the birth narratives of Matthew 1 and Luke 1-2, which states that Jesus Christ was conceived of the Holy Spirit and born of the virgin Mary. The whole concept of the Incarnation (as well as Jesus' divine and human natures) focuses upon this historical event as its foundation. At the same time, rationalists and literary critics deny this miracle, stating that it was created by the early Christians.

PAGAN PARALLELS TO THE VIRGIN BIRTH
Some critics of the virgin birth argue that the early church first propounded the belief that Jesus was the Son of God and then proved it by using Hellenistic parallels. In Greek mythology Zeus, as well as the other gods, bore many children by human mothers, including Perseus and Hercules. These offspring were also men of heroic proportion. In addition, there were tales of the miraculous births of great historical figures, such as Plato (whose father was Apollo) or Alexander the Great (whose father, Philip of Macedon, was kept from consummating his marriage until the child, conceived of Zeus, was born). Interestingly, the church fathers often used these stories in their polemic against their Greek opponents to show that the idea of the virgin birth was not really so incredible to the Greek mind. However, the differences between the pagan and Christian forms are too great. For one thing, the lustful promiscuity of the gods starkly contrasts with the sexual restraint commanded by the NT. Also, in the pagan stories the concept of "virgin" hardly has any stress. In all cases, it is simply a physical union between a god and a human, not a spiritual conception, as in the case of Jesus.

The same is true of the birth of Buddha, for the oldest records state that the entrance of the "white elephant" (representing the spirit of childbirth) into Gautama's mother took place in a dream, and the story of an actual virgin birth is post-Christian. As for the Persian myths of the birth of Zoroaster or the birth of Mithras from a rock, there is no concept of a virgin birth. Babylonian tales do involve the goddess-mother Ishtar, but again virginity has no emphasis and is actually doubtful.

The Old Testament Prophecy The KJV of Isaiah 7:14 says that a "virgin" shall "conceive and bear a son . . . Immanuel," and Matthew 1:22-23 expressly states that this was fulfilled in Jesus' birth. This passage has been greatly debated, especially since the RSV changed the KJV "virgin" to "young woman," based on the ambiguity of the term in the original manuscripts. The Hebrew *'almah* refers generally to a young girl who has passed puberty and thus is of marriageable age. Another Hebrew word (*bethulah*) specifies a woman who is a virgin. The Septuagint translators, nevertheless, translated *'almah* as *parthenos*, which does denote a virgin.

From these linguistic considerations come the following four interpretations:

1. The "virgin" (Is 7:14) was Ahaz's new wife and the son was Hezekiah. But Hezekiah was nine years old when Ahaz began to reign, so this prophecy must look to the future.

2. She was Isaiah's wife and the son was Maher-shalal-hash-baz. Many scholars support this interpretation because the definite article with *'almah* seems to indicate that "the woman" was known to Isaiah and Ahaz and because Isaiah 7:14-16 seems to indicate that the prophecy was to be fulfilled in Isaiah's time. The difficulty here is that Isaiah's wife already had a son and so she could not be called *'almah.*

3. The prophecy is purely messianic. This is the traditional evangelical position, based on the name of the child Immanuel, "God with us," and the reference (Is 9:6-7; 11:1-5), which points to a divine person.

4. Many evangelicals recently have opted for a fourth interpretation, which accepts the arguments for the historical fulfillment (in Isaiah's day) and for the futuristic fulfillment. This view takes into account the historical fulfillment intended in Isaiah 7:15-16 while seeing the future as being fulfilled through the virgin birth of Jesus, as indicated in Matthew 1:22-23.

The Gospel Records Neither Mark nor John provides an account of the birth of Christ; the actual event is chronicled only in Matthew and Luke. Both agree that a "virgin," Mary, conceived of the Holy Spirit and bore a son, Jesus. Matthew's account is simpler and more direct, attributing the birth of the Messiah to divine origins and highlighting the christological significance. Jesus is called the "Christ [or Messiah]," the son of David (Mt 1:1), who comes to inaugurate the kingdom of God. As evidenced both by the fulfillment of Isaiah's prophecy (vv 22-23) and by the nature of his conception (vv 18-20), Jesus is "God with us," now come to "save his people from their sins" (v 21). The scene where Joseph decides to privately divorce Mary is added to give even greater stress to the miraculous conception.

Luke told the Nativity story from the perspective of Mary. The angel Gabriel visited her and announced that she would give birth to the Messiah (Lk 1:26-38). She conceived miraculously by the Holy Spirit, as was foretold by the angel Gabriel: "The Holy Spirit will come upon you; therefore the child to be born will be called holy, the Son of God" (v 35, RSV). Mary was portrayed by Luke as being devoutly submissive to the purposes of God.

Theological Significance for the Church From the very beginning of the church, the doctrine of the virgin birth became the foundation of an exalted Christology. Some of the earliest church fathers stressed this more than any other event in Jesus' life as proof of the incarnation and deity of Christ. Justin Martyr and Ignatius defended the virgin birth against opponents at the beginning of the second century, and even at that early date it appeared to be a fixed doctrine. In the debates of the next three centuries, the virgin birth became a prominent issue. Gnostics such as Marcion contended that Christ descended directly from heaven and so was never truly human. On the other hand, those groups that denied his deity, such as the Arians, also denied the virgin birth, stating that at his baptism Jesus was "adopted" as Son of God. The Council of Nicaea in AD 325 affirmed that Jesus was truly God, and then the Council of Chalcedon in AD 451 stated that Jesus was at the same time human and divine, a "hypostatic union" of the true natures. These were summarized in the Apostles' Creed of the fifth century, which declares, "I believe in . . . Jesus Christ, his only Son, our Lord, conceived of the Holy Ghost, born of the Virgin Mary." In most of the creeds the virgin birth is also connected to Jesus' sinlessness, inasmuch as his incarnate, divine nature is the source of his sinlessness.

From the beginning, as attested in Matthew and Luke as well as the early patristic writers, the virgin birth has been a central doctrine of the church. As such, it is a living symbol of the twofold nature of Jesus: born of the Holy Spirit and

of woman, he is the incarnate God-man. *See* Christology; Incarnation; Jesus Christ, Life and Teachings of; Virgin.

VISION, VISIONS Visual experiences of any kind, but in the Bible the word usually refers to supernatural revelations of a prophet. In early OT prophecy there are cases of extraordinary sight, which was regarded as evidence of the visionary endowment of a prophet. Samuel was a "seer" or visionary; he was able to "see" where Saul's lost donkeys were and to tell him their whereabouts (1 Sm 9:19-20). Elisha was able to follow Gehazi's wrongful actions "in spirit" and confront him on his return (2 Kgs 5:26). This psychic gift was given only to the prophets.

Apart from these kinds of visions of present happenings occurring elsewhere on earth, there are revelatory visions—visions concerning the future that are given by God to various prophets. Sometimes God communicated these visions through dreams. Both experiences are legitimate channels of divine revelation. Presumably visions are distinguished from dreams as being daytime experiences.

There are different types of revelatory vision. At one end of the spectrum is the ecstatic vision of Ezekiel. He experienced a psychic trance that could supernaturally transport him to other places (Ez 8:3; 40:2). Daniel's vision (Dn 8) was probably of the same type, and so perhaps was Jeremiah's experience (Jer 13:4-7). At the other end of the spectrum is what has been called symbolical perception. In this, a prophet sees an ordinary object that is part of the natural world, but sees it with a heightened significance. The basket of summer fruit that God "caused" Amos "to see" (Am 8:1-2) seems to fall into this category, and so probably do Jeremiah's visions of the almond branch and the tilting pot (Jer 1:11-13). An intermediate type includes the pictorial heavenly visions that Isaiah received (1 Kgs 22:19-22; Is 6), as well as those of the apostle John, when he wrote the book of Revelation.

Actually, prophecy could come via either an auditory or a visual experience. Typically, in the course of a vision a verbal message was communicated, so that the seeing and hearing took place within the same supernatural experience. This was the case with Isaiah, who both "saw the Lord" and heard his voice. But an auditory experience could itself be called a vision, for the divine word is a revelation from God. It is often difficult to know whether the term "vision" includes a predominant element of hearing or is used in the wider sense of revelation (e.g., Ez 12:21-28). Often "vision" is apparently used simply as a technical term for a verbal communication from God. Thus Samuel's call is literally called a "vision" (1 Sm 3:15). Several of the prophetic books have the word "vision" in their headings (Is 1:1; Ob 1:1; Na 1:1). Nathan's prophecy of God's covenant with David is described as a vision (2 Sm 7:17; 1 Chr 17:15; Ps 89:19). In Daniel 9:24 "to seal both vision and prophet" means to authenticate the prophecy of Jeremiah referred to in verse 2. In the famous proverb traditionally rendered "Where there is no vision, the people perish" (Prv 29:18, KJV), the term "vision" refers to prophetic revelation, the divine gift of prophecy that was intended to be a guiding influence in Israel's life. *See* Apocalypse; Dreams; Prophecy.

VOPHSI Man appointed by Moses from Naphtali's tribe to spy out the land of Canaan (Nm 13:14).

VOW, VOWS Serious promises or pledges made to God. The making of vows to God is a religious practice frequently mentioned in Scripture. Most references to vows are found in the OT, especially in the Psalms, but there are a few in the NT.

Unlike tithing, sacrifices and offerings, Sabbath keeping, and circumcision, vow making was not something commanded by the Mosaic law. For example, Psalm 50:14 says, "Offer to God a sacrifice of thanksgiving, and pay your vows to the Most High" (RSV). The command is to "pay," that is, to keep or fulfill a pledge that has already been made. No order is given to make such promises in the first place. The practice is accepted and regulated but not demanded.

The purpose of a vow is to win a desired favor from the Lord, to express gratitude to him for some deliverance or benefit, or simply to prove absolute devotion to him by way of certain abstinences. Dedication of oneself and separation to the Lord were the primary features of the Nazirite vow. Samson, Samuel, and John the Baptist are the most familiar examples of those who took this type of vow. Numbers 6:1-8 prescribes the conditions of this commitment, and verses 13-21 tell how release from the vow may be obtained. Women, as well as men, might take this vow of separation (v 2), which could be of limited duration. The Recabite clan pledged themselves to an ascetic and nomadic life. They constitute a compelling illustration of loyalty to the God of Israel (Jer 35).

Frequently, however, vows were taken as a type of bargain with God. At Bethel, Jacob promised God worship and the tithe if he would protect him and supply his needs (Gn 28:20-22). Hannah pledged that if God would give her a son, she would return him to God (1 Sm 1:11, 27-28). In the Psalms, payment of vows is often associated with thanksgiving for deliverance from danger or affliction (e.g., Pss 22:24-25; 56:12-13).

Most important is that once a vow is made, the obligation is serious. To refrain from making any vow is no sin (Dt 23:22), but once declared, the vow must be kept (Dt 23:21-23; see also Nm 30:2; Eccl 5:4-6).

The term "vow" occurs just twice in the NT, both times in association with the apostle Paul (Acts 18:18; 21:23-24). But the same principle is involved in the case of the word "Corban" (Mk 7:11-13; cf. Mt 15:5-6). In these two passages Jesus severely rebuked those who made a vow that served as a clever escape from meeting obligations to care for aged parents. A monetary figure was involved in such a "gift" or "offering." But Jesus declared that God did not want a gift designed to deprive someone.

In the case of Paul, he may have entered into his vows for the very purpose of averting objections that either antagonistic Jews or Jewish-Christian believers had to his removing the yoke of Mosaic regulations from the shoulders of gentile believers. Paul was in Jerusalem under the keen surveillance of Jewish authorities. He made it a point to join with four other Jewish believers in the payment of vows in the temple. This action, however, was misconstrued by his enemies, who charged that he was bringing Gentiles into the holy temple.

See also Covenant; Oath.

VULGATE*, The The Latin version of the Bible, commonly identified as the work of Jerome. *See* Bible, Versions of the (Ancient).

VULTURE *See* Birds.

W

WADI* Intermittent stream or torrent in the arid and semiarid regions of the Middle East. Although the streambeds were usually dry, they could attain flood stage during spring runoff or after heavy rainfalls. The most significant wadi in the Bible was the Wadi of Egypt ("Brook of Egypt" in modern versions), which served as the southwestern border of Canaan according to God's instructions to Moses (Nm 34:5; Jos 15:4, 47; 1 Kgs 8:65; Is 27:12). During the dry periods, wadis were important as roadways.

WAGES Payment received by a laborer in return for his work. Usually wages are calculated in terms of a medium of exchange, such as money, but they can be paid in any kind of goods or services. Jacob worked seven years in return for Laban's younger daughter, Rachel (Gn 29:18-20), and then had to work another seven years when Laban did not honor his agreement. Later, Jacob's wages were sheep and goats (30:31-32; 31:8). Nebuchadnezzar was given the country of Egypt as wages for his work in capturing the city of Tyre (Ez 29:18-20).

Usually wages were agreed upon by employer and employee (Gn 29:15-19; Mt 20:2), but sometimes the pay was at the discretion of the employer (Mt 20:4). A fair wage for honest work is a biblical principle (Lk 10:7; 1 Tm 5:18). The Lord established laws to cover this principle and judged those who violated it. Wages were to be paid promptly (Lv 19:13); the holding back of wages is condemned in the Scripture (Mal 3:5; Jas 5:1-6).

Wages were often a source of discontent and dispute between employer and employee. When soldiers came to John the Baptist to be baptized and asked about their future conduct, he urged them to be content with their wages (Lk 3:14). Jacob and Laban had disagreements about wages and twice Jacob complained, "You have changed my wages ten times" (Gn 31:7, 41).

The Bible also speaks of ill-gotten wages. The wages of a prostitute could not be brought into the house of the Lord (Dt 23:18), and people are warned against the error of Balaam, who corrupted Israel because he "loved the wages of unrighteousness" (2 Pt 2:15).

See also Money; Banker, Banking; Poor, The; Riches; Work.

WAHEB Town in the area of Suphah (Nm 21:14). *See* Suphah.

WALNUT* *See* Plants.

WANDERINGS IN THE WILDERNESS *See* Wilderness Wanderings.

WAR*, Holy Warfare as described in the book of Deuteronomy, especially in chapter 20. Not merely a human enterprise fought by kings with trained soldiers and military equipment, it is God's war in which he himself is involved together with his covenant people who are selected to fight in his name. The size of the army is not important; indeed, sometimes the numbers were pared down to dramatize the fact that the victory was gained,

not by military superiority, but by the action of God against his enemies. When Israel lived in obedience to God as his covenant people and went into battle under his direction, war was within the will of God, commanded by him, and accomplished through trust in him. God was known as "a man of war," and it is declared that "the battle is the Lord's" (1 Sm 17:47; cf. 18:17; 25:28). With this faith on the part of the Jews, it is easy to see how a concept of holy war developed, especially when they had the conviction that their enemies were God's enemies and that they were the people through whom God would carry out his saving purposes for the world.

Moses believed that God declared war and sent his people into battle (Ex 17:16; Nm 31:3). On several occasions, at crucial points in warfare, the "terror of the Lord" fell upon the enemy, enabling the numerically inferior army of Israel to gain an easy victory over vastly superior forces (Jos 10:10-14; Jgs 4:12-16; 2 Sm 5:24-25). In a time of acute military crisis, Elisha was enabled to see the heavenly army of Yahweh drawn up on the hills around Samaria, ready to defeat the fierce, invading armies of Syria. In response to Elisha's prayer, the Syrian soldiers were struck with blindness and rendered helpless against the Israelites (2 Kgs 6:15-23). Various means were used to determine the will of God and to assure his active participation in war. In addition to the word of the prophet (1 Kgs 22:5-23), Urim and Thummim (Ex 28:30; Lv 8:8), the ephod (1 Sm 30:7), and the ark of the covenant were employed for this purpose. The leaders of God's troops constantly sought his direction for military strategy during the progress of battle, for no step was to be taken without divine approval and guidance (2 Sm 5:19-23).

Since God gave Palestine to his own people, the Jews, the land was indeed the Promised Land; it belonged by divine covenant to Israel and was in that sense "the Holy Land." Any defense of that land against foreign invasion was a holy war. The invading enemy was trespassing upon sacred territory that belonged to God's people by immutable decree and thus incurred the divine wrath. From this perspective the complete destruction of Israel's enemies was necessary, particularly when the enemy was pagan and morally corrupt. A characteristic Hebrew word used for this concept, *herem*, originally meant "devoted" and came to mean "devoted to destruction" as something hostile to the rule of God (Jos 6:17-18). The divine plan must not be thwarted, obstructed, or aborted by any debasing idolatry or corrupting immorality (Dt 7). Enemy cities within the boundaries of the land promised to the Jews were to be utterly destroyed—a practice known as "the ban." Only silver, gold, and vessels of bronze and iron were to be spared. They were to be placed in the treasury of the Lord as sacred to him (Jos 6:17-21; 1 Sm 15:3).

There was a distinctly teleological aspect to the concept of holy war. It looked beyond the triumphs of God in specific battles to the conclusion of all hostilities and to a final time of peace that will vindicate the righteousness and sovereignty of God's saving purposes and display his concern and goal for his own people. The final consummation will

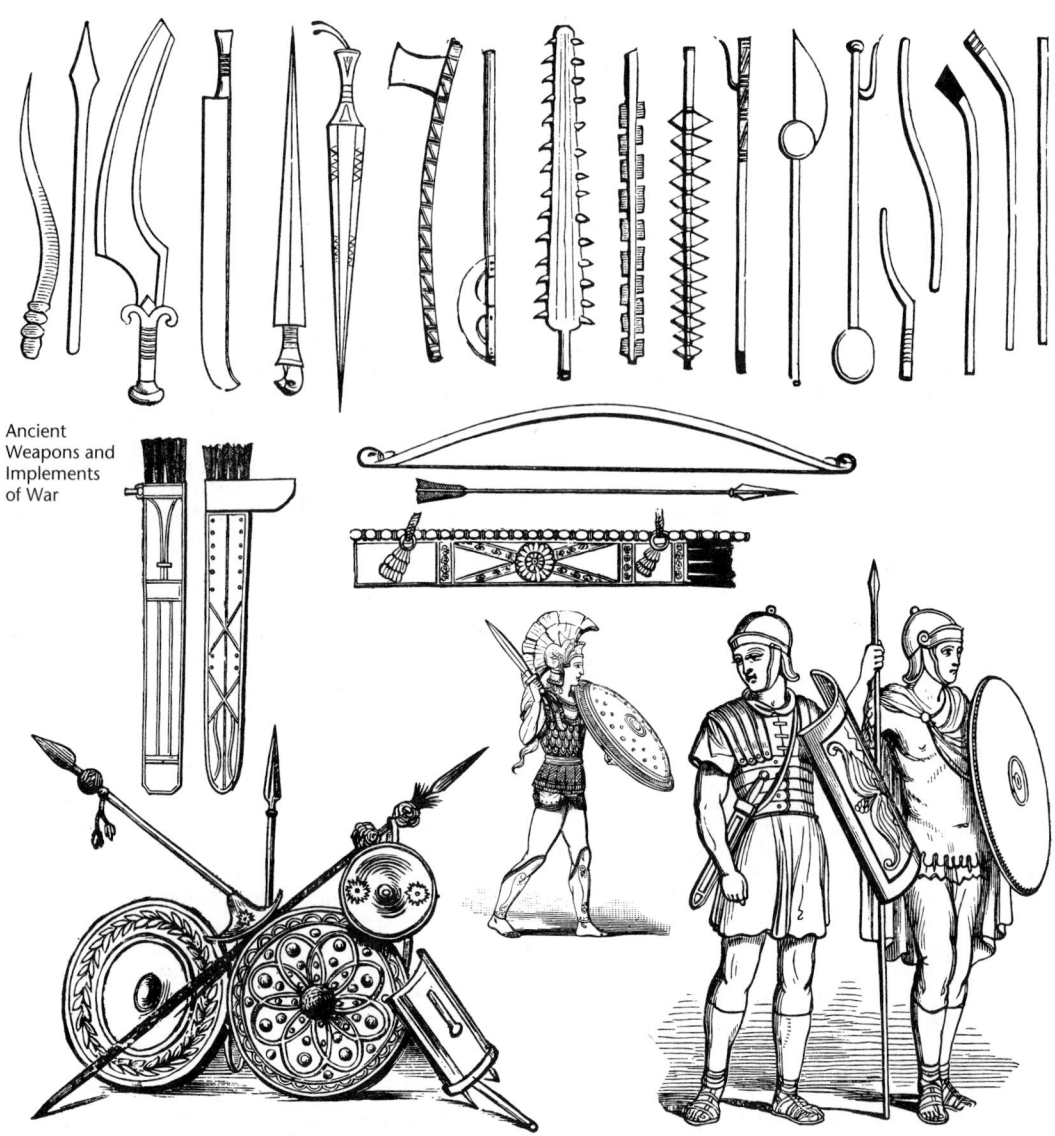

Ancient
Weapons and
Implements
of War

be preceded by a massive holy war, after which the weapons of warfare will be transformed into implements of peace (Is 2:4; Mi 4:3) under the reign of the Messiah, the Prince of Peace (Is 9:6), who will subdue all God's enemies in a triumphant Day of the Lord (Ps 110; Dn 7; Zec 14).

WARFARE The means by which one nation seeks to impose its will upon another by force. An index to the importance of warfare in antiquity is provided by the amount of technical skill directed to perfecting devices for destruction and defense.

Methods of Warfare

Standard Combat Cavalry units were introduced at the close of the second millennium BC and the beginning of the first. The cavalry charge provided a shock force to the great armies, and the cavalry's mobility permitted concentration of firepower at decisive points. When the Assyrians coordinated their infantry, cavalry, and chariot corps into a powerful battle machine, smaller neighboring nations

were more and more compelled to retreat behind their fortifications. They could not hope to engage the massive Assyrian army in standard combat in open terrain. No period is richer in illustrated monuments than Iron Age II; the Assyrian war reliefs present detailed illustrations of their conquests and the size of fortified cities. The few scenes depicting standard combat in open terrain show chariots charging from all directions and engaging the enemy at all stages of a battle. Other formations carry out mopping-up operations, finishing off pockets of enemy resistance remaining after the chariot charge.

The factor of terrain was always very important. In standard combat on open terrain it became conventional to place the best troops on the right side of the line. A Greek commander, Epaminodas (d. 362 BC), introduced the variant of a slanting attack by a strengthened left wing, taking the Spartan army completely by surprise. Philip of Macedon and his son Alexander continued to surprise their enemies with variations on a plan of attack based on the phalanx.

Helmets and Armor in Bible Times

Battle in Open Terrain: The Duel During certain periods in the ancient Near East, the duel presented an alternative to standard combat. The duel was a contest between two champions who represented the contending forces. The two armies would agree in advance to abide by the outcome of the fight. The duel was meant to avoid the heavy casualties of full-scale warfare. The earliest detailed written account of this unique form of warfare occurs in the Tale of Sinuhe. A chamberlain in the royal court of the 12th dynasty, Sinuhe voluntarily went into exile and traveled to northern Palestine and Syria, where he lived among Semitic tribes. There he was challenged to a duel by a local champion, whom he defeated and whose goods he then plundered.

Although the duel was common among other armies in subsequent periods, it was evidently unknown to Israel before the encounter between David and Goliath (1 Sm 17). The Philistine army had penetrated Judah as far as Socoh and were arrayed on one hill. Drawn up against them on an opposite hill was the army of Saul. The valley of Elah separated the two camps. The Israelites were challenged daily by the Philistine champion, Goliath, who proposed that the battle be decided through combat between two warriors. David accepted his pro-

posal, but when he killed Goliath, the Philistines fled, unwilling to honor the terms of the prior agreement. The Israelite army then entered the contest, pursuing the Philistines and inflicting heavy casualties.

Assaults on Fortified Cities Most cities in the ancient Near East were located at sites that could be defended against attack and that possessed economic advantages. An assault on a fortified city presented opposite problems for attacker and defender. The actions of one were a direct response to the actions of the other. Systems of defense were intended to thwart methods of attack, which in turn were designed to penetrate systems of defense.

There were five possible ways of conquering a fortified city: penetration from above the fortifications; direct penetration through the fortifications; penetration from below the fortifications; siege; and penetration by ruse. On many occasions, a combination of two or more methods was necessary to breach the defensive network.

The biblical narrative of the conquest of Shechem by Abimelech (Jgs 9) gives an account of an assault on a fortified city in the period of the judges (Iron Age I). When the people of Shechem and their allies rebelled against

Abimelech, he retaliated by attacking the city, advancing his army of mercenaries by night and launching an assault from ambush positions at dawn (9:32-35). The men of Shechem engaged in open battle outside the city gates but were forced to retreat behind the security of the city walls. The next day Abimelech directed his assault against the city itself. Dividing his forces into three groups, he assumed direct command of one, which he committed to an attack on the city gates at the decisive moment of battle (vv 43-44). The gate was breached and the main walls seized, but the city's surviving defenders fled to an inner citadel, the temple of Baal-berith.

Many reliefs depict groups of soldiers defending an inner citadel after a city's wall was breached. Archaeological excavations at Shechem confirm that its temple, like those in other Canaanite cities, was built in the form of a fortified tower, supported by stout bastions near the entrance. The tower of Shechem was thus strongly fortified and occupied only a small area, enabling its defenders to concentrate their firepower on Abimelech's troops. Since it could not be taken by storm, Abimelech ordered his soldiers to use their battle-axes to cut brushwood, which was piled against the stronghold and set on fire (Jgs 9:48-49). All of the defenders within the tower died.

An assault on an inner citadel was always a hazardous undertaking for an attacking army, as shown in the sequel to the capture of Shechem's tower. Abimelech turned his attention next to the city of Thebez and followed the same plan of assault that had proved successful at Shechem. But as he was preparing to burn the door of the tower to which the defenders had fled, his skull was crushed by a piece of millstone dropped on him by a woman (Jgs 9:50-53). The incident was remembered and became proverbial for the danger of approaching too closely the walls of a fortified tower (2 Sm 11:19-21).

Communications and Intelligence From the patriarchal period (middle Bronze period), we have detailed written information on the use of communications systems in wartime. The documents from Mari on the Euphrates provide evidence for a well-developed communications system based on signaling. Signals were flashed by torches or firebrands at night in accordance with a prearranged code. The system was widely used in Mesopotamia and elsewhere to call for immediate help when a city was under attack.

In the late Bronze period horsemen were sometimes employed for isolated communication functions. Intelligence services played a role in planning and executing military operations. The importance of intelligence and the use of spies or scouts is stressed in the biblical accounts of the conquest of the land of Canaan. Before entering the land, Moses sent men on an espionage mission. He instructed them to gather information on the topography of the land, to observe the relative strength of its inhabitants, to determine whether the land was fertile, to survey the cities and see if they were fortified, and to report on the character of the land—whether it was capable of sustaining a large population (Nm 13:17-20).

Tactical intelligence was very important. Joshua dispatched spies to Jericho and to Ai before beginning military operations against them (Jos 2:1; 7:2). The reports he received about the offensive spirit and strength of the Canaanites enabled him to formulate an attack plan. In the period of the judges the conquest of Bethel (Jgs 1:22-26) was due directly to intelligence gathered by a reconnaissance patrol. The tribes of Joseph sent out scouts to keep the city under observation. It was strongly fortified and seemed impregnable. The scouts captured a man who emerged from the city—presumably not through the main gate, which was shut tight, but

through a concealed postern or tunnel. In exchange for his own life and the safety of his family, he disclosed the location of the passage leading beneath the walls. The city was penetrated through the tunnel and captured.

Attack and Penetration: The Breach Direct penetration through the fortifications of an ancient city meant breaching the gate or the main walls by using hammers, axes, pikes, spears, swords, or a battering ram. Illustrated monuments and written documents indicate that early in the middle Bronze period fortified cities were being attacked with battering rams. The earliest known illustration of a ram appears in a siege scene in the wall paintings from Beni Hasan (20th century BC). The ram pictured is a relatively simple device, consisting of a hutlike structure with a slightly pointed roof, which could be moved near a fortress with the help of two parallel crossbars. The structure provided cover for two or three soldiers who operated by hand a very long pole with a sharp tip, presumably of metal.

The Mari documents provide information for the period 200 years later. They mention the effectiveness of battering rams constructed largely of wood. Although very heavy, the siege weapon could be moved over long distances. One document speaks of the use of a wagon drawn by draft animals and of a boat to transport a battering ram to the site of a besieged city.

Moving a battering ram into position always exposed the demolition unit to heavy fire from defenders on the walls above them. Its heaviness made it cumbersome to move. Moreover, the ground adjacent to the walls was usually rough, rocky, and steep. When the chosen point of penetration was a section of the wall, an assault force had to construct an earthen ramp, occasionally strengthened on the top surface and sides with wooden planks or stones. The ramp provided a track along which the battering ram could be moved from the foot of the slope to the outer wall. Once moved into operational position, the ram had to be braked to prevent it from rolling back. The building of such a ramp was evidently necessary in Joab's campaign against the fortified city of Abel in Beth-maacah (2 Sm 20:15). The biblical account indicates that some sort of battering ram was in use in Israel under King David during the early monarchy.

The earliest Assyrian reliefs show that protection of the penetration units was a major consideration. High, mobile assault towers constructed of wood operated in tandem with a battering ram. Such towers, moved into position near a breach operation and manned by archers, provided covering fire directed against the defenders on the wall. Siege towers neutralized the defenders' advantage in firepower and drew fire away from the crew engaged in breaching the walls.

The details of the Assyrian reliefs make it possible to visualize clearly the fate of Jerusalem, as announced to the prophet Ezekiel (Ez 4:1-3; 21:22). The gate was the focal point of attack because it was the weakest point in the wall. Moreover, the path leading up to the gate made construction of a special ramp unnecessary. In the demolition of a gate, swords were sometimes used to pry the doors loose and to tear down hinges. Wooden doors unprotected by metal were often set on fire.

The battering ram continued to be used as an engine for breaching walls in the Hellenistic-Roman period. In 63 BC the Roman commander Pompey brought up battering rams from Tyre against the defenders of Jerusalem, and with them penetrated the fortified wall that enclosed the temple. The siege machine shown on Trajan's column had a beam with an iron head shaped like a ram. It was moved up to a wall in a frame protected by a wooden roof covered with clay or hides. A variation equipped for boring into a wall was used by Titus when besieging Jerusalem in AD 70.

The battering ram was not the only device used to effect a breach in a wall. Troops trained as sappers would tear down a section of the wall by using sharp-headed levers (pikes, swords, spears) or even sledgehammers (cf. Ez 26:8-9). In Ashurnasirpal's army such men were issued full-length coats of mail to cover their whole bodies. Under later Assyrian kings, they were protected by both round and rectangular shields, which they carried on their backs when engaged in demolition. Later, Ashurbanipal relied exclusively on such sappers for direct penetration of a fortified city. He designed for their protection a huge shield, the curved head of which could be propped against the wall, screening the sapper from missiles while he worked beneath it.

Scaling the Walls A battle scene depicted on limestone in the tomb of Anta at Dashashe in Upper Egypt (24th century BC) provides the earliest known representation of siege activities. It shows the Egyptians raising a scaling ladder against the walls of a fortified city. By the time of Sargon, the thickness of walls was increased considerably, which permitted construction of much higher walls, more resistant to scaling. Such solid, massive walls also tended to blunt the effectiveness of a battering ram. Sargon, and especially his successor Ashurbanipal, responded by constructing longer scaling ladders, some of which could reach a height of from 25 to 30 feet (7.6 to 9.1 meters), judging from the number of rungs.

Penetration beneath the Walls A tunneling operation could be started beyond the range of any weapons at the disposal of the defenders. Once underground, the penetration unit was shielded from enemy fire. The tunneling could be accomplished under cover of night, so that the element of surprise could be exploited to the maximum. It was, however, a lengthy process requiring considerable technical skill. Moreover, if the operation was detected by the defenders before its completion, they could destroy the penetration unit as it emerged from the tunnel. Attempts to penetrate fortified cities by tunneling beneath the walls was a characteristic feature of warfare in Iron Age II. That is confirmed by reliefs, written documents, and archaeological excavation of sites dating to this period, where the remains of attack tunnels have been discovered.

Siege Particularly when a walled city was situated on a high hill, an extended siege provided an alternate method of conquering it. By encircling the city and preventing aid or supplies from reaching its defenders, the attacking army could starve the inhabitants out. That procedure minimized the element of risk for the attacking army. Its success depended upon their capacity to prevent outside assistance from reaching the city and the defenders from leaving it. An army would generally resort to siege when a city's fortifications were too powerful for direct penetration. The siege of Samaria by the Assyrians lasted for three years (2 Kgs 18:9-10).

The peculiar conditions of siege produced the catapult, a major innovation of Greek artillery and a logical improvement on the bow and the sling. Designed originally as a strengthened bow mounted on a stand and used to fire arrows only, it was introduced around 400 BC by Demetrius I. He may have borrowed the idea from the Phoenicians at Carthage.

In the course of time the instrument was improved. The perfect weapon, called the torsion catapult, derived its power from many tightly twisted strands of elastic material, frequently supplied by women's hair, which could be tightened with a windlass and then released suddenly. Firing arrows, large stones, or fire-baskets with an effective range of 200 yards (182.9 meters), a catapult could clear a wall of its defenders while a battering ram breached it or a boarding party attacked from a mobile tower.

For those in a besieged city, the critical problems were food and water supplies. The horror of famine is stressed in the biblical account of the siege of Samaria by the Syrian Ben-hadad in the days of the prophet Elisha. On that occasion women were reduced to eating their children (2 Kgs 6:26-29). A besieging army would do everything in its power to aggravate such conditions. In one of the siege reliefs of Ashurnasirpal II, a defender has lowered a bucket from the wall to draw water from a stream below; an Assyrian soldier is shown cutting the rope with his dagger.

Ruses and Stratagems Various ruses and stratagems could draw the defenders out of a city or infiltrate troops into the city. If a small force could enter a city by a cunning stratagem, it could overpower the guards and open the city gates to an attacking army. A city's fortifications were of little value once an enemy had entered the city. Moreover, penetrating a city's defenses at any one point frequently caused the entire defense system to collapse. The story of the Trojan horse is probably the most celebrated account of a stratagem circumventing the defense of a strongly fortified ancient city.

In the biblical account of the siege of Samaria by Ben-hadad, a sudden lifting of the Syrian siege led Joram, the king of Israel, to suspect a ruse. He refused to believe the report of four lepers that the Syrians had gone, leaving behind large food supplies (2 Kgs 7:12). That was the same kind of tactic that Joshua had employed at Ai (Jos 8:3-8).

On other occasions, powerful armies sought to break down resistance by psychological warfare, as in the unsuccessful attempt by Sennacherib to capture Jerusalem in the time of Hezekiah (2 Kgs 18–19). The dialogue between the Assyrian general and Hezekiah's delegates reveals that the Assyrian was trying to shake the confidence of the city's defenders.

The ambush was a type of ruse used to trap and destroy an enemy at a moment when he was least able to counter a sudden, unexpected blow. Its effectiveness depended almost entirely on the element of surprise. By taking advantage of good intelligence, knowledge of the terrain, and the cover of night, a small force could stage a devastating ambush against vastly superior numbers.

The ambush was a standard method of combat during the period of the conquest of Canaan. The fall of Ai, for example, was due directly to the tactical success of an ambush (Jos 8:1-23). Under cover of night, Joshua was able to move a large force to a concealed position behind the city. He then led the remainder of the Israelite army to the edge of a valley north of the fortified city, giving the appearance of a planned assault on the city. The diversion, as calculated, drew the main force of Ai away from the city to engage Israel on the plain of Arabah. When the Israelites fell back, appearing to be badly beaten, the remaining defenders of the city were summoned to pursue Joshua's fleeing army. With the city left undefended, the main Israelite strike force rose from its ambush position, poured into the city, and set it on fire. Too late, the men of Ai saw the smoke from their burning city and realized the stratagem. Joshua's army turned to counterattack their pursuers, who found themselves trapped between two bodies of Israelite forces. Assaulted from both front and rear, the king of Ai's army was annihilated, victim of an effectively laid ambush.

Fortifications and Defense The earliest known fortifications in the world, dated by some to about 7000 BC, were discovered in 1954 at Jericho. They were impressive in conception and construction. The core of the defense system was a wall, part of which, bordering the western edge of the ancient city, was still standing to a height of 21 feet (6.4 meters). Further excavation uncovered a large moat that had been carved out of solid rock at the base of the wall, 27 feet (8.2 meters) wide and 9 feet (2.7 meters) deep. How that feat was accomplished when the only tools assumed to have been available were made of stone is a complete mystery. A third component of Jericho's defense system was a huge stone circular tower 30 feet (9.1 meters) high, once evidently attached to the inner side of the western part of the wall. The exact purpose of the tower has not yet been determined, but Neolithic Jericho provides the earliest evidence of a fortified city supported by a wall, tower, and moat.

By the middle Bronze period, there were four components in a standard defense system: a moat, an advance (outer) wall, the main (inner) wall, and a well-fortified gate structure. The moat, advance wall, and subsidiary fortifications protecting the steep slope and lower portion of the main wall were intended to prevent breaching by a battering ram.

City Walls Erection of a simple wall could halt a hostile advance only temporarily, since walls could be scaled or breached. Walls therefore provided a firing platform so defenders could repel attacks. The wall system consisted of three principal components: the wall itself, constituting the barrier; an upper structure, which provided the firing platform and cover for the defenders; and a series of obstacles and traps erected in front of the wall to keep archers at a distance and to prevent operation of a battering ram.

The battlement—a parapet built along the outer top edge of the wall—provided the defenders with a measure of security, freedom for mobility, and openings through which fire could be directed. From a distance the square notches looked like a row of teeth with gaps between them. The teeth, called merlons, provided a protective barrier against hostile missiles. The gaps, called embrasures or crenels, supplied openings through which the defenders could discharge their weapons. Special towers protruded from the outer face of the wall, spaced at a distance no greater than the double range of a bow. Such towers enabled the defenders to fire at troops who managed to reach the walls. One way of protecting the main wall was to construct an outer or advance wall that could be breached or climbed only under heavy fire from defending units on the battlements of the main wall. Another method was to dig a wide, deep moat around the base of the main wall. A moat kept the enemy from using a battering ram unless they could bridge the moat or fill it up at certain points, under concentrated fire from the defenders.

Casemate fortifications, introduced in the middle Bronze period, were developed from double walls built of dressed stones. The space between the walls was divided into chambers, or casemates, used for storage or dwellings. The Hittite casemate system, introduced into Palestine at least as early as the time of Saul, was widely adopted in Syria and Palestine. A fine example has been discovered at Gibeah, where Saul's citadel was located, dating to the end of the 11th century BC. The overall thickness of the double walls, including the casemates, reaches 15 feet (4.6 meters). The same type of construction has been found in excavations of three Solomonic cities—Hazor, Gezer, and Megiddo (cf. 1 Kgs 9:15)—where the casemate walls have an overall thickness of 18 feet (5.5 meters).

Although the divided kingdoms of Judah and Israel were not noted for technical advancements in offensive warfare, a number of their kings worked at improving fortifications and means of defense. Uzziah was especially

remembered for his accomplishments in defensive warfare. Along with other measures, "he produced machines mounted on the walls of Jerusalem, designed by brilliant men to shoot arrows and hurl stones from the towers and the corners of the wall" (2 Chr 26:15, NLT). Those "machines" were special protective structures built to facilitate the task of the archers and to permit huge stones to be dropped on the heads of assaulting troops.

Gate It was inevitable that the gate would be the focus of action in any assault on a fortified city. City gates were therefore designed to expose an attacking army to the greatest risk while providing maximum security to the defenders. The road approaching a city on a hill would wind up the slope, climbing obliquely to the left or the right. Such roads were usually laid out to reach the gate from the right, so an attacker would have to expose the right side of his body to the defenders on the wall. Since he carried his shield in his left hand, that made him more vulnerable.

To prevent the heavy wooden doors of the gate from being set on fire, they were usually plated with metal. A gate wide enough for chariots required double doors, making the line at the center where the two doors met the weakest point in the barrier. Double doors were therefore fitted with huge bolts and fortified with a heavy beam running across the back of both door panels and held in place by sockets set in the doorposts.

Another component in the defense complex at a gate consisted of towers erected on either side of the gate and protruding from the outer face of the wall. Enemy soldiers trying to smash the doors with axes or set them on fire with torches were thus exposed to heavy flanking fire from defensive units on the towers. From a roof over the gate having a balcony, concentrated firepower could be poured down on attackers' heads. The addition of such auxiliary structures transformed a gate into a small fortress.

Inner Citadel A major weakness of a city's walls and gate was the magnitude of the circumference. An average-size city might have a perimeter of half a mile (.8 kilometer); a larger city, a perimeter of over a mile (1.6 kilometers). Yet the entire wall had to be defended against breaching, scaling, or tunneling. An attacking army would use diversionary tactics to keep defenders dispersed along the entire perimeter but concentrate their primary assault at one point in the wall. Once the wall was breached, perimeter fortifications served no further defensive purpose. Therefore, internal walls were often added to subdivide a city into several sections, each capable of independent defense. Also, on the highest point of land within the city a citadel would be constructed as a self-contained defensive unit.

The earliest examples of such fortifications, called migdols, are found in the late Bronze Age. They were originally small citadels built to guard important military targets such as sources of water, strategic routes, cultivated farmlands, or frontiers. A migdol of that type was discovered in Israel, not far from Ashdod, in 1960. It was square in plan, with rectangular bastions, and was two stories high, just like structures depicted in Egyptian reliefs from the same period. The same design was used to fortify temples inside of cities. Such fortified temples served as places of refuge and as a city's final defense once its walls had been breached (cf. Jgs 9:45-51).

In a later period an inner citadel could embrace a complex consisting of the fortified palace of the governor, dwellings of his chief ministers, and sometimes the temple. Such citadels resembled fortified cities, possessing a main wall, a gateway, an outer wall, and occasionally a moat. Being small in area and heavily fortified, citadels could be defended in a final effort by the governor and remaining inhabitants. Presumably Zimri could have held out against Omri's army for an extended period in the citadel of Tirzah, had he not committed suicide by setting it on fire (1 Kgs 16:17-18).

Water Supply under Siege Unless provision was made to keep a city's inhabitants supplied with food and water during a protracted siege, no defense system could be effective. Several Judean kings made efforts to solve the food-storage problem. Rehoboam, for example, fortified a number of cities located on the western, eastern, and southern borders of his kingdom and made them centers for the storage of food, oil, and wine (2 Chr 11:5-11).

Storage of food was easier than storage of water. Cisterns built to collect rainwater were a partial answer, but cisterns often ran dry, particularly in times of drought. Cities were sometimes built on the banks of a stream or river, using the stream as part of the city's defense system. But for a city built on a hill, the source of water might be a spring located at the foot of the slope and outside the city walls. Sometimes the mouth of the spring could be blocked and its location concealed from the enemy while still allowing access by the inhabitants. At Megiddo a vertical shaft 100 feet (274.3 meters) deep was connected by a horizontal tunnel about 200 feet (548.6 meters) long to the water supply at the western end of the city, beyond the fortifications. The work was undertaken in the time of either Solomon or Ahab.

The most celebrated measures to guarantee a supply of fresh water in a time of siege were those taken by Hezekiah at Jerusalem. That engineering achievement is recalled in all the summaries of his reign, both in the Bible and in the "Praise of Famous Men" in the apocryphal book of Ecclesiasticus (2 Kgs 20:20; 2 Chr 32:30; Ecclus 48:17). The prodigious feat commemorated in those references was the sealing of the spring of Gihon and the cutting of an 1,800-foot (548.6-meter) channel through solid rock in order to bring water into a reservoir in the city. How it was accomplished was reported by Hezekiah himself in the famous Siloam inscription. Two crews, working with hammers, wedges, and pickaxes, began at opposite ends. The crew that began at the spring was able to take advantage of the older tunnel (cf. Is 22:11). They turned due south, in the direction of the city. The other crew, starting from the reservoir, began in a northeasterly direction. They then turned southeast until they reached the north-south line followed by the crew tunneling from the spring, when they turned due north to meet them. The two crews almost passed each other, being about five feet (1.5 meters) apart, but a shout from one was heard through a crevice in the rock by the other. Both parties turned sharply right, and the tunnel was completed. Hezekiah's precautionary step, taken before Sennacherib's invasion of Judah, helps to explain why the Assyrians were unable to subdue Jerusalem by the siege tactics that had earlier subdued Samaria in the time of Sargon.

Hebrew Military Organization

Tribal Army In their exodus from Egypt the Israelites were organized by tribes and divisions. That systematic arrangement for their trek through the wilderness provided a precedent for military organization. After the sojourn at Mt Sinai, the 12 tribes were divided into divisions or army corps, and certain grades in military rank began to appear. The "officers of the army" (Nm 31:14) had command over units of 1,000 or 100 men, which suggests that the tribal army was divided into decimal units. At a later period there is reference to units of 1,000 (the division), 100 (the company), 50 (the platoon), and 10 (the section). Except for the Levites, who were assigned as a tribe to the care of the tabernacle (Nm 2:33), men from 20 years of age who were physically

able to fight were assigned to a unit in the tribal army. Certain individuals, however, were exempted from military service (cf. Dt 20:5-9; 24:5; Jgs 7:3).

Until after the conquest of Canaan, the tribal army was essentially a militia recruited in an emergency. Internal organization of the militia was the responsibility of the tribe; each clan and family sent their quota of warriors when summoned to battle by tribal leaders. Because the clan formed the basic unit, recruits were under the command of their own leaders. David's brothers, for example, served in a division composed of the fighting men from their clan under the command of a captain (1 Sm 17:18; 18:13). When the emergency passed, the militia was disbanded and the soldiers returned to their home districts.

Because the land was divided among the tribes, no tribal or clan leader before Saul commanded the entire tribal confederation (cf. 1 Sm 11:1-11). In fact, tribal jealousies and rivalries threatened national solidarity and jeopardized united action even in a critical period. On some occasions, however, the severity of a crisis caused the armies of the various tribes to unite in common action. The multitribal armies were divided into companies of 1,000, 100, and 50, and still further into families under appointed officers. There is evidence of organization into units according to weaponry (1 Chr 12:24-38). Benjamin's tribe specialized in the bow and sling. The tribes of Gad, Judah, and Naphtali were expert with the spear and shield.

Provisioning the tribal army was the responsibility of each tribe (Jgs 20:9-10). One out of every ten soldiers was appointed to secure food for the others, either from wealthy landowners (cf. 1 Sm 25) or from the natural resources of the land. In that early stage of military organization, a soldier's pay generally consisted only of supplies and a portion of the spoils of battle (cf. 30:21-25).

Professional Army Not until the time of the united monarchy did Israel have a regular army. Transition from a people's militia to a professional army took place under Saul, whose reign changed the tribal confederacy into a monarchy (1 Sm 13:2). Philistine harassment of Israel encouraged establishment of a strong standing army. The army, however, was not large; it consisted of 3,000 men organized in three formations of 1,000 each (1 Sm 13:2; 24:2). Pay for those career soldiers was sometimes in the form of a land grant (8:14) as well as a share of booty. In the organization of Saul's army, Abner, Jonathan, and David were given particular responsibilities. Abner was named commander of the army (17:55) and was probably also given direct command of one of the divisions. David's band of valorous men, "the thirty," provided the leadership core for his own military organization when he became king.

David continued the practice of maintaining a professional army. But he also developed a national militia of 12 regiments, each being called up for duty for one month of the year under professional officers (1 Chr 27:1-15). Each regiment, recruited across tribal lines, consisted of 24,000 soldiers. David's innovation provided him with a large reserve force that could be mustered for war in times of emergency. The reserves, and presumably the professional army as well, were organized into units of 1,000, 100, 50, and 10. Joab, a specialist in siege warfare (2 Sm 20:15), commanded the professional army, and Amasa was over the citizens' militia. David, however, remained commander-in-chief of the military organization.

The Israelite group in King David's professional army was an outgrowth of the small band of fighting men who had served with him during the period of conflict with Saul. That veteran group consisted of David's family and clansmen, and others who felt themselves oppressed by the central authority under Saul (1 Sm 22:1-2). It ranged in size between 400 and 600 men (1 Sm 22:2; 23:13; 27:2). The presence of mercenaries in David's army is clearly recorded. Uriah the Hittite and Ittai of Gath are conspicuous examples, along with many career soldiers of Philistine origin, such as the Cherethites and the Pelethites under Benaiah (2 Sm 8:18; 15:19-22; 23:22-23).

The Davidic dynasty maintained a permanent mercenary army until 701 BC, after which it was considered too costly. The oppressive cost of maintaining a professional army, financed by burdensome taxes and forced labor, was in fact a major factor contributing to the disruption of the monarchy after Solomon's death (cf. 1 Kgs 10:26-29; 12:4-19). After Sennacherib's invasion in 701 BC, the southern kingdom of Judah depended entirely on a citizens' militia for its defense. It is commonly held that the northern kingdom of Israel did not employ a professional army, but it is evident that King Ahab used at least some mercenary soldiers in his defense against Ben-hadad of Syria (1 Kgs 20:15-20).

See also Armor and Weapons.

GOD AND WAR
Modern readers of the Bible often have difficulty with the military emphasis of the OT, asking, "How could God be a God of love and yet lead his chosen people into bloody wars?" The fact is that the Israelites were no more belligerent than the people who came before them or after them. God wanted to introduce new concepts of love and justice into the world through his people, but it was necessary for them to survive in order to do that. He did not take them out of their world—a world where resources were scarce and life precarious—but helped them fight for survival among far more brutal and acquisitive powers. Yet through the prophet Isaiah, God gave to his people the vision of a day when the art of warfare would be forgotten (Is 2:2-5).

The centuries that followed were characterized by a series of crises precipitated by intrigue and war. Persia, Macedonia, Parthia, and Rome successively established a military presence in the land. No display of military prowess, however, could dim the prophetic vision. No experience of an imposed peace could satisfy its terms. Indeed, Christians believe that at a time when Israel was under total military domination by Rome, God brought forth a Ruler, his Messiah, the "Prince of Peace," to establish a peace that will never end (Is 9:6-7). The promise that nations will one day beat their swords into plowshares and their spears into pruning hooks accounts for the rebirth of hope in the hearts of God's people—even when war or the threat of warfare looms imminent, or when a nation's leadership directs its attention to arms and warfare. The accomplishment of Isaiah's prophecy ultimately depends not on the ingenuity or intention of human beings but on the will of the sovereign God.

WAR OF THE SONS OF LIGHT AGAINST THE SONS OF DARKNESS*

Scroll found in Cave One at Qumran (1947–48). It casts light on military regulations of the Jewish forces, on the religious life of the sectarians at Qumran, and particularly on their eschatological expectations. It was probably written about the middle of the first century BC or the beginning of the first century AD. Professor Sukenik of Hebrew University purchased the scroll, consisting of 19 sheets, from an antiquities dealer in Bethlehem (*see* page 178), then edited the scroll. It was published posthumously in 1954.

The sectarians at Qumran divided all mankind into two camps: the Sons of Light and the Sons of Darkness. Only those in fellowship with the community at Qumran were reckoned to belong to the Sons of Light, and all other Jews, together with the Gentiles, belonged to Satan and his hosts. The scroll expresses the hope that the day of victory over the forces of darkness is approaching. The rule of the Romans (Kittim) "shall come to an end and iniquity shall be vanquished, leaving no remnants; [for the sons] of darkness there shall be no escape." The Sons of Light will participate in the last battle.

In order to fight the Lord's battle in the manner of the Lord, the Sons of Light have to be familiar with the rules of war. This scroll was written to indoctrinate the faithful in the biblical rules of war. Since the sabbatical years of rest must be observed, the faithful will fight against the evil forces only 35 out of 40 years.

Six priests in special dress were to proceed ahead of the forces while blowing a trumpet. On each of the trumpets is an inscription that bears out the belief that the battle is the Lord's and that those who are called are summoned to avenge themselves on the enemies of the Lord and thus to vindicate his holiness. The priests, together with the Levites, blowing their horns, would confound the enemy. In the description of the ordering of the battle divisions, the priests again take up a prominent role. The priests and Levites were to go ahead of the battle formations. They were God's appointed ministers, as representatives of God's presence among the fighting forces. In the end, it was expected that God would conquer evil on behalf of the faithful remnant: "This is the day appointed by him for the defeat and overthrow of the Prince of the kingdom of wickedness, and he will send eternal succor to the company of his redeemed by the might of the princely Angel of the kingdom of Michael."

WARS OF THE LORD, Book of the

Document mentioned once in the OT (Nm 21:14); it is found in a description of Moab's border at the Arnon. The book was used as a source but is no longer extant. It probably contained a record of Israel's conquest in Transjordan and may be identical to the "Book of the Upright [Jashar]" (Jos 10:13; 2 Sm 1:18). The passage in Numbers 21 has a poetic style and pertains to Israel's conquest and warfare. However, the extent of the quotation is debatable. Some limit it to verse 14, others include verse 15, and still others include verses 27-30.

WATCH

Time unit for the division of the night in both the OT and NT. During the OT period, the night was divided into three military watches. The beginning or evening watch ran from sunset to roughly 10:00 PM (Lam 2:19); the middle or night watch was from 10:00 PM to 2:00 AM (Jgs 7:19); and the morning watch was from approximately 2:00 AM until sunrise (Ex 14:24; 1 Sm 11:11). During the Roman period, the number of watches was increased from three to four. These were either described by number (first, second, etc.) or as evening, midnight, cock-crowing, and morning (Mt 14:25; Mk 6:48). The respective watches ended at roughly 9:00 PM, midnight, 3:00 AM, and 6:00 AM. *See* Night.

WATCHMAN

Military or civil security person who had the responsibility to protect ancient towns or military installations from surprise attack or civil disasters (1 Sm 14:16; 2 Sm 18:24-27; 2 Kgs 9:17-20; Is 21:6-9). Watchmen also had the responsibility of announcing the dawning of a new day (Ps 130:6; Is 21:11-12). In a passage describing the function and responsibilities of the prophets, Ezekiel reported the watchman's parallel responsibility to warn of impending danger. If the watchman (or prophet) failed in his task, he would be guilty of the blood of the people (Ez 33:2-9; cf. Jer 6:17; Ez 3:17; Hos 9:8). In contrast to the faithful prophets, Isaiah compared the leaders of Israel to blind watchmen who lacked the ability to see Israel's danger, much less lead the people to repentance (Is 56:10; Mi 7:4). The prophets who served as Israel's watchmen were the ones who first saw the coming destruction of Israel and also the ones who first announced their return to the land (Is 21:11-12; 52:8).

WATCHTOWER Platform from which farmers protected their land and livestock and from which soldiers guarded their cities. Watchtowers were built in the vineyards of Palestine. From the tower the watchman was assigned to oversee the vineyard, protecting it from wild animals and thieves (Is 5:2; Mt 21:33; Mk 12:1). Such structures are still used for similar purposes in Palestine and serve as the living quarters for the vineyard workers. Some watchtowers, like the tower of Eder (Gn 35:21), were constructed in wilderness areas. They provided a protected shelter for shepherds to watch their flocks and a fortified outpost for sentinels to guard a city and to safeguard its commerce from marauding bandits (2 Kgs 18:8; 2 Chr 20:24; Is 32:14).

WATER One of the essentials of life, which covers much of the earth's surface and is the primary component of the human body. Life cannot be sustained more than a few days without it.

In the beginning, water covered the earth. Then God brought up the dry land from the water (Gn 1:9-10). As Peter said, "God made the heavens by the word of his command, and he brought the earth up from the water and surrounded it with water" (2 Pt 3:5, NLT).

When the Lord created the Garden of Eden, he made a river to water it. This river divided into four rivers, of which two are identified with certainty, the Euphrates and the Tigris, which have sustained agricultural life in the Mesopotamian area both in antiquity and today (Gn 2:10-14). The Bible also relates that early in the history of the earth there was no rain but only a mist that watered the earth (vv 5-6). In the time of Noah, the Lord used an overwhelming mass and movement of water to destroy "the world that then existed" (2 Pt 3:6), as punishment for its wickedness.

In the Near East, water is of special importance, for much of the area receives only moderate amounts of rainfall. In Egypt, for example, only two to four inches (5.1 to 10.2 centimeters) of rain falls in the area of Cairo, and at Aswan the average annual rainfall is zero. Egypt is dependent upon the Nile, which is supplied by equatorial rains. By contrast, Palestine is watered well by "the rain from heaven" (Dt 11:10-11).

Water has many symbolic usages in Scripture (quoted below mostly from the NLT). The righteous man is like a tree planted by streams of water (Ps 1:3; Jer 17:8). The longing of the soul after God is likened to thirst for water: "My soul thirsts for you; my whole body longs for you in this parched and weary land where there is no water" (Ps 63:1); "I thirst for you as parched land thirsts for rain" (143:6). Jesus fulfills this need and declares, "If you are thirsty, come to me! If you believe in me, come and drink!" (Jn 7:37-38). And Jesus said, "The water I give them takes away thirst altogether. It becomes a perpetual spring within them, giving them eternal life" (4:14). The Spirit of Jesus is that spiritual water that satisfies the thirst of the human spirit (7:38-39). The Word of God is also presented as water by which spiritual cleansing is effected. The Lord speaks of the cleansing of the church by "the

washing of water with the word" (Eph 5:26). And Paul said that people are saved "by the washing of regeneration and renewal in the Holy Spirit" (Ti 3:5).

In the closing chapters of the Bible the Lord declares, "To all who are thirsty I will give the springs of the water of life without charge!" (Rv 21:6, NLT). Even in the description of the heavenly Jerusalem there is mention of water—the river of the water of life: "The angel showed me a pure river with the water of life, clear as crystal, flowing from the throne of God and of the Lamb, coursing down the center of the main street" (22:1-2). The final invitation of Scripture comes to us in similar terms: "Let the thirsty ones come—anyone who wants to. Let them come and drink the water of life without charge" (v 17).

WATER GATE One of the principal gates on the east side of Jerusalem. It was rebuilt during Nehemiah's day and served as the location for Ezra's reading of the law (Neh 3:26; 8:3, 16; 12:37).

WATER HEN* Designation for several birds living near water, such as the marsh hen, swan, or even the horned owl. *See* Animals; Birds.

WATER LILY* *See* Plants.

WATERS OF MEROM *See* Merom, Waters of.

WAVE OFFERING* *See* Offerings and Sacrifices.

WAY, The One of the names applied to the early Christian community (Acts 9:2). It was apparently used by both the Jewish and the secular community and appeared in both positive and negative assessments of the church (19:9, 23; 22:4; 24:14, 22). Paul's use of the term in his defense before Felix suggests that the name had at least quasiofficial acceptance (24:14, 22). Quite likely, the term came from Jesus' own statement, "I am the way, the truth, and the life" (Jn 14:6).

FOLLOWERS OF THE WAY
Early Christianity was far from being an abstract belief; it was a whole way of life. The new way of living was obvious to those around Christians and to the Christians themselves, for they were following Jesus' lifestyle, the way he had lived and taught. Soon the term "this Way" or "the Way" meant Christian. Thus Saul (the pre-Christian name of Paul) was sent to Damascus to arrest anyone belonging to "the Way" (Acts 9:2). Christians may also have used the term to describe themselves; Luke referred to the Christian movement as "the Way" (Acts 19:9, 23; 24:22). It may be the only name Christians and non-Christians both used for the new movement.

WEALTH Abundance, usually of money or material goods, whose value is ordinarily expressed in terms of some understood unit, such as a national currency. It is virtually synonymous with riches, and both may refer to family, friends, or even moral qualities.

In the OT riches are a mark of favor with God (Ps 112:3), and he gives power to acquire wealth (Dt 8:18). Both the piety and the wealth of Job are well known (Jb 1:1-3). Solomon was perhaps the richest man who ever lived; God granted him "riches, possessions, and honor" because Solomon had asked for wisdom and discernment rather than material things (1 Kgs 3:10-13; 2 Chr 1:11-12). But the Bible makes it clear that a person's life does not consist in the abundance of his possessions (Lk 12:15).

In the NT wealthy men are often seen as godless—for example, the rich farmer (Lk 12:16-21) and the rich man who neglected the beggar Lazarus (16:19-31). The wealthy are condemned for oppression and greed (Jas 5:1-6). Luke 6:24 pronounces woe against the rich, and all three synoptic Gospels speak of the dangers of riches (Mt 13:22; Mk 4:19; Lk 8:14). But not all rich men were bad. Jesus was buried in the tomb of a rich man from Arimathea, named Joseph (Mt 27:57). Nicodemus, who provided lavishly for the burial of Jesus (Jn 19:39), was "a ruler of the Jews" (3:1) and probably a man of wealth.

See also Mammon; Money; Poor, The; Riches; Wages.

WEAPONS *See* Armor and Weapons; Warfare.

WEASEL* *See* Animals.

WEAVING *See* Cloth and Cloth Manufacturing.

WEDDING *See* Marriage, Marriage Customs.

WEEDS *See* Plants (Darnel Grass).

WEEK *See* Calendars, Ancient and Modern.

WEEKS*, Feast of Celebration of the beginning of the wheat harvest (Ex 23:14-17; Dt 16:16), occurring seven weeks after Passover on the sixth day of Sivan (June); also known as the Feast of Pentecost. *See* Feasts and Festivals of Israel.

WEIGHTS AND MEASURES

PREVIEW
•Introduction
•Weight Measures
•Linear Measures in the Old Testament
•Linear Measures in the New Testament
•Capacity (Dry Measure) in the Old Testament
•Capacity (Dry Measure) in the New Testament
•Liquid Measures in the Old Testament
•Liquid Measures in the New Testament

Introduction Units of measure in the ancient world were largely based on practical standards: the length of an arm, a day's journey, how much a donkey could carry, and so forth. While this was a convenient system, it also suffered from a lack of standardization. Some arms were longer than others, and some donkeys could carry more than others. The history of weights and measures, therefore, becomes the story of seeking standards. This was not achieved in the OT but began to take place under Greek and Roman influences in NT times.

In the OT the measures that were used are frequently attested to in Mesopotamian, Egyptian, and Canaanite literature as well. The Israelites did not have their own unique set of measurements. Yet while the terms are shared, it is not unusual to find a particular term having one value in Israel and a noticeably different value in one of the other cultures.

By the time of the NT, other variables were added. The Israelites of this period were still using many of the measures that had been used and developed throughout the OT period. But added to that were the Greek and Roman systems of measurement. Sometimes these terms were adopted wholesale, while at other times Hebrew terms were adapted to Greco-Roman standards. On still other occasions, the Roman terms were apparently used when dealing with the government, whereas Hebrew terms were still used in everyday practice.

In most of the kinds of measurement, the base unit (i.e., the one that all of the others are fractions or multiples of) is the one about which there is the most uncertainty. So the cubit (length), the shekel (weight), the homer (dry volume), and the bath (liquid volume) are all to some degree uncertain. This makes all of the other measures based on them equally uncertain.

Weight Measures The terms used for weights have benefited most from archaeological discoveries. Excavations provide stone weights that are occasionally inscribed with the unit they represent. When the stones are weighed, they frequently give a range of weights that have only a general consistency. However, comparing this data with that provided by the text has given the basis for fairly accurate determinations. The relative scale in any given location is more important than absolute values.

TABLE OF WEIGHTS AND MEASURES

Weight

talent	75 pounds	34 kilograms
mina	1.25 pounds	600 grams
shekel	.4 ounce	11.4 grams
pim	.25 ounce	8 grams
beka	.2 ounce	5.7 grams
gerah	.02 ounce	.6 gram
litra	12 ounces	327 grams

Distance

long cubit	20.5 inches	52.1 centimeters
cubit	17.5 inches	44.5 centimeters
span	8.75 inches	22.2 centimeters
handbreadth	3 inches	7.6 centimeters
fathom	6 feet	1.8 meters
furlong/stadium	200 yards	182.9 meters
Roman mile	1620 yards	1.4 kilometers

Capacity

Dry Measure

cor/homer	5 bushels	182 liters
lethek	2.5 bushels	91 liters
ephah	.5 bushel	17.6 liters
seah	5 quarts	6 liters
omer/issaron	2 quarts	2 liters
cab, kab	1 quart	1.3 liters
choinix	1 quart	1.1 liters
modius	1 peck	8.5 liters
saton	5 quarts	6 liters

Liquid Measure

bath	5.5 gallons	20.8 liters
hin	1 gallon	3.8 liters
log	.3 quart	.3 liter
metretes	10 gallons	37.9 liters
sextarius/xestes	1.2 pints	552 milliliters

There was standardization of weight measures, but precision was difficult to attain. The Israelite system is similar to that used by the Mesopotamians and the Canaanites. For most of the OT period, the weights system provided the monetary system. Minted coinage was the invention of the Persians. Up until that time, silver or gold or any other trading commodity had to be weighed out so that bartering or purchasing could take place. This made the weights system the core of the ancient economy. It also explains why the Scriptures speak so seriously against the use of false weights (Lv 19:36; Dt 25:13; Prv 16:11; 20:10, 23; Mi 6:11; Hos 12:7; Am 8:5).

Stone weights were used on a set of balances for conducting business in the ancient marketplace. Scales or balances are mentioned half a dozen times in the OT, but none of those are in actual economic contexts (Jb 6:2; 31:6; Ps 62:9; Is 40:12; Ez 5:1; Dn 5:27). The scales used were generally of the beam-balance type with dishes on each end.

Talent According to Exodus 38:25-26 the talent must have been equal to 3,000 shekels. (A hundred talents would then have been equal to 300,000 shekels, and if that is added to the 1,175 shekels in verse 25, the total is 301,775, or half a shekel for each of the 603,550 men—as verse 26 states.) Excavated talents weigh from about 65 to 80 pounds (29.5 to 36.3 kilograms). In the OT the talent is used only for precious metals, usually silver or gold. According to 1 Kings 10:14, the annual tribute income of Solomon's kingdom was 666 talents, which apparently was considered quite extravagant. David bequeathed 100,000 talents of gold and 1,000,000 talents of silver to Solomon for the building of the temple (1 Chr 22:14).

Mina In the Canaanite material from Ugarit the mina equals 50 shekels, while in Babylon the mina equals 60 shekels. In Ezekiel 45:12, the mina is set at 60 shekels, but it is unclear whether this represents a change from previous standards.

Shekel The shekel was the basic unit of weight. Besides the regular shekel, there was a "royal" shekel (2 Sm 14:26). Calculating by weights that have been excavated and found labeled as "beka" (one-half shekel), the shekel has been estimated to be about .4 ounce (11.4 grams).

The shekel is used in Scripture almost exclusively in contexts dealing with monetary value. Whether silver, gold, barley, or flour, the shekel valuation assigns the commodity a relative value in the economy. Exceptions to this are Goliath's armor and spear (1 Sm 17:5-7), which are described in terms of their shekel weight.

Pim The only reference to this unit is in 1 Samuel 13:21, where it is the price charged to the Israelites by the Philistines for sharpening a plowshare. Excavated weights range from .25 to .3 ounce (7.1 to 8.5 grams), suggesting that the pim was two-thirds of a shekel.

Beka Seven stones inscribed with this label range in weight from .2 to .23 ounce (5.7 to 6.5 grams). In Exodus 38:26 it is the amount levied on each individual for the census tax. There it is the equivalent of one-half shekel.

Gerah Equal to one-twentieth of a shekel, or .02 ounce (.6 gram). The term is used five times (Ex 30:13; Lv 27:25; Nm 3:47; 18:16; Ez 45:12) and on each occasion is used to give a valuation to the shekel. Its use is strictly monetary in these contexts.

Litra The NT uses the same weights that have already been identified in the OT usage, particularly the shekel, mina, and talent. There is one additional unit used: the litra, which is used in John 12:3 and 19:39 with regard to spices. In Greek literature one litra is approximately 12 ounces (327 grams).

Linear Measures in the Old Testament Measurements of length and depth generally were derived from a part of the body used to make the measurement. The basic unit was the cubit, and most others were related to it. Precise measurements of geographic distance are lacking in the OT and was most frequently stated in terms of the number of days it would take to arrive at a destination. A single day's journey was mostly likely 20 to 25 miles (32.2 to 40.2 kilometers). A "pace" was equal to a "step"—about a yard (2 Sm 6:13).

Cubit The length from the tip of the forefinger to the elbow. There are both long and short cubits, which are used not only in Israel but in Mesopotamia and Egypt as well. Ezekiel 40:5 identifies the long cubit as being the equivalent of a cubit plus a handbreadth (about 20 to 21 inches, or 50.8 to 53.3 centimeters). The inscription found inside the Siloam tunnel built by Hezekiah (715–686 BC) indicates that the tunnel is 1,200 cubits long. The actual length of the tunnel was determined to be 1,749 feet (533.1 meters). This would yield a cubit of 17.49 inches (44.4 centimeters). All things considered, 17.5 inches (44.5 centimeters) is a good estimation of the length of the cubit in Israel. This would set the long cubit at approximately 20.5 inches (52.1 centimeters). The cubit was most frequently used to give the dimensions of buildings or objects (e.g., curtains, pillars, pieces of furniture, etc.). The largest structure measured in cubits was the ark that Noah built, which was 300 cubits long (Gn 6:15).

Span The distance measured by the stretch of the hand from fingertip to fingertip, equal to one-half a cubit, or eight and three-quarters inches (22.2 centimeters). It is used only seven times in the OT, and four of those are to describe the dimensions of the high priest's breastplate (Ex 28:15-16; 39:8-9).

Handbreadth The width of the hand at the base, equal to one-sixth of a cubit, one-third of a span, or just under three inches (7.6 centimeters). The term is used only five times and gives the width of the rim around the table of showbread (Ex 25:25) and Solomon's molten sea (1 Kgs 7:26).

Linear Measurements in the New Testament In the NT some of the units of length and depth represent Greco-Roman standards, while others are those used in the OT. Like the OT, the NT frequently uses imprecise designations for distance, such as a stone's throw or a day's journey. There are, however, a few occurrences of precise terms borrowed from Roman culture.

Cubit For the Romans, the cubit was set at one and a half times their standard foot of 11.66 inches, equaling 17.5 inches (44.5 centimeters), just as the OT cubit.

Fathom The distance between the fingertips of the left and right hand when the arms were outstretched. It is used only in Acts 27:28 and is considered to be about six feet (1.8 meters).

Furlong/Stadium The length of the ancient Greek racecourse, equal to one-eighth of a Roman mile, or a little over 200 yards (182.9 meters). It is usually used to give approximate distance, but in Revelation 21:16 it is used to give the dimensions of the New Jerusalem and is measured with a measuring rod.

Mile The only occurrence of this term, Matthew 5:41, has reference to the Roman mile of 1,620 yards, about nine-tenths of a modern mile (1.4 kilometers).

Capacity (Dry Measure) in the Old Testament Amounts of dry goods were oriented toward practical matters such as typical donkey loads, how much seed could be sown in a day, or how much seed would be needed to sow a certain size plot. As with the other types of measures, these then became standardized.

Cor/Homer The most common dry commodity measure and the equivalent of one donkey load. Estimates of its standard size vary greatly, ranging from 3.8 bushels to 7.5 bushels (133.9 to 264.3 liters). Other than the seven occurrences in Ezekiel 45:11-14, the term occurs only four times in the OT. Three of these contexts feature seed or barley (Lv 27:16; Is 5:10; Hos 3:2), while the fourth is in the context of Israelites gathering quail in the wilderness. A cor is used nine times and occurs with a variety of commodities, including oil, flour, wheat, and barley, in multiples all the way up to 20,000 (1 Kgs 5:11).

Lethek Unit occurring only in Hosea 3:2. The early versions of the Bible identified it as one-half of a cor, or homer.

Ephah This is equal to one-tenth of a homer (Ez 45:11), or one-half of a bushel (17.6 liters). The term occurs dozens of times with all sorts of agricultural products. It seems to have been the unit most used in trading and selling. According to Zechariah 5:6-10, the ephah refers to a container that would hold an ephah of produce, much like the modern-day bushel basket.

Seah A fraction of the homer, which has a very wide range. The term measures flour, seed, barley, and grain, and is roughly one-third of an ephah. A bushel was about five seahs (1 Sm 25:18, NLT mg).

Omer/Issaron The omer occurs only in the account of the collecting of manna by the Israelites (Ex 16:22). It represents a day's ration of manna and is identified as one-tenth of an ephah (Ex 16:36). The issaron is a term that means a tenth. Its 25 occurrences are all in Exodus, Leviticus, and Numbers (mostly in Nm 28–29); it refers only to measures of fine flour.

Cab, Kab This unit occurs only in 2 Kings 6:25. The estimate given by Josephus, one-eighteenth of an ephah (or about one-half of an omer), is usually accepted.

Capacity (Dry Measure) in the New Testament
The following dry measures are used in the NT.

Choinix Occurring only in Revelation 6:6 (see NLT mg), the choinix is a little more than a quart (1.1 liters). In Greek literature it was considered the amount of one man's daily allowance of corn.

Modius This is the "bushel" under which one's lamp should not be hid (Mt 5:15; Mk 4:21; Lk 11:33). It is actually equal to about a peck, 7.68 dry quarts (8.5 liters).

Saton This is the equivalent of the OT seah and can therefore also be approximated at about a peck. It is used only twice in the NT in parallel passages of the parable of the leaven, which is like the kingdom of God (Mt 13:33; Lk 13:21).

Liquid Measures in the Old Testament Three basic measures were used for liquids in the OT.

Bath The base unit for the measurement of liquids. The biblical data (Ez 45:11-14) sets it as the liquid equivalent to the dry measure, the ephah. It is one-tenth of a homer. Archaeology has also been able to provide some data for this determination. Jars inscribed as "bath of the king" were found at Lachish and Tell en-Nasbeh, and jars marked "bath" were found at Tell Beit Mirsim. The jars are not complete, so their capacity must be calculated based on a reconstruction. Using this data, the bath was approximately 5.5 gallons (20.8 liters). This estimate would provide acceptable results when factored into the information given in 1 Kings 7:23-26, where the "molten sea" of Solomon's temple is described as being 30 cubits in circumference, 10 cubits in diameter, 5 cubits deep, and capable of holding 2,000 baths of water.

Hin One-sixth of a hin of water was considered a person's minimum daily requirement (Ez 4:11). A hin is equal to one-sixth of a bath, approximately one gallon (3.8 liters). It is used for a measure of oil, wine, and water, but no context ever mentions more than one hin. Rather, fractions of a hin are used. Occurrences are limited to Exodus, Leviticus, Numbers, and Ezekiel and are therefore most commonly attested in the context of sacrificial libations.

Log This unit occurs only in Leviticus 14:10-24 and equals one-twelfth of a hin, so about .3 quart or .3 liter.

Liquid Measures in the New Testament The following liquid measures occur in the NT.

Bath This is used only once (Lk 16:6) and is the same as the OT bath.

Metretes This is used only in John 2:6, where it describes the containers in which water was turned to wine. Josephus identifies it as equivalent to a Hebrew bath, but in Greek usage it was the equivalent of about ten gallons (37.9 liters).

Sextarius/Xestes A measure of capacity equal to about one and one-sixth pints (552 milliliters). In Mark 7:4 the word is translated "pitcher" (NLT) or "pot" (KJV, see mg).

WELL Man-made reservoir fed either by subterranean springs or by rainwater. Because the majority of the biblical world ranges from arid to semiarid, wells were a critical source of water for humans, livestock, and the irrigation of crops. Unfortunately, most wells did not offer a reliable source of water, being dependent on the scarce rainfall or intermittent springs (Prv 25:26). The discovery of a reliable source of water was therefore the cause of much rejoicing (Nm 21:17-18) and frequent conflict (Gn 21:25-30; 26:19-22; 2 Kgs 3:19). Successfully digging a well and defending one's water rights often served as an important determinant of property rights (Gn 21:25-30; 29:2-3).

Good wells were generally considered signs of God's providence (Gn 16:14; 21:19; Nm 21:16-18). Biblical writers therefore compared the water of spring-fed wells to God's provision of salvation for his people (Is 12:3; Jn 4:14). The distinction between the relatively poor quality of water in cisterns that captured rainwater and the high quality of those wells that tapped springs of "living" (i.e., flowing) water helps clarify the dialogue between Jesus and the Samaritan woman when Jesus offered her "living water" (Jn 4:10-15).

See also Cistern; Jacob's Well.

WESTERN TEXT* According to the classification of B. F. Wescott and F. J. A. Hort, one of the four principal text types of the Greek New Testament. *See* Bible, Manuscripts and Text of the (New Testament).

WHALE* *See* Animals.

WHEAT *See* Agriculture; Food and Food Preparation; Plants.

WHEEL Device originating in the region of Mesopotamia, probably dating from about 3500 BC. The earliest known form is the two-wheeled cart of Sumer. The first wheels were probably just discs cut from trees, but later wheels were made by clamping three shaped planks together by copper clamps extending the length of the wheel. After 2000 BC wheels with spokes appeared in northern Mesopotamia.

In the Bible, four Hebrew words are used to identify a number of types and usages of the wheel. These include the potter's wheel (Jer 18:3), chariot wheels (Ex 14:25), and wheels for grinding grain (Is 28:28). The most frequent and most important usage of the word "wheel" in the Bible, however, is in connection with Ezekiel's vision of the chariot of God (Ez 1, 10). Associated with the cloud appearing in a stormy wind (1:4) are fire, creatures, and wheels. Ezekiel draws the reader's attention to each of these phenomena. The wheels move in the direction the creatures take them. The significance of the wheel in Ezekiel is the shape. The wheel is compound, a wheel within a wheel. This is not to say that two wheels are on the same axis. It rather signifies a wheel set in a wheel in such a way that its rim makes a 90-degree angle with the rim of the wheel in which it is set. The wheel has mobility;

it can roll from east to west and from north to south. Wherever the living creatures go, it will follow. This speaks of God's universal judgment, which no one can escape.

See also Ezekiel, Book of.

WHIRLWIND Term descriptive of any strong, potentially destructive wind (Jb 27:20; Ps 77:18; Dn 11:40). While whirlwinds are relatively common in the arid regions of the Middle East (e.g., dust devils), the apparent fury and destructiveness of the biblical "whirlwinds" makes it unlikely that the relatively harmless dust devils are intended (cf. Am 1:14; Hb 3:14). Sirocco winds from the eastern deserts are occasionally cyclonic in form, but the winds in Scripture may not be whirlwinds in the technical sense.

Biblical whirlwinds were often associated with divine activity. Elijah was taken into heaven by a whirlwind (one case where "whirlwind" may properly be translated as such; 2 Kgs 2:1, 11). God frequently spoke out of the whirlwind (Jb 38:1; 40:6; Ps 77:18). The description of the sudden destruction of divine judgment was frequently associated with storms, tempests, and whirlwinds (Hos 8:7; Am 1:14; Na 1:3; Hb 3:14).

WHITE *See* Color.

WHORE *See* Prostitute, Prostitution.

WICKEDNESS *See* Sin.

WIDOW A woman whose husband has died. In the Scriptures, widows are often listed with the fatherless and orphans (Dt 14:29; 16:11; 24:19-20; 26:12; Ps 94:6). Laws were passed to make special provision for this group and to protect them against the unscrupulous. The primary law had to do with levirate marriage—i.e., the closest kin would marry the widow (if she was without a son) to continue the family line (see discussion under Marriage).

The plight of the widow was recognized in the number of laws designed for her protection and even survival. God was her legal protector (Ps 68:5) and saw that she was provided with the essentials of food and clothing (Dt 10:18). Those who denied her justice were cursed by God (27:19). At harvesttime the widow might glean the grain in the fields, as well as some grapes and olives (Dt 24:19; Ru 2:2, 7, 15-19), and she was also eligible for some assistance from the third-year tithe. Nevertheless, the poverty of widows and the cruel treatment extended to them was so widespread that frequent reference is made to it (Jb 24:21; Ps 94:6; Is 1:23; Mal 3:5). A special law provided that the widow's garment could not be used as security for a loan (Dt 24:17).

In the early Christian church there was a recognized group of widows eligible to receive charity. They were generally those over 60 years of age who had been faithful to their husband, were in poverty, had no relatives to support them, and had lived blameless lives filled with Christian good works (1 Tm 5:9-16).

See also Family Life and Relations; Marriage.

WIFE *See* Family Life and Relations.

WILDERNESS Land that is basically wild and sparsely inhabited or unfit for permanent human settlement. It may be desert, mountains, forest, or marsh.

In the Near East the wilderness is characteristically dry, desolate, and mostly rock and sand. It is rough, uneven, and interlaced with dry watercourses. The wilderness is not completely barren but provides seasonal pasture for flocks, depending on the rainfall.

Joel 2:22 declares that "the pastures of the wilderness are green," and Psalm 65:12 states that the pastures of the wilderness drip with richness. But Jeremiah says that "the pastures of the wilderness are dried up" (Jer 23:10; cf. Jl 1:20). And Job refers to the wilderness as a land where no human can live (Jb 38:26); it is a place for various animals and birds, such as wild asses, jackals, vultures, and owls (Ps 102:6; Jer 2:24; Is 13:22; 34:13-15).

Certain wilderness tracts are identified by name and are related to definite cities, persons, or events. Hagar wandered in the wilderness of Beersheba (Gn 21:14). In the exodus from Egypt, the Israelites traversed the following wildernesses: Shur (Ex 15:22), Etham (Nm 33:8), Sin (Ex 16:1), Sinai (19:1-2), Zin (Nm 13:21; 20:1), Paran (13:26), Kadesh (Ps 29:8), Moab (Dt 2:8), and Kedemoth (v 26). When David was fleeing from Saul, David hid in the hill country of the wilderness of Ziph (1 Sm 23:14-15), in the wilderness of Maon (vv 24-25), and in the wilderness of En-gedi (24:1).

In spite of the comparative desolation of the wilderness, villages or towns are sometimes associated with a wilderness setting. Joshua 15:61-62 lists the names of six cities and their villages "in the wilderness." The future joy of the towns of the desert is proclaimed by Isaiah (Is 42:11).

The wilderness is associated with both austerity and temptation. Elijah, by his way of life and his dress, is often thought of in connection with the wilderness. His successor, Elisha, had occasion to minister in the wilderness of Edom (2 Kgs 3:4-27).

Isaiah prophesied of the message of John the Baptist, who preached in the wilderness of Judea (Is 40:3; Mt 3:1-3; Mk 1:2-4; Lk 3:1-6; Jn 1:23). Jesus, full of the Holy Spirit, was led by the Spirit into the wilderness for 40 days. There he was tempted by the devil (cf. Lk 4:1-2), but there also angels ministered to him (Mk 1:13). The anchorites (hermits) of Egypt and the Qumran community near the Dead Sea used the wilderness as an escape from the evils of urban life. Jesus, however, used the wilderness as a place of prayer and communion with the Father (Lk 5:16).

See Desert; Wilderness Wanderings.

WILDERNESS WANDERINGS* When the Israelites came out of Egypt, they spent some 40 years wandering in the wildernesses of the Sinai Peninsula and the Negev. Then they moved on to conquer the Promised Land. The most significant events in this period are described in the books of Exodus, Leviticus, and Numbers.

According to the Bible, their experiences during these hard years in the desert molded the various tribes of former Egyptian slaves into a nation. In Sinai they became one people with one God and one national goal, the conquest of Canaan.

Numbers 33:38 and Deuteronomy 1:3 describe the wilderness wanderings as lasting 40 years. Though 40 is sometimes used in the Bible as a large round number, the exactness of many of the dates in these narratives implies it should be taken literally. However, it is hard to know when this period began and ended.

According to 1 Kings 6:1, Solomon started to build the temple 480 years after the Israelites left Egypt. The building of the temple began about 960 BC, which would mean the exodus must have taken place about 1440 BC and the conquest about 1400 BC. However, contemporary scholars generally date the exodus and conquest more than a century later (1290–1250 BC) on the grounds that this agrees with archaeological discoveries. But as yet, convincing proof for either position is lacking. Within the 40-year period of wanderings, there are full details of the first year and a half spent in the desert, from the exodus to the return of the spies (Ex 12–Nm 14), and of the final year or so that involved the conquest of Transjordan (Nm 20–Dt 34). Little is known of the intervening years when the tribes camped in the desert near such oases as Kadesh-barnea. The episodes described in Numbers 15–17 presumably date from this little-known period.

See also Chronology of the Bible (Old Testament); Exodus, The; Israel, History of; Sina, Sinai; Sin, Wilderness of; Zin, Wilderness of.

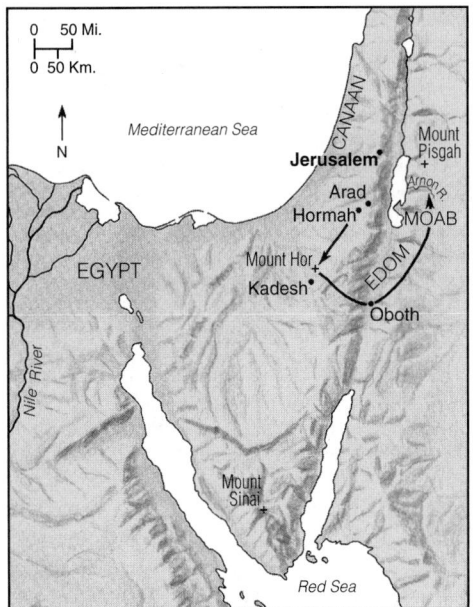

The Israelites Wander in the Wilderness

WILD OX *See* Animals.

WILD VINE *See* Plants (Vine); Vines, Vineyard; Wine.

WILL OF GOD Important NT term indicating God's choice and determination, emanating from desire.

Paul used a Greek word in Ephesians 1:5, 9, and 11 that conveys the idea of desire, even heart's desire. The word is usually translated as "will"—"the will of God." But the English word "will" sublimates the primary meaning. The Greek word (*thelema*) is primarily an emotional word and only secondarily is it volitional. "God's will" is not so much "God's intention" as it is "God's heart's desire." God does have an intention, a purpose, a plan. It is called *prothesis* in Greek (see Eph 1:11), and it literally means "a laying out beforehand" (like a blueprint). This plan was created by God's counsel (called *boule* in Greek, Eph 1:11). However, behind the plan and the counsel was not just a mastermind but a heart—a heart of love and of good pleasure. Therefore, Paul talked about "the good pleasure of God's heart" (Eph 1:5). Paul also said, "He made known to us the mystery of his heart's desire, according to his good pleasure which he purposed in him" (v 9). Indeed, God operated all things according to the counsel of his heart's desire or will (v 11).

The impetus of God's eternal purpose came from a heart's desire, and that heart's desire was to have many sons and daughters made like his only Son (see Rom 8:26-28). In love, he predestined many people to participate in this—not by their own merits but by virtue of being

in the Son (Eph 1:4-5). Notice how often in Ephesians 1 Paul speaks of the believers' position "in him." Outside of him (the Son), no one could be a son or daughter of God and no one could be pleasing to the Father. The many sons and daughters owe all their divine privileges to the Beloved, as ones graced in him and selected in him (v 6). Thus, predestination and election are issues of God's will.

See also Elect, Election; Predestination.

WILLOW *See* Plants (Aspen).

WILLOWS, Ravine of the Ravine by which Moab's abundance would be carried off (Is 15:7, NIV "Ravine of the Poplars"). Isaiah's language suggests that it marked the southern border of Moab.

WINE Beverage made from fermented grape juice.

Origin Noah was among the first to produce wine (Gn 9:21), presumably on the slopes of Mt Ararat. But wine making was not confined to that region, because Egypt, and later Greece, had a fondness for the juice. In fact, wine making was known to have existed in the prehistoric period of Mesopotamia and was brought to Egypt before 3000 BC.

The word "wine" may be identified with words for vine, vineyard, and black grapes. The vine, which brings forth the wine, was often identified in the Near Eastern world with the "tree of life." In both Egypt and Mesopotamia a goddess was thought to protect the vine. The "mistress of the heavenly tree of life," the goddess Siris, lived in the mountains of northwestern Assyria. First Enoch 32:4 calls the vine the tree of knowledge. According to Jewish tradition, the vine was saved from the Flood by Noah.

Production of Wine Few ancient documents are extant on the art of wine making. Experience and the interests of a few early botanists appear to be the only source of knowledge available about the early vine growers. Aristotle's gifted student Theophrastus of Eresos wrote a book entitled *Enquiry into Plants* showing a blend of practical experience and theory. Later, he followed with *On the Life of Plants*, a work giving detailed observations about wine making. His ideas on when to plant, how to prune, statements against grafting, and how to care for the vine demonstrate the Greek genius. They raised viticulture to a science that has changed little in the last 2200 years.

Great care was taken by Greek vine growers to ensure the success of their crops. The vines were close to the ground instead of being propped. In view of this, mice and foxes were especially undesirable, and much hoeing was needed to keep the soil free of weeds. But their method, overall, was very effective.

In early September the grapes were collected in the plains, and at the end of the month in the hills. With an initial festival of song and dance, the workers brought the bunches of grapes to the winepresses, low cement vats inclined toward one corner. After this, workers trod the grapes. The first *must* (juice from the crushing) was highly valued because it provided the choicest wines. The remaining juice was extracted by wringing the trodden grapes in a bag press usually made of cloth. A third class of wine was produced by mixing or even cooking the remaining grapes with some water and expressing the mixture. This type of wine was drunk only by the poor.

At a later time the Greeks invented a beam press in which a long beam, having a turning portion at one end and heavy stones on the other, compressed layers of grapes. The ancient Near East had these different methods of extracting wine, but the treading of grapes, even in Greece, was always the favorite method.

In Greece the fermentation period was usually six

months, during which the liquid was constantly skimmed. However, in the ancient Near East the fermentation process was usually over in three or four days, the optimum growth temperature being 77 degrees. The ancients knew that any further fermentation would produce acid.

After desired fermentation, the wine was transferred to skins or pottery jars for transport or sale. The handles and stoppers were stamped to indicate the brand, the origin, and the vintage. At this time the wine was strained through perforated metal sieves or cloth to eliminate contaminates such as grit or insects.

Kinds of Wine Ancient poets discuss many different brands of wine, with Athenaeus mentioning 85 different varieties. Galen cites 60; Pliny mentions 150; and Strabo, 30. Wines are distinguished by different colors (black, red, white, or yellow) and by their taste (dry, harsh, light, or sweet). The biblical account enumerates various kinds of wine, such as the wines of Lebanon and Helbon. Hebron and Samaria were famous for their wine making. The Hebrew language has at least nine different words for wine, and the Greek has four that are mentioned in the NT.

Nature of Wine Few would question that at least some wine of the OT was fermented. Some scholars argue, however, that certain forms of wine in the ancient world were unfermented. They contrast two Hebrew words for wine, concluding that one particular Hebrew word that refers to fresh wine meant only grape juice (Prv 3:10; Hos 9:2; Jl 2:24; Mi 6:15). The inconclusiveness of these arguments may be seen from the following points: (1) the Hebrew word is found in primarily neutral contexts; (2) often that particular word is found in contexts definitely including a fermented beverage (e.g., Gn 27:28; Hos 4:11; Mi 6:15); (3) the Ugaritic parallel to the term in question refers with certainty to a fermented wine; (4) the Septuagint equivalents refer to fermented wine; (5) fermentation in the ancient Near East, unlike Greece, took only about three days; and (6) the Mishnah provides no such evidence of the practice of having unfermented wine. There seems to have been no attempts to preserve wine in an unfermented state; it may have been a near-impossible task. A careful examination of all the Hebrew words (as well as their Semitic cognates) and the Greek words for wine demonstrates that the ancients knew little, if anything, about unfermented wine.

Ample evidence is available to demonstrate that wine, though always fermented, was usually mixed with water in the classical and Hellenistic world. The wine was stored in large jugs called *amphorae*, from which the wine was poured through a strainer into a large mixing bowl called a *krater*. In the krater the wine was mixed with water. Then the drinking bowls or cups were filled.

The amount of wine per volume varied. The mixture that represented the greatest amount of water to wine was 20 to 1, apparently because the wine was so strong (Homer, *Odyssey* 10.208).

In the western Mediterranean world, the term "wine" referred to the mixture of wine and water. If one desired to mention wine without water, it was necessary to add the word "unmixed." For the Greeks, to drink wine unmixed was regarded as barbaric. The evidence, however, seems to indicate that in the OT era wine was used without being mixed with water. The terminology of mixing water and wine is strikingly unattested. Wine diluted with water was symbolic of spiritual adulteration (Is 1:22). By Roman times, this attitude had changed. The Mishnah assumes a ratio of two parts of water to one part wine; however, later Talmudic sources speak of three to one. A natural, nondistilled wine could reach as high

as 15 percent alcohol content. If watered down three parts water to one part wine, the alcohol content would be 5 percent and still fairly potent.

Wine was mixed not only with water but also with other ingredients, similar to mixed drinks today. An example of this is seen in the Homeric "Hymn to Demeter," where the goddess rejects straight wine and desires the drink mixed with meal, water, and a soft mint. Often strong wine was mixed into weak wine, resulting in a stronger drink. This is what is meant by "mixture" in the Bible (Ps 75:8; Is 5:22; Rv 18:6; 19:13-15). At times the fresh wine, high in sugar content, was evaporated, and this concentrated *must* was mixed with wine to obtain a higher alcohol content.

There is no mention of wine being mixed with water to make it safe for drinking, as is commonly accepted. Modern examples of pollution were not common in the ancient world, although this problem appeared occasionally. Examples are myriad concerning the fresh wells, springs, and moving bodies of water in biblical times, and methods were available to purify any impure water.

Wine in the Old Testament The evidence, as seen above, suggests that wine in the OT was not mixed with water and was looked on with favor when taken in moderation. Judges 9:13 presents wine as that "which cheers God and men." Psalm 104:15 portrays wine similarly: "wine which makes man's heart glad" (cf. also Est 1:10; Eccl 10:19; Is 55:1-2; Zec 10:7). The temperate use of wine was a normal and accepted part of life (Gn 14:18; Jgs 19:19; 1 Sm 16:20). Levitical priests in service at the temple (Lv 10:8-9), Nazirites (Nm 6:3), and the Recabites (Jer 35:1-6) were forbidden to drink wine.

Wine had many uses in the OT world. The "drink offering" was wine (Ex 29:40; Lv 23:13), and the worshiper regularly brought wine when offering sacrifice (1 Sm 1:24). In addition, a supply of wine was kept in the temple for sacrificial purposes (1 Chr 9:29). At times, wine was used in helping the weak and sick (2 Sm 16:2; Prv 31:6).

The strong drink of the OT seems to be closely related to Mesopotamian date wine. This same date wine, high in sugar content, must have also been high in alcohol content. One Hebrew word is consistently used as strong drink (Lv 10:9; Dt 29:6; 1 Sm 1:15; Prv 20:1; 31:6; Is 29:9). There is an equivalent word to this in Ugaritic, translated "drunk," which parallels the normal word for wine.

Negative reactions to intemperate wine drinking abound in the OT. Isaiah condemned those who drank wine to excess (Is 28:1-8). Many admonitions of drinking wine in excess are given in the Scriptures (Prv 20:1; 21:17; 23:20-21; 23:32-34).

Wine in the New Testament Wine in the NT was a fermented beverage that was mixed with various amounts of water. It was also mixed with gall (Mt 27:34) and myrrh (Mk 15:23). Evidence strongly suggests that the wine used at the Lord's Supper was a mixture of water and wine, probably three to one in agreement with the dictates of the Mishnah. The phrase "fruit of the vine" (Mt 26:27-29) is often interpreted to mean fresh grape juice. However, fresh grape juice would be all but impossible to find.

The NT, as the OT, argues forcefully against the unrestrained use of wine. The biblical admonition is not to be drunk with wine (Eph 5:18; 1 Pt 4:3). Leaders in the church were to practice moderation in the use of wine (1 Tm 3:3, 8; Ti 1:7); the Greek says that they should "not be addicted to wine."

See also Vines, Vineyard; Winepress.

WINEPRESS A sunken area (Jgs 6:11) into which the grape harvest was thrown and then trodden with bare feet, amid shouts of joy and traditional vintage work songs (Jer 48:33; cf. Is 65:8). The red juice flowed through spouts into jars. Full winepresses meant prosperity; deserted ones spoke of destitution. The common winepress was a natural landmark (Jgs 7:25; Zec 14:10); a privately owned one indicated the special care and efficiency of the vineyard's owner (Is 5:2; Mt 21:33).

Grape treading provided a dramatic metaphor for the ruthless trampling by invading armies (Lam 1:15). This vivid metaphor of battle is mingled with divine judgment (Is 63:1-6) and anticipates the Lord's final judgment, spoken of as "the winepress of the wrath of God" (Rv 14:18-20).

See also Vines, Vineyard; Wine.

One Kind of Winepress

WINESKINS Containers made of animal hide for keeping wine. The term is prominent in Jesus' maxim that new wine cannot be put in old wineskins but must be put in new wineskins because the new wine, when it ferments and expands, will break the old wineskins and spill out. New wine must be put into new wineskins, so that both can be preserved. This image indicates that Jesus' new teachings and new kind of spiritual life could not be put into old Judaism. They required a new container—namely, the living church.

WINNOWER One who removes chaff from grain. *See* Agriculture.

WISDOM The ability to direct one's mind toward a full understanding of human life and toward its moral fulfillment. Wisdom is thus a special capacity, necessary for full human living; it can be acquired through education and the application of the mind.

Divine Wisdom Although the term "wisdom" is used primarily in the OT with reference to human beings, all wisdom is ultimately rooted and grounded in God. In wisdom forms a central part of the nature of God. In wisdom God created the universe (Prv 3:19) and human beings (Ps 104:24). Thus wisdom, in its positive connotations, is something inherent in God, reflected in creation, and a part of the reason for human existence.

Wisdom in creation is reflected in the form and order that emerged out of primeval chaos. The wisdom of God expressed in the creation of humanity means that human life may also be marked by form and order, and that meaning in life may be found in the created world, which contains marks of divine wisdom. The wisdom of God is creative, purposeful, and good; it is not merely the intellectual activity of God. The potential for human wisdom is rooted in the creation of mankind. Created by

divine wisdom, human beings have within them the God-given capacity for wisdom. Thus, it is impossible to understand human wisdom without first grasping its necessary antecedent, divine wisdom.

Human Wisdom The word "wisdom," with reference to human beings, is used in a variety of different ways in the OT. The word is often used as virtually synonymous with the term "knowledge," but in its general and secular uses it commonly indicates applied knowledge, skill, or even cunning. Wisdom could be defined as either "superior mental capacity" or "superior skill." Thus, wisdom is used to describe both the cunning of King Solomon (1 Kgs 2:1-6) and the skill of the craftsman Bezalel (Ex 35:33). But it was also used to describe mental capacities and skills that had a moral component—the capacity to understand and to do good. Thus, when Moses delegated some of his authority to newly appointed judges, he chose men who were wise, understanding, and experienced (Dt 1:13). Such men were considered the wise men in ancient Israel. Human wisdom, in this special sense, was not merely a gift from God, inherent at birth; it had to be developed consciously during a life lived in relationship with God.

Thus this positive and special kind of wisdom in human beings cannot be understood apart from God. A frequent theme of the Wisdom Literature in the OT is that the "fear of the Lord is the beginning of wisdom" (Prv 9:10; see also Jb 28:28; Ps 111:10; Prv 1:7; 15:33). In several ways, this theme sets a perspective for understanding true human wisdom.

First, human wisdom is possible only because of the divine wisdom present in creation; the potential for wisdom exists only because God created it. Second, if wisdom is to be developed in a human being, the starting point must be God—specifically, one must revere or fear God. This Hebraic concept of wisdom is strikingly different from the Greek concept. The Ionian philosophers, with remarkable power, developed a system of thought that began without the assumption of the existence of deity. They attempted to develop wisdom through human reason alone. But Hebrew wisdom, though it sought to develop both the reason and the intellect as did the Greeks, could start only with God. The mind and its capacities were God-given; thus, however secular in appearance the wisdom of the Hebrews might seem, it had God as its starting point. The reverence of God—namely the acknowledgment that God existed, created, and was important in human life—lay behind all the developments of Hebrew wisdom.

Human wisdom, in the Hebrew conception, is thus a development of the mind, an expansion of knowledge, and an understanding of both the meaning of life and how that life must be lived. It is thoroughly intellectual but has a powerful moral result. Wisdom was sought not for its own sake but always for its application to the meaning of life, because life—like wisdom—was God's gift. This emphasis in Hebrew wisdom meant that the virtues of the wise man or woman were never described in intellectual terms alone. The wise are not the intelligentsia of Israelite society, but as the book of Proverbs makes clear, they were those whose lives were characterized by understanding, patience, diligence, trustworthiness, self-control, modesty, and similar virtues. In a word, the wise man was the God-fearing man; his wisdom lay not just in a static attitude of reverence but rather in the conscious development of the mind toward wisdom in the context of godly living.

From this general conception of wisdom there emerged in ancient Israel a special category of men, the wise men. Though wisdom was not limited to them, they were responsible for the growth and communication of wisdom in Israel. The wise men formed one of three classes of religious personnel. First, there were priests and Levites, whose responsibilities lay primarily within the context of established religion. They were the servants of the temple and the leaders of worship and also had certain responsibilities in the area of religious education. Second, there were the prophets, the spokesmen of God to the people of God. Third, there were the wise men. From a certain perspective, they possessed the most secular task among the three groups. They were involved in a variety of tasks, from governmental administration to moral and secular education. As moral educators, they instructed the young people of their day, not in how to make a living, but in how to live. Something of their curriculum has survived in the book of Proverbs. The books of Job and Ecclesiastes also reflect the thought of the wise men.

Wisdom in the New Testament The word "wisdom" is used in the NT both of the wisdom of God and the wisdom of humans. The continuation of the OT wisdom tradition is found in the NT's use of the word in conjunction with God and in the positive connotations of the word in relation to human beings. But the NT also speaks negatively of human wisdom. Thus, Paul described his message as being "not in the plausible words of wisdom, but in demonstration of the Spirit and of power" (1 Cor 2:4). Purely human wisdom has no ultimate merit of its own, and Paul quotes the OT to demonstrate that God would destroy human wisdom (1 Cor 1:19; cf. Is 29:14). A clear distinction between good and evil wisdom is provided in the Letter of James (Jas 3:13-18). A person whose life reflects jealousy and selfish ambition does not have the true wisdom of God but is earthly-minded and unspiritual. But true wisdom is God-given; this wisdom is "first pure, then peaceable, gentle, open to reason, full of mercy and good fruits, without uncertainty or insincerity" (v 17).

As wisdom was the primary possession of God, so too it was reflected in the life and ministry of Jesus. Jesus, during the years of his growth, reflected in his life the increase of wisdom (Lk 2:40, 52), and his opponents, as well as his friends, recognized the wisdom in his teaching (Mt 13:54).

Since wisdom is rooted and grounded in God, true and spiritual wisdom is God's gift. It could be seen in the lives and words of the servants of God such as Stephen (Acts 6:10) and Paul (2 Pt 3:15). Spiritual wisdom, which provided the knowledge enabling a person to live fully the life given by God, was to be desired for oneself and prayed for in others (Col 1:9).

The most central aspect of wisdom in the NT is in the gospel of the crucified Christ. In his first letter to the Corinthian church, Paul contrasted vividly the positive and negative senses of wisdom in proclaiming the death of Jesus Christ. The world did not know God by their own wisdom (1 Cor 1:21); that is, the true revelation of God and his redemption of mankind were not revealed to those who sought such truth through wisdom alone, namely, through the Greek approach to wisdom and philosophy. The gospel was declared in preaching, which was, from a strictly philosophical or wisdom perspective, a kind of foolishness. And yet the gospel of Jesus Christ was both the power of God and the wisdom of God (1 Cor 1:24). Jesus, for those who believed, became the ultimate source of that wisdom that could come from God alone (1 Cor 1:30).

See also Wisdom Literature.

WISDOM LITERATURE* Literature in the OT that has wisdom as its central theme. It comprises principally the books of Job, Proverbs, and Ecclesiastes and may also be found in portions of the Psalms and Prophets. The Wis-

dom Literature contains both the moral substance of true wisdom (as in Proverbs) and also the intellectual explorations of wise men seeking to understand the fundamental problems of human existence (as in Job, Ecclesiastes).

Wisdom Literature forms an important part of the OT. It falls within the third division of the Hebrew canon, called the Writings, and comprises basically three books: Proverbs, Ecclesiastes (or Koheleth), and Job. There are also wisdom psalms (e.g., Pss 1, 32, 34, 37) and wisdom-type passages in the Prophets (such as the parables of Isaiah). In the Greek OT (and the English Apocrypha), two additional books of wisdom are found. There is Ecclesiasticus, a second-century BC work of Jesus ben Sirach, which has certain similarities to the book of Proverbs, and the Wisdom of Solomon, an anonymous work representing the flowering of Jewish wisdom in the Hellenistic period.

Proverbs The starting point for an understanding of OT Wisdom Literature is Proverbs. Its wisdom concerns morality—the knowledge of how to live properly. It has a theological foundation, though much of its wisdom is secular in form. The starting point, as for all wisdom, is the reverence of God. But for the most part, the concern of the book is to convey the fundamentals of morality, the virtues of integrity, discipline, justice, and common sense, and to show by way of contrast the failure in life that awaits the fool. The book has a strongly didactic nature. Nowadays it can be read as a piece of literature, though its wisdom was designed to be learned, memorized even, by the young persons who received their education at the feet of the wise men. For those who learned its truth, for whom the short poetic sayings became a part of the subconscious mind, the wisdom of the proverbs served as a moral and spiritual guide throughout life. There was a way to live successfully, a way governed by morality, and success lay in the fact that the morally good life was the life lived according to the wisdom of the Creator of all life. Thus, the wise men of the proverbs functioned as guides, in both their teaching and their writing; they provided no new philosophical theories, no advanced intellectual speculation, but communicated that most valuable of all human kinds of knowledge: wisdom on how to live. Wisdom is "more precious than jewels, and nothing you desire can compare with her. Long life is in her right hand; in her left hand are riches and honor. Her ways are ways of pleasantness, and all her paths are peace" (Prv 3:15-17, RSV).

Ecclesiastes Ecclesiastes reflects the wisdom of a man who had lived long and seen the world from all perspectives. His faith was not the superficial faith of a man who lived easily and believed lightly. The man had seen that the righteous do not always prosper and the wicked suffer. Too often the righteous suffer, with no relief from their suffering, and the wicked enjoy their lives in carefree abandon. The writer of Ecclesiastes sought justice, but as he observed the world through honest and objective eyes, he could not see that justice was always done. More than justice, he sought truth, but even truth in its ultimate perspectives eluded him. All was vanity, a grasping after wind! Yet for all the skeptical and apparently negative tenor of Ecclesiastes, it is a magnificent monument of faith, a faith that held on to God despite the agony and pointlessness of a world filled with evil and vanity. This wise man could not soar with hope like that of the prophets, but he could hold on to the fundamental truth of God when all else, including understanding, failed. So the book of Ecclesiastes may become an intimate companion to those who see the world as it really is, in all its agony and apparent vanity.

Job Whereas the writer of Ecclesiastes described the grief and sadness of the world from the perspective of an observer,

Job grasped the problems from within, from the perspective of the sufferer. Job knew the ancient proverbial wisdom and had lived his life by that wisdom, but he had an experience that called into question conventional morality and wisdom. He was a pious man, an upright man, whose life embodied the precepts of Proverbs. Prior to his experience, he had no cause to doubt a simple interpretation of proverbial wisdom: righteousness led to prosperity and happiness. But then Job's world collapsed, and with it the wisdom by which he had lived. The loss of possessions, property, and prestige; the death of his children; the pain and suffering of terrible illness—all these things conspired to raise an enormous question as to the validity of traditional morality. But the wisdom of the book of Job raises an even more fundamental question than the validity of morality; Job questioned the premise of all wisdom, God himself. In what sense can God be just in the face of such apparent injustice? In what sense can God be just, when unjust men flourish and prosper (Jb 21:7-15)? Does God's creation really reflect structure, order, and goodness, if the experience of Job is the measure of human life? Such are the radical questions evoked by Job, and they receive no simple solution. Yet in the great climax of the book of Job, namely, the encounter between God and Job (chs 38–42), wisdom is set in its proper perspective. There remains always a mystery in God and in God's ways that lies beyond the grasp of the human mind. Wisdom is pursuit of the knowledge of God, but wisdom as intellectual knowledge can never grasp ultimate truth in all its depth, for God is always greater than the human mind and human wisdom. Yet Job adds a further truth to the knowledge of conventional wisdom. While Job's questions were not explicitly answered, they were effectively removed; it was the encounter of God with Job that transformed the man. Thus, the ultimate wisdom lies not in finding an answer to the ultimate questions but rather in the encounter with the living God.

Conclusion The teaching of the Wisdom Literature has manifold dimensions and in its totality is a compound of the various perspectives on the truth contained in Proverbs, Ecclesiastes, and Job. There is a fundamental knowledge and morality that is vital to proper and successful living and that must be communicated to the young as their basic rule of life. It will lead not always to material prosperity but to that more profound prosperity that transcends adversity—the prosperity of the person whose life is lived in reverence of God. With the passage of time and advancement of years, there comes to those educated in conventional wisdom the understanding that life and the world are not so simple. Faced with the temptation to jettison conventional morality and wisdom, a person may find that the more worldly wisdom of Ecclesiastes provides an anchor. Life may seem pointless, the world may seem to be essentially a place of vanity, but the truth of God and reverence for God must be maintained in the face of radical doubt (Eccl 12:13-14). To those who experience in some fashion the plight of Job, wisdom reaches its limits and points beyond itself; humans cannot always find an answer to the questions, and the last resort is simply the experience of the living God.

WISDOM OF JESUS BEN SIRACH Deuterocanonical book that is also known as Ecclesiasticus (to be distinguished from the canonical book Ecclesiastes). The author is generally referred to as Jesus ben Sirach; however, in recently discovered Hebrew manuscripts, his name is given as Simon son of Jesus son of Eleazar ben Sirach. He was a Hebrew sage who lived in the beginning of the second century BC and who taught in Jerusalem (Ecclus 50:27; cf. 51:23ff.). The work bears the imprint of a man steeped in a tradition later known as Sadducean.

This work was valued highly by both Jews and Christians. The author was a scribe who wished to give his teachings a more permanent form, for which he utilized the canonical Proverbs as a model. His instruction adheres closely to Jewish orthodoxy. The book was probably written about 180 BC.

WISDOM OF SOLOMON Deuterocanonical work containing a treasury of wisdom. A theological and/or philosophical treatise, the Wisdom of Solomon seeks to blend the piety of orthodox Judaism with the best of Greek philosophy.

The book tries to give the impression that the whole is the work of Solomon (see Wisd of Sol 8:9-21; 9:7-2), but this is simply a device to gain authority for the statements of the book concerning wisdom. Originally composed in Greek rather than in Hebrew, it is likely the production of a cultivated Jew deeply influenced by Greek culture and ideas, familiar with the Septuagint, and writing at Alexandria probably in the first century BC.

The book was regarded as canonical by some of the early church fathers, including such notable figures as Origen, Eusebius of Caesarea, and Augustine of Hippo; it was even incorporated into the Muratorian Canon of the second century. Historically, it has been favorably regarded by Protestants, although not considered canonical. The Roman Catholic Church gave it official recognition as Scripture at the Council of Trent in AD 1546.

The author sought to rekindle the religious zeal of his fellow Jews who have departed from the faith of their fathers, to encourage and fortify them for a life of faith and godliness in the midst of perplexities and persecutions and to demonstrate the folly of idolatry and the truth of Judaism. The book begins with the author being exhorted to "love righteousness, . . . think of the Lord with uprightness, and seek him with sincerity of heart" (1:1). From there on in, the book encourages people to become religious and to know God. By knowing God and conforming to his will, a person can attain immortality (15:3).

WISE MEN *See* Magi.

WITCH*, WITCHCRAFT *See* Sorcery; Magic.

WITHERED HAND* *See* Deformity.

WITNESS One who tells what he or she has seen or personally experienced, often in a court of law. The term may also refer to the testimony the person has given.

Witness in the Old Testament In the judicial procedure outlined in the OT, one witness was not adequate for personal testimony against anyone, but two or three witnesses were required (Dt 17:6; 19:15). This principle was incorporated into Jewish law and is reiterated in the NT (cf. Mt 18:16; 2 Cor 13:1).

The truth of testimony is so important that the Bible expressly forbids false witness in the ninth commandment (Ex 20:16; Dt 5:20; cf. Mk 10:19; Lk 18:20). The practical wisdom of Proverbs speaks out frequently against the false witness (e.g., Prv 6:19; 14:5; 25:18). Nevertheless, false witnesses did arise (Pss 27:12; 35:11), and there are notable examples of the bringing of more than one witness in order to bring about the death of an innocent person. The case of Naboth and his vineyard is notorious; here Jezebel, wife of King Ahab, bribed two men to bear false witness against Naboth so that he would be stoned to death and her wicked husband could take the vineyard he coveted so intensely (1 Kgs 21).

Witnesses could be tested by the judges. If the testimony of an accuser was found to be false, that person was subjected to the punishment he had sought to have executed on the defendant (Dt 19:16-21). Proverbs also speaks of the punishment of the false witness (Prv 19:5, 9; 21:28).

The OT records several accounts of legal proceedings in which witnesses are mentioned. Most of these involve the purchase or transfer of property. Ruth 4:7-12 relates the redemption of a field from Naomi by Boaz. Isaiah found "reliable witnesses" concerning a property title written on a large tablet (Is 8:1-2). To confirm the prophecy of the return of the exiles from Babylon, Jeremiah bought and paid for a field in the presence of witnesses, who also signed the deed for the property (Jer 32:6-15).

At the conclusion of his farewell message at Shechem, Joshua declared that the Israelites themselves were witnesses that they had chosen to serve the Lord; then he set up a large stone and declared that it also was a witness (Jos 24:22-27). The people of Israel themselves were declared God's witnesses (Is 43:10; 44:8-9). They were witnesses to the existence of God, to his uniqueness, holiness, power, and love. When they failed to acknowledge his uniqueness and holiness and turned to idolatry, he sent them into captivity, as he had warned, for they had failed in their witness and had given opportunity for the enemies of God to blaspheme.

Witness in the New Testament In the NT the various words for witness are mainly related to the verb *martureo*, meaning "to bear witness, be a witness." The word "martyr" shows the ultimate form of witness in that Christians have sacrificed their lives because of their witness for Jesus Christ.

John the Baptist was both a witness and a martyr. As the forerunner of the Messiah, his mission was to bear witness to the light and to identify the Lamb of God (Jn 1:7-8, 19-36). The followers of Jesus, and particularly the 12 apostles, were witnesses to the person and character of Jesus. They knew him intimately, heard his teachings and observed his miracles; three were witnesses of his transfiguration (Mt 17:1-2; 2 Pt 1:17-18) and many were witnesses to his resurrection (Lk 24:48; 1 Cor 15:4-8). At the time of his ascension, the disciples were specifically commissioned to be his witnesses (Acts 1:8).

WITNESS, Altar of Altar built by the Reubenites, the Gadites, and the half-tribe of Manasseh in the frontier of Israel near the Jordan (Jos 22:10-34). The building of the altar incited the remainder of Israel to threaten war for the presumed treachery. After the Transjordanian tribes explained their motives and Phinehas mediated the conflict, the altar was called "Witness" as a memorial of the resulting treaty.

WIZARD* *See* Magic.

WOE An exclamation denoting pain or displeasure. Less frequently, it occurs as a noun denoting a disaster or calamity. For example, in Revelation 9:12, following the release of the demonic locusts from the abyss and their scourge upon those who follow the Beast, John announces, "The first woe is past; two other woes are yet to come" (NIV). Again, in Revelation 11:14, immediately before the seventh trumpet is sounded John writes, "The second woe has passed; the third woe is coming soon" (NIV). The woes that Revelation describes are equivalent to the plagues of the OT, although somewhat more intense in that they are demonic in origin.

The Greek word is onomatopoeic: *ouai* (cf. the Hebrew *oi* and *hoi*). It is not necessarily a pronouncement of judgment in every case. At times it is an expression of regret or

sorrow about the miserable situation that prompted the exclamation. In each case the context needs to be taken into consideration. In Matthew 11:21 (Lk 10:13) when Jesus says, "Woe to you, Korazin! Woe to you, Bethsaida!" he was reproaching the people of those cities for their unbelief. The same is true in Luke 17:2 where Jesus pronounces woe upon the one who causes another to sin: "It would be better for him to be thrown into the sea with a millstone tied around his neck" (NIV). In the Lucan Sermon on the Plain, the Beatitudes are followed by four woe statements. These statements are not so much threats as they are expressions of regret or compassion.

WOLF *See* Animals.

WOMAN Man's companion created by God.

Her Creation Genesis provides two accounts of the creation of the first man and woman. In the first, Genesis 1:26-28, God created humans in his image, as male and female. Hence, the female shares with the male the image of God, reflects his power and majesty on earth, and is commanded to multiply and bring dominion to the earth. From Genesis 1:26-28 there is no suggestion of inferiority of the female to the male, nor is there any suggestion of her submission to his dominance. Rather, they are pictured together, the male and the female, as the representation of their Maker.

Genesis 2:20-25 is the second portrayal of the creation of the first woman. In Genesis 2 the male was made before the female, a point that seems to give him some precedence. This may not be pressed too far, however, as the pattern in the creation texts is to move progressively from the lesser to the finer work! Yet it is because of his prior creation that the male is given the prerogative to name the female (Gn 2:23). In Semitic thought, the giving of names signifies dominion or ownership. This means that Adam's naming of his wife was an act of lordship. However, the name that he gives her is the equivalent to his own, meaning the male affirmed her equality with him. Paradoxically, then, this hierarchical relationship is also a relationship of equals.

The situation in Genesis 1 and 2 reveals a balanced relationship between the man and the woman who were the parents of all mankind: two persons who were altogether equal in status as coheirs of the mystery of the image of God and yet who dwell in a delicate one-to-one relationship in which one is the leader of the other. In Eden before the fall, this delicate balance was possible.

Her Downfall and Plight Genesis 3, the story of the fall of mankind, speaks of the breaking of the delicate balance between the man and the woman and the ensuing struggles that have been passed down through the ages. In God's words to the woman, he announced the pain that would accompany her childbearing (Gn 3:16) and the conflict of interests that would affect her relationship with her husband: "Your desire will be for your husband, and he will rule over you" (NIV). The Hebrew term "desire" (*teshuqah*) in the Genesis 3 and 4 passages is not a sexual longing but a desire to control, to master, to be in charge (the use of *teshuqah* meaning sexual desire is seen in Sg 7:10). Consequently, after the fall, the desire of woman has been to dominate her husband. Her determination to reject his leadership in their relationship of equals is a breaking of the balance in their relationship. For his part, the man tends to tyrannize the woman.

To the women who attempt to dominate their husbands, the apostle Paul says, "Wives, submit to your husbands as to the Lord" (Eph 5:22, NIV). Her natural inclination needs transformation, so that she can submit to her husband as she submits to the Lord. For, Paul argues, the husband is to the wife as Christ is to the church (v 23). The husbands who tend to dominate their wives also need transformation so that they can love their wives, "just as Christ loved the church and gave himself up for her" (v 25, NIV). By these words, the apostle Paul was presenting a means whereby couples could regain the bliss in their relationship that was the mark of Eden before the fall. Paul's citation of Genesis 2:24 in Ephesians 5:31 is a case in point: here a couple may regain the original oneness that God intended for them. The relationship of equal persons in a hierarchy of responsiveness is stated in the context of mutual submission, which is a mark of their greater submission to the Lord Jesus.

Her Role in Life according to the Bible A woman is a person in every respect as a man; she shares in the image of God and has the potential of varied ranges of response to culture, community, and life about her. It is a fact of Scripture that women are regularly associated with, and find their sense of worth in, childbearing. Yet the same Scriptures show that the nature of woman is not exhausted by associations with childbearing: she has her own identity in the community, in the church, and before the Lord in the whole of her life, not just when (or if) she bears and nourishes a child. Further, the biblical concept of childbearing always involves the husband, who is her partner at conception, at her side during delivery, and partner with her in the ongoing task of nourishing the child.

The image of the woman as the childbearer begins with the promise of God in Genesis 3:15, where he announced the ultimate victory over the evil one, Satan, by the offspring of the woman. This promise respecting the offspring of the woman became the universal blessing of God upon woman as the childbearer. Ultimately, through one born of a woman, there would come the final deliverance. There is a sense in which each birth experience is a participation in the continuity of this promise (see 1 Tm 2:15 and its possible relationship to this continuity of women, salvation, and childbearing).

Further, in the culture of the OT world, a woman's genuine worth was solely, or largely, perceived in terms of childbearing. Yet it is not in childbearing alone that she finds worth and dignity before God. For the woman, as for the man, the issue of faith in the Lord is central. A woman who has a household of children but no faith in God might regard herself as a fulfilled person. Yet her care of her children is no substitute for piety to God. A woman who has no children, and perhaps no husband, may have her full identity and worth in her relationship with the God in whose image she is made and whose tasks she is commissioned by him to do. The gifts of God in a woman's life may lead her to find opportunities in the community to express her devotion to God. Women apparently had the same opportunities as men to take a Nazirite vow (Nm 6:2; see also ch 30).

Certain notable women in the Bible led lives of public service. Miriam, the sister of Moses and Aaron (Ex 15:20-21), was a prophetess, musician, and national leader (Nm 12). Long after her time, God spoke through his prophets of the gift he had given to Israel in the person of the national leader Miriam (Mi 6:4). There were other magnificent women who had exemplary lives: Deborah, the prophetess of God and the only named woman judge of Israel (Jgs 4–5); Esther, the Hebrew queen of Xerxes who saved her people from the rash acts of the Persian king, a result of a frightful conspiracy; and Huldah, the prophetess who was the agent of the Lord's word to Josiah at the inception of his revival (2 Chr 34:22-28). Huldah's reception and transmission of the word of the Lord is the more remarkable because she was a contemporary with

Jeremiah and Zephaniah. In this case God chose to speak through a woman.

In the NT, certain women were noted for their public ministries: the daughters of Philip, Phoebe, Priscilla, Junias, Tryphena, Tryphosa, Persis, Euodia, and Syntyche. These women mark the beginning of the fulfillment of Joel's prophecy of a day in which women as well as men would be the instruments of the outpouring of the Holy Spirit (Jl 2:28-29). Women such as Sarah, Ruth, and Hannah exercised their faith in God in the context of the home and family as well. And preeminently there is Mary, mother of Jesus, in whom the ideal of womanhood is conjoined to the fulfillment of the ancient promise to Eve that she would one day be the great victor over the enemy of mankind.

See also Eve; Man.

WONDERS *See* Miracle; Sign.

WOOL Important commodity of the ancient Near East. King Mesha of Moab, a sheep breeder, annually sent the wool of 100,000 rams as tribute to King Ahab of Israel (2 Kgs 3:4), and the people of Damascus traded wool with Tyre's merchants (Ez 27:18). Woolen garments were commonly worn by the Israelites (Lv 13:47-59; Is 51:8; Hos 2:5, 9), though woolen garments mingled with linen fabric were forbidden (Dt 22:11). In fact, wearing wool was prohibited entirely for Israelite priests serving in the sanctuary's inner court (Ez 44:17).

Wool is sometimes a biblical symbol for whiteness and purity, it is a simile for redemption (Is 1:18), for the hair of the Ancient of Days (Dn 7:9), and for the hair and head of the Son of Man (Rv 1:14).

See also Cloth and Cloth Manufacturing.

WORD, WORD OF GOD, WORDS OF GOD A "word" is an expression that communicates. On the level of human communication, "words "usually refer to verbal expression. When God "spoke" over the centuries, though, he communicated in various ways (Heb 1:1), culminating in that epitome of all divine expression, Jesus Christ, his Son.

The Importance of Words In a mainly nonliterary society the dependability of the spoken word was all-important in law, trade, religion, marriage, and reputation. Receipts, agreements, and records had little usefulness. Personal integrity and sincere speech were essential to communication and, for most people, to self-expression and stable relationships. The words of poets, prophets, storytellers, and instructors were carefully preserved.

Words were diligently tested. Foolish words, flattery, deceit, words of enticement, lies, rumor, scandal, and blasphemous speech were all recognized as evil. The oath had to be inviolable in commercial, judicial, and civic affairs. The spoken blessing had power within itself and could not be withdrawn (Gn 27:30-38; Mt 10:12-13); so also the vow (Jgs 11:34-35) and the curse (Gn 27:12-13). Equally powerful was the word of command—of priestly, judicial, or royal authority (Eccl 8:4).

This estimate of human words lingers in the NT. The word reveals the inner self, and so every careless, hurtful, deceitful word will be judged (Mt 12:34-37; 5:22), as will blasphemy (Lk 12:10). Paul (Eph 4:29; 5:4) and James (Jas 3:1-12) preserve this Hebrew reverence for the spoken word.

The Words of God God's spoken word has been preserved in Scripture. His word came to and through the prophets (1 Kgs 12:22; 1 Chr 17:3; cf. Lk 3:2), who spoke and acted "by the word of the Lord." His word also came in the law, which God "spoke" on Sinai (Ex

20:1); hence, "statutes," "command-ments," and "precepts" are synonyms for God's "word" (e.g., Ps 119).

Periods when no such divine communication came constituted "famine" (1 Sm 3:1; Am 8:11). Mingled with warnings and injunctions were divine promises. All God's words were dependable (Is 31:2), firmly fixed in heaven (Ps 119:89; Is 40:8), and backed up by divine oath (Jer 1:12; Ps 110:4; Ez 12:25, 28). A word, expressing the divine mind, was not threatening or burdensome; it was a delight, hope, joy, and protection against sin (Pss 1; 119; Jer 15:16). Men can live by it (Dt 8:3; Mt 4:4).

God's word has power to execute his will. It will not return to him "empty" but accomplish that which he purposes (Is 55:11). By his speech alone, God created the world, and his word upholds it (Gn 1; Ps 33:6; cf. Heb 1:2; 11:3; 2 Pt 3:5). Eventually, this divine revelation was put into writing, which makes the Bible also "the word of God" (Mk 7:13; cf. Lk 16:29-31; Jn 5:39).

Jesus spoke the word of God. He was "mighty in word" (Lk 24:19); he taught with authority (Mk 1:22, 27), exercising power over the sea, disease, demons, and death (Mt 8:8, 13). His "word of the kingdom" is the living seed, which, planted in the good soil of receptive hearts, bears fruit for God (Mt 13:19; Mk 4:14). The word that Christ gives to his disciples cleanses them and frees them (Jn 8:31; 12:48; 15:3; 17:14). The word of faith the church preaches (Rom 10:8-9, 17) is variously described as the word of salvation, the word of grace, the word of reconciliation, the word of the gospel, the word of righteousness, and the word of life.

**The Title "Word"
in John 1:1** The first lines of John's Gospel, showing the Greek title Λογος (Logos) in Bodmer Papyrus XIV–XV (c. 200)—P75.

The Word of God Deliberately recalling Genesis 1, the Gospel writer, John, named the Son of God "the Word." As the Word, the Son of God fully conveys and communicates God. The Greek term is *logos*; it was used in two ways by the Greeks. The word might be thought of as remaining within a person, when it denoted his thought or reason. Or it might refer to the word going forth from a person, when it denoted the expression of his thought, i.e., speech. As a philosophical term, the *logos* denoted the principle of the universe, even the creative energy that generated the universe. In both the Jewish conception and the Greek, the *logos* was associated with the idea of beginnings—the world began through the origination and instrumentality of the Word (Gn 1:3ff., where the expression "God said" is used again and again). John may have had these ideas in mind, but most likely he originated a new term to identify the Son of God as the divine expression in human form (Jn 1:14). He is the image of the invisible God (Col 1:15), the express image of God's substance (Heb 1:3). In the Godhead, the Son functions as the revealer of God and the reality of God, which is a central theme throughout John's Gospel. John used a similar title in his first epistle: "the Word of life" (1 Jn 1:1-3). And in Revelation 19:11-16, Jesus is presented as the King of kings and Lord of lords, who has a name on him: "the Word of God."

See also Bible; John, Gospel of; Logos; Revelation.

WORK A term referring either to God's activity or to people's regular occupation or employment.

The Value of Work The Bible's positive outlook on work is rooted in its teaching about God. Unlike other ancient religious writings, which regarded creation as something beneath the dignity of the Supreme Being, Scripture unashamedly describes God as a worker. Like a manual laborer, he made the universe as "the work of his fingers" (Ps 8:3). He worked with his raw material just as a potter works with the clay (Is 45:9). The intricate development of the unborn child in the womb and the vast, magnificent spread of the sky both display his supreme craftsmanship (Pss 139:13-16; 19:1). In fact, all creation bears witness to his wisdom and skill (104:24). The almighty Creator even had his rest day (Gn 2:2-3) and enjoyed job satisfaction when surveying his achievements at the end of the week (1:31).

This vivid biblical description of a working God reaches its climax with the incarnation of Jesus. The "work" that Jesus was given to do (Jn 4:34) was, of course, the unique task of redemption. But he was also a worker in the ordinary sense. His contemporaries knew him as "a carpenter" (Mk 6:3). In NT times carpentry and joinery were muscle-building trades. So the Jesus who stormed through the temple, overturning tables and driving out the men and animals (Jn 2:14-16), was no pale weakling but a workingman whose hands had been hardened by years of toil with the ax, saw, and hammer. Hard, physical labor was not beneath the dignity of the Son of God.

If the Bible's teaching about God enhances work's dignity, its account of mankind's creation gives all human labor the mark of normality. God "took the man and put him in the Garden of Eden to till it and keep it" (Gn 2:15). And God's first command, to "fill the earth and subdue it" (1:28), implied a great deal of work for both man and woman. In an important sense, people today are obeying that command of their Creator when they do their daily work, whether they acknowledge him or not. Work did not, therefore, arrive in the world as a direct result of the fall into sin (though sin did spoil working conditions, 3:17-19). Work was planned by God from the dawn of history for mankind's good—as natural to men and women as sunset is to day (Ps 104:19-23).

With this firm emphasis on the dignity and normality of labor, it is no surprise to find that Scripture strongly condemns idleness. "Go to the ant, O sluggard; consider her ways, and be wise" (Prv 6:6, RSV). Paul is equally blunt: "If any one will not work, let him not eat" (2 Thes 3:10, RSV). He set a good example (Acts 20:33-35; 1 Thes 2:9). Those who refuse to work, he insists, even for spiritual reasons, earn no respect from non-Christian onlookers by depending on others to pay their bills (1 Thes 4:11-12). Wage earners, on the other hand, have the material resources of Christian service (Eph 4:28).

Vocations In biblical times the Greeks and Romans catalogued jobs according to importance or desirability. Routine manual labor, for example, was considered inferior to work involving mental activity.

Jewish teaching contrasts strongly with this attitude. "Hate not laborious work," taught the rabbis (Ecclus 7:15). Even the scholar had to spend some time in manual work. A few trades, like that of the tanner, were regarded as undesirable (a taboo broken very quickly by the early church—see Acts 9:43), but there is no indication in the Bible that some jobs are more worthwhile than others in God's sight. The Lord calls craftsmen into his service (Ex 31:1-11), just as much as prophets (Is 6:8-9). So Amos was summoned from his fruit-picking to prophesy (Am 7:14-15), but with no suggestion that he was being promoted to a superior role. The important thing was not the nature of the occupation but the readiness to obey God's call and to witness faithfully to him, whatever the job.

The Bible has some poignant things to say about the relationship between employer and employee. The OT prophets voice the strongest criticism. God is especially concerned to see that the weak get justice (Is 1:17; Mi 6:8). So, naturally, his spokesmen declare his anger when employers exploit their laborers and cheat them of their wages (Jer 22:13; Mal 3:5; cf. Jas 5:4). A person who wants to please God must "stop oppressing those who work for [him] and treat them fairly and give them what they earn" (Is 58:6, TLB).

In Bible times, the scales were weighted heavily in favor of the employer. But Scripture is not blind to the existence of selfish, greedy employees. Every worker deserves a just wage (Lk 10:7), but those with special power must not try to increase their pay by threats and violence (3:14).

Working for Christ God is a working God who is pleased when his people work hard and conscientiously. That conviction lies at the heart of the Bible's teaching about Christian attitudes toward secular employment. And quite naturally, the NT extends the same positive emphasis to cover all Christian service, paid or unpaid. The world is God's harvest field, said Jesus, waiting for Christian reapers to move in and evangelize (Mt 9:37-38). Paul used the same agricultural illustration and added another from the building trade to describe the Lord's work of evangelism and teaching (1 Cor 3:6-15). Church leaders must work especially hard, he said (1 Thes 5:12), to stimulate *all* God's people to be involved in the Lord's work (1 Cor 15:58). All Christians should see themselves as "God's coworkers" (3:9).

WORLD An important NT term from the Greek word *kosmos* (meaning that which is ordered or arranged), having five different meanings:

1. The universe created by God with design and order (e.g., Mt 13:35; Jn 17:24; Acts 17:24).
2. The planet earth (e.g., Jn 11:9). This includes the idea of earth as the dwelling place of human beings (16:21) and of earth as contrasted with heaven (6:14; 12:46).
3. The total of humanity (Mt 5:14; Jn 3:16; 1 Cor 4:13).
4. The total of human existence in this present life, with all of its experience and possessions (Mt 16:26; 1 Cor 7:33).
5. The world order as alienated from God, in rebellion against him, and condemned for its godlessness. It is "this world" (Jn 8:23; 12:25; 1 Cor 3:19), as opposed to "that which is to come." The ruler of this world is the devil (Jn 12:31; 14:30; 16:11; 1 Cor 5:10)—as John said it, "The whole world is under the control of the evil one" (1 Jn 5:19, NIV). Christians are not of this world (Jn 15:19; 17:16), even though they live in the world and participate in its activities (17:11). The believer is regarded as dead to the world (Gal 6:14; cf. Col 3:2-3). The Christian is to be separated from the world (Jas 1:27).

One's relationship with the world is an indicator of one's relationship with God. Those who love the world are void of love for God the Father (1 Jn 2:15). The Scripture points out that "all that is in the world, the lust of the flesh and the lust of the eyes and the pride of life, is not of the Father but is of the world" (v 16, RSV). The world and its desires or lusts are transient, passing away, but the doer of God's word abides forever (1 Jn 2:17; cf. 2 Cor 4:18). Friendship with the world is enmity toward God (Jas 4:4).

The discourse of Jesus on the night before his crucifixion contains much teaching about the world. The world cannot receive the Spirit of truth (Jn 14:17). Christ gives a peace that the world cannot give (v 27). Jesus offers love, while the world gives hatred and persecution (15:19-20). The world's hatred of God is also directed against the followers of Christ (vv 18-21). Although the disciples of Jesus have tribulation "in this world," they are to be of good cheer, for Jesus has overcome the world (16:33).

Another Greek word sometimes translated "world" is *aion*, which emphasizes the temporal aspect of the world. It is used of time without end, eternity (e.g., Rom 1:25; 2 Cor 11:31; Phil 4:20). *See* Age.

WORM *See* Animals.

WORMWOOD* Strong, bitter-tasting plant that symbolized bitterness and sorrow (Prv 5:4; Jer 9:15; Rv 8:11). *See* Plants.

WORSHIP Expression of reverence and adoration of God.

Worship in the Old Testament The 1,500 years from the days of Abraham to the time of Ezra (c. 1900–450 BC) saw many significant changes in the form of worship in ancient Israel. Abraham, the wandering nomad, built altars and offered sacrifices wherever God appeared to him. In Moses' time the tabernacle served as a portable sanctuary for the Israelite tribes journeying through the wilderness. Solomon built a temple in Jerusalem that lasted more than three centuries until its destruction by the Babylonians in 586 BC. When the Jews returned from exile, they built a new temple, which was later renovated and enlarged by Herod the Great. Though all the temple buildings were destroyed by the Romans in AD 70, the

foundations remained. Jews still pray by the Western Wall (called the Wailing Wall).

If the form of worship changed with times and situations, its heart and center did not. God revealed himself to Abraham, promising that his children would inherit the land of Canaan. Abraham demonstrated his faith through prayer and sacrifice. Throughout the biblical period listening to God's Word, prayer, and sacrifice constituted the essence of worship. The promises to Abraham were constantly recalled as the basis of Israel's existence as a nation and its right to the land of Canaan.

From time to time every family visited the temple in Jerusalem. Eight days after a baby boy was born, he was circumcised to mark his membership in Israel. Then, a month or two later, the baby's mother went to the temple to offer sacrifice (Lv 12; cf. Lk 2:22-24).

Animals were sacrificed in the lambing and calving season. The first lamb or calf born to every ewe or cow was presented in sacrifice (Ex 22:30). Similarly, at the beginning of the harvest season, a basket of the first fruits was offered, and at the end, a tenth of all the harvest, the tithe, was given to the priests as God's representatives (Nm 18:21-32). Deuteronomy 26:5-15 gives a typical prayer for use on such occasions.

Sometimes a person would decide to offer a sacrifice for more personal reasons. In a crisis, vows could be made and sealed with a sacrifice (Gn 28:18-22; 1 Sm 1:10-11). Then when the prayer was answered, a second sacrifice was customarily offered (Gn 35:3, 14; 1 Sm 1:24-25). Serious sin or serious sickness were also occasions for sacrifice (Lv 4–5, 13–15).

The worshiper brought the animal into the temple court. Standing before the priest, he placed one hand on its head, thereby identifying himself with the animal, and confessed his sin or explained the reason for offering the sacrifice. Then the worshiper killed the animal and cut it up for the priest to burn on the great bronze altar. Some sacrifices (burnt offerings) involved the whole animal being burnt on the altar. In others, some of the meat was set aside for the priests, while the rest was shared by the worshiper and his family. But in every case the worshiper killed the animal from his own flock with his own hands. These sacrifices expressed in a vivid and tangible way the cost of sin and the worshiper's responsibility. As the worshiper killed the animal, he recalled that sin would have caused his own death, had God not provided an escape through animal sacrifice.

Three times a year all adult men went to the temple to celebrate the national festivals (Ex 23:17; Dt 16:16): Passover (held in April), the Feast of Weeks (held in May), and the Feast of Booths (in October). When possible, the whole family accompanied the men. But if they lived a long way from Jerusalem, they would go up for only one of the festivals (1 Sm 1:3; Lk 2:41).

These festivals were tremendous occasions. Hundreds of thousands of people converged on Jerusalem. They would stay with relatives or camp in tents outside the city. The temple courts would be thronged with worshipers. The temple choirs sang psalms appropriate for the festival, while the priests and Levites offered hundreds (at Passover, thousands) of animals in sacrifice. Groups of worshipers carried away with emotion would break forth into dancing. Those of more sober temperament were content to join in the singing or simply pray quietly.

The major festivals were joyful occasions, for they celebrated the deliverance of Israel from Egypt. At Passover each family ate roasted lamb and bitter herbs to reenact the last meal their forefathers ate before leaving Egypt (Ex 12). At the Feast of Booths, they built shelters of branches and lived in them for a week, as a reminder that the Israelites camped in tents during the 40 years of wandering in the wilderness (Lv 23:39-43). These great festivals served as reminders of how God had delivered them from slavery in Egypt and had given them the land of Canaan as he had promised to Abraham.

Each of these three festivals lasted a week, but there was one day in the year that was totally different, the Day of Atonement, when everyone fasted and mourned for their sins. On this day the high priest confessed the nation's sins as he pressed his hand on the head of a goat. Then the goat was led away into the wilderness, symbolizing the removal of sin from the people (Lv 16).

Sometime after the destruction of the first temple, synagogues developed for public worship. The services were more like modern church worship, consisting exclusively of prayer, Bible reading, and preaching. There were no sacrifices made in the synagogues. When the second temple was destroyed in AD 70, synagogues became the only places where Jews could worship in public. Then there were no more sacrifices at all. The NT pictures this as fitting, for Jesus is the true Lamb of God (Jn 1:29); because of his death, there is no need for further animal sacrifice (Heb 10:11-12).

Worship in the New Testament The Jews had become far too dependent on a physical place, the temple, for their worship. When Jesus arrived on the scene, he proclaimed that he himself was the temple of God; in resurrection, he would provide the spiritual dwelling where God the Spirit and people, in spirit, could have spiritual communion (see Mt 12:6; Jn 2:19-22). In other words, worship would no longer be in a place but in a person—through Jesus Christ and his Spirit the worshipers could come directly to God (see Jn 14:6; Heb 10:19-20).

This shift in worship—from physical to spiritual—is the theme of John 4, a chapter that recounts Jesus' visit to the Samaritans. After Jesus' encounter with the Samaritan woman, she acknowledged that he must be a prophet, and then she launched into a discussion concerning the religious debate between the Jews and the Samaritans over which place of worship was the right one—Jerusalem or Mt Gerizim. The Samaritans had set up a place for worship on Mt Gerizim in accordance with Deuteronomy 11:26-29 and 27:1-8, while the Jews had followed David and Solomon in making Jerusalem the center of Jewish worship. The Scriptures affirmed Jerusalem as the true center for worship (Dt 12:5; 2 Chr 6:6; 7:12; Ps 78:67-68). But Jesus told her that a new age had come in which the issue no longer concerned a physical site. God the Father would no longer be worshiped in either place. A new age had come in which the true worshipers (Jew, Samaritan, or Gentile) must worship the Father in spirit and in truth.

"In spirit" corresponds to Jerusalem, and "in truth" corresponds to the Samaritans' unknowledgeable ideas of worship, God, etc. Formerly, God was worshiped in Jerusalem, but now the true Jerusalem would be in a person's spirit. Indeed, the church is called "the habitation of God in spirit" (Eph 2:22). True worship required a people to contact God, the Spirit, in their spirit, as well as a people who knew the truth. New Testament worship must be in spirit and in truth. Since "God is Spirit," he must be worshiped in spirit. Human beings possess a human spirit, the nature of which corresponds to God's nature, which is spirit. Therefore, people can have fellowship with God and worship God in the same sphere that God exists in.

In a sense, John 4 anticipates Revelation 21 and 22,

where God provides the rivers of the water of life to all the believers and where the Lamb and God are the temple in the New Jerusalem. The believers receive life from God and they worship in God. There is a profound, even mystical connection between drinking of the Spirit and worshiping God in the Spirit (see 1 Cor 12:13). This is also described in Ezekiel 47, which pictures the river flowing from God's temple as a symbol of God's never-ending supply. In John 4, Jesus provides the living waters to all who receive the gift of God, and he directs people to a new temple, a spiritual one, where God is worshiped in spirit.

WRATH OF GOD A term for God's displeasure with human beings and their sinful actions. The word "wrath" is a concept represented by many different words and idioms in the original languages of the Bible, all of which express the notion of justifiable anger for unjust actions.

In the Old Testament In the OT God is said to be angry with nations, sinners, and even with his covenant people. God's anger is first expressed toward the covenant community of Israel for having refused to believe his word about entering into the Promised Land. After they had been rescued from Egypt, had received the Ten Commandments and the covenant, and had seen his glory (Nm 11:10; 12:9; 22:22; 32:10-14), they still disbelieved. Consequently, God in his wrath condemned the Israelites to wander in the wilderness until they died. The major reason for the Lord's anger in the OT was that his own people constantly broke the covenant. They provoked him by their idolatry (Dt 2:15; 4:25; 9:7-8, 19; Jgs 2:14; 1 Kgs 11:9; 14:9, 15; 2 Kgs 17:18), by their mixing paganism with the worship of the Lord (Is 1:10-17; Jer 6:20; Hos 6:6; Am 5:21-27); by their wanton rebellion (1 Kgs 8:46), their unbelief (Nm 11:33; 14:11, 33; Ps 95:10-11), and their disregard for his concern for love, justice, righteousness, and holiness (Ex 22:22-24; Is 1:15-17; Am 5:7-12; Mi 3:1).

The wrath of God also extends to all humanity (Na 1:2). The concept of the Day of the Lord was developed by the prophets to warn Israel and the nations that no one can escape the righteous expression of God's wrath (Am 5:18-20). The Day of the Lord is the day of his wrath (Zep 1:15).

The OT presents the concept of the wrath of God in balance with three other doctrines: his forbearance, his love, and his readiness to forgive. First, God is patient. The Hebrew word for "patient" is related to the word for "wrath" and means "length of wrath"; that is, God does not quickly become angry. He is longsuffering (Ex 34:6). Second, God is full of compassion and fidelity (Ex 34:6). Even when his children sin against him, he is like a father who is full of compassion and love. He is always faithful to his children. Third, he is ready to forgive those who sin against him when they atone for and are cleansed from their sins (Ex 34:6). The pleasure of his love is so much greater than his wrath (Ps 30:5). Micah prayed that the Lord may soon forgive and restore his people on the ground that he cannot be angry forever (7:18; cf. Ps 89:46; Jer 3:5). In Psalm 103:8-13, the psalmist likens God's love and forgiveness to that of a father who does not harbor his anger continually, nor does he vex his children with discipline, so great is his love for those who fear him.

The purpose of God's wrath is not to destroy humanity (Hos 11:9). His wrath is neither a vindictive, emotional overreaction, nor is it unpredictable. In his wrath he sovereignly imposes limits on nations (Babylon, Assyria) and disciplines his own people with the desired end that they return to him (Jl 2:13-14). The OT presentation of the Day of the Lord doesn't end with God's anger; it concludes with the restoration of the earth, when the whole earth will be filled with knowledge of God (Is 11:9; Hb 2:14) and wickedness will be no more (Is 65:25).

In the New Testament The NT also teaches the wrath of God side by side with the doctrine of his grace, love, and forbearance (Mt 3:7; Lk 21:23; Jn 3:36; Rom 1:18; Eph 5:6; Rv 14:10). Those who do not profess faith in the risen Christ remain in their sins and will be subject to God's wrath, whereas those who believe in him are delivered from God's wrath (Eph 2:3; 1 Thes 1:10). The good news of the NT is that Jesus has come to deliver us from the wrath of God (Rom 5:9). Those who have been delivered are reconciled with God (v 10) because they no longer are under condemnation (8:1).

See also Death; Hell; Judgment; Last Judgment; Love.

WRITER Professional scribe and/or secretary; religious scribe and/or secretary.

Professional Scribes and Secretaries Scribes were employed as secretaries in Palestine, Egypt, Mesopotamia, and the Greco-Roman Empire. Court scribes would sometimes rise to positions of social prestige and considerable political influence, much as a secretary of state today.

There were schools for the training of such scribes. To master the difficult art of writing on clay probably required as much time then as it takes students now to develop the ability to read and write. Would-be scribes could either enter a regular school or work as an apprentice under a private teacher, though most of them apparently followed the latter procedure. Scribes who were willing to teach could be found everywhere, even in the smaller towns. In fact, most of the scribes had at least one apprentice, who was treated like a son while learning the profession. Such students learned not only from private tutoring but also from the example of their teacher. This kind of education was sufficient to equip young scribes for the normal commercial branches of the craft. They were fully prepared to handle the necessary formulas for the various kinds of legal and business documents, and they could easily take dictation for private correspondence.

For additional study and training, however, it was necessary to attend the regular schools. The schools were attached to temples, and only these schools had the proper facilities to teach the sciences (including mathematics) and literature, which the more advanced scribes had to master. There a budding scribe could study to become even a priest or a "scientist." In the ruins of ancient cities archaeologists have discovered "textbooks" used by the pupils. Excavators have also uncovered schoolrooms with benches on which the students sat. Some of the ancient Near Eastern texts that have been unearthed are nothing but schoolboy exercises or student copies of originals. These copies are usually not as beautiful or as legible as the originals, which were written by master scribes.

When the teacher wanted to give the students an assignment, he had available in the temple school virtually every type of text imaginable. For elementary work he could have the students practice writing a list of cuneiform signs, much like our learning the letters of the alphabet—except that there were some 600 signs! Another simple assignment would have been to copy dictionaries containing lists of stones, cities, animals, and gods. After such preparatory work, the students could then move on to literary texts and, for example,

accurately reproduce a portion of one of the great epics, a hymn, or a prayer. Through arduous study and a lengthy program of instruction and practice, a gifted student could become qualified for scribal service in almost any field.

Religious Scribe The scribe in Israel undertook a wide range of writing tasks. Often the scribe sat at the gate of the city or in an open area undertaking numerous kinds of writing tasks for illiterate citizens, correspondence, writing of receipts, and contracts. More officially, he kept records and wrote annals. Religious scribes copied the Scriptures. Several of these men are mentioned in the OT: Shebna (2 Kgs 18:18, 37), Shaphan (2 Kgs 22:8-12), Ezra (Ezr 7:6, 11; Neh 8:1, 9, 13; 12:26, 36), Baruch (Jer 36:26, 32), and Jonathan (Jer 37:15, 20).

Paul made use of secretaries or scribes (called amanuenses) when he composed his epistles. The usual procedure for a dictated epistle was for the amanuensis to take down the speaker's words and produce a transcript, which the author would then review and edit. Taking the edited copy, the amanuensis would produce a final draft, which the author would sign in his own handwriting. Two NT epistles provide the name of an amanuensis: Tertius for Romans (Rom 16:22) and Silvanus for 1 Peter (1 Pt 5:12). Some of Paul's epistles indicate that he provided the concluding salutation in his own handwriting: 1 Corinthians (1 Cor 16:21), Galatians (Gal 6:11), Colossians (Col 4:18), and 2 Thessalonians (2 Thes 3:17). This indicates that these epistles were penned by someone else—Paul's amanuensis—prior to his signing off. By contrast, John penned his own epistles (1 Jn 1:4; 2:1, 7-8, 12-14; 2 Jn 1:12; 3 Jn 1:9, 13).

See also Letter Writing, Ancient; Writing.

WRITING The process that goes into producing books.

Books have been written for many centuries but have not always been produced in the familiar form in which they are known today. If a book is defined as any written record of thoughts or acts, the production of books goes back to a very early period in the history of civilization. The Sumerians produced written documents and primers on clay tablets as early as 2500 BC. The Sumerian civilization went into decline after its conquest by the Akkadians (2300 BC). In the 21st century BC, however, there occurred a revival of Sumerian culture that produced a number of important literary works, including the first known written codified system of law. Today a rich collection of Sumerian material exists. It includes legal, mythological, and commercial documents as well as written material produced in the process of training scribes. A large collection of cuneiform tablets was found in the library of the Assyrian king Ashurbanipal, which was established in the seventh century BC. The library contained many records of religious and scientific knowledge.

We have many ancient manuscripts of the books of the Bible. As for the books of the Hebrew Bible, scribes used quill, ink, and leather scrolls to make copies of individual books. Some of the scrolls, made of several treated animal hides stitched together, could be as long as 35 to 40 feet (10.7 to 12.2 meters) when unrolled. As scrolls wore out, or if there was a need for copies in various synagogues, Jewish scribes would make additional copies—and they did so with painstaking care. Prior to the Dead Sea Scroll discoveries, museums housed several manuscripts of the Hebrew Bible dated between the eighth and tenth centuries. The Dead Sea Scrolls are dated between 100 BC and AD 100, which makes them a thousand years earlier than these other mauscripts. The

Dead Sea Scrolls contain significant portions of the OT. Every book except Esther is represented. The largest portions come from the Pentateuch (especially Deuteronomy—25 manuscripts), the Major Prophets (especially Isaiah—18 manuscripts), and Psalms (27 manuscripts). As for the books of the NT, we have nearly 6,000 manuscripts prior to the time of the printing press (c. 1500). About 200 of these manuscripts date between the early second and late fourth century. Most of the NT manuscripts were written on papyrus or vellum, and all of the NT manuscripts were written in the codex form.

Writing Materials

Clay The Sumerian, Babylonian, and Assyrian clay tablets are well known. Baked clay tablets were preserved easily in almost any climate. They were suitable, however, only for a straight-line form of writing such as cuneiform, and were therefore not appropriate for the rounded Aramaic form of Hebrew script.

Papyrus The papyrus rolls of Egypt have been used as a writing surface since the early third millennium BC. The Greeks adopted papyrus around 900 BC, and the Romans adopted its use later. The oldest extant Greek rolls of papyrus date from the fourth century BC. The inner pith of the papyrus plant was called *byblos*. From this comes the Greek word *biblion* ("book") and the English word "bible." The word "paper" is derived from "papyrus."

Unfortunately, papyrus is perishable, requiring a dry climate for its preservation. That is why few papyri have been discovered anywhere other than in the desert sands of Egypt. Some papyrus fragments have also been found in the caves near the Dead Sea, where the climate is likewise sufficiently dry.

Potsherds Broken pieces of pottery furnished an inexpensive writing material because the supply was so abundant. The Samaria and Lachish ostraca are examples.

Wood Wooden tablets covered with stucco or wax were sometimes used as a writing surface. A NT example is Luke 1:63.

Leather, Parchment, and Vellum These are all made from animal skins. Leather (tanned skins), the forerunner of parchment, has been in use about as long as papyrus, but it was rarely used because papyrus was so abundant. The ancient Hebrews probably used leather and papyrus for writing materials. The Dead Sea Scrolls were sheets of leather sewed together with linen thread. Metal scrolls also existed (e.g., copper).

Parchment, made in the beginning from sheep and goat skins, began to replace leather as early as the third century BC, though actual parchment codices date from the second century AD. To prepare parchment or refined leather, the hair was removed from the skins and the latter rubbed smooth. The most common form of book for OT and NT documents was evidently a roll or scroll of papyrus, leather, or parchment. The average length of a scroll was about 30 feet (9.1 meters), though the famous Harris Papyrus was 133 feet (40.5 meters) long. Scrolls were often stored in pottery jars (Jer 32:14) and were frequently sealed (Rv 5:1).

Vellum had a finer quality than parchment and was prepared from the skins of calves, lambs, or kids. In the fourth century AD, vellum or parchment as a material and the codex as a form became the norm.

Paper Paper, made from wood, rags, and certain grasses, began to replace vellum and parchment as early as the tenth century AD in the Western world, though it was used considerably earlier in China and Japan. By the 15th century, paper manuscripts were common.

Kinds of Books

Scroll The scroll is a roll of papyrus, parchment, or leather used for writing a document or literary work. The papyrus scroll of Egypt can be traced as far back as 2500 BC. One of the most famous literary productions of ancient Egypt is the Book of the Dead. Jews used leather scrolls for writing the books of the Old Testament. Most of the scrolls discovered from the Dead Sea area were written on leather, with a few having been written on papyrus.

Codex An important development in the evolution of book production occurred with the advent of the codex in the middle of the first century. A codex was constructed much like our modern books by folding sheets of papyrus or vellum (treated animal hide) in the middle and then sewing them together at the spine. This kind of book was advantageous because it enabled the scribe to write on both sides; it facilitated easier access to particu-

Ancient Codex of Paul's Epistles Two leaves of Romans in Chester Beatty Papyrus II (late second century)—P46.

lar passages (as opposed to a scroll, which had to be unrolled); and it enabled Christians to bind together all four Gospels or all Paul's epistles or any other such combination.

Writing Utensils and Ink Different kinds of writing implements were used, depending on the writing surfaces in use at various periods of history. Metal chisels and gravers were used for inscribing stone and metal. A stylus was used for writing cuneiform ("wedge-shaped" characters) on clay tablets. For writing on ostraca (potsherds), papyrus, and parchment, a reed was split or cut to act as a brush. In Egypt rushes were used to form a brush. Later, reeds were cut to a point and split like a quill pen. Apparently this was the type of pen or "calamus" used in NT times (3 Jn 1:13).

Ink (cf. 2 Jn 1:12) was usually a black carbon (charcoal) mixed with gum or oil for use on parchment or mixed with a metallic substance for papyrus. It was kept in an inkhorn as a dried substance, on which the scribe would dip or rub his moistened pen. It could be erased by washing (Nm 5:23) or with a penknife, which was also used for sharpening pens and trimming or cutting scrolls (Jer 36:23).

See also Hieroglyphics; Inscriptions; Lachish Letters; Letter Writing, Ancient; Scribe; Writer.

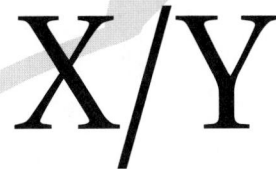

X/Y

XANTHICUS* Name of the month in the Macedonian calendar corresponding to the Hebrew month Nisan (March–April); mentioned in 2 Maccabees 11:27-38. *See* Calendars, Ancient and Modern.

XERXES NIV and NLT rendering of Ahasuerus in Ezra 4:6 and the book of Esther. *See* Ahasuerus #1.

XESTES* Liquid measure equivalent to about one and one-sixth pints (552 milliliters). *See* Weights and Measures.

YAHWEH* (YHWH) Most holy name for God in the OT, usually translated "Lord." *See* God, Names of (Yahweh).

YEAR *See* Calendars, Ancient and Modern.

YEAST *See* Leaven.

YELLOW *See* Color.

YIRON One of the fortified cities of Naphtali's tribe (Jos 19:38). Some have identified Yiron with the present village of Jarun, southeast of Bint Jebeil.

YOKE The wooden bar that allowed two (or more) draft animals to be coupled (yoked) so that they might effectively work together (Nm 19:2; 1 Kgs 19:19; Jb 1:3). In addition to this literal usage, the Bible frequently uses the term metaphorically to refer to work or bondage (Lv 26:13). The yoke of bondage was applied not only by foreign oppressors but often by Israel's own kings as well (1 Kgs 12:4-14; 2 Chr 10:4-14). In prophetic writings, the yoke of bondage was generally associated with divine judgment (Lam 1:14), so that deliverance was represented as God breaking the yoke that had enslaved Israel (Is 9:4; 10:27; 14:25; 58:6; Jer 2:20; 5:5). The yoke of bondage figured prominently in Jeremiah's dispute with Hananiah's prophecy concerning Judah's imminent release from Babylonian captivity (Jer 27:8-11; 28:1-17). In the NT, Jesus transforms "yoke" into a positive term by calling on people to take up his yoke, which is not burdensome, and he will give them rest for their souls (Mt 11:29-30).

YOM KIPPUR* One of the feast days of Israel involving atonement for the sins of the nation (Lv 23:26-32). *See* Feasts and Festivals of Israel.

Pairs of Oxen Linked with Yokes

Z

ZAANAIM* KJV spelling of Zaanannim in Judges 4:11. *See* Zaanannim.

ZAANAN Village mentioned in Micah's lament over Jerusalem (Mi 1:11). Zaanan is probably a play on the Hebrew word *yatsa'*, "to come forth." The village was in the Shephelah; it is probably the same place as Zenan.
    See also Zenan.

ZAANANNIM One of the markers of the border of Naphtali listed between Heleph and Adami-nekeb (Jos 19:33). Judges 4:11 puts it near Kedesh. There Sisera took refuge in the tent of Heber the Kenite and was killed by Jael (vv 11-21). While the precise location is not known, it was west of Lake el-Huleh (modern Merom) in a region that was probably marshy in ancient times. Though the KJV translates the text as "plain of Zaanaim," it is more likely "Oak of Zaanannim" (RSV, NIV, NLT). Since many terebinth trees are located in the region, the text is probably referring to a terebinth set aside as a sacred tree.

ZAAVAN Second son of Ezer, a Horite clan chief (Gn 36:27; 1 Chr 1:42).

ZABAD
1. Son of Nathan (1 Chr 2:36) and a descendant of Ahlai the daughter of Sheshan (vv 30, 34-36).
2. Tahath's son and the father of Shuthelah from Ephraim's tribe (1 Chr 7:21).
3. One of David's mighty men, listed as a son of Ahlai (1 Chr 11:41); he is perhaps the same as #1 above.
4. One of the assassins of King Joash, listed as the son of Shimeath the Ammonitess (2 Chr 24:26). He is identical to Jozacar (alternately "Jozabad") in 2 Kings 12:21. Zabad was a palace official who was likely the agent of a powerful conspiracy against Joash.
    See also Jozacar, Jozachar.
5–7. Three priests variously descended from Zattu, Hashum, and Nebo, who renounced their foreign wives at Ezra's request during the postexilic period (Ezr 10:27, 33, 43).

ZABBAI
1. Bebai's son and one of the priests who divorced his foreign wife at Ezra's command (Ezr 10:28).
2. Father of Baruch. Baruch repaired a section of the Jerusalem wall during Nehemiah's day (Neh 3:20).

ZABBUD* KJV form of Zaccur, Bigvai's descendant, in Ezra 8:14. *See* Zaccur #5.

ZABDI
1. Zerah's descendant from Judah's tribe (Jos 7:1). Achan was a Zerahite of the family of Zabdi (Jos 7:17-18); alternately called Zimri (NLT mg, 1 Chr 2:6).
2. Shimei's son and a descendant of Ehud from Benjamin's tribe (1 Chr 8:19).
3. David's officer over the produce of the vineyards for the

wine cellars (1 Chr 27:27). He is called a Shiphmite, which likely means that he was a native of Shepham.
4. One of the temple musicians of the order of Asaph (Neh 11:17); alternately called Zicri (1 Chr 9:15).

ZABDIEL
1. Father of Jashobeam, the commander of the first division of David's army (1 Chr 27:2).
2. Priest and overseer of 128 "mighty men of valor" (RSV, Neh 11:14). The notation that he was a "son of Haggedolim" might indicate that he was a "son of the mighty men."
3. Arab who beheaded Alexander (Balas) Epiphanes and sent the head to Ptolemy (1 Macc 11:17).

ZABUD Priest in Solomon's court and the "king's friend" (1 Kgs 4:5). The phrase "king's friend" may be an official title given to one of the king's advisers. Hushai the Archite had a similar title in David's court (2 Sm 15:37; 16:16).

ZABULON* KJV spelling of Zebulun in Matthew 4:13-15 and Revelation 7:8. *See* Zebulun, Tribe of.

ZACCAI Forefather of a family who returned with Zerubbabel to Judah following the exile (Ezr 2:9; Neh 7:14).

ZACCHAEUS Jewish tax collector who collected taxes for the Romans at Jericho. He probably secured this position by purchasing the exclusive right to collect revenue in that region or by working as a subcontractor for another affluent official. In either case, Zacchaeus himself accrued great wealth (largely by illegitimate means) from his customs enterprise. Jericho, a significant center of commerce, was situated along a major trade route connecting Jerusalem and its environs with the lands east of the Jordan.
    In his Gospel, Luke records Zacchaeus's encounter with Jesus (Lk 19:2-8). Seeking Jesus, but unable to see him over the crowd because of his small stature, Zacchaeus climbed a sycamore tree to get a better view when Jesus passed by. To his astonishment, Jesus stopped under the tree and after calling him down, invited himself to the publican's house for the night. Subsequently, Zacchaeus repented and followed Jesus, promising to restore fourfold to those whom he had wrongfully exploited and give to the poor. According to Clement of Alexandria, Zacchaeus later became the bishop of Caesarea (*Homily* 3.63).

ZACCHUR* KJV spelling of Zaccur, Hammuel's son, in 1 Chronicles 4:26. *See* Zaccur #2.

ZACCUR
1. Reubenite and father of Shammua, one of the 12 spies in the reconnaissance of Canaan (Nm 13:4).
2. Simeonite who was the son of Hammuel and the father of Shimei (1 Chr 4:26).

3. One of the descendants of Merari in the record of the divisions of the priests (1 Chr 24:27).
4. One of the sons of Asaph who was assigned responsibility for the temple service (1 Chr 25:2). Zaccur and his sons and brothers were assigned the third lot among the various duties for the temple musicians (1 Chr 25:10). Descendants of Zaccur were present at the dedication of the city wall following the exile (Neh 12:35).
5. One of the descendants of Bigvai who returned to Jerusalem with Ezra (Ezr 8:14).
6. Son of Imri who worked on repairing Jerusalem's wall in the vicinity of the Sheep Gate (Neh 3:2).
7. One of the Levites who signed Nehemiah's covenant to obey the law of God (Neh 10:12).
8. Son of Mattaniah and father of Hanan, the assistant to the storehouse treasurers during Nehemiah's time (Neh 13:13). Some have suggested that he is the same as #7 above.

ZACHARIAH*

1. KJV spelling of Zechariah, king of Israel, in 2 Kings 14:29 and 15:8, 11. See Zechariah (Person) #1.
2. KJV spelling of Zechariah, King Hezekiah's maternal grandfather, in 2 Kings 18:2. See Zechariah (Person) #2.

ZACHARIAS*

1. KJV spelling of Zechariah, Jehoiada's son, in Matthew 23:35 and Luke 11:51. See Zechariah (Person) #14.
2. KJV spelling of Zechariah, John the Baptist's father, in Luke 1:5-67. See Zechariah (Person) #31.
3. KJV spelling of Zechariah, a proposed name for John the Baptist, in Luke 1:59. See John the Baptist; Zechariah (Person) #32.

ZACHER* KJV form of Zechariah, or Zeker, in 1 Chronicles 8:31. See Zechariah (Person) #5.

ZADOK Common OT name meaning "righteous one."

1. David's priest, probably the most famous and influential of Israel's high priests apart from Aaron. He first appeared at the time of Absalom's revolt, when he and his fellow priest Abiathar showed their loyalty to David by coming to him with the ark, fully prepared to share his exile (2 Sm 15:24-29). David refused their offer and sent them back to Jerusalem to act in his interests.

In 2 Samuel 8:17, Zadok is listed as the son of Ahitub, who is noted in 1 Samuel 14:3 as the grandson of Eli. In the genealogies of Chronicles, Zadok's descent through Ahitub is traced back to Eleazar, the eldest son of Aaron (1 Chr 6:1-8, 50-53; Ezr 7:2-5), but with no reference to Eli. A slight problem emerges in that Zadok replaces the banished Abiathar, a descendant of Eli. This is regarded as the fulfillment of an earlier prophecy that the tenure of the high priestly office by Eli's family would be broken in favor of a different branch of Aaron's family (1 Sm 2:30-36; 1 Kgs 2:26-27).

In both summaries of David's court officials (2 Sm 8:17; 20:25), Zadok is listed as one of David's two principal priests, an office held throughout the latter part of David's reign. When David was near death, a power struggle over the throne was precipitated by Adonijah, David's oldest surviving son. With the support of Joab, the commander of the army, and the priest Abiathar, David's long-standing friend, Adonijah declared himself king (1 Kgs 1:5-10). Nathan the prophet promptly

intervened with Bathsheba as Solomon's advocate. Zadok and Benaiah, the captain of the mercenary troops, supported Solomon. Adonijah's cause was hopeless once David had indicated his approval of Nathan's plans. Consequently, the discredited Abiathar was banished (2:26-27), leaving the loyal Zadok as Solomon's chief priest (2:35; 4:4).

In the centuries that followed, the descendants of Zadok preserved this dominance, and as Jerusalem's prestige increased, so did their status. Azariah, the chief priest in Hezekiah's reign, was a Zadokite (2 Chr 31:10). Ezekiel restricted the main priestly functions to the "sons of Zadok," demoting the Levites generally to the rank of "temple caretakers" because of their apostasy during the monarchy (Ez 44:10-16). When the Jews came under Seleucid domination in the early second century BC, the high priesthood, regarded as a political appointment, was taken away from the Zadokites. Conservative elements, however, like the Qumran covenanters, continued to look for its restoration.

See also David; Israel, History of.

2. Father-in-law of Uzziah and grandfather of Jotham, kings of Judah (2 Kgs 15:32-33; 2 Chr 27:1).
3. Descendant of Zadok, David's priest (1 Chr 6:12; 9:11; Neh 11:11).
4. Young man of exceptional courage, the leader of a contingent that joined David at Hebron against Saul (1 Chr 12:28).
5. Son of Baana, who helped to repair the wall of Jerusalem in Nehemiah's time (Neh 3:4).
6. Son of Immer, who also shared in Nehemiah's rebuilding operations (Neh 3:29).
7. Signatory to Nehemiah's covenant (Neh 10:21) and perhaps identifiable with #5 or #6 above.
8. One of three treasurers appointed by Nehemiah during his second term of office, called the scribe (Neh 13:13).
9. Ancestor of Christ (Mt 1:14). See Genealogy of Jesus Christ.

ZAHAM One of Rehoboam's sons by his wife Mahalath (2 Chr 11:19).

ZAIR Place where Joram attacked and defeated the Edomites (2 Kgs 8:21). In the parallel passage of 2 Chronicles 21:9, the phrase "to Zair" is replaced by the phrase "with his commanders" (the Hebrew words are similar). Many have therefore suggested that a copyist revision appeared in 2 Chronicles because the location of Zair was unknown. Others have suggested that Zair should be identified with Zoar on the southeast end of the Dead Sea, or with Seir in Edom. In any case, it was located in Transjordan on a principal road to Edom.

ZALAPH Hanun's father. Hanun repaired a section of the Jerusalem wall during Nehemiah's day (Neh 3:30).

ZALMON (Person) One of David's mighty men (2 Sm 23:28); alternately called Ilai the Ahohite in 1 Chronicles 11:29.

ZALMON (Place) Mountain from which Abimelech took brush to burn down the tower of Shechem (Jgs 9:48). Since the mountain obviously was close to Shechem, it tentatively has been identified with es-Sulemiyeh (the modern name for the southeastern portion of Mt Ebal) or one of its surrounding hills. Zalmon is also mentioned in connection with the defeat of Israel's enemies in Psalm 68:14. Because of the mention of snowfall and the "mighty mountain of Bashan" in the following verse, the Septuagint and some commentators consider this Zalmon to be Mt Hermon in Lebanon. However, seasonal snowfalls also occur in the region of Mt Ebal.

ZALMONAH Place where the Israelites camped after they set out from Mt Hor (Nm 33:41-42). The name suggests that it was a gloomy valley leading up to the Edomite plateau.

ZALMUNNA *See* Zebah and Zalmunna.

ZAMZUMMIM*, ZAMZUMMITES Ammonite name for the Rephaim, who are described as a "people great and many, and tall as the Anakim" (Dt 2:20). The Zamzummites were displaced by the Ammonites, just as the Horites were displaced by the Edomites and the Avvim by the Caphtorim. The comparison with the Anakim, the Rephaim, and the Emim makes it evident that the Zamzummites were a race of giants who lived in Transjordan. While their precise origin is unknown, they probably resided in the vicinity of Rabbath-ammon.

See also Giants; Rephaim.

ZANOAH (Person) Descendant of Caleb from Judah's tribe (1 Chr 4:18). Zanoah was the son of Jekuthiel and, depending on the translation of the Hebrew text, may have been related to Bithiah, the daughter of Pharaoh. Some have interpreted the text as indicating that Jekuthiel was the founder or principal settler of the city named Zanoah. In any case, Zanoah's descendants may well have been connected with the city of that name.

ZANOAH (Place)
1. One of the cities "in the lowland" that was part of Judah's inheritance (Jos 15:34). The inhabitants of Zanoah worked with Hanun to rebuild the Valley Gate as well as about 1,500 feet (457.2 meters) of the city wall during the restoration of Jerusalem (Neh 3:13; 11:30). The city is probably identifiable with Zanu'a, which is located approximately 10 miles (16.1 kilometers) west of Jerusalem.
2. One of the cities in the Judean highlands south of Hebron that was part of Judah's inheritance (Jos 15:56). It was probably inhabited by the descendants of Zanoah, Jekuthiel's son.

ZAPHENATH-PANEAH Name given to Joseph by Pharaoh when Joseph assumed his governmental responsibilities in Egypt (Gn 41:45). The name most likely means "says the god, he will live." *See* Joseph #1.

ZAPHON Town located east of the Jordan River (Jos 13:27) and included as part of the inheritance of Gad's tribe (v 24). Egyptian records (13th century BC) refer to a town known as *Dapuna*, while an Amarna text spells the name *Sapuna*.

ZARA*, ZARAH* KJV alternate forms of Zerah, Judah's son, in Genesis 38:30, 46:12, and Matthew 1:3. *See* Zerah #2.

ZAREAH*, ZAREATHITE* KJV spelling of Zorah and Zorathite in Nehemiah 11:29 and 1 Chronicles 2:53, respectively. *See* Zorah, Zorathite.

ZARED* KJV spelling for the valley of Zered in Numbers 21:12. *See* Zered.

ZAREPHATH Village where the woman who provided food and lodging for Elijah lived (1 Kgs 17:9-10; Lk 4:26). Obadiah later prophesied that the Israelite exiles of Halah would "possess Phoenicia as far as Zarephath" (Ob 1:20). Zarephath was under the control of Sidon at the time Elijah visited, thus serving as a safe haven from King Ahab of Israel. Zarephath is likely identifiable with modern Surafend, where a chapel marks the traditional site for the widow's house.

ZARETHAN City or region near the Jordan River north of Jericho. It is first mentioned in connection with the "cutting off" of the waters of the Jordan that occurred at Adam, "the city that is beside Zarethan" (Jos 3:16). Its location is more precisely defined in the list of Solomon's administrative districts as being in the vicinity of Beth-shan below Jezreel (1 Kgs 4:12). Bronze utensils for Solomon's temple were cast near there (7:46; 2 Chr 4:17, "Zeredah").

ZARETH-SHAHAR* KJV spelling of Zereth-shahar, a Reubenite city, in Joshua 13:19. *See* Zereth-shahar.

ZARHITE*
1. KJV spelling of Zerahite, a descendant of Zerah's family in Simeon's tribe, in Numbers 26:13. *See* Zerah #3.
2. KJV spelling of Zerahite, a descendant of Zerah's family in Judah's tribe, in Numbers 26:20. *See* Zerah #2.

ZARTANAH*, ZARTHAN* KJV alternate forms of Zarethan in 1 Kings 4:12 and 7:46, respectively. *See* Zarethan.

ZATTHU* KJV rendering of Zattu in Nehemiah 10:14. *See* Zattu #2.

ZATTU
1. Clan chief with whom 945 people returned with Zerubbabel (Ezr 2:8; Neh 7:13 cites 845 returnees). Of the priests who renounced their foreign wives, six are listed as "sons" of Zattu (Ezr 10:27).
2. One of the chiefs of the people who signed Nehemiah's covenant (Neh 10:14); perhaps the same person as #1 above.

ZAVAN* KJV spelling of Zaavan, Ezer's son, in 1 Chronicles 1:42. *See* Zaavan.

ZAZA Jonathan's son, in the family of Jerahmeel, a member of Judah's tribe (1 Chr 2:33).

ZEALOT Term used for the second Simon among the Twelve to distinguish him from Simon Peter (Lk 6:15; Acts 1:13). Matthew (Mt 10:4) and Mark (Mk 3:18) use "Cananaean"—Greek and Aramaic equivalents for "zealous defender, enthusiast, one eager to acquire, fanatic" (from root words meaning "burn with zeal, or jealousy; desire eagerly"; Ex 34:14; 2 Macc 4:2). In this general sense, Christ showed zeal for God's house. Some were "zealots" for spiritual gifts, good works, goodness, and the law, as Paul was for the tradition of the fathers and for God (Jn 2:17; Acts 21:20; 22:3; 1 Cor 14:12; Gal 1:14; Ti 2:14). So, Simon was distinguished from Peter and the others by his religious zeal.

By the time Luke wrote, the title "Zealot" had become attached especially to a militant, anti-Roman, revolutionary faction, equally religious and political in motivation. This party may have been founded in AD 6, following the death of Herod the Great, by Judas the Galilean and Zadduk the Pharisee. The movement was rooted in Maccabean resistance to foreign rule and infiltration

(1 Macc 2:15-28). Zealot opposition to Roman rule was rooted in zeal for the Torah and for God the only King. The Zealot regarded himself as an agent of divine judgment and redemption, resolutely and fearlessly contending against idolatry, apostasy, and collaboration. The Zealots thought that the Messiah would become their leader.

As hostility between Rome and Judea sharpened, the religious motivation was channeled by nationalist feeling into a "holy war." Whereas the Maccabees had been forced to take arms in self-defense, the Zealots became increasingly militaristic. Josephus (*Antiquities* 18.1.1-6; *War* 4.3.9), with some prejudice, calls them brigands and robbers. Their Latin name was *sicarii*, assassins, but supporters would call them patriotic guerrillas. They reached preeminence in the revolt against Rome (AD 66–70). Their last refuge and stronghold, at Masada, was overcome in AD 73, when the surviving 960 committed suicide.

Simon probably was, or had been, a member of this movement's earlier phase, around AD 30. It is less probable that Judas Iscariot (possibly Sicarius) and the "sons of thunder" (Mk 3:17) were. Judas the Galilean (Acts 5:37-38), and even Paul (21:38), were considered Zealots.

See also First Jewish Revolt; Judaism.

ZEALOT, Simon the *See* Simon #5.

ZEBADIAH

1. One of the sons of Beriah from Benjamin's tribe (1 Chr 8:15).
2. One of the sons of Elpaal from Benjamin's tribe (1 Chr 8:17).
3. One of the sons of Jeroham of Gedor, who came to David's support at Ziklag (1 Chr 12:7).
4. Korahite Levite descended from Asaph, third of Meshelemiah's seven sons and a temple gatekeeper (1 Chr 26:2).
5. Son of Asahel, Joab's brother, who was the commander of the fourth division of David's army (1 Chr 27:7).
6. One of the Levites sent by Jehoshaphat into the cities of Judah to teach the law (2 Chr 17:8).
7. Ishmael's son and one of the leaders of the Levites whom Jehoshaphat appointed as governor of civil affairs for the house of Judah (2 Chr 19:11).
8. Michael's son from Shephatiah's house, who returned with Ezra to Jerusalem following the exile (Ezr 8:8).
9. One of the sons of Immer who renounced his foreign wife at Ezra's command (Ezr 10:20).

ZEBAH AND ZALMUNNA

Two Midianite kings who slaughtered Gideon's brothers at Tabor. Gideon subsequently killed them in order to avenge his brothers' deaths (Jgs 8:18-21).

During Gideon's day, Midianite camel raiders annually made forays into Israelite territory at harvesttime, stealing crops and livestock (Jgs 6:3). So complete were their raids that nothing was left in Israel, including crops, sheep, oxen, or donkeys.

In this state of affairs God called Gideon to deliver Israel (Jgs 6:16). His well-known victory over Midian near Mt Moreh was an important step toward realization of this divine commission (7:1-23). In the operations following the battle, Ephraimite warriors captured and assassinated two Midianite leaders named Zeeb and Oreb (7:24–8:3).

Gideon determined to capture Zebah and Zalmunna, the kings of the Midianite forces. In tracking them down,

he crossed the Jordan River and traveled more than 100 miles (160.9 kilometers) from the site of the original battle. Along the way, two successive towns, Succoth and Penuel, refused to help Gideon and his men, doubtless fearing reprisal from the Midianite raiders should Gideon fail to defeat them.

Gideon routed the remaining Midianite warriors and captured Zebah and Zalmunna (Jgs 8:12). Because Zebah and Zalmunna had killed his brothers, Gideon killed the two Midianite kings (vv 19-21). Psalm 83:11 indicates that Zebah, Zalmunna, and the Midianites were the enemies not merely of Israel but also of God.

ZEBAIM*

KJV rendering of a place mentioned in Ezra 2:57 and Nehemiah 7:59. *See* Pochereth-Hazzebaim, Pochereth of Zebaim.

ZEBEDEE

Father of the disciples James and John (Mt 26:37; Mk 3:17; 10:35). Zebedee was in the fishing business and may have been wealthy, considering that he had servants and apparent connections with the high priest (Jn 18:15). Although he personally appears only once in the narrative (Mt 4:21; Mk 1:19-20), his wife, Salome, appears frequently as one of the pious women who followed Christ.

ZEBIDAH

Mother of Jehoiakim, king of Judah, Josiah's wife and the daughter of Pedaiah (2 Kgs 23:36).

ZEBINA

Nebo's son, who obeyed Ezra's exhortation to divorce his foreign wife after the exile (Ezr 10:43).

ZEBOIIM

One of the "cities of the plain" that was destroyed with Sodom and Gomorrah (Dt 29:23; Hos 11:8). Zeboiim is first mentioned, with Sodom, Gomorrah, and Admah, as one of the Canaanite cities in the "table of nations" in Genesis 10:19. It later appears confederated with the same states (including Zoar) in the battle against Amraphel king of Shinar, Arioch king of Ellasar, Kedorlaomer king of Elam, and Tidal king of Goiim (Gn 14:2, 8).

See also Cities of the Plain.

ZEBOIM

1. KJV spelling of Zeboiim in Genesis 10:19, Deuteronomy 29:23, and Hosea 11:8. *See* Zeboiim.
2. Valley where one of the raiding parties of the Philistines turned toward the border of the wilderness (1 Sm 13:18). It may be identified with Shuk ed-Dubba.
3. One of the villages outside of Jerusalem where the Benjaminites settled after the exile (Neh 11:34).

ZEBUDAH*

KJV spelling of Zebidah, King Josiah's wife, in 2 Kings 23:36. *See* Zebidah.

ZEBUL

Ruler of Shechem who served as an officer of Abimelech (Jgs 9:28-30). Zebul apparently obtained his position when Abimelech was crowned king at Shechem. When Gaal the son of Ebed incited the Shechemites to rebel against Abimelech, Zebul played an instrumental role in Abimelech's victory. After he goaded Gaal into attacking Abimelech outside of the city, Zebul shut Gaal out of the city, preventing retreat into its confines. It is difficult to determine Zebul's fate when Abimelech later attacked and destroyed the city, but it is possible that he too met a treacherous fate.

ZEBULUN (Person)

One of Jacob's 12 sons (Gn 35:23; 1 Chr 2:1). He was the sixth and last son borne to Jacob by Leah, who named the boy Zebulun, meaning "abode, dwelling," for she said, "Now my husband will *dwell with* me, because I have borne him six sons" (Gn 30:20, NASB, emphasis added). Later, he settled his family in Egypt with Jacob and his brothers (Ex 1:3). Jacob foretold that Zebulun's descendants would become a maritime people with their border touching Sidon (Gn 49:13). Though Zebulun's tribe was separated from the Mediterranean by Asher's tribe and from the Sea of Galilee by Naphtali, it prospered greatly in trade with the Canaanite cities of the coastal plains. Zebulun fathered three sons (Gn 46:14) and founded one of Israel's 12 tribes (Nm 1:30-31).

See also Zebulun, Tribe of.

ZEBULUN, Tribe of Tribe descended from Zebulun, the tenth son of Jacob and the sixth borne to him by Leah (Gn 30:19-20). His tribe was divided into three clans named after his three sons: the Seredites, the Elonites, and the Jahleelites (Gn 46:14; Nm 26:27). At the census taken on the plains of Moab, the number of men in the tribe over 20 years of age and fit for military service was 60,500 (Nm 26:26-27).

The territory allotted to Zebulun's tribe was in central Canaan and included the valley of Jezreel, but the boundary lines given in Joshua 19:10-16 are difficult to trace because only the tribe's southeastern and eastern borders are indicated. The western border on the Mediterranean side is not clearly defined. In the blessing of Moses (Dt 33:18-19), Zebulun, along with Issachar, "shall draw out [lit. suck] the abundance of the sea," which would seem to indicate that Zebulun would have access to the sea (Mediterranean) and therefore to the mercantile and maritime trade.

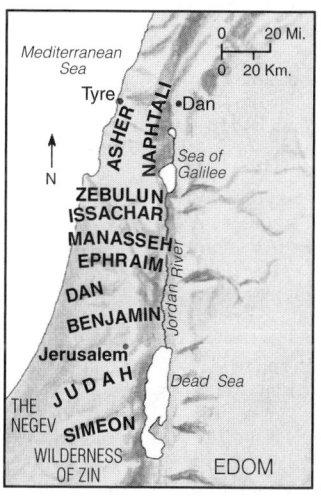

Location of Zebulun This map shows the location of Zebulun in relation to the other tribes west of the Jordan.

The boundary details, however, do not bring Zebulun in touch geographically with the sea, in apparent contradiction to Genesis 49:13. But this reference may not imply actual contact with the Mediterranean. Zebulun's position did enable it to profit by maritime trade because the great caravan route to the sea passed through Zebulunite territory. In addition, Zebulun's "lot," with its fruitful fields and valleys, ensured olive groves, vineyards, and splendid harvests. In 1 Chronicles 12:40 the tribe was able to provide rich provisions for David. Throughout the centuries the tribe maintained its identity.

Clearly, then, the tribe of Zebulun held a strong position among its tribal neighbors around Galilee and was settled more securely. In contrast to the tribes of Asher and Naphtali, who continued to live among the Canaanites

(Jgs 1:32-33), the Canaanites constituted a minority in Zebulun. Throughout the period of the judges the tribe was very active. For example, the victorious army in the battle of Kishon was composed of men of Zebulun and Naphtali (4:6-10); in the Song of Deborah, Zebulun is praised as a people that puts its life in jeopardy to the point of death (5:18). According to Judges 6:35, the men of Zebulun took part in Gideon's struggle with the Midianites on the plain of Jezreel and fought with outstanding valor. The judge Elon belonged to the tribe of Zebulun (12:11-12), and since Galilee was in the territory of Zebulun (Jos 19:15), Ibzan of Bethlehem was probably also a Zebulunite. Another indication of the strength and importance of Zebulun's tribe within the united kingdom period is found in the mention of Zebulun's fighting force as the largest of the western tribal armies that fought under King David (1 Chr 12:33).

In the NT there are two references to Zebulun. The first notes Zebulun as a region into which Jesus, the great light, made an appearance (Mt 4:13-15). The second mention of Zebulun appears in the list of the 12 tribes in Revelation 7:8 after Issachar.

See also Zebulun (Person).

ZEBULUNITE* Descendant of Zebulun, Jacob's son (Nm 26:27; Jgs 12:11-12). See Zebulun, Tribe of.

ZECHARIAH (Person) Extremely popular name in the Bible; it means "the Lord remembers."

1. Son of King Jeroboam II; the 15th king of Israel and the last of Jehu's dynasty. Beginning his rule in 753 BC, the 38th year of Azariah's reign in Judah (792–740 BC), Zechariah ruled in Samaria for only six months before he was murdered at Ibleam in a conspiracy masterminded by Shallum, his successor (2 Kgs 14:29; 15:8-11). The Lord's promise to Jehu, that his descendants would rule to the fourth generation (10:30), was fulfilled with Zechariah's reign.
2. Father of Abi (or Abijah, 2 Chr 29:1). Abi was the mother of Hezekiah, who later ruled Judah for 29 years (2 Kgs 18:2).
3. Reubenite and leader of his tribe (1 Chr 5:7).
4. Korahite Levite, firstborn of Meshelemiah's seven sons and a wise counselor, selected by lot to oversee the gatekeepers of the sanctuary's northern entrance during David's reign (1 Chr 9:21; 26:2, 14).
5. Benjaminite and descendant of Jeiel (1 Chr 9:37). He is alternately called Zeker, perhaps an abbreviation of Zechariah, in 1 Chronicles 8:31.
6. One of the eight Levites assigned to play a harp before the ark of God in the procession led by David when the ark was brought from Obed-edom's house to Jerusalem (1 Chr 15:18, 20; 16:5).
7. One of the priests assigned to blow a trumpet in the procession led by David when the ark was brought to Jerusalem (1 Chr 15:24).
8. Levite and a descendant of Isshiah, who served in the sanctuary during David's reign (1 Chr 24:25).
9. Merarite Levite and Hosah's son, who served as one of the gatekeepers of the sanctuary's western entrance, at the gate of Halleketh, during David's reign (1 Chr 26:11-12, 16).
10. Father of Iddo. Iddo was the chief officer of the half-tribe of Manasseh in Gilead during David's reign (1 Chr 27:21).
11. One of the officials sent by King Jehoshaphat (872–848 BC) to teach the law in the cities of Judah (2 Chr 17:7).
12. Gershonite Levite and Jahaziel's father (2 Chr 20:14).

13. One of King Jehoshaphat's seven sons and the brother of Jehoram. Jehoram became sole regent of Judah (848–841 BC) at his father's death (2 Chr 21:2).

14. Son of Jehoiada the priest, who rebuked the princes of Judah for turning against the Lord and worshiping false gods. Enraged by Zechariah's rebuff, they conspired against him, and at King Joash's command, stoned him to death in the court of the sanctuary (2 Chr 24:20-22). The Lord, however, avenged Zechariah's death by allowing the Syrians to defeat Judah, kill the princes, and severely wound Joash, who was subsequently killed by two of his own servants.

In his castigation of his own generation of Jewish leaders, Jesus alluded to Zechariah's shameful murder in the temple's sacred precincts: "You will become guilty of murdering all the godly people from righteous Abel to Zechariah son of Barachiah, whom you murdered in the Temple between the altar and the sanctuary" (Mt 23:35, NLT). Abel was the first and Zechariah the last of the recorded prophets of God who were unjustly slain, according to the OT.

15. Man who counseled King Uzziah of Judah to walk in the fear of God (2 Chr 26:5).

16. Abijah's father. Abijah was the mother of King Hezekiah of Judah (2 Chr 29:1).

17. Gershonite Levite descended from Asaph, who along with Mattaniah his kinsman was chosen by King Hezekiah to help cleanse the house of the Lord (2 Chr 29:13).

18. Kohathite Levite who was appointed to oversee the repair of the temple during King Josiah's reign (2 Chr 34:12).

19. One of the chief officers of the house of God who generously gave animals to the priests for the celebration of the Passover feast during King Josiah's reign (2 Chr 35:8).

20. Prophet, Berechiah's son and the grandson of Iddo, who began prophesying as a young man in 520 BC during the reign of King Darius I of Persia (Zec 1:1; cf. 2:4). Little is known about the prophet. He ministered with Haggai, his contemporary, in postexilic Jerusalem during the days of Zerubbabel, the governor, and Jeshua, the high priest (Ezr 5:1). He exhorted the Jews to finish building the second temple (6:14) and headed Iddo's priestly family during Joiakim's term as high priest (Neh 12:16). Like Jeremiah and Ezekiel, Zechariah served as both priest and prophet (Zec 1:1, 7; 7:1, 8).

Numerous suggestions have been offered to resolve the discrepancy of Zechariah's pedigree. In the Ezra and Nehemiah passages, Iddo is listed as his father, whereas in Zechariah, Berechiah is the father. Some conclude that Berechiah and Iddo were different names for the same person, or that Berechiah's name (Zec 1:1, 7) was a later scribal emendation that confused Jeberechiah's son with Iddo's son (cf. Is 8:2). A more plausible theory identifies Iddo as Zechariah's grandfather, the renowned head of his family, who returned to Jerusalem from exile in 538 BC. Either by Berechiah's early death or by the precedence of his grandfather's name, Zechariah was considered Iddo's successor.

See also Prophet, Prophetess; Zechariah, Book of.

21. Parosh's descendant and the head of his father's household. He returned with Ezra to Judah following the exile during the reign of King Artaxerxes I of Persia (Ezr 8:3).

22. Bebai's son and the head of a household. He returned with Ezra to Judah following the exile during the reign of King Artaxerxes I of Persia (Ezr 8:11).

23. One of the Jewish leaders whom Ezra sent to Iddo, the man in charge at Casiphia, to gather Levites and temple servants for the caravan of Jews returning to Palestine from Babylon (Ezr 8:15-17).

24. One of the six descendants of Elam who was encouraged by Ezra to divorce his foreign wife during the postexilic period (Ezr 10:26).

25. One of the men who stood to Ezra's left when Ezra read the law to the people (Neh 8:4).

26. Descendant of Perez and an ancestor of a Judahite family headed by Athaiah living in Jerusalem during the postexilic period (Neh 11:4).

27. Descendant of Shelah and an ancestor of a Judahite family headed by Maaseiah living in Jerusalem during the postexilic era (Neh 11:5).

28. Priest, descendant of Malkijah and an ancestor of a family of priests headed by Adaiah living in Jerusalem during the postexilic period (Neh 11:12).

29. Jonathan's son, a descendant of Asaph. He led a group of the priestly musicians who played trumpets at the dedication of the Jerusalem wall in Nehemiah's day (Neh 12:35).

30. Priest who played a trumpet at the Jerusalem wall's dedication (Neh 12:41).

31. Jeberechiah's son and undoubtedly a man of distinction who, along with Uriah the priest, publicly witnessed Isaiah's writing of the puzzling expression "Maher-shalal-hash-baz," which later prophetically revealed God's intended judgment on Damascus and Samaria (Is 8:2).

32. John the Baptist's father, priest of Abijah's division, and the husband of Elizabeth, a woman of priestly descent. His story is recounted in Luke 1. They lived in the Judean hill country during King Herod the Great's reign (37–4 BC; Lk 1:5). Zechariah and Elizabeth both lived righteous and pious lives; however, they were advanced in years and still had no children.

As priest, Zechariah was one of the men chosen to represent his division in its yearly appointed session of service in the Jerusalem temple (the priests of Israel were divided into 24 orders, each being assigned an annual two-week period of service in the temple). One day while serving in Jerusalem, Zechariah was selected by lot to burn incense in the temple's Holy Place, a privilege granted to a priest only once in his lifetime. While performing this temple duty, the angel Gabriel appeared to him, telling him that Elizabeth his wife, though barren, would bear him a son, whose name would be called John and who would prepare the way for the Messiah. As a sign confirming the angel's report, Zechariah was made mute for his disbelief that, in their old age, he and Elizabeth would produce a child. When Zechariah returned to the temple court, the gathered multitude perceived that the gesturing priest had seen a vision.

Elizabeth became pregnant as promised and in her sixth month was visited by her relative Mary, who was also with child. Later, shortly after the baby's birth, Zechariah affirmed that his son's name would be John, at which time his speech was restored and he was filled with the Holy Spirit, prophesying and praising God for the work that he was about to do in Israel.

33. Original name proposed for John the Baptist after his father's name (Lk 1:59). *See* John the Baptist.

ZECHARIAH, Book of Longest book of the Minor Prophets and the most difficult to understand. One reason for this difficulty is the numerous visions that call for an interpreter. At times an interpreting angel is present to tell what the vision means (Zec 1:9-10, 19-20;

4:1-6; 5:5-6), but at other times, when an interpretation is really needed, there is no angel to give one. The obscure meaning of many passages has spawned numerous theories concerning the date, authorship, unity, and interpretation of this book. One thing that makes the book of Zechariah significant for the Christian is its use in the NT. The last part of Zechariah (chs 9–11) is the most quoted section of the Prophets in the Gospel Passion narratives, and, other than Ezekiel, Zechariah influenced the book of Revelation more than any other OT book.

PREVIEW
• Author
• Date
• Background
• Purpose and Message
• Content

Author The name Zechariah probably means "the Lord remembers" or "the Lord is renowned." Zechariah is a common name in the OT and NT. At least 30 different people in the OT are named Zechariah. There is a problem in identifying the prophet's father. In Zechariah 1:1 and 1:7, the prophet is called "the son of Berechiah, the son of Iddo," but in Ezra 5:1 and 6:14 he is called simply "the son of Iddo." There was another Zechariah in Isaiah's time whose father was named Jeberechiah (Is 8:2). Another prophet by the name of Zechariah, the son of Jehoiada the priest, lived much earlier during the reign of Joash, king of Judah (835–796 BC). This prophet was stoned to death because he proclaimed that the Lord had forsaken his people because of their sins (2 Chr 24:20-22). Jesus seemed to refer to this or a similar unrecorded incident, but he calls the prophet the son of Berechiah, the last of the martyrs among the prophets (Mt 23:35). However, Luke's account of what Jesus said about Zechariah (Lk 11:51) does not include the words "the son of Berechiah." Since Jesus was quoting 2 Chronicles, which was the last book in the Hebrew Bible, he was simply indicating the sweep of time from the first murder (Abel) to the last (Zechariah, the son of Jehoiada). There is no evidence that the prophet of the book of Zechariah was martyred; therefore, the best solution to the problem is to consider Berechiah the father, and Iddo the grandfather, of this prophet.

Date The first part of the book of Zechariah (chs 1–8) is easy to date. The first date is in the first verse, "the eighth month of the second year of Darius." This was Darius, king of Persia (521–486 BC). The eighth month of Darius's second year would be October 520 BC. This date seems to be the first time the "word of the Lord" came to Zechariah. The second date in Zechariah is in 1:7: "On the twenty-fourth day of the eleventh month which is the month of Shebat, in the second year of Darius . . ." (RSV). This date would be February 15, 519 BC. The word of the Lord that came to Zechariah on this date seems to include the account of eight night visions, along with some oracles, from an angel who talked with him. The third date in Zechariah is in 7:1: "In the fourth year of King Darius . . . on the fourth day of the ninth month, which is Chislev . . ." (RSV). This date would be the equivalent of December 7, 518 BC.

There are no dates in Zechariah 9–14. Zechariah's name is never mentioned, and neither is Darius or any king. A period of relative peace and stability gives place to war. The temple is standing (11:13; 14:20), and evidently Greek soldiers are present (9:13). Any attempt to

assign specific dates to Zechariah 9–14 would be speculation.

Background The temple in Jerusalem was destroyed by Nebuchadnezzar, king of Babylon, in 586 BC. Nebuchadnezzar made several raids against Jerusalem before and after it fell, taking many captives to Babylon (cf. 2 Kgs 24:1-17; Dn 1:1). On two occasions, Jeremiah had predicted that captivity would last 70 years (Jer 25:11; 29:10; cf. Dn 9:2). In the time of Zechariah, the period of 70 years since the fall of Jerusalem was coming to an end (Zec 1:12; 7:5). It had been 66 years since Jerusalem fell, when the first "word of the Lord" came to Zechariah in the second year of Darius (520 BC). The Babylonian Empire had fallen to the Persians in 538 BC, and Cyrus the first king of Persia signed a decree permitting all captives to return to their homes (2 Chr 36:23; Ezr 1:1-4). Evidently, the first contingent of Jewish captives returned to Jerusalem with Zerubbabel and Joshua the priest about 536 BC. One of the first objectives of the returnees was to rebuild the temple (Ezr 1:3), but internal strife and external opposition from the Samaritans prohibited the immediate rebuilding of the temple. After Darius I became king of Persia in 521 BC, a wave of expectation and enthusiasm swept over the Jewish communities in Jerusalem and Babylon. Two prophets, possibly from the Babylonian exiles, Haggai and Zechariah, began preaching so powerfully that work on the second temple began in 520 BC and was finished in 516 BC (Ezr 5:1, 14-15; Hg 1–2; Zec 1–8).

The book of Zechariah opens in the second year of Darius (520 BC). Some of the captives had been back in Jerusalem for 16 years, but nothing was being done about rebuilding the temple. Zechariah's first message called for the people to repent and not repeat the mistake of their fathers, whose sins and refusal to repent led to the exile and destruction of the temple (Zec 1:1-6). Then a series of eight night visions follows (1:7–6:8), assuring the people that the temple would be rebuilt by Zerubbabel (1:16; 4:9; 6:15). Two verses in Zechariah speak volumes concerning the hardships and difficulties in Jerusalem before the temple was rebuilt: "This is what the LORD Almighty says: Take heart and finish the task! You have heard what the prophets have been saying about building the Temple of the LORD Almighty ever since the foundation was laid. Before the work on the Temple began, there were no jobs and no wages for either people or animals. No traveler was safe from the enemy, for there were enemies on all sides. I had turned everyone against each other" (8:9-10, NLT).

The first eight chapters of Zechariah are set against the social, political, and religious situations in Jerusalem from 520 to 518 BC. But beginning with chapter 9, historical moorings are lost. Chapter 9 opens with an oracle against Syria, including Damascus, Tyre, and Sidon, and against Philistia. Each of these places will be conquered and cleansed and will become like a clan in Judah. There is the promise of a new king coming triumphantly to Jerusalem, yet humbly riding on a donkey. His reign will be peaceful and universal. The next oracle speaks of setting the captives free, but this may not refer to the Babylonian captives, because of a reference to the Greeks. Zechariah 9–12 is almost wholly concerned with the future. Some scholars call this part apocalyptic literature. The nations attack Jerusalem and are defeated (chs 12, 14). The temple is standing (11:13), but it does not seem to have a place of great prominence in the new Jerusalem and in the kingdom of God (14:6-9).

Purpose and Message The purpose of the book is to reassure and encourage. The restored Jewish community of 520 BC needed the assurance that the temple would be rebuilt, and later groups of God's people needed to know that ultimately the kingdom of God would come in its fullness. There are three messages in the book of Zechariah: the need for repentance (1:1–5:11); the eight night visions (1:7–6:8) signifying that the temple would be rebuilt and God's glory would return to Jerusalem; and the coming kingdom of God (chs 9–14).

Content The book of Zechariah may be divided into two main parts: chapters 1–8 and 9–14. The first part is dated between 520 BC and 518 BC. It consists of oracles and visions of Zechariah the son of Berechiah. Mainly prose, its primary concern is to assure the restored Jewish community that the temple will be rebuilt. The second part (chs 9–14) is undated. There are no references to Zechariah. The temple is standing, and much of the language is eschatological and apocalyptic. The second part itself has two parts: chapters 9–11 and 12–14. Chapters 9 and 12 begin essentially the same way: "The oracle of the word of the Lord."

The first part of Zechariah (chs 1–8) has four main sections: superscription and first oracle (1:1-6); eight night visions and related oracles (1:7–6:8); the symbolic crowning of Joshua (6:9-15); and the question about fasting and morality (7:1–8:23).

The Superscription (1:1) This section is dated specifically "in the eighth month" of the Babylonian calendar, which was from mid-October to mid-November. The second year of Darius, king of Persia, was 520 BC. The date is important in relating the work of Zechariah to that of Haggai (cf. Hg 1:1, 15; 2:1, 10, 18-20) and to the reconstruction of the temple under Zerubbabel. The first oracle concerns the need for repentance. The first message of Zechariah came between Haggai's second and third message. He, like Haggai, probably attributed the failure of the crops and other hardships to a failure to rebuild the temple (cf. Hg 1:6-11). Zechariah calls for the people to repent so that they can persevere with work on the temple.

The Eight Night Visions and Related Oracles (1:7–6:8) These visions that Zechariah saw in Jerusalem all seem to have been given on the night of the 24th day of the 11th month (Shebat) in the second year of Darius (mid-January to mid-February 519 BC). Seven of the eight visions have essentially the same form. Four of the visions begin with the words "Then I looked up and saw" (1:18; 2:1; 5:1; 6:1). One begins, "In a vision during the night" (1:8). Another begins, "Then the angel who had been talking with me returned and woke me, as though I had been asleep. 'What do you see now?' he asked" (4:1-2, NLT). Still another (the seventh) vision begins, "Then the angel who was talking with me came forward and said . . ." (5:5). However, the fourth vision is different from the other seven. It begins, "Then he showed me" (3:1, cf. Am 7:1, 4, 7). This message in the third person contains no interpreting angel nor any direct message to Zechariah, as if he were merely an observer. This fourth vision is so different from the other seven that it was not a part of the original series of eight.

An overall pattern to the eight visions is not evident. Some scholars have seen some significance in the fact that the visions move from the evening or night in the first vision to the sunrise in the last vision. Others have detected some relationships in pairs of visions. The first and last visions involve horses and riders or chariots. The second and third visions involve the restoration of Judah and Jerusalem (1:18-21; 2:1-5). The fourth and fifth deal with the place of the two leaders in the

restored community: Joshua will be cleansed and restored as the high priest (3:1-5) and Zerubbabel the governor will complete the temple (4:1-14). The sixth and seventh visions involve the cleansing of the land. A flying scroll enters the house of every thief and false witness and consumes it (5:1-4). Wickedness personified as a woman will be carried in an ephah (basket) to the land of Shinar (vv 5-11). Interspersed in the vision accounts are four oracles (1:14-17; 2:8-13; 3:6-10; 4:8-14). Each of these passages begins with the messenger formula, "Thus says the Lord," or the expression "Cry out" (1:14, 17). The first oracle assures the people that the temple, the cities, and the choice of Jerusalem will be renewed. The second oracle exhorts any exiles remaining in Babylon to return to Judah and Jerusalem (2:7-12). Zechariah 2:12-13 are interesting. Verse 12 is the only OT reference to Palestine as "the Holy Land," and verse 13 is similar to the call to worship in Habakkuk 2:20: "Be silent before the LORD, all humanity, for he is springing into action from his holy dwelling" (Zec 2:13, NLT). The third oracle in the visionary accounts concerns Joshua the high priest as a sign of the coming of God's servant, the Branch who removes the guilt of the land in a single day (3:6-10).

The Symbolic Crowning of Joshua (6:9-15) Zechariah is told to go into the house of Josiah son of Zephaniah, take silver and gold from some returnees from Babylon, make a crown, and put it on the head of Joshua the priest as a symbol of the royal and priestly king, the Branch, the builder of the temple. After the ceremony the crown is to be hung in the temple as a memorial of those who gave the silver and the gold. The last verse (6:15) seems to say that just as gold and silver from exiles was used to symbolize the crowning of the coming king of the kingdom, so exiles, "those who are far off," will also participate in the completion of the temple. Then Zechariah's hearers will know God sent him to prophesy. This will all take place when and if they will diligently obey the voice of the Lord.

The Question about Fasting and Morality (7:1–8:23) A delegation from Bethel (10 miles or 16.1 kilometers north of Jerusalem) came to Jerusalem in the fourth year of Darius (518 BC). Work on the temple had been going on for two years. The purpose of this visit was to entreat the favor of the Lord (7:2) and to ask the priests and the prophets if they should continue to fast as they had done since the temple was destroyed 70 years earlier (v 3). The Lord told Zechariah to ask why they were fasting—for the Lord or for selfish motives? The answer to the question of fasting seems to be that God desires truth, justice, and covenant-love more than fasting. Zechariah reiterates the message the Lord had already given his people by the former prophets. The last section in the first part of Zechariah is a decalogue of promises (8:1-23). The ten promises begin with the words "Thus says the Lord" or "The word of the Lord came to me." The last word of God is not judgment but promise, hope, forgiveness, and restoration.

The Oracles of the Lord (chs 9–12) The last half of the book of Zechariah (chs 9–14) falls into two nearly equal parts: chapters 9–11 (46 verses) and chapters 12–14 (44 verses). Each part begins with the words "An oracle" (9:1; 12:1). Both "oracles" are primarily eschatological. The first part (chs 9–11) is concerned with the restoration of the tribes to Palestine (9:11-17; 10:6-12). In order to accomplish this, the Lord will rid Palestine and Syria of opponents to his rule (9:1-8; 11:1-3), remove the evil shepherds (rulers; 10:2b-5; 11:4-17), and the Prince of Peace will come (9:9-10). The last "oracle" of

Zechariah (12:1–14:21) is also eschatological. This time the concern is primarily that of Jerusalem and Judah. Twice Jerusalem is attacked by the nations (12:1-8; 14:1-5). Each time the Lord fights for Jerusalem, Judah, and the house of David. Jerusalem weeps and mourns for an unidentified martyr (12:10-14). The martyr could be called the "good" shepherd who is killed and his sheep scattered (13:7-9). Jesus referred to this passage in connection with his arrest (Mt 26:31; Mk 14:27). A fountain will be opened for the house of David, and the inhabitants of Jerusalem will be cleansed from sin, idolatry, and false prophets (Zec 13:1-6). The new Jerusalem will remain aloft on its site and the land around it will be turned into a plain (14:10-11). There will be no night nor extreme temperatures in the new Jerusalem. Living waters will flow from Jerusalem, and the Lord will become King of all the earth. Those who fight against Jerusalem will be destroyed, but those who survive will worship the Lord year by year by keeping the Feast of Booths.

The last scene in the book of Zechariah is a picture of the world after Armageddon, a new world cleansed of sin. It will be a time of peace and security. When God comes to reign, everything will become holy. The warhorses will become as holy as the priest's turban, and the ordinary cooking vessel will be as temple vessels. The Canaanite or trader will be eliminated. There will be no difference between Jew and Gentile, as long as one worships the Lord of Hosts as King.

See also Israel, History of; Postexilic Period; Prophecy; Prophet, Prophetess; Zechariah (Person) #20.

ZECHER*, ZEKER* Alternate form of Zechariah, Gibeon's son, in 1 Chronicles 8:31. *See* Zechariah (Person) #5.

ZEDAD One of the geographical landmarks of Israel's northern boundary, mentioned between Hamath and Ziphron (Nm 34:8; Ez 47:15).

ZEDEKIAH

1. Judah's last king and a key political figure in the fateful final decade of the southern kingdom. His reign (597–586 BC) spanned Nebuchadnezzar's two attacks on Jerusalem, in 597 and 586. The first attack was in reprisal for the rebellion of Josiah's son, Jehoiakim (609–598 BC), against Nebuchadnezzar; however, by the time his forces captured Jerusalem, Jehoiakim was dead and had been succeeded by his 18-year-old son Jehoiachin. Nebuchadnezzar deposed the young king and deported him to Babylon, along with the elite of the nation: government officials, army officers, and craftsmen. As Jehoiachin's replacement, Nebuchadnezzar appointed his uncle Mattaniah, a younger brother of Jehoiakim and of the earlier, short-lived King Jehoahaz (609 BC). Mattaniah was thus the third son of Josiah to occupy the throne of Judah. The Babylonian king named him Zedekiah, which means "the Lord is my righteousness."

Zedekiah found himself in a difficult position as Judah's king. Many evidently still regarded Jehoiachin as the real king (cf. Jer 28:1-4). Certainly the Judeans deported to Babylonia dated events by reference to Jehoiachin (2 Kgs 25:27; Ez 1:2). Though the Babylonians exacted from Zedekiah an oath of loyalty (2 Chr 36:13; Ez 17:13-18), evidence suggests that they too viewed Zedekiah's predecessor as the legitimate king and Zedekiah as regent. They may have been holding him in reserve for possible restoration to power, should events require it.

Judah was filled with a false optimism that could hardly have helped the new king. It was confidently expected that the deportation of the leading citizens would be only temporary; prophets were guaranteeing that Babylon's power would be broken within two years (Jer 28:2-4). They were opposed by a few prophets led by Jeremiah, whose message found little support.

Pressure both from within the nation and from without was put on Zedekiah to change his political allegiance. In the fourth year of his reign (593 BC), the neighboring states of Ammon, Moab, Tyre, and Sidon formed a coalition to fight for independence from Babylon. Envoys were sent to Zedekiah (Jer 27:1-3). However, Jeremiah advised the king not to get involved. In the same year, according to Jeremiah 51:59, Zedekiah visited Babylon. He may have been summoned to affirm his loyalty and to explain his role in the political situation. The planned rebellion did not occur, perhaps because aid from Egypt failed to materialize.

Within the Judean court a strong pro-Egyptian party existed. This party saw Egypt as an ally for breaking away from their eastern master, just like the advisers of King Hezekiah a century before (cf. Is 31:1-3; 36:6). Zedekiah, finding it difficult to resist this political pressure, eventually transferred his allegiance to Egypt.

Hophra (589–570 BC), Psammetichus's heir to the Egyptian throne, organized a joint rebellion in the west against Babylon. According to Ezekiel 21:18-32 and 25:12-17, Judah and Ammon supported him, while Edom and Philistia shrewdly abstained. Zedekiah was rebuked by the prophet Ezekiel (Ez 17:13-18) for breaking his oath to Nebuchadnezzar (cf. 2 Chr 36:13) and rebelling against him by sending envoys to Egypt to negotiate for military support.

In the face of this western uprising engineered by his Egyptian rival, Nebuchadnezzar was forced to march westward. Setting up headquarters at Riblah in northern Syria, he decided to make Jerusalem his prime target (Ez 21:18-23). The ensuing siege of Jerusalem was temporarily lifted due to an Egyptian attack but afterward was resumed until the city fell. Zedekiah, fleeing eastward with his troops, was caught near Jericho and taken north to Nebuchadnezzar at Riblah. There he was put on trial for breaking his promises of vassalage. By way of punishment, his sons were killed before his eyes. This tragic sight was the last he ever saw, since his eyes were then put out. He was taken in chains to Babylon, where he eventually died in prison (2 Kgs 25:5-7; Jer 39:7; 52:8-11; cf. Ez 12:13).

See also Chronology of the Bible (Old Testament); Israel, History of.

2. Kenaanah's son and one of the prophets who spoke falsely to kings Ahab of Israel and Jehoshaphat of Judah, telling them that the Lord would give Ahab victory over the Syrians at Ramoth-gilead (1 Kgs 22:11). After hearing Micaiah's contrary prediction that Ahab would in fact be killed in the battle, Zedekiah, in anger, struck Micaiah (v 24).

3. Jeconiah's son and a descendant of David through Solomon's line (1 Chr 3:16).

4. Leading priest who affirmed Nehemiah's covenant during the postexilic era (Neh 10:1).

5. Maaseiah's son, who, according to Jeremiah, King Nebuchadnezzar of Babylon would kill by roasting in fire for his adultery and lying words (Jer 29:21-23).

6. Hananiah's son and a prince in Judah during King Jehoiakim's reign (Jer 36:12).

ZEEB One of two Midianite princes executed by Gideon's army (Jgs 7:25).

ZELA, ZELAH* City of Benjamin's tribe where the bones of Saul and Jonathan were buried (Jos 18:28; 2 Sm 21:14). Zela was probably the native town of Saul's father, Kish, and may well have been Saul's home before he was anointed king.

ZELEK Ammonite warrior among David's mighty men (2 Sm 23:37; 1 Chr 11:39).

ZELOPHEHAD Hepher's son from Manasseh's tribe. He fathered five daughters but no sons (Nm 26:33). Because Zelophehad had no sons, his daughters petitioned Moses to give them their father's inheritance (27:1). Moses' subsequent ruling provided that daughters should receive the inheritance in such cases, providing that they marry within their tribe so that the tribal allotments would remain constant (Nm 27:7; 36:2; Jos 17:3).

ZELOTES* KJV spelling of "Zealot," the surname of Simon, one of the 12, in Luke 6:15 and Acts 1:13. *See* Simon #5.

ZELZAH Place near Rachel's tomb where Saul met two men in fulfillment of Samuel's prophecy concerning the events that would confirm Saul's anointing (1 Sm 10:2). Rachel's tomb is traditionally located at the northern border of Benjamin, but no precise identification of Zelzah has been made. Some have argued that Zelzah and Zela are the same place, but this is unlikely.

ZEMARAIM
1. Town near the northern border of the territory of Benjamin (Jos 18:22). The most likely location is Ras ez-Zeimara, about five miles (8 kilometers) northeast of Bethel in the hill country between et-Taiyibeh and Rammum.
2. Mountain in the hill country of Ephraim (2 Chr 13:4) and the scene of Abijah's speech of rebuke against Jeroboam and the Israelites.

ZEMARITES One of the families of the Canaanites in the ethnological lists of Genesis 10 (v 18) and 1 Chronicles 1 (v 16). The Zemarites were a Hamitic tribe mentioned in connection with the Arvadites and the Hamathites. They were probably located near the Mediterranean in the vicinity of Tripoli.

ZEMIRAH Beker's firstborn son, from Benjamin's tribe (1 Chr 7:8).

ZENAN One of the cities of the Shephelah inherited by Judah (Jos 15:37).

ZENAS Lawyer whom Paul requested Titus to help with his travels in Crete (Ti 3:13).

ZEPHANIAH (Person)
1. Priest during the reign of Zedekiah who was executed at Riblah by the king of Babylon (2 Kgs 25:18; Jer 52:24). He was the second priest under Seraiah the chief priest and served as Zedekiah's envoy to Jeremiah during the period prior to the fall of Jerusalem (Jer 21:1; 29:25-29; 37:3).
2. Ancestor of Heman who was among the Kohathite Levites whom David placed in charge of the service of music in the house of the Lord (1 Chr 6:33-36).

Zephaniah is listed as the father of Azariah and the son of Tahath.
3. Author of the book of Zephaniah (Zep 1:1). Though little is known about Zephaniah, it is possible that his ancestor Hezekiah is the same as the king by that name. *See* Zephaniah, Book of.
4. Father of Josiah in whose house Joshua was crowned as high priest (Zec 6:10-14).

ZEPHANIAH, Book of One of the books of the Minor Prophets in the OT.

P R E V I E W
• Author
• Date, Origin, and Destination
• Background
• Purpose and Teaching
• Content

Author According to the editorial heading (Zep 1:1), Zephaniah prophesied during the reign of Josiah (640–609 BC). His family tree is given in an unusually full form. Some scholars have suggested that his great-great-grandfather was King Hezekiah (715–686 BC). But remarkably there is no Jewish or Christian tradition to support the suggestion, which there probably would have been if it had been true. His own name, meaning "he whom the Lord protects or hides," was not uncommon and was a testimony to the keeping power of God.

Date, Origin, and Destination Zephaniah probably prophesied around 630 BC. The fall of Nineveh (612 BC) had not yet occurred (2:13-15). Josiah's reign falls into two periods, dividing at 622 BC. In that year, while the temple was being cleared of pagan articles, the Book of the Law was found, which gave momentum to Josiah's religious reforms (2 Kgs 22). The unreformed state of affairs described by Zephaniah (Zep 1:4-12; 3:1-4) points to a date before 622, at least for his denunciations. The prophet addressed Judah, the southern kingdom, and in particular the civil and religious authorities in Jerusalem. He most probably prophesied during the reign of Josiah, who came to the throne at the age of eight.

The negative parts of the book concerning the sin and punishment of Judah—now fulfilled—would serve as a serious warning against disobedience to God. Moreover, the fulfillment of Zephaniah's prophetic threats would serve to enhance the positive side of the book, confirming the hope of completion in the experience of a fresh generation of God's people.

Background Politically, the Assyrian Empire had spread westward and held Palestine in its grip. The long reign of Manasseh (696–642 BC) had been a period of total subservience to Assyria. Political subservience as an Assyrian vassal meant religious subservience to the gods of Assyria, especially worship of the heavenly bodies (2 Kgs 21:5). Zephaniah complained of this sin (Zep 1:5). When the door opened to one foreign religion, others naturally came in. Once the exclusiveness of the worship of the God of Israel was abandoned, Palestinian cults were openly accepted. The Canaanite Baal was blatantly worshiped (2 Kgs 21:3), as Zephaniah attested (Zep 1:4). Zephaniah condemned the worshipers of Molech (v 5), who sacrificed children to the Ammonite god (1 Kgs 11:7; 2 Kgs 23:10). International imperialism meant a weakening of national culture, so that foreign customs were practiced, probably with religious overtones (Zep 1:8-9).

The reign of Josiah brought changes, marking a political and religious turning point. Assyria, preoccupied with troubles on the eastern and northern frontiers and unable to consolidate its acquisitions, became unable to reinforce its authority in the west. This weakness induced Josiah to launch a national liberation movement. He threw off the yoke of Assyria and expanded his sphere of influence northward into the territory of the old northern kingdom. From a religious standpoint, he completely dissociated himself and his country from the religions that prevailed in Judah and recalled the nation to a pure and exclusive faith in the God of Israel. The book of Zephaniah shows that there was at least one person who shared his ideals. His prophetic ministry undoubtedly paved the way for Josiah's subsequent reformation. He was a contemporary of Jeremiah, at least for the early part of that prophet's career (Jeremiah began prophesying in 627 BC).

Scholars have suggested that Zephaniah's prophesying was prompted in part by attacks of the Scythians. The Greek historian Herodotus tells how the barbaric Scythians overran western Asia and reached as far south as the Egyptian frontier at about the time that Zephaniah prophesied. There is now much less inclination to believe Herodotus's tale and relate Zephaniah's prophetic ministry to it. There is no objective evidence for Scythian attacks on so large a scale as Herodotus claimed. Probably Zephaniah spoke simply out of a theological necessity, as he himself claimed (e.g., 1:17). From his inspired standpoint, he foresaw that a clash involving divine intervention and human downfall was unavoidable.

Purpose and Teaching As Zephaniah prophesied in God's name, he denounced the religious sins of Judah and the corruption rampant among both civil and religious authorities. He foretold the downfall of the nation that actually occurred in 586 BC. The moral and religious landslide could only culminate in a political avalanche of destruction that would engulf the nation. This avalanche is called by Zephaniah "the Day of the Lord." It was not a new term, and the prophet knew that it would arouse terror in the hearts of his hearers. Amos used it, and even in his time it was well established (Am 5:18-20). Isaiah was the first to use the expression in the southern kingdom (Is 2:6-22, see v 12). In this, as in a number of respects, Zephaniah was a latter-day Isaiah called by God to reapply truths earlier prophesied by Isaiah to a later generation.

The theme of the Day of the Lord refers to a time when the Lord would decisively intervene in the world to establish his sovereignty. Hostile elements would be swept aside. The enemies of God, sinners against his moral will, would be exposed and punished. It was associated with judgment upon those who did not acknowledge God's sovereignty—especially Gentiles, but also sinful Israel. The emphasis on the suffering of God's people was intended to correct the popular assumption that other nations would be the sole target of divine judgment.

The "day" also would vindicate those who were loyal to God. It guaranteed the rehabilitation of his oppressed supporters. Zephaniah developed this two-sided phenomenon in order to communicate the truth of God to his own generation. It is "a day of the wrath of God" (Zep 1:15, 18; 2:2), when his reaction to human sin would be demonstrated. Its target was not only other nations but Judah as well, both Jerusalem, the capital (1:10-13), and the other cities of Judah.

Zephaniah also had a positive message for the people of Judah. For the prophets, the message of salvation did not cancel the message of doom. Judgment would come

first, then salvation would follow. But the period of tribulation could not be avoided. The prophet's grim descriptions of "the day of wrath" are interpreted as dire warnings and implicit pleas to the people of Judah to abandon their complacent, sinful ways.

Clearly, Zephaniah's role under God was to reapply earlier truths sadly forgotten by his own generation. Zephaniah was able to foresee God's judgment of Judah and the world. But he also proclaimed permanent truths concerning the nature of God and his providential relationship to the world and concerning the responsibilities of the people of God.

The importance of the book of Zephaniah for the NT lies in the phraseology about the Day of the Lord. There are a number of allusions to this aspect of his message (Mt 13:41 [Zep 1:3]; Rv 6:17 [1:14]; 14:5 [3:13]; 16:1 [3:8]). These echoes stress Zephaniah's importance beyond his own time. He contributed to the total biblical picture of a God who intervenes in human history and will establish his kingdom. Zephaniah's descriptions are a pattern for events that will mark the end of history.

Content The heading (Zep 1:1) introduces Zephaniah, gives the historical setting, and above all stresses his meditation on the divine word.

The first major part of the book is 1:2–2:3. It subdivides into four units: verses 2-7, 8-13, 14-18; 2:1-3. Verses 2-7 include Judah in a forecast of universal destruction. Zephaniah used traditional material to stress that God's people were by no means exempt, as they often chose to believe (cf. Am 5:18-20). The prophet supported his startling revelation with reasoned statements regarding the religious deviations practiced in Jerusalem. The image of sacrifice was used ironically, portraying Judah as the victim.

The national administration and members of the royal family were guilty (Zep 1:8-13). Superstitions were punctiliously observed, yet basic divine commands against stealing and fraudulent gain went unheeded. Zephaniah saw the enemy attack on the north side of Jerusalem as an illustration of God's punishment of dishonest traders (cf. Am 8:5-6; Mi 6:10-11).

There follows a shocking and terrifying description of the grimness of the coming "Day" (Zep 1:14-18). The prophet stirred up a complacent people who did not want to hear God's message. He frightened them into reality with a monotonous drumbeat of doom and destruction. Judah would be the demoralized target of God's wrath. Their wealth had secured luxurious imports but could not prevent divine judgment.

The prophet completed his sermon with an appeal for repentance (2:1-3). Having emotionally stirred his audience from their apathy, he was able to bring the good news that all was not yet lost. A penitential assembly at the temple and the intercession of the spiritually minded and obedient among God's people might prevent destruction. God's punishment of foreign nations is described in the second main part of the book (2:4-15). Representative states are named to the west, east, south, and north of Judah. In the context of the previous material, it amplifies the universal nature of the Day of the Lord. Like the first part, it subdivides into four passages: verses 2:4-7, 8-11, 12, and 13-15.

The subject of the first passage is the Philistines. In the case of the cities of Gaza and Ekron, there is a play on words typical of Hebrew prophecy. Both names contain doom within their very sound. The Philistines are labeled as trespassers because they were illegal immigrants from Crete into the Promised Land, which was intended for God's own people.

Zephaniah predicted that Moab and Ammon would suffer attack for their overbearing attitude and their annexation of Judean territory (2:8-11). God would come to the aid of his covenant people.

The first two main sections have spelled out at length a message of judgment for both Judah and the surrounding nations. This twofold message is now repeated in a much shorter form in the third main section (3:1-8). Zephaniah criticized Jerusalem in its combined role of political capital and religious center. The responsibility of being God's representatives rested too lightly on the shoulders of government and temple officials. Civil leaders abused their powers by demanding bribes and even killing their political opponents. Instead of being the shepherds of the people (cf. Ez 34), they were beasts of prey (cf. Ez 22:25-27). The prophets misused their gifts for their own selfish interests, while the priests broke the strict regulations of the temple. The lessons of history went unheeded; they had not learned caution and reverence. The conclusion is clear: Judah could not escape punishment in the coming Day of the Lord but would suffer with other nations.

The outworking of God's will for both Judah and the nations is in view in the final main section (Zep 3:9-20), but this time from a quite different aspect. Punishment was not God's last word for his own people or even for the nations at large. Ultimately God's will is not destruction but salvation (2 Pt 3:9). The section has three parts: Zephaniah 3:9-10, 11-13, and 14-20. Verses 9-10 deal with the conversion of the nations. This remarkable passage looks forward with divinely guaranteed certainty to the willing submission of Gentiles to the God of Israel. Their turning to God would not be based on human initiative but would originate in the providential activity of God. Lips defiled by worship of pagan gods would be purified and devoted solely to the adoration of the God of Israel. People from remote parts of the earth, here illustrated as the remote south beyond the Ethiopian Nile, would come as suppliants, as if they were scattered Jews returning home.

God's own people would be marked by a change of heart (3:11-13). By now they would have been purged of the proud people who put themselves before God in the sphere of politics and religion. They would be a purified people who humbly trusted in God. To them were promised the blessings of paradise.

The last passage speaks of coming joys (3:14-20). The prophet projects himself into the future, to the time when God's judgment would be over and the time of salvation had dawned. God's people would rejoice in the presence of their Lord. Fear and demoralization would be canceled by God's powerful presence and radiant joy. His joy would infectiously communicate itself to them so that they too would rejoice. Moreover, his joy would be a reaction to the transformation he was working in the lives of his people (v 17; "he will renew you in his love," RSV). A necessary part of this transformation would feature the vindication of God's suffering people. They would be brought to a position of honor, as the visible representatives of the God of glory. Ultimately, God's power would be revealed through a people of power.

See also Israel, History of; Josiah #1.

ZEPHATH Canaanite city conquered by Judah and Simeon and subsequently renamed Hormah (Jgs 1:17). Zephath (Hormah) was the site of Israel's first abortive attempt to enter Canaan when they violated Moses' command and were, as a result, defeated by the Amalekites and the Canaanites (Nm 14:45).

See also Hormah.

ZEPHATHAH* Valley where Asa defeated Zerah the Ethiopian (2 Chr 14:10). The valley of Zephathah is located in the vicinity of Mareshah and thus in southwestern Judah.

ZEPHO Eliphaz's son and a descendant of Esau (Gn 36:11, 15; 1 Chr 1:36).

ZEPHON Firstborn son of Gad and the father of the Zephonite family (Gn 46:16; Nm 26:15).

ZER One of the fortified cities of Naphtali's tribe (Jos 19:35). From the surrounding names in the list, it may be inferred that it was located on the southwest side of the Sea of Galilee.

ZERAH
1. One of the chiefs of the Edomites (Gn 36:17; 1 Chr 1:37), listed as the son of Reuel, Esau's son by his wife Basemath, and likely the ancestor of Jobab, who later assumed the position of king of the Edomites (Gn 36:13, 33).
2. One of the twin sons of Judah by his daughter-in-law Tamar (Gn 38:30; 46:12; Mt 1:3). Although Zerah thrust out his hand first, he retracted it, allowing his brother, Perez, to be born first. The descendants of Zerah (the Zerahites) became one of the most influential clans of Judah (Nm 26:20; Jos 7:1, 18; 22:20; 1 Chr 2:4-6; 9:6). Because Ethan and Heman are listed as sons of Zerah in 1 Chronicles 2:6, the Ezrahites mentioned in 1 Kings 4:31 and the titles to Psalms 88 and 89 are also considered to be Zerahites. However, Ethan and Heman are listed as Levites in 1 Chronicles 15:17, thus making it more likely that the Ezrahites were a Levite clan.
3. One of the sons of Simeon from whom the Zerahite clan descended (Nm 26:13; 1 Chr 4:24); alternately called Zohar in Genesis 46:10 and Exodus 6:15.
4. One of the sons of Iddo, from the Gershonite branch of Levi's tribe (1 Chr 6:21).
5. One of the ancestors of Asaph from Levi's tribe, listed as the son of Adaiah and the father of Ethni (1 Chr 6:41). Several believe him to be the same individual as #4 above.
6. Commander of the Ethiopians (Cushites) who fought against Asa, king of Judah (2 Chr 14:9). It is difficult to identify this individual or the historical event with any certainty. The most common identification has been with Usarkon II of Egypt. The account of the battle agrees with the chronology of Usarkon's reign in Egypt, as do the number and nationalities of the troops involved in the conflict.

ZERAHIAH
1. Uzzi's son and ancestor of Ezra from the priestly line of Eleazar (1 Chr 6:6, 51; Ezr 7:4).
2. Father of Eliehoenai, who was head of a family who returned to Jerusalem with Ezra (Ezr 8:4).

ZERAHITE
1. Descendant of Zerah, Simeon's son (Nm 26:13). See Zerah #3.
2. Descendant of Zerah, Judah's son by Tamar (Nm 26:20). See Zerah #2.
   See also Izrahite.

ZERED Valley and brook by which the Israelites encamped, listed between Iye-abarim and a stopping place near the Arnon River to the north (Nm 21:12). Though its exact location remains in question, Zered is probably identifiable with the modern Wadi el-Hesa, a streambed that formed a natural border between the ancient countries of Moab and Edom and, following a northwestward course, emptied into the southern end of the Dead Sea. The crossing of the Zered Brook by the Israelites marked 38 years since Israel rebelled against God at Kadesh-barnea (Dt 2:13-14).

ZEREDA* KJV spelling of Zeredah in 1 Kings 11:26. *See* Zeredah #1.

ZEREDAH
1. Birthplace (or hometown) of Jeroboam, Israel's first king during the period of the divided kingdom (1 Kgs 11:26).
2. City in the Jordan Valley (2 Chr 4:17; 1 Kgs 7:46 "Zarethan"). *See* Zarethan.

ZEREDATHAH* KJV rendering of Zeredah in 2 Chronicles 4:17. *See* Zeredah #2.

ZERERAH City mentioned in connection with Gideon's defeat of the Midianites (Jgs 7:22); perhaps also identifiable with Zarethan.

ZERESH Wife of Haman the Agagite who advised him to build the gallows for hanging Mordecai (Est 5:10, 14).

ZERETH Asshur's son by his wife Helah from Judah's tribe (1 Chr 4:7).

ZERETH-SHAHAR One of the cities inherited by Reuben's tribe (Jos 13:19), described as being on "the hill of the valley."

ZERI One of the sons of Jeduthun who prophesied with the lyre in thanksgiving to the Lord (1 Chr 25:3). He may be the same person as Izri (v 11).

ZEROR Benjaminite, Becorath's son, the father of Abiel, and an ancestor of King Saul (1 Sm 9:1).

ZERUAH Mother of Israel's King Jeroboam I (1 Kgs 11:26).

ZERUBBABEL Babylonian-born Jew who returned to Palestine in 538 BC to serve as governor of Jerusalem under Persian rule. The name presumably means "seed [offspring] of Babylon," referring to someone born in Babylon.

The exact identity of Zerubbabel's biological father is uncertain. All biblical references except one mention Shealtiel as his father (Ezr 3:2, 8; 5:2; Neh 12:1; Hg 1:1, 12-14; 2:2, 23; Mt 1:12-13; Lk 3:27). This would make Zerubbabel the grandson of the Davidic king Jehoiachin. However, 1 Chronicles 3:19 identifies Pedaiah, the brother of Shealtiel, as Zerubbabel's father.

Two solutions have been proposed. Many scholars have assumed that Shealtiel died before fathering an heir. His brother, Pedaiah, would then have fathered Zerubbabel by Shealtiel's widow. Hence, Zerubbabel would have retained the name of Shealtiel rather than Pedaiah in accordance with the law of levirate marriage (Dt 25:5-10). This solution is weakened by its lack of textual support; similarly, the Chronicler would hardly have failed to state such an important piece of information if he had been desirous of "correcting" an error pertaining to Zerubbabel's parentage.

A simpler solution is obtained by reading the Septuagint text of 1 Chronicles 3:19, which lists Salathiel (Shealtiel) as the father of Zerubbabel. In this way, the single reference to 1 Chronicles may be harmonized with the other verses cited above.

In either case, whether Shealtiel or Pedaiah was Zerubbabel's biological father, it is clear that Zerubbabel was of Davidic lineage and was viewed by members of the Israelite community as a viable candidate for leading them back to a position of power.

Following the edict of Cyrus in 538 BC, Jews were permitted to return to Palestine and reclaim their former homeland. Zerubbabel was appointed governor, and probably by the decade of 529–520 had started work on the reconstruction of the Jerusalem temple. However, because of several discouraging events, little was accomplished until the year 520 BC.

The writings of Haggai and Zechariah reveal much information about Zerubbabel's standing in the community. These two prophets evidently viewed Jeshua and Zerubbabel as the two men chosen by God for the task. Accordingly, in many of their oracles, support for one or both men is openly stated (e.g., Hg 2:21-23; Zec 3:8; 4:6-7; 6:12). The prophets viewed Jeshua and Zerubbabel's work as being messianic. This is most clearly seen in the vision of Zechariah (Zec 4:11-14). In the vision, two olive branches, one on either side of the lampstand, are identified as "the two anointed who stand by the Lord of the whole earth." As the context clearly shows, none other than Jeshua (or Joshua; named in 3:1-9) and Zerubbabel (named in 4:6-10) are meant. Because of his association with the rebuilding of the temple in Jerusalem, Zerubbabel had been accorded a place of great honor in Jewish tradition.

Some hold that Zerubbabel was known to the Persians as Sheshbazzar. *See* Sheshbazzar.

ZERUIAH Nahash's daughter and the sister of Abigail (2 Sm 17:25). Zeruiah eventually bore three sons: Joab, Abishai, and Asahel, all of whom were David's friends during his reign (2 Sm 2:18; 3:39; 8:16; 18:2).

ZETHAM One of Ladan's descendants, a Gershonite, in charge of the temple treasuries (1 Chr 23:8; 26:22).

ZETHAN Bilhan's son from Benjamin's tribe (1 Chr 7:10).

ZETHAR One of King Ahasuerus's seven chamberlains, who was commanded to bring Queen Vashti before the king for public display of her beauty (Est 1:10).

ZEUS Chief god of the Greek pantheon (Roman Jupiter). Zeus was initially worshiped as part of an animistic cult, as the sky god with thunder as his principal manifestation. Well before the time of Homer, however, Zeus had become the preeminent personal god of the Greek residents of Thessaly, with Mt Olympus serving as the focal point of the cult. By NT times, Zeus was considered the Greek father god who possessed supreme powers. The quotation Paul used in Acts 17:28 from Cleanthes (and/or Aratus) was originally ascribed to Zeus ("in him we live and move and have our being").

Zeus is most significant in biblical writings as a result of Paul and Barnabas's encounter with the priest of Zeus at Lystra (Acts 14:8-18). Because Paul and Barnabas had healed a lame man, the residents of Lystra attempted to worship them, identifying Barnabas with Zeus and Paul with Hermes, the messenger of the gods. It was not unusual that this misidentification should take place, since the Greek gods were frequently represented as taking on human appearances and intervening directly in human affairs. Unlike the true God, Zeus and his consorts were often viewed as capriciously bestowing favor or disfavor. The attribution of "divinity" to Paul and Barnabas allowed them to identify the key differences between Greek and Christian theology.

ZIA One of the clan leaders of Gad's tribe dwelling in Bashan (1 Chr 5:13).

ZIBA Former servant of Saul whom David commissioned to find survivors of the house of Saul so that he might "show them kindness" (2 Sm 9:2-12). In the period following Saul's death, Ziba apparently had not only gained his freedom but had also become a successful landowner. This status was lost as a result of the discovery of Mephibosheth, Jonathan's crippled son. Ziba later became involved in a controversy with Mephibosheth concerning Mephibosheth's failure to accompany David when he fled during Absalom's rebellion (2 Sm 16:1-4; 19:17, 24-29). Most commentators have blamed Ziba with duplicity and slander in the affair, but the text allows no certain conclusion as to who was guilty. On Mephibosheth's behalf, it is unlikely that he would have believed that he could inherit the throne, as Ziba had claimed (2 Sm 16:3). Mephibosheth also seems to have been loyal to David (though it is possible that David brought him to Jerusalem to ensure that he would be under protective surveillance). In Ziba's defense, it is notable that David did believe without question that Mephibosheth might have had aspirations for the throne. Ziba also appears consistently as a loyal supporter of David in spite of the fact that David's decision had cost him his independent status (2 Sm 16:1; 19:17). Of course, Ziba's displeasure at his loss of independence might have motivated him to defame Mephibosheth. In any case, David appears to have had reason to doubt both versions of the truth. Rather than supporting either claim, he chose to divide the land between them (2 Sm 19:29).

ZIBEON Ancestor of Oholibamah, the Canaanite wife of Esau (Gn 36:2, 14). He is listed as a Hivite in Genesis 36:2 but is probably the same as Zibeon the son of Seir the Horite (Gn 36:20, 29; 1 Chr 1:38). Possibly "Hivite" designated his tribal affiliation, while "Horite" indicated the fact that he dwelt in caves. It is also possible that "Hivite" is a transmission error in Genesis 36:2.

ZIBIA One of the seven sons borne to Shaharaim by his wife Hodesh (1 Chr 8:9).

ZIBIAH Mother of King Jehoash of Judah, from the town of Beersheba (2 Kgs 12:1; 2 Chr 24:1).

ZICHRI*, ZICRI
1. Kohathite Levite and a descendant of Izhar (Ex 6:21).
2. One of Shimei's sons from Benjamin's tribe (1 Chr 8:19).
3. One of Shashak's sons from Benjamin's tribe (1 Chr 8:23).
4. One of Jeroham's sons from Benjamin's tribe (1 Chr 8:27).
5. Ancestor of Mattaniah. Mattaniah returned with Zerubbabel to Israel following the exile (1 Chr 9:15); Zicri is probably identifiable with Zabdi in Nehemiah 11:17.
6. Descendant of Eliezer, the son of Moses. His son, Shelomoth, was in charge of the treasuries of the dedicated gifts (1 Chr 26:25).
7. Father of Eliezer, the chief officer of the Reubenites during David's reign (1 Chr 27:16).
8. Father of Amasiah, a volunteer in charge of 200,000 men during Jehoshaphat's reign (2 Chr 17:16).

9. Father of Elishaphat, a participant in the conspiracy against Athaliah led by Jehoiada (2 Chr 23:1).
10. Mighty man of Ephraim who participated in Pekah's subjugation of Judah. Zicri killed Ahaz's son Maaseiah, Azrikam the commander of the palace, and Elkanah the king's deputy (2 Chr 28:7).
11. Father of Joel, overseer of the Benjaminites who returned to Jerusalem following the exile (Neh 11:9).
12. Levite who served as a priest and the head of the clan of Abijah during the days of Joiakim the high priest (Neh 12:17).

ZIDDIM Fortified city in the land assigned to Naphtali's tribe (Jos 19:35).

ZIDKIJAH* KJV form of Zedekiah, a priest in Nehemiah 10:1. See Zedekiah #4.

ZIDON*, ZIDONIAN* KJV forms of Sidon and Sidonian, a city and its inhabitants in Asher's territory. See Sidon (Place), Sidonian.

ZIF* KJV form of Ziv, the name of the Hebrew month, corresponding to about mid-April to mid-May (1 Kgs 6:1, 37). See Calendars, Ancient and Modern.

ZIGGURAT* Term meaning "temple tower"; a ziggurat was similar in profile to the step pyramid of Egypt and was used for worship. They were frequent in the major cities of Mesopotamia. The Tower of Babel (Gn 11:1-9) is believed to have been of this construction. It was widely believed that deities dwelt above, in high places. Therefore, worship was more appropriate on hills or mountains. There are no hills in Mesopotamia, nor is there building stone. Consequently, the inhabitants built with mud brick. The ziggurats of mud brick were constructed as substitutes for hills, where the worshiper or priest could get closer to the gods. Like the pyramids of Egypt, these temple towers were square. Instead of having sloping sides, there was a succession of terraces, each smaller than the one below. Access to each level was by stairways or ramps. The shrine or altar was on top, where the priests would officiate at sacrifices, incantations, and prayers. The great seven-story ziggurat at Babylon measured nearly 300 feet (91.4 meters) on a side at the base and rose to about the same height.

The Ziggurat or Stepped Pyramid of Saqqarah, Egypt

ZIHA
1. Ancestor of a family of temple servants who returned to Jerusalem with Zerubbabel after the exile (Ezr 2:43; Neh 7:46).
2. Overseer of the temple servants living at Ophel during

the postexilic era (Neh 11:21). If Ziha is simply a family name, then this person is likely the same as #1 above.

ZIKLAG Philistine city ruled by David for 16 months before he moved to Hebron to become the king of Judah. Ziklag was deeded to David by Achish of Gath, presumably to ensure David's continued neutrality (1 Sm 27:6; 1 Chr 12:1). The location of Ziklag is difficult to determine despite its prominence in the early history of Israel. In the record of the land allotments following the Conquest, Ziklag appears to be located in the extreme south of Judah (Jos 15:31). It is later described as part of the allotment within western Judah that was granted to Simeon (Jos 19:5; 1 Chr 4:30). Ziklag was most likely located somewhere on the frontier between Philistia and Judah, southeast of Gaza (possibly Tell el-Khuweilfeh).

ZILLAH Second wife of Lamech and mother of Tubal-cain and Naamah (Gn 4:19-23).

ZILLETHAI
1. One of Shimei's sons from Benjamin's tribe (1 Chr 8:20).
2. One of the "chiefs of thousands" who deserted Saul and came to David at Ziklag (1 Chr 12:20).

ZILPAH Mother of Jacob's sons Gad and Asher. Laban had given her to his daughter Leah as a handmaid (Gn 29:24; 46:18). Later, at Leah's insistence, she became Jacob's concubine for the purpose of bearing sons (30:9; 37:2).

ZILTHAI* KJV spelling of Zillethai in 1 Chronicles 8:20 and 12:20. *See* Zillethai #1 and #2.

ZIMMAH Gershonite Levite and ancestor of Joah (1 Chr 6:20); possibly the same Joah who assisted Hezekiah (2 Chr 29:12).

ZIMRAN One of the sons of Abraham by Keturah (Gn 25:2; 1 Chr 1:32). Unlike the other sons of Abraham by Keturah, there is little evidence that Zimran is associated with a later tribal group.

ZIMRI (Person)
1. Clan chief of Simeon's tribe who was killed by Phinehas for consorting with a Midianite woman at

Peor (Nm 25:14). Zimri's sin was magnified by the fact that he did it openly, that he was a leader within his tribe, and that the woman was the daughter of an important Midianite prince.
2. King of Israel for seven days (885 BC) following his assassination of Elah and the rest of the family of Baasha (1 Kgs 16:9-12). Zimri, commander of half of the chariot forces, failed to gain the support of the people, who supported Omri, the commander of the army. When Omri marched against Zimri at Tirzah, Zimri committed suicide by burning his palace down (16:15-18). The cruelty of Zimri's coup is reflected in Jezebel's later taunt against Jehu, when she compared his duplicity to that of Zimri (2 Kgs 9:31).
3. One of the sons of Zerah, the son of Judah by Tamar (1 Chr 2:6); alternately called Zabdi in the parallel passage in Joshua 7:1, 17. *See* Zabdi #1.
4. Descendant of Saul from Benjamin's tribe, listed as the son of Jehoaddah and the father of Moza (1 Chr 8:36). He is likely the same as Zimri the son of Jadah (9:42).

ZIMRI (Place) Place and peoples of the East, listed along with Elam and Media, against whom God's wrath would fall (Jer 25:25). Zimri's location and history are unknown; some identify its progenitor with Zimran, Abraham and Keturah's son (Gn 25:2).

ZIN, Wilderness of Area lying in the northern portion of the Sinai Peninsula, while the wilderness of Sin lies in the southern portion. It is one of the four or five "wildernesses" of the Sinai Peninsula, the others being the wilderness of Paran (Gn 21:21), the wilderness of Shur (Ex 15:22), and the wilderness of Sinai (Nm 9:1) and the wilderness of Sin (Nm 33:11). These areas are not clearly defined, and there is probably some overlap.

The area identified as the wilderness of Zin is associated with the village of Zin (Nm 34:4). The wilderness was west of Edom, southwest of the Dead Sea, and south of Judah. Within this arid area were four copious springs or oases, including Kadesh-barnea. Most of the 38 years the Israelites spent in the Sinai Desert were spent in this area. From the wilderness of Zin the spies were dispatched to spy out the land of Canaan (Nm 13:1-26; 32:8). Here also the rebels were sentenced to die because of their unbelief (14:22-23). Moses sinned by failing to give God the credit for bringing water out of the rock (20:1-13; 27:14), and Miriam, his sister, died and was buried here (20:1). This area was remembered as the "great and terrible wilderness" (Dt 1:19; 8:15).

See also Wilderness Wanderings.

ZINA* Alternate form of Ziza, Shimei's son, in 1 Chronicles 23:10. *See* Ziza.

ZINC* *See* Minerals and Metals.

ZION The Jebusite fortress in Jerusalem conquered by David. Thereafter, Zion was used by biblical writers to identify other areas of Jerusalem and was used as a designation of the entire city. Zion was also used to describe, spiritually speaking, the eternal city of God.

Geographical Sites

The Jebusite Fortress The first occurrence of the word "Zion" is in the narrative of David's conquest of Jerusalem (2 Sm 5:6-10; 1 Chr 11:4-9). David captured the "fortress of Zion," which was thereafter known as the "city of David." The "fortress of Zion" may refer to the entire walled perimeter of the approximately 11-acre

Zion

(4.5-hectare) site on the southeastern ridge (the Ophel Ridge), or to a smaller fortified area within that site.

The Temple Mount Changes in the perimeter of the city by incorporating more territory within the walls extend the term Zion. When Solomon built the temple and his palace and extended the walls north of the Ophel Ridge to encompass the threshing floor of Ornan the Jebusite (2 Sm 24:16-18; 1 Chr 21:15-18, 28), the name Zion was applied to these areas as well. The transfer of the ark "from the city of David which is Zion" (1 Kgs 8:1; 2 Chr 5:2) to the temple hill brought both an extension and a reduction of the territory embraced by the term "Zion." The whole city could still be called Zion, but from this point on, there would be a close identification between Zion and the temple hill. The temple precincts became the primary Zion; references to Zion in the poetic books and the preaching of the prophets are primarily to the temple area as the dwelling place of God.

The Entire City The word "Zion" can be used as a designation of the entire city or its population without any particular reference to the temple area. This use is clearest in poetic passages where Zion is the parallel term to Jerusalem (Pss 51:18; 76:2; 102:21; 135:21; 147:12; Is 2:3; 30:19; 33:20; 37:32; 40:9; 41:27; 62:1; Jer 26:18; 51:35; Am 1:2; Zep 3:14) or to the villages of Judah (Pss 69:35; 97:8; Is 40:9).

Theological Motifs

In the Old Testament Many theological motifs attach to the Zion theme as it develops in redemptive history. The dominant motif of Zion as the dwelling place of God, the place where God is in the midst of his people, is conjoined to the larger theme of Immanuel, "God in our midst." Just as the pillar of fire and cloud stood above the tabernacle during the wilderness wandering, so once Israel had attained the place of God's choosing (Dt 12:5-14), he would dwell there. When Jerusalem became David's capital and Solomon had completed the temple, the glory cloud filled the temple (1 Kgs 8:10; 2 Chr 5:13-14) and Jerusalem became the dwelling place of God (Pss 74:2; 76:2; 135:21; Is 8:18; Jl 3:17-21). The Lord loved and chose Zion (Pss 78:68; 132:13). His glorious presence was there, and from there he would speak (50:1-2). His fire was in Zion, his furnace in Jerusalem (Is 31:8-9). There he was enthroned above the cherubim (Pss 9:11; 99:1-2) and ruled over his people and the nations (Is 24:23). His chosen king ruled from that holy hill (Pss 2:6; 48:1).

Though the size of the site of ancient Jerusalem is not particularly impressive and ordinarily would not be considered a large hill, for the psalmist Zion is God's holy hill (Ps 99:9). The prophets describe it as "chief among the mountains, raised above the hills" (Is 2:2; Mi 4:1). The Canaanite god Baal was thought to dwell on a great mountain to the north, Mt Zaphon, so the psalmist describes Zion as "beautiful in its loftiness, like the utmost heights of Mt Zaphon" (Ps 48:1-2). God's sanctuary is "like the high mountains" (Ps 78:68; Ez 40:2).

An adequate water supply has been a problem for Jerusalem throughout its history. During the OT period, the city's water came from one small spring. But in the eyes of the poets and prophets, Zion is gladdened by a great river that brings life wherever it flows (Ps 46:4; Ez 47:1-12; Jl 3:18; Zec 13:1; 14:8; see Rv 22:1-2). The threatening waters of chaos cannot shake the city of God (Ps 46:1-3).

Because Zion is the city of God, it is the object of pilgrims, Jew and Gentile alike, who thirst to be in the presence of God in Zion's temple (Pss 42:1-2; 63:1). The pilgrim psalms give vivid expression to their longing (84;

122; 125–128). All humanity will come to God in Zion (65:1-4). The Gentiles will make annual pilgrimages bringing gifts (Ps 76; Is 18:7; Zep 3:9-10); even former enemies will be regarded as native-born citizens of Zion (Ps 87; Is 60:14; Zec 14:21). The nations will stream into Jerusalem to inaugurate an era of peace (Is 2:1-5; Mi 4:1-8). Year after year the festivals of Israel will be celebrated in Zion by Gentiles (Zec 14:16-19).

In the New Testament The NT further develops the emphasis on both the heavenly and the eschatological Zion. For example, the author of Hebrews said that the OT saints looked "forward to the city with foundations, whose architect and builder is God . . . longing for a better country—a heavenly one" (Heb 11:10, 16, NIV), but none of them received the promises because God had planned something even better (vv 39-40). The church now enjoys what believers of the old covenant could never know: unlimited access to the presence of God in that Holy City, "Mount Zion, the heavenly Jerusalem, the city of the living God" (12:22; see vv 18-24). Earthly Zion is but a shadow of the heavenly reality. The present city of Jerusalem is likened to a slave woman, but the heavenly Jerusalem is free and the mother of both Jew and Gentile (Gal 4:21-27; see Is 49:14-23; 54:1). The NT also looks forward to the eschatological expectation of the re-creation of heaven and earth and the revelation of the new Jerusalem (Rv 21:2). It is a city on a great high mountain (Rv 21:10; see Pss 48:1-2; 78:68; Is 2:2; Ez 40:2; Mi 4:1), and a river of life flows within (Rv 22:1-2).

See also Jerusalem; Jerusalem, New.

ZION, Daughter of Term used primarily in prophetic literature to designate the inhabitants of Jerusalem (Zion) and its surrounding regions. The term was further applied to those in Babylon who had been exiled from Jerusalem and the Judean countryside (Is 1:8; Jer 4:31; 6:2, 23). Since ancient cities were considered metaphorically to be the mother of their inhabitants, referring to the people of Jerusalem as "daughters of Zion" was entirely appropriate, particularly in poetic literature. While Israel was to be the "virgin daughter" of spiritual Zion (2 Kgs 19:21; Is 37:22; Lam 2:13), many of the prophetic contexts proclaim judgment on the unfaithful "daughters" (Is 3:16-17; 4:4; Mi 1:13). Although the "daughters of Zion" were judged for their unfaithfulness, the ultimate promise was that God would deliver them (Is 52:2; 62:11; Zec 9:9; Mt 21:5; Jn 12:15).

See also Zion.

ZIOR One of the cities of the hill country allotted to Judah's tribe for an inheritance (Jos 15:54). Since it is associated with Hebron in the text, Zior is likely identified with modern Sa'ir, the traditional location for Esau's tomb.

ZIPH (Person)
1. Descendant of Caleb from Judah's tribe (1 Chr 2:42).
2. One of the sons of Jehallelel from Judah's tribe (1 Chr 4:16).

ZIPH (Place)
1. One of the cities in the extreme south assigned to Judah's tribe for an inheritance (Jos 15:24).
2. One of the cities in the hill country belonging to Judah's tribe (Jos 15:55), mentioned with Maon, Carmel, Jezreel, and most prominently with Hebron (cf. 1 Chr 2:42). Ziph has been identified with a site three miles (4.8 kilometers) south of Hebron. The sur-

rounding wilderness region is probably the "wilderness of Ziph" where David hid from Saul (1 Sm 23:14-15; 26:2). The Ziphites who betrayed David to Saul were residents of this city and the surrounding region (1 Sm 23:19; 26:1; Ps 54 title). Ziph is later mentioned as one of the cities fortified by Rehoboam (2 Chr 11:8).

ZIPHAH Jehallelel's second son (or possibly daughter, since the form is feminine), listed in 1 Chronicles 4:16.

ZIPHIMS* KJV rendering of Ziphites, the inhabitants of Ziph, in the title of Psalm 54. See Ziph (Place) #2.

ZIPHITE Inhabitant of Ziph (1 Sm 23:19; 26:1; Ps 54 title). See Ziph (Place) #2.

ZIPHRON Geographical landmark defining the northern boundary of the Canaanite land to be possessed by Israel (Nm 34:9).

ZIPPOR Father of the Moabite king Balak. Balak called on Balaam to curse Israel (Nm 22:2, 10, 16; 23:18; Jos 24:9; Jgs 11:25).

ZIPPORAH Wife of Moses and mother of his sons Gershom and Eliezer (Ex 2:21). Though she is listed as the daughter of Reuel (v 18), Reuel was probably the father of Hobab (Nm 10:29; also called Jethro, Ex 3:1; 4:18), who in turn was the father of Zipporah. Zipporah circumcised Gershom to prevent Moses' death prior to his return to Egypt (Ex 4:25). Apparently at that point Zipporah and the children left Moses and went back to live with her father, returning later during the wilderness wanderings (18:2).

ZITHER See Musical Instruments.

ZITHRI* KJV spelling of Sithri, Uzziel's son, in Exodus 6:22. See Sithri.

ZIV* Name of the Hebrew month corresponding to about mid-April to mid-May (1 Kgs 6:1, 37). See Calendars, Ancient and Modern.

ZIZ, Ascent of Mountain pass going up from the Dead Sea to the Judean highlands. This ascent was the route used by the Ammonites and the Moabites prior to their defeat by Jehoshaphat as prophesied by Jehaziel (2 Chr 20:16). It is likely that Ziz should be identified with Ain Jidy, a pass that still provides an important route from the Dead Sea into the Judean interior.

ZIZA
1. Chief of Simeon's tribe descending from Shemaiah (1 Chr 4:37).
2. Son of Rehoboam and Maacah (2 Chr 11:20).
3. Second of Shimei's sons and a clan chief within the Gershonite branch of Levi's tribe (1 Chr 23:11); perhaps the same as Zina in 1 Chronicles 23:10.

ZOAN One of the principal cities in the delta region of ancient Egypt. Zoan, which was variously known as Zoan, Tanis, Avaris, and possibly Rameses (the towns were either the same or contiguous), was located on the south shore of Lake Menzaleh at the northeastern edge of the Egyptian Delta. Zoan was rebuilt during or shortly before the Hyksos period (c. 1730 BC; Nm 13:22). Because of its strategic location on the Tanitic branch of the Nile and near Egypt's northeastern frontier, Zoan was an important military and political base during the entire period of Egyptian native rule. It served as the capital city during the Hyksos period, as well as serving as the effective capital during the 21st through the 23d dynasties (c. 1090–718 BC) and as the northern capital during the 25th dynasty (c. 712–663 BC).

Zoan was significant to the Israelites during each of its periods of ascendancy. Whether the exodus occurred early (c. 1441 BC) or late (1290 BC), the Israelite settlement in Egypt would have been in the general vicinity of Zoan. The Israelites built the store cities of Pithom and Rameses, and possibly the latter should be identified with Zoan. In the account of the exodus in Psalm 78, the city of Zoan is poetically parallel to Egypt, indicating that it was either the capital or at least a significant city. During the period of Isaiah, Zoan was again significant, being designated as the home of the "princes" and "officials" of Egypt (Is 19:11-13; Ez 30:14).

See also Rameses (Place).

ZOAR One of the "cities of the plain" confederate with Sodom, Gomorrah, Admah, and Zeboiim (Gn 14:2, 8). Zoar, also known by its earlier name Bela, is best known as the town that served as a temporary refuge for Lot and his daughters during the destruction of Sodom and the other cities of the plain (19:22-23, 30). Despite the fact that Zoar was evidently a small town (v 22; Zoar means "little"), this place was evidently considered a significant geographical landmark in ancient times. When Abraham and Lot divided the land, Lot selected the land close to Zoar (13:10). When Moses surveyed the Promised Land from Mt Pisgah, Zoar was reckoned as the southern terminus of the plain of the valley of Jericho (Dt 34:3). During the prophetic period, Zoar was evidently considered to be on the southern boundary of Moab (Is 15:5; Jer 48:4, 34).

See also Cities of the Plain.

ZOBAH Aramean nation suffering military defeat from Israel during the early kingdom period. King Saul defeated the kings of Zobah (1 Sm 14:47). Soon after David became king of Israel, he defeated Hadadezer the son of Rehob, king of Zobah (2 Sm 8:3-5, 12; 1 Chr 18:3-10; Ps 60 title). Later, the Ammonites hired 20,000 "Syrians of Zobah" for an anticipated attack by David's forces. The coalition of Ammonites and hired mercenaries was defeated by soldiers led by Joab (2 Sm 10:6-14). When Hadadezer's army counterattacked, they were again defeated decisively by David (2 Sm 10:15-19; 1 Chr 19:16-19).

ZOBEBAH One of the sons of Koz (or possibly a daughter, since the noun is feminine) from Judah's tribe (1 Chr 4:8). The genealogy is obscure.

ZODIAC* See Astrology.

ZOHAR
1. Father of Ephron the Hittite. Abraham bought the cave of Machpelah from Ephron (Gn 23:7-9; 25:9).
2. Alternate spelling of Zerah, Simeon's son, in Genesis 46:10 and Exodus 6:15. See Zerah #3.
3. Alternate spelling of Izhar in 1 Chronicles 4:7.

ZOHELETH, Stone of Alternate rendering for "Serpent's Stone" in 1 Kings 1:9. See Serpent's Stone.

ZOHETH Ishi's son from Judah's tribe (1 Chr 4:20).

ZOPHAH Helem's son from Asher's tribe (1 Chr 7:35-36).

ZOPHAI Alternate form of Zuph, one of Samuel's ancestors, in 1 Chronicles 6:26. *See* Zuph (Person).

ZOPHAR One of the "counselors" of Job who is listed as a Naamathite (Jb 2:11; 11:1; 20:1). He offers the most direct accusations against Job but later offers sacrifice for Job as commanded by the Lord (42:9).

ZOPHIM Place from which Balaam pronounced his second blessing upon Israel (Nm 23:13-16). Zophim must have been on or near Mt Pisgah.

ZORAH, ZORATHITE A city of the Shephelah and its people, attributed to both the tribe of Dan and of Judah (Jos 15:33; 19:41). It was part of Judah's original allocation but was settled by Danites until they established their own territory near Laish (Jgs 18:1-11). Originally Zorah and nearby Eshtaol seem to have been settled by residents of Kiriath-jearim (1 Chr 2:53; 4:2). The city was the home of Manoah, the father of Samson (Jgs 13:2). Samson's ministry was focused in the region surrounding Zorah and Eshtaol, and he was ultimately buried there. Zorah is traditionally identified with Tell Sur'ah, which is strategically located at the entrance to a large valley leading toward the Mediterranean plain.

ZORITES Descendants of Salma from Judah's tribe (1 Chr 2:54). They possibly represent half of the Manahathite clan.

ZOROBABEL* KJV form of Zerubbabel, Jerusalem's governor after the exile, in Matthew 1:12-13 and Luke 3:27. *See* Zerubbabel.

ZUAR Father of Nethanel, the leader of Issachar's tribe at the start of Israel's wilderness wanderings (Nm 1:8; 2:5; 7:18, 23; 10:15).

ZUPH (Person) Ancestor of Elkanah, the father of the prophet Samuel (1 Sm 1:1). Zuph was a member of the Kohathite branch of Levites and is listed as the son of Elkanah (different than above) and the father of Toah (1 Chr 6:35). He is the same as Zophai listed in 1 Chron-icles 6:26. It is evident that Zuph was a Levite, even though he is listed as an Ephraimite in the 1 Samuel passage.

ZUPH (Place) Place where Saul looked for his father's donkeys prior to his meeting with Samuel (1 Sm 9:5). It was near the tomb of Rachel, which is traditionally placed near the northern border of Benjamin. Zuph is apparently linked with Samuel, as one of his ancestors bore the name (see 1 Sm 1:1; 1 Chr 6:35), and his native town was called Ramathaim-zophim.

ZUR
1. Midianite prince who was the father of Cozbi, the Midianite woman who was killed by Phinehas for consorting with Zimri after the incident at Baal-peor (Nm 25:15). He was one of the five "kings" of Midian who (with Balaam) were later killed by the Israelites (31:8). Apparently, he was a vassal of the Amorite king Sihon, since he is listed as one of his "princes" (Jos 13:21).
2. Son of Jeiel, the founder of Gibeon (1 Chr 8:30; 9:36). He was a Benjaminite and a distant relative of Saul.

ZURIEL Son of Abihail and the head of the Merari family of Levites during the wilderness wanderings (Nm 3:35).

ZURISHADDAI Father of Shelumiel, the leader of Simeon's tribe at the start of Israel's wilderness wanderings (Nm 1:6; 2:12; 7:36, 41; 10:19).

ZUZIM*, ZUZITES One of the kingdoms attacked and defeated by Kedorlaomer's confederation (Gn 14:5), mentioned as residents of Ham. They were likely located somewhere north of the Arnon River, since the general path of Kedorlaomer was from north to south along the King's Highway. Possibly these Zuzites are associated with the Zamzummites of Deuteronomy 2:20, since both are linked to the same geographical proximity. Furthermore, both passages speak of them in connection with races of giants, including the Horites, the Emim, and the Rephaim.

Look for other books in:

THE TYNDALE REFERENCE LIBRARY
Bible Resources for Everyone's Library

Tyndale Bible Dictionary
Tyndale Handbook of Bible Charts and Maps
Tyndale Concise Bible Commentary

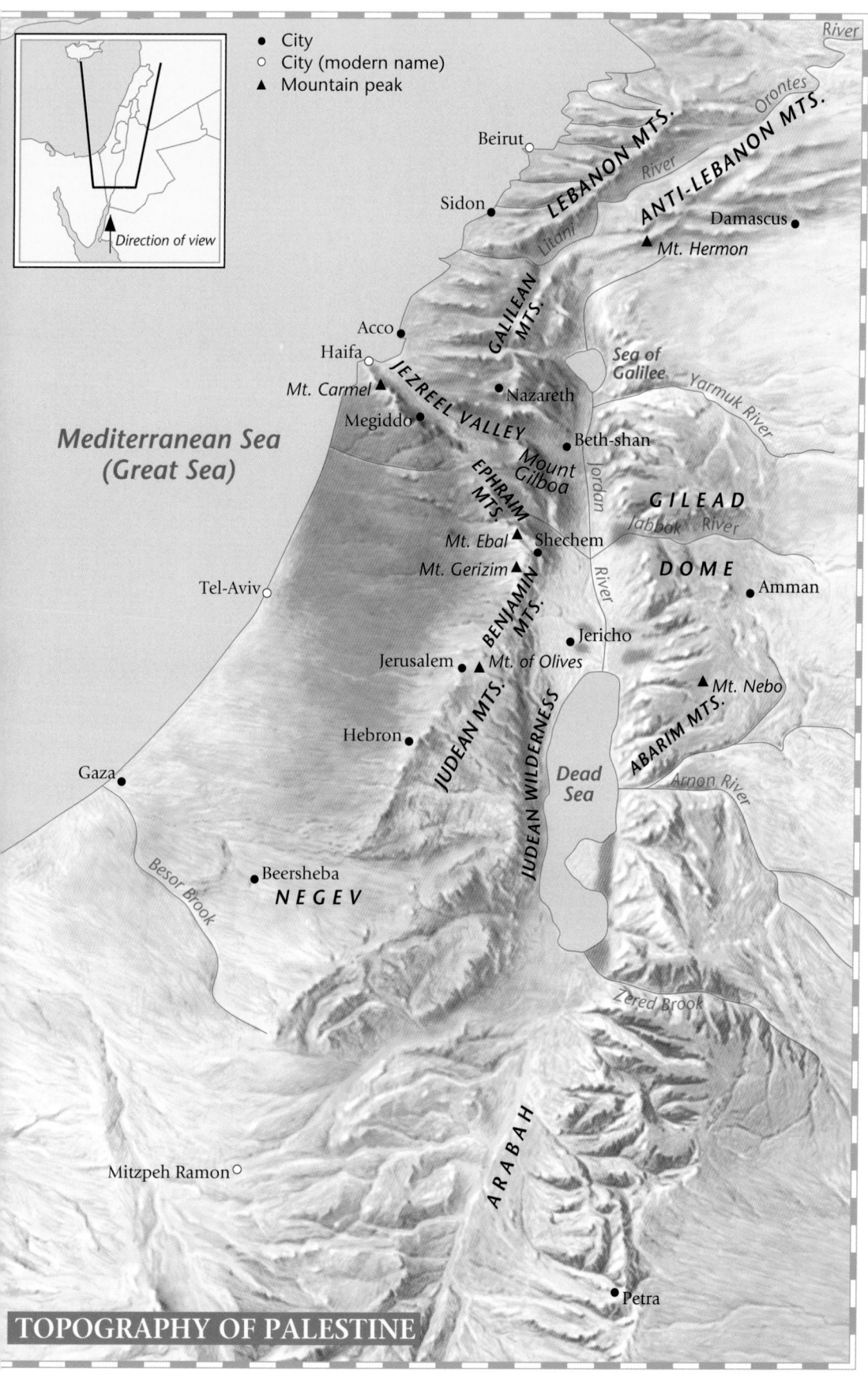

City
City (modern name)
Mountain peak

Direction of view

Beirut

Sidon

LEBANON MTS.

ANTI-LEBANON MTS.

Orontes River

Damascus

▲ Mt. Hermon

GALILEAN MTS.

Acco

Haifa

Sea of Galilee

Litani

Mt. Carmel ▲

JEZREEL VALLEY

Nazareth

Yarmuk River

Megiddo

Mediterranean Sea
(Great Sea)

Beth-shan

Mount Gilboa

EPHRAIM MTS.

GILEAD

Jordan

Jabbok River

Mt. Ebal ▲ Shechem

Mt. Gerizim ▲

DOME

Tel-Aviv

BENJAMIN MTS.

River

Amman

Jericho

Jerusalem ▲ Mt. of Olives

▲ Mt. Nebo

Hebron

JUDEAN MTS.

JUDEAN WILDERNESS

ABARIM MTS.

Gaza

Dead Sea

Arnon River

Besor Brook

Beersheba

NEGEV

Zered Brook

Mitzpeh Ramon

ARABAH

Petra

TOPOGRAPHY OF PALESTINE

Copyright © 1996 Tyndale House Publishers, Inc.

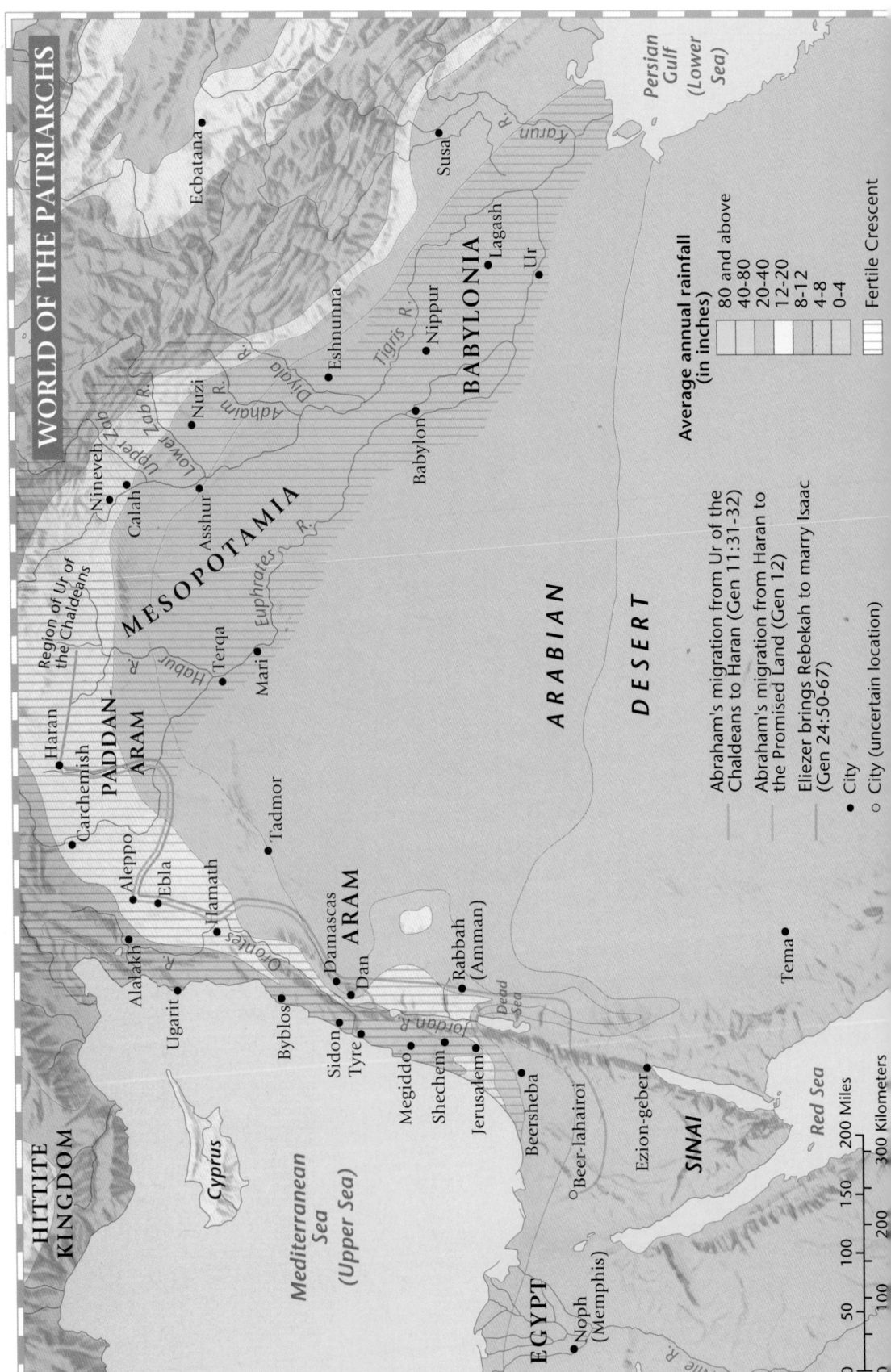

WORLD OF THE PATRIARCHS

HITTITE KINGDOM

Ecbatana

Nineveh
Calah
Asshur
Nuzi
Eshnunna

Upper Zab R.
Lower Zab R.
Adhaim R.
Diyala R.
Tigris R.

MESOPOTAMIA

Region of Ur of the Chaldeans

Carchemish
Haran

PADDAN-ARAM

Nippur
Babylon
Lagash
Ur

BABYLONIA

Susa

Karun R.

Persian Gulf (Lower Sea)

Euphrates R.
Habur R.
Terqa
Mari

Tadmor

Cyprus

Mediterranean Sea (Upper Sea)

Ugarit
Alalakh
Aleppo
Ebla
Hamath
Orontes R.

ARAM
Damascas
Dan

Byblos
Sidon
Tyre

Megiddo
Shechem
Jerusalem

Rabbah (Amman)

Dead Sea
Jordan R.

Beersheba
Beer-lahairoi
Ezion-geber

ARABIAN

DESERT

Tema

SINAI

EGYPT
Noph (Memphis)
Nile R.

Red Sea

Average annual rainfall (in inches)

80 and above
40-80
20-40
12-20
8-12
4-8
0-4

Fertile Crescent

——— Abraham's migration from Ur of the Chaldeans to Haran (Gen 11:31-32)

——— Abraham's migration from Haran to the Promised Land (Gen 12)

——— Eliezer brings Rebekah to marry Isaac (Gen 24:50-67)

● City

○ City (uncertain location)

0   50   100   150   200 Miles
0   100   200   300 Kilometers

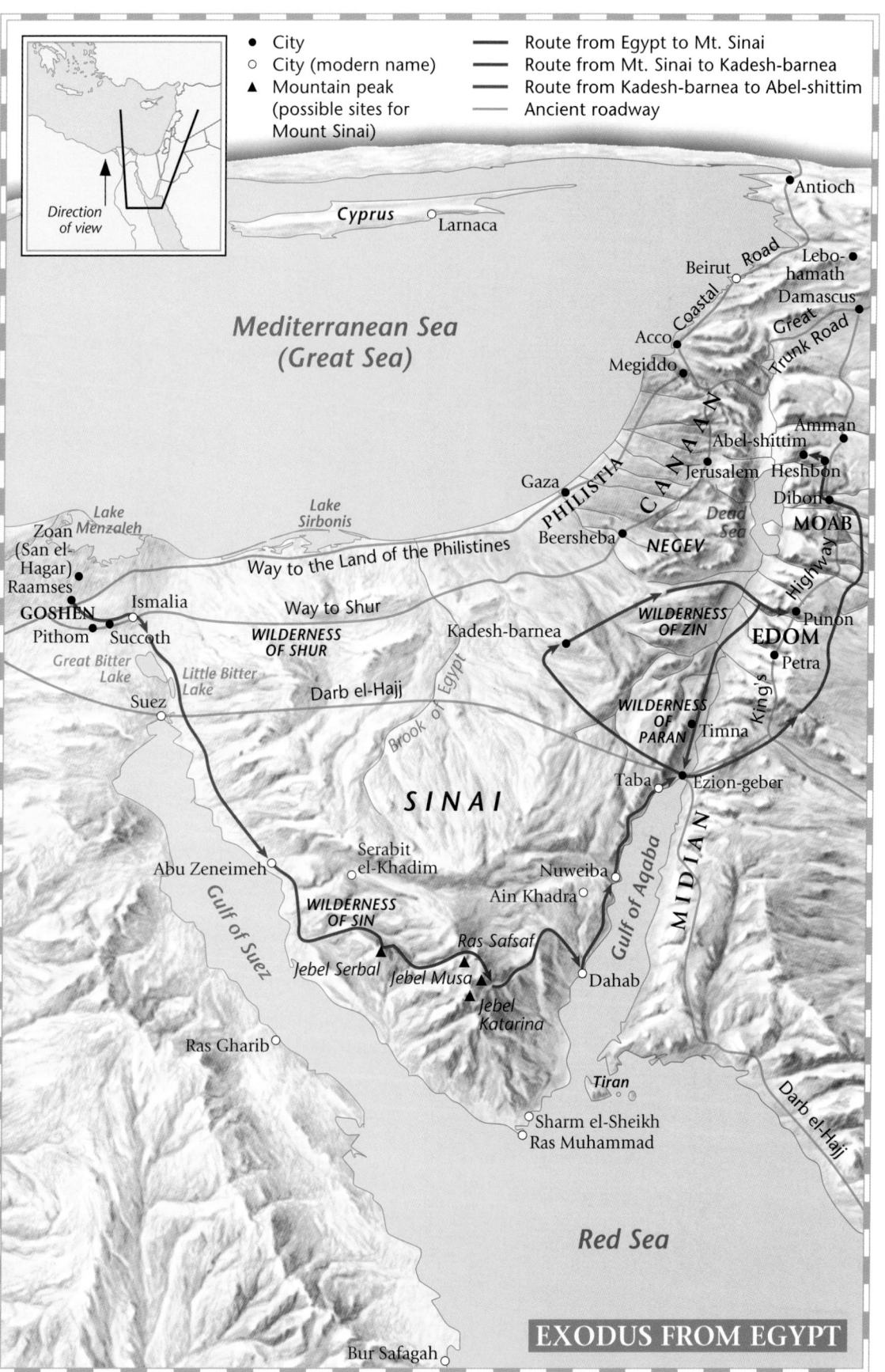

EXODUS FROM EGYPT

Legend:
- City
- City (modern name)
- Mountain peak (possible sites for Mount Sinai)
- Route from Egypt to Mt. Sinai
- Route from Mt. Sinai to Kadesh-barnea
- Route from Kadesh-barnea to Abel-shittim
- Ancient roadway

Direction of view

Cyprus
Larnaca

Mediterranean Sea (Great Sea)

Antioch
Beirut
Lebo-hamath
Damascus
Coastal Road
Great Trunk Road
Acco
Megiddo
CANAAN
Amman
Abel-shittim
Heshbon
Jerusalem
Dibon
Gaza
PHILISTIA
MOAB
Lake Menzaleh
Lake Sirbonis
Zoan (San el-Hagar)
Raamses
GOSHEN
Pithom
Succoth
Ismalia
Way to the Land of the Philistines
Beersheba
NEGEV
Dead Sea
Punon
EDOM
King's Highway
Way to Shur
WILDERNESS OF SHUR
Kadesh-barnea
WILDERNESS OF ZIN
Petra
Great Bitter Lake
Little Bitter Lake
Suez
Darb el-Hajj
Brook of Egypt
WILDERNESS OF PARAN
Timna
SINAI
Taba
Ezion-geber
Abu Zeneimeh
Serabit el-Khadim
Nuweiba
Ain Khadra
Gulf of Aqaba
MIDIAN
WILDERNESS OF SIN
Jebel Serbal
Ras Safsaf
Jebel Musa
Jebel Katarina
Dahab
Gulf of Suez
Ras Gharib
Tiran
Sharm el-Sheikh
Ras Muhammad
Darb el-Hajj
Red Sea
Bur Safagah

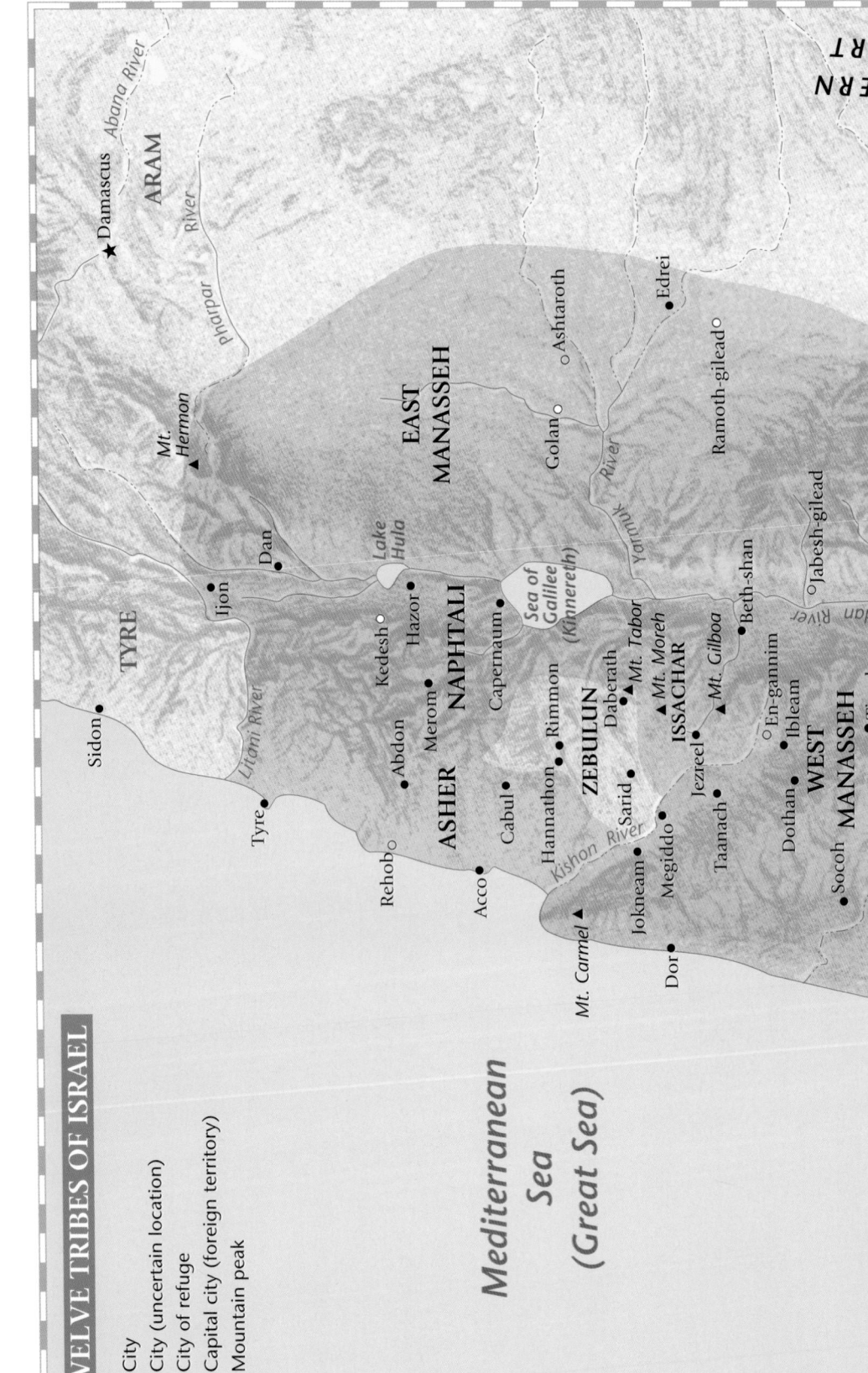

TWELVE TRIBES OF ISRAEL

- • City
- ○ City (uncertain location)
- ○ City of refuge
- ★ Capital city (foreign territory)
- ▲ Mountain peak

Mediterranean Sea (Great Sea)

Sidon •

Tyre •

Rehob ○

Acco •

Litani River

TYRE

ASHER

Abdon •

Kedesh ○

Merom •

Hazor •

Cabul •

Hannathon •

Rimmon •

NAPHTALI

Lake Hula

Dan •

Ijon •

Kishon River

Jokneam •

Mt. Carmel ▲

Dor •

Megiddo •

Sarid •

ZEBULUN

Daberath •

▲ Mt. Tabor

Capernaum •

Sea of Galilee (Kinnereth)

Mt.
Hermon ▲

ARAM

Damascus ★

Abana River

Pharpar River

EAST
MANASSEH

○ Ashtaroth

Golan ○

• Edrei

Ramoth-gilead ○

Yarmuk River

▲ Mt. Moreh

Jezreel •

ISSACHAR

Taanach •

▲ Mt. Gilboa

○ En-gannim

Iblean •

Beth-shan •

Jordan River

○ Jabesh-gilead

Dothan •

WEST
MANASSEH

Tirzah •

Socoh •

Samaria •

Mt. Ebal ▲

STERN
SERT

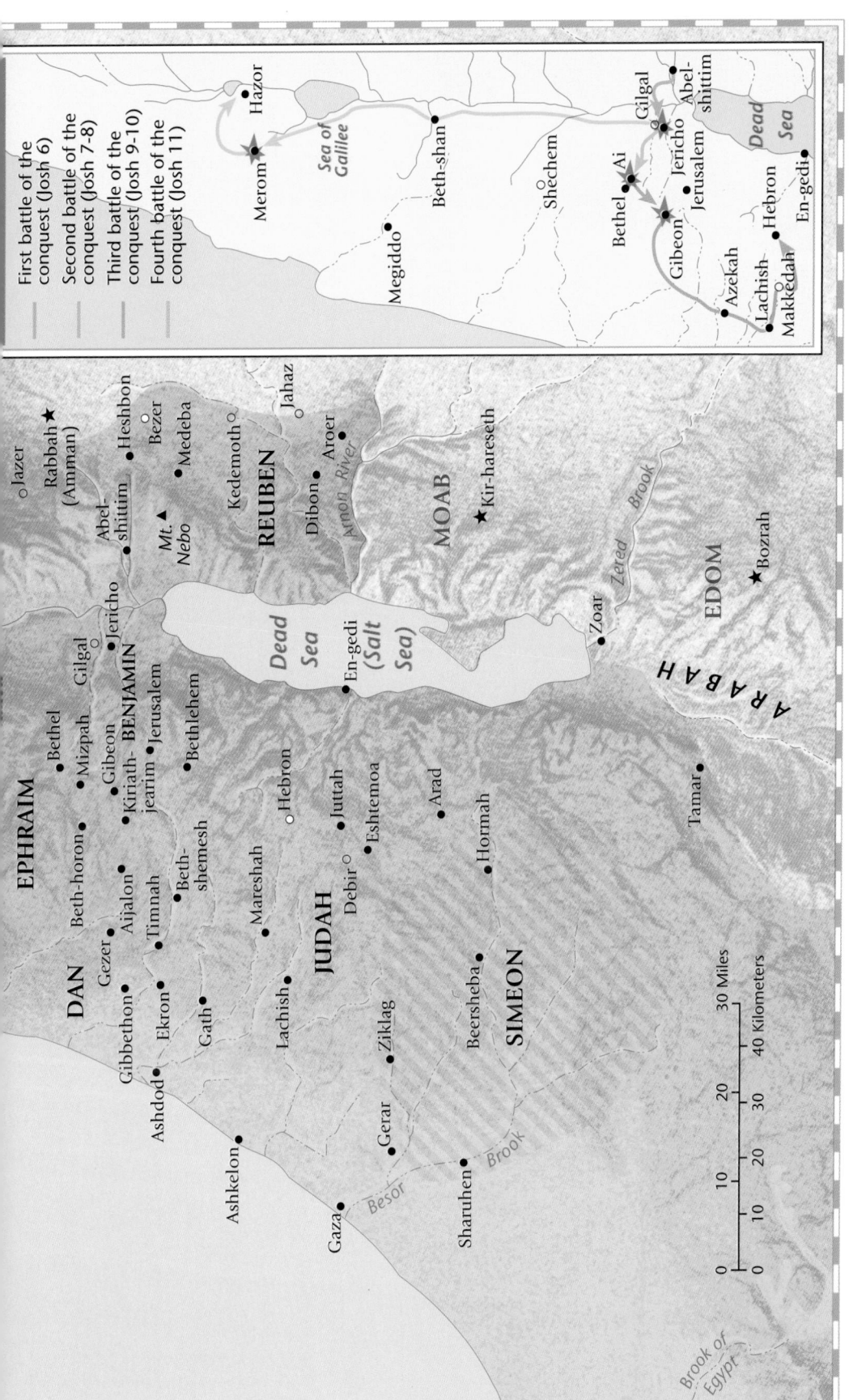

First battle of the
conquest (Josh 6)
Second battle of the
conquest (Josh 7-8)
Third battle of the
conquest (Josh 9-10)
Fourth battle of the
conquest (Josh 11)

Hazor
Merom
Sea of Galilee
Beth-shan
Shechem
Gilgal
Abel-shittim
Bethel
Ai
Jericho
Jerusalem
Gibeon
Hebron
En-gedi
Megiddo
Azekah
Lachish
Makkedah
Dead Sea

Jazer
Rabbah (Amman)
Heshbon
Bezer
Medeba
Abel-shittim
Kedemoth
Mt. Nebo
Jahaz
REUBEN
Aroer
Dibon
Arnon River
MOAB
Kir-hareseth
Zered Brook
Zoar
EDOM
Bozrah
ARABAH

EPHRAIM
Bethel
Mizpah
Beth-horon
Gilgal
Gibeon
Jericho
BENJAMIN
Kiriath-jearim
Jerusalem
Bethlehem
DAN
Gezer
Aijalon
Timnah
Beth-shemesh
Gibbethon
Ekron
Gath
Mareshah
Lachish
Ashdod
Hebron
Juttah
Eshtemoa
Debir
Arad
Dead Sea (Salt Sea)
En-gedi
JUDAH
Hormah
Ashkelon
Gaza
Gerar
Ziklag
Beersheba
Sharuhen
Besor Brook
SIMEON
Tamar
Brook of Egypt

0   10   20   30 Miles
0 10 20 30 40 Kilometers

UNITED KINGDOM

0 40 Miles
0 40 Kilometers

Cyprus

Mediterranean Sea (Great Sea)

Aleppo
YAMHAD
Tiphsah
Euphrates R.
Hamath
HAMATH
Tadmor
Arvad
Byblos
PHOENICIA
Lebo-hamath
Damascus
Tyre
ARAM
Dan
Hazor
Sea of Galilee (Kinnereth)
Dor
Jordan R.
Megiddo
Shechem
AMMON
Joppa
Gezer
Rabbah (Amman)
PHILISTIA
Jerusalem
Gaza
Dead Sea (Salt Sea)
Raphia
Beersheba
MOAB
AMALEK
Petra
EDOM
Kadesh-barnea
Ezion-geber
Gulf of Aqaba
SINAI

EASTERN DESERT

Kingdom of Saul
Kingdom of David
Kingdom of Solomon

DIVIDED KINGDOM

0 25 50 Miles
0 25 50 Kilometers

Great Trunk Road

Mediterranean Sea (Great Sea)

Hamath
HAMATH
Qatna
Arvad
Kadesh
Byblos
Coastal Road
Sadad
Lebo-hamath
Orontes R.
Berothai
Sidon
Litani R.
Tyre
Dan
Damascus
Kedesh
ARAM
Hazor
Acco
Sea of Galilee (Kinnereth)
Ashtaroth
Dor
Ramoth-gilead
Salecah
Megiddo
Beth-shan
Jordan R.
Jabbok R.
Shechem
ISRAEL
Rabbah (Amman)
Joppa
AMMON
Gezer
Gibeah
Ashdod
Jerusalem
Medeba
Gath
Dead Sea (Salt Sea)
Lachish
Gaza
Hebron
Aroer
JUDAH
Raphia
PHILISTIA
Great Trunk Road
MOAB
Beersheba
Kir-hareseth (Kir-moab)
NEGEV
Brook of Egypt
Kadesh-barnea
Bozrah
Petra
King's Highway
EDOM
Territory periodically contested by Edom and Judah
WILDERNESS OF ZIN
Ezion-geber
EASTERN DESERT
Gulf of Aqaba
SINAI

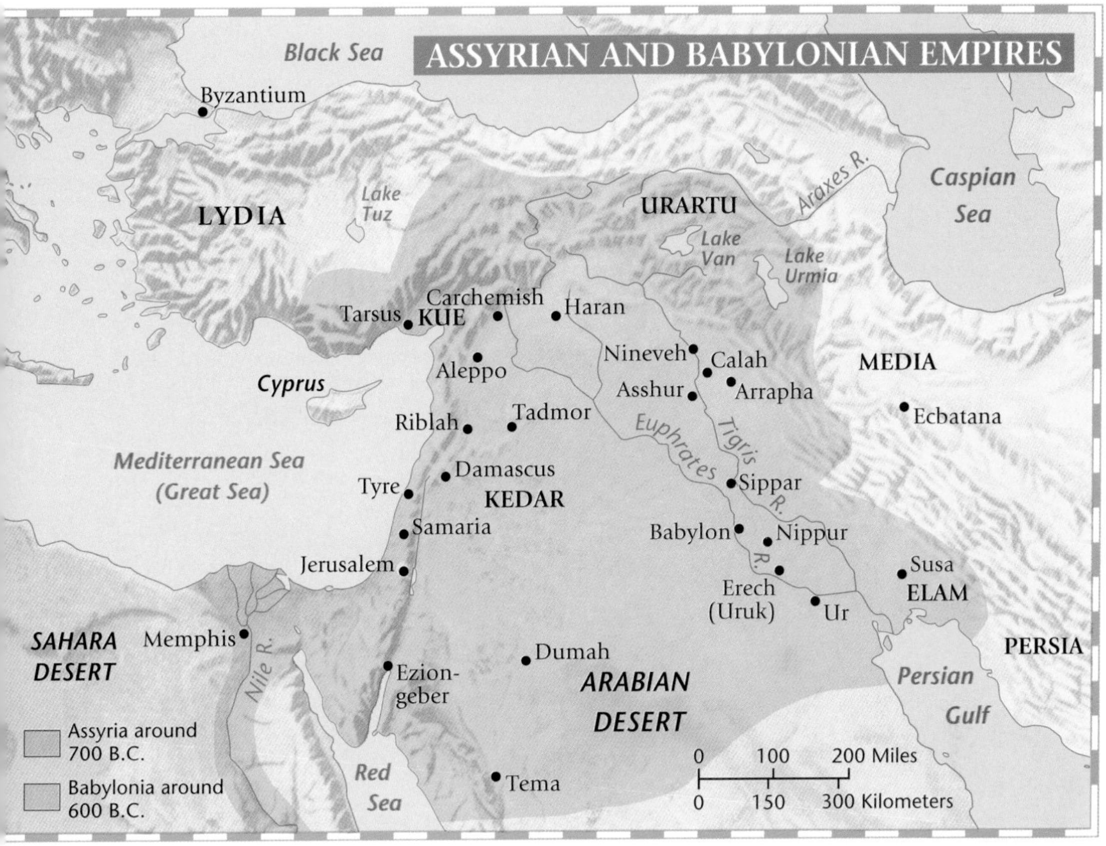
ASSYRIAN AND BABYLONIAN EMPIRES
Black Sea
Byzantium
LYDIA
Lake Tuz
URARTU
Araxes R.
Caspian Sea
Lake Van
Lake Urmia
Tarsus
KUE
Carchemish
Haran
Nineveh
Calah
MEDIA
Aleppo
Cyprus
Asshur
Arrapha
Riblah
Tadmor
Ecbatana
Euphrates
Tigris
Mediterranean Sea
(Great Sea)
Damascus
Tyre
KEDAR
Sippar
R.
Samaria
Babylon
Nippur
R.
Jerusalem
Susa
Erech
(Uruk)
Ur
ELAM
SAHARA DESERT
Memphis
Nile R.
PERSIA
Ezion-geber
Dumah
ARABIAN DESERT
Persian Gulf
Assyria around 700 B.C.
Babylonia around 600 B.C.
Red Sea
Tema
0 100 200 Miles
0 150 300 Kilometers

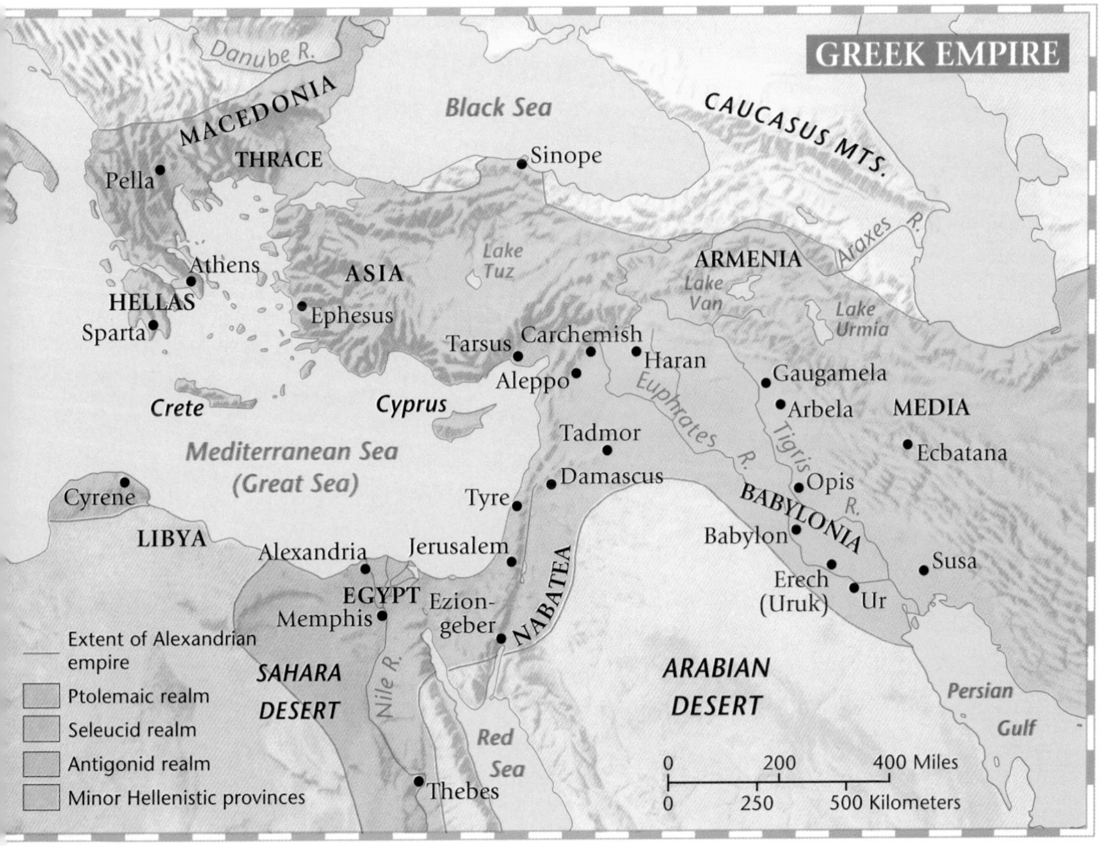
GREEK EMPIRE
Danube R.
MACEDONIA
Black Sea
CAUCASUS MTS.
THRACE
Sinope
Pella
Araxes R.
ARMENIA
Athens
HELLAS
ASIA
Lake Tuz
Lake Van
Lake Urmia
Ephesus
Sparta
Tarsus
Carchemish
Haran
Aleppo
Gaugamela
Crete
Cyprus
Arbela
MEDIA
Euphrates R.
Tigris R.
Tadmor
Mediterranean Sea
(Great Sea)
Ecbatana
Damascus
Opis
Cyrene
Tyre
BABYLONIA
LIBYA
Babylon
Alexandria
Jerusalem
Susa
NABATEA
Erech
(Uruk)
Ur
EGYPT
Ezion-geber
Memphis
Extent of Alexandrian empire
SAHARA DESERT
ARABIAN DESERT
Ptolemaic realm
Nile R.
Persian Gulf
Seleucid realm
Red Sea
Antigonid realm
Minor Hellenistic provinces
Thebes
0 200 400 Miles
0 250 500 Kilometers

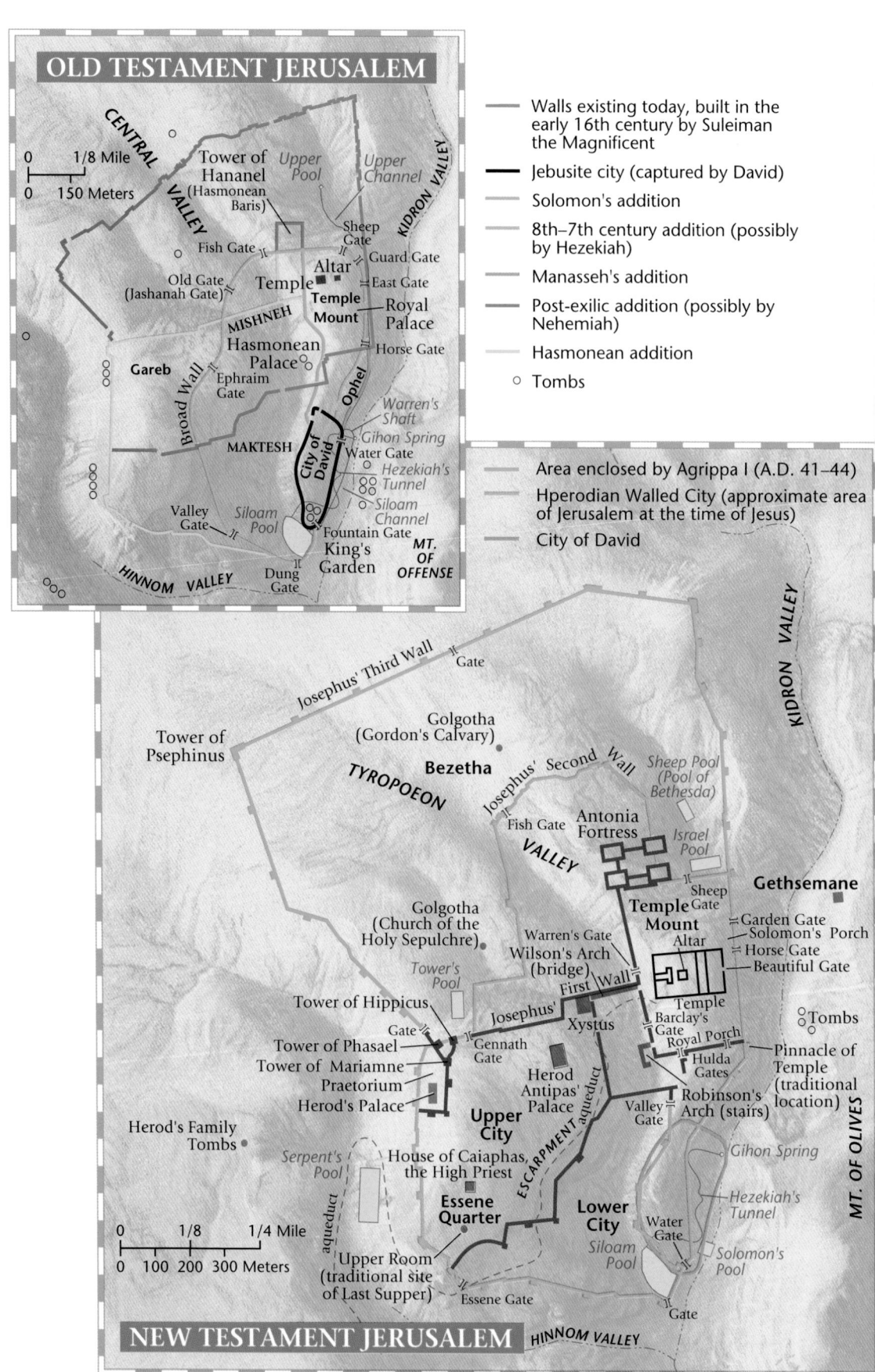

OLD TESTAMENT JERUSALEM

0   1/8 Mile
0   150 Meters

CENTRAL VALLEY

KIDRON VALLEY

Tower of Hananel (Hasmonean Baris)

Upper Pool

Upper Channel

Sheep Gate

Fish Gate

Guard Gate

Old Gate (Jashanah Gate)

Altar

East Gate

Temple

Temple Mount

Royal Palace

MISHNEH

Hasmonean Palace

Horse Gate

Gareb

Ephraim Gate

Broad Wall

MAKTESH

Ophel

Warren's Shaft

Gihon Spring

City of David

Water Gate

Hezekiah's Tunnel

Siloam Channel

Valley Gate

Siloam Pool

Siloam

King's Garden

Fountain Gate

MT. OF OFFENSE

HINNOM VALLEY

Dung Gate

--- Walls existing today, built in the early 16th century by Suleiman the Magnificent

--- Jebusite city (captured by David)

--- Solomon's addition

--- 8th–7th century addition (possibly by Hezekiah)

--- Manasseh's addition

--- Post-exilic addition (possibly by Nehemiah)

--- Hasmonean addition

○ Tombs

--- Area enclosed by Agrippa I (A.D. 41–44)

--- Hperodian Walled City (approximate area of Jerusalem at the time of Jesus)

--- City of David

Josephus' Third Wall

Gate

Golgotha (Gordon's Calvary)

Tower of Psephinus

TYROPOEON

Bezetha

Josephus' Second Wall

Sheep Pool (Pool of Bethesda)

Fish Gate

Antonia Fortress

Israel Pool

VALLEY

Sheep Gate

Gethsemane

Golgotha (Church of the Holy Sepulchre)

Temple Mount

Garden Gate
Solomon's Porch
Horse Gate
Beautiful Gate

Tower's Pool

Warren's Gate

Wilson's Arch (bridge)

Altar

First Wall

Temple

Tower of Hippicus

Josephus' First Wall

Xystus

Barclay's Gate

Royal Porch

Tombs

Gate

Gennath Gate

Tower of Phasael

Tower of Mariamne

Praetorium

Herod's Palace

Herod Antipas' Palace

Hulda Gates

Pinnacle of Temple (traditional location)

Robinson's Arch (stairs)

Valley Gate

KIDRON VALLEY

Gihon Spring

MT. OF OLIVES

Upper City

ESCARPMENT

aqueduct

Hezekiah's Tunnel

Herod's Family Tombs

Serpent's Pool

House of Caiaphas, the High Priest

Essene Quarter

Lower City

Water Gate

aqueduct

Siloam Pool

Solomon's Pool

0   1/8   1/4 Mile
0   100 200 300 Meters

Upper Room (traditional site of Last Supper)

Essene Gate

Gate

NEW TESTAMENT JERUSALEM

HINNOM VALLEY

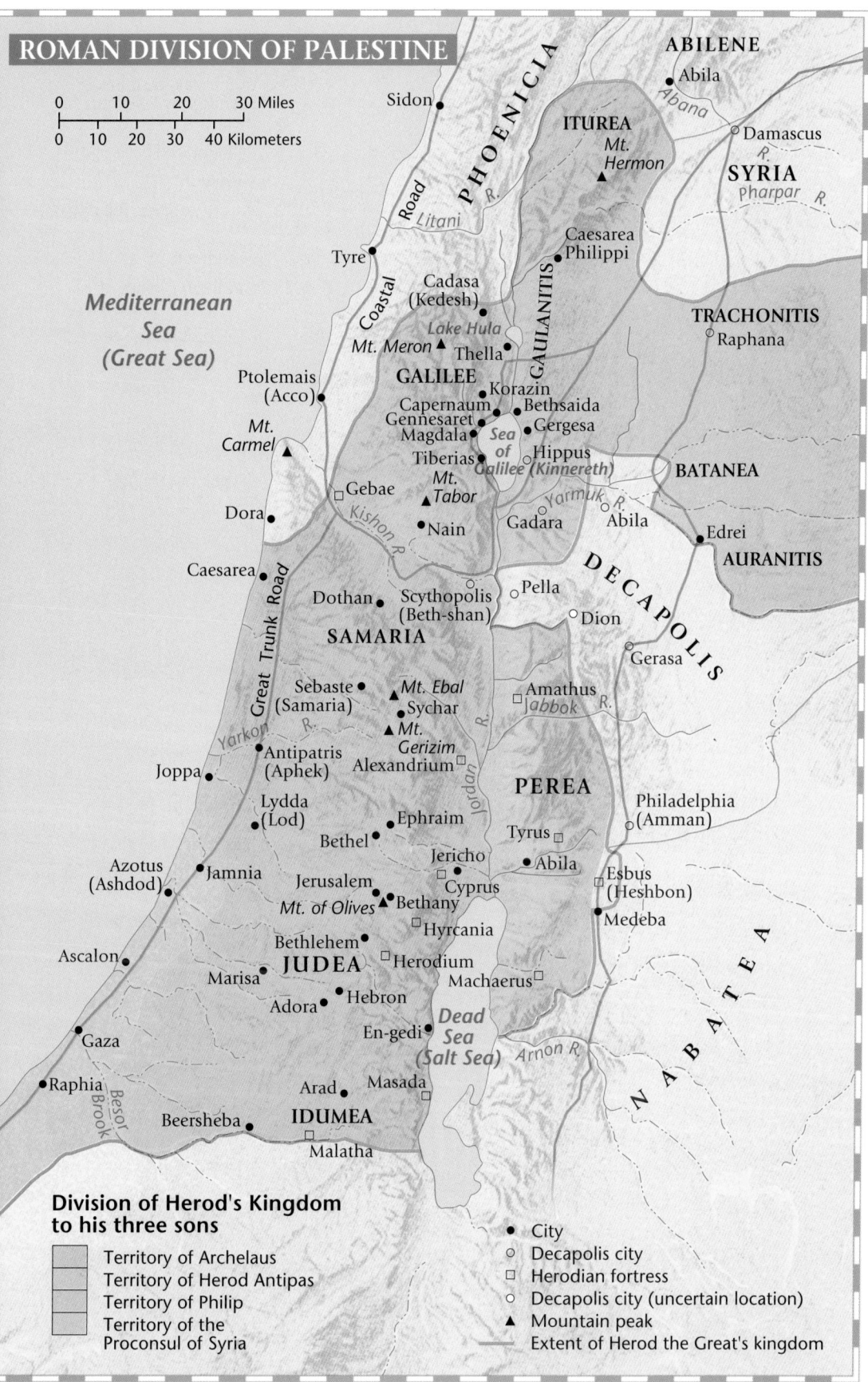

ROMAN DIVISION OF PALESTINE

0   10   20   30 Miles
0 10 20 30 40 Kilometers

Mediterranean Sea (Great Sea)

ABILENE

Abila

Sidon

Abana R.

PHOENICIA

ITUREA

Mt. Hermon ▲

Damascus

SYRIA

Pharpar R.

Road

Litani R.

Caesarea Philippi

Tyre

Coastal

Cadasa (Kedesh)

GAULANITIS

TRACHONITIS

Raphana

Lake Hula

Mt. Meron ▲ Thella

GALILEE

Korazin

Ptolemais (Acco)

Capernaum
Gennesaret
Magdala
Bethsaida
Gergesa

Mt. Carmel ▲

Tiberias
Sea of Galilee (Kinnereth)

Hippus

BATANEA

Mt. Tabor ▲

Dora

Kishon R.

Gebae □

Nain

Gadara

Yarmuk R.

Abila

Edrei

AURANITIS

Caesarea

Great Trunk Road

Dothan

Scythopolis (Beth-shan)

Pella

DECAPOLIS

Dion

SAMARIA

Gerasa

Yarkon R.

Sebaste (Samaria)

Mt. Ebal ▲
Sychar
Mt. Gerizim ▲

Amathus □
Jabbok R.

Joppa

Antipatris (Aphek)

Alexandrium □

Lydda (Lod)

Ephraim

PEREA

Philadelphia (Amman)

Bethel

Jordan R.

Tyrus □

Azotus (Ashdod)

Jamnia

Jericho □

Abila

Esbus (Heshbon)

Jerusalem
Cyprus □

Mt. of Olives ▲ Bethany
Hyrcania □

Medeba

Ascalon

Bethlehem

Herodium □

JUDEA

Marisa

Machaerus □

Adora Hebron

Dead Sea (Salt Sea)

Gaza

En-gedi

Arnon R.

N A B A T E A

Raphia

Besor Brook

Arad Masada □

Beersheba

IDUMEA

Malatha □

Division of Herod's Kingdom to his three sons

- Territory of Archelaus
- Territory of Herod Antipas
- Territory of Philip
- Territory of the Proconsul of Syria

- ● City
- ○ Decapolis city
- □ Herodian fortress
- ◌ Decapolis city (uncertain location)
- ▲ Mountain peak
- — Extent of Herod the Great's kingdom

MINISTRY OF JESUS

Chronologically speaking, it is not possible to sequentially arrange the events in the life of Christ in any definitive way; none of the New Testament gospels follows an overtly chronological pattern. Accordingly, the arrangement here follows a geographic order, basically proceeding from north to south on the map. Because the gospel of Matthew most frequently contains information cited here, and because it is the most geographically particularistic gospel, synoptic passages are keyed to the book of Matthew, except where they are unattested there or where more pertinent information about the event cited is available in another gospel.

A. *Region of Tyre:* Gentile woman's daughter healed (Mt 15:21-28)

B. *Caesarea Philippi:* Peter's great declaration (Mt 16:13-20)

C. *Mt. Meron/Mt. Tabor/Mt. Hermon:* (1) possible location of Transfiguration (Mt 17:1-13); (2) demon-possessed boy healed nearby (Mt 17:14-21)

D. *Cana of Galilee:* (1) water changed to wine (Jn 2:1-11); (2) Capernaum official's son healed (Jn 4:46-54)

E. *Gennesaret:* (1) possible location of feeding of multitudes (Mt 14:13-21; 15:32-39); (2) many healings (Mk 6:53-56)

F. *Area of Korazin:* (1) judgment pronounced on the cities of Korazin, Bethsaida, and Capernaum (Mt 11:20-24); (2) possible area of Sermon on the Mount (Mt 5-7)

G. *Capernaum:* (1) catch of fish (Lk 5:1-11); (2) evil spirit cast out (Mk 1:21-28); (3) Sermon on the Mount (Mt 5-7); (4) Peter's mother-in-law healed (Mt 8:5-13); (5) Roman officer's servant healed (Mt 8:5-13); (6) paralyzed man healed (Mk 2:1-12); (7) woman with a hemorrhage healed (Mk 5:25-34); (8) Jairus's daughter raised (Lk 8:40-56); (9) two blind men healed (Mt 9:27-31); (10) a mute, demon-possessed man healed (Mt 9:32-34); (11) the twelve apostles sent out (Mt 10:1-15); (12) man with deformed hand healed (Mt 12:9-13); (13) another demon-possessed man healed (Mt 12:22-37); (14) Temple tax provided (Mt 17:24-27); (15) Bread of Life discourse (Jn 6:22-59)

H. *Bethsaida:* (1) possible location of feeding of multitudes (Mt 14:13-21; 15:32-39); (2) blind man healed (Mk 8:22-26)

I. *Sea of Galilee near Bethsaida:* walking on water (Mt 14:22-33)

J. *Sea of Galilee:* storm quieted (Mt 8:23-27)

K. *Gergesa/Gadara:* possible location of casting out demons, which enter pigs; the pigs then rush down a steep bank and drown (Lk 8:26-39)

L. *Nazareth:* (1) childhood home (Mt 2:19-23); (2) rejected by townspeople (Lk 4:16-30)

M. *Nain:* widow's son raised (Lk 7:11-17)

N. *Region of Galilee:* (1) leper cleansed (Mk 1:40-45); (2) post-resurrection appearances to the disciples (Mt 28:16-20)

O. *Region of Ten Towns:* many healings (Mt 15:29-31; Mk 7:31-37)

P. *Region between Galilee and Samaria:* (1) refused entry into village (Lk 9:51-56); (2) ten lepers healed (Lk 17:11-19)

Q. *Sychar:* woman at the well of Samaria (Jn 4:1-42)

R. *Ephraim:* enters into seclusion with the disciples (Jn 11:54)

S. *Region of Perea:* (1) teaching on marriage (Mt 19:1-12); (2) possible location of healing of woman with infirmity (Lk 13:10-13); (3) possible location of healing of man with swollen limbs (Lk 14:1-6); (4) possible location of the rich young ruler (Lk 18:18-30)

T. *Jericho:* (1) Bartimaeus healed (Mk 10:46-52); (2) Zacchaeus converted (Lk 19:1-10)

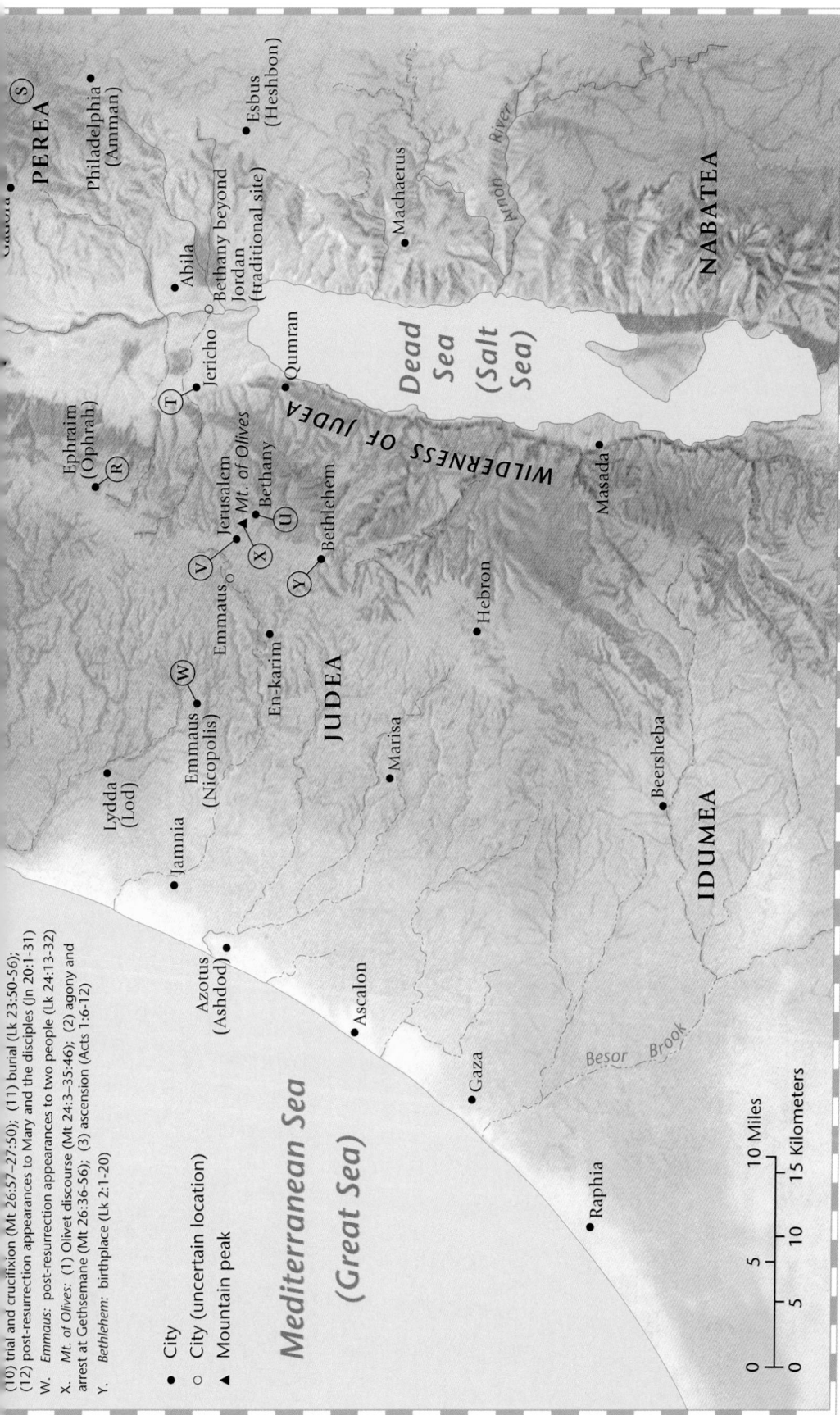

(10) trial and crucifixion (Mt 26:57–27:50); (11) burial (Lk 23:50-56);
(12) post-resurrection appearances to Mary and the disciples (Jn 20:1-31)
W. *Emmaus:* post-resurrection appearances to two people (Lk 24:13-32)
X. *Mt. of Olives:* (1) Olivet discourse (Mt 24:3-35-46); (2) agony and
arrest at Gethsemane (Mt 26:36-56); (3) ascension (Acts 1:6-12)
Y. *Bethlehem:* birthplace (Lk 2:1-20)

● City
○ City (uncertain location)
▲ Mountain peak

Mediterranean Sea
(Great Sea)

PEREA

Philadelphia
(Amman)

Esbus
(Heshbon)

Machaerus

Abila

Bethany beyond
Jordan
(traditional site)

Qumran

Jericho

Ephraim
(Ophrah)

NABATEA

Dead
Sea
(Salt
Sea)

WILDERNESS OF JUDEA

Masada

Jerusalem
Mt. of Olives
Bethany

Bethlehem

Emmaus

En-karim

Hebron

JUDEA

Marisa

Emmaus
(Nicopolis)

Lydda
(Lod)

Jamnia

Beersheba

IDUMEA

Azotus
(Ashdod)

Ascalon

Besor Brook

Gaza

Raphia

0   5   10 Miles
0   5   10   15 Kilometers

Copyright © 1996 Tyndale House Publishers, Inc.

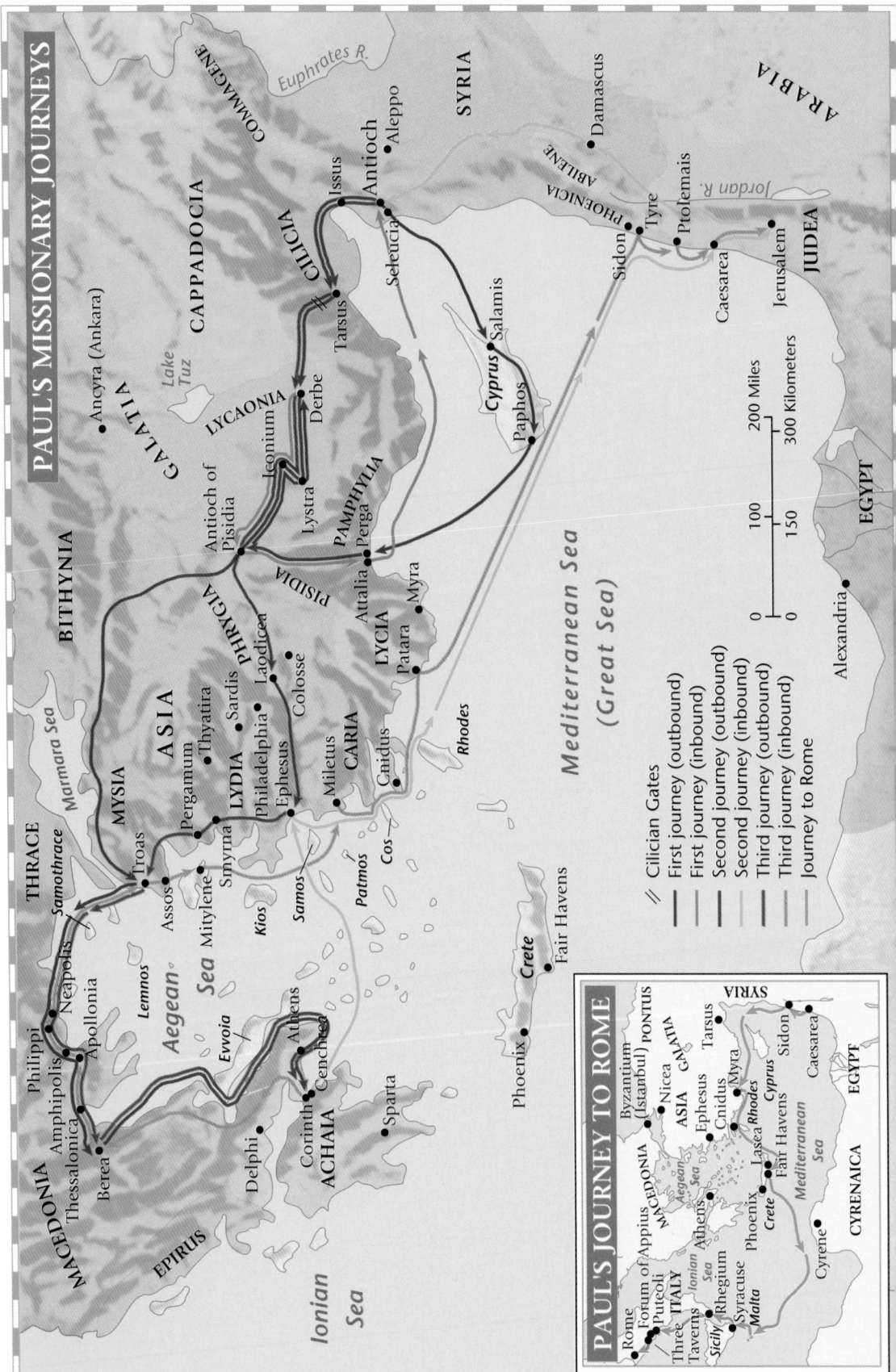

PAUL'S MISSIONARY JOURNEYS

COMMAGENE

Euphrates R.

SYRIA

ARABIA

Damascus

Aleppo

Antioch

Issus

CILICIA

Seleucia

PHOENICIA

ABILENE

Jordan R.

Tyre

Ptolemais

Sidon

Caesarea

CAPPADOCIA

Tarsus

Salamis

Cyprus

Paphos

Jerusalem

JUDEA

Ancyra (Ankara)

Lake Tuz

GALATIA

LYCAONIA

Derbe

Iconium

Antioch of Pisidia

Lystra

PAMPHYLIA

PISIDIA

Perga

Attalia

LYCIA

Patara

Myra

BITHYNIA

PHRYGIA

Laodicea

Colosse

Sardis

Thyatira

ASIA

LYDIA

Philadelphia

Ephesus

Pergamum

Miletus

CARIA

Cnidus

Cos

Rhodes

Mediterranean Sea
(Great Sea)

MYSIA

Troas

Assos

Mitylene

Smyrna

Kios

Samos

Patmos

THRACE

Marmara Sea

Neapolis

Apollonia

Samothrace

Lemnos

Aegean
Sea

Evvoia

Philippi

Amphipolis

Thessalonica

Berea

MACEDONIA

Athens

Cenchrea

Corinth

ACHAIA

Delphi

Sparta

EPIRUS

Ionian
Sea

Crete

Phoenix

Fair Havens

Alexandria

EGYPT

Scale

0	100	200 Miles
0	150	300 Kilometers

Legend:

// Cilician Gates
— First journey (outbound)
— First journey (inbound)
— Second journey (outbound)
— Second journey (inbound)
— Third journey (outbound)
— Third journey (inbound)
— Journey to Rome

PAUL'S JOURNEY TO ROME

Rome
Forum of Appius
Puteoli
Three Taverns
ITALY
Rhegium
Sicily
Syracuse
Malta
CYRENAICA
Cyrene
Phoenix
Crete
Lasea
Fair Havens
Mediterranean
Sea
Athens
MACEDONIA
Aegean
Sea
Byzantium
(Istanbul)
Nicea
GALATIA
PONTUS
ASIA
Ephesus
Cnidus
Rhodes
Myra
Cyprus
Tarsus
Sidon
Caesarea
SYRIA
EGYPT

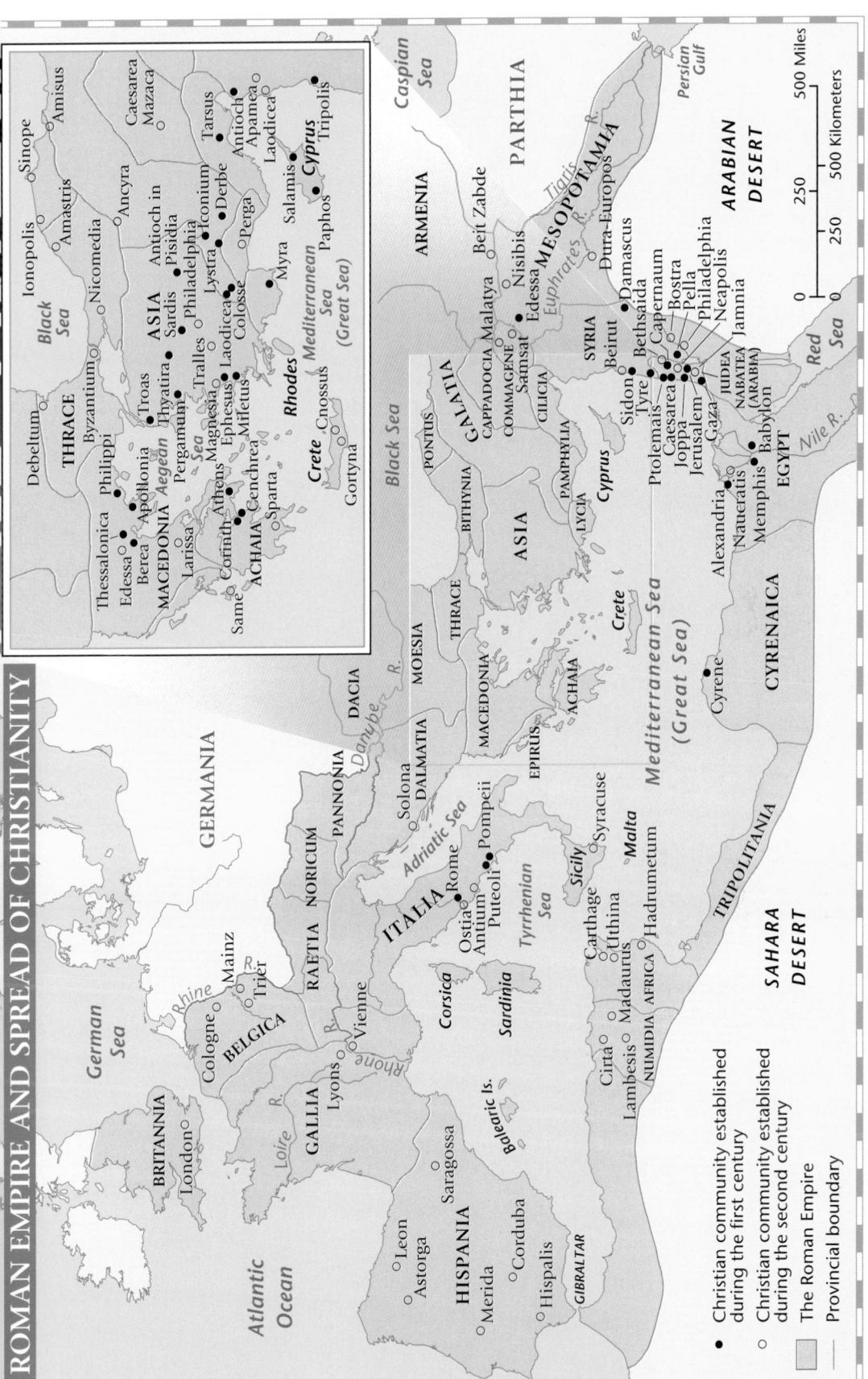

ROMAN EMPIRE AND SPREAD OF CHRISTIANITY

Legend:

● Christian community established during the first century

○ Christian community established during the second century

▢ The Roman Empire

— Provincial boundary

Inset map labels:

Amisus, Sinope, Ionopolis, Amastris, Caesarea Mazaca, Nicomedia, Ancyra, Tarsus, Antioch, Apamea, Laodicea, Tripolis, Cyprus, Salamis, Paphos, Byzantium, Iconium, Derbe, Perga, Myra, Antioch in Pisidia, Lystra, Philadelphia, Sardis, Laodicea, Colosse, Thyatira, Pergamum, Ephesus, Miletus, Tralles, Magnesia, Troas, Apollonia, Athens, Cenchrea, Sparta, Philippi, Thessalonica, Edessa, Berea, Larissa, Corinth, Same, Crete, Cnossus, Gortyna, Rhodes, Debeltum, Mediterranean Sea (Great Sea), Black Sea, Aegean Sea, THRACE, MACEDONIA, ACHAIA, ASIA

Main map labels:

Caspian Sea, PARTHIA, ARMENIA, Persian Gulf, ARABIAN DESERT, Beit Zabde, MESOPOTAMIA, Nisibis, Edessa, Samsat, Dura-Europos, Tigris R., Euphrates R., CAPPADOCIA, Malatya, COMMAGENE, CILICIA, PAMPHYLIA, LYCIA, GALATIA, PONTUS, BITHYNIA, ASIA, THRACE, MOESIA, DACIA, Danube R., PANNONIA, NORICUM, RAETIA, GERMANIA, DALMATIA, Solona, Adriatic Sea, MACEDONIA, EPIRUS, ACHAIA, Crete, Mediterranean Sea (Great Sea), SYRIA, Beirut, Damascus, Sidon, Tyre, Capernaum, Bethsaida, Bostra, Pella, Philadelphia, Neapolis, Jamnia, Ptolemais, Caesarea, Joppa, Jerusalem, Gaza, JUDEA, NABATEA (ARABIA), Babylon, Memphis, Naucratis, Alexandria, EGYPT, Nile R., Red Sea, Cyprus, Cyrene, CYRENAICA, Pompeii, Rome, Ostia, Antium, Puteoli, ITALIA, Corsica, Sardinia, Tyrrhenian Sea, Sicily, Syracuse, Malta, Carthage, Uthina, Madaurus, Hadrumetum, AFRICA, NUMIDIA, Cirta, Lambesis, TRIPOLITANIA, SAHARA DESERT, Mainz, Trier, Cologne, Rhine R., BELGICA, Vienne, Lyons, GALLIA, Rhone R., Loire R., London, BRITANNIA, German Sea, Atlantic Ocean, Leon, Astorga, Saragossa, Balearic Is., HISPANIA, Merida, Corduba, Hispalis, GIBRALTAR, Black Sea

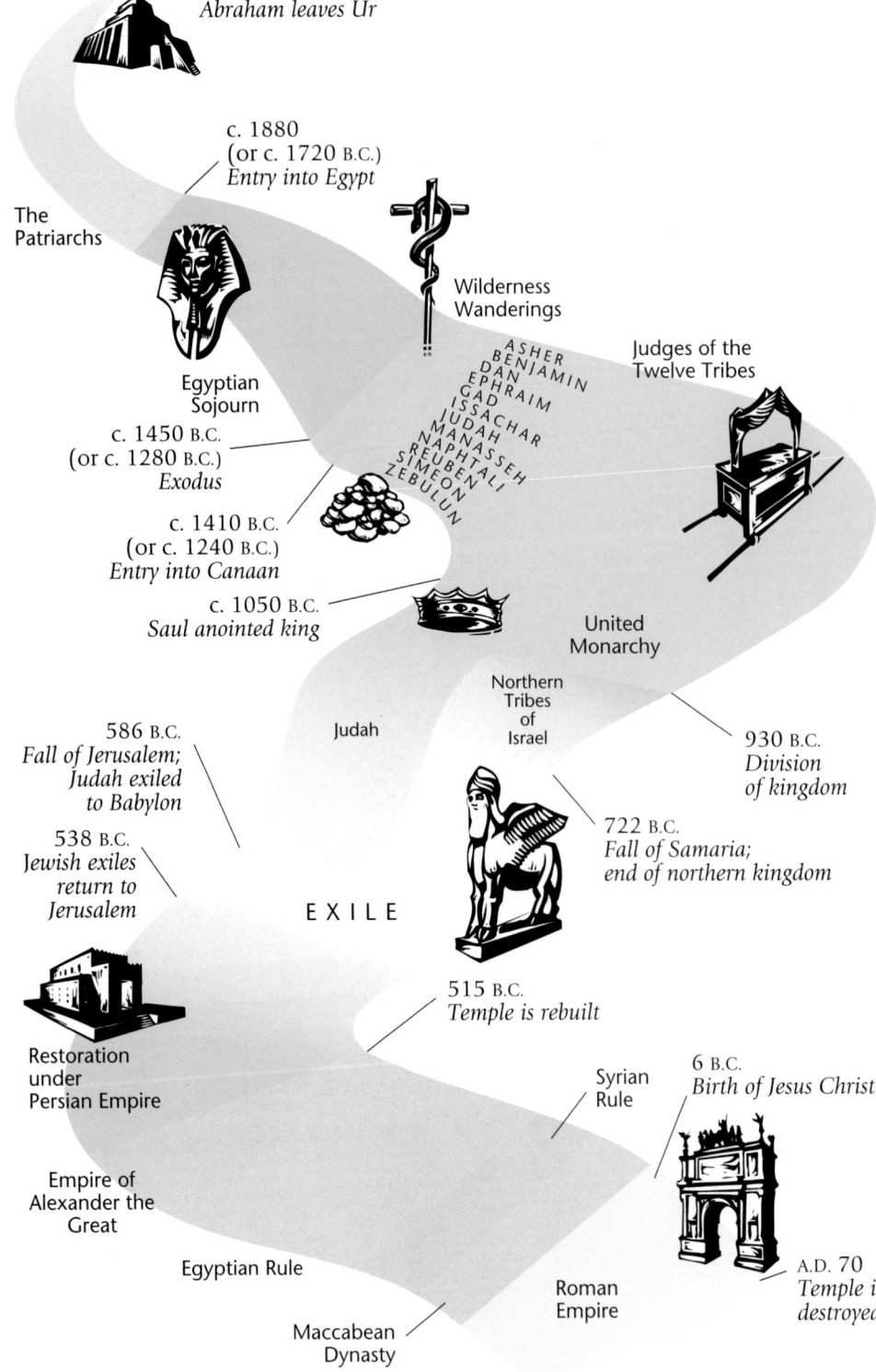

TIMELINE OF BIBLICAL EVENTS

c. 2170
(or c. 2000 B.C.)
Abraham leaves Ur

c. 1880
(or c. 1720 B.C.)
Entry into Egypt

The
Patriarchs

Wilderness
Wanderings

ASHER
BENJAMIN
DAN
EPHRAIM
GAD
ISSACHAR
JUDAH
MANASSEH
NAPHTALI
REUBEN
SIMEON
ZEBULUN

Judges of the
Twelve Tribes

Egyptian
Sojourn

c. 1450 B.C.
(or c. 1280 B.C.)
Exodus

c. 1410 B.C.
(or c. 1240 B.C.)
Entry into Canaan

c. 1050 B.C.
Saul anointed king

United
Monarchy

Northern
Tribes
of
Israel

586 B.C.
*Fall of Jerusalem;
Judah exiled
to Babylon*

Judah

930 B.C.
*Division
of kingdom*

538 B.C.
*Jewish exiles
return to
Jerusalem*

722 B.C.
*Fall of Samaria;
end of northern kingdom*

E X I L E

515 B.C.
Temple is rebuilt

Restoration
under
Persian Empire

Syrian
Rule

6 B.C.
Birth of Jesus Christ

Empire of
Alexander the
Great

Egyptian Rule

Maccabean
Dynasty

Roman
Empire

A.D. 70
*Temple is
destroyed*

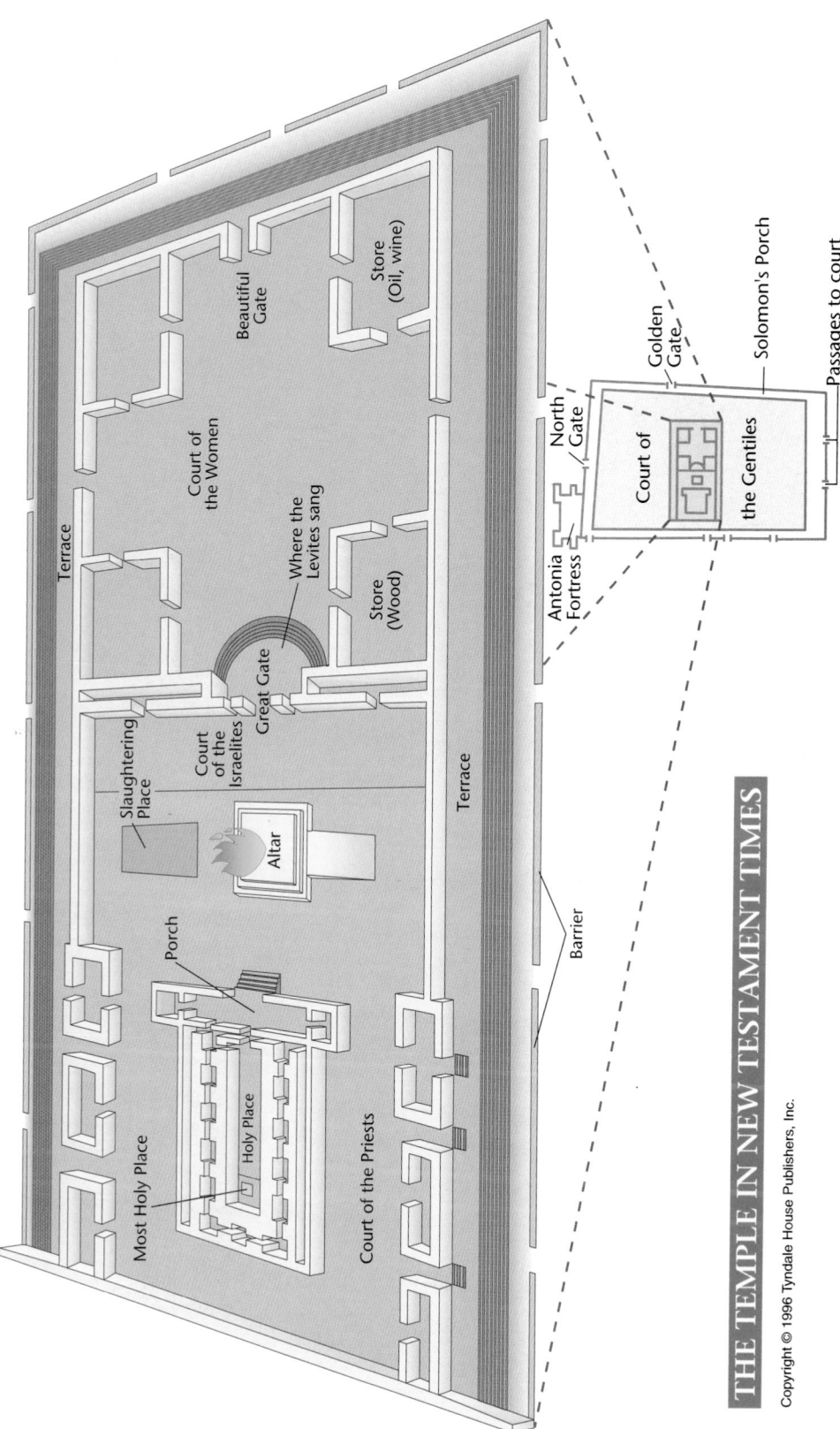

THE TEMPLE IN NEW TESTAMENT TIMES

Terrace

Beautiful Gate

Store
(Oil, wine)

Court of
the Women

Where the
Levites sang

Store
(Wood)

Great Gate

Terrace

Slaughtering
Place

Court of
the Israelites

Altar

Porch

Most Holy Place

Holy Place

Court of the Priests

Barrier

Antonia
Fortress

North
Gate

Golden
Gate

Court of

Solomon's Porch

the Gentiles

Passages to court

ISRAEL AND THE MIDDLE EAST TODAY

ROMANIA • Odessa UKRAINE
• Bucharest
• Sofia
BULGARIA
Black Sea
RUSSIA KAZAKSTAN
UZBEKISTAN

GEORGIA Caspian Sea
Istanbul
GREECE AZERBAIJAN
ARMENIA • Baku
TURKMENISTAN
Ankara Halys R.
Mt. Ararat ▲
Izmir (Smyrna) TURKEY
Tabriz
Maimana •
Oxus R.

• Aleppo Tehran •
AFGHANISTAN
CYPRUS Mosul •
SYRIA Tigris R.
LEBANON • Beirut Euphrates R.
• Damascus • Baghdad IRAN
Mediterranean Sea
Jerusalem • • Amman IRAQ
PAKISTAN
JORDAN Basra •
• Shiraz
Alexandria
Cairo • SINAI Kuwait
KUWAIT City
Bandar Abbas

SAHARA DESERT
Nile R.
EGYPT SAUDI ARABIA Persian Gulf
Doha • QATAR
Arabian Sea
• Medina Riyadh •
Aswan • Red Sea

LEBANON Mt. Hermon ▲
• Tyre SYRIA
Kiryat Shemona
GOLAN HEIGHTS
Mediterranean Sea Acco • Safed •
Haifa • Tiberias • Sea of Galilee
Megiddo • Nazareth •
SUDAN Jenin • Beth-shan •
Netanya •
Khartoum • Tulkarm •
ERITREA Nablus •
Tel Aviv • WEST BANK Amman
Ramallah • Jericho •
Jerusalem • Qumran •

0 200 400 Miles
0 200 400 600 Kilometers
ETHIOPIA

Gaza • Hebron • Dead Sea
Khan Yunis • En-gedi •
GAZA STRIP • Beersheba
• El-Arish Dimona •
ISRAEL JORDAN

AL SC
GA
Atlantic Ocean
FL
Gulf of Mexico

Mizpe Ramon •

EGYPT • Petra

Note the comparative size of
Israel to the state of Florida

SINAI

Eilat •
Red Sea